1990 edition
standard catalog of
WORLD COINS

by Chester L. Krause and Clifford Mishler · Colin R. Bruce II, Editor

Marian S. Moe
Coordinating Editor

Thomas Michael
Market Analyst

Robert Wilhite
US Market Analyst

Fred J. Borgmann
New Issues Editor

Alan Herbert
Special Consultant

Denny Kurir
Special Consultant

Joan Melum
Project Coordinator

UNCIRCULATED VALUATIONS

The Uncirculated valuations represented in this edition are for typical quality specimens; for some of the more popularly collected series, superior quality examples may easily command 10% to 50% premiums, or even greater where particularly popular or rare types or dates are concerned. **Exceptions:** The MS-60 and MS-63 designations are represented in the Canadian listings while MS-60, MS-63, MS-64 and MS-65 grades are indicated in selected areas of the United States section.

BULLION VALUE (BV) MAKET VALUATIONS

Valuations for all platinum, gold, palladium or silver coins of the more common, basically bullion types, or those possessing only modest numismatic premiums, are presented in this edition based on market levels of $550 per ounce for platinum, $400 for gold, $150 for palladium and $6.00 per ounce for silver. Where the letters "BV" — Bullion Value — appear in a value column, that particular issue in the condition indicated generally trades at or near the bullion value of its precious metal content. Further information on using this catalog to evaluate platinum, gold, palladium or silver coins amid fluctuating precious metal market conditions is presented on page 32.

Riches amassed in haste will diminish, but those collected by little and little will multiply. — *Goethe*.

sixteenth edition
standard catalog of
WORLD COINS

krause publications
IOLA, WISCONSIN 54990

COPYRIGHT MCMLXXXIX by KRAUSE PUBLICATIONS, INC.
Library of Congress Catalog Card Number: 79-640940
International Standard Book Number: 0-87341-123-4

WANTED

COINS of the WORLD

Attention Dealers & Collectors!

We are always in the market for material cataloging $10 & up. Gold, silver, copper, minors, & crowns; what do you have to offer? Ship insured for our top offer. Same day check. We are one of the largest advertisers in "World Coin News". We can pay more.

Coin Net

BLACKBURN & BLACKBURN LTD.

P.O. Box 424, Killen, Alabama 35645   (205) 757-5332

ACKNOWLEDGMENTS

Many hundreds of individuals have contributed countless valuable contributions which have been incorporated in this sixteenth edition. While all can not be acknowledged, special appreciation is extended to the following principal contributors and organizations who have exhibited a special dedication — revising and verifying historical and technical data and coin listings, reviewing market valuations and loaning coins for photographing — for this edition.

Jan Olav Aamlid
Esko Ahlroth
Kevin Akin
Stephen Album
Antonio Alessandrini
Sam Alexander
Norman I. Applebaum
Luis A. Asbun-Karmy
George Azuma
Don Bailey
Cem Barlock
Nessin Bassan M.
Michael Bates
George M. Beach
Dr. Anton Belcev
Lauren Benson
Jack Beymer
C.H. Blackburn
Col. Joseph Boling
Al Boulanger
Bruce B. Braun
Saul Braun
B.F. Brekke
Ken Bressett
Michael L. Briley
Glen W. Brogden
Michael Broome
Irv Brotman
John T. Bucek
Davis Burnett, Jr.
Theodore V. Buttrey
Ralph A. Cannito
David L. Cannon
Francisco Capuano
Jim Carr
Douglas S. Cass
K.H. Chan
Peter A. Chase
Daniel K.E. Ching
Wm. B. Christensen
Bill Church
Ritchie Clay
John L. Cobb
Edward E. Cohen
Scott E. Cordry
Douglas D. Cox
Freeman Craig, Jr.
Jerry Crain
Jed Crump
George Cucu
Raymond E. Czahor
John S. Davenport
Dolores H. Davis
Gordon De Mars

C.J. Denton
J.B. Desai
John S. Deyell
Robert Diedrich
Jean-Paul Divo
Richard Doty
Frank Draskovic
F. Droulers
Michael J. Druck
Graham P. Dyer
Jan M. Dyroff
Stephen D. Eccles
Arnaldo Efron
Wilhelm Eglseer
Esko Ekman
Lester J. Elliott
Jean Elsen
Steve Eyer
Steve I. Fass
Dr. Gerald M. Feigen
Guvendik Fisekcioglu
Thomas F. Fitzgerald
Horace Flatt
Richard Ford
Greg Franke
Arthur Friedberg
Victor Gadoury
Albert Galloway
Edward J. Ganister
Paul Garner
Francesco Giacalone
Dennis Gill
Ronald J. Gillio
Dr. Alfred R. Globus
Joseph J. Goldberg
Lawrence S. Goldberg
Mark Goldberg
Alberto Gomes
Stan Goran
Ralph C. Gordan
David R. Gotkin
Albert A. Goulet
Dr. G.R. Gruber
Hakim Hamidi
Peter Hamilton
Brian Hannon
David Hastings
M.R. Hayter
Sergio Heise F.
Leon Hendrickson
Hans Herrli
Anton Holt
Charles R. Hosch
Terris C. Howard

Serge Huard
Clyde Hubbard
Louis Hudson
Charles L. Huff
John G. Humphris
Curtis Iverson
Larry Jackson
Dr. Norman Jacobs
Ton Jacobs
B. Johnson (deceased)
Chester R. Johnson
James J. Johnson
Werner H. Jorg
Art Jorgensen
William M. Judd
Robert W. Julian
William S. Kable
Michael Kaplan
John Keogh
Ketab Corp
Andy Kornafel
Peter Kraneveld
Harold Kritzman
Col. Robert F. Kriz
Kurt R. Krueger
Russell Kruzell
Prashant P. Kulkarni
Guntis Kuskevics
Samuel Lachman
Eng. Gergely Lajos
Peter Last
Lee Shin Song
George Lill III
Jan Lingen
David Lisot
Richard Lobel
James Lorah
Rudi Lotter
Alan Luedeking
Odd Lund
Ma Tok Wo
Kenneth MacKenzie
Ranko Mandic
Harrington Manville
Richard Margolis
Virg Marshall III
Ivan Maxwell
Robert T. McIntire
Dr. Wayne McKim
Don Medcalf
Balazs Meekesh
Jurgen Mikeska
Mario Gutierrez Minera

Dr. William J. Mira
Robert Mish
Lazar Mishev
Michael Mitchiner
Dr. Richard Montrey
Mohammad Abdul Munin
R. Paul Nadin-Davis
Hitoshi Nagai
Oen Nelson
Richard A. Nelson
N. Douglas Nicol
William O'Connor
Tony Oliver
Charles Panish
Krzysztof Panuciak
Gus A. Pappas
Jim Payette
Robert A. Perrin
Michael Peykar
Thomas Pierce
Colin Pitchfork
Richard J. Plant
Derek Pobjoy
J.J. Polczyk
Rick Ponterio
M. Mukund Prabhu
Miguel Angel Pratt Mayans
Paul Puckett
Dr. S.K. Punshi
Sidky Rabie
Bill Randel
Leo Reich
Jerome H. Remick
Nicholas Rhodes
Alistair F. Robb
G.N. Robbins (deceased)
Dana Roberts
M.R. Roberts
Frank S. Robinson
Dr. Kerry A. Rodgers
Jay Roe
Carl Rosenblum
Maurice Rosen
Landon T. Ross
Russell Rulau
Arnaldo Russo
John Sacher
Godwin Said
John Saunders
Harry S. Scherzer
Hans Schlumberger
Gerhard Schon
David E. Seelye

Scott Semans
Narendra Sengar
R.C. Senior
Dale Seppa
Denver W. Sherry
H. S. Monte Sherwin
Ross B. Shields
Frovin Sieg
Ladislav Sin
M.R. Singer
Saran Singh
Ing. Evzen Sknouril
Arlie R. Slabaugh
Art Smith
Bruce W. Smith
Prof. David S. Smith
Marian C. Smith
Lester D. Snell
Wm. F. Spengler
Robert Steinberg
Larry Stevens
A.A. Sumana
James O. Sweeny
Steven Tan
M. Louis Teller
Gunnar Thesen
Albert A. Tom
Guillermo Triana Aguiar
Antonio M. Trigueiros
Warren Tucker
Anastasios Tzamalis
Willem Van Alsenoy
A.G. van der Dussen
Jan W. Vandersande
J.J. Van Grover
E.J. Van Loon
J. Ferraro Vaz
Zdenek Vesely
Edmundo F. Vicente
Holland Wallace
Justin C. Wang
William B. Warden, Jr.
R.B. White
Raymond E. Whyborn
John Wilkison
Augusto Wing
Lt. Col. Barrie J. Winsor
Richard Wright
Ertekin Yenisey
R.S. Yeoman (deceased)
Joseph Zaffern
Ran Zander
M. Zerder (deceased)

AUCTION HOUSES

Bowers and Merena, Inc.
Adolph Hess AG-Lucerne

Fritz Rudolf Kunker
H.D. Rauch

Sotheby's
Stack's

Superior Galleries
Swiss Bank Corporation

SOCIETIES and INSTITUTIONS

American Numismatic Association
American Numismatic Society

Hong Kong Numismatic Society
John Hopkins University

Numismatics International
Smithsonian Institution

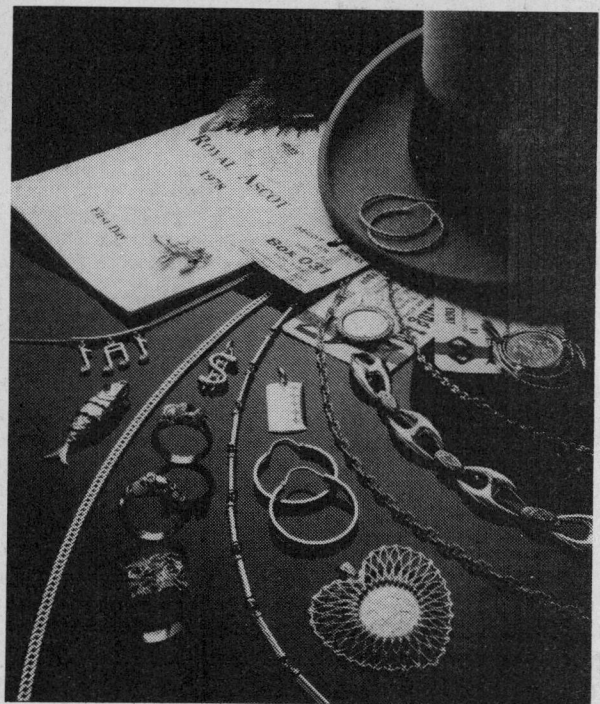
Specialty items, jewelry and knickknacks.

Custom minting

fit for Kings, Princes, Distributors, Commoners and Collectors

**Pobjoy Mint Ltd.
Sutton, England**
Producers of the Noble, the world's first widely circulated PLATINUM coin. Producers of the world's first large circulation PALLADIUM coins.

Contractors to Princes, Kings, Commoners and Savvy Distributors.
Official minters to foreign governments.
Suppliers of coins, medals and precious metal art objects.
Creators of regalia for Royalty and Nobility.

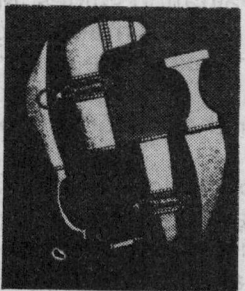
*Etched daggers and swords.
1970 Commemorative Arab dagger for Oman.*

Anniversary Nuptial Cup in silver and gold.

The world's best selling Platinum coin.

America's fastest growing Gold Bullion coin.

**Official Minters to Foreign Governments
MINT OFFICES**

Pobjoy Mint (Canada)
P.O. Box 37
St. Catharines, Ontario
Canada L2R 6R4

Pobjoy Mint Ltd. (England)
92 Oldfields Road
Sutton, Surrey SM1 1BR
Great Britain

Pobjoy Mint Ltd. (U.S.)
P.O. Box 153
Iola, WI 54945
715-445-3581

INTRODUCTION

This 16th edition covering a period of 190 years includes the greatest share of the world's most popularly collected modern coinage. This edition has been produced in a more economical package in response to thousands of requests received over and over throughout the past 5 years. This handy, easy to carry - easy to use edition will maintain its integrity throughout the world as the "tool of the industry" and "bible of modern numismatics".

Hundreds of new coinage types, dates and varieties issued over the past year have been included in this edition in a sophisticated process that allows for inclusion of new issues just days before the printing presses begin to roll. The cataloging staff constantly monitors the world's mints for new issues through a broadly based communications network developed worldwide among collectors, dealers, mints and authorized agents, national banks and treasuries.

The base on which the new features and expanded areas are built consists of the many traditional presentations which have been associated with the Standard Catalog of World Coins in its first fifteen editions, starting, of course, with the valuation guides. Market values throughout have been carefully reviewed and revised in light of current market conditions in up to four of the most collectible grades in any particular issue. The expertise of hundreds of the world's top numismatists and analysts played a vital role in setting updated market prices. A quick check of the values listed in this book can spare the reader the misfortune of buying above or selling below current market levels.

Where appropriate within the listings, detailed explanations of the various specialized dating systems used on the coin of some countries and eras have been provided. The Instant Identifier and Monograms sections are keyed to instant visual identification by matching state symbols and heraldry. Actual silver weight (ASW), actual gold weight (AGW) and actual platinum weights (APW) are provided for precious metal coinage to determine intrinsic value and act as a guide toward ascertaining authenticity.

Coins OF THE WORLD

We make a market in coins of the world. Whether you're buying or selling.... it'll pay you to contact our office.

Quality collector material
Modern Issues • *Gold* •
Silver • *Platinum*

Canadian Maple Leaf

Featuring Platinum Coins For Investors

The Isle of Man Noble

The Australian Koala

We keep in touch with the market at over fifty major coin shows worldwide each year, and offer you up to the minute information through the FACTS teletype network and Coin Net.

31-15 Peachtree Road, N.E.
Atlanta, Georgia 30305
404-262-1810
Telex: 522-371
FAX: 404-231-3137

**Call Toll Free
800-272-8022**
For
additional information
No Obligation — Ever!

ADVERTISEMENT

STANDARD INTERNATIONAL NUMERAL SYSTEMS

PREPARED ESPECIALLY FOR THE **STANDARD CATALOG OF WORLD COINS** © 1989 BY KRAUSE PUBLICATIONS

WESTERN	0	½	1	2	3	4	5	6	7	8	9	10	50	100	500	1000
ROMAN			I	II	III	IV	V	VI	VII	VIII	IX	X	L	C	D	M
ARABIC-TURKISH	٠	١/٢	١	٢	٣	٤	٥	٦	٧	٨	٩	١٠	٥٠	١٠٠	٥٠٠	١٠٠٠
MALAY—PERSIAN	٠	١/٢	١	٢	٣	۴	۵	۶	٧	٨	٩	١٠	۵٠	١٠٠	۵٠٠	١٠٠٠
EASTERN ARABIC	0	½	1	2	3	4	5	6	7	8	9	10	40	100	400	1000
HYDERABAD ARABIC	0	١/٢	1	2	3	4	5	6	7	8	9	10	50	100	500	1000
INDIAN (Sanskrit)	0	८/२	१	२	३	४	५	६	७	८	९	१०	४०	१००	४००	१०००
ASSAMESE	0	৬/২	১	২	৩	৪	৫	৯	৭	৮	৯	১০	৫০	১০০	৫০০	১০০০
BENGALI	0	১/২	১	২	৩	8	৫	৬	৭	৮	৯	১০	৫০	১০০	৫০০	১০০০
GUJARATI	0	૨/૨	૧	૨	૩	૪	૫	૬	૭	૮	૯	૧૦	૪૦	૧૦૦	૪૦૦	૧૦૦૦
KUTCH	0	1/2	1	2	3	8	4	६	9	८	९	10	40	100	400	1000
DEVAVNAGRI	0	૨/૨	૧	2	3	૪	૫	૬	૭	૮	૯	૧૦	૪૦	૧૦૦	૪૦૦	૧૦૦૦
NEPALESE	0	१/२	१९	२	३	४	५	६	७	८	९	१०	४०	१००	४००	१०००
TIBETAN	༠	༧/༢	༡	༢	༣	༤	༥	༦	༧	༨	༩	༡༠	༤༠	༡༠༠	༤༠༠	༡༠༠༠
MONGOLIAN	0	༡/༢	༡	༢	༣	༤	༥	༦	༧	༨	༩	༡༠	༤༠	༩༠༠	༤༠༠	༩༠༠༠
BURMESE	၀	၁/၂	၁	၂	၃	၄	၅	၆	၇	၈	၉	၁၀	၅၀	၁၀၀	၅၀၀	၁၀၀၀
THAI-LAO	๐	๑/๒	๑	๒	๓	๔	๕	๖	๗	๘	๙	๑๐	๔๐	๑๐๐	๔๐๐	๑๐๐๐
JAVANESE	0		꧑	꧒	꧓	꧔	꧕	꧖	꧗	꧘	꧙	꧑꧐	꧕꧐	꧑꧐꧐	꧕꧐꧐	꧑꧐꧐꧐
ORDINARY CHINESE JAPANESE-KOREAN	零	半	一	二	三	四	五	六	七	八	九	十	十五	百	百五	千
OFFICIAL CHINESE			壹	貳	參	肆	伍	陸	柒	捌	玖	拾	拾伍	佰	佰伍	仟
COMMERCIAL CHINESE			〡	〢	〣	〤	〥	〦	〧	〨	〩	十	〥十	百	〥百	千
KOREAN		반	일	이	삼	사	오	육	칠	팔	구	십	오십	백	오백	천
GEORGIAN			ა	ბ	გ	დ	ე	ვ	ზ	ჱ	თ	ი	⁶⁰ⱽ	რ	ს	ჰ
			¹¹	²⁰	³⁰ⱽ	⁴⁰ⱽ	⁵⁰ⱽ	⁶⁰ⱽ	⁷⁰ⱽ	⁸⁰ⱽ	⁹⁰ⱽ	¹⁰⁰	²⁰⁰	³⁰⁰	⁴⁰⁰	⁷⁰⁰	⁸⁰⁰
ETHIOPIAN	♦		፩	፪	፫	፬	፭	፮	፯	፰	፱	፲	፶	፻	፭፻	፲፻
				²⁰	³⁰	⁴⁰		⁶⁰	⁷⁰	⁸⁰	⁹⁰						
HEBREW			א	ב	ג	ד	ה	ו	ז	ח	ט	י	ק	תק			
				²⁰	³⁰	⁴⁰		⁶⁰	⁷⁰	⁸⁰	⁹⁰		²⁰⁰	³⁰⁰	⁴⁰⁰	⁶⁰⁰	⁷⁰⁰	⁸⁰⁰
				כ	ל	מ		ס	ע	פ	צ		ר	ש	ת	תת	תש	תת
GREEK			A	B	Γ	Δ	E	Σ	T	Z	H	Θ	I	N	P	O	Λ
				²⁰	³⁰	⁴⁰		⁶⁰	⁷⁰	⁸⁰		²⁰⁰	³⁰⁰	⁴⁰⁰	⁶⁰⁰	⁷⁰⁰	⁸⁰⁰
				K	Λ	M	Ξ	O	Π		Σ	T	Y	X	Ψ		Ω

NUMERAL SYSTEMS 8

WE ARE BUYING

We have more than 3000 active foreign coin buyers and several times as many United States coin, stamp and currency collectors buying from us.

Our average foreign coin pricelist has 5000 separate coins listed - in real terms that's about 20 double row red and black stock boxes, priced from 10 cents to 5,000 dollars, we need coins for these lists. I can't hatch them. I need to buy them.

If that isn't enough motivation for you to sell to us, then send the coins just for the money.

If you are not in a selling frame of mind, please send us your name, address and collecting specialty. We'll sell to you.

WE ARE SELLING

100 Mixed World Coins $9.95	100 Mixed Silver Coins $89.95	1000 Mixed USA Wheat Cents $27.50	1000 1939 & Earlier Wheat Cents $59.00
100 Mixed World Coins (at least 20% Silver) $19.95	100 USA 1943 Steel Cents $6.50	2500 Mixed USA Wheat Cents $59.00	5000 Wheat Cents, Mixed $109.00

We accept American Express, Discover, Visa and MasterCard.
Postage: Orders under $25.00 add $2.50; $25.00 and over add $4.00.
Foreign orders will be charged additional postage.

SEQUOIA NUMISMATICS

Bill Clark
P.O. Box 338
Clementon, NJ 08021

Store Address:
Store 305, Berlin Market Shopping Center
Berlin, NJ 08009

Life Member

PCGS Authorize Dealer

Member: International Society of Appraisers

Foreign Exchange Table

The foreign exchange fixed rates below apply to trade with banks in the country of origin. Courtesy of Texas Foreign Exchange Inc., Houston, Texas as of May 3, 1989. The three letter codes are used in international transactions.

Country	Code	US $	#/$
Abu Dhabi uses U.A.E. Dirham			
Afghanistan (Afghani)	AFA	0.017	58.8
Ajman uses U.A.E. Dirham			
Albania (Lek)	ALL	0.1678	6
Alderney (Pound)	ALP	1.6851	0.6
Algeria (Dinar)	DZD	0.1431	4.8
Andorra uses French Franc and Spanish Peseta			
Angola (Kwanza)	AOK	0.0338	29.6
Antigua uses E.C.T. Dollar			
Argentina (Austral)	ARA	0.0116	86.2
Aruba (Florin)		0.5618	1.8
Australia (Dollar)	ALD	0.7964	1.3
Austria (Schilling)	ATS	0.0752	13.3
Azores uses Portuguese Escudo			
Bahamas (Dollar)	BSD	1.00	1
Bahrain Is. (Dinar)	BHD	2.6511	0.38
Bangladesh (Taka)	BDT	0.032	31.3
Barbados (Dollar)	BBD	0.5	2
Belgium (Franc)	BEF	0.0252	39.7
Belize (Dollar)	BZD	0.50	2
Benin (Franc)	XOF	0.0031	322.6
Bermuda (Dollar)	BMD	1.00	1
Bhutan (Ngultrum)	BTN	0.0628	15.9
Bolivia (Boliviano)	BOP	0.3906	2.6
Botswana (Pula)	BWP	0.4896	2
Brazil (Cruzado)	BRC	0.9737	1
British Virgin Islands uses U.S.A Dollar			
Brunei Daressalam (Dollar)	BND	0.5139	1.9
Bulgaria (Lev)	BGL	1.1716	0.9
Burkina Faso (Franc)	XOF	0.0031	322.6
Burma (Kyat)	BUK	0.149	6.7
Burundi (Franc)	BIF	0.0064	156.3
Cambodia (Riel)	CMR	0.01	100
Cameroon (Franc)	XAF	0.0031	322.6
Canada (Dollar)	CAD	0.8457	1.2
Cape Verde (Escudo)	CVE	0.0131	76.3
Cayman Is. (Dollar)	KYD	1.2005	0.8
Central African Rep. (Franc)	XAF	0.0031	322.6
Chad (Franc)	XAF	0.0031	322.6
Chile (Peso)	CLP	0.004	250
China, P.R. (R. Yuan)	CNY	0.2693	3.7
Colombia (Peso)	COP	0.0028	357.1
Comoros (Franc)	KMF	0.0031	322.6
Congo P.R. (Franc)	XAF	0.0031	322.6
Cook Islands (Dollar)	CID	0.6195	1.6
Costa Rica (Colon)	CRC	0.0124	80.6
Cuba (Peso)	CUP	1.3139	0.8
Cyprus (Pound)	CYP	2.034	0.5
Czech. (Koruna)	CSK	0.1018	9.8
Denmark (Krone)	DKK	0.1361	7.3
Djibouti (Franc)	DJF	0.0056	178.6
Dominica uses E.C.T. Dollar			
Dom. Rep. (Peso)	DOP	0.1577	6.3
Dubai uses U.A.E. Dirham			
East Caribbean Terr. (Dollar)	XCD	0.3704	2.7
Ecuador (Sucre)	ECS		
Floating		0.0021	476.2
Official		0.01489	67.2
Egypt (Pound)	EGP	0.3984	2.5
El Salvador (Colon)	SVC	0.2	5
Equatorial Guinea (Franc)	XAF	0.0031	322.6
Ethiopia (Birr)	ETB	0.4864	2.1
Faeroe Islands (Krone)		0.1361	7.3
Falkland Is. (Pound)	FKP	1.6851	0.6
Fiji Islands (Dollar)	FJD	0.69	1.4
Finland (Markka)	FIM	0.2372	4.2
France (Franc)	FRF	0.1568	6.4
French Polynesia (Franc)	XPF	0.0086	133.8
Fujairah uses U.A.E. Dirham			
Gabon (Franc)	XAF	0.0031	322.6
Gambia (Dalasi)	GMD	0.1576	6.3
Germany, W. (Mark)	DEM	0.5295	1.9
Germany, E. (Mark)	DDM	0.5295	1.9
Ghana (New Cedi)	GHC	0.0038	263.2
Gibraltar (Pound)	GIP	1.6851	0.6
Great Britain (Pound)	GBP	1.6851	0.6
Greece (Drachma)	GRD	0.0062	142.9
Greenland uses Danish Krone			
Guadeloupe uses French Franc			
Guatemala (Quetzal)	GTQ	0.3676	2.7
Guernsey (Pound)		1.6851	0.6
Guinea (Franc)		0.0033	303
Guinea-Bissau (Peso)	GWP	0.0015	666.7
Guyana (Dollar)	GYD	0.0303	33
Haiti (Gourde)	HTG	0.20	5
Honduras (Lempira)	HNL	0.50	2
Hong Kong (Dollar)	HKD	0.1285	7.8
Hungary (Forint)	HUF	0.0165	60.6
Iceland (New Krona)	ISK	0.0188	53.2
India (Rupee)	INR	0.0629	15.9
Indonesia (Rupiah)	IDR	0.0057	1754.4
Iran (Rial)	IRR	0.0139	71.9
Iraq (Dinar)	IOD	3.2249	0.3
Ireland Rep. (Punt)	IEP	1.4148	0.7
Ireland, N. (Pound)		1.6851	0.6
Isle of Man (Pound)		1.6851	0.6
Israel (Shekel-new)	ILS	0.5618	1.8
Italy (Lira)	ITL	0.00072	1388.9
Ivory Coast (Franc)	XOF	0.0031	322.6
Jamaica (Dollar)	JMD	0.1845	5.461
Japan (Yen)	JPY	0.0075	133.3
Jersey (Pound)		1.6851	0.6
Jordan (Dinar)	JOD	1.6667	0.6
Keeling Cocos uses Australian Dollar			
Kenya (Shilling)	KES	0.0514	19.5
Kirabati uses Australian Dollar			
Korea-North (Won)	KPW	1.0316	1
Korea-South (Won)	KRW	0.0015	887.9
Kuwait (Dinar)	KWD	3.4376	0.3
Laos (Kip)	LAK	0.0023	434.8
Lebanon (Pound)	LBP	0.0022	454.5
Lesotho (Maloti)	LSM	0.3899	2.6
Liberia (Dollar)	LRD	1.00	1
Libya (Dinar)	LYD	3.5051	0.3
Liechtenstein uses Swiss Franc			
Luxembourg (Franc)	LUF	0.0252	39.7
Macao (Pataca)	MOP	0.1245	8
Malagasy (Franc)	MGF	0.00069	1449.3
Malawi (Kwacha)	MWK	0.3745	2.7
Malaysia (Dollar)	MYR	0.3712	2.7
Maldive Is. (Rufiyaa)	MVR	0.1149	8.7
Mali (Franc)	MLF	0.0031	322.6
Malta (Lira)	MTL	2.884	0.3
Marshall Islands	MIS	1.00	1
Martinique uses French Franc			
Mauritania (Ouguiya)	MRO	0.0133	75.2
Mauritius (Rupee)	MUR	0.0678	14.7
Mexico (Peso) Floating	MXP	0.00042	2381
Monaco uses French Franc			
Mongolia (Tughrik)	MNT	0.298	3.4
Montserrat uses E.C.T. Dollar			
Morocco (Dirham)	MAD	0.1195	8.4
Mozambique (Metica)	MZM	0.0014	714.3
Nauru uses Australian Dollar			
Nepal (Rupee)	NPR	0.0417	24
Netherlands (Gulden)	NLG	0.4696	2.1
Netherlands Antilles (Gulden)	ANG	0.5618	1.8
New Caledonia (Franc)	XPF	0.0086	116.3
New Zealand (Dollar)	NZD	0.6195	1.6
Nicaragua (Cordoba)	NIC	0.00014	7142.9
Niger (Franc)	XOF	0.0031	322.6
Nigeria (Naira)	NGN	0.1351	7.4
Norway (Krone)	NOK	0.146	6.8
Oman (Rial)	OMR	2.5967	0.4
Pakistan (Rupee)	PKR	0.0501	20
Palau uses U.S.A. Dollar			
Panama (Balboa)	PAB	1	1
Papua-New Guinea (Kina)	PGK	1.175	1
Paraguay (Guarani)	PYG	0.00099	1010.1
Peru (Inti)	PEI	0.00061	1639.3
Philippines (Peso)	PHP	0.0467	21.4
Poland (Zloty)	PLZ	0.0015	666.7
Portugal (Escudo)	PTE	0.0064	156.3
Puerto Rico uses U.S.A. Dollar			
Qatar (Riyal)	QAR	0.2746	3.6
Ras Al Khaima uses U.A.E.Dirham			
Reunion uses French Franc			
Romania (Leu)	ROL	0.1143	8.7
Rwanda (Franc)	RWF	0.0126	79.4
St. Helena (Pound)		1.6851	0.6
St. Kitts uses E.C.T. Dollar			
St. Lucia uses E.C.T. Dollar			
St. Pierre & Miquelon uses French Franc			
St. Thomas & Prince (Dobra)	STD	0.0098	102
St. Vincent uses E.C.T. Dollar			
San Marino uses Italian Lira			
Saudi Arabia (Riyal)	SAR	0.2667	3.7
Scotland (Pound)		1.6851	0.6
Senegal (Franc)	XOF	0.0031	322.6
Seychelles (Rupee)	SCR	0.1825	5.5
Sierra Leone (Leone)	SLL	0.0159	62.9
Singapore (Dollar)	SGD	0.5128	2
Solomon Is. (Dollar)	SBD	0.4508	2.2
Somalia (Somali)	SOS	0.0042	238.1
South Africa (Rand)	ZAR	0.3899	2.6
Spain (Peseta)	ESP	0.0085	117.6
Spanish West Africa uses Spanish Peseta			
Sri Lanka (Rupee)	LKR	0.0296	33.8
Sudan (Pound)	SDP	0.2222	4.5
Surinam (Gulden)	SRG	0.5618	1.8
Swaziland (Lilangeni)	SZL	0.3899	2.6
Sweden (Krona)	SEK	0.156	6.4
Switzerland (Franc)	CHF	0.5949	1.7
Syria (Pound)	SYP	0.0478	20.9
Tahiti (Franc)	XPF	0.0086	116.3
Taiwan (Dollar)	TWD	0.0389	25.7
Tanzania (Shilling)	TZS	0.0073	137
Thailand (Baht)	THB	0.0396	25.3
Togo (Franc)	XOF	0.0031	322.6
Tonga (Pa'anga)	TOP	0.7951	1.3
Trinidad & Tobago (Dollar)	TTD	0.2353	4.2
Tristan Da Cunha uses Great Britain Pound			
Tunisia (Dinar)	TND	1.0578	0.9
Turkey (Lira)	TRL	0.00049	2040.8
Turks & Caicos uses U.S.A. Dollar			
Tuvalu uses Australian Dollar			
Uganda (New Shilling)	UGS	0.005	200
Umm Al Qawain uses U.A.E. Dirham			
U.S.S.R. (Ruble)	SUR	1.5815	0.6
United Arab Emirates (Dirham)	AED	0.2723	3.7
Uruguay (New Peso)	UYP	0.0019	526.3
Vanuatu (Vatu)	VUV	0.0095	105.3
Vatican City uses Italian Lira			
Venezuela (Bolivar)	VEB		
Floating		0.027	37
Official		0.1333	7.5
Vietnam (Dong)	VND	0.00022	4545.5
Western Samoa (Tala)	WST	0.4541	2.2
Yemen Arab Rep. (Rial)	YER	0.1053	9.5
Yemen, P.D.R. (Dinar)	YDD	2.9155	0.3
Yugoslavia (Dinar)	YUD	0.0001	10000
Zaire (Zaire)	ZRZ	0.0028	357.1
Zambia (Kwacha)	ZMK	0.0988	10.1
Zimbabwe (Dollar)	ZWD	0.4926	2

One of America's Most Active Dealers in World Coins

David L. Cannon is actively buying all choice and rare coins of the world.

We urgently need the following for our large & ever growing list of clients.

Single rarities from any country.

Entire specialized and general collections.

Entire dealer's stocks.

Bulk Lots — quantities of single coins.
All Modern Gold — Proof.
Bank Note Deals — quantities of high value notes.

AUSTRALIA
All rare Gold
All BU 1910-1935
All keys — ½P 1922, 1P 1930, 3P 1922/1, FL 1934-35, and 1938 Crowns.
All pre-decimal Proofs 1955-1963.
All decimal Mint sets 1966-1974.
All decimal Proof sets 1966-1974, 1985.

AUSTRIA
All coins cataloging $50 or more.
Complete 2 Shilling sets.
2 Groschen 1967 Proof (and sets).
25 Sch & 50 Sch 1955-1964 Proof.
1964 Proof sets.

BAHAMAS
1966-1986 Proof and Mint sets. $10 "Ships" & "Flowers"

BELGIUM
All rare dates VF-BU.

CANADA
$5 and $10 Gold 1912-1914.
5¢ 1916-C.
Key dates all grades.
1858-1935 Choice and Gem BU.
$1 1935-1949 VF Gem BU.
$1 1961-66 Gem BU Business Strikes
All cased Dollars — Double Dollar sets — Proof sets.
Rolls and bags quantities.
Olympic sets.

CAYMAN ISLANDS
$25 and Proof sets.

CHINA
All rare coins.

CRETE
All in BU.

DANISH WEST INDIES
1 Skilling 1740.
2 Skilling 1740.
All BU and Proof.

DENMARK
Any Choice and/or rare.

EGYPT
Any coin cataloging $50 or more.

FALKLAND ISLANDS
25£ 1985 Proof.

FINLAND
Any coin cataloging $50 or more.

FRANCE
Louis XIII Coinage.
Crowns 1792-1878.
Coppers pre-1898 Full and BU.
Silver pre-1898 Mint State.
Rare dates all grades.
French Mint sets 1964-1986, quantities required.

GERMAN NEW GUINEA
1 Pfg thru 20 Mark Gold all grades.

GERMANY
All rare dates and types.
5 Mk 1952-U Museum thru 1964-J Fichte EF, BU, Proof.

GERMAN STATES
All early Thalers.
Thalers 1800-1871 VF-Unc.
2-3-5 Mk Fine-Gem BU.

GREAT BRITAIN
Pre-1910 Silver Choice to Gem BU.
All rare dates and types.
£ 1 Pieforts.
Gem Gold — Trade $1's — Maundy Sets.

GREECE
All coinage 1828-1855.

HAWAII
All coinage.

HONG KONG
All rare dates.
Pre-1911 Silver Mint State.

IRELAND
Hammered coinage.
1 Penny 1940 Full Red BU.
Florin and ½ Crown 1943.

ITALY
Any coin that books $20.00 or more.
Rare dates and top grades.

JAPAN
All Silver coins 1870-1914 in all grades.
Any better dates.
All Gold coins any grade.
1000 Yen 1964 Olympic.
Mint Sets 1969-1972 (clean holders only).

KEELING-COCOS ISLANDS
All 1913-1977 coinage wanted.

KOREA
All coins cataloging $20 or more.
Proof Sets 1970 Silver & Gold.

LUXEMBOURG
20-50-100 Fr 1946 Sets.
100 Frs 1963, 1964.
250 Frs 1963.

MEXICO
Rare dates, all denominations, all grades.
Top grades.
Bulk lots.

MONACO
All 16th Century coinage.

NETHERLANDS
All scarce and high grade.
All pre-1900 Gold.

NEW ZEALAND
1935 Waitangi Crowns and Proof Sets

NORWAY
All better coins 1874 to date.
Strong prices.

PANAMA
5¢ 1916.
Pre-1947 Silver Choice Gem BU.
1904 Proof Sets.
Proof Sets 1966-1986.
20 Balboas BU and Proof.

PHILIPPINES
All Spanish Colonial 1865-1897.
Choice Proof Sets 1905-1906-1908.
Peso 1906-S any grades.
All key dates and Gem BU's.

PORTUGAL
All Mint State pre-1898.

PUERTO RICO
All 5¢ - 10¢ - 20¢ - 40¢ - Peso all grades.

ROMANIA
Mint State Silver pre-1900.

SOUTH AFRICA
Rare dates.

SPAIN
All better coins.

SWEDEN
Any key dates or choice grades.

SWITZERLAND
Any coin that catalogs $20 or more.
All Gold 10 Frs - 20 Frs - 100 Frs.

THAILAND
All coins that catalog $100 or more.

UNITED STATES
All Gold.
Any coin that books $50 or more.
Rarities in the $1000 to $100,000 class.
Large lots.

VATICAN CITY
All coins 1943-1946.
5¢ & 10¢ 1938.
All Mint Sets 1929-1946, 1959, 1963.
All Gold 100 Lires 1929-1959.

VENEZUELA
All pre-1935 Silver in BU.

ZANZIBAR
Crowns and 1908 10¢ & 20¢.

SELLING
Send for our current price list featuring coins from $5 to $5000 from our constantly changing inventory.

AUCTIONS
We hold five to ten mail bid sales a year.
Always looking for better consignments.

DAVID L. CANNON
Telephone 513-931-7254 (11-8 EST)
Fax 513-931-0519

Box 31129   Cincinnati, OH 45231

COUNTRY INDEX

A

Aargau	1572
Abyssinia	531
Aden-Protectorate States	1830
Afghanistan	65
Aguascalientes	1281
Ahom Kingdom	853
Ahualulco	1279
Ajman	1716
Akita	1127
Albania	88
Algeria	92, 94
Algiers	92
Alwar	868
Ameca	1279
Amecameca	1286
Amescua	1279
Ancona	1784
Anconna	1784
Andorra	96
Angola	98
Anguilla	101
Anhalt-Bernburg	588
Anhalt-Cothen	589
Anhalt-Dessau	590
Anhui	300, 318
Anhwei	300, 318
Anjouan Sultanate	424
Annam	1810
Antigua & Barbuda	102
Antwerp	577
Anvers	577
Appenzell	1573
Arenys de Mar	1540
Argau	1572
Argentina	103
Argovie	1572
Armavir	1708
Aruba	112
Ascension Island	1468
Assam	853
Asturias and Leon	1540
Atencinco	1279
Atlixtac	1284
Atotonilco	1279
Auersberg	150
Auersperg	150
Augsburg	591
Aurangabad	911
Ausser Rhoden	1573
Australia	113
Austria	123
Austrian States	150
Awadh	869
Azerbaijan S.S.R.	1709
Azores	152

B

Baden	591
Baden-Durlach	591
Bahamas	155
Bahawalpur	873
Bahrain	163
Balearic Islands	1537
Baltic Regions	164
Bamberg	599
Banaras	966
Bangladesh	167
Banswara	875
Barbados	168
Barcelona	1537
Barinas	1804
Barmawal	952
Baroda	875
Basel	1574
Basilea	1574
Batavian Republic	1000, 1329, 1340
Bavaria	599
Bela	881
Belgen	169
Belges	169
Belgian Congo	1846
Belgie	169
Belgique	169
Belgium	169
Belize	181, 183
Bengal Presidency	966
Benin	188
Berg	612
Bermuda	189
Bern	1574
Beylah	881
Bharatpur	881
Bhaunagar	883
Bhinda	944
Bhopal	883
Bhopal Feudatory	885
Bhutan	193
Biafra	1357
Biberach	612
Bikanir	885
Bindraban	887
Birkenfeld	613
Bohemia-Moravia	463
Bolivia	196
Bombay Presidency	969
Botswana	206
Brandenburg-Ansbach-Bayreuth	613
Brazil	208
Bremen	613
British East Caribbean Territories	488
British East India Co.	1467
British Guiana	811
British Guiana and West Indies	811
British Honduras	181
British India Government	1195
British North Borneo	1198
British Virgin Islands	228
British West Africa	234
British West Indies	237
Brunei	237
Brunswick-Luneburg-Calenberg-Hannover	614
Brunswick-Wolfenbuttel	616
Buenos Aires	104
Bukhara	1711
Bulgaria	239
Bundi	887
Burma	248
Burundi	251

C

Cabo Blanco	1810
Cacahuatepec	1284
Cacalotepec	1284
Calcutta	967
Cambay	889
Cambodia	1138
Cameroon	252
Campeche	1279
Campo Morado	1284
Canada	254
Cannanore	890
Cape Verde	271
Caracas	1804
Cartagena	407
Catalonia	1538
Catorce	1279
Cattaro	1842
Cayenne	579
Cayman Islands	272
Cazalla de Sierra	1542
Ceara	215
Celaya	1279
Central African Republic	279
Central African States	280
Central American Republic	281
Ceylon	1543
Chad	283
Chamba	890
Cheh-Kiang	300
Chekiang	300, 321
Chhota Udaipur	890
Chiconcuautla	1289
Chihli	300, 323
Chihuahua	1231, 1281
Chilchota	1279
Chile	284
Chiloe	286, 289
Chilpancingo	1285
China	298
China-Foreign Enclaves	405
China-Japanese Puppet States	388
China-People's Republic	390
Chinese Soviet Republic	300, 390
Ching-Kiang	300, 326
Chingkiang	300, 326, 351
Chitung	300
Cis-Sutlej States	891
Cisalpine Republic	1073
Colima	1279
Colombia	405
Colony of Cayenne	579
Commonwealth of Australia	114
Comoros	424
Concepcion	289
Confederacion Argentina	104
Confoederatio Helvetica	1587
Congo Democratic Republic	1784
Congo People's Republic	425
Congress Kingdom of Poland	1426
Cooch Behar	854
Cook Islands	426
Copiapo	297
Cordoba	105
Costa Rica	430
Cotija	1280
Crab Island	1455
Crete	784
Croatia	1843
Cuba	440
Cuiaba	212
Culion Leper Colony	1424
Cundinamarca	407
Curacao	1340
Cyprus	450
Czechoslovak Socialist Republic	455
CCCP (U.S.S.R.)	1699

D

Dagestan	1709
Daghestan A.S.S.R.	1709
Dahomey	188
Dai Nam	1810
Daman	961
Damao	961
Danish Royal Colony	959
Danish West Indies	464
Danzig	1440
Darfur	1553
Datia	893
Denmark	466
Dera	865
Derajat	865
Dewas Junior Branch	894
Dewas Senior Branch	894
Dhar	894
Dholpur	895
Distrito Federal	1286
Diu	961
Djibouti	476, 478
Dominica	478
Dominican Republic	480
Dungarpur	895
Durango	1231, 1282

E

East Africa	485
East Africa & Uganda Protectorate	485
East Africa Protectorate	485
East Caribbean States	488
East Caribbean Territories	489
East Friesland	620
East Germany	739
East Hopei	388
East India Company	850, 858, 869, 933, 966, 976, 1004, 1195
East Prussia	1441
East Timor	1008
Ecuador	490
Egypt	495
El Arahal	1542
El Salvador	521
Elichpur	912
Emilia	1073
Emilia-Romagna	1073
Empire of Iturbide	1245
Empire of Maximilian	1261
Empire of Mexico	821
Entre Rios	106
Equatorial African States	280

Country	Page
Equatorial Guinea	527
Erfurt	621
Eritrea	535
Essequibo & Demerary	810
Estado de Mexico	1270, 1286
Estados Unidos de Colombia	412
Estados Unidos de Nueva Granada	412
Estonia S.S.R.	164
Ethiopia	531
Etruria	1087
Euzkadi	1541

F

Country	Page
Faeroe Islands	476
Falkland Islands	536
Farrukhabad	856, 967
Fengtien	300, 326
Fiji Islands	538
Filipinas	1413
Finland	542
Foo-Kien	300
Fort St. David	974
France	548
Frankfurt	621
Freiburg	1576
French Afars & Issas	477
French Cochin China	1813
French Colonies	577
French Equatorial Africa	578
French Guiana	579
French Indo-China	579
French Oceania	582
French Polynesia	582
French Somaliland	477
French West Africa	583
Freyburg	1576
Fribourg	1576
Friburg	1576
Friedberg	624
Fujairah	1717
Fujian	300, 328
Fukien	300, 328
Fukien-Chekiang-Kiangsi	391
Fun-tien	300
Fung-tien	300
Furstenberg	625
Furstenberg-Stuhlingen	625
Further Austria	625

G

Country	Page
Gabon	584
Galapagos Islands	495
Gambia, The	584
Gansu	300, 342
Garhwal	856
Gelderland	1000
Geneva	1577
Genoa	1073
Georgian S.S.R.	1709
German East Africa	1598
German New Guinea	1384
German States	587
Germany	716
Germany, East	739
Germany, West	728
Gerona	1539
Ghana	747
Ghurfah	1830
Gibraltar	749
Glarus	1578
Goa	961
Gold Coast	747
Gorizia	1074
Gorz	1074
Gran Colombia	1805
Granadine Confederation	412
Grand Duchy of Warsaw	1426
Graubunden	1578
Great Britain	751
Greece	777
Greenland	786
Grenada	786
Guadalajara	1232, 1286
Guadeloupe	787
Guanajuato	1233
Guangdong	300, 356
Guangxi	300, 355
Guatemala	789
Guayana	1805
Guernsey	802
Guerrero	1283
Guinea	805
Guinea-Bissau	808, 809

Country	Page
Guizhou	300, 359
Gurk	150
Gurkha Kingdom	856
Guyana	810, 811
Gwalior	895

H

Country	Page
Haidarabad	905
Haiti	813
Hakodate	1128
Hamburg	625
Hannover	628
Hansi	891
Harar	536
Hawaii	1776
Hebei	300, 323
Heilongjiang	300, 332
Heilungkiang	300, 332
Hejaz	1486
Hejaz & Nejd	1488
Helvetian Republic	1587
Henan	300, 332
Hesse-Cassel	635
Hesse-Darmstadt	638
Hesse-Homburg	643
Hessen-Kassel	635
Hill Tipperah	957
Hispaniola	813
Hohenlohe	644
Hohenlohe-Kirchberg	644
Hohenlohe-Neuenstein-Oehringen	644
Hohenzollern Under Prussia	646
Hohenzollern-Hechingen	644
Hohenzollern-Sigmaringen	645
Holland	1000
Honan	300, 332
Honduras	821
Hong Kong	405, 826
Hopeh	300
Hopei	300, 322
Hosokura	1128
House of Savoy	1092
Hsiang-O-Hsi Soviet	391
Hsinkiang	362
Hu Poo	300
Hu Pu	300
Huatla	1239
Hubei	300, 339
Hunan	300, 335
Hunan Soviet	391
Hungary	830
Hupeh	300, 339
Hupeh-Honan-Anhwei Soviet	391
Hupei	300
Hyderabad	905
Hyderabad Feudatories	911

I

Country	Page
Ibi	1541
Iceland	847
Ico	216
India Republic	990
India-British	966
India-Danish	959
India-French	960
India-Independent Kingdoms-British	856
India-Independent Kingdoms-Mughal	853
India-Portuguese	961
India, Mughal Empire	850
Indian Enclaves	959
Indian Princely States	867
Indonesia	1000, 1005
Indore	912
Ionian Islands	784
Iran	1009
Iraq	1030
Ireland	1036
Irian Barat	1008
Irian Jaya	1008
Irish Free State	1037
Isenburg	646
Isla de Providencia	1810
Isle de Bourbon	1457
Isle de France et Bonaparte	1227
Isle of Man	1039
Israel	1057
Italian Somaliland	1504
Italian States	1072
Italy	1092
Ivory Coast	1104

J

Country	Page
Jaipur	917

Country	Page
Jaipur Feudatory States	921
Jaisalmir	921
Jalisco	1286
Jamaica	1105
Janjira Island	922
Jaora	922
Japan	1115
Jaring	1605
Jering	1605
Jersey	1130
Jhabua	923
Jhalawar	923
Jiangsu	300, 349
Jiangxi	300, 347
Jilin	300, 352
Jind	891
Jodhpur	924
Jodhpur Feudatory States	928
Jordan	1135
Junagadh	928

K

Country	Page
Kachar	854
Kaga	1128
Kalat	929
Kalayani	912
Kallian	912
Kampuchea	1138, 1141
Kansu	300, 342
Karabagh	1709
Karauli	929
Kasadi of Mukalla	1830
Kashmir	930
Katanga	1849
Kedah	1192
Keeling-Cocos Islands	123
Kelantan	1192
Kelat	929
Kemasin	1192
Kenya	1142
Khanbayat	889
Khelat	929
Khetri	921
Khiva	1713
Khmer Republic	1141
Khoqand	1714
Khwarezm Soviet People's Republic	1714
Kiangnan	300, 343
Kiangsee	300, 347
Kiangsi	300, 347
Kiangsi-West Hupeh	391
Kiangsoo	300, 349
Kiangsu	300, 349
Kiau Chau	405
Kingdom of Abyssinia	531
Kingdom of Ethiopia	532
Kingdom of Holland	1003, 1329
Kingdom of Naples	1079
Kingdom of Napoleon	1074
Kingdom of Netherlands	1001, 1004, 1330
Kingdom of Sardinia	1092
Kingdom of Serbs, Croats and Slovenes	1833
Kiribati	1144
Kirin	300, 352
Kishangarh	932
Knyphausen	646
Kolhapur	933
Korea	1145
Korea, North	1156
Korea, South	1157
Kotah	933
Krakow	1441
Kuchawan	928
Kumaon	856
Kutch	934
Kuwait	1162
Kwangchowan	405
Kwangsea	300, 355
Kwangsi	300, 355
Kwangtung	300, 356
Kwantung	405
Kweichow	300, 359

L

Country	Page
L'Ametlla del Valles	1541
La Puebla de Cazalla	1542
La Rioja	106
Ladakh	941
Lagos	1280
Lahej	1830
Langkat	1605
Laos	1164
Las Bela	881

COUNTRY INDEX 14

Latvian S.S.R.	165
Lauenburg	646
Lazareto	1809
Lebanon	1166
Legeh	1605
Leiningen	647
Lerida	1539
Lesotho	1168
Liaoning	300, 326
Liberia	1172
Libya	1175, 1178
Liechtenstein	1180
Ligeh	1605
Ligor	1605
Ligurian Republic	1073
Lippe-Detmold	647
Lithuanian S.S.R.	166
Liu-Kiu	1129
Lombardy-Venetia	1075
Loo-Choo	1129
Lora del Rio	1542
Lowenstein-Wertheim	648
Lubeck	648
Luca	1078
Lucca	1078
Lucca and Piombino	1078
Lucensis	1078
Lucerne	1579
Lunavada	942
Luxembourg	1181
Luzern	1579

M

Macao	405, 1184
Madagascar	1187
Madeira	1188
Madras Presidency	971
Majorca	1537
Makrai	943
Malabar Coast	971
Malacca	1192
Malagasy Republic	1187
Malawi	1189
Malaya	1199
Malaya & British Borneo	1199
Malaysia	1191, 1200
Maldive Islands	1204
Maler Kotla	891
Mali	1207
Malolos	1418
Malta	1208
Malta, Order of	1213
Manchukuo	300, 389
Manchurian Provinces	300, 327, 360
Manipur	855
Maracaibo	1805
Maracaibo Lazareto Nacional	1809
Maranhao	215
Maratha Confederacy	857, 943
Marchena	1542
Marshall Islands	1221
Martinique	1222
Mato Grosso	212
Mauritania	1223
Mauritius	1224
Mauritius & Reunion	1220
Mecca	1485
Mecklenburg-Schwerin	649
Mecklenburg-Strelitz	651
Mendoza	107
Meng-Chiang	390
Mengchiang	301
Menorca	1541
Merida	1280
Mesopotamia	1030
Mewar	943
Mexico	1228
Mexico, Estado de	1286
Mimasaka	1128
Min-Che-Kan Soviet	391
Minas Gerais	213
Mombasa	1142
Monaco	1290
Mongolia	1293
Montenegro	1843
Montserrat	1296
Morelia	1234
Morelos	1287
Morioka	1128
Morocco	1296
Mozambique	1304
Mukalla	1830
Munster	652
Murshidabad	968
Muscat & Oman	1368
Mutawwakkilite	1823
Mysore	945

N

Nabha	892
Najibabad	865
Naples & Sicily	1079
Narayanpett	912
Narsinghgarh	885
Nassau	653
Nassau-Usingen	654
Nassau-Weilburg	654
Nassau-Weilburg & Nassau-Usingen	653
Navanagar	947
Navarre	1539
Nawanagar	947
Nejd	1487
Nepal	1309
Netherlands	1328
Netherlands Antilles	1339, 1341
Netherlands East Indies	1000
Netherlands New Guinea	1008
Neuchatel	1580
Nevis	1470
New Brunswick	269
New Caledonia	1344
New Guinea	1384
New Hebrides	1782
New South Wales	113
New Zealand	1345
Newfoundland	268
Nicaragua	1352
Nidwalden	1584
Niger	1356
Nigeria	1357
Niue	1358
Nor Peruano	1401
North China	301
North Korea	1156
North Peru	1401
North Vietnam	1814
Northwest Anhwei	393
Norway	1359
Nova Scotia	270
Nueva Galicia	1237
Nueva Granada	408
Nueva Viscaya	1233
Nulles	1541
Nurnberg	657

O

Oaxaca	1233, 1238, 1287
Ober-Greiz	670
Ober-Hessen	638
Obwalden	1584
Okinawa	1129
Oldenburg	657
Olmutz	150
Olot	1542
Oman	1368, 1370
Orchha	948
Order of Malta	1213
Osnabruck	659
Oudh	869
Overyssel	1001

P

P'ing Chiang County Soviet	391
Pahang	1193
Pakistan	1371
Palestine	1057
Palma Nova	1091
Palo Seco	1383
Panama	1375
Panay	1417
Papua New Guinea	1384
Para	215
Paraguay	1387
Parma	1085
Partabgarh	948
Patani	1192, 1605
Patiala	892
Pattani	1192, 1605
Pazcuaro	1280
Pei Yang	300, 360
Penang	1193
People's Republic of China	301, 393
Perak	1194
Perlis	1194
Peru	1395
Peru-North	1401
Peru-South	1401
Pfalz	659
Philippines	1413
Piedmont Republic	1086
Piratini	215
Poland	1426
Pomerania	659
Popayan	407
Portugal	1442
Portuguese Guinea	808
Posen	1441
Pratapgarh	948
Prince of Wales Island	1193
Prince Edward Island	270
Progreso	1280
Province of Cayenne	579
Province of Santander	423
Province of Trinidad	440
Provincias Del Rio de la Plata	103
Provisional Government of China	390
Prussia	659
Pudukkottai	859
Pudukota	859
Puebla	1239, 1289
Puerto Rico	1455
Pula Penang	1193
Pyrmont	670
PCФCP (R.S.F.S.R.)	1699

Q

Qatar	1456
Qatar & Dubai	1457
Quaiti State	1830
Quitupan	1280

R

Radhanpur	949
Ragusa	1842
Rampur	950
Ras Al Khaima	1718
Ratisbon	670
Ratlam	951
Real Del Catorce	1233
Reformed Government Republic of China	390
Regensburg	670
Reman	1606
Repubblica Genuensis	1073
Repubblica Ligure	1073
Repubblica Romana	1784
Republic of China	301, 403
Republic of Colombia	408
Republic of Nueva Granada	409
Republic of Piratini	215
Republic of Zaire	1849
Reunion	1457
Reuss	670
Reuss-Ebersdorf	672
Reuss-Greiz	670
Reuss-Lobenstein	672
Reuss-Lobenstein-Ebersdorf	672
Reuss-Schleiz	673
Rewa	951
Rhaman	1606
Rheinpfalz	659
Rhenish Confederation	674
Rhenish Palatinate	659
Rhodesia	1855
Rhodesia & Nyasaland	1854
Riau Archipelago	1007
Rochefort	648
Rohilkhand	859, 951
Roman Republic	1784
Romania	1458
Rostock	674
Ruanda-Urundi	1848
Russia	1686
Russian Caucasia	1708
Russian Socialist Federated Soviet Republic	1699
Russian Turkestan	1711
Rwanda	1464
Rwanda-Burundi	1465
Ryukyu Islands	1129

S

Saarland	739
Sai	1606
Saiburi	1606
Sailana	951
Sailana Feudatory States	952
Saint Eustatius	1339
Saint Martin	1340
Salta	107

Salumba ... 945
Salzburg ... 150
San Bernardo de Maypo ... 297
San Fernando de Bexar ... 1233
San Luis Potosi ... 1233
San Marino ... 1476
Santa Marta ... 407
Santa Tereza Leper Colony ... 227
Santander ... 423
Santander, Palencia & Burgos ... 1542
Santiago ... 289
Santiago del Estero ... 108
Santo Domingo ... 480
Sarawak ... 1197
Sardinia ... 1086
Saudi Arabia ... 1485, 1488
Saxe-Altenburg ... 675
Saxe-Coburg-Gotha ... 677
Saxe-Coburg-Saalfeld ... 676
Saxe-Hildburghausen ... 681
Saxe-Meiningen ... 681
Saxe-Weimar-Eisenach ... 685
Saxony ... 687
Schaffhausen ... 1582
Schamakhi ... 1710
Schaumburg-Hessen ... 698
Schaumburg-Lippe ... 698
Schleswig-Holstein ... 699
Schwarzburg-Rudolstadt ... 700
Schwarzburg-Sondershausen ... 702
Schwytz ... 1582
Schwyz ... 1582
Segarra de Gaia ... 1542
Seiyun & Tarim ... 1831
Selangor ... 1194
Sendai ... 1129
Senegal ... 1491
Serbia ... 1844
Serena ... 289
Seychelles ... 1492
Shaanxi ... 300, 362
Shahpur ... 945
Shandong ... 300, 361
Shanghai ... 352, 405
Shangtung ... 300
Shansi ... 300, 360
Shantung ... 300, 361
Shanxi ... 300, 360
Sharjah ... 1719
Sheki ... 1710
Shensi ... 300, 362
Shensi-North Soviet ... 392
Shorapur ... 912
Sichuan ... 300, 377
Sicily ... 1086
Sierra de Pinos ... 1233
Sierra Leone ... 1496
Sikh Empire ... 859
Sikh Feudatory States ... 865
Sikhs ... 952
Sikkim ... 865, 952
Silesia ... 702
Sinaloa ... 1289
Sind ... 866, 952
Sindhia ... 895
Singapore ... 1498
Sinkiang ... 300, 362
Sirmur ... 952
Sirmur Nahan ... 952
Sirohi ... 952
Sitamau ... 952
Slovakia ... 463
Socialist Ethiopia ... 534
Soleure ... 1582
Solodornensis ... 1582
Solomon Islands ... 1502
Solothurn ... 1582
Somalia ... 1504
Sombrerete ... 1233
South Africa ... 1508
South Arabia ... 1832
South Australia ... 114
South Korea ... 1157
South Peru ... 1401
South Vietnam ... 1814
Southern Rhodesia ... 1852
Spain ... 1520
Spain, Civil War ... 1540
Spain, Local ... 1537
Sri Lanka ... 1543, 1546
St. Bartholomew ... 1466
St. Christopher & Nevis ... 1470
St. Croix ... 1466
St. Gall ... 1581
St. Gallen ... 1581
St. Helena & Ascension ... 1467
St. Helena-Ascension ... 1468
St. Kitts ... 1469
St. Kitts & Nevis ... 1469
St. Lucia ... 1471
St. Pierre & Miquelon ... 1472
St. Thomas & Prince ... 1472
St. Vincent ... 1475
Stolberg-Rossla ... 703
Stolberg-Wernigerode ... 703
Straits Settlements ... 1194
Subalpine Republic ... 1086
Subsilvania ... 1584
Sud ... 1238
Sud Peruano ... 1401
Sudan ... 1541
Suitensis ... 1582
Sumatra ... 1004
Sungarei ... 300
Suriana ... 1285
Surinam ... 1553
Swaziland ... 1555
Sweden ... 1558
Swiss Cantons ... 1572
Switzerland ... 1587
Syria ... 1595
Szechuan ... 300, 377
Szechuan-Shensi Soviet ... 392

T

Tacambaro ... 1280
Taiwan ... 300, 382, 405
Tajima ... 1129
Tannu Tuva ... 1710
Tanzania ... 1598, 1600
Tarapaca ... 297
Taretan ... 1280
Tarim ... 1831
Tarragona ... 1539
Taxco ... 1285
Tegnapatam ... 974
Tellicherry ... 971
Teluban ... 1606
Tenancingo ... 1286
Terceira Island ... 152
Tessin ... 1584
Tetela del Oro y Ocampo ... 1289
Teutonic Order ... 703
Thailand ... 1602, 1606
Thicurinae ... 1586
Thurgau ... 1583
Thurgovie ... 1583
Thuricensis ... 1586
Tibet ... 1618
Ticino ... 1584
Ticurinae ... 1586
Tierra Caliente ... 1239
Timor ... 1008
Timur ... 1008
Tirol ... 152
Tlazasalca ... 1280
Togo ... 1623
Tokelau Islands ... 1624
Toluca ... 1286
Tonga ... 1625
Tonk ... 952
Tonkin ... 1814
Tortola ... 228
Tortosa ... 1540
Tosa ... 1129
Town of Le Cap ... 813
Tranquebar ... 959
Transpadane Republic ... 1073
Travancore ... 954
Trengganu ... 1194
Trinidad ... 1632
Trinidad & Tobago ... 1632
Tripoli ... 1175
Tripura ... 957
Tristan da Cunha ... 1637
Tsing-Kiang ... 300
Tucuman ... 108
Tugiensis ... 1586
Tugium ... 1586
Tung San ... 300
Tunis ... 1638
Tunisia ... 1638, 1643
Tunk ... 952
Turicensis ... 1586
Turkey ... 1649
Turks & Caicos Islands ... 1677
Tuscany ... 1087
Tuvalu ... 1682
Two Sicilies ... 1079
Tyrol ... 152

U

Uganda ... 1683
Uighuristan Republic ... 374
Umarda ... 944
Umm Al Qaiwain ... 1720
Union of Burma ... 251
Union of Soviet Socialist Republics ... 1686
United Arab Emirates ... 1716, 1721
United Provinces of Nueva Granada ... 408
United States of America ... 1722
Unterwalden ... 1584
Uranie ... 1584
Uri ... 1584
Uruguay ... 1777

V

Valdivia ... 287, 289
Valencia ... 1540
Valladolid Michoacan ... 1234
Valparaiso ... 289
Vanuatu ... 1782
Varanasi ... 966
Vatican City ... 1794
Vatican Papal City States ... 1784
Vatican Papal States ... 1785
Vaud ... 1585
Venezia ... 1091
Venezuela ... 1804
Venice ... 1091
Veracruz ... 1239
Vieque ... 1455
Vietnam ... 1814
Vietnam-Annam ... 1810
Vietnam-French Cochin China ... 1813
Vietnam-Tonkin ... 1814
Virneburg & Rochefort ... 648
Viscayan Republic ... 1541
Vorderoesterreich ... 625

W

Waadt ... 1585
Waldeck ... 703
Waldeck-Pyrmont ... 703
Wallmoden-Gimborn ... 705
Wan-Hsi-Pei Soviet ... 393
Wanparti ... 912
War of Independence ... 1231
West African States ... 1817
West Germany ... 728
West Irian ... 1008
Western Samoa ... 1818
Westphalia ... 705
Wismar ... 708
Wurttemberg ... 708
Wurzburg ... 715

X

Xalostotitlan ... 1280
Xinjiang ... 300, 362

Y

Yemen ... 1830
Yemen Arab Republic ... 1823
Yemen Democratic Republic ... 1832
Yonezawa ... 1129
Yugoslavia ... 1833
Yunnan ... 300, 383
Yunnan-Burma ... 388
Yunnan-Sichuan ... 300, 388
Yunnan-Szechuan ... 300, 388

Z

Zacatecas ... 1234
Zacatlan ... 1239
Zaire ... 1846
Zambia ... 1850
Zamora ... 1280
Zamosc ... 1441
Zanzibar ... 1599
Zapotlan ... 1281
Zara ... 1842
Zhejiang ... 300, 321
Zimbabwe ... 1852
Zongolica ... 1239
Zug ... 1586
Zuid Afrikaansche Republic ... 1508
Zurich ... 1586

Silver Bullion Chart

Oz.	5.000	5.500	6.000	6.500	7.000	7.500	8.000	8.500	9.000	9.500	10.000	10.500	11.000	11.500	12.000	12.500	Oz.
0.001	0.005	0.006	0.006	0.007	0.007	0.008	0.008	0.009	0.009	0.010	0.010	0.011	0.011	0.012	0.012	0.013	0.001
0.002	0.010	0.011	0.012	0.013	0.014	0.015	0.016	0.017	0.018	0.019	0.020	0.021	0.022	0.023	0.024	0.025	0.002
0.003	0.015	0.017	0.018	0.020	0.021	0.023	0.024	0.026	0.027	0.029	0.030	0.032	0.033	0.035	0.036	0.038	0.003
0.004	0.020	0.022	0.024	0.026	0.028	0.030	0.032	0.034	0.036	0.038	0.040	0.042	0.044	0.046	0.048	0.050	0.004
0.005	0.025	0.028	0.030	0.033	0.035	0.038	0.040	0.043	0.045	0.048	0.050	0.053	0.055	0.058	0.060	0.063	0.005
0.006	0.030	0.033	0.036	0.039	0.042	0.045	0.048	0.051	0.054	0.057	0.060	0.063	0.066	0.069	0.072	0.075	0.006
0.007	0.035	0.039	0.042	0.046	0.049	0.053	0.056	0.060	0.063	0.067	0.070	0.074	0.077	0.081	0.084	0.088	0.007
0.008	0.040	0.044	0.048	0.052	0.056	0.060	0.064	0.068	0.072	0.076	0.080	0.084	0.088	0.092	0.096	0.100	0.008
0.009	0.045	0.050	0.054	0.059	0.063	0.068	0.072	0.077	0.081	0.086	0.090	0.095	0.099	0.104	0.108	0.113	0.009
0.010	0.050	0.055	0.060	0.065	0.070	0.075	0.080	0.085	0.090	0.095	0.100	0.105	0.110	0.115	0.120	0.125	0.010
0.020	0.100	0.110	0.120	0.130	0.140	0.150	0.160	0.170	0.180	0.190	0.200	0.210	0.220	0.230	0.240	0.250	0.020
0.030	0.150	0.165	0.180	0.195	0.210	0.225	0.240	0.255	0.270	0.285	0.300	0.315	0.330	0.345	0.360	0.375	0.030
0.040	0.200	0.220	0.240	0.260	0.280	0.300	0.320	0.340	0.360	0.380	0.400	0.420	0.440	0.460	0.480	0.500	0.040
0.050	0.250	0.275	0.300	0.325	0.350	0.375	0.400	0.425	0.450	0.475	0.500	0.525	0.550	0.575	0.600	0.625	0.050
0.060	0.300	0.330	0.360	0.390	0.420	0.450	0.480	0.510	0.540	0.570	0.600	0.630	0.660	0.690	0.720	0.750	0.060
0.070	0.350	0.385	0.420	0.455	0.490	0.525	0.560	0.595	0.630	0.665	0.700	0.735	0.770	0.805	0.840	0.875	0.070
0.080	0.400	0.440	0.480	0.520	0.560	0.600	0.640	0.680	0.720	0.760	0.800	0.840	0.880	0.920	0.960	1.000	0.080
0.090	0.450	0.495	0.540	0.585	0.630	0.675	0.720	0.765	0.810	0.855	0.900	0.945	0.990	1.035	1.080	1.125	0.090
0.100	0.500	0.550	0.600	0.650	0.700	0.750	0.800	0.850	0.900	0.950	1.000	1.050	1.100	1.150	1.200	1.250	0.100
0.110	0.550	0.605	0.660	0.715	0.770	0.825	0.880	0.935	0.990	1.045	1.100	1.155	1.210	1.265	1.320	1.375	0.110
0.120	0.600	0.660	0.720	0.780	0.840	0.900	0.960	1.020	1.080	1.140	1.200	1.260	1.320	1.380	1.440	1.500	0.120
0.130	0.650	0.715	0.780	0.845	0.910	0.975	1.040	1.105	1.170	1.235	1.300	1.365	1.430	1.495	1.560	1.625	0.130
0.140	0.700	0.770	0.840	0.910	0.980	1.050	1.120	1.190	1.260	1.330	1.400	1.470	1.540	1.610	1.680	1.750	0.140
0.150	0.750	0.825	0.900	0.975	1.050	1.125	1.200	1.275	1.350	1.425	1.500	1.575	1.650	1.725	1.800	1.875	0.150
0.160	0.800	0.880	0.960	1.040	1.120	1.200	1.280	1.360	1.440	1.520	1.600	1.680	1.760	1.840	1.920	2.000	0.160
0.170	0.850	0.935	1.020	1.105	1.190	1.275	1.360	1.445	1.530	1.615	1.700	1.785	1.870	1.955	2.040	2.125	0.170
0.180	0.900	0.990	1.080	1.170	1.260	1.350	1.440	1.530	1.620	1.710	1.800	1.890	1.980	2.070	2.160	2.250	0.180
0.190	0.950	1.045	1.140	1.235	1.330	1.425	1.520	1.615	1.710	1.805	1.900	1.995	2.090	2.185	2.280	2.375	0.190
0.200	1.000	1.100	1.200	1.300	1.400	1.500	1.600	1.700	1.800	1.900	2.000	2.100	2.200	2.300	2.400	2.500	0.200
0.210	1.050	1.155	1.260	1.365	1.470	1.575	1.680	1.785	1.890	1.995	2.100	2.205	2.310	2.415	2.520	2.625	0.210
0.220	1.100	1.210	1.320	1.430	1.540	1.650	1.760	1.870	1.980	2.090	2.200	2.310	2.420	2.530	2.640	2.750	0.220
0.230	1.150	1.265	1.380	1.495	1.610	1.725	1.840	1.955	2.070	2.185	2.300	2.415	2.530	2.645	2.760	2.875	0.230
0.240	1.200	1.320	1.440	1.560	1.680	1.800	1.920	2.040	2.160	2.280	2.400	2.520	2.640	2.760	2.880	3.000	0.240
0.250	1.250	1.375	1.500	1.625	1.750	1.875	2.000	2.125	2.250	2.375	2.500	2.625	2.750	2.875	3.000	3.125	0.250
0.260	1.300	1.430	1.560	1.690	1.820	1.950	2.080	2.210	2.340	2.470	2.600	2.730	2.860	2.990	3.120	3.250	0.260
0.270	1.350	1.485	1.620	1.755	1.890	2.025	2.160	2.295	2.430	2.565	2.700	2.835	2.970	3.105	3.240	3.375	0.270
0.280	1.400	1.540	1.680	1.820	1.960	2.100	2.240	2.380	2.520	2.660	2.800	2.940	3.080	3.220	3.360	3.500	0.280
0.290	1.450	1.595	1.740	1.885	2.030	2.175	2.320	2.465	2.610	2.755	2.900	3.045	3.190	3.335	3.480	3.625	0.290
0.300	1.500	1.650	1.800	1.950	2.100	2.250	2.400	2.550	2.700	2.850	3.000	3.150	3.300	3.450	3.600	3.750	0.300
0.310	1.550	1.705	1.860	2.015	2.170	2.325	2.480	2.635	2.790	2.945	3.100	3.255	3.410	3.565	3.720	3.875	0.310
0.320	1.600	1.760	1.920	2.080	2.240	2.400	2.560	2.720	2.880	3.040	3.200	3.360	3.520	3.680	3.840	4.000	0.320
0.330	1.650	1.815	1.980	2.145	2.310	2.475	2.640	2.805	2.970	3.135	3.300	3.465	3.630	3.795	3.960	4.125	0.330
0.340	1.700	1.870	2.040	2.210	2.380	2.550	2.720	2.890	3.060	3.230	3.400	3.570	3.740	3.910	4.080	4.250	0.340
0.350	1.750	1.925	2.100	2.275	2.450	2.625	2.800	2.975	3.150	3.325	3.500	3.675	3.850	4.025	4.200	4.375	0.350
0.360	1.800	1.980	2.160	2.340	2.520	2.700	2.880	3.060	3.240	3.420	3.600	3.780	3.960	4.140	4.320	4.500	0.360
0.370	1.850	2.035	2.220	2.405	2.590	2.775	2.960	3.145	3.330	3.515	3.700	3.885	4.070	4.255	4.440	4.625	0.370
0.380	1.900	2.090	2.280	2.470	2.660	2.850	3.040	3.230	3.420	3.610	3.800	3.990	4.180	4.370	4.560	4.750	0.380
0.390	1.950	2.145	2.340	2.535	2.730	2.925	3.120	3.315	3.510	3.705	3.900	4.095	4.290	4.485	4.680	4.875	0.390
0.400	2.000	2.200	2.400	2.600	2.800	3.000	3.200	3.400	3.600	3.800	4.000	4.200	4.400	4.600	4.800	5.000	0.400
0.410	2.050	2.255	2.460	2.665	2.870	3.075	3.280	3.485	3.690	3.895	4.100	4.305	4.510	4.715	4.920	5.125	0.410
0.420	2.100	2.310	2.520	2.730	2.940	3.150	3.360	3.570	3.780	3.990	4.200	4.410	4.620	4.830	5.040	5.250	0.420
0.430	2.150	2.365	2.580	2.795	3.010	3.225	3.440	3.655	3.870	4.085	4.300	4.515	4.730	4.945	5.160	5.375	0.430
0.440	2.200	2.420	2.640	2.860	3.080	3.300	3.520	3.740	3.960	4.180	4.400	4.620	4.840	5.060	5.280	5.500	0.440
0.450	2.250	2.475	2.700	2.925	3.150	3.375	3.600	3.825	4.050	4.275	4.500	4.725	4.950	5.175	5.400	5.625	0.450
0.460	2.300	2.530	2.760	2.990	3.220	3.450	3.680	3.910	4.140	4.370	4.600	4.830	5.060	5.290	5.520	5.750	0.460
0.470	2.350	2.585	2.820	3.055	3.290	3.525	3.760	3.995	4.230	4.465	4.700	4.935	5.170	5.405	5.640	5.875	0.470
0.480	2.400	2.640	2.880	3.120	3.360	3.600	3.840	4.080	4.320	4.560	4.800	5.040	5.280	5.520	5.760	6.000	0.480
0.490	2.450	2.695	2.940	3.185	3.430	3.675	3.920	4.165	4.410	4.655	4.900	5.145	5.390	5.635	5.880	6.125	0.490
0.500	2.500	2.750	3.000	3.250	3.500	3.750	4.000	4.250	4.500	4.750	5.000	5.250	5.500	5.750	6.000	6.250	0.500
0.510	2.550	2.805	3.060	3.315	3.570	3.825	4.080	4.335	4.590	4.845	5.100	5.355	5.610	5.865	6.120	6.375	0.510
0.520	2.600	2.860	3.120	3.380	3.640	3.900	4.160	4.420	4.680	4.940	5.200	5.460	5.720	5.980	6.240	6.500	0.520
0.530	2.650	2.915	3.180	3.445	3.710	3.975	4.240	4.505	4.770	5.035	5.300	5.565	5.830	6.095	6.360	6.625	0.530
0.540	2.700	2.970	3.240	3.510	3.780	4.050	4.320	4.590	4.860	5.130	5.400	5.670	5.940	6.210	6.480	6.750	0.540
0.550	2.750	3.025	3.300	3.575	3.850	4.125	4.400	4.675	4.950	5.225	5.500	5.775	6.050	6.325	6.600	6.875	0.550
0.560	2.800	3.080	3.360	3.640	3.920	4.200	4.480	4.760	5.040	5.320	5.600	5.880	6.160	6.440	6.720	7.000	0.560
0.570	2.850	3.135	3.420	3.705	3.990	4.275	4.560	4.845	5.130	5.415	5.700	5.985	6.270	6.555	6.840	7.125	0.570
0.580	2.900	3.190	3.480	3.770	4.060	4.350	4.640	4.930	5.220	5.510	5.800	6.090	6.380	6.670	6.960	7.250	0.580
0.590	2.950	3.245	3.540	3.835	4.130	4.425	4.720	5.015	5.310	5.605	5.900	6.195	6.490	6.785	7.080	7.375	0.590
0.600	3.000	3.300	3.600	3.900	4.200	4.500	4.800	5.100	5.400	5.700	6.000	6.300	6.600	6.900	7.200	7.500	0.600
0.610	3.050	3.355	3.660	3.965	4.270	4.575	4.880	5.185	5.490	5.795	6.100	6.405	6.710	7.015	7.320	7.625	0.610
0.620	3.100	3.410	3.720	4.030	4.340	4.650	4.960	5.270	5.580	5.890	6.200	6.510	6.820	7.130	7.440	7.750	0.620
0.630	3.150	3.465	3.780	4.095	4.410	4.725	5.040	5.355	5.670	5.985	6.300	6.615	6.930	7.245	7.560	7.875	0.630
0.640	3.200	3.520	3.840	4.160	4.480	4.800	5.120	5.440	5.760	6.080	6.400	6.720	7.040	7.360	7.680	8.000	0.640
0.650	3.250	3.575	3.900	4.225	4.550	4.875	5.200	5.525	5.850	6.175	6.500	6.825	7.150	7.475	7.800	8.125	0.650
0.660	3.300	3.630	3.960	4.290	4.620	4.950	5.280	5.610	5.940	6.270	6.600	6.930	7.260	7.590	7.920	8.250	0.660
0.670	3.350	3.685	4.020	4.355	4.690	5.025	5.360	5.695	6.030	6.365	6.700	7.035	7.370	7.705	8.040	8.375	0.670
0.680	3.400	3.740	4.080	4.420	4.760	5.100	5.440	5.780	6.120	6.460	6.800	7.140	7.480	7.820	8.160	8.500	0.680
0.690	3.450	3.795	4.140	4.485	4.830	5.175	5.520	5.865	6.210	6.555	6.900	7.245	7.590	7.935	8.280	8.625	0.690
0.700	3.500	3.850	4.200	4.550	4.900	5.250	5.600	5.950	6.300	6.650	7.000	7.350	7.700	8.050	8.400	8.750	0.700
0.710	3.550	3.905	4.260	4.615	4.970	5.325	5.680	6.035	6.390	6.745	7.100	7.455	7.810	8.165	8.520	8.875	0.710
0.720	3.600	3.960	4.320	4.680	5.040	5.400	5.760	6.120	6.480	6.840	7.200	7.560	7.920	8.280	8.640	9.000	0.720
0.730	3.650	4.015	4.380	4.745	5.110	5.475	5.840	6.205	6.570	6.935	7.300	7.665	8.030	8.395	8.760	9.125	0.730
0.740	3.700	4.070	4.440	4.810	5.180	5.550	5.920	6.290	6.660	7.030	7.400	7.770	8.140	8.510	8.880	9.250	0.740
0.750	3.750	4.125	4.500	4.875	5.250	5.625	6.000	6.375	6.750	7.125	7.500	7.875	8.250	8.625	9.000	9.375	0.750
0.760	3.800	4.180	4.560	4.940	5.320	5.700	6.080	6.460	6.840	7.220	7.600	7.980	8.360	8.740	9.120	9.500	0.760
0.770	3.850	4.235	4.620	5.005	5.390	5.775	6.160	6.545	6.930	7.315	7.700	8.085	8.470	8.855	9.240	9.625	0.770
0.780	3.900	4.290	4.680	5.070	5.460	5.850	6.240	6.630	7.020	7.410	7.800	8.190	8.580	8.970	9.360	9.750	0.780
0.790	3.950	4.345	4.740	5.135	5.530	5.925	6.320	6.715	7.110	7.505	7.900	8.295	8.690	9.085	9.480	9.875	0.790
0.800	4.000	4.400	4.800	5.200	5.600	6.000	6.400	6.800	7.200	7.600	8.000	8.400	8.800	9.200	9.600	10.000	0.800
0.810	4.050	4.455	4.860	5.265	5.670	6.075	6.480	6.885	7.290	7.695	8.100	8.505	8.910	9.315	9.720	10.125	0.810
0.820	4.100	4.510	4.920	5.330	5.740	6.150	6.560	6.970	7.380	7.790	8.200	8.610	9.020	9.430	9.840	10.250	0.820
0.830	4.150	4.565	4.980	5.395	5.810	6.225	6.640	7.055	7.470	7.885	8.300	8.715	9.130	9.545	9.960	10.375	0.830
0.840	4.200	4.620	5.040	5.460	5.880	6.300	6.720	7.140	7.560	7.980	8.400	8.820	9.240	9.660	10.080	10.500	0.840
0.850	4.250	4.675	5.100	5.525	5.950	6.375	6.800	7.225	7.650	8.075	8.500	8.925	9.350	9.775	10.200	10.625	0.850
0.860	4.300	4.730	5.160	5.590	6.020	6.450	6.880	7.310	7.740	8.170	8.600	9.030	9.460	9.890	10.320	10.750	0.860
0.870	4.350	4.785	5.220	5.655	6.090	6.525	6.960	7.395	7.830	8.265	8.700	9.135	9.570	10.005	10.440	10.875	0.870
0.880	4.400	4.840	5.280	5.720	6.160	6.600	7.040	7.480	7.920	8.360	8.800	9.240	9.680	10.120	10.560	11.000	0.880
0.890	4.450	4.895	5.340	5.785	6.230	6.675	7.120	7.565	8.010	8.455	8.900	9.345	9.790	10.235	10.680	11.125	0.890
0.900	4.500	4.950	5.400	5.850	6.300	6.750	7.200	7.650	8.100	8.550	9.000	9.450	9.900	10.350	10.800	11.250	0.900
0.910	4.550	5.005	5.460	5.915	6.370	6.825	7.280	7.735	8.190	8.645	9.100	9.555	10.010	10.465	10.920	11.375	0.910
0.920	4.600	5.060	5.520	5.980	6.440	6.900	7.360	7.820	8.280	8.740	9.200	9.660	10.120	10.580	11.040	11.500	0.920
0.930	4.650	5.115	5.580	6.045	6.510	6.975	7.440	7.905	8.370	8.835	9.300	9.765	10.230	10.695	11.160	11.625	0.930
0.940	4.700	5.170	5.640	6.110	6.580	7.050	7.520	7.990	8.460	8.930	9.400	9.870	10.340	10.810	11.280	11.750	0.940
0.950	4.750	5.225	5.700	6.175	6.650	7.125	7.600	8.075	8.550	9.025	9.500	9.975	10.450	10.925	11.400	11.875	0.950
0.960	4.800	5.280	5.760	6.240	6.720	7.200	7.680	8.160	8.640	9.120	9.600	10.080	10.560	11.040	11.520	12.000	0.960
0.970	4.850	5.335	5.820	6.305	6.790	7.275	7.760	8.245	8.730	9.215	9.700	10.185	10.670	11.155	11.640	12.125	0.970
0.980	4.900	5.390	5.880	6.370	6.860	7.350	7.840	8.330	8.820	9.310	9.800	10.290	10.780	11.270	11.760	12.250	0.980
0.990	4.950	5.445	5.940	6.435	6.930	7.425	7.920	8.415	8.910	9.405	9.900	10.395	10.890	11.385	11.880	12.375	0.990
1.000	5.000	5.500	6.000	6.500	7.000	7.500	8.000	8.500	9.000	9.500	10.000	10.500	11.000	11.500	12.000	12.500	1.000

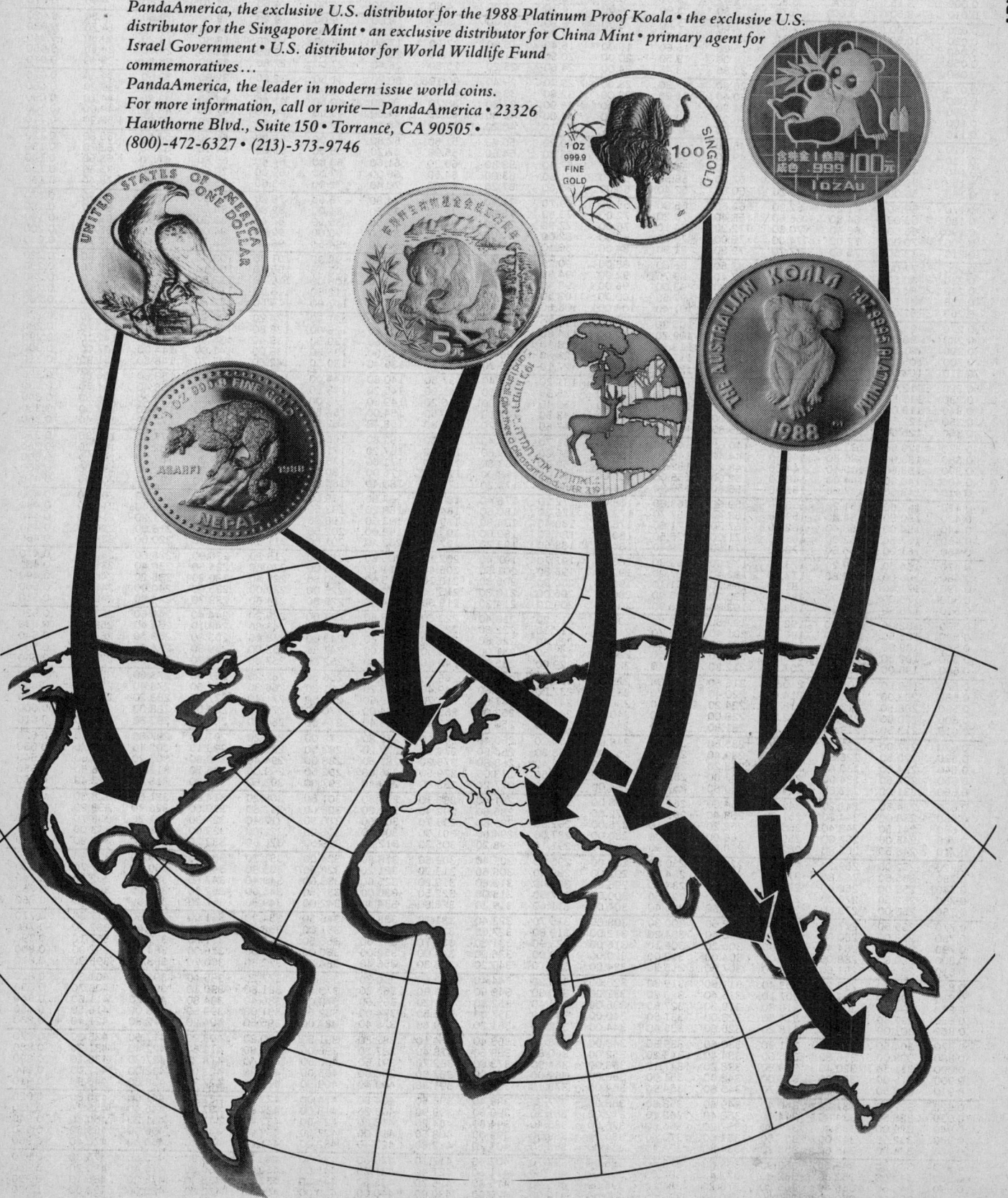

Gold and Platinum Bullion Chart

oz.	350.00	360.00	370.00	380.00	390.00	400.00	410.00	420.00	430.00	440.00	450.00	460.00	470.00	480.00	490.00	
0.001	0.35	0.36	0.37	0.38	0.39	0.40	0.41	0.42	0.43	0.44	0.45	0.46	0.47	0.48	0.49	0.001
0.002	0.70	0.72	0.74	0.76	0.78	0.80	0.82	0.84	0.86	0.88	0.90	0.92	0.94	0.96	0.98	0.002
0.003	1.05	1.08	1.11	1.14	1.17	1.20	1.23	1.26	1.29	1.32	1.35	1.38	1.41	1.44	1.47	0.003
0.004	1.40	1.44	1.48	1.52	1.56	1.60	1.64	1.68	1.72	1.76	1.80	1.84	1.88	1.92	1.96	0.004
0.005	1.75	1.80	1.85	1.90	1.95	2.00	2.05	2.10	2.15	2.20	2.25	2.30	2.35	2.40	2.45	0.005
0.006	2.10	2.16	2.22	2.28	2.34	2.40	2.46	2.52	2.58	2.64	2.70	2.76	2.82	2.88	2.94	0.006
0.007	2.45	2.52	2.59	2.66	2.73	2.80	2.87	2.94	3.01	3.08	3.15	3.22	3.29	3.36	3.43	0.007
0.008	2.80	2.88	2.96	3.04	3.12	3.20	3.28	3.36	3.44	3.52	3.60	3.68	3.76	3.84	3.92	0.008
0.009	3.15	3.24	3.33	3.42	3.51	3.60	3.69	3.78	3.87	3.96	4.05	4.14	4.23	4.32	4.41	0.009
0.010	3.50	3.60	3.70	3.80	3.90	4.00	4.10	4.20	4.30	4.40	4.50	4.60	4.70	4.80	4.90	0.010
0.020	7.00	7.20	7.40	7.60	7.80	8.00	8.20	8.40	8.60	8.80	9.00	9.20	9.40	9.60	9.80	0.020
0.030	10.50	10.80	11.10	11.40	11.70	12.00	12.30	12.60	12.90	13.20	13.50	13.80	14.10	14.40	14.70	0.030
0.040	14.00	14.40	14.80	15.20	15.60	16.00	16.40	16.80	17.20	17.60	18.00	18.40	18.80	19.20	19.60	0.040
0.050	17.50	18.00	18.50	19.00	19.50	20.00	20.50	21.00	21.50	22.00	22.50	23.00	23.50	24.00	24.50	0.050
0.060	21.00	21.60	22.20	22.80	23.40	24.00	24.60	25.20	25.80	26.40	27.00	27.60	28.20	28.80	29.40	0.060
0.070	24.50	25.20	25.90	26.60	27.30	28.00	28.70	29.40	30.10	30.80	31.50	32.20	32.90	33.60	34.30	0.070
0.080	28.00	28.80	29.60	30.40	31.20	32.00	32.80	33.60	34.40	35.20	36.00	36.80	37.60	38.40	39.20	0.080
0.090	31.50	32.40	33.30	34.20	35.10	36.00	36.90	37.80	38.70	39.60	40.50	41.40	42.30	43.20	44.10	0.090
0.100	35.00	36.00	37.00	38.00	39.00	40.00	41.00	42.00	43.00	44.00	45.00	46.00	47.00	48.00	49.00	0.100
0.110	38.50	39.60	40.70	41.80	42.90	44.00	45.10	46.20	47.30	48.40	49.50	50.60	51.70	52.80	53.90	0.110
0.120	42.00	43.20	44.40	45.60	46.80	48.00	49.20	50.40	51.60	52.80	54.00	55.20	56.40	57.60	58.80	0.120
0.130	45.50	46.80	48.10	49.40	50.70	52.00	53.30	54.60	55.90	57.20	58.50	59.80	61.10	62.40	63.70	0.130
0.140	49.00	50.40	51.80	53.20	54.60	56.00	57.40	58.80	60.20	61.60	63.00	64.40	65.80	67.20	68.60	0.140
0.150	52.50	54.00	55.50	57.00	58.50	60.00	61.50	63.00	64.50	66.00	67.50	69.00	70.50	72.00	73.50	0.150
0.160	56.00	57.60	59.20	60.80	62.40	64.00	65.60	67.20	68.80	70.40	72.00	73.60	75.20	76.80	78.40	0.160
0.170	59.50	61.20	62.90	64.60	66.30	68.00	69.70	71.40	73.10	74.80	76.50	78.20	79.90	81.60	83.30	0.170
0.180	63.00	64.80	66.60	68.40	70.20	72.00	73.80	75.60	77.40	79.20	81.00	82.80	84.60	86.40	88.20	0.180
0.190	66.50	68.40	70.30	72.20	74.10	76.00	77.90	79.80	81.70	83.60	85.50	87.40	89.30	91.20	93.10	0.190
0.200	70.00	72.00	74.00	76.00	78.00	80.00	82.00	84.00	86.00	88.00	90.00	92.00	94.00	96.00	98.00	0.200
0.210	73.50	75.60	77.70	79.80	81.90	84.00	86.10	88.20	90.30	92.40	94.50	96.60	98.70	100.80	102.90	0.210
0.220	77.00	79.20	81.40	83.60	85.80	88.00	90.20	92.40	94.60	96.80	99.00	101.20	103.40	105.60	107.80	0.220
0.230	80.50	82.80	85.10	87.40	89.70	92.00	94.30	96.60	98.90	101.20	103.50	105.80	108.10	110.40	112.70	0.230
0.240	84.00	86.40	88.80	91.20	93.60	96.00	98.40	100.80	103.20	105.60	108.00	110.40	112.80	115.20	117.60	0.240
0.250	87.50	90.00	92.50	95.00	97.50	100.00	102.50	105.00	107.50	110.00	112.50	115.00	117.50	120.00	122.50	0.250
0.260	91.00	93.60	96.20	98.80	101.40	104.00	106.60	109.20	111.80	114.40	117.00	119.60	122.20	124.80	127.40	0.260
0.270	94.50	97.20	99.90	102.60	105.30	108.00	110.70	113.40	116.10	118.80	121.50	124.20	126.90	129.60	132.30	0.270
0.280	98.00	100.80	103.60	106.40	109.20	112.00	114.80	117.60	120.40	123.20	126.00	128.80	131.60	134.40	137.20	0.280
0.290	101.50	104.40	107.30	110.20	113.10	116.00	118.90	121.80	124.70	127.60	130.50	133.40	136.30	139.20	142.10	0.290
0.300	105.00	108.00	111.00	114.00	117.00	120.00	123.00	126.00	129.00	132.00	135.00	138.00	141.00	144.00	147.00	0.300
0.310	108.50	111.60	114.70	117.80	120.90	124.00	127.10	130.20	133.30	136.40	139.50	142.60	145.70	148.80	151.90	0.310
0.320	112.00	115.20	118.40	121.60	124.80	128.00	131.20	134.40	137.60	140.80	144.00	147.20	150.40	153.60	156.80	0.320
0.330	115.50	118.80	122.10	125.40	128.70	132.00	135.30	138.60	141.90	145.20	148.50	151.80	155.10	158.40	161.70	0.330
0.340	119.00	122.40	125.80	129.20	132.60	136.00	139.40	142.80	146.20	149.60	153.00	156.40	159.80	163.20	166.60	0.340
0.350	122.50	126.00	129.50	133.00	136.50	140.00	143.50	147.00	150.50	154.00	157.50	161.00	164.50	168.00	171.50	0.350
0.360	126.00	129.60	133.20	136.80	140.40	144.00	147.60	151.20	154.80	158.40	162.00	165.60	169.20	172.80	176.40	0.360
0.370	129.50	133.20	136.90	140.60	144.30	148.00	151.70	155.40	159.10	162.80	166.50	170.20	173.90	177.60	181.30	0.370
0.380	133.00	136.80	140.60	144.40	148.20	152.00	155.80	159.60	163.40	167.20	171.00	174.80	178.60	182.40	186.20	0.380
0.390	136.50	140.40	144.30	148.20	152.10	156.00	159.90	163.80	167.70	171.60	175.50	179.40	183.30	187.20	191.10	0.390
0.400	140.00	144.00	148.00	152.00	156.00	160.00	164.00	168.00	172.00	176.00	180.00	184.00	188.00	192.00	196.00	0.400
0.410	143.50	147.60	151.70	155.80	159.90	164.00	168.10	172.20	176.30	180.40	184.50	188.60	192.70	196.80	200.90	0.410
0.420	147.00	151.20	155.40	159.60	163.80	168.00	172.20	176.40	180.60	184.80	189.00	193.20	197.40	201.60	205.80	0.420
0.430	150.50	154.80	159.10	163.40	167.70	172.00	176.30	180.60	184.90	189.20	193.50	197.80	202.10	206.40	210.70	0.430
0.440	154.00	158.40	162.80	167.20	171.60	176.00	180.40	184.80	189.20	193.60	198.00	202.40	206.80	211.20	215.60	0.440
0.450	157.50	162.00	166.50	171.00	175.50	180.00	184.50	189.00	193.50	198.00	202.50	207.00	211.50	216.00	220.50	0.450
0.460	161.00	165.60	170.20	174.80	179.40	184.00	188.60	193.20	197.80	202.40	207.00	211.60	216.20	220.80	225.40	0.460
0.470	164.50	169.20	173.90	178.60	183.30	188.00	192.70	197.40	202.10	206.80	211.50	216.20	220.90	225.60	230.30	0.470
0.480	168.00	172.80	177.60	182.40	187.20	192.00	196.80	201.60	206.40	211.20	216.00	220.80	225.60	230.40	235.20	0.480
0.490	171.50	176.40	181.30	186.20	191.10	196.00	200.90	205.80	210.70	215.60	220.50	225.40	230.30	235.20	240.10	0.490
0.500	175.00	180.00	185.00	190.00	195.00	200.00	205.00	210.00	215.00	220.00	225.00	230.00	235.00	240.00	245.00	0.500
0.510	178.50	183.60	188.70	193.80	198.90	204.00	209.10	214.20	219.30	224.40	229.50	234.60	239.70	244.80	249.90	0.510
0.520	182.00	187.20	192.40	197.60	202.80	208.00	213.20	218.40	223.60	228.80	234.00	239.20	244.40	249.60	254.80	0.520
0.530	185.50	190.80	196.10	201.40	206.70	212.00	217.30	222.60	227.90	233.20	238.50	243.80	249.10	254.40	259.70	0.530
0.540	189.00	194.40	199.80	205.20	210.60	216.00	221.40	226.80	232.20	237.60	243.00	248.40	253.80	259.20	264.60	0.540
0.550	192.50	198.00	203.50	209.00	214.50	220.00	225.50	231.00	236.50	242.00	247.50	253.00	258.50	264.00	269.50	0.550
0.560	196.00	201.60	207.20	212.80	218.40	224.00	229.60	235.20	240.80	246.40	252.00	257.60	263.20	268.80	274.40	0.560
0.570	199.50	205.20	210.90	216.60	222.30	228.00	233.70	239.40	245.10	250.80	256.50	262.20	267.90	273.60	279.30	0.570
0.580	203.00	208.80	214.60	220.40	226.20	232.00	237.80	243.60	249.40	255.20	261.00	266.80	272.60	278.40	284.20	0.580
0.590	206.50	212.40	218.30	224.20	230.10	236.00	241.90	247.80	253.70	259.60	265.50	271.40	277.30	283.20	289.10	0.590
0.600	210.00	216.00	222.00	228.00	234.00	240.00	246.00	252.00	258.00	264.00	270.00	276.00	282.00	288.00	294.00	0.600
0.610	213.50	219.60	225.70	231.80	237.90	244.00	250.10	256.20	262.30	268.40	274.50	280.60	286.70	292.80	298.90	0.610
0.620	217.00	223.20	229.40	235.60	241.80	248.00	254.20	260.40	266.60	272.80	279.00	285.20	291.40	297.60	303.80	0.620
0.630	220.50	226.80	233.10	239.40	245.70	252.00	258.30	264.60	270.90	277.20	283.50	289.80	296.10	302.40	308.70	0.630
0.640	224.00	230.40	236.80	243.20	249.60	256.00	262.40	268.80	275.20	281.60	288.00	294.40	300.80	307.20	313.60	0.640
0.650	227.50	234.00	240.50	247.00	253.50	260.00	266.50	273.00	279.50	286.00	292.50	299.00	305.50	312.00	318.50	0.650
0.660	231.00	237.60	244.20	250.80	257.40	264.00	270.60	277.20	283.80	290.40	297.00	303.60	310.20	316.80	323.40	0.660
0.670	234.50	241.20	247.90	254.60	261.30	268.00	274.70	281.40	288.10	294.80	301.50	308.20	314.90	321.60	328.30	0.670
0.680	238.00	244.80	251.60	258.40	265.20	272.00	278.80	285.60	292.40	299.20	306.00	312.80	319.60	326.40	333.20	0.680
0.690	241.50	248.40	255.30	262.20	269.10	276.00	282.90	289.80	296.70	303.60	310.50	317.40	324.30	331.20	338.10	0.690
0.700	245.00	252.00	259.00	266.00	273.00	280.00	287.00	294.00	301.00	308.00	315.00	322.00	329.00	336.00	343.00	0.700
0.710	248.50	255.60	262.70	269.80	276.90	284.00	291.10	298.20	305.30	312.40	319.50	326.60	333.70	340.80	347.90	0.710
0.720	252.00	259.20	266.40	273.60	280.80	288.00	295.20	302.40	309.60	316.80	324.00	331.20	338.40	345.60	352.80	0.720
0.730	255.50	262.80	270.10	277.40	284.70	292.00	299.30	306.60	313.90	321.20	328.50	335.80	343.10	350.40	357.70	0.730
0.740	259.00	266.40	273.80	281.20	288.60	296.00	303.40	310.80	318.20	325.60	333.00	340.40	347.80	355.20	362.60	0.740
0.750	262.50	270.00	277.50	285.00	292.50	300.00	307.50	315.00	322.50	330.00	337.50	345.00	352.50	360.00	367.50	0.750
0.760	266.00	273.60	281.20	288.80	296.40	304.00	311.60	319.20	326.80	334.40	342.00	349.60	357.20	364.80	372.40	0.760
0.770	269.50	277.20	284.90	292.60	300.30	308.00	315.70	323.40	331.10	338.80	346.50	354.20	361.90	369.60	377.30	0.770
0.780	273.00	280.80	288.60	296.40	304.20	312.00	319.80	327.60	335.40	343.20	351.00	358.80	366.60	374.40	382.20	0.780
0.790	276.50	284.40	292.30	300.20	308.10	316.00	323.90	331.80	339.70	347.60	355.50	363.40	371.30	379.20	387.10	0.790
0.800	280.00	288.00	296.00	304.00	312.00	320.00	328.00	336.00	344.00	352.00	360.00	368.00	376.00	384.00	392.00	0.800
0.810	283.50	291.60	299.70	307.80	315.90	324.00	332.10	340.20	348.30	356.40	364.50	372.60	380.70	388.80	396.90	0.810
0.820	287.00	295.20	303.40	311.60	319.80	328.00	336.20	344.40	352.60	360.80	369.00	377.20	385.40	393.60	401.80	0.820
0.830	290.50	298.80	307.10	315.40	323.70	332.00	340.30	348.60	356.90	365.20	373.50	381.80	390.10	398.40	406.70	0.830
0.840	294.00	302.40	310.80	319.20	327.60	336.00	344.40	352.80	361.20	369.60	378.00	386.40	394.80	403.20	411.60	0.840
0.850	297.50	306.00	314.50	323.00	331.50	340.00	348.50	357.00	365.50	374.00	382.50	391.00	399.50	408.00	416.50	0.850
0.860	301.00	309.60	318.20	326.80	335.40	344.00	352.60	361.20	369.80	378.40	387.00	395.60	404.20	412.80	421.40	0.860
0.870	304.50	313.20	321.90	330.60	339.30	348.00	356.70	365.40	374.10	382.80	391.50	400.20	408.90	417.60	426.30	0.870
0.880	308.00	316.80	325.60	334.40	343.20	352.00	360.80	369.60	378.40	387.20	396.00	404.80	413.60	422.40	431.20	0.880
0.890	311.50	320.40	329.30	338.20	347.10	356.00	364.90	373.80	382.70	391.60	400.50	409.40	418.30	427.20	436.10	0.890
0.900	315.00	324.00	333.00	342.00	351.00	360.00	369.00	378.00	387.00	396.00	405.00	414.00	423.00	432.00	441.00	0.900
0.910	318.50	327.60	336.70	345.80	354.90	364.00	373.10	382.20	391.30	400.40	409.50	418.60	427.70	436.80	445.90	0.910
0.920	322.00	331.20	340.40	349.60	358.80	368.00	377.20	386.40	395.60	404.80	414.00	423.20	432.40	441.60	450.80	0.920
0.930	325.50	334.80	344.10	353.40	362.70	372.00	381.30	390.60	399.90	409.20	418.50	427.80	437.10	446.40	455.70	0.930
0.940	329.00	338.40	347.80	357.20	366.60	376.00	385.40	394.80	404.20	413.60	423.00	432.40	441.80	451.20	460.60	0.940
0.950	332.50	342.00	351.50	361.00	370.50	380.00	389.50	399.00	408.50	418.00	427.50	437.00	446.50	456.00	465.50	0.950
0.960	336.00	345.60	355.20	364.80	374.40	384.00	393.60	403.20	412.80	422.40	432.00	441.60	451.20	460.80	470.40	0.960
0.970	339.50	349.20	358.90	368.60	378.30	388.00	397.70	407.40	417.10	426.80	436.50	446.20	455.90	465.60	475.30	0.970
0.980	343.00	352.80	362.60	372.40	382.20	392.00	401.80	411.60	421.40	431.20	441.00	450.80	460.60	470.40	480.20	0.980
0.990	346.50	356.40	366.30	376.20	386.10	396.00	405.90	415.80	425.70	435.60	445.50	455.40	465.30	475.20	485.10	0.990
1.000	350.00	360.00	370.00	380.00	390.00	400.00	410.00	420.00	430.00	440.00	450.00	460.00	470.00	480.00	490.00	1.000

CHRISTIE'S

International Auctioneers of Coins, Medals, Banknotes and Tokens

Christie, Manson &
Woods, Int'l.
502 Park Avenue
New York, NY
10002 U.S.A.
212/546-1056

Christie's
International Ltd.
8 King Street
St. James's, London
SW1Y 6QT ENGLAND
01/839-9060

Christie's
International S.A.
8 Place de la Taconnerie
1204 Geneva
SWITZERLAND
(4122) 28 25 44

Christie's
International S.A.
Palazzo Massimo Lancellotti
Piazza Navona 114, Rome 00186
ITALY
(396) 654-1217

Christie's
Amsterdam B.V.
Cornelis Schuytstraat 57
1071 JG Amsterdam
THE NETHERLANDS
(3120) 64 20 11

Gold and Platinum Bullion Chart

500.00	510.00	520.00	530.00	540.00	550.00	560.00	570.00	580.00	590.00	600.00	610.00	620.00	630.00	640.00	650.00	oz.
0.50	0.51	0.52	0.53	0.54	0.55	0.56	0.57	0.58	0.59	0.60	0.61	0.62	0.63	0.64	0.65	0.001
1.00	1.02	1.04	1.06	1.08	1.10	1.12	1.14	1.16	1.18	1.20	1.22	1.24	1.26	1.28	1.30	0.002
1.50	1.53	1.56	1.59	1.62	1.65	1.68	1.71	1.74	1.77	1.80	1.83	1.86	1.89	1.92	1.95	0.003
2.00	2.04	2.08	2.12	2.16	2.20	2.24	2.28	2.32	2.36	2.40	2.44	2.48	2.52	2.56	2.60	0.004
2.50	2.55	2.60	2.65	2.70	2.75	2.80	2.85	2.90	2.95	3.00	3.05	3.10	3.15	3.20	3.25	0.005
3.00	3.06	3.12	3.18	3.24	3.30	3.36	3.42	3.48	3.54	3.60	3.66	3.72	3.78	3.84	3.90	0.006
3.50	3.57	3.64	3.71	3.78	3.85	3.92	3.99	4.06	4.13	4.20	4.27	4.34	4.41	4.48	4.55	0.007
4.00	4.08	4.16	4.24	4.32	4.40	4.48	4.56	4.64	4.72	4.80	4.88	4.96	5.04	5.12	5.20	0.008
4.50	4.59	4.68	4.77	4.86	4.95	5.04	5.13	5.22	5.31	5.40	5.49	5.58	5.67	5.76	5.85	0.009
5.00	5.10	5.20	5.30	5.40	5.50	5.60	5.70	5.80	5.90	6.00	6.10	6.20	6.30	6.40	6.50	0.010
10.00	10.20	10.40	10.60	10.80	11.00	11.20	11.40	11.60	11.80	12.00	12.20	12.40	12.60	12.80	13.00	0.020
15.00	15.30	15.60	15.90	16.20	16.50	16.80	17.10	17.40	17.70	18.00	18.30	18.60	18.90	19.20	19.50	0.030
20.00	20.40	20.80	21.20	21.60	22.00	22.40	22.80	23.20	23.60	24.00	24.40	24.80	25.20	25.60	26.00	0.040
25.00	25.50	26.00	26.50	27.00	27.50	28.00	28.50	29.00	29.50	30.00	30.50	31.00	31.50	32.00	32.50	0.050
30.00	30.60	31.20	31.80	32.40	33.00	33.60	34.20	34.80	35.40	36.00	36.60	37.20	37.80	38.40	39.00	0.060
35.00	35.70	36.40	37.10	37.80	38.50	39.20	39.90	40.60	41.30	42.00	42.70	43.40	44.10	44.80	45.50	0.070
40.00	40.80	41.60	42.40	43.20	44.00	44.80	45.60	46.40	47.20	48.00	48.80	49.60	50.40	51.20	52.00	0.080
45.00	45.90	46.80	47.70	48.60	49.50	50.40	51.30	52.20	53.10	54.00	54.90	55.80	56.70	57.60	58.50	0.090
50.00	51.00	52.00	53.00	54.00	55.00	56.00	57.00	58.00	59.00	60.00	61.00	62.00	63.00	64.00	65.00	0.100
55.00	56.10	57.20	58.30	59.40	60.50	61.60	62.70	63.80	64.90	66.00	67.10	68.20	69.30	70.40	71.50	0.110
60.00	61.20	62.40	63.60	64.80	66.00	67.20	68.40	69.60	70.80	72.00	73.20	74.40	75.60	76.80	78.00	0.120
65.00	66.30	67.60	68.90	70.20	71.50	72.80	74.10	75.40	76.70	78.00	79.30	80.60	81.90	83.20	84.50	0.130
70.00	71.40	72.80	74.20	75.60	77.00	78.40	79.80	81.20	82.60	84.00	85.40	86.80	88.20	89.60	91.00	0.140
75.00	76.50	78.00	79.50	81.00	82.50	84.00	85.50	87.00	88.50	90.00	91.50	93.00	94.50	96.00	97.50	0.150
80.00	81.60	83.20	84.80	86.40	88.00	89.60	91.20	92.80	94.40	96.00	97.60	99.20	100.80	102.40	104.00	0.160
85.00	86.70	88.40	90.10	91.80	93.50	95.20	96.90	98.60	100.30	102.00	103.70	105.40	107.10	108.80	110.50	0.170
90.00	91.80	93.60	95.40	97.20	99.00	100.80	102.60	104.40	106.20	108.00	109.80	111.60	113.40	115.20	117.00	0.180
95.00	96.90	98.80	100.70	102.60	104.50	106.40	108.30	110.20	112.10	114.00	115.90	117.80	119.70	121.60	123.50	0.190
100.00	102.00	104.00	106.00	108.00	110.00	112.00	114.00	116.00	118.00	120.00	122.00	124.00	126.00	128.00	130.00	0.200
105.00	107.10	109.20	111.30	113.40	115.50	117.60	119.70	121.80	123.90	126.00	128.10	130.20	132.30	134.40	136.50	0.210
110.00	112.20	114.40	116.60	118.80	121.00	123.20	125.40	127.60	129.80	132.00	134.20	136.40	138.60	140.80	143.00	0.220
115.00	117.30	119.60	121.90	124.20	126.50	128.80	131.10	133.40	135.70	138.00	140.30	142.60	144.90	147.20	149.50	0.230
120.00	122.40	124.80	127.20	129.60	132.00	134.40	136.80	139.20	141.60	144.00	146.40	148.80	151.20	153.60	156.00	0.240
125.00	127.50	130.00	132.50	135.00	137.50	140.00	142.50	145.00	147.50	150.00	152.50	155.00	157.50	160.00	162.50	0.250
130.00	132.60	135.20	137.80	140.40	143.00	145.60	148.20	150.80	153.40	156.00	158.60	161.20	163.80	166.40	169.00	0.260
135.00	137.70	140.40	143.10	145.80	148.50	151.20	153.90	156.60	159.30	162.00	164.70	167.40	170.10	172.80	175.50	0.270
140.00	142.80	145.60	148.40	151.20	154.00	156.80	159.60	162.40	165.20	168.00	170.80	173.60	176.40	179.20	182.00	0.280
145.00	147.90	150.80	153.70	156.60	159.50	162.40	165.30	168.20	171.10	174.00	176.90	179.80	182.70	185.60	188.50	0.290
150.00	153.00	156.00	159.00	162.00	165.00	168.00	171.00	174.00	177.00	180.00	183.00	186.00	189.00	192.00	195.00	0.300
155.00	158.10	161.20	164.30	167.40	170.50	173.60	176.70	179.80	182.90	186.00	189.10	192.20	195.30	198.40	201.50	0.310
160.00	163.20	166.40	169.60	172.80	176.00	179.20	182.40	185.60	188.80	192.00	195.20	198.40	201.60	204.80	208.00	0.320
165.00	168.30	171.60	174.90	178.20	181.50	184.80	188.10	191.40	194.70	198.00	201.30	204.60	207.90	211.20	214.50	0.330
170.00	173.40	176.80	180.20	183.60	187.00	190.40	193.80	197.20	200.60	204.00	207.40	210.80	214.20	217.60	221.00	0.340
175.00	178.50	182.00	185.50	189.00	192.50	196.00	199.50	203.00	206.50	210.00	213.50	217.00	220.50	224.00	227.50	0.350
180.00	183.60	187.20	190.80	194.40	198.00	201.60	205.20	208.80	212.40	216.00	219.60	223.20	226.80	230.40	234.00	0.360
185.00	188.70	192.40	196.10	199.80	203.50	207.20	210.90	214.60	218.30	222.00	225.70	229.40	233.10	236.80	240.50	0.370
190.00	193.80	197.60	201.40	205.20	209.00	212.80	216.60	220.40	224.20	228.00	231.80	235.60	239.40	243.20	247.00	0.380
195.00	198.90	202.80	206.70	210.60	214.50	218.40	222.30	226.20	230.10	234.00	237.90	241.80	245.70	249.60	253.50	0.390
200.00	204.00	208.00	212.00	216.00	220.00	224.00	228.00	232.00	236.00	240.00	244.00	248.00	252.00	256.00	260.00	0.400
205.00	209.10	213.20	217.30	221.40	225.50	229.60	233.70	237.80	241.90	246.00	250.10	254.20	258.30	262.40	266.50	0.410
210.00	214.20	218.40	222.60	226.80	231.00	235.20	239.40	243.60	247.80	252.00	256.20	260.40	264.60	268.80	273.00	0.420
215.00	219.30	223.60	227.90	232.20	236.50	240.80	245.10	249.40	253.70	258.00	262.30	266.60	270.90	275.20	279.50	0.430
220.00	224.40	228.80	233.20	237.60	242.00	246.40	250.80	255.20	259.60	264.00	268.40	272.80	277.20	281.60	286.00	0.440
225.00	229.50	234.00	238.50	243.00	247.50	252.00	256.50	261.00	265.50	270.00	274.50	279.00	283.50	288.00	292.50	0.450
230.00	234.60	239.20	243.80	248.40	253.00	257.60	262.20	266.80	271.40	276.00	280.60	285.20	289.80	294.40	299.00	0.460
235.00	239.70	244.40	249.10	253.80	258.50	263.20	267.90	272.60	277.30	282.00	286.70	291.40	296.10	300.80	305.50	0.470
240.00	244.80	249.60	254.40	259.20	264.00	268.80	273.60	278.40	283.20	288.00	292.80	297.60	302.40	307.20	312.00	0.480
245.00	249.90	254.80	259.70	264.60	269.50	274.40	279.30	284.20	289.10	294.00	298.90	303.80	308.70	313.60	318.50	0.490
250.00	255.00	260.00	265.00	270.00	275.00	280.00	285.00	290.00	295.00	300.00	305.00	310.00	315.00	320.00	325.00	0.500
255.00	260.10	265.20	270.30	275.40	280.50	285.60	290.70	295.80	300.90	306.00	311.10	316.20	321.30	326.40	331.50	0.510
260.00	265.20	270.40	275.60	280.80	286.00	291.20	296.40	301.60	306.80	312.00	317.20	322.40	327.60	332.80	338.00	0.520
265.00	270.30	275.60	280.90	286.20	291.50	296.80	302.10	307.40	312.70	318.00	323.30	328.60	333.90	339.20	344.50	0.530
270.00	275.40	280.80	286.20	291.60	297.00	302.40	307.80	313.20	318.60	324.00	329.40	334.80	340.20	345.60	351.00	0.540
275.00	280.50	286.00	291.50	297.00	302.50	308.00	313.50	319.00	324.50	330.00	335.50	341.00	346.50	352.00	357.50	0.550
280.00	285.60	291.20	296.80	302.40	308.00	313.60	319.20	324.80	330.40	336.00	341.60	347.20	352.80	358.40	364.00	0.560
285.00	290.70	296.40	302.10	307.80	313.50	319.20	324.90	330.60	336.30	342.00	347.70	353.40	359.10	364.80	370.50	0.570
290.00	295.80	301.60	307.40	313.20	319.00	324.80	330.60	336.40	342.20	348.00	353.80	359.60	365.40	371.20	377.00	0.580
295.00	300.90	306.80	312.70	318.60	324.50	330.40	336.30	342.20	348.10	354.00	359.90	365.80	371.70	377.60	383.50	0.590
300.00	306.00	312.00	318.00	324.00	330.00	336.00	342.00	348.00	354.00	360.00	366.00	372.00	378.00	384.00	390.00	0.600
305.00	311.10	317.20	323.30	329.40	335.50	341.60	347.70	353.80	359.90	366.00	372.10	378.20	384.30	390.40	396.50	0.610
310.00	316.20	322.40	328.60	334.80	341.00	347.20	353.40	359.60	365.80	372.00	378.20	384.40	390.60	396.80	403.00	0.620
315.00	321.30	327.60	333.90	340.20	346.50	352.80	359.10	365.40	371.70	378.00	384.30	390.60	396.90	403.20	409.50	0.630
320.00	326.40	332.80	339.20	345.60	352.00	358.40	364.80	371.20	377.60	384.00	390.40	396.80	403.20	409.60	416.00	0.640
325.00	331.50	338.00	344.50	351.00	357.50	364.00	370.50	377.00	383.50	390.00	396.50	403.00	409.50	416.00	422.50	0.650
330.00	336.60	343.20	349.80	356.40	363.00	369.60	376.20	382.80	389.40	396.00	402.60	409.20	415.80	422.40	429.00	0.660
335.00	341.70	348.40	355.10	361.80	368.50	375.20	381.90	388.60	395.30	402.00	408.70	415.40	422.10	428.80	435.50	0.670
340.00	346.80	353.60	360.40	367.20	374.00	380.80	387.60	394.40	401.20	408.00	414.80	421.60	428.40	435.20	442.00	0.680
345.00	351.90	358.80	365.70	372.60	379.50	386.40	393.30	400.20	407.10	414.00	420.90	427.80	434.70	441.60	448.50	0.690
350.00	357.00	364.00	371.00	378.00	385.00	392.00	399.00	406.00	413.00	420.00	427.00	434.00	441.00	448.00	455.00	0.700
355.00	362.10	369.20	376.30	383.40	390.50	397.60	404.70	411.80	418.90	426.00	433.10	440.20	447.30	454.40	461.50	0.710
360.00	367.20	374.40	381.60	388.80	396.00	403.20	410.40	417.60	424.80	432.00	439.20	446.40	453.60	460.80	468.00	0.720
365.00	372.30	379.60	386.90	394.20	401.50	408.80	416.10	423.40	430.70	438.00	445.30	452.60	459.90	467.20	474.50	0.730
370.00	377.40	384.80	392.20	399.60	407.00	414.40	421.80	429.20	436.60	444.00	451.40	458.80	466.20	473.60	481.00	0.740
375.00	382.50	390.00	397.50	405.00	412.50	420.00	427.50	435.00	442.50	450.00	457.50	465.00	472.50	480.00	487.50	0.750
380.00	387.60	395.20	402.80	410.40	418.00	425.60	433.20	440.80	448.40	456.00	463.60	471.20	478.80	486.40	494.00	0.760
385.00	392.70	400.40	408.10	415.80	423.50	431.20	438.90	446.60	454.30	462.00	469.70	477.40	485.10	492.80	500.50	0.770
390.00	397.80	405.60	413.40	421.20	429.00	436.80	444.60	452.40	460.20	468.00	475.80	483.60	491.40	499.20	507.00	0.780
395.00	402.90	410.80	418.70	426.60	434.50	442.40	450.30	458.20	466.10	474.00	481.90	489.80	497.70	505.60	513.50	0.790
400.00	408.00	416.00	424.00	432.00	440.00	448.00	456.00	464.00	472.00	480.00	488.00	496.00	504.00	512.00	520.00	0.800
405.00	413.10	421.20	429.30	437.40	445.50	453.60	461.70	469.80	477.90	486.00	494.10	502.20	510.30	518.40	526.50	0.810
410.00	418.20	426.40	434.60	442.80	451.00	459.20	467.40	475.60	483.80	492.00	500.20	508.40	516.60	524.80	533.00	0.820
415.00	423.30	431.60	439.90	448.20	456.50	464.80	473.10	481.40	489.70	498.00	506.30	514.60	522.90	531.20	539.50	0.830
420.00	428.40	436.80	445.20	453.60	462.00	470.40	478.80	487.20	495.60	504.00	512.40	520.80	529.20	537.60	546.00	0.840
425.00	433.50	442.00	450.50	459.00	467.50	476.00	484.50	493.00	501.50	510.00	518.50	527.00	535.50	544.00	552.50	0.850
430.00	438.60	447.20	455.80	464.40	473.00	481.60	490.20	498.80	507.40	516.00	524.60	533.20	541.80	550.40	559.00	0.860
435.00	443.70	452.40	461.10	469.80	478.50	487.20	495.90	504.60	513.30	522.00	530.70	539.40	548.10	556.80	565.50	0.870
440.00	448.80	457.60	466.40	475.20	484.00	492.80	501.60	510.40	519.20	528.00	536.80	545.60	554.40	563.20	572.00	0.880
445.00	453.90	462.80	471.70	480.60	489.50	498.40	507.30	516.20	525.10	534.00	542.90	551.80	560.70	569.60	578.50	0.890
450.00	459.00	468.00	477.00	486.00	495.00	504.00	513.00	522.00	531.00	540.00	549.00	558.00	567.00	576.00	585.00	0.900
455.00	464.10	473.20	482.30	491.40	500.50	509.60	518.70	527.80	536.90	546.00	555.10	564.20	573.30	582.40	591.50	0.910
460.00	469.20	478.40	487.60	496.80	506.00	515.20	524.40	533.60	542.80	552.00	561.20	570.40	579.60	588.80	598.00	0.920
465.00	474.30	483.60	492.90	502.20	511.50	520.80	530.10	539.40	548.70	558.00	567.30	576.60	585.90	595.20	604.50	0.930
470.00	479.40	488.80	498.20	507.60	517.00	526.40	535.80	545.20	554.60	564.00	573.40	582.80	592.20	601.60	611.00	0.940
475.00	484.50	494.00	503.50	513.00	522.50	532.00	541.50	551.00	560.50	570.00	579.50	589.00	598.50	608.00	617.50	0.950
480.00	489.60	499.20	508.80	518.40	528.00	537.60	547.20	556.80	566.40	576.00	585.60	595.20	604.80	614.40	624.00	0.960
485.00	494.70	504.40	514.10	523.80	533.50	543.20	552.90	562.60	572.30	582.00	591.70	601.40	611.10	620.80	630.50	0.970
490.00	499.80	509.60	519.40	529.20	539.00	548.80	558.60	568.40	578.20	588.00	597.80	607.60	617.40	627.20	637.00	0.980
495.00	504.90	514.80	524.70	534.60	544.50	554.40	564.30	574.20	584.10	594.00	603.90	613.80	623.70	633.60	643.50	0.990
500.00	510.00	520.00	530.00	540.00	550.00	560.00	570.00	580.00	590.00	600.00	610.00	620.00	630.00	640.00	650.00	1.000

Sell your coins for the highest price!
AUCTIONS BY
BOWERS AND MERENA, INC.

THINKING OF SELLING?

Thinking of selling? We offer you an unequaled record of auction success. Of the top ten world's record auction prices for coins, we hold nine, including all seven of the top seven. Similarly, when the world's most valuable coin collection was auctioned ($25,000,000 Garrett Collection for The Johns Hopkins University), we were the auctioneers. Similarly, we have the record for the second most valuable collection (The Norweb Collection sold for $20,000,000). Let us put our expertise and proven record of success to work for you! For one low commission rate to you, the seller, plus our normal charge to the buyer, your coins can be offered to our worldwide clientele of collectors, investors, dealers, and others.

THINKING OF SELLING YOUR WORLD COINS?

We are leading auctioneers of fine collections of world gold coins, crowns, and minors, from all countries and eras. Over the years we have auctioned such landmark collections as the Guia Collection of World Gold Coins, the Stanislaw Herstal Collection of Polish Coins, the Dundee Collection of Scottish Coins, the Ibero-American Collection of Coins of Latin America, the Dr. Richard P. Ariagno Collection of World Coins, the Abe Kosoff Collection, and many other properties. Our specialist in world coins, Michael Hodder is available to help you plan the most profitable way of selling your collection. He is just a telephone call or a letter away.

THINKING OF SELLING UNITED STATES COINS?

Let us sell your scarce and rare United States coins, medals, and currency. For 36 years we have maintained close relationships with major European, Asian, and other auction houses and dealerships, and for them we have auctioned United States numismatic material in the active American market. Our sales are held in New York City and Los Angeles on a regularly scheduled basis. Dr. Richard Bagg, our Auction Director, will assist you with any questions you have. He is just a telephone call or a letter away. All sale purchases will be paid for in U.S. dollar funds, or any other agreeable arrangement you propose.

THINKING OF SELLING?
Telephone, write, or use the convenient coupon below.
It may well be the best financial decision you have ever made.

Dear Rick Bagg:
Please tell me how I can include my coins in one of your forthcoming New York City sales. I understand that all information will be kept confidential.

Name _____

Street _____

City _____ State or Country _____ Code _____

Check here: ☐ I am thinking about selling my coins. Please contact me.

Brief description of holdings: _____

Telephone _____ Daytime Telephone _____

AUCTIONS BY BOWERS AND MERENA, INC.
Attention: Dr Richard Bagg
Box 1224
Wolfeboro, NH 03894 U.S.A.
(603) 569-5095 • Fax (603) 569-5319

Auctions held in New York City and other metropolitan centers

"When great collections are sold, Bowers and Merena sells them"
Chairman: Q. David Bowers (who was also Chairman of Bowers and Ruddy, our predecessor firm), President: Raymond N. Merena.
Members: Professional Numismatists Guild, IAPN, ICTA, Life Members ANA, with a tradition of serving numismatists for 36 years, since 1953.

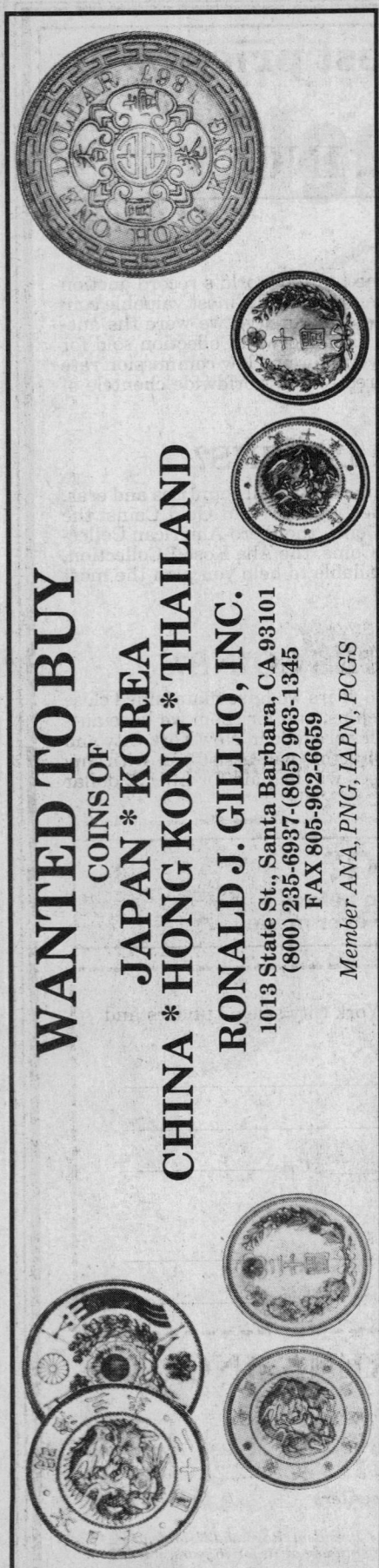

HOW TO USE THIS CATALOG

This catalog is designed to serve the needs of both the novice and advanced collectors. It provides a comprehensive guide to more than 180 years of world coinage. It is generally arranged so that persons with no more than a basic knowledge of world history after 1800 and a casual acquaintance with coin collecting can consult it with confidence and ease. The following explanations summarize the general practices used in preparing this catalog's listings. However, because of specialized requirements which may vary by country and era, these must not be considered ironclad. Where these standards have been set aside, appropriate notations of the variations are incorporated.

ARRANGEMENT

All coin listings are alphabetically arranged in a historical-geographic approach according to the current identity of the sovereign government concerned. Thus, the coins of Persia can be located by referring to the listings for Iran, or the Imperial issues of Russia by turning to Union of Soviet Socialist Republics (U.S.S.R.) This approach has also resulted in combining the coin listings for such issuing entities as Annam, French Cochin China, Tonkin, North and South Vietnam as sub-groupings under the historical- geographic identity of Vietnam. Likewise, coins of North and South Korea will be found grouped under Korea, those of the Congo Free State, Belgian Congo, Congo Democratic Republic, Katanga and Zaire, under the latter identity.

Coins of each country are generally arranged by denomination from lowest to highest, except where arrangement by ruler, mint of issue, type or period makes a series easier to understand. The non-circulating legal tender (NCLT) coins are integrated in the listings. Exceptions which are not readily adaptable to this traditional North American cataloging style are generally found in the more complicated series, most notably those encompassing the early issues of Afghanistan, Mughal issues of India, Indian Princely States, Iran, Nepal and the areas under the influence of the late Ottoman Empire, which are listed by ruler.

Strict date sequence of listings is also interrupted in a number of countries which have been subjected to major monetary reforms or conversion to decimal or other new currency systems. Where these considerations apply, appropriate headings are incorporated to introduce the change from one standard to another.

IDENTIFICATION

The most important step in the identification of a coin is the determination of the nation of origin. This is generally easily accomplished where English-speaking lands are concerned, however, use of the country index is sometimes required. The coins of Great Britain provide an interesting challenge. For hundreds of years the only indication of the country of origin was in the abbreviated Latin legends. In recent times there have been occasions when there has been no indication of origin. Only through the familiarity of the monarchical portraits, symbols and legends or indication of currency system are they identifiable.

The coins of many countries beyond the English-language realm, such as those of French, Italian or Spanish heritage, are also quite easy to identify through reference to their legends, which appear in the national languages based on Western alphabets. In many instances the name is spelled exactly the same in English as in the national language, such as France; while in other cases it varies only slightly, like Italia for Italy, Belgique or Belgie for Belgium, Brasil for Brazil and Danmark for Denmark.

This is not always the case, however, as in Norge for Norway, Espana for Spain, Sverige for Sweden and Helvetia for Switzerland. Some other examples include:
DEUTSCHES REICH - Germany 1873-1945
BUNDESREPUBLIK DEUTSCHLAND - Federal Republic of Germany (West Germany).
DEUTSCHE DEMOKRATISCHE REPUBLIK - Germany Democratic Republic (East Germany).
EMPIRE CHERIFIEN MAROC - Morocco.
ESTADOS UNIDOS MEXICANOS - United Mexican States (Mexico).
ETAT DU GRAND LIBAN - State of Great Lebanon (Lebanon).

Thus it can be seen there are instances in which a little schooling in the rudiments of foreign languages can be most helpful. In general, colonial possessions of countries using the Western alphabet are similarly identifiable as they often carry portraits of their current rulers, the familiar lettering, sometimes in combination with a companion designation in the local language.

Collectors have the greatest difficulty with coins that do not bear legends or dates in the Western systems. These include coins bearing Cyrillic lettering, attributable to the Soviet lands, the Slavic states and Balkan area, or Mongolia, the Greek script peculiar to Greece, Crete and the Ionian Islands; the Amharic characters of Ethiopia, or Hebrew in the case of Israel. Dragons and sunbursts, along with the distinctive word characters, attribute a coin to the Oriental countries of China, Japan, Korea, Vietnam, Tibet and their component parts.

The most difficult coins to identify are those bearing only Persian or Arabic script and its derivatives, found on the issues of nations stretching in a wide swath across North Africa and East Asia, from Morocco to Indonesia, and the Indian subcontinent coinages which surely are more confusing in their vast array of Nagari, Sanskrit, Ahom, Assamese and other local dialects found on the local issues of the Indian Princely States. Although the task of identification on the more modern issues of these lands is often eased by the added presence of Western alphabet legends, a feature sometimes adopted as early as the late 19th Century, for the earlier pieces it is often necessary for the uninitiated to laboriously seek and find.

Except for the cruder issues, however, it

will be found that certain characteristics and symbols featured in addition to the predominant legends are typical coins from a given country or group of countries. The toughra monogram, for instance, occurs on some of the coins of Afghanistan, Egypt, the Sudan, Pakistan, Turkey and other areas of the late Ottoman Empire. A predominant design feature on the coins of Nepal is the trident; while neighboring Tibet features a lotus blossom or lion on many of their issues.

To assist in identification of the more difficult coins, we have assembled the *Instant Identifier* and monogram sections presented on the pages following. They are designed to provide a point of beginning for collectors by allowing them to compare unidentified coins with photographic details from typical issues. We also suggest reference to the *Index of Coin Denominations* presented here also and the comprehensive *Country Index*, where the inscription will be found listed just as it appears on the coin for nations using the Western alphabet.

DENOMINATIONS

The second basic consideration to be met in the attribution of a coin is the determination of denomination. Since denominations are usually expressed in numeric, rather than word form on a coin, this is usually quite easily accomplished on coins from nations which use Western numerals, except in those instances where issues are devoid of any mention of face value, and denomination must be attributed by size, metallic composition or weight. Coins listed in this volume are generally illustrated in actual size. Where size is critical to proper attribution, the coin's millimeter size is indicated.

The sphere of countries stretching from North Africa through the Orient, on which numeric symbols generally unfamiliar to Westerners are employed, often provide the collector with a much greater challenge. This is particularly true on nearly all pre-20th Century issues. On some of the more modern issues, and increasingly so as the years progress, Western style numerals, usually presented in combination with the local numeric system, are becoming more commonplace on these coins.

Determination of a coin's currency system can also be valuable in attributing the issue to its country of origin. A comprehensive alphabetical index of currency names, applicable to the countries as cataloged in this volume, with all individual nations of use for each, is presented in this section.

The included table of *Standard International Numeral Systems* presents charts of the basic numeric designations found on coins of non-Western origin. Although denomination numerals are generally prominently displayed on coins, it must be remembered that these are general representations of characters which individual coin engravers may have rendered in widely varying styles. Where numeric or script denominations designation forms peculiar to a given coin or country apply, such as the script used on some Persian (Iranian) issues, they are so indicated or illustrated in conjunction with the appropriate listings.

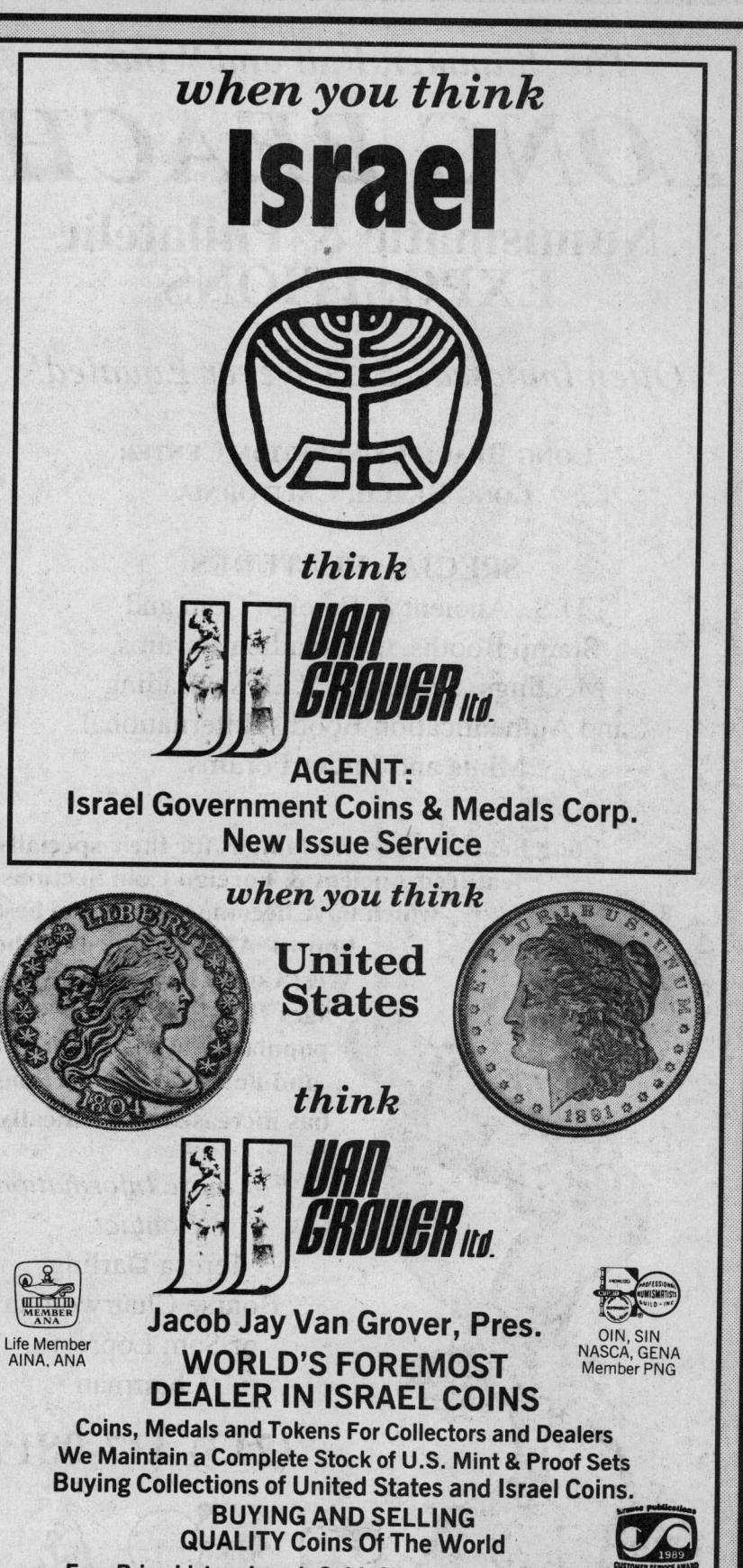

The Summer, Fall and Winter
LONG BEACH
Numismatic & Philatelic EXPOSITIONS

Often Imitated...BUT Never Equaled!

Long Beach Convention Center
Long Beach, California

SPECIAL FEATURES
U.S., Ancient & Foreign Coin and Stamp Booths, Outstanding Forums, Meetings, Seminars, V.I.P.'s, Grading and Authentication Booths, International Mints and Junior Forums.

Long Beach Expos are famous for their specially featured Ancient & Foreign Coin Sections, which have become some of the best known AND attended on the West Coast. Each Expo averages 7000 Plus visitors. The popularity of these Ancient and Foreign Coin Sections has increased dramatically.

For more Information Contact:
Teresa Darling, Bourse Chairwoman
or Sam Lopresto, Chairman

(213) 437-0819

Sam Lopresto

Largest Ever in TV, Radio & Print Coverage

DATING

Coin dating is the final basic attribution consideration. Here, the problem can be more difficult because the reading of a coin date is subject not only to the vagaries of numeric styling, but to calendar variations caused by the observance of various religious eras or regal periods from country to country, or even within a country. Here again, with the exception of the sphere from North Africa through the Orient, it will be found that most countries rely on Western date numerals and Christian (AD) era reckoning, although in a few instances, coin dating has been tied to the year of a reign or government. The Vatican, for example, dates its coinage according to the year of reign of the current pope, in addition to the Christian-era date.

Countries in the Arabic sphere generally date their coins to the Mohammedan era (AH), which commenced on July 16, 622 AD (Julian calendar), when the prophet Mohammed fled from Mecca to Medina. As their calendar is reckoned by the lunar year of 354 days, which is about three percent (precisely 2.98%) shorter than the Christian year, a formula is required to convert AH dating to its Western equivalent. To convert an AH date to the approximate AD date, subject three percent of the AH date (round to the closest whole number) from the AH date, then add 622. A chart for all AH years from 1088 (March 6, 1677) to 1411 (July 24, 1990) which fully encompasses the scope of this catalog, is presented on page 25 of this volume.

The Mohammedan calendar is not always based on the lunar year (AH), however, causing some confusion, particularly in Afghanistan and Iran, where a calendar based on the solar year (SH) was introduced around 1920. These dates can be converted to AD by simply adding 621. In 1976 the government of Iran implemented a new solar calendar based on the foundation of the Iranian monarchy in 559 BC. The first year observed on the new calendar was 2535 (MS), which commenced March 20, 1976. A reversion to the traditional SH dating standards occurred a few years later.

Several different eras of reckoning, including Christian and Mohammedan (AH), have been used to date coins of the Indian subcontinent. The two basic systems are the Vikrama Samvat (VS), which dates from Oct. 18, 58 BC, and the Saka era, the origin of which is reckoned from March 3, 78 AD. Dating according to both eras appears on various coins of the area.

Coins of Thailand (Siam) are found dated by three different eras. The most predominant is the Buddhist era (BE) which originated in 543 BC. Next is the Bangkok or Ratanakosindsok (RS) era, dating from 1781 AD; followed by the Chula-Sakarat (CS) era, dating from 638 AD. The latter era originated in Burma and is used on that country's coins.

Other calendars include that of the Ethiopian era (EE) which commenced seven years, eight months after AD dating; and that of the Jewish people, which commenced on Oct. 7, 3761 BC. Korea claims a legendary dating from 2333 BC, which is

HEJIRA DATE CONVERSION CHART

HEJIRA (Hijra, Hegira), the name of the Mohammedan era (A.H. - Anno Hegirae) dates back to the Christian year 622 when Mohammed "fled" from Mecca, escaping to Medina to avoid persecution from the Koreish tribesmen. Based on a lunar year the Mohammedan year is 11 days shorter.

* - Leap Year (Christian Calendar)

AH Hejira	AD Christian Date
1089	1678, February 23
1090	1679, February 12
1091	1680, February 2*
1092	1681, January 21
1093	1682, January 10
1094	1682, December 31
1095	1683, December 20
1096	1684, December 8*
1097	1685, November 28
1098	1686, November 17
1099	1687, November 7
1100	1688, October 26*
1101	1689, October 15
1102	1690, October 5
1103	1691, September 24
1104	1692, September 12*
1105	1693, September 2
1106	1694, August 22
1107	1695, August 12
1108	1696, July 31*
1109	1697, July 20
1110	1698, July 10
1111	1699, June 29
1112	1700, June 18
1113	1701, June 8
1114	1702, May 28
1115	1703, May 17
1116	1704, May 6*
1117	1705, April 25
1118	1706, April 15
1119	1707, April 4
1120	1708, March 23*
1121	1709, March 18
1122	1710, March 2
1123	1711, February 19
1124	1712, February 9*
1125	1713, January 28
1126	1714, January 17
1127	1715, January 7
1128	1715, December 27
1129	1716, December 16*
1130	1717, December 5
1131	1718, November 24
1132	1719, November 14
1133	1720, November 2*
1134	1721, October 22
1135	1722, October 12
1136	1723, October 1
1137	1724, September 29*
1138	1725, September 9
1139	1726, August 29
1140	1727, August 19
1141	1728, August 7*
1142	1729, July 27
1143	1730, July 17
1144	1731, July 6
1145	1732, June 24*
1146	1733, June 14
1147	1734, June 3
1148	1735, May 24
1149	1736, May 12*
1150	1737, May 1
1151	1738, April 21
1152	1739, April 10
1153	1740, March 29*
1154	1741, March 19
1155	1742, March 8
1156	1743, February 25
1157	1744, February 15*
1158	1745, February 3
1159	1746, January 24
1160	1747, January 13
1161	1748, January 2
1162	1748, December 22*
1163	1749, December 11
1164	1750, November 30
1165	1751, November 20
1166	1752, November 8*
1167	1753, October 29
1168	1754, October 18
1169	1755, October 7
1170	1756, September 26*
1171	1757, September 15
1172	1758, September 4
1173	1759, August 25
1174	1760, August 13*
1175	1761, August 2
1176	1762, July 28
1177	1763, July 12
1178	1764, July 1*
1179	1765, June 20
1180	1766, June 9
1181	1767, May 30
1182	1768, May 18*
1183	1769, May 7
1184	1770, April 27
1185	1771, April 16
1186	1772, April 4*
1187	1773, March 25
1188	1774, March 14

AH Hejira	AD Christian Date
1189	1775, March 4
1190	1776, February 21*
1191	1777, February 9
1192	1778, January 30
1193	1779, January 19
1194	1780, January 8*
1195	1780, December 28*
1196	1781, December 17
1197	1782, December 7
1198	1783, November 26
1199	1784, November 14*
1200	1785, November 4
1201	1786, October 24
1202	1787, October 13
1203	1788, October 2*
1204	1789, September 21
1205	1790, September 10
1206	1791, August 31
1207	1792, August 19*
1208	1793, August 9
1209	1794, July 29
1210	1795, July 18
1211	1796, July 7*
1212	1797, June 26
1213	1798, June 15
1214	1799, June 5
1215	1800, May 25
1216	1801, May 14
1217	1802, May 4
1218	1803, April 23
1219	1804, April 12*
1220	1805, April 1
1221	1806, March 21
1222	1807, March 11
1223	1808, February 28*
1224	1809, February 16
1225	1810, February 6
1226	1811, January 26
1227	1812, January 16*
1228	1813, January 4
1229	1813, December 24
1230	1814, December 14
1231	1815, December 3
1232	1816, November 21*
1233	1817, November 11
1234	1818, October 31
1235	1819, October 20
1236	1820, October 9*
1237	1821, September 28
1238	1822, September 18
1239	1823, September 7
1240	1824, August 26*
1241	1825, August 16
1242	1826, August 5
1243	1827, July 25
1244	1828, July 14*
1245	1829, July 3
1246	1830, June 22
1247	1831, June 12
1248	1832, May 31*
1249	1833, May 21
1250	1834, May 10
1251	1835, April 29
1252	1836, April 18*
1253	1837, April 7
1254	1838, March 27
1255	1839, March 17
1256	1840, March 5*
1257	1841, February 23
1258	1842, February 12
1259	1843, February 1
1260	1844, January 22*
1261	1845, January 10
1262	1845, December 30
1263	1846, December 20
1264	1847, December 9
1265	1848, November 27*
1266	1849, November 17
1267	1850, November 6
1268	1851, October 27
1269	1852, October 15*
1270	1853, October 4
1271	1854, September 24
1272	1855, September 13
1273	1856, September 1*
1274	1857, August 22
1275	1858, August 11
1276	1859, July 31
1277	1860, July 20*
1278	1861, July 9
1279	1862, June 29
1280	1863, June 18
1281	1864, June 6*
1282	1865, May 27
1283	1866, May 16
1284	1867, May 5
1285	1868, April 24*
1286	1869, April 13
1287	1870, April 3
1288	1871, March 23
1289	1872, March 11*
1290	1873, March 1
1291	1874, February 18
1292	1875, February 7
1293	1876, January 28*
1294	1877, January 16
1295	1878, January 5
1296	1878, December 26
1297	1879, December 15
1298	1880, December 4*
1299	1881, November 23

AH Hejira	AD Christian Date
1300	1882, November 12
1301	1883, November 2
1302	1884, October 21*
1303	1885, October 10
1304	1886, September 30
1305	1887, September 19
1306	1888, September 7*
1307	1889, August 28
1308	1890, August 17
1309	1891, August 7
1310	1892, July 26*
1311	1893, July 15
1312	1894, July 5
1313	1895, June 24
1314	1896, June 12*
1315	1897, June 2
1316	1898, May 22
1317	1899, May 12
1318	1900, May 1
1319	1901, April 20
1320	1902, April 10
1321	1903, March 30
1322	1904, March 18*
1323	1905, March 8
1324	1906, February 25
1325	1907, February 14
1326	1908, February 4*
1327	1909, January 23
1328	1910, January 13
1329	1911, January 2
1330	1911, December 22
1331	1912, December 11*
1332	1913, November 30
1333	1914, November 19
1334	1915, November 9
1335	1916, October 28*
1336	1917, October 17
1337	1918, October 7
1338	1919, September 26
1339	1920, September 15*
1340	1921, September 4
1341	1922, August 24
1342	1923, August 14
1343	1924, August 2*
1344	1925, July 22
1345	1926, July 12
1346	1927, July 1
1347	1928, June 20*
1348	1929, June 9
1349	1930, May 29
1350	1931, May 19
1351	1932, May 7*
1352	1933, April 26
1353	1934, April 16
1354	1935, April 5
1355	1936, March 24*
1356	1937, March 14
1357	1938, March 3
1358	1939, February 21
1359	1940, February 10*
1360	1941, January 29
1361	1942, January 19
1362	1943, January 8
1363	1943, December 28
1364	1944, December 17*
1365	1945, December 6
1366	1946, November 25
1367	1947, November 15
1368	1948, November 3*
1369	1949, October 24
1370	1950, October 13
1371	1951, October 2
1372	1952, September 21*
1373	1953, September 10
1374	1954, August 30
1375	1955, August 20
1376	1956, August 8*
1377	1957, July 29
1378	1958, July 18
1379	1959, July 7
1380	1960, June 25*
1381	1961, June 14
1382	1962, June 4
1383	1963, May 25
1384	1964, May 13*
1385	1965, May 2
1386	1966, April 22
1387	1967, April 11
1388	1968, March 31*
1389	1969, March 20
1390	1970, March 9
1391	1971, February 27
1392	1972, February 16*
1393	1973, February 4
1394	1974, January 25
1395	1975, January 14
1396	1976, January 3*
1397	1976, December 23*
1398	1977, December 12
1399	1978, December 2
1400	1979, November 21
1401	1980, November 9*
1402	1981, October 30
1403	1982, October 19
1404	1983, October 8
1405	1984, September 27*
1406	1985, September 16
1407	1986, September 6
1408	1987, August 26
1409	1988, August 14*
1410	1989, August 3
1411	1990, July 24

Central Ohio's Leading Buyer and Seller of United States and World-Wide...

- ...Coins, Currency and Stamps •
- • Gold, Silver and Platinum •
- • Pocket Watches and Wrist Watches •
- • Antique Jewelry and Masonic Jewelry •
- • Picture Postcards and Baseball Cards •
- • Indian Relics • Political Buttons •
- • Hummels • Doultons •
- • Old Toys, Banks and Dolls •

We Buy and Sell Nearly Everything Collectable

Send For Our FREE Price List

COIN SHOP INC.

EST. 1960

"The Higher Buyer"

Life Member

MasterCard VISA

#1 Cherri Park Square
399 S. State St.
Westerville, OH 43081
1-614-882-3937
Toll Free 1-800-848-3966

---

acknowledged in some of its coin dating. Some coin issues of the Indonesian area carry dates determined by the Javanese Aji Saka era (AS), a calendar of 354 days (100 Javanese years equals 97 Christian or Gregorian calendar years) which can be matched to AD dating by comparing it to AH dating.

The following table indicates the year dating for the various eras which correspond to 1990 in Christian calendar reckoning, but it must be remembered that there are overlaps between the eras in some instances:

Christian era (AD)	1990
Mohammedan era (AH)	AH1411
Solar year (SH)	SH1369
Monarchic Solar era (MS)	MS2549
Vikrama Samvat (VS)	VS2047
Saka era (SE)	SE1912
Buddhist era (BE)	BE2533
Bangkok era (RS)	RS209
Chula-Sakarat era (CS)	CS1352
Ethiopian era (EE)	EE1982
Jewish era	5750
Korean era	4323
Javanese Aji Saka era (AS)	AS1923
Fasli era (FE)	FE1400

Coins of Oriental origin - principally Japan, Korea, China, Turkestan and Tibet and some modern gold issues of Turkey - are generally dated to the year of the government, dynasty, reign or cyclic eras, with the dates indicated in Oriental characters which usually read from right to left. In recent years, however, some dating has been according to the Christian calendar and in Western numerals. In Japan, Oriental character dating was reversed to read from left to right in Showa year 23 (1948 AD).

More detailed guides to less prevalent coin dating systems which are strictly local in nature are presented with the appropriate listings.

Some coins carry dates according to both locally observed and Christian eras. This is particularly true in the Arabic world, where the Hejira date may be indicated in Arabic numerals and the Christian date in Western numerals, or both dates represented in either form.

The date actually carried on a given coin is generally cataloged here in the first column (Date) to the right of the catalog number. If the date is not by AD reckoning, the next column (Year) indicates the date by the conventional calendar which applies, generally Christian. If an AD date appears in either column, the AD is not necessarily indicated. Era abbreviations appearing in the dating table in this section are generally shown in conjunction with the listings of coins dated in those eras.

Dates listed in either column which does not actually appear on a given coin is generally enclosed by parentheses. Undated coins are indicated by the letters ND in the date column and the estimated year of issue in parentheses.

Timing differentials between some era of reckoning particularly the 354-day Mohammedan and 365-day Christian years, cause situations whereby coins which carry dates for both eras exist bearing two year dates from one calendar combined with a single date from another.

NUMISMATIC SOCIETIES

A great many numismatic organizations exist today. They offer their members a wide variety of services and benefits. Foremost among these are their publications which present information often previously unpublished. Many sponsor major educational programs at large conventions, maintain extensive libraries, and prepare regular auctions for their membership. Assistance with research is an important hallmark of some societies. Locating other collectors with similar interests may also be easily achieved through membership in such groups.

Listed here are some of the national and international organizations and societies active at this time:

AMERICAN NUMISMATIC ASSOCIATION
P.O. Box 2366
Colorado Springs, Colorado 80901, U.S.A.

AMERICAN NUMISMATIC SOCIETY
Broadway at 155th Street
New York, New York 10032, U.S.A.

ASOCIACION NUMISMATICA ESPAÑOLA
Gran via de las Corts
Catalanes, 627, pral. 1ª
08010 Barcelona, Spain

CANADIAN NUMISMATIC ASSOCIATION
Box 226
Barrie, Ontario, Canada L4M 4T2

CLUBE NUMISMATIC DE PORTUGAL
Rua Angelina Vidal, 40
1100 Lisbon — Portugal

COMMISSION INTERNATIONALE NUMISMATIQUE (C.I.N.)
Rutimeyer Strasse 12
CH-4054 Basel
Switzerland

HONG KONG NUMISMATIC SOCIETY
GPO Box 8977
Hong Kong

INDIAN INSTITUTE OF RESEARCH IN NUMISMATIC STUDIES
507, Raheja Centre
214, Nariman Point
Bombay, India 400021

LA SOCIETE AMERICAINE POUR L'ETUDE DE LA NUMISMATIQUE FRANCAISE
5140 East Boulevard N.W.
Canton, Ohio 44718, U.S.A.

LITHUANIAN NUMISMATIC ASSOCIATION
(The Knight)
P.O. Box 612
Columbia, Maryland 21045, U.S.A.

MALAYSIA NUMISMATIC SOCIETY
P.O. Box 12367
Kuala Lumpur, 50776
Malaysia

NUMISMATIC ASSOCIATION OF AUSTRALIA
Box 1920R
GPO Melbourne
Victoria 3001, Australia

NUMISMATIC ASSOCIATION OF THAILAND
Royal Mint
11017 Pradipat Road
Bangkok, Thailand

NUMISMATICS INTERNATIONAL
P.O. Box 670013
Dallas, Texas 75367, U.S.A.

NUMISMATIC SOCIETY OF INDIA
P.O. Hindu University
Varanasi, India 221-005

ORIENTAL NUMISMATIC SOCIETY
30 Warren Road
Woodley, Reading, Berks.
United Kingdom RG5 3AR

ORIENTAL NUMISMATIC SOCIETY
American Section
P.O. Box 356
New Hope, Pennsylvania 18938, U.S.A.

ROYAL NUMISMATIC SOCIETY
Dept. Coins/Medals
British Museum
London, England WC1B306

ROYAL NUMISMATIC SOCIETY OF NEW ZEALAND
G.P.O. Box 2023
Wellington, New Zealand

RUSSIAN NUMISMATIC SOCIETY
P.O. Box F334
Akron, Ohio 44308, U.S.A.

SOCIEDAD NUMISMATICA DE BOLIVIA
Casilla 6592
La Paz, Bolivia

SOCIEDAD NUMISMATICA DE MEXICO, A.C.
Eugenia 13-301
México 18, D.F. México

SOCIETY OF INTERNATIONAL NUMISMATISTS
4214 West 238th Street
Torrance, California 90505, U.S.A.

SOUTH AFRICAN NUMISMATIC SOCIETY
P.O. Box 1689
Cape Town 8000
South Africa

TURKISH NUMISMATIC SOCIETY
P.K. 258 Osmanbey
Istanbul, Turkey

VERBAND DER DEUTSCHEN MUNZVEREINE
(Association of German Numismatic Societies)
Reisenbergstr 58A
8000 Munich 60, West Germany

NETHERLANDS

"SELL YOUR DUTCH COINS WHERE THEY BELONG."

"SELL THEM DIRECTLY TO THE NETHERLANDS."

We buy all Dutch coins at attractive prices.

Also consignments accepted for our auctions.

Please feel free to call, write or FAX and offer us your coins.

THEO PETERS
Rosmarijnsteeg 7
1012 RP
Amsterdam/Holland
Telephone: 31-20-222530
Telefax: 31-20-222454

WANTED
PAYING TOP PRICES!

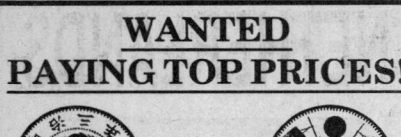

* **Japan**
  * All Coins & Banknotes
  * Proof & Mint Sets
  * Military Medals

* **Korea**
  * 1970 6 Pc. Silver Proof Set
  * 12 Pc. Gold & Silver Proof Set

* **Thailand** * **Franklin Mint**
  & World Gold
  * **Military Payment Certificates**

Arrow International offers not only **TOP BUYING PRICES**, but, we will do our best to fill most any need from the above areas. Should you require a single coin or banknote, even those special books which you have been trying to locate for your library, contact Herb Cook. You will receive immediate attention, no matter what your needs. **NO INQUIRY GOES UNANSWERED.**

Arrow International
A Numismatic Trading Company

#703 Ichibankan
4-35-11 Higashi Nippori
Arakawa-ku, Tokyo, JAPAN 116
Tel. (03) 805-2064
FAX: (03) 802-6380

NUMBERING SYSTEM

Many catalog numbers assigned in this volume are based on established references. This practice has been observed for two reasons: First, when world coins are listed chronologically they are basically self-cataloging; second, there was no need to confuse collectors with totally new numeric designations where appropriate systems already existed. As time progressed we found many of these established systems incomplete and inadequate and are now replaced with new KM numbers with appropriate cross-referencing.

The majority of the coins listed in this catalog are identified or cross referenced by numbers assigned by R.S. Yeoman (Y#), or slight adaptations thereof, in his *Modern World Coins*, and *Current Coins of the World*. For the pre-Yeoman dated issues, the numbers assigned by William D. Craig (C#) in his *Coins of the World (1750-1850 period)*, 3rd edition, have generally been applied.

In some countries, listings are frequently cross-referenced to Robert Friedberg's (Fr#) *Gold Coins of the World* or *Coins of the British World*. Major Fred Pridmore's (P#) studies of British colonial coinage are also referenced frequently, as are W.H. Valentine's (V#) references on the *Modern Copper Coins of the Muhammadan States*. Coins issued under the Chinese sphere of influence are frequently assigned numbers from E. Kann's (K#) *Illustrated Catalog of Chinese Coins* and T.K. Hsu's (Su) work of similar title.

MINTAGES

Quantities minted of each date are indicated where that information is available, generally stated in millions, rounded off to the nearest 10,000 pieces. On quantities of a few thousand or less, actual mintages are generally indicated, a fact that can be determined by the presence of a comma, rather than a decimal point, in the stated figure. The following mintage conversion formulas have been observed:

10,000,000 - 10.000
1,000,000 - 1.000
100,000 - .100
10,000 - .010
9,999 - 9,999
1,000 - 1,000
842 - 842 pcs. (Pieces)
27 - 27 pcs.

The abbreviation "Inc. Ab." or "I.A." means Included Above, while the abbreviation "Inc. Be." or "I.B." means Included Below. An "*" listing beside a mintage figure indicates the number given is an estimate or mintage limit.

MINT AND PRIVY MARKS

The presence of distinctive, but frequently inconspicuously placed, mint marks indicates the mint of issue for many of the coins listed in this catalog. An appropriate designation in the date listings notes the presence, if any, of a mint mark on a particular coin type by incorporating the letter or letters of the mint mark adjoining the date, i.e., 1950D or 1927R.

The presence of mint and/or mintmaster's privy marks on a coin in non-letter form is indicated by incorporating the mint letter in lower case within parentheses adjoining the date; i.e., 1927 (a). The corresponding mark is illustrated or identified in the introduction of the country.

A listing format by mints of issue has been adopted for some countries - including France, Germany, Spain and Mexico - to allow for a more logical arrangement. In these instances, the name of the mint and its mint mark letter or letters is presented at the beginning of each series.

Where listings incorporate mintmaster initials, they are always presented in capital letters separated from the date; i.e., 1850 MF. The different mint mark and mintmaster letters found on the coins of any country, state or city of issue are always shown at the beginning of listings.

METALS

At the beginning of each date listing, the metallic composition of each coin denomination is listed, and thereafter, whenever a change in metal occurs. The traditional coinage metals and their symbolic chemical abbreviations used in this catalog are:

Platinum - (PT)	Copper - (Cu)
Gold - (Au)	Brass -
Silver - (Ag)	Copper-nickel - (CN)
Billon -	Lead - (Pb)
Nickel - (Ni)	Steel -
Zinc - (Zn)	Tin - (Sn)
Bronze - (Ae)	Aluminum - (Al)

During the 18th and 19th Centuries, most of the world's coins were struck of copper or bronze, silver and gold. Commencing in the early years of the 20th Century, however, numerous new coinage metals, primarily non-precious metal alloys, were introduced. Gold has not been widely used for circulation coinages since World War I, although silver remained a popular coinage metal in most parts of the world until after World War II. With the disappearance of silver for circulation coinage, numerous additional compositions were introduced to coinage applications.

Most recent is the development of clad or plated planchets in order to maintain circulation life and extend the life of a set of production dies as used in the production of the copper-nickel clad copper 50 Centesimos of Panama or in the latter case to reduce production costs of the planchets and yet provide a coin quite similar in appearance to its predecessor as in the case of the copper plated zinc core United States 1983 cent.

OFF-METAL STRIKES

Off-metal strikes are designated by "(OMS)" following the listed metal. The term includes the wide range of coinage issues struck in other than their officially authorized compositions for purposes of presentation, sale to collectors and trade. The designation is not meant to cover those issues struck as true patterns or genuine minting errors. Examples of off-metal strikes include the Dutch duits, struck normally in copper, but also produced in limited quantities in gold and

Germanic coinage may be familiar with the term "Abschlag" for off-metal strikes.

Closely related are "trial strikes," the first coins or uniface impressions produced from a new set of dies, often in softer metals other than that used for normal circulation.

PRECIOUS METAL WEIGHTS

Listings of weight, fineness and actual silver (ASW), gold (AGW), platinum or palladium (APW) content of most machine-struck silver, gold, platinum and palladium coins are provided in this edition. These designations will be found incorporated in the listings immediately beneath illustrations or in conjunction with type changes wherever these factors could be determined.

The ASW, AGW and APW figures were determined by multiplying the gross weight of a given coin by its known or tested fineness and converting the resulting gram or grain weight to troy ounces, rounded to the nearest ten-thousandth of an ounce. A silver coin with a 24.25 gram weight and .875 fineness, for example, would have a fine weight of approximately 21.2188 grains, or a .6822 ASW, a factor that can be used to accurately determine the intrinsic value for multiple examples.

The ASW, AGW or APW figure can be multiplied by the spot price of each precious metal to determine the current intrinsic value of any coin accompanied by these designations.

WEIGHTS AND FINENESSES

Coin weights are indicated in grams (abbreviated "g") along with fineness where the information is of value in differentiating between types. These weights are based on 31.103 grams per troy (scientific) ounce, as opposed to the avoirdupois (commercial) standard of 28.35 grams. Actual coin weights are generally shown in hundredths or thousandths of a gram; i.e., .500 SILVER, 2.92 g.

As the silver and gold bullion markets have advanced and declined sharply in recent years, the fineness and total fine precious metal content of coins has become especially significant where bullion coins - issues which trade on the basis of their intrinsic metallic content rather than numismatic value - are concerned. In many instances, such issues have become worth more in bullion form than their nominal collector values or denominations indicate.

Establishing the weight of a coin can also be valuable for determining its denomination. Actual weight is also necessary to ascertain the specific gravity of the coin's metallic content, an important factor in determining authenticity.

TROY WEIGHT STANDARDS
24 Grains = 1 Pennyweight
480 Grains = 1 Ounce
31.103 Grams = 1 Ounce

UNIFORM WEIGHTS
15.432 Grains = 1 Gram
0.0648 Gram = 1 Grain

TWO FOR THE HOBBY

A GUIDE BOOK OF MEXICAN COINS

5th edition (1989)
By T.V. Buttrey and Clyde Hubbard
304 pages. 5"x8" $14.95

Let this handbook work as your personal guide through all regular issue and commemorative coinages by denominations and date, from 1822 to 1985, complete with valuations for all mintmark and assayer initial combinations.

A comprehensive introduction reviews Mexican coinage beginning with the opening of the first mint and leads you through that country's rich and vibrant history. It's a must for those interested in coinage from the Western hemisphere.

Full coverage of the Iturbide (first) Empire, the Mexican Republic real/escudo issues, the Maximilian (second) Empire and Mexican Republic decimal system issues adds to the expansive nature of this value-packed guidebook.

SPINK'S CATALOGUE OF BRITISH COLONIAL AND COMMONWEALTH COINS

1st edition
By Andre P. de Clermont and John Wheeler
704 pages. 7½"x9¼" $40.00

Experience, in complete pictorial detail, an inspiring collection of coinage for Great Britain's overseas possessions from 1601 to the present. Every issue struck under the auspices of the crown outside of the United Kingdom during the last three centuries is compiled here for your collecting pleasure.

You'll regard this easy-to-use, streamlined catalogue as a practical and valuable collecting tool. Updated Krause/Mishler cataloguing system numbers appear with references to Friedberg numbers where our experts deemed necessary or helpful. Pricing data reflects current market conditions in up to six grades of preservation to help you pinpoint values for the essential components of your British coin collection.

( ) Yes! Send me _____ copies of Spink's Catalogue of British Colonial and Commonwealth Coins, listed at $40.00 each.

( ) Yes! Send me _____ copies of A Guide Book of Mexican Coins, 1822 to Date, 5th edition, at $14.95 each.

(Payable in U.S. funds. U.S. addresses send $2.50 per book, shipping and handling. Non-U.S. addresses enclose $5.50 per book.)

Total Amt. for Books $ _____

Total Shipping $ _____

Total Amt. Enclosed $ _____

( ) Check or money order
(to Krause Publications)

( ) MasterCard/VISA

Name _____
Address _____
City _____
State _____ Zip _____
Country _____
Credit Card No. _____
Expires: Mo. _____ Yr. _____
Signature _____
Phone No. _____

Mail with payment to
Krause Publications, Book Dept.,
700 E. State St., Iola, WI 54990

Bernstein, McCaffrey & Lee
INCORPORATED
International Trading in Bullion and Rare Coins

Members of A.N.A. & F.U.N.

"We specialize in the buying and selling of the most rare coins in the world, focusing on coins from China. We seek to provide the scarcest and most desirable coins to our clientele."

For additional information inquiries can be made to:
BERNSTEIN, McCAFFREY & LEE, INC.
"The Exchange Building", 401 Cleveland St., Clearwater, FL 34615
or Call us toll free at 1 (800) 343-2968 or Call Direct (813) 447-5088

AVOIRDUPOIS STANDARDS

27-11/32 Grains = 1 Dram
437-1/2 Grains = 1 Ounce
28.350 Grams = 1 Ounce

BULLION VALUE CHARTS

Universal silver, gold, and platinum bullion value charts are provided for use in combination with the ASW, AGW and APW factors to determine approximate intrinsic values of listed coins. By adding the component weights as shown in troy ounces on each chart, the approximate intrinsic value of any silver, gold or platinum coins' precious metal content can be determined.

Again referring to the examples presented in the above section, the intrinsic value of a silver coin with a .6822 ASW would be indicated as $4.43 + based on the application of the silver bullion chart. This result is obtained by moving across the top to the $6.50 column, then moving down to the line indicated .680 in the far left hand corner, which reveals a bullion value of $4.420. To determine the value of the remaining .0022 of ASW, return up the same column to the .002 line, the closest factor available, where a $ .0130 value is indicated. The two factors total to $4.433, which would be slightly less than actual value.

The silver bullion chart provides silver values in thousandths from .001 to .009 troy ounce, and in hundredths from .01 to 1.00 in 50¢ value increments from $5.00 to $12.50. If the market value of silver exceeds $16.50, doubling the increments presented will provide valuations in $1 steps from $18.00 to $33.00.

The gold/platinum bullion chart is similarly arranged in $10 increments from $400 to $750, and by doubling the increments presented, $20 steps from $800 to $1500 can be determined.

Valuations for most of the silver, gold, platinum and palladium coins listed in this edition are based on assumed market values of $6.00 per troy ounce for silver, $400 for gold, $550 for platinum, and $150 for palladium. To arrive at accurate current market indications for these issues, increase or decrease the valuations appropriately based on any variations in these indicated levels.

PHOTOGRAPHS

To assist the reader in coin identification, every effort has been made to present actual size photographs of every coinage type listed. Obverse and reverse are illustrated, except when a change in design is restricted to one side, and the coin has a diameter of 39mm or larger, in which case only the side, required for identification of the type is generally illustrated. All coins up to 60mm are illustrated actual size, to the nearly 1/2mm up to 25mm, and to the nearest 1mm thereafter. Coins larger than 60mm diameter are illustrated in reduced size, with the actual size noted thereunder. Where slight change in size is important to coin type identification, actual millimeter measurements are stated.

COIN vs. MEDAL ALIGNMENT

Coins are traditionally struck with obverse and reverse aligned at a rotation of 180 degrees from each other. When a coin is held for vertical viewing with the obverse design aligned upright and the index finger and thumb at the top and bottom, upon rotation from left to right for viewing the reverse, the latter will be upside down. Such alignment is called "coin rotation". Some coins are struck with the obverse and reverse designs mated on an alignment of zero or 360 degrees. If such a piece is held and rotated as described, the reverse will appear upright. This is the alignment which is generally observed in the striking of medals, and for that reason coins produced in this manner are termed to have been struck in "medal rotation". In some instances certain coin issues have been struck to both alignment standards, creating interesting collectible varieties which will be found noted in some listings.

RESTRIKES, COUNTERFEITS

Deceptive restrike and counterfeit (both contemporary and modern) examples exist of some coin issues. Where possible, the existence of restrikes is noted. Warnings are also incorporated in instances where particularly deceptive counterfeits are known to exist. Collectors who are uncertain about the authenticity of a coin held in their collection, or being offered for sale, should take the precaution of having it authenticated by the American Numismatic Association Certification Service, 818 N. Cascade, Colorado Springs, CO 80903. Their reasonably-priced certification tests are widely accepted by collectors and dealers alike.

COUNTERMARKS/COUNTERSTAMPS

There is some confusion among collectors over the terms "countermark" and "counterstamp" when applied to a coin bearing an additional mark or change of design and/or denomination.

To clarify, a countermark might be considered similar to the "hall mark" applied to a piece of silverware, by which a silversmith assured the quality of the piece. In the same way, a countermark assures the quality of the coin on which it is placed, as, for example, when the royal crown of England was countermarked (punched into) on segmented Spanish reales, allowing them to circulate in commerce in the British West Indies. An additional countermark indicating the new denomination may also be encountered on these coins.

Countermarks are generally applied singularly and in most cases indiscriminately on either side of the "host" coin.

Counterstamped coins are more extensively altered. The counterstamping is done with a set of dies, rather than a hand punch. The coin being counterstamped is placed between the new dies and struck as if it were a blank planchet as found with the Manila 8 reales issue of the Philippines. A more unusual application where the counterstamp dies were smaller than the host coin is in the revalidated 50 centimos and 1 colon of Costa Rica issued in 1923.

STANDARD INTERNATIONAL GRADING TERMINOLOGY AND ABBREVIATIONS

U.S. and ENGLISH SPEAKING LANDS	PROOF	UNCIRCULATED	EXTREMELY FINE	VERY FINE	FINE	VERY GOOD	GOOD	POOR
Abbreviation	PRF	UNC	EF or XF	VF	F	VG	G	PR
BRAZIL	—	(1) FDC or FC	(3) S	(5) MBC	(7) BC	(8) BC/R	(9) R	UTGeG
DENMARK	M	0	01	1+	1	1÷	2	3
FINLAND	00	0	01	1+	1	1?	2	3
FRANCE	FB	FDC	SUP	TTB or TB	TB or B	B	TBC	BC
GERMANY	PP	I/STGL	II/VZGL	III/SS	IV/S	V/S.g.E.	VI/G.e.	G.e.s.
ITALY	FS	FDC	SPL	BB	MB	B	M	—
JAPAN	—	未使用	極美品	美品	並品	—	—	—
NETHERLANDS	—	FDC	Pr.	Z.F.	Fr.	Z.g.	G	—
NORWAY	M	0	01	1+	1	1÷	2	3
PORTUGAL	—	Soberba	Bela	MBC	BC	MREG	REG	MC
SPAIN	Prueba	SC	EBC	MBC	BC+	BC	RC	MC
SWEDEN	Polerad	0	01	1+	1	1?	2	—

CONDITIONS/GRADING

Wherever possible, coin valuations are given in four grades of preservation. The following standards have been observed to provide continuity in grouping grade ranges in this catalog. However, because they cannot be universally applied, appropriate variations have been incorporated and noted: 1) Good, Very Good, Fine and Very Fine - used for crude "dump" or similar issues; 2) Very Good, Very Fine and Extremely Fine - used for early machine-minted issues of Europe (early 1800s), Latin America (up to the mid-1800s), the present. Listings in three grades of preservation will also be found, usually in cases of modern issues.

There are almost no grading guides for world coins. What follows is an attempt to help bridge that gap until a detailed, illustrated guide becomes available.

In grading world coins, there are two elements to look for: 1) Overall wear, and 2) loss of design details, such as strands of hair, feathers on eagles, designs on coats of arms, etc.

The age, rarity or type of a coin should not be a consideration in grading.

Grade each coin by the weaker of the two sides. This method appears to give results most nearly consistent with conservative American Numismatic Association standards for U.S. coins. Split grades, i.e., F/VF for obverse and reverse, respectively, are normally no more than one grade apart. If the two sides are more than one grade apart, the series of coins probably wears differently on each side and should then be graded by the weaker side alone.

Grade by the amount of overall wear and loss of detail evident in the main design on each side. On coins with a moderately small design element which is prone to early wear, grade by that design alone. For example, the 5-ore (Y-46) of Sweden has a crown above the monogram on which the beads on the arches show wear most clearly. So, grade by the crown alone.

For **Uncirculated** (Unc.) grades there will be no visible signs of wear or handling, even under a 30-power microscope. Bag marks may be present.

For **Almost Uncirculated** (AU), all detail will be visible. There will be wear only on the highest point of the coin. There will often be half or more of the original mint luster present.

On the **Extremely Fine** (XF or EF) coin, there will be about 95% of the original detail visible. Or, on a coin with a design with no inner detail to wear down, there will be a light wear over nearly all the coin. If a small design is used as the grading area, about 90% of the original detail will be visible. This latter rule stems from the logic that a smaller amount of detail needs to be present because a small area is being used to grade the whole coin.

The **Very Fine** (VF) coin will have about 75% of the original detail visible. Or, on a coin with no inner detail, there will be moderate wear over the entire coin. Corners of letters and numbers may be weak. A small grading area will have about 66% of the original detail.

For **Fine** (F), there will be about 50% of the original detail visible. Or, on a coin with no inner detail, there will be fairly heavy wear over all of the coin. Sides of letters will be weak. A typically uncleaned coin will often appear as dirty or dull. A small grading area will have just under 50% of the original detail.

On the **Very Good** (VG) coin, there will be about 25% of the original detail visible. There will be heavy wear on all of the coin.

The **Good** (G) coin's design will be clearly outlined but with substantial wear. Some of the larger detail may be visible. The rim may have a few weak spots of wear.

On the **About Good** (AG) coin, there will typically be only a silhouette of a large design. The rim will be worn down into the letters if any.

Strong or weak strikes, partially weak strikes, damage, corrosion, attractive or unattractive toning, dipping or cleaning should be described along with the above grades. These factors affect the quality of the coin just as do wear and loss of detail, but are easier to describe.

The "Official A.N.A. Grading Standards for United States Coins" is utilized in the presentation of these listings and is explained on page 34. It is commonly referred to as the "MS" or "Mint State" numeric grading system.

NON-CIRCULATING LEGAL TENDER COINS

Coins of non-circulating legal tender (NCLT) origin are individually listed and integrated by denomination into the regular listings for each country. These coins fall outside the customary definitions of coin-of-the-realm issues, but were created and sold by, or under authorization of, agencies of sovereign governments expressly for collectors. These are primarily individual coins and sets of a commemorative nature, marketed at prices substantially in excess of face value, and most often do not have counterparts released for circulation.

The eight criteria applied in assigning coins (other than regular issue proof or mint sets) to the NCLT category are: 1) Intrinsic value of the content of the coin is of greater value than its unlike metallic nominal denomination. 2) Both proof and "circulation" issues, if any, are of very low mintage. 3) All specimens distributed at prices in excess of face value. 4) Metallic composition unlike that of normal circulation issues. 5) Circulation unlikely because of excessively high face value or physical size. 6) Currency unit not in general use. 7) Prohibitions against circulation or sale of coins in country of issue. 8) Only non-government agencies distribute the coin.

SETS

Listings in this catalog for specimen, proof and mint sets are for official, government-produced sets. In many instances privately packaged sets also exist.

Mint Sets/Fleur de Coin Sets: Specially prepared by worldwide mints to provide banks, collectors and government dignitaries with examples of current coinage. Usually subjected to rigorous inspection to insure that top quality specimens of selected business strikes are provided. The most popular mint set is that given out by the monarch of Great Britain each year on Maundy Thursday. This set contains four special coins in denominations of 1, 2, 3 and 4 pence, struck in silver and contained in a little pouch. They have been given away in a special ceremony for the poor for more than two centuries.

The Paris Mint introduced polyvinyl plastic cases packed within a cardboard box for homeland and colonial Fleur de Coin sets of the 1960s. British colonial sets were issued in velvet-lined metal cases similar to those used for proof sets. For its client nations, the Franklin Mint introduced a sealed composition of cardboard and specially-molded hard clear plastic protective container inserted in a soft plastic wallet. Recent discovery that soft polyvinyl packaging has proved hazardous to coins has resulted in a change to the use of hard, inert plastics for virtually all mint sets.

Some of the highest quality mint sets ever produced were those struck by the Franklin Mint during 1972-74. In many cases matte finish dies were used to strike a polished proof planchet. Later on, from 1975, sets contained highly polished, glassy-looking coins similar to those struck by the Bombay Mint for collectors over a period of 12 years.

Specimen Sets: Forerunners of today's proof sets. In most cases the coins were specially struck, perhaps even double struck, to produce a very soft or matte finish on the effigies and fields, along with high, sharp "wire" rims. The finish is rather dull to the naked eye.

The original purpose of these sets was to provide VIPs, monarchs and mintmasters around the world with samples of the highest quality workmanship of a particular mint. These were usually housed in elaborate velvet-lined leather and metal cases.

Proof-like Sets: A relative late-comer to the field of numismatics. During the mid 1950s the Royal Canadian Mint furnished the hobby with specially selected early business strike coins that exhibited some qualities similar to proof coinage. However, the "proof-like" fields are generally flawed and the edges are rounded. These pieces are not double struck. These are commonly encountered in cardboard holders, later in soft plastic or pliofilm packaging. Of late, the Royal Canadian Mint packages such sets in rigid plastic cases.

Many worldwide officially-issued proof sets would in reality fall into this category upon careful examination of the quality of the coins' finish.

Another term encountered in this category is "Special Select", used to describe the crowns of the Union of South Africa and 100-schilling coins produced for collectors in the late 1970s by the Austrian Mint.

Proof Sets: This is undoubtedly among the most misused terms in the hobby, not only by collectors and dealers, but also by many of the world mints.

A true proof set must be at least double-struck on specially prepared polished planchets and struck using dies (often themselves polished) of the highest quality.

Modern-day proof quality consists of frosted effigies surrounded by absolute mirror-like fields.

Listings for proof sets in this catalog are for officially-issued proof sets so designated by the issuing authority, and may or may not possess what are considered modern proof quality standards.

It is necessary for collectors to acquire the knowledge to allow them to differentiate true proof sets from would-be proof sets and proof-like sets which may be encountered.

TRADE COINS

From approximately 1750-1940, a number of nations, particularly European colonial powers and commercial traders, minted trade coins to facilitate commerce with local populace of Africa, the Arab countries, the Indian sub-continent, Southeast Asia and the Far East. Such coins generally circulated at a value based on the weight and fineness of their silver or gold content, rather than their stated denomination. Examples include the silver trade dollars of Great Britain, Japan and the United States, the Spanish Colonial 8 reales, a very successful world trade coin being very popular in the orient right into the 20th century, the gold ducat issues of Austria, Hungary and the Netherlands, and the Maria Theresa talers of Austria, another of the world's most successful trade coins especially in Africa and the Middle East. Trade coinage will be found listed at the end of the domestic issues.

HOMELAND TYPES

The era of global empires established by Europe's colonial powers found the homeland coinage types, particularly in the case of Great Britain, of specific dates and denominations being minted exclusively or primarily for circulation in certain overseas possessions. Identical in design and indistinguishable except for the date of issue or less frequently by denomination from the homeland coinages, these issues also circulated freely, if on a somewhat restricted basis, in other colonies, ports of call and even the homeland. A modern example is the French 1 Centime which are used solely in the French Colonies in Africa.

In a departure from established cataloging practice, which incorporated listings of these issues under the designated area of circulation, in this catalog they will be found incorporated under the homelands. Appropriate references note the intended areas of distribution for these somewhat puzzling issues, which range in date from the early 1800s until after World War II.

VALUATIONS

Values quoted in this catalog represent the current market and are compiled from recommendations provided and verified through various source documents and specialized consultants. **It should be stressed, however, that this book is intended to serve only as an aid for evaluating coins, actual market conditions are constantly changing and additional influences,** such as particularly strong local demand for certain coin series, fluctuation of international exchange rates and worldwide collecting patterns must also be considered. Publication of this catalog is not intended as a solicitation by the publisher, editors or contributors to buy or sell the listed coins at the prices indicated.

All valuations are stated in U.S. dollars, based on careful assessment of the varied international money market. Valuations for coins priced below $1,000.00 are generally stated in full amounts - i.e. 37.50 or 950.00 - while valuations at or above that figure are rounded off in even dollars - i.e., $1250.00 is expressed as 1250. A comma is added to indicate tens of thousands of dollars in value.

For the convenience of overseas collectors and for U.S. collectors doing business with overseas dealers, the base exchange rate for the national currencies of approximately 180 countries are presented in the foreign exchange table.

It should be noted that when particularly select uncirculated or proof-like examples of uncirculated coins become available, they can be expected to command proportionately high premiums. Such examples in reference to choice Germanic Thalers are referred to as "erst schlage" or first strikes.

NEW ISSUES

All newly released coins that have been physically observed by our staff and those that have been confirmed by press time have been incorporated in this edition. Certain exceptions exist in such countries as West Germany where current date coin production lags far behind and other countries whose fiscal year actually begins in the latter half of the current year.

Collectors and dealers alike are kept up to date with worldwide new issues having newly assigned catalog reference numbers and releases of mintage figures of previous years presented in the weekly feature "World Coin Roundup" in *World Coin News*. Direct ordering instructions from worldwide mints and authorized institutions is also provided through new releases and the "Mint Data" column in *World Coin News*. A free sample copy will be sent upon request. Overseas requests should include 1 international postal reply coupon for surface mail or 2 international postal reply coupons for air mail dispatch: Write to *World Coin News*, 700 East State St., Iola, WI 54990 USA.

ANA MEMBERSHIP CAN DO YOUR COINS A WORLD OF GOOD

When you join the American Numismatic Association, you become a member of the **WORLD'S** largest, nonprofit, educational numismatic organization chartered by Congress.

As a member, you can give your coins the **WORLD'S** best certification and grading service—ANACS.

ANACS' service can make a **WORLD** of difference.

A **WORLD** of quality control is inherent in every grade. Speed is not our sole criterion.

We recognize eye appeal as a major factor in grading your **WORLD** coin.

Consistent, expert opinions from **WORLD**-class coin graders deliver the optimum grade, while our skilled photographers capture every **WORLDLY** dimension.

Do your **WORLD** coins a favor. Become a member of ANA's **WORLD**.

Call toll free and join today.
800-367-9723

American Numismatic ASSOCIATION
818 North Cascade Avenue
Colorado Springs, CO 80903-3279

OFFICIAL ANA GRADING STANDARDS

For United States Coins

The following grading system as adopted by the American Numismatic Association is utilized in our presentation of the United States coinage.

For descriptive and illustrative analysis refer to the *Official A.N.A. Grading Standards for United States Coins*, Second Edition, as compiled by Ken Bressett and A. Kosoff, copyright American Numismatic Association and Whitman Publishing, 1977, 1981.

PROOF COINS

The term "Proof" refers to a manufacturing process which results in a special surface or finish on coins made for collectors. Most familiar are modern brilliant Proofs. These coins are struck at the mint by a special process. Carefully prepared dies, sharp in all features, are made. Then the flat surfaces of the dies are given a high mirrorlike polish. Specially prepared planchets are fed into low-speed coining presses. Each Proof coin is slowly and carefully struck more than once to accentuate details. When striking is completed the coin is taken from the dies with care and not allowed to come into contact with other pieces. The result is a coin with mirrorlike surface. The piece is then grouped together with other denominations in a set and offered for sale to collectors.

From 1817 through 1857 inclusive, Proof coins were made only on special occasions and not for general sale to collectors. They were made available to visiting foreign dignitaries, government officials, and those with connections at the mint. Earlier (pre-1817) United States coins may have prooflike surfaces and many Proof characteristics (1796 silver coins are a good example), but they were not specifically or intentionally struck as Proofs. These are sometimes designated as "specimen strikings."

Beginning in 1858, Proofs were sold to collectors openly. In that year 80 silver Proof sets (containing silver coins from the three-cent piece through the silver dollar), plus additional pieces of the silver dollar denomination, were produced as well as perhaps 200 (the exact number is not known) copper-nickel cents and a limited number of Proof gold coins.

The traditional or "brilliant" type of Proof finish was used on all American Proof coins of the nineteenth century. During the twentieth century, cents through the 1909 Indian, nickels through the 1912 Liberty, regular issue silver coins through 1915, and gold coins through 1907 were of the brilliant type. When modern Proof coinage was resumed in 1936 and continued through 1942, then 1950-1964, and 1968 to date, the brilliant finish was used. While these types of Proofs are referred to as "brilliant Proofs," actual specimens may have toned over the years. The mirrorlike surface is still evident however.

From 1908 through 1915, Matte Proofs and Sandblast Proofs (the latter made by directing fine sand particles at high pressure toward the coin's surface) were made of certain gold coins (exceptions are 1909-1910 Proofs with Roman finish). While characteristics vary from issue to issue, generally all of these pieces have extreme sharpness of design detail and sharp, squared-off rims. The surfaces are without luster and have a dullish matte surface. Sandblast Proofs were made of certain commemoratives also, such as the 1928 Hawaiian issue.

Roman finish Proof gold coins were made in 1909 and 1910. These pieces are sharply struck, have squared-off-edges, and have a satin-like surface finish, not too much different from an Uncirculated coin (which causes confusion among collectors today, and which at the time of issue was quite unpopular as collectors resented having to pay a premium for a coin without a distinctly different appearance).

Matte Proofs were made of Lincoln cents 1909-1917 and Buffalo nickels 1913-1917. Such coins have extremely sharp design detail, squared-off rims, "brilliant" (mirrorlike) edges, but a matte or satin-like (or even satin surface, not with flashy mint luster) surface. In some instances Matte Proof dies may have been used to make regular circulation strikes once the requisite number of Matte Proofs were made for collectors. So, it is important that a Matte Proof, to be considered authentic, have squared-off rims and mirrorlike perfect edges in addition to the proper surface characteristics.

Additional Points Concerning Proofs: Certain regular issues or business strike coins have nearly full prooflike surfaces. These were produced in several ways. Usually regular issue dies (intended to make coins for circulation) were polished to remove surface marks or defects for extended use. Coins struck from these dies were produced at high speed, and the full Proof surface is not always evident. Also, the pieces are struck on ordinary planchets. Usually such pieces, sometimes called "first strikes" or "prooflike Uncirculated," have patches of Uncirculated mint frost. A characteristic in this regard is the shield on the reverse (on coins with this design feature). The stripes within the shield on Proofs are fully brilliant, but on prooflike non-proofs the stripes usually are not mirrorlike. Also, the striking may be weak in areas and the rims might not be sharp.

The mirrorlike surface of a brilliant Proof coin is much more susceptible to damage than are the surfaces of an Uncirculated coin. For this reason, Proof coins which have been cleaned often show a series of fine hairlines or minute striations. Also, careless handling has resulted in certain Proofs acquiring marks, nicks, and scratches.

Some Proofs, particularly nineteenth century issues, have "lintmarks." When a Proof die was wiped with an oily rag, sometimes threads, bits of hair, lint, and so on would remain. When a coin was struck from such a die, an incuse or recessed impression of the debris would appear on the piece. Lintmarks visible to the unaided eye should be specifically mentioned in a description.

Proofs are divided into the following classifications:

Proof-70. A Proof-70 or Perfect Proof is a coin with no hairlines, handling marks, or other defects; in other words, a flawless coin. Such a coin may be brilliant or may have natural toning.

Proof-67. A grade midway between Proof-70 and Proof-65. Such a coin would be very close to Proof-70 and would be noticeably finer than Proof-65.

Proof-65. Proof-65 or Choice Proof refers to a Proof which may show some very fine hairlines, usually from friction-type cleaning or friction-type drying or rubbing after dipping. To the unaided eye, a Proof-65 or a Choice Proof will appear to be virtually perfect. However, 4x magnification will reveal some minute lines. Such hairlines are best seen under strong incandescent light.

Proof-63. A coin which is midway between Proof-65 and Proof-60.

Proof-60. Proof-60 refers to a Proof with some scattered handling marks and hairlines which will be visible to the unaided eye.

Impaired Proofs; Other Comments. If a Proof has been excessively cleaned, has many marks, scratches, dents or other defects, it is described as an impaired Proof. If the coin has seen extensive wear then it will be graded one of the lesser grades — Proof-55, Proof-45, or whatever. It is not logical to describe a slightly worn Proof as "AU" (Almost Uncirculated) for it never was "Uncirculated" to begin with — in the sense that Uncirculated describes a top grade normal production strike. So, the term "impaired Proof" is appropriate. It is best to describe fully such a coin, examples being: "Proof with extensive hairlines and scuffing," or "Proof with numerous nicks and scratches in the field," or "Proof-55, with light wear on the higher surfaces."

UNCIRCULATED COINS

The term "Uncirculated," interchangeable with "Mint State," refers to a coin which has never seen circulation. Such a piece has no wear of any kind. A coin as bright as the time it was minted or with very light natural toning can be described as "Brilliant Uncirculated." A coin which has natural toning can be described as "Toned Uncirculated." Except in the instance of copper coins, the presence or absence of light toning does not affect an Uncirculated coin's grade. Indeed, among silver coins, attractive natural toning often results in the coin bringing a premium.

The quality of luster or "mint bloom" on an Uncirculated coin is an essential element in correctly grading the piece, and has a bearing on its value. Luster may in time become dull, frosty, spotted or discolored. Unattractive luster will normally lower the grade.

With the exception of certain Special Mint Sets made in recent years for collectors, Uncirculated or normal production strike coins were produced on high speed presses, stored in bags together with other coins, run through counting machines, and in other ways handled without regard to numismatic posterity. As a result, it is the rule and not the exception for an Uncirculated coin to have bag marks and evidence of coin-to-coin contact, although the piece might not have seen actual commercial circulation. The amount of such marks will depend upon the coin's size. Differences in criteria in this regard are given in the individual sections under grading descriptions for different denominations and types.

Uncirculated coins can be divided into five major categories:

MS-70. MS-70 or Perfect Uncirculated is the finest quality available. Such a coin under 4x magnification will show no bag marks, lines, or other evidence of handling or contact with other coins.

A brilliant coin may be described as "MS-70, Brilliant" or "Perfect Brilliant Uncirculated." A lightly toned nickel or silver coin may be described as "MS-70, toned" or "Perfect Toned Uncirculated." Or, in the case of particularly attractive or unusual toning, additional adjectives may be in order such as "Perfect Uncirculated with attractive iridescent toning around the borders."

Copper and bronze coins: To qualify as MS-70 or Perfect Uncirculated, a copper or bronze coin must have its full luster and natural surface color, and may not be toned brown, olive, or any other color. (Coins with toned surfaces which are otherwise perfect should be described as MS-65, rather than MS-67.

MS-67. This refers to a coin which is midway between MS-70 and MS-65. The coin may be either brilliant or toned (except for a copper coin, for which a toned piece should be described as MS-65).

MS-65. This refers to an above Uncirculated coin which may be brilliant or toned (and described accordingly) and which has fewer bag marks than usual; scattered occasional bag marks on the surface or perhaps one or two very light rim marks.

MS-63. A coin which is midway between MS-65 and MS-60.

MS-60. MS-60 or Uncirculated (typical Uncirculated without any other adjectives) refers to a coin which has a moderate number of bag marks on its surface. Also present may be a few minor edge nicks and marks, although not of a serious nature. Unusually deep bag marks, nicks, and the like must be described separately. A coin may be either brilliant or toned.

Grading Standard Interpretations

The "official" A.N.A. grading standards in the "Mint State" range as described have been adapted in assigning the market valuations presented for U.S. issues, to conform to concensus interpretations prevailing in the marketplace.

The numeric grades, along with their prevailing adjectival grades and descriptions are as follows:

MS-63: (Choice Uncirculated) — Choice quality specimens with minimal weaknesses or blemishes readily evident.

MS-64 — Choice quality specimens with eye appeal and only the smallest distracting weakness, blemish or bagmarks.

MS-65 (Gem Uncirculated) — Sharply struck, hairline-free coins with full lustre and no distracting blemishes.

MS-67 — Described as "Gem" according to "official" A.N.A. criteria, is not presently associated with an adjectival equivalent. There is also not a concensus description that is associated with this grade.

Striking and Minting Peculiarities on Uncirculated Coins

Certain early United States gold and silver coins have mint-caused planchet or adjustment marks, a series of parallel striations. If these are visible to the naked eye they should be described adjectivally in addition to the numerical or regular descriptive grade. For example: "MS-60 with adjustment marks," or "MS-65 with adjustment marks," or "Perfect Uncirculated with very light adjustment marks," or something similar.

If an Uncirculated coin exhibits weakness due to striking or die wear, or unusual (for the variety) die wear, this must be adjectivally mentioned in addition to the grade. Examples are: "MS-60, lightly struck," or "Choice Uncirculated, lightly struck," and "MS-70, lightly struck."

CIRCULATED COINS

Once a coin enters circulation it begins to show signs of wear. As time goes on the coin becomes more and more worn until, after a period of many decades, only a few features may be left.

Dr. William H. Sheldon devised a numerical scale to indicate degrees of wear. According to this scale, a coin in condition 1 or "Basal State" is barely recognizable. At the opposite end, a coin touched by even the slightest trace of wear (below MS-60) cannot be called Uncirculated.

While numbers from 1 through 59 are continuous, it has been found practical to designate specific intermediate numbers to define grades. Hence, this text uses the following descriptions and their numerical equivalents:

Choice About Uncirculated-55. Abbreviation: AU-55. Only a small trace of wear is visible on the highest points of the coin.

About Uncirculated-50. Abbreviation: AU-50. With traces of wear on nearly all of the highest areas. At least half of the original mint luster is present.

Choice Extremely Fine-45. Abbreviation: EF-45. With light overall wear on the coin's highest points. All design details are very sharp. Mint luster is usually seen only in protected areas of the coin's surface such as between the star points and in the letter spaces.

Extremely Fine-40. Abbreviation: EF-40. with only slight wear but more extensive than the preceding, still with excellent overall sharpness. Traces of mint luster may still show.

Choice Very Fine-30. Abbreviation: VF-30. With light even wear on the surface; design details on the highest points lightly worn, but with all lettering and major features sharp.

Very Fine-20. Abbreviation: VF-20. As preceding but with moderate wear on highest parts.

Fine-12. Abbreviation: F-12. Moderate to considerable even wear. Entire design is bold. All lettering, including the word LIBERTY (on coins with this feature on the shield or headband), visible, both with some weaknesses.

Very Good-8. Abbreviation: VG-8. Well worn. Most fine details such as hair strands, leaf details, and so on are worn nearly smooth. The word LIBERTY, if on a shield or headband, is only partially visible.

Good-4. Abbreviations: G-4. Heavily worn. Major designs visible, but with faintness in areas. Head of Liberty, wreath, and other major features visible in outline form without center detail.

About Good-3. AG-3. Very heavily worn with portions of the lettering, date, and legends being worn smooth. The date barely readable. *Note:* The exact descriptions of circulated grades vary widely from issue to issue, so the preceding commentary is only of a very general nature.

COIN DENOMINATION INDEX

A

ABAZI - Russian Caucasia
ABBASI - Afghanistan, Iran, Russian Caucasia
ACKEY - Gold Coast (Ghana)
ADHIO - Indian Princely States
ADLI ALTIN - Turkey
AFGHANI - Afghanistan
AGORA - Israel
AGOROT - Israel
AHMADI RIYAL - Yemen Arab Republic
AKCE - Turkey
AKCHEH - Egypt, U.S.S.R.
ALBERTIN - Belgian States
ALBERTUS DALER - Denmark
ALBUS - German States, Swiss- Cantons
ALEX D'OR - German States
ALTIN - Egypt, Turkey
ALTINLIK - Turkey
ALTMISHLIK - U.S.S.R.
AMANI - Afghanistan
ANANTARAYA - Indian Princely States
ANGEL - Great Britain, Isle of Man
ANGSTER - Swiss- Cantons
ANNA - India, India-British, India-Independent Kingdom, Indian Princely States, Kenya, Mombasa, Muscat & Oman, Oman, Pakistan, Yemen
ANANTARAYA - Indian States
ARDITE - Navarre (Spain)
ARGENTINO - Argentina
ARIARY - Madagascar
ASARPHI - Nepal
ASHRAFI - Afghanistan, Egypt, Indian Princely States
ASHRAPI - Nepal
ASPER - Algeria, Egypt, Libya, Tunisia, Turkey
ASSES - Luxembourg
ATIA - India-Portuguese
ATRIBUO - German States-Frankfurt
ATT - Cambodia, Laos, Thailand
AURAR - Iceland
AVOS - Macao, Timor

B

BAHT - Thailand
BAIOCCHI - Vatican-Papal States
BAIOCCO - Vatican-Papal States
BAISA - Muscat & Oman, Oman
BAIZA - Kuwait
BAIZA - Oman
BALBOA - Panama
BAN - Romania
BANI - Romania
BANU - Romania
BARBONE - Italian States
BARILLA - Philippines
BASTARDO - India-Portuguese
BATZEN - Swiss- Cantons, Switzerland
BAZARUCOS - India-Portuguese
BAZARUK - India-Dutch
BELGA - Belgium
BENDUQI - Morocco
BESA - Somalia
BESE - Somalia
BESHLIK - U.S.S.R.
BESLIK - Turkey
BEZZO - Italian States
BICHE - India-French
BIPKWELE - Equatorial Guinea
BIRR - Ethiopia
BIRBUCHUK TUGHRALI ALTIN - Egypt
BISTI - Russian Caucasia
BIT - British Virgin Islands, Danish West Indies, Dominica, Essequibo & Demerary (Guyana), Grenada, Martinique, Montserrat, Trinidad & Tobago
BLACK DOG - Nevis
BLUZGER - Swiss-Cantons
BOLIVAR - Venezuela
BOLIVIANO - Bolivia
BOLOGNINO - Italian States, Vatican-Papal States
BU - Japan
BUDJU - Algeria
BUQSHA - Yemen Arab Republic
BURBE - Tunisia
BURBENS - Tunisia
BUTUT - Gambia

C

CACHE - India-French
CAGLIARESI - Italian States
CANDAREENS - China
CARLINI - Italian States, Order of Malta, Vatican Papal States
CARLINO - Italian States, Vatican-Papal States
CAROLIN - Austrian States, German States, Sweden
CASH - China, India-Dutch, India-British, Indian Princely States, Vietnam-Annam
CASSATHALER - German States
CAURIS - Guinea
CAVALIER D'OR - Netherlands
CAVALLI - Italian States
CEDI - Ghana
CEDID MAHMUDIYE - Turkey
CENT - Aruba, Australia, Bahamas, Barbados, Belize, Bermuda, Botswana, British East Caribbean Territories, British Honduras, British North Borneo, British Virgin Islands, Brunei, Canada, Cayman Islands, Ceylon, China, Cook Islands, Curacao, Cyprus, Danish West Indies, East Africa, East Caribbean States, Ethiopia, Fiji, French Cochin China, French Indo-China, Guyana, Hawaii, Hong Kong, Indonesia, Jamaica, Keeling-Cocos Islands, Kenya, Kiao Chau, Kiribati, Laos, Liberia, Malawi, Malaya & British Borneo, Malaysia, Malta, Mauritius, Netherlands, Netherlands Antilles, Netherlands East Indies, New Brunswick, New Zealand, Newfoundland, Nova Scotia, Palo Seco, Panama, Prince Edward Island, Rhodesia, Sarawak, Seychelles, Sierra Leone, Singapore, Solomon Islands, South Africa, Sri Lanka, Straits Settlement, Surinam, Swaziland, Tanzania, Trinidad & Tobago, Tuvalu, Uganda, United States of America, Zanzibar, Zimbabwe
CENTAI - Baltic Regions-Lithuania
CENTAS - Baltic Regions-Lithuania
CENTAVO - Angola, Argentina, Bolivia, Brazil, Cape Verde, Chile, Colombia, Costa Rica, Cuba, Dominican Republic, Ecuador, El Salvador, Guatemala, Guinea-Bissau, Honduras, India-Portuguese, Indonesia, Mexico, Mozambique, Nicaragua, Paraguay, Peru, Philippines, Portugal, Portuguese Guinea, Puerto Rico, St. Thomas & Prince, Timor, Venezuela
CENTECIMO - Bolivia
CENTESIMI - Eritrea, Ethiopia, Italian States, Italy, San Marino, Somalia, Vatican City
CENTESIMO - Bolivia, Chile, Dominican Republic, Italian States, Italy, Panama, Paraguay, Somalia, Uruguay, Vatican City- Papal States
CENTIME - Algeria, Antwerp, Belgian Congo, Belgium, Cambodia, Cameroon, Comoros, Djibouti, France, French Cochin China, French Colonies, French Equatorial Africa, French Guiana, French Indo China, French Oceania, French Polynesia, French West Africa, German States, Germany, Ghent, Guadeloupe, Haiti, Laos, Luxembourg, Madagascar, Martinique, Monaco, Morocco, New Caledonia, Reunion, Ruanda-Urundi, Senegal, Swiss- Cantons, Togo, Tunisia, Vietnam, Yugoslavia, Zaire, Zara
CENTIMO - Costa Rica, Mozambique, Paraguay, Peru, Philippines, Puerto Rico, St. Thomas & Prince, Spain, Venezuela
CENTIMS - Andorra
CENTU - Baltic Regions-Lithuania
CHERVONETZ - U.S.S.R.
CHETRUM - Bhutan
CHIAO - China-Jap. Puppet States
CHI'EN - China
CHIO - China
CHOMSIH - Ghurfah, Mukulla, Quati State, Seiyun & Tarim, Yemen
CHOMSIHI - Yemen
CHON - Korea, Korea-North
CHRISTIAN D'OR - Denmark
CHUCKRAM - Indian Princely States
COLON - Costa Rica, El Salvador
CONDOR - Chile, Ecuador
CORDOBA - Nicaragua
CORNADO - Spain
CORONA - Austria, French States
COURONNE D'OR - Belgian States
CROCIONE - Italian States
CROWN - Australia, Bermuda, Ghana, Gibraltar, Great Britain, Ireland, Isle of Man, Malawi, New Zealand, Nigeria, Rhodesia & Nyasaland, Saint Helena-Ascension, Southern Rhodesia, Turks & Caicos Island, Tristan Da Cunha, Zimbabwe
CRUZADO - Brazil, Portugal
CRUZEIRO - Brazil

D

DALA - Hawaii
DALASI - Gambia
DALER - Danish West Indies, Denmark
DALER S.M. - Sweden
DAM - Afghanistan, India, Nepal
DECIME - France, Monaco
DECIMO - Argentina, Chile, Colombia, Ecuador, Galapagos Islands
DENAR - Hungary
DENARI - Italian States, Swiss- Cantons
DENGA - U.S.S.R.
DENGI - Romania
DENIERS - France, French Colonies, Guadeloupe, Haiti,

Swiss-Cantons
DEUTSCHE MARK - Germany
DHABU - Indian Princely States
DHINGLO - Indian Princely States
DHOFARI RIYAL - Muscat & Oman, Oman
DIME - United States of America
DINAR - Afghanistan, Algeria, Bahrain, Iran, Iraq, Jordan, Kuwait, Libya, Serbia, Tunisia, Yugoslavia, Yemen Dem. Republic
DINARA - Serbia, Yugoslavia
DINAR HASHIMI - Hejaz
DINER - Andorra
DINERO - Peru, Spain
DIO - India-Portuguese
DIRHAM - Jordan, Libya, Morocco, United Arab Emirates
DIRHEM - Morocco, Qatar, Qatar & Dubai
DIU - India-Portuguese
DOBRA - St. Thomas & Prince
DOIT - India-Dutch, Indonesia
DOKDA - Indian Princely States
DOKDO - Indian Princely State
DOLLAR - Anguilla, Antigua & Barbuda, Australia, Bahamas, Barbados, Belize, Bermuda, British Virgin Islands, British West Indies, Brunei, Canada, Cayman Islands, China, Cook Islands, Danish West Indies, Dominica, East Caribbean States, East Caribbean Territories, Ethiopia, Fiji, Great Britain, Grenada, Guyana, Hawaii, Hong Kong, Indonesia, Jamaica, Japan, Kiribati, Liberia, Malaysia, Marshall Islands, Mauritius, Montserrat, New South Wales, New Zealand, Newfoundland, Niue, Palo Seco, Panama, Saint Christopher & Nevis, Saint Kitts, Saint Lucia, Saint Vincent, Sierra Leone, Singapore, Solomon Islands, Straits Settlements, Trinidad & Tobago, Tuvalu, United States of America, Zimbabwe
DOLYA - U.S.S.R.
DONG - Annam, Vietnam, Vietnam-North, Vietnam-South
DOPPIA - German States, Italian States, Italy, Vatican-Papal States
DOPPIETTA - Italian States
DOUBLE - Guernsey
DOUDOU - India-French
DRACHMA - Crete, Greece
DRACHMAI - Crete, Greece
DREILING - German States
DUB - India-British
DUCAT - Austria, Austrian States, Baltic Regions, Bulgaria, Czechoslovakia, Danish West Indies, French States, Denmark, German States, Hungary, Italian States, Indonesia, Liechtenstein, Liege, Netherlands, Poland, Romania, Sweden, Swiss-Cantons, U.S.S.R., Yugoslavia
DUCATI - Italian States, Yugoslavia
DUCATO - Italian States, Yugoslavia
DUCATON - Belgium, Netherlands
DUCATONE - Italian States
DUDU - India-British
DUETTO - Italian States
DUIT - German States, Indonesia, Netherlands, Netherlands East Indies, Sri Lanka
DUKAT - Bulgaria, Czechoslovakia, Hungary, Sweden, Yugoslavia
DUKATO - Czechoslovakia, Yugoslavia
DUKATY - Czechoslovakia
DUPLONE - Swiss- Cantons
DURO - Spain

E

ECU - Belgium, France
ECU D'OR - Belgian States, French States
EKUELE - Equatorial Guinea
EKWELE - Equatorial Guinea
EMALANGENI - Swaziland
ESCALIN - Belgium, Guadeloupe, Haiti, Liege, Martinique
ESCUDO - Angola, Argentina, Azores, Bolivia, Cape Verde, Central American Republic, Chile, Colombia, Costa Rica, Ecuador, Guadeloupe, Guatemala, India-Portuguese, Maderia, Mexico, Mozambique, Peru, Portugal, Portuguese Guinea, Spain, St. Thomas & Prince, Timor
EYRIR - Iceland

F

FALUS - Afghanistan, China, India-Independent Kingdom, Indian Princely States, Iran, Morocco, Russian Turkestan
FANAM - India-British, India-Mughal, India-Dutch, Indian Princely States, Sri Lanka
FANO - India-Danish
FANON - India-French
FARTHING - Antigua & Barbuda, Ceylon, Great Britain, Ireland, Isle of Man, Jamaica, Malta, South Africa, Sri Lanka
FELS - Algeria
FEN - China, China-Jap. Puppet States
FENIG - Poland
FENIGOW - Poland
FILIPPO - Italian States
FILS - Bahrain, Iraq, Jordan, Kuwait, South Arabia, United Arab Emirates, Yemen, Yemen Arab Republic
FILLER - Hungary
FIORINO - Italian States
FLORIN - Aruba, Australia, Austria, Belgium, Brazil, East Africa, Fiji Islands, Great Britain, Ireland, Malawi, Netherlands, New Zealand, South Africa, Swiss-Cantons
FLORIN D'OR - Belgian States, French States, Netherlands
FORINT - Hungary
FRANC - Algeria, Austria, Belgian Congo, Belgium, Benin, Burma, Burundi, Cambodia, Cameroon, Cattaro, Central African Republic, Central African States, Chad, Comoros, Congo, Dahomey, Danish West Indies, Djibouti, Equatorial African States, France, French Afars & Issas, French Equatorial Africa, French Oceania, French Polynesia, French Somaliland, French West Africa, Gabon, Guadeloupe, Guinea, Hungary, Italian States, Ivory Coast,

Katanga, Luxembourg, Madagascar, Malagasy Republic, Mali, Martinique, Monaco, Morocco, New Caledonia, New Hebrides, Niger, Reunion, Ruanda-Urundi, Rwanda, Rwanda & Burundi, St. Pierre & Miquelon, Senegal, Swiss-Cantons, Switzerland, Togo, Tunisia, West African States, Yugoslavia, Zaire, Zara
FRANCESCONE - Italian States
FRANCHI - Italian States, Swiss- Cantons
FRANCO - Dominican Republic, Ecuador, Equatorial Guinea, Italian States, Swiss- Cantons
FRANCOIS D'OR - French States
FRANG - Luxembourg
FRANK - German States, Liechtenstein, Swiss-Cantons
FRANGA AR - Albania
FRANKEN - Belgium, German States, Ghent, Liechtenstein, Saarland, Swiss-Cantons, Switzerland
FREDERIK D'OR - Denmark, German States
FRIEDRICH D'OR - German States
FUANG - Burma, Cambodia, Thailand
FUENG - Thailand
FUN - Japan, Korea

G

GAZETTA - Ionian Islands
GENEVOISE - Swiss-Cantons
GERSH - Ethiopia
GHIRSH - Hejaz, Hejaz & Nejd, Nejd, Saudi Arabia, Sudan
GIFTE RUMI - Egypt
GIN - Japan
GIRSH - Hejaz, Saudi Arabia
GIULIO - Italian States, Vatican Papal States
GOLD CROWN - Denmark
GOLDE - Sierra Leone
GOLDGULDEN - Austria, Austrian States, Belgian States, French States, German States, Swiss-Cantons
GORYO BAN - Japan
GOURDE - Haiti
GRAMOS - Bolivia
GRAMS - Afghanistan
GRANA - Italian States
GRANI - Order of Malta
GRANO - Italian States, Mexico, Order of Malta
GRESCHL - Romania, Transylvania
GROAT - Great Britain
GROESCHL - Bohemia
GROSCHEL - German States
GROSCHEN - Austria, Danzig, East Prussia, German States, Poland, Posen, Swiss-Cantons
GROSHEN - Austria, German States
GROSSETTI - Ragusa, Yugoslavia
GROSSI - Poland
GROSSO - Italian States, Vatican-Papal States
GROSSUS - Baltic Regions-Courland, Poland
GROSZ - Poland
GROSZE - Poland
GROSZY - Baltic Regions-Courland, Krakow, Poland, Zomosc
GROTE - German States
GROTEN - Romania
GUARANI - Paraguay
GUARANIES - Paraguay
GUERCHE - Egypt
GUILDERS - British Guiana, Curacao, Essequibo & Demerary, Surinam
GUINEA - Great Britain, Saudi Arabia
GULDEN - Austria, Curacao, Danzig, Denmark, German States, Indonesia, Netherlands, Netherlands Antilles, Netherlands East Indies, Surinam, Swiss-Cantons
GUTE GROSHEN - German States
GUTERPFENNIG - German States

H

HABIBI - Afghanistan
HALALA - Saudi Arabia, Yemen
HALBAG - German States-Frankfurt
HALER - Czechoslovakia
HALERE - Czechoslovakia
HALERU - Bohemia-Moravia, Czechoslovakia
HALIEROV - Slovakia
HALLER - Switzerland - Cantons
HAO - China, Vietnam-North, Vietnam
HAPAHA - Hawaii
HAPULA - Hawaii
HAU - Tonga
HAYRIYE ALTIN - Iraq, Turkey
HELLER - Austria, Austrian States, German East Africa, German States
HSIEN - China
HWAN - Korea-South

I

IKILIK - U.S.S.R.
IMADI RIYAL - Yemen Arab Republic
INTI - Peru
ISCHAL - U.S.S.R.

J

JA'U - Indian Princely States
JAWA - Nepal
JIAO - People's Republic (China)
JEDID - Egypt
JOKOH - Kelantan (Malaysia)

K

KAPANG - Malaysia, Sarawak
KAROLIN - German States

KAS - India-Danish
KAZBEG - Russian Caucasia
KENETA - Hawaii
KEPING - Indonesia, Malaysia, Sumatra
KHARUB - Algeria, Tunisia
KHARUBA - Algeria
KHAYRIYA - Egypt
KHOUM - Mauritania
KIN - Japan
KINA - Papua New Guinea
KIP - Laos
KOBAN - Japan
KOBO - Nigeria
KOPEJEK - Tanna Tuva, U.S.S.R.
KOPEK - Baltic Regions-Livonia & Estonia, Germany, Poland, Romania, Spitzbergen, U.S.S.R.
KORI - Indian Princely States
KORONA - Hungary
KORTLING - German States
KORUN - Czechoslovakia, Slovakia
KORUNA - Bohemia-Moravia, Czechoslovakia, Slovakia
KORUNY - Czechoslovakia
KOULA - Tonga
KRAJCZAR - Hungary
KRAN - Iran, Persia
KREUTZER - Austria, German States
KREUZER - Austria, Austrian States, Czechoslovakia, German States, Hungary, Liechtenstein, Poland, Romania, Swiss-Cantons
KRONA - Iceland, Sweden
KRONE - Austria, Denmark, German States, Greenland, Liechtenstein, Norway
KRONEN - Austria, Liechtenstein
KRONENTHALER - Austrian Netherlands
KRONER - Denmark, Greenland, Norway
KRONOR - Sweden
KRONUR - Iceland
KROON - Baltic Regions-Estonia
KROONI - Baltic Regions-Estonia
KRUGERRAND - South Africa
KUNA - Yugoslavia-Croatia
KUNE - Yugoslavia-Croatia
KUPANG - Malaysia, Thailand
KURUS - Turkey
KWACHA - Malawi, Zambia
KWANZA - Angola
KYAT - Burma
KYRMIS - USSR

L

LAARI - Maldive Islands
LANG - Annam (Vietnam)
LARI - Maldive Islands
LARIAT - Maldive Islands
LARIN - Maldive Islands
LATI - Baltic Regions-Latvia
LATS - Baltic Regions-Latvia
LAUREL - Great Britain
LEI - Romania
LEK - Albania
LEKE - Albania
LEKU - Albania
LEMPIRA - Honduras
LEONE - Sierra Leone
LEOPOLD D'OR - French States
LEPTA - Crete, Greece, Ionian Islands
LEPTON - Crete, Greece, Ionian Islands
LEU - Romania
LEV - Bulgaria
LEVA - Bulgaria
LI - China, China-Jap. Puppet States
LIANG - China, French Indo-China
LIARD - Belgium, France, Luxembourg
LIBERTAD - Mexico
LIBRA - Peru
LICENTE - Lesotho
LIKUTA - Congo (Zaire)
LILANGENI - Swaziland
LION D'OR - Austrian Netherlands, Belgian States
LIRA - Eritrea, Israel, Italian States, Italy, San Marino, Syria, Turkey, Vatican-Papal States, Vatican City
LIRE - Eritrea, Italian Somaliland, Italian States, Italy, San Marino, Somalia, Vatican-Papal City States, Vatican-Papal States, Vatican City
LIROT - Israel
LIS D'OR - France
LISENTE - Lesotho
LITAI - Baltic Regions-Lithuania
LITAS - Baltic Regions-Lithuania
LITU - Baltic Regions-Lithuania
LIVRE - France, Guadeloupe, Lebanon, Martinique, Mauritius & Reunion
LOTI - Lesotho
LOUIS D'OR - France, French States
LUHLANGA - Swaziland
LWEI - Angola

M

MACE - China
MACUTA - Angola
MAHALEKI - Ethiopia
MAHALLAK - Harar (Ethiopia)
MAHBUB - Egypt, Libya, Tripoli, Turkey
MAHMUDI - Mecca (Saudi Arabia)
MAHMUDIYE - Turkey
MAKUTA - Congo (Zaire)

MALOTI - Lesotho
MANGHIR - Krim
MARAVEDI - Spain
MARCK - German States
MARIEN GROSCHEN - German States
MARK - Baltic Regions-Estonia, Denmark, German States, German New Guinea, Germany, Germany-East, Germany—West, Norway, Poland, Sweden
MARKA - Baltic Regions-Estonia
MARKKA - Finland
MARKKAA - Finland
MAS - Malaysia
MAT - Burma
MATHBU - Morocco
MATICAS - Mozambique
MATONAS - Ethiopia
MATTIER - German States
MAXIMILLIAN D'OR - German States
MAZUNA - Morocco
MEDIN - Egypt
MELGAREJO - Bolivia
MEMDUHIYE ALTIN - Turkey
METICA - Mozambique
METICAIS - Mozambique
METICAL - Mozambique
MIL - Cyprus, Hong Kong, Israel, Malta, Palestine
MILESIMA - Spain
MILLIEME - Egypt, Libya
MILLIM - Sudan, Tunisia
MILREIS - Brazil
MISCALS - China
MISRIYA - Egypt
MOHAR - Nepal
MOHUR - Afghanistan, India-Mughal, India-British, India-Independent Kingdom, Indian Princely States, Indonesia, Maldive Islands
MOMME - Japan
MON - Japan, Ryukyu Islands (Japan)
MONGO - Mongolia
MU - Burma
MUDRA - Indian Princely State
MUN - Korea
MUNZGULDEN - Swiss-Cantons
MUZUNA - Algeria

N

NASRIYA - Egypt
NAYA PAISA - Bhutan, India
NAZARANA MOHUR - India-British, India-Mughal, Indian Princely States
NAZARANA PAISA - Indian Princely States
NAZARANA RUPEE - India-British, India-Independent Kingdom, India-Mughal, Indian Princely States
NEU-GROSCHEN - German States
NEW AGORA - Israel
NEW AGOROT - Israel
NEW ALTIN - Turkey
NEW PENCE - Gibraltar, Great Britain, Guernsey, Isle of Man, Jersey
NEW PENNY - Great Britain, Guernsey, Isle of Man, Jersey
NEW PESO - Uruguay
NEW SHEQALIM - Israel
NEW SHEQEL - Israel
NGULTRUM - Bhutan
NGWEE - Zambia
NICKEL - United States of America
NISAR - Afghanistan, India
NISFIYA - Egypt
NOBLE - Isle of Man
NOUSF - Egypt

O

OBAN - Japan
OBOL - Greece, Ionian Islands
OCHAVO - Spain
OCTAVO - Mexico, Philippines
OMANI RIALS - Oman
ONCA - Mozambique
ONCIA - Italian States
ONLIK - Krim (U.S.S.R.)
ONLUK - Turkey
ONZA - Bolivia, Chile, Costa Rica, Mexico
OR - Sweden
ORE - Denmark, Faeroe Islands, Greenland, Norway, Sweden
OUGUIYA - Mauritania

P

PA'ANGA - Tonga
PAGODA - India-Independent Kingdoms, Indian Princely States, India-British, India-French
PAGODE - India-Danish
PAHLAVI - Iran
PAI - Indian Princely States, Siam, Thailand
PAISA - Afghanistan, Bhutan, India, India-British, India-Independent Kingdom, India-Mughal, Indian Princely States, Nepal, Pakistan
PANA - India-Independent Kingdom
PANCHIA - India-British
PAOLI - Italian States, Vatican-Papal States
PAOLO - Italian States
PARA - Egypt, Greece, Ionian Islands, Iraq, Krim, Libya, Montenegro, Nejd, Romania, Saudi Arabia, Serbia, Sudan, Syria, Turkey, U.S.S.R., Yugoslavia
PARDAO - India-Portuguese
PARE - Serbia, Yugoslavia
PATACA - Macao

PATACO - Portugal
PATAGON - Belgium
PAVALI - Indian Princely States
PAYALO - Indian Princely States
PE - Burma, Cambodia
PECA - Portugal
PENCE - Australia, Biafra, British Guiana, British Virgin Islands, British West Africa, Ceylon, Falkland Islands, Fiji, Gambia, Ghana, Gibraltar, Great Britain, Guernsey, Ireland, Isle of Man, Jamaica, Jersey, Malawi, Montserrat, New Guinea, New South Wales, New Zealand, Nigeria, Rhodesia, Rhodesia & Nyasaland, St. Helena & Ascension, St. Kitts, South Africa, Southern Rhodesia, Sri Lanka, Trinidad & Tobago, Tristan Da Cunha, Zambia, Zimbabwe
PENGO - Hungary
PENNI - Finland
PENNIA - Finland
PENNY - Australia, Bahamas, Barbados, Bermuda, British West Africa, Canada, Falkland Islands, Fiji, Gambia, Ghana, Gibraltar, Great Britain, Guernsey, Ireland, Isle of Man, Jamaica, Jersey, Malawi, New Brunswick, New Guinea, New Zealand, Nigeria, Nova Scotia, Rhodesia & Nyasaland, St. Helena & Ascension, Sierra Leone, South Africa, Southern Rhodesia, Trinidad & Tobago, Zambia, Zimbabwe
PERPER - Yugoslavia-Montenegro
PERPERA - Yugoslavia-Montenegro
PERPERO - Ragusa, Yugoslavia-Montenegro
PESA - German East Africa (Tanzania)
PESETA - Andorra, Equatorial Guinea, Peru, Spain
PESEWA - Ghana
PESO - Argentina, Bolivia, Cambodia, Chile, Colombia, Costa Rica, Cuba, Dominican Republic, El Salvador, Guatemala, Guinea-Bissau, Honduras, Mexico, Netherlands Antilles, Nicaragua, Paraguay, Peru, Philippines, Puerto Rico, Uruguay, Venezuela
PESO BOLIVIANO - Bolivia
PESO FUERTES - Paraguay
PESSA - Lahej (Yemen)
PFENNIG - Austria, Bohemia, Danzig, German New Guinea, German States, Germany, Germany-East, Germany-West, Poland, Salzburg, Swiss-Cantons
PFENNIGE - German States
PFENNING - Austrian States, German States
PHOENIX - Greece
PIASTRA - Italian States
PIASTRE - Cambodia, Cyprus, Denmark, Egypt, French Cochin China, French Indo China, Hejaz, Iraq, Lebanon, Libya, Nejd, Saudi Arabia, Sudan, Syria, Tonkin, Tripoli, Tunisia, Turkey, U.S.S.R., Vietnam-Annam, Yemen
PICCIOLI - Order of Malta
PICCOLI - Italian States
PICE - Bhutan, Ceylon, East Africa, India, India-British, Indian Princely States, Kenya, Malaysia, Mombasa, Pakistan
PIE - India-British, Indian Princely States, Pakistan
PILON - Mexico
PINTO - Portugal
PISO - Philippines
PISTOLE - French States, German States, Ireland, Swiss-Cantons
PISTOLET - French States
PITIS - Brunei, Indonesia, Malaysia, Thailand
POISHA - Bangladesh
POLTINA - U.S.S.R.
POLTURA - Hungary, Romania
POLUPOLTINNIK - U.S.S.R.
POLUSHKA - U.S.S.R.
POND - Zuid Afrikaansche Republic
PORTUGALOSER - Denmark, German States
POUND - Australia, Biafra, Cyprus, Egypt, Falkland Islands, Ghana, Gibraltar, Great Britain, Guernsey, Iran, Isle of Man, Israel, Jersey, Malta, Nigeria, Rhodesia, Saint Helena-Ascension, Saudi Arabia, South Africa, South Australia, Southern Rhodesia, Sudan, Syria, Tristan da Cunha
PROTEA - South Africa
PRUTA - Israel
PRUTOT - Israel
PUFFIN - Lundy
PUL - Afghanistan, China, Russian Turkestan, U.S.S.R.
PULA - Botswana
PULI - Russian Caucasia
PULTORAK - Poland
PYA - Burma
PYSA - Zanzibar, (Tanzania)

Q

QINDAR AR - Albania
QINDARKA - Albania
QINDAR LEKU - Albania
QIRAN - Afghanistan
QIRSH - Egypt
QUAN - Annam (Vietnam)
QUART - Gibraltar, Swiss-Cantons
QUARTER DOLLAR - United States of America
QUARTINHO - Portugal
QUARTO - Ecuador, Mexico, Philippines, Spain
QUATTRINI - Italian States
QUATTRINO - Italian States, Vatican Papal States
QUETZAL - Guatemala

R

RAND - South Africa
RAPPEN - Swiss-Cantons, Switzerland
RASI - India-Dutch
REAAL - Curacao (Netherlands Antilles)
REAL - Argentina, Bolivia, Central American Republic, Chile, Colombia, Costa Rica, Dominican Republic, Ecuador, El Salvador, Guatemala, Honduras, Malaysia, Mexico, Mozambique, Paraguay, Peru, Philippines, Santo Domingo, Spain, Venezuela
REAL BATU - Indonesia
REAL DE VELLON - Spain
REALE - Italian States
REALES - Argentina, Belize, Bolivia, Central American Republic, Chile, Colombia, Costa Rica, Cuba, Dominican Republic, Ecuador, El Salvador, Guatemala, Honduras, Mexico, Paraguay, Peru, Santo Domingo, Spain, Venezuela
REICHSMARK - Germany
REICHSPFENNIG - Germany
REICHSTHALER - German States
REIS - Angola, Azores, Brazil, India-Portuguese, Madeira, Mozambique, Portugal, St. Thomas & Prince, Terceira Island
REISE DALER - Denmark
RENTENPFENNIG - Germany
RIAL - Iran, Morocco, Oman, Persia, Yemen Arab Republic
RIEL - Kampuchea, Khmer
RIGSBANKDALER - Denmark
RIGSBANKSKILLING - Denmark
RIGSDALER - Denmark, Norway
RIGSDALER SPECIES - Denmark
RIGSMONTSKILLING - Denmark
RIJKSDAALER - Netherlands
RIKSDALER - Sweden
RIKSDALER RIKSMYNT - Sweden
RIKSDALER SPECIE - Sweden
RIN - Japan
RINGGIT - Malaysia
RIXDOLLAR - Ceylon (Sri Lanka)
RIYAL - Ajman, Fujairah, Hejaz & Nejd, Iran, Iraq, Muscat & Oman, Saudi Arabia, Sharjah, Umm Al Qaiwain, Yemen Arab Republic
ROSE NOBLE - Denmark, Netherlands
ROSE RYAL - Baltic Regions, Great Britain
ROUBLE - Russian Caucasia, Russian Turkestan, U.S.S.R.
ROYALIN - India-Danish
RUB - Ethiopia
RUBIYA - Egypt
RUBLE - Poland
RUFIYAA - Maldive Islands
RUMI ALTIN - Turkey
RUPEE - Afghanistan, Andaman Islands, Bhutan, Burma, Ceylon, China, India, India-Mughal, India-British, India-French, India-Independent Kingdom, Indian Princely States, Indonesia, Iran, Keeling-Cocos Islands, Kenya, Mauritius, Mombasa, Nepal, Netherlands East Indies, Pakistan, Saudi Arabia, Seychelles, Sharjah, Sri Lanka, Tanzania, Tibet, United Arab Emirates, Yemen
RUPIA - India-Portuguese, Italian Somaliland, Somalia
RUPIAH - Indonesia
RUPIE - German East Africa
RUPIEN - German East Africa
RUSPONE - Italian States
RYAL - Hejaz, Oman, Persia, Quaiti State, Saudi Arabia, Zanzibar
RYO - Japan

S

SAIDI RIYAL - Muscat & Oman, Oman
SALU'NG - Thailand
SANAR - Afghanistan
SANTA CROCE - Italian States
SANTIM - Morocco
SANTIMAT - Morocco
SANTIMI - Baltic Regions-Latvia
SANTIMS - Baltic Regions-Latvia
SANTIMU - Baltic Regions-Latvia
SAPEQUE - Annam, French Cochin China, French Indo China
SAR - Sinkiang
SATANG - Thailand
SCELLINO - Somalia
SCHILLING - Austria, Danzig, East Prussia, German States, Poland, Swiss-Cantons
SCHWAREN - German States
SCUDI - Order of Malta
SCUDO - Bolivia, Italian States, Italy, Mexico, Order of Malta, San Marino, Vatican Papal States
SCUDI - San Marino
SECHSLING - German States
SEL - India-Independent Kingdom
SEN - Brunei, Cambodia, China, Indonesia, Irian Barat, Japan, Kampuchea, Malaysia, Riau Archipelago, Thailand, West Irian, West New Guinea
SENE - Western Samoa
SENGI - Congo (Zaire)
SENITI - Tonga
SENT - Baltic Regions-Estonia
SENTE - Lesotho
SENTI - Baltic Regions-Estonia, Somalia, Tanzania
SENTIMO - Philippines
SERTUM - Bhutan
SESINO - Italian States
SESTINO - Italian States
SHAHI - Afghanistan, Iran, U.S.S.R.
SHEQEL - Israel
SHEQALIM - Israel
SHILIN - Somalia
SHILINGI - Tanzania
SHILLING - Australia, Biafra, British Virgin Islands, British West Africa, Canada-Prince Edward Island, Cyprus, East Africa, Fiji, Gambia, Ghana, Great Britain, Grenada, Guernsey, Ireland, Isle of Man, Jamaica, Jersey, Kenya, Malawi, New Guinea, New Zealand, Nigeria, Rhodesia, Rhodesia & Nyasaland, Scotland, Somalia, South Africa, Southern Rhodesia, Trinidad & Tobago, Uganda, Zambia, Zimbabwe

SHO - Nepal, Tibet
SHU - Japan
SIK - Thailand
SILBERGROSCHEN - German States
SIO - Thailand
SKAR - Tibet
SKILLING - Danish West Indies, Denmark, Norway, Sweden
SKILLINGRIGSMONT - Denmark
SOL - Argentina, Belgium, Bolivia, France, Haiti, Luxembourg, Mauritius & Reunion, Peru, Swiss-Cantons, Windward Islands
SOLDI - Italian States, Italy, Swiss-Cantons, Vatican-Papal States, Yugoslavia
SOLDO - Italian States, Vatican-Papal States
SOLES - Argentina, Bolivia, Peru
SOLIDUS - Baltic Regions-Courland, Poland
SOMALO - Somalia
SOUS - Canada, French Colonies, French Guiana, Guadeloupe, Mauritius, Mauritius & Reunion, Spain
SOUVERAIN D'OR - Austrian Netherlands, Belgian States
SOVEREIGN - Andorra, Australia, Canada, Falkland Islands, Great Britain, India-British, Indian Princely States, Isle of Man, Saudi Arabia, South Africa
SOVRANO - Italian States
SPECIEDALER - Denmark, Norway
SPECIES DUCAT - Denmark
SPUR RYAL - Great Britain
SRANG - Tibet
STAMPEE - French Colonies
STIVER - Ceylon, Essequibo & Demerary, Indonesia, Netherlands, Netherlands East Indies, Sri Lanka
STOTINKA - Bulgaria
STOTINKI - Bulgaria
STUBER - German States
STUIVER - Curacao, Indonesia, Netherlands, Netherlands-Antilles, Netherlands East Indies, Sri Lanka
STUVER - German States
SU - Vietnam-South
SUCRE - Ecuador, Galapagos Islands
SUELDO - Bolivia, Spain
SUKUS - Indonesia
SULTANI - Algeria, Egypt, Libya, Tripoli, Tunisia-Tunis
SURRE ALTIN - Turkey
SYLI - Guinea

T

TACKOE - Gold Coast (Ghana)
TAEL - China, French Indo-China
TAKA - Bangladesh
TALA - Tokelau, Western Samoa
TALAR - Poland
TALARA - Poland
TALER - German States, Poland, Swiss-Cantons
TALLERO - Eritrea, Italian States, Yugoslavia-Ragusa
TAMBALA - Malawi
TAMLUNG - Thailand
TANGA - India-Portuguese
TANGKA - Tibet
TANKA - Nepal
TANKAH - Burma
TARI - Italian States, Order of Malta
TEK ALTIN - Turkey
TEK RUMI - Egypt
TENGA - China, Russian Turkestan
THALER - Austria, Austrian States, Baltic Regions-Courland, Czechoslovakia, German States, Hungary, Liechtenstein, Poland, Romania, Switzerland
THEBE - Botswana
THELER - German States-Frankfurt
TICAL - Cambodia, Thailand
TIEN - Annam (Vietnam)
TILLA - Afghanistan, Russian Turkestan, Sinkiang
TIMASHA - Afghanistan, India-Independent Kingdom
TLACO - Mexico
TOEAS - Papua New Guinea
TOLA - India-British, Nepal
TOMAN - Iran, Persia, Russian Caucasia
TORNESE - Italian States
TORNESI - Italian States
TOSTAO - Portugal
TRADE DOLLAR - Japan, United States of America
TRA - Malaysia
TRAMBIYO - Indian Princely States
TUKHRIK - Mongolia
TYMPF - Poland

U

UNGHERO - Italian States
UNIT - French West Africa
UNITE - Great Britain

V

VAN - Vietnam-Annam
VATU - Vanuatu
VENEZOLANO - Venezuela
VIERER - Swiss-Cantons
VINTEN - Portugal
VIRARAYA FANAM - India-Princely States

W

WERK - Ethiopia
WARN - Korea
WHAN - Korea
WILLIAM D'OR - German States
WON - Korea, Korea-South

MINT INDEX

COIN DENOMINATIONS 38

X

XERAFIN - India-Portuguese
XU - Vietnam-North, Vietnam-South, Vietnam

Y

YANG - Korea
YARIM - Turkey
YARIM ALTIN - Egypt, Turkey
YARIM ZINJINLI ALTIN - Egypt
YEN - Japan
YIRMILIK - Turkey, U.S.S.R.
YUAN - China
YUZLUK - Turkey

Z

ZAIRE - Congo Democratic Republic, Zaire
ZALAT - Yemen Arab Republic
ZECCHINO - French States, Italian States, Order of Malta, Vatican-Papal States
ZELAGH - Morocco
ZERI MAHBUB - Egypt, Libya, Turkey
ZERI NAHBUB NISFIYE - Egypt
ZINJINLI ALTIN - Egypt
ZLOTE - Poland
ZLOTY - Krakow, Poland, Zamosc
ZLOTYCH - Poland, U.S.S.R.
ZOLOTA - Turkey
ZOLOTNIKS - U.S.S.R.

A

A - Ackroyd & Best (Morley)
A - Alamos (Mexico)
A - Ancona (Italy)
A - Angra (Portugal)
A - Antioquia (Colombia)
A - Beaumont-le-Roger (France)
A - Berlin (E. Germany)
A - Clausthal (German States)
A - Hall (Austria)
A - Paris (France)
A - Vienna (Austria)
AA - Metz (France)
AARGAU - Swiss Canton
AB - Geneva (Swiss Canton)
AB - Strassburg (France)
ABUSHAHR - Iran
ACKROYD & BEST - East Africa
AD - (Akcionarno Drustvo) Belgrade (Yugoslavia)
A-D - Diu (India-Portuguese)
ADRIANOPLE - Turkey
AE - (Ligate) Aix and Marseilles (France)
AEGINA - Greece
AHLUWALIA - India-Independent Kingdom
AHMADABAD - India-British, India-Independent Kingdom, India-Mughal, Indian Princely States
AHMADNAGAR-FARRUKHABAD - Afghanistan, India-Independent Kingdom
AHMADPUR - Afghanistan, Indian Princely States
AHMADSHAHI - Afghanistan
AIX - France
AIZU - Japan
AJMER - India-Independent Kingdom, India-Mughal, Indian Princely States
AKBARABAD - India-British, India-Mughal, Indian Princely States
AKSU - China
ALAMOS - Mexico
ALGIERS - Algeria
ALLAHABAD - India-British, India-Mughal, Indian Princely States
ALLOTE - Indian Princely States
ALMORA - India-Independent Kingdom
ALTONA - Danish West Indies, Denmark, German States, Philippines
AM - Anninsk, U.S.S.R.- Russia-Empire
AM - Bogota (Colombia)
AMARAVATI - Indian Princely States
AMBERG - German States
AMIENS - France
AMRELI - Indian Princely States
AMRITSAR - India-Independent Kingdom
AMSTERDAM - Netherlands East Indies
ANANDGARH - India-Independent Kingdom
ANCONA - Papal States
ANGERS - France
ANHWEI - China
ANNINSK - U.S.S.R.-Russia-Empire
ANTIOQUIA - Colombia
ANTWERP - Austrian Netherlands
ANWALA - Afghanistan, India-Independent Kingdom, India-Mughal
AP - Goa (India-Portuguese)
AR - Arras (France)
ARCOT - India-British, India-French
ARDABIL - Iran
AREQ - Arequipa, Peru, South Peru
AREQUIPA - Peru, South Peru
AREZZO - Order of Malta
ARKAT - India-British, India-French, India-Mughal, Indian Princely States
ARZI-I-AKDAS - Iran
As - Alamos (Mexico)
ASAFABAD - India-Mughal, Indian Princely States
ASAFNAGAR - India-Independent Kingdom, Indian Princely States
ASHIO - Japan
ASTARABAD - Iran
ATHENS - Greece
ATTOCK - Afghanistan
AURANGABAD - India-Mughal, Indian Princely States
AURANGNAGAR - India-Independent Kingdom
AURICH - German States
AVESTA - Sweden
AWADH - India-Mughal, Indian Princely States
AYACUCHO - Peru
AZIMABAD - India-British, India-Mughal, Indian Princely States

B

B - Bacaim (India)
B - Bahia (Brazil)
B - Barcelona (Spain)
B - Basel (Swiss Cantons)
B - Bayreuth (German States)
B - Beaumont-le-Roger (France)
B - Berne (Switzerland)
B - Bogota (Colombia)
B - Bologna (Italy)
B - Bombay (India-British)
B - Breslau (Poland)
B - Brunswick (German States)
B - Brussels (Belgium)
B - Bucharest (Romania)
B - Budapest (Hungary)
B - Buenos Aires (Argentina)
B - Burgos (Spain)
B - Bydgoszcz (Poland)
B - Dieppe (France)
B - Dresden (E. Germany)
B - Freiburg (Swiss Cantons)
B - Hannover (German States)
B - Kormoczbanya (Czechoslovakia)
B - Kremnitz (Czechoslovakia)
B - Luzern (Swiss Cantons)
B - Regensburg (German States)
B - Rouen (France)
B - Schwyz (Swiss Cantons)
B - Vienna-(Germany 1938-45)
B - Zurich (Swiss Cantons)
B and acorn - Bologna (Italy)
BA - Bahia (Brazil)
BA - Barcelona (Spain)
BA - (ligate) Basel (Switzerland)
BA - Buenos Aires (Argentina)
B.AS. - Buenos Aires (Argentina)
Ba - Bogota (Colombia)
BADAKHSHAN - Afghanistan
Bs - Buenos Aires (Argentina)
BAGALKOT - India-Independent Kingdom
BAGCHIH-SERAI - U.S.S.R.-Krim
BAGHDAD - Mesopotamia
BAHAWALPUR - Afghanistan, Indian Princely States
BAHIA - Brazil
BAHRAIN - Bahrain
BAJRANGGARH - Indian Princely States
BALHARI - India-Independent Kingdom
BALK - Afghanistan, India-Mughal
BALKH - Afghanistan
BAMBERG - German States
BANARAS - India-British, Indian Princely States
BANDAR ABBAS - Iran
BANGALORE - Indian Princely States
BANGKO SENTRAL PILIPINAS - Philippines
BARCELONA - Spain
BARELI - Afghanistan, India-Independent Kingdom, India-Mughal, Indian Princely States
BARODA - Indian Princely States
BASEL - Swiss Cantons, Switzerland
BASODA - Indian Princely States
BAYONNE - France
BAYREUTH - German States
BB - Strasbourg (France)
BCCR - Philadelphia (USA)
BD - Pau (France)
Be - Berlin (Germany)
BEAUMONT-LE-ROGER - France, French Indo-China
BEHBEHAN - Iran
BEL - Basel (Swiss Cantons)
BEL - Freiburg (Swiss Cantons)
BEL - Lausanne (Swiss Cantons)
BELGRADE - Yugoslavia
BENARES - India-British
BENGAL - India-British
BENGALUR - India-Independent Kingdom
BERGA - Spain
BERLIN - Brazil, Bulgaria, Danzig, Dominican Republic, East Prussia, German East Africa, German New Guinea, German States, Germany, Germany-East, Italy, Laos, Morocco, Posen, Uruguay
BERNE - Botswana, Israel, Liberia, Liechtenstein, Swiss Cantons, Switzerland
BESANCON - France
BGA - Brega (Libya)
B.H. FRANKFURT - German States
B (rosette) H - German States
BHAKHAR - Afghanistan, India-Independent Kingdom, India- Mughal
BHARATPUR - Indian Princely States
BHILSA - India-Mughal, Indian Princely States
BHINDA - Indian Princely States
BHOPAL - Indian Princely States
BHUJ - Indian Princely States
BI - (ligate) Birmingham (Great Britain)
BICR - Philadelphia (USA)
BIKANIR - Indian Princely States
BILBAO - Spain
BINDRABAN - Indian Princely States
BIRMm - Birmingham
BIRMINGHAM H - British Honduras, British North Borneo, British West Africa, Bulgaria, Canada, Ceylon, Colombia, Costa Rica, Cyprus, Dominican Republic, East Africa, Ecuador, Egypt, El Salvador, Finland, French Indo-China, Great Britain, Greece, Guernsey, Haiti, Hong Kong, Italy, Jamaica, Jersey, Kenya, Liberia, Malaya & British Borneo, Mauritius, Mombasa, Morocco, Newfoundland, Nicaragua, Oman, Romania, Sarawak, Serbia, Straits Settlements, Thailand, Uruguay, Venezuela
BIRMINGHAM K,KN - British West Africa, East Africa, Great Britain, Greece, Hong Kong, Malaya & British

Borneo, Romania
BISAULI - India-Independent Kingdom
BM - Warsaw (Poland)
BNCR - London (England)
BNCR - San Jose (Costa Rica)
BNT - Turin (Italy)
Bo - Bilbao (Spain)
BOARD OF PUBLIC WORKS - China
BOARD OF REVENUE - China
BOGOTA - Colombia, Estados Unidos De Nueva Granada, Granadine Confederation, Lazareto, Republic of Colombia, Republic of Nueva Granada, United Provinces of Nueva Granada
BOLOGNA - Italian States, Italy, Papal States
BOLSHAYA KAZNA - U.S.S.R.
BOMBAY - Australia, Ceylon, East Africa, India, India-British, Iraq, Malaya, Straits Settlements
BOMBAY (Mumbai) - India-British
BON - Bologna
BON DOCET - Bologna
BONON DOCET - Bologna
BORDEAUX - France, French Cochin China, Greece
BORUJERD - Iran
BOURGES - France
BP - Budapest (Hungary)
BRAJ INDRAPUR - Indian Princely States
BREGA - Libya
BRESLAU - German States, Posen
BROACH - Indian Princely States
BRUGES - Austrian Netherlands
BRUNSWICK - German States
BRUSSELS - Austrian Netherlands, Belgium, Brazil, Burundi, Congo Democratic Republic, France, Luxembourg, Netherlands, Peru, Philippines, Romania, Rwanda, Spain, Switzerland, U.S.S.R.
BSP - Bangko Sentral Pilipinas
BUCHAREST - Romania
BUDAPEST - Bulgaria, Egypt, Hungary, Serbia
BUENOS AIRES - Argentina
BUKHARA - Russian Turkestan
BUNDI - Indian Princely States
BURHANABAD - Indian Princely State
BURHANPUR - India-Mughal, Indian Princely States
BURGOS - Spain
BURSA - Turkey
BURUJERD - Iran
BUSHIRE - Iran

C

C - Bucharest (Romania)
C - Caen (France)
C - Calcutta (India)
C - Calcutta (India-British)
C - Canadian (Winnipeg)
C - Cassel (W. Germany)
C - Castelsarrasin (France)
C - Catalonia (Spain)
C - Cayenne (French Guiana)
C - Ceuta (Spain)
C - Charlotte (U.S.A.)
C - Chihuahua (Mexico)
C - Civitavecchia (Italy)
C - Clausthal (German States)
C - Cuenca (Spain)
C - Cuiaba (Brazil)
C - Culiacan (Mexico)
C - Dresden (E. Germany)
C - Frankfurt Am Main (German States)
C - Gunzburg (Austria)
C - Karlsburg (Romania)
C - Ottawa (Canada)
C - Prague (Czechoslovakia)
C - Saint Lo (France)
C - Spoleto (Yugoslavia)
C - Surabaya (Indonesia)
C - Vienna (Austria)
C crowned - Cadiz (Spain)
C and eagle head - Cassel (German States)
C and lion - Geneva (Swiss Cantons)
C-A - Carlsburg (Austria)
CA - Camora
Ca - Chihuahua (Mexico)
CA - Cuenca (Spain)
CA - Vienna (Austria)
CA - Zaragoza (Mexico)
CADIZ - Spain
CALCUTTA - Australia, India, India-British, Kenya, Malaya, Mombasa
C.A.M. - San Salvador
CANBERRA - Australia, New Zealand
CANTON - China
CARLSBURG - Austria, Austrian Netherlands
CASSEL - German States
CASTELSARRASIN - France, French Indo-China
CATALONIA - Spain
CC - (First C is backward) Besancon (France)
CC - Carson City (U.S.A.)
CC - Genoa (Italy)
CE - Ceuta (Morocco)
Ce - Real del Catorce (Mexico)
CENTRAL AMERICAN - El Salvador
CH - Chalons (France)
CH - Chihuahua (Mexico)
CH - Pressburg (Hungary)
CHALONS - France
CHAMPANER - India-Independent Kingdom

CHANDA - India-Independent Kingdom
CHANDERI - Indian Princely States
CHANDOR - Indian Princely States
CHANGSHA - China
CHANGTE - China
CHE - China
CHEKIANG - China
CHENGTU - China
CHHACHRAULI - India-Mughal
CHHATARPUR - Indian Princely States
CHI - China
CHI - Valcambi (Switzerland)
CHICHOW - China
CHIHUAHUA - Mexico
CHIHLI - China
CHINAN - China
CHINAPATTAN - India-British, India-Mughal
CHINCHWAR - India-Independent Kingdom
CHING - China
CHING CHOW - China
CHITARKOT - Indian Princely States
CHITOR - India-Mughal, Indian Princely States
CL - Chihuahua (Mexico)
CL - Genoa (Italy)
CL and prow - Genoa (Italy)
CLAUSTHAL - German States
CLERMONT - France
C/M - Calcutta (India-British)
CM - St. Petersburg (U.S.S.R.-Russia-Empire)
CM - Sestroretsk (U.S.S.R.-Russia-Empire)
CM - Souzan (U.S.S.R.-Russia-Empire)
Cn - Culiacan (Mexico)
Co - Coimbra (Portugal)
Co - Cuzco (Peru)
CONSTANTINE - Algeria
CONSTANTINOPLE - Turkey
COPENHAGEN - Danish West Indies, Denmark, Finland, Greenland, Iceland
COQUIMBO - Chile
CORDOBA - Argentina
CORDOVA - Argentina
CR - San Jose (Costa Rica)
CUENCA - Spain
CUIABA - Brazil
CULIACAN - Mexico
CUTTACK - India-Independent Kingdom
CUZ or CUZO plain - Cuzco (Peru)
CUZCO - Peru, South Peru
CUZO monogram - Cuzco (Peru)

D

D - Aurich (German States)
D - Dahlonega (U.S.A.)
D - Damao (India-Portuguese)
D - Denver (U.S.A.)
D - Durango (Mexico)
D - Dusseldorf (German States)
D - Graz (Austria)
D - Lyon (France)
D - Munich (W. Germany)
D - Salzburg (Austria)
D - Surabaya (Indonesia)
D - Stuttgart (Swiss Cantons)
DACCA - India-British
DALIPNAGAR - India Princely States
DAMASCUS - Syria
DAR AL-ISLAM - India Princely States
DARBAND - Iran
DARMSTADT - German States, Germany
DAULATABAD - India-Mughal, Indian Princely States
DB - Schwyz (Swiss Cantons)
D-B - Damao (India-Portuguese)
D-D - Diu (India-Portuguese)
DEHLI - Afghanistan, India-Mughal
DENVER - Australia, Ecuador, Liberia, Netherlands, Philippines
DEOGARH - Indian Princely States
DERA - Afghanistan
DERAJAT - Afghanistan, India-Mughal
DEZFUL - Iran
DHOLPUR - Indian Princely States
DI - Diu (India-Portuguese)
DIG - Indian Princely States
DIJON - France
DIO - Diu (India-Portuguese)
D-O - Diu (India-Portuguese)
Do - Durango (Mexico)
DODE - Tibet
DODPAL - Tibet
DOHAD - Indian Princely States
DORDRECHT - Netherlands, Netherlands East Indies
DRESDEN - German States, Germany
DURANGO - Mexico
DUSSELDORF - German States
DVOR ZAMOSKVORETSKY - U.S.S.R.

E

E - Carlsburg (Austria)
E - Dresden (E. Germany)
E - Ekaterinburg (U.S.S.R.)
E - Karlsburg (Romania)
E - Konigsberg (German States)
E - Muldenhutten (Germany)
E - Tours (France)
EDIRNE - Turkey
EKATERINBURG - U.S.S.R.-Russia-Empire

ELICHPUR - India-Mughal, Indian Princely States
EM - Ekaterinburg (U.S.S.R.-Russia-Empire)
EM - Essaouir Mogador (Morocco)
ENKHUIZEN - Netherlands, Netherlands East Indies
EoMo - Estado de Mexico (Mexico)
ERAVAN - Iran
ESSAOUIR MOGADOR - Morocco
ESTADO DE MEXICO - Mexico

F

F - Angers (France)
F - Cassel
F - Dresden (E. Germany)
F - Feres (Romania)
F - Florence (Italy)
F - Gunzburg (Austria)
F - Hall (Austria)
F - Magdeburg (German States)
F - Stuttgart (Germany)
FAIZ HISAR - India-Independent Kingdom
FARKHANDA BUNYAD - India-Mughal, Indian Princely States
FARRUKHABAD - India-British, India-Mughal
FARRUKHI - India-Independent Kingdom
FARRUKHYAB - India-Independent Kingdom
FENGTIEN - China
FEODESIA - U.S.S.R. Russia-Empire
FERES - Romania
FERGANA - U.S.S.R. Russian Turkestan-Khoqand
FES HAZRAT - Morocco
FEZ - Morocco
FF - Altona (Germany)
FF - Stuttgart (Germany)
FH - Fes Hazrat (Morocco)
FLORENCE - Italian States, Italy
FM monogram - Franklin Mint
FOUMAN - Iran
FRANKFURT - German States, Germany
FRANKLIN MINT - Bahamas, Barbados, Belize, Bermuda, British Virgin Islands, Cayman Islands, Cook Islands, Ethiopia, Guyana, Jamaica, Jordan, Liberia, Malaysia, Malta, Netherlands Antilles, Panama, Papua New Guinea, Philippines, Romania, Solomon Islands, Surinam, Trinidad & Tobago, Tunisia
FRIBOURG - Swiss Cantons
FS - Fez (Morocco)
FS - Santa Fe-Nuevo Reino (Colombia)
FU - China
FUCHOU - China
FUCHOW - China
FUKAGAWA - Japan
FUKIEN - China

G

G - Dresden (E. Germany)
G - Galle (Sri Lanka)
G - J.R. Gaunt & Sons (Birmingham)
G - Geneva (Switzerland)
G - Glatz (Poland)
G - Goa (India-Portuguese)
G - Goias (Brazil)
G - Graz (Austria)
G - Guadalajara (Mexico)
G - Guanajuato (Mexico)
G - Guatemala
G - Gunzburg (Austria)
G - Harderwijk (Gelderland-Netherlands)
G - Karlsruhe (Germany)
G - Nagybanya (Austria, Hungary)
G - Poitiers (France)
G - Schwerin (German State)
G - Stettin (German State)
G-A - Goa (India-Portuguese)
Ga - Guadalajara (Mexico)
GADWAL - Indian Princely States
GANJAH - Iran
GARHAKOTA - Indian Princely States
GAUNT & SONS - British West Africa
GC - Gualalupe y Calvo (Mexico)
GCR - Philadelphia (USA)
GCR - San Jose (Costa Rica)
GEL - Harderwijk (Gelderland-Netherlands)
GENEVA - France, Swiss Cantons
GENOA - France, Italian States, Italy
GHAZNI - Afghanistan
GHENT - Ghent
GIAMDA - Tibet
GIJON - Spain
GILAN - Iran
GLATZ - East Prussia, German States
G.M. - Mantua (Italian States)
GN - Nagybanya (Romania)
GN-BW - Bamberg
Go - Guanajuato (Mexico)
GOHAD - India-Mughal, Indian Princely States
GOIAS - Brazil
GOKULGARH - India-Mughal
GOOTY - India-Independent Kingdom
GORHAM MFG. CO. - Serbia
GR - Graz (Austria)
GRAZ - Austria, Italian States
GRENOBLE - France
GUADALAJARA - Mexico
GOKUL - Indian Princely State
GUADALUPE Y CALVO - Mexico
GUANAJUATO - Mexico

GUATEMALA - Central American Republic, Guatemala
GUERNICA - Spain
GULSHANABAD - India-Independent Kingdom, India-Mughal
GUNZBURG - Austria, Austrian Netherlands, Burgau, German States, Italian States, Luxembourg
GWALIAR - India-Mughal, Indian Princely States
GWALIOR FORT - Indian Princely States
GYF - Karlsburg (Romania)

H

H - Amsterdam (Netherlands)
H - Birmingham (England)
H - Darmstadt (Germany)
H - Dresden (E. Germany)
H - Geneva (Swiss Cantons)
H - Gunzburg (Austria)
H - Hall (Austria)
H - Heaton (England)
H - Hermosillo (Mexico)
H - La Rochelle (France)
H - Schwyz (Swiss Cantons)
HA - Hall (Austria)
HAIDARABAD - India-Mughal, Indian Princely States
HAIDARABAD SIND - Afghanistan
HAIDARNAGAR - India-Independent Kingdom
HALEB (ALEPPO) - Syria
HALL - Austria, Austrian Netherlands, Austrian States, Hungary, Italian States
HAMADAN - Iran
HAMBURG - German East Africa, German States, Germany, Germany-West, Romania
HANCHENG - China
HANGCHOW - China
HANNOVER - German States, Germany
HANOI - French Indo-China
HARDERWIJK - Netherlands, Netherlands East Indies
HATHRAS - Indian Princely States
HAVANA - Afghanistan, Cuba, Kampuchea, Laos, Vietnam
HEATON - Australia, Belgian Congo, Bolivia, British North Borneo, British West Africa, Bulgaria, Canada, Ceylon, Costa Rica, Cyprus, Dominican Republic, East Africa, Ecuador, Egypt, El Salvador, Finland, French Indo China, Great Britain, Greece, Guatemala, Guernsey, Haiti, Hong Kong, India, Jamaica, Jersey, Kenya, Liberia, Malaya, Malaya & British North Borneo, Mauritius, Nicaragua, Paraguay, Romania, Sarawak, Serbia, Straits Settlements, Thailand, Uruguay, Venezuela
HELSINKI - Finland
HERAT - Afghanistan, Iran
HERMOSILLO - Mexico
HF - LeLocle (Switzerland)
HINGANGHAT - India-Independent Kingdom
HIROSHIMA - Japan
HK - Rostock
Ho - China
Ho - Hermosillo (Mexico)
HOCHENG - China
HOL - Holland (Netherlands)
HOLL - Holland (Netherlands)
HONAN - China
HOORN - Netherlands, Netherlands East Indies
HQ - China
HOTAN - China
HOTIEN - China
HU - China
HUGUENIN - LA LOCOLE - Romania
HUI YUAN - China
HUNAN - China
HUPEH - China
HWEIYUAN - China
HYDERABAD - India, Indian Princely States
HYDERABAD SIND - India-Independent Kingdom

I

I - Bombay (India-British)
I - Calcutta (India)
I - Graz (Austria)
I - Hamburg (Germany)
I - Limoges (France)
ILI - China
IMPERIAL NAVAL YARD - China
INDORE - Indian Princely States
I/P - Potosi (Mexico)
IRAVAN - Iran, Ottoman Empire
ISAGARH - Indian Princely States
ISE - Japan
ISFAHAN - Iran
ISLAMBUL - Turkey
ITAWA - India-Independent Kingdom, India-Mughal, Indian Princely States
IZHORA - U.S.S.R. Russia-Empire

J

J - Hamburg (Germany)
J - Jubia (Spain)
J - Paris
J - Surabaya (Indonesia)
J and horse head - Cassel (German States)
J and horse head - Paris
JA - Jubia (Spain)
J'AFARABAD URF CHANDOR - Indian Princely States
JAIPUR SUWAI - Indian Princely States
JAISALMIR - Indian Princely States
JALAUN - India-Independent Kingdom
JAMMU - Indian Princely States
JAORA - Indian Princely States
JAWAD - Indian Princely States
JAZA-IR - Algeria
JAZA'IR GARP - Algeria
JAZA-IRIYAT - Algeria
JEHOL - China
JERUSALEM - Israel
JHABUA - Indian Princely States
JHALAWAR - Indian Princely States
JHANG - India-Independent Kingdom
JHANSI - India-Independent Kingdom, India-Mughal, Indian Princely States
JODHPUR - Indian Princely States
JOHN PINCHES - Bahamas
JP - John Pinches (England)
JUBIA - Spain
JUNAGADH - Indian Princely States

K

K - Bordeaux (France)
K - King's Norton (Great Britain)
K - Kormoczbanya (Czechoslovakia)
K - Kremnitz (Czechoslovakia)
K - St. Gall (Swiss Cantons)
KABUL - Afghanistan, India-Mughal
KADAPA - Indian Princely States
KAFFA - U.S.S.R.-Krim
KAIFENG - China
KALAT - Indian Princely States
KALAYANI - Indian Princely States
KALCUTTA - India-British, India-Mughal
KALIKUT - India-Independent Kingdom
KALPI - India-Independent Kingdom
KAMPEN - Netherlands, Netherlands East Indies
KANAUJ - Indian Princely States
KANSU - China
KARA AMID - Turkey
KARAULI - Indian Princely States
KARLSBURG - Hungary, Transylvania
KARLSRUHE - German States, Germany, Germany-West
KASHAN - Iran
KASHGAR - China
KASHI - China
KASHMIR - Afghanistan, India-Independent Kingdom, India-Mughal, Indian Princely States
KB - Berlin (Germany)
KB - Kormoczbanya (Bulgaria)
K-B or K.B. - Kremnitz (Czechoslovakia)
KERMAN - Iran
KERMANSHAHAN - Iran
KH - Kitaoua Hazrat (Morocco)
KHALIQABAD - India-Independent Kingdom
KHALSA - India-Independent Kingdom
KHANBAYAT - Indian Princely States
KHANABAD - Afghanistan
KHANPUR - Indian Princely States
KHETRI - Indian Princely States
KHARTOUM - Sudan
KHOQAND - U.S.S.R. Russian Turkestan
KHOTAN - China
KHOY - Iran
KHURSHED-SAWAD - India-Independent Kingdom
KHUY - Iran
KHWAREZM- USSR - Russian Turkestan
KIANGSI - China
KIANGSU - China
KING'S NORTON - Angola, Bolivia, British West Africa, EastAfrica, Egypt, Great Britain, Greece, Hong Kong, Romania
KIRIN - China
KIRMAN - Iran
KIRMANSHAHAN - Iran
KISHANGARH - Indian Princely States
KITAOUA HAZRAT - Morocco
KM - Copenhagen (Denmark)
KM - Kaschau (Czechoslovakia)
KM - Kolpina (U.S.S.R.)
KM - Kolyvan (U.S.S.R.)
KN - King's Norton (Great Britain)
KOLPINA - U.S.S.R. Russia-Empire
KOLYVAN - U.S.S.R. Russia-Empire, Russia-Siberia
KONIGSBERG - East Prussia, German States
KORA - India-Independent Kingdom, India-Mughal, Indian Princely States
KORMOCZBANYA - Bulgaria
KOSOVA - Turkey
KOTAH - Indian Princely States
KOTSHA - China
KOVNICA - Yugoslavia
KRASHNY DVOR - U.S.S.R.
KREMNITZ - Austria, Austrian Netherlands, Hungary, Italian States
KUCHA - China
KUCHAR - China
KUCHE - China
KUELIN - China
KULDJA - China
KULDSHA - China
KUMBER - Indian Princely States
KUNAR - India-Independent Kingdom
KUNCH - India-Independent Kingdom, India Princely States
KUNGCHANG - China
KUTCH - Indian Princely States
KWANGSI - China
KWANGTUNG - China
KWEICHOW - China
KWEIYANG - China
KWLJA - China

L

L - Bayonne (France)
L - Lahore (India)
L - Leipzig (German States)
L - Lima (Peru)
L - Lisbon (Portugal)
L - London (England)
LADAKH - Afghanistan, Indian Princely States
LAHIJAN - Iran
LAHORE - Afghanistan, India-British, India-Independent Kingdom, India-Mughal
LANCHOW - China
LA PAZ - Bolivia
LA PLATA - Bolivia
LARACHE - Morocco
LA ROCHELLE - France, French Colonies, Windward Islands
LASHKAR - Indian Princely States
LAUSANNE - Swiss Cantons
LEIPZIG - German States
LELOCLE - Ecuador, Paraguay, Romania
LENINGRAD - Laos, Russia
LILLE - France
LIMA - Chile, Ecuador, Peru, Peru-North
LIMAE monogram - Lima (Peru)
LIMOGES - France
LISBON - Brazil, Portugal
LIVORNO - Italian States
LJUSNEDAL - Sweden
LLANTRISANT - New Zealand, Philippines
LM monogram - Lima (Peru)
Ln - London (Great Britain)
LONDON - Albania, Australia, Bahamas, Costa Rica, France, Great Britain, Greece, Iceland, Liberia, Morocco, Peru, Russia, Yugoslavia
LOTUS - Madras (India-British)
LPA - La Plata (Bolivia)
Lr - Larache (Morocco)
LUCKNOW - Indian Princely States
LUZERN - Swiss Cantons
LYON - France, French Colonies, Uruguay

M

M - Aargau (Swiss Cantons)
M - Madras (India-British)
M - Madrid (Spain)
M - Manila (Philippines)
M - Maranhao (Brazil)
M - Medellin (Colombia)
M - Melbourne (Australia)
M - Mendoza (Argentina)
M - Mexico
M - Meyer (Danzig)
M - Milan (Italy)
M - Minas Gerais (Brazil)
M - Monaco
M - Moscow (U.S.S.R.)
M - Munich (Germany)
M - Salzburg (Austria)
M - Toulouse (France)
M crowned - Madrid (Spain)
Ma - Manila (Philippines)
MA - (ligate) Marseilles (France)
MACHILIPATNAM - India-British
MADHOPUR SAWAI - Indian Princely States
MADRAS - India-British
MADRIS - India-British, Indian Princely States
MADRID - France, Philippines, Spain
MADURAL - Indian Princely States
MAGDEBURG - German States
MAHE INDRAPUR - Indian Princely States
MAHESHWAR - Indian Princely States
MAHOBA - India-Independent Kingdom
MALHARNAGAR - Indian Princely States
MALKARIAN - India-Independent Kingdom
MANDISOR - Indian Princely States
MANILA - Philippines, Culion Leper Colony
MANISTIR - Turkey
MANTUA - Austria
MARAGHEH - Iran
MARAKESH HAZRAT - Morocco
MARRAKESH - Morocco
MARSEILLES - France
MASCARA - Algeria
MASHAD - Afghanistan, Iran
MASULIPATAM - India British
MASULIPATNAM - India-British, India-Dutch, India-French
MATHURA - Indian Princely States
MAZANDARAN - Iran
MAZULIPATAM - French
MB - (ligate) Birmingham (Great Britain)
MC - Brunswick
MC - Monaco
MD - Madrid (Spain)
MECCA - Saudi Arabia
MEDEA - Algeria
MEDELLIN - Colombia
MEDEMBLIK - Netherlands
MEKHA - Saudi Arabia
MEKYI - Tibet
MEKNES - Morocco
MELBOURNE - Australia

MERTA - Indian Princely States
METZ - France, French Colonies
MEXICO CITY - Dominican Republic, Ecuador, El Salvador, Mexico, Nicaragua, Uruguay
MEYER - Danzig
MH - Marakesh Hazrat (Morocco)
MH - Vienna (Austria)
MIDDELBURG - Netherlands
MIKNASAH - Morocco
MILAN - Austria, Danzig, Eritrea, Italian States, Italy, San Marino
MINAS GERAIS - Brazil
MIRAJ - India-Independent Kingdom
MISR - Egypt
MITO - Japan
MK - Meknes (Morocco)
MM - Moscow, U.S.S.R.-Russia-Empire
Mo - Mexico City (Mexico)
MONTE CARLO - Monaco
MONTPELLIER - France
MORIOKA - Japan
MOSCOW - U.S.S.R.-Russia-Empire
MR - Marrakesh (Morocco)
MUHAMMABAD - India-Mughal, Indian Princely States
MUKDEN - China
MULDENHUTTEN - German States, Germany, Germany-East
MULTAN - Afghanistan, India-Mughal, India-Independent Kingdom
MUNICH - German States, Germany, Germany-West, Leichtenstein, Paraguay
MURADABAD - Afghanistan, India-Independent Kingdom, India-Mughal, Indian Princely States
MURSHIDABAD - British-India, India-French, India-Mughal
MUSTAFABAD - India-Independent Kingdom
MV or MW - Warsaw (Poland)
Mx* - Mexico
MYSORE - India-Independent Kingdom, Indian Princely States

N

N - Bern (Swiss Cantons)
N - Montpellier (France)
N - Nagybanya (Romania)
N - Naples (Italy)
N above VOC - Negapatnam (India)
NABHA - Indian Princely States
NABEREZHNY DVOR - U.S.S.R.
NAGAR - India-Independent Kingdom, Indian Princely States
NAGASAKI - Japan
NAGOR - Indian Princely States
NAGPUR - India-Independent Kingdom
NAGYBANYA - Austria, Austrian Netherlands, Hungary, Italian States, Transylvania
NAHTARNAGAR - Indian Princely States
NAJAFGARH - India-Independent Kingdom
NAJIBABAD - Afghanistan, India-Independent Kingdom, Indian Princely States
NAKHCHAWAN - Iran
NANCHANG - China
NANTES - France
NAPLES - Italy
NARBONNE - France
NARWAR - Indian Princely States
NASIRI - Iran
NASRULLANAGAR - India-Independent Kingdom
NAZARBAR - India-Independent Kingdom
N-B or N.B. - Nagybanya (Romania)
NG - Nueva Guatemala
NIHAWAND - Iran
NIMAK - India-Independent Kingdom
NIPANI - India-Independent Kingdom
NoRo - Santa Fe-Nuevo Reino (Colombia)
NR - Santa Fe-Nuevo Reino (Colombia)
NUEVA GUATEMALA - Guatemala
NUEVA VIZCAYA - Mexico
NUEVO REINO (Bogota) - Colombia
NUKHA - Russian Caucasia
NUKHWI - Iran

O

O - Clermont (France)
O - New Orleans (U.S.A.)
O - Oaxaca (Mexico)
O - Oravicza (Romania)
O crowned between pillars - Oaxaca (Mexico)
O - Riom (France)
Oa - Oaxaca (Mexico)
OAXACA - Mexico
OM - Strasbourg (France)
OMDURMAN - Sudan
OR - Oruro (Bolivia)
ORAVICZA - Austria
ORAVITZA - Italian States
ORLEANS - France
ORURO - Bolivia
OSAKA - French Indo-China, Japan
OTTAWA (RCM) - Canada, Iceland, Jamaica, Newfoundland, New Zealand

P

P - Dijon (France)
P - Pamplona (Spain)
P - Parma (Italy)
P - Pernambuco (Brazil)
P - Perth (Australia)
P - Perugia (Italy)
P - Philadelphia (U.S.A.)
P - Popayan (Colombia)
P - Porto (Portugal)
P - Potosi (Mexico)
P - Prague (Austria)
P - Pretoria (South Africa)
P - Semur (France)
PA - Pamplona (Spain)
Pa - Paris (France)
PALERMO - Italian States
PALI - Indian Princely States
PAMPLONA - Spain
PANAHABAD - Iran, U.S.S.R. Russian Caucasia-Karabegh
PAOTING - China
PARIS - Bolivia, Cochin China, Colombia, Comoros, Crete, Dominican Republic, Ethiopia, France, French Cochin China, French Colonies, French Guiana, French Indo-China, German States, Greece, Haiti, Honduras, Italy, Luxembourg, Monaco, Portugal, Serbia, Switzerland, Tunis, Tunisia, U.S.S.R., Uruguay, Venezuela
PARIS - Privy Marks Only - Algeria, Bolivia, Brazil, Bulgaria, Cambodia, Cameroon, Central African Republic, Central African States, Chad, Comoros, Congo People's Republic, Crete, Equatorial African States, Ethiopia, France, French Afars & Issas, French Equatorial Africa, French Indo-China, French Oceania, French Polynesia, French Somaliland, French West Africa, Gabon, Greece, Haiti, Italy, Laos, Lebanon, Luxembourg, Madagascar, Malagasy Republic, Mali, Malta (Order of), Monaco, Montenegro, Morocco, New Caledonia, New Hebrides, Reunion, Romania, Rwanda, Saarland, St. Pierre & Miquelon, Serbia, South Korea, South Vietnam, Syria, Togo, Tonkin, Tunis, Tunisia, U.S.S.R., Uruguay, Venezuela, West African States, Yugoslavia
PARTABGARH - Indian Princely States
PASCO - Peru
PATAN - India-Independent Kingdom
PATHANKOT - India-Independent Kingdom
PATNA - East India Company, India-British, India-Mughal
PAU - France
PAZ - Bolivia, Peru
PEIYANG ARSENAL - China
PEKING - China
PERNAMBUCO - Brazil
PERPIGNAN - France, French Colonies
PERTH - Australia
PESHAWAR - Afghanistan, India-Independent Kingdom, India-Mughal
PETLAD - Indian Princely States
PETROGRAD - Russia
PHILADELPHIA - Canada, Costa Rica, Ecuador, Netherlands, Peru, Surinam
PI - San Luis Potosi (Mexico)
PINCHES - Bahamas
PISA - Italian States
PL - London (England)
PL - Pamplona (Spain)
PM - Manila (Philippines)
PM - Pobjoy (England)
PN or Pn - Popayan (Colombia)
PO - Pasco (Peru)
POBJOY - Ascension Islands, Isle of Man, Tristan Da Cunha
POISSY - Bulgaria, France, French Equatorial Africa, French Indo-China, Gabon, Greece, Monaco, Morocco, Romania, Uruguay, Yugoslavia
POITTERS - France
PONDICHERY - India-French
POONA - India-Independent Kingdom
POPAYAN - Colombia
PORTO - Portugal
POTOSI - Argentina, Bolivia, Chile
PP - Pamplona (Spain)
PR - Dusseldorf
P-R - Gunzburg (Austria)
PRAGUE - Austria, Austrian Netherlands, Bohemia
PRESSBURG - Hungary
PRETORIA - British West Africa, Cameroon, East Africa, French Equatorial Africa, India-British, Madagascar, Mauritius, South Africa
PTA monogram - La Plata
PTS monogram - Potosi
PUEBLA - Mexico

Q

Q - Narbonne (France)
Q - Perpignan (France)
QANDAHAR - Afghanistan, India-Mughal
QASBAH PANIPAT - India-Independent Kingdom
QAZWIN - Iran
QUITO - Ecuador
QILA MUQAM - Indian Princely States
QUM - Iran
QUSANTINAH - Algeria

R

R - London (England)
R - Orleans (France)
R - Rio de Janeiro (Brazil)
R - Rioja (Argentina)
R - Rome (Italy)
R - Saint Andre (France)
R crowned - Rome (Italy)
RA - Rioja (Argentina)
RABAT - Morocco
RABAT AL-FATH - Morocco
RADHANPUR - Indian Princely States
RAJGARH - Indian Princely States
RAJOD - Indian Princely States
RAMNOD - Indian Princely States
RAMPUR - Indian Princely States
RA'NASH - Iran
RASHT - Iran
RATHAMBHOR - Indian Princely States
RATHGARH - Indian Princely States
RAVISHNAGAR - India-Independent Kingdom
Rb - Rabat (Morocco)
REAL DE CATORCE - Mexico
REGENSBURG - German States
REKAB - Iran
RENNES - France
REZA'IYEH - Iran
RF - Rabat al-Fath (Morocco)
RIKAB - Afghanistan, Iran
RIO DE JANEIRO - Brazil, Mozambique
RIOJA - Argentina
RIOM - France
RIOXA - Argentina
ROME - Albania, Eritrea, France, Italian Somaliland, Italy, Malta (Order of), Papal States, San Marino
ROSTOCK - German States
ROUEN - France, French Colonies
ROYAL MINT (London & Llantrisant) - Bahamas, Barbados, Belize, British West Africa, Canada, Fiji, Great Britain, Jamaica, Malaya, Malaya & British Borneo, Philippines
Rs - Brussels (Belgium)
RS - Brussels (Belgium)
Rs - Rio de Janeiro (Brazil)

S

S - Dresden (E. Germany)
S - Durlach (German States)
S - Gunzburg (Austria)
S - Hall in Tyrol (Austria)
S - Hannover (Germany)
S - Helsinki (Finland)
S - Reims (France)
S - San Francisco (U.S.A.)
S - Santiago (Chile)
S - Schmollnitz (Hungary)
S - Seville (Spain)
S - Solothurn (Switzerland)
S - Sydney (Australia)
S - Troyes (France)
S - Utrecht (Indonesia)
S crowned between pillars - Sombrerete de Vargas
SA - Pretoria (South Africa)
Sa - Surabaya
Sa - Utrecht
SACHE - China
SADO - Japan
SAGAR - East India Company, India-British
SAGUR - Sagur
SAHARANPUR - India-British, India-Mughal
SAHIBABAD - Indian Princely States
SAINT ANDRE - France
SAINT LO - France
SAINT MALO - France
SALAMABAD - India-Independent Kingdom
SALONIKA - Turkey
SALZBURG - Austria
SANA - Yemen
SAN FRANCISCO - Australia, El Salvador, Fiji, French Indo-China, Liberia, Netherlands, Peru, Philippines
SANGLI - India-Independent Kingdom
SAN JOSE - Central American Republic, Costa Rica
SAN LUIS POTOSI - Mexico
SAN SALVADOR (C.A.M.) - El Salvador
SANTANDER - Spain
SANTIAGO - Bolivia, Chile, Ecuador, Peru, Uruguay
SAO PAULO - Brazil
SARAKHS - Iran
SAHRIND - Afghanistan
SARI - Iran
SAR-I-POL - Afghanistan
SASHTI - India-Independent Kingdom
SAUGAR - India-Independent Kingdom
SA'UJBULAGH - Iran
SCHMOLLNITZ - Austria, Galicia & Lodomeria, Hungary, Italian States
SCHWERIN - German States
SCHWYZ - Swiss Cantons
SD - Santo Domingo (Dominican Republic)
SE - Santiago del Estero (Chile)
SEGOVIA - Spain
SEMLAN - Sweden
SEMUR - France
SENDAI - Japan
SERINGAPATAN - India-Independent Kingdom
SER-KHANG - Tibet
SESTRORETSK - U.S.S.R. Russia-Empire
SEVILLE - Spain
SF - Santa Fe-Nuevo Reino (Colombia)
SGV - Madrid (Spain)
Sh - Suwairah (Morocco)
SHADORAH - Indian Princely States
SHAHABAD - Indian Princely States
SHAHJAHANABAD - Afghanistan, India-Mughal
SHAMAKHI - U.S.S.R. Russian Caucasia
SHAN - China
SHANSI - China
SHANTUNG - China

MINT INDEX 41

SHAW - Heaton (England)
SHENSI - China
SHEOPUR - Indian Princely States
SHERRITT - Nicaragua, Philippines
SHIKARPUR - India-Independent Kingdom
SHIRAZ - Iran
SHUFU - China
SHUSHTAR - Iran
SI - Sijilmasah (Morocco)
SIAN - China
SIBER - Lausanne (Swiss Cantons)
SIJILMASAH - Morocco
SIMNAN - Iran
SIND - Afghanistan, India-Independent Kingdom, India-Mughal
SINKIANG - China
SIPRI - Indian Princely States
SIRHIND - Indian Princely States
SIRONJ - India-Mughal, Indian Princely States
SL - Seville (Spain)
SLAN - China
SLP - San Luis Potosi (Mexico)
SM - Santa Marta (Colombia)
SM - St. Petersburg (U.S.S.R.-Russia-Empire)
S-M-O-M - Malta (Order of)
So - (O above S) Santiago (Chile)
SOCHE - China
SOHO - Straits Settlements
SOLOTHURN - Switzerland
SOMBRETE - Mexico
SOURABAYA - Indonesia
SOUTHERN CONCAN - India-British
SOUZAN - U.S.S.R. Russia-Empire
SP - Sao Paulo (Brazil)
SR - Santander (Spain)
SR - Suwair (Morocco)
SRINAGAR - India-Independent Kingdom, India-Mughal, Indian Princely States
STETTIN - German States
ST. GALLEN - Swiss Cantons
ST. PETERSBURG - U.S.S.R. Russia-Empire
STRASBOURG - France, Greece, Italy, Switzerland
STUTTGART - German States, Germany, Germany-West, Israel, Poland, Swiss Cantons
SU - China
SUCHOW - China
SUJAT - Indian Princely States
SULTANABAD - Iran
SURABAYA - Netherlands East Indies
SURAT - India-French, India-British, India-Mughal
SUS - Morocco
SUWAIRAH - Morocco
SY - Sydney (Australia)
SYDNEY - Australia, Surinam
SZECHUAN - China, Tibet

T

T - Nantes (France)
T - Tabora (Tanzania)
T - Tegucigalpa (Honduras)
T - Toledo (Spain)
T - Tucuman (Argentina)
T - Turin (Italy)
TABARISTAN - Iran
TABORA - German East Africa
TABRIZ - Iran
TAI - China
TAIWAN - China
TAIYUAN - China
TAKU - China
TANDA - Indian Princely States
TANJAH - Morocco
TANJORE - Indian Princely States
TAPCHI - Tibet
TAQIDEMT - Algeria
TARABALUS - Libya-Tripoli
TARABALUS GHARB - Libya-Tripoli
TASHQURGHAN - Afghanistan
TATTA - Afghanistan, India-Independent Kingdom, India-Mughal
Te - Tetuan (Morocco)
TEGUCIGALPA - Central American Republic, Honduras
TEH - China
TEHRAN - Iran
TE
TETUAN - Morocco
TG - Tanjah (Morocco)
TIENTSIN - China
TIERRA DEL FUEGO - Argentina
TIFLIS - U.S.S.R. Russian Caucasia-Georgia
TIHWA - China
TILIMSAN - Algeria
TINNEVELLY - Indian Princely States
TIP ARSENAL - Tibet
TM - Feodosia (U.S.S.R.-Russia-Empire)
TM - Tucuman (Argentina)
TOKAT - Turkey
TO - Toledo (Spain)
TOKYO - Japan
TOLE - Toledo (Spain)
TOLEDO - Spain
TONK - Indian Princely States
TORAGAL - India-Independent Kingdom, India-Mughal
TOULOUSE - France
TOURS - France
TOWER OF LONDON - Bahamas

TRA - Utrecht (Netherlands)
TRAI - Utrecht (Netherlands)
TRAIECTUM - Utrecht (Netherlands)
TRANSI - Overijsel (Netherlands)
TRICHINOPOLY - Indian Princely States
TRIPOLI - Tripoli, Libya
TROYES - France
TUNG - China
TUNG CH'UAN - China
TUNIS - Tunis
TURIN - France, Italian States, Italy
TUYSERKAN - Iran

U

U - Turin (Italy)
U and St Eric - Stockholm (Sweden)
UDAIPUR - India-Mughal, Indian Princely States
UJJAIN - India-Mughal, Indian Princely States
URUMCI - China
URUMI - Iran
URUMQI - China
USHI - China
UTRECHT - France, Lebanon, Luxembourg, Netherlands, Netherlands Antilles, Netherlands East Indies, Surinam, Uruguay

V

V - Surabaya (Indonesia)
V - Valencia (Spain)
V - Valona (Albania)
V - Venice (Italy)
V - Vienna (Austria)
V between C-O - Negapatnam (India)
V over VOC monogram - Pulicat (India)
VA - Valencia (Spain)
VAL - Valencia (Spain)
VALCAMBI - Panama
VALENCIA - Spain
VALONA - Albania
VENICE - Austria, Italian States
VEREINIGTE DEUTSCHE METALL WERKS - Philippines
VIENNA - Austria, Austrian Netherlands, Bohemia, Galicia & Lodomeria, Germany, Greece, Hungary, Italian States, Liechtenstein, Romania, Serbia, Uruguay, Yugoslavia

W

W - Lille (France)
W - Soho (Malaysia)
W - Surabaya (Indonesia)
W - Vienna (Austria)
W - Watt & Co. (Romania)
W - West Point (U.S.A.)
W - Wratislawis (Poland)
WARSAW - Poland, U.S.S.R. Russia-Empire
WATERBURY - Peru
WATT & CO. - Romania
WESTF - Westfriesland (Netherlands)
WESTRI - Westfriesland (Netherlands)
WI - Vienna (Austria)
WIESBADEN - German States
WINNIPEG - Canada, India
WRATISLAWIA - German States
W.M. - Warsaw (Poland), U.S.S.R.-Russia-Empire
WU - China
WUCH'ANG - China
WUSHI - China
WUSHIH - China

X

X - Amiens (France)

Y

Y - Bourges (France)
YAMANOUCHI - Japan
YANGHISSAR - China
YARKAND - China
YAZD - Iran
YENGISAR - China
YENISHEHIR - Turkey
YERKIM - China
YUN - China
YUNNAN - China
YUNNANFU - China

Z

Z - Batavia (Indonesia)
Z - Grenoble (France)
Z - Harderwijk (Netherlands)
Z - Surabaya (Indonesia)
Z - Zacatecas (Mexico)
Z - Zongolica (Mexcio)
ZACATECAS - Mexico
ZAFARABAD - India-Independent Kingdom, India-Mughal
ZANJAN - Iran
ZEL - Zeeland (Netherlands)
ZEELANDIA - Netherlands
Zs - Zacatecas (Mexico)
ZURICH - Swiss Cantons
Z.V. - Zecca Venezia (Venice)

SYMBOLS

ANCHOR - Genoa (Italy)
ANGEL HEAD - Brussels (Belgium)
ANGEL HEAD - Turin (Italy)
APPLE - Altona (W. Germany)
ARROW - Warsaw (Poland)

AQUEDUCT - Segovia (Spain)
CADUCEUS - Utrecht (Netherlands)
CHILD or STAR - Utrecht (Netherlands)
COCK - Harderwijk (Netherlands)
COW - Pau (France)
CRESCENT - India-Independent Kingdom, Pondichery (India-French)
CROSS - Harderwijk (Netherlands)
CROSSED HAMMERS - Kongsberg (Germany)
CROWN - Bombay (India-British), Copenhagen (Denmark)
DIAMOND - Hyderabad (Indian Princely States)
EAGLE - Hall (Austria)
EAGLE - Kampen (Netherlands)
EAGLE'S HEAD - Turin (Italy)
FLAG - Utrecht (Netherlands)
HAND - Antwerp (Belgium)
HAND - Austrian Netherlands
HEART - Copenhagen (Denmark)
KEY ABOVE STAR - Havana (Cuba)
MERCURY STAFF - Utrecht (Netherlands)
ORB - Altona (W. Germany)
OWL - Aegina, Athens (Greece)
POMEGRANATE - Granada (Nicaragua)
ROSE - Calcutta (India)
ROSETTE - Dordrecht (Netherlands)
ROSETTE - Harderwijk (Netherlands)
SHIELD - Vienna (Austria)
STAR - Dresden (German State)
STAR - Einkhuizen (Netherlands)
STAR - Harderwijk (Netherlands)
STAR - Hoorn (Netherlands)
STAR - Hyderabad
STAR - Luzern (Switzerland)
STAR - Madrid (Spain)
STAR (on rim) - Paris for U.S.S.R.
2 STARS (on rim) - Brussels for U.S.S.R.
TOWER - Middleburg in Zeeland
ZIGZAG LINE - Poissy (France)
¢ - Aix (France)
9 - Rennes (France)
9 - Saint Malo (France)
ИМ - Ichora (U.S.S.R.)
ММД - Moscow (U.S.S.R.)
БМ - St. Petersburg (U.S.S.R.)
СП - St. Petersburg (U.S.S.R.)
СПБ - St. Petersburg (U.S.S.R.)
СПМ - St. Petersburg (U.S.S.R.)

Pave your hobby success with
GOLD

Introducing the all-new 2nd edition

Standard Catalog of

World Gold Coins

from 1601 to date

**Greatly expanded
Totally updated**

- Identify coin issues quickly and easily
- Determine rare coin values with accuracy
- Verify current prices at a glance
- Four centuries of all world gold issues.

Platinum and palladium issues incorporated in this new edition for the first time ever!

- 704 pages • 11,500 actual-size photos • 39,500 coin listings • 675 coin-issuing authorities • your complete date-by-date chronicle of world gold coinage from 1601 to the present

Credit Card Orders (U.S. Only) - Call Toll-Free
(800) 258-0920

8 am to 5 pm CST

Please have order and credit card information ready
Telephone: 715-445-2214
Telex: 55-6461
Facsimile: 715-445-4087

700 East State St.   Iola, WI 54990

Return with proper remittance to:
**Krause Publications, Department DFM,
700 E. State, Iola, WI 54990**

Please send me ____ copy(ies) of the new 2nd edition STANDARD CATALOG OF WORLD GOLD COINS, priced at $45, plus $2.50 postage and handling. (Outside the U.S. add $5.50 for additional postage and handling).

Name _____

Address _____

City _____

State _____ Zip _____

Country _____
DFM

( ) Check enclosed for $ _____, payable to Krause Publications

( ) Charge MasterCard/VISA

Signature _____

Account Number _____

Expiration Date: Month _____ Year _____

Telephone _____

ADVERTISEMENT 43

INSTANT IDENTIFIER

 Aachen (German States)
 Albania
 Austria
 Baden (German States)
 Brandenburg-Ansbach (German States)
 Finland
 Jever (German States)

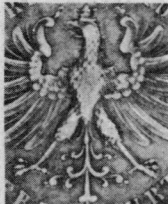 Frankfurt (German States)
 Furstenberg (German States)
 Geneva (Swiss Cantons)
 German Empire
 Montenegro (Yugoslavia)
 Nurnberg (German States)
 Milan (Italian States)

 Prussia (German States)
 Russia (Czarist) Russian Poland
 Schwarzburg-Rudolstadt (German States)
 Schwarzburg-Sondershausen (German States)
 Serbia (Yugoslavia)
 Teutonic Order (German States)
 Genoa (Italian States)

 United Arab Republic (Egypt, Syria)
 Yemen Arab Republic
 Bulgaria
 Burma
 Ethiopia
 Finland
 Norway

 Gorizia (Italian States)
 Hannover (German States)
 Hesse-Darmstadt (German States)
 Iran (Persia)
 Morocco
 Japan

 Hohenlohe-Neuenstein-Oehringen (German States)

 Siberia (U.S.S.R.)
 Tibet (China)
 Tibet (China)
Nepal
 Morocco (AH1320=1902AD)
 Morocco (AH1371=1951AD)

INSTANT IDENTIFIER

 Hanau-Munzenberg (German States)
 Nassau (German States)
 Hesse-Cassel (German States)
 Sri Lanka (Ceylon)
 Tibet (China)
 Utrecht (Netherlands)
 Venice (Italian States)

 Neuchatel (Swiss Cantons)
 China (Empire-Provincial)
 China (Empire-Provincial)
 Japan
 Japan
 African States
 Bretzenheim (German States)

 Hall in Swabia (German States)
 Greenland
 German New Guinea (Papua New Guinea)
 Lithuania (Baltic Regions)
 Mongolia
 Sudan
 Algeria

 Lowenstein-Wertheim (German States)
 Maldive Islands
 Afghanistan
 Ireland
 Israel
 Lebanon
 Papal States (Vatican)

 Regensburg (German States)
 Sweden
 North Korea
 CCCP-USSR
 CCCP-USSR
 Yugoslavia
 Formosa (Rep. of China)

 Mainz (German States)
 Solms-Laubach (German States)
 Ticino (Swiss Cantons)
 Fugger (German States)
 Naples & Sicily (Italian States)
 Saxe-Saalfield (German States)
 Stolberg-Stolberg (German States)

INSTANT IDENTIFIER

 French Colonial

 French Colonial

 French Colonial

 Bangladesh

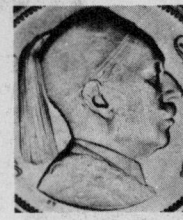 Isle of Man Sicily

 Libya

Anhalt-Bernberg (German States)

 Aargau (Swiss Cantons)

 Augsburg (German States)

 Basel (Swiss Cantons)

 Bavaria (German States)

 Brazil

 Bremen (German States)

 Luzern (Swiss Cantons)

 Chur Pfalz (German States)

 Fulda (German States)

 Glarus (Swiss Cantons)

 Grand Duchy Of Warsaw (Poland)

 Graubunden (Swiss Cantons)

 Hamburg (German States)

 Lucca (Italian States)

 Hesse-Cassel (German States)

 Hesse-Homburg (German States)

 Hildesheim (German States)

 Hohenzollern-Hechingen (German States)

 Hungary

 Julich-Berg (German States)

 Gelderland (Netherlands)

 Lippe-Detmold (German States)

 Lubeck (German States)

 Mecklenburg-Strelitz (German States)

 Oldenburg (German States)

 Passau (German States)

 Portugal

 Vaud (Swiss Cantons)

 Anhalt (Joint Coinage) (German States)

 Oldenburg (German States)

 Schwarzenberg (German States)

 Schaffhausen (Swiss Cantons)

 Paderborn (German States)

 Thurgau (Swiss Cantons)

 Westfrisia (Netherlands)

INSTANT IDENTIFIER

 Arenberg (German States)
 Rhenish Confederation (German States)
 Reuss-Greiz (German States)
 Sardinia (Italian States)
 Saxony (German States)
 Schaumburg-Lippe (German States)
 Schleswig-Holstein (German States)

 St. Gall (Swiss Cantons)
 Slovakia (Czechoslovakia)
 Solothurn (Swiss Cantons)
 Unterwalden (Nidwalden) (Swiss Cantons)
 Wurttemberg (German States)
 Wurzburg (German States)
 Zurich (Swiss Cantons)

 Waldeck-Pyrmont (German States)
 Iraq
 Pakistan
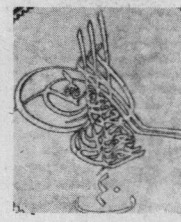 Turkey, Egypt, Sudan, Algeria
 Muscat & Oman, Oman
 Saudi Arabia
 Tunisia

 Wismar (German States)
 Order of Malta
 Bamberg
 Brunswick-Wolfenbuttel
 Brunswick-Luneburg
 Erfurt Mainz
 Hannover

 Eichstadt (German States)
 Greece
 Serbia (Yugoslavia)
 Switzerland
 Albania
 Thailand (Siam)
 Israel
Japan (Dai Nippon)
 South Korea (Korea)

 Sitten (Swiss Cantons)
 Rostock (German States)
 Saint Alban (German States)
 English East India Co. (Sumatra)
 China, Japan, Annam, Korea (All holed 'cash' coins look quite similar.)
 Japan
 Korea

MONOGRAMS

MJ
Maximilian IV Joseph
Berg

FI
Frederick IX & Ingrid
Denmark

F VI R
Fred. VI Denmark
Tranquebar

FVII
Frederick VII
Denmark

FF8
Frederick VIII
Denmark

F IX R
Frederick IX
Denmark

FVII
Ferdinand VII
Mexico

PI
Paul I
Russia-Empire
(U.S.S.R.)

FVII
Ferdinand VII
Mexico

FW
Friedrich Wilhelm III
Prussia

GA IV
Gustav Adolf IV
Sweden

HI
Nicholas I
Russia

HC
Henri Christophe
Haiti

HVII
Haakon VII
Norway

HN
Hieronymus
Napoleon
Westphalia

J
Joachim (Murat)
Berg

E(K)I II
Katherine II
Russia

L
Ludwig
Hesse-Darmstadt

L
Leopold
Belgium

LL III
Leopold III
Belgium

LL
Louis XVIII
Antwerp

C XIVJ
Carl XIV Johann
Norway

M
Morelos
Revolutionary
Mexico

M 2 R
Margrethe II Regina
Denmark

NII
Nicholas II
Russia

NI
Nicholas I
Russia

NFP
Nicholas Friedrich
Peter
Oldenburg

OII
Oscar II
Norway

E
Ernest I
Saxe-Coburg-Gotha

O V
Olav V
Norway

P I
Paul I
Russia

P III
Peter III
Russia

R
Rainier III
Monaco

WL
Wilhelm Landgraf
Hesse-Cassel

WR
William Rex
Hannover

PFA
Peter Friedrich
August
Oldenburg

OII
Oscar II
Sweden

GR
Georgius Rex
Hannover

FRVI
Frederik VI Rex
Tranquebar

PF
Paul Friedrich
Mecklenburg-
Schwerin

FII
Friedrich II
Wurttemberg

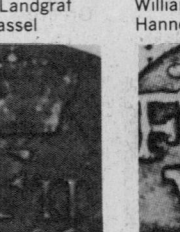
FER VII
Ferdinand VII
(Spain) Gerona

MONOGRAMS

MJ
Maximilian IV Joseph
Berg

CC99
Christian IX
Danish West Indies

V OC
Dutch East India
Co. (Indonesia)

CVII
Christian VII
Danish West Indies

CCX
Christian X
Danish West Indies

G
Georg
Mecklenburg-Strelitz

CWF
Carl Wilhelm
Ferdinand
Brunswick-
Wolfenbuttel

H7
Haakon VII
Norway

A
Albert I
Belgium

GRI
Georgius Rex
Imperator
New Guinea

L
Leopold II
Belgium

EAR
Ernest August Rex
Hannover

FRVI
Frederik VI Rex
Denmark

CX
Christian X
Denmark

A
Albert I
Belgium

AF
Adolpf Frederick IV
Mecklenburg-Strelitz

B
Baudouin I
Belgium

C
Cayenne
French Guiana

CL
Carl & Louise
Saxe-Meiningen

CR
Christian VIII (Denmark)
Tranquebar

FW
Friedrich Wilhelm
Mecklenburg-Strelitz

C7
Christian VII
Tranquebar

C7
Christian VII
Denmark

CIX
Christian IX
Denmark

CCX
Christian X
Denmark

CCXIII
Charles XIII
Sweden

CLXIV
Carl XIV Johann
Norway

CXIV
Carl XIV Johann
Sweden

EP
Elizabeth-Philip
Great Britain

ERI
Edward Rex
Imperator
New Guinea

EIIR
Elizabeth II Regina
Cook Isl.

FA
Friedrich August
Lubeck Bishopric

FF
Friedrich Franz
Mecklenburg-
Schwerin

FJI
Franz Joseph I
Austria

O
Oscar I
Sweden

AFC
Alexius Friedrich
Christian
Anhalt-Bernburg

NII
Nicholas II
Russia-Empire
(U.S.S.R.)

FRVII
Frederik VII Rex
Danish West Indies
Denmark

FC
Friedrich Christian
Brandenburg-
Bayreuth

AIII
Alexander III
Russia-Empire
(U.S.S.R.)

W
William I
Netherlands

LLX
Ludwig X
Hesse-Darmstadt

ILLUSTRATED GUIDE TO EASTERN MINT NAMES

PREPARED ESPECIALLY FOR THE STANDARD CATALOG OF WORLD COINS © 1989 BY KRAUSE PUBLICATIONS

Compiled by Harry S. Scherzer. Arabic typesetting by Mideast Business Exchange

Eastern mint names are basically composed of the Arabic alphabet which in fact covers a number of languages — Arabic is Semitic; Persian is Indo-European; and Malayan is in the Malayo-Polynesian group. Differences are not just of dialect, they are of basic structure. However, Arabic itself is the really important one, bearing a relationship to other Oriental languages not unlike that of Latin to the languages of Europe. Just as medieval European coins are inscribed in Latin, so are the majority of the coins of North African, Turkish, Persian, and Indian origin inscribed until very recent times in Arabic. A limited knowledge of Persian will also be necessary for unravelling the Persian poetic couplets found on Indian and Persian coins particularly during the seventeenth and eighteenth centuries A.D.

(Courtesy of Richard J. Plant)

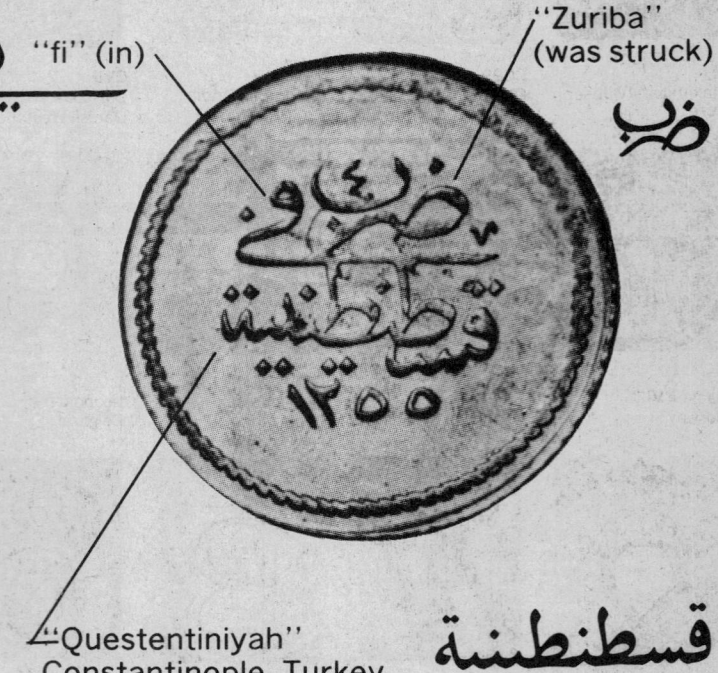

"fi" (in) — "Zuriba" (was struck) — "Questentiniyah" Constantinople, Turkey

ANKARA Turkey	انقره	AKSU China-Sinkiang	اقصو
EL-'ARAISH "Larache", Morocco	العرايش	ALGERIA See "El-Jaza'Iriyat"	—
EL-'ARAISHAN "Larache", Morocco	العرايشة	BI-ANGLAND "In England" (Birmingham) For Morocco	بانكلند
ABUSHAHR "Bushire", Iran	ابو شهر	BI-ANGLAND "In England" (London) For Morocco	بانكلند
ADRANAH "Edirne", Turkey	ادرنة	DAULAT ANJAZANCHIYAH "The State of Anjazanchiyah" See Comoros	دولة انجزنجية
AFGHANISTAN	افغانستان		
AHMADABAD Bombay, India-British	احمد اباد	ANWALA "Aonla", Afghanistan	انوله
AHMADNAGAR-FARRUK Afghanistan	احمدنكر فرخ اباد	EL-ARABIYAT ES-SA'UDIYAT "Saudi-Arabian", Saudi Arabia	العربية السعودية
AHMADPUR See "Bahawalpur", Afghanistan	احمد پور	ARDEBIL Iran	اردبيل
AHMADSHAHI See "Ashraf Al-Bilad" and "Qandahar", Afghanistan	احمد شاهى	ARKAT "Arcot", India-French	اركات
AJMAN See "United Arab Emirates"	اجمان	ASHRAF AL-BILAD "Most Noble of Cities" See "Ahmadshahi", Afghanistan	اشرف البلاد

ILLUSTRATED GUIDE TO EASTERN MINT NAMES

ASTARABAD
Iran
استراباد

ATCHEH
Indonesia
اجه

ATTOCK
Afghanistan
اتك

AZIMABAD
See "Patna", Bengal, India-British
عظیم اباد

BACAIM (no legends)
See "India-Portuguese"
—

BADAKHSHAN
See Afghanistan
بردخشان

BAGCHIH-SERAI
See "Krim", U.S.S.R.-Russian Caucasia
باغجه سراي

BAGHDAD
Iraq
بغداد

BAHAWALPUR
See "Ahmadpur" and "Dar Es-Surur", Afghanistan
بهاولپور

BAHRAIN
See "El-Bahrain"
بحرين

EL-BAHRAIN
"Of the Two Seas", Bahrain
البحرين

BALKH
See "Umm Al-Bilad", Afghanistan
بلخ

BANARAS
"Awadh", Bengal, India-British
بنارس

BANDAR ABBAS
Iran
بندر عباس

BANJARMASIN
Indonesia
بنجرمسن

BARELI
Afghanistan
بريلي

BI BARIZ
"In Paris"
For Morocco
بباريز

BEHBEHAN
Iran
بهبهان

BERLIN
For Morocco
برلين

BHAKHAR
Afghanistan
بهكر

BOMBAY
See "Mumbai", Bombay, India-British
—

BORUJERD
Iran
بروجرد

NEGRI BRUNEI
"State of Brunei", Brunei
نكري بروني

BRUSAH
"Bursa", Turkey
بروسة

BUKHARA
See U.S.S.R.-Russian Turkestan
بخارا

BUSHIRE
See "Abushahr", Iran
—

CALCUTTA
See "Kalkatah", Bengal, India-British
كلكته

COCHIN
See India-Dutch and "V.O.C.", India-Dutch
—

COMOROS
See "Anjazanchiyah", "The Largest of the Islands", Comoros
كموز

DACCA
See "Jahangirnagar", Bengal, India-British
—

DAMAO (no legends)
See India-Portuguese
—

DAR AL-AMAN
"Abode of Security" (honorific)
See "Multan"
دار الامان

DAR AL-ISLAM
See Bahawalpur, India Princely States
دار الاسلام

DAR AL-MULK
"Abode of the King" (honorific)
See "Kabul"
دار لملك

DAR AL-NUSRAT
"Abode of the New (Town?)" (honorific)
See "Herat"
دارالنصرت

DAR EL-KHILAFAT
"Abode of the Caliphate" (honorific)
See "Tehran" and "Yemen"
دار الخلافة

DAR ES-SALAM
"Abode of Peace" (honorific)
See "Ligkeh", Thailand
دار السلام

DAR AS-SULTANAT
"Abode of the Sultanate" (honorific)
See "Herat" and "Kabul", Afghanistan
دار السلطنة

DAR AS-SURUR
"Abode of Happiness" (honorific)
See "Bahawalpur", Afghanistan
دار السرور

DARBAND
Iran
دربند

ILLUSTRATED GUIDE TO EASTERN MINT NAMES

DARFUR
   See "Al-Fasher", Sudan   الفشير

DEHLI
   See "Shajahanabad", Afghanistan   دهلي

DELI
   Indonesia   دلي

DERA
   "Dera Ghazi Khan", Afghanistan   ديره

DERAJAT
   "Dera Ishmael Khan", Afghanistan   ديره جات

DEZFUL
   Iran   دزفول

DIU (no legends)
   See India-Portuguese   ——

DJIBOUTI
   See "Jaibuti"   ——

EDIRNE
   See "Adranah", Turkey   ——

EGYPT
   See "Misr" and "El-Misriyat"   ——

ERAVAN
   Iran   ايروان

FARRUKHABAD
   Bengal, India-British   فرخ اباد

AL-FASHER
   See "Darfur", Sudan   الفشير

FES
   "Fez", Morocco   فاس

FERGANA
   See "Khoqand", U.S.S.R.-Russian Turkestan   فرغانة

FILASTIN
   "Palestine", Israel   فلسطين

AL-FUJAIRAH
   See "United Arab Emirates"   الفجيره

GANJAH
   Iran   كنجه

GERMAN EAST AFRICA
   See "Sharakat Almaniyah", Tanzania   شراكة المانيا

GHAZNI
   Afghanistan   غزني

GOA (no legends)
   See India-Portuguese   ——

HAIDARABAD SIND MINT
   Afghanistan   حيدر آباد سند

HALEB
   "Allepo", Syria   حلب

HAMADAN
   Iran   همدان

EL-HARAR
   Ethiopia-Eritrea   الهرر

AL-HEJAZ
   Saudi Arabia-Hejaz   الحجاز

HERAT
   See "Dar Al-Nushat" and "Dar Es-Sultanat", Afghanistan   هرات

HERAT
   Iran   هرات

ILI
   China-Sinkiang   الي

IRAN   ايران

EL-IRAQ
   "Iraq"   العراق

EL-IRAQIYAT
   "Iraqi", Iraq   العراقية

ISFAHAN
   Iran   اصفهان

ISLAMBUL
   Turkey   اسلامبول

ITALIAN SOMALILAND
   See "Al-Somal Al-Italianiah", Somalia   الصومال الايطالينية

JAHANGIRNAGAR
   See "Dacca", Bengal, India-British   جهانكيرنكر

BI-JAIBUTI
   "In Djibouti", Djibouti   بجيبوتي

JAVA
   Indonesia   جاوا

JAZA'IR
   Algeria-Algiers   جزاير

EL-JAZA'IRIYAT
   Algeria-Algiers   الجزايرة

JERING
   "Jaring", Thailand   جريج

EL-JOMHURIYAT EL-IRAQIYAT
   "The Iraqi Republic" Iraq   الجمهورية العرقية

EL-JOMHURIYAT EL-LUBNANIYAT
   "The Lebanese Republic", Lebanon   الجمهورية البنانية

ILLUSTRATED GUIDE TO EASTERN MINT NAMES

EL-JOMHURIYAT EL-MUTTAHIDAH EL-ARABIYAT
"United Arab Republic"
See "Egypt, Syria and Yemen"
الجمهورية المتحدة العربية

EL-JOMHURIYAT ES-SUDAN
"The Sudanese Republic", Sudan
الجمهورية السودان

EL-JOMHURIYAT ES-SURIYAT
"The Syrian Republic", Syria
الجمهورية السورية

EL-JOMHURIYAT AL-TUNISIAT
"The Tunisian Republic", Tunisia
الجمهورية التونسية

EL-JOMHURIYAT EL-TURKIYAH
"The Turkish Republic", Turkey
الجمهورية توركية

JORDON
See "El-Urduniyat" and "El-Mamlakat, etc.", Jordan

KABUL
See "Dar Al-Mulk" > AH1163 and "Dar Es-Sultanat" >AH1164, Afghanistan
كابل

KAFFA
Krim, U.S.S.R.- Russian Caucasia
كفه

KALKATAH
"Calcutta", Bengal, India-British
كلكته

KASHAN
Iran
كاشان

KASHMIR
Afghanistan
كشمير

KASHQUAR
China-Sinkiang
كشقر

KEDAH
See "Bilad Kedah" and "Bilad Al-Perlis Kedah", Malaysia
كداه

KELANTAN
See "Khalifat Al-Mu'Minin" and "Negri Kelantin", Malaysia
كلنتن

KEMASIN
Malaysia
كماسن

KERMAN
Iran
كرمان

KERMANSHAHAN
See "Kermanshah", Iran
كرمانشاهان

KHALIFAT AL-MU'MININ
"Commander of the Faithful" (honorific)
See "Kelantin" and "Trengganu"
خليفة المؤمنين

KHALIFAT AL-KARAM
"Noble Caliph" (honorific)
See "Patani"
خليفة الكرم

KHANABAD
Afghanistan
خان اباد

KHOQAND
See "U.S.S.R.-Russian Turkestan"
خوقند

KHUI
See "Khoy", Iran
خوى

AL-KHURFAH
See "Yemen"
الخرفاه

KHUTAN
China-Sinkiang
خوتن

KHWAREZM
U.S.S.R.-Russian Turkestan-Khiva
خوارزم

KOSOVAH
Turkey
قوصوه

KOTSHA
China-Sinkiang
كوتشر

AL-KUWAIT
Kuwait
الكويت

LADAKH
Afghanistan
لداخ

LAHEJ
See "Yemen"
لحج

LAHIJAN
See "Gilan", Iran
لاهيجان

LAHORE
Afghanistan
لابهور

LEBANON
See "El-Lubnaniyat" and "Jomhuriyat, etc."

EL-LIBIYAT
"Libyan", Libya
الليبية

LIBYA
See "El-Libyat" and "Mamlakat, etc."
ليبيا

NEGRI LIGKEH
"State of Ligeh (or Ligor)"
See "Dar Es-Salam", Thailand
نكري لغكه

ILLUSTRATED GUIDE TO EASTERN MINT NAMES

EL-LUBNANIYAT
"Lebanese", Lebanon

اللبنلية

MACHHLIPATAN
See "Mazulipatam", India-French
"Masulipatam", India-Madras

مچهلي بتن

MACHHLIPATAN-BANDAR
See "Machhlipatan", India-Madras

مچهلي پتن بندر

EL-MAGHRIBIYAT
"Moroccan", Morocco

المغربية

TANAH MALAYU
"Land of the Malays"
See "Sumatra", Indonesia and
"Malacca", Malaysia

تانه ملايو

PULU MALAYU
"Island of the Malays"
See "Sumatra", Indonesia

فولو ملايو

MALUKA
Indonesia

ملوك

EL-MAMLAKAT EL-ARABIYAT EL-SA'UDIYAT
"The Kingdom of Saudi Arabia"

المملكة العربية السعودية

EL-MAMLAKAT EL-LIBIYAT
"The Kingdom of Libya"

المملكة الليبية

EL-MAMLAKAT EL-MAGHRIBIYAT
"The Kingdom of Morocco"

المملكة المغربية

EL-MAMLAKAT EL-MUTAWAKELIYAT EL-YEMENIAT
"The Mutawakelite Kingdom of Yemen"

المملكة المتوكلية اليمنية

EL-MAMLAKAT EL-MISRIYAT
"The Kingdom of Egypt"

المملكة المصرية

EL-MAMLAKAT EL-URDUNIYAT EL-HASHEMIYAT
"The Hashemite Kingdom of Jordan"

المملكة الاردنية الهاشمية

MANASTIR
Turkey

مناستر

MARAGHEH
Iran

مراغه

MARAKESH
"Marrakech", Morocco

مراكش

AL-MASCARA
Algeria-Algiers

المعسكر

MASH'HAD
Afghanistan

مشهد

MASH'HAD
Iran

مشهد

MASULIPATAM
See "Machhlipatan", India-Madras

—

MAZANDARAN
Iran

مازندران

MAZULIPATAM
See "Machhlipatan", India-French

—

MEDEA
Algeria-Algiers

مديه

MEKHA
"Mecca", Saudi-Arabia

مكة

MENANGKABAU
Indonesia

منفكابو

MIKNAS
"Meknes", Morocco

مكناس

MIKNASAH
"Meknes", Morocco

مكناسة

MISR
Egypt

مصر

EL-MISRIYAT
"Egyptian", Egypt

المصرية

EL-MOHAMMEDIYAT ESH-SHERIFATE
"The Mohammedan Sherifate" or
"Empire Cherifien" (French), Morocco

المحمدية الشريفة

MOMBASA
Kenya

ممباسه

MOROCCO
See "El-Maghribyat" and
"El-Mohammediyat Esh-Sherifate"

—

MOXOUDABAT
See "Murshidabad", India-French

—

MUBARAK
"Auspicious" (honorific)
See "Rikab"

مبارك

AL-MAKALA
"Mukalla"
See "Yemen"

المكلا

MULTAN
See "Dar Al-Aman", Afghanistan

ملتان

ILLUSTRATED GUIDE TO EASTERN MINT NAMES

MUNBAI
See "Bombay", India-British
منبي

MURADABAD
Afghanistan
مراد اباد

MURSHIDABAD
See "Moxoudabat", India-French
مرشد اباد

MURSHIDABAD
Bengal, India-British
مرشد اباد

MUSCAT
Oman
مسقط

NAJIBABAD
Afghanistan
نجيب اباد

NAKAPATTANAM (Tamil legends)
"Negapatnam", India-Dutch
நகபட்டணம்

NAKHCHAWAN
Iran
نخجوان

NEGAPATNAM
See "Nakappattanam"
—

NEJD
Saudi Arabia
نجد

NIHAWAND
Iran
نهاوند

NUKHWI
"Sheki", Iran
نخوى

NUKHWI
See "Sheki", U.S.S.R.-
Russian Caucasia
نخوي

OMAN
عمان

OMDURMAN
Sudan
ام درمان

PAHANG
"Pahang Company", Malaysia
فاحغ

PAKISTAN
باكستان

PALEMBANG
Indonesia
فلمبغ

PALESTINE
See "Filastin", Israel
—

PANA'HABAD
"Shusha"
See "Karabagh", U.S.S.R.-
Russian Caucasia
بناه باد

AL-PATANI
See "Khalifat Al-Karam",
"Khalifat Al-Mu'Minin" and
"Bilad Al-Patani", Thailand
الفطاني

PATNA
See "Azimabad", Bengal,
India-British
بتنه

PULU PENANG
"Prince of Wales Island", Malaysia
فولو فنيغ

NEGRI PERAQ
"State of Perak", Malaysia
نكري فيرق

PULU PERCHA
"Island of Sumatra", Indonesia
فولو فرج

PERLIS
See "Kedah", Malaysia
—

PESHAWAR
Afghanistan
پشاور

PHALICHERY
SEE "Pondichery", India-French
بهلجري

PONDICHERY
See "Phalichery", India-French
—

PONTIANAQ (no legends)
Indonesia
—

PULICAT (no legends)
See "India-Dutch"
—

QANDAHAR
See "Ashraf Al-Bilad" and
"Ahmadshahi", Afghanistan
قندهار

QATAR WA DUBAI
"Qatar and Dubai", Qatar
قطرودبي

DAULAT QATAR
"State of Qatar", Qatar
—

QAZWIN
Iran
قزوين

QUAITI
Yemen
قيطي

QUM
Iran
قم

QUSANTINAT
"Constantine", Algeria-Algiers
قسنطينة

QUSTINTINIYAH
"Constantinople", Turkey
قسطنطينية

RA'NASH
Iran
رعنش

ILLUSTRATED GUIDE TO EASTERN MINT NAMES

RABAT
See "Rabat Al-Fath", Morocco
رباط

RABAT AL-FATH
"Rabat", Morocco
رباط الفتح

RAS AL-KHAIMA
See "United Arab Emirates"
راس الخيمه

RASHT
Iran
رشت

REHMAN
Thailand
رحمن

REZA'IYEH
See "Urumi", Iran
رظاعيه

RIKAB
See "Mubarak", Afghanistan
ركاب

RIKAB
Iran
ركاب

SA'UJBALAQ
Iran
ساوج بلاق

SAGAR
Bengal, India-British
ساكر

SAHRIND
Afghanistan
شهرند

AL-SAIWI
See "Bilad Al-Saiwi", "Sai", "Saiburi" and "Teluban", Thailand
السيوي

SAN'A
See "Yemen", Yemen Arab Republic
سنة

SARAKHS
Iran
سرخس

SARHIND
See "Sahrind", Afghanistan
—

SARI
Iran
ساري

SARI POL
Afghanistan
سربل

SAUDI ARABIA
See "Al-Hejaz", "Nejd" and "El-Arabiyat Es-Sa'udiya", Saudi Arabia
—

NEGRI SELANGHUR
"State of Selangor", Malaysia
نكري سلاغور

SELANIK
"Salonika", Turkey
سلانيك

SHAJAHANABAD
See "Dehli", Afghanistan
شاجهان اباد

SHAMAKHI
U.S.S.R.-Russian Caucasia
شماخ

SHAMAKHA
U.S.S.R.-Russian Caucasia
سماخه

SHARAKAT ALMANIYAH
"German Company" or "German East Africa", Tanzania
شراكتة المانيا

ES-SHARJAH
See "United Arab Emirates"
الشارجة

SHIRAZ
Iran
شيراز

SHUSHTAR
Iran
شوشتر

NEGRI SIAK
"State of Siak", Indonesia
نكري سيك

SIMNAN
Iran
سمنان

SIND
Afghanistan
سند

AL-SOMAL AL-ITALIANIYAH
"Italian Somaliland", Somalia
الصومال الايطليانية

SULTANABAD
Iran
سلطاناباد

SUMENEP
Indonesia
سمنف

SURAT
See "Surate", India-French
سورت

SURAT
Bombay, India-British
سورت

ES-SURIYAT
"Syrian", Syria
السورية

AL-SUWAIR
"Essaouira Mogador", Morocco
الصوير

AL-SUWAIRAH
"Essaouira Mogador", Morocco
الصويرة

SYRIA
See "Haleb", "Es-Suriyat", "Jomhuriyat, etc.", Syria
—

TABARISTAN
Iran
طبرستان

TABRIZ
Iran
تبريز

ILLUSTRATED GUIDE TO EASTERN MINT NAMES

TANGIER
　See "Tanjah", Morocco

TANJAH
　"Tangier", Morocco　　　　　　　طنجة

TAQIDEMT
　Algeria-Algiers　　　　　　　تاقدمت

TARABALUS GHARB
　"Tripoli West", Libya　　　طرابلس غرب

TARIM
　See "Yemen"　　　　　　　　تريم

NEGRI TARUMON
　"State of Tarumon", Indonesia　نكري ترومن

TASHQURGHAN
　Afghanistan　　　　　　تاش قورغان

TATTA
　Afghanistan　　　　　　　　تته

TEGNAPATAM (no legends)
　"Fort St. David", Madras, India-British

TEHRAN
　See "Dar El-Khilafat", Iran　　طهران

TELLICHERY
　Bombay, India-British　　　　تلچري

TETUAN
　Morocco　　　　　　　　تطوان

TIFLIS
　See "U.S.S.R.-Russian Caucasia-
　Georgian S.S.R.　　　　　　تفليس

TRANQUEBAR (no legends)
　See "India-Danish"

TRENGKANU
　See "Khalifat Al-Mu'Minin",
　Malaysia　　　　　　　　ترغكانو

TUNIS
　Tunisia　　　　　　　　　تونس

TUNISIA
　See "Tunis", "El-Tunisiyat",
　"Jomhuriyat, etc."

EL-TUNISIYAT
　"Tunisian", Tunisia　　　　التونسية

TURKEY
　See "Turkiyah",
　"Jomhuriyat, etc."

EL-TURKIYAT
　"Turkish", Turkey　　　　　التوركية

TUTICORIN (degenerate Nagari legends)
　See "India-Dutch"

TUYSERKAN
　Iran　　　　　　　　توى سركان

TANAH UGI
　"Land of the Bugis", Indonesia　تانه اغيسى

UMM AL-BILAD
　"Mother of Cities"
　See "Balkh", Afghanistan　　ام البلاد

UMM AL-QAIWAIN
　See "United Arab Emirates"　ام القوين

UNITED ARAB EMIRATES
　　　　　　الامارات العربية المتحدة

UNITED ARAB REPUBLIC
　See "El-Jomhuriyat El-Arabiyat
　El-Muttahidah"

EL-URDUNIYAT
　"Jordanian", Jordan　　　　الاردنية

URUMCHI
　China-Sinkiang　　　　　　ارومجي

URUMI
　See "Reza'iyeh", Iran　　　　ارومى

USHI
　China-Sinkiang　　　　　　اوش

WAN
　"Van", Turkey　　　　　　　وان

YARKHAND
　China-Sinkiang　　　　　　يارقند

YARKHISSARMARAN
　"Yanghissar"
　China-Sinkiang　　　　ياركسارمرن

YAZD
　Iran　　　　　　　　　　يزد

YEMEN
　See "Sana", "Dar El-Khilafat",
　El-Yemeniyat", Mamlakat, etc."

EL-YEMENIYAT
　"The Yemen"　　　　　　اليمنية

ZANJAN
　Iran　　　　　　　　　　زنجان

ZANJIBARA
　"Zanzibar", Tanzania　　　　زنجباره

LEGEND ABBREVIATIONS

A

A.D.J. - Amecameca de Juarez

A Deo et Caesare From God and emperor - (Frankfurt)

A.V. & O.S. Steph. R.A.M.C. Eq. U.S.C.R.A.M.A.I. Cons. Conf. M. & S.A. Praef Knight both of the Golden Fleece and of the Order of the Great Cross of the Apostolic King St. Stephen, present privy counselor of their sacred, imperial, royal and apostolic majesties, conference minister, and high prefect of the court - (Khevenhuller-Metsch)

Abb. S.G.E.S.I.A.V.E. Abbot of St. Gallen and St. John, Knight of the Virgin of the Annunciation - (St. Gall)

Ad Legem Conventionis To the law of the convention - (Furstenberg)

Ad Normam Conventionis According to the convention standard

Ad Normam Talerorum Alberti According to the Albertus taler standard - (Prussia)

Ad Usam Luxemburgi CC Vallati For the use of the 200,000 besieged Luxemburgians - (Luxembourg)

Adalbertus D.G. Epis. et Abb. Fuld. S.R.I.Pr. Adalbert by the grace of God bishop and abbot of Fulda, prince of the Holy Roman Empire - (Fulda)

Ad(am) Fri(deric) D.G. Ep. Bam. et Wirc(eb). S.R.I. Pr(in) Fr. Or. Dux Adam Friedrich by the grace of God bishop of Bamberg and Wurzburg, prince of the Holy Roman Empire, duke of Eastern Franconia - (Bamberg, Wurzburg)

Adam Frid. D.G. Franc. Orient. Dux Adam Friedrich by the grace of God, duke of Eastern Franconia - (Wurzburg)

Adolphus Frid. D.G. Rex Sveciae Adolf Frederick D.G. king of Sweden - (Sweden)

Adventus Optimi Principis The coming of the noblest prince - (Papal States)

Alexander D.G. March. Brand. Alexander by the grace of God, margrave of Brandenburg - (Brandenburg-Ansbach)

Alexander D.G.M.B.D.B. & S. (B.N.) Alexander by the grace of God, margrave of Brandenburg, duke of Prussia and Silesia, burgrave of Nuremberg - (Brandenburg-Ansbach)

Amalia Tutrix Reg. Sax. Vinar & Isenac. Amalia ruling regent of Saxe-Weimar and Eisenach - (Saxe- Weimar-Eisenach)

Anselmus D.G.S.R.I. Abbas Werdinensis & Helmstad. Anselm by the grace of God, of the Holy Roman Empire Abbot of Werden and Helmstedt - (Werden & Helmstedt)

Ant. Ign. D.G.S.R.I. Princeps Praep. Ae. Dom. Elvancensis Anton Ignaz by the grace of God, prince of the Holy Roman Empire, provost and lord of Ellwangen - (Ellwangen)

Anton. Ignat. D.G. Episc. Ratisbon. Anton Ignaz by the grace of God, bishop of Regensburg - (Regensburg-Bishopric)

Ant. Theodor D.G. Prim. A. Ep. Olomu. Dux Anton Theodor D.G. first archbishop of Olmutz, duke - (Olmutz)

Antonius I Barbiani Belgiojoso et S.R.I. Princeps Antonio I Barbiani of Belgiojoso, prince of the Holy Roman Empire - (Belgiojoso)

Apres les tenebres la lumiere After the shadows, the light - (Geneva)

Ar(c). Au. Dux Bu. Medi. Pr. Tran. Co. Ty. Archduke of Austria, duke of Burgundy and Milan, prince of Transylvania, count of Tyrol - (Austria)

Arch. Aus(t). Dux Burg. Brab. C. Fl. Archduke of Austria, duke of Burgundy and Brabant, count of Flanders - (Austrian Netherlands)

Arch. Aust. Dux Burg Loth. Brab. Com. Flan. Archduke of Austria, duke of Burgundy, Lorraine, Brabant, count of Flanders - (Austria, Austrian Netherlands, Milan)

Arch(idux) Aust. D(ux) Burg. (et) Loth. M(ag) D(ux) Het(r). Archduke of Austria, duke of Burgundy and Lorraine, grandduke of Tuscany - (Austria)

Archid. Aust. D. Burg. Marggr. Burgoviae Archduke of Austria, duke of Burgundy, margrave of Burgau - (Burgau)

Archid(ux) Aust(riae) Dux Bur(gundiae) Com. Ty(rolis) Archduke of Austria, duke of Burgundy, count of Tyrol - (Austria)

Archiep. Vien. S.R.I.P. Ep. Vacien, Adm. S. Steph. R.A.M.C.E. Archbishop of Vienna, prince of the Holy Roman Empire, administrator of Waitzen bishopric, knight of the Grand Cross of the Apostolic King St. Stephen - (Vienna)

Augustus D.G. Ep. Spir. S.R.I.P. et Praep. Weiss. August by the grace of God, bishop of Speyer, prince of the Holy Roman Empire and provost of Weissenburg - (Speyer)

Auxilium de Sancto Aid from the Sanctuary - (Papal States)

Avr. Vel. Equ. SS.CC.RR.MM. Act. Int. et Conferent. Consil. et Supr. Camer. Knight of the Golden Fleece, present privy and conference chancellor of their sacred, imperial, royal majesties, and High Chamberlain - (Khevenhuller-Metsch)

B

Barbarae Qvirini Sponsae Dulcissimae Moribvs Ingenio Praeclarae Intempestiva Morte Perempte Die XXIII Oct. Thomas Obicivs Moerens Memoriam Perennat A.S. MDCCXCVI To his betrothed Barbara Quirini, most sweet in character and illustrious in her genius, carried away - (Orciano)

Basilea - Basel

Beda D.G. S.R.I.P. Beda D.G. prince of the Holy Roman Empire - (St. Gall)

Britanniarum Regina Fid. Def. Queen of the Britains, Defender of the Faith - (Great Britain)

Bruns et Lun. Dux. S.R.I. Archithes of Elect. Duke of Brunswick - Luneburg, archtreasurer and elector of the Holy Roman Empire - (Brunswick-Luneburg)

Burggravie Norimberg. Supperioris & Inferioris Principatus Burgraves of Nuremberg, of the upper and lower state - (Brandenburg-Ansbach)

C

C.B. - Chur Bavaria

C.G.F.Z.S.S. - Christian Gunther, Prince of Schwarzburg-Sonderhausen

C.M.L.M. - Electorate of Mainz Land-Munze

C.P. - Chur Pfalz

C.S.T. - Colony of Santa Tereza - (Brazil)

Cai. & Car. Com. de Fugger in Zin. & Norn. Sen. & Adm. Fam. Cajetan and Karl counts of Fugger in Zinnenberg and Nordendorf, lords and administrators of the family - (Fugger)

Capit. Cath. Ecclesia Monasteriensis Sede Vacante The Chapter of the cathedral church of Munster, the seat being vacant - (Munster)

Capit. Eccle. Metropolit. Colon. Sede Vacante The Chapter of the metropolitan church of Cologne, the seat being vacant - (Cologne)

Capit(ulum) Cath(edrale) Monasterien(se). Sede Vacante The Cathedral Chapter, Munster. The seat being vacant - (Munster)

Capitulum Brixense Regnans Sede Vacante The Chapter of Brixen governing, the seat being vacant - (Brixen)

Capitulum Eystettense Regnans Sede Vacante The Chapter of Eichstedt governing, the seat being vacant - (Eichstadt)

Capitulum Regnans Sede Vacante The Chapter governing, the seat being vacant - (Eichstadt)

Car. Albertus D. G. Rex Sard. Cyp. et Hier. Charles Albert by the Grace of God King of Sardinia, Cyprus and Jerusalem - (Sardinia)

Car. August D.G.S.R.I. Princeps de Brezenheim Karl August by the grace of God, of the Holy Roman Empire prince of Bretzenheim - (Bretzenheim)

Car. Em. D.G. Rex Sar. Cyp. et Ier. Charles Emanuele D.G. king of Sardinia, Cyprus, and Jerusalem - (Sardinia)

Car. Felix D.G. Rex Sar. Cyp. et Hier Charles Felix by the grace of God King of Sardinia, Cyprus, and Jerusalem - (Sardinia)

Car. Theodor. D.G.C.P.R.S.R.I.A.T. & El Karl Theodore by the grace of God, count palatine of the Rhine, arch treasurer and elector of the Holy Roman Empire - (Julich-Berg, Pfalz-Sulzbach)

Car. Th(eodor) D.G.C.P.R. Utr. Bav. Dux S.R.I.A.D. & El. D.I.C.M. Karl Theodore by the grace of God, count palatine of the Rhine, duke of both Bavarias, archidapifer and elector of the Holy Roman Empire, duke of Julich, Cleves, and Berg - (Bavaria)

Carl Ludw. U.H. Christ Fried. Graf. z. Stolb. Karl Ludwig and Heinrich Christian Friedrich counts of Stolberg - (Stolberg)

Carl August Furst zu Anhalt Schaumburg Karl Ludwig prince of Anhalt Schaumburg - (Anhalt-Schaumburg)

Carol. D.G. S.R. Imp. Princ. in (de) Lowenst. & Werth. Karl by the grace of God, of the Holy Roman Empire prince of Lowenstein-Wertheim - (Lowenstein-Wertheim-Rochefort)

Carol S.R.I. Princ. de Batthyan. P.I.N.U. & S. Com. Aur. V.E.C.C.P.S.U.S.C. Karl, of the Holy Roman Empire, prince of Batthyani, hereditary count in Nemet-Ujvar and Siklos, knight of the Golden Fleece, hereditary in the county of Eisenburg, full supreme count of Simega (Somogy) - (Batthyani)

Carol. Christ. Erdm. Dux Wurtemb. Olsn. & Berolst. Karl Christian Erdmann, duke of Wurttemberg, Oels, and Berolstadt - (Wurttemberg- Oels)

Carol Lud. S.R.I. Com. in Loewenst. Werth. Karl Ludwig of the Holy Roman Empire count of Loewenstein- Wertheim - (Lowenstein- Wertheim- Virneburg)

Carola Magna Ducissa Feliciter Regnante Grand duchess Charlotte, happily reigning - (Luxembourg)

Carolus IIII Dei G. Charles IV D.G. - (Spain, Spanish America)

Carolus D.G. Dux Brunsvic. et Luneb. Karl by the grace of God, duke of Brunswick-Luneburg - (Brunswick-Wolfenbuttel)

Carolus D.G. Dux Wurt. & T(ec) Karl by the grace of God, duke of Wurttemberg and Teck - (Wurttemberg)

Carolus D.G. Hass. Landg. Karl by the grace of God, landgrave of Hesse - (Hanau- Munzenberg)

Carolus Frid(ericus) D.G. Marchio Bad. & (et) H(ochb.) Karl Friedrich by the grace of God, margrave of Baden and Hochberg - (Baden)

Carolus Guil. Ferd. Dux Brunsv. et Lun. Karl Wilhelm Ferdinand, duke of Brunswick-Luneburg - (Brunswick-Wolfenbuttel)

Carolus Ioachim D.G. Princ Furstenberg Karl Ioachim by the grace of God, Prince of Furstenberg - (Furstenberg)

Carolus Lud. D.G. Rex Etr(uriae) & M. Aloysia R(egina) Rectrix I. I. H. H. Charles Louis by the grace of God, King of Etruria and Maria Luisa Queen Regent, Prince and Princess of Spain - (Tuscany)

Charta Magna Bavariae Magna Carta of Bavaria - (Bavaria)

Christ. Fr. Car. D.G.S.R.I. Princ. Hohenl. Kirchb. Christian Friedrich Karl by the grace of God, of the Holy Roman Empire prince of Hohenlohe- Kirchberg - (Hohenlohe-Kirchberg)

Christ. Lud. Com. Wed. Isenb. & Crich. Charl. Soph. Aug. Com. Sayn & Witg. Christian Ludwig count of Wied, Isenburg and Crichingen, Charlotte Sophie Auguste countess of Sayn and Wittgenstein - (Wied)

Christian den VII Danmarks og Norges Konge Christian VII king of Denmark and Norway - (Denmark)

Christian IV D.G.C.P.R. Bav. D(ux) Christian IV by the grace of God, count palatine of the Rhine, duke of Bavaria - (Pfalz-Birkenfeld-Zweibrucken)

Christianus VII D.G. Dan. Norv. V.G. Rex Christian VII D.G. king of Denmark, Norway, Vendalia, Gothland - (Denmark)

Christianus VIII D.G. Daniae V.G. Rex Christian VIII by the grace of God, King of Denmark, Vendalia, and Gothland - (Denmark)

Christianus IX D.G. Daniae V.G. Rex Christian IX by the grace of God, King of Denmark, Vendalia, and Gothland - (Denmark)

Christoph Frank Bischof zu Bamberg des H.R.R. Furst Christopher Franz bishop of Bamberg, prince of the Holy Roman Empire - (Bamberg)

Christophorus D.M.S.R.E. Cardinalis de Migazzi Christopher, by the mercy of God, Cardinal Migazzi of the Holy Roman Church - (Vienna)

Chur Mainz Electorate of Mainz - (Mainz)

Civibus Quorum Pietas Coniuratione Die III Mai MDCCXCI Obrutan et Deletam Libertate Polona Tueri Conabatur Respublica Resurgens To the citizens whose piety the resurgent commonwealth tried to protect. Poland overturned and deprived of liberty by the conspiracy of the 3rd day of May 1791 - (Poland)

Civit Imperialis Muhlhusinae Imperial city of Muhlhausen - (Muhlhausen)

Civitas Lucemborgensis Millesimum Ovans Expletannum Completing the celebration of 1000 years of the city of Luxemburg - (Luxembourg)

Clem. Wenc. D.G.A. Ep. & El. Trev. Ep. Aug. P. Pr. Elv. Adm. Prum. P.P.R. Pol. D. Sax. Clemens Wenceslaus by the grace of God, archbishop and elector of Trier, bishop of Augsburg, provost and prince of Ellwangen, perpetual administrator of Pruem, royal prince of Poland, duke of Saxony - (Trier)

Clem. Wenc. D.G.A. Ep(isc) Trev. S.R.I.A.C. & El. Clemens Wenceslaus by the grace of God, archbishop of Trier, arch chancellor and elector of the Holy Roman Empire - (Trier)

Clemens XIII Pont. Max. Clement XIII Pope - (Papal States)

Com. in Theng. S.C.M. Intim. Cons. et Supr. Stabuli Praefect Count of Thengen, privy counselor of his sacred, imperial majesty and High Constable - (Auersperg)

Com(es) in Thengen et Sup(remus) Haer (editarius) Prov(inciae) Carn(iolae) Maresch(allus) Count in Thengen and Supreme Hereditary Marshal in the Province of Carniola - (Auersperg)

Comes Cunii Lugi March. Grumelli Count of Cuneo, Lugio, marquis of Grumellio - (Belgiojoso)

Communitas et Senatus Bonon. The city and Senate of Bologna - (Bologna)

Concordia Patriae Nutrix. Peace, the nurse of the fatherland - (Waldeck)

Concordia Res Parvae Crescunt Little things grow through concord - (Batavian Republic)

Concordia Res Parvae Crescunt, Discordia Dilabuntur By concord small things increase, by discord they fall apart - (Lowenstein- Wertheim- Virneburg)

Concordia Stabili With lasting peace - (Hildesheim)

Confoederatio Helvetica Helvetian Confederation - (Switzerland)

Conjuncto Felix Fortunate in his connection - (Solms)

Consilio et Aequitate With deliberation and justice - (Fulda)

Cum Deo et Iure With God and the law - (Wurttemberg)

Custos Regni Deus God the Guardian of the Realm - (Naples & Sicily)

D

D.G. (Dei Gratia) By the grace of God

D.G.F.A.P.A. - By the grace of God, Friedrich August, Prince of Anhalt

D.G.F.A.P.A.D.S.A. & W.C.A.D.S.B.I. & K. & By the grace of God, Friedrich August, Prince of Anhalt, Duke of Saxony, Angria and Westphalia, Count Ascania, Lord of Zerbst, Bernburg, Jever and Knyphausen etc.

D.G. Car. Th(eodor) C.P.R.S.R.I.A.T. & El(ect) By the grace of God, Karl Theodore count palatine of the Rhine, arch-treasurer and elector of the Holy Roman Empire - (Pfalz-Sulzbach)

D.G. Carolus Dux Brunsvic. & Luneburg By the grace of God, Karl Duke of Brunswick-Luneburg - (Brunswick-Wolfenbuttel)

D.G. Christ. Gunth. Pr. Schwarzb. Sondersh. By the grace of God, Christian Gunther prince of Schwarzburg-Sondershausen - (Schwarzburg-Sonderhausen)

D.G. Clemens Wenc. A. Ep. Trev. S.R.I.P. Gal. & R. Arel. A. Canc. & P. El. Ep. Aug. Adm. Prum. P.P. By the grace of God, Clemens Wenceslaus archbishop of Trier, arch chancellor and prince elector of the Holy Roman Empire for Gaul and the kingdom of Arles, bishop of Augsburg, administrator provost of Pruem - (Trier)

D.G. Dan. Nor(v). Van(d). Got(h). Rex By the grace of God, king of Denmark, Norway, Vendalia, Gothland - (Denmark)

D.G. Ep. Lub. Haer. Norw. Dux S.H. St. & D. Dux Regn. Old. By the grace of God, Bishop of Lubeck, heir of Norway, duke of Schleswig-Holstein, Stormarn and Ditmarsh, reigning duke of Oldenburg - (Lubeck-Bishopric)

D.G. Frid. August P. Anhalt D.S.A. & W.C.A.D.S.B.I. & K. By the grace of God, Friedrich August prince of Anhalt - (Anhalt-Zerbst)

D.G. Frid. Carolus Pr. Schwarzb. Rud. Dom. Schwarzb. Senior By the grace of God, Friedrich Karl prince of Schwarzburg-Rudolstadt, senior lord of Schwarzburg - (Schwarzburg-Rudolstadt)

D.G. Frid. Christ. Pr. R. Pol. & L. Dux Sax. By the grace of

God, Friedrich Christian royal prince of Poland and Lithuania, duke of Saxony - (Saxony)

D.G. Leop. Ernest S.R.E. Praesb. Card. de Firmian By the grace of God, Leopold Ernst Presbyter of the Holy Roman Church, cardinal of Firmian - (Passau)

D.G. Ludovicus Guntherus Pr. Schwarzburg Rud. Dom. Schw. Senior By the grace of God, Ludwig Gunther prince of Schwarzburg- Rudolstadt, senior lord of Schwarzburg - (Schwarzburg - Rudolstadt)

D.G. Ludovicus Rudolphus Dux Br. & Lun. By the grace of God, Ludwig Rudolph duke of Brunswick-Luneburg - (Brunswick-Wolfenbuttel)

D.G. Max. Ios. C.P.R.V.B.D.S.R.I.A. & El.D.I.C. & M. By the grace of God, Maximilian Joseph count palatine of the Rhine, duke of both Bavarias, archidapifer and elector of the Holy Roman Empire, duke of Julich, Cleves, and Berg - (Bavaria)

D.G. Max. Ios. U.B.D.S.R.I.A. & El. L.L. By the grace of God, Maximillin Joseph duke of both Bavarias, archidapifer and elector of the Holy Roman Empire, landgrave of Leuchtenberg - (Bavaria)

D.G. Max. Ios. Ut. Bav. & P.S.D. Co. Pa. R. By the grace of God, Maximilian Joseph duke of both Bavarias and the Upper Palatinate, count palatine of the Rhine - (Bavaria)

D.G. Parmae Plac(et). Vast. Dux By the grace of God, Duke of Parma, Piacenza and Guastalla - (Parma)

D.G. Petrus in Liv. Curl. et Semgal. Dux By the grace of God, Peter duke of Livonia, Curland, and Semigalia - (Courland)

D.G. Rex Dan. Nor. Van. Go. Dux Sl. Hols. St. Dit. & Old. By the grace of God, king of Denmark, Norway, Vendalia, Gothland, duke of Schleswig-Holstein, Stormark, Ditmarsh, and Oldenburg - (Denmark)

D. in Furst(enberg) et Furstenav ex L.B. de Rost Lord in Furstenberg and Furstenau, late free baron von Rost - (Chur)

Decreto Reipublicae Nexu Confederationis Iunctae die V Xbris MDCCXCII Stanislao Augusto Regnante By decree of the state in conjunction with the joint federation on the 5th day of Dec. 1792, Stanislaus August ruling - (Poland)

Deo Conservatori Pacis To God, preserver of peace - (Brandenburg-Ansbach)

Deo O.M. Auspice Suaviter et Fortiter sed Iuste nec Sibi sed Suis Under the auspices of God, greatest and best, pleasantly and bravely but justly, not for himself but for his people - (Speyer)

Deus Providebit God will provide - (Lowenstein - Wertheim- Virneburg)

Dextera Domini Exaltavit Me The right hand of the Lord has exalted me - (Modena, Spain)

Dirige Domine Gressos Meos Direct, O Lord my steps - (Tuscany)

Dominabitur Gentium et Ipse He himself too will be lord of the nation - (Austrian Netherlands)

Domini Conserva Nos in Pace Lord, preserve us in peace - (Basel)

Domini est Regnum The kingdom is the Lord's - (Austrian Netherlands)

Dominus providebit The Lord will provide - (Bern)

Dominus Spes Populi Sui The Lord, the hope of his people - (Luzern)

Ducat et Sem. Reip. Rhac(v). 1-1/2 ducats of the republic of Ragusa - (Ragusa)

Ducatus Venetus Ducat of Venice - (Venice)

Duce Deo Fide et Just. Faith and Justice with God our guide - (Ragusa)

Dux et Gub(ernatores) Reip. Gen(u). Duke and governors of the republic of Genoa - (Genoa)

Dux Sab(aud) et Montisf(er). Princ. Ped(em) Duke of Savoy and Montferrat, prince of Piedmont - (Sardinia)

E

E & D - Essequibo & Demerara - (British Guiana)

E.I.D.G.S.S.M.A.E.S.R.I.P.G.A.O.P.E.E.W. - Emeric Joseph, Archbishop of the Holy See of Mainz, Archchancellor of the Holy Roman Empire of the German Nation, Prince, Bishop of Worms

Eccl. S. Barbarae Patronae Fodin. Kuttenbergensium Duo Flor. Arg. Puri The Church of Saint Barbara, Patron of the Kuttenberg Mines Two florins of pure silver - (Hungary)

Edwardus VII Dei Gra. Britt. Omn. Rex Fid. Def. Ind. Imp. Edward VII by the grace of God King of all the Britains, Defender of the Faith, Emperor of India - (Great Britain)

Electorus Saxoniae Administrator Elector, administrator of Saxony - (Saxony)

Elizabeth II Dei Gratia Britt. Omn. Regina Fidei Defensor Elizabeth II by the grace of God Queen of Great Britain, Defender of the Faith - (Great Britain)

Elizabeth II Regina Elizabeth II Queen - (South Africa)

Emanuel II Portug. et Algarb. Rex Manuel II, King of Portugal and Algarve - (Portugal)

Emeric Joseph D.G. A. Ep. Mog. S.R.I.P.G.A. Can. P. El. (Ep. W.) Emeric Joseph by the grace of God, archbishop of Mainz, prince of the Holy Roman Empire, arch chancellor in Germany, elector, bishop of Worms - (Mainz)

Ep. Fris. & Ratisb. Ad. Prum. Pp. Coad. Aug. Bishop of Freising and Regensburg, administrator of Pruem, prince-provost, coadjutant bishop of Augsburg - (Trier)

Episc(op) Aug. A.P.P. Co(ad) Elv(ang) Bishop of Augsburg, administrator of Pruem, provost coadjutant of Elwangen - (Trier)

Episc. et S.R.I. Princ. Exemtae Eccle. Passav. Bishop and prince of the Holy Roman Empire, of the freed church of Passau - (Passau)

Episc. Wratisl. Pr. Niss. et Dux Grottkov Bishop of Breslau, prince of Neisse, duke of Grottkau - (Breslau)

Ern. Frid. Car. D.G. Dux Saxon. Ernst Friedrich Karl by the grace of God, duke of Saxony - (Saxe-Hildburghausen)

Ernestus D.G. Gothan Saxonum Dux Ernst by the grace of God, duke of Saxe-Gotha - (Saxe-Gotha-Altenburg)

Ernestus Fridericus D.G.D.S. Coburg Saalfeld Ernst Friedrich by the grace of God, duke of Saxe-Coburg-Saalfeld - (Saxe-Saalfeld)

Et in Minimus Integer Faithful even in the smallest things - (Olmutz)

Ex Avro Argentea resurgit From gold it arises, again silver - (Sicily)

Ex Flammis Orior I arise from flames - (Hohenlohe-Neuenstein- Ohringen)

Ex Fodinis Bipontino Seelbergensibus From the Seelberg mines of Zweibrucken - (Pfalz-Birkenfeld-Zweibrucken)

Ex Uno Omnis Nostra Salus From one is all our salvation - (Eichstadt)

Ex Vasis Argent Cleri. Mogunt. Pro Aris et Focis From the silver vessels of the clergy of Mainz for altars and for hearths - (Mainz)

Ex Vasis Argenteis in Usum Patriae sine Censibus Datis Aciero et Privatis From the silver vessels given without cost for the fatherland by the nobles and citizens - (Trier)

Ex Visceribus Fodinae Bieber From the veins of the Bieber mine - (Hanau- Munzenberg)

Exemtae Eccle. Passav. Episc. et S.R.I. Princ Bishop of the freed church of Passau, prince of the Holy Roman Empire - (Passau)

F

F.A.B.S.M. - Prince of Anhalt-Bernburg Scheide-Munze

F.A.Z.L.M. - Prince of Anhalt-Zerbst Land-Munze

F.B.L.M. - Prince of Baden Land- Munze

F.B.U.C.L.Gr.Z.STOLB.K.R.W.U.H. - Friedrich Botho and Carl Ludwig, Counts of Stolberg, Konigstein, Rochefort, Wernigerode and Hohnstein

F.F.L.M. - Prince of Fulda Land-Munze

F.L.W.S.M. - Prince of Lowenstein-Wertheim Scheide-Munze

F.R.P.LOB.S.M. - Prince of Reuss-Plauen- Lobenstein Scheide- Munze

F.R.PL.G.L.M. - Prince of Reuss-Plauen-Greiz Land-Munze

F.S.R.L.M. - Prince of Schwarzburg-Rudolstadt Land-Munze

F.S.W.V.E.O.V.M. Princely Saxe-Weimar and Eisenach chief-guardianship money - (Saxe-Weimar-Eisenach)

F. Emmanuel de Rohan M.M. (H.SS.) Brother Emanuel de Rohan, Grand Master of the Hospital and the Holy Sepulchre - (Malta)

F. Emmanuel Pinto M.M.H.S.S. Brother Emanuel Pinto, Grand Master of the Hospital and the Holy Sepulchre - (Malta)

F. Ferdinandus Hompesch M.M. Brother Ferdinand Hompesch, Grand Master - (Malta)

Fecunditas Fertility - (Naples & Sicily)

Felix Coniunctio Happy union - (Brandenburg-Ansbach)

Ferd(inandus) I D. G. Aust(riae) Imp(erator) Hung(ariae) B(ohemiae) Rex H(ujus) N(ominis) V R(ex) L(ombardiae) V(enetiae) D(almatiae) G(aliciae) L(odomeriae) I(llyriae) A.A. Ferdinand I by the grace of God, Emperor of Austria, King of Hungary and Bohemia, Fifth of this name, King of Lombardy, Venice, Dalmatia, Galicia, Lodomeria, Illyria, Archduke of Austria - (Hungary)

Ferd. I D.G. Austr. Imp. Hung. Boh. R(ex) H(etruriae) N(eapolis) V(enetiae) Ferdinand I by the grace of God, Emperor of Austria, King of Hungary and Bohemia, Tuscany, Naples, Venice - (Austria)

Ferd. I.D.G. Regni Siciliarum et Hier Rex Ferdinand I by the grace of God King of the Sicilies and Jerusalem - (Naples & Sicily)

Ferd(inandus) D.G. H(ungariae) et B(ohemiae) Reg(ius) Pr(inceps) A. A. S(acri) R(omani) I(mperii) Pr(inceps) El(ector) Salisb(urgensis) Ferdinand by the grace of God Royal Prince of Hungary and Bohemia, Archduke of Austria, Prince of the Holy Roman Empire, Elector of Salzburg - (Salzburg)

Ferd. Hu. et Bo. Reg. Pr. A.A.S.R.I.Pr. El. Salisb. Ferdinand, Royal Prince of Hungary and Bohemia, Archduke of Austria, Prince of the Holy Roman Empire, Elector of Salzburg - (Salzburg)

Ferd. IV D.G. Utr. Sic. et Hier, Rex Ferdinand IV by the grace of God King of the Two Sicilies and Jerusalem - (Naples & Sicily)

Ferdin. VII Dei G. Ferdinand VII by the grace of God - (Spain)

Ferdinan(dus) D.G. Sicil. et Hier. Rex Ferdinand by the grace of God, king of Sicily and Jerusalem - (Sicily)

Ferdinan. III D.G. Sicil. et Hier. Rex Ferdinand III by the grace of God, King of Sicily and Jerusalem (Naples & Sicily)

Ferdinan. IV D.G. Siciliar, et Hie Rex Ferdinand IV by the grace of God, King of the Sicilies and Jerusalem - (Naples & Sicily)

Ferdinandus Rex Maria Carolina Regina Ferdinand king, Maria Carolina queen - (Naples & Sicily)

Ferdinandus I D.G. Austriae Imperator Ferdinand I by the grace of God, Emperor of Austria - (Austria)

Ferdinandus I Hisp. Infans Ferdinand I, prince of Spain - (Parma)

Ferdinandus II Dei Gratia Rex Ferdinand II by the grace of God, King - (Naples & Sicily)

Ferdinandus III D.G. P(rinceps) R(egius) H(ungariae) et B(ohemiae) A.A. M(agnus) D(ux) Etrur(iae) Ferdinand III by the grace of God, Royal Prince of Hungary and Bohemia, Archduke of Austria, Grand duke of Tuscany - (Tuscany)

Ferdinandus III D.G. Rex Ferdinand III King by the grace of God - (Naples & Sicily)

Ferdinandus IV D.G. Rex Ferdinand IV, King by the grace of God - (Naples & Sicily)

Ferdinan(dus) IV D.G. Siciliar et Hier. Rex Ferdinand IV by the grace of God, king of Sicily and Jerusalem - (Naples & Sicily)

Ferdinandus IV et M. Carolina Undiq. Felices Ferdinand IV and Maria Carolina, blessed on all sides - (Naples & Sicily)

Ferdinandus IV et Maria Carolina Ferdinand IV and Maria Carolina - (Naples & Sicily)

Ferdinandus IV Neap. et Sic. Rex Ferdinand IV, king of Naples and Sicily - (Roman Republic)

Ferdinandus IV Utr. Sic. Rex Ferdinand IV, king of the Two Sicilies - (Roman Republic)

Ferdinandus VII Dei G(ratia) Ferdinand VII by the grace of God - (Spain)

Fid. Def. Ind. Imp. Defender of the Faith, Emperor of India - (Great Britain)

Fideliter et Constanter Faithfully and steadfastly - (Saxe-Coburg- Gotha)

Fr. D. Franciscus Ximenez de Texada Brother Don Francisco Ximenez de Texada - (Malta)

Fr. Ios. Max. Pr. de Lobk. Dux Raud. Pr. Com. in Sternst. Franz Josef Maximilian, prince of Lobkowitz, duke of Raudnitz, prince, count in Sternstein - (Lobkowitz)

Fran. Con. Tit. S. Ma. De Pop. Card. de Rodt Epis. Const. S.R.I. Prin. Franz Konrad, with the title of Holy Mary of the People, cardinal of Rodt, bishop of Constance, prince of the Holy Roman Empire - (Constance-Bishopric)

Franc. D.G. Ep. Princ Gurc Antiq. Com. de Salm Reifferscheid Francis by the grace of God Prince-Bishop of Gurk, Count of Reifferscheid - (Gurk)

Franc. D.G. Hu. Bo. Ga. Lod. Rex A.A D.B. et L.M.D. Hetr. Franz by the grace of God, king of Hungary, Bohemia, Galica, Lodomeria, archduke of Austria duke of Burgundy and Lorraine, grand duke of Tuscany - (Hungary)

Franc. I D.G. Aust. Imp. Hung. B.L.V.G.L.Il. Rex A.A. Francis I by the grace of God Emperor of Austria, King of Hungary and Bohemia, Lombardy, Venice, Galicia, Lodomeria, Illyria, Archduke of Austria - (Hungary)

Franc. II D.G.R.I.S.A. Conservator Castri Francis II by the grace of God Emperor of Rome, ever august, protector of the city - (Friedberg)

Franc. II D.G.R. Imp. S.A. Ge. Hu. Bo. Rex A.A.D.B.L. M.D.H. Franz II by the grace of God, emperor of Rome, ever august, king of Germany, Hungary, Bohemia, archduke of Austria, duke of Burgundy and Lorraine, grand duke of Tuscany - (Hungary)

Franc. II D.G.R. Imp. S.A. Ger. Hier. Hung. Boh. Rex Franz II by the grace of God, emperor of Rome, ever august, king of Germany, Jerusalem, Hungary, Bohemia - (Austrian Netherlands)

Franc. Gund. S.R.I.P. Colloredo Mannsfeld C. in Walds. V.C. in Mels M. in S. Soph. S.R.I. Pro. Canc. Franz Gundacker, prince of Holy Roman Empire of Colloredo-Mannsfeld, count in Waldsee, viscount of Mels, marquis of St. Sophia, vice chancellor of Holy Roman Empire - (Colloredo-Mansfeld)

Franc. Ios. I D.G. Austrie Imperator Francis Joseph I by the grace of God Emperor of Austria - (Austria)

Franc Ios. I D.G. Austr. Imp. Hung. Boh. Rex Francis Joseph I by the grace of God Emperor of Austria, King of Hungary and Bohemia - (Austria)

Franc Ios. I D.G. Austr. Imp. et Hung. Rex Ap. Elisabetha Imp. et Reg. Francis Joseph I by the grace of God Emperor of Austria and Apostolic King of Hungary, Elizabeth Empress and Queen - (Austria)

Franc. Ios. I D.G. Imp. Austr. Rex Boh. Gal. Ill. etc. Ap. Rex Hung. Francis Joseph I by the grace of God Emperor of Austria, King of Bohemia, Galicia and Illyria and King of Hungary - (Austria)

Franc Lavredano Dux Venetiar Francisco Lauredano, doge of Venice - (Venice)

Franc. Ludov. D.G. Ep. (Bamb. et) Wirc. S.R.I. Pr. Fr. Or. Dux Franz Ludwig by the grace of God, bishop of Bamberg and Wurzburg, prince of the Holy Roman Empire, duke of Eastern Franconia - (Wurzburg)

Fr(anc) Xav. Com. de Montfort Franz Xaver count of Montfort - (Montfort)

Francis D. Gratia Roman Imperat. S.A. Franz II by the grace of God, emperor of Rome, ever august - (Austrian Netherlands)

Francisc. II D.G.R.I.S.A. Ger. Hie. Hun. Boh. Rex Franz II by the grace of God, emperor of Rome, ever august, king of Germany, Jerusalem, Hungary, Bohemia - (Milan)

Francisc. Ios. I D.G. Austriae Imp. et Elisabetha Max. in Bavar. Ducis Fil. Francis Joseph I by the grace of God Emperor of Austria and Elizabeth, daughter of Maximilian Duke of Bavaria - (Austria)

Franciscus I Dei Gratia Rex Francis I, King by the grace of God - (Tuscany)

Franciscus I D.G. Austriae Imperator Francis I by the grace of God Emperor of Austria - (Austria)

Franciscus II D.G.R. Imp. S.A. Germ. Hu. Bo. Rex Francis II by the grace of God, emperor of the Romans, ever august, King of Germany, Hungary, Bohemia - (Austria)

Franciscus II D.G. Rom. et Haer. Aust. Imp. Francis II by the grace of God Emperor of the Romans and Hereditary Emperor of Austria - (Austria)

Franciscus II Dei Gratia Rex Francis II, King by the grace of God - (Naples & Sicily)

Franciscus II D.G. Rom. Imp. Semp. Aug. Francis II by the grace of God, Emperor of Rome, ever august - (Regensburg)

Franciscus II D.G.R. Imp. S.A. Germ. (Hie). Hu(n) Bo(h). Rex Franz II by the grace of God, emperor of Rome, ever august, king of Germany, Jerusalem, Hungary, Bohemia - (Austria)

Franciscus D.G. Hungar. Bohem. Gallic. Lodom. Rex Franz D.G. king of Hungary, Bohemia, Galicia, Lodomeria - (Hungary)

Franciscus Iosias D.G.D.S. Coburg Saalfeld Franz Josias by the grace of God, duke of Saxe-Coburg-Saalfeld - (Saxe-Saalfeld)

Franciscus Ursin, S.R.I. Princeps Rosenberg Franz Orsini, prince of the Holy Roman Empire of Rosenberg - (Orsini-Rosenberg)

Franz. Ios. D.G.S.R.I.Pr. & Gub. Dom. de Liechtenstein Franz Joseph by the grace of God, prince of the Holy Roman Empire, ruling lord of Liechtenstein - (Liechtenstein)

Franz Joseph I V.G.G. Kaiser V. Oesterreich Francis Joseph I by the grace of God Kaiser of Austria - (Austria)

Franz Ludwig B. zu Bamberg u. Wurzb. D.H.R.R. Furst Herzog z. Franken Franz Ludwig bishop of Bamberg and Wurzburg, prince of the Holy Roman Empire, duke of Franconia - (Bamberg)

Fredericus VI D.G. Dan. V.G. Rex Frederick VI by the grace of God King of Denmark, Vendalia, and Gothland - (Denmark)

Fredericus VII D.G. Daniae V.G. Rex Frederick VII by the grace of God King of Denmark, Vendalia, and Gothland - (Denmark)

Frid. Aug. Rex Sax(oniae) Dux Varsov Frederick August, King of Saxony, Duke of Warsaw - (Duchy of Warsaw)

Frid. August D.G. Dux Sax. Elector Frederick August by the grace of God, Duke and Elector of Saxony (Saxony)

Frid. Aug(ust) D.G. Dux Sax. Elector & Vicarius Imperii Friedrich August by the grace of God, duke of Saxony, elector and vicar of the empire - (Saxony)

Frid. August D.G. Rex Saxoniae Frederick August by the grace of God, King of Saxony - (Saxony)

Frid. August D.G. Saxoniae Elector Friedrich August by the grace of God, elector of Saxony - (Saxony)

Frid. Car. Ios. Aep. et El. Mog. Ep. Wor. Friedrich Karl Joseph archbishop and elector of Mainz, bishop of Worms - (Mainz)

Frid. Car. Ios. D.G. A.E. Mog. S.R.I.P.G.A.C. et El. E.W. Friedrich Karl Joseph by the grace of God, archbishop of Mainz, prince of the Holy Roman Empire, arch chancellor of Germany and elector, bishop of Worms - (Mainz)

Frid. Christ. D.G.M.B.D.P. et S.B.N. Friedrich Christian by the grace of God, margrave of Brandenburg, duke of Prussia and Silesia, burgrave of Nuremberg - (Brandenburg- Bayreuth)

Frid. Christian March. Brand. D.G.&S. Friedrich Christian margrave of Brandenburg, duke of Prussia and Silesia - (Brandenburg- Bayreuth)

Frid. Eug. D.G. Dux Wirtemb. et T. Friedrich Eugene by the grace of God, duke of Wurttemberg and Teck - (Wurttemberg)

Frid. Wilh. D.G. Ep. Hild. S.R.I.P. Friedrich Wilhelm by the grace of God, bishop of Hildesheim, prince of the Holy Roman Empire - (Hildesheim)

Frid. (III) D.G. Pr. A. Salm Kyrb. Com. Rh. & Sylv. Friedrich III by the grace of God, prince of Salm- Kyrburg, count of the Rhine and the Forest - (Salm)

Frider. Wilhelm Boruss. Rex Friedrich Wilhelm king of Prussia - (Prussia)

Frider. III (D.G.) Gothanus Saxonum Dux Friedrich III by the grace of God, duke of Saxe-Gotha - (Saxe- Gotha-Altenburg)

Fridericus Borussorum Rex Friedrich king of Prussia - (Prussia)

Fridericus D.G. Rex Wurt(t)emberg(iae) Frederick by the grace of God, king of Wurttemberg - (Wurttemberg)

Fridericus Pr. Waldecciae Com. Pyr. Frederick, Prince of Waldeck, Count of Pyrmont - (Waldeck)

Fridericus Wurtembergiae Rex Frederick, King of Wurttemberg - (Wurttemberg)

Fridericus II D.G. Dux Wurt. S.R.I. Ar. Vex. et Elector Frederick II by the grace of God, Duke of Wurttemberg, Archmarshall, Standard Bearer, and Elector of the Holy Roman Empire - (Wurttemberg)

Fridericus II D.G. Dux Wirtemb. et T. Friedrich II by the grace of God, duke of Wurttemberg and Teck - (Wurttemberg)

Fridericus II D.G. Hass Landg. Han Com. Friedrich II by the grace of God, landgrave of Hesse, count of Hanau - (Hesse-Cassel)

Fridericus Carolus D.G.H.N.D.S.H.S. et D.C. in O. et D. Frederick Karl by the grace of God, heir of Norway, duke of Schleswig- Holstein, Stormark and Ditmarch, count in Oldenburg and Delmenhorst - (Holstein)

Fried. Aug. D.G. Haer. N. Ep. Lub. Dux S.H. St. & D. Dux Regn. Old. Friedrich August by the grace of God, heir of Norway, bishop of Lubeck, duke of Schleswig-Holstein, Stormarn, and Ditmarsh, reigning duke of Oldenburg - (Lubeck- Bishopric)

Fried. Aug. Soph. Princ. Anh. Dyn. Iever Admin. Frederika Augusta Sophia, princess of Anhalt, line of Jever, administrator - (Jever)

Fried. D.G. Pr. Wald. C.P.E.R. Friedrich by the grace of God, prince of Waldeck, count of Pyrmont and Rappolstein - (Waldeck)

Fried. Lud. S.R.I. Com in Lowenst. Werth Friedrich Ludwig count of Lowenstein- Wertheim of the Holy Roman Empire - (Lowenstein- Wertheim- Virneburg)

G

G.H.K.M. - Grand Duchy of Hesse Copper Munze

G.H.L.M. - Grand Duchy of Hesse Land-Munze

G.H.S.M. - Grand Duchy of Hesse Scheide-Munze

G.H.S.W.E. - Grand Duchy of Saxe-Weimar - Eisenach

G.R.P.E.L.M. - County of Reuss-Plauen-Ebersdorf Land-Munze

G.R.P.V.G.L.M. - County of Reuss-Plauen Unter-Greiz Land- Munze

G.R.PL.L.L.M. - County of Reuss-Plauen-Lobenstein Land-Munze

Gen. C. Mar. V.L. Dim. Col. U.S.C. & R.A.M.A.I. Cons. & S. Conf. M. General field marshal, colonel of the only dragoon regiment, present privy counselor of both their sacred, imperial and royal apostolic majesties, and state conference minister - (Batthyani)

Georgius III Dei Gratia Rex George III, King by the grace of God - (Great Britain)

Georgius III D.G. Britanniarum Rex F.D. George III by the grace of God King of Britain, Defender of the Faith - (Great Britain, Gold Coast)

Georg. III D.G. Mag. Brit. Fr. et Hib. Rex F.Def. (Br. & L. Dux S.R.I. A. Th. & El.) George III by the grace of God, king of Great Britain, France, and Ireland, defender of the faith, duke of Brunswick- Luneburg, archtreasurer and elector of the Holy Roman Empire - (Brunswick-Luneburg)

Georgius IIII D.G. Britanniar. Rex F.D. George IV by the grace of God King of the Britains, Defender of the Faith - (Great Britain)

Georgius V Dei Gra. Britt. Omn. Rex George V by the grace of God King of Great Britain - (Great Britain)

Georgius V D.G. Britt. Omn. Rex F.D. Ind. Imp. George V by the grace of God King of Great Britain, Defender of the Faith, Emperor of India - (Great Britain)

Georgius V. Dei. Gra. Rex et Ind Imp George V, by the grace of God, King and Emperor of India - (Cyprus)

Georgius VI D.G. Br. Omn. Rex George VI by the grace of God King of Great Britain - (Great Britain)

Georgius VI D.G. Br. Omn. Rex. D.F. Imp. Ind George VI, by the grace of God, King of Great Britain; defender of the faith, emperor of India - (Australia)

Georgius VI D.G. Br. Omn. Rex F.D. George VI D.G. King of Great Britain, Defender of the Faith - (Great Britain)

Georgius VI Rex Imperator George VI, king, emperor - (South Africa)

Georgius Sextus Rex George VI, king - (South Africa)

Georg. Carol. D.G. Ep. Wirc. S.R.I. Pr. Fr. Or. Dux George Karl by the grace of God, bishop of Wurzburg, prince of the Holy Roman Empire, duke of Eastern Franconia - (Wurzburg)

Georg. Frid. & Alexander March. Brand. George Friedrich and Alexander margraves of Brandenburg - (Brandenburg-Ansbach)

Germ. Hun. Boh. Rex A.A.D. Loth. Ven. Sal. King of Germany, Hungary, Bohemia, Archduke of Austria, Duke of Lorraine, Venice, Salzburg - (Austria)

Germ. Jero. Rex Loth. Bar. Mag. Het. Dux King of Germany, Jerusalem, Lorraine, Bar, grand duke of Tuscany - (Austrian Netherlands)

Germania Voti Compos MDCCLXXVIIII D. XIII May Germany sharing the vows, 13 May 1779 - (Brandenburg-Ansbach)

Gloria ex Amore Patriae Glory from love of country - (Denmark)

Glori in Excelsis Deo Glory to God in the highest - (Sweden)

Gratitudo concivibus exemplum posteritati Gratitude to fellow citizens, an example to posterity - (Poland)

Guilelmus II Imperator William II Emperor - (German East Africa)

Gustaf IV Aldolph Sv. G. och W. Konung Gustaf IV, king of Sweden, Gothland, and Vendalia - (Sweden)

Gustavus III D.G. Rex Sveciae Gustaf III, king of Sweden - (Sweden)

H

H.III S.L.R.T.ST.S.C. & D.D.P.D.G.C.G.S. & L. - Heinrich III of the eldest line of the entire house of Reuss, oldest count and lord of Plauen, Lord of Greiz, Kranichfeld, Gera, Schleiz and Lobenstein

H.XI S.L.R.C. & D.D.PL.DG.C.G.S.&.L. - Heinrich XI of the eldest line of Reuss, Count and Lord of Plauen, Lord of Greiz, Kranichfeld, Gera, Schleiz and Lobenstein

H.D. - Hesse-Darmstadt

H.D.L.M. - Hesse-Darmstadt Land-Munze

H.H. - Duchy of Hildburghausen

H.S.C. - Duchy of Saxe-Coburg

H.S.C.G. - Duchy of Saxe- Coburg- Gotha

H.S.C.L.M. - Duchy of Saxe-Coburg Land-Munze

H.S.C.M. - Duchy of Saxe-Coburg-Meiningen

H.S.C.S. - Duchy of Saxe-Coburg-Saalfeld

H.S.C.S.L.M. - Duchy of Saxe-Coburg-Saalfeld Land-Munze

H.S.C.S.M. - Duchy of Saxe-Coburg Scheide-Munze

H.S.C.S.S.M. - Duchy of Saxe-Coburg-Saalfeld Scheide-Munze

H.S.H.H. - Duchy of Saxe-Hildburghausen

H.S.H.S.M. - Duchy of Saxe-Hildburghausen Scheide-Munze

Hac Nitimur Hanc Tuemur With this we strive, this we will defend - (Batavian Republic)

Hac Sub Tutila Under this protection - (Eichstadt)

Hanc tuemur, had nitimur This we defend, by this we strive - (Gelderland, Holland, Overijssel, Utrecht, West Friesland)

Henri S.R.I.P.C. Mansfeld Ae. N.D. in Held. Seeb. & Schrapplau Heinrich, prince of the Holy Roman Empire, count of Mansfeld, and noble lord in Heldrungen, Seeburg and Schraplau - (Mansfeld)

Henricus D.G. Epis. et Abb. Fuld. S.R.I. Pr. Henry by the grace of God, bishop and abbot of Fulda, prince of the Holy Roman Empire - (Fulda)

Henricus S.R.I. Princeps Avrsperg Dux Minsterberg Henry, prince of the Holy Roman Empire of Auersperg, duke of Munsterberg - (Auersperg)

Hercules III D.G. Mut. Reg. Mir. Ec. Dux Ercole III by the grace of God, duke of Modena, Reggio and Mirandola - (Modena)

Herman Frider. Otto D.G. Princ. de Hohenzollern Heching. Herman Frederick Otto by the grace of God, Prince of Hohenzollern- Hechingen - (Hohenzollern-Hechingen)

Hic est qui Multum Orat Pro Populo Here is he who prays much for the people - (Paderborn)

Hieronymus D.G.A. & P.S.A.S.L.N.G. Prim. Jerome D.G. archbishop and prince of Salzburg, legate of the Apostolic See, born Primate of Germany - (Salzburg)

Hispaniar(um) Infans Prince of Spain - (Naples & Sicily)

Hispaniarum et Ind. Rex King of Spain and the Indies - (Spain)

Hispaniarum Rex King of Spain - (Spain)

Honi Soit Qui Mal Y Pense Evil to him who thinks evil - (Great Britain)

Hospita(lis) et S. Sep(ul) Hierus(al) Hospital and Holy Sepulchre of Jerusalem - (Malta)

Hun. Boh. Gal. Rex A.A.D. Lo. Sal. Wirc. King of Hungary, Bohemia, Galicia, Archduke of Austria, Dalmatia, Lodomeria, Salzburg, and Wurzburg - (Austria)

Hun. Boh. Gal. Rex A.A. Lo Wi. et in Fr. Dux King of Hungary, Bohemia, Galicia, Archduke of Austria, Lodomeria, Wurzburg, and in Franconia Duke - (Austria)

Hun(g) Boh. Lomb. et Ven. Gal. Lod. Il(l) Rex A.A. King in Hungary, Bohemia, Lombardy, and Venice, Galicia, Lodomeria, Illyria, Archduke of Austria - (Austria)

Hungar. Bohem. Gal. Lod. Ill. Rex. A.A. King in Hungary, Bohemia, Galicia, Lodomeria, Illyria, Archduke of Austria - (Austria)

I

In Hoc Signo Vinces In this sign thou shalt conquer - (Portugal)

In Memor. Vindicatae Libere. ac Relig. In memory of the establishment of liberty and religion - (Sweden)

In Memoriam Coniunctionis ultriusque Burgraviatus Norice D. XX Ian. MDCCLXIX In memory of the union of both burgraviates in peace 20 Jan. 1769 - (Brandenburg-Ansbach)

In Memoriam/Connub. Felicias. Inter/Princ. Her. Frider Carol/et Dub. Sax/August Louis Frideric/Rodae D. 28 Nov. 1780/ Celebrati In commemoration of the most happy marriage between the hereditary prince Friedrich Karl and the duchess of Saxony, Auguste Louisa Frederika Roda, celebrated on 28 Nov. 1780 - (Schwarzburg-Rudolstadt)

In Memoriam Felicissimus Matrimonii In memory of the most happy marriage - (Wied)

In Memoriam Pacis Teschinensis In memory of the Peace of Teschen - (Brandenburg- Ansbach)

In te Domine Speravi In thee have I hoped, O Lord - (Gurk)

In Terra Pax Peace in the land - (Papal States)

Insignia Capituli Brixinensis The insignia of the Chapter of Brixen - (Brixen)

Intima Candent The innermost parts glow - (Eichstadt)

Io. Ios. Kevenhuller ab Aichelberg S.R.I. Pr. A. Metsch Johann Josef Khevenhuller of Aichelberg, Prince of the Holy Roman Empire of Metsch - (Khevenhuller)

Ioan. Philip D.G. Ar. Ep. (& El.) Trevir. S.R.I. Prin. El (Ep. Worm) Admi. Prum. Pp. Johann Philip by the grace of God, bishop and elector of Trier, prince of the Holy Roman Empire, bishop of Worms, administrator of Pruem, provost - (Trier)

Ioann. Frid. Com. de Hohenl. et Gleich. Dom. in Langenb. et Cranichf. Senior et Feud. Administrator Aetat S. 77 Johann Friedrich, count of Hohenlohe and Gleichen, lord in Langenburg and Kranichfeld, lord and administrator of the fief, age 77 - (Hohenlohe- Neuenstein- Ohringen)

Ioannes Fridericus D.G. P.S. Rud. D.S. Senior Johann Friedrich by the grace of God, prince of Schwarzburg-Rudolstadt, senior lord in Schwarzburg - (Schwarzburg-Rudolstadt)

Ioh. D.G.S.R.I. Princeps in Schwarzenburg Johann by the grace of God, prince of the Holy Roman Empire in Schwarzenberg - (Scwarzenberg)

Ioh. Lud. Vollrath (S.R.I.) Com. in Loew. Wertheim Johann Ludwig Vollrath (of the Holy Roman Empire) count of Lowenstein- Wertheim - (Lowenstein-Wertheim-Virneburg)

Ioh. Wen. S.R. Imp. Princeps a Paar Johann Wenzel, prince of the Holy Roman Empire of Paar - (Paar)

Ios. II D.G.R.I(mp). S.A.G.H.B.R (ex) A.A.D.B. et (&) L. Joseph II by the grace of God, emperor of Rome, ever august, king of Germany, Hungary, Bohemia, archduke of Austria, duke of Burgundy and Lorraine - (Hungary)

Ios. Conr. D.G. Ep. Frising & Ratisb. Praep. Berchtesg. S.R.I. Princ. Joseph Conrad by the grace of God, bishop of Freising and Regensburg, provost of Berchtesgaden, prince of the Holy Roman Empire - (Freising)

Ios. Wenc. D.G.S.R.I. Pr. & Gub. Dom. de Liechtenstein Joseph Wenceslaus by the grace of God, prince of the Holy Roman Empire and ruling Lord in Liechtenstein - (Liechtenstein)

Ios. Wilh. D.G. Pr. de Hohenzollern. Burgg. N. Joseph Wilhelm by the grace of God, prince of Hohenzollern, burgrave of Nuremberg - (Hohenzollern- Hechingen)

Ios. Wilh. Ernest S.R.I. Princ in (de) Furstenberg Landgrav. in Baar & Stuhlingen Joseph Wilhelm Ernst, prince of the Holy Roman Empire in Furstenberg, landgrave in Baar and Stuhlingen - (Furstenberg)

Ioseph Nap. Dei Gratia Joseph Napoleon by the grace of God - (Spain)

Ioseph Napol. D.G. Utr. Sicil. Rex Joseph Napoleon

by the grace of God King of the Two Sicilies - (Naples & Sicily)

Ioseph D.G. S.R.I. Prin. in Schwarzenberg Joseph by the grace of God, prince of the Holy Roman Empire in Schwarzenberg - (Schwarzenberg)

Ioseph II D.G.R.S.I.A. Cor. & Her. R.H.B. & C. Joseph II by the grace of God, Roman emperor ever august, co-regent and heir to kingdom of Hungary, Bohemia etc. - (Muhlhausen)

Ioseph II D.G.R.I.S.A. Cor. Her. R.H.B. Joseph II by the grace of God, emperor of Rome, ever august, co-regent and heir of the kingdoms of Hungary and Bohemia - (Austria)

Ioseph II D.G. R.I.S.A. Germ. (Hie.) Hu(n). Bo(h). Rex Joseph II by the grace of God, emperor of Rome, ever august, king of Germany, Jerusalem, Hungary, Bohemia - (Hungary, Milan)

Ioseph II. Rom. Imp. Semper August Joseph II Roman emperor, ever august - (Fugger)

Ioseph. Ex. Prin. de Aversberg S.R. Eccl. Cardin. Joseph of the princes of Auersberg, cardinal of the Holy Roman Church - (Passau)

Iosephus D.G. Episc. Evstettensis S.R.I.P. Joseph by the grace of God, bishop of Eichstedt, prince of the Holy Roman Empire - (Eichstadt)

Iosephus M.B. Furst zu Furstenberg L.I.D.B.U.Z.St. H.Z. Hausen I. Kinz. Thal. Joseph Maria Benedict, prince of Furstenberg, landgrave in Baar, and of Stuhlingen, duke of the line of Kinzigthal - (Furstenberg)

Iosephus I D.G. Port. et Alg. Rex Joseph I by the grace of God, king of Portugal and Algarve - (Portugal)

Iosephus II D.G. Rom. Imp. Semp. Aug. Joseph II by the grace of God, emperor of Rome, ever august - (Chur)

Iosephus Wenceslaus S.R.I.Princeps de Furstenberg Joseph Wenceslaus prince of the Holy Roman Empire of Furstenberg - (Furstenberg)

Isti Sunt Patres Tui Verique Pastores These are your fathers and true shepherds - (Papal States)

Ivl. Cl. & Mont. D.L.L.P.M.M.M.A.Z.C.V.S.M. & R.D.I.R. Duke of Julich, Cleves, and Berg, landgrave of Leuchtenberg, prince of Mors, margrave of Berg-op-Zoom, count of Veldenz, Sponheim, Mark and Ravensberg, lord in Ravenstein - (Bavaria)

Iul. Cl. Mont. A. & W.S.R.I. Archim. & Elector Julich, Cleves, Berg, Angria and Westphalia, arch marshall and elector - (Saxony)

Iuste et Constanter Justly and constantly - (Paderborn)

Iustirt Adjusted - (Hesse-Cassel)

Iustitia et Concordia Justice and harmony - (Zurich)

Iustitia et Mansuetudine Justice and mildness - (Cologne)

Iustitia Regn(orum) Fundamentum Justice the foundation for kingdoms - (Austria)

J

Joannes D.G. P(rinceps) Portugaliae et Alg (arbiae) John by the grace of God Prince of Portugal and Algarve - (Portugal)

Joannes D.G. Port. et Alg. P. Regens John by the grace of God Prince Regent of Portugal and Algarve - (Portugal)

Joannes VI D.G. Portug. Brasil et Algarb. Rex John VI by the grace of God King of Portugal, Brazil and Algarve - (Portugal)

Josephus I D.G. Port. et Alg. Rex Joseph I by the grace of God, king of Portugal and Algarve - (Portugal)

Josephus. I. D.G. Rex P. et D. Guineae Joseph I, by the grace of God, king of Portugal and lord of Guinea - (Angola)

K

K.S.P.L.M. - Royal Swedish-Pomerania Land-Munze

K.S.S.M. - Kingdom of Saxony Scheide-Munze

L

L.W. - Lowenstein-Wertheim

Landgr. in Cleggov. Com. in Sulz Dux Crum Landgrave of Klettgau, count of Sulz, duke of Krumlau - (Schwarzburg-Sonderhausen)

Lege et Fide By law and faith - (Austria)

Lege Vindice Supported by law - (Nuremberg)

Leo XII Pon(tifex) Max(imus) Leo XII Pope (Papal States)

Leop. II D.G. Hu. Bo. Ga. Lod. Rex A.A.D.B. et L.M.D. Hetr. Leopold II D.G. king of Hungary, Bohemia, Galicia, Lodomeria, archduke of Austria, duke of Burgundy and Lorraine, grandduke of Tuscany - (Hungary)

Leop. Ern. D.G. Exemp. Eccl. Patavi. Eps. Leopold Ernst by the grace of God, bishop of the freed church of Passau - (Passau)

Leop. Hen. Schlik S.R.I.C. de Passaun & Weiskerchen Leopold Heinrich, count of the Holy Roman Empire of Schlick, of Passaun and Weiskirchen - (Schlick)

Leopold II D.G. R.I.S.A. Ger. Hie. Hun. Boh. Rex Leopold II by the grace of God, emperor of Rome, ever August, king of Germany, Jerusalem, Hungary, Bohemia - (Milan)

Leopold II D.G. Rom. Imp. Semp. Aug. Leopold II by the grace of God, Roman emperor ever August - (Regensburg)

Leopoldus D.G. P.I.A. P(rinceps) R(egius) H(ungariae) et B(ohemiae) A.A. Magn(us) Dux Etr(uriae) Leopold II by the grace of God Prince of Imperial Austria, Prince Regent of Hungary and Bohemia, Archduke of Austria, Grand Duke of Tuscany - (Tuscany)

Leopoldus II D.G. H. et B. Rex A.A.M.D.E. Leopold II by the grace of God, king of Hungary and Bohemia, archduke of Austria, grandduke of Tuscany - (Tuscany)

Leopoldus II D.G. Hungar. Bohem. Galic. Lodom. Rex Leopold II by the grace of God, king of Hungary, Bohemia, Galicia, Lodomeria - (Hungary)

Leopoldus II D.G. R.I.S.A. Ger. H. et H. Rex A.A.M.D. Etr. Leopold II by the grace of God, emperor of Rome, ever august, king of Germany, Jerusalem, and Hungary, archduke of Austria, grandduke of Tuscany - (Tuscany)

Leop(oldus) II D.G. R. Imp. S.A. Germ. (Hie.) Hun(n). Bo(h). Rex Leopold II by the grace of God, emperor of Rome, ever august, king of Germany, Jerusalem, Hungary, Bohemia - (Austria)

Lex tua Veritas Thy law is the truth - (Tuscany)

Louise Eleonore Herz. Z.S.C. Mein. Geb. Furst z. Hohenl. Louise Eleonore duchess of Saxe- Coburg- Meiningen, born princess of Hohenlohe - (Saxe-Meiningen)

Lud. Const. D.G. Epus. et P PS. Argentl. Lan. Al. Ludwig Constantine by the grace of God, bishop and prince-provost of Strassburg, landgrave of Alsace - (Strasbourg)

Lud. Eng. D.G. Dux Arenbergae S.R.I.P. Ludwig Engelhardt by the grace of God, duke of Arenberg, prince of the Holy Roman Empire - (Arenberg)

Lud. Frid. Carol. D.G. Princ Ab. Hohenl. Com. de Gleich. D. in Langenb. & Cranichfeld Ludwig Friedrich Karl by the grace of God. prince of Hohenlohe, count of Gleichen, lord of Langenburg and Kranichfeld - (Hohenlohe- Neuenstein-Ohringen)

Ludov. Eugen. D.G. Dux Wirtemb. & T. Ludwig Eugen by the grace of God, duke of Wurttemberg and Teck - (Wurttemberg)

Ludovico Manin Dux Venetiar Ludovico Manin, doge of Venice - (Venice)

Ludovicus S.R.I. Princeps de Batthyan. Strattmann Ludwig, prince of the Holy Roman Empire of Batthyani Strattmann - (Batthyani)

Ludovicus I D.G. (Hisp(aniarum) Inf(ans) Rex Etruriae Par(mae) Plac(entiae) and Prince Louis I by the grace of God Prince of Spain, King of Tuscany, Prince of Parma and Piacenza - (Tuscany)

Ludovicus VIII D.G. Landgravius Hass. Ludwig VIII by the grace of God, landgrave of Hesse - (Hesse- Darmstadt)

Ludovicus IX D.G. Landgravius Hass. Ludwig IX by the grace of God, landgrave of Hesse - (Hesse-Darmstadt)

Ludovicus X D.G. Landgravius Hass. Ludwig X by the grace of God, landgrave of Hesse - (Hesse- Darmstadt)

Ludovicus et Philippus Christianus et Carolus Henricus, etc. Ludwig and Philip Christian and Karl Heinrich and August, sprung from these brothers, happy in union, and are the heads of the line of Hohenlohe- Langenburg. May their union ever endure - (Hohenlohe- Langenburg)

Lumen ad Revelationem Gentium Light and revelation for the peoples - (Papal States)

M

M. Theresia D.G. R. Imp. (Ge.) Hu. Bo. Reg. (A.A.) Maria Theresia by the grace of God, empress of Rome, queen of Germany, Hungary, Bohemia, archduchess of Austria - (Austria)

M. Theresia Nata Non. Iuni Maria Theresia born June 5 - (Naples & Sicily)

Magnus ab Integro Saeclorum Nascitur Ordo The great order of the centuries is born anew - (Bavaria)

Manibus Ne Laedar Avris Lest I be injured by greedy hands - (Sweden)

Mar. Bran. Sac. Rom. Imp. Arcam. et Elec. Sup. Dux Siles Margrave of Brandenburg, arch chamberlain of the Holy Roman Empire and elector, ranking duke of Silesia - (Prussia)

Marcus Foscarenus Dux Venetiar Marco Foscarino, doge of Venice - (Venice)

Maria D.G. Landgr. Has. N. Pr. M. B. Fr. & H. T. & Com. Han. Administer Maria by the grace of God, landgravine of Hesse, born princess of Great Britain, France and Ireland, regent and administrator of the county of Hanau - (Hanau-Munzenberg)

Maria I D.G. Port. et Alg. Regina Maria I by the grace of God, queen of Portugal and Algarve - (Portugal)

Maria I D. G. Regina P. et D. Guineae Maria I, by the grace of God, queen of Portugal and lord of Guinea - (Angola)

Maria I et Petrus III D.G. Port. et Alg. Reges Maria I and Peter III by the grace of God, rulers of Portugal and Algarve - (Portugal)

Maria I et Petrus III D.G. Reges P. E.D.D. Guineae Maria I and Peter III, by the grace of God, rulers of Portugal and lords of Guinea - (Angola)

Maria II D.G. Portug. et Alg. Regina Maria II by the grace of God Queen of Portugal and Algarve - (Portugal)

Maria II Portug. et Algarb Regina Maria II, Queen of Portugal and Algarve - (Portugal)

Maria Luigia Princ(ipissa) Imp. Arcid. d'Austria Marie Louise Imperial Princess Archduchess of Austria - (Parma)

Matrimonio Conjuncti Joined in wedlock - (Austria)

Max. Frid. D.G. Ar. Ep. & Elect. Col. E. & P. M. W. & A. D. Maximilian Friedrich by the grace of God, archbishop and elector of Cologne, bishop and prince of Munster, duke of Westphalia and Angria - (Cologne)

Maximilian Frider. Ar. Ep. et Elect. Col. Maximilian Friedrich archbishop and elector of Cologne - (Cologne)

Maximilianus Iosephus Bavariae Rex Maximilian Joseph, King of Bavaria - (Bavaria)

Mediolani Dux Duke of Milan - (Milan)

Mediolani et Mant. Dux Duke of Milan and Mantua - (Milan)

Memor. Ero Tui Iustina Vir(go) I will be mindful of you, Justina, Virgin - (Venice)

Merces Laborum Wages of labor - (Wurzburg)

Michael I D.G. Portug. et Algarb. Rex Michael I by the grace of God King of Portugal and Algarve - (Portugal)

Mo(neta) Arg(entiae) Ord. Faed. Belg(ii) Holl. Silver money of the federated Belgian union - Holland (Province) - (Batavian Republic)

Mo. Arg. Ord. Foe. Belg. D. Gel. & C.Z. Silver money of the order of the Belgian Federation, duchy of Gelders, county of Zutphen - (Gelderland)

Mo. Arg. Pro. Con(foe) Belg. D. Gel. & C.Z. Silver money of the provinces of the Belgian Federation, duchy of Gelders, county of Zutphen - (Gelderland)

Mo. No. Arg. Con. Foe. Belg. Pro. Hol. New silver money of the Belgian Federation, province of Holland - (Holland)

Mo. No. Arg. Pro. Confoe. Belg. Trai Holl. New silver money of the Confederated Belgian Provinces - Utrecht or Holland (provinces) - (Batavian Republic)

Mo(n) No(v) Arg. Pro. Con. Foe(d). Belg. Com. Ze(e)l. New silver money of the provinces of the Belgian Federation, county of Zeeland - (Zeeland)

Mon. Lib. Reip. Bremens. Money of the free republic of Bremen - (Bremen)

Mon. Nova Arg. Duc. Curl. Ad Normam Tal. Alb. New silver money, duchy of Courland, according to the Albertus taler standard - (Courland)

Mon. Nov. Castri Imp. Friedberg New money of the free city of Friedberg - (Friedberg)

Moneta Bipont. Money of Zweibrucken - (Pfalz- Birkenfeld-Zweibrucken)

Moneta Capit. Cathedr. Fuld. Sede Vacante Money of the cathedral chapter of Fulda, the seat being vacant - (Fulda)

Moneta Livoesthonica Money of Livonia-Estonia - (Livonia)

Moneta Nov. Arg. Regis Daniae New silver money of the kingdom of Denmark - (Denmark)

Moneta Nova ad Normam Conventionis New money according to the Convention standard - (Orsini-Rosenberg)

Moneta Nova Capil. Leod. Sede Vacante New money of the Chapter of Liege, the seat being vacant - (Liege)

Moneta Nova Castri Imp. Fridberg in Wetter New money of the imperial castle of Friedberg in Wetterau - (Friedberg)

Moneta Nova Lubecensis New money of Lubeck - (Lubeck)

Moneta Nova Reipublicae Halae Suevicae New money of the republic of Hall in Swabia - (Hall in Swabia)

Moneta Reipub. Basileensis Money of the Republic of Basel - (Basel)

Moneta Reipub. Lucernen Money of the Republic of Luzern - (Luzern)

Moneta Reipubl. Francofurt ad Legem Conventionis Money of the republic of Frankfurt after the laws of the convention - (Frankfurt)

Moneta Reipubl. Norimberg Money of the republic of Nuremberg - (Nuremberg)

Moneta Reipublicae Ratisbonensis Money of the republic of Regensburg - (Regensburg)

N

Navigare Necesse Est It is necessary to navigate - (Germany)

Nec Aspera Terrent Nor do difficulties terrify - (Brunswick)

Nec Temere Nec Timide Neither rashly nor timidly - (Danzig)

Nicol. S.R.I. Princ. Eszterhazy de Galantha Perp. Com. in Frak. Nikolaus, prince of the Holy Roman Empire of Eszerhazy of Galantha, hereditary count of Forchtenstein - (Eszerhazy)

Nobilissum Dom. Ac. Com. in Lipp. & St. Most noble lord and count in Lippe and Sternberg - (Schaumburg- Lippe)

Nomen Domini Turris Fortissima The name of the Lord is the strongest tower - (Frankfurt)

Non Relinquam Vox Orphanos I shall not leave you as orphans - (Papal States)

Non surrexit major None greater has arisen - (Genoa, Malta)

Noremberga Nuremberg

Nunquam Retrorsum Never backwards - (Brunswick-Wolfenbuttel)

Nurnberg Nuremberg

O

O.L.M. - Oldenburg Land-Munze

Omnia Cum Deo Everything with God - (Reuss-Greiz)

Opp. & Carn. Dux Com. Rittb. S.C.M. Cons. Int. & Campi. Mareschal Duke of Troppau and Carnovia, count of Rietberg, privy counselor of his sacred, imperial majesty, Field Marshal - (Liechtenstein)

Opp. & Carn. Dux Com. Rittb. S.C.M. Cons. Int. Aur. Velleris Eques Same as above with Knight of the Golden Fleece - (Liechtenstein)

P

P.Z. - Pfalz-Zweibrucken

P. Leop(oldus) D.G. P.R.H. et B.A.A.M.D. E(truriae) Peter Leopold by the grace of God, royal prince of Hungary and Bohemia, archduke of Austria, grandduke of Tuscany - (Tuscany)

Palma Sub Pondere Crescit The palm grows under its weight - (Waldeck)

Patria Si Dreptul Meu The country and my right - (Romania)

Patrimon. Henr. Frid. Sorte Divisum . . The heritage of Heinrich Friedrich divided by lot - (Hohenlohe-Langenburg)

Patrona Bavaria Patron of Bavaria - (Bavaria)

Patrona Bavariae Patroness of Bavaria - (Bavaria)

Patrona Franconiae Patron of Franconia - (Wurzburg)

Paulus Rainerius Dux Venetiar Paolo Renier, doge of Venice - (Venice)

Per Aspera-Ad Astra Through difficulties to the stars - (Mecklenburg- Schwerin)

Perpetuus in Nemet Vivar S.C.R.A.M. Act. Cam. Inc. Com. Cast. Perp. et Supr. Com. Hereditary count in Nemt-Ujvar,

present chamberlain of his sacred, imperial, royal, apostolic majesty, privy counselor, hereditary and supreme count of Eisenburg - (Batthyani)

Petrus IV D.G. Portug. Algarb. Rex Peter IV by the grace of God King of Portugal and Algarve - (Portugal)

Phil. Gotthard D.G. Pr. de Schaffgotsch Philip Gotthard by the grace of God, prince of Schaffgotsch - (Breslau)

Pius Sextus Pont. M(ax). Pius VI Pope - (Papal States)

Pius VI Pon(t). Max. Pius VI Pope - (Papal States)

Pius VI Pont. Max. Anno Iubeliae Pius VI Pope, Jubilee year - (Papal States)

Pius VII Pon(tifex) M(aximus) Pius VII Pope - (Papal States)

Pius VIII Pont. Max. Pius VIII Pope - (Papal States)

Pius IX Pont. Max. Pius IX Pope - (Papal States)

Pons Civit. Castellana The bridge of Castellana - (Papal States)

Populus et Senatus Bon(on). The people and Senate of Bologna - (Bologna)

Post Tenebras Lux After darkness light - (Geneva)

Praep. & D. Elvac. S.R.I. Pr. C. Fugger Provost and lord of Ellwangen, prince of the Holy Roman Empire, count of Fugger - (Regensburg Bishopric)

Praesidium et Decus Protection and ornament - (Bologna)

Primitiae Fodin Kuttenb. ab Aerari. Iterum Susceptarum First results dug from the Kuttenberg mines in a renewed undertaking - (Austria)

Princ Aichst. Passau et Berchtolsgad Prince of Eichstadt, Passau and Berchtesgaden - (Salzburg)

Princ Aichst. Pas. et Ber. S.R.I.P. Elector Prince of Eichstadt, Passau and Berchtesgaden, Prince of the Holy Roman Empire, Elector - (Salzburg)

Princ. Gallic Magn. Elect. Imp. Prince of France, Grand Imperial Elector - (Naples & Sicily)

Princeps Pius Iustus Clemens. Natus 17 Iul. 1708. Obiit 20 Ian. 1769. Aetatis LX Prince pius, just, clement, born July 17, 1708, died Jan. 20, 1769, age 60 - (Brandenburg-Bayreuth)

Pro Deo et Patria For God and fatherland - (Fulda)

Pro Deo et Populo For God and the people - (Bavaria)

Pro Ecclesia et Pro Patria For the church and fatherland - (Constance)

Pro Fausio PP. Reditur V.S. For happy returns of the princes of the Two Sicilies - (Naples & Sicily)

Proxima Fisica Finis Nearest to natural end - (Orciano)

Proxima Soli Nearest the sun - (Modena)

Pro Maxima Dei Gloria et Bono Publico For the greatest glory of God and the good of the people - (Wurttemberg)

Pro Patria For the fatherland - (Wurzburg)

Provide et Constanter Wisely and firmly - (Wurttemberg)

Providentia et Pactis Through foresight and pacts - (Brandenburg- Ansbach)

Providentia Optimi Principis With the forethought of the wisest leaders - (Naples & Sicily)

Q

Quem/Quadragesies et/Semel Patriae/Natum Essg/ Gratulamur/ d. XI Jun./ MDCCLXVII Whom we congratulate for the fortyfirst time on the 12th of June 1767 for being born for the fatherland - (Lippe-Detmold)

Quin Matrimonii Lustrum Celebrant XXIV Aprilis MDCCCLXXXIX They celebrate the 25th wedding anniversary April 24, 1879 - (Austria)

R

Raim, Antonius D.G. Ep. Eyst. S.R.I.P. Raimund Anton by the grace of God, bishop of Eichstadt, prince of the Holy Roman Empire - (Eichstadt)

Recta Tueri (or Tveri) Defend the right - (Austria, Hungary)

Rector Reip. Rhacusin Rector of the Republic of Ragusa - (Ragusa)

Redeunt Antiqui Gaudia Moris There return the joys of ancient custom - (Regensburg)

Reg. Pr. Pol. et Lith. Saxon Dux Royal prince of Poland and Lithuania duke of Saxony - (Trier)

Regia Boruss. Societas Asiat. Embdae Royal Prussian Asiatic Society of Emden - (Prussia)

Regnans Capitulum Ecclesiae Cathedralis Ratisbonensis, Sede Vacante Administering the chapter of the cathedral church at Regensburg, the seat being vacant - (Regensburg)

Regni Vtr. Sic. et Hier. Of the Kingdom of the Two Sicilies and Jerusalem - (Naples & Sicily)

Relinquo vos Liberos ab Utroque Homine I leave you as children of each man - (San Marino)

Rep(ublica) Romana Roman Republic

Resp. Gosl. Republic of Goslar

Respubl. Rhacus(i) Republic of Ragusa - (Ragusa)

Respublica Basiliensis Republic of Basel - (Basel)

Respublica Bernensis Republic of Bern - (Bern)

Respublica Genevensis Republic of Geneva - (Geneva)

Respublica Lucernensi Republic of Luzern - (Luzern)

Respublica Veneta Republic of Venice - (Venice)

Rex Lomb. et Ven. Dalm. Gal. Lod. III. A.A. King of Lombardy and Venice, Dalmatia, Galicia, Lodomeria, Illyria, Archduke of Austria - (Austria)

Roberto I D. Di Par. Piac. Ecc. E Luisa M. Di Borb. Regg. Robert I, Duke of Parma, Piacenza, etc. and Luisa Maria of Bourbon, Regent - (Parma)

Rudolph Joan D.G. Case. A.R. Hun. Boh. Princ. A.A. Rudolph John by the grace of God Imperial and Royal Prince of Hungary and Bohemia, Archduke of Austria - (Olmutz)

S

S.H. - Saxe-Hildburghausen

S.M. - Saxe-Meiningen

S.W.E. - Saxe-Weimar-Eisenach

S.W.u.E. - Saxe-Weimar und Eisenach

S. Annae Fundgruben Ausb. Tha. In N. Oe. St. Anne mine, mining taler in Lower Austria - (Austria)

S. Ap. S. Leg. Nat(us) Germ. Primas Legate of the Holy Apostolic See, born Primate of Germany - (Salzburg)

S. Carol(us) Magnus Fundator Charlemagne founder - (Munster)

S.I. Aul. Reg. Her. & P. Ge. H. Post. Mag. Supreme of the Imperial court of the hereditary kingdom and provinces, general hereditary postmaster - (Paar)

S. Kilianus (cum Socys) Francorum Apostli(us) Saint Kilian, apostle of the Franks with companions - (Wurzburg)

S. Lambertus Patronus Leodiensis St. Lambert, patron of Liege - (Liege)

S. Liborius Patr. Paderb. Saint Liborus, patron of Paderborn - (Paderborn)

S.M.V (enetu) Aloy. Mocenico Dux St. Mark of Venice, Alvise Mocenigo, doge - (Venice)

S.M.V. Franc Lavredano Dux St. Mark of Venice, Francesco Loredan, doge - (Venice)

S.M.V. Ludov(i) Manin Dux St. Mark of Venice, Lodovico Manin, doge - (Venice)

S.M.V. M(arc) Foscarenus D(ux) St. Mark of Venice, Marco Foscarini, doge - (Venice)

S.M.V. Paul Rainerius D(ux) St. Mark of Venice, Paolo Renier, doge - (Venice)

S. Maria Mater Dei Patrona Hung. Holy Mary, Mother of God, patron of Hungary - (Hungary)

S. Petron(io) Prot(ector) Bon(on) St. Peter, protector of of Bologna - (Papal States)

S.R.I. Archid. & (El(ector) Dux I. Cl. & M. Archidapifer and elector of the Holy Roman Empire, duke of Julich, Cleves & Berg - (Bavaria)

S.R.I. Pr. Re. Cap. Boh. & A. Colloredo & Wald. Co. Prince of the Holy Roman Empire, count of the royal chapel of Bohemia, and of Colloredo and Waldsee - (Olmutz)

S.R.I. Pr. Salisb. S.S. Ap. Leg. Nat. Germ. Primas Prince of the Holy Roman Empire of Salzburg, legate of the Holy Apostolic See, born primate of Germany - (Salzburg)

Sac. Nupt. Celeb. Berol. For the holy matrimony celebrated at Berlin - (Brandenburg- Ansbach)

Sac. Rom. Imp. Archie. et Elect. Arch-chancellor and elector of the Holy Roman Empire - (Prussia)

Sac. Rom. Imp. Archid. & Elect. Land. Leucht. Archidapifer and elector of the Holy Roman Empire, landgrave of Leuchtenberg - (Bavaria)

Sac. Rom. Imp. Provisor Iterum Administrator of the Holy Roman Empire for the second time - (Saxony)

Salus Populi The safety of the people - (Spain)

Salus Publica Salus Mea Public safety, my safety - (Sweden)

Salus Reipublicae Suprema Lex Supreme law is the safety of the state - (Poland)

Salvam Fac Rempublicam Tuam Your state safe in union - (San Marino)

Sanctus Leodegarius St. Leodegran - (Luzern)

Sanctus Marcus Venet. St. Mark of Venice - (Venice)

Securitati Publicae For the public safety - (Brandenburg-Ansbach)

Sigismundus D.G. Archiepiscop(us) Sigismund by the grace of God, archbishop - (Salzburg)

Simon August Com. & Nob. D. Lipp. S.D.V. & A.B.H. Ultr. Simon August, count and most noble lord of Lippe, supreme lord of Vianen and Ameiden, hereditary burgrave of Utrecht - (Lippe- Detmold)

Simon Henrich Adolph Com. & N.D. Lipp. Simon Heinrich Adolph count and most noble lord of Lippe - (Lippe-Detmold)

Sincere et Constanter Truthfully and steadfastly - (Hesse-Darmstadt)

Sit Nomen Domini Benedictum Blessed be the name of the Lord - (Strasbourg)

Sit Unio Haec Perennis May this union be everlasting - (Hohenlohe- Langenburg)

Solemnium/A. MDLXXXVI/per Actorum/ Memoriam/ Patrum Patriae/ Indulgentia /Celebrant/ Sagatarii Ratisb./ A. MDCCLXXXVIII etc. With the approval of the fatherland the archers of Ratisbon in the year 1788 celebrate the memory of the solemn acts of the fathers in the year 1576 - (Regensburg)

Soli Reduci To Him, the only one restored - (Naples & Sicily)

Stadt Franckfurt City of Frankfurt - (Frankfurt)

Stanislaus Augustus D.G. Rex Pol(on) M.D. Lith(u) or Lit(uan) Stanislaus August, by the grace of God, king of Poland, grandduke of Lithuania - (Poland)

Sub Tuum Praesidium Confug. We flee to Thy protection - (Salzburg)

Sub Umbra Alarum Tuarum Under the shadow of Thy wings - (Jever)

Subditorum Salus Felicitas Summa The safety of the subjects is the highest happiness - (Lubeck- Bishopric)

Supra Firmam Petram Upon a firm rock - (Papal States)

Susceptor Noster Deus God is our defense - (Tuscany)

Sydera Favent Industriae The stars favor industry - (Furstenberg)

Sylvarum Culturae Praemium Prize for the culture of the forest - (Brandenburg- Ansbach)

T

Tert. Ducat Secular Third centennial of the duchy - (Wurtemberg)

Thomas Orciani F.T. S.R.I. Marchio Un. Cr. Bo. Com. & Thomas Orciano F.T. Marquis of the Holy Roman Empire and count of Hungary, Croatia, Bohemia - (Orciano)

Traiectum ad Mosam The crossing of the Meuse - (Maastricht)

Tueatur Unita Deus, Anno Dom 1847 May God guard these United (Kingdoms) in the year of our Lord 1847 - (Great Britain)

Tut. Mar. Gab. Pr. Vid. de Lobk. Nat. Pr. Sab. Car. et Aug. Pr. de Lobk. Regency of Maria Gabriele, widow of the prince of Lobkowitz, born princess of Savoy-Carignan, and August prince of Lobkowitz - (Lobkowitz)

U

Ubi Uvlt Spirat He breathes where he will - (Papal States)

Urbe Obsessa The city is besieged - (Maastricht)

U.S.C. & R.A.M. Cons. Int. Gen. C. Mar. & Nob. Praet. H. Turmae Capit. Privy counselor of both their holy imperial and royal apostolic majesties, general field marshal and captain of the noble praetorian Hungarian squadrons - (Eszterhazy)

Ut sit suo Pondere Tutus That he may be safe by his own weight - (Nassau)

U(V)tr. Sic. Hier. Hisp. Inf(ans) Of the Two Sicilies and Jerusalem, Prince of Spain - (Naples & Sicily)

V

V.E.I.C. - United East India Company

V.G.G.GR.HZ.V.M.S. - By the grace of God, Grand Duke of Mecklenburg- Schwerin

V.G.G.H.Z.M. - By the Grace of God, Duke of Mecklenburg

V.O.C. - Vereenigde Oostindische Compagnie (United East India Company)

V.G.G. Ioseph Fried. (II) H. Z(u). S(achsen) & Obervormund u. Landes Regent By the grace of God, Joseph Friedrich II, duke of Saxony and chief guardian and regent of the land - (Saxe- Hildburghausen)

Vasculis Avlae Argenteis Patriae Indigenti Ministravit Auxilia With the silver vessels of the court aid was brought to the needy fatherland - (Eichstadt)

Veni Lumen Cordium Come light of hearts - (Papal States)

Verbum Dni Manet in Aeternum The word of the Lord abides forever - (Hesse- Darmstadt)

Veritas Lex Tua The truth is your law - (Salzburg)

Vic. Am. D.G. Rex Sar. Cyp. et Ier. Victor Amadeus by the grace of God, king of Sardinia, Cyprus, and Jerusalem - (Sardinia)

Vic. Em. D.G. Rex Sar. Cyp. et Ier. Victor Emmanuel by the grace of God King of Sardinia, Cyprus, and Jerusalem - (Sardinia)

Victoria Dei Gratia Victoria by the grace of God - (Great Britain)

Victoria Dei Gratia Britanniar. Reg. F.D. Victoria by the grace of God Queen of the Britains, Defender of the Faith - (Great Britain)

Victoria Dei Gra. Britt. Regina Fid. Def. Ind. Imp. Victoria by the grace of God Queen of Britain, Defender of the Faith, Empress of India - (Great Britain)

Victoria D.G. Britt. Reg. F.D. Victoria by the grace of God Queen of Britain, Defender of the Faith - (Great Britain)

Victorius Emmanuel II D.G. Rex Sard. Cyp. et Hier. Victor Emmanuel II by the grace of God, King of Sardinia, Cyprus, and Jerusalem - (Sardinia)

Videant Pauperes et Laetentur Let the poor see and rejoice - (Tuscany)

Viribus Unitis With men united - (Austria)

Virtute et Fidelitate By virtue and faithfulness - (Hesse-Cassel)

Virtute et Prudentia With virtue and prudence - (Auersperg)

Virtute Viam Dimetiar I shall mark the way with valour - (Waldeck)

Vox de Throno A voice from the throne - (Papal States)

W

W.E.Z.H. - Wilhelm, hereditary Prince of Hesse

W.K. - Wilhelm Elector (Hesse)

Wenceslaus S. Rom. Imp. Princeps a Paar Wenceslaus, prince of the Holy Roman Empire of Paar - (Paar)

Wilhelm(us) D.G. Landgr. & Pr. Her. Hass. Com. Han. Wilhelm by the grace of God, landgrave and hereditary prince of Hesse, count of Hanau - (Hanau- Munzenberg)

Wilhelmus S(acri) R(omani) I(mperii) Pr(inceps) Auersperg Dux de Gotshee William, Prince of the Holy Roman Empire and Auersperg, Duke of Gotschee - (Auersperg)

Wilhelmus I Dei Grat. C. Reg. in Schaumb. Wilhelm I by the grace of God, reigning count in Schaumburg - (Schaumburg-Lippe)

Wilhelmus I D.G. Elect. Landg. Hass. William I by the grace of God, Elector and landgrave of Hesse - (Hesse- Cassel)

Wilhelmus IX D.G. Hass. Landgr. Com. Han. Wilhelm IX by the grace of God landgrave of Hesse, count of Hanau - (Hesse-Cassel)

Wilh(elmus) Ant(onius) D.G. Eps. Paderb. S.R.I. Pr. Com. Pyrm. Wilhelm Anton by the grace of God, bishop of Paderborn, prince of the Holy Roman Empire, count of Pyrmont - (Paderborn)

X

Xaverius D.G. Reg. Pr. Pol. & Lith. Dux Sax. (El. Adm.) Xaver by the grace of God, royal prince of Poland and Lithuania, duke of Saxony, elector, administrator - (Saxony)

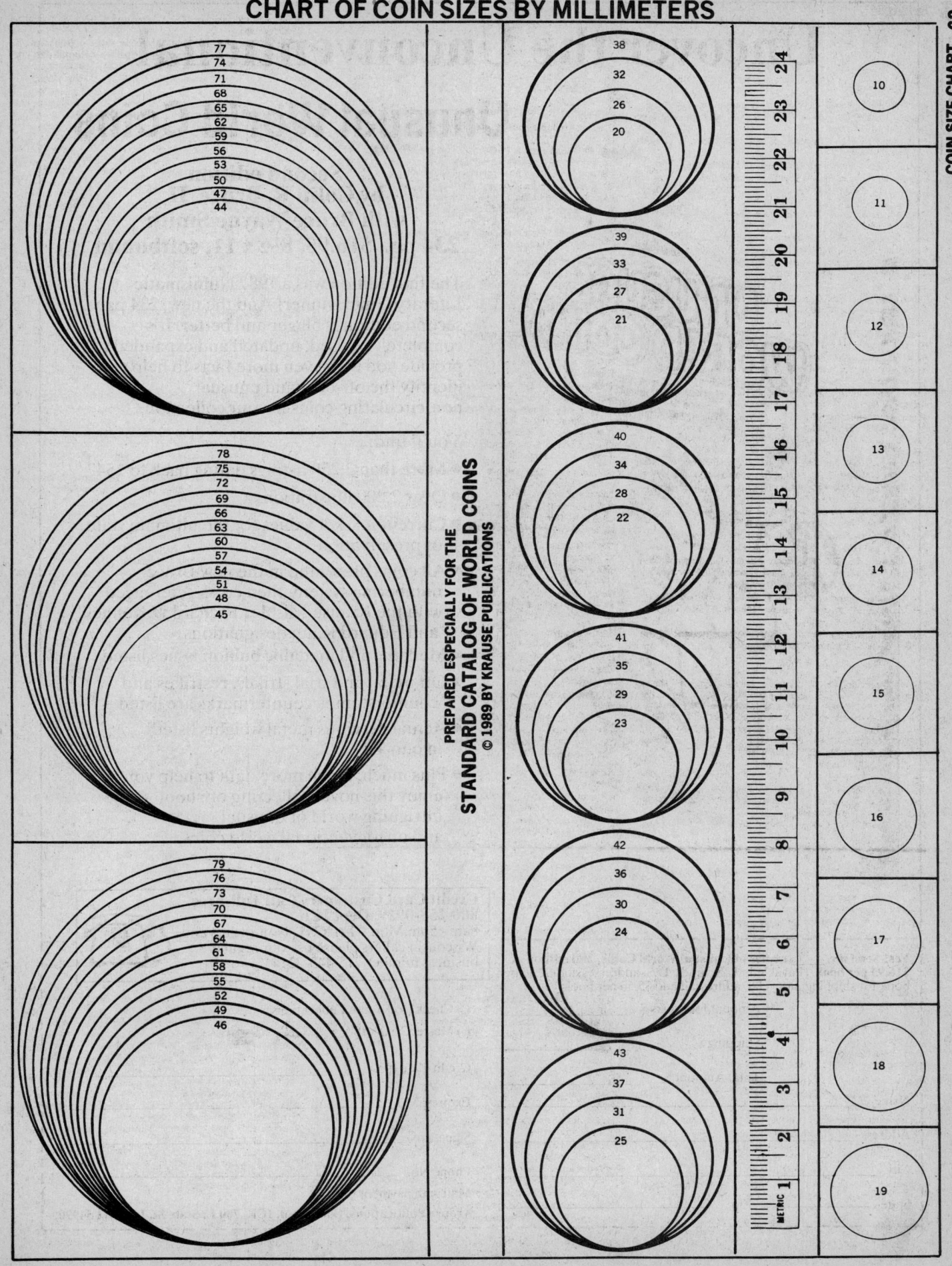

Uncover the Unconventional

Unusual World Coins

Second edition
by Colin R. Bruce II
with Bruce Wayne Smith
234 pg., $16.95, 8½ x 11, softbound

The first edition was a 1987 Numismatic Literary Guild winner! And the new, 234 page, second edition is bigger and better. It's completely revised, updated and expanded to provide you with even more facts to help you identify the off-beat and unusual non-circulating coins in your collection.

You'll find:

- More than 2,250 listings dating back to 1547
- Over 2,200 illustrations
- Current market values for the ultimate state of preservation
- All coins presented in the new Bruce numbering system, then cross-referenced with the Krause/Mishler, Richard D. Kenney and Eduard Kann designations
- Medallic and medallic bullion issues listed
- Off metal and trial strikes, restrikes and counterstamps/countermarks are listed
- Actual precious metal weights listed in ounces
- Plus much, much more data to help you enjoy this novel collecting offshoot — the intriguing world of unusual and unconventional world coins.

Credit Card Customers Call Toll-Free
800-258-0929, Dept ICK
8am - 5pm, Mon. - Fri. CST. Non-orders and Wisconsin callers please use our regular business number 715-445-2214.

Yes! Send me _____ copies of Unusual World Coins, 2nd edition at $16.95 per book. (Payable in U.S. funds. U.S. addresses add $2.50 per book for shipping; non-U.S. addressed add $5.50 per book)

Amount for books $ _____

Shipping $ _____

Total Amount $ _____

Name _____

Address _____

City _____

State _____ Zip _____   ICK

( ) Check (to Krause Publications)
( ) MasterCard/VISA

Credit Card No. _____

Expires: Mo. _____ Yr. _____

Signature _____

Phone No. _____

Mail with payment to:
Krause Publications, Book Dept. ICK, 700 E. State St., Iola, WI 54990

This Catalog brings you a tremendous amount of valuable information about "The Coins of the Past" —

This Card can bring you valuable information about "The Coins of the Future" —

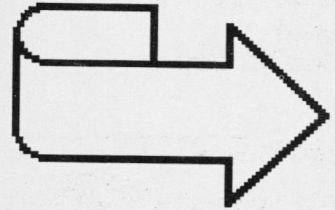

Detach along here

Place postage here or send in envelope if you prefer.

THE MONEY COMPANY
5959 Tampa Avenue
Tarzana, CA 91356 USA

The Money Company's "Wonderful World of Coins"

- **NEW ISSUES** — The Money Company will be leading the way in exciting "Low Mintage" Gold and Silver Legal Tender Commemorative Coin issues. These issues will range over the entire globe. But many of these issues will be sold out before release date — so ask for our exclusive "Priority One" service below, so that you will not miss out!

- **RARE COIN AND BANKNOTE AUCTIONS** — The Word's most interesting, unusual and informative Auction Catalogs are created by The Money Company. If you are not already one of our auction clients you are missing fun and opportunity — so please check the card below to receive a special offer on our next exciting Auction Catalog.

- **INTERNATIONAL NUMISMATIC EXPOSITIONS** — The Money Company are the creators and sponsors of the World Famous "Hong Kong International Coin Expo", and have made it possible for so many collectors, dealers and their families to visit exciting and exotic foreign destinations. Check the card below for information about Hong Kong and other International Expositions.

- **EXCITING NUMISMATIC PUBLICATIONS** — Besides producing the World's most interesting Auction Catalogs, The Money Company also publishes "A Closer Look", "China Coin Investment News" (for Chinese Readers) and will soon debut it's major new publication "China Numismatic Quarterly". CNQ will be fully published in both English and Chinese — and through it's incorporated feature "The Far East Numismatic News" will actually cover the entire important Asian market. A special subscription offer is yours if you check number 4 below.

- **IF YOU HAVE RARE COINS TO SELL** — Through their Auctions and Publications, the Money Company reaches not only buyers from the Americas and Europe, but also the important and affluent Far Eastern market. Whether by consignment to Auction or Direct Sale, some "Straight Talk" with The Money Company about your Rare Coin holdings would be in your best interests.

YOUR KEY TO THE NUMISMATIC FUTURE:
THE MONEY COMPANY GIVES YOU CHOICES

1. ( ) "Priority One" Service: New Issue Advance Notification Service. No cost or obligation - but only active buyers will continue to receive this service.
2. ( ) Rare Coin and Banknote Auctions - check here to receive special catalog offer.
3. ( ) International Numismatic Expositions - check here for ( ) bourse or ( ) travel information.
4. ( ) China Numismatic Quarterly. Check here for special subscription offer.
5. ( ) I have Rare Coins that I may want to sell or consign to Auction. Please contact me.

Name _____
Address _____
City _____ State ____ Zip ____ Phone _____
I am: ( ) Collector   ( ) Investor   ( ) Dealer.   Interested in _____
2X

charter member

THE MONEY COMPANY
'The Innovators'
Phone: (818) 609-7666   Telex: 69-1647
Fax: (818) 609-9725   Coinnet: CA71
5959 Tampa Avenue
Tarzana, CA. 91356 USA

- In Hong Kong we're located at:
Suite 502, Supreme House
2A Hart Avenue, Tsim Sha Tsui
Kowloon, Hong Kong

AFGHANISTAN

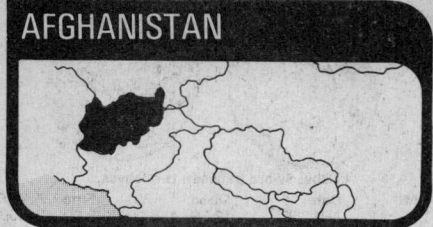

The Democratic Republic of Afghanistan, which occupies a mountainous region of Southwest Asia, has an area of 250,000 sq. mi. (647,497 sq. km.) and a population of about 15 million, over a fourth of whom are presently living in exile as refugees. Capital: Kabul. It is bordered by Iran, Pakistan, the USSR, and China's Sinkiang Province. Agriculture and herding are the principal industries; textile mills and cement factories are recent additions to the industrial sector. Cotton, wool, fruits, nuts, sheepskin coats and hand-woven carpets are normally exported but foreign trade has been interrupted since 1979.

Because of its strategic position astride the ancient land route to India, Afghanistan -- formerly known as Aryana and Khorasan -- was invaded by Darius I, Alexander the Great, various Scythian tribes, the Arabs, the Turks, Genghis Khan, Tamerlane, the Mughals, the Persians, and in more recent times by Great Britain. It was a powerful empire under the Kushans, Hephthalites, Ghaznavids and Ghorids. Afghanistan's new name dates only from the middle of the 18th century when Ahmad Shah Abdali defeated the Persians AH1160 (1747AD) and established his Durrani dynasty. Later, family feuds plagued his successors and resulted in a new dynasty, the Barakzai.

A constitution approved by the General Assembly in 1964 established Afghanistan as a constitutional monarchy, and began moving the country toward parliamentary democracy. The last king was Muhammad Zahir Shah, who ascended the throne Nov. 8, 1933. On July 17, 1973, Muhammad Daud, the king's cousin, seized power in a coup d'etat, and proclaimed Afghanistan a republic with himself as president and premier. Daud was killed in a military coup which established a Marxist regime on April 28, 1978. Internal conflict mounted and in December, 1979 the U.S.S.R. invaded and occupied the country, installing puppet regimes. A civil war ensued which has caused the flight of about five million refugees into neighboring Pakistan and Iran. Soviet Russian armed forces withdrew, effective February 15, 1989, by agreement under United Nations auspices, leaving the remaining Marxist regime to face mounting internal resistance.

Coinage reflects Persian, Turkish and Indian influences. Inscriptions are in Dari and Pushtu, with Pushtu being employed exclusively after A.D. 1950. Dating is by the Muhammadan lunar calendar (A.H.) and solar calendar (S.H.), the lunar calendar being employed prior to A.D. 1920 and during A.D. 1929-31. Decimal coinage was introduced in 1926.

RULERS

Names of rulers are shown in Perso-Arabic script in the style usually found on their coins, but are not always in a straight line.

DURRANI DYNASTY

Shah Shuja al-Mulk, 1st reign,

AH1216/1801AD (no coins)
Mahmud Shah, 1st reign,

AH1216-1218/1801-1803AD
Qaisar Shah,

AH1218/1803AD
Shah Shuja al-Mulk, 2nd reign,
  AH1218-1224/1803-1808AD
Mahmud Shah, 2nd reign,
  AH1224-1233/1808-1817AD
Ayyub Shah, Puppet of Dost Muhammad,

AH1233-1245/1817-1826AD
Sultan Muhammad, at Peshawar
  AH1247-1250/1831-1834AD
Kohandil Khan, at Qandahar
  AH1256-1271/1840-1855AD
Shah Shuja al-Mulk, as nominee of British East India Co., 3rd reign,
  AH1255-1258/1839-1842AD
Fath Jang

AH1258/1842AD
Shahpur Shah

AH1258/1842AD
Succession at Kashmir, AH1221-1234

Qaisar Shah,
  AH1221-1223/1806-1808AD
Ata Muhammad, called Shah Nur al-Din on coins,

AH1223-1228/1808-1813AD
Azim Khan, coins in name of Mahmud Shah,
  AH1228-1234/1813-1818AD

Succession at Herat, AH1216-1298

Mahmud Shah,
  AH1216-1245/1801-1829AD
Kamran Shah,

AH1245-1258/1829-1842AD
Yar Muhammad Khan Barakzai,
  AH1258-1267/1842-1851AD
Muhammad Yusuf Khan Sadozai,
  AH1267-1272/1851-1856AD
Iranian Occupation of Herat (coins in name of Nasir al-Din Shah):
  AH1272-1280/1856-1863AD

Sher Ali, AH1280-1296/1863-1879AD
Muhammad Yaqub,
  AH1296-1298/1879-1881AD
thereafter, as in the rest of Afghanistan

BARAKZAI DYNASTY

Dost Muhammad, 1st reign, anonymous coinage

AH1239-1255/1824-1839AD
British Occupation
  AH1255-1258/1839-1842AD
Dost Muhammad, 2nd reign, "Akbar Amir" (Great King) in center of obv.
  AH1258-1280/1842-1863AD
Sher Ali, 1st reign,

AH1280-1283/1863-1866AD
Muhammad Afzal,

AH1283-1284/1866-1867AD
Muhammad A'zam,

AH1283-1285/1866-1868AD
Sher Ali, 2nd reign,
  AH1285-1296/1868-1879AD
Muhammad Yaqub,

AH1296-1297/1879-1880AD
Wali Muhammad, at Kabul
  AH1297/1880AD
Wali Sher Ali, at Qandahar

AH1297/1880AD
Abdur Rahman,

AH1297-1319/1880-1901AD
Muhammad Ishaq, rebel at Balkh,

AH1305-1306/1889AD
Habibullah,

AH1319-1337/1901-1919AD
Amanullah,

AH1337, SH1298-1307/1919-1929AD
Habibullah (rebel, known as Baccha-i-Saqao),

AH1347-1348/1929AD
Muhammed Nadir Shah

AH1348-1350, SH1310-1312
1929-1933AD
Muhammad Zahir Shah,

SH1312-1352/1933-1973AD
Republic, SH1352-1358/1973-1979AD
Democratic Republic, SH1358- /1979- AD

MINTNAMES

Hammered coins were struck at numerous mints in Afghanistan and adjacent lands. These are listed below, together with their honorific titles, and shown in the style ordinarily found on the coins.

Afghanistan

Ahmadpur Mint
  See Bahawalpur Mint

Ahmadshahi Mint
  See Qandahar Mint

'Ashraf al-Bilad'
  Most Noble of Cities

Badakhshan Mint

Bahawalpur Mint

'Dar as-Surur'
  Abode of Happiness

Balkh Mint

'Umm al-Bilad'
  Mother of Cities

Bhakhar Mint

Dera Mint
  Dera Ghazi Khan

Derajat Mint
  Dera Isma'il Khan

Ghazni Mint

Herat Mint

Dar al-Nusrat
  Seat of Victory

'Dar as-Sultanat'
  Abode of the Sultanate

Kabul Mint

'Dar al-Mulk'
  Abode of the King

'Dar as-Sultanat' (see Herat)

Kashmir Mint

Khanabad Mint

Ladakh Mint
(Not usually clear on coins)

Mashhad Mint

Multan Mint

'Dar al-Aman'
  Abode of Security

AFGHANISTAN 66

Peshawar Mint   پشاور

Qandahar Mint   قندهار
See Ahmadshahi Mint

Sar-i Pol Mint   سَرِ پل

Tashqurghan Mint   تاش قورغان

ANONYMOUS HAMMERED COPPER COINAGE

Afghan copper coins, prior to the beginning of machine-struck coinage in 1891, were not regulated by the central authorities. Mintmasters produced many types of hand-struck coinage including the use of old Afghan coins as blanks. Consequently, weights are quite random, and there are no denominations in the true sense of the term. All were known as 'Falus', and lots of mixed sizes were accounted by weight. Every few years, sometimes every year, coppers were recalled and recoined, at a fee, often substantial, which was paid to the mintmaster and formed his salary. This accounts for the large number of overstruck pieces, which are generally less desirable than clear singly struck specimens.

Hundreds of varieties were issued at the principal mints of Kabul and Ahmadshahi/Qandahar, and the following listing is only a representation of what exists. It is arranged chronologically by mint, to the extent that coins bear dates. A more detailed, but still very fragmentary listing is given by W.H. Valentine, in 'Modern Copper Coins of the Muhammadan States'. No attempt at a complete listing has ever been undertaken.

Prices are for well-struck specimens with clear design and date. Partial or overstruck coins are worth considerably less. Unrepresented types are worth about the same as listed pieces of the same mint.

IMPORTANT: Most types were used at one time or other at all mints. The type cannot therefore be used to determine the mint, which can ordinarily only be ascertained by reading the Persian inscription.

NOTE: Copper coins bearing the name of the issuing ruler are included under "Named Hammered Coinage", below, by mint. For later anonymous issues, see the local coppers listed after the milled coinage.

Ahmadshahi Mint
(See also Qandahar)

Obv: Sword within 4 circles.

KM#	Date	Good	VG	Fine	VF
10	AH1211	10.00	25.00	40.00	80.00

11	**Obv: Lion right.**				
11	AH1227	2.00	4.00	6.50	10.00

Obv: Eight-petalled flower.
| 14 | AH1240 | 3.50 | 6.50 | 11.00 | 16.50 |

Obv: Leaf between swords.
| 15 | AH1240 | 4.00 | 7.00 | 12.00 | 18.00 |

Obv: Flower between swords.
KM#	Date	Good	VG	Fine	VF
16	AH1241	4.00	7.00	12.00	18.00

Obv: Three flowers on one stem.
| 18 | AH1245 | 4.00 | 7.00 | 12.00 | 18.00 |

Obv: Three swords.
| 20 | AH1249 | 5.00 | 8.00 | 15.00 | 25.00 |

Obv: Flower.
| 21 | AH1252 | 2.00 | 4.00 | 7.00 | 11.00 |

Obv: Sunface.
| 22 | AH1253 | 1.50 | 3.00 | 5.00 | 8.00 |

Obv: Crossed swords.
| 23 | ND | 2.50 | 5.00 | 8.00 | 12.00 |
| | AH1253 | 3.00 | 6.00 | 10.00 | 15.00 |

Obv: Leaf between two swords.
| 24 | AH1254 | 3.00 | 6.00 | 10.00 | 15.00 |

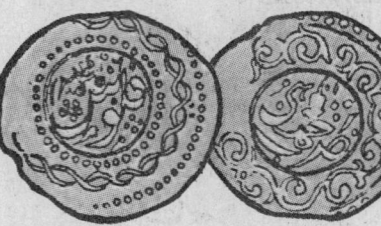

Obv: Ornate borders.
| 25 | AH1255 | 5.00 | 8.00 | 15.00 | 25.00 |

Obv: Two bladed sword.
| 26 | AH1255 | 2.50 | 5.00 | 7.00 | 12.00 |

Obv: Sword between two leaves.
KM#	Date	Good	VG	Fine	VF
27	AH1256	2.50	5.00	8.00	12.00
	1257	2.50	5.00	8.00	12.00

Obv: Bird.
| 28 | ND | 2.00 | 4.00 | 7.00 | 11.00 |

Badakhshan Mint

Obv: Badakhshan
| 30 | ND | 6.00 | 12.50 | 20.00 | 40.00 |

Balkh Mint

Obv: Flower between two swords.
32	AH1228	2.00	4.00	7.00	11.00
	1233	2.00	4.00	7.00	11.00
	1234	2.00	4.00	7.00	11.00
	1238	2.00	4.00	7.00	11.00

Obv: Lion right.
| 35 | AH1267 | 2.50 | 5.00 | 8.00 | 12.00 |

Obv: Plant between two swords.
| 37 | AH1274 | 3.00 | 6.00 | 10.00 | 15.00 |
| | 1277 | 4.00 | 8.00 | 15.00 | 22.50 |

Obv: Small lion and inscriptions.
| 38 | AH1295 | 1.50 | 3.00 | 5.00 | 8.00 |

NOTE: This type struck by machine over a number of years without change of date. Lion usually faces right, rarely left.

Ghazni Mint

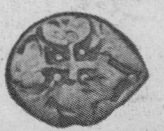 

Obv: Floral design.
| 40 | ND | 3.00 | 6.00 | 10.00 | 15.00 |

Herat Mint

Obv: Leaf and two swords.

KM#	Date	Good	VG	Fine	VF
43	AH1224	2.00	4.00	7.00	11.00
	1226	2.00	4.00	7.00	11.00

Obv: Sunface.

| 44 | AH1227 | 2.00 | 4.00 | 7.00 | 11.00 |

Obv: Crab.

| 45 | AH(12)95 | 2.00 | 4.00 | 7.00 | 11.00 |

Obv: Fish ?

| 47 | AH1297 | 2.00 | 4.00 | 7.00 | 11.00 |

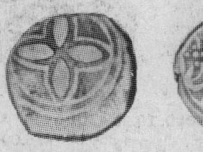 

Obv: 4 ovals in the shape of a cross within double circle.

| 50 | AH1305 | 5.00 | 9.00 | 15.00 | 25.00 |

Kabul Mint

Obv: Leaf and swords, J in center, large size.

| 54 | AH1229 | 2.50 | 5.00 | 8.00 | 12.00 |

Obv: Flower.

| 55 | AH1232 | 3.00 | 6.50 | 12.00 | 18.00 |

Obv: Crossed swords.

KM#	Date	Good	VG	Fine	VF
56	AH1234	2.50	5.00	8.00	12.00

Obv: Crossed swords.

| 58 | AH1236 | 3.00 | 6.00 | 10.00 | 15.00 |

Obv: Star between two swords.

| 59 | AH1236 | 4.00 | 7.00 | 12.00 | 18.00 |
| | ND | 3.00 | 6.00 | 10.00 | 15.00 |

Obv: Flower between two leaves.

| 60 | AH1236 | 4.00 | 7.00 | 12.00 | 18.00 |

Obv: Floral pattern.

| 66 | AH12xx | 2.00 | 4.00 | 7.00 | 11.00 |
| | ND | 2.00 | 4.00 | 7.00 | 11.00 |

Obv: Sword and stars.

68	AH1252	2.00	4.00	7.00	11.00
	126x	2.00	4.00	7.00	11.00
	ND	2.00	4.00	7.00	11.00

Obv: Sword right.

| 69 | AH1258 | — | — | — | — |

Obv: Sword and floral ornaments.

| 70 | AH1254 | 2.00 | 4.00 | 7.00 | 11.00 |
| | 1258 | 3.00 | 6.00 | 10.00 | 15.00 |

 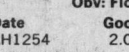

Obv: Flower.

KM#	Date	Good	VG	Fine	VF
71	AH1254	2.00	4.00	7.00	11.00

Obv: Flower and swords.

| 72 | AH1254-8 | 2.00 | 4.00 | 7.00 | 11.00 |
| | 1256 | 2.00 | 4.00 | 7.00 | 11.00 |

Obv: Sword.

| 73 | AH1254 | 2.50 | 5.00 | 8.00 | 12.00 |

Obv: Flower and swords.

| 75 | AH1261 | 2.50 | 5.00 | 8.00 | 12.00 |
| | 1265 | 2.50 | 5.00 | 8.00 | 12.00 |

Obv: Flower within chevron border.

| 76 | AH1261 | 4.50 | 8.00 | 13.50 | 20.00 |

Obv: Floral spray.

| 77 | AH1267 | 5.00 | 9.00 | 15.00 | 25.00 |

Obv: Flower.

| 78 | AH1268 | 2.00 | 4.00 | 7.00 | 11.00 |

Obv: Flower.

| 79 | ND | 4.00 | 7.00 | 12.00 | 18.00 |

Khanabad Mint

| 80 | AH1301 | 10.00 | 18.50 | 28.50 | 40.00 |
| | 1302 | 10.00 | 18.50 | 28.50 | 40.00 |

AFGHANISTAN 68

Qandahar Mint
(See also Ahmadshahi)

Obv: Large date and legend.

KM#	Date	Good	VG	Fine	VF
85	AH1228	2.00	4.00	7.00	11.00

Obv: Four petaled flower within swords.

| 87 | ND | 2.00 | 4.00 | 7.00 | 11.00 |

Obv: Three flowers on one stem. Rev: Sword.

| 88 | ND | 4.00 | 7.00 | 12.00 | 18.00 |

Obv: Flower within wreath.

| 90 | AH1294 | 3.00 | 6.00 | 10.00 | 15.00 |

Obv: Hand of Ali?

| 91 | AH1295 | 2.25 | 4.50 | 7.50 | 11.50 |

Obv: Leaf between two swords.

| 92 | AH1295 | 2.50 | 5.00 | 8.00 | 12.00 |

***Adl* (Justice) in hexagram.**

| 95 | AH1296 | 1.00 | 2.00 | 3.50 | 6.00 |

Obv: Peacock.

| 96 | AH1297 | 1.50 | 2.50 | 3.50 | 5.50 |

Obv: Flower.

| 97 | AH1300 | 2.50 | 5.00 | 8.00 | 12.00 |

British Occupation

Obv: Crown.

KM#	Date	Good	VG	Fine	VF
94	AH1296	15.00	30.00	50.00	80.00

NOTE: Issued during the British occupation of Qandahar 1878-79. Crude elongated varieties exist.

| 101 | AH1296 | — | — | — |

Sar-i Pol Mint

Obv: Lion.

| 98 | AH1297 | 10.00 | 15.00 | 20.00 | 30.00 |
| | ND | 10.00 | 15.00 | 20.00 | 30.00 |

Tashqurghan Mint

Obv: Stem with leaves.

| 99 | AH1300 | 10.00 | 18.50 | 28.50 | 40.00 |

Obv: Flower.

| 100 | AH1300 | 12.50 | 22.50 | 35.00 | 50.00 |

NAMED HAMMERED COINAGE

Unlike the anonymous copper coinage, which was purely local, the silver and gold coins, as well as some of the early copper coins, bear the name or characteristic type of the ruler. Because the sequence of rulers often varied at different mints, each ruled by different princes, the coins are best organized according to mint. Each mint employed characteristic types and calligraphy, which continued from one ruler to the next. It is hoped that this system will facilitate identification of these coins.

The following listings include not only the mints situated in contiguous territories under Durrani and Barakzai rule for extended periods of time, but also mints in Kashmir or in other parts of India which the Afghans occupied for relatively brief intervals.

Ahmadpur Mint
(In Bahawalpur)

MAHMUD SHAH
AH1216-1218/1801-1803AD

LIGHT RUPEE

SILVER, 8.20-8.40 g

KM#	Date	Year	VG	Fine	VF	XF
108	AH1217	48	22.00	40.00	50.00	60.00
	—	49	22.00	40.00	50.00	60.00

Posthumous issue. Reverse only shown.

Ahmadshahi/Qandahar Mint
Ashraf-al-Bilad

Until AH1273, this mint was almost always given on the coins as *Ahmadshahi*, a name given it by Ahmad Shah in honor of himself in AH1171, often with the honorific *Ashraf al-Bilad* (meaning 'Most Noble of Cities'). On later issues, after AH1271, the traditional name *Qandahar* is generally used.

MAHMUD SHAH
AH1216-1218/1801-1803AD, 1st reign

RUPEE

SILVER, 11.40-11.60 g

KM#	Date	Year	VG	Fine	VF	XF
143	AH1216	—	15.00	30.00	45.00	60.00
	1217	2	15.00	30.00	45.00	60.00
	1217	3	15.00	30.00	45.00	60.00
	1218	3	15.00	30.00	45.00	60.00

ASHRAFI

GOLD, 25mm, 3.50 g

| 144 | AH1218 | 3 | — | 275.00 | 400.00 | 500.00 |

MOHUR

GOLD, 10.90 g

| 145 | AH1218 | 3 | — | 275.00 | 350.00 | 400.00 |

QAISAR SHAH
AH1218/1803AD

RUPEE

SILVER, 11.50-11.60 g

| 148 | AH1218 | — | 20.00 | 50.00 | 70.00 | 85.00 |

MOHUR

GOLD, 10.90 g

| 149 | AH1218 | — | — | 350.00 | 475.00 | 600.00 |

SHAH SHUJA AL-MULK
AH1218-1224/1803-1808AD, 2nd reign

1/4 RUPEE

SILVER, 2.80-3.00 g

| 151 | AH1218 | 2 | 20.00 | 40.00 | 60.00 | 90.00 |

RUPEE

SILVER, 11.40-11.60 g

153	AH1218	—	7.50	15.00	20.00	27.50
	1219	1	7.50	15.00	20.00	27.50
	1220	2	7.50	15.00	20.00	27.50
	1221	3	7.50	15.00	20.00	27.50
	1222	—	7.50	15.00	20.00	27.50
	1223	—	7.50	15.00	20.00	27.50
	1224	—	7.50	15.00	20.00	27.50

NOTE: Varieties of the obverse exist.

ASHRAFI

AFGHANISTAN 69

GOLD, 3.00-3.50 g

KM#	Date	Year	VG	Fine	VF	XF
154	AH1220	—	—	175.00	200.00	350.00
	1222	—	—	175.00	200.00	350.00

MOHUR

GOLD, 10.90 g

155	AH—	2	—	—	300.00	375.00
	AH1220	3	—	—	325.00	400.00
	1222	—	—	—	325.00	400.00

MAHMUD SHAH
AH1224-1233/1808-1817AD, 2nd reign

1/2 RUPEE

SILVER, 5.40-5.80 g

| 156 | AH1224 | — | 20.00 | 45.00 | 65.00 | 85.00 |

RUPEE

SILVER, 11.40-11.60 g
Rev: In cartouche or circle.

157	AH1222 (error date)
	—	—	7.00	14.00	20.00	30.00
	1224	—	7.00	14.00	20.00	28.00
	1225	—	7.00	14.00	20.00	28.00
	1226	—	7.00	14.00	20.00	28.00
	1227	—	7.00	14.00	20.00	28.00
	1228	—	7.00	14.00	20.00	28.00
	1230	—	7.00	14.00	20.00	28.00
	1232	—	7.00	14.00	20.00	28.00

10.20-10.40 g
Rev: In toughra.

158.1	AH1229	—	—	10.00	16.00	25.00
	1230	—	—	10.00	16.00	25.00
	1231	—	—	10.00	16.00	25.00
	1232	—	—	10.00	16.00	25.00

Rev: Legend in a circle.

158.2	AH1232	—	8.00	15.00	25.00	35.00
	1233	—	8.00	15.00	25.00	35.00
	1234	—	8.00	15.00	25.00	35.00

ASHRAFI
GOLD, 28mm, 2.40 g

| 159 | AH1224 | — | — | — | Rare | — |

AYYUB SHAH
AH1233-1245/1817-1826AD

RUPEE

SILVER, 11.20-11.60 g

163	AH1235	—	15.00	30.00	40.00	50.00
	1236	—	—	Reported, not confirmed		
	1237	—	15.00	30.00	40.00	50.00
	1239	—	15.00	30.00	40.00	50.00

NOTE: Reverses differ each year. Coins dated AH1239 are struck in debased metal.

ANONYMOUS COINAGE
During the reign of Dost Muhammad
AH1239-1255/1824-1839AD, 1st reign

RUPEE

SILVER
Obv: Kalimah.

KM#	Date	Year	VG	Fine	VF	XF
168	AH1243	—	10.00	20.00	30.00	40.00
	1244	—	7.00	15.00	20.00	30.00
	1245	—	—	10.00	15.00	25.00
	1246	—	—	10.00	15.00	25.00
	1247	—	—	10.00	15.00	25.00
	1248	—	—	10.00	15.00	25.00
	1249	—	—	9.00	14.00	23.00
	1250	—	—	9.00	14.00	23.00
	1251	—	—	9.00	14.00	23.00
	1252	—	7.00	13.00	20.00	30.00
	1253	—	7.00	13.00	20.00	30.00
	1254	—	7.00	13.00	20.00	30.00

NOTE: Minor variations exist on both sides.

SHAH SHUJA AL-MULK
AH1255-1258/1839-1842AD, 3rd reign

1/4 RUPEE

SILVER, 2.30 g

| 171 | AH1255 | — | 25.00 | 32.50 | 45.00 | 60.00 |

RUPEE

SILVER, 9.00-9.20 g

173	AH1255	—	10.00	20.00	25.00	35.00
	1256	—	12.50	30.00	40.00	50.00

FATH JANG
AH1258/1842AD

RUPEE

SILVER, 9.15-9.35 g

| 178 | AH1258 | — | 20.00 | 50.00 | 75.00 | 100.00 |

ANONYMOUS COINAGE
During the reign of Kohandil Khan
AH1256-1271/1840-1855AD

1/2 RUPEE

SILVER

182	AH1260	—	4.00	10.00	14.00	20.00
	1261	—	4.00	10.00	14.00	20.00
	1262	—	4.00	10.00	14.00	20.00
	1263	—	4.00	10.00	14.00	20.00
	1264	—	4.00	10.00	14.00	20.00
	1265	—	4.00	10.00	14.00	20.00
	1267	—	5.00	12.00	19.00	25.00
	1268	—	6.50	16.00	25.00	35.00
	1269	—	6.50	16.00	25.00	35.00
	1270	—	6.50	16.00	25.00	35.00
	1271	—	6.50	16.00	25.00	35.00
	1272	—	6.50	16.00	25.00	35.00

NOTE: Both obverse and reverse have legends differently arranged in different years.

RUPEE

SILVER

KM#	Date	Year	VG	Fine	VF	XF
183	AH1259	—	12.50	27.50	35.00	50.00

RAHAMDIL KHAN
AH1271-1272/1855-1856AD

1/2 RUPEE

SILVER
Mintname: *Ahmadshahi*

| 184 | AH1272 | — | 15.00 | 35.00 | 50.00 | 70.00 |

DOST MUHAMMAD
AH1258-1280/1842-1863AD, 2nd reign
Issues bearing name of Amir and his late son, Akbar Khan

1/2 RUPEE

SILVER
Mintname: *Ahmadshahi*
Dated on both sides.

186	AH1272	—	3.00	6.00	10.00	15.00
	1273	—	3.00	6.00	10.00	15.00

Mintname: *Qandahar*
Dated on both sides.

187	AH1273	—	3.00	6.00	8.50	13.50
	1274	—	3.00	6.00	8.50	13.50
	1275	—	3.00	6.00	8.50	13.50
	1277	—	3.00	6.00	9.00	15.00
	1278	—	3.00	6.00	9.00	15.00
	1279	—	—	Reported, not confirmed		

RUPEE

SILVER
Mintname: *Ahmadshahi*
Dated on both sides.

188	AH1272	—	10.00	25.00	35.00	50.00
	1273	—	10.00	25.00	35.00	50.00

SHER ALI
AH1280-1283/1863-1866, 1st reign

1/2 RUPEE

SILVER
Obv: Couplet. Rev: Title of ruler and mint.

191	AH1280	—	5.00	10.00	17.00	30.00
	1281	—	6.00	13.00	20.00	30.00
	1282	—	5.00	8.00	15.00	30.00

AFGHANISTAN 70

Obv: Couplet. Rev: Mint only.

KM#	Date	Year	VG	Fine	VF	XF
192	AH1283	—	10.00	20.00	30.00	40.00

NOTE: Arrangement of rev. legend varies.

TILLA

GOLD

194	AH1283	—	150.00	200.00	250.00
	1284	—	150.00	200.00	250.00
	1285	—	150.00	200.00	250.00

MUHAMMAD AFZAL
AH1283-1284/1866-1867AD
1/2 RUPEE

SILVER

| 196 | AH1283 | — | 25.00 | 50.00 | 75.00 | 100.00 |

MUHAMMAD A'ZAM
AH1283-1285/1866-1868AD
1/2 RUPEE

SILVER

| 201 | AH1283 | — | 25.00 | 50.00 | 75.00 | 100.00 |
| | 1284 | — | 25.00 | 50.00 | 75.00 | 100.00 |

SHER ALI
AH1285-1296/1868-1879AD, 2nd reign
1/2 RUPEE

SILVER

| 205.1 | AH1284 | — | 6.00 | 13.00 | 20.00 | 30.00 |
| | 1285 | — | 6.00 | 13.00 | 20.00 | 30.00 |

NOTE: Resumption of type identical to KM#191 of first reign.

| 205.2 | AH1287 | — | 12.50 | 20.00 | 30.00 | 40.00 |

NOTE: Formerly listed as uncertain mint, KM#792.

206	AH1277 (error) for 1288
		—	5.50	12.50	20.00	30.00
	1288	—	4.00	7.00	10.00	15.00
	1289	—	5.00	12.50	20.00	30.00

| 207.1 | AH1290 | — | 3.00 | 6.00 | 10.00 | 15.00 |

KM#	Date	Year	VG	Fine	VF	XF
207.1	1291	—	3.00	6.00	10.00	15.00
	1292	—	3.00	6.00	10.00	15.00
	1293	—	3.00	6.00	10.00	15.00

Obv: Teardrop design.

| 207.2 | AH1294 | — | 3.00 | 6.00 | 10.00 | 15.00 |
| | 1295 | — | 3.00 | 6.00 | 10.00 | 15.00 |

| 208 | AH1295 | — | 3.50 | 13.50 | 22.50 | 37.50 |

MUHAMMAD YAQUB
AH1296-1297/1879-1880AD
1/2 RUPEE

SILVER

| 212 | AH1296 | — | 6.00 | 16.00 | 25.00 | 35.00 |
| | 1297 | — | 12.00 | 25.00 | 35.00 | 45.00 |

RUPEE
SILVER

| 213 | AH1298 | — | — | Reported, not confirmed |

WALI SHER ALI
AH1297/1880AD
1/2 RUPEE

SILVER
Dated on both sides.

| 217 | AH1297 | — | 8.50 | 17.50 | 25.00 | 35.00 |

RUPEE

SILVER
Type of half Rupee

| 218 | AH1297 | — | 15.00 | 30.00 | 40.00 | 60.00 |

TILLA

GOLD

| 219 | AH1297 | — | — | — | Rare | — |

ANONYMOUS COINAGE
1/2 RUPEE

SILVER
Dated on both sides.
Obv: Al-Mulk Lillah.

| 221 | AH1297 | — | 10.00 | 20.00 | 30.00 | 40.00 |

NOTE: It is not known under whose authority this type was struck.

ABDUR RAHMAN
AH1297-1319/1880-1901AD
1/2 RUPEE

SILVER
Mintname: *Ahmadshahi*

KM#	Date	Year	VG	Fine	VF	XF
222	AH1298	—	15.00	30.00	40.00	50.00

Mintname: *Qandahar*

| 225 | AH1298 | — | 20.00 | 35.00 | 50.00 | 70.00 |
| (KM-A223) |

RUPEE

SILVER
Mintname: *Ahmadshahi*

| 227 | ND(AH1298) | — | — | — | — | — |
| (KM-B223) |

Mintname: *Qandahar*

| 223 | AH1298 | — | 35.00 | 60.00 | 85.00 | 120.00 |

NOTE: Variety with only one leaf on obverse exists.

224	AH1298	—	7.50	12.50	20.00	30.00
	1299	—	10.00	16.00	25.00	40.00
	1300	—	10.00	16.00	25.00	40.00
	1301	—	10.00	16.00	25.00	40.00
	1302	—	10.00	16.00	25.00	40.00
	1303	—	6.00	10.00	15.00	25.00
	1304	—	—	6.00	10.00	17.50
	1305	—	—	6.00	10.00	17.50
	1306	—	—	6.00	10.00	17.50
	1307	—	—	6.00	10.00	17.50
	1308	—	—	6.00	10.00	17.50

TILLA

GOLD

| 226 | AH1298 | — | — | — | Rare | — |

Bahawalpur Mint
Dar as-Surur

NOTE: Most Bahawalpur coins have crude oblique milling on the edge.

MAHMUD SHAH
AH1216-1218/1801-1803AD, 1st reign

RUPEE

SILVER, 11.40-11.60 g
Rev: Mint and epithet.

KM#	Date	Year	VG	Fine	VF	XF
242	AH1217	—	30.00	65.00	80.00	100.00

Rev: Mint and *Julus* formula.

243	AH1217	1	30.00	50.00	65.00	
	1217	2	30.00	50.00	65.00	
	1218	2	30.00	50.00	65.00	

2 RUPEES

SILVER, 23.00-23.20 g

244	AH1217	1	85.00	140.00	200.00	275.00

NOTE: Regnal year written as numeral, not *AHAD*.

MOHUR

GOLD, 11.00 g

| 245 | AH1218 | 2 | — | — | 400.00 | 500.00 |

2 MOHURS

GOLD, 22.00-22.20 g

246	AH1217	1	—	—	750.00	1000.
	1217	2	—	—	750.00	1000.
	1218	2	—	—	750.00	1000.

SHAH SHUJA AL-MULK
AH1218-1224/1803-1808AD, 2nd reign

RUPEE

SILVER, 11.20-11.60 g

253	AH1218	1	—	30.00	50.00	65.00
	1218	2	—	30.00	50.00	65.00
	1219	1	—	30.00	50.00	65.00
	1222	—	—	30.00	50.00	65.00
	1212 (error for 1221 ?)			35.00	55.00	75.00

2 RUPEES

SILVER, 23.00 g

| 254 | AH1218 | 1 | 50.00 | 100.00 | 200.00 | 275.00 |

MOHUR

GOLD, 11.00 g

| 255 | AH1218 | 1 | — | — | 350.00 | 450.00 |

2 MOHURS

GOLD, 22.00 g

KM#	Date	Year	VG	Fine	VF	XF
256	AH1218	1	—	—	850.00	1100.

MAHMUD SHAH
AH1224-1233/1808-1817AD, 2nd reign

RUPEE

SILVER, 21.5-26mm, 11.00-11.20 g

263	AH1224	1	25.00	55.00	75.00	110.00
	1239	—	15.00	30.00	40.00	60.00
	1240	—	15.00	30.00	40.00	60.00
	1241	—	15.00	30.00	40.00	60.00
	1242	—	15.00	30.00	40.00	60.00
	1244	—	15.00	30.00	40.00	60.00
	1244 (1245 on reverse)					
		—	15.00	30.00	40.00	60.00
	1249	—	15.00	30.00	40.00	60.00
	1249 (1250 on reverse)					
	1250	—	15.00	30.00	40.00	60.00

NOTE: Coins dated after AH1233 are struck in Mahmud's name by the virtually independent Nawabs of Bahawalpur.

MOHUR

GOLD, 21.5mm, 11.00 g

| 265 | AH1225 | 1 | — | — | Rare | |

Bhakhar Mint

NOTE: The mint is found variously spelled, as Bhakhar (most common), Bakhar, and Bakkar.

MAHMUD SHAH
AH1216-1218/1801-1803AD, 1st reign

RUPEE

SILVER, 11.40-11.60 g
Broad flan, nazarana style.

| 308 | ND | — | 40.00 | 90.00 | 150.00 | 200.00 |

SHAH SHUJA AL-MULK
AH1218-1224/1803-1808AD, 2nd reign

RUPEE

SILVER, 11.40-11.60 g

309.1	AH1218	—	15.00	25.00	35.00	50.00
	1220	—	15.00	25.00	35.00	50.00
	1221	12	15.00	25.00	35.00	50.00
	1222	—	15.00	25.00	35.00	50.00
	1223	—	15.00	25.00	35.00	50.00
	1224	—	15.00	25.00	35.00	50.00
	ND	—	6.00	12.00	18.00	25.00

Obv: King's name circled within couplet.

| 309.2 | AH1223 | — | 50.00 | 100.00 | 150.00 | 180.00 |

MAHMUD SHAH
AH1224-1233/1809-1817AD, 2nd reign

RUPEE

SILVER, 11.40-11.60 g

| 307 | AH1228 | — | 15.00 | 25.00 | 35.00 | 50.00 |

KM#	Date	Year	VG	Fine	VF	XF
(KM-1229	—	15.00	25.00	35.00	50.00
A310)	ND	—	6.00	10.00	18.00	25.00

Dera Mint
Dera Ghazi Khan

The mint of Dera was located at Dera Ghazi Khan, taken by the Sikhs in AH1235 (1819AD), and now within Pakistan.

MAHMUD SHAH
AH1216-1218/1801-1803AD, 1st reign

RUPEE

SILVER, 11.40-11.60 g

| 338 | AH1216 | 1 | 12.50 | 32.50 | 45.00 | 60.00 |
| | — | 2 | 12.50 | 32.50 | 45.00 | 60.00 |

SHAH SHUJA AL-MULK
AH1218-1224/1803-1808AD, 2nd reign

RUPEE

SILVER, 11.40-11.60 g

343	—	1	12.50	32.50	45.00	60.00
	—	4	12.50	32.50	45.00	60.00
	—	5	12.50	32.50	45.00	60.00

MOHUR

GOLD

| 345 | AH1218 | 1 | — | — | 400.00 | 450.00 |

Derajat Mint
Dera Ismail Khan

The mint of Derajat was located at Dera Ismail Khan, which fell to the Sikhs in (AH1236) 1820-21AD. Issues in the name of Mahmud Shah dated AH1236 and later are actually Sikh issues. The Sikhs formally annexed Derajat in 1835AD (AH1281).

MAHMUD SHAH
AH1216-1218/1801-1803AD, 1st reign

RUPEE

SILVER, 11.00-11.20 g

| 363 | AH1216 | 1 | 18.00 | 38.00 | 50.00 | 70.00 |
| | 1217 | 2 | 18.00 | 38.00 | 50.00 | 70.00 |

SHAH SHUJA AL-MULK
AH1218-1224/1803-1808AD, 2nd reign

RUPEE

SILVER, 20-21.5mm, 10.80-11.20 g

368	AH1218	1	12.50	20.00	30.00	40.00
	1218	2	12.50	20.00	30.00	40.00
	1219	2	12.50	20.00	30.00	40.00
	1220	2	12.50	20.00	30.00	40.00
	1220	3	12.50	20.00	30.00	40.00
	1221	4	12.50	20.00	30.00	40.00
	1221	5	12.50	20.00	30.00	40.00
	—	6	12.50	20.00	30.00	40.00

MAHMUD SHAH
AH1224-1233/1808-1817AD, 2nd reign

RUPEE

SILVER, 10.60-11.20 g

KM#	Date	Year	VG	Fine	VF	XF
373	AH1224	1	12.50	30.00	40.00	50.00
	1226	3	12.50	30.00	40.00	50.00
	1227	3	12.50	30.00	40.00	50.00
	1228	4	12.50	30.00	40.00	50.00
	1231	4	7.50	15.00	25.00	35.00
	1234	—	7.50	15.00	25.00	35.00
	1236	—	7.50	15.00	25.00	35.00
	1237	—	7.50	15.00	25.00	35.00
	1238	14	7.50	15.00	25.00	35.00
	1240	—	7.50	15.00	25.00	35.00
	1241	—	7.50	15.00	25.00	35.00
	1242	—	7.50	15.00	25.00	35.00
	1244	—	7.50	15.00	25.00	35.00
	1245	—	7.50	15.00	25.00	35.00
	1246	—	7.50	15.00	25.00	35.00
	1247	—	7.50	15.00	25.00	35.00
	1248	—	7.50	15.00	25.00	35.00
	1250	—	7.50	15.00	25.00	35.00
	1251	—	7.50	15.00	25.00	35.00

NOTE: Coins after AH1235 were issued under Sikh protectorate.

Herat Mint

Dar as-Sultanat

After AH1254, rupees ceased to be coined at Herat. Later emissions, beginning with anonymous issues of Yar Muhammad Khan, were half rupees. From AH1272-1280 (1856-63AD), Herat was occupied by the Persians, who struck coins there in the name of Nasir al-Din Shah. The mint was closed in AH1308 (1891AD), except for a few later coins in copper.

MAHMUD SHAH

AH1216-1245/1801-1829AD

1/12 RUPEE

SILVER, 0.90 g

KM#	Date	Year	VG	Fine	VF	XF
392	AH1230	—	15.00	35.00	50.00	65.00

1/6 RUPEE

SILVER, 1.80 g

KM#	Date	Year	VG	Fine	VF	XF
393	AH1225	—	15.00	35.00	50.00	70.00
	1238	—	15.00	35.00	50.00	70.00

1/4 RUPEE

SILVER, 11.5mm, 2.80 g

KM#	Date	Year	VG	Fine	VF	XF
395	AH1242	—	25.00	55.00	75.00	100.00

1/2 RUPEE

SILVER, 5.00-5.60 g

KM#	Date	Year	VG	Fine	VF	XF
396	AH1242	—	25.00	45.00	60.00	85.00
	1243	—	25.00	45.00	60.00	85.00

RUPEE

SILVER, 11.00-11.60 g

KM#	Date	Year	VG	Fine	VF	XF
398.1	AH1216	—	—	6.00	9.00	15.00
	1217	—	—	6.00	9.00	15.00
	1218	—	—	6.00	9.00	15.00

KM#	Date	Year	VG	Fine	VF	XF
398.2	AH1219	—	—	6.00	9.00	15.00
	1220	—	—	6.00	9.00	15.00
	1221	—	—	6.00	9.00	15.00
	1222	—	—	6.00	9.00	15.00
	1223	—	—	6.00	9.00	15.00
	1224	—	—	6.00	9.00	15.00
	1225	—	—	6.00	9.00	15.00
	1226	—	—	6.00	9.00	15.00
	1227	—	—	6.00	9.00	15.00
	1228	—	—	6.00	9.00	15.00
	1229	—	—	6.00	9.00	15.00
	1230	—	—	6.50	10.00	16.50
	1231	—	6.00	11.50	18.00	28.00
	1232	—	6.00	11.50	18.00	28.00
	1233	—	6.00	11.50	18.00	28.00
	1234	—	6.00	11.50	18.00	28.00
	1235	—	6.00	11.50	18.00	28.00
	1236	—	6.00	11.50	18.00	28.00
	1237	—	6.00	11.50	18.00	28.00
	1238	—	6.00	11.50	18.00	28.00
	1240	—	6.00	11.50	18.00	28.00
	1242	—	8.00	14.00	20.00	30.00

KM#	Date	Year	VG	Fine	VF	XF
398.3	AH1244	—	8.00	14.00	20.00	30.00
	1254 (error date)	—	8.00	14.00	20.00	30.00

KAMRAN SHAH

AH1245-1258/1829-1842AD

1/6 RUPEE

SILVER, 1.80 g

KM#	Date	Year	VG	Fine	VF	XF
400	AH1257	—	25.00	55.00	80.00	100.00

1/4 RUPEE

SILVER, 2.60-2.80 g

KM#	Date	Year	VG	Fine	VF	XF
401	AH1248	—	35.00	75.00	100.00	135.00

1/2 RUPEE

SILVER, 5.20-5.60 g

KM#	Date	Year	VG	Fine	VF	XF
402	AH125x	—	20.00	30.00	45.00	75.00

RUPEE

SILVER, 10.20-11.00 g

KM#	Date	Year	VG	Fine	VF	XF
403	AH1244	—	30.00	65.00	100.00	125.00
	1245	—	30.00	65.00	100.00	125.00
	1246	—	30.00	65.00	100.00	125.00
	1248	—	30.00	65.00	100.00	125.00
	1249	—	30.00	65.00	100.00	125.00
	1252	—	30.00	65.00	100.00	125.00
	1255	—	30.00	65.00	100.00	125.00

YAR MUHAMMAD KHAN SADOZAI

AH1258-1267/1842-1851AD

Anonymous coinage struck with the Kalima on obv. and mint and date on rev.

1/2 RUPEE

SILVER

KM#	Date	Year	VG	Fine	VF	XF
405	AH1261	—	10.00	25.00	35.00	50.00
	1263	—	10.00	25.00	35.00	50.00
	1264	—	10.00	25.00	40.00	60.00
	1265	—	10.00	25.00	40.00	60.00
	1269(sic)	—	12.50	30.00	50.00	70.00

MUHAMMAD YUSUF KHAN SADOZAI

AH1267-1272/1851-1856AD

1/2 RUPEE

SILVER

KM#	Date	Year	VG	Fine	VF	XF
	Rev: Mint in circular area.					
406	AH1271	—	35.00	60.00	80.00	100.00
	Rev: Mint in square.					
407	AH1271	—	40.00	70.00	90.00	125.00

TILLA

GOLD

KM#	Date	Year	VG	Fine	VF	XF
409	AH1272	—	—	—	450.00	500.00

SHER ALI

AH1280-1296/1863-1879AD

1/2 RUPEE

SILVER

Obv: ***Amir*** **at top. Rev: Date.**

KM#	Date	Year	VG	Fine	VF	XF
411	AH1281	—	10.00	20.00	35.00	50.00

Obv: ***Amir*** **at bottom, date both sides.**

KM#	Date	Year	VG	Fine	VF	XF
412	AH1281	—	8.00	15.00	25.00	40.00
	1282	—	8.00	15.00	25.00	40.00
	1283	—	8.00	15.00	25.00	40.00
	1284	—	8.00	15.00	25.00	40.00
	1287	—	8.00	15.00	25.00	40.00

Obv: ***Amir*** **at top, legend rearranged.**

KM#	Date	Year	VG	Fine	VF	XF
414	AH1287	—	15.00	30.00	45.00	65.00
	1288	—	10.00	23.00	40.00	55.00
	1290	—	10.00	23.00	40.00	55.00

Obv: Shorter inscription (Ruler's name only).

KM#	Date	Year	VG	Fine	VF	XF
413	AH1292	—	12.50	20.00	30.00	40.00
	1295	—	—	5.00	10.00	16.00

NOTE: Several varieties exist.

NOTE: A tilla dated AH1284 of Sher Ali has been reported.

MUHAMMAD YAQUB

AH1296-1298/1879-1881AD

1/6 RUPEE

SILVER, 11mm, 1.80 g

KM#	Date	Year	VG	Fine	VF	XF
415	AH1297	—	—	—	Rare	—

1/2 RUPEE

SILVER

KM#	Date	Year	VG	Fine	VF	XF
417	AH1296	—	3.00	5.00	7.00	13.50
	1297	—	3.00	5.00	7.00	13.50
	1298	—	3.00	5.00	7.00	13.50

ABDUR RAHMAN
AH1297-1319/1880-1901AD

1/8 RUPEE

SILVER, 13mm

| 418 | AH1307 | — | — | — | Rare | |

1/2 RUPEE

SILVER

419	AH1297	—	3.00	5.00	8.00	14.00
	1298	—	5.00	10.00	15.00	25.00
	1299	—	8.00	14.00	20.00	30.00
	1300	—	2.50	5.00	8.00	14.00
	1301	—	2.50	5.00	8.00	14.00
	1302	—	2.50	5.00	8.00	14.00
	1303	—	1.50	3.00	6.00	12.00
	1304	—	1.50	3.00	6.00	12.00
	1305	—	1.50	3.00	6.00	12.00
	1306	—	1.50	3.00	6.00	12.00
	1307	—	1.50	3.00	6.00	12.00
	1308	—	1.50	3.00	6.00	12.00

NOTE: Many coins of this type KM#419 are found with blundered dates. Such coins are worth the same as normal dates. Mulings of dates exist.

Kabul Mint
Dar al-Mulk (until AH1163)
Dar as-Sultanat (after AH1164)

MAHMUD SHAH
AH1216-1218/1801-1803AD, 1st reign

RUPEE

SILVER, 11.40-11.60 g

448	AH1216	1	11.00	25.00	35.00	45.00
	1217	1	11.00	25.00	35.00	45.00
	1217	2	11.00	25.00	35.00	45.00
	1218	2	11.00	25.00	35.00	45.00

MOHUR

GOLD, 10.80-11.00 g

| 450 | AH1218 | 3 | — | — | 350.00 | 400.00 |

QAISAR SHAH
AH1218/1803AD

RUPEE

SILVER, 11.65 g
As Rebel

| 453 | AH1222 | 1 | 45.00 | 100.00 | 150.00 | 200.00 |

MOHUR

GOLD, 11.00 g

| 455 | AH1222 | — | — | — | Rare | — |

SHAH SHUJA AL-MULK
AH1218-1224/1803-1808AD, 2nd reign

RUPEE

SILVER, 11.50-11.60 g

KM#	Date	Year	VG	Fine	VF	XF
457	AH1218	1	13.50	30.00	40.00	55.00
	1219	2	13.50	30.00	40.00	55.00
	1220	—	13.50	30.00	40.00	55.00
	1222	—	13.50	30.00	40.00	55.00
	1223	—	13.50	30.00	40.00	55.00

MOHUR

GOLD, 10.95 g

| 459 | AH1223 | — | — | — | 350.00 | 400.00 |

MAHMUD SHAH
AH1224-1233/1808-1817AD, 2nd reign

RUPEE

SILVER, 10.75-11.60 g
Rev: Mint name as on previous reign (KM#457).

461	AH1225	2	10.00	20.00	30.00	40.00
	1226	3	10.00	20.00	30.00	40.00
	1227	4	10.00	20.00	30.00	40.00
	122x	6	10.00	20.00	30.00	40.00

Rev: Mint in small circle.

| 462 | AH1228 | 5 | 9.00 | 18.00 | 25.00 | 35.00 |

Rev: Mint in toughra form.

463	AH(122)6	—	10.00	20.00	30.00	40.00
	1231	8	10.00	20.00	30.00	40.00
	1233	—	10.00	20.00	30.00	40.00

2 RUPEES

SILVER, 23.00-23.20 g

| 464 | AH1225 | 1 | 65.00 | 115.00 | 150.00 | 200.00 |

MOHUR

GOLD, 10.90-11.00 g

KM#	Date	Year	VG	Fine	VF	XF
465	AH1224	2	—	—	300.00	375.00
	122x	8	—	—	300.00	375.00

AYYUB SHAH
AH1233-1245/1817-1826AD

RUPEE

SILVER, 10.70-11.40 g

468	AH1234	1	12.50	30.00	40.00	50.00
	1234	2	12.50	30.00	40.00	50.00
	1235	2	12.50	30.00	40.00	50.00
	1236	2	12.50	30.00	40.00	50.00
	1237	3	12.50	30.00	40.00	50.00
	1238	3	12.50	30.00	40.00	50.00

NOTE: Various arrangements of obverse legend.

ANONYMOUS COINAGE

RUPEE

SILVER, 11.00-11.40 g
Obv: Kalima

| 473 | AH123x | — | 15.00 | 35.00 | 50.00 | 70.00 |

DOST MUHAMMAD
AH1239-1255/1824-1839AD, 1st reign
In the name of Mahmud Shah Durrani

RUPEE

SILVER

| 475 | AH1239 | — | 20.00 | 50.00 | 75.00 | 100.00 |

Anonymous, with title Sultan al-Zaman

| 476 | AH1239 | — | 20.00 | 50.00 | 75.00 | 100.00 |

Anonymous, with title Sahib al-Zaman

Rev: Mint in toughra form.

477	AH1240	1	8.50	12.50	20.00	30.00
	1241	2	8.50	12.50	20.00	30.00

Obv: Cartouche in center.

478	AH1241	—	6.00	10.00	15.00	22.50
	1242	—	6.00	10.00	15.00	22.50
	1243	—	6.00	10.00	15.00	22.50
	1244	—	6.00	10.00	15.00	22.50

AFGHANISTAN 73

AFGHANISTAN 74

Rev: Mint in ordinary form.

KM#	Date	Year	VG	Fine	VF	XF
479	AH1244	—	8.00	15.00	22.50	35.00
	1245	—	8.00	15.00	22.50	35.00

In the name of his father, Payinda Khan.

480.1	AH1245	—	5.00	8.00	12.00	20.00
	1246	—	5.00	8.00	12.00	20.00
	1247	—	5.00	8.00	12.00	20.00
	1248	—	5.00	8.00	12.00	20.00
	1249	—	5.00	8.00	12.00	20.00
	1250	—	5.00	8.00	12.00	20.00

NOTE: Various arrangements of obverse couplet and various borders on reverse.

480.2	AH1247	—	5.00	8.00	12.00	20.00
	1248	—	5.00	8.00	12.00	20.00

In his own name

481	AH1250	—	4.50	8.00	12.00	20.00
	1251	—	4.50	8.00	12.00	20.00
	1252	—	4.50	8.00	12.00	20.00
	1253	—	4.50	8.00	12.00	20.00
	1254	—	4.50	8.00	12.00	20.00
	1255	—	4.50	8.00	12.00	20.00

SHAH SHUJA AL-MULK
AH1255-1258/1839-1842AD, 3rd reign

RUPEE

SILVER, 11.50 g
Obv: Short inscription, title *Sultan*. **Broad flan.**

482	AH1255	—	—	—	Rare	—

9.20 g
Obv: Long inscription.

483	AH1255	—	10.00	18.00	25.00	35.00

9.20-9.50 g
Obv: Short inscription, title *Sultan*.

KM#	Date	Year	VG	Fine	VF	XF
484.1	AH1255	—	—	6.50	10.00	17.00
	1256	—	—	6.50	10.00	17.00
	1257	—	6.00	12.00	18.00	28.00
	1258	—	6.00	12.00	18.00	28.00

NOTE: Varieties exist, some on broad planchets.

Obv: *Dur-e-Duran* **above** *Sultan*.

484.2	AH1255	—	6.00	12.00	18.00	28.00

Anonymous in name of Sahib al-Zaman

485	AH1257	—	12.50	25.00	36.00	50.00

In the name of Shah Zaman

486	AH1258	—	16.00	35.00	50.00	70.00

MOHUR

GOLD, 10.70-10.80 g

487	AH1255	—	—	—	285.00	350.00
	1258	—	—	—	285.00	350.00

FATH JANG
AH1258/1842AD

RUPEE

SILVER, 9.30-9.40 g
Obv: Couplet, name *Fath Jung* **at top.**

488.1	AH1258	—	18.00	38.00	60.00	80.00

Obv: Couplet, name *Fath Jung* **in center.**

488.2	AH1258	—	25.00	50.00	70.00	100.00

Obv: Name only w/title *Durr-i Durran*.

488.3	AH1258	—	18.00	38.00	60.00	80.00

Obv: Name only w/title *Padshah-i Ghazi*.

KM#	Date	Year	VG	Fine	VF	XF
488.4	AH1258	—	18.00	38.00	60.00	80.00

SHAHPUR SHAH
AH1258/1842AD

RUPEE

SILVER, 9.40 g

489	AH1258	—	35.00	65.00	100.00	150.00

DOST MUHAMMAD
AH1258-1280/1842-1863AD, 2nd reign
Anonymous

RUPEE

SILVER
Obv: Kalimah

493	AH1258	—	9.00	16.00	25.00	35.00

In his own name

Obv: Long couplet.

496	AH1259	—	13.50	30.00	40.00	55.00

Obv: Couplet ending *Khaliq-i-Akbar*
Many varieties

497	AH1262	—	7.00	11.00	15.00	25.00
	1263	—	4.50	7.00	10.00	18.00
	1264	—	—	—	—	—
	1265	—	—	5.00	8.00	16.00
	1266	—	—	5.00	8.00	16.00
	1267	—	—	5.00	8.00	16.00
	1268	—	4.50	7.00	12.00	20.00
	1269	—	4.50	7.00	10.00	18.00
	1270	—	—	5.00	8.00	16.00
	1271	—	—	5.00	8.00	16.00
	1272	—	—	5.00	8.00	16.00
	1273	—	—	5.00	8.00	16.00
	1274	—	—	5.00	8.00	16.00
	1275	—	—	5.00	8.00	16.00
	1276	—	4.00	7.00	10.00	18.00
	1277	—	4.00	7.00	10.00	18.00
	1278	—	4.00	7.00	10.00	18.00
	1279	—	4.00	7.00	10.00	18.00
	1280	—	12.50	20.00	30.00	40.00

NOTE: Mulings exist with different dates on obverse and reverse.

TILLA
GOLD

499	AH1269	—	—	—	235.00	300.00

SHER ALI
AH1280-1283/1863-1866AD, 1st reign

AFGHANISTAN 75

RUPEE

SILVER
Obv: New couplet, *Bi-Valayi Amir*.

KM#	Date	Year	VG	Fine	VF	XF
502	AH1280	—	—	—	Rare	—

Obv: Couplet starting *Za Aini Marhamat*. . .

503	AH1280	—	5.00	9.00	13.00	20.00
	1281	—	5.00	9.00	13.00	20.00
	1282	—	5.00	9.00	13.00	20.00

NOTE: Two varieties of obv. exist.

Anonymous, with title Sahib al-Zaman

504	AH1282	—	12.50	25.00	35.00	50.00

MUHAMMAD AFZAL
AH1283-1284/1866-1867AD

RUPEE

SILVER

507	AH1283	—	9.00	15.00	20.00	30.00
	1284	—	9.00	15.00	20.00	30.00

NOTE: 2 varieties are known dated AH1283.

MUHAMMAD A'ZAM
AH1283-1285/1866-1868AD

RUPEE

SILVER

508.1	AH1284	—	10.00	15.00	20.00	30.00
	1285	—	10.00	15.00	20.00	30.00

508.2	AH1284	—	15.00	30.00	45.00	60.00

509	AH1285	—	13.00	25.00	35.00	45.00

SHER ALI
AH1285-1296/1868-1879AD, 2nd reign

1/6 RUPEE

SILVER, 1.50 g

KM#	Date	Year	VG	Fine	VF	XF
511	AH1287	—	25.00	50.00	65.00	85.00

1/2 RUPEE

NOTE: KM#512, which was reported for AH1288, 1292, 1293 and 1294, is a misreading of the Qandahar Mint.

SILVER
Large, thin planchet; fine engraving.

513	AH1292	—	—	5.00	10.00	18.00

Small, thick planchet; coarse engraving.

514	AH1295	—	—	4.00	8.00	15.00

RUPEE

SILVER
Obv: Couplet starting *Za Iltifat-i*. . .

516	AH1285	—	7.50	12.50	20.00	30.00

Obv: 3-stem toughra.

517	AH1285	—	6.00	10.00	15.00	25.00
	1286	—	3.00	6.00	10.00	20.00
	1286/87	—	6.00	10.00	15.00	25.00
	1287	—	6.00	10.00	15.00	25.00

Obv: 5-stem toughra.

518	AH1286	—	25.00	40.00	60.00	100.00

519	AH1287	—	3.50	6.00	10.00	18.00
	1288	—	—	5.00	7.50	15.00
	1289	—	—	5.00	7.50	15.00
	1290	—	—	5.00	7.50	15.00
	1291	—	—	5.00	7.50	15.00
	1292	—	—	5.00	7.50	15.00
	1293	—	—	5.00	7.50	15.00
	1294	—	—	5.00	7.50	15.00
	1295	—	—	5.00	7.50	15.00
	1295 dated 1296 on rev.					
		—	—	5.00	7.50	15.00
	1296 date on both sides					
		—	5.00	7.50	12.50	20.00

NOTE: Other examples bearing different obverse and reverse dates exist.

Fine style

KM#	Date	Year	VG	Fine	VF	XF
520	AH1292	—	4.50	9.00	15.00	25.00
	1293	—	4.50	9.00	15.00	25.00

Coarse style

521	AH1293	—	3.50	6.00	10.00	18.00
	1294	—	3.50	6.00	10.00	18.00
	1295	—	3.50	6.00	10.00	18.00

TILLA

GOLD

524	AH1294	—	—	180.00	225.00	275.00
	1295	—	—	165.00	200.00	250.00
	1296	—	—	165.00	200.00	250.00

MOHUR

GOLD

525	AH1288	—	—	225.00	300.00	400.00

MUHAMMAD YAQUB
AH1296-1297/1879-1880AD

1/3 RUPEE

SILVER

531	AH1296	—	25.00	55.00	75.00	100.00

RUPEE

SILVER

533	AH1296	—	—	5.00	8.00	16.00
	1297	—	6.00	12.50	20.00	30.00

WALI MUHAMMAD
AH1297/1880AD

RUPEE

SILVER

538	AH1297	—	10.00	16.00	25.00	40.00

ABDUR RAHMAN
AH1297-1319/1880-1901AD

AFGHANISTAN 76

1/3 RUPEE

SILVER, 15mm

KM#	Date	Year	VG	Fine	VF	XF
541	AH1298	—	30.00	60.00	75.00	100.00

RUPEE

SILVER
Obv: Rudimentary toughra.

543	AH1297	—	25.00	45.00	60.00	85.00

Obv: Name of ruler in fancy border.

A544	AH1297	—	20.00	40.00	55.00	75.00

Obv: Ornate toughra.

B544	AH1298	—	30.00	60.00	80.00	120.00

Obv: Name of ruler in plain border.

544	AH1297	—	4.00	6.00	10.00	18.00
	1298	—	7.50	10.00	13.00	22.50
	1299	—	12.50	20.00	30.00	45.00
	1300	—	12.50	18.00	25.00	35.00
	1301	—	3.00	6.00	10.00	18.00
	1302	—	3.50	6.00	10.00	18.00
	1303	—	—	4.00	7.00	15.00
	1304	—	—	4.00	7.00	15.00
	1305	—	—	2.75	6.00	15.00
	1306	—	—	4.00	7.00	15.00
	1307	—	—	4.00	7.00	15.00
	1308	—	7.00	10.00	15.00	25.00

NOTE: Obverses are often muled with reverses bearing a different date. For machine struck coins dated AH1303/4 and 1304/4 see KM#862.
NOTE: The year AH1297 has been observed struck over an 1876 British India 1/4 rupee, probably a mint sport.

NAZARANA RUPEE

SILVER
Similar to 1 Rupee, KM#544 but broader flan.

545	AH1303	—	25.00	50.00	75.00	100.00

MUHAMMAD ISHAQ
AH1305-1306/1889AD

RUPEE

SILVER
Struck at Balkh, but inscribed *Kabul*.
W/o title of *Khan*.

KM#	Date	Year	VG	Fine	VF	XF
548	AH1305	—	—	Reported, not confirmed		
	1306	—	30.00	55.00	75.00	100.00

Title *Khan* added.

549	AH1305	—	35.00	70.00	100.00	125.00
	1306	—	35.00	70.00	100.00	125.00

Kashmir Mint
MAHMUD SHAH
AH1216-1218/1801-1803AD, 1st reign
AH1223-1233/1808-1818AD, 2nd reign

FRACTIONAL FALUS

COPPER, 3.80-4.40 g
First Reign

KM#	Date	Year	Good	VG	Fine	VF
580	AH1217	2	3.00	4.00	5.00	7.00

20mm, 7.20-7.80 g
Second Reign
Obv: King's name in toughra style.

581	AH—	1	3.00	4.00	5.00	7.00

FALUS

COPPER, 25.5mm, 10.20 g
First Reign

583	AH1216	1	4.00	7.00	10.00	16.00

20mm, 9.40-9.80 g
Second Reign
Obv: Toughra style. Rev: Legend.

584	AH—	1	3.00	4.50	7.00	10.00
	1229	—	3.00	4.50	7.00	10.00
	1230	6	3.00	4.50	7.00	10.00

10.00 g
Rev: Swords and plume.

585	AH1233	11	4.00	7.00	10.00	15.00

1/4 RUPEE

SILVER, 2.50-2.60 g

KM#	Date	Year	VG	Fine	VF	XF
586	AH1217	2	18.50	40.00	60.00	80.00

RUPEE

SILVER, 10.80-11.00 g
1st Reign

588	AH1216	1	8.50	15.00	25.00	35.00
	1217	2	8.50	15.00	25.00	35.00
	1218	3	8.50	15.00	25.00	35.00

KM#	Date	Year	VG	Fine	VF	XF
589	AH1218	3	10.00	20.00	30.00	45.00

591	AH1228	6	4.50	9.00	14.00	20.00
	1229	6	4.50	9.00	14.00	20.00
	1229	7	4.50	9.00	14.00	20.00
	1230	7	4.50	9.00	14.00	20.00
	1230	8	4.50	9.00	14.00	20.00
	1230	10	4.50	9.00	14.00	20.00
	1232	10	4.50	9.00	14.00	20.00
	1233	10	6.50	12.50	20.00	30.00
	1233	11	6.50	12.50	20.00	30.00

The sequence of regnal years at Kashmir is very confused.

SHAH SHUJA AL-MULK
AH1218-1223/1803-1808AD, 2nd reign

FALUS

COPPER, 7.40-9.00 g
Rev: Sword.

KM#	Date	Year	Good	VG	Fine	VF
594	AH1218	1	2.50	3.50	5.00	7.00
	—	2	3.00	4.50	6.50	9.00

Rev: Two swords.

A595	AH1219	—	5.00	8.50	15.00	22.50

Rev: Crossed swords.

595	AH(12)19	—	3.00	4.00	6.00	8.50
596	AH1220	3	3.00	4.00	6.00	8.50

Rev: Sword.

597	AH1221	4	3.50	5.00	7.50	10.00

Reign in Kashmir
AH1227-1228/1812-1813AD

RUPEE

SILVER, 10.80-11.20 g

KM#	Date	Year	VG	Fine	VF	XF
598	AH1218	1	—	6.00	10.00	17.50
	1219	2	—	6.00	10.00	17.50
	1220	3	—	6.00	10.00	17.50
	1221	4	—	6.00	10.00	17.50
	1222	5	—	6.00	10.00	17.50
	1223	6	4.50	7.50	12.50	20.00

QAISAR SHAH
AH1222-1223/1807-1808AD

RUPEE

SILVER, 11.00-11.20 g

KM#	Date	Year	VG	Fine	VF	XF
600	AH1222	1	20.00	40.00	60.00	80.00
	1223	1	20.00	40.00	60.00	80.00
	1223	2	20.00	40.00	60.00	80.00

ATA MUHAMMAD BAMIZAI KHAN
Rebel governor of Kashmir
AH1223-1228/1808-1813AD

In the name of Shah Nur al-Din, the patron 'saint' of Kashmir.

FALUS

COPPER, 16.5mm, 7.50 g

KM#	Date	Year	Good	VG	Fine	VF
601	AH1225	3	8.00	15.00	22.50	35.00
	1228	—	8.00	15.00	22.50	35.00

RUPEE

SILVER, 10.70-11.10 g

KM#	Date	Year	VG	Fine	VF	XF
603	AH1223	1	6.50	12.50	20.00	30.00
	1224	1	6.50	12.50	20.00	30.00
	1224	2	6.50	12.50	20.00	30.00
	1225	2	6.50	12.50	20.00	30.00
	1225	3	6.50	12.50	20.00	30.00
	1226	4	6.50	12.50	20.00	30.00
	1227	4	6.50	12.50	20.00	30.00
	1227	5	6.50	12.50	20.00	30.00
	1228	5	6.50	12.50	20.00	30.00

HEAVY RUPEE
(1-1/4 Rupee)

SILVER, 14.50 g

604	AH1223	1	—	200.00	250.00	300.00

2 MOHURS

GOLD, 21.60-21.80 g

607	AH1225	2	—	—	5000.	6500.

608	AH1225	3	—	—	Rare	

MUHAMMAD A'ZIM
Governor for Ayub Shah
AH1228-1234/1813-1819AD

FALUS

COPPER, 7.50 g

KM#	Date	Year	Good	VG	Fine	VF
609	AH1228	1	5.00	9.00	16.00	25.00

AYYUB SHAH
AH1233-1245/1818-1829AD

FALUS

COPPER, 7.00-8.00 g

610	AH1233	—	7.00	12.00	18.00	27.50

RUPEE

SILVER, 11.00-11.20 g
Rev: Mint name and regnal year.

KM#	Date	Year	VG	Fine	VF	XF
613	AH1234	1	12.50	25.00	40.00	60.00

Rev: Mint, regnal year and *Julus* formula.

614	AH1234	2	15.00	30.00	50.00	75.00

Kashmir fell to the Sikhs in AH1234 (1819AD), ending the Durrani dominion in India.

Ladakh Mint
Mint name is written *Botan* on the coins.

MAHMUD SHAH
AH1216-1218/1801-1803AD
AH1223-1233/1808-1818AD

In the name of Aqabat Mahmud Khan

TIMASHA

SILVER

616	ND	—	20.00	45.00	60.00	80.00

In the name of Mahmud Shah

Rev: Legend.

617	ND	—	10.00	14.00	20.00	30.00

Rev: Legend and *Katar*.

KM#	Date	Year	VG	Fine	VF	XF
618	ND	—	10.00	14.00	20.00	30.00

Mashhad Mint
Mashhad, entitled Muqaddas (holy), was the chief city of Iranian Khorasan. From 1161/1748 until 1218/1803, it was the capital of the Afsharid principality, which remained under nominal Durrani suzerainty from 1163/1750 onwards. Coins were struck in the name of Durrani rulers in 1163, 1168-1186, 1198-1218. Issues in the name of Iranian rulers will be listed in a future edition of this catalog under Iran.

MAHMUD SHAH
AH1216-1218/1801-1803AD, First Reign

RUPEE
SILVER, 11.00-11.50 g

G640	AH1218	—	60.00	125.00	160.00	200.00

In AH1218/1803AD, Mashhad was seized by Fath Ali Shah and permanently annexed to Iran.

Multan Mint
Known as *Dar al-Aman*, ('Abode of Security'), Multan was annexed by Ahmad Shah in AH1165/1752AD, and held under Afghan rule until lost to the Sikhs in AH1233/1818AD, except for an interval of Maratha control in AH1173/1759AD and Sikh control from AH1185-1194/1771-1780AD.

MAHMUD SHAH
AH1216-1218/1801-1803AD, 1st reign

RUPEE

SILVER, 11.50-11.60 g

668	AH1216	1	20.00	40.00	60.00	85.00
	1218	1	20.00	40.00	60.00	85.00

SHAH SHUJA AL-MULK
AH1218-1224/1803-1808AD, 2nd reign

RUPEE

SILVER, 20.5mm, 11.40-11.60 g

673	AH1218	1	20.00	40.00	60.00	85.00
	1219	1	20.00	40.00	60.00	85.00

MOHUR

GOLD, 10.90-11.00 g

675	AH1218	1	—	—	Rare	
	1224	8	—	—	Rare	

NOTE: Multan fell to the Sikhs in AH1233 (1818AD).

MAHMUD SHAH
AH1224-1233/1808-1817AD, 2nd reign

FALUS

COPPER, 11.60-12.80 g

KM#	Date	Year	Good	VG	Fine	VF
677	AH1226	1	3.75	7.50	10.00	16.50
	1227	1	3.75	7.50	10.00	16.50
	1227	2	3.75	7.50	10.00	16.50
	1228	3	3.75	7.50	10.00	16.50
	1228	5	3.75	7.50	10.00	16.50
	1230	7	3.75	7.50	10.00	16.50
	1231	7	3.75	7.50	10.00	16.50
	1235	—	3.75	7.50	10.00	16.50
	1253	—	3.75	7.50	10.00	16.50
	1254	—	3.75	7.50	10.00	16.50

AFGHANISTAN

KM#	Date	Year	Good	VG	Fine	VF
677	1257	—	3.75	7.50	10.00	16.50
	1263	—	3.75	7.50	10.00	16.50
	1264	—	3.75	7.50	10.00	16.50
	1270	—	3.75	7.50	10.00	16.50

NOTE: Issues dated after AH1233 are posthumous issues struck by the Sikhs.

AYYUB SHAH
AH1233-1245/1817-1826AD

RUPEE

SILVER, 11.20-11.40 g
Obv: Kalima, mint and date.

680	AH1239	—	—	—	Rare	—

Peshawar Mint

Peshawar passed to Ahmad Shah after the death of Nadir Shah Afshar, who had seized it from the Mughals in AH1151/1738AD. It was lost to the Sikhs in AH1250/1834AD. Although the winter capital of the Durranis, it was never granted an honorific epithet.

MAHMUD SHAH
AH1216-1218/1801-1803AD, 1st reign

RUPEE

SILVER, 11.40-11.60 g
Rev: Mint name w/Julus formula.

KM#	Date	Year	VG	Fine	VF	XF
718	AH1216	1	10.00	13.50	20.00	30.00

Rev: Mint name.

719	AH1217	2	10.00	13.50	20.00	30.00
	1218	3	10.00	13.50	20.00	30.00

SHAH SHUJA AL-MULK
AH1218-1224/1803-1808AD, 2nd reign

1/10 RUPEE

SILVER, 1.00 g
As local ruler at Peshawar

720	AH1227	7	—	—	Rare	—

RUPEE

SILVER, 11.40-11.60 g

722	AH1218	1	7.00	12.00	18.00	28.00
	1219	2	7.00	12.00	18.00	28.00
	1220	3	7.00	12.00	18.00	28.00
	1221	4	7.00	12.00	18.00	28.00
	1222	5	7.00	12.00	18.00	28.00
	1223	6	7.00	12.00	18.00	28.00

As local ruler at Peshawar

723	AH1227	1	40.00	70.00	100.00	130.00

Shah Shuja briefly at Peshawar in AH1233/1818AD.

KM#	Date	Year	VG	Fine	VF	XF
724	AH1233	1	40.00	70.00	100.00	130.00

NOTE: This coin may be distinguished from KM#722 and 723 by the octagon and calligraphy of the rev. and by the date.

MAHMUD SHAH
AH1224-1233/1808-1817AD, 2nd reign

FALUS

COPPER, 11.40 g

726	AH123x	—	—	—	Rare	—

RUPEE

SILVER, 10.60-11.50 g
Obv: Linear legends.

727.1	AH1225	1	—	11.00	18.00	26.00
	1226	2	—	11.00	18.00	26.00
	1227	2	—	11.00	18.00	26.00
	—	3	—	11.00	18.00	26.00

727.2	AH1227	3	—	11.00	18.00	26.00
	1227	4	—	11.00	18.00	26.00
	1228	4	—	11.00	18.00	26.00
	1228	5	—	11.00	18.00	26.00
	1229	5	—	11.00	18.00	26.00
	1229	6	—	11.00	18.00	26.00
	1230	6	—	11.00	18.00	26.00
	1230	7	—	11.00	18.00	26.00
	1231	7	—	11.00	18.00	26.00
	1231	8	—	11.00	18.00	26.00

Obv: Circular legend around central cartouche.

728	AH1232	8	10.00	20.00	30.00	40.00
	1232	9	10.00	20.00	30.00	40.00
	1233	9	10.00	20.00	30.00	40.00
	1233	10	10.00	20.00	30.00	40.00

AYYUB SHAH
AH1233-1245/1817-1826AD

FALUS

COPPER, 10.40-12.20 g

KM#	Date	Year	Good	VG	Fine	VF
730	AH1236	4	6.00	10.00	17.50	30.00
	1237	—	5.00	8.50	15.00	25.00
	1238	6	5.00	8.50	15.00	25.00
	124-	—	6.50	11.00	18.00	32.50

RUPEE

SILVER, 10.40-10.60 g
Obv: Ruler's name in fancy diamond.

KM#	Date	Year	VG	Fine	VF	XF
732	AH1233	1	23.00	45.00	65.00	85.00

Obv: Couplet in 3 lines.

733	AH1233	1	8.00	13.00	20.00	30.00
	1233	2	8.00	13.00	20.00	30.00
	1234	2	8.00	13.00	20.00	30.00
	(123)4	6	8.00	13.00	20.00	30.00
	1235	2	8.00	13.00	20.00	30.00
	1235	3	8.00	13.00	20.00	30.00
	1236	3	8.00	13.00	20.00	30.00
	1236	4	8.00	13.00	20.00	30.00
	1237	4	8.00	13.00	20.00	30.00
	1237	5	8.00	13.00	20.00	30.00
	1238	5	8.00	13.00	20.00	30.00
	1238	6	8.00	13.00	20.00	30.00
	1239	6	8.00	13.00	20.00	30.00
	1239	7	8.00	13.00	20.00	30.00
	1240	6	8.00	13.00	20.00	30.00
	1240	7	8.00	13.00	20.00	30.00
	1240	8	8.00	13.00	20.00	30.00
	1241	7	8.00	13.00	20.00	30.00
	1242	9	8.00	13.00	20.00	30.00
	1243	9	8.00	13.00	20.00	30.00
	1243	10	8.00	13.00	20.00	30.00
	1244	11	8.00	13.00	20.00	30.00
	1245	11	5.00	8.50	14.00	20.00

Obv: Name in foliated diamond.

734	AH124x	12	25.00	45.00	65.00	85.00

MOHUR

GOLD, 21.5mm, 10.50-10.60 g

735	AH—	6	—	—	325.00	375.00
	—	7	—	—	325.00	375.00

DOST MUHAMMAD
AH1239-1255/1824-1839AD, 1st reign

RUPEE

SILVER, 23mm, 10.40 g

738	AH1246	—	22.50	50.00	75.00	120.00
	1249	—	22.50	50.00	75.00	120.00

SULTAN MUHAMMAD
AH1247-1250/1831-1834AD at Peshawar
Anonymous couplet type.

RUPEE

SILVER

KM#	Date	Year	VG	Fine	VF	XF
739	AH1247	—	12.50	25.00	35.00	60.00
	1248	—	12.50	25.00	35.00	60.00
	1249	—	12.50	25.00	35.00	60.00

NOTE: Peshawar fell to the Sikhs in AH1250 (AD1834). For later issues, see India, Sikhs.

Qandahar Mint

Issues of this mint are listed together with those of Ahmadshahi, which was a name of Qandahar granted in honor of Ahmad Shah, founder of the Durrani Kingdom.

MILLED COINAGE
MONETARY SYSTEM

10 Dinar = 1 Paisa
5 Paisa = 1 Shahi
2 Shahi = 1 Sanar
2 Sanar = 1 Abbasi
1-1/2 Abbasi = 1 Qiran
2 Qiran = 1 Kabuli Rupee

PAISA

BRONZE, 24-25mm

KM#	Date	Mintage	VG	Fine	VF	XF
800	AH1309	—	25.00	40.00	120.00	200.00

20mm dies on 25mm planchet

| 801 | AH1309 | — | 20.00 | 30.00 | 50.00 | 70.00 |

BRONZE or BRASS, 20mm

802	AH1309	—	2.50	5.00	7.50	20.00
	1312	—	2.00	4.00	6.50	15.00
	1313	—	2.50	5.00	7.50	20.00
	1314	—	2.00	4.00	6.50	15.00
	1316	—	3.00	5.00	7.50	20.00
	1317	—	4.00	6.00	10.00	30.00

NOTE: Coins dated AH1313 and 1317 are known in two varieties. 3 varieties are known for AH1314.

| 827 | AH1317 | — | 3.50 | 6.00 | 12.00 | 35.00 |

NOTE: 2 varieties are known.

Mule. Obv: KM#827. Rev: KM#802.

| 828 | AH1317 | — | 10.00 | 15.00 | 30.00 | 50.00 |

| 848 | AH1329 | — | 6.00 | 12.00 | 20.00 | 30.00 |
| | 1329/17 on KM#828 obverse die | | 8.00 | 15.00 | 30.00 | 50.00 |

21mm

849	AH1329	—	2.00	4.00	7.50	15.00
	1331	—	2.00	4.00	7.50	15.00
	1332	—	2.50	4.75	9.00	16.00
	1334	—	3.00	6.00	11.50	20.00

Thick flan, reduced size: 19mm

KM#	Date	Mintage	VG	Fine	VF	XF
854	AH1336	—	2.50	5.00	10.00	25.00

Thin flan

| 855 | AH1336 | — | 1.75 | 3.00 | 5.00 | 12.50 |
| | 1337 | — | 1.75 | 3.00 | 5.00 | 12.50 |

Thick flan, 20mm

| 857 | AH1337 | — | 6.50 | 10.00 | 20.00 | 35.00 |

Thin flan, 19-20mm

KM#	Date	Year	VG	Fine	VF	XF
858	AH1337	—	3.00	6.00	10.00	20.00
	SH1298	(1919)	4.50	8.00	15.00	32.50

NOTE: 3 varieties are known dated AH1337.

880	SH1299	(1920)	1.75	4.00	8.00	12.50
	1300	(1921)	2.50	5.00	9.00	15.00
	1301	(1922)	2.50	5.00	9.00	15.00
	1302	(1923)	1.75	4.00	8.00	12.50
	1303	(1924)	1.75	4.00	8.00	12.50

NOTE: 2 varieties are known dated AH1301.

SHAHI
(5 Paisa)

COPPER or BRASS

KM#	Date	Mintage	VG	Fine	VF	XF
803	AH1309	—	15.00	25.00	55.00	125.00

Thick flan

| 859 | AH1337 | — | 9.00 | 16.00 | 25.00 | 55.00 |

Thin flan

| 860 | AH1337 | — | 8.00 | 15.00 | 22.50 | 40.00 |

100 DINAR
(10 Paisa)

COPPER

KM#	Date	Mintage	VG	Fine	VF	XF
809	AH1311	—	125.00	200.00	350.00	600.00

SANAR
(10 Paisa)

1.5500 g, .500 SILVER, .0249 oz ASW
Obv: Date in loop of toughra.

| 823 | AH1315 | — | 7.00 | 10.00 | 20.00 | 40.00 |
| | ND | — | 8.50 | 13.00 | 25.00 | 45.00 |

Rev: Date below mosque.

| 824 | AH1315 | — | 9.00 | 14.00 | 25.00 | 45.00 |
| | ND | — | 8.50 | 13.50 | 25.00 | 45.00 |

846	AH1325	—	10.00	20.00	35.00	60.00
	1326	—	5.00	7.50	12.50	20.00
	1328	—	5.00	7.50	12.50	20.00
	1329	—	5.75	8.50	14.00	25.00

850	AH1329	—	4.00	7.00	11.00	16.00
	1330	—	3.00	6.00	10.00	15.00
	1331	—	3.00	6.00	10.00	15.00
	1333	—	3.00	5.00	9.00	14.00
	1335	—	3.00	5.00	9.00	14.00
	1337	—	3.00	6.00	10.00	15.00

NOTE: Coins dated AH1333 and 1337 are known in 2 varieties.

COPPER or BRASS
Thick flan

| 861 | AH1337 | — | 10.00 | 17.50 | 30.00 | 50.00 |

Thin flan

| 862 | AH1337 | — | 9.00 | 14.00 | 20.00 | 35.00 |

10 PAISA

COPPER

| 901 | AH1348 | — | 5.00 | 9.00 | 17.50 | 30.00 |

3 SHAHI
(15 Paisa)

COPPER, 32-33mm
Rev: W/o Al-Ghazi.

KM#	Date	Year	VG	Fine	VF	XF
863	AH1337	—	3.00	7.00	14.00	20.00

NOTE: 3 varieties are known.

AFGHANISTAN 80

Obv: *Shamsi, w/o Al Ghazi.*

KM#	Date	Year	VG	Fine	VF	XF
869	SH1298	(1919)	2.00	4.00	8.00	13.00

NOTE: *Shamsi* (= Solar) is an additional word written on some of the coins dated SH1298, to show the change from a lunar to solar calendar.

Obv: *Al-Ghazi, w/o Shamsi.*
Rev: Mosque in 8-pointed star.

870	SH1298	(1919)	3.00	5.00	8.00	13.00
	1299	(1920)	—	Reported, not confirmed		
	1300	(1921)	—	Reported, not confirmed		

Thick flan, 11.5 g.
Obv: *Al-Ghazi, Shamsi.*

871.1	SH1298	(1919)	10.00	14.00	18.00	24.00

Thin flan, 9 g.

871.2	SH1298	(1919)	2.00	4.00	8.00	14.00

Obv: *Shamsi.*
Rev: Mosque in 7-pointed star.

872	SH1298	(1919)	2.00	4.00	8.00	14.00

Obv: *W/o Shamsi.*

881	SH1298	(1919)	4.00	15.00	22.00	25.00
	1299	(1920)	2.00	4.00	7.00	15.00
	1300	(1921)	2.00	4.00	7.00	15.00
	1302	(1923)	2.00	4.00	7.00	15.00

NOTE: 4 varieties for date 1299 and 3 varieties for date 1300 are known.

Obv. and rev: 8 stars around perimeter.

891	SH1300	(1921)	—	—	—	—

BRASS

892	SH1300	(1921)	4.00	8.00	12.00	20.00

COPPER

893	SH1300	(1921)	1.25	3.00	5.00	10.00
	1301 (2 vars.)					
		(1922)	1.25	3.00	5.00	10.00
	1303	(1924)	1.25	3.00	5.00	10.00

ABBASI
(20 Paisa)
3.1100 g, .500 SILVER, .0499 oz ASW
Rev: Date below mosque.

KM#	Date	Mintage	VG	Fine	VF	XF
811	AH1313	—	10.00	17.50	27.50	40.00

Rev: New style mosque.

816	AH1314	—	4.00	8.00	15.00	25.00

837	AH1320	—	12.50	22.50	35.00	50.00
845	AH1324	—	7.00	12.00	18.00	30.00
	1328	—	7.00	12.00	18.00	30.00

851	AH1329	—	6.00	11.00	16.00	22.50
	1330	—	4.00	7.00	10.00	15.00
	1333	—	3.00	6.00	9.00	14.00
	1334	—	3.00	6.00	9.00	14.00
	1335	—	3.00	5.00	8.00	13.00
	1337	—	3.00	5.00	8.00	13.00

BILLON

KM#	Date	Year	VG	Fine	VF	XF
874	SH1298	(1919)	50.00	75.00	100.00	140.00

25mm

882	SH1299	(1920)	15.00	30.00	50.00	75.00

COPPER or BILLON

883	SH1299	(1920)	2.00	5.00	10.00	20.00
	1300	(1921)	2.00	5.00	10.00	20.00
	1301	(1922)	2.00	5.00	10.00	20.00
	1302	(1923)	2.00	5.00	10.00	20.00
	1303	(1924)	2.00	5.00	10.00	20.00

NOTE: Varieties exist.

20 PAISA

BRONZE or BRASS

KM#	Date	Mintage	VG	Fine	VF	XF
895	AH1347	—	3.00	5.00	7.50	17.50

QIRAN
(1/2 Rupee)

4.6500 g, .500 SILVER, .0747 oz ASW
Rev: Star above mosque.

804	AH1308	—	5.00	7.50	10.00	20.00
	1309	—	5.00	8.00	12.00	25.00
	1310	—	5.00	8.00	12.00	25.00

Rev: *Kabul* **above mosque.**

KM#	Date	Mintage	VG	Fine	VF	XF
812	AH1313	—	6.00	8.50	12.50	27.50

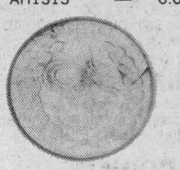

Rev: *Yak Mesqhal* **above mosque.**

817	AH1314	—	7.50	13.50	20.00	55.00

NOTE: The half rupee dated AH1314 bears the denomination of 1 Qiran; all others have Half Rupee.

Rev: Crossed swords and cannons below mosque.

825	AH1316	—	4.50	8.50	15.00	30.00
	1317	—	Reported, not confirmed			
	1318	—	Reported, not confirmed			

Rev: Crossed cannons below mosque.

831	AH1319	—	14.00	25.00	40.00	60.00

Obv: Date below toughra.

838	AH1320	—	8.00	14.00	22.50	35.00
	1325	—	7.00	11.00	18.00	27.50

Obv: Date at upper right of toughra.

841	AH1321	—	7.00	10.00	14.00	22.50

Rev: Dated AH1320

844	AH1323	—	3.00	6.00	9.00	17.00
	1324	—	4.00	6.00	9.00	15.00
	1326	—	4.00	6.00	9.00	15.00
	1327	—	4.00	6.00	9.00	15.00
	1328	—	4.00	6.00	9.00	15.00
	1329	—	4.00	6.00	10.00	18.00

NOTE: 2 varieties are known.

4.6000 g, .500 SILVER, .0739 oz ASW

852	AH1329	—	3.50	5.50	8.50	12.50
	1333	—	3.50	5.50	8.50	12.50
	1334	—	4.50	7.50	12.50	20.00
	1335	—	4.50	7.50	12.50	20.00
	1337	—	3.50	5.50	8.50	12.50

5.00 g
Obv: Name of Habibullah.
Rev: Star of Solomon.

864	AH1335	—	—	300.00	500.00	—

Obv: Uncircled inscription.

KM#	Date	Year	VG	Fine	VF	XF
865	AH1337	—	4.00	9.00	13.00	20.00

NOTE: 5 varieties are known.

AFGHANISTAN 81

25mm
Obv: Inscription within circle and wreath.

KM#	Date	Year	VG	Fine	VF	XF
866	AH1337	—	150.00	300.00	500.00	700.00

4.7500 g, .500 SILVER, .0763 oz ASW
Obv: Star above inscription, *Shamsi*.

| 875 | SH1298 | (1919) | 3.00 | 5.00 | 8.00 | 14.00 |

NOTE: 2 varieties are known.
Obv: *Al-Ghazi* above inscription, *Shamsi*.

| 876 | SH1298 | (1919) | 15.00 | 30.00 | 50.00 | 75.00 |

Obv: W/o *Shamsi*.

| 884 | SH1299 | (1920) | 3.00 | 4.00 | 7.00 | 12.00 |
| | 1300 | (1921) | 3.00 | 4.00 | 7.00 | 12.00 |

NOTE: 2 varieties are known dated 1299.

894	SH1300	(1921)	2.00	4.00	7.00	11.00
	1301	(1922)	2.00	4.00	7.00	10.00
	1302	(1923)	2.00	4.00	7.00	10.00
	1303	(1924)	2.00	4.00	7.00	10.00

4.7000 g, .500 SILVER, .0755 oz ASW

KM#	Date	Mintage	VG	Fine	VF	XF
896	AH1347	—	4.00	7.00	12.00	20.00

| 902 | AH1348 | — | 14.00 | 25.00 | 35.00 | 50.00 |

RUPEE

SILVER

805	AH1304(1303 on rev.)					
		—	25.00	40.00	60.00	110.00
	1304(1304 on rev.)					
		—	25.00	40.00	60.00	110.00

NOTE: Similar to KM#544 these machine struck Rupees were produced by the Birmingham Mint as patterns.

9.2000 g, .900 SILVER, .2662 oz ASW
Obv: Star above toughra.
Rev: Star above, *Kabul* below mosque.

Toughra of Abdur Rahman Khan. Above the toughra between the ends of the wreath, appear stars, a single star, the name *Kabul* or a blank space.

806	AH1308	—	5.00	8.00	14.00	25.00
	1309	—	4.00	6.00	10.00	20.00
	1310/09	—	4.00	6.00	10.00	25.00
	1310	—	5.00	8.00	14.00	25.00
	1311	—	4.00	6.00	10.00	20.00
	1311/09	—	4.00	6.00	10.00	20.00
	1312/1/9	—	4.00	7.00	14.00	25.00
	1312/1	—	4.00	6.00	10.00	20.00
	1312	—	4.00	6.00	10.00	20.00
	1313	—	4.00	6.00	10.00	20.00
	1391(error)	12.00	15.00	17.50	25.00

NOTE: 2 varieties are known with dates AH1311, 1312 and 1313.

Rev: *Kabul* to right of mosque.

KM#	Date	Mintage	VG	Fine	VF	XF
813	AH1313	—	5.00	7.50	10.00	20.00

Rev: *Kabul* above mosque.

| 814 | AH1312 | — | 10.00 | 20.00 | 50.00 | 75.00 |
| | 1313 | — | 5.00 | 7.00 | 9.00 | 20.00 |

Rev: *Du Mesqal* above mosque.

| 818 | AH1314 | — | 6.00 | 10.00 | 20.00 | 40.00 |

Obv: *Kabul* above toughra, undivided dates.

| 819.1 | AH1314 | — | 4.00 | 10.00 | 17.50 | 35.00 |
| | 1315 | — | 4.00 | 5.50 | 8.50 | 20.00 |

819.2	AH1315	—	20.00	50.00	100.00	150.00
	1316	—	4.00	5.50	8.50	20.00
	1317	—	20.00	50.00	100.00	150.00

Obv: Date to right of toughra.

| 819.3 | AH1317 | — | 15.00 | 40.00 | 60.00 | 100.00 |

Obv: 3 stars above toughra.

| 829 | AH1317 | — | 6.00 | 10.00 | 25.00 | 50.00 |

Obv: Date to right of toughra.
Rev: New style mosque.

| 830 | AH1318 | — | 5.00 | 8.50 | 12.50 | 20.00 |

Obv: Toughra of Habibullah in wreath, star above.

KM#	Date	Mintage	VG	Fine	VF	XF
832	AH1319	—	8.00	12.00	25.00	70.00

NOTE: 2 varieties are known.

Obv: *Afghanistan* above small toughra.
Rev: Large inverted pyramid dome.

833	AH1319	—	4.00	5.50	10.00	25.00
	1320	—	4.00	5.50	8.50	20.00
	1325	—	4.00	5.50	10.00	40.00

NOTE: 2 varieties exist. One w/star right of toughra and one w/o star.

Obv: *Afghanistan* divided by a star above large toughra.
Rev: Inverted pyramid dome.

| 839 | AH1320 | — | 4.00 | 6.00 | 10.00 | 20.00 |

Rev: Small dome mosque.

| 840.1 | AH1320 | — | 5.00 | 8.00 | 15.00 | 35.00 |

Obv: Date in loop of toughra.

| 840.2 | AH1321 | — | 10.00 | 15.00 | 25.00 | 50.00 |

Rev: *Afghanistan* above mosque, crossed swords and cannons.

| 842.1 | AH1321 | — | 4.00 | 7.00 | 10.50 | 22.00 |
| | 1322 | — | 4.00 | 7.00 | 10.50 | 22.00 |

Rev: Crossed cannons.

842.2	AH1322	—	4.00	5.00	7.50	15.00
	1324	—	4.00	5.00	7.50	15.00
	1325	—	5.00	8.00	12.00	25.00
	1326	—	4.00	6.00	10.00	16.50
	1327	—	4.00	6.00	10.00	20.00
	1328	—	6.00	8.00	15.00	30.00
	1329	—	5.00	7.50	12.50	25.00

NOTE: 2 varieties for dates AH1321 and 1328.

Rev: Large dome mosque w/o *Afghanistan.*

KM#	Date	Mintage	VG	Fine	VF	XF
847	AH1328	—	7.00	12.00	20.00	40.00

NOTE: Varieties exist.

Obv: Name and titles of Habibullah in wreath.
Rev: Mosque w/pulpit within sunburst.

853	AH1329	—	4.00	6.00	10.00	17.50
	1330	—	4.00	6.00	9.00	15.00
	1331	—	4.00	6.00	9.00	15.00
	1332	—	4.00	6.00	9.00	15.00
	1333	—	4.00	6.00	9.00	15.00
	1334	—	4.00	6.00	9.00	15.00
	1335	—	4.00	6.00	9.00	15.00
	1337	—	4.00	6.00	10.00	17.50

NOTE: 5 varieties are known.

Similar to KM#853, but name and titles of Amanullah on obv., star above inscription.

KM#	Date	Year	VG	Fine	VF	XF
867	AH1337	—	6.00	10.00	18.00	30.00

NOTE: 7 varieties are known.

9.0000 g, .900 SILVER, .2604 oz ASW
Obv: Al-Ghazi above inscription.

877	SH1298	(1919)	4.50	6.50	9.00	15.00
	1299	(1920)	4.50	6.50	9.00	15.00

NOTE: 4 varieties are known dated SH1298. 2 varieties are known dated SH1299.

9.2500 g, .900 SILVER, .2676 oz ASW
Obv: Toughra of Amanullah.

885	SH1299	(1920)	4.00	5.00	7.50	15.00
	1300	(1921)	4.00	5.00	7.50	15.00
	1301	(1922)	4.00	5.00	7.50	15.00
	1302	(1923)	4.00	5.00	7.50	15.00
	1303	(1924)	4.00	5.00	7.50	15.00

9.1000 g, .900 SILVER, .2633 oz ASW
Obv: Name and titles of Amir Habibullah (The Usurper).

KM#	Date	Mintage	VG	Fine	VF	XF
897	AH1347	—	5.00	9.00	15.00	30.00

Obv: Title in circle.

898	AH1347	—	30.00	40.00	60.00	80.00

2-1/2 RUPEES

22.9200 g, .900 SILVER, .6632 oz ASW

KM#	Date	Year	VG	Fine	VF	XF
878	SH1298	(1919)	12.50	16.50	20.00	40.00
	1299	(1920)	8.50	12.50	16.50	30.00
	1300	(1921)	8.50	12.50	16.50	30.00
	1301	(1922)	8.50	12.50	15.00	30.00
	1302	(1923)	8.50	12.50	15.00	35.00
	1303	(1924)	8.50	12.50	15.00	40.00

NOTE: 2 varieties are known for dates SH1298, 1299 and 1300.

5 RUPEES

46.0500 g, .900 SILVER, 1.3325 oz ASW

KM#	Date	Mintage	VG	Fine	VF	XF
820	AH1314	—	20.00	27.50	50.00	100.00

45.6000 g, .900 SILVER, 1.3194 oz ASW
Obv: Similar to KM#820.

826	AH1316	—	17.50	27.50	40.00	90.00

Rev: Similar to KM#826.

KM#	Date	Mintage	VG	Fine	VF	XF
834	AH1319	—	25.00	45.00	85.00	150.00

NOTE: Two varieties exist.

843	AH1322	—	20.00	25.00	35.00	75.00
	1323	—	Reported, not confirmed			
	1324	—	15.00	20.00	30.00	70.00
	1326	—	15.00	20.00	30.00	70.00
	1327/6	—	15.00	20.00	30.00	70.00
	1328	—	22.50	30.00	42.50	85.00
	1329	—	25.00	40.00	60.00	110.00

NOTE: Most dates are recut dies. 2 varieties are known for dates AH1324 and 1327.

1/2 AMANI
(5 Rupees)

2.2750 g, .900 GOLD, .0658 oz AGW

KM#	Date	Year	VG	Fine	VF	XF
886	SH1299	(1920)	BV	50.00	70.00	110.00

TILLA
(10 Rupees)

4.6000 g, .900 GOLD, 22mm, .1331 oz AGW
Rev. leg: *Allah Akbar* **above mosque.**

KM#	Date	Mintage	VG	Fine	VF	XF
807	AH1309	—	BV	75.00	125.00	225.00

19mm
Rev. leg: *Allah Akbar* **above.**

815	AH1313	—	75.00	100.00	150.00	300.00

AFGHANISTAN 83

Rev: Date below throne.

KM#	Date	Mintage	VG	Fine	VF	XF
821	AH1314	—	BV	75.00	100.00	150.00
	1316	—	BV	85.00	110.00	175.00

Obv: Date below toughra.

822	AH1314	—	BV	85.00	110.00	175.00
	1316	—	BV	75.00	100.00	175.00

Obv: Star above toughra.

835	AH1319	—	75.00	100.00	150.00	250.00

Obv: Star divides leg: *Afghanistan* above toughra.

836.1	AH1319	—	75.00	100.00	150.00	250.00

Obv. leg: *Afghanistan* above toughra w/star to right.

836.2	AH1320	—	75.00	100.00	150.00	250.00

Obv: Date divided.

A856	AH1325	—	—	450.00	700.00	900.00

Obv. leg: Name of *Habibullah*.

856	AH1335	—	200.00	220.00	275.00	350.00
	1336	—	100.00	120.00	175.00	250.00
	1337	—	110.00	130.00	180.00	225.00

Obv. leg: Name of *Amanullah*.
Rev: Crossed swords below throne.

868.1	AH1337	—	100.00	125.00	160.00	225.00

Rev: Six-pointed star below throne.

868.2	AH1337	—	100.00	135.00	175.00	250.00

AMANI
(10 Rupees)

4.5500 g, .900 GOLD, 22mm, .1316 oz AGW

KM#	Date	Year	VG	Fine	VF	XF
887	SH1299	(1920)	BV	60.00	80.00	140.00

2 TILLAS
(20 Rupees)

9.2000 g, .900 GOLD, 22mm, .2661 oz AGW

KM#	Date	Mintage	VG	Fine	VF	XF
808	AH1309	—	BV	150.00	220.00	280.00

KM#	Date	Year		Fine	VF	Unc
879	SH1298	(1919)	BV	150.00	250.00	400.00

2 AMANI
(20 Rupees)

9.1000 g, .900 GOLD, .2633 oz AGW

KM#	Date	Year	VG	Fine	VF	XF
888	SH1299	(1920)	BV	150.00	225.00	300.00
	1300	(1921)	BV	150.00	225.00	300.00
	1301	(1922)	BV	150.00	225.00	300.00
	1302	(1923)	BV	150.00	225.00	300.00
	1303	(1924)	BV	150.00	225.00	300.00

HABIBI
(30 Rupees)

4.6000 g, .900 GOLD, .1331 oz AGW

KM#	Date	Mintage	VG	Fine	VF	XF
899	AH1347	—	75.00	125.00	200.00	325.00

Obv: Small star replaces '30 Rupees' in leg.

900	AH1347	—	75.00	125.00	200.00	325.00

5 AMANI
(50 Rupees)

22.7500 g, .900 GOLD, 34mm, .6583 oz AGW
Obv: Persian 5 above toughra; *Al Ghazi* to right.
Rev. leg: *Amaniya* above throne.

KM#	Date	Year	VG	Fine	VF	XF
889	SH1299	(1920)	BV	350.00	600.00	1500.

Obv: Star above toughra. Rev: Persian 5 above throne.

890	SH1299	(1920)	BV	350.00	600.00	1500.

60 RUPEES
GOLD

903	AH1337	—	—	600.00	800.00	1600.

DECIMAL COINAGE
100 Pul = 1 Afghani
20 Afghani = 1 Amani

PUL

BRONZE or BRASS

KM#	Date	Year		Fine	VF	XF	Unc
A922 (922)	AH1349	—	.75	1.25	1.75	2.50

Obv: Toughra.

922	AH1349	—	100.00	250.00	300.00	400.00

NOTE: On this and many other Afghan copper coins, various alloys were used quite indiscriminately, depending upon what was immediately at hand. Thus one finds bronze, brass, and various shades in between. For this reason, bronze and brass coins are not given separate types, but are indicated as a single listing.

2 PUL

BRONZE or BRASS, 2.00 g

905	SH1304	(1925)	2.00	3.00	4.50	10.00
	1305	(1926)	2.00	3.00	4.50	10.00

917	AH1348	—	1.25	2.50	3.50	8.00

928	SH1311	(1932)	2.00	3.00	4.00	12.00
	1312	(1933)	1.50	2.25	3.00	10.00
	1313	(1934)	1.75	2.75	3.75	10.00
	1314	(1935)	2.00	3.00	4.00	12.00

BRONZE

936	SH1316	(1937)	.15	.20	.35	1.00

3 PUL

BRONZE

937	SH1316	(1937)	.50	.75	1.00	2.50

5 PUL

BRONZE or BRASS, 3.00 g

906	SH1304	(1925)	1.75	3.50	6.00	12.00
	1305	(1926)	1.50	3.00	5.50	12.00

923	AH1349	—	1.75	2.75	4.50	10.00
	1350	—	1.25	2.25	3.50	10.00

NOTE: 2 varieties are known dated AH1350.

AFGHANISTAN 84

KM#	Date	Year	Fine	VF	XF	Unc
929	SH1311	(1932)	2.00	3.50	5.00	15.00
	1312	(1933)	2.00	3.50	5.00	15.00
	1313	(1934)	2.00	3.50	5.00	15.00
	1314	(1935)	2.00	3.50	5.00	15.00

BRONZE
| 938 | SH1316 | (1937) | .25 | .30 | .40 | 2.50 |

10 PUL

COPPER, 6.00 g
907	SH1304	(1925)	2.00	3.50	5.50	15.00
	1305	(1926)	2.50	4.00	6.00	20.00
	1306	(1927)	2.50	4.00	6.00	20.00
	ND	—	—	Reported, not confirmed

COPPER or BRASS
918	AH1348	—	2.00	3.50	5.00	15.00
	1349 (2 vars.)		2.25	4.00	5.50	15.00

NOTE: Illustration shows an example struck off-center; prices are for properly struck specimens.

BRASS
930	SH1311	(1932)	1.50	2.50	4.00	15.00
	1312	(1933)	1.50	2.50	4.00	15.00
	1313	(1934)	1.50	2.50	4.00	15.00
	1314	(1935)	1.50	2.50	4.00	15.00

COPPER-NICKEL
| 939 | SH1316 | (1937) | .40 | .60 | .90 | 2.50 |

20 PUL

BILLON, 2.00 g
908	SH1304	(1925)	75.00	95.00	125.00	170.00
	ND	—	60.00	85.00	110.00	160.00

COPPER or BRASS
KM#	Date	Year	Fine	VF	XF	Unc
919	AH1348	—	2.00	4.00	10.00	15.00
	1349	—	3.00	5.00	12.00	18.00

25 PUL

COPPER or BRASS
KM#	Date	Mintage	Fine	VF	XF	Unc
924	AH1349	—	2.00	3.50	9.00	14.00

NOTE: 2 varieties are known dated AH1349.

BRONZE or BRASS
KM#	Date	Year	Fine	VF	XF	Unc
931	SH1312	(1933)	1.50	2.50	9.00	15.00
	1313	(1934)	1.50	2.50	9.00	15.00
	1314	(1935)	1.75	2.75	12.00	17.50
	1315	(1936)	—	Reported, not confirmed
	1316	(1937)	1.75	2.75	4.00	17.50

COPPER-NICKEL
| 940 | SH1316 | (1937) | .60 | .75 | 1.00 | 3.00 |

BRONZE
941	SH1330	(1951)	.15	.25	.50	1.00
	1331	(1952)	.15	.25	.50	1.00
	1332	(1953)	.15	.25	.50	1.00

NICKEL-CLAD STEEL, 20mm, reeded edge
943	SH1331	(1952)	1.00	2.00	3.50	6.00
	1332	(1953)	1.50	3.00	5.00	7.50

Plain edge
944	SH1331	(1952)	.30	.50	.60	1.00
	1332	(1953)	.30	.50	.60	1.00
	1333	(1954)	.30	.50	.60	1.00
	1334	(1955)	.30	.50	.60	1.50

ALUMINUM, 24mm
| 945 | SH1331 | (1952) | .50 | .75 | 3.00 | 20.00 |

NOTE: Struck on oversize 2 Afghani KM#949 planchets in 1970.

1/2 AFGHANI
(50 Pul)

5.0000 g, .500 SILVER, .0803 oz ASW
Obv: Date below toughra.
909	SH1304	7	2.00	3.50	6.50	20.00
	1305	8	2.00	3.50	6.50	20.00
	1306	9	2.00	3.50	6.50	20.00

NOTE: 2 varieties are known dated SH1304.

Rev: Date below mosque.
| 915 | SH1307 | 10 | 3.00 | 5.50 | 10.00 | 30.00 |

KM#	Date	Year	Fine	VF	XF	Unc
920	AH1348	1	1.50	2.25	4.00	12.50
(919)	1349	2	1.50	2.25	4.00	12.50
	1350	3	1.50	2.25	4.00	12.50

4.7500 g, .500 SILVER, .0763 oz ASW
926	SH1310	(1931)	1.50	2.25	4.00	12.50
	1311	(1932)	1.50	2.25	4.00	12.50
	1312	(1933)	1.50	2.25	4.00	12.50

932.1	SH1312	(1933)	1.50	2.25	4.00	12.50
	1313	(1934)	1.50	2.25	4.00	12.50
	1314	(1935)	1.50	2.25	4.00	12.50
	1315	(1936)	1.50	2.25	4.00	12.50
	1316	(1937)	1.50	2.25	4.00	12.50

Obv: Smaller dotted circle.
| 932.2 | AH1312 | (1933) | 1.75 | 2.50 | 4.50 | 13.00 |

BRONZE, 21.5mm
Obv: Denomination in numerals.
| 942.1 | SH1330 | (1951) | .35 | .50 | .75 | 1.25 |

24mm
| 942.2 | SH1330 | (1951) | 20.00 | 30.00 | 40.00 | 50.00 |

NICKEL-CLAD STEEL
946	SH1331	(1952)	.15	.25	.40	.75
	1332	(1953)	.15	.25	.40	.75
	1333	(1954)	.20	.30	.50	.80
	1334	(1955)	.15	.25	.40	.75

Obv: Denomination in words.
| 947 | SH1331 | 1952 | .40 | .65 | .85 | 1.25 |

AFGHANI
(100 Pul)

AFGHANISTAN 85

10.0000 g, .900 SILVER, .2893 oz ASW
Obv: Date below toughra.

KM#	Date	Year	Fine	VF	XF	Unc
910	SH1304	7	3.00	4.50	8.50	20.00
	1305	8	3.00	4.50	8.50	20.00
	1305	9	3.00	4.50	8.50	20.00
	1306	9	3.00	4.50	8.50	20.00

NOTE: 3 varieties are known dated SH1304. 2 varieties are known for dates SH1305 and 1306.

Rev: Date under mosque.

| 916 | SH1307 (1928) | — Reported, not confirmed |

9.9500 g, .900 SILVER, .2879 oz ASW

921	AH1348	1	3.00	4.50	9.00	16.50
	1349	2	3.00	4.50	9.00	16.50
	1350	3	3.00	4.50	9.00	16.50

10.0000 g, .900 SILVER, .2893 oz ASW

| 927.1 | SH1310 (1931) | 50.00 | 65.00 | 80.00 | 120.00 |
| | 1311 (1932) | 110.00 | 160.00 | 190.00 | 250.00 |

Thick flan, 22.5mm

| 927.2 | SH1310 (1931) | 250.00 | 375.00 | 500.00 | 700.00 |

NICKEL-CLAD STEEL

| 953 | SH1340 (1961) | .15 | .20 | .30 | .50 |

2 AFGHANI

ALUMINUM

| 949 | SH1337 (1958) | .60 | 1.00 | 1.50 | 2.00 |

NOTE: The above issue was withdrawn and demonetized due to extensive counterfeiting.

NICKEL-CLAD STEEL

| 954 | SH1340 (1961) | .20 | .30 | .50 | .75 |

NOTE: 2 varieties, normal coin type and medallic die orientation.

2-1/2 AFGHANI

25.0000 g, .900 SILVER, .7234 oz ASW

KM#	Date	Year	Fine	VF	XF	Unc
913	SH1305	8	15.00	22.50	40.00	115.00
	1306	9	15.00	20.00	30.00	70.00

NOTE: 2 varieties are known for above dates.

5 AFGHANI

ALUMINUM

| 950 | SH1337 (1958) | 1.00 | 1.75 | 2.25 | 3.00 |

NOTE: The above issue was withdrawn and demonetized due to extensive counterfeiting.

NICKEL-CLAD STEEL

| 955 | SH1340 AH1381 | .25 | .40 | .75 | 1.50 |

10 AFGHANI

ALUMINUM

| 948 | SH1336 (1957) | — | — | 900.00 |

1/2 AMANI

3.0000 g, .900 GOLD, .0868 oz AGW

911	SH1304	7	BV	50.00	75.00	100.00
	1305	8	BV	50.00	75.00	100.00
	1306	9	BV	50.00	75.00	100.00

4 GRAMS

4.0000 g, .900 GOLD, .1157 oz AGW

KM#	Date	Year	Fine	VF	XF	Unc
935	SH1315 (1936)	BV	75.00	110.00	170.00
	1317 (1938)	BV	75.00	110.00	170.00

AMANI

6.0000 g, .900 GOLD, .1736 oz AGW

912	SH1304	7	BV	90.00	110.00	160.00
	1305	8	BV	90.00	130.00	200.00
	1306	9	BV	90.00	110.00	160.00

20 AFGHANI

6.0000 g, .900 GOLD, .1736 oz AGW

925	AH1348	—	125.00	175.00	200.00	300.00
	1349	2	BV	110.00	165.00	240.00
	1350	3	BV	110.00	165.00	240.00

6 GRAMS

6.0000 g, .900 GOLD, .1736 oz AGW

| 933 | SH1313 (1934) | 125.00 | 150.00 | 175.00 | 250.00 |

8 GRAMS

8.0000 g, .900 GOLD, .2314 oz AGW

934	SH1314 (1935)	BV	130.00	175.00	240.00
	1315 (1936)	BV	130.00	175.00	240.00
	1317 (1938)	BV	130.00	175.00	240.00

| 952 | SH1339 AH1380 200 pcs. | — | 300.00 | 800.00 |

NOTE: Struck for royal presentation purposes. Specimens struck with the same dies (including the "8 grams"), but on thin planchets weighing 3.9-4 grams, are reported. They are regarded as "mint sports". Market value $200.00 in unc.

2-1/2 AMANI

15.0000 g, .900 GOLD, 30mm, .4340 oz AGW

| 914 | SH1306 | 9 | — | — | 2850. | 3500. |

LOCAL COINAGE

With the inception of machine struck coinage in AH1308/AD1891, the provincial mints were closed and all minting was centralized at Kabul. However, few base metal coins were struck at Kabul, and old copper coins, as well as foreign copper coins, circulated in Afghanistan. After nine years, the Kabul Mint suspended the production of copper coins (AH1317/AD1900). The consequence was the sanctioning of private striking at Herat and Qandahar, where coins were struck from about AH1322 until AH1333. Royal coinage in copper and brass resumed in AH1329/AD1911, and the private mints were soon afterwards suppressed. Further private strikings took place in AH1337-38/SH1298-99. The minting place, probably Kabul, is not shown on these coins. The local coinage is quite crude, and is usually counterstruck on older Afghan and foreign coins. The listings below may be incomplete.

Herat
PAISA

COPPER, round or irregular flan

KM#	Date	Good	VG	Fine	VF
956.1	AH1322	2.50	4.00	7.50	12.50
	1328	2.50	4.00	7.50	12.50
	1329	2.50	4.00	7.50	12.50
	1330	2.50	4.00	7.50	12.50
	1331	2.50	4.00	7.50	12.50
	1332	2.50	4.00	7.50	12.50
	Date off flan	1.50	2.50	5.00	8.00

Obv: In a rayed circle.
| 956.2 | AH1332 | 3.00 | 5.00 | 8.50 | 15.00 |

Rev: Scroll symbol.
| 956.3 | AH1325 | 3.00 | 5.00 | 8.50 | 15.00 |

Struck over Iran, 50 Dinars, Y#4.
| 957 | AH1322 | 4.00 | 6.50 | 12.50 | 16.00 |
| | 1328 | 3.00 | 5.00 | 10.00 | 12.50 |

Obv: Dar al-Nusrat added, date above.
| 958.1 | AH1331 | 2.50 | 4.00 | 7.50 | 12.50 |

Rev: Date below mosque.
| 958.2 | AH1331 | 3.50 | 5.00 | 8.50 | 15.00 |

2 PAISA
COPPER
Similar to Paisa, KM#956, but inscribed *Do Paisa* below mosque.
| 959 | AH1329 | 3.00 | 5.00 | 8.50 | 13.50 |

5 PAISA

BRASS
In the name of Baccha-i-Saqao
KM#	Date	Good	VG	Fine	VF
969	AH1347	5.00	8.50	15.00	22.50

10 PAISA

BRASS
In the name of Baccha-i-Saqao
| 970 | AH1347 | 6.00 | 10.00 | 16.50 | 25.00 |

20 PAISA

BRASS
In the name of Baccha-i-Saqao
| 972 | AH1347 | 7.50 | 12.50 | 20.00 | 30.00 |

Qandahar
PAISA

COPPER
| 960 | AH1322 | 4.50 | 7.50 | 12.50 | 17.50 |

Struck over Iran, 50 Dinars, Y#4.
| 961 | AH1321 | 3.50 | 6.00 | 10.00 | 15.00 |
| | 1322 | 3.00 | 5.00 | 8.00 | 12.50 |

Struck over Muscat & Oman, 1/4 Anna, KM#4.
| 962 | AH1322 | 3.75 | 6.50 | 10.00 | 15.00 |

Struck over British East India Co., 1/4 Anna.
| 963 | AH1322 | 3.75 | 6.50 | 10.00 | 15.00 |

964	AH1320	2.00	3.50	6.00	10.00
	1333	2.00	3.50	6.00	10.00
	1334	2.00	3.50	6.00	10.00

Without Mint Name
Believed struck at Kabul

PAISA

COPPER, crudely struck.

KM#	Date	Year	Good	VG	Fine	VF
965	SH1298	(1919)	4.50	7.50	12.50	20.00
	1299	(1920)	4.50	7.50	12.50	20.00

Rev: *Amanullah* added.
| 966 | SH1299 | (1920) | 6.00 | — | 16.50 | 24.00 |

5 PAISA
(1 Shahi)

COPPER, crudely struck.
Rev: Both denominations.
967.1	SH1298	AH1338	6.00	10.00	16.50	24.00
	1299	1338	7.50	12.50	20.00	30.00
	1299	1339	6.00	10.00	16.50	24.00

Rev: X in place of 5 Paisa.
| 967.2 | SH1299 | — | 7.50 | 12.50 | 20.00 | 30.00 |

Rev: *Amanullah* added.
| 968 | SH1299 | (1920) | 6.00 | 10.00 | 16.50 | 24.00 |

15 PAISA

BRASS
In the name of Baccha-i-Saqao
KM#	Date	Good	VG	Fine	VF
971	AH1347	7.50	12.50	20.00	30.00

NOTE: KM#969 and 972 previously listed here are now listed under the Herat Mint.

ABBASI

3.1100 g, .500 SILVER, .0499 oz ASW
Obv: Date above toughra.
KM#	Date	Mintage	VG	Fine	VF	XF
810	AH1313	—	3.00	5.00	8.00	14.00

BILLON, 20mm
Obv: Leg. in wreath.
KM#	Date	Year	VG	Fine	VF	XF
873	SH1298	(1919)	—	—	—	—

QIRAN

AFGHANISTAN 87

BILLON

KM#	Date	Year	VG	Fine	VF	XF
973	SH1298	(1919)	—	—	—	—

REPUBLIC
SH1352-1357/1973-1978AD
25 PUL

BRASS CLAD STEEL

KM#	Date	Mintage	Fine	VF	XF	Unc
975	SH1352	45,950	.25	.50	1.00	2.50

50 PUL

COPPER CLAD STEEL

| 976 | SH1352 | 24,750 | .75 | 1.50 | 2.50 | 5.00 |

5 AFGHANI

COPPER-NICKEL CLAD STEEL

| 977 | SH1352 | 34,750 | 1.75 | 3.50 | 5.00 | 10.00 |

250 AFGHANI

28.5700 g, .925 SILVER, .8496 oz ASW
Conservation Series
Rev: Snow Leopard.

| 978 | 1978 | 4,370 | — | — | — | 25.00 |

28.2800 g, .925 SILVER, .8410 oz ASW

| 979 | 1978 | 4,387 | — | — | Proof | 35.00 |

500 AFGHANI

35.3000 g, .925 SILVER, 1.0498 oz ASW
Conservation Series
Obv: Similar to 250 Afghani, KM#978.
Rev: Siberian Crane.

KM#	Date	Mintage	Fine	VF	XF	Unc
980	1978	4,374	—	—	—	25.00

35.0000 g, .925 SILVER, 1.0408 oz ASW

| 981 | 1978 | 4,218 | — | — | Proof | 35.00 |

10,000 AFGHANI

33.4370 g, .900 GOLD, .9676 oz AGW
Conservation Series
Obv: Similar to 250 Afghani, KM#978.
Rev: Marco Polo Sheep.

| 982 | 1978 | 694 pcs. | — | — | — | 500.00 |
| | 1978 | 181 pcs. | — | — | Proof | 900.00 |

DEMOCRATIC REPUBLIC
SH1357- /1978- AD
25 PUL

ALUMINUM-BRONZE

KM#	Date	Year	Fine	VF	XF	Unc
990	SH1357	(1978)	.25	.50	1.00	2.50

Obv: Similar to 5 Afghanis, KM#1000.
Rev: Similar to KM#990.

| 996 | SH1359 | (1980) | .25 | .50 | 1.00 | 2.50 |

50 PUL

ALUMINUM-BRONZE, 3.00 g

| 992 | SH1357 | (1978) | .50 | .80 | 1.50 | 3.00 |

| 997 | SH1359 | (1980) | .25 | .50 | 1.00 | 2.00 |

AFGHANI

COPPER-NICKEL

| 993 | SH1357 | (1978) | .60 | 1.00 | 1.75 | 3.50 |

| 998 | SH1359 | (1980) | .50 | .80 | 1.50 | 2.50 |

2 AFGHANIS

COPPER-NICKEL

| 994 | SH1357 | (1978) | 1.00 | 1.50 | 2.00 | 4.00 |

Obv: Similar to 1 Afghani, KM#998.

KM#	Date	Year	Fine	VF	XF	Unc
999	SH1359	(1980)	.60	1.00	1.50	3.00

5 AFGHANIS

COPPER-NICKEL, 7.40 g

| 995 | SH1357 | (1978) | 1.00 | — | 4.00 | 6.00 |

| 1000 | SH1359 | (1980) | 1.00 | 1.50 | 2.00 | 3.50 |

BRASS
World Food Day

| 1001 | SH1360 | (1981) | .25 | .50 | 1.00 | 1.50 |

50 AFGHANIS

COPPER-NICKEL
World Wildlife Fund-Leopard

KM#	Date	Mintage	Fine	VF	XF	Unc
1006	1987					

500 AFGHANIS

9.0600 g, .900 SILVER, .2622 oz ASW
World Food Day

KM#	Date	Year	Fine	VF	XF	Unc
1002	SH1360	1981	—	—	Proof	25.00

12.0000 g, .999 SILVER, .3855 oz ASW

AFGHANISTAN 88

100th Anniversary of the Automobile

KM#	Date	Mintage	Fine	VF	XF	Unc
1003	1986	2,000	—	—	—	20.00

1988 Winter Olympics

| 1004 | ND(1986) | — | — | — | — | 20.00 |

Wildlife Preservation - Leopard

| 1005 | 1986 | *5,000 | — | — | — | 20.00 |

Listings For
AJMAN: refer to United Arab Emirates

ALBANIA

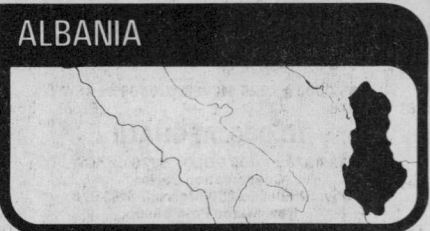

The People's Socialist Republic of Albania, a Balkan communist republic bounded by Yugoslavia, Greece, and the Adriatic Sea, has an area of 11,100 sq. mi. (28,748 sq. km.) and a population of 2.8 million. Capital: Tirana. The country is predominantly agricultural, although recent progress has been made in the manufacturing and mining sectors. Petroleum, chrome, iron, copper, cotton textiles, tobacco and wood products are exported.

Since it had been part of the Greek and Roman empires, little is known of the early history of Albania. After the disintegration of the Roman Empire, Albania was overrun by Goths, Byzantines, Venetians, and Turks. Skanderbeg, the national hero, resisted the Turks and established an independent Albania in 1443, but in 1468 the country again fell to the Turks and remained part of the Ottoman Empire for more than 400 years.

Independence was re-established by revolt in 1912, and the present borders established in 1913 by a conference of European powers which, in 1914, placed Prince William of Wied on the throne; popular discontent forced his abdication within months. In 1920, following World War I occupancy by several nations, a republic was set up. Ahmed Zogu seized the presidency in 1925, and in 1928 proclaimed himself king with the title of Zog I. King Zog fled when Italy occupied Albania in 1939 and enthroned King Victor Emanuel of Italy. Upon the surrender of Italy to the Allies in 1943, German troops occupied the country. They withdrew in 1944, and communist partisans seized power, naming Gen. Enver Hoxha provisional president. In 1946, following a victory by the communist front in the 1945 elections, a new constitution modeled on that of the USSR was adopted. In accordance with the constitution of Dec. 28, 1976, the official name of Albania was changed from the People's Republic of Albania to the People's Socialist Republic of Albania.

RULERS
Ahmed Bey Zogu - King Zog I, 1928-1939
Vittorio Emanuele III, 1939-1943

MINT MARKS
L - London
R - Rome
V - Valona

MONETARY SYSTEM
100 Qindar Leku = 1 Lek
100 Qindar Ari = 1 Franga Ari
 = 5 Lek

KINGDOM

5 QINDAR LEKU

BRONZE

KM#	Date	Mintage	Fine	VF	XF	Unc
1	1926R	.512	15.00	35.00	50.00	100.00

QINDAR AR

BRONZE

| 14 | 1935R | 2.000 | 2.00 | — | 5.00 | 10.00 | 20.00 |

10 QINDAR LEKU

BRONZE

| 2 | 1926R | .511 | 10.00 | 20.00 | 40.00 | 85.00 |

---

2 QINDAR AR

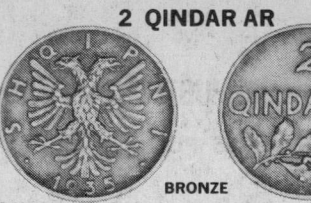

BRONZE

KM#	Date	Mintage	Fine	VF	XF	Unc
15	1935R	1.500	3.00	8.00	15.00	32.00

1/4 LEKU

NICKEL

| 3 | 1926R | .506 | 3.00 | 6.00 | 14.00 | 32.00 |
| | 1927R | .756 | 3.00 | 6.00 | 12.00 | 30.00 |

1/2 LEK

NICKEL

| 4 | 1926R | 1.002 | 2.50 | 5.00 | 10.00 | 22.00 |

13	1930V	.500	2.00	4.00	8.00	16.00
	1931L	.500	2.00	4.00	8.00	16.00
	1931L	—	—	—	Proof	—

LEK

NICKEL

5	1926R	1.004	2.50	5.00	10.00	25.00
	1927R	.506	2.50	7.50	15.00	30.00
	1930V	1.250	2.50	5.00	10.00	25.00
	1931L	1.000	2.50	5.00	10.00	25.00
	1931L	—	—	—	Proof	—

FRANG AR

5.0000 g, .835 SILVER, .1342 oz ASW

6	1927R	.100	50.00	75.00	120.00	250.00
	1927V	.050	—	Reported, not confirmed		
	1928R	.060	50.00	85.00	140.00	280.00

| 16 | 1935R | .700 | 6.00 | 10.00 | 22.00 | 60.00 |
| | 1937R | .600 | 6.00 | 10.00 | 22.00 | 60.00 |

ALBANIA 89

Independence Commemorative

KM#	Date	Mintage	Fine	VF	XF	Unc
18	1937R	.050	10.00	15.00	30.00	60.00

2 FRANGA AR

10.0000 g, .835 SILVER, .2684 oz ASW

7	1926R	.050	45.00	85.00	140.00	240.00
	1927R	.050	55.00	100.00	150.00	260.00
	1928R	.060	45.00	85.00	135.00	240.00

17	1935R	.150	10.00	22.50	45.00	100.00

Independence Commemorative

19	1937R	.025	15.00	27.50	50.00	120.00

5 FRANGA AR

25.0000 g, .900 SILVER, .7234 oz ASW

8.1	1926R	.060	60.00	130.00	260.00	480.00
	1927V	*.040	70.00	160.00	320.00	600.00

Obv: Star below bust.

8.2	1926R	Inc. Ab.	115.00	250.00	360.00	650.00

10 FRANGA AR

3.2258 g, .900 GOLD, .0933 oz AGW

KM#	Date	Mintage	Fine	VF	XF	Unc
9	1927R	6,000	100.00	140.00	220.00	300.00

20 FRANGA AR

6.4516 g, .900 GOLD, .1867 oz AGW

10	1926R	—	120.00	150.00	280.00	350.00
	1927R	6,000	120.00	150.00	280.00	400.00

George Kastrioti "Skanderbeg"

12	1926R	5,900	125.00	160.00	290.00	450.00
	1926 fasces *100 pcs.	—	—	3000.	5000.
	1927V	5,053	—	135.00	225.00	300.00

*NOTE: 90 pieces were reported melted.

25th Anniversary of Independence

20	1937R	2,500	—	150.00	300.00	450.00

King Zog Marriage

22	1938R	2,500	—	150.00	250.00	500.00

King Zog 10th Anniversary of Reign

24	1938R	1,000	—	200.00	320.00	700.00

NOTE: This piece was restruck in 1969 from new dies and is possibly counterfeit.

50 FRANGA AR

16.1290 g, .900 GOLD, .4667 oz AGW
King Zog 10th Anniversary of Reign

25	1938R	600 pcs.	—	600.00	1250.	2000.

NOTE: This piece was restruck in 1969 from new dies and is possibly counterfeit.

100 FRANGA AR

32.2580 g, .900 GOLD, .9335 oz AGW

11.1	1926R	6,614	—	600.00	900.00	1200.

Obv: Star below bust.

KM#	Date	Mintage	Fine	VF	XF	Unc
11.2	1926R	Inc. Ab.	—	600.00	900.00	1200.

Obv: 2 stars below bust.

11.3	1926R	Inc. Ab.	—	600.00	900.00	1200.

11a.1	1927R	5,000	—	600.00	900.00	1200.

Obv: Star below bust.

11a.2	1927R	Inc. Ab.	—	650.00	950.00	1250.

Obv: Two stars below bust.

11a.3	1927R	Inc. Ab.	—	650.00	950.00	1250.

25th Anniversary of Independence

21	1937R	500 pcs.	—	850.00	1600.	2400.

King Zog Marriage

23	1938R	500 pcs.	—	800.00	1400.	1600.

ALBANIA 90

King Zog 10th Anniversary of Reign

KM#	Date	Mintage	Fine	VF	XF	Unc
26	1938R	500 pcs.	—	800.00	1400.	1600.

NOTE: This piece was restruck in 1969 from new dies and is possibly counterfeit.

ITALIAN OCCUPATION WW II
MONETARY SYSTEM
1 Lek = 1 Lira

0.05 LEK

ALUMINUM-BRONZE

27	1940R	1.400	1.00	3.00	8.00	15.00
	1941R	.200	3.00	8.00	20.00	50.00

0.10 LEK

ALUMINUM-BRONZE

28	1940R	.800	2.00	5.00	8.00	18.00
	1941R	.250	17.50	35.00	65.00	110.00

0.20 LEK

NOTE: KM#29, 30, 31, 32 exist in two types, magnetic and non-magnetic, the latter being the scarcer.

STAINLESS STEEL

29	1939R	.900	1.00	2.00	2.25	6.00
	1940R	.700	1.00	2.00	3.25	7.00
	1941R	1.400	1.00	2.50	4.00	8.00

0.50 LEK

STAINLESS STEEL

30	1939R	.100	1.25	3.00	7.00	12.00
	1940R	.500	1.25	2.50	5.00	11.00
	1941R	.900	1.25	5.00	5.50	12.00

LEK

STAINLESS STEEL

31	1939R	2.100	.50	1.25	3.50	10.00
	1940R	—	60.00	120.00	220.00	350.00
	1941R			Rare		

NOTE: Coins dated after 1939 were not struck for circulation.

2 LEK

STAINLESS STEEL

KM#	Date	Mintage	Fine	VF	XF	Unc
32	1939R	1.300	—	5.00	5.00	15.00
	1940R	—	60.00	130.00	230.00	400.00
	1941R			Rare		

NOTE: Coins dated after 1939 were not struck for circulation.

5 LEK

5.0000 g, .835 SILVER, .1342 oz ASW

33	1939R	1.350	5.00	10.00	22.50	55.00

10 LEK

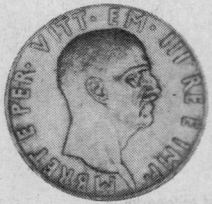 

10.0000 g, .835 SILVER, .2684 oz ASW

34	1939R	.175	30.00	60.00	80.00	180.00

PEOPLES' SOCIALIST REPUBLIC
MONETARY SYSTEM
100 Qindarka = 1 Lek

5 QINDARKA

ALUMINUM

39	1964	—	.10	.25	.50	1.00

25th Anniversary of Liberation

44	1969	—	.10	.20	.30	.50

10 QINDARKA

ALUMINUM

40	1964	—	.15	.30	.60	1.25

25th Anniversary of Liberation

45	1969	—	.10	.20	.35	.60

KM#	Date	Mintage	Fine	VF	XF	Unc
60	1988	—	—	—	—	1.25

20 QINDARKA

ALUMINUM

41	1964	—	.20	.40	.60	1.25

25th Anniversary of Liberation

46	1969	—	.15	.30	.50	1.00

1/2 LEKU

ZINC

35	1947	—	.30	.60	1.25	2.25
	1957	—	.30	.60	1.25	2.00

50 QINDARKA

ALUMINUM

42	1964	—	.50	.75	2.00	4.00

25th Anniversary of Liberation

47	1969	—	.30	.50	1.00	2.50

LEK

ZINC

36	1947	—	.50	.75	2.00	4.50
	1957	—	.30	.60	1.50	3.50

ALUMINUM

43	1964	—	.50	1.00	2.00	3.50

ALBANIA 91

25th Anniversary of Liberation

KM#	Date	Mintage	Fine	VF	XF	Unc
48	1969	—	.35	.75	1.25	3.00

2 LEKE

ZINC

37	1947	—	.35	.75	1.50	3.50
	1957	—	.30	.60	1.35	2.50

5 LEKE

ZINC

38	1947	—	.60	1.25	2.50	4.00
	1957	—	.50	1.00	2.25	3.00

16.7500 g, .999 SILVER, .5385 oz ASW

49	1968	8,540	—	—	Proof	17.50
	1969	1,500	—	—	Proof	25.00
	1970	500 pcs.	—	—	Proof	30.00

COPPER-NICKEL
Seaport of Durazzo

57	1987	*.050	—	—	—	5.00

Railroad
Similar to 50 Leke, KM#62 but w/o hole in coin.

61	1988	.020	—	—	—	5.50

10 LEKE

32.8000 g, .999 SILVER, 1.0545 oz ASW
Rev: Similar to 5 Leke, KM#49.

KM#	Date	Mintage	Fine	VF	XF	Unc
50	1968	8,540	—	—	Proof	38.00
	1969	1,500	—	—	Proof	45.00
	1970	500 pcs.	—	—	Proof	100.00

20 LEKE

3.9500 g, .900 GOLD, .1143 oz AGW

51	1968	2,920	—	—	Proof	80.00
	1968 Paris	24 pcs.	—	—	—	300.00
	1969	650 pcs.	—	—	Proof	80.00
	1970	500 pcs.	—	—	Proof	100.00

25 LEKE

82.8000 g, .999 SILVER, 2.6621 oz ASW
Rev: Similar to 5 Leke, KM#49.

52	1968	8,540	—	—	Proof	85.00
	1969	1,500	—	—	Proof	95.00
	1970	500 pcs.	—	—	Proof	130.00

50 LEKE

9.8700 g, .900 GOLD, .2856 oz AGW

53	1968	3,120	—	—	Proof	160.00
	1969	500 pcs.	—	—	Proof	175.00
	1970	100 pcs.	—	—	Proof	200.00

168.1500 g, .925 SILVER, 5.0012 oz ASW
Reduced. Actual size: 65mm.
Obv: Similar to 5 Leke, KM#57.
Seaport of Durazzo

KM#	Date	Mintage	Fine	VF	XF	Unc
58	1987	*.015	—	—	Proof	130.00

Reduced. Actual size: 65mm
Railroad

62	1988	7,500	—	—	Proof	135.00

100 LEKE

19.7500 g, .900 GOLD, .5715 oz AGW

54	1968	3,470	—	—	Proof	325.00
	1969	450 pcs.	—	—	Proof	350.00
	1970	Inc. Ab.	—	—	Proof	350.00

6.4500 g, .900 GOLD, .1866 oz AGW
Seaport of Durazzo
Similar to 5 Leke, KM#57.

59	1987	*5,000	—	—	Proof	180.00

Railroad
Similar to 50 Leke, KM#62 but w/o hole in coin.

63	1988	2,000	—	—	Proof	185.00

ALBANIA 92

200 LEKE

39.4900 g, .900 GOLD, 1.1427 oz AGW
Rev: Similar to 5 Leke, KM#49.

KM#	Date	Mintage	Fine	VF	XF	Unc
55	1968	2,170	—	—	Proof	600.00
	1969	200 pcs.	—	—	Proof	650.00
	1970	Inc. Ab.	—	—	Proof	650.00

500 LEKE

98.7400 g, .900 GOLD, 2.8574 oz AGW
Rev: Similar to 5 Leke, KM#49.

56	1968	1,520	—	—	Proof	1600.
	1969	200 pcs.	—	—	Proof	1800.
	1970	Inc. Ab.	—	—	Proof	1800.

7500 LEKE

483.7500 g, .900 GOLD, 13.9992 oz AGW
Railroad
Similar to 50 Leke, KM#62.

64	1988	50 pcs.	—	—	Proof	10,000.

PROOF SETS (PS)

KM#	Date	Mintage	Identification	Issue Price	Mkt. Val.
PS1	1968(5)	1,540	KM51,53-56	470.00	2765.
PS2	1968(3)	8,540	KM49,50,52	44.00	145.00
PS3	1969(5)	—	KM51,53-56	470.00	3065.
PS4	1969(3)	1,500	KM49,50,52	45.00	170.00
PS5	1970(5)	—	KM51,53-56	516.00	3100.
PS6	1970(3)	500	KM49,50,52	45.00	260.00

ALGERIA

The Democratic and Popular Republic of Algeria, a North African country fronting on the Mediterranean Sea between Tunisia and Morocco, has an area of 919,595 sq. mi. (2,381,741 sq. km.) and a population of 21 million. Capital: Algiers. Most of the country's working population is engaged in agriculture although a recent industrial diversification, financed by oil revenues, is making steady progress. Wines, fruits, iron and zinc ores, phosphates, tobacco products, liquified natural gas, and petroleum are exported.

Algiers, the capital and chief seaport of Algeria, was the site of Phoenician and Roman settlements before the present Moslem city was founded about 950. Nominally part of the sultanate of Tilimsan, Algiers had a large measure of independence under amirs of its own. In 1492 the Jews and Moors who had been expelled from Spain settled in Algiers and enjoyed an increasing influence until the imposition of Turkish control in 1518. For the following three centuries Algiers was the headquarters of the notorious Barbary pirates as Turkish control became more and more nominal. The French took Algiers in 1830, and after a long and wearisome war completed the conquest of Algeria and annexed it to France, 1848, becoming a colony, then a territory, and finally, in the northern provinces, French departments. The inability to obtain equal rights with Frenchmen led to an organized revolt which began on Nov. 1, 1954 and lasted until a ceasefire was signed on July 1, 1962. Independence was proclaimed on July 3, 1962, following a self-determination referendum, and the Republic was declared on September 25, 1962.

RULERS
Ottoman, until 1830
Abd-el-Kader (rebel)
AH1250-1264/1834-1847AD

ALGIERS
MINTNAMES

Jaza'Ir جزاير

El Jaza'Ir Garp الجزايرة
AH1012-1115/1603-1703AD

El-Jaza' Iriyat جزايرعرب
Until AH1246/1830AD

Al Mascara المعسكر
During revolt of Abd-el-Kader
AH1250-1264/1834-1847AD

Medea مديه
AH1246/1830AD

Qusantinah
Constantine قسنطينة
AH1245-1253/1830-1836AD

Taqidemt تاقدمت
During revolt of Abd-el-Kader
AH1250-1264/1834-1847AD

Tilimsan تلمسان
AH964-1026/1556-1617AD

NOTE: The dots above and below the letters are integral parts of the letters, but for stylistic reasons, are occasionally omitted.

MONETARY SYSTEM
(Until 1847)
14-1/2 Asper (Akcheh,
  Dirham Saghir) = 1 Kharub
2 Kharuba = 1 Muzuna
24 Muzuna = 1 Budju

NOTE: Coin denominations are not expressed on the coins, and are best determined by size and weight. The silver Budju weighed about 13.5 g until AH1236/1821AD, when it was reduced to about 10.0 g. The fractional pieces varied in proportion to the Budju. They had secondary names, which are given in the text. In 1829 three new silver coins were introduced and Budju became Tugrali-rial, Tugrali-batlaka = 1/3 Rial = 8 Mazuna and Tugrali-nessflik = 1/2 Batlaka = 4 Mazuna. The gold Sultani was officially valued at 108 Mazuna, but varied in accordance with the market price of gold expressed in silver. It weighed 3.20-3.40 g.

OTTOMAN COINAGE
SELIM III
AH1203-1222/1789-1807AD

1/8 BUDJU
(3 Mazuna)
SILVER, 1.65-1.70 g
Mintname: *Jaza'Ir*

KM#	Date	Mintage	VG	Fine	VF	XF
40	AH1216	—	20.00	40.00	60.00	100.00
	1218	—	20.00	40.00	60.00	100.00
	1220	—	20.00	40.00	60.00	100.00

Rev: Leg. within hexagram.

47	AH1221	—	40.00	60.00	125.00	175.00
	1222	—	40.00	60.00	125.00	175.00

1/4 BUDJU
SILVER, 3.40 g
Mintname: *Jaza'Ir*

42	AH1216	—	20.00	40.00	75.00	120.00
	1217	—	20.00	40.00	75.00	120.00
	1218	—	20.00	40.00	75.00	120.00
	1219	—	20.00	40.00	75.00	120.00
	1220	—	20.00	40.00	75.00	120.00

Rev: Leg. within octagram.

48	AH1221	—	40.00	75.00	125.00	175.00
	1222	—	40.00	75.00	125.00	175.00

1/2 BUDJU

SILVER, 5.80-6.80 g
Mintname: *Jaza'Ir*

45	AH1216	—	30.00	50.00	150.00	225.00
	1217	—	30.00	50.00	150.00	225.00
	1218	—	30.00	50.00	150.00	225.00
	1219	—	30.00	50.00	150.00	225.00
	1220	—	30.00	50.00	150.00	225.00

1/4 SULTANI
GOLD, 16mm, 0.85 g
Mintname: *Jaza'Ir*
Obv. leg: 2 lines. Rev: Mint overdate.

44	AH1217	—	65.00	100.00	200.00	250.00
	1219	—	65.00	100.00	200.00	250.00

Rev: Leg. within octagram.

49	AH1221	—	150.00	225.00	300.00	375.00
	1222	—	150.00	225.00	300.00	375.00

1/2 SULTANI

GOLD, 1.70 g
Mintname: *Jaza'Ir*

46	AH1215	—	100.00	150.00	200.00	275.00
	1216	—	100.00	150.00	200.00	275.00
	1217	—	100.00	150.00	200.00	275.00
	1218	—	100.00	150.00	200.00	275.00
	1219	—	100.00	150.00	200.00	275.00

Rev: Leg. within octagram.

50	AH1221	—	200.00	275.00	375.00	500.00
	1222	—	200.00	275.00	375.00	500.00

Algiers/ALGERIA 93

SULTANI

GOLD, 3.40 g
Mintname: *Jaza'Ir*

KM#	Date	Mintage	VG	Fine	VF	XF
41	AH1216	—	200.00	275.00	375.00	500.00
	1217	—	200.00	275.00	375.00	500.00
	1218	—	200.00	275.00	375.00	500.00
	1219	—	200.00	275.00	375.00	500.00
	1220	—	200.00	275.00	375.00	500.00
	1221	—	200.00	275.00	375.00	500.00

3.10 g
Rev: Leg. within octagon.

KM#	Date	Mintage	VG	Fine	VF	XF
51	AH1221	—	—	—	Rare	—
	1222	—	—	—	Rare	—

MUSTAFA IV

AH1222-1223/1807-1808AD

1/8 BUDJU

SILVER, 16mm, 1.48 g
Mintname: *Jaza'Ir*

KM#	Date	Mintage	VG	Fine	VF	XF
53	AH1222	—	100.00	150.00	250.00	350.00
	1223	—	100.00	150.00	250.00	350.00

1/4 BUDJU

SILVER, 2.88-3.40 g
Mintname: *Jaza'Ir*

KM#	Date	Mintage	VG	Fine	VF	XF
54	AH1222	—	100.00	150.00	250.00	350.00
	1223	—	100.00	150.00	250.00	350.00

1/4 SULTANI

GOLD, 0.80 g
Mintname: *Jaza'Ir*

KM#	Date	Mintage	VG	Fine	VF	XF
55	AH1222	—	—	—	Rare	—
	1223	—	—	—	Rare	—

1/2 SULTANI

GOLD, 1.60-1.73 g
Mintname: *Jaza'Ir*

KM#	Date	Mintage	VG	Fine	VF	XF
56	AH1222	—	—	—	Rare	—
	1223	—	—	—	Rare	—

SULTANI

GOLD, 3.15-3.40 g
Mintname: *Jaza'Ir*

KM#	Date	Mintage	VG	Fine	VF	XF
57	AH1222	—	—	—	Rare	—
	1223	—	—	—	Rare	—

MAHMUD II

AH1223-1253/1808-1837AD

ASPER

(Akcheh or Dirham Saghir)

COPPER, square, often silver washed

KM#	Date	Mintage	Good	VG	Fine	VF
69	AH1230	—	30.00	45.00	60.00	—

2 ASPERS

COPPER, 0.80 g
Mintname: *Jaza'Ir*

KM#	Date	Mintage	Good	VG	Fine	VF
70	AH1237	—	5.00	10.00	25.00	35.00
	1238	—	5.00	10.00	25.00	35.00
	1240	—	5.00	10.00	25.00	35.00
	1242	—	5.00	10.00	25.00	35.00
	1243	—	5.00	10.00	25.00	35.00
	1244	—	5.00	10.00	25.00	35.00

Mintname: *Constantine*

KM#	Date	Mintage	Good	VG	Fine	VF
81	AH1247	—	25.00	50.00	80.00	135.00

5 ASPERS

(Valued at 1/3 Kharuba)

COPPER, 1.80-2.20 g
Mintname: *Jaza'Ir*

KM#	Date	Mintage	Good	VG	Fine	VF
71	AH1237	—	4.00	6.50	11.50	17.50
	1238	—	4.00	6.50	11.50	17.50
	1239	—	4.00	6.50	11.50	17.50
	1240	—	4.00	7.00	12.50	18.50
	1244	—	3.50	5.50	10.00	16.50

NOTE: The 5 Aspers formerly listed as C#140 is probably an example of the 1/8 Budju, KM#74, of very base metal.

10 ASPERS

COPPER

KM#	Date	Mintage	Good	VG	Fine	VF
72	AH1237	—	—	Rare, Unc. 1500.		

NOTE: Possibly a pattern issue.

KHARUB

BILLON, 14mm, 0.70-0.80 g
Mintname: *Jaza'Ir*

KM#	Date	Mintage	VG	Fine	VF	XF
73	AH1237	—	10.00	15.00	30.00	75.00
	1238	—	10.00	15.00	30.00	75.00
	1240	—	10.00	15.00	30.00	75.00
	1242	—	10.00	15.00	30.00	75.00

0.70-0.90 g
Mintname: *Constantine*

KM#	Date	Mintage	VG	Fine	VF	XF
76	AH1245	—	35.00	55.00	75.00	150.00
	1246	—	50.00	100.00	175.00	275.00
	1247	—	50.00	100.00	175.00	275.00
	1250	—	50.00	100.00	175.00	275.00
	1252	—	50.00	100.00	175.00	275.00

1/8 BUDJU

(Temin Budju = 3 Muzuna)

SILVER, 1.65-1.70 g
Mintname: *Jaza'Ir*

KM#	Date	Mintage	VG	Fine	VF	XF
61	AH1225	—	25.00	45.00	75.00	125.00
	1226	—	25.00	45.00	75.00	125.00
	1227	—	25.00	45.00	75.00	125.00
	1228	—	25.00	45.00	75.00	125.00
	1229	—	25.00	45.00	75.00	125.00
	1230	—	25.00	45.00	75.00	125.00
	1231	—	25.00	45.00	75.00	125.00
	1232	—	25.00	45.00	75.00	125.00
	1233	—	25.00	45.00	75.00	125.00
	1234	—	25.00	45.00	75.00	125.00

Reduced standard, 1.20-1.30 g

KM#	Date	Mintage	VG	Fine	VF	XF
74	AH1237	—	5.00	10.00	17.50	30.00
	1238	—	5.00	10.00	17.50	30.00
	1239	—	5.00	10.00	17.50	30.00
	1240	—	5.00	10.00	17.50	30.00
	1242	—	5.00	10.00	17.50	30.00
	1243	—	5.00	10.00	17.50	30.00
	1244	—	5.00	10.00	17.50	30.00
	1245	—	5.00	15.00	20.00	35.00

1/6 BUDJU

(Tugrali-ness-flik)
(4 Muzuna = 1/2 Batlaka)

SILVER, 1.50 g

KM#	Date	Mintage	VG	Fine	VF	XF
77	AH1245	—	7.50	15.00	30.00	75.00

SILVER or BILLON, 18-19mm, 1.40-1.50 g
Mintname: *Constantine*

KM#	Date	Mintage	VG	Fine	VF	XF
82	AH1247	—	50.00	100.00	175.00	250.00
	1248	—	50.00	100.00	175.00	250.00
	1252	—	50.00	100.00	175.00	250.00

1/4 BUDJU

(6 Muzuna = Rebi Budju)

SILVER, 20mm, 3.40 g
Mintname: *Jaza'Ir*
Octagram type

KM#	Date	Mintage	VG	Fine	VF	XF
59	AH1223	—	40.00	75.00	125.00	200.00
	1224	—	40.00	75.00	125.00	200.00

KM#	Date	Mintage	VG	Fine	VF	XF
62	AH1225	—	35.00	60.00	100.00	150.00
	1226	—	35.00	60.00	100.00	150.00
	1227	—	35.00	60.00	100.00	150.00
	1228	—	35.00	60.00	100.00	150.00
	1229	—	35.00	60.00	100.00	150.00
	1230	—	35.00	60.00	100.00	150.00
	1231	—	35.00	60.00	100.00	150.00
	1232	—	35.00	60.00	100.00	150.00
	1233	—	35.00	60.00	100.00	150.00
	1234	—	35.00	60.00	100.00	150.00
	1235	—	35.00	60.00	100.00	150.00

Reduced standard, 2.40 g

KM#	Date	Mintage	VG	Fine	VF	XF
67	AH1236	—	10.00	15.00	25.00	45.00
	1237	—	7.00	12.50	20.00	35.00
	1238	—	7.50	12.50	20.00	35.00
	1239	—	7.50	12.50	20.00	35.00
	1240	—	7.50	12.50	20.00	35.00
	1241	—	7.50	12.50	20.00	35.00
	1242	—	7.50	12.50	20.00	35.00
	1243	—	7.50	12.50	20.00	35.00
	1244	—	7.50	12.50	20.00	35.00
	1245	—	10.00	15.00	22.50	40.00
	1246	—	15.00	20.00	30.00	50.00

Mintname: *Medea*

KM#	Date	Mintage	VG	Fine	VF	XF
80	AH1246	—	—	—	Rare	—

Algiers/ALGERIA

1/3 BUDJU
(Tugrali-batlaka)

SILVER, 3.10 g
Toughra type

KM#	Date	Mintage	VG	Fine	VF	XF
78	AH1245	—	20.00	35.00	65.00	135.00

BUDJU

SILVER, 9.80-10.10 g
Mintname: *Jaza'Ir*

68	AH1236	—	12.50	20.00	35.00	75.00
	1237	—	12.50	20.00	30.00	60.00
	1238	—	12.50	20.00	30.00	60.00
	1239	—	12.50	20.00	30.00	60.00
	1240	—	12.50	20.00	30.00	60.00
	1241	—	12.50	20.00	30.00	60.00
	1242	—	12.50	20.00	35.00	75.00
	1243	—	12.50	25.00	35.00	75.00
	1244	—	25.00	40.00	75.00	150.00
	1245	—	—	Reported, not confirmed		

(Tugrali-rial)

Mintname: *Jaza'Ir*

79	AH1245	—	100.00	200.00	350.00	700.00

SILVER or BILLON, 7.90-9.80 g
Mintname: *Constantine*

83	AH1247	—	150.00	250.00	600.00	1250.
	1248	—	150.00	250.00	600.00	1250.
	1249	—	150.00	300.00	650.00	1500.
	1253	—	150.00	250.00	600.00	1250.

2 BUDJU
(Zudj Budju)

SILVER, 19.50-20.00 g
Mintname: *Jaza'Ir*

KM#	Date	Mintage	VG	Fine	VF	XF
75	AH1237	—	25.00	40.00	65.00	100.00
	1238	—	25.00	40.00	65.00	100.00
	1239	—	25.00	40.00	65.00	100.00
	1240	—	27.50	45.00	75.00	110.00
	1241	—	25.00	40.00	65.00	100.00
	1242	—	25.00	40.00	65.00	100.00
	1243	—	30.00	50.00	85.00	150.00
	1244	—	50.00	75.00	150.00	250.00

NOTE: Varieties exist.

1/4 SULTANI
GOLD, 14-15mm, 0.85 g
Mintname: *Jaza'Ir*
Obv: *Sultan Mahmud.*

63.1	AH1228	—	—	—	Rare	—
	1234	—	—	—	Rare	—

Obv: *Sultan Mahmud Han.*

63.2	AH1231	—	85.00	125.00	175.00	250.00
	1240	—	85.00	125.00	175.00	250.00
	1243	—	85.00	125.00	175.00	250.00

1/2 SULTANI

GOLD, 1.60 g
Mintname: *Jaza'Ir*

65	AH1231	—	100.00	140.00	200.00	275.00
	1232	—	100.00	140.00	200.00	275.00
	1236	—	100.00	140.00	200.00	275.00
	1237	—	100.00	140.00	200.00	275.00
	1238	—	100.00	140.00	200.00	275.00
	1239	—	100.00	140.00	200.00	275.00
	1240	—	100.00	140.00	200.00	275.00

SULTANI
GOLD, 24mm, 3.20 g
Mintname: *Jaza'Ir*
Rev: Year in fourth line.

60	AH1223	—	250.00	350.00	450.00	575.00
	1224	—	250.00	350.00	450.00	575.00
	1225	—	250.00	350.00	450.00	575.00
	1226	—	250.00	350.00	450.00	575.00
	1228	—	250.00	350.00	450.00	575.00
	1231	—	250.00	350.00	450.00	575.00

Rev: Year in third line.

66	1235	—	165.00	225.00	300.00	400.00
	1236	—	165.00	225.00	300.00	400.00
	1237	—	165.00	225.00	300.00	400.00
	1238	—	165.00	225.00	300.00	400.00
	1239	—	165.00	225.00	300.00	400.00
	1240	—	165.00	225.00	300.00	400.00
	1241	—	165.00	225.00	300.00	400.00
	1243	—	165.00	225.00	300.00	400.00
	3421(error)	—	165.00	225.00	300.00	400.00
	1244	—	165.00	225.00	300.00	400.00

REVOLUTIONARY COINAGE
ABDEL KADER
AH1250-1264/1834-1847AD

5 ASPERS/KHARUBA
(Mohammadiya)

COPPER-BILLON, .73-1.30 g
Mintname: *Taqidemt*
12-18mm

KM#	Date	Mintage	Good	VG	Fine	VF
85	AH1250	—	6.00	10.00	17.50	35.00
	1252	—	6.00	10.00	17.50	35.00
	1253	—	6.00	10.00	17.50	35.00
	1254, Arabic '4'					
		—	3.50	6.00	10.00	25.00
	1254, Persian '4'					
		—	3.50	6.00	10.00	25.00
	1255	—	3.00	6.00	10.00	25.00
	1256	—	3.00	6.00	10.00	25.00
	1257	—	4.50	7.50	12.50	35.00

Reduced size. 8mm, 0.40 g

86	AH1258	—	6.50	11.50	17.50	50.00

KHARUBA
BILLON
Mintname: *Al Mascara*

KM#	Date	Mintage	VG	Fine	VF	XF
87	AH125x	—	70.00	100.00	150.00	250.00

1/8 BUDJU
(3 Muzuna-Nasfia)

BILLON, 1.00 g
Mintname: *Taqidemt*

88	AH1254	—	100.00	150.00	275.00	450.00

BUDJU
SILVER, 27-28mm, 5.57-6.03 g
Mintname: *Taqidemt*
Denomination uncertain
Obv: 3 lines. Rev: 4 lines.

89	AH1256	—	150.00	250.00	525.00	800.00

NOTE: This coin has also been considered to be a 1/2 Budju, but its weight apparently indicates a reduced Budju in debased metal. Varieties exist.

ALGERIA
FRENCH OCCUPATION
MINT MARKS
(a) Paris - Privy marks only
MONETARY SYSTEM
100 Centimes = 1 Franc

20 FRANCS

COPPER-NICKEL

KM#	Date	Mintage	Fine	VF	XF	Unc
91	1949(a)	25.566	.25	.50	1.25	5.00
	1956(a)	7.500	.25	.50	1.25	5.00

50 FRANCS

COPPER-NICKEL

92	1949(a)	18.000	2.00	4.00	7.50	12.50

100 FRANCS

COPPER-NICKEL

KM#	Date	Mintage	Fine	VF	XF	Unc
93	1950(a)	22.189	1.00	2.50	4.00	15.00
	1952(a)	12.000	1.00	2.50	5.00	20.00

NOTE: During World War II homeland coins were struck at the Paris Mint and the France 2 Francs, Y#89 were struck at the Philadelphia Mint for use in Africa.

REPUBLIC
MONETARY SYSTEM
100 Centimes = 1 Dinar

CENTIME

ALUMINUM

KM#	Date	Year	Mintage	VF	XF	Unc
94	AH1383	1964	35.000	—	—	.10

2 CENTIMES

ALUMINUM

| 95 | AH1383 | 1964 | 50.000 | — | .10 | .25 |

5 CENTIMES

ALUMINUM

| 96 | AH1383 | 1964 | 40.000 | — | .10 | .25 |

F.A.O. Issue

KM#	Date	Mintage	VF	XF	Unc
101	1970/73	10.000	—	.15	.50

F.A.O. Issue

| 106 | 1974/77 | 10.000 | — | .15 | .50 |

F.A.O. Issue

| 113 | ND | — | — | .10 | .35 |

KM#	Date	Mintage	VF	XF	Unc
116	1985/89	—	—	.10	.35

10 CENTIMES

ALUMINUM-BRONZE

KM#	Date	Year	Mintage	VF	XF	Unc
97	AH1383	1964	—	.10	.20	.25

ALUMINUM

KM#	Date	Mintage	VF	XF	Unc
115	1984	—	—	.10	.25

20 CENTIMES

ALUMINUM-BRONZE

KM#	Date	Year	Mintage	VF	XF	Unc
98	AH1383	1964	—	.10	.25	.50

BRASS
F.A.O. Issue

KM#	Date	Mintage	VF	XF	Unc
103	1972	20.000	.10	.25	.65

ALUMINUM-BRONZE
F.A.O. Issue

| 107.1 | 1975 | 50.000 | .15 | .30 | 1.25 |

Obv: Small flower above 20.

| 107.2 | 1975 | Inc. Ab. | .15 | .30 | 1.00 |

50 CENTIMES

ALUMINUM-BRONZE

KM#	Date	Year	Mintage	VF	XF	Unc
99	AH1383	1964	—	.20	.30	.65

COPPER-NICKEL-ZINC

| 102 | AH1391 | 1971 | 10.000 | .15 | .20 | .40 |
| | 1393 | 1973 | | .15 | .20 | .40 |

BRASS
30th Anniversary French-Algerian Clash

KM#	Date	Mintage	VF	XF	Unc
109	ND(1975)	18.000	.20	.50	2.00

ALUMINUM-BRONZE
Hegira Issue

KM#	Date	Year	Mintage	VF	XF	Unc
111	AH1400	1980	—	.20	.50	2.50

DINAR

COPPER-NICKEL

| 100 | AH1383 | 1964 | 15.000 | .50 | 1.00 | 1.50 |

F.A.O. Issue

KM#	Date	Mintage	VF	XF	Unc
104.1	1972	20.000	.35	.75	2.00

Legend touches inner circle.

| 104.2 | 1972 | Inc. Ab. | .35 | .75 | 2.00 |

ALGERIA 96

20th Anniversary of Independence

KM#	Date	Mintage	VF	XF	Unc
112	1983	—	.50	1.00	3.50

5 DINARS

12.0000 g, .750 SILVER, .2893 oz ASW
10th Anniversary & F.A.O. Issue

| 105 | 1972(a) | — | — | — | 15.00 |

NICKEL

| 105a | 1972(a) | — | 4.00 | 7.50 | 15.00 |

NOTE: Varieties exist with the mintmark pointing toward the oil derrick and away from the derrick.

20th Anniversary of Revolution

| 108 | 1974 | — | 4.00 | 8.00 | 12.50 |

30th Anniversary of Revolution

| 114 | 1984 | — | 1.50 | 3.00 | 10.00 |

10 DINARS

BRONZE, 11.37 g

| 110 | 1979 | 25.001 | 2.75 | 4.00 | 6.00 |
| | 1981 | — | 2.75 | 4.00 | 6.00 |

14.6000 g, .925 SILVER, .4342 oz ASW

| 110a | 1979 | 1,000 | — | — | 25.00 |

24.5000 g, .900 GOLD, .7090 oz AGW

| 110b | 1979 | 100 pcs. | — | — | 1250. |

ANDORRA

Principality of Andorra (Principat d'Andorra), situated on the southern slopes of the Pyrenees Mountains between France and Spain, has an area of 175 sq. mi. (453 sq. km.) and a population of 30,600. Capital: Andorra la Vella. Tourism is the chief source of income. Timber, cattle and derivatives, and furniture are exported.

According to tradition, the independence of Andorra derives from a charter Charlemagne granted the people of Andorra in 806 in recognition of their help in battling the Moors. An agreement between the Count of Foix (France) and the Bishop of Seo de Urgel (Spanish) in 1278 to recognize each other as Co-Princes of Andorra gave the state what has been its political form and territorial extent continuously to the present day. Over the years, the title on the French side passed to the Kings of Navarre, then to the Kings of France, and is now held by the President of France. In 1806 Napoleon declared Andorra a republic, but today it is referred to as a principality.

NOTE: Previous listings KM#1-13 are considered medals.

MONETARY SYSTEM
100 Centims = 1 Diner

25 CENTIMS

BRONZE

KM#	Date	Mintage	Fine	VF	XF	Unc
33	1986	.010	—	—	—	3.50

DINER

BRASS

| 14 | 1983 | .030 | — | — | — | 4.50 |

CAST COPPER - ZINC

| 15 | 1984 | .010 | — | — | — | 2.50 |

BRASS

| 35 | 1986 | .010 | — | — | — | 1.75 |

2 DINERS

COPPER-NICKEL RING, BRONZE CENTER

Wildlife - Bear

KM#	Date	Mintage	Fine	VF	XF	Unc
19	1984	5,000	—	—	—	6.00

Wildlife - Squirrel

| 20 | 1984 | 5,000 | — | — | — | 6.00 |

Wildlife - Ibex

| 21 | 1984 | 5,000 | — | — | — | 6.00 |

1988 Winter Olympics - Skier

| 27 | 1985 | .015 | — | — | — | 6.00 |

1988 Summer Olympics - High Jumper

| 28 | 1985 | .015 | — | — | — | 6.00 |

BRASS

| 36 | 1986 | .010 | — | — | — | 3.50 |

COPPER-NICKEL
1988 Summer Olympics - Tennis

| 40 | 1987 | .020 | — | — | — | 14.00 |

ANDORRA 97

1992 Winter Olympics - Kayak & Skier

KM#	Date	Mintage	Fine	VF	XF	Unc
46	1987	—	—	—	—	13.50

5 DINERS

CAST COPPER

16	1984	.010	—	—	—	5.00

2nd Congress of the Catalan Language

29	1986	.010	—	—	—	Proof 5.00

BRONZE

37	1986	.010	—	—	—	8.50

10 DINERS

8.0000 g, .900 CAST SILVER, .2315 oz ASW

17	1984	.010	—	—	—	12.50

World Cup Soccer Games

34	1986	.010	—	—	—	P/L 30.00

7.9300 g, .900 SILVER, .2295 oz ASW

KM#	Date	Mintage	Fine	VF	XF	Unc
38	1986	.010	—	—	—	17.50

20 DINERS

16.0000 g, .835 SILVER, .4296 oz ASW
Wildlife - Bear

22	1984	.010	—	—	—	Proof 25.00

Protection of Nature - Squirrel

23	1984	.010	—	—	—	Proof 25.00

Protection of Nature - Ibex
Obv: Similar to KM#23.

24	1984	.010	—	—	—	Proof 25.00

16.0000 g, .900 SILVER, .4630 oz ASW
Los Angeles Olympics

25	1984	.010	—	—	—	20.00
	1984		—	—	—	Proof 30.00

Christmas

KM#	Date	Mintage	Fine	VF	XF	Unc
26	1985	7,000	—	—	—	Proof 20.00

Olympic Tennis

39	1987	.010	—	—	—	40.00

16.0000 g, .999 SILVER, .4501 oz ASW
Seoul Olympics - Stadium

43	1988	.012	—	—	—	

25 DINERS

20.0000 g, .900 SILVER, .5787 oz ASW

18	1984	4,350	—	—	—	30.00
	1984	650 pcs.	—	—	—	Proof 35.00

ANDORRA

Latin Legends

KM#	Date	Mintage	Fine	VF	XF	Unc
32	1983	1,500	—	—	—	180.00

MINT SETS (MS)

KM#	Date	Mintage	Identification	Issue Price	Mkt. Val.
MS1	1986(5)	—	KM33,35-38	31.00	31.00

Andorra's Governing Charter

KM#	Date	Mintage	Fine	VF	XF	Unc
44	1988	3,000	—	—	Proof	30.00

100 DINERS

5.0000 g, .999 GOLD, .1607 oz AGW

41	1987	2,000	—	—	—	80.00

42	1988	2,000	—	—	—	80.00

250 DINERS

12.0000 g, .999 GOLD, .3858 oz AGW
Andorra's Governing Charter

45	1988	3,000	—	—	Proof	200.00

SOVEREIGN

8.0000 g, .918 GOLD, .2361 oz AGW
Latin Legend

30	1982	1,500	—	—	—	180.00

Catalan Legend

31	1982	1,500	—	—	—	180.00

ANGOLA

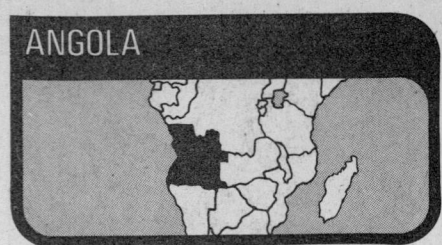

The People's Republic of Angola, a country on the west coast of southern Africa bounded by Zaire, Zambia, and Namibia (South-West Africa), has an area of 481,354 sq. mi. (1,246,700 sq. km.) and a population of 7.2 million, predominantly Bantu in origin. Capital: Luanda. Most of the people are engaged in subsistence agriculture. However, important oil and mineral deposits make Angola potentially one of the richest countries in Africa. Iron and diamonds are exported.

Angola was discovered by Portuguese navigator Diogo Cao in 1482. Portuguese settlers arrived in 1491, and established Angola as a major slaving center which sent about 3 million slaves to the New World.

A revolt, characterized by guerrilla warfare, against Portuguese rule began in 1961 and continued until 1974, when a new regime in Portugal offered independence. The independence movement was actively supported by three groups, the National Front, based in Zaire, the Soviet-backed Popular Movement, and the moderate National Union. Independence was proclaimed on Nov. 11, 1975, and the Portuguese departed, leaving the Angolan people to work out their own political destiny. Within hours, each of the independence groups proclaimed itself Angola's sole ruler. A bloody intertribal civil war erupted in which the Communist Popular Movement, assisted by Soviet arms and Cuban mercenaries, was the eventual victor.

RULERS
Portuguese until 1975

MINT MARKS
KN - King's Norton

MONETARY SYSTEM
(Until 1860)
50 Reis = 1 Macuta
(Commencing 1910)
100 Centavos = 20 Macutas = 1 Escudo

1/4 MACUTA

COPPER

KM#	Date	Mintage	VG	Fine	VF	XF
38	1814	—	5.00	10.00	15.00	35.00
	1815	—	15.00	30.00	60.00	125.00
	1816	—	—	Reported, not confirmed		

1/2 MACUTA

COPPER

39	1814	—	3.00	6.00	10.00	25.00
	1815	.018	75.00	150.00	300.00	500.00
	1819	—	—	—	Rare	

42	1848	.417	5.00	10.00	15.00	35.00
	1851	.104	2.00	4.00	7.50	20.00
	1853	.143	2.00	4.00	7.50	20.00
43	1858	.226	1.50	3.00	5.00	15.00
	1860	.398	1.50	3.00	5.00	15.00

MACUTA

KM#	Date	Mintage	VG	Fine	VF	XF
40	1814	—	2.00	3.50	7.50	17.50
	1816	6,110	25.00	45.00	90.00	175.00
	1819				Rare	

NOTE: Lightweight coins dated 1814 exist weighing 10.96 g.

Similar to 1/2 Macuta, KM#42.
| 44 | 1860 | — | 2.50 | 4.00 | 7.50 | 20.00 |

2 MACUTAS
COPPER
Similar to 1 Macuta, KM#40.
41	1815	—	25.00	50.00	90.00	175.00
	1816	—	35.00	65.00	120.00	250.00
	1819	3,175	—	—	Rare	

COUNTERMARKED COINAGE

In 1814 various copper coins were countermarked with the crowned arms of Portugal to double their face value.

10 REIS
COPPER
c/m: Crowned arms on V Reis, KM#7.

KM#	Date	Year	Good	VG	Fine	VF
45	(1814)	1752	4.00	7.50	15.00	30.00
		1753	1.50	3.00	5.00	10.00
		1757	2.00	4.00	7.50	15.00

20 REIS
COPPER
c/m: Crowned arms on X Reis, KM#8.
46	(1814)	1752	4.50	7.50	12.50	25.00
		1753	4.50	7.50	12.50	25.00
		1757	5.50	10.00	15.00	30.00

1/2 MACUTA

COPPER
c/m: Crowned arms on 1/4 Macuta, KM#10.
49	(1814)	1762	3.00	6.50	14.00	27.50
		1763	2.00	4.00	7.50	15.00
		1770	2.00	4.00	7.50	15.00
		1771	6.50	12.50	20.00	40.00

c/m: Crowned arms on 1/4 Macuta, KM#27.
| 53 | (1814) | 1785 | 2.50 | 5.00 | 10.00 | 20.00 |

c/m: Crowned arms on 1/4 Macuta, KM#29.
| 55 | (1814) | 1789 | 2.50 | 5.00 | 10.00 | 20.00 |

40 REIS
COPPER
c/m: Crowned arms on XX Reis, KM#9.

KM#	Date	Year	Good	VG	Fine	VF
47	(1814)	1752	4.00	7.50	15.00	30.00
		1753	2.00	4.00	7.50	15.00
		1757	2.00	4.00	7.50	15.00

MACUTA

COPPER
c/m: Crowned arms on 1/2 Macuta, KM#11.
50	(1814)	1762	15.00	25.00	40.00	80.00
		1763	3.00	6.00	10.00	20.00
		1770	3.00	6.00	10.00	20.00

c/m: Crowned arms on 1/2 Macuta, KM#28.
| 54 | (1814) | 1785 | 5.00 | 9.00 | 14.00 | 27.50 |
| | | 1786 | 5.00 | 9.00 | 14.00 | 27.50 |

c/m: Crowned arms on 1/2 Macuta, KM#30.
| 56 | (1814) | 1789 | 5.00 | 8.00 | 14.00 | 27.50 |

80 REIS
COPPER
c/m: Crowned arms on XL Reis, KM#9.
| 48 | (1814) | 1753 | 8.00 | 15.00 | 25.00 | 45.00 |
| | | 1757 | 8.00 | 15.00 | 25.00 | 45.00 |

2 MACUTAS
COPPER
c/m: Crowned arms on 1 Macuta, KM#12.
51	(1814)	1762	25.00	40.00	60.00	120.00
		1763	7.50	10.00	15.00	30.00
		1770	5.00	7.50	10.00	20.00

c/m: Crowned arms on 1 Macuta, KM#20.
52	(1814)	1783	40.00	65.00	90.00	175.00
		1785	5.00	10.00	15.00	35.00
		1786	7.50	12.50	20.00	45.00

c/m: Crowned arms on 1 Macuta, KM#31.
KM#	Date	Year	Good	VG	Fine	VF
57	(1814)	1789	5.00	10.00	15.00	35.00

c/m: Crowned arms on 1 Macuta, KM#40.
| 58 | (1814) | 1814 | — | — | Rare | |
| | | 1816 | — | — | Rare | |

4 MACUTAS
COPPER
c/m: Crowned arms on 2 Macutas, KM#41.
| 59 | (1814) | 1815 | — | — | Rare | |
| | | 1816 | — | — | Rare | |

DECIMAL COINAGE
100 Centavos = 1 Escudo

CENTAVO

BRONZE
KM#	Date	Mintage	Fine	VF	XF	Unc
60	1921	1.360	7.50	12.50	25.00	50.00

2 CENTAVOS

BRONZE
| 61 | 1921 | .530 | 10.00 | 15.00 | 35.00 | 85.00 |

5 CENTAVOS
(1 Macuta)

BRONZE
62	1921	.720	5.00	8.50	15.00	45.00
	1922	5.680	4.00	7.50	12.50	35.00
	1923	5.840	4.00	7.50	12.50	35.00
	1924	—	12.00	20.00	40.00	75.00

NICKEL-BRONZE
| 66 | 1927 | 2.002 | 1.50 | 3.00 | 7.00 | 12.50 |

10 CENTAVOS
(2 Macutas)

COPPER-NICKEL
63	1921	.160	7.50	12.50	22.50	60.00
	1922	.340	5.00	10.00	17.50	40.00
	1923	2.960	3.00	6.00	12.00	30.00

| 67 | 1927 | 2.003 | 1.25 | 3.25 | 7.00 | 15.00 |
| | 1928 | 1.000 | 1.25 | 3.25 | 7.00 | 15.00 |

ANGOLA 100

KM#	Date	Mintage	BRONZE Fine	VF	XF	Unc
70	1948	10.000	.75	2.00	3.00	5.00
	1949	10.000	.20	.50	1.00	2.00

			ALUMINUM			
82 (82a)	1974	4.000	—	—	—	8.00

NOTE: Not released for circulation, but relatively available.

20 CENTAVOS

			COPPER-NICKEL			
64	1921	2.115	3.00	7.00	15.00	35.00
	1922	1.730	3.00	7.00	15.00	35.00

			NICKEL-BRONZE			
68	1927	2.001	2.25	4.00	7.00	10.00
	1928	.500	3.00	5.00	10.00	15.00

			BRONZE			
71	1948	7.850	.40	.75	1.00	2.50
	1949	2.150	4.00	7.50	12.50	20.00

| 78 | 1962 | 3.000 | — | — | .50 | 1.00 |

50 CENTAVOS

			NICKEL			
65	1922	6.000	2.50	7.50	12.50	35.00
	1923 KN	6.000	—	—	225.00	375.00
	1923 Inc. Ab.		2.50	7.50	12.50	35.00

			NICKEL-BRONZE			
69	1927	1.608	2.50	6.00	15.00	50.00
	1928	1.600	2.50	6.00	15.00	50.00

| 72 | 1948 | 4.000 | .35 | .75 | 2.00 | 4.00 |
| | 1950 | 4.000 | .35 | .75 | 2.00 | 4.00 |

KM#	Date	Mintage	BRONZE	VF	XF	Unc
75	1953	5.000		.20	.40	1.00
	1954	11.731		.20	.35	.70
	1955	1.126		2.00	3.00	6.00
	1957	8.873		.20	.40	1.00
	1958	17.520		.15	.30	.60
	1961	8.750		.20	.40	1.00

			COPPER-NICKEL			
75a	1974	150 pcs.	—	100.00	150.00

NOTE: Not released for circulation.

ESCUDO

			BRONZE			
76	1953	2.001	.25	.75	2.50
	1956	2.989	.25	.75	2.00
	1963	5.000	.25	.75	1.50
	1965	5.000	.25	.75	1.50
	1972	10.000	.20	.40	1.00
	1974	6.214	.50	1.25	2.50

			COPPER-NICKEL			
76a	1972	—	—	Rare	—
	1974	—	—	Rare	—

NOTE: Not released for circulation.

2-1/2 ESCUDOS

			COPPER-NICKEL			
77	1953	6.008	.35	.75	1.50
	1956	9.992	.35	.75	1.50
	1967	6.000	.35	.75	1.50
	1968	5.000	.35	.75	1.50
	1969	5.000	.35	.75	1.50
	1974	19.999	.25	.50	1.00

5 ESCUDOS

			COPPER-NICKEL			
81	1972	8.000	7.00	12.00	20.00
	1974	*3.343	—	—	50.00

*NOTE: Not released for circulation.

10 ESCUDOS

5.0000 g, .720 SILVER, .1157 oz ASW

| 73 | 1952 | 2.023 | 2.50 | 4.00 | 6.50 |
| | 1955 | 1.977 | 2.50 | 4.00 | 6.50 |

KM#	Date	Mintage	COPPER-NICKEL	VF	XF	Unc
79	1969	3.022		1.50	3.00	6.00
	1970	.978		2.00	4.00	7.00

20 ESCUDOS

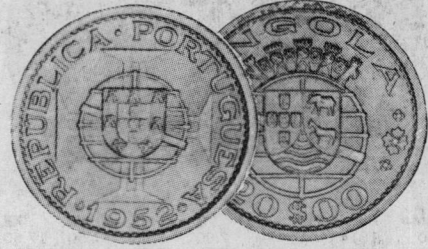

10.0000 g, .720 SILVER, .2315 oz ASW

| 74 | 1952 | 1.003 | 2.50 | 5.00 | 8.50 |
| | 1955 | .997 | 2.50 | 4.00 | 7.50 |

			COPPER-NICKEL			
80	1971	1.572	.75	2.00	4.00
	1972	.428	1.00	2.50	5.00

PEOPLE'S REPUBLIC

MONETARY SYSTEM
100 Lwei = 1 Kwanza

50 LWEI

			COPPER-NICKEL		
90 (82)	ND	—	.10	.30	.85
	1979	—	.10	.30	.85

KWANZA

			COPPER-NICKEL		
83	ND	—	.30	.50	1.00
	1978	—	.25	.40	1.00
	1979	—	.25	.40	1.00

2 KWANZAS

			COPPER-NICKEL		
84	ND	—	.40	.60	1.25

5 KWANZAS

			COPPER-NICKEL		
85	ND	—	.75	1.00	2.00

10 KWANZAS

COPPER-NICKEL

KM#	Date	Mintage	VF	XF	Unc
86	ND	—	1.00	1.50	2.75
	1978	—	1.00	1.50	2.75

20 KWANZAS

COPPER-NICKEL

87	1978	—	1.50	2.50	5.00

500 KWANZAS

SILVER

88	1979	7,500	—	—	25.00

1000 KWANZAS

SILVER

89	1979	7,500	—	—	35.00

ANGUILLA

The British colony of Anguilla, a self-governing British territory situated in the east Caribbean Sea about 60 miles (100 km.) northwest of St. Kitts, has an area of 35 sq. mi. (91 sq. km.) and a population of 6,832. Capital: The Valley. In recent years, tourism has replaced the traditional fishing, stock raising and salt production as the main industry.

Anguilla was discovered by Columbus in 1493 and became a British colony in 1650. In March 1967, Anguilla was joined politically with St. Christopher (St. Kitts) and Nevis to form a British associated state.

On June 16, 1967, the Provisional Government of Anguilla unilaterally declared its independence and seceded from the Federation. Later, on July 11, 1967, a vote of confidence was taken and the results favored independence. Britain refused to accept the declaration (nor did any other country recognize it) and appointed a British administrator whom Anguilla accepted. However, in Feb. 1969 Anguilla ousted the British emissary, voted to sever all ties with Britain, and established the Republic of Anguilla. The following month Britain landed a force of paratroopers and policemen. This bloodless counteraction ended the self-proclaimed republic and resulted in the installation of a governing commissioner. The troops were withdrawn in Sept. 1969, and the Anguilla Act of July 1971 placed Anguilla directly under British control. A new constitution in 1976 established Anguilla as a self-governing British colony. Britain retains power over defense, police and civil service, and foreign affairs.

RULERS

British

PROVISIONAL GOVERNMENT
1967, 1969

COUNTERMARKED COINAGE
LIBERTY DOLLAR

c/m: ANGUILLA LIBERTY DOLLAR JULY 11, 1967 on various crown-sized coins.

KM#	Date	Mintage	Identification	Issue Price	Mkt. Val.
1	1967	5,987	c/m on Mexico KM467	10.00	15.00

NOTE: 4,000 of the above pieces were remelted.

2	1967	1,530	c/m on Mexico KM465	10.00	25.00
3	1967	1,531	c/m on Peru KM218.1	10.00	25.00

3A	1967	Inc. KM4	c/m on Yemen Y31	10.00	35.00
4	1967	494 pcs.	c/m on Yemen Y17	10.00	80.00
5	1967	340 pcs.	c/m on Philippines KM172	10.00	65.00

6	1967	250 pcs.	c/m on Mexico KM474	10.00	75.00
7	1967	91 pcs.	c/m on Panama KM13	10.00	100.00
8	1967	21 pcs.	c/m on Ecuador KM79	—	150.00
9	1967	15 pcs.	c/m on Mexico KM409	—	200.00
10	1967	10 pcs.	c/m on China, assorted Yuan Shih Kai Dollars	—	225.00
11	1967	2 pcs.	c/m on Mexico KM468	—	400.00
12	1967	1 pc.	c/m on Gr. Britain Y-T5	—	400.00

NOTE: The c/m was done in San Francisco, California.

100 LIBERTY DOLLARS
GOLD
c/m: 100 LIBERTY DOLLARS

KM#	Date	Mintage	Identification	Issue Price	Mkt. Val.
14	1967	2 pcs.	c/m on Mexico KM481	—	3000.

NOTE: The c/m was done in San Francisco, California.

DECIMAL COINAGE
1/2 DOLLAR

3.6100 g, .999 SILVER, .1160 oz ASW

KM#	Date	Mintage	VF	XF	Unc
15	1969	4,200	—	Proof	10.00
	1970	Inc. Ab.	—	Proof	10.00

DOLLAR

7.1800 g, .999 SILVER, .2308 oz ASW

16	1969	—	—	Proof	12.50
	1970	Inc. Ab.	—	Proof	12.50

2 DOLLARS

14.1400 g, .999 SILVER, .4546 oz ASW

17	1969	4,150	—	Proof	17.50
	1970	Inc. Ab.	—	Proof	17.50

4 DOLLARS

28.4800 g, .999 SILVER, .9156 oz ASW

18	1969	5,100	—	Proof	70.00
	1970	Inc. Ab.	—	Proof	70.00

5 DOLLARS

2.4600 g, .900 GOLD, .0711 oz AGW

20	1969	1,925	—	Proof	75.00
	1970	Inc. Ab.	—	Proof	75.00

ANGUILLA

10 DOLLARS

4.9300 g, .900 GOLD, .1426 oz AGW

KM#	Date	Mintage	VF	XF	Unc
21	1969	1,615	—	Proof	125.00
	1970	Inc. Ab.	—	Proof	125.00

20 DOLLARS

9.8700 g, .900 GOLD, .2856 oz AGW

22	1969	1,395	—	Proof	225.00
	1970	Inc. Ab.	—	Proof	225.00

100 DOLLARS

49.3700 g, .900 GOLD, 1.4287 oz AGW

23	1969	710 pcs.	—	Proof	950.00
	1970	Inc. Ab.	—	Proof	950.00

PROOF SETS (PS)

KM#	Date	Mintage	Identification	Issue Price	Mkt. Val.
PS1	1969(8)	—	KM15-18,20-23	225.50	1500.
PS2	1969(4)	—	KM15-18	25.50	115.00
PS3	1969(4)	—	KM20-23	200.00	1375.
PS4	1970(8)	—	KM15-18,20-23	225.50	1500.
PS5	1970(4)	—	KM15-18	25.50	115.00
PS6	1970(4)	—	KM20-23	200.00	1375.

Listings For
ANNAM: refer to Vietnam

ANTIGUA & BARBUDA

The Independent State of Antigua and Barbuda, located on the eastern edge of the Leeward Islands in the Caribbean Sea, has an area of 171 sq. mi. (442 sq. km.) and a population of 77,004. Capital: St. John's. Prior to 1967 Antigua and its dependencies, Barbuda and Redonda, comprised a presidency of the Leeward Islands. The mountainous island produces sugar, molasses, rum, cotton and fruit. Tourism is making an increasingly valuable contribution to the economy.

Antigua was discovered by Columbus in 1493, settled by the British in 1632, occupied by the French in 1666, and ceded to Britain in 1667. It became an associated state on February 27, 1967. On November 1, 1981 it became independent as Antigua and Barbuda.

Spanish silver coinage was used throughout the islands' early history, however, late in the seventeeth century the introduction of British tin farthings was attempted with complete lack of success.

From 1825 to 1955, Antigua was on the sterling standard and used British coins. Coins of the British Caribbean Territories (Eastern Group) and East Caribbean States, and banknotes of East Caribbean Currency Authority are now used on the island.

RULERS
British

MONETARY SYSTEM
100 Cents = 1 Dollar

4 DOLLARS

COPPER-NICKEL
F.A.O. Issue

KM#	Date	Mintage	VF	XF	Unc
1	1970	.014	—	5.00	8.00
	1970	2,000	—	Proof	25.00

NOTE: For similar issues see Barbados, Dominica, Grenada, Montserrat, St. Kitts, St. Lucia and St. Vincent.

10 DOLLARS

COPPER-NICKEL
Royal Visit

5	1985	.100	—	—	5.00

28.2800 g, .925 SILVER, .8409 oz ASW

5a	1985	5,000	—	Proof	35.00

47.5400 g, .917 GOLD, 1.4013 oz AGW

KM#	Date	Mintage	VF	XF	Unc
5b	1985	250 pcs.	—	Proof	1300.

30 DOLLARS

31.1000 g, .500 SILVER, .5000 oz ASW
George Washington - Artillery

2	1982	1,200	—	Proof	45.00

George Washington - Row Boat
Obv: Similar to KM#2.

3	1982	1,125	—	Proof	45.00

George Washington - With Horse
Obv: Similar to KM#2.

4	1982	675 pcs.	—	Proof	50.00

500 DOLLARS

47.5400 g, .917 GOLD, 1.4011 oz AGW
Obv: Queen Elizabeth II. Rev: Arms.

6	1985	250 pcs.	—	Proof	1300.

ARGENTINA

The Argentine Republic, located in southern South America, has an area of 1,068,301 sq. mi. (2,766,889 sq. km.) and a population of 31.5 million. Capital: Buenos Aires. Its varied topography ranges from the subtropical lowlands of the north to the towering Andean Mountains in the west and the wind-swept Patagonian steppe in the south. The rolling, fertile pampas of central Argentina are ideal for agriculture and grazing, and support most of the republic's population. Meat packing, flour milling, textiles, sugar refining and dairy products are the principal industries. Oil is found in Patagonia, but most mineral requirements must be imported.

Argentina was discovered in 1516 by the Spanish navigator Juan de Solis. A permanent Spanish colony was established at Buenos Aires in 1580, but the colony developed slowly. When Napoleon conquered Spain, the Argentines set up their own government on May 25, 1810. Independence was formally declared on July 9, 1816. A strong tendency toward local autonomy, fostered by difficult transportation, resulted in a federalized union with much authority left to the states or provinces, which resulted in the coinage of 1817-1867.

Internal conflict through the first half century of Argentine independence resulted in a limited national coinage supplemented by provincial issues.

RULERS
Spanish until 1810

MINT MARKS
BA, Bs, B.AS. = Buenos Aires
CORDOBA, CORDOVA
Potosi monogram (Bolivia)
R, RA, RIOJA, RIOXA
SE = Santiago del Estero
T, TM = Tucuman

In Colonial times, Potosi-struck coinage was used in Argentina and the mint was captured in 1813 by Argentine forces. The coinage of the Independence forces was struck there until 1815 when the mint was retaken by a Spanish army. With independence secured, the Argentine states turned elsewhere for their coinage.

MONETARY SYSTEM
8 Reales = 8 Soles = 1/2 Escudo
16 Reales or Soles = 1 Escudo
100 Decimos (de Real) = 10 Reales = 1/2 Escudo
100 Centavos = 1 Peso
10 Pesos = 1 Argentino
       (Commencing 1970)
100 Old Pesos = 1 New Peso
       (Commencing June 1983)
10,000 New Pesos = 1 Peso Argentino
1,000 Pesos Argentino = 1 Austral

PROVINCIAS DEL RIO DE LA PLATA

1/2 REAL
SILVER
Mint mark: Potosi monogram
Obv: Facing sun, leg: PROVINCIAS DEL RIO DE LA PLATA, w/o denomination. Rev: Arms in branches.

KM#	Date	Mintage	Good	VG	Fine	VF
1	1813 J	—	5.00	8.50	14.00	27.50
	1815 F	—	6.00	9.00	14.00	27.50

1/2 SOL

SILVER
Mint mark: Potosi monogram

10	1815 FL	—	8.00	13.50	25.00	55.00

REAL

SILVER
Mint mark: Potosi monogram
Similar to 1/2 Sol, KM#10.

KM#	Date	Mintage	Good	VG	Fine	VF
2	1813 J	—	6.00	8.50	14.00	27.50
	1815 F	—	6.00	8.50	14.00	27.50

Mint mark: RA
Similar to 2 Soles, KM#18.

17	1824 DS	—	5.00	8.50	15.00	30.00
	1825 CA	—	—	—	Rare	

SOL
SILVER
Mint mark: Potosi monogram
Similar to 1/2 Sol, KM#10.

11	1815 FL	—	7.50	15.00	35.00	65.00

2 REALES

SILVER
Mint mark: Potosi monogram

3	1813 J	—	6.50	14.00	27.50	55.00
	1815 F	—	6.50	14.00	27.50	55.00

2 SOLES
SILVER
Mint mark: Potosi monogram
Similar to 2 Reales, KM#3.

12	1815 FL	—	8.00	14.00	30.00	65.00

Mint mark: RA

18	1824 DS	—	6.00	12.00	17.50	25.00
	1825 CA	—	13.00	25.00	45.00	75.00
	1825 CA. DE B. AS.					
		—	7.50	14.00	25.00	47.50
	1826/5 P	—	8.00	15.00	27.50	55.00
	1826 P	—	7.50	14.00	25.00	50.00
	1826 'P' omitted from rev. leg.					
		—	4.50	9.00	14.00	25.00

4 REALES
SILVER
Mint mark: Potosi monogram
Similar to 2 Soles, KM#18.

4	1813 J	—	15.00	28.00	50.00	85.00
	1815 F	—	15.00	28.00	55.00	90.00

4 SOLES

SILVER
Mint mark: Potosi monogram

13	1815 FL	—	20.00	32.50	65.00	125.00

Mint mark: RA
Similar to 2 Soles, KM#18.

22	1828 P	—	10.00	20.00	32.50	50.00
	1832 P	—	10.00	20.00	32.50	50.00

8 REALES

SILVER
Mint mark: Potosi monogram
Obv: Flame tips end clockwise.

KM#	Date	Mintage	VG	Fine	VF	XF
5	1813 J	—	40.00	65.00	100.00	175.00
	1813 J PRORVINCIAS (error)					
		—	—	—	Rare	—

Obv: Flame tips end counterclockwise.

14	1815 F	—	40.00	65.00	100.00	175.00
	1815 F PROVICIAS (error)					
		—	75.00	125.00	200.00	350.00

Mint mark: RA

20	1826 P	—	35.00	80.00	160.00	280.00
	1827 P	—	35.00	75.00	120.00	200.00
	1828 P	—	35.00	90.00	240.00	360.00
	1830 P	—	50.00	115.00	320.00	600.00
	1831/0 P	—	38.50	105.00	280.00	480.00
	1831 P	—	38.50	100.00	260.00	400.00
	1832 P	—	35.00	80.00	160.00	320.00
	1833 P	—	35.00	75.00	120.00	200.00
	1834 P	—	35.00	75.00	120.00	200.00
	1835 P	—	35.00	95.00	160.00	280.00
	1836 P	—	35.00	95.00	160.00	280.00
	1837 P	—	35.00	75.00	120.00	240.00

ARGENTINA 104

8 SOLES

SILVER
Mint mark: Potosi monogram

KM#	Date	Mintage	VG	Fine	VF	XF
15	1815 FL	—	50.00	100.00	150.00	225.00
	1815 FL S/R	—	80.00	150.00	250.00	400.00

ESCUDO

3.3750 g, .875 GOLD, .0949 oz AGW
Mint mark: Potosi monogram

| 6 | 1813 J | — | — | — | Rare | — |

2 ESCUDOS

6.7500 g, .875 GOLD, .1899 oz AGW
Mint mark: Potosi monogram

| 7 | 1813 J | — | — | — | Rare | — |

Mint mark: RA

19	1824 DS	—	175.00	275.00	400.00	650.00
	1825 CA. DE B. AS.					
		—	175.00	275.00	400.00	650.00
	1826 P	—	175.00	275.00	400.00	650.00
	1826 P omitted from rev. leg.					
		—	175.00	275.00	400.00	650.00

4 ESCUDOS

13.5000 g, .875 GOLD, .3798 oz AGW
Mint mark: Potosi monogram

| 8 | 1813 J | — | — | — | Reported, not confirmed |

8 ESCUDOS

27.0000 g, .875 GOLD, .7596 oz AGW
Mint mark: Potosi monogram

| 9 | 1813 J | — | 3000. | 5000. | 8500. | 12,000. |

Mint mark: RA

KM#	Date	Mintage	VG	Fine	VF	XF
21	1826 P	—	750.00	1400.	2250.	3000.
	1828 P	—	750.00	1400.	2250.	3000.
	1829 P	—	—	—	Unique	—
	1830 P	—	1500.	3000.	4500.	6000.
	1831/0	—	—	—	Rare	—
	1831 P	—	750.00	1400.	2250.	3000.
	1832 P	—	650.00	1400.	2250.	3000.
	1833 P	—	750.00	1600.	2600.	3600.
	1834 P	—	750.00	1400.	2250.	3200.
	1835 P	—	750.00	1400.	2250.	3200.

CONFEDERACION ARGENTINA
CENTAVO

COPPER

| 23 | 1854 | — | 2.50 | 5.00 | 14.00 | 32.50 |

2 CENTAVOS

COPPER

| 24 | 1854 | — | 3.00 | 7.50 | 16.00 | 42.50 |

4 CENTAVOS

COPPER

| 25 | 1854 | — | 4.00 | 11.00 | 22.00 | 70.00 |

PROVINCIAL COINAGE
BUENOS AIRES

Buenos Aires, a city and province in eastern Argentina, was the first province to have coins made outside the country. Governor Martin Rodriguez initiated negotiations with Boulton & Watt (Soho Mint) in 1821. The Banco Nacional was dissolved in 1836 and the Casa de Moneda took its place.

NOTE: National Bank 5/10 reales are frequently struck over Soho decimos of 1822-1823.

DECIMO

COPPER

| 1 | 1822 | — | 1.25 | 3.00 | 8.50 | 17.50 |
| | 1823 | — | .75 | 2.00 | 6.50 | 14.00 |

NOTE: Officially retired in 1827, in favor of Banco Nacional issues, KM#2-5.

1/4 REAL
COPPER
Obv: Fraction in shaded circle.
Rev: BUENOS AYRES 1827 within branches.

KM#	Date	Mintage	VG	Fine	VF	XF
2	1827	—	13.50	23.50	42.50	80.00

5/10 REAL

COPPER

3	1827	—	.75	2.50	5.00	15.00
	1828	—	.75	2.50	5.00	15.00
	1830	—	3.00	5.00	9.50	27.50
	1831/27	—	—	—	—	—
	1831	—	1.00	3.00	6.00	20.00

| 6 | 1840 | — | 3.75 | 10.00 | 22.50 | 55.00 |

10 DECIMOS

COPPER

4	1827	—	3.00	7.50	17.50	35.00
	1828	—	10.00	22.50	45.00	70.00
	1830	—	3.00	7.50	17.50	35.00

REAL

COPPER

| 7 | 1840 | — | .75 | 3.00 | 6.00 | 13.00 |

| 10 | 1854 | — | 4.00 | 10.00 | 15.00 | 35.00 |

20 DECIMOS

COPPER

5	1827	—	3.50	7.00	17.50	50.00
	1830	—	2.50	4.50	15.00	40.00
	1831	—	12.50	30.00	50.00	100.00

2 REALES

COPPER

KM#	Date	Mintage	VG	Fine	VF	XF
8	1840	—	2.00	4.00	11.00	22.50
	1844	—	2.00	4.00	11.00	22.50

9	1853	—	1.00	2.50	6.00	15.00
	1854	—	1.00	2.75	7.50	17.50
	1855	—	1.00	2.50	6.00	15.00
	1856	—	2.00	4.00	9.50	25.00

11	1860	—	1.50	3.50	9.00	17.50
	1861	—	1.50	3.50	9.00	17.50

CORDOBA

Cordoba, a city and province in central Argentina, was the most prolific of the provincial issuers. The provincial government contracted with concessionaires to make coins. The contractors for 1833 are not known, but all the private makers' coinage is relatively crude and replete with variations, die-sinking in conguities and minor errors.

On February 2, 1844 a provincial mint was authorized by Governor Manuel Lopez. It operated from 1844 to 1852.

CONCESSIONAIRES

Letter	Date	Name
PP, PNP	1839-41	Pedro Nolasco Pizarro
JPP	1841-44	Jose Policarpo Patino

1/4 REAL

SILVER
Obv: Castle, date below.
Rev: Sun face.

KM#	Date	Mintage	VG	Fine	VF	XF
1	1833	—	15.00	25.00	45.00	75.00
	1838	—	15.00	25.00	45.00	75.00

Obv: Castle flanked by P-P, date below.

2	1839 PP	—	6.00	12.50	22.50	45.00
	1840 PP	—	10.00	22.50	45.00	70.00
	1841 PP	—	15.00	27.50	60.00	100.00

NOTE: Many legend and die varieties exist.

Obv: Fraction.

| 33 | ND(1853-54) | — | 8.00 | 13.50 | 25.00 | 50.00 |

NOTE: Die varieties exist.

1/2 REAL

SILVER
Obv: Arms in wreath, leg: EN UNION Y LIBERTAD.
Rev: Sun face, leg: PROVINCIA DE CORDOVA.

3	1839 PNP	—	22.50	50.00	65.00	125.00
	1839 PNP LIVERTAD

KM#	Date	Mintage	VG	Fine	VF	XF
3		—	25.00	55.00	75.00	150.00
	1839 PNP CORDOBA on rev.
		—	25.00	55.00	75.00	150.00
	1840 PNP LIVERTAD
		—	15.00	37.50	60.00	115.00

Obv. leg: EN UNION Y LIVERTAD.
Rev. leg: CONFEDERADA.

| 4 | 1839 PNP | — | 22.50 | 50.00 | 70.00 | 125.00 |

Obv. leg: CONFEDERADA.
Rev. leg: PROVINCIA DE CORDOVA.

| 5 | 1840 PNP | — | 25.00 | 50.00 | 70.00 | 125.00 |

Obv. leg: PROVINCIA DE CORDOV.
Rev. leg: PROVINCIA DE CORDOV.

15	1841 PNP	—	22.50	50.00	70.00	125.00
	1841	—	22.50	50.00	70.00	125.00

Obv: Banner over castle; date below, leg: CORDOVA.
Rev: Sun face, leg: CONFEDERADA.

6	1840 PNP crossed lances below castle
	—	25.00	55.00	90.00	150.00

Obv. leg: CONFEDERADA.
Rev. leg: PROVINCIA DE CORDOVA.

16	1841 PNP	—	22.50	50.00	70.00	125.00
	1841	—	22.50	50.00	70.00	125.00

Obv: Denomination. Rev: Sun face.

29	1850	—	5.50	12.00	20.00	45.00
	1850 error: CONFEDRRADA
		—	5.50	12.00	20.00	45.00
	1851	—	30.00	75.00	120.00	225.00
	1853	—	5.50	12.00	20.00	45.00
	1854	—	5.50	12.00	20.00	45.00

NOTE: Many legend and die varieties exist.

REAL

SILVER
Obv: Arms (shaded) in wreath; date below, leg: PROVINCIA DE CORDOVA.
Rev: Sun face, leg: CONFEDERADA.

7	1840 PNP	—	3.50	6.00	13.50	25.00
	1841/0 PNP
	1841 PNP	—	3.25	6.00	13.50	25.00
	1841 PNP CORDOBA
		—	32.50	55.00	90.00	200.00
	1841 PNP CORDOBA & inverted 4
		—	42.50	72.50	95.00	200.00
	1841 JPP	—	3.25	6.00	13.50	25.00
	1842 JPP	—	3.25	6.00	13.50	25.00
	1842 JPP PROVINCI
		—	5.00	10.00	22.50	50.00
	1842 JPP PROVINCA
		—	5.00	10.00	17.50	45.00
	1843 JPP	—	3.50	7.00	11.50	22.50
	1843 JPP inverted 3
		—	4.50	8.75	16.00	32.50
	3481 JPP (error for 1843)
		—	8.50	20.00	32.50	70.00
	1843 JPP PROVICIA
		—	5.00	11.00	18.00	40.00
	1843 JPP CORDOV
		—	3.25	6.25	17.50	22.50
	4481 JPP (error for 1844)
		—	40.00	70.00	100.00	200.00

NOTE: Many legend and die varieties exist.

Obv. leg: PROVINCIA DE CORDOVA.
Rev. leg: PROVINCIA DE CORDOVA.

8	1840 PNP	—	15.00	35.00	65.00	110.00
	1841 PNP	—	15.00	35.00	65.00	110.00

Obv. leg: PROVINCIA DE CORDOVA.
Rev. leg: EN UNION Y LIBERTAD.

9	1840 PNP	—	3.25	6.50	13.50	30.00
	1841 PNP	—	3.50	7.50	15.00	32.50
	1841 PNP CORDOBA
		—	30.00	50.00	80.00	115.00

Obv. leg: CONFEDERADA.
Rev. leg: CONFEDERADA.

| 10 | 1840 PNP | — | 30.00 | 50.00 | 80.00 | 120.00 |

Obv. leg: CONFEDERADA.
Rev. leg: PROVINCIA DE CORDOVA.

| 11 | 1840 PNP | — | 30.00 | 50.00 | 80.00 | 120.00 |

Obv. leg: EN UNION Y LIBERTAD.
Rev. leg: PROVINCIA DE CORDOVA.

| 12 | 1840 PNP | — | 30.00 | 50.00 | 80.00 | 120.00 |

Obv. leg: EN UNION Y LIBERTAD.
Rev. leg: PROVINCIA DE CORDOVA.

| 13 | 1840 PNP | — | 30.00 | 50.00 | 80.00 | 120.00 |

Obv. leg: PROVINCIA DE CORDOVA, arms w/o shading and 2 rosettes. Rev. leg: CONFEDERADA, sun face.

| 17 | 1841 PNP | — | 2.75 | 6.00 | 11.00 | 25.00 |

KM#	Date	Mintage	VG	Fine	VF	XF
17	1843 JPP	—	2.75	6.00	11.00	25.00
	1843 JPP PROVINCI
		—	2.75	6.00	11.00	25.00
	1843 JPP CONFEDERDA
		—	2.75	6.00	11.00	25.00
	1843 JPP CORDOV
		—	2.75	6.00	11.00	25.00

Rev. leg: LIBRE YNDEPENDIENTE.

| 20 | 1843 JPP | — | 11.00 | 20.00 | 40.00 |

Obv. leg: PROVINCIA DE CORDOVA; banner over castle.
Rev. leg: CONFEDERADA, sun face.

14	1840 PNP	—	50.00	80.00	120.00	180.00
	1841 PNP	—	6.00	11.00	22.50	45.00
	1841 PNP CORDOBA
		—	35.00	60.00	100.00	150.00
	1841 PNP CORDOV, inverted 4
		—	3.50	8.00	17.50	37.50
	1841 PNP inverted 4
		—	3.50	8.00	17.50	37.50
	1841 PNP CORDOV
		—	7.50	15.00	27.50	50.00

NOTE: Many legend and die varieties exist.

Obv. leg: PROVINCIA DE CORDOVA.
Rev. leg: EN UNION Y LIBERTAD.

| 18 | 1841 PNP | — | 12.50 | 22.50 | 40.00 | 75.00 |

Obv. leg: PROVINCIA DE CORDOVA.
Rev. leg: PROVINCIA DE CORDOVA.

19	1841 PNP rosette below castle
	—	22.50	45.00	75.00	135.00

Obv. leg: PROVINCIA DE CORDOVA, arms w/o shading; date below. Rev. leg: CONFEDERADA, sun face.

21	1843 JPP	—	3.75	6.50	11.00	22.50
	1843 JPP CONFEDERDA
		—	3.75	6.50	11.00	22.50
	1843 JPP CORDOV
		—	3.75	6.50	11.00	22.50
	1843 JPP CORDOV & CONFEDERDA
		—	3.75	6.50	11.00	22.50
	1843 JPP CORDOV & PROVINCI
		—	5.50	10.00	17.50	35.00
	1843 JPP CORDO
		—	3.75	6.50	11.00	22.50
	1843 JPP CORDO & CONFEDERDA
		—	3.75	6.50	11.00	22.50
	1844 JPP CORDOV
		—	22.50	45.00	80.00	130.00

NOTE: Many legend and die varieties exist.

Obv. leg: PROVINCIA DE CORDOVA.
Rev. leg: LIBRE YNDEPENDIENTE.

| 22 | 1843 JPP | — | 7.00 | 12.50 | 18.00 | 37.50 |

NOTE: Many legend and die varieties exist.

Obv. leg: PROVINCIA DE CORDOBA, denomination.
Rev. leg: CONFEDERADA, sun face, date below.

| 26 | 1848 | — | 6.50 | 11.00 | 17.50 | 35.00 |

NOTE: Many legend and die varieties exist.

2 REALES

.750 SILVER
Obv: Castle among flags in sprays, leg: PROVINCIA DE CORDOBA.
Rev: Sun face in sprays, date below, leg: CONFEDERADA.

23	1844	—	6.00	11.00	20.00	37.50
	1844 CONFEDRADA
		—	18.00	37.50	75.00	135.00
	1845	—	5.50	11.00	18.00	27.50

NOTE: Many legend and die varieties exist.

Cordoba/ARGENTINA 105

Cordoba / ARGENTINA 106

KM#	Date	Mintage	VG	Fine	VF	XF
25	1846	—	7.00	13.00	20.00	32.50
	1848	—	—	—	—	Rare

NOTE: Many legend and die varieties exist.

| 27 | 1849 | — | 6.00 | 11.00 | 20.00 | 32.50 |

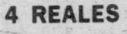

| 28 | 1849 | — | 6.00 | 11.00 | 20.00 | 32.50 |
| | 1850 | — | 6.00 | 11.00 | 20.00 | 32.50 |

NOTE: Many legend and die varieties exist.

Similar to 4 Reales, KM#31.

| 30 | 1852 | — | 15.00 | 30.00 | 45.00 | 85.00 |
| | 1854 | — | 15.00 | 30.00 | 45.00 | 85.00 |

4 REALES

.750 SILVER
Obv: Castle among flags over spray.
Rev: Sun face, date below.

24	1844	—	100.00	200.00	325.00	575.00
	1845	—	22.50	40.00	70.00	115.00
	1846 die of 1845	—	80.00	130.00	180.00	300.00
	1846	—	47.50	85.00	115.00	175.00
	1847	—	15.00	25.00	50.00	90.00
	1850	—	15.00	25.00	50.00	90.00
	1851	—	15.00	25.00	50.00	90.00

NOTE: Many legend, die and edge varieties exist.

| 31 | 1852 | — | 30.00 | 50.00 | 80.00 | 150.00 |

8 REALES

.750 SILVER
Obv: High spear tips at left.

KM#	Date	Mintage	VG	Fine	VF	XF
32.1	1852	—	30.00	50.00	115.00	200.00

Obv: Low spear tips at left.

| 32.2 | 1852 | — | 30.00 | 50.00 | 115.00 | 200.00 |

ENTRE RIOS

Entre Rios (Colonia San Jose) was a settlement of Swiss and Italian families in northeast Argentina on the Uruguayan border. General Urquiza (deposer of Rosas) was a political power in the province. As governor, during the war with Paraguay, he authorized an Italian, Pablo Cataldi, to make coins for the settlement during a coin shortage in 1867.

1/2 REAL

SILVER

| 1 | 1867 | — | 50.00 | 75.00 | 125.00 | 225.00 |

LA RIOJA

La Rioja (Rioxa), a city and province in northwest Argentina, was the source of rich mineral wealth. Governor Nicolas Davila, authorized a mint at Chilecito to take advantage of the rich mines at Famatina in 1820. The mint made "cob" types, with and without the name RIOXA from 1821 to 1823. The cobs were officially called-in in 1824.

In Chilecito, another city in La Rioja province, gold 1 Escudos and silver 1 Reales were struck in 1823. This mint was transferred to La Rioja in 1824, where coins were struck until 1860.

*NOTE: Virtually all of the early pieces are false. All pieces dated between 1820 and 1824 should only be bought with certification of two or more authorities.

1/2 REAL

SILVER
Cob type w/RIOXA.

KM#	Date	Mintage	Good	VG	Fine	VF
3	1822*	—	—	—	Rare	—

Obv: Arms in branches. Rev: Sun over mountain.

| 18 | 1844 B | — | 3.50 | 6.50 | 15.00 | 25.00 |

Obv. leg: REPUB. ARGENT. CONFEDERADA.
Rev. leg: PROV. DE LA. RIOJA.

| 22 | 1854 B | — | 1.50 | 2.50 | 6.00 | 12.50 |

Rev. leg: CRED. PUB. DE LA RIOJA.

| 23 | 1854 B | — | 2.00 | 4.00 | 10.00 | 17.50 |

Obv. leg: CONFEDERACION ARGENTINA.
Rev. leg: PROV. DE LA. RIOJA.

| 24 | 1854 B | — | 1.50 | 2.50 | 6.00 | 12.50 |

| 25 | 1854 B | — | 1.50 | 2.50 | 6.00 | 12.50 |
| | 1860 B | — | 2.50 | 5.00 | 12.50 | 25.00 |

REAL

SILVER
Chilecito Mint
Cob type w/RIOXA.

| 4 | 1822* | — | — | — | Rare | — |

NOTE: 1821 dated coins are false.

La Rioja Mint
Obv: Sun above arms. Rev. leg: SVR AMERICA RIOXA.

| 5 | ND (1823)* | — | 100.00 | 150.00 | 250.00 | 400.00 |

Rev. leg: SUD AMERICA 1823 RIOXA

| 6 | 1823* | — | — | — | Rare | — |

2 REALES

SILVER
Cob Type

KM#	Date	Mintage	Good	VG	Fine	VF
1	(1)821*	—	75.00	150.00	225.00	350.00
	(1)822*	—	75.00	150.00	225.00	350.00
	(1)823*	—	—	—	Rare	—

| 12 | 1842 | — | 15.00 | 25.00 | 42.50 | 85.00 |

Mountain type

| 15 | 1843 RB | — | 6.00 | 12.50 | 22.50 | 35.00 |

Mountain and sun type

| 16 | 1843 RB | — | 6.00 | 13.50 | 30.00 | 60.00 |
| | 1844 RB | — | 5.00 | 10.00 | 20.00 | 45.00 |

| 26 | 1859 B | — | 17.50 | 32.50 | 50.00 | 80.00 |
| | 1860 B | — | 3.50 | 6.50 | 13.50 | 25.00 |

4 REALES

SILVER
Obv: Castles & lions. Rev: Pillars, RIOXA, date.

2	(1)821*	—	100.00	200.00	330.00	480.00
	(1)822*	—	—	—	Rare	—
	(1)823 w/o RIOXA*	—	125.00	250.00	375.00	550.00

Salta / ARGENTINA 107

KM#	Date	Mintage	VG	Fine	VF	XF
11	1840	—	850.00	1250.	2000.	3250.

Bust type
| 14 | 1842 | 2-4 pcs. known | — | Rare | — |

KM#	Date	Mintage	VG	Fine	VF	XF
20	1846 RV	—	15.00	27.50	40.00	65.00
	1849 RV	—	—	—	—	—
	1849 RB	—	12.50	25.00	37.50	60.00
	1850 RB	—	20.00	30.00	50.00	85.00

KM#	Date	Mintage	VG	Fine	VF	XF
10	1840 R	—	150.00	250.00	375.00	650.00

ESCUDO
3.3750 g, .875 GOLD, .0949 oz AGW
Obv: Sun over arms in branches.
Rev. leg: SUD AMERICA 1823 RIOXA in wreath.

| 7 | 1823* | — | — | — | Unique | — |

2 ESCUDOS

6.7500 g, .875 GOLD, .1899 oz AGW
| 13 | 1842 | — | 200.00 | 400.00 | 650.00 | 1000. |

| 17 | 1843 B | — | 200.00 | 325.00 | 500.00 | 750.00 |

| 21 | 1852 B | — | 55.00 | 85.00 | 130.00 | 200.00 |

8 REALES

8 ESCUDOS

27.0000 g, .875 GOLD, .7596 oz AGW
9	1836	2-4 pcs.	—	—	—	—
	1838	—	600.00	1000.	1500.	2500.
	1840	—	750.00	1150.	1750.	2750.

SILVER
8	1838 R	—	30.00	60.00	100.00	150.00
	1839 R	—	30.00	60.00	100.00	150.00
	1840 R	—	30.00	60.00	125.00	200.00

| 19 | 1845 B | — | 1250. | 1750. | 2500. | 4000. |

MENDOZA

Mendoza, a province in western Argentina, was one of the first to make coins designed to resemble the Spanish Colonial cobs of Potosi.

In 1835 Molina saw that coins were needed, and decided to award contracts for production rather than have the provincial mint make them. Abel Bucci and Manuel Espeys, who had the contract failed to supply any volume of coinage for circulation and were retired in 1836.

1/8 REAL
COPPER
Obv: Provincial arms, date below.
Rev: Fraction in dotted circle in wreath.

KM#	Date	Mintage	Good	VG	Fine	VF
5	1835	—	—	—	Unique	—

1/4 REAL
SILVER
Obv: Arms divide value.
Rev: Small animal.

| 6 | 1836 | — | — | — | Unique | — |

SALTA

Salta, a province in northwest Argentina, was a frequent battleground during the War of Independence. Governor Martin Guemes fought the Spaniards without help from the patriotic forces in Buenos Aires. There was no money with which to pay the troops and what was circulating was counterfeit. Low morale and frequent desertions were one result. In desperation, Guemes decided to countermark the false coins with the word PATRIA and to guarantee them as genuine.

When this action became known to the patriot government, in Buenos Aires, it was declared to be a violation of national laws and all the pieces were to be withdrawn.

Meanwhile, Guemes had gained valuable time, culminating with a victory at Castanares which finally rid the north of Spanish influence.

All genuine Salta countermarks are only found on counterfeit Potosi cobs.

PATRIA

c/m: PATRIA monogram in wreath.

2 REALES
SILVER
c/m: PATRIA monogram in wreath on Potosi Mint cobs.
| 2 | ND(1817) | — | 50.00 | 100.00 | 150.00 | — |

4 REALES
SILVER
c/m: PATRIA monogram in wreath on Potosi Mint

Salta / ARGENTINA 108

KM#	Date	Mintage	cobs. Good	VG	Fine	VF
3	ND(1817)	—	—	—	Rare	—

8 REALES
All known specimens are considered fantasies.

SANTIAGO DEL ESTERO
Santiago del Estero is a province in north central Argentina. In 1823, during the governorship of Felipe Ibarra, coinage began in an effort to replace the fast-disappearing cob coins of the Potosi mint. The pieces were not well received and coining was soon halted. Another effort, in 1836, faired no better.

1/2 REAL
SILVER
Obv: SoEo in angles of crossed arrows, date below.
Rev: Sun in branches.

1	(1)823 So Eo	—	—	—	—	—

Obv: S E in angles of crossed arrows, date below.

| 2 | (1)823 | — | 75.00 | 150.00 | 225.00 | 300.00 |

REAL
SILVER
Obv: SoEo in angles of crossed arrows, date below.
Rev: Cross.

| 3 | (1)823 | — | — | — | Unique | — |

Rev: Sun in branches.

| 4 | (1)823 | — | 100.00 | 200.00 | 350.00 | 600.00 |

Obv: S E in angles of crossed arrows, date below.

| 5 | (1)823 | — | 50.00 | 100.00 | 150.00 | 250.00 |

Rev: Sun over Liberty cap in branches.

| 6 | (1)836 | — | 35.00 | 75.00 | 125.00 | 200.00 |

TUCUMAN
Tucuman is a province in northwestern Argentina. Due to the large quantity of false Potosi cobs circulating in the province, Governor Bernabe Araoz established a mint in 1823 to make cobs that would be distinctive to the area. Their circulation was brief due to the introduction of Confederation coins.

2 REALES
SILVER
Mint mark: TN
Similar to Potosi Cob 2 Reales.

| 1 | ND(1823) | — | 35.00 | 75.00 | 100.00 | 125.00 |

NOTE: Most coins exist without the TN mint mark. Those with ficticious dates are attributed to Venezuela.

REPUBLIC
Decimal Coinage
100 Centavos = 1 Peso
5 Pesos = 1 Argentino

CENTAVO

BRONZE

KM#	Date	Mintage	Fine	VF	XF	Unc
7	1882	.108	6.50	13.50	22.50	35.00
	1883	.786	.75	1.75	4.50	18.00
	1884	4.604	.50	1.00	2.50	6.50
	1885	1.314	.50	1.00	3.50	9.00
	1886	.444	.75	1.75	4.50	20.00
	1888	.413	.75	2.25	5.50	22.50
	1889	.568	.75	2.25	5.50	22.50
	1890	2.137	.50	1.00	2.50	6.50
	1891	.605	.75	1.75	4.50	18.00
	1892	.205	1.00	2.25	5.50	22.50
	1893	.754	.50	1.75	4.50	18.00
	1894	.532	1.00	1.75	4.50	18.00
	1895	.423	.75	2.25	5.50	18.00
	1896	.174	4.50	11.00	15.50	27.00

| 12 | 1939 | 3.488 | .15 | .35 | .70 | 1.50 |

KM#	Date	Mintage	Fine	VF	XF	Unc
12	1940	3.140	.15	.35	.70	1.50
	1941	4.572	.15	.35	.70	1.50
	1942	.496	.30	.75	1.50	7.50
	1943	1.294	.20	.50	1.00	2.00
	1944	3.104	.10	.25	.50	1.25

COPPER
Cruder diework

12a	1945	.420	.20	.50	1.00	4.00
	1946	4.450	.15	.35	.50	1.00
	1947	5.630	.15	.35	.50	1.00
	1948	4.420	.15	.35	.50	1.00

2 CENTAVOS

BRONZE

8	1882	.088	6.00	13.50	22.50	54.00
	1883	1.389	.75	1.75	3.50	13.50
	1884	5.667	.75	1.75	2.50	6.50
	1885	3.065	.75	1.75	3.00	9.00
	1887	.363	4.50	11.50	18.00	32.50
	1888	.659	1.75	3.50	7.00	21.50
	1889	2.391	.75	1.75	3.00	9.00
	1890	3.609	.75	1.75	3.00	9.00
	1891	8.050	.50	1.75	3.00	6.50
	1892	3.497	.75	1.75	3.00	9.00
	1893	5.473	.75	1.75	3.00	9.00
	1894	2.233	.75	1.75	3.00	9.00
	1895	.593	1.25	3.50	7.00	21.50
	1896	.596	1.75	4.50	8.00	25.00

13	1939	5.490	.10	.25	.50	1.25
	1940	4.625	.10	.25	.50	1.75
	1941	4.567	.10	.25	.50	1.75
	1942	2.082	.10	.25	.50	1.75
	1944	.387	.25	.50	1.00	6.50
	1945	4.585	.10	.25	.50	1.75
	1946	3.395	.10	.25	.50	1.75
	1947	4.395	.10	.25	.50	1.75

COPPER
Cruder diework

13a	1947	Inc. Ab.	.15	.30	.50	1.50
	1948	3.645	.15	.30	.50	1.50
	1949	7.290	.15	.30	.50	1.50
	1950	.903	.25	.65	1.25	3.00

5 CENTAVOS

COPPER-NICKEL

9	1896	1.499	.75	2.00	5.00	15.00
	1897	3.981	.50	1.00	4.00	10.00
	1898	2.661	.50	1.00	4.00	10.00
	1899	2.835	.25	.50	3.00	7.50
	1903	2.502	.25	.50	3.00	7.50
	1904	2.518	.25	.50	3.00	7.50
	1905	4.359	.25	.50	3.00	7.50
	1906	3.939	.25	.50	3.00	7.50
	1907	1.682	.50	1.00	5.00	15.00
	1908	1.693	.50	1.00	5.00	15.00
	1909	4.650	.25	.50	3.00	7.50
	1910	1.469	.75	2.00	5.00	17.50
	1911	1.431	.25	.50	4.00	10.00
	1912	2.377	.25	.75	4.00	10.00
	1913	1.477	.25	.75	4.00	10.00
	1914	1.097	.25	1.00	5.00	15.00

KM#	Date	Mintage	Fine	VF	XF	Unc
9	1915	1.903	.30	.75	3.50	10.00
	1916	1.310	.30	.75	3.50	7.50
	1917	1.009	.75	1.50	4.00	8.50
	1918	2.387	.25	.50	3.00	5.00
	1919	2.476	.25	.50	3.00	5.00
	1920	5.235	.25	.50	3.00	5.00
	1921	7.040	.20	.35	2.00	4.00
	1922	9.427	.20	.35	2.00	4.00
	1923	6.256	.20	.35	2.00	4.00
	1924	6.355	.20	.35	2.00	4.00
	1925	3.955	.20	.35	2.00	4.00
	1926	3.560	.20	.35	2.00	4.00
	1927	5.650	.20	.35	2.00	4.00
	1928	6.380	.20	.35	2.00	4.00
	1929	11.831	.20	.35	2.00	4.00
	1930	7.110	.20	.35	2.00	4.00
	1931	.506	.75	1.50	4.00	12.50
	1933	5.537	.10	.25	1.00	2.50
	1934	1.288	.25	.50	3.00	5.00
	1935	3.052	.10	.25	1.00	2.50
	1936	7.175	.10	.25	1.00	2.50
	1937	7.063	.10	.25	1.00	2.50
	1938	10.252	.10	.25	1.00	2.50
	1939	7.171	.10	.25	1.00	2.50
	1940	10.191	.10	.25	1.00	2.50
	1941	.951	.25	.75	2.00	6.50
	1942	8.692	.10	.25	1.00	2.50

ALUMINUM-BRONZE

15	1942	2.130	.15	.35	1.00	3.00
	1943	15.778	.10	.25	.50	2.00
	1944	21.081	.10	.25	.50	2.00
	1945	21.600	.10	.25	.50	2.00
	1946	20.460	.10	.25	.50	2.00
	1947	22.520	.10	.25	.50	2.00
	1948	42.790	.10	.25	.50	2.00
	1949	35.470	.10	.25	.50	2.00
	1950	13.500	.10	.25	.50	2.00

COPPER-NICKEL

| 18 | 1950 | 3.460 | .20 | .50 | .75 | 2.50 |

Reeded edge

21	1951	34.994	—	.20	.30	.50
	1952	33.110	—	.20	.30	.50
	1953	20.129	—	.20	.30	.50

COPPER-NICKEL-CLAD STEEL
Plain edge

| 21a | 1953 | 56.300 | — | .15 | .20 | .30 |

Rev: Smaller head.

25	1954	50.640	—	.15	.20	.30
	1955	42.200	—	.15	.20	.30
	1956	36.870	—	.15	.20	.30

28	1957	26.930	—	.15	.20	.30
	1958	13.108	—	.15	.20	.30
	1959	14.971	—	.15	.20	.30

10 CENTAVOS

2.5000 g, .900 SILVER, .0723 oz ASW

1	1881	1.020	50.00	100.00	150.00	250.00
	1882	.778	4.00	7.50	15.00	32.50
	1883	2.786	2.50	5.00	10.00	17.50

ARGENTINA 109

KM#	Date	Mintage	Fine	VF	XF	Unc
29	1957	52.810	—	.10	.15	.25
	1958	41.916	—	.10	.15	.25
	1959	29.183	—	.10	.15	.25

20 CENTAVOS

COPPER-NICKEL

KM#	Date	Mintage	Fine	VF	XF	Unc
10	1896	1.877	1.00	2.50	5.00	22.50
	1897	8.582	.50	1.50	4.00	8.00
	1898	8.534	.50	1.50	4.00	8.00
	1899	8.889	.50	1.50	4.00	8.00
	1905	3.785	.50	1.00	3.50	7.50
	1906	3.854	.50	1.00	3.50	7.50
	1907	2.355	.50	1.00	4.00	8.00
	1908	2.280	.50	1.00	4.00	8.00
	1909	3.738	.50	1.00	3.50	7.50
	1910	3.026	.50	1.00	3.50	7.50
	1911	2.142	.75	2.00	4.50	10.00
	1912	2.993	.75	2.00	4.50	10.00
	1913	1.828	1.00	2.50	5.00	12.50
	1914	.751	1.00	2.50	5.00	12.50
	1915	2.607	.50	1.00	3.50	7.50
	1916	.835	1.00	2.50	5.00	12.00
	1918	3.897	.50	1.00	3.50	7.50
	1919	2.517	.50	1.00	3.50	7.50
	1920	7.509	.25	.75	2.50	7.00
	1921	11.564	.25	.60	2.00	3.75
	1922	6.542	.20	.50	1.50	3.50
	1923	5.301	.20	.50	1.50	3.50
	1924	3.489	.20	.50	1.50	3.50
	1925	5.415	.20	.50	1.50	3.50
	1926	5.055	.15	.35	1.00	3.00
	1927	5.205	.15	.35	1.00	3.00
	1928	8.255	.15	.35	1.00	3.00
	1929	2.501	.15	.35	1.00	3.00
	1930	14.586	.15	.35	1.00	2.50
	1931	.893	.50	1.00	2.50	7.50
	1933	5.394	.15	.35	1.00	2.50
	1934	3.319	.15	.35	1.00	2.50
	1935	1.018	.30	.75	2.00	5.00
	1936	3.000	.15	.35	1.00	4.50
	1937	11.766	.15	.35	1.00	2.00
	1938	10.494	.15	.35	1.00	2.00
	1939	5.585	.15	.35	1.00	3.00
	1940	3.955	.15	.35	1.00	3.00
	1941	4.101	.15	.35	1.00	3.00
	1942	2.962	.15	.25	1.00	3.00

5.0000 g, .900 SILVER, .1446 oz ASW

2	1881	2,018	40.00	70.00	100.00	150.00
	1882	.762	6.50	11.50	20.00	45.00
	1883/2 inverted 2					
		1.511	8.00	17.50	35.00	75.00
	1883	Inc. Ab.	4.50	9.00	15.00	30.00

COPPER-NICKEL

11	1896	2.030	.75	2.00	5.00	12.50
	1897	5.263	.75	2.00	5.00	12.50
	1898	1.264	1.50	4.00	8.00	20.00
	1899	.840	2.75	6.00	12.00	32.50
	1905	4.455	.75	2.00	5.00	12.50
	1906	4.331	.75	2.00	5.00	12.50
	1907	3.730	1.00	3.00	7.00	17.50
	1908	.719	2.25	5.00	10.00	20.00
	1909	1.329	.50	1.50	4.00	10.00
	1910	1.845	.50	1.50	4.00	10.00
	1911	1.110	.50	1.50	4.00	10.00
	1912	2.402	.50	1.50	4.00	10.00
	1913	1.579	.50	1.00	2.50	7.50
	1914	.527	2.25	5.00	10.00	30.00
	1915	1.921	.50	1.00	2.50	7.50
	1916	.985	.50	1.25	2.50	17.50
	1918	1.638	.40	.75	2.00	7.50
	1919	2.280	.40	.75	2.00	7.50
	1920	7.572	.40	.75	2.00	6.25
	1921	5.286	.25	.60	1.75	5.00
	1922	2.324	.25	.60	1.75	5.00
	1923	4.416	.25	.60	1.75	5.00
	1924	3.676	.25	.60	1.75	5.00
	1925	3.799	.25	.60	1.75	5.00
	1926	3.250	.25	.50	1.25	3.75
	1927	2.880	.25	.50	1.25	3.75
	1928	2.886	.25	.50	1.25	3.75
	1929	8.361	.25	.50	1.25	3.00
	1930	8.281	.25	.50	1.25	3.00
	1931	.315	2.25	5.00	10.00	20.00
	1935	1.127	.25	.60	1.75	5.00
	1936	.855	.50	1.25	2.50	12.50
	1937	3.314	.25	.50	1.50	3.75
	1938	6.449	.25	.50	1.25	3.00
	1939	3.555	.25	.50	1.25	3.00
	1940	4.465	.25	.50	1.25	3.00
	1941	.600	.50	1.00	2.00	10.00
	1942	4.844	.25	.50	1.25	3.00

ALUMINUM-BRONZE

17	1942	10.255	.15	.25	.75	2.00
	1943	13.775	.15	.25	.75	2.00
	1944	12.225	.15	.25	.75	2.00
	1945	13.340	.15	.25	.75	2.00
	1946	14.625	.15	.25	.75	2.00
	1947	23.165	.15	.25	.75	2.00
	1948	32.245	.15	.25	.75	2.00
	1949	67.115	.15	.25	.75	2.00
	1950	40.071	.15	.25	.75	2.00

COPPER-NICKEL

| 20 | 1950 | 86.770 | .25 | .50 | .75 | 2.00 |

ALUMINUM-BRONZE

16	1942	15.541	.15	.25	.75	2.00
	1943	13.916	.15	.25	.75	2.00
	1944	16.411	.15	.25	.75	2.00
	1945	12.500	.15	.25	.75	2.00
	1946	15.790	.15	.25	.75	2.00
	1947	36.430	.15	.25	.75	2.00
	1948	54.685	.15	.25	.75	2.00
	1949	57.740	.15	.25	.75	2.00
	1950	42.825	.15	.25	.75	2.00

COPPER-NICKEL

| 19 | 1950 | 17.505 | .30 | .75 | 1.00 | 2.50 |

22	1951	98.521	—	.20	.30	.50
	1952	67.328	—	.20	.30	.50

NICKEL-CLAD STEEL

22a	1952	33.240	—	.10	.15	.25
	1953	106.685	—	.10	.15	.25

Obv: Smaller head.

26	1954	117.200	—	.10	.15	.25
	1955	97.045	—	.10	.15	.25
	1956	122.630	—	.10	.15	.25

KM#	Date	Mintage	Fine	VF	XF	Unc
23	1951	85.782	.10	.20	.30	.50
	1952	69.796	.10	.20	.30	.50

NICKEL CLAD STEEL

23a	1952	12.863	—	.15	.40	1.00
	1953	36.893	—	.15	.25	.50

Head size reduced slightly

27	1954	52.563	—	.15	.20	.25
	1955	46.952	—	.15	.20	.25
	1956	35.995	—	.15	.20	.25

30	1957	89.365	—	.15	.20	.25
	1958	52.710	—	.15	.20	.25
	1959	56.585	—	.15	.20	.25
	1960	21.254	—	.15	.20	.25
	1961	2.083	—	.25	.50	1.50

50 CENTAVOS

12.5000 g, .900 SILVER, .3617 oz ASW

3	1881	1,020	125.00	225.00	350.00	500.00
	1882	.476	16.50	27.50	50.00	100.00
	1883	2.273	10.00	18.50	32.50	60.00

NICKEL

| 14 | 1941 | 10.961 | .40 | 1.00 | 1.25 | 2.00 |

NICKEL-CLAD STEEL

24	1952	29.736	.10	.20	.35	.75
	1953	62.814	.10	.20	.35	.75
	1954	132.224	.10	.20	.35	.75
	1955	75.490	.10	.20	.35	.75
	1956	19.120	.10	.20	.45	1.00

31	1957	18.139	—	.10	.25	.30
	1958	51.750	.10	.20	.30	.40
	1959	13.997	—	.10	.20	.30
	1960	26.038	.10	.20	.30	.40
	1961	11.106	—	.10	.20	.35

PESO

25.0000 g, .900 SILVER, .7234 oz ASW

KM#	Date	Mintage	Fine	VF	XF	Unc
4	1881	.062	100.00	150.00	200.00	325.00
	1882	.414	40.00	65.00	110.00	225.00
	1883	.098	100.00	150.00	250.00	380.00

NICKEL-CLAD STEEL

KM#	Date	Mintage	Fine	VF	XF	Unc
32	1957	118.118	.10	.20	.40	.75
	1958	118.151	.10	.20	.40	.75
	1959	237.733	.10	.20	.30	.50
	1960	75.048	.10	.30	.50	1.00
	1961	76.897	.10	.30	.50	1.00
	1962	30.006	.10	.30	.50	1.00

Provisional Government

33	1960	98.751	.20	.50	.75	1.25

1/2 ARGENTINO

4.0322 g, .750 GOLD, .0972 oz AGW

5	1881	9 pcs.	—	—	Rare	—
	1884	421 pcs.	1000.	1500.	2000.	2750.

5 PESOS

NICKEL-CLAD STEEL

34	1961	37.423	.10	.20	.30	.50
	1962	42.362	.10	.20	.30	.50
	1963	71.769	.10	.20	.30	.50
	1964	12.302	.15	.25	.40	.75
	1965	19.450	.10	.20	.30	.50
	1966	17.259	.10	.20	.30	.50
	1967	17.806	.10	.20	.30	.50
	1968	12.634	.10	.20	.30	.50

ARGENTINO

8.0645 g, .750 GOLD, .1944 oz AGW

KM#	Date	Mintage	Fine	VF	XF	Unc
6	1881	.037	150.00	200.00	250.00	375.00
	1882	.252	100.00	135.00	175.00	300.00
	1883	.906	100.00	135.00	175.00	300.00
	1884	.448	100.00	135.00	175.00	300.00
	1885	.204	100.00	135.00	175.00	300.00
	1886	.398	100.00	135.00	175.00	300.00
	1887	1.835	100.00	125.00	150.00	300.00
	1888	1.663	100.00	125.00	150.00	300.00
	1889	.404	175.00	275.00	400.00	550.00
	1896	.197	100.00	135.00	175.00	300.00

10 PESOS

NICKEL-CLAD STEEL

35	1962	57.401	.10	.20	.30	.50
	1963	136.792	.10	.20	.30	.50
	1964	46.576	.10	.20	.30	.50
	1965	40.640	—	.15	.30	.50
	1966	50.733	.10	.20	.30	.50
	1967	43.050	.10	.20	.30	.75
	1968	36.588	—	.15	.30	.50

Declaration of Independence

37	1966	29.336	.10	.15	.35	.75

25 PESOS

NICKEL-CLAD STEEL

36	1964	20.485	.10	.25	.50	1.00
	1965	14.884	.10	.25	.50	1.00
	1966	16.426	.10	.25	.50	1.00
	1967	15.734	.10	.25	.50	1.00
	1968	4.446	.10	.25	.75	1.50

80th Anniversary of Death of Domingo Sarmiento

38	1968	15.804	.25	.60	.85	1.25

MONETARY REFORM
100 Old Pesos = 1 New Peso

CENTAVO

ALUMINUM

39	1970	47.801	—	—	.10	.20
	1971	44.644	—	—	.10	.20
	1972	92.430	—	—	.10	.20
	1973	29.515	—	—	.10	.20
	1974	5.162	—	—	.10	.25
	1975	3.840	—	.10	.20	.50
	1983	19.959	—	—	.10	.25

5 CENTAVOS

ALUMINUM

KM#	Date	Mintage	Fine	VF	XF	Unc
40	1970	56.174	—	.10	.15	.25
	1971	3.798	.10	.20	.35	.50
	1972	84.250	—	.10	.15	.25
	1973	113.912	—	.10	.15	.25
	1974	18.150	—	.10	.15	.25
	1975	6.940	.10	.20	.35	.50
	1983	59.870	—	.10	.15	.25

10 CENTAVOS

BRASS

41	1970	52.903	—	.10	.15	.25
	1971	135.623	—	.10	.15	.25
	1973	19.930	—	.10	.15	.25
	1974	79.156	—	.10	.15	.25
	1975	31.270	—	.10	.15	.25
	1976	.730	.10	.20	.35	1.00
	1983	191.577	—	.10	.15	.25

20 CENTAVOS

BRASS

42	1970	27.029	—	.10	.15	.25
	1971	32.211	—	.10	.15	.25
	1972	.220	2.00	6.00	10.00	20.00
	1973	9.676	—	.10	.15	.25
	1974	41.024	—	.10	.15	.25
	1975	26.540	—	.10	.15	.25
	1976	.960	—	.10	.15	.25

50 CENTAVOS

BRASS

43	1970	44.748	.10	.15	.30	.50
	1971	34.947	.10	.15	.30	.50
	1972	40.960	.10	.15	.30	.50
	1973	69.472	.10	.15	.30	.50
	1974	63.063	.10	.15	.30	.50
	1975	64.859	.10	.15	.30	.50
	1976	9.768	.10	.15	.30	.50
	1983	115.859	.10	.15	.30	.50
	1984	57.968	.10	.15	.30	.50

PESO

ALUMINUM-BRASS

44	1974	77.292	—	.10	.25	.50
	1975	658.200	—	.10	.20	.50

Slightly modified design.

45	1975	Inc. Ab.	—	.10	.20	.50
	1976	365.075	—	.10	.25	.50
	1984	63.525	—	.10	.25	.50

5 PESOS

ALUMINUM-BRONZE

KM#	Date	Mintage	Fine	VF	XF	Unc
46	1976	118.353	—	.10	.20	.60
	1977	64.738	—	.10	.20	.60
	1978	13.367	—	.10	.20	.60
	1984	185.691	—	.10	.20	.60

Admiral G. Brown Bicentennial

48	1977	Inc. Ab.	.10	.15	.25	.50

10 PESOS

ALUMINUM-BRONZE

47	1976	128.965	.10	.15	.35	1.00
	1977	248.959	.10	.15	.35	1.00
	1978	253.863	.10	.15	.35	1.00
	1979	5.561	.10	.15	.35	1.00
	1984	11.206	.10	.15	.35	1.00

Admiral G. Brown Bicentennial

49	1977	Inc. Ab.	.10	.20	.50	1.00

20 PESOS

COPPER-ALUMINUM-NICKEL
World Soccer Championship 1978

50	1977	1.506	.15	.35	.75	1.25
	1978	2.000	.10	.25	.50	1.00

50 PESOS

COPPER-ALUMINUM-NICKEL
World Soccer Championship 1978

51	1977	1.506	.15	.35	.75	1.25
	1978	2.000	.10	.25	.50	1.00

200th Anniversary of Birth of Jose de San Martin

56	1978	40.601	.20	.50	1.00	2.00

ALUMINUM-BRONZE
Jose de San Martin

KM#	Date	Mintage	Fine	VF	XF	Unc
58	1979	103.491	.10	.25	.75	1.50
	1980	94.730	.10	.25	.75	1.50

BRONZE CLAD STEEL

58a	1980	Inc. Ab.	.10	.25	.75	1.50
	1981	4.372	.10	.25	.75	1.50
	1984	16.528	.10	.25	.75	1.50

Conquest of Patagonia Centennial

59	1979	Inc. Ab.	.10	.25	.75	1.50

100 PESOS

COPPER-ALUMINUM-NICKEL
World Soccer Championship 1978

52	1977	1.506	.25	.50	1.00	1.50
	1978	2.000	.25	.50	1.00	1.50

200th Anniversary of Birth of Jose de San Martin

57	1978	113.826	—	.50	1.00	2.00

ALUMINUM-BRONZE
Jose de San Martin

60	1979	207.572	.15	.30	.75	1.50
	1980	154.260	.15	.30	.75	1.50
	1981	145.680	.15	.30	.75	1.50

BRONZE CLAD STEEL

60a	1980	Inc. Ab.	—	.10	.20	.40
	1981	Inc. Ab.	—	.10	.20	.40

Conquest of Patagonia Centennial

61	1979	Inc. Ab.	.15	.30	.75	1.50

1000 PESOS

10.0000 g, .900 SILVER, .2893 oz ASW
World Soccer Championship 1978

KM#	Date	Mintage	Fine	VF	XF	Unc
53	1977	.106	—	—	5.00	7.50
	1977	1,000	—	—	Proof	17.50
	1978	.141	—	—	5.00	7.50
	1978	1,750	—	—	17.50	20.00

2000 PESOS

15.0000 g, .900 SILVER, .4340 oz ASW
World Soccer Championship 1978

54	1977	.106	—	—	7.50	10.00
	1977	1,000	—	—	Proof	22.50
	1978	.141	—	—	7.50	10.00
	1978	1,750	—	—	Proof	22.50

3000 PESOS

25.0000 g, .900 SILVER, .7234 oz ASW
World Soccer Championship 1978

55	1977	.106	—	—	10.00	15.00
	1977	1,000	—	—	Proof	35.00
	1978	.141	—	—	10.00	15.00
	1978	1,750	—	—	Proof	35.00

MONETARY REFORM

10,000 Pesos = 1 Peso Argentino
100 Centavos = 1 Peso Argentino

CENTAVO

ALUMINUM

62	1983	19.959	—	—	—	.10

5 CENTAVOS

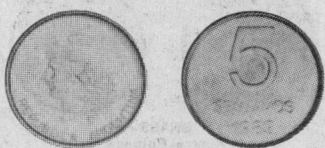

ALUMINUM

63	1983	869.688	—	—	—	.10

10 CENTAVOS

ARGENTINA 112

ALUMINUM

KM#	Date	Mintage	Fine	VF	XF	Unc
64	1983	245.545	—	—	—	.10

50 CENTAVOS

ALUMINUM

| 65 | 1983 | 179.384 | — | — | — | .20 |

PESO

ALUMINUM
National Congress

| 66 | 1984 | 199.782 | — | — | — | .20 |

5 PESOS

BRASS
Buenos Aires City Hall

| 67 | 1984 | 11.206 | — | — | — | .35 |
| | 1985 | 52.248 | — | — | — | .35 |

10 PESOS

BRASS
Tucuman Provincial Capital

| 68 | 1984 | 16.528 | — | — | — | .50 |
| | 1985 | 33.214 | — | — | — | .50 |

50 PESOS

ALUMINUM-BRONZE
50th Anniversary of Central Bank

| 69 | 1985 | 26.400 | — | — | — | .75 |

MONETARY REFORM
1000 Pesos Argentinos = 1 Austral
100 Centavos = 1 Austral

1/2 CENTAVO

BRASS
Austral Coinage

| 70 | 1985 | 7.915 | — | — | — | .10 |

CENTAVO

BRASS

| 71 | 1985 | 76.082 | — | — | — | .10 |

KM#	Date	Mintage	Fine	VF	XF	Unc
71	1986	18.934	—	—	—	.10
	1987	76.582	—	—	—	.10

5 CENTAVOS

BRASS

72	1985	36.924	—	—	—	.15
	1986	66.414	—	—	—	.15
	1987	13.188	—	—	—	.15

10 CENTAVOS

BRASS

73	1985	23.268	—	—	—	.30
	1986	158.427	—	—	—	.30
	1987	67.108	—	—	—	.30

50 CENTAVOS

BRASS

74	1985	13.884	—	—	—	1.25
	1986	59.074	—	—	—	1.25
	1987	16.097	—	—	—	1.25

MINT SETS (MS)

KM#	Date	Mintage	Identification	Issue Price	Mkt. Val.
MS1	1970(5)	—	KM39-43	—	2.00
MS2	1977(6)	—	KM50-55	—	37.50
MS3	1978(6)	—	KM50-55	—	37.50
MS4	1983(4)	—	KM62-65	—	2.00

PROOF SETS (PS)

| PS1 | 1977(3) | 1,000 | KM53-55 | — | 75.00 |
| PS2 | 1978(3) | 1,750 | KM53-55 | 153.00 | 75.00 |

Listings For
ASCENSION ISLANDS: refer to St. Helena

ARUBA

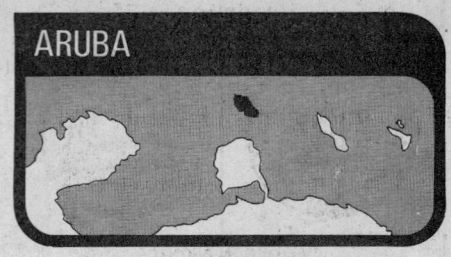

Aruba, formerly a part of the Netherlands Antilles, achieved on Jan. 1, 1986 a special status "status aparte" as the third state under the Dutch crown, together with the Netherlands and the remaining five islands of the Netherlands Antilles. On Dec. 15, 1954 the Netherlands Antilles were given complete domestic autonomy and granted equality within the Kingdom of the Netherlands. The "status aparte" is a step towards total independence of Aruba, scheduled for 1996. Aruba was the second largest island of the Netherlands Antilles and is situated near the Venezuelan coast. The island has an area of 74-1/2 sq. mi. (193 sq. km.) and a population of 60,000. Capital is Oranjestad, named after the Dutch royal family. Chief industry is tourism.

For earlier issues see Curacao and the Netherlands Antilles.

RULERS
Dutch

MINT MARKS
(u) Utrecht - Privy marks only

MONETARY SYSTEM
100 Cents = 1 Florin

5 CENTS

NICKEL BONDED STEEL

KM#	Date	Mintage	Fine	VF	XF	Unc
1	1986(u)	.240	—	—	.10	.15
	1987(u)	.200	—	—	—	.10
	1988(u)	—	—	—	—	.10

10 CENTS

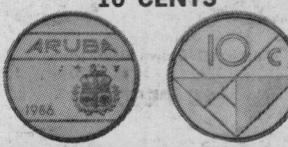

NICKEL BONDED STEEL

2	1986(u)	.320	—	—	.10	.25
	1987(u)	.200	—	—	—	.25
	1988(u)	—	—	—	—	.25

25 CENTS

NICKEL BONDED STEEL

3	1986(u)	.320	—	—	.20	.50
	1987(u)	.200	—	—	—	.50
	1988(u)	—	—	—	—	.50

50 CENTS

NICKEL BONDED STEEL

4	1986(u)	.200	—	—	.40	.75
	1987(u)	.100	—	—	—	.75
	1988(u)	—	—	—	—	.75

FLORIN

NICKEL BONDED STEEL

KM#	Date	Mintage	Fine	VF	XF	Unc
5	1986(u)	.300	—	—	.75	1.25
	1987(u)	.200	—	—	—	1.25
	1988(u)		—	—	—	1.25

2-1/2 FLORIN

NICKEL BONDED STEEL

KM#	Date	Mintage	Fine	VF	XF	Unc
6	1986(u)	.050	—	—	1.75	2.50
	1987(u)	.010	—	—	—	2.50
	1988(u)		—	—	—	2.50

25 FLORIN

25.0200 g, .925 SILVER, .7441 oz ASW
Commonwealth of Aruba
Obv: Similar to 2-1/2 Florin, KM#6.

7	1986	5,000	—	—	—	30.00
	1986(u)	.010	—	—	Proof	40.00

MINT SETS (MS)

KM#	Date	Mintage	Identification	Issue Price	Mkt. Val.
MS1	1986(6)	36,200	KM1-6	8.95	10.00
MS2	1987(6)	21,447	KM1-6	9.95	11.00
MS3	1988(6)	—	KM1-6	12.95	13.00

AUSTRALIA

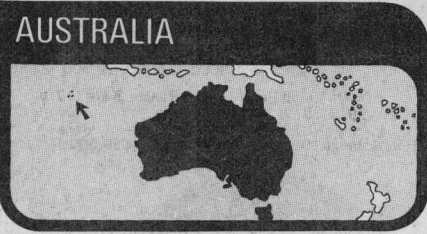

The Commonwealth of Australia, the smallest continent and largest island in the world, is located south of Indonesia between the Indian and Pacific oceans. It has an area of 2,967,909 sq. mi. (7,686,848 sq. km.) and a population of 14.7 million. Capital: Canberra. Due to its early and sustained isolation, Australia is the habitat of such curious and unique fauna as the kangaroo, koala, platypus, wombat, echidna and frilled-necked lizard. The continent possesses extensive mineral deposits, the most important of which are gold, coal, silver, nickel, uranium, lead and zinc. Livestock raising, mining and manufacturing are the principal industries. Chief exports are wool, meat, wheat, iron ore, coal and nonferrous metals.

The first whites to see Australia probably were Portuguese and Spanish navigators of the late 16th century. In 1770, Captain James Cook explored the east coast and annexed it for Great Britain. New South Wales was founded as a penal colony following the loss of British North America by Capt. Arthur Phillip on January 26, 1788, a date now celebrated as Australia Day. Dates of creation of the six colonies that now comprise the states of the Australian Commonwealth are: New South Wales, 1823; Tasmania, 1825; Western Australia, 1838; South Australia, 1842; Victoria, 1851; Queensland, 1859. A constitution providing for federation of the colonies was approved by the British Parliament in 1900; the Commonwealth of Australia came into being in 1901. Australia passed the Statute of Westminster Adoption Act on October 9, 1942, which officially established Australia's complete autonomy in external and internal affairs, thereby formalizing a situation that had existed for years. Australia is a member of the Commonwealth of Nations. The Queen of England is Chief of State.

Australia's currency system was changed from Pounds-Shillings-Pence to a decimal system of Dollars and Cents on Feb. 14, 1966.

RULERS
British

MINT MARKS

Abbr.	Mint	Mint Marks and Locations
(b)	Bombay	"I" under bust; dots before and after HALF PENNY, 1942-43
(b)	Bombay	"I" under bust dots before and after PENNY, 1942-43
(c)	Calcutta	"I" above date, 1916-18
D	Denver	"D" above date 1/-& 2/-, under date on 3d
D	Denver	"D" under date on 6d
H	Heaton	"H" below date on silver coins, 1914-15
H	Heaton	"H" above date on bronze coins
(L)	London	None, 1910-1915, 1966
M	Melbourne	"M" under date on silver coins, 1916-21
M	Melbourne	"M" above date on the ground on gold coins w/St. George
(m)	Melbourne	Dot below scroll on penny, 1919-20
(m)	Melbourne	Two dots; under lower scroll and above upper, 1919-20
P	Perth	"P" above date on the ground on gold coins w/St. George
(p)	Perth	Dot between KG (designer's Initials), 1940-41
(p)	Perth	Dot after PENNY, 1941-51 1954-64
(p)	Perth	Dot after AUSTRALIA, 1952-53
(p)	Perth	Dot before SHILLING, 1946
(p)	Perth	None, 1922 penny, 1966
P	Perth	Nuggets, 1986
PL	London	"PL" after PENNY in 1951
PL	London	"PL" on bottom folds of ribbon, 1951 threepence
PL	London	"PL" over date on sixpence, 1951
S	San Francisco	"S" above or below date, 1942-44
S	Sydney	"S" above date on the ground on gold coins w/St. George
(sy)	Sydney	Dot above bottom scroll on penny 1920
(c)	Canberra	None, 1966 to date
(m)	Melbourne	None, 1922-1964
(sy)	Sydney	None, 1919-1926

Mint designations are shown in ( ). Ex. 1878(m).
Mint marks are shown after date. Ex. 1878M.

MONETARY SYSTEM
12 Pence = 1 Shilling
2 Shillings = 1 Florin
5 Shillings = 1 Crown
20 Shillings = 1 Pound

NEW SOUTH WALES

CUT AND COUNTERSTAMPED COINAGE
15 PENCE

Cross

A

Crown band
Mira type A/1. Rev: FIFTEEN/4.5mm/PENCE.
.903 SILVER
Struck over center plugs of cut Spanish or Spanish Colonial 8 Reales.

KM#	Date	Mintage	Good	VG	Fine	VF
1.1	1813	*.026	500.00	1000.	2000.	3500.

Cross
C

Crown band
Mira type C/4.
Obv: Pearls in band of crown diamond shaped.

1.2	1813	*1,600	1000.	3500.	4500.	7500.

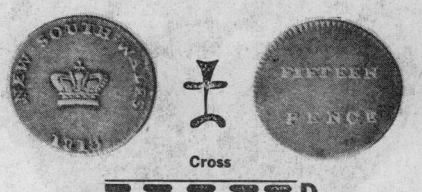

Cross
D

Crown band
Mira type D/2. Rev: FIFTEEN/5.0mm/PENCE.

1.3	1813	*8,000	750.00	1500.	3000.	4500.

Cross
E

Crown band
Mira type E/3. Rev: FIFTEEN/3.0mm/PENCE.

1.4	1813	*4,400	1200.	2500.	4000.	6500.

NOTE: *Estimated original mintage.
REFERENCE: "A Classification of the New South Wales Dumps", 1977 by Dr. W. J. D. Mira.

'HOLEY DOLLAR'
(5 Shillings)

.903 SILVER
c/s: NEW SOUTH WALES-1813/FIVE SHILLINGS on holed Bolivia, Potosi 8 Reales KM#55.

2.1	1813(1773-89)					
	*.040	3000.	6500.	12,500.	25,000.	

New South Wales / AUSTRALIA

c/s: On holed Bolivia, Potosi 8 Reales KM#73.

KM#	Date	Mintage	Good	VG	Fine	VF
2.3	1813(1791-1808)	—	2000.	4000.	10,000.	20,000.

c/s: On holed Mexico City 8 Reales, KM#104.

2.5	1813(1757)	1 known	—	—	Rare	—

M. R. Roberts 1988 sale, unique, realized A $45,000.

c/s: On holed Mexico City 8 Reales, KM#106.

2.6	1813(1772-89)	Inc. Ab.	2500.	4000.	10,000.	18,000.

c/s: On holed Mexico City 8 Reales, KM#107.

2.7	1813(1789-90)	Inc. Ab.	2500.	4000.	10,000.	18,000.

c/s: On holed Mexico City 8 Reales, KM#109.

2.9	1813(1791-1808)	Inc. Ab.	2250.	3750.	7500.	15,000.

c/s: On holed Mexico City 8 Reales, KM#110.

2.10	1813(1809-10)	Inc. Ab.	2500.	4000.	10,000.	18,000.

c/s: On holed Peru, Lima 8 Reales, KM#117.1.

2.11	1813(1772-89)	Inc. Ab.	3000.	6000.	12,500.	22,500.

c/s: On holed Peru, Lima 8 Reales, KM#117.1.

KM#	Date	Mintage	Good	VG	Fine	VF
2.13	1813(1791-1808)	Inc. Ab.	3000.	6000.	12,500.	22,500.

c/s: On holed Peru, Lima 8 Reales, KM#117.1.

2.14	1813(1810)	2 known	—	—	Rare	—

M. R. Roberts 1988 sale, AEF realized A $50,000.

c/s: On holed Spain, Madrid 8 Reales C#71.1.

2.15	1813(1788-1808)	Inc. Ab.	7500.	12,500.	25,000.	30,000.

M. R. Roberts 1988 sale, EF realized A $65,000.

c/s: On holed Spain, Seville 8 Reales, C#71.2.

2.16	1813(1788-1803)	Inc. Ab.	7500.	12,500.	25,000.	30,000.

SOUTH AUSTRALIA
ADELAIDE POUND

8.7500 g, .917 GOLD, .2579 oz AGW

KM#	Date	Mintage	Fine	VF	XF	Unc
1	1852	*20-50 pcs.	—	22,500.	32,500.	45,000.

Rev: Dentilated inner circle.

2	1852	.025	3500.	5000.	8500.	12,750.

COMMONWEALTH OF AUSTRALIA
1/2 PENNY

BRONZE

KM#	Date	Mintage	Fine	VF	XF	Unc
22	1911(L)	2.832	.30	5.00	30.00	130.00
	1912H	2.400	.30	5.00	30.00	155.00
	1913(L)	2.160	.35	7.50	40.00	200.00
	1914(L)	1.440	2.50	10.00	60.00	200.00

KM#	Date	Mintage	Fine	VF	XF	Unc
22	1914H	1.200	4.00	10.00	65.00	270.00
	1915H	.720	15.00	60.00	275.00	1200.
	1916-I(c)	3.600	.25	1.75	17.50	110.00
	1917-I(c)	5.760	.25	2.00	17.50	110.00
	1918-I(c)	1.440	4.00	40.00	150.00	1000.
	1919(sy)	3.326	.20	2.25	20.00	100.00
	1920(sy)	4.114	.65	4.00	18.00	275.00
	1921(sy)	5.280	.25	1.50	14.00	95.00
	1922(sy)	6.924	.25	1.75	20.00	100.00
	1923(sy)	Disputed	225.00	375.00	600.00	10,000.
	1923(sy)	—	—	—	Proof	15,000.
	1924(m)	.682	4.00	8.00	70.00	350.00
	1924(m)	—	—	—	Proof	1750.
	1925(m)	1.147	1.00	3.50	40.00	275.00
	1925(m)	—	—	—	Proof	2750.
	1926(m&sy)	4.139	.20	1.50	30.00	150.00
	1926(m)	—	—	—	Proof	1500.
	1927(m)	3.072	.20	1.00	30.00	120.00
	1927(m)	50 pcs.	—	—	Proof	1500.
	1928(m)	2.318	1.25	3.50	50.00	350.00
	1928(m)	—	—	—	Proof	1500.
	1929(m)	2.635	.20	1.00	25.00	140.00
	1929(m)	—	—	—	Proof	1500.
	1930(m)	.638	5.00	8.00	50.00	300.00
	1930(m)	—	—	—	Proof	10,000.
	1931(m)	.370	7.00	8.50	75.00	300.00
	1931(m)	—	—	—	Proof	1500.
	1932(m)	2.554	.20	1.00	17.50	75.00
	1933(m)	4.608	.20	1.00	12.50	65.00
	1933(m)	—	—	—	Proof	1000.
	1934(m)	3.816	.20	1.00	15.00	75.00
	1934(m)	100 pcs.	—	—	Proof	650.00
	1935(m)	2.916	.20	1.00	10.00	65.00
	1935(m)	100 pcs.	—	—	Proof	650.00
	1936(m)	2.562	.20	1.00	10.00	65.00
	1936(m)	—	—	—	Proof	1000.

Mule. Obv: India 1/4 Anna, Y#37. Rev: Y#5.

30	1916-I(c)	*10	2000.	3000.	6000.	8000.

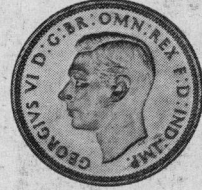 

35	1938(m)	3.014	.20	.50	2.50	32.50
	1938(m)	250 pcs.	—	—	Proof	650.00
	1939(m)	4.382	.20	.50	5.00	32.50
	1939(m)	—	—	—	Proof	1250.

41	1939(m)	.504	5.00	8.00	70.00	300.00
	1939(m)	100 pcs.	—	—	Proof	1500.
	1940(m)	2.294	.20	1.75	12.50	55.00
	1940(m)	—	—	—	Proof	1000.
	1941(m)	5.011	.20	.75	4.25	25.00
	1942(m)	.720	2.00	5.00	20.00	90.00
	1942(m)	—	—	—	Proof	1000.
	1942(p)	4.334	.20	.50	2.00	20.00
	1942-I(b)	6.000	.15	.25	2.50	30.00
	1943(m)	33.989	.15	.25	1.50	9.00
	1943-I(b)	6.000	.20	.35	4.00	18.00
	1944(m)	.720	2.00	4.00	30.00	125.00
	1944(m)	—	—	—	Proof	1000.
	1945(p)	3.033	.90	3.50	10.00	50.00
	1945(p) w/o dot	Inc. Ab.	1.00	5.00	8.50	40.00
	1945(p)	—	—	—	Proof	750.00
	1946(p)	13.747	.15	.25	2.00	12.00
	1946(p)	—	—	—	Proof	750.00
	1947(p)	9.293	.15	.25	2.00	16.50
	1947(p)	—	—	—	Proof	750.00
	1948(m)	4.608	.25	1.00	6.00	30.00
	1948(p)	25.553	.15	.25	2.00	11.00
	1948(p)	—	—	—	Proof	750.00

Obv. leg: IND:IMP: dropped.

42	1949(p)	22.310	.15	.25	2.75	10.00
	1950(p)	12.014	.15	.50	5.00	20.00
	1950(p)	—	—	—	Proof	750.00
	1951(p)	29.422	.15	.25	2.00	9.00
	1951(p)	—	—	—	Proof	750.00
	1951(p) w/o dot					

AUSTRALIA 115

KM#	Date	Mintage	Fine	VF	XF	Unc
42		Inc. Ab.	.15	.50	3.00	18.50
	1951PL	17.040	.15	.35	3.00	8.50
	1951PL	—	—	—	Proof	1000.
	1952(p)	1.832	.50	3.00	8.00	25.00
	1952(p)	—	—	—	Proof	750.00

***NOTE:** 5.040 Struck at the Birmingham Mint.

KM#	Date	Mintage	Fine	VF	XF	Unc
49	1953(p)	23.967	.15	.25	1.00	5.25
	1953(p)	16 pcs.	—	—	Proof	750.00
	1954(p)	21.963	.15	.25	1.00	5.25
	1954(p)	—	—	—	Proof	750.00
	1955(p)	9.343	.15	.25	1.00	5.00
	1955(p)	301 pcs.	—	—	Proof	400.00

Obv. leg: F:D: added.

KM#	Date	Mintage	Fine	VF	XF	Unc
61	1959(m)	10.166	.10	.15	.25	2.00
	1959(m)	1,506	—	—	Proof	40.00
	1960(p)	17.812	.10	.15	.25	1.00
	1960(p)	1,030	—	—	Proof	50.00
	1961(p)	20.183	.10	.15	.25	.75
	1961(p)	1,040	—	—	Proof	50.00
	1962(p)	10.259	.10	.15	.25	.75
	1962(p)	1,064	—	—	Proof	45.00
	1963(p)	16.410	.10	.15	.25	.75
	1963(p)	1,060	—	—	Proof	45.00
	1964(p)	18.230	.10	.15	.25	.75
	1964(p)	1 known	—	—	Proof	3000.

PENNY

Bronze

KM#	Date	Mintage	Fine	VF	XF	Unc
23	1911(L)	3.768	2.00	5.00	25.00	155.00
	1912H	3.600	2.00	5.00	30.00	175.00
	1913(L)	2.520	2.50	10.00	40.00	250.00
	1914(L)	.720	10.00	40.00	100.00	475.00
	1915(L)	.960	6.00	30.00	85.00	600.00
	1915H	1.320	5.00	15.00	85.00	500.00
	1916-I(c)	3.324	1.00	2.00	40.00	200.00
	1917-I(c)	6.240	.75	1.50	27.50	150.00
	1918-I(c)	1.200	5.00	20.00	100.00	700.00
	1919(m) w/o dots	5.810	1.00	3.00	30.00	300.00
	1919(m) dot below bottom scroll	Inc. Ab.	2.00	4.00	60.00	275.00
	1919(m) dots below bottom scroll and above upper	I.A.	15.00	40.00	150.00	1000.
	1920(m&sy) w/o dots	8.250	1.25	9.00	150.00	1500.
	1920(m) dot below bottom scroll	Inc. Ab.	5.00	12.00	75.00	400.00
	1920(sy) dot above bottom scroll	Inc. Ab.	5.00	12.00	75.00	400.00
	1920(m) dots below bottom scroll and above upper	I.A.	10.00	50.00	200.00	1000.
	1921(m&sy)	7.438	.40	2.50	40.00	235.00
	1922(m&p)	12.697	.40	2.00	32.50	200.00
	1923(m)	5.654	.40	2.00	35.00	235.00
	1923(m)	—	—	—	Proof	1500.
	1924(m&sy)	4.656	.40	2.00	37.50	225.00
	1924(m)	—	—	—	Proof	1250.
	1925(m)	1.639	25.00	45.00	200.00	3500.
	1925(m)	—	—	—	Proof	8000.
	1926(m&sy)	1.859	1.50	8.00	50.00	475.00
	1926(m)	—	—	—	Proof	2000.
	1927(m)	4.922	.50	5.00	20.00	235.00
	1927(m)	50 pcs.	—	—	Proof	1000.
	1928(m)	3.038	.50	7.50	35.00	275.00
	1928(m)	—	—	—	Proof	1700.
	1929(m)	2.599	.50	3.25	35.00	275.00
	1929(m)	—	—	—	Proof	1750.
	1930(m)	*3,000	3000.	4750.	8500.	30,000.
	1930(m)	—	—	—	Proof	75,000.
	1931(m)	.494	2.50	7.00	100.00	625.00
	1931(m)	—	—	—	Proof	1750.
	1932(m)*	2.117	.50	3.50	65.00	100.00
	1933/2(m)	5.818	4.00	15.00	80.00	400.00

KM#	Date	Mintage	Fine	VF	XF	Unc
23	1933(m)	Inc. Ab.	.25	2.00	20.00	100.00
	1933(m)	—	—	—	Proof	1000.
	1934(m)	5.808	.25	1.00	18.50	90.00
	1934(m)	100 pcs.	—	—	Proof	850.00
	1935(m)	3.725	.25	1.25	15.00	95.00
	1935(m)	100 pcs.	—	—	Proof	850.00
	1936(m)	9.890	.25	1.00	11.00	50.00
	1936(m)	—	—	—	Proof	750.00

KM#	Date	Mintage	Fine	VF	XF	Unc
36	1938(m)	5.552	.25	.50	5.50	27.50
	1938(m)	250 pcs.	—	—	Proof	750.00
	1939(m)	6.240	.25	.50	5.50	30.00
	1939(m)	—	—	—	Proof	1000.
	1940(m)	4.075	.50	1.50	9.00	50.00
	1940(p)K.G	1.114	3.00	6.00	50.00	300.00
	1941(m)	1.588	.50	1.25	12.50	50.00
	1941(p)K.G	12.794	1.00	3.00	30.00	100.00
	1941(p)	—	—	—	Proof	1750.
	1941(p)Y.	I.A.	.25	1.00	9.00	50.00
	1941 high dot after 'Y'	Inc. Ab.	25.00	1.00	10.00	60.00
	1942(p)	12.245	.15	.75	8.00	40.00
	1942-I(b)	9.000	.15	.50	5.00	25.00
	1942(b) w/o 'I'	Inc. Ab.	2.00	5.00	15.00	75.00
	1942(b)	—	—	—	Proof	1000.
	1943(m)	11.112	.20	.50	5.00	25.00
	1943(p)	33.086	.15	.50	5.00	20.00
	1943(p)	—	—	—	Proof	1000.
	1943-I(b)	9.000	.20	.50	6.50	30.00
	1943-I(b) w/o (I)	Inc. Ab.	2.00	5.00	10.00	75.00
	1943(b)	—	—	—	Proof	600.00
	1944(m)	2.112	.50	2.50	25.00	150.00
	1944(p)	27.830	.15	.50	5.00	22.50
	1944(p)	—	—	—	Proof	1000.
	1945(p)	15.173	.20	.50	5.00	30.00
	1945(p)	—	—	—	Proof	1000.
	1945-I(b)	6 pcs.	—	—	Rare	—
	1945(m)	—	—	—	—	15,000.
	1946(m)	.240	15.00	30.00	125.00	1000.
	1947(m)	6.864	.15	.40	2.75	15.00
	1947(p)	4.49	.50	1.50	9.50	55.00
	1947(p)	—	—	—	Proof	1000.
	1948(m)	26.616	.15	.40	2.75	12.50
	1948(p)	1.534	1.00	4.00	50.00	200.00
	1948(p)	—	—	—	Proof	1000.

Obv. leg: IND:IMP. dropped.

KM#	Date	Mintage	Fine	VF	XF	Unc
43	1949(m)	27.065	.15	.25	2.50	14.00
	1950(m)	36.359	.15	.25	2.50	14.00
	1950(p)	21.488	.20	.30	2.75	30.00
	1950(p)	—	—	—	Proof	750.00
	1951(m)	21.240	.15	.20	1.25	10.00
	1951(p)	12.888	.20	.40	1.75	22.50
	1951(p)	—	—	—	Proof	750.00
	1951PL	18.000	.15	.25	1.00	9.00
	1951PL	—	—	—	Proof	1000.
	1952(m)	12.408	.15	.30	1.25	9.00
	1952(p)	45.514	.15	.30	1.25	10.00
	1952(p)	—	—	—	Proof	1000.

KM#	Date	Mintage	Fine	VF	XF	Unc
50	1953(m)	6.936	.20	1.00	4.75	22.50
	1953(p)	6.203	.20	.90	2.75	13.50
	1953(p)	16 pcs.	—	—	Proof	1000.

Obv. leg: F:D: added.

KM#	Date	Mintage	Fine	VF	XF	Unc
56	1955(m)	6.336	.25	1.25	3.25	20.00
	1955(m)	1,200	—	—	Proof	60.00
	1955(p)	11.110	.10	.20	1.00	7.50
	1955(p)	301 pcs.	—	—	Proof	600.00
	1956(m)	13.872	.10	.20	1.00	6.00
	1956(m)	1,500	—	—	Proof	50.00
	1956(p)	12.121	.10	.20	1.00	6.00
	1956(p)	417 pcs.	—	—	Proof	500.00
	1957(p)	15.978	.10	.20	1.00	4.00
	1957(p)	1,112	—	—	Proof	90.00
	1958(m)	10.012	.10	.20	1.00	5.00
	1958(m)	1,506	—	—	Proof	50.00
	1958(p)	14.428	.10	.20	1.00	4.00
	1958(p)	1,028	—	—	Proof	90.00
	1959(m)	1.617	2.00	4.00	10.00	40.00
	1959(m)	1,506	—	—	Proof	50.00
	1959(p)	14.428	.10	.20	1.00	8.00
	1959(p)	1,030	—	—	Proof	90.00
	1960(p)	20.515	.10	.20	1.00	3.00
	1960(p)	1,030	—	—	Proof	60.00
	1961(p)	30.607	.10	.20	.50	2.00
	1961(p)	1,040	—	—	Proof	60.00
	1962(p)	34.851	.10	.20	.40	1.25
	1962(p)	1,064	—	—	Proof	60.00
	1963(p)	10.258	.10	.20	.40	1.25
	1963(p)	1,100	—	—	Proof	60.00
	1964(p)	54.590	.10	.20	.50	1.25
	1964(m)	49.130	.10	.20	.50	1.25
	1964(p)	1 known	—	—	Proof	3000.

THREEPENCE

1.4100 g, .925 SILVER, .0419 oz ASW

KM#	Date	Mintage	Fine	VF	XF	Unc
18	1910(L)	4.000	5.00	10.00	25.00	68.00

KM#	Date	Mintage	Fine	VF	XF	Unc
24	1911(L)	2.000	10.00	20.00	75.00	250.00
	1911(L)	—	—	—	Proof	5000.
	1912(L)	2.400	10.00	20.00	75.00	300.00
	1914(L)	1.600	15.00	35.00	125.00	525.00
	1915(L)	.800	20.00	75.00	250.00	800.00
	1916M	1.913	10.00	20.00	80.00	350.00
	1916M	25 pcs.	—	—	Proof	900.00
	1917M	3.808	2.00	8.00	27.00	145.00
	1918M	3.119	2.00	10.00	32.00	145.00
	1919M	3.201	3.00	12.50	45.00	200.00
	1920M	4.196	10.00	20.00	75.00	350.00
	1921M	7.378	2.00	6.00	20.00	175.00
	1921(m)plain	I.A.	10.00	20.00	75.00	275.00
	1922/1(m)	5.531	1250.	3500.	10,000.	20,000.
	1922(m)	Inc. Ab.	2.00	7.50	20.00	125.00
	1923(m)	.815	10.00	40.00	125.00	550.00
	1924(m&sy)	2.014	10.00	20.00	50.00	150.00
	1924(m)	—	—	—	Proof	650.00
	1925(m&sy)	4.347	1.50	7.50	20.00	125.00
	1925(m)	—	—	—	Proof	650.00
	1926(m&sy)	6.158	1.50	3.75	20.00	80.00
	1926(m)	—	—	—	Proof	650.00
	1927(m)	6.720	1.50	3.00	20.00	75.00
	1927(m)	50 pcs.	—	—	Proof	650.00
	1928(m)	5.000	1.50	3.00	25.00	90.00
	1928(m)	—	—	—	Proof	600.00
	1934/3(m)	1.616	12.50	40.00	200.00	500.00
	1934(m)	Inc. Ab.	1.50	4.00	17.50	90.00
	1934(m)	100 pcs.	—	—	Proof	300.00
	1935(m)	2.800	1.50	3.00	15.00	75.00
	1935(m)	—	—	—	Proof	300.00
	1936(m)	3.600	1.00	2.00	15.00	70.00
	1936(m)	—	—	—	Proof	600.00

KM#	Date	Mintage	Fine	VF	XF	Unc
37	1938(m)	4.560	.75	2.00	9.00	20.00
	1938(m)	250 pcs.	—	—	Proof	200.00
	1939(m)	3.856	.75	2.50	12.00	45.00
	1939(m)	—	—	—	Proof	350.0C
	1940(m)	3.840	.75	2.50	9.00	30.C

116 AUSTRALIA

KM#	Date	Mintage	Fine	VF	XF	Unc
37	1941(m)	7.584	.75	1.75	5.50	15.00
	1942(m)	.528	10.00	20.00	125.00	425.00
	1942D	16.000	BV	.50	1.25	5.00
	1942S	8.000	BV	1.00	1.50	6.00
	1943(m)	24.912	BV	.50	1.00	4.00
	1943D	16.000	BV	.50	1.25	4.50
	1943S	8.000	BV	1.00	1.50	7.50
	1944S	32.000	BV	.50	1.00	4.25

1.4100 g, .500 SILVER, .0226 oz ASW

KM#	Date	Mintage	Fine	VF	XF	Unc
37a	1947(m)	4.176	1.00	2.50	10.00	30.00
	1948(m)	26.208	BV	.50	1.25	5.00

Obv. leg: IND:IMP. dropped.

KM#	Date	Mintage	Fine	VF	XF	Unc
44	1949(m)	26.400	BV	.50	1.25	5.00
	1950(m)	35.456	BV	.50	1.25	5.00
	1951(m)	15.856	BV	1.00	3.00	10.00
	1951PL	40.000	BV	.25	1.25	5.50
	1951PL	—	—	—	Proof	400.00
	1952(m)	21.560	BV	.25	1.50	5.50

KM#	Date	Mintage	Fine	VF	XF	Unc
51	1953(m)	7.664	.25	2.00	6.50	20.00
	1954(m)	2.672	2.00	4.00	10.00	50.00
	1954(m)	—	—	—	Proof	400.00

Obv. leg: F:D: added.

KM#	Date	Mintage	Fine	VF	XF	Unc
57	1955(m)	27.088	BV	.25	1.50	5.00
	1955(m)	1,040	—	—	Proof	35.00
	1956(m)	14.088	BV	.25	1.50	5.00
	1956(m)	1,500	—	—	Proof	30.00
	1957(m)	26.704	BV	.25	1.00	5.00
	1957(m)	1,256	—	—	Proof	30.00
	1958(m)	11.248	BV	.25	2.00	5.00
	1958(m)	1,506	—	—	Proof	25.00
	1959(m)	19.888	BV	.25	1.00	2.00
	1959(m)	1,506	—	—	Proof	25.00
	1960(m)	19.600	BV	.25	.75	2.00
	1960(m)	1,509	—	—	Proof	25.00
	1961(m)	33.840	BV	.25	.75	1.50
	1961(m)	1,506	—	—	Proof	20.00
	1962(m)	15.968	BV	.25	.75	1.50
	1962(m)	2,016	—	—	Proof	20.00
	1963(m)	44.016	BV	.25	.50	1.50
	1963(m)	5,042	—	—	Proof	10.00
	1964(m)	20.320	BV	.25	.50	1.50

SIXPENCE

2.8200 g, .925 SILVER, .0838 oz ASW

KM#	Date	Mintage	Fine	VF	XF	Unc
19	1910(L)	3.046	7.50	20.00	45.00	150.00

KM#	Date	Mintage	Fine	VF	XF	Unc
25	1911(L)	1.000	15.00	40.00	160.00	500.00
	1911(L)	—	—	—	Proof	2500.
	1912(L)	1.600	20.00	50.00	200.00	650.00
	1914(L)	1.800	10.00	20.00	80.00	300.00
	1916M	1.769	10.00	27.50	175.00	650.00
	1916M	25 pcs.	—	—	Proof	2000.
	1917M	1.632	10.00	27.50	175.00	600.00
	1918M	.915	25.00	75.00	250.00	850.00
	1919M	1.521	10.00	20.00	90.00	450.00
	1920M	1.476	20.00	50.00	200.00	800.00
	1921(m)	—	—	—	Proof	2000.
	1921(m&sy)	3.795	7.50	15.00	55.00	300.00
	1922(sy)	1.488	25.00	60.00	225.00	700.00
	1923(m&sy)	1.458	12.50	32.50	175.00	500.00
	1924(m)	—	—	—	Proof	2000.
	1924(m&sy)	1.038	15.00	50.00	150.00	450.00
	1925(m)	—	—	—	Proof	750.00
	1925(m&sy)	3.266	4.00	15.00	35.00	130.00
	1926(m)	—	—	—	Proof	750.00
	1926(m&sy)	3.609	2.50	8.50	30.00	130.00
	1927(m)	3.592	2.50	8.50	30.00	130.00
	1927(m)	50 pcs.	—	—	Proof	750.00

KM#	Date	Mintage	Fine	VF	XF	Unc
25	1928(m)	2.721	2.50	8.50	30.00	135.00
	1928(m)	—	—	—	Proof	750.00
	1934(m)	1.024	3.50	9.00	45.00	175.00
	1934(m)	100 pcs.	—	—	Proof	700.00
	1935(m)	.392	8.00	20.00	100.00	350.00
	1935(m)	—	—	—	Proof	800.00
	1936(m)	1.800	2.00	5.00	20.00	100.00
	1936(m)	—	—	—	Proof	750.00

KM#	Date	Mintage	Fine	VF	XF	Unc
38	1938(m)	2.864	1.75	3.50	12.50	40.00
	1938(m)	250 pcs.	—	—	Proof	325.00
	1939(m)	1.600	1.75	4.00	25.00	90.00
	1940(m)	1.600	1.75	4.00	20.00	75.00
	1941(m)	2.912	1.50	2.50	8.00	30.00
	1942(m)	8.968	BV	1.75	5.00	20.00
	1942D	12.000	BV	.75	2.75	10.00
	1942S	4.000	BV	.75	2.75	15.00
	1943D	8.000	BV	.75	2.75	12.00
	1943S	4.000	BV	.75	2.75	15.00
	1944S	4.000	BV	1.75	3.50	17.50
	1945(m)	10.096	BV	1.75	5.00	20.00

2.8200 g, .500 SILVER, .0453 oz ASW

KM#	Date	Mintage	Fine	VF	XF	Unc
38a	1946(m)	10.024	BV	1.00	5.00	17.50
	1948(m)	1.584	.50	2.00	6.00	20.00

Obv. leg: IND:IMP. dropped.

KM#	Date	Mintage	Fine	VF	XF	Unc
45	1950(m)	10.272	BV	2.50	5.00	22.50
	1951(m)	13.760	BV	2.00	4.00	17.50
	1951PL	20.024	BV	.50	2.50	12.00
	1951PL	—	—	—	Proof	550.00
	1952(m)	2.112	2.00	6.00	25.00	200.00

KM#	Date	Mintage	Fine	VF	XF	Unc
52	1953(m)	1.152	4.00	7.00	20.00	120.00
	1954(m)	7.672	BV	1.50	2.25	7.50
	1954(m)	—	—	—	Proof	700.00

Obv. leg: F:D: added.

KM#	Date	Mintage	Fine	VF	XF	Unc
58	1955(m)	14.248	BV	.75	2.50	9.00
	1955(m)	1,200	—	—	Proof	45.00
	1956(m)	7.904	.50	3.00	6.00	25.00
	1956(m)	1,500	—	—	Proof	35.00
	1957(m)	13.752	BV	.50	1.00	6.00
	1957(m)	1,256	—	—	Proof	35.00
	1958(m)	17.944	BV	.50	1.00	4.00
	1958(m)	1,506	—	—	Proof	30.00
	1959(m)	11.728	BV	.50	1.00	5.00
	1959(m)	1,506	—	—	Proof	30.00
	1960(m)	18.592	BV	.50	1.00	4.00
	1960(m)	1,509	—	—	Proof	30.00
	1961(m)	9.152	BV	.50	1.75	2.50
	1961(m)	1,506	—	—	Proof	25.00
	1962(m)	44.816	BV	.50	.75	1.75
	1962(m)	2,016	—	—	Proof	25.00
	1963(m)	25.056	BV	.50	.75	2.00
	1963(m)	5,042	—	—	Proof	15.00

SHILLING

5.6500 g, .925 SILVER, .1680 oz ASW

KM#	Date	Mintage	Fine	VF	XF	Unc
20	1910(L)	2.536	10.00	25.00	90.00	225.00

KM#	Date	Mintage	Fine	VF	XF	Unc
26	1911(L)	1.700	20.00	45.00	225.00	600.00
	1911(L)	—	—	—	Proof	6000.
	1912(L)	1.000	35.00	125.00	350.00	875.00
	1913(L)	1.200	25.00	75.00	225.00	850.00
	1914(L)	3.300	8.00	25.00	100.00	325.00
	1915(L)	.800	35.00	135.00	400.00	2500.
	1915H	.500	65.00	185.00	600.00	3250.
	1916M	5.141	4.00	12.00	75.00	275.00
	1916M	25 pcs.	—	—	Proof	1250.
	1917M	5.274	4.00	12.00	75.00	275.00
	1918M	3.761	8.00	17.50	55.00	250.00
	1919M	6 pcs.	—	—	—	15,000.
	1920M	.520	10.00	35.00	140.00	450.00
	1920 star(m)	—	—	—	—	15,000.
	1921star(sy)	1.641	50.00	150.00	550.00	2000.
	1921star(sy)	—	—	—	Proof	8000.
	1922(m)	2.040	15.00	30.00	115.00	400.00
	1924(m&sy)	.674	20.00	55.00	300.00	650.00
	1924(m)	—	—	—	Proof	3000.
	1925/3(m&sy)	1.448	4.00	15.00	50.00	170.00
	1925(m)	—	—	—	Proof	1500.
	1926(m&sy)	2.352	4.00	12.50	40.00	150.00
	1926(m)	—	—	—	Proof	1500.
	1927(m)	1.146	6.00	15.00	45.00	160.00
	1927(m)	50 pcs.	—	—	Proof	1250.
	1928(m)	.664	15.00	50.00	200.00	550.00
	1928(m)	—	—	—	Proof	3000.
	1931(m)	1.000	6.00	12.50	60.00	175.00
	1931(m)	—	—	—	Proof	2000.
	1933(m)	.220	60.00	125.00	500.00	2000.
	1934(m)	.480	10.00	25.00	150.00	400.00
	1934(m)	100 pcs.	—	—	Proof	750.00
	1935(m)	.500	7.50	15.00	50.00	180.00
	1935(m)	—	—	—	Proof	950.00
	1936(m)	2.000	4.00	10.00	40.00	170.00
	1936(m)	—	—	—	Proof	1250.

KM#	Date	Mintage	Fine	VF	XF	Unc
39	1938(m)	1.484	3.00	6.00	15.00	70.00
	1938(m)	250 pcs.	—	—	Proof	500.00
	1939(m)	1.520	3.00	6.00	17.50	85.00
	1939(m)	—	—	—	Proof	2000.
	1940(m)	.760	7.00	15.00	50.00	200.00
	1941(m)	3.040	BV	5.00	10.00	45.00
	1942(m)	1.380	BV	4.00	8.00	25.00
	1942S	4.000	BV	2.00	5.00	15.00
	1943(m)	2.720	4.00	8.00	20.00	85.00
	1943S	16.000	BV	2.00	4.00	10.00
	1944(m)	14.576	BV	3.00	8.00	22.50
	1944S	8.000	BV	2.00	4.00	12.50

5.6500 g, .500 SILVER, .0908 oz ASW

KM#	Date	Mintage	Fine	VF	XF	Unc
39a	1946(m)	10.072	BV	3.50	7.00	17.50
	1946(p)	1.316	6.00	15.00	40.00	150.00
	1948(m)	4.132	2.00	4.00	8.00	20.00

Obv. leg: IND:IMP. dropped.

KM#	Date	Mintage	Fine	VF	XF	Unc
46	1950(m)	7.188	BV	3.50	7.00	17.50
	1952(m)	19.644	BV	3.00	5.00	10.00

KM#	Date	Mintage	Fine	VF	XF	Unc
53	1953(m)	12.204	BV	2.75	6.00	14.00
	1954(m)	16.188	BV	2.50	5.00	12.00

AUSTRALIA 117

Obv. leg: F:D: added.

KM#	Date	Mintage	Fine	VF	XF	Unc
59	1955(m)	7.492	BV	2.00	5.00	18.00
	1955(m)	1,200	—	—	Proof	45.00
	1956(m)	6.064	BV	1.00	4.00	20.00
	1956(m)	1,500	—	—	Proof	35.00
	1957(m)	12.668	BV	.75	2.50	9.00
	1957(m)	1,256	—	—	Proof	35.00
	1958(m)	7.412	BV	.75	2.00	8.00
	1958(m)	1,506	—	—	Proof	30.00
	1959(m)	10.876	BV	.75	1.75	6.00
	1959(m)	1,506	—	—	Proof	30.00
	1960(m)	14.512	—	BV	1.50	4.50
	1960(m)	1,509	—	—	Proof	30.00
	1961(m)	31.864	—	BV	.75	3.00
	1961(m)	1,506	—	—	Proof	25.00
	1962(m)	6.592	—	BV	.75	3.00
	1962(m)	2,016	—	—	Proof	25.00
	1963(m)	10.072	—	BV	1.50	4.50
	1963(m)	5,042	—	—	Proof	15.00

FLORIN

11.3100 g, .925 SILVER, .3363 oz ASW

| 21 | 1910(L) | 1.259 | 50.00 | 175.00 | 500.00 | 1250. |

27	1911(L)	.950	60.00	250.00	1000.	2000.
	1911(L)	—	—	—	Proof	9000.
	1912(L)	1.000	60.00	225.00	950.00	2500.
	1913(L)	1.200	60.00	200.00	750.00	1850.
	1914(L)	2.300	15.00	30.00	180.00	500.00
	1914H	.500	75.00	300.00	1000.	4500.
	1915(L)	.500	100.00	275.00	800.00	3000.
	1915H	.750	60.00	150.00	650.00	2000.
	1916M	2.752	17.50	45.00	200.00	950.00
	1916M	25 pcs.	—	—	Proof	3000.
	1917M	4.305	15.00	40.00	145.00	750.00
	1918M	2.095	15.00	40.00	160.00	750.00
	1919M	1.677	50.00	150.00	600.00	2000.
	1920 star(m)	—	—	—	—	40,000.
	1921(m)	1.247	25.00	100.00	500.00	1600.
	1922(m)	2.058	20.00	80.00	300.00	1250.
	1923(m)	1.038	25.00	100.00	475.00	1750.
	1924(m)	—	—	—	Proof	3000.
	1924(m&sy)	1.582	20.00	75.00	250.00	1250.
	1925(m&sy)	2.960	12.50	35.00	150.00	550.00
	1926(m&sy)	2.487	10.00	40.00	135.00	500.00
	1926(m)	—	—	—	Proof	3000.
	1927(m)	3.420	10.00	20.00	130.00	450.00
	1927(m)	50 pcs.	—	—	Proof	2000.
	1928(m)	1.962	15.00	35.00	150.00	450.00
	1928(m)	—	—	—	Proof	2000.
	1931(m)	3.129	10.00	20.00	100.00	300.00
	1931(m)	—	—	—	Proof	2000.
	1932(m)	.188	200.00	500.00	2000.	5500.
	1933(m)	.488	60.00	275.00	800.00	3000.
	1934(m)	1.674	10.00	25.00	125.00	400.00
	1934(m)	100 pcs.	—	—	Proof	1250.
	1935(m)	.915	8.00	17.50	100.00	350.00
	1935(m)	—	—	—	Proof	1250.
	1936(m)	2.382	5.00	10.00	50.00	200.00
	1936(m)	—	—	—	Proof	1500.

Parliament House, Canberra

| 31 | 1927(m) | 2.000 | 5.00 | 8.00 | 15.00 | 60.00 |
| | 1927(m) | 400 pcs. | — | — | Proof | 1500. |

Centennial of Victoria and Melbourne

KM#	Date	Mintage	Fine	VF	XF	Unc
33	"1934-35"	*.054	100.00	150.00	250.00	400.00

*NOTE: 21,000 pcs. were melted.

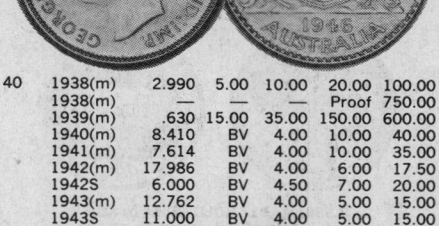

40	1938(m)	2.990	5.00	10.00	20.00	100.00
	1938(m)	—	—	—	Proof	750.00
	1939(m)	.630	15.00	35.00	150.00	600.00
	1940(m)	8.410	BV	4.00	10.00	40.00
	1941(m)	7.614	BV	4.00	10.00	35.00
	1942(m)	17.986	BV	—	6.00	17.50
	1942S	6.000	BV	4.50	7.00	20.00
	1943(m)	12.762	BV	4.00	5.00	15.00
	1943S	11.000	BV	4.00	5.00	15.00
	1944(m)	22.440	BV	4.00	5.00	15.00
	1944S	11.000	BV	4.00	5.00	15.00
	1945(m)	11.970	BV	5.00	10.00	40.00

11.3100 g, .500 SILVER, .1818 oz ASW

| 40a | 1946(m) | 22.154 | BV | 2.50 | 5.50 | 20.00 |
| | 1947(m) | 39.292 | BV | 2.50 | — | 18.00 |

50th Year Jubilee

| 47 | 1951(m) | 2.000 | BV | 3.00 | 5.00 | 15.00 |

COPPER-NICKEL

| 47a | 1951(L) | — | — | — | Proof | 3000. |

11.3100 g, .500 SILVER, .1818 oz ASW
Obv. leg: IND:IMP. dropped.

| 48 | 1951(m) | 10.068 | 3.00 | 5.00 | 8.00 | 27.50 |
| | 1952(m) | 10.044 | 4.00 | 6.00 | 15.00 | 35.00 |

54	1953(m)	12.658	BV	4.50	7.50	20.00
	1954(m)	15.366	BV	4.50	7.50	20.00
	1954(m)	—	—	—	Proof	1000.

Royal Visit

| 55 | 1954(m) | 4.000 | BV | 2.50 | 5.00 | 10.00 |

Obv. leg: F:D: added.

KM#	Date	Mintage	Fine	VF	XF	Unc
60	1956(m)	8.090	2.00	—	4.00	10.00	35.00
	1956(m)	1,500	—	—	Proof	45.00
	1957(m)	9.278	BV	3.00	4.00	10.00
	1957(m)	1,256	—	—	Proof	45.00
	1958(m)	8.972	BV	3.00	4.00	10.00
	1958(m)	1,506	—	—	Proof	40.00
	1959(m)	3.500	BV	3.00	4.00	10.00
	1959(m)	1,506	—	—	Proof	35.00
	1960(m)	15.760	BV	2.50	3.00	7.00
	1960(m)	1,509	—	—	Proof	35.00
	1961(m)	9.452	BV	3.00	4.00	8.00
	1961(m)	1,506	—	—	Proof	30.00
	1962(m)	13.748	BV	2.50	3.50	7.50
	1962(m)	2,016	—	—	Proof	30.00
	1963(m)	12.002	BV	2.50	3.50	5.50
	1963(m)	5,042	—	—	Proof	20.00

CROWN

28.2800 g, .925 SILVER, .8411 oz ASW

34	1937(m)	1.008	7.00	11.00	22.50	85.00
	1937(m)	100 pcs.	—	—	Proof	1500.
	1938(m)	.102	50.00	80.00	150.00	500.00
	1938(m)	250 pcs.	—	—	Proof	2000.

TRADE COINAGE

MINT MARKS

M - Melbourne
P - Perth
S - Sydney
(sy) - Sydney

1/2 SOVEREIGN

3.9940 g, .917 GOLD, .1177 oz AGW
Obv: Fillet head.

KM#	Date	Mintage	Fine	VF	XF	Unc
1	1855(sy)	.021	5000.	12,500.	27,500.	50,000.
	1856(sy)	.478	500.00	1750.	4000.	10,000.

Obv: Hair tied with banksia wreath.

3	1857(sy)	.537	200.00	600.00	1250.	3500.
	1857(sy)	—	—	—	Proof	25,000.
	1858(sy)	.483	200.00	600.00	1500.	4500.
	1859(sy)	.341	200.00	600.00	1750.	6500.
	1860(sy)	.156	350.00	1500.	3000.	10,000.
	1861(sy)	.186	200.00	600.00	1750.	4500.
	1862(sy)	.210	250.00	675.00	1750.	4500.
	1863(sy)	.348	200.00	600.00	1500.	4500.

118 AUSTRALIA

KM#	Date	Mintage	Fine	VF	XF	Unc
3	1864(sy)	.141	200.00	600.00	1750.	4000.
	1865(sy)	.062	300.00	700.00	1750.	5000.
	1866(sy)	.154	200.00	600.00	1500.	5000.
	1866(sy)	—	—	—	Proof	20,000.

HALF SOVEREIGN MINT MARKS

KM#5 & #9: S or M on reverse below shield.

All others have S, M or P (from 1900) on reverse on ground below dragon.

Obv: Young head.

KM#	Date	Mintage	Fine	VF	XF	Unc
5	1871S	.180	100.00	175.00	500.00	1500.
	1871S	—	—	—	Proof	12,500.
	1872S	.356	100.00	175.00	500.00	1500.
	1873M	.165	100.00	175.00	500.00	1750.
	1875S	.252	100.00	175.00	500.00	1500.
	1877M	.140	125.00	200.00	500.00	1750.
	1879S	.220	100.00	175.00	400.00	1250.
	1880S	.080	100.00	250.00	600.00	2000.
	1880S	—	—	—	Proof	10,000.
	1881S	.062	100.00	250.00	600.00	2000.
	1881M	.042	150.00	250.00	800.00	2500.
	1881M	—	—	—	Proof	10,000.
	1882S	.052	150.00	250.00	800.00	3000.
	1882M	.106	150.00	250.00	600.00	1500.
	1883S	.220	100.00	175.00	350.00	1000.
	1883S	—	—	—	Proof	10,000.
	1884M	.048	150.00	250.00	600.00	2000.
	1884M	—	—	—	Proof	10,000.
	1885M	.011	300.00	575.00	1750.	5000.
	1886S	.082	100.00	175.00	500.00	1500.
	1886M	.038	125.00	250.00	600.00	2000.
	1886M	—	—	—	Proof	10,000.
	1887S	.134	100.00	175.00	500.00	1500.
	1887S	—	—	—	Proof	10,000.
	1887M	.064	175.00	300.00	1000.	3500.

Obv: Jubilee head.

KM#	Date	Mintage	Fine	VF	XF	Unc
9	1887S	Inc. Ab.	95.00	175.00	250.00	700.00
	1887S	—	—	—	Proof	8000.
	1887M	Inc. Ab.	100.00	175.00	300.00	800.00
	1887M	—	—	—	Proof	8000.
	1888M	—	—	—	Proof	10,000.
	1889S	.064	100.00	175.00	400.00	1000.
	1889M	—	—	—	Proof	10,000.
	1890M	—	—	—	Proof	10,000.
	1891S	.154	100.00	175.00	400.00	1000.
	1891M	—	—	—	Proof	10,000.
	1892S	—	—	—	Proof	10,000.
	1892M	—	—	—	Proof	10,000.
	1893S	—	—	—	Proof	10,000.
	1893M	.110	100.00	175.00	400.00	1000.
	1893M	—	—	—	Proof	8500.

Obv: Old head.

KM#	Date	Mintage	Fine	VF	XF	Unc
12	1893S	.250	85.00	125.00	300.00	750.00
	1893S	—	—	—	Proof	8500.
	1893M	2 known	1000.	—	—	—
	1893M	—	—	—	Proof	10,000.
	1894M	—	—	—	Proof	10,000.
	1895M	—	—	—	Proof	10,000.
	1896M	.218	100.00	175.00	400.00	1000.
	1896M	—	—	—	Proof	8500.
	1897S	.230	75.00	100.00	250.00	600.00
	1897M	—	—	—	Proof	10,000.
	1898M	—	—	—	Proof	8500.
	1899M	.090	100.00	150.00	400.00	1000.
	1899M	—	—	—	Proof	8500.
	1899P	One known		—	Proof	20,000.
	1900S	.260	75.00	125.00	250.00	500.00
	1900M	.113	100.00	175.00	400.00	1000.
	1900M	—	—	—	Proof	7000.
	1900P	.119	100.00	150.00	400.00	1000.
	1901M	—	—	—	Proof	10,000.
	1901P	—	—	—	Proof	20,000.
14	1902S	.084	80.00	125.00	200.00	500.00
	1902S	—	—	—	Proof	10,000.
	1903S	.231	70.00	100.00	150.00	450.00
	1904P	.060	125.00	200.00	400.00	1000.
	1906S	.308	70.00	100.00	125.00	325.00
	1906M	.082	75.00	100.00	125.00	350.00
	1907M	.400	70.00	90.00	125.00	325.00
	1908S	.538	70.00	90.00	125.00	325.00
	1908M	Inc. 1907M	70.00	90.00	125.00	325.00

KM#	Date	Mintage	Fine	VF	XF	Unc
14	1908P	.025	130.00	250.00	450.00	1000.
	1909M	.186	70.00	90.00	125.00	350.00
	1909P	.044	125.00	250.00	425.00	900.00
	1910S	.474	70.00	90.00	125.00	325.00

KM#	Date	Mintage	Fine	VF	XF	Unc
28	1911S	.252	70.00	70.00	90.00	140.00
	1911S	—	—	—	Proof	10,000.
	1911P	.130	65.00	70.00	100.00	150.00
	1912S	.278	65.00	70.00	90.00	130.00
	1914S	.322	65.00	70.00	80.00	110.00
	1915S	.892	65.00	70.00	80.00	110.00
	1915M	.125	65.00	70.00	80.00	120.00
	1915P	.138	65.00	70.00	80.00	150.00
	1916S	.448	65.00	70.00	80.00	110.00
	1918P	*200-250 pcs.	300.00	500.00	700.00	900.00

SOVEREIGN

7.9881 g, .917 GOLD, .2354 oz AGW
Obv: Fillet head.

KM#	Date	Mintage	Fine	VF	XF	Unc
2	1855(sy)	.502	1250.	3000.	9000.	18,000.
	1856(sy)	.981	1250.	3000.	8000.	16,000.

Obv: Hair tied with banksia wreath.

KM#	Date	Mintage	Fine	VF	XF	Unc
4	1855(sy)	—	—	—	Proof	55,000.
	1856(sy)	—	—	—	Proof	50,000.
	1857(sy)	.499	275.00	500.00	1500.	3750.
	1857(sy) (plain or milled edge)				Proof	30,000.
	1858(sy)	1.101	275.00	600.00	2000.	5000.
	1859(sy)	1.050	225.00	400.00	1500.	3750.
	1860(sy)	1.573	375.00	800.00	2500.	6000.
	1861(sy)	1.626	175.00	350.00	1000.	2750.
	1862(sy)	2.477	250.00	450.00	1500.	4000.
	1863(sy)	1.255	200.00	400.00	1250.	3000.
	1864(sy)	2.698	175.00	275.00	800.00	2500.
	1865(sy)	2.130	175.00	300.00	900.00	3000.
	1866(sy)	2.911	175.00	250.00	600.00	1500.
	1866(sy)	—	—	—	Proof	25,000.
	1867(sy)	2.370	175.00	250.00	700.00	1500.
	1868(sy)	3.522	175.00	250.00	700.00	1500.
	1870(sy)	1.220	150.00	225.00	500.00	1500.
	1870(sy)	—	—	—	Proof	50,000.

NOTE: 1,202,600 pcs. reported in 1869 are dated 1868.

SOVEREIGN MINT MARKS

KM#6: S or M on obverse below head.

All others have S, M or P from 1899 on reverse on ground below dragon.

Obv: Young head.

NOTE: Mintage figures include St. George and shield types. No separate mintage figures are known.

KM#	Date	Mintage	Fine	VF	XF	Unc
6	1871S	2.814	BV	135.00	225.00	500.00
	1871S	—	—	—	Proof	12,500.
	1872S	1.815	BV	135.00	200.00	500.00
	1872/1M	.748	150.00	200.00	375.00	1200.
	1872M	Inc. Ab.	BV	135.00	200.00	500.00
	1873S	1.478	BV	135.00	200.00	500.00
	1873M	3 pcs.	—	—	Rare	—
	1874M	1.373	BV	135.00	200.00	500.00
	1875S	2.122	BV	135.00	200.00	400.00
	1875S	—	—	—	Proof	10,000.
	1877S	1.590	BV	135.00	200.00	400.00
	1878S	1.259	BV	135.00	200.00	400.00
	1879S	1.366	BV	135.00	200.00	400.00
	1879M	1 pc.	—	—	Rare	—
	1880S	1.459	BV	135.00	200.00	400.00
	1880S	—	—	—	Proof	10,000.
	1880M	3.053	500.00	1000.	2500.	7000.
	1880M	—	—	—	Proof	10,000.
	1881S	1.360	BV	135.00	200.00	400.00
	1881M	2.324	BV	150.00	250.00	1000.

KM#	Date	Mintage	Fine	VF	XF	Unc
6	1882S	1.298	BV	135.00	200.00	400.00
	1882M	2.466	BV	135.00	200.00	400.00
	1883S	1.108	BV	135.00	200.00	400.00
	1883S	—	—	—	Proof	10,000.
	1883M	2.050	150.00	350.00	1000.	2000.
	1883M	—	—	—	Proof	10,000.
	1884S	1.595	BV	135.00	200.00	400.00
	1884M	2.942	BV	135.00	200.00	400.00
	1884M	—	—	—	Proof	10,000.
	1885S	1.486	BV	135.00	200.00	400.00
	1885M	2.957	BV	135.00	200.00	400.00
	1885M	—	—	—	Proof	10,000.
	1886S	1.677	BV	135.00	200.00	400.00
	1886S	—	—	—	Proof	10,000.
	1886M	2.902	1500.	2500.	5000.	8000.
	1886M	—	—	—	Proof	12,500.
	1887S	1.000	BV	150.00	300.00	450.00
	1887S	—	—	—	Proof	10,000.
	1887M	1.915	600.00	800.00	2000.	4500.
	1887M	—	—	—	Proof	10,000.

Obv: Young head.

NOTE: Mintage figures include St. George and shield types. No separate mintage figures are known.

KM#	Date	Mintage	Fine	VF	XF	Unc
7	1871S	2.814	—	BV	200.00	600.00
	1871S	—	—	—	Proof	12,500.
	1872S	1.815	—	BV	175.00	600.00
	1872M	.748	—	175.00	250.00	1000.
	1873S	1.478	—	BV	175.00	500.00
	1873M	.752	—	BV	225.00	425.00
	1873M	—	—	—	Proof	10,000.
	1874S	1.899	—	BV	150.00	375.00
	1874M	1.373	—	BV	150.00	375.00
	1874M	—	—	—	Proof	10,000.
	1875S	2.122	—	BV	150.00	375.00
	1875M	1.888	—	BV	150.00	375.00
	1875M	—	—	—	Proof	10,000.
	1876S	1.613	—	BV	150.00	375.00
	1876M	2.124	—	BV	150.00	375.00
	1877S	2 pcs.	—	—	Rare	—
	1877M	1.487	—	BV	150.00	375.00
	1878M	2.171	—	BV	150.00	375.00
	1879S	1.366	—	BV	200.00	600.00
	1879M	2.740	—	BV	150.00	375.00
	1880S	1.459	—	BV	150.00	375.00
	1880S	—	—	—	Proof	10,000.
	1880M	3.053	—	BV	150.00	325.00
	1881S	1.360	—	BV	150.00	325.00
	1881M	2.324	—	BV	150.00	325.00
	1881M	—	—	—	Proof	10,000.
	1882S	1.298	—	BV	150.00	325.00
	1882M	2.466	—	BV	150.00	325.00
	1883S	1.108	—	BV	150.00	325.00
	1883M	2.050	—	BV	150.00	325.00
	1883M	—	—	—	Proof	10,000.
	1884S	1.595	—	BV	150.00	325.00
	1884M	2.942	—	BV	150.00	325.00
	1884M	—	—	—	Proof	10,000.
	1885S	1.486	—	BV	150.00	325.00
	1885M	2.957	—	BV	150.00	325.00
	1885M	—	—	—	Proof	10,000.
	1886S	1.677	—	BV	150.00	325.00
	1886M	2.902	—	BV	150.00	325.00
	1886M	—	—	—	Proof	10,000.
	1887S	1.000	—	BV	150.00	325.00
	1887M	1.915	—	BV	150.00	325.00
	1887M	—	—	—	Proof	10,000.

NOTE: Designer's initials on reverse omitted on some pieces 1880S-1882S and 1881M-1882M.

Obv: Jubilee head.

KM#	Date	Mintage	Fine	VF	XF	Unc
10	1887S	1.002	BV	130.00	200.00	500.00
	1887S	—	—	—	Proof	8500.
	1887M	.940	—	BV	140.00	250.00
	1887M	—	—	—	Proof	8500.
	1888S	2.187	—	BV	140.00	275.00
	1888M	2.830	—	BV	140.00	225.00
	1888M	—	—	—	Proof	8500.
	1889S	3.262	—	BV	130.00	225.00
	1889M	2.732	—	BV	130.00	225.00
	1889M	—	—	—	Proof	8500.
	1890S	2.808	—	BV	140.00	250.00
	1890M	2.473	—	BV	130.00	250.00
	1890M	—	—	—	Proof	8500.
	1891S	2.596	—	BV	130.00	250.00
	1891M	2.749	—	BV	130.00	250.00
	1892S	2.837	—	BV	130.00	250.00
	1892M	3.488	—	BV	130.00	250.00
	1893S	1.498	—	BV	130.00	250.00
	1893S	—	—	—	Proof	8500.
	1893M	1.649	—	BV	130.00	250.00
	1893M	—	—	—	Proof	8500.

AUSTRALIA

Obv: Old head.

KM#	Date	Mintage	Fine	VF	XF	Unc
13	1893S	1.346	—	BV	120.00	150.00
	1893S	—	—	—	Proof	8500.
	1893M	1.914	—	BV	120.00	160.00
	1893M	—	—	—	Proof	8500.
	1894S	3.067	—	BV	120.00	175.00
	1894S	—	—	—	Proof	8500.
	1894M	4.166	—	BV	120.00	160.00
	1894M	—	—	—	Proof	8500.
	1895S	2.758	—	BV	120.00	175.00
	1895M	4.165	—	BV	120.00	160.00
	1895M	—	—	—	Proof	8500.
	1896S	2.544	—	BV	120.00	175.00
	1896M	4.456	—	BV	120.00	160.00
	1896M	—	—	—	Proof	8500.
	1897S	2.532	—	BV	120.00	300.00
	1897M	5.130	—	BV	120.00	160.00
	1897M	—	—	—	Proof	8500.
	1898S	2.548	—	BV	120.00	160.00
	1898M	5.509	—	BV	120.00	160.00
	1898M	—	—	—	Proof	8500.
	1899S	3.259	—	BV	120.00	160.00
	1899M	5.579	—	BV	120.00	160.00
	1899M	—	—	—	Proof	8500.
	1899P	.690	BV	125.00	175.00	275.00
	1899P	—	—	—	Proof	10,000.
	1900S	3.586	—	BV	120.00	160.00
	1900M	4.305	—	BV	120.00	160.00
	1900M	—	—	—	Proof	8500.
	1900P	1.886	—	BV	120.00	175.00
	1901S	3.012	—	BV	120.00	160.00
	1901M	3.987	—	BV	120.00	160.00
	1901M	—	—	—	Proof	8500.
	1901P	2.889	—	BV	120.00	175.00
	1901P	—	—	—	Proof	8500.
15	1902S	2.813	—	—	BV	125.00
	1902S	—	—	—	Proof	10,000.
	1902M	4.267	—	—	BV	125.00
	1902P	4.289	—	—	BV	125.00
	1902P	—	—	—	Proof	8500.
	1903S	2.806	—	—	BV	125.00
	1903M	3.521	—	—	BV	125.00
	1903P	4.674	—	—	BV	125.00
	1904S	2.986	—	—	BV	125.00
	1904M	3.743	—	—	BV	125.00
	1904M	—	—	—	Proof	8500.
	1904P	4.506	—	—	BV	125.00
	1905S	2.778	—	—	BV	125.00
	1905M	3.633	—	—	BV	125.00
	1905P	4.876	—	—	BV	125.00
	1906S	2.792	—	—	BV	125.00
	1906M	3.657	—	—	BV	125.00
	1906P	4.829	—	—	BV	125.00
	1907S	2.539	—	—	BV	125.00
	1907M	3.332	—	—	BV	125.00
	1907P	4.972	—	—	BV	125.00
	1908S	2.017	—	—	BV	125.00
	1908M	3.080	—	—	BV	125.00
	1908P	4.875	—	—	BV	125.00
	1909S	2.057	—	—	BV	125.00
	1909M	3.029	—	—	BV	125.00
	1909P	4.524	—	—	BV	125.00
	1910S	2.135	—	—	BV	125.00
	1910M	3.054	—	—	BV	125.00
	1910M	—	—	—	Proof	8500.
	1910P	4.690	—	—	BV	125.00

KM#	Date	Mintage	Fine	VF	XF	Unc
29	1911S	2.519	—	—	—	BV	120.00
	1911S	—	—	—	—	Proof	12,500.
	1911M	2.851	—	—	—	BV	120.00
	1911M	—	—	—	—	Proof	12,500.
	1911P	4.373	—	—	—	BV	120.00
	1912S	2.227	—	—	—	BV	120.00
	1912M	2.467	—	—	—	BV	120.00
	1912P	4.278	—	—	—	BV	120.00
	1913S	2.249	—	—	—	BV	120.00
	1913M	2.323	—	—	—	BV	120.00
	1913P	4.635	—	—	—	BV	120.00
	1914S	1.774	—	—	—	BV	120.00
	1914S	—	—	—	—	Proof	10,000.
	1914M	2.012	—	—	—	BV	120.00
	1914P	4.815	—	—	—	BV	120.00
	1915S	1.346	—	—	—	BV	120.00
	1915M	1.637	—	—	—	BV	120.00
	1915P	4.373	—	—	—	BV	120.00
	1916S	1.242	—	—	—	BV	120.00
	1916M	1.277	—	—	—	BV	120.00
	1916P	4.906	—	—	—	BV	120.00
	1917S	1.666	—	—	—	BV	120.00
	1917M	.934	—	—	—	BV	120.00
	1917P	4.110	—	—	—	BV	120.00
	1918S	3.716	—	—	—	BV	120.00
	1918M	4.969	—	—	—	BV	120.00
	1918P	3.812	—	—	—	BV	120.00
	1919S	1.835	—	—	—	BV	120.00
	1919M	.514	BV	125.00	175.00	250.00
	1919P	2.995	—	—	—	BV	120.00
	1920S	.360	3000.	4000.	7000.	10,000.
	1920M	.530	300.00	1000.	1500.	2500.
	1920P	2.421	—	—	—	BV	120.00
	1921S	.839	250.00	750.00	1000.	1500.

KM#	Date	Mintage	Fine	VF	XF	Unc
29	1921M	.240	750.00	2500.	5000.	7000.
	1921P	2.314	—	—	—	BV	120.00
	1922S	.578	1500.	2500.	5000.	7000.
	1922M	.608	300.00	1500.	3500.	6000.
	1922P	2.298	—	—	—	BV	120.00
	1923S	.416	300.00	1000.	3000.	5000.
	1923M	.510	BV	120.00	150.00	200.00
	1923P	2.124	—	—	—	BV	120.00
	1924S	.394	200.00	500.00	1000.	1500.
	1924M	.278	BV	120.00	150.00	200.00
	1924P	1.464	—	—	BV	120.00	130.00
	1925S	5.632	—	—	—	BV	120.00
	1925M	3.311	—	—	—	BV	120.00
	1925P	1.837	—	—	—	BV	125.00	150.00
	1926S	1.031	1500.	3000.	6000.	10,000.
	1926S	—	—	—	—	Proof	20,000.
	1926M	.211	—	BV	150.00	200.00
	1926P	1.131	—	—	BV	120.00	150.00
	1927M	.310	4500.	5500.	6500.	9000.
	1927P	1.383	—	—	—	BV	125.00	150.00
	1928M	.413	500.00	850.00	1250.	1800.
	1928P	1.333	—	—	—	BV	125.00	150.00

Obv: Smaller head.

KM#	Date	Mintage	Fine	VF	XF	Unc
32	1929M	.436	250.00	650.00	1250.	1800.
	1929M	—	—	—	—	Proof	8500.
	1929P	1.606	—	—	BV	125.00	150.00
	1930M	.077	100.00	125.00	200.00	275.00
	1930M	—	—	—	—	Proof	8500.
	1930P	1.915	—	—	BV	125.00	150.00
	1931M	.057	150.00	200.00	300.00	500.00
	1931M	—	—	—	—	Proof	8500.
	1931P	1.173	—	—	BV	125.00	150.00

2 POUNDS
15.9761 g, .917 GOLD, .4707 oz AGW

KM#	Date	Mintage	Fine	VF	XF	Unc
8	1887S	*11 pcs.	—	—	Proof	30,000.
16	1902S	*3 pcs.	—	—	Proof	40,000.

5 POUNDS
39.9403 g, .917 GOLD, 1.1771 oz AGW

KM#	Date	Mintage	Fine	VF	XF	Unc
11	1887S	*3 pcs.	—	—	Proof	Rare
17	1902S	*3 pcs.	—	—	Proof	Rare

DECIMAL COINAGE
100 Cents = 1 Dollar

CENT

BRONZE

KM#	Date	Mintage	Fine	VF	XF	Unc
62	1966	146.457	—	—	.10	.50
	1966	.018	—	—	Proof	4.00
	1966(m) blunted whisker on right
		238.990	—	.10	.20	1.50
	1966(p) blunted second whisker from right
		26.620	.10	.25	1.50	8.00
	1967	110.055	—	.10	.20	2.00
	1968	19.930	—	.10	.50	5.00
	1969	87.680	—	—	.10	.50
	1969	.013	—	—	Proof	4.25
	1970	72.560	—	—	.10	.50
	1970	.015	—	—	Proof	4.25
	1971	102.455	—	—	.10	.50
	1971	.005	—	—	Proof	5.00
	1972	82.400	—	—	.10	.50
	1972	.006	—	—	Proof	4.75
	1973	140.710	—	—	.10	.30
	1973	.010	—	—	Proof	5.75
	1974	131.720	—	—	.10	.30
	1974	.010	—	—	Proof	5.00
	1975	134.775	—	—	—	.10
	1975	.023	—	—	Proof	1.00
	1976	172.935	—	—	—	.10
	1976	.021	—	—	Proof	1.75
	1977	149.430	—	—	—	.10
	1977	.055	—	—	Proof	1.50
	1978	97.253	—	—	—	.10
	1978	.039	—	—	Proof	1.00
	1979	130.339	—	—	—	.10
	1979	.036	—	—	Proof	1.00
	1980	136.855	—	—	—	.10
	1980	.068	—	—	Proof	1.00
	1981	224.020	—	—	—	.10
	1981	.086	—	—	Proof	1.00
	1982	134.486	—	—	—	.10
	1982	.100	—	—	Proof	1.00
	1983	239.082	—	—	—	.10
	1983	.080	—	—	Proof	1.25

KM#	Date	Mintage	Fine	VF	XF	Unc
62	1984	74.781	—	—	—	.10
	1984	.061	—	—	Proof	1.50
78	1985	12.413	—	—	—	.10
	1985	.074	—	—	Proof	1.00
	1986	.180	—	—	—	2.50
	1986	.067	—	—	Proof	3.00
	1987	—	—	—	—	.10
	1987	—	—	—	Proof	1.00
	1988	—	—	—	—	.10

2 CENTS

BRONZE

KM#	Date	Mintage	Fine	VF	XF	Unc
63	1966	145.226	—	—	.10	.50
	1966	.018	—	—	Proof	9.00
	1966(m) blunted third left claw
		66.575	—	.10	.30	2.50
	1966(p) blunted first right claw
		217.735	—	.10	.20	1.50
	1967	73.250	—	.10	.25	2.75
	1968	17.000	—	.10	.50	3.00
	1969	12.940	—	.10	.25	1.00
	1969	.013	—	—	Proof	6.25
	1970	39.872	—	—	.10	.75
	1970	.015	—	—	Proof	7.75
	1971	60.735	—	—	.10	.75
	1971	.005	—	—	Proof	7.75
	1972	72.267	—	—	.10	.50
	1972	.006	—	—	Proof	7.75
	1973	94.058	—	—	.10	.40
	1973	.010	—	—	Proof	8.75
	1974	177.723	—	—	.10	.40
	1974	.010	—	—	Proof	8.75
	1975	100.045	—	—	.10	.25
	1975	.023	—	—	Proof	1.50
	1976	121.882	—	—	.10	.15
	1976	.021	—	—	Proof	2.50
	1977	102.000	—	—	—	.10
	1977	.055	—	—	Proof	1.50
	1978	88.253	—	—	—	.10
	1978	.038	—	—	Proof	1.50
	1979	69.705	—	—	.10	.15
	1979	.036	—	—	Proof	1.50
	1980	142.470	—	—	—	.10
	1980	.068	—	—	Proof	1.50
	1981	188.191	—	—	—	.10
	1981	.086	—	—	Proof	1.50
	1982	121.907	—	—	—	.10
	1982	.100	—	—	Proof	1.50
	1983	208.770	—	—	—	.10
	1983	.080	—	—	Proof	1.50
	1984	66.688	—	—	—	.10
	1984	.061	—	—	Proof	2.00
79	1985	6.293	—	—	—	.10
	1985	.074	—	—	Proof	1.00
	1986	.180	—	—	—	2.75
	1986	.067	—	—	Proof	4.00
	1987	—	—	—	—	.10
	1987	—	—	—	Proof	1.00
	1988	—	—	—	—	.10

5 CENTS

COPPER-NICKEL

KM#	Date	Mintage	Fine	VF	XF	Unc
64	1966	45.427	—	.10	.20	1.50
	1966	.018	—	—	Proof	7.00
	1966(L)	30.000	—	.10	.20	1.50
	1966(L)	—	—	—	Proof	15.00
	1967	62.144	—	.10	.30	2.50
	1968	67.336	—	—	.35	3.00
	1969	22.146	—	—	.15	1.00
	1969	.013	—	—	Proof	12.00
	1970	46.058	—	—	.10	1.00
	1970	.015	—	—	Proof	16.00
	1971	39.516	—	—	.20	2.00

119

AUSTRALIA

KM#	Date	Mintage	Fine	VF	XF	Unc
64	1971	.005	—	—	Proof	16.00
	1972	8.256	.10	.25	1.25	17.00
	1972	.006	—	—	Proof	15.00
	1973	48.816	—	.10	.15	.75
	1973	.010	—	—	Proof	17.00
	1974	64.248	—	.10	.15	.75
	1974	.010	—	—	Proof	14.00
	1975	44.256	—	—	.10	.40
	1975	.023	—	—	Proof	3.00
	1976	113.180	—	—	.10	.30
	1976	.021	—	—	Proof	4.50
	1977	109.173	—	—	.10	.30
	1977	.055	—	—	Proof	3.75
	1978	25.210	—	—	.10	.20
	1978	.038	—	—	Proof	2.00
	1979	44.533	—	—	.10	.20
	1979	.036	—	—	Proof	2.75
	1980	100.720	—	—	.10	.20
	1980	.068	—	—	Proof	2.75
	1981	162.384	—	—	.10	.20
	1981	.086	—	—	Proof	3.25
	1982	139.664	—	—	.10	.20
	1982	.100	—	—	Proof	2.25
	1983	165.025	—	—	.10	.20
	1983	.080	—	—	Proof	3.25
	1984	74.496	—	—	.10	.20
	1984	.061	—	—	Proof	4.00
80	1985	.170	(in mint sets only)			
	1985	—	—	—	—	20.00
	1985	.074	—	—	Proof	25.00
	1986	.180	(in mint sets only)			
	1986	—	—	—	—	3.00
	1986	.067	—	—	Proof	5.00
	1987	—	—	—	—	.20
	1987	—	—	—	Proof	2.25
	1988	—	—	—	—	.20

10 CENTS

COPPER-NICKEL

KM#	Date	Mintage	Fine	VF	XF	Unc
65	1966	13.700	—	.10	.25	2.00
	1966	.018	—	—	Proof	15.00
	1966(L)	30.000	—	.10	.25	2.00
	1966(L)	—	—	—	Proof	16.00
	1967	49.316	—	.10	.50	5.00
	1968	57.194	—	.10	.40	4.00
	1969	22.146	—	.10	.20	1.50
	1969	.013	—	—	Proof	11.00
	1970	22.306	—	.10	.20	1.50
	1970	.015	—	—	Proof	14.00
	1971	20.726	—	.10	.25	2.00
	1971	.005	—	—	Proof	14.00
	1972	12.502	—	.10	.25	2.50
	1972	.006	—	—	Proof	14.00
	1973	27.320	—	.10	.15	1.00
	1973	.010	—	—	Proof	14.00
	1974	46.550	—	.10	.15	1.00
	1974	.010	—	—	Proof	14.00
	1975	50.900	—	.10	.15	.70
	1975	.023	—	—	Proof	2.50
	1976	57.060	—	.10	.15	.70
	1976	.021	—	—	Proof	3.75
	1977	24.065	—	.10	.15	.65
	1977	.055	—	—	Proof	3.00
	1978	36.652	—	.10	.15	.40
	1978	.038	—	—	Proof	2.50
	1979	36.950	—	.10	.15	.40
	1979	.036	—	—	Proof	2.50
	1980	55.418	—	.10	.15	.40
	1980	.068	—	—	Proof	2.50
	1981	106.066	—	.10	.15	.40
	1981	.086	—	—	Proof	2.75
	1982	61.688	—	.10	.15	.35
	1982	.100	—	—	Proof	2.00
	1983	115.775	—	.10	.15	.35
	1983	.080	—	—	Proof	3.00
	1984	23.861	—	.10	.15	.30
	1984	.061	—	—	Proof	3.50
81	1985	—	—	—	.10	.20
	1985	—	—	—	Proof	1.00
	1986	—	—	—	—	3.50

KM#	Date	Mintage	Fine	VF	XF	Unc
81	1986	—	—	—	Proof	8.00
	1987	—	—	—	—	.20
	1987	—	—	—	Proof	2.25
	1988	—	—	—	—	.20

20 CENTS

COPPER-NICKEL

KM#	Date	Mintage	Fine	VF	XF	Unc
66	1966	28.223	—	.15	.90	7.50
	1966	.018	—	—	Proof	10.00
	1966(L)	30.000	—	.15	.70	8.00
	1966(L)	—	—	—	Proof	10.00
	1967	83.848	—	.15	1.25	13.00
	1968	40.537	—	.15	1.00	10.00
	1969	16.502	—	.15	1.00	10.00
	1969	.013	—	—	Proof	12.50
	1970	23.271	—	.15	.50	5.00
	1970	.015	—	—	Proof	18.00
	1971	8.947	—	.15	.75	8.00
	1971	.005	—	—	Proof	17.50
	1972	16.643	—	.15	.50	6.00
	1972	.006	—	—	Proof	17.50
	1973	23.356	—	.15	.45	5.00
	1973	.010	—	—	Proof	17.50
	1974	33.548	—	.15	.45	5.00
	1974	.010	—	—	Proof	17.50
	1975	53.300	—	.15	.20	1.00
	1975	.023	—	—	Proof	3.25
	1976	59.774	—	.15	.20	.90
	1976	.021	—	—	Proof	4.50
	1977	41.272	—	.15	.20	.80
	1977	.055	—	—	Proof	3.75
	1978	38.781	—	.15	.20	.80
	1978	.038	—	—	Proof	3.00
	1979	22.300	—	.15	.20	1.00
	1979	.036	—	—	Proof	3.00
	1980	81.070	—	.15	.20	.40
	1980	.068	—	—	Proof	3.25
	1981	164.223	—	.15	.20	.40
	1981	.086	—	—	Proof	3.25
	1982	76.800	—	.15	.20	.40
	1982	.100	—	—	Proof	2.50
	1983	88.570	—	.15	.20	.40
	1983	.080	—	—	Proof	3.50
	1984	31.453	—	.15	.20	.35
	1984	.061	—	—	Proof	5.00

NOTE: Some 1981 dated coins were struck on a Hong Kong 2 Dollar planchet, KM#37. 6 pcs. are reported.

KM#	Date	Mintage	Fine	VF	XF	Unc
82	1985	2.701	—	.15	.20	.30
	1985	—	—	—	Proof	2.00
	1986	—	—	—	—	4.00
	1986	—	—	—	Proof	10.00
	1987	—	—	—	—	.30
	1987	—	—	—	Proof	2.50
	1988	—	—	—	—	.30

50 CENTS

13.2800 g, .800 SILVER, .3416 oz ASW

KM#	Date	Mintage	Fine	VF	XF	Unc
67	1966	36.454	—	—	BV	7.50
	1966	.018	—	—	Proof	80.00

COPPER-NICKEL

KM#	Date	Mintage	Fine	VF	XF	Unc
68	1969	14.020	—	.40	1.00	8.50
	1969	.013	—	—	Proof	45.00
	1971	7.530	—	.40	2.00	12.50
	1971	5.080	—	—	Proof	19.00
	1972	8.030	—	.40	2.00	12.50
	1972	5.861	—	—	Proof	30.00
	1973	4.230	—	.40	1.50	10.00
	1973	.010	—	—	Proof	32.00
	1974	1.287	—	.40	.75	5.00
	1974	.010	—	—	Proof	30.00
	1975	14.680	—	.40	.50	1.00
	1975	.023	—	—	Proof	18.00
	1976	27.280	—	.40	.50	1.00
	1976	.021	—	—	Proof	21.00
	1978	25.765	—	.40	.50	.85
	1978	.038	—	—	Proof	16.00
	1979	24.886	—	.40	.50	.85
	1979	.036	—	—	Proof	17.00
	1980	35.067	—	.40	.50	.80
	1980	.068	—	—	Proof	7.00
	1981	44.374	—	.40	.50	.75
	1981	.086	—	—	Proof	10.00
	1983	82.380	—	—	.40	.50
	1983	.080	—	—	Proof	10.00
	1984	22.849	—	—	.40	.50
	1984	.061	—	—	Proof	15.00

Cook Commemorative

KM#	Date	Mintage	Fine	VF	XF	Unc
69	1970	17.100	—	.40	1.50	5.00
	1970	.015	—	—	Proof	45.00

Queen's Silver Jubilee

KM#	Date	Mintage	Fine	VF	XF	Unc
70	1977	25.243	—	.40	.50	1.00
	1977	.055	—	—	Proof	15.00

Wedding of Prince Charles and Lady Diana

KM#	Date	Mintage	Fine	VF	XF	Unc
72	1981	—	—	.40	.50	1.00

XII Commonwealth Games Brisbane

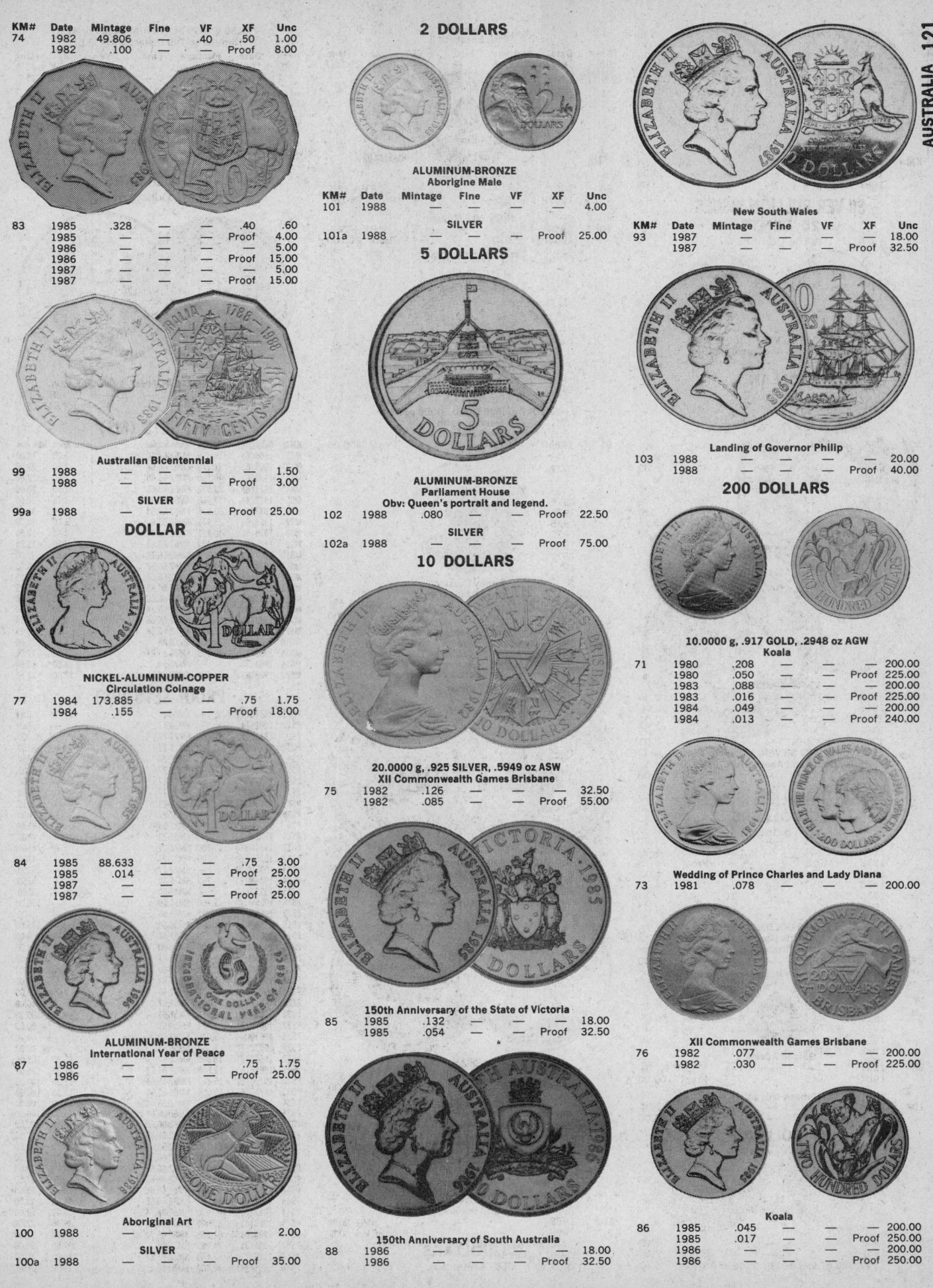

AUSTRALIA 122

Arthur Phillip

KM#	Date	Mintage	Fine	VF	XF	Unc
94	1987	—	—	—	—	200.00
	1987	—	—	—	Proof	265.00

SILVER BULLION ISSUES
25 CENTS
(The Dump)

7.7750 g, .999 SILVER, .2500 oz ASW
Holey Dollar and Aboriginal Culture

| 113 | 1988 | — | — | — | — | 12.00 |

DOLLAR

31.1000 g, .999 SILVER, 1.0000 oz ASW
Holey Dollar and Aboriginal Culture

| 112 | 1988 | — | — | — | — | 30.00 |

GOLD BULLION ISSUES
15 DOLLARS
(1/10 Ounce)

3.1103 g, .999 GOLD, .1000 oz AGW
Little Hero
Obv: Elizabeth II

| 89 | 1986P | .015 | — | — | Proof | 100.00 |

Golden Aussie

| 95 | 1987 | — | — | — | BV + 15% |
| | 1987P | .015 | — | — | Proof | 100.00 |

Jubilee Nugget

| 104 | 1988 | — | — | — | BV + 15% |
| | 1988P | *.010 | — | — | Proof | 100.00 |

25 DOLLARS
(1/4 Ounce)

7.7508 g, .999 GOLD, .2500 oz AGW

Gold Eagle
Obv: Elizabeth II

KM#	Date	Mintage	Fine	VF	XF	Unc
90	1986P	.015	—	—	Proof	200.00

Father's Day

| 96 | 1987 | — | — | — | BV + 12% |
| | 1987P | .015 | — | — | Proof | 250.00 |

Ruby Well Nugget

| 105 | 1988 | — | — | — | BV + 12% |
| | 1988P | *.010 | — | — | Proof | 200.00 |

50 DOLLARS
(1/2 Ounce)

15.5017 g, .999 GOLD, .5000 oz AGW
Hand of Faith
Obv: Elizabeth II

| 91 | 1986P | .015 | — | — | Proof | 400.00 |

Bobby Dazzler
Obv: Elizabeth II

| 97 | 1987 | — | — | — | BV + 7% |
| | 1987P | .015 | — | — | Proof | 400.00 |

Welcome Nugget

| 106 | 1988 | — | — | — | BV + 7% |
| | 1988P | *.010 | — | — | Proof | 400.00 |

100 DOLLARS
(Ounce)

31.1035 g, .999 GOLD, 1.0000 oz AGW
Welcome Stranger

| 92 | 1986P | .015 | — | — | Proof | 600.00 |

Poseidon

| 98 | 1987 | — | — | — | BV + 5% |
| | 1987P | .015 | — | — | Proof | 600.00 |

Pride of Australia Nugget

| 107 | 1988 | — | — | — | BV + 5% |
| | 1987P | *.010 | — | — | Proof | 600.00 |

PLATINUM BULLION ISSUES
15 DOLLARS
(1/10 Ounce)

3.1370 g, .999 PLATINUM, .1000 oz APW
Similar to 100 Dollars, KM#111.

| 108 | 1988 | — | — | — | BV + 20% |
| | 1988 | — | — | — | Proof BV + 20% |

25 DOLLARS
(1/4 Ounce)

7.8150 g, .999 PLATINUM, .2500 oz APW
Similar to 100 Dollars, KM#111.

KM#	Date	Mintage	Fine	VF	XF	Unc
109	1988	—	—	—	BV + 15%
	1988	—	—	—	Proof BV + 15%

50 DOLLARS
(1/2 Ounce)

15.6050 g, .999 PLATINUM, .5000 oz APW
Similar to 100 Dollars, KM#111.

| 110 | 1988 | — | — | — | BV + 8% |
| | 1988 | — | — | — | Proof BV + 8% |

100 DOLLARS
(1 Ounce)

31.1850 g, .999 PLATINUM, 1.0000 oz APW

| 111 | 1988 | — | — | — | BV + 6% |
| | 1988 | — | — | — | Proof BV + 6% |

MINT SETS (MS)

KM#	Date	Mintage	Identification	Issue Price	Mkt. Val.
MS1	1966(6)	16,359	KM62-67 (Card)	2.00	17.00
MS2	1969(6)	31,176	KM62-66,68	2.50	33.00
MS3	1970(6)	40,230	KM62-66,69	2.50	23.00
MS4	1971(6)	28,572	KM62-66,68	2.50	33.00
MS5	1972(6)	39,068	KM62-66,68	2.75	36.00
MS6	1973(6)	30,928	KM62-66,68	3.40	30.00
MS7	1974(6)	25,948	KM62-66,68	3.60	30.00
MS8	1975(6)	30,121	KM62-66,68	3.30	12.50
MS9	1976(6)	40,004	KM62-66,68	3.80	11.25
MS10	1977(6)	128,000	KM62-66,68	4.20	9.00
MS11	1978(6)	70,000	KM62-66,68	4.20	6.00
MS12	1979(6)	70,000	KM62-66,68	4.50	5.25
MS13	1980(6)	100,000	KM62-66,68	5.75	5.25
MS14	1981(6)	120,010	KM62-66,68	6.50	4.00
MS15	1982(6)	195,950	KM62-66,74	6.50	4.00
MS16	1983(6)	155,700	KM62-66,68	5.00	6.50
MS17	1984(6)	131,016	KM62-66,68	7.00	5.25
MS18	1985(7)	170,000	KM78-84	4.00	25.00
MS19	1986(7)	180,000	KM78-83,87	5.50	22.00
MS20	1987(7)	—	KM78-84	8.00	12.00
MS21	1988(8)	—	KM78-82,99-101	12.00	12.50

PROOF SETS (PS)

PSA1	1887S(4)	—	KM8-11	—	Rare
PS1	1902S(4)	—	KM14-17	—	Rare
PS2	1911L(4)	—	KM24-27	—	20,000.
PS3	1916M(4)	25	KM24-27	—	6250.
PS4	1925M(5)	—	KM22-26	—	13,650.
PS5	1926M(5)	—	KM22-27	—	9400.
PS6	1927M(6)	50	KM22-27	—	7150.
PS7	1928M(6)	—	KM22-27	—	9550.
PS8	1929M(2)	—	KM22-23	—	3250.
PSA9	1931m(4)	—	KM22-27	—	7000.
PS9	1930M(2)	—	KM22-23	—	85.00
PS10	1933M(2)	—	KM22-23	—	2000.
PS11	1934M(6)	100	KM22-27	—	4500.
PS12	1935M(6)	100	KM22-27	—	4800.
PS13	1936M(6)	—	KM22-27	—	6350.
PS14	1938M(6)	250	KM35-40	—	5150.
PS15	1953P(2)	—	KM49-50	—	3500.
PS16	1955M(4)	1,200	KM56-59	—	150.00
PS17	1955P(2)	301	KM49,56	—	1000.
PS18	1956M(5)	1,500	KM56-60	—	175.00
PS19	1957M(4)	1,256	KM57-60	—	150.00
PS20	1958M(5)	1,506	KM56-60	—	165.00
PS21	1959M(6)	1,506	KM56-61	—	175.00
PS22	1959M(4)	1,509	KM57-60	—	100.00
PS23	1960P(2)	1,030	KM56,61	—	90.00
PS24	1961M(4)	1,506	KM57-60	—	100.00
PS25	1961P(2)	1,040	KM56,61	—	90.00
PS26	1962M(4)	2,016	KM57-60	—	100.00
PS27	1962P(2)	1,064	KM56,61	—	90.00
PS28	1963M(4)	5,042	KM57-60	—	60.00
PS29	1963P(2)	1,064	KM56,61	—	90.00
PS30	1966C(6)	18,000	KM62-67	15.70	125.00
PS31	1969C(6)	12,696	KM62-66,68	11.25	125.00
PS32	1970C(6)	15,112	KM62-66,69	11.30	100.00
PS33	1971C(6)	10,066	KM62-66,68	11.30	100.00
PS34	1972C(6)	10,272	KM62-66,68	14.00	100.00
PS35	1973C(6)	10,090	KM62-66,68	15.50	100.00
PS36	1974(6)	11,103	KM62-66,68	18.00	100.00
PS37	1975(6)	23,021	KM62-66,68	17.00	27.50
PS38	1976(6)	21,200	KM62-66,68	20.00	32.50
PS39	1977(6)	55,000	KM62-66,70	20.20	22.50
PS40	1978(6)	38,513	KM62-66,68	—	27.50
PS41	1979(6)	36,000	KM62-66,68	—	27.50
PS42	1980(6)	68,000	KM62-66,68	—	13.50
PS43	1981(6)	86,008	KM62-66,68	48.00	13.50
PS44	1982(6)	100,000	KM62-66,74	50.00	12.00
PS45	1983(6)	80,000	KM62-66,68	39.00	22.50
PS46	1984(6)	61,398	KM62-66,77	39.00	37.50
PS47	1985(7)	74,089	KM78-84	27.50	90.00
PS48	1986(7)	67,000	KM78-83,87	40.00	70.00
PS49	1986P(4)	12,000	KM89-92	1445.	1800.

KM#	Date	Mintage	Identification	Issue Price	Mkt. Val.
PS50	1986P(2)	3,000	KM89,90	305.00	350.00
PS51	1987(7)	—	KM78-84	40.00	53.00
PS52	1987(4)	12,000	KM95-98	1440.	1700.
PS53	1987(2)	3,000	KM95,96	305.00	350.00
PS54	1988(4)	9,000	KM104-107	—	1400.
PS55	1988(2)	1,000	KM104-105	—	200.00
PS56	1988(2)	—	KM112-113	50.00	42.50

KEELING-COCOS ISLANDS

The Territory of Cocos (Keeling) Islands, an Australian territory, comprises a group of 27 coral islands located (see arrow on map of Australia) in the Indian Ocean 1,300 miles northwest of Australia. Only Direction and Home Islands are regularly inhabited. The group has an area of 5.4 sq. mi. and a population of about 1,237. Calcium, phosphate, and coconut products are exported.

The islands were discovered by Capt. William Keeling of the British East India Co. in 1609. Alexander Hare, an English adventurer, established a settlement on one of the southern islands in 1823, but it lasted less than a year. A permanent settlement was established on Direction Island in 1827 by Hare and Capt. John Clunies Ross, a Scot, for the purpose of storing East Indian spices for reshipment to Europe during periods of shortage. When the experiment in spice futures did not develop satisfactorily, Hare left the islands (1829 or 1830), leaving Ross as sole owner. The coral group became a British protectorate in 1856; was attached to the colony of Ceylon in 1878; and was placed under the administration of the Straits Settlements in 1882. In 1903 the group was annexed to the Straits Settlements and incorporated into the colony of Singapore until Nov. of 1955, when it was placed under the administration of Australia.

RULERS
British

MONETARY SYSTEM
100 Cents = 1 Rupee

5 CENTS

BRONZE

KM#	Date	Mintage	VF	XF	Unc
1	1977	—	.10	.20	.50

10 CENTS

BRONZE

| 2 | 1977 | — | .15 | .25 | .75 |

25 CENTS

BRONZE

| 3 | 1977 | — | .15 | .25 | .75 |

50 CENTS

BRONZE

| 4 | 1977 | — | .20 | .50 | 1.00 |

RUPEE

COPPER-NICKEL

| 5 | 1977 | — | .50 | 1.00 | 2.00 |

2 RUPEES

COPPER-NICKEL

KM#	Date	Mintage	VF	XF	Unc
6	1977	—	.75	1.50	3.00

5 RUPEES

COPPER-NICKEL

| 7 | 1977 | — | 1.50 | 3.00 | 5.00 |

10 RUPEES

6.5000 g, .925 SILVER, .1933 oz ASW

| 8 | 1977 | 6,000 | — | — | 7.50 |
| | 1977 | 4,000 | — | Proof | 12.50 |

25 RUPEES

16.2500 g, .925 SILVER, .4833 oz ASW

| 9 | 1977 | 6,000 | — | — | 15.00 |
| | 1977 | 4,000 | — | Proof | 22.50 |

150 RUPEES

.750 GOLD

| 10 | 1977 | 2,000 | — | — | — |
| | 1977 | 2,000 | — | Proof | — |

NOTE: The entire issue of KM#10 was stolen with only 290 pieces being recovered.

8.4800 g, .916 GOLD, .2497 oz AGW

| 10a | 1977 | 2,000 | — | — | 150.00 |
| | 1977 | 2,000 | — | Proof | 300.00 |

MINT SETS (MS)

KM#	Date	Mintage	Identification	Issue Price	Mkt. Val.
MS1	1977(7)	—	KM1-7	—	12.00
MS2	1977(2)	6,000	KM8-9	—	22.50

PROOF SETS (PS)

| PS1 | 1977(2) | 4,000 | KM8-9 | 28.00 | 35.00 |

AUSTRIA

AUSTRALIA 123

The Republic of Austria, a parliamentary democracy located in mountainous central Europe, has an area of 32,374 sq. mi. (83,849 sq. km.) and a population of 7.5 million. Capital: Vienna. Austria is primarily an industrial country. Machinery, iron and steel, textiles, yarns and timber are exported.

The territories later to be known as Austria, were overrun in pre-Roman times by various tribes, including the Celts. Upon the fall of the Roman Empire, the country became a margravate of Charlemagne's Empire. Premysl Otakar, King of Bohemia, gained possession in 1252, only to lose the territory to Rudolf of Hapsburg in 1276. Thereafter, until World War I, the story of Austria was that of the ruling Hapsburgs.

During World War I, the Austro-Hungarian Empire was one of the Central Powers with Germany, Bulgaria and Turkey. At the end of the war, the Empire was dismembered and Austria established as an independent republic. In March, 1938, Austria was incorporated into Hitler's short-lived Greater German Reich. Allied forces of both East and West occupied Austria in April, 1945, and subsequently divided it into four zones of military occupation. On May 15, 1955, the four powers formally recognized Austria as a 'sovereign independent democratic state'.

A number of coin-issuing entities that were or are a part of Austria continue to be of interest to collectors of world coins.

Francis I died on August 18, 1765. His wife Maria Theresa, decreed on July 21, 1766 that coins would be issued with the portrait of Francis and bearing the year of his death (1765). Also to be included were letters of the alphabet to indicate the actual year of issue: i.e. A-1766, G-1772, P-1780.

The posthumous coins were issued rather erratically as to denominations, years and mints. 5 denominations were made and 7 mints were used. Only the Ducat and 20 Kreuzer were made until 1780, the year of Maria Theresa's death. The other denominations were 3, 10 and 17 Kreuzer.

RULERS
Franz II (I), 1792-1835
  (as Franz I, Austrian Emperor, 1804-1835)
Ferdinand I, 1835-1848
Franz Joseph I, 1848-1916
Karl I, 1916-1918

MINT MARKS
A, W, WI - Vienna
(a) - Vienna
B, K, K-B - Kremnitz
C - Prague (Bohemia)
C-A,E - Carlsburg
D - Salzburg
D,G,GR - Graz
F, HA - Hall
GM - Mantua
H,P-R - Gunzburg
(h) Shield - Vienna
M - Milan (Lombardy)
N-B-Nagybanya (Hungary)
O - Oravicza (Hungary)
P - Prague (Bohemia)
S - Schmollnitz (Hungary)
V - Venice (Venetia)
(v) Eagle - Hall

MINTMASTERS INITIALS
SALZBURG MINT

Initials	Years	Mintmaster
M	1803-1806	Franz Xaver Matzenkopf

MONETARY SYSTEM
Before 1857
8 Heller = 4 Pfennig = 1 Kreuzer
60 Kreuzer = 1 Florin (Gulden)
2 Florin = 1 Species or Convention Thaler
1857-1892
100 Kreuzer = 1 Florin (Gulden)
1-1/2 Florin = 1 Vereinsthaler

1/4 KREUZER

COPPER
Mint mark: A

KM#	Date	Mintage	Fine	VF	XF	Unc
476.1	1812	—	2.00	4.00	8.00	25.00

AUSTRIA

KM#	Date	Mintage	Fine	VF	XF	Unc
			Mint mark: B			
476.2 (C171.2)	1812	1.725	3.00	6.00	12.50	35.00
			Mint mark: S			
476.3 (C171.3)	1812	—	—	Reported, not confirmed		

KM#	Date	Mintage	Fine	VF	XF	Unc
			Mint mark: A			
483.1 (C175.1)	1816	—	1.50	2.50	5.00	30.00
			Mint mark: B			
483.2 (C175.2)	1816	6.652	1.50	2.50	5.00	30.00
			Mint mark: E			
483.3 (C175.3)	1816	—	—	—	Rare	—
			Mint mark: G			
483.4 (C175.4)	1816	—	—	—	Rare	—
			Mint mark: O			
483.5 (C175.5)	1816	—	3.00	6.00	12.00	35.00
			Mint mark: S			
483.6 (C175.6)	1816	—	1.00	2.00	4.00	25.00

NOTE: The above 6 issues struck until 1852 w/1816 date.

KM#	Date	Mintage	Fine	VF	XF	Unc
			Mint mark: A			
540.1 (C197.1)	1851	—	.50	1.00	2.00	7.50
			Mint mark: B			
540.2 (C197.2)	1851	9.637	1.00	3.50	6.00	10.00
			Mint mark: G			
540.3 (C197.3)	1851	—	10.00	30.00	60.00	120.00

1/2 KREUZER

COPPER
Mint mark: A

KM#	Date	Mintage	Fine	VF	XF	Unc
477.1 (C172.1)	1812	—	2.00	6.00	12.00	40.00
			Mint mark: B			
477.2 (C172.2)	1812	—	—	—	Rare	—
			Mint mark: S			
477.3 (C172.3)	1812	—	3.00	8.00	20.00	50.00

			Mint mark: A			
484.1 (C176.1)	1816	—	1.00	2.00	4.00	25.00
			Mint mark: B			
484.2 (C176.2)	1816	6.652	1.50	5.00	10.00	40.00
			Mint mark: E			
484.3 (C176.3)	1816	—	—	—	Rare	—
			Mint mark: G			
484.4 (C176.4)	1816	—	—	—	Rare	—
			Mint mark: O			
484.5 (C176.5)	1816	—	2.00	8.00	20.00	50.00

			Mint mark: S			
484.6 (C176.6)	1816	—	2.00	6.00	12.50	40.00

NOTE: The above 6 issues were struck until 1852 w/1816 date.

			Mint mark: A			
541.1 (C198.1)	1851	—	1.00	2.00	4.00	10.00
			Mint mark: B			
541.2 (C198.2)	1851	27.733	1.00	2.00	5.00	11.00
			Mint mark: C			
541.3 (C198.3)	1851	—	100.00	150.00	300.00	600.00
			Mint mark: G			
541.4 (C198.4)	1851	—	10.00	20.00	40.00	100.00

5/10 KREUZER

COPPER, 1.67 g
Mint mark: A
Obv: Small eagle.

KM#	Date	Mintage	Fine	VF	XF	Unc
559.1 (Y6.1)	1858	—	1.50	3.00	6.00	9.00
	1859	—	.75	1.50	3.00	7.00
	1860	—	1.00	3.00	7.50	15.00
	1861	—	5.00	10.00	25.00	50.00
	1864	—	2.00	5.00	10.00	25.00
	1865	—	2.00	5.00	10.00	20.00
	1866	—	2.00	5.00	10.00	20.00

			Mint mark: B			
559.2 (Y6.2)	1858	11.058	2.00	3.00	6.50	10.00
	1859	13.397	3.50	6.50	10.00	20.00
	1861	3.474	3.50	7.50	15.00	30.00
	1863	—	6.00	12.00	20.00	40.00
	1864	7.598	2.00	5.00	10.00	20.00
	1865	7.182	6.50	13.50	22.50	50.00

			Mint mark: E			
559.3 (Y6.3)	1858	—	15.00	35.00	60.00	130.00
	1859	—	15.00	30.00	60.00	120.00
	1860	—	15.00	30.00	60.00	120.00

			Mint mark: M			
559.4 (Y6.4)	1858	—	3.50	8.00	20.00	35.00
	1859	—	8.00	16.00	24.00	40.00

			Mint mark: V			
559.5 (Y6.5)	1858	—	10.00	20.00	40.00	—
	1859	—	15.00	30.00	60.00	100.00
	1860	—	5.00	7.50	18.00	40.00
	1864	—	15.00	30.00	60.00	100.00

Mint: Vienna - w/o mint mark.
Reduced weight, 1.60 g

600 (Y6a)	1877	—	5.00	10.00	15.00	25.00
	1881	4.200	2.00	4.00	6.00	10.00
	1885	2.000	.75	1.50	3.00	7.00

Obv: Large eagle.

604 (Y6b)	1885	Inc. Ab.	.50	1.00	2.00	5.00
	1891	2.000	3.00	6.00	12.50	15.00

KREUZER

COPPER
Mint mark: A

478.1 (C173.1)	1812	—	3.00	6.00	15.00	40.00

Mint mark: B

478.2 (C173.2)	1812	92.163	3.00	6.00	12.00	30.00

Mint mark: C

478.3 (C173.3)	1812	—	—	Reported, not confirmed		

KM#	Date	Mintage	Fine	VF	XF	Unc
			Mint mark: E			
478.4 (C173.4)	1812	—	2.50	5.00	10.00	30.00
			Mint mark: G			
478.5 (C173.5)	1812	—	3.00	8.00	20.00	40.00
			Mint mark: O			
478.6 (C173.6)	1812	—	6.00	20.00	35.00	60.00
			Mint mark: S			
478.7 (C173.7)	1812	—	1.50	4.00	10.00	30.00

			Mint mark: A			
485.1 (C177.1)	1816	—	1.00	2.00	4.00	25.00
			Mint mark: B			
485.2 (C177.2)	1816	54.516	1.00	2.00	5.00	25.00
			Mint mark: E			
485.3 (C177.3)	1816	—	7.50	15.00	25.00	40.00
			Mint mark: G			
485.4 (C177.4)	1816	—	2.00	6.00	12.00	30.00
			Mint mark: O			
485.5 (C177.5)	1816	—	2.00	6.00	12.00	30.00
			Mint mark: S			
485.6 (C177.6)	1816S	—	2.00	6.00	12.00	30.00
	1816S.	—	2.00	6.00	12.00	30.00

NOTE: The above 6 issues were struck until 1852 w/1816 date.

			Mint mark: A			
542.1 (C199.1)	1851	—	.50	.75	1.50	5.00
			Mint mark: B			
542.2 (C199.2)	1851	106.458	1.00	1.50	3.00	6.00
			Mint mark: C			
542.3 (C199.3)	1851	—	40.00	60.00	120.00	250.00
			Mint mark: E			
542.4 (C199.4)	1851	—	8.00	15.00	30.00	80.00
			Mint mark: G			
542.5 (C199.5)	1851 sm.G	—	2.00	5.00	20.00	60.00
	1851 lg.G	—	2.00	5.00	20.00	60.00

			Mint mark: A			
			Obv: Small eagle			
560.1 (Y7.1)	1858	—	.50	1.00	2.00	4.00
	1859	—	.50	1.00	2.00	4.00
	1860	—	.50	1.00	2.00	4.00
	1861	—	.75	1.50	2.50	5.00
	1873	—	2.00	4.00	7.00	15.00
			Mint mark: B			
560.2 (Y7.2)	1858	23.497	1.00	2.00	3.00	5.00
	1859	93.406	1.00	2.00	3.50	6.00
	1860	87.955	.50	2.00	4.00	5.00
	1861	54.201	.50	1.00	3.00	5.00
	1862	11.599	5.00	10.00	25.00	50.00
			Mint mark: E			
560.3 (Y7.3)	1858	—	5.00	10.00	20.00	45.00
	1859	—	2.50	5.00	10.00	17.50
	1860	—	5.00	10.00	20.00	45.00
	1861	—	2.50	6.00	12.50	27.50
	1862	—	10.00	20.00	40.00	90.00
	1863	—	15.00	35.00	75.00	160.00
			Mint mark: M			

KM#	Date	Mintage	Fine	VF	XF	Unc
560.4 (Y7.4)	1858	—	4.00	7.00	15.00	40.00
	1859	—	2.50	5.00	12.00	20.00

Mint mark: V

560.5 (Y7.5)	1858	—	11.00	20.00	40.00	75.00
	1859	—	7.00	14.00	25.00	45.00
	1860	—	4.00	9.00	20.00	35.00

Mint: Vienna - w/o mint mark.

560.6 (Y7.6)	1878	—	.50	1.00	2.00	3.00
	1879	—	.50	1.00	2.00	4.00
	1881	37.900	.25	.50	1.50	3.00

Obv: Large eagle.

605 (Y7.7)	1885	29.000	.25	.50	1.25	3.00
	1891	23.800	.25	.50	1.25	3.00

2 KREUZER

COPPER
Mint mark: A
Revolution 1848-1849

531 (C196)	1848	7.755	5.00	10.00	17.50	45.00

543.1 (C200.1)	1851	—	3.00	7.50	15.00	30.00

Mint mark: B

543.2 (C200.2)	1851	22.419	3.50	8.00	16.00	32.50

Mint mark: C

543.3 (C200.3)	1851	—	300.00	500.00	700.00	1000.

Mint mark: G

543.4 (C200.4)	1851 lg. G	—	8.00	15.00	30.00	85.00
	1851 sm. G	—	8.00	15.00	30.00	85.00

3 KREUZER

COPPER
Mint mark: A

KM#	Date	Mintage	Fine	VF	XF	Unc
479.1 (C174.1)	1812	—	15.00	25.00	40.00	100.00

Mint mark: B

479.2 (C174.2)	1812	13.594	2.00	4.00	8.00	25.00
	1812(error)U.H.		5.00	10.00	20.00	40.00

KM#	Date	Mintage	Fine	VF	XF	Unc

Mint mark: E

479.3 (C174.3)	1812	—	9.00	15.00	30.00	65.00

Mint mark: G

479.4 (C174.4)	1812	—	6.00	12.50	20.00	50.00

Mint mark: O

479.5 (C174.5)	1812	—	6.00	12.50	20.00	50.00

Mint mark: S

479.6 (C174.6)	1812	—	3.00	5.00	10.00	30.00

1.7000 g, .344 SILVER, .0188 oz ASW
Mint mark: A

480.1 (C180.1)	1814	—	—	—	Rare	—
	1815	—	7.50	15.00	30.00	60.00

Mint mark: B

480.2 (C180.2)	1815	—	10.00	20.00	40.00	90.00

Mint mark: V

480.3 (C180.3)	1815	—	7.50	15.00	30.00	60.00

.346 SILVER
Mint mark: A

488.1 (C180a.1)	1817	—	50.00	80.00	150.00	300.00
	1819	—	12.00	25.00	50.00	100.00
	1820	—	7.50	15.00	30.00	55.00
	1821	—	7.50	15.00	30.00	60.00
	1822	.079	12.00	25.00	50.00	100.00
	1823	.035	25.00	45.00	75.00	150.00
	1824	.037	—	—	Rare	—

Mint mark: B

488.2 (C180a.2)	1818	.538	12.00	25.00	40.00	90.00
	1820	1.457	7.50	15.00	30.00	55.00
	1821	4.894	7.50	15.00	30.00	60.00
	1823	Inc.C180a.1	—	—	Rare	—

Mint mark: V

488.3 (C180a.3)	1818	—	—	—	Rare	—
	1820	—	—	—	—	—

Mint mark: G

488.4 (C180a.4)	1820	—	—	—	Rare	—
	1821	—	25.00	50.00	75.00	175.00
	1824	Inc.C180a.1	25.00	50.00	75.00	175.00

Mint mark: E

488.5 (C180a.5)	1821	—	25.00	50.00	75.00	200.00

Mint mark: A

495.1 (C180b.1)	1825	.051	25.00	50.00	75.00	175.00
	1826	—	8.00	15.00	30.00	50.00
	1827	.118	40.00	80.00	150.00	250.00
	1828	—	8.00	15.00	30.00	50.00
	1829	—	8.00	15.00	30.00	50.00
	1830	—	8.00	15.00	30.00	55.00
	1831		* Reported, not confirmed			

Mint mark: B

495.2 (C180b.2)	1826	.375	8.00	15.00	30.00	60.00
	1827	—	45.00	75.00	150.00	250.00
	1828	.965	8.00	15.00	30.00	60.00
	1829	.133	22.50	40.00	75.00	160.00
	1830	.076	40.00	80.00	150.00	250.00

Mint mark: E

495.3 (C180b.3)	1826	—	25.00	40.00	75.00	175.00
	1828	—	35.00	60.00	120.00	200.00
	1829	—	17.50	30.00	60.00	140.00
	1830	—	40.00	70.00	140.00	225.00

Mint mark: G

495.4 (C180b.4)	1828	—	40.00	70.00	140.00	225.00
	1829	—	40.00	70.00	140.00	225.00

Mint mark: A
Struck in a collar, short braids.

KM#	Date	Mintage	Fine	VF	XF	Unc
502 (C180d)	1831	—	40.00	75.00	130.00	225.00

Obv: Larger head

503.1 (C180c.1)	1831	—	—	Reported, not confirmed		
	1832	—	5.00	10.00	20.00	50.00
	1833	—	5.00	10.00	20.00	50.00
	1834	—	20.00	40.00	70.00	130.00
	1835	—	20.00	40.00	70.00	130.00

Mint mark: C

503.2 (C180c.2)	1833	—	8.00	15.00	30.00	60.00
	1834	—	30.00	50.00	80.00	175.00

Mint mark: A
Obv: Head of Ferdinand I right.
Rev: Eagle, value on chest.

515.1 (C188.1)	1835	—	20.00	30.00	65.00	140.00
	1836	—	10.00	20.00	40.00	80.00

Mint mark: E

515.2 (C188.2)	1835	—	30.00	50.00	100.00	250.00
	1836	—	25.00	40.00	90.00	240.00

Mint mark: A

523.1 (C188a.1)	1837	—	3.50	7.50	15.00	40.00
	1838	—	3.50	7.50	15.00	45.00
	1839	—	4.00	8.00	15.00	40.00
	1840	—	2.50	5.00	10.00	30.00
	1841	—	15.00	25.00	50.00	110.00
	1842	—	6.00	12.00	20.00	50.00
	1843	—	10.00	15.00	30.00	80.00
	1844	—	6.00	10.00	20.00	50.00
	1845	—	3.00	7.50	15.00	35.00
	1846	—	2.50	5.00	12.50	30.00
	1847	—	2.50	5.00	12.50	30.00
	1848/5	—	3.50	7.00	15.00	35.00
	1848	—	2.50	5.00	12.50	30.00

Mint mark: C

523.2 (C188a.2)	1837	—	25.00	40.00	75.00	150.00
	1838	—	10.00	20.00	35.00	75.00
	1839	—	12.50	25.00	50.00	100.00
	1847	—	5.00	10.00	20.00	45.00

Mint mark: E

523.3 (C188a.3)	1837	—	25.00	40.00	75.00	150.00
	1838	—	15.00	25.00	50.00	110.00
	1839	—	12.50	25.00	50.00	100.00
	1840	—	12.50	25.00	45.00	90.00
	1841	—	35.00	60.00	100.00	175.00
	1842	—	15.00	25.00	50.00	110.00
	1843	—	15.00	25.00	50.00	110.00
	1844	—	15.00	25.00	50.00	110.00
	1845	—	15.00	30.00	55.00	120.00
	1846	—	15.00	30.00	55.00	120.00
	1847	—	15.00	30.00	55.00	120.00
	1848	—	22.50	40.00	75.00	150.00

Mint mark: B

523.4 (C188a.4)	1838	.130	15.00	25.00	40.00	100.00

Mint mark: G-M

532 (C188b)	1848 swan above mint mark					
	—	200.00	350.00	700.00	1200.	
	1848 w/o swan above mint mark					
	—	200.00	350.00	700.00	1200.	

NOTE: The above issue was struck in Mantua by the Austrian garrison under General Josef Radetzky during the siege of March 18-22, 1848 by Italian rebels.

COPPER
Mint mark: A

544.1 (C201.1)	1851	—	5.00	10.00	20.00	50.00

Mint mark: B

544.2 (C201.2)	1851	7.173	5.00	10.00	20.00	50.00

Mint mark: C

544.3 (C201.3)	1851	36 pcs.	300.00	400.00	700.00	1300.

Mint mark: G

544.4 (C201.4)	1851	—	10.00	20.00	50.00	150.00

NOTE: Varieties of size of mint mark exist.

4 KREUZER

COPPER

Mint mark: A

KM#	Date	Mintage	Fine	VF	XF	Unc
567.1	1860	—	2.00	6.00	12.00	30.00
(Y8.1)	1861	—	2.00	6.00	12.00	30.00

Mint mark: B

567.2	1860	—	2.00	6.00	12.00	30.00
(Y8.2)	1861	18.470	2.00	6.00	12.00	30.00
	1862	.383	2.50	8.00	15.00	35.00
	1864	6.666	2.50	8.00	15.00	35.00
	1865	.224	2.50	8.00	15.00	35.00

Mint mark: E

567.3	1860	—	10.00	25.00	50.00	150.00
(Y8.3)	1861	—	5.00	15.00	40.00	115.00

5 KREUZER

.438 SILVER

KM#	Date	Mintage	Fine	VF	XF	Unc
482	1815	—	7.50	15.00	25.00	55.00
(C181)						

Mint mark: A

489.1	1817	—	25.00	40.00	75.00	175.00
(C181a.1)	1818	—	10.00	20.00	30.00	75.00
	1819	—	—	—	Rare	—
	1820	—	10.00	20.00	30.00	75.00
	1821	—	10.00	20.00	30.00	75.00
	1823	—	30.00	50.00	75.00	125.00
	1824	—	—	—	Rare	—

Mint mark: B

489.2	1818	.538	10.00	20.00	30.00	75.00
(C181a.2)	1820	1.457	10.00	20.00	30.00	75.00
	1821	4.894	10.00	25.00	40.00	90.00

Mint mark: G

489.3	1820	—	—	—	Rare	—
(C181a.3)	1821	—	20.00	40.00	70.00	140.00
	1822	1 known		—	Rare	—
	1824	1 known		—	Rare	—

Mint mark: V

489.4	1820	—	15.00	35.00	60.00	125.00
(C181a.4)						

Mint mark: E

489.5	1821	—	25.00	50.00	75.00	175.00
(C181a.5)	1822	5,791	—	—	Rare	—

Mint mark: A
Obv: Bust w/short hair, 1 ribbon on neck.

496.1	1825	.015	75.00	100.00	200.00	400.00
(C181b.1)	1826	.053	60.00	90.00	175.00	350.00
	1827	.018	—	—	Rare	—
	1828	.044	60.00	90.00	175.00	350.00
	1830	—	—	—	—	—

Mint mark: E

496.2	1826					
(C181b.2)	Inc.KM496.1		—	—	Rare	—

Mint mark: A
Obv: Bust w/short hair, both ribbons on neck.

504	1831	—	—	—	—	—
(C181d)						

Obv: Larger head

512	1832	—	20.00	35.00	60.00	125.00
(C181c)	1833	.029	20.00	40.00	70.00	150.00
	1834	.031	20.00	35.00	60.00	125.00
	1835	—	15.00	25.00	50.00	100.00

KM#	Date	Mintage	Fine	VF	XF	Unc
516	1835	—	25.00	50.00	100.00	185.00
(C189)	1836	—	12.50	25.00	50.00	110.00

524.1	1837	—	5.00	10.00	20.00	45.00
(C189a.1)	1838	—	5.00	10.00	20.00	45.00
	1839	—	5.00	10.00	20.00	45.00
	1840	—	5.00	12.50	25.00	60.00
	1842	—	15.00	30.00	60.00	125.00
	1844	—	10.00	20.00	40.00	80.00
	1846	—	5.00	12.50	30.00	60.00
	1847	—	7.50	15.00	30.00	70.00
	1848	90.472	5.00	10.00	20.00	50.00

Mint mark: B

524.2	1838	.130	—	Reported, not confirmed		
(C189a.2)						

Mint mark: C

524.3	1839	—	7.50	15.00	30.00	60.00
(C189a.3)	1840	—	5.00	10.00	20.00	45.00

1.3333 g, .375 SILVER, .0161 oz ASW
Mint mark: A

KM#	Date	Mintage	Fine	VF	XF	Unc
561.1	1858	—	2.00	3.50	7.50	15.00
(Y9.1)	1859	—	1.00	2.00	4.00	10.00
	1860	—	—	—	—	—
	1863	1.013	5.00	8.00	16.00	40.00
	1864	1.922	1.50	3.00	6.00	12.50

Mint mark: B

561.2	1858	851 pcs.	250.00	350.00	600.00	1100.
(Y9.2)	1860	851 pcs.	250.00	350.00	600.00	1100.

Mint mark: V

561.3	1858	—	200.00	300.00	450.00	750.00
(Y9.3)	1859	—	10.00	15.00	25.00	40.00
	1860	—	50.00	75.00	100.00	175.00

Mint mark: M

561.4	1859	—	10.00	15.00	25.00	40.00
(Y9.4)						

Mint mark: A
Obv: Head w/heavier whiskers.

580	1867	.069	90.00	125.00	200.00	500.00
(Y9a)						

6 KREUZER

2.2300 g, .428 SILVER, .0306 oz ASW
Mint mark: A
Revolution 1848-1849

533.1	1848	90.400	3.00	5.00	10.00	20.00
(C202.1)						

Mint mark: B

533.2	1848	—	20.00	30.00	50.00	90.00
(C202.2)						

Mint mark: C

533.3	1848	—	4.00	7.50	15.00	40.00
(C202.3)						

1.9100 g, .438 SILVER, .0268 oz ASW
Mint mark: A

539.1	1849	—	1.00	2.00	3.00	10.00
(C202a.1)						

Mint mark: B

539.2	1849	—	15.00	25.00	40.00	90.00
(C202a.2)						

Mint mark: C

539.3	1849	—	4.00	7.50	15.00	40.00
(C202a.3)						

NOTE: The above 1849 dated issues were struck from 1849-1852 and 1859-1870.

7 KREUZER

4.6800 g, .250 SILVER, .0376 oz ASW
Mint mark: A

KM#	Date	Mintage	Fine	VF	XF	Unc
457.1	1802	—	5.00	10.00	20.00	50.00
(C154.1)						

Mint mark: B

457.2	1802	102.034	5.00	10.00	20.00	50.00
(C154.2)						

Mint mark: C

457.3	1802	—	5.00	10.00	25.00	75.00
(C154.3)						

Mint mark: E

457.4	1802	—	12.50	25.00	40.00	110.00
(C154.4)						

Mint mark: F

457.5	1802	—	25.00	50.00	80.00	185.00
(C154.5)						

Mint mark: G

457.6	1802	—	17.50	35.00	60.00	130.00
(C154.6)						

NOTE: The above 6 issues were overstruck on 1795 dated 12 Kreuzer pieces.

10 KREUZER

.500 SILVER
Mint mark: A
Rev. leg. ends: D. LO. SAL. WIRC.

KM#	Date	Mintage	Fine	VF	XF	Unc
470	1809	—	40.00	75.00	160.00	275.00
(C182)	1810	—	35.00	70.00	140.00	225.00

Rev. leg. ends: LO: WI: ET IN FR: D:

481.1	1814	—	—	—	Rare	—
(C182a.1)	1815	—	15.00	30.00	60.00	120.00

Mint mark: B

481.2	1815	1.800	15.00	30.00	60.00	120.00
(C182a.2)						

Mint mark: C

481.3	1815	—	20.00	40.00	75.00	160.00
(C182a.3)						

Mint mark: A
Rev. leg. ends: GAL. LOD. IL. REX. A. A.

490.1	1817	—	45.00	80.00	150.00	275.00
(C182b.1)	1818	—	—	—	Rare	—
	1819	.012	—	—	Rare	—
	1820	—	—	—	Rare	—
	1823	—	30.00	50.00	80.00	175.00
	1824	—	30.00	60.00	100.00	200.00

Mint mark: B

490.2	1818	—	—	—	Rare	—
(C182b.2)	1820	—	—	—	Rare	—
	1821	—	—	—	Rare	—

Mint mark: G

490.3	1818	—	—	—	Rare	—
(C182b.3)	1820	—	—	—	Rare	—
	1821	—	50.00	90.00	150.00	275.00
	1822	—	—	—	Rare	—
	1823	—	30.00	60.00	120.00	225.00
	1824	—	—	—	Rare	—

Mint mark: V

490.4	1818	—	25.00	50.00	100.00	175.00
(C182b.4)	1821	—	—	—	Rare	—

Mint mark: A
Obv: Older head of Franz I right, 1 ribbon on neck.
Rev: Eagle, value below.

497.1	1825	—	—	—	Rare	—
(C182c.1)	1826	—	35.00	70.00	140.00	225.00
	1827	—	35.00	70.00	140.00	225.00
	1828	—	35.00	70.00	140.00	200.00
	1829	.020	—	—	Rare	—
	1830	—	35.00	75.00	150.00	250.00

Mint mark: E

497.2	1828	—	45.00	90.00	175.00	300.00
(C182c.2)	1829					
		Inc.KM497.1	35.00	75.00	150.00	250.00
	1830	—	40.00	80.00	160.00	265.00

Mint mark: B

497.3	1830	.045	150.00	275.00	350.00	450.00
(C182c.3)						

Mint mark: A
Obv: Both ribbons on neck.

505	1831	—	—	Reported, not confirmed		
(C182e)						

Obv: Larger head

513	1832	—	20.00	30.00	60.00	135.00
(C182d)	1833	—	20.00	30.00	65.00	150.00
	1834	—	20.00	30.00	70.00	160.00
	1835	—	35.00	60.00	120.00	250.00

AUSTRIA 127

Obv: Head of Ferdinand I right.
Rev: Eagle, value below.

KM#	Date	Mintage	Fine	VF	XF	Unc
517.1 (C190.1)	1835	—	20.00	35.00	70.00	175.00
	1836/5	—	20.00	30.00	60.00	160.00
	1836	—	10.00	20.00	40.00	120.00

Mint mark: E

517.2 (C190.2)	1835	—	—	—	Rare	—
	1836	—	—	—	Rare	—

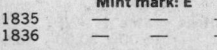

Mint mark: A

525.1 (C190a.1)	1837	—	7.00	15.00	30.00	60.00
	1838	—	17.50	35.00	65.00	150.00
	1839	—	7.50	15.00	30.00	60.00
	1840	—	5.00	12.50	25.00	60.00
	1842	—	5.00	12.50	25.00	60.00
	1843	—	5.00	10.00	20.00	50.00
	1844	—	5.00	10.00	20.00	50.00
	1845	—	5.00	10.00	20.00	50.00
	1846	—	5.00	10.00	20.00	50.00
	1847	—	7.00	15.00	30.00	60.00
	1848	—	20.00	40.00	70.00	160.00

Mint mark: C

525.2 (C190a.2)	1837	—	10.00	20.00	40.00	80.00
	1838	—	8.00	20.00	40.00	70.00
	1839	—	5.00	10.00	20.00	50.00

Mint mark: E

525.3 (C190a.3)	1837	—	17.50	35.00	65.00	150.00
	1840	—	15.00	30.00	50.00	120.00
	1841	—	17.50	35.00	65.00	150.00
	1842	—	15.00	30.00	65.00	150.00
	1843	—	17.50	35.00	65.00	150.00
	1844	—	17.50	35.00	65.00	150.00
	1845	—	10.00	25.00	50.00	100.00
	1846	—	15.00	30.00	50.00	120.00
	1847	—	12.00	25.00	50.00	100.00
	1848	—	20.00	40.00	70.00	160.00

2.1600 g, .900 SILVER, .0625 oz ASW
Mint mark: A

545.1 (C206.1)	1852	—	10.00	20.00	40.00	60.00
	1853	—	7.50	15.00	30.00	50.00
	1854	—	15.00	30.00	50.00	120.00
	1855	—	7.50	15.00	25.00	50.00

Mint mark: B

545.2 (C206.2)	1853	.031	25.00	50.00	100.00	160.00

2.0000 g, .500 SILVER, .0322 oz ASW
Mint mark: A

KM#	Date	Mintage	Fine	VF	XF	Unc
562.1 (Y10.1)	1858	—	6.00	12.00	25.00	37.50
	1859	—	—	—	—	—
	1863	—	7.00	15.00	30.00	45.00
	1864	1.050	10.00	20.00	30.00	65.00

Mint mark: V

562.2 (Y10.2)	1858	—	100.00	150.00	250.00	500.00
	1859	—	8.00	16.00	30.00	60.00
	1860	—	9.00	18.00	40.00	75.00
	1861	—	15.00	30.00	50.00	110.00
	1862	—	30.00	50.00	80.00	180.00
	1864	.036	150.00	250.00	400.00	650.00
	1865	1.198	10.00	20.00	30.00	80.00

Mint mark: M

562.3 (Y10.3)	1859	—	5.00	10.00	20.00	40.00

Mint mark: A
Obv: Head of Franz Joseph I right w/heavier whiskers.

581 (Y10a)	1867	.059	100.00	200.00	300.00	550.00

1.6667 g, .400 SILVER, .0214 oz ASW
Mint: Vienna - w/o mint mark.

KM#	Date	Mintage	Fine	VF	XF	Unc
587 (Y11)	1868	12.000	.75	1.00	3.00	8.00
	1869	30.000	.75	1.00	3.00	10.00
	1870	35.000	.75	1.00	2.50	8.00
	1871	2.000	10.00	20.00	40.00	90.00
	1872	70.000	.25	.50	1.00	6.00

15 KREUZER

COPPER
Mint mark: A

KM#	Date	Mintage	Fine	VF	XF	Unc
466.1 (C178.1)	1807	—	3.00	5.00	10.00	50.00

Mint mark: B

466.2 (C178.2)	1807	22.007	3.00	5.00	10.00	50.00
	1087 (error for 1807)	—	45.00	90.00	150.00	300.00

Mint mark: E

466.3 (C178.3)	1807	—	10.00	20.00	40.00	110.00

Mint mark: G

466.4 (C178.4)	1807	—	10.00	17.50	30.00	100.00

Mint mark: S

466.5 (C178.5)	1807	—	3.00	5.00	10.00	55.00

20 KREUZER

6.6800 g, .583 SILVER, .1252 oz ASW
Mint mark: A

434.1 (C157.1)	1802	—	9.00	20.00	40.00	90.00
	1803	—	7.00	15.00	27.50	55.00
	1804	—	9.00	20.00	40.00	80.00

Mint mark: B

434.2 (C157.2)	1802	1.359	7.00	15.00	27.50	60.00
	1803	8.469	7.00	15.00	27.50	60.00
	1804	5.693	7.00	15.00	27.50	60.00

Mint mark: E

434.3 (C157.3)	1802	—	15.00	35.00	60.00	120.00
	1803	—	7.00	15.00	30.00	75.00
	1804	—	7.00	15.00	27.50	65.00

Mint mark: H

434.4 (C157.4)	1802	—	9.00	20.00	40.00	85.00
	1803	—	12.00	25.00	50.00	100.00

Mint mark: F

434.5 (C157.5)	1803	—	7.00	15.00	30.00	70.00
	1804	.651	7.00	15.00	30.00	70.00

Mint mark: G

434.6 (C157.6)	1802	—	12.00	25.00	50.00	90.00
	1803	—	9.00	20.00	40.00	80.00
	1804	—	7.00	15.00	30.00	60.00

Mint mark: C

434.7 (C157.7)	1802	—	7.00	15.00	27.50	60.00
	1803	5.925	7.00	15.00	30.00	70.00
	1804	.566	7.00	15.00	30.00	70.00

Mint mark: A
Rev. leg. ends: D. LOTH. VEN. SAL.

KM#	Date	Mintage	Fine	VF	XF	Unc
458.1 (C166.1)	1804	—	25.00	45.00	80.00	175.00
	1805	—	6.00	12.00	25.00	60.00
	1806	—	5.00	10.00	20.00	55.00

Mint mark: F

458.2 (C166.2)	1804	Inc.KM434.5	—	—	—	—

Mint mark: H

458.3 (C166.3)	1804	—	—	—	Rare	—

Mint mark: B

458.4 (C166.4)	1805	8.402	5.00	10.00	20.00	60.00
	1806	19.090	5.00	10.00	20.00	60.00

Mint mark: C

458.5 (C166.5)	1805	1.993	7.00	15.00	30.00	80.00
	1806	2.977	6.00	12.00	25.00	60.00

Mint mark: E

458.6 (C166.6)	1805	—	7.00	15.00	25.00	60.00
	1806	—	—	—	Rare	—

Mint mark: G

458.7 (C166.7)	1805	—	10.00	20.00	40.00	90.00
	1806	—	10.00	20.00	40.00	90.00

Mint mark: D

458.8 (C166.8)	1806	—	10.00	20.00	40.00	85.00

Mint mark: A
Rev. leg. ends: D. LO. SAL. WIRC.

463.1 (C183.1)	1806	—	7.00	15.00	30.00	75.00
	1807	—	7.00	15.00	30.00	75.00
	1808	—	5.00	10.00	20.00	55.00
	1809	—	5.00	10.00	20.00	55.00
	1810	—	5.00	10.00	20.00	50.00

Mint mark: B

463.2 (C183.2)	1806	Inc.C166.4	15.00	30.00	60.00	120.00
	1807	6.723	12.00	25.00	45.00	95.00
	1808	3.235	7.00	15.00	30.00	75.00
	1809	7.239	7.00	15.00	27.50	65.00

Mint mark: C

463.3 (C183.3)	1806	—	25.00	55.00	100.00	175.00
	1807	2.421	12.00	25.00	45.00	95.00
	1808	1.188	5.00	10.00	20.00	55.00
	1809	2.381	7.00	15.00	27.50	60.00
	1810	.714	—	—	—	—
	1812	.092	—	—	—	—
	1813	.055	—	—	—	—
	1814	—	12.00	25.00	50.00	100.00

Mint mark: D

463.4 (C183.4)	1807	—	12.00	25.00	45.00	100.00
	1808	—	10.00	20.00	40.00	80.00
	1809	—	12.00	25.00	50.00	100.00

Mint mark: E

463.5 (C183.5)	1808	—	7.00	15.00	35.00	80.00
	1809	—	7.00	15.00	35.00	80.00
	1810	—	50.00	100.00	150.00	200.00

Mint mark: G

463.6 (C183.6)	1808	—	7.00	15.00	30.00	70.00
	1809	—	5.00	10.00	20.00	50.00
	1810	—	12.00	25.00	50.00	100.00

Mint mark: A
Rev. leg. ends: LO WI: ET IN FR D.

471.1	1811	—	5.00	10.00	20.00	45.00

KM#	Date	Mintage	Fine	VF	XF	Unc
(C183a.1)	1812	—	5.00	10.00	20.00	45.00
	1813	—	5.00	10.00	20.00	50.00
	1814	—	5.00	10.00	20.00	45.00
	1815	—	5.00	10.00	20.00	45.00

Mint mark: B

KM#	Date	Mintage	Fine	VF	XF	Unc
471.2	1811	.580	9.00	20.00	40.00	80.00
(C183a.2)	1812	.774	20.00	40.00	80.00	120.00
	1813	1.103	6.00	12.00	25.00	50.00
	1814	1.021	7.00	15.00	35.00	70.00
	1815	1.043	4.00	8.00	15.00	45.00
	1816	5.773	10.00	20.00	40.00	80.00

Mint mark: E

KM#	Date	Mintage	Fine	VF	XF	Unc
471.3	1811	—	12.00	25.00	50.00	100.00
(C183a.3)	1812	—	10.00	20.00	40.00	80.00
	1813	—	6.00	12.00	25.00	55.00
	1814	—	10.00	20.00	40.00	80.00
	1815	—	7.00	15.00	30.00	65.00

Mint mark: G

KM#	Date	Mintage	Fine	VF	XF	Unc
471.4	1812	—	10.00	20.00	40.00	80.00
(C183a.4)	1813	—	100.00	150.00	200.00	300.00
	1814	—	7.00	15.00	35.00	70.00
	1815	—	6.00	12.00	25.00	50.00

Mint mark: C

KM#	Date	Mintage	Fine	VF	XF	Unc
471.5	1814	—	7.00	15.00	30.00	60.00
(C183a.5)	1815	.128	6.00	12.00	25.00	50.00
	1816	.785	Reported, not confirmed			

Mint: Vienna - w/o mint mark.

KM#	Date	Mintage	Fine	VF	XF	Unc
471.6	1815	—	15.00	30.00	60.00	120.00
(C183a.6)						

.583 SILVER

Mint mark: A

Rev. leg. ends: GAL. LOD. IL. REX. A. A.

KM#	Date	Mintage	Fine	VF	XF	Unc
491.1	1817	—	5.00	10.00	20.00	45.00
(C183b.1)	1818	—	5.00	10.00	20.00	45.00
	1819	—	5.00	10.00	20.00	45.00
	1820	—	5.00	10.00	20.00	45.00
	1821	—	6.00	12.00	25.00	55.00
	1822	—	6.00	12.00	25.00	55.00
	1823	—	5.00	10.00	20.00	45.00
	1824	—	5.00	10.00	20.00	45.00

Mint mark: B

KM#	Date	Mintage	Fine	VF	XF	Unc
491.2	1818	2.703	5.00	10.00	20.00	55.00
(C183b.2)	1820	1.118	12.00	25.00	50.00	100.00
	1821	1.075	10.00	20.00	40.00	80.00
	1822	.269	10.00	20.00	40.00	80.00
	1823	.324	25.00	45.00	75.00	140.00
	1824	.014	40.00	60.00	90.00	175.00

Mint mark: C

KM#	Date	Mintage	Fine	VF	XF	Unc
491.3	1818	.033	10.00	20.00	40.00	80.00
(C183b.3)	1819	.081	25.00	45.00	75.00	140.00
	1820	.028	10.00	20.00	40.00	80.00
	1821	.116	20.00	40.00	70.00	130.00
	1822	.165	20.00	40.00	70.00	130.00
	1823	.096	30.00	50.00	90.00	150.00

Mint mark: E

KM#	Date	Mintage	Fine	VF	XF	Unc
491.4	1818	—	7.00	15.00	30.00	60.00
(C183b.4)	1819	—	8.00	15.00	30.00	60.00
	1820	—	7.00	15.00	30.00	65.00
	1821	—	7.00	15.00	30.00	70.00
	1822	—	7.00	15.00	30.00	75.00
	1823	—	6.00	12.00	25.00	55.00
	1824	—	6.00	12.00	25.00	60.00

Mint mark: G

KM#	Date	Mintage	Fine	VF	XF	Unc
491.5	1818	—	10.00	20.00	40.00	80.00
(C183b.5)	1820	—	25.00	45.00	75.00	140.00
	1821	—	25.00	45.00	75.00	140.00
	1822	—	12.00	25.00	45.00	85.00
	1823	—	12.00	25.00	50.00	100.00
	1824	—	6.00	12.00	25.00	55.00

Mint mark: V

KM#	Date	Mintage	Fine	VF	XF	Unc
491.6	1818	—	6.00	12.00	25.00	55.00
(C183b.7)	1818 (error FNANCISCUS)					
		—	60.00	100.00	150.00	375.00

Mint mark: M

KM#	Date	Mintage	Fine	VF	XF	Unc
491.7	1819	—	7.00	15.00	25.00	50.00
(C183b.6)						

Mint mark: A

Obv: Small bust w/short hair.

KM#	Date	Mintage	Fine	VF	XF	Unc
498.1	1825	—	3.50	7.00	15.00	35.00
(C183c.1)	1826	—	3.50	7.00	15.00	35.00
	1827	—	3.50	7.00	15.00	35.00
	1828	—	3.50	7.00	15.00	35.00

Mint mark: B

KM#	Date	Mintage	Fine	VF	XF	Unc
498.2	1825	.373	20.00	40.00	70.00	120.00
(C183c.2)	1826	—	6.00	12.00	25.00	50.00
	1827	1.053	7.00	15.00	30.00	60.00
	1828	2.402	6.00	12.00	25.00	50.00

Mint mark: E

KM#	Date	Mintage	Fine	VF	XF	Unc
498.3	1825	—	6.00	12.00	25.00	50.00
(C183c.3)	1826	—	6.00	12.00	25.00	50.00
	1827	—	6.00	12.00	25.00	50.00
	1828	—	6.00	12.00	25.00	50.00

Mint mark: G

KM#	Date	Mintage	Fine	VF	XF	Unc
498.4	1826	—	—	—	Rare	—
(C183c.4)	1827	—	7.00	15.00	30.00	60.00

Mint mark: C

KM#	Date	Mintage	Fine	VF	XF	Unc
498.5	1827	.924	5.00	10.00	20.00	40.00
(C183c.5)						

Mint mark: A

Obv: Large bust w/short hair.

KM#	Date	Mintage	Fine	VF	XF	Unc
501.1	1829	—	3.00	6.00	12.00	30.00
(C183e.1)	1830	—	3.00	6.00	12.00	30.00

Mint mark: B

KM#	Date	Mintage	Fine	VF	XF	Unc
501.2	1829	2.319	4.00	8.00	16.00	40.00
(C183e.2)	1830 small mm					
		2.348	3.00	6.00	12.00	25.00
	1830 large mm					
		Inc. Ab.	3.00	6.00	12.00	25.00

Mint mark: E

KM#	Date	Mintage	Fine	VF	XF	Unc
501.3	1829	—	5.00	10.00	20.00	40.00
(C183e.3)	1830	—	3.50	7.00	15.00	35.00

Mint mark: C

KM#	Date	Mintage	Fine	VF	XF	Unc
501.4	1830	1.754	3.00	6.00	12.00	25.00
(C183e.4)						

Mint mark: A

Obv: Ribbons on wreath forward across neck.

KM#	Date	Mintage	Fine	VF	XF	Unc
506	1831	—	20.00	40.00	80.00	200.00
(C183d)						

Obv: Ribbons on wreath behind neck.

KM#	Date	Mintage	Fine	VF	XF	Unc
507.1	1831	—	3.00	6.00	12.00	30.00
(C183f.1)	1832	—	3.00	6.00	12.00	25.00
	1833	—	6.00	12.00	25.00	50.00
	1834	—	3.50	7.00	15.00	40.00
	1835	—	5.00	10.00	20.00	45.00

Mint mark: C

KM#	Date	Mintage	Fine	VF	XF	Unc
507.2	1831	—	10.00	20.00	40.00	80.00
(C183f.2)	1832	5.122	5.00	10.00	20.00	45.00
	1833	1.818	6.00	12.00	25.00	50.00
	1834	1.517	6.00	12.00	25.00	50.00
	1835	1.489	6.00	12.00	25.00	50.00

Mint mark: M

KM#	Date	Mintage	Fine	VF	XF	Unc
507.3	1831	—	6.00	12.00	25.00	50.00
(C183f.3)	1832	—	7.00	15.00	30.00	60.00

Mint mark: V

KM#	Date	Mintage	Fine	VF	XF	Unc
507.4	1831	—	7.00	15.00	30.00	55.00
(C183f.4)						

Mint mark: B

KM#	Date	Mintage	Fine	VF	XF	Unc
507.5	1832	—	100.00	150.00	250.00	400.00
(C183f.5)	1833	—	7.00	15.00	30.00	60.00
	1834	—	6.00	12.00	25.00	50.00
	1835	—	5.00	10.00	20.00	45.00

Mint mark: E

KM#	Date	Mintage	Fine	VF	XF	Unc
507.6	1833	—	12.00	25.00	45.00	90.00
(C183f.6)	1834	—	6.00	12.00	25.00	50.00
	1835	—	5.00	10.00	20.00	45.00

Mint mark: A

KM#	Date	Mintage	Fine	VF	XF	Unc
518.1	1835	—	15.00	30.00	60.00	120.00
(C191.1)	1836	—	10.00	20.00	45.00	90.00

Mint mark: C

KM#	Date	Mintage	Fine	VF	XF	Unc
518.2	1835	.295	15.00	30.00	60.00	130.00
(C191.2)						

Mint mark: E

KM#	Date	Mintage	Fine	VF	XF	Unc
518.3	1835	—	35.00	75.00	125.00	250.00
(C191.3)	1836	—	25.00	50.00	100.00	225.00

Mint mark: A

KM#	Date	Mintage	Fine	VF	XF	Unc
526.1	1837	—	5.00	10.00	20.00	45.00
(C191a.1)	1838	—	5.00	10.00	20.00	45.00
	1839	—	5.00	10.00	20.00	45.00
	1840	—	2.50	4.00	8.00	30.00
	1841	—	2.50	4.00	8.00	30.00
	1842	—	2.50	5.00	10.00	35.00
	1843	—	20.00	40.00	70.00	130.00
	1844	—	2.50	4.00	8.00	30.00
	1845	—	2.50	5.00	10.00	35.00
	1846	—	2.50	5.00	10.00	35.00
	1847	—	2.50	4.00	8.00	30.00
	1848	13.632	2.50	4.00	8.00	30.00

Mint mark: B

KM#	Date	Mintage	Fine	VF	XF	Unc
526.2	1837	—	7.50	15.00	30.00	60.00
(C191a.2)	1838	—	5.00	10.00	20.00	45.00
	1839	—	8.00	18.00	35.00	70.00

Mint mark: C

KM#	Date	Mintage	Fine	VF	XF	Unc
526.3	1837	.484	10.00	20.00	40.00	80.00
(C191a.3)	1838	.625	10.00	20.00	40.00	80.00
	1839	.220	15.00	30.00	60.00	120.00
	1840	1.122	3.00	7.00	15.00	35.00
	1841	2.543	5.00	10.00	20.00	45.00
	1842	.644	5.00	10.00	20.00	45.00
	1843	1.257	5.00	10.00	20.00	45.00
	1844	1.492	5.00	10.00	20.00	45.00
	1845	1.461	3.00	6.00	14.00	35.00
	1846	1.549	3.00	6.00	14.00	35.00
	1847	1.528	3.00	6.00	15.00	35.00
	1848	2.241	3.00	6.00	10.00	30.00

Mint mark: E

KM#	Date	Mintage	Fine	VF	XF	Unc
526.4	1837	—	10.00	22.00	45.00	100.00
(C191a.4)	1838/7	—	8.00	16.50	35.00	80.00
	1838	—	6.00	12.00	25.00	60.00
	1839	—	4.00	9.00	20.00	60.00
	1840	—	10.00	20.00	40.00	80.00
	1841	—	4.00	9.00	20.00	60.00
	1842	—	12.00	25.00	50.00	100.00
	1843	—	5.00	15.00	30.00	80.00
	1844	—	4.00	9.00	20.00	80.00
	1845	—	9.00	18.00	35.00	90.00
	1846/5	—	15.00	35.00	60.00	135.00
	1846	—	13.50	27.50	50.00	120.00
	1847	—	7.00	15.00	30.00	70.00
	1848	—	12.00	25.00	45.00	100.00

Mint mark: M

KM#	Date	Mintage	Fine	VF	XF	Unc
526.5	1837	—	30.00	60.00	100.00	225.00
(C191a.5)	1838	—	30.00	60.00	100.00	225.00
	1840	—	25.00	50.00	90.00	160.00
	1842	—	10.00	20.00	40.00	80.00
	1843	—	5.00	10.00	20.00	45.00
	1844	—	7.00	15.00	30.00	60.00
	1845	—	7.00	15.00	30.00	60.00
	1846	—	7.00	15.00	35.00	70.00
	1847	—	14.00	30.00	60.00	100.00

Mint mark: G-M

Obv: Head of Ferdinand I right.

KM#	Date	Mintage	Fine	VF	XF	Unc
534	1848	7,799	125.00	250.00	350.00	800.00
(C191b)						

NOTE: The above issue was struck in Mantua by the Austrian garrison under General Josef Radetzky during the siege of March 18-22, 1848 by Italian rebels.

AUSTRIA 129

Mint mark: A

KM#	Date	Mintage	Fine	VF	XF	Unc
546.1 (C203.1)	1852	—	25.00	50.00	100.00	150.00

Mint mark: C

546.2 (C203.2)	1852	.114	60.00	100.00	200.00	400.00

4.3200 g, .900 SILVER, .1250 oz ASW
Mint mark: A

547.1 (C207.1)	1852	—	4.00	8.00	18.00	30.00
	1853	—	4.00	8.00	18.00	35.00
	1854	—	4.00	8.00	18.00	30.00
	1855	—	4.00	8.00	18.00	35.00
	1856	—	20.00	35.00	50.00	100.00

Mint mark: B

547.2 (C207.2)	1852	4.926	5.00	8.00	15.00	32.00
	1854	2.287	5.00	8.00	15.00	36.00
	1855	2.198	5.00	8.00	15.00	30.00
	1856	3.654	5.00	8.00	15.00	30.00
	1869	3.224	5.00	8.00	15.00	30.00
	1870	9.487	5.00	8.00	15.00	30.00
	1871	4.092	5.00	8.00	15.00	30.00
	1872	.335	5.00	8.00	15.00	30.00
	1873	1.286	5.00	8.00	15.00	30.00

Mint mark: C

547.3 (C207.3)	1852	1.687	50.00	100.00	150.00	325.00
	1853	1.590	5.50	11.00	22.00	45.00
	1854	2.098	6.50	13.00	24.00	45.00
	1855	1.904	10.00	20.00	30.00	47.50
	1856	.048	35.00	75.00	100.00	135.00

Mint mark: E

547.4 (C207.4)	1852	—	40.00	80.00	150.00	275.00
	1853	—	12.50	25.00	50.00	75.00
	1854	—	10.00	20.00	40.00	60.00
	1855	—	7.00	15.00	22.50	35.00
	1856	—	10.00	20.00	37.50	65.00

2.6667 g, .500 SILVER, .0429 oz ASW
Mint: Vienna - w/o mint mark.

588 (Y12)	1868	30.000	1.00	2.00	4.00	15.00
	1869	30.000	1.00	2.00	4.00	13.00
	1870	30.000	1.00	2.00	4.00	10.00
	1872	.576	15.00	30.00	50.00	85.00

1/4 FLORIN

5.3450 g, .520 SILVER, .0893 oz ASW
Mint mark: A

KM#	Date	Mintage	Fine	VF	XF	Unc
555.1 (Y13.1)	1857	—	7.50	15.00	25.00	40.00
	1858	31.197	4.50	9.00	15.00	25.00

Mint mark: B

555.2 (Y13.2)	1857	—	12.00	22.50	37.50	60.00
	1858	2.982	6.50	13.00	25.00	50.00

Mint mark: E

555.3 (Y13.3)	1857	—	35.00	70.00	100.00	140.00
	1858	Inc.Y13.1	6.50	13.00	20.00	35.00

Mint mark: M

555.4 (Y13.4)	1857	—	50.00	75.00	125.00	250.00
	1858	Inc.Y13.1	45.00	80.00	115.00	160.00
	1859	27.415	45.00	75.00	115.00	200.00

Mint mark: V

555.5 (Y13.5)	1857	—	22.00	40.00	60.00	140.00
	1858	Inc.Y13.1	15.00	30.00	50.00	130.00

Mint mark: A

KM#	Date	Mintage	Fine	VF	XF	Unc
565.1 (Y14.1)	1859	27.415	3.00	8.00	15.00	25.00
	1860	—	11.50	23.00	40.00	55.00
	1861	—	3.00	6.00	15.00	45.00
	1862	—	3.00	6.00	15.00	45.00
	1863	—	15.00	35.00	60.00	120.00
	1864	4.843	3.00	7.00	15.00	30.00
	1865	.080	27.50	50.00	80.00	135.00

Mint mark: B

565.2 (Y14.2)	1859	13.109	3.00	6.00	10.00	25.00
	1860	21.247	2.00	4.00	6.50	20.00
	1861	1.656	30.00	50.00	80.00	120.00
	1862	2.796	7.50	15.00	25.00	75.00

Mint mark: E

565.3 (Y14.3)	1859	—	4.00	8.00	15.00	25.00
	1860	—	35.00	60.00	90.00	180.00
	1861	—	90.00	180.00	250.00	425.00
	1862	—	8.00	16.00	30.00	75.00

Mint mark: M

565.4 (Y14.4)	1859	—	30.00	60.00	125.00	300.00

Mint mark: V

565.5 (Y14.5)	1859	—	9.00	20.00	40.00	80.00
	1860	—	10.00	20.00	40.00	80.00
	1861	—	15.00	40.00	70.00	150.00
	1862	—	10.00	20.00	40.00	90.00
	1863	.800	17.50	35.00	60.00	140.00
	1864	.165	17.50	30.00	50.00	120.00

Mint mark: A
Obv: Head of Franz Joseph I right w/heavier side whiskers. Rev: Eagle, value below.

571.1 (Y14a.1)	1866	—	150.00	250.00	400.00	850.00

Mint mark: V

571.2 (Y14a.2)	1866	—	120.00	225.00	400.00	950.00

Mint mark: A
Rev. leg: HUNGAR, BOHEM. GAL. - LOD. ILL. REX. A.A.

582 (Y14b)	1867	—	75.00	150.00	250.00	500.00
	1868	—	65.00	110.00	200.00	315.00
	1869	—	55.00	90.00	150.00	250.00
	1870	7.956	120.00	200.00	400.00	700.00
	1871	—	100.00	175.00	300.00	600.00

Mint: Vienna - w/o mint mark.

592 (Y14c)	1872	.100	50.00	100.00	200.00	375.00
	1873	.050	40.00	75.00	150.00	300.00
	1874	.100	80.00	150.00	250.00	425.00
	1875	.020	100.00	250.00	350.00	550.00

30 KREUZER

COPPER

KM#	Date	Mintage	Fine	VF	XF	Unc
467.1 (C179.1)	1807	—	4.00	8.00	15.00	40.00

Mint mark: B

467.2 (C179.2)	1807	15.787	4.00	8.00	15.00	40.00
	1807 (error inverted C in ERBLAENDISCH)		40.00	70.00	100.00	200.00

Mint mark: E

467.3 (C179.3)	1807	—	15.00	30.00	50.00	100.00

Mint mark: G

467.4 (C179.4)	1807	—	10.00	20.00	40.00	80.00

Mint mark: S

467.5 (C179.5)	1807	—	4.00	8.00	15.00	40.00

NOTE: The above 5 issues struck until 1811.

GULDEN

12.9900 g, .900 SILVER, .3758 oz ASW
Mint mark: A

KM#	Date	Mintage	Fine	VF	XF	Unc
553 (C210)	1854	—	20.00	30.00	50.00	140.00

FLORIN

12.3400 g, .900 SILVER, .3571 oz ASW
Mint mark: A

556.1 (Y15.1)	1857	—	20.00	35.00	70.00	150.00
	1858	—	7.50	15.00	22.50	35.00
	1859	—	5.00	7.00	14.00	30.00
	1860	—	3.00	5.00	10.00	25.00
	1861	—	3.00	5.00	10.00	25.00
	1862	—	6.00	10.00	15.00	27.50
	1863	—	7.00	12.00	17.50	35.00
	1864	—	15.00	30.00	50.00	120.00
	1865	—	15.00	30.00	50.00	120.00

Mint mark: B

556.2 (Y15.2)	1857	—	100.00	210.00	350.00	600.00
	1858	1.920	9.00	18.00	27.50	45.00
	1859	7.537	6.00	11.00	25.00	40.00
	1860	1.883	12.50	25.00	40.00	70.00
	1861	.815	75.00	150.00	300.00	500.00
	1862	.314	11.00	25.00	50.00	90.00
	1863	.287	17.50	35.00	60.00	100.00
	1864	.340	40.00	75.00	140.00	350.00
	1865	.291	20.00	35.00	65.00	110.00

Mint mark: E

556.3 (Y15.3)	1857	—	100.00	225.00	375.00	675.00
	1858	—	15.00	25.00	40.00	75.00
	1859	—	10.00	20.00	35.00	60.00
	1860	—	10.00	20.00	35.00	50.00
	1861	—	15.00	30.00	60.00	120.00
	1862	—	60.00	150.00	225.00	450.00
	1863	—	17.50	32.50	65.00	95.00
	1864	.150	40.00	100.00	175.00	275.00
	1865	—	15.00	32.50	70.00	100.00

Mint mark: V

556.4 (Y15.4)	1857	—	135.00	240.00	400.00	775.00
	1858	—	14.00	30.00	60.00	120.00
	1859	—	12.50	25.00	45.00	90.00
	1860	—	17.50	30.00	60.00	120.00
	1861	—	20.00	35.00	75.00	150.00
	1862	—	25.00	60.00	95.00	190.00
	1863	—	17.50	37.50	65.00	130.00
	1864	.130	55.00	110.00	200.00	400.00
	1865	.031	120.00	240.00	400.00	675.00

Mint mark: M

556.5 (Y15.5)	1858	—	20.00	45.00	90.00	200.00
	1859	—	12.00	18.00	45.00	125.00

NOTE: Varieties exist.

Mint mark: A
Obv: Head of Franz Joseph I right w/heavier side whiskers. Rev: Eagle, value below.

572.1 (Y15a.1)	1866	—	25.00	50.00	85.00	150.00

Mint mark: B

572.2 (Y15a.2)	1866	.359	27.50	60.00	90.00	150.00

Mint mark: E

572.3 (Y15a.3)	1866	—	70.00	150.00	250.00	450.00

Mint mark: V

572.4 (Y15a.4)	1866	—	80.00	150.00	250.00	450.00

Mint mark: A
Rev. leg: HUNGAR, BOHEN. GAL. - LOD. ILL. REX. A.A.

AUSTRIA 130

KM#	Date	Mintage	Fine	VF	XF	Unc
583.1 (Y15b.1)	1867	—	25.00	40.00	80.00	150.00
	1868	—	30.00	50.00	90.00	160.00
	1869	—	22.50	35.00	70.00	150.00
	1870	—	15.00	30.00	50.00	90.00
	1871	—	12.50	25.00	40.00	70.00
	1872	—	150.00	250.00	400.00	800.00

Mint mark: B

| 583.2 (Y15b.2) | 1867 | .714 | 15.00 | 30.00 | 50.00 | 85.00 |

Mint mark: E

| 583.3 (Y15b.3) | 1867 | — | 150.00 | 250.00 | 400.00 | 650.00 |

Mint: Vienna - w/o mint mark.

593 (Y15c)	1872	4.725	12.50	25.00	40.00	100.00
	1873	7.880	10.00	20.00	35.00	85.00
	1874	2.479	22.50	40.00	70.00	100.00
	1875	5.053	6.00	10.00	15.00	30.00
	1876	7.283	6.00	9.00	14.00	27.50
	1877	13.963	5.00	8.00	13.00	25.00
	1878	18.963	5.00	8.00	13.00	25.00
	1878 plain edge					
	1879	37.485	5.00	8.00	13.00	25.00
	1880	6.505	7.50	12.00	20.00	35.00
	1881	6.128	7.50	12.00	20.00	35.00
	1882	5.476	9.00	15.00	25.00	45.00
	1883	6.036	7.00	10.00	14.00	25.00
	1884	4.303	7.00	10.00	14.00	25.00
	1885	3.395	7.00	12.00	16.00	25.00
	1886	6.710	6.00	10.00	14.00	25.00
	1887	5.692	6.00	10.00	14.00	25.00
	1888	6.572	6.00	10.00	14.00	25.00
	1889	5.053	6.00	10.00	14.00	25.00
	1890	4.164	6.00	10.00	14.00	25.00
	1891	4.235	6.00	10.00	14.00	25.00
	1892	2.504	11.00	15.00	25.00	50.00

Pribram Mine

| 599 (Y17) | 1875 | 8,000 | 150.00 | 200.00 | 250.00 | 500.00 |

1/2 THALER

14.0300 g, .833 SILVER, .3757 oz ASW
Obv. leg: FRANCISCVS II. D. G. R. IMP., etc.

435 (C159)	1801	—	60.00	100.00	150.00	225.00
	1802	—	60.00	100.00	150.00	225.00
	1803	—	100.00	175.00	275.00	350.00
	1804	—	60.00	100.00	150.00	225.00

Obv. leg: FRANCISCVS II. D. G. ROM ET, etc.

KM#	Date	Mintage	Fine	VF	XF	Unc
459.1 (C167.1)	1804	—	150.00	250.00	400.00	750.00
	1805	—	—	—	Rare	—
	1806	—	120.00	225.00	375.00	700.00

Mint mark: V

| 459.2 (C167.2) | 1805 | — | — | — | — | — |

Mint mark: A
Obv. leg: FRANCISCVS I. D. G. AVSTRIAE, etc.
Rev. leg. ends: D. LO. SAL. WIRC.

468.1 (C184.1)	1807	—	—	—	Rare	—
	1808	—	125.00	200.00	400.00	675.00
	1809	—	125.00	200.00	400.00	675.00
	1810	—	150.00	225.00	450.00	750.00

Mint mark: C

| 468.2 (C184.2) | 1809 | — | 150.00 | 225.00 | 450.00 | 750.00 |

Mint mark: A
Rev. leg. ends: LO: WI: ET IN. FR: DVX

472.1 (C184a.1)	1811	2,186	60.00	100.00	150.00	250.00
	1812	1,930	65.00	110.00	175.00	275.00
	1813	1,718	65.00	110.00	175.00	275.00
	1814	1,533	50.00	80.00	125.00	225.00
	1815	7,849	30.00	50.00	90.00	150.00

Mint mark: B

| 472.2 (C184a.2) | 1815 | .057 | 40.00 | 70.00 | 130.00 | 200.00 |

Mint mark: A
Rev. leg. ends: GAL. LOD. IL. REX. A. A.

492.1 (C184b.1)	1817	.012	40.00	70.00	115.00	175.00
	1818	3,695	50.00	80.00	125.00	185.00
	1819	—	40.00	65.00	110.00	165.00
	1820	—	40.00	70.00	115.00	175.00
	1821	—	40.00	70.00	115.00	175.00
	1822	—	35.00	60.00	100.00	150.00
	1823	—	35.00	60.00	100.00	150.00
	1824	—	35.00	60.00	100.00	150.00

Mint mark: B

492.2 (C184b.2)	1818	—	50.00	80.00	125.00	185.00
	1819	.015	—	—	Rare	—
	1820	.023	—	—	Rare	—
	1821	9,650	40.00	70.00	115.00	175.00
	1822	.013	—	—	Rare	—
	1823	.015	50.00	80.00	125.00	185.00
	1824	.013	40.00	70.00	115.00	175.00

Mint mark: V

| 492.3 (C184b.3) | 1818 | — | 35.00 | 60.00 | 100.00 | 150.00 |
| | 1821 | — | — | — | Rare | — |

Mint mark: C

| 492.4 (C184b.4) | 1819 | — | 45.00 | 75.00 | 125.00 | 185.00 |
| | 1820 | — | 40.00 | 70.00 | 115.00 | 175.00 |

KM#	Date	Mintage	Fine	VF	XF	Unc
492.4	1821	—	35.00	60.00	100.00	150.00
	1822	—	40.00	70.00	115.00	175.00
	1823	—	50.00	80.00	125.00	185.00
	1824	—	30.00	55.00	100.00	135.00

Mint mark: E

492.5 (C184b.5)	1819	—	—	—	Rare	—
	1820	—	50.00	80.00	125.00	185.00
	1821	—	50.00	80.00	125.00	185.00
	1822	—	50.00	80.00	125.00	185.00
	1823	—	50.00	80.00	125.00	185.00

Mint mark: G

492.6 (C184b.6)	1819	—	50.00	80.00	135.00	200.00
	1820	—	—	—	Rare	—
	1821	—	50.00	80.00	125.00	185.00
	1822	—	50.00	80.00	125.00	185.00
	1823	—	35.00	65.00	110.00	165.00
	1824	—	65.00	115.00	150.00	225.00

Mint mark: A
Obv: Bust w/short hair.

499.1 (C184c.1)	1825	—	50.00	80.00	125.00	185.00
	1826	—	30.00	50.00	80.00	125.00
	1827	—	25.00	40.00	60.00	120.00
	1828	—	30.00	55.00	85.00	130.00
	1829	—	30.00	50.00	80.00	125.00
	1830	—	25.00	45.00	75.00	112.00

Mint mark: B

499.2 (C184c.2)	1825	.015	50.00	80.00	125.00	185.00
	1826	.013	40.00	70.00	115.00	175.00
	1827	5,230	—	—	Rare	—

Mint mark: C

499.3 (C184c.3)	1825	—	50.00	80.00	125.00	185.00
	1826	—	35.00	60.00	100.00	150.00
	1827	—	60.00	100.00	175.00	250.00

Mint mark: G

| 499.4 (C184c.4) | 1826 | — | 80.00 | 150.00 | 250.00 | 450.00 |

Mint mark: E

| 499.5 (C184c.5) | 1830 | — | — | — | Rare | — |

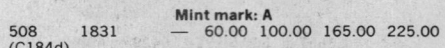

Mint mark: A

| 508 (C184d) | 1831 | — | 60.00 | 100.00 | 165.00 | 225.00 |

514.1 (C184e.1)	1832	—	40.00	75.00	125.00	200.00
	1832 plain edge					
	1833	—	40.00	75.00	125.00	200.00
	1833 plain edge					
	1834	—	40.00	75.00	125.00	200.00
	1835	—	35.00	60.00	100.00	175.00

Mint mark: E

AUSTRIA 131

KM#	Date	Mintage	Fine	VF	XF	Unc
514.2 (C184e.2)	1833	—	—	—	Rare	—

Mint mark: A
Obv: Head of Ferdinand I right. Rev: Eagle.

KM#	Date	Mintage	Fine	VF	XF	Unc
519.1 (C192.1)	1835	—	250.00	400.00	600.00	1200.
	1836	—	250.00	400.00	600.00	1200.

Mint mark: C

| 519.2 (C192.2) | 1835 | — | — | — | Rare | — |
| | 1836 | — | 275.00 | 550.00 | 1100. | 1700. |

Mint mark: A

527 (C192a)	1837	—	50.00	100.00	200.00	400.00
	1838	—	50.00	100.00	200.00	400.00
	1839	—	45.00	90.00	175.00	350.00
	1840	—	30.00	65.00	135.00	275.00
	1841	—	45.00	90.00	175.00	350.00
	1842	—	40.00	80.00	160.00	300.00
	1843	—	40.00	80.00	160.00	300.00
	1844	—	45.00	90.00	175.00	350.00
	1845	—	40.00	80.00	160.00	300.00
	1846	—	30.00	65.00	135.00	275.00
	1847	—	30.00	65.00	135.00	275.00
	1848	3,964	50.00	100.00	225.00	500.00

Mint mark: G-M

| 535 (C192b) | 1848 | 3,947 | 275.00 | 450.00 | 675.00 | 1350. |

NOTE: The above issue was struck in Mantua by the Austrian garrison under General Josef Radetzky during the siege of March 18-22, 1848 by Italian rebels.

Mint mark: A
Obv: Young head of Franz Joseph I left.

536 (C204)	1848	—	700.00	1450.	2000.	3250.
	1849	—	700.00	1450.	2000.	3250.
	1850	—	850.00	1750.	2250.	3750.
	1851	—	650.00	1250.	1800.	3000.

.900 SILVER
Obv: Young head of Franz Joseph I right.
Edge lettering: VIRIBVS VNITIS.

548.1 (C208)	1852	—	125.00	250.00	400.00	800.00
	1853	—	200.00	375.00	500.00	1000.
	1854	—	200.00	375.00	500.00	1000.
	1855	—	150.00	325.00	450.00	950.00
	1856	—	150.00	325.00	425.00	900.00

Edge lettering: VIRIBUS-VIRIBUS

| 548.2 (C208a) | 1856 | — | 150.00 | 275.00 | 450.00 | 750.00 |

ZWEI (2) GULDEN

25.9900 g, .900 SILVER, .7520 oz ASW
Mint mark: A
Denomination on edge

KM#	Date	Mintage	Fine	VF	XF	Unc
554 (C211)	1854	—	50.00	100.00	175.00	300.00

2 FLORINS

24.6900 g, .900 SILVER, .7145 oz ASW
Mint mark: A

566.1 (Y16.1)	1859	—	75.00	125.00	175.00	275.00
	1860	—	550.00	950.00	1500.	2250.
	1861					
	1862	.015	100.00	180.00	300.00	450.00
	1863	.024	50.00	90.00	150.00	250.00
	1864	.031	50.00	90.00	150.00	250.00
	1865	.072	50.00	90.00	150.00	250.00
	1866	—	Reported, not confirmed			

Mint mark: B

| 566.2 (Y16.2) | 1859 | .511 | 40.00 | 70.00 | 120.00 | 200.00 |

Mint mark: V

| 566.3 (Y16.3) | 1860 | — | 175.00 | 350.00 | 700.00 | 1100. |

Mint mark: A
Rev: Similar to KM#566.1.

| 573 (Y16a) | 1866 | .011 | 175.00 | 350.00 | 700.00 | 1100. |

Rev: Similar to KM#566.1.

584 (Y16b)	1867	.045	50.00	100.00	150.00	250.00
	1868	—	50.00	100.00	150.00	250.00
	1869	—	40.00	75.00	125.00	200.00
	1870	—	40.00	75.00	125.00	200.00
	1871	—	50.00	100.00	150.00	250.00
	1872	—	75.00	150.00	250.00	375.00

Mint: Vienna - w/o mint mark.

KM#	Date	Mintage	Fine	VF	XF	Unc
594 (Y16c)	1872	.045	35.00	65.00	110.00	200.00
	1873	.099	35.00	65.00	120.00	225.00
	1874	.079	25.00	50.00	80.00	150.00
	1875	.106	30.00	60.00	85.00	150.00
	1876	.092	35.00	65.00	90.00	170.00
	1877	.105	25.00	55.00	80.00	150.00
	1878	.147	30.00	60.00	80.00	150.00
	1879	.501	25.00	50.00	70.00	150.00
	1880	.083	30.00	60.00	80.00	140.00
	1881	.104	25.00	50.00	80.00	140.00
	1882	.121	25.00	50.00	70.00	130.00
	1883	.070	35.00	65.00	95.00	160.00
	1884	.087	25.00	50.00	70.00	130.00
	1885	.078	25.00	50.00	70.00	140.00
	1886	.093	25.00	50.00	70.00	140.00
	1887	.117	25.00	50.00	70.00	140.00
	1888	.073	25.00	50.00	70.00	140.00
	1889	.147	35.00	65.00	90.00	170.00
	1890	.104	25.00	65.00	90.00	150.00
	1891	.117	35.00	65.00	90.00	150.00
	1892	.032	30.00	60.00	70.00	140.00

22.0000 g, .900 SILVER, .6366 oz ASW
Vienna Shooting Fest
Rev: F. GAUL below eagle.

| 597 (Y18) | 1873 | — | 500.00 | 800.00 | 1250. | 1600. |
| | 1873 | — | — | — | Proof | 1750. |

NOTE: The Kremnica Mint struck reproductions with 'R.1973-KOLARSKY' below eagle, 24.31 g.

24.6900 g, .900 SILVER, .7145 oz ASW
Silver Wedding Anniversary

| 602 (Y19) | 1879 | .275 | 20.00 | 30.00 | 50.00 | 125.00 |

NOTE: Varieties exist w/and w/o dots in legend.

First Federal Shooting Festival

| 603 | 1880 | — | 50.00 | 100.00 | 150.00 | 225.00 |

AUSTRIA 132

Reopening Of Kuttenberg Mines

KM#	Date	Mintage	Fine	VF	XF	Unc
606 (Y20)	1887	400 pcs.	1500.	2150.	2900. Proof	4500. 4800.

COPPER (OMS)

606a	1887	—	800.00	1350.	2150.	3050.

BRONZE (OMS)

606b	1887	—	—	—	—	—

NOTE: The Kremnica Mint struck reproductions with R74 below church left of shield.

THALER

28.0600 g, .833 SILVER, .7514 oz ASW
Mint mark: A
Obv. leg: FRANCISCVS II. D.G.R. IMP. S.A. . . .

437 (C161)	1801	—	85.00	175.00	325.00	650.00
	1802	—	110.00	225.00	450.00	850.00
	1803	—	125.00	250.00	475.00	950.00
	1804	—	75.00	150.00	275.00	550.00

Obv. leg: FRANCISCVS II D.G. ROM. ET. . . .

460 (C168)	1804	—	60.00	125.00	250.00	475.00
	1805	—	60.00	125.00	250.00	475.00
	1806	—	60.00	125.00	250.00	475.00

Obv. leg: FRANCISCVS I.D.G. AVSTRIAE. . . .
Rev. leg. ends: D. LO. SAL. WIRC.

KM#	Date	Mintage	Fine	VF	XF	Unc
464.1 (C185.1)	1806	—	—	—	Rare	—
	1807	—	40.00	80.00	160.00	325.00
	1808	—	40.00	80.00	160.00	325.00
	1809	—	40.00	80.00	160.00	325.00
	1810	—	30.00	60.00	120.00	150.00

NOTE: 1810A exists as a klippe.

Mint mark: B

464.2 (C185.2)	1809 (restrike 1841)	— — — Rare —

Mint mark: C

464.3 (C185.3)	1809	—	35.00	70.00	140.00	275.00

Mint mark: A
Rev. leg. ends: LO: WI: ET IN. FR...

KM#	Date	Mintage	Fine	VF	XF	Unc
473.1 (C185a.1)	1811	—	30.00	65.00	130.00	250.00
	1812	—	175.00	350.00	725.00	1100.
	1813	—	50.00	100.00	200.00	—
	1814	—	25.00	50.00	100.00	—
	1815	—	25.00	50.00	100.00	—

Mint mark: C

473.2 (C185a.2)	1811	—	30.00	65.00	130.00	250.00
	1812	—	50.00	100.00	200.00	400.00
	1813	—	50.00	100.00	200.00	400.00
	1814	—	40.00	80.00	160.00	325.00
	1815	—	35.00	75.00	150.00	250.00

Mint mark: G

473.3 (C185a.3)	1813	—	55.00	100.00	200.00	325.00
	1814	—	55.00	100.00	200.00	325.00

Mint mark: B

473.4 (C185a.4)	1814	—	—	—	Rare	—
	1815	—	50.00	110.00	225.00	325.00

Mint mark: A
Rev. leg. ends: GAL. LOD. IL. REX. A. A.

493.1 (C185b.1)	1817	—	25.00	50.00	100.00	250.00
	1818	—	25.00	50.00	100.00	250.00
	1819	—	35.00	70.00	135.00	300.00
	1820	—	20.00	40.00	80.00	200.00
	1821	—	25.00	50.00	100.00	250.00
	1822	—	20.00	40.00	80.00	200.00
	1823	—	20.00	40.00	80.00	200.00
	1824	—	25.00	50.00	100.00	250.00

Mint mark: B

493.2 (C185b.2)	1818	—	30.00	55.00	110.00	200.00
	1819	.153	—	—	Rare	—
	1820	.250	—	—	Rare	—
	1821	.150	20.00	40.00	85.00	150.00
	1822	.215	25.00	50.00	100.00	200.00
	1823	.201	25.00	50.00	100.00	200.00
	1824	.282	25.00	50.00	100.00	200.00

Mint mark: V

493.3 (C185b.3)	1818	—	35.00	70.00	150.00	275.00
	1821	—	45.00	80.00	175.00	275.00
	1822	—	—	—	Rare	—

Mint mark: C

493.4 (C185b.4)	1819	—	35.00	70.00	150.00	275.00
	1820	—	30.00	55.00	100.00	200.00
	1821	—	20.00	40.00	85.00	150.00
	1822	—	25.00	50.00	100.00	200.00
	1823	—	35.00	70.00	150.00	275.00
	1824	—	30.00	60.00	125.00	250.00

Mint mark: E

493.5 (C185b.5)	1819	—	35.00	70.00	150.00	275.00
	1820	—	50.00	100.00	200.00	325.00

KM#	Date	Mintage	Fine	VF	XF	Unc
493.5	1821	—	27.50	55.00	125.00	225.00
	1822	—	30.00	60.00	125.00	250.00
	1823	—	30.00	60.00	125.00	250.00
	1824	—	35.00	70.00	150.00	275.00

Mint mark: G

493.6 (C185b.6)	1819	—	30.00	60.00	125.00	250.00
	1820	—	65.00	130.00	250.00	375.00
	1821	—	25.00	50.00	100.00	200.00
	1822	—	25.00	50.00	100.00	200.00
	1823	—	30.00	60.00	125.00	250.00
	1824	—	30.00	60.00	125.00	250.00

Mint mark: M

493.7 (C185b.7)	1819	—	45.00	90.00	180.00	300.00
	1820	—	30.00	60.00	125.00	250.00
	1821	—	50.00	100.00	200.00	300.00
	1822	—	50.00	100.00	200.00	400.00

Mint mark: A
Rev: Similar to KM#493.1.

494.1 (C185c.1)	1824	—	40.00	80.00	155.00	250.00
	1825	—	30.00	60.00	125.00	250.00
	1826	—	25.00	55.00	100.00	225.00
	1827	—	30.00	60.00	125.00	250.00
	1828	—	25.00	50.00	100.00	225.00
	1829	—	25.00	50.00	100.00	225.00
	1830	—	20.00	40.00	80.00	175.00

Mint mark: C

494.2 (C185c.2)	1824	—	—	—	—	—
	1825	—	35.00	70.00	145.00	270.00
	1826	—	30.00	60.00	125.00	250.00
	1827	—	25.00	50.00	100.00	200.00

Mint mark: B

494.3 (C185c.3)	1825	.336	30.00	60.00	125.00	250.00
	1826	.269	30.00	60.00	125.00	250.00
	1827	.089	80.00	175.00	325.00	475.00

Mint mark: G

494.4 (C185c.4)	1825	—	30.00	60.00	125.00	250.00
	1826	—	35.00	70.00	145.00	275.00

Mint mark: E

494.5 (C185c.5)	1830	—	75.00	150.00	275.00	425.00

Mint mark: A
Obv: Ribbons on wreath forward across neck.

509 (C185d)	1831	—	40.00	80.00	175.00	325.00

Obv: Ribbons of wreath hang behind neck.

510.1 (C185e.1)	1831	—	400.00	800.00	1200.	1600.
	1832	—	40.00	80.00	175.00	325.00
	1833	—	50.00	100.00	200.00	350.00
	1833 (error edge reads: FUNDAMENIUM)					
		—	100.00	200.00	325.00	525.00
	1834	—	42.50	85.00	175.00	325.00
	1835	—	50.00	100.00	200.00	350.00

Mint mark: B

510.2 (C185e.2)	1833	—	75.00	150.00	325.00	650.00

Mint mark: E

510.3 (C185e.3)	1833	—	50.00	100.00	200.00	350.00

Mint mark: A
Ferdinandus I
Obv: Oval loop in knot of wreath.

520.1 (C193.1)	1835	—	125.00	250.00	400.00	800.00
	1836	—	75.00	150.00	250.00	500.00

Mint mark: C

520.2 (C193.2)	1835	—	—	—	Rare	—
	1836	—	250.00	400.00	800.00	1500.

AUSTRIA 133

Mint mark: A
Obv: Sharp cornered loop in knot of wreath.

KM#	Date	Mintage	Fine	VF	XF	Unc
521 (C193b)	1835	—	375.00	600.00	1100.	1700.

528.1 (C193a.1)	1837	—	50.00	100.00	200.00	350.00
	1838	—	50.00	100.00	200.00	350.00
	1839	—	50.00	100.00	200.00	350.00
	1840	—	45.00	90.00	175.00	325.00
	1841	—	40.00	80.00	150.00	275.00
	1842	—	40.00	80.00	150.00	275.00
	1843	—	40.00	80.00	150.00	275.00
	1844	—	40.00	80.00	150.00	275.00
	1845	—	40.00	80.00	150.00	275.00
	1846	—	40.00	80.00	150.00	275.00
	1847	—	40.00	80.00	150.00	275.00
	1848	.119	30.00	60.00	100.00	225.00

Mint mark: M

528.2 (C193a.2)	1837	—	275.00	500.00	1000.	1700.
	1838	—	550.00	1150.	1750.	2400.

Mint mark: A
Obv. leg: FRANC.IOS.I.D.G.AVSTR.IMP.HVNG.BOH.REX.
Rev: Similar to KM#528.1.

537 (C205)	1848	—	500.00	1000.	1500.	2250.
	1849	—	500.00	1000.	1500.	2250.
	1850	—	700.00	1350.	1950.	2650.
	1851	—	500.00	1000.	1500.	2250.

Obv. leg: FRANC.IOS.I.D.G.AVSTRIAE.IMPERATOR.
Rev: Similar to KM#528.1.

549 (C205a)	1852	—	600.00	1250.	2250.	3000.

25.9900 g, .900 SILVER, .7520 oz ASW
Rev: Similar to KM#528.1.
Edge lettering: VIRIBVS VNITIS.

KM#	Date	Mintage	Fine	VF	XF	Unc
550.1 (C209.1)	1852	—	60.00	120.00	225.00	350.00
	1853	—	45.00	100.00	200.00	300.00
	1854	—	45.00	100.00	200.00	375.00
	1855	—	40.00	90.00	175.00	325.00
	1856	—	40.00	90.00	175.00	325.00

Mint mark: B

550.2 (C209.2)	1853	—	160.00	275.00	450.00	700.00

Mint mark: A
Edge lettering: VIRIBUS-VIRIBUS.

550.3 (C209a)	1856	—	—	—	—	—

(Vereins)

18.5186 g, .900 SILVER, .5359 oz ASW

KM#	Date	Mintage	Fine	VF	XF	Unc
557.1 (Y1.1)	1857	9.154	15.00	30.00	60.00	100.00
	1858	Inc. Ab.	15.00	30.00	60.00	100.00
	1859	4.949	20.00	40.00	70.00	125.00
	1860	1.620	20.00	40.00	70.00	150.00
	1861	3.140	20.00	40.00	70.00	150.00
	1862	.998	25.00	50.00	90.00	175.00
	1863	2.209	20.00	40.00	70.00	125.00
	1864	2.636	17.50	35.00	65.00	110.00
	1865	2.085	17.50	35.00	65.00	110.00

NOTE: Varieties in asterisk size on edge exist on 1863 and 1864 dated coins.

Mint mark: B

557.2 (Y1.2)	1857	—	50.00	100.00	200.00	425.00
	1858	—	20.00	40.00	80.00	150.00
	1859	—	20.00	40.00	80.00	150.00
	1861	—	20.00	40.00	75.00	150.00
	1862	—	25.00	50.00	85.00	175.00
	1863	—	25.00	50.00	85.00	175.00
	1864	—	27.50	55.00	100.00	200.00
	1865	—	20.00	40.00	75.00	125.00

Mint mark: E

557.3 (Y1.3)	1857	—	40.00	80.00	165.00	325.00
	1858	—	50.00	100.00	200.00	425.00
	1859	—	40.00	80.00	160.00	350.00
	1861	—	20.00	40.00	75.00	150.00
	1863	—	25.00	50.00	90.00	175.00
	1864	.556	17.50	35.00	65.00	125.00
	1865	—	17.50	35.00	60.00	100.00

Mint mark: V

557.4 (Y1.4)	1857	—	75.00	150.00	300.00	550.00
	1858	—	37.50	75.00	150.00	300.00
	1860	.043	37.50	75.00	150.00	300.00
	1861	—	25.00	50.00	100.00	175.00
	1862	—	25.00	50.00	100.00	175.00
	1863	—	25.00	50.00	100.00	175.00
	1864	.107	62.50	125.00	250.00	450.00
	1865	—	75.00	150.00	275.00	525.00

Mint mark: M

557.5 (Y1.5)	1858	—	37.50	75.00	150.00	300.00
	1859	—	37.50	75.00	150.00	300.00

Mint mark: A
Obv: Head w/heavier whiskers.

Rev: Similar to KM#577.1.

KM#	Date	Mintage	Fine	VF	XF	Unc
574.1 (Y1a.1)	1866	1.236	25.00	50.00	90.00	150.00
	1867	.850	30.00	60.00	110.00	200.00

Mint mark: B

574.2 (Y1a.2)	1866	Inc. Ab.	35.00	60.00	100.00	175.00
	1867	Inc. Ab.	40.00	85.00	150.00	275.00

Mint mark: E

574.3 (Y1a.3)	1866	Inc. Ab.	40.00	80.00	150.00	275.00
	1867	Inc. Ab.	40.00	80.00	150.00	275.00
	1868	.168	—	Reported, not confirmed		

(Fein)

Mint: Vienna - w/o mint mark.
3rd German Shooting Festival

589 (Y-A16)	1868	—	30.00	60.00	125.00	200.00

(Gedenk)

Opening of Mt. Raxalpe Inn

601 (Y-A20)	1877	100 pcs.	1500.	2250.	3500.	5500.

2 THALERS
(Vereins)

37.0371 g, .900 SILVER, 1.0718 oz ASW
Mint mark: A
Opening of Vienna-Trieste Railway
Obv: Similar to 1 Thaler, KM#557.1.

558 (Y3)	1857	1,644	400.00	800.00	1500.	2250.

NOTE: Varieties exist.

Rev: Similar to KM#575.

570 (Y2)	1865	7,425	350.00	600.00	1000.	1800.

AUSTRIA 134

KM#	Date	Mintage	Fine	VF	XF	Unc
575 (Y2a)	1866	.010	175.00	350.00	500.00	850.00
	1867	8,300	175.00	350.00	500.00	850.00

1/2 KRONE

5.5555 g, .900 GOLD, .1608 oz AGW
Mint mark: A

KM#	Date	Mintage	Fine	VF	XF	Unc
563.1 (Y4.1)	1858	.020	350.00	650.00	950.00	1400.
	1859	.402	275.00	600.00	800.00	1300.
	1860	.201	175.00	325.00	575.00	850.00
	1861	2,868	525.00	875.00	1250.	1800.
	1863	40 pcs.	2000.	4000.	8000.	10,000.
	1864	980 pcs.	1000.	1500.	2000.	2500.
	1865	2,690	750.00	1250.	1750.	2250.

Mint mark: E

563.2 (Y4.2)	1858	.025	300.00	525.00	800.00	1200.
	1859	.017	350.00	700.00	1100.	1600.
	1861	.055	275.00	500.00	700.00	1150.

Mint mark: V

563.3 (Y4.3)	1858	947 pcs.	1300.	1800.	2250.	3000.

Mint mark: B

563.4 (Y4.4)	1859	4,376	350.00	700.00	1100.	1600.
	1860	.043	325.00	600.00	875.00	1400.
	1861	.018	350.00	700.00	1100.	1600.

Mint mark: A

576 (Y4a)	1866	4,000	425.00	700.00	1100.	1600.

KRONE

11.1111 g, .900 GOLD, .3215 oz AGW
Mint mark: A

564.1 (Y5.1)	1858	.047	450.00	800.00	1150.	2250.
	1859	.010	350.00	650.00	825.00	1750.
	1860	557 pcs.	875.00	1400.	1750.	3000.
	1861	2,010	650.00	1100.	1500.	2750.
	1863	1,000	700.00	1250.	1750.	3000.
	1864	1,530	650.00	1100.	1400.	2750.
	1865	2,800	650.00	1100.	1400.	2750.

Mint mark: E

564.2 (Y5.2)	1858	.031	350.00	575.00	850.00	1500.

Mint mark: V

KM#	Date	Mintage	Fine	VF	XF	Unc
564.3 (Y5.3)	1858	600 pcs.	1750.	2500.	3500.	4500.
	1859	1,885	1250.	2000.	2750.	3500.

Mint mark: M

564.4 (Y5.4)	1859	3,974	650.00	1250.	1750.	3000.

Mint mark: A
Obv: Large bust.

577 (Y5a)	1866	3,000	875.00	1500.	2000.	3500.

MONETARY REFORM
1892-1918
100 Heller = 1 Corona

HELLER

BRONZE

610 (Y26)	1892	—	30.00	40.00	80.00	180.00
	1893	29.000	.20	.35	.50	4.00
	1894	30.100	.20	.35	.50	4.00
	1895	49.500	.20	.35	.50	2.00
	1896	15.600	.35	1.50	3.00	6.00
	1897	12.400	.35	2.00	4.00	8.00
	1898	6.780	5.00	10.00	20.00	35.00
	1899	1.901	3.00	12.00	25.00	45.00
	1900	26.981	.20	.50	1.50	4.00
	1901	52.096	.20	.35	.50	2.00
	1902	20.553	.20	.50	1.25	3.00
	1903	13.779	.20	.35	.50	2.50
	1909	12.668	.20	.35	.50	2.50
	1910	21.900	.20	.35	.50	2.50
	1911	18.387	.20	.35	.50	2.50
	1912	27.053	.20	.35	.50	2.50
	1913	8.782	.20	.35	.50	2.50
	1914	9.906	.20	.35	.50	2.50
	1915	5.670	.20	.35	.75	2.50
	1916	12.484	.35	.75	1.50	4.00

Obv: Austrian shield on eagle's breast.

633 (Y27)	1916	Inc. Ab.	4.00	6.00	10.00	17.50

2 HELLER

BRONZE

611 (Y28)	1892	.260	50.00	80.00	150.00	300.00
	1893	41.507	.20	.50	1.75	5.00
	1894	78.036	.15	.25	.75	2.50
	1895	25.610	.20	.50	2.25	6.25
	1896	43.080	.15	.25	.75	3.00
	1897	98.000	.15	.25	.75	2.50
	1898	10.720	.75	1.50	4.00	8.00
	1899	42.734	.15	.25	.75	3.00
	1900	7.942	.50	1.00	3.00	8.00
	1901	12.157	2.00	3.00	6.00	12.50
	1902	18.760	.15	.50	1.50	3.00
	1903	26.983	.50	1.50	3.00	8.00
	1904	12.863	.15	.50	1.75	4.00
	1905	6.679	.75	2.75	5.50	12.50
	1906	20.104	.50	1.00	3.00	8.00
	1907	23.804	.15	.25	.75	3.00
	1908	21.984	.15	.25	.75	3.00
	1909	25.975	.15	.25	.75	3.00
	1910	28.406	.50	1.00	3.00	8.00
	1911	50.007	.15	.25	.50	2.00
	1912	74.234	.15	.20	.25	3.00
	1913	27.432	.35	.75	2.25	6.00
	1914	60.674	.15	.20	.25	2.00
	1915	7.870	.15	.20	.25	2.00

IRON
Obv: Austrian shield on eagle's breast.

KM#	Date	Mintage	Fine	VF	XF	Unc
634 (Y33)	1916	61.909	.50	1.00	2.00	6.00
	1917	81.186	.25	.50	.75	4.00
	1918	66.353	.25	.50	.75	4.00

10 HELLER

NICKEL

612 (Y29)	1892	—	100.00	175.00	250.00	375.00
	1892	—	—	—	Proof	650.00
	1893	43.524	.25	.50	1.50	3.00
	1894	45.558	.25	.50	1.25	3.00
	1895	79.918	.25	.50	1.00	2.50
	1907	8.662	.25	.50	1.00	3.00
	1908	7.772	.75	1.50	2.50	5.00
	1909	20.462	.15	.25	.75	2.00
	1910	10.100	.15	.25	.75	2.00
	1911	3.634	1.00	2.00	3.50	7.50

COPPER-NICKEL-ZINC

632 (Y31)	1915	18.366	.15	.25	.50	1.50
	1916	27.487	.15	.25	.50	1.50

Obv: Austrian shield on eagle's breast.

635 (Y32)	1916	14.804	.50	1.00	2.00	4.00

20 HELLER

NICKEL

613 (Y30)	1892	1.500	7.50	15.00	35.00	75.00
	1892	—	—	Proof	250.00
	1893	41.457	.25	.50	1.00	3.00
	1894	50.116	.25	.50	1.00	3.00
	1895	32.927	.25	.35	.50	2.50
	1907	7.650	.75	1.50	3.00	10.00
	1908	7.469	.75	1.25	2.50	8.00
	1909	7.592	1.00	2.00	4.00	10.00
	1911	19.560	.25	.35	.50	2.00
	1914	2.342	5.00	15.00	25.00	50.00

IRON
Obv: Austrian shield on eagle's breast.

636 (Y34)	1916	130.770	.50	1.00	1.50	5.00
	1917	127.420	.50	1.00	1.50	5.00
	1918	48.985	.25	.50	.75	4.00

CORONA

5.0000 g, .835 SILVER, .1342 oz ASW

614 (Y35)	1892	.235	80.00	160.00	250.00	425.00
	1893	50.124	1.75	3.00	5.00	10.00
	1894	28.003	1.75	3.00	5.00	12.00
	1895	15.115	3.75	6.00	12.00	20.00
	1896	3.068	7.50	15.00	25.00	50.00
	1897	2.142	20.00	30.00	60.00	100.00
	1898	5.855	2.50	5.00	8.00	15.00
	1899	11.820	1.75	2.75	5.00	10.00

KM#	Date	Mintage	Fine	VF	XF	Unc
(Y35)	1900	3.745	2.50	5.00	8.00	14.00
	1901	10.387	1.75	2.75	5.00	10.00
	1902	2.947	2.00	4.25	7.50	14.00
	1903	2.198	2.00	4.25	7.50	14.00
	1904	.993	4.00	8.50	17.50	25.00
	1905	.505	10.00	25.00	50.00	75.00
	1906	.165	80.00	125.00	200.00	300.00
	1907	.244	30.00	60.00	100.00	200.00

60th Anniversary of Reign

| 618 (Y36) | 1908 | 4.784 | 2.00 | 3.00 | 5.00 | 10.00 |

630 (Y37)	1912	8.457	1.50	2.00	3.00	8.00
	1913	9.345	1.50	2.00	3.00	7.00
	1914	37.897	1.50	2.00	3.00	6.00
	1915	23.000	1.50	2.00	3.00	6.00
	1916	12.415	1.50	2.00	3.00	6.00

2 CORONA

10.0000 g, .835 SILVER, .2684 oz ASW

| 631 (Y38) | 1912 | 10.245 | 3.50 | 5.00 | 7.00 | 11.00 |
| | 1913 | 7.256 | 3.50 | 5.00 | 7.00 | 11.00 |

ALUMINUM (OMS)

| 631a (Y38a) | 1913 | — | — | — | — | 100.00 |

5 CORONA

24.0000 g, .900 SILVER, .6945 oz ASW

617 (Y39)	1900	8.525	8.00	12.50	25.00	75.00
	1907	1.539	10.00	15.00	30.00	90.00
	1907	—	—	—	Proof	500.00

60th Anniversary of Reign

KM#	Date	Mintage	Fine	VF	XF	Unc
619 (Y40)	1908	5.090	8.00	12.50	25.00	65.00
	1908				Proof	500.00

Obv: Large head.

| 623 (Y41) | 1909 | 1.709 | 10.00 | 15.00 | 35.00 | 110.00 |

Obv: Similar to KM#619.
Rev: Similar to KM#617.

| 624 (Y-A41) | 1909 | 1.776 | 10.00 | 15.00 | 35.00 | 85.00 |

10 CORONA

3.3875 g, .900 GOLD, .0980 oz AGW
Obv: Laureate head of Franz Joseph I right.
Rev: Eagle w/value and date below.

615 (Y42)	1892	—	1000.	1500.	2500.	3500.
	1893				Rare	
	1896	.211	BV	55.00	60.00	80.00
	1897	1.803	BV	55.00	60.00	90.00
	1905	1.933	BV	55.00	60.00	90.00
	1906	1.081	BV	55.00	60.00	90.00

Jubilee
Obv: Small plain head of Franz Joseph I right.
Rev: Eagle, value below, 2 dates above.

| 620 (Y44) | 1908 | .654 | BV | 60.00 | 70.00 | 100.00 |

Obv: Small head.
Rev: Eagle, value and date below.

| 625 (Y47) | 1909 | 2.320 | BV | 55.00 | 60.00 | 80.00 |

Obv: Large head.

626 (Y49)	1909	.192	55.00	60.00	80.00	100.00
	1910	1.005	BV	50.00	60.00	80.00
	1911	1.286	BV	50.00	60.00	80.00
	1912	(restrike)	—	—	BV + 10%	

20 CORONA

6.7751 g, .900 GOLD, .1960 oz AGW

616 (Y43)	1892	.653	—	BV	125.00	150.00
	1893	7.872	—	BV	100.00	115.00
	1894	6.714	—	BV	100.00	115.00

KM#	Date	Mintage	Fine	VF	XF	Unc
(Y43)	1895	2.266	—	BV	100.00	115.00
	1896	6.868	—	BV	100.00	115.00
	1897	5.133	—	BV	100.00	115.00
	1898	1.874	—	BV	100.00	115.00
	1899	.098	100.00	110.00	130.00	150.00
	1900	.027	200.00	400.00	600.00	800.00
	1901	.049	150.00	225.00	325.00	400.00
	1902	.441	BV	110.00	140.00	160.00
	1903	.323	BV	110.00	140.00	160.00
	1904	.494	BV	110.00	140.00	160.00
	1905	.146	100.00	120.00	150.00	170.00

Jubilee
Rev: 2 dates above eagle.

| 621 (Y45) | 1908 | .188 | 100.00 | 125.00 | 150.00 | 200.00 |

| 627 (Y48) | 1909 | .228 | 450.00 | 750.00 | 1250. | 1750. |

628 (Y50)	1909	.102	575.00	850.00	1250.	1750.
	1910	.386	120.00	150.00	250.00	350.00
	1911	.059	125.00	175.00	275.00	375.00
	1912	4.460	250.00	325.00	400.00	500.00
	1913	.028	350.00	500.00	750.00	1000.
	1914	.082	135.00	225.00	300.00	500.00
	1915	(restrike)	—	—	BV + 5%	
	1916	.072	2500.	3500.	5500.	7500.

Rev: Austrian shield on eagle.

| 637 (Y52) | 1916 | Inc. Ab. | 450.00 | 550.00 | 900.00 | 1200. |

Obv: Head of Kaiser Karl I. Rev: Similar to KM#628.

| 638 | 1918 | 1 pc. | — | — | Unique | |

100 CORONA

33.8753 g, .900 GOLD, .9803 oz AGW
Jubilee

| 622 (Y46) | 1908 | .016 | 500.00 | 600.00 | 900.00 | 1300. |
| | 1908 | — | — | — | Proof | 1750. |

| 629 | 1909 | 3.203 | 500.00 | 650.00 | 950.00 | 1400. |

KM#	Date	Mintage	Fine	VF	XF	Unc
(Y51)	1910	3,074	500.00	650.00	950.00	1400.
	1911	11,165	500.00	650.00	950.00	1400.
	1912	3,591	550.00	850.00	1150.	1900.
	1913	2,696	500.00	800.00	1200.	1650.
	1914	1,195	500.00	650.00	1000.	1500.
	1915	(restrike)	—	—		BV + 2%
	1915	(restrike)	—	—	Proof	—

TRADE COINAGE

THALER

28.0668 g, .833 SILVER, .7517 oz ASW

T1 (Y55)	1780 SF	(restrike-1853-present)	—	—	—	7.00
	1780 SF	(restrike)		—	Proof	9.00

An unofficial trade dollar, the final date of the famous Maria Theresa Thaler has been restruck intermittently since 1781 to modern times at many world mints. It has been used in many areas that lacked a firm local coinage, particularly in north and east Africa and the Near East. Gunzburg Mint was where the original talers were struck. (Listings for these can be found under Burgau-Austrian States, C#14). Since then the talers have been restruck at the following mints, Vienna, Prague, Milan, Venice, Gunzburg, London, Paris, Brussels, Kremnitz, Karlsburg, Rome, Bombay and Florence with an estimated 800 million struck to date. For original Thaler listings refer to BURGAU.

Period	Mintage	Mint
1920-1937	52,069,465	Vienna
1935-1939	19,496,729	Rome
1935-1957	11,809,956	Paris
1936-1961	20,159,070	London
1937-1957	10,995,024	Brussels
1940-1941	18,864,576	Bombay
1949-1955	3,488,500	Birmingham
1956-1975	9,924,151	Vienna

4 FLORIN-10 FRANCS

3.2258 g, .900 GOLD, .0933 oz AGW
Mint: Vienna - w/o mint mark.

KM#	Date	Mintage	Fine	VF	XF	Unc
590	1870	7,440	60.00	100.00	160.00	250.00
(Y21)	1871	6,665	60.00	100.00	160.00	250.00
	1872	4,960	60.00	90.00	140.00	225.00
	1877	3,004	80.00	160.00	250.00	350.00
	1878	6,820	55.00	90.00	140.00	225.00
	1881	8,370	55.00	90.00	140.00	200.00
	1883	3,720	65.00	120.00	180.00	325.00
	1884	7,518	55.00	90.00	115.00	200.00
	1885	.038	55.00	60.00	110.00	165.00
	1888	4,145	55.00	100.00	140.00	250.00
	1889	5,707	55.00	90.00	135.00	225.00
	1890	2,947	65.00	120.00	180.00	300.00
	1891	.011	55.00	65.00	90.00	175.00
	1892	(restrike)	—	—	BV	55.00

DUCAT

3.4909 g, .986 GOLD, .1106 oz AGW
Mint mark: A
Obv. leg: FRANC. II. D. G. R. . . . . . .

KM#	Date	Mintage	Fine	VF	XF	Unc
439.1	1801	—	120.00	200.00	290.00	450.00
(C163.1)	1802	—	110.00	180.00	260.00	400.00
	1803	—	120.00	200.00	290.00	450.00
	1804	—	110.00	180.00	260.00	400.00

Mint mark: B

KM#	Date	Mintage	Fine	VF	XF	Unc
439.2 (C163.2)	1802	—	100.00	160.00	250.00	375.00

Mint mark: E

439.3 (C163.3)	1804	—	100.00	160.00	250.00	375.00

Mint mark: G

439.4 (C163.4)	1802	—	110.00	170.00	250.00	375.00

Mint mark: A
Obv. leg: FRANCISCVS II D. G. ROM. . . . .
Rev. leg: . . . . .D. LOTH. VEN. SAL.

461.1	1804	—	325.00	650.00	1000.	1750.
(C169.1)	1805	—	325.00	650.00	1000.	1750.
	1806	—	300.00	600.00	900.	1600.

Mint mark: B

461.2 (C169.2)	1806	—	325.00	650.00	1000.	1750.

Mint mark: C

461.4	1806	—	750.00	1500.	2250.	3000.

Mint mark: D

461.3 (C169.3)	1806	—	325.00	650.00	1000.	1750.

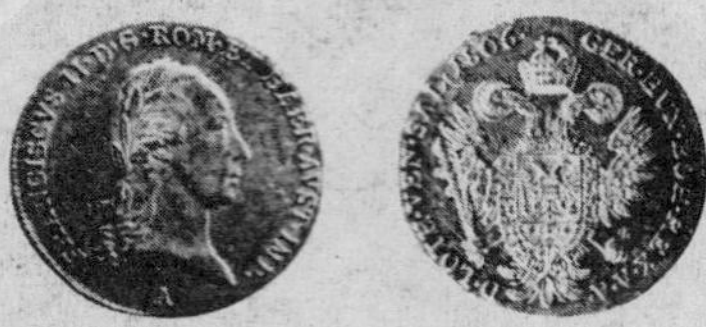

Mint mark: A
Rev. leg: . . . . . D. LO. SAL. WIRC.

465.1	1806	—	160.00	250.00	375.00	550.00
(C186.1)	1807	—	125.00	200.00	275.00	450.00
	1808	—	125.00	200.00	275.00	450.00
	1809	—	125.00	200.00	275.00	450.00
	1810	—	125.00	200.00	275.00	450.00

Mint mark: D

465.2	1806	—	750.00	1250.	1500.	2000.
(C186.2)	1808	—		—	Rare	—
	1809	—	500.00	700.00	950.00	1200.

Mint mark: C

465.3 (C186.3)	1807	—	180.00	275.00	425.00	650.00

Mint mark: B

465.4 (C186.4)	1809	—	160.00	250.00	375.00	575.00

Mint mark: A
Rev. leg: . . . . . .LO: WI: ET IN. FR: DVX.

474.1	1811	—	80.00	120.00	200.00	300.00
(C186a.1)	1812	—	80.00	120.00	200.00	300.00
	1813	—	100.00	140.00	225.00	325.00
	1814	—	80.00	120.00	200.00	300.00
	1815	—	80.00	120.00	200.00	300.00

Mint mark: B

474.2	1811	—	80.00	120.00	200.00	300.00
(C186a.2)	1812	—	80.00	120.00	200.00	300.00
	1813	—	80.00	120.00	200.00	300.00
	1814	—	100.00	140.00	225.00	325.00
	1815	—	80.00	120.00	200.00	300.00

Mint mark: G

474.3	1812	—		—	Rare	—
(C186a.3)	1813	—		—	Rare	—
	1814	—		—	Rare	—
	1815	—	100.00	140.00	225.00	325.00

Mint mark: E

474.4	1813	—	100.00	140.00	225.00	325.00
(C186a.4)	1814	—	100.00	140.00	225.00	325.00
	1815	—	80.00	120.00	200.00	300.00

Mint mark: A
Rev. leg: . . . . . .GAL. LOB. IL. REX. A. A.

486.1	1816	—	100.00	140.00	225.00	350.00
(C186b.1)	1817	—	100.00	140.00	225.00	350.00
	1818	—	100.00	140.00	225.00	350.00
	1819	—	100.00	140.00	225.00	350.00
	1820	—	100.00	140.00	225.00	350.00
	1821	—	100.00	140.00	225.00	350.00
	1822	—	100.00	140.00	225.00	350.00
	1823	—	100.00	140.00	225.00	350.00
	1824	—	100.00	140.00	225.00	350.00

Mint mark: B

KM#	Date	Mintage	Fine	VF	XF	Unc
486.2	1818	—	100.00	140.00	225.00	350.00
(C186b.2)	1819	—	110.00	160.00	250.00	375.00
	1820	—	100.00	140.00	225.00	350.00
	1821	—	100.00	140.00	225.00	350.00
	1822	—	100.00	140.00	225.00	350.00
	1823	—	100.00	140.00	225.00	350.00
	1824	—	100.00	140.00	225.00	350.00

Mint mark: E

486.3	1818	—	100.00	140.00	225.00	350.00
(C186b.3)	1819	—	100.00	140.00	225.00	350.00
	1820	—	100.00	140.00	225.00	350.00
	1821	—	100.00	140.00	225.00	350.00
	1822	—	100.00	140.00	225.00	350.00
	1823	—	100.00	140.00	225.00	350.00
	1824	—	100.00	140.00	225.00	350.00

Mint mark: G

486.4	1818	—	110.00	160.00	275.00	375.00
(C186b.4)	1819	—	110.00	160.00	275.00	375.00
	1820	—	100.00	140.00	225.00	350.00
	1821	—	100.00	140.00	225.00	350.00
	1822	—	100.00	140.00	225.00	350.00
	1823	—	100.00	140.00	225.00	350.00
	1824	—	110.00	160.00	275.00	375.00

Mint mark: V

486.5	1819	—	350.00	525.00	700.00	1050.
(C186b.5)	1824	—	250.00	375.00	550.00	800.00

Mint mark: A
Obv: Ribbons on wreath forward across neck.

500.1	1825	—	80.00	120.00	200.00	300.00
(C186c.1)	1826	—	80.00	120.00	200.00	300.00
	1827	—	80.00	120.00	200.00	300.00
	1828	—	100.00	130.00	225.00	325.00
	1829	—	80.00	120.00	180.00	275.00
	1830	—	80.00	120.00	180.00	275.00
	1831	—	1100.	1600.	2400.	3200.

Mint mark: B

500.2	1825	—	100.00	130.00	225.00	325.00
(C186c.2)	1826	—	110.00	160.00	250.00	375.00
	1827	—	110.00	160.00	250.00	375.00
	1828	—	100.00	130.00	200.00	300.00
	1829	—	100.00	130.00	200.00	300.00
	1830	—	100.00	130.00	200.00	300.00

Mint mark: E

500.3	1825	—	110.00	160.00	250.00	375.00
(C186c.3)	1826	—	90.00	130.00	200.00	300.00
	1827	—	110.00	160.00	250.00	375.00
	1828	—	90.00	130.00	200.00	300.00
	1829	—	90.00	130.00	200.00	300.00
	1830	—	90.00	130.00	200.00	300.00

Mint mark: G

500.4	1825	—	—	—	—	—
(C186c.4)	1826	—	—	—	Rare	—

Mint mark: A
Obv: Ribbons on wreath behind neck.

511.1	1831	—	110.00	160.00	250.00	375.00
(C186d.1)	1832	—	100.00	130.00	200.00	300.00
	1833	—	100.00	130.00	200.00	300.00
	1834	—	100.00	130.00	200.00	300.00
	1835	—	100.00	130.00	200.00	300.00

Mint mark: B

511.2	1832	—	100.00	130.00	225.00	325.00
(C186d.2)	1833	—	100.00	130.00	200.00	300.00
	1834	—	100.00	130.00	200.00	300.00
	1835	—	100.00	130.00	200.00	300.00

Mint mark: E

511.3	1833	—	110.00	160.00	250.00	375.00
(C186d.3)	1834	—	110.00	160.00	250.00	375.00
	1835	—	110.00	160.00	250.00	375.00

Mint mark: A
Obv. leg: . . . . . .AVSTRIAE IMPERATOR.

522.1	1835	—	275.00	500.00	800.00	1200.
(C194.1)	1836	—	160.00	275.00	450.00	650.00

Mint mark: E

522.2	1835	—	275.00	500.00	800.00	1200.
(C194.2)	1836	—	200.00	325.00	525.00	800.00

Mint mark: A
Obv. leg: . . . . .AVSTRI. IMP.

KM#	Date	Mintage	Fine	VF	XF	Unc
529.1 (C194a.1)	1837	—	60.00	80.00	130.00	200.00
	1838	—	60.00	80.00	200.00	275.00
	1839	—	60.00	80.00	130.00	200.00
	1840	—	60.00	80.00	130.00	200.00
	1841	—	60.00	80.00	130.00	200.00
	1842	—	65.00	100.00	160.00	250.00
	1843	—	60.00	80.00	110.00	180.00
	1844	—	60.00	80.00	110.00	180.00
	1845	—	60.00	80.00	110.00	180.00
	1846	—	60.00	80.00	130.00	200.00
	1847	—	60.00	80.00	110.00	180.00
	1848	—	60.00	80.00	110.00	180.00

Mint mark: B

KM#	Date	Mintage	Fine	VF	XF	Unc
529.2 (C194a.2)	1837	—	80.00	115.00	200.00	275.00
	1838	—	80.00	115.00	200.00	275.00
	1839	—	80.00	115.00	200.00	275.00
	1840	—	60.00	80.00	130.00	200.00
	1841	—	60.00	80.00	110.00	180.00
	1842	—	100.00	130.00	200.00	350.00
	1843	—	60.00	80.00	130.00	200.00
	1844	—	60.00	80.00	110.00	180.00
	1845	—	60.00	80.00	110.00	180.00
	1846	—	60.00	80.00	130.00	200.00
	1847	—	60.00	80.00	110.00	180.00
	1848	—	60.00	80.00	110.00	180.00

Mint mark: E

KM#	Date	Mintage	Fine	VF	XF	Unc
529.3 (C194a.3)	1837	—	80.00	115.00	200.00	275.00
	1838	—	80.00	115.00	200.00	275.00
	1839	—	80.00	115.00	200.00	275.00
	1840	—	60.00	80.00	140.00	225.00
	1841	—	60.00	80.00	110.00	180.00
	1842	—	60.00	80.00	110.00	180.00
	1843	—	60.00	80.00	130.00	200.00
	1844	—	60.00	80.00	110.00	180.00
	1845	—	60.00	80.00	130.00	200.00
	1846	—	60.00	80.00	130.00	200.00
	1847	—	80.00	100.00	180.00	250.00
	1848	—	60.00	80.00	110.00	180.00

Mint mark: V

KM#	Date	Mintage	Fine	VF	XF	Unc
529.4 (C194a.4)	1840	—	475.00	650.00	975.00	1275.
	1841	—	250.00	350.00	525.00	725.00
	1842	—	200.00	275.00	700.00	1000.
	1843	—	200.00	275.00	700.00	1350.
	1844	—	200.00	275.00	700.00	1350.
	1845	—	200.00	275.00	700.00	1200.
	1846	—	200.00	275.00	700.00	1000.
	1847	—	250.00	350.00	550.00	775.00
	1848	—	60.00	80.00	110.00	180.00

Mint mark: A

KM#	Date	Mintage	Fine	VF	XF	Unc
551.1 (C212.1)	1852	—	80.00	100.00	160.00	225.00
	1853	—	90.00	120.00	180.00	250.00
	1854	—	60.00	80.00	120.00	180.00
	1855	—	60.00	80.00	120.00	180.00
	1856	—	60.00	80.00	140.00	200.00
	1857	—	60.00	80.00	130.00	180.00
	1858	—	60.00	80.00	110.00	160.00
	1859	—	60.00	80.00	110.00	160.00

Mint mark: B

KM#	Date	Mintage	Fine	VF	XF	Unc
551.2 (C212.2)	1853	.114	90.00	110.00	180.00	250.00
	1854	.087	110.00	135.00	225.00	350.00
	1855	.133	160.00	225.00	350.00	550.00
	1856	.121	80.00	110.00	180.00	250.00
	1857	.086	60.00	80.00	130.00	200.00
	1858	.071	100.00	130.00	180.00	250.00
	1859	.034	60.00	80.00	140.00	200.00

Mint mark: E

KM#	Date	Mintage	Fine	VF	XF	Unc
551.3 (C212.3)	1853	—	100.00	130.00	200.00	250.00
	1854	—	100.00	130.00	200.00	250.00
	1855	—	90.00	110.00	180.00	250.00
	1856	—	60.00	80.00	140.00	200.00
	1857	—	100.00	140.00	225.00	350.00
	1858	—	90.00	110.00	180.00	250.00
	1859	—	60.00	80.00	110.00	180.00

Mint mark: V

KM#	Date	Mintage	Fine	VF	XF	Unc
551.4 (C212.4)	1854	—	250.00	450.00	800.00	1200.
	1855	—	250.00	450.00	800.00	1200.
	1856	—	250.00	450.00	800.00	1200.
	1857	—	250.00	450.00	800.00	1200.
	1858	—	250.00	450.00	800.00	1200.
	1859	—	250.00	450.00	800.00	1200.

Mint mark: M

KM#	Date	Mintage	Fine	VF	XF	Unc
551.5 (C212.5)	1858	—	275.00	800.00	1750.	2500.

Mint mark: A

KM#	Date	Mintage	Fine	VF	XF	Unc
568.1 (Y23.1)	1860	—	70.00	100.00	140.00	225.00
	1861	—	60.00	80.00	120.00	200.00
	1862	—	60.00	80.00	120.00	225.00
	1863	—	60.00	80.00	120.00	225.00
	1864	—	60.00	100.00	160.00	250.00
	1865	—	60.00	100.00	160.00	250.00

Mint mark: B

KM#	Date	Mintage	Fine	VF	XF	Unc
568.2 (Y23.2)	1860	.056	80.00	120.00	180.00	275.00
	1861	.121	60.00	100.00	160.00	250.00
	1862	.068	60.00	90.00	140.00	225.00
	1863	.058	60.00	80.00	120.00	225.00
	1864	.099	75.00	120.00	180.00	275.00
	1865	.081	60.00	100.00	160.00	250.00

Mint mark: E

KM#	Date	Mintage	Fine	VF	XF	Unc
568.3 (Y23.3)	1860	—	100.00	140.00	200.00	325.00
	1861	—	90.00	120.00	200.00	325.00
	1862	—	60.00	100.00	160.00	225.00
	1863	—	60.00	80.00	120.00	225.00
	1864	—	60.00	100.00	160.00	250.00
	1865	—	60.00	100.00	160.00	250.00

Mint mark: V

KM#	Date	Mintage	Fine	VF	XF	Unc
568.4 (Y23.4)	1860	—	250.00	400.00	800.00	1200.
	1861	—	325.00	800.00	1750.	2500.
	1862	—	200.00	400.00	800.00	1200.
	1863	—	175.00	375.00	600.00	1000.
	1864	—	275.00	800.00	1750.	2500.
	1865	—	250.00	475.00	800.00	1200.

Mint mark: A
Obv: Head of Franz Joseph I right w/heavier side whiskers.

KM#	Date	Mintage	Fine	VF	XF	Unc
578.1 (Y23a.1)	1866	—	75.00	115.00	200.00	350.00

Mint mark: B

KM#	Date	Mintage	Fine	VF	XF	Unc
578.2 (Y23a.2)	1866	.076	75.00	140.00	225.00	400.00

Mint mark: E

KM#	Date	Mintage	Fine	VF	XF	Unc
578.3 (Y23a.3)	1866	—	75.00	115.00	200.00	350.00

Mint mark: V

KM#	Date	Mintage	Fine	VF	XF	Unc
578.4 (Y23a.4)	1866	—	275.00	575.00	1100.	1700.

Mint mark: A

KM#	Date	Mintage	Fine	VF	XF	Unc
585.1 (Y23b.1)	1867	—	60.00	90.00	130.00	180.00
	1868	—	60.00	90.00	130.00	180.00
	1869	—	60.00	90.00	130.00	180.00
	1870	—	60.00	90.00	130.00	180.00
	1871	—	60.00	90.00	130.00	180.00
	1872	—	60.00	90.00	130.00	180.00

Mint mark: B

KM#	Date	Mintage	Fine	VF	XF	Unc
585.2 (Y23b.2)	1867	.112	60.00	100.00	140.00	200.00

Mint mark: E

KM#	Date	Mintage	Fine	VF	XF	Unc
585.3 (Y23b.3)	1867	—	70.00	110.00	160.00	225.00

Mint: Vienna - w/o mint mark.

KM#	Date	Mintage	Fine	VF	XF	Unc
595 (Y23c)	1872	.460	60.00	100.00	125.00	175.00
	1873	.516	60.00	100.00	125.00	175.00
	1874	.353	60.00	100.00	125.00	175.00
	1875	.184	60.00	100.00	125.00	175.00
	1876	.680	60.00	80.00	125.00	150.00
	1877	.823	60.00	80.00	125.00	175.00
	1878	.281	60.00	80.00	125.00	175.00
	1879	.362	60.00	80.00	125.00	175.00
	1880	.341	60.00	100.00	150.00	225.00

KM#	Date	Mintage	Fine	VF	XF	Unc
(Y23c)	1881	.477	60.00	80.00	125.00	175.00
	1882	.390	60.00	100.00	125.00	175.00
	1883	.409	60.00	100.00	125.00	175.00
	1884	.238	60.00	80.00	125.00	175.00
	1885	.257	60.00	80.00	125.00	150.00
	1886	.291	60.00	80.00	125.00	150.00
	1887	.223	60.00	80.00	100.00	150.00
	1888	.309	60.00	80.00	100.00	150.00
	1889	.335	60.00	80.00	100.00	150.00
	1890	.374	60.00	80.00	100.00	150.00
	1891	.325	60.00	80.00	100.00	150.00
	1892	.361	60.00	80.00	100.00	150.00
	1893	.285	60.00	80.00	100.00	150.00
	1894	.293	60.00	80.00	100.00	150.00
	1895	.330	60.00	80.00	100.00	150.00
	1896	.414	60.00	80.00	100.00	150.00
	1897	.256	60.00	80.00	100.00	150.00
	1898	.350	60.00	80.00	100.00	150.00
	1899	.412	60.00	80.00	100.00	150.00
	1900	.356	60.00	100.00	125.00	175.00
	1901	.349	60.00	100.00	125.00	175.00
	1902	.311	60.00	100.00	125.00	175.00
	1903	.380	60.00	100.00	125.00	175.00
	1904	.517	60.00	100.00	125.00	175.00
	1905	.392	60.00	125.00	150.00	200.00
	1906	.492	60.00	125.00	150.00	200.00
	1907	.554	60.00	125.00	175.00	250.00
	1908	.409	60.00	80.00	125.00	175.00
	1909	.366	60.00	80.00	100.00	150.00
	1910	.440	60.00	80.00	100.00	150.00
	1911	.591	60.00	80.00	100.00	125.00
	1912	.495	60.00	80.00	100.00	125.00
	1913	.320	60.00	80.00	100.00	125.00
	1914	.378	60.00	80.00	100.00	125.00
	1915 (restrike)*		—	—		*BV + 10%*
	1951 (error for 1915)	—	75.00	125.00	150.00	225.00

NOTE: 996,721 pieces were struck from 1920-1936.

Mint mark: A
50th Jubilee
Rev: Second date below eagle.

KM#	Date	Mintage	Fine	VF	XF	Unc
538 (Y24)	1848/1898	.027	150.00	250.00	350.00	500.00
	1849/1898	2,292	500.00	1000.	1300.	1800.
	1850/1898	2,292	500.00	1000.	1300.	1800.
	1851/1898	2,292	500.00	1000.	1300.	1800.

8 FLORIN-20 FRANCS

6.4516 g, .900 GOLD, .1867 oz AGW
Mint: Vienna - w/o mint mark.

KM#	Date	Mintage	Fine	VF	XF	Unc
591 (Y22)	1870	.025	BV	100.00	175.00	250.00
	1871	.034	BV	100.00	150.00	200.00
	1872	5,185	100.00	175.00	275.00	375.00
	1873	.023	BV	100.00	175.00	250.00
	1874	.042	BV	100.00	150.00	200.00
	1875	.086	BV	100.00	150.00	200.00
	1876	.146	BV	100.00	150.00	200.00
	1877	.125	BV	100.00	150.00	200.00
	1878	.125	BV	100.00	150.00	200.00
	1879	.043	BV	100.00	175.00	250.00
	1880	.062	BV	100.00	150.00	200.00
	1881	.062	BV	100.00	150.00	200.00
	1882	.115	BV	100.00	150.00	200.00
	1883	.031	BV	100.00	150.00	200.00
	1884	.091	BV	100.00	150.00	200.00
	1885	.178	BV	100.00	150.00	200.00
	1886	.140	BV	100.00	150.00	200.00
	1887	.174	BV	100.00	150.00	200.00
	1888	.114	BV	100.00	150.00	200.00
	1889	.208	BV	100.00	150.00	175.00
	1890	.043	BV	100.00	150.00	200.00
	1891	.019	100.00	150.00	225.00	325.00
	1892	(restrike)	—	—	BV	110.00

2 DUCATS

7.0000 g, .986 GOLD, .2219 oz AGW
Mint mark: A
Obv: Head right. Rev: Crowned double-headed eagle.

KM#	Date	Mintage	Fine	VF	XF	Unc
444 (C164)	1803	—	—	—	Rare	—

Similar to 1 Ducat, KM#461.1.

KM#	Date	Mintage	Fine	VF	XF	Unc
449	1804	—	—	—	Rare	—

AUSTRIA 138

4 DUCATS

14.0000 g, .986 GOLD, .4438 oz AGW
Mint mark: A
Obv. leg: FRANCISCVS II. D. G. R. IMP. . . .
Rev. leg: . . . . .LOTH. M. D. HET.

KM#	Date	Mintage	Fine	VF	XF	Unc
440	1801	—	300.00	750.00	1800.	2500.
(C165)	1802	—	300.00	800.	2000.	3000.
	1803	—	300.00	750.00	1800.	2500.
	1804	—	300.00	750.00	1800.	2500.

Obv. leg: FRANCISCVS II. D. G. ROM. ET. . . .
Rev. leg: . . . . .D. LOTH. VEN. SAL.

KM#	Date	Mintage	Fine	VF	XF	Unc
462	1804	—	325.00	900.00	2200.	3000.
(C170)	1805	—	325.00	900.00	2200.	3000.
	1806	—	300.00	750.00	1800.	2500.

Obv. leg: . . . . .AVSTRIAE IMPERATOR.
Rev. leg: . . . . .D. LO. SAL. WIRC.

469	1807	—	350.00	1000.	2250.	3200.
(C187)	1808	—	325.00	900.00	2200.	3000.
	1809	—	300.00	750.00	1800.	2500.
	1810	—	350.00	1000.	2250.	3200.

Rev. leg: . . . . .LO: WI: ET IN. FR: DVX.

475	1811	—	300.00	750.00	1600.	2200.
(C187a)	1812	—	350.00	800.00	1800.	2500.
	1813	—	300.00	750.00	1600.	2200.
	1814	—	350.00	800.00	1800.	2500.
	1815	—	300.00	750.00	1600.	2200.

Rev. leg: . . . . .GAL. LOD. IL. REX. A. A.

KM#	Date	Mintage	Fine	VF	XF	Unc
487	1816	—	300.00	550.00	1500.	2500.
(C187b)	1817	—	300.00	550.00	1500.	2500.
	1818	—	325.00	675.00	1800.	2750.
	1819	—	300.00	550.00	1500.	2500.
	1820	—	300.00	550.00	1500.	2500.
	1821	—	300.00	550.00	1500.	2500.
	1822	—	300.00	550.00	1500.	2500.
	1823	—	300.00	550.00	1500.	2500.
	1824	—	300.00	550.00	1500.	2500.
	1825	—	250.00	500.00	1200.	2000.
	1826	—	300.00	550.00	1500.	2500.
	1827	—	300.00	550.00	1500.	2500.
	1828	—	250.00	500.00	1275.	2000.
	1829	—	250.00	500.00	1275.	2000.
	1830	—	250.00	500.00	1275.	2000.

13.9636 g, .986 GOLD, .4430 oz AGW

530.1	1835	—	—	—	Rare	—
(C195.1)	1837	—	250.00	400.00	1000.	2000.
	1838	—	250.00	400.00	1000.	2000.
	1839	—	250.00	400.00	1000.	2000.
	1840	—	250.00	400.00	1000.	2000.
	1841	—	250.00	400.00	1000.	2000.
	1842	—	250.00	400.00	1000.	2000.
	1843	—	250.00	400.00	1000.	2000.
	1844	—	250.00	400.00	1000.	2000.
	1845	—	250.00	400.00	1000.	2000.
	1846	—	250.00	400.00	1000.	2000.
	1847	—	250.00	400.00	1000.	2000.
	1848	4,411	250.00	400.00	1000.	2000.

Mint mark: E

530.2	1848	—	250.00	500.00	1250.	2500.
(C195.2)						

Mint mark: A

552.1	1852			No specimens known		

KM#	Date	Mintage	Fine	VF	XF	Unc
(C213.1)	1853	—	—	No specimens known		
	1854	—	250.00	500.00	1250.	2500.
	1855	—	250.00	500.00	1250.	2500.
	1856	—	250.00	500.00	1250.	2500.
	1857	—	250.00	400.00	1000.	2000.
	1858	—	250.00	400.00	1000.	2000.
	1859	.013	250.00	400.00	1000.	2000.

Obv: Laurel wreath w/o berries.

552.3	1854	—	350.00	850.00	1750.	2100.
	1855	—	—	—	Rare	—

Mint mark: V

552.2	1857	—	800.00	1600.	3000.	4000.
(C213.2)						

Mint mark: A

KM#	Date	Mintage	Fine	VF	XF	Unc
569.1	1860	6,303	250.00	600.00	1500.	2750.
(Y25.1)	1861	7,664	250.00	600.00	1500.	2750.
	1862	8,944	250.00	500.00	1250.	2250.
	1863	.022	250.00	400.00	1000.	2000.
	1864	.045	250.00	400.00	1000.	2000.
	1865	.013	250.00	400.00	1000.	2000.

Mint mark: V

569.2	1864	4,463	400.00	800.00	1750.	2750.
(Y25.2)	1865	.010	250.00	400.00	1000.	2000.

Mint mark: A
Obv: Laureate bust w/heavier side whiskers.

579	1866	8,463	250.00	500.00	1250.	2250.
(Y25a)						

586	1867	.016	250.00	400.00	1000.	2000.
(Y25b)	1868	.017	250.00	400.00	1000.	2000.
	1869	.019	250.00	400.00	1000.	2000.
	1870	.012	250.00	400.00	1000.	2000.
	1871	.019	250.00	400.00	1000.	2000.
	1872	*.012	250.00	400.00	1000.	2000.

Mint: Vienna - w/o mint mark.

598	1873	—	600.00	1200.	2500.	3500.
(Y-A18)	1873	—	—	—	Proof	7000.

AUSTRIA 139

Obv: Similar to KM#569.1, but w/o mint mark.

KM#	Date	Mintage	Fine	VF	XF	Unc
596	1872	*.012	250.00	525.00	725.00	1200.
(Y25c)	1873	.024	225.00	400.00	600.00	1000.
	1874	.015	225.00	325.00	600.00	1000.
	1875	.012	225.00	325.00	600.00	1000.
	1876	5,243	250.00	450.00	800.00	1300.
	1877	5,970	250.00	450.00	800.00	1300.
	1878	.023	225.00	325.00	550.00	800.00
	1879	.029	225.00	325.00	550.00	800.00
	1880	.023	225.00	325.00	550.00	800.00
	1881	.035	225.00	325.00	550.00	800.00
	1882	.029	225.00	325.00	550.00	800.00
	1883	.037	225.00	325.00	550.00	800.00
	1884	.035	225.00	325.00	550.00	800.00
	1885	.028	225.00	325.00	550.00	800.00
	1886	.018	225.00	300.00	525.00	800.00
	1887	.027	225.00	300.00	525.00	800.00
	1888	.036	225.00	300.00	525.00	800.00
	1889	.031	225.00	300.00	525.00	800.00
	1890	.047	225.00	300.00	525.00	750.00
	1891	.054	225.00	300.00	525.00	750.00
	1892	.058	225.00	300.00	525.00	750.00
	1893	.054	225.00	275.00	550.00	800.00
	1894	.035	225.00	275.00	550.00	800.00
	1895	.040	225.00	275.00	550.00	800.00
	1896	.049	225.00	250.00	500.00	800.00
	1897	.035	225.00	275.00	550.00	800.00
	1898	.054	225.00	250.00	500.00	800.00
	1899	.054	225.00	250.00	500.00	600.00
	1900	.047	225.00	250.00	500.00	600.00
	1901	.052	225.00	250.00	450.00	600.00
	1902	.069	225.00	250.00	400.00	600.00
	1903	.073	225.00	250.00	400.00	600.00
	1904	.080	225.00	250.00	400.00	600.00
	1905	.091	225.00	250.00	400.00	550.00
	1906	.123	225.00	250.00	300.00	450.00
	1907	.104	225.00	250.00	300.00	500.00
	1908	.080	225.00	250.00	450.00	600.00
	1909	.084	225.00	250.00	375.00	500.00
	1910	.101	225.00	250.00	275.00	400.00
	1911	.142	225.00	250.00	275.00	350.00
	1912	.151	225.00	250.00	275.00	350.00
	1913	.119	225.00	250.00	275.00	350.00
	1914	.102	225.00	250.00	275.00	350.00
	1915 (restrike)*		—	—		*BV + 8%*

NOTE: 496,501 pieces were struck from 1920-1936.

REPUBLIC

MONETARY SYSTEM

10,000 Kronen = 1 Schilling

20 KRONEN

6.7751 g, .900 GOLD, .1960 oz AGW

KM#	Date	Mintage	Fine	VF	XF	Unc
640	1923	6,988	700.00	1500.	2000.	2500.
(Y80)	1924	10,337	700.00	1500.	2000.	2500.

100 KRONEN

33.8753 g, .900 GOLD, .9802 oz AGW

KM#	Date	Mintage	Fine	VF	XF	Unc
641	1923	617 pcs.	750.00	1250.	2000.	2500.
(Y81)	1923	—	—	—	Proof	2750.
	1924	2,851	750.00	1250.	2000.	2500.

BRONZE

KM#	Date	Mintage	Fine	VF	XF	Unc
642	1923	6.404	4.00	8.00	15.00	30.00
(Y56)	1924	43.014	.25	.50	1.50	4.00

200 KRONEN

BRONZE

KM#	Date	Mintage	Fine	VF	XF	Unc
643	1924	57.160	.50	1.00	2.00	6.00
(Y57)						

1000 KRONEN

COPPER-NICKEL

KM#	Date	Mintage	Fine	VF	XF	Unc
644	1924	72.353	.75	1.50	3.00	7.50
(Y58)						

PRE WWII DECIMAL COINAGE

100 Groschen = 1 Schilling

GROSCHEN

BRONZE

KM#	Date	Mintage	Fine	VF	XF	Unc
645	1925	30.465	.10	.20	.50	2.00
(646)	1926	15.487	.10	.30	.75	2.00
	1927	9.318	.10	.30	.75	2.50
	1928	17.189	.10	.30	.75	2.50
	1929	11.400	.10	.30	.75	2.50
	1930	8.893	.10	.30	.75	2.50
	1931	.971	10.00	20.00	30.00	60.00
	1932	3.040	1.00	2.50	5.00	7.50
	1933	3.940	.50	1.00	2.00	6.00
	1934	4.232	.15	.50	1.00	4.00
	1935	3.740	.15	.50	1.00	4.00
	1936	6.020	.50	1.00	3.00	9.00
	1937	5.830	.50	1.00	2.00	7.50
	1938	1.650	2.00	3.00	6.00	15.00

2 GROSCHEN

BRONZE

KM#	Date	Mintage	Fine	VF	XF	Unc
647	1925	29.892	.10	.25	.50	1.50
(Y61)	1926	17.700	.10	.30	.75	2.00
	1927	7.757	.20	.75	2.00	5.00
	1928	19.478	.10	.30	.75	2.00
	1929	16.184	.10	.30	.75	2.00
	1930	5.709	.20	.60	1.50	4.00
	1934	.812	7.00	12.00	15.00	25.00
	1935	3.148	.20	.60	1.50	4.00
	1936	4.410	.15	.30	1.00	3.00
	1937	3.790	.20	.40	1.25	3.50
	1938	.860	2.50	4.00	6.50	12.50

5 GROSCHEN

COPPER-NICKEL

KM#	Date	Mintage	Fine	VF	XF	Unc
656	1931	16.631	.15	.40	.80	2.00
(Y62)	1932	4.700	.25	1.00	2.00	5.00
	1934	3.210	.30	1.00	2.50	6.00
	1936	1.240	2.00	4.00	7.50	15.00
	1937	1.540	20.00	30.00	45.00	80.00
	1938	.870	125.00	175.00	250.00	425.00

10 GROSCHEN

COPPER-NICKEL

KM#	Date	Mintage	Fine	VF	XF	Unc
648	1925	66.199	.10	.25	.50	3.00
(Y63)	1928	11.468	.50	1.00	4.00	12.00
	1929	12.000	.40	.75	1.50	4.00

1/2 SCHILLING

3.0000 g, .640 SILVER, .0617 oz ASW

KM#	Date	Mintage	Fine	VF	XF	Unc
649	1925	18.370	1.00	2.00	3.00	7.50
(Y67)	1926	12.943	2.50	4.00	6.00	11.00

50 GROSCHEN

COPPER-NICKEL

KM#	Date	Mintage	Fine	VF	XF	Unc
660	1934	8.225	20.00	35.00	50.00	90.00
(Y64)	1934	Inc. Ab.	—	—	Proof	125.00

KM#	Date	Mintage	Fine	VF	XF	Unc
664	1935	11.435	.50	.75	1.50	3.00
(Y65)	1935	Inc. Ab.	—	—	Proof	80.00
	1936	1.000	30.00	40.00	60.00	115.00
	1936	Inc. Ab.	—	—	Proof	140.00

SCHILLING

7.0000 g, .800 SILVER, .1800 oz ASW

KM#	Date	Mintage	Fine	VF	XF	Unc
645	1924	11.086	1.25	2.00	3.00	7.00
(Y59)						

6.0000 g, .640 SILVER, .1235 oz ASW

KM#	Date	Mintage	Fine	VF	XF	Unc
650	1925	38.209	1.25	2.00	3.00	6.00
(Y68)	1926	20.157	1.25	2.00	4.00	8.00
	1932	.700	30.00	40.00	60.00	100.00

COPPER-NICKEL

KM#	Date	Mintage	Fine	VF	XF	Unc
661	1934	30.641	.75	1.50	3.00	7.00
(Y66)	1934	—	—	—	Proof	150.00
	1935	11.987	3.00	6.00	12.50	30.00

AUSTRIA 140

2 SCHILLING

12.0000 g, .640 SILVER, .2469 oz ASW
Franz Schubert

KM#	Date	Mintage	Fine	VF	XF	Unc
653	1928	6.900	4.00	5.00	6.00	10.00
(Y69)	1928	Inc. Ab.	—	—	Proof	275.00

Dr. Theodor Billroth

654	1929	2.000	6.00	8.00	14.00	27.50
(Y70)						

von der Vogelweide

655	1930	.500	6.00	6.00	7.50	12.50
(Y71)	1930	Inc. Ab.	—	—	Proof	115.00

Mozart

657	1931	.500	8.00	14.00	18.00	27.50
(Y72)	1931	Inc. Ab.	—	—	Proof	200.00

Haydn

658	1932	.300	20.00	30.00	50.00	80.00
(Y73)	1932	Inc. Ab.	—	—	Proof	350.00

Dr. Seipel

659	1932	.400	10.00	15.00	25.00	45.00
(Y74)	1932	Inc. Ab.	—	—	Proof	300.00

Dr. Dollfuss

KM#	Date	Mintage	Fine	VF	XF	Unc
662	1934	1.500	7.00	11.00	16.00	27.50
(Y75)	1934	Inc. Ab.	—	—	Proof	190.00

Dr. Lueger

665	1935	.500	8.00	12.50	17.50	32.50
(Y76)	1935	Inc. Ab.	—	—	Proof	180.00

Prince Eugen

668	1936	.500	6.00	9.00	13.00	22.50
(Y77)	1936	Inc. Ab.	—	—	Proof	160.00

St. Charles Church

669	1937	.500	6.00	9.00	13.00	22.50
(Y78)	1937	Inc. Ab.	—	—	Proof	135.00

5 SCHILLING

15.0000 g, .835 SILVER, .4027 oz ASW
Madonna of Maria Zell

663	1934	3.066	12.50	20.00	25.00	45.00
(Y79)	1934	—	—	—	Proof	200.00
	1935	5.377	12.50	20.00	25.00	45.00
	1936	1.557	40.00	75.00	100.00	180.00

25 SCHILLING

5.8810 g, .900 GOLD, .1702 oz AGW

651	1926	.276	85.00	95.00	110.00	140.00
(Y82)	1927	.073	85.00	95.00	125.00	175.00
	1928	.134	85.00	95.00	110.00	140.00
	1929	.243	85.00	95.00	110.00	140.00
	1930	.130	85.00	95.00	110.00	140.00
	1931	.169	85.00	95.00	110.00	140.00

KM#	Date	Mintage	Fine	VF	XF	Unc
(Y82)	1933	4,944	—	—	1300.	1750.
	1934	.011	—	—	450.00	575.00

St. Leopold

666	1935	2,880	—	—	500.00	600.00
(Y84)	1936	7,260	—	—	450.00	550.00
	1937	7,660	—	—	450.00	550.00
	1938	1,360	—	—	11,000.	15,000.

100 SCHILLING

23.5245 g, .900 GOLD, .6806 oz AGW

652	1926	.064	—	—	375.00	500.00
(Y83)	1927	.069	—	—	375.00	500.00
	1928	.040	—	—	375.00	500.00
	1929	.075	—	—	375.00	500.00
	1930	.025	—	—	375.00	500.00
	1931	.102	—	—	375.00	500.00
	1933	4,700	—	—	800.00	1200.
	1934	9,383	—	—	375.00	525.00

Madonna of Maria Zell

667	1935	951 pcs.	—	—	1750.	2500.
(Y85)	1936	.012	—	—	900.00	1400.
	1937	2,900	—	—	1000.	1500.
	1938	1,400	—	—	8000.	12,000.

GERMAN OCCUPATION
1938-1945
MONETARY SYSTEM
150 Schillings = 100 Reichsmark
NOTE: During this time period German Reichsmark coins and banknotes circulated.

POST WWII DECIMAL COINAGE
100 Groschen = 1 Schilling

GROSCHEN

ZINC

673	1947	23.574	—	.10	.25	1.00
(Y86)						

2 GROSCHEN

AUSTRIA

2 GROSCHEN

ALUMINUM

KM#	Date	Mintage	VF	XF	Unc
676	1950	21.600	.10	.25	.50
(Y89)	1950	—	—	Proof	15.00
	1951	7.370	.20	.50	1.00
	1951	—	—	Proof	30.00
	1952	37.800	.10	.25	.50
	1952	—	—	Proof	15.00
	1954	20.000	.10	.25	.50
	1954	—	—	Proof	30.00
	1957	21.300	.10	.25	.50
	1957	—	—	Proof	30.00
	1962	5.430	.15	.25	.50
	1962	—	—	Proof	17.50
	1964	.173	—	Proof	3.00
	1965	14.475	.10	.15	.25
	1965	—	—	Proof	2.00
	1966	7.454	.10	.15	.25
	1966	—	—	Proof	4.00
	1967	.013	—	Proof	50.00
	1968	1.803	.10	.15	.25
	1968	.022	—	Proof	.75
	1969	.057	—	Proof	.75
	1970	.260	—	Proof	.50
	1971	.145	—	Proof	.50
	1972	2.763	—	.10	.20
	1972	.132	—	Proof	.50
	1973	5.883	—	.10	.20
	1973	.149	—	Proof	.50
	1974	1.387	—	.10	.20
	1974	.093	—	Proof	.50
	1975	1.394	—	.10	.20
	1975	.052	—	Proof	.50
	1976	3.309	—	—	.10
	1976	.045	—	Proof	.50
	1977	3.674	—	—	.10
	1977	.047	—	Proof	.50
	1978	1.560	—	—	.10
	1978	—	—	Proof	.50
	1979	2.473	—	—	.10
	1979	—	—	Proof	.50
	1980	1.861	—	—	.10
	1980	.048	—	Proof	.50
	1981	.981	—	—	.10
	1981	.049	—	Proof	.50
	1982	3.967	—	—	.10
	1982	.050	—	Proof	.50
	1983	2.665	—	—	.10
	1983	.065	—	Proof	.50
	1984	.564	—	—	.10
	1984	—	—	Proof	.50
	1985	—	—	—	.10
	1985	—	—	Proof	.50
	1986	—	—	—	.10
	1986	—	—	Proof	.50
	1987	—	—	—	.10
	1987	—	—	Proof	.50
	1988	—	—	—	.10
	1988	—	—	Proof	.50

5 GROSCHEN

ZINC

KM#	Date	Mintage	VF	XF	Unc
675	1948	17.200	.15	.50	1.25
(Y87)	1950	19.400	.15	.50	1.25
	1950	—	—	Proof	10.00
	1951	12.400	.15	.50	1.25
	1951	—	—	Proof	10.00
	1953	84.900	.10	.50	1.00
	1955	17.000	.10	.50	1.00
	1957	20.700	.10	.50	1.00
	1957	—	—	Proof	20.00
	1961	3.420	.15	.75	1.50
	1961	—	—	Proof	15.00
	1962	5.990	.15	.50	1.50
	1963	13.295	.10	.25	1.00
	1963	—	—	Proof	10.00
	1964	4.659	.10	.25	1.00
	1964	—	—	Proof	.50
	1965	13.704	.10	.15	.25
	1965	—	—	Proof	.50
	1966	9.348	.10	.15	.25
	1966	—	—	Proof	3.00
	1967	4.404	.10	.15	.25
	1967	—	—	Proof	3.00
	1968	31.422	—	.10	.15
	1968	.016	—	Proof	2.00
	1969	—	—	.10	.25
	1969	.040	—	Proof	2.00
	1970	—	—	.10	.25
	1970	.144	—	Proof	.50
	1971	—	—	.10	.25
	1971	.125	—	Proof	.50
	1972	10.879	—	—	.10
	1972	.116	—	Proof	.50
	1973	10.336	—	—	.10
	1973	.120	—	Proof	.50
	1974	2.911	—	—	.10
	1974	.087	—	Proof	.50
	1975	7.559	—	—	.10
	1975	.051	—	Proof	.50
	1976	12.230	—	—	.10
	1976	.045	—	Proof	.50
	1977	3.200	—	—	.10

KM#	Date	Mintage	VF	XF	Unc
(Y87)	1977	.045	—	Proof	.50
	1978	2.690	—	—	.10
	1978	—	—	Proof	.50
	1979	4.966	—	—	.10
	1979	—	—	Proof	.50
	1980	3.068	—	—	.10
	1980	.048	—	Proof	.50
	1981	.481	—	—	.10
	1981	.049	—	Proof	.50
	1982	3.967	—	—	.10
	1982	.050	—	Proof	.50
	1983	.501	—	—	.10
	1983	.065	—	Proof	.50
	1984	1.052	—	—	.10
	1984	—	—	Proof	.50
	1985	—	—	—	.10
	1985	—	—	Proof	.50
	1986	—	—	—	.10
	1986	—	—	Proof	.50
	1987	—	—	—	.10
	1987	—	—	Proof	.50
	1988	—	—	—	.10
	1988	—	—	Proof	.50

10 GROSCHEN

ZINC

KM#	Date	Mintage	Fine	VF	XF	Unc
674	1947	6.840	.50	1.50	3.00	10.00
(Y88)	1947	—	—	—	Proof	20.00
	1948	66.200	—	.10	.50	3.00
	1948	—	—	—	Proof	30.00
	1949	51.200	—	.10	.50	3.00
	1949	—	—	—	Proof	35.00

ALUMINUM

KM#	Date	Mintage	VF	XF	Unc
678	1951	9.570	.20	.50	2.25
(Y90)	1951	—	—	Proof	75.00
	1952	45.900	.10	.25	1.00
	1952	—	—	Proof	20.00
	1953	39.000	.10	.25	1.00
	1953	—	—	Proof	75.00
	1955	27.500	.10	.25	1.00
	1955	—	—	Proof	15.00
	1957	33.500	.10	.20	1.00
	1957	—	—	Proof	50.00
	1959	80.700	.10	.20	.75
	1959	—	—	Proof	30.00
	1961	11.100	.10	.25	.75
	1961	—	—	Proof	—
	1962	24.600	.10	.20	.75
	1962	—	—	Proof	25.00
	1963	38.062	.10	.20	.60
	1963	—	—	Proof	10.00
	1964	34.928	.10	.20	.45
	1964	—	—	Proof	.50
	1965	40.615	.10	.20	.40
	1965	—	—	Proof	.50
	1966	24.991	.10	.15	.35
	1966	—	—	Proof	3.00
	1967	32.553	—	.15	.30
	1967	—	—	Proof	2.00
	1968	42.396	—	.10	.25
	1968	.016	—	Proof	2.00
	1969	19.953	—	.10	.25
	1969	.027	—	Proof	.75
	1970	36.998	—	.10	.25
	1970	.102	—	Proof	.50
	1971	57.450	—	.10	.25
	1971	.082	—	Proof	.50
	1972	75.661	—	.10	.25
	1972	.081	—	Proof	.50
	1973	60.244	—	.10	.25
	1973	.097	—	Proof	.50
	1974	55.924	—	.10	.15
	1974	.078	—	Proof	.50
	1975	70.196	—	.10	.15
	1975	.049	—	Proof	.50
	1976	42.379	—	.10	.15
	1976	.044	—	Proof	.50
	1977	107.264	—	.10	.15
	1977	.044	—	Proof	.50
	1978	57.890	—	.10	.15
	1978	—	—	Proof	.50
	1979	103.724	—	—	.15
	1979	—	—	Proof	.50
	1980	79.816	—	—	.15
	1980	.048	—	Proof	.50
	1981	92.299	—	—	.15
	1981	.049	—	Proof	.50
	1982	99.967	—	—	.15
	1982	.050	—	Proof	.50

KM#	Date	Mintage	VF	XF	Unc
(Y90)	1983	93.768	—	—	.15
	1983	.065	—	Proof	.50
	1984	86.667	—	—	.15
	1984	—	—	Proof	.50
	1985	—	—	—	.15
	1985	—	—	Proof	.50
	1986	—	—	—	.15
	1986	—	—	Proof	.50
	1987	—	—	—	.15
	1987	—	—	Proof	.50
	1988	—	—	—	.15
	1988	—	—	Proof	.50

20 GROSCHEN

ALUMINUM-BRONZE

KM#	Date	Mintage	Fine	VF	XF	Unc
677	1950	1.610	.10	.25	.50	6.50
(Y95)	1950	—	—	—	Proof	25.00
	1951	7.780	.10	.25	.50	2.00
	1951	—	—	—	Proof	25.00
	1954	5.340	.10	.25	.50	2.00
	1954	—	—	—	Proof	100.00

50 GROSCHEN

ALUMINUM

KM#	Date	Mintage	VF	XF	Unc
670	1946	13.000	.10	.25	.50	1.75
(Y91)	1946	—	—	—	Proof	60.00
	1947	26.900	.10	.25	.50	1.25
	1947	—	—	—	Proof	20.00
	1952	7.450	.40	1.00	2.00	5.00
	1952	—	—	—	Proof	35.00
	1955	10.500	.20	.40	.75	3.50
	1955	—	—	—	Proof	30.00

ALUMINUM-BRONZE

KM#	Date	Mintage	VF	XF	Unc
685	1959	14.100	.10	.20	.50
(Y103)	1959	—	—	Proof	15.00
	1960	22.400	.10	.20	.50
	1960	—	—	Proof	35.00
	1961	19.800	.10	.20	.50
	1961	—	—	Proof	30.00
	1962	10.000	.10	.25	.75
	1962	—	—	Proof	30.00
	1963	9.483	.10	.15	.50
	1963	—	—	Proof	15.00
	1964	5.331	.10	.25	.75
	1964	—	—	Proof	.75
	1965	15.007	—	.15	.40
	1965	—	—	Proof	1.00
	1966	7.322	.10	.15	.40
	1966	—	—	Proof	5.00
	1967	8.237	.10	.10	.40
	1967	—	—	Proof	7.00
	1968	7.742	—	.10	.25
	1968	.015	—	Proof	3.00
	1969	7.076	—	.10	.25
	1969	.026	—	Proof	1.00
	1970	2.994	—	.10	.20
	1970	.129	—	Proof	.50
	1971	14.217	—	.10	.15
	1971	.084	—	Proof	.50
	1972	17.367	—	.10	.15
	1972	.080	—	Proof	.50
	1973	17.902	—	.10	.15
	1973	.090	—	Proof	.50
	1974	15.852	—	.10	.15
	1974	.076	—	Proof	.50
	1975	9.916	—	.10	.15
	1975	.049	—	Proof	.50
	1976	12.396	—	.10	.15
	1976	.044	—	Proof	.50
	1977	14.516	—	.10	.15
	1977	.044	—	Proof	.50
	1978	12.440	—	.10	.15
	1978	—	—	Proof	.50
	1979	16.389	—	—	.15
	1979	—	—	Proof	.50
	1980	29.852	—	—	.15
	1980	.048	—	Proof	.50
	1981	13.024	—	—	.15
	1981	.049	—	Proof	.50

AUSTRIA

KM#	Date	Mintage	VF	XF	Unc
(Y103)	1982	9.967	—	—	.15
	1982	.050	—	Proof	.50
	1983	15.182	—	—	.15
	1983	.065	—	Proof	.50
	1984	20.806	—	—	.15
	1984	—	—	Proof	.50
	1985	—	—	—	.15
	1985	—	—	Proof	.50
	1986	—	—	—	.15
	1986	—	—	Proof	.50
	1987	—	—	—	.15
	1987	—	—	Proof	.50
	1988	—	—	—	.15
	1988	—	—	Proof	.50

SCHILLING

ALUMINUM

KM#	Date	Mintage	Fine	VF	XF	Unc
671	1946	27.300	.20	.35	.50	1.50
(Y92)	1946	—	—	—	Proof	135.00
	1947	35.800	.20	.35	.50	1.50
	1947	—	—	—	Proof	25.00
	1952	23.300	.25	.50	.75	2.50
	1952	—	—	—	Proof	50.00
	1957	28.600	.25	.50	.75	3.00
	1957	—	—	—	Proof	90.00

ALUMINUM-BRONZE

KM#	Date	Mintage	VF	XF	Unc
686	1959	46.700	.15	.25	.75
(Y104)	1959	—	—	Proof	10.00
	1960	46.100	.15	.25	.75
	1960	—	—	Proof	25.00
	1961	51.100	.15	.25	.75
	1961	—	—	Proof	20.00
	1962	9.300	.20	.35	1.00
	1962	—	—	Proof	25.00
	1963	24.845	.15	.25	.75
	1963	—	—	Proof	20.00
	1964	11.709	.20	.35	1.00
	1964	—	—	Proof	1.50
	1965	23.925	.15	.20	.40
	1965	—	—	Proof	1.50
	1966	18.688	.15	.20	.75
	1966	—	—	Proof	7.00
	1967	22.214	.10	.15	.40
	1967	—	—	Proof	9.00
	1968	30.860	.10	.15	.35
	1968	.017	—	Proof	5.00
	1969	10.285	.10	.15	.35
	1969	.028	—	Proof	3.00
	1970	10.679	.10	.15	.25
	1970	.100	—	Proof	1.00
	1971	27.974	.10	.15	.20
	1971	.082	—	Proof	.75
	1972	54.577	.10	.15	.20
	1972	.078	—	Proof	.75
	1973	41.332	.10	.15	.20
	1973	.090	—	Proof	.75
	1974	43.712	.10	.15	.20
	1974	.077	—	Proof	.75
	1975	18.564	.10	.15	.20
	1975	.049	—	Proof	.75
	1976	37.642	.10	.15	.20
	1976	.044	—	Proof	.75
	1977	39.172	.10	.15	.20
	1977	.044	—	Proof	.75
	1978	35.665	—	.10	.20
	1978	—	—	Proof	.75
	1979	64.840	—	.10	.20
	1979	—	—	Proof	.75
	1980	49.823	—	.10	.20
	1980	.048	—	Proof	2.50
	1981	37.533	—	.10	.20
	1981	.049	—	Proof	1.50
	1982	29.967	—	—	.20
	1982	.050	—	Proof	.75
	1983	38.186	—	—	.20
	1983	.065	—	Proof	.75
	1984	31.995	—	—	.20
	1984	—	—	Proof	.75
	1985	—	—	—	.20
	1985	—	—	Proof	.75
	1986	—	—	—	.20
	1986	—	—	Proof	.75
	1987	—	—	—	.20
	1987	—	—	Proof	.75
	1988	—	—	—	.20
	1988	—	—	Proof	1.50

2 SCHILLING

ALUMINUM

KM#	Date	Mintage	Fine	VF	XF	Unc
672	1946	10.082	.35	.75	1.00	5.00
(Y93)	1946	—	—	—	Proof	100.00
	1947	20.140	.35	.75	1.00	4.50
	1947	—	—	—	Proof	35.00
	1952	.149	55.00	80.00	135.00	215.00
	1952	—	—	—	Proof	600.00

5 SCHILLING

ALUMINUM

KM#	Date	Mintage	Fine	VF	XF	Unc
679	1952	29.873	.75	1.25	2.00	7.50
(Y94)	1952	—	—	—	Proof	50.00
	1957	.240	65.00	125.00	200.00	300.00
	1957	—	—	—	Proof	400.00

5.2000 g, .640 SILVER, .1070 oz ASW
Reeded edge

KM#	Date	Mintage	VF	XF	Unc
689	1960	12.618	—	BV	2.50 5.00
(Y106)	1960	1.000	—	—	Proof 55.00
	1961	17.902	—	BV	2.50 4.00
	1961	—	—	—	Proof 25.00
	1962	6.771	—	BV	2.50 4.00
	1962	—	—	—	Proof 20.00
	1963	1.811	BV	2.00	4.00 7.50
	1963	—	—	—	Proof 80.00
	1964	4.030	—	BV	2.25 4.00
	1964	—	—	—	Proof 4.00
	1965	4.759	—	BV	2.25 4.00
	1965	—	—	—	Proof 4.00
	1966	4.481	—	BV	2.25 4.00
	1966	—	—	—	Proof 6.00
	1967	1.900	BV	2.00	4.00 5.00
	1967	—	—	—	Proof 7.50
	1968	4.792	—	BV	2.25 4.00
	1968	.020	—	—	Proof 6.50

COPPER-NICKEL
Plain edge

KM#	Date	Mintage	VF	XF	Unc
689a	1968	2.075	.60	.75	2.00
(Y106a)	1969	41.222	—	.40	.75
	1969	.021	—	Proof	3.00
	1970	15.771	—	.40	.75
	1970	.092	—	Proof	2.00
	1971	21.422	—	.40	.75
	1971	.084	—	Proof	2.00
	1972	5.430	—	.40	.75
	1972	.075	—	Proof	2.00
	1973	8.259	—	.40	.50
	1973	.087	—	Proof	1.00
	1974	17.973	—	.40	.50
	1974	.076	—	Proof	1.00
	1975	6.898	—	.40	.50
	1975	.049	—	Proof	1.00
	1976	1.949	—	.40	.50
	1976	.044	—	Proof	1.00
	1977	12.846	—	.40	.50
	1977	.044	—	Proof	1.00
	1978	9.940	—	.40	.50
	1978	—	—	Proof	1.00
	1979	11.645	—	.40	.50
	1979	—	—	Proof	1.00
	1980	14.866	—	.40	.50
	1980	.048	—	Proof	3.00
	1981	13.868	—	.40	.50
	1981	.049	—	Proof	2.00
	1982	4.967	—	.40	.50
	1982	.050	—	Proof	1.00
	1983	9.268	—	.40	.50
	1983	.065	—	Proof	1.00
	1984	13.827	—	.40	.50
	1984	—	—	Proof	1.00

KM#	Date	Mintage	VF	XF	Unc
(Y106a)	1985	—	—	.40	.50
	1985	—	—	Proof	1.00
	1986	—	—	—	.50
	1986	—	—	Proof	1.00
	1987	—	—	—	.50
	1987	—	—	Proof	1.00
	1988	—	—	—	.50
	1988	—	—	Proof	2.00

10 SCHILLING

7.5000 g, .640 SILVER, .1543 oz ASW

KM#	Date	Mintage	Fine	VF	XF	Unc
682	1957	15.636	—	BV	2.50	6.00
(Y99)	1957	—	—	—	Proof	60.00
	1958	27.280	—	BV	2.50	8.00
	1958	—	—	—	Proof	315.00
	1959	4.740	—	BV	2.50	9.00
	1959	—	—	—	Proof	30.00
	1964	.187	7.00	10.00	15.00	25.00
	1964	.027	—	—	Proof	8.00
	1965	1.721	—	BV	2.50	5.00
	1965	—	—	—	Proof	4.00
	1966	3.392	—	BV	2.50	4.00
	1966	—	—	—	Proof	7.50
	1967	1.394	—	BV	2.50	4.00
	1967	—	—	—	Proof	8.00
	1968	1.525	—	BV	2.50	4.00
	1968	.015	—	—	Proof	7.00
	1969	1.200	—	BV	2.50	4.00
	1969	—	—	—	Proof	7.00
	1970	4.600	—	BV	2.50	4.00
	1970	—	—	—	Proof	5.00
	1971	7.100	—	BV	2.50	4.00
	1971	—	—	—	Proof	5.00
	1972	14.300	—	BV	2.50	4.00
	1972	—	—	—	Proof	5.00
	1973	14.600	—	BV	2.50	4.00
	1973	—	—	—	Proof	5.00

COPPER-NICKEL

KM#	Date	Mintage	VF	XF	Unc
718	1974	79.000	—	.80	1.50
(Y-A99)	1974	—	—	Proof	3.50
	1975	16.941	—	.80	1.50
	1975	.049	—	Proof	2.50
	1976	15.970	—	.80	1.50
	1976	.044	—	Proof	2.50
	1977	7.652	—	.80	1.50
	1977	.044	—	Proof	2.50
	1978	6.846	—	.80	1.50
	1978	—	—	Proof	2.50
	1979	11.740	—	.80	1.00
	1979	—	—	Proof	2.50
	1980	10.852	—	.80	1.00
	1980	.048	—	Proof	4.50
	1981	8.021	—	.80	1.00
	1981	.049	—	Proof	4.00
	1982	4.967	—	.80	1.00
	1982	.050	—	Proof	2.50
	1983	8.993	—	.80	1.00
	1983	.065	—	Proof	2.50
	1984	8.000	—	.80	1.00
	1984	—	—	Proof	2.50
	1985	—	—	.80	1.00
	1985	—	—	Proof	2.50
	1986	—	—	—	1.00
	1986	—	—	Proof	2.50
	1987	—	—	—	1.00
	1987	—	—	Proof	2.50
	1988	—	—	—	1.00
	1988	—	—	Proof	4.50

20 SCHILLING

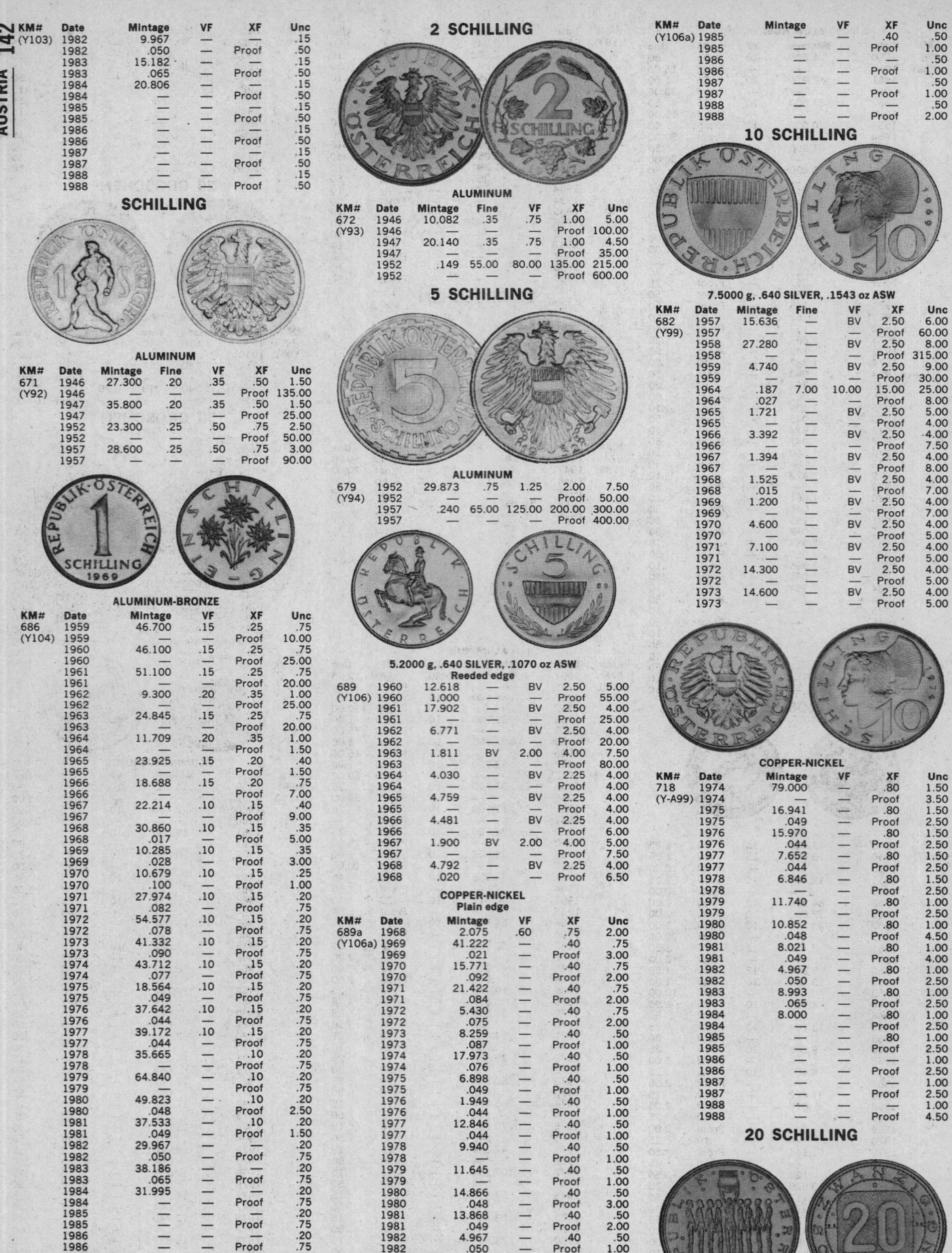

AUSTRIA 143

COPPER-ALUMINUM-NICKEL

KM#	Date	Mintage	VF	XF	Unc
746	1980	7.298	—	1.75	2.25
(Y165)	1980	.048	—	Proof	3.00
	1981	2.987	—	1.75	2.25
	1981	.049	—	Proof	3.00

Joseph Haydn
755	1982	3.107	—	1.75	2.25
(Y171)	1982	.050	—	Proof	3.00

Hochosterwitz Castle
760	1983	1.002	—	1.75	2.25
(Y175)	1983	.065	—	Proof	3.00

Grafenegg Palace
765	1984	12.667	—	1.75	2.25
(Y181)	1984	—	—	Proof	3.00

ALUMINUM-BRONZE
200th Anniversary of Diocese of Linz
770	1985	.400	—	1.75	2.25
(Y186)	1985	—	—	Proof	3.00

Georgenberger Treaty
775	1986	—	—	1.75	2.25
	1986	—	—	Proof	3.00

COPPER-ALUMINUM-NICKEL
Salzburg's Archbishop Thun
780	1987	—	—	—	2.50
	1987	—	—	Proof	3.00

25 SCHILLING

13.0000 g, .800 SILVER, .3344 oz ASW
Reopening of the National Theater in Vienna

KM#	Date	Mintage	Fine	VF	XF	Unc
680	1955	1.499	BV	7.50	10.00	20.00
(Y96)	1955	*5,000	—	—	Proof	60.00

Birth of Mozart Bicentennial
681	1956	4.999	—	BV	3.50	5.00
(Y97)	1956	*1,500	—	—	Proof	200.00

Maria Zell Cathedral
683	1957	4.999	—	BV	3.50	5.00
(Y98)	1957	*1,500	—	—	Proof	175.00

Birth of von Welsbach Centennial
684	1958	4.999	—	BV	3.50	5.00
(Y100)	1958	*500 pcs.	—	—	Proof	1300.

Death of Archduke Johann Centennial
687	1959	1.899	—	BV	3.50	5.00
(Y102)	1959	*1,000	—	—	Proof	200.00

40th Anniversary of Carinthian Plebescite
690	1960	1.599	—	BV	3.50	5.00
(Y105)	1960	*900 pcs.	—	—	Proof	200.00

40th Anniversary of Burgenland
KM#	Date	Mintage	Fine	VF	XF	Unc
691	1961	1.399	—	BV	3.50	5.00
(Y107)	1961	*1,200	—	—	Proof	175.00

Anton Bruckner
692	1962	2.399	—	BV	3.50	5.00
(Y108)	1962	*3,000	—	—	Proof	100.00

300th Anniversary of Birth of Prince Eugen
693	1963	1.994	—	BV	3.50	5.00
(Y109)	1963	5.931	—	—	Proof	75.00

Franz Grillparzer
695.1	1964	1.664	—	BV	3.50	5.00
(Y112)	1964	.036	—	—	Proof	5.00

9 shield obverse (error)
695.2	1964	3.660	—	—	Proof	250.00
(Y112a)						

Vienna Technical School Sesquicentennial
697	1965	1.563	—	BV	3.50	5.00
(Y113)	1965	.037	—	—	Proof	8.00

AUSTRIA 144

Ferdinand Raimund

KM#	Date	Mintage	Fine	VF	XF	Unc
699	1966	1.388	—	BV	3.50	5.00
(Y115)	1966	11.800	—	—	Proof	35.00

250th Anniversary of Birth of Maria Theresa

701	1967	2.472	—	BV	3.50	5.00
(Y117)	1967	.028	—	—	Proof	12.50

300th Anniversary of Birth of Von Hildebrandt

703	1968	1.258	—	BV	3.50	6.50	8.00
(Y119)	1968	.042	—	—	—	Proof	10.00

Peter Rosegger

705	1969	1.356	—	BV	3.50	5.00
(Y121)	1969	.044	—	—	Proof	10.00

Birth of Franz Lehar Centennial

707	1970	1.661	—	BV	3.50	5.00
(Y123)	1970	.139	—	—	Proof	6.00

200th Anniversary of Vienna Bourse

710	1971	1.804	—	BV	3.50	5.00
(Y126)	1971	.196	—	—	Proof	6.00

50th Anniversary of Death of Carl M. Ziehrer

KM#	Date	Mintage	Fine	VF	XF	Unc
712	1972	1.955	—	BV	3.50	5.00
(Y128)	1972	.145	—	—	Proof	6.00

Birth of Max Reinhardt Centennial

715	1973	2.323	—	BV	3.50	5.00
(Y131)	1973	.177	—	—	Proof	6.00

50 SCHILLING

20.0000 g, .900 SILVER, .5787 oz ASW
Andreas Hofer

KM#	Date	Mintage	VF	XF	Unc
688	1959	2.999	4.00	—	8.50
(Y101)	1959	*800 pcs.	—	Proof	375.00

600th Anniversary Union with Tirol

694	1963	2.994	4.00	5.00	6.50
(Y110)	1963	6.000	—	Proof	100.00

Winter Olympics

696	1964	2.832	4.00	5.00	6.50
(Y111)	1964	.068	—	Proof	10.00

600th Anniversary Vienna University

KM#	Date	Mintage	VF	XF	Unc
698	1965	2.163	4.00	5.00	6.50
(Y114)	1965	.037	—	Proof	8.00

National Bank Sesquicentennial

700	1966	1.782	4.00	5.00	6.50
(Y116)	1966	17.400	—	Proof	45.00

Blue Danube Waltz Centennial

702	1967	2.974	4.00	5.00	6.50
(Y118)	1967	.026	—	Proof	40.00

50th Anniversary Republic
Matte surface between pillars

704.1	1968	1.660	4.00	5.00	6.50
(Y120)	1968	.040	—	Proof	20.00

Proof surface between pillars

704.2	1968	—	—	Proof	75.00
(Y120v)					

450th Anniversary of Death of Maximilian I

706	1969	2.045	4.00	5.00	6.50
(Y122)	1969	.055	—	Proof	10.00

300th Anniversary of University of Innsbruck

708	1970	2.087	4.00	5.00	6.50
(Y124)	1970	.113	—	Proof	7.50

AUSTRIA 145

100 SCHILLING

Birth of Dr. Karl Renner Centennial

KM#	Date	Mintage	VF	XF	Unc
709	1970	2.214	4.00	5.00	6.50
(Y125)	1970	.286	—	Proof	7.50

80th Anniversary of Birth of Julius Raab

| 711 | 1971 | 2.317 | 4.00 | 5.00 | 6.50 |
| (Y127) | 1971 | .183 | — | Proof | 7.50 |

350th Anniversary Salzburg University

| 713 | 1972 | 2.863 | 4.00 | 5.00 | 6.50 |
| (Y129) | 1972 | .136 | — | Proof | 7.50 |

100th Anniversary Agricultural University

| 714 | 1972 | 1.891 | 4.00 | 5.00 | 6.50 |
| (Y130) | 1972 | .109 | — | Proof | 7.50 |

500th Anniversary of Bummerlhaus

| 716 | 1973 | 2.842 | 4.00 | 5.00 | 6.50 |
| (Y132) | 1973 | .158 | — | Proof | 7.50 |

Centennial Birth of Dr. Theodor Korner

| 717 | 1973 | 2.868 | 4.00 | 5.00 | 6.50 |
| (Y133) | 1973 | .132 | — | Proof | 7.50 |

20.0000 g, .640 SILVER, .4115 oz ASW
International Garden Exhibition

KM#	Date	Mintage	VF	XF	Unc
719	1974	2.279	—	4.00	5.00
(Y134)	1974	.221	—	Proof	6.50

125th Anniversary of Austrian Police Force

| 720 | 1974 | 2.259 | — | 4.00 | 5.00 |
| (Y135) | 1974 | .241 | — | Proof | 6.50 |

1200th Anniversary of Salzburg Cathedral

| 721 | 1974 | 2.293 | — | 4.00 | 5.00 |
| (Y136) | 1974 | .207 | — | Proof | 6.50 |

50th Year Austrian Broadcasting

| 722 | 1974 | 2.290 | — | 4.00 | 5.00 |
| (Y137) | 1974 | .210 | — | Proof | 6.50 |

150th Anniversary of Death of Schubert

| 737 | 1978 | 1.868 | — | 4.00 | 5.00 |
| (Y152) | 1978 | .132 | — | Proof | 6.50 |

23.9300 g, .640 SILVER, .4924 oz ASW
150th Anniversary of Birth of Johann Strauss

KM#	Date	Mintage	VF	XF	Unc
723	1975	2.646	—	—	8.00
(Y138)	1975	.209	—	Proof	9.00

20th Anniversary of State Treaty

| 724 | 1975 | 3.215 | — | — | 8.00 |
| (Y139) | 1975 | .225 | — | Proof | 9.00 |

50th Anniversary of Schilling

| 725 | 1975 | 3.234 | — | — | 8.00 |
| (Y140) | 1975 | .201 | — | Proof | 9.00 |

Winter Olympics I

| 726 | 1976 | 2.826 | — | — | 8.00 |
| (Y141) | 1976 | .374 | — | Proof | 9.00 |

Mint mark: Shield.
Winter Olympics II

| 727.1 | 1976 | 2.718 | — | — | 8.00 |
| (Y142.1) | 1976 | .232 | — | Proof | 9.00 |

Mint mark: Eagle.

| 727.2 | 1976 | 2.692 | — | — | 8.00 |
| (Y142.2) | 1976 | .223 | — | Proof | 9.00 |

AUSTRIA 146

Mint mark: Shield.
Winter Olympics III

KM#	Date	Mintage	VF	XF	Unc
728.1	1976	2.641	—	—	8.00
(Y143.1)	1976	.184	—	Proof	9.00

Mint mark: Eagle.

| 728.2 | 1976 | 2.636 | — | — | 8.00 |
| (Y143.2) | 1976 | .179 | — | Proof | 9.00 |

Mint mark: Shield.
Winter Olympics IV

| 729.1 | 1976 | 2.627 | — | — | 8.00 |
| (Y144.1) | 1976 | .188 | — | Proof | 9.00 |

Mint mark: Eagle.

| 729.2 | 1976 | 2.611 | — | — | 8.00 |
| (Y144.2) | 1976 | .179 | — | Proof | 9.00 |

Burgtheater Bicentennial

| 730 | 1976 | 1.630 | — | — | 8.00 |
| (Y145) | 1976 | .220 | — | Proof | 9.00 |

1000th Anniversary of Carinthia

| 731 | 1976 | 1.632 | — | — | 8.00 |
| (Y146) | 1976 | .168 | — | Proof | 9.00 |

Johann Nestroy

| 732 | 1976 | 1.761 | — | — | 8.00 |
| (Y147) | 1976 | .139 | — | Proof | 9.00 |

1200th Anniversary of Kremsmunster Monastery

KM#	Date	Mintage	VF	XF	Unc
734	1977	1.865	—	—	8.00
(Y149)	1977	.135	—	Proof	10.00

900th Anniversary of Hohensalzburg Fortress

| 735 | 1977 | 1.878 | — | — | 8.00 |
| (Y150) | 1977 | .122 | — | Proof | 10.00 |

500th Anniversary of Mint at Hall

| 736 | 1977 | 1.868 | — | — | 8.00 |
| (Y151) | 1977 | .132 | — | Proof | 15.00 |

700th Anniversary of Gmunden

| 738 | 1978 | 1.870 | — | — | 8.00 |
| (Y153) | 1978 | .130 | — | Proof | 9.00 |

700th Anniversary Battle of Durnkrut and Jedenspeigen

| 739 | 1978 | 1.677 | — | — | 8.00 |
| (Y154) | 1978 | .123 | — | Proof | 10.00 |

1100th Anniversary of Founding of Villach

KM#	Date	Mintage	VF	XF	Unc
740	1978	1.569	—	—	8.00
(Y155)	1978	.131	—	Proof	9.00

Opening of Arlberg Tunnel

| 741 | 1978 | 1.844 | — | — | 8.00 |
| (Y156) | 1978 | .156 | — | Proof | 9.00 |

Cathedral of Wiener Neustadt Centennial

| 742 | 1979 | 1.866 | — | — | 8.00 |
| (Y157) | 1979 | .134 | — | Proof | 9.00 |

200th Anniversary of Inn District

| 743 | 1979 | 1.870 | — | — | 8.00 |
| (Y158) | 1979 | .130 | — | Proof | 9.00 |

Vienna International Center

| 744 | 1979 | 1.855 | — | — | 8.00 |
| (Y159) | 1979 | .145 | — | Proof | 9.00 |

AUSTRIA 147

		Festival and Congress Hall at Bregenz						800th Anniversary of Verduner Altar						500 Years of Austrian Printing			
KM#	Date	Mintage	VF	XF	Unc	KM#	Date	Mintage	VF	XF	Unc	KM#	Date	Mintage	VF	XF	Unc
745	1979	1.573	—	—	8.00	751	1981	.950	—	—	40.00	757	1982	.632	—	—	40.00
(Y160)	1979	.161	—	Proof	9.00	(Y166)	1981	.200	—	Proof	45.00	(Y172)	1982	.118	—	Proof	45.00

500 SCHILLING

23.9600 g, .640 SILVER, .4930 oz ASW
Millenium of City of Steyr

								Anton Wildgans						825 Years of the Maria Zell Shrine			
747	1980	.888	—	—	41.00	752	1981	.983	—	—	40.00	758	1982	.632	—	—	40.00
(Y161)	1980	.111	—	Proof	50.00	(Y167)	1981	.167	—	Proof	45.00	(Y173)	1982	.118	—	Proof	45.00

		25th Anniversary of Austrian State Treaty						Otto Bauer						80th Birthday of Leopold Figl			
748	1980	.866	—	—	40.00	753	1981	.994	—	—	40.00	759	1982	.384	—	—	40.00
(Y162)	1980	.134	—	Proof	45.00	(Y168)	1981	.156	—	Proof	45.00	(Y174)	1982	.116	—	Proof	45.00

		Bicentennial of Death of Maria Theresa						200th Anniversary of Religious Tolerance				23.9600 g, .925 SILVER, .7125 oz ASW World Cup Horse Jumping Championship					
749	1980	.928	—	—	40.00	754	1981	.852	—	—	40.00	761	1983	.368	—	—	40.00
(Y163)	1980	.172	—	Proof	45.00	(Y169)	1981	.148	—	Proof	45.00	(Y176)	1983	.132	—	Proof	45.00

		Centennial of Austrian Red Cross						St. Severin						Vienna City Hall			
750	1980	.950	—	—	40.00	756	1982	.880	—	—	40.00	762	1983	.466	—	—	40.00
(Y164)	1980	.200	—	Proof	45.00	(Y170)	1982	.120	—	Proof	45.00	(Y177)	1983	.134	—	Proof	45.00

AUSTRIA 148

Catholic Day - Pope's Visit

KM#	Date	Mintage	VF	XF	Unc
763	1983	.660	—	—	40.00
(Y178)	1983	.140	—	Proof	45.00

Fanny Eissler

KM#	Date	Mintage	VF	XF	Unc
769	1984	.462	—	—	40.00
(Y184)	1984	.138	—	Proof	45.00

St. Florian's Cathedral

KM#	Date	Mintage	VF	XF	Unc
776	1986	.400	—	—	40.00
	1986	Inc. Ab.	—	Proof	45.00

Parliament Building

764	1983	.463	—	—	40.00
(Y179)	1983	.137	—	Proof	45.00

University of Graz

771	1985	.600	—	—	40.00
(Y185)	1985	.122	—	Proof	45.00

First Thaler Coin Struck at Hall Mint

777	1986	.500	—	—	40.00
	1986	Inc. Ab.	—	Proof	45.00

Tirolean Revolution of 1809

766	1984	.454	—	—	40.00
(Y180)	1984	.146	—	Proof	45.00

40 Years of Peace in Austria

772	1985	.500	—	—	40.00
(Y187)	1985	.118	—	Proof	45.00

Prince Eugene of Savoy

778	1986	—	—	—	40.00
	1986	—	—	Proof	45.00

100th Anniversary Commercial Shipping on Lake Constance

767	1984	.455	—	—	40.00
(Y182)	1984	.145	—	Proof	45.00

500th Anniversary of Canonization of Leopold III

773	1985	.500	—	—	40.00
(Y188)	1985	.113	—	Proof	45.00

European Conference on Security and Cooperation

779	1986	—	—	—	40.00
	1986	—	—	Proof	45.00

700th Anniversary of Stams Stift in Tirol

768	1984	.459	—	—	40.00
(Y183)	1984	.141	—	Proof	45.00

2000th Anniversary of Bregenz

774	1985	.500	—	—	40.00
	1985	.116	—	Proof	45.00

Austrian Railroad

781	1987	.300	—	—	40.00
	1987	Inc. Ab.	—	Proof	45.00

Salzburg's Archbishop von Raitenau

KM#	Date	Mintage	VF	XF	Unc
782	1987	.300	—	—	40.00
	1987	Inc. Ab.	—	Proof	45.00

Holy Cross Church

783	1987	.300	—	—	40.00
	1987	Inc. Ab.	—	Proof	45.00

St. Georgenberg Abbey

784	1988	.300	—	—	40.00
	1988	Inc. Ab.	—	Proof	45.00

Pope's Visit to Austria

785	1988	.300	—	—	40.00
	1988	Inc. Ab.	—	Proof	45.00

1000 SCHILLING

13.5000 g, .900 YELLOW GOLD, .3906 oz AGW
Austrian Millenium

KM#	Date	Mintage	VF	XF	Unc
733 (Y148)	1976	1.800	—	—	250.00

13.5000 g, .900 RED GOLD, .3906 oz AGW

733a (Y148a)	1976	Inc. Ab.	—	—	250.00

SPECIAL SELECTS (S/S)

NOTE: These are proof-like in appearance.

KM#	Date	Mintage	Identification	Issue Price	Mkt. Val.
723	1975	—	100 Schilling, Strauss	—	10.00
724	1975	—	100 Schilling, State Treaty	—	10.00
725	1975	—	100 Schilling, 50th Anniversary of Schilling	—	10.00
727.1	1976	—	100 Schilling, Winter Olympics II, Vienna Mint	—	10.00
727.2	1976	—	100 Schilling, Winter Olympics II, Hall Mint	—	10.00
728.1	1976	—	100 Schilling, Winter Olympics III, Vienna Mint	—	10.00
728.2	1976	—	100 Schilling, Winter Olympics III, Hall Mint	—	10.00
729.1	1976	—	100 Schilling, Winter Olympics IV, Vienna Mint	—	10.00
729.2	1976	—	100 Schilling, Winter Olympics IV, Hall Mint	—	10.00
730	1976	—	100 Schilling, Burgtheater	—	10.00
731	1976	—	100 Schilling, Herzogstuhl	—	10.00
732	1976	—	100 Schilling, Nestroy	—	10.00
734	1977	—	100 Schilling, Kremsmunster	—	10.00
735	1977	—	100 Schilling, Hohensalzb	—	10.00
736	1977	—	100 Schilling, Hall Mint	—	10.00
738	1978	—	100 Schilling, Gmunder	—	10.00
739	1978	—	100 Schilling, Durnkrut	—	10.00
740	1978	—	100 Schilling, Villach	—	10.00
741	1978	80,000	100 Schilling, Arlberg	—	10.00
742	1979	70,000	100 Schilling, Wiener Neustadt	—	10.00
743	1979	75,000	100 Schilling, Inn District	8.50	10.00
744	1979	75,000	100 Schilling, Vienna Center	—	10.00
745	1979	75,000	100 Schilling, Bregenz Hall	—	10.00
747	1980	63,000	500 Schilling, Steyr	—	40.00
748	1980	79,000	500 Schilling, Treaty	—	40.00
749	1980	86,400	500 Schilling, Maria Theresa	—	40.00
750	1980	90,000	500 Schilling, Red Cross	—	40.00
751	1981	85,000	500 Schilling, Verdun	—	40.00
752	1981	72,000	500 Schilling, Anton Wildgans	—	40.00
753	1981	65,000	500 Schilling, Otto Bauer	38.00	40.00
754	1981	60,000	500 Schilling, Religious Tolerance	—	40.00
756	1982	42,600	500 Schilling, St. Severin	—	40.00
757	1982	42,200	500 Schilling, Printing	—	40.00
758	1982	41,600	500 Schilling, Maria Zell Shrine	—	40.00
759	1982	39,600	500 Schilling, Leopold Figl	—	40.00
763	1983	60,000	500 Schilling, Pope's Visit	—	40.00

PROOF SETS (PS)

PS#	Date	Mintage	Identification	Issue Price	Mkt. Val.
PS1	1959(2)	1,000	KM687-688	—	575.00
PS2	1964(9)	69,731	KM675-676,678,682,685-686,689, 695.1,696	—	25.00
PS3	1964(9)	2,700	KM675-676,678,682,685-686,689, 695.2,696 (error set)	—	275.00
PS4	1964(7)	—	KM675-676,678,682,685-686,689	—	12.00
PS5	1965(7)	83,000	KM675-676,678,682,685-686,689	—	7.00
PS6	1965(4)	38,000	KM682,689,697-698	5.00	25.00
PS7	1966(9)	1,765	KM675-676,678,682,685-686,689, 699-700	—	100.00
PS8	1966(7)	—	KM675-676,678,682,685-686,689	—	15.00
PS9	1967(9)	1,163	KM675-676,678,682,685-686,689 701-702	5.50	100.00
PS10	1967(7)	—	KM675-676,678,682,685-686,689	—	40.00
PS11	1968(9)	15,200	KM675-676,678,682,685-686,689, 703,704.1	5.75	40.00
PS12	1968(7)	—	KM675-676,678,682,685-686,689	—	15.00
PS13	1969(9)	20,000	KM675-676,678,682,685-686,689a, 705-706	7.50	30.00
PS14	1969(7)	—	KM675-676,678,682,685-686,689a	—	11.00
PS15	1970(9)	—	KM675-676,678,682,685-686,689a 707-708	8.25	20.00
PS16	1970(9)	—	KM675-676,678,682,685-686,689a, 707,709	8.25	20.00
PS17	1970(7)	—	KM675-676,678,682,685-686,689a	—	8.50
PS18	1970(3)	—	KM707-709	7.00	20.00
PS19	1971(9)	—	KM675-676,678,682,685-686,689a, 710-711	8.25	17.50
PS20	1971(7)	—	KM675-676,678,682,685-686,689a	—	8.50
PS21	1972(9)	—	KM675-676,678,682,685-686,689a 712-713	8.50	20.00
PS22	1972(9)	—	KM675-676,678,682,685-686,689a, 712,714	8.50	20.00
PS23	1972(7)	—	KM675-676,678,682,685-686,689a	—	8.50
PS24	1972(3)	—	KM712-714	7.50	20.00
PS25	1973(10)	—	KM675-676,678,682,685-686,689a, 715-717	—	25.00
PS26	1973(7)	—	KM675-676,678,682,685-686,689a	—	8.50
PS27	1973(3)	—	KM712-714	—	20.00
PS28	1974(12)	—	KM675-676,678,685-686,689a, 718-723	29.70	35.00
PS29	1974(8)	—	KM675-676,678,685-686,689a, 718,721	—	10.00
PS30	1974(7)	—	KM675-676,678,685-686,689,718	—	7.50
PS31	1974(5)	—	KM719-723	27.00	30.00
PS32	1975(10)	—	KM675-676,678,685-686,689a, 718,724-726	30.00	30.00
PS33	1975(7)	—	KM675-676,678,685-686,689a,718	—	6.50
PS34	1975(3)	—	KM724-726	27.00	25.00
PS35	1976(7)	—	KM675-676,678,685-686,689a, 718	3.00	6.50
PS36	1977(7)	—	KM675-676,678,685-686,689a, 718	3.15	6.50
PS37	1977(6)	—	KM730-732,734-736	27.00	60.00
PS38	1978(7)	—	KM675-676,678,685-686,689a,718	—	6.50
PS39	1979(7)	44,000	KM675-676,678,685-686,689a,718	—	6.50
PS40	1980(8)	—	KM675-676,678,685-686,689a,718, 746	—	12.50
PS41	1980(7)	48,000	KM675-676,678,685-686,689a,718	—	12.00
PS42	1981(8)	49,000	KM675-676,678,685-686,689a,718, 746	—	12.50
PS43	1982(8)	50,000	KM675-676,678,685-686,689a,718, 755	—	9.00
PS44	1983(8)	—	KM675-676,678,685-686,689a,718, 760	—	9.00
PS45	1984(8)	—	KM675-676,678,685-686,689a,718, 765	—	9.00
PS46	1985(8)	—	KM675-676,678,685-686,689a,718, 770	—	9.00
PS47	1986(8)	—	KM675-676,678,685-686,689a,718, 775	—	9.00
PS48	1987(8)	—	KM675-676,678,685-686,689a,718, 780	—	9.00
PS49	1988(7)	—	KM675-676,678,685-686,689a,718	—	14.00

AUSTRIAN STATES 150

AUERSPERG
Auersberg

The Auersperg princes were princes of estates in Austrian Carniola, a former duchy with estates in Laibach and Silesia, a former province in southwestern Poland and Swabia, one of the stem-duchies of medieval Germany. They were elevated to princely rank in 1653, and the following year were made dukes of Muensterberg, which they ultimately sold to Prussia.

RULERS
Wilhelm, 1800-1822

MONETARY SYSTEM
120 Kreuzer = 1 Convention Thaler

THALER
(Convention)

SILVER

C#	Date	Mintage	VG	Fine	VF	XF
3	1805	—	80.00	175.00	275.00	500.00

GURK

A bishopric in the Austrian Alpine province of Carinthia, was founded in 1071. In 1806 it was mediatized and assigned to Austria.

RULERS
Franz Xavier, Count V. Salm - Reifferscheid (later Prince) 1783-1822

20 KREUZER

SILVER

	Date	Mintage				
1	1806	—	37.50	75.00	90.00	125.00

THALER
(Convention)

SILVER

C#	Date	Mintage	VG	Fine	VF	XF
2	1801	—	90.00	150.00	200.00	375.00

TRADE COINAGE
DUCAT

3.5000 g, .986 GOLD, .1109 oz AGW
Obv: Bust of Franz Xavier right.
Rev: Crowned and mantled arms.

3	1806	—	200.00	375.00	700.00	1750.

OLMUTZ
IN MORAVIA

Olmutz (Olomouc), a principality in north-central Czechoslovakia which was, until 1640, the recognized capital of Moravia, obtained the right to mint a coinage in 1141, but exercised it sparingly until the 17th century.

RULERS
Anton Theodor 1777-1811
Rudolph Johann, Archduke of Austria, 1819-1831

20 KREUZER

SILVER

10	1820	—	15.00	25.00	40.00	60.00

1/2 CONVENTION THALER

SILVER

11	1820	—	50.00	90.00	150.00	200.00

CONVENTION THALER

SILVER

C#	Date	Mintage	VG	Fine	VF	XF
12	1820	—	75.00	175.00	325.00	550.00

TRADE COINAGE
DUCAT

3.5000 g, .986 GOLD, .1109 oz AGW
Rudolph Johann.

13	1820	—	175.00	250.00	500.00	800.00

SALZBURG

A town on the Austro-Bavarian frontier which grew up around a monastery and bishopric that was founded circa 700. It was raised to the rank of archbishopric in 798. In 1803 Salzburg was secularized and given to the archduke of Austria. In 1805 it was annexed to Austria but years later passed to Bavaria, returning to Austria in 1813. It became a crownland in 1849, remaining so until becoming part of the Austrian Republic in 1918.

RULERS
Hieronymus, 1772-1803
Ferdinand, Elector, 1803-1805

ENGRAVERS INITIALS
FMF, FMK - Franz Xavier Matzenkopf, Sr. 1738-1755
FM, M - Franz Xavier Matzenkopf, Jr. 1755-1805

MONETARY SYSTEM
4 Pfenning = 1 Kreutzer
120 Kreutzer = 1 Convention Thaler

EIN (1) PFENNING

COPPER

KM#	Date	Mintage	VG	Fine	VF	XF
474 (C87b)	1801	—	3.00	5.00	9.00	18.00
	1802	—	3.00	5.00	9.00	18.00

480 (C88)	1802	—	5.00	7.00	10.00	20.00

Rev: 1 PFENNING.

488 (C115)	1804	—	5.00	7.00	10.00	20.00

KM#	Date	Mintage	VG	Fine	VF	XF
489	1804	—	1.50	3.00	5.00	15.00
(C115a)	1805	—	1.50	3.00	5.00	15.00

ZWEI (2) PFENNING

COPPER

472	1801	—	3.00	6.00	12.00	25.00
(C90a)						

481	1802	—	5.00	8.50	17.00	35.00
(C91)						

Rev: II PFENNING.

490	1804	—	4.50	8.50	17.00	35.00
(C116)						

Rev: ZWEI PFENNING.

493	1805	—	3.50	7.50	15.00	30.00
(C116a)	1806	—	3.50	7.50	15.00	30.00

EIN (1) KREUZER

COPPER

470	1801	—	2.00	3.00	5.00	10.00
(C93a)	1802	—	2.00	3.00	5.00	10.00

482	1802	—	4.50	6.50	10.00	20.00
(C93b)						

491	1804	—	3.00	6.00	12.00	25.00
(C117)	1805	—	1.50	3.00	6.00	12.00
	1806	—	1.50	4.00	10.00	20.00

3 KREUZER

BILLON

KM#	Date	Mintage	VG	Fine	VF	XF
483	1803	—	10.00	20.00	40.00	80.00
(C119)	1804	—	10.00	20.00	40.00	80.00

Rev: Date in lozenge.

494	1805	—	10.00	20.00	40.00	85.00
(C119a)						

NOTE: Varieties exist with and without mint mark.

5 KREUZER

BILLON

477	1801	—	7.50	20.00	50.00	130.00
(C96c)	1802	—	7.50	20.00	50.00	130.00

6 KREUZER

BILLON

484	1803	—	10.00	30.00	65.00	130.00
(C121)	1804	—	10.00	30.00	60.00	120.00
	1805	—	10.00	25.00	50.00	100.00

Rev: Date in lozenge.

495	1805	—	10.00	25.00	50.00	100.00
(C121a)	1806	—	10.00	25.00	50.00	100.00

10 KREUZER

3.8900 g, .500 SILVER, .0625 oz ASW

464	1801 M	—	15.00	30.00	55.00	110.00
(C99a)	1802 M	—	15.00	30.00	55.00	110.00

20 KREUZER

6.6800 g, .583 SILVER, .1252 oz ASW

460	1801 M	—	3.00	6.00	15.00	30.00
(C103a)	1802 M	—	3.00	6.00	15.00	30.00
	1803 M	—	5.00	15.00	20.00	50.00

NOTE: Varieties exist.

KM#	Date	Mintage	VG	Fine	VF	XF
492	1804 M	—	10.00	20.00	40.00	90.00
(C123)						

496	1805 M	—	10.00	25.00	50.00	100.00
(C123a)	1806 M	—	10.00	25.00	50.00	100.00

1/2 THALER

14.0300 g, .833 SILVER, .3757 oz ASW

461	1802 M	—	15.00	30.00	60.00	150.00
(C104a)						

THALER

28.0000 g, .833 SILVER, .7515 oz ASW

KM#	Date	Mintage	Fine	VF	XF	Unc
465	1801 M	—	65.00	110.00	150.00	325.00
(C107a)	1802 M	—	75.00	110.00	150.00	325.00
	1803 M	—	75.00	110.00	150.00	325.00

NOTE: Varieties exist.

Salzburg / AUSTRIAN STATES 152

KM#	Date	Mintage	Fine	VF	XF	Unc
485 (C125)	1803	—	100.00	175.00	400.00	750.00

| 497 (C125a) | 1805 M | — | 150.00 | 250.00 | 450.00 | 850.00 |

Rev. leg: . . . PAS ETBER S R IP ELECTOR.

| 499 (C125b) | 1806 M | — | 150.00 | 250.00 | 450.00 | 850.00 |

TRADE COINAGE
DUCAT
3.5000 g, .986 GOLD, .1109 oz AGW
Obv: Bust right. Rev: Crowned, mantled arms.

KM#	Date	Mintage	VG	Fine	VF	XF
463	1801 M	—	80.00	125.00	250.00	375.00
(C111a)	1802 M	—	80.00	125.00	250.00	375.00

Similar to KM#463.

| 486 (C111b) | 1803 M | — | — | — | Rare | |

NOTE: Varieties exist.

| 487 (C126) | 1803 M | — | 100.00 | 250.00 | 700.00 | 1100. |
| | 1804 M | — | 125.00 | 275.00 | 800.00 | 1250. |

| 498 (C126a) | 1805 M | — | 100.00 | 250.00 | 600.00 | 1000. |
| | 1806 M | — | 100.00 | 250.00 | 600.00 | 1000. |

TYROL
Tirol

A prince-bishopric situated in Austria between Germany and Italy. In 1363 Margaret Maultasch, countess of Tyrol, handed over Tyrol to Rudolph, Duke of Austria. Except for a period of Bavarian occupation, 1805-14, Tyrol remained a Hapsburg possession until the breakup of the Austrian Empire at the end of World War I. The world's first dollar-size silver crown was struck at Hall, Tyrol, in 1486.

RULERS
Napoleon, (France) 1805-1809
Maximilian Joseph I, (Bavaria) 1805-1814
Andreas Hofer, Rebellion, 1809
Franz I, (Austria), 1814-1835
Ferdinand, (Austria), 1835-1848
Franz Joseph, (Austria), 1848-1916

MINT MARKS
F, FH, G, H - Hall

EIN (1) KREUZER

COPPER
Insurrection Issue of Andreas Hofer

KM#	Date	Mintage	VG	Fine	VF	XF
148 (C41)	1809	—	10.00	15.00	35.00	80.00

NOTE: Varieties exist.

20 KREUZER

SILVER
Insurrection Issue of Andreas Hofer

| 149 (C42) | 1809 | — | 15.00 | 20.00 | 35.00 | 70.00 |

NOTE: Three varieties exist.

AZORES

The Azores, an archipelago of nine islands of volcanic origin, are located in the Atlantic Ocean 740 miles (1,190 km.) west of Cape de Roca, Portugal. They are under the administration of Portugal, and have an area of 902 sq. mi. (2,336 sq. km.) and a population of 254,160 Principal City: Ponta Delgada. The natives are mainly of Portuguese descent and earn their livelihood by fishing, wine making, basket weaving, and the growing of fruit, grains and sugar cane. Pineapples are the chief item of export. The climate is particularly temperate, making the islands a favorite winter resort.

The Azores were discovered about 1427 by the Portuguese navigator Diogo de Silves. Portugal secured the islands in the 15th century and established the first settlement, on Santa Maria, about 1439. From 1580 to 1640 the Azores were subject to Spain.

Angra on Terceira Island became the capital of the captaincy-general of the Azores in 1766 and it was here in 1826 that the constitutionalists set up a pro-Pedro government in opposition to King Miguel in Lisbon. The whole Portuguese fleet attacked Terceira and was repelled at Praia, after which Azoreans, Brazilians and British mercenaries defeated Miguel in Portugal. Maria de Gloria, Pedro's daughter, was proclaimed queen of Portugal on Terceira in 1828.

A U.S. naval base was established at Ponta Delgada in 1917.

After World War II, the islands acquired a renewed importance as a refueling stop for transatlantic air transport. The United States maintains defense bases in the Azores as part of the collective security program of NATO.

In 1976 the archipelago became the Autonomous Region of Azores.

RULERS
Portuguese

MONETARY SYSTEM
1000 Reis (Insulanos) = 1 Milreis

TERCEIRA ISLAND

MARIA II IN EXILE
1828-1833

In 1828 Pedro declined the Portuguese throne in favor of his daughter, Maria da Gloria, who was therefore forced to live in exile 1828-1834 until Miguel was completely defeated.

5 REIS

COPPER

KM#	Date	Mintage	VG	Fine	VF	XF
5	1830	—	.75	1.50	3.00	8.00

10 REIS

COPPER

| 6 | 1830 | — | 1.00 | 2.00 | 3.50 | 10.00 |

80 REIS

CAST GUN OR BELL METAL
Rev: Large leg. and large stars.

KM#	Date	Mintage	VG	Fine	VF	XF
4.1	1829	—	30.00	50.00	80.00	140.00

Rev: Small leg. and small stars.

KM#	Date	Mintage	VG	Fine	VF	XF
4.2	1829	—	15.00	30.00	45.00	75.00

AZORES
PROVINCIAL COINAGE
5 REIS
COPPER

KM#	Date	Mintage	VG	Fine	VF	XF
10	1843	—	1.50	3.00	6.00	12.00

KM#	Date	Mintage	Fine	VF	XF	Unc
13	1865	.090	2.00	3.00	5.00	12.00
	1866	.060	3.00	4.50	7.00	27.50
	1880	.400	1.00	2.50	5.00	10.00

KM#	Date	Mintage	Fine	VF	XF	Unc
16	1901	.800	1.00	2.00	5.00	10.00

10 REIS

COPPER

KM#	Date	Mintage	VG	Fine	VF	XF
11	1843	—	1.50	3.50	6.00	12.00

KM#	Date	Mintage	Fine	VF	XF	Unc
14	1865	.525	1.00	2.00	5.00	10.00
	1866	Inc. Ab.	20.00	30.00	40.00	70.00

KM#	Date	Mintage	Fine	VF	XF	Unc
17	1901	.600	1.00	2.00	5.00	10.00

20 REIS

COPPER

KM#	Date	Mintage	VG	Fine	VF	XF
12	1843	—	1.00	3.00	6.00	12.00

KM#	Date	Mintage	Fine	VF	XF	Unc
15	1865	.178	1.00	2.00	3.00	22.00
	1866	.273	1.00	2.00	5.00	30.00

COUNTERMARKED COINAGE
Decree of June 14, 1871

This first decree ordained that the circulating Brazilian Patacas of 2000 Reis, including the fractions of 1000, 500 and 200 Reis, which at the time locally had a value of 1200, 600, 300 and 120 Reis (Portuguese) respectively, were to be countermarked with a royal crown. These were eventually to be replaced or exchanged by current Portuguese coinage upon their entry into the public treasury. This countermark is also known on copper coins and on various silver coins of other nations that were circulating at the time. The following list is a basic guide with samples of known examples. Grades noted are for the basic coin as the countermark is normally found in better condition.

20 REIS
COPPER
c/m: Crown on Portuguese and Colonies X (10) Reis.

KM#	Date	Good	VG	Fine	VF
18	ND	10.00	20.00	30.00	60.00

40 REIS
COPPER
c/m: Crown on Mozambique 40 Reis, KM#19.

KM#	Date	Good	VG	Fine	VF
22	ND(1819)	10.00	20.00	30.00	60.00
	ND(1825)	10.00	20.00	30.00	60.00

120 REIS
SILVER
c/m: Crown on Brazilian 200 Reis, KM#469.

KM#	Date	Good	VG	Fine	VF
19.1	ND(1854-67)	10.00	20.00	30.00	50.00

c/m: Crown on Brazilian 200 Reis, KM#471.

KM#	Date	Good	VG	Fine	VF
19.2	ND(1867-69)	10.00	20.00	30.00	50.00

300 REIS
SILVER
c/m: Crown on Brazilian 500 Reis, KM#458.

KM#	Date	Good	VG	Fine	VF
20.1	ND(1848-52)	12.50	25.00	40.00	60.00

c/m: Crown on Brazilian 500 Reis, KM#464.

KM#	Date	Good	VG	Fine	VF
20.2	ND(1853-67)	12.50	25.00	40.00	60.00

c/m: Crown on Brazilian 500 Reis, KM#472.

KM#	Date	Good	VG	Fine	VF
20.3	ND(1867-68)	12.50	25.00	40.00	60.00

600 REIS
SILVER
c/m: Crown on Brazilian 1000 Reis, KM#459.

KM#	Date	Good	VG	Fine	VF
28.1	ND(1849-52)	15.00	27.50	45.00	65.00

c/m: Crown on Brazilian 1000 Reis, KM#465.

KM#	Date	Good	VG	Fine	VF
28.2	ND(1853-66)	15.00	27.50	45.00	65.00

c/m: Crown on Brazilian 1000 Reis, KM#476.

KM#	Date	Good	VG	Fine	VF
28.3	ND(1869)	17.50	30.00	50.00	75.00

1200 REIS

SILVER
c/m: Crown on Austria Burgau Maria Theresa Thaler, C#14b.

KM#	Date	Good	VG	Fine	VF
21.1	ND(1780)	30.00	50.00	75.00	125.00

c/m: Crown on Brazilian 2000 Reis, KM#462.

KM#	Date	Good	VG	Fine	VF
21.2	ND(1851-52)	17.50	30.00	50.00	75.00

c/m: Crown on Brazilian 2000 Reis, KM#466.

KM#	Date	Good	VG	Fine	VF
21.3	ND(1853-57)	15.00	27.50	45.00	65.00

Decree of March 31, 1887

**Countermark crowned G.P., 8mm.
Illustration is twice normal size.**

This second decree ordained that all foreign silver and copper coinage circulating in the Azores was to be countermarked with a crowned G.P. (Governo Portugues) within a circle. These also were eventually to be replaced or exchanged by current Portuguese coinage upon their entry into the public treasury. This countermark for general use is found on a profusion of Portuguese, Brazilian, and foreign issues. The largest crown or dollar size includes the Portuguese 1000 Reis, Brazilian 2000 Reis, obsolete 960 Reis, 1200 Reis, Austrian Thaler, English 5 Shilling or Crown, Spanish American 8 Reales and Spanish 2 Escudos for comparison to the United States dollar. This countermark has been heavily counterfeited and should be approached with caution. The following list is a basic guide with samples of known examples. Grades noted are for the basic coin and the countermark is normally found in better condition than the coin bearing it.

15 REIS
COPPER
c/m: Crowned G.P. on Portuguese India (Goa) 15 Reis, KM#263.

KM#	Date	Good	VG	Fine	VF
23	ND	10.00	20.00	30.00	60.00

120 REIS
SILVER
c/m: Crowned G.P. on Portuguese 80 Reis, KM#238.

| 24 | ND | 15.00 | 25.00 | 40.00 | 70.00 |

300 REIS
SILVER
c/m: Crowned G.P. on Spanish or Spanish Colonial 2 Reales.

| 25 | ND | 20.00 | 30.00 | 50.00 | 80.00 |

600 REIS

SILVER
c/m: Crowned G.P. on Bolivia 4 Reales, KM#54.

| 26.1 | ND(1773-89) | 30.00 | 50.00 | 75.00 | 125.00 |

c/m: Crowned G.P. on Portuguese 400 Reis, KM#331.

| 26.2 | ND(1802-16) | 25.00 | 45.00 | 70.00 | 110.00 |

c/m: Crowned G.P. on Portuguese 400 Reis, KM#386.

| 26.3 | ND(1828-34) | 35.00 | 60.00 | 100.00 | 150.00 |

1200 REIS

SILVER
c/m: Crowned G.P. on Brazilian (Minas Gerais) 960 Reis, KM#242.

KM#	Date	Good	VG	Fine	VF
29.1	ND(1791-1808)	55.00	90.00	135.00	200.00

c/m: Crowned G.P. on Brazilian 960 Reis, KM#307.1.

KM#	Date	VG	Fine	VF	XF
29.2	ND(1809-18)	40.00	60.00	100.00	150.00

c/m: Crowned G.P. on Peru 8 Reales, KM#142.3.

| 29.3 | ND(1828-40) | 40.00 | 60.00 | 100.00 | 150.00 |

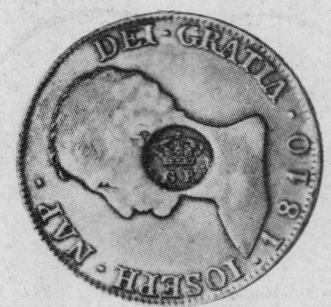

c/m: Crowned G.P. on Spain 20 Reales, C#92.

KM#	Date	Good	VG	Fine	VF
29.4	ND(1808-13)	65.00	95.00	175.00	300.00

NOTE: The above examples as noted are listed only to determine relative size and do not reflect a current price for other foreign types found with genuine countermarks.

REPUBLIC
25 ESCUDOS

COPPER-NICKEL
Regional Autonomy

KM#	Date	Mintage	VF	XF	Unc
43 (33)	1980	.250	—	1.00	2.00

11.0000 g, .925 SILVER, .3272 oz ASW

| 43a (33a) | 1980 | .012 | — | Proof | 15.00 |

100 ESCUDOS

COPPER-NICKEL
Regional Autonomy

KM#	Date	Mintage	VF	XF	Unc
44 (34)	1980	.750	—	1.50	3.00

16.5000 g, .925 SILVER, .4908 oz ASW

| 44a (34a) | 1980 | .012 | — | Proof | 35.00 |

COPPER-NICKEL
10th Anniversary of Regional Autonomy - Flower

| 45 | 1986 | .750 | — | — | 1.50 |

16.5000 g, .925 SILVER, .4908 oz ASW

| 45a | 1986 | .020 | — | — | 18.50 |
| | 1986 | .010 | — | Proof | 32.50 |

PROOF SETS (PS)

KM#	Date	Mintage	Identification	Issue Price	Mkt. Val.
PS1	1980	12,000	KM43a-44a	40.00	50.00

BAHAMAS

The Commonwealth of the Bahamas is an archipelago of about 3,000 islands, cays and rocks located in the Atlantic Ocean east of Florida and north of Cuba. The total land area of the 800 mile (1,287 km.) long chain of islands is 5,380 sq. mi. (13,935 sq. km.). They have a population of 244,692. Capital: Nassau. The Bahamas import most of their food and manufactured products and export cement, refined oil, pulpwood and lobsters. Tourism is the principal industry.

The Bahamas were discovered by Columbus in October, 1492, but Spain made no attempt to settle them. British influence began in 1626 when Charles I granted them to the lord proprietors of Carolina. They continued under British proprietors until 1717, when, as the result of political and economic mismanagement, the civil and military governments were surrendered to the King and the islands designated a British Crown Colony. The Bahamas obtained complete internal self-government under the constitution of Jan. 7, 1964. Full independence was achieved on July 10, 1973. The Bahamas is a member of the Commonwealth of Nations. The Queen of England is Chief of State.

The coinage of Great Britain was legal tender in the Bahamas from 1825 to the issuing of a definitive coinage in 1966.

RULERS
British

MINT MARKS
Through 1969 all decimal coinage of the Bahamas was executed at the Royal Mint in England. Since that time issues have been struck at both the Royal Mint and at the Franklin Mint (FM) in the U.S.A. While the mint mark of the latter appears on coins dated 1971 and subsequently, it is missing from the 1970 issues.

JP - John Pinches, London
None - Royal Mint
(t) - Tower of London
FM - Franklin Mint, U.S.A.*

*NOTE: From 1975 the Franklin Mint has produced coinage in up to 3 different qualities. Qualities of issue are designated in ( ) after each date and are defined as follows:

(M) MATTE - Normal circulation strike or a dull finish produced by sandblasting special uncirculated (polish finish) or proof quality dies.

(U) SPECIAL UNCIRCULATED - Polished or proof-like in appearance without any frosted features.

(P) PROOF - The highest quality obtainable having mirror-like fields and frosted features.

MONETARY SYSTEM
100 Cents = 1 Dollar

PENNY

COPPER
KM#	Date	Mintage	Fine	VF	XF	Unc
1	1806 engrailed edge					
		.120	30.00	60.00	120.00	250.00
	1806 engrailed edge	—	—	Proof	250.00	
	1806 plain edge	(restrike)	—	Proof	150.00	
	1807 engrailed edge	—	—	Proof	3000.	

GILT
| 1a | 1806 engrailed edge | (restrike) | — | Proof | 350.00 |

DECIMAL COINAGE
CENT

NICKEL-BRASS
KM#	Date	Mintage	VF	XF	Unc
2	1966	7.312	—	.10	.15
	1968	.800	—	.10	.25
	1969	4.036	—	.10	.15
	1969	.010	—	Proof	.50

BRONZE
| 15 | 1970 | .125 | .10 | .25 | .50 |
| | 1970 | .023 | — | Proof | .50 |

NOTE: Proof specimens of this date are struck in 'special brass' which looks like a pale bronze.

16	1971FM	1.007	—	.10	.15
	1971FM(P)	.031	—	Proof	.50
	1972FM	1.037	—	.10	.15
	1972FM(P)	.035	—	Proof	.50
	1973	7.000	—	.10	.15
	1973FM	1.040	—	.10	.15
	1973FM(P)	.035	—	Proof	.50

BRASS
59	1974	.011	—	.10	.25
	1974FM	.071	—	.10	.20
	1974FM(P)	.094	—	Proof	.50
	1975FM(M)	.060	—	.10	.15
	1975FM(U)	3,845	—	.10	.50
	1975FM(P)	.029	—	Proof	.50
	1976FM(M)	.060	—	.10	.20
	1976FM(U)	1,453	—	.10	.50
	1976FM(P)	.023	—	Proof	.50
	1977	3.000	—	.10	.15
	1977FM(M)	.060	—	.10	.20
	1977FM(U)	713 pcs.	—	.50	1.50
	1977FM(P)	.011	—	Proof	.50
	1978FM(M)	.060	—	.10	.20
	1978FM(U)	767 pcs.	—	.50	1.50
	1978FM(P)	6,931	—	Proof	.75
	1979	—	—	.10	.15
	1979FM(P)	2,053	—	Proof	1.00
	1980	4.000	—	.10	.15
	1980FM(P)	2,084	—	Proof	1.00
	1981	5.000	—	.10	.15
	1981FM(M)	—	—	.10	.15
	1981FM(P)	1,980	—	Proof	1.00
	1982	5.000	—	.10	.15
	1982FM(M)	—	—	.10	.15
	1982FM(P)	1,217	—	Proof	1.00
	1983	8.000	—	.10	.15
	1983FM(P)	1,020	—	Proof	1.00
	1984	—	—	.10	.15
	1984FM(P)	7,500	—	Proof	.75
	1985	1.036	—	.10	.15
	1985FM(P)	7,500	—	Proof	.50

COPPER PLATED ZINC
| 59a | 1987 | — | — | — | — |

5 CENTS

COPPER-NICKEL
3	1966	2.571	—	.10	.20
	1968	.600	—	.10	.30
	1969	2.026	—	.10	.20
	1969	.075	—	Proof	.50

KM#	Date	Mintage	VF	XF	Unc
3	1970	.026	—	.10	.30
	1970	.023	—	Proof	.50

NOTE: The obverse of the above also comes muled with the reverse of a New Zealand 2-cent piece KM#32. The undated 1967 error is listed as New Zealand KM#33.

17	1971FM	.013	—	.10	.35
	1971FM(P)	.031	—	Proof	.50
	1972FM	.011	—	.10	.35
	1972FM(P)	.035	—	Proof	.50
	1973FM	.021	—	.10	.35
	1973FM(P)	.035	—	Proof	.50

Obv. leg: THE COMMONWEALTH OF THE BAHAMAS
| 38 | 1973 | 1.000 | — | .10 | .30 |

60	1974FM	.023	—	.10	.25
	1974FM(P)	.094	—	Proof	.50
	1975	—	—	.10	.30
	1975FM(M)	.012	—	.10	.25
	1975FM(U)	3,845	—	.15	.50
	1975FM(P)	.029	—	Proof	.50
	1976FM(M)	.012	—	.10	.25
	1976FM(U)	1,453	—	.15	.75
	1976FM(P)	.023	—	Proof	.50
	1977FM(M)	.012	—	.10	.35
	1977FM(U)	713 pcs.	—	.50	1.50
	1977FM(P)	.011	—	Proof	.50
	1978FM(M)	.012	—	.10	.35
	1978FM(U)	767 pcs.	—	.50	1.50
	1978FM(P)	6,931	—	Proof	.50
	1979FM(P)	2,053	—	Proof	.75
	1980FM(P)	2,084	—	Proof	.75
	1981	—	—	.10	.25
	1981FM(P)	1,980	—	Proof	.75
	1982FM(P)	1,217	—	Proof	.75
	1983	2.000	—	.10	.25
	1983FM(P)	1,020	—	Proof	.75
	1984	—	—	.10	.25
	1984FM(P)	1,036	—	Proof	.75
	1985FM(P)	7,500	—	Proof	.75

10 CENTS

COPPER-NICKEL
4	1966	2.198	—	.10	.25
	1968	.550	—	.50	4.00
	1969	2.026	—	.10	.25
	1969	.010	—	Proof	.50
	1970	.027	—	.10	.35
	1970	.023	—	Proof	.50

18	1971FM	.013	—	.15	.50
	1971FM(P)	.031	—	Proof	.50
	1972FM	.011	—	.15	.50
	1972FM(P)	.035	—	Proof	.50
	1973FM	.015	—	.15	.50
	1973FM(P)	.035	—	Proof	.50

Obv. leg: THE COMMONWEALTH OF THE BAHAMAS
| 39 | 1973 | 1.000 | — | .10 | .35 |

BAHAMAS 156

KM#	Date	Mintage	VF	XF	Unc
61	1974FM	.017	—	.10	.35
	1974FM(P)	.094	—	Proof	.50
	1975	3.000	—	.10	.25
	1975FM(M)	6,000	—	.15	.50
	1975FM(U)	3,845	—	.15	.50
	1975FM(P)	.029	—	Proof	.50
	1976FM(M)	6,000	—	.15	.50
	1976FM(U)	1,453	—	.25	1.00
	1976FM(P)	.023	—	Proof	.50
	1977FM(M)	6,000	—	.15	.50
	1977FM(U)	713 pcs.	—	.50	1.50
	1977FM(P)	.011	—	Proof	.50
	1978FM(M)	6,000	—	.15	.50
	1978FM(U)	767 pcs.	—	.50	1.50
	1978FM(P)	6,931	—	Proof	.75
	1979FM(P)	2,053	—	Proof	1.00
	1980	2.500	—	.10	.35
	1980FM(P)	2,084	—	Proof	1.00
	1981FM(P)	1,980	—	Proof	1.00
	1982	2.000	—	.10	.35
	1982FM(P)	1,217	—	Proof	1.00
	1983FM(P)	1,020	—	Proof	1.00
	1984FM(P)	1,036	—	Proof	1.00
	1985	—	—	.10	.35
	1985FM(M)	—	—	.15	.50
	1985FM(P)	7,500	—	Proof	.75

15 CENTS

COPPER-NICKEL

KM#	Date	Mintage	VF	XF	Unc
5	1966	.930	—	.15	.35
	1969	1.026	—	.15	.35
	1969	.010	—	Proof	.50
	1970	.028	—	.15	.35
	1970	.023	—	Proof	.50

19	1971FM	.013	—	.15	.35
	1971FM(P)	.031	—	Proof	.50
	1972FM	.011	—	.15	.35
	1972FM(P)	.035	—	Proof	.50
	1973FM	.014	—	.15	.35
	1973FM(P)	.035	—	Proof	.50

62	1974FM	.015	—	.15	.35
	1974FM(P)	.094	—	Proof	.50
	1975FM(M)	3,500	—	.20	1.00
	1975FM(U)	3,845	—	.20	1.00
	1975FM(P)	.029	—	Proof	.50
	1976FM(M)	3,500	—	.20	1.00
	1976FM(U)	1,453	—	.25	1.50
	1976FM(P)	.023	—	Proof	.50
	1977FM(M)	3,500	—	.20	1.00
	1977FM(U)	713 pcs.	—	.50	2.00
	1977FM(P)	.011	—	Proof	.50
	1978FM(M)	3,500	—	.20	1.00
	1978FM(U)	767 pcs.	—	.50	2.00
	1978FM(P)	6,931	—	Proof	.75
	1979FM(P)	2,053	—	Proof	1.00
	1980FM(P)	2,084	—	Proof	1.00
	1981FM(P)	1,980	—	Proof	1.00
	1982FM(P)	1,217	—	Proof	1.25
	1983FM(P)	1,020	—	Proof	1.25
	1984FM(P)	1,036	—	Proof	1.25
	1985FM(P)	7,500	—	Proof	.75

25 CENTS

NICKEL

KM#	Date	Mintage	VF	XF	Unc
6	1966	3.685	—	.25	.50
	1969	1.026	—	.25	.50
	1969	.010	—	Proof	.75
	1970	.026	—	.25	.50
	1970	.023	—	Proof	.75

20	1971FM	.013	—	.25	.50
	1971FM(P)	.031	—	Proof	.75
	1972FM	.011	—	.25	.50
	1972FM(P)	.035	—	Proof	.75
	1973FM	.012	—	.25	.50
	1973FM(P)	.035	—	Proof	.75

63	1974FM	.013	—	.25	.50
	1974FM(P)	.094	—	Proof	.75
	1975FM(M)	2,400	—	.25	1.00
	1975FM(U)	3,845	—	.25	1.00
	1975FM(P)	.029	—	Proof	.75
	1976FM(M)	2,400	—	.25	1.00
	1976FM(U)	1,453	—	.30	1.25
	1976FM(P)	.023	—	Proof	.75
	1977	—	—	.25	.50
	1977FM(M)	2,400	—	.25	1.00
	1977FM(U)	713 pcs.	—	.50	3.00
	1977FM(P)	.011	—	Proof	.75
	1978FM(M)	2,400	—	.25	1.00
	1978FM(U)	767 pcs.	—	.50	3.00
	1978FM(P)	6,931	—	Proof	1.00
	1979	—	—	.25	.50
	1979FM(P)	2,053	—	Proof	1.25
	1980FM(P)	2,084	—	Proof	1.25
	1981	1.600	—	.25	.50
	1981FM(P)	1,980	—	Proof	1.25
	1982FM(P)	1,217	—	Proof	1.50
	1983FM(P)	1,020	—	Proof	1.50
	1984FM(P)	1,036	—	Proof	1.50
	1985FM(P)	7,500	—	Proof	1.00

50 CENTS

10.3700 g, .800 SILVER, .2667 oz ASW

7	1966	.701	BV	2.50	3.50
	1969	.026	BV	2.50	3.50
	1969	.010	—	Proof	4.25
	1970	.025	BV	2.50	3.50
	1970	.023	—	Proof	4.25

21	1971FM	.014	BV	2.50	3.50
	1971FM(P)	.031	—	Proof	4.25
	1972FM	.012	BV	2.50	3.50
	1972FM(P)	.035	—	Proof	4.25

KM#	Date	Mintage	VF	XF	Unc
21	1973FM	.011	BV	2.50	3.50
	1973FM(P)	.035	—	Proof	4.25

COPPER-NICKEL

64	1974FM	.012	—	.50	1.25
	1975FM(M)	1,200	—	.75	5.00
	1975FM(U)	3,828	—	.50	2.00
	1976FM(M)	1,200	—	.75	5.00
	1976FM(U)	1,453	—	.65	4.00
	1977FM(M)	1,200	—	.75	5.00
	1977FM(U)	713 pcs.	—	1.00	6.00
	1978FM(M)	1,200	—	.75	5.00
	1978FM(U)	767 pcs.	—	1.00	6.00
	1981FM(P)	1,980	—	Proof	3.00
	1982FM(P)	1,217	—	Proof	3.50
	1983FM(P)	1,020	—	Proof	3.50
	1984FM(P)	1,036	—	Proof	3.50
	1985FM(P)	7,500	—	Proof	2.50

10.3700 g, .800 SILVER, .2667 oz ASW

64a	1974FM(P)	.094	—	Proof	4.25
	1975FM(P)	.029	—	Proof	4.25
	1976FM(P)	.023	—	Proof	4.25
	1977FM(P)	.011	—	Proof	4.25
	1978FM(P)	6,931	—	Proof	5.00
	1979FM(P)	2,053	—	Proof	6.00
	1980FM(P)	2,084	—	Proof	6.00

DOLLAR

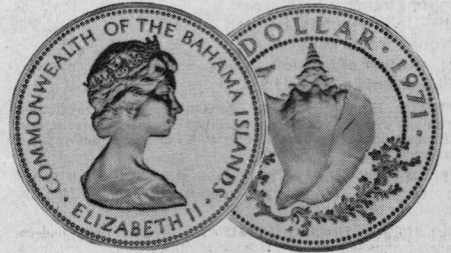

18.1400 g, .800 SILVER, .4666 oz ASW

8	1966	.406	BV	3.00	5.00
	1969	.026	BV	3.00	5.00
	1969	.010	—	Proof	6.00
	1970	.027	BV	3.00	5.00
	1970	.023	—	Proof	6.00

22	1971FM	.015	BV	3.00	5.00
	1971FM(P)	.031	—	Proof	6.00
	1972FM	.018	BV	3.00	5.00
	1972FM(P)	.035	—	Proof	6.00
	1973FM	.010	BV	3.00	5.00
	1973FM(P)	.035	—	Proof	6.00

COPPER-NICKEL

65	1974FM	.012	—	1.00	3.00
	1975FM(M)	600 pcs.	—	7.50	20.00
	1975FM(U)	3,845	—	1.00	3.00
	1976FM(M)	600 pcs.	—	7.50	20.00
	1976FM(U)	1,453	—	1.00	3.50
	1977FM(M)	600 pcs.	—	7.50	20.00
	1977FM(U)	713 pcs.	—	4.00	10.00
	1978FM(U)	1,367	—	1.50	5.00

18.1400 g, .800 SILVER, .4666 oz ASW

KM#	Date	Mintage	VF	XF	Unc
65a	1974FM(P)	.094	—	Proof	6.00
	1975FM(P)	.029	—	Proof	6.00
	1976FM(P)	.023	—	Proof	6.00
	1977FM(P)	.011	—	Proof	6.00
	1978FM(P)	6,931	—	Proof	7.00
	1979FM(P)	2,053	—	Proof	8.00
	1980FM(P)	2,084	—	Proof	8.00

COPPER-NICKEL, 32mm

65b	1981FM(P)	1,980	—	Proof	8.00

Poinciana Flower
Obv: Similar to KM#65.

89	1982FM(P)	1,217	—	Proof	10.00

10th Anniversary of Independence

93	1983FM(P)	1,020	—	Proof	12.50

Bougainvillea Flower

104	1984FM(P)	1,036	—	Proof	12.50
	1985FM(P)	7,500	—	Proof	7.50

2 DOLLARS

29.8000 g, .925 SILVER, .8863 oz ASW
Obv: Similar to 1 Dollar, KM#8.

9	1966	.104	BV	6.00	9.50
	1969	.026	BV	6.00	9.50
	1969	.010	—	Proof	11.00
	1970	.032	BV	6.00	9.50
	1970	.023	—	Proof	11.00

Rev: Similar to KM#9.

23	1971FM	.088	BV	6.00	9.50
	1971FM(P)	.060	—	Proof	11.00

KM#	Date	Mintage	VF	XF	Unc
23	1972FM	.065	BV	6.00	9.50
	1972FM(P)	.059	—	Proof	11.00
	1973FM	.043	BV	6.00	9.50
	1973FM(P)	.050	—	Proof	11.00

COPPER-NICKEL
Rev: Similar to KM#9.

66	1974FM	.037	—	2.00	5.00
	1975FM(M)	300 pcs.	—	9.00	25.00
	1975FM(U)	8,810	—	2.00	5.50
	1976FM(M)	300 pcs.	—	9.00	25.00
	1976FM(U)	4,381	—	2.00	6.00
	1977FM(M)	300 pcs.	—	9.00	25.00
	1977FM(U)	946 pcs.	—	3.00	10.00
	1978FM(U)	1,067	—	3.00	10.00
	1979FM	300 pcs.	—	7.50	25.00

29.8000 g, .925 SILVER, .8863 oz ASW

66a	1974FM(P)	.129	—	Proof	11.00
	1975FM(P)	.045	—	Proof	11.00
	1976FM(P)	.035	—	Proof	11.00
	1977FM(P)	.015	—	Proof	12.00
	1978FM(P)	.011	—	Proof	12.00
	1979FM(P)	2,053	—	Proof	18.00
	1980FM(P)	2,084	—	Proof	18.00

COPPER-NICKEL, 34mm

66b	1981FM(P)	1,980	—	Proof	10.00

Bahama Swallows
Obv: Similar to KM#66.

90	1982FM(P)	1,217	—	Proof	15.00

10th Anniversary of Independence

94	1983FM(P)	1,020	—	Proof	15.00

Flamingo Birds

105	1984FM(P)	1,036	—	Proof	15.00
	1985FM(P)	7,500	—	Proof	12.50

5 DOLLARS

42.1200 g, .925 SILVER, 1.2527 oz ASW
Obv: Similar to 1 Dollar, KM#8.

KM#	Date	Mintage	VF	XF	Unc
10	1966	.100	BV	10.00	12.00
	1969	.036	BV	10.00	12.00
	1969	.010	—	Proof	13.00
	1970	.043	BV	10.00	12.00
	1970	.023	—	Proof	13.00

Rev: Similar to KM#10.

24	1971FM	.029	BV	10.00	12.00
	1971FM(P)	.031	—	Proof	14.00

Obv: Similar to KM#24.

33	1972FM	.032	BV	8.00	12.00
	1972FM(P)	.035	—	Proof	14.00
	1973FM	.032	BV	8.00	12.00
	1973FM(P)	.035	—	Proof	14.00

BAHAMAS 158

KM#	Date	Mintage	VF	XF	Unc
67	1974FM	.032	—	—	6.50
	1975FM(M)	200 pcs.	—	—	40.00
	1975FM(U)	7,058	—	—	7.50
	1976FM(M)	200 pcs.	—	—	40.00
	1976FM(U)	2,591	—	—	10.00
	1977FM(M)	200 pcs.	—	—	40.00
	1977FM(U)	801 pcs.	—	—	18.00
	1978FM(U)	1,244	—	—	15.00

42.1200 g, .925 SILVER, 1.2527 oz ASW

67a	1974FM(P)	.094	—	Proof	13.00
	1975FM(P)	.029	—	Proof	13.00
	1976FM(P)	.023	—	Proof	13.00
	1977FM(P)	.011	—	Proof	15.00
	1978FM(P)	6,931	—	Proof	17.50
	1979FM(P)	2,053	—	Proof	22.50
	1980FM(P)	2,084	—	Proof	22.50

42.1200 g, .500 SILVER, .6771 oz ASW
Reduced diameter.

67b	1981FM(P)	1,980	—	Proof	27.50

Columbus Memorial
Obv: Similar to KM#67.

91	1982FM(P)	1,217	—	Proof	50.00

10th Anniversary of Independence

95	1983FM(P)	1,020	—	Proof	50.00

Historical Map

106	1984FM(P)	1,036	—	Proof	45.00

Christopher Columbus

KM#	Date	Mintage	VF	XF	Unc
107	1985FM(P)	7,847	—	Proof	30.00

10 DOLLARS

3.9943 g, .917 GOLD, .1177 oz AGW

11	1967	6,200	—	—	60.00
	1967	850 pcs.	—	Proof	90.00

25	1971	.023	—	—	60.00
	1971(t)	1,250	—	Proof	90.00

Rev: Hallmark and fineness stamped near bottom.

26	1971	—	—	—	70.00

NOTE: The above coins were struck by the Gori & Zucchi Mint, Italy.

3.1950 g, .917 GOLD, .0940 oz AGW

34	1972	.011	—	—	60.00
	1972	1,250	—	Proof	70.00

1.4500 g, .750 GOLD, .0349 oz AGW
Rev: W/o fineness and date.

40	1973	—	—	—	25.00
	1973	—	—	Proof	45.00

1.4500 g, .585 GOLD, .0272 oz AGW
Rev: .585 fineness

41	1973	9,960	—	—	25.00
	1973	1,260	—	Proof	45.00

49.7500 g, .925 SILVER, 1.4795 oz ASW
Independence Commemorative
Obv: Similar to 5 Dollars, KM#24.

42	1973FM	.028	—	—	18.00
	1973FM(P)	.063	—	Proof	22.50

COPPER-NICKEL
First Anniversary of Independence
Obv: Similar to 5 Dollars, KM#67.

KM#	Date	Mintage	VF	XF	Unc
68	1974FM	4,825	—	—	12.00

50.4200 g, .925 SILVER, 1.4994 oz ASW

68a	1974FM(P)	.043	—	Proof	14.00

COPPER-NICKEL
Second Anniversary of Independence
Obv: Similar to 5 Dollars, KM#67.

76	1975FM(M)	100 pcs.	—	—	100.00
	1975FM(U)	5,325	—	—	12.50
	1976FM(M)	100 pcs.	—	—	100.00
	1976FM(U)	100 pcs.	—	—	100.00
	1977FM(M)	100 pcs.	—	—	100.00
	1977FM(U)	369 pcs.	—	—	45.00

49.1000 g, .925 SILVER, 1.4602 oz ASW

76a	1975FM(P)	.063	—	Proof	19.00
	1976FM(P)	.010	—	Proof	21.00
	1977FM(P)	4,424	—	Proof	22.50

45.3600 g, .500 SILVER, .7291 oz ASW
Fifth Anniversary of Independence
Obv: Similar to 5 Dollars, KM#67.

78.1	1978	.050	—	Proof	18.00

BAHAMAS 159

Rev: Tower mint mark after DOLLARS.
KM#	Date	Mintage	VF	XF	Unc
78.2	1978(t)	—	—	Proof	18.00

Fifth Anniversary of Independence
Obv: Arms.
| 79 | 1978 | .050 | — | Proof | 16.00 |

30.2800 g, .500 SILVER, .4868 oz ASW
Tenth Anniversary Caribbean Development Bank
| 84 | 1980FM(P) | .010 | — | Proof | 20.00 |

28.2800 g, .925 SILVER, .8410 oz ASW
Wedding of Prince Charles and Lady Diana
| 85 | 1981 | .039 | — | Proof | 18.00 |

30.2800 g, .500 SILVER, .4867 oz ASW
30th Anniversary of Coronation of Queen Elizabeth II
KM#	Date	Mintage	VF	XF	Unc
96	1983FM(P)	3,374	—	Proof	25.00

23.3300 g, .925 SILVER, .6939 oz ASW
10th Anniversary of Independence
| 97 | 1983 | 800 pcs. | — | Proof | 42.50 |

H.R.H. Prince Charles
Obv: Similar to KM#67.
Rev: Prince Charles standing w/flag of Bahamas behind.
| 102 | 1983 | .010 | — | Proof | 17.50 |

Los Angeles Olympics - Sprinter
| 114 | 1984 | 2,100 | — | Proof | 42.50 |

28.2800 g, .925 SILVER, .8411 oz ASW
Royal Visit
KM#	Date	Mintage	VF	XF	Unc
109	1985	*5,000	—	Proof	27.50

47.5400 g, .917 GOLD, 1.4013 oz AGW
| 109a | 1985 | *250 pcs. | — | Proof | 1000. |

28.2800 g, .500 SILVER, .4546 oz ASW
Commonwealth Games
| 113 | 1986 | .050 | — | Proof | 17.50 |

28.2800 g, .925 SILVER, .8411 oz ASW
| 113a | 1986 | .020 | — | Proof | 27.50 |

Queen Isabella and Columbus
Similar to 250 Dollars, KM#121.
| 120 | 1987 | *.010 | — | Proof | 60.00 |

Columbus Discovering America
Obv: Queen Elizabeth. Rev: Columbus sighting America.
| 123 | 1988 | *.010 | — | Proof | 45.00 |

20 DOLLARS

7.9880 g, .917 GOLD, .2355 oz AGW
| 12 | 1967 | 6,200 | — | — | 130.00 |
| | 1967 | 850 pcs. | — | Proof | 170.00 |

| 27 | 1971 | .022 | — | — | 135.00 |
| | 1971(t) | 1,250 | — | Proof | 150.00 |

Rev: Hallmark and fineness stamped at bottom
| 28 | 1971 | | — | — | 130.00 |

NOTE: The above coins were struck by the Gori & Zucchi Mint, Italy.

6.4800 g, .917 GOLD, .1880 oz AGW
| 35 | 1972 | .010 | — | — | 110.00 |
| | 1972 | 1,250 | — | Proof | 140.00 |

BAHAMAS 160

2.9000 g, .750 GOLD, .0699 oz AGW
Rev: W/o fineness and date.

KM#	Date	Mintage	VF	XF	Unc
43	1973	—	—	—	45.00
	1973	—	—	Proof	55.00

2.9000 g, .585 GOLD, .0545 oz AGW
Rev: .585 fineness.

| 44 | 1973 | 8,660 | — | — | 40.00 |
| | 1973 | 1,260 | — | Proof | 60.00 |

25 DOLLARS

37.3800 g, .925 SILVER, 1.1117 oz ASW
250th Anniversary of Parliament
Obv: Similar to 10 Dollars, KM#96.

| 82 | 1979FM | 3,002 | — | Proof | 45.00 |

120.0000 g, .925 SILVER, 3.5687 oz ASW
Columbus' Discovery of America
Obv: Similar to 10 Dollars, KM#113.

| 110 | 1985 | *.020 | — | Proof | 75.00 |

129.6000 g, .925 SILVER, 3.8547 oz ASW
Bird Conservation - Flamingos
Obv: Similar to 10 Dollars, KM#113.

| 115 | 1985 | *.010 | — | Proof | 80.00 |

Queen Isabella and Columbus
Similar to 250 Dollars, KM#121.

KM#	Date	Mintage	VF	XF	Unc
118	1987	*.010	—	Proof	80.00

136.0000 g, .925 SILVER, 5.0000 oz ASW
Columbus Discovering America
Obv: Queen Elizabeth. Rev: Columbus sighting America.

| 124 | 1988 | — | — | Proof | 160.00 |

50 DOLLARS

19.9710 g, .917 GOLD, .5888 oz AGW

| 13 | 1967 | 1,200 | — | — | 300.00 |
| | 1967 | 850 pcs. | — | Proof | 325.00 |

| 29 | 1971 | 6,800 | — | — | 300.00 |
| | 1971(t) | 1,250 | — | Proof | 325.00 |

Rev: Hallmark and fineness stamped at bottom

| 30 | 1971 | — | — | — | 300.00 |

NOTE: The above coins were struck by the Gori & Zucchi Mint, Italy.

15.9700 g, .917 GOLD, .4708 oz AGW

| 36 | 1972 | 2,250 | — | — | 250.00 |
| | 1972 | 1,250 | — | Proof | 275.00 |

7.2700 g, .750 GOLD, .1753 oz AGW
Rev: W/o fineness, date below lobster.

| 45 | 1973 | — | — | — | 90.00 |
| | 1973 | — | — | Proof | 110.00 |

7.2700 g, .585 GOLD, .1367 oz AGW
Rev: .585 fineness to left, date to right.

| 46 | 1973 | 5,160 | — | — | 80.00 |
| | 1973 | 1,260 | — | Proof | 90.00 |

Rev: W/o date or fineness

| 47 | 1973 | — | — | — | 90.00 |

15.6448 g, .500 GOLD, .2515 oz AGW
Independence Commemorative

| 48 | 1973JP | .023 | — | — | 125.00 |
| | 1973JP | .018 | — | Proof | 135.00 |

2.7300 g, .917 GOLD, .0804 oz AGW
Rev: W/o fineness

| 69 | 1974 | .034 | — | — | 50.00 |
| | 1974 | .020 | — | Proof | 60.00 |

KM#	Date	Mintage	VF	XF	Unc
69	1975	.026	—	—	50.00
	1975	.015	—	Proof	60.00
	1976	2,207	—	—	50.00
	1976	Inc. Ab.	—	Proof	60.00
	1977	1,090	—	—	75.00
	1977	—	—	Proof	75.00

Rev: .917 fineness

| 70 | 1974 | — | — | — | 60.00 |

2.6800 g, .500 GOLD, .0430 oz AGW

| 86 | 1981FM(P) | 2,050 | — | Proof | 80.00 |

Marlin (Swordfish)

| 92 | 1982FM(P) | 841 pcs. | — | Proof | 100.00 |

30th Anniversary of Independence

| 98 | 1983FM(P) | 962 pcs. | — | Proof | 100.00 |

Golden Allamanda

| 103 | 1984FM(P) | 3,716 | — | Proof | 85.00 |

Santa Maria

| 108 | 1985FM(P) | 1,786 | — | Proof | 85.00 |

100 DOLLARS

39.9400 g, .917 GOLD, 1.1776 oz AGW

| 14 | 1967 | 1,200 | — | — | 625.00 |
| | 1967 | 850 pcs. | — | Proof | 650.00 |

| 31 | 1971 | 6,800 | — | — | 625.00 |
| | 1971(t) | 1,250 | — | Proof | 650.00 |

BAHAMAS 161

Rev: Hallmark and fineness at bottom right.

KM#	Date	Mintage	VF	XF	Unc
32	1971	—	—	—	625.00

NOTE: The above coins were struck by the Gori & Zucchi Mint, Italy.

31.9500 g, .917 GOLD, .9420 oz AGW

37	1972	2,250	—	—	475.00
	1972	1,250	—	Proof	550.00

NOTE: The 1972 proof $100 is serially numbered on the edge.

14.5400 g, .750 GOLD, .3506 oz AGW
Rev: W/o fineness, date at bottom.

49	1973	—	—	—	185.00
	1973	—	—	Proof	195.00

14.5400 g, .585 GOLD, .2735 oz AGW
Rev: .585 fineness to left, date to right.

50.1	1973	4,660	—	—	145.00
	1973 serial no. on reverse	1,260	—	Proof	155.00

Rev: Date and fineness at right, serial no. at left.

50.2	1973	—	—	—	170.00

18.0145 g, .500 GOLD, .2896 oz AGW
First Anniversary of Independence

71	1974	4,486	—	—	155.00
	1974	4,153	—	Proof	195.00

5.4600 g, .917 GOLD, .1609 oz AGW
Rev: Broken waves behind flamingos legs.

72	1974	.029	—	—	100.00
	1975	—	—	—	115.00

Rev: Unbroken waves behind flamingos legs.

KM#	Date	Mintage	VF	XF	Unc
73	1974	.017	—	Proof	115.00
	1975	—	—	Proof	115.00
	1976	—	—	—	100.00
	1976	—	—	Proof	115.00
	1977	—	—	—	100.00
	1977	—	—	Proof	115.00

Rev: .917 fineness in oval.

74	1974	—	—	—	115.00

18.0145 g, .500 GOLD, .2896 oz AGW
Second Anniversary of Independence

77	1975	3,694	—	—	175.00
	1975	3,145	—	Proof	225.00
	1976	761 pcs.	—	Proof	250.00
	1977	2,023	—	—	225.00

13.6000 g, .963 GOLD, .4211 oz AGW
Fifth Anniversary of Independence
Obv: Arms. Rev: Portrait of H.R.H. Prince Charles.

80	1978	3,275	—	Proof	210.00

Fifth Anniversary of Independence
Obv: Arms. Rev: Portrait of Sir Milo B. Butler.

81	1978	.025	—	Proof	210.00

6.4800 g, .900 GOLD, .1875 oz AGW
Wedding of Prince Charles and Lady Diana

87	1981	.010	—	Proof	135.00

10th Anniversary of Independence

99	1983	400 pcs.	—	Proof	195.00

Columbus' Discovery of America

111	1985	450 pcs.	—	—	220.00

Queen Isabella and Christopher Columbus
Similar to 250 Dollars, KM#121.

119	1987	*5,000	—	Proof	

Columbus Discovering America
Obv: Queen Elizabeth. Rev: Columbus sighting America.

125	1988	*5,000	—	Proof	260.00

150 DOLLARS

8.1900 g, .917 GOLD, .2414 oz AGW

KM#	Date	Mintage	VF	XF	Unc
51	1973	—	—	—	165.00
	1973	—	—	Proof	165.00
	1974	7,128	—	—	165.00
	1974	4,787	—	Proof	165.00
	1975	3,141	—	—	165.00
	1975	2,770	—	Proof	165.00
	1976	168 pcs.	—	Proof	230.00
	1977	327 pcs.	—	Proof	180.00

Rev: Waves under crawfish extend to its two front legs.

52	1973	—	—	Proof	200.00

Rev: .917 fineness in oval.

53	1973	—	—	—	175.00

200 DOLLARS

10.9200 g, .917 GOLD, .3219 oz AGW

54	1973	—	—	—	200.00
	1973	—	—	Proof	215.00
	1974	5,528	—	—	200.00
	1974	3,587	—	Proof	215.00
	1975	1,545	—	—	200.00
	1975	1,570	—	Proof	220.00
	1976	168 pcs.	—	Proof	275.00
	1977	321 pcs.	—	Proof	245.00

55	1973	—	—	Proof	215.00

Rev: .917 fineness in oval.

56	1973	—	—	—	200.00

Rev: .916 fineness at left,
serial number stamped below arms.

57	1973	—	—	—	200.00

Rev: W/o fineness, serial number to left.

58	1973	—	—	—	200.00

BAHAMAS 162

250 DOLLARS

10.5800 g, .900 GOLD, .3061 oz AGW
250th Anniversary of Parliament

KM#	Date	Mintage	VF	XF	Unc
83	1979	1,835	—	Proof	300.00

47.5400 g, .917 GOLD, 1.4017 oz AGW
Commonwealth Games
Similar to 10 Dollars, KM#113.

| 117 | 1986 | 150 pcs. | — | Proof | 975.00 |

41.4700 g, .900 GOLD, 1.2001 oz AGW
America's Cup Challenge

KM#	Date	Mintage	VF	XF	Unc
100	1983	300 pcs.	—	Proof	950.00

2500 DOLLARS

Queen Isabella and Columbus

| 121 | 1987 | *250 pcs. | — | Proof | 1625. |

Columbus Discovering America
Obv: Queen Elizabeth. Rev: Columbus sighting America.

| 126 | 1988 | *250 pcs. | — | Proof | 1300. |

500 DOLLARS

407.2600 g, .917 GOLD, 12.0082 oz AGW
Obv: Similar to KM#101.
Illustration is reduced, actual size: 72mm

| 75 | 1974 | 204 pcs. | — | Proof | 8500. |
| | 1977 | 168 pcs. | — | Proof | 9000. |

Columbus' Discovery of America
Illustration is reduced, actual size: 72mm

KM#	Date	Mintage	VF	XF	Unc
112	1985	37 pcs.	—	Proof	10,000.

25.9200 g, .900 GOLD, .7500 oz AGW
Wedding of Prince Charles and Lady Diana

| 88 | 1981 | 5,000 | — | Proof | 550.00 |

1000 DOLLARS

10th Anniversary of Independence
Illustration is reduced, actual size: 72mm

| 101 | 1983 | 55 pcs. | — | Proof | 10,000. |

Columbus and Isabella
Illustration is reduced, actual size: 72mm

| 116 | 1987 | 200 pcs. | — | — | 8500. |

Columbus
Obv: Queen Elizabeth.

Rev: Columbus sighting "New World."

KM#	Date	Mintage	VF	XF	Unc
122	1988	100 pcs.	—	Proof	9750.

MINT SETS (MS)

KM#	Date	Mintage	Identification	Issue Price	Mkt. Val.
MS1	1966(9)	75,050	KM2-10	16.00	25.00
MS2	1966(7)	500,000	KM2-8	5.25	9.00
MS3	1967(4)	1,200	KM11-14	180.00	1150.
MS4	1969(9)	26,221	KM2-10	20.25	30.00
MS5	1970(9)	25,135	KM3-10,15	20.25	30.00
MS6	1971(9)	12,895	KM16-24	20.25	25.00
MS7	1971(4)	6,800	KM25,27,29,31	185.00	1150.
MS8	1972(9)	10,128	KM16-23,33	22.75	25.00
MS9	1972(4)	2,250	KM34-37	185.00	950.00
MS10	1973(9)	9,853	KM16-23,33	23.75	25.00
MS11	1973(4)	4,660	KM41,44,46,50	—	310.00
MS12	1973(2)	—	KM40,43	—	85.00
MS13	1974(9)	11,004	KM59-67	22.50	15.00
MS14	1974(4)	5,528	KM51,54,69,72	—	530.00
MS15	1974(2)	—	KM68,71	—	170.00
MS16	1975(9)	3,845	KM59-67	27.00	20.00
MS17	1975(4)	1,545	KM51,54,69,72	—	535.00
MS18	1976(9)	1,453	KM59-67	27.00	30.00
MS19	1977(9)	731	KM59-67	27.00	55.00
MS20	1978(9)	767	KM59-67	27.00	50.00

PROOF SETS (PS)

PS1	1967(4)	850	KM11-14	252.00	1245.
PS2	1969(9)	10,381	KM2-10	35.00	35.00
PS3	1970(9)	22,827	KM3-10,15	35.00	35.00
PS4	1971(9)	30,507	KM16-24	35.00	35.00
PS5	1971(4)	1,250	KM25,27,29,31	298.00	1220.
PS6	1972(9)	34,789	KM16-23,33	35.00	35.00
PS7	1972(4)	1,250	KM34-37	565.00	1000.
PS8	1973(9)	34,815	KM16-23,33	35.00	35.00
PS9	1973(4)	1,260	KM41,44,46,50	402.00	355.00
PS10	1974(9)	93,776	KM59-63,64a-67a	45.00	35.00
PS11	1974(4)	3,587	KM51,54,69,73	1000.	550.00
PS12	1975(9)	29,095	KM59-63,64a-67a	59.00	35.00
PS13	1975(4)	1,570	KM51,54,69,73	1000.	555.00
PS14	1976(9)	22,570	KM59-63,64a-67a	59.00	35.00
PS15	1976(4)	—	KM51,54,69,73	1000.	695.00
PS16	1977(9)	10,812	KM59-63,64a-67a	59.00	38.00
PS17	1977(4)	—	KM51,54,69,73	—	625.00
PS18	1978(9)	6,931	KM59-63,64a-67a	59.00	45.00
PS19	1979(9)	2,053	KM59-63,64a-67a	115.00	65.00
PS20	1979(2)	—	KM82-83	445.00	300.00
PS21	1980(9)	2,084	KM59-63,64a-67a	145.00	65.00
PS22	1981(9)	1,980	KM59-66,65b-67b	62.00	55.00
PS23	1982(9)	—	KM59-64,89-91	67.00	80.00
PS24	1983(9)	1,009	KM59-64,93-95	67.00	80.00
PS25	1984(9)	7,500	KM59-64,104-106	72.00	80.00
PS26	1985(9)	—	KM59-64,104,105,107	—	50.00

BAHRAIN

The State of Bahrain, a group of islands in the Persian Gulf off Saudi Arabia, has an area of 240 sq. mi. (622 sq. km.) and a population of 443,597. Capital: Manama. Prior to the depression of the 1930s, the economy was based on pearl fishing. Petroleum and aluminum industries and transit trade are the vital factors in the economy today.

The Portuguese occupied the islands in 1507 but were driven out in 1602 by Arab subjects of Persia. They in turn were ejected by Arabs of the Ataiba tribe from the Arabian mainland who have maintained possession up to the present time. The ruling sheikh of Bahrain entered into relations with Great Britain in 1805 and concluded a binding treaty of protection in 1861. In 1968 Great Britain decided to terminate treaty relations with the Persian Gulf sheikhdoms. Unable to agree on terms of union with the other sheikhdoms, Bahrain decided to seek independence as a separate entity and became fully independent on August 14, 1971.

The coinage of the State of Bahrain was struck at the Royal Mint, London, England.

RULERS
Isa Bin Sulman, 1961-

MINT MARKS
Bahrain بحرين

El Bahrain
of the Two Seas البحرين

MONETARY SYSTEM
1000 Fils = 1 Dinar

FIL

BRONZE

KM#	Date	Year	Mintage	VF	XF	Unc
1	AH1385	1965	1.500	.10	.15	.30
	1385	1965	1,719	—	Proof	1.00
	1386	1966	1.500	.10	.15	.30
	1386	1966	—	—	Proof	2.00

1.5000 g, .925 SILVER, .0446 oz ASW
| 1a | AH1403 | 1983 | *.015 | — | Proof | 3.00 |

5 FILS

BRONZE
2	AH1385	1965	8.000	.10	.15	.25
	1385	1965	.012	—	Proof	1.00

2.0000 g, .925 SILVER, .0595 oz ASW
| 2a | AH1403 | 1983 | *.015 | — | Proof | 3.00 |

10 FILS

BRONZE
3	AH1385	1965	8.500	.10	.15	.35
	1385	1965	.012	—	Proof	1.50

4.7500 g, .925 SILVER, .1413 oz ASW
| 3a | AH1403 | 1983 | *.015 | — | Proof | 4.00 |

25 FILS

COPPER NICKEL

KM#	Date	Year	Mintage	VF	XF	Unc
4	AH1385	1965	11.250	.15	.25	.50
	1385	1965	.012	—	Proof	2.00

1.7500 g, .925 SILVER, .0521 oz ASW
| 4a | AH1403 | 1983 | *.015 | — | Proof | 4.00 |

50 FILS

COPPER-NICKEL
5	AH1385	1965	6.909	.20	.40	.75
	1385	1965	.012	—	Proof	2.50

3.1000 g, .925 SILVER, .0922 oz ASW
| 5a | AH1403 | 1983 | *.015 | — | Proof | 5.00 |

100 FILS

COPPER-NICKEL
6	AH1385	1965	8.300	.25	.50	1.00
	1385	1965	.012	—	Proof	3.00

6.5000 g, .925 SILVER, .1933 oz ASW
| 6a | AH1403 | 1983 | *.015 | — | Proof | 6.00 |

250 FILS

COPPER-NICKEL
F.A.O. Issue
7	AH1385	1965	.012	—	Proof	5.00
	1389	1969	.050	.75	1.25	3.00
	1389	1969	—	—	Proof	5.00
	1403	1983	—	.75	1.25	3.00

15.0000 g, .925 SILVER, .4461 oz ASW
| 7a | AH1403 | 1983 | *.015 | — | Proof | 10.00 |

500 FILS

18.3000 g, .800 SILVER, .4707 oz ASW
Opening of Isatown
| 8 | AH1385 | 1965 | .012 | — | Proof | 12.50 |

BAHRAIN 164

KM#	Date	Year	Mintage	VF	XF	Unc
8	1388	1968	.050	2.00	4.00	7.00
	1388	1968		—	Proof	12.50

18.0600 g, .925 SILVER, .5372 oz ASW

| 8a | AH1403 | 1983 | *.015 | — | Proof | 25.00 |

5 DINARS

19.4400 g, .925 SILVER, .5782 oz ASW
Wildlife - Gazelle

| 13 | AH1406 | 1986 | *.025 | — | Proof | 20.00 |

10 DINARS

16.0000 g, .917 GOLD, .4717 oz AGW
Opening of Isatown

| 9 | AH1388 | 1968 | 3,000 | — | — | 350.00 |

Independence Commemorative

| 10 | AH1391 | 1971 | 3,000 | — | — | 350.00 |

50 DINARS

15.9800 g, .917 GOLD, .4712 oz AGW

| 11 | AH1398 | 1978 | 5,000 | — | Proof | 350.00 |

100 DINARS

31.9600 g, .917 GOLD, .9424 oz AGW

| 12 | AH1398 | 1978 | 5,000 | — | Proof | 750.00 |

PROOF SETS (PS)

KM#	Date	Mintage	Identification	Issue Price	Mkt. Val.
PS1	Mixed (8)	20,000	KM1-6,1965;KM7,1969;KM8, 1968	32.00	22.50
PS2	1983 (7)	15,000	KM1a-8a	99.00	60.00

BALTIC REGIONS

ESTONIAN S.S.R.

The former free state of Estonia (now the Estonian Soviet Socialist Republic of the U.S.S.R.) is the northernmost of the three Baltic States in Eastern Europe. It has an area of 17,413 sq. mi. (45,100 sq. km.) and a population of 1.4 million. Capital: Tallinn. Agriculture and dairy farming are the principal industries. Butter, eggs, bacon, timber and petroleum are exported.

This small and ancient Baltic state has enjoyed but two decades of independence since the 13th century. After having been conquered by the Danes, the Livonian Knights, the Teutonic Knights of Germany (who reduced the people to serfdom), the Swedes, the Poles and Russia, Estonia declared itself an independent republic on Feb. 24, 1918 but was not freed until Feb. 1919. The peace treaty was signed Feb. 2, 1920. Shortly after the start of World War II, it was again occupied by Russia and incorporated as the 16th state of the U.S.S.R. Germany occupied the tiny state from 1941 to 1944, after which it was retaken by Russia. Most of the nations of the world, including the United States and Great Britain, have not recognized Estonia's incorporation into the Soviet Union.

The coinage, issued during the country's brief independence, is obsolete.

REPUBLIC COINAGE

MONETARY SYSTEM
100 Marka = 1 Kroon

MARK

COPPER-NICKEL

KM#	Date	Mintage	Fine	VF	XF	Unc
1	1922	5.025	1.50	3.00	5.00	9.00

NICKEL-BRONZE

| 1a | 1924 | 1.985 | 2.00 | 4.00 | 6.00 | 11.00 |

| 5 | 1926 | 3.979 | 3.00 | — | 9.00 | 20.00 |

3 MARKA

COPPER-NICKEL

| 2 | 1922 | 2.089 | 2.00 | 3.50 | 5.00 | 10.00 |

NICKEL-BRONZE

| 2a | 1925 | 1.134 | 4.00 | 7.00 | 12.00 | 22.50 |

| 6 | 1926 | .903 | 17.50 | 32.50 | 50.00 | 90.00 |

5 MARKA

COPPER-NICKEL

KM#	Date	Mintage	Fine	VF	XF	Unc
3	1922	3.983	2.50	4.00	6.00	17.50

NICKEL-BRONZE

| 3a | 1924 | 1.335 | 3.00 | 5.00 | 7.00 | 20.00 |

| 7 | 1926 | 1.038 | 75.00 | 150.00 | 200.00 | 350.00 |

10 MARKA

NICKEL-BRONZE

| 4 | 1925 | 2.200 | 3.00 | 6.00 | 10.00 | 22.50 |
| 8 | 1926 | *2.789 | 400.00 | 700.00 | 900.00 | 1000. |

*NOTE: Most of this issue were melted down. Not released to circulation.

MONETARY REFORM

100 Senti = 1 Kroon

SENT

BRONZE

| 10 | 1929 | 23.553 | .50 | 1.00 | 1.50 | 3.00 |

1mm thick planchet

| 19.1 | 1939 | 5.000 | 5.00 | 10.00 | 15.00 | 25.00 |

0.9mm thick planchet

| 19.2 | 1939 | Inc. Ab. | 5.00 | 10.00 | 15.00 | 27.50 |

2 SENTI

BRONZE

| 15 | 1934 | 5.838 | 1.00 | 2.00 | 4.00 | 8.00 |

5 SENTI

BRONZE

| 11 | 1931 | 11.000 | 1.00 | 2.00 | 4.00 | 8.00 |

10 SENTI

NICKEL-BRONZE

KM#	Date	Mintage	Fine	VF	XF	Unc
12	1931	4.089	1.00	2.00	4.00	8.00

20 SENTI

NICKEL-BRONZE

| 17 | 1935 | 4.250 | 1.00 | 2.00 | 4.00 | 12.00 |

25 SENTI

NICKEL-BRONZE

| 9 | 1928 | 2.025 | 3.00 | 6.00 | 10.00 | 20.00 |

50 SENTI

NICKEL-BRONZE

| 18 | 1936 | 1.256 | 3.00 | 6.00 | 12.00 | 25.00 |

KROON

6.0000 g, .500 SILVER, .0965 oz ASW
Tenth Singing Festival

| 14 | 1933 | .350 | 8.00 | 12.50 | 27.50 | 55.00 |

ALUMINUM-BRONZE

| 16 | 1934 | 3.304 | 4.00 | 7.00 | 13.00 | 27.50 |

2 KROONI

12.0000 g, .500 SILVER, .1929 oz ASW
Tallinn Castle

| 20 (10) | 1930 | 1.276 | 3.00 | 6.00 | 14.00 | 30.00 |

University of Tartu Tercentenary

KM#	Date	Mintage	Fine	VF	XF	Unc
13	1932	.100	—	15.00	30.00	40.00

LATVIAN S.S.R.

The Latvian Soviet Socialist Republic of the U.S.S.R., the central Baltic state in east Europe, has an area of 24,595 sq. mi. (43,601 sq. km.) and a population of 2.5 million. Capital: Riga. Livestock raising and manufacturing are the chief industries. Butter, bacon, fertilizers and telephone equipment are exported.

The Latvians, of Aryan descent, were nomadic tribesmen who settled along the Baltic prior to the 13th century. Lacking a central government, they were easily conquered by the German Teutonic Knights, Russia, Sweden and Poland. Following the third partition of Poland by Austria, Prussia and Russia in 1795, Latvia came under Russian domination and did not experience autonomy until the Russian Revolution of 1917 provided an opportunity for freedom. The Latvian Republic was established on Nov. 18, 1918. The republic was occupied by Soviet troops and annexed to the Soviet Union in 1940. Following the German occupation of 1941-44, it was retaken by Russia and reestablished as a member republic of the Soviet Union. Western countries, including the United States, have not recognized Latvia's incorporation into the Soviet Union.

The coinage, issued during Latvia's short tenure as a republic, is obsolete.

REPUBLIC COINAGE

MONETARY SYSTEM
100 Santimu = 1 Lats

SANTIMS

BRONZE

1						
	1922	5.000	.65	1.40	2.75	8.00
	1924	4.990	.65	1.40	2.75	8.00
	1926	5.000	.65	1.40	2.75	8.00
	1928 designer's name below ribbon					
		5.000	.65	1.40	2.75	8.00
	1928 w/o designer's name below ribbon					
	Inc. Ab.		2.00	5.00	10.00	32.50
	1932	5.000	.65	1.40	2.75	8.00
	1932	—	—	—	Proof	—
	1935	5.000	.65	1.40	2.75	8.00

10	1937	2.700	.65	1.40	2.75	8.00
	1938	1.900	.65	1.40	2.75	10.00
	1939	*3.400	.50	1.00	2.00	3.00

*NOTE: Most were never placed into circulation.

2 SANTIMI

BRONZE

2						
	1922 designer's name on rev.					
		10.000	1.00	2.00	4.00	9.00
	1922 w/o designer's name					
	Inc. Ab.		5.00	10.00	17.50	35.00
	1926	5.000	.90	2.00	4.00	9.00
	1928	5.000	.90	2.00	4.00	9.00
	1932	5.000	.90	2.00	4.00	9.00
	1932	—	—	—	Proof	—

19mm

| 11.1 | 1937 | .045 | 8.00 | 15.00 | 25.00 | 50.00 |

19.5mm

KM#	Date	Mintage	Fine	VF	XF	Unc
11.2	1939	*5.000	1.00	2.00	3.00	5.50

*NOTE: Most were never placed into circulation.

5 SANTIMI

BRONZE

3	1922 designer's name on reverse					
		15.000	.50	1.00	3.00	8.00
	1922 w/o designer's name					
	Inc. Ab.		3.00	6.00	10.00	20.00

10 SANTIMU

NICKEL

| 4 | 1922 | 15.000 | .50 | 1.00 | 3.00 | 5.00 |

20 SANTIMU

NICKEL

| 5 | 1922 | 15.000 | .50 | 1.00 | 3.00 | 8.00 |

50 SANTIMU

NICKEL

| 6 | 1922 | 9.000 | 1.00 | 3.00 | 5.00 | 10.00 |

LATS

5.0000 g, .835 SILVER, .1342 oz ASW

7	1923	—	—	—	—	900.00
	1924	10.000	2.00	3.00	5.00	20.00

2 LATI

10.0000 g, .835 SILVER, .2684 oz ASW

8	1925	6.386	2.50	3.00	5.00	30.00
	1926	1.114	2.50	3.00	5.00	30.00

5 LATI

25.0000 g, .835 SILVER, .6712 oz ASW

KM#	Date	Mintage	Fine	VF	XF	Unc
9	1929	1.000	9.00	14.00	20.00	40.00
	1929	—	—	—	Proof	
	1931	2.000	9.00	14.00	20.00	40.00
	1931	—	—	—	Proof	
	1932	.600	9.00	14.00	20.00	40.00
	1932	—	—	—	Proof	

LITHUANIAN S.S.R.

The Lithuanian Soviet Federated Socialist Republic, southernmost of the Baltic states in east Europe, has an area of 25,174 sq. mi. (65,201 sq. km.) and a population of 3.4 million. Capital: Vilnius. The economy is based on livestock raising and manufacturing. Hogs, cattle, hides and electric motors are exported.

Lithuania emerged as a grand duchy in the 14th century. In the 15th century it was a major power of central Europe, stretching from the Baltic to the Black Sea. It was joined with Poland in 1569. Following the third partition of Poland by Austria, Prussia and Russia, 1795, Lithuania came under Russian domination and did not regain its independence until shortly before the end of World War I when it declared itself a sovereign republic. The republic was occupied by Soviet troops and annexed to the U.S.S.R. in 1940. Following the German occupation of 1941-44, it was retaken by Russia and reestablished as a member republic of the Soviet Union. Western countries, including the United States, have not recognized Lithuania's incorporation into the Soviet Union.

The coinage issued during Lithuania's short tenure as a republic, is obsolete.

REPUBLIC COINAGE
MONETARY SYSTEM
100 Centu = 1 Litas

CENTAS

ALUMINUM-BRONZE

| 71 (Y1) | 1925 | 5.000 | 3.00 | 6.00 | 10.00 | 25.00 |

BRONZE

| 79 (Y9) | 1936 | 9.995 | 2.00 | 4.50 | 9.00 | 20.00 |

2 CENTAI

BRONZE

| 80 (Y10) | 1936 | 4.951 | 5.00 | 10.00 | 15.00 | 35.00 |

5 CENTAI

ALUMINUM-BRONZE

KM#	Date	Mintage	Fine	VF	XF	Unc
72 (Y2)	1925	12.000	2.00	4.00	10.00	20.00

BRONZE

| 81 (Y11) | 1936 | 4.800 | 3.00 | 6.00 | 14.00 | 25.00 |

10 CENTU

ALUMINUM-BRONZE

| 73 (Y3) | 1925 | 12.000 | 2.00 | 4.00 | 10.00 | 22.50 |

20 CENTU

ALUMINUM-BRONZE

| 74 (Y4) | 1925 | 8.000 | 3.00 | 5.00 | 12.00 | 25.00 |

50 CENTU

ALUMINUM-BRONZE

| 75 (Y5) | 1925 | 5.000 | 7.50 | 12.00 | 20.00 | 45.00 |

LITAS

2.7000 g, .500 SILVER, .0434 oz ASW

| 76 (Y6) | 1925 | 5.985 | 2.00 | 5.00 | 12.00 | 30.00 |

2 LITU

5.4000 g, .500 SILVER, .0868 oz ASW

| 77 (Y7) | 1925 | 3.000 | 6.00 | 9.00 | 12.00 | 25.00 |

5 LITAI

13.5000 g, .500 SILVER, .2170 oz ASW

KM#	Date	Mintage	Fine	VF	XF	Unc
78 (Y8)	1925	1.000	BV	6.00	10.00	30.00
	1925	—	—	—	Proof	500.00

9.0000 g, .750 SILVER, .2170 oz ASW
Obv: Designer's initials below bust, lettered edge

| 82 (Y12) | 1936 | 2.612 | 3.00 | 5.00 | 8.00 | 25.00 |

10 LITU

18.0000 g, .750 SILVER, .4340 oz ASW
Lettered edge

| 83 (Y13) | 1936 | .720 | 7.00 | 12.50 | 18.00 | 30.00 |

20th Anniversary of Founding

| 84 (Y14) | 1938 | .170 | 15.00 | 25.00 | 30.00 | 50.00 |

MINT SETS (MS)

KM#	Date	Mintage	Identification	Issue Price	Mkt. Val.
MS1	1925(10)	—	KM71-75	—	800.00

BANGLADESH

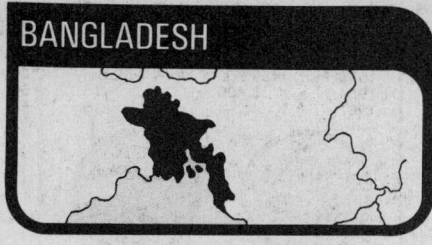

The People's Republic of Bangladesh (formerly East Pakistan), a parliamentary democracy located on the Bay of Bengal bordered by India and Burma, has an area of 55,598 sq. mi. (143,998 sq. km.) and a population of 89.8 million. Capital: Dacca. The economy is predominantly agricultural. Jute products, jute and tea are exported.

British rule over the vast Indian sub-continent ended in 1947 when British India attained independence and was partitioned into the two successor states of India and Pakistan. Pakistan consisted of East and West Pakistan, two areas united by the Moslem religion but separated by culture and 1,000 miles of Indian territory. Restive under the de facto rule of the militant but fewer West Pakistanis, the East Pakistanis unsuccessfully demanded greater economic benefits and political reforms. The inability of the leaders of East and West Pakistan to resolve a political breakdown occasioned by the East Pakistan success in the general elections of 1970 precipitated massive civil disobedience in East Pakistan which West Pakistan sought to suppress militarily. East Pakistan seceded from Pakistan, March 26, 1971, and with the support of India declared an independent People's Republic of Bangladesh.

Bangladesh is a member of the Commonwealth of Nations. The president is the Head of State and of Government.

MONETARY SYSTEM
100 Poisha = 1 Taka

DATING
Christian era using Bengali numerals.

POISHA

ALUMINUM

KM#	Date	Mintage	VF	XF	Unc
5	1974	300.000	—	.10	.15

5 POISHA

ALUMINUM

KM#	Date	Mintage	VF	XF	Unc
1	1973	*47.088	—	.10	.20

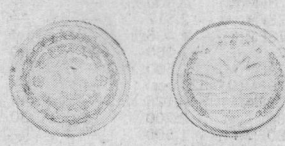

F.A.O. Issue

6	1974	5.000	—	.10	.20
	1975	3.000	—	.10	.20
	1976	3.000	—	.10	.20

F.A.O. Issue

10	1977	90.000	—	.10	.15
	1978	52.432	—	.10	.15
	1979	120.096	—	.10	.15
	1980	127.008	—	.10	.15
	1981	72.992	—	.10	.15

10 POISHA

ALUMINUM

KM#	Date	Mintage	VF	XF	Unc
2	1973	*21.500	—	.10	.30

F.A.O. Issue

7	1974	5.000	—	.15	.30
	1975	4.000	—	.15	.30
	1976	4.000	—	.15	.30
	1977	4.000	—	.15	.30
	1978	141.744	—	.15	.30
	1979	—	—	.15	.25

11	1977	48.000	—	.15	.25
	1978	77.518	—	.15	.25
	1979	170.112	—	.15	.25
	1980	200.000	—	.15	.25
	1983	142.848	—	.15	.25
	1984	57.152	—	.15	.25

25 POISHA

STEEL

3	1973	*25.072	—	.25	.50

F.A.O. Issue

8	1974	5.000	—	.20	.50
	1975	6.000	—	.20	.50
	1976	6.000	—	.20	.50
	1977	51.300	—	.15	.25
	1978	66.750	—	.15	.25

COPPER-NICKEL

12	1977	45.300	—	.15	.40
	1978	66.750	—	.15	.40
	1979	56.704	—	.15	.40
	1980	228.992	—	.15	.40
	1981	45.072	—	.15	.40
	1983	96.128	—	.15	.25
	1984	203.872	—	.15	.25

50 POISHA

COPPER-NICKEL

4	1973	18.000	—	.40	1.00

F.A.O. Issue

KM#	Date	Mintage	VF	XF	Unc
13	1977	12.700	—	.20	.50
	1978	37.300	—	.20	.50
	1979	2.208	—	.20	.50
	1980	124.512	—	.20	.50
	1981	36.680	—	.20	.50
	1983	31.392	—	.20	.50
	1984	168.608	—	.20	.50

TAKA

COPPER-NICKEL

9	1975	4.000	.15	.45	1.00
	1976	—	.15	.45	1.00
	1977	—	.15	.45	1.00

BARBADOS

Barbados, an independent state within the British Commonwealth, is located in the Windward Islands of the West Indies east of St. Vincent. The coral island has an area of 166 sq. mi. (431 sq. km.) and a population of 255,043. Capital: Bridgetown. The economy is based on sugar and tourism. Sugar, petroleum products, molasses, and rum are exported.

Barbados was named by the Portuguese who achieved the first landing on the island in 1563. British sailors landed at the site of present-day Holetown in 1624. Barbados was under uninterrupted British control from the time of the first British settlement in 1627 until it obtained independence on Nov. 30, 1966. It is a member of the Commonwealth of Nations. The Queen of England is Chief of State.

Unmarked 'side cut' pieces of Spanish and Spanish Colonial 1, 2 and 8 reales were the principal coinage medium of 18th-century Barbados. The "Neptune" tokens issued by Sir Phillip Gibbs, a local plantation owner, circulated freely but were never established as legal coinage. The coinage and banknotes of the British Caribbean Territories (Eastern Group) were employed prior to 1973 when Barbados issued a decimal coinage.

RULERS

British, until 1966

MINT MARKS

FM - Franklin Mint, U.S.A.*

None - Royal Mint

***NOTE:** From 1975 the Franklin Mint has produced coinage in up to 3 different qualities. Qualities of issue are designated in ( ) after each date and are defined as follows:

(M) MATTE - Normal circulation strike or a dull finish produced by sandblasting special uncirculated (polish finish) or proof quality dies.

(U) SPECIAL UNCIRCULATED - Polished or proof-like in appearance without any frosted features.

(P) PROOF - The highest quality obtainable having mirror-like fields and frosted features.

MONETARY SYSTEM

100 Cents = 1 Dollar

CENT

BRONZE

KM#	Date	Mintage	VF	XF	Unc
10	1973	5.000	—	.10	.25
	1973FM(M)	7,500	—	—	1.00
	1973FM(P)	.097	—	Proof	.50
	1974	7.000	—	.10	.25
	1974FM(M)	8,708	—	—	1.00
	1974FM(P)	.036	—	Proof	.50
	1975	8.000	—	.10	.25
	1975FM(M)	5,000	—	—	.75
	1975FM(U)	1,360	—	—	1.00
	1975FM(P)	.020	—	Proof	.50
	1977FM(M)	2,102	—	—	.75
	1977FM(U)	468 pcs.	—	—	3.00
	1977FM(P)	5,014	—	Proof	.50
	1978	4.807	—	—	—
	1978FM(M)	2,000	—	—	1.00
	1978FM(U)	2,517	—	—	1.50
	1978FM(P)	4,436	—	Proof	1.00
	1979	5.606	—	.10	.25
	1979FM(M)	1,500	—	—	1.00
	1979FM(U)	523 pcs.	—	—	2.50
	1979FM(P)	4,126	—	Proof	1.00
	1980	14.400	—	.10	.25
	1980FM(M)	1,500	—	—	1.00
	1980FM(U)	649 pcs.	—	—	2.00
	1980FM(P)	2,111	—	Proof	1.50
	1981	10.160	—	.10	.25
	1981FM(M)	1,500	—	—	1.00
	1981FM(U)	327 pcs.	—	—	2.00
	1981FM(P)	943 pcs.	—	Proof	1.50
	1982	5.040	—	.10	.25
	1982FM(U)	1,500	—	—	1.25
	1982FM(P)	843 pcs.	—	Proof	1.50
	1983FM(M)	1,500	—	—	1.00
	1983FM(U)	—	—	—	1.25
	1983FM(P)	459 pcs.	—	Proof	1.50
	1984	5.008	—	.10	.25
	1984FM(M)	868 pcs.	—	—	1.25
	1985	—	—	.10	.25
	1986	—	—	.10	.25
	1987	—	—	.10	.25

10th Anniversary of Independence

KM#	Date	Mintage	VF	XF	Unc
19	1976	6.406	—	.10	.15
	1976FM(M)	5,000	—	—	.50
	1976FM(U)	996 pcs.	—	—	1.00
	1976FM(P)	.012	—	Proof	.50

5 CENTS

BRASS

KM#	Date	Mintage	VF	XF	Unc
11	1973	3.000	.10	.15	.35
	1973FM(M)	7,500	—	—	1.25
	1973FM(P)	.097	—	Proof	.75
	1974	4.600	.10	.15	.35
	1974FM(M)	8,708	—	—	1.25
	1974FM(P)	.036	—	Proof	.75
	1975FM(M)	5,000	—	—	1.00
	1975FM(U)	1,360	—	—	1.25
	1975FM(P)	.020	—	Proof	.75
	1977FM(M)	2,100	—	—	2.00
	1977FM(U)	468 pcs.	—	—	3.00
	1977FM(P)	5,014	—	Proof	.75
	1978FM(M)	2,000	—	—	.75
	1978FM(U)	2,517	—	—	2.75
	1978FM(P)	4,436	—	Proof	1.25
	1979	4.800	.10	.15	.35
	1979FM(M)	1,500	—	—	.75
	1979FM(U)	523 pcs.	—	—	2.75
	1979FM(P)	4,126	—	Proof	1.25
	1980FM(M)	1,500	—	—	1.00
	1980FM(U)	649 pcs.	—	—	2.25
	1980FM(P)	2,111	—	Proof	1.75
	1981FM(M)	1,500	—	—	1.00
	1981FM(U)	327 pcs.	—	—	2.25
	1981FM(P)	943 pcs.	—	Proof	1.75
	1982	2.100	.10	.15	.35
	1982FM(U)	1,500	—	—	1.50
	1982FM(P)	843 pcs.	—	Proof	1.75
	1983FM(M)	1,500	—	—	1.50
	1983FM(U)	—	—	—	1.50
	1983FM(P)	459 pcs.	—	Proof	1.75
	1984FM	1,737	—	—	1.50
	1986	—	—	—	.25

10th Anniversary of Independence

KM#	Date	Mintage	VF	XF	Unc
20	1976FM(M)	5,000	—	—	1.00
	1976FM(U)	996 pcs.	—	—	1.25

10 CENTS

COPPER-NICKEL

KM#	Date	Mintage	VF	XF	Unc
12	1973	4.000	.10	.15	.50
	1973FM(M)	5,000	—	—	1.50
	1973FM(P)	.097	—	Proof	1.00
	1974	4.000	.10	.15	.50
	1974FM(M)	6,208	—	—	1.50
	1974FM(P)	.036	—	Proof	1.00
	1975FM(M)	2,500	—	—	1.00
	1975FM(U)	1,360	—	—	1.50
	1975FM(P)	.020	—	Proof	1.00
	1977FM(M)	2,100	—	—	1.00
	1977FM(U)	468 pcs.	—	—	4.00
	1977FM(P)	5,014	—	Proof	1.00
	1978FM(M)	2,000	—	—	1.00
	1978FM(U)	2,517	—	—	3.00
	1978FM(P)	4,436	—	Proof	1.50
	1979	2.500	.10	.20	.60
	1979FM(M)	1,500	—	—	2.50
	1979FM(U)	523 pcs.	—	—	3.00
	1979FM(P)	4,126	—	Proof	1.50
	1980	3.500	.10	.15	.50
	1980FM(M)	1,500	—	—	1.00
	1980FM(U)	649 pcs.	—	—	2.50
	1980FM(P)	2,111	—	Proof	2.00
	1981FM(M)	1,500	—	—	1.00
	1981FM(U)	327 pcs.	—	—	2.50
	1981FM(P)	943 pcs.	—	Proof	2.00
	1982FM(U)	1,500	—	—	1.75
12	1982FM(P)	843 pcs.	—	Proof	2.00
	1983FM(M)	1,500	—	—	1.75
	1983FM(U)	—	—	—	1.75
	1983FM(P)	459 pcs.	—	Proof	2.00
	1984	3.400	.10	.15	.50
	1987	—	.10	.15	.50

10th Anniversary of Independence

KM#	Date	Mintage	VF	XF	Unc
21	1976FM(M)	2,500	—	—	.75
	1976FM(U)	996 pcs.	—	—	1.50
	1976FM(P)	.012	—	Proof	1.00

25 CENTS

COPPER-NICKEL

KM#	Date	Mintage	VF	XF	Unc
13	1973	6.000	.15	.30	.60
	1973FM(M)	4,300	—	—	1.75
	1973FM(P)	.097	—	Proof	1.25
	1974	1.000	.20	.40	.80
	1974FM(M)	5,508	—	—	1.75
	1974FM(P)	.036	—	Proof	1.25
	1975FM(M)	1,800	—	—	1.25
	1975FM(U)	1,360	—	—	1.75
	1975FM(P)	.020	—	Proof	1.25
	1977FM(M)	2,100	—	—	1.00
	1977FM(U)	468 pcs.	—	—	4.25
	1977FM(P)	5,014	—	Proof	1.25
	1978	2.407	.20	.40	.80
	1978FM(M)	2,000	—	—	1.00
	1978FM(U)	2,517	—	—	3.25
	1978FM(P)	4,436	—	Proof	1.75
	1979	1.200	.20	.40	.80
	1979FM(M)	1,500	—	—	1.00
	1979FM(U)	523 pcs.	—	—	3.00
	1979FM(P)	4.126	—	Proof	1.75
	1980	2.700	.15	.30	.60
	1980FM(M)	1,500	—	—	3.00
	1980FM(U)	649 pcs.	—	—	2.75
	1980FM(P)	2,111	—	Proof	2.25
	1981	4.365	.15	.30	.60
	1981FM(M)	1,500	—	—	3.00
	1981FM(U)	327 pcs.	—	—	2.75
	1981FM(P)	943 pcs.	—	Proof	2.25
	1982FM(U)	1,500	—	—	2.00
	1982FM(P)	843 pcs.	—	Proof	2.25
	1983FM(M)	1,500	—	—	2.00
	1983FM(U)	—	—	—	2.00
	1983FM(P)	459 pcs.	—	Proof	2.25
	1984FM	868 pcs.	—	—	2.00
	1987	—	—	—	2.00

10th Anniversary of Independence

KM#	Date	Mintage	VF	XF	Unc
22	1976FM(M)	1,800	—	—	1.25
	1976FM(U)	996 pcs.	—	—	1.75
	1976FM(P)	.012	—	Proof	1.25

DOLLAR

COPPER-NICKEL

KM#	Date	Mintage	VF	XF	Unc
14	1973	—	.60	.75	1.00
	1973FM(M)	3,000	—	—	2.00
	1973FM(P)	.097	—	Proof	1.00
	1974	2.000	.60	.75	1.00
	1974FM(M)	4,208	—	—	2.00
	1974FM(P)	.036	—	Proof	1.00
	1975FM(M)	500 pcs.	—	—	3.50
	1975FM(U)	1,360	—	—	2.00
	1975FM(P)	.020	—	Proof	1.00
	1977FM(M)	600 pcs.	—	—	5.00
	1977FM(U)	468 pcs.	—	—	4.50
	1977FM(P)	5,014	—	Proof	1.50

KM#	Date	Mintage	VF	XF	Unc
14	1978FM(U)	1,017	—	—	3.50
	1978FM(P)	4,436	—	Proof	2.00
	1979	2.000	.75	1.25	1.75
	1979FM(M)	600 pcs.	—	—	3.00
	1979FM(U)	523 pcs.	—	—	3.50
	1979FM(P)	4,126	—	Proof	2.00
	1980FM(M)	600 pcs.	—	—	3.50
	1980FM(U)	649 pcs.	—	—	3.50
	1980FM(P)	2,111	—	Proof	2.50
	1981FM(M)	600 pcs.	—	—	3.00
	1981FM(U)	327 pcs.	—	—	3.50
	1981FM(P)	943 pcs.	—	Proof	2.50
	1982FM(M)	600 pcs.	—	—	2.25
	1982FM(P)	843 pcs.	—	Proof	2.50
	1983FM(M)	600 pcs.	—	—	2.25
	1983FM(U)	—	—	—	2.25
	1983FM(P)	459 pcs.	—	Proof	2.50
	1984FM	469 pcs.	—	—	2.25
	1985	—	—	—	1.00

10th Anniversary of Independence

23	1976FM(M)	500 pcs.	—	—	4.00
	1976FM(U)	996 pcs.	—	—	2.00
	1976FM(P)	.012	—	Proof	1.50

2 DOLLARS

COPPER-NICKEL

15	1973FM(M)	3,000	—	—	2.25
	1973FM(P)	.097	—	Proof	2.50
	1974FM(M)	4,208	—	—	2.25
	1974FM(P)	.036	—	Proof	2.50
	1975FM(M)	500 pcs.	—	—	4.00
	1975FM(U)	1,360	—	—	2.25
	1975FM(P)	.020	—	Proof	2.50
	1977FM(M)	600 pcs.	—	—	3.50
	1977FM(U)	468 pcs.	—	—	4.75
	1977FM(P)	5,014	—	Proof	2.50
	1978FM(U)	1,017	—	—	3.75
	1978FM(P)	4,436	—	Proof	2.50
	1979FM(M)	600 pcs.	—	—	3.50
	1979FM(U)	523 pcs.	—	—	3.75
	1979FM(P)	4,126	—	Proof	2.50
	1980FM(M)	600 pcs.	—	—	3.50
	1980FM(U)	649 pcs.	—	—	3.25
	1980FM(P)	2,111	—	Proof	2.75
	1981FM(M)	600 pcs.	—	—	3.00
	1981FM(U)	327 pcs.	—	—	3.25
	1981FM(P)	943 pcs.	—	Proof	2.75
	1982FM(M)	600 pcs.	—	—	2.50
	1982FM(P)	843 pcs.	—	Proof	2.75
	1983FM(U)	—	—	—	2.50
	1983FM(P)	459 pcs.	—	Proof	2.75
	1984FM	473 pcs.	—	—	2.50

10th Anniversary of Independence
Rev: Similar to KM#15.

24	1976FM(M)	500 pcs.	—	—	3.00
	1976FM(U)	996 pcs.	—	—	2.25
	1976FM(P)	.012	—	Proof	2.50

4 DOLLARS

COPPER-NICKEL
F.A.O. Issue

KM#	Date	Mintage	VF	XF	Unc
9	1970	.030	—	2.50	4.00
	1970	2,000	—	Proof	12.00

5 DOLLARS

COPPER-NICKEL
Obv: Similar to 2 Dollars, KM#15.

16	1974FM(M)	3,958	—	—	5.00
	1975FM(M)	250 pcs.	—	—	8.00
	1975FM(U)	1,360	—	—	5.00
	1977FM(M)	600 pcs.	—	—	5.00
	1977FM(U)	468 pcs.	—	—	5.00
	1978FM(U)	1,017	—	—	5.00
	1979FM(M)	600 pcs.	—	—	5.00
	1979FM(U)	523 pcs.	—	—	5.00
	1980FM(M)	600 pcs.	—	—	5.00
	1980FM(U)	649 pcs.	—	—	5.00
	1981FM(M)	600 pcs.	—	—	5.00
	1981FM(U)	1,156	—	—	5.00
	1982FM(M)	600 pcs.	—	—	5.00
	1982FM(P)	843 pcs.	—	Proof	5.00
	1983FM(M)	600 pcs.	—	—	5.00
	1983FM(U)	261 pcs.	—	—	5.00
	1984FM	470 pcs.	—	—	5.00

31.1000 g, .800 SILVER, .7999 oz ASW

16a	1973FM(M)	2,750	—	—	12.50
	1973FM(P)	.097	—	Proof	10.00
	1974FM(P)	.036	—	Proof	10.00
	1975FM(P)	.020	—	Proof	10.00
	1977FM(P)	5,014	—	Proof	12.50
	1978FM(P)	4,436	—	Proof	12.50
	1979FM(P)	4,126	—	Proof	12.50
	1980FM(P)	2,111	—	Proof	15.00
	1981FM(P)	835 pcs.	—	Proof	25.00
	1982FM(P)	658 pcs.	—	Proof	30.00
	1983FM(P)	130 pcs.	—	Proof	40.00
	1984FM(P)	—	—	Proof	20.00

COPPER-NICKEL
10th Anniversary of Independence
Rev: Similar to KM#16.

25	1976FM(M)	250 pcs.	—	—	25.00
	1976FM(U)	996 pcs.	—	—	12.50

31.1000 g, .800 SILVER, .7999 oz ASW

25a	1976FM(P)	.012	—	Proof	15.00

10 DOLLARS

COPPER-NICKEL
Obv: Similar to 2 Dollars, KM#15.

KM#	Date	Mintage	VF	XF	Unc
17	1974FM(M)	3,958	—	—	10.00
	1975FM(M)	250 pcs.	—	—	20.00
	1975FM(U)	1,360	—	—	12.50
	1977FM(M)	600 pcs.	—	—	12.50
	1977FM(U)	468 pcs.	—	—	12.50
	1978FM(U)	1,017	—	—	12.50
	1979FM(M)	600 pcs.	—	—	12.50
	1979FM(U)	523 pcs.	—	—	12.50
	1980FM(M)	600 pcs.	—	—	12.50
	1980FM(U)	649 pcs.	—	—	12.50
	1981FM(M)	600 pcs.	—	—	12.50
	1981FM(U)	1,156	—	—	12.50

37.9000 g, .925 SILVER, 1.1271 oz ASW

17a	1973FM(M)	2,750	—	—	15.00
	1973FM(P)	.097	—	Proof	12.50
	1974FM(P)	.057	—	Proof	12.50
	1975FM(P)	.029	—	Proof	12.50
	1977FM(P)	7,212	—	Proof	15.00
	1978FM(P)	7,079	—	Proof	15.00
	1979FM(P)	6,534	—	Proof	15.00
	1980FM(P)	3,618	—	Proof	20.00
	1981FM(P)	835 pcs.	—	Proof	35.00

COPPER-NICKEL
10th Anniversary of Independence
Rev: Similar to KM#17.

26	1976FM(M)	250 pcs.	—	—	30.00
	1976FM(U)	996 pcs.	—	—	15.00

37.9000 g, .925 SILVER, 1.1271 oz ASW

26a	1976FM(P)	.016	—	Proof	14.00

COPPER-NICKEL
10th Anniversary of the Central Bank of Barbados
Obv: Similar to KM#26.

34	1982FM(U)	600 pcs.	—	—	20.00

35.5200 g, .925 SILVER, 1.0564 oz ASW

34a	1982FM(P)	851 pcs.	—	Proof	40.00

BARBADOS 170

COPPER-NICKEL
Pelican

KM#	Date	Mintage	VF	XF	Unc
36	1983FM(M)	600 pcs.	—	—	20.00
	1983FM(U)	141 pcs.	—	—	35.00

35.5200 g, .925 SILVER, 1.0564 oz ASW
| 36a | 1983FM(P) | 679 pcs. | — | Proof | 60.00 |

Dolphins
| 40 | 1984FM(P) | 469 pcs. | — | Proof | 60.00 |

20 DOLLARS

23.3300 g, .925 SILVER, .6938 oz ASW
Decade For Women
| 46 | 1985 | .020 | — | Proof | 20.00 |

25 DOLLARS

28.2800 g, .925 SILVER, .8410 oz ASW
Coronation Jubilee
Obv: Portrait of Queen Elizabeth II.
27	1978FM(M)	300 pcs.	—	—	60.00
	1978FM(U)	69 pcs.	—	—	230.00
	1978FM(P)	8,728	—	Proof	30.00

30.2800 g, .500 SILVER, .4868 oz AGW
10th Anniversary of Caribbean Development Bank
KM#	Date	Mintage	VF	XF	Unc
30	1980FM(P)	2,345	—	Proof	30.00

Caribbean Festival of Arts
Obv: Similar to KM#30.
| 31 | 1981FM(P) | 1,008 | — | Proof | 35.00 |

30th Anniversary of Queen Elizabeth II
| 37 | 1983FM(P) | 2,951 | — | Proof | 35.00 |

28.2800 g, .925 SILVER, .8410 oz ASW
Royal Visit
| 43 | 1985 | *5,000 | — | Proof | 35.00 |

47.5400 g, .917 GOLD, 1.4013 oz AGW
| 43a | 1985 | *250 pcs. | — | Proof | 900.00 |

28.2800 g, .500 SILVER, .4546 oz ASW
Commonwealth Games
KM#	Date	Mintage	VF	XF	Unc
44	1986	*.050	—	—	20.00

28.2800 g, .925 SILVER, .8410 oz ASW
| 44a | 1986 | *.020 | — | Proof | 30.00 |

50 DOLLARS

27.3500 g, .500 SILVER, .4397 oz ASW
F.A.O. Issue
| 32 | 1981FM(U) | 6,012 | — | — | 27.50 |

16.8500 g, .500 SILVER, .2709 oz ASW
F.A.O. Issue - Four Wing Flying Fish
| 42 | 1984FM(P) | 3,600 | — | Proof | 27.50 |

100 DOLLARS

6.2100 g, .500 GOLD, .0998 oz AGW
350th Anniversary
18	1975FM(M)	50 pcs.	—	—	250.00
	1975FM(U)	.016	—	—	65.00
	1975FM(P)	.023	—	Proof	100.00

4.0600 g, .900 GOLD, .1174 oz AGW
Human Rights
| 28 | 1978 | 1,114 | — | — | 100.00 |

5.0500 g, .900 GOLD, .1461 oz AGW
| 28a | 1978 | Inc. Ab. | — | Proof | 125.00 |

Neptune, God of the Sea

KM#	Date	Mintage	VF	XF	Unc
38	1983FM(U)	3 pcs.	—	—	
	1983FM(P)	484 pcs.	—	Proof	165.00

Triton, Son of Neptune

39	1984FM(P)	1,103	—	Proof	150.00

Amphitrite, Wife of Neptune

41	1985FM(P)	1,276	—	Proof	150.00

150 DOLLARS

7.1300 g, .500 GOLD, .1146 oz AGW
National Flower - Poinciana

33	1981FM(U)	7 pcs.	—	—	
	1981FM(P)	1,140	—	Proof	175.00

200 DOLLARS

8.1200 g, .900 GOLD, .2349 oz AGW
Year of the Child

29	1979	1,121	—	—	200.00

10.1000 g, .900 GOLD, .2922 oz AGW

29a	1979	Inc. Ab.	—	Proof	250.00

250 DOLLARS

6.6000 g, .900 GOLD, .1910 oz AGW
250th Anniversary of Birth of George Washington

35	1982FM(P)	802 pcs.	—	Proof	185.00

47.5400 g, .917 GOLD, 1.4017 oz AGW
Commonwealth Games
Similar to 25 Dollars, KM#44.

45	1986	150 pcs.	—	Proof	1200.

MINT SETS (MS)

KM#	Date	Mintage	Identification	Issue Price	Mkt. Val.
MS1	1973(8)	2,500	KM10-15,16a,17a	25.00	25.00
MS2	1974(8)	3,708	KM10-17	25.00	20.00
MS3	1975(8)	1,360	KM10-17	27.50	25.00
MS4	1976(8)	996	KM19-26	27.50	30.00
MS5	1977(8)	468	KM10-17	27.50	30.00
MS6	1978(8)	517	KM10-17	29.00	30.00
MS7	1979(8)	523	KM10-17	29.00	30.00
MS8	1980(8)	649	KM10-17	30.00	30.00
MS9	1981(8)	327	KM10-17	30.00	35.00
MS10	1982(8)	—	KM10-16,34	35.00	50.00
MS11	1983(8)	141	KM10-16,36	35.50	70.00

PROOF SETS (PS)

PS1	1973(8)	97,454	KM10-15,16a,17a	37.50	20.00
PS2	1974(8)	35,600	KM10-15,16a,17a	50.00	20.00
PS3	1975(8)	20,458	KM10-15,16a,17a	55.00	20.00
PS4	1976(8)	11,929	KM19-24,25a,26a	55.00	25.00
PS5	1977(8)	5,014	KM10-15,16a,17a	55.00	27.50
PS6	1978(8)	4,436	KM10-15,16a,17a	58.00	27.50
PS7	1979(8)	4,126	KM10-15,16a,17a	60.00	27.50
PS8	1980(8)	2,011	KM10-15,16a,17a	117.00	35.00
PS9	1980(2)	—	KM16a,17a	115.00	30.00
PS10	1981(8)	943	KM10-15,16a,17a	117.00	75.00
PS11	1982(8)	—	KM10-15,16a,34a	117.00	75.00
PS12	1983(8)	315	KM10-15,16a,36a	—	75.00
PS13	1984(8)	—	KM10-15,16a,40	132.00	75.00

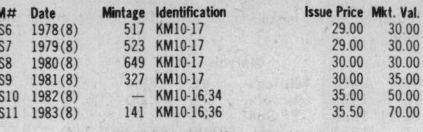

Listings For
BELGIAN CONGO: refer to Zaire

BELGIUM

The Kingdom of Belgium, a constitutional monarchy in northwest Europe, has an area of 11,781 sq. mi. (30,513 sq. km.) and a population of 9.9 million, chiefly Dutch-speaking Flemish and French-speaking Walloons. Capital: Brussels. Agriculture, dairy farming, and the processing of raw materials for re-export are the principal industries. Beurs voor Diamant in Antwerp is the world's largest diamond trading center. Iron and steel, machinery, motor vehicles, chemicals, textile yarns and fabrics comprise the principal exports.

The Celtic tribe called 'Belgae', from which Belgium derived its name, was described by Caesar as the most courageous of all the tribes of Gaul. The Belgae eventually capitulated to Rome and the area remained for centuries as a part of the Roman Empire known as Belgica.

As Rome began its decline Frankish tribes migrated westward and established the Merovingian, and subsequently, the Carolingian empires. At the death of Charlemagne Europe was divided among his three sons Karl, Lothar and Ludwig. The eastern part of today's Belgium lies in the Duchy of Lower Lorraine while much of the western parts eventually became the County of Flanders. After further divisions the area came under the control of the Duke of Burgundy from whence it passed under Hapsburg control when Marie of Burgundy married Maximilian of Austria. Phillip I (the Fair), son of Maximilian and Marie then added Spain to the Hapsburg empire by marrying Johanna, daughter of Ferdinand and Isabella. Charles and Ferdinand, sons of Phillip and Johanna, began the separate Spanish and Austrian lines of the Hapsburg family. The Burgundian lands, along with the northern provinces which make up present day Netherlands, became the Spanish Netherlands. The northern provinces successfully rebelled and broke away from Hapsburg rule in the late 16th century and early 17th century. The southern provinces along with the Duchy of Luxembourg remained under the influence of Spain until the year 1700 when Charles II, last of the Spanish Hapsburg line, died without leaving an heir and the Spanish crown went to the Bourbon family of France. The Spanish Netherlands then reverted to the control of the Austrian line of Hapsburgs and became the Austrian Netherlands. The Austrian Netherlands along with the Bishopric of Liege fell to the French Republic in 1794.

At the Congress of Vienna in 1815 the area was reunited with the Netherlands, but in 1830 independence was gained and the constitutional monarchy of Belgium was established. A large part of the Duchy of Luxembourg was incorporated into Belgium and the first king was Leopold I of Saxe-Coburg-Gotha.

Belgian coins are inscribed either in Flemish, French or both. The language used is best told by noting the spelling of the name of the country.

LEGENDS

(Fr) French: BELGIQUE or BELGES
(Fl) Flemish: BELGIE or BELGEN

RULERS

Leopold I, 1831-1865
Leopold II, 1865-1909
Albert I, 1909-1934
Leopold III, 1934-1950
Baudouin I, 1951-

MINT MARKS

Angel head - Brussels

MONETARY SYSTEM

100 Centimes = 1 Franc
43 Francs = 1 Ecu

CENTIME

COPPER
Wide rims.

KM#	Date	Mintage	VG	Fine	VF	XF
1.1	1832	—	20.00	50.00	150.00	300.00
(C1.1)	1833/2	5.007	2.50	12.00	40.00	80.00
	1833	Inc. Ab.	2.00	10.00	30.00	60.00
	1835/2	4.367	3.00	14.00	50.00	95.00
	1835	Inc. Ab.	2.50	10.00	35.00	90.00

NOTE: Until 1836 these were commonly struck over Netherlands 1/2 Cent, KM#51. If the date of the Netherlands coin is still visible, add up to 50 percent to the value.

Narrow rims.

1.2	1835	Inc. Ab.	1.25	4.00	15.00	20.00
(C1.2)	1836/2	4.256	1.25	4.50	20.00	37.50
	1836	Inc. Ab.	1.25	4.50	15.00	32.50
	1837	—	22.50	65.00	200.00	400.00
	1838	—	22.50	65.00	200.00	400.00

KM#	Date	Mintage	VG	Fine	VF	XF
(C1.2)	1841	—	22.50	65.00	200.00	400.00
	1844	1.822	2.75	10.00	35.00	70.00
	1845	8.324	.75	3.00	10.00	35.00
	1846	8.241	.75	3.50	12.50	35.00
	1847	5.138	.75	3.50	12.50	35.00
	1848	.383	70.00	150.00	230.00	425.00
	1849	1.218	1.50	12.50	45.00	100.00
	1850	2.309	1.50	5.00	20.00	35.00
	1855	—	50.00	100.00	250.00	400.00
	1856	2.428	.75	5.00	20.00	40.00
	1857	.948	3.00	10.00	35.00	50.00
	1858	.916	3.00	10.00	35.00	50.00
	1859	.982	3.00	10.00	35.00	50.00
	1860	1.581	1.00	3.00	9.00	20.00
	1861	1.696	1.00	3.00	9.00	20.00
	1862	11.907	.50	1.50	4.00	10.00
	1863	—	40.00	75.00	175.00	375.00

Obv. French leg: DES BELGES

KM#	Date	Mintage	Fine	VF	XF	Unc
33	1869	5.064	1.00	3.00	10.00	20.00
(Y1.1)	1870	3.930	1.00	3.00	10.00	20.00
	1873	2.036	1.00	3.00	10.00	20.00
	1874	3.907	1.00	3.00	10.00	20.00
	1875	2.970	1.00	3.00	10.00	20.00
	1876	2.966	1.00	3.00	10.00	20.00
	1882	5.000	1.00	1.50	3.50	12.50
	1899	2.500	1.00	1.50	3.50	12.50
	1901/801 near 1					
		3.743	.50	1.50	4.00	12.50
	1901/801 far 1					
		Inc. Ab.	.50	1.50	4.00	12.50
	1901	Inc. Ab.	.50	1.50	4.00	12.50
	1902/802 near 2					
		2.847	1.00	3.00	7.50	20.00
	1902/802 far 2					
		Inc. Ab.	1.00	3.00	7.50	20.00
	1902/801	I.A.	1.00	3.00	7.50	20.00
	1902/1	I.A.	1.00	3.00	7.50	20.00
	1902	Inc. Ab.	.35	.50	1.00	3.50
	1907	3.967	.35	.50	1.00	3.50

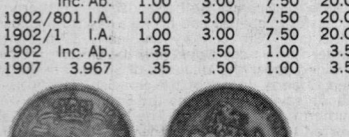

Obv. Flemish leg: DER BELGEN

KM#	Date	Mintage	Fine	VF	XF	Unc
34	1882	Inc. Ab.	50.00	150.00	325.00	550.00
(Y1.2)	1887	5.000	1.00	1.50	3.00	12.00
	1892	—	50.00	150.00	300.00	500.00
	1894	5.000	.50	1.25	3.00	7.00
	1899	2.500	.50	1.25	3.00	7.00
	1901/899	I.A.	.75	3.00	4.50	7.00
	1901	Inc. Ab.	.25	.50	1.50	3.50
	1902/1	2.482	1.25	3.50	9.00	15.00
	1902	Inc. Ab.	.20	.75	1.00	3.50
	1907	3.966	.20	.75	1.00	3.50

Obv. French leg: DES BELGES

KM#	Date	Mintage	Fine	VF	XF	Unc
76	1912	2.540	.20	.50	1.00	2.50
(Y22.1)	1914	.870	.25	.75	1.25	4.00

Obv. Flemish leg: DER BELGEN

KM#	Date	Mintage	Fine	VF	XF	Unc
77	1912	2.542	.20	.50	1.00	2.50
(Y22.2)						

2 CENTIMES

COPPER
Wide rims.

KM#	Date	Mintage	VG	Fine	VF	XF
4.1	1833	16.748	1.50	5.00	17.50	27.50
(C2.1)	1834	3.268	3.00	7.00	25.00	50.00
	1835	26.774	2.50	6.00	22.50	42.50

NOTE: Until 1836 these were commonly struck over Netherlands 1 Cent, KM#47. If the date of the Netherlands coin is still visible, add up to 50 percent to the value.

Narrow rims.

KM#	Date	Mintage	VG	Fine	VF	XF
4.2	1835	Inc. Ab.	.75	2.00	8.00	14.00
(C2.2)	1836	27.084	.75	2.00	8.00	14.00
	1837	—	30.00	65.00	210.00	375.00
	1838	—	30.00	65.00	210.00	375.00
	1841	2.226	1.50	6.00	15.00	25.00
	1842	2.823	1.50	7.00	15.00	30.00
	1844	1.802	1.00	6.00	15.00	25.00
	1845	8.324	.75	2.50	10.00	17.50
	1846	8.088	.75	2.50	10.00	17.50
	1847	3.432	1.00	3.50	12.00	20.00
	1848	.420	8.00	20.00	45.00	75.00
	1849	3.690	1.00	3.50	12.00	20.00
	1850	.404	8.00	20.00	50.00	80.00
	1851	2.407	.75	3.00	10.00	15.50
	1852	.731	5.00	15.00	40.00	65.00
	1853	.466	12.00	30.00	75.00	120.00
	1855	.171	22.00	50.00	100.00	200.00
	1856	6.255	.75	2.00	8.00	15.00
	1857	4.612	.75	2.00	8.00	17.00
	1858/47	3.177	1.50	3.00	15.00	25.00
	1858/57	I.A.	1.50	3.00	15.00	25.00
	1858	Inc. Ab.	.75	2.00	8.00	17.00
	1859	4.074	.75	2.00	8.00	17.00
	1860	3.070	.75	2.00	8.00	17.00
	1861	2.924	.75	2.00	8.00	15.00
	1862	6.589	.50	2.00	8.00	15.00
	1863/2	18.621	.75	2.50	12.00	20.00
	1863	Inc. Ab.	.50	1.00	4.00	6.00
	1864	16.840	.50	1.00	4.00	6.00
	1865	2.447	.50	2.00	8.00	15.00

Obv. French leg: DES BELGES

KM#	Date	Mintage	Fine	VF	XF	Unc
35	1869	2.972	2.50	14.00	30.00	60.00
(Y2.1)	1870	5.654	.75	1.50	4.00	10.00
	1870/1	I.A.	1.25	2.00	12.50	30.00
	1871	Inc.1870	1.25	3.00	15.00	40.00
	1873	7.491	.75	1.50	4.00	10.00
	1874	7.876	.75	1.50	4.00	10.00
	1875	7.932	.75	1.50	4.00	10.00
	1876	10.472	.50	1.50	4.00	10.00
	1902	2.490	.50	1.50	4.00	10.00
	1905	4.981	.50	1.00	2.00	6.00
	1909/0	4.983	.75	1.50	2.50	7.00
	1909	Inc. Ab.	.50	1.00	2.00	6.00

Obv. Flemish leg: DER BELGEN

KM#	Date	Mintage	Fine	VF	XF	Unc
36	1902	2.488	.50	1.50	3.00	10.00
(Y2.2)	1905	4.986	.50	1.00	2.00	6.00
	1909	.565	1.00	3.00	9.00	20.00

Obv. French leg: DES BELGES

KM#	Date	Mintage	Fine	VF	XF	Unc
64	1911	.645	2.50	4.00	8.00	17.50
(Y23.1)	1912	4.928	.25	.50	1.00	3.50
	1914	.491	2.50	4.00	8.00	17.50
	1919/4	5.000	3.00	6.00	12.00	50.00
	1919	Inc. Ab.	.25	.50	1.00	3.00

Obv. Flemish leg: DER BELGEN

KM#	Date	Mintage	Fine	VF	XF	Unc
65	1910	1.248	.50	.75	1.75	5.00
(Y23.2)	1911	6.441	.25	.50	1.00	3.50
	1912	1.602	.75	1.00	2.00	6.00
	1919	4.998	.25	.50	.75	3.00

5 CENTIMES

COPPER

KM#	Date	Mintage	VG	Fine	VF	XF
5	1811 (error)	—	60.00	120.00	350.00	800.00
(C3)	1833	4.437	2.50	6.00	20.00	55.00
	1834	2.515	3.00	7.00	25.00	50.00
	1835	—	60.00	120.00	275.00	550.00
	1837	12.038	1.00	3.00	10.00	25.00
	1838	—	60.00	175.00	450.00	800.00
	1841/11	2.509	2.50	7.00	20.00	35.00

KM#	Date	Mintage	VG	Fine	VF	XF
(C3)	1841 narrow 1					
		Inc. Ab.	2.50	7.00	20.00	35.00
	1841 wide 1					
		Inc. Ab.	2.50	7.00	20.00	35.00
	1842	5.537	1.00	4.00	12.00	25.00
	1847	1.131	4.00	10.00	25.00	45.00
	1848	1.845	2.50	7.00	25.00	45.00
	1849	1.447	2.50	7.00	25.00	45.00
	1850 5 w/ball top, round 0 w/wide center					
		2.689	1.50	5.00	18.00	30.00
	1850 5 w/less curved top, 0 tall w/narrow center					
		Inc. Ab.	1.50	5.00	18.00	30.00
	1851	2.381	1.50	5.00	18.00	30.00
	1852	1.943	1.50	5.00	18.00	30.00
	1853	.705	10.00	40.00	110.00	175.00
	1855	.265	40.00	85.00	200.00	400.00
	1856	5.656	1.00	2.00	7.00	20.00
	1857	2.299	1.50	4.00	12.50	25.00
	1858	2.712	1.50	4.00	12.50	25.00
	1859	2.591	1.50	4.00	12.50	25.00
	1860	.199	60.00	175.00	300.00	550.00
	1861	—	70.00	200.00	350.00	650.00

COPPER-NICKEL

KM#	Date	Mintage	VG	Fine	VF	XF
21	1861	8.259	.25	.60	2.00	5.00
(C6)	1862/1	14.149	.25	.60	2.00	5.00
	1862	Inc. Ab.	.25	.50	1.50	4.00
	1863/2	16.055	.25	1.00	2.50	7.50
	1863	Inc. Ab.	.25	.60	2.00	5.00
	1864	2.513	7.50	20.00	40.00	70.00

Obv. French leg: DES BELGES

KM#	Date	Mintage	Fine	VF	XF	Unc
40	1894	3.111	1.00	2.50	5.00	15.00
(Y3.1)	1895	3.693	1.00	2.50	5.00	15.00
	1898	1.004	12.50	22.00	35.00	55.00
	1900/891					
		1.666	12.50	22.00	35.00	55.00
	1900	Inc. Ab.	10.00	15.00	30.00	45.00

Rev: Lion of different design.

KM#	Date	Mintage	Fine	VF	XF	Unc
44	1901	2.494	5.00	12.00	30.00	42.50
(Y3.2)						

Obv. Flemish leg: DER BELGEN

KM#	Date	Mintage	Fine	VF	XF	Unc
41	1894	1.658	1.00	2.50	5.00	15.00
(Y3.3)	1895	4.957	1.00	2.50	5.00	15.00
	1898	.985	10.00	22.00	30.00	55.00
	1900	1.670	8.00	15.00	30.00	45.00

Rev: Lion of different design

KM#	Date	Mintage	Fine	VF	XF	Unc
45	1901	2.491	5.00	12.00	30.00	42.50
(Y3.4)						

Obv. French leg: BELGIQUE, small date

KM#	Date	Mintage	Fine	VF	XF	Unc
46	1901	.202	25.00	37.50	47.50	80.00
(Y12.1)	1902/1	1.416	.50	1.00	5.00	12.00
	1902	Inc. Ab.	.25	.75	2.50	7.00
	1903	.864	.25	1.00	5.50	12.00

Obv: Large date

KM#	Date	Mintage	Fine	VF	XF	Unc
54	1904	5.814	.15	.25	2.00	7.00
(Y12.2)	1905/4	9.575	.30	.50	3.00	12.00
	1905	Inc. Ab.	.15	.25	2.00	7.00
	1906/5	8.463	.30	.50	3.00	12.00
	1906	Inc. Ab.	.15	.25	2.00	7.00
	1907	.993	.25	.50	3.00	12.00

Obv. Flemish leg: BELGIE, small date

KM#	Date	Mintage	Fine	VF	XF	Unc
47	1902	1.485	.15	.25	2.50	7.00
(Y12.3)	1903	1.002	.35	.75	5.00	12.00

BELGIUM 173

Obv: Large date

KM#	Date	Mintage	Fine	VF	XF	Unc
55	1904	5.812	.15	.25	2.00	7.00
(Y12.4)	1905/4	7.002	.30	.50	3.00	12.00
	1905	Inc. Ab.	.15	.25	2.00	7.00
	1906	11.016	.15	.25	2.00	7.00
	1907	.998	.15	.25	3.00	12.00

Obv. French leg: BELGIQUE

KM#	Date	Mintage	Fine	VF	XF	Unc
66	1910	8.011	.10	.25	1.25	5.00
(Y24.1)	1913/0	5.005	.10	.25	2.25	10.00
	1913	Inc. Ab.	.10	.25	1.50	5.00
	1914	1.004	.10	.50	4.00	12.00
	1920/10	10.040	.10	.25	1.00	5.00
	1920	Inc. Ab.	.10	.25	.75	4.00
	1922/0	12.640	.10	.25	1.00	4.00
	1922/1	I.A.	.10	.25	1.25	5.00
	1922	Inc. Ab.	.10	.25	.75	4.00
	1923/13	9.000	.10	.25	2.00	6.00
	1923	Inc. Ab.	.10	.25	.75	4.00
	1925/13	15.860	.10	.25	1.00	4.00
	1925	Inc. Ab.	.10	.25	.75	4.00
	1926/5	7.000	.10	.25	1.00	4.00
	1926	Inc. Ab.	.10	.25	.75	4.00
	1927	2.000	.10	.25	1.00	4.00
	1928	12.507	.10	.25	.75	4.00
	1932	—	5.00	12.50	25.00	80.00

Obv. Flemish leg: BELGIE

KM#	Date	Mintage	Fine	VF	XF	Unc
67	1910	8.033	.10	.25	1.25	7.00
(Y24.2)	1914	6.040	.10	.25	1.25	7.00
	1920/10	10.030	.10	.25	1.25	7.00
	1920	Inc. Ab.	.10	.25	.75	5.00
	1921/11	4.200	.10	.25	1.25	7.00
	1921	Inc. Ab.	.10	.25	1.25	7.00
	1922/12	13.180	.10	.25	2.50	8.00
	1922/0	I.A.	.10	.25	1.25	7.00
	1922	Inc. Ab.	.10	.25	1.25	5.00
	1923/13	3.530	.10	.25	1.25	7.00
	1923	Inc. Ab.	.10	.25	1.25	5.00
	1924/11	5.260	.10	.25	1.25	5.00
	1924/14	I.A.	.10	.25	1.25	5.00
	1924	Inc. Ab.	.10	.25	1.25	5.00
	1925/13	13.000	.10	.25	1.25	5.00
	1925/15 high 2	Inc. Ab.	.10	.25	2.00	6.00
	1925/15 level 2	Inc. Ab.	.10	.25	2.00	6.00
	1925/3	I.A.	.10	.25	2.00	6.00
	1925	Inc. Ab.	.10	.25	.75	4.00
	1926/5	I.A.	.10	.25	1.25	5.00
	1927	6.938	.10	.25	.75	4.00
	1928/3	6.252	.10	.25	1.25	5.00
	1928	Inc. Ab.	.10	.25	.75	4.00
	1930	—	5.00	12.50	25.00	80.00
	1931	—	7.50	15.00	30.00	100.00

ZINC
German Occupation WW I
Obv. French leg: BELGIQUE-BELGIE

KM#	Date	Mintage	Fine	VF	XF	Unc
80	1915	10.199	.15	.50	3.00	10.00
(Y38)	1916 dots	45.464	.10	.30	2.00	5.00

NICKEL-BRASS
Obv. French leg: BELGIQUE
Rev: Star added above 5

KM#	Date	Mintage	Fine	VF	XF	Unc
93 (Y24a.1)	1932	5.520	.10	.20	.35	3.00

Obv. Flemish leg: BELGIE

KM#	Date	Mintage	Fine	VF	XF	Unc
94	1930	3.000	.10	.20	.35	3.00
(Y24a.2)	1931	7.430	.10	.20	.35	3.00

NOTE: KM#93 and 94 coins dated 1906 and 1922 with stars are restrikes.

Obv. French leg: BELGIQUE-BELGIE

KM#	Date	Mintage	Fine	VF	XF	Unc
110 (Y42.1)	1938	4.970	.10	.20	.75	2.00

Obv. Flemish leg: BELGIE-BELGIQUE

KM#	Date	Mintage	Fine	VF	XF	Unc
111	1939	3.000	.10	.20	.75	2.00
(Y42.2)	1940	1.970	.20	.40	1.00	3.00

ZINC
German Occupation WW II
Obv. French leg: BELGIQUE-BELGIE

KM#	Date	Mintage	Fine	VF	XF	Unc
123	1941	10.000	.10	.20	.30	3.00
(Y51.1)	1943	7.606	.10	.20	.30	3.00

Obv. Flemish leg: BELGIE-BELGIQUE

KM#	Date	Mintage	Fine	VF	XF	Unc
124	1941	4.000	.15	.20	.60	3.00
(Y51.2)	1942	18.430	.10	.20	.30	3.00

10 CENTIMES

COPPER

KM#	Date	Mintage	VG	Fine	VF	XF
2	1832	.993	9.00	30.00	100.00	160.00
(C4)	1833	.994	9.00	30.00	100.00	160.00
	1835	—	125.00	250.00	750.00	1500.
	1838	—	125.00	250.00	750.00	1500.
	1841	—	125.00	250.00	750.00	1500.
	1847/37	.135	16.00	50.00	130.00	250.00
	1847	Inc. Ab.	16.00	50.00	130.00	250.00
	1848/38	.777	20.00	55.00	140.00	200.00
	1848	Inc. Ab.	20.00	55.00	140.00	200.00
	1849	Inc. Ab.	125.00	150.00	500.00	1200.
	1855	.191	50.00	100.00	175.00	300.00
	1856	Inc. Ab.	100.00	200.00	400.00	1000.

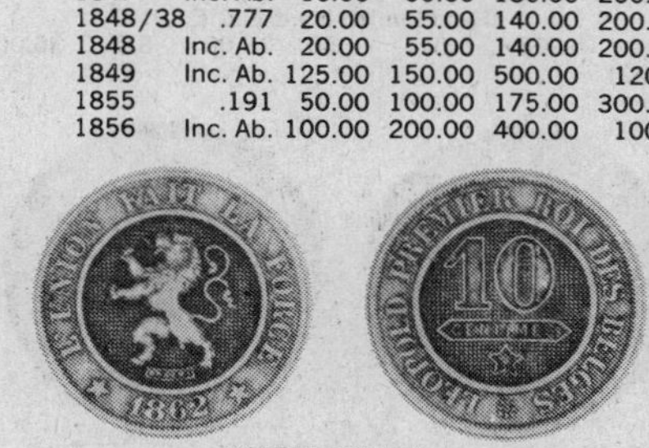

COPPER-NICKEL

KM#	Date	Mintage	VG	Fine	VF	XF
22	1861	9.080	.25	.75	1.50	5.00
(C7)	1862/61	15.129	.35	1.00	2.00	8.00
	1862	Inc. Ab.	.10	.50	1.25	4.00
	1863	14.482	.10	.50	1.25	4.00
	1864	3.202	3.00	6.00	12.50	27.50

Obv. French leg: DES BELGES

KM#	Date	Mintage	Fine	VF	XF	Unc
42	1894	18.886	.75	3.00	5.00	15.00
(Y4.1)	1895	.736	30.00	60.00	125.00	160.00
	1898	3.499	3.00	6.00	12.00	30.00
	1901	.556	20.00	30.00	90.00	200.00

Obv. Flemish leg: DER BELGEN

KM#	Date	Mintage	Fine	VF	XF	Unc
43	1894	9.209	.75	3.00	5.00	15.00
(Y4.2)	1895/4	3.529	2.00	3.50	10.00	30.00
	1895	Inc. Ab.	1.00	3.50	7.50	25.00
	1898	3.500	3.00	6.00	15.00	30.00
	1901	.556	20.00	40.00	95.00	200.00

Obv. French leg: BELGIQUE, small date.

KM#	Date	Mintage	Fine	VF	XF	Unc
48	1901	.582	6.00	15.00	25.00	45.00
(Y13.1)	1902/1	5.866	.50	1.25	7.00	15.00
	1902	Inc. Ab.	.15	.40	2.00	9.00
	1903	.763	1.00	3.00	7.00	15.00

Obv: Large date

KM#	Date	Mintage	Fine	VF	XF	Unc
52	1903	Inc. Ab.	2.00	6.00	15.00	40.00
(Y13.2)	1904	16.354	.15	.25	1.50	7.50
	1905/4	14.392	.25	.50	3.00	10.00
	1905	Inc. Ab.	.15	.25	1.50	7.00
	1906/5	1.483	.50	.75	4.00	10.00
	1906	Inc. Ab.	.25	.50	2.00	8.00

Obv. Flemish leg: BELGIE, small date.

KM#	Date	Mintage	Fine	VF	XF	Unc
49	1902	1.560	.20	.50	2.00	8.00
(Y13.3)	1903	5.658	.15	.25	1.50	7.00

Obv: Large date

KM#	Date	Mintage	Fine	VF	XF	Unc
53	1903	Inc. Ab.	1.00	4.00	10.00	20.00
(Y13.4)	1904	16.834	.20	.35	1.50	7.00
	1905/3	13.758	.30	.70	2.00	8.00
	1905	Inc. Ab.	.20	.35	1.50	7.00
	1906/5 point above center of 6	2.017	.50	.75	4.00	12.50
	1906/5 point above right side of 6	Inc. Ab.	.50	.75	4.00	12.50
	1906	Inc. Ab.	.10	.30	1.75	8.00

ZINC
German Occupation
Obv. French leg: BELGIQUE-BELGIE

KM#	Date	Mintage	Fine	VF	XF	Unc
81	1915	9.681	.25	.50	2.50	10.00
(Y39)	1916	37.382	.15	.25	1.50	8.00
	1917	1.447	17.50	25.00	35.00	85.00

COPPER-NICKEL
Obv. French leg: BELGIQUE

KM#	Date	Mintage	Fine	VF	XF	Unc
85	1920	6.520	.15	.20	.75	3.00
(Y25.1)	1921	7.215	.15	.20	.75	3.00
	1923	20.625	.10	.20	.75	3.00
	1926/3	6.916	.20	.25	1.00	3.00
	1926/5	I.A.	.20	.25	1.00	3.00
	1926	Inc. Ab.	.15	.20	.75	3.00
	1927	8.125	.15	.20	.75	3.00
	1928/3	6.895	.20	.25	1.00	3.00
	1928/5	I.A.	.20	.25	1.00	3.00
	1928	Inc. Ab.	.15	.20	.75	3.00
	1929	12.260	.15	.20	.75	3.00

Obv. Flemish leg: BELGIE

KM#	Date	Mintage	Fine	VF	XF	Unc
86	1920	5.050	.15	.20	.75	3.00

BELGIUM 174

KM#	Date	Mintage	Fine	VF	XF	Unc
(Y25.2)	1921	7.580	.15	.20	.75	3.00
	1922	6.250	.15	.20	.75	3.00
	1924	5.825	.15	.20	.75	3.00
	1925/3	8.160	.20	.25	1.00	3.00
	1925/4	I.A.	.15	.25	1.00	3.00
	1925	Inc. Ab.	.10	.20	.75	3.00
	1926/3	6.250	.20	.25	1.00	3.00
	1926/5	I.A.	.20	.25	1.00	3.00
	1926	Inc. Ab.	.15	.20	.75	3.00
	1927	10.625	.15	.20	.75	3.00
	1928	6.750	.15	.20	.75	3.00
	1929	4.668	.15	.20	.75	3.00

NICKEL-BRASS
Obv. French leg: BELGIQUE
Rev: Star added above 10

KM#	Date	Mintage	Fine	VF	XF	Unc
95	1930	2.000	50.00	100.00	175.00	250.00
(Y25a.1)	1931	6.270	3.00	5.00	8.00	15.00
	1932	1.270	65.00	100.00	175.00	250.00

Obv. Flemish leg: BELGIE

| 96 | 1930 | 1.581 | .30 | .75 | 2.00 | 6.00 |
| (Y25a.2) | 1931 | 5.000 | 40.00 | 80.00 | 140.00 | 190.00 |

Obv. French leg: BELGIQUE-BELGIE

| 112 | 1938 | 6.000 | .10 | .25 | .50 | 1.50 |
| (Y43.1) | 1939 | 7.000 | .50 | 1.00 | 3.00 | 5.00 |

Obv. Flemish leg: BELGIE-BELGIQUE

| 113 | 1939 | 8.425 | .10 | .25 | .50 | 1.50 |
| (Y43.2) | | | | | | |

ZINC
German Occupation WW II
Obv. French leg: BELGIQUE-BELGIE

125	1941	10.000	.15	.25	1.00	1.50
(Y52.1)	1942	17.000	.15	.25	1.00	1.50
	1943	22.500	.15	.25	1.00	1.50

Obv. Flemish leg: BELGIE-BELGIQUE

126	1941	7.000	.15	.25	1.00	1.50
(Y52.2)	1942	21.000	.15	.25	1.00	1.50
	1943	22.000	.15	.25	1.00	1.50
	1944	28.140	.15	.25	1.00	1.50
	1945	8.000	.15	.25	1.00	1.50
	1946	5.370	.15	.25	1.00	1.50

20 CENTIMES

1.0000 g, .900 SILVER, 0289 oz ASW

KM#	Date	Mintage	VG	Fine	VF	XF
19	1852	.301	8.00	20.00	50.00	125.00
(C14)	1853	1.965	3.00	8.00	30.00	75.00
	1858	.865	40.00	125.00	350.00	600.00

COPPER-NICKEL

| 20 | 1860 | 1.804 | 10.00 | 20.00 | 70.00 | 100.00 |
| (C8) | 1861 | Inc. Ab. | 1.00 | 3.00 | 10.00 | 22.50 |

BRONZE
Obv. French leg: BELGIQUE

KM#	Date	Mintage	Fine	VF	XF	Unc
146	1953	14.150	—	.10	.20	.50
(Y62.1)	1954		—	400.00	600.00	800.00
	1957	13.300	—	—	.10	.25
	1958	8.700	—	—	.10	.25
	1959	19.670	—	—	.10	.25

KM#	Date	Mintage	Fine	VF	XF	Unc
(Y62.1)	1962	.410	—	6.00	10.00	12.50
	1963	2.550	.10	.20	.50	1.00

Obv. Flemish leg: BELGIE

| 147 | 1954 | 50.130 | — | — | .10 | .20 |
| (Y62.2) | 1960 | 7.530 | — | — | .10 | .25 |

1/4 FRANC

1.2500 g, .900 SILVER, .0362 oz ASW

KM#	Date	Mintage	VG	Fine	VF	XF
8	1834 signature					
(C9)		.762	15.00	30.00	75.00	130.00
	1834 w/o signature					
		Inc. Ab.	20.00	40.00	110.00	175.00
	1835 signature					
		.640	15.00	35.00	100.00	170.00
	1835 w/o signature					
		Inc. Ab.	24.00	55.00	150.00	225.00
	1841	—	175.00	250.00	725.00	1500.
	1843	8.000	50.00	100.00	200.00	450.00
	1844	.966	20.00	70.00	110.00	

| 14 | 1849 | — | 200.00 | 750.00 | 1500. | 2000. |
| (C15) | 1850 | .101 | 85.00 | 250.00 | 600.00 | 1500. |

25 CENTIMES

COPPER-NICKEL
Obv. French leg: BELGIQUE

KM#	Date	Mintage	Fine	VF	XF	Unc
62	1908	4.007	.50	1.00	12.50	35.00
(Y14.1)	1909	1.998	.50	1.50	15.00	50.00

Obv. Flemish leg: BELGIE

| 63 | 1908 | 4.011 | .50 | — | 8.00 | 35.00 |
| (Y14.2) | | | | | | |

Obv. French leg: BELGIQUE

68	1913	2.011	.15	.30	2.50	7.50
(Y26.1)	1920	2.844	.15	.25	2.00	5.00
	1921	7.464	.10	.15	1.00	4.00
	1922	7.600	.10	.20	1.00	4.00
	1923	11.356	.15	.25	1.00	4.00
	1926/3	1.300	1.00	2.50	7.50	17.50
	1926	Inc. Ab.	1.00	2.50	7.50	17.50
	1927/3	8.800	.20	.30	1.00	4.00
	1927/6	I.A.	.20	.30	1.00	4.00
	1927	Inc. Ab.	.15	.25	1.00	4.00
	1928	4.351	.10	.15	1.00	4.00
	1929	9.600	.10	.15	1.00	4.00

Obv. Flemish leg: BELGIE

KM#	Date	Mintage	Fine	VF	XF	Unc
69	1910	2.006	.15	.30	2.50	7.50
(Y26.2)	1913	2.010	.15	.30	2.00	5.00
	1921	11.173	.15	.25	1.00	4.00
	1922/1					
		14.200	.20	.30	1.00	4.00
	1922	Inc. Ab.	.15	.25	1.00	4.00
	1926	6.400	.10	.20	1.00	4.00
	1927	3.799	.10	.15	1.00	4.00
	1928	9.200	.15	.25	1.00	4.00
	1929	8.980	.15	.25	1.00	4.00
	1930/20					
		1.176	.20	.30	1.00	4.00

ZINC
German Occupation WW I
Obv. French leg: BELGIQUE-BELGIE

82	1915	8.080	.25	1.25	4.00	12.50
(Y40)	1916	10.671	.25	1.25	4.00	12.50
	1917	3.555	1.50	5.00	10.00	22.50
	1918	5.489	.50	2.50	7.00	15.00

NICKEL-BRASS
Obv. French leg: BELGIQUE-BELGIE

| 114 | 1938 | 7.200 | — | .15 | 1.00 | 2.50 |
| (Y44.1) | 1939 | 7.732 | — | .15 | 1.00 | 3.00 |

Obv. Flemish leg: BELGIE-BELGIQUE

| 115 | 1938 | 14.932 | — | .15 | 1.00 | 2.50 |
| (Y44.2) | | | | | | |

ZINC
German Occupation WW II
Obv. French leg: BELGIQUE-BELGIE

131	1942	14.400	—	.10	.75	2.00
(Y53.1)	1943	21.600	—	.10	.75	2.00
	1946	21.428	—	.10	.75	2.00

Obv: Flemish leg: BELGIE-BELGIQUE

KM#	Date	Mintage	Fine	VF	XF	Unc
132	1942	14.400	—	.10	.75	2.00
(Y53.2)	1943	21.600	—	.10	.75	2.00
	1944	25.960	—	.10	.75	2.00
	1945	8.200	—	.10	.75	2.00
	1946	11.652	—	.10	.75	2.00

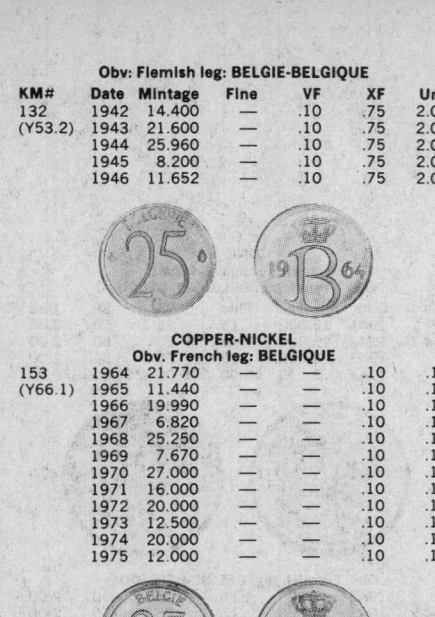

COPPER-NICKEL
Obv. French leg: BELGIQUE

KM#	Date	Mintage	Fine	VF	XF	Unc
153	1964	21.770	—	—	.10	.15
(Y66.1)	1965	11.440	—	—	.10	.15
	1966	19.990	—	—	.10	.15
	1967	6.820	—	—	.10	.15
	1968	25.250	—	—	.10	.15
	1969	7.670	—	—	.10	.15
	1970	27.000	—	—	.10	.15
	1971	16.000	—	—	.10	.15
	1972	20.000	—	—	.10	.15
	1973	12.500	—	—	.10	.15
	1974	20.000	—	—	.10	.15
	1975	12.000	—	—	.10	.15

Obv. Flemish leg: BELGIE

KM#	Date	Mintage	Fine	VF	XF	Unc
154	1964	21.300	—	—	.10	.15
(Y66.2)	1965	7.900	—	—	.10	.15
	1966	23.420	—	—	.10	.15
	1967	7.720	—	—	.10	.15
	1968	22.750	—	—	.10	.15
	1969	25.190	—	—	.10	.15
	1970	12.000	—	—	.10	.15
	1971	16.000	—	—	.10	.15
	1972	20.000	—	—	.10	.15
	1973	12.500	—	—	.10	.15
	1974	20.000	—	—	.10	.15
	1975	12.000	—	—	.10	.15

1/2 FRANC

2.5000 g, .900 SILVER, .0723 oz ASW

KM#	Date	Mintage	VG	Fine	VF	XF
6	1833	.058	50.00	120.00	275.00	700.00
(C10)	1834	1.578	15.00	40.00	125.00	250.00
	1835	.805	20.00	50.00	150.00	300.00
	1838	.550	30.00	60.00	165.00	400.00
	1840	.347	30.00	60.00	165.00	400.00
	1841	—	300.00	450.00	1000.	2000.
	1843	.346	30.00	65.00	175.00	450.00
	1844	1.584	15.00	40.00	125.00	200.00

KM#	Date	Mintage	VG	Fine	VF	XF
15	1849	—	150.00	450.00	1000.	2000.
(C16)	1850	.210	125.00	325.00	700.00	1500.

50 CENTIMES

2.5000 g, .835 SILVER, .0671 oz ASW
Obv. French leg: DES BELGES

KM#	Date	Mintage	Fine	VF	XF	Unc
26	1866	6.806	2.00	10.00	40.00	100.00
(Y5.1)	1867	1.014	12.00	40.00	120.00	225.00
	1868	1.076	50.00	110.00	400.00	700.00
	1881/61	.200	90.00	300.00	700.00	1100.
	1881/66	I.A.	80.00	225.00	550.00	900.00
	1881	Inc. Ab.	70.00	225.00	550.00	900.00
	1886/66	1.250	12.00	30.00	80.00	125.00
	1886	Inc. Ab.	2.00	12.00	40.00	110.00
	1898	.499	2.00	15.00	45.00	135.00
	1899	.500	2.00	15.00	45.00	135.00

Obv. Flemish leg: DER BELGEN

KM#	Date	Mintage	Fine	VF	XF	Unc
27	1886	3.750	2.00	7.00	35.00	110.00
(Y5.2)	1898	.501	2.50	12.00	45.00	135.00
	1899/86	.500	2.50	17.00	75.00	225.00
	1899	Inc. Ab.	2.50	12.00	45.00	110.00

Obv. French leg: DES BELGES

KM#	Date	Mintage	Fine	VF	XF	Unc
50	1901	3.000	1.00	5.00	15.00	35.00
(Y15.1)						

Obv. Flemish leg: DER BELGEN

KM#	Date	Mintage	Fine	VF	XF	Unc
51	1901	3.000	1.00	5.00	15.00	35.00
(Y15.2)						

Obv. French leg: DES BELGES

KM#	Date	Mintage	Fine	VF	XF	Unc
60	1907	.545	3.00	10.00	25.00	40.00
(Y16.1)	1909	2.503	2.00	4.00	9.00	25.00

Obv. Flemish leg: DER BELGEN

KM#	Date	Mintage	Fine	VF	XF	Unc
61	1907	.545	3.00	10.00	25.00	40.00
(Y16.2)	1909	2.510	2.00	4.00	9.00	25.00

Obv. French leg: DES BELGES

KM#	Date	Mintage	Fine	VF	XF	Unc
70	1910	1.900	1.00	3.00	7.00	12.50
(Y33.1)	1911	2.063	1.00	3.00	7.00	17.50
	1912	1.000	.75	1.50	3.00	6.00
	1914	.240	5.00	10.00	25.00	45.00

Obv. Flemish leg: DER BELGEN

KM#	Date	Mintage	Fine	VF	XF	Unc
71	1910	1.900	1.00	3.00	7.00	20.00
(Y33.2)	1911	2.063	.75	1.50	3.00	6.00
	1912	1.000	.75	1.50	3.00	6.00
	1914	—	—	—	Rare	—

ZINC
German Occupation WW I
Obv. Flemish leg: BELGIE-BELGIQUE

KM#	Date	Mintage	Fine	VF	XF	Unc
83	1918	7.394	.50	2.00	5.00	15.00
(Y41)						

NICKEL
Obv. French leg: BELGIQUE

KM#	Date	Mintage	Fine	VF	XF	Unc
87	1922	6.180	.15	.25	.50	1.50
(Y27.1)	1923	8.820	.15	.25	.50	1.50
	1927	1.750	.15	.30	.50	1.50
	1928	3.000	.15	.25	.75	2.50
	1929	1.000	.25	1.50	3.50	10.00
	1930	1.000	.25	1.50	3.50	10.00
	1932	2.530	.15	.30	.75	3.00
	1933	2.861	.15	.25	.75	2.50

Obv. Flemish leg: BELGIE

KM#	Date	Mintage	Fine	VF	XF	Unc
88	1923	15.000	.20	.25	.50	1.50
(Y27.2)	1928/3	10.000	.25	.50	.90	4.00
	1928	Inc. Ab.	.20	.25	.50	1.50
	1930/20	2.252	.50	2.00	3.50	7.00
	1930	Inc. Ab.	.20	.30	.75	3.00
	1932	2.000	.20	.30	.75	2.50
	1933	1.189	1.00	4.00	6.00	12.00
	1934	.935	50.00	90.00	120.00	180.00

Obv. French leg: BELGIQUE-BELGIE

KM#	Date	Mintage	Fine	VF	XF	Unc
118	1939	15.500	175.00	300.00	400.00	600.00
(Y27.3)						

NOTE: Striking interrupted by the war. Never officially released into circulation.

BRONZE
Obv. French leg: BELGIQUE. Rev: Large head.

KM#	Date	Mintage	Fine	VF	XF	Unc
144	1952	3.520	—	.10	.25	1.00
(Y63.1)	1953	22.620	—	—	.10	.35

Rev: Smaller head.

KM#	Date	Mintage	Fine	VF	XF	Unc
148	1955	29.160	—	—	.10	.25
(Y63.2)	1958	9.750	—	—	.10	.25
	1959	17.350	—	—	.10	.20
	1962	6.160	—	—	.10	.15
	1964	5.860	—	—	.10	.15
	1965	10.320	—	—	.10	.15
	1966	11.040	—	—	.10	.15
	1967	7.200	—	—	.10	.15
	1968	2.000	—	—	.10	.20
	1969	10.000	—	—	.10	.15
	1970	16.000	—	—	.10	.15
	1971	1.250	—	—	.10	.20
	1972	3.000	—	—	.10	.15
	1973	3.000	—	—	.10	.15
	1974	5.000	—	—	.10	.15
	1975	7.000	—	—	.10	.15
	1976	8.000	—	—	.10	.15
	1977	13.000	—	—	.10	.15
	1978	2.500	—	—	.10	.15
	1979	20.000	—	—	.10	.15
	1980	20.000	—	—	.10	.15
	1981	2.000	—	—	.10	.15
	1982	7.000	—	—	.10	.15
	1983	14.100	—	—	.10	.15
	1985	6.000	—	—	.10	.15
	1987	9.000	—	—	.10	.15

Obv. Flemish leg: BELGIE. Rev: Large head.

KM#	Date	Mintage	Fine	VF	XF	Unc
145	1952	5.830	—	.10	.25	1.00
(Y63.3)	1953	22.930	—	—	.10	.35
	1954	15.730	—	—	.10	.35

Rev: Smaller head

KM#	Date	Mintage	Fine	VF	XF	Unc
149	1956	5.640	—	—	.10	.25
(Y63.4)	1957	13.800	—	—	.10	.25
	1958	19.480	—	—	.10	.20
	1962	4.150	—	—	.10	.15
	1963	1.110	—	—	.10	.15
	1964	10.340	—	—	.10	.15
	1965	9.590	—	—	.10	.15
	1966	6.930	—	—	.10	.15
	1967	6.970	—	—	.10	.15
	1968	2.000	—	—	.10	.20
	1969	10.000	—	—	.10	.15
	1970	12.000	—	—	.10	.15
	1971	1.250	—	—	.10	.20
	1972	7.000	—	—	.10	.15
	1973	3.000	—	—	.10	.15
	1974	5.000	—	—	.10	.15
	1975	7.000	—	—	.10	.15
	1976	8.000	—	—	.10	.15
	1977	13.000	—	—	.10	.15
	1978	2.500	—	—	.10	.15
	1979	40.000	—	—	.10	.15
	1980	20.000	—	—	.10	.15
	1981	2.000	—	—	.10	.15

KM#	Date	Mintage	Fine	VF	XF	Unc
(Y63.4)	1982	7.000	—	—	.10	.15
	1983	14.100	—	—	.10	.15
	1985	6.000	—	—	.10	.15
	1987	9.000	—	—	.10	.15

FRANC

5.0000 g, .900 SILVER, .1447 oz ASW

KM#	Date	Mintage	VG	Fine	VF	XF
7	1833	.061	110.00	225.00	500.00	1000.
(C11)	1834	.482	30.00	50.00	150.00	300.00
	1835	.831	35.00	70.00	160.00	350.00
	1838	.525	35.00	75.00	180.00	400.00
	1840	.261	40.00	80.00	210.00	450.00
	1841	—	135.00	375.00	1100.	2000.
	1843	—	65.00	165.00	550.00	1100.
	1844	2.196	18.00	35.00	110.00	175.00

KM#	Date	Mintage	VG	Fine	VF	XF
16	1849	.041	150.00	350.00	1000.	2200.
(C17)	1850	.162	125.00	300.00	700.00	2000.

5.0000 g, .835 SILVER, .1342 oz ASW
Obv. French leg: DES BELGES

KM#	Date	Mintage	Fine	VF	XF	Unc
28	1866	3.041	3.00	15.00	65.00	150.00
(Y6.1)	1867	6.652	2.00	10.00	40.00	130.00
	1868*	.675	—	Reported, not confirmed		
	1869	1.394	5.00	30.00	130.00	350.00
	1881	.119	75.00	225.00	600.00	1250.
	1886/66	1.250	4.00	20.00	55.00	175.00
	1886	Inc. Ab.	3.00	15.00	35.00	120.00

*NOTE: Mintage probably dated 1867.

Obv. Flemish leg: DER BELGEN

KM#	Date	Mintage	Fine	VF	XF	Unc
29	1886	1.026	3.00	15.00	45.00	130.00
(Y6.2)	1887	2.724	2.00	7.50	25.00	100.00

50th Anniversary Independence

KM#	Date	Mintage	Fine	VF	XF	Unc
38	1880	.545	8.00	20.00	65.00	120.00
(Y9)						

Obv. French leg: DES BELGES

KM#	Date	Mintage	Fine	VF	XF	Unc
56	1904	.803	3.00	7.00	20.00	55.00
(Y17.1)	1909	2.250	1.25	3.00	9.00	35.00

Obv. Flemish leg: DER BELGEN

KM#	Date	Mintage	Fine	VF	XF	Unc
57	1904	.803	3.00	7.00	20.00	55.00
(Y17.2)	1909	2.250	1.25	3.00	9.00	35.00

Obv. French leg: DES BELGES

KM#	Date	Mintage	Fine	VF	XF	Unc
72	1910	2.190	1.00	3.00	6.00	15.00
(Y34.1)	1911	2.810	1.00	2.50	5.00	12.00
	1912	3.250	1.00	2.00	3.00	7.00
	1913	3.000	1.00	2.00	3.00	7.00
	1914	10.563	1.00	2.00	3.00	7.00
	1917	8.540	—	—	—	2000.
	1918	1.469	—	—	—	2000.

Obv. Flemish leg: DER BELGEN

KM#	Date	Mintage	Fine	VF	XF	Unc
73	1910	2.750	1.00	3.00	6.00	15.00
(Y34.2)	1911	2.250	1.00	2.50	5.00	12.00
	1912	3.250	1.00	2.00	3.00	7.00
	1913	3.000	1.00	2.00	3.00	7.00
	1914	10.222	1.00	2.00	3.00	7.00
	1918	—	—	—	—	2000.

NICKEL
Obv. French leg: BELGIQUE

KM#	Date	Mintage	Fine	VF	XF	Unc
89	1922	14.000	.15	.25	.75	3.00
(Y28.1)	1923	22.500	.15	.25	.75	3.00
	1928/3	5.000	.20	.75	2.00	5.00
	1928/7	I.A.	.20	.75	2.00	5.00
	1928	Inc. Ab.	.15	.25	.75	3.00
	1929	7.415	.15	.25	.75	3.50
	1930	5.365	.20	.50	1.00	3.50
	1931	—	250.00	450.00	900.00	1500.
	1933	1.998	.50	1.50	3.50	9.00
	1934/24	10.263	.20	.75	2.00	5.00
	1934	Inc. Ab.	.15	.25	.75	3.00

Obv. Flemish leg: BELGIE

KM#	Date	Mintage	Fine	VF	XF	Unc
90	1922	19.000	.15	.25	.75	3.00
(Y28.2)	1923/2	17.500	.20	.75	2.00	4.00
	1923	Inc. Ab.	.15	.25	.75	3.00
	1928/3	4.975	.20	.75	2.00	4.00
	1928/7	I.A.	.20	.75	2.00	4.00
	1928	Inc. Ab.	.15	.25	1.50	4.00
	1929	10.365	.15	.25	.75	3.00
	1933	.786	200.00	300.00	450.00	750.00
	1934/24	8.025	.20	.75	2.00	5.00
	1934	Inc. Ab.	.15	.25	.75	3.00
	1935/23	2.238	.35	.75	2.50	7.50
	1935	Inc. Ab.	.30	.50	2.00	6.00

Obv. French leg: BELGIQUE-BELGIE

KM#	Date	Mintage	Fine	VF	XF	Unc
119	1939	46.865	.15	.25	.50	1.50
(Y45.1)						

Obv. Flemish leg: BELGIE-BELGIQUE

KM#	Date	Mintage	Fine	VF	XF	Unc
120	1939	36.000	.15	.25	.50	1.50
(Y45.2)	1940	10.865	.20	.40	.75	2.50

ZINC
German Occupation WW II
Obv. French leg: BELGIQUE-BELGIE

KM#	Date	Mintage	Fine	VF	XF	Unc
127	1941	16.000	.15	.25	.50	2.00
(Y54.1)	1942	25.000	.15	.25	.50	2.00
	1943	28.000	.15	.25	.50	2.00
	1947	3.175	60.00	100.00	250.00	375.00

Obv. Flemish leg: BELGIE-BELGIQUE

KM#	Date	Mintage	Fine	VF	XF	Unc
128	1942	42.000	.15	.25	.50	2.00
(Y54.2)	1943	28.000	.15	.25	.50	2.00
	1944	24.190	.15	.25	.50	2.00
	1945	15.930	.15	.25	.50	2.00
	1946	36.000	.15	.25	.50	2.00
	1947	3.000	30.00	60.00	100.00	175.00

COPPER-NICKEL
Obv. French leg: BELGIQUE

KM#	Date	Mintage	Fine	VF	XF	Unc
142	1950	13.630	—	—	.10	3.00
(Y57.1)	1951	51.025	—	—	.10	2.00
	1952	53.205	—	—	.10	2.00
	1954	4.980	—	.10	.25	4.00
	1955	3.960	—	.10	.25	4.00
	1956	10.000	—	—	.10	1.00
	1958	31.750	—	—	.10	1.00
	1959	9.000	—	—	.10	1.00
	1960	10.000	—	—	.10	.15
	1961	5.030	—	—	.10	.15
	1962	12.250	—	—	.10	.15
	1963	18.700	—	—	.10	.15
	1964	10.110	—	—	.10	.15
	1965	10.185	—	—	.10	.15
	1966	16.430	—	—	.10	.15
	1967	32.945	—	—	.10	.15
	1968	8.000	—	—	.10	.15
	1969	21.950	—	—	.10	.15
	1970	35.500	—	—	.10	.15
	1971	10.000	—	—	.10	.15
	1972	35.000	—	—	.10	.15
	1973	42.500	—	—	.10	.15
	1974	30.000	—	—	.10	.15
	1975	80.000	—	—	.10	.15
	1976	18.000	—	—	.10	.15
	1977	68.500	—	—	.10	.15
	1978	47.500	—	—	.10	.15
	1979	25.000	—	—	.10	.15
	1980	66.500	—	—	.10	.15
	1981	2.000	—	—	.10	.15

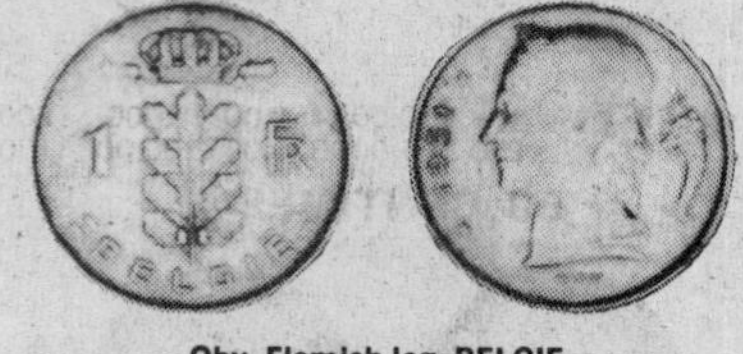

Obv. Flemish leg: BELGIE

KM#	Date	Mintage	Fine	VF	XF	Unc
143	1950	10.000	—	—	.10	3.00
(Y57.2)	1951	53.750	—	—	.10	2.00
	1952	49.145	—	—	.10	2.00
	1953	9.915	—	—	.10	2.00
	1954	4.940	—	.10	.25	4.00
	1955	3.960	—	.10	.25	4.00
	1956	10.040	—	—	.10	1.00
	1957	18.315	—	—	.10	1.00
	1958	17.365	—	—	.10	1.00
	1959	5.830	—	—	.10	1.00
	1960	5.555	—	—	.10	.15
	1961	9.350	—	—	.10	.15
	1962	10.720	—	—	.10	.15
	1963	23.460	—	—	.10	.15
	1964	7.430	—	—	.10	.15
	1965	11.190	—	—	.10	.15
	1966	20.990	—	—	.10	.15
	1967	27.470	—	—	.10	.15
	1968	8.170	—	—	.10	.15
	1969	21.730	—	—	.10	.15

BELGIUM 177

KM#	Date	Mintage	Fine	VF	XF	Unc
(Y57.2)	1970	35.730	—	—	.10	.15
	1971	10.000	—	—	.10	.15
	1972	35.000	—	—	.10	.15
	1973	42.500	—	—	.10	.15
	1974	30.000	—	—	.10	.15
	1975	80.000	—	—	.10	.15
	1976	18.000	—	—	.10	.15
	1977	68.500	—	—	.10	.15
	1978	47.500	—	—	.10	.15
	1979	50.000	—	—	.10	.15
	1980	66.500	—	—	.10	.15
	1981	2.000	—	—	.10	.15
	1988	—	—	—	.10	.15

2 FRANCS

10.0000 g, .900 SILVER, .2894 oz ASW

KM#	Date	Mintage	VG	Fine	VF	XF
9	1834	.276	75.00	165.00	600.00	1400.
(C12)	1834	—	—	—	Proof	4500.
	1835	.225	100.00	225.00	700.00	1600.
	1838	.300	125.00	275.00	800.00	2000.
	1840	.236	100.00	225.00	700.00	1500.
	1841	—	200.00	600.00	—	2200.	3800.
	1843	.735	60.00	200.00	500.00	1300.
	1844	.483	90.00	250.00	650.00	1500.

10	1848	(restrike)	—	—	—	—
(C18)	1849	—	400.00	900.00	2800.	4700.
	1865	—	450.00	1100.	3200.	5200.

NOTE: The above type was not officially released into circulation.

10.0000 g, .835 SILVER, .2685 oz ASW
Obv. French leg: DES BELGES

KM#	Date	Mintage	Fine	VF	XF	Unc
30	1866	1.942	7.00	25.00	160.00	400.00
(Y7.1)	1867	3.789	5.00	20.00	150.00	350.00
	1868	2.164	7.00	30.00	175.00	400.00

Obv. Flemish leg: DER BELGEN

31	1887	.150	75.00	300.00	1000.	2000.
(Y7.2)						

50th Anniversary Independence
Rev. French leg: DE BELGIQUE

39	1880	.118	30.00	100.00	225.00	500.00
(Y10)						

Obv. French leg: DES BELGES

58	1904	.400	6.00	15.00	45.00	90.00
(Y18.1)	1909	1.088	2.50	7.50	25.00	45.00

Obv. Flemish leg: DER BELGEN

KM#	Date	Mintage	Fine	VF	XF	Unc
59	1904	.400	5.00	15.00	45.00	90.00
(Y18.2)	1909	1.088	2.50	7.50	25.00	45.00

Obv. French leg: DES BELGES

74	1910	.800	4.00	8.00	17.00	40.00
(Y35.1)	1911	1.000	2.50	7.00	15.00	35.00
	1912	.375	5.00	12.00	22.00	40.00

Obv. Flemish leg: DER BELGEN

75	1911	1.775	2.50	7.00	15.00	35.00
(Y35.2)	1912	.375	5.00	12.00	22.00	40.00

NICKEL
Obv. French leg: BELGIQUE

91	1923	7.500	.25	1.00	2.00	10.00
(Y29.1)	1930/20	1.250	22.50	40.00	70.00	135.00
	1930 Inc. Ab.	17.50	35.00	60.00	115.00

Obv. Flemish leg: BELGIE

92	1923	6.500	.25	1.00	2.00	10.00
(Y29.2)	1924	1.000	12.50	25.00	40.00	75.00
	1930/20	1.252	20.00	35.00	65.00	125.00
	1930 Inc. Ab.	15.00	30.00	55.00	110.00

ZINC COATED STEEL
Allied Occupation Issue
Obv. French leg: BELGIQUE-BELGIE

133	1944	25.000	.25	.50	.75	3.00
(Y56)						

NOTE: Made in U.S.A. on blanks for 1943 cents.

2-1/2 FRANCS

12.5000 g, .900 SILVER, .3617 oz ASW
Obv. French leg: ROI DES BELGES

KM#	Date	Mintage	VG	Fine	VF	XF
11	1848	.559	45.00	165.00	250.00	400.00
(C19.1)	1849	2.003	30.00	100.00	225.00	300.00

Larger head

12	1848	—	125.00	350.00	1200.	2000.
(C19.2)	1849	—	30.00	110.00	275.00	550.00
	1849	—	—	—	Proof	1500.
	1850	.065	175.00	400.00	700.00	1500.
	1865	—	350.00	750.00	2000.	3250.

NOTE: Coins dated 1865 were not released into circulation.

5 FRANCS

25.0000 g, .900 SILVER, .7234 oz ASW
Incuse lettered edge.

3.1	1832	.037	60.00	150.00	350.00	800.00
(C13.1)	1833	1.126	16.00	30.00	100.00	325.00
	1834	.350	45.00	100.00	250.00	475.00
	1835	.370	45.00	100.00	250.00	475.00
	1838	5.203	450.00	1000.	2000.	4000.
	1840	—	500.00	1700.	3400.	6300.
	1841	—	500.00	1700.	3400.	6300.
	1844	.080	60.00	135.00	275.00	850.00

Raised lettered edge.

3.2	1847	.700	20.00	40.00	110.00	250.00
(C13.2)	1848	2.516	12.00	30.00	65.00	135.00
	1849	3.014	10.00	17.50	45.00	115.00

17	1849	3.909	12.50	17.50	35.00	45.00
(C20)	1850 dot above date	5.265	12.50	17.50	35.00	45.00
	1850 w/o dot above date Inc. Ab.	10.00	17.50	30.00	45.00
	1850	—	—	—	Proof	500.00
	1851/0	3.708	15.00	20.00	40.00	60.00
	1851 dot above date Inc. Ab.	10.00	17.50	30.00	45.00
	1851 w/o dot above date					
	1852/1	4.605	15.00	25.00	35.00	75.00
	1852 Inc. Ab.	10.00	17.50	30.00	45.00
	1853	2.427	15.00	20.00	30.00	45.00	75.00
	1858	.018	60.00	200.00	300.00	550.00
	1865/55 broken M in PREMIER					
		.907	15.00	25.00	60.00	110.00

BELGIUM

KM#	Date	Mintage	VG	Fine	VF	XF
(C20)	1865/55	I.A.	15.00	25.00	60.00	110.00
	1865	Inc. Ab.	10.00	20.00	45.00	90.00
	1865 dot after F on reverse					
		Inc. Ab.	15.00	30.00	65.00	100.00

Obv: Smaller head, engravers name near rim, below truncation.

KM#	Date	Mintage	Fine	VF	XF	Unc
24	1865	Inc. 1867	100.00	225.00	350.00	650.00
(Y8.1)	1866	Inc. 1867	175.00	250.00	425.00	725.00
	1866 dot after F on reverse					
		Inc. 1867	175.00	325.00	525.00	800.00
	1867	3.693	7.50	15.00	35.00	70.00
	1867 dot after F on reverse					
		Inc. Ab.	10.00	35.00	50.00	100.00
	1868	6.751	7.50	12.50	30.00	75.00
	1869	12.658	7.50	10.00	20.00	75.00
	1870	10.486	7.50	10.00	20.00	75.00
	1871	4.783	7.50	12.50	30.00	75.00
	1872	2.045	7.50	15.00	35.00	80.00
	1873	22.341	6.50	7.50	15.00	60.00
	1874	2.400	7.50	10.00	30.00	80.00
	1875	2.981	7.50	10.00	30.00	80.00
	1876	2.160	7.50	10.00	30.00	80.00
	1878	3 known	—	—	Rare	—

Obv: Larger head, engravers name below truncation.

KM#	Date	Mintage	Fine	VF	XF	Unc
25	1865	—	450.00	900.00	1350.00	2500.
(Y8.2)	1866	—	550.00	1150.	1800.	3400.
	1867	—	400.00	800.00	1100.	2300.
	1868	—	550.00	1100.	1650.	3100.

(Un (1) Belga)

NICKEL
Obv. French leg: DES BELGES
Rev. value: UN BELGA

KM#	Date	Mintage	Fine	VF	XF	Unc
97	1930	1.600	1.00	2.50	5.00	15.00
(Y30.1)	1931	9.032	.75	2.00	3.00	10.00
	1932	3.600	4.00	7.00	10.00	20.00
	1933	1.387	8.00	15.00	25.00	40.00
	1934	1.000	45.00	75.00	110.00	175.00

Obv. Flemish leg: DER BELGEN
Rev. value: EEN BELGA

KM#	Date	Mintage	Fine	VF	XF	Unc
98	1930	5.086	1.00	2.50	5.00	12.50
(Y30.2)	1931	5.336	1.00	2.50	5.00	12.50
	1932	3.683	1.50	3.00	7.50	20.00
	1933	2.514	8.00	10.00	20.00	40.00

Rev. French leg: BELGIQUE

KM#	Date	Mintage	Fine	VF	XF	Unc
108	1936	.650	6.00	17.50	25.00	50.00
(Y47.1)	1937	1.848	6.00	17.50	25.00	50.00

Rev. Flemish leg: BELGIE

109	1936	2.498	4.00	15.00	20.00	45.00
(Y47.2)						

Obv. French leg: BELGIQUE-BELGIE

116	1938 edge lettering separated by a crown					
(Y46.1)		11.419	.10	.50	1.50	4.00
	1938 milled edge w/o lettering					
		Inc. Ab.	30.00	50.00	100.00	175.00

Obv. Flemish leg: BELGIE-BELGIQUE

117	1938 edge lettering separated by a crown					
(Y46.2)		3.200	15.00	35.00	50.00	65.00
	1938 edge lettering separated by a star					
		Inc. Ab.	15.00	35.00	50.00	65.00
	1939 edge lettering separated by a crown					
		8.219	15.00	35.00	50.00	65.00
	1939 edge lettering separated by a star					
		Inc. Ab.	.10	.75	1.50	9.00
	1939 reeded edge w/o edge lettering					
		Inc. Ab.	—	—	—	—

ZINC
German Occupation WW II
Obv. French leg: DES BELGES

129	1941	15.200	.35	.75	1.50	5.00
(Y55.1)	1943	16.236	.35	.75	1.50	5.00
	1944	1.868	.75	2.00	5.00	12.00
	1945	3.200	.50	1.00	2.50	7.50
	1946	4.452	1.00	2.50	5.00	12.00
	1947	3.100	30.00	65.00	110.00	190.00

Obv. Flemish leg: DER BELGEN

130	1941	27.544	.30	.75	1.50	5.00
(Y55.2)	1945	3.200	40.00	70.00	110.00	190.00
	1946	4.000	—	—	Rare	—
	1947	.036	125.00	250.00	375.00	650.00

COPPER-NICKEL
Obv. French leg: BELGIQUE

KM#	Date	Mintage	Fine	VF	XF	Unc
134	1948	5.304	—	.10	.15	4.00
(Y58.1)	1949	38.752	—	.10	.15	2.00
	1950	23.948	—	.10	.15	2.00
	1958	9.088	—	.10	.15	1.00
	1961	6.000	—	.10	.15	.50
	1962	6.576	—	.10	.15	.50
	1963	11.144	—	.10	.15	.30
	1964	3.520	—	.10	.15	.40
	1965	11.988	—	.10	.15	.30
	1966	6.772	—	.10	.15	.40
	1967	13.268	—	.10	.15	.30
	1968	5.192	—	.10	.15	.40
	1969	22.235	—	.10	.15	.30
	1970	2.000	—	.10	.15	.45
	1971	15.000	—	.10	.15	.30
	1972	17.500	—	.10	.15	.30
	1973	10.000	—	.10	.15	.30
	1974	25.000	—	.10	.15	.30
	1975	34.000	—	.10	.15	.30
	1976	7.500	—	.10	.15	.40
	1977	22.500	—	.10	.15	.30
	1978	27.500	—	.10	.15	.30
	1979	5.000	—	.10	.15	.40
	1980	11.000	—	.10	.15	.30
	1981	2.000	—	.10	.15	.40

Obv. Flemish leg: BELGIE

135	1948	4.800	—	.10	.15	4.00
(Y58.2)	1949	31.500	—	.10	.15	2.00
	1950	34.728	—	.10	.15	2.00
	1958	2.672	—	.10	.15	4.00
	1960	5.896	—	.10	.15	.75
	1961	4.120	—	.10	.15	.50
	1962	7.624	—	.10	.15	.50
	1963	6.136	—	.10	.15	.40
	1964	8.128	—	.10	.15	.40
	1965	9.956	—	.10	.15	.40
	1966	7.136	—	.10	.15	.40
	1967	16.132	—	.10	.15	.30
	1968	3.200	—	.10	.15	.40
	1969	21.500	—	.10	.15	.30
	1970	2.000	—	.10	.15	.45
	1971	15.000	—	.10	.15	.30
	1972	17.500	—	.10	.15	.30
	1973	10.000	—	.10	.15	.30
	1974	25.000	—	.10	.15	.30
	1975	34.000	—	.10	.15	.30
	1976	7.500	—	.10	.15	.40
	1977	22.500	—	.10	.15	.30
	1978	27.500	—	.10	.15	.30
	1979	5.000	—	.10	.15	.30
	1980	11.000	—	.10	.15	.30
	1981	2.000	—	.10	.15	.40

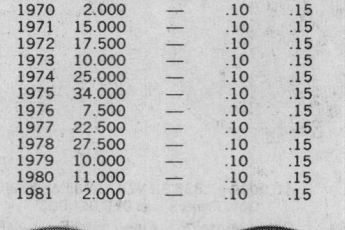

BRASS or ALUMINUM-BRONZE
Rev: French leg: BELGIQUE.

163	1986	152.060	—	—	—	.50
	1987	—	—	—	—	.50

Rev: Flemish leg: BELGIE.

164	1986	208.500	—	—	—	.50
	1987	—	—	—	—	.50

10 FRANCS

3.2258 g, .900 GOLD, .0933 oz AGW

KM#	Date	Mintage	Fine	VF	XF	Unc
18	1849	.037	500.00	1200.	2500.	3750.
(C24)	1850	.063	400.00	1000.	2000.	3000.

NOTE: 54,890 pcs. dated 1849 and 1850 were withdrawn from circulation.

(Deux or Twee (2) Belgas)
NICKEL
Independence Centennial
Rev. French leg: BELGIQUE

99	1930	2.699	25.00	50.00	80.00	110.00
(Y31.1)						

Rev. Flemish leg: BELGIE

100	1930	3.000	30.00	60.00	90.00	125.00
(Y31.2)						

Rev. French leg: BELGIQUE

155	1969	22.235	—	—	.30	.60
(Y67.1)	1970	9.500	—	—	.30	.60
	1971	15.000	—	—	.30	.60
	1972	10.000	—	—	.30	.60
	1973	10.000	—	—	.30	.60
	1974	5.000	—	—	.30	.60
	1975	5.000	—	—	.30	.60
	1976	7.500	—	—	.30	.60
	1977	7.000	—	—	.30	.60
	1978	2.500	—	—	.30	.60
	1979	—	—	—	.30	.60

Rev. Flemish leg: BELGIE

156	1969	21.500	—	—	.30	.60
(Y67.2)	1970	10.000	—	—	.30	.60
	1971	15.000	—	—	.30	.60
	1972	10.000	—	—	.30	.60
	1973	10.000	—	—	.30	.60
	1974	5.000	—	—	.30	.60
	1975	5.000	—	—	.30	.60
	1976	7.500	—	—	.30	.60
	1977	7.000	—	—	.30	.60
	1978	2.500	—	—	.30	.60
	1979	10.000	—	—	.30	.60

20 FRANCS

6.4516 g, .900 GOLD, .1867 oz AGW

23	1864	—	1500.	3000.	5000.	8000.
(C26)	1865	1.026	BV	95.00	125.00	200.00
	1865 (error: engraver-Winner)					
		Inc. Ab.	BV	120.00	150.00	200.00

NOTE: 1864 dated coins were not released for circulation and are considered patterns.

KM#	Date	Mintage	Fine	VF	XF	Unc
32.1	1866	—	1000.	2000.	5000.	8000.
(Y19.1)	1867	1.341	—	BV	95.00	110.00
	1868	1.382	—	BV	95.00	110.00
	1869	1.234	—	BV	95.00	110.00
	1870	3.191	—	BV	95.00	110.00

NOTE: 1866 dated coins were not released for circulation and are considered patterns.

32.2	1869	Inc. Ab.	100.00	175.00	250.00	325.00

Obv: Smaller bust.

37.1	1870	Inc. Ab.	—	BV	95.00	110.00
(Y19.2)	1871	2.259	—	BV	95.00	110.00
	1874	3.046	—	BV	95.00	110.00
	1875	4.134	—	BV	95.00	110.00
	1876	2.070	—	BV	95.00	110.00
	1877	5.906	—	BV	95.00	110.00
	1878	2.505	—	BV	95.00	110.00
	1882	.522	—	BV	95.00	110.00

Inverted edge lettering.

37.2	1876	Inc. Ab.	250.00	400.00	550.00	1000.
	1878	Inc. Ab.	550.00	1100.	1650.	2200.

Obv. French leg: DES BELGES

78.1	1914	.125	—	BV	100.00	140.00
(Y37.1)						

Inverted edge lettering.

78.2	1914	Inc. Ab.	375.00	500.00	625.00	750.00

Obv. Flemish leg: DER BELGEN

79.1	1914	.125	—	BV	100.00	140.00
(Y37.2)						

Inverted edge lettering.

79.2	1914	Inc. Ab.	BV	110.00	150.00	175.00

(Vier or Quatre Belgas)

NICKEL
Obv. French leg: DES BELGES

101	1931	3.957	30.00	45.00	75.00	125.00
(Y32.1)	1932	5.472	25.00	55.00	70.00	120.00

Obv. Flemish leg: DER BELGEN

102	1931	2.600	30.00	60.00	75.00	125.00
(Y32.2)	1932	6.950	25.00	55.00	70.00	120.00

11.0000 g, .680 SILVER, .2405 oz ASW
Obv. French leg: DES BELGES

103	1933	.200	22.50	45.00	80.00	135.00
(Y36.1)	1934	12.300	BV	3.50	5.00	9.00

Obv. Flemish leg: DER BELGEN

KM#	Date	Mintage	Fine	VF	XF	Unc
104	1933	.200	17.50	40.00	60.00	85.00
(Y36.2)	1934	12.300	BV	3.00	4.50	8.00

105	1934	1.250	4.00	7.00	10.00	20.00
(Y49)	1935	10.760	BV	3.00	6.00	8.00

8.0000 g, .835 SILVER, .2148 oz ASW
Obv. French leg: BELGIQUE

140	1949	4.600	BV	2.50	5.00	8.00
(Y59.1)	1950	12.957	BV	2.50	5.00	8.00
	1953	3.953	BV	3.50	6.00	10.00
	1954	4.835	12.00	20.00	55.00	90.00
	1955	1.730	150.00	275.00	400.00	650.00

Obv. Flemish leg: BELGIE

141	1949	5.545	BV	2.50	5.00	8.00
(Y59.2)	1950	—	150.00	400.00	600.00	1000.
	1951	7.885	BV	2.50	5.00	8.00
	1953	6.625	BV	3.00	6.00	10.00
	1954	5.323	8.00	14.00	25.00	45.00
	1955	3.760	10.00	35.00	100.00	150.00

BRONZE
Rev. French leg: BELGIQUE

159	1980	30.000	—	—	.60	.90
(Y-A67.1)	1981	60.000	—	—	.60	.90
	1982	54.000	—	—	.60	.90

Rev. Flemish leg: BELGIE

160	1980	30.000	—	—	.60	.90
(Y-A67.2)	1981	60.000	—	—	.60	.90
	1982	54.000	—	—	.60	.90

BELGIUM 180

25 FRANCS

8.0645 g, .900 GOLD, .2333 oz AGW

KM#	Date	Mintage	Fine	VF	XF	Unc
13	1848	.321	650.00	1500.	2200.	3000.
(C25)	1849	.150	750.00	2000.	4000.	5000.
	1850	.074	850.00	2000.	4000.	5000.

50 FRANCS

22.0000 g, .680 SILVER, .4810 oz ASW
Brussels Exposition And Railway Centennial
Obv. leg: DE BELGIQUE.
Rev. French leg: DE FER BELGES.

KM#	Date	Mintage	Fine	VF	XF	Unc
106 (Y48.1)	1935	.140	45.00	90.00	130.00	200.00

Obv. leg: BELGIE.
Rev. Flemish leg: DER BELGISCHE.

| 107 (Y48.2) | 1935 | .140 | 50.00 | 120.00 | 160.00 | 240.00 |

20.0000 g, .835 SILVER, .5369 oz ASW
Obv. French leg: BELGIQUE: BELGIE

| 121 (Y50.1) | 1939 | 1.000 | BV | 7.00 | 11.00 | 18.00 |
| | 1940 | .631 | BV | 10.00 | 20.00 | 32.50 |

Obv. Flemish leg: BELGIE: BELGIQUE

| 122 (Y50.2) | 1939 | 1.000 | BV | 8.00 | 12.00 | 18.00 |
| | 1940 | .631 | BV | 10.00 | 20.00 | 32.50 |

12.5000 g, .835 SILVER, .3356 oz ASW
Obv. French leg: BELGIQUE

136 (Y60.1)	1948	2.000	BV	2.50	5.00	9.00
	1949	4.354	BV	2.50	5.00	9.00
	1951	2.904	BV	2.50	5.00	10.00
	1954	3.232	BV	6.00	12.00	25.00

Obv. Flemish leg: BELGIE

KM#	Date	Mintage	Fine	VF	XF	Unc
137 (Y60.2)	1948	3.000	BV	2.50	5.00	9.00
	1950	4.110	BV	2.50	5.00	9.00
	1951	1.698	BV	2.50	5.50	10.00
	1954	2.978	BV	2.50	5.00	9.00

Brussels Fair
Obv. French leg: DES BELGES

| 150 (Y64.1) | 1958 | .476 | BV | 6.00 | 7.00 | 12.00 |

Obv. Flemish leg: DER BELGEN

| 151 (Y64.2) | 1958 | .382 | BV | 6.00 | 7.00 | 12.00 |

King Baudouin Marriage

| 152 (Y65) | 1960 | .500 | BV | 4.00 | 6.00 | 10.00 |

NICKEL
Rev. French leg: BELGIQUE

| 168 | 1987 | 30.000 | — | — | — | 4.00 |

Rev. Flemish leg: BELGIE

| 169 | 1987 | 30.000 | — | — | — | 4.00 |

100 FRANCS

18.0000 g, .835 SILVER, .4832 oz ASW
Obv. French leg: BELGIQUE

KM#	Date	Mintage	Fine	VF	XF	Unc
138 (Y61.1)	1948	1.000	BV	4.00	8.00	12.00
	1949	.106	12.50	20.00	30.00	50.00
	1950	2.807	BV	4.00	7.00	10.00
	1954	2.517	BV	4.00	7.00	10.00

Obv. Flemish leg: BELGIE

139 (Y61.2)	1948	1.000	BV	4.00	8.00	12.00
	1949	2.271	BV	4.00	7.00	12.00
	1950	—	300.00	500.00	650.00	800.00
	1951	4.691	BV	4.00	7.00	10.00

250 FRANCS

25.0000 g, .835 SILVER, .6711 oz ASW
Obv. French leg: ROI DES BELGES, reeded edge.

| 157.1 (Y68.1) | 1976 | 1.000 | — | BV | 7.00 | 10.00 |

Stars on edge

| 157.2 (Y68.2) | 1976 | .100 | — | — | P/L | 20.00 |

Obv. Flemish leg: KONING DER BELGEN, reeded edge.

| 158.1 (Y68.3) | 1976 | 1.000 | — | BV | 7.00 | 10.00 |

Stars on edge

| 158.2 (Y68.4) | 1976 | .100 | — | — | P/L | 20.00 |

500 FRANCS

25.0000 g, .200 SILVER, .1608 oz ASW
SILVER CLAD COPPER-NICKEL
150th Anniversary of Independence
Rev: French legend.

KM#	Date	Mintage	Fine	VF	XF	Unc
161 (Y69.1)	1980	1.000	—	—	—	15.00

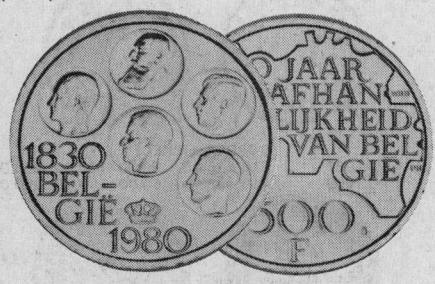

Rev: Flemish legend

| 162 (Y69.2) | 1980 | 1.000 | — | — | — | 15.00 |

25.0000 g, .510 SILVER, .4099 oz ASW
Rev: French legend.

| 161a (Y69.3) | 1980 | .053 | — | — | Proof | 30.00 |

Rev: Flemish legend.

| 162a (Y69.4) | 1980 | .052 | — | — | Proof | 30.00 |

Mule. Obv: KM#161. Rev: KM#162.

| 165 | 1980 | — | — | — | Rare | — |

EUROPEAN CURRENCY UNITS
5 ECU

22.8500 g, .833 SILVER, .6120 oz ASW

166	1987	.850	—	—	—	20.00
	1987	.015	—	—	Proof	50.00
	1988	—	—	—	—	20.00
	1988	—	—	—	Proof	50.00

50 ECU

17.2800 g, .900 GOLD, .5000 oz AGW

167	1987	.911	—	—	—	235.00
	1987	.015	—	—	Proof	350.00
	1988	—	—	—	—	235.00
	1988	—	—	—	Proof	315.00

FLEUR DE COIN SETS (SS)

KM#	Date	Mintage	Identification	Issue Price	Mkt. Val.
SS1	1970(5)	5,000	KM135,143,149,154,156 FL	.60	35.00
SS2	1970(5)	5,000	KM134,142,148,153,155 FR	.60	35.00
SS3	1971(5)	20,000	KM135,143,149,154,156 FL	.63	12.50
SS4	1971(5)	20,000	KM134,142,148,153,155 FR	.63	12.50
SS5	1972(5)	10,000	KM135,143,149,154,156 FL	.70	25.00
SS6	1972(5)	10,000	KM134,142,148,153,155 FR	.70	25.00
SS7	1973(5)	31,773	KM135,143,149,154,156 FL	.80	12.50
SS8	1973(5)	31,773	KM134,142,148,153,155 FR	.80	12.50
SS9	1974(5)	39,609	KM135,143,149,154,156 FL	1.10	6.00
SS10	1974(5)	39,609	KM134,142,148,153,155 FR	1.10	6.00
SS11	1975(10)	100,000	KM135,143,149,154,156 FL, 134,142,148,153,155 FR	2.50	6.00
SS12	1976(10)	15,000	KM135,143,149,154,156 FL, 134,142,148,153,155 FR	20.75	70.00
SS13	1977(8)	50,000	KM135,143,149,156 FL, 134,142,148,155 FR	2.65	6.00
SS14	1978(8)	50,000	KM135,143,149,156 FL 134,142,148,155 FR	4.00	6.00
SS15	1979(8)	50,000	KM135,143,149,156 FL 134,142,148,155 FR	4.00	6.00
SS16	1980(8)	60,000	KM135,143,149,160 FL, 134,142,148,159 FR	4.00	6.00
SS17	1981(8)	62,000	KM135,143,149,160 FL, 134,142,148,159 FR	3.25	6.00

PROOF SETS (PS)

| PS1 | 1987(2) | .015 | KM166-167 | 395.00 | 400.00 |

BELIZE

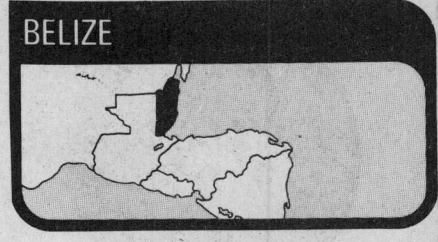

Belize, formerly British Honduras, but now an independent member of the British Commonwealth, is situated in Central America south of Mexico and east and north of Guatemala, with an area of 8,867 sq. mi. (22,965 sq. km.) and a population of 164,777. Capital: Belmopan. Tourism now augments Belize's economy, in addition to sugar, citrus fruits, chicle and hard woods which are exported.

The area, site of the ancient Mayan civilization, was sighted by Columbus in 1502, and settled by shipwrecked English seamen in 1638. British buccaneers settled the former capital of Belize in the 17th century. Britain claimed administrative right over the area after the emancipation of Central America from Spain, and declared it a colony subordinate to Jamaica in 1862. It was established as the separate Crown Colony of British Honduras in 1884. The anti-British People's United Party, which attained power in 1954, won a constitution, effective in 1964 which established self-government under a British appointed governor. British Honduras became Belize on June 1, 1973, following the passage of a surprise bill by the People's United Party, but the constitutional relationship with Britain remained unchanged.

In Dec. 1975, the U.N. General Assembly adopted a resolution supporting the right of the people of Belize to self-determination, and asking Britain and Guatemala to renew their negotiations on the future of Belize. They obtained independence on Sept. 21, 1981.

RULERS
British

MINT MARKS
H - Birmingham Mint
No mm - Royal Mint

MONETARY SYSTEM
Commencing 1884
100 Cents = 1 Dollar

BRITISH HONDURAS
COUNTERMARKED COINAGE
1810-1818
6 SHILLINGS 1 PENCE

.916 SILVER
c/m: Crowned script GR in rectangular indent on Mexico City 8 Reales, KM#109.

KM#	Date	Good	VG	Fine	VF
1	ND(1791-1808)	75.00	150.00	250.00	400.00

c/m: Crowned script GR in rectangular indent on Peru (Lima) 8 Reales, KM#97.

| 5 | ND(1791-1808) | 75.00 | 150.00 | 250.00 | 400.00 |

British Honduras / BELIZE 182

c/m: Crowned script GR in oval indent on Mexico City 8 Reales, KM#111.

KM#	Date	Good	VG	Fine	VF
2	ND(1811-1818)	60.00	120.00	200.00	325.00

c/m: Crowned script GR in oval indent on France 5 Francs, C#138.

3	ND(L'an 4-11)	100.00	175.00	300.00	500.00

c/m: Incuse crowned script GR on Mexico City 8 Reales, KM#111.

4	ND(1811-1818)	75.00	150.00	250.00	400.00

NOTE: KM#4 is considered a local issue. The c/m crowned GR in octagonal indent is considered a modern fabrication. Refer to "UNUSUAL WORLD COINS", second edition, Krause Publications, 1988.

DECIMAL COINAGE
CENT

BRONZE

KM#	Date	Mintage	Fine	VF	XF	Unc
6	1885	.072	4.00	10.00	25.00	65.00
	1885	—	—	—	Proof	250.00
	1888	.100	3.00	8.50	25.00	75.00
	1888	—	—	—	Proof	275.00
	1889	.050	4.00	10.00	25.00	60.00
	1889	—	—	—	Proof	275.00
	1894	.050	8.00	20.00	50.00	275.00
	1894	*25 pcs.	—	—	Proof	300.00

11	1904	.050	6.00	15.00	35.00	70.00
	1904	—	—	—	Proof	200.00
	1904	—	—	—	Matte Proof	550.00
	1906	.050	8.00	22.50	65.00	225.00
	1906	—	—	—	Proof	300.00
	1909	.025	35.00	80.00	150.00	350.00

KM#	Date	Mintage	Fine	VF	XF	Unc
15	1911	.050	50.00	85.00	150.00	350.00
	1912H	.050	85.00	160.00	225.00	400.00
	1913	.025	75.00	135.00	200.00	350.00

19	1914	.175	2.25	7.50	25.00	120.00
	1916H	.125	2.50	8.50	27.50	125.00
	1918	.040	5.00	15.00	40.00	95.00
	1919	.050	5.00	15.00	40.00	150.00
	1924	.050	4.00	12.00	35.00	100.00
	1924	—	—	—	Proof	250.00
	1926	.050	4.00	12.00	35.00	125.00
	1926	—	—	—	Proof	225.00
	1936	.040	2.00	5.00	20.00	70.00
	1936	50 pcs.	—	—	Proof	150.00

21	1937	.080	.50	4.00	12.00	75.00
	1937	—	—	—	Proof	150.00
	1939	.050	.50	2.00	10.00	25.00
	1939	—	—	—	Proof	100.00
	1942	.050	1.00	5.00	15.00	150.00
	1942	—	—	—	Proof	125.00
	1943	.100	.50	2.50	12.00	125.00
	1943	—	—	—	Proof	135.00
	1944	.100	.50	5.00	15.00	150.00
	1944	—	—	—	Proof	200.00
	1945	.130	.50	1.00	7.50	50.00
	1945	—	—	—	Proof	120.00
	1947	.100	.50	1.00	10.00	70.00
	1947	—	—	—	Proof	150.00

Obv. leg: W/o EMPEROR OF INDIA

24	1949	.100	.60	1.25	3.50	15.00
	1949	—	—	—	Proof	150.00
	1950	.100	.40	1.00	2.50	5.00
	1950	—	—	—	Proof	90.00
	1951	.100	.60	1.50	4.00	15.00
	1951	—	—	—	Proof	90.00

27	1954	.200	.50	.75	1.00	5.00
	1954	—	—	—	Proof	90.00

30	1956	.200	.10	.25	.50	3.50
	1956	—	—	—	Proof	85.00
	1958	.400	.50	1.00	5.00	30.00
	1958	—	—	—	Proof	85.00
	1959	.200	.50	1.00	5.00	50.00
	1959	—	—	—	Proof	125.00
	1961	.800	—	.15	.25	.50
	1961	—	—	—	Proof	75.00

KM#	Date	Mintage	Fine	VF	XF	Unc
30	1964	.300	—	.10	.30	.90
	1965	.400	—	—	.10	.50
	1966	.100	—	—	.10	.50
	1967	.400	—	—	.10	.50
	1968	.200	—	—	.10	.50
	1969	.520	—	—	.10	.40
	1970	.120	—	—	.10	.40
	1971	.800	—	—	.10	.40
	1972	.800	—	—	.10	.40
	1973	.400	—	—	.10	.40

5 CENTS

1.1620 g, .925 SILVER, .0346 oz ASW

7	1894	.128	5.00	15.00	30.00	75.00
	1894	*25 pcs.	—	—	Proof	400.00

COPPER-NICKEL

14	1907	.010	25.00	60.00	100.00	225.00
	1909	.010	25.00	50.00	100.00	250.00

16	1911	.010	10.00	30.00	75.00	175.00
	1912H	.020	5.00	22.50	55.00	150.00
	1912H	—	—	—	Proof	550.00
	1916H	.020	5.00	20.00	55.00	170.00
	1918	.020	5.00	18.00	50.00	150.00
	1919	.020	4.00	15.00	50.00	150.00
	1936	.060	2.00	5.00	20.00	75.00
	1936	50 pcs.	—	—	Proof	200.00

22	1939	.020	3.00	5.00	20.00	50.00
	1939	—	—	—	Proof	225.00

NICKEL-BRASS

22a	1942	.030	5.00	15.00	65.00	200.00
	1942	—	—	—	Proof	300.00
	1943	.040	1.50	7.50	35.00	130.00
	1944	.050	1.50	10.00	50.00	175.00
	1944	—	—	—	Proof	275.00
	1945	.065	1.00	5.00	15.00	75.00
	1945	—	—	—	Proof	150.00
	1947	.040	1.50	5.00	15.00	85.00
	1947	—	—	—	Proof	185.00

Obv. leg: W/o EMPEROR OF INDIA

25	1949	.040	1.00	2.00	7.50	35.00
	1949	—	—	—	Proof	100.00
	1950	.225	.40	1.00	4.00	30.00
	1950	—	—	—	Proof	100.00
	1952	.100	.50	1.00	5.00	25.00
	1952	—	—	—	Proof	200.00

31	1956	.100	.20	.50	3.00	75.00
	1956	—	—	—	Proof	185.00
	1957	.100	.30	.75	1.50	10.00
	1957	—	—	—	Proof	185.00
	1958	.200	.30	1.00	7.50	90.00
	1958	—	—	—	Proof	125.00
	1959	.100	.30	1.00	5.00	75.00
	1959	—	—	—	Proof	185.00
	1961	.100	.30	.75	2.50	35.00
	1961	—	—	—	Proof	120.00
	1962	.200	.15	.35	.65	2.00

KM#	Date	Mintage	Fine	VF	XF	Unc
31	1962	—	—	—	Proof	110.00
	1963	.100	.10	.20	.50	1.50
	1963	—	—	—	Proof	120.00
	1964	.100	.10	.15	.35	1.00
	1965	.150	—	.10	.25	.75
	1966	.150	—	.10	.20	.60
	1968	.200	—	.10	.15	.50
	1969	.540	—	.10	.15	.50
	1970	.240	—	.10	.15	.50
	1971	.450	—	.10	.15	.50
	1972	.200	—	.10	.15	.50
	1973	.210	—	.10	.15	.75

10 CENTS

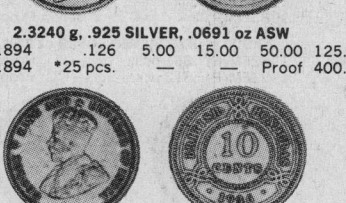

2.3240 g, .925 SILVER, .0691 oz ASW

KM#	Date	Mintage	Fine	VF	XF	Unc
8	1894	.126	5.00	15.00	50.00	125.00
	1894	*25 pcs.	—	—	Proof	400.00

20	1918	.010	10.00	25.00	100.00	350.00
	1919	.010	10.00	25.00	100.00	350.00
	1936	.030	4.00	10.00	25.00	100.00
	1936	50 pcs.	—	—	Proof	250.00

23	1939	.020	3.00	7.00	20.00	60.00
	1939	—	—	—	Proof	250.00
	1942	.010	3.50	12.00	60.00	150.00
	1943	.020	3.00	6.00	45.00	250.00
	1944	.030	2.50	5.00	40.00	150.00
	1944	—	—	—	Proof	250.00
	1946	.010	3.50	8.00	35.00	175.00
	1946	—	—	—	Proof	250.00

COPPER-NICKEL

32	1956	.100	.40	1.00	2.00	7.50
	1956	—	—	—	Proof	200.00
	1959	.100	.60	1.50	2.00	37.50
	1959	—	—	—	Proof	135.00
	1961	.050	.30	.75	1.25	3.00
	1961	—	—	—	Proof	135.00
	1963	.050	.20	.50	.75	2.00
	1963	—	—	—	Proof	135.00
	1964	.060	.15	.25	.50	1.00
	1965/6	.200	5.00	10.00	20.00	40.00
	1965	Inc. Ab.	—	.10	.15	.50
	1970	—	—	.10	.15	.75

25 CENTS

5.8100 g, .925 SILVER, .1728 oz ASW

9	1894	8.00	20.00	65.00	285.00
	1894	*25 pcs.	—	—	Proof	550.00
	1895	.047	10.00	25.00	75.00	300.00
	1897	.040	10.00	25.00	85.00	350.00
	1901	.020	15.00	30.00	100.00	350.00
	1901	30 pcs.	—	—	Proof	750.00

12	1906	.030	10.00	30.00	100.00	350.00
	1907	.060	7.50	25.00	95.00	325.00

KM#	Date	Mintage	Fine	VF	XF	Unc
17	1911	.014	15.00	40.00	125.00	350.00
	1919	.040	6.00	15.00	75.00	250.00

26	1952	.075	1.40	3.50	25.00	225.00
	1952	—	—	—	Proof	400.00

COPPER-NICKEL

29	1955	.075	.40	1.00	3.50	15.00
	1955	—	—	—	Proof	150.00
	1960	.075	.40	1.00	5.00	120.00
	1960	—	—	—	Proof	250.00
	1962	.050	.30	.50	1.00	2.50
	1962	—	—	—	Proof	150.00
	1963	.050	.30	.50	2.00	8.00
	1963	—	—	—	Proof	150.00
	1964	.100	.30	.50	.75	1.50
	1965	.075	—	.50	1.00	2.00
	1966	.075	.30	.75	1.50	6.00
	1968	.125	.25	.50	1.00	2.00
	1970	—	.20	.35	.75	1.50
	1971	.150	.20	.30	.50	1.50
	1972	.200	.20	.30	.50	1.50
	1973	.100	.20	.30	.60	1.75

50 CENTS

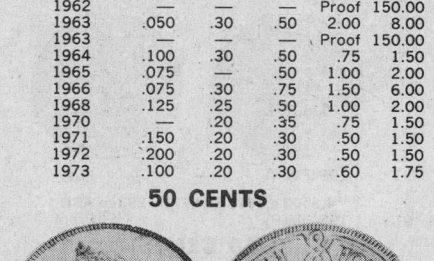

11.6200 g, .925 SILVER, .3456 oz ASW

10	1894	.038	12.00	25.00	85.00	375.00
	1894	*25 pcs.	—	—	Proof	1350.
	1895	.036	15.00	30.00	135.00	500.00
	1897	.020	12.00	30.00	150.00	550.00
	1901	.010	22.50	50.00	175.00	800.00
	1901	30 pcs.	—	—	Proof	1400.

13	1906	.015	15.00	50.00	150.00	450.00
	1907	.019	15.00	60.00	170.00	450.00

18	1911	.012	20.00	50.00	150.00	700.00
	1919	.040	8.00	20.00	100.00	400.00
	1919	—	—	—	Proof	1000.

KM#	Date	Mintage	Fine	VF	XF	Unc
28	1954	.075	.30	.50	1.00	3.00
	1954	—	—	—	Proof	175.00
	1962	.050	.30	.50	1.50	3.50
	1962	—	—	—	Proof	200.00
	1964	.050	.30	.50	1.50	2.50
	1965	.025	1.00	3.00	5.00	25.00
	1966	.025	.50	1.50	3.00	15.00
	1971	.030	.50	1.50	3.00	2.50

PROOF SETS (PS)

KM#	Date	Mintage	Identification	Issue Price	Mkt. Val.
PS1	1894(5)	*25	KM6-10	—	3000.
PS2	1901(2)	30	KM9,10	—	2000.
PS3	1936(3)	50	KM16,19,20	—	600.00
PS4	1939(3)	—	KM21-23	—	500.00
PS5	1949(2)	—	KM24,26	—	200.00
PS6	1950(2)	—	KM24,26	—	200.00
PS7	1954(2)	—	KM27,28	—	250.00
PS8	1956(3)	—	KM30-32	—	350.00
PS9	1958(2)	—	KM30,31	—	250.00

BELIZE

MINT MARKS

No mm - Royal Mint
FM - Franklin Mint, U.S.A.*

***NOTE:** From 1975 the Franklin Mint has produced coinage in 3 different qualities. Qualities of issue are designated in ( ) after each date and are defined as follows:

(M) MATTE - Normal circulation strike or a dull finish produced by sandblasting special uncirculated (polish finish) or proof quality dies.

(U) SPECIAL UNCIRCULATED - Polished or proof-like in appearance without any frosted features.

(P) PROOF - The highest quality obtainable having mirror-like fields and frosted features.

CENT

BRONZE

KM#	Date	Mintage	VF	XF	Unc
33	1973	.400	—	.10	.25
	1974	2.000	—	.10	.20
	1975	Inc. Ab.	—	.10	.15
	1976	3.000	—	.10	.15

ALUMINUM

33a	1976	2.050	—	.10	.15
	1979	2.505	—	.10	.15
	1980	1.505	—	.10	.15
	1982	—	—	.10	.15
	1986	—	—	.10	.15

BRONZE

38	1974FM(M)	.225	—	.40	1.00
	1974FM(P)	.021	—	Proof	1.25

3.0200 g, .925 SILVER, .0898 oz ASW

38a	1974FM(P)	.031	—	Proof	2.50

BRONZE

46	1975FM(M)	.118	—	.10	.75
	1975FM(U)	1,095	—	.20	1.00
	1975FM(P)	8,794	—	Proof	1.00
	1976FM(M)	.126	—	.10	.75
	1976FM(U)	759 pcs.	—	.20	1.00
	1976FM(P)	4,893	—	Proof	1.00

3.0200 g, .925 SILVER, .0898 oz ASW

BELIZE 184

KM#	Date	Mintage	VF	XF	Unc
46a	1975FM(P)	.013	—	Proof	1.50
	1976FM(P)	5,897	—	Proof	1.50
	1977FM(P)	3,197	—	Proof	1.50
	1978FM(P)	3,342	—	Proof	1.50
	1979FM(P)	2,445	—	Proof	1.50
	1980FM(P)	1,826	—	Proof	1.50
	1981FM(P)	643 pcs.	—	Proof	2.00

ALUMINUM

KM#	Date	Mintage	VF	XF	Unc
46b	1977FM(U)	.126	—	.10	.15
	1977FM(P)	2,107	—	Proof	1.00
	1978FM(U)	.125	—	.10	.15
	1978FM(P)	1,671	—	Proof	1.00
	1979FM(U)	808 pcs.	—	.15	.75
	1979FM(P)	1,287	—	Proof	1.00
	1980FM(U)	761 pcs.	—	.15	.75
	1980FM(P)	920 pcs.	—	Proof	1.00
	1981FM(U)	297 pcs.	—	.15	.75
	1981FM(P)	643 pcs.	—	Proof	1.00

83	1982FM(U)	—	—	.15	.75
	1982FM(P)	—	—	Proof	1.00
	1983FM(U)	—	—	.15	.75
	1983FM(P)	—	—	Proof	1.00

3.0200 g, .925 SILVER, .0898 oz ASW

83a	1982FM(P)	381 pcs.	—	Proof	3.00
	1983FM(P)	336 pcs.	—	Proof	3.00

ALUMINUM

90	1984FM(P)	—	—	Proof	1.00

3.0200 g, .925 SILVER, .0898 oz ASW

90a	1984FM(P)	—	—	Proof	3.00

5 CENTS

NICKEL-BRASS

34	1973	.210	—	.10	.40
	1974	.210	—	.10	.40
	1975	.420	—	.10	.40
	1976	.570	—	.10	.40

ALUMINUM

34a	1976	1.000	—	.10	.20
	1979	.960	—	.10	.20
	1980	1.040	—	.10	.20
	1986	—	—	.10	.20

NICKEL-BRASS

39	1974FM(M)	.050	—	.25	1.25
	1974FM(P)	.021	—	Proof	1.50

4.3500 g, .925 SILVER, .1293 oz ASW

39a	1974FM(P)	.031	—	Proof	3.00

NICKEL-BRASS

47	1975FM(M)	.024	—	.25	1.50
	1975FM(U)	1,095	—	.25	1.50
	1975FM(P)	8,794	—	Proof	1.25
	1976FM(M)	.025	—	.25	1.50
	1976FM(U)	759 pcs.	—	.25	1.50
	1976FM(P)	4,893	—	Proof	1.25

4.3500 g, .925 SILVER, .1293 oz ASW

47a	1975FM(P)	.013	—	Proof	2.00
	1976FM(P)	5,897	—	Proof	2.00
	1977FM(P)	3,197	—	Proof	2.00
	1978FM(P)	3,342	—	Proof	2.00

KM#	Date	Mintage	VF	XF	Unc
47a	1979FM(P)	2,445	—	Proof	2.00
	1980FM(P)	1,826	—	Proof	2.00
	1981FM(P)	643 pcs.	—	Proof	2.50

ALUMINUM

47b	1977FM(U)	.026	—	.10	.50
	1977FM(P)	2,107	—	Proof	1.50
	1978FM(U)	.025	—	.10	.50
	1978FM(P)	1,671	—	Proof	1.50
	1979FM(U)	808 pcs.	—	.15	.75
	1979FM(P)	1,287	—	.25	1.75
	1980FM(U)	761 pcs.	—	.15	.75
	1980FM(P)	920 pcs.	—	Proof	1.75
	1981FM(U)	297 pcs.	—	.15	.75
	1981FM(P)	643 pcs.	—	Proof	1.75

84	1982FM(U)	—	—	.15	.75
	1982FM(P)	—	—	Proof	1.75
	1983FM(U)	—	—	.15	.75
	1983FM(P)	—	—	Proof	1.75

4.3500 g, .925 SILVER, .1293 oz ASW

84a	1982FM(P)	381 pcs.	—	Proof	5.00
	1983FM(P)	479 pcs.	—	Proof	5.00

ALUMINUM
World Food Day

64	1981	—	—	.10	.35

91	1984FM(P)	—	—	Proof	1.75

4.3500 g, .925 SILVER, .1293 oz ASW

91a	1984FM(P)	—	—	Proof	5.00

10 CENTS

COPPER-NICKEL

35	1974	.100	.15	.30	.60
	1975	.200	.10	.20	.50
	1976	.700	.10	.15	.45
	1979	.800	.10	.15	.35
	1980	—	.10	.15	.35

40	1974FM(M)	.027	—	.50	2.00
	1974FM(P)	.021	—	Proof	1.75

2.7900 g, .925 SILVER, .0829 oz ASW

40a	1974FM(P)	.031	—	Proof	3.50

COPPER-NICKEL

48	1975FM(M)	.012	—	.25	1.50
	1975FM(U)	1,095	—	.30	2.00
	1975FM(P)	8,794	—	Proof	1.50
	1976FM(M)	.013	—	.25	1.50
	1976FM(U)	759 pcs.	—	.35	2.50
	1976FM(P)	4,893	—	Proof	1.50
	1977FM(U)	.014	—	.25	2.00
	1977FM(P)	2,107	—	Proof	2.00
	1978FM(U)	.013	—	.25	1.50
	1978FM(P)	1,671	—	Proof	2.00
	1979FM(U)	808 pcs.	—	.25	1.50
	1979FM(P)	1,287	—	Proof	2.50
	1980FM(U)	761 pcs.	—	.25	1.50
	1980FM(P)	920 pcs.	—	Proof	1.50
	1981FM(U)	297 pcs.	—	.25	1.50
	1981FM(P)	643 pcs.	—	Proof	2.50

2.7900 g, .925 SILVER, .0829 oz ASW

KM#	Date	Mintage	VF	XF	Unc
48a	1975FM(P)	.013	—	Proof	2.50
	1976FM(P)	5,897	—	Proof	2.50
	1977FM(P)	3,197	—	Proof	2.50
	1978FM(P)	3,342	—	Proof	2.50
	1979FM(P)	2,445	—	Proof	2.50
	1980FM(P)	1,826	—	Proof	2.50
	1981FM(P)	643 pcs.	—	Proof	3.50

COPPER-NICKEL

85	1982FM(U)	—	—	.25	1.50
	1982FM(P)	—	—	Proof	2.50
	1983FM(U)	—	—	.25	1.50
	1983FM(P)	—	—	Proof	2.50

2.7900 g, .925 SILVER, .0829 oz ASW

85a	1982FM(P)	381 pcs.	—	Proof	6.00
	1983FM(P)	312 pcs.	—	Proof	6.00

COPPER-NICKEL

92	1984FM(P)	—	—	Proof	2.50

2.7900 g, .925 SILVER, .0829 oz ASW

92a	1984FM(P)	—	—	Proof	6.00

25 CENTS

COPPER-NICKEL

36	1974	.100	.35	.65	1.25
	1975	.200	.20	.35	.75
	1976	.790	.20	.35	.75
	1979	.500	.20	.35	.75
	1980	—	.20	.35	.75
	1981	—	.20	.35	.75

41	1974FM(M)	.013	—	1.00	3.50
	1974FM(P)	.021	—	Proof	2.50

6.6000 g, .925 SILVER, .1962 oz ASW

41a	1974FM(P)	.031	—	Proof	5.00

COPPER-NICKEL

49	1975FM(M)	4,716	—	.55	5.00
	1975FM(U)	1,095	—	.40	3.00
	1975FM(P)	8,794	—	Proof	2.50
	1976FM(M)	5,000	—	.50	4.00
	1976FM(U)	759 pcs.	—	.45	3.50
	1976FM(P)	4,893	—	Proof	2.50
	1977FM(U)	5,520	—	.30	2.00
	1977FM(P)	2,107	—	Proof	2.75
	1978FM(U)	5,458	—	.30	2.00
	1978FM(P)	1,671	—	Proof	2.75
	1979FM(U)	808 pcs.	—	.40	3.00
	1979FM(P)	1,287	—	Proof	3.00
	1980FM(U)	761 pcs.	—	.40	3.00
	1980FM(P)	920 pcs.	—	Proof	3.00
	1981FM(U)	297 pcs.	—	.40	3.00
	1981FM(P)	643 pcs.	—	Proof	3.00

6.6000 g, .925 SILVER, .1962 oz ASW

49a	1975FM(P)	.013	—	Proof	3.50
	1976FM(P)	5,897	—	Proof	3.50
	1977FM(P)	3,197	—	Proof	3.50
	1978FM(P)	3,342	—	Proof	3.50
	1979FM(P)	2,445	—	Proof	3.50
	1980FM(P)	1,826	—	Proof	3.50
	1981FM(P)	643 pcs.	—	Proof	5.00

BELIZE 185

KM#	Date	Mintage	VF	XF	Unc
50	1978FM(U)	2,958	—	.45	3.50
	1978FM(P)	1,671	—	Proof	3.50
	1979FM(U)	808 pcs.	—	.55	5.00
	1979FM(P)	1,287	—	Proof	3.50
	1980FM(U)	761 pcs.	—	.55	5.00
	1980FM(P)	920 pcs.	—	Proof	5.00
	1981FM(U)	297 pcs.	—	.55	5.00
	1981FM(P)	643 pcs.	—	Proof	5.00

9.9400 g, .925 SILVER, .3197 oz ASW

50a	1975FM(P)	.013	—	Proof	6.50
	1976(P)	5,897	—	Proof	6.50
	1977FM(P)	3,197	—	Proof	6.50
	1978FM(P)	3,342	—	Proof	6.50
	1979FM(P)	2,445	—	Proof	6.50
	1980FM(P)	1,826	—	Proof	6.50
	1981FM(P)	643 pcs.	—	Proof	8.50

COPPER-NICKEL

KM#	Date	Mintage	VF	XF	Unc
88	1982FM(U)	—	—	1.50	8.50
	1982FM(P)	—	—	Proof	8.50
	1983FM(U)	—	—	1.50	8.50
	1983FM(P)	—	—	Proof	8.50

19.8900 g, .925 SILVER, .5915 oz ASW

88a	1982FM(P)	381 pcs.	—	Proof	17.50
	1983FM(P)	1,589	—	Proof	17.50

KM#	Date	Mintage	VF	XF	Unc
86	1982FM(U)	—	—	.40	3.00
	1982FM(P)	—	—	Proof	3.00
	1983FM(U)	—	—	.40	3.00
	1983FM(P)	—	—	Proof	3.00

6.6000 g, .925 SILVER, .1962 oz ASW

86a	1982FM(P)	381 pcs.	—	Proof	8.50
	1983FM(P)	314 pcs.	—	Proof	8.50

COPPER-NICKEL

93	1984FM(P)	—	—	Proof	3.00

6.6000 g, .925 SILVER, .1962 oz ASW

93a	1984FM(P)	—	—	Proof	8.50

COPPER-NICKEL

87	1982FM(U)	—	—	.55	5.00
	1982FM(P)	—	—	Proof	5.00
	1983FM(U)	—	—	.55	5.00
	1983FM(P)	—	—	Proof	5.00

9.9400 g, .925 SILVER, .3197 oz ASW

87a	1982FM(P)	381 pcs.	—	Proof	12.50
	1983FM(P)	312 pcs.	—	Proof	12.50

95	1984FM(P)	—	—	Proof	8.50

19.8900 g, .925 SILVER, .5915 oz ASW

95a	1984FM(P)	—	—	Proof	17.50

5 DOLLARS

World Forestry Congress

77	1985	—	.15	.25	.85

50 CENTS

COPPER-NICKEL

94	1984FM(P)	—	—	Proof	5.00

9.9400 g, .925 SILVER, .3197 oz ASW

94a	1984FM(P)	—	—	Proof	12.50

DOLLAR

COPPER-NICKEL

37	1974	.123	.40	.75	2.00
	1975	Inc. Ab.	.40	.75	2.00
	1976	.312	.40	.75	2.00
	1979	.125	.40	.75	1.75
	1980	—	.40	.75	1.75

42	1974FM(M)	8,806	—	.40	4.00
	1974FM(P)	.021	—	Proof	3.50

9.9400 g, .925 SILVER, .3197 oz ASW

42a	1974FM(P)	.031	—	Proof	7.50

COPPER-NICKEL

50	1975FM(M)	2,358	—	.65	6.00
	1975FM(U)	1,095	—	.45	4.00
	1975FM(P)	8,794	—	Proof	3.50
	1976FM(M)	3,259	—	.55	5.00
	1976FM(U)	759 pcs.	—	.55	5.00
	1976FM(P)	4,893	—	Proof	3.50
	1977FM(U)	3,540	—	.45	3.50
	1977FM(P)	2,107	—	Proof	3.50

COPPER-NICKEL

43	1974FM(M)	6,656	—	.75	6.00
	1974FM(P)	.021	—	Proof	4.00
	1975FM(M)	1,182	—	1.50	10.00
	1975FM(U)	1,095	—	.75	6.00
	1975FM(P)	8,794	—	Proof	5.00
	1976FM(M)	1,250	—	1.50	9.00
	1976FM(U)	759 pcs.	—	1.25	7.50
	1976FM(P)	4,893	—	Proof	5.00
	1977FM(U)	1,770	—	1.00	6.50
	1977FM(P)	2,107	—	Proof	6.50
	1978FM(U)	1,708	—	1.00	6.50
	1978FM(P)	1,671	—	Proof	6.50
	1979FM(U)	808 pcs.	—	1.25	7.50
	1979FM(P)	1,287	—	Proof	6.50
	1980FM(U)	761 pcs.	—	1.25	7.50
	1980FM(P)	920 pcs.	—	Proof	6.50
	1981FM(U)	297 pcs.	—	1.50	8.50
	1981FM(P)	643 pcs.	—	Proof	8.50

19.8900 g, .925 SILVER, .5915 oz ASW

43a	1974FM(P)	.031	—	Proof	11.50
	1975FM(P)	.013	—	Proof	11.50
	1976FM(P)	5,897	—	Proof	12.50
	1977FM(P)	3,197	—	Proof	12.50
	1978FM(P)	3,342	—	Proof	12.50
	1979FM(P)	2,445	—	Proof	12.50
	1980FM(P)	1,826	—	Proof	12.50
	1981FM(P)	643 pcs.	—	Proof	13.50

COPPER-NICKEL
Obv: Similar to 1 Dollar, KM#43.

44	1974FM(M)	4,936	—	2.75	10.00
	1974FM(P)	.021	—	Proof	7.50
	1975FM(M)	237 pcs.	—	5.00	22.50
	1975FM(U)	1,095	—	2.75	9.00
	1975FM(P)	8,794	—	Proof	7.50
	1976FM(M)	250 pcs.	—	5.00	20.00
	1976FM(U)	759 pcs.	—	2.75	10.00
	1976FM(P)	4,893	—	Proof	7.50
	1977FM(U)	720 pcs.	—	2.75	10.00
	1977FM(P)	2,107	—	Proof	8.50
	1978FM(U)	708 pcs.	—	2.75	15.00
	1978FM(P)	1,671	—	Proof	8.50
	1979FM(U)	808 pcs.	—	2.75	10.00
	1979FM(P)	1,287	—	Proof	8.50
	1980FM(U)	761 pcs.	—	2.75	10.00
	1980FM(P)	920 pcs.	—	Proof	8.50
	1981FM(U)	297 pcs.	—	2.75	12.00
	1981FM(P)	643 pcs.	—	Proof	10.00

26.4000 g, .925 SILVER, .7851 oz ASW

44a	1974FM(P)	.031	—	Proof	9.00
	1975FM(P)	.013	—	Proof	10.00
	1976FM(P)	5,897	—	Proof	12.00
	1977FM(P)	3,197	—	Proof	12.00
	1978FM(P)	3,342	—	Proof	12.00
	1979FM(P)	2,445	—	Proof	12.00
	1980FM(P)	1,826	—	Proof	12.00
	1981FM(P)	643 pcs.	—	Proof	20.00

COPPER-NICKEL

BELIZE 186

KM#	Date	Mintage	VF	XF	Unc
89	1982FM(U)	—	—	1.50	10.00
	1982FM(P)	—	—	Proof	10.00
	1983FM(U)	—	—	1.50	10.00
	1983FM(P)	—	—	Proof	10.00

26.4000 g, .925 SILVER, .7851 oz ASW

89a	1982FM(P)	381 pcs.	—	Proof	25.00
	1983FM(P)	311 pcs.	—	Proof	25.00

COPPER-NICKEL

96	1984FM(P)	—	—	Proof	10.00

26.4000 g, .925 SILVER, .7851 oz ASW

96a	1984FM(P)	—	—	Proof	20.00

10 DOLLARS

COPPER-NICKEL

45	1974FM(M)	4,726	—	3.50	15.00
	1974FM(P)	.021	—	Proof	8.00
	1975FM(M)	117 pcs.	—	12.50	50.00
	1975FM(U)	1,095	—	3.50	15.00
	1975FM(P)	8,794	—	Proof	10.00
	1976FM(M)	125 pcs.	—	10.00	40.00
	1976FM(U)	759 pcs.	—	4.00	17.50
	1976FM(P)	4,893	—	Proof	12.00
	1977FM(U)	645 pcs.	—	4.00	17.50
	1977FM(P)	2,107	—	Proof	15.00
	1978FM(U)	583 pcs.	—	5.00	20.00
	1978FM(P)	1,671	—	Proof	15.00

29.8000 g, .925 SILVER, .8863 oz ASW

45a	1974FM(P)	.031	—	Proof	12.00
	1975FM(P)	.013	—	Proof	13.00
	1976FM(P)	5,897	—	Proof	14.00
	1977FM(P)	3,197	—	Proof	15.00
	1978FM(P)	3,342	—	Proof	15.00

COPPER-NICKEL
Jabiru

KM#	Date	Mintage	VF	XF	Unc
57	1979FM(U)	808 pcs.	—	5.00	25.00
	1979FM(P)	1,287	—	Proof	25.00

29.8000 g, .925 SILVER, .8863 oz ASW

57a	1979FM(P)	2,445	—	Proof	40.00

COPPER-NICKEL
Scarlet Ibis

60	1980FM(U)	761 pcs.	—	5.00	25.00
	1980FM(P)	920 pcs.	—	Proof	25.00

25.5000 g, .925 SILVER, .7583 oz ASW

60a	1980FM(P)	1,826	—	Proof	45.00

COPPER-NICKEL
Roseate Spoonbill
Obv: Similar to 1 Dollar, KM#43.

65	1981FM(U)	297 pcs.	—	7.50	30.00
	1981FM(P)	643 pcs.	—	Proof	30.00

25.5000 g, .925 SILVER, .7583 oz ASW

65a	1981FM(P)	643 pcs.	—	Proof	60.00

COPPER-NICKEL
Parrot
Obv: Similar to KM#80.

69	1982FM(U)	—	—	7.50	30.00
	1982FM(P)	—	—	Proof	30.00

25.5000 g, .925 SILVER, .7583 oz ASW

69a	1982FM(P)	381 pcs.	—	Proof	50.00

COPPER-NICKEL
Ringed King Fisher

KM#	Date	Mintage	VF	XF	Unc
71	1983FM(U)	—	—	5.00	25.00
	1983FM(P)	334 pcs.	—	Proof	25.00

25.5000 g, .925 SILVER, .7583 oz ASW

71a	1983FM(P)	—	—	Proof	50.00

COPPER-NICKEL
Laughing Falcon

75	1984FM(P)	—	—	Proof	25.00

25.5000 g, .925 SILVER, .7583 oz ASW

75a	1984FM(P)	—	—	Proof	50.00

COPPER-NICKEL
Mule. Obv: KM#69. Rev: KM#45.

80	1982	—	—	—	—

20 DOLLARS

23.3300 g, .925 SILVER, .6938 oz ASW
Los Angeles Olympics

KM#	Date	Mintage	VF	XF	Unc
79	1984	1,050	—	Proof	35.00

Decade For Women

| 82 | 1985 | *.020 | — | Proof | 25.00 |

25 DOLLARS

27.8100 g, .925 SILVER, .8270 oz ASW
Coronation Jubilee

| 54 | 1978FM(U) | 352 pcs. | — | 12.50 | 50.00 |
| | 1978FM(P) | 8,438 | — | Proof | 25.00 |

30.2800 g, .500 SILVER, .4686 oz ASW
10th Anniversary of Caribbean Development Bank

KM#	Date	Mintage	VF	XF	Unc
61	1980FM(P)	2,647	—	Proof	27.50

30th Anniversary of Coronation of Queen Elizabeth II

| 72 | 1983FM(P) | 2,944 | — | Proof | 27.50 |

28.2800 g, .925 SILVER, .8409 oz ASW
Royal Visit

| 78 | 1985 | *5,000 | — | Proof | 25.00 |

47.5400 g, .917 GOLD, 1.4013 oz AGW

| 78a | 1985 | *250 pcs. | — | Proof | 1200. |

50 DOLLARS

1.5000 g, .500 GOLD, .0241 oz AGW
White-necked Jacobin Hummingbird

| 66 | 1981FM(U) | 200 pcs. | | | 50.00 |
| | 1981FM(P) | 2,873 | — | Proof | 50.00 |

129.6000 g, .925 SILVER, 3.8547 oz ASW
Bird Conservation - Redfooted Booby
Obv: Similar to 25 Dollars, KM#72.

| 81 | 1985 | *.010 | — | Proof | 45.00 |

100 DOLLARS

6.2100 g, .500 GOLD, .0998 oz AGW
30th Anniversary of United Nations

KM#	Date	Mintage	VF	XF	Unc
51	1975FM(M)	100 pcs.	—	—	200.00
	1975FM(U)	2,028	—	—	65.00
	1975FM(P)	8,126	—	Proof	100.00

Ancient Mayan Symbols

| 52 | 1976FM(M) | 216 pcs. | — | — | 175.00 |
| | 1976FM(P) | .011 | — | Proof | 100.00 |

Kinich Ahau, Mayan Sun God

53	1977FM(M)	200 pcs.	—	—	150.00
	1977FM(U)	51 pcs.	—	—	350.00
	1977FM(P)	7,859	—	Proof	100.00

Itzamna Mayan God

| 55 | 1978FM(U) | 351 pcs. | — | — | 150.00 |
| | 1978FM(P) | 7,178 | — | Proof | 100.00 |

Queen Angelfish

| 58 | 1979FM(U) | 400 pcs. | — | — | 150.00 |
| | 1979FM(P) | 4,465 | — | Proof | 100.00 |

6.4700 g, .500 GOLD, .1040 oz AGW
Star of Bethlehem

| 59 | 1979FM(U) | — | — | — | 100.00 |
| | 1979FM(P) | — | — | Proof | 110.00 |

6.2100 g, .500 GOLD, .0998 oz AGW

BELIZE 188

Moorish Idol Reef Fish
KM#	Date	Mintage	VF	XF	Unc
62	1980FM(U)	400 pcs.	—	—	100.00
	1980FM(P)	3,993	—	Proof	110.00

Orchids
63	1980FM(U)	250 pcs.	—	—	125.00
	1980FM(P)	2,454	—	Proof	110.00

Yellow Swallowtail Butterfly
67	1981FM(U)	200 pcs.	—	—	175.00
	1981FM(P)	1,658	—	Proof	250.00

National Independence
68	1981FM(U)	50 pcs.	—	—	300.00
	1981FM(P)	1,401	—	Proof	150.00

Kinkajou
70	1982FM(U)	10 pcs.	—	—	450.00
	1982FM(P)	586 pcs.	—	Proof	175.00

Margay Jungle Cat
73	1983FM(U)	20 pcs.	—	—	400.00
	1983FM(P)	494 pcs.	—	Proof	175.00

White-tail Deer
74	1984FM(P)	2,500	—	Proof	150.00

Ocelot
76	1985FM(P)	899 pcs.	—	Proof	150.00

250 DOLLARS

8.8100 g, .900 GOLD, .2549 oz AGW
Jaguar Commemorative

KM#	Date	Mintage	VF	XF	Unc
56	1978FM(U)	200 pcs.	—	—	350.00
	1978FM(P)	*3,399	—	Proof	450.00

*NOTE: 1,712 pieces were used in First Day Covers.

MINT SETS (MS)
KM#	Date	Mintage	Identification	Issue Price	Mkt. Val.
MS1	1974(8)	4,506	KM38-45	20.00	20.00
MS2	1975(8)	1,095	KM43-50	27.50	27.50
MS3	1976(8)	759	KM43-50	27.50	35.00
MS4	1977(8)	—	KM43-45,46b-47b,48-50	27.50	35.00
MS5	1978(8)	458	KM43-45,46b-47b,48-50	28.50	35.00
MS6	1979(8)	808	KM43-44,46b-47b,48-50,57	28.50	35.00
MS7	1980(8)	761	KM43-44,46b-47b,48-50,60	29.50	35.00
MS8	1981(8)	297	KM43-44,46b-47b,48-50,65	29.50	60.00
MS9	1982(8)	—	KM43-44,46b-47b,48-50,69	29.50	60.00
MS10	1983(8)	—	KM43-44,46b-47b,48-50,71	29.50	60.00

PROOF SETS (PS)
PS1	1974(8)	21,470	KM38-45	35.00	15.00
PS2	1974(8)	31,368	KM38a-45a	100.00	40.00
PS3	1975(8)	8,794	KM43-50	37.50	17.50
PS4	1975(8)	13,275	KM43a-50a	110.00	40.00
PS5	1976(8)	4,893	KM43-50	37.50	20.00
PS6	1976(8)	5,897	KM43a-50a	110.00	50.00
PS7	1977(8)	2,107	KM43-50	37.50	30.00
PS8	1977(8)	3,197	KM43a-50a	110.00	50.00
PS9	1978(8)	1,671	KM43-50	39.50	35.00
PS10	1978(8)	3,342	KM43a-50a	110.00	50.00
PS11	1979(8)	1,287	KM43-44,46b-47b,48-50,57	41.50	45.00
PS12	1979(8)	2,445	KM43a-44a,46a-50a,57a	112.00	75.00
PS13	1980(8)	920	KM43-44,46b-47b,48-50,60	41.50	45.00
PS14	1980(8)	1,826	KM43a-44a,46a-50a,60a	222.00	85.00
PS15	1981(8)	643	KM43-44,46b-47b,48-50,65	41.50	60.00
PS16	1981(8)	615	KM43a-44a,46a-50a,65a	—	110.00
PS17	1982(8)	—	KM43-44,46b-47b,48-50,69	49.50	60.00
PS18	1982(8)	381	KM43a-44a,46a-50a,69a	222.00	130.00
PS19	1983(8)	306	KM43-44,46b-47b,48-50,71	37.00	60.00
PS20	1983(8)	241	KM43a-44a,46a-50a,71a	197.00	135.00
PS21	1984(8)	—	KM43-44,46b-47b,48-50,75	37.00	50.00
PS22	1984(8)	—	KM43a-44a,46a-50a,75a	197.00	125.00

BENIN (Dahomey)

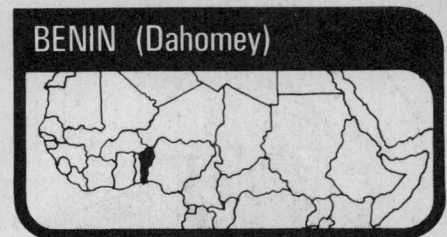

The People's Republic of Benin (formerly the Republic of Dahomey), located on the south side of the African bulge between Togo and Nigeria, has an area of 43,484 sq. mi. (112,622 sq. km.) and a population of 3.6 million. Capital: Porto-Novo. The principal industry of Benin, one of the poorest countries of West Africa, is the processing of palm oil products. Palm kernel oil, peanuts, cotton, and coffee are exported.

Porto-Novo, on the Bight of Benin, was founded as a trading post by the Portuguese in the 17th century. At that time, Benin was composed of an aggregation of mutually suspicious tribes, the majority of which were tributary to the powerful northern Kingdom of Abomey. In 1863, the King of Porto-Novo petitioned France for protection from Abomey. The French subjugated other militant tribes as well, and in 1892 organized the area as a protectorate of France; in 1904 it was incorporated into French West Africa as the Territory of Dahomey. After the establishment of the Fifth French Republic, the Territory at Dahomey became an autonomous state within the French community. On Aug. 1, 1960, it became the fully independent Republic of Dahomey. In 1974, the republic began a transition to a socialist society with Marxism-Leninism as its revolutionary philosophy. On Nov. 30, 1975, the name of the Republic of Dahomey was changed to the People's Republic of Benin.

DAHOMEY
100 FRANCS

5.1000 g, .999 SILVER, .1638 oz ASW

KM#	Date	Mintage	VF	XF	Unc
1	1971	4,650	—	Proof	7.50

200 FRANCS

10.2500 g, .999 SILVER, .3292 oz ASW

2	1971	5,150	—	Proof	12.50

500 FRANCS

25.2000 g, .999 SILVER, .8094 oz ASW

KM#	Date	Mintage	VF	XF	Unc
3	1971	5,550	—	Proof	30.00

1000 FRANCS

51.5000 g, .999 SILVER, 1.6542 oz ASW
Obv: Similar to 500 Francs, KM#3.

| 4 | 1971 | 6,500 | — | Proof | 75.00 |

2500 FRANCS

8.8800 g, .900 GOLD, .2569 oz AGW

| 6 | 1971 | 960 pcs. | — | Proof | 200.00 |

5000 FRANCS

17.7700 g, .900 GOLD, .5142 oz AGW
Obv: Similar to 2500 Francs, KM#6.

| 7 | 1971 | 610 pcs. | — | Proof | 500.00 |

10,000 FRANCS

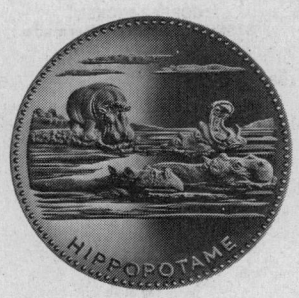

35.5500 g, .900 GOLD, 1.0287 oz AGW
Obv: Similar to 2500 Francs, KM#6.

| 8 | 1971 | 470 pcs. | — | Proof | 900.00 |

25,000 FRANCS

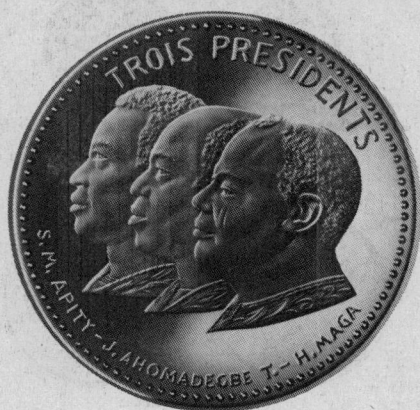

88.8800 g, .900 GOLD, 2.5720 oz AGW
Obv: Similar to 2500 Francs, KM#6.

KM#	Date	Mintage	VF	XF	Unc
9	1971	380 pcs.	—	Proof	1500.

PROOF SETS (PS)

KM#	Date	Mintage	Identification	Issue Price	Mkt. Val.
PS1	1971(8)	380	KM1-4,6-9	—	3400.
PS2	1971(4)	4,600	KM1-4	36.00	125.00
PS3	1971(4)	2,000	KM6-9	—	3100.

BERMUDA

The Parliamentary British Colony of Bermuda, situated in the western Atlantic Ocean 660 miles (1,062 km.) east of North Carolina, has an area of 20.5 sq. mi. (53 sq. km.) and a population of 59,909. Capital: Hamilton. Concentrated essences, beauty preparations, and cut flowers are exported. Most Bermudians derive their livelihood from tourism.

Bermuda was discovered by Juan de Bermudez, a Spanish navigator, in 1503. British influence dates from 1609 when a group of Virginia-bound British colonists under the command of Sir George Somers was shipwrecked on the islands for 10 months. The islands were settled in 1612 by 60 British colonists from the Virginia Colony and became a crown colony in 1684. Internal autonomy was obtained by the constitution of June 8, 1968.

In February, 1970, Bermuda converted from its former currency, which was sterling, to a decimal currency, the dollar unit which is equal to one U.S. dollar. On July 31, 1972, Bermuda severed its monetary link with the British pound sterling and pegged its dollar to be the same gold value as the U.S. dollar.

RULERS
British

MINT MARKS
FM - Franklin Mint, U.S.A.*

*NOTE: From 1975 the Franklin Mint has produced coinage in up to 3 different qualities. Qualities of issue are designated in ( ) after each date and are defined as follows:

(M) MATTE -Normal circulation strike or a dull finish produced by sandblasting special uncirculated (polish finish) or proof quality dies.
(U) SPECIAL UNCIRCUALTED - Polished or proof-like in appearance without any frosted features.
(P) PROOF - The highest quality obtainable having mirror-like fields and frosted features.

MONETARY SYSTEM
12 Pence = 1 Shilling
20 Shillings = 1 Pound

CROWN

28.2800 g, .925 SILVER, .8411 oz ASW

KM#	Date	Mintage	Fine	VF	XF	Unc
13	1959	.100	BV	6.00	10.00	13.50
	1959	6-10 pcs.	—	—	Matte Proof	1000.

22.6200 g, .500 SILVER, .3636 oz ASW

| 14 | 1964 | .470 | — | — | BV | 4.00 |
| | 1964 | .030 | — | — | Proof | 6.00 |

DECIMAL COINAGE
100 Cents = 1 Dollar

CENT

BRONZE

KM#	Date	Mintage	Fine	VF	XF	Unc
15	1970	5.500	—	—	.10	.20
	1970	.011	—	—	Proof	.50
	1971	4.256	—	—	.10	.20
	1972	—	Reported, not confirmed			
	1973	2.144	—	—	.10	.20
	1974	.856	—	—	.10	.25
	1975	1.000	—	—	.10	.20
	1976	1.000	—	—	.10	.20
	1977	2.000	—	—	.10	.20
	1978	3.160	—	—	.10	.20
	1980	3.520	—	—	.10	.20
	1981	3.200	—	—	.10	.20
	1982	.320	—	—	.10	.15
	1983	.800	—	—	.10	.15
	1983	.010	—	—	Proof	1.50
	1984	.800	—	—	.10	.15
	1985	—	—	—	.10	.15

KM#	Date	Mintage	Fine	VF	XF	Unc
44	1986	.960	—	—	.10	.15
	1986	Inc. Ab.	—	—	Proof	2.50
	1987	—	—	—	.10	.15

5 CENTS

COPPER-NICKEL

KM#	Date	Mintage	Fine	VF	XF	Unc
16	1970	2.190	—	—	.10	.25
	1970	.011	—	—	Proof	.50
	1974	.310	—	—	.10	.25
	1975	.500	—	—	.10	.25
	1977	.500	—	—	.10	.25
	1979	.500	—	—	.10	.25
	1980	1.100	—	—	.10	.25
	1981	.900	—	—	.10	.25
	1982	.200	—	—	.10	.30
	1983	.800	—	—	.10	.25
	1983	.010	—	—	Proof	2.00
	1984	.500	—	—	.10	.20
	1985	—	—	—	.10	.20

KM#	Date	Mintage	Fine	VF	XF	Unc
45	1986	.700	—	—	.10	.15
	1986	Inc. Ab.	—	—	Proof	2.50
	1987	—	—	—	.10	.15

10 CENTS

COPPER-NICKEL

KM#	Date	Mintage	Fine	VF	XF	Unc
17	1970	2.500	—	.10	.15	.25
	1970	.011	—	—	Proof	.50
	1971	2.000	—	.10	.15	.25
	1978	.500	—	.10	.15	.25
	1979	.800	—	.10	.15	.30
	1980	1.100	—	.10	.15	.25
	1981	1.300	—	.10	.15	.25
	1982	.400	—	.10	.15	.30
	1983	1.000	—	.10	.15	.25
	1983	.010	—	—	Proof	2.50
	1984	.500	—	.10	.15	.25
	1985	—	—	.10	.15	.25

KM#	Date	Mintage	Fine	VF	XF	Unc
46	1986	.350	—	—	.10	.30
	1986	Inc. Ab.	—	—	Proof	5.00

25 CENTS

COPPER-NICKEL

KM#	Date	Mintage	Fine	VF	XF	Unc
18	1970	1.500	—	.30	.40	.75
	1970	.011	—	—	Proof	1.50
	1973	1.000	—	.30	.40	.75
	1979	.570	—	.30	.40	.75
	1980	1.120	—	.30	.40	.75
	1981	2.200	—	.30	.40	.75
	1982	.160	—	.30	.40	1.00
	1983	.600	—	.30	.40	.75
	1983	.010	—	—	Proof	3.50
	1984	.400	—	.30	.40	.75
	1985	—	—	.30	.40	.75

375th Anniversary of Bermuda
Obv: Similar to KM#18.

KM#	Date	Mintage	Fine	VF	XF	Unc
32	1984	—	—	—	.50	2.25

5.9600 g, .925 SILVER, .1772 oz ASW

| 32a | 1984 | 1,750 | — | — | Proof | 18.00 |

COPPER-NICKEL
375th Anniversary of Bermuda
City of Hamilton
Obv: Similar to KM#18.

| 33 | 1984 | — | — | — | .50 | 2.25 |

5.9600 g, .925 SILVER, .1772 oz ASW

| 33a | 1984 | 1,750 | — | — | Proof | 18.00 |

COPPER-NICKEL
375th Anniversary of Bermuda
Town of St. George
Obv: Similar to KM#18.

| 34 | 1984 | — | — | — | .50 | 2.25 |

5.9600 g, .925 SILVER, .1772 oz ASW

| 34a | 1984 | 1,750 | — | — | Proof | 18.00 |

COPPER-NICKEL
375th Anniversary of Bermuda
Warwick Parish
Obv: Similar to KM#18.

| 35 | 1984 | — | — | — | .50 | 2.25 |

5.9600 g, .925 SILVER, .1772 oz ASW

| 35a | 1984 | 1,750 | — | — | Proof | 18.00 |

COPPER-NICKEL
375th Anniversary of Bermuda
Smith's Parish
Obv: Similar to KM#18.

KM#	Date	Mintage	Fine	VF	XF	Unc
36	1984	—	—	—	.50	2.25

5.9600 g, .925 SILVER, .1772 oz ASW

| 36a | 1984 | 1,750 | — | — | Proof | 18.00 |

COPPER-NICKEL
375th Anniversary of Bermuda
Devonshire Parish
Obv: Similar to KM#18.

| 37 | 1984 | — | — | — | .50 | 2.25 |

5.9600 g, .925 SILVER, .1772 oz ASW

| 37a | 1984 | 1,750 | — | — | Proof | 18.00 |

COPPER-NICKEL
375th Anniversary of Bermuda
Sandy's Parish
Obv: Similar to KM#18.

| 38 | 1984 | — | — | — | .50 | 2.25 |

5.9600 g, .925 SILVER, .1772 oz ASW

| 38a | 1984 | 1,750 | — | — | Proof | 18.00 |

COPPER-NICKEL
375th Anniversary of Bermuda
Hamilton Parish
Obv: Similar to KM#18.

| 39 | 1984 | — | — | — | .50 | 2.25 |

5.9600 g, .925 SILVER, .1772 oz ASW

| 39a | 1984 | 1,750 | — | — | Proof | 18.00 |

COPPER-NICKEL
375th Anniversary of Bermuda
Southampton Parish
Obv: Similar to KM#18.

| 40 | 1984 | — | — | — | .50 | 2.25 |

5.9600 g, .925 SILVER, .1772 oz ASW

| 40a | 1984 | 1,750 | — | — | Proof | 18.00 |

COPPER-NICKEL
375th Anniversary of Bermuda
Pembroke Parish
Obv: Similar to KM#18.

| 41 | 1984 | — | — | — | .50 | 2.25 |

BERMUDA 191

5.9600 g, .925 SILVER, .1772 oz ASW

KM#	Date	Mintage	Fine	VF	XF	Unc
41a	1984	1,750	—	—	Proof	18.00

COPPER-NICKEL
375th Anniversary of Bermuda Paget Parish
Obv: Similar to KM#18.

| 42 | 1984 | — | — | — | .50 | 2.25 |

5.9600 g, .925 SILVER, .1772 oz ASW

| 42a | 1984 | 1,750 | — | — | Proof | 18.00 |

COPPER-NICKEL

| 47 | 1986 | .560 | — | .30 | .40 | .75 |
| | 1986 | Inc. Ab. | — | — | Proof | 10.00 |

50 CENTS

COPPER-NICKEL

19	1970	1.000	—	—	.75	1.00
	1970	.011	—	—	Proof	2.00
	1978	.200	—	.60	.85	1.25
	1980	.060	—	.60	.85	1.50
	1981	.100	—	.60	.85	1.25
	1982	.080	—	.60	.85	1.50
	1983	.060	—	.60	.85	1.50
	1983	.010	—	—	Proof	5.50
	1984	.040	—	.60	.85	1.50
	1985	—	—	.60	.85	1.50

| 48 | 1986 | .060 | — | .60 | .85 | 1.50 |
| | 1986 | Inc. Ab. | — | — | Proof | 15.00 |

DOLLAR

28.2800 g, .800 SILVER, .7273 oz ASW

| 20 | 1970 | .011 | — | — | Proof | 18.00 |

28.2800 g, .500 SILVER, .4546 oz ASW
Silver Wedding Anniversary
Obv: Similar to 50 Cents, KM#19.

KM#	Date	Mintage	Fine	VF	XF	Unc
22	1972	.075	—	—	—	8.00

28.2800 g, .925 SILVER, .8411 oz ASW

| 22a | 1972 | .015 | — | — | Proof | 12.50 |

COPPER-NICKEL
Wedding of Prince Charles and Lady Diana
Obv: Similar to 50 Cents, KM#19.

| 28 | 1981 | .065 | — | — | — | 2.50 |

28.2800 g, .925 SILVER, .8411 oz ASW

| 28a | 1981 | .016 | — | — | Proof | 15.00 |

NICKEL-BRASS

| 30 | 1983 | .250 | — | — | — | 2.00 |
| | 1983 | .010 | — | — | Proof | 6.00 |

COPPER-NICKEL
Cruise Ship Tourism

| 43 | 1985 | .011 | — | — | — | 3.00 |

28.2800 g, .925 SILVER, .8411 oz ASW

| 43a | 1985 | 2,500 | — | — | — | 10.00 |
| | 1985 | 4,000 | — | — | Proof | 18.00 |

COPPER-NICKEL
Wildlife

KM#	Date	Mintage	Fine	VF	XF	Unc
49	1986	—	—	—	—	3.00

28.2800 g, .925 SILVER, .8411 oz ASW

| 49a | 1986 | *.010 | — | — | — | 17.50 |
| | 1986 | *.025 | — | — | Proof | 22.50 |

BRASS
Obv: Similar to KM#43. Rev: Seagull over Bermuda.

| 50 | 1986 | — | — | — | — | 2.00 |
| | 1986 | — | — | — | Proof | 15.00 |

COPPER-NICKEL
50th Anniversary of Commercial Aviation

| 52 | 1987 | — | — | — | — | 3.00 |

28.2800 g, .925 SILVER, .8411 oz ASW

| 52a | 1987 | 4,000 | — | — | — | 25.00 |
| | 1987 | 5,000 | — | — | Proof | 40.00 |

COPPER-NICKEL
Railroad
Obv: Similar to KM#43.

| 55 | 1988 | — | — | — | — | 3.00 |

28.2800 g, .925 SILVER, .8411 oz ASW

| 55a | 1988 | — | — | — | — | 25.00 |
| | 1988 | — | — | — | Proof | 40.00 |

COPPER-NICKEL
Circulation Type

| 56 | 1988 | — | — | — | — | 1.50 |

8.4000 g, .925 SILVER, .2498 oz ASW

| 56a | 1988 | *3,000 | — | — | Proof | 25.00 |

5 DOLLARS

NICKEL-BRASS

KM#	Date	Mintage	Fine	VF	XF	Unc
31	1983	.100	—	—	—	6.00
	1983	.010	—	—	Proof	8.00

BRASS
Obv: Similar to 1 Dollar, KM#43.
Rev: Onion superimposed over Bermuda map.

51	1986	—	—	—	—	6.00
	1986	—	—	—	Proof	15.00

20 DOLLARS

7.9881 g, .917 GOLD, .2355 oz AGW

21	1970	1,000	—	—	Proof	275.00

25 DOLLARS

COPPER-NICKEL
Royal Visit
Obv: Bust of Queen Elizabeth

23	1975FM(M) 1.193	—	—	—	20.00
	1975FM(U) 100 pcs.	—	—	—	60.00

48.7000 g, .925 SILVER, 1.4483 oz ASW

23a	1975FM(P) .015	—	—	Proof	30.00

54.7500 g, .925 SILVER, 1.6283 oz ASW
Queen's Silver Jubilee

KM#	Date	Mintage	Fine	VF	XF	Unc
25	1977	.011	—	—	—	35.00
	1977	.011	—	—	Proof	45.00
	1977 w/o mm	—	—	—	Proof	—

50 DOLLARS

4.0500 g, .900 GOLD, .1172 oz AGW
Queen's Silver Jubilee

26	1977	4,470	—	—	—	75.00
	1977	4,650	—	—	Proof	125.00

100 DOLLARS

7.0300 g, .900 GOLD, .2034 oz AGW
Royal Visit

24	1975FM(M) 25 pcs.	—	—	—	300.00
	1975FM(U) .019	—	—	—	135.00
	1975FM(P) .027	—	—	Proof	200.00

8.1000 g, .900 GOLD, .2344 oz AGW
Queen's Silver Jubilee

27	1977	8,537	—	—	—	150.00
	1977	7,500	—	—	Proof	250.00

250 DOLLARS

15.9760 g, .917 GOLD, .4710 oz AGW
Wedding of Prince Charles and Lady Diana
Obv: Similar to 20 Dollars, KM#21.

29	1981	217 pcs.	—	—	—	350.00
	1981	790 pcs.	—	—	Proof	350.00

SILVER BULLION ISSUES
5 DOLLARS

155.5150 g, .999 SILVER, 5.0000 oz ASW
Sailing Ship
Reduced. Actual size: 65mm
Obv: Similar to 1 Dollar, KM#43.

KM#	Date	Mintage	Fine	VF	XF	Unc
54	1987	*.020	—	—	Proof	100.00

PALLADIUM BULLION ISSUES
25 DOLLARS

31.1000 g, .999 PALLADIUM, 1.0000 oz APW
Ship - Sea Venture
Obv: Queen Elizabeth II portrait.
Rev: Ship, denomination and metallic content.

53	1987	*.020	—	—	Proof	275.00

MINT SETS (MS)

KM#	Date	Mintage	Identification	Issue Price	Mkt. Val.
MS1	1970(5)	90,000	KM15-19	3.25	2.00
MS2	1977(3)	4,470	KM25-27	175.00	275.00
MS3	1977(2)	—	KM26-27	150.00	250.00
MS4	1984(11)	3,350	KM32-42	24.95	200.00
MS5	1985(5)	—	KM15-19	—	7.50

PROOF SETS (PS)

PS1	1970(6)	10,000	KM15-20	24.00	27.50
PS2	1970(7)	1,000	KM15-21	216.00	225.00
PS3	1977(3)	4,650	KM25-27	245.00	300.00
PS4	1977(2)	—	KM26-27	210.00	250.00
PS5	1981(3)	500	KM28a,29(P1) numbered set	1500.	725.00
PS6	1983(7)	6,474	KM15-19,30,31	30.00	25.00
PS7	1984(11)	1,750	KM32a-42a	250.00	—
PS8	1986(7)	4,000	KM44-48,50-51	—	65.00
PS9	1986(5)	4,000	KM44-48	45.00	45.00

BHUTAN

The Kingdom of Bhutan, a landlocked Himalayan country bordered by Tibet and India, has an area of 18,147 sq. mi. (47,000 sq. km.) and a population of 1.3 million. Capital: Thimphu. Virtually the entire population is engaged in agricultural and pastoral activities. Rice, wheat, barley, and yak butter are produced in sufficient quantity to make the country self-sufficient in food. The economy of Bhutan is primitive and many transactions are conducted on a barter basis.

Bhutan's early history is obscure, but is thought to have resembled that of rural medieval Europe. The country was conquered by Tibet, in the 9th century, and a dual temporal and spiritual rule developed which operated until the mid-19th century, when the southern part of the country was occupied by the British and annexed to British India. Bhutan was established as a hereditary monarchy in 1907, and in 1910 agreed to British control of its external affairs. In 1949, India and Bhutan concluded a treaty whereby India assumed Britain's role in subsidizing Bhutan and guiding its foreign affairs. In 1971 Bhutan became a full member of the United Nations.

RULERS
Ugyen Wangchuck, 1907-1926
Jigme Wangchuck, 1926-1952
Jigme Dorji Wangchuck, 1952-1972
Jigme Singye Wangchuck, 1972-

DEB (1/2) RUPEE

NOTE: Prior to their own issues the coins (1/2 Rupees) of Cooch-Behar circulated freely. After the Cooch Behar Mint closed in 1789, Bhutan began to strike copies of the Cooch Behar coins. As time went on these coins were remelted and increasing amounts of debasing alloys were used until we have a copper or brass issue, some with a slight silver wash.

Period I
C.1790-1820AD
'Ma'

SILVER

KM#	Date	Mintage	Good	VG	Fine	VF
1	ND	—	4.00	6.50	8.50	12.50

'Sa'

| 2 | ND | — | 4.00 | 6.50 | 8.50 | 12.50 |

Period II
C1820-1835AD
"Ma-tam"

'Sa'
SILVER, LEAD alloying

| 3 | ND | — | 3.50 | 4.50 | 6.00 | 8.00 |

SILVER, COPPER alloying

| 4 | ND | — | 3.50 | 4.50 | 6.00 | 8.00 |

Dot
KM#	Date	Mintage	Good	VG	Fine	VF
4a	ND	—	3.50	4.50	6.00	8.00

Obv: Leaf spray.
| 5 | ND | — | 3.50 | 4.50 | 6.00 | 8.00 |

Obv: Swastika. Rev: Center inscription retrograde.
| 6 | ND | — | 3.50 | 5.00 | 7.50 | 10.00 |

Period III
1835-1910 AD
"Ma-tam"

'Sa'

COPPER or BRASS
| A7 | ND | — | 1.00 | 2.25 | 3.50 | 5.00 |

'Sa'

| 7 | ND | — | 1.00 | 1.50 | 2.25 | 3.50 |

Obv. and rev. leg: Retrograde.
| A8 | ND | — | 1.00 | 2.00 | 2.75 | 3.50 |

Obv: X above crescent.
| 8.1 | ND | — | 1.00 | 1.50 | 2.25 | 3.50 |

Obv: 2 dots in center inscription.
| 8.2 | ND | — | .50 | 1.00 | 1.75 | 2.50 |

'+'
| A9 | ND | — | 1.00 | 2.00 | 2.75 | 3.50 |

Obv: Swastika.
KM#	Date	Mintage	Good	VG	Fine	VF
9	ND	—	2.00	3.00	5.00	7.50

'Wang'

| 10 | ND | — | 3.00 | 5.00 | 7.00 | 10.00 |

'Sa dar'

| 11 | ND | — | 3.00 | 5.00 | 7.00 | 10.00 |

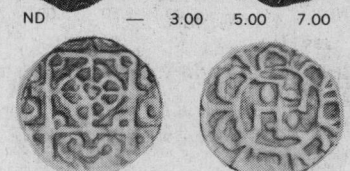

| 11a | ND | — | 3.00 | 5.00 | 7.00 | 10.00 |

| 11b | ND | — | 3.00 | 5.00 | 7.00 | 10.00 |

Obv: Rosette. Rev: Swastika.
| 12 | ND | — | 3.00 | 5.00 | 7.00 | 10.00 |

Obv: Rosette. Rev: Two fish.
| 13 | ND | — | 3.00 | 5.00 | 7.00 | 10.00 |

Rev: Two fish.
| 14 | ND | — | 2.00 | 3.00 | 5.00 | 7.50 |

Obv: Knot. Rev: Conch shell.
| 15 | ND | — | 1.50 | 2.50 | 3.50 | 5.00 |

Period IV
C.1910-1927AD

| 16 | ND | — | 2.00 | 3.50 | 7.00 | 10.00 |

BHUTAN 193

BHUTAN 194

			SILVER			
KM#	Date	Mintage	Good	VG	Fine	VF
17	ND	—	10.00	15.00	25.00	30.00
			COPPER			
17a	ND	—	2.00	3.50	5.00	7.50

			SILVER			
18	ND	—	10.00	15.00	25.00	30.00
			COPPER			
18a	ND	—	2.00	3.50	5.00	7.50
			BRASS			
18b	ND	—	2.00	3.50	5.00	7.50

			SILVER			
19	ND	—	10.00	15.00	25.00	30.00
			COPPER			
19a	ND	—	2.00	3.50	5.00	7.50

			SILVER			
20	ND	—	10.00	15.00	25.00	30.00
			COPPER			
20a	ND	—	3.00	4.50	6.00	8.50

21	ND	—	1.50	2.50	3.50	5.00

Obv. and rev: Interlacing opposite of KM#21.

22	ND	—	1.50	2.50	3.50	5.00

RUPEE
Period I
C.1790-1820AD
'Ma'

			SILVER			
A23	ND	—	—	—	—	250.00

MODERN COINAGE
64 Pice (Paisa) = 1 Rupee
CYCLICAL DATES

Earth-Dragon   Iron-Tiger

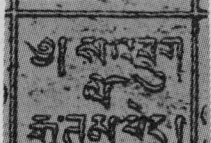

(1928)   (1950)
OBVERSE LEGENDS

Normal   Modified

PICE

			BRONZE			
KM#	Date	Mintage	Fine	VF	XF	Unc
23	1928	.010	30.00	40.00	50.00	75.00
	1928	—	—	—	Proof	100.00

27	ND	*1.260	.75	1.15	1.75	2.50

*NOTE: Actually struck in 1951 and 1955.

1/2 RUPEE

SILVER, 5.83-5.85 g
24	ND(1928)*	.050	10.00	15.00	22.50	35.00
	ND(1928)	—	—	—	Proof	100.00

NOTE: Actually struck in 1929.

Obv: Leg. modified.
25	ND(1928)	I.A.	10.00	15.00	22.50	35.00

NOTE: Actually struck in 1930.

NICKEL, 5.78-5.90 g
Obv: Leg. normal.
26	ND(1928)*	.020	2.00	3.00	4.50	7.00
	ND(1950)**	.202	1.50	2.50	3.00	4.50

*NOTE: Actually struck in 1951.
**NOTE: Actually struck in 1955.

NICKEL, reduced wgt., 5.08 g
Obv: Leg. normal.
28	ND(1950)***					
		10.000	.75	1.00	1.75	2.50

***NOTE: Actually struck in 1967/68.

DECIMAL COINAGE
1957-1974
100 Naye Paisa = 1 Rupee
100 Rupees = 1 Sertum

25 NAYA PAISA

COPPER-NICKEL
40th Anniversary Accession of Jigme Wangchuk
KM#	Date	Mintage	VF	XF	Unc
29	1966	.010	.20	.40	.75
	1966	6,000	—	Proof	1.00

50 NAYA PAISA

COPPER-NICKEL
40th Anniversary Accession of Jigme Wangchuk
30	1966	.010	.25	.50	1.00
	1966	6,000	—	Proof	1.50

RUPEE

COPPER-NICKEL
40th Anniversary Accession of Jigme Wangchuk
31	1966	.010	.50	.75	1.50
	1966	6,000	—	Proof	1.50

3 RUPEES

COPPER-NICKEL
40th Anniversary Accession of Jigme Wangchuk
32	1966	5,826	—	—	4.00
	1966	6,000	—	Proof	4.00

28.2800 g, .925 SILVER, .8411 oz ASW
32a	1966	—	—	—	375.00
	1966	2,000	—	Proof	27.50
	1966	—	—	Matte Proof	375.00

SERTUM

7.9800 g, .917 GOLD, .2352 oz AGW
33	1966	2,300	—	—	150.00
	1966	598 pcs.	—	Proof	175.00

9.8400 g, .950 PLATINUM, .3005 oz APW
33a	1966	72 pcs.	—	Proof	350.00

7.9800 g, .917 GOLD, .2352 oz AGW
36	1970	—	—	—	150.00

2 SERTUMS

15.9800 g, .917 GOLD, .4711 oz AGW

KM#	Date	Mintage	VF	XF	Unc
34	1966	800 pcs.	—	—	250.00
	1966	598 pcs.	—	Proof	300.00

19.6700 g, .950 PLATINUM, .6008 oz APW

| 34a | 1966 | 72 pcs. | — | Proof | 650.00 |

5 SERTUMS

39.9400 g, .917 GOLD, 1.1776 oz AGW

35	1966	800 pcs.	—	—	600.00
	1966	598 pcs.	—	—	900.00

49.1800 g, .950 PLATINUM, 1.5022 oz APW

| 35a | 1966 | 72 pcs. | — | Proof | 1500. |

MONETARY REFORM
Commencing 1974
100 Chetrums (Paisa) =
1 Ngultrum (Rupee)
100 Ngultrums = 1 Sertum

5 CHETRUMS

ALUMINUM

37	1974	—	.10	.20	.50
	1974	1,000	—	Proof	1.00
	1975	—	.10	.15	.20
	1975	—	—	Proof	1.00

5 CHHERTUM

BRONZE

45	1979	—	.10	.20	.50
	1979	—	—	Proof	1.00

10 CHETRUMS

ALUMINUM

38	1974	—	.15	.25	.50
	1974	1,000	—	Proof	1.25

F.A.O. Issue and International Women's Year

KM#	Date	Mintage	VF	XF	Unc
43	1975	4.000	.15	.25	.75
	1975	—	—	Proof	2.50

10 CHHERTUM

BRONZE

46	1979	—	.15	.30	1.00
	1979	—	—	Proof	2.00

20 CHETRUMS

ALUMINUM-BRONZE
F.A.O. Issue

39	1974	1.194	.15	.25	.50
	1974	1,000	—	Proof	1.50

25 CHETRUMS

COPPER-NICKEL

40	1974	—	.10	.20	.75
	1974	1,000	—	Proof	2.50
	1975	—	.10	.20	.50
	1975	—	—	Proof	2.50

25 CHHERTUM

COPPER-NICKEL

47	1979	—	.25	.50	1.25
	1979	—	—	Proof	4.00

50 CHHERTUM

COPPER-NICKEL

48	1979	—	.25	.65	1.50
	1979	—	—	Proof	5.00

NGULTRUM

COPPER-NICKEL

KM#	Date	Mintage	VF	XF	Unc
41	1974	—	.20	.50	1.25
	1974	1,000	—	Proof	4.00
	1975	—	.20	.50	1.25
	1975	—	—	Proof	4.00

49	1979	—	.30	.75	2.00
	1979	—	—	Proof	5.00

3 NGULTRUMS

COPPER-NICKEL

50	1979	—	1.00	2.00	3.50
	1979	—	—	Proof	7.50

28.2800 g, .925 SILVER, .8411 oz ASW

| 50a | 1979 | — | — | — | 27.50 |

15 NGULTRUMS

22.3000 g, .500 SILVER, .3584 oz ASW
F.A.O. Issue

42	1974	.030	—	—	8.00
	1974	1,000	—	Proof	45.00

25 NGULTRUMS

COPPER-NICKEL
International Games - Boxing

| 59 | 1984 | — | — | Proof | 15.00 |

30 NGULTRUMS

25.0000 g, .500 SILVER, .4018 oz ASW
F.A.O. Issue and International Women's Year

KM#	Date	Mintage	VF	XF	Unc
44	1975	.014	—	—	10.00
	1975	—	—	Proof	20.00

50 NGULTRUMS

28.2800 g, .925 SILVER, .8411 oz ASW
World Food Day

54	1981	.015	—	—	25.00
	1981	5,000	—	Proof	35.00

100 NGULTRUMS

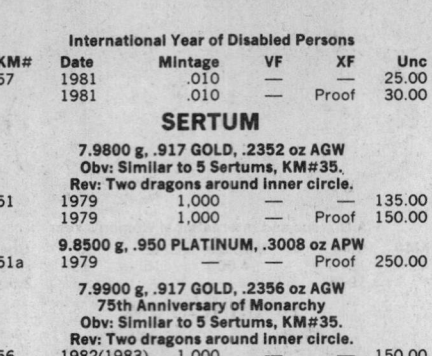

23.3300 g, .925 SILVER, .6938 oz ASW
Decade For Women

58	1984	1,050	—	Proof	35.00

200 NGULTRUMS

28.2800 g, .925 SILVER, .8411 oz ASW
75th Anniversary of Monarchy

55	1982(1983)	.010	—	—	25.00
	1982(1983)	5,000	—	Proof	35.00

International Year of Disabled Persons

KM#	Date	Mintage	VF	XF	Unc
57	1981	.010	—	—	25.00
	1981	.010	—	Proof	30.00

SERTUM
7.9800 g, .917 GOLD, .2352 oz AGW
Obv: Similar to 5 Sertums, KM#35.
Rev: Two dragons around inner circle.

51	1979	1,000	—	—	135.00
	1979	1,000	—	Proof	150.00

9.8500 g, .950 PLATINUM, .3008 oz APW

51a	1979	—	—	Proof	250.00

7.9900 g, .917 GOLD, .2356 oz AGW
75th Anniversary of Monarchy
Obv: Similar to 5 Sertums, KM#35.
Rev: Two dragons around inner circle.

56	1982(1983)	1,000	—	—	150.00
	1982(1983)	1,000	—	Proof	175.00

2 SERTUMS
15.9800 g, .917 GOLD, .4711 oz AGW
Obv: Similar to 5 Sertums, KM#35.
Rev: Two dragons around inner circle.

52	1979	1,000	—	—	225.00
	1979	1,000	—	Proof	300.00

19.7000 g, .950 PLATINUM, .6017 oz APW

52a	1979	—	—	Proof	500.00

5 SERTUMS
39.9400 g, .917 GOLD, 1.1776 oz AGW
Obv: Similar to 5 Sertums, KM#35.
Rev: Two dragons around inner circle.

53	1979	1,000	—	—	600.00
	1979	1,000	—	Proof	650.00

49.2000 g, .950 PLATINUM, 1.5022 oz APW

53a	1979	—	—	Proof	1000.

MINT SETS (MS)

KM#	Date	Mintage	Identification	Issue Price	Mkt. Val.
MS1	1966(3)	300	KM33-35	175.00	850.00
MS2	1974(2)	—	KM39,42	4.00	10.00
MS3	1974(4)	—	KM37-38,40-41	6.00	3.00
MS4	1979(3)	1,000	KM51-53	1575.	950.00

PROOF SETS (PS)

PS1	1966(4)	6,000	KM29-32	11.50	7.50
PS2	1966(3)	598	KM33-35	300.00	1350.
PS3	1966(3)	72	KM33a-35a	685.00	2500.
PS4	1974(6)	1,000	KM37-42	18.00	55.00
PS5	1975(5)	—	KM37,40-41,43-44	—	Rare
PS6	1979(5)	.020	KM45-49	30.00	15.00
PS7	1979(3)	1,000	KM51-53	2100.	1050.
PS8	1979(3)	—	KM51a-53a	2400.	1750.

Listings For
BIAFRA: refer to Nigeria
BOHEMIA & MORAVIA: refer to Czechoslovak

BOLIVIA

The Republic of Bolivia, a landlocked country in west-central South America, has an area of 424,165 sq. mi. (1,098,581 sq. km.) and a population of 6 million. Its Capitals are: La Paz (administrative) and Sucre (constitutional). Principal exports are tin, zinc, antimony, tungsten, petroleum, natural gas, cotton and coffee.

Much of present day Bolivia was first dominated by the been incorporated into the Inca Empire by 1440AD prior to the arrival of the Spanish in 1535 who reduced the Indian population to virtual slavery. When Napoleon was placed upon the throne of occupied Spain in 1809, a fervor of revolutionary activity quickened throughout Alto Peru culminating with the 1809 proclamation of liberty. Sixteen bloody years of struggle ensued before the republic, named for the famed liberator Simon Bolivar, was established on August 6, 1825. Since then Bolivia has suffered through more than 11 constitutions, 60 Presidents and 70 revolutions.

The Imperial City of Potosi, founded by Villaroel in 1546, was established in the midst of what is estimated to have been the world's richest silver mines. While the productivity of the "Casa de Moneda", was enormous, the quality of the coinage was at times so poor that several mint officials were even put to death by their superiros.

Most pre-decimal coinage of independent Bolivia carry the assayer's initials on the reverse near the rim to the right of the date in 4 to 5 o'clock position. The mint mark or name appears in the 7 to 8 o'clock area.

RULERS
Spanish until 1825

MINT MARKS
A - Paris
H - Heaton
KN - Kings' Norton
LA PLATA monogram - Chuquisaca
ORURO monogram - Oruro
PAZ - La Paz
P or PTS monogram - Potosi

ASSAYER'S INITIALS

Letter	Date	Name
J	1803-1859	Juan Palomo Sierra
L	1825	?
P	1776-1802	Pedro de Mazondo
P	1795-1834	Pedro Martin de Albizu

*NOTE: These names are based on data put forth by Dr. E.A. Sellschopp in *Las Acunadiones de las Cecas de Lima, La Plata Y Potosi* and J. Pelliceri Bru in *Glosario de Maestros de Ceca y Ensayedores*.

COLONIAL MILLED COINAGE
1/4 REAL

.8500 g, .903 SILVER, .0247 oz ASW
Mint mark: PTS monogram
Obv: Castle. Rev: Lion.

KM#	Date	Mintage	VG	Fine	VF	XF
82	1801	—	15.00	35.00	75.00	200.00
	1802	—	7.50	12.50	20.00	50.00
	1803	—	10.00	15.00	30.00	65.00
	1804	—	20.00	50.00	150.00	300.00
	1805	—	20.00	50.00	150.00	300.00
	1806	—	7.50	12.50	32.50	60.00
	1807	—	12.50	25.00	50.00	125.00
	1808	—	7.50	12.50	20.00	60.00

NOTE: There is a variety of 1802 with base of 2 not struck up and frequently miscataloged as 1809.

1/2 REAL
1.6500 g, .903 SILVER, .0479 oz ASW
Mint mark: PTS monogram
Obv. leg: CAROLUS IIII. . . ., bust.

69	1801 PP	—	4.00	7.00	16.00	30.00
	1802 PP	—	4.00	7.00	16.00	30.00
	1803 PJ	—	4.00	7.00	16.00	30.00
	1804 PJ	—	4.00	7.00	16.00	30.00
	1805 PJ	—	4.00	7.00	16.00	30.00
	1806 PJ	—	4.00	7.00	16.00	30.00
	1807 PJ	—	4.00	7.00	16.00	30.00
	1808 PJ	—	4.00	7.00	16.00	30.00
	1809 PJ	—	20.00	32.50	45.00	85.00

Obv. leg: FERDIN VII. . . ., bust.

BOLIVIA 197

KM#	Date	Mintage	VG	Fine	VF	XF
90	1814 PJ	—	12.50	20.00	75.00	100.00
	1815 PJ	—	10.00	17.50	70.00	100.00
	1816 PJ	—	4.00	8.00	18.50	55.00
	1817 PJ	—	4.00	7.00	18.50	35.00
	1818 PJ	—	3.50	6.00	17.50	35.00
	1819 PJ	—	3.50	6.00	17.50	35.00
	1820 PJ	—	3.50	6.00	17.50	35.00
	1821 PJ	—	3.50	6.00	17.50	35.00
	1822 PJ	—	3.50	6.00	17.50	35.00
	1823 PJ	—	3.50	6.00	17.50	35.00
	1823 JL	—	3.50	6.00	20.00	50.00
	1824 PJ	—	3.50	6.00	17.50	35.00
	1825 JL	—	3.50	6.00	17.50	35.00

REAL
3.2500 g, .903 SILVER, .0943 oz ASW
Mint mark: PTS monogram
Obv. leg: CAROLUS IIII. . . ., bust.

KM#	Date	Mintage	VG	Fine	VF	XF
70	1801 PP	—	4.00	6.50	12.50	37.50
	1802 PP	—	4.00	7.00	15.00	45.00
	1803 PP	—	5.00	8.00	25.00	60.00
	1803 PJ	—	4.00	7.00	15.00	35.00
	1804 PJ	—	4.00	6.50	12.50	27.50
	1805 PJ	—	4.00	7.00	15.00	40.00
	1806 PJ	—	4.00	7.00	15.00	40.00
	1807 PJ	—	4.00	7.00	15.00	40.00
	1808 PJ	—	4.00	6.50	15.00	35.00
	1808/9 PJ	—	17.50	30.00	60.00	125.00
	1809 PJ	—	22.50	40.00	75.00	100.00

Obv. leg: FERDIN. VII. . . ., bust.

87	1813 PJ	—	6.50	10.00	25.00	40.00
	1816 PJ	—	4.00	6.50	12.50	25.00
	1817 PJ	—	4.00	6.50	12.50	25.00
	1818 PJ	—	4.00	6.50	12.50	25.00
	1819 PJ	—	4.00	6.50	12.50	25.00
	1820 PJ	—	4.00	6.50	12.50	25.00
	1821 PJ	—	4.00	6.50	12.50	25.00
	1822 PJ	—	4.00	6.50	12.50	25.00
	1823 PJ	—	4.00	6.50	12.50	25.00
	1824 PJ	—	4.00	6.50	12.50	25.00
	1825 JL	—	4.00	6.50	12.50	25.00

2 REALES
6.5000 g, .903 SILVER, .1886 oz ASW
Mint mark: PTS monogram
Obv. leg: CAROLUS IIII. . . ., bust.

71	1801 PP	—	4.00	7.00	20.00	40.00
	1802 PP	—	4.00	7.00	20.00	40.00
	1803/2 PJ	—	4.00	7.00	22.50	60.00
	1803 PJ	—	4.00	7.00	20.00	40.00
	1804 PJ	—	4.00	7.00	20.00	40.00
	1805 PJ	—	4.00	7.00	20.00	40.00
	1806 PJ	—	4.00	7.00	20.00	40.00
	1807 PJ	—	4.00	7.00	20.00	40.00
	1808 PJ	—	4.00	7.00	20.00	40.00

Obv. leg: FERDIN VII. . . ., bust.

83	1808 PJ	—	10.00	15.00	40.00	60.00
	1809 PJ	—	4.00	8.00	25.00	40.00
	1813 PJ	—	4.00	8.00	25.00	40.00
	1814 PJ	—	4.00	8.00	30.00	40.00
	1816 PJ	—	4.00	8.00	25.00	45.00
	1817 PJ	—	4.00	8.00	25.00	45.00
	1818 PJ	—	4.00	8.00	25.00	45.00
	1819 PJ	—	4.00	8.00	25.00	40.00
	1820 PJ	—	4.00	8.00	25.00	45.00
	1821 PJ	—	4.00	8.00	25.00	40.00
	1822 PJ	—	4.00	8.00	25.00	40.00
	1823 PJ	—	4.00	8.00	25.00	40.00
	1824 PJ	—	4.00	8.00	25.00	40.00
	1825 PJ	—	7.50	25.00	50.00	100.00
	1825 J	—	25.00	50.00	150.00	250.00
	1825 JL	—	10.00	15.00	40.00	75.00

4 REALES

13.0000 g, .903 SILVER, .3773 oz ASW
Mint mark: PTS monogram
Obv. leg: CAROLUS IIII. . . ., bust.

72	1801 PP	—	15.00	25.00	45.00	90.00
	1802 PP	—	17.50	30.00	50.00	90.00
	1803 PJ	—	17.50	30.00	50.00	90.00
	1804 PJ	—	17.50	30.00	50.00	90.00
	1805 PJ	—	30.00	50.00	75.00	100.00
	1806 PJ	—	15.00	25.00	50.00	90.00
	1807 PJ	—	15.00	25.00	50.00	90.00
	1808 PJ	—	15.00	25.00	50.00	90.00

KM#	Date	Mintage	VG	Fine	VF	XF
72	1808/9 PJ	—	15.00	25.00	50.00	90.00
	1809 PJ	—	30.00	50.00	75.00	150.00

Obv. leg: FERDIN. . . ., bust.

88	1813 PJ	—	—	Reported, not confirmed		
	1814 PJ	—	—	Reported, not confirmed		
	1815 PJ	—	—	Reported, not confirmed		
	1816 PJ	—	17.50	30.00	50.00	90.00
	1817 PJ	—	17.50	30.00	50.00	90.00
	1818 PJ	—	20.00	35.00	60.00	100.00
	1819 PJ	—	20.00	35.00	60.00	100.00
	1820 PJ	—	20.00	35.00	60.00	100.00
	1821 PJ	—	30.00	50.00	75.00	125.00
	1822 PJ	—	20.00	35.00	60.00	100.00
	1823 PJ	—	17.50	30.00	50.00	90.00
	1824 PJ	—	30.00	50.00	75.00	125.00
	1825 PJ	—	225.00	350.00	475.00	650.00
	1825 JL	—	15.00	25.00	50.00	90.00
	1825 J	—	175.00	275.00	375.00	500.00

8 REALES

27.0000 g, .903 SILVER, .7837 oz ASW
Mint mark: PTS monogram
Obv. leg: CAROLUS IIII. . . ., bust.
Rev: Crowned arms between pillars.

73.1	1801 PP	—	20.00	27.50	40.00	85.00
	1802 PP	—	20.00	27.50	40.00	85.00
	1803 PJ	—	20.00	27.50	40.00	85.00
	1804 PJ	—	20.00	27.50	40.00	85.00
	1805 PJ	—	20.00	27.50	40.00	85.00
	1806/5 PJ	—	22.50	32.50	45.00	100.00
	1806 PJ	—	20.00	27.50	40.00	85.00
	1807 PJ	—	20.00	27.50	40.00	85.00
	1808 PJ	—	20.00	27.50	40.00	85.00

Rev: Similar to KM#89.

84	1808 PJ	—	25.00	40.00	70.00	175.00
	1809 PJ	—	25.00	40.00	70.00	135.00
	1813 PJ	—	20.00	27.50	40.00	100.00
	1814/13 PJ	—	20.00	27.50	45.00	110.00
	1814 PJ	—	20.00	27.50	40.00	85.00
	1815 PJ	—	22.00	30.00	45.00	100.00
	1816 PJ	—	20.00	27.50	40.00	75.00
	1817 PJ	—	20.00	27.50	40.00	75.00
	1818 PJ	—	20.00	27.50	40.00	75.00
	1819 PJ	—	20.00	27.50	45.00	100.00
	1820 PJ	—	20.00	27.50	40.00	75.00
	1821 PJ	—	20.00	27.50	40.00	75.00
	1822 PJ	—	20.00	27.50	40.00	75.00
	1823 PJ	—	20.00	27.50	40.00	75.00
	1823 JP	—	25.00	35.00	75.00	175.00
	1824 PJ	—	40.00	65.00	100.00	200.00
	1824 J	—	100.00	200.00	350.00	650.00
	1825 J	—	75.00	150.00	300.00	550.00
	1825 JL	—	20.00	27.50	40.00	75.00

NOTE: 1825 JL are also struck with medal rotation.

Obv. leg: FERDIN IIV (error).

KM#	Date	Mintage	VG	Fine	VF	XF
89	1813 PJ	—	250.00	450.00	750.00	1200.

ESCUDO
3.4000 g, .875 GOLD, .0956 oz AGW
Mint mark: PTS monogram
Obv. leg: CAROL IIII. . . ., bust.

78	1801 PP	—	150.00	200.00	250.00	400.00
	1802 PP	—	150.00	200.00	250.00	400.00
	1803 PJ	—	150.00	200.00	250.00	500.00
	1804 PJ	—	150.00	200.00	250.00	500.00
	1805 PJ	—	150.00	200.00	250.00	500.00
	1806 PJ	—	150.00	200.00	250.00	500.00
	1807 PJ	—	150.00	200.00	250.00	500.00
	1808 PJ	—	150.00	200.00	250.00	500.00

Obv. leg: FERDIN VII. . . ., bust.

92	1822 PJ	—	200.00	300.00	400.00	1000.
	1823 PJ	—	250.00	400.00	600.00	1200.
	1824 PJ	—	300.00	500.00	750.00	1450.

2 ESCUDOS

6.8000 g, .875 GOLD, .1913 oz AGW
Mint mark: PTS monogram
Obv. leg: CAROL IIII, bust.

79	1801 PP	—	250.00	400.00	475.00	900.00
	1802 PP	—	400.00	550.00	650.00	1100.
	1804 PJ	—	325.00	450.00	475.00	950.00
	1805 PJ	—	325.00	475.00	650.00	1100.
	1806 PJ	—	400.00	550.00	725.00	1100.
	1807 PJ	—	250.00	350.00	475.00	700.00
	1808 PJ	—	325.00	475.00	650.00	900.00

4 ESCUDOS
13.5000 g, .875 GOLD, .3798 oz AGW
Mint mark: PTS monogram
Obv. leg: CAROL IIII. . . ., bust. Rev: Arms.

80	1801 PP	—	400.00	525.00	800.00	1600.
	1802 PP	—	475.00	600.00	900.00	1400.
	1803 PP	—	800.00	1100.	1450.	2700.
	1804 PJ	—	950.00	1300.	1600.	2700.
	1804 PP	—	950.00	1300.	1600.	2700.
	1805 PJ	—	550.00	725.00	900.00	1500.
	1806 PJ	—	400.00	525.00	725.00	1500.
	1807 PJ	—	475.00	600.00	800.00	1500.
	1808 PJ	—	475.00	600.00	800.00	1500.

8 ESCUDOS

BOLIVIA 198

27.0000 g, .875 GOLD, .7596 oz AGW
Mint mark: PTS monogram
Obv. leg: CAROL IIII.... Rev: Bust.

KM#	Date	Mintage	VG	Fine	VF	XF
81	1801 PP	—	375.00	450.00	600.00	900.00
	1802 PP	—	375.00	450.00	600.00	900.00
	1803 PJ	—	375.00	450.00	600.00	900.00
	1804 PJ	—	375.00	450.00	600.00	900.00
	1805 PJ	—	375.00	450.00	600.00	900.00
	1806 PJ	—	375.00	450.00	600.00	900.00
	1807 PJ	—	375.00	450.00	600.00	900.00
	1808 PJ	—	375.00	450.00	600.00	900.00

Obv. leg: FERDIN VII...., uniformed bust.

| 86 | 1809 PJ | — | — | — | Rare | — |

Obv. leg: FERDIN. VII...., bust.

91	1817 PJ	—	675.00	900.00	1500.	4000.
	1822 PJ	—	375.00	450.00	600.00	1000.
	1823 PJ	—	500.00	750.00	1125.	3000.
	1824 PJ	—	400.00	550.00	900.00	1500.

REPUBLIC

MINT MARKS

A - Paris
(a) - Paris, privy marks only
H - Heaton
PTA monogram - La Plata
OR monogram - Oruro
PAZ - La Paz
PTS monogram - Potosi
So - Santiago

MONETARY SYSTEM

8 Soles = 1 Peso
16 Soles = 1 Scudo

1/4 SOL

.8500 g, .667 SILVER, .0182 oz ASW
Obv: Llama in plain field, POTOSI below.

| 111 | 1852 | — | 6.00 | 12.00 | 30.00 | 55.00 |

Obv: Branches flank Llama.

| 117 | 1853 | — | 30.00 | 40.00 | 80.00 | 155.00 |

1/2 SOL

1.5000 g, .903 SILVER, .0435 oz ASW
Mint mark: PTS monogram

93	1827 JM	—	2.50	4.00	7.50	27.00
	1828/7 JM	—	3.00	5.00	8.00	27.50
	1828 JM	—	1.50	3.00	5.00	22.50
	1829 JM	—	2.00	3.50	6.00	22.50
	1830 J	—	2.50	4.00	7.50	27.00
	1830 JF	—	2.50	4.00	7.00	25.00
	1830 JL wide date					
		—	1.00	2.00	3.50	18.00
	1830 JL narrow date					
		—	1.00	2.00	3.50	18.00

1.5000 g, .667 SILVER, .0322 oz ASW

KM#	Date	Mintage	VG	Fine	VF	XF
93a	1830 J	—	—	—	—	—
	1830 JF	—	—	—	—	—
	1830 JL wide date	—	—	—	—	—
	1830 JL narrow date	—	—	—	—	—

Obv: W/o denomination.
Rev: BOLIVAR on truncation.

118.1	1853 FP	—	2.50	5.50	10.00	28.00
	1854 FP	—	2.00	3.00	6.00	18.00
	1855 MJ	—	2.50	5.50	10.00	28.00
	1856 FJ	—	4.50	5.50	11.00	35.00
	1856 MJ	—	5.00	6.50	11.00	35.00

Obv: Denomination added.

118.2	1856 FJ	—	3.00	5.50	10.00	22.50
	1857/6 FJ	—	3.50	7.00	11.00	25.00
	1857 FJ	—	1.50	3.50	7.50	18.00
	1858/7 FJ	—	3.50	7.50	13.50	32.00
	1858 FJ	—	2.50	5.50	10.00	22.50

NOTE: Varieties exist.

Rev: BOLIVAR below truncation.

118.3	1859	—	8.00	12.00	30.00	70.00
	1859 (error) BOLIVAR spelled BOLIVRA
		—	11.00	17.50	45.00	100.00

Mint mark: PAZ
Rev: Crude "La Paz style" head.

127	1855 P	—	7.50	12.50	25.00	65.00
	1856/5 P	—	10.00	15.00	30.00	75.00
	1856 P	—	10.00	15.00	30.00	75.00

Rev: Crude so-called "ugly head".

| 132 | 1858/7 P | — | 10.00 | 17.50 | 40.00 | 80.00 |
| | 1858 P | — | 8.00 | 15.00 | 35.00 | 70.00 |

1.3000 g, .667 SILVER, .0279 oz ASW
Mint mark: PTS monogram
Rev. weight: PESO 25 Gs.

| 133.1 | 1859 FJ | — | 5.00 | 10.00 | 25.00 | 45.00 |

1.3000 g, .903 SILVER, .0377 oz ASW
Rev. weight: 25 G. or Gs.

133.2	1859 FJ	—	5.00	7.50	15.00	65.00
	1860 FJ	—	5.00	7.50	15.00	45.00
	1861 FJ	—	5.00	7.50	15.00	45.00
	1862 FP	—	5.00	7.50	15.00	60.00
	1863 FP	—	5.00	7.50	15.00	45.00

SOL

3.0000 g, .903 SILVER, .0871 oz ASW
Mint mark: PTS monogram

94	1827 JM	—	6.00	12.00	25.00	45.00
	1828 JM	—	6.00	12.00	25.00	45.00
	1829 JM	—	5.00	10.00	20.00	40.00
	1830 J	—	5.00	10.00	20.00	40.00
	1830 JL	—	2.50	3.50	6.00	15.00

3.0000 g, .667 SILVER, .0643 oz ASW

| 94a | 1830 J | — | — | — | — | — |
| | 1830 JL | — | — | — | — | — |

2.6-3.6 g, .667 SILVER, .056-.077 oz ASW
Mint mark: Oruro monogram
Obv. leg: .....SOCABON.

KM#	Date	Mintage	VG	Fine	VF	XF
200.1	1849 JM	—	40.00	60.00	90.00	165.00

Obv. leg: .....SOCN.

| 200.2 | 1849 JM | — | 40.00 | 60.00 | 90.00 | 165.00 |

NOTE: Unholed specimens command a substantial premium.

3.0000 g, .667 SILVER, .0643 oz ASW
Obv: W/o denomination.
Rev: BOLIVAR on truncation.

| 119.1 | 1853 FP | — | 4.00 | 6.00 | 12.00 | 25.00 |
| | 1854 MJ | — | 5.00 | 7.50 | 15.00 | 35.00 |

Obv: Denomination added.

119.2	1855 MJ	—	4.50	8.00	17.50	35.00
	1856/5 FJ/MJ
		—	5.00	12.00	27.50	55.00
	1856 FJ	—	4.00	8.00	17.50	35.00
	1857 FJ	—	4.00	8.00	15.00	35.00
	1858/7 FJ	—	4.00	8.00	15.00	35.00
	1858 FJ	—	4.00	8.00	15.00	35.00

Rev: BOLIVAR below truncation.

| 119.3 | 1859 | — | 13.50 | 20.00 | 45.00 | 70.00 |

Mint mark: PAZ
Rev: "Potosi style" laureate head.

| 120 | 1855 P | — | 10.00 | 17.50 | 35.00 | 65.00 |
| | 1855 F | — | 10.00 | 17.50 | 35.00 | 65.00 |

Rev: Crude "La Paz style" head.

| 128 | 1855 F | — | 20.00 | 50.00 | 75.00 | 130.00 |
| | 1856 P | — | 15.00 | 25.00 | 45.00 | 75.00 |

Rev: Crude so-called "ugly head".

131	1857 P	—	15.00	30.00	60.00	90.00
	1858/7 PAZ	—	15.00	25.00	50.00	80.00
	1858 P	—	—	—	—	—
	1859/7 P	—	30.00	75.00	150.00	250.00
	1859 P	—	15.00	25.00	50.00	80.00

2.5000 g, .667 SILVER, .0536 oz ASW
Mint mark: PTS monogram

| 134.1 | 1859 FJ | — | 10.00 | 15.00 | 35.00 | 70.00 |

2.5000 g, .903 SILVER, .0726 oz ASW
W/o denomination, only weight indicated as 50 Gs.

134.2	1860 FJ	—	3.00	5.00	15.00	15.00
	1860 FJ/JJ	—	4.00	7.00	10.00	20.00
	1861 FJ	—	3.00	5.00	7.50	15.00

KM#	Date	Mintage	VG	Fine	VF	XF
134.2	1862/1 FP	—	—	—	—	—
	1862 FJ	—	—	—	—	—
	1862 FP	—	3.00	5.00	7.50	15.00
	1863/2 FP	—	4.00	6.00	10.00	20.00
	1863 FP	—	3.00	5.00	7.50	15.00

2 SOLES

6.2000 g, .903 SILVER, .1799 oz ASW
Mint mark: PTS monogram

KM#	Date	Mintage	VG	Fine	VF	XF
95	1827 JM	—	8.00	15.00	32.00	62.50
	1828/7 JM	—	25.00	40.00	65.00	115.00
	1828 JM	—	5.00	7.50	15.00	32.00
	1829 JM	—	12.50	20.00	35.00	60.00
	1830/27 J	—	20.00	35.00	45.00	90.00
	1830 J	—	6.00	10.00	15.00	32.00
	1830 JF	—	10.00	18.00	27.50	55.00
	1830 JL	—	4.00	6.00	10.00	22.50
	1831 J	—	—	—	Rare	—

6.2000 g, .667 SILVER, .1324 oz ASW

95a	1830/27 J	—	—	—	—	—
	1830 J	—	—	—	—	—
	1830 JF	—	—	—	—	—
	1830 JL	—	—	—	—	—
	1831 J	—	—	—	—	—

Obv: W/o denomination.

121.1	1853 FP	—	20.00	35.00	70.00	110.00

Obv: Denomination added.

121.2	1854 MJ	—	5.00	10.00	32.00	60.00
	1855 MJ	—	5.00	10.00	32.00	60.00
	1856 FJ	—	7.50	12.50	40.00	80.00
	1856/5 MJ	—	7.50	12.50	40.00	80.00
	1857 MJ	—	7.50	12.50	40.00	80.00
	1857 FJ	—	5.00	10.00	32.00	60.00
	1858 FJ	—	7.50	12.50	40.00	80.00

Rev: BOLIVAR below truncation.

121.3	1859/7 FJ	—	15.00	20.00	40.00	90.00
	1859 FJ	—	15.00	20.00	40.00	90.00

Mint mark: PAZ
Rev: Bare head

122	1853	—	500.00	750.00	1000.	1500.

Rev: "Potosi style" laureate head.

126	1854 F	—	75.00	125.00	250.00	400.00

Rev: Crude "La Paz style" head.

129	1855 F	—	75.00	150.00	250.00	400.00
	1856 P	—	75.00	150.00	250.00	400.00

Mint mark: PTS monogram
Rev: Weight indicated as PESO 100 Gs.

KM#	Date	Mintage	VG	Fine	VF	XF
135.1	1859 FJ	—	20.00	40.00	80.00	150.00

4.5000 g, .903 SILVER, .1306 oz ASW
Rev: Weight indicated as 100 Gs.

135.2	1859 FJ	—	—	Reported, not confirmed		
	1860 FJ	—	5.00	8.00	12.50	25.00
	1861 FJ	—	7.50	12.50	20.00	35.00
	1862/1 FJ	—	—	—	—	—
	1862 FJ	—	5.00	8.00	12.50	25.00
	1862 FP	—	4.00	7.00	10.00	20.00
	1863/2 FP	—	7.50	12.50	20.00	35.00
	1863 FP	—	5.00	8.00	12.50	25.00

4 SOLES

13.5000 g, .903 SILVER, .3918 oz ASW
Mint mark: PTS monogram
Reeded edge,
incuse lettering: AYACUCHO*SUCRE *1824*.

96	1827 JM	—	12.50	17.50	30.00	65.00
	1828 JM	—	12.50	17.50	30.00	65.00
	1829 JM	—	12.50	17.50	30.00	65.00
	1830 J	—	10.00	15.00	20.00	50.00
	1830/27 JL	—	8.00	12.50	17.50	35.00
	1830 JL	—	4.00	6.00	8.00	15.00

NOTE: Many die varieties exist.

13.5000 g, .667 SILVER, .2895 oz ASW

96a	1830 J	—	—	—	—	—
	1830/27 JL	—	—	—	—	—
	1830 JL	—	—	—	—	—

Obv: W/o denomination

123.1	1853 FP	—	10.00	15.00	25.00	50.00

Obv: Denomination added

123.2	1853 MF	—	8.00	16.00	25.00	40.00
	1854 MF	—	8.00	16.00	25.00	40.00
	1854 MJ	—	8.00	16.00	25.00	40.00
	1855 MJ (error: CONSTITUCIN)					
		—	8.00	16.00	35.00	55.00
	1855 FJ	—	8.00	16.00	25.00	40.00
	1856 FJ	—	8.00	16.00	25.00	40.00
	1856/5 MJ	—	8.00	16.00	25.00	40.00
	1856 MJ	—	8.00	16.00	25.00	40.00

BOLIVIA 199

KM#	Date	Mintage	VG	Fine	VF	XF
123.2	1857 FJ	—	8.00	16.00	25.00	40.00
	1857 FJ (error) V in BOLIVIANA is inverted A					
		—	—	—	—	—
	1857 FJ (error) CONSTITUCIO					
		—	—	—	—	—
	1858 FJ	—	10.00	20.00	35.00	55.00

Rev: BOLIVAR below truncation.

123.3	1859 FJ	—	10.00	20.00	35.00	55.00

Mint mark: PAZ

124.1	1853 J	—	75.00	125.00	175.00	275.00

Mint mark: LA PLATA monogram.

124.2	1853 J	—	600.00	1200.	2100.	—

Rev: "Potosi style" laureate head.

125	1853 J	—	15.00	20.00	50.00	110.00
	1854 J	—	—	Reported, not confirmed		
	1854 F	—	15.00	20.00	50.00	110.00
	1855 F	—	10.00	25.00	40.00	95.00

Rev: Crude "La Paz style" head.

130	1855 F	—	12.50	20.00	35.00	80.00
	1856/5 P/F	—	15.00	25.00	45.00	90.00
	1856 P	—	12.50	20.00	35.00	80.00
	1857/6 P	—	30.00	45.00	65.00	95.00
	1857 P	—	100.00	200.00	300.00	500.00
	1858 P	—	100.00	200.00	300.00	500.00

NOTE: Varieties exist.

136	1859 P	—	150.00	225.00	300.00	400.00

NOTE: Several distinct bust varieties exist.

BOLIVIA 200

13.5000 g, .903 SILVER, .3918 oz ASW
Mint mark: PTS monogram
W/o denomination, only weight indicated as 200 Gs.

KM#	Date	Mintage	VG	Fine	VF	XF
139	1860 FJ	—	30.00	50.00	65.00	100.00

8 SOLES

27.0000 g, .903 SILVER, .7836 oz ASW
Reeded edge,
incuse lettering: AYACUCHO*SUCRE *1824*.

KM#	Date	VG	Fine	VF	XF
97	1827 JM	10.00	15.00	25.00	60.00
	1828 JM	10.00	15.00	25.00	60.00
	1829 JM	10.00	15.00	25.00	60.00
	1830/20 JF	17.50	25.00	40.00	80.00
	1830 JF	10.00	15.00	25.00	60.00
	1830 JF/J	30.00	50.00	90.00	120.00
	1830 J	20.00	30.00	45.00	90.00
	1830 L	30.00	50.00	90.00	120.00
	1831 JF	10.00	15.00	25.00	60.00
	1831 JL	10.00	15.00	25.00	60.00
	1832 JL	10.00	15.00	25.00	60.00
	1833 L	150.00	225.00	325.00	450.00
	1833 LM	10.00	15.00	25.00	60.00
	1834 LM	10.00	15.00	25.00	60.00
	1835 LM	17.50	25.00	40.00	80.00
	1836/5 LM	17.50	25.00	40.00	80.00
	1836 LM	10.00	15.00	25.00	60.00
	1837 LM	10.00	15.00	25.00	60.00
	1838 LM	10.00	15.00	25.00	60.00
	1839 LM	10.00	15.00	25.00	60.00
	1839 LR	20.00	30.00	45.00	90.00
	1840 LR	10.00	15.00	25.00	60.00

NOTE: Varieties exist.

103	1841 LR	—	10.00	15.00	25.00	60.00
	1841 LR (error: CONSTITUCIN)					
		—	150.00	250.00	350.00	600.00
	1842 LR	—	10.00	15.00	25.00	60.00
	1843/2 LR	—	17.50	30.00	45.00	90.00
	1843 LR	—	15.00	22.50	40.00	70.00
	1844 R	—	15.00	22.50	40.00	70.00
	1845 R	—	10.00	15.00	25.00	60.00
	1846/5 R	—	20.00	35.00	60.00	135.00
	1846 R	—	15.00	22.50	40.00	70.00
	1847 R	—	15.00	22.50	40.00	70.00
	1848 R	—	25.00	40.00	80.00	145.00
	1848 M	—	100.00	150.00	200.00	350.00

NOTE: Varieties exist.

Obv: w/o denomination.

KM#	Date Mintage	VG	Fine	VF	XF
109	1848 FM	15.00	22.50	35.00	70.00
	1849 FM	12.50	22.50	35.00	70.00
	1850 FM	10.00	20.00	32.50	65.00
	1851/50 FM	17.50	25.00	45.00	90.00
	1851 FM	10.00	20.00	32.50	65.00
	1851 FR	75.00	125.00	175.00	300.00

112.1	1852 FM	—	17.50	25.00	45.00	90.00
	1853 FP	—	40.00	80.00	125.00	200.00
	1854 M	—	40.00	80.00	125.00	200.00
	1856 FJ	—	25.00	45.00	85.00	140.00

Obv: Denomination added.

112.2	1854 MJ	—	17.50	27.50	50.00	90.00
	1855/4 MJ	—	17.50	25.00	50.00	90.00
	1855 MJ	—	12.50	20.00	35.00	75.00

NOTE: Varieties exist.

| 137 | 1859 FJ | — | 400.00 | 600.00 | 1250. | 1750. |

20.0000 g, .903 SILVER, .5807 oz ASW
Mint mark: PTS monogram
Rev. leg: PESO (weight).

138.1	1859 F.J.	—	30.00	60.00	125.00	275.00
	1859 FJ.	—	60.00	70.00	140.00	375.00

Space between CONSTITUCION 400 Gs wider.
Rev. leg: PESO over Po

| 138.2 | 1859F.J. | — | 25.00 | 40.00 | 65.00 | 110.00 |

Rev. leg: PESO changed to Po.

KM#	Date	Mintage	VG	Fine	VF	XF
138.3	1859 FJ	—	200.00	350.00	600.00	1000.

Rev. leg: W/o PESO or Po.

| 138.4 | 1859 FJ | — | 200.00 | 350.00 | 500.00 | 900.00 |

Obv: Tree divides 10Ds-20Gs.
Rev. leg: Po w/o L10D20Gs.

| 138.5 | 1860 FJ | — | 150.00 | 250.00 | 500.00 | 850.00 |

Obv: Tree divides 10Ds.–20Gs. Rev. leg: W/o Po

138.6	1859 FJ	—	75.00	125.00	200.00	350.00
	1860 FJ	—	9.00	12.50	25.00	50.00
	1861 FJ	—	9.00	12.50	25.00	50.00
	1862/1 FJ	—	9.00	12.50	25.00	50.00
	1862 FJ	—	9.00	12.50	25.00	50.00
	1862 FP	—	9.00	12.50	25.00	50.00
	1863/2 FP	—	9.00	12.50	25.00	50.00
	1863 FP	—	9.00	12.50	25.00	50.00

NOTE: Varieties exist.

1/2 SCUDO

1.7000 g, .875 GOLD, .0478 oz AGW

100	1834 LM	—	—	—	Rare	
	1838 LM	—	80.00	140.00	190.00	350.00
	1839 LM	—	80.00	130.00	185.00	325.00
	1840 LR	—	80.00	140.00	190.00	350.00

104	1841 LR/PR	—	65.00	85.00	110.00	175.00
	1841 LR	—	65.00	85.00	110.00	175.00
	1842 LR	—	65.00	85.00	110.00	175.00
	1842 LR (error) "BOLIAR" under bust					
		—	65.00	85.00	110.00	175.00
	1843 LR	—	65.00	85.00	110.00	175.00
	1844 R	—	65.00	85.00	110.00	175.00
	1845 R	—	65.00	85.00	110.00	175.00
	1846 R	—	65.00	85.00	110.00	175.00
	1847 R	—	65.00	85.00	110.00	175.00

KM#	Date	Mintage	Fine	VF	XF	Unc
113	1852 MJ	—	100.00	150.00	225.00	400.00
	1852 FP	—	85.00	125.00	200.00	375.00
	1853 FP	—	85.00	125.00	200.00	375.00
	1854 FP	—	100.00	150.00	225.00	400.00
	1855 MF/FJ	—	85.00	125.00	200.00	375.00

KM#	Date	Mintage	Fine	VF	XF	Unc
113	1855 FP	—	85.00	125.00	200.00	375.00
	1855 M	—	85.00	125.00	200.00	375.00
	1855 FS	—	85.00	125.00	200.00	375.00
	1856 FS	—	85.00	125.00	200.00	375.00
	1857 FP	—	225.00	350.00	500.00	750.00

| 140 | 1868 FE | — | 300.00 | 500.00 | 600.00 | 900.00 |

SILVER (OMS)

| 140a | 1868 FE | — | — | — | — | 450.00 |

SCUDO

3.4000 g, .875 GOLD, .0956 oz AGW

KM#	Date	Mintage	VG	Fine	VF	XF
98	1831 JL	—	95.00	130.00	225.00	250.00
	1832 JL	—	95.00	130.00	225.00	275.00
	1833 JL	—	95.00	130.00	225.00	275.00
	1834 JL	—	75.00	115.00	225.00	275.00
	1834 LM	—	95.00	130.00	225.00	275.00
	1835 LM	—	95.00	130.00	225.00	275.00
	1837 LM	—	95.00	130.00	225.00	275.00
	1838 LM	—	95.00	130.00	225.00	275.00
	1839 LM	—	95.00	130.00	225.00	275.00

105	1841 LR	—	100.00	140.00	180.00	250.00
	1842 LR	—	100.00	140.00	180.00	250.00
	1846 R	—	100.00	140.00	180.00	250.00

KM#	Date	Mintage	Fine	VF	XF	Unc
114	1852 FP	—	100.00	140.00	200.00	325.00
	1853 FP	—	100.00	140.00	200.00	325.00
	1855 LM/J	—	100.00	140.00	200.00	325.00
	1856 FJ	—	100.00	140.00	200.00	325.00

| 141 | 1868 FE | — | 200.00 | 275.00 | 425.00 | 650.00 |

| 143 | 1887 FE | — | — | Rare | — | — |

2 SCUDOS

6.8000 g, .875 GOLD, .1913 oz AGW

KM#	Date	Mintage	VG	Fine	VF	XF
101	1834 LM	—	250.00	375.00	550.00	750.00
	1835 JM	—	—	Reported, not confirmed		
	1835 LM	—	225.00	325.00	500.00	650.00
	1839 JM	—	—	Reported, not confirmed		
	1839 LM	—	—	Reported, not confirmed		

KM#	Date	Mintage	VG	Fine	VF	XF
106	1841 LR	—	400.00	550.00	750.00	1200.

4 SCUDOS

13.5000 g, .875 GOLD, .3798 oz AGW

| 102 | 1834 JL | — | 650.00 | 1000. | 1500. | 2750. |
| | 1834 LM | — | — | — | Rare | |

| 107 | 1841 LR | — | 900.00 | 1500. | 2250. | 3000. |

8 SCUDOS

27.0000 g, .875 GOLD, .7596 oz AGW

99	1831 JL	—	550.00	650.00	950.00	1500.
	1832 JL	—	550.00	650.00	950.00	1500.
	1833 JL	—	550.00	650.00	950.00	1500.
	1833 LM	—	550.00	650.00	950.00	1500.
	1834 JL	—	550.00	650.00	950.00	1500.
	1834 JM	—	650.00	750.00	1000.	1600.
	1834 LM	—	550.00	650.00	950.00	1500.
	1835 JM	—	550.00	650.00	950.00	1500.
	1835 LM	—	550.00	650.00	950.00	1500.
	1836 LM	—	650.00	750.00	1000.	1600.
	1837 LM	—	500.00	600.00	900.00	1350.
	1838 LM	—	600.00	650.00	950.00	1500.
	1839 LM	—	500.00	600.00	900.00	1350.
	1840 LR	—	500.00	600.00	900.00	1350.

108	1841 LR	—	550.00	600.00	725.00	1100.
	1842 LR	—	550.00	600.00	725.00	1100.
	1843 LR	—	550.00	600.00	725.00	1100.
	1844 LR	—	550.00	600.00	725.00	1100.
	1844 R	—	700.00	750.00	950.00	1500.
	1845 R	—	700.00	750.00	950.00	1500.
	1846 R	—	700.00	750.00	950.00	1500.
	1847 R	—	700.00	750.00	950.00	1500.

KM#	Date	Mintage	VG	Fine	VF	XF
110	1851 MF	—	900.00	1500.	2500.	4000.

KM#	Date	Mintage	Fine	VF	XF	Unc
115	1852 FP	—	3500.	6000.	8500.	12,500.

116	1852 FP	—	475.00	700.00	1200.	2200.
	1853 FP	—	475.00	700.00	1200.	2200.
	1854 M	—	475.00	700.00	1200.	1750.
	1854 MJ	—	475.00	700.00	1200.	1750.
	1855 LM	—	475.00	700.00	1200.	1750.
	1855 MJ	—	475.00	700.00	1200.	1750.
	1856 FJ/MJ	—	—	—	—	1750.
	1856 FJ	—	475.00	700.00	1200.	1750.
	1857/6 FJ	—	475.00	700.00	1200.	1750.
	1857 FJ	—	475.00	700.00	1200.	1750.

ONZA

GOLD
Obv: Value in wreath.
Rev: Arms set against weapons and flags.

| 142 | 1868 FE | — | — | — | *Rare | — |
| | 1868 FP | — | — | — | Rare | — |

*NOTE: Stack's Hammel sale 9-82 AU realized $13,000., Pacific Coast Auction Galleries, Long Beach sale 6-86 AU realized $15,500.

SILVER (OMS)

| 142a | 1868 FE | — | — | — | — | 2000. |

MELGAREJO COINAGE
1/4 MELGAREJO

.666 SILVER

KM#	Date	Mintage	VG	Fine	VF	XF
144	1865	—	8.00	15.00	25.00	100.00

NOTE: Varieties exist.

COPPER (OMS)

| 144a | 1865 | — | — | — | — | 30.00 |

BOLIVIA 202

1/2 MELGAREJO

.666 SILVER

KM#	Date	Mintage	VG	Fine	VF	XF
145	1865*	—	10.00	20.00	30.00	100.00
	1868	—	—	—	Rare	—

*NOTE: Varieties exist.

COPPER (OMS)

| 145a | 1865 | — | — | — | 50.00 | |

MELGAREJO

.666 SILVER

146	1865 FP*	—	40.00	60.00	95.00	250.00
	1866	—	—	Reported, not confirmed		

NOTE: Varieties exist:

DECIMAL COINAGE

100 Centecimos (Centavos) = 1 Boliviano
NOTE: In 1870 the weight of the silver coins was modified by adjusting it to the metric system.

CENTECIMO

COPPER

KM#	Date	Mintage	Fine	VF	XF	Unc
147	1864	.010	50.00	75.00	180.00	300.00

CENTAVO

COPPER

| 162 | 1878 | — | 20.00 | 40.00 | 80.00 | 175.00 |

Obv: Denomination under condor.
Rev: 'LA UNION ES LA FUERZA' in wreath, date below.

| 163 | 1878 | — | 100.00 | 200.00 | 350.00 | 650.00 |

| 167 | 1883A | .500 | 3.50 | 7.50 | 15.00 | 35.00 |

2 CENTECIMOS

COPPER

KM#	Date	Mintage	Fine	VF	XF	Unc
148	1864	.150	75.00	125.00	180.00	260.00

2 CENTAVOS

COPPER

| 164 | 1878 | — | 30.00 | 60.00 | 90.00 | 175.00 |

Denomination under condor.

| 165 | 1878 | — | 150.00 | 250.00 | 400.00 | 800.00 |

| 168 | 1883A | .250 | 3.50 | 7.50 | 15.00 | 50.00 |

1/20 BOLIVIANO

1.2500 g, .900 SILVER, .0361 oz ASW

149	1864 FP	—	6.50	12.50	20.00	70.00
	1865/4 FP	—	10.00	17.50	27.50	100.00
	1865 FP	—	8.00	15.00	22.50	70.00

5 CENTAVOS

1.2500 g, .900 SILVER, .0361 oz ASW
Obv: 11 stars at bottom.
Rev. leg: LA UNION HACE LA FUERZA, w/weight.

156.1	1871/0 ER	—	20.00	30.00	70.00	120.00
	1871 ER	—	125.00	—	—	—
	1871 FP	—	60.00	120.00	175.00	—

1.1500 g, .900 SILVER, .0333 oz ASW
Obv: 11 stars at bottom. Rev: W/o weight.

156.2	1871 ER	—	5.00	8.00	20.00	45.00
	1872 ER	—	95.00	185.00	—	—
	1872/1 FE	—	5.00	8.00	12.50	25.00
	1872 FE	—	6.50	10.00	20.00	45.00

Obv: 9 stars at bottom.

| 156.3 | 1872 FE | — | 4.00 | 7.00 | 15.00 | 40.00 |

Rev. leg: LA UNION ES LA FUERZA

157.1	1872 FE	—	2.00	3.50	6.00	12.50
	1873 FE	—	1.50	2.50	5.00	10.00
	1874 FE	—	2.00	4.00	7.50	15.00
	1875 FE	—	1.50	2.50	5.00	10.00
	1876 FE	—	2.00	3.00	6.00	12.00
	1877 FE	—	2.00	3.00	6.00	12.00
	1878 FE	—	2.50	3.50	6.00	12.00
	1878 FE V inverted A					
		—	5.00	10.00	17.50	40.00

KM#	Date	Mintage	Fine	VF	XF	Unc
157.1	1879 FE	—	3.50	5.00	10.00	17.50
	1879 FE V inverted A					
		—	5.00	10.00	17.50	40.00
	1880 FE	—	5.00	10.00	17.50	40.00
	1881 FE	—	2.00	3.50	5.00	12.50
	1882 FE	—	3.75	6.50	10.00	25.00
	1883 FE	—	3.50	4.75	9.00	15.00
	1884 FE	—	4.00	6.00	10.00	20.00
	1884/3 FE	—	7.00	12.50	22.50	55.00

NOTE: Varieties exist.

Reduced size lettering

157.2	1884 FE	—	—	—	—	—
	1885 FE	—	3.00	5.00	7.50	17.50
	1886 FE	—	2.75	4.00	6.00	15.00
	1887 FE	—	2.75	4.00	6.00	15.00
	1888 FE	—	3.00	5.00	7.50	17.50
	1889/8 FE	—	7.50	15.00	20.00	27.50
	1889 FE	—	5.00	8.00	11.50	20.00
	1890 CB	—	2.00	5.00	7.50	15.00
	1891 CB	—	3.00	6.50	10.00	17.50
	1893 CB	.070	2.00	3.50	6.00	12.00
	1895 ES	.020	5.00	15.00	20.00	35.00
	1899 MM	—	2.00	3.50	6.00	12.00
	1900 MM	.050	2.00	5.00	7.50	12.00

NOTE: Varieties exist.

| 169.1 | 1883A | 1.420 | 7.50 | 12.50 | 20.00 | 40.00 |

COPPER-NICKEL

| 169.2 | 1883A | .390 | 2.50 | 5.00 | 10.00 | 25.00 |

NOTE: KM#169.2 was converted from 169.1 by officially punching a center hole to prevent confusion with the silver 10 Centavos.

| 171 | 1892H | 2.000 | 3.00 | 5.00 | 10.00 | 25.00 |

NOTE: Medal rotation strike.

173	1893	2.500	3.50	6.00	12.00	27.50
	1893	—	—	—	Proof	100.00
	1895	2.000	1.00	1.75	4.00	12.00
	1897	1.500	1.00	1.75	4.00	12.00
	1899	2.000	1.00	1.75	4.00	12.00
	1902	2.000	1.00	1.75	4.00	12.00
	1907	2.000	1.75	3.75	6.50	20.00
	1908	3.000	.50	1.00	3.00	12.00
	1909	4.000	.50	1.00	3.00	12.00
	1918	.530	1.25	2.00	4.50	12.00
	1919	4.370	3.00	5.00	10.00	25.00

NOTE: The 1893, 1918 and 1919 dated coins have a medal rotation.

| 178 | 1935 | 5.000 | .50 | 1.00 | 2.00 | 5.00 |

1/10 BOLIVIANO

2.5000 g, .900 SILVER, .0723 oz ASW

KM#	Date	Mintage	VG	Fine	VF	XF
150	1864 FP	—	4.00	6.50	10.00	20.00

KM#	Date	Mintage	VG	Fine	VF	XF
150	1865 FP	—	4.00	6.00	10.00	20.00
	1866 FP	—	—	Reported, not confirmed		
	1867 FP	—	22.50	45.00	75.00	125.00

10 CENTAVOS

2.5000 g, .900 SILVER, .0723 oz ASW
Obv: 11 stars at bottom.
Rev. leg: LA UNION HACE LA FUERZA, weight in grams.

KM#	Date	Mintage	VG	Fine	VF	XF
153.1	1870 ER	—	1.50	3.00	6.00	12.00
	1871 ER	—	2.00	4.00	7.00	15.00
	1871 FP	—	3.00	6.00	12.00	20.00

NOTE: Varieties exist.

2.3000 g, .900 SILVER, .0666 oz ASW
Obv: 11 stars at bottom. Rev: W/o weight.

KM#	Date	Mintage	VG	Fine	VF	XF
153.2	1871 ER	—	2.00	5.00	10.00	17.50

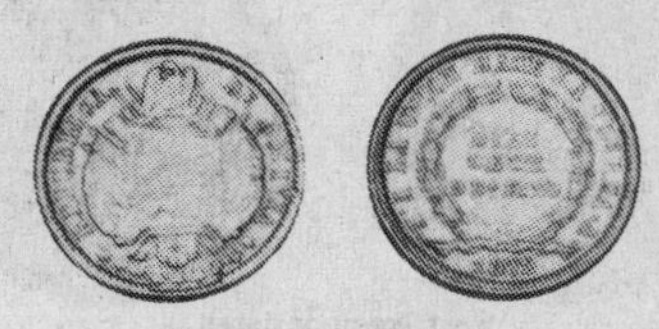

Obv: 9 stars at bottom.

KM#	Date	Mintage	VG	Fine	VF	XF
153.3	1872 FE	—	1.50	3.00	6.00	15.00

Rev. leg: LA UNION ES LA FUERZA.

KM#	Date	Mintage	VG	Fine	VF	XF
158.1	1872 FE	—	3.00	6.00	10.00	15.00
	1873 FE line below CENTS	—	3.00	6.00	10.00	15.00
	1873 FE w/o line below CENTS	—	1.25	2.25	4.50	9.00
	1874 FE line below CENTS	—	3.00	6.00	10.00	15.00
	1874 FE w/o line below CENTS	—	1.25	2.25	4.50	9.00
	1875 FE	—	1.25	2.00	4.00	8.00
	1876 FE	—	1.25	2.00	4.00	8.00
	1877 FE	—	1.25	2.00	4.00	8.00
	1878 FE	—	1.50	2.50	5.00	10.00
	1879 FE	—	1.25	2.00	4.00	8.00
	1880 FE	—	1.25	2.25	4.50	9.00
	1881 FE	—	1.25	2.00	4.00	8.00
	1882 FE	—	1.50	2.50	5.00	10.00
	1883 FE line below CENTS	—	1.50	2.50	5.00	10.00
	1883 FE w/o line below CENTS	—	1.50	2.50	5.00	10.00
	1883/2 FE w/o line below CENTS	—	1.50	2.50	5.00	10.00
	1884/3 FE line below CENTS	—	3.00	5.00	10.00	17.50
	1884/3 FE w/o line below CENTS	—	3.00	5.00	10.00	17.50

Reduced size lettering

KM#	Date	Mintage	VG	Fine	VF	XF
158.2	1884 FE	—	3.00	6.00	10.00	15.00
	1885 FE	—	1.50	2.50	5.00	10.00
	1886 FE	—	1.25	2.00	4.00	8.00
	1887 FE	—	5.00	8.00	15.00	27.50
	1888 FE	—	10.00	15.00	25.00	42.50
	1889 FE	—	2.50	5.00	10.00	17.50
	1890 FE	—	2.50	5.00	10.00	17.50
	1890 CB	—	2.50	5.00	10.00	17.50
	1891 CB	—	1.50	3.00	6.00	12.00
	1893 CB	.050	1.50	3.00	6.00	12.00
	1895 ES	.020	4.00	7.00	13.50	20.00
	1899 MM	—	1.50	3.00	6.00	12.00
	1900 MM	.030	2.00	4.00	7.50	15.00

COPPER-NICKEL

KM#	Date	Mintage	Fine	VF	XF	Unc
170.1	1883A	.140	3.75	7.50	15.00	45.00

KM#	Date	Mintage	Fine	VF	XF	Unc
170.2	1883A	.320	3.00	6.00	12.50	30.00

NOTE: KM#170.2 was converted from 170.1 by officially punching a center hole to prevent confusion with the silver 20 Centavos.

KM#	Date	Mintage	Fine	VF	XF	Unc
172	1892H	1.000	2.25	5.00	10.00	35.00

NOTE: Medal rotation strike.

KM#	Date	Mintage	Fine	VF	XF	Unc
174	1893	1.250	5.00	10.00	15.00	30.00
	1893	—	—	—	Proof	125.00
	1895	1.000	4.00	8.00	17.50	30.00
	1897	2.250	1.00	2.00	4.00	12.00
	1899	3.000	1.00	2.00	4.00	12.00
	1901	—	17.50	27.50	45.00	75.00
	1902	8.500	.50	1.00	3.00	12.00
	1907/2	4.000	1.25	2.50	5.00	15.00
	1907	Inc. Ab.	.50	1.00	3.00	12.00
	1908	6.000	.50	1.00	3.00	12.00
	1909	8.000	.50	1.00	3.00	12.00
	1918	1.335	1.00	2.00	4.00	12.00
	1919	6.165	.50	1.00	3.00	12.00

NOTE: Coins dated 1893, 1918 and 1919 are struck w/medal rotation.

Rev: Wide 0 in value.

KM#	Date	Mintage	Fine	VF	XF	Unc
179.1	1935	10.000	.25	.50	1.50	3.00
	1936	10.000	.25	.50	1.50	3.00

NOTE: Coins are struck with medal rotation.

Rev: Narrow 0 in value.

KM#	Date	Mintage	Fine	VF	XF	Unc
179.2	1939	—	1.25	1.50	2.00	3.00

NOTE: Coins are struck w/medal rotation.

KM#	Date	Mintage	Fine	VF	XF	Unc
180	1937	20.000	.25	.50	1.25	2.50

NOTE: Medal rotation strike.

ZINC

KM#	Date	Mintage	Fine	VF	XF	Unc
179a	1942	10.000	.75	1.25	2.00	3.50

NOTE: Medal rotation strike.

1/5 BOLIVIANO

5.0000 g, .900 SILVER, .1446 oz ASW
Obv: Large stars.

KM#	Date	Mintage	VG	Fine	VF	XF
151.1	1864 FP	—	5.00	10.00	20.00	45.00

NOTE: Varieties exist in the space between stars.

Obv: Small, closely spaced stars.

KM#	Date	Mintage	VG	Fine	VF	XF
151.2	1865 FP	—	3.50	7.50	15.00	35.00
	1866 FP	—	3.50	7.50	15.00	35.00
	1866/5 FP	—	5.00	10.00	20.00	45.00

20 CENTAVOS

5.0000 g, .900 SILVER, .1446 oz ASW
Obv: 11 stars at bottom.
Rev. leg: LA UNION HACE LA FUERZA, weight.

KM#	Date	Mintage	VG	Fine	VF	XF
154.1	1870 ER	—	20.00	30.00	50.00	80.00
	1871 ER	—	10.00	22.00	40.00	65.00

4.6000 g, .900 SILVER, .1331 oz ASW
Obv: 11 stars. Rev: W/o weight.

KM#	Date	Mintage	VG	Fine	VF	XF
154.2	1871 ER	—	12.00	25.00	50.00	85.00

Obv: 9 stars at bottom

KM#	Date	Mintage	VG	Fine	VF	XF
154.3	1871 ER	—	8.00	15.00	25.00	45.00
	1872 ER	—	10.00	20.00	35.00	55.00
	1872 FE	—	2.50	5.00	10.00	25.00

Rev. leg: LA UNION ES LA FUERZA

KM#	Date	Mintage	VG	Fine	VF	XF
159.1	1872 FE	—	3.00	4.50	7.00	15.00
	1873 FE	—	1.50	3.00	6.00	10.00
	1874 FE	—	3.00	4.50	7.00	15.00
	1875 FE	—	2.25	3.00	5.00	8.00
	1876 FE	—	2.25	3.00	6.00	9.00
	1877 FE	—	2.25	3.00	5.00	8.00
	1878 FE	—	2.25	3.00	5.00	8.00
	1879 FE	—	2.25	3.00	5.00	8.00
	1880 FE	—	2.25	3.00	5.00	8.00
	1881 FE	—	2.25	3.00	5.00	8.00
	1882 FE	—	2.25	3.00	5.00	8.00
	1883 FE	—	2.25	3.00	5.00	8.00
	1883 EF	—	12.50	20.00	30.00	50.00
	1884/3 FE	—	4.00	6.00	12.50	20.00
	1884 FE	—	2.25	3.00	5.00	8.00
	1885/75 FE	—	5.00	7.50	15.00	25.00
	1885 FE	—	5.00	7.50	10.00	15.00

Daza Commemorative

KM#	Date	Mintage	VG	Fine	VF	XF
166	1879	—	22.50	37.50	55.00	80.00

NOTE: Varieties exist.

BOLIVIA 204

Reduced size lettering

KM#	Date	Mintage	VG	Fine	VF	XF
159.2	1885 FE	—	2.25	3.00	5.00	8.00
	1886 FE	—	2.25	3.00	6.00	9.00
	1887 FE	—	2.25	3.00	5.00	8.00
	1888 FE	—	2.25	3.00	5.00	8.00
	1889 FE	—	2.25	3.00	5.00	8.00
	1889/8 FE	—	2.50	4.00	6.50	10.00
	1890 FE	—	2.25	3.00	5.00	8.00
	1890 CB	—	2.25	3.00	5.00	8.00
	1891 CB	—	2.25	3.50	6.00	9.00
	1892/82 CB	—	3.00	5.00	10.00	17.50
	1892 CB	—	2.25	3.50	6.00	9.00
	1893 CB	.500	2.25	3.00	5.00	8.00
	1894 ES	.490	2.25	4.50	7.00	15.00
	1895 ES	—	2.25	3.50	6.00	9.00
	1896 ES	.100	2.25	3.00	5.00	8.00
	1896 CB Inc. Ab.		4.50	8.00	15.00	25.00
	1897 CB	.170	2.25	3.00	5.00	8.00
	1898 CB	—	10.00	15.00	25.00	35.00
	1899 CB	—	—	—	Rare	—
	1899 MM	—	2.25	3.50	6.00	9.00
	1900 MM	.170	2.25	3.50	6.00	9.00
	1901 MM	.040	2.50	4.50	8.00	12.00
	1901 MM/MW		2.50	5.00	13.50	20.00
	1902 MM	—	6.50	10.00	20.00	30.00
	1903 MM	.010	10.00	15.00	25.00	40.00
	1904 MM	—	7.00	12.00	20.00	30.00
	1907 MM	—	50.00	100.00	150.00	250.00

NOTE: Varieties exist.

4.0000 g, .833 SILVER, .1071 oz ASW

| 176 | 1909H | 1.500 | 1.50 | 4.00 | 6.00 | 9.00 |

ZINC

| 183 | 1942 | 10.000 | .75 | 1.50 | 3.00 | 6.00 |

NOTE: Medal rotation strike.

50 CENTAVOS
(1/2 Boliviano)

12.5000 g, .900 SILVER, .3617 oz ASW
Rev. leg: 12 GS. 500 MS. 9 DS. FINO
| 161.1 | 1873 FE | — | 5.50 | 7.00 | 12.00 | 20.00 |

Rev. leg: 12 GMS 500 MMS
| 161.2 | 1873 FE | — | 20.00 | 30.00 | 50.00 | 125.00 |

Rev: W/o 50 Cents and weight.
| 161.3 | 1879/7 FE | — | 75.00 | 125.00 | 225.00 | 350.00 |
| | 1882 FE | — | 75.00 | 125.00 | 200.00 | 275.00 |

11.5000 g, .900 SILVER, .3328 oz ASW
Rev: Reduced size lettering w/weight.
161.4	1884 FE	—	—	—	Rare	—
	1887 FE	—	—	—	Rare	—
	1889 MM	—	—	—	Rare	—

KM#	Date	Mintage	VG	Fine	VF	XF
161.4	1891 CB(error)	—	40.00	60.00	100.00	225.00

Rev: Reduced size lettering w/o weight.
161.5	1891 CB	—	BV	3.50	6.00	11.00
	1892 CB	—	BV	3.50	6.00	11.00
	1893 CB	3.150	BV	3.50	6.00	11.00
	1894/1 CB	2.470	BV	3.50	6.00	11.00
	1894 CB	I.A.	BV	3.50	6.00	11.00
	1894/84 ES	—	—	—	—	—
	1894 ES	I.A.	BV	3.50	6.00	11.00
	1895 ES	3.390	BV	3.50	6.00	11.00
	1896 ES	2.980	BV	3.50	6.00	11.00
	1897 CB	2.300	BV	3.50	6.00	11.00
	1897 ES	—	BV	3.50	6.00	11.00
	1898 CB	—	BV	3.50	6.00	11.00
	1899 CB	—	BV	3.50	6.00	11.00
	1899 MM	—	BV	3.50	6.00	11.00
	1900 MM	3.820	BV	3.50	6.00	11.00

175.1	1900 MM	I.A.	BV	3.50	6.00	12.00
	1901/0 MM	2.000	BV	3.50	6.00	11.00
	1901 MM	I.A.	BV	3.50	6.00	11.00
	1902 MM	1.530	BV	3.50	6.00	11.00
	1903 MM	.690	BV	3.50	6.00	11.00
	1904 MM	1.290	BV	3.50	6.00	11.00
	1905 MM	1.690	BV	3.50	6.00	11.00
	1905 AB	I.A.	BV	3.50	6.00	11.00
	1906 MM	.630	BV	3.50	6.00	11.00
	1906 AB	5.500	BV	3.50	6.00	11.00
	1907 MM	.050	BV	3.50	6.00	11.00
	1908 MM	—	BV	3.50	6.00	11.00
	1908 MM inverted 8		BV	7.00	18.00	35.00

| 175.2 | 1900So | .900 | BV | 6.50 | 9.00 | 17.50 |

.900 GOLD (OMS)
| 175.2a | 1900So | — | — | 3500. | 5000. | |

10.0000 g, .833 SILVER, .2678 oz ASW
| KM# | Date | Mintage | Fine | VF | XF | Unc |
| 177 | 1909H | 1.400 | BV | 5.00 | 7.50 | 15.00 |

COPPER-NICKEL
| 181 | 1937 | 8.000 | 10.00 | 20.00 | 30.00 | 60.00 |

NOTE: Most remelted upon receipt in Bolivia.

KM#	Date	Mintage	Fine	VF	XF	Unc
182	1939	—	.25	.50	.75	3.00

NOTE: Medal rotation strike.

BRONZE
| 182a.1 | 1942 | 10.000 | .25 | .50 | 1.00 | 4.00 |

NOTE: Medal rotation strike.

Restrike-poor detail
| 182a.2 | 1942 | 5.310 | .25 | .50 | 1.00 | 4.00 |

NOTE: Medal rotation strike.

BOLIVIANO

25.0000 g, .900 SILVER, .7234 oz ASW
Obv: 9 stars

KM#	Date	Mintage	VG	Fine	VF	XF
152.1	1864 FP	—	12.50	17.50	30.00	65.00
	1864 FP inverted P		15.00	30.00	50.00	100.00
	1865/1 FP	—	15.00	25.00	45.00	90.00
	1865/4 FP	—	15.00	25.00	45.00	90.00
	1865 FP	—	10.00	15.00	25.00	55.00
	1866/5 FP	—	—	—	Rare	—
	1866 FP	—	10.00	15.00	25.00	55.00
	1866 PF	—	—	—	Rare	—
	1867/6 FP	—	12.50	20.00	35.00	70.00
	1867 FP	—	12.50	17.50	30.00	65.00
	1868 FP	—	—	—	Rare	—

Obv: Larger shield.
| 152.2 | 1864 FP | — | 30.00 | 60.00 | 90.00 | 135.00 |

Obv: 11 stars. Rev: Similar to KM#152.1.
152.3	1867/6 FP	—	7.50	12.50	22.50	45.00
	1867/6 FE/P	—	10.00	15.00	25.00	55.00
	1867 FE	—	7.50	12.50	18.00	35.00
	1867 FE/P	—	—	—	—	—
	1867 FP	—	12.50	20.00	35.00	70.00
	1868/7 FE	.720	12.50	20.00	35.00	70.00
	1868 FE Inc. Ab.		7.50	12.50	18.00	35.00
	1869 FE	.260	12.50	20.00	35.00	70.00
	1869 FP	—	—	—	—	—

Rev: Large wreath, leg: 25 GMS 9DS FINO.
| 155.1 | 1870 ER* | — | 10.00 | 12.50 | 20.00 | 27.50 |

BOLIVIA 205

Rev. leg: LA UNION HACE LA FUERZA, small wreath.

KM#	Date	Mintage	VG	Fine	VF	XF
155.2	1870 ER*	—	10.00	12.50	20.00	35.00
	1871 ER*	—	10.00	12.50	20.00	35.00
	1871 FP*	—	12.50	15.00	25.00	40.00

Obv: 9 stars at bottom. Rev: Similar to KM#155.1.

155.3	1870 ER*	—	15.00	25.00	35.00	65.00
	1871 ER*	—	12.50	18.50	25.00	55.00
	1871 FP*	—	12.50	18.50	25.00	55.00
	1871 EF	—	12.50	18.50	25.00	55.00
	1872 FE	—	20.00	32.50	50.00	85.00
	1872 FE (error: EA FUERZA)					
		—	60.00	100.00	200.00	—

Rev: Large wreath, leg: 25 G 9D FINO.

155.4	1870 ER	—	40.00	60.00	120.00	180.00

*NOTE: Several varieties exist.

Rev. leg: LA UNION ES LA FUERZA

160.1	1872 FE	—	10.00	12.50	20.00	27.50
	1873 FE	—	10.00	12.50	20.00	27.50
	1874 FE stars widely spaced					
		—	10.00	12.50	20.00	27.50
	1874 FE stars closely spaced					
		—	12.50	17.50	30.00	65.00
	1875 FE	—	12.50	15.00	25.00	27.50
	1877/6 FE	—	100.00	175.00	300.00	500.00
	1877 FE	—	40.00	60.00	120.00	180.00

Rev. leg: 25 GS instead of GMS.

160.2	1879 F.E.	—	60.00	120.00	225.00	375.00

Rev. leg: 25 GMS, horizontal bar between denomination and weight.

160.3	1884 FE	—	—	—	Rare	—
	1887 FE	—	—	—	Rare	—
	1893 CB	—	—	—	Rare	—
	1893 FE	—	40.00	60.00	120.00	180.00

BRONZE

KM#	Date	Mintage	Fine	VF	XF	Unc
184	1951	10.000	.10	.20	.40	1.00
	1951	10 pcs.	—	—	Proof	175.00
	1951H	15.000	.10	—	.40	1.50
	1951KN	15.000	.25	.50	1.00	3.00

NOTE: Medal rotation strike.

5 BOLIVIANOS

BRONZE

185	1951	7.000	.25	.50	.75	2.00
	1951	—	—	—	Proof	—
	1951H	15.000	.25	.50	.75	2.50
	1951KN	15.000	.60	.90	1.25	3.50

NOTE: Medal rotation strike.

10 BOLIVIANOS
(1 Bolivar)

BRONZE

186	1951	40.000	.75	1.25	2.00	4.00
	1951	—	—	—	Proof	—

NOTE: Medal rotation strike.

MONETARY REFORM
100 Centavos = 1 Peso Boliviano

5 CENTAVOS

COPPER-CLAD STEEL

187	1965	10.000	.10	.20	.40	1.00
	1970	.100	.20	.30	.65	1.50

10 CENTAVOS

COPPER-CLAD STEEL

188	1965	10.000	.10	.25	.50	1.00
	1967	—	.10	.20	.40	1.00
	1969	5.700	.10	.20	.40	1.00
	1971	.200	.15	.25	.50	1.00
	1972	.100	.20	.40	.80	1.50
	1973	6.000	.10	.20	.40	1.00

20 CENTAVOS

NICKEL-CLAD STEEL

189	1965	5.000	.20	.40	.60	1.50
	1967	—	.20	.40	.60	1.00
	1970	.400	.20	.40	.75	2.00
	1971	.400	.20	.40	.75	2.00
	1973	5.000	.20	.40	.60	1.50

25 CENTAVOS

NICKEL-CLAD STEEL

193	1971	—	.15	.30	.60	1.00
	1972	9.998	.10	.15	.25	.50

50 CENTAVOS

NICKEL-CLAD STEEL

KM#	Date	Mintage	Fine	VF	XF	Unc
190	1965	10.000	—	.10	.40	1.00
	1967	—	—	.10	.40	1.00
	1972	—	—	.10	.40	1.00
	1973	5.000	—	.10	.40	1.00
	1974	15.000	—	.10	.40	1.00
	1978	5.000	—	.10	.40	1.00
	1980	3.600	—	.10	.40	1.00

PESO BOLIVIANO

NICKEL-CLAD STEEL
F.A.O. Issue

191	1968	.040	—	3.00	5.00	10.00

192	1968	10.000	.20	.35	.75	1.50
	1969	—	.20	.35	.75	1.50
	1970	10.000	.15	.25	.75	1.50
	1972	—	.20	.35	.75	1.50
	1973	5.000	.15	.25	.75	1.50
	1974	15.000	.15	.25	.75	1.50
	1978	10.000	.15	.25	.75	1.50
	1980	2.993	.15	.25	.75	1.50

5 PESOS BOLIVIANOS

NICKEL-CLAD STEEL

197	1976	20.000	1.25	1.75	2.50	5.00
	1978	10.000	1.25	1.75	2.50	5.00
	1980	5.231	1.25	1.75	2.50	5.00

100 PESOS BOLIVIANOS

10.0000 g, .933 SILVER, .3000 oz ASW
Sesquicentenario Commemorative

194	1975	.160	—	—	5.00	8.00

BOLIVIA

200 PESOS BOLIVIANOS

23.3300 g, .925 SILVER, .6938 oz ASW
International Year of the Child

KM#	Date	Mintage	Fine	VF	XF	Unc
198	1979	.576	—	—	Proof	30.00

250 PESOS BOLIVIANOS

15.0000 g, .933 SILVER, .4500 oz ASW
Sesquicentenario Commemorative

| 195 | 1975 | .140 | — | — | 6.00 | 12.00 |

500 PESOS BOLIVIANOS

22.0000 g, .933 SILVER, .6600 oz ASW
Sesquicentenario Commemorative

| 196 | 1975 | .100 | — | — | 8.50 | 18.00 |

4000 PESOS BOLIVIANOS

17.1700 g, .900 GOLD, .4968 oz AGW
International Year of the Child

| 199 | 1979 | 6,315 | — | — | Proof | 275.00 |

MONETARY REFORM

1,000,000 Peso Bolivianos = 1 Boliviano
100 Centavos = 1 Boliviano

2 CENTAVOS

STAINLESS STEEL

| 200 | 1987 | — | — | — | — | .25 |

5 CENTAVOS

STAINLESS STEEL

| 201 | 1987 | — | — | — | — | .25 |

10 CENTAVOS

STAINLESS STEEL

KM#	Date	Mintage	Fine	VF	XF	Unc
202	1987	—	—	—	—	.25

20 CENTAVOS

STAINLESS STEEL

| 203 | 1987 | — | — | — | — | .25 |

50 CENTAVOS

STAINLESS STEEL

| 204 | 1987 | — | — | — | — | .50 |

BOLIVIANO

STAINLESS STEEL

| 205 | 1987 | — | — | — | — | 1.00 |

BOTSWANA

The Republic of Botswana (formerly Bechuanaland), located in south central Africa between Southwest Africa (Namibia) and Zimbabwe, has an area of 231,805 sq. mi. (600,372 sq. km.) and a population of 800,323. Capital: Gaborone. Botswana is a member of a Customs Union with South Africa, Lesotho, and Swaziland. The economy is primarily pastoral with a rapidly developing mining industry, of which diamonds, copper and nickel are the chief elements. Meat products and diamonds comprise 85 percent of the exports.

Little is known of the origin of the peoples of Botswana. The early inhabitants, the Bushmen, did not develop a recorded history and are now dying out. The ancestors of the present Botswana residents probably arrived about 1600AD in Bantu migrations from the north and east. Bechuanaland was first united early in the 19th century under Chief Khama III to more effectively resist incursions by the Boer trekkers from Transvaal and by the neighboring Matabeles. As the Boer threat intensified, appeals for protection were made to the British Government, which proclaimed the whole of Bechuanaland a British protectorate in 1885. In 1895, the southern part of the protectorate was annexed to Cape Province. The northern part, known as the Bechuanaland Protectorate, remained under British administration until it became the independent Republic of Botswana on Sept. 30, 1966. Botswana is a member of the Commonwealth of Nations. The president is Chief of State and Head of Government.

MINT MARKS

B - Berne

MONETARY SYSTEM

100 Cents = 1 Thebe

50 CENTS

10.0000 g, .800 SILVER, .2572 oz ASW
Independence Commemorative

KM#	Date	Mintage	VF	XF	Unc
1	1966B	40,200	2.50	3.50	5.50
	1966B	—	—	Proof	8.00

10 THEBE

11.3000 g, .900 GOLD, .3270 oz AGW
Independence Commemorative

| 2 | 1966B | 5,100 | — | Proof | 200.00 |

MONETARY REFORM

100 Thebe = 1 Pula

THEBE

ALUMINUM

3	1976	15.000	.10	.15	.25
	1976	.026	—	Proof	.75
	1981	.010	—	Proof	1.00
	1983	5.000	.10	.15	.20
	1984	5.000	.10	.15	.20

2 THEBE

BRONZE
F.A.O. Issue

KM#	Date	Mintage	VF	XF	Unc
14	1981	9.990	—	—	.35
	1981	.010	—	Proof	1.00

5 THEBE

BRONZE

4	1976	3.000	.10	.20	.40
	1976	.026	—	Proof	1.00
	1977	.250	.10	.20	.40
	1979	.200	.10	.20	.40
	1980	1.000	.10	.20	.40
	1981	4.990	.10	.20	.40
	1981	.010	—	Proof	1.25
	1984	2.000	.10	.20	.40

10 THEBE

COPPER-NICKEL

5	1976	1.500	.15	.25	.60
	1976	.026	—	Proof	1.50
	1977	.500	.15	.25	.50
	1979	.750	.15	.25	.50
	1980	—	.15	.25	.50
	1981	2.590	Reported, not confirmed		
	1981	.010	—	Proof	1.75
	1984	4.000	.15	.25	.50

25 THEBE

COPPER-NICKEL

6	1976	1.500	.25	.50	1.20
	1976	.026	—	Proof	2.00
	1977	.265	.25	.50	1.30
	1980	—	.25	.50	1.30
	1981	.740			confirmed
	1981	.010	—	Proof	2.50
	1982	.400	.25	.50	1.30
	1984	2.000	.25	.50	1.30

50 THEBE

COPPER-NICKEL

7	1976	.266	.50	1.00	2.00
	1976	.026	—	Proof	3.00
	1977	.250	.50	1.00	2.00
	1980	—	.50	1.00	2.00
	1981	—	Reported, not confirmed		
	1981	.010	—	Proof	3.50
	1984	2.000	.50	1.00	2.00

PULA

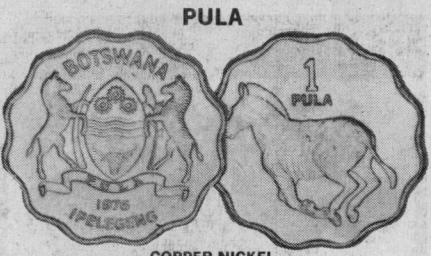

COPPER-NICKEL

KM#	Date	Mintage	VF	XF	Unc
8	1976	.166	1.00	1.50	3.75
	1976	.026	—	Proof	5.00
	1977	.500	1.00	1.50	3.00
	1981	—	1.00	1.50	3.00
	1981	.010	—	Proof	5.50

2 PULA

28.2800 g, .500 SILVER, .4546 oz ASW
Commonwealth Games

| 17 | 1986 | *.050 | — | — | 12.00 |

28.2800 g, .925 SILVER, .8411 oz ASW

| 17a | 1986 | *.020 | — | Proof | 20.00 |

Wildlife - Slaty Egret

| 18 | 1986 | *.025 | — | Proof | 20.00 |

5 PULA

28.2800 g, .500 SILVER, .4546 oz ASW
10th Anniversary of Independence

KM#	Date	Mintage	VF	XF	Unc
9	1976	.031	—	—	15.00

28.2800 g, .925 SILVER, .8411 oz ASW

| 9a | 1976 | .022 | — | Proof | 25.00 |

28.5000 g, .500 SILVER, .4582 oz ASW
Conservation Series
Obv: Similar to 150 Pula, KM#13.
Rev: Gemsbok.

| 11 | 1978 | 4,026 | — | — | 30.00 |

28.5000 g, .925 SILVER, .8477 oz ASW

| 11a | 1978 | 4,172 | — | Proof | 35.00 |

International Year of Disabled Persons

| 15 | 1981 | .013 | — | — | 20.00 |
| | 1981 | .011 | — | Proof | 30.00 |

15.9800 g, .917 GOLD, .4711 oz AGW
Wildlife - Red Lechwes

| 19 | 1986 | *5,000 | — | Proof | 475.00 |

COPPER-NICKEL
Pope's Visit

| 20 | 1988 | *.050 | — | — | 8.00 |

28.2800 g, .925 SILVER, .8411 oz ASW

| 20a | 1988 | *5,000 | — | Proof | 45.00 |

COPPER-NICKEL
Olympics - Runners

| 21 | 1988 | — | — | — | 4.00 |

BOTSWANA 208

28.2800 g, .925 SILVER, .8411 oz ASW

KM#	Date	Mintage	VF	XF	Unc
21a	1988	*.025	—	Proof	45.00

10 PULA

35.0000 g, .500 SILVER, .5627 oz ASW
Conservation Series
Obv: Similar to 150 Pula, KM#13.
Rev: Klipspringer.

| 12 | 1978 | 4,088 | — | — | 35.00 |

35.0000 g, .925 SILVER, 1.0408 oz ASW

| 12a | 1978 | 3,989 | — | Proof | 45.00 |

150 PULA

15.9800 g, .917 GOLD, .4711 oz AGW
10th Anniversary of Independence

| 10 | 1976 | 2,520 | — | — | 225.00 |
| | 1976 | 2,000 | — | Proof | 275.00 |

33.4370 g, .900 GOLD, .9676 oz AGW
Conservation Series
Rev: Brown Hyaena.

| 13 | 1978 | 664 pcs. | — | — | 550.00 |
| | 1978 | 219 pcs. | — | Proof | 800.00 |

15.9800 g, .917 GOLD, .4711 oz AGW
International Year of Disabled Persons

| 16 | 1981 | 4,158 | — | — | 275.00 |
| | 1981 | 4,155 | — | Proof | 400.00 |

MINT SETS (MS)

KM#	Date	Mintage	Identification	Issue Price	Mkt. Val.
MS1	1978(2)	—	KM11,12	—	65.00

PROOF SETS (PS)

PS1	1976(6)	20,000	KM3-8	18.00	14.00
PS2	1978(2)	5,850	KM11a,12a	—	85.00
PS3	1981(7)	10,000	KM3-8,16	33.00	16.00

BRAZIL

The Federative Republic of Brazil, which comprises half the continent of South America and is the only Latin American country deriving its culture and language from Portugal, has an area of 3,286,488 sq. mi. (8,511,965 sq. km.) and a population of 127.7 million. Capital: Brasilia. The economy of Brazil is as varied and complex as any in the developing world. Agriculture is a mainstay of the economy, although but 4 percent of the area is under cultivation. Known mineral resources are almost unlimited in variety and size of reserves. A large, relatively sophisticated industry ranges from basic steel and chemical production to finished consumer goods. Coffee, cotton, iron ore and cocoa are the chief exports.

Brazil was discovered and claimed for Portugal by Admiral Pedro Alvares Cabral in 1500. Portugal established a settlement in 1532 and proclaimed the area a royal colony in 1549. During the Napoleonic Wars, Dom Joao VI established the seat of Portuguese government in Rio de Janeiro. when he returned to Portugal, his son Dom Pedro I declared Brazil's independence on Sept. 7, 1822, and became emperor of Brazil. The Empire of Brazil was maintained until 1889 when the federal republic was established. The Federative Republic that exists today was established in 1946 by terms of a constitution drawn up by a constituent assembly.

RULERS
Dutch
Maria I, Widow, 1786-1805
 As Regent, 1799-1805
Joao, Prince Regent, 1799-1818
Joao VI, 1818-1822
 Brazilean
Pedro I, 1822-1831
Pedro II, 1831-1889

MINT MARKS
(a) - Paris, privy marks only
A - Berlin 1913
B - Bahia 1714-1831
C - Cuiaba (Mato Grosso) 1823-1833
G - Goias 1823-1833
M - Minas Gerais 1823-1828
P - Pernambuco (supposedly all counterfeit)
R - Rio de Janeiro 1703-1834
Rs - Rio de Janeiro 1869
Rs. - Brussels 1869
SP - Sao Paulo 1825-1832
W/o mintmark - Lisbon 1715-1805

MONETARY SYSTEM
(Until 1833)
120 Reis = 1 Real
6400 Reis 1 Peca (Dobra = Johannes (Joe)
 = 4 Escudos
(1833-1942)
1000 Reis = 1 Milreis
(1942-1967)
100 Centavos = 1 Cruzeiro

COLONIAL COINAGE
X (10) REIS

COPPER
Mint: Lisbon, w/o mint mark.

Obv. leg: JOANNES.D.G.P.E. BRASILIAE....

KM#	Date	Mintage	VG	Fine	VF	XF
232.1	1802	.612	1.00	3.00	5.00	10.00
(C80.1)	1803	1.167	1.00	3.00	5.00	10.00
	1805	1.248	1.00	3.00	5.00	10.00

Mint mark: R

232.2	1805	—	1.00	3.00	5.00	12.00
(C80.2)	1806	—	3.00	8.00	12.00	20.00
	1812	—	—	—	Rare	—
	1814	—	3.00	8.00	12.00	20.00
	1815	—	1.00	3.00	5.00	12.00

Mint mark: B

232.3	1815	—	2.00	4.00	6.00	15.00
(C80.3)	1816	—	2.00	4.00	6.00	15.00
	1818	—	3.00	7.00	10.00	30.00

Mint mark: R
Obv. leg: JOANNES VI.D.G.PORT....

314.1	1818	—	1.10	2.75	4.75	11.50
(C105.1)	1819	—	.75	2.00	3.75	8.50
	1820	—	.75	2.00	3.75	8.50
	1821	—	.65	1.75	3.25	7.50
	1822	—	.65	1.75	3.25	7.50

Mint mark: B

314.2	1821	—	.75	2.00	5.00	10.00
(C105.2)	1822	—	1.25	3.00	7.00	15.00
	1823	—	1.25	3.00	7.00	16.00

XX (20) REIS
COPPER
Mint: Lisbon, w/o mint mark.
Obv. leg: JOANNES D.G.PORT.ET.BRAS.P.REGENS

| 233.1 | 1802 | .788 | 1.10 | 2.75 | 4.50 | 10.00 |
| (C81.1) | 1803 | 1.920 | 1.10 | 2.75 | 4.50 | 10.00 |

Mint mark: B

233.2	1812	—	1.50	3.75	7.50	15.00
(C81.2)	1813	—	1.10	2.75	5.00	10.00
	1815	—	1.25	3.00	5.00	10.00
	1816	—	1.25	3.00	5.00	10.00

Mint mark: R

233.3	1812	—	4.00	8.00	18.00	25.00
(C81.3)	1813	—	3.00	6.00	12.00	16.00
	1814	—	3.00	6.00	12.00	16.00
	1815	—	3.00	6.00	12.00	16.00
	1817	—	4.00	8.00	18.00	25.00
	1818	—	4.00	8.00	18.00	25.00

Obv. leg: JOANNES D.G.PORT.BRAS.ET ALG.

| 309 | 1816 | — | 4.00 | 8.00 | 16.00 | 25.00 |
| (C82) | | | | | | |

Minted for Goias and Mato Grosso
Obv. leg: JOANNES D.G.P.E..... crowned value.
Rev. leg: PECUNIA.TOTUM.CIRCUMIT.... globe.

| 315 | 1818 | — | 4.00 | 7.00 | 17.00 | 25.00 |
| (C86) | | | | | | |

Obv. leg: JOANNES. VI. D.G.PORT.....

316.1	1818	—	1.50	3.75	7.50	15.00
(C106.1)	1819	—	1.00	2.50	5.00	10.00
	1820	—	1.00	2.50	5.00	10.00
	1821	—	2.50	6.00	10.00	20.00
	1822	—	1.00	2.50	5.00	10.00

Mint mark: B

| 316.2 | 1820 | — | 1.50 | 3.75 | 7.50 | 15.00 |
| (C106.2) | 1821 | — | 1.50 | 3.75 | 7.50 | 15.00 |

37-1/2 REIS

COPPER
Mint mark: M
Minted for Minas Gerais

Obv. leg: JOANNES.VI.D.G.PORT.BRAS...crowned value
Rev. leg: PECUNIA.TOTUM.CIRCUMIT...globe

KM#	Date	Mintage	VG	Fine	VF	XF
317.1	1818	—	8.00	20.00	40.00	60.00
(C109.1)	1819	—	8.00	20.00	40.00	60.00
	1821	—	8.00	20.00	40.00	60.00

Mint mark: R

317.2	1818	—	20.00	40.00	110.00	180.00
(C109.2)						

XL (40) REIS

COPPER
Mint mark: B
Rev: Similar to 10 Reis, KM#232.1.

234.1	1802	.584	1.50	3.75	7.50	15.00
(C83.1)	1803	1.143	1.50	3.75	7.50	15.00
234.2	1809	—	2.50	6.00	10.00	20.00
(C83.2)	1810	—	2.50	6.00	10.00	20.00
	1811	—	1.75	4.50	8.50	17.50
	1812	—	1.50	3.75	7.50	15.00
	1814	—	1.50	3.75	7.50	15.00
	1816	—	1.50	3.75	7.50	15.00

Mint mark: R

234.3	1812	—	2.50	6.00	10.00	20.00
(C83.3)	1813	—	2.50	6.00	10.00	20.00
	1815	—	2.50	6.00	12.50	25.00
	1816	—	2.50	6.00	10.00	20.00
	1817	—	6.00	15.00	25.00	45.00

Mint mark: B
Obv. leg: JOANNES.D.G.P.ET.BRAS.P.REGENS., smaller crown.

310	1816	—	3.00	10.00	20.00	40.00
(C83.4)						

Mint mark: R
Obv. leg: JOANNES D.G. PORT.BRAS...

311	1816	—	3.00	7.50	15.00	30.00
(C84)						

Minted for Goias and Mato Grosso
Obv. leg: JOANNES.D.G.P.E....crowned value.
Rev. leg: PECUNIA.TOTUM.CIRCUMIT....globe.

318	1818	—	15.00	40.00	160.00	200.00
(C87)						

Similar to 20 Reis, KM#316.1.

319.1	1818	—	1.50	3.50	8.00	15.00
(C107.1)	1819	—	3.00	7.50	20.00	40.00
	1820	—	1.25	3.00	8.00	15.00
	1821	—	1.25	3.00	8.00	15.00
	1822	—	1.25	3.00	8.00	15.00

Mint mark: B

319.2	1820	—	3.00	7.50	20.00	30.00
(C107.2)	1821	—	3.50	8.50	22.00	35.00
	1822	—	3.50	8.50	22.00	35.00
	1823	—	3.50	8.50	25.00	50.00

Minted for Goias and Mato Grosso
Obv. leg: JOANNES.VI.D.G.PORT.BRAS.

340	1820	—	5.00	35.00	100.00	150.00
(C111)						

75 REIS

COPPER
Mint mark: M
Minted for Minas Gerais
Obv. leg: JOANNES.VI.D.G.PORT.BRAS...
Rev. leg: PECUNIA.TOTUM.CIRCUMIT. .arms on globe.

320	1818	—	10.00	20.00	40.00	60.00
(C110)	1819	—	12.50	25.00	50.00	75.00
	1821	—	10.00	20.00	40.00	60.00

LXXX (80) REIS

2.2400 g, .917 SILVER, .0660 oz ASW
Mint mark: R
Obv. leg: JOANNES.D G.PORT.P.REGENS....

KM#	Date	Mintage	VG	Fine	VF	XF
305	1810	—	—	—	Rare	—
(C90)	1814	—	30.00	70.00	150.00	300.00
	1816	—	25.00	50.00	120.00	200.00

COPPER
Similar to 10 Reis, KM#232.2.

308	1811	—	7.50	20.00	30.00	80.00
(C85)	1812	—	7.50	20.00	30.00	80.00

Mint mark: B
Minted for Goias and Mato Grosso
Obv. leg: JOANNES.D.G.PORT...crowned value.
Rev. leg: PECUNIA.TOTUM.CIRCUMIT...globe.

321.1	1818	—	1.50	5.00	10.00	30.00
(C88.1)						

Mint mark: R

321.2	1818	—	4.00	10.00	20.00	30.00
(C88.2)						

2.2400 g, .917 SILVER, .0660 oz ASW
Obv: Crowned 80 within wreath, leg: JOANNES.VI. D.G.PORT. BRAS.....

322.1	1818	—	25.00	50.00	90.00	200.00
(C113.1)						

Mint mark: B

322.2	1821	—	20.00	50.00	80.00	220.00
(C113.2)						

COPPER
Minted for Goias and Mato Grosso
Obv. leg: JOANNES.VI.D.G.PORT... crowned value.
Rev: Arms on globe.

341	1820	—	4.00	10.00	17.50	30.00
(C112)						

Mint mark: B

342.1	1820	—	1.50	4.00	8.50	20.00
(C108.1)	1821	—	1.50	4.00	8.50	20.00
	1822/1	—	3.00	7.50	12.50	25.00
	1822	—	2.50	6.00	10.00	22.50
	1823	—	2.50	6.00	10.00	22.50

Mint mark: R

342.2	1821	—	1.25	3.00	7.50	17.50
(C108.2)	1822	—	1.50	4.00	8.50	20.00

160 REIS

4.4800 g, .917 SILVER, .1320 oz ASW
Mint mark: R
Obv. leg: JOANNES.D.G.PORT.P. REGENS....

306.1	1810	—	17.50	35.00	80.00	160.00
(C91.1)	1813	—	6.00	10.00	25.00	50.00
	1813R/B	—	8.50	17.50	30.00	50.00
	1815	—	12.50	25.00	35.00	60.00

Mint mark: B

306.2	1811	—	150.00	300.00	600.00	900.00
(C91.2)	1812	—	20.00	70.00	150.00	700.00

4.4509 g, .917 SILVER, .1312 oz ASW
Mint mark: R
Obv. leg: JOANNES.VI.D.G.PORT.BRAS....

KM#	Date	Mintage	VG	Fine	VF	XF
323.1	1818	—	10.00	20.00	40.00	60.00
(C114.1)	1820	—	100.00	200.00	350.00	700.00

Mint mark: B

323.2	1821	5,639	75.00	125.00	225.00	275.00
(C114.2)						

320 REIS

8.9018 g, .917 SILVER, .2623 oz ASW
Mint mark: R
Obv. leg: MARIA.I.D.G.PORT.REGINA....

221.2	1802	—	11.00	20.00	27.50	45.00
(C72.2)						

8.9600 g, .917 SILVER, .2641 oz ASW
Obv. leg: JOANNES.D.G.PORT.P.REGENS....

255.1	1809	—	11.50	22.50	30.00	45.00
(C92.1)	1812	—	9.00	15.00	20.00	40.00
	1813	—	9.00	15.00	20.00	40.00
	1817	—	15.00	30.00	50.00	75.00

Mint mark: B

255.2	1810	—	17.50	25.00	65.00	160.00
(C92.2)	1816	—	65.00	110.00	200.00	350.00

Mint mark: M

255.3	1812	—	60.00	100.00	220.00	460.00
(C92.3)	1814	—	65.00	190.00	300.00	600.00
	1816	—	70.00	200.00	400.00	800.00

Obv. leg: JOANNES.VI.D.G.PORT.BRAS....

324.1	1818	—	250.00	375.00	550.00	1500.
(C115a)						

Mint mark: R

324.2	1818	—	11.00	20.00	35.00	80.00
(C115.1)	1819	—	17.50	35.00	45.00	90.00
	1820	—	9.00	15.00	20.00	35.00

Mint mark: B

324.3	1821	—	18.50	37.50	55.00	100.00
(C115.2)						

640 REIS

17.7600 g, .917 SILVER, .5233 oz ASW
Mint mark: R
Similar to KM#231.2 but obv. leg: MARIA.I.D.G. PORT. REGINA.....

222.2	1802	—	20.00	35.00	45.00	65.00
(C73.2)						

BRAZIL 209

BRAZIL 210

Mint mark: B

KM#	Date	Mintage	VG	Fine	VF	XF
231.2	1801	—	18.50	25.00	35.00	50.00
(C73.4)	1802	—	18.50	25.00	35.00	50.00
	1803	—	18.50	25.00	35.00	50.00
	1804	—	18.50	25.00	35.00	50.00
	1805	—	35.00	60.00	85.00	250.00

17.9200 g, .917 SILVER, .5280 oz ASW
Obv. leg: JOANNES.D.G.PORT.P.REGENS....

KM#	Date	Mintage	VG	Fine	VF	XF
237	1806	—	25.00	50.00	75.00	250.00
(C93.1)	1807	—	25.00	50.00	75.00	250.00
	1808/7	—	20.00	35.00	60.00	75.00
	1808	—	16.50	25.00	35.00	50.00
256.1	1809	—	16.50	25.00	35.00	50.00
(C93.2)	1810	—	16.50	25.00	35.00	50.00
	1816	—	—	—	Rare	—

Mint mark: R

256.2	1809	—	18.50	35.00	45.00	65.00
(C93.3)	1811	—	18.50	35.00	45.00	75.00
	1812	—	25.00	80.00	150.00	300.00
	1813	—	50.00	125.00	250.00	400.00
	1814	—	55.00	150.00	300.00	600.00
	1815	—	55.00	150.00	300.00	600.00
	1816	—	55.00	150.00	300.00	600.00

Mint mark: M

256.3	1810	—	—	—	Rare	—
(C93.4)	1811	—	35.00	100.00	180.00	300.00
	1812	—	70.00	120.00	200.00	420.00
	1813	—	70.00	120.00	280.00	600.00
	1816	—	70.00	150.00	400.00	800.00

19.3200 g, .917 SILVER, .5693 oz ASW
Obv. leg: JOANNES.VI.

325.1	1818	—	200.00	500.00	1000.	1800.
(C116a)						

Mint mark: R

325.2	1818	—	16.50	35.00	75.00	180.00
(C116.1)	1819	—	25.00	60.00	90.00	240.00
	1820	—	16.00	18.50	30.00	60.00
	1821	—	17.50	30.00	35.00	60.00
	1822	—	21.50	50.00	100.00	300.00

Mint mark: B

325.3	1821	—	40.00	75.00	150.00	300.00
(C116.2)						

960 REIS

26.8900 g, .896 SILVER, .7746 oz ASW
Mint mark: B

KM#	Date	Mintage	VG	Fine	VF	XF
307.1	1810	—	17.50	27.50	40.00	55.00
(C94.1)	1810 small crown					
		—	—	—	Rare	—
	1810..P.REGENS...					
		—	30.00	60.00	80.00	120.00
	1811	—	25.00	40.00	60.00	100.00
	1812	—	17.50	27.50	35.00	60.00
	1813	—	17.50	27.50	35.00	60.00
	1813..P.REGENS...					
		—	50.00	80.00	100.00	200.00
	1814	—	17.50	27.50	35.00	60.00
	1815	—	17.50	27.50	35.00	60.00
	1816	—	17.50	27.50	35.00	60.00

Mint mark: M

307.2	1810	—	—	—	Rare	—
(C94.2)	1816	—	—	—	Rare	—

Mint mark: R

307.3	1810	—	17.50	27.50	35.00	60.00
(C94.3)	1811	—	17.50	27.50	35.00	60.00
	1812	—	17.50	27.50	35.00	60.00
	1813/2	—	17.50	27.50	35.00	60.00
	1813	—	17.50	27.50	35.00	60.00
	1814	—	17.50	27.50	35.00	60.00
	1815	—	17.50	27.50	35.00	60.00
	1815..STAB.NATA...					
		—	—	—	Rare	—
	1816	—	17.50	25.00	35.00	60.00
	1817	—	17.50	25.00	35.00	60.00
	1818	—	17.50	25.00	35.00	60.00

27.0700 g, .903 SILVER, .7859 oz ASW
Obv. leg. ends: .BRAS.ET.ALG.P.REGENS.....

313	1816	—	30.00	50.00	75.00	150.00
(C94a)						

Rev: Similar to KM#307.1.

326.1	1818	—	17.50	22.50	35.00	60.00

KM#	Date	Mintage	VG	Fine	VF	XF
(C117.1)	1819	—	17.50	22.50	35.00	60.00
	1820	—	17.50	22.50	35.00	60.00
	1820 small castle within zero of denomination					
		—	—	—	Rare	—
	1821	—	17.50	22.50	35.00	60.00
	1822	—	25.00	35.00	50.00	85.00

Mint mark: B

326.2	1819	—	—	—	Rare	—
(C117.2)	1820/19	—	—	—	Rare	—
	1820	—	17.50	22.50	35.00	60.00
	1820...BARS.ET...					
		—	25.00	40.00	60.00	90.00
	1821/0	—	20.00	35.00	45.00	70.00
	1821	—	17.50	22.50	35.00	60.00
	1822	—	375.00	800.00	1800.	2800.

NOTE: KM#307.1-307.3, 313 and 326.1-326.2 are usually found struck over Spanish Colonial 8 Reales. Specimens having the original date and mint mark visible command a premium.

4000 REIS

8.0600 g, .917 GOLD, .2376 oz AGW
Mint: Lisbon w/o mint mark.
Obv. leg: MARIA I.D.G...

KM#	Date	Mintage	Fine	VF	XF	Unc
225	1801	3,705	150.00	275.00	550.00	800.00
(C78)	1802	7,738	150.00	275.00	500.00	750.00
	1803	7,807	150.00	275.00	500.00	750.00
	1804/2	Inc. Ab.	150.00	275.00	500.00	750.00
	1805/2	Inc. Be.	150.00	275.00	500.00	750.00

Mint mark: B
Obv. leg: JOANNES,D.G....
Rev: Dots on either side of date.

235.1	1805	.010	125.00	225.00	375.00	500.00
(C101)	1806	.012	125.00	225.00	375.00	500.00
	1807	7,725	125.00	225.00	375.00	500.00
	1808	.037	125.00	225.00	375.00	500.00
	1809/8	.019	125.00	225.00	375.00	500.00
	1809	Inc. Ab.	125.00	225.00	375.00	500.00
	1810	.018	125.00	225.00	375.00	500.00
	1811	.019	125.00	225.00	375.00	500.00
	1812	.010	125.00	225.00	375.00	500.00
	1813	.011	125.00	225.00	375.00	500.00
	1814	9,494	125.00	225.00	375.00	500.00
	1815	—	125.00	225.00	375.00	500.00
	1816	7,522	125.00	225.00	375.00	500.00

Mint mark: R
Rev: Flower on either side of date.

235.2	1808	.128	125.00	225.00	375.00	500.00
(C101b)	1809/08	.094	125.00	225.00	375.00	500.00
	1809	Inc. Ab.	125.00	225.00	375.00	500.00
	1810/09	.066	125.00	225.00	375.00	500.00
	1810	Inc. Ab.	125.00	225.00	375.00	500.00
	1811/10	.087	125.00	225.00	375.00	500.00
	1811	Inc. Ab.	125.00	225.00	375.00	500.00
	1812	.124	125.00	225.00	375.00	500.00
	1813/2	.148	125.00	225.00	375.00	500.00
	1813	Inc. Ab.	125.00	225.00	375.00	500.00
	1814/3	.102	125.00	225.00	375.00	500.00
	1814	Inc. Ab.	125.00	225.00	375.00	500.00
	1815	.083	125.00	225.00	375.00	500.00
	1816	.091	125.00	225.00	375.00	500.00
	1817	.071	125.00	225.00	375.00	500.00

Rev. leg: ...PRINCEPS.REGENS....

312	1816	Inc. Ab.	175.00	350.00	550.00	800.00
(C101a)						

Mint mark: R
Obv: 6-petal flower on either side of date.

KM#	Date	Mintage	Fine	VF	XF	Unc
327.1	1818	.064	140.00	275.00	450.00	650.00
(C119)	1819	.049	140.00	400.00	650.00	900.00
	1820	.087	140.00	275.00	450.00	650.00
	1821/0	.035	140.00	275.00	450.00	650.00
	1821	Inc. Ab.	140.00	275.00	450.00	650.00
	1822/0	.054	150.00	300.00	500.00	700.00
	1822/1	Inc. Ab.	150.00	300.00	500.00	700.00
	1822	Inc. Ab.	150.00	300.00	500.00	700.00

Obv: 4-petal flower on either side of date.
| 327.2 | 1819 | Inc. Ab. | 200.00 | 400.00 | 650.00 | 900.00 |
| (C119b) | | | | | | |

Mint mark: B
Obv: Date between crosses.
| 327.3 | 1819 | 1,864 | 300.00 | 600.00 | 1000. | 1500. |
| (C119a) | 1820 | 4,374 | 350.00 | 700.00 | 1200. | 1700. |

6400 REIS
14.3400 g, .917 GOLD, .4228 oz AGW
Mint mark: R
Obv: Bust right w/bejeweled headdress.
Rev: Crowned arms.

226.1	1801	.185	225.00	300.00	450.00	600.00
(C75.1)	1802	.168	225.00	300.00	450.00	600.00
	1803	.176	225.00	300.00	450.00	600.00
	1804	.128	225.00	300.00	450.00	600.00
	1805	.109	225.00	300.00	450.00	600.00

Mint mark: B
226.2	1801	.012	250.00	400.00	750.00	1000.
(C75.2)	1802	3,324	250.00	400.00	750.00	1000.
	1803	3,743	250.00	400.00	750.00	1000.
	1804	3,539	250.00	400.00	750.00	1000.

Mint mark: R
Obv. leg: JOANNES.D.G.PORT.ET.ALG.P.REGENS.

236.1	1805	Inc. Ab.	200.00	300.00	500.00	800.00
(C100)	1806	.096	200.00	300.00	500.00	800.00
	1807	.059	200.00	300.00	500.00	800.00
	1808/7	.133	200.00	300.00	500.00	800.00
	1808	Inc. Ab.	200.00	300.00	500.00	800.00
	1809/8	.188	200.00	300.00	500.00	800.00
	1809	Inc. Ab.	200.00	300.00	500.00	800.00
	1810	.159	200.00	300.00	500.00	800.00
	1811/10	.082	225.00	350.00	550.00	900.00
	1811	Inc. Ab.	225.00	350.00	550.00	900.00
	1812	.064	225.00	350.00	550.00	900.00
	1813	.053	225.00	450.00	650.00	900.00
	1814/3	.042	275.00	450.00	750.00	1000.
	1814	Inc. Ab.	275.00	450.00	750.00	1000.
	1815	.040	275.00	450.00	750.00	1000.
	1816	.039	300.00	500.00	1000.	2000.
	1817	.032	300.00	500.00	1000.	2000.

Obv. leg. ends: . . .PORT.BRAS.ET.ALG.P.REG.
| 236.2 | 1816 | Inc. Ab. | 500.00 | 1000. | 1800. | 2600. |
| (C100a) | | | | | | |

Obv. leg: JOANNES.VI.D.G.PORT.BRAS.ET.ALG.REX.
KM#	Date	Mintage	Fine	VF	XF	Unc
328	1818	.014	600.00	1200.	2000.	2800.
(C118)	1819	9,227	625.00	1250.	2250.	3250.
	1820	3,286	825.00	1650.	2800.	4000.
	1821	2,122	—	—	Unique	—
	1822	599 pcs.	—	—	Rare	—

COUNTERMARKED COINAGE
Shield Countermark

Authorized on April 18, 1809.

The purpose of the shield countermark was to double the value of the earlier Colonial copper coinage and raise the value of the earlier silver coinage. Other Portuguese and Portuguese Colonial coins are known with this countermark.

75 - 80 Reis   300 - 320 Reis
150 - 160 Reis   600 - 640 Reis

10 REIS
COPPER
c/m: Shield on V (5) Reis, KM#142.5.

KM#	Date	Year	Good	VG	Fine	VF
260	(1809)	1749	—	1.00	3.00	5.00	10.00

c/m: Shield on V (5) Reis, KM#173.1.
261	(1809)	1752	10.00	20.00	70.00	140.00
(C1a)		1753	2.00	3.50	5.50	10.00
		1768	1.00	2.00	4.00	8.00
		1773	1.00	2.00	4.00	8.00
		1774	1.00	2.00	4.00	8.00

c/m: Shield on V (5) Reis, KM#188.
262	(1809)	1762B	2.50	4.50	7.50	12.50
(C2a)		1763B	2.50	4.50	7.50	12.50
		1764B	2.00	3.50	5.50	8.50
		1766B	2.00	3.50	5.50	8.50
		1767B	1.50	2.50	4.50	7.50
		1768B	1.50	2.50	4.50	7.50
		1769B	1.50	2.50	4.50	7.50

c/m: Shield on V (5) Reis, KM#200.
263	(1809)	1778	1.25	2.00	5.00	10.00
(C41a)		1781	1.25	2.00	5.00	10.00
		1782	1.25	2.00	5.00	10.00
		1784	1.25	2.00	5.00	10.00

c/m: Shield on V (5) Reis, w/low flat arch crown, KM#214.1.
264.1	(1809)	1786	1.50	5.00	12.00	18.00
(C60a)		1787	1.50	3.00	10.00	18.00
		1790	1.50	3.00	10.00	18.00
		1791	1.50	3.00	10.00	18.00
		1797	5.00	8.50	15.00	32.00

c/m: Shield on V (5) Reis, w/high full arch crown, KM#214.2.
264.2	(1809)	1786	1.50	5.00	12.00	18.00
(C60a)		1787	1.50	3.00	10.00	18.00
		1790	1.50	3.00	10.00	18.00
		1791	1.50	3.00	10.00	18.00

20 REIS
COPPER
c/m: Shield on X (10) Reis, KM#71.
265	(1809)	1694 P	10.00	25.00	45.00	75.00
		1696 P	8.00	15.00	25.00	45.00
		1697 P	6.00	10.00	20.00	35.00
		1699 P	6.00	10.00	20.00	35.00

c/m: Shield on X (10) Reis, KM#107.
| 266 | (1809) | ND | 30.00 | 45.00 | 85.00 | 160.00 |

c/m: Shield on X (10) Reis, KM#108.
267	(1809)	1715	1.00	1.50	3.00	5.00
		1718	1.00	1.50	3.00	5.00
		1719	1.00	1.50	3.00	5.00
		1720	1.00	1.50	3.00	5.00

c/m: Shield on X (10) Reis, KM#142.1.
268.1	(1809)	1729 B	1.00	1.50	3.00	6.00
		1730 B	1.00	1.50	3.00	6.00
		1731 B	1.00	1.50	3.00	6.00

c/m: Shield on X (10) Reis, KM#142.2.
268.2	(1809)	1729	1.50	2.00	3.50	7.00
		1730	1.50	2.00	3.50	7.00
		1731	1.50	2.00	3.50	7.00
		1732	1.50	2.00	3.50	7.00
		1747	8.00	17.00	20.00	30.00
		1748	20.00	40.00	70.00	130.00

c/m: Shield on X (10) Reis, KM#142.3.
268.3	(1809)	1735	1.00	1.50	3.00	5.00
		1736	1.00	1.50	3.00	5.00
		1746	1.00	1.50	3.00	5.00

c/m: Shield on X (10) Reis, KM#142.4.
| 268.4 | (1809) | 1746 | 1.50 | 2.50 | 3.50 | 5.50 |

c/m: Shield on X (10) Reis, KM#142.5.
| 268.5 | (1809) | 1749 | 1.50 | 2.50 | 3.50 | 5.50 |

c/m: Shield on X (10) Reis, KM#165.1.
| 269 | (1809) | 1751 | 18.00 | 27.00 | 65.00 | 110.00 |
| (C3a) | | | | | | |

c/m: Shield on X (10) Reis, KM#174.1.
KM#	Date	Year	Good	VG	Fine	VF
270	(1809)	1752	4.00	10.00	20.00	30.00
(C4a)		1753	1.00	1.75	3.00	5.00
		1773	3.00	10.00	20.00	30.00
		1774	.75	1.50	2.50	3.50
		1775	.85	1.50	2.50	3.50
		1776	.85	1.50	2.50	3.50

c/m: Shield on X (10) Reis, KM#174.2.
| 271 | (1809) | 1762B | 1.25 | 2.00 | 3.50 | 6.00 |
| (C5a) | | | | | | |

c/m: Shield on X (10) Reis, KM#201.
272	(1809)	1778	.75	1.25	2.50	4.00
(C42a)		1781	.85	1.50	3.00	5.00
		1782	.85	1.50	3.00	5.00
		1784	.85	1.50	3.00	5.00
		1785	.85	1.50	3.00	5.00

c/m: Shield on X (10) Reis, w/low flat arch crown, KM#215.1.
273.1	(1809)	1786	1.25	2.00	3.50	6.00
(C61a)		1787	1.25	2.00	3.50	6.00
		1790	1.25	2.00	3.50	6.00
		1796	1.25	2.00	3.50	6.00

c/m: Shield on X (10) Reis, w/high full arch crown, KM#215.2.
273.2	(1809)	1786	1.25	2.00	3.50	6.00
(C61a)		1787	1.75	3.00	4.50	8.00
		1790	1.25	2.00	3.50	6.00

c/m: Shield on X (10) Reis, KM#228.
| 274 | (1809) | 1799 | 1.00 | 2.00 | 3.50 | 6.00 |
| (C65a) | | | | | | |

40 REIS
COPPER
c/m: Shield on XX (20) Reis, KM#70.
275	(1809)	1693 P	15.00	30.00	50.00	90.00
		1694 P	7.50	15.00	30.00	40.00
		1695 P	5.00	10.00	22.00	30.00
		1697 P	5.00	10.00	22.00	28.00
		1698 P	5.00	10.00	22.00	28.00
		1699 P	5.00	10.00	22.00	28.00

c/m: Shield on XX (20) Reis, KM#109.
276	(1809)	1715	1.00	2.00	3.00	4.50
		1718	1.00	2.00	3.00	4.50
		1719	1.00	2.00	3.00	4.50
		1729	1.00	2.00	3.00	4.50

c/m: Shield on XX (20) Reis, KM#110.
| 277 | (1809) | 1722 | 1.00 | 2.00 | 3.00 | 6.00 |

c/m: Shield on XX (20) Reis, KM#143.1.
278.1	(1809)	1729 B	1.00	2.00	4.00	6.00
		1730 B	1.00	2.00	4.00	6.00
		1731 B	1.00	2.00	4.00	6.00
		1748 B	17.00	35.00	65.00	135.00

c/m: Shield on XX (20) Reis, KM#143.2.
278.2	(1809)	1729 B	1.50	2.50	4.00	5.00
		1730 B	1.50	2.50	4.00	5.00
		1731 B	1.50	2.50	4.00	5.00

c/m: Shield on XX (20) Reis, KM#143.3.
| 278.3 | (1809) | 1735 | 1.00 | 2.00 | 3.50 | 5.00 |
| | | 1736 | 1.00 | 2.00 | 3.50 | 5.00 |

c/m: Shield on XX (20) Reis, KM#143.4.
278.4	(1809)	1735	1.00	1.50	3.00	4.00
		1736	1.00	1.50	3.00	4.00
		1746	1.00	1.50	3.00	4.00

c/m: Shield on XX (20) Reis, KM#143.5.
| 278.5 | (1809) | 1749 | 1.00 | 2.00 | 3.50 | 5.00 |

c/m: Shield on XX (20) Reis, KM#166.1.
| 279 | (1809) | 1751 | 10.00 | 25.00 | 45.00 | 70.00 |
| (C6a) | | 1752 | 3.00 | 6.00 | 12.00 | 17.50 |

c/m: Shield on XX (20) Reis, KM#175.1.
| 280 | (1809) | 1752 | 2.00 | 4.00 | 7.00 | 12.00 |
| (C7a) | | 1753 | 1.00 | 1.75 | 3.00 | 5.00 |

BRAZIL 212

KM#	Date	Year	Good	VG	Fine	VF
(C7a)		1774	1.00	1.75	3.00	5.00
		1775	1.00	1.75	3.00	5.00
		1776	1.00	1.75	3.00	5.00

c/m: Shield on XX (20) Reis, KM#175.2.
| 281 (C8a) | (1809) 1761B | 1.00 | 1.50 | 3.00 | 4.50 |

c/m: Shield on XX (20) Reis, KM#202.
282 (C43a)	(1809) 1778	1.25	3.00	4.50	7.00
	1781	1.25	3.00	4.50	7.00
	1782	1.25	3.00	4.50	7.00
	1784	1.25	3.00	4.50	7.00

c/m: Shield on XX (20) Reis w/low flat arch crown, KM#216.1.
283.1 (C62a)	(1809) 1786	1.50	2.50	4.00	6.50
	1787	1.00	1.75	3.00	5.00
	1790	2.00	3.50	5.50	8.50
	1796	2.00	3.50	5.50	8.50
	1799	2.00	3.50	5.50	8.50

c/m: Shield on XX (20) Reis w/high full arch crown, KM#216.2.
283.2 (C62c)	(1809) 1786	2.00	3.75	5.75	9.00
	1787	2.00	3.75	5.75	9.00
	1790	2.00	3.75	5.75	9.00
	1799	2.00	4.00	6.00	10.00

c/m: Shield on XX (20) Reis, KM#229.
| 284 (C66a) | (1809) 1799 | 1.50 | 2.50 | 4.00 | 6.50 |

c/m: Shield on XX (20) Reis, KM#233.1.
| 285 (C81a) | (1809) 1802 | 1.00 | 2.00 | 3.50 | 6.00 |
| | 1803 | 1.00 | 2.00 | 3.50 | 6.00 |

80 REIS
COPPER
c/m: Shield on XL (40) Reis, KM#111.
| 286 | (1809) 1722 | — | — | — | 6.00 |

c/m: Shield on XL (40) Reis, KM#184.1.
287 (C9a)	(1809) 1753	.85	1.50	3.00	5.00
	1760	1.00	2.00	4.00	7.00
	1774	—	—	—	8.00

c/m: Shield on XL (40) Reis, KM#189.
| 288 (C10a) | (1809) 1762B | 1.50 | 2.50 | 4.00 | 6.00 |

c/m: Shield on XL (40) Reis, KM#203.
289 (C44a)	(1809) 1778	2.00	3.50	5.00	8.00
	1781	2.00	3.50	5.00	8.00
	1784	2.00	3.50	5.00	8.00

c/m: Shield on XL (40) Reis w/low flat arch crown, KM#217.1.
KM#	Date	Year	Good	VG	Fine	VF
290.1 (C63a)	(1809) 1786	2.75	4.50	6.50	10.00
	1790	3.25	5.50	8.50	13.50
	1791	9.00	15.00	20.00	30.00
	1796	3.25	5.50	8.50	13.50

c/m: Shield on XL (40) Reis w/high full arch crown, KM#217.2.
290.2 (C63a.1)	(1809) 1786	3.00	5.00	8.50	13.00
	1787	3.00	5.00	8.50	13.00
	1790	3.00	5.00	8.50	13.00
	1791	3.00	5.00	8.50	13.00

c/m: Shield on XL (40) Reis, KM#230.
| 291 (C67a) | (1809) 1799 | 1.50 | 2.50 | 4.00 | 7.00 |

c/m: Shield on XL (40) Reis, KM#234.1.
| 292 (C83a) | (1809) 1802 | 1.50 | 3.00 | 4.50 | 7.00 |
| | 1803 | 1.50 | 3.00 | 4.50 | 7.00 |

2.2600 g, .917 SILVER, .0666 oz ASW
c/m: Shield on 75 Reis, KM#176.1.
293 (C21a)	(1809) 1752B	50.00	150.00	350.00	600.00
	1753B	7.00	—	50.00	100.00
	1754B	7.00	—	50.00	100.00

c/m: Shield on 75 Reis, KM#176.2.
294 (C22a)	(1809) 1754R	20.00	45.00	65.00	100.00
	1755R	20.00	45.00	65.00	100.00
	1760R	27.00	55.00	120.00	400.00

160 REIS

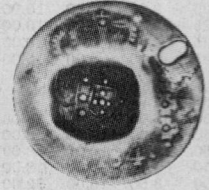 

4.5200 g, .917 SILVER, .1332 oz ASW
c/m: Shield on 150 Reis, KM#177.
295 (C23a)	(1809) 1752B	9.00	40.00	100.00	250.00
	1753B	9.00	30.00	50.00	100.00
	1754B	9.00	30.00	50.00	100.00
	1756B	10.00	35.00	70.00	130.00
	1768B	—	—	Rare	—

c/m: Shield on 150 Reis, KM#185.
296 (C24a)	(1809) 1754R	9.00	20.00	50.00	100.00
	1754 R ATAN NGIS				
		10.00	15.00	25.00	50.00
	1755R	9.00	15.00	25.00	60.00
	1758R	9.00	15.00	25.00	60.00
	1760R	40.00	85.00	150.00	300.00
	1771R	30.00	50.00	100.00	200.00

320 REIS

9.0500 g, .917 SILVER, .2668 oz ASW
c/m: Shield on 300 Reis, KM#178.
297 (C25a)	(1809) 1752B	25.00	45.00	85.00	160.00
	1753B	19.00	35.00	65.00	120.00
	1754B	19.00	35.00	65.00	120.00
	1756B	25.00	45.00	85.00	160.00
	1757B	25.00	50.00	90.00	180.00
	1768B	—	—	Rare	—

c/m: Shield on 300 Reis, KM#186.
298 (C26a)	(1809) 1754R	12.50	20.00	30.00	50.00
	1755R	12.50	20.00	30.00	50.00
	1756R	12.50	20.00	30.00	50.00
	1757R	12.50	20.00	30.00	50.00
	1758R	12.50	20.00	30.00	50.00
	1764R	12.50	20.00	30.00	50.00
	1771R	15.00	25.00	45.00	85.00

640 REIS
18.1100 g, .917 SILVER, .5339 oz ASW
c/m: Shield on 600 Reis, KM#179.
KM#	Date	Year	Good	VG	Fine	VF
299 (C27a)	(1809) 1752B	100.00	350.00	500.00	800.00
	1754B	30.00	60.00	105.00	160.00
	1756B	30.00	60.00	105.00	160.00
	1757B	35.00	65.00	110.00	180.00
	1758B	30.00	60.00	100.00	150.00
	1760B	50.00	200.00	350.00	550.00
	1768B	—	—	Rare	—

c/m: Shield on 600 Reis, KM#187.
300 (C28a)	(1809) 1754R	25.00	30.00	40.00	65.00
	1755R	30.00	40.00	55.00	90.00
	1756R	30.00	40.00	55.00	90.00
	1758R	30.00	40.00	55.00	90.00
	1760R	80.00	150.00	250.00	400.00
	1764R	25.00	30.00	40.00	65.00
	1765R	65.00	95.00	140.00	220.00
	1770R	40.00	50.00	65.00	120.00
	1771R	30.00	40.00	60.00	95.00
	1774R	30.00	40.00	60.00	95.00

REGIONAL COINAGE
CUIABA

Cuiaba is the present capital of the Mato Grosso state. In 1820 this city name appeared as "CUYABA" or "C" on a counterstamp appearing on Spanish-American 8 Reales coins. This is the rarest Brazilian counterstamp.

COUNTERSTAMPED COINAGE
Authorized 1820
Obv. c/s: Crowned shield above CUYABA.
Rev. c/s: Banded globe.

960 REIS
SILVER
c/s: On Spanish Colonial 8 Reales.
KM#	Date	Year	VG	Fine	VF	XF
345 (C98)	ND(1820)	—	—	—	Rare	—

MATO GROSSO
A large state in the center of Brazil. One of the issuers of the counterstamps of the 1808 law. The name of the province appears under the arms on the obverse.

COUNTERSTAMPED COINAGE
TYPE A
Authorized November 4, 1818
c/s: Crowned shield above MATO GROSSO.
Rev. c/s: Banded globe.
NOTE: The c/s having the crown made up of close large pearls is considered a counterfeit.

960 REIS
SILVER
c/s: Type A on Argentina 8 Reales, KM#5.
| 330 (C97.1) | ND (1813-15) | — | — | Rare | — |

c/s: Type A on Bolivia 8 Reales, KM#73.
| 331.1 (C97.2) | ND (1791-1808) | — | — | Rare | — |

c/s: Type A on Bolivia 8 Reales, KM#84.
| 331.2 | ND (1808-18) | — | — | Rare | — |

TYPE B
Authorized in January, 1821.
Obv. c/s: Crowned 960/C (C. or C.) within branches.
Rev. c/s: Shield on globe.

c/s: Type B on Argentina 8 Reales, KM#5.
| 351 (C99.2) | ND (1813-15) | 450.00 | 850.00 | 1500. | 2000. |

BRAZIL 213

		c/s: On Peru 8 Reales, KM#97.			
KM#	Date	Year Mintage	Fine	VF	XF
251 (C96.12)	ND (1791-1808)	—	60.00	100.00	150.00

c/s: On Spanish 8 Reales.

| 252 (C96.13) | ND | — | — | — | Rare | — |

UNITED KINGDOM
Copper Coinage

The imperial copper coins of Brazil (1823-1833) Were struck to several different standards simultaneously, each intended for a different part of the empire. The following table shows the standards used at each mint:

Weights of Imperial Brazilian copper coins in oitavos:

MINT MARK DENOMINATION (REIS)

	MARK	10	20	40	80	37½	75
Rio De Janeiro	R	1	2	4	8	—	—
Bahia	B	1	2	4	8	—	—
Goias	G	—	1	2	4	—	4
Cuiaba	C	—	1	2	4	—	—
Minas Gerais	M	—	—	—	—	2	—
Sao Paulo	SP	—	—	—	5⅓	—	—

NOTE: 1 Oitavo = 3.586 g.; 8 Oitavos = 1 Onza (28.68 g); thus 5-1/3 Oitavos plus 1 Escropalo) is precisely 2/3 Onza (ounce).

Lightweight Coins: Many coppers are found as much as 15 percent or more below the official weights, and even heavy specimens are occasionally observed. Most of the above coins were counterfeited, as their face value exceeded the cost of the metal and minting. Though usually crude and carelessly engraved, some counterfeits are of decent workmanship, and entirely undistinguishable from government issues. Brazilian collectors generally accept these contemporary counterfeits as collectable, due to their historical value. Before Pedro I began his regular coinage, colonial coppers were revalued with a special countermark, probably in 1822.

Imperial Countermarks

These countermarks consist of a crowned 20, 40 or 80 within a wreath in a circle and opposite a shield in a circle is used.

20 REIS
COPPER
c/m: Crowned 20 in sprays on various Colonial X (10) Reis.

KM#	Date	Year	Good	VG	Fine	VF
355 (C120)	Various	—	—	—	Rare	—

NOTE: Many authorities consider all known examples of KM#355 to be counterfeit.

40 REIS
COPPER
c/m: Crowned 40 in sprays on various Colonial XX (20) Reis.

| 356 (C121) | Various | — | — | — | Rare | — |

NOTE: Three of eight known dies are believed counterfeit.

80 REIS

COPPER
c/m: Crowned 80 in sprays on various Colonial XL (40) Reis.

| 357 (C122) | Various | — | — | — | Rare | — |

NOTE: One of 11 known dies are believed counterfeit.

Regular Coinage

CAUTION: Prices are for specimens without any countermark. Countermarked pieces follow these listings.

10 REIS
COPPER
Mint mark: R

KM#	Date	Mintage	Good	VG	Fine	VF
371.1 (C125.1)	1824	.235	1.00	3.50	8.00	15.00

Mint mark: B

| 371.2 | 1827 | .104 | 3.00 | 7.50 | 15.00 | 30.00 |
| (C125.2) | 1828 | .728 | 2.00 | 5.00 | 12.00 | 20.00 |

SILVER
c/s: On Bolivia 8 Reales, KM#55.

KM#	Date	Year Mintage	Fine	VF	XF
240 (C96.1)	ND (1773-89)	—	70.00	160.00	200.00

c/s: On Bolivia 8 Reales, KM#64.

| 241 (C96.2) | ND (1789-91) | — | 30.00 | 60.00 | 100.00 |

c/s: Type B on Bolivia 8 Reales, KM#73.

KM#	Date	Year	VG	Fine	VF	XF
350 (C99.1)	ND (1791-1808)		450.00	850.00	1500.	2000.

c/s: On Bolivia 8 Reales, KM#73.

| 242 (C96.3) | ND (1791-1808) | — | 20.00 | 40.00 | 80.00 |

c/s: On Chile 8 Reales.

| 243 (C96.4) | ND | — | 150.00 | 250.00 | 450.00 |

c/s: On Guatemala 8 Reales.

| 244 (C96.5) | ND | — | — | Rare | — |

c/s: Type B on Bolivia 8 Reales, KM#84.

| 352 (C99.3) | ND (1808-18) | 350.00 | 650.00 | 1000. | 1700. |

MINAS GERAIS

Minas Gerais is a state in eastern Brazil. In September of 1808 an edict was issued for the authorization of various counterstamps to be used on the many circulating Spanish 8 reales in the country. The Minas Gerais counterstamp was issued both with and w/o the M on the reverse. The silver value was 750 to 800 Reis per coin but they were marked and passed at 960 Reis giving the government a nice profit.

COUNTERSTAMPED COINAGE

Authorized Sept. 1, 1808 until 1810
Obv. c/s: Crowned shield in branches/960.
Rev. c/s: Banded globe with cross.

960 REIS

c/s: On Mexico City 8 Reales, KM#105.

| 245 (C96.6) | ND (1760-72) | 100.00 | 150.00 | 250.00 | 450.00 |

c/s: On Mexico City 8 Reales, KM#106.

| 246 (C96.7) | ND (1772-89) | — | 150.00 | 250.00 | 450.00 |

c/s: On Mexico City 8 Reales, KM#107.

| 247 (C96.8) | ND (1789-90) | — | 100.00 | 200.00 | 350.00 |

c/s: On Mexico City 8 Reales, KM#109.

| 248 (C96.9) | ND (1791-1808) | — | 100.00 | 200.00 | 300.00 |

c/s: On Peru 8 Reales, KM#78.

| 249 (C96.10) | ND (1772-89) | — | 60.00 | 100.00 | 150.00 |

c/s: On Peru 8 Reales, KM#87.

| 250 (C96.11) | ND (1789-91) | — | 60.00 | 100.00 | 150.00 |

20 REIS

COPPER
Mint mark: R
PEDRO I, weight: 2 oitavos, 7.17 g

KM#	Date	Mintage	Good	VG	Fine	VF
360.1	1822		Counterfeit			
(C126.1)	1823	1.700	.75	1.25	2.00	6.00
	1824	4.956	.75	1.25	2.00	6.00
	1825	9.054	.50	1.25	2.00	6.00
	1826	4.419	.50	1.25	2.00	6.00
	1827	4.648	.50	1.25	2.00	6.00
	1828	4.474	.75	1.75	3.00	6.00
	1829	6.806	.50	1.25	2.00	6.00
	1830	—	.75	1.25	2.00	6.00
	1831		Counterfeit	—	—	

Mint mark: B

360.2	1825	.582	1.60	4.00	7.50	12.50
(C126.2)	1827	.044	1.60	4.00	7.50	12.50
	1828	.585	1.50	3.50	8.00	15.00
	1830	.316	1.65	4.00	7.50	12.50

Mint mark: C
PEDRO I, reduced weight: 1 oitavo – 3.59 g

375.1	1825	—	15.00	30.00	80.00	150.00
(C129.1)						

Mint mark: G

375.2	1829		Counterfeit	—	—	
(C129.2)						

Mint mark: R
PEDRO II, reduced weight: 2 oitavos – 7.17 g

380	1832	.014	25.00	60.00	100.00	175.00
(C145)						

37-1/2 REIS

COPPER
Mint mark: M
PEDRO I, weight: 2 oitavos – 7.17 g

362	1823	—	10.00	20.00	40.00	60.00
(C130)	1824	—	7.50	15.00	30.00	50.00
	1825	—	7.50	15.00	30.00	50.00
	1826	—	7.50	15.00	30.00	50.00
	1827	—	7.50	15.00	30.00	50.00
	1828	—	7.50	15.00	30.00	50.00

40 REIS

COPPER
Mint mark: R
PEDRO I, weight: 4 oitavos – 14.34 g

KM#	Date	Mintage	Good	VG	Fine	VF
363.1	1823	.920	1.00	2.25	5.00	10.00
(C127.1)	1824	9.170	.50	1.25	3.00	6.00
	1825	6.774	.75	2.00	3.00	6.00
	1826	10.507	.75	2.00	3.00	6.00
	1827	17.892	.75	2.00	3.00	6.00
	1828	15.570	.75	2.00	3.00	6.00
	1829	8.924	.75	2.00	3.00	6.00
	1830	—	.75	2.00	3.00	6.00
	1831/0	—				
	1831	—	.75	2.00	3.00	6.00

Mint mark: B

363.2	1824	.230	2.00	5.00	10.00	15.00
(C127.2)	1825	Inc. Ab	2.00	5.00	10.00	15.00
	1827	.161	2.00	5.00	10.00	15.00
	1828	.051	2.00	5.00	10.00	15.00
	1829	2.052	2.00	5.00	10.00	15.00
	1830	1.032	2.00	5.00	10.00	15.00

NOTE: Most known examples of 1828R, 1829R, and 1830R are counterfeit!

Mint mark: C
PEDRO I, reduced weight: 2 oitavos – 7.17 g

364.1	1823	—	6.00	10.00	15.00	30.00
(C131.1)	1824	—	1.25	3.00	8.00	15.00
	1825	—	1.00	2.50	8.00	15.00
	1826	—	1.25	3.00	8.00	15.00
	1827	—	1.25	3.00	8.00	15.00
	1828	—	1.00	2.50	8.00	15.00
	1829	—	2.00	4.00	8.00	15.00
	1830	—	2.00	4.00	8.00	15.00
	1831	—	6.00	10.00	15.00	30.00

Mint mark: G

364.2	1823	—	5.00	10.00	20.00	30.00
(C131.2)	1825	—	2.50	5.00	12.50	20.00
	1826	—	5.00	10.00	20.00	30.00
	1827	—	2.50	5.00	8.00	20.00
	1828	—	2.50	5.00	8.00	20.00
	1829	—	2.50	5.00	8.00	20.00
	1830	—	2.50	5.00	8.00	20.00

NOTE: 1823C is considered a counterfeit by many authorities.

Mint mark: R
PEDRO II, weight: 4 oitavos – 14.34 g

378	1831		Counterfeit	—	—	
(C146)	1832	.816	1.50	3.00	5.00	10.00

NOTE: 1833R exists as a pattern.

Mint mark: G
PEDRO II, reduced weight: 2 oitavos – 7.17 g

381.1	1832 Petrus II					
(C148.1)		—	3.00	5.00	8.00	20.00
	1832 Petrus 2.o					
		—	3.00	5.00	8.00	20.00

Mint mark: C

381.2	1833	—	5.00	8.00	15.00	20.00
(C148.2)						

75 REIS

COPPER
Mint mark: G
PEDRO I, weight: 4 oitavos – 14.34 g

365	1823	—	20.00	40.00	85.00	175.00
(C132)						

80 REIS

COPPER
Mint mark: R
PEDRO I, weight: 8 oitavos – 28.69 g

KM#	Date	Mintage	Good	VG	Fine	VF
366.1	1823	.100	.65	1.75	3.00	8.00
(C128.1)	1824	.825	.65	1.75	3.00	8.00
	1825	1.027	.75	1.75	3.00	8.00
	1826	10.507	.65	1.75	3.00	8.00
	1827	17.892	.65	1.75	3.00	8.00
	1828	26.524	.65	1.75	3.00	8.00
	1829	20.180	.65	1.75	3.00	8.00
	1830	—	.65	1.75	3.00	8.00
	1831	—	.75	1.75	3.00	8.00

Mint mark: B

366.2	1824	.879	1.25	3.00	6.00	12.00
(C128.2)	1825	Inc. Ab.	1.25	3.00	6.00	12.00
	1826	.695	1.25	3.00	6.00	12.00
	1827	.352	1.25	3.00	6.00	12.00
	1828	2.539	1.25	3.00	6.00	12.00
	1829	3.993	1.25	3.00	6.00	12.00
	1830	.359	1.25	3.00	6.00	12.00
	1831		Counterfeits exist			—

NOTE: Coins with P mint mark are all counterfeit.

Mint mark: SP
PEDRO I, weight: 5 1/3 oitavos – 19.13 g

376	1825	—	3.00	5.00	10.00	20.00
(C128b)	1828	—	1.50	3.00	6.00	12.00
	1829	—	1.50	3.00	6.00	12.00

NOTE: Many varieties of the Sao Paulo coins exist.

Mint mark: C
PEDRO I, weight: 4 oitavos – 14.34 g

377.1	1826	—	2.00	5.00	10.00	20.00
(C133.1)	1827	—	15.00	25.00	50.00	100.00
	1828	—	3.00	6.00	15.00	25.00
	1830	—	10.00	30.00	60.00	100.00

Mint mark: G

377.2	1826	—	4.00	7.50	15.00	20.00
(C133.2)	1828	—	2.00	6.00	12.00	18.00
	1829	—	2.00	6.00	12.00	18.00
	1830	—	2.00	6.00	12.00	18.00
	1831	—	4.00	9.00	18.00	30.00

NOTE: Coins dated 1826G are believed to be all counterfeit.

Mint mark: R
PEDRO II, weight: 8 oitavos – 28.69 g
Rev: Similar to KM#366.1

379	1831	—	1.75	2.50	5.00	10.00
(C147)	1832	6.119	1.75	2.50	5.00	10.00
	1833	—	Reported, not confirmed			

Mint mark: SP
PEDRO II, weight: 5 1/3 oitavos – 19.13 g

382	1832	—	30.00	60.00	100.00	150.00
(C147b)						

NOTE: The 1832SP is considered a counterfeit by many authorities.

Mint mark: G
PEDRO II, weight: 4 oitavos – 14.34 g

383	1832	—	3.00	5.00	10.00	20.00
(C149)	1833	—	3.00	5.00	10.00	20.00
	1833 Petrus I (error)					
		—	12.00	25.00	50.00	100.00

REGIONAL COUNTERMARKS

NOTE: Due to variations in value from one part of the country to another, copper coins tended to flow to areas where their buying power was greatest. To prevent the outflow, some districts ordered coinage countermarked and reduced in value. There is speculation that silver coins were also ordered to be countermarked, but no documentation is available to substantiate this claim. The

following issues are recognized as genuine. Prices are for countermarks on common coins of each variety. Countermarked rare dates bring a premium.

CEARA

Ceara is a state in northeastern Brazil. Due to coin shortages a law was passed October 3, 1833 that copper coins would be countermarked and pass for 1/2 of their face value. In November of 1834 legislation was passed to stop the star countermarks.

Coins of 20, 40, and 80 Reis were countermarked CEARA in a 5-pointed star to indicate a 50 percent reduction in value (to 10, 20, and 40 Reis).

10 REIS
COPPER
c/m: Star on various 20 Reis.

KM#	Date	Year	Good	VG	Fine	VF
396 (C150)	ND	(1834)	3.00	7.00	10.00	20.00

20 REIS

COPPER
c/m: Star on various 40 Reis.

| 397 (C151) | ND | (1834) | 1.50 | 5.00 | 7.50 | 10.00 |

40 REIS

COPPER
c/m: Star on various 80 Reis.

| 398 (C152) | ND | (1834) | 1.50 | 5.50 | 8.00 | 15.00 |

NOTE: A few silver coins bearing this c/m are considered trial pieces and are rare. Many imitations of this c/m exist on various silver coins and are listed in "Unusual World Coins."

MARANHAO

Maranhao is a state in northeastern Brazil. Coin shortages caused 2 issues of countermarked coins. The first was to make the coins pass for 1/4 their face value. These had M and the new value. The second issue was to make the coins pass for 1/2 the face value. These were countermarked with an M. These too were soon recalled.

FIRST SERIES (1834)
M and denomination in Roman numerals within a rectangle.

5 REIS
COPPER
c/m: M/V on various 20 Reis.

| 401 (C154) | ND | (1834) | 5.00 | 10.00 | 20.00 | 30.00 |

10 REIS
COPPER
c/m: M/X on various 40 Reis.

KM#	Date	Year	Good	VG	Fine	VF
402 (C155)	ND	(1834)	3.25	8.00	15.00	25.00

20 REIS

COPPER
c/m: M/XX on various 80 Reis.

| 403 (C156) | ND | (1834) | 2.00 | 4.50 | 10.00 | 15.00 |

SECOND SERIES (1835)
Large M on reverse of coin.

10 REIS
COPPER
c/m: M on various 20 Reis.

| 404 (C157) | ND | (1835) | 3.00 | 7.00 | 12.00 | 25.00 |

20 REIS

COPPER
c/m: M on various 40 Reis.

| 405 (C158) | ND | (1835) | 3.00 | 7.00 | 12.00 | 25.00 |

40 REIS

COPPER
c/m: M on various 80 Reis.

| 406 (C159) | ND | (1835) | 3.00 | 7.00 | 12.00 | 25.00 |

NOTE: Second series countermarks are found struck over coins which already have the first series countermark. They are worth about 50 percent more than ordinary second series coins.

PARA

Para is a state in northern Brazil. Two series of countermarks were issued from this state. On January 14, 1835 Governor Malcher authorized a law for the countermarking of the recently withdrawn Mato Grosso coppers to 1/4 of their previous value. On March 6, 1835 Governor Vinagre authorized the countermarking of coppers at 1/2 their face value. Although heavily counterfeited because of their crudeness these coins stayed in circulation until 1868 and even later.

Crude Arabic 10, 20, or 40 countermarked on obverse of coins weighing 2, 4, and 8 oitavos, respectively. The numerals are quite crude and styles vary and are easily distinguished from the general countermarks. Examples of the Para marks are:

10 REIS

COPPER
c/m: 10 on various Colonial XX (20) Reis.

KM#	Date	Year	Good	VG	Fine	VF
407 (C160.1)	ND	(1835)	3.00	4.50	8.00	12.00

c/m: 10 on Imperial 20 Reis, R or B mints.

| 408 (C160.2) | ND | (1835) | 3.00 | 4.50 | 8.00 | 12.00 |

c/m: 10 on Imperial 40 Reis, C or G mints.

| 409 (C161) | ND | (1835) | 4.00 | 6.00 | 10.00 | 15.00 |

20 REIS
COPPER
c/m: 20 on Colonial XL (40) Reis.

| 410 (C162) | ND | (1835) | 3.00 | 4.50 | 8.00 | 12.00 |

c/m: 20 on Imperial 40 Reis, R or B mints.

| 411 (C164) | ND | (1835) | 3.00 | 4.50 | 8.00 | 12.00 |

c/m: 20 on Imperial 80 Reis, C or G mints.

| 412 (C163) | ND | (1835) | 4.00 | 6.00 | 12.00 | 20.00 |

40 REIS
COPPER
c/m: 40 on Colonial LXXX (80) Reis.

| 413 (C165.1) | ND | (1835) | 3.00 | 4.50 | 8.00 | 12.00 |

c/m: 40 on Imperial 80 Reis, R or B mints.

| 414 (C165.2) | ND | (1835) | 3.00 | 4.50 | 8.00 | 12.00 |

REPUBLIC OF PIRATINI

As a result of a revolt in 1835 in the southern Brazilian state of Rio Grande do Sol the "Republic of Piratini" was briefly established and all coins then circulating in the province were countermarked with the arms of the new republic. This series is probably the most counterfeited of all of the elaborate countermarks.

1835-1845

Two hands grasping a sword with Liberty cap on point within oval. Similar countermarks with either the date 1835 or PIRATINI at the bottom or date divided are considered to be fantasies.

20 REIS
COPPER

Republic of Piratini / BRAZIL

KM#	Date	Year	VG	Fine	VF	XF
A415	ND	c/m: On various 20 Reis.	—	10.00	18.00	27.00	40.00

40 REIS
COPPER

KM#	Date	c/m: On various 40 Reis.				
B415	ND	—	10.00	18.00	27.00	40.00

80 REIS
COPPER

KM#	Date	c/m: On various 80 Reis.				
C415	ND	—	10.00	18.00	27.00	40.00

240 REIS

SILVER
c/m: On Argentina 2 Soles, KM#18.

KM#	Date					
D415	ND(1826)	—	—	—	Rare	—

320 REIS

SILVER
c/m: On 320 Reis, KM#374.

KM#	Date					
E415	1825R	—	—	—	Rare	—

960 REIS

SILVER
c/m: On 960 Reis, KM#307.

| 415.1 | ND (1810-18) | — | — | — | Rare | — |

c/m: On 960 Reis, KM#368.
| 415.2 | ND(1823-28) | — | — | — | Rare | — |

c/m: On Colombia-Cundinamarca 8 Reales, KM#6.
| 415.3 | ND(1820-21) | — | — | — | Rare | — |

c/m: On Spain 8 Reales, C#93.
| 415.4 | ND(1809-10) | — | — | — | Rare | — |

ICO

Ico is a city in the state of Ceara in northeastern Brazil. It was the center of a revolutionary movement from 1829-1832. Various copper and silver coins countermarked ICO, YCO, JGO and IGO are all considered counterfeit, countermarked after the suppression of the revolt. They have little value, but are collected as curiosities. Average value, about $4.00.

NOTE: In addition to local countermarks, over 280 private countermarks are known. A list of these is given by Kurt Prober, in his "Catalogo das Moedas Brasileiras".

National Countermarks

In order to prevent chaotic conditions resulting from local and private countermarking, the government passed law #54 of 6 October 1835 ordering all coppers countermarked according to the following standards:

- 2 Oitavos = 7.18 g = 10 Reis
- 4 Oitavos = 14.34 g = 20 Reis
- 8 Oitavos = 28.69 g = 40 Reis

The countermarks consist of neat numerals within a circle, having a plain or shaded field. These countermarks were applied to various Brazilian coinage from 1799 to 1833. In addition, wrong countermarks are occasionally found, as well as various Portuguese, Angolan, San Tome, Mozambiquean and pre-1799 Brazilian coins.

10 REIS
COPPER

Mint: Lisbon - w/o mint mark.
c/m: 10 on XX (20) Reis, KM#229.

KM#	Date	Year	Good	VG	Fine	VF
416 (C66b)	ND(1835)	1799	3.00	7.50	15.00	25.00

c/m: 10 on XX (20) Reis, KM#233.1.
417.1 (C81b.1)	ND(1835)	1802	2.00	4.00	7.00	11.00
		1803	2.00	4.00	7.00	11.00
		1805	2.00	4.00	7.00	11.00

Mint mark: B
417.2 (C81b.2)	ND(1835)	1812	3.50	6.00	10.00	18.00
		1813	2.50	4.50	7.00	15.00
		1815	2.50	4.50	7.00	15.00
		1816	2.50	4.50	7.00	15.00

Mint mark: R
417.3 (C81b.3)	ND(1835)	1812	3.00	6.00	13.00	25.00
		1813	3.00	6.00	13.00	25.00
		1814	3.00	6.00	13.00	25.00
		1815	3.00	6.00	13.00	25.00

c/m: 10 on XX (20) Reis, KM#309.
418 (C82a)	ND(1835)	1816	3.00	6.00	13.00	25.00
		1817	3.00	6.00	13.00	25.00
		1818	4.00	8.00	15.00	30.00

c/m: 10 on XL (40) Reis, KM#318.
| 419 (C87a) | ND(1835) | 1818 | 12.50 | 18.50 | 27.50 | 40.00 |

c/m: 10 on XX (20) Reis, KM#316.1.
420.1 (C106a.1)	ND(1835)	1818	1.00	2.00	3.50	5.50
		1819	1.00	2.00	3.50	5.50
		1820	1.00	2.00	3.50	5.50
		1821	1.00	2.00	3.50	5.50
		1822	1.00	2.00	3.50	5.50

Mint mark: B
| 420.2 (C106a.2) | ND(1835) | 1820 | 3.00 | 6.00 | 11.00 | 17.50 |
| | | 1821 | 3.00 | 6.00 | 11.00 | 17.50 |

Mint mark: M
c/m: 10 on 37-1/2 Reis, KM#317.1.
421.1 (C109a.1)	ND(1835)	1818	2.50	8.00	15.00	22.00
		1819	2.50	8.00	15.00	22.00
		1819	3.00	medal strike	17.50	25.00
				10.00		
		1821	2.50	8.00	15.00	22.00
		1821	medal strike			
			2.50	8.00	15.00	22.00

Mint mark: R
| 421.2 (C109a.2) | ND(1835) | 1818 | 12.50 | 30.00 | 50.00 | 110.00 |

Mint: Lisbon - w/o mint mark.
c/m: 10 on XL (40) Reis, KM#340.
| 422 (C111a) | ND(1835) | 1820 | 25.00 | 75.00 | 150.00 | — |

Mint mark: R
c/m: 10 on 20 Reis, Pedro I, KM#360.1.
423.1 (C126a.1)	ND(1835)	1823	1.50	3.00	5.00	7.00
		1824	1.00	2.00	4.00	7.00
		1825	1.00	2.00	4.00	7.00
		1826	1.00	2.00	4.00	7.00
		1827	1.00	2.00	5.00	7.00
		1828	1.00	2.00	5.00	7.00
		1829	1.00	2.00	5.00	7.00
		1830	1.00	2.00	5.00	7.00

Mint mark: B
423.2 (C126a.2)	ND(1835)	1825	2.00	4.00	7.00	12.00
		1827	2.00	4.00	7.00	12.00
		1828	2.00	4.00	7.00	12.00
		1830	2.00	4.00	7.00	12.00

Mint mark: C
c/m: 10 on 20 Reis of Pedro I, KM#375.1.
| 424.1 (C129a.1) | ND(1835) | 1825 | 50.00 | 100.00 | 150.00 | 240.00 |

Mint mark: G
| 424.2 (C129a.2) | ND(1835) | 1827 | 20.00 | 32.50 | 50.00 | 100.00 |

NOTE: The above two pieces were not supposed to have been countermarked, as they only weigh one oitavo-3.59 g.

Mint mark: R
c/m: 10 on 20 Reis of Pedro II, KM#380.
| 425 (C145a) | ND(1835) | 1832 | 30.00 | 60.00 | 100.00 | 150.00 |

Mint mark: M
c/m: 10 on 37-1/2 Reis of Pedro I.
426 (C130a)	ND(1835)	1823	7.50	20.00	40.00	75.00
		1824	7.50	20.00	40.00	75.00
		1825	7.50	20.00	40.00	75.00
		1826	7.50	20.00	40.00	75.00
		1827	7.50	20.00	40.00	75.00
		1828	7.50	20.00	40.00	75.00

Mint mark: C
c/m: 10 on 40 Reis of Pedro I, KM#364.1.

KM#	Date	Year	Good	VG	Fine	VF
427.1 (C131a.1)	ND(1835)	1823	2.50	4.50	7.50	15.00
		1824	1.50	3.00	6.00	10.00
		1825	1.50	3.00	6.00	10.00
		1826	1.50	3.00	6.00	10.00
		1827	1.50	3.00	6.00	10.00
		1828	1.50	3.00	6.00	10.00
		1829	1.50	3.00	6.00	10.00
		1830	1.50	3.00	6.00	10.00
		1831	1.50	3.00	6.00	10.00

Mint mark: G
427.2 (C131a.2)	ND(1835)	1823	2.50	5.00	7.50	20.00
		1825	2.50	5.00	7.50	20.00
		1826	2.50	5.00	7.50	20.00
		1827	1.50	3.00	5.00	12.00
		1828	1.50	3.00	5.00	12.00
		1829	1.50	3.00	5.00	12.00
		1830	1.50	3.00	5.00	12.00

c/m: 10 on 40 Reis of Pedro II, KM#381.1.
428.1 (C148a.1)	ND(1835)	1832	PETRUS II			
			3.00	4.50	7.50	12.00
		1832	Petrus 2.o			
			2.00	3.00	5.00	10.00

Mint mark: C
| 428.2 (C148a.2) | ND(1835) | 1833 | 2.00 | 4.00 | 6.00 | 10.00 |

c/m: 10 on Mozambique 40 Reis, KM#19.
429 (C55a)	ND(1835)	1819	3.00	7.00	12.50	25.00
		1820	3.00	7.00	12.50	25.00
		1821	3.00	7.00	12.50	25.00
		1821	4.00	9.00	17.50	35.00
		1822	4.00	9.00	17.50	35.00
		1825	4.00	9.00	17.50	35.00

20 REIS
COPPER

Mint: Lisbon - w/o mint mark.
c/m: 20 on XL (40) Reis, KM#230.
| 430 (C67b) | ND(1835) | 1799 | — | 3.00 | 7.50 | 15.00 |

c/m: 20 on XL (40) Reis, KM#234.1.
| 431.1 (C83b.1) | ND(1835) | 1802 | 1.00 | 3.00 | 5.00 | 10.00 |
| | | 1803 | 1.00 | 3.00 | 5.00 | 10.00 |

Mint mark: B
431.2 (C83b.2)	ND(1835)	1809	2.50	5.00	8.00	20.00
		1810	2.50	5.00	10.00	20.00
		1811	2.00	4.00	8.00	16.00
		1812	2.00	4.00	8.00	16.00
		1814	1.25	2.50	5.00	10.00
		1816	1.25	2.50	5.00	10.00

Mint mark: R
431.3 (C83b.3)	ND(1835)	1812	2.00	5.00	10.00	20.00
		1813	2.00	5.00	10.00	20.00
		1815	2.00	5.00	10.00	20.00

c/m: 20 on XL (40) Reis, KM#311.
| 432 (C84a) | ND(1835) | 1816 | 2.00 | 5.00 | 8.00 | 20.00 |
| | | 1817 | 2.00 | 5.00 | 8.00 | 20.00 |

c/m: 20 on XL (40) Reis, KM#319.1.
433.1 (C107a.1)	ND(1835)	1818	1.50	3.50	7.00	15.00
		1819	1.50	3.50	7.00	15.00
		1820	1.50	3.50	7.00	15.00
		1821	1.50	3.50	7.00	15.00
		1822	1.50	3.50	7.00	15.00

Mint mark: B
433.2 (C107a.2)	ND(1835)	1820	2.50	4.50	9.00	18.00
		1821	2.50	4.50	9.00	18.00
		1822	2.50	4.50	9.00	18.00
		1823	6.00	12.50	—	25.00

Mint mark: M
c/m: 20 on 75 Reis, KM#320.
434 (C110a)	ND(1835)	1818	3.00	5.00	12.00	25.00
		1819	3.00	5.00	12.00	25.00
		1819	medal strike			
			4.00	7.50	30.00	
		1821	3.00	5.00	12.00	25.00

Mint: Lisbon - w/o mint mark.
c/m: 20 on LXXX (80) Reis, KM#341.
| 435 (C112a) | ND(1835) | 1820 | 4.00 | 8.00 | 15.00 | 25.00 |

Mint mark: R
c/m: 20 on 40 Reis of Pedro I, KM#363.1.
436.1 (C127a.1)	ND(1835)	1823	1.00	1.25	2.50	5.00
		1824	1.00	1.25	2.50	5.00
		1825	1.00	1.25	2.50	5.00
		1826	1.00	1.25	2.50	5.00
		1827	1.00	1.25	2.50	5.00

Ico/BRAZIL 217

KM#	Date	Year	Good	VG	Fine	VF
436.1		1828	1.00	1.25	2.50	5.00
		1829	1.00	1.25	2.50	5.00
		1830	1.00	1.25	2.50	5.00
		1831	1.00	1.25	2.50	5.00

Mint mark: B

436.2 (C127a.2)	ND(1835)	1824	2.00	3.00	5.00	12.00
		1825	2.00	3.00	5.00	12.00
		1827	2.00	3.00	5.00	12.00
		1828	2.00	3.00	5.00	12.00
		1829	2.00	3.00	5.00	12.00
		1830	2.00	3.00	5.00	12.00

Mint mark: R
c/m: 20 on 40 Reis of Pedro II, KM#378.

| 437 (C146a) | ND(1835) | 1831 | .75 | 1.50 | 3.00 | 4.50 |
| | | 1832 | .75 | 1.50 | 3.00 | 4.50 |

Mint mark: G
c/m: 20 on 75 Reis of Pedro I, KM#365.

| 438 (C132a) | ND(1835) | 1823 | 5.00 | 8.00 | 15.00 | 25.00 |

Mint mark: C
c/m: 20 on 80 Reis of Pedro I, KM#377.1.

439.1 (C133a.1)	ND(1835)	1826	1.75	3.00	4.75	7.00
		1827	6.00	9.00	16.00	30.00
		1828	3.00	5.00	8.50	12.50
		1830	2.50	4.50	7.50	11.50

Mint mark: G

439.2 (C133a.2)	ND(1835)	1826	2.00	5.00	7.50	12.00
		1828	1.00	2.00	3.00	4.50
		1829	1.50	2.50	4.00	6.00
		1830	1.50	2.50	4.00	6.00
		1831	6.00	10.00	17.50	40.00

c/m: 20 on 80 Reis of Pedro II, KM#383.

440 (C149a)	ND(1835)	1832	2.00	3.00	6.00	10.00
		1833	2.00	3.00	6.00	10.00
		1833 Petrus I				
			10.00	22.00	45.00	95.00

c/m: 20 on Mozambique 80 Reis, KM#20.

| 441 (C56a) | ND(1835) | 1819 | 6.00 | 12.00 | 23.00 | 45.00 |
| | | 1820 | 6.00 | 12.00 | 23.00 | 45.00 |

40 REIS
COPPER
Mint mark: R
c/m: 40 on LXXX (80) Reis, KM#308.

| 442 (C85a) | ND(1835) | 1811 | 4.00 | 7.00 | 13.00 | 25.00 |
| | | 1812 | 4.00 | 7.00 | 13.00 | 25.00 |

Mint mark: B
c/m: 40 on LXXX (80) Reis, KM#342.1.

443.1 (C108a.1)	ND(1835)	1820	1.00	2.00	4.50	9.00
		1821	1.00	2.00	4.50	9.00
		1822	1.00	2.00	4.50	9.00
		1823	2.00	3.50	7.50	15.00

Mint mark: R

| 443.2 (C108a.2) | ND(1835) | 1821 | 2.00 | 4.50 | 7.50 | 15.00 |
| | | 1822 | 2.00 | 4.50 | 7.50 | 15.00 |

c/m: 40 on 80 Reis of Pedro I, KM#366.1.

444.1 (C128a.1)	ND(1835)	1823	1.50	3.00	5.00	10.00
		1824	.80	1.00	3.00	4.50
		1825	.80	1.00	2.00	3.00
		1826	.85	1.50	2.75	4.00
		1827	.80	1.00	2.00	3.00
		1828	.80	1.00	2.00	3.00
		1829	.80	1.00	2.00	3.00
		1830	.80	1.00	2.00	3.00
		1831	.85	1.50	2.75	4.00

Mint mark: B

444.2 (C128a.2)	ND(1835)	1824	1.00	2.00	4.50	8.00
		1825	1.00	2.00	4.50	8.00
		1826	1.00	2.00	4.50	8.00
		1827	1.00	2.00	4.50	8.00
		1828	1.00	2.00	4.50	8.00
		1829	1.00	2.00	4.50	8.00
		1830	1.25	2.00	4.50	8.00
		1831			Counterfeit	—

Mint mark: SP
c/m: 40 on 80 Reis of Pedro I, KM#376.

445 (C128c)	ND(1835)	1825	2.00	5.00	10.00	20.00
		1828	2.00	5.00	10.00	20.00
		1829	2.00	5.00	10.00	20.00

Mint mark: R
c/m: 40 on 80 Reis of Pedro II, KM#379.

KM#	Date	Year	Good	VG	Fine	VF
446 (C147a)	ND(1835)	1831	1.00	2.00	5.00	7.50
		1832	.50	2.00	5.00	7.50

Mint mark: SP
c/m: 40 on 80 Reis of Pedro II, KM#382.

| 447 (C147c) | ND(1835) | 1832 | 35.00 | 60.00 | 100.00 | 150.00 |

EMPIRE
80 REIS
2.2400 g, .917 SILVER, .0660 oz ASW
Mint mark: R
Obv. leg: PETRUS I D.G. around value in floral circle.
Rev: Crowned arms in branches.

KM#	Date	Mintage	Fine	VF	XF	Unc
372	1824	—	400.00	750.00	1500.	2000.
(C134)	1826	—	300.00	600.00	1200.	1600.

Obv. leg: PETRUS II D.G.

| 388 (C178) | 1833 | 418 pcs. | 400.00 | 600.00 | 1000. | 2000. |

160 REIS

4.4800 g, .917 SILVER, .1320 oz ASW
Mint mark: R
Obv. leg: PETRUS I D.G.

| 373 | 1824 | — | 400.00 | 600.00 | 900.00 | 1500. |
| (C135) | 1826 | — | 400.00 | 600.00 | 900.00 | 1500. |

Obv. leg: PETRUS II D.G.

| 389 (C179) | 1833 | 492 pcs. | 750.00 | 1200. | 1500. | 2000. |

320 REIS

8.9600 g, .917 SILVER, .2640 oz ASW
Mint mark: R
Obv. leg: PETRUS I D.G.

374	1824	642 pcs.	500.00	800.00	1200.	1800.
(C136)	1825	.018	20.00	40.00	80.00	175.00
	1826	—	100.00	300.00	800.00	1500.
	1827	—			Unique	
	1830	8,542	—	—	Rare	

Obv. leg: PETRUS II D.G.

| 390 (C180) | 1833 | 22 pcs. | — | — | Rare | |

640 REIS

17.9200 g, .917 SILVER, .5280 oz ASW
Mint mark: R
Obv. leg: PETRUS I D.G.

KM#	Date	Mintage	Fine	VF	XF	Unc
367	1823	—		Counterfeit		
(C137)	1824/3	.080	15.00	30.00	80.00	150.00
	1824	Inc. Ab.	15.00	30.00	80.00	150.00
	1825	.353	15.00	30.00	50.00	150.00
	1826	9,472	200.00	400.00	900.00	1200.
	1827	Inc. Ab.	200.00	400.00	900.00	1200.

Obv. leg: PETRUS II D.G.

| 384 | 1832 | 118 pcs. | — | — | Rare | |
| (C181) | 1833 | 5 pcs. | — | — | Rare | |

960 REIS

26.8900 g, .896 SILVER, .7746 oz ASW
Mint mark: R

368.1	1823 SIGNO above crown					
(C138.1)		.395	17.50	35.00	75.00	150.00
	1823 IGNO above crown					
		Inc. Ab.	100.00	150.00	300.00	550.00
	1824	.600	17.50	35.00	75.00	150.00
	1825 small 960					
		.600	20.00	40.00	80.00	175.00
	1825 large 960					
		Inc. Ab.	100.00	200.00	350.00	700.00
	1826	.500	20.00	40.00	80.00	175.00
	1827	.018	—	—	Rare	
	1828	—		Counterfeit		

Mint mark: B

368.2	1824	—	45.00	75.00	150.00	225.00
(C138.2)	1825	—	50.00	85.00	150.00	225.00
	1826	—	250.00	500.00	1100.	2000.

NOTE: KM#368 is occasionally found struck over Spanish Colonial 8 Reales. Specimens having the original date and mint mark visible command a premium.

Mint mark: R

385	1832	3,039	—	—	Rare	
(C182)	1833	Inc. Ab.	—	—	Rare	
	1834	154 pcs.	—	—	Rare	

BRAZIL 218

4000 REIS

8.2000 g, .917 GOLD, .2417 oz AGW
Mint mark: R

KM#	Date	Mintage	Fine	VF	XF	Unc
369.1	1823	.021	250.00	500.00	850.00	1200.
(C140.1)	1824	.038	250.00	500.00	850.00	1200.
	1825	.020	250.00	500.00	850.00	1200.
	1826	8,966	250.00	500.00	900.00	1400.
	1827/6	7,771	—	—	Rare	—
	1827	Inc. Ab.	1100.	2100.	3200.	4500.

Mint mark: B

369.2	1825	—	1100.	2100.	3600.	5200.
(C140.2)	1826	—	1150.	2300.	3900.	5600.
	1828	—	1250.	2500.	4100.	5800.

Mint mark: R

| 386.1 | 1832 | 64 pcs. | 1200. | 2500. | 3750. | 5400. |
| (C202.1) | 1833/2 | 257 pcs. | 1000. | 2100. | 3500. | 5200. |

Obv: AZEVEDO below bust.

| 386.2 | 1832 | 5 known | — | — | Rare | — |
| (C202.2) | | | | | | |

6400 REIS

14.3400 g, .917 GOLD, .4228 oz AGW
Mint mark: R
Pedro I Coronation

| 361 | 1822 | 64 pcs. | — | — | Rare | — |
| (C139) | | | | | | |

370.1	1823	931 pcs.	950.00	1900.	3200.	4600.
(C141.1)	1824	235 pcs.	1200.	4500.	6000.	8000.
	1825	776 pcs.	950.00	1900.	3200.	4600.
	1827	637 pcs.	950.00	1900.	3200.	4600.
	1828	650 pcs.	1200.	2400.	3500.	5000.
	1830					Unique

Mint mark: B

370.2	1825	—	1200.	3000.	4500.	6000.
(C141.2)	1826	—	1200.	3000.	4500.	6000.
	1828	423 pcs.	1200.	3000.	4500.	6000.

Mint mark: R

| 387.1 | 1832 | .030 | 300.00 | 600.00 | 1000. | 1500. |
| (C203.1) | 1833 | .011 | 300.00 | 600.00 | 1000. | 1500. |

Obv: AZEVEDO below bust.

KM#	Date	Mintage	Fine	VF	XF	Unc
387.2	1832	4,101	500.00	1000.	1750.	2750.
(C203.2)						

MONETARY REFORM

10 REIS

BRONZE

473	1868	89.604	.50	2.00	4.00	7.00
(Y-A11)	1869 Rs. (Brussels)					
		Inc. Ab.	.50	2.00	4.00	7.00
	1869 Rs (w/o period, Rio de Janeiro)					
		Inc. Ab.	—	—	—	7.00
	1870	—	.50	2.00	5.00	8.00

20 REIS

BRONZE

474	1868	90.360	1.50	2.25	4.00	7.00
(Y-A12)	1869 Rs. (Brussels)					
		Inc. Ab.	1.50	2.25	4.00	7.00
	1869 Rs (w/o period, Rio de Janeiro)					
		Inc. Ab.	1.75	2.75	4.00	7.00
	1870	—	1.75	3.50	7.50	20.00

40 REIS

BRONZE

479	1873	3.750	1.00	2.50	5.00	17.50
(Y-A13)	1874	.890	1.00	2.50	6.00	25.00
	1875	1.208	1.00	2.50	5.00	17.50
	1876	.549	1.00	4.00	12.00	50.00
	1877	.465	1.00	3.00	10.00	40.00
	1878	1.223	1.00	2.50	6.00	25.00
	1879	2.771	1.00	2.50	5.00	17.50
	1880	1.569	1.00	2.50	5.00	17.50

50 REIS

COPPER-NICKEL

482	1886	.590	1.00	2.00	7.00	17.50
(Y-A16)	1887	Inc. Ab.	1.00	2.50	7.00	20.00
	1888	.153	1.00	2.50	7.00	35.00

100 REIS

2.2400 g, .917 SILVER, .0660 oz ASW
Obv: Value in floral circle.
Rev: Crowned arms in branches.

452	1834	7,709	20.00	35.00	65.00	200.00
(C183)	1835	Inc. Ab.	20.00	35.00	65.00	200.00
	1836	5,592	400.00	700.00	1000.	2750.
	1837	9,562	20.00	35.00	65.00	200.00
	1840	910 pcs.	125.00	175.00	250.00	500.00
	1844	—	—	—	Rare	—

KM#	Date	Mintage	Fine	VF	XF	Unc
(C183)	1846	4,699	20.00	35.00	65.00	200.00
	1847/4	682 pcs.	125.00	200.00	350.00	600.00
	1848	486 pcs.	300.00	450.00	700.00	1750.

COPPER-NICKEL

477	1871	4.000	.50	1.25	3.00	30.00
(Y-A14)	1872	100 pcs.	600.00	900.00	1800.	3000.
	1874	—	.75	2.50	12.00	30.00
	1875	—	5.00	30.00	150.00	450.00
	1876	—	2.50	20.00	150.00	450.00
	1877	—	.75	2.50	12.00	30.00
	1878	—	1.00	3.00	15.00	50.00
	1879	—	1.00	2.50	12.00	30.00
	1880	—	1.50	5.00	50.00	300.00
	1881	—	.75	2.50	12.00	30.00
	1882	—	.75	2.50	12.00	30.00
	1883	2,700	.75	2.50	12.00	30.00
	1884	—	.75	2.50	12.00	30.00
	1885	—	.75	2.50	12.00	30.00

483	1886	.877	.75	2.00	9.50	30.00
(Y-A17)	1887	—	.75	2.00	9.50	30.00
	1888	1.696	.75	2.00	9.50	30.00
	1889	.862	.75	2.00	9.50	30.00

200 REIS

4.4800 g, .917 SILVER, .1320 oz ASW

455	1835	4,894	20.00	50.00	100.00	300.00
(C184)	1837	5,007	20.00	50.00	100.00	300.00
	1840	624 pcs.	125.00	300.00	500.00	800.00
	1844	893	100.00	200.00	300.00	500.00
	1846	406 pcs.	150.00	300.00	450.00	500.00
	1847	2,936	25.00	45.00	125.00	300.00
	1848/7	501 pcs.	250.00	450.00	900.00	1350.
	1848	Inc. Ab.	250.00	400.00	800.00	1000.

2.5200 g, .917 SILVER, .0742 oz ASW

469	1854	.037	6.00	10.00	30.00	100.00
(Y-A6)	1855	.228	3.00	6.00	12.00	30.00
	1856/5	.103	6.00	10.00	17.50	50.00
	1856	Inc. Ab.	3.00	6.00	10.00	25.00
	1857	.128	3.00	6.00	12.00	30.00
	1858	.245	3.00	6.00	15.00	35.00
	1859	.152	3.00	6.00	15.00	35.00
	1860	.028	3.00	6.00	10.00	20.00
	1861	—	4.00	7.50	15.00	60.00
	1862	—	3.00	6.00	10.00	25.00
	1863	—	3.00	6.00	10.00	25.00
	1864	—	3.00	6.00	10.00	25.00
	1865	—	3.00	6.00	10.00	25.00
	1866	—	3.00	6.00	12.00	27.50
	1867	—	3.00	6.00	10.00	25.00

2.5000 g, .835 SILVER, .0671 oz ASW

471	1867	—	2.50	4.00	9.00	25.00
(Y-A19)	1868	—	2.50	4.00	9.00	25.00
	1869	—	5.00	10.00	20.00	50.00

KM#	Date	Mintage	Fine	VF	XF	Unc
478	1871	3.650	.50	1.25	4.00	30.00
(Y-A15)	1874	—	1.00	2.00	5.00	35.00
	1875	—	3.00	10.00	20.00	75.00
	1876	—	1.00	2.00	5.00	30.00
	1877	—	1.00	2.00	5.00	30.00
	1878	—	1.00	2.50	7.00	50.00
	1880	—	1.00	3.00	6.00	30.00
	1882	—	1.00	3.50	6.00	30.00
	1884	—	1.00	1.25	6.00	30.00

COPPER-NICKEL

484	1886	.177	4.50	18.00	65.00	200.00
(Y-A18)	1887	—	1.00	2.00	6.00	20.00
	1888	.967	1.00	2.00	6.00	20.00
	1889	.511	1.50	2.50	7.00	22.50

400 REIS

8.9600 g, .917 SILVER, .2640 oz ASW
Obv: Value in floral circle.
Rev: Crowned arms in branches.

453	1834	6,197	50.00	100.00	175.00	400.00
(C185)	1835	Inc. Ab.	50.00	100.00	175.00	400.00
	1837	7,837	50.00	100.00	175.00	400.00
	1840	—	300.00	600.00	1200.	2000.
	1841	—	300.00	600.00	1200.	2000.
	1843	161 pcs.	700.00	1000.	2000.	3000.
	1844	649 pcs.	200.00	400.00	1000.	2000.
	1845	179 pcs.	500.00	750.00	1400.	2000.
	1847/0	878 pcs.	125.00	250.00	500.00	1000.
	1847	Inc. Ab.	60.00	125.00	200.00	400.00
	1848	510 pcs.	300.00	6000.	1200.	2000.

500 REIS

6.3700 g, .917 SILVER, .1877 oz ASW

458	1848	—	—	—	Rare	
(Y-A1)	1849	.026	25.00	50.00	80.00	200.00
	1850	.067	7.50	10.00	20.00	75.00
	1851	.095	7.50	10.00	18.00	50.00
	1852	.167	7.50	10.00	18.00	50.00

464	1853	.241	5.00	8.50	10.00	35.00
(Y-A7)	1854	.317	5.00	8.50	10.00	35.00
	1855	.212	5.00	8.50	10.00	35.00
	1856	.223	5.00	8.50	10.00	35.00
	1857	.265	5.00	7.50	10.00	35.00

KM#	Date	Mintage	Fine	VF	XF	Unc
(Y-A7)	1858	.791	5.00	7.50	10.00	35.00
	1859	.152	5.00	7.50	10.00	35.00
	1860/50	*.108	5.00	7.50	10.00	50.00
	1860	Inc. Ab.	5.00	7.50	10.00	35.00
	1861	—	5.00	7.50	10.00	35.00
	1862	—	5.00	7.50	10.00	35.00
	1863	—	5.00	7.50	10.00	35.00
	1864	—	5.00	7.50	10.00	35.00
	1865	—	5.00	7.50	10.00	35.00
	1866	—	5.00	7.50	10.00	35.00
	1867	—	5.00	7.50	10.00	35.00

*NOTE: The 1860 mintage figure includes only first six month's production.

6.2500 g, .835 SILVER, .1678 oz ASW
Obv: C.L. under truncation.

472	1867	—	5.00	7.50	10.00	35.00
(Y-A20)	1868	—	5.00	7.50	10.00	35.00

6.3750 g, .917 SILVER, .1879 oz ASW
Obv: W/o C.L. Rev. leg: DECRETO DE 1870.

480	1876	.076	4.50	7.00	10.00	50.00
(Y-A23)	1886	5,283	50.00	100.00	150.00	300.00
	1887	768 pcs.	600.00	900.00	1250.	1750.
	1888	.333	—	7.00	10.00	35.00
	1889	.278	4.50	7.00	10.00	35.00

800 REIS

17.9300 g, .917 SILVER, .5283 oz ASW

456	1835	1,698	600.00	800.00	1600.	2500.
(C186)	1838	497 pcs.	650.00	1000.	2000.	3000.
	1840	145 pcs.	1000.	1700.	2400.	3750.
	1843	127 pcs.	2750.	3750.	5000.	6500.
	1844	628 pcs.	700.00	1100.	1800.	3250.
	1846	672 pcs.	700.00	1100.	2000.	3500.

1000 REIS

12.7500 g, .917 SILVER, .3757 oz ASW

459	1849	965 pcs.	600.00	1000.	1500.	2500.
(Y-A2)	1850	.169	6.00	8.00	15.00	60.00
	1851	.099	6.00	8.00	15.00	65.00
	1852	.196	6.00	8.00	15.00	60.00

465	1853	.266	6.00	8.00	20.00	40.00
(Y-A8)	1854	.228	6.00	8.00	20.00	40.00
	1855	.312	6.00	8.00	20.00	40.00
	1856	.426	6.00	8.00	20.00	40.00
	1857	.512	6.00	8.00	20.00	40.00
	1858	.430	6.00	8.00	20.00	40.00

KM#	Date	Mintage	Fine	VF	XF	Unc
(Y-A8)	1859	.996	6.00	8.00	20.00	40.00
	1860/50	.387	8.00	12.00	30.00	60.00
	1860	Inc. Ab.	6.00	8.00	20.00	40.00
	1861	—	6.00	8.00	20.00	40.00
	1862	—	6.00	8.00	20.00	40.00
	1863	—	6.00	8.00	20.00	40.00
	1864	—	6.00	8.00	20.00	40.00
	1865	—	6.00	8.00	20.00	40.00
	1866	—	6.00	8.00	20.00	40.00

12.5000 g, .900 SILVER, .3617 oz ASW
Obv: LUSTER F. under truncation.

476	1869	—	15.00	25.00	50.00	85.00
(Y-A21)						

12.7500 g, .917 SILVER, .3759 oz ASW
Obv: W/o LUSTER F. Rev. leg: DECRETO DE 1870.

481	1876	.194	7.50	12.50	20.00	60.00
(Y-A24)	1877	.012	17.50	30.00	30.00	100.00
	1878	.047	12.50	17.50	30.00	90.00
	1879	.035	12.50	17.50	30.00	85.00
	1880	.020	12.50	17.50	30.00	90.00
	1881	.020	20.00	30.00	45.00	140.00
	1882	.018	25.00	40.00	75.00	175.00
	1883	.031	12.50	17.50	30.00	80.00
	1884	.022	20.00	30.00	65.00	150.00
	1885	.011	30.00	40.00	75.00	175.00
	1886	.048	8.50	15.00	30.00	100.00
	1887	9,875	35.00	60.00	80.00	175.00
	1888	.100	7.50	12.50	20.00	65.00
	1889	.089	50.00	70.00	90.00	200.00

1200 REIS

26.8900 g, .917 SILVER, .7924 oz ASW

454	1834	891 pcs.	75.00	250.00	500.00	1250.
(C187)	1835	.010	75.00	180.00	450.00	1250.
	1837	6,304	75.00	175.00	450.00	1250.
	1839	186 pcs.			Rare	—
	1840/37	633 pcs.	250.00	425.00	900.00	2000.
	1840	Inc. Ab.	225.00	450.00	700.00	1500.
	1843	1,803	100.00	450.00	500.00	1250.
	1845	292 pcs.	375.00	750.00	1250.	2500.
	1846	1,898	225.00	450.00	900.00	2250.
	1847	.010	75.00	175.00	500.00	1250.

NOTE: The above coins dated 1841 and 1842 are counterfeit.

2000 REIS

25.5000 g, .917 SILVER, .7514 oz ASW

462	1851	.256	10.00	15.00	30.00	100.00
(Y-A3)	1852	.277	10.00	15.00	30.00	100.00

BRAZIL 219

BRAZIL 220

KM#	Date	Mintage	Fine	VF	XF	Unc
466	1853	.145	10.00	20.00	35.00	80.00
(Y-A9)	1854	.086	20.00	30.00	60.00	125.00
	1855	.300	10.00	20.00	35.00	100.00
	1856	.229	10.00	20.00	35.00	80.00
	1857	.105	20.00	30.00	50.00	80.00
	1858	.022	35.00	65.00	100.00	200.00
	1859	.041	400.00	800.00	1250.	1750.
	1863	—	10.00	20.00	35.00	80.00
	1864	—	35.00	65.00	100.00	300.00
	1865	—	20.00	30.00	50.00	80.00
	1866	—	400.00	800.00	1250.	1750.
	1867	—	400.00	800.00	1250.	1750.

25.0000 g, .900 SILVER, .7234 oz ASW
Obv: LUSTER F. under truncation.

475	1868	—	20.00	30.00	80.00	200.00
(Y-A22)	1869	—	15.00	—	—	150.00

25.5000 g, .917 SILVER, .7515 oz ASW

475a	1875	—	15.00	25.00	50.00	150.00
(Y-A22a)	1876	—	75.00	125.00	200.00	500.00

Obv: W/o LUSTER F. Rev. leg: DECRETO DE 1870.

485	1886	1,190	400.00	600.00	1000.	1400.
(Y-A25)	1887	.043	15.00	25.00	45.00	125.00
	1888	.906	10.00	15.00	25.00	60.00
	1889	—	10.00	15.00	25.00	60.00

5000 REIS

4.4824 g, .917 GOLD, .1321 oz AGW

470	1854	.021	75.00	100.00	125.00	200.00
(Y-A26)	1855	.047	90.00	120.00	150.00	250.00
	1856	.027	75.00	100.00	125.00	200.00
	1857	4,631	150.00	400.00	1150.	1350.
	1858	1,146	250.00	1000.	1750.	2500.
	1859	493	350.00	2000.	2500.	3500.

10,000 REIS

14.3400 g, .917 GOLD, .4228 oz AGW

451	1833	7,304	250.00	500.00	700.00	1000.
(C204)	1834	5,617	250.00	500.00	700.00	1000.
	1835	.013	250.00	500.00	700.00	1000.

KM#	Date	Mintage	Fine	VF	XF	Unc
(C204)	1836	.011	300.00	500.00	750.00	1800.
	1838	482 pcs.	500.00	1000.	2000.	3000.
	1839	567 pcs.	500.00	1000.	2000.	3000.
	1840	4,462	300.00	600.00	1500.	2000.

Obv: Military bust

457	1841	3,454	350.00	800.00	1500.	2000.
(C205)	1842	1,146	500.00	1200.	2000.	3000.
	1843	544 pcs.	500.00	1500.	2200.	3500.
	1844	1,989	500.00	1000.	2000.	3000.
	1845	3,834	250.00	600.00	1000.	2000.
	1847	.026	225.00	600.00	1000.	2000.
	1848	4,567	500.00	1000.	2000.	3000.

8.9648 g, .917 GOLD, .2643 oz AGW
Reduced size, 26mm.

460	1849	1,678	300.00	750.00	1000.	1500.
(Y-A4)	1850	7,359	150.00	250.00	400.00	700.00
	1851	.011	150.00	250.00	400.00	700.00

467	1853	.040	BV	130.00	160.00	400.00
(Y-A27)	1854	.163	BV	130.00	160.00	400.00
	1855	.041	BV	130.00	160.00	400.00
	1856	.208	BV	130.00	160.00	400.00
	1857	.098	BV	130.00	160.00	400.00
	1858	.055	BV	130.00	160.00	400.00
	1859	.016	150.00	350.00	1850.	3000.
	1861	—	BV	130.00	160.00	450.00
	1863	—	150.00	350.00	1850.	3000.
	1865	—	BV	130.00	160.00	400.00
	1866	—	BV	130.00	160.00	400.00
	1867	—	BV	130.00	160.00	400.00
	1871	—	BV	160.00	200.00	500.00
	1872	—	BV	160.00	200.00	500.00
	1873	—	BV	160.00	200.00	500.00
	1874	—	BV	160.00	200.00	500.00
	1875	—	BV	160.00	200.00	500.00
	1876	.020	BV	160.00	200.00	500.00
	1877	3,441	BV	200.00	300.00	650.00
	1878	.010	BV	150.00	200.00	650.00
	1879	6,431	BV	150.00	200.00	650.00
	1880	9,806	BV	200.00	300.00	650.00
	1882	4,671	BV	220.00	350.00	700.00
	1883	.010	BV	200.00	250.00	600.00
	1884	.011	BV	160.00	200.00	600.00
	1885	7,955	100.00	300.00	650.00	1250.
	1886	3,782	BV	220.00	350.00	700.00
	1887	1,180	100.00	300.00	650.00	1250.
	1888	5,359	BV	250.00	400.00	800.00
	1889	—	BV	220.00	350.00	700.00

20,000 REIS

17.9296 g, .917 GOLD, .5286 oz AGW

461	1849	6,464	275.00	600.00	800.00	1000.
(Y-A5)	1850	.042	260.00	300.00	500.00	700.00
	1851	.303	260.00	300.00	500.00	700.00

KM#	Date	Mintage	Fine	VF	XF	Unc
463	1851	Inc. Ab.	260.00	300.00	400.00	550.00
(Y-A10)	1852	.186	260.00	300.00	400.00	550.00

Obv: Larger bust

468	1853	.246	BV	260.00	350.00	700.00
(Y-A28)	1854	.026	BV	320.00	450.00	900.00
	1855	.048	BV	260.00	300.00	650.00
	1856	.262	BV	260.00	300.00	650.00
	1857/6	.315	BV	260.00	350.00	700.00
	1857	Inc. Ab.	BV	260.00	350.00	700.00
	1858	.032	BV	260.00	350.00	700.00
	1859	.047	BV	275.00	400.00	850.00
	1860	—	BV	275.00	400.00	800.00
	1861	—	BV	275.00	375.00	750.00
	1862	—	—	—	Rare	
	1863	—	425.00	550.00	800.00	1300.
	1864	—	300.00	550.00	800.00	1300.
	1865	—	BV	275.00	500.00	800.00
	1867	—	BV	260.00	350.00	700.00
	1889	—	BV	260.00	300.00	600.00

REPUBLIC
20 REIS

BRONZE

490	1889	.630	.40	1.00	2.50	15.00
(Y1)	1893	.250	.40	1.00	2.50	15.00
	1894	Inc. Ab.	.75	1.50	3.00	25.00
	1895	2.118	.50	1.00	2.50	15.00
	1896	.490	5.00	40.00	80.00	200.00
	1897	.273	3.00	8.00	12.50	40.00
	1898	.300	3.00	8.00	12.50	40.00
	1899	1.065	3.00	8.00	12.50	40.00
	1900	1.718	.40	1.00	3.00	20.00
	1901	.713	.50	1.00	3.00	20.00
	1904	.850	.50	1.00	3.00	20.00
	1905	1.075	4.00	8.00	15.00	50.00
	1906	.215	2.00	5.00	10.00	30.00
	1908	4.558	.40	1.00	3.00	20.00
	1909	1.215	5.00	15.00	45.00	100.00
	1910	.828	.75	1.50	3.00	20.00
	1911	1.545	.75	1.50	3.00	20.00
	1912	.480	.85	1.75	4.00	25.00

COPPER-NICKEL

516	1918	.373	.25	.50	2.00	5.00
(Y27)	1919	2.870	.25	.50	1.00	4.00
	1920	.825	.25	.50	1.25	5.00
	1921	1.020	.25	.50	1.25	5.00
	1927	.053	5.00	10.00	30.00	80.00
	1935	100 pcs.	200.00	350.00	700.00	1000.

40 REIS

BRONZE

KM#	Date	Mintage	Fine	VF	XF	Unc
491	1889	1.781	.50	1.00	2.00	15.00
(Y2)	1893	1.085	1.50	3.00	5.00	22.50
	1894	.770	1.50	3.00	5.00	22.50
	1895	Inc. Ab.	2.00	3.50	6.00	25.00
	1896	.191	25.00	50.00	100.00	300.00
	1897	1.236	.75	2.00	3.50	17.50
	1898	.300	12.50	40.00	75.00	200.00
	1900	2.115	.75	2.50	4.50	20.00
	1901	.525	.75	2.00	3.50	15.00
	1907	.218	.75	2.00	3.50	15.00
	1908	4.639	.75	2.00	3.50	15.00
	1909	4.226	.75	2.00	3.50	17.50
	1910	.848	.75	2.00	4.00	20.00
	1911	1.660	.75	2.00	4.00	20.00
	1912	.819	1.00	2.50	4.50	22.50

50 REIS

COPPER-NICKEL

KM#	Date	Mintage	Fine	VF	XF	Unc
517	1918	.558	.15	.35	.75	6.00
(Y28)	1919	.558	.15	.35	.75	6.00
	1920	.072	.40	1.00	4.00	18.00
	1921	.682	.15	.35	.75	6.00
	1922	.176	.40	1.00	4.00	18.00
	1925	.128	.40	1.50	5.00	20.00
	1926	.194	.40	1.50	5.00	20.00
	1931	.020	2.00	10.00	30.00	80.00
	1935	100 pcs.	125.00	300.00	450.00	1000.

100 REIS

COPPER-NICKEL

KM#	Date	Mintage	Fine	VF	XF	Unc
492	1889	7.686	.75	3.00	8.50	30.00
(Y3)	1893	3.589	1.00	3.00	8.50	30.00
	1894	1.881	1.00	3.00	8.50	30.00
	1895	2.308	1.00	3.00	8.50	30.00
	1896	3.390	1.00	3.00	8.50	30.00
	1897	2.875	3.00	6.50	12.00	40.00
	1898	3.685	3.00	6.50	12.00	40.00
	1899	2.990	3.00	6.50	12.00	40.00
	1900	.539	8.00	20.00	60.00	200.00

Date: MCMI – 1901.

503	1901	15.775	.40	1.00	2.00	8.00
(Y12)						

518	1918	.600	.40	1.00	1.50	4.00
(Y29)	1919	1.219	.40	1.00	1.50	4.00
	1920	1.251	.40	1.00	1.50	4.00
	1921	.853	.40	1.00	1.50	4.00
	1922	.347	.40	1.00	2.00	8.00
	1923	.956	1.00	2.00	2.00	8.00
	1924	1.478	1.00	2.00	5.00	10.00
	1925	2.502	.30	.75	1.25	4.00
	1926	1.807	.50	1.00	2.00	8.00
	1927	1.451	.30	.75	1.25	4.00
	1928	1.514	.30	.75	1.25	4.00

KM#	Date	Mintage	Fine	VF	XF	Unc
(Y29)	1929	2.503	.30	.75	1.25	4.00
	1930	2.398	.30	.75	1.25	4.00
	1931	2.500	.25	.50	1.00	4.00
	1932	.948	.25	.50	1.00	4.00
	1933	1.314	.25	.50	1.00	4.00
	1934	3.614	.25	.50	1.00	4.00
	1935	3.442	.25	.50	1.00	4.00

Cazique Tibercia
400th Anniversary of Colonization

527	1932	1.012	.50	1.00	2.50	8.00
(Y39)						

Tamandare Commemorative

536	1936	3.928	.20	.50	1.50	3.50
(Y45)	1937	7.905	.10	.25	1.00	3.00
	1938	8.618	.10	.25	1.00	3.00

Getulio Vargas Government

544	1938	8.106	.10	.20	.50	1.50
(Y57)	1940	8.797	.10	.20	.50	1.50
	1942	1.285	.10	.20	.50	1.50

NOTE: The 1942 issue has a yellow cast due to higher copper content.

200 REIS

COPPER-NICKEL

493	1889	4.829	1.50	3.00	7.50	45.00
(Y4)	1893	2.586	2.00	4.50	10.00	45.00
	1894	1.562	2.00	4.50	10.00	45.00
	1895	1.633	2.00	4.50	10.00	50.00
	1896	2.850	2.50	5.00	12.50	50.00
	1897	2.405	2.50	5.50	15.00	50.00
	1898	3.925	2.50	5.00	12.50	50.00
	1899	2.724	3.00	6.00	17.50	50.00
	1900	.330	15.00	50.00	100.00	300.00

Date: MCMI – 1901.

504	1901	12.625	.60	1.50	2.00	7.50
(Y13)						

519	1918	.625	.35	.75	1.25	7.50
(Y30)	1919	.882	.35	.75	1.00	7.50
	1920	1.657	.35	.75	1.00	7.50
	1921	1.135	.35	.75	1.00	7.50
	1922	.678	.35	.75	1.00	7.50
	1923	1.655	.35	.75	1.00	7.50
	1924	1.750	.35	.75	1.00	7.50
	1925	2.082	.35	.75	1.00	7.50

KM#	Date	Mintage	Fine	VF	XF	Unc
(Y30)	1926	.324	1.00	3.00	8.00	22.50
	1927	1.806	.35	.75	1.00	6.00
	1928	.782	.35	.75	1.00	6.00
	1929	2.440	.25	.50	.75	5.00
	1930	1.697	.25	.50	.75	5.00
	1931	1.830	.25	.50	.75	5.00
	1932	.761	.25	.50	.75	5.00
	1933	.173	.35	.75	1.00	6.00
	1934	.612	.25	.50	.75	5.00
	1935	1.329	.25	.50	.75	5.00

400th Anniversary of Colonization

528	1932	.596	.75	2.00	5.00	10.00
(Y40)						

Maua Commemorative

537	1936	2.256	.30	.50	1.00	4.00
(Y46)	1937	6.506	.30	.50	1.00	4.00
	1938	5.787	.30	.50	1.00	4.00

Getulio Vargas Government

545	1938	7.666	.20	.50	1.00	3.00
(Y58)	1940	10.161	.15	.40	.60	2.50
	1942	1.966	.15	.40	.60	2.50

NOTE: The 1942 issue has a yellow cast due to higher copper content.

300 REIS

COPPER-NICKEL
Carlos Gomes

538	1936	3.029	.30	.75	1.50	5.00
(Y47)	1937	4.507	.30	.75	1.50	5.00
	1938	3.753	.30	.75	1.50	5.00

Getulio Vargas Government

546	1938	12.080	.20	.35	.50	3.00
(Y59)	1940	8.124	.20	.35	.50	3.00
	1942	2.020	.25	.40	.75	4.00

NOTE: The 1942 issue has a yellow cast due to higher copper content.

400 REIS

5.1000 g, .917 SILVER, .1503 oz ASW
400th Anniversary of Discovery

499	1900	.055	20.00	35.00	50.00	100.00
(Y8)						

BRAZIL 221

BRAZIL 222

COPPER-NICKEL
Obv: Date: MCMI - 1901.

KM#	Date	Mintage	Fine	VF	XF	Unc
505 (Y14)	1901	5.531	1.25	2.50	6.25	25.00

KM#	Date	Mintage	Fine	VF	XF	Unc
515 (Y-B14)	1914	.646	15.00	30.00	60.00	100.00

NOTE: This is considered a pattern by many authorities.

KM#	Date	Mintage	Fine	VF	XF	Unc
520 (Y31)	1918	.491	.75	1.50	3.00	6.00
	1919	.891	.75	1.50	3.00	6.00
	1920	1.521	.75	1.50	3.00	6.00
	1921	.871	.50	1.00	3.00	6.00
	1922	1.275	.50	1.00	3.00	6.00
	1923	.764	.50	1.00	3.00	6.00
	1925	2.048	.50	1.00	3.00	6.00
	1926	1.034	.50	1.00	3.00	6.00
	1927	.738	.50	1.00	3.00	6.00
	1929	.869	.50	1.00	3.00	6.00
	1930	1.031	.50	1.00	3.00	6.00
	1931	1.431	.50	1.00	3.00	6.00
	1932	.588	.50	1.00	3.00	6.00
	1935	.225	.50	1.00	3.00	6.00

400th Anniversary of Colonization
KM#	Date	Mintage	Fine	VF	XF	Unc
529 (Y41)	1932	.416	1.00	3.00	6.00	12.00

Oswaldo Cruz
KM#	Date	Mintage	Fine	VF	XF	Unc
539 (Y48)	1936	2.079	.50	.90	1.50	7.50
	1937	3.111	.50	.90	1.50	7.50
	1938	2.681	.50	.90	1.50	7.50

Getulio Vargas Government

KM#	Date	Mintage	Fine	VF	XF	Unc
547 (Y60)	1938	10.620	.25	.50	.75	3.00
	1940	7.312	.25	.50	.75	3.00
	1942	1.496	.25	.50	1.00	3.50

NOTE: The 1942 issue has a yellow cast due to higher copper content.

500 REIS

6.3750 g, .917 SILVER, .1879 oz ASW

KM#	Date	Mintage	Fine	VF	XF	Unc
494 (Y5)	1889	4.541	2.50	4.50	8.00	25.00

5.0000 g, .900 SILVER, .1446 oz ASW

KM#	Date	Mintage	Fine	VF	XF	Unc
506 (Y15)	1906	.352	BV	3.00	5.00	15.00
	1907	1.282	BV	3.00	5.00	15.00
	1908	.498	BV	3.00	5.00	15.00
	1911	8.000	20.00	30.00	50.00	80.00
	1912	*.222	20.00	30.00	60.00	90.00

KM#	Date	Mintage	Fine	VF	XF	Unc
509 (Y18)	1912	*Inc. Ab.	3.50	7.50	15.00	40.00

KM#	Date	Mintage	Fine	VF	XF	Unc
512 (Y21)	1913A	—	1.50	3.00	6.00	17.50

ALUMINUM-BRONZE
Independence Centennial
KM#	Date	Mintage	Fine	VF	XF	Unc
521.1 (Y34)	1922	13.744	.25	.60	1.25	5.00

Error: BBASIL instead of BRASIL
| 521.2 (Y34a) | 1922 | Inc. Ab. | 17.50 | 35.00 | 55.00 | 120.00 |

KM#	Date	Mintage	Fine	VF	XF	Unc
524 (Y32)	1924	7.400	.30	.75	1.25	4.00
	1927	2.725	.30	.75	1.25	4.00
	1928	9.432	.30	.75	1.25	4.00
	1930	.146	1.00	2.00	4.00	10.00

Joao Ramalho
400th Anniversary of Colonization
KM#	Date	Mintage	Fine	VF	XF	Unc
530 (Y42)	1932	.034	1.50	5.00	7.50	15.00

Diego Feijo
4.00 g
| 533 (Y49) | 1935 | .014 | 2.00 | 7.50 | 10.00 | 17.00 |

5.00 g
540 (Y50)	1936	1.326	.60	.90	1.25	4.00
	1937	Inc. Ab.	.60	.90	1.25	4.00
	1938	—	.60	.90	1.25	4.00

Joachim Machado de Assis
| 549 (Y61) | 1939 | 5.928 | .50 | .75 | 1.00 | 4.00 |

1000 REIS

12.7500 g, .917 SILVER, .3758 oz ASW
| 495 (Y6) | 1889 | .296 | 10.00 | 15.00 | 35.00 | 80.00 |

400th Anniversary of Discovery
| 500 (Y9) | 1900 | .033 | 50.00 | 75.00 | 100.00 | 150.00 |

10.0000 g, .900 SILVER, .2894 oz ASW
507 (Y16)	1906	.420	BV	4.00	7.50	24.00
	1907	1.282	BV	4.00	7.50	24.00
	1908	1.624	BV	4.00	7.50	24.00

BRAZIL 223

KM#	Date	Mintage	Fine	VF	XF	Unc
(Y16)	1909	.816	BV	4.00	7.50	24.00
	1910	2.354	BV	4.00	7.50	24.00
	1911	2.810	BV	4.00	7.50	24.00
	1912	*1.570	BV	4.00	7.50	24.00

510	1912	*Inc. Ab.	4.00	6.00	10.00	35.00
(Y19)	1913	2.525	4.00	6.00	10.00	35.00

513	1913A	—	BV	3.50	7.00	20.00
(Y22)						

ALUMINUM-BRONZE
Independence Centennial

522.1	1922	16.698	.40	.60	2.00	5.00
(Y35)						

Error: BBASIL instead of BRASIL

522.2	1922	Inc. Ab.	2.50	4.00	10.00	22.50
(Y35a)						

525	1924	9.354	.50	1.25	2.50	7.00
(Y33)	1925	6.205	.50	1.25	2.50	7.00
	1927	35.817	.50	1.25	2.50	7.00
	1928	1.899	.50	1.25	2.50	7.00
	1929	.083	2.50	7.50	15.00	60.00
	1930	.045	2.50	7.50	15.00	60.00
	1931	.200	1.00	5.00	8.50	12.50

Martim Affonso da Sousa
400th Anniversary of Colonization

531	1932	.056	3.00	5.00	8.00	14.00
(Y43)						

Jose de Anchieta

KM#	Date	Mintage	Fine	VF	XF	Unc
534	1935	.138	1.00	3.00	5.00	12.00
(Y51)						

Size reduced

541	1936	.926	.50	1.00	2.00	6.00
(Y52)	1937	Inc. Ab.	.50	1.00	2.00	6.00
	1938	—	.50	1.00	2.00	6.00

Tobias Barreto

550	1939	9.586	.25	.50	1.25	5.00
(Y62)						

2000 REIS

25.5000 g, .917 SILVER, .7515 oz ASW

498	1891	.040	500.00	1000.	2000.	3000.
(Y7)	1896	.010	500.00	1000.	2000.	3000.
	1897	.160	175.00	350.00	500.00	1500.

400th Anniversary of Discovery

501	1900	.020	100.00	150.00	250.00	350.00
(Y10)						

20.0000 g, .900 SILVER, .5787 oz ASW

508	1906	.256	4.50	9.00	17.50	55.00
(Y17)	1907	2.863	BV	6.00	9.00	45.00
	1908	1.707	BV	6.00	9.00	45.00
	1910	.585	4.50	9.00	17.50	55.00
	1911	1.929	BV	6.00	9.00	45.00
	1912	.741	4.50	9.00	17.50	55.00

KM#	Date	Mintage	Fine	VF	XF	Unc
511	1912	Inc. Ab.	6.50	12.50	25.00	60.00
(Y20)	1913	.395	6.50	12.50	25.00	60.00

514	1913A	—	4.50	9.00	13.00	40.00
(Y23)						

7.9000 g, .900 SILVER, .2285 oz ASW
Independence Centennial

523	1922	1.560	BV	3.00	4.00	8.00
(Y38)						

7.9000 g, .500 SILVER, .1269 oz ASW

523a	1922	Inc. Ab.	BV	3.00	4.00	8.00
(Y38a)						

*NOTE: Struck in both .900 and .500 fine silver, but can only be distinguished by analysis (and color, on worn specimens).

 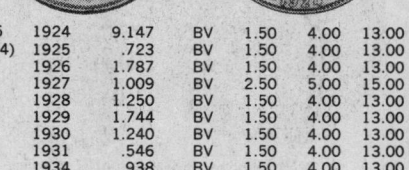

526	1924	9.147	BV	1.50	4.00	13.00
(Y24)	1925	.723	BV	1.50	4.00	13.00
	1926	1.787	BV	1.50	4.00	13.00
	1927	1.009	BV	2.50	5.00	15.00
	1928	1.250	BV	1.50	4.00	13.00
	1929	1.744	BV	1.50	4.00	13.00
	1930	1.240	BV	1.50	4.00	13.00
	1931	.546	BV	1.50	4.00	13.00
	1934	.938	BV	1.50	4.00	13.00

John III
400th Anniversary of Colonization

532	1932	.695	2.00	2.50	5.00	15.00
(Y44)						

Duke of Caxias

535	1935	2.131	BV	1.50	4.00	13.00
(Y55)						

BRAZIL 224

ALUMINUM-BRONZE
Duke of Caxias
Reeded edge.

KM#	Date	Mintage	Fine	VF	XF	Unc
542	1936	.665	.50	.75	2.00	6.00
(Y53)	1937	Inc. Ab.	.50	.75	2.00	6.00
	1938	—	2.50	4.50	12.50	30.00

Plain edge, polygonal planchet

| 548 | 1937 | — | 25.00 | 50.00 | 125.00 | 300.00 |
| (Y54) | 1938 | — | .75 | 1.50 | 3.50 | 8.00 |

Floriano Peixoto

| 551 | 1939 | 5.048 | .50 | .75 | 2.00 | 6.00 |
| (Y63) | | | | | | |

4000 REIS

51.0000 g, .917 SILVER, 1.5030 oz ASW
400th Anniversary of Discovery
Obv: Star w/16 rays.

| 502.1 | 1900 | 6,850 | 225.00 | 400.00 | 600.00 | 800.00 |
| (Y11.1) | | | | | | |

Obv: Star w/20 rays.

| 502.2 | 1900 | Inc. Ab. | 225.00 | 400.00 | 600.00 | 800.00 |
| (Y11.2) | | | | | | |

5000 REIS

10.0000 g, .600 SILVER, .1929 oz ASW
Santos Dumont

| 543 | 1936 | 1.986 | BV | 2.00 | 3.00 | 8.00 |

KM#	Date	Mintage	Fine	VF	XF	Unc
(Y56)	1937	.414	BV	2.00	3.00	8.00
	1938	.994	BV	2.00	3.00	8.00

10,000 REIS

8.9645 g, .917 GOLD, .2643 oz AGW

496	1889	7,302	150.00	250.00	500.00	900.00
(Y25)	1892	2,289	—	—	Rare	—
	1893	—	150.00	250.00	500.00	900.00
	1895	306 pcs.	150.00	250.00	600.00	1000.
	1896	383 pcs.	—	—	Rare	—
	1897	421 pcs.	150.00	250.00	600.00	1000.
	1898	216 pcs.	250.00	500.00	1500.	2000.
	1899	238 pcs.	150.00	250.00	600.00	1000.
	1901	111 pcs.	150.00	250.00	500.00	900.00
	1902	—	—	—	Unique	—
	1903	391 pcs.	150.00	250.00	600.00	1000.
	1904	541 pcs.	150.00	250.00	600.00	1000.
	1906	572 pcs.	150.00	250.00	600.00	1000.
	1907	878 pcs.	150.00	250.00	500.00	900.00
	1908	689 pcs.	150.00	250.00	500.00	900.00
	1909	1,069	150.00	250.00	500.00	900.00
	1911	137 pcs.	175.00	350.00	750.00	1150.
	1914	969 pcs.	250.00	500.00	1500.	2000.
	1915	4,314	250.00	500.00	1500.	2000.
	1916	4,720	150.00	250.00	600.00	1000.
	1919	526 pcs.	150.00	250.00	600.00	1000.
	1921	2,435	150.00	250.00	500.00	900.00
	1922	6 pcs.	—	—	Rare	—

20,000 REIS

17.9290 g, .917 GOLD, .5286 oz AGW

497	1889	.091	BV	300.00	450.00	900.00
(Y26)	1892	7,738	—	—	Rare	—
	1893	4,303	BV	300.00	450.00	900.00
	1894	4,267	BV	300.00	450.00	900.00
	1895	4,811	BV	300.00	450.00	900.00
	1896	7,043	BV	300.00	450.00	900.00
	1897	.011	BV	300.00	450.00	900.00
	1898	.014	BV	300.00	450.00	900.00
	1899	9,558	BV	300.00	450.00	900.00
	1900	7,551	BV	300.00	450.00	900.00
	1901	784 pcs.	BV	350.00	650.00	1100.
	1902	884 pcs.	BV	350.00	650.00	1100.
	1903	675 pcs.	BV	350.00	650.00	1100.
	1904	444 pcs.	BV	350.00	650.00	1100.
	1906	396 pcs.	375.00	750.00	1500.	3000.
	1907	3,310	BV	300.00	450.00	900.00
	1908	6,001	BV	300.00	450.00	900.00
	1909	4,427	BV	300.00	450.00	900.00
	1910	5,119	BV	300.00	450.00	900.00
	1911	8,467	BV	300.00	450.00	900.00
	1912	4,878	BV	300.00	450.00	900.00
	1913	5,182	BV	300.00	500.00	1000.
	1914	1,980	BV	300.00	500.00	1000.
	1917	2,269	BV	300.00	500.00	1000.
	1918	1,216	BV	300.00	500.00	1000.
	1921	5,924	BV	300.00	500.00	1000.
	1922	2,681	BV	300.00	500.00	1000.

MONETARY REFORM
1942-1967
100 Centavos = 1 Cruzeiro

10 CENTAVOS

COPPER-NICKEL
Getulio Vargas

KM#	Date	Mintage	VF	XF	Unc
555	1942	3.826	.35	.50	1.00
(Y64)	1943	13.565	.25	.35	.75

ALUMINUM-BRONZE

555a	1944	12.617	.25	.60	1.00
(Y64a)	1945	24.674	.25	.60	1.00
	1946	35.159	.25	.60	1.00
	1947	20.664	.25	.35	.75

NOTE: KM#555 has a very light yellowish appearance while KM#555b is a deeper yellow.

KM#	Date	Mintage	VF	XF	Unc
555b	1943	Inc. Ab.	.25	.35	.75
(Y64b)					

Jose Bonifacio

561	1947	Inc. Ab.	.15	.20	.35
(Y73)	1948	45.041	.15	.20	.35
	1949	21.763	.15	.20	.35
	1950	16.330	.15	.20	.35
	1951	15.561	.10	.15	.35
	1952	10.966	.10	.20	.50
	1953	25.883	.10	.15	.35
	1954	17.031	.10	.15	.35
	1955	25.172	.10	.15	.35

ALUMINUM

564	1956	.741	.10	.15	.50
(Y76)	1957	25.311	.10	.15	.25
	1958	5.813	.10	.15	.25
	1959	2.611	.10	.15	.25
	1960	.624	.10	.15	.50
	1961	.951	.10	.15	.50

20 CENTAVOS

COPPER-NICKEL
Getulio Vargas

| 556 | 1942 | 3.007 | .25 | .50 | 1.00 |
| (Y65) | 1943 | 13.392 | .15 | .40 | .75 |

NOTE: KM#556 has a very light yellowish appearance while KM#556a is a deeper yellow.

ALUMINUM-BRONZE

556a	1943	Inc. Ab.	.15	.35	.75
(Y65a)	1944	12.673	.15	.35	.75
	1945	61.632	.15	.35	.60
	1946	31.526	.15	.35	.60
	1947	36.422	.15	.35	.75
	1948	39.671	.15	.35	.75

Rui Barbosa

562	1948	Inc. Ab.	.15	.25	.50
(Y74)	1949	24.805	.15	.25	.50
	1950	15.145	.15	.25	.50
	1951	14.964	.15	.25	.50
	1952	10.942	.15	.25	.50
	1953	25.585	.15	.25	.50
	1954	16.477	.15	.25	.50
	1955	25.122	.15	.25	.50
	1956	6.716	.15	.25	.50

ALUMINUM
National arms

565	1956	Inc. Ab.	.10	.25	.50
(Y77)	1957	27.110	.10	.20	.40
	1958	8.552	.10	.20	.40
	1959	4.810	.10	.20	.40
	1960	.510	.10	.25	.50
	1961	2.332	.10	.20	.40

NOTE: Varieties exist in the thickness of the planchet for year 1956.

50 CENTAVOS

COPPER-NICKEL
Getulio Vargas

KM#	Date	Mintage	VF	XF	Unc
557	1942	2.358	.40	.75	1.50
(Y66)	1943	13.392	.35	.50	1.00

NOTE: Y66 has a very light yellowish appearance while Y66a is a deeper yellow.

ALUMINUM-BRONZE

557a	1943	Inc. Ab.	.30	.50	1.00
(Y66a)	1944	12.102	.30	.50	1.00
	1945	73.222	.30	.50	1.00
	1946	13.941	.30	.50	1.00
	1947	23.588	.20	.50	1.00

Presidente Dutra

563	1948	32.023	.15	.25	.50
(Y75)	1949	11.392	.15	.25	.50
	1950	7.804	.15	.35	.75
	1951	7.523	.15	.35	.75
	1952	6.863	.15	.35	.75
	1953	17.372	.15	.25	.50
	1954	11.353	.15	.25	.50
	1955	27.150	.15	.25	.50
	1956	32.130	.15	.25	.50

National arms

566	1956	Inc. Ab.	.10	.20	.40
(Y78)					

ALUMINUM

569	1957	49.350	.10	.20	.35
(Y81)	1958	59.815	.10	.20	.35
	1959	32.891	.10	.20	.35
	1960	15.997	.10	.20	.35
	1961	18.456	.10	.15	.25

CRUZEIRO

ALUMINUM-BRONZE

558	1942	.381	.50	1.00	3.00
(Y67)	1943	2.728	.25	.50	1.00
	1944	3.820	.25	.50	1.00
	1945	32.544	.25	.50	.75
	1946	49.794	.25	.50	1.00
	1947	15.391	.25	.50	1.00
	1949	7.889	.25	.50	1.00
	1950	5.163	.25	.50	1.00
	1951	3.757	.25	.50	1.00
	1952	1.769	.50	1.00	2.00
	1953	5.195	.25	.50	1.00
	1954	1.145	.25	.50	1.50
	1955	1.758	.25	.50	1.00
	1956	.668	4.00	6.00	10.00

567	1956	Inc. Ab.	.15	.25	.50
(Y79)					

ALUMINUM

KM#	Date	Mintage	VF	XF	Unc
570	1957	11.849	.10	.15	.30
(Y82)	1958	15.443	.10	.15	.30
	1959	25.010	.10	.15	.30
	1960	35.267	.10	.15	.30
	1961	22.181	.10	.15	.30

2 CRUZEIROS

ALUMINUM-BRONZE

559	1942	.276	.75	1.50	4.00
(Y68)	1943	1.929	.25	.50	1.00
	1944	3.820	.25	.50	1.00
	1945	32.544	.20	.40	1.00
	1946	33.650	.20	.40	1.00
	1947	9.908	.20	.40	1.00
	1949	11.252	.20	.40	1.00
	1950	7.754	.25	.50	1.00
	1951	.390	.40	1.00	3.00
	1952	1.456	1.00	2.00	5.00
	1953	3.582	.20	.40	1.00
	1954	1.197	.25	1.00	2.00
	1955	1.838	.20	.50	1.00
	1956	—	.35	1.00	3.50

568	1956	Inc. Ab.	.20	.40	1.50
(Y80)					

ALUMINUM

571	1957	.194	.25	.50	1.50
(Y83)	1958	13.687	.15	.25	.50
	1959	20.894	.15	.25	.50
	1960	19.624	.15	.25	.50
	1961	24.924	.15	.25	.50

5 CRUZEIROS

ALUMINUM-BRONZE

560	1942	.115	.75	1.50	8.00
(Y69)	1943	.222	.50	1.00	6.50

10 CRUZEIROS

ALUMINUM

572	1965	19.656	.10	.15	.25
(Y84)					

20 CRUZEIROS

ALUMINUM

573	1965	25.930	.15	.20	.35
(Y85)					

50 CRUZEIROS

COPPER-NICKEL

KM#	Date	Mintage	VF	XF	Unc
574	1965	18.001	.15	.25	.50
(Y86)					

MONETARY REFORM
1967-1985
1000 Old Cruzeiros = 1 New Cruzeiro
100 Centavos = 1 (New) Cruzeiro

CENTAVO

STAINLESS STEEL

575.1	1967	57.499	—	—	.10
(Y87)					

Thinner planchet

575.2	1969	243.855	—	—	.10
(Y87a)	1975		—	—	.10

F.A.O. Issue

585	1975	31.700	—	.10	.20
(Y98)	1976	18.355	—	.10	.10
	1977	.100	—	.10	.10
	1978	.050	—	.10	.15

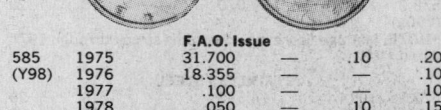

589	1979	.100	—	.10	.25
(Y101)	1980	.060	.10	.25	.75
	1981	.100	.10	.25	.75
	1982	.100	.10	.25	.75

2 CENTAVOS

STAINLESS STEEL

576.1	1967	65.226	—	—	.10
(Y88)					

Thinner planchet

576.2	1969	*134.298	—	—	.10
(Y88a)	1975		—	.10	.20

*NOTE: Mintage figure includes coins struck through 1974 dated 1969.

F.A.O. Issue

586	1975	31.400	—	—	.10
(Y99)	1976	18.754	—	—	.10
	1977	.100	—	—	.10
	1978	.050	—	.10	.20

5 CENTAVOS

STAINLESS STEEL

577.1	1967	69.304	—	.10	.15
(Y89)					

Thinner planchet

577.2	1969	*345.071	—	.10	.15
(Y89a)	1975		—	.10	.15

BRAZIL 225

BRAZIL 226

*NOTE: Mintage figure includes coins struck through 1974 dated 1969.

F.A.O. Issue
Rev: Plain 5

KM#	Date	Mintage	VF	XF	Unc
587.1 (Y100)	1975	44.500	—	.10	.15
	1976	134.267	—	.10	.15
	1977	85.360	—	.10	.15
	1978	34.090	—	.10	.20

Rev: 5 over wavy lines.

| 587.2 (Y100.1) | 1975 | Inc. Ab. | — | .10 | .15 |
| | 1976 | Inc. Ab. | — | .10 | .15 |

10 CENTAVOS

COPPER-NICKEL

| 578.1 (Y90) | 1967 | 22.420 | — | .10 | .30 |

Thinner planchet

| 578.2 (Y90a) | 1970 | *134.070 | — | .10 | .20 |

*NOTE: Mintage figure includes coins struck through 1974 dated 1970.

STAINLESS STEEL

578.1a (Y90b)	1974	114.598	—	.10	.20
	1975	—	—	.10	.20
	1976	—	—	.10	.20
	1977	225.213	—	.10	.20
	1978	225.000	—	.10	.20
	1979	.100	—	.10	.20

20 CENTAVOS

COPPER-NICKEL

| 579.1 (Y91) | 1967 | 123.610 | — | .10 | .25 |
| | 1970 | — | — | .10 | .25 |

Thinner planchet

| 579.2 (Y91a) | 1970 | *384.894 | — | .10 | .30 |

*NOTE: Mintage figure includes coins struck through 1974 dated 1970.

STAINLESS STEEL

579.1a (Y91b)	1975	102.367	—	.10	.25
	1976	—	—	.10	.25
	1977	240.001	—	.10	.25
	1978	255.000	—	.10	.25
	1979	.116	—	.10	.25

50 CENTAVOS

NICKEL

| 580 (Y92) | 1967 | 12.987 | .25 | .50 | 1.00 |

COPPER-NICKEL

| 580a (Y92a) | 1970 | 503.895 | .20 | .35 | .75 |
| | 1975 | — | .20 | .35 | .75 |

STAINLESS STEEL

580b (Y92b)	1975	79.062	.20	.35	.75
	1976	—	.20	.35	1.00
	1977	160.019	.20	.35	1.00
	1978	200.000	.20	.35	.75
	1979	.104	.20	.35	.75

CRUZEIRO

NICKEL

KM#	Date	Mintage	VF	XF	Unc
581 (Y93)	1970	*48.930	.25	.50	1.00
	1970	.018	—	Proof	3.00
	1974	24.135	.20	.35	.75

*NOTE: Mintage figure includes coins struck through 1972 dated 1970.

COPPER-NICKEL

581a (Y93a)	1975	21.613	.20	.35	.75
	1976	—	.20	.35	.75
	1977	.098	.20	.35	.75
	1978	.077	.20	.35	.75

NICKEL
150 Year Commemorative

582 (Y94)	1972 lettered edge	5.600	.35	.75	1.25
	1972 plain edge Inc. Ab.	.35	.75	1.25
	1972 lettered edge	—	—	Proof	3.00
	1972 plain edge	—	—	Proof	3.00

STAINLESS STEEL

590 (Y102)	1979	.596	.10	.20	.50
	1980	690.497	.10	.20	.50
	1981	560.000	.10	.20	.50
	1982	300.000	.10	.20	.50
	1983	.100	.10	.20	.50
	1984	62.100	.10	.20	.50

F.A.O. Issue

| 598 | 1985 | — | — | .10 | .40 |

5 CRUZEIROS

STAINLESS STEEL

591 (Y103)	1980	288.200	.25	.35	.60
	1981	82.000	.25	.35	.60
	1982	108.000	.25	.35	.60
	1983	113.400	.25	.35	.60
	1984	243.000	.25	.35	.60

F.A.O. Issue

| 599 | 1985 | — | .15 | .35 | .75 |

10 CRUZEIROS

11.3000 g, .800 SILVER, .2906 oz ASW

KM#	Date	Mintage	VF	XF	Unc
588 (Y97)	1975	.020	—	—	55.00

STAINLESS STEEL

592 (Y104)	1980	100.010	—	.40	.50
	1981	200.000	—	.40	.50
	1982	331.000	—	.40	.50
	1983	390.000	—	.40	.50
	1984	390.000	—	.40	.50
	1985	—	—	.40	.50
	1986	—	—	.40	.50

20 CRUZEIROS

18.0000 g, .900 SILVER, .5208 oz ASW, 34mm
150th Anniversary of Independence

| 583.1 (Y95) | 1972(a) | .250 | BV | 4.00 | 5.00 |

35mm

| 583.2 (Y95a) | 1972(a) | Inc. Ab. | BV | 4.00 | 5.00 |

STAINLESS STEEL

593 (Y105)	1981	88.297	—	.10	.50
	1982	158.200	—	.10	.50
	1983	312.000	—	.10	.50
	1984	226.000	—	.10	.50
	1985	—	—	.10	.50
	1986	—	—	.10	.50

50 CRUZEIROS

STAINLESS STEEL

594 (Y106)	1981	57.000	—	.10	.50
	1982	134.000	—	.10	.50
	1983	181.800	—	.10	.50
	1984	292.418	—	.10	.50
	1985	—	—	.10	.50
	1986	—	—	.10	.50

Santa Tereza Leper Colony / BRAZIL 227

100 CRUZEIROS

STAINLESS STEEL

KM#	Date	Mintage	VF	XF	Unc
595	1985	—	—	.10	.25
	1986	—	—	—	.25

200 CRUZEIROS

STAINLESS STEEL

596	1985	—	—	.15	.50
	1986	—	—	—	.50

300 CRUZEIROS

16.6500 g, .920 GOLD, .4925 oz AGW
150th Anniversary of Independence

584 (Y96)	1972(a)	.030	—	—	300.00

500 CRUZEIROS

STAINLESS STEEL

597	1985	—	—	.35	.75
	1986	—	—	.35	.75

MONETARY REFORM
1986-1989
1,000 New Cruzeiros = 1 Cruzado
100 Centavos = 1 Cruzado

CENTAVO

STAINLESS STEEL

600	1986	—	—	—	.10
	1987	—	—	—	.10
	1988	—	—	—	.10

5 CENTAVOS

STAINLESS STEEL

601	1986	—	—	—	.10
	1987	—	—	—	.10
	1988	—	—	—	.10

10 CENTAVOS

STAINLESS STEEL

602	1986	—	—	—	.10
	1987	—	—	—	.10
	1988	—	—	—	.10

20 CENTAVOS

STAINLESS STEEL

KM#	Date	Mintage	VF	XF	Unc
603	1986	—	—	—	.10
	1987	—	—	—	.10
	1988	—	—	—	.10

50 CENTAVOS

STAINLESS STEEL

604	1986	—	—	—	.15
	1987	—	—	—	.15
	1988	—	—	—	.15

CRUZADO

STAINLESS STEEL

605	1986	—	—	—	.25
	1987	—	—	—	.25
	1988	—	—	—	.25

5 CRUZADOS

STAINLESS STEEL

606	1986	—	—	—	.35
	1987	—	—	—	.35
	1988	—	—	—	.35

10 CRUZADOS

STAINLESS STEEL

607	1987	—	—	—	.50
	1988	—	—	—	.50

100 CRUZADOS

STAINLESS STEEL
Abolition of Slavery Centennial - Male

608	1988	.200	—	1.00	2.00

Abolition of Slavery Centennial - Female

KM#	Date	Mintage	VF	XF	Unc
609	1988	.200	—	1.00	2.00

Abolition of Slavery Centennial - Child

610	1988	.200	—	1.00	2.00

MONETARY REFORM
1989-
1,000 Old Cruzados = 1 New Cruzado

SANTA TEREZA LEPER COLONY

All the following tokens have plain edges. Obverse letters C.S.T. abbreviation for Colonia Santa Tereza.

TOKEN ISSUES (Tn)
100 REIS

BRASS

Tn1	ND	—	—	Rare	—

200 REIS

BRASS

Tn2	ND	—	—	Rare	—

300 REIS

BRASS

Tn3	ND	—	—	Rare	—

500 REIS

BRASS

Tn4	ND	—	—	Rare	—

1000 REIS

BRASS

KM#	Date	Mintage	VF	XF	Unc
Tn5	ND	—	—	Rare	—

BRITISH VIRGIN IS.

The Colony of the Virgin Islands, a British colony situated in the Caribbean Sea northeast of Puerto Rico and west of the Leeward Islands, has an area of 59 sq. mi. (153 sq. km.) and a population of 14,024. Capital: Road Town. The principal islands of the 36-island group are Tortola, Virgin Gorda, Anegada, and Jost Van Dyke. The chief industries are fishing and stock raising. Fish, livestock and bananas are exported.

The Virgin Islands were discovered by Columbus in 1493, and named by him, Las Virgenes, in honor of St. Ursula and her companions. The British Virgin Islands were formerly part of the administration of the Leeward Islands but received a separate administration as a Crown Colony in 1950. A new constitution promulgated in 1967 provided for a ministerial form of government headed by the Governor.

The Government of the British Virgin Islands issued the first official coinage in its history on June 30, 1973, in honor of 300 years of constitutional government in the islands. U.S. coins and currency continue to be accepted as a medium of exchange.

TORTOLA

Tortola, which has an area of about 24 sq. mi. (62 sq. km.), is the largest of thirty-six islands which comprise the British Virgin Islands. It was settled by the Dutch in 1648 and was occupied by the British in 1666. They have held it ever since.

MONETARY SYSTEM
8 Shillings, 3 Pence = 11 Bits = 8 Reales

COUNTERMARKED COINAGE
Tortola

Type I: TORTOLA in odd shaped rectangle.
NOTE: Market valuations listed for "TORTOLA" c/m issues are just for the "TORTOLA" c/m and do not take into consideration any other c/m that may be encountered on the same piece.

1-1/2 PENCE
Black Dog

BILLON
c/m: Incuse 'T' on French Colonial 2 Sous.

KM#	Date	Year	Good	VG	Fine	VF
3	ND	(1801)	22.50	32.50	47.50	80.00

9 PENCE or 1 BIT

SILVER
c/m: Type I on 1/2 cut of Spanish or Spanish Colonial 2 Reales.

| 4 | ND | (1801) | 40.00 | 75.00 | 130.00 | 175.00 |

SHILLING
SILVER
c/m: Type I on 1/8 cut of Spanish or Spanish Colonial 8 Reales.

| 5 | ND | (1801) | 70.00 | 100.00 | 140.00 | 190.00 |

2 SHILLINGS

SILVER
c/m: Type I on 1/4 cut of Spanish or Spanish Colonial 8 Reales.

| 6 | ND | (1801) | 75.00 | 100.00 | 150.00 | 200.00 |

4 SHILLINGS, 1-1/2 PENCE

SILVER
c/m: Type I on 1/2 cut of Spanish or Spanish Colonial 8 Reales.

KM#	Date	Year	Good	VG	Fine	VF
7	ND	(1801)	100.00	150.00	200.00	250.00

Type II: TORTOLA in rectangle

SHILLING
SILVER
c/m: Type II on 1/8 cut of Spanish or Spanish Colonial 8 Reales.

| 8 | ND | (1801-05) | 70.00 | 100.00 | 140.00 | 190.00 |

2 SHILLINGS

SILVER
c/m: Type II on 1/4 cut of Spanish or Spanish Colonial 8 Reales.

| 9 | ND | (1801-05) | 32.50 | 60.00 | 90.00 | 120.00 |

4 SHILLINGS, 1-1/2 PENCE

SILVER
c/m: Type II on 1/2 cut of Spanish or Spanish Colonial 8 Reales.

| 10 | ND | (1801-05) | 40.00 | 75.00 | 125.00 | 165.00 |

PRIVATE COUNTERMARKED ISSUES
Hodge Plantation
1-1/2 PENCE
Black Dog

c/m: Small 3mm incuse 'H' in square indent on French Colonial 2 Sous.

KM#	Date	Year	VG	Fine	VF	XF
11	ND (1801-1811)		7.50	12.50	22.50	40.00

c/m: Large 5mm incuse 'H' in square indent on French Colonial 2 Sous.

KM#	Date	Year	Good	VG	Fine	VF
12	ND (1801-1811)		7.50	12.50	22.50	40.00

Tirtila

Type III: TIRTILA

Type IV: TIRTILA w/inverted V for A.

NOTE: Market valuations listed for TIRTILA c/m issues are just for the TIRTILA c/m and do not take into consideration any other c/m that may be encountered on the same piece.

9 PENCE or 1 BIT

SILVER
c/m: Type III on 1/2 cut of Spanish or Spanish Colonial 2 Reales.

| 13 | ND | (1805-24) | 22.50 | 32.50 | 50.00 | 80.00 |

c/m: Type IV on 1/2 cut of Spanish or Spanish Colonial 2 Reales.

| 14 | ND | (1805-24) | 26.50 | 38.50 | 62.50 | 100.00 |

Listings For
BRITISH EAST CARIBBEAN TERRITORIES: refer to East Caribbean States
BRITISH GUIANA: refer to Guyana
BRITISH HONDURAS: refer to Belize
BRITISH NORTH BORNEO: refer to Malaysia

SHILLING
SILVER
c/m: Type III on 1/8 cut of Spanish or Spanish Colonial 8 Reales.

KM#	Date	Year	Good	VG	Fine	VF
15	ND	(1805-24)	22.50	32.50	50.00	80.00

c/m: Type IV on 1/8 cut of Spanish or Spanish Colonial 8 Reales.

| 16 | ND | (1805-24) | 22.50 | 32.50 | 50.00 | 80.00 |

2 SHILLINGS

SILVER
c/m: Type III on 1/4 cut of Spanish or Spanish Colonial 8 Reales.

| 17 | ND | (1805-24) | 22.50 | 32.50 | 50.00 | 80.00 |

c/m: Type IV on 1/4 cut of Spanish or Spanish Colonial 8 Reales.

| 18 | ND | (1805-24) | 22.50 | 32.50 | 50.00 | 80.00 |

4 SHILLINGS, 1-1/2 PENCE

SILVER
c/m: Type III on 1/2 cut of Spanish or Spanish Colonial 8 Reales.

| 19 | ND | (1805-24) | 22.50 | 32.50 | 50.00 | 80.00 |

c/m: Type IV on 1/2 cut of Spanish or Spanish Colonial 8 Reales.

| 20 | ND | (1805-24) | 22.50 | 32.50 | 50.00 | 80.00 |

BRITISH VIRGIN ISLANDS

RULERS
British

MINT MARKS
FM - Franklin Mint, U.S.A.*

*NOTE: From 1975 the Franklin Mint has produced coinage in up to 3 different qualities. Qualities of issue are designated in ( ) after each date and are defined as follows:

(M) MATTE - Normal circulation strike or a dull finish produced by sandblasting special uncirculated (polish finish) or proof quality dies.

(U) SPECIAL UNCIRCULATED - Polished or proof-like in appearance without any frosted features.

(P) PROOF - The highest quality obtainable having mirror-like fields and frosted features.

MONETARY SYSTEM
100 Cents = 1 Dollar

CENT

BRONZE
Green-Throated Carib and Antillean Crested Hummingbird

KM#	Date	Mintage	VF	XF	Unc
1	1973FM	.053	—	.10	.50
	1973FM(P)	.181	—	Proof	1.00
	1974FM	.022	—	.10	.50
	1974FM(P)	.094	—	Proof	1.00
	1975FM(M)	6,000	—	.10	.75
	1975FM(U)	2,351	—	.10	.50
	1975FM(P)	.032	—	Proof	1.00
	1976FM(M)	.012	—	.10	.50
	1976FM(U)	996 pcs.	—	.10	.50
	1976FM(P)	.015	—	Proof	1.00
	1977FM(M)	500 pcs.	—	.25	2.00
	1977FM(U)	782 pcs.	—	.10	.50
	1977FM(P)	7,218	—	Proof	1.00
	1978FM(U)	1,443	—	.10	.50

1	1978FM(P)	7,059	—	Proof	1.00
	1979FM(U)	680 pcs.	—	.10	.50
	1979FM(P)	5,304	—	Proof	1.00
	1980FM(U)	1,007	—	.10	.50
	1980FM(P)	3,421	—	Proof	1.00
	1981FM(U)	472 pcs.	—	.10	.50
	1981FM(P)	1,124	—	Proof	1.00
	1982FM(U)	—	—	.10	.50
	1982FM(P)	—	—	Proof	1.50
	1983FM(U)	—	—	.10	.50
	1983FM(P)	—	—	Proof	1.50
	1984FM(P)	—	—	Proof	1.50

1.7500 g, .925 SILVER, .0520 oz ASW
Queen's Silver Jubilee

| 9 | 1977FM(P) | .017 | — | Proof | 2.50 |

Coronation Jubilee
Similar to KM#1.

| 16 | 1978FM(P) | 6,196 | — | Proof | 3.50 |

BRONZE
Hawksbill Turtle

| 42 | 1985FM(P) | — | — | Proof | 1.00 |

1.7500 g, .925 SILVER, .0520 oz ASW

| 42a | 1985FM(P) | 1,474 | — | Proof | 3.00 |

5 CENTS

COPPER-NICKEL
Zenaida Dove

2	1973FM	.026	—	.15	.75
	1973FM(P)	.181	—	Proof	1.25
	1974FM	.018	—	.15	.75
	1974FM(P)	.094	—	Proof	1.25
	1975FM(M)	3,800	—	.20	1.00
	1975FM(U)	2,351	—	.15	.75
	1975FM(P)	.032	—	Proof	1.25
	1976FM(M)	4,800	—	.20	1.00
	1976FM(U)	996 pcs.	—	.15	.75
	1976FM(P)	.015	—	Proof	1.25
	1977FM(M)	500 pcs.	—	.35	3.50
	1977FM(U)	782 pcs.	—	.15	.75
	1977FM(P)	7,218	—	Proof	1.25
	1978FM(U)	1,443	—	.15	.75
	1978FM(P)	7,059	—	Proof	1.25
	1979FM(U)	680 pcs.	—	.15	.75
	1979FM(P)	5,304	—	Proof	1.25
	1980FM(U)	1,007	—	.15	.75
	1980FM(P)	3,421	—	Proof	1.25
	1981FM(U)	472 pcs.	—	.15	.75
	1981FM(P)	1,124	—	Proof	1.25
	1982FM(U)	—	—	.15	.75
	1982FM(P)	—	—	Proof	1.25
	1983FM(U)	—	—	.15	.75
	1983FM(P)	—	—	Proof	1.25
	1984FM(P)	—	—	Proof	1.25

3.5500 g, .925 SILVER, .1055 oz ASW
Queen's Silver Jubilee

| 10 | 1977FM(P) | .017 | — | Proof | 3.00 |

Coronation Jubilee

| 17 | 1978FM(P) | 6,196 | — | Proof | 4.50 |

COPPER-NICKEL
Bonito Fish

KM#	Date	Mintage	VF	XF	Unc
43	1985FM(P)	—	—	Proof	1.00

3.5550 g, .925 SILVER, .1055 oz ASW

| 43a | 1985FM(P) | 1,473 | — | Proof | 4.00 |

10 CENTS

COPPER-NICKEL
Belted Kingfisher

3	1973FM(U)	.023	—	.20	1.00
	1973FM(P)	.181	—	Proof	1.50
	1974FM(U)	.013	—	.20	1.00
	1974FM(P)	.094	—	Proof	1.50
	1975FM(M)	2,000	—	.20	1.25
	1975FM(U)	2,351	—	.20	1.00
	1975FM(P)	.032	—	Proof	1.50
	1976FM(M)	3,000	—	.20	1.25
	1976FM(U)	996 pcs.	—	.20	1.00
	1976FM(P)	.015	—	Proof	1.50
	1977FM(M)	500 pcs.	—	.45	4.00
	1977FM(U)	782 pcs.	—	.20	1.00
	1977FM(P)	7,218	—	Proof	1.50
	1978FM(U)	1,443	—	.20	1.00
	1978FM(P)	7,059	—	Proof	1.50
	1979FM(U)	680 pcs.	—	.20	1.00
	1979FM(P)	5,304	—	Proof	1.50
	1980FM(U)	1,007	—	.20	1.00
	1980FM(P)	3,421	—	Proof	1.50
	1981FM(U)	472 pcs.	—	.20	1.00
	1981FM(P)	1,124	—	Proof	1.50
	1982FM(U)	—	—	.20	1.00
	1982FM(P)	—	—	Proof	1.50
	1983FM(U)	—	—	.20	1.00
	1983FM(P)	—	—	Proof	1.50
	1984FM(P)	—	—	Proof	1.50

6.4000 g, .925 SILVER, .1903 oz ASW
Queen's Silver Jubilee

| 11 | 1977FM(P) | .017 | — | Proof | 5.00 |

Coronation Jubilee

| 18 | 1978FM(P) | 6,196 | — | Proof | 6.50 |

COPPER-NICKEL
Great Barracuda

| 44 | 1985FM(P) | — | — | Proof | 1.00 |

6.4000 g, .925 SILVER, .1903 oz ASW

| 44a | 1985FM(P) | 1,474 | — | Proof | 5.00 |

BRITISH VIRGIN ISLANDS 230

25 CENTS

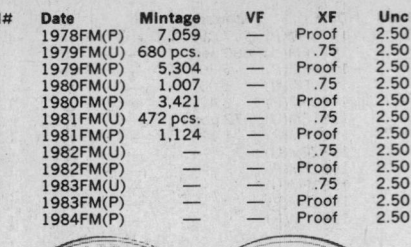

COPPER-NICKEL
Mangrove Cuckoo

KM#	Date	Mintage	VF	XF	Unc
4	1973FM	.021	—	.30	1.50
	1973FM(P)	.181	—	Proof	1.75
	1974FM	.012	—	.30	1.50
	1974FM(P)	.094	—	Proof	1.75
	1975FM(M)	1,000	—	.35	3.00
	1975FM(U)	2,351	—	.30	1.50
	1975FM(P)	.032	—	Proof	1.75
	1976FM(M)	2,000	—	.30	2.00
	1976FM(U)	996 pcs.	—	.30	1.50
	1976FM(P)	.015	—	Proof	1.75
	1977FM(M)	500 pcs.	—	.50	5.00
	1977FM(U)	782 pcs.	—	.30	1.50
	1977FM(P)	7,218	—	Proof	1.75
	1978FM(U)	1,443	—	.30	1.50
	1978FM(P)	7,059	—	Proof	1.75
	1979FM(U)	680 pcs.	—	.30	1.50
	1979FM(P)	5,304	—	Proof	1.75
	1980FM(U)	1,007	—	.30	1.50
	1980FM(P)	3,421	—	Proof	1.75
	1981FM(U)	472 pcs.	—	.30	1.50
	1981FM(P)	1,124	—	Proof	1.75
	1982FM(U)	—	—	.30	1.50
	1982FM(P)	—	—	Proof	1.75
	1983FM(U)	—	—	.30	1.50
	1983FM(P)	—	—	Proof	1.75
	1984FM(P)	—	—	Proof	1.75

8.8100 g, .925 SILVER, .2620 oz ASW
Queen's Silver Jubilee

12	1977FM(P)	.017	—	Proof	7.00

Coronation Jubilee

19	1978FM(P)	6,196	—	Proof	8.50

COPPER-NICKEL
Blue Marlin

45	1985FM(P)	—	—	Proof	1.50

8.8100 g, .925 SILVER, .2620 oz ASW
45a	1985FM(P)	1,480	—	Proof	7.00

50 CENTS

COPPER-NICKEL
Brown Pelican

5	1973FM	.020	—	.75	2.50
	1973FM(P)	.181	—	Proof	2.50
	1974FM	.012	—	.75	2.00
	1974FM(P)	.094	—	Proof	2.50
	1975FM(M)	1,000	—	1.00	5.00
	1975FM(U)	2,351	—	.75	2.50
	1975FM(P)	.032	—	Proof	2.50
	1976FM(M)	2,000	—	.75	3.00
	1976FM(U)	996 pcs.	—	.75	2.50
	1976FM(P)	.015	—	Proof	2.50
	1977FM(M)	600 pcs.	—	1.00	6.00
	1977FM(U)	782 pcs.	—	.75	2.50
	1977FM(P)	7,218	—	Proof	2.50
	1978FM(U)	1,543	—	.75	2.50

KM#	Date	Mintage	VF	XF	Unc
5	1978FM(P)	7,059	—	Proof	2.50
	1979FM(U)	680 pcs.	—	.75	2.50
	1979FM(P)	5,304	—	Proof	2.50
	1980FM(U)	1,007	—	.75	2.50
	1980FM(P)	3,421	—	Proof	2.50
	1981FM(U)	472 pcs.	—	.75	2.50
	1981FM(P)	1,124	—	Proof	2.50
	1982FM(U)	—	—	.75	2.50
	1982FM(P)	—	—	Proof	2.50
	1983FM(U)	—	—	.75	2.50
	1983FM(P)	—	—	Proof	2.50
	1984FM(P)	—	—	Proof	2.50

16.7200 g, .925 SILVER, .4972 oz ASW
Queen's Silver Jubilee

13	1977FM(P)	.017	—	Proof	10.00

Coronation Jubilee

20	1978FM(P)	6,196	—	Proof	12.50

COPPER-NICKEL
Dolphin

46	1985FM(P)	—	—	Proof	2.00

16.7200 g, .925 SILVER, .4972 oz ASW
46a	1985FM(P)	1,406	—	Proof	10.00

DOLLAR

COPPER-NICKEL
Magnificent Frigate
Obv: Similar to 50 Cents, KM#5.

6	1974FM(M)	.012	—	8.00	9.00
	1975FM(M)	800 pcs.	—	2.50	7.50
	1975FM(U)	2,351	—	2.50	6.00
	1976FM(M)	1,800	—	2.50	6.00
	1976FM(U)	996 pcs.	—	2.50	7.50
	1977FM(M)	800 pcs.	—	2.50	7.50
	1977FM(U)	782 pcs.	—	2.50	7.50
	1978FM(U)	1,743	—	2.50	6.00
	1979FM(U)	680 pcs.	—	2.50	7.50
	1980FM(U)	1,007	—	2.50	6.00
	1981FM(U)	472 pcs.	—	2.50	7.50
	1982FM(U)	—	—	2.50	6.00
	1983FM(U)	—	—	2.50	7.50

25.7000 g, .925 SILVER, .7643 oz ASW
6a	1973FM(M)	.020	—	8.00	9.00
	1973FM(P)	.181	—	Proof	7.00
	1974FM(P)	.094	—	Proof	9.00
	1975FM(P)	.032	—	Proof	9.00
	1976FM(P)	.015	—	Proof	9.00
	1977FM(P)	7,218	—	Proof	9.00

KM#	Date	Mintage	VF	XF	Unc
6a	1978FM(P)	7,059	—	Proof	9.00
	1979FM(P)	5,304	—	Proof	10.00
	1980FM(P)	3,421	—	Proof	12.00
	1981FM(P)	1,124	—	Proof	12.00
	1982FM(P)	1,865	—	Proof	12.00
	1983FM(P)	478 pcs.	—	Proof	30.00
	1984FM(P)	—	—	Proof	12.00

Queen's Silver Jubilee
Rev: Similar to KM#6.

14	1977FM(P)	.017	—	Proof	15.00

Coronation Jubilee

21	1978FM(P)	6,196	—	Proof	17.50

COPPER-NICKEL
Butterfly Fish

47	1985FM(P)	—	—	Proof	20.00

24.7400 g, .925 SILVER, .7358 oz ASW
47a	1985FM(P)	1,372	—	Proof	25.00

5 DOLLARS

COPPER-NICKEL
Snowy Egret
Obv: Similar to 50 Cents, KM#13.

24	1979FM(U)	680 pcs.	—	—	25.00

40.5000 g, .925 SILVER, 1.2044 oz ASW
24a	1979FM(P)	5,304	—	Proof	25.00

BRITISH VIRGIN ISLANDS 231

COPPER-NICKEL
Great Blue Heron
Obv: Similar to 50 Cents, KM#13.

KM#	Date	Mintage	VF	XF	Unc
26	1980FM(U)	1,007	—	—	25.00

40.5000 g, .925 SILVER, 1.2044 oz ASW
| 26a | 1980FM(P) | 3,421 | — | Proof | 25.00 |

COPPER-NICKEL
Royal Tern
Obv: Similar to 50 Cents, KM#13.

| 30 | 1981FM(U) | 472 pcs. | — | — | 25.00 |

40.5000 g, .925 SILVER, 1.2044 oz ASW
| 30a | 1981FM(P) | 1,124 | — | Proof | 30.00 |

COPPER-NICKEL
White-Tailed Tropic Birds
Obv: Similar to 50 Cents, KM#13.

| 33 | 1982FM(U) | — | — | — | 25.00 |

40.5000 g, .925 SILVER, 1.2044 oz ASW
| 33a | 1982FM(P) | 1,865 | — | Proof | 30.00 |

COPPER-NICKEL
Yellow Warblers
Obv: Similar to 50 Cents, KM#13.

| 35 | 1983FM(U) | — | — | — | 25.00 |

40.5000 g, .925 SILVER, 1.2044 oz ASW
| 35a | 1983FM(P) | 478 pcs. | — | Proof | 50.00 |
| | 1984FM(P) | — | — | Proof | 45.00 |

10 DOLLARS

30.2800 g, .500 SILVER, .4868 oz ASW
30th Anniversary of Coronation of Queen Elizabeth II

KM#	Date	Mintage	VF	XF	Unc
36	1983FM(P)	2,957	—	Proof	25.00

20 DOLLARS

19.0900 g, .925 SILVER, .5678 oz ASW
Crossed Cannons
| 48 | 1985FM(P) | — | — | Proof | 26.00 |

Porcelain Cup
Obv: Similar to KM#48.
| 49 | 1985FM(P) | — | — | Proof | 26.00 |

Sextant
Obv: Similar to KM#48.
| 50 | 1985FM(P) | — | — | Proof | 26.00 |

Emerald and Gold Ring
Obv: Similar to KM#48.
| 51 | 1985FM(P) | — | — | Proof | 26.00 |

Gold Doubloon of 1702
Obv: Similar to KM#48.

KM#	Date	Mintage	VF	XF	Unc
52	1985FM(P)	—	—	Proof	26.00

Anchor
Obv: Similar to KM#48.
| 53 | 1985FM(P) | — | — | Proof | 26.00 |

Brass Nocturnal
Obv: Similar to KM#48.
| 54 | 1985FM(P) | — | — | Proof | 26.00 |

Sword Guillon
Obv: Similar to KM#48.
| 55 | 1985FM(P) | — | — | Proof | 26.00 |

Gold Bar
Obv: Similar to KM#48.
| 56 | 1985FM(P) | — | — | Proof | 26.00 |

BRITISH VIRGIN ISLANDS 232

Gold Escudo
Obv: Similar to KM#48. Rev: Obv. and rev. of gold escudo of 1733.

KM#	Date	Mintage	VF	XF	Unc
57	1985FM(P)	—	—	Proof	26.00

Astrolable
Obv: Similar to KM#48.

KM#	Date	Mintage	VF	XF	Unc
62	1985FM(P)	—	—	Proof	26.00

Ship's Stern Lantern
Obv: Similar to KM#48.

KM#	Date	Mintage	VF	XF	Unc
67	1985FM(P)	—	—	Proof	26.00

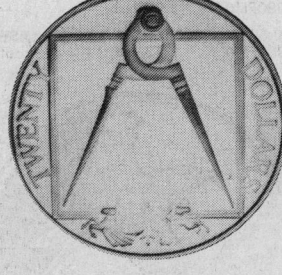

Ivory Sundial
Obv: Similar to KM#48.
58 1985FM(P)   —   —   Proof   26.00

Bells
Obv: Similar to KM#48.
63 1985FM(P)   —   —   Proof   26.00

Brass Dividers
Obv: Similar to KM#48.
68 1985FM(P)   —   —   Proof   26.00

Gold Monstrance
Obv: Similar to KM#48.
59 1985FM(P)   —   —   Proof   26.00

Porcelain Bottle
Obv: Similar to KM#48.
64 1985FM(P)   —   —   Proof   26.00

Gold Cross
Obv: Similar to KM#48.
69 1985FM(P)   —   —   Proof   26.00

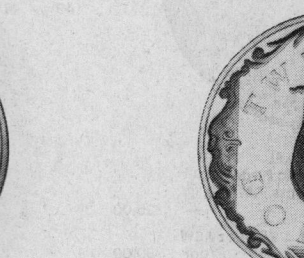

Teapot
Obv: Similar to KM#48.
60 1985FM(P)   —   —   Proof   26.00

Dutch Cannon
Obv: Similar to KM#48.
65 1985FM(P)   —   —   Proof   26.00

Perfurme Bottle
Obv: Similar to KM#48.
70 1985FM(P)   —   —   Proof   26.00

Brass Religious Medallion
Obv: Similar to KM#48.
61 1985FM(P)   —   —   Proof   26.00

8 Reales Cob
Obv: Similar to KM#48.
66 1985FM(P)   —   —   Proof   26.00

Pocket Watch
Obv: Similar to KM#48.
71 1985FM(P)   —   —   Proof   26.00

BRITISH VIRGIN ISLANDS 233

Gold Bracelet and Button
Obv: Similar to KM#48.

KM#	Date	Mintage	VF	XF	Unc
72	1985FM(P)	—	—	Proof	26.00

25 DOLLARS

28.1000 g, .925 SILVER, .8356 oz ASW
Coronation Jubilee
Obv: Portrait of Queen.

| 22 | 1978FM(P) | 8,438 | — | Proof | 25.00 |

1.5000 g, .500 GOLD, .0241 oz AGW
Diving Osprey

| 27 | 1980FM(P) | .011 | — | Proof | 50.00 |

Caribbean Sparrow Hawk

| 31.1 | 1981FM(P) | 2,513 | — | Proof | 50.00 |

Error. Rev: W/o FM mint mark.

| 31.2 | 1981(P) | — | — | Proof | 60.00 |

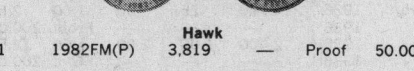

Hawk

| 41 | 1982FM(P) | 3,819 | — | Proof | 50.00 |

Merlin Hawk

| 37 | 1983FM(P) | 5,949 | — | Proof | 50.00 |

Peregrine Falcon

| 40 | 1984FM(P) | 97 pcs. | — | Proof | 100.00 |

Marsh Hawk

| 73 | 1985FM(P) | 1,294 | — | Proof | 60.00 |

50 DOLLARS

2.6800 g, .500 GOLD, .0430 oz AGW
Golden Dove of Christmas

KM#	Date	Mintage	VF	XF	Unc
28	1980	6,379	—	Proof	75.00

100 DOLLARS

7.1000 g, .900 GOLD, .2054 oz AGW
Royal Tern

7	1975FM(M)	10 pcs.	—	Rare	—
	1975FM(U)	.013	—	—	110.00
	1975FM(P)	*.023	—	Proof	225.00

*NOTE: Includes 8,754 in First Day Covers.

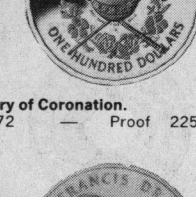

50th Birthday

8	1976FM(M)	10 pcs.	—	Rare	—
	1976FM(U)	1,752	—	—	125.00
	1976FM(P)	.012	—	Proof	225.00

Queen's Silver Jubilee

| 15 | 1977FM(U) | 10 pcs. | — | Rare | — |
| | 1977FM(P) | 6,715 | — | Proof | 225.00 |

25th Anniversary of Coronation.

| 23 | 1978FM(P) | 5,772 | — | Proof | 225.00 |

Sir Francis Drake

| 25 | 1979FM(P) | 3,216 | — | Proof | 225.00 |

400th Anniversary of Drake's Voyage

| 29 | 1980FM(P) | 5,412 | — | Proof | 225.00 |

Knighting of Sir Francis Drake

KM#	Date	Mintage	VF	XF	Proof	Unc
32	1981FM(P)	1,321	—	—	Proof	225.00

30th Anniversary of Queen Elizabeth II Reign

| 34 | 1982FM(P) | 620 pcs. | — | Proof | 250.00 |

30th Anniversary of Coronation of Queen Elizabeth II

| 38 | 1983FM(P) | 624 pcs. | — | Proof | 250.00 |

Flora - Ginger Thomas

| 39 | 1984FM(P) | 25 pcs. | — | Proof | 600.00 |

Sir Francis Drake's West Indian Voyage

| 74 | 1985FM(P) | 772 pcs. | — | Proof | 300.00 |

MINT SETS (MS)

KM#	Date	Mintage	Identification	Issue Price	Mkt. Val.
MS1	1973(6)	18,402	KM1-6	11.50	8.00
MS2	1974(6)	9,474	KM1-6	10.00	8.00
MS3	1975(6)	2,351	KM1-6	12.50	10.00
MS4	1976(6)	996	KM1-6	13.50	15.00
MS5	1977(6)	782	KM1-6	12.50	15.00
MS6	1978(6)	943	KM1-6	13.00	15.00
MS7	1979(7)	680	KM1-6,24	20.00	27.50
MS8	1980(7)	1,007	KM1-6,26	21.00	27.50
MS9	1981(7)	472	KM1-6,30	20.00	30.00
MS10	1982(7)	—	KM1-6,33	28.50	35.00
MS11	1983(7)	203	KM1-6,35	22.00	50.00

PROOF SETS (PS)

PS1	1973(6)	*146,581	KM1-5,6a	15.00	10.00

*NOTE: Includes 34,418 proofs in First Day Covers.

PS2	1974(6)	93,555	KM1-5,6a	20.00	15.00
PS3	1975(6)	32,244	KM1-5,6a	25.00	15.00
PS4	1976(6)	15,003	KM1-5,6a	25.00	15.00
PS5	1977(6)	7,218	KM1-5,6a	26.00	15.00
PS6	1977(6)	17,366	KM9-14	60.00	50.00
PS7	1978(6)	7,059	KM1-5,6a	25.00	15.00
PS8	1978(6)	6,196	KM16-21	—	50.00
PS9	1979(7)	5,304	KM1-5,6a,24a	39.50	40.00
PS10	1980(7)	3,421	KM1-5,6a,26a	97.00	50.00
PS11	1981(7)	1,124	KM1-5,6a,30a	97.00	55.00
PS12	1982(7)	—	KM1-5,6a,33a	97.00	55.00
PS13	1983(7)	478	KM1-5,6a,35a	77.00	75.00
PS14	1984(7)	5,000	KM1-5,6a,35a	77.00	55.00
PS12	1985(6)	—	KM42-47	20.50	26.50
PS16	1985(6)	—	KM42a-46a,47	76.00	50.00

BRITISH WEST AFRICA

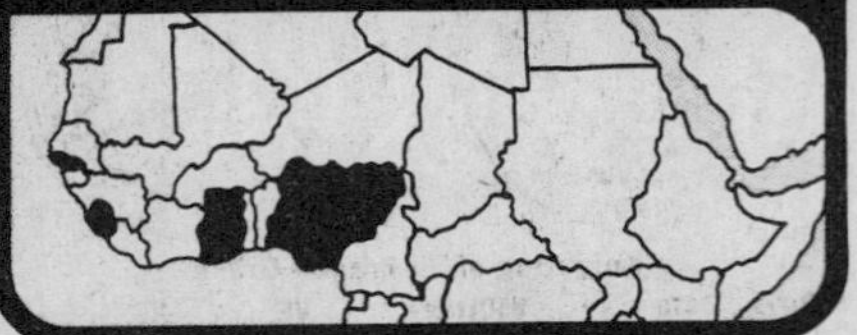

British West Africa was an administrative grouping of the four former British West African colonies of Gambia, Sierra Leone, Nigeria and Gold Coast (now Ghana). All are now independent republics and members of the British Commonwealth of Nations. See separate entries for individual statistics and history.

The four colonies were supplied with a common coinage and banknotes by the West African Currency Board from 1907 through 1958. From 1907 through 1911, the coinage bore the inscription, NIGERIA-BRITISH WEST AFRICA; from 1912 through 1958, BRITISH WEST AFRICA. The coinage, which includes three denominations of 1936 bearing the name of Edward VIII, is obsolete.

For later coinage see Gambia, Ghana, Sierra Leone and Nigeria.

RULERS

British until 1958

MINT MARKS

G-J.R. Gaunt & Sons, Birmingham
H - Heaton Mint, Birmingham
K, KN - King's Norton, Birmingham
SA - Pretoria, South Africa
No mm - Royal Mint

MONETARY SYSTEM

12 Pence = 1 Shilling
20 Shillings = 1 Pound

1/10 PENNY

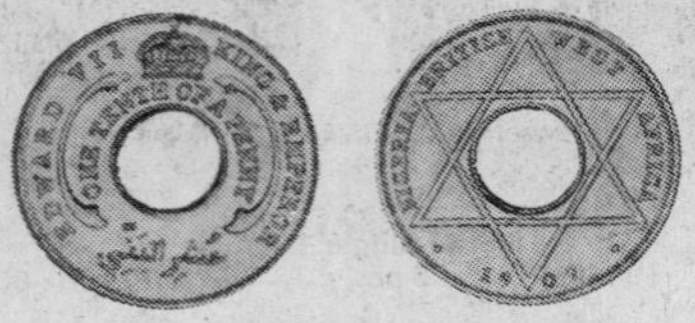

ALUMINUM

KM#	Date	Mintage	Fine	VF	XF	Unc
1	1906	—	—	—	Rare	—
	1907	1.254	2.00	4.00	7.00	17.50
	1908	8.363	1.00	3.00	5.00	12.50
	1908	—	—	—	Proof	250.00

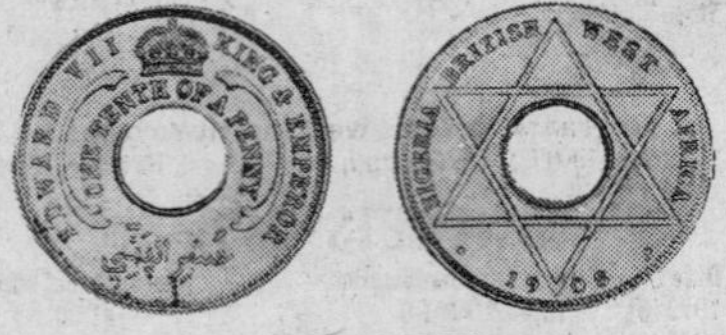

COPPER-NICKEL

KM#	Date	Mintage	Fine	VF	XF	Unc
3	1908	9.600	.30	.50	1.00	2.00
	1909	4.800	.40	.75	1.50	6.00
	1910	7.200	.50	1.00	2.00	7.50

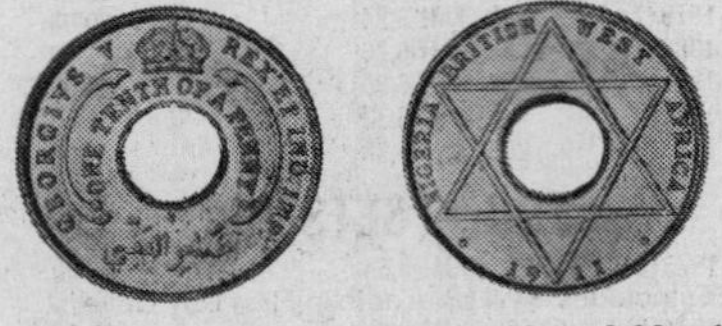

KM#	Date	Mintage	Fine	VF	XF	Unc
4	1911H	7.200	1.00	2.00	3.00	10.00

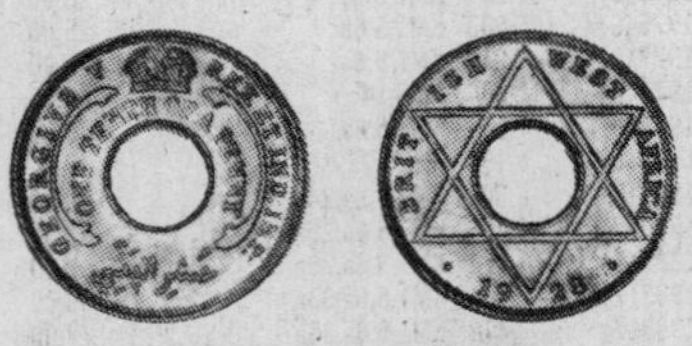

Rev. leg: W/o NIGERIA

KM#	Date	Mintage	Fine	VF	XF	Unc
7	1912H	10.800	.30	.75	1.50	4.00
	1913	4.632	1.00	2.50	5.00	7.50
	1913H	1.080	.30	.75	1.50	3.50
	1914	1.200	3.00	6.00	10.00	22.50
	1914H	20.088	.50	1.25	3.00	5.00
	1915H	10.032	.30	.75	1.50	5.00
	1916H	.480	50.00	85.00	125.00	200.00
	1917H	9.384	2.50	4.50	7.50	15.00
	1919H	.912	1.25	2.00	4.00	7.50
	1919KN	.480	10.00	25.00	50.00	80.00
	1920H	1.560	2.00	3.00	5.00	10.00
	1920KN	12.996	.40	1.00	3.00	5.00
	1920KN	—	—	—	Proof	125.00

KM#	Date	Mintage	Fine	VF	XF	Unc
7	1922KN	7.265	1.00	1.75	4.50	12.00
	1923KN	12.000	.30	.75	1.50	5.00
	1925	2.400	5.00	10.00	20.00	40.00
	1925H	12.000	2.50	4.50	7.50	15.00
	1925KN	12.000	.75	1.50	3.00	8.00
	1926	12.000	.75	1.50	3.00	6.00
	1927	3.984	.20	.50	1.50	3.00
	1927	—	—	—	Proof	150.00
	1928	11.760	.20	.50	1.50	3.00
	1928	—	—	—	Proof	150.00
	1928H	2.964	.20	.50	1.50	3.00
	1928KN	3.151	2.00	3.00	5.00	15.00
	1930	9.600	1.75	3.00	6.00	15.00
	1930	—	—	—	Proof	150.00
	1931	9.840	.20	.50	1.00	3.00
	1931	—	—	—	Proof	150.00
	1932	3.600	.20	.50	1.50	5.00
	1932	—	—	—	Proof	150.00
	1933	7.200	.20	.50	5.00	3.50
	1933	—	—	—	Proof	150.00
	1934	4.800	.75	1.50	3.00	6.00
	1934	—	—	—	Proof	150.00
	1935	13.200	.75	1.50	3.00	7.50
	1935	—	—	—	Proof	150.00
	1936	9.720	.30	.50	1.50	3.00
	1936	—	—	—	Proof	150.00

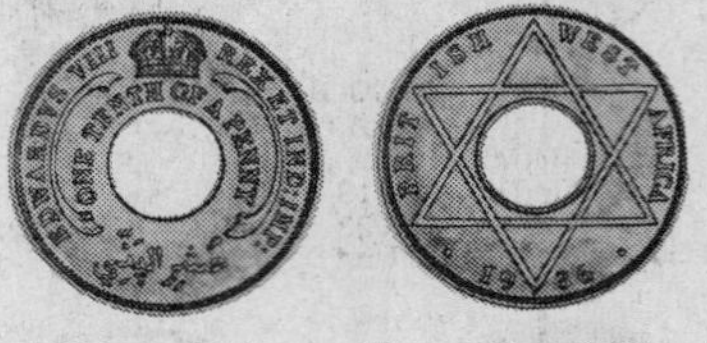

KM#	Date	Mintage	Fine	VF	XF	Unc
14	1936	5.880	.25	.50	1.00	2.50
	1936	—	—	—	Proof	200.00
	1936H	1.404	45.00	85.00	125.00	225.00
	1936H	—	—	—	Proof	350.00
	1936KN	3.000	1.00	2.00	3.50	9.00
	1936KN	—	—	—	Proof	200.00

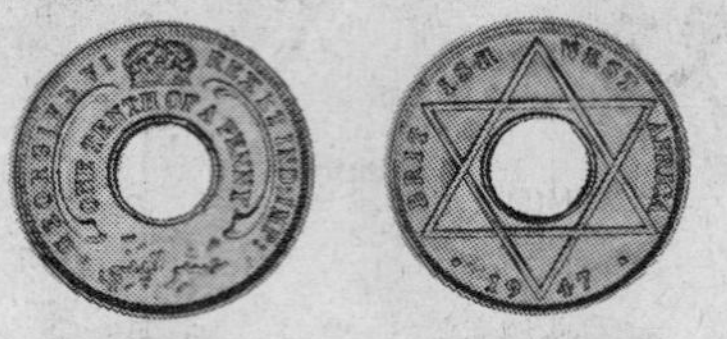

KM#	Date	Mintage	Fine	VF	XF	Unc
20	1938	12.000	.10	.25	.50	1.50
	1938	—	—	—	Proof	125.00
	1938H	1.596	5.00	9.00	12.50	25.00
	1938H	—	—	—	Proof	100.00
	1939	9.840	.25	.50	1.00	3.50
	1939	—	—	—	Proof	200.00
	1940	13.920	.25	.50	1.00	2.00
	1940	—	—	—	Proof	125.00
	1941	16.560	1.50	2.50	4.50	10.00
	1941	—	—	—	Proof	125.00
	1942	12.360	1.00	2.50	4.50	10.00
	1942	—	—	—	Proof	125.00
	1943	22.560	1.00	2.50	5.00	10.00
	1944	10.440	1.00	2.50	5.00	10.00
	1945	25.706	.50	1.00	1.75	6.00
	1945	—	—	—	Proof	125.00
	1946	2.803	1.00	2.00	3.50	9.00
	1946	—	—	—	Proof	125.00
	1946H	5.004	1.00	2.00	4.00	9.00
	1946KN	1.152	.25	.50	1.00	3.00
	1947	4.202	.25	.50	1.50	3.50
	1947	—	—	—	Proof	125.00
	1947KN	3.900	200.00	300.00	500.00	600.00

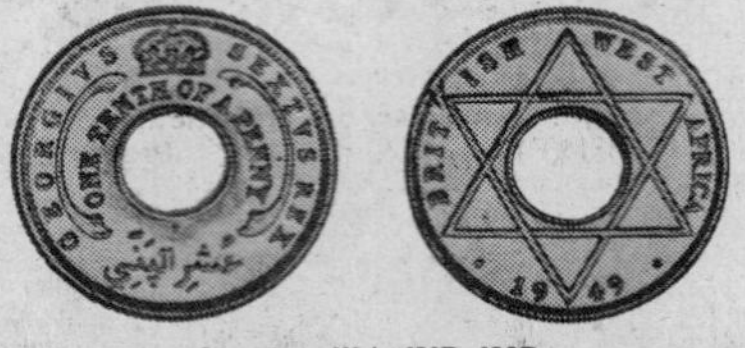

Obv. leg: W/o IND: IMP:

KM#	Date	Mintage	Fine	VF	XF	Unc
26	1949H	3.700	1.00	2.00	3.00	7.50
	1949KN	3.036	1.00	2.00	3.00	5.00
	1950KN	13.200	.25	.50	1.00	3.00

BRONZE

KM#	Date	Mintage	Fine	VF	XF	Unc
26a	1952	15.060	.50	1.00	2.00	6.00
	1952	—	—	—	Proof	150.00

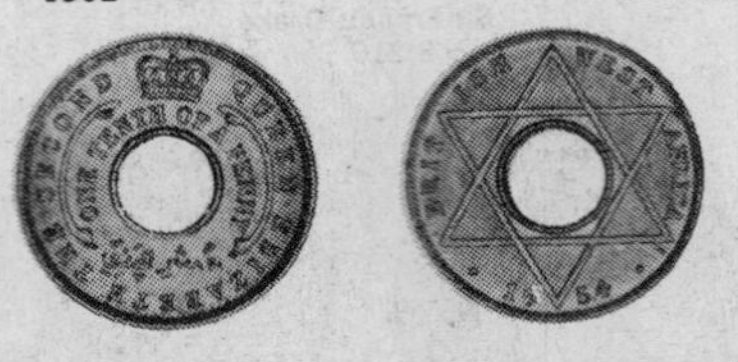

KM#	Date	Mintage	Fine	VF	XF	Unc
32	1954	4.800	.50	1.00	2.00	5.00
	1954	—	—	—	Proof	150.00
	1956	2.400	—	—	Rare	—
	1956	—	—	—	Proof	750.00
	1957	7.200	75.00	150.00	275.00	450.00
	1957	—	—	—	Proof	600.00

1/2 PENNY

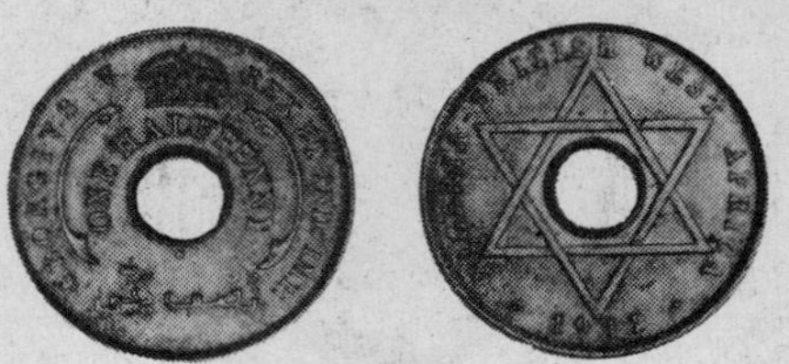

COPPER-NICKEL

KM#	Date	Mintage	Fine	VF	XF	Unc
5	1911H	3.360	3.00	7.50	15.00	35.00

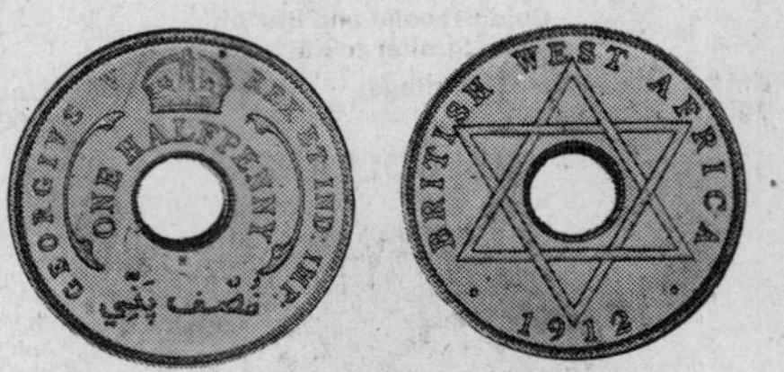

Rev. leg: W/o NIGERIA

KM#	Date	Mintage	Fine	VF	XF	Unc
8	1912H	3.120	2.00	5.00	7.00	20.00
	1913	—	175.00	250.00	350.00	600.00
	1913H	.216	5.00	10.00	17.50	30.00
	1914	1.622	10.00	20.00	35.00	60.00
	1914H	.586	10.00	20.00	35.00	60.00
	1914K	3.360	3.00	6.00	17.50	30.00
	1914K*	—	—	—	Proof	225.00
	1915H	3.577	1.00	2.00	4.00	15.00
	1916H	4.046	1.00	3.00	5.00	15.00
	1917H	.214	6.00	12.00	20.00	50.00
	1918H	.490	2.50	5.00	10.00	30.00
	1919H	4.950	1.25	2.50	6.00	20.00
	1919KN	3.861	1.25	2.50	7.50	25.00
	1920H	26.285	1.50	3.00	7.50	15.00
	1920KN	13.844	.50	2.00	3.50	15.00
	1922KN	5.817	500.00	800.00	1200.	1800.
	1927	.528	10.00	20.00	45.00	120.00
	1927	—	—	—	Proof	225.00
	1929	.336	6.00	10.00	17.50	85.00
	1929	—	—	—	Proof	225.00
	1931	.096	500.00	1000.	1200.	1500.
	1931	—	—	—	Proof	225.00
	1932	.960	2.50	5.00	15.00	50.00
	1932	—	—	—	Proof	225.00
	1933	2.122	2.00	3.50	12.00	95.00
	1933	—	—	—	Proof	225.00
	1934	1.694	2.50	5.00	12.50	65.00
	1934	—	—	—	Proof	225.00
	1935	3.271	1.00	3.00	10.00	35.00
	1935	—	—	—	Proof	225.00
	1936	5.400	2.50	5.00	12.00	30.00
	1936	—	—	—	Proof	225.00

***NOTE:** The 1914K was issued with East Africa KM#11 in a double (4 pc.) specimen set.

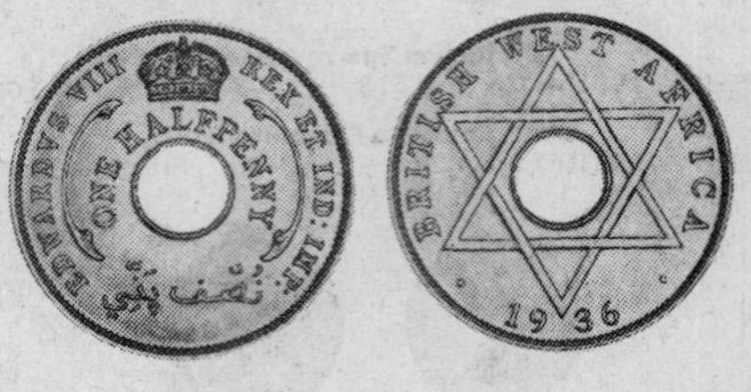

KM#	Date	Mintage	Fine	VF	XF	Unc
15	1936	14.760	.25	.50	1.00	2.50
	1936	—	—	—	Proof	200.00
	1936H	2.400	1.00	2.00	5.00	12.50
	1936H	—	—	—	Proof	200.00
	1936KN	2.298	.65	1.25	2.25	4.00
	1936KN	—	—	—	Proof	200.00

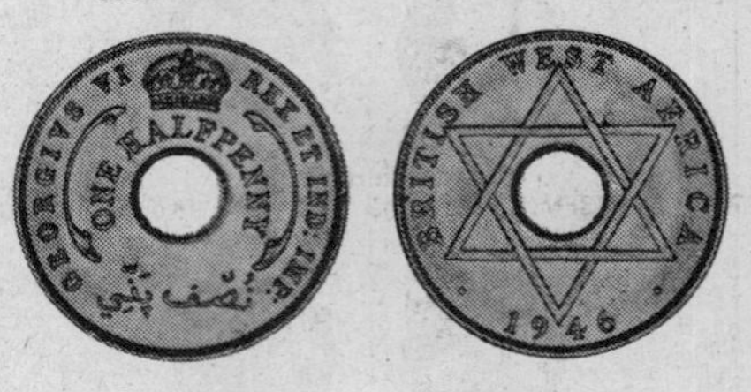

KM#	Date	Mintage	Fine	VF	XF	Unc
18	1937H	4.800	.40	.85	1.50	4.00
	1937H	—	—	—	Proof	125.00
	1937KN	5.577	.40	.85	3.00	5.00
	1940KN	2.410	1.25	2.50	5.00	15.00
	1940KN	—	—	—	Proof	125.00
	1941H	2.400	.40	2.00	4.00	12.00
	1942	4.800	.40	.85	2.00	8.50
	1943	3.360	.50	1.00	5.00	10.00
	1944	3.600	1.00	3.00	7.00	20.00
	1944	—	—	—	Proof	125.00
	1946	3.600	.25	1.00	3.00	7.00
	1946	—	—	—	Proof	125.00
	1947H	15.218	.35	.75	1.25	5.00
	1947KN	12.000	.40	.85	2.00	6.00

Obv. leg: W/o IND: IMP:

KM#	Date	Mintage	Fine	VF	XF	Unc
27	1949H	5.909	1.00	2.00	5.00	20.00
	1949KN	3.413	1.00	2.00	8.00	25.00
	1951	3.468	1.00	3.50	9.00	25.00
	1951	—	—	—	Proof	250.00

BRONZE

27a	1952	11.332	.25	.50	1.50	5.50
	1952	—	—	—	Proof	150.00
	1952H	27.603	.20	.35	.75	2.00
	1952KN	4.800	.50	1.00	3.00	7.50

PENNY

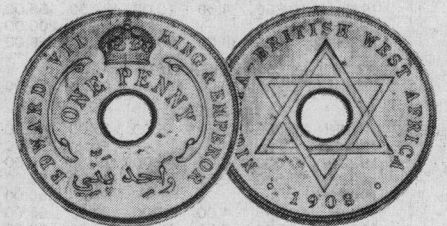

COPPER-NICKEL

2	1906	2 known	—	—	Rare	—
	1907	.863	1.35	3.50	7.00	17.50
	1908	3.217	1.35	2.75	6.00	14.00
	1909	.960	3.00	7.50	15.00	40.00
	1910	2.520	2.50	5.00	10.00	25.00

6	1911H	1.920	10.00	25.00	60.00	100.00

Rev. leg: W/o NIGERIA

9	1912H	1.560	1.50	3.00	7.50	22.50
	1913	1.680	10.00	20.00	30.00	75.00
	1913H	.144	5.00	10.00	17.50	35.00
	1914	3.000	2.50	5.00	10.00	22.50
	1914H	.072	30.00	45.00	80.00	175.00
	1915H	3.295	1.25	2.00	5.00	15.00
	1916H	3.461	1.25	2.00	7.00	14.00
	1917H	.444	3.50	7.00	15.00	45.00
	1918H	.994	5.00	15.00	30.00	65.00
	1919H	21.864	1.25	2.50	5.00	15.00
	1919KN	.264	7.50	14.50	25.00	50.00
	1920H	37.870	1.00	1.75	3.50	12.50
	1920KN	20.685	1.00	2.00	5.00	17.50
	1922KN	3.971	350.00	700.00	1000.	1500.
	1926	8.040	2.00	4.00	10.00	30.00
	1927	.792	25.00	45.00	85.00	200.00
	1927	—	—	—	Proof	225.00
	1928	6.672	2.00	4.00	10.00	25.00
	1928	—	—	—	Proof	225.00
	1929	.636	3.00	5.00	15.00	70.00
	1929	—	—	—	Proof	225.00
	1933	2.806	2.00	4.00	12.50	65.00
	1933	—	—	—	Proof	225.00
	1934	2.640	2.00	4.00	15.00	55.00
	1934	—	—	—	Proof	225.00
	1935	8.551	1.25	3.00	7.50	45.00
	1935	—	—	—	Proof	225.00
	1936	7.368	1.00	2.00	4.50	16.00
	1936	—	—	—	Proof	225.00

BRASS (OMS)

9a	1920KN	—	500.00	750.00	1000.	1250.

COPPER-NICKEL

KM#	Date	Mintage	Fine	VF	XF	Unc
16	1936	7.992	.50	1.00	3.50	7.00
	1936	—	—	—	Proof	250.00
	1936H	12.600	.35	.75	1.50	3.50
	1936H	—	—	—	Proof	250.00
	1936KN	12.512	.35	.75	1.00	3.50
	1936KN	—	—	—	Proof	250.00

Mule. Obv: East Africa, KM#24. Rev: KM#16.

17	1936H	—	125.00	150.00	225.00	350.00

19	1937H	11.999	.50	.75	1.25	2.00
	1937H	—	—	—	Proof	200.00
	1937KN	11.999	.50	.75	1.25	2.00
	1937KN	—	—	—	Proof	200.00
	1940	3.840	.50	.75	1.25	2.00
	1940	—	—	—	Proof	—
	1940H	2.400	.50	.75	3.00	8.00
	1940KN	2.400	.75	1.50	4.50	10.00
	1941	6.960	.35	.75	1.25	3.50
	1941	—	—	—	Proof	—
	1942	18.840	.30	.60	1.00	3.00
	1943	28.920	.30	.60	1.00	3.00
	1943H	7.140	2.00	5.00	10.00	20.00
	1944	19.440	.30	.60	1.00	4.00
	1945	6.072	.45	.90	1.75	5.00
	1945	—	—	—	Proof	150.00
	1945H	9.000	1.00	2.00	4.50	10.00
	1945KN	9.557	.75	1.50	3.00	7.00
	1946H	10.446	.85	1.75	3.75	8.00
	1946KN	11.976	.30	.60	1.00	5.00
	1946SA	1.020	250.00	500.00	750.00	1200.
	1947H	12.443	.30	.60	1.00	5.00
	1947KN	9.829	.30	.60	1.00	5.00
	1947SA	58.980	.30	.60	1.00	4.50

BRONZE (OMS)

19a	1937H	—	—	—	—	400.00

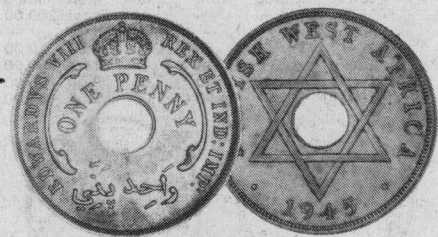

COPPER-NICKEL
Mule. Obv: KM#16. Rev: KM#19.

25	1945H	—	900.00	1500.	2000.	2750.

Obv. leg: W/o IND: IMP:

KM#	Date	Mintage	Fine	VF	XF	Unc
30	1951	1.258	5.00	10.00	22.50	40.00
	1951	—	—	—	Proof	250.00
	1951KN	2.692	4.00	8.00	15.00	30.00

BRONZE

30a	1952	10.542	.75	1.50	3.00	8.50
	1952	—	—	—	Proof	175.00
	1952H	30.794	.20	.40	.60	3.00
	1952KN	45.398	.20	.40	.60	3.00
	1952 KN	—	—	—	Proof	175.00

33	1956	—	.75	1.50	3.00	9.00
	1956H	13.503	.75	1.50	3.00	7.00
	1956KN	13.500	.30	.60	2.00	6.00
	1957	9.000	.75	1.50	5.00	10.00
	1957	—	—	—	Proof	150.00
	1957H	5.340	1.00	2.50	6.50	15.00
	1957KN	5.600	1.00	2.50	5.00	12.50
	1958	12.200	.75	1.50	3.50	10.00
	1958	—	—	—	Proof	150.00
	1958KN	Inc. Ab.	.75	1.50	2.50	8.00

Mule. Obv: KM#30. Rev: KM#33.

34	1956H	—	60.00	80.00	100.00	250.00

3 PENCE

1.4138 g, .925 SILVER, .0420 oz ASW

10	1913	.240	3.50	7.50	12.50	30.00
	1913	—	—	—	Proof	125.00
	1913H	.496	2.00	4.00	7.50	25.00
	1914H	1.560	1.00	2.00	7.50	25.00
	1915H	.270	15.00	20.00	40.00	85.00
	1916H	.820	10.00	15.00	22.50	65.00
	1917H	3.600	1.50	2.50	7.50	25.00
	1918H	1.722	1.75	3.50	8.00	20.00
	1919H	19.826	1.00	2.00	6.00	15.00
	1919H	—	—	—	Proof	200.00

1.4138 g, .500 SILVER, .0227 oz ASW

10a	1920H	3.616	25.00	40.00	65.00	140.00

TIN-BRASS

10b	1920KN	19.000	1.00	2.50	6.50	25.00
	1920KN	—	—	—	Proof	75.00
	1920KN*	—	—	—	Unique	—
	1925	8.800	1.50	3.00	9.00	40.00
	1926	1.600	10.00	25.00	35.00	85.00
	1927	.800	20.00	40.00	75.00	175.00
	1928	1.760	8.00	20.00	45.00	100.00
	1928	—	—	—	Proof	175.00
	1933	2.800	2.00	4.00	8.00	35.00
	1933	—	—	—	Proof	200.00
	1934	6.400	—	2.50	6.00	30.00
	1934	—	—	—	Proof	200.00
	1935	11.560	1.00	2.50	6.00	30.00
	1935	—	—	—	Proof	200.00
	1936	17.160	1.00	2.00	5.00	25.00
	1936	—	—	—	Proof	200.00
	1936H	1.000	20.00	30.00	50.00	100.00
	1936H	—	—	—	Proof	200.00
	1936KN	2.038	10.00	15.00	30.00	65.00

*NOTE: Mint mark on obverse below bust.

COPPER-NICKEL

21	1938H	7.000	.30	.60	2.00	7.50
	1938H	—	—	—	Proof	200.00
	1938KN	9.056	.35	.75	2.00	8.00
	1938KN	—	—	—	Proof	300.00
	1939H	16.500	.30	.60	2.00	6.00

236 BRITISH WEST AFRICA

KM#	Date	Mintage	Fine	VF	XF	Unc
21	1939H	—	—	—	Proof	300.00
	1939KN	15.500	.30	.60	1.75	8.00
	1939KN	—	—	—	Proof	200.00
	1940H	3.862	.50	1.00	2.00	7.50
	1940KN	10.000	.30	.60	1.50	5.00
	1941H	5.032	1.00	.85	2.00	9.00
	1943H	5.106	1.00	.85	2.00	15.00
	1943KN	9.502	1.00	.85	2.00	9.00
	1944KN	2.536	1.00	.85	2.50	15.00
	1945H	.998	2.00	2.50	5.00	20.00
	1945KN	3.000	1.00	.85	2.00	12.50
	1946KN	7.488	.40	.85	2.00	9.00
	1947H	10.000	.35	.75	2.00	8.00
	1947KN	11.248	.40	.85	2.00	8.00

KM#	Date	Mintage	Fine	VF	XF	Unc
35	1957H	.800	30.00	65.00	125.00	200.00

6 PENCE

2.8276 g, .925 SILVER, .0841 oz ASW

KM#	Date	Mintage	Fine	VF	XF	Unc
11	1913	.560	3.00	5.00	8.00	27.50
	1913	—	—	—	Proof	175.00
	1913H	.400	3.00	5.00	9.00	32.50
	1914H	.952	2.75	5.00	12.50	35.00
	1916H	.400	5.00	10.00	15.00	55.00
	1917H	2.400	3.00	5.00	10.00	32.50
	1918H	1.160	2.00	5.00	10.00	35.00
	1919H	8.676	2.00	3.50	7.50	20.00
	1919H	—	—	—	Proof	200.00
	2.8276 g, .500 SILVER, .0454 oz ASW					
11a	1920H	2.948	12.50	30.00	50.00	175.00
	1920H	—	—	—	Proof	275.00
	TIN-BRASS					
11b	1920KN	12.000	1.00	5.00	20.00	37.50
	1920KN	—	—	—	Proof	125.00
	1923H	2.000	5.00	12.50	40.00	95.00
	1924	1.000	15.00	30.00	60.00	150.00
	1924H	1.000	12.50	27.50	60.00	125.00
	1924KN	1.000	15.00	30.00	60.00	150.00
	1925	2.800	3.50	7.00	17.50	60.00
	1928	.400	20.00	35.00	85.00	200.00
	1928	—	—	—	Proof	200.00
	1933	1.000	15.00	30.00	80.00	150.00
	1933	—	—	—	Proof	225.00
	1935	4.000	5.00	12.50	25.00	50.00
	1935	—	—	—	Proof	225.00
	1936	10.400	7.50	15.00	25.00	50.00
	1936	—	—	—	Proof	225.00
	1936H	.480	25.00	50.00	75.00	200.00
	1936H	—	—	—	Proof	225.00
	1936KN	2.696	15.00	25.00	35.00	70.00
	1936KN	—	—	—	Proof	225.00

NICKEL-BRASS

KM#	Date	Mintage	Fine	VF	XF	Unc
22	1938	12.114	.50	1.00	2.00	8.00
	1938	—	—	—	Proof	200.00
	1940	17.829	.75	1.50	2.00	10.00
	1940	—	—	—	Proof	200.00
	1942	1.600	1.75	3.50	7.50	18.00
	1943	10.586	.75	1.75	4.00	11.00
	1944	1.814	2.00	3.00	10.00	32.50
	1945	4.000	1.00	2.00	7.50	25.00
	1945	—	—	—	Proof	200.00
	1946	4.000	2.50	5.00	17.50	50.00
	1946	—	—	—	Proof	225.00
	1947	6.120	.50	1.50	5.00	15.00
	1947	—	—	—	Proof	175.00

Obv. leg: W/o IND: IMP:

KM#	Date	Mintage	Fine	VF	XF	Unc
31	1952	2.544	7.50	15.00	25.00	55.00
	1952	—	—	—	Proof	300.00

SHILLING

5.6552 g, .925 SILVER, .1682 oz ASW

KM#	Date	Mintage	Fine	VF	XF	Unc
12	1913	8.800	2.75	4.00	7.50	22.50
	1913	—	—	—	Proof	200.00
	1913H	3.540	2.75	4.00	7.50	30.00
	1914	3.000	2.75	4.00	12.50	35.00
	1914H	11.292	2.75	4.00	10.00	30.00
	1915H	.254	12.50	20.00	37.50	100.00
	1916H	11.838	2.75	4.00	10.00	35.00
	1917H	15.018	2.75	5.50	10.00	32.50
	1918H	9.486	2.75	5.50	12.00	35.00
	1918H	—	—	—	Proof	200.00
	1919	2.000	10.00	15.00	30.00	55.00
	1919H	.992	15.00	22.50	50.00	100.00
	1919H	—	—	—	Proof	200.00
	1920	.828	22.50	40.00	70.00	150.00
	TIN-BRASS					
12a	1920G	.016	1400.	2000.	2600.	3500.
	1920KN	38.800	1.50	5.00	12.50	32.50
	1920KN	—	—	—	Proof	200.00
	1920KN*	—	—	—	Unique	—
	1922KN	32.324	2.00	6.50	20.00	70.00
	1923H	24.384	4.00	7.50	17.50	45.00
	1923KN	5.000	8.00	15.00	35.00	90.00
	1924	17.000	2.00	6.50	17.50	60.00
	1924H	9.567	10.00	20.00	50.00	125.00
	1924KN	7.000	7.50	15.00	30.00	80.00
	1925	19.800	4.00	8.00	18.00	45.00
	1926	19.952	2.00	5.00	10.00	40.00
	1927	22.248	1.50	3.50	7.50	30.00
	1927	—	—	—	Proof	225.00
	1928	10.000	15.00	30.00	60.00	200.00
	1928	—	—	—	Proof	300.00
	1936	70.200	3.00	6.50	11.00	32.50
	1936	—	—	—	Proof	225.00
	1936H	10.920	12.50	22.50	45.00	75.00
	1936KN	14.962	2.00	5.00	15.00	45.00
	1936KN	—	—	—	Proof	200.00

*NOTE: Mint mark on obverse below bust.

SILVER (OMS)

KM#	Date	Mintage	Fine	VF	XF	Unc
12b	1936KN	—	Reported, not confirmed			

NICKEL-BRASS

KM#	Date	Mintage	Fine	VF	XF	Unc
23	1938	57.806	.50	1.25	2.50	10.00
	1938	—	—	—	Proof	200.00
	1939	55.472	.50	1.25	2.50	15.00
	1939	—	—	—	Proof	200.00
	1940	40.311	.50	1.25	2.50	12.50
	1940	—	—	—	Proof	200.00
	1942	42.000	.50	1.25	2.50	15.00
	1943	133.600	.50	1.25	2.50	12.50
	1945	8.010	1.00	1.50	6.00	20.00
	1945	—	—	—	Proof	200.00
	1945H	12.864	2.00	3.50	10.00	30.00
	1945KN	11.120	1.00	2.00	4.00	20.00
	1946	37.350	1.00	2.00	4.50	30.00
	1946	—	—	—	Proof	200.00
	1946H	—	—	—	Rare	—
	1947	99.200	.50	1.00	2.50	10.00
	1947	—	—	—	Proof	200.00
	1947H	10.000	1.50	3.00	9.00	25.00
	1947KN	10.384	.50	1.00	2.50	14.00

TIN-BRASS
Obv. leg: W/o IND: IMP:

KM#	Date	Mintage	Fine	VF	XF	Unc
28	1949	70.000	.50	1.00	4.00	20.00
	1949	—	—	—	Proof	175.00
	1949H	10.000	1.25	2.50	7.50	22.50
	1949KN	10.016	1.25	2.50	7.50	22.50
	1949KN	—	—	—	Proof	200.00
	1951	35.346	1.25	2.50	7.50	25.00
	1951	—	—	—	Proof	175.00
	1951H	10.000	1.25	2.50	7.50	25.00
	1951KN	16.832	1.25	2.50	7.50	25.00
	1952	98.654	.50	1.00	3.00	7.50
	1952	—	—	—	Proof	225.00
	1952H	44.096	.50	1.00	2.00	6.00
	1952KN	41.653	.50	1.00	2.00	5.00
	1952KN	—	—	—	Proof	175.00

2 SHILLINGS

11.3104 g, .925 SILVER, .3364 oz ASW

KM#	Date	Mintage	Fine	VF	XF	Unc
13	1913	2.100	5.00	8.00	15.00	37.50
	1913	—	—	—	Proof	250.00
	1913H	1.176	6.00	12.00	17.50	50.00
	1914	.330	15.00	30.00	75.00	200.00
	1914H	.637	10.00	25.00	35.00	75.00
	1915H	.066	15.00	27.50	40.00	150.00
	1916H	9.824	5.00	8.00	17.50	50.00
	1917H	1.059	15.00	30.00	50.00	150.00
	1917H	—	—	—	Proof	300.00
	1918H	7.294	5.00	12.00	17.50	50.00
	1919	2.000	6.00	12.50	25.00	75.00
	1919H	10.866	4.50	10.00	22.50	55.00
	1919H	—	—	—	Proof	200.00
	1920	.683	30.00	60.00	175.00	250.00
	11.3104 g, .500 SILVER, .1818 oz ASW					
13a	1920H	1.926	30.00	55.00	100.00	275.00
	TIN-BRASS					
13b	1920KN	15.856	2.50	5.00	15.00	40.00
	1920KN	—	—	—	Proof	250.00
	1922	10.000	3.00	9.00	17.50	55.00
	1922KN	5.500	6.00	15.00	30.00	75.00
	1922KN	—	—	—	Proof	250.00
	1923H	12.696	4.00	12.00	22.50	65.00
	1924	1.500	7.50	15.00	35.00	90.00
	1925	3.700	4.00	12.00	25.00	70.00
	1926	11.500	4.50	11.00	30.00	80.00
	1927	11.100	4.00	12.00	45.00	100.00
	1927	—	—	—	Proof	250.00
	1928	7.900	—	—	Rare	—
	1928	—	—	—	Proof	350.00
	1936	32.940	5.00	10.00	20.00	50.00
	1936	—	—	—	Proof	250.00
	1936H	8.703	6.00	12.00	35.00	60.00
	1936KN	8.794	6.00	12.00	35.00	75.00

NICKEL-BRASS

KM#	Date	Mintage	Fine	VF	XF	Unc
24	1938H	32.000	1.00	2.00	4.00	15.00
	1938KN	27.852	1.00	2.00	4.00	15.00
	1939H	5.750	1.25	2.50	5.50	25.00
	1939KN	6.250	1.00	2.00	4.00	25.00
	1939KN	—	—	—	Proof	200.00
	1942KN	10.000	1.25	2.50	5.50	25.00
	1946H	10.500	1.25	2.50	5.50	22.50
	1946KN	4.800	1.25	3.00	9.00	35.00
	1947H	5.055	1.00	2.25	5.00	32.50
	1947KN	4.200	1.25	2.75	6.00	35.00

Obv. leg: W/o IND: IMP:

KM#	Date	Mintage	Fine	VF	XF	Unc
29	1949H	7.500	1.25	3.00	8.50	35.00
	1949KN	7.576	1.25	3.00	8.50	30.00
	1951H	6.566	1.25	3.00	8.50	35.00
	1951H	—	—	—	Proof	250.00
	1952H	4.410	2.00	3.50	8.50	35.00
	1952KN	1.236	3.50	6.00	15.00	45.00

SPECIMEN SETS (SS)

KM#	Date	Mintage	Identification	Issue Price	Mkt. Val.
SS1	1913(8)	14	KM10-13, double set	—	1500.
SS2	1913(4)	200	KM10-13	—	750.00
SS3	1919H(8)	2 known	KM10-13, double set	—	1500.
SS4	1920KN(8)	36	KM10b,11b,12a,13b,double set	—	1350.
SS5	1928(4)	—	KM10b,11b,12a,13b	—	1000.
SS6	1936H(3)	—	KM14-16	—	500.00
SS7	1952(4)	—	KM26a,27a,30a,31	—	800.00

BRITISH WEST INDIES

The 'Anchor Coins' catalogued under this heading do not bear a particular place identification. They were issued for use in various British colonies in both the New World and the Orient. Coins of this type dated 1820 are traditionally assigned to Mauritius and other holdings in the Indian Ocean. Those of 1822 were initially struck for Mauritius but after the introduction of sterling as the denomination of public accounts in Mauritius, they found their widest circulation in Canada and colonies in the Caribbean Sea. In Jamaica they were limited to military transactions only. In the Leeward Islands they were used on all the islands except the Virgin Islands, Windward Islands, Barbados, Tobago and Trinidad.

RULERS
British

ANCHOR COINAGE
1/16 DOLLAR

.892 SILVER

KM#	Date	Mintage	Fine	VF	XF	Unc
1	1820	.162	10.00	25.00	50.00	125.00
	1820	—	—	—	Proof	350.00
	1822/1	.142	12.50	27.50	55.00	135.00
	1822	Inc. Ab.	6.00	12.50	25.00	100.00
	1822	—	—	—	Proof	350.00

1/8 DOLLAR

.892 SILVER

2	1820	.120	12.50	30.00	60.00	180.00
	1820	—	—	—	Proof	350.00
	1822/0	.142	10.00	25.00	50.00	160.00
	1822/1	Inc. Ab.	7.50	17.50	40.00	145.00
	1822	Inc. Ab.	6.00	15.00	35.00	130.00
	1822	—	—	—	Proof	350.00

1/4 DOLLAR

.892 SILVER

3	1820	.100	30.00	50.00	100.00	275.00
	1820	—	—	—	Proof	400.00
	1822/1	.071	7.50	17.50	45.00	225.00
	1822	Inc. Ab.	6.00	15.00	40.00	200.00
	1822	—	—	—	Proof	400.00

1/2 DOLLAR

.892 SILVER

4	1821	—	—	—	Proof	Unique
	1822/1	.089	100.00	200.00	500.00	750.00
	1822	Inc. Ab.	85.00	175.00	300.00	600.00
	1822	—	—	—	Proof	800.00

BRUNEI

The state of Brunei Darussalam (Negeri Brunei), an independent sultanate on the northwest coast of the island of Borneo, has an area of 2,226 sq. mi. (5,765 sq. km.) and a population of 213,003. Capital: Bandar Seri Begawan. Crude oil and rubber are exported.

Magellan was the first European to visit Brunei in 1521. It was a powerful state, ruling over northern Borneo and adjacent islands from the 16th to the 19th century. Brunei became a British protectorate in 1888 and a British dependency in 1905. The Constitution of 1959 restored control over internal affairs to the sultan, while delegating responsibility for defense and foreign affairs to Britain.

The island of Labuan (formerly Sultana), located 6 miles off the northwest coast of Borneo, has an area of 35 sq. mi. and a population of 10,000. It is now part of Sabah (British North Borneo), and consequently of Malaysia. The East India Co. sought to make Labuan a trading station in 1775, but the island reverted to a pirate refuge. In 1846 it was ceded by the sultan of Brunei to Britain. Labuan was a crown colony from 1848 to 1890, when its administration was handed over to British North Borneo, which ruled it until 1905, when it became part of the Straits Settlements. Labuan became a part of Sabah in 1946. On January 1, 1984 it became independent.

TITLES

Negri Brunei

RULERS
Sultan Abdul Mumin, 1852-1885
Sultan Hashim Jelal, 1885-1906
British 1906-1950
Sultan Sir Omar Ali Saifuddin III, 1950-1967
Sultan Hassanal Bolkiah I, 1967-

MONETARY SYSTEM
100 Cents = 1 Straits Dollar
100 Sen = 1 Dollar

1/2 PITIS

TIN, 24mm

KM#	Date	Mintage	Good	VG	Fine	VF
1	AH1285	—	17.50	27.50	45.00	75.00

PITIS

TIN
Obv: Flag at top to right.

| 2.1 | AH1285 | — | 12.50 | 20.00 | 32.50 | 55.00 |

Obv: Flag at top to left.

| 2.2 | AH1285 | — | 12.50 | 20.00 | 32.50 | 55.00 |

CENT

BRONZE

KM#	Date	Mintage	Fine	VF	XF	Unc
3	AH1304	1.000	10.00	20.00	50.00	125.00
	1304	—	—	—	Proof	400.00

DECIMAL COINAGE
100 Sen = 1 Dollar (Ringgit)

SEN

BRONZE

KM#	Date	Mintage	VF	XF	Unc
4	1967	1.000	.10	.20	.50

9	1968	.060	.25	.50	1.50
	1970	.140	.10	.20	.50
	1970	3,234	—	Proof	2.50
	1971	.400	.10	.15	.40
	1973	.120	.10	.30	1.25
	1974	.640	—	.10	.30
	1976	.140	—	.10	.30
	1977	.140	—	.10	.30

Obv. leg: W/o numeral 'I' in title.

15	1977	.280	—	.10	.20
	1978	.269	—	.10	.15
	1979	.250	.10	.20	.50
	1979	.010	—	Proof	.90
	1980	.260	—	.10	.15
	1981	.540	—	.10	.15
	1982	.100	—	.20	1.00
	1983	.500	—	.10	.15
	1984	.400	—	.10	.15
	1984	3,000	—	Proof	1.00
	1985	.200	—	.10	.15
	1985	—	—	Proof	1.00
	1986	.101	—	—	.15
	1986	7,000	—	Proof	1.00
	1987	—	—	—	.15
	1987	—	—	Proof	1.00

5 SEN

COPPER-NICKEL

| 5 | 1967 | 1.160 | .20 | .35 | 1.25 |

10	1968	.320	.10	.20	.80
	1970	.760	.10	.25	.60
	1970	3,234	—	Proof	2.50
	1971	.320	.10	.20	.70
	1973	.128	.10	.15	1.85
	1974	.576	.10	.15	.40
	1976	.384	.10	.15	.45
	1977	.384	.10	.15	.45

Obv. leg: W/o numeral 'I' in title.

16	1977	.920	—	.10	.20
	1978	.640	—	.10	.20
	1979	.650	.10	.20	.50
	1979	.010	—	Proof	1.25
	1980	.640	—	.10	.15
	1981	.960	—	.10	.15
	1982	.240	—	.30	1.45
	1983	1.280	—	.10	.15
	1984	.800	—	.10	.15
	1984	3,000	—	Proof	1.25
	1985	.800	—	.10	.15
	1985	—	—	Proof	1.25
	1986	.189	—	—	.15
	1986	7,000	—	Proof	1.25
	1987	—	—	—	.15
	1987	—	—	Proof	1.25

BRUNEI 238

10 SEN

COPPER-NICKEL

KM#	Date	Mintage	VF	XF	Unc
6	1967	3.510	.10	.20	.50

11	1968	.580	.10	.25	.60
	1970	1.360	.10	.20	.50
	1970	3,234	—	Proof	2.50
	1971	.420	.10	.20	.50
	1973	.300	.10	.25	.60
	1974	1.410	.10	.20	.50
	1976	.920	.10	.20	.50
	1977	.920	—	.15	.40

Obv. leg: W/o numeral 'I' in title.

17	1977	1.800	.10	.15	.40
	1978	1.080	—	.10	.30
	1979	2.050	—	.10	.30
	1979	.010	—	Proof	1.35
	1980	2.840	—	.10	.20
	1981	.976	—	.10	.20
	1983	1.080	—	.10	.20
	1984	1.400	—	.10	.20
	1984	3,000	—	Proof	1.50
	1985	1.540	—	—	.20
	1985	—	—	Proof	1.50
	1986	2.181	—	—	.20
	1986	7,000	—	Proof	1.50
	1987	—	—	—	.20
	1987	—	—	Proof	1.50

20 SEN

COPPER-NICKEL

7	1967	2.130	.25	1.25	2.00

12	1968	.510	.20	.60	1.25
	1970	.850	.15	.40	1.00
	1970	3,234	—	Proof	2.50
	1971	.450	.20	.60	1.25
	1973	.450	.20	.60	1.25
	1974	.700	.15	.40	1.00
	1976	.640	.15	.40	1.00
	1977	.640	.15	.40	1.00

Obv. leg: W/o numeral 'I' in title.

18	1977	1.200	.10	.25	.60
	1978	.720	.15	.40	1.00
	1979	1.060	.20	.50	1.25
	1979	.010	—	Proof	2.00
	1980	1.540	.10	.20	.50
	1981	2.140	.10	.20	.50
	1982	.120	1.00	4.00	8.00
	1983	1.350	.10	.15	.35
	1984	.750	.10	.15	.35
	1984	3,000	—	Proof	2.25
	1985	1.000	.10	.15	.35

KM#	Date	Mintage	VF	XF	Unc
18	1985	—	—	Proof	2.25
	1986	2.639	—	—	.35
	1986	7,000	—	Proof	2.25
	1987	—	—	—	.35
	1987	—	—	Proof	2.25

50 SEN

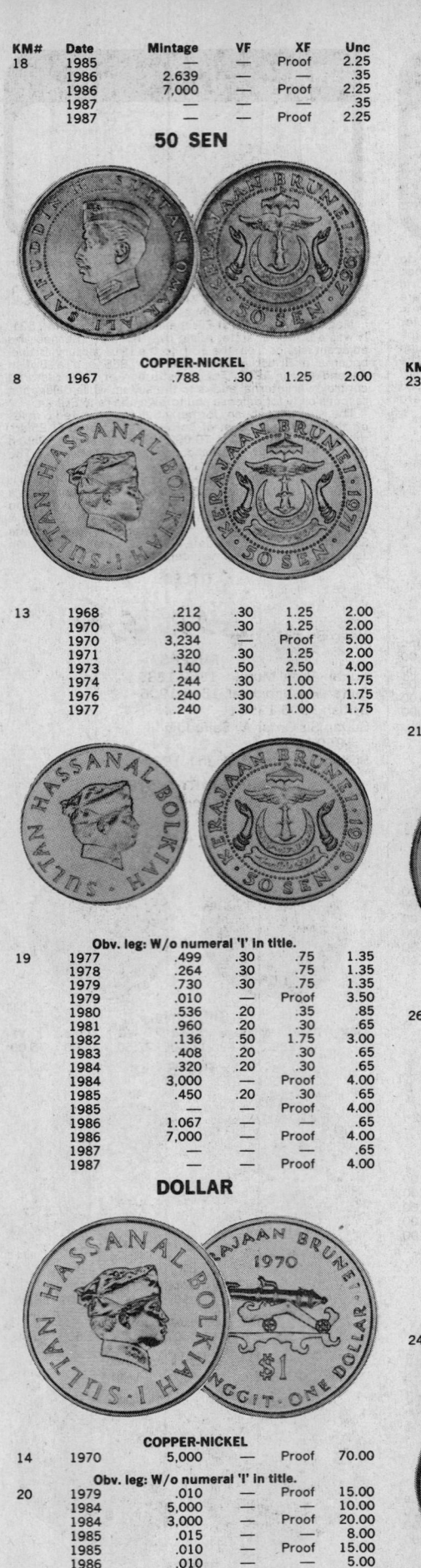

COPPER-NICKEL

8	1967	.788	.30	1.25	2.00

13	1968	.212	.30	1.25	2.00
	1970	.300	.30	1.25	2.00
	1970	3,234	—	Proof	5.00
	1971	.320	—	1.25	2.00
	1973	.140	.50	2.50	4.00
	1974	.244	.30	1.00	1.75
	1976	.240	.30	1.00	1.75
	1977	.240	.30	1.00	1.75

Obv. leg: W/o numeral 'I' in title.

19	1977	.499	.30	.75	1.35
	1978	.264	.30	.75	1.35
	1979	.730	.30	.75	1.35
	1979	.010	—	Proof	3.50
	1980	.536	.20	.35	.85
	1981	.960	.20	.30	.65
	1982	.136	.50	1.75	3.00
	1983	.408	.20	.30	.65
	1984	.320	.20	.30	.65
	1984	3,000	—	Proof	4.00
	1985	.450	.20	.30	.65
	1985	—	—	Proof	4.00
	1986	1.067	—	—	.65
	1986	7,000	—	Proof	4.00
	1987	—	—	—	.65
	1987	—	—	Proof	4.00

DOLLAR

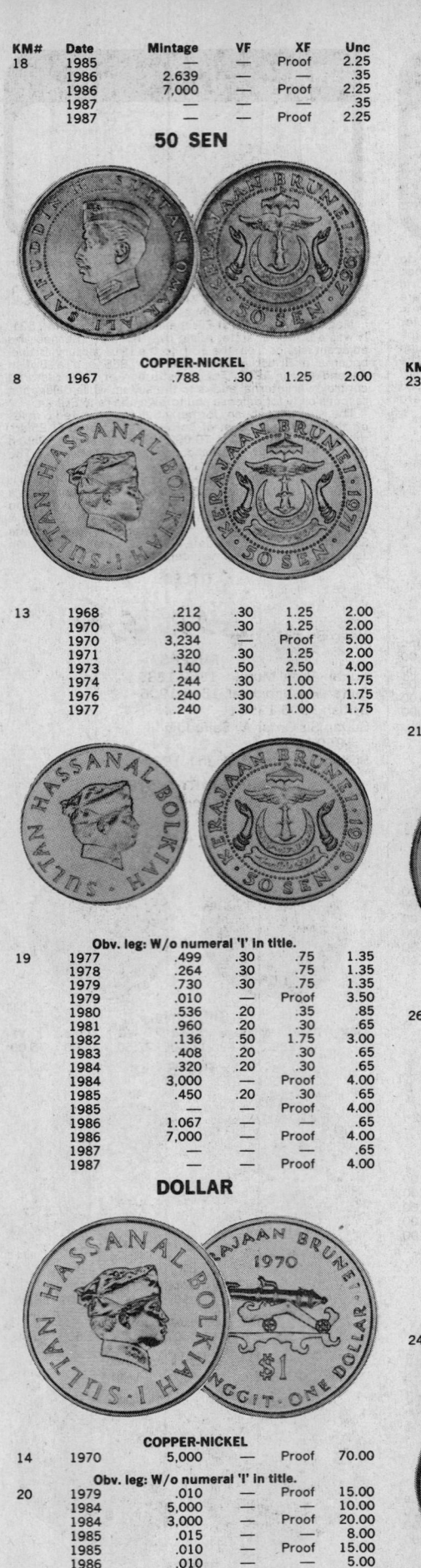

COPPER-NICKEL

14	1970	5,000	—	Proof	70.00

Obv. leg: W/o numeral 'I' in title.

20	1979	.010	—	Proof	15.00
	1984	5,000	—	—	10.00
	1984	3,000	—	Proof	20.00
	1985	.015	—	—	8.00
	1985	.010	—	Proof	15.00
	1986	.010	—	—	5.00
	1986	7,000	—	Proof	20.00
	1987	—	—	—	5.00
	1987	—	—	Proof	20.00

5 DOLLARS

COPPER-NICKEL
Year of Hejira, 1400
Obv: Similar to 50 Sen, KM#19.

KM#	Date	Mintage	VF	XF	Unc
23	1980	.010	3.00	12.00	20.00

10 DOLLARS

28.2800 g, .925 SILVER, .8411 oz ASW
10th Anniversary of Brunei Currency Board
Obv: Similar to 50 Sen, KM#19.

21	1977	.010	—	Proof	80.00

COPPER-NICKEL
Independence Day

26	1984	.015	—	—	18.00
	1984	5,000	—	Proof	40.00

50 DOLLARS

28.2800 g, .925 SILVER, .8411 oz ASW
Year of Hejira 1400
Obv: Similar to 50 Sen, KM#19.

24	1980	3,000	—	Proof	100.00

100 DOLLARS

28.2800 g, .925 SILVER, .8411 oz ASW

KM#	Date	Mintage	VF	XF	Unc
27	1984	5,000	—	100.00	
	1984	2,000	—	Proof	125.00

750 DOLLARS

15.9800 g, .917 GOLD, .4711 oz AGW
Year of Hejira 1400

25	1980	1,000	—	Proof	600.00

1000 DOLLARS

50.0000 g, .917 GOLD, 1.4742 oz AGW
10th Anniversary of Sultan's Coronation

22	1978	1,000	—	Proof	1500.

Independence Day
Similar to 100 Dollars, KM#27.

28	1984	4,000	—	—	1000.
	1984	1,000	—	Proof	1325.

SPECIMEN/MINT SETS (MS)

KM#	Date	Mintage	Identification	Issue Price	Mkt. Val.
MS1	1970(5)	4,000	KM9-13	6.60	22.00
MS2	1984(6)	5,000	KM15-20	—	15.00
MS3	1984(3)	500	KM26-28	—	1250.
MS4	1985(6)	15,000	KM15-20	10.00	20.00
MS5	1986(6)	7,000	KM15-20	10.00	20.00
MS6	1987(6)	5,000	KM15-20	—	20.00

PROOF SETS (PS)

PS1	1979(6)	10,000	KM15-20	30.00	70.00
PS2	1984(6)	3,000	KM15-20	—	60.00
PS3	1984(3)	500	KM26-28	—	1500.
PS4	1985(6)	10,000	KM15-20	30.00	60.00
PS5	1986(6)	5,000	KM15-20	30.00	60.00
PS6	1987(6)	2,000	KM15-20	—	60.00

Listings For
BUKHARA: refer to Union of Soviet Socialist Republics-Russian Turkestan

---

BULGARIA

The People's Republic of Bulgaria, a Balkan country on the Black Sea in southeastern Europe, has an area of 42,823 sq. mi. (110,912 sq. km.) and a population of 8.9 million. Capital: Sofia. Agriculture remains a key component of the economy but industrialization, particularly heavy industry, has been emphasized since the late 1940s. Machinery, tobacco and cigarettes, wines and spirits, clothing and metals are the chief exports.

The area now occupied by Bulgaria was conquered by the Bulgars, an Asiatic tribe, in the 7th century. Bulgarian kingdoms continued to exist on the Bulgarian peninsula until it came under Turkish rule in 1395. In 1878, after nearly 500 years of Turkish rule, Bulgaria was made a principality under Turkish suzerainty. Union seven years later with Eastern Rumelia created a Balkan state with borders approximating those of present-day Bulgaria. A Bulgarian kingdom fully independent of Turkey was proclaimed Sept. 22, 1908. That monarchy was abolished by plebiscite in 1946 and Bulgaria became a People's Republic on the Soviet pattern.

Coinage of the People's Republic features a number of politically oriented commemoratives.

RULERS
Alexander I, 1879-1886
Ferdinand I, as Prince, 1887-1908
  As King, 1908-1918
Boris III, 1918-1943

MINT MARKS
A - Berlin
(a) Cornucopia & torch - Paris
BP - Budapest
H - Heaton Mint, Birmingham
KB - Kormoczbanya
(p) Poissy - Thunderbolt

MONETARY SYSTEM
100 Stotinki = 1 Lev

STOTINKA

BRONZE

KM#	Date	Mintage	Fine	VF	XF	Unc
22	1901	20.000	1.00	2.50	5.00	12.00
(Y16)	1912	20.000	.75	1.25	2.00	6.00

2 STOTINKI

BRONZE
Rev: HEATON below wreath

1	1881	5.000	3.00	6.00	15.00	32.00
(Y1)	1881	—	—	—	Proof	85.00

23	1901(a)	40.000	1.00	2.00	4.00	9.00
(Y17)	1912	40.000	.75	1.25	2.00	6.00

2-1/2 STOTINKI

COPPER-NICKEL

8	1888	12.000	2.00	4.00	8.00	20.00
(Y8)	1888	—	—	—	Proof	60.00

---

5 STOTINKI

BRONZE
Rev: HEATON below wreath

KM#	Date	Mintage	Fine	VF	XF	Unc
2	1881	10.000	2.00	4.00	10.00	25.00
(Y2)	1881	—	—	—	Proof	110.00

COPPER-NICKEL

9	1888	14.000	1.00	3.00	7.00	16.00
(Y9)	1888	—	—	—	Proof	55.00

24	1906	14.000	.20	.50	1.75	5.00
(Y18)	1912	14.000	.20	.50	1.50	4.50
	1913	20.000	.20	.30	1.00	4.00

ZINC

24a	1917	53.200	.50	1.00	2.00	5.00
(Y18a)						

10 STOTINKI

BRONZE
Rev: HEATON below wreath

3	1881	15.000	2.00	4.50	9.00	22.00
(Y3)	1881	—	—	—	Proof	75.00

COPPER-NICKEL

10	1888	10.000	1.50	3.50	8.00	16.00
(Y10)						

25	1906	13.000	.50	1.00	2.00	5.00
(Y19)	1912	13.000	.20	.40	1.25	4.50
	1913	20.000	.20	.30	1.00	4.00

ZINC

25a	1917	59.100	.25	1.00	2.00	4.50
(Y19a)						

20 STOTINKI

COPPER-NICKEL

11	1888	5.000	2.00	4.00	8.00	18.00
(Y11)						

BULGARIA 240

KM#	Date	Mintage	Fine	VF	XF	Unc
26 (Y20)	1906	10.000	.50	1.00	2.00	7.00
	1912	10.000	.20	.40	2.00	5.00
	1913	5.000	.20	.40	1.00	5.00
			ZINC			
26a (Y20a)	1917	40.000	.35	1.25	2.00	6.50

50 STOTINKI

2.5000 g, .835 SILVER, .0671 oz ASW

6 (Y4)	1883	3.000	2.00	4.00	9.00	30.00

12 (Y12)	1891KB	2.000	2.00	4.00	10.00	32.00

LEV

5.0000 g, .835 SILVER, .1342 oz ASW

4 (Y5)	1882	4.500	2.50	5.00	10.00	40.00

13 (Y13)	1891KB	4.000	2.50	5.00	10.00	42.00

16 (Y13a)	1894	1.000	3.00	5.50	11.00	45.00

2 LEVA

10.0000 g, .835 SILVER, .2685 oz ASW

5 (Y6)	1882	2.000	5.00	7.50	15.00	60.00

KM#	Date	Mintage	Fine	VF	XF	Unc
14 (Y14)	1891	1.500	5.00	7.50	16.00	65.00

17 (Y14a)	1894KB	1.000	5.00	7.50	18.00	75.00
	1894KB	—	—	—	Proof	300.00

5 LEVA

25.0000 g, .900 SILVER, .7234 oz ASW

7 (Y7)	1884	.512	12.00	17.50	45.00	200.00
	1885	1.426	12.00	17.50	40.00	185.00

15 (Y15)	1892	1.000	12.00	15.00	30.00	180.00

Obv. leg. rearranged.

18 (Y15a)	1894	1.800	12.00	15.00	25.00	160.00

10 LEVA

3.2258 g, .900 GOLD, .0933 oz AGW

19 (Y21)	1894KB	.075	50.00	85.00	130.00	250.00

20 LEVA

6.4516 g, .900 GOLD, .1867 oz AGW

KM#	Date	Mintage	Fine	VF	XF	Unc
20 (Y22)	1894KB	.100	100.00	125.00	180.00	320.00

100 LEVA

32.2580 g, .900 GOLD, .9334 oz AGW

21 (Y23)	1894KB	2.500	525.00	725.00	1200.	2250.

KINGDOM
50 STOTINKI

2.5000 g, .835 SILVER, .0671 oz ASW

27 (Y24)	1910	.400	1.75	3.50	7.00	20.00

30 (Y27)	1912	2.000	1.50	3.00	6.00	14.00
	1913	3.000	1.50	2.50	5.00	13.00
	1916	4.562	50.00	90.00	140.00	200.00

ALUMINUM-BRONZE

46 (Y41)	1937	60.200	.10	.25	.50	3.00

LEV

5.0000 g, .835 SILVER, .1342 oz ASW

28 (Y25)	1910	3.000	2.25	4.50	8.00	22.00

31 (Y28)	1912	2.000	2.25	4.50	8.00	18.00
	1913	3.500	2.25	4.50	7.50	17.50
	1916	4.569	100.00	200.00	300.00	400.00

BULGARIA 241

ALUMINUM

KM#	Date	Mintage	Fine	VF	XF	Unc
35	1923	40.000	3.00	6.00	12.00	35.00
(Y32)	1923H	—	—	—	Rare	—

COPPER-NICKEL

37	1925	35.000	.15	.30	.75	2.00
(Y34)	1925(p)	35.000	.15	.30	.75	2.00

NOTE: The Poissy issue bears the thunderbolt mint mark.

IRON

37a	1941	10.000	3.00	6.00	14.00	30.00
(Y34a)						

2 LEVA

10.0000 g, .835 SILVER, .2685 oz ASW

29	1910	.400	4.50	9.00	15.00	45.00
(Y26)						

32	1912	1.000	4.50	8.00	14.00	32.00
(Y29)	1913	.500	4.50	9.00	15.00	35.00
	1916	2.286	125.00	250.00	345.00	450.00

ALUMINUM

36	1923	20.000	4.00	8.00	15.00	38.00
(Y33)	1923H	—	—	—	Rare	—

COPPER-NICKEL

38	1925	20.000	.20	.50	1.00	2.50
(Y35)	1925(p)	20.000	.20	.50	1.00	2.50

NOTE: The Poissy issue bears the thunderbolt mint mark.

IRON

38a	1941	15.000	.50	1.00	3.00	9.00
(Y35a)						

49	1943	35.000	.50	1.00	4.00	12.00
(Y-A45)						

5 LEVA

COPPER-NICKEL

KM#	Date	Mintage	Fine	VF	XF	Unc
39	1930	20.001	.50	1.00	2.00	5.00
(Y36)						

IRON

39a	1941	15.000	1.00	3.00	5.00	18.00
(Y36a)						

NICKEL-CLAD STEEL

39b	1943	36.000	.40	1.00	1.75	4.50
(Y36b)						

10 LEVA

COPPER-NICKEL

40	1930	15.001	.60	1.25	2.50	9.00
(Y37)						

IRON

40a	1941	2.200	7.50	15.00	28.00	60.00
(Y37a)						

NICKEL-CLAD STEEL

40b	1943	25.000	.60	1.50	4.00	10.00
(Y37b)						

20 LEVA

6.4516 g, .900 GOLD, .1867 oz AGW
25th Year Jubilee

33	1912	.075	100.00	125.00	200.00	350.00
(Y30)						

4.0000 g, .500 SILVER, .0643 oz ASW

41	1930BP	10.016	1.00	1.50	2.50	8.00
(Y38)						

COPPER-NICKEL

47	1940A	6.650	.50	.75	1.50	4.00
(Y42)						

50 LEVA

10.0000 g, .500 SILVER, .1607 oz ASW

42	1930BP	9.029	2.00	4.00	6.00	10.00
(Y39)						

Similar to 100 Leva, KM#45.

KM#	Date	Mintage	Fine	VF	XF	Unc
44	1934	3.000	2.50	4.50	6.50	12.50
(Y44)	1934	—	—	—	Proof	—

COPPER-NICKEL

48	1940A	12.340	.50	1.00	2.00	6.00
(Y43)						

NICKEL-CLAD STEEL

48a	1943A	15.000	.75	1.75	2.50	7.50
(Y43a)						

100 LEVA

32.2580 g, .900 GOLD, .9334 oz AGW
25th Year Jubilee

34	1912	5,000	600.00	900.00	2000.	3000.
(Y31)						

20.0000 g, .500 SILVER, .3215 oz ASW

43	1930BP	1.556	BV	4.00	8.50	20.00
(Y40)						

45	1934	2.508	BV	3.50	6.00	14.00
(Y45)	1934	—	—	—	Proof	—
	1937	2.207	BV	3.50	—	12.00

TRADE COINAGE
4 DUKAT

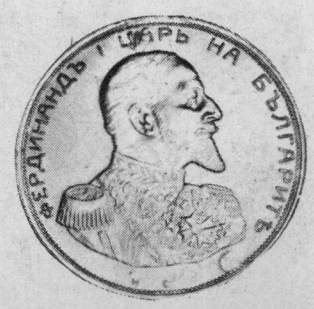

BULGARIA 242

13.9600 g, .986 GOLD, .4425 oz AGW
c/m: Crown and government mark.

KM#	Date	Mintage	Fine	VF	XF	Unc
T1	1910	—	225.00	250.00	275.00	500.00
	1911	—	250.00	275.00	300.00	525.00
	1912	—	225.00	250.00	275.00	500.00
	1914	—	275.00	400.00	500.00	900.00
	1917	—	275.00	400.00	500.00	900.00
	1918	—	250.00	275.00	300.00	525.00

c/m: Crown and government mark.

| T2 | 1926 | — | 275.00 | 350.00 | 450.00 | 625.00 |

NOTE: Values above are for holed or holed and plugged specimens. Unholed specimens command 5 times the values indicated.

PEOPLE'S REPUBLIC
STOTINKA

BRASS

| 50 (Y46) | 1951 | — | — | — | .10 | .25 |

| 59 (Y53) | 1962 | — | — | — | .10 | .25 |
| | 1970 | — | — | — | — | 2.00 |

Obv: 2 dates on arms, '681-1944'

84 (Y53a)	1974	—	—	—	.10	.15
	1979	2,000	—	—	Proof	1.00
	1980	2,000	—	—	Proof	1.00
	1981	—	—	—	Proof	1.00
	1988	—	—	—	.10	.15

1300th Anniversary of Bulgaria

| 111 (Y53b) | 1981 | — | — | .10 | .20 | .50 |
| | 1981 | — | — | — | Proof | — |

2 STOTINKI

BRASS

| 60 (Y54) | 1962 | — | — | — | .10 | .25 |

Obv: 2 dates on arms, '681-1944'

KM#	Date	Mintage	Fine	VF	XF	Unc
85 (Y54a)	1974	—	—	—	.10	.25
	1979	2,000	—	—	Proof	2.00
	1980	2,000	—	—	Proof	2.00
	1988	—	—	—	.10	.25

1300th Anniversary of Bulgaria

| 112 (Y54b) | 1981 | — | — | .10 | .20 | .50 |
| | 1981 | — | — | — | Proof | — |

3 STOTINKI

BRASS

| 51 (Y47) | 1951 | — | — | — | .10 | .25 | .50 |

5 STOTINKI

BRASS

| 52 (Y48) | 1951 | — | — | .10 | .15 | .20 | .35 |

| 61 (Y55) | 1962 | — | — | — | .10 | .15 | .25 |

Obv: 2 dates on arms '681-1944'

86 (Y55a)	1974	—	—	—	.10	.15	.25
	1979	2,000	—	—	Proof	2.00
	1980	2,000	—	—	Proof	2.00
	1981	—	—	—	Proof	2.00
	1988	—	—	—	.15	.25

1300th Anniversary of Bulgaria

| 113 (Y55b) | 1981 | — | — | — | .10 | .25 | .60 |
| | 1981 | — | — | — | Proof | — |

10 STOTINKI

COPPER-NICKEL

| 53 (Y49) | 1951 | — | — | — | .10 | .20 | .30 |

KM#	Date	Mintage	Fine	VF	XF	Unc

NICKEL-BRASS

| 62 (Y56) | 1962 | — | — | — | .10 | .15 | .25 |

Obv: 2 dates on arms, '681-1944'

87 (Y56a)	1974	—	—	—	.10	.15	.25
	1979	2,000	—	—	Proof	3.00
	1980	2,000	—	—	Proof	3.00
	1988	—	—	—	.15	.25

COPPER-NICKEL
1300th Anniversary of Bulgaria

| 114 (Y56b) | 1981 | — | — | .15 | .30 | 1.00 |
| | 1981 | — | — | — | Proof | — |

20 STOTINKI

COPPER-NICKEL

| 55 (Y-A49) | 1952 | — | 1.00 | 2.00 | 3.50 | 10.00 |
| | 1954 | — | .10 | .20 | .30 | .50 |

NICKEL-BRASS

| 63 (Y57) | 1962 | — | .10 | .20 | .30 | .50 |

Obv: 2 dates on arms, '681-1944'

88 (Y57a)	1974	—	.10	.20	.30	.50
	1979	2,000	—	—	Proof	2.50
	1980	2,000	—	—	Proof	2.50
	1988	—	—	—	.75	.50

COPPER-NICKEL
1300th Anniversary of Bulgaria

| 115 (Y57b) | 1981 | — | — | — | .25 | .50 | 1.50 |
| | 1981 | — | — | — | Proof | — |

25 STOTINKI

COPPER-NICKEL

| 54 (Y50) | 1951 | — | .10 | .20 | .50 | 1.00 |

50 STOTINKI

COPPER-NICKEL

KM#	Date	Mintage	Fine	VF	XF	Unc
56 (Y51)	1959	—	.10	.20	.40	.75

| 64 (Y58) | 1962 | — | .10 | .40 | .65 | 1.00 |

NICKEL-BRASS
Obv: 2 dates on arms, '681-1944'

89 (Y58a)	1974	—	.10	.40	.65	1.00
	1979	2,000	—	—	Proof	3.00
	1980	2,000	—	—	Proof	3.00
	1988	—	—	—	.50	1.00

COPPER-NICKEL
Sofia University

| 98 (Y86) | 1977 | 2,000 | .15 | .50 | .75 | 1.50 |

1300th Anniversary of Bulgaria

| 116 (Y58b) | 1981 | — | — | .25 | .50 | 1.50 |
| | 1981 | — | — | — | Proof | |

LEV

COPPER-NICKEL

| 57 (Y52) | 1960 | — | .10 | .25 | .60 | 1.00 |

NICKEL-BRASS

| 58 (Y59) | 1962 | — | — | .50 | 1.00 | 1.50 |

Obv: 2 dates on arms, '681-1944'

90 (Y59a)	1974	—	—	.50	1.00	1.50
	1979	2,000	—	—	Proof	4.50
	1980	2,000	—	—	Proof	4.50
	1988	—	—	—	.75	1.50

25th Anniversary of Socialist Revolution

KM#	Date	Mintage	Fine	VF	XF	Unc
74 (Y69)	1969	3.700	.20	.60	1.20	2.50

90th Anniversary Liberation From Turks

| 76 (Y71) | 1969 | 2.150 | .20 | .60 | 1.20 | 2.50 |

BRONZE
100th Anniversary of the April Uprising Against the Turks

| 94 (Y82) | 1976 | .300 | .25 | .60 | 1.50 | 3.00 |
| | 1976 | — | — | — | Proof | 8.00 |

COPPER-NICKEL
World Cup Soccer Games

| 107 (Y94) | 1980 | .220 | — | .40 | 1.00 | 2.00 |
| | 1980 | .030 | — | — | Proof | 5.00 |

1300th Anniversary of Bulgaria

| 117 (Y59b) | 1981 | — | — | .50 | 1.00 | 1.50 |
| | 1981 | — | — | — | Proof | |

International Hunting Exposition

| 118 (Y99) | 1981 | — | — | .50 | 1.25 | 3.00 |
| | 1981 | — | — | — | Proof | 6.00 |

Russo-Bulgarian Friendship

KM#	Date	Mintage	Fine	VF	XF	Unc
119 (Y105)	1981	—	—	.50	1.25	3.00
	1981	1,000	—	—	Proof	6.00

2 LEVA

8.8889 g, .900 SILVER, .2572 oz ASW
1100th Anniversary Slavic Alphabet

| 65 (Y60) | 1963 | .010 | — | — | Proof | 8.00 |

20th Anniversary People's Republic

| 69 (Y64) | 1964 | .020 | — | — | Proof | 7.00 |

COPPER-NICKEL
1050th Anniversary Death of Ochridsky

| 73 (Y68) | 1966 | .506 | — | .50 | 1.50 | 3.00 |

25th Anniversary of Socialist Revolution

| 75 (Y70) | 1969 | 1.500 | — | .50 | 1.50 | 3.00 |

90th Anniversary Liberation From Turks

| 77 (Y72) | 1969 | 1.900 | — | .50 | 1.50 | 3.00 |

NICKEL-BRASS
100th Anniversary of Birth of Dobri Chintu Lov

| 80 (Y75) | 1972 | .100 | — | .75 | 2.00 | 4.00 |

BULGARIA 244

COPPER-NICKEL
100th Anniversary of the April Uprising Against the Turks

KM#	Date	Mintage	Fine	VF	XF	Unc
95.1	1976	*.300	—	.75	2.00	4.00
(Y83)	1976	—	—	—	Proof	10.00

Lettered edge.

| 95.2 | 1976 | 138 pcs. | — | — | — | — |

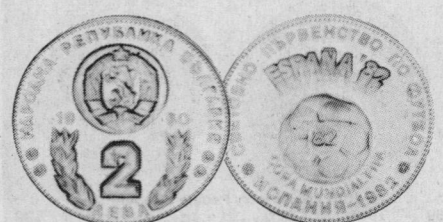

World Cup Soccer Games

| 108 | 1980 | .220 | — | .50 | 1.00 | 3.00 |
| (Y95) | 1980 | .030 | — | — | Proof | 6.00 |

Centennial of Yordan Yovkov Birth

| 110 | 1980 | .200 | — | — | 2.50 | 6.00 |
| (Y98) | | | | | | |

International Hunting Exposition

| 120 | 1981 | — | — | .75 | 2.00 | 4.00 |
| (Y100) | 1981 | — | — | — | Proof | 8.00 |

1300th Anniversary of Nationhood
Rev: Equestrian Figure

| 121 | 1981 | — | — | — | — | 6.00 |
| (Y102) | | | | | | |

1300th Anniversary of Nationhood
Rev: Mother and child.

| 122 | 1981 | — | — | — | Proof | 14.00 |
| (Y106) | | | | | | |

1300th Anniversary of Nationhood
Rev: Dimitrov.

KM#	Date	Mintage	Fine	VF	XF	Unc
123	1981	—	—	—	—	8.00
(Y113)	1981	—	—	—	Proof	10.00

1300th Anniversary of Nationhood
Rev: King and saint.

| 124 | 1981 | — | — | — | — | 8.00 |
| (Y114) | 1981 | — | — | — | Proof | 10.00 |

1300th Anniversary of Nationhood
Rev: Soldier.

| 125 | 1981 | — | — | — | — | 10.00 |
| (Y116) | 1981 | — | — | — | Proof | 12.00 |

1300th Anniversary of Nationhood
Rev: Clandestine meeting.

| 126 | 1981 | — | — | — | Proof | 10.00 |
| (Y117) | | | | | | |

1300th Anniversary of Nationhood
Rev: Cyrillic alphabet.

| 127 | 1981 | — | — | — | — | 8.00 |
| (Y124) | 1981 | — | — | — | Proof | 10.00 |

1300th Anniversary of Nationhood
Rev: Rila Monastary.

| 128 | 1981 | — | — | — | — | 8.00 |
| (Y125) | 1981 | — | — | — | Proof | 10.00 |

1300th Anniversary of Nationhood
Rev: Russky Monument.

KM#	Date	Mintage	Fine	VF	XF	Unc
129	1981	—	—	—	Proof	10.00
(Y126)						

1300th Anniversary of Nationhood
Rev: Bojana Church.

| 130 | 1981 | 3,000 | — | — | Proof | 8.00 |

1300th Anniversary of Nationhood and the Oboriste Assembly

| 161 | 1981 | — | — | — | Proof | 8.00 |

1300th Anniversary of Nationhood and Uprising of Assen and Peter

| 162 | 1981 | — | — | — | Proof | 8.00 |

100th Anniversary of Serbo - Bulgarian War

| 163 | 1985 | — | — | — | Proof | 6.00 |

Soccer

| 155 | 1986 | .100 | — | — | — | 7.00 |

BULGARIA 245

World Championship of Eurythmics

KM#	Date	Mintage	Fine	VF	XF	Unc
158	1987	—	—	—	Proof	8.00

Winter Olympics - Skier

| 159 | 1987 | — | — | — | Proof | 8.00 |

5 LEVA

16.6667 g, .900 SILVER, .4823 oz ASW
1100th Anniversary Slavic Alphabet

| 66 (Y61) | 1963 | 5,000 | — | — | Proof | 15.00 |

20th Anniversary People's Republic

| 70 (Y65) | 1964 | .010 | — | — | Proof | 15.00 |

20.5000 g, .900 SILVER, .5932 oz ASW
120th Anniversary Ivan Vazov

| 78 (Y73) | 1970 | .370 | — | 2.00 | 4.00 | 12.50 |
| | 1970 | .110 | — | — | Proof | 22.50 |

150th Anniversary of Birth of Georgi S. Rakovski

| 79 (Y74) | 1971 | .300 | — | — | Proof | 15.00 |

250th Anniversary of Birth of Paisii Hilendarski

KM#	Date	Mintage	VF	XF	Unc
81 (Y76)	1972	.200	—	Proof	15.00

Death of Vasil Levski Centennial

| 82 (Y77) | 1973 | .200 | — | Proof | 15.00 |

50th Anniversary Anti-Fascist Uprising

| 83 (Y78) | 1973 | .200 | — | Proof | 15.00 |

50th Anniversary of Death of Alexander Stamboliiski

| 91 (Y79) | 1974 | .200 | — | Proof | 17.50 |

30th Anniversary Socialist Revolution

| 92 (Y80) | 1974 | .200 | — | Proof | 15.00 |

100th Anniversary of Death of Khristo Botev

KM#	Date	Mintage	VF	XF	Unc
96 (Y84)	1976	.200	—	Proof	15.00

20.5000 g, .500 SILVER, .3295 oz ASW
100th Anniversary of the April Uprising Against the Turks

| 97 (Y85) | 1976 | .200 | — | Proof | 15.00 |

150th Anniversary of Birth of Petko Slaveykov

| 99 (Y87) | 1977 | .200 | — | Proof | 14.50 |

100th Anniversary of Birth of Peio Javoroff

| 100 (Y88) | 1978 | .200 | — | Proof | 14.50 |

100th Anniversary of National Library

| 101 (Y90) | 1978 | .200 | — | Proof | 14.50 |

BULGARIA 246

100th Anniversary of Communications Systems

KM#	Date	Mintage	VF	XF	Unc
103	1979	.035	—	—	10.00
(Y91)	1979	.015	—	Proof	14.50

COPPER-NICKEL
World Cup Soccer Games

109	1980	.220	—	—	6.50
(Y96)	1980	.030	—	Proof	14.00

International Hunting Exposition

131	1981	—	—	—	6.50
(Y101)	1981	—	—	Proof	14.00

1300th Anniversary of Bulgarian Statehood

132	1981	—	—	—	9.00
(Y115)					

100th Anniversary of Dimitrov

140	1982	3,000	—	Proof	10.00
(Y107)					

Ljudmila Jivkowa

KM#	Date	Mintage	VF	XF	Unc
141	1982	—	—	Proof	10.00
(Y108)					

2nd International Childrens Assembly

142	1982	—	—	Proof	9.00
(Y109)					

3rd International Children's Assembly

| 151 | 1985 | 2,500 | — | Proof | 8.00 |

90th Anniversary of Tourism Movement

| 152 | 1985 | — | — | Proof | 9.00 |

4th Anniversary of UNESCO

| 153 | 1985 | — | — | Proof | 9.00 |

Young Inventors Exposition

| 154 | 1985 | — | — | Proof | 9.00 |

10 LEVA

8.4444 g, .900 GOLD, .2443 oz AGW
1100th Anniversary Slavic Alphabet

67	1963	7,000	—	Proof	150.00
(Y62)					

20th Anniversary People's Republic

KM#	Date	Mintage	VF	XF	Unc
71	1964	.010	—	Proof	140.00
(Y66)					

29.9500 g, .900 SILVER, .8666 oz ASW
10th Olympic Congress
Edge inscription in Latin

93.1	1975	.050	—	Proof	35.00
(Y81)					

Edge inscription in Cyrillic

93.2	1975	.050	—	Proof	35.00
(Y81a)					

29.8500 g, .500 SILVER, .4798 oz ASW
100th Anniversary Liberation from Turks

102	1978	.200	—	Proof	20.00
(Y89)					

23.3280 g, .925 SILVER, .6938 oz ASW
International Year of the Child

104	1979	.020	—	Proof	25.00
(Y92)					

BULGARIA 247

14.0000 g, .500 SILVER, .2251 oz ASW, 32mm
Bulgarian-Soviet Cosmonaut Flight

KM#	Date	Mintage	VF	XF	Unc
105 (Y97)	1979	.035	—	—	35.00

23.8500 g, .900 SILVER, .6901 oz ASW, 38mm

| 105a (Y97a) | 1979 | .025 | — | Proof | 25.00 |

18.8800 g, .500 SILVER, .3035 oz ASW
Soccer Games

| 143 (Y111) | 1982 | 1,000 | — | Proof | 30.00 |

Soccer Games

| 144 (Y112) | 1982 | 1,000 | — | Proof | 30.00 |

COPPER-NICKEL
Winter Olympics

KM#	Date	Mintage	VF	XF	Unc
146 (Y123)	1984	—	—	Proof	18.00

23.3300 g, .925 SILVER, .6939 oz ASW

| 146a (Y123a) | 1984 | 1,500 | — | Proof | 40.00 |

COPPER-NICKEL
Summer Olympics
Obv: Similar to KM#146.

| 147 (Y128) | 1984 | 2,000 | — | Proof | 20.00 |

23.3300 g, .925 SILVER, .6939 oz ASW

| 147a (Y128a) | 1984 | 300 pcs. | — | Proof | 55.00 |

International Decade for Women

| 149 | 1984 | .018 | — | Proof | 20.00 |

18.7500 g, .640 SILVER, .3858 oz ASW
Cosmonauts
Obv: Cosmonaut symbol above denomination.
Rev: Portraits of 5 cosmonauts, stars and legend.

| 157 | 1986 | 2,500 | — | Proof | 30.00 |

20 LEVA

16.8889 g, .900 GOLD, .4887 oz AGW
1100th Anniversary Slavic Alphabet

KM#	Date	Mintage	Fine	VF	XF	Unc
68 (Y63)	1963	3,000	—	—	Proof	320.00

20th Anniversary People's Republic

KM#	Date	Mintage	Fine	VF	XF	Unc
72 (Y67)	1964	5,000	—	—	Proof	280.00

21.8000 g, .500 SILVER, .3505 oz ASW, 37mm
Centennial of Sophia as Capital

| 106 (Y93) | 1979 | .035 | — | Proof | 25.00 |

32.0000 g, .900 SILVER, .9260 oz ASW, 42mm

| 106a (Y93a) | 1979 | .015 | — | Proof | 20.00 |

14.0000 g, .500 SILVER, .2250 oz ASW
Ljudmila Jivkowa
Similar to 5 Leva, KM#141.

| 133 (Y122) | 1981 | — | — | Proof | 30.00 |

25 LEVA

14.0000 g, .500 SILVER, .2250 oz ASW
1300th Anniversary of Nationhood
Similar to 2 Leva, KM#122.

| 134 (Y118) | 1981 | — | — | Proof | 20.00 |

100th Anniversary of National Independence

| 145 (Y110) | 1982 | .015 | — | Proof | 20.00 |

40th Anniversary of People's Republic

| 148 (Y127) | 1984 | — | — | Proof | 20.00 |

BULGARIA 248

23.3300 g, .925 SILVER, .6939 oz ASW
Soccer

KM#	Date	Mintage	Fine	VF	XF	Unc
156	1986	.010	—	—	Proof	50.00

Winter Olympics - Skier
Similar to 2 Leva, KM#159.

| 160 | 1987 | .015 | — | — | Proof | 50.00 |

50 LEVA
20.5000 g, .900 SILVER, .5932 oz ASW
1300th Anniversary of Nationhood
Similar to 2 Leva, KM#121.

| 135 (Y103) | 1981 | 1,000 | — | — | Proof | 30.00 |

1300th Anniversary of Nationhood
Rev: Dimitrov.

| 136 (Y104) | 1981 | 1,000 | — | — | Proof | 30.00 |

1300th Anniversary of Nationhood
Similar to 2 Leva, KM#122.

| 137 (Y119) | 1981 | — | — | — | Proof | 30.00 |

1300th Anniversary of Nationhood
Similar to 2 Leva, KM#124.

| 138 (Y121) | 1981 | — | — | — | Proof | 35.00 |

100 LEVA

8.0000 g, .900 GOLD, .2315 oz AGW
International Womens Decade

| 150 | 1984 | .014 | — | — | Proof | 275.00 |

1000 LEVA

16.8800 g, .900 GOLD, .4885 oz AGW
1300th Anniversary of Nationhood
Obv: Similar to 5 Leva, KM#132.

| 139 (Y120) | 1981 | — | — | — | Proof | 400.00 |

PROOF SETS (PS)

KM#	Date	Mintage	Identification	Issue Price	Mkt. Val.
PS1	1912(2)	5,000	KM33-34	—	1500.
PS2	1963(2)	5,000	KM65-66	—	20.00
PS3	1964(2)	10,000	KM69-70	—	20.00
PS4	1963/73(8)		KM65-66,69-70,78-79,81-82 mixed date set, REPUBLIQUE DE BULGARIE		75.00
PS5	1979(7)	2,000	KM84-90	—	15.00
PS6	1980(7)	2,000	KM84-90	—	15.00

BURMA

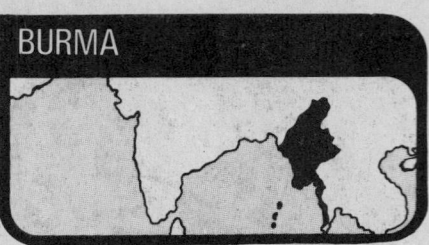

The Socialist Republic of the Union of Burma, a country of Southeast Asia fronting on the Bay of Bengal and the Andaman Sea, has an area of 261,218 sq. mi. (676,552 sq. km.) and a population of 34 million. Capital: Rangoon. Burma is an agricultural country heavily dependent on its leading product (rice) which occupies two-thirds of the cultivated area and accounts for 40 per cent of the value of exports. Mineral resources are extensive, but production is low. Petroleum, lead, tin, silver, zinc, nickel cobalt, and precious stones are exported.

The first European to reach Burma, about 1435, was Nicolo Di Conti, a merchant of Venice. During the beginning of the reign of Bodawpaya (1781-1819AD) the kingdom comprised most of the same area as it does today including Arakan which was taken over in 1784-85. The British East India Company, while unsuccessful in its 1612 effort to establish posts along the Bay of Bengal, was enabled by the Anglo-Burmese Wars of 1824-86 to expand to the whole of Burma and to secure its annexation to British India. In 1937, Burma was separated from India, becoming a separate British colony with limited self-government. Burma became an independent nation outside the British Commonwealth on Jan. 4, 1948, the constitution of 1948 providing for a parliamentary democracy and the nationalization of certain industries. However, political and economic problems persisted, and on March 2, 1962, Gen. Ne Win took over the government, suspended the constitution, installed himself as chief of state, and pursued a socialistic program with nationalization of nearly all industry and trade. On Jan. 4, 1974, a new constitution adopted by referendum established Burma as a 'socialist republic' under one-party rule.

The coins issued by kings Mindon and Thibaw between 1852 and 1885 circulated in Upper Burma. Indian coins were current in Lower Burma, which was annexed in 1852. Burmese coins are frequently known by the equivalent Indian denominations, although their values are inscribed in Burmese units. Upper Burma was annexed in 1885 and the Burmese coinage remained in circulation until 1889, when Indian coins became current throughout Burma. Coins were again issued in the old Burmese denominations after independence in 1948, but these were replaced by decimal issues in 1952. The Chula-Sakarat (CS) dating is sometimes referred to as BE-Burmese Era and began in 638AD.

RULERS
Bodawpaya, CS1143-1181/ 1782-1819AD
Bagyidaw, CS1181-1198/ 1819-1837AD
Tharawaddy, CS1198-1207/ 1837-46AD
Pagan, CS1207-1214/1846-53AD
Mindon, CS1214-1240/1853-78AD
Thibaw, CS1240-1248/1880-85AD

British, 1886-1948

MONETARY SYSTEM
(Until 1952)

4 Pyas = 1 Pe
2 Pe = 1 Mu
2 Mu = 1 Mat
5 Mat = 1 Kyat

NOTE: Originally 10 light Mu = 1 Kyat but later on 8 heavy Mu = 1 Kyat.

Indian Equivalents
1 Silver Kyat = 1 Rupee = 16 Annas
1 Gold Kyat = 1 Mohur = 16 Rupees

1/8 PYA

LEAD

KM#	Date	Year	Good	VG	Fine	VF
22.1	BE1230	(1868)	—	—	Rare	—

Obv: Legend closer together.

| 22.2 | BE1231 | (1869) | 17.50 | 27.50 | 45.00 | 75.00 |

1/4 PYA
LEAD, 21-22mm
Obv: Hare crouching left. Rev: Leg. in wreath.

KM	Date	Year	Good	VG	Fine	VF
23	CS1231	(1869)	15.00	25.00	35.00	60.00

1/4 PE
(Pice)

COPPER

| 17 | CS1227 | (1865) | 2.50 | 4.50 | 7.50 | 13.50 |

Rev: W/o stars above and below leg.

| 18 | CS1227 | (1865) | 2.50 | 4.50 | 7.50 | 15.00 |

IRON

| 18a | CS1227 | (1865) | 22.50 | 35.00 | 55.00 | 85.00 |

COPPER
Rev: Flower petals at top of wreath upright.

| 25.1 | CS1240 | (1878) | 2.50 | 4.50 | 10.00 | 25.00 |

Rev: Flower petals at top of wreath diagonal.

| 25.2 | CS1240 | (1878) | 2.50 | 4.50 | 10.00 | 25.00 |

BRASS

| 25a | CS1240 | (1878) | 7.50 | 12.50 | 22.50 | 35.00 |

TIN

| 25b | CS1240 | (1878) | — | — | — | — |

2 PYAS

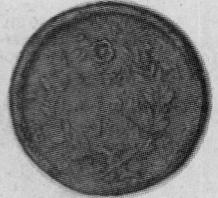

COPPER

| 24 | CS1231 | (1869) | 17.50 | 30.00 | 50.00 | 75.00 |

PE

0.7300 g, .917 SILVER, .0215 oz ASW

KM#	Date	Year	Fine	VF	XF	Unc
6.1	CS1214	(1852)	15.00	27.50	65.00	100.00

Accent mark omitted from value.
| 6.2 | CS1214 | (1852) | 15.00 | 27.50 | 65.00 | 100.00 |

Figure J omitted from date.
| 6.3 | CS1214 | (1852) | 15.00 | 27.50 | 65.00 | 100.00 |

Two dots omitted from value.
| 6.4 | CS1214 | (1852) | 15.00 | 27.50 | 65.00 | 100.00 |

Accent marks and two dots omitted.
| 6.5 | CS1214 | (1852) | 15.00 | 27.50 | 60.00 | 100.00 |

MU

1.4600 g, .917 SILVER, .0430 oz ASW
| 7.1 | CS1214 | (1852) | 5.00 | 10.00 | 17.50 | 90.00 |

Rev: Dot above top left character in denomination.
| 7.2 | CS1214 | (1852) | — | — | Proof | — |

MAT

2.9200 g, .917 SILVER, .0860 oz ASW
| 8.1 | CS1214 | (1852) | 7.50 | 12.50 | 50.00 | 100.00 |
| | 1214 | (1852) | — | — | Proof | — |

Tail omitted from last digit of date.
| 8.2 | CS1214 | (1852) | 7.50 | 12.50 | 50.00 | 100.00 |

5 MU
(1/2 Rupee)

5.8300 g, .917 SILVER, .1718 oz ASW
| 9 | CS1214 | (1852) | 12.50 | 22.50 | 70.00 | 150.00 |
| | CS1214 | (1852) | — | — | Proof | — |

COPPER (OMS)
| 9a | CS1214 | (1852) | — | — | Proof | — |

KYAT
(Rupee)

11.6600 g, .917 SILVER, .3436 oz ASW
| 10 | CS1214 | (1852) | 7.50 | 12.50 | 45.00 | 150.00 |
| | CS1214 | (1852) | — | — | Proof | — |

GOLD (OMS)
| 10a | CS1214 | (1852) | (restrike) | — | — | — |

SILVER, 16.23 g
Obv: Peacock w/spread tail, flanked by two groups of 5 rosettes.

KM#	Date	Year	Good	VG	Fine	VF
11	CS1214	(1852)	150.00	350.00	500.00	850.00

Obv: Peacock in full display w/circular feather ends.
| 12 | CS1214 | (1852) | 250.00 | 500.00 | 1000. | 1500. |

SILVER, 39mm, 16.45 g
Obv: Shwepyizoe bird. Rev: Leg. over date.
| 15 | BE2396 | (1853) | — | — | — | — |

SILVER, 32mm, 15.75 g
Obv: Peacock w/folded tail flanked by floral garlands.
| 16 | CS1222 | (1860) | — | — | — | — |

PE
.900 GOLD
Obv: Facing peacock. Rev: Value in wreath.
| 13 | CS1214 | (1852) | 35.00 | 60.00 | 85.00 | 135.00 |

GOLD, 0.67 g
| 19 | CS1228 | (1866) | 35.00 | 60.00 | 95.00 | 175.00 |

MU

.900 GOLD
Obv: Facing peacock. Rev: Value in wreath.
| 14 | CS1214 | (1852) | 60.00 | 100.00 | 150.00 | 200.00 |

2 MU 1 PE

GOLD, 2.75 g
KM#	Date	Year	VG	Fine	VF	XF
20	CS1228	(1866)	125.00	175.00	250.00	400.00

5 MU
(1/2 Mohur)

GOLD, 5.85 g
KM#	Date	Year	Good	VG	Fine	VF
26	CS1240	(1878)	—	—	Rare	—

KYAT
(Mohur)

GOLD, 11.94 g
| 21 | CS1228 | (1866) | — | — | Rare | — |

REPUBLIC
2 PYAS

COPPER-NICKEL
KM#	Date	Mintage	Fine	VF	XF	Unc
27	1949	7.000	.25	.50	1.00	3.00
	1949	100 pcs.	—	—	Proof	100.00

PE

COPPER-NICKEL
28	1949	8.000	.35	.75	1.50	4.00
	1949	100 pcs.	—	—	Proof	100.00
	1950	9.500	.35	.75	1.50	4.00
	1950	—	—	—	Proof	—
	1951	6.500	.50	1.00	2.00	5.00
	1951	—	—	—	Proof	—

2 PE

COPPER-NICKEL
29	1949	7.100	.50	1.00	2.00	5.00
	1949	100 pcs.	—	—	Proof	100.00
	1950	8.500	.50	1.00	2.00	5.00
	1950	—	—	—	Proof	—
	1951	7.480	.50	1.00	2.00	5.00
	1951	—	—	—	Proof	—

4 PE

NICKEL
30	1949	6.500	1.25	2.50	5.00	15.00
	1949	100 pcs.	—	—	Proof	100.00
	1950	6.120	1.00	2.00	4.00	12.00

BURMA 250

8 PE

NICKEL

KM#	Date	Mintage	Fine	VF	XF	Unc
31	1949	3.270	1.50	3.00	6.00	25.00
	1949	100 pcs.	—	Proof		100.00
	1950	3.900	1.25	2.50	5.00	20.00
	1950	—	—	Proof		

COPPER-NICKEL

31a	CS1314(1952)					
		1.642	50.00	100.00	150.00	200.00
	1314(1952)	—	—	Proof		—

DECIMAL COINAGE
100 Pyas - 1 Kyat

PYA

BRONZE

32	1952	.500	.10	.15	.20	.35
	1952	100 pcs.	—	—	Proof	60.00
	1953	14.000	.10	.15	.20	.35
	1953	—	—	—	Proof	
	1955	30.000	.10	.15	.20	.35
	1955	—	—	—	Proof	
	1956	100 pcs.	—	—	Proof	60.00
	1962	100 pcs.	—	—	Proof	60.00
	1965	15.000	.10	.15	.20	.35
	1965	—	—	—	Proof	

ALUMINUM
General Ne Win

| 38 | 1966 | 8.000 | .10 | .15 | .25 | .50 |

5 PYAS

COPPER-NICKEL

33	1952	20.000	.10	.15	.25	.50
	1952	100 pcs.	—	—	Proof	65.00
	1953	59.700	.10	.15	.35	.50
	1953	—	—	—	Proof	
	1955	40.272	.10	.15	.25	.50
	1955	—	—	—	Proof	
	1956	20.000	.10	.15	.25	.50
	1956	100 pcs.	—	—	Proof	65.00
	1961	12.000	.10	.15	.25	.50
	1961	—	—	—	Proof	
	1962	10.000	.10	.15	.25	.50
	1962	100 pcs.	—	—	Proof	65.00
	1963	40.400	.10	.15	.25	.50
	1963	—	—	—	Proof	
	1965	43.600	.10	.15	.20	.30
	1965	—	—	—	Proof	
	1966	20.000	.10	.15	.20	.30
	1966	—	—	—	Proof	

ALUMINUM

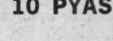

General Ne Win

KM#	Date	Mintage	Fine	VF	XF	Unc
39	1966	—	.10	.20	.35	.60

10 PYAS

COPPER-NICKEL

34	1952	20.000	.10	.20	.35	.60
	1952	100 pcs.	—	—	Proof	70.00
	1953	37.250	.10	.20	.35	.60
	1953	—	—	—	Proof	
	1955	22.750	.10	.20	.35	.60
	1955	—	—	—	Proof	
	1956	35.000	.10	.15	.35	.75
	1956	100 pcs.	—	—	Proof	70.00
	1962	6.000	.10	.20	.35	.60
	1962	100 pcs.	—	—	Proof	70.00
	1963	10.750	.10	.20	.35	.60
	1963	10.750	—	—	—	
	1965	32.620	.10	.20	.35	.60
	1965	—	—	—	Proof	

 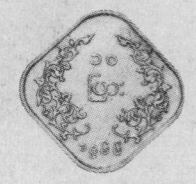

ALUMINUM
General Ne Win

| 40 | 1966 | — | .10 | .25 | .50 | 1.00 |

BRASS
F.A.O. Issue

| 49 | 1983 | | .10 | .25 | .50 | 1.00 |

25 PYAS

COPPER-NICKEL

35	1952	13.540	.10	.20	.50	1.00
	1952	100 pcs.	—	—	Proof	75.00
	1954	18.000	.10	.20	.50	1.00
	1954	—	—	—	Proof	
	1955	—	—	—	Proof	75.00
	1956	14.000	.10	.20	.50	1.00
	1956	100 pcs.	—	—	Proof	75.00
	1959	6.000	.10	.20	.50	1.00
	1959	—	—	—	Proof	
	1961	4.000	.10	.20	.50	1.00
	1961	—	—	—	Proof	
	1962	3.200	.10	.20	.50	1.00
	1962	100 pcs.	—	—	Proof	75.00
	1963	16.000	.10	.15	.30	.60
	1963	—	—	—	Proof	
	1965	26.000	.10	.15	.30	.60
	1965	—	—	—	Proof	

ALUMINUM
General Ne Win

| 41 | 1966 | — | .10 | .20 | .50 | 1.00 |

BRONZE
F.A.O. Issue

KM#	Date	Mintage	Fine	VF	XF	Unc
48	1980	—	.20	.35	.75	1.25

Circulation Coinage

| 50 | 1986 | | | | | .10 |

50 PYAS

COPPER-NICKEL

36	1952	2.500	.20	.50	.75	1.50
	1952	100 pcs.	—	—	Proof	80.00
	1954	12.000	.20	.50	.75	1.50
	1954	—	—	—	Proof	
	1956	8.000	.20	.50	.75	1.50
	1956	100 pcs.	—	—	Proof	80.00
	1961	2.000	.15	.40	.75	1.50
	1961	—	—	—	Proof	
	1962	.600	.25	.75	1.25	2.25
	1962	100 pcs.	—	—	Proof	80.00
	1963	4.800	.15	.25	.60	1.00
	1963	—	—	—	Proof	
	1965	2.800	.15	.40	.75	1.50
	1965	—	—	—	Proof	
	1966	3.400	.10	.30	.75	1.50
	1966	—	—	—	Proof	

ALUMINUM
General Ne Win

| 42 | 1966 | — | .15 | .35 | 1.00 | 2.00 |

BRASS
F.A.O. Issue

46	1975		.25	.40	.85	1.50
	1976		.25	.40	.85	1.50

KYAT

COPPER-NICKEL

37	1952	2.500	.35	.75	1.50	3.00
	1952	100 pcs.	—	—	Proof	85.00
	1953	7.500	.25	.50	1.00	2.00
	1953	—	—	—	Proof	
	1956	3.500	.35	.75	1.50	3.00
	1956	100 pcs.	—	—	Proof	85.00
	1962	100 pcs.	—	—	Proof	85.00
	1965	1.000	.35	.75	1.50	3.00
	1965	—	—	—	Proof	

F.A.O. Issue

KM#	Date	Mintage	Fine	VF	XF	Unc
47	1975	20.000	.25	.50	1.00	2.00

UNION OF BURMA
Patriotic Liberation Army
MU

2.0000 g, 1.000 GOLD, .0643 oz AGW
Obv: UNION OF BURMA GOVERNMENT 1970-1971 around peacock. Rev. leg: U NU in star SHWE MUZI below.

KM#	Date	Mintage	VF	XF	Unc
43	1970-71	—	—	—	100.00

2 MU

4.0000 g, 1.000 GOLD, .1286 oz AGW

| 44 | 1970-71 | — | — | — | 300.00 |

4 MU

8.0000 g, 1.000 GOLD, .2572 oz AGW

| 45 | 1970-71 | — | — | — | 500.00 |

PROOF SETS (PS)

KM#	Date	Mintage	Identification	Issue Price	Mkt. Val.
PS1	1949(5)	100	KM27-31	—	500.00
PS2	1952(6)	100	KM32-37	—	435.00
PS3	1956(6)	100	KM32-37	—	435.00
PS4	1962(6)	100	KM32-37	—	435.00

BURUNDI

The Republic of Burundi, a landlocked country in central Africa, was a kingdom with a feudalistic society, caste system and Mwami (king) for more than 400 years before independence. It has an area of 10,747 sq. mi. (27,834 sq. km.) and a population of 3.9 million. Capital: Bujumbura. Plagued by poor soil, irregular rainfall and a single-crop economy, coffee, Burundi is barely able to feed itself. Coffee and tea are exported.

Although the area was visited by European explorers and missionaries in the latter half of the 19th century, it wasn't until the 1890s that it, together with Rwanda, fell under European domination as part of German East Africa. Following World War I, the territory was mandated to Belgium by the League of Nations and administered with the Belgian Congo. After World War II it became a U.N. Trust Territory. Limited self-government was established by U.N.-supervised elections in 1961. Burundi gained independence as a kingdom under Mwami Mwambutsa IV on July 1, 1962. The republic was established by military coup in 1966.

For earlier coinage see Belgian Congo, and Rwanda and Burundi. For previously listed coinage dated 1966 refer to UNUSUAL WORLD COINS, 2nd edition, Krause Publications, 1988.

RULERS
Mwambutsa IV, 1962-1966
Ntare V, 1966

MINT MARKS
(b) - Privy Marks, Brussels

MONETARY SYSTEM
100 Centimes = 1 Franc

KINGDOM
FRANC

BRASS

KM#	Date	Mintage	Fine	VF	XF	Unc
6	1965	10.000	—	.60	1.00	2.00

5 FRANCS

COPPER-NICKEL
Burundi Independence

| 1 | 1962 | — | — | — | — | — |
| | 1962 | — | — | — | Proof | 15.00 |

10 FRANCS

3.2000 g, .900 GOLD, .0926 oz AGW

Burundi Independence

KM#	Date	Mintage	Fine	VF	XF	Unc
2	1962	7,500	—	—	Proof	75.00

3.0000 g, .900 GOLD, .0868 oz AGW
50th Anniversary of Reign of Mwambutsa IV

| 7 | 1965 | — | — | — | — | 55.00 |
| | 1965 | 5,000 | — | — | Proof | 75.00 |

25 FRANCS

8.0000 g, .900 GOLD, .2315 oz AGW
Burundi Independence

| 3 | 1962 | 15,000 | — | — | Proof | 150.00 |

7.5000 g, .900 GOLD, .2170 oz AGW
50th Anniversary of Reign of Mwambutsa IV

| 8 | 1965 | — | — | — | — | 125.00 |
| | 1965 | 5,000 | — | — | Proof | 150.00 |

50 FRANCS

16.0000 g, .900 GOLD, .4630 oz AGW
Burundi Independence

| 4 | 1962 | 3,500 | — | — | Proof | 300.00 |

15.0000 g, .900 GOLD, .4340 oz AGW
50th Anniversary of Reign of Mwambutsa IV

| 9 | 1965 | — | — | — | — | 225.00 |
| | 1965 | 5,000 | — | — | Proof | 300.00 |

100 FRANCS

BURUNDI 252

32.0000 g, .900 GOLD, .9260 oz AGW
Burundi Independence

KM#	Date	Mintage	Fine	VF	XF	Unc
5	1962	2,500	—	—	Proof	600.00

30.0000 g, .900 GOLD, .8681 oz AGW
50th Anniversary of Reign of Mwambutsa IV

10	1965	—	—	—	—	500.00
	1965	5,000	—	—	Proof	600.00

REPUBLIC
FRANC

ALUMINUM

18	1970	10.000	1.00	2.50	4.50	7.00

19	1976	5.000	—	.30	.75	1.25
	1980	—	—	.15	.50	1.00

5 FRANCS

ALUMINUM

16	1968(b)	2.000	—	.25	.80	1.75
	1969(b)	2.000	—	.25	.80	1.75
	1971(b)	2.000	—	.25	.80	1.75

20	1976	2.000	—	.25	.75	1.50
	1980	—	—	.25	.75	1.50

10 FRANCS
.900 GOLD
Micombero Commemorative

KM#	Date	Mintage	Fine	VF	XF	Unc
11	1967	—	—	—	—	60.00

COPPER-NICKEL
F.A.O. Issue

17	1968	2.000	—	.75	1.50	2.50
	1971	2.000	—	.75	1.50	2.50

20 FRANCS
.900 GOLD
Micombero Commemorative

12	1967	—	—	—	—	100.00

25 FRANCS
.900 GOLD
Micombero Commemorative

13	1967	—	—	—	—	125.00

50 FRANCS

.900 GOLD
Micombero Commemorative

14	1967	—	—	—	—	250.00

100 FRANCS
.900 GOLD
Micombero Commemorative

15	1967	—	—	—	—	540.00

PROOF SETS (PS)

KM#	Date	Mintage	Identification	Issue Price	Mkt. Val.
PS1	1962(4)	2,500	KM2-5	—	1125.
PS2	1965(4)	5,000	KM7-10	—	1125.

CAMEROON

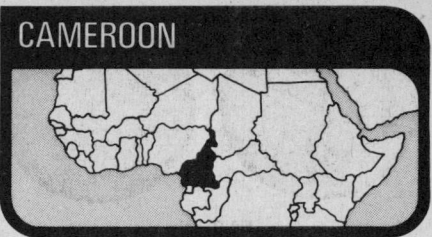

The Republic of Cameroon, located in west-central Africa on the Gulf of Guinea, has an area of 183,569 sq. mi. (475,442 sq. km.) and a population of 8.5 million. Capital: Yaounde. About 90 percent of the labor force is employed on the land; cash crops account for 80 percent of the country's export revenue. Cocoa, coffee, aluminum, cotton, rubber, and timber are exported.

European contact with what is now the United Republic of Cameroon began in the 16th century with the voyage of Portuguese navigator Fernando Po. The following three centuries saw continuous activity by Spanish, Dutch, and British traders and missionaries. The land was spared colonial rule until 1884, when treaties with tribal chiefs brought German domination. In 1919, the League of Nations divided the Cameroons between Great Britain and France, with the larger eastern area going to France. The French and British mandates were converted into United Nations trusteeships in 1946. French Cameroon became the independent Cameroon Republic on Jan. 1, 1960. The federation of East (French) and West (British) Cameroon was established in 1961 when the southern part of British Cameroon voted for reunification with the Cameroon Republic, and the northern part for union with Nigeria.

Coins of French Equatorial Africa and of the monetary unions identified as the Equatorial African States and Central African States are also current in Cameroon.

MINT MARKS
(a) - Paris, privy marks only
SA - Pretoria, 1943

MONETARY SYSTEM
100 Centimes = 1 Franc

50 CENTIMES

ALUMINUM-BRONZE

KM#	Date	Mintage	Fine	VF	XF	Unc
1	1924(a)	4.000	1.50	3.50	12.00	50.00
	1925(a)	2.500	2.00	5.00	15.00	55.00
	1926(a)	7.800	1.00	2.00	8.00	40.00

BRONZE

4	1943	4.000	1.50	3.00	6.00	15.00

Obv. leg: LIBRE added

6	1943	4.000	—	5.00	10.00	18.00

FRANC

ALUMINUM-BRONZE

2	1924(a)	3.000	2.00	4.00	8.00	55.00
	1925(a)	1.722	3.00	6.00	17.50	75.00
	1926(a)	11.928	1.00	2.00	8.00	45.00

CAMEROON 253

BRONZE

KM#	Date	Mintage	Fine	VF	XF	Unc
5	1943	3.000	2.00	4.00	15.00	35.00

Obv. leg: LIBRE added

| 7 | 1943 | 3.000 | 2.00 | 4.00 | 15.00 | 35.00 |

ALUMINUM

| 8 | 1948(a) | 8.000 | .10 | .25 | .75 | 1.25 |

2 FRANCS

ALUMINUM-BRONZE

| 3 | 1924(a) | .500 | 4.00 | 8.00 | 30.00 | 100.00 |
| | 1925(a) | .100 | 5.00 | 12.00 | 35.00 | 125.00 |

ALUMINUM

| 9 | 1948(a) | 5.000 | .20 | .50 | .75 | 2.00 |

50 FRANCS

COPPER-NICKEL
Independence Commemorative

| 13 | 1960(a) | 1.154 | 1.50 | 3.00 | 4.00 | 6.50 |

100 FRANCS

NICKEL

14	1966(a)	9.950	1.50	2.50	5.00	10.00
	1967(a)	10.000	1.50	2.50	5.00	10.00
	1968(a)	11.000	1.50	2.50	5.00	10.00

NOTE: KM#14 was issued double thick and should not be considered a Piefort.

KM#	Date	Mintage	Fine	VF	XF	Unc
15	1971(a)	15.000	2.00	3.00	5.00	10.00
	1972(a)	20.000	2.00	3.00	5.00	10.00

NOTE: For earlier issues of similar coinage with 'Cameroun' in the legends see French Equatorial Africa. Refer also to Equatorial African States and Central African States.

Obv: KM#17. Rev: KM#15.

| 16 | 1972(a) | — | 17.50 | 30.00 | 40.00 | 70.00 |

17	1975(a)	—	1.00	1.50	2.50	4.00
	1980(a)	—	.75	1.50	2.50	4.00
	1983(a)	—	.75	1.50	2.50	3.50
	1984(a)	—	.75	1.25	2.00	3.00
	1986(a)	—	—	—	—	—

500 FRANCS

COPPER-NICKEL

| 23 | 1985(a) | — | 1.75 | 2.50 | 4.00 | 10.00 |

1000 FRANCS

3.5000 g., .900 GOLD, .1012 oz AGW
10th Anniversary of Independence

| 18 | 1970 | 4,000 | — | — | Proof | 85.00 |

3000 FRANCS

10.5000 g., .900 GOLD, .3038 oz AGW
10th Anniversary of Independence

| 19 | 1970 | 4,000 | — | — | Proof | 260.00 |

NOTE: With or without cornucopia mint mark on reverse.

5000 FRANCS

17.5000 g., .900 GOLD, .5064 oz AGW
10th Anniversary of Independence

KM#	Date	Mintage	Fine	—	VF	XF	Unc
20	1970	4,000	—	—	Proof	425.00

10,000 FRANCS

35.0000 g., .900 GOLD, 1.0128 oz AGW
10th Anniversary of Independence

| 21 | 1970 | 4,000 | — | — | Proof | 950.00 |

20,000 FRANCS

70.0000 g., .900 GOLD, 2.0257 oz AGW
10th Anniversary of Independence
Obv: Similar to 10,000 Francs, KM#21.

| 22 | 1970 | 4,000 | — | — | Proof | 1600. |

PROOF SETS (PS)

KM#	Date	Mintage	Identification	Issue Price	Mkt. Val.
PS1	1970(5)	4,000	KM18-22	—	3325.

1858-59 (5¢ & 10¢ to 1901)   1870-1901
VICTORIA

1902-1910
EDWARD VII

1911   1912-1936
GEORGE V

1937-1947   1948-1952
GEORGE VI

1953-1964 (without straps)   (with straps)   1965 to Date

1973 and 1988 Olympics   1978 Games
ELIZABETH II

Canadian Coins

The history of Canadian coinage parallels that of the United States in many respects, although in several aspects it also contrasts quite sharply. Canadian coins are widely collected in the U.S., particularly in the northern tier of states, where at times the issues of our northern neighbors have been encountered in substantial circulating quantities.

This is a most logical situation, as when the dollar was established as the monetary unit of Canada, in 1857 it was given the same intrinsic value as the U.S. dollar. Through the years the Canadian dollar has traded on an approximate par with the U.S. dollar, although from time to time one or the other units has traded at a slight premium.

The first Canadian decimal coins were issued in 1858 — 1, 5, 10 and 20 cents — in the name of the Province of Canada (Upper and Lower Canada, or the provinces of Ontario and Quebec as we know them today). The first truly Canadian coinage was offered in 1870 — 5, 10, 25 and 50 cents — following the confederation of these provinces with Nova Scotia and New Brunswick in 1867. Both of the latter had offered their own distinctive coinages in the early 1860s.

Prince Edward Island also offered a single issue of a one cent coin in 1871, prior to its 1873 entry into the confederation. A coinage of Newfoundland was also initiated during this period, in 1865, which continued through 1947, with the British dependency moving into the confederation in 1949.

In contrast to the .900 fine standard of American silver coins, Canada's coinage was originally launched with a .925 fine silver content, and as a result slightly smaller coin sizes. In 1920 the standard was reduced to .800 fine, remaining there until mid-1967 when it was lowered to .500 fine, then abandoned in favor of pure nickel a year later. Another contrast with U.S. coinage was evident in the issue of the large cent from 1858 to 1920, when a small cent of similar size, content and weight to the U.S. cent was introduced.

When Canada's dominion coin issue of 1870 was introduced, the 1858 provincial issue of a decimal 20 cent piece was abandoned in favor of a quasi-decimal 25 cent piece. This move was made, in part, because of the confusion between the 20 cent piece and the U.S. 25 cent piece, which also circulated in Canada, forecasting the similar fate which would befall the U.S. 20 cent piece a few years later. Although tentative steps aimed at the creation of a dollar coin were instituted in 1911, it was not until 1935, the year the issue of silver dollars was halted in the U.S., that Canada launched the issue of a silver dollar.

The first dollar was a commemorative of the silver jubi-

lee of the reign of George V, while the other George V dollar coin (1936) utilized dies which had been prepared at the Royal Mint in London in anticipation of the 1911 dollar which did not materialize. From the beginning, Canada's dollar series has been frequently employed as a vehicle for the commemoration of national events. In addition, a 1951 nickel commemorated the 200th anniversary of the isolation of nickel, of which Canada is the world's leading producer, while the entire 1967 series commemorates the centennial of Canadian confederation.

In the early years, Canada's coins were struck in England at London's Royal Mint or at the Heaton Mint in Birmingham. Issues struck at the Royal Mint do not bear a mint mark, but those produced by Heaton carry an "H". All Canadian coins have been struck since January 2, 1908, at the Royal Canadian Mints at Ottawa and recently at Winnipeg except for some 1968 pure nickel dimes struck at the U.S. Mint in Philadelphia, and do not bear mint marks. Ottawa's mint mark (C) does not appear on some 20th century Newfoundland issues, however, as it does on English type sovereigns struck there from 1908 through 1918.

Canadian coins are graded on standards similar to those used for the U.S. series. The points of greatest wear are generally found on the obverses in the bands of the crowns, the sprays of laurel around the head and in the hairlines above or over the ear. The susceptibility of these varying points to wear has decreed that Canadian coins are almost exclusively graded accordingly, with little concentration on the reverses, unless they are abnormally worn.

Those who become seriously interested in the collecting of Canadian coins will find membership in the Canadian Numismatic Association beneficial. The organization publishes a scholarly monthly journal for its members. Full details on membership may be obtained by writing to:

**General Secretary
Canadian Numismatic Association
P.O. Box 226
Barrie, Ontario, L4M 4T2 Canada**

LARGE CENTS

SMALL CENTS

KM#	Date	Mintage	VG-8	F-12	VF-20	XF-40	MS-60	MS-63
	1858-1910		BRONZE		1911-1920			
1	1858	421,000	25.00	30.00	40.00	60.00	140.00	395.00
	1859	9,579,000	1.00	1.50	2.25	3.25	20.00	65.00
	1859/8 narrow 9	Inc. Ab.	100.00	150.00	200.00	300.00	500.00	900.00
	1859/8 wide 9	Inc. Ab.	20.00	27.50	35.00	60.00	125.00	310.00
	1859 narrow 9	Inc. Ab.	20.00	27.50	35.00	60.00	125.00	310.00
7	1876H	4,000,000	1.00	2.00	2.75	4.75	30.00	145.00
	1881H	2,000,000	2.00	2.75	4.25	7.25	43.00	150.00
	1882H	4,000,000	1.00	1.75	2.25	4.00	26.00	90.00
	1884	2,500,000	1.50	2.50	3.50	5.75	35.00	140.00
	1886	1,500,000	2.75	3.50	5.00	9.25	43.00	185.00
	1887	1,500,000	2.00	2.75	4.25	6.50	35.00	145.00
	1888	4,000,000	1.00	1.50	2.00	3.50	24.00	90.00
	1890H	1,000,000	3.50	6.50	9.00	16.00	85.00	265.00
	1891 lg. date	1,452,000	3.00	5.00	8.00	15.00	60.00	225.00
	1891 S.D.L.L.	I.A.	37.50	45.00	65.00	85.00	300.00	760.00
	1891 S.D.S.L.	I.A.	25.00	35.00	45.00	65.00	190.00	525.00
	1892	1,200,000	2.25	4.25	6.00	8.50	27.50	120.00
	1893	2,000,000	1.25	2.00	3.50	5.75	25.00	90.00
	1894	1,000,000	4.25	6.50	9.00	14.00	85.00	200.00
	1895	1,200,000	2.50	4.25	5.75	7.25	60.00	150.00
	1896	2,000,000	1.25	1.75	2.25	4.00	25.00	85.00
	1897	1,500,000	1.25	2.00	2.50	4.50	25.00	85.00
	1898H	1,000,000	2.75	4.25	5.75	7.25	60.00	200.00
	1899	2,400,000	1.25	1.75	2.50	4.00	25.00	85.00
	1900	1,000,000	4.25	6.50	9.00	12.50	60.00	165.00
	1900H	2,600,000	1.00	1.75	2.25	3.75	20.00	75.00
	1901	4,100,000	1.00	1.25	1.75	3.25	18.50	65.00
8	1902	3,000,000	.90	1.25	1.75	2.50	12.00	40.00
	1903	4,000,000	1.00	1.50	2.00	3.00	17.50	50.00
	1904	2,500,000	2.00	3.00	4.00	5.00	20.00	75.00
	1905	2,000,000	2.50	3.75	5.00	6.50	27.50	110.00
	1906	4,100,000	1.00	1.50	2.00	3.50	17.00	50.00
	1907	2,400,000	1.50	2.50	3.25	4.75	18.50	90.00
	1907H	800,000	8.00	10.00	16.00	30.00	70.00	220.00
	1908	2,401,506	2.00	2.75	3.75	5.00	18.00	60.00
	1909	3,973,339	1.00	1.25	2.00	3.00	18.00	55.00
	1910	5,146,487	.90	1.25	1.75	2.75	14.00	50.00
15	1911	4,663,486	1.00	1.25	2.00	3.25	15.00	50.00
21	1912	5,107,642	.75	1.00	1.50	2.50	15.00	55.00
	1913	5,735,405	.75	1.00	1.50	2.50	12.00	45.00
	1914	3,405,958	1.00	1.25	2.00	3.50	28.00	85.00
	1915	4,932,134	.75	1.00	1.75	2.75	15.00	56.00
	1916	11,022,367	.45	.65	.90	2.00	12.00	40.00
	1917	11,899,254	.45	.65	.90	1.50	8.00	30.00
	1918	12,970,798	.45	.65	.90	1.50	8.00	30.00
	1919	11,279,634	.45	.65	.90	1.50	8.00	30.00
	1920	6,762,247	.45	.65	.90	1.50	10.00	35.00

KM#	Date	Mintage	VG-8	F-12	Dot VF-20	XF-40	MS-60	MS-63
		BRONZE						
28	1920	15,483,923	.15	.25	.90	1.50	8.50	30.00
	1921	7,601,627	.30	.50	1.75	5.00	12.00	55.00
	1922	1,243,635	8.00	10.00	13.00	20.00	100.00	300.00
	1923	1,019,002	12.50	15.00	20.00	30.00	175.00	550.00
	1924	1,593,195	3.50	5.00	6.50	10.00	70.00	245.00
	1925	1,000,622	11.00	13.00	17.00	27.50	145.00	450.00
	1926	2,143,372	1.50	2.00	3.00	7.00	55.00	200.00
	1927	3,553,928	.60	.85	1.75	3.50	22.50	95.00
	1928	9,144,860	.10	.20	.50	1.50	10.00	37.00
	1929	12,159,840	.10	.20	.50	1.50	10.00	37.00
	1930	2,538,613	1.50	1.75	2.50	5.50	27.50	100.00
	1931	3,842,776	.60	.85	1.75	3.50	22.50	80.00
	1932	21,316,190	.10	.20	.40	1.50	9.00	35.00
	1933	12,079,310	.10	.20	.40	1.50	9.00	35.00
	1934	7,042,358	.10	.20	.40	1.50	9.00	32.00
	1935	7,526,400	.10	.20	.40	1.50	9.00	32.00
	1936	8,768,769	.10	.20	.40	1.50	8.00	27.50
	1936 dot below dt	678,823	—	—	—	—	Unique	
	1936 dot below dt	4 known	—	—	—	—	Specimen	—

Maple Leaves

KM#	Date	Mintage	VG-8	F-12	Maple Leaf VF-20	XF-40	MS-60	MS-63
32	1937	10,040,231	.10	.20	.35	1.10	2.00	4.50
	1938	18,365,608	.10	.15	.25	.50	2.00	7.00
	1939	21,600,319	.10	.15	.25	.50	2.00	5.00
	1940	85,740,532	—	.10	.20	.40	1.50	3.50
	1941	56,336,011	—	.10	.25	.70	10.00	37.00
	1942	76,113,708	—	.10	.20	.70	9.00	27.00
	1943	89,111,969	—	.10	.20	.40	3.00	9.00
	1944	44,131,216	—	.10	.20	1.25	9.00	25.00
	1945	77,268,591	—	.10	.20	.35	1.25	4.00
	1946	56,662,071	—	.20	.30	1.00	2.00	5.00
	1947	31,093,901	—	.10	.20	.35	1.50	5.00
	1947ML	47,855,448	—	.10	.20	.35	1.25	3.50
41	1948	25,767,779	.10	.20	.35	.60	2.00	7.00
	1949	33,128,933	—	.10	.15	.25	1.25	2.75
	1950	60,444,992	—	.10	.15	.25	1.25	2.75
	1951	80,430,379	—	.10	.15	.25	.75	2.25
	1952	67,631,736	—	.10	.15	.25	.75	2.25
49	1953 w/o strap	67,806,016	—	.10	.15	.25	.75	1.75
	1953 w/strap	Inc. Ab.	.45	.90	1.25	2.75	12.50	30.00
	1954 w/ strap	22,181,760	.10	.15	.30	.50	1.75	4.50
	1954 w/o strap	Inc. Ab.	Proof-Like Only	—	125.00	225.00
	1955 w/strap	56,403,193	—	.10	.15	.20	.50	1.00
	1955 w/o strap	Inc. Ab.	30.00	45.00	80.00	130.00	325.00	800.00

CANADA 256

KM#	Date	Mintage	VG-8	F-12	VF-20	XF-40	MS-60	MS-63
49	1956	78,658,535	—	—	—	.10	.50	.80
	1957	100,601,792	—	—	—	.10	.30	.70
	1958	59,385,679	—	—	—	.10	.30	.70
	1959	83,615,343	—	—	—	.10	.30	.70
	1960	75,772,775	—	—	—	.10	.30	.70
	1961	139,598,404	—	—	—	—	.15	.40
	1962	227,244,069	—	—	—	—	.10	.25
	1963	279,076,334	—	—	—	—	.10	.25
	1964	484,655,322	—	—	—	—	.10	.25

New Elizabeth II Effigy

KM#	Date	Mintage	VG-8	F-12	VF-20	XF-40	MS-60	MS-63
59	1965 sm. beads, pointed 5	304,441,082	—	—	—	.10	.45	.90
	1965 sm. beads, blunt 5 I.A.	—	—	—	—	.10	.20	
	1965 lg. beads, pointed 5 I.A.	—	—	1.50	5.00	15.00	25.00	
	1965 lg. beads, blunt 5 I.A.	—	—	—	.10	.20	.35	
	1966	184,151,087	—	—	—	—	.10	.15
	1968	329,695,772	—	—	—	—	.10	.15
	1969	335,240,929	—	—	—	—	.10	.15
	1970	311,145,010	—	—	—	—	.10	.15
	1971	298,228,936	—	—	—	—	.10	.15
	1972	451,304,591	—	—	—	—	.10	.15
	1973	457,059,852	—	—	—	—	.10	.15
	1974	692,058,489	—	—	—	—	.10	.15
	1975	642,318,000	—	—	—	—	.10	.15
	1976	701,122,890	—	—	—	—	.10	.15
	1977	453,762,670	—	—	—	—	.10	.15
	1978	911,170,647	—	—	—	—	.10	.15

Confederation Centennial

KM#	Date	Mintage	VG-8	F-12	VF-20	XF-40	MS-60	MS-63
65	1967	345,140,645	—	—	—	—	.10	.15

Smaller Bust

| 123 | 1979 | 754,394,064 | — | — | — | — | .10 | .15 |

Reduced Weight

127	1980	912,052,318	—	—	—	—	.10	.15
	1981	1,209,468,500	—	—	—	—	.10	.15
	1981	199,000	—	—	—	—	Proof	1.00

KM#	Date	Mintage	VG-8	F-12	VF-20	XF-40	MS-60	MS-63
132	1982	911,001,000	—	—	—	—	.10	.15
	1982	180,908	—	—	—	—	Proof	1.00
	1983	975,510,000	—	—	—	—	.10	.15
	1983	168,000	—	—	—	—	Proof	1.00
	1984	838,225,000	—	—	—	—	.10	.15
	1984	—	—	—	—	—	Proof	1.00
	1985	782,752,500	—	—	—	—	.10	.15
	1985	—	—	—	—	—	Proof	1.00
	1986	740,335,000	—	—	—	—	.10	.15
	1986	—	—	—	—	—	Proof	1.00
	1987	918,549,000	—	—	—	—	.10	.15
	1987	—	—	—	—	—	Proof	1.00
	1988	—	—	—	—	—	.10	.15
	1988	—	—	—	—	—	Proof	1.00

FIVE CENTS

Round 0's / Oval 0's

1.1620 g, .925 SILVER, .0346 oz ASW

KM#	Date	Mintage	VG-8	F-12	VF-20	XF-40	MS-60	MS-63
2	1858 sm. date	1,500,000	7.25	11.00	15.00	25.00	225.00	470.00
	1858 lg. date over sm. date	Inc. Ab.	90.00	135.00	225.00	300.00	850.00	1750.
	1870 flat rim	2,800,000	6.00	9.00	15.00	27.50	200.00	400.00
	1870 wire rim	Inc. Ab.	6.50	10.00	18.00	30.00	220.00	450.00
	1871	1,400,000	6.00	9.00	15.00	27.50	185.00	400.00
	1872H	2,000,000	4.75	7.25	12.00	20.00	175.00	375.00
	1874H plain 4	800,000	13.00	20.00	30.00	65.00	420.00	1000.
	1874H crosslet 4	Inc. Ab.	7.25	11.00	15.00	25.00	330.00	800.00
	1875H lg. date	1,000,000	80.00	125.00	200.00	375.00	1450.	3000.
	1875H sm. date	Inc. Ab.	65.00	110.00	175.00	300.00	1150.	2500.
	1880H	3,000,000	3.00	5.50	7.25	15.00	140.00	365.00
	1881H	1,500,000	3.50	6.00	9.50	18.00	165.00	400.00
	1882H	1,000,000	4.25	6.50	11.00	20.00	195.00	420.00
	1883H	600,000	10.00	15.00	20.00	35.00	350.00	950.00
	1884	200,000	65.00	100.00	175.00	350.00	1850.	3200.
	1885	1,000,000	4.75	7.25	12.00	25.00	300.00	900.00
	1886	1,700,000	3.50	6.00	9.50	18.00	200.00	500.00
	1887	500,000	10.00	15.00	25.00	40.00	300.00	700.00
	1888	1,000,000	3.00	4.75	7.25	14.00	165.00	300.00

KM#	Date	Mintage	VG-8	F-12	VF-20	XF-40	MS-60	MS-63
2	1889	1,200,000	15.00	20.00	35.00	75.00	450.00	1000.
	1890H	1,000,000	3.50	5.50	9.00	18.00	175.00	350.00
	1891	1,800,000	2.50	4.00	6.00	11.00	140.00	285.00
	1892	860,000	3.50	6.00	10.00	20.00	225.00	375.00
	1893	1,700,000	2.50	4.25	6.50	12.00	160.00	300.00
	1894	500,000	9.00	15.00	25.00	40.00	300.00	750.00
	1896	1,500,000	3.00	4.75	7.25	12.00	145.00	285.00
	1897	1,319,283	3.00	4.75	7.25	12.00	145.00	285.00
	1898	580,717	6.00	9.50	15.00	27.50	200.00	500.00
	1899	3,000,000	1.75	3.00	4.50	9.00	120.00	225.00
	1900 oval 0's	1,800,000	1.75	3.00	4.50	10.00	140.00	285.00
	1900 round 0's	Inc. Ab.	13.00	25.00	35.00	50.00	350.00	800.00
	1901	2,000,000	1.75	2.50	3.50	7.25	110.00	210.00
9	1902	2,120,000	1.50	2.00	3.00	6.50	35.00	70.00
	1902 lg. broad H	2,200,000	2.00	2.75	4.25	7.75	40.00	80.00
	1902 sm. narrow H	Inc. Ab.	7.00	12.00	18.00	40.00	165.00	275.00
13	1903	1,000,000	4.00	6.00	10.00	18.00	225.00	495.00
	1903H	2,640,000	1.75	3.00	4.50	9.00	110.00	220.00
	1904	2,400,000	1.75	3.00	4.50	9.00	120.00	250.00
	1905	2,600,000	1.75	3.00	4.50	9.00	90.00	210.00
	1906	3,100,000	1.50	2.00	3.00	6.00	80.00	165.00
	1907	5,200,000	1.50	2.00	3.00	6.00	80.00	150.00
	1908	1,220,524	4.25	6.50	11.00	20.00	120.00	240.00
	1909	1,983,725	1.75	2.25	4.50	9.00	175.00	375.00
	1910	3,850,325	1.25	1.75	3.00	5.50	70.00	130.00
16	1911	3,692,350	1.25	3.00	5.00	9.00	120.00	245.00
22	1912	5,863,170	1.25	2.00	3.00	4.50	70.00	125.00
	1913	5,488,048	1.25	2.00	3.00	4.50	35.00	65.00
	1914	4,202,179	1.25	2.00	3.25	5.00	65.00	135.00
	1915	1,172,258	7.00	12.00	18.00	40.00	270.00	500.00
	1916	2,481,675	2.75	4.75	6.50	15.00	110.00	250.00
	1917	5,521,373	1.25	1.75	2.50	4.00	50.00	100.00
	1918	6,052,298	1.25	1.75	2.50	4.00	40.00	85.00
	1919	7,835,400	1.25	1.75	2.50	4.00	40.00	85.00

1.1664 g, .800 SILVER, .0300 oz ASW

| 22a | 1920 | 10,649,851 | 1.25 | 1.75 | 2.50 | 4.50 | 35.00 | 80.00 |
| | 1921 | 2,582,495 | 1500. | 2000. | 3000. | 5000. | 13,500. | 20,000. |

NOTE: Approximately 460 known, balance remelted.

Near 6 / NICKEL / Far 6

KM#	Date	Mintage	VG-8	F-12	VF-20	XF-40	MS-60	MS-63
29	1922	4,794,119	.20	.40	2.00	6.00	40.00	80.00
	1923	2,502,279	.30	.80	2.50	8.00	85.00	220.00
	1924	3,105,839	.20	.40	2.25	5.50	65.00	150.00
	1925	201,921	22.00	30.00	50.00	140.00	800.00	1500.
	1926 near 6	938,162	2.25	3.50	13.00	45.00	245.00	550.00
	1926 far 6	Inc. Ab.	70.00	95.00	135.00	285.00	1350.	2600.
	1927	5,285,627	.20	.40	2.00	5.00	55.00	120.00
	1928	4,577,712	.20	.40	2.00	5.00	50.00	90.00
	1929	5,611,911	.20	.40	2.00	5.00	55.00	120.00
	1930	3,704,673	.20	.40	2.00	6.00	75.00	150.00
	1931	5,100,830	.20	.40	2.00	5.00	70.00	185.00
	1932	3,198,566	.20	.40	2.00	5.00	70.00	185.00
	1933	2,597,867	.35	.75	2.25	10.00	90.00	275.00
	1934	3,827,304	.20	.40	2.00	5.00	80.00	200.00
	1935	3,900,000	.20	.40	2.00	4.50	80.00	175.00
	1936	4,400,450	.20	.40	2.00	5.00	40.00	85.00

KM#	Date	Mintage	VG-8	F-12	VF-20	XF-40	MS-60	MS-63
33	1937 dot	4,593,263	.15	.35	1.75	3.00	13.00	25.00
	1938	3,898,974	.15	.75	2.25	8.50	80.00	145.00
	1939	5,661,123	.15	.35	1.75	4.50	45.00	85.00
	1940	13,920,197	.10	.20	.50	1.50	20.00	45.00
	1941	8,681,785	.10	.25	.75	2.00	22.50	50.00
	1942 round	6,847,544	.10	.25	.75	2.00	20.00	45.00

Tombac (BRASS)

KM#	Date	Mintage	VG-8	F-12	VF-20	XF-40	MS-60	MS-63
39	1942 - 12 sided	3,396,234	.20	.40	.60	1.20	3.20	7.00

1947 1947
Dot Maple leaf

NICKEL

KM#	Date	Mintage	VG-8	F-12	VF-20	XF-40	MS-60	MS-63
39a	1946	6,952,684	.10	.15	.25	2.00	10.00	22.50
	1947	7,603,724	.10	.15	.25	1.00	6.00	12.00
	1947 dot	Inc. Ab.	12.00	15.00	25.00	40.00	350.00	700.00
	1947 maple leaf	9,595,124	.10	.15	.25	1.00	6.00	12.00

Tombac (BRASS)
Victory

KM#	Date	Mintage	VG-8	F-12	VF-20	XF-40	MS-60	MS-63
40	1943	24,760,256	.15	.25	.35	.60	2.00	4.50

CHROMIUM-PLATED STEEL

| 40a | 1944 | 11,532,784 | .10 | .15 | .20 | .50 | 2.50 | 4.00 |
| | 1945 | 18,893,216 | .10 | .15 | .20 | .50 | 2.50 | 4.00 |

NICKEL

42	1948	1,810,789	.50	.70	1.40	3.50	20.00	32.50
	1949	13,037,090	.10	.15	.20	.40	4.00	8.00
	1950	11,970,521	.10	.15	.20	.40	4.00	8.00

CHROMIUM-PLATED STEEL

42a	1951 low relief*	4,313,410	.10	.20	.50	1.00	3.00	6.00
	1951 high relief**	Inc. Ab.	20.00	40.00	75.00	120.00	500.00	1000.
	1952	10,891,148	.10	.20	.50	1.00	3.00	4.50

*NOTE: A in GRATIA points between denticles.
**NOTE: A in GRATIA points to the denticle.

NICKEL
Nickel Industry

KM#	Date	Mintage	VG-8	F-12	VF-20	XF-40	MS-60	MS-63
48	1951	9,028,507	.10	.15	.25	.50	1.75	3.50

CHROMIUM-PLATED STEEL

50	1953 w/o strap	16,635,552	.10	.15	.20	.50	3.00	5.00
	1953 w/strap	Inc.Ab.	.10	.15	.25	.75	4.00	7.50
	1954	6,998,662	.10	.15	.30	1.00	4.50	9.00

NICKEL

50a	1955	5,355,028	.10	.15	.25	.55	3.00	5.00
	1956	9,399,854	—	.10	.20	.45	1.75	3.00
	1957	7,387,703	—	—	.15	.30	1.25	2.75
	1958	7,607,521	—	—	.15	.30	1.25	2.75
	1959	11,552,523	—	—	—	.20	.75	1.25
	1960	37,157,433	—	—	—	.15	.25	.50
	1961	47,889,051	—	—	—	—	.20	.40
	1962	46,307,305	—	—	—	—	.20	.40

KM#	Date	Mintage	VG-8	F-12	VF-20	XF-40	MS-60	MS-63
57	1963	43,970,320					.20	.30
	1964	78,075,068					.20	.30
	1964 XWL		6.00	8.00	10.00	12.50	25.00	35.00

New Elizabeth II Effigy

60	1965	84,876,018					.20	.30
	1966	27,976,648					.20	.30
	1968	101,930,379					.20	.30
	1969	27,830,229					.20	.30
	1970	5,726,010				.25	.55	.75
	1971	27,312,609					.20	.30
	1972	62,417,387					.20	.30
	1973	53,507,435					.20	.30
	1974	94,704,645					.20	.30
	1975	138,882,000					.20	.30
	1976	55,140,213					.20	.30
	1977	89,120,791					.20	.30
	1978	137,079,273					.20	.30
	1979	186,295,825					.20	.30
	1980	134,878,000					.20	.30
	1981	99,107,900					.20	.30
	1981	199,000					Proof	1.00

COPPER-NICKEL

KM#	Date	Mintage	VG-8	F-12	VF-20	XF-40	MS-60	MS-63
60a	1982	64,924,400					.20	.30
	1982	180,908					Proof	1.00
	1983	72,596,000					.20	.30
	1983	168,000					Proof	1.00
	1984	84,088,000					.20	.30
	1984						Proof	1.00
	1985	126,618,000					.20	.30
	1985						Proof	1.00
	1986	156,104,000					.20	.30
	1986						Proof	1.00
	1987	106,299,000					.10	.15
	1987						Proof	1.00
	1988						.10	.15
	1988						Proof	1.00

Confederation Centennial

KM#	Date	Mintage	VG-8	F-12	VF-20	XF-40	MS-60	MS-63
66	1967	36,876,574					.20	.30

TEN CENTS

1858-1901 2.3240 g, .925 SILVER, .0691 oz ASW **1902-1910**

KM#	Date	Mintage	VG-8	F-12	VF-20	XF-40	MS-60	MS-63
3	1858/5	Inc. Below	—	—	—	—	Rare	
	1858	1,250,000	8.50	15.50	30.00	60.00	275.00	550.00
	1870 narrow 0	1,600,000	7.50	13.50	30.00	60.00	300.00	575.00
	1870 wide 0	Inc. Ab.	8.00	16.50	32.50	65.00	325.00	600.00
	1871	800,000	9.50	18.00	35.00	75.00	350.00	650.00
	1871H	1,870,000	12.00	20.00	45.00	80.00	475.00	800.00
	1872H	1,000,000	50.00	85.00	145.00	285.00	950.00	2000.
	1874H	600,000	5.00	13.00	30.00	60.00	300.00	500.00
	1875H	1,000,000	135.00	225.00	360.00	750.00	2400.	4500.
	1880H	1,500,000	4.75	9.00	18.00	40.00	275.00	500.00
	1881H	950,000	6.00	12.00	25.00	55.00	350.00	600.00
	1882H	1,000,000	5.50	10.00	20.00	50.00	325.00	585.00
	1883H	300,000	12.50	25.00	50.00	110.00	800.00	1500.
	1884	150,000	100.00	200.00	350.00	750.00	2800.	6000.
	1885	400,000	9.00	18.00	40.00	100.00	950.00	2250.
	1886 sm. 6	800,000	7.75	13.50	30.00	60.00	400.00	775.00
	1886 lg. 6	Inc. Ab.	9.00	18.00	40.00	110.00	500.00	875.00
	1887	350,000	12.50	25.00	60.00	150.00	1200.	2500.
	1888	500,000	3.50	6.00	15.00	35.00	275.00	480.00
	1889	600,000	300.00	500.00	950.00	1650.	5750.	9500.
	1890H	450,000	7.75	14.00	30.00	65.00	400.00	675.00
	1891 21 leaves	800,000	8.50	15.00	32.50	80.00	450.00	800.00
	1891 22 leaves	Inc. Ab.	7.75	14.00	30.00	70.00	400.00	800.00
	1892/1	520,000	75.00	125.00	—	—	—	—
	1892	Inc. Ab.	6.00	12.00	25.00	60.00	400.00	750.00
	1893 flat top 3	500,000	9.00	18.00	40.00	85.00	475.00	950.00
	1893 rd. top 3	Inc. Ab.	375.00	600.00	1200.	2750.	6000.	9500.
	1894	500,000	6.00	12.00	25.00	60.00	400.00	750.00
	1896	650,000	4.25	7.75	15.00	37.50	300.00	525.00
	1898	720,000	4.25	7.75	15.00	37.50	300.00	525.00
	1899 sm. 9's	1,200,000	3.50	6.00	12.00	32.50	275.00	475.00
	1899 lg. 9's	Inc. Ab.	6.00	12.00	25.00	60.00	385.00	750.00
	1900	1,100,000	2.25	4.75	10.00	30.00	200.00	365.00
	1901	1,200,000	2.25	4.75	10.00	30.00	200.00	365.00
10	1902	720,000	4.00	7.00	14.50	35.00	200.00	500.00
	1902H	1,100,000	2.25	4.75	10.00	32.00	130.00	250.00
	1903	500,000	7.50	18.00	30.00	65.00	625.00	1450.
	1903H	1,320,000	2.25	4.75	10.00	35.00	225.00	500.00
	1904	1,000,000	3.50	7.00	18.00	50.00	325.00	600.00
	1905	1,000,000	3.00	6.00	12.50	40.00	375.00	700.00
	1906	1,700,000	1.75	3.50	9.00	25.00	225.00	450.00
	1907	2,620,000	1.75	3.00	7.50	20.00	170.00	350.00
	1908	776,666	3.50	7.00	18.00	45.00	320.00	700.00
	1909 Victorian leaves, similar to 1902-1908 coinage							
		1,697,200	2.25	5.25	12.00	35.00	350.00	680.00
	1909 broad leaves similar to 1910-1912 coinage							
		Inc. Ab.	4.25	7.50	20.00	50.00	375.00	700.00
	1910	4,468,331	1.75	3.50	7.00	20.00	180.00	350.00
17	1911	2,737,584	5.00	8.00	15.00	50.00	220.00	380.00

Small leaves **Broad leaves**

KM#	Date	Mintage	VG-8	F-12	VF-20	XF-40	MS-60	MS-63
23	1912	3,235,557	1.75	2.25	6.00	14.00	185.00	425.00
	1913 sm. leaves	3,613,937	1.00	2.25	5.25	12.00	185.00	425.00
	1913 lg. leaves	Inc. Ab.	75.00	125.00	250.00	450.00	2750.	4200.
	1914	2,549,811	1.25	2.50	5.00	11.00	185.00	425.00

CANADA 258

KM#	Date	Mintage	VG-8	F-12	VF-20	XF-40	MS-60	MS-63
23	1915	688,057	5.00	9.00	25.00	90.00	700.00	1250.
	1916	4,218,114	1.25	2.00	4.00	8.00	150.00	295.00
	1917	5,011,988	1.00	1.75	3.00	6.25	90.00	160.00
	1918	5,133,602	1.00	1.75	3.00	6.25	90.00	150.00
	1919	7,877,722	1.00	1.75	3.00	6.25	90.00	150.00

2.3328 g, .800 SILVER, .0600 oz ASW

KM#	Date	Mintage	VG-8	F-12	VF-20	XF-40	MS-60	MS-63
23a	1920	6,305,345	1.00	1.75	3.25	6.50	90.00	140.00
	1921	2,469,562	1.75	2.50	4.25	8.00	100.00	220.00
	1928	2,458,602	1.00	2.25	4.25	8.00	95.00	180.00
	1929	3,253,888	1.00	2.00	4.00	6.00	85.00	170.00
	1930	1,831,043	1.50	2.50	4.50	10.00	100.00	200.00
	1931	2,067,421	1.00	2.25	4.25	8.00	90.00	160.00
	1932	1,154,317	1.75	3.00	5.50	12.50	125.00	225.00
	1933	672,368	2.25	3.50	7.25	20.00	185.00	400.00
	1934	409,067	3.50	5.50	10.00	40.00	500.00	1250.
	1935	384,056	4.25	6.50	14.00	60.00	500.00	1000.
	1936	2,460,871	1.00	1.75	3.25	6.50	60.00	90.00
	1936 dot on rev.	4 known	—	—	—	Specimen		

Maple Leaf

KM#	Date	Mintage	VG-8	F-12	VF-20	XF-40	MS-60	MS-63
34	1937	2,500,095	1.50	2.25	3.50	6.00	18.00	30.00
	1938	4,197,323	1.00	2.25	3.50	9.00	60.00	125.00
	1939	5,501,748	1.00	2.25	3.50	9.00	60.00	125.00
	1940	16,526,470	BV	1.00	2.00	4.00	26.00	40.00
	1941	8,716,386	BV	1.00	3.00	7.00	55.00	115.00
	1942	10,214,011	BV	1.00	2.00	5.50	40.00	70.00
	1943	21,143,229	BV	1.00	2.00	4.25	18.00	30.00
	1944	9,383,582	BV	1.00	2.00	5.00	35.00	60.00
	1945	10,979,570	BV	1.00	2.00	4.25	18.00	30.00
	1946	6,300,066	BV	1.00	2.50	5.50	30.00	55.00
	1947	4,431,926	BV	1.50	3.00	8.00	45.00	70.00
	1947 maple leaf	9,638,793	BV	1.00	2.00	3.50	15.00	25.00
43	1948	422,741	3.50	5.00	10.00	22.50	80.00	160.00
	1949	11,336,172	—	BV	1.25	2.00	8.00	20.00
	1950	17,823,075	—	BV	1.25	2.00	7.00	10.00
	1951	15,079,265	—	BV	1.25	2.00	7.00	10.00
	1952	10,474,455	—	BV	1.25	2.00	7.00	10.00
51	1953 w/o straps	17,706,395	—	BV	1.00	1.50	5.00	8.00
	1953 w/straps	Inc. Ab.	—	BV	1.25	2.00	7.00	10.00
	1954	4,493,150	—	BV	1.50	3.00	10.00	18.00
	1955	12,237,294	—	BV	.75	1.50	5.00	7.00
	1956	16,732,844	—	BV	.75	1.50	3.50	6.00
	1956 dot below date	Inc. Ab.	1.50	2.75	4.25	5.50	14.00	20.00
	1957	16,110,229	—	—	BV	.60	2.00	2.75
	1958	10,621,236	—	—	BV	.60	2.00	2.75
	1959	19,691,433	—	—	BV	.50	1.25	2.25
	1960	45,446,835	—	—	—	BV	.75	1.00
	1961	26,850,859	—	—	—	BV	.75	1.00
	1962	41,864,335	—	—	—	BV	.75	1.00
	1963	41,916,208	—	—	—	BV	.75	1.00
	1964	49,518,549	—	—	—	BV	.75	1.00

New Elizabeth II Effigy

KM#	Date	Mintage	VG-8	F-12	VF-20	XF-40	MS-60	MS-63
61	1965	56,965,392	—	—	—	BV	.75	1.00
	1966	34,567,898	—	—	—	BV	.75	1.00

Confederation Centennial

KM#	Date	Mintage	VG-8	F-12	VF-20	XF-40	MS-60	MS-63
67	1967	62,998,215	—	—	—	BV	.75	1.00

2.3328 g, .500 SILVER, .0375 oz ASW

KM#	Date	Mintage	VG-8	F-12	VF-20	XF-40	MS-60	MS-63
67a	1967	Inc. Ab.	—	—	—	BV	.75	1.00

KM#	Date	Mintage	VG-8	F-12	VF-20	XF-40	MS-60	MS-63
72	1968 Ottawa	70,460,000	—	—	—	BV	.60	.75

NICKEL

KM#	Date	Mintage	VG-8	F-12	VF-20	XF-40	MS-60	MS-63
72a	1968 Ottawa	87,412,930	—	—	—	.15	.25	.30

OTTAWA-Reeding-PHILADELPHIA

KM#	Date	Mintage	VG-8	F-12	VF-20	XF-40	MS-60	MS-63
73	1968 Philadelphia	85,170,000	—	—	—	.15	.25	.30
	1969 lg date, lg ship	3 known	—	—	6500	—	—	—

Redesigned Smaller Ship

KM#	Date	Mintage	VG-8	F-12	VF-20	XF-40	MS-60	MS-63
77	1969	55,833,929	—	—	—	.15	.25	.30
	1970	5,249,296	—	—	—	.25	.65	.95
	1971	41,016,968	—	—	—	.15	.25	.30
	1972	60,169,387	—	—	—	.15	.25	.30
	1973	167,715,435	—	—	—	.15	.25	.30
	1974	201,566,565	—	—	—	.15	.25	.30
	1975	207,680,000	—	—	—	.15	.25	.30
	1976	95,018,533	—	—	—	.15	.25	.30
	1977	128,452,206	—	—	—	.15	.25	.30
	1978	170,366,431	—	—	—	.15	.25	.30
	1979	237,321,321	—	—	—	.15	.25	.30
	1980	170,111,533	—	—	—	.15	.25	.30
	1981	123,912,900	—	—	—	.15	.25	.30
	1981	199,000	—	—	—	—	Proof	1.50
	1982	93,475,000	—	—	—	.15	.25	.30
	1982	180,908	—	—	—	—	Proof	1.50
	1983	111,065,000	—	—	—	.15	.25	.30
	1983	168,000	—	—	—	—	Proof	1.50
	1984	119,080,000	—	—	—	.15	.25	.30
	1984	—	—	—	—	—	Proof	1.50
	1985	143,025,000	—	—	—	.15	.25	.30
	1985	—	—	—	—	—	Proof	1.50
	1986	168,620,000	—	—	—	.15	.25	.30
	1986	—	—	—	—	—	Proof	1.50
	1987	147,309,000	—	—	—	.15	.25	.30
	1987	—	—	—	—	—	Proof	1.50
	1988	—	—	—	—	.15	.25	.30
	1988	—	—	—	—	—	Proof	1.50

TWENTY CENTS

4.6480 g, .925 SILVER, .1382 oz ASW

KM#	Date	Mintage	VG-8	F-12	VF-20	XF-40	MS-60	MS-63
4	1858	750,000	40.00	60.00	80.00	175.00	1000.	2000.

TWENTY-FIVE CENTS

5.8100 g, .925 SILVER, .1728 oz ASW

KM#	Date	Mintage	VG-8	F-12	VF-20	XF-40	MS-60	MS-63
5	1870	900,000	8.50	14.50	35.00	85.00	800.00	1300.
	1871	400,000	10.00	18.00	45.00	140.00	1000.	1850.
	1871H	748,000	12.00	20.00	50.00	145.00	900.00	1450.
	1872H	2,240,000	5.00	9.00	18.00	60.00	575.00	975.00
	1874H	1,600,000	5.00	9.00	18.00	60.00	600.00	1100.
	1875H	1,000,000	150.00	400.00	900.00	1750.	5400.	11,000.
	1880H narrow 0	400,000	25.00	50.00	125.00	250.00	1150.	2200.
	1880H wide 0	Inc. Ab.	70.00	135.00	285.00	550.00	2500.	5000.
	1880H wide/narrow 0	Inc. Ab.	90.00	150.00	300.00	600.00	—	—
	1881H	820,000	8.50	15.00	35.00	110.00	800.00	1250.
	1882H	600,000	11.00	18.00	45.00	135.00	850.00	1400
	1883H	960,000	7.00	12.00	30.00	110.00	850.00	1350.
	1885	192,000	75.00	125.00	275.00	500.00	3000.	5500
	1886/3	540,000	9.00	18.00	50.00	135.00	1050.	2000.
	1886	Inc. Ab.	8.00	15.00	45.00	135.00	1050.	2000.
	1887	100,000	50.00	100.00	225.00	500.00	3000.	5500.
	1888	400,000	9.00	15.00	35.00	95.00	700.00	1100.
	1889	66,324	75.00	150.00	300.00	700.00	3500.	6500.
	1890H	200,000	12.00	20.00	50.00	150.00	1200.	1950.
	1891	120,000	35.00	65.00	150.00	300.00	1500.	2400.
	1892	510,000	7.00	12.00	30.00	100.00	700.00	1150.
	1893	100,000	55.00	100.00	200.00	425.00	1750.	2850.
	1894	220,000	10.00	20.00	45.00	135.00	1000.	1600.
	1899	415,580	4.00	7.00	18.00	60.00	600.00	950.00
	1900	1,320,000	3.00	6.00	15.00	55.00	450.00	800.00
	1901	640,000	3.00	6.00	15.00	50.00	475.00	825.00
11	1902	464,000	4.00	8.00	20.00	65.00	600.00	1000.
	1902H	800,000	2.75	5.50	13.00	40.00	300.00	500.00
	1903	846,150	4.00	8.00	20.00	70.00	600.00	1000.
	1904	400,000	9.00	18.00	60.00	150.00	1050.	2200.
	1905	800,000	4.75	9.00	25.00	85.00	850.00	1800.
	1906 lg. crown	1,237,843	3.25	6.00	15.00	45.00	450.00	825.00
	1906 sm. crown	Inc. Ab.	—	—	—	—	Rare	—
	1907	2,088,000	3.25	6.00	15.00	45.00	410.00	800.00
	1908	495,016	5.50	13.00	30.00	90.00	600.00	900.00
	1909	1,335,929	4.00	8.00	20.00	75.00	600.00	950.00
	1910	3,577,569	2.75	5.50	13.00	40.00	300.00	500.00
18	1911	1,721,341	9.00	18.00	40.00	90.00	475.00	850.00
24	1912	2,544,199	3.25	4.75	9.50	30.00	400.00	750.00
	1913	2,213,595	3.25	4.75	9.50	27.50	325.00	650.00
	1914	1,215,397	3.25	5.00	12.50	40.00	500.00	1000.
	1915	242,382	12.00	25.00	90.00	250.00	2500.	4200.
	1916	1,462,566	2.50	4.75	9.00	25.00	280.00	500.00
	1917	3,365,644	2.25	3.25	7.50	20.00	165.00	300.00
	1918	4,175,649	2.25	3.25	7.50	20.00	150.00	250.00
	1919	5,852,262	2.25	3.25	7.50	20.00	150.00	250.00

KM#	Date	Mintage	VG-8	F-12	VF-20	XF-40	MS-60	MS-63
24a	1920	5.8319 g, .800 SILVER, .1500 oz ASW						
	1920	1,975,278	2.25	3.75	9.00	25.00	200.00	375.00
	1921	597,337	9.00	20.00	60.00	175.00	1450.	2200.
	1927	468,096	20.00	32.50	80.00	200.00	1450.	2200.
	1928	2,114,178	2.25	3.25	7.50	25.00	200.00	325.00
	1929	2,690,562	2.25	3.25	7.50	25.00	175.00	325.00
	1930	968,748	3.25	4.75	9.50	30.00	275.00	500.00
	1931	537,815	3.25	4.75	10.00	32.50	325.00	650.00
	1932	537,994	3.25	5.25	12.50	35.00	300.00	525.00
	1933	421,282	4.00	6.25	14.00	40.00	325.00	525.00
	1934	384,350	4.75	7.50	17.50	50.00	400.00	700.00
	1935	537,772	4.75	6.50	15.00	45.00	330.00	550.00
	1936	972,094	2.25	3.25	7.50	20.00	150.00	250.00

KM#	Date	Mintage	VG-8	F-12	VF-20	XF-40	MS-60	MS-63
24a	1936 dot	153,322	30.00	70.00	175.00	375.00	1450.	2750.

KM#	Date	Mintage	VG-8	F-12	VF-20	XF-40	MS-60	MS-63
					Maple Leaf Variety			
35	1937	2,690,176	BV	2.50	4.25	6.00	20.00	40.00
	1938	3,149,245	BV	2.50	4.25	9.00	100.00	170.00
	1939	3,532,495	BV	2.50	4.25	9.00	90.00	150.00
	1940	9,583,650	BV	2.00	3.00	5.00	20.00	35.00
	1941	6,654,672	BV	2.00	3.00	5.00	30.00	40.00
	1942	6,935,871	BV	2.00	3.00	5.00	30.00	40.00
	1943	13,559,575	BV	2.00	3.00	5.00	27.50	35.00
	1944	7,216,237	BV	2.00	3.00	5.25	45.00	70.00
	1945	5,296,495	BV	2.00	3.00	5.00	20.00	32.50
	1946	2,210,810	BV	2.25	3.50	7.25	65.00	110.00
	1947	1,524,554	BV	2.25	3.50	8.25	70.00	120.00
	1947 dot after 7	Inc. Ab.	20.00	40.00	60.00	90.00	375.00	750.00
	1947 maple leaf	4,393,938	BV	2.00	3.00	4.00	20.00	32.00
44	1948	2,564,424	BV	2.25	3.50	7.25	70.00	120.00
	1949	7,988,830	—	BV	2.00	3.00	15.00	20.00
	1950	9,673,335	—	BV	2.00	3.00	12.00	17.50
	1951	8,290,719	—	BV	2.00	3.00	8.00	15.00
	1952	8,859,642	—	BV	2.00	3.00	8.00	15.00
52	1953 lg. date	10,546,769	—	BV	2.00	3.00	6.00	10.00
	1953 sm. date	Inc. Ab.	—	BV	2.00	3.00	8.00	12.00
	1954	2,318,891	BV	2.00	3.00	6.75	30.00	40.00
	1955	9,552,505	—	—	BV	1.50	6.00	9.00
	1956	11,269,353	—	—	BV	1.25	4.50	6.00
	1957	12,770,190	—	—	BV	1.00	3.00	5.00
	1958	9,336,910	—	—	BV	1.00	2.50	4.00
	1959	13,503,461	—	—	—	BV	2.50	4.00
	1960	22,835,327	—	—	—	BV	2.00	3.00
	1961	18,164,368	—	—	—	BV	2.00	3.00
	1962	29,559,266	—	—	—	BV	2.00	3.00
	1963	21,180,652	—	—	—	BV	2.00	3.00
	1964	36,479,343	—	—	—	BV	2.00	3.00
62	1965	44,708,869	—	—	—	BV	2.00	2.75
	1966	25,626,315	—	—	—	BV	2.00	2.75

KM#	Date	Mintage	VG-8	F-12	VF-20	XF-40	MS-60	MS-63
		Confederation Centennial						
68	1967	48,855,500	—	—	—	BV	2.00	2.75
		5.8319 g, .500 SILVER, .0937 oz ASW						
68a	1967	Inc. Ab.	—	—	—	BV	1.50	2.25
62a	1968	71,464,000	—	—	—	BV	1.50	2.25
		NICKEL						
74	1968	88,686,931	—	—	—	.30	.50	.65
	1969	133,037,929	—	—	—	.30	.50	.65
	1970	10,302,010	—	—	—	.30	.75	1.45
	1971	48,170,428	—	—	—	.30	.50	.65

KM#	Date	Mintage	VG-8	F-12	VF-20	XF-40	MS-60	MS-63
74	1972	43,743,387	—	—	—	.30	.50	.65
	1974	192,360,598	—	—	—	.30	.50	.65
	1975	141,148,000	—	—	—	.30	.50	.65
	1976	86,898,261	—	—	—	.30	.50	.65
	1977	99,634,555	—	—	—	.30	.50	.65
	1978	176,475,408	—	—	—	.30	.50	.65
	1979	131,042,905	—	—	—	.30	.50	.65
	1980	76,178,000	—	—	—	.30	.50	.65
	1981	131,580,272	—	—	—	.30	.50	.65
	1981	199,000	—	—	—	—	Proof	2.00
	1982	171,926,000	—	—	—	.30	.50	.65
	1982	180,908	—	—	—	—	Proof	2.00
	1983	13,162,000	—	—	—	.30	.50	.65
	1983	168,000	—	—	—	—	Proof	2.00
	1984	119,212,000	—	—	—	.30	.50	.65
	1984	—	—	—	—	—	Proof	2.00
	1985	158,734,000	—	—	—	.30	.50	.65
	1985	—	—	—	—	—	Proof	2.00
	1986	132,220,000	—	—	—	.30	.50	.65
	1986	—	—	—	—	—	Proof	2.00
	1987	53,408,000	—	—	—	.30	.50	.65
	1987	—	—	—	—	—	Proof	2.00
	1988	—	—	—	—	.30	.50	.65
	1988	—	—	—	—	—	Proof	2.00

KM#	Date	Mintage	VG-8	F-12	VF-20	XF-40	MS-60	MS-63
		Obv: 120 beads.						
81.1	1973	134,958,587	—	—	—	.30	.50	.65
		Obv: 132 beads.						
81.2	1973	—	20.00	35.00	50.00	65.00	100.00	130.00

FIFTY CENTS

	1870-1901	11.6200 g, .925 SILVER, .3456 oz ASW			1902-1936			
KM#	Date	Mintage	VG-8	F-12	VF-20	XF-40	MS-60	MS-63
6	1870	450,000	500.00	950.00	2150.	2700.	12,500.	18,500.
	1870 LCW	Inc. Ab.	25.00	60.00	75.00	225.00	3500.	7500.
	1871	200,000	40.00	100.00	250.00	460.00	3850.	7500.
	1871H	45,000	75.00	160.00	275.00	550.00	5000.	8750.
	1872H	80,000	20.00	45.00	160.00	300.00	3850.	7500.
	1872H inverted A for V in VICTORIA							
		Inc. Ab.	70.00	135.00	265.00	650.00	—	—
	1881H	150,000	35.00	70.00	110.00	250.00	3500.	7000.
	1888	60,000	115.00	185.00	325.00	750.00	4300.	7750.
	1890H	20,000	650.00	975.00	2250.	4000.	18,500.	25,500.
	1892	151,000	45.00	85.00	210.00	325.00	3500.	7500.
	1894	29,036	180.00	325.00	750.00	1450.	8700.	12,500.
	1898	100,000	60.00	150.00	275.00	550.00	3500.	7000.
	1899	50,000	90.00	185.00	325.00	750.00	5800.	10,500.
	1900	118,000	22.50	50.00	145.00	225.00	3500.	6800.
	1901	80,000	35.00	60.00	150.00	240.00	3500.	7000.

		Victorian Leaves			Edwardian Leaves			
KM#	Date	Mintage	VG-8	F-12	VF-20	XF-40	MS-60	MS-63
12	1902	120,000	15.00	32.00	90.00	160.00	1550.	2750.
	1903H	140,000	18.00	40.00	135.00	245.00	2150.	4000.
	1904	60,000	85.00	160.00	320.00	625.00	5800.	8500.
	1905	40,000	90.00	180.00	400.00	800.00	7300.	11,000.
	1906	350,000	8.00	30.00	65.00	150.00	1700.	2850.
	1907	300,000	12.00	20.00	55.00	140.00	1700.	2850.
	1908	128,119	25.00	45.00	120.00	250.00	1950.	3650.
	1909	302,118	15.00	35.00	95.00	225.00	1900.	3650.
	1910 Victorian lvs.	649,521	6.50	22.50	55.00	145.00	1500.	2650.
	1910 Edwardian lvs.	Inc. Ab.	6.50	22.50	55.00	145.00	1500.	2650.
19	1911	209,972	12.00	60.00	235.00	550.00	2000.	3200.
25	1912	285,867	6.50	20.00	70.00	200.00	2300.	4000.
	1913	265,889	6.00	20.00	70.00	190.00	2300.	4000.
	1914	160,128	17.50	40.00	175.00	560.00	3600.	6200.
	1916	459,070	5.50	20.00	60.00	135.00	1100.	1900.
	1917	752,213	5.00	12.00	35.00	110.00	700.00	1350.
	1918	754,989	5.00	10.00	30.00	95.00	650.00	1250.
	1919	1,113,429	5.00	8.00	28.00	85.00	550.00	1100.

CANADA 260

11.6638 g, .800 SILVER, .3000 oz ASW

KM#	Date	Mintage	VG-8	F-12	VF-20	XF-40	MS-60	MS-63
25a	1920	584,691	5.00	18.00	35.00	125.00	900.00	1500.
	1921	75 to 100 pcs.known	10,000.	13,000.	16,500.	22,000.	31,000.	48,500.
	1929	228,328	5.00	12.50	30.00	115.00	850.00	1550.
	1931	57,581	8.00	20.00	60.00	175.00	1600.	2850.
	1932	19,213	42.50	95.00	200.00	425.00	2300.	3850.
	1934	39,539	16.00	27.50	95.00	225.00	1600.	3000.
	1936	38,550	17.50	28.00	100.00	225.00	1150.	2000.

1937-1958 / **1959-1964**

KM#	Date	Mintage	VG-8	F-12	VF-20	XF-40	MS-60	MS-63
36	1937	192,016	5.00	6.00	7.50	15.00	32.50	70.00
	1938	192,018	5.00	6.50	25.00	40.00	130.00	300.00
	1939	287,976	5.00	6.00	10.00	20.00	175.00	250.00
	1940	1,996,566	BV	5.00	6.00	8.00	35.00	55.00
	1941	1,714,874	BV	4.50	5.00	6.50	30.00	55.00
	1942	1,974,164	BV	4.50	5.00	6.50	30.00	55.00
	1943	3,109,583	BV	4.00	5.00	6.00	25.00	55.00
	1944	2,460,205	BV	4.00	5.00	6.00	30.00	52.00
	1945	1,959,528	BV	4.00	5.00	7.50	30.00	52.00
	1946	950,235	BV	5.00	6.50	9.00	75.00	120.00
	1946 hoof in 6	Inc. Ab.	15.00	20.00	35.00	100.00	1000.	1750.
	1947 straight 7	424,885	3.00	5.00	7.00	12.00	150.00	250.00
	1947 curved 7	Inc. Ab.	3.00	5.00	7.00	12.00	150.00	250.00
	1947ML straight 7	38,433	15.00	20.00	40.00	55.00	250.00	420.00
	1947ML curved 7	Inc. Ab.	975.00	1250.	1500.	1900.	4000.	5500.
45	1948	37,784	32.50	45.00	65.00	85.00	225.00	375.00
	1949	858,991	3.00	4.00	6.50	8.00	50.00	100.00
	1949 hoof over 9	Inc. Ab.	7.50	12.50	22.50	65.00	400.00	700.00
	1950	2,384,179	4.00	6.50	10.00	18.00	230.00	385.00
	1950 lines in 0	Inc. Ab.	BV	2.50	3.00	5.00	12.50	25.00
	1951	2,421,730	BV	2.50	3.00	3.75	10.00	20.00
	1952	2,596,465	BV	2.50	3.00	3.75	10.00	20.00
53	1953 sm. date	1,630,429	BV	2.50	3.00	3.50	9.00	15.00
	1953 lg.dt,straps	Inc. Ab.	BV	3.00	3.50	5.00	25.00	40.00
	1953 lg.dt,w/o straps	I.A.	4.00	6.00	12.50	17.50	125.00	200.00
	1954	506,305	2.25	3.25	4.75	8.00	28.50	45.00
	1955	753,511	BV	2.50	4.00	6.00	20.00	30.00
	1956	1,379,499	—	BV	2.00	3.50	7.50	15.00
	1957	2,171,689	—	—	BV	2.50	5.00	7.00
	1958	2,957,266	—	—	BV	2.00	4.50	5.50
56	1959	3,095,535	—	—	—	BV	4.00	5.25
	1960	3,488,897	—	—	—	BV	2.75	3.50
	1961	3,584,417	—	—	—	BV	2.75	3.50
	1962	5,208,030	—	—	—	BV	2.75	3.50
	1963	8,348,871	—	—	—	BV	2.75	3.50
	1964	9,377,676	—	—	—	BV	2.75	3.50

1965-1966 / **1967**

New Elizabeth II Effigy

KM#	Date	Mintage	VG-8	F-12	VF-20	XF-40	MS-60	MS-63
63	1965	12,629,974	—	—	—	BV	2.75	3.50
	1966	7,920,496	—	—	—	BV	2.75	3.50

Confederation Centennial

| 69 | 1967 | 4,211,392 | — | — | — | BV | 3.00 | 4.00 |

1968-76 / **1977** / **1978-**

NICKEL

KM#	Date	Mintage	VG-8	F-12	VF-20	XF-40	MS-60	MS-63
75	1968	3,966,932	—	—	—	.50	.85	1.00
	1969	7,113,929	—	—	—	.50	.85	1.00
	1970	2,429,526	—	—	—	.50	.85	1.00
	1971	2,166,444	—	—	—	.50	.85	1.00
	1972	2,515,632	—	—	—	.50	.85	1.00
	1973	2,546,096	—	—	—	.50	.85	1.00
	1974	3,436,650	—	—	—	.50	.85	1.00
	1975	3,710,000	—	—	—	.50	.85	1.00
	1976	2,940,719	—	—	—	.50	.85	1.00
	1977	709,839	—	—	.40	1.25	2.25	2.75

KM#	Date	Mintage	VG-8	F-12	VF-20	XF-40	MS-60	MS-63
75	1978 square beads	3,341,892	—	—	—	.50	.85	1.00
	1978 round beads	Inc. Ab.	—	—	.40	3.00	3.50	4.00
	1979	3,425,000	—	—	—	.50	.85	1.00
	1980	1,574,000	—	—	—	.50	.85	1.00
	1981	2,690,272	—	—	—	.50	.85	1.00
	1981	199,000	—	—	—	—	Proof	3.00
	1982	2,236,674	—	—	—	.50	.85	1.00
	1982	180,908	—	—	—	—	Proof	3.00
	1983	1,177,000	—	—	—	.50	.85	1.00
	1983	168,000	—	—	—	—	Proof	3.00
	1984	1,502,989	—	—	—	.50	.85	1.00
	1984	—	—	—	—	—	Proof	3.00
	1985	2,188,374	—	—	—	.50	.85	1.00
	1985	—	—	—	—	—	Proof	3.00
	1986	781,400	—	—	—	.50	.85	1.00
	1986	—	—	—	—	—	Proof	3.00
	1987	373,000	—	—	—	.50	.85	1.00
	1987	—	—	—	—	—	Proof	3.00
	1988	—	—	—	—	.50	.85	1.00
	1988	—	—	—	—	—	Proof	3.00

VOYAGEUR DOLLARS

23.3276 g, .800 SILVER, .6000 oz ASW

KM#	Date	Mintage	F-12	VF-20	XF-40	AU-50	MS-60	MS-63
31	1936	306,100	10.00	13.00	15.00	22.00	45.00	85.00

Pointed 7 / **Blunt 7** / **Maple Leaf (blunt 7 only)**

KM#	Date	Mintage	F-12	VF-20	XF-40	AU-50	MS-60	MS-63
37	1937	241,002	10.00	14.00	17.00	22.00	40.00	75.00
	1937				Matte Proof		—	400.00
	1938	90,304	25.00	32.50	40.00	55.00	145.00	325.00
	1945	38,391	65.00	100.00	120.00	140.00	325.00	500.00
	1945					Specimen		2750.
	1946	93,055	16.00	30.00	40.00	55.00	145.00	350.00
	1947 pointed 7	Inc. Bl.	75.00	115.00	145.00	225.00	500.00	1000.
	1947 blunt 7	65,595	35.00	60.00	70.00	100.00	225.00	375.00
	1947 maple leaf	21,135	120.00	160.00	200.00	275.00	400.00	750.00
46	1948	18,780	450.00	550.00	650.00	775.00	1000.	1350.
	1950 w/4 water lines	261,002	7.00	8.00	11.00	13.00	20.00	40.00
	1950 w/4 water lines (1 known)			Matte Proof				
	1950 Arnprior w/1-1/2 w.l. I.A.	15.00	18.00	22.00	35.00	50.00	100.00
	1951 w/4 water lines	416,395	6.00	7.00	8.00	11.00	18.00	25.00
	1951 w/4 water lines					—	Proof	400.00
	1951 Arnprior w/1-1/2 w.l. I.A.	22.00	30.00	35.00	70.00	120.00	225.00
	1952 Arnprior	I.A.					Rare	
	1952 Arnprior					—	Proof	Rare
	1952 w/o water lines	I.A.	7.50	8.00	11.00	16.00	24.00	35.00

KM#	Date	Mintage	VF-20	XF-40	AU-50	MS-60	MS-63
54	1953 w/o strap, wire rim	1,074,578	6.50	7.50	8.50	12.50	20.00
	1953 w/strap, flat rim	Inc. Ab.	6.50	7.50	8.50	12.50	20.00
	1954	246,606	7.00	8.00	10.00	18.00	32.00
	1955 w/4 water lines	268,105	7.00	8.00	10.00	18.00	32.00
	1955 Arnprior w/1-1/2 w.l.*	I.A.	70.00	85.00	110.00	130.00	185.00
	1956	209,092	11.00	12.00	14.00	30.00	45.00
	1957 w/4 water lines	496,389	6.50	7.50	9.00	12.00	20.00
	1957 w/1 water line	I.A.	10.00	12.50	15.00	20.00	32.50
	1959	1,443,502	BV	5.25	6.00	7.50	9.00
	1960	1,420,486	BV	5.25	6.00	7.00	8.00
	1961	1,262,231	BV	5.25	6.00	7.00	8.00
	1962	1,884,789	BV	5.25	6.00	7.00	8.00
	1963	4,179,981	BV	5.25	6.00	7.00	8.00

*****NOTE:** All genuine circulation strike 1955 Arnprior dollars have a die break running along the top of TI in the word GRATIA on the obverse.

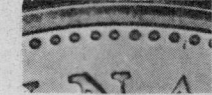 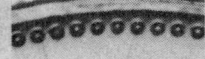 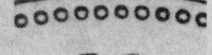

Small Beads / **Medium Beads** / **Large Beads**

New Elizabeth II Effigy

KM#	Date	Mintage	VF-20	XF-40	AU-50	MS-60	MS-63
64	1965 sm. beads, pointed 5	10,768,569	BV	5.25	6.00	7.00	8.00
	1965 sm. beads, blunt 5	Inc. Ab.	BV	5.25	6.00	7.00	8.00
	1965 lg. beads, blunt 5	Inc. Ab.	BV	5.25	6.00	7.00	8.00
	1965 lg. beads, pointed 5	Inc. Ab.	BV	5.25	6.50	9.00	12.00
	1965 med. beads, pointed 5	Inc. Ab.	7.00	8.00	10.00	15.00	25.00
	1966 lg. beads	9,912,178	BV	5.25	6.00	7.00	8.00
	1966 sm. beads	*485 pcs.			—	1300.	1500.

NICKEL, 32mm

KM#	Date	Mintage	MS-63	Mintage	P/L	Spec.
76.1	1968	5,579,714	1.50	1,408,143	2.50	—
	1969	4,809,313	1.50	594,258	2.50	—
	1972	2,676,041	1.75	405,865	2.50	—
	1975	3,256,000	2.00	322,325	3.25	—
	1976	2,498,204	2.50	274,106	4.00	—

23.3276 g, .500 SILVER, .3750 oz ASW, 36mm

KM#	Date	Mintage	MS-63	Mintage	P/L	Spec.
76.1a	1972	—	—	341,598	—	15.00
(76a)	1976	2,498,204	2.00	274,106	5.00	—
76.2	1975 mule w/1976 obv.	Inc. Ab.			*	

*NOTE: Only known in proof-like sets w/1976 obv. slightly modified.

117.1	1977 attached jewel	1,393,745	7.00	—	8.00	—
117.2	1977 detached jewel	Inc. Ab.	2.50	—	4.50	—
120	1978	2,948,488	2.00	—	3.50	—
	1979	2,954,842	2.00	—	5.50	—
	1980	3,291,221	2.00	—	9.00	—

KM#	Date	Mintage	MS-63	P/L	Proof
	1981	2,778,900	2.50	5.00	6.50
	1982	1,098,500	2.00	5.50	10.00
	1983	2,267,525	2.00	6.00	15.00
	1984	1,223,486	2.00	6.00	15.00
	1985	3,104,092	2.00	7.00	35.00
	1986	3,089,225	2.00	12.00	30.00
	1987	—	2.00	8.00	30.00

LOON DOLLARS

AUREATE NICKEL

KM#	Date	Mintage	MS-63	P/L	Proof
157	1987	199,300,000	1.50	3.25	—
	1987	178,120	—	—	20.00
	1988	—	1.25	2.50	10.00

COMMEMORATIVE DOLLARS

23.3276 g, .800 SILVER, .6000 oz ASW

KM#	Date	Mintage	F-12	VF-20	XF-40	AU-50	MS-60	MS-63
30	1935 Jubilee	428,707	10.00	15.00	18.00	25.00	45.00	85.00

KM#	Date	Mintage	F-12	VF-20	XF-40	AU-50	MS-60	MS-63
38	1939 Royal Visit	1,363,816	6.00	7.00	8.00	11.00	18.00	32.50
	1939 Royal Visit	—					Specimen	600.00
	1939 Royal Visit	—					Proof	2500.
47	1949 Newfoundland	672,218	9.00	12.00	15.00	20.00	35.00	50.00
	1949 Newfoundland	—					Specimen	425.00

 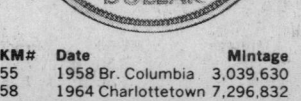 

KM#	Date	Mintage	F-12	VF-20	XF-40	AU-50	MS-60	MS-63
55	1958 Br. Columbia	3,039,630	BV	5.00	6.00	7.50	10.00	13.00
58	1964 Charlottetown	7,296,832	—	BV	5.00	6.00	7.00	8.00

KM#	Date	Mintage	MS-63	P/L	Spec.
70	1967 Goose, Confederation Centennial	6,767,496	8.00	12.00	550.00
78	1970 Manitoba (Nickel, 32mm)	4,140,058	1.50	—	—
		645,869	—	(c) 2.75	—

KM#	Date	Mintage	MS-63	P/L	Spec.
79	1971 Br. Columbia (Nickel, 32mm)	4,260,781	1.50	—	—
		468,729	—	(c) 2.50	—

23.3276 g, .500 SILVER, .3750 oz ASW*

80	1971 Br. Columbia (.500 Silver, 36mm)	585,674	—	—	(c) 9.00

*NOTE: Silver dollars dated 1971 and after are minted to this standard.

KM#	Date	Mintage	MS-63	P/L	Spec.
82	1973 Pr. Edward Island (Nickel, 32mm)	3,196,452	2.50	—	—
		466,881	—	(c) 3.25	—
83	1973 Mountie (.500 Silver, 36mm)	1,031,271	—	—	(c) 8.50
83v	1973 Mountie, with metal crest on case	Inc. Ab.	—	—	(c) 13.00

KM#	Date	Mintage	MS-63	P/L	Spec.
88	1974 Winnipeg (Nickel, 32mm)	2,799,363	2.75	—	—
		363,786	—	(c) 5.00	—
88a	1974 Winnipeg (.500 Silver, 36mm)	728,947	—	—	(c) 7.25
97	1975 Calgary (.500 Silver, 36mm)	930,956	—	—	(c) 7.25

KM#	Date	Mintage	MS-63	P/L	Spec.
106	1976 Parliament Library (.500 Silver, 36mm)	578,708	—	—	7.25
118	1977 Silver Jubilee	744,848	—	—	7.25

CANADA 262

KM#	Date	Mintage	MS-63	P/L	Spec.
121	1978 XI Games (.500 Silver, 36mm)	709,602	—	—	7.25
124	1979 Griffon (.500 Silver, 36mm)	826,695	—	— (c)	12.50

KM#	Date	Mintage	MS-63	P/L	Proof
149	1986 Vancouver (.500 Silver, 36mm)	124,574 672,642	11.50 —	— —	— 18.50
154	1987 John Davis (.500 Silver, 36mm)	117,147 587,102	11.50 —	— —	— 18.50

KM#	Date	Mintage	MS-63	P/L	Spec.
128	1980 Arctic Territories (.500 Silver, 36mm)	539,617	—	—	25.00

KM#	Date	Mintage	MS-63	P/L	Proof
130	1981 Railroad (.500 Silver, 36mm)	699,494	19.00	—	42.50

KM#	Date	Mintage	MS-63	P/L	Proof
161	1988 Ironworks (.500 Silver, 36mm)	—	11.50	—	17.50

NOTE: (c) Individually cased Proof-likes (P/L), Proofs or Specimens or from broken up Proof-like or specimen sets.

5 DOLLARS

8.3592 g, .900 GOLD, .2419 oz AGW

KM#	Date	Mintage	F-12	VF-20	XF-40	AU-50	MS-60	MS-63
26	1912	165,680	120.00	140.00	170.00	200.00	300.00	550.00
	1913	98,832	120.00	140.00	170.00	200.00	300.00	550.00
	1914	31,122	200.00	300.00	400.00	500.00	725.00	1500.

Olympic Commemoratives

KM#	Date	Mintage	MS-63	P/L	Proof
133	1982 Bison Skull (.500 Silver, 36mm)	903,888	13.50	— (c)	17.50
134	1982 Constitution (Nickel, 32mm)	9,709,422	2.00	—	—

24.3000 g, .925 SILVER, .7227 oz ASW
Series I

KM#	Date	Mintage	MS-63	Proof
84	1973 Sailboats (Kingston)	—	5.50	7.25
85	1973 North America Map	—	5.50	7.25

KM#	Date	Mintage	MS-63	P/L	Proof
138	1983 Edmonton University Games (.500 Silver, 36mm)	159,450 340,068	11.50 —	— —	— 17.50
140	1984 Toronto Centennial (.500 Silver, 36mm)	133,610 570,940	11.00 —	— —	— 17.50

KM#	Date	Mintage	MS-63	P/L	Proof
141	1984 Cartier (Nickel, 32mm)	7,009,323 87,760	2.50 —	— —	— 9.00
143	1985 National Parks -Moose- (.500 Silver, 36mm)	162,873 727,247	11.50 —	— —	— 17.50

Series II

KM#	Date	Mintage	MS-63	Proof
89	1974 Olympic Rings	—	5.50	7.25
90	1974 Athlete with torch	—	5.50	7.25

10 DOLLARS

CANADA 263

KM#	Date	Mintage	F-12	VF-20	XF-40	AU-50	MS-60	MS-63
		16.7185 g, .900 GOLD, .4838 oz AGW						
27	1912	74,759	215.00	340.00	415.00	500.00	750.00	1500.
	1913	149,232	215.00	340.00	415.00	500.00	750.00	1500.
	1914	140,068	230.00	440.00	500.00	625.00	925.00	1850.

Series III

KM#	Date	Mintage	MS-63	Proof
91	1974 Rowing	—	5.50	7.25
92	1974 Canoeing	—	5.50	7.25

Olympic Commemoratives

48.6000 g, .925 SILVER, 1.4454 oz ASW

Series I

KM#	Date	Mintage	MS-63	Proof
86	1973 World Map	—	11.50	14.00
	1974 World Map (Error-Mule)	—	320.00	—
87	1973 Montreal Skyline	—	10.50	14.00

Series IV

KM#	Date	Mintage	MS-63	Proof
98	1975 Marathon	—	5.50	7.25
99	1975 Ladies' javelin	—	5.50	7.25

Series V

KM#	Date	Mintage	MS-63	Proof
100	1975 Swimmer	—	5.50	7.25
101	1975 Diver	—	5.50	7.25

Series II

KM#	Date	Mintage	MS-63	Proof
93	1974 Head of Zeus	—	10.50	14.00
94	1974 Temple of Zeus	—	10.50	14.00

Series VI

KM#	Date	Mintage	MS-63	Proof
107	1976 Fencing	—	5.50	10.00
108	1976 Boxing	—	5.50	10.00

Series VII

KM#	Date	Mintage	MS-63	Proof
109	1976 Olympic Village	—	5.50	11.50
110	1976 Olympic flame	—	5.50	11.50

Series III

KM#	Date	Mintage	MS-63	Proof
95	1974 Cycling	—	10.50	14.00
96	1974 Lacrosse	—	10.50	14.00

CANADA 264

KM#	Date	Series IV	Mintage	MS-63	Proof
102	1975 Men's hurdles		—	10.50	14.00
103	1975 Ladies' shot put		—	10.50	14.00

KM#	Date	Series V	Mintage	MS-63	Proof
104	1975 Sailing		—	10.50	14.00
105	1975 Paddler		—	10.50	14.00

KM#	Date	Series VI	Mintage	MS-63	Proof
111	1976 Football		—	10.50	17.50
112	1976 Field Hockey		—	10.50	17.50

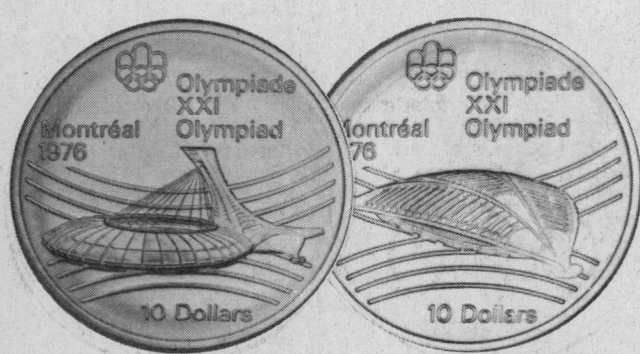

KM#	Date	Series VII	Mintage	MS-63	Proof
113	1976 Olympic Stadium		—	10.50	18.50
114	1976 Olympic Velodrome		—	10.50	18.50

20 DOLLARS

18.2733 g, .900 GOLD, .5288 oz AGW

KM#	Date	Mintage	MS-63	Proof
71	1967 Centennial	337,688	—	260.00

33.6300 g, .925 SILVER, 1.0000 oz ASW

KM#	Date	Mintage	MS-63	Proof
145	1985 Winter Olympics, Downhill Skier	359,522	—	32.50
146	1985 Winter Olympics, Speed Skater*	311,830	—	32.50

KM#	Date	Mintage	MS-63	Proof
147	1986 Winter Olympics, Biathlon*	280,188	—	32.50
148	1986 Winter Olympics, Hockey	345,203	—	32.50

KM#	Date	Mintage	MS-63	Proof
150	1986 Winter Olympics, Cross Country Skier	267,790	—	32.50
151	1986 Winter Olympics, Free Style Skier	263,820	—	32.50

*NOTE: Errors of these two types have been reported with plain instead of lettered edges.

34.1070 g, .925 SILVER, 1.0000 oz ASW

KM#	Date	Mintage	MS-63	Proof
155	1987 Winter Olympics, Figure Skater	283,720	—	32.50
156	1987 Winter Olympics, Curling	253,220	—	32.50

KM#	Date		Mintage	MS-63	Proof
159	1987 Winter Olympics, Ski Jumper		246,651	—	32.50
160	1987 Winter Olympics, Bobsled		216,709	—	32.50

100 DOLLARS

13.3375 g, .583 GOLD, .2500 oz AGW

KM#	Date	Mintage	MS-63	Proof
115	1976 Olympics, beaded borders, 27mm	650,000	140.00	—

16.9655 g, .917 GOLD, .5000 oz AGW

116	1976 Olympics, reduced size, 25mm, plain borders	337,342	—	265.00
119	1977 Queen's Silver Jubilee	180,396	—	300.00

KM#	Date	Mintage	MS-63	Proof
122	1978 Canadian Unification	200,000	—	265.00
126	1979 Year of the Child	250,000	—	265.00
129	1980 Arctic Territories	300,000	—	275.00

KM#	Date	Mintage	MS-63	Proof
131	1981 National Anthem	102,000	—	275.00
137	1982 New Constitution	121,708	—	265.00
139	1983 St. John's Newfoundland	83,128	—	275.00

KM#	Date	Mintage	MS-63	Proof
142	1984 Jacques Cartier	67,662	—	300.00
144	1985 National Parks - Big horn sheep	61,332	—	325.00
152	1986 Peace	76,255	—	285.00

KM#	Date	Mintage	MS-63	Proof
158	1987 1988 Olympics - Torch and logo	134,652	—	210.00
162	1988 Whales	*95,000	—	210.00

SOVEREIGN

1908-1910 **7.9881 g, .917 GOLD, .2354 oz AGW** **1911-1919**
C mint mark below horse's rear hooves

KM#	Date	Mintage	F-12	VF-20	XF-40	AU-50	MS-60	MS-63
14	1908C	636 pcs.	1000.	1700.	2300.	2800.	3300.	4100.
	1909C	16,273	175.00	250.00	325.00	450.00	875.00	1400.
	1910C	28,012	125.00	175.00	250.00	325.00	600.00	1100.
20	1911C	256,946	110.00	115.00	120.00	130.00	150.00	200.00
	1911C					Specimen		5500.
	1913C	3,715	350.00	475.00	650.00	850.00	1150.	1600.
	1914C	14,871	175.00	300.00	375.00	500.00	700.00	1200.
	1916C	Rare	*About 20 known		17,500.	22,500.	32,500.	
	1917C	58,845	110.00	115.00	120.00	130.00	150.00	225.00
	1918C	106,516	110.00	115.00	120.00	130.00	150.00	225.00
	1919C	135,889	110.00	115.00	120.00	130.00	150.00	225.00

SILVER BULLION ISSUES
5 DOLLARS

31.1000 g, .9999 SILVER, 1.0000 oz ASW

KM#	Date	Mintage	MS-63	Proof
163	1988 Maple leaf	—	10.50	—
	1989 Maple leaf	—	9.00	—

GOLD BULLION ISSUES
5 DOLLARS

3.1200 g, .9999 GOLD, .1000 oz AGW

KM#	Date	Mintage	MS-63	Proof
135	1982 Maple leaf	246,000	BV + 15%	—
	1983 Maple leaf	198,000	BV + 15%	—
	1984 Maple leaf	262,000	BV + 15%	—
	1985 Maple leaf	398,000	BV + 15%	—
	1986 Maple leaf	529,516	BV + 15%	—
	1987 Maple leaf	459,000	BV + 15%	—
	1988 Maple leaf	—	BV + 15%	—

10 DOLLARS

7.7850 g, .9999 GOLD, .2500 oz AGW

KM#	Date	Mintage	MS-63	Proof
136	1982 Maple leaf	184,000	BV + 11%	—
	1983 Maple leaf	192,000	BV + 11%	—
	1984 Maple leaf	312,800	BV + 11%	—
	1985 Maple leaf	620,000	BV + 11%	—
	1986 Maple leaf	915,200	BV + 11%	—
	1987 Maple leaf	276,800	BV + 11%	—
	1988 Maple leaf	—	BV + 11%	—

20 DOLLARS

15.5515 g, .9999 GOLD, .5000 oz AGW

KM#	Date	Mintage	MS-63	Proof
153	1986 Maple leaf	529,200	BV + 7%	—
	1987 Maple leaf	332,800	BV + 7%	—
	1988 Maple leaf	—	BV + 7%	—

50 DOLLARS

31.1030 g, .999 GOLD, 1.0000 oz AGW
Rev: 999. Maple Leaf. 999.

KM#	Date	Mintage	MS-63	Proof
125.1	1979 Maple leaf	1,000,000	BV + 5%	—
	1980 Maple leaf	1,251,500	BV + 5%	—
	1981 Maple leaf	863,000	BV + 5%	—
	1982 Maple leaf	883,000	BV + 5%	—

31.1030 g, .9999 GOLD, 1.0000 oz AGW
Rev: 9999 Maple Leaf 9999

KM#	Date	Mintage	MS-63	Proof
125.2	1983 Maple leaf	776,000	BV + 5%	—
	1984 Maple leaf	1,089,000	BV + 5%	—
	1985 Maple leaf	1,908,000	BV + 5%	—
	1986 Maple leaf	779,115	BV + 5%	—
	1987 Maple leaf	978,000	BV + 5%	—
	1988 Maple leaf	—	BV + 5%	—

PLATINUM BULLION ISSUES
5 DOLLARS

3.1203 g, .9995 PLATINUM, .1000 oz APW

KM#	Date	Mintage	MS-63	Proof
164	1988 Maple leaf	—	BV + 17%	—

10 DOLLARS

7.7857 g, .9995 PLATINUM, .2500 oz APW

KM#	Date	Mintage	MS-63	Proof
165	1988 Maple leaf	—	BV + 12%	—

20 DOLLARS

15.5519 g, .9995 PLATINUM, .5000 oz APW

KM#	Date	Mintage	MS-63	Proof
166	1988 Maple leaf	—	BV + 8%	—

50 DOLLARS

31.1030 g, .9995 PLATINUM, 1.0000 oz APW

KM#	Date	Mintage	MS-63	Proof
167	1988 Maple leaf	—	BV + 6%	—

PROOF-LIKE DOLLARS

23.3276 g, .800 SILVER, .6000 oz ASW

KM#	Date	Mintage	Identification	Issue Price	Mkt Value
D3	1953	1,200	KM54, Canoe w/shoulder fold	—	500.00
D4	1954	5,300	KM54, Canoe	1.25	165.00
D5	1955	7,950	KM54, Canoe	1.25	145.00
D5a	1955	Inc. Ab.	KM54, Arnprior	1.25	275.00
D6	1956	10,212	KM54, Canoe	1.25	90.00
D7	1957	16,241	KM54, Canoe	1.25	32.50
D8	1958	33,237	KM55, British Columbia	1.25	30.00
D9	1959	45,160	KM54, Canoe	1.25	13.50
D10	1960	82,728	KM54, Canoe	1.25	12.50
D11	1961	120,928	KM54, Canoe	1.25	11.00
D12	1962	248,901	KM54, Canoe	1.25	10.00
D13	1963	963,525	KM54, Canoe	1.25	9.00
D14	1964	2,862,441	KM58, Charlottetown	1.25	9.00
D15	1965	2,904,352	KM64, Canoe	—	9.00
D16	1966	672,514	KM64, Canoe	—	9.00
D17	1967	1,036,176	KM70, Confederation	—	12.00

MINT SETS (MS)
Olympic Commemoratives

KM#	Date	Mintage	Identification	Issue Price	Mkt Value
MS1	1973(4)	—	KM84-87, Series I	45.00	32.00
MS2	1974(4)	—	KM89-90,93-94, Series II	48.00	32.00
MS3	1974(4)	—	KM91-92,95-96, Series III	48.00	32.00
MS4	1975(4)	—	KM98-99,102-103, Series IV	48.00	32.00
MS5	1975(4)	—	KM100-101,104-105, Series V	60.00	32.00
MS6	1976(4)	—	KM107-108,111-112, Series VI	60.00	32.00
MS7	1976(4)	—	KM109-110,113-114, Series VII	60.00	35.00

SPECIMEN SETS (SS)

NOTE: Some authorities list these as proof sets. However, the Canadian Mint does not. The coins are double struck with higher than usual pressure, but are considered to have the same quality as proof issue from the Royal Mint, London.

	Date	Mintage	Identification		Mkt Value
SS1	1858(4)	—	KM1-4 Reeded Edge	—	6000.
SS2	1858(4)	—	KM1-4 Plain Edge	—	6000.
SS3	1858(8)	—	KM1-4 Double Set	—	12,500.
SS4	1858(8)	—	KM1(overdate),2-4 Double Set	—	14,000.
SS5	1870(4)	100*	KM2,3,5,6 (reeded edges)	—	12,500.
SS6	1870(8)	—	KM2,3,5,6 Double Set (plain edges)	—	25,000.
SS7	1872H(4)	—	KM2,3,5,6	—	12,500.
SS8	1875H(3)	—	KM2(Large Date),3,5	—	20,000.
SS9	1880H(3)	—	KM2,3,5(Narrow 0)	—	7000.
SS10	1881H(5)	—	KM7,2,3,5,6	—	12,000.
SS11	1892(2)	—	KM3,5	—	10,000.
SS12	1902(5)	100*	KM8-12	—	10,000.
SS13	1902H(3)	—	KM9(Large H),10,11	—	6500.
SS14	1903H(3)	—	KM10,12,13	—	7000.

NOTE: A 1903H double set has been reported on display in Bombay, India.

SS15	1908(5)	1,000*	KM8,10-13	—	2800.
SS16	1911(5)	1,000*	KM15-19	—	6000.
SS17	1911/12(8)	5	KM15-20,26-27	—	40,000.
SS18	1921(5)	—	KM22-25,28	—	80,000.
SS19	1922(2)	—	KM28,29	—	800.00
SS20	1923(2)	—	KM28,29	—	800.00
SS21	1924(2)	—	KM28,29	—	800.00
SS22	1925(2)	—	KM28,29	—	1800.
SS23	1926(2)	—	KM28,29 (Near 6)	—	1800.
SS24	1927(3)	—	KM24a,28,29	—	3200.
SS25	1928(5)	—	KM23a,24a,28,29	—	2800.
SS26	1929(5)	—	KM23a-25a,28,29	—	10,000.
SS27	1930(4)	—	KM23a,24a,28,29	—	6500.
SS28	1931(5)	—	KM23a-25a,28,29	—	8500.
SS29	1932(5)	—	KM23a-25a,28,29	—	10,000.
SS30	1934(5)	—	KM23-25,28,29	—	8500.
SS31	1936(5)	—	KM23-25,28,29	—	8500.
SS32	1936(6)	—	KM23a(dot),24a,25a,28(dot),29,30	—	Rare
SS33	1937(6)	1025*	KM32-37 Matte Finish	—	800.00
SS34	1937(4)	—	KM32-35 Mirror Fields	—	500.00
SS35	1937(6)	75*	KM32-37 Mirror Fields	—	1500.
SS36	1938(6)	—	KM32-37	—	15,000.
SS-A36	1939(6)	—	KM32-35,38 Matte Finish	—	—
SS-B36	1939(6)	—	KM32-35,38 Mirror Fields	—	—
SS-C36	1942(2)	—	KM32,33	—	300.00
SS-D36	1943(2)	—	KM32,40	—	300.00
SS37	1944(5)	3	KM32,34-37,40a	—	15,000.
SS-A37	1944(2)	—	KM32,40a	—	300.00
SS38	1945(6)	6	KM32,34-37,40a	—	4000.

KM#	Date	Mintage	Identification	Issue Price	Mkt Value
SS-A38	1945(2)	—	KM32,40a	—	300.00
SS39	1946(6)	15	KM32,34-37,39a	—	4000.
SS40	1947(6)	—	KM32,34-36(7 curved),37(pointed 7), 39a	—	6000.
SS41	1947(6)	—	KM32,34-36(7 curved),37(blunt 7),39a	—	6000.
SS42	1947ML(6)	—	KM32,34-36(7 curved right),37,39a	—	6500.
SS43	1948(6)	30	KM41-46	—	6500.
SS44	1949(6)	20	KM41-45,47	—	2000.
SS44A	1949(2)	—	KM47	—	1000.
SS45	1950(6)	12	KM41-46	—	2000.
SS46	1950(6)	—	KM41-45,46(Arnprior)	—	2200.
SS47	1951(7)	12	KM41,48,42a,43-46 (w/water lines)	—	2000.
SS48	1952(6)	2,317	KM41,42a,43-46 (water lines)	—	2200.
SS48A	1952(6)	—	KM41,42a,43-46 (w/o water lines)	—	2200.
SS49	1953(6)	28	KM49 w/o straps,50-54	—	1200.
SS50	1953(6)	—	KM49 w/straps,50-54	—	1200.
SS51	1964(6)	—	KM49,51,52,56-58	—	450.00
SS52	1965(6)	—	KM59-64	—	450.00
SS56	1971(7)	66,860	KM59,60,74,75,77,79(2 pcs.)	12.00	12.75
SS57	1972(7)	36,349	KM59,60,74,75,76(2 pcs.),77	12.00	57.50
SS58	1973(7)	119,819	KM59,60,75,77,81.1,82,83	12.00	13.50
SS59	1973(7)	Inc. Ab.	KM59,60,75,77,81.2,82,83	—	150.00
SS60	1974(7)	85,230	KM59,60,74,75,77,88,88a	15.00	13.50
SS61	1975(7)	97,263	KM59,60,74,77,97	15.00	13.50
SS62	1976(7)	87,744	KM59,60,74-77,106	16.00	18.00
SS63	1977(7)	142,577	KM59,60,74,75,77,117.1,118	16.50	13.50
SS64	1978(7)	147,000	KM59,60,74,75,77,120,121	16.50	13.50
SS65	1979(7)	155,698	KM59,60,74,75,77,120,124	18.50	20.00
SS66	1980(7)	162,875	KM59,60,74,75,77,120,128	30.50	32.50
SS67	1981(7)	71,300	KM60,74,75,77,120,123	10.00	10.00
SS68	1982(6)	62,298	KM60a,74,75,77,120,123	11.50	10.00
SS69	1983(6)	60,329	KM60a,74,75,77,120,132	—	10.00
SS70	1984(6)	60,440	KM60a,74,75,77,120,132	10.00	10.00
SS71	1985(6)	61,553	KM60a,74,75,77,120,132	10.00	10.00
SS73	1986(6)	67,152	KM60a,74,75,77,120,132	10.00	10.00
SS72	1987(6)	75,194	KM60a,74,75,77,120,132	11.00	10.00
SS73	1988(6)	—	KM60a,74,75,77,132,157	12.30	12.30

NOTE: *Estimated.

V.I.P. SPECIMEN SETS (VS)

NOTE: A very limited number of cased Specimen sets were produced by the Mint beginning in 1969 for presentation to dignitaries visiting the Royal Canadian Mint or other parts of Canada. (A small quantity of 1970 cased Specimen sets were sold to the public for $13.00 each.) The coins, 1¢ to $1.00 were cased in long narrow leather cases (black and other colors).

KM#	Date	Mintage	Identification	Issue Price	Mkt Value
VS1	1969	2 known	—	—	1700.
VS2	1970	100	KM59,60,74,75,77,78	—	475.00
VS3	1971	69	KM59,60,74,75,77,79(2 pcs.)	—	375.00
VS4	1972	25	KM59,60,74,75,76(2 pcs.),77	—	435.00
VS5	1973	26	KM59,60,75,77,81.1,82,83	—	435.00
VS6	1974	72	KM59,60,74,75,77,88,88a	—	375.00
VS7	1975	94	KM59,60,74-77,97	—	375.00
VS8	1976	—	KM59,60,74-77,106	—	375.00

PROOF-LIKE SETS (PL)

NOTE: These sets do not have the quality of the Proof or Specimen Set, but are specially produced and packaged.

KM#	Date	Mintage	Identification	Issue Price	Mkt Value
PL1	1953(6)	1,200	KM49 w/o straps, 50-54	2.20	1200.
PL2	1953(6)	Inc. Ab.	KM49-54	2.20	700.00
PL3	1954(6)	3,000	KM49-54	2.50	290.00
PL4	1954(6)	Inc. Ab.	KM49 w/o straps, 50-54	2.50	450.00
PL5	1955(6)	6,300	KM49,50a,51-54	2.50	220.00
PL6	1955(6)	Inc. Ab.	KM49,50a,51-54,Arnprior	2.50	325.00
PL7	1956(6)	6,500	KM49,50a,51-54	2.50	120.00
PL8	1957(6)	11,862	KM49,50a,51-54	2.50	55.00
PL9	1958(6)	18,259	KM49,50,51-53,55	2.50	50.00
PL10	1959(6)	31,577	KM49,50a,51,52,54,56	2.50	27.50
PL11	1960(6)	64,097	KM49,50a,51,52,54,56	3.00	17.50
PL12	1961(6)	98,373	KM49,50a,51,52,54,56	3.00	15.00
PL13	1962(6)	200,950	KM49,50a,51,52,54,56	3.00	13.00
PL14	1963(6)	673,006	KM49,51,52,54,56,57	3.00	12.00
PL15	1964(6)	1,653,162	KM49,51,52,56-58	3.00	12.00
PL16	1965(6)	2,904,352	KM59-64	4.00	12.00
PL17	1966(6)	672,514	KM59-64	4.00	12.00

KM#	Date	Mintage	Identification	Issue Price	Mkt Value
PL18	1967(6)	963,714	KM65-70 (pliofilm flat pack)	4.00	14.00
PL18A	1967(6)	337,514	KM65-70 and Silver Medal (red box)	12.00	18.00
PL18B	1967(7)	Inc. Ab.	KM65-71 (black box)	40.00	275.00

KM#	Date	Mintage	Identification	Issue Price	Mkt Value
PL19	1968(6)	521,641	KM59,60,72,74-76	4.00	2.25
PL20	1969(6)	326,203	KM59,60,74-77	4.00	3.00
PL21	1970(6)	349,120	KM59,60,74,75,77,78	4.00	5.00
PL22	1971(6)	253,311	KM59,60,74,75,77,79	4.00	3.75
PL23	1972(6)	224,275	KM59,60,74-77	4.00	3.25
PL24	1973(6)	243,695	KM59,60,74,75 obv. 120 beads, 77,81.1,82	4.00	3.75
PL25	1973(6)	Inc. Ab.	KM59,60,74,75 obv. 132 beads, 77,81.1,82	4.00	150.00
PL26	1974(6)	213,589	KM59,60,74,75,77,88	5.00	3.75
PL27.1	1975(6)	197,372	KM59,60,74,75,76.1,77	5.00	3.75
PL27.2	1975(6)	Inc. Ab.	KM59,60,74,75,76.2,77	5.00	—
PL28	1976(6)	171,737	KM59,60,74-77	5.15	5.50
PL29	1977(6)	225,307	KM59,60,74,75,77,117.1	5.15	5.00
PL30	1978(6)	260,000	KM59,60,74,75,77,120	—	3.25
PL31	1979(6)	187,624	KM59,60,74,75,77,120	6.25	6.50
PL32	1980(6)	410,842	KM59,60,74,75,77,120	6.50	11.00
PL33	1981(6)	186,250	KM60,74,75,77,120,123	8.50	8.00
PL34	1982(6)	180,908	KM60a,74,75,77,120,123	6.00	6.50
PL35	1982(6)	Inc. Ab.	KM60a,74,75,77,120,132	—	6.50
PL36	1983(6)	190,838	KM60a,74,75,77,120,132	—	10.00
PL37	1984(6)	181,249	KM60a,74,75,77,120,132	5.25	7.00
PL38	1985(6)	173,924	KM60a,74,75,77,120,132	5.25	6.00
PL40	1986(6)	167,338	KM60a,74,75,77,120,132	5.25	6.00
PL39	1987(6)	212,064	KM60a,74,75,77,120,132	5.25	6.00
PL41	1988(6)	—	KM60a,74,75,77,132,157	6.05	6.50

CUSTOM PROOF-LIKE SETS (CPL)

KM#	Date	Mintage	Identification	Issue Price	Mkt Value

Each set contains two 1 cent pieces.

CPL1	1971(7)	33,517	KM59(2 pcs.),60,74,75,77,79	6.50	5.75
CPL2	1972(7)	38,198	KM59(2 pcs.),60,74-77	6.50	5.75
CPL3	1973(7)	35,676	KM59(2 pcs.),60,75 obv. 120 beads, 77,81.1,82	6.50	5.75
CPL4	1973(7)	Inc. Ab.	KM56(2 pcs.),60,75 obv. 132 beads, 77,81.1,82	6.50	160.00
CPL5	1974(7)	44,296	KM59(2 pcs.),60,74,75,77,88	8.00	5.75
CPL6	1975(7)	36,851	KM59(2 pcs.),60,74-77	8.00	5.75
CPL7	1976(7)	28,162	KM59(2 pcs.),60,74-77	8.00	8.75
CPL8	1977(7)	44,198	KM59(2 pcs.),60,74,75,77,117	8.15	10.00
CPL9	1978(7)	41,000	KM59(2 pcs.),60,74,75,77,120	—	5.75
CPL10	1979(7)	31,174	KM59(2 pcs.),60,74,75,77,120	10.75	8.75
CPL11	1980(7)	41,447	KM59(2 pcs.),60,74,75,77,120	10.75	11.50

PROOF SETS (PS)

KM#	Date	Mintage	Identification	Issue Price	Mkt Value
PS1	1981(7)	199,000	KM60,74,75,77,120,123,130	36.00	50.00
PS2	1982(7)	180,908	KM60a,74,75,77,120,123,133	36.00	25.00
PS3	1983(7)	166,779	KM60a,74,75,77,120,132,138	36.00	27.50
PS4	1984(7)	161,545	KM60a,74,75,77,120,132,140	30.00	40.00
PS5	1985(7)	153,950	KM60a,74,75,77,120,132,143	30.00	40.00
PS7	1986(7)	176,224	KM60a,74,75,77,120,132,149	30.00	40.00
PS6	1987(7)	179,004	KM60a,74,75,77,120,132,154	34.00	40.00
PS7	1988(7)	—	KM60a,74,75,77,132,157,161	37.50	37.50

Olympic Commemoratives (OCP)

KM#	Date	Mintage	Identification	Issue Price	Mkt Value
OCP1	1973(4)	—	KM84-87,Series I	78.50	42.50
OCP2	1974(4)	—	KM89,90,93,94,Series II	88.50	42.50
OCP3	1974(4)	—	KM91,92,95,96,Series III	88.50	42.50
OCP4	1975(4)	—	KM98,99,102,103,Series IV	88.50	42.50
OCP5	1975(4)	—	KM100,101,104,105,Series V	88.50	42.50
OCP6	1976(4)	—	KM107,108,111,112,Series VI	88.50	55.00
OCP7	1976(4)	—	KM109,110,113,114,Series VII	88.50	60.00

NEWFOUNDLAND

LARGE CENTS

1865-1896 BRONZE 1904-1936

KM#	Date	Mintage	VG-8	F-12	VF-20	XF-40	MS-60	MS-63
1	1865	240,000	1.50	2.25	3.75	11.25	150.00	450.00
	1872H	200,000	1.50	2.25	3.75	11.25	100.00	200.00
	1872H	—	—	—	—	—	Proof	600.00
	1873	200,025	1.50	2.25	3.75	11.25	150.00	500.00
	1873	—	—	—	—	—	Proof	600.00
	1876H	200,000	1.50	2.25	3.75	11.25	150.00	500.00
	1876H	—	—	—	—	—	Proof	600.00
	1880 round O, even date	400,000	1.00	2.00	4.00	11.25	125.00	375.00
	1880 round O, low O	Inc. Ab.	1.50	2.25	4.50	11.25	150.00	425.00
	1880 oval 0	Inc. Ab.	60.00	70.00	95.00	150.00	650.00	1500.
	1885	40,000	12.75	15.00	25.00	55.00	300.00	750.00
	1888	50,000	11.25	13.50	18.75	40.00	225.00	675.00
	1890	200,000	1.50	2.25	3.00	6.75	125.00	325.00
	1894	200,000	1.50	2.25	3.00	6.75	125.00	325.00
	1896	200,000	1.50	2.25	3.00	6.75	125.00	325.00
9	1904H	100,000	4.50	6.75	12.00	25.00	225.00	650.00
	1907	200,000	1.00	1.75	3.00	8.25	130.00	325.00
	1909	200,000	1.00	1.75	3.00	8.25	130.00	325.00
	1909	—	—	—	—	—	Proof	400.00
16	1913	400,000	.75	1.50	2.25	5.25	50.00	165.00
	1917C	702,350	.75	1.50	2.25	5.25	50.00	165.00
	1919C	300,000	.75	1.50	2.25	5.25	70.00	200.00
	1919C	—	—	—	—	—	Proof	150.00
	1920C	302,184	.75	1.50	2.25	5.25	70.00	185.00
	1929	300,000	.75	1.50	2.25	5.25	50.00	165.00
	1929	—	—	—	—	—	Proof	125.00
	1936	300,000	.75	1.50	2.25	5.25	35.00	90.00
	1936	—	—	—	—	—	Proof	250.00

SMALL CENTS

BRONZE

KM#	Date	Mintage	VG-8	F-12	VF-20	XF-40	MS-60	MS-63
18	1938	500,000	.25	.50	1.00	2.25	20.00	50.00
	1938	—	—	—	—	—	Proof	65.00
	1940	300,000	1.00	2.25	3.25	7.50	45.00	120.00
	1940 re-engraved date	—	10.00	15.00	20.00	35.00	150.00	400.00
	1941C	827,662	.20	.25	.50	1.50	15.00	30.00
	1941C re-engraved date	—	10.00	15.00	20.00	35.00	150.00	400.00
	1942	1,996,889	.20	.25	.50	1.50	12.50	25.00
	1943C	1,239,732	.20	.25	.50	1.50	12.50	25.00
	1944C	1,328,776	.75	1.75	2.50	3.50	35.00	90.00
	1947C	313,772	.50	.75	1.00	1.50	30.00	150.00

FIVE CENTS

1.1782 g, .925 SILVER, .0350 oz ASW

KM#	Date	Mintage	VG-8	F-12	VF-20	XF-40	MS-60	MS-63
2	1865	80,000	25.00	37.50	65.00	165.00	1100.	2000.
	1870	40,000	37.50	50.00	90.00	225.00	1300.	2750.
	1870	—	—	—	—	—	Proof	3900.
	1872H	40,000	25.00	37.50	65.00	165.00	1000.	1500.
	1873	44,260	37.50	50.00	100.00	240.00	1500.	3200.
	1873H	Inc. Ab.	725.00	1100.	1650.	2600.	—	—
	1876H	20,000	70.00	100.00	165.00	350.00	2500.	4000.
	1880	40,000	30.00	45.00	85.00	165.00	1200.	2400.
	1881	40,000	18.00	35.00	50.00	135.00	1100.	2000.
	1882H	60,000	12.50	20.00	40.00	100.00	900.00	1600.
	1882H	—	—	—	—	—	Proof	2800.
	1885	16,000	100.00	150.00	240.00	450.00	3100.	5500.
	1888	40,000	20.00	30.00	60.00	150.00	900.00	1400.
	1890	160,000	8.00	15.00	35.00	90.00	700.00	1400.
	1890	—	—	—	—	—	Proof	2100.
	1894	160,000	8.00	15.00	35.00	90.00	700.00	1400.
	1896	400,000	5.00	10.00	20.00	55.00	500.00	1250.
7	1903	100,000	4.00	9.00	22.50	50.00	600.00	1100.
	1904H	100,000	3.75	6.75	15.00	45.00	450.00	750.00
	1908	400,000	3.00	6.00	12.50	37.50	300.00	600.00
13	1912	300,000	1.75	3.25	9.00	25.00	325.00	550.00
	1917C	300,319	1.75	3.25	9.00	25.00	325.00	550.00
	1919C	100,844	2.50	6.00	15.00	37.50	475.00	900.00
	1929	300,000	1.50	3.00	7.50	22.50	225.00	400.00
	1929	—	—	—	—	—	Proof	750.00
19	1938	100,000	1.00	1.50	2.50	5.00	100.00	225.00
	1938	—	—	—	—	—	Proof	350.00
	1940C	200,000	1.00	1.50	2.25	4.50	60.00	145.00
	1941C	621,641	.75	1.00	1.50	3.25	25.00	50.00
	1942C	298,348	1.00	1.50	2.50	5.00	35.00	80.00
	1943C	351,666	.75	1.00	1.50	3.25	25.00	50.00

1.1664 g, .800 SILVER, .0300 oz ASW

19a	1944C	286,504	1.00	1.75	2.50	4.50	60.00	145.00
	1945C	203,828	.75	1.00	1.50	3.25	25.00	50.00
	1945C	—	—	—	—	—	Proof	250.00
	1946C	2,041	200.00	275.00	350.00	525.00	2250.	3750.
	1946C	—	—	—	—	—	Proof	4000.
	1947C	38,400	4.50	6.50	9.50	15.00	90.00	180.00
	1947C	—	—	—	—	—	Proof	400.00

TEN CENTS

1865-1896 2.3564 g, .925 SILVER, .0701 oz ASW 1903-1947

KM#	Date	Mintage	VG-8	F-12	VF-20	XF-40	MS-60	MS-63
3	1865	80,000	15.00	30.00	75.00	200.00	1500.	3200.
	1865 plain edge	—	—	—	—	—	Proof	5500.
	1870	30,000	100.00	150.00	350.00	750.00	4500.	9500.
	1872H	40,000	15.00	25.00	60.00	165.00	1300.	2400.
	1873 flat 3	23,614	18.00	32.50	85.00	240.00	2400.	4000.
	1873 round 3	Inc. Ab.	18.00	32.50	85.00	240.00	2400.	4000.
	1876H	10,000	30.00	50.00	120.00	325.00	3000.	4800.
	1880/70	10,000	30.00	50.00	120.00	325.00	3000.	4800.
	1882H	20,000	15.00	30.00	65.00	165.00	1300.	2400.
	1882H	—	—	—	—	—	Proof	3400.
	1885	8,000	65.00	125.00	300.00	675.00	3200.	6000.
	1888	30,000	16.00	30.00	75.00	200.00	1800.	3300.
	1890	100,000	6.00	12.50	30.00	100.00	1100.	2000.
	1890	—	—	—	—	—	Proof	3200.
	1894	100,000	6.00	12.50	30.00	100.00	1000.	1750.
	1894	—	—	—	—	—	Proof	1750.
	1896	230,000	5.00	10.00	25.00	80.00	900.00	1600.
8	1903	100,000	5.00	10.00	30.00	90.00	1000.	1700.
	1904H	100,000	4.50	9.50	25.00	75.00	550.00	950.00
14	1912	150,000	2.25	5.00	12.50	45.00	550.00	950.00
	1917C	250,805	1.75	3.75	9.00	25.00	500.00	850.00
	1919C	54,342	3.00	6.00	15.00	50.00	375.00	600.00
20	1938	100,000	1.00	2.25	4.75	10.00	125.00	250.00
	1938	—	—	—	—	—	Proof	500.00
	1940	100,000	1.00	2.25	4.50	8.00	100.00	225.00
	1941C	483,630	1.00	1.75	3.25	6.75	30.00	85.00
	1942C	293,736	1.00	1.75	3.25	6.75	35.00	90.00
	1943C	104,706	1.00	1.75	3.25	6.75	50.00	100.00

2.3328 g, .800 SILVER, .0600 oz ASW

20a	1944C	151,471	1.00	1.75	3.75	7.50	75.00	175.00
	1945C	175,833	1.00	1.75	3.00	6.75	45.00	95.00
	1946C	38,400	4.00	6.50	12.50	25.00	175.00	325.00
	1947C	61,988	2.25	3.75	7.50	17.50	90.00	175.00

TWENTY CENTS

1865-1900 4.7127 g, .925 SILVER, .1401 oz ASW 1904-1912

KM#	Date	Mintage	VG-8	F-12	VF-20	XF-40	MS-60	MS-63
4	1865	100,000	10.00	15.00	40.00	165.00	1600.	2800.
	1865 plain edge	—	—	—	—	—	Proof	4500.
	1870	50,000	18.00	30.00	75.00	200.00	1750.	3600.
	1872H	90,000	10.00	17.00	35.00	130.00	1300.	2600.
	1873	45,797	12.50	22.50	60.00	165.00	1800.	3700.
	1876H	50,000	15.00	25.00	65.00	185.00	1900.	4000.
	1880/70	30,000	15.00	30.00	80.00	225.00	1900.	4000.
	1881	60,000	6.00	13.00	32.50	110.00	1100.	2200.
	1882H	100,000	5.00	10.00	25.00	100.00	1100.	2200.
	1882H	—	—	—	—	—	Proof	3700.
	1885	40,000	9.00	17.00	40.00	130.00	1600.	3200.
	1888	75,000	6.00	12.00	35.00	110.00	1200.	2400.
	1890	100,000	4.50	9.00	22.50	80.00	900.00	1800.
	1890	—	—	—	—	—	Proof	2750.
	1894	100,000	4.50	9.00	22.50	80.00	700.00	1600.
	1896 small 96	125,000	4.50	9.00	25.00	75.00	700.00	1600.
	1896 large 96	Inc. Ab.	6.00	12.00	32.50	100.00	1000.	2000.
	1899 small 99	125,000	6.00	12.00	32.50	100.00	1000.	2000.
	1899 large 99	Inc. Ab.	4.50	9.00	25.00	75.00	700.00	1600.
	1900	125,000	4.50	7.50	18.00	65.00	600.00	1400.
10	1904H	75,000	10.00	22.50	60.00	150.00	1000.	2400.
	1904H	—	—	—	—	—	Proof	3250.
15	1912	350,000	2.50	4.50	13.00	45.00	550.00	1200.

TWENTY-FIVE CENTS

5.8319 g, .925 SILVER, .1734 oz ASW

KM#	Date	Mintage	VG-8	F-12	VF-20	XF-40	MS-60	MS-63
17	1917C	464,779	2.25	3.75	7.50	15.00	125.00	280.00
	1919C	163,939	2.25	3.75	8.25	18.00	200.00	425.00

FIFTY CENTS

1870-1900   11.7818 g, .925 SILVER, .3504 oz ASW   1904-1919

KM#	Date	Mintage	VG-8	F-12	VF-20	XF-40	MS-60	MS-63
6	1870	50,000	12.00	18.00	55.00	185.00	2000.	4800.
	1870 plain edge	—	—	—	—	—	Proof	5500.
	1872H	48,000	12.00	18.00	55.00	185.00	1750.	4000.
	1873	37,675	15.00	22.50	55.00	200.00	2200.	5800.
	1874	80,000	12.00	18.00	50.00	190.00	2200.	5400.
	1876H	28,000	18.00	30.00	85.00	325.00	2800.	5600.
	1880	24,000	21.00	32.50	95.00	350.00	2800.	5600.
	1881	50,000	12.00	20.00	65.00	240.00	2200.	5400.
	1882H	100,000	10.00	17.00	45.00	185.00	1400.	3250.
	1882H	—	—	—	—	—	Proof	5500.
	1885	40,000	12.00	18.00	50.00	200.00	2200.	5400.
	1888	20,000	12.00	22.50	65.00	300.00	2400.	5800.
	1894	40,000	9.00	15.00	45.00	185.00	1800.	4200.
	1896	60,000	7.50	11.00	37.50	150.00	1600.	3200.
	1898	76,607	7.50	11.00	37.50	150.00	1600.	3200.
	1899 wide 9's	150,000	6.00	10.00	30.00	135.00	1600.	3200.
	1899 narrow 9's	Inc. Ab.	6.00	10.00	30.00	135.00	1600.	3200.
	1900	150,000	6.00	10.00	30.00	115.00	1500.	3000.
11	1904H	140,000	5.00	7.50	18.00	60.00	400.00	900.00
	1907	100,000	6.00	9.00	25.00	70.00	450.00	1100.
	1908	160,000	5.00	7.50	18.00	50.00	300.00	675.00
	1909	200,000	5.00	7.50	18.00	50.00	300.00	675.00
12	1911	200,000	4.00	7.50	18.00	50.00	400.00	800.00
	1917C	375,560	4.00	6.00	12.00	30.00	250.00	550.00
	1918C	294,824	4.00	6.00	12.00	30.00	300.00	600.00
	1919C	306,267	4.00	6.00	12.00	30.00	250.00	550.00

TWO DOLLARS

3.3284 g, .917 GOLD, .0981 oz AGW

KM#	Date	Mintage	F-12	VF-20	XF-40	AU-50	MS-60	MS-63
5	1865	10,000	175.00	225.00	350.00	650.00	1400.	3000.
	1865 plain edge	about 10 known	—	—	—	—	Proof	10,000.
	1870	10,000	175.00	225.00	350.00	675.00	1450.	3100.
	1870 plain edge	—	—	—	—	—	Proof	10,000.
	1872	6,050	225.00	350.00	500.00	950.00	2750.	5250.
	1880	2,500	1000.	1500.	2000.	2800.	6000.	10,000.
	1880	—	—	—	—	—	Proof	18,500.
	1881	10,000	120.00	180.00	225.00	340.00	800.00	1600.
	1882H	25,000	110.00	160.00	200.00	300.00	700.00	1450.
	1882H	—	—	—	—	—	Proof	6000.
	1885	10,000	120.00	190.00	235.00	350.00	800.00	1600.
	1888	25,000	110.00	160.00	200.00	300.00	700.00	1450.

NEW BRUNSWICK
HALF PENNY

COPPER

KM#	Date	Mintage	VG-8	F-12	VF-20	XF-40	MS-60	MS-63
1	1843	480,000	1.00	2.00	3.50	8.00	30.00	100.00
	1843	—	—	—	—	—	Proof	600.00

KM#	Date	Mintage	VG-8	F-12	VF-20	XF-40	MS-60	MS-63
3	1854	864,000	1.00	2.00	3.50	8.00	32.00	100.00

ONE PENNY

COPPER

KM#	Date	Mintage	VG-8	F-12	VF-20	XF-40	MS-60	MS-63
2	1843	480,000	1.50	2.50	4.50	9.00	50.00	120.00
	1843	—	—	—	—	—	Proof	450.00

KM#	Date	Mintage	VG-8	F-12	VF-20	XF-40	MS-60	MS-63
4	1854	432,000	1.50	2.50	4.50	9.00	55.00	120.00

DECIMAL COINAGE
HALF CENT

BRONZE

KM#	Date	Mintage	VG-8	F-12	VF-20	XF-40	MS-60	MS-63
5	1861	222,800	50.00	65.00	90.00	120.00	400.00	1200.
	1861	—	—	—	—	—	Proof	2000.

ONE CENT

BRONZE

KM#	Date	Mintage	VG-8	F-12	VF-20	XF-40	MS-60	MS-63
6	1861	1,000,000	1.75	2.50	4.50	9.00	70.00	225.00
	1861	—	—	—	—	—	Proof	450.00
	1864 short 6	1,000,000	1.75	2.50	4.50	9.00	70.00	225.00
	1864 long 6	Inc. Ab.	1.75	2.50	4.50	9.00	70.00	200.00

FIVE CENTS

1.1620 g, .925 SILVER, .0346 oz ASW

KM#	Date	Mintage	VG-8	F-12	VF-20	XF-40	MS-60	MS-63
7	1862	100,000	25.00	55.00	100.00	225.00	1450.	2400.
	1862	—	—	—	—	—	Proof	2000.
	1864 small 6	100,000	25.00	55.00	100.00	225.00	1500.	2500.
	1864 large 6	Inc. Ab.	25.00	55.00	100.00	225.00	1450.	2400.

TEN CENTS

2.3240 g, .925 SILVER, .0691 oz ASW

KM#	Date	Mintage	VG-8	F-12	VF-20	XF-40	MS-60	MS-63
8	1862	150,000	25.00	50.00	100.00	225.00	1250.	2200.
	1862 recut 2	Inc. Ab.	25.00	50.00	100.00	225.00	1250.	2200.
	1862	—	—	—	—	—	Proof	2000.
	1864	100,000	25.00	50.00	100.00	225.00	1250.	2200.

TWENTY CENTS

4.6480 g, .925 SILVER, .1382 oz ASW

KM#	Date	Mintage	VG-8	F-12	VF-20	XF-40	MS-60	MS-63
9	1862	150,000	12.50	20.00	40.00	165.00	1250.	2200.
	1862	—	—	—	—	—	Proof	2000.
	1864	150,000	12.50	20.00	40.00	165.00	1250.	2200.

NOVA SCOTIA STERLING COINAGE
HALF PENNY

COPPER

KM#	Date	Mintage	VG-8	F-12	VF-20	XF-40	MS-60	MS-63
1	1823	400,000	1.50	3.00	7.00	12.00	50.00	125.00
	1823 w/o hyphen	Inc. Ab.	5.00	10.00	18.00	24.00	100.00	300.00
	1824	118,636	2.00	4.00	10.00	17.50	75.00	175.00
	1832	800,000	1.00	2.50	6.00	10.00	40.00	125.00
1a	1382(error)	—	125.00	275.00	475.00	—	—	—
	1832/1382	—	500.00	700.00	—	—	—	—
	1832 (imitation)	—	3.25	5.00	8.00	12.50	50.00	100.00

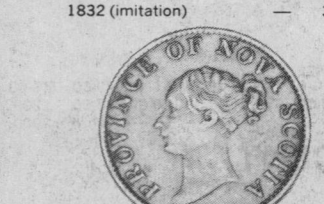

KM#	Date	Mintage	VG-8	F-12	VF-20	XF-40	MS-60	MS-63
3	1840 small 0	300,000	3.25	4.75	8.00	12.50	55.00	125.00
	1840 medium 0	Inc. Ab.	2.50	4.00	6.50	11.00	45.00	165.00
	1840 large 0	Inc. Ab.	4.00	5.50	10.00	16.00	52.50	175.00
	1843	300,000	2.00	3.00	5.00	10.00	40.00	125.00

KM#	Date	Mintage	VG-8	F-12	VF-20	XF-40	MS-60	MS-63
5	1856 w/o LCW	720,000	2.00	4.00	7.50	10.00	55.00	175.00
	1856 w/o LCW	—	—	—	—	—	Proof	600.00
	1856 w/o LCW, inverted A for V in PROVINCE	—	—	—	—	—	Proof	600.00

BRONZE

5a	1856 w/LCW	—	—	—	—	—	Proof	600.00

ONE PENNY

COPPER

KM#	Date	Mintage	VG-8	F-12	VF-20	XF-40	MS-60	MS-63
2	1824	217,776	2.50	5.00	8.00	17.50	75.00	200.00
	1832	200,000	1.50	3.50	6.00	12.50	60.00	180.00
2a	1832 (imitation)	—	5.50	16.00	24.00	40.00	—	—

KM#	Date	Mintage	VG-8	F-12	VF-20	XF-40	MS-60	MS-63
4	1840	150,000	1.50	3.50	6.00	12.50	60.00	175.00
	1843/0	150,000	8.00	11.00	16.00	26.00	70.00	—
	1843	Inc. Ab.	2.50	5.00	8.00	15.00	60.00	175.00

KM#	Date	Mintage	VG-8	F-12	VF-20	XF-40	MS-60	MS-63
6	1856 w/o LCW	360,000	2.00	4.00	8.00	11.00	50.00	125.00
	1856 w/LCW	Inc. Ab.	2.00	4.00	7.00	10.00	45.00	115.00

BRONZE

6a	1856	—	—	—	—	—	Proof	400.00

DECIMAL COINAGE
HALF CENT

BRONZE

KM#	Date	Mintage	VG-8	F-12	VF-20	XF-40	MS-60	MS-63
7	1861	400,000	3.00	5.00	8.00	12.50	45.00	110.00
	1864	400,000	3.00	5.00	8.00	12.50	45.00	110.00
	1864	—	—	—	—	—	Proof	300.00

ONE CENT

BRONZE

KM#	Date	Mintage	VG-8	F-12	VF-20	XF-40	MS-60	MS-63
8	1861	800,000	1.50	2.25	4.50	10.00	75.00	150.00
	1862	(Est.) 100,000	15.00	25.00	45.00	100.00	350.00	900.00
	1864	800,000	1.50	2.25	4.50	10.00	75.00	150.00

NOTE: The Royal Mint Report records mintage of 1,000,000 for 1862 which is considered incorrect.

PRINCE EDWARD ISLAND
ONE CENT

BRONZE

KM#	Date	Mintage	VG-8	F-12	VF-20	XF-40	MS-60	MS-63
4	1871	1,000,000	1.25	2.00	3.50	8.50	90.00	225.00
	1871	—	—	—	—	—	Proof	2000.

CAPE VERDE

The Republic of Cape Verde, Africa's smallest republic, is located in the Atlantic Ocean, about 370 miles (595 km.) west of Dakar, Senegal, off the coast of Africa. The 14-island republic has an area of 1,557 sq. mi. (4,033 sq. km.) and a population of 329,175. Capital: Praia. The refueling of ships and aircraft is the chief economic function of the country. Fishing is important and agriculture is widely practiced, but the Cape Verdes are not self-sufficient in food. Fish products, salt, bananas, and shellfish are exported.

The date of discovery of the islands is uncertain. Possibly they were visited by Venetian captain Alvise Cadamosto in 1456. Portuguese navigator Diogo Gomes claimed them for Portugal in May of 1460. Settlement began two years later. The early importance and wealth of the islands, which caused them to be attacked by Sir Francis Drake and the Dutch, resulted from the monopoly of the Guinea slave trade granted the inhabitants in 1466. Poverty and famine occasioned by frequent periods of severe drought have marked the history of the country since abolition of the slave trade in 1876.

After 500 years of Portuguese rule, the Cape Verdes became independent on July 5, 1975. At the first general election, all seats of the new national assembly were won by the Party for the Independence of Guinea-Bissau and Cape Verde (PAIGC). The PAIGC plans to link the two former colonies into one state.

RULERS
Portuguese, until 1975

MONETARY SYSTEM
100 Centavos = 1 Escudo

COLONIAL COINAGE
5 CENTAVOS

BRONZE

KM#	Date	Mintage	VF	XF	Unc
1	1930	1.000	1.00	2.25	5.00

10 CENTAVOS

BRONZE

| 2 | 1930 | 1.500 | 1.25 | 2.50 | 5.25 |

20 CENTAVOS

BRONZE

| 3 | 1930 | 1.500 | 1.50 | 3.00 | 6.00 |

50 CENTAVOS

NICKEL-BRONZE

| 4 | 1930 | 1.000 | 12.00 | 35.00 | 165.00 |

KM#	Date	Mintage	VF	XF	Unc
6	1949	1.000	.50	1.50	4.00

BRONZE

| 11 | 1968 | 1.000 | .35 | .75 | 1.50 |

ESCUDO

NICKEL-BRONZE

| 5 | 1930 | .050 | 20.00 | 50.00 | 200.00 |

| 7 | 1949 | .500 | 1.50 | 3.00 | 7.00 |

BRONZE

| 8 | 1953 | .250 | 1.25 | 2.50 | 5.00 |
| | 1968 | .500 | .75 | 1.25 | 3.00 |

2-1/2 ESCUDOS

NICKEL-BRONZE

| 9 | 1953 | .500 | .75 | 1.50 | 3.25 |
| | 1967 | .400 | .50 | 1.25 | 3.00 |

5 ESCUDOS

NICKEL-BRONZE

| 12 | 1968 | .200 | 1.00 | 2.00 | 4.00 |

10 ESCUDOS

5.0000 g, .720 SILVER, .1158 oz ASW

KM#	Date	Mintage	VF	XF	Unc
10	1953	.400	2.50	4.00	8.00

REPUBLIC
20 CENTAVOS

ALUMINUM

| 15 | 1977 | — | .25 | .40 | .60 |

50 CENTAVOS

ALUMINUM

| 16 | 1977 | — | .35 | .75 | 1.00 |

ESCUDO

NICKEL-BRONZE
F.A.O. Issue

| 17 | 1977 | 1.000 | .50 | 1.00 | 2.00 |
| | 1980 | — | .50 | .75 | 1.25 |

BRASS
10th Anniversary of Independence

| 23 | 1985 | — | — | — | 2.00 |

SILVER

| 23a | 1985 | — | — | Proof | — |

GOLD

| 23b | 1985 | 50 pcs. | — | Proof | — |

2-1/2 ESCUDOS

NICKEL-BRONZE
F.A.O. Issue

| 18 | 1977 | 1.200 | .50 | 1.25 | 2.00 |
| | 1982 | — | .50 | .75 | 1.25 |

CAPE VERDE 272

10 ESCUDOS

COPPER-NICKEL

KM#	Date	Mintage	VF	XF	Unc
19	1977	—	.50	1.00	2.00
	1982	—	.50	.75	1.25

10th Anniversary of Independence

24	1985	—	—	—	2.00
		SILVER			
24a	1985	—	—	Proof	—
		GOLD			
24b	1985	50 pcs.	—	Proof	—

20 ESCUDOS

COPPER-NICKEL

20	1977	—	1.00	2.00	3.00
	1982	—	.75	1.50	2.00

50 ESCUDOS

COPPER-NICKEL

21	1977	—	1.00	2.50	5.00

F.A.O. World Fisheries Conference

KM#	Date	Mintage	VF	XF	Unc
22	1984	*.115	—	—	5.00

16.0000 g, .925 SILVER, .4759 oz ASW

22a	1984	*.020	—	Proof	35.00

27.0000 g, GOLD

22b	1984	*100 pcs.	—	Proof	1500.

250 ESCUDOS

16.4000 g, .900 SILVER, .4745 oz ASW
1st Anniversary of Independence

13	1976	.013	—	—	17.50
	1976	3,525	—	Proof	45.00

2500 ESCUDOS

8.0000 g, .900 GOLD, .2315 oz AGW
1st Anniversary of Independence

14	1976	3,409	—	Proof	145.00

CAYMAN ISLANDS

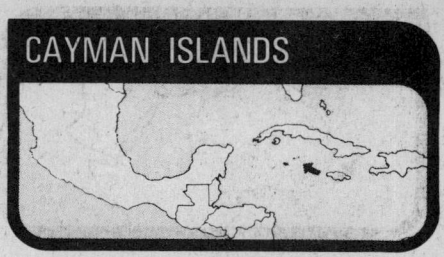

The Cayman Islands, a British dependency situated about 180 miles (290 km.) northwest of Jamaica, consists of three islands: Grand Cayman, Little Cayman, and Cayman Brac. The islands have an area of 100 sq. mi. (259 sq. km.) and a population of 10,419. Capital: Georgetown. Seafaring, commerce, banking, and tourism are the principal industries. Rope, turtle shells, and shark skins are exported.

The islands were discovered by Columbus in 1503, and named by him Tortugas (Spanish for 'turtles') because of the great number of turtles in the nearby waters. They were colonized from Jamaica by the British and remained dependencies of Jamaica until 1959, when they became a unit territory within the West Indies Federation. They became a separate colony when the Federation was dissolved in 1962. Since 1972 a form of self-government has existed, with the Governor responsible for defense and certain other affairs.

Cayman issued its first national coinage in 1972. The $25 gold and silver commemorative coins issued in 1972 to celebrate the silver wedding anniversary of Queen Elizabeth II and Prince Philip are the first coins in 300 years of Commonwealth coinage to portray a member of the British royal family other than the reigning monarch.

RULERS
British

MINT MARKS
FM - Franklin Mint, U.S.A.*

MONETARY SYSTEM
100 Cents = 1 Dollar

CENT

BRONZE

KM#	Date	Mintage	VF	XF	Unc
1	1972	2.155	—	.10	.25
	1972	.011	—	Proof	.50
	1973	9.988	—	Proof	.50
	1974	.030	—	Proof	.50
	1975	7,175	—	Proof	.50
	1976	3,044	—	Proof	.50
	1977	1.200	—	.10	.25
	1977FM	1,970	—	Proof	1.00
	1979FM	4,247	—	Proof	.50
	1980FM	1,215	—	Proof	1.25
	1981FM	865 pcs.	—	Proof	1.50
	1982FM	589 pcs.	—	Proof	1.50
	1982	—	—	.10	.25
	1983FM	—	—	Proof	1.50
	1984FM	—	—	Proof	1.50
	1986	1,000	—	Proof	1.50

25th Anniversary of Coronation

26	1978	.600	—	.10	.25
	1978	1,303	—	Proof	2.00

87	1987	*500 pcs.	—	Proof	3.00
	1988	*500 pcs.	—	Proof	3.00

5 CENTS

COPPER-NICKEL

2	1972	.300	—	.10	.25
	1972	.012	—	Proof	.50
	1973	.200	—	.10	.25
	1973	9.988	—	Proof	.50
	1974	.030	—	Proof	.50

KM#	Date	Mintage	VF	XF	Unc
2	1975	7,175	—	Proof	.50
	1976	3,044	—	Proof	.50
	1977	.400	—	.10	.20
	1977	1,980	—	Proof	.50
	1979FM	4,247	—	Proof	.50
	1980FM	—	—	Proof	2.00
	1981FM	—	—	Proof	2.50
	1982	—	—	.10	.20
	1982FM	—	—	Proof	2.50
	1983FM	—	—	Proof	2.50
	1984FM	—	—	Proof	2.50
	1986	1,000	—	Proof	2.50

NOTE: 1973 Uncs. were not released to circulation.

25th Anniversary of Coronation
Rev: Similar to KM#2.

27	1978	.200	—	.10	.25
	1978	1,303	—	Proof	3.00

88	1987	*500 pcs.	—	Proof	4.50
	1988	*500 pcs.	—	Proof	4.50

10 CENTS

COPPER-NICKEL

3	1972	.550	.15	.20	.50
	1972	.011	—	Proof	.75
	1973	.200	.15	.20	.50
	1973	9,988	—	Proof	.75
	1974	.030	—	Proof	.75
	1975	7,175	—	Proof	.75
	1976	3,044	—	Proof	.75
	1977	.560	.15	.20	.50
	1977	1,980	—	Proof	.75
	1979FM	4,247	—	Proof	.75
	1980FM	1,215	—	Proof	3.00
	1981FM	865 pcs.	—	Proof	3.00
	1982	—	.15	.20	.50
	1982FM	589 pcs.	—	Proof	3.00
	1983FM	—	—	Proof	3.00
	1984FM	—	—	Proof	3.00
	1986	1,000	—	Proof	3.00

NOTE: 1973 Uncs. were not released to circulation.

25th Anniversary of Coronation

28	1978	.400	.15	.20	.60
	1978	1,304	—	Proof	3.50

89	1987	*500 pcs.	—	Proof	5.00
	1988	*500 pcs.	—	Proof	5.00

25 CENTS

COPPER-NICKEL

4	1972	.350	.30	.50	1.00
	1972	.011	—	Proof	1.00
	1973	.100	.30	.50	1.00
	1973	9,988	—	Proof	1.00
	1974	.030	—	Proof	1.00
	1975	7,175	—	Proof	1.00

KM#	Date	Mintage	VF	XF	Unc
4	1976	3,044	—	Proof	1.00
	1977	.320	.30	.50	1.00
	1977	1,980	—	Proof	1.00
	1979FM	4,247	—	Proof	1.00
	1980FM	1,215	—	Proof	3.50
	1981FM	865 pcs.	—	Proof	4.00
	1982	—	—	.30	.50
	1982FM	589 pcs.	—	Proof	4.00
	1983FM	—	—	Proof	4.00
	1984FM	—	—	Proof	4.00
	1986	1,000	—	Proof	4.00

NOTE: 1973 Uncs. were not released to circulation.

25th Anniversary of Coronation
Rev: Similar to KM#4.

29	1978	.200	.35	.60	1.25
	1978	1,303	—	Proof	4.00

90	1987	*500 pcs.	—	Proof	6.00
	1988	*500 pcs.	—	Proof	6.00

50 CENTS

10.3000 g, .925 SILVER, .3063 oz ASW

5	1972	500 pcs.	—	—	12.50
	1972	.011	—	Proof	3.00
	1973	9,988	—	Proof	3.00
	1974	.030	—	Proof	3.00
	1975	7,175	—	Proof	3.00
	1976	3,044	—	Proof	4.00
	1977	1,980	—	Proof	4.00
	1979FM	4,247	—	Proof	4.00
	1980FM	1,215	—	Proof	5.00
	1981FM	865 pcs.	—	Proof	6.00
	1982FM	589 pcs.	—	Proof	6.00

25th Anniversary of Coronation

30	1978	2,169	—	Proof	8.00

Obv: Similar to KM#5.

73	1983FM	—	—	Proof	9.00
	1984FM	411 pcs.	—	Proof	9.00
	1986	1,000	—	Proof	9.00

Obv: Similar to 5 Dollars, KM#81.

91	1987	*500 pcs.	—	Proof	13.50
	1988	*500 pcs.	—	Proof	13.50

DOLLAR

18.0000 g, .925 SILVER, .5353 oz ASW

KM#	Date	Mintage	VF	XF	Unc
6	1972	500 pcs.	—	—	15.00
	1972	.011	—	Proof	6.00
	1973	9,988	—	Proof	6.00
	1974	.030	—	Proof	6.00
	1975	7,175	—	Proof	6.00
	1976	3,044	—	Proof	6.50
	1977	1,980	—	Proof	6.50
	1979FM	4,247	—	Proof	6.50
	1980FM	1,215	—	Proof	10.00
	1981FM	865 pcs.	—	Proof	12.00
	1982FM	589 pcs.	—	Proof	12.00

25th Anniversary of Coronation

31	1978	2,168	—	Proof	12.50

Obv: Similar to 50 Cents, KM#5.

74	1983FM	1,686	—	Proof	12.50
	1984FM	—	—	Proof	12.50
	1986	1,000	—	Proof	12.50

Obv: Similar to 5 Dollars, KM#81.

92	1987	*500 pcs.	—	Proof	20.00
	1988	*500 pcs.	—	Proof	20.00

2 DOLLARS

29.4500 g, .925 SILVER, .8758 oz ASW
Obv: Similar to 50 Cents, KM#5.

7	1972	500 pcs.	—	—	20.00
	1972	.011	—	Proof	9.00
	1973	9,988	—	Proof	9.00
	1974	.030	—	Proof	9.00
	1975	5,390	—	Proof	10.00
	1976	3,044	—	Proof	12.50
	1977	1,980	—	Proof	12.50
	1979FM	4,247	—	Proof	12.50
	1980FM	1,215	—	Proof	20.00
	1981FM	865 pcs.	—	Proof	22.50
	1982FM	589 pcs.	—	Proof	22.50
	1986	1,000	—	Proof	20.00

CAYMAN ISLANDS 274

25th Anniversary of Coronation
Rev: Similar to KM#7.

KM#	Date	Mintage	VF	XF	Unc
32	1978	2,169	—	Proof	22.50

150th Anniversary of Parliamentary Government
Obv: Similar to 50 Cents, KM#5.

KM#	Date	Mintage	VF	XF	Unc
70	1982FM	1,105	—	Proof	30.00

Queen Elizabeth II and Philip's 40th Wedding Anniversary

KM#	Date	Mintage	VF	XF	Unc
85	ND(1987)	*2,000	—	Proof	40.00

35.6400 g, .925 SILVER, 1.0560 oz ASW, 42mm
| 85a | ND(1987) | *500 pcs. | — | Proof | 120.00 |

Obv: Similar to 50 Cents, KM#5.
| 75 | 1983FM | 409 pcs. | — | Proof | 30.00 |
| | 1984FM | — | — | Proof | 25.00 |

Obv: Similar to 5 Dollars, KM#81. Rev: Similar to KM#7.
| 93 | 1987 | *500 pcs. | — | Proof | 30.00 |
| | 1988 | *500 pcs. | — | Proof | 30.00 |

5 DOLLARS

35.5000 g, .925 SILVER, 1.0557 oz ASW
Obv: Similar to 50 Cents, KM#5.
8	1972	500 pcs.	—	—	35.00
	1972	.011	—	Proof	11.00
	1973	.017	—	Proof	11.00
	1974	.026	—	Proof	11.00
	1975	7,753	—	Proof	12.00
	1976	5,177	—	Proof	12.00
	1977	3,525	—	Proof	12.00
	1979FM	—	—	Proof	18.00
	1980FM	—	—	Proof	20.00
	1981FM	—	—	Proof	22.00
	1984FM	—	—	Proof	22.00
	1986	1,000	—	Proof	22.00

25th Anniversary of Coronation
Rev: Similar to KM#8.
| 33 | 1978 | 2,168 | — | Proof | 27.50 |

Queen's Royal Visit
| 76 | 1983FM | 419 pcs. | — | Proof | 35.00 |

28.2800 g, .500 SILVER, .4547 oz ASW
Commonwealth Games
Obv: Similar to KM#81.
| 80 | 1986 | *.050 | — | — | 12.50 |

28.2800 g, .925 SILVER, .8411 oz ASW
| 80a | 1986 | *.020 | — | Proof | 15.00 |

250th Anniversary of Royal Land Grant
| 81 | 1985 | *1,000 | — | Proof | 35.00 |

Seoul Olympics
| 94 | 1988 | .020 | — | Proof | 15.00 |

35.6400 g, .925 SILVER, 1.0560 oz ASW
| 94a | 1988 | *500 pcs. | — | Proof | 120.00 |

28.2800 g, .925 SILVER, .8411 oz ASW
World Wildlife Fund - Cuban Amazon
| 95 | 1987 | — | — | Proof | 45.00 |

500th Anniversary of Columbus' Discovery of America
| 96 | 1988 | *.010 | — | Proof | 45.00 |

10 DOLLARS

28.2800 g, .925 SILVER, .8411 oz ASW
Wedding of Prince Charles and Lady Diana
| 68 | 1981 | .040 | — | Proof | 20.00 |

CAYMAN ISLANDS 275

27.8900 g, .925 SILVER, .8295 oz ASW
International Year of the Child
Obv: Similar to 50 Cents, KM#5.

KM#	Date	Mintage	VF	XF	Unc
72	1982	6,616	—	Proof	25.00

23.4500 g, .925 SILVER, .6975 oz ASW
Queen's Royal Visit
Obv: Similar to 50 Cents, KM#5.

| 77 | 1983FM | .010 | — | Proof | 40.00 |

25 DOLLARS

51.3500 g, .925 SILVER, 1.5271 oz ASW
Silver Wedding Anniversary
Obv: Similar to KM#9a.

| 9 | 1972 | .186 | — | — | 30.00 |
| | 1972 | .026 | — | Proof | 32.50 |

15.7500 g, .500 GOLD, .2532 oz AGW
Silver Wedding Anniversary

| 9a | 1972 | 7,706 | — | — | 125.00 |
| | 1972 | .021 | — | Proof | 150.00 |

51.3500 g, .925 SILVER, 1.5271 oz ASW
Churchill Centenary

KM#	Date	Mintage	VF	XF	Unc
10	1974	1,200	—	—	35.00
	1974	.012	—	Proof	32.50

NOTE: 4300 sets were issued in proof containing KM#10 and Turks & Caicos Islands 20 Crowns KM#2 with an issue price of $80.00.

Queen's Silver Jubilee
Obv: Similar to KM#9a.

| 14 | 1977 | 3,600 | — | — | 40.00 |
| | 1977 | 7,854 | — | Proof | 40.00 |

Queen Mary I
Obv: Similar to KM#9a.

| 16 | 1977 | 2,720 | — | Proof | 40.00 |

Queen Elizabeth I
Obv: Similar to KM#9a.

| 17 | 1977 | 2,677 | — | Proof | 40.00 |

Queen Mary II
Obv: Similar to KM#9a.

KM#	Date	Mintage	VF	XF	Unc
18	1977	2,653	—	Proof	40.00

Queen Anne
Obv: Similar to KM#9a.

| 19 | 1977 | 2,630 | — | Proof | 40.00 |

Queen Victoria
Obv: Similar to KM#9a.

| 20 | 1977 | 2,623 | — | Proof | 40.00 |

25th Anniversary of Coronation
Obv: Similar to KM#9a. Rev: Ampulla.

| 36 | 1978 | 5,000 | — | Proof | 35.00 |

CAYMAN ISLANDS

25th Anniversary of Coronation
Obv: Similar to KM#9a. Rev: Orb.

KM#	Date	Mintage	VF	XF	Unc
37	1978	5,000	—	Proof	35.00

House of Plantagenet - I
Obv: Similar to KM#9a.

KM#	Date	Mintage	VF	XF	Unc
50	1980	.012	—	Proof	32.50

House of Tudor
Obv: Similar to KM#9a.

KM#	Date	Mintage	VF	XF	Unc
54	1980	.012	—	Proof	32.50

25th Anniversary of Coronation
Obv: Similar to KM#9a. Rev: St. Edward's crown.

38	1978	5,000	—	Proof	35.00

25th Anniversary of Coronation
Obv: Similar to KM#9a. Rev: Coronation chair.

39	1978	5,000	—	Proof	35.00

25th Anniversary of Coronation
Obv: Similar to KM#9a. Rev: Royal scepter.

40	1978	5,000	—	Proof	35.00

25th Anniversary of Coronation
Obv: Similar to KM#9a. Rev: Spoon.

41	1978	5,000	—	Proof	35.00

House of Plantagenet - II.
Obv: Similar to KM#9a.

51	1980	.012	—	Proof	32.50

House of Stuart & Orange
Obv: Similar to KM#9a.

55	1980	.012	—	Proof	32.50

35.6400 g, .500 SILVER, .5729 oz ASW
Saxon Kings
Obv: Similar to KM#9a.

48	1980	.012	—	Proof	32.50

House of Lancaster.
Obv: Similar to KM#9a.

52	1980	.012	—	Proof	32.50

House of Hanover
Obv: Similar to KM#9a.

56	1980	.012	—	Proof	32.50

House of Normandy
Obv: Similar to KM#9a.

49	1980	.012	—	Proof	32.50

House of York.
Obv: Similar to KM#9a.

53	1980	.012	—	Proof	32.50

House of Saxe-Coburg and Windsor.
Obv: Similar to KM#9a.

57	1980	.012	—	Proof	32.50

CAYMAN ISLANDS 277

64.8000 g, .925 SILVER, 1.9273 oz ASW
Queen's Royal Visit
Obv: Similar to 50 Cents, KM#5.

KM#	Date	Mintage	VF	XF	Unc
78	1983FM	5,000	—	Proof	45.00

50 DOLLARS

64.9400 g, .925 SILVER, 1.9314 oz ASW
Sovereign Queens of England
Obv: Similar to KM#21.

12	1975	.033	—	—	60.00
	1975	7,800	—	Proof	65.00
	1976	1,292	—	—	65.00
	1976	2,843	—	Proof	65.00
	1977	2,400	—	—	65.00
	1977	Inc. Ab.	—	Proof	65.00

Rev: Coronation Anniversary legend added.
| 34 | 1978 | 5,775 | — | Proof | 70.00 |

11.3400 g, .500 GOLD, .1823 oz AGW
Queen Mary I
| 21 | 1977 | 1,999 | — | Proof | 180.00 |

Queen Elizabeth I
| 22 | 1977 | 1,969 | — | Proof | 180.00 |

Queen Mary II
| 23 | 1977 | 1,961 | — | Proof | 180.00 |

Queen Anne
KM#	Date	Mintage	VF	XF	Unc
24	1977	1,938	—	Proof	180.00

Queen Victoria
| 25 | 1977 | 1,932 | — | Proof | 180.00 |

25th Anniversary of Coronation
Obv: Similar to KM#21. Rev: Ampulla.
| 42 | 1978 | 771 pcs. | — | Proof | 180.00 |

25th Anniversary of Coronation
Obv: Similar to KM#21. Rev: Orb.
| 43 | 1978 | 771 pcs. | — | Proof | 180.00 |

25th Anniversary of Coronation
Obv: Similar to KM#21. Rev: St. Edward's crown.
| 44 | 1978 | 771 pcs. | — | Proof | 180.00 |

25th Anniversary of Coronation
Obv: Similar to KM#21. Rev: Chair.
| 45 | 1978 | 771 pcs. | — | Proof | 180.00 |

25th Anniversary of Coronation
Obv: Similar to KM#21. Rev: Scepter.
| 46 | 1978 | 771 pcs. | — | Proof | 180.00 |

25th Anniversary of Coronation
Obv: Similar to KM#21. Rev: Spoon.
| 47 | 1978 | 771 pcs. | — | Proof | 180.00 |

Saxon Kings
Obv: Similar to KM#21.
| 58 | 1980 | .010 | — | Proof | 200.00 |

House of Normandy
Obv: Similar to KM#21.

KM#	Date	Mintage	VF	XF	Unc
59	1980	.010	—	Proof	200.00

House of Plantagenet - I
Obv: Similar to KM#21.
| 60 | 1980 | .011 | — | Proof | 200.00 |

House of Plantagenet - II
Obv: Similar to KM#21.
| 61 | 1980 | .011 | — | Proof | 200.00 |

House of Lancaster
Obv: Similar to KM#21.
| 62 | 1980 | .011 | — | Proof | 200.00 |

House of York
Obv: Similar to KM#21.
| 63 | 1980 | .011 | — | Proof | 200.00 |

House of Tudor
Obv: Similar to KM#21.
| 64 | 1980 | .011 | — | Proof | 200.00 |

House of Stuart and Orange
Obv: Similar to KM#21.
| 65 | 1980 | .011 | — | Proof | 200.00 |

CAYMAN ISLANDS 278

House of Hanover
Obv: Similar to KM#21.

KM#	Date	Mintage	VF	XF	Unc
66	1980	.011	—	Proof	200.00

House of Saxe-Coburg and Windsor
Obv: Similar to KM#21.

| 67 | 1980 | .011 | — | Proof | 200.00 |

5.0000 g, .900 GOLD, .1447 oz AGW
150th Anniversary of Parliamentary Government

| 71 | 1982FM | 585 pcs. | — | Proof | 125.00 |

5.1900 g, .917 GOLD, .1530 oz AGW
Obv: Similar to KM#71.
Rev: Similar to 25 Dollars, KM#78.

| 79 | 1983 | 5,000 | — | Proof | 125.00 |

129.6000 g, .925 SILVER, 3.8547 oz ASW
Bird Conservation - Snowy Egret

| 83 | 1985 | *.010 | — | Proof | 75.00 |

100 DOLLARS

22.6801 g, .500 GOLD, .3646 oz AGW
Churchill Centenary

KM#	Date	Mintage	VF	XF	Unc
11	1974	1,400	—	—	180.00
	1974	6,300	—	Proof	200.00

Sovereign Queens of England
Obv: Similar to 50 Dollars, KM#21.

13	1975	8,053	—	—	200.00
	1975	4,950	—	Proof	250.00
	1976	2,028	—	—	200.00
	1976	3,560	—	Proof	250.00
	1977	—	—	—	200.00
	1977	2,845	—	Proof	250.00

Queen's Silver Jubilee

| 15 | 1977 | 562 pcs. | — | — | 200.00 |
| | 1977 | 4,386 | — | Proof | 225.00 |

Rev: Coronation Anniversary legend.

| 35 | 1978 | 1,973 | — | Proof | 225.00 |

8.0352 g, .917 GOLD, .2369 oz AGW
Wedding of Prince Charles and Lady Diana

| 69 | 1981 | .011 | — | Proof | 175.00 |

15.9800 g, .917 GOLD, .4708 oz AGW
500th Anniversary of Columbus' Discovery of America

| 97 | 1988 | *500 pcs. | — | Proof | 500.00 |

250 DOLLARS

47.5400 g, .917 GOLD, 1.4001 oz AGW

250th Anniversary of Royal Land Grant
Similar to 5 Dollars, KM#81.

KM#	Date	Mintage	VF	XF	Unc
82	1985	*250 pcs.	—	Proof	1200.

Commonwealth Games
Similar to 5 Dollars, KM#80.

| 84 | 1986 | *150 pcs. | — | Proof | 1400. |

Queen Elizabeth II and Philip's 40th Wedding Anniversary
Rev: Similar to 5 Dollars, KM#85.

| 86 | ND(1987) | 75 pcs. | — | Proof | 1500. |

PROOF SETS (PS)

KM#	Date	Mintage	Identification	Issue Price	Mkt. Val.
PS1	1972(8)	10,757	KM1-8	40.00	28.00
PS2	1973(8)	9,988	KM1-8	40.00	28.00
PS3	1974(8)	15,387	KM1-8	40.00	28.00
PS4	1974(2)	2,400	KM10-11	245.00	200.00
PS5	1975(8)	5,390	KM1-8	54.50	25.00
PS6	1975(6)	1,785	KM1-6	31.50	10.00
PS7	1975(2)	3,650	KM12,13	293.00	235.00
PS8	1976(8)	3,044	KM1-8	54.50	30.00
PS9	1976(2)	1,531	KM12,13	293.00	265.00
PS11	1977(8)	1,970	KM1-8	52.50	35.00
PS12	1977(8)	2,445	KM12,16-20	315.00	265.00
PS13	1977(6)	1,932	KM13,21-25	651.00	700.00
PS14	1977(2)	223	KM14,15	290.00	210.00
PS15	1978(6)	1,303	KM26-33	79.50	80.00
PS16	1978(6)	5,000	KM36-41	306.00	210.00
PS17	1978(6)	771	KM42-47	600.00	750.00
PS18	1979(8)	4,247	KM1-8	117.00	50.00
PS19	1980(8)	1,215	KM1-8	147.00	65.00
PS20	1981(8)	865	KM1-8	147.00	75.00
PS21	1982(8)	589	KM1-7,70	147.00	75.00
PS22	1983(8)	348	KM1-4,73-76	157.00	75.00
PS23	1984(8)	—	KM1-4,8,73-75	159.00	80.00
PS24	1986(8)	*1,000	KM1-4,7-8,73-74	150.00	75.00
PS25	1987(8)	*500	KM85a,87-93	160.00	200.00
PS26	1988(8)	*500	KM87-93,94a	170.00	200.00

CENTRAL AFRICAN REP.

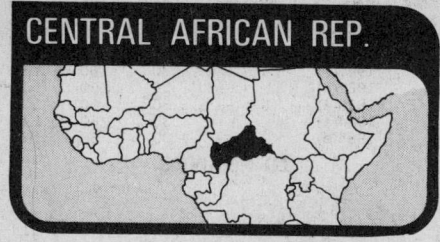

The Central African Republic, a landlocked country in Central Africa, bounded by Chad on the north, Cameroon on the west, Congo (Brazzaville) and Zaire on the south, and The Sudan on the east, has an area of 240,535 sq. mi. (622,984 sq. km.) and a population of 2.5 million. Capital: Bangui. Deposits of uranium, iron ore, manganese and copper remain to be developed. Diamonds, cotton, timber and coffee are exported.

The area that is now the Central African Republic was constituted as the French territory of Ubangi-Shari in 1894. It was united with Chad in 1905 and joined with Middle Congo and Gabon in 1910, becoming one of the four territories of French Equatorial Africa. Upon dissolution of the federation on Dec. 1, 1958, the constituent territories became fully autonomous members of the French Community. Ubangi-Shari proclaimed its complete independence as the Central African Republic on Aug. 13, 1960.

On Jan. 1, 1966, Col. Jean-Bedel Bokassa, Chief of Staff of the Armed Forces, overthrew the government of President David Dacko and assumed power as president of the republic. President Bokassa abolished the constitution of 1959 and dissolved the National Assembly. In 1975 the Congress of the sole political party appointed Bokassa president for life. The republic became a constitutional monarchy on Dec. 4, 1976; President Bokassa was named Emperor Bokassa I. Bokassa was ousted as Central African emperor in a bloodless takeover of the government led by former president David Dacko on Sept. 20, 1979, and the African nation proclaimed once again a republic.

NOTE: Also see French Equatorial Africa and Equatorial African States.

RULERS
French, until 1960
Marshal Jean-Bedel Bokassa, 1976-1979

MINT MARKS
(a) - Paris, privy marks only

MONETARY SYSTEM
100 Centimes = 1 Franc

100 FRANCS

NICKEL

KM#	Date	Mintage	Fine	VF	XF	Unc
6	1971(a)	3.500	4.50	7.00	12.00	27.50
	1972(a)	—	4.50	7.00	12.00	27.50
	1974(a)	—	4.50	7.00	12.00	27.50

7	1975(a)	—	2.50	6.50	10.00	15.00
	1976(a)	—	1.50	2.50	4.00	7.50
	1979(a)	—	2.50	6.50	10.00	15.00
	1983(a)	—	1.00	1.50	3.00	5.00

Obv. leg: EMPIRE CENTRAFRICAIN

8	1978(a)	—	—	50.00	75.00	125.00

NOTE: Not released for circulation.

500 FRANCS

COPPER-NICKEL

KM#	Date	Mintage	Fine	VF	XF	Unc
11	1985	—	2.00	3.00	4.50	6.50

1000 FRANCS

3.5000 g, .900 GOLD, .1012 oz AGW
10th Anniversary of Independence
Obv: Bust of Pres. Jean Bedel Bokasso.

| 1 | 1970 | 4,000 | — | — | Proof | 85.00 |

3000 FRANCS

10.5000 g, .900 GOLD, .3038 oz AGW
10th Anniversary of Independence

| 2 | 1970 | 4,000 | — | — | Proof | 200.00 |

5000 FRANCS

17.5000 g, .900 GOLD, .5064 oz AGW
10th Anniversary of Independence
Obv: Similar to 3000 Francs, KM#2.

| 3 | 1970 | 4,000 | — | — | Proof | 325.00 |

10,000 FRANCS

35.0000 g, .900 GOLD, 1.0128 oz AGW
10th Anniversary of Independence
Obv: Similar to 3000 Francs, KM#2.

| 4 | 1970 | 4,000 | — | — | Proof | 650.00 |

20,000 FRANCS

70.0000 g, .900 GOLD, 2.0257 oz AGW
10th Anniversary of Independence

KM#	Date	Mintage	Fine	VF	XF	Unc
5	1970	4,000	—	—	Proof	1200.

PROOF SETS (PS)

KM#	Date	Mintage	Identification	Issue Price	Mkt. Val.
PS1	1970(5)	4,000	KM1-5	375.00	2460.

CENTRAL AFRICAN STATES

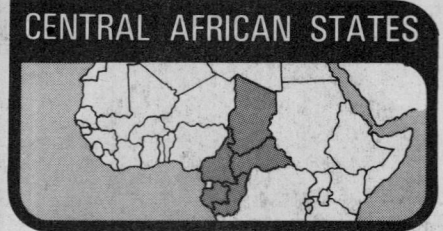

The Central African States, a monetary union comprising the former French possessions and now independent states of the Republic of Congo (Brazzaville), Gabon, Central African Republic, Chad and Cameroon, issues a common currency for the member states from a common central bank. The monetary unit, the African Financial Community Franc, is tied to and supported by the French franc.

In 1960, an abortive attempt was made to form a union of the newly independent republics of Chad, Congo, Central Africa and Gabon. The proposal was discarded when Chad refused to become a constituent member. The four countries then linked into an Equatorial Customs Unit, to which Cameroon became an associate member in 1961. A more extensive cooperation of the five republics, identified as the Central African Customs and Economic Union, was entered into force at the beginning of 1966.

In 1974 the Central Bank of the Equatorial African States, which had issued coins and paper currency in its own name and with the names of the constituent member nations, changed its name to the Bank of the Central African States.

For earlier coinage see French Equatorial Africa.

EQUATORIAL AFRICAN STATES

MINT MARKS
(a) - Paris, privy marks only

MONETARY SYSTEM
100 Centimes = 1 Franc (C.F.A.)

FRANC

ALUMINUM

KM#	Date	Mintage	Fine	VF	XF	Unc
6	1969(a)	2.500	.20	.50	.75	1.25
	1971(a)	3.000	.20	.50	.75	1.25

5 FRANCS

ALUMINUM-BRONZE

1	1961(a)	10.000	.35	1.00	1.50	2.50
	1962(a)	5.000	.35	1.00	1.50	2.50
	1965(a)	2.010	.35	1.00	1.50	2.50
	1967(a)	5.795	.35	1.00	1.25	2.00
	1968(a)	5.000	.35	1.00	1.25	2.00
	1969(a)	—	.35	1.00	1.25	2.00
	1970(a)	9.000	.35	1.00	1.25	2.00
	1972(a)	31.010	.35	1.00	1.25	2.00
	1973(a)	5.010	.35	1.00	1.25	2.00

10 FRANCS

ALUMINUM-BRONZE

2	1961(a)	10.000	.40	1.00	1.75	3.00
	1962(a)	5.000	.40	1.00	1.75	3.00
	1965(a)	7.000	1.00	1.75	2.75	5.00
	1967(a)	8.000	.40	1.00	1.75	3.00
	1968(a)	2.000	1.50	2.25	3.50	6.00
	1969(a)	10.000	.40	1.00	1.75	3.00
	1972(a)	23.500	.40	1.00	1.75	3.00
	1973(a)	5.000	.75	1.50	2.50	4.50

25 FRANCS

ALUMINUM-BRONZE

KM#	Date	Mintage	Fine	VF	XF	Unc
4	1962(a)	6.000	.50	1.25	2.25	4.00
	1968(a)	—	1.25	2.50	4.00	7.50
	1969(a)	—	1.25	2.50	4.00	7.50
	1970(a)	3.019	.50	1.25	2.25	4.00
	1972(a)	18.516	.50	1.25	2.00	3.00
	1973(a)	—	1.25	2.50	4.00	7.50

50 FRANCS

COPPER-NICKEL

3	1961(a)	5.000	3.00	5.00	7.50	12.00
	1963(a)	5.000	3.00	5.00	7.50	12.00

100 FRANCS

NICKEL

5	1966(a)	9.948	2.00	5.00	7.50	12.00
	1967(a)	11.000	2.00	5.00	7.50	12.00
	1968(a)	—	2.00	5.00	7.50	12.00

NOTE: For later 100-Francs issues see individual listings under Central African Republic, Congo Peoples' Republic, Gabon, Chad, Cameroun and Equatorial Guinea.

CENTRAL AFRICAN STATES

COUNTRY CODE LETTERS
The country in which the coin is intended to circulate in is designated by the following additional code letters.
- A = Chad
- B = Central African Republic
- C = Congo
- D = Gabon
- E = Cameroon

FRANC

ALUMINUM

KM#	Date	Mintage	VF	XF	Unc
8	1974(a)	—	.60	1.00	3.00
	1976(a)	—	.60	1.00	3.00
	1978(a)	—	.40	.80	2.50
	1979(a)	—	.40	.80	2.50
	1982(a)	—	.40	.80	2.50

5 FRANCS

ALUMINUM-BRONZE

7	1973(a)	—	.30	.60	1.75
	1975(a)	—	.30	.60	1.75
	1976(a)	—	.30	.60	1.75
	1977(a)	—	.30	.60	1.75

KM#	Date	Mintage	VF	XF	Unc
7	1978(a)	—	.30	.60	1.75
	1979(a)	—	.30	.60	1.50
	1980(a)	—	.30	.60	1.50
	1981(a)	—	.30	.60	1.50
	1982(a)	—	.30	.60	1.50
	1983(a)	—	.30	.60	1.50
	1984(a)	—	.30	.60	1.50
	1985(a)	—	.30	.60	1.50

10 FRANCS

ALUMINUM-BRONZE

9	1974(a)	—	.40	.75	2.00
	1975(a)	—	.40	.75	2.00
	1976(a)	—	.40	.75	2.00
	1977(a)	—	.40	.75	2.00
	1978(a)	—	.40	.75	2.00
	1979(a)	—	.40	.75	2.00
	1980(a)	—	.40	.75	1.50
	1981(a)	—	.40	.75	1.50
	1982(a)	—	.40	.75	1.50
	1983(a)	—	.40	.75	1.50
	1984(a)	—	.40	.75	1.50
	1985(a)	—	.40	.75	1.50

25 FRANCS

ALUMINUM-BRONZE

10	1975(a)	—	1.00	1.75	3.00
	1976(a)	—	1.00	1.50	2.75
	1978(a)	—	1.00	1.50	2.75
	1982(a)	—	.75	1.25	2.50
	1983(a)	—	.75	1.25	2.50
	1984(a)	—	.75	1.25	2.50
	1985(a)	—	.75	1.25	2.50

50 FRANCS

NICKEL

11	1976A(a)	10.000	2.50	4.50	8.00
	1976B(a)	Inc. Ab.	2.50	4.50	8.00
	1976C(a)	Inc. Ab.	2.50	4.50	8.00
	1976D(a)	Inc. Ab.	2.50	4.50	8.00
	1976E(a)	Inc. Ab.	2.50	4.50	8.00
	1977A(a)	—	2.50	4.50	8.00
	1977B(a)	—	2.50	4.50	8.00
	1977D(a)	—	2.50	4.50	8.00
	1977E(a)	—	2.50	4.50	8.00
	1978A(a)	—	2.50	4.50	8.00
	1978B(a)	—	2.50	4.50	8.00
	1978C(a)	—	2.50	4.50	8.00
	1978D(a)	—	2.50	4.50	8.00
	1979E(a)	—	2.50	4.50	8.00
	1980A(a)	—	1.75	3.75	6.50
	1982A(a)	—	1.75	3.75	6.50
	1983D(a)	—	1.75	3.75	6.50
	1983E(a)	—	1.75	3.75	6.50
	1984D(a)	—	1.75	3.75	6.50
	1985D(a)	—	1.75	3.75	6.50

500 FRANCS

COPPER-NICKEL

12	1976A(a)	4.000	7.50	12.00	18.50
	1976B(a)	Inc. Ab.	7.50	12.00	18.50
	1976C(a)	Inc. Ab.	7.50	12.00	18.50
	1976D(a)	Inc. Ab.	7.50	12.00	18.50

KM#	Date	Mintage	VF	XF	Unc
12	1976E(a)	Inc. Ab.	7.50	12.00	18.50
	1977A(a)	—	7.50	12.00	18.50
	1977B(a)	—	7.50	12.00	18.50
	1977C(a)	—	7.50	12.00	18.50
	1977D(a)	—	7.50	12.00	18.50
	1977E(a)	—	7.50	12.00	18.50
	1979D(a)	—	7.50	11.00	15.00
	1982D(a)	—	7.50	11.00	15.00
	1984A(a)	—	6.00	9.50	13.50
	1984E(a)	—	6.00	9.50	13.50

CENTRAL AMERICAN REP.

The Central American Republic (Provincias Unidas del Centro de America, Republic of the United States of Central America, Central American Union) was an 1823-39 confederation of the former sections of the Captaincy General of Guatemala - Guatemala, Honduras, El Salvador, Nicaragua and Costa Rica - formed after the downfall of the short-lived Mexican empire of Augustin de Iturbide. The confederation, which occupied all of Central America between Mexico and Panama, had a population of fewer than 1.5 million. There was no permanent capital.

On Sept. 15, 1821, the leaders of the Captaincy General that governed the five provinces of Central America for Spain, declared Central America independent from Spain. The following year, Iturbide crowned himself Augustin I of Mexico and invited the Central Americans to join his empire. Guatemala, Honduras, Nicaragua and Costa Rica did so. El Salvador, which desired to become a part of the United States, refused and was invaded and conquered for Mexico by Vicente Filisola, the military governor Iturbide had sent to Guatemala. But almost before El Salvador had been forced into the Mexican empire, Iturbide was ousted and sent into exile by Antonio Lopez de Santa Anna. Filisola then reconvened the National Constituent Assembly that had been called into existence by the Central American declaration of independence of 1821. On July 1, 1823, the Assembly issued a second declaration of independence, from Mexico as well as Spain, and established the Central American Republic.

Historically the confederation, which lasted 15 years, was a triumph of rhetoric over reality. It had neither permanent capital, army nor treasury and was all but powerless to raise funds. The political leaders managed to write a constitution, but it was as ineffectual as the first constitution of the United States, the Articles of Confederation. The citizens of the Central American Republic had no sense of nationhood and were divided by geography as well as religious and class animosity. By 1827 the entire confederation was embroiled in a civil war. By the end of 1838 every state but El Salvador had seceded from the ill-advised union; however, Costa Rica, Guatemala and Honduras continued to strike coins of the confederation style until 1850, 1851 and 1861 respectively. The concept of a unified nation of Central America continues to inspire some interest to this day.

MINT MARKS
CR - San Jose, Costa Rica
G - Guatemala
NG - Guatemala
T - Tegucigalpa, Honduras

MONETARY SYSTEM
16 Reales = 1 Escudo

1/4 REAL

.8500 g, .903 SILVER, .0246 oz ASW
Mint mark: G

KM#	Date	Mintage	VG	Fine	VF	XF
1	1824	—	5.00	12.00	20.00	40.00
	1826	—	3.00	7.50	12.50	25.00
	1828	—	—	—	Rare	—
	1831	—	3.00	7.50	12.50	25.00
	1833	—	—	—	Rare	—
	1837	—	2.00	6.00	12.50	25.00
	1838	—	5.00	12.00	20.00	40.00
	1840/30	—	2.00	5.00	10.00	20.00
	1841	—	—	—	Rare	—

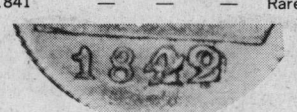

1842/29

	1842/29	—	2.00	4.00	9.00	17.50
	1842/37	—	2.00	4.00	9.00	17.50
	1843	—	2.00	4.50	10.00	18.50
	1844	—	2.00	—	9.00	17.50
	1845	—	40.00	70.00	125.00	250.00
	1846	—	4.00	9.00	15.00	27.50
	1847	—	—	—	Rare	—
	1850	—	7.00	17.50	35.00	60.00
	1851	—	—	—	Rare	—

Mint mark: CR

| 23 | 1845 | — | 35.00 | 60.00 | 110.00 | 225.00 |

1/2 REAL

1.6900 g., .903 SILVER, .0490 oz ASW
Mint mark: NG

KM#	Date	Mintage	VG	Fine	VF	XF
2	1824 M	—	6.50	13.50	27.50	70.00

Mint mark: T
Similar to KM#20.

18	1830 F	—	—	—	Rare	—
	1831 F	—	—	Reported, not confirmed		

Mint mark: CR

20	1831 E	—	6.00	15.00	35.00	60.00
	1831 F	—	5.50	13.50	25.00	42.50
	1843 M	—	4.00	8.00	22.50	40.00
	1845 B	—	12.50	25.00	40.00	90.00

1.6900 g, .750 SILVER, .0407 oz ASW

20a	1846 JB CRESCA					
		—	6.00	15.00	30.00	60.00
	1846 JB CREZCA					
		—	22.50	47.50	85.00	175.00
	1847 JB CRESCA					
		—	22.50	47.50	85.00	175.00
	1847 JB CREZCA					
		—	6.00	13.50	30.00	60.00
	1848 JB	—	4.00	9.00	22.50	47.50
	1849 JB	—	17.50	32.50	55.00	100.00

REAL

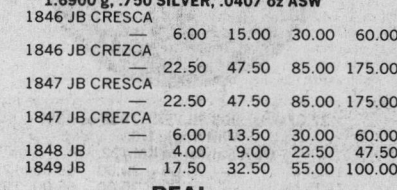

3.3800 g, .903 SILVER, .0981 oz ASW
Mint mark: NG

3	1824 M	—	7.50	15.00	32.50	55.00
	1828 M	—	18.50	40.00	85.00	150.00

Mint mark: T
Similar to KM#21.

19	1830 F	—	5.00	10.00	25.00	60.00
	1831 F	—	—	Reported, not confirmed		

Mint mark: CR

21	1831 E	—	13.50	22.50	60.00	125.00
	1831 F	—	10.00	20.00	40.00	85.00
	1848 JB	—	—	—	—	—

3.3800 g, .750 SILVER, .0815 oz ASW

21a	1848 JB	—	30.00	65.00	130.00	250.00
	1849 JB	—	15.00	32.50	60.00	100.00

2 REALES

6.7700 g, .903 SILVER, .1965 oz ASW
Mint mark: T

9	1825 M	—	—	—	Rare	—
	1831 F	—	4.50	9.00	20.00	35.00
	1832 F	—	7.50	15.00	32.50	55.00

.917 SILVER

KM#	Date	Mintage	Good	VG	Fine	VF
10	1825T NR	—	85.00	150.00	375.00	600.00

CENTRAL AMERICAN REPUBLIC 282

6.5000 g, .750 SILVER, .1567 oz ASW
Mint mark: CR

KM#	Date	Mintage	VG	Fine	VF	XF
24	1848 JB	—	—	Reported, not confirmed		
	1849 JB	—	—	Rare	—	

8 REALES

27.0700 g, .903 SILVER, .7859 oz ASW
Mint mark: NG
Obv: Similar to KM#22.

	Date	Mintage	VG	Fine	VF	XF
4	1824 M	—	14.00	30.00	65.00	125.00
	1825 M	—	14.00	30.00	65.00	125.00
	1826 M	—	14.00	30.00	65.00	125.00
	1827 M	—	14.00	32.50	75.00	150.00
	1828 M	—	17.50	37.50	85.00	175.00
	1829 M	—	14.00	30.00	65.00	125.00
	1830 M	—	150.00	250.00	500.00	900.00
	1831 M	—	200.00	400.00	750.00	1250.
	1834 M	—	65.00	120.00	200.00	350.00
	1835 M	—	14.00	30.00	65.00	125.00
	1836 M	—	14.00	30.00	65.00	125.00
	1836 BA	—	17.50	37.50	75.00	150.00
	1837 BA	—	14.00	30.00	65.00	125.00
	1838 BA	—	—	Reported, not confirmed		
	1839/7 MA/BA					
		—	35.00	75.00	150.00	300.00
	1840/37 MA/BA					
		—	15.00	37.50	80.00	150.00
	1840/39 MA	—	14.00	30.00	65.00	125.00
	1840 MA	—	14.00	30.00	65.00	125.00
	1841/37 MA/BA					
		—	60.00	125.00	250.00	500.00
	1841 MA	—	50.00	100.00	200.00	400.00
	1842/37 MA/BA					
		—	15.00	32.50	75.00	150.00
	1842/0 MA	—	15.00	32.50	75.00	150.00
	1842 MA	—	14.00	30.00	65.00	125.00
	1846 MA	—	15.00	32.50	75.00	150.00
	1846/2 AE	—	65.00	120.00	200.00	350.00
	1846 AE/MA w/CREZCA over CRESCA					
		—	65.00	120.00	200.00	350.00
	1846 A	—	15.00	35.00	80.00	150.00
	1847/6 A	—	25.00	50.00	110.00	225.00
	1847 A	—	20.00	40.00	100.00	200.00

Mint mark: CR

	Date	Mintage	VG	Fine	VF	XF
22	1831 E	—	1000.	2000.	4000.	7500.
	1831 F	—	300.00	500.00	800.00	1600.

1/2 ESCUDO

1.6875 g, .875 GOLD, .0474 oz AGW
Mint mark: NG

KM#	Date	Mintage	VG	Fine	VF	XF
5	1824 M	—	45.00	90.00	150.00	300.00
	1825/4 M	—	50.00	100.00	175.00	275.00
	1825 M	—	45.00	75.00	150.00	225.00
	1826 M	—	50.00	100.00	175.00	275.00
	1843 M	—	100.00	200.00	350.00	550.00

Mint mark: CR
Provisional Issue

| 11 | 1825 | 2 known | — | — | Rare | — |

13	1828 F	4,435	75.00	125.00	200.00	350.00
	1843 M	593	90.00	180.00	360.00	600.00
	1846 JB	.013	30.00	50.00	80.00	135.00
	1847 JB	.023	30.00	50.00	80.00	135.00
	1848 JB	.014	30.00	50.00	80.00	135.00
	1849 JB Inc. Ab.	90.00	180.00	350.00	550.00	

ESCUDO

3.3750 g, .875 GOLD, .0949 oz AGW
Mint mark: NG

| 6 | 1824 M | — | 100.00 | 200.00 | 400.00 | 600.00 |
| | 1825 M | — | 75.00 | 125.00 | 200.00 | 400.00 |

Mint mark: CR

14	1828 F	—	—	—	Rare	—
	1833 E	.010	50.00	100.00	150.00	250.00
	1833 F	Inc. Ab.	90.00	150.00	225.00	350.00
	1844 M	6,353	50.00	100.00	150.00	240.00
	1845 JB	8,672	90.00	150.00	250.00	375.00
	1846 JB	2,722	50.00	100.00	150.00	240.00
	1847 JB	3,510	50.00	80.00	150.00	225.00
	1848 JB	.010	50.00	80.00	150.00	225.00
	1849 JB	.013	50.00	90.00	150.00	225.00
	1850 JB	—	100.00	175.00	250.00	450.00

2 ESCUDOS

6.7500 g, .875 GOLD, .1899 oz AGW
Mint mark: NG

12	1825 M	—	135.00	180.00	320.00	450.00
	1826 M	—	135.00	180.00	320.00	450.00
	1827 M	—	135.00	180.00	320.00	450.00
	1828 M	—	135.00	180.00	320.00	450.00
	1830 M	—	200.00	250.00	400.00	550.00
	1834 M	—	225.00	375.00	750.00	1000.
	1835 M	—	125.00	190.00	320.00	450.00
	1836 M	—	150.00	200.00	400.00	500.00
	1837 BA	—	150.00	200.00	425.00	750.00
	1842 MA	—	150.00	200.00	400.00	725.00
	1844 B	—	150.00	200.00	425.00	750.00
	1846 A	—	150.00	200.00	400.00	550.00
	1847 A	—	150.00	200.00	400.00	625.00

Mint mark: CR

KM#	Date	Mintage	VG	Fine	VF	XF
15	1828 F	2,750	100.00	190.00	350.00	700.00
	1835 F	5,452	100.00	170.00	275.00	550.00
	1843 F	4,482	100.00	190.00	350.00	700.00
	1848 JB	—	125.00	250.00	425.00	850.00
	1850 JB	7,432	100.00	125.00	225.00	450.00

4 ESCUDOS

13.5000 g, .875 GOLD, .3798 oz AGW
Mint mark: NG

7	1824 M	—	900.00	1800.	3200.	5500.
	1825 M	—	1200.	2100.	3500.	6000.
	1826 M	—	—	—	Rare	—

Mint mark: CR

16	1828 F	3,048	500.00	750.00	1500.	3500.
	1835 F	697 pcs.	350.00	625.00	1250.	3250.
	1837 E	.011	350.00	650.00	1400.	3750.
	1837 F	Inc. Ab.	—	—	Rare	—
	1849 JB	441 pcs.	1500.	2500.	4500.	7000.

8 ESCUDOS

27.0000 g, .875 GOLD, .7596 oz AGW
Mint mark: NG
Obv: Similar to KM#17.

| 8 | 1824 M | — | 1750. | 3500. | 7000. | 12,000. |
| | 1825 M | — | 1750. | 3500. | 7000. | 12,000. |

NOTE: Stack's Hammel sale 9-82 Unc 1824 M realized $27,000.

Mint mark: CR

KM#	Date	Mintage	VG	Fine	VF	XF
17	1828 F	5,302	900.00	1500.	2500.	3500.
	1833 F	4,459	900.00	1500.	2500.	3500.
	1837 E	2,028	950.00	1550.	3250.	5500.
	1837 F	Inc. Ab.	1200.	2100.	4000.	6500.

NOTE: Stack's Hammel sale 9-82 AU 1828 F realized $9500.

CHAD

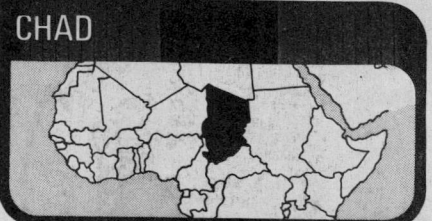

The Republic of Chad, a landlocked country of central Africa, is the largest country of former French Equatorial Africa. It has an area of 495,755 sq. mi. (1,284,000 sq. km.) and a population of 4.7 million. Capital: N'Djamena. An expanding livestock industry produces camels, cattle and sheep. Cotton (the chief product), ivory and palm oil are important exports.

Although supposedly known to Ptolemy, the Chad area was first visited by white men in 1823. Exaggerated estimates of its economic importance led to a race for its possession (1890-93) which resulted in the territory being divided by treaty between Great Britain, France and Germany. As a consequence of World War I, the German area was mandated to France in 1919. Chad was absorbed into the colony of French Equatorial Africa, as part of Ubangi-Shari, in 1910 and became a separate colony in 1920. Upon dissolution of French Equatorial Africa in 1959, the component states became autonomous members of the French Union. Chad became an independent republic on Aug. 11, 1960.

NOTE: For earlier and related coinage see French Equatorial Africa and the Equatorial African States.

MINT MARKS
(a) - Paris, privy marks only

COMMEMORATIVE EDGE INSCRIPTION
1960 LIBERTE PROGRESS SOLIDARITE
1970/REPUBLIQUE DU TCHAD

100 FRANCS

5.0000 g, .925 SILVER, .0957 oz ASW
10th Anniversary of Independence
Robert Francis Kennedy

KM#	Date	Mintage	Fine	VF	XF	Unc
1	1970	975 pcs.	—	—	Proof	100.00

NICKEL

2	1971(a)	5,000	7.00	15.00	22.00	40.00
	1972(a)	5,000	7.00	15.00	22.00	40.00

3	1975(a)	—	6.00	10.00	15.00	25.00
	1978(a)	—	5.00	8.00	10.00	20.00
	1980(a)	—	3.00	6.00	8.00	15.00

200 FRANCS

15.0000 g, .925 SILVER, .4461 oz ASW
10th Anniversary of Independence
Martin Luther King, Jr.

Obv: Similar to 300 Francs, KM#7.

KM#	Date	Mintage	Fine	VF	XF	Unc
4	1970	952 pcs.	—	—	Proof	100.00

15.0000 g, .800 SILVER, .3858 oz ASW
10th Anniversary of Independence
General De Gaulle

| 5 | 1970 | 442 pcs. | — | — | Proof | 200.00 |

President Nasser

| 6 | 1970 | 435 pcs. | — | — | Proof | 200.00 |

300 FRANCS

25.0000 g, .925 SILVER, .8922 oz ASW
10th Anniversary of Independence
John Fitzgerald Kennedy

| 7 | 1970 | 504 pcs. | — | — | Proof | 400.00 |

500 FRANCS

COPPER-NICKEL
Obv: Denomination, local flora and legend.
Rev: Native woman and legend.

| 13 | 1985(a) | — | 2.50 | 5.00 | 7.00 | 10.00 |

1000 FRANCS

3.5000 g, .900 GOLD, .1012 oz AGW
10th Anniversary of Independence
Commandant Lamy

| 8 | 1970 | 4,000 | — | — | Proof | 75.00 |

3000 FRANCS

10.5000 g, .900 GOLD, .3038 oz AGW
10th Anniversary of Independence
Governor Eboue

| 9 | 1970 | 4,000 | — | — | Proof | 225.00 |

Listings For
CEYLON: refer to Sri Lanka

CHAD

5000 FRANCS

17.5000 g, .900 GOLD, .5064 oz AGW
10th Anniversary of Independence
General Leclerc

KM#	Date	Mintage	Fine	VF	XF	Unc
10	1970	4,000	—	—	Proof	350.00

10,000 FRANCS

70.0000 g, .900 GOLD, 2.0257 oz AGW
10th Anniversary of Independence
Francois Tombalbaye

KM#	Date	Mintage	Fine	VF	XF	Unc
12	1970	4,000	—	—	Proof	1350.

PROOF SETS (PS)

KM#	Date	Mintage	Identification	Issue Price	Mkt. Val.
PS1	1970(5)	4,000	KM8-12	412.50	2900.
PS2	1970(3)	—	KM1,4,7	33.00	600.00

36.0000 g, .900 GOLD, 1.0128 oz AGW
10th Anniversary of Independence
General DeGaulle

11	1970	90 pcs.	—	—	Proof 900.00

President Nasser

14	1970	205 pcs.	—	—	Proof 700.00

20,000 FRANCS

CHILE

The Republic of Chile, a ribbon-like country on the Pacific coast of southern South America, has an area of 292,258 sq. mi. (756,945 sq. km.) and a population of 11.4 million. Capital: Santiago. Historically, the economic base of Chile has been the rich mineral deposits of its northern provinces. Copper, of which Chile has 25 percent of the free world's reserves, has accounted for more than 75 percent of Chile's export earnings in recent years. Other important exports are iron ore, iodine and nitrate of soda.

Diego de Almargo was the first Spaniard to attempt to wrest Chile from the Incas and Araucanian tribes in 1536. He failed, and was followed by Pedro de Valdivia, a favorite of Pizarro, who founded Santiago in 1541. When the Napoleonic Wars involved Spain, leaving the constituent parts of the Spanish Empire to their own devices, Chilean patriots formed a national government and proclaimed the country's independence, Sept. 18, 1810. Independence however, was not secured until Feb. 12, 1818, after a bitter struggle led by Bernardo O'Higgins and San Martin.

In 1960, the peso was replaced by the escudo, valued at 1,000 pesos. In 1975, the peso was reintroduced, valued at 1,000 escudos.

RULERS
Spanish until 1818

MINT MARKS
So - Santiago

MINTMASTER'S INITIALS

Letter	Date	Name
AJ	1800-1801	Agustin de Infante y Prado and Jose Maria de Bobadilla
D		Domingo Eizaguirre
F		Francisco Rodriguez Brochero
FJ, JF	1803-1817	Francisco Rodriguez Brochero and Jose Maria de Bobadilla

MONETARY SYSTEM
16 Reales = 1 Escudo

COLONIAL MILLED COINAGE
1/4 REAL

.8462 g, .896 SILVER, .0243 oz ASW
Mint mark: So

KM#	Date	Mintage	VG	Fine	VF	XF
63	1801	.057	10.00	15.00	35.00	75.00
	1802	.056	10.00	15.00	35.00	75.00
	1803	.054	10.00	15.00	35.00	75.00
	1804	.056	10.00	15.00	35.00	75.00
	1805	.056	10.00	15.00	35.00	75.00
	1806/5	.054	10.00	15.00	35.00	75.00
	1806	Inc. Ab.	10.00	15.00	35.00	75.00
	1807	.057	10.00	15.00	35.00	75.00
	1808	.057	10.00	15.00	35.00	75.00

Obv: Lion. Rev: Castle.

73	1809	.054	15.00	25.00	50.00	100.00
	1810	.054	10.00	15.00	35.00	75.00
	1811	.054	10.00	15.00	35.00	75.00
	1812	.071	10.00	15.00	35.00	75.00
	1813	.063	10.00	15.00	35.00	75.00
	1814	.067	10.00	15.00	35.00	75.00
	1815	.054	10.00	15.00	35.00	75.00
	1816/5	.082	10.00	15.00	35.00	75.00
	1816	Inc.Ab.	10.00	15.00	35.00	75.00
	1817	—	10.00	15.00	35.00	75.00

1/2 REAL
1.6925 g, .896 SILVER, .0487 oz ASW
Obv. leg: CAROLUS IIII. . . ., bust of Charles IIII.
Rev: Similar to KM#64.

57	1801 AJ	.059	8.00	12.00	22.00	55.00
	1802 JJ	.078	8.00	12.00	22.00	55.00
	1803 FJ	.036	20.00	40.00	75.00	150.00
	1804/3 FJ	.058	10.00	15.00	30.00	70.00

KM#	Date	Mintage	VG	Fine	VF	XF
57	1804/3 FJ	.058	10.00	15.00	30.00	70.00
	1804 FJ	I.A.	8.00	12.00	22.00	70.00
	1805 FJ	.028	12.00	20.00	40.00	80.00
	1806 FJ	.059	8.00	12.00	22.00	55.00
	1807 FJ	.040	8.00	12.00	22.00	55.00
	1808/7 FJ	.058	10.00	15.00	30.00	60.00
	1808 FJ	I.A.	8.00	12.00	22.00	55.00

Obv. leg: FERDIN VII, bust of Charles IV.

KM#	Date	Mintage	VG	Fine	VF	XF
64	1808 FJ Inc. Ab.		8.00	12.00	25.00	60.00
	1809/8 FJ	.051	12.00	18.00	35.00	65.00
	1809 FJ Inc. Ab.		10.00	17.00	28.00	55.00
	1810 FJ	.050	10.00	17.00	28.00	55.00
	1811 FJ	.018	10.00	17.00	28.00	55.00
	1812 FJ	.125	10.00	17.00	28.00	55.00
	1813 FJ	.218	10.00	17.00	28.00	55.00
	1814 FJ	.077	9.00	14.00	20.00	50.00
	1815 FJ	.099	9.00	14.00	20.00	50.00
	1816 FJ	.119	9.00	14.00	20.00	50.00
	1817 FJ	—	10.00	15.00	30.00	65.00
	1817 FD	—	10.00	15.00	30.00	65.00
	1817 FI	—	—	—	Rare	

REAL
3.3834 g, .896 SILVER, .0974 oz ASW
Obv. leg: CAROLUS IIII...., bust of Charles IIII.
Rev: Similar to KM#65.

58	1801 AJ	.053	8.00	18.00	30.00	60.00
	1802 JJ	.081	7.50	15.00	27.00	55.00
	1803 FJ	.018	100.00	200.00	—	—
	1804 FJ	.035	7.50	15.00	27.00	55.00
	1804 FJ/AJ	I.A.	12.00	30.00	45.00	100.00
	1805 FJ	.019	8.00	20.00	35.00	75.00
	1806 FJ	.038	9.00	20.00	45.00	90.00
	1807/6 FJ	.023	12.00	30.00	45.00	100.00
	1807 FJ Inc. Ab.		9.00	20.00	45.00	80.00
	1808/7 FJ	.034	—	—	—	—
	1808 FJ	I.A.	9.00	20.00	35.00	65.00

Obv. leg: FERDIN. VII...., bust of Charles IV.

65	1808 FJ	I.A.	25.00	50.00	100.00	200.00
	1809/8 FJ	.029	10.00	20.00	30.00	90.00
	1809 FJ	I.A.	10.00	20.00	30.00	90.00
	1810 FJ	.079	10.00	20.00	30.00	90.00
	1811 FJ	.020	12.00	25.00	50.00	125.00
	1812/1 FJ	.043	15.00	30.00	65.00	135.00
	1812 FJ Inc. Ab.		10.00	20.00	30.00	90.00
	1813 FJ	.213	10.00	20.00	30.00	90.00
	1814 FJ	.054	10.00	20.00	30.00	90.00
	1815 FJ	.041	10.00	20.00	30.00	90.00
	1816 FJ	.123	10.00	20.00	30.00	90.00
	1817 FJ	—	10.00	20.00	30.00	90.00

2 REALES

6.7680 g, .903 SILVER, .1965 oz ASW
Obv. leg: CAROLUS IIII...., bust of Charles IIII.

59	1801 AJ	.039	15.00	30.00	80.00	—
	1802 JJ	.028	15.00	30.00	80.00	—
	1803 FJ	.025	15.00	30.00	80.00	—
	1803 FJ/JJ	I.A.	18.00	40.00	95.00	—
	1804 FJ	.028	15.00	30.00	80.00	—
	1804 FJ/inverted mm					
	Inc. Ab.		20.00	40.00	95.00	—
	1805 FJ	.024	15.00	30.00	80.00	—
	1806/5 FJ	.066	18.00	40.00	95.00	—
	1806 FJ inverted mm					
	Inc. Ab.		20.00	40.00	95.00	—
	1806 FJ	I.A.	15.00	30.00	80.00	—
	1807 FJ	.042	15.00	30.00	80.00	—
	1808 FJ	.054	15.00	30.00	80.00	—

Obv. leg: FERDIN. VII...., bust of Charles IV.

KM#	Date	Mintage	VG	Fine	VF	XF
66	1808 FJ	I.A.	20.00	40.00	80.00	—
	1809 FJ	.041	20.00	40.00	80.00	—

Obv. leg: FERDIN. VII...., imaginary laureate military bust.

74	1810 FJ	.045	25.00	50.00	100.00	—
	1810 FJ inverted A for V in VII					
	Inc. Ab.		50.00	100.00	—	—
	1811 FJ	.027	30.00	60.00	120.00	—

Obv. leg: FERDIN. VII...., bust of Ferdinand.

79	1812 FJ	.069	12.00	20.00	40.00	—
	1813 FJ	.136	10.00	18.00	35.00	—
	1813 FJ/inverted mm					
	Inc. Ab.		12.00	20.00	40.00	—
	1814 FJ	.004	40.00	75.00	150.00	—
	1815 FJ	.024	15.00	30.00	65.00	—
	1816 FJ	.067	10.00	18.00	35.00	—
	1817 FJ	—	12.00	20.00	40.00	—

4 REALES

13.5360 g, .896 SILVER, .3899 oz ASW

60	1801 AJ	2,000	150.00	300.00	480.00	—
	1802 JJ	.018	65.00	150.00	240.00	—
	1803 FJ	9,000	80.00	200.00	320.00	—
	1804/3 FJ	6,000	70.00	150.00	240.00	—
	1804 FJ	I.A.	37.50	75.00	150.00	275.00
	1805 FJ	9,000	75.00	125.00	250.00	400.00
	1806 FJ	.020	32.50	50.00	125.00	250.00
	1807 FJ	.048	32.50	50.00	125.00	250.00
	1808/7 FJ	.025	37.50	75.00	150.00	275.00
	1808 FJ	I.A.	50.00	100.00	175.00	350.00

Obv. leg: FERDIN. VII...., bust of Charles IV.

KM#	Date	Mintage	VG	Fine	VF	XF
67	1808/7 FJ inverted J					
	Inc. Ab.	32.50	60.00	125.00	275.00	
	1808 FJ	I.A.	32.50	60.00	125.00	275.00
	1808 FJ/inverted J					
	Inc. Ab.	32.50	60.00	125.00	275.00	
	1809 FJ	.015	125.00	200.00	375.00	600.00
	1810 FJ	.010	75.00	100.00	175.00	350.00
	1811 FJ	6,000	75.00	100.00	175.00	350.00
	1811 FJ/inverted J					
	Inc. Ab.	75.00	100.00	175.00	350.00	
	1812 FJ	.027	32.50	50.00	150.00	250.00
	1813 FJ	.034	32.50	50.00	100.00	225.00
	1813 FJ/inverted J					
	Inc. Ab.	32.50	50.00	100.00	225.00	
	1814 FJ	850 pcs.	—	Reported, not confirmed		
	1815 FJ	.010	100.00	200.00	400.00	600.00

8 REALES

27.0730 g, .896 SILVER, .7799 oz ASW
Obv. leg: CAROLUS IIII...., bust of Charles IIII.

51	1801 AJ	.185	100.00	150.00	200.00	400.00
	1802 JJ	.160	100.00	150.00	200.00	400.00
	1803/2 FJ/JJ	.111	150.00	275.00	400.00	600.00
	1803 FJ	I.A.	250.00	400.00	600.00	800.00
	1804 FJ	.129	100.00	150.00	200.00	400.00
	1805 FJ	.159	250.00	450.00	550.00	750.00
	1806/5 FJ	.155	250.00	400.00	500.00	700.00
	1806 FJ	I.A.	250.00	400.00	500.00	700.00
	1807 FJ	.094	250.00	400.00	500.00	750.00
	1808 FJ	.134	250.00	400.00	500.00	750.00

Obv. leg: FERDIN. VII...., imaginary military bust.
Rev: Similar to 2 Reales, KM#66.

68	1808 FJ	I.A.	400.00	700.00	1100.	1600.
	1809 FJ	.123	100.00	200.00	300.00	500.00

CHILE 286

Obv. leg: FERDIN. VII..., imaginary laureate military bust. Rev: Similar to 2 Reales, KM#74.

KM#	Date	Mintage	VG	Fine	VF	XF
75	1810 FJ	.126	100.00	200.00	300.00	500.00
	1811 FJ	.097	100.00	200.00	300.00	500.00

Obv. leg: FERDIN. VII.., bust of Ferdinand.

80	1812 FJ	.307	90.00	130.00	175.00	300.00
	1813 FJ	.415	90.00	130.00	175.00	300.00
	1814 FJ	.368	90.00	130.00	175.00	300.00
	1815 FJ	.388	90.00	130.00	175.00	300.00
	1816 FJ	.386	90.00	130.00	175.00	300.00
	1816/6 FJ	I.A.	100.00	200.00	300.00	500.00
	1817 FJ	*.132	600.00	1000.	1500.	2250.

ESCUDO
3.3834 g, .901 GOLD, .0980 oz AGW
Obv. leg: CAROL VII..., bust of Charles IIII. Rev: Arms, order chain.

61	1801 AJ	1,088	175.00	250.00	500.00	750.00
	1802 JJ	748 pcs.	275.00	425.00	600.00	850.00
	1803 FJ	1,156	225.00	325.00	500.00	750.00
	1804 FJ	1,428	225.00	325.00	500.00	750.00
	1805 FJ	816 pcs.	225.00	325.00	500.00	750.00
	1806 FJ	544 pcs.	275.00	425.00	600.00	850.00
	1807 FJ	544 pcs.	275.00	425.00	600.00	850.00
	1808 FJ	2,448	175.00	250.00	375.00	600.00

Obv. leg: FERDIN. VII..., imaginary military bust. Rev: Arms.

69	1808	3,986	—	—	Rare	—
	1809	5,026	—	—	Rare	—

Obv. leg: FERDIN. VII.D.G..., bust of Charles IV.

76	1810 FJ	816 pcs.	175.00	375.00	500.00	750.00
	1811 FJ	680 pcs.	175.00	375.00	500.00	750.00
	1812 FJ	952 pcs.	175.00	375.00	500.00	750.00
	1813 FJ	4,556	125.00	175.00	250.00	400.00
	1814 FJ	1,152	175.00	375.00	500.00	750.00
	1815 FJ	816 pcs.	175.00	375.00	500.00	750.00
	1816 FJ	408 pcs.	225.00	450.00	600.00	900.00
	1817 FJ	.022	125.00	175.00	250.00	400.00
	1817 JF	Inc. Ab.	150.00	250.00	325.00	500.00

NOTE: An additional 17,860 pcs. were struck between 1818-1823; the actual date on the coin is unknown.

2 ESCUDOS
6.7667 g, .875 GOLD, .1904 oz AGW
Obv. leg: CAROL IIII..., bust of Charles III. Rev: Arms.

53	1801 AJ	680 pcs.	500.00	850.00	1250.	1750.
	1802 JJ	374 pcs.	650.00	1000.	1400.	2000.
	1803 FJ	578 pcs.	500.00	850.00	1250.	1750.
	1804 FJ	544 pcs.	500.00	850.00	1250.	1750.
53	1805 FJ	646 pcs.	500.00	850.00	1250.	1750.
	1806 FJ	306 pcs.	650.00	1000.	1400.	2000.
	1807 FJ	340 pcs.	650.00	1000.	1400.	2000.
	1808 FJ	1,020	500.00	850.00	1250.	1750.
	1810 FJ	510 pcs.	500.00	850.00	1250.	1750.
	1811 FJ	340 pcs.	500.00	850.00	1250.	1750.
	1812 FJ	476 pcs.	450.00	650.00	1000.	1500.
	1813 FJ	2,958	450.00	650.00	1000.	1500.

Obv. leg: FERDIN.VII., imaginary military bust.

70	1808 FJ	Inc. Ab.	—	—	Rare	—
	1809 FJ	Inc. Ab.	—	—	Rare	—
	1810 FJ	Inc. Ab.	—	—	Rare	—
	1811 FJ	Inc. Ab.	—	—	Rare	—

Obv. leg: FERDIN. VII..., bust of Charles IV.

81	1814 FJ	682 pcs.	300.00	475.00	700.00	1250.
	1815 FJ	408 pcs.	400.00	600.00	900.00	1500.
	1816 FJ	608 pcs.	400.00	600.00	900.00	1500.
	1817 FJ	168 pcs.	550.00	750.00	1150.	1800.

NOTE: An additional 19,876 pcs. were struck between 1818-1823, the actual date of the coin is unknown.

4 ESCUDOS
13.5334 g, .901 GOLD, .3920 oz AGW
Obv. leg: CAROL IIII..., bust of Charles IIII. Rev: Arms.

62	1801 AJ	340 pcs.	500.00	750.00	1000.	1250.
	1802 JJ	374 pcs.	500.00	750.00	1000.	1250.
	1803 FJ	476 pcs.	500.00	750.00	1000.	1250.
	1804 FJ	255 pcs.	575.00	850.00	1250.	1500.
	1805 FJ	323 pcs.	575.00	850.00	1250.	1500.
	1806 FJ	204 pcs.	575.00	850.00	1250.	1500.
	1807 FJ	187 pcs.	600.00	900.00	1500.	1750.
	1808/7 FJ	1,207	550.00	800.00	1200.	1500.
	1808 FJ	I.A.	500.00	750.00	1000.	1250.

Obv. leg: FERDIN. VII..., bust of Ferdinand. Rev: Arms.

71	1808 FJ	Inc. Ab.	—	—	Rare	—
	1809 FJ	Inc. Ab.	—	—	Rare	—

Obv. leg: FERDIN. VII..., bust of Charles IV.

77	1810 FJ	272 pcs.	425.00	700.00	1250.	1750.
	1811 FJ	170 pcs.	750.00	1250.	1750.	2500.
	1812 FJ	254 pcs.	425.00	700.00	1250.	1750.
	1813 FJ	1,462	375.00	650.00	1100.	1600.
	1814 FJ	340 pcs.	425.00	700.00	1250.	1750.
	1815 FJ	290 pcs.	425.00	700.00	1250.	1750.
	1816 FJ	100 pcs.	650.00	1000.	1500.	2000.
	1817 FJ	68 pcs.	1000.	1500.	2000.	—

NOTE: An additional 6,560 pcs. were struck between 1818-1823; the actual date on the coin is unknown.

8 ESCUDOS

27.0674 g, .901 GOLD, .7842 oz AGW
Obv. leg: CAROL IIII..., bust of Charles III. Rev: Similar to KM#78.

54	1801 AJ	.046	375.00	550.00	675.00	900.00
54	1802 JJ	.049	375.00	550.00	675.00	900.00
	1803 FJ	.044	375.00	550.00	675.00	900.00
	1804 FJ	.040	375.00	550.00	675.00	900.00
	1805 FJ	.044	375.00	550.00	675.00	900.00
	1806 FJ	.040	375.00	550.00	675.00	900.00
	1806 JF	I.A.	375.00	550.00	675.00	900.00
	1807 FJ	.039	375.00	550.00	725.00	1100.
	1807 JF	I.A.	375.00	550.00	725.00	1100.
	1808 FJ	.039	375.00	550.00	675.00	900.00

Obv. leg: FERDIN. VII..., imaginary military bust.

72	1808 FJ	I.A.	700.00	1200.	1500.	2500.
	1809 FJ	.041	400.00	650.00	1000.	1500.
	1810 FJ	.055	400.00	650.00	1000.	1500.
	1811 FJ	—	400.00	650.00	1000.	1500.

Obv. leg: FERDIN. VII..., bust of Charles IIII.

78	1811 FJ	.044	900.00	1500.	2400.	4500.
	1812 FJ	.048	375.00	550.00	675.00	900.00
	1813/2 FT	.037	375.00	550.00	675.00	900.00
	1813 FJ	Inc. Ab.	375.00	550.00	675.00	900.00
	1814 FJ	.029	375.00	550.00	675.00	900.00
	1815 FJ	.039	375.00	550.00	675.00	900.00
	1816 FJ	.030	375.00	400.00	500.00	900.00
	1817/6 FJ	.011	375.00	425.00	500.00	900.00
	1817/7/8 FJ	Inc. Ab.	400.00	800.00	1500.	2500.
	1817 FJ	Inc. Ab.	375.00	425.00	500.00	900.00

ROYALIST COINAGE
CHILOE

An island off the southwest coast of Chile. The island was the last outpost of the Spanish in their war with Chile. Antonio Quintanilla had the emergency coins cast to show that the empire of Ferdinand VII of Spain still exerted power in the New World.

COUNTERMARKED COINAGE
(Issued by Antonio Quintanilla)
8 REALES
CAST SILVER
Lima Mint
c/m: Chi-loe on cast 8 Reales of Ferdinand VII

KM#	Date	Mintage	Good	VG	Fine	VF
1	1818	—	350.00	500.00	800.00	1250.

Potosi Mint
c/m: Chi-loe on cast 8 Reales of Ferdinand VII.

KM#	Date	Mintage	Good	VG	Fine	VF
2	1822	—	350.00	500.00	800.00	1250.
	1825	—	350.00	500.00	800.00	1250.

VALDIVIA

Emergency coinage issued by Don Antonio Adriazola by order of the Governor.

REAL

BILLON

1.1	1822	—	50.00	75.00	125.00	200.00

c/m: APDLVA monogram.

1.2	1822	—	50.00	75.00	125.00	200.00

2 REALES

BILLON

2.1	1822	—	75.00	100.00	150.00	225.00

c/m: APDLVA monogram.

2.2 (3)	1822	—	75.00	100.00	150.00	225.00

8 REALES

BILLON

KM#	Date	Mintage	Good	VG	Fine	VF
3.1 (4)	1822	—	250.00	350.00	450.00	550.00

c/m: APDLVA monogram.

3.2 (5)	1822	—	250.00	350.00	450.00	550.00

REPUBLIC

MONETARY SYSTEM
8 Reales = 1 Peso
16 Reales = 1 Escudo

UN QUART (1/4) REAL

.903 SILVER
Obv: Lion. Rev: Castle.

KM#	Date	Mintage	VG	Fine	VF	XF
83	1818/6	.403	6.25	12.50	25.00	50.00
	1818	Inc. Ab.	6.25	12.50	25.00	50.00

NOTE: Dies of KM#83 used by Republic.

.900 SILVER

89	1832/1	.054	15.00	25.00	50.00	100.00
	1832	Inc. Ab.	15.00	25.00	50.00	100.00
	1833	.082	15.00	25.00	50.00	100.00
	1834	.134	75.00	125.00	175.00	350.00

1/2 REAL

.900 SILVER

90	1833 I	.014	12.00	20.00	37.50	80.00
	1834/3 I	.022	15.00	25.00	42.50	90.00
	1834 I	Inc. Ab.	12.00	20.00	37.50	80.00

98.1	1838 IJ	.015	15.00	32.00	50.00	90.00
	1840 IJ	.014	15.00	32.00	50.00	90.00
	1841 IJ	.016	15.00	32.00	50.00	90.00
	1842 IJ	.027	12.00	30.00	45.00	80.00

98.2	1844 IJ	—	3.00	7.50	15.00	25.00
	1845 IJ	—	3.00	7.50	15.00	25.00
	1846 IJ	—	3.00	7.50	15.00	25.00
	1847 IJ	—	3.00	7.50	15.00	25.00
	1848 JM	—	75.00	150.00	225.00	—
	1849 ML	—	3.00	7.50	15.00	25.00
	1850 LA	—	—	Reported, not confirmed		
	1851 LA	—	3.00	7.50	15.00	25.00

UN (1) REAL

3.2000 g, .900 SILVER, .0925 oz ASW

KM#	Date	Mintage	VG	Fine	VF	XF
91	1834 IJ	.016	7.50	15.00	30.00	65.00

94.1	1838 IJ	.012	10.00	20.00	40.00	85.00
	1840 IJ	6,800	10.00	20.00	30.00	65.00
	1841 IJ	7,928	10.00	20.00	30.00	65.00
	1842 IJ	4,768	10.00	20.00	30.00	65.00

94.2	1843 IJ	—	3.75	7.50	15.00	25.00
	1844 IJ	—	3.75	7.50	15.00	25.00
	1845 IJ	—	3.75	7.50	15.00	25.00
	1846 IJ	—	3.75	7.50	15.00	25.00
	1847 IJ	—	3.75	7.50	15.00	25.00
	1848/7/6 JM	—	—	—	—	—
	1848/7 JM	—	—	—	—	—
	1848 JM	—	3.75	7.50	15.00	25.00
	1849 ML	—	10.00	20.00	35.00	60.00
	1850 LA	—	3.75	7.50	15.00	25.00

2 REALES

.900 SILVER

92	1834 IJ	3,740	20.00	35.00	65.00	100.00

24.5mm

100.1	1843 IJ	—	5.00	10.00	20.00	40.00

23mm

100.2	1843 IJ	—	—	—	—	—
	1844 IJ	—	3.00	6.00	10.00	20.00
	1845/4 IJ	—	16.00	30.00	40.00	—
	1845 IJ	—	3.00	6.00	10.00	20.00
	1846/5 IJ	—	—	—	—	—
	1846/6 IJ	—	12.00	30.00	40.00	—
	1846 IJ	—	3.00	6.00	10.00	20.00
	1847 IJ	—	3.00	6.00	10.00	20.00
	1848 JM	—	2.50	5.00	8.00	15.00
	1849 ML	—	5.00	10.00	15.00	27.50
	1850/49 LA/ML	—	10.00	20.00	35.00	50.00
	1850 LA	—	8.00	12.50	18.00	30.00
	1850 LA/ML	—	8.00	12.50	18.00	30.00
	1851 LA	—	10.00	17.50	25.00	40.00
	1852 LA	—	10.00	17.50	25.00	40.00

CHILE 288

UN (1) PESO

.900 SILVER
Rev: Y above pillar.

KM#	Date	Mintage	Good	VG	Fine	VF
82.1	1817	—	65.00	110.00	180.00	550.00

Rev: Y to left of pillar.

82.2	1817 FJ	—	15.00	30.00	60.00	125.00
	1817 FD	—	28.00	55.00	120.00	260.00
	1818/7 FD	.371	32.00	65.00	135.00	300.00
	1818 FD Inc. Ab.		32.00	65.00	135.00	300.00
	1819 FD	.236	28.00	55.00	110.00	260.00
	1820 FD	.116	20.00	40.00	85.00	190.00
	1821 FD	.126	70.00	145.00	325.00	675.00
	1822 FI	.148	18.00	32.00	75.00	160.00
	1823 FI	.045	28.00	55.00	115.00	230.00
	1824 I	.011	75.00	155.00	335.00	610.00
	1825 I	3,400	65.00	125.00	300.00	535.00
	1826 I	6,111	—	—	Rare	—
	1830 I	6,868	80.00	165.00	365.00	695.00
	1831 I	.051	32.00	65.00	135.00	270.00
	1832 I	.040	28.00	55.00	110.00	230.00
	1833 I	.088	18.00	30.00	75.00	160.00
	1834 I	.043	45.00	80.00	180.00	360.00
	1834 IJ Inc. Ab.	52.50	110.00	245.00	475.00	

Coquimbo Mint
Rev: Similar to KM#82.2.

88	1828TH	—	—	—	8000.

8 REALES

27.0700 g, .900 SILVER, .7853 oz ASW, 39mm

KM#	Date	Mintage	VG	Fine	VF	XF
96.1	1837 IJ	5,404	—	—	Rare	—
	1839 I	.205	45.00	75.00	125.00	350.00
	1840 IJ	4,556	—	—	Rare	—

Rev: Similar to KM#96.1 but w/larger leg.
Reduced size, 38.5mm, same weight and fineness

KM#	Date	Mintage	VG	Fine	VF	XF
96.2	1848 JM	—	30.00	55.00	80.00	300.00
	1849 ML	—	40.00	70.00	100.00	360.00

ESCUDO

3.4000 g, .875 GOLD, .0956 oz AGW
Obv: Sun over mountains in wreath.
Rev: Crossed flags behind pillar in wreath, date below.

85	1824 I	3,400	95.00	135.00	170.00	275.00
	1825 I	2,920	95.00	135.00	170.00	275.00
	1826 I	4,280	95.00	135.00	170.00	275.00
	1827 I	408 pcs.	150.00	240.00	300.00	375.00
	1828 I	4,488	95.00	135.00	170.00	275.00
	1830 I	3,328	95.00	135.00	170.00	275.00
	1832 I	2,338	95.00	135.00	170.00	275.00
	1833/0 I	2,620	130.00	200.00	250.00	350.00
	1833 I	Inc. Ab.	115.00	180.00	215.00	300.00
	1834 I	10,614	115.00	180.00	215.00	300.00

Obv: Plumed and supported arms, date below.
Rev: Hand on book under sun rays.

99	1838 IJ	6,122	125.00	175.00	225.00	375.00

Rev: Liberty standing, column at left, fasces and cornucopia at right.

101.1	1839 IJ	4,946	100.00	135.00	175.00	250.00
	1840 IJ	4,312	100.00	135.00	175.00	250.00
	1841 IJ	3,992	100.00	135.00	175.00	250.00
	1842 IJ	5,076	100.00	135.00	175.00	250.00
	1843 IJ	4,632	100.00	135.00	175.00	250.00
	1844 IJ	—	100.00	135.00	175.00	250.00
	1845 IJ	—	100.00	135.00	175.00	250.00

Rev: Liberty standing scene rendered on smaller scale.

101.2	1847 IJ	—	125.00	175.00	225.00	375.00
	1848 JM	—	100.00	135.00	200.00	350.00
	1849 ML	—	100.00	135.00	200.00	350.00
	1850 LA	—	100.00	135.00	200.00	350.00
	1851 LA	—	125.00	175.00	225.00	375.00

2 ESCUDOS

6.8000 g, .875 GOLD, .1913 oz AGW

86	1824 I	1,700	150.00	190.00	300.00	450.00
	1825 I	1,460	150.00	190.00	300.00	450.00
	1826 I	1,936	150.00	190.00	300.00	450.00
	1827 I	204 pcs.	200.00	275.00	400.00	550.00
	1832 I	493 pcs.	200.00	275.00	400.00	550.00
	1833 I	224 pcs.	150.00	190.00	325.00	475.00
	1834 IJ	4,648	150.00	190.00	325.00	475.00

97	1837 IJ	331 pcs.	200.00	255.00	400.00	600.00
	1838 IJ	3,449	150.00	200.00	250.00	450.00

102.1	1839 IJ	3,064	225.00	275.00	425.00	550.00
	1840 IJ	2,396	225.00	275.00	425.00	550.00

KM#	Date	Mintage	VG	Fine	VF	XF
102.1	1841 IJ	2,552	180.00	235.00	375.00	500.00
	1842 IJ	2,986	180.00	235.00	375.00	500.00
	1843 IJ	2,464	180.00	235.00	375.00	500.00
	1844 IJ	—	180.00	235.00	375.00	500.00
	1845 IJ	—	180.00	235.00	375.00	500.00

Rev: Liberty standing scene rendered on smaller scale.

102.2	1846 IJ	—	150.00	225.00	300.00	375.00
	1847 IJ	—	150.00	225.00	300.00	375.00
	1848 JM	—	150.00	225.00	300.00	375.00
	1849 ML	—	150.00	225.00	300.00	375.00
	1850 LA	—	150.00	225.00	300.00	375.00
	1851 LA	—	150.00	225.00	300.00	375.00

4 ESCUDOS

13.5000 g, .875 GOLD, .3798 oz AGW

87	1824 FD	1,530	325.00	450.00	700.00	1100.
	1825 I	986 pcs.	350.00	525.00	875.00	1250.
	1826 I	1,326	325.00	450.00	700.00	1100.
	1833 IJ	321 pcs.	350.00	525.00	875.00	1250.
	1834 I	2,564	325.00	450.00	700.00	1100.

95	1836 IJ	1,389	275.00	375.00	575.00	950.00
	1837 IJ	321 pcs.	350.00	500.00	750.00	1150.

103	1839 IJ	—	—	—	Rare	—
	1840 IJ	108 pcs.	—	—	Rare	—
	1841 IJ	100 pcs.	—	—	Rare	—

8 ESCUDOS

27.0000 g, .875 GOLD, .7596 oz AGW

84	1818 FD	.029	375.00	425.00	575.00	800.00
	1819 FD	.037	375.00	425.00	575.00	800.00
	1820 FD	.035	375.00	425.00	575.00	800.00
	1821 FD	.016	375.00	425.00	575.00	800.00
	1822 FD	.031	375.00	425.00	575.00	800.00
	1823 FD	.019	375.00	425.00	575.00	800.00
	1824 FD	.010	375.00	425.00	575.00	800.00
	1825 I	8,483	375.00	425.00	575.00	750.00

KM#	Date	Mintage	VG	Fine	VF	XF
84	1826 I	7,607	375.00	425.00	575.00	750.00
	1827 I	2,176	375.00	425.00	575.00	750.00
	1828/7 I	4,250	475.00	675.00	1125.	2000.
	1828 I	Inc. Ab.	375.00	425.00	575.00	800.00
	1829 I	—	375.00	425.00	575.00	750.00
	1830 I	3,068	375.00	425.00	575.00	750.00
	1831 I	1,745	375.00	450.00	625.00	850.00
	1832/1 I	.011	375.00	425.00	575.00	750.00
	1832 I	Inc. Ab.	375.00	425.00	575.00	750.00
	1833 I	.025	375.00	425.00	575.00	750.00
	1834 IJ	.031	375.00	425.00	575.00	750.00

93	1835 IJ	.028	375.00	425.00	575.00	800.00
	1836 IJ	.027	375.00	425.00	575.00	800.00
	1837 IJ	.017	375.00	425.00	575.00	800.00
	1838 IJ	.033	375.00	425.00	575.00	800.00

Reeded edge

104.1	1839 IJ	.027	375.00	425.00	575.00	725.00
	1840 IJ	.025	375.00	425.00	575.00	725.00
	1841 IJ	.025	375.00	425.00	575.00	725.00
	1842 IJ	.027	375.00	425.00	575.00	725.00
	1843/2 IJ	.027	375.00	425.00	575.00	725.00
	1843 IJ	Inc. Ab.	375.00	425.00	575.00	725.00

Lettered edge

104.2	1844 IJ	—	400.00	500.00	600.00	800.00
	1845 IJ	—	400.00	500.00	600.00	800.00

105	1846 IJ	—	375.00	425.00	575.00	750.00
	1847 IJ	—	375.00	425.00	575.00	750.00
	1848 JM	—	375.00	425.00	575.00	750.00
	1849 ML	—	375.00	425.00	575.00	750.00
	1850 LA	—	375.00	425.00	575.00	750.00
	1851 LA	—	375.00	425.00	575.00	750.00

COUNTERMARKED COINAGE

NOTE: On March 29, 1833, the government ordered the legal circulation of the Argentinian 8 Reales struck at Potosi. The coins struck at Potosi must have the countermark of the coat of arms of Chile and the abbreviation of the place where the countermark was applied.

CHILOE
8 REALES
SILVER
c/m: Mountains/CHIL on Argentina 8 Reales, KM#5.

KM#	Date	Good	VG	Fine	VF
106	ND(1833)	1150.	1750.	2250.	2750.

CONCEPCION
8 REALES
SILVER
c/m: Mountains/CON on Argentina 8 Reales, KM#5.

107	ND(1833)	900.00	1500.	2000.	2500.

SANTIAGO
8 REALES
SILVER

c/m: Mountains/SAN on Argentina 8 Reales, KM#5.

KM#	Date	Good	VG	Fine	VF
108	ND(1833)	1150.	1750.	2250.	2750.

SERENA
4 REALES

SILVER
c/m: Mountains/SER on Argentina 4 Soles, KM#13.
113	ND(1833)	—	—	—	—

8 REALES

SILVER
c/m: Mountains/SER on Argentina 8 Reales, KM#5.
109	ND(1833)	135.00	225.00	375.00	550.00

VALDIVIA
4 REALES

SILVER
c/m: Mountains/VALD on Argentina 4 Reales, KM#4.
110	ND(1833)	180.00	300.00	550.00	900.00

8 REALES
SILVER
c/m: Mountains/VALD on Argentina 8 Reales, KM#5.
111.1	ND(1833)	180.00	300.00	550.00	900.00

c/m: Mountains/VALD on Mexico 8 Reales, KM#304.
111.2	ND(1822)	—	—	Rare	—

VALPARAISO
8 REALES
SILVER
c/m: Mountains/VALP on Argentina 8 Reales, KM#5.

KM#	Date	Good	VG	Fine	VF
112	ND(1833)	180.00	300.00	550.00	900.00

DECIMAL COINAGE
10 Centavos = 1 Decimo
10 Decimos = 1 Peso
10 Pesos = 1 Condor

MEDIO (1/2) CENTAVO

COPPER

KM#	Date	Mintage	VG	Fine	VF	XF
114	1835	2.000	1.00	2.00	3.50	20.00
	1835	Inc. Ab.	—	—	Proof	—

Flat star, stars flank date.
117	1851	1.620	2.00	4.00	6.00	25.00

Raised star, dots flank date.
118	1851	2.200	1.00	2.00	4.00	20.00

126	1853	2.667	1.00	2.00	4.00	20.00

COPPER-NICKEL
148	1871	.133	1.75	4.25	8.50	15.50
	1872/1	.506	1.75	4.25	8.50	15.50
	1872	Inc. Ab.	2.50	5.00	10.00	18.00
	1873	1.265	1.75	4.25	8.50	15.50

COPPER
148a	1883/73	.714	1.50	3.00	4.25	10.00
	1883	Inc. Ab.	1.00	2.00	3.50	8.00
	1884	.104	1.50	3.00	5.00	12.50
	1885	.132	1.00	2.00	3.50	8.00
	1886	.469	1.00	2.00	3.50	8.00
	1888/78	.294	1.25	2.50	4.25	10.00
	1888	Inc. Ab.	1.50	3.00	5.00	12.50
	1890/70	.070	—	—	—	—
	1890/73	I.A.	2.50	4.25	8.50	18.00
	1890	Inc. Ab.	3.25	6.00	10.00	22.50
	1893/88	.071	—	—	—	—
	1893	I.A.	2.00	4.00	6.00	14.50
	1894	.251	1.00	2.00	3.50	8.00

UN (1) CENTAVO

COPPER, thick flan, 18.01 g

KM#	Date	Mintage	VG	Fine	VF	XF
115	1835	2.000	2.00	4.00	8.00	22.50
	1835	—	—	—	Proof	100.00

Thin flan, 13.35 g

| 116 | 1835 | Inc. Ab. | 2.00 | 4.00 | 8.00 | 22.50 |

Obv: Flat star, stars flank date.
Rev: W/o diamond below wreath.

| 119 | 1851 | 2.430 | 2.50 | 5.00 | 12.50 | 30.00 |

Obv: Raised star, dots flank date.
Rev: Diamond below wreath.

| 120 | 1851 | 3.300 | 3.00 | 8.00 | 17.50 | 45.00 |

Rev: Different sprays.

| 127 | 1853 | 2.667 | 2.00 | 5.00 | 15.00 | 35.00 |
| | 1853 | — | — | — | Proof | 150.00 |

NOTE: The 1853 coins were struck with coin and medal rotation.

COPPER-NICKEL

146	1870/60	—	—	—	—	—
	1871	1.687	1.00	2.00	3.00	6.00
	1872/1	.690	1.75	3.50	5.00	10.00
	1872	Inc. Ab.	1.50	3.00	4.00	8.00
	1873/1	.779	—	—	—	—
	1873	Inc. Ab.	1.50	3.00	4.00	8.00
	1874	.263	1.90	3.75	4.00	8.00
	1875/1	.113	—	—	—	—
	1875	Inc. Ab.	2.25	4.50	5.00	10.00
	1876	.022	3.25	6.50	10.00	20.00
	1877	.016	3.50	7.00	10.00	20.00

COPPER

146a	1878	.177	1.50	3.00	6.00	12.00
	1879	.793	1.10	2.25	3.75	7.50
	1880/70	.478	—	—	—	—
	1880/79	I.A.	—	—	—	—
	1880	Inc. Ab.	1.10	2.25	3.75	7.50
	1881	.318	1.25	2.50	4.00	8.00
	1882	.492	1.10	2.25	3.75	7.50
	1883	.274	1.50	3.00	5.00	10.50
	1884/3	.171	1.75	3.50	6.00	12.00
	1884	Inc. Ab.	1.50	3.00	5.00	10.50
	1885	.205	1.10	2.25	3.75	7.50
	1886	.510	1.10	2.25	3.75	7.50
	1887/4	.231	—	—	—	—
	1887	Inc. Ab.	1.10	2.25	3.50	7.00
146a	1888	.141	1.50	3.00	5.00	9.00
	1890	.047	4.25	8.50	15.00	28.00
	1891	.099	2.50	5.00	10.00	18.00
	1893	.115	1.00	2.00	3.75	8.00
	1894	.244	.75	1.50	3.00	6.00
	1895	.449	.75	1.50	2.50	5.50
	1895 1 over inverted 1					
	Inc. Ab.	—	—	—	—	
	1896	.139	1.25	2.50	4.00	8.00
	1898	1.605	.50	1.00	1.50	4.50

NOTE: Varieties exist.

161	1904	.970	.50	1.00	2.00	5.00
	1908	.174	.65	1.25	2.00	7.00
	1919	.173	.25	.50	2.00	7.00

DOS (2) CENTAVOS

COPPER-NICKEL

KM#	Date	Mintage	Fine	VF	XF	Unc
147	1870/60	—	—	—	—	—
	1871	.639	2.50	6.00	9.00	15.00
	1872/1	.207	—	—	—	—
	1872	Inc. Ab.	2.50	6.00	9.00	15.00
	1873	.461	2.50	6.00	9.00	15.00
	1874	.263	4.00	6.50	9.00	17.50
	1875	.294	4.00	6.50	9.00	17.50
	1876	.108	10.00	15.00	20.00	30.00
	1877	.021	15.00	35.00	50.00	120.00

COPPER

147a	1878	.112	3.00	7.50	11.00	26.00
	1879	.479	1.60	4.00	6.00	15.00
	1880	.278	1.60	4.00	6.00	15.00
	1881	.172	2.00	5.00	7.50	18.00
	1882	.361	1.60	4.00	6.00	15.00
	1883	.405	1.20	3.00	5.00	12.00
	1884	.182	1.60	4.00	6.00	15.00
	1885	.146	1.60	4.00	6.00	15.00
	1886	.494	1.20	3.00	5.00	12.00
	1887	.106	1.60	4.00	6.00	15.00
	1888	.186	2.00	5.00	7.50	18.00
	1890	.155	3.00	7.50	9.00	20.00
	1891	.089	8.00	20.00	30.00	60.00
	1893/1	.141	1.20	3.00	5.00	12.00
	1893	Inc. Ab.	1.00	2.50	4.00	10.00
	1894	.190	2.00	5.00	7.50	18.00

| 164 | 1919 | .147 | 1.00 | 2.50 | 4.00 | 8.00 |

DOS I MEDIO (2-1/2) CENTAVOS

COPPER

150	1886	.381	1.50	3.00	8.00	22.50
	1887/6	.500	3.00	8.00	15.00	35.00
	1887	Inc. Ab.	1.60	4.00	8.00	22.50
	1895	.366	1.50	3.00	8.00	22.50
	1896	.172	1.60	4.00	8.00	27.50
	1898/88	2.177	—	—	—	—
	1898	Inc. Ab.	1.50	3.00	8.00	22.50

KM#	Date	Mintage	Fine	VF	XF	Unc
162	1904	.277	1.60	4.00	8.00	22.50
	1906	.161	2.00	5.00	7.50	20.00
	1907	.262	1.60	4.00	7.00	20.00
	1908	.201	1.20	3.00	6.50	20.00

NOTE: Varieties exist for 1907 dated coins.

MEDIO (1/2) DECIMO

1.2500 g, .900 SILVER, .0361 oz ASW

KM#	Date	Mintage	VG	Fine	VF	XF
121	1851	.233	150.00	250.00	350.00	500.00
	1853	Inc. Ab.	2.00	4.00	7.00	17.50
	1854	.122	4.00	8.00	12.50	32.50
	1855	1.257	2.00	4.00	7.00	17.50
	1856/5	.767	3.00	6.00	11.00	30.00
	1856	Inc. Ab.	2.50	5.00	9.00	25.00
	1857	1.655	2.00	4.00	7.00	17.50
	1858	.318	2.50	5.00	9.00	25.00
	1859/8	.041	—	—	—	—
	1859	Inc. Ab.	10.00	20.00	30.00	60.00

1.1500 g, .900 SILVER, .0332 oz ASW

121a	1860/59	.372	10.00	20.00	27.50	55.00
	1860	Inc. Ab.	8.50	17.50	25.00	50.00
	1861	.338	7.50	15.00	22.50	45.00
	1862	4,400	—	—	Rare	—

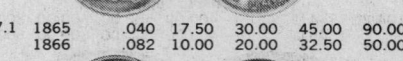

| 137.1 | 1865 | .040 | 17.50 | 30.00 | 45.00 | 90.00 |
| | 1866 | .082 | 10.00 | 20.00 | 32.50 | 50.00 |

137.2	1867	.028	4.00	8.00	12.50	25.00
	1868	.181	2.00	4.00	6.00	12.50
	1869	.293	1.50	3.00	4.75	9.50
	1870/69	.540	1.25	2.50	4.00	8.00
	1870	Inc. Ab.	1.25	2.00	3.25	6.50
	1871/0	.171	1.50	3.00	5.00	10.00
	1871	Inc. Ab.	3.00	5.00	7.50	15.00
	1872	.286	2.00	4.00	7.00	12.50
	1873	.170	3.00	5.00	7.50	15.00
	1874/3	.588	3.00	7.00	15.00	20.00
	1874	Inc. Ab.	2.00	4.00	7.00	12.50
	1875/2	.097	—	—	—	—
	1875/3	I.A.	—	—	—	—
	1875	Inc. Ab.	5.00	8.00	12.50	25.00
	1876	.082	3.00	7.00	12.00	16.00
	1877	.327	2.00	6.00	9.00	14.00
	1878	.306	2.00	6.50	10.00	15.00
	1880	.194	3.00	7.00	12.00	16.00
	1881	.264	3.00	7.00	12.00	16.00

COPPER (OMS)

| 137.2a | 1868 | — | — | — | — | 50.00 |

1.2500 g, .500 SILVER, .0200 oz ASW
Obv. leg: 0.5 added.

KM#	Date	Mintage	Fine	VF	XF	Unc
137.3	1879	.916	2.00	3.00	6.00	20.00
	1880	1.205	1.50	3.00	5.00	15.00
	1881/0	1.687	1.50	3.00	5.00	15.00
	1881	Inc. Ab.	1.50	3.00	5.00	15.00
	1882	.235	2.50	5.00	8.00	20.00
	1883	.117	3.75	7.50	12.50	24.00
	1884	.664	2.50	3.50	6.50	20.00
	1885/3	.489	2.00	3.00	5.00	15.00
	1885/4	I.A.	2.00	3.00	5.00	15.00
	1885	Inc. Ab.	2.00	3.00	5.00	15.00
	1887	3.081	1.50	3.00	5.00	15.00
	1888/7	2.448	2.50	3.50	6.50	20.00
	1888	Inc. Ab.	1.50	3.00	5.00	15.00

KM#	Date	Mintage	Fine	VF	XF	Unc
137.3	1892/72	1.684	2.50	3.50	7.50	20.00
	1892/82	I.A.	2.50	3.50	6.50	20.00
	1892/82/72	Inc. Ab.	—	—	—	—
	1892/88	I.A.	—	—	—	—
	1892	Inc. Ab.	2.50	5.00	7.00	20.00
	1893/73	.850	—	—	—	—
	1893/83	I.A.	—	—	—	—
	1893/2	I.A.	2.00	4.00	6.00	20.00
	1893	Inc. Ab.	1.50	3.00	5.00	15.00
	1894/73	.784	2.00	4.50	7.50	18.00
	1894/84	Inc. Ab.	2.00	4.50	7.50	18.00
	1894/3	Inc. Ab.	—	—	—	—
	1894	Inc. Ab.	2.00	4.00	7.00	16.00

Mule. Obv: KM#137.3. Rev: KM#137.2.

KM#	Date	Mintage	Fine	VF	XF	Unc
149	1884	—	—	—	20.00	50.00

CINCO (5) CENTAVOS

1.0000 g, .835 SILVER, .0268 oz ASW

KM#	Date	Mintage	Fine	VF	XF	Unc
155.1	1896	.888	3.00	6.00	10.00	20.00

1.0000 g, .500 SILVER, .0160 oz ASW
Obv: 0.5 below condor.

KM#	Date	Mintage	Fine	VF	XF	Unc
155.2	1899	1.794	2.00	3.00	5.00	15.00
	1901/891	2.109	—	—	—	—
	1901	Inc. Ab.	2.00	3.00	5.00	15.00
	1904/1	2.527	3.50	7.00	12.50	27.50
	1904	Inc. Ab.	2.00	3.00	5.00	15.00
	1906	.713	2.00	3.00	6.00	17.00
	1907	2.791	2.00	3.00	5.00	15.00
	1909/899	—	2.50	4.00	7.00	18.50

NOTE: Varieties exist for 1906 dated coins w/0.5, 0.5. and 05. below condor.

1.0000 g, .400 SILVER, .0128 oz ASW

KM#	Date	Mintage	Fine	VF	XF	Unc
155.2a	1908	3.642	2.00	3.00	5.00	10.00
	1909/8	1.177	—	—	—	—
	1909	Inc. Ab.	2.00	4.00	6.00	12.50
	1910/01	1.587	—	—	—	—
	1910	Inc. Ab.	2.00	3.00	5.00	10.00
	1911	.847	2.00	4.00	6.00	12.50
	1913/2	2.573	2.00	5.00	10.00	20.00
	1913	Inc. Ab.	2.00	3.00	5.00	10.00
	1919	Inc. Be.	1.50	3.00	5.00	10.00

1.0000 g, .450 SILVER, .0144 oz ASW
Obv: 0.45 below condor.

KM#	Date	Mintage	Fine	VF	XF	Unc
155.3	1915	2.250	1.50	3.00	5.00	10.00
	1916/1	4.337	1.50	3.50	6.00	12.00
	1916/5	I.A.	—	—	—	—
	1916	Inc. Ab.	1.50	3.00	5.00	10.00
	1919/1	1.494	3.00	5.00	10.00	20.00
	1919/5	I.A.	3.00	5.00	10.00	20.00
	1919	Inc. Ab.	2.00	4.00	6.00	12.00

COPPER-NICKEL

KM#	Date	Mintage	Fine	VF	XF	Unc
165	1920	.718	1.00	1.50	3.00	6.50
	1921	2.406	.50	1.25	2.00	5.00
	1922	3.872	.50	1.25	2.00	5.00
	1923	2.150	.50	1.25	2.00	5.00
	1925	.994	.50	1.25	2.00	5.00
	1926	.594	1.50	2.50	3.00	6.50
	1927	1.276	.50	1.00	2.00	5.00
	1928	5.197	.50	1.00	2.00	5.00
	1933	3.000	5.00	10.00	17.50	35.00
	1934	Inc. Ab.	.25	.50	1.00	2.00
	1936	2.000	.25	.50	1.00	2.00
	1937	2.000	.25	.50	1.00	2.00
	1938	2.000	.25	.50	1.00	2.00

UN (1) DECIMO

2.5000 g, .900 SILVER, .0723 oz ASW

KM#	Date	Mintage	VG	Fine	VF	XF
124	1852	.211	3.00	7.00	20.00	50.00
	1853	Inc. Ab.	3.00	7.00	20.00	50.00
	1855	.585	3.00	7.00	20.00	50.00
	1856/5	.580	3.00	7.00	20.00	50.00
	1856	Inc. Ab.	3.00	7.00	15.00	35.00
	1857	1.481	3.00	7.00	15.00	35.00
	1858	.540	3.00	7.00	20.00	50.00
	1859	.020	40.00	65.00	100.00	—
	1860/50	—	—	—	—	—
	1860/59	—	3.00	7.00	20.00	40.00

2.3000 g, .900 SILVER, .0665 oz ASW

KM#	Date	Mintage	VG	Fine	VF	XF
124a	1860	.382	3.50	7.00	15.00	30.00
	1861	.236	3.50	7.00	15.00	30.00
	1862	.095	8.00	12.00	20.00	40.00

KM#	Date	Mintage	VG	Fine	VF	XF
136.1	1864 thick flan	.096	5.50	9.00	15.00	30.00
	1864 thin flan	Inc. Ab.	—	—	—	—
	1865/4	.222	6.00	9.00	15.00	30.00
	1865/inverted 5	Inc. Ab.	6.00	9.00	15.00	30.00
	1865	Inc. Ab.	6.00	9.00	15.00	30.00
	1866	.096	5.50	9.00	15.00	30.00

KM#	Date	Mintage	VG	Fine	VF	XF
136.2	1867	.020	7.00	12.00	20.00	40.00
	1868	.207	2.00	2.50	4.00	8.00
	1869/8	.245	—	—	—	—
	1869	Inc. Ab.	2.00	2.50	4.00	8.00
	1870/60	.192	2.75	3.75	6.00	12.50
	1870	Inc. Ab.	2.50	3.50	5.00	10.00
	1871	.091	2.50	3.50	5.00	10.00
	1872/1	.288	—	—	—	—
	1872	Inc. Ab.	2.00	2.50	4.00	8.00
	1873/2	.305	—	—	—	—
	1873/9	I.A.	—	—	—	—
	1873	Inc. Ab.	2.00	2.50	4.00	8.00
	1874/64	.271	—	—	—	—
	1874	Inc.Ab.	2.00	2.50	4.00	8.00
	1875/4	.050	—	—	—	—
	1875	Inc. Ab.	5.00	10.00	20.00	40.00
	1876	.100	2.25	2.75	4.50	9.50
	1877	.096	2.25	2.75	4.50	9.50
	1878	.512	2.00	2.50	4.00	8.00
	1880	.243	2.00	2.50	4.00	8.00

COPPER (OMS)

KM#	Date	Mintage	VG	Fine	VF	XF
136.2a	1868	—	—	—	—	100.00

2.5000 g, .500 SILVER, .0401 oz ASW
Rev. leg: 0.5 added.

KM#	Date	Mintage	Fine	VF	XF	Unc
136.3	1879/8	1.268	1.25	2.25	3.50	8.00
	1879	Inc. Ab.	1.00	2.00	3.00	7.50
	1880/70	.705	1.50	3.00	5.00	10.00
	1880	Inc. Ab.	1.00	2.00	5.00	10.00
	1881	2.186	1.00	2.00	5.00	10.00
	1882	.233	1.00	2.00	5.00	10.00
	1882/2	I.A.	2.00	5.00	10.00	15.00
	1883	.178	1.00	2.00	5.00	10.00
	1884/2	.319	5.00	10.00	17.00	25.00
	1884	Inc. Ab.	1.00	2.00	5.00	10.00
	1885	.116	6.00	12.00	18.00	25.00
	1887/6	1.514	1.25	2.25	3.50	8.00
	1887	Inc. Ab.	1.00	2.00	3.00	7.50
	1891	—	—	—	Rare	—
	1892/82	.994	1.00	2.00	5.00	10.00
	1892/0	Inc. Ab.	3.00	6.00	12.00	20.00
	1892	Inc. Ab.	1.00	2.00	3.00	7.50
	1893/83	.516	1.25	2.25	3.50	8.00
	1893/inverted 3	Inc. Ab.	3.50	5.50	10.00	18.00
	1893	Inc. Ab.	1.00	2.00	3.00	7.50
	1894/84	.826	1.00	2.00	3.00	7.50
	1894/3	I.A.	1.00	2.00	3.00	7.50
	1894/3 E/R in REPUBLICA	Inc. Ab.	1.25	2.25	3.50	8.00
	1894	Inc. Ab.	1.00	2.00	3.00	7.50

2.0000 g, .500 SILVER, .0321 oz ASW

KM#	Date	Mintage	Fine	VF	XF	Unc
136.3a	1891/81	.264	25.00	60.00	125.00	250.00
	1891	I.A.	25.00	60.00	125.00	250.00

DIEZ (10) CENTAVOS

2.0000 g, .835 SILVER, .0536 oz ASW

KM#	Date	Mintage	Fine	VF	XF	Unc
156.1	1896	2.561	2.00	3.50	6.00	10.00

2.0000 g, .500 SILVER, .0321 oz ASW
Obv: 0.5 below condor.

KM#	Date	Mintage	Fine	VF	XF	Unc
156.2	1899	2.013	2.00	3.50	6.00	10.00
	1900	.104	20.00	35.00	50.00	85.00
	1901	Inc. Ab.	10.00	20.00	28.00	35.00
	1904/899	.779	2.00	3.00	5.00	10.00
	1904	Inc. Ab.	2.00	3.50	6.00	10.00
	1906	.139	2.50	4.50	7.50	12.00
	1907	3.151	2.00	3.50	6.00	10.00

NOTE: Varieties exist for 1907 dated coins w/0.5, 0,5 or 0.5/9 below condor.

1.5000 g, .400 SILVER, .0192 oz ASW

KM#	Date	Mintage	Fine	VF	XF	Unc
156.2a	1908	4.149	1.00	2.00	3.50	7.00
	1909	2.964	1.00	2.00	3.50	7.00
	1913	1.269	1.50	3.00	5.00	10.00
	1919	.883	2.50	5.00	7.50	15.00
	1920	2.109	1.00	2.00	3.50	7.00

NOTE: Varieties exist.

1.5000 g, .450 SILVER, .0217 oz ASW
Obv: 0.45 below condor.

KM#	Date	Mintage	Fine	VF	XF	Unc
156.3	1915	1.620	1.00	1.50	2.50	4.00
	1916	2.855	1.00	1.50	2.50	4.00
	1917	.736	1.50	2.50	4.00	8.00
	1918	Inc. Ab.	1.50	2.50	4.00	8.00

COPPER-NICKEL

KM#	Date	Mintage	Fine	VF	XF	Unc
166	1920	.451	1.50	3.50	5.00	10.00
	1921	2.654	.50	.75	1.50	3.00
	1922	4.017	.50	.75	1.50	3.00
	1923	3.356	.50	.75	1.50	3.00
	1924	1.445	.50	.75	1.50	3.00
	1925	2.665	.50	.75	1.50	3.00
	1927	.523	1.00	2.00	3.00	6.00
	1928	3.052	.50	.75	1.50	3.00
	1932	1.500	.75	1.00	2.00	4.00
	1933	5.800	.25	.50	1.00	2.00
	1934	.900	.50	.75	1.50	3.00
	1935	1.500	.50	.75	1.50	3.00
	1936	3.300	.25	.50	1.00	2.00
	1937	2.000	.25	.50	1.00	2.00
	1938	5.000	.25	.50	1.00	2.00
	1939	1.200	.25	.50	1.00	2.00
	1940	6.100	.25	.50	1.00	2.00
	1941	.900	1.00	2.00	3.00	6.00

VEINTE (20) CENTAVOS

5.0000 g, .900 SILVER, .1446 oz ASW

KM#	Date	Mintage	VG	Fine	VF	XF
125	1852	.077	10.00	15.00	20.00	35.00
	1853	.906	5.00	6.50	11.00	20.00
	1854	.417	5.00	6.50	11.00	20.00
	1855	.325	5.00	6.50	12.00	22.50
	1856/5	.396	6.00	8.00	12.50	22.50
	1856	Inc, Ab.	5.00	6.50	11.00	20.00
	1857	.748	5.00	6.50	11.00	20.00

CHILE 292

KM#	Date	Mintage	VG	Fine	VF	XF
125	1858	.532	7.50	15.00	15.00	25.00
	1859/8	.120	15.00	25.00	50.00	75.00
	1859	Inc. Ab.	50.00	75.00	—	—

4.60000 g, .900 SILVER, .1331 oz ASW

KM#	Date	Mintage	VG	Fine	VF	XF
125a	1860/59	.388	3.00	6.00	10.00	20.00
	1860	Inc. Ab.	3.00	6.00	10.00	20.00
	1861/51	1.471	5.00	7.00	10.00	24.00
	1861/58	I.A.	5.00	7.00	10.00	24.00
	1861/91	I.A.	5.00	7.00	10.00	22.50
	1861	Inc. Ab.	5.00	7.00	10.00	22.50
	1862/52	.324	5.00	7.00	10.00	24.00
	1862	Inc. Ab.	5.00	7.00	10.00	22.50

135	1863	.160	5.00	7.50	10.00	18.00
	1864	.226	4.50	6.00	10.00	16.00
	1865	1.505	3.00	5.00	5.00	8.00
	1866	4.298	2.00	3.00	5.00	8.00
	1867	Inc. Be.	10.00	15.00	25.00	40.00

Obv: Smaller sprays.

138.1	1867	.286	4.50	6.00	8.00	12.50
	1868	.197	2.00	3.50	5.00	7.50
	1869/8	.163	3.00	5.00	7.00	10.00
	1869	Inc. Ab.	2.00	3.50	5.00	7.50
	1870/60	.992	3.00	5.00	7.00	10.00
	1870	Inc. Ab.	2.00	3.50	5.00	7.50
	1871	1.144	2.00	3.50	5.00	7.50
	1872	1.979	2.00	3.50	5.00	7.50
	1873/2	.846	—	—	—	—
	1873	Inc. Ab.	2.00	3.50	5.00	7.50
	1874	1.256	2.00	3.50	5.00	7.50
	1875	.120	5.00	7.50	15.00	25.00
	1876	.749	2.75	4.50	6.00	8.50
	1877	.549	2.75	4.50	6.00	8.50
	1878	2.639	2.75	4.50	6.00	8.50
	1879	9.645	60.00	100.00	175.00	250.00

5.0000 g, .500 SILVER, .0803 oz ASW
Obv. leg: 0.5 added.

138.2	1879	5.073	2.50	4.00	6.00	9.00
	1880/70	6.846	2.75	4.50	7.00	11.00
	1880/79	I.A.	2.75	4.50	7.00	11.00
	1880	Inc. Ab.	2.50	4.00	6.00	9.00
	1881	6.408	2.50	4.00	6.00	9.00
	1892/82	3.719	2.75	4.50	7.00	11.00
	1892	Inc. Ab.	2.50	4.00	6.00	9.00
	1893	1.397	2.50	4.00	6.00	9.00

4.0000 g, .500 SILVER, .0643 oz ASW

138.2a	1891	2.953	6.00	9.00	15.00	25.00

5.0000 g, .200 SILVER, .0321 oz ASW
Obv. leg: 0.2 added.

138.3	1891	.787	10.00	15.00	20.00	50.00

4.0000 g, .835 SILVER, .1073 oz ASW

151.1	1895	.146	12.50	20.00	30.00	60.00

4.0000 g, .500 SILVER, .0643 oz ASW
Obv: 0.5 below condor.

KM#	Date	Mintage	Fine	VF	XF	Unc
151.2	1899	4.343	1.00	2.00	3.00	6.50
	1899/sideways 9		—	—	—	—
		Inc. Ab.				
	1900/899	.334	60.00	80.00		
	1900	Inc. Ab.	30.00	40.00	80.00	150.00
	1906/896	.866				
	1906	Inc. Ab.	2.00	3.50	4.50	9.00
	1907/895					
		7.625	2.00	3.00	4.00	8.00
	1907	Inc. Ab.	1.00	2.00	3.00	6.50

3.0000 g, .400 SILVER, .0385 oz ASW
Obv: W/o 0.5 below condor.

151.3	1907	1.201	1.00	1.50	3.00	7.00
	1908	5.869	.75	1.25	2.50	6.00
	1909	1.080	.75	1.25	2.50	6.00
	1913/1	3.507	1.50	2.50	4.00	9.00
	1913	Inc. Ab.	.75	1.25	2.50	6.00
	1919	3.749	.75	1.25	2.50	6.00
	1920	4.189	.75	1.25	2.50	6.00

3.0000 g, .450 SILVER, .0434 oz ASW
Obv: 0.45 below condor.

151.4	1916	3.377	2.00	3.00	4.50	9.50

COPPER-NICKEL
Obv: W/o designer's name. Rev: Large 20.

167.1	1920	.499	1.00	2.50	5.00	12.00
	1921	6.547	.25	.50	1.00	3.50
	1922	8.261	.25	.50	1.00	3.50
	1923	5.439	.25	.50	1.00	3.50
	1924	16.096	.25	.50	1.00	3.50
	1925	9.830	.25	.50	1.00	3.50
	1929	9.685	.25	.50	1.00	3.50

Obv: O.ROTY.

167.4	1929		.25	.50	5.00	10.00

Obv: W/o designer's name. Rev: Small 20.

167.2	1932	—	.50	1.00	2.00	4.50
	1933	5.900	.25	.50	1.00	3.50
	1937	1.000	.50	1.00	2.00	4.50

Obv: O. ROTY.

167.3	1932		.25	.50	1.00	3.50
	1933/inverted 33					
		1.000	1.00	1.50	2.50	6.00
	1933	Inc. Ab.	.25	.50	1.00	3.50
	1937	—	.25	.50	1.00	3.50
	1938	3.043	.25	.50	1.00	3.50
	1939	5.283	.25	.50	1.00	3.50
	1940	9.300	.25	.50	1.00	3.00
	1941	3.000	.25	.50	1.00	3.00

COPPER

177	1942	30.000	.15	.25	.50	1.50
	1943	39.600	.15	.25	.50	1.50
	1944	29.100	.15	.25	.50	1.50
	1945	11.400	.15	.25	.50	1.50
	1946	13.800	.15	.25	.50	1.50
	1947	15.700	.15	.25	.50	1.50
	1948	15.200	.15	.25	.50	1.50
	1949	14.700	.15	.25	.50	1.50
	1950	15.200	.15	.25	.50	1.50
	1951	14.700	.15	.25	.50	1.00
	1952	15.500	.15	.25	.50	1.00
	1953	7.800	.15	.25	.50	1.00

40 CENTAVOS

6.0000 g, .400 SILVER, .0771 oz ASW

KM#	Date	Mintage	Fine	VF	XF	Unc
163	1907	.056	15.00	25.00	50.00	100.00
	1908	1.452	2.50	6.00	10.00	20.00

50 CENTAVOS

12.5000 g, .900 SILVER, .3617 oz ASW

KM#	Date	Mintage	VG	Fine	VF	XF
128	1853	.769	7.50	10.00	20.00	65.00
	1854	.551	7.50	10.00	20.00	65.00
	1855	1.354	7.50	10.00	20.00	65.00
	1856	.606	7.50	10.00	20.00	65.00
	1856 1/inverted 1					
		Inc. Ab.				
	1858	.245	13.00	18.00	25.00	90.00
	1859	.489	9.00	13.00	22.00	70.00
	1860	.020	250.00	350.00	450.00	600.00
	1862	.123	13.00	18.00	35.00	100.00

Obv: Large sprays. Rev: Eagle w/shield.

134	1862	Inc. Ab.	22.00	30.00	45.00	90.00
	1863/2	.080	13.00	22.00	30.00	52.00
	1863	Inc. Ab.	13.00	22.00	30.00	50.00
	1864/3	.068	13.00	22.00	30.00	50.00
	1864	Inc. Ab.	13.00	22.00	30.00	50.00
	1865/4	.287	7.00	12.00	20.00	32.50
	1865	Inc. Ab.	6.50	11.00	18.00	30.00
	1866/5	.200	6.50	11.00	18.00	30.00
	1866	Inc. Ab.	9.00	13.00	22.00	35.00
	1867	.047	22.00	35.00	55.00	80.00

Obv: Smaller sprays.

139	1867	Inc. Ab.	15.00	22.00	30.00	50.00
	1868	.147	7.00	9.00	11.00	20.00
	1870/68	.271	5.50	7.50	9.00	16.50
	1870	Inc. Ab.	5.50	7.00	9.00	15.00
	1872/0	.104	7.00	9.00	11.00	20.00
	1872	Inc. Ab.	7.00	9.00	11.00	20.00

10.0000 g, .700 SILVER, .2250 oz ASW

KM#	Date	Mintage	Fine	VF	XF	Unc
160	1902	2.022	3.50	6.00	10.00	25.00
	1903	1.111	3.50	6.00	10.00	25.00
	1905	1.075	3.50	6.00	10.00	25.00
	1906	.142	—	Reported, not confirmed		

COPPER

KM#	Date	Mintage	Fine	VF	XF	Unc
178	1942	4.715	.50	1.00	2.00	5.00

UN (1) PESO

25.0000 g, .900 SILVER, .7234 oz ASW

KM#	Date	Mintage	VG	Fine	VF	XF
129	1853	.394	14.00	24.00	42.00	65.00
	1854	.567	14.00	24.00	42.00	65.00
	1855	.683	14.00	24.00	42.00	65.00
	1856/5	.406	24.00	38.00	62.00	145.00
	1856	Inc. Ab.	18.50	28.50	50.00	95.00
	1858	.051	55.00	95.00	145.00	285.00
	1859/8	.330	18.50	28.50	50.00	70.00
	1859	Inc. Ab.	14.00	24.00	42.00	65.00
	1862	.103	45.00	90.00	200.00	335.00

1.5235 g, .900 GOLD, .0441 oz AGW
Crude style.

KM#	Date	Mintage	Fine	VF	XF	Unc
133	1860	.156	35.00	50.00	75.00	110.00
	1861	.176	35.00	50.00	75.00	110.00
	1862	.011	40.00	60.00	80.00	125.00
	1863	.055	35.00	50.00	75.00	110.00
	1864	.029	40.00	60.00	80.00	125.00

Fine style.

| 140 | 1867 | 949 pcs. | 75.00 | 100.00 | 250.00 | 400.00 |
| | 1873 | .016 | 40.00 | 60.00 | 80.00 | 125.00 |

25.0000 g, .900 SILVER, .7234 oz ASW
Obv. value: 1 PESO. Rev: Eagle w/shield.

| 141 | 1867 | Inc. Be. | 1200. | 2800. | 4000. | 6000. |

Obv. value: UN PESO

142.1	1867	.220	20.00	40.00	60.00	95.00
	1868	1.037	10.00	15.00	25.00	80.00
	1869	.467	12.50	20.00	32.50	80.00
	1870/69	.556	12.50	20.00	32.50	85.00
	1870	Inc. Ab.	12.50	20.00	32.50	80.00
	1871	.795	25.00	45.00	60.00	120.00
	1872	Inc. Ab.	12.50	20.00	32.50	80.00
	1873/2	.323	20.00	35.00	65.00	100.00
	1873	Inc. Ab.	10.00	15.00	25.00	70.00
	1874	1.204	10.00	15.00	25.00	70.00
	1875	2.128	10.00	15.00	25.00	70.00
	1876	1.508	10.00	15.00	25.00	70.00
	1877	1.930	10.00	15.00	25.00	70.00
	1878	.950	10.00	15.00	25.00	70.00
	1879	.780	10.00	15.00	25.00	70.00
	1880	.693	10.00	15.00	25.00	70.00
	1881	.109	10.00	15.00	25.00	70.00
	1882/1	1.648	12.50	20.00	32.50	80.00
	1882	Inc. Ab.	10.00	15.00	25.00	70.00
	1883 round top 3					
		1.397	10.00	15.00	25.00	70.00

KM#	Date	Mintage	Fine	VF	XF	Unc
142.1	1884	1.812	10.00	15.00	25.00	70.00
	1885/3	.528	12.50	20.00	40.00	115.00
	1885	Inc. Ab.	10.00	15.00	30.00	95.00
	1886	.966	10.00	15.00	25.00	70.00
	1887	.023	400.00	800.00	1200.	1800.
	1889	.241	20.00	35.00	50.00	145.00
	1890/89	.109	25.00	45.00	65.00	190.00
	1890	Inc. Ab.	20.00	35.00	50.00	145.00
	1891	.109	50.00	100.00	200.00	400.00

Flat top 3, obv. not inverted w/respect to rev.
| 142.2 | 1883(1925).150 | — | 150.00 | 300.00 | 465.00 |

Flat top 3, obv. inverted w/respect to rev.
| 142.3 | 1883(1926) I.A. | — | 150.00 | 300.00 | 465.00 |

Above issue minted in 1925-6 and most coins were subsequently melted down.

20.0000 g, .835 SILVER, .5369 oz ASW

152.1	1895	6.086	8.00	12.50	16.50	40.00
	1896	1.556	10.00	15.00	28.00	55.00
	1897	.037	25.00	40.00	55.00	90.00

NOTE: 1895 dated coins exist w/TASSET left of rock and O'ROTY on rock.

20.0000 g, .700 SILVER, .4501 oz ASW
Obv: 0.7 below condor.

152.2	1902	.178	8.00	17.50	35.00	65.00
	1903	.372	6.00	12.50	16.50	40.00
	1905	.429	6.00	12.50	16.50	40.00

12.0000 g, .900 SILVER, .3472 oz ASW
Obv: 0.9 below condor.

| 152.3 | 1910 | 2.166 | 4.00 | 6.00 | 12.00 | 22.50 |

9.0000 g, .720 SILVER, .2083 oz ASW
Obv: 0.72 below condor.

| 152.4 | 1915 | 6.032 | 3.75 | 5.00 | 6.50 | 15.00 |
| | 1917 | 3.033 | 4.00 | 5.50 | 8.00 | 17.50 |

9.0000 g, .500 SILVER, .1446 oz ASW
Obv: 0.5 below condor.

KM#	Date	Mintage	Fine	VF	XF	Unc
152.5	1921	2.287	2.25	3.50	5.00	9.00
	1922	2.718	2.25	3.50	5.00	9.00

NOTE: Struck with coin rotation.

| 152.6 | 1924 | 1.748 | 2.25 | 3.50 | 5.00 | 9.00 |
| | 1925 | 2.037 | 2.25 | 3.50 | 5.00 | 9.00 |

NOTE: Struck with medal rotation. Varieties of 1925 dated coins exist w/flat and curved tops.

Mule. Obv: KM#152.5. Rev: KM#171.

| A171.1 | 1927 | — | 15.00 | 30.00 | 45.00 | 90.00 |

Obv: 0.5 FINO.
Rev: Smaller letters in denomination.

| 171.1 | 1927 | 4.099 | 4.00 | 6.00 | 10.00 | 18.00 |

Obv: 0,5 FINO.

| 171.2 | 1927 | — | 4.00 | 6.00 | 10.00 | 18.00 |

6.0000 g, .400 SILVER, .0771 oz ASW

| 174 | 1932 | 4.000 | 1.75 | 2.75 | 3.50 | 6.50 |

COPPER-NICKEL

| 176.1 | 1933 | 29.976 | .20 | .50 | 1.00 | 2.00 |

NICKEL (OMS)

| 176.1a | 1933 | — | — | — | — | — |

COPPER-NICKEL
Obv: O ROTY incuse on rock base.

| 176.2 | 1940 | .150 | 1.50 | 2.00 | 2.50 | 4.00 |

COPPER

179	1942	15.150	.10	.35	1.00	4.00
	1943	16.900	.10	.35	1.00	4.00
	1944	12.050	.10	.35	1.00	5.00
	1945	7.600	.10	.35	1.00	5.00
	1946	2.050	.10	.35	1.50	7.50
	1947	2.200	.10	.35	1.50	7.50
	1948	5.900	.10	.25	.75	3.75
	1949	7.100	.10	.20	.45	2.25
	1950	7.250	.10	.20	.45	2.25
	1951	8.150	.10	.20	.45	2.25
	1952	10.400	.10	.20	.45	2.25
	1953	17.200	.10	.20	.40	1.50
	1954	7.566	.10	.20	.40	1.50

ALUMINUM

179a	1954	43.550	.10	.15	.25	.40
	1955	69.050	.10	.15	.25	.40
	1956	58.250	.10	.15	.25	.40
	1957	49.250	.10	.15	.25	.40
	1958	29.900	.10	.15	.25	.40

CHILE 294

DOS (2) PESOS

3.0506 g, .900 GOLD, .0882 oz AGW
Crude style.

KM#	Date	Mintage	Fine	VF	XF	Unc
132	1857	.207	BV	50.00	75.00	125.00
	1858/7	.056	BV	65.00	100.00	150.00
	1858	Inc. Ab.	BV	50.00	75.00	125.00
	1859	.097	BV	50.00	75.00	125.00
	1860	.078	BV	50.00	75.00	125.00
	1862	.010	BV	50.00	75.00	125.00
	1865	—	—	—	Rare	—

Fine style.

KM#	Date	Mintage	Fine	VF	XF	Unc
143	1867	841 pcs.	—	—	Rare	—
	1873	.054	BV	50.00	75.00	100.00
	1874	.061	BV	50.00	75.00	100.00
	1875	.037	45.00	60.00	80.00	120.00

18.0000 g, .500 SILVER, .2893 oz ASW

KM#	Date	Mintage	Fine	VF	XF	Unc
172	1927	1.112	BV	4.00	8.00	17.50

CINCO (5) PESOS

7.6265 g, .900 GOLD, .2207 oz AGW
Crude style.

KM#	Date	Mintage	Fine	VF	XF	Unc
122	1851	3.735	BV	135.00	160.00	250.00
	1852	.020	BV	125.00	150.00	225.00
	1853	5.987	BV	135.00	160.00	250.00

Fine style.

KM#	Date	Mintage	Fine	VF	XF	Unc
130	1854	953 pcs.	—	—	Rare	—
	1855	7.609	BV	135.00	160.00	250.00
	1856	4.753	BV	135.00	160.00	250.00
	1857	.025	BV	125.00	150.00	225.00
	1858	1.100	BV	125.00	150.00	225.00
	1859/8	.066	BV	125.00	150.00	225.00
	1859	Inc. Ab.	BV	125.00	150.00	225.00
	1862	6.738	BV	135.00	160.00	250.00
	1865	5.110	BV	135.00	160.00	250.00
	1866	6.249	BV	135.00	160.00	250.00
	1867	.010	BV	125.00	150.00	225.00

Modified arms.

KM#	Date	Mintage	Fine	VF	XF	Unc
144	1868	4.065	BV	135.00	160.00	250.00
	1869	5.913	BV	135.00	160.00	250.00
	1870	.013	BV	125.00	150.00	225.00
	1872	.023	BV	125.00	150.00	225.00
	1873	.050	BV	125.00	150.00	225.00

2.9955 g, .917 GOLD, .0883 oz AGW

KM#	Date	Mintage	Fine	VF	XF	Unc
153	1895	3.026	BV	50.00	60.00	90.00
	1896	—	75.00	100.00	250.00	375.00

KM#	Date	Mintage	Fine	VF	XF	Unc
159	1898	.426	BV	55.00	85.00	100.00
	1900	1.267	60.00	100.00	120.00	150.00
	1911	—	—	—	200.00	300.00

25.0000 g, .900 SILVER, .7234 oz ASW
Obv: 0.9 FINO

KM#	Date	Mintage	Fine	VF	XF	Unc
173.1	1927	.976	10.00	12.50	17.50	50.00

Obv: 0,9 FINO

KM#	Date	Mintage	Fine	VF	XF	Unc
173.2	1927	Inc. Ab.	10.00	12.50	17.50	50.00

ALUMINUM

KM#	Date	Mintage	Fine	VF	XF	Unc
180	1956	1.600	.15	.35	.50	.75

22.0500 g, .999 SILVER, .7082 oz ASW
Obv: Similar to 50 Pesos, KM#184.

KM#	Date	Mintage	VF	XF	Unc
182	1968	1,200	—	Proof	20.00

DIEZ (10) PESOS

15.2530 g, .900 GOLD, .4414 oz AGW
Crude style.

KM#	Date	Mintage	Fine	VF	XF	Unc
123	1851	.050	BV	225.00	275.00	350.00
	1852	.135	BV	225.00	275.00	350.00
	1853	.206	BV	225.00	250.00	300.00

Fine style.

KM#	Date	Mintage	Fine	VF	XF	Unc
131	1854	.195	BV	225.00	275.00	350.00
	1855	.061	BV	225.00	275.00	350.00
	1856	.066	BV	225.00	275.00	350.00
	1857	.020	BV	225.00	275.00	350.00
	1858	.052	BV	225.00	275.00	350.00
	1859	.281	BV	225.00	275.00	350.00
	1860	.031	BV	225.00	275.00	350.00
	1861	.015	BV	225.00	275.00	350.00
	1862	.021	BV	225.00	275.00	350.00
	1863	.025	BV	225.00	275.00	350.00
	1864	.026	BV	225.00	275.00	350.00
	1865	.045	BV	225.00	275.00	350.00
	1866	.066	BV	225.00	275.00	350.00
	1867	.121	BV	225.00	275.00	350.00

Obv: Modified arms design.

KM#	Date	Mintage	Fine	VF	XF	Unc
145	1868	.054	BV	225.00	275.00	350.00
	1869	.036	BV	225.00	275.00	350.00
	1870	.076	BV	225.00	275.00	350.00

KM#	Date	Mintage	Fine	VF	XF	Unc
145	1871	.041	BV	225.00	275.00	350.00
	1872	.235	BV	225.00	275.00	350.00
	1873	.112	BV	225.00	275.00	350.00
	1874	1.277	BV	235.00	285.00	375.00
	1876	2.106	BV	235.00	285.00	375.00
	1877	8.208	BV	235.00	285.00	375.00
	1878	7.983	BV	235.00	285.00	375.00
	1879	9.805	BV	235.00	285.00	375.00
	1880	.011	BV	225.00	275.00	350.00
	1881	.013	BV	225.00	275.00	350.00
	1882	.014	BV	225.00	275.00	350.00
	1883	8.381	BV	235.00	285.00	375.00
	1884	9.888	BV	235.00	285.00	375.00
	1885	7.758	BV	235.00	285.00	375.00
	1886	3.721	BV	235.00	285.00	375.00
	1887	5.236	BV	235.00	285.00	375.00
	1888	4.217	BV	235.00	285.00	375.00
	1889	4.650	BV	235.00	285.00	375.00
	1890	2.344	BV	235.00	285.00	375.00
	1892	1.192	BV	235.00	285.00	375.00

5.9910 g, .917 GOLD, .1766 oz AGW

KM#	Date	Mintage	Fine	VF	XF	Unc
154	1895	.808	—	BV	100.00	160.00

KM#	Date	Mintage	Fine	VF	XF	Unc
157	1896	1.438	—	BV	100.00	125.00
	1898	—	—	BV	100.00	150.00
	1900	—	Reported, not confirmed			
	1901	1.651	BV	100.00	125.00	200.00

ALUMINUM

KM#	Date	Mintage	Fine	VF	XF	Unc
181	1956	13.100	.15	.35	.50	.75
	1957	28.800	.15	.35	.50	.75
	1958	44.500	.15	.35	.50	.75
	1959	10.220	.25	.50	1.00	1.50

44.5000 g, .999 SILVER, 1.4292 oz ASW
Obv: Similar to 50 Pesos, KM#184.

KM#	Date	Mintage	VF	XF	Unc
183	1968	1,215	—	Proof	75.00

VEINTE (20) PESOS

11.9821 g, .917 GOLD, .3532 oz AGW

KM#	Date	Mintage	Fine	VF	XF	Unc
158	1896	.149	—	BV	200.00	250.00
	1906	.041	—	BV	200.00	300.00
	1907	.012	—	BV	200.00	300.00
	1908	.025	—	BV	200.00	300.00

KM#	Date	Mintage	Fine	VF	XF	Unc
158	1910	.027	—	BV	200.00	300.00
	1911	.017	—	BV	200.00	300.00
	1913/11	.018	—	BV	200.00	300.00
	1913	Inc. Ab.	—	BV	200.00	300.00
	1914	.022	—	BV	200.00	300.00
	1915	.065	—	BV	200.00	300.00
	1916	.035	—	BV	200.00	300.00
	1917	.717	—	BV	200.00	300.00

4.0679 g, .900 GOLD, .1177 oz AGW

168	1926	.085	—	BV	60.00	90.00
	1958	500 pcs.	BV	60.00	125.00	200.00
	1959	.025	—	—	BV	80.00
	1961	.020	—	—	BV	80.00
	1964	—	—	—	BV	80.00
	1976	.099	—	—	BV	80.00
	1977	.038	—	—	BV	80.00
	1979	.030	—	—	BV	80.00
	1980	.030	—	—	BV	80.00

Rev: Coat of arms on ornamental vines.

| 188 | 1976 | Inc. Ab. | — | BV | 70.00 | 100.00 |

CINCUENTA (50) PESOS

10.1698 g, .900 GOLD, .2943 oz AGW

169	1926	.126	—	BV	150.00	200.00
	1958	.010	—	—	BV	200.00
	1961	.020	—	—	BV	200.00
	1962	.030	—	—	BV	200.00
	1965	—	—	—	BV	200.00
	1966	—	—	—	BV	200.00
	1967	—	—	—	BV	200.00
	1968	—	—	—	BV	200.00
	1969	—	—	—	BV	200.00
	1974	Inc. Ab.	—	—	BV	200.00

10.1600 g, .900 GOLD, .2940 oz AGW
150th Anniversary of Military Academy

| 184 | 1968 | 2,515 | — | — | Proof | 200.00 |

CIEN (100) PESOS

20.3397 g, .900 GOLD, .5886 oz AGW

| 170 | 1926 | .678 | — | BV | 325.00 | 375.00 |

KM#	Date	Mintage	Fine	VF	XF	Unc
175	1932	9,315	—	BV	350.00	450.00
	1946	.380	—	—	BV	350.00
	1947	.500	—	—	BV	350.00
	1948	.405	—	—	BV	350.00
	1949	.245	—	—	BV	350.00
	1950	.020	—	—	BV	350.00
	1951	.190	—	—	BV	350.00
	1952	.240	—	—	BV	350.00
	1953	.150	—	—	BV	350.00
	1954	.250	—	—	BV	350.00
	1955	.085	—	—	BV	350.00
	1956	.070	—	—	BV	350.00
	1957	.020	—	—	BV	350.00
	1958	.178	—	—	BV	350.00
	1959	.100	—	—	BV	350.00
	1960	.345	—	—	BV	350.00
	1961	.195	—	—	BV	350.00
	1962	.250	—	—	BV	350.00
	1963	.145	—	—	BV	350.00
	1964	—	—	—	BV	350.00
	1968	—	—	—	BV	350.00
	1969	—	—	—	BV	350.00
	1970	—	—	—	BV	350.00
	1971	—	—	—	BV	350.00
	1972	—	—	—	BV	350.00
	1973	—	—	—	BV	350.00
	1974	—	—	—	BV	350.00
	1976	.172	—	—	BV	350.00
	1977	.025	—	—	BV	350.00
	1979	.100	—	—	BV	350.00
	1980	.050	—	—	BV	350.00

20.3300 g, .900 GOLD, .5883 oz AGW
150th Anniversary of National Coinage

| 185 | 1968 | 1,815 | — | — | Proof | 400.00 |

200 PESOS

40.6700 g, .900 GOLD, 1.1769 oz AGW
150th Anniversary of San Martin's Passage through Andes Mountains
Obv: Similar to 50 Pesos, KM#184.

| 186 | 1968 | 965 pcs. | — | — | Proof | 1000. |

101.6900 g, .900 GOLD, 2.9427 oz AGW
Obv: Liberty facing left w/flag.
Rev: Similar to 50 Pesos, KM#184.

| 187 | 1968 | — | — | — | Proof | 2250. |

MONETARY REFORM
10 Pesos = 1 Centesimo
100 Centesimos = 1 Escudo

1/2 CENTESIMO

CHILE 295

ALUMINUM

KM#	Date	Mintage	VF	XF	Unc
192	1962	3.750	.10	.30	.50
	1963	8.100	.10	.30	.50

CENTESIMO

ALUMINUM

189	1960	20.160	.35	.75	1.25
	1961	Inc. Ab.	.15	.30	.50
	1962	26.320	.15	.30	.50
	1963	51.360	.15	.30	.50

2 CENTESIMOS

ALUMINUM-BRONZE

193	1960*	—	—	—	50.00
	1964	4.050	—	.10	1.00
	1965	32.550	—	.10	1.00
	1966	31.800	—	.10	1.00
	1967	34.750	—	.10	1.00
	1968	29.400	—	.10	1.00
	1969	—	—	—	6.00
	1969	—	—	Proof	50.00
	1970	20.250	—	.10	1.00

*NOTE: Not released for circulation.

5 CENTESIMOS

ALUMINUM-BRONZE

190	1960	—	—	Proof	100.00
	1961	.012	2.50	5.00	10.00
	1962	Inc. Be.	.10	.15	1.00
	1963	17.280	.10	.15	1.00
	1964	16.628	.10	.15	1.00
	1965	37.680	.10	.15	1.00
	1966	32.360	.10	.15	1.00
	1967	17.640	.10	.15	1.00
	1968	4.338	.10	.15	1.00
	1968	—	—	Proof	50.00
	1969	—	—	—	7.50
	1969	—	—	Proof	50.00
	1970	30.680	.10	.15	1.00

10 CENTESIMOS

ALUMINUM-BRONZE

191	1960	—	2.00	3.50	6.50
	1961	57.068	.10	.20	1.00
	1962	1.480	.10	.20	1.00
	1963	10.920	.10	.20	1.00
	1964	27.020	.10	.20	1.00
	1965	49.480	.10	.20	1.00
	1966	60.360	.10	.20	1.00
	1967	60.680	.10	.25	1.00
	1968	8.040	.10	.20	1.00

CHILE 296

KM#	Date	Mintage	VF	XF	Unc
191	1969	—			7.50
	1970	42.080	.10	.20	1.00
194	1971	99.700	—	.10	.15

20 CENTESIMOS
ALUMINUM-BRONZE

KM#	Date	Mintage	VF	XF	Unc
195	1971	89.200	—	.10	.20
	1972	—	.10	.20	1.00

50 CENTESIMOS
ALUMINUM-BRONZE

196	1971	58.300	.10	.15	.25

ESCUDO
COPPER-NICKEL

197	1971	160.900	.10	.20	.40
	1972	Inc. Ab.	.10	.20	.40
	1972	—	—	Proof	50.00

2 ESCUDOS
COPPER-NICKEL

198	1971*	106 pcs.	—	—	125.00
	1971	—	—	Proof	50.00

*NOTE: Not released for circulation.

5 ESCUDOS
COPPER-NICKEL

199	1971	—	.10	.25	.75
	1972	—	.10	.25	.75
	1972	—	—	Proof	50.00

ALUMINUM

199a	1972	—	.10	.15	.20

10 ESCUDOS

ALUMINUM

200	1974	33.750	.10	.15	.20
	1974	—	—	Proof	50.00

50 ESCUDOS
NICKEL-BRASS

KM#	Date	Mintage	VF	XF	Unc
201	1974	6.000	.15	.25	.60
	1975	20.300	.15	.20	.50

100 ESCUDOS
NICKEL-BRASS

202	1974	32.100	.20	.35	.75
	1975	65.600	.20	.35	.75

MONETARY REFORM
100 Centavos = 1 Peso
1000 Old Escudos = 1 Peso

CENTAVO
ALUMINUM

203	1975	2.000	.10	.15	.50

5 CENTAVOS
ALUMINUM-BRONZE

204	1975	12.000	—	.10	.15

ALUMINUM

204a	1976	5.000	—	.10	.15

10 CENTAVOS
ALUMINUM-BRONZE

205	1975	17.600	—	.10	.15

ALUMINUM

205a	1976	6.600	—	.10	.20
	1977	57.800	—	.10	.15
	1978	58.050	—	.10	.15
	1979	101.950	—	.10	.15

50 CENTAVOS
COPPER-NICKEL

206	1975	38.000	—	.10	.20
	1976	1.000	.50	1.00	2.00
	1977	10.000	—	.10	.20

ALUMINUM-BRONZE

206a	1978	19.250	—	.10	.20
	1979	28.000	—	.10	.20

PESO
COPPER-NICKEL
Obv. leg: BERNARD O'HIGGINS.

KM#	Date	Mintage	VF	XF	Unc
207	1975	51.000	.10	.15	.25

Obv. leg: LIBERTADOR. B.O'HIGGINS.

208	1976	30.000	—	.10	.25
	1977	20.000	—	.10	.25

ALUMINUM-BRONZE

208a	1978	39.700	—	.10	.25
	1979	63.000	—	.10	.25

Reduced size, 17mm.

216	1981	40.000	—	.10	.20
	1984	60.000	—	.10	.20
	1985	—	—	.10	.20
	1986	—	—	.10	.20
	1987	—	—	.10	.20
	1988	—	—	.10	.20

5 PESOS
COPPER-NICKEL
3rd Anniversary of New Government

209	1976	2.100	.15	.25	2.00
	1977	28.300	.15	.25	2.00
	1978	11.700	.15	.25	2.00
	1980	8.000	.15	.25	2.00

NICKEL-BRASS, 19mm

217	1981	17.000	—	.10	.50
	1982	20.000	—	.10	.50
	1984	12.000	—	.10	.50
	1985	—	—	.10	.50
	1986	—	—	.10	.50
	1987	—	—	.10	.50
	1988	—	—	.10	.50

10 PESOS
COPPER-NICKEL
3rd Anniversary of New Government

210	1976	2.100	.10	.20	1.25
	1977	30.000	.10	.20	1.00
	1978	20.000	—	.20	1.00
	1979	7.000	—	.20	1.00
	1980	20.000	.10	.20	1.00

100 PESOS

20.3000 g, .900 GOLD, .5874 oz AGW
3rd Anniversary of New Government

KM#	Date	Mintage	VF	XF	Unc
213	1976	2,900	—	—	350.00
	1976	100 pcs.	—	Proof	825.00

50 CENTAVOS

SILVER
Obv: COPIAPO-CHILE around shield. Rev: Date.

KM#	Date	Mintage	VG	Fine	VF	XF
3	1865	6 known	—	—	350.00	500.00

NOTE: All known 50 Centavos are restrikes made from original dies circa 1909 by Medina.

PESO

ALUMINUM-BRONZE

226	1981	10.000	.50	.75	2.50
	1984	8.000	.50	.75	2.50
	1985	15.000	.50	.75	2.50
	1986	—	.50	.75	2.50
	1987	—	.50	.75	2.50

500 PESOS

102.2700 g, .900 GOLD, 2.9595 oz AGW
3rd Anniversary of New Government
Similar to 100 Pesos, KM#213.

214	1976	500 pcs.	—	—	1650.
	1976	700 pcs.	—	Proof	1650.

PROOF SETS (PS)

KM#	Date	Mintage	Identification	Issue Price	Mkt. Val.
PS1	1968(6)*	—	KM182-187	560.00	2200.
PS2	1968(4)*	—	KM184-187	528.00	3850.
PS3	1968(2)*	—	KM182,183	31.50	95.00
PS4	1971/72(3)	—	KM197(1972),KM198(1971), KM199(1972)	—	150.00

*Total of 12,000 coins struck for each denomination, including those available singly.

4	1865	—	—	25.00	50.00	75.00

COPPER, 32mm

| 4a | 1865* | Unique? | — | 7000. | — | — |

***NOTE:** This coin is either a pattern or an original Peso.

SAN BERNARDO DE MAYPO

1/4 REAL

COPPER
Obv: Mountains (volcano in center) in circle.
Rev: View of Canal de San Bernardo.

| 1 | 1821 | — | 150.00 | 300.00 | 500.00 | 800.00 |

NOTE: Struck to pay canal workers.

TARAPACA

Tarapaca is the northernmost province of Chile. It was annexed to Chile from Peru in 1885 after a war between those two countries, in which Chile was the victor. In that same year the Liberal Party came to power in Chile, instituting reforms. In response to these reforms the Conservative Party rebelled and formed a provisional government, and within a few years defeated the Liberals.

NECESSITY COINAGE

COPIAPO

Revolution of 1859

Issued by Don Pedro Leon Gallo.

50 CENTAVOS

SILVER, uniface

KM#	Date	Mintage	VG	Fine	VF	XF
1	ND	—	25.00	35.00	50.00	70.00

PESO

SILVER, uniface

| 2 | ND | — | 20.00 | 30.00 | 40.00 | 50.00 |

NOTE: Denomination appears as either "I.P" or "I.P".

Blockade of Puerto de Caldera

Issued during the War of 1865 with Spain.

REVOLUTIONARY COINAGE

Struck at Iquique by the revolutionary Junta.

PESO

25.0000 g, .620 SILVER, .4983 oz ASW, 37.5mm
Rev. leg: 25 GRs/620 FINO.

KM#	Date	Mintage	Fine	VF	XF	Unc
1	1891	—	250.00	500.00	1000.	1750.

COPPER

| 1a | 1891 | — | — | — | Rare | — |

44.8000 g, .999 SILVER, 1.4390 oz ASW
3rd Anniversary of New Government

KM#	Date	Mintage	VF	XF	Unc
211	1976	1,000	—	Proof	100.00

NICKEL-BRASS

218	1981	55.000	.10	.20	.50
	1982	45.000	.10	.20	.50
	1984	30.000	.10	.20	.50
	1985	.400	.50	1.50	3.50
	1986	—	.10	.20	.50
	1987	—	.10	.20	.50
	1988	—	.10	.20	.50

50 PESOS

10.1500 g, .900 GOLD, .2937 oz AGW
3rd Anniversary of New Government

212	1976	1,900	—	—	200.00
	1976	Inc. Ab.	—	Proof	225.00

ALUMINUM-BRONZE

219	1981	12.000	.25	.50	1.25
	1982	14.000	.25	.50	1.25
	1985	.400	.60	1.50	3.50
	1986	—	.25	.50	1.25
	1987	—	.25	.50	1.25
	1988	—	.25	.50	1.25

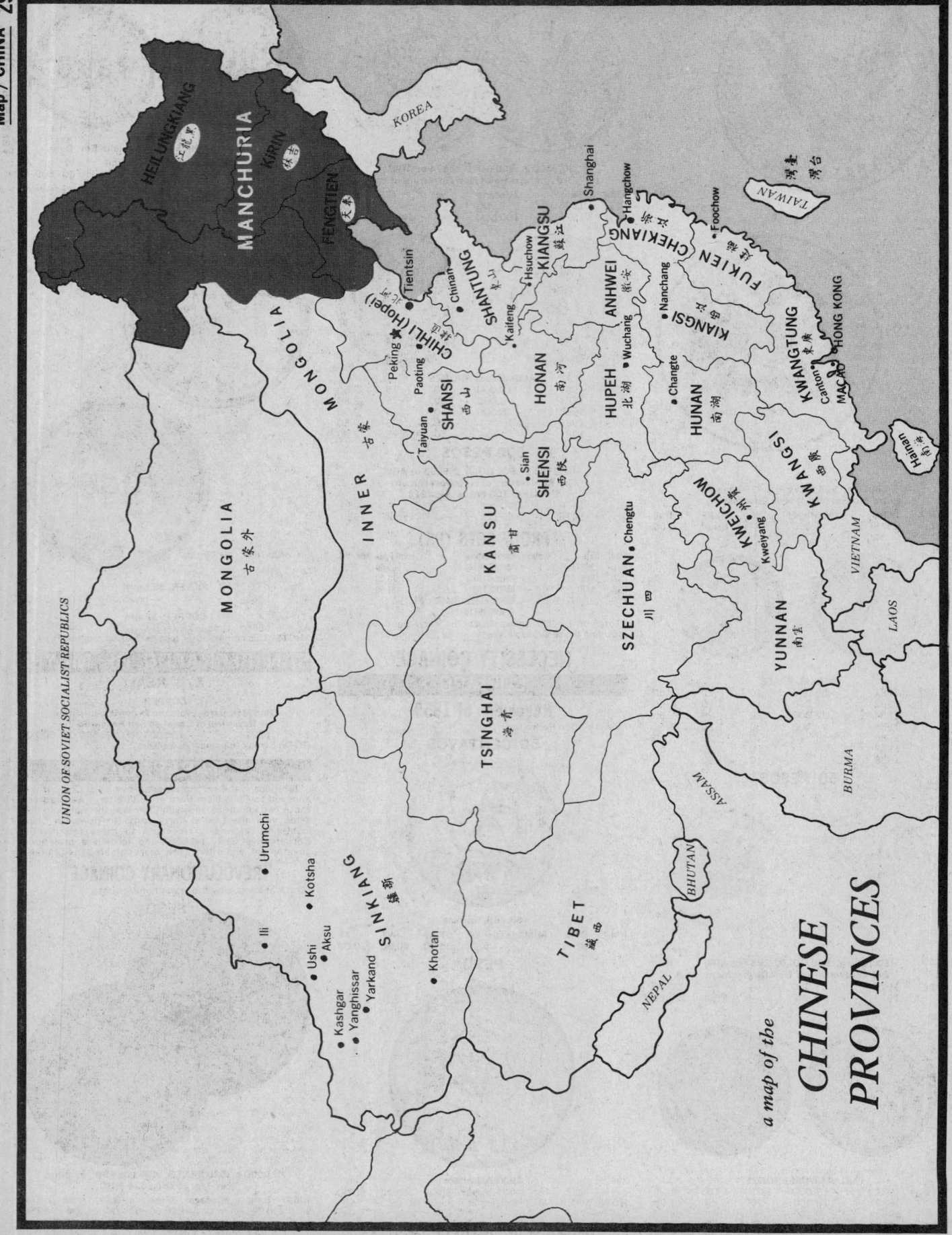

CHINA

Before 1912, China was ruled by an imperial government. The republican administration which replaced it was itself supplanted on the Chinese mainland by a communist government in 1949, but it has remained in control of Taiwan and other offshore islands in the China Sea with a land area of approximately 14,000 square miles and a population of more than 14 million. The People's Republic of China administers some 3.7 million square miles and an estimated 942 million people. This communist government officially established on October 1, 1949, was admitted to the United Nations, replacing its nationalist predecessor, the Republic of China, in 1971.

Cast coins in base metals were used in China many centuries before the Christian era, but locally struck coinages of the western type in gold, silver, copper and other metals did not appear until 1888. In spite of the relatively short time that modern coins have been in use, the number of varieties is exceptionally large.

Both Nationalist and Communist China, as well as the pre-revolutionary Imperial government and numerous provincial or other agencies, including some foreign-administered agencies and governments, have issued coins in China. Most of these have been in dollar (yuan) or dollar-fraction denominations, based on the internationally-used Mexican Pillar Dollar, but coins in tael denominations were issued in the 1920's and earlier. The striking of coins nearly ceased in the late 1930's through the 1940's due to the war effort and a period of uncontrollable inflation while vast amounts of paper currency were issued by the Nationalist, Communist and Japanese occupation institutions.

EMPERORS
OBVERSE TYPES

NOTE: Obverse Type B, *Chung-pao* and Type C *Yuan-pao* were normally used for multiple-cash issues.

JEN TSUNG 仁宗
1796-1820

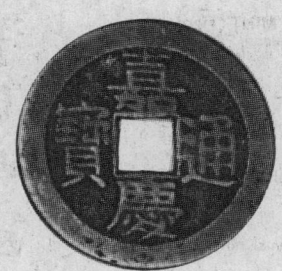

Type A
Reign title: Chia Ch'ing 嘉 慶

Chia-ch'ing T'ung-pao 嘉慶通寶

Chia-ch'ing - Born November 13, 1760, in Peking, he was proclaimed emperor and assumed the reign title in 1796. The White Lotus Rebellion, 1796-1804, broke out in central and western China. Capable generals were appointed to quell the rebellion, but it took the depleted Ch'ing armies five years to put it down. Chia-ch'ing made efforts to restore the finances of the imperial treasury but corruption may have increased as a result of the practice of selling high office as a means of collecting more revenue. Chia-ch'ing died on September 2, 1820, as one of the most unpopular emperors of the Ch'ing dynasty.

HSUAN TSUNG 宣宗
1821-1851

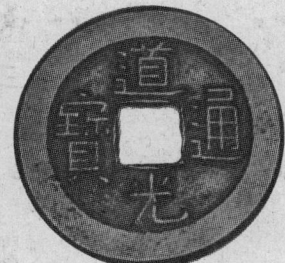

Type A
Reign title: Tao Kuang 道 光

Tao-kuang T'ung-pao 道光通寶

Tao-kuang - The sixth emperor of the Ch'ing dynasty, born September 16, 1782, in Peking, ascended the throne in 1820. He tried to restore the nation's finances by personal austerity. In 1838 the Emperor's attempts to stop the opium trade carried out by Western merchants resulted in the first Opium War between Britain and China, 1839-42. Tao-kuang died February 25, 1850 just as the Taiping Rebellion (1850-64) was beginning to sweep South China.

WEN TSUNG 文宗
1851-1861

Type A
Reign title: Hsien Feng 咸 豐

Hsien-feng T'ung-pao 咸豐通寶

Type B-1
Hsien-feng Chung-pao 咸豐重寶

Type B-2
Left character *Pao* in another style.
Hsien-feng Chung-pao 咸豐重寶

Type C
Hsien-feng Yuan-pao 咸豐元寶

Hsien-feng - The 7th emperor in the Ch'ing dynasty was born in 1831, the 4th son of Tao-Kuang. He took Yehonala as his concubine and she later became the Empress Dowager Tzu-hsi. Her son T'ung-chih was Hsien-feng's successor. The Taiping Rebellion (1850-1864) occurred during his reign. The Treaty of Tientsin in 1858 opened 11 ports in the war with England. He fled to Jehol in 1860.

MU TSUNG 穆宗
1861

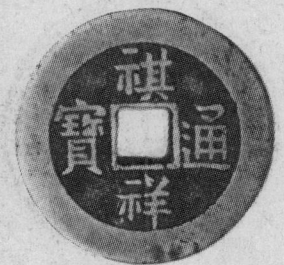

Type A-1
1st reign title: Ch'i Hsiang 祺祥

Ch'i-hsiang T'ung-pao 祺祥通寶

Type B-1
Ch'i-hsiang Chung-pao 祺祥重寶

MU TSUNG 穆宗
1862-1875

Type A-2
2nd reign title: T'ung Chih 同治

T'ung-chih T'ung-pao 同治通寶

Type B-2
T'ung-chih Chung-pao 同治重寶

T'ung-chih - Born on April 27, 1856, T'ung-chih ascended the throne at the age of six with the reign-title Ch'i-hsiang and very few coins were struck with this title. He ruled under the regency of a triumvirate headed by his mother, the Empress Dowager Tz'u-hsi (1835-1908) who made him change to nien-hao T'ung-chih. In the first years of his reign the Taiping rebels were suppressed and the government began attempts to understand and deal with the West. He assumed personal control of the government in 1873 when he was 17. T'ung-chih was a weak ruler whose affairs were constantly scrutinized by the Empress Dowager. He died January 12, 1875, in Peking.

TE TSUNG 1875-1908 德宗

Type A

Reign title: Kuang Hsu 光緒
Kuang-hsu T'ung-pao 光緒通寶

Type B

Kuang-hsu Chung-pao 光緒重寶

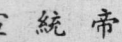
Type C

Kuang-hsu Yuan-pao 光緒元寶

Kuang-hsu - When the previous emperor died, his mother, the Empress Dowager Tz'u-hsi chose her four year old nephew, born August 14, 1871, as emperor. She adopted the boy so that she could act as regent and on February 25, 1875, the young prince ascended the throne, taking the reign title of Kuang-hsu. In 1898 he tried to assert himself and collected a group of progressive officials around him. He issued a series of edicts for revamping of the military, abolition of civil service examinations, improvement of agriculture and restructing of administrative procedures. During Kuang-hsu's reign (1875-1908) the Empress Dowager totally dominated the government. She confined the emperor to his palace and spread rumors that he was deathly ill. Foreign powers let it be known they would not take kindly to the Emperor's death. This saved his life but thereafter he had no power over the government. On November 15, 1908, Tz'u-hsi died under highly suspicious circumstances and the usually healthy emperor was announced as having died the previous day.

HSUAN T'UNG 宣統帝 1908-1911

Ti (Hsun Ti) 遜帝

Type A

Reign title: Hsuan T'ung 宣統
Hsuan-t'ung T'ung-pao 宣統通

Hsuan-t'ung - The last emperor of the Ch'ing dynasty in China and Japan's puppet emperor in Manchukuo from 1934 to 1945, was born on February 7, 1906. He succeeded to the throne at the age of three on November 14, 1908. He reigned under a regency for three years but on February 12, 1912, was forced to abdicate the throne. He was permitted to continue living in the palace in Peking until he left secretly in 1924. On March 9, 1932, he was installed as president, and from 1934 to 1945 was emperor of Manchukuo under the reign title of K'ang-te. He was taken prisoner by the Russians in August of 1945 and returned to China as a war criminal in 1950. He was pardoned in 1959 and went to live in Peking where he worked in the repair shop of a botanical garden.

Although Hsuan T'ung became Emperor in 1908, all the coins of his reign are based on an Accession year of 1909.

YUAN SHIH KAI
Dec. 15, 1915 - March 21, 1916

Reign title: Hung Hsien 憲洪
Hung-hsien Tung-pao 憲洪通寶

Hung-hsien (more popularly known as Yuan Shih Kai) - Born in 1859 in Honan Province, he was the first Han Chinese to hold a viceroyalty and become a grand councillor without any academic qualifications. In 1885 he was made Chinese commissioner at Seoul. During the Boxer Rebellion of 1900, the division under his command was the only remnant of China's army to survive. He enjoyed the trust and support of the dowager empress, Tz'u-hsi, and at her death he was stripped of all his offices. However, when the tide of the revolution threatened to engulf the Manchus Yuan appeared as the only man who could lead the country to peace and unity. Both the Emperor and the provisional president recommended that Yuan be the first president of China. He contrived to make himself president for life and boldly tried to create a new imperial dynasty in 1915-1916. He died of uremia on June 6, 1916.

NOTE: For other legend types refer to Rebel Issues listed after Yunnan-Szechuan.

PROVINCIAL NAMES
(and other source indicators)

	Single Character (1)	Full Names (Right to left reading)
ANHWEI Also An-hwi, Anhui, now Anhui	(Huan) 皖	徽安
CHEKIANG Also Cheh-kiang, now Zhejiang	(Che) 浙	江浙
CHIHLI Also Hopei (after 1928) now Hebei	(Chih) 直	隸直
CH'ING DYNASTY		清大
CHING-KIANG Also Tsing-Kiang	(Huai) 淮	江清
FUKIEN Also Foo-kien, F.K., now Fujian	(Min) 閩	建福
FENGTIEN Also Fung-tien, Fun-tien Manchurian Provinces, now Liaoning	(Feng) 奉	天奉
HEILUNGKIANG Also Hei Lung Kiang, now Heilongjiang		江龍黑
HONAN Also Ho-nan, now Henan(Pien)		汴南河
HOPEH Also Chihli, Hopei, now Hebei		北河
HUNAN Also Hu-nan, now Hunan	(Hsiang) 湘	南湖
HUPEH Also Hupei, Hu-peh, now Hubei		鄂 北湖
HU PU (Board of Revenue) Also Hu Poo	(Hu)	戶 部戶
KANSU Now Gansu		甘肅
KIANGNAN Also Kiang Nan	(Ning) 寧	南江
KIANGSI Also Kiang-si, Kiang-see, (Kan) now Jiangxi	贛	西江
KIANGSI (Alternate)		頴
KIANGSU Also Kiang-soo, now Jiangsu	(Su) 蘇	蘇江
KIRIN Now Jilin	(Chi) 吉	林吉
KWANGSI Also Kwang-si, now Guangxi	(Kuei) 桂	西廣
KWANGTUNG Also Kwang-tung, now Guangdong	(Yueh) 粵	東廣
KWEICHOW Also Kweichou, now Guizhou	(Ch'ien) 黔	州貴
PEIYANG MINT (Tientsin) Also Pei-uang, Pei Yang		洋北
SINKIANG (Chinese Turkestan) Also Sin-kiang, Sungarei, now Xinjiang		疆新
SHANSI Now Shanxi	(Shan) 山	西山
SHENSI Also Shen-si, now Shaanxi	(Shan) 陝	西陝
SHANTUNG, SHAN-TUNG Also Shang-tung, now Shandong	(Tung) 東	東山
SZECHUAN Now Sichuan	(Ch'uan) 川	川四
TAIWAN Also Tai-wan, now Taiwan		灣臺
TAIWAN (Alternate)		灣台
YUNNAN Also Yun-nan, now Yunnan	(Yun) 雲	南雲
YUNNAN (Alternate)	(Tien) 滇	南雲 三
TUNG SAN		東 滇川
YUNNAN-SZECHUAN		

GOVERNMENTAL NAMES
(and other source indicators)

	Full Names (Right to left reading)
CHITUNG (Japanese puppet)	府政東冀
CHINESE SOVIET REPUBLIC	國和共埃維蘇華中
MANCHUKUO (Japanese puppet)	國洲滿大

Introduction / CHINA 301

MENGCHIANG (Japanese puppet)	行銀疆蒙	(2)
PEOPLES REPUBLIC OF CHINA (Communist)	中華人民共和國	(3)
REPUBLIC OF CHINA (Nationalist)	國民華中	
NORTH CHINA (Japanese puppet)	行銀備準合聯國中	

(1) Single-character designators for provincial or regional mints are used primarily on copper coins of the Tai Ching Ti Kuo series.
(2) Vertical readings predominate.
(3) Reads left to right.
(4) For lists of mints in Sinkiang, see that section.

ADDITIONAL CHARACTERS

The additional characters illustrated and defined below are usually found on the reverse of cast bronze cash coins above the square center hole. In the period covered by this catalog the following mints produced cash coins with these additional marks: Board of Revenue and Board of Works in Peking, Kweichow, Aksu and Ili in Sinkiang, Szechuan, and all three mints listed in Yunnan.

MINT MARK IDENTIFIER

There are more than 30 different mints covered in the following text. For ease in identification the more common varieties are illustrated with the Manchu legend.

Boo-Ciowan (Peking)
BOARD OF REVENUE

Boo Yuwan (Peking)
BOARD OF PUBLIC WORKS

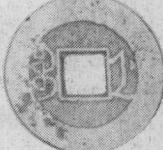
Boo Je
Che Mint
Hangchow
CHEKIANG

Boo Ji
Chihli Mint
Paoting
CHIHLI

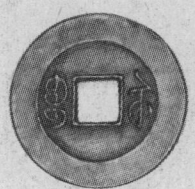
Boo Hu
Hu Mint
ANHWEI

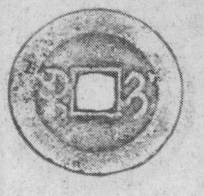
Boo Su
Su Mint
Suchow
KIANGSU

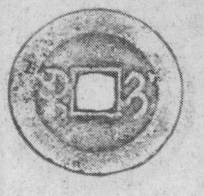
Boo Gi
Chi Mint
KIRIN

Boo Gi
Chi Mint
Chichow
CHIHLI

Boo Jiyen
Ching Mint
Tientsin
CHIHLI

Boo Gui
Kuelin
KWANGSI

Boo Guwang
Canton
KWANGTUNG

Boo Fung
FENGTIEN

Boo Fu
Fu Mint
Fuchou
FUKIEN

Boo Giyan
Kweiyang
KWEICHOW

Boo Jin
Taiyuan
SHANSI

Boo Ho
Ho Mint
K'aifeng
HONAN

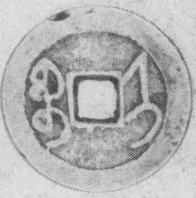
Boo Ji
Chinan
SHANTUNG

Boo Cuwan
Chengtu
SZECHUAN

Boo Ho
Ho Mint
K'aifeng
HUNAN

Boo San
Shan Mint
Sian
SHENSI

Boo De
Teh Mint
Changte
HUNAN

Boo U
Wu Mint
Wuch'ang
HUPEH

Aksu (Hocheng)
SINKIANG

Ili (Hweiyuan)
SINKIANG

Boo Gung
Kungchang
KANSU

Nanchang
KIANGSI

Kotsha (Kuche)
SINKIANG

Introduction / CHINA 302

Kashgar (Shufu) SINKIANG   Khotan (Hotien) SINKIANG

 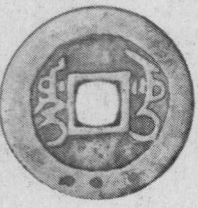

Urumchi (Tihwa) SINKIANG   Ushi (Wushih) SINKIANG

Yarkand (Soche) SINKIANG   Tai Mint TAIWAN

 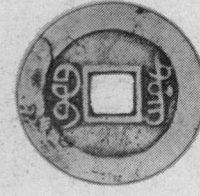

Boo Yon Yun Mint Yunnanfu YUNNAN   Boo Dong Tung Mint Tungch'uan YUNNAN

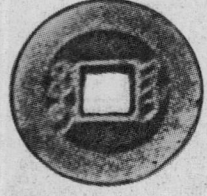 

Ching Mint Location unknown   Fu Mint Location uncertain (Refer to Yunnan)

NON-CIRCULATING ISSUES

Along with regular circulation coinage produced by the various mints certain cash types were cast with the emperor's reign title on the obverse but with various characters and/or symbols not found in our mint identifiers. This listing is not complete but it will benefit the collector as an aide to proper identification.

PALACE ISSUES

Rev: *Tien-hsia T'ai-p'ing*
"An Empire at Peace"
The market value is about $40.00-60.00 in VF condition.

Obv: Chia Ching
Tao Kuang
Hsien Feng
Mu Tsung
Kuang Hsu

Rev: *I-t'ung T'ien-hsia*
"One Government (altogether) at Peace"
The market value is about $50.00-70.00 in VF condition.

Obv: Hsien Feng

BIRTHDAY CASH

壽 福

These issues have the normal reign title on the obverse but the reverse has two Chinese characters 'Fu' or happiness at right and 'Shou' or birthday at left. The market value is about $40.00-60.00 in VF condition.

Hsien Feng

Mu Tsung

Kuang Hsu

AMULETS

Rev: *Eight Trigrams*

Hsien Feng

The eight trigrams (Pa Kua) of the Book of Changes (I Ching). This book, one of the Five Classics, consists of a set of sixty-four figures known as "trigrams". The trigram is composed of combinations of pairs of eight trigrams each of which represents some power in nature, either active or passive, such as fire, water, thunder, earth, etc. These trigrams are said to have been invented 2000 years and more B.C. by the legendary monarch Fu Hsi, who copied them from the back of a tortoise. Attached to each hexagram are explanatory notes and expository comments. The notes are said to have been written by the Chou King Wen Wang and the comments by Confucius. The notes are made in symbolic language which only mystics could understand, but the comments are written in plain language. These comments have lifted the Book of Changes from a primitive book of divination and oracles to an ethical and philosophical importance. The market value is about $30.00-40.00 in VF condition.

MULTIPLE CASH

The size and weight of multiple cash coins cannot be used to determine the correct denomination as these were issued on various standards. The weights decreased considerably in later years. The values are given in various manners.

4 CASH

Ili Mint, Sinkiang

5 CASH

Board of Public Works Mint, Peking

8 CASH

Tihwa Mint, Sinkiang

10 CASH

Normal Ten
Board of Public Works Mint, Peking

Official Ten
Board of Revenue Mint, Peking

Fukien Mint

20 CASH

Fukien Mint

30 CASH

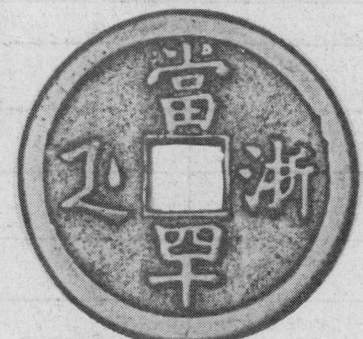

Kiangsu Mint

40 CASH

Chekiang Mint

50 CASH

Fukien Mint
(Weighing) 2 Tael 5 Mace (on rim)

Fukien Mint

100 CASH

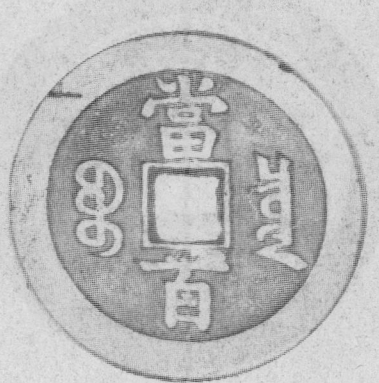

Board of Revenue Mint, Peking

500 CASH

Board of Revenue Mint, Peking

1000 CASH

Board of Revenue Mint, Peking

VARIETIES OF DENOMINATIONS
The denominations for multiple cash may appear in at least three methods. The 50 Cash of Fukien previously illustrated has the 5 above and the 10 below the center hole. The 50 Cash of Kwangsi has the denomination written horizontally below the center hole while the 50 cash of Chekiang has the denomination written vertically below the center hole.

50 CASH

Kwangsi Mint

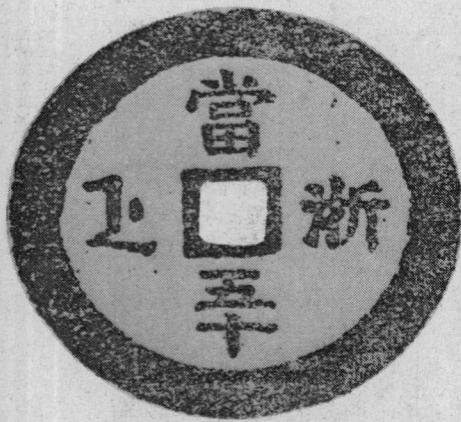

Chekiang Mint

NUMERALS

NUMBER	CONVENTIONAL	FORMAL	COMMERCIAL
1	一 元	壹 弋	丨
2	二	弍 貳	丨丨
3	三	叁 弎	丨丨丨
4	四	肆	乂
5	五	伍	丨
6	六	陸	丄
7	七	柒	丄
8	八	捌	丰
9	九	玖	夂
10	十	拾 什	十
20	十二 or 廿	拾貳	丨丨十
25	五十二 or 五廿	伍拾貳	丨丨十乂
30	十三 or 卅	拾叁	丨丨丨十
100	百一	佰壹	丨百
1,000	千一	仟壹	丨千
10,000	萬一	萬壹	丨万
100,000	萬十 億一	萬拾 億壹	十万
1,000,000	萬百一	萬佰壹	丨百万

NOTE: This table has been adapted from *Chinese Bank Notes* by Ward Smith and Brian Matravers.

MONETARY UNITS

Dollar Amounts

DOLLAR (Yuan)	元 or 員	圓 or 圜	
HALF DOLLAR (Pan Yuan)	圓半	元中	
50¢ (Chiao/Hao)	角伍	毫伍	
10¢ (Chiao/Hao)	角壹	毫壹	
1¢ (Fen/Hsien)	分壹	仙壹	

Copper and Cash Coin Amounts

COPPER (Mei)	枚	CASH (Wen)	文

Tael Amounts

1 TAEL (Liang)	兩
HALF TAEL (Pan Liang)	兩半
5 MACE (Wu Ch'ien)	錢伍
1 MACE (I Ch'ien)	錢壹
1 CANDEREEN (I Fen)	分壹

Common Prefixes

COPPER (T'ung)	銅	GOLD (Chin)	金
SILVER (Yin)	銀	Ku Ping (Tael)*	平庫

NOTE: This table has been adapted from *Chinese Bank Notes* by Ward Smith and Brian Matravers.

MONETARY SYSTEM

Cash Coin System

800-1600 Cash = 1 Tael

In theory, 1000 cash were equal to a tael of silver, but in actuality the rate varied from time to time and place to place.

Dollar System

10 Cash (Wen, Ch'ien) = 1 Cent (Fen, Hsien)
10 Cents = 1 Chiao (Hao)
100 Cents = 1 Dollar (Yuan)
1 Dollar = 0.72 Tael

Imperial silver coins normally bore no denomination, but were inscribed with their weights as follows:

1 Dollar = 7 Mace and 2 Candareens
50 Cents = 3 Mace and 6 Candareens
20 Cents = 1 Mace and 4.4 Candareens
10 Cents = 7.2 Candareens
5 Cents = 3.6 Candareens

Tael System

10 Li = 1 Fen (Candareen)
10 Fen (Candareen) = 1 Ch'ien (Mace)
10 Ch'ien (Mace) = 1 Liang (Tael)

DATING

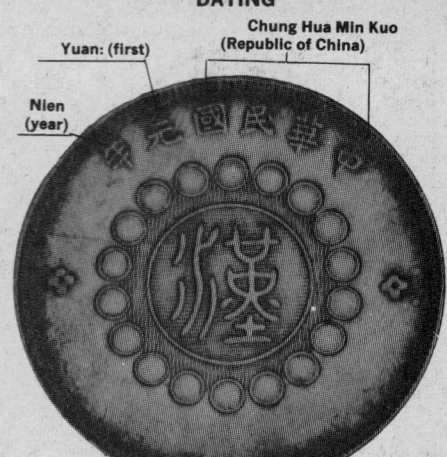

Most struck Chinese coins are dated by year within a given period, such as the regnal eras or the republican periods. A 1907 issue, for example, would be dated in the 33rd year of the Kuang Hsu era (1875 + 33 - 1 = 1907) or a 1926 issue is dated in the 15th year of the Republic (1912 + 15 - 1 = 1926). The mathematical discrepancy in both instances is accounted for by the fact that the first year is included in the elapsed time. Modern Chinese Communist coins are dated in western numerals using the western calendar, but earlier issues use conventional Chinese numerals. Still another method is a 60-year, repeating cycle, outlined in the table below. The date is shown by the combination of two characters, the first from the top row and the second from the column at left. In this catalog, when a cyclical date is used, the abbreviation CD appears before the AD date.

Dates not in parenthesis are those which appear on the coins. For undated coins, dates appearing in parenthesis are the years in which the coin was actually minted. Undated coins for which the year of minting is unknown are listed with ND (No Date) in the date or year column.

CYCLICAL DATES

	庚	辛	壬	癸	甲	乙	丙	丁	戊	己
戌	1850 1910		1862 1922		1874 1934		1886 1946		1838 1898	
亥		1851 1911		1863 1923		1875 1935		1887 1947		1839 1899
子	1840 1900		1852 1912		1864 1924		1876 1936		1888 1948	
丑		1841 1901		1853 1913		1865 1925		1877 1937		1889 1949
寅	1830 1890		1842 1902		1854 1914		1866 1926		1878 1938	
卯		1831 1891		1843 1903		1855 1915		1867 1927		1879 1939
辰	1880 1940		1832 1892		1844 1904		1856 1916		1868 1928	
巳		1881 1941		1833 1893		1845 1905		1857 1917		1869 1929
午	1870 1930		1882 1942		1834 1894		1846 1906		1858 1918	
未		1871 1931		1883 1943		1835 1895		1847 1907		1859 1919
申	1860 1920		1872 1932		1884 1944		1836 1896		1848 1908	
酉		1861 1921		1873 1933		1885 1945		1837 1897		1849 1909

NOTE: This table has been adapted from *Chinese Bank Notes* by Ward Smith and Brian Matravers.

GRADING

Chinese coins should not be graded entirely by western standards. In addition to Fine, Very Fine, Extremely Fine (XF), and Uncirculated, the type of strike should be considered weak, medium or sharp strike. China had no rigid minting rules as we know them. For instance, Kirin (Jilin) and Sinkiang (Xinjiang) Provinces used some dies made of iron - hence, they wore out rapidly. Some communist army issues were apparently struck by crude hand methods on soft dies (it is hard to find two coins of the same die!) In general, especially for some minor coins, dies were used until they were worn well beyond western standards. Subsequently, one could have an uncirculated coin struck from worn dies with little of the design or letters still visible, but still uncirculated! All prices quoted are for well struck (sharp struck) well centered specimens. Most silver coins can be found from very fine to uncirculated. Some copper coins are difficult to find except in poorer grades.

NOTE: The following references have been used for this section:

K - Edward Kann - Illustrated Catalog of Chinese Coins.
Hsu - T.K. Hsu - Illustrated Catalog of Chinese Coins, 1981 edition.
W - A.M. Tracey Woodward - The Minted Ten-Cash Coins of China.

NOTE: The die struck 10 and 20 Cash coins are often found silver plated. This was not done at the mint. They were apparently plated to be passed to the unwary as silver coins.

IDENTIFICATION

Board of Revenue
Cyclical Date
(1905)

Cash | 10 | Standard Coin | Equal To

Province Indicator (Mintmark)

DRAGON TYPES
(Chinese Imperial Coins)

Side View Dragon (Silver Coins)
First used by the Kwangtung Mint in 1889. This was the standard (though not the only) dragon used on silver coins. Normally there is no circle around the dragon. Note the fireball beneath the dragon's chin. Normally there are seven flames on the fireball.

Side View Dragon (Copper Coins)
First used on copper coins in 1901 or 1902. The dragon may be circled or uncircled. Many varieties exist, with three to seven flames on the fireball.

Flying Dragon
Introduced in 1901. Copied from the dragon on Japanese coins. China used this dragon only on copper coins (with one rare exception). Note that the clouds around the dragon's body are curly and snake-like instead of puffy like those around the side view dragon. The fireball now appears as a pearl which the dragon is about to grasp, and normally has no flames. This dragon is normally circled.

Front View Dragon
Introduced about 1904, this type of dragon was not used by many mints. The dragon is usually uncircled and has few clouds around its body. Note the tiny mountain under the cloud beneath the fireball.

Tai Ch'ing Ti Kuo Dragon
In 1905 China carried out a coinage reform which standardized the designs of copper coins. All mints were ordered to use the same obverse and reverse designs, but to place a mint mark in the center of the obverse.

SYCEE (INGOTS)

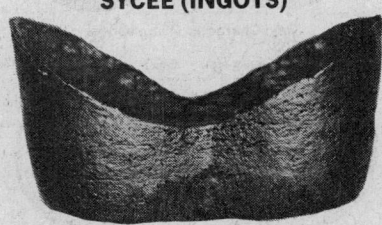

Prior to 1889 the only coinage issued by the Chinese government was the brass cash coin. Despite occasional shortlived experiments with silver and gold coinage, and disregarding paper money which tended to be unreliable, the government expected the people to get by solely with cash coins. This system worked well for individuals making purchases for themselves, but was unsatisfactory for trade and large business transactions, since a dollar's worth of cash coins weighed about four pounds. As a result, a private currency consisting of silver ingots crudely stamped by the firm which made them came into use. These were the sycee ingots.

It is not known when these ingots first came into use. Some sources date them to the Yuan (Mongol) dynasty but they are certainly much older. Examples are known from as far back as the Han dynasty (206 BC - 220 AD) but prior to the Sung era (960 - 1280AD) they were used mainly for hoarding wealth. The development of commerce by the Sung dynasty, however, required the use of silver or gold to pay for large purchases. By the Mongol period (1280-1368) silver ingots and paper money had become the dominant currencies, especially for trade. The western explorers who traveled to China during this period (such as Marco Polo) mention both paper money and sycee but not a single one refers to cash coins.

During the Ming dynasty (1368-1644) trade fell off and the use of silver decreased. But towards the end of that dynasty, Dutch and British ships began a new China trade and sycee once again became common. During the 19th and early 20th centuries, the trade in sycee became enormous. Most of the sycee around today are from this period. In 1935 the Chinese government banned the use of sycee and it soon disappeared.

The word sycee (pronounced "sigh - see") is a western corruption of the Chinese words hsi ssu ("fine silk") or sai ssu ("fine silver") and is first known to have appeared in the English language in the late 1600's. By the early 1700's the word appeared regularly in the records of the British East India Company. Westerners also called these ingots "boat money" or "shoe money" due to the fact that the most common type of ingot resembles a Chinese shoe. The Chinese, however, called the ingots by a variety of names, the most common of which were yuan pao, wen yin and yin ting.

The ingots were cast in molds (giving them their characteristic shapes) and while the metal was still semi-liquid, the inscription was impressed. It was due to this procedure that the sides of some sycee are higher than the center. The manufacturers were usually silver firms, often referred to as lu fang's, and after the sycee was finished it was tested and marked by the kung ku (public assayer).

Sycee were not circulated as we understand it. One didn't usually carry a sycee to market and spend it. Usually the ingots were used as a means of carrying a large amount of money on trips (as we would carry $100 bills instead of $5 bills) or for storing wealth. Large transactions between merchants or banks were paid by means of crates of sycee - each containing 60 fifty tael ingots.

Sycee are known in a variety of shapes the most common of which are the shoe or boat shaped, drum shaped, and loaf shaped (rectangular or hourglass-shaped, with a generally flat surface). Other shapes include one that resembles a double headed axe (this is the oldest type known), one that is square and flat, and others that are "fancy" (in the form of fish, butterflies, leaves, etc.).

Sycee have no denominations as they were simply ingots that passed by weight. Most are in more or less standard weights, however, the most common being 1, 5, 10 and 50 taels. Other weights known include 1/10, 1/5, 1/4, 1/3, 1/2, 2/3, 72/100 (this is the weight of a dollar), 3/4, 2, 3, 4, 6, 7 and 8 taels. Most of the pieces weighing less than 5 taels were used as gifts or souvenirs.

The actual weight of any given value of sycee varied considerably due to the fact that the tael was not a single weight but a general term for a wide range of local weight standards. The weight of the tael varied depending upon location and type of tael in question. For example in one town, the weight of a tael of rice, of silver and of stones may each be different. In addition, the fineness of silver also varied depending upon location and type of tael in question. It was not true, as westerners often wrote, that sycee were made of pure silver. For most purposes, a weight of 37 grams may be used for the tael.

Weights and Current Market Value of Sycee
(Weights are approximate)

1/2 tael	17-19 grams	26.00
72/100 tael	25-27 grams	36.00
1 tael	35-38 grams	46.00
2 taels	70-75 grams	70.00
3 taels	100-140 grams	85.00
5 taels	175-190 grams	110.00
7 taels	240-260 grams	125.00
10 taels	350-380 grams	175.00
25 taels	895-925 grams	650.00
50 taels	1790-1850 grams	950.00
50 taels, square	1790-1850 grams	1600.

SZECHUAN WARLORD ISSUE
200 CASH

Obv: Mirror image of normal coin, Y#459.
NOTE: Certain coins found with degenerate or reversed English legends are usually considered to be local warlord issues while some authorities insist on referring to them as contemporary counterfeits.

GENERAL ISSUE

EMPIRE
Board of Revenue Mint
(Peking)

CASH
CAST BRASS, 21-26mm
Obv: Type A

C#	Date	Emperor	Good	VG	Fine	VF
1-2	(1796-1820)	Chia Ch'ing	.10	.20	.35	.65

28-30mm

1-2.1	(1796-1820)	Chia Ch'ing	2.50	3.50	5.00	7.50

Rev: Dot Above.

C#	Date	Emperor	Good	VG	Fine	VF
1-2.2	(1796-1820)	Chia Ch'ing	1.25	2.00	3.00	5.00

Rev: Dot below.

1-2.3	(1796-1820)	Chia Ch'ing	1.25	2.00	3.00	5.00

CAST BRASS, 20-26 mm
Obv: Type A

1-3	(1821-51)	Tao Kuang	.15	.25	.40	.75

28-30mm

1-3.1	(1821-51)	Tao Kuang	5.00	7.00	10.00	15.00

Rev: Dot above.

1-3.2	(1821-51)	Tao Kuang	1.75	3.00	4.00	6.00

Rev: Dot below.

1-3.3	(1821-51)	Tao Kuang	1.75	3.00	4.50	8.00

Obv: Type A

1-4	(1851-61)	Hsien Feng	.60	1.00	2.00	3.50

CAST IRON

1-4a	(1851-61)	Hsien Feng	7.50	12.50	20.00	30.00

CAST ZINC

1-4b	(1851-61)	Hsien Feng	—	Rare	—	—

CAST IRON
Obv: Character *Pao* in different form like Type B-2.

1-4.1	(1851-61)	Hsien Feng				

CAST BRASS
Obv: Type A-1

1-12	(1861)	Ch'i Hsiang	—	—	Rare	—

Obv: Type A-2

1-14	(1862-74)	T'ung Chih	3.50	5.50	8.50	15.00

Obv: Type A

1-16	(1875-1908)	Kuang Hsu	1.25	1.75	2.50	4.50

Rev: Character *Chih* above.

1-16.1	(1875-1908)	Kuang Hsu	6.00	9.00	13.50	18.50

Rev: Character *Chou* above.

1-16.2	(1875-1908)	Kuang Hsu	6.00	9.00	13.50	18.50

Rev: Character *Jih* above.

C#	Date	Emperor	Good	VG	Fine	VF
1-16.3	(1875-1908)	Kuang Hsu	6.00	9.00	13.50	18.50

Rev: Character *Lai* above.

1-16.4	(1875-1908)	Kuang Hsu	6.00	9.00	13.50	18.50

Rev: Character *Lieh* above.

1-16.5	(1875-1908)	Kuang Hsu	6.00	9.00	13.50	18.50

Rev: Character *Wang* above.

1-16.6	(1875-1908)	Kuang Hsu	6.00	9.00	13.50	18.50

Rev: Character *Yu* above.

1-16.7	(1875-1908)	Kuang Hsu	6.00	9.00	13.50	18.50

NOTE: Refer to the 'Additional Characters' chart in the introduction to China.

Rev: Dot below.

1-16.8	(1875-1908)	Kuang Hsu	1.75	3.00	4.00	6.00

Rev: Dot above.

1-16.9	(1875-1908)	Kuang Hsu	1.75	3.00	4.00	6.00

Rev: Character *Shou* above.

1-16.10	(1875-1908)	Kuang Hsu	6.00	9.00	13.50	18.50

19mm
Obv: Type A

1-19	(1909-11)	Hsuan T'ung	3.00	5.00	7.00	10.00

24mm

C#	Date	Emperor	Good	VG	Fine	VF
1-19.1	(1909-11)	Hsuan T'ung	9.00	13.00	18.00	25.00

5 CASH

CAST BRASS
Obv: Type B-1

1-5	(1851-61)	Hsien Feng	—	—	Rare	—

10 CASH

CAST BRASS, 36-39mm
Obv: Type B-1

1-6	(1851-61)	Hsien Feng	4.00	5.00	7.00	10.00

CAST IRON, 37.5mm

1-6a	(1851-61)	Hsien Feng	15.00	18.00	28.00	42.00

CAST BRASS, 29-34mm

1-6.1	(1851-61)	Hsien Feng	3.00	4.00	5.00	7.50

CAST IRON, 29-34mm

1-6.1a	(1851-61)	Hsien Feng	35.00	50.00	70.00	100.00

Obv: Type B-2

1-6.2	(1851-61)	Hsien Feng	100.00	150.00	225.00	275.00

CAST BRASS
Obv: Type B-1

1-13	(1861)	Ch'i Hsiang	500.00	650.00	800.00	1000.

28-33mm
Obv: Type B-2

1-15	(1862-74)	T'ung Chih	1.50	2.25	3.50	6.00

23-26mm

1-15.1	(1862-74)	T'ung Chih	1.00	2.00	3.00	5.00

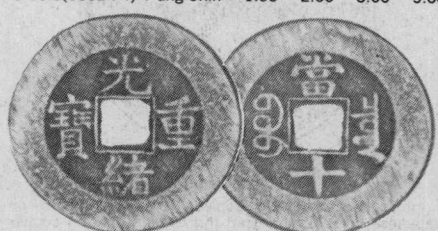

Obv: Type B-1
Rev: Normal character for 10 below.

1-17	(1875-1908)	Kuang Hsu	3.00	5.00	8.50	12.50

28mm
Rev: Official character for 10 below.

C#	Date	Emperor	Good	VG	Fine	VF
1-18	(1875-1908)	Kuang Hsu	4.50	7.50	10.00	13.50

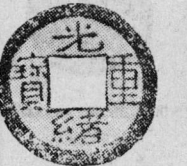 

22mm
1-18.1 (1875-1908)
Kuang Hsu — — — —

50 CASH

CAST BRASS, 54-58mm
Obv: Type B-1
1-7 (1851-61) Hsien Feng 12.00 17.00 20.00 30.00
40-48mm
1-7.1 (1851-61) Hsien Feng 10.00 15.00 18.00 35.00

Rev: Dot to upper right and crescent to upper left.
1-7.2 (1851-61) Hsien Feng 15.00 25.00 35.00 50.00
NOTE: This is one of a series of coins from this mint marked with a dot and crescent to indicate that they were issued by Ching Hui, the Hereditary Prince of K'o Ch'in.
CAST IRON
1-7a (1851-61) Hsien Feng — — Rare —

100 CASH

CAST BRASS
Obv: Type C
1-8 (1851-61) Hsien Feng 7.50 10.00 18.00 28.00

Rev: Dot and crescent similar to 50 Cash, C#1-7.2.
C#	Date	Emperor	Good	VG	Fine	VF
1-8.1	(1851-61)	Hsien Feng	30.00	45.00	55.00	85.00

CAST IRON
1-8a (1851-61) Hsien Feng — — Rare —

200 CASH

CAST BRASS
Obv: Type C
1-9 (1851-61) Hsien Feng 75.00 125.00 150.00 225.00
Rev: Dot and crescent similar to 50 Cash, C#1-7.2.
1-9.1 (1851-61) Hsien Feng 125.00 175.00 225.00 300.00

500 CASH

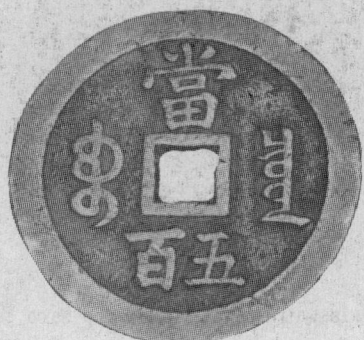

CAST BRASS
Obv: Type C
1-10 (1851-61) Hsien Feng 20.00 30.00 50.00 75.00
58mm
1-10.1 (1851-61) Hsien Feng 25.00 35.00 55.00 85.00
Rev: Dot and crescent similar to 50 Cash, C#1-7.2.
1-10.2 (1851-61) Hsien Feng 35.00 60.00 100.00 150.00

1000 CASH

CAST BRASS
Obv: Type C
1-11 (1851-61) Hsien Feng 50.00 75.00 125.00 175.00
Rev: Dot and crescent similar to 50 Cash, C#1-7.2.
1-11.1 (1851-61) Hsien Feng 125.00 175.00 225.00 300.00

FANTASY ISSUES

NOTE: Coins of this mint in denominations of 6, 9, 20, 30, 90, 300, 400, 600, 700, 800, 900, 4000 and 5000 Cash are considered fantasy issues.

Board of Public Works Mint
(Peking)
CASH

CAST BRASS
Obv: Type A
2-2 (1796-1820)
Chia Ch'ing .15 .25 .40 .75
Rev: Dot above.
2-2.1 (1796-1820)
Chia Ch'ing 2.50 4.00 6.00 7.50

Rev: Dot below.
C#	Date	Emperor	Good	VG	Fine	VF
2-2.2	(1796-1820)	Chia Ch'ing	2.50	4.00	6.00	7.50

CAST BRASS
Obv: Type A
2-3 (1821-51) Tao Kuang .15 .25 .35 .50
Rev: Dot above.
2-3.1 (1821-51) Tao Kuang 2.50 4.00 6.00 7.50
Rev: Dot below.
2-3.2 (1821-51) Tao Kuang 2.50 4.00 6.00 7.50
Obv: Type A
Wide borders, 27mm.
2-4 (1851-61) Hsien Feng 3.00 5.00 9.00 14.00

20-24mm
2-4.1 (1851-61) Hsien Feng .85 1.50 3.00 4.00
CAST ZINC
2-4.2 (1851-61) Hsien Feng — — Rare —
CAST IRON
2-4.3 1851-61 Hsien Feng 50.00 60.00 75.00 100.00

CAST BRASS
Obv: Type A-1
2-11 (1861) Ch'i Hsiang 250.00 325.00 400.00 500.00

Obv: Type A-2
2-13 (1862-74) T'ung Chih 40.00 60.00 90.00 120.00

Obv: Type A
2-15 (1875-1908)
Kuang Hsu 1.50 2.50 4.00 5.00
Rev: Character Chou above.
2-15.1 (1875-1908)
Kuang Hsu 6.00 10.00 15.00 20.00
Rev: Character Lai above.
2-15.2 (1875-1908)
Kuang Hsu 6.00 10.00 15.00 20.00
Rev: Character Lieh above.
2-15.3 (1875-1908)
Kuang Hsu 6.00 10.00 15.00 20.00
Rev: Character Yu above.
2-15.4 (1875-1908)
Kuang Hsu 6.00 10.00 15.00 20.00

Rev: Character *Jih* above.

C#	Date	Emperor	Good	VG	Fine	VF
2-15.5	(1875-1908)	Kuang Hsu	6.00	10.00	15.00	20.00

NOTE: For a machine-struck cash with this mint mark, refer to Szechuan.

Rev: Character *Wang* above.

| 2-15.6 | (1875-1908) | Kuang Hsu | 6.00 | 10.00 | 15.00 | 20.00 |

5 CASH

CAST BRASS, 28-32mm
Obv: Type B-1

2-5	(1851-61)	Hsien Feng	10.00	12.50	17.50	30.00

23-25mm

| 2-5.1 | (1851-61) | Hsien Feng | 12.50 | 20.00 | 30.00 | 50.00 |

CAST IRON

| 2-5a | (1851-61) | Hsien Feng | | Reported, not confirmed | | |

CAST BRASS

| 2-16 | (1875-1908) | Kuang Hsu | 200.00 | 350.00 | 500.00 | 700.00 |

10 CASH

CAST BRASS, 33-38mm
Obv: Type B-1

| 2-6 | (1851-61) | Hsien Feng | 2.50 | 4.50 | 6.00 | 10.00 |

29-31mm

| 2-6.1 | (1851-61) | Hsien Feng | 2.50 | 4.50 | 6.00 | 10.00 |

CAST IRON

| 2-6a | (1851-61) | Hsien Feng | — | Rare | — | |

CAST BRASS
Obv: Type B-1

| 2-12 | (1861) | Ch'i Hsiang | 450.00 | 600.00 | 700.00 | 900.00 |

Obv: Type B-2

| 2-14 | (1862-74) | T'ung Chih | 4.50 | 7.50 | 10.00 | 15.00 |

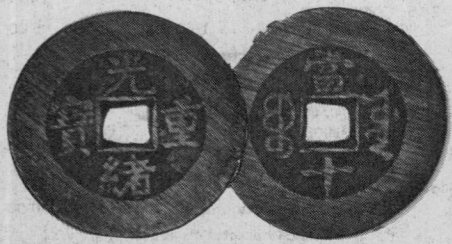

Obv: Type B
Rev: Normal character for 10 below.

C#	Date	Emperor	Good	VG	Fine	VF
2-17	(1875-1908)	Kuang Hsu	4.50	7.50	10.00	20.00

Rev: Official character for 10 below.

| 2-18 | (1875-1908) | Kuang Hsu | 6.00 | 10.00 | 15.00 | 30.00 |

50 CASH

CAST BRASS, 51-57mm
Obv: Type B-1

| 2-7 | (1851-61) | Hsien Feng | 15.00 | 20.00 | 35.00 | 55.00 |

42-45mm

| 2-7.1 | (1851-61) | Hsien Feng | 10.00 | 15.00 | 22.50 | 30.00 |

100 CASH

CAST BRASS
Obv: Type C

| 2-8 | (1851-61) | Hsien Feng | 13.50 | 18.00 | 22.50 | 40.00 |

500 CASH

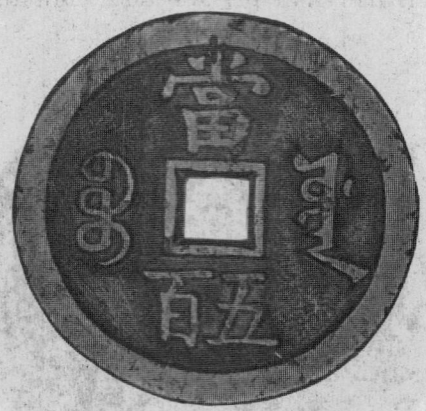

CAST BRASS
Obv: Type C

| 2-9 | (1851-61) | Hsien Feng | 30.00 | 50.00 | 75.00 | 120.00 |

CAST COPPER

| 2-9.1 | (1851-61) | Hsien Feng | 32.50 | 55.00 | 85.00 | 130.00 |

1000 CASH

CAST BRASS
Obv: Type C

| 2-10 | (1851-61) | Hsien Feng | 50.00 | 80.00 | 115.00 | 160.00 |

FANTASY ISSUES

NOTE: Coins of this mint in denominations of 6, 9, 30, 80 and 90 Cash are considered fantasy issues.

MILLED COINAGE

A Central mint opened at Tientsin in 1905, was made responsible for producing most of the dies for the Tai Ch'ing coinage and for the 1910 and 1911 unified coinage. The mint was burned down in 1912 but resumed operations in 1914 with Yuan Shih-kai dollar issues. It continued producing dies for selected branch mints until 1921. It was superseded as the Central mint of China by Nanking in 1927 and by the new Nationalist Government mint at Shanghai in 1933.

CASH

BRASS, struck
Obv: Type A

Rev: Two Manchu characters *Pao-chuan*. (Board of Revenue Mint)

Hsu#	Date	Emperor	Fine	VF	XF	Unc
2	ND(1899)	Kuang Hsu	—	Rare		

Y#	Date	Mintage	VG	Fine	VF	XF
7	CD1908	—	.50	1.50	3.00	7.50

| 18 | CD1909 | Inc. Y25 | 15.00 | 35.00 | 60.00 | 100.00 |

| 25 | ND | 92.126 | 1.00 | 1.50 | 2.00 | 3.00 |

2 CASH

COPPER

8	CD1905	—	2.00	4.50	10.00	17.50
	CD1906	—	3.00	7.50	12.00	25.00
	CD1907	—	5.00	10.00	20.00	35.00

Obv: Date, 4 dots divide legend.

| 8.1 | CD1907 | | | | | |
| A18 | CD1909 | 13.353 | — | — | Rare | — |

5 CASH

COPPER

| 3 | ND(1903-05) | 3.671 | 6.50 | 12.00 | 20.00 | 35.00 |

Rev. leg: Smaller English letters.

| 3.1 | ND(1903-05) | — | — | Reported, not confirmed | | |

9	CD1905	—	5.00	10.00	20.00	35.00
	CD1906	—	—	—	Rare	—
	CD1907	—	16.50	40.00	75.00	125.00

Obv: Characters *Hsuan Tung*.

| 19 | CD1909 | 2.170 | — | — | 750.00 | 1100. |

10 CASH

COPPER

Y#	Date	Mintage	VG	Fine	VF	XF
4	ND(1903-05)	281.171	.40	1.00	2.00	3.50

Rev: Smaller English letters and different rosettes.

4.1	ND(1903-05)	Inc. Ab.	.40	1.00	2.00	3.50

10	CD1905	Inc. Ab.	.60	1.50	3.00	5.00

Rev: Larger English letters and different dragon.

10.1	CD1905	—	10.00	22.00	45.00	80.00

10.2	CD1906	—	.30	.75	1.50	3.00

Obv: W/o dots. Rev leg: W/o dot after KUO.

10.3	CD1907	—	.20	.50	1.25	2.50

Rev. leg: Dot after KUO.

10.4	CD1907	—	.20	.50	1.25	2.50

BRASS
Obv: W/o dots.

10.4a	CD1907	—	2.50	5.50	15.00	30.00

COPPER
Obv: Dots between leg.

Y#	Date	Mintage	VG	Fine	VF	XF
10.5	CD1907	—	.20	.50	1.25	2.50

BRASS

10.5a	CD1907	—	2.50	5.50	12.00	25.00

COPPER
Mule. Obv: Y#10.5. Rev: Kiangnan Y#138.1.

W277	CD1907	—	45.00	95.00	200.00	260.00

NOTE: Other mules exist. Refer to Kiangnan.

Rev: Waves under dragon.

20	CD1909	—	.40	1.00	2.00	4.00

Rev: Rosette under dragon, U of KUO inverted A.

20.1	CD1909	—	2.50	5.50	12.00	25.00

NOTE: Although this coin bears no indication of its origin, it was minted in the Manchurian Provinces ca. 1922.

20x	CD1909	—	7.00	17.50	30.00	60.00

NOTE: Although this coin bears no indication of its origin, it was minted in Kirin Province.

BRONZE

Y#	Date	Mintage	Fine	VF	XF	Unc
27	Yr.3(1911)	95.585	2.50	4.00	8.00	30.00
	Yr.3(1911)	—	—	Proof	Rare	

BRASS

27a	Yr.3(1911)	—	30.00	42.50	85.00	125.00

20 CASH

COPPER

Y#	Date	Mintage	VG	Fine	VF	XF
5	(1917)	—	.20	.50	1.50	5.00

NOTE: This coin was struck in 1917 from unused dies made in 1903.

Obv: 4-point rosette in center.

5.1	ND	—	2.50	6.00	12.00	25.00

Rev: Head of dragon and clouds redesigned.

5.2	ND	—	2.50	6.00	12.00	25.00

Rev: Dragon in circle of dots.

5a	ND(1903-05)	—	35.00	50.00	85.00	125.00

11	CD1905	—	12.50	30.00	50.00	75.00

11.1	CD1906	—	12.50	30.00	50.00	75.00

Obv: Dots around date, 1.2-1.7mm thick.

11.2	CD1907	—	.60	1.50	2.00	4.00

2.0-2.3mm thick

11.3	CD1907	—	2.50	6.00	12.00	25.00

BRASS

11.3a	CD1907	—	4.00	8.00	15.00	30.00

COPPER
Obv: W/o dots around date.

Y#	Date	Mintage	VG	Fine	VF	XF
11.4	CD1907	—	—	Reported, not confirmed		

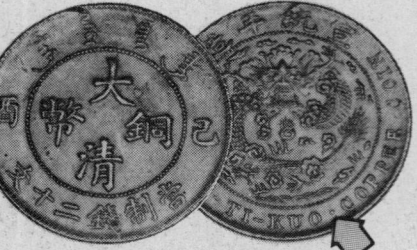

Rev. leg: Dot between KUO and COPPER, six waves beneath dragon.

| 21 | CD1909 | — | .75 | 2.00 | 5.00 | 8.00 |

1.2-1.7mm thick
Rev. leg: W/o dot between KUO and COPPER, six waves beneath dragon.

| 21.1 | CD1909 | — | 1.25 | 3.00 | 6.00 | 10.00 |

2.0-2.3mm thick

| 21.2 | CD1909 | — | 1.25 | 3.00 | 6.00 | 10.00 |

Rev: Rosette beneath dragon.

| 21.3 | CD1909 | — | 3.00 | 7.50 | 20.00 | 30.00 |

NOTE: Although this coin bears no indication of its origin, it was minted in the Manchurian Provinces ca. 1922.

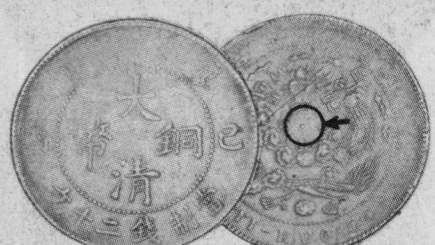

Rev: Dot below dragon's chin.

| 21.4 | CD1909 | — | 3.50 | 8.50 | 16.00 | 30.00 |

NOTE: Although this coin bears no indication of its origin, it was minted in the Manchurian Provinces ca. 1922.

Rev: Five crude waves beneath dragon w/ redesigned forehead.
Inner circle of large dots on obv. and rev.

| 21.5 | CD1909 | — | 1.20 | 3.00 | 6.00 | 12.00 |

10 CENTS
2.7000 g, .820 SILVER, .0712 oz ASW
Similar to Y#12.

K#	Date	Mintage	Fine	VF	XF	Unc
215	CD1907	—	35.00	85.00	150.00	300.00

Y#	Date	Mintage	VG	Fine	VF	XF
12	ND(1908)	—	20.00	40.00	75.00	125.00

3.2000 g, .650 SILVER, .0669 oz ASW
Similar to 50 Cents, Y#23.

K#	Date	Mintage	VG	Fine	VF	XF
222	ND(1910)	—	60.00	125.00	250.00	500.00
	ND(1910)	—	—	—	Proof	600.00

NICKEL (OMS)

| 222x | ND(1910) | — | — | — | — | — |

Rev: Larger characters.

| 222y | ND(1910) | — | — | — | — | — |

SILVER, 2.70 g

Y#	Date	Mintage	Fine	VF	XF	Unc
28	Yr.3(1911)	—	10.00	20.00	50.00	120.00

NOTE: Refer to Hunan Republic 10 Cents, K#762.

20 CENTS

5.5000 g, .820 SILVER, .1450 oz ASW

K#	Date	Mintage	Fine	VF	XF	Unc
214	CD1907	—	40.00	80.00	150.00	300.00

5.30 g

Y#	Date	Mintage	Fine	VF	XF	Unc
13	ND(1908)	—	85.00	115.00	150.00	200.00

(Error) Rev. leg: "COPPER COIN"

K#	Date	Mintage	Fine	VF	XF	Unc
217w	ND(1908)	—	—	—	Rare	

NICKEL (OMS)
Milled edge.

| 217x | ND(1908) | — | — | — | — | — |

Plain edge.

| 217y | ND(1908) | — | — | — | — | — |

SILVER, 5.40 g

Y#	Date	Mintage	Fine	VF	XF	Unc
29	Yr.3(1911)	—	25.00	50.00	150.00	250.00

25 CENTS

6.7000 g, .800 SILVER, .1724 oz ASW

K#	Date	Mintage	Fine	VF	XF	Unc
221	ND(1910)	1.410	—	—	Proof	2000.

50 CENTS

13.6000 g, .860 SILVER, .3761 oz ASW

K#	Date	Mintage	Fine	VF	XF	Unc
213	CD1907	—	100.00	225.00	375.00	750.00

13.4000 g, .800 SILVER, .3447 oz ASW

Y#	Date	Mintage	Fine	VF	XF	Unc
23	ND(1910)	1.571	25.00	50.00	100.00	300.00

| 30 | Yr.3 (1911) | I.A. | 200.00 | 400.00 | 650.00 | 1000. |
| | Yr.3 (1911) | — | — | — | Proof | 1200. |

DOLLAR

26.9000 g, .900 SILVER, .7785 oz ASW

K#	Date	Mintage	Fine	VF	XF	Unc
212	CD1907	—	150.00	275.00	400.00	600.00

COPPER (OMS)

| 212x | CD1907 | — | — | — | — | — |

26.9000 g, .900 SILVER, .7785 oz ASW

Y#	Date	Mintage	Fine	VF	XF	Unc
14	ND(1908)	—	15.00	20.00	50.00	225.00

Empire-Rebel Issue / CHINA 311

K#	Date	Mintage	Fine	VF	XF	Unc
219	ND(1910)	—	125.00	250.00	350.00	525.00
	ND(1910)	—	—	—	Proof	2100.

Y#	Date	Mintage	Fine	VF	XF	Unc
31	Yr.3 (1911)	77.153	10.00	15.00	30.00	150.00

Rev: Mint mark "dot" after DOLLAR.

| 31.1 | Yr.3 (1911) I.A. | 15.00 | 20.00 | 35.00 | 160.00 |

REBEL COINAGE
CHAO CHIN LUNG
CASH

CAST COPPER or BRASS, uniface
Obv: *Chin Lung T'ung Pao*

KM#	Date	Emperor	Good	VG	Fine	VF
1	ND(1832)	—	—	—	Rare	

T'AI P'ING REBELLION

A radical political and religious upheaval that lasted from 1850 to 1864. It ravaged 17 provinces and took an estimated 20,000,000 lives. The rebellion began under the leadership of Hung Hsiu-ch'uan (1814-64), a disappointed civil service examination candidate who believed himself to be the son of God, the younger brother of Jesus Christ, sent to reform China.

Their slogan -- to share property in common -- attracted many famine-stricken peasants, workers, and miners, as did their propaganda against the foreign Manchu rulers of China. Under the Taipings, the Chinese language was simplified, and equality between men and women was decreed. All property was to be held in common, and equal distribution of the land according to a form of communism was planned. Both the Chinese Communists and the Chinese Nationalists trace their origin to the Taipings.

HUNG HSIU-CH'UAN
CASH

CAST COPPER or BRASS
Obv: *T'ai P'ing T'ien Kuo* (top-bottom-right-left).
Rev: *Sheng Pao* (right-left). 24-25mm.

C#	Date	Good	VG	Fine	VF
38-8	ND(1853-64)	10.00	15.00	25.00	35.00

31-35mm.
| 38-7 | ND(1853-64) | 20.00 | 35.00 | 50.00 | 75.00 |

42-45mm.
| 38-6 | ND(1853-64) | 25.00 | 45.00 | 70.00 | 100.00 |

Rev: *Sheng Pao* (top-bottom).
24-26mm. Narrow rims.
| 38-5 | ND(1853-64) | 10.00 | 25.00 | 35.00 | 50.00 |

28mm. Wide rims.
| 38-5.1 | ND(1853-64) | 10.00 | 13.00 | 20.00 | 30.00 |

31-33mm. Narrow rims.
| 38-4 | ND(1853-64) | 20.00 | 35.00 | 50.00 | 75.00 |

35mm. Wide rims.
| 38-4.1 | ND(1853-64) | 22.50 | 40.00 | 60.00 | 90.00 |

IRON
| 38-4.1a | ND(1853-64) | — | — | 1000. | — |

BRONZE
38-42mm. Narrow rims.
| 38-3 | ND(1853-64) | 60.00 | 100.00 | 150.00 | 220.00 |

47-48mm. Wide rims.
| 38-3.1 | ND(1853-64) | 85.00 | 150.00 | 225.00 | 350.00 |

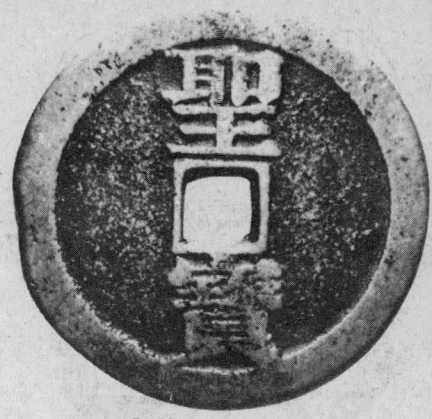

54-56mm. Narrow rims.
C#	Date	Good	VG	Fine	VF
38-2	ND(1853-64)	100.00	175.00	250.00	400.00

Obv: *T'ai P'ing Sheng Pao* (top-bottom-right-left).
Rev: *T'ien Kuo* (right-left).
| 38-12 | ND(1853-64) | 15.00 | 20.00 | 30.00 | 40.00 |

Obv: *T'ien Kuo T'ai P'ing* (top-bottom-right-left).
Rev: *Sheng Pao* (right-left). 25-26mm.
| 38-14 | ND(1853-64) | 20.00 | 30.00 | 40.00 | 60.00 |

Obv: *T'ien Kuo Sheng Pao* (top-bottom-right-left).
Rev: *T'ai P'ing* (right-left). 21-23mm.
| 38-13 | ND(1853-64) | 10.00 | 15.00 | 25.00 | 40.00 |

Obv: *T'ien Kuo* (top-bottom)
Rev: *Sheng Pao* (top-bottom). 24-25mm.
| 38-11 | ND(1853-64) | 30.00 | 40.00 | 50.00 | 60.00 |

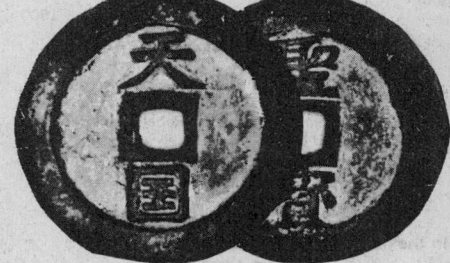

38mm. Large characters.
| 38-10 | ND(1853-64) | 20.00 | 35.00 | 50.00 | 75.00 |

36mm. Small characters.
| 38-10.1 | ND(1853-64) | 50.00 | 70.00 | 90.00 | 110.00 |

BRASS
Obv: *T'ai P'ing T'ung Pao*.
Rev: Crescent above and character *Ming* below.
| 39-1 | ND(1853-64) | 20.00 | 30.00 | 40.00 | 50.00 |

Rev: Dot above and crescent below.
| 39-2 | ND(1853-64) | 20.00 | 30.00 | 45.00 | 65.00 |

Rev: Character *Wen* above.
| 39-3 | ND(1853-64) | 20.00 | 30.00 | 40.00 | 50.00 |

Rev: Character *Wen* at the right of hole.
| 39-4 | ND(1853-64) | 20.00 | 30.00 | 40.00 | 50.00 |

Empire-Rebel Issue / CHINA 312

 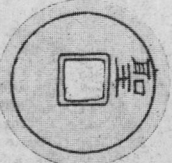

Obv: Huang Ti T'ung Pao.
Rev: Character Sheng at right (sideways).

C#	Date	Good	VG	Fine	VF
39-5	ND(1853-64)	20.00	30.00	40.00	50.00

Obv: Huang Ti T'ung Pao.
Rev: Characters Che-Pao (right-left).

| 39-6 | ND(1853-64) | 20.00 | 30.00 | 40.00 | 50.00 |

NOTE: There are numerous other Cash coins issued by Taiping supporters and military units.

1/4 TAEL

SILVER

KM#	Date	Mintage	Good	VG	Fine	VF
2	ND(1853-64)	5 known	—	—	—	2500.

1/2 TAEL

SILVER

| 3 | ND(1853-64) | 10 known | — | — | — | 1500. |

5 TAELS

GOLD

| 4 | ND(1853-64) | 1 known | — | — | — | — |

NOTE: For additional listings of Rebel Coins, refer to Sinkiang (Xinjiang) Province.

REPUBLIC
Transitional Coinage
In the name of the Republic

CASH

CAST COPPER or BRASS

| 5 | ND(1912) | — | 10.00 | 20.00 | 30.00 | 45.00 |

10 CASH

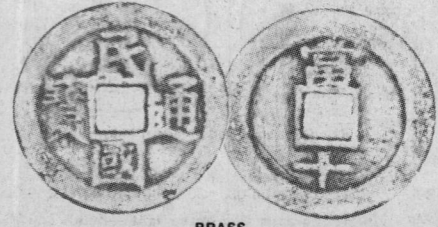

BRASS

| 4 | ND (1912) | — | 8.00 | 15.00 | 30.00 | 45.00 |

In the name of Hung Hsien

5 CASH

COPPER
Obv: Type A.

KM#	Date	Mintage	Good	VG	Fine	VF
1	ND (1916)	—	—	—	Rare	—

10 CASH

COPPER or BRASS, uniface
Obv: Type A.

| 2 | ND (1916) | — | — | — | — | — |

NOTE: Questionable, believed to be a fantasy by some authorities.

Regular Coinage
1/2 CENT

BRONZE

Y#	Date	Mintage	Fine	VF	XF	Unc
323	Yr.5 (1916)	—	5.00	10.00	20.00	40.00

| 346 | Yr.25 (1936) | 64.720 | .60 | 1.50 | 3.00 | 7.50 |

10 CASH (1 CENT OR 1 FEN)

NOTE: Some sources date these 10 Cash pieces bearing crossed flags ca. 1912, but many were not struck until the 1920's.

COPPER
Rev: Double circle w/small rosettes separating leg.

| 301 | ND | — | .20 | .50 | 1.00 | 8.00 |

BRASS

| 301a | ND | — | — | — | — | — |

COPPER
Obv: Second character from right in bottom leg. is rounded. **Rev:** Double circle w/three dots separating leg.

Y#	Date	Mintage	Fine	VF	XF	Unc
301.1	ND	—	1.00	2.00	5.00	18.00

Obv: Second character from right in bottom leg. rounded. **Rev:** Double circle w/two dots separating leg.

| 301.2 | ND | — | .30 | .75 | 1.50 | 10.00 |

Obv: Small star on flag. **Rev:** Double circle w/six-pointed stars separating leg.

| 301.3 | ND | — | .60 | 1.50 | 3.00 | 15.00 |

Obv: Large star on flag extending to edges of flag.
Rev: Double circle w/six-pointed stars separating leg.

| 301.4 | ND | — | 10.00 | 15.00 | 20.00 | 50.00 |

BRASS

| 301.4a | ND | — | — | — | — | — |

COPPER
Obv: Flower w/many stems. **Rev:** Single circle.

| 301.5 | ND | — | .50 | 1.25 | 3.00 | 15.00 |

Obv: Flower w/fewer stems. **Rev:** Single circle.

| 301.6 | ND | — | .50 | 1.25 | 3.00 | 15.00 |

Rev: Vine above leaf at 12 o'clock. Wreath tied at bottom. M-shaped leaves at base of wheat ears.

| 302 | ND | — | — | .40 | 2.00 | 8.50 |

BRASS

| 302a | ND | — | — | — | — | — |

Republic-General Issue / CHINA 313

COPPER
Rev: Larger wheat ears.

Y#	Date	Mintage	Fine	VF	XF	Unc
302.1	ND	—	1.20	3.00	7.50	20.00

Rev: Vine beneath leaf at 12 o'clock. Wreath not tied at bottom. W/o M-shaped leaves at base of wheat ears.

| 302.2 | ND | — | 1.60 | 4.00 | 8.00 | 20.00 |

Rev: Leaves pointing clockwise.

| 302.3 | ND | — | 45.00 | 50.00 | 75.00 | 100.00 |

Obv: Small star shaped rosettes.
Rev: Small four-pointed rosettes separating leg.

| 303 | ND | — | .30 | .70 | 2.00 | 10.00 |

Obv: Left flag's star in relief.

| 303.1 | ND | — | .30 | .70 | 2.00 | 10.00 |

BRASS
Obv: Stars replace rosettes.

| 303a | ND | — | 1.60 | 4.00 | 8.00 | 20.00 |

COPPER
Obv: Large rosettes replace stars.
Rev: Stars separating leg.

| 303.3 | ND | — | 1.00 | 3.00 | 8.00 | 25.00 |

Obv: Very small pentagonal rosettes.

Y#	Date	Mintage	Fine	VF	XF	Unc
303.4	ND	—	.75	1.50	3.00	10.00

BRASS

| 303.4a | ND | — | 3.00 | 6.25 | 12.50 | 25.00 |

COPPER
Obv: Circled flag flanked by pentagonal rosettes.

| 304 | ND | — | 11.50 | 21.50 | 42.50 | 85.00 |

Rev: Chrysanthemum.

| 305 | ND | — | 15.00 | 25.00 | 50.00 | 100.00 |

| 306.1 | ND | — | .40 | 1.00 | 2.00 | 7.50 |

BRASS

| 306b | ND | — | 1.00 | 2.50 | 5.00 | 15.00 |

COPPER
Obv: Y#306.1, Rev: Y#306.4

| 306.1b | ND | — | 2.00 | 3.50 | 7.00 | 25.00 |

Obv: Dot on either side of upper legend.

| 306.2 | ND | — | 1.00 | — | 3.50 | 11.00 |

BRASS

| 306.2b | ND | — | 1.25 | 3.00 | 5.00 | 15.00 |

COPPER
Obv: Star between flags.

| 306.3 | ND | — | 20.00 | 40.00 | 75.00 | — |

Obv: Elongated rosettes, different characters in bottom leg. Rev: Thin leaf blade between lower wheat ears.

Y#	Date	Mintage	Fine	VF	XF	Unc
306.4	ND	—	17.50	35.00	70.00	150.00

Obv: Five characters in lower leg.

| 306a | ND | — | 5.00 | 12.00 | 25.00 | 65.00 |

Obv: One large rosette on either side.
Rev: Slender leaves and short ribbon.

| 307 | ND | 421.138 | .50 | 1.00 | 2.00 | 5.00 |

Rev: Larger leaves and longer ribbon.

| 307.1 | ND | Inc. Ab. | 8.00 | 20.00 | 40.00 | 100.00 |

Obv: Three rosettes on either side, ornate right flag.
Rev: Long ribbon.

| 307a | ND | Inc. Ab. | 1.00 | 2.00 | 4.00 | 12.50 |

Rev: Short ribbon and smaller wheat ears.

| 307a.1 | ND | Inc. Ab. | 20.00 | 50.00 | 100.00 | 200.00 |

| 309 | ND | — | 8.00 | 20.00 | 40.00 | 80.00 |

NOTE: Pieces w/L. GIORGI near rim are patterns.

Republic-General Issue / CHINA 314

BRONZE

Y#	Year	Date	Fine	VF	XF	Unc
324	5	(1916)	1.00	2.50	4.25	12.00

NOTE: Pieces w/L. GIORGI near rim are patterns.

COPPER

| 311 | 13 | (1924) | 175.00 | 350.00 | 500.00 | 750.00 |

BRASS

| 337 | 17 | (1928) | 100.00 | 150.00 | 200.00 | 300.00 |

NOTE: This coin is always found with small punchmarks near center on obverse and reverse.

BRONZE

| 324a | 22 | (1933) | 12.50 | 25.00 | 60.00 | 125.00 |

Y#	Date	Mintage	Fine	VF	XF	Unc
347	Yr.25 (1936)	311.780	.20	.50	1.00	2.50
	Yr.26 (1937)	307.198	.25	.60	1.25	3.00
	Yr.27 (1938)	12.000	1.00	2.00	4.00	8.00
	Yr.28 (1939)	75.000	2.00	4.00	8.00	17.50

Y#	Year	Date	Fine	VF	XF	Unc
353	28	(1939)	20.00	45.00	75.00	110.00

ALUMINUM

Y#	Date	Mintage	Fine	VF	XF	Unc
355	Yr.29 (1940)	150.000	.10	.25	.50	1.50

BRASS

Y#	Date	Mintage	Fine	VF	XF	Unc
357	Yr.29 (1940)	50.000	.30	.75	1.00	2.50

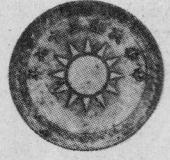 

BRONZE

Y#	Year	Date	Fine	VF	XF	Unc
363	37	(1948)	4.00	10.00	15.00	20.00

'PORTRAIT' TEN CASH

NOTE: A number of ten Cash pieces exist with portraits of Yuan Shih-kai, Sun Yat-sen, Li Yuan-hung or Ni Su-chung and are considered fantasies. Refer to "Unusual World Coins" c. 1987 Krause Publications.

20 CASH (2 CENTS or 2 FEN)

NOTE: Some sources date these 20 Cash pieces bearing crossed flags ca. 1912, but many were not struck until the 1920's.

COPPER

Y#	Date	Mintage	Fine	VF	XF	Unc
308	Yr.8 (1919)	200.861	1.00	2.50	6.00	30.00

| 308a | Yr.10 (1921) I.A. | | 1.00 | 2.50 | 6.00 | 30.00 |

| 310 | ND | — | 17.50 | 35.00 | 60.00 | 125.00 |

NOTE: This coin is usually found weakly struck.

Y#	Year	Date	Fine	VF	XF	Unc
312	13	(1924)	7.00	17.50	35.00	100.00

NOTE: This coin is usually found weakly struck.

Nationalist Commemorative

Hsu#	Date	Mintage	Fine	VF	XF	Unc
9	ND(1927/8)	—	450.00	900.00	1200.	1500.

BRASS

Y#	Date	Mintage	Fine	VF	XF	Unc
338	Yr.17(1928)	—	275.00	425.00	600.00	750.00

NOTE: This coin has always been found with small punchmarks near center on obverse and reverse.

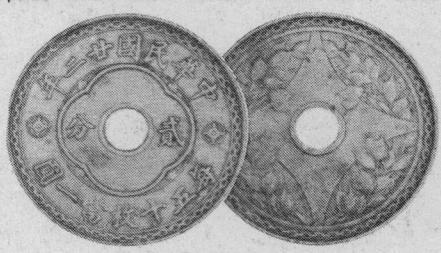

BRONZE

| 325a | Yr.22(1933) | — | 90.00 | 150.00 | 250.00 | 450.00 |

BRASS

Y#	Date	Mintage	Fine	VF	XF	Unc
354	Yr.28 (1939)	300.000	3.50	7.50	13.00	22.50

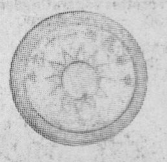 

| 358 | Yr.29 (1940) | — | .25 | .50 | .75 | 1.50 |

5 CENTS (5 FEN)

NICKEL

348	Yr.25 (1936)	72.844	.25	.60	1.00	3.00
	Yr.27 (1938)	34.325	.60	1.50	3.00	8.00
	Yr.28 (1939)	6.000	4.00	10.00	15.00	30.00

Rev: A mint mark below spade (Vienna)

| 348.1 | Yr.25 (1936) | 20.000 | .50 | 1.00 | 3.25 | 10.00 |

Obv: Character P'ing on both sides of portrait.

Y#	Year	Date	Fine	VF	XF	Unc
348.2	25	(1936)	20.00	50.00	100.00	150.00

Obv: Character Ch'ing on both sides of portrait.

| 348.3 | 25 | (1936) | 20.00 | 50.00 | 100.00 | 150.00 |

COPPER (OMS)

348a	25	(1936)	—	—	—	—
	27	(1938)	—	—	—	—
	28	(1939)	—	—	—	—

BRASS (OMS)

| 348b | 28 | (1939) | — | — | — | — |

ALUMINUM

Y#	Date	Mintage	Fine	VF	XF	Unc
356	Yr.29 (1940)	350.000	.10	.25	.50	1.00

COPPER-NICKEL

| 359 | Yr.29 (1940) | 57.000 | .25 | 1.50 | 2.50 | 5.00 |
| | Yr.30 (1941) | 96.000 | .25 | 1.50 | 2.50 | 6.00 |

10 CENTS (10 FEN)

SILVER, 2.30 g
Similar to 1 Dollar, Y#318, vertical reeding.

K#	Date	Mintage	Fine	VF	XF	Unc
602	ND(1912)	—	100.00	225.00	350.00	500.00

Edge engrailed with circles.

| 602b | ND(1912) | — | — | 250.00 | 400.00 | 575.00 |

2.7000 g, .700 SILVER, .0607 oz ASW

Y#	Year	Date	Fine	VF	XF	Unc
326	3	(1914)	1.50	3.50	7.00	25.00
	5	(1916)	20.00	40.00	80.00	175.00

COPPER (OMS)

| 326a | 3 | (1914) | — | — | — | — |

NICKEL (OMS)

| 326b | 3 | (1914) | — | — | — | — |

SILVER
Pu Yi Wedding

| 334 | 15 | (1926) | 2.50 | 5.00 | 10.00 | 30.00 |

COPPER (OMS)

| 334a | 15 | (1936) | — | — | — | — |

LEAD (OMS)

| 334b | 15 | (1936) | — | — | — | — |

SILVER, 2.50 g
Death of Sun Yat-sen

| 339 | 16 | (1927) | 15.00 | 30.00 | 50.00 | 125.00 |

COPPER (OMS)

| 339a | 16 | (1927) | — | — | — | — |

GOLD (OMS)

| 339b | 16 | (1927) | — | — | — | — |

NICKEL

Y#	Date	Mintage	Fine	VF	XF	Unc
349	Yr.25 (1936)	73.866	.40	.60	1.00	3.00
	Yr.27 (1938)	110.203	.80	1.25	3.00	7.50
	Yr.28 (1939)	68.000	.80	1.25	3.00	7.50

NON-MAGNETIC NICKEL ALLOY

| 349a | Yr.25 (1936) | 1.000 | 18.00 | 25.00 | 30.00 | 45.00 |

All of the Y#349 coins were supposed to have been minted in pure nickel at the Shanghai Mint. However in 1936 the Tientsin Mint produced about one million 10 Cent pieces of heavily alloyed nickel. The result is that the Shanghai pieces are attracted to a magnet while the Tientsin pieces are not.

NICKEL
Rev: A mint mark below spade (Vienna Mint)

| 349.1 | Yr.25 (1936)A | 60.000 | .50 | 1.00 | 2.50 | 6.50 |

COPPER (OMS)

Y#	Year	Date	Fine	VF	XF	Unc
349b	25	(1936)	—	—	—	—
	27	(1938)	—	—	—	—

ALUMINUM (OMS)

Y#	Date	Mintage	Fine	VF	XF	Unc
349c	25	(1936)	—	—	—	—

ALUMINUM-BRONZE (OMS)

Y#	Date	Fine	VF	XF	Unc
349d	25	(1936)	—	—	—	—

LEAD (OMS)

| 349e | 25 | (1936) | — | — | — | — |

COPPER-NICKEL
Reeded edge.

Y#	Date	Mintage	Fine	VF	XF	Unc
360	Yr.29 (1940)	68.000	.50	1.50	2.50	6.00
	Yr.30 (1941)	254.000	.50	1.50	2.50	5.00
	Yr.31 (1942)	10.000	10.00	20.00	35.00	50.00

Plain edge.

| 360.1 | Yr.29(1940) I.A. | — | — | — | Rare | — |
| | Yr.30(1941) I.A. | 2.00 | 5.00 | 7.50 | 12.50 |

COPPER (OMS)

Y#	Year	Date	Fine	VF	XF	Unc
360a	30	(1941)	—	—	—	—
	31	(1942)	—	—	—	—

BRASS (OMS)

| 360b | 30 | (1941) | — | — | — | — |
| | 31 | (1941) | — | — | — | — |

20 CENTS (20 FEN)

SILVER, 5.20 g
Founding of the Republic

Y#	Date	Mintage	Fine	VF	XF	Unc
317	ND(1912)	.155	10.00	15.00	20.00	45.00

GOLD, 19.30 g (OMS)

| 317a | ND(1912) | — | — | 1200. | 1500. | |

5.4000 g, .700 SILVER, .1215 oz ASW

Y#	Year	Date	Fine	VF	XF	Unc
327	3	(1914)	1.00	2.00	5.00	20.00
	5	(1916)	2.00	3.00	10.00	50.00
	9	(1920)	100.00	200.00	250.00	400.00

COPPER (OMS)

Y#	Year	Date	Fine	VF	XF	Unc
327a	3	(1914)	—	—	—	—
	5	(1916)	—	—	—	—

NICKEL (OMS)

| 327b | 3 | (1914) | — | — | — | — |

PEWTER (OMS)

| 327c | 3 | (1914) | — | — | — | — |

SILVER, 5.20 g
Pu Yi Wedding

| 335 | 15 | (1926) | 5.00 | 7.50 | 15.00 | 40.00 |

COPPER (OMS)

| 335a | 15 | (1926) | — | — | — | — |

SILVER, 5.30 g
Death of Sun Yat-sen

| 340 | 16 | (1927) | 15.00 | 22.50 | 37.50 | 85.00 |

NICKEL

Y#	Date	Mintage	Fine	VF	XF	Unc
350	Yr.25 (1936)	49.620	.20	.50	2.00	3.50
	Yr.27 (1938)	61.248	1.00	2.00	4.50	8.00
	Yr.28 (1939)	38.000	1.00	2.00	4.50	9.00

Rev: A mint mark below spade (Vienna Mint)

| 350.1 | Yr.25 (1936) | 40.000 | 1.00 | 2.00 | 3.50 | 6.00 |

COPPER (OMS)

Y#	Year	Date	Fine	VF	XF	Unc
350a	25	(1936)	—	—	—	—
	27	(1936)	—	—	—	—

ALUMINUM (OMS)

| 350b | 25 | (1936) | — | — | — | — |

ALUMINUM-BRONZE (OMS)

| 350c | 25 | (1936) | — | — | — | — |

PEWTER (OMS)

| 350d | 25 | (1936) | — | — | — | 75.00 |
| | 27 | (1938) | — | — | — | 150.00 |

COPPER-NICKEL

Y#	Date	Mintage	Fine	VF	XF	Unc
361	Yr.31 (1942)	32.300	.40	1.00	2.25	4.00

COPPER (OMS)

Y#	Year	Date	Fine	VF	XF	Unc
361a	31	(1942)	—	—	—	—

500 CASH

COPPER
Nationalist Commemorative

Hsu#	Date	Mintage	Fine	VF	XF	Unc
445a	ND(1927/8)	12 pcs. (8 known)	—	—	Rare	—

50 CENTS

13.6000 g, .700 SILVER, .3060 oz ASW

Y#	Year	Date	Fine	VF	XF	Unc
328	3	(1914)	5.00	10.00	16.00	65.00

10.0000 g, .720 SILVER, .2315 oz ASW

K#	Date	Mintage	Fine	VF	XF	Unc
633	Yr.25 (1936)S	*6.480	250.00	450.00	650.00	1000.

*NOTE: All but a few pieces were melted.

COPPER-NICKEL

Y#	Date	Mintage	Fine	VF	XF	Unc
362	Yr.31 (1942)	57.000	.40	.80	1.50	4.00
	Yr.32 (1943)	4.000	2.50	7.50	15.00	27.50

COPPER (OMS)

Y#	Year	Date	Fine	VF	XF	Unc
362a	31	(1942)	—	—	—	200.00
	32	(1943)	—	—	—	200.00

BRONZE (OMS)

| 362b | 31 | (1942) | — | — | — | 200.00 |
| | 32 | (1943) | — | — | — | 200.00 |

SILVER (OMS)

Y#	Year	Date	Fine	VF	XF	Unc
362c	31	(1942)	—	—	—	500.00

DOLLAR (YUAN)

26.9000 g, .900 SILVER, .7785 oz ASW
Sun Yat-sen Founding of the Republic
Rev: Two 5-pointed stars dividing leg. at top.

Y#	Date	Mintage	Fine	VF	XF	Unc
318	ND(1912)	—	40.00	80.00	125.00	200.00

GOLD (OMS)

| 318b | ND(1912) | | | | | |

26.9000 g, .900 SILVER, .7785 oz ASW
Obv: Dot below ear.

| 318.1 | ND | | | | | |

NOTE: For similar issue with rosettes see Y#318a (1927).

27.3000 g, .900 SILVER, .7900 oz ASW
Obv: Similar to Y#318.

| 319 | ND(1912) | — | 60.00 | 100.00 | 150.00 | 175.00 |

GOLD (OMS)

K#	Date	Mintage	Fine	VF	XF	Unc
1550	ND(1912)	—	—	—	4500.	6500.

SILVER, 26.50 g
Li Yuan-hung Founding of Republic
Rev: Similar to Y#319.

Y#	Date	Mintage	Fine	VF	XF	Unc
320	ND(1912)	—	100.00	175.00	275.00	375.00

Rev. leg: OE for OF.

| 320.1 | ND(1912) | — | 100.00 | 175.00 | 275.00 | 375.00 |

Rev. leg: CIIINA for CHINA.

| 320.2 | ND(1912) | — | 175.00 | 275.00 | 400.00 | 500.00 |

Li Yuan-hung Founding of Republic
Rev: Similar to Y#319.

| 321 | ND(1912) | — | 20.00 | 40.00 | 65.00 | 85.00 |

Rev. leg: H of 'THE' engraved as I I, w/o crossbar.

Y#	Date	Mintage	Fine	VF	XF	Unc
321.1	ND(1912)	—	30.00	50.00	75.00	100.00

39mm, thickness 2.5mm
Yuan Shih-kai Founding of Republic

| 322 | ND(1914) | .020 | — | 100.00 | 150.00 | 275.00 |

39.5mm, thickness 3.25mm

| 322.1 | ND | — | 100.00 | 150.00 | 300.00 | |

NOTE: A restrike made about 1918 for collectors.

COPPER (OMS)

| 322a | ND(1914) | — | — | — | 350.00 | 500.00 |

BRASS (OMS)

| 322b | ND(1914) | — | — | — | 400.00 | 600.00 |

26.4000 g, .890 SILVER, .7555 oz ASW
Obv: 6 characters above head.
Vertical reeding.

Y#	Year	Date	Fine	VF	XF	Unc
329	3	(1914)	5.00	6.00	7.50	14.00

Edge engrailed w/circles.

| 329.1 | 3 | (1914) | 30.00 | 75.00 | 150.00 | 300.00 |

Edge ornamented w/alternating T's.

| 329.2 | 3 | (1914) | 30.00 | 75.00 | 150.00 | 400.00 |

Plain edge.

| 329.3 | 3 | (1914) | 20.00 | 40.00 | 60.00 | 80.00 |

Tiny circle in ribbon bow. This is a mint mark, but it is not clear what mint is indicated.

| 329.4 | 3 | (1914) | 15.00 | 25.00 | 40.00 | 75.00 |

Obv: 7 characters above head.

329.6	8	(1919)	10.00	15.00	25.00	75.00
	9	(1920)	6.00	7.00	8.00	15.00
	10	(1921)	6.00	7.00	8.00	15.00

Oblique edge reeding.

| 329.5 | 10 | (1921) | 17.50 | 30.00 | 35.00 | 50.00 |

NOTE: Although bearing dates of Yr. 3 (1914) and Yr. 8-10

(1919-21), these Yuan Shi-Kai Dollars were struck for years afterwards. Coins dated Yr. 3 (1914) were struck continuously through 1929 and were also later restruck by the Chinese Communists. Later again in the 1950's this coin was struck for use in Tibet. Coins with dates Yr. 9 and 10 (1920 and 1921) were struck at least until 1929. The total mintage of all four dates of Y#329 is estimated at more than 750 million pieces.

GOLD (OMS)

Y#	Year	Date	Fine	VF	XF	Unc
329a	3	(1914)	—	—	—	—

COPPER (OMS)

| 329b | 3 | (1914) | — | — | 250.00 | 400.00 |

BRASS (OMS)

| 329c | 3 | (1914) | — | — | 250.00 | 400.00 |

SILVER, 26.80 g
Inauguration of Hung Hsien Regime
Obv: Similar to Y#322.

| 332 | ND | (1916) | — | 150.00 | 200.00 | 475.00 |

NOTE: Struck in 1917.

GOLD (OMS)

| 332a | ND | (1916) | — | — | 3500. | 5500. |

WHITE METAL (OMS)

| 332b | ND | (1916) | — | — | — | — |

SILVER, 26.50 g
President Hsu Shih-chang
Reeded edge

K#	Year	Date	Fine	VF	XF	Unc
676	10	(1921)	—	175.00	200.00	450.00

Plain edge

| 676.1 | 10 | (1921) | — | 200.00 | 250.00 | 500.00 |

GOLD (OMS)

| 676a | 10 | (1921) | — | — | 5000. | 6500. |

SILVER, 26.70 g
President Tsao Kun

K#	Date	Mintage	Fine	VF	XF	Unc
677	ND(1923)	.050	—	150.00	200.00	350.00

GOLD, 37.50 g (OMS)

| 1572 | ND(1923) | | — | — | 3000. | 4500. |

COPPER (OMS)

| 677x | ND(1923) | | | | | |

BRASS (OMS)

| 677y | ND(1923) | | | | | |

SILVER, 26.80 g
Pu Yi Wedding
Rev: Value in small characters.

Y#	Year	Date	Fine	VF	XF	Unc
336	12	(1923)	—	225.00	300.00	550.00

GOLD (OMS)

| 336a | 12 | (1923) | — | — | 4500. | 6500. |

COPPER (OMS)

| 336b | 12 | (1923) | | | | |

SILVER, 26.80 g
Rev: Value in large characters.

| 336.1 | 12 | (1923) | — | 350.00 | 500.00 | 1000. |

GOLD (OMS)

| 336.1a | 12 | (1923) | — | — | — | — |

SILVER
President Tuan Chi-jui

K#	Date	Mintage	Fine	VF	XF	Unc
683	ND(1924)		—	150.00	200.00	275.00

GOLD (OMS)

| 1577 | ND(1924) | | — | — | 3500. | 5000. |

COPPER (OMS)

| 683x | ND(1924) | | | | | |

PEWTER (OMS)

| 683y | ND(1924) | | | | | |

27.0000 g, .890 SILVER, .7727 oz ASW
Incuse edge reeding
Rev: Two rosettes dividing leg. at top.

Y#	Date	Mintage	Fine	VF	XF	Unc
318a.1	ND(1927)		6.00	7.00	8.00	15.00

Edge reeding in relief.

| 318a.2 | ND(1927) | | 6.00 | 7.00 | 8.00 | 15.00 |

NOTE: Varieties exist with errors in the English legend. For similar coins with 5 pointed stars dividing legends, see Y#318 (1912). In 1949 the Canton Mint restruck Memento dollars.

GOLD, 42.00 g (OMS)

| 318c | ND(1927) | | — | — | — | — |

COPPER (OMS)

| 318d | ND(1927) | | — | — | — | 225.00 |

NOTE: There are modern restrikes in red copper and brass.

SILVER, 26.50 g
General Chu Yu-pu

K#	Year	Date	Fine	VF	XF	Unc
690	16	(1927)	—	—	3500.	5000.

27.00 g
Sun Yat-sen Memorial

K#	Date	Mintage	Fine	VF	XF	Unc
609	Yr.16 (1927)	480 pcs.	400.00	800.00	1250.	2600.

26.7000 g, .880 SILVER, .7555 oz ASW
Rev: Birds over junk.

Y#	Date	Mintage	Fine	VF	XF	Unc
344	Yr.21 (1932)	2.260	40.00	80.00	120.00	250.00

COPPER (OMS)

Y#	Year	Date	Fine	VF	XF	Unc
344a	21	(1932)	—	—	125.00	250.00

26.7000 g, .880 SILVER, .7555 oz ASW
Obv: Similar to Y#344.

Y#	Date	Mintage	Fine	VF	XF	Unc
345	Yr.22 (1933)	46.400	7.00	9.50	12.50	25.00
	Yr.23 (1934)	128.740	6.00	7.00	8.00	15.00

NOTE: In 1949, three U.S. mints restruck a total of 30 million "Junk Dollars" dated Year 23.

COPPER (OMS)

Y#	Year	Date	Fine	VF	XF	Unc
345a	22	(1933)	—	—	—	—
	23	(1934)	—	—	—	—
	24	(1935)	—	—	—	—

20.0000 g, .720 SILVER, .4630 oz ASW

K#	Date	Mintage	Fine	VF	XF	Unc
632	Yr.26 (1936)S	3.240	—	—	2500.	3500.

10 DOLLARS

RED GOLD, 7.05 g
Hung Hsien

Y#	Year	Date	Fine	VF	XF	Unc
333	1	(1916)	—	2000.	3000.	4500.

YELLOW GOLD, 7.05 g

333a	1	(1916)	—	2000.	3000.	4500.

SILVER (OMS)

Y#	Year	Date	Fine	VF	XF	Unc
333b	1	(1916)	—	—	—	—

COPPER (OMS)

333c	1	(1916)	—	—	250.00	375.00

8.1500 g, .850 GOLD, .2227 oz AGW

330	8	(1919)	—	—	2250.	3000.

COPPER (OMS)

330a	8	(1919)	—	—	175.00	300.00

BRASS (OMS)

330b	8	(1919)	—	—	—	—

20 DOLLARS

16.3000 g, .850 GOLD, .4456 oz AGW

331	8	(1919)	—	—	4500.	6000.

COPPER (OMS)

331a	8	(1919)	—	—	250.00	450.00

PROVINCIAL COINAGE
ANHWEI PROVINCE
Anhui

A province located in eastern China. Made a separate province during the Manchu dynasty in the 17th century. Principally agricultural with some mining of coal and iron ore. Spanish-American 8 Reales saw wide circulation in this province until the end of World War I. The provincial mint at Anking began operations in 1897, closed in 1899, and later reopened in 1902. The primary production of the mint was Cash coins but included a series of silver coinage.

EMPIRE
CASH

CAST BRASS
Obv: Type A-1

C#	Date	Emperor	Good	VG	Fine	VF
—	ND (1796-1820) Chia Ch'ing	—	—	Rare		

Obv: Type A

| — | ND (1820-51) Tao Kuang | — | — | Rare | | |

NOTE: Not to be confused with similar coins from the Changsha Mint in Hunan Province. The Changsha Mint coins have an extra dot or vertical stroke to the left of the mint mark at right of the center hole.

NOTE: For previously listed 3-1, 3-1.1 and 3-1.1a, refer to Chihli (Hebei) Province.

MILLED COINAGE
5 CASH

COPPER
Rev: Circled dragon, leg: AN-HWEI.

Y#	Date	VG	Fine	VF	XF
35	ND (1902)	125.00	175.00	250.00	350.00

Rev: Uncircled dragon, leg: AN-HUI.

Y#	Date	VG	Fine	VF	XF
35.1	ND	—	—	—	Rare

10 CASH

COPPER
Rev: Letter A inverted, denomination ONE SEN.

34a	ND (1902)	50.00	80.00	125.00	350.00

Rev: Letter A corrected.

34a.1	ND (1902)	40.00	65.00	100.00	250.00

Rev. denomination: ONE CEN

34	ND (1902)	35.00	50.00	85.00	135.00

NOTE: May show various stages of recutting of 'C' in CEN.

Rev: Rosettes around dragon close together.
Letter N backwards in AN-HWEI.

36	ND (1902-06)	6.00	12.00	20.00	40.00

Obv: Small Manchu characters in center.
Rev: Rosettes close together. Letter N corrected.

36.1	ND (1902-06)	.75	2.00	3.00	8.00

Obv: Smaller redesigned rosettes.
Larger Manchu characters in center.
Rev: Rosettes close together.

Larger clouds around redesigned dragon.
Y#	Date	VG	Fine	VF	XF
36.2	ND (1902-06)	.75	2.00	3.00	8.00

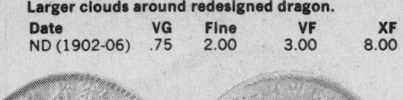

Obv: Rosettes crude and heavy.
Rev: Rosettes close together. Dragon's head redesigned.
| 36.3 | ND (1902-06) | 5.00 | 10.00 | 17.50 | 35.00 |

Rev: Rosettes far apart.
| 36.4 | ND (1902-06) | .75 | 2.00 | 5.00 | 8.00 |

Obv: Small rosette at center with five characters at bottom. Rev: Large English leg. above dragon, w/o TEN CASH.
| 36a | ND (1902-06) | .75 | 2.00 | 3.00 | 8.00 |

Obv: Small rosette.
Rev: Small English leg. above dragon.
| 36a.1 | ND (1902-06) | 1.50 | 3.50 | 7.50 | 15.00 |

Rev: Small English leg. w/larger clouds around dragon and only one cloud below dragon's tail.
| 36a.2 | ND (1902-06) | 1.50 | 3.50 | 7.50 | 15.00 |

Obv: Large rosette at center w/two characters at bottom.
| 36a.3 | ND (1902-06) | .75 | 2.00 | 3.00 | 6.00 |

Obv: Large rosette at center w/five characters at bottom.
| 36a.4 | ND (1902-06) | 1.25 | 2.50 | 3.50 | 7.00 |

Obv: Two characters at bottom.
Rev: Small English leg. above dragon.
Y#	Date	VG	Fine	VF	XF
36a.5	ND (1902-06)	3.50	7.50	15.00	30.00

Obv: Slightly smaller rosette at center w/right Manchu character slightly higher than on Y#36a.5.
Rev: Small English leg. above dragon.
| 36a.6 | ND (1902-06) | .75 | 2.00 | 3.50 | 7.00 |

Obv: Two characters at bottom.
Rev: Ten spelled TOEN.
| 38a | ND (1902-06) | 8.00 | 15.00 | 30.00 | 50.00 |

Obv: Five characters at bottom.
Rev: Ten spelled TOEN.
| 38a.1 | ND (1902-06) | 35.00 | 70.00 | 150.00 | 250.00 |

Obv: Two characters at bottom.
Rev: W/o TEN CASH.
| 38b | ND (1902-06) | 5.00 | 11.00 | 22.50 | 45.00 |

Obv: Five characters at bottom.
| 38b.1 | ND (1902-06) | 15.00 | 35.00 | 50.00 | 120.00 |

Rev: Rosettes at sides and AN-HUI above dragon.
Y#	Date	VG	Fine	VF	XF
39	ND (1902-06)	—	—	Rare	—

Rev: Stars at sides and AN-HUI above dragon.
| 39.1 | ND (1902-06) | — | — | Rare | — |

Square holed center, AN-HUI, upright dragon.
| 39.2 | (1902-06) | — | — | Rare | — |

Obv: Large mint mark at center.
Y#	Date	Mintage	VG	Fine	VF	XF
10a	CD1906	—	.75	2.00	3.00	6.00

Obv: Small mint mark at center.
| 10a.1 | CD1906 | — | .60 | 1.50 | 2.50 | 5.00 |

Obv. and rev: More finely engraved.
Rev: Cloud near dragon's lower foot shaped like a 3.
| 10a.2 | CD1906 | — | .60 | 1.50 | 2.50 | 5.00 |

| 20a | CD1909 | — | 12.00 | 25.00 | 50.00 | 100.00 |

Rev: Dot after COIN.
| 20a.1 | CD1909 | — | 35.00 | 65.00 | 130.00 | 225.00 |

Anhwei / CHINA
320

20 CASH

COPPER

Y#	Date	Mintage	VG	Fine	VF	XF
37	ND (1902)	—	375.00	750.00	1100.	1500.

| 11a | CD1906 | — | 37.50 | 75.00 | 150.00 | 250.00 |

5 CENTS

1.3300 g, .820 SILVER, .0351 oz ASW

Y#	Date	Mintage	Fine	VF	XF	Unc
41	ND (1897)	—	40.00	75.00	130.00	240.00

Y#	Year	Date	Fine	VF	XF	Unc
41.1	25	(1899)	35.00	55.00	90.00	160.00

10 CENTS

2.6500 g, .820 SILVER, .0699 oz ASW
Obv: Rosettes divide leg.

Y#	Date	Mintage	Fine	VF	XF	Unc
42	ND (1897)	—	12.00	25.00	50.00	120.00

Obv: W/o rosettes dividing leg.

Y#	Year	Date	Fine	VF	XF	Unc
42.1	24	(1898)	10.00	20.00	40.00	80.00

Obv: Rosettes divide leg.

| 42.2 | 24 | (1898) | 10.00 | 20.00 | 40.00 | 80.00 |

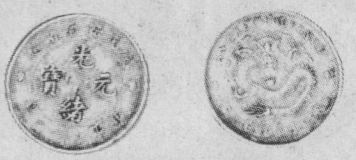

Obv: A S T C in field.

| 42.3 | 24 | (1898) | 10.00 | 22.50 | 45.00 | 90.00 |

Obv: Six characters at top.

Y#	Date	Mintage	Fine	VF	XF	Unc
42.4	CD1898	—	12.00	25.00	50.00	100.00

20 CENTS

5.3000 g, .820 SILVER, .1397 oz ASW
Rev: Large dragon and small English leg.

Y#	Date	Mintage	Fine	VF	XF	Unc
43	ND (1897)	—	15.00	35.00	70.00	140.00

Rev: Smaller dragon and larger English leg.

43.1	ND (1897)	—	15.00	35.00	70.00	140.00
43.2	23 (1897)					
	Two known	—				

Y#	Year	Date	Fine	VF	XF	Unc
43.3	24	(1898)	15.00	35.00	70.00	140.00

Obv: A S T C in field.

| 43.4 | 24 | (1898) | 15.00 | 35.00 | 70.00 | 140.00 |

| 43.5 | 27 | (1901) | One known | — | | |

50 CENTS

13.5000 g, .860 SILVER, .3733 oz ASW

| 44 | 24 | (1898) | 70.00 | 130.00 | 200.00 | 450.00 |

BRASS (OMS)

| 44a | 24 | (1898) | | | | 1000. |

13.5000 g, .860 SILVER, .3733 oz ASW
Obv: A S T C in field.

| 44.1 | 24 | (1898) | 65.00 | 130.00 | 200.00 | 400.00 |

DOLLAR

27.1000 g, .900 SILVER, .7842 oz ASW

Y#	Date	Mintage	Fine	VF	XF	Unc
45	ND (1897)	—	75.00	150.00	250.00	550.00

Y#	Year	Date	Fine	VF	XF	Unc
45.1	23	(1897)	—	—	17,500.	25,000.

SILVER PLATED BRONZE (OMS)

| 45.1a | 23 | (1897) | | | — | 8500. |

27.1000 g, .900 SILVER, .7842 oz ASW
Obv: Tall Chinese character '4' in date.
Rev: Similar to Y#45.

| 45.2 | 24 | (1898) | 80.00 | 125.00 | 200.00 | 575.00 |

Obv: Short Chinese character '4' in date.
Rev: Similar to Y#45.

| 45.5 | 24 | (1898) | 80.00 | 125.00 | 200.00 | 550.00 |

Obv: A S T C in field. Rev: Similar to Y#45.

| 45.3 | 24 | (1898) | 80.00 | 125.00 | 200.00 | 500.00 |

26.90 g
Obv: Six characters at top.

Y#	Date	Mintage	Fine	VF	XF	Unc
45.4	CD1898	—	150.00	225.00	350.00	800.00

Rev: Similar to Y#45.1

CHEKIANG PROVINCE
Zhejiang

A province located along the east coast of China. Although the smallest of the Chinese mainland provinces, it is one of the most densely populated. Mostly agricultural with iron and coal mining and some fishing. A small mint opened in 1897. This was replaced by a larger mint which operated briefly 1898-99. Other mints opened in 1903 and 1905. These were merged with the Fukien Mint in 1906-07.

EMPIRE
CASH

CAST BRASS
Obv: Type A
Rev: Large mint mark and normal rims.

C#	Date	Emperor	Good	VG	Fine	VF
4-2	ND (1796-1820)	Chia Ch'ing	.25	.50	.75	1.50

Rev: Small mint mark and wide rims.

4-2.1 ND (1796-1820)
　　　Chia Ch'ing　.25　.50　.75　1.50

CAST IRON

4-2.1a ND (1796-1820)
　　　Chia Ch'ing　—　—　Rare　—

Rev: Dot at bottom.

4-2.2 ND (1796-1820)
　　　Chia Ch'ing　2.00　3.50　5.00　10.00

CAST BRASS
Obv: Type A
Rev: Large mint mark. 23-25mm.

4-3 ND (1820-51)
　　Tao Kuang　.25　.50　.75　1.50

Rev: Small mint mark. 21-23mm.

4-3.1 ND (1820-51)
　　　Tao Kuang　.25　.50　.75　1.50

21-25mm
Obv: Type A

4-3.5 ND (1851-61)
　　　Hsien Feng　1.00　2.00　3.00　6.00

16-20mm

4-3.6 ND (1851-61)
　　　Hsien Feng　1.00　2.00　3.00　6.00

CAST IRON

4-3.6a ND (1851-61)
　　　Hsien Feng　6.50　12.50　25.00　50.00

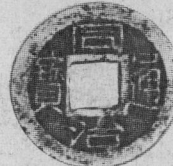 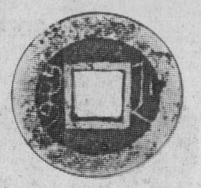

CAST BRASS
Obv: Type A-2

C#	Date	Emperor	Good	VG	Fine	VF
4-17	ND (1862-74)	T'ung Chih	1.00	2.00	3.00	6.00

Obv: Type A
Rev: Mint mark as C#4-1.

4-19 ND (1875-1908)
　　　Kuang Hsu　1.00　2.00　3.00　6.00

Rev: Mint mark as C#4-1.1.

4-19.1 ND (1875-1908)
　　　Kuang Hsu　1.00　2.00　3.00　6.00

CAST ZINC

4-19a ND (1875-1908)
　　　Kuang Hsu　—　—　Rare　—

10 CASH

CAST BRASS
Obv: Type B-1
Rev: Manchu mint mark to right as above. Denomination at bottom in Chinese.

4-4 ND (1851-61)
　　Hsien Feng　3.00　4.50　6.00　10.00

Rev: Chinese character '10' at top.

4-9 ND (1851-61)
　　Hsien Feng　15.00　25.00　40.00　70.00

Rev: Manchu mint mark left and Chinese mint mark right. Denomination at bottom.

4-11 ND (1851-61)
　　　Hsien Feng　20.00　35.00　60.00　100.00

4-18 ND (1862-74)
　　　T'ung Chih　—　—　Rare　—

Obv: Type A

4-20 ND (1875-1908)
　　　Kuang Hsu　—　—　Rare　—

20 CASH

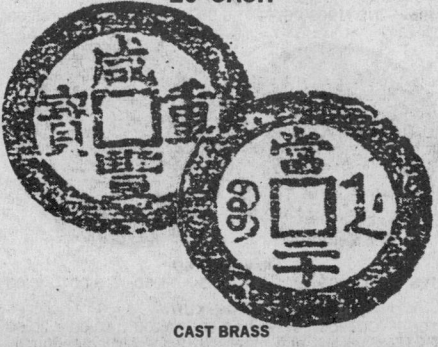

CAST BRASS

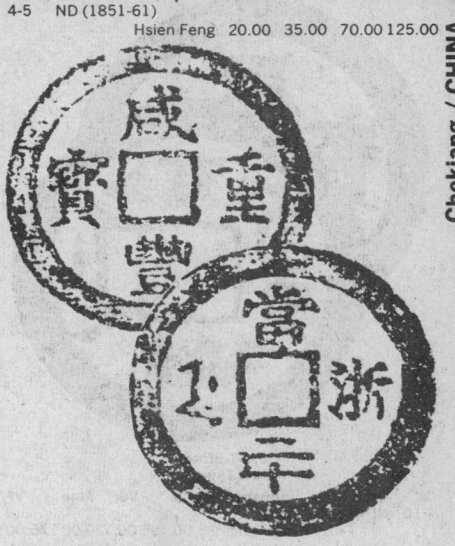

Obv: Type B-1

C#	Date	Emperor	Good	VG	Fine	VF
4-5	ND (1851-61)	Hsien Feng	20.00	35.00	70.00	125.00

4-12 ND (1851-61)
　　　Hsien Feng　20.00　35.00　70.00　125.00

30 CASH

CAST BRASS
Obv: Type B-1
Rev: Similar to 10 Cash, C#4-4.

4-6 ND (1851-61)
　　　Hsien Feng　35.00　65.00　120.00　175.00

Rev: Similar to 40 Cash, C#4-14.

4-13 ND (1851-61)
　　　Hsien Feng　35.00　65.00　120.00　175.00

40 CASH

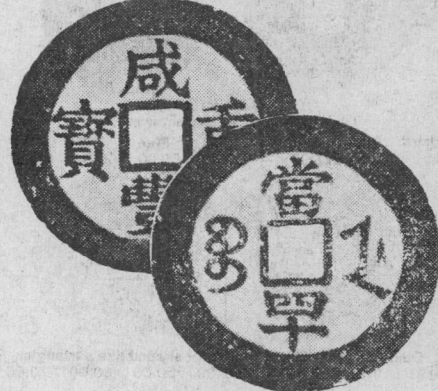

CAST BRASS
Obv: Type B-1
Rev: Similar to 10 Cash, C#4-4.

4-7 ND (1851-61)
　　　Hsien Feng　35.00　65.00　130.00　225.00

4-14 ND (1851-61)
　　　Hsien Feng　35.00　65.00　130.00　250.00

50 CASH

CAST BRASS
Obv: Type B-1
Rev: Similar to 10 Cash, C#4-4.

4-8 ND (1851-61)
　　　Hsien Feng　25.00　40.00　70.00　110.00

Rev: Similar to 40 Cash, C#4-14.

4-15 ND (1851-61)
　　　Hsien Feng　25.00　40.00　70.00　110.00

Chekiang / CHINA 322

100 CASH

CAST BRASS
Obv: Type B-1

C#	Date	Emperor	Good	VG	Fine	VF
4-10	ND (1851-61)	Hsien Feng	35.00	65.00	120.00	175.00

Rev: Similar to 40 Cash, C#4-14.

| 4-16 | ND (1851-61) | Hsien Feng | 25.00 | 40.00 | 70.00 | 110.00 |

FANTASY ISSUES
NOTE: Coins of this mint in denominations of 400 Cash are considered fantasy issues.

MILLED COINAGE
CASH

BRASS, struck
Obv: Type A, large character at left.

Hsu#	Date	Mintage	VG	Fine	VF	XF
151	ND(1897-98)	—	35.00	50.00	65.00	80.00

Obv: Top part of right character shaped like a triangle.
| 151.1 | ND(1897-98) | — | 35.00 | 50.00 | 60.00 | 70.00 |

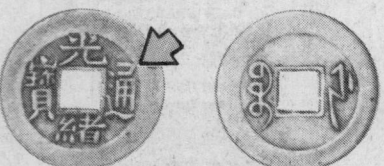

Obv: Top part of right character shaped like a box.
| 151.2 | ND(1897-98) | — | 35.00 | 50.00 | 60.00 | 80.00 |

2 CASH

COPPER

Y#	Date	Mintage	VG	Fine	VF	XF
8b	CD1906	—	7.50	12.50	20.00	35.00

5 CASH

COPPER
| 9b | CD1906 | — | 5.00 | 10.00 | 16.00 | 35.00 |

10 CASH

COPPER
Obv: Ball in circle in center.

Y#	Date	Mintage	VG	Fine	VF	XF
49	ND (1903-06)	—	.50	1.00	2.00	4.00

Obv: Rosette at center and large Manchu character at left.
| 49.1 | ND (1903-06) | — | .25 | .50 | 1.25 | 2.50 |

BRASS
| 49.1a | ND (1903-06) | — | 2.00 | 4.00 | 8.00 | 15.00 |

COPPER
Similar to Y#49.1a
| 49.2 | ND (1903-06) | — | .75 | 1.50 | 3.00 | 6.00 |

Obv: Rosette at center and small Manchu character at left. Rev: Small cramped dragon w/few clouds around body.
| 49.3 | ND (1903-06) | — | .75 | 1.50 | 3.00 | 6.00 |

Rev: W/o ball in center circle.
| 49.4 | ND (1903-06) | — | 1.25 | 2.50 | 5.00 | 10.00 |

BRASS
Obv: Four characters at bottom.
| 49a | ND (1903-06) | — | 3.00 | 6.00 | 11.00 | 20.00 |

COPPER
| 49b | ND (1903-06) | — | 6.00 | 12.00 | 25.00 | 45.00 |

Rev. leg: KIIO
| 10b | CD1906 | — | .75 | 1.50 | 3.00 | 6.00 |

Rev. leg: KUO
| 10b.1 | CD1906 | — | 2.50 | 5.00 | 10.00 | 20.00 |

NOTE: Chekiang and other 10 Cash coin types found struck over Korean 5 Fun coins are counterfeits.

20 CASH

COPPER

Y#	Date	Mintage	VG	Fine	VF	XF
50	ND (1903-04)	—	50.00	100.00	150.00	225.00

NOTE: Exists in two different size planchets.

| 11b | CD1906 | — | 40.00 | 75.00 | 125.00 | 200.00 |

5 CENTS

1.3500 g, .820 SILVER, .0356 oz ASW
Rev. leg: CHEH-KIANG, 3.2 CANDAREENS.

Y#	Date	Mintage	Fine	VF	XF	Unc
51	ND (1898-99)	—	10.00	20.00	30.00	70.00

10 CENTS
2.7000 g, .820 SILVER, .0712 oz ASW
Rev. leg: CHEH-KIANG

Y#	Year	Date	Fine	VF	XF	Unc
52	22	(1896)	50.00	100.00	150.00	250.00

Rev. leg: N's backwards.
| 52.1 | 22 | (1896) | 55.00 | 110.00 | 175.00 | 300.00 |

Rev: Denomination reads 2.7 instead of 7.2.
| 52.2 | 22 | (1896) | 50.00 | 100.00 | 150.00 | 250.00 |
| 52.3 | 23 | (1897) | 65.00 | 125.00 | 225.00 | 350.00 |

Y#	Date	Mintage	Fine	VF	XF	Unc
52.4	ND (1898-99)	—	10.00	20.00	30.00	60.00

20 CENTS

5.4000 g, .820 SILVER, .1424 oz ASW
Rev: Six rows of scales on dragon.

Y#	Year	Date	Fine	VF	XF	Unc
53	22	(1896)	75.00	150.00	250.00	350.00

Rev. leg: Letter E backwards in CHEH-KIANG.
| 53.1 | 22 | (1896) | 75.00 | 150.00 | 250.00 | 350.00 |

Rev. leg: Additional cross-strokes in letter H in CHEH-KIANG. Eight rows of scales on dragon.
| 53.2 | 22 | (1896) | 75.00 | 150.00 | 250.00 | 350.00 |

Rev. leg: W/o hyphen in CHEH KIANG.
| 53.3 | 22 | (1896) | 75.00 | 150.00 | 250.00 | 350.00 |

Rev. leg: Dot in CHEH.KIANG.
| 53.4 | 22 | (1896) | 75.00 | 150.00 | 250.00 | 350.00 |

Rev: Rosettes made of seven dots dividing leg.

Y#	Year	Date	Fine	VF	XF	Unc
53.5	23	(1897)	55.00	110.00	175.00	275.00

**Rev: Rosettes replaced by a cross;
leg: MACE spelled NACE.**

| 53.6 | 23 | (1897) | 55.00 | 110.00 | 175.00 | 275.00 |

Rev. leg: CHEH-KIANG

Y#	Date	Mintage	Fine	VF	XF	Unc
53.7	ND (1898-99)	—	10.00	20.00	40.00	95.00

50 CENTS

13.5000 g, .860 SILVER, .3733 oz ASW
Rev. leg: CHEH-KIANG

| 54 | ND (1898-99) | — | 125.00 | 275.00 | 500.00 | 950.00 |

DOLLAR

27.5000 g, .900 SILVER, .7958 oz ASW
Rev. leg: CHEH-KIANG

| 56 | Yr.23 (1897) | — | — | — | 20,000. | 30,000. |

| 55 | ND(1898-99) | — | — | — | 8500. | 13,500. |

REPUBLIC
10 CENTS

2.6500 g, .650 SILVER, .0554 oz ASW

Y#	Date	Mintage	Fine	VF	XF	Unc
371	Yr.13 (1924)	4.464	2.00	5.00	7.00	20.00

20 CENTS
SILVER, 5.30 g
Rev: Large 20

Y#	Year	Date	Fine	VF	XF	Unc
373	13	(1924)	300.00	500.00	700.00	1100.

CHIHLI PROVINCE
Hebei, Hopei

A province located in northeastern China which contains the eastern end of the Great Wall. An important producer of coal and some iron ore. In 1928 the provincial name was changed from Chihli to Hopei. The Paoting mint was established in 1745 and only produced cast cash coins.

A mint for struck cash was established in 1888 and the mint for the Peiyang silver coinage was added in 1896. This was destroyed during the Boxer Rebellion. A replacement mint was built in 1902 for the provincial coinage and merged with the Tientsin Central mint in 1910.

EMPIRE

Included here are coins inscribed PEI YANG. These were produced by the mint in the Peiyang Arsenal in Tientsin. For coins inscribed PEKING, see General Issues.

Changte Mint
(Jehol)
CASH
**CAST BRASS
Obv: Type A.**

C#	Date	Emperor	Good	VG	Fine	VF
6-1	ND(1851-61)	Hsien Feng	20.00	30.00	40.00	50.00

5 CASH

CAST BRASS

| 6-2 | ND(1851-61) | Hsien Feng | 40.00 | 70.00 | 100.00 | 150.00 |

CAST IRON

| 6-2a | ND(1851-61) | Hsien Feng | 25.00 | 45.00 | 70.00 | 100.00 |

10 CASH

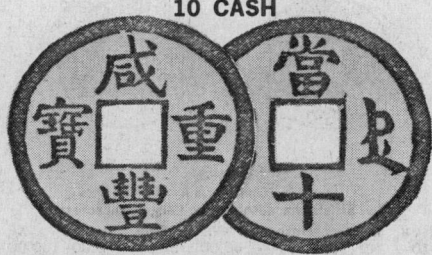

**CAST BRASS
Obv: Type B-1.**

C#	Date	Emperor	Good	VG	Fine	VF
6-3	ND(1851-61)	Hsien Feng	40.00	70.00	100.00	150.00

CAST IRON

| 6-3a | ND(1851-61) | Hsien Feng | 40.00 | 70.00 | 100.00 | 150.00 |

50 CASH
**CAST BRASS
Obv: Type B-1.**

| 6-4 | ND(1851-61) | Hsien Feng | 150.00 | 165.00 | 200.00 | 400.00 |

100 CASH
CAST BRASS

| 6-5 | ND(1851-61) | Hsien Feng | — | — | Rare | |

FANTASY ISSUES
NOTE: Coins of this mint in denominations of 500 and 1000 Cash are considered fantasy issues.

Chichow Mint
5 CASH

**CAST BRASS
Obv: Type B-1**

| 7-1 | ND (1851-61) | Hsien Feng | 30.00 | 50.00 | 75.00 | 110.00 |

CAST IRON

| 7-1a | ND (1851-61) | Hsien Feng | 40.00 | 60.00 | 85.00 | 120.00 |

10 CASH
**CAST BRASS
Large size, 35mm.**

| 7-2 | ND (1851-61) | Hsien Feng | 30.00 | 50.00 | 75.00 | 100.00 |

Small size, 27mm.

| 7-2.1 | ND (1851-61) | Hsien Feng | 25.00 | 42.50 | 65.00 | 90.00 |

CAST IRON

| 7-2a | ND (1851-61) | Hsien Feng | 25.00 | 40.00 | 65.00 | 125.00 |

50 CASH
CAST BRASS

| 7-3 | ND (1851-61) | Hsien Feng | 25.00 | 40.00 | 60.00 | 90.00 |

100 CASH
CAST BRASS

| 7-4 | ND (1851-61) | Hsien Feng | 25.00 | 40.00 | 65.00 | 100.00 |

NOTE: This mint mark was later transferred to the Kirin Mint; the Chichow Mint operated only during the reign of Hsien'Feng.

Paoting Mint
CASH
**CAST BRASS
Obv: Type A**

| 5-2 | ND (1796-1820) | Chia Ch'ing | .25 | .50 | 1.00 | 2.00 |

Obv: Type A

| 5-3 | ND (1820-51) | Tao Kuang | .25 | .50 | 1.00 | 2.00 |

Rev: Dot below.

| 5-3.1 | ND (1820-51) | Tao Kuang | 1.50 | 3.00 | 6.00 | 10.00 |

Obv: Type A

| 5-4 | ND (1851-61) | Hsien Feng | 1.50 | 3.00 | 6.00 | 10.00 |

CAST IRON

| 5-4a | ND (1851-61) | Hsien Feng | 6.50 | 12.50 | 25.00 | 50.00 |

**CAST BRASS
Obv: Type A-2**

| 5-8 | ND (1862-74) | T'ung Chih | 2.00 | 4.00 | 8.00 | 16.00 |

Obv: Type A

| 5-10 | ND (1875-1908) | Kuang Hsu | 2.00 | 4.00 | 8.00 | 16.00 |

Rev: Dot above.

| 5-10.1 | ND (1875-1908) | Kuang Hsu | 2.25 | 4.50 | 9.00 | 18.50 |

Rev: Crescent above.

| 5-10.2 | ND (1875-1908) | Kuang Hsu | 2.50 | 5.00 | 10.00 | 20.00 |

Chihli / CHINA 324

NOTE: The crescent is known in various positions above the center hole.

Rev: Circle above.
C#	Date	Emperor	Good	VG	Fine	VF
5-10.3	ND (1875-1908) Kuang Hsu		2.50	5.00	10.00	20.00

Rev: Dot below.
| 5-10.4 | ND (1875-1908) Kuang Hsu | 2.00 | 4.00 | 8.00 | 16.00 |

Rev: Circle below.
| 5-10.5 | ND (1875-1908) Kuang Hsu | 2.50 | 5.00 | 10.00 | 20.00 |

Rev: Dash above.
| 5-10.6 | ND (1875-1908) Kuang Hsu | 2.50 | 5.00 | 10.00 | 20.00 |

Rev: Dash below.
| 5-10.7 | ND (1875-1908) Kuang Hsu | 2.50 | 5.00 | 10.00 | 20.00 |

10 CASH

CAST BRASS
Obv: Type B-1
| 5-5 | ND (1851-61) Hsien Feng | 10.00 | 15.00 | 20.00 | 50.00 |

CAST IRON
| 5-5a | ND (1851-61) Hsien Feng | 30.00 | 45.00 | 65.00 | 100.00 |

CAST BRASS
Rev: Dot above.
| 5-5.1 | ND (1851-61) Hsien Feng | 17.50 | 27.50 | 37.50 | 60.00 |

| 5-9 | ND (1862-74) T'ung Chih | — | — | Rare | |

| 5-11 | ND (1875-1908) Kwang Hsu | — | — | Rare | |

50 CASH

CAST BRASS
Obv: Type B-1
| 5-6 | ND (1851-61) Hsien Feng | 30.00 | 50.00 | 75.00 | 110.00 |

Rev: Dot at upper right; crescent upper left.
| 5-6.1 | ND (1851-61) Hsien Feng | 35.00 | 55.00 | 85.00 | 120.00 |

100 CASH

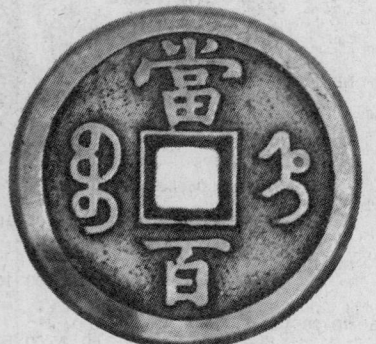

CAST BRASS
Obv: Type C.
| 5-7 | ND (1851-61) Hsien Feng | 50.00 | 75.00 | 100.00 | 175.00 |

1000 CASH
CAST BRASS
| A5-7 | ND (1851-61) Hsien Feng | Reported, not confirmed |

Peiyang Arsenal Mint
(Tientsin)

CASH

CAST BRASS
Obv: Type A
C#	Date	Emperor	Good	VG	Fine	VF
8-1	ND (1875-1908) Kuang Hsu	1.50	3.00	6.00	12.00

Rev: Dot above.
| 8-1.1 | ND (1875-1908) Kuang Hsu | 1.65 | 3.25 | 6.50 | 13.00 |

Rev: Dot below.
| 8-1.2 | ND (1875-1908) Kuang Hsu | 1.25 | 2.50 | 5.00 | 10.00 |

Rev: Two dots below.
| 8-1.3 | ND (1875-1908) Kuang Hsu | 2.00 | 3.75 | 7.50 | 15.00 |

Rev: Circle above.
| 8-1.4 | ND (1875-1908) Kuang Hsu | 2.00 | 3.75 | 7.50 | 15.00 |

Rev: Circle below.
| 8-1.5 | ND (1875-1908) Kuang Hsu | 2.00 | 3.75 | 7.50 | 15.00 |

Rev: Crescent above.
| 8-1.6 | ND (1875-1908) Kuang Hsu | 2.00 | 3.75 | 7.50 | 15.00 |

Rev: Crescent below.
| 8-1.7 | ND (1875-1908) Kuang Hsu | 2.00 | 3.75 | 7.50 | 15.00 |

Rev: Dash below.
| 8-1.8 | ND (1875-1908) Kuang Hsu | 2.00 | 3.75 | 7.50 | 15.00 |

NOTE: 4 other varieties exist, each with dot in a different corner on reverse.

MILLED COINAGE
CASH

BRASS
Obv: Type A
Obv: Small characters. Rev: Large characters.
Hsu#	Date	Mintage	VG	Fine	VF	XF
410	ND (1888-89)	—	40.00	50.00	75.00	100.00

Obv: Large characters. Rev: Small characters.
| 410.1 | ND (1888-89) | — | 40.00 | 50.00 | 75.00 | 100.00 |

Obv: and rev: Small characters.
Hsu#	Date	Mintage	VG	Fine	VF	XF
410.2	ND (1888-89)	—	7.50	12.50	20.00	30.00

Obv: and rev: Large characters.
| 410.3 | ND (1888-89) | — | 40.00 | 50.00 | 75.00 | 100.00 |

Y#	Date	Mintage	VG	Fine	VF	XF
66	ND	—	1.50	3.00	5.50	10.00

| 7c | CD1908 | — | 2.50 | 4.50 | 7.50 | 13.50 |

5 CASH

COPPER
| 9c | CD1906 | — | 4.50 | 8.50 | 15.00 | 27.50 |

10 CASH

COPPER
Rev: Hole in center of rosettes, square mouth dragon.
| 67 | ND | — | .50 | 1.00 | 1.75 | 3.00 |

NOTE: Mulings exist with obverse of Kwangtung (Guangdong) Y#192 and reverse of Chihli Y#67. Refer to Kwangtung listings.

Rev: Round mouth dragon.
| 67.1 | ND | — | .50 | 1.00 | 1.75 | 3.00 |

Rev: Dot in center of rosettes, square mouth dragon.
| 67.2 | ND | — | .50 | 1.00 | 1.75 | 3.00 |

Rev: Round mouth dragon.
| 67.3 | ND | — | .50 | 1.00 | 1.75 | 3.00 |

Rev: Redesigned dragon with smaller body and smaller English legends.
| 67.4 | ND | — | 1.50 | 3.50 | 7.00 | 15.00 |

Chihli / CHINA 325

Y#	Date	Mintage	VG	Fine	VF	XF
10c	CD1906	—	.50	1.00	2.00	4.00

20 CASH

			COPPER			
68	ND	—	7.50	15.00	27.50	65.00
			BRASS			
68a	ND		10.00	20.00	40.00	80.00
			COPPER			
			Rev: Smaller lettering.			
68.1	ND	—	10.00	20.00	40.00	80.00

| 11c | CD1906 | — | 15.00 | 30.00 | 60.00 | 120.00 |

5 CENTS

1.3200 g, .820 SILVER, .0348 oz ASW

Y#	Date	Mintage	Fine	VF	XF	Unc
61	Yr.22 (1896)	7,000	200.00	250.00	300.00	500.00
	Yr.23 (1897)	Inc. Ab.	25.00	50.00	100.00	200.00

Rev: Redesigned dragon.
| 61.1 | Yr.23 (1897) | .039 | 12.00 | 25.00 | 50.00 | 100.00 |
| | Yr.24 (1898) | .231 | 9.00 | 17.50 | 35.00 | 75.00 |

69	Yr.25 (1899)	.097	12.00	25.00	50.00	100.00
	Yr.26 (1900)	—	90.00	175.00	350.00	700.00
		COPPER (OMS)				
69a	Yr.25 (1899)	—	—	—	—	—

10 CENTS

2.6500 g, .820 SILVER, .0699 oz ASW
Y#	Date	Mintage	Fine	VF	XF	Unc
62	Yr.22 (1896)	5,000	50.00	100.00	150.00	300.00
	Yr.23 (1897)	.148	10.00	20.00	40.00	85.00
	Yr.24 (1898)	.614	5.00	10.00	30.00	75.00
70	Yr.25 (1899)	.153	15.00	35.00	50.00	95.00

20 CENTS

5.3000 g, .820 SILVER, .1397 oz ASW
63	Yr.22 (1896)	.012	100.00	225.00	400.00	700.00
	Yr.23 (1897)	.147	12.00	25.00	45.00	90.00
	Yr.24 (1898)	.350	10.00	20.00	40.00	80.00

| 71 | Yr.25 (1899) | .152 | 25.00 | 50.00 | 80.00 | 150.00 |
| | Yr.26 (1900) | — | 500.00 | 650.00 | 900.00 | 1250. |

| 71a | Yr.31 (1905) | .161 | 35.00 | 75.00 | 150.00 | 250.00 |

50 CENTS

13.3000 g, .860 SILVER, .3678 oz ASW
64	Yr.22 (1896)	2,500	400.00	800.00	1500.	2500.
	Yr.23 (1897)	.021	30.00	65.00	125.00	250.00
	Yr.24 (1898) I.A.		30.00	65.00	125.00	250.00

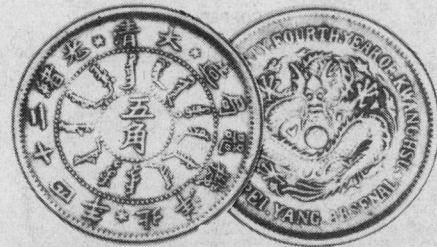

Rev: Redesigned dragon.
| 64.1 | Yr.24 (1898) | .176 | 20.00 | 50.00 | 90.00 | 200.00 |

Y#	Date	Mintage	Fine	VF	XF	Unc
72	Yr.25 (1899)	.056	75.00	140.00	225.00	500.00

DOLLAR

26.7000 g, .900 SILVER, .7727 oz ASW
| 65 | Yr.22 (1896) | 3,000 | 850.00 | 1850. | 3250. | 5000. |

Rev: Dragon w/beady eyes.
| 65.1 | Yr.23 (1897) | 1.120 | 30.00 | 65.00 | 130.00 | 400.00 |

Rev: Dragon w/eyelids.
| 65.2 | Yr.24 (1898) | 2.806 | 30.00 | 60.00 | 90.00 | 300.00 |

Chihli / CHINA

Obv: Similar to Y#73.2.

Y#	Date	Mintage	Fine	VF	XF	Unc
73	Yr.25 (1899)	1.566	15.00	30.00	50.00	300.00
	Yr.26 (1900)	—	40.00	75.00	125.00	600.00
	Yr.29 (1903)	22.018	8.00	12.00	32.50	200.00

BRASS (OMS)
| 73a | Yr.29 (1903) | — | — | — | — | — |

26.7000 g, .900 SILVER, .7727 oz ASW
Rev: Period after PEI YANG.
| 73.1 | Yr.29 (1903) I.A. | 8.00 | 12.00 | 30.00 | 175.00 |

Rev: Thinner dragon.
| 73.2 | Yr.33 (1907) | 2.341 | 8.00 | 12.00 | 35.00 | 225.00 |
| | Yr.34 (1908) | — | 8.00 | 12.00 | 25.00 | 125.00 |

Rev: Short center spine to tail.
| 73.3 | Yr.34 (1908) | — | 8.00 | 12.00 | 25.00 | 135.00 |

Rev: Crosslet 4 in date.
| 73.4 | Yr.34 (1908) | — | 45.00 | 100.00 | 150.00 | 450.00 |

NOTE: The 1907 issue has the year as '33th'. The 34th year (1908) issue was restruck during Republican times.

TAEL

SILVER, 51.20 g
Y#	Year	Date	Fine	VF	XF	Unc
74	33	(1907)	—	3250.	4500.	8000.

Rev: 3 dots on pearl arranged ··· (horizontally).
| 74.1 | 33 | (1907) | — | 3250. | 4500. | 8000. |

Rev: 3 dots on pearl arranged ∴ (in arc).
| 74.2 | 33 | (1907) | — | 3250. | 4500. | 8000. |

CHINGKIANG
For coins of Chingkiang refer to listings under Kiangsu.

Taku Mint
(Imperial Naval Yard)
CASH

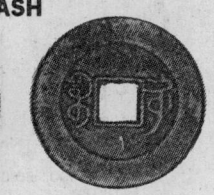

CAST BRASS
Obv: Type A. Rev: Type 2 mint mark.
C#	Date	Emperor	Good	VG	Fine	VF
3-1.1	ND (1896-1900)	Kuang Hsu	30.00	55.00	75.00	125.00

Obv: Type A. Rev: Type 2 mint mark.
| 3-1.2 | ND(1896-1900) | Kuang Hsu | 15.00 | 27.50 | 37.50 | 60.00 |

FENGTIEN PROVINCE
Liaoning

The southern most province of the Three Eastern Provinces was known by a variety of names including Fengtien, Shengching, and Liaoning. The modern Mukden (Fengtien Province) Mint operated from 1897 to 1931.

EMPIRE
CASH

CAST BRASS
Obv: Type A.
| 9-1 | ND (1875-1908) | Kuang Hsu | — | — | Rare | — |

MILLED COINAGE
5 CASH

COPPER
Y#	Date	Mintage	VG	Fine	VF	XF
19e	CD1909	—	37.50	75.00	125.00	175.00

10 CASH

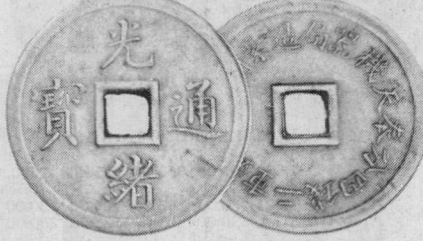

COPPER
Obv: Type A.
| 81 | ND | — | 40.00 | 60.00 | 90.00 | 140.00 |

NOTE: Seven varieties exist.

BRASS
Province spelled FEN-TIEN.
Y#	Date	Mintage	VG	Fine	VF	XF
88	CD1903	—	25.00	75.00	135.00	225.00

COPPER (OMS)
| 88a | CD1903 | — | — | — | Rare | — |

BRASS
Province spelled FUNG-TIEN.
89	CD1903	—	3.75	7.50	15.00	30.00
	CD1904	—	1.25	3.00	5.00	12.00
	CD1905	—	1.25	3.00	5.00	12.00
	CD1906	35.036	3.00	6.00	12.00	25.00

Obv: Manchu characters in center reversed.
| 89.1 | CD1903 | — | 35.00 | 85.00 | 150.00 | 250.00 |

Rev: Large pearl.
| 89.2 | CD1905 | — | 1.00 | 2.00 | 4.00 | 8.00 |

COPPER (OMS)
89a	CD1903	—	—	—	Rare	—
	CD1904	—	—	—	Rare	—
	CD1905	—	—	—	Rare	—

COPPER
Rev: Small pearl.
| 10e | CD1905 | — | 2.00 | 4.00 | 8.00 | 15.00 |

Rev: Large pearl.
| 10e.1 | CD1905 | — | 2.00 | 4.00 | 8.00 | 15.00 |

Obv: Mint mark on spherical disc in center.
| 10e.2 | CD1907 | 130.000 | 1.00 | 1.50 | 3.00 | 6.00 |

Obv: Mint mark on flat disc in center.
| 10e.3 | CD1907 Inc. Ab. | 1.00 | 1.50 | 3.00 | 6.00 |

Fengtien / CHINA 327

Y#	Date	Mintage	VG	Fine	VF	XF
20e	CD1909	—	4.00	8.00	17.50	30.00

20 CASH

BRASS

Y#	Date	Mintage	VG	Fine	VF	XF
90	CD1903	—	75.00	100.00	125.00	150.00
	CD1904	—	5.50	11.00	22.50	45.00
	CD1905	—	4.50	9.00	17.50	35.00

COPPER (OMS)

90a	CD1903	—	85.00	125.00	150.00	200.00
	CD1905	—				Rare

COPPER

11e	CD1904	—	5.50	10.00	20.00	40.00
	CD1905	—	5.50	10.00	20.00	40.00
	CD1907	—	6.00	12.00	25.00	50.00

21e	CD1909	—	25.00	60.00	110.00	175.00

5 CENTS

SILVER, 1.20 g

Y#	Year	Date	Fine	VF	XF	Unc
83	25	(1899)	14.00	27.50	50.00	150.00

10 CENTS

SILVER

84	24	(1898)	15.00	30.00	55.00	150.00

20 CENTS

SILVER, 5.20 g
Rev: 4 rows of scales on dragon.
Clockwise spiral on pearl.

Y#	Year	Date	Fine	VF	XF	Unc
85	24	(1898)	14.00	27.50	50.00	125.00

Rev: 5 rows of scales on dragon.
Counter-clockwise spiral on pearl.

85.1	24	(1898)	14.00	27.50	50.00	125.00

24mm, 8 rows of scales on dragon.

Y#	Date	Mintage	Fine	VF	XF	Unc
91	CD1904	—	6.00	10.00	25.00	60.00

25mm, 5 rows of scales on dragon.

91.1	CD1904	—	9.00	16.00	30.00	70.00

50 CENTS

SILVER, 13.10 g

86	Yr.32(1897)*	—	—	—	Rare	—
	Yr.24(1898)	—	60.00	120.00	190.00	350.00
	Yr.25(1899)	—	200.00	350.00	500.00	750.00

*NOTE: (error) year 32 should read year 23 (1897).

DOLLAR

26.4000 g, .850 SILVER, .7215 oz ASW

Y#	Year	Date	Fine	VF	XF	Unc
87	24	(1898)	35.00	75.00	150.00	400.00
	25	(1899)	300.00	400.00	500.00	800.00

Obv: Two center Chinese characters within double circle, one of dots around one solid.

Y#	Year	Date	Fine	VF	XF	Unc
87.1	25	(1899)	200.00	375.00	500.00	750.00

Y#	Date	Mintage	Fine	VF	XF	Unc
92	CD1903	.262	50.00	120.00	225.00	400.00

Obv: Manchu characters in center are reversed.

92.1	CD1903 Inc. Ab.	40.00	100.00	225.00	425.00

MANCHURIAN PROVINCES

Since the 17th century, Manchuria has been divided into three provinces. The two northern provinces were called Heilungkiang and Kirin. Together the three provinces of Manchuria were known as the Manchurian Provinces in English or the Three Eastern Provinces in Chinese.

10 CENTS

2.6000 g, .890 SILVER, .0744 oz ASW

209	Yr.33 (1907)					
		1.079	12.00	25.00	40.00	100.00

20 CENTS

5.2000 g, .890 SILVER, .1488 oz ASW
Obv: One rosette at either side.

Y#	Year	Date	Fine	VF	XF	Unc
210	33	(1907)	6.00	12.00	20.00	60.00

Obv: Three rosettes at either side.

210.1	33	(1907)	9.00	15.00	35.00	70.00

Obv: Dots replace rosettes.

210.2	33	(1907)	15.00	30.00	60.00	125.00

5.2000 g, .820 SILVER, .1371 oz ASW
Hsuan T'ung
Obv: Two small stars flanking one large star at either side.
Rev: Date given as FIRST YEAR.

Y#	Date	Mintage	Fine	VF	XF	Unc
213	Yr.1 (1909)					
		249.219	4.00	7.50	12.50	25.00

Fengtien / CHINA 328

Obv: One small star at sides.

Y#	Date	Mintage	Fine	VF	XF	Unc
213.1	Yr.1 (1909)	I.A.	4.00	8.50	15.00	30.00

Obv: One large six-pointed rosette at either side.
Rev: Date as 1ST YEAR.

| 213.2 | ND (1909) | I.A. | 4.00 | 8.50 | 15.00 | 30.00 |

Obv: Manchu characters at center.

| 213a | ND (1910) | I.A. | 4.00 | 8.50 | 15.00 | 30.00 |

5.2000 g, .700 SILVER, .1170 oz ASW
Obv: Five-petalled rosette in center w/dot in center of rosette. Dot under side rosettes.

| 213a.1 | ND (1914) | I.A. | 4.00 | 8.50 | 15.00 | 30.00 |

Obv: W/o dot under side rosettes.

| 213a.2 | ND (1914) | I.A. | 4.00 | 8.50 | 15.00 | 30.00 |

Obv: W/o dot in center of 5-petalled rosette.

| 213a.3 | ND (1914) | I.A. | 4.00 | 8.50 | 15.00 | 30.00 |

Obv: W/o rosette in center.
Rev: Few clouds around dragon.

| 213a.4 | ND (1912) | I.A. | 5.00 | 10.00 | 20.00 | 40.00 |

Rev: Head of dragon redesigned, heavier clouds around dragon, rosettes at sides of dragon elongated.

| 213a.6 | ND (1912) | I.A. | 5.00 | 10.00 | 20.00 | 40.00 |

50 CENTS

13.1000 g, .890 SILVER, .3749 oz ASW

Y#	Year	Date	Fine	VF	XF	Unc
211	33	(1907)	80.00	200.00	300.00	500.00

DOLLAR

26.4000 g, .890 SILVER, .7555 oz ASW

| 212 | 33 | (1907) | 150.00 | 350.00 | 550.00 | 1000. |

REPUBLIC
CENT

COPPER

| 434 | 18 | (1929) | 2.00 | 3.00 | 5.00 | 15.00 |

FUKIEN PROVINCE
Fujian

A province located on the southeastern coast of China. Important agricultural area, also forestry and some mining, particularly iron ore and coal. The Foochow Mint operated throughout the Manchu dynasty. For struck coinage the Viceroy's or City mint was opened in 1896. Two other mints were established in 1905; the Mamoi Arsenal Mint which struck the Custom-House issues until closed in 1906, and the West Mint which later became the main Fukien (Fujian) Mint. It was closed between 1914 and 1920. Various subsidiary mints were in operation 1924-5.

EMPIRE
Fuchow Mint
CASH

LEAD
Obv: Type A

C#	Date	Emperor	Good	VG	Fine	VF
10-2	ND (1796-1820)	Chia Ch'ing	.25	.50	1.00	3.00

Rev: Thin Manchu at right.

| 10-2.1 | ND (1796-1820) | Chia Ch'ing | .25 | .50 | 1.25 | 3.50 |

Rev: Different Manchu at right.

C#	Date	Emperor	Good	VG	Fine	VF
10-2.2	ND (1796-1820)	Chia Ch'ing	.25	.50	1.50	4.00

CAST COPPER or BRASS
Obv: Type A

| 10-3 | ND (1821-51) | Tao Kuang | .50 | 1.00 | 2.00 | 4.50 |

Obv: Type A
Rev: Dot right of mint mark. 22-24mm.

| 10-4 | ND (1851-61) | Hsien Feng | 2.50 | 4.00 | 6.50 | 10.00 |

Rev: Line right of mint mark. 26mm.

| 10-4.1 | ND (1851-61) | Hsien Feng | 2.50 | 5.00 | 7.50 | 12.50 |

CAST IRON

| 10-4a.1 | ND (1851-61) | Hsien Feng | 20.00 | 35.00 | 50.00 | 65.00 |

Larger size. Wide rims.

| 10-4a.2 | ND (1851-61) | Hsien Feng | 20.00 | 35.00 | 50.00 | 65.00 |

CAST BRASS
Obv: Type A-2

| 10-22 | ND (1862-74) | T'ung Chih | 1.25 | 2.50 | 4.00 | 6.00 |

Obv: Type A

| 10-25 | ND (1875-1908) | Kuang Hsu | 1.00 | 2.00 | 3.00 | 4.50 |

Rev: Dot at top of hole.

| 10-25.1 | ND (1875-1908) | Kuang Hsu | 2.50 | 4.00 | 6.50 | 10.00 |

5 CASH

BRASS, 31mm
Rev: Weight on the rim similar to 20 Cash, C#10-12.

| 10-5 | ND (1851-61) | Hsien Feng | 40.00 | 70.00 | 110.00 | 150.00 |

10 CASH

CAST BRASS, 35-40mm.
Obv: Type A

C#	Date	Emperor	Good	VG	Fine	VF
10-6	ND (1851-61)	Hsien Feng	4.00	8.00	12.00	20.00

Rev: Characters *Ta Ching* appear at upper left and right.

10-6.1 ND (1851-61) Hsien Feng — — — Rare

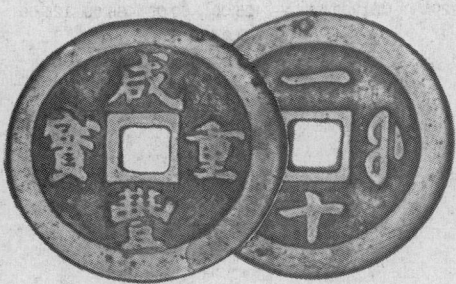

Obv: Type B-1
10-7 ND (1851-61) Hsien Feng 8.50 15.00 18.50 30.00

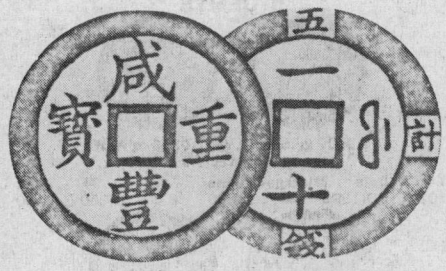

Rev: Four characters appearing on rim.
10-8 ND (1851-61) Hsien Feng 12.50 20.00 30.00 60.00

CAST IRON
10-8a ND (1851-61) Hsien Feng — — — Rare

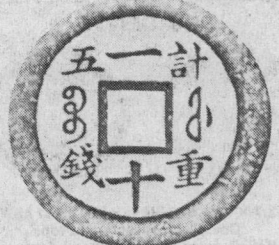

CAST BRASS
10-9 ND (1851-61) Hsien Feng 70.00 110.00 150.00 225.00

42mm
Rev: Four characters at top, four different characters at bottom. Mint mark (at right) has a crescent at right instead of a dot.
10-9.1 ND (1851-61) Hsien Feng — — — Rare

35mm. Rev: Chinese mint mark at right, Manchu mint mark at left.
10-9.2 ND (1851-61) Hsien Feng — — — Rare

10-23 ND (1862-74) T'ung Chih — — — Rare

10-26 ND (1875-1908) Kuang Hsu — — — Rare

20 CASH

CAST BRASS, 45-46mm
Obv: Type A

C#	Date	Emperor	Good	VG	Fine	VF
10-10	ND (1851-61)	Hsien Feng	5.50	10.00	16.50	28.00

CAST IRON
10-10a ND (1851-61) Hsien Feng Reported, not confirmed

CAST BRASS, 44mm
Obv: Type B-1. Rev: Similar to C10-10.
10-11 ND (1851-61) Hsien Feng 13.50 22.50 30.00 45.00

Rev: Four characters appearing on rim.
10-12 ND (1851-61) Hsien Feng 30.00 50.00 75.00 115.00

CAST IRON
10-12a ND (1851-61) Hsien Feng Reported, not confirmed

CAST COPPER, 46mm
Rev: Eight characters in the field.
10-13 ND (1851-61) Hsien Feng 100.00 175.00 250.00 350.00

CAST IRON
10-13a ND (1851-61) Hsien Feng — — — —

50 CASH

CAST COPPER, 55mm
Obv: Type A. Rev: Four characters.
10-14 ND (1851-61) Hsien Feng 15.00 25.00 30.00 45.00

65mm
Rev: Mint mark w/long vertical stroke at right instead of dot.
10-14.1 ND (1851-61) Hsien Feng — — — Rare

Obv: Type B-1. Rev: Four characters.
10-15 ND (1851-61) Hsien Feng 25.00 40.00 55.00 90.00

Fukien / CHINA 329

Rev: Four characters appearing on rim.

C#	Date	Emperor	Good	VG	Fine	VF
10-16	ND (1851-61)	Hsien Feng	60.00	130.00	175.00	250.00

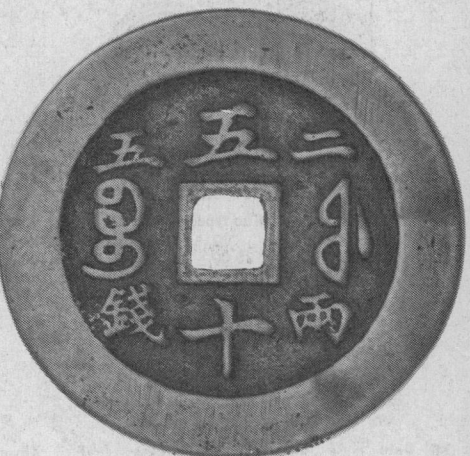

Rev: Eight characters in field.
10-17 ND (1851-61) Hsien Feng 200.00 325.00 475.00 600.00

100 CASH

CAST COPPER, 70mm
Obv: Type A. Rev: Four characters.
10-18 ND (1851-61) Hsien Feng 35.00 50.00 75.00 100.00

74mm
Rev: Mint mark w/long vertical stroke at right instead of dot.
10-18.1 ND (1851-61) Hsien Feng — — — Rare

CAST ZINC
Rev: Four characters.
10-18a ND (1851-61) Hsien Feng — — — Rare

NOTE: Composition of this coin is reportedly a mixture of zinc, lead and tin. The coin is blue-gray in color and has a large mint mark, written differently from any of the above.

Fukien / CHINA 330

CAST COPPER
Obv: Type B-1. Rev: Four characters.

C#	Date	Emperor	Good	VG	Fine	VF
10-19	ND(1851-61)	Hsien Feng	25.00	40.00	55.00	80.00

72mm
Rev: Four characters appearing on rim and small characters in field.

| 10-20 | ND(1851-61) | Hsien Feng | 75.00 | 125.00 | 175.00 | 250.00 |

78mm
Rev: Larger characters in field.

| 10-20.1 | ND(1851-61) | Hsien Feng | 35.00 | 50.00 | 75.00 | 100.00 |

Rev: Eight characters in field.

| 10-21 | ND(1851-61) | Hsien Feng | Reported, not confirmed |

FANTASY ISSUES
NOTE: 30, 40, 500 and 1000 Cash pieces are reported for this mint, but their existence is doubtful and would most likely be considered fantasies.

MILLED COINAGE
CASH

BRASS
Obv: Type A

Y#	Date	Emperor	VG	Fine	VF	XF
95	ND(1908)	Kuang Hsu	9.00	20.00	32.50	50.00

Tai Ching Ti Kuo type, Hsu#259.

Y#	Date	Mintage	VG	Fine	VF	XF
7f	CD1908	—	35.00	75.00	110.00	165.00

Obv: Type A

Y#	Date	Emperor	VG	Fine	VF	XF
106	ND(1909/11)	Hsuan-Tung	20.00	40.00	70.00	100.00

2 CASH

BRASS

Y#	Date	Mintage	VG	Fine	VF	XF
8f	CD1906	—	2.50	5.00	9.00	20.00

5 CASH

COPPER

| 99 | ND(1901-03) | .590 | 6.00 | 12.00 | 17.50 | 27.50 |

BRASS

| 99a | ND(1901-03) | | 12.00 | 25.00 | 50.00 | 75.00 |

10 CASH

COPPER
Obv: Large characters at left and right.

| 97 | ND(1901-05) | 417.031 | .60 | 1.50 | 2.50 | 8.00 |

Obv: Small characters at left and right sides.

Y#	Date	Mintage	VG	Fine	VF	XF
97.1	ND(1901-05)	Inc. Ab.	.80	2.00	4.00	10.00

Rev: FOO-KIEN CUSTOM.

| 98 | ND(1901-05) | Inc. Ab. | 45.00 | 100.00 | 150.00 | 225.00 |

Rev: One cloud left of pearl.

| 100 | ND(1901-05) | Inc. Ab. | .80 | 2.00 | 4.00 | 7.00 |

Rev: Three clouds left of pearl and w/o cloud above tip of dragons tail.

| 100.1 | ND(1901-05) | Inc. Ab. | .80 | 2.00 | 4.00 | 7.00 |

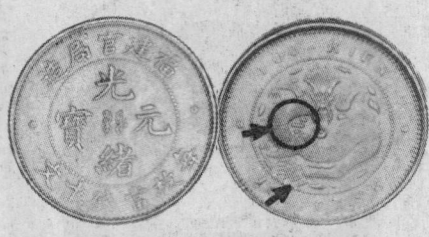

Rev: Three clouds left of pearl and a cloud above tip of dragon's tail.

| 100.2 | ND(1901-05) | Inc. Ab. | .40 | 1.00 | 2.00 | 4.00 |

Rev. denomination: 10 CASHES.

| 100.3 | ND(1901-05) | Inc. Ab. | 6.00 | 15.00 | 25.00 | 45.00 |

Y#	Date	Mintage	VG	Fine	VF	XF
10f	CD1906	—	.30	.75	1.50	3.00

| 20f | CD1909 | — | 25.00 | 50.00 | 85.00 | 125.00 |

20 CASH

COPPER

| 101 | ND(1901-02) | .018 | 12.00 | 30.00 | 45.00 | 75.00 |

5 CENTS

1.3500 g, .820 SILVER, .0356 oz ASW
Obv: Five characters at top.

Y#	Date	Mintage	Fine	VF	XF	Unc
102	ND(1896-1903)		4.00	8.00	17.50	40.00

Obv: Four characters at top.
Rev: Rosette at either side of redesigned dragon.

| 102.1 | ND(1898-1903) | | 3.00 | 5.00 | 11.00 | 30.00 |

Rev: Rosette above dragon.

| 102.2 | ND(1898-1903) | | 6.00 | 12.00 | 22.50 | 40.00 |

10 CENTS

2.7000 g, .820 SILVER, .0712 oz ASW
Obv: Five characters at top.
Rev: Rosette at either side of dragon.

| 103 | ND(1896-1908) | 13.425 | 5.00 | 9.00 | 17.50 | 35.00 |

Rev: Dot at either side of dragon.

| 103.1 | ND(1896-1908) | Inc. Ab. | 8.00 | 15.00 | 30.00 | 60.00 |

Obv: Four characters at top.

| 103.2 | ND(1898-1908) | Inc. Ab. | 3.00 | 6.00 | 12.00 | 25.00 |

COPPER (OMS)

| 103.2a | ND(1898-1908) | — | — | — | — | — |

20 CENTS

5.4000 g, .820 SILVER, .1424 oz ASW
Obv: Five characters at top.
Rev: Dot at either side of dragon.

Y#	Date	Mintage	Fine	VF	XF	Unc
104	ND(1896-1908)	31.772	3.00	6.00	12.50	30.00

Rev: Rosette at either side of dragon.
| 104.1 | ND(1898-1908) | Inc. Ab. | 3.00 | 6.00 | 12.50 | 30.00 |

Obv: Four characters at top. Rev: Redesigned dragon.
| 104.2 | ND(1898-1908) | Inc. Ab. | 3.00 | 6.00 | 12.50 | 30.00 |

COPPER (OMS)
| 104a | ND(1896-1908) | — | — | — | — | — |

DOLLAR

SILVER, 25.70 g
Obv: Four characters at top.

K#	Date	Mintage	VG	Fine	VF	XF
6	ND(ca.1844)	—	1800.	2500.	3000.	4500.

27.20 g
Obv: Lower character written in different style.
| 5 | ND(ca.1844) | — | 3000. | 4000. | 5000. | 7500. |

26.20 g
Obv. and rev.: Two rosettes.

Obv: Two characters at top.
K#	Date	Mintage	VG	Fine	VF	XF
7	ND(ca.1844)	—	225.00	500.00	800.00	1750.

Obv: Two rosettes and two 5-petalled flowers.
| 7c | ND(ca.1844) | — | 850.00 | 1250. | 1500. | 3000. |

Kann #5-7 above were issued by military authorities at the city of Chang Chow. Though Kann dates these pieces in the 1860's they were already circulating in the 1840's.

27.00 g
Y#	Date	Mintage	Fine	VF	XF	Unc
105	ND(ca.1899)	—	—	—	Rare	—

REPUBLIC
CASH
CAST BRASS
Rev: Five stripes on right flag.
Y#	Date	Mintage	Good	VG	Fine	VF
374	ND(c.1912)	—	70.00	175.00	250.00	350.00

Rev: Six stripes on right flag.
| 374.1 | ND(c.1912) | — | 100.00 | 175.00 | 250.00 | 350.00 |

2 CASH
CAST BRASS
Rev: Five stripes on right flag.
| 375 | ND(c.1912) | — | 12.00 | 22.50 | 35.00 | 60.00 |

Rev: Six stripes on right flag, left flag redesigned.
| 375.1 | ND(c.1912) | — | 50.00 | 75.00 | 100.00 | 150.00 |

MILLED COINAGE
10 CASH

COPPER
Y#	Date	Mintage	Fine	VF	XF	Unc
379	ND(ca.1912)	—	3.00	7.00	15.00	30.00

BRASS
| 379a | ND(ca.1912) | — | 42.50 | 60.00 | 87.50 | 125.00 |

10 CENTS

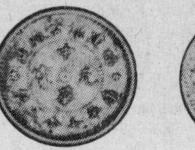 

SILVER, 2.60 g
Y#	Date	Mintage	Fine	VF	XF	Unc
380	ND(ca.1912)	—	30.00	50.00	80.00	150.00

| 382 | ND(ca.1913) | — | 2.50 | 5.00 | 9.00 | 20.00 |

Similar to Y#380. Obv: Different leg. in center.
| 380a | CD1924 | — | 12.00 | 30.00 | 50.00 | 100.00 |

Canton Martyrs
Y#	Year	Date	Fine	VF	XF	Unc
388	17	(1928)	5.00	12.50	25.00	40.00
	20	(1931)	7.00	17.50	30.00	50.00

Canton Martyrs
| 390 | 21 | (1932) | 125.00 | 175.00 | 250.00 | 350.00 |

20 CENTS

 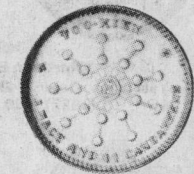

SILVER, 5.00 g
Y#	Date	Mintage	Fine	VF	XF	Unc
377	CD1911	—	9.00	20.00	35.00	100.00

| A381 | ND(1912) | — | 3.50 | 7.00 | 15.00 | 25.00 |

| 383 | ND | — | 3.00 | 5.00 | 10.00 | 22.50 |

NOTE: Kann dates this coin 1913, but evidence suggests that it was struck in 1923.

Fuklen / CHINA 332

5.70 g

Y#	Year	Date	Fine	VF	XF	Unc
383a	13	(1924)	35.00	50.00	70.00	90.00

5.30 g
Obv. and rev: Rosettes at sides.
Obv: Dot in middle of rosette center.

Y#	Date	Mintage	Fine	VF	XF	Unc
381	CD1923	—	3.50	7.00	10.00	25.00

Rev. leg: MADE spelled MAIE.
| 381.1 | CD1923 | — | 3.50 | 7.50 | 12.50 | 30.00 |

Rev. leg: MADEIN FOO-KIENMINT.
| 381.2 | CD1923 | — | 3.50 | 7.50 | 12.50 | 30.00 |

Obv: W/o dot in middle of center rosette,
Five-pointed star at sides in place of rosette.
| 381.3 | CD1923 | — | 10.00 | 12.50 | 17.50 | 35.00 |

Obv: Different leg. in center.
| 381.4 | CD1924 | — | 5.00 | 8.00 | 15.00 | 32.50 |

Northern Expedition
Y#	Year	Date	Fine	VF	XF	Unc
384	16	(1927)	200.00	300.00	400.00	600.00

5.00 g
Northern Expedition
| 385 | 16 | (1927) | 600.00 | 950.00 | 1150. | 1750. |

Canton Martyrs
Obv: 2 rows of bricks at right of gate.
| 389.1 | 17 | (1928) | 5.00 | 7.50 | 12.50 | 30.00 |
| | 20 | (1931) | 6.00 | 10.00 | 15.00 | 40.00 |

BRASS (OMS)
| 389.1a | 17 | (1928) | — | — | — | — |

SILVER, 5.00 g
Obv: Half brick in 3rd row of bricks at right of gate.
| 389.2 | 17 | (1928) | — | — | — | — |

SILVER, 5.30 g
Canton Martyrs
Y#	Year	Date	Fine	VF	XF	Unc
391	21	(1932)	46.00	65.00	115.00	225.00

BRASS (OMS)
| 391a | 21 | (1932) | — | — | — | — |

HEILUNGKIANG PROVINCE
Heilongjiang

The northwestern-most of the former Three Eastern Provinces, bordering on Siberia. Though very large in extent, it is only sparsely populated, for wide areas are desert land. Economically the district was always backward. Heilungkiang (Heilongjiang) Province had no mint of its own, and seemingly no silver money bearing its name was ever placed in circulation although Imperial patterns in the standard dragon design exist for at least the dollar and 50 cent denominations. During the beginning of the 20th century it was suggested to contract for silver coins from the Berlin Mint.

HONAN PROVINCE
Henan

A province in east central China. As well as being one of the most densely populated provinces it is also one of the most important agriculturally. It is the area of earliest settlement in China and has housed the capital during various dynasties. The Kaifeng Mint issued coins from its opening in 1647 through most of the rulers of the Manchu dynasty. A second modern mint was opened at Chengchow in 1926.

EMPIRE
CASH

CAST BRASS
Obv: Type A. Rev: Type 1.
C#	Date	Emperor	Good	VG	Fine	VF
11-1	ND(1851-61)	Hsien Feng	20.00	30.00	40.00	50.00

Rev: Crescent above.
| 11-1.1 | ND(1851-61) | Hsien Feng | 20.00 | 30.00 | 40.00 | 50.00 |

Rev: Circle above.
| 11-1.2 | ND(1851-61) | Hsien Feng | 20.00 | 30.00 | 40.00 | 50.00 |

CAST IRON
| 11-1a | ND(1851-61) | Hsien Feng | 12.50 | 20.00 | 30.00 | 50.00 |

CAST BRASS
Obv: Type A.
| 11-9 | ND(1875-1908) | Kuang Hsu | 5.00 | 9.00 | 13.50 | 20.00 |

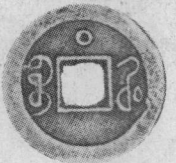

Rev: Circle above.
| 11-9.1 | ND(1875-1908) | Kuang Hsu | 5.00 | 9.00 | 13.50 | 20.00 |

Rev: Circle below.
| 11-9.2 | ND(1875-1908) | Kuang Hsu | 5.00 | 9.00 | 13.50 | 20.00 |

Rev: Crescent above.
C#	Date	Emperor	Good	VG	Fine	VF
11-9.3	ND(1875-1908)	Kuang Hsu	5.00	9.00	13.50	20.00

Rev: Crescent below.
| 11-9.4 | ND(1875-1908) | Kuang Hsu | 5.00 | 9.00 | 13.50 | 20.00 |

Rev: Crescent above, dot below.
| 11-9.5 | ND(1875-1908) | Kuang Hsu | 5.00 | 9.00 | 13.50 | 20.00 |

Rev: Dot above.
| 11-9.6 | ND(1875-1908) | Kuang Hsu | 5.00 | 9.00 | 13.50 | 20.00 |

Rev: Dot below.
| 11-9.7 | ND(1875-1908) | Kuang Hsu | 5.00 | 9.00 | 13.50 | 20.00 |

CAST ZINC
| 3-1.1a | ND(1875-1908) | Kuang Hsu | — | — | Rare | — |

10 CASH

CAST BRASS
Obv: Type B-1
| 11-2 | ND(1851-61) | Hsien Feng | 6.00 | 12.00 | 20.00 | 30.00 |

50 CASH

CAST BRASS
Obv: Type B-1
| 11-5 | ND(1851-61) | Hsien Feng | 8.00 | 15.00 | 25.00 | 35.00 |

100 CASH

CAST BRASS
Obv: Type C

C#	Date	Emperor	Good	VG	Fine	VF
11-6	ND(1851-61)	Hsien Feng	10.00	22.00	32.00	48.00

Rev: Larger Manchu.
11-6.1 ND(1851-61)
　　　　Hsien Feng 10.00 25.00 35.00 50.00

500 CASH
CAST BRASS
Obv: Type C
11-7 ND(1851-61)
　　　Hsien Feng 25.00 50.00 75.00 125.00

1000 CASH
CAST BRASS
Obv: Type C
11-8 ND(1851-61)
　　　Hsien Feng — — — —

FANTASY ISSUES
Coins of this mint in denominations of 20 (C#11-3), 30 (C#11-4), 40 and 70 cash are considered fantasy issues.

MILLED COINAGE
CASH

BRASS

Y#	Date	Mintage	VG	Fine	VF	XF
7g	CD1908	—	10.00	25.00	40.00	65.00

5 CASH
BRASS
19g CD1909 — — — — —

10 CASH

COPPER
Rev: Circled dragon w/o mountain below pearl with 3 flames.

Y#	Date	Mintage	VG	Fine	VF	XF
108	ND(1905)	—	4.00	10.00	20.00	40.00

Rev: 5 flames on pearl.
108.1 ND(1905) — .75 1.50 3.00 6.00

Rev: Mountain below pearl, very small English lettering.
108.2 ND(1905) — 6.00 15.00 30.00 50.00

Rev: Large English legend.
108.3 ND(1905) — 2.50 6.00 10.00 20.00

BRASS
Obv: Raised sphere Yin-Yang in center.
Rev: Uncircled dragon, Honan spelled HOU-NAN.
108a ND(1905) — — — Rare

COPPER
Rev: Uncircled dragon.
108a.1 ND(1905) — .80 2.00 4.00 8.00

Honan / CHINA 333

Obv: Curved line on raised Yin-Yang slanted more.

Y#	Date	Mintage	VG	Fine	VF	XF
108a.2	ND(1905)	—	.80	2.00	4.00	8.00

Obv: Flat Yin-Yang. Rev: Plain pearl.
108a.3 ND(1905) — .40 1.00 2.00 4.00
BRASS
108a.3a ND(1905) — 2.50 5.00 10.00 17.50

COPPER
Rev: Incuse swirl in pearl.
108a.4 ND(1905) — 1.00 2.00 4.00 8.00

Rev: Period after COIN.
10g CD1906 132.000 .60 1.50 2.50 5.00
Rev: Period after COPPER.
10g.1 CD1906 — 1.20 3.00 6.00 10.00

20g CD1909 — 20.00 40.00 60.00 100.00
　　　1911 — 5.00 15.00 25.00 50.00
NOTE: Normally encountered with weak legends.

REPUBLIC
10 CASH

COPPER
A392 ND(ca.1913) — .40 1.00 2.00 6.00

Honan / CHINA 334

Obv: W/o lines above and below rosettes.

Y#	Date	Mintage	VG	Fine	VF	XF
A392.1	ND(ca.1913)	—	.40	1.00	2.00	6.00

Rev: TEN CASH in larger letters

| 392 | ND | — | .30 | .75 | 1.50 | 4.00 |

Obv: Rosette in center higher in relation to heart shaped leaves below.

| 392.1 | ND | — | .80 | 2.00 | 3.50 | 6.00 |

Rev: Letter S in CASH backwards.

| 392.2 | ND | — | 4.50 | 10.00 | 17.50 | 30.00 |

20 CASH

COPPER
Obv: Six characters at bottom.

Y#	Date	Mintage	Good	VG	Fine	VF
393	ND	—	1.25	2.50	5.00	10.00

Obv: Five characters at bottom.

| 393.1 | ND | — | 1.00 | 2.00 | 4.00 | 6.00 |

Rev: CHINA replaces HO-NAN.

Y#	Date	Mintage	Good	VG	Fine	VF
393.2	ND(1921)	—	12.00	25.00	45.00	200.00

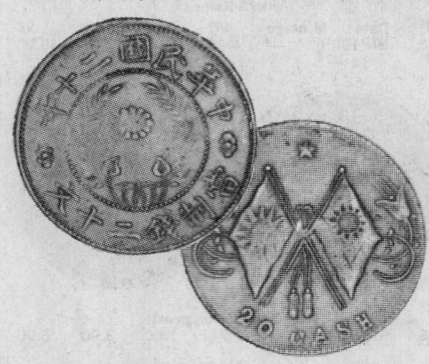

Rev: Star above flags.

| A397 | Yr.20 (1931) | 1 known | — | — | Rare | — |

50 CASH

COPPER
Rev: Short flag poles.

| 394 | ND | — | 2.00 | 3.75 | 6.50 | 15.00 |

Rev: Long flag poles.

| 394.1 | ND | — | 2.00 | 3.75 | 6.50 | 15.00 |

BRASS

| 394b | ND | — | 20.00 | 40.00 | 60.00 | 100.00 |

Rev: CHINA replaces HONAN.

Y#	Date	Mintage	Good	VG	Fine	VF
394a	ND	—	6.50	12.50	25.00	50.00

Y#	Year	Date	Good	VG	Fine	VF
397	20	(1931)	25.00	50.00	90.00	135.00

100 CASH

COPPER
Rev: Small star in right flag, tassels 4mm long.

Y#	Date	Mintage	Good	VG	Fine	VF
395	ND ca.1928	—	3.00	5.00	10.00	22.00

Rev: Tassels 5mm long.

| 395.1 | ND ca.1928 | — | 3.75 | 6.50 | 12.50 | 25.00 |

Rev: Large star in right flag.

| 395.2 | ND ca.1928 | — | — | — | — | — |

Y#	Year	Date	Good	VG	Fine	VF
398	20	(1931)	10.00	17.50	35.00	70.00

200 CASH

COPPER

Rev: Large square inside right flag.

Y#	Date	Mintage	Good	VG	Fine	VF
396	ND ca.1928	—	3.00	5.00	10.00	25.00

Rev: Small square and small star inside right flag.
| 396.1 | ND ca.1928 | — | 2.50 | 4.50 | 9.00 | 22.00 |

Rev: Small square and large star inside right flag.
| 396.2 | ND | — | 2.50 | 4.50 | 9.00 | 22.00 |

BRASS
| 396a | ND ca.1928 | — | 6.00 | 15.00 | 22.50 | 45.00 |

NOTE: The Republican coins of Honan (Henan) are usually found weakly struck. Crudely struck specimens with die variations, misspelled leg. are considered war lord issues.

HUNAN PROVINCE

A province in south-central China. Mining of coal, antimony, tungsten and tin is important as well as raising varied agricultural products. The Changsha Mint produced Cash coins from early in the Manchu dynasty. Its facility for struck coinage opened in 1897, and two further copper mints were added in 1905. All three mints were closed down in 1907, but one mint was reopened at a later date and produced vast quantities of republican copper coinage until 1926.

EMPIRE
Changsha Mint
CASH
CAST BRASS
Obv: Type A.

C#	Date	Emperor	Good	VG	Fine	VF
12-2	ND(1796-1820)	Chia Ch'ing	.50	1.00	2.00	4.00

Obv: Type A.
| 12-3 | ND(1821-50) | Tao Kuang | 2.00 | 4.00 | 6.50 | 10.00 |

Obv: Type A.
| 12-4 | ND(1851-61) | Hsien Feng | 2.00 | 4.00 | 6.50 | 10.00 |

Obv: Type A-2.
| 12-5 | ND(1862-74) | T'ung Chih | 3.50 | 8.00 | 12.50 | 20.00 |

Obv: Type A.
| 12-7 | ND(1875-1908) | Kuang Hsu | 2.50 | 5.00 | 7.50 | 12.00 |

10 CASH
CAST BRASS
| 12-6 | ND(1862-74) | T'ung Chih | — | — | Rare | — |
| 12-8 | ND(1875-1908) | Kuang Hsu | — | — | Rare | — |

MILLED COINAGE
NOTE: 2, 5 and 20 Cash Tai Ching Ti Kuo type patterns are reported, not confirmed.

10 CASH

COPPER
Obv: Rosette in center w/center of petals depressed. Manchu characters at sides.
Rev: Narrow spacing in HU-NAN above dragon.

Y#	Date	Mintage	VG	Fine	VF	XF
112	ND(1902-06)		.40	1.00	2.00	5.00

Rev: Wide spacing in HU-NAN.
| 112.1 | ND(1902-06) | | .50 | 1.25 | 2.00 | 5.00 |
Obv: Petals of rosette not depressed.
| 112.2 | ND(1902-06) | | .60 | 1.50 | 2.50 | 6.00 |

Obv: Two Manchu characters in center.
| 112.3 | ND(1902-06) | | 1.20 | 3.00 | 6.00 | 10.00 |

Rev: Narrow spacing in HU-NAN.
| 112.4 | ND(1902-06) | | .60 | 1.50 | 2.50 | 6.00 |

Obv: Rosette in center. Rev: Ring around pearl.
| 112.5 | ND(1902-06) | | .50 | 1.25 | 2.00 | 4.00 |
Obv: Centers of petals on rosette depressed.
| 112.6 | ND(1902-06) | | .60 | 1.50 | 2.50 | 6.00 |

Obv: Two Manchu characters in center.
Rev: Ring around pearl.
| 112.7 | ND(1902-06) | | .75 | 1.50 | 2.50 | 6.00 |

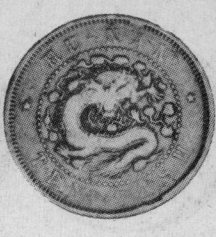

Obv: Larger characters at left and right, and different characters below. **Rev:** Dragon redesigned and small star at either side.

Y#	Date	Mintage	VG	Fine	VF	XF
112.8	ND(1902-06)		2.00	5.00	10.00	17.50

Obv: Rosette in center, four characters at bottom.
Rev: Redesigned dragon w/o pearl; rosette at either side.
| 112.9 | ND(1902-06) | | 2.00 | 5.00 | 10.00 | 17.50 |

Obv: Two Manchu characters in center w/dot between; two characters at bottom.
| 112.10 | ND(1902-06) | | .50 | 1.00 | 2.00 | 4.00 |
Obv: W/o dot between Manchu characters.
| 112.11 | ND(1902-06) | | .50 | 1.00 | 2.00 | 4.00 |

Obv: Smaller inner circle.
| 112.12 | ND(1902-06) | | 30.00 | 60.00 | 125.00 | 250.00 |

Obv: Six characters at bottom.
Rev: Flying dragon. Reeded edge.
| 113 | ND(1902-06) | | 1.75 | 4.00 | 8.00 | 15.00 |

Rev: Inverted U in HU-NAN. Reeded edge.
| 113.1 | ND(1902-06) | | 5.00 | 12.00 | 25.00 | 45.00 |

Hunan / CHINA

BRASS
Obv: Three characters at bottom.

Y#	Date	Mintage	VG	Fine	VF	XF
113a	ND(1904-06)	—	2.00	3.50	6.00	12.50

COPPER
Obv: Upper and lower parts of character HU connected.
Rev: Dot between Chinese characters above dragon.

10h	CD1906	—	12.50	17.50	35.00	70.00

Obv: Upper and lower part of Hu not connected. Rev: Dot between Chinese characters at top.

10h.1	CD1906	—	12.50	17.50	35.00	70.00

Obv: Similar to Y#10h.1.
Rev: Seven flames on pearl.

10h.2	CD1906	—	.75	2.00	4.00	8.00

Rev: 7-flame pearl ornamented w/toothlike projections.

10h.3	CD1906	—	.50	1.00	2.00	4.00

Rev: Four flames on pearl.

10h.4	CD1906	—	.75	2.00	4.00	8.00

Rev: Redesigned dragon w/high waves beneath.

Y#	Date	Mintage	VG	Fine	VF	XF
10h.5	CD1906	—	5.00	12.00	20.00	40.00

Obv: Character Hu connected.
Rev: Redesigned dragon; dot between COPPER COIN.

10h.6	CD1906	—	5.00	12.00	20.00	40.00

Rev: Redesigned dragon, w/five flames on pearl (Woodward #342 and 343).

10h.7	CD1906	—	12.00	30.00	45.00	75.00

5 CENTS
1.3000 g, .820 SILVER, .0343 oz ASW
Similar to 20 Cents, Y#116.

Y#	Date	Mintage	Fine	VF	XF	Unc
—	ND(1897)	—	—	—	Rare	—

10 CENTS
2.5000 g, .820 SILVER, .0659 oz ASW
Obv: Two rosettes at both sides.

115	ND(1897)	—	7.00	15.00	25.00	70.00

Obv: One rosette at both sides.

115.1	ND(1897)	—	14.00	25.00	45.00	90.00
	CD1898	—	17.50	35.00	60.00	125.00
	CD1899	—	22.50	45.00	75.00	150.00

ANTIMONY (OMS)

115.1a	ND(1897)					

20 CENTS

5.3000 g, .820 SILVER, .1397 oz ASW

116	ND(1897)	—	20.00	40.00	65.00	125.00

TAEL SYSTEM
The following coins, in Tael and Mace (Liang and Ch'ien) denominations, are often called Hunan cakes because of their thickness. Three basic series exist; those issued under provincial authority, those issued by the Ta Ch'ing Bank, and those issued by Changsha merchants.

CH'IEN (MACE)

SILVER, 3.70 g
Provincial Type
Obv: Four characters. Rev: Two characters.

K#	Date	Mintage	VG	Fine	VF	XF
951	ND(ca.1906)	—	30.00	50.00	70.00	100.00

3.80 g
Merchant Type
Obv: Six vertical characters. Rev: Six horizontal characters.

971	ND(ca.1908)	—	30.00	50.00	70.00	100.00

Merchant Type
Obv: Four characters. Rev: Two vertical characters.

973	ND(ca.1908)	—	30.00	50.00	70.00	100.00

Merchant Type
Obv: Six horizontal characters.

Rev: Two vertical characters.

K#	Date	Mintage	VG	Fine	VF	XF
984/5	ND(ca.1908)	—	30.00	50.00	70.00	100.00

2 CH'IEN (MACE)

SILVER, 7.30 g
Provincial Type
Obv. and rev: Four characters.

950	ND(ca.1906)	—	35.00	55.00	75.00	110.00

Provincial Type
Obv: Six vertical characters. Rev: Four characters.

960	ND(ca.1906)	—	35.00	55.00	75.00	110.00

Ta Ch'ing Bank Type
Obv: Six vertical characters.
Rev: Six horizontal characters.

970	ND(ca.1908)	—	35.00	55.00	75.00	110.00

Merchant Type
Obv. and rev: Four characters.

972	ND(ca.1908)	—	35.00	55.00	75.00	110.00

Merchant Type
Obv: Six horizontal characters. Rev: Four characters.

982/3	ND(ca.1908)	—	35.00	55.00	75.00	110.00

3 CH'IEN (MACE)

SILVER, 10.70 g
Provincial Type
Obv. and rev: Six horizontal characters.

949	ND(ca.1906)	—	37.50	60.00	85.00	120.00

Provincial Type
Obv: Six vertical characters.
Rev: Six horizontal characters.

959	ND(ca.1906)	—	37.50	60.00	85.00	120.00

Ta Ch'ing Bank Type
Obv: Six vertical characters.
Rev: Six horizontal characters.

969	ND(ca.1908)	—	37.50	60.00	85.00	120.00

Merchant Type
Obv. and rev: Six horizontal characters.

981	ND(ca.1908)	—	37.50	60.00	85.00	120.00

Merchant Type
"Official" character for "Three".

981a	ND(ca.1908)	—	37.50	60.00	85.00	120.00

4 CH'IEN (MACE)

Hunan / CHINA 337

SILVER, 14.3000 g
Provincial Type
Obv. and rev: Six horizontal characters.

K#	Date	Mintage	VG	Fine	VF	XF
948	ND(ca.1906)	—	40.00	65.00	90.00	125.00

Provincial Type
Obv: Six vertical characters.
Rev: Six horizontal characters.

| 958 | ND(ca.1906) | — | 40.00 | 65.00 | 90.00 | 125.00 |

Ta Ch'ing Bank Type
Obv: Six vertical characters.
Rev: Six horizontal characters.

| 968 | ND(ca.1908) | — | 40.00 | 65.00 | 90.00 | 125.00 |

Merchant Type
Obv. and rev: Six horizontal characters.

| 980 | ND(ca.1908) | — | 40.00 | 65.00 | 90.00 | 125.00 |

5 CH'IEN (MACE)

SILVER, 18.30 g
Provincial Type
Obv. and rev: Six horizontal characters.

| 947 | ND(ca.1906) | — | 42.50 | 70.00 | 100.00 | 140.00 |

Provincial Type
Obv: Six vertical characters.
Rev: Six horizontal characters.

| 957 | ND(ca.1906) | — | 42.50 | 70.00 | 100.00 | 140.00 |

Ta Ch'ing Bank Type
Obv: Six vertical characters.
Rev: Six horizontal characters.

| 967 | ND(ca.1908) | — | 42.50 | 70.00 | 100.00 | 140.00 |

Merchant Type
Obv. and rev: Six horizontal characters.

| 979 | ND(ca.1908) | — | 42.50 | 70.00 | 100.00 | 140.00 |

6 CH'IEN (MACE)

SILVER, 21.40 g
Provincial Type
Obv. and rev: Six horizontal characters.

| 946 | ND(ca.1906) | — | 45.00 | 75.00 | 110.00 | 150.00 |

Provincial Type
Obv: Six vertical characters.
Rev: Six horizontal characters.

| 956 | ND(ca.1906) | — | 45.00 | 75.00 | 110.00 | 150.00 |

Ta Ch'ing Bank Type
Obv: Six vertical characters.
Rev: Six horizontal characters.

| 966 | ND(ca.1908) | — | 45.00 | 75.00 | 110.00 | 150.00 |

Merchant Type
Obv. and rev: Six horizontal characters.

| 978 | ND(ca.1908) | — | 45.00 | 75.00 | 110.00 | 150.00 |

7 CH'IEN (MACE)

SILVER, 25.90 g
Provincial Type
Obv. and rev: Six horizontal characters.

K#	Date	Mintage	VG	Fine	VF	XF
945	ND(ca.1906)	—	45.00	75.00	110.00	150.00

Provincial Type
Obv: Six vertical characters.
Rev: Six horizontal characters.

| 955 | ND(ca.1906) | — | 45.00 | 75.00 | 110.00 | 150.00 |

Ta Ch'ing Bank Type
Obv: Six vertical characters.
Rev: Six horizontal characters.

| 965 | ND(ca.1908) | — | 45.00 | 75.00 | 110.00 | 150.00 |

Merchant Type
Obv. and rev: Six horizontal characters.

| 977 | ND(ca.1908) | — | 45.00 | 75.00 | 110.00 | 150.00 |

8 CH'IEN (MACE)

SILVER, 29.20 g
Provincial Type
Obv. and rev: Six horizontal characters.

| 944 | ND(ca.1906) | — | 47.50 | 72.50 | 120.00 | 165.00 |

Provincial Type
Obv: Six vertical characters.
Rev: Six horizontal characters.

| 954 | ND(ca.1906) | — | 47.50 | 72.50 | 120.00 | 165.00 |

Ta Ch'ing Bank Type
Obv: Six vertical characters.
Rev: Six horizontal characters.

| 964 | ND(ca.1908) | — | 47.50 | 72.50 | 120.00 | 165.00 |

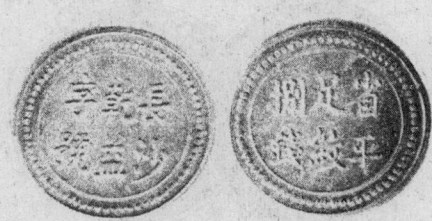

Merchant Type
Obv. and rev: Six horizontal characters.

| 976 | ND(ca.1908) | — | 47.50 | 72.50 | 120.00 | 165.00 |

9 CH'IEN (MACE)

SILVER, 32.70 g
Provincial Type
Obv. and rev: Six horizontal characters.

K#	Date	Mintage	VG	Fine	VF	XF
943	ND(ca.1906)	—	50.00	75.00	125.00	175.00

Provincial Type
Obv: Six vertical characters.
Rev: Six horizontal characters.

| 953 | ND(ca.1906) | — | 50.00 | 75.00 | 125.00 | 175.00 |

Ta Ch'ing Bank Type
Obv: Six vertical characters.
Rev: Six horizontal characters.

| 963 | ND(ca.1908) | — | 50.00 | 75.00 | 125.00 | 175.00 |

Merchant Type

| 975 | ND(ca.1908) | — | 50.00 | 75.00 | 125.00 | 175.00 |

LIANG (TAEL)

SILVER, 35.90 g
Provincial Type
Obv. and rev: Six horizontal characters.

| 942 | ND(ca.1906) | — | 60.00 | 100.00 | 150.00 | 225.00 |

Obv: Twelve characters. Rev: Blank.

| 942r | ND(ca.1908) | — | — | — | Rare | — |

Provincial Type
Obv: Six vertical characters.
Rev: Six horizontal characters.

| 952 | ND(ca.1906) | — | 60.00 | 100.00 | 140.00 | 200.00 |

Hunan / CHINA 338

Ta Ch'ing Bank Type
Obv: Six vertical characters.
Rev: Six horizontal characters.

K#	Date	Mintage	VG	Fine	VF	XF
962	ND(ca.1908)	—	45.00	75.00	110.00	150.00

Merchant Type
Obv. and rev: Six horizontal characters.

974	ND(ca.1908)	—	90.00	150.00	225.00	325.00

TRANSITIONAL COINAGE
In the name of Hung Hsien
10 CASH

COPPER

Y#	Year	Date	VG	Fine	VF	XF
401.1	1	(1915)	15.00	30.00	45.00	75.00

NOTE: This coin is dated first year of Hung Hsien which corresponds to 1915.

Rev: Wider spacing in legend.
| 401.2 | 1 | (1915) | 10.00 | 20.00 | 30.00 | 45.00 |

REPUBLIC
10 CASH

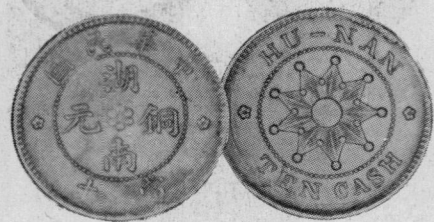

COPPER
Obv: Large rosette. Rev: Center of star convex.

Y#	Date	Mintage	VG	Fine	VF	XF
399	ND	—	1.00	2.00	4.00	7.50

BRASS
| 399a | ND | — | 2.25 | 5.00 | 10.00 | 17.50 |

COPPER
Obv: Small rosette. Rev: Center of star convex.
| 399.1 | ND | — | 1.00 | 2.00 | 4.00 | 7.00 |

Rev: Center of star concave. Star outlined.
| 399.2 | ND | — | 1.00 | 2.25 | 4.50 | 8.50 |

Rev: Star not outlined.
| 399.3 | ND | — | 1.00 | 2.25 | 4.50 | 8.50 |

Obv: Large rosette. Rev: Center of star concave.
| 399.4 | ND | — | 1.00 | 2.25 | 4.50 | 8.50 |

Mule. Obv: General Issue, Y#306.
| 399.5 | — | — | — | — | — | — |

Provincial Constitution
Rev: Rosette above flags.

Y#	Year	Date	VG	Fine	VF	XF
402	11	(1922)	9.00	17.50	27.50	40.00

Rev: Star above flags.
| 402.1 | 11 | (1922) | 7.00 | 15.00 | 20.00 | 35.00 |

20 CASH

COPPER
Obv: Rosette above flags, 5 characters at bottom.

Y#	Date	Mintage	VG	Fine	VF	XF
400	ND	—	1.20	3.00	7.50	15.00

BRASS
| 400b | ND | — | 1.60 | 4.00 | 10.00 | 20.00 |

COPPER
Obv: Dot in rosette above flags, 6 characters at bottom.
Rev: 11 curls in ribbon at base of plant.
| 400.2 | ND | — | — | .40 | 2.00 | 4.00 |

Rev: 25 small curls in ribbon at base of plant.

Y#	Date	Mintage	VG	Fine	VF	XF
400.3	ND	—	.40	1.00	2.00	4.00

Obv: Floral ornament at left smaller.
Rev: Smaller rice grains.
| 400.4 | ND | — | .40 | 1.00 | 2.00 | 4.00 |

Rev: Thin ribbon at base of plant.
| 400.5 | ND | — | .40 | 1.00 | 2.00 | 4.00 |

Obv: Small pentagonal rosette above flags.
| 400.6 | ND | — | .40 | 1.00 | 2.00 | 4.00 |

Obv: Small star-shaped rosette above flags.
| 400.7 | ND | — | .80 | 2.00 | 3.00 | 5.00 |

BRASS
| 400.7b | ND | — | 1.60 | 4.00 | 8.00 | 15.00 |

COPPER
Obv: Larger star-shaped rosette above flags.
| 400.8 | ND | — | 1.00 | 2.50 | 4.00 | 7.00 |

Hupeh / CHINA 339

Obv: Sharp-pointed star above flags.

Y#	Date	Mintage	VG	Fine	VF	XF
400.9	ND	—	1.00	2.50	4.00	7.00

Obv: Sharp pointed star over rosette above flags.

| 400.10 | ND | — | 20.00 | 25.00 | 30.00 | 35.00 |

Rev. denomination: 20 CASH.

| 400a | ND | — | 30.00 | 70.00 | 100.00 | 150.00 |

Provincial Constitution

Y#	Year	Date	VG	Fine	VF	XF
403	11	(1922)	11.00	20.00	30.00	50.00

Obv: Wreath similar to 1 Dollar, Y#404.

| A404 | 11 | (1922) | — | Rare | — | |

10 CENTS

SILVER
Hung Hsien

K#	Date	Mintage	Fine	VF	XF	Unc
762	ND(1915)	—	250.00	550.00	900.00	1200.

NICKEL (OMS)
Plain Edge

| 762x | ND(1915) | | | | | |

COPPER (OMS)
Plain edge

| 762y | ND(1915) | | — | — | 350.00 | 450.00 |

Though Kann calls this coin an Essay, contemporary reports indicate that the coin actually circulated briefly in 1915. Not to be confused with Y#28, the obverse of which has a different legend in Chinese. (See General Issues - Empire).

DOLLAR

SILVER, 27.40 g
Provincial Constitution

Y#	Year	Date	Fine	VF	XF	Unc
404	11	(1922)	125.00	175.00	250.00	400.00

HUPEH PROVINCE

Hubei

A province located in east-central China. Hilly, with some lakes and swamps it has rich coal and iron deposits plus a varied agricultural program. The Wuchang Mint had been active from early in the Manchu dynasty and its modern equipment began operations in 1895. It probably closed in 1929.

EMPIRE
CASH

CAST BRASS
Obv: Type A

C#	Date	Emperor	Good	VG	Fine	VF
13-2	ND(1796-1820)	Chia Ch'ing	1.00	2.00	3.00	5.00

Rev: Crescent above.

| 13-2.1 | ND(1796-1820) | Chia Ch'ing | 2.50 | 5.00 | 6.00 | 8.50 |

Obv: Type A

| 13-3 | ND(1821-50) | Tao Kuang | .75 | 1.50 | 2.50 | 4.00 |

Obv: Type A

| 13-4 | ND(1851-61) | Hsien Feng | 1.60 | 4.00 | 5.00 | 7.50 |

Obv: Type A-2

| 13-9 | ND(1862-74) | T'ung Chih | 3.50 | 7.50 | 11.50 | 16.50 |

Obv: Type A

| 13-11 | ND(1875-1908) | Kuang Hsu | 3.50 | 7.50 | 11.50 | 16.50 |

5 CASH

CAST BRASS
Obv: Type B-1

| 13-5 | ND(1851-61) | Hsien Feng | 40.00 | 70.00 | 100.00 | 130.00 |

10 CASH

CAST BRASS
Obv: Type B-1

| 13-6 | ND(1851-61) | Hsien Feng | 2.50 | 5.00 | 10.00 | 20.00 |

Rev: Crescent in upper right corner.

| 13-6.1 | ND(1851-61) | Hsien Feng | 10.00 | 20.00 | 30.00 | 50.00 |

Obv: Type B

| 13-10 | ND(1862-74) | T'ung Chih | — | — | Rare | |

Obv: Type B

| 13-12 | ND(1875-1908) | Kuang Hsu | — | — | Rare | |

50 CASH

CAST BRASS
Obv: Type B
Obv: and rev: Large characters.

C#	Date	Emperor	Good	VG	Fine	VF
13-7	ND(1851-61)	Hsien Feng	10.00	20.00	25.00	40.00

Rev: Crescent in upper right corner.

| 13-7.1 | ND(1851-61) | Hsien Feng | 52.50 | 85.00 | 110.00 | 150.00 |

Obv: and rev: Small characters.

| 13-7.2 | ND(1851-61) | Hsien Feng | 35.00 | 55.00 | 75.00 | 100.00 |

100 CASH

CAST BRASS
Obv: Type C

| 13-8 | ND(1851-61) | Hsien Feng | 10.00 | 20.00 | 30.00 | 50.00 |

Rev: Crescent in upper right corner.

| 13-8.1 | ND(1851-61) | Hsien Feng | 35.00 | 55.00 | 75.00 | 100.00 |

Ching Chow Mint
CASH

CAST BRASS
Obv: Type A

| 13-11.1 | ND(1875-1908) | Kuang Hsu | 13.50 | 17.50 | 22.50 | 30.00 |

MILLED COINAGE
CASH

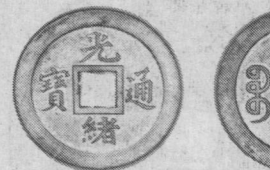

BRASS, struck
Obv: Small characters, 22.5mm.

Hsu#	Date	Mintage	VG	Fine	VF	XF
181	ND(1898)	—	22.50	40.00	50.00	65.00

Obv: Larger characters, 20.5mm.

| 182 | ND(1898) | — | 17.50 | 25.00 | 35.00 | 55.00 |

Y#	Date	Mintage	VG	Fine	VF	XF
121	ND(1906)	66.474	3.00	5.00	9.00	15.00

Obv: Small mint mark on small disc in center.

| 7j | CD1908 | Inc. Ab. | 3.50 | 8.00 | 15.00 | 25.00 |

Obv: Large mint mark on small disc in center.

| 7j.1 | CD1908 | Inc. Ab. | 3.50 | 8.00 | 15.00 | 25.00 |

2 CASH

COPPER

| 8j | CD1906 | .844 | 50.00 | 80.00 | 125.00 | 175.00 |

5 CASH

COPPER, 24mm

| 9j | CD1906 | 9.846 | 5.00 | 9.00 | 15.00 | 30.00 |

Dragon redesigned, 23mm.

| 9j.1 | CD1906 | Inc. Ab. | 6.00 | 11.00 | 17.50 | 35.00 |

10 CASH

COPPER
Obv: Eight-petal rosette. Rev: Circled dragon.

Y#	Date	Mintage	VG	Fine	VF	XF
120	ND(1902-05)	4.475	2.00	5.00	8.00	15.00

Rev: Uncircled dragon.

| 120a | ND(1902-05) | Inc. Ab. | 1.40 | 3.50 | 7.00 | 13.50 |

Rev: Slightly larger English letters; wide face on dragon.

| 120a.1 | ND(1902-05) | Inc. Ab. | .20 | .50 | 1.00 | 2.50 |

Rev: Large pearl w/many spines, narrower face on dragon.

| 120a.2 | ND(1902-05) | Inc. Ab. | .20 | .50 | 1.00 | 2.50 |

Rev: Smaller pearl w/fewer spines on dragon.

| 120a.3 | ND(1902-05) | Inc. Ab. | .25 | .60 | 1.25 | 2.75 |

NOTE: Commonly found with medal alignment and also exists with coin alignment.

Obv: Five-petal rosette, small Manchu character at right. Rev: Four dots in shape of cross at either side of dragon, Province spelled PHOVINCE, with V as inverted A.

| 120a.4 | ND(1902-05) | Inc. Ab. | .30 | .75 | 1.50 | 3.00 |

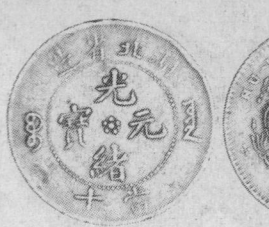

Obv: Large Manchu at right.
Rev: R in PROVINCE inverted, V an inverted A.

Y#	Date	Mintage	VG	Fine	VF	XF
120a.5	ND(1902-05)	Inc. Ab.	.30	.75	1.50	3.00

Rev: Six-pointed star at either side of dragon. Hyphen in HU-PEH.

| 120a.6 | ND(1902-05) | Inc. Ab. | .30 | .75 | 1.50 | 3.00 |

Rev: W/o hyphen in HU PEH.

| 120a.7 | ND(1902-05) | Inc. Ab. | .60 | 1.50 | 3.00 | 6.00 |

Obv: Five-petal rosette and small Manchu. Rev: Very small pearl.

| 120a.8 | ND(1902-05) | Inc. Ab. | .60 | 1.50 | 2.50 | 5.00 |

Obv: Square in circle. Rev: Hyphen in HU-PEH.

| 120a.9 | ND(1902-05) | Inc. Ab. | .60 | 1.50 | 2.50 | 5.00 |

Rev: W/o hyphen in HU PEH.

| 120a.10 | ND(1902-05) | Inc. Ab. | .60 | 1.50 | 2.50 | 5.00 |

Hupeh / CHINA 341

Obv: Second character from right at top is larger, six-petal rosette. Rev: Front view dragon.

Y#	Date	Mintage	VG	Fine	VF	XF
122	ND(1902-05)	Inc. Ab.	.25	.60	.85	2.25

Obv: 2nd character from right *Pei* smaller.
122.1 ND(1902-05)
 Inc. Ab. .20 .50 .75 2.00

BRASS
Rev: W/o dot at either side of mountain beneath pearl.
122b ND(1902-05)
 Inc. Ab. — — Rare —

WHITE BRONZE
W#	Date	Mintage	VG	Fine	VF	XF
518	ND(1902-05)	—	—	Rare	—	

COPPER
Rev: Clouds above dragons head; two clouds below pearl instead of one.
Y#	Date	Mintage	VG	Fine	VF	XF
122.3	ND(1902-05)	Inc. Ab.	.80	2.00	5.00	10.00

Rev: Small circle around lower part of pearl; w/o dots on either side of mountain.
122.4 ND(1902-05)
 Inc. Ab. .80 2.00 5.00 10.00

Rev: Larger circle around larger pearl; larger English letters.
122.5 ND(1902-05)
 Inc. Ab. .80 2.00 5.00 10.00

Rev: Circled front view dragon.
122a ND(1902-05) 125.00 175.00 225.00 300.00

Rev. leg: TAI CH'ING TI KUO, dragon, seven flames on pearl.
Y#	Date	Mintage	VG	Fine	VF	XF
10j	CD1906	1865.558	.30	.75	1.00	2.00

Rev: Redesigned dragon with wide lips; cloud shaped bar under pearl w/five flames, 28-29mm.
10j.1 CD1906 Inc. Ab. .80 2.00 5.00 10.00
30mm
10j.2 CD1906 Inc. Ab. .80 2.00 5.00 10.00

Rev: Different dragon w/hook-shaped cloud beneath, pearl w/four flames; large incuse swirl on pearl.
10j.3 CD1906 Inc. Ab. .20 .50 .75 1.50

Rev: Small incuse swirl on pearl w/four flames.
10j.4 CD1906 Inc. Ab. .20 .50 .75 1.50

Rev: Swirl on pearl in relief w/four flames.
10j.5 CD1906 Inc. Ab. .30 .75 1.00 2.00

Rev: Large incuse swirl on pearl.
20j CD1909
 371.577 .60 1.50 3.00 6.00

Rev: Small swirl in relief on pearl.
Y#	Date	Mintage	VG	Fine	VF	XF
20j.1	CD1909	Inc. Ab.	.60	1.50	3.00	6.00

Obv: CD1909 over CD1906.
20j.2 CD1909/1906 — — Rare —

Rev: Characters *Hsuan T'ung* re-engraved over characters *Kuang Hsu*.
20j.3 CD1909 — — Rare —

20 CASH

COPPER
11j CD1906 3.710 — 250.00 375.00 600.00

5 CENTS

1.3500 g, .820 SILVER, .0356 oz ASW
Y#	Date	Mintage	Fine	VF	XF	Unc
123	ND(1895-1905)	4.278	50.00	100.00	200.00	325.00

COPPER (OMS)
123a ND(1895-1905) — — — —

10 CENTS
2.7000 g, .820 SILVER, .0712 oz ASW
Rev: Character at either side of dragon *Pen Sheng* indicating coin was for provincial use.
124 ND(1894) — 300.00 700.00 1200. 1750.

Rev: W/o characters beside dragon. Two varieties of edge milling.
124.1 ND(1895-1907) — 1.00 4.00 7.50 20.00

COPPER (OMS)
124.1a ND(1895-1907) — — — —

Hupeh / CHINA   342

SILVER
Hsuan T'ung

Y#	Date	Mintage	Fine	VF	XF	Unc
129	ND(1909)	—	12.00	30.00	55.00	100.00

20 CENTS
5.3000 g, .820 SILVER, .1397 oz ASW
Rev: Character at either side of dragon *Pen Sheng* indicating coin was for provincial use.

| 125 | ND(1894) | — | 1500. | 3500. | 4000. | 5000. |

Rev: W/o characters beside dragon.
| 125.1 | ND(1895-1907) | | 3.00 | 6.00 | 10.00 | 25.00 |

COPPER (OMS)
| 125.1a | ND(1895-1907) | — | — | — | — | |

SILVER
Hsuan T'ung
| 130 | ND(1909) | — | 150.00 | 350.00 | 500.00 | 700.00 |

50 CENTS
13.5000 g, .860 SILVER, .3733 oz ASW
| 126 | ND(1895-1905) | | 20.00 | 35.00 | 50.00 | 140.00 |

COPPER (OMS)
| 126a | ND(1895-1905) | — | — | — | — | |

DOLLAR

26.7000 g, .900 SILVER, .7727 oz ASW
Obv: Similar to Y#127.1.
Rev: Characters at either side of dragon *Pen Sheng* indicating coin was for provincial use.
| 127 | ND(1894) | — | 7500. | 10,000. | 15,000. | 25,000. |

Rev: W/o *Pen Sheng* at either side of dragon.
| 127.1 | ND(1895-1907) | 19.935 | 10.00 | 15.00 | 25.00 | 125.00 |

COPPER (OMS)
| 127.1a | ND(1895-1907) | — | — | — | 350.00 | |

27.0000 g, .900 SILVER, .7814 oz ASW
Hsuan T'ung
Y#	Date	Mintage	Fine	VF	XF	Unc
131	ND(1909-11)	2.703	10.00	15.00	22.50	100.00

TAEL SYSTEM
TAEL

37.7000 g, .877 SILVER, 1.0631 oz ASW
Obv: Large central characters.
| 128.1 | Yr.30 (1904) | .648 | 90.00 | 160.00 | 200.00 | 450.00 |

Obv: Smaller central characters.
| 128.2 | Yr.30 (1904) | Inc. Ab. | 65.00 | 85.00 | 120.00 | 200.00 |

REPUBLIC
20 CASH

BRASS
Y#	Date	Mintage	VG	Fine	VF	XF
A405	ND	—	40.00	85.00	115.00	165.00

Attribution is uncertain. Probably minted in Szechuan (Sichuan). Former Y#471.

50 CASH
COPPER OR BRASS
Crude Strike

Y#	Year	Date	Good	VG	Fine	VF
405	3	(1914)	375.00	575.00	850.00	1100.
	7	(1918)	375.00	575.00	850.00	1100.

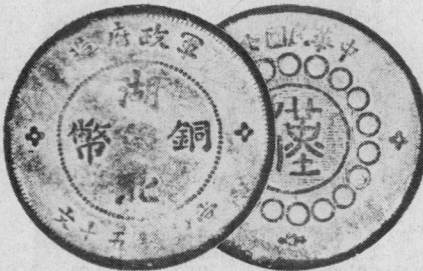

Machine Strike
| 405.1 | 7 | (1918) | 375.00 | 575.00 | 850.00 | 1100. |

NOTE: Not to be confused with Szechuan (Sichuan) Y#449.

20 CENTS

SILVER, 5.20 g

Obv: Characters at left and right of bust.
Y#	Year	Date	Fine	VF	XF	Unc
406	9	(1920)	75.00	125.00	200.00	450.00

NOTE: Do not confuse with Y#327 (See Republic-General issues.)

KANSU PROVINCE
Gansu

A province located in north central China with a contrast of mountains and sandy plains. The west end of the Great Wall with its branches lies in Kansu (Gansu). Kansu (Gansu) was the "Silk Road" that led to central and western Asia. Two mints issued Cash coins. It has been reported, but not confirmed, that the Lanchow Mint operated as late as 1949.

EMPIRE
CASH

CAST BRASS
Obv: Type A
C#	Date	Emperor	Good	VG	Fine	VF
14-1	ND(1851-61)	Hsien Feng	5.00	10.00	15.00	22.50
14-8	ND(1862-74)	T'ung Chih	6.00	12.00	18.00	25.00

5 CASH

CAST BRASS
Obv: Type B-1
| 14-2 | ND(1851-61) | Hsien Feng | 30.00 | 40.00 | 50.00 | 75.00 |

Rev: Large Manchu
| 14-2.1 | ND(1851-61) | Hsien Feng | 30.00 | 40.00 | 50.00 | 75.00 |

Obv: Type B
| 14-9 | ND(1862-74) | T'ung Chih | 30.00 | 40.00 | 50.00 | 75.00 |

10 CASH

CAST BRASS
Obv: Type B
| 14-3 | ND(1851-61) | Hsien Feng | 7.00 | 10.00 | 20.00 | 35.00 |

Obv: Type B
| 14-10 | ND(1862-74) | T'ung Chih | 25.00 | 40.00 | 50.00 | 60.00 |

50 CASH

CAST BRASS, 48mm.
Obv: Type B-1

C#	Date	Emperor	Good	VG	Fine	VF
14-4	ND(1851-61)					
		Hsien Feng	50.00	70.00	100.00	150.00

43mm

| 14-4.1 | ND(1851-61) | | | | | |
| | | Hsien Feng | 40.00 | 55.00 | 75.00 | 125.00 |

100 CASH
CAST BRASS
Obv: Type C

| 14-5 | ND(1851-61) | | | | | |
| | | Hsien Feng | 25.00 | 35.00 | 50.00 | 70.00 |

500 CASH
CAST BRASS
Obv: Type C

| 14-6 | ND(1851-61) | | | | | |
| | | Hsien Feng | 80.00 | 110.00 | 150.00 | 250.00 |

1000 CASH
CAST BRASS
Obv: Type C

| 14-7 | ND(1851-61) | | | | | |
| | | Hsien Feng | 160.00 | 220.00 | 300.00 | 500.00 |

REPUBLIC
50 CASH

COPPER

Y#	Date	Mintage	VG	Fine	VF	XF
408	Yr.15 (1926)	2.564	100.00	175.00	275.00	450.00

100 CASH

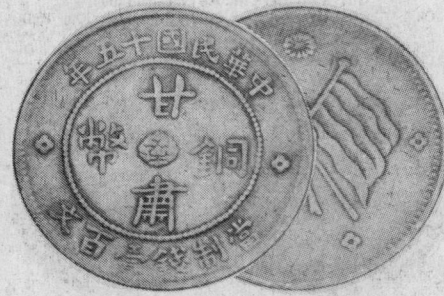

COPPER

Y#	Year	Date	VG	Fine	VF	XF
409	15	(1926)	40.00	75.00	125.00	200.00

DOLLAR

SILVER, 26.60 g

Y#	Year	Date	Fine	VF	XF	Unc
407	3	(1914)	100.00	200.00	300.00	650.00

| 410 | 17 | (1928) | 150.00 | 275.00 | 375.00 | 750.00 |

KIANGNAN

A district in eastern China made up of Anhwei (Anhui) and Kiangsu (Jiangsu) provinces. In 1667 the province of Kiangnan was divided into the present provinces of Anhwei (Anhui) and Kiangsu (Jiangsu). In 1723 Nanking, formerly the capital of Kiangnan, was made the capital of Liang-Chiang (an administrative area consisting of Anhwei (Anhui), Kiangsu (Jiangsu) and Kiangsi (Jiangxi) provinces.

Always highly regarded because of location, agriculture and manufacturing, Kiangnan has frequently been sought after by contending forces.

The Nanking Mint had been active during imperial times. Modern minting facilities began operations in 1897 at the Kiangnan Arsenal in Nanking. A second mint was opened in 1905 in northern Kiangsu for the production of coppers only. A third mint was planned for in Shanghai in 1921 and a fourth at Soochow saw limited service. The Nanking Mint, the most important of the group, burned down in 1929. The Nationalist Government Central Mint was opened in Shanghai in 1933.

EMPIRE
MILLED COINAGE
CASH

COPPER
Obv: Type A

Hsu#	Date	Mintage	VG	Fine	VF	XF
261	ND(1898)	—	15.00	25.00	35.00	50.00

NOTE: This coin has been erroneously attributed to Ningpo in Chekiang (Zhejang) and to Changchow in Fukien. The coin was minted at Nanking from dies produced by the Heaton Mint.

Obv: Smaller characters.
Rev: Mint mark written differently.

Y#	Date	Mintage	VG	Fine	VF	XF
—	ND	—	90.00	135.00	200.00	300.00

BRASS

Obv: Bottom horizontal stroke in mint mark extends beyond outside vertical strokes.

Y#	Date	Mintage	VG	Fine	VF	XF
7k	CD1908	25.450	2.50	4.50	8.50	16.00

Obv: Bottom horizontal stroke in mint mark does not extend beyond outside vertical strokes.

| 7k.1 | CD1908 Inc. Ab. | 3.50 | 6.50 | 12.50 | 21.50 |

2 CASH

 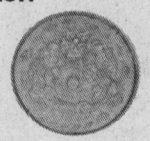

COPPER

| 8k | CD1906 | — | — | — | — |

5 CASH

COPPER
Obv: Mint mark incused on raised disk.

| 9k.1 | CD1906 | — | 35.00 | 65.00 | 100.00 | 150.00 |

BRASS

| 9k.1a | CD1906 | — | 45.00 | 90.00 | 125.00 | 200.00 |

COPPER
Obv: Mint mark in relief at center w/o disc.

| 9k.2 | CD1906 | — | 45.00 | 90.00 | 125.00 | 200.00 |

10 CASH

COPPER
Reeded edge

| 135 | ND | — | 15.00 | 30.00 | 60.00 | 100.00 |

Plain edge

| 135.1 | ND | — | 15.00 | 30.00 | 60.00 | 100.00 |

Obv: Small Manchu characters in center.

| 135.2 | CD1902 | — | .75 | 1.50 | 3.00 | 5.00 |

Obv: Large Manchu characters in center.

| 135.3 | CD1902 | — | 2.50 | 6.00 | 12.00 | 25.00 |

Kiangnan / CHINA

Y#	Date	Mintage	VG	Fine	VF	XF
135.4	CD1903	—	.50	1.00	2.00	4.00

Rev: Cloud above letter T looks like number 3.

135.5	CD1904					
		351.974	.50	1.00	2.00	4.00

Rev: Cloud above T redesigned. Cash spelled GASH.

| 135.6 | CD1904 | I.A. | 2.00 | 4.50 | 10.00 | 17.50 |

Rev: Third design of cloud above letter T, thin tailed dragon.

| 135.7 | CD1904 | I.A. | .50 | 1.00 | 2.00 | 4.00 |

Rev: Fewer clouds around dragon, scales on dragons body different, pearl smaller.

| 135.8 | CD1904 | I.A. | 2.00 | 4.50 | 9.00 | 17.50 |

NOTE: The above coin is believed to be counterfeit.

Rev: Small rosette at either side of dragon.

135.9	CD1905					
		496.020	.30	.75	1.50	3.00

Rev: Large oblong rosettes at either side of dragon.

Y#	Date	Mintage	VG	Fine	VF	XF
135.10	CD1905	I.A.	.75	1.50	3.00	5.00

Obv: Rosette in center. Rev. denomination: TEN-CASH.

| 138 | CD1905 | I.A. | 1.50 | 3.50 | 6.00 | 12.00 |

Rev: W/o hyphen in TEN CASH.

| 138.1 | CD1905 | I.A. | .30 | .75 | 1.50 | 3.00 |

Mule. Obv: Y#10k. Rev: Y#138. raised or incused mint mark.

| 140 | CD1906 | I.A. | 1.50 | 3.50 | 9.00 | 17.50 |

Mule. Obv: Y#10k.2. Rev: Y#138.

| A140 | CD1906 | I.A. | 10.00 | 25.00 | 40.00 | 60.00 |

Mule. Obv: Y#138. Rev: Y#10k.

| B140 | CD1905 | I.A. | 15.00 | 30.00 | 50.00 | 70.00 |

Mule. Obv: Kiangnan. Rev: Kiangsu. Often confused w/Y#162.

| C140 | ND | | 65.00 | 100.00 | 150.00 | 250.00 |

Mule. Obv: Y#138.1. Rev: Y#135.

Y#	Date	Mintage	VG	Fine	VF	XF
D140	CD1905	I.A.	25.00	50.00	100.00	200.00

Other Kiangnan mules exist, dated 1902 and 1903.

Obv: Mint mark in relief on raised disc.
Rev: Dragon w/wide face and incuse eyes.

10k	CD1906					
		504.800	.75	1.25	2.50	5.00

Rev: Dragon w/narrower face and raised dots for eyes.

| 10k.1 | CD1906 | I.A. | .75 | 1.25 | 2.50 | 5.00 |

Obv: Mint mark in relief in field w/o raised disc.
Rev: Dragon w/wide face and incuse eyes.

| 10k.2 | CD1906 | I.A. | .25 | .75 | 1.50 | 3.00 |

Rev: Dragon w/narrow face and raised dots for eyes.

| 10k.3 | CD1906 | I.A. | .25 | .75 | 1.50 | 3.00 |

Obv: Mint mark incuse on raised disc.

| 10k.4 | CD1906 | I.A. | 5.00 | 12.00 | 25.00 | 45.00 |

BRASS

| 10K.4a | CD1906 | — | — | — | — |

COPPER
Obv: Mint mark incuse on raised disc.
Rev: Dragon w/wide face. Seven flames on pearl.

10k.5	CD1907					
		552.000	.60	1.50	3.00	5.00

Rev: Different dragon w/narrow face and small mouth, five flames on pearl, dot after COIN.

Y#	Date	Mintage	VG	Fine	VF	XF
10k.6	CD1907	I.A.	.20	.50	1.00	2.50

BRASS

| 10k.6a | CD1907 | I.A. | 3.50 | 9.00 | 17.50 | 30.00 |

COPPER

Rev: Dragon w/large mouth and redesigned head, flame below pearl has long tail which touches dragon's body, Kuo spelled KIIO.

| 10k.7 | CD1907 | I.A. | .25 | .75 | 1.50 | 3.00 |

Rev: Tail of flame below pearl does not touch body, dash after word COIN. Kuo spelled KUO.

| 10k.8 | CD1907 | I.A. | .25 | .75 | 1.50 | 3.00 |

Rev: Dragon w/square mouth, letter K in KUO larger than other letters, w/o dot or dash after COIN.

| 10k.9 | CD1907 | I.A. | .20 | .50 | 1.00 | 2.50 |

Rev: Large, flat faced dragon.

| 10k.9a | CD1907 | | | | | |

Obv: Mint mark incuse on raised disc. **Rev:** Dragon w/ small mouth, five-flame pearl, dot after COIN, Kuo spelled KUO.

| 10k.10 | CD1908 | | | | | |
| | | 442.750 | .20 | .50 | 1.00 | 2.50 |

Rev: Dragon has large mouth and redesigned head, tail on cloud beneath pearl touches dragon's body, Kuo spelled KIIO.

| 10k.11 | CD1908 | I.A. | .40 | 1.00 | 2.00 | 4.00 |

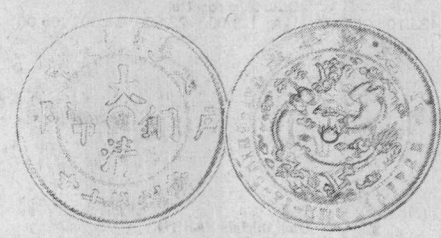

Rev: Dash after COIN. Kuo spelled KUO.

Y#	Date	Mintage	VG	Fine	VF	XF
10k.12	CD1908	I.A.	.20	.50	1.00	2.50

Rev: Dragon's head redesigned. W/o dot or dash after COIN. Kuo spelled KIIO.

| 10k.13 | CD1908 | I.A. | .40 | 1.00 | 2.00 | 4.00 |

NOTE: Most of the 1907 and 1908 ten Cash above have copper spelled GOPPER.

5 CENTS

1.3000 g, .820 SILVER, .0343 oz ASW
Rev: Circled dragon.

Y#	Date	Mintage	Fine	VF	XF	Unc
141	ND(1898)	.100	18.00	30.00	55.00	150.00
	ND(1898)				Proof	700.00

Rev: W/o circle around dragon.

141a	ND(1898)	I.A.	7.00	12.00	18.00	40.00
	CD1899	3,812	11.00	20.00	30.00	65.00
	CD1900	.618	7.00	12.00	18.00	40.00
	CD1901	—	10.00	22.00	35.00	70.00

10 CENTS

2.6000 g, .820 SILVER, .0686 oz ASW
Rev: Circled dragon.

| 142 | ND(1898) | 8.000 | 12.00 | 25.00 | 50.00 | 150.00 |
| | ND(1898) | | | | Proof | 700.00 |

| 142.1 | CD1898 | Inc. Ab. | 7.00 | 15.00 | 25.00 | 45.00 |

Rev: W/o circle around dragon w/small rosettes at sides.

| 142a | CD1898 | I.A. | 3.50 | 7.00 | 15.00 | 30.00 |

Rev: Large rosettes at sides of dragons.

| 142a.1 | CD1898 | I.A. | 3.50 | 7.00 | 15.00 | 30.00 |

Obv: Large characters in center, small characters in outer ring.

| 142a.2 | CD1899 | | | | | |
| | | 10.784 | 2.25 | 4.50 | 9.00 | 20.00 |

Obv: Small characters in center, large characters in outer ring.

| 142a.3 | CD1899 | I.A. | 2.25 | 4.50 | 9.00 | 20.00 |

Kiangnan / CHINA **345**

Y#	Date	Mintage	Fine	VF	XF	Unc
142a.4	CD1900	5.460	2.50	5.00	10.00	22.00

Obv: W/o initials. **Rev:** Large English letters.

| 142a.5 | CD1901 | 7.794 | 2.25 | 4.50 | 9.00 | 20.00 |

Rev: Small English letters.

| 142a.6 | CD1901 | I.A. | 2.25 | 4.50 | 9.00 | 20.00 |

Obv: Initials HAH.
Rev: Large rosettes beside dragon.

| 142a.7 | CD1901 | I.A. | 3.50 | 6.50 | 12.50 | 25.00 |

Rev: Small rosettes beside dragon.

| 142a.8 | CD1901 | I.A. | 3.50 | 6.50 | 12.50 | 25.00 |

Rev: Large stars beside dragon.

| 142a.9 | CD1902 | 3.778 | 2.25 | 4.50 | 9.00 | 20.00 |

Rev: Small stars beside dragon.

| 142a.10 | CD1902 | I.A. | 2.25 | 4.50 | 9.00 | 20.00 |

Obv: Large rosette.

| 142a.11 | CD1903 | 1.161 | 3.50 | 6.50 | 12.50 | 25.00 |

Obv: Small rosette.

| 142a.12 | CD1903 | I.A. | 3.50 | 6.50 | 12.50 | 25.00 |

Obv: Initials HAH TH.

| 142a.13 | CD1904 | .897 | 3.75 | 7.50 | 15.00 | 30.00 |

Obv: Initials SY upside down.

| 142a.14 | CD1905 | .681 | 3.50 | 6.50 | 12.50 | 25.00 |

Obv: W/o initials.

| 142a.15 | CD1905 | I.A. | 3.50 | 6.50 | 12.50 | 25.00 |

| 146 | ND(1911) | *.820 | 7.50 | 15.00 | 30.00 | 60.00 |

*****NOTE:** Includes 590,000 pieces struck in debased silver in 1916.

20 CENTS

5.3000 g, .820 SILVER, .1397 oz ASW
Obv: Rosettes at 2 and 10 o'clock.

Kiangnan / CHINA

Rev: Circle around dragon.

Y#	Date	Mintage	Fine	VF	XF	Unc
143	ND(1898)	7.000	17.50	40.00	70.00	140.00

143.1	CD1898	I.A.	15.00	35.00	65.00	110.00

Obv: Large characters in outer ring. Rev: Large English letters, w/o circle around dragon.

143a	CD1898	I.A.	3.75	5.50	11.50	22.50

Obv: Small characters in outer ring. Rev: Small English letters.

143a.1	CD1898	I.A.	3.75	5.50	11.50	22.50

Rev: Old type dragon w/long face, flanked by short rosettes.

143a.2	CD1899	11.096	3.50	5.00	10.00	21.50

Rev: New type dragon w/shorter face and larger forehead, flanked by long rosettes.

143a.3	CD1899	I.A.	3.50	5.00	10.00	21.50

Rev: Old type dragon w/long face, flanked by long rosettes.

143a.4	CD1900	5.796	5.00	10.00	20.00	40.00

Rev: New type dragon w/shorter face and larger forehead.

143a.5	CD1900	I.A.	5.00	10.00	20.00	40.00

Obv: W/o initials.

143a.6	CD1901	47.114	3.50	5.00	10.00	21.50

Obv: Initials HAH.

143a.7	CD1901	I.A.	3.50	5.00	10.00	21.50
143a.8	CD1902	15.754	4.00	6.50	12.50	25.00

Obv: Rosette in outer leg.

Y#	Date	Mintage	Fine	VF	XF	Unc
143a.9	CD1903	2.432	7.00	17.50	30.00	55.00

Obv: W/o rosette.

143a.10	CD1903	I.A.	9.00	22.50	35.00	65.00

Obv: Initials HAH TH.

143a.11	CD1904	1.172	15.00	35.00	55.00	100.00

Obv: W/o initials.

143a.12	CD1905	.828	7.00	17.50	30.00	55.00

Obv: Initials SY.

143a.13	CD1905	I.A.	9.00	22.50	35.00	70.00

147	ND(1911)	2.320	12.00	30.00	50.00	90.00

NOTE: Includes 2,005,000 pieces struck in debased silver in 1916.

50 CENTS

13.2000 g, .860 SILVER, .3650 oz ASW
Rev: Circled dragon

144	ND(1898)	.100	175.00	325.00	500.00	875.00
	ND(1898)	—	—	—	Proof	2000.

Rev: W/o circle around dragon.

144a	CD1899					
		155 pcs.	—	800.00	1200.	2000.
	CD1900	—	300.00	800.00	1150.	1700.

DOLLAR

27.0000 g, .900 SILVER, .7814 oz ASW
Rev: Circled dragon. Normal edge reeding.

145	ND(1898)	1.603	175.00	300.00	500.00	1000.

Ornamented edge

Y#	Date	Mintage	Fine	VF	XF	Unc
145.1	ND(1898)	I.A.	85.00	125.00	250.00	750.00

Rev: W/o circle around old style dragon.

145a.1	CD1898	I.A.	25.00	75.00	120.00	375.00

Similar to Y#145a.1 but w/smaller letters.

145a.2	CD1898	I.A.	25.00	75.00	120.00	450.00
(Y145a)	CD1899	2.039	22.50	50.00	125.00	500.00

Obv: Chinese date characters *Wu Shu* reversed.

145a.18	CD1898	I.A.	1500.	2750.	—	—

Rev: Redesigned dragon w/shorter face and larger forehead, similar to 1900.

145a.3	CD1899	I.A.	75.00	115.00	185.00	650.00
(Y145a.1)						

Rev: Large scales on dragon.

145a.4	CD1900	2.531	30.00	75.00	150.00	300.00
(Y145a.2)						

Rev: Small scales on dragon.

145a.20	CD1900	I.A.	22.50	50.00	125.00	300.00

Obv: W/o initials.

145a.5	CD1901	2.377	120.00	200.00	300.00	1000.
(Y145a.3)						

Obv: Fine initials HAH w/o rosette. Rev: Similar to Y#145a.6.

145a.21	CD1901	I.A.	65.00	125.00	200.00	450.00

Obv: Bold initials HAH w/o rosette. Rev: Petals of rosettes separated from each other.

145a.6	CD1901	I.A.	65.00	120.00	200.00	450.00
(Y145a.4)						

Obv: Cross of 6 dots at upper right. Rev: Similar to Y#145a.6.

145a.22	CD1901	I.A.	100.00	165.00	285.00	850.00

Obv: Initials HAH and rosette. Rev: Petals of rosettes run together.

145a.7	CD1901	I.A.	20.00	35.00	65.00	250.00
(Y145a.5)						

Obv: Small date, small HAH.
Rev: Similar to Y#145a.4

Y#	Date	Mintage	Fine	VF	XF	Unc
145a.8 (Y145a.6)	CD1902	3.562	25.00	50.00	75.00	150.00

Obv: Larger date, larger HAH.

| 145a.9 (Y145a.7) | CD1902 | I.A. | 25.00 | 50.00 | 75.00 | 150.00 |

Obv: HAH and rosette in outer ring.

| 145a.10 (Y145a.8) | CD1903 | 1.489 | 40.00 | 85.00 | 175.00 | 350.00 |

Obv: W/o rosette in outer ring.

| 145a.11 (Y145a.9) | CD1903 | I.A. | 400.00 | 600.00 | 900.00 | 2000. |

Obv: Initials HAH and CH, w/o dots or rosettes.
Rev: Similar to Y#145a.4

| 145a.12 (Y145a.10) | CD1904 | 44.725 | 10.00 | 16.00 | 25.00 | 125.00 |

Obv: Dot at either side.

| 145a.13 (Y145a.11) | CD1904 | I.A. | 10.00 | 16.00 | 30.00 | 200.00 |

Obv: Dot at either side, w/o 4 central characters.

| 145a.19 (Y145a.18) | CD1904 | — | — | — | — | — |

Rev: Dot to left of numeral 7.

| 145a.14 (Y145a.12) | CD1904 | I.A. | 10.00 | 16.00 | 30.00 | 200.00 |

Obv: Four point rosette at either side HAH and CH.

| 145a.15 (Y145a.13) | CD1904 | I.A. | 50.00 | 125.00 | 200.00 | 500.00 |

Obv: Initials HAH and TH.

| 145a.16 (Y145a.14) | CD1904 | I.A. | 100.00 | 200.00 | 500.00 | 1000. |

Obv: Initials SY.
Rev: Similar to Y#145a.10.

Y#	Date	Mintage	Fine	VF	XF	Unc
145a.17 (Y145a.15)	CD1905	.634	35.00	65.00	125.00	350.00

NOTE: The initials HAH, SY, CH and TH are those of mint officials and were placed on the coins as a guarantee of the coin's fineness. The 5, 10 and 20 Cent coins are often found without a decimal point between the numbers on the reverse. The 1904 dated dollar was restruck during Republican times.

KIANGSI PROVINCE

Jiangxi, Kiangsee

A province located in southeastern China. Mostly hilly with some mountains on borders that produce coal and tungsten. Some of China's finest porcelain comes from this province. Kiangsi was visited by Marco Polo. A mint was opened in Nanchang in 1729, closed in 1733, reopened in 1736 and operated with reasonable continuity from that time. Modern machinery was introduced in 1901 although it only produced copper coins. The mint closed amidst internal problems in the 1920's.

EMPIRE
CASH
CAST BRASS
Obv: Type A

C#	Date	Emperor	Good	VG	Fine	VF
15-2	ND(1796-1820)	Chia Ch'ing	.20	.50	1.00	1.50

Rev: Dot in upper left corner.

| 15-2.1 | ND(1796-1820) | Chia Ch'ing | 3.50 | 5.00 | 7.00 | 10.00 |

Obv: Type A

| 15-3 | ND(1821-51) | Tao Kuang | .35 | .85 | 1.50 | 2.00 |

CAST ZINC

| 15-3a | ND(1821-51) | Tao Kuang | — | — | Rare | — |

CAST BRASS
Obv: Type A

| 15-4 | ND(1851-61) | Hsien Feng | .80 | 2.00 | 3.00 | 4.00 |

 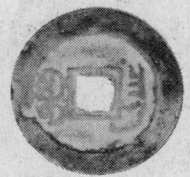

Obv: Type A

| 15-7 | ND(1862-74) | T'ung Chih | 1.20 | 3.00 | 4.00 | 5.00 |

Obv: Type A. Rev: Type 1 mint mark.

| 15-9 | ND(1875-1908) | Kuang Hsu | 4.50 | 6.50 | 9.00 | 13.50 |

10 CASH

CAST BRASS
Obv: Type B-1

C#	Date	Emperor	Good	VG	Fine	VF
15-5	ND(1851-61)	Hsien Feng	3.00	6.00	10.00	20.00

Obv: Type B

| 15-8 | ND(1862-74) | T'ung Chih | — | — | Rare | — |

Obv: Type B

| 15-10 | ND(1875-1908) | Kuang Hsu | — | — | Rare | — |

50 CASH
CAST COPPER
Obv: Type B-1

| 15.6 | ND(1851-61) | Hsien Feng | 8.00 | 15.00 | 20.00 | 35.00 |

CAST BRASS

| 15-6.1 | ND(1851-61) | Hsien Feng | 5.00 | 10.00 | 15.00 | 20.00 |

MILLED COINAGE

Horizontal rosette   Vertical rosette

10 CASH

COPPER
Obv: Vertical rosette at center.
Rev: Name of province spelled KIANG-SEE.

Y#	Date	Mintage	VG	Fine	VF	XF
149	ND	—	3.25	8.00	12.50	22.50

Obv: Horizontal rosette at center.

| 149.1 | ND | — | 3.25 | 8.00 | 12.50 | 22.50 |

Obv: Different Manchu character at right. Rev: Circled dragon.

| 149.2 | ND | — | — | — | Rare | — |

NOTE: May be a pattern.

Kiangsi / CHINA   348

Obv: Manchu reading *Pao Yuan.*
Rev: Name of province spelled KIANG-SI, two stars at either side of dragon.

Y#	Date	Mintage	VG	Fine	VF	XF
150	ND	—	2.50	6.00	11.00	17.50

Obv: Manchu reading *Pao Ch'ang* **at center and Chinese reading** *Ku P'ing* **at 3 and 9 o'clock.**

| 150.1 | ND | — | 1.00 | 3.00 | 6.00 | 12.00 |

Obv: Manchu reading *Pao Ch'ang* **at 3 and 9 o'clock, horizontal rosette in center.**

150.2	ND	—	.50	1.00	2.00	4.00
		BRASS				
150.2a	ND	—	2.00	5.00	10.00	20.00
		COPPER				

Obv: Vertical rosette in center.

| 150.3 | ND | — | .50 | 1.00 | 2.00 | 4.00 |

Obv: Horizontal rosette. Rev: One star at either side of dragon, large English lettering.

150.4	ND	—	.50	1.00	2.00	4.00
		BRASS				
150.4a	ND	—	2.00	5.00	9.00	17.50
		COPPER				

Obv: Vertical rosette.

| 150.5 | ND | — | .50 | 1.00 | 2.00 | 4.00 |

Rev: Smaller English lettering, one star at either side of dragon.

| 150.6 | ND | — | .50 | 1.00 | 2.00 | 4.00 |

Obv: Small rosette center.
Rev: One star at either side of dragon.

| 150.7 | ND | — | 2.50 | 6.00 | 11.00 | 17.50 |

Rev: Three stars at either side of dragon.

Y#	Date	Mintage	VG	Fine	VF	XF
150.8	ND	—	5.00	12.00	20.00	30.00

Obv: Manchu *Pao Ch'ang* **at 3 and 9 o'clock.**
Rev: Name of province spelled KIANG-SI, front view dragon, mountain below pearl.

| 152 | ND | — | 2.50 | 4.00 | 6.00 | 12.00 |

Obv: Horizontal rosette in center and Manchu *Pao Ch'ang* **at 3 and 9 o'clock.**

| 152.1 | ND | — | 2.50 | 4.00 | 6.00 | 12.00 |

Obv: Horizontal rosette in center and Manchu *Pao Ch'ang* **at 3 and 9 o'clock, small character '10'.**

| 152.2 | ND | — | 5.00 | 12.00 | 17.50 | 27.50 |

Obv: Horizontal rosette in center and Manchu *Pao Ch'ang* **at 3 and 9 o'clock, large character '10'.**
Rev: W/o mountain below dragon.

| 152.3 | ND | — | 3.50 | 8.00 | 12.00 | 17.50 |

Obv: Small character '10'.

| 152.4 | ND | — | 3.50 | 8.00 | 12.00 | 17.50 |

Obv: Manchu *Pao Ch'ang* **in center, Chinese** *K'u P'ing* **at 3 and 9 o'clock. Rev: W/o mountain below pearl, dragon's body repositioned.**

| 152.5 | ND | — | 3.50 | 8.00 | 12.00 | 17.50 |

Rev: Mountain under dragon.

| 152.6 | ND | — | 3.25 | 7.50 | 11.00 | 16.00 |

Rev: Front view dragon w/KIANG-SEE PROVINCE above.

Y#	Date	Mintage	VG	Fine	VF	XF
153	ND	—	2.00	4.50	7.00	11.00

Obv: Manchu *Pao Ch'ang* **at center and Chinese** *K'u P'ing* **at 3 and 9 o'clock.**

| 153.1 | ND | — | .80 | 2.00 | 3.50 | 7.00 |

Obv: Manchu *Pao Ch'ang* **at 3 and 9 o'clock and horizontal rosette in center.**

| 153.2 | ND | — | .80 | 2.00 | 3.50 | 7.00 |

Obv: Small vertical rosette in center.

| 153.3 | ND | — | .80 | 2.00 | 3.50 | 7.00 |

NOTE: All four varieties of Y#153 are found with and without a swirl on the pearl below dragon's mouth.

Rev: Flying dragon w/KIANG-SI above.

| 154 | ND | — | 17.50 | 40.00 | 70.00 | 100.00 |

Rev: Eyes of dragon in relief

| 10m | CD1906 | — | 1.25 | 3.00 | 6.00 | 12.00 |

Rev: Dragon's eyes incuse

| 10m.1 | CD1906 | — | 1.25 | 3.00 | 6.00 | 12.00 |

Rev: Dragon redesigned, small faint cloud beneath pearl.

Y#	Date	Mintage	VG	Fine	VF	XF
10m.2	CD1906	—	5.00	12.00	17.50	30.00

REPUBLIC
10 CASH
COPPER
Obv: Mint mark incused on raised-disc center, w/ Chinese characters on four sides *Ta Han T'ung Pi*. Five character value in outer ring at bottom. **Rev:** Ring of nine balls w/o inscription.

| 411 | CD1911 | — | — | — | Rare |

Obv: Date appears at 3 and 9 o'clock. **Rev:** Nine pointed star inside circle and five-petal rosette at 3 and 9 o'clock.

| 412 | CD1912 | — | 150.00 | 200.00 | 325.00 | 450.00 |

Obv: Horizontal rosette in center, w/Chinese characters *Chiang Hsi* above and below. **Rev:** Six-petal rosette at either side.

| 412a | CD1912 | — | 1.25 | 3.00 | 5.00 | 9.00 |

Obv: Small vertical rosette in center.

| 412a.1 | CD1912 | — | 1.25 | 3.00 | 5.00 | 9.00 |

Obv: Large vertical rosette, thick, large center characters. **Rev:** Small five-petal rosettes at either side.

| 412a.2 | CD1912 | — | 6.00 | 12.00 | 17.50 | 27.50 |

Obv: Large vertical rosette in center, thin center characters.

| 412a.3 | CD1912 | — | 1.25 | 3.00 | 5.00 | 10.00 |

NOTE: Many Kiangsi coins have a six-petal rosette in the center of the obverse, arranged so that two sides of the rosette are formed by two petals in line with each other. The remaining two sides have a single petal, standing out from the rest. The direction that these single petals point, determines whether the rosette is horizontal or vertical. A horizontal rosette has the single petals pointing left and right, while the single petals of the vertical rosette point up and down.

KIANGSU/KIANGSOO PROVINCE
Jiangsu

A province located on the east coast of China. One of the smallest and most densely populated of all Chinese provinces. A mint opened in Soochow in 1667, but closed shortly after in 1670. A new mint opened in 1734 for producing cast coins and had continuous operation until about 1870. Modern equipment was introduced in 1898 and a second mint was opened in 1904. Both mints closed down production in 1906. Taels were produced in Shanghai by local silversmiths as early as 1856. These saw limited circulation in the immediate area.

EMPIRE
Kiangsu Mint
CASH
CAST BRASS
Obv: Type A

C#	Date	Emperor	Good	VG	Fine	VF
16-2	ND(1796-1820)	Chia Ch'ing	.20	.50	1.25	2.50

Narrow rims.

| 16-3 | ND(1821-51) | Tao Kuang | .75 | 1.50 | 2.50 | 4.00 |

Wide rims.

| 16-3.1 | ND(1821-51) | Tao Kuang | — | — | Rare | — |

Narrow rims.
Obv: Type A

| 16-4 | ND(1851-61) | Hsien Feng | 1.00 | 2.00 | 3.00 | 4.50 |

Wide rims.

| 16-4.1 | ND(1851-61) | Hsien Feng | — | — | Rare | — |

Rev: Crescent above.

| 16-4.2 | ND(1851-61) | Hsien Feng | 4.25 | 8.50 | 17.50 | 35.00 |

Obv: Type A-2

| 16-11 | ND(1862-74) | T'ung Chih | 1.00 | 2.00 | 3.00 | 4.00 |

Obv: Type A

| 16-12 | ND(1875-1908) | Kuang Hsu | 1.20 | 3.00 | 6.50 | 9.00 |

Rev: Circle above.

| 16-12.1 | ND(1875-1908) | Kuang Hsu | 3.00 | 7.50 | 10.00 | 13.50 |

Rev: Crescent above.

C#	Date	Emperor	Good	VG	Fine	VF
16-12.2	ND(1875-1908)	Kuang Hsu	3.00	7.50	10.00	13.50

5 CASH
CAST BRASS
Obv: Type B-1

| 16-5 | ND(1851-61) | Hsien Feng | 30.00 | 45.00 | 65.00 | 100.00 |

CAST IRON

| 16-5a | ND(1851-61) | Hsien Feng | 40.00 | 55.00 | 80.00 | 120.00 |

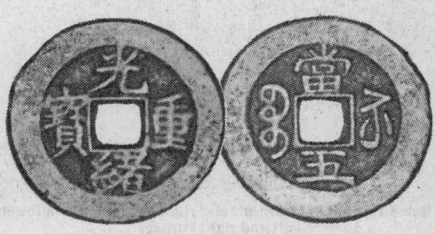

CAST BRASS
Obv: Type B

| 16-13 | ND(1875-1908) | Kuang Hsu | 30.00 | 40.00 | 50.00 | 75.00 |

10 CASH
CAST BRASS, 36-40mm
Obv: Type B-1

| 16-6 | ND(1851-61) | Hsien Feng | 5.00 | 7.50 | 10.00 | 20.00 |

30-34mm

| 16-6.1 | ND(1851-61) | Hsien Feng | 5.00 | 7.50 | 10.00 | 20.00 |

CAST IRON

| 16-6a | ND(1851-61) | Hsien Feng | 27.50 | 50.00 | 75.00 | 100.00 |

CAST BRASS
Obv: Type B

| 16-14 | ND(1875-1908) | Kuang Hsu | — | — | Rare | — |

20 CASH

CAST BRASS, 39mm
Obv: Type B-1

| 16-7 | ND(1851-61) | Hsien Feng | 30.00 | 45.00 | 65.00 | 100.00 |

30 CASH

CAST BRASS, 46mm
Obv: Type B-1

C#	Date	Emperor	Good	VG	Fine	VF
16-8	ND(1851-61)					
		Hsien Feng	100.00	150.00	175.00	300.00

Rev: Crescent in upper left and right corners; dot in lower
left and right corners.

16-8.1	ND(1851-61)					
		Hsien Feng	250.00	350.00	500.00	750.00

50 CASH

CAST COPPER, 50mm
Obv: Type B-1. Rev: Small characters.

16-9.1	ND(1851-61)					
		Hsien Feng	8.00	22.00	35.00	50.00

CAST BRASS, 55mm
Rev: Large characters.

16-9.2	ND(1851-61)					
		Hsien Feng	8.00	22.00	35.00	50.00

100 CASH

CAST BRASS
Obv: Type C
Obv: and rev: Small characters.

C#	Date	Emperor	Good	VG	Fine	VF
16-10	ND(1851-61)					
		Hsien Feng	10.00	25.00	35.00	75.00

Obv: and rev: Large characters.

16-10.1	ND(1851-61)					
		Hsien Feng	10.00	25.00	35.00	75.00

Milled Coinage
CASH

BRASS
Obv: Type A
Obv. and rev: Narrow rims.

Hsu#	Date	Mintage	VG	Fine	VF	XF
85	ND ca.1890	—	20.00	35.00	55.00	90.00

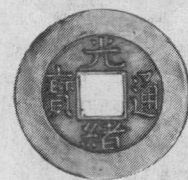

Obv. and rev: Wide rims.
| 85.1 | ND ca.1890 | — | — | — | Rare | — |

5 CASH

COPPER
Rev: Side view dragon, EIVE for FIVE.

Y#	Date	Mintage	VG	Fine	VF	XF
158	ND(1901)	—	20.00	32.50	55.00	100.00

BRASS
| 9n | CD1906 | | 35.00 | 75.00 | 125.00 | 200.00 |

10 CASH
BRASS

Y#	Date	Mintage	Fine	VF	XF	Unc
—	ND(1898)	—	—	—	Rare	—

COPPER
Rev: Cloud under all three letters of SOO.

Y#	Date	Mintage	VG	Fine	VF	XF
160	ND(1904-05)		1.50	2.50	4.00	8.00

Rev: Cloud under first two letters of SOO, Manchu
character at 9 o'clock higher, dragons body thinner.
| 160.1 | ND(1904-05) | | 1.50 | 2.50 | 4.00 | 8.00 |

Obv: Manchu characters at center, w/o rosettes.
Reeded edge.
| 162 | ND | — | .50 | 1.00 | 2.00 | 4.00 |

Obv: Manchu in center, rosettes at 2 and 10 o'clock.
| 162.1 | ND | | .50 | 1.00 | 2.00 | 4.00 |

Unreeded edge.
| 162.2 | ND | | .50 | 1.00 | 2.00 | 4.50 |

Obv. and rev: Tiny rosettes.
Reeded edge.
| 162.3 | ND | | .60 | 1.25 | 2.50 | 5.00 |

Obv: Rosette center, Manchu at 3 and 9 o'clock.
| 162.4 | ND | — | .30 | .75 | 1.50 | 3.50 |

Plain edge.
| 162.5 | ND | | .30 | .75 | 1.50 | 3.50 |

Obv: Rosette center, large Manchu at 3 and 9 o'clock,
higher than on Y#162.4. Reeded edge.
| 162.6 | ND | | .60 | 1.50 | 2.50 | 5.00 |

Plain edge.
| 162.7 | ND | | .60 | 1.50 | 2.50 | 5.00 |

BRASS
| 162.7a | ND | | — | — | Rare | — |

Kiangsu / Kiangsoo / CHINA   351

COPPER
Obv: Manchu characters at center, reeded edge.

Y#	Date	Mintage	VG	Fine	VF	XF
162.8	CD1902	—	.80	2.00	4.00	7.50

Plain edge.
| 162.13 | CD1902 | — | — | — | — | — |

Obv: Manchu characters at center, reeded edge.
| 162.9 | CD1903 | — | 2.00 | 5.00 | 7.50 | 12.00 |

Obv: Rosette center, small Manchu at 3 and 9 o'clock.
Unreeded edge.
| 162.10 | CD1905 | — | .50 | 1.00 | 2.00 | 4.50 |

Obv: Larger Manchu characters.
| 162.11 | CD1905 | — | 1.00 | 2.50 | 5.00 | 8.00 |

Rev: Kiangsu spelled KIANG-COO.
| 162.12 | CD1905 | — | 100.00 | 250.00 | 500.00 | 750.00 |

NOTE: Y#162.12 is considered a contemporary counterfeit by some authorities.

Mule. Obv: Kiangsu Y#162. Rev: Kiangnan Y#135.
| A162 | ND | — | 60.00 | 90.00 | 150.00 | 250.00 |

Mule. Obv: Kiangsu Y#162.8. Rev: Kiangnan Y#135.
| B162 | CD1902 | — | 60.00 | 90.00 | 150.00 | 250.00 |

Mule. Obv: Kiangsu Y#162.9. Rev: Kiangnan Y#135.
| C162 | CD1903 | — | 60.00 | 90.00 | 150.00 | 250.00 |

Obv: Mint mark incused on raised disc. Plain edge.
Y#	Date	Mintage	VG	Fine	VF	XF
10n	CD1906	—	1.00	2.50	5.00	10.00

Reeded edge.
| 10n.1 | CD1906 | — | 2.25 | 6.00 | 11.00 | 17.50 |

Obv: Mint mark in relief in field at center; w/o raised disc. Plain edge.
| 10n.2 | CD1906 | — | 2.25 | 6.00 | 11.00 | 17.50 |

20 CASH

COPPER
| 163 | ND | — | 17.50 | 32.50 | 45.00 | 65.00 |

BRASS
| 163a | ND | — | 30.00 | 45.00 | 70.00 | 110.00 |

COPPER
| 11n.1 | CD1906 | — | 25.00 | 40.00 | 60.00 | 90.00 |

BRASS
| 11n.1a | CD1906 | — | 35.00 | 60.00 | 90.00 | 150.00 |

Chingkiang Coinage

Chingkiang was a city in Kiangsu (Jiangsu) province. Some of the coins issued by the mint have the name spelled Tsing-Kiang in English. This is not an error as both spellings were acceptable at the time.

10 CASH

COPPER
Obv: Large character at 3 o'clock. Reeded edge.
| 77 | ND(1905) | — | 1.00 | 2.50 | 4.00 | 7.50 |

Plain edge.
| 77.1 | ND(1905) | — | 1.00 | 2.50 | 4.00 | 7.50 |

Obv: Ring around center dot in rosette.
Reeded edge.
| 77.2 | ND(1905) | — | 1.20 | 3.00 | 5.00 | 10.00 |

Plain edge.
| 77.3 | ND(1905) | — | 1.20 | 3.00 | 5.00 | 10.00 |

Obv: Smaller character at 3 o'clock. Reeded edge.
Y#	Date	Mintage	VG	Fine	VF	XF
77.4	ND(1905)	—	1.40	3.50	6.00	12.00

Plain edge.
| 77.5 | ND(1905) | — | 1.40 | 3.50 | 6.00 | 12.00 |

Obv: W/o rosette. Reeded edge.
| 77.6 | ND(1905) | — | 1.20 | 3.00 | 5.00 | 10.00 |

Plain edge.
| 77.7 | ND(1905) | — | 1.20 | 3.00 | 5.00 | 10.00 |

Obv: Large character at 3 o'clock. Reeded edge.
| 78 | ND(1905) | — | .60 | 1.50 | 3.00 | 5.00 |

Plain edge.
| 78.1 | ND(1905) | — | 1.20 | 3.00 | 5.00 | 10.00 |

Obv: Small character at 3 o'clock. Reeded edge.
| 78.2 | ND(1905) | — | .40 | 1.00 | 1.50 | 4.50 |

Plain edge.
| 78.3 | ND(1905) | — | .30 | .75 | 1.25 | 4.00 |

Obv: W/o rosette. Reeded edge.
| 78.4 | ND(1905) | — | 1.40 | 3.50 | 6.00 | 15.00 |

Obv: Small mint mark in center, w/o center raised disc.
Rev: Five flames on pearl.
| 10d | CD1906 | — | 15.00 | 25.00 | 50.00 | 100.00 |

Kirin / CHINA 352

Obv: Small mint mark. Rev: Seven flames on pearl.

Y#	Date	Mintage	VG	Fine	VF	XF
10d.1	CD1906	—	.60	1.50	2.50	5.00

Rev: Nine flames on pearl.

| 10d.2 | CD1906 | — | .40 | 1.00 | 2.00 | 4.00 |

Obv: Large mint mark. Rev: Five flames on pearl.

| 10d.3 | CD1906 | — | .60 | 1.50 | 2.50 | 5.00 |

Rev: Seven flames on pearl.

| 10d.4 | CD1906 | — | .60 | 1.50 | 2.50 | 5.00 |

Rev: Nine flames on pearl.

| 10d.5 | CD1906 | — | .60 | 1.50 | 2.50 | 5.00 |

Obv: Mint mark incused on raised disc.

| 10d.6 | CD1906 | — | — | — | Rare | — |

NOTE: A trial piece.

NOTE: The 10 Cash coins of Kiangsu (Jiangsu) and Chingkiang are often found plated with a silvery material. This was not done at the mint. Apparently they were plated to be passed to the unwary as silver coins.

Shanghai Coinage

NOTE: An important port city in Kiangsu (Jiangsu) province. Although there was no mint in Shanghai prior to the 1930's a number of coins were minted for Shanghai by silversmiths.

5 CH'IEN
SILVER, 18.40 g
Issued by Wang Yung-sheng. Engraved by Wan Ch'uan.
Similar to K#902.

K#	Year	Date	VG	Fine	VF	XF
908	6	(1856)	—	—	450.00	650.00

Issued by Yu Shen-sheng. Engraved by Wang Shou.

K#	Year	Date	VG	Fine	VF	XF
907	6	(1856)	—	—	350.00	500.00

Issued by Ching Cheng-chi. Engraved by Wan Ch'uan.

| 910 | 6 | (1856) | — | — | 350.00 | 500.00 |

LIANG (TAEL)

SILVER, 36.70 g
Issued by Wang Yung-sheng. Engraved by Wan Ch'uan.

| 900 | 6 | (1856) | — | — | 950.00 | 1200. |

Issued by Yu Sen-sheng. Engraved by P'ing Cheng.

| 902 | 6 | (1856) | — | — | 700.00 | 1000. |

Issued by Yu Sen-sheng. Engraved by Feng Nien.

| 901 | 6 | (1856) | — | — | 700.00 | 1000. |

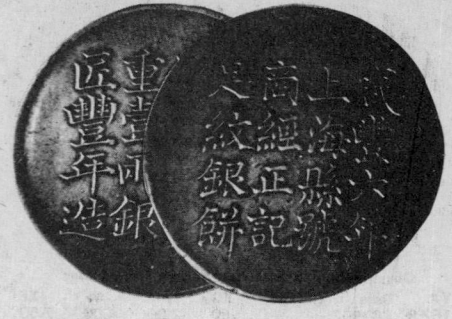

Issued by Ching Cheng-chi. Engraved by Feng Nien.

K#	Year	Date	VG	Fine	VF	XF
903	6	(1856)	—	—	700.00	1000.

K#900-910 above are known as "Silversmith" Taels because each bears the name of a silver smelting firm in Shanghai. The coins were authorized by the taotai (a government official) of Shanghai to facilitate foreign trade and to replace the vanishing Mexican 8 Reales which had become very scarce due to hoarding.

KIRIN PROVINCE
Jilin

A province of northeast China that was formed in 1945. Before that it was one of the three original provinces of Manchuria. Besides growing corn, wheat and tobacco, there is also coal mining. An arsenal in Kirin (Jilin) opened in 1881 and was chosen as a source for coinage attempts. In 1884 Tael trials were struck and regular coinage began in 1895. Modern equipment was installed in a new mint in Kirin (Jilin) in 1901. The issues of this mint were very prolific and many varieties exist due to the use of hand cut dies for the earlier issues. The mint burned down in 1911.

EMPIRE
CASH

CAST BRASS
Obv: Type A

C#	Date	Emperor	Good	VG	Fine	VF
17-1	(1875-1908)	Kuang Hsu	15.00	25.00	30.00	45.00

10 CASH

CAST BRASS
Obv: Type C

| 17-2 | (1875-1908) | Kuang Hsu | — | — | Rare | — |

MILLED COINAGE

NOTE: It has been estimated there are over 2500 die varieties of Kirin (Jilin) silver coins and more than 1000 varieties of copper 10 Cash. Listed here are basic types and major varieties only.

CASH

BRASS, struck
Obv: Type A

Hsu#	Date	Mintage	Fine	VF	XF	Unc
481	ND	—	200.00	250.00	300.00	400.00

NOTE: This coin is sometimes erroneously attributed to Chichou in Chihli (Hebei) province.

2 CASH

COPPER

Y#	Date	Mintage	VG	Fine	VF	XF
175	ND	—	70.00	110.00	150.00	200.00

10 CASH

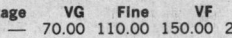

COPPER

Y#	Date	Mintage	VG	Fine	VF	XF
174	ND	—	110.00	200.00	325.00	425.00

| 176 | ND | — | 35.00 | 60.00 | 90.00 | 125.00 |

Rev: Thinner dragon.

| 176.1 | ND | — | 35.00 | 60.00 | 90.00 | 125.00 |

Obv: Small rosette. Rev: Large rosette.

| 177 | ND | — | 5.00 | 10.00 | 15.00 | 25.00 |

Rev: Small star.

| 177.1 | ND | — | 5.00 | 10.00 | 15.00 | 25.00 |

Obv: Small star. Rev: Large rosette.

| 177.2 | ND | — | 5.00 | 10.00 | 17.50 | 30.00 |

Obv. and rev: Small stars.

Y#	Date	Mintage	VG	Fine	VF	XF
177.3	ND	—	5.00	10.00	15.00	25.00

BRASS

| 177.3a | ND | — | 5.00 | 10.00 | 17.50 | 30.00 |

COPPER
Obv. and rev: Large stars.

| 177.4 | ND | — | 4.00 | 7.00 | 12.00 | 17.50 |

Obv: Large star. Rev: Large rosette.

| 177.5 | ND | — | 4.00 | 7.00 | 12.00 | 17.50 |

Obv: Medium rosettes.

| 177.6 | ND | — | 4.00 | 7.00 | 12.00 | 17.50 |

Rev. denomination spelled: CASHIS

| 177.7 | ND | — | 60.00 | 100.00 | 160.00 | 250.00 |

NOTE: It is difficult to differentiate the stars and rosettes on worn coins. The rosettes have a raised dot in the center while the stars have a hole in the center. It has been estimated that 1000 varieties of Y#177 exist.

Obv: Very small mint mark.

| 20p | CD1909 | — | 8.00 | 15.00 | 25.00 | 40.00 |

Obv: Larger mint mark. Rev: Head of dragon redesigned w/more whiskers.

| 20p.1 | CD1909 | — | 10.00 | 17.50 | 30.00 | 45.00 |

Obv: Larger mint mark. Rev: Dragon similar to Y#20p.

| 20p.2 | CD1909 | — | 10.00 | 17.50 | 30.00 | 45.00 |

NOTE: For YY20x refer to General Issues-Empire.

20 CASH

COPPER

Y#	Date	Mintage	VG	Fine	VF	XF
178	ND	—	35.00	65.00	100.00	150.00

Obv: Manchu in center, eight characters below.

| A176 | ND | — | 80.00 | 200.00 | 400.00 | 700.00 |

Obv: Rosette in center, three characters below.

| A176.1 | ND | — | 80.00 | 225.00 | 425.00 | 725.00 |

| 21p | CD1909 | — | 120.00 | 250.00 | 450.00 | 750.00 |

50 CASH

BRASS

Y#	Date	Mintage	Good	VG	Fine	VF
B176	CD1901	—	Rare			

NOTE: A similar 20 Cash and silver 50 Cent have been reported.

5 CENTS

SILVER, 1.27 g
Obv: Flower vase center.
Rev: Cross before and after denomination.

Y#	Date	Mintage	Fine	VF	XF	Unc
179	ND	—	9.00	18.50	37.50	75.00

Rev: W/o crosses.

179.1	ND	—	5.00	10.00	20.00	40.00
	CD1899	—	6.50	12.50	25.00	50.00
	CD1900	—	7.50	15.00	30.00	60.00

Kirin / CHINA

Y#	Date	Mintage	Fine	VF	XF	Unc
179.1	CD1906	—	6.50	12.50	25.00	50.00
	CD1907	—	6.50	12.50	25.00	50.00
	CD1908	—	—	—	Rare	—

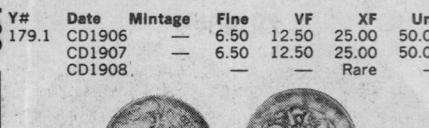

Obv: Yin-yang center.

179a	CD1900	—	7.50	15.00	30.00	60.00
	CD1901	—	5.50	11.50	22.50	45.00
	CD1902	—	6.50	12.50	25.00	50.00
	CD1903	—	12.50	25.00	50.00	100.00
	CD1904	—	5.50	11.50	22.50	45.00
	CD1905	—	7.50	15.00	30.00	60.00

10 CENTS

SILVER, 2.55 g
Obv: Small flower vase center.
Rev: Cross before and after denomination.

| 180 | ND | — | 5.50 | 11.50 | 22.50 | 45.00 |

Obv: Large flower vase center.
Rev: W/o cross flanking denomination.

180.1	ND	—	5.50	11.50	22.50	45.00
	CD1899	—	6.50	12.50	25.00	50.00
	CD1900	—	6.50	12.50	25.00	50.00
	CD1906	—	6.50	12.50	25.00	50.00
	CD1907	—	45.00	90.00	150.00	250.00

Obv: Yin-yang center.

180a	CD1900	—	7.50	15.00	30.00	60.00
	CD1901	—	5.50	11.50	22.50	45.00
	CD1902	—	7.50	15.00	30.00	60.00
	CD1903	—	9.00	18.50	37.50	75.00
	CD1904	—	10.00	20.00	40.00	80.00
	CD1905	—	5.50	11.50	22.50	45.00

Obv: Numeral 1 in center.

| 180c | CD1908 | — | 35.00 | 65.00 | 110.00 | 175.00 |

20 CENTS

SILVER, 5.10 g
Obv: Flower vase center.

181	ND	—	7.50	15.00	30.00	60.00
	CD1899	—	6.50	12.50	25.00	50.00
	CD1900	—	7.50	15.00	30.00	60.00
	CD1906	Inc. Be.	6.50	12.50	25.00	50.00
	CD1907	Inc. Be.	6.50	12.50	25.00	50.00
	CD1908	Inc. Be.	87.50	175.00	300.00	500.00

Obv: Yin-yang center.

181a	CD1900	—	7.50	15.00	30.00	60.00
	CD1901	22.508	6.50	12.50	25.00	50.00
	CD1902	Inc.Ab.	6.50	12.50	25.00	50.00
	CD1903	Inc.Ab.	6.50	12.50	25.00	50.00
	CD1904	Inc.Ab.	6.50	12.50	25.00	50.00
	CD1905	Inc.Ab.	6.50	12.50	25.00	50.00

Obv: Manchu characters center.

Y#	Date	Mintage	Fine	VF	XF	Unc
181b	CD1908	Inc.Ab.	35.00	70.00	120.00	225.00

Obv: Numeral 2 center.

| 181c | CD1908 | Inc.Ab. | 25.00 | 50.00 | 85.00 | 150.00 |

ZINC (OMS)

| 181d | CD1908 | — | — | — | — | — |

SILVER, 5.10 g
Obv: Mint mark in relief on raised disc at center.

| 22 | (1909) | — | 35.00 | 70.00 | 125.00 | 225.00 |

Obv: Mint mark incuse on raised disc at center.

| 22.1 | (1909) | — | 35.00 | 70.00 | 125.00 | 225.00 |

Obv: Mint mark in circle at center.

| 22.2 | (1909) | — | 35.00 | 70.00 | 125.00 | 225.00 |

50 CENTS

SILVER, 13.10 g
Obv: Flower vase center w/rosette at either side. Rev: W/o crosses flanking denomination.

| 182 | ND | — | 15.00 | 25.00 | 50.00 | 125.00 |

Obv: Rosette at either side. Rev: Crosses before and after denomination.

| 182.1 | ND | — | 15.00 | 25.00 | 50.00 | 125.00 |

Obv: W/o rosettes. Rev: W/o crosses.

182.2	ND	—	15.00	25.00	50.00	125.00
	CD1899	—	25.00	45.00	80.00	200.00
	CD1900	—	20.00	32.50	60.00	150.00
	CD1906	—	20.00	32.50	60.00	150.00

182.3	CD1907	—	20.00	32.50	60.00	150.00
	CD1908	—	47.50	80.00	125.00	300.00

Obv: Figure '8' Yin-yang in center.

Y#	Date	Mintage	Fine	VF	XF	Unc
182a	CD1900	—	20.00	32.50	60.00	150.00

Obv: Redesigned Yin-yang in center.

182a.1	CD1901	—	20.00	32.50	60.00	150.00
	CD1902	—	20.00	32.50	60.00	150.00
	CD1903	—	21.50	35.00	65.00	165.00
	CD1904	—	20.00	32.50	60.00	150.00
	CD1905	—	17.50	30.00	50.00	125.00

Obv: Manchu characters in center.

| 182b | CD1908 | — | 75.00 | 150.00 | 275.00 | 450.00 |

BRASS (OMS)

| 182c | CD1902 | — | — | — | — | — |

DOLLAR

SILVER, 26.10 g
Obv: Flower vase center.
Rev: Small rosettes before and after denomination.

183	ND	—	30.00	55.00	125.00	300.00
	CD1899	—	35.00	65.00	125.00	350.00
	CD1900	—	35.00	75.00	150.00	500.00
	CD1906	—	32.50	60.00	125.00	275.00
	CD1907	—	100.00	135.00	175.00	500.00
	CD1908	—	350.00	750.00	1500.	3000.

Obv: Large rosettes.
Rev: W/o rosettes before and after denomination.

| 183.1 | ND | — | 750.00 | 1350. | 2500. | 4500. |

Rev. leg: 3.2 CAINDARINS 2 (error).

| 183.2 | CD1906 | — | 100.00 | 135.00 | 175.00 | 475.00 |

Kirin / CHINA 355

Obv: Small rosettes.
Rev: Small rosettes before and after denomination.
Y#	Date	Mintage	Fine	VF	XF	Unc
183.3	ND	—	100.00	135.00	175.00	500.00

Obv: Small leaves out of left of basket.
Rev: Similar to Y#183.2.
| 183.4 | ND | — | 35.00 | 70.00 | 150.00 | 400.00 |

Obv: Figure '8' Yin-yang in center.
| 183a | CD1900 | — | 75.00 | 125.00 | 350.00 | 850.00 |

Obv: Redesigned Yin-yang in center.
Rev: Coarse scaled dragon.
| 183a.1 | CD1901 | — | 35.00 | 75.00 | 175.00 | 500.00 |
| | CD1902 | — | 35.00 | 70.00 | 150.00 | 350.00 |

Rev: Fine scaled dragon.
183a.2	CD1902	—	35.00	70.00	150.00	350.00
	CD1903	—	30.00	65.00	135.00	300.00
	CD1904	—	30.00	55.00	125.00	250.00
	CD1905	—	30.00	55.00	125.00	250.00

Obv: Manchu characters in center.
| 183b | CD1908 | — | 300.00 | 650.00 | 1150. | 2500. |

Obv: Numeral II in center.
Y#	Date	Mintage	Fine	VF	XF	Unc
183c	CD1908	—	350.00	850.00	1650.	2750.

NOTE: Errors in the English legends are common on Kirin (Jilin) coinage.

TAEL SERIES
CH'IEN (MACE)

SILVER, 3.60 g
Rev.: Numeral 1 in simple Chinese.
K#	Year	Date	Fine	VF	XF	Unc
919	10	(1884)	—	—	500.00	750.00

Rev: Different, more complicated character for 1.
| 920 | 10 | (1884) | — | — | 400.00 | 650.00 |

WHITE METAL (OMS)
| 920y | 10 | (1884) | — | — | — | — |

3 CH'IEN

SILVER, 10.80 g
Vertical edge reeding.
| 918 | 10 | (1884) | — | — | 500.00 | 750.00 |

Diagonal edge reeding.
| 918b | 10 | (1884) | — | — | 500.00 | 750.00 |

WHITE METAL (OMS)
| 918y | 10 | (1884) | — | — | — | — |

BRASS (OMS)
| 918z | 10 | (1884) | — | — | 850.00 | 1500. |

5 CH'IEN
(1/2 Tael)

SILVER, 17.80 g
| 917 | 10 | (1884) | — | — | 850.00 | 1500. |

WHITE METAL (OMS)
| 917y | 10 | (1884) | — | — | — | — |

7 CH'IEN

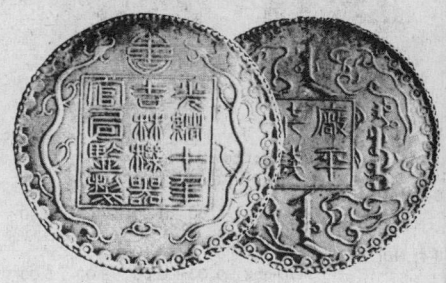

SILVER, 25.40 g
K#	Year	Date	Fine	VF	XF	Unc
916	10	(1884)	—	—	3500.	5000.

WHITE METAL (OMS)
| 916y | 10 | (1884) | — | — | — | — |

TAEL

SILVER, 35.50 g
| 915 | 10 | (1884) | — | — | 7500. | 10,000. |

WHITE METAL (OMS)
| 915y | 10 | (1884) | — | — | — | — |

KWANGSI/KWANGSEA
Guangxi

A hilly region in southeast China with many forests. Large amounts of rice are grown adjacent to the many rivers. A mint opened in Kweilin in 1667, closed in 1670, reopened in 1679, closed again in 1681. It reopened in the mid-1700's and was a rather prolific issuer of Cash coins. In 1905 the government allowed modern mints to be established in some of the southern regions. Three were established in Kwangsi (Guangxi)-Nanning (1905), Kweilin (1905), and Wuchow (1920). The Nanning Mint began operation in 1919 and closed in 1921. The nature and amount of activity of the other two mints is questionable.

EMPIRE
CASH
CAST BRASS
Obv: Type A
C#	Date	Emperor	Good	VG	Fine	VF
18-2	ND(1796-1820)	Chia Ch'ing	.20	.50	.85	1.25

Obv: Type A
| 18-3 | ND(1821-51) | Tao Kuang | .30 | .85 | 1.50 | 2.50 |

Kwangsi / CHINA   356

Rev: Dot below left.

C#	Date	Emperor	Good	VG	Fine	VF
18-3.1	ND(1821-51)	Tao Kuang	.60	1.00	2.00	3.00

Obv: Type A

| 18-4 | ND(1851-61) | Hsien Feng | 1.00 | 2.00 | 3.00 | 5.00 |

Obv: Type A-2
Rev: Large Manchu characters.

| 18-7 | ND(1862-74) | T'ung Chih | 2.50 | 3.50 | 6.50 | 9.00 |

Rev: Small Manchu characters.

| 18-7.1 | ND(1862-74) | T'ung Chih | 2.50 | 3.50 | 6.50 | 9.00 |

Rev: Circle above.

| 18-7.2 | ND(1862-74) | T'ung Chih | 5.50 | 8.50 | 13.50 | 20.00 |

Obv: Type A

| 18-9 | ND(1875-1908) | Kuang Hsu | 5.50 | 8.50 | 13.50 | 20.00 |

10 CASH

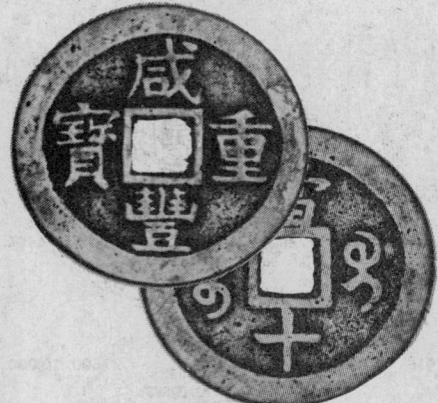

CAST BRASS
Obv: Type B-1

| 18-5 | ND(1851-61) | Hsien Feng | 3.00 | 7.00 | 9.00 | 12.00 |

Obv: Type B-2

| 18-8 | ND(1862-74) | T'ung Chih | — | Rare | | |

Obv: Type B

| 18-10 | ND(1875-1908) | Kuang Hsu | — | Rare | | |

50 CASH

CAST BRASS
Obv: Type B-1

| 18-6 | ND(1851-61) | Hsien Feng | 40.00 | 60.00 | 80.00 | 120.00 |

REPUBLIC
MILLED COINAGE
CENT

BRASS
Rev. leg: KWANG-SEA.

Y#	Year	Date	Fine	VF	XF	Unc
413	8	(1919)	40.00	100.00	175.00	350.00

Rev. leg: KWANG-SI.

| 413a | 8 | (1919) | 17.50 | 37.50 | 55.00 | 150.00 |

Rev: Large *Kuei* mint mark below PU.

| 347 | 28 | (1939) | — | — | Rare | — |

Rev: Small *Kuei* mint mark below PU.

| 347.1 | 28 | (1939) | — | — | Rare | — |

10 CENTS

SILVER, 2.70 g

| 414 | 9 | (1920) | 35.00 | 75.00 | 125.00 | 175.00 |

20 CENTS

SILVER, 5.30 g
Rev: KWANG-SEA.

415	8	(1919)	40.00	70.00	100.00	175.00
	9	(1920)	65.00	100.00	150.00	250.00
	13	(1924)	65.00	100.00	150.00	250.00

Rev: KWANG-SI.

415a	8	(1919)	8.00	15.00	40.00	125.00
	9	(1920)	6.00	17.50	45.00	100.00
	11	(1922)	6.00	15.00	40.00	100.00
	12	(1923)	4.00	9.00	20.00	40.00
	13	(1924)	4.00	7.50	12.50	25.00
	14	(1925)	4.00	7.50	12.50	25.00

Rev: Wreath added around '20'.

| 415b | 15 | (1926) | 3.50 | 6.50 | 10.00 | 20.00 |
| | 16 | (1927) | 3.50 | 6.50 | 13.00 | 22.50 |

Obv: Character *Kuei* in center instead of dot.

| 415a.1 | 13 | (1924) | 35.00 | 55.00 | 75.00 | 150.00 |

Rev: Elephant Nose Rock at Kueilin.

Y#	Year	Date	Fine	VF	XF	Unc
416	38	(1949)	50.00	75.00	125.00	200.00

KWANGTUNG PROVINCE
Guangdong

A province located on the southeast coast of China. Kwangtung (Guangdong) lies mostly in the tropics and has both mountains and plains. Its coastline is nearly 800 miles long and provides many good harbors. Because of the location of Guangzhou (Canton) in the province, Kwangtung (Guangdong) was the first to be visited by foreign traders. Hong Kong was ceded to Great Britain after the First Opium War in 1841. Kowloon was later ceded to Britain in 1860 (100 year lease in 1898) and Macao to Portugal in 1887, Kwangchowan was leased to France in 1898 (a property that was restored in 1946). A modern mint opened in Guangzhou (Canton) in 1889 with Edward Wyon as superintendent. The mint was a large issuer of coins until it closed in 1931. The Nationalists reopened the mint briefly in 1949, striking a few silver dollars, before abandoning the mainland for their retreat to Taiwan.

EMPIRE
CASH

CAST BRASS
Obv: Type A

C#	Date	Emperor	Good	VG	Fine	VF
19-2	ND(1796-1820)	Chia Ch'ing	.30	.75	1.50	2.50

CAST IRON

| 19-2a | ND(1796-1820) | Chia Ch'ing | — | — | Rare | — |

CAST BRASS
Obv: Type A

| 19-3 | ND(1821-51) | Tao Kuang | .20 | .50 | 1.00 | 2.00 |

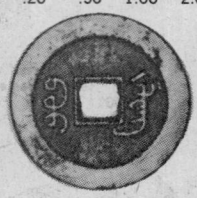

Obv: Type A

| 19-4 | ND(1851-61) | Hsien Feng | 1.50 | 2.50 | 3.50 | 5.00 |

Obv: Type A-2

| 19-5 | ND(1862-74) | T'ung Chih | 2.00 | 3.00 | 4.00 | 6.00 |

Obv: Type A

| 19-7 | ND(1875-1908) | Kuang Hsu | 5.00 | 8.00 | 11.00 | 15.00 |

10 CASH

CAST BRASS
Obv: Type B-2

| 19-6 | ND(1862-74) | T'ung Chih | — | — | Rare | — |

Obv: Type B

| 19-8 | ND(1875-1908) | Kuang Hsu | — | — | Rare | — |

MILLED COINAGE
CASH

BRASS, struck
Obv: Type A

Y#	Date	Mintage	Fine	VF	XF	Unc
189	ND(1889)	—	.25	.45	.85	3.00
	ND(1889)	—	—	—	Proof	—

Obv: *Kuang* in a different style.

Y#	Date	Mintage	Fine	VF	XF	Unc
189.1	ND(1889)	—	20.00	25.00	40.00	60.00

| 190 | ND(1890-1908) | 1059.253 | — | .10 | .20 | .50 |

| 191 | ND(1906-08) | — | — | .10 | .20 | .50 |

Obv: Type A

| 204 | ND (1909-11) | — | .50 | .75 | 1.00 | 3.00 |

CENT (10 CASH)

COPPER
Obv: Six characters at bottom. Rev: ONE CENT.

Y#	Date	Mintage	VG	Fine	VF	XF
192	ND(1900-06)	—	.30	.75	1.50	3.00

Mule. Obv: Y#192. Rev: Chihli 10 Cash Y#67.
| A192 | ND | — | 15.00 | 25.00 | 35.00 | 50.00 |

Obv: Seven characters at bottom. Rev: TEN CASH.
| 193 | ND(1900-06) | — | .50 | 1.00 | 2.00 | 4.00 |

Mule. Obv: Y#192. Rev: Y#193.
| A193 | ND | — | 12.50 | 20.00 | 28.50 | 40.00 |

Mule. Obv: Y#193. Rev: Y#192.
| B193 | ND | — | 12.50 | 20.00 | 28.50 | 40.00 |

W#	Date	Mintage	VG	Fine	VF	XF
896	—	—	65.00	100.00	150.00	225.00

Y#	Date	Mintage	VG	Fine	VF	XF
10r	CD1906	79.000	.40	1.00	2.00	4.00
	CD1907	46.000	.40	1.00	2.00	4.00
	CD1908	62.736	.40	1.00	2.00	4.00

Y#	Date	Mintage	VG	Fine	VF	XF
20r	CD1909	—	.60	1.50	3.00	5.00

5 CENTS

1.3000 g, .820 SILVER, .0343 oz ASW
Obv: 3.65 CANDAREENS.
Rev: Chinese characters around dragon.

Y#	Date	Mintage	Fine	VF	XF	Unc
194	ND(1889)	—	150.00	300.00	450.00	650.00

Obv: 3.6 CANDAREENS.
| 194.1 | ND(1889) | — | 275.00 | 550.00 | 850.00 | 1200. |

Rev: English legend around dragon.
| 199 | ND(1890-1905) | — | 2.00 | 3.50 | 6.00 | 12.00 |

COPPER (OMS)
| 199a | ND(1890-1905) | | | | | |

10 CENTS

2.7000 g, .820 SILVER, .0712 oz ASW
Obv: 7 3/10 CANDAREENS.

| 195 | ND(1889) | — | 90.00 | 175.00 | 275.00 | 450.00 |
| | ND(1889) | — | — | — | Proof | |

COPPER (OMS)
| 195a | ND(1889) | | | | | |

SILVER
Obv: 7.2 CANDAREENS.
| 195.1 | ND(1889) | — | 2000. | 3000. | 4500. | |

Rev: English legends around dragon.
| 200 | ND(1890-1900) | — | 2.25 | 3.00 | 4.00 | 12.00 |

COPPER (OMS)
| 200a | ND(1890-1900) | | | | | |

BRASS (OMS)
| 200b | ND(1890-1900) | | | | | |

20 CENTS

5.3000 g, .820 SILVER, .1397 oz ASW
Obv: 1 MACE AND 4 3/5 CANDAREENS.
| 196 | ND(1889) | — | 125.00 | 225.00 | 375.00 | 600.00 |
| | ND(1889) | — | — | — | Proof | |

COPPER (OMS)
| 196a | ND(1889) | — | — | — | 300.00 | |

SILVER
Obv: 1 MACE AND 4.4 CANDAREENS.
| 196.1 | ND(1889) | — | 2500. | 3500. | 5000. | |

Rev: English legends around dragon.

Y#	Date	Mintage	Fine	VF	XF	Unc
201	ND(1890-1908)	—	1.25	2.25	3.50	10.00
	ND(1890-1908)	10 known	—	—	Proof	400.00

COPPER (OMS)
| 201a | ND(1890-1908) | | | | | |

BRASS (OMS)
| 201b | ND(1890-1908) | | | | | |

5.5000 g, .800 SILVER, .1415 oz ASW
| 205 | ND(1909-11) | 94.774 | 4.50 | 6.00 | 9.00 | 20.00 |

NOTE: Two varieties of edge reeding known.

50 CENTS

13.8000 g, .860 SILVER, .3816 oz ASW
Obv: 3 MACE AND 6-1/2 CANDAREENS.
| 197 | ND(1889) | — | 325.00 | 625.00 | 900.00 | 1400. |

COPPER (OMS)
| 197a | ND(1889) | — | — | — | Rare | |

SILVER
Obv: 3 MACE AND 6 CANDAREENS.
| 197.1 | ND(1889) | — | — | 6500. | 10,000. | 15,000. |

COPPER (OMS)
| 197.1a | ND(1889) | — | — | — | Rare | |

13.5000 g, .860 SILVER, .3733 oz ASW
Rev: English legends around dragon.
| 202 | ND(1890-1905) | — | 15.00 | 25.00 | 50.00 | 125.00 |
| | ND(1890-1905) | — | — | — | Proof | 500.00 |

COPPER (OMS)
| 202a | ND(1890-1905) | — | — | — | Rare | |

Kwangtung / CHINA 358

DOLLAR

27.4000 g, .900 SILVER, .7929 oz ASW
Obv: 7 MACE AND 3 CANDAREENS

Y#	Date	Mintage	Fine	VF	XF	Unc
198	ND(1889)	—	1250.	1750.	2500.	4500.
	ND(1889)	—	—	—	Proof	10,000.

Obv: 7 MACE AND 2 CANDAREENS.
198.1 ND(1889) — — — — 35,000.
NOTE: Considered a pattern.

COPPER (OMS)
198.1a ND(1889) — — — Rare —

27.0000 g, .900 SILVER, .7814 oz ASW
Rev: English legends around dragon.

Y#	Date	Mintage	Fine	VF	XF	Unc
203	ND(1890-1908)		7.00	10.00	22.50	150.00
	ND(1890-1908)		—	—	Proof	750.00

COPPER (OMS)
203a ND(1890-1908) — — — — 450.00

27.0000 g, .900 SILVER, .7814 oz ASW
Obv: Different characters at top and bottom.
206 ND(1909-11) 10.00 15.00 30.00 150.00

REPUBLIC
CENT

COPPER

417	Yr.1 (1912)				
		18.836	1.50	2.25	5.00	17.50
	Yr.3 (1914)				
		14.750	1.50	2.25	5.00	17.50
	Yr.4 (1915)				
		6.350	4.00	6.00	15.00	35.00
	Yr.5 (1916)				
		18.388	2.00	3.00	7.50	22.50
	Yr.7 (1918)	—	7.50	12.50	20.00	45.00

BRASS

417a	Yr.3 (1914) I.A.	2.00	5.00	10.00	25.00
	Yr.4 (1915) I.A.	3.00	7.50	15.00	30.00
	Yr.5 (1916) I.A.	1.25	3.00	6.00	20.00
	Yr.7 (1918) —	4.00	10.00	20.00	45.00

2 CENTS

BRASS
418 Yr.7 (1918) — 30.00 50.00 90.00 175.00
COPPER
418a Yr.7 (1918) — — — Rare —

5 CENTS

COPPER-NICKEL

Y#	Date	Mintage	Fine	VF	XF	Unc
420	Yr.8 (1919)	.916	.50	1.25	2.25	4.00

| 421 | Yr.10 (1921) | | | | | |
| | | .666 | 1.25 | 3.00 | 6.50 | 12.50 |

| 420a | Yr.12 (1923) | | | | | |
| | | .480 | .50 | 1.25 | 2.25 | 4.00 |

10 CENTS

SILVER, 2.70 g

422	Yr.2 (1913)					
		8.798	1.25	2.50	4.00	8.00
	Yr.3 (1914)	I.A.	1.75	3.00	4.50	9.00
	Yr.11 (1922)	—	2.00	4.00	6.50	12.50

COPPER (OMS)
422a Yr.3 (1914) — — — — —

SILVER, 2.50 g

| 425 | Yr.18 (1929) | | | | | |
| | | 48.960 | 1.50 | 2.25 | 3.25 | 7.00 |

20 CENTS

SILVER, 5.40 g

423	Yr.1 (1912)					
		88.000	BV	2.50	6.00	12.00
	Yr.2 (1913)					
		109.974	BV	2.50	6.00	12.00
	Yr.3 (1914)					
		41.691	BV	2.50	6.00	12.00
	Yr.4 (1915)					
		22.332	4.00	10.00	30.00	100.00
	Yr.7 (1918)	—	BV	2.50	5.00	10.00
	Yr.8 (1919)					
		195.000	BV	1.25	2.50	5.00
	Yr.9 (1920)					
		197.000	BV	1.25	2.50	5.00
	Yr.10 (1921)					
		402.250	BV	1.25	2.50	5.00
	Yr.11 (1922)					
		350.000	BV	1.25	2.50	5.00
	Yr.12 (1923)					
		4.400	2.00	3.50	7.00	12.50
	Yr.13 (1924)					
		55.109	2.00	3.50	8.25	16.50

NOTE: The fineness of many of these 20 cent pieces especially those dated Yr.13 (1924) is as low as .500. In 1924 the Anhwei (Anhui) Mint secretly produced quantities of Kwangtung (Guangdong) 20 cent pieces which were only .400 fine.

COPPER (OMS)
423a	Yr.8 (1919)	—	—	—	—
	Yr.9 (1920)	—	—	—	—
	Yr.10 (1921)	—	—	—	—

SILVER, 5.30 g

Y#	Date	Mintage	Fine	VF	XF	Unc
424	Yr.13 (1924)	I.A.	8.50	17.50	32.50	60.00

GOLD (OMS)

| 424a | Yr.13 (1924) | — | — | — | — | — |

SILVER, 5.30 g

426	Yr.17 (1928)	28.530	15.00	37.50	65.00	110.00
	Yr.18 (1929)	779.738	BV	2.25	3.25	6.50

COPPER (OMS)

426a	Yr.17 (1928)	—	—	—	—	—
	Yr.18 (1929)	—	—	—	—	—

GOLD (OMS)

| 426b | — | — | — | 800.00 | — | — |

SPECIMEN SETS (SS)

KM#	Date	Mintage	Identification	Issue Price	Mkt. Val.
SS1	1889(10)	—	Y189,195-198 (2 each)	—	—
SS2	1890(?)	—	Y189-190,199-203	—	2000.

KWEICHOW PROVINCE
Guizhou

A province located in southern China. It is basically a plateau region that is somewhat remote from the general traffic of China. The Kweichow Mint opened in 1730 and produced Cash coins until the end of the reign of Kuang Hsu. The Republic issues for this province are enigmatic as to their origin, as a mint supposedly did not exist in Kweichow (Guizhou) at this time.

EMPIRE
CASH
CAST BRASS
Obv: Type A

C#	Date	Emperor	Good	VG	Fine	VF
20-2	ND(1796-1820)	Chia Ch'ing	.40	1.00	1.25	1.75

Rev: Dot above.

| 20-2.1 | ND(1796-1820) | Chia Ch'ing | .80 | 2.00 | 3.00 | 4.00 |

Rev: Character Erh (two) above.

| 20-2.2 | ND(1796-1820) | Chia Ch'ing | 5.50 | 8.50 | 13.50 | 20.00 |

Obv: Type A

| 20-3 | ND(1821-50) | Tao Kuang | .60 | 1.50 | 2.00 | 3.00 |

Rev: Crescent above.

| 20-3.1 | ND(1821-50) | Tao Kuang | 3.50 | 6.00 | 9.00 | 13.50 |

Rev: Circle above.

| 20-3.2 | ND(1821-50) | Tao Kuang | 3.50 | 6.00 | 9.00 | 13.50 |

Rev: Dot inside circle above.

| 20-3.3 | ND(1821-50) | Tao Kuang | 2.50 | 5.00 | 6.50 | 9.00 |

Rev: Dot above.

| 20-3.4 | ND(1821-50) | Tao Kuang | 2.50 | 5.00 | 6.50 | 9.00 |

Rev: An X above.

| 20-3.5 | ND(1821-50) | Tao Kuang | 5.50 | 8.50 | 13.50 | 20.00 |

Rev: A triangle above.

| 20-3.6 | ND(1821-50) | Tao Kuang | 5.50 | 8.50 | 13.50 | 20.00 |

Rev: Character Yi (one) above.

| 20-3.7 | ND(1821-50) | | | | | |

Rev: Character Ta (large) above.

C#	Date	Emperor	Good	VG	Fine	VF
20-3.8	ND(1821-50)	Tao Kuang	5.50	8.50	13.50	20.00

Rev: Crescent below.

| 20-3.9 | ND(1821-50) | Tao Kuang | 3.50 | 6.00 | 9.00 | 13.50 |

Rev: An X below.

| 20-3.10 | ND(1821-50) | Tao Kuang | 5.50 | 50 | 13.50 | 20.00 |

Rev: Dot below.

| 20-3.11 | ND(1821-50) | Tao Kuang | 3.00 | 5.50 | 8.00 | 11.50 |

Rev: Inverted triangle below.

| 20-3.12 | ND(1821-50) | Tao Kuang | 5.50 | 8.50 | 13.50 | 20.00 |

Rev: Yi (one) below.

| 20-3.13 | ND(1821-50) | Tao Kuang | 5.50 | 8.50 | 13.50 | 20.00 |

Rev: Liu (six) above.

| 20-3.14 | ND(1821-50) | Tao Kuang | 5.50 | 8.50 | 13.50 | 20.00 |

Rev: Chi (seven) below.

| 20-3.15 | ND(1821-50) | Tao Kuang | 5.50 | 8.50 | 13.50 | 20.00 |

Obv: Type A

| 20-4 | ND(1851-61) | Hsien Feng | 1.50 | 2.50 | 4.00 | 6.00 |

Rev: Dot above.

| 20-4.1 | ND(1851-61) | Hsien Feng | 2.50 | 4.00 | 5.00 | 7.00 |

Rev: Two vertical lines above.

| 20-4.2 | ND(1851-61) | Hsien Feng | 5.50 | 8.50 | 13.50 | 20.00 |

Rev: Three vertical lines above.

| 20-4.3 | ND(1851-61) | Hsien Feng | 5.50 | 8.50 | 13.50 | 20.00 |

Rev: An "X" above.

C#	Date	Emperor	Good	VG	Fine	VF
20-4.4	ND(1851-61)	Hsien Feng	5.50	8.50	13.50	20.00

Rev: Character Chi (seven) above.

| 20-4.5 | ND(1851-61) | Hsien Feng | 5.50 | 8.50 | 13.50 | 20.00 |

Rev: Character Shih (ten) above.

| 20-4.6 | ND(1851-61) | Hsien Feng | 5.50 | 8.50 | 13.50 | 20.00 |

Rev: Character Wen (unit) lying on its side above.

| 20-4.7 | ND(1851-61) | Hsien Feng | 5.50 | 8.50 | 13.50 | 20.00 |

Rev: Character Shih above and crescent below.

| 20-4.8 | ND(1851-61) | Hsien Feng | 5.50 | 8.50 | 13.50 | 20.00 |

Obv: Type A-2

| 20-7 | ND(1862-74) | T'ung Chih | — | — | Rare | — |

Obv: Type A

| 20-9 | ND(1875-1908) | Kuang Hsu | 4.00 | 7.50 | 10.00 | 14.00 |

Rev: Dot above.

| 20-9.1 | ND(1875-1908) | Kuang Hsu | 5.00 | 9.00 | 12.50 | 17.50 |

Rev: Character Kung above.

| 20-9.2 | ND(1875-1905) | Kuang Hsu | 8.50 | 11.50 | 16.50 | 25.00 |

10 CASH

CAST BRASS, 38mm
Obv: Type B-1

| 20-5 | ND(1851-61) | Hsien Feng | 18.00 | 25.00 | 35.00 | 50.00 |

25mm

| 20-5.1 | ND(1851-61) | Hsien Feng | 35.00 | 55.00 | 75.00 | 100.00 |

Obv: Type B-2

| 20-8 | ND(1862-74) | T'ung Chih | — | — | Rare | — |

Obv: Type B

| 20-10 | ND(1875-1908) | Kuang Hsu | — | — | Rare | — |

50 CASH
CAST BRASS
Obv: Type B-1

| 20-6 | ND(1851-61) | Hsien Feng | 60.00 | 85.00 | 110.00 | 150.00 |

Kweichow / CHINA 360

MILLED COINAGE
50 CENTS

K#	Year	Date	VG	Fine	VF	XF
10	14	(1888)	—	—	Rare	—

DOLLAR

SILVER, 24.80 g

9	14	(1888)	—	—	Rare	—

(11)	14	(1888)	—	—	Rare	—

22.60 g

12	16	(1890)	—	—	Rare	—

K#	Year	Date	VG	Fine	VF	XF
13	16	(1890)	—	—	Rare	—

NOTE: The Kweichow (Guizhou) coins above, obviously copied from contemporary Japanese coins, are still a mystery. Even as late as the 1920's Kweichow (Guizhou) was a very primitive area. It is highly unlikely that the coins were made there in the 1880's and 1890's. It is possible that they were minted elsewhere, possibly in one of the central coastal provinces.

REPUBLIC
1/2 CENT

COPPER

Y#	Year	Date	VG	Fine	VF	XF
A429	38	1949	450.00	750.00	—	—

BRASS

A429a	38	1949	325.00	550.00	—	—

10 CENTS

ANTIMONY

429	20	(1931)	225.00	425.00	625.00	925.00

20 CENTS

SILVER

Y#	Year	Date	Fine	VF	XF	Unc
430	38	(1949)	100.00	175.00	275.00	400.00

431	38	(1949)	300.00	575.00	900.00	1500.

50 CENTS

SILVER

Y#	Year	Date	Fine	VF	XF	Unc
432	38	(1949)	275.00	500.00	1000.	1500.

DOLLAR

SILVER, 25.80 g
First Road in Kweichow

Y#	Date	Mintage	Fine	VF	XF	Unc
428	Yr.17 (1928)	.648	150.00	300.00	600.00	3000.

NOTE: This coin is known as the 'Auto Dollar' as it purports to portray the governor's automobile. Minor varieties exist in Chinese legends and automobile design.

26.40 g

Y#	Year	Date	Fine	VF	XF	Unc
433	38	(1949)	300.00	600.00	800.00	2000.

NOTE: This coin is known as the 'Bamboo Dollar.'

MANCHURIAN PROVINCES

For coins of Manchuria refer to listings under Fengtien (Liaoning).

PEI YANG

For coins of Pei Yang refer to listings under Chihli (Hebei).

SHANSI PROVINCE
Shanxi

A province located in northeastern China that has some of the richest coal deposits in the world. Parts of the Great Wall cross the province. Extensive agriculture of early China started here. Cited as a "model province" in the new Chinese Republic. Intermittently active mint from 1645. The modern mint was established in 1919. It operated until the mid-1920's and closed because of the public's resistance against the coins that were being produced.

EMPIRE
CASH

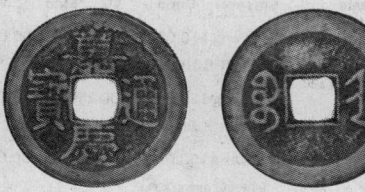

CAST BRASS
Obv: Type A

C#	Date	Emperor	Good	VG	Fine	VF
21-2	ND(1796-1820)	Chia Ch'ing	.25	.50	1.00	1.50

Obv: Type A

| 21-3 | ND(1821-50) | Tao Kuang | 1.25 | 2.50 | 3.00 | 6.00 |

Obv: Type A

| 21-4 | ND(1851-61) | Hsien Feng | 18.50 | 27.50 | 35.00 | 45.00 |

Obv: Type A-2

| 21-6 | ND(1862-74) | T'ung Chih | 8.50 | 17.50 | 25.00 | 35.00 |

Obv: Type A

| 21-8 | ND(1875-1908) | Kuang Hsu | 6.50 | 11.50 | 17.50 | 25.00 |

10 CASH

CAST BRASS
Obv: Type B-1

| 21-5 | ND(1851-61) | Hsien Feng | 12.00 | 20.00 | 27.50 | 40.00 |

Obv: Type B-2

| 21-7 | ND(1862-74) | T'ung Chih | — | — | Rare | — |

Obv: Type B

| 21-9 | ND(1875-1908) | Kuang Hsu | — | — | Rare | — |

REPUBLIC
MILLED COINAGE
10 CASH (1 CENT)

COPPER

Y#	Date	Mintage	Fine	VF	XF	Unc
A435	ND	—	100.00	175.00	225.00	275.00

20 CENTS

SILVER, 4.80 g

Y#	Date	Mintage	VG	Fine	VF	XF
217	ND (ca.1913)	—	100.00	175.00	300.00	400.00

NOTE: Several varieties exist similar to Y#217, but struck cruder, base metal and with different Chinese legends at top of obverse. English legends are usually blundered. Struck about 1913 and thought to be war lord issues. Do not confuse with coins of Fengtien (Liaoning), from which this was copied.

SHANTUNG PROVINCE
Shandong

A province located on the northeastern coast of China. Confucius was born in this province. Parts of the province were leased to Great Britain and to Germany. Farming, fishing and mining are the chief occupations. A mint was opened at Tsinan in 1647 and was an intermittent producer for the empire. A modern mint was opened at Tsinan in 1905, but later closed in 1906. Patterns were prepared between 1926-1933 in anticipation of a new coinage, but none were struck for circulation.

EMPIRE
CASH

CAST BRASS
Obv: Type A

C#	Date	Emperor	Good	VG	Fine	VF
22-2	ND(1851-61)	Hsien Feng	16.50	30.00	45.00	60.00

Obv: Type A-2

| 22-5 | ND(1862-74) | T'ung Chih | 10.00 | 18.50 | 27.50 | 40.00 |

Obv: Type A. Rev: Type 1 mint mark.

| 22-6 | ND(1875-1908) | Kuang Hsu | 10.00 | 18.50 | 27.50 | 40.00 |

MILLED COINAGE
2 CASH

COPPER

Y#	Date	Mintage	VG	Fine	VF	XF
8s	CD1906	—	12.00	25.00	35.00	70.00

10 CASH

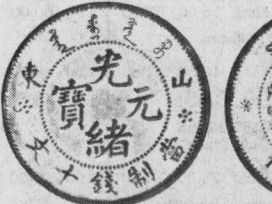 

COPPER

| 220 | ND(1904-05) | — | 4.00 | 8.00 | 15.00 | 30.00 |

Obv: Thin Manchu characters in center.
Rev: SHANTUNG.

Y#	Date	Mintage	VG	Fine	VF	XF
221	ND(1904-05)	3.50	7.00	11.00	17.50

Obv: Thick Manchu in center.

| 221.1 | ND(1904-05) | 1.75 | 3.50 | 7.00 | 14.00 |

Obv: Smaller stars.

| 221.2 | ND(1904-05) | 1.75 | 3.50 | 7.00 | 14.00 |

Obv: Similar to Y#220. Rev: Similar to Y#221.

| 221.3 | ND(1904-05) | 65.00 | 125.00 | 200.00 | 300.00 |

Obv: Thick Manchu in center. Rev: SHANG-TUNG.

| 221a | ND(1904-05) | 1.50 | 2.50 | 4.00 | 7.50 |

Obv: Thin Manchu.

| 221a.1 | ND(1904-05) | 2.50 | 5.00 | 10.00 | 17.50 |

BRASS
Rev: Six large waves under dragon.

| 10s | CD1906 | — | 3.00 | 6.00 | 10.00 | 17.50 |

COPPER

| 10s.1 | CD1906 | — | 3.50 | 7.00 | 12.00 | 25.00 |

Shantung / CHINA 362

Y#	Date	Mintage	VG	Fine	VF	XF
10s.1a	CD1906	—	2.50	5.00	10.00	17.50

Rev: Five small waves under dragon.

Rev: Dragon w/larger forehead and narrower face, pearl redesigned.

10s.2a	CD1906	—	4.00	8.00	15.00	30.00

SHENSI PROVINCE
Shaanxi

A province located in central China that is a rich agricultural area. A very important province in the early development of China. An active imperial mint was located at Sian (Xian).

EMPIRE
CASH

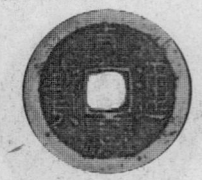

CAST BRASS or COPPER
Obv: Type A

C#	Date	Emperor	Good	VG	Fine	VF
23-2	ND(1796-1820)	Chia Ch'ing	1.50	3.00	4.00	6.00

23-3	ND(1821-50)	Tao Kuang	2.00	4.00	6.00	8.50

Obv: Type A

23-4	ND(1851-61)	Hsien Feng	2.50	5.00	7.50	12.50

CAST IRON

23-4a	ND(1851-61)	Hsien Feng	—	—	Rare	—

CAST BRASS
Obv: Type A-2

23-11	ND(1862-74)	T'ung Chih	—	—	Rare	—

Obv: Type A

23-13	ND(1875-1908)	Kuang Hsu	20.00	35.00	50.00	75.00

10 CASH

CAST BRASS, 43mm
Obv: Type B-1

C#	Date	Emperor	Good	VG	Fine	VF
23-5	ND(1851-61)	Hsien Feng	10.00	15.00	25.00	40.00

36mm

23-5.1	ND(1851-61)	Hsien Feng	18.50	30.00	50.00	75.00

Rev: Character *Shen* (for Shensi) above center hole.

23-6	ND(1851-61)	Hsien Feng	40.00	65.00	90.00	125.00

Obv: Type B-2

23-12	ND(1862-74)	T'ung Chih	—	—	Rare	—

Obv: Type B

23-14	ND(1875-1908)	Kuang Hsu	—	—	Rare	—

50 CASH

CAST BRASS
Obv: Type B-1

23-7	ND(1851-61)	Hsien Feng	10.00	17.50	25.00	40.00

100 CASH

CAST BRASS, 57mm
Obv: Type C

23-8.1	ND(1851-61)	Hsien Feng	35.00	55.00	75.00	100.00

50mm

23-8.2	ND(1851-61)	Hsien Feng	10.00	17.50	25.00	40.00

500 CASH

CAST BRASS
Obv: Type C

23-9	ND(1851-61)	Hsien Feng	75.00	110.00	150.00	200.00

Rev: Character *Kuan* (official) cast on rim.

23-9.1	ND(1851-61)	Hsien Feng	125.00	175.00	250.00	350.00

1000 CASH

CAST BRASS
Obv: Type C

C#	Date	Emperor	Good	VG	Fine	VF
23-10	ND(1851-61)	Hsien Feng	110.00	165.00	225.00	300.00

CAST COPPER

23-10a	ND(1851-61)	Hsien Feng	120.00	175.00	250.00	350.00

Rev: Character *Kuan* cast on rim.

23-10.1	ND(1851-61)	Hsien Feng	150.00	220.00	300.00	400.00

REPUBLIC

Obv. legends:
IMTYPIF; I MEI TA YUAN PI I FEN
(One Piece Great Dollar Coin - 1 Cent)
IMTYPEF: Ehr Fen or 2 Fen

CENT

COPPER

Y#	Date	Mintage	VG	Fine	VF	XF
435	ND ca.1928	—	75.00	125.00	225.00	300.00

2 CENTS

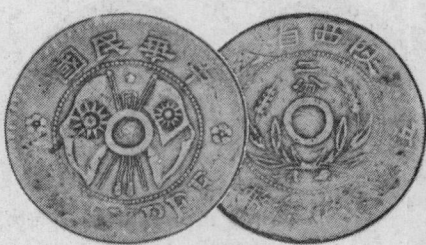

COPPER
Obv: Star between flags.

436	ND ca.1928	—	35.00	60.00	90.00	150.00

Obv: W/o star between flags.

436.1	ND ca.1928	—	25.00	50.00	80.00	125.00

Obv. and rev: Star in center.

436.2	ND ca.1928	—	60.00	100.00	150.00	250.00

SINKIANG PROVINCE
Hsinkiang, Xinjiang
"New Dominion"

An autonomous region in western China. High mountains surround 2000 ft. tableland on three sides with a large desert in center of this province. Many salt lakes, mining and some farming and oil. Inhabited by early man and was referred to as the "Silk Route" to the West. Sinkiang (Xinjiang) has been historically, under the control of many factions, including Genghis Khan. It became a province in 1884. China has made claim to Sinkiang (Xinjiang) for many, many years. This rule has been more nominal than actual. Sinkiang (Xinjiang) had eight imperial mints, only three of which were in operation towards the end of the reign of Kuang Hsu. Only two mints operated during the early years of the republic. In 1949, due to a drastic coin shortage and lack of confidence in the inflated paper money, it was planned to mint some dollars in Sinkiang (Xinjiang). These did not see much circulation however due to the defeat of the nationalists, though they have recently appeared in considerable numbers in

today's market.

PATTERNS

NOTE: A number of previously listed cast coins of Sinkiang Province are now known to be patterns - "mother" cash or "seed" cash for which no circulating issues are known. The following coins are, therefore, no longer listed Most were probably manufactured in Beijing. They are generally made of brass rather than the purer copper usual to Sinkiang. The following coins are, therefore, no longer listed here: 30-9, 30-11a, 30-12a, 30-14, 30-15a, 30-16, 30-17, 28-4.1, 28-8a, 28-9a, 28-9c, 28-10, 31-1a, 31-1v, 31-2, 32-4, 32-5, 33-12, 33-21, 34-2, 34-3, 35-5a, 35-6 and 38-8.

MONETARY SYSTEM

2 Pul = 1 Cash
2 Cash = 5 Li
4 Cash = 10 Li = 1 Fen
25 Cash = 10 Fen = 1 Miscal = 1 Ch'ien, Mace, Tanga
10 Miscals (Mace) = 1 Liang (Tael or Sar)
20 Miscals (Tangas) = 1 Tilla

MINT NAME
LOCAL MINT NAMES AND MARKS

MINT	CHINESE	TURKI	MANCHU
Aksu	阿城	اقصو	
Ili	伊犁	الي	
Kashgar now Kashi	喀什	كشقر	
Khotan now Hotan	和闐	خوتن	
Kotsha		كوتشر	
Kuche	庫車		
Urumchi now Urumqi	廸化	ارومجي	
Ushi now Wushih	烏什	اوش	
Yanghissar now Yengisar	英吉沙		
Yarkand now Sache	葉爾羌	يارقند	

GENERAL COINAGE
EMPIRE
CASH
CAST COPPER
Rev: *Boo Chiowan* (Manchu for Pao Chuan - Board of Revenue)

KM#	Date	Emperor	Good	VG	Fine	VF
10	ND (1875-1908)	Kuang Hsu	1.50	3.00	5.00	8.50

Rev: Similar to KM#10 but *Boo* in mirror image.
| 11 | ND (1875-1908) | Kuang Hsu | 3.50 | 6.00 | 9.00 | 13.50 |

Rev: Similar to KM#10 but *Boo Chiowan* in mirror image.
| 12 | ND (1875-1908) | Kuang Hsu | 1.50 | 3.00 | 5.00 | 8.50 |

Rev: *Boo Chaun* or *Yaun* (illiterate Manchu).
KM#	Date	Emperor	Good	VG	Fine	VF
13	ND (1875-1908)	Kuang Hsu	1.50	3.00	5.00	8.50

Rev: *Boo Choan* (illiterate Manchu).
| 14 | ND (1875-1908) | Kuang Hsu | 1.50 | 3.00 | 5.00 | 8.50 |

NOTE: The five one-cash varieties listed above could be confused with Beijing issues C1-16 or C2-15, but they are much more crudely cast, and are made of red copper rather than brass. See Landon Ross, 1986, Numismatics International Bulletin 20(3) for a more detailed review.

10 CASH
CAST COPPER
Rev: *Pao Yuan?* w/*Hsin* (new) above.
| 3 | ND(1821-50) | Tao Kuang | 8.50 | 15.00 | 25.00 | 40.00 |

Rev: *Pao Yuan?* w/*Hsin* (new) above.
| 5 | ND(1862-74) | | | | | |
| (C33-15) | | T'ung Chih | 8.50 | 15.00 | 25.00 | 40.00 |

NOTE: All of the above were probably cast in the reign of Kuang Hsu (1875-1908).

Obv: **Type A**
Rev: *Pao Yuan?* w/*K'a* (for Kashgar) above.
| 6 | ND(1875-1908) | | | | | |
| (C33-25) | | Kuang Hsu | 2.50 | 3.50 | 5.00 | 12.50 |

Rev: *Pao Yuan?* w/*K'u* (for Kuche) above.
| 7.1 | ND(1875-1908) | Kuang Hsu | 2.50 | 3.50 | 5.00 | 10.00 |

Rev: *Pao* at left reversed.
| 7.2 | ND(1875-1908) | Kuang Hsu | 7.50 | 13.50 | 22.50 | 35.00 |

Rev: *Pao Yuan?* w/*Hsin* (new) above.
| 8 | ND(1875-1908) | | | | | |
| (C33-20) | | Kuang Hsu | 3.50 | 5.00 | 7.50 | 15.00 |

Rev: *Pao Hsin* (for Sinkiang - New Territory) w/ *Hsin* (new) above.
| 9 | ND(1875-1908) | | | | | |
| (C33-24) | | Kuang Hsu | 3.50 | 5.00 | 7.50 | 15.00 |

Rev: *Pao Yuan?* w/*A* (for Aksu) above.
| 15 | ND (1875-1908) | Kuang Hsu | 12.00 | 15.00 | 21.50 | 28.50 |

Obv: *Kuang Hsu Ting Wu*.
Rev: *Pao Yuan?* w/*Hsin* (new) above.
| 16 | CD1907 | Kuang Hsu | 17.50 | 23.50 | 30.00 | 45.00 |

Obv: *Kuang Hsu Mou Shen*.
| 17 | CD1908 | Kuang Hsu | 23.50 | 32.50 | 45.00 | 60.00 |

HAMMERED COINAGE
1/2 MISCAL (5 FEN)

SILVER, 1.45 g
Obv: *On gumush*.
Rev: *Besh Fen* (5 Fen), w/o mint name.

Y#	Date	Mintage	Good	VG	Fine	VF
A7.1	ND	—	5.00	7.00	10.00	15.00
(Y-A7.2)	AH1294	—	5.00	7.00	10.00	15.00
	1295	—	5.00	7.00	10.00	15.00

Obv: *Kang Hsu Beg*.
Rev: *Fourth year* in Turki script.
| A7.2 | Yr.4 (1878) | — | 5.50 | 10.00 | 15.00 | 20.00 |
| (Y-A7.3) | AH1295 | — | 5.50 | 10.00 | 15.00 | 20.00 |

Obv. leg: Turki. Rev. leg: Manchu.
| A7.3 | ND | — | — | Rare | — | — |
| (K995) | | | | | | |

MILLED COINAGE
Fen and Li Series
FEN, 5 LI

COPPER
| 1 | ND | — | 150.00 | 200.00 | 350.00 | 550.00 |

NOTE: Two varieties are reported.

Obv: **Small dots in circle, dotted rims**.
Y#	Date	Mintage	Fine	VF	XF	Unc
1a	ND	(modern copy)			25.00	35.00

NOTE: The legend on this coin states that it is valued at 1 Fen 5 Li of silver (about 15 Cash). The coin is the size of a normal 10 Cash piece of Sinkiang (Xinjiang), but these pieces are usually larger than those of the other provinces. For this reason, it is assumed the coin was overvalued to benefit the government.

2 FEN, 5 LI

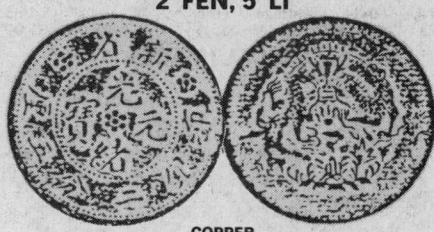

COPPER
Y#	Date	Mintage	Good	VG	Fine	VF
A1	ND	—	—	—	Rare	—

NOTE: This denomination was recalled shortly after issue and the dies re-engraved 1 Fen and 5 Li to produce Y#1. Do not confuse poorly re-engraved Chinese numeral 2 examples of Y#1 for Y#A1. Note the difference in spacing of the Chinese characters below the rosettes between Y#1 and Y#A1.

| B1 | ND | — | — | — | Rare | — |

NOTE: Status unknown.

Sinkiang / CHINA
364 Cash Series

10 CASH

COPPER
Rev: W/o Chinese leg. above dragon.

Y#	Date	Mintage	Good	VG	Fine	VF
2.1	ND	—	25.00	42.50	75.00	175.00

Rev: Chinese leg. w/*Nien* (year) added above dragon.

2.2	CD1910	—	25.00	42.50	75.00	175.00
	1911	—	30.00	50.00	100.00	200.00

Obv: Double ring around star in center.
2.3	CD1911	—	30.00	50.00	100.00	200.00

Obv: Large characters within center circle.

Y#	Date	Mintage	Fine	VF	XF	Unc
2a	CD1910 (modern copy)	—	25.00	35.00		

MISCAL (MACE)

SILVER
K#	Date	Mintage	VG	Fine	VF	XF
1000	ND	—	150.00	250.00	425.00	700.00

Kann #1000 was minted at the Arsenal of Lanchowfu in Gansu (Kansu) by order of General Tso Tsung-tang when he was campaigning against Yakub Beg's Sinkiang (Xinjiang) armies.

3.50 g
Obv. outer leg: Turki w/o dot in center.
Rev: W/o Turki leg.

Y#	Date	Mintage	VG	Fine	VF	XF
3	ND	—	30.00	60.00	100.00	175.00

Obv. outer leg: Turki w/ dot in center.
Rev: W/o Turki leg.
Y#	Date	Mintage	VG	Fine	VF	XF
3.1	ND	—	70.00	150.00	225.00	375.00

Obv: W/o outer Turki leg. Rev. leg: Turki.
3.2	ND	—	100.00	200.00	325.00	550.00

Obv. & rev: W/o outer Turki leg.
3.3	ND	—	22.00	45.00	70.00	125.00

Rev. leg: SUNGAREI above dragon, 1 MACE below.
10	ND	—	110.00	225.00	400.00	650.00

2 MISCALS (2 MACE)

SILVER, 7.20 g
Obv. outer leg: Turki. Rev: W/o Turki leg.
4	—	20.00	40.00	85.00	150.00

Obv. outer leg: Continuous Turki. Rev: W/o Turki leg.
| 4.1 | — | 25.00 | 50.00 | 100.00 | 200.00 |

Obv: W/o outer Turki leg. Rev. leg: Turki.
| 4.2 | ND | — | — | Rare |

 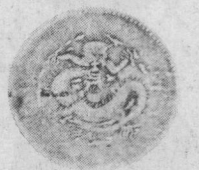

Rev: Redesigned dragon w/o Turki legends.
4.3	ND	—	25.00	50.00	100.00	200.00

Rev. leg: SUNGAREI above dragon, 2 MACE below.
| 11 | ND | — | 200.00 | 425.00 | 850.00 | 1350. |

4 MISCALS (4 MACE)

SILVER, 14.20 g
| 5 | ND | — | 60.00 | 100.00 | 175.00 | 300.00 |

5 MISCALS (5 MACE)

SILVER, 17.90 g
Obv: W/o dot or rosette in center.
Rev: Uncircled dragon.
| 6 | ND | — | 40.00 | 80.00 | 90.00 | 150.00 |

Rev: Circled dragon, w/o rosettes.
Y#	Date	Mintage	VG	Fine	VF	XF
6.1	ND	—	15.00	25.00	50.00	90.00

Rev: Large rosettes at sides of dragon.
| 6.2 | ND | — | 15.00 | 25.00 | 50.00 | 90.00 |

Obv: Dot in center. Rev: W/o rosettes, circled dragon.
| 6.3 | ND | — | 15.00 | 25.00 | 50.00 | 90.00 |

Obv: Cross in center.
| 6.4 | ND | — | 15.00 | 25.00 | 50.00 | 90.00 |

Obv: Large rosette in center, middle of which is depressed.
| 6.5 | ND | — | 15.00 | 25.00 | 50.00 | 90.00 |

Obv: Eight-petal rosette in center, middle of which is raised. Rev: Small rosettes at sides of dragon.
| 6.6 | ND | — | 15.00 | 25.00 | 50.00 | 90.00 |

Rev: Bat above dragon's head, K#1012-i.
| 6.7 | ND | — | 175.00 | 300.00 | 450.00 | 700.00 |

Rev: Turki leg. around uncircled dragon.
| 6.8 | ND | — | 400.00 | 600.00 | — | — |

Rev. leg: SUNGAREI above uncircled dragon, 5 MACE below.
| 6.9 | ND | — | — | — | — | Rare |

NOTE: Some authorities consider this coin a fantasy.

Rev: W/o SUNGAREI w/4 bats and many clouds around dragon.
| 6.10 | ND | — | — | — | — | Rare |

Obv: Turki leg. rotated. Rev: Bat above dragon's head.
| 6.11 | ND | — | — | — | — | Rare |

SAR (TAEL)

Sinkiang / CHINA 365

SILVER, 35.50 g
Obv: W/o outer Turki leg. Rev: W/o Turki leg.,
rosettes at sides of uncircled dragon.

Y#	Date	Mintage	VG	Fine	VF	XF
7	ND	—	25.00	40.00	60.00	125.00

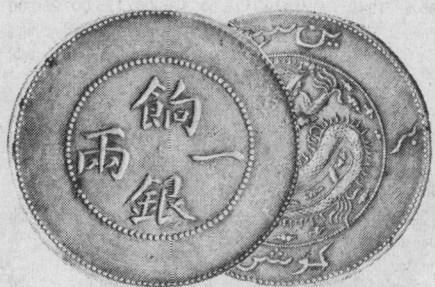

Rev: Turki leg. around circled dragon, w/o rosettes.
| 7.1 | ND | — | 40.00 | 65.00 | 100.00 | 300.00 |

Rev: Turki leg. around uncircled dragon.
| 7.2 | ND | — | 500.00 | 850.00 | 1250. | 1600. |

Obv: Outer Turki leg., rosette in center.
Rev: W/o Turki leg., w/rosettes at sides of
uncircled dragon.
| 7.3 | ND | — | 35.00 | 50.00 | 70.00 | 140.00 |

GOLD MISCAL (MACE)

GOLD, 3.90 g
Rev: Turki leg. around uncircled dragon.
Y#	Date	Mintage	Fine	VF	XF	Unc
8	ND	—	300.00	700.00	1250.	2000.

Rev: W/o Turki leg. around uncircled dragon.
| 8.1 | ND | — | 1150. | 1850. | 2750. | 4000. |

GOLD 2 MISCALS

GOLD, 7.80 g
Obv: Narrow spaced Chinese "2".
Rev: Turki leg. around uncircled dragon.
Y#	Date	Mintage	Fine	VF	XF	Unc
9	ND	—	750.00	1350.	2000.	3000.

Obv: Wide spaced Chinese "2".
Rev: Redesigned dragon.
| 9.1 | ND | — | 750.00 | 1350. | 2000. | 3000. |

Similar to 2 Miscals (Silver) Y#11.
K#	Date	Mintage	Fine	VF	XF	Unc
1505	ND	—	Reported, not confirmed			

Republic
10 CASH

COPPER
Obv: Large character *Shih* (ten).
Y#	Date	Mintage	Good	VG	Fine	VF
B39.1	ND	—	8.50	15.00	25.00	37.50

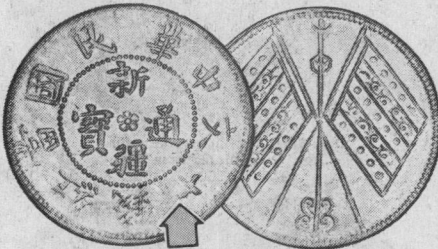

Obv: Small character *Shih* (ten).
Rev: Small crossed flags.
| B39.2 | ND | — | 12.50 | 25.00 | 35.00 | 50.00 |

Rev: Large crossed flags w/vertical stripes.
Y#	Year	Date	Good	VG	Fine	VF
A39.1	1	(1912)	7.50	13.50	18.50	28.00

Rev: Small crossed flags w/vertical stripes.
Y#	Year	Date	Good	VG	Fine	VF
A39.2	1	(1912)	7.00	12.00	16.50	25.00

Y#	Date	Mintage	Good	VG	Fine	VF
C39	CD1921	—	—	—	Rare	
NOTE: Status unknown.

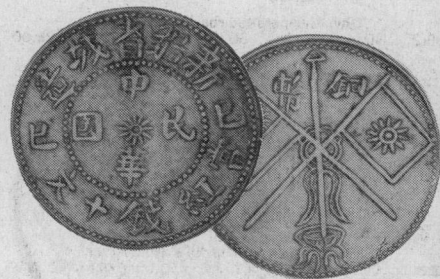

Obv: Chinese leg. *Chung Hwa Min Kuo* in inner circle
w/*Hsin Kiang* at upper right.
Rev: Flags w/solid sunbursts w/inner circles.
| 40.1 | CD1929 | — | 7.00 | 12.00 | 16.50 | 25.00 |
| | 1930 | — | — | — | Rare | |
NOTE: The cyclical date character at left exists closed and open for CD1929.

Obv: Large starburst in center.
Rev: Long streamers.
| 40.2 | CD1929 | — | 7.00 | 12.00 | 16.50 | 25.00 |
NOTE: Y#40 inscribed "Sheng Ch'eng" in upper legend may refer to Tihwa (Urumchi now Urumqi).

Obv. leg: Cyclical date at upper right.
| 40.3 | CD1930 | — | — | — | Rare | |

366 Sinkiang / CHINA

20 CASH

COPPER
Obv: Eight-petalled rosette in center.
Rev: Two stripes in flags have arabesques.

Y#	Date	Mintage	VG	Fine	VF	XF
39.1	ND	—	10.00	16.50	20.00	27.50

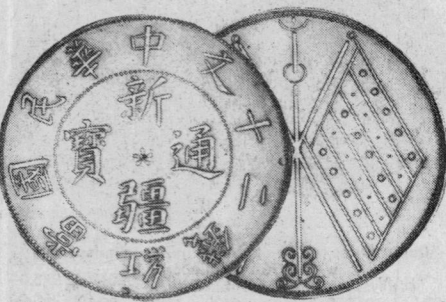

Obv: Five-petalled rosette in center.
39.2 ND   —   50.00 100.00 150.00 225.00

Rev: W/o arabesques in flags.

Y#	Date	Mintage	Fine	VF	XF	Unc
39.3	ND	(restrike)	—	—	50.00	75.00

Obv: Chinese leg. *Chung Hwa Min Kuo* in inner circle w/*Hsin Kiang* at upper right.

Y#	Date	Mintage	Good	VG	Fine	VF
A41.1	CD1929	—	75.00	125.00	200.00	300.00
	1930	—	85.00	140.00	225.00	335.00

NOTE: Y#A41.1 inscribed "Sheng Ch'eng" in upper legend may refer to Tihwa (Urumchi now Urumqi).

Obv. leg: Cyclical date at upper right.
A41.2 CD1930   —   —   —   Rare   —

5 MISCALS (5 MACE)

SILVER, 17.90 g
Rev: Two stripes in flags have arabesques.

Y#	Year	Date	VG	Fine	VF	XF
41	1	(1912)	40.00	65.00	150.00	200.00

Rev: Four stripes in flags have arabesques.
41a 1 (1912) 40.00 65.00 150.00 200.00

DOLLAR
SILVER

Obv: Similar to Y#46.2 but w/larger Chinese characters.
Rev: Thick pointed base "1".
46 38 1949 10.00 20.00 30.00 45.00

Obv: Similar to Y#46.2 but w/larger Chinese characters.
Rev: Thick pointed base "1" w/large serif.
46.1 38 1949 10.00 20.00 30.00 45.00

Obv: Smaller Chinese characters.
Rev: Thin pointed base "1".
46.2 38 1949 10.00 20.00 30.00 50.00

Rev: Square based "1".
46.3 38 1949 15.00 25.00 45.00 80.00

Obv: Outlined Chinese characters *Ee Yuan* in center.

Y#	Year	Date	VG	Fine	VF	XF
46.4	38	1949	15.00	25.00	60.00	100.00

Obv: Chinese characters *Min Kuo 38 Nien* (year) replaced by Chinese numerals 9-4-9-1 (1949) at bottom.
46.5 1949 75.00 125.00 175.00 250.00

SAR (TAEL)

SILVER, 35.90 g
Rev: Two stripes in flags have arabesques.
42 1 (1912) 60.00 100.00 200.00 350.00

Obv: Similar to Y#42.
Rev: Four stripes in flags have arabesques.
42a 1 (1912) 60.00 100.00 200.00 350.00

LOCAL COINAGE
Aksu (Hocheng) Mint
EMPIRE
CASH

CAST COPPER
Obv: Type A

C#	Date	Emperor	Good	VG	Fine	VF
30-5	ND(1796-1820)	Chia Ching	1.00	1.75	2.75	5.50

Obv: Type A

C#	Date	Emperor	Good	VG	Fine	VF
30-6	ND(1821-50)	Tao Kuang	1.00	1.75	2.75	5.50

5 CASH

 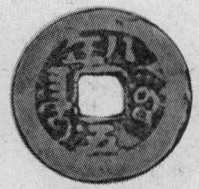

CAST COPPER
Obv: Type A
Rev: Characters *Pa Nien* above.

30-7	Yr.8 (1828)	Tao Kuang	1.50	3.00	5.50	10.00
30-10	ND(1851-61)	Hsien Feng	6.00	12.00	22.50	35.00

30-A15	ND(1862-74)	T'ung Chih	75.00	95.00	120.00	150.00

10 CASH

CAST COPPER
Obv: Type A-1
Rev: *Tang* above.

30-2.1	ND(1736-95)	Ch'ien Lung	7.00	10.00	15.00	25.00

Rev: Character *K'a* (Kashgar) above.

30-2.2	ND(1736-95)	Ch'ien Lung	1.75	3.50	4.50	9.00

Rev: Character *A* (for Aksu) above.

30-3	ND(1736-95)	Ch'ien Lung	1.25	2.50	3.50	7.00

NOTE: C#30-2, 30-3 and 30-4 (1 Cash) though bearing the reign title of Ch'ien Lung, were cast during the Kuang Hsu era, (1875-1908).

Obv: Type A
Rev: Characters *Pa Nien* (= year 8 - 1828) above.

C#	Date	Emperor	Good	VG	Fine	VF
30-8	Yr.8 (1828)	Tao Kuang	1.00	1.75	2.75	5.50

NOTE: C#30-7 and 30-8 are commemoratives marking the supression of a revolt in Sinkiang in 1828.

25 mm
Obv: Type A

30-11	ND(1851-61)	Hsien Feng	1.00	1.75	2.75	5.50

CAST COPPER, 25mm
Obv: Type A

30-15	ND(1862-74)	T'ung Chih	1.50	2.50	4.00	8.00

CAST COPPER
Rev: Character *A* (for Aksu) above center hole, *Aksu* in Turki at right, in Manchu at left.

30-18	ND(1875-1908)	Kuang Hsu	1.50	2.50	4.00	8.00

Rev: *Aksu* in Manchu at right, in Turki at left.

30-18.1	ND(1875-1908)	Kuang Hsu	7.50	12.50	19.00	27.50

Rev: Character *K'a* (for Kashgar) above.

30-19	ND(1875-1908)	Kuang Hsu	2.00	4.50	6.50	13.50

50 CASH

CAST COPPER, 37mm

30-12	ND(1851-61)	Hsien Feng	100.00	150.00	200.00	300.00

100 CASH

CAST COPPER, 45mm

30-13	ND(1851-61)	Hsien Feng	140.00	200.00	275.00	400.00

40-41mm

30-13.1	ND(1851-61)	Hsien Feng	30.00	55.00	85.00	150.00

Hammered Coinage
1/2 MISCAL (5 FEN)

SILVER, 1.45 g
Obv. and rev: Turki script.

Y#	Date	Mintage	Good	VG	Fine	VF
A7.4	ND	—	6.00	12.00	15.00	30.00
(Y-A7.5)	AH1296	—	6.00	12.00	15.00	30.00

Obv: Square in center. Rev: Turki leg.

A7.5	AH1296	—	7.50	13.50	18.50	35.00
(Y-A7)	1297	—	7.50	13.50	18.50	35.00
	1298/1297 (mule)					
		—	7.50	13.50	18.50	35.00
	1298	—	7.50	13.50	18.50	35.00

Milled Coinage
MISCAL (MACE)

SILVER, 3.50 g
Similar to 3 Miscals, Y#14.

Y#	Date	Mintage	VG	Fine	VF	XF
A13	AH1311				Rare	

2 MISCALS (2 MACE)

SILVER, 7.20 g
Similar to 3 Miscals, Y#14.

13	AH1310	—	40.00	80.00	150.00	225.00
	1311	—	30.00	60.00	100.00	165.00
	1312	—	40.00	80.00	150.00	225.00

3 MISCALS (3 MACE)

SILVER, 10.50 g

14	AH1310	—	40.00	80.00	140.00	225.00
	1311	—	32.50	65.00	110.00	200.00
	1313	—	32.50	65.00	110.00	200.00
	1315	—	40.00	80.00	140.00	225.00

5 MISCALS (5 MACE)

SILVER, 17.50 g

15	AH1310	—	55.00	110.00	190.00	325.00
	1311	—	50.00	100.00	165.00	275.00
	1312	—	40.00	80.00	150.00	250.00
	1315	—	50.00	100.00	165.00	275.00

REPUBLIC
10 CASH

CAST COPPER, 32mm.

Y#	Date	Mintage	Good	VG	Fine	VF
37.1	ND	—	35.00	55.00	80.00	125.00

Reduced size, 29mm.

37.2	ND	—	35.00	55.00	80.00	125.00

MILLED COINAGE
10 CASH

COPPER
Obv: Chinese characters *Shih Wen* (10 Wen) at lower left.
Rev: Upper Turki leg. Inverted.

Y#	Date	Mintage	Good	VG	Fine	VF
F38	AH1332	—	35.00	65.00	85.00	125.00

Ili Mint
(Hui Yuan, Kuldja, Kuldsha, Kwlja)

EMPIRE
CASH

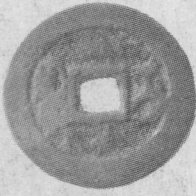

CAST COPPER

C#	Date	Emperor	Good	VG	Fine	VF
28-2	ND(1796-1820)	Chia Ch'ing	25.00	42.50	70.00	100.00

Rev: Vertical line below.
| 28-2.1 | ND(1796-1820) | Chia Ch'ing | 30.00 | 50.00 | 85.00 | 125.00 |

Rev: Vertical line above.
| 28-2.2 | ND(1796-1820) | Chia Ch'ing | 30.00 | 50.00 | 85.00 | 125.00 |

Obv: Type A
| 28-3 | ND(1821-50) | Tao Kuang | 25.00 | 35.00 | 50.00 | 85.00 |

Rev: Dot above.
| 28-3.1 | ND(1821-50) | Tao Kuang | 30.00 | 50.00 | 85.00 | 125.00 |

Rev: Vertical line above.
| 28-3.2 | ND(1821-50) | Tao Kuang | 30.00 | 50.00 | 85.00 | 125.00 |

Rev: Character *Shih* (meaning 10) above.
| 28-3.3 | ND(1821-50) | Tao Kuang | 60.00 | 75.00 | 110.00 | 150.00 |

Rev: Short vertical lines above and below.
| 28-3.4 | ND(1821-50) | Tao Kuang | 35.00 | 55.00 | 95.00 | 140.00 |

CAST BRASS
Obv: Type A
Narrow rims.
| 28-4 | ND(1851-61) | Hsien Feng | — | — | — | 500.00 |

4 CASH

CAST COPPER

C#	Date	Emperor	Good	VG	Fine	VF
28-5	ND(1851-61)	Hsien Feng	25.00	35.00	50.00	85.00

Obv: Type B-2
| 28-9 | ND(1862-74) | T'ung Chih | — | — | — | 500.00 |

10 CASH
CAST COPPER
| 28-6 | ND(1851-61) | Hsien Feng | — | — | — | 500.00 |

50 CASH
CAST COPPER
| 28-7 | ND(1851-61) | Hsien Feng | 100.00 | 150.00 | 220.00 | 300.00 |

100 CASH

CAST COPPER
Obv: Type C
| 28-8 | ND(1851-61) | Hsien Feng | 20.00 | 30.00 | 45.00 | 70.00 |

NOTE: Numerous counterfeits of C28-8, presumably contemporary, have recently come on the market. Refer to page 39 of Ch'en Hung-hsi's 1987 *Hsin Chiang Hung Ch'ien Chia Ko Mu Lu* for illustrations.

CAST BRASS
| 28-8a | ND(1851-61) | Hsien Feng | 35.00 | 55.00 | 75.00 | 100.00 |

500 CASH
CAST COPPER or BRASS
| 28-11 | ND(1851-61) | Hsien Feng | 250.00 | 325.00 | 400.00 | 500.00 |

Kashgar (Shufu) now Kashi Mint
10 CASH

CAST COPPER
Obv: Type A

C#	Date	Emperor	Good	VG	Fine	VF
32-2	ND(1851-61)	Hsien Feng	11.50	18.00	22.50	45.00

Obv: Type A
Rev: Kashgar in Turki at left; in Manchu at right, K'e (Kashgar) above.
| 32-6 | ND(1875-1908) | Kuang Hsu | 5.00 | 7.50 | 13.50 | 20.00 |

Rev: *Kashgar Pao* (right-left).
| 32-6.1 | ND(1875-1908) | Kuang Hsu | 5.00 | 7.50 | 13.50 | 20.00 |

50 CASH
CAST COPPER
| 32-3 | ND(1851-61) | Hsien Feng | 135.00 | 225.00 | 350.00 | 500.00 |

100 CASH

CAST COPPER, 52mm
| 32-4 | ND(1851-61) | Hsien Feng | 150.00 | 250.00 | 375.00 | 550.00 |

Hammered Coinage
1/2 MISCAL (5 FEN)

SILVER, 1.45 g
Obv. leg: Manchu and Chinese w/outer border of S's at rim w/o square in center.
Rev: Turki leg.

Y#	Date	Mintage	Good	VG	Fine	VF
A7.6	ND	—	4.50	6.50	8.00	17.50
(Y-A7.1)	AH(12)95	—	4.50	6.50	8.00	17.50

Obv. & rev: Square in center.
Rev. leg: In Manchu, Chinese and Turki.
| A7.7 | ND | — | 4.50 | 6.50 | 8.00 | 17.50 |
| (Y-A7.2) | AH(12)95 | — | 4.50 | 6.50 | 8.00 | 17.50 |

Obv. & rev: W/o square in center.
Obv. leg: Turki. Rev. leg: Chinese for 5 Fen.
| A7.8 | AH1313 | — | 125.00 | 250.00 | 350.00 | 500.00 |
| (K1064) | | | | | | |

Y#	Date	Mintage	Good	VG	Fine	VF
A7.9 (K1064a)	ND	—	125.00	250.00	350.00	500.00

**Obv: Arabesque, wreath and flower replaces Turki leg.
Rev. leg: Chinese for 5 Fen.**

A7.10 (K1064b)	ND	—	125.00	250.00	350.00	500.00

A7.19	ND(1875-1908) Kwang Hsu	—	—	Rare	—

MISCAL (MACE)

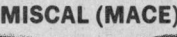

**SILVER, 2.90 g
Rev. leg: In Chinese, Turki and Manchu.**

B7	AH1295	—	—	Rare	—

Milled Coinage
MISCAL (MACE)

**SILVER, 3.50 g
Obv: Six characters. Rev: Wreath around Turki leg.**

Y#	Date	Mintage	VG	Fine	VF	XF
16	ND	—	30.00	60.00	100.00	165.00
	AH1309	—	30.00	60.00	100.00	165.00
	1311	—	30.00	60.00	100.00	165.00

Obv: Like Y#A16. Rev: Like Y#16.

D16	AH1310	—	35.00	70.00	125.00	200.00

Obv: Four characters. Rev: W/o wreath.

A16	ND	—	30.00	60.00	100.00	165.00
	AH1310	—	30.00	60.00	100.00	165.00

Obv: Kashgar at right.

B16	AH1322	—	30.00	60.00	100.00	165.00
	1331 (error for 1321)	—	30.00	60.00	100.00	165.00

Obv: Kashgar in Chinese at right and left.

C16	AH1322	—	35.00	70.00	125.00	200.00

Obv: Date at lower left.

A20.1	AH1323	—	85.00	165.00	275.00	450.00

Obv: Date at lower right.

Y#	Date	Mintage	VG	Fine	VF	XF
A20.2	AH1323	—	85.00	165.00	275.00	450.00

2 MISCALS (2 MACE)

SILVER, 7.20 g

17	AH1310	—	15.00	25.00	35.00	50.00
	1311	—	10.00	14.00	20.00	35.00
	1312	—	16.00	27.50	40.00	65.00
	1313	—	17.50	30.00	45.00	75.00

Obv: Chinese characters K'e Shih at right.

17a	AH1313	—	12.50	22.50	32.50	50.00
	1314	—	12.50	22.50	32.50	50.00
	1315	—	12.50	22.50	32.50	50.00
	1319	—	12.50	22.50	32.50	50.00
	1320	—	17.50	30.00	45.00	75.00

Obv: Chinese characters K'e Tsao at right.

17a.1	AH1320	—	—	—	Rare	—
	1321	—	17.50	30.00	45.00	75.00
	1322	—	20.00	35.00	55.00	100.00

**Obv: Chinese and Turki leg.
Rev: Dragon, w/o leg.**

B20	AH1323	—	65.00	135.00	225.00	350.00

Rev: Dragon in circle surrounded by wreath.

23	AH1325	—	20.00	40.00	65.00	110.00
	1326	—	20.00	40.00	65.00	110.00
	1327	—	25.00	50.00	80.00	150.00
	1329	—	35.00	65.00	110.00	175.00

Obv: Turki leg. around Chinese within a beaded circle. Rev: Double ring around small dragon, floral pattern outside, w/o leg.

29	AH1329	—	25.00	50.00	100.00	165.00

**Obv: Chinese leg. within circle w/o Turki leg.
Rev: Turki leg. around larger dragon within single circle.**

Y#	Date	Mintage	VG	Fine	VF	XF
29.1	AH1329	—	100.00	200.00	325.00	550.00

3 MISCALS

SILVER, 10.50 g

	AH1307	—	—	—	Rare	—

18	AH1310	—	10.00	20.00	30.00	50.00
	1311	—	17.50	30.00	45.00	75.00
	1312	—	20.00	35.00	55.00	100.00

Obv: Chinese characters K'e Shih to right.

18a	AH1313	—	10.00	20.00	32.50	65.00
	1314	—	10.00	20.00	32.50	65.00
	1315	—	10.00	20.00	32.50	65.00
	1316	—	10.00	20.00	32.50	65.00
	1317	—	10.00	20.00	32.50	65.00
	1319	—	10.00	20.00	32.50	65.00
	1320	—	10.00	20.00	32.50	65.00

Obv: Chinese characters K'e Tsao to right.

18a.1	AH1320	—	10.00	20.00	32.50	65.00
	1321	—	10.00	20.00	32.50	65.00
	1322	—	10.00	20.00	32.50	65.00

Obv: Normal 3 in Chinese at bottom.

20	AH1323	—	85.00	175.00	275.00	450.00

Sinkiang / CHINA 370

Obv: Official 3 in Chinese at bottom, date at upper left.

Y#	Date	Mintage	VG	Fine	VF	XF
20.1	AH1323	—	100.00	200.00	325.00	550.00

Obv: Official 3 in Chinese at bottom, date at lower right.

| 20.2 | AH1323 | — | 100.00 | 200.00 | 365.00 | 600.00 |

Rev: Small, circled dragon, Arabic legend.

| 30 | AH1329 | — | 125.00 | 265.00 | 450.00 | 750.00 |

5 MISCALS

SILVER, 17.20 g
Obv. leg. in Turki, Chinese and Manchu.

K#	Date	Mintage	VG	Fine	VF	XF
1040	AH1307	—	250.00	500.00	775.00	1400.

Y#	Date	Mintage	VG	Fine	VF	XF
19	AH1310	—	17.50	30.00	55.00	100.00
	1311	—	10.00	20.00	35.00	70.00
	1312	—	15.00	27.50	45.00	90.00
	1313	—	15.00	27.50	45.00	90.00
	1315	—	15.00	27.50	45.00	90.00

Obv: Chinese characters K'e Shih at right.

19a	AH1313	—	17.50	25.00	40.00	70.00
	1314	—	17.50	25.00	40.00	70.00
	1315	—	17.50	25.00	40.00	70.00
	1316	—	17.50	25.00	40.00	70.00
	1317	—	17.50	25.00	40.00	70.00
	1319	—	17.50	25.00	40.00	70.00
	1320	—	17.50	25.00	40.00	70.00

Obv: Chinese characters K'e Tsao at right.

Y#	Date	Mintage	VG	Fine	VF	XF
19a.1	AH1321	—	10.00	17.50	30.00	60.00
	1322	—	10.00	17.50	30.00	60.00

Obv: Official Chinese and standard Turki leg., date at upper left.
Rev: Dragon's tail points to right.

| 21 | AH1323 | — | 20.00 | 30.00 | 45.00 | 75.00 |

Obv: Date at lower right.

| 21.1 | AH1323 | — | 20.00 | 30.00 | 45.00 | 75.00 |

Obv: Date at upper right.

| 21.7 | AH1323 | — | 20.00 | 30.00 | 45.00 | 75.00 |

Obv: Inverted Turki leg., date at lower right.

| 21.2 | AH1323 | — | 22.50 | 35.00 | 60.00 | 100.00 |

Obv: Simple 5 in Chinese, date at lower right.

| 21.3 | AH1323 | — | — | — | — | Rare |

Obv: Official Chinese and standard Turki leg., date at upper left.
Rev: Dragon's tail points to left.

| 21.4 | AH1323 | — | 15.00 | 25.00 | 45.00 | 90.00 |

Obv: Date at lower right.

| 21.5 | AH1323 | — | 15.00 | 25.00 | 50.00 | 90.00 |

Obv: Inverted Turki leg., date at lower right.

| 21.6 | AH1323 | — | 20.00 | 35.00 | 80.00 | 135.00 |

Obv: Three Chinese characters at top between standard Turki leg.

| 25 | ND | — | 22.50 | 40.00 | 85.00 | 150.00 |

Obv: Date at upper left.

Y#	Date	Mintage	VG	Fine	VF	XF
25.1	AH1325	—	22.50	40.00	85.00	150.00
	1326	—	22.50	40.00	85.00	150.00

Obv: Date at upper right.

| 25.5 | AH1326 | — | 22.50 | 40.00 | 85.00 | 150.00 |

Similar to Y#21.1 w/date at lower right.

| 25.2 | AH1327 | — | 22.50 | 40.00 | 85.00 | 150.00 |

Obv: Date at left.

| 25.6 | AH1327 | — | 22.50 | 40.00 | 85.00 | 150.00 |

Obv: Inverted Turki leg., date at lower right.

| 25.3 | AH1325 | — | 17.50 | 25.00 | 75.00 | 110.00 |
| | 1328 | — | 17.50 | 25.00 | 75.00 | 110.00 |

Obv: Date at right.

| 25.7 | AH1325 | — | 17.50 | 25.00 | 75.00 | 110.00 |

Obv: Date at upper left.

| 25.8 | AH1325 | — | 17.50 | 25.00 | 75.00 | 110.00 |

Obv: Two Chinese characters at top between standard Turki leg. w/date at upper right.

| 25.4 | AH1325 | — | 50.00 | 100.00 | 165.00 | 275.00 |

Sinkiang / CHINA 371

Obv: Similar to Y#25.4.
Rev: Floral sprays reversed.

Y#	Date	Mintage	VG	Fine	VF	XF
25.9	AH1325	—	50.00	100.00	165.00	275.00

Obv: Three Chinese characters at top, star in center.

27	AH1327	—	20.00	30.00	65.00	110.00
	1328	—	25.00	50.00	90.00	150.00

Obv: Official 5 at right, dot in center.

27.1	AH1328	—	35.00	65.00	150.00	225.00

Obv: Rosette in center.

27.2	AH1329	—	50.00	100.00	200.00	275.00

Obv: Two Chinese characters at top, simple 5 at right, star in center.

27.3	AH1329	—	17.50	25.00	75.00	110.00

Obv: Dot in center.

27.4	AH1329	—	17.50	25.00	75.00	110.00

Obv: Rosette in center.

27.5	AH1329	—	17.50	25.00	75.00	110.00

Obv: Official 5 at right, leg: *Kashgar*.

27.6	AH1329	—	17.50	25.00	75.00	110.00

Obv: Dot in center, leg: *made in Kashgar*.

31	AH1329	—	25.00	50.00	110.00	175.00

Obv: Star in center. **Rev:** Stars in outer field.

Y#	Date	Mintage	VG	Fine	VF	XF
31.1	AH1321 (error for 1331)					
		—	20.00	40.00	100.00	150.00
	1329	—	20.00	40.00	100.00	150.00
	1330	—	20.00	40.00	100.00	150.00
	1331	—	20.00	40.00	100.00	150.00

Rev: Rosettes in outer field.

31.2	AH1329	—	50.00	100.00	165.00	275.00

Obv: Rosette in center.

31.3	AH1329	—	22.50	75.00	100.00	150.00

SAR (TAEL)

SILVER, 35.20 g
Obv: Two Chinese characters at top.

26	AH1325	—	100.00	225.00	475.00	850.00

Obv: Three Chinese characters at top.

26.1	AH1325	—	450.00	1100.	1650.	2200.

REPUBLIC
5 CASH

COPPER
Obv: Large Chinese leg.

Y#	Date	Mintage	Good	VG	Fine	VF
A36.1	ND	—	275.00	375.00	500.00	700.00

Obv: Small Chinese leg.

A36.2	ND	—	275.00	375.00	500.00	700.00

36	AH1331	—	100.00	135.00	225.00	350.00

10 CASH

COPPER
Obv: Large Chinese leg.

B36.1	ND	—	25.00	37.50	50.00	70.00

Rev: Small Chinese leg.

B36.2	ND	—	25.00	37.50	50.00	70.00

Obv: Chinese leg. *Shih Wen* (10 Wen) at upper left.
Rev: Date at upper center.

38.1	ND	—	7.50	15.00	20.00	35.00
	AH1331	—	12.50	22.50	35.00	50.00
	1332	—	7.50	15.00	20.00	35.00
	1333	—	7.50	15.00	20.00	35.00
	1334	—	7.50	15.00	20.00	35.00

Sinkiang / CHINA 372

Rev: Modified Turki leg. w/date at bottom.

Y#	Date	Mintage	Good	VG	Fine	VF
38.2	AH1331	—	8.50	12.50	17.50	30.00
	1332	—	8.50	12.50	17.50	30.00
	1334	—	8.50	12.50	17.50	30.00
	1335	—	8.50	12.50	17.50	30.00
	1339	—	8.50	12.50	17.50	30.00

Obv: 2 lower right Chinese characters different. Rev: AH date at top.

Y#	Date	Year	Good	VG	Fine	VF
38.3	AH133-4	1916	50.00	75.00	125.00	200.00

Obv: Chinese leg. Hung Hsien T'ung Pi in inner dotted circle.

Y#	Date	Mintage	Good	VG	Fine	VF
A38.1	AH1334	—	20.00	35.00	50.00	100.00

Rev: Smaller Turki leg. in florals.

| A38.2 | AH1334 | — | 20.00 | 35.00 | 50.00 | 100.00 |

NOTE: Y#A38.1 and A38.2 were issued for the brief reign of Yuan Shih-kai as Emperor Hung Hsien (1916).

Obv: Chinese date at upper right w/rosette. Chinese leg. Chung Hwa Min Kuo in inner circle.

Y#	Date	Year	Good	VG	Fine	VF
38a.1	AH1339	10	5.00	10.00	15.00	25.00
	1340	10	5.00	10.00	15.00	25.00

Obv: Outer Chinese leg. w/o Shih of Kashgar at upper left.

Y#	Date	Year	Good	VG	Fine	VF
38a.2	AH134x	11	5.00	10.00	15.00	25.00

Rev: Turki leg. rearranged.

| 38a.3 | AH1339 | 10 | 5.00 | 10.00 | 15.00 | 25.00 |
| | 134x | 10 | 5.00 | 10.00 | 15.00 | 25.00 |

Obv: Outer Chinese leg. w/o Shih of Kashgar at lower left. Rev: Turki leg. in florals w/Zarb Kashgar at top, similar to Y#A38.2.

| 38a.4 | AH1334 | — | 37.50 | 60.00 | 100.00 | 150.00 |

Obv: Crowded Chinese year '11'.

| 38a.5 | AH1334 | 11 | 25.00 | 40.00 | 65.00 | 100.00 |

Obv: Chinese leg. Min Kuo T'ung Yuan in inner circle w/ Kashgar at right.

Y#	Date	Mintage	Good	VG	Fine	VF
38b.1	AHxxxx	—	15.00	30.00	40.00	65.00

Obv: Outer Chinese leg. rotated.

| 38b.2 | AH13x4 | — | 15.00 | 30.00 | 40.00 | 65.00 |

Rev: Chinese character Jih in solid sunburst.

Y#	Date	Mintage	Good	VG	Fine	VF
B38c.1	CD1928	—	175.00	275.00	425.00	600.00

Obv: Like B38c.1. Rev: Chinese character Jih in rayed sunburst.

| B38c.2 | CD1928 | — | 175.00 | 275.00 | 425.00 | 600.00 |

Obv: Like B38d. Rev: Like B38c.1.

| B38c.3 | CD1928 | — | 175.00 | 275.00 | 425.00 | 600.00 |

Obv. leg: Cyclic date at left and right like B38.4.

| B38c.4 | CD1928 | — | 175.00 | 275.00 | 425.00 | 600.00 |

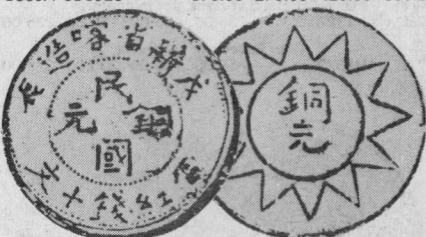

Obv: Chinese leg. Min Kuo T'ung Yuan in inner circle. Rev: Chinese characters T'ung Yuan in solid sunburst.

| B38d | CD1928 | — | 125.00 | 175.00 | 300.00 | 400.00 |

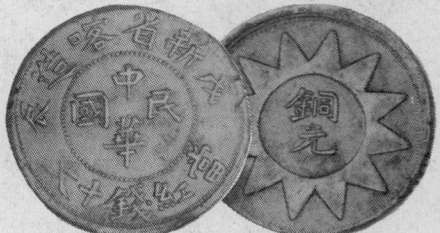

Obv: Chinese leg. Chung Hwa Min Kuo in inner circle. Chinese date part of upper leg. Rev: Chinese characters T'ung Yuan in solid sunburst.

| B38.1 | CD1928 | — | 17.50 | 32.50 | 45.00 | 75.00 |

Obv: Upper leg: Hsin Sheng. Rev: Small Chinese characters T'ung Yuan in outlined sunburst.

| B38.2 | CD1928 | — | 15.00 | 23.00 | 30.00 | 50.00 |

Sinkiang / CHINA 373

Obv: Upper leg. *Hsin Kiang.*
Rev: Large Chinese characters *T'ung Yuan* in outlined sunburst.

Y#	Date	Mintage	Good	VG	Fine	VF
B38.3	CD1928	—	15.00	23.00	30.00	50.00

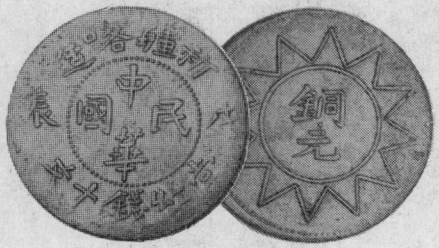

Obv: Chinese date at left and right.
Rev: Chinese characters *T'ung Yuan* in outlined sunburst.

B38.4	CD1928	—	3.00	5.50	8.00	16.00
	1929	—	5.00	7.50	15.00	25.00

Rev: Chinese characters *T'ung Yuan* in outlined and finely rayed sunburst.

B38.5	CD1928	—	35.00	50.00	65.00	100.00

Obv: 5 Chinese characters at top w/ *Kashgar* at upper left.

B38.6	CD1929	—	9.50	16.50	32.50	45.00

Obv: Chinese leg. *Min Kuo T'ung Yuan* in inner circle.
Rev: Turki leg. in solid sunburst.

B38b.1	CD1928 AH1346	125.00	175.00	300.00	400.00

Obv: Similar to Y#B38d. Rev: Similar to Y#B38b.1.

B38b.2	CD1928 AH1346	150.00	200.00	350.00	500.00

Obv: Chinese characters for date to left and right of *Chung Hwa Min Kuo* in inner circle.
Rev: Turki leg. in outlined sunburst.

B38a.1	CD1929	—	100.00	165.00	250.00	350.00

Obv: Upper Chinese leg. *Hsin Kiang Kashgar.* (10) at upper left.

Y#	Date	Mintage	Good	VG	Fine	VF
B38a.2	CD1929	—	75.00	100.00	125.00	150.00

Y#	Date	Year	Good	VG	Fine	VF
A44.1	(1922)	11	50.00	75.00	100.00	125.00

Flags reversed.

A44.2	(1922)	11	50.00	75.00	100.00	125.00

Obv: Chinese leg. *Hsin Kiang Kashgar* at top.
Rev: Flags w/wide outlined sunbursts. Flag at right w/inner circle.

44.1	CD1929	—	5.00	8.50	17.50	32.50

Obv: Small eight-petalled rosette in center.
Rev: Flag at right w/o inner circle.

44.2	CD1929	—	4.50	7.50	12.00	16.00
	CD1930	—	4.50	7.50	12.00	16.00

Obv: Star w/rays in center.

44.3	CD1930	—	8.50	17.50	22.50	37.50

Eight-petalled rosette in center.
Rev: Flags w/narrow outlined sunbursts.

Y#	Date	Year	Good	VG	Fine	VF
44.4	CD1930	—	10.00	20.00	35.00	55.00

Reduced size
Rev: Flags w/solid sunbursts.

44.5	CD1933	—	4.00	8.00	15.00	20.00

Rev: Reversed flags w/large solid sunbursts.

44.6	CD1929	—	3.00	7.00	13.00	18.00
	1930	—	4.00	8.00	15.00	20.00

Rev: Reversed flags w/small solid sunbursts.

44.7	CD1930	—	25.00	50.00	100.00	165.00

Obv: leg. 4 Chinese characters at top.

44.8	CD1929	—	75.00	100.00	125.00	150.00

20 CASH

Sinkiang / CHINA

Y#	Date	Year	Good	VG	Fine	VF
48	AH1334(?)	10			Rare	

5 MISCALS

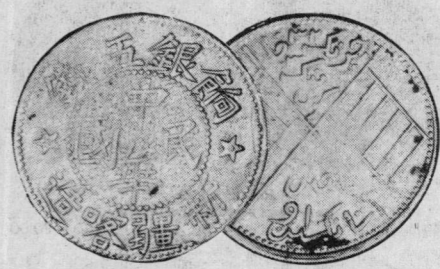

SILVER, 17.30 g
Obv: Stars dividing Chinese legends.
Rev: Crossed flags dividing Turki leg.

Y#	Date	Mintage	VG	Fine	VF	XF
43	AH1331	—	40.00	75.00	160.00	275.00
	1332	—	40.00	75.00	160.00	275.00

Obv: Rosettes dividing Chinese leg.

43.1	AH1331	—	35.00	65.00	135.00	225.00
	1332	—	35.00	65.00	135.00	225.00
	13-32	—	35.00	65.00	135.00	225.00

NOTE: Varieties exist.

Obv: Rosettes dividing Chinese leg.
Rev: Different Turki leg.

43.2	AH1334	—	45.00	85.00	185.00	325.00
	133-4	—	45.00	85.00	185.00	325.00

NOTE: Varieties exist.

Obv: Rosette in center, floral arrangements dividing Chinese leg.

43.3	AH13-32	—	40.00	75.00	160.00	275.00
	133-4	—	45.00	85.00	185.00	325.00

NOTE: Varieties exist.

Obv: Stars divide rotated outer Chinese leg.

Y#	Date	Mintage	VG	Fine	VF	XF
43.4	AHx13x	—	—	—	—	—

Uighuristan Republic
AH1352/1933-1934

10 CASH

COPPER
Rev: Flag at right w/o fringe.

Y#	Date	Mintage	Good	VG	Fine	VF
D38.1	AH1352	—	17.50	35.00	55.00	75.00

Rev: Flag at right w/partial fringe.

D38.2	AH1352	—	17.50	35.00	55.00	75.00

Rev: Flag at right w/full fringe.

D38.3	AH1352	—	17.50	35.00	55.00	75.00

20 CASH

COPPER

E38.1	AH1352	—	50.00	100.00	150.00	200.00

Flags reversed.

E38.2	AH1352	—	50.00	100.00	150.00	200.00

REBEL COINAGE
Yakub Beg

Most of these coins were struck at Kashgar (Kashi) in the name of the Ottoman Sultan Abdul Aziz by the rebel Yakub Beg, who controlled much of Sinkiang (Xinjiang) between 1865 and 1877.

In the name of Abdul Aziz

FALUS

COPPER
Obv. and rev: Date.

C#	Date	Good	VG	Fine	VF
37.4	AH1290	20.00	32.50	40.00	50.00
	1292	20.00	32.50	40.00	50.00

Obv: Date.

37.5	AH1291	20.00	32.50	40.00	50.00
	1293	20.00	32.50	40.00	50.00
	1294	20.00	32.50	40.00	50.00

Rev: Date.

37.6	AH1292	20.00	32.50	40.00	50.00

Obv. and rev: W/o date.

37.7	ND	15.00	21.50	30.00	40.00

1/2 MISCAL (MACE)

SILVER

37-1.1	AH1290/91	1.00	3.00	5.00	8.00
	1291	1.00	3.00	5.00	8.00
	1291/92	1.00	3.00	5.00	8.00
	1292	1.00	3.00	5.00	8.00
	1293	1.00	3.00	5.00	8.00
	1294	1.00	3.00	5.00	8.00
	ND	1.00	3.00	5.00	8.00

Legends arranged differently.

37-1.2	AH1292	3.00	5.50	7.50	10.00
	1292/93	3.00	5.50	7.50	10.00
	1293	3.00	5.50	7.50	10.00
	1293/94	3.00	5.50	7.50	10.00
	1294	3.00	5.50	7.50	10.00
	ND	3.00	5.50	7.50	10.00

TILLA

GOLD, 4.50 g
Rev. leg: *Zarb Mahrusah Kashgar.*

C#	Date	VG	Fine	VF	XF
37-2.1	AH1290	175.00	250.00	500.00	800.00

3.70 g
Rev. leg: *Zarb Daru-S-Sultanat Kashgar.*

37-2.2	AH1291/1290 (mule)				
		175.00	250.00	500.00	800.00
	1291	100.00	150.00	350.00	600.00

Obv. leg. within dotted border within circles.
Rev. leg. within circle.

C#	Date	VG	Fine	VF	XF
37-2.3	AH1291	100.00	150.00	350.00	600.00

Rev. leg. within segmented circles.

| 37-2.4 | AH1291 | 100.00 | 150.00 | 350.00 | 600.00 |

Obv. leg. within dotted border within circles w/loop.
Rev. leg. within dotted border within circles.

| 37-2.5 | AH1292 | 125.00 | 175.00 | 400.00 | 700.00 |

Obv. leg. within segmented circles w/loop.
Rev. leg. within segmented circles.

| 37-2.6 | AH1292 | 100.00 | 150.00 | 300.00 | 500.00 |
| | 1293 | 125.00 | 200.00 | 400.00 | 700.00 |

In the name of Abdulhamid II

| 37-3 | — | — | — | — | — |

Khotan (Hotien) now Hotan Mint
Hammered Coinage
1/2 MISCAL

SILVER, 1.45 g
Rev: *Kho-tan* in Arabic. Retrograde and inverted Chinese '5'.

Y#	Date	Mintage	Good	VG	Fine	VF
A7.11	ND (1875-1908)	—	10.00	22.00	30.00	50.00
(K1184)						

Rev: *Zarb Khotan* in Arabic.

| A7.12 | ND (1875-1908) | — | 10.00 | 22.00 | 30.00 | 50.00 |
| (K1184v) | | | | | | |

Rebel Coinage
Ghazi Rashid

A rebel in Sinkiang (Xinjiang) about whom little is known. He was in power from 1862 until his death in 1867.

TENGA

SILVER

C#	Date	VG	Fine	VF	XF
36-5	AH1283	—	—	Rare	—

Kuche (Kucha) Mint
(Also called Ningyuansen)
Kuche is west north-west of Aksu and has sometimes been confused with Kulja (Kuldja).

EMPIRE
CASH
CAST COPPER
Rev: Characters *Boo Yuan* left and right, *Ku* above.

C#	Date	Emperor	Good	VG	Fine	VF
33-20	ND(1862-74)	Tung Chih	10.00	20.00	30.00	50.00

5 CASH

CAST COPPER
Obv: Type A

| 33-8 | ND(1851-61) | Hsien Feng | 50.00 | 75.00 | 100.00 | 150.00 |

Obv: Type A-2.

| 33-22 | ND(1862-74) | T'ung Chih | 135.00 | 225.00 | 350.00 | 500.00 |

10 CASH
CAST COPPER
Rev: Character *K'u* (Kuche) above.

| 33-6 | ND(1821-50) | Tao Kuang | 3.50 | 5.00 | 7.50 | 15.00 |

Rev: Character *Hsin* (Sinkiang) above.

| 33-7 | ND(1821-50) | Tao Kuang | 2.50 | 4.00 | 6.50 | 13.00 |

NOTE: C#33-6 and 33-7 were cast during a later reign.

Obv: Type A

| 33-9 | ND(1851-61) | Hsien Feng | 2.00 | 3.00 | 4.50 | 8.00 |

Obv: Type A-2

| 33-13 | ND(1862-74) | T'ung Chih | 1.50 | 2.50 | 3.50 | 7.00 |

Rev: Character *K'u* (Kuche) above.

| 33-14 | ND(1862-74) | T'ung Chih | 1.50 | 2.50 | 3.50 | 7.00 |

Obv: Type A

| 33-16 | ND(1875-1908) | Kuang Hsu | 10.00 | 20.00 | 30.00 | 50.00 |

Rev: Characters *Chiu Nien* (year 9 – 1883) above.

| 33-17 | ND(1883) | Kuang Hsu | 10.00 | 17.50 | 25.50 | 45.00 |

Rev: Character *K'u* above.

C#	Date	Emperor	Good	VG	Fine	VF
33-18	ND(1875-1908)	Kuang Hsu	1.50	2.50	3.50	7.00

Rev: Semi-circle at lower right.

| 33-18.1 | ND(1875-1908) | Kuang Hsu | 7.50 | 13.50 | 22.50 | 35.00 |

| 33-19 | ND(1875-1908) | Kuang Hsu | 1.50 | 2.50 | 3.50 | 7.00 |

NOTE: Other varieties are reported for T'ung Chih and Kuang Hsu reigns.

50 CASH
CAST COPPER

| 33-10 | ND(1851-61) | Hsien Feng | 100.00 | 150.00 | 250.00 | 400.00 |

100 CASH

CAST COPPER

| 33-11 | ND(1851-61) | Hsien Feng | 100.00 | 125.00 | 150.00 | 225.00 |

Hammered Coinage
1/2 MISCAL (5 FEN)

SILVER, 1.45 g

Y#	Date	Mintage	Good	VG	Fine	VF
A7.13	ND(1875-1908)	—	—	—	Rare	—

Urumchi (Tihwa) now Urumqi Mint
EMPIRE
8 CASH

CAST COPPER
Obv: Type B-1

C#	Date	Emperor	Good	VG	Fine	VF
29-1	ND(1851-61)	Hsien Feng	21.50	35.00	50.00	75.00

Sinkiang / CHINA 376

10 CASH

CAST COPPER
Obv: Type B-1

C#	Date	Emperor	Good	VG	Fine	VF
29-2	ND(1851-61)	Hsien Feng	5.00	8.00	15.00	25.00

50 CASH
CAST COPPER

29-3	ND(1851-61)	Hsien Feng	Reported, not confirmed

80 CASH
CAST COPPER

29-5	ND(1851-61)	Hsien Feng	Reported, not confirmed

100 CASH
CAST COPPER

29-4	ND(1851-61)	Hsien Feng	—	Rare	—

Milled Coinage
2 MISCALS (2 MACE)

SILVER, 6.60 g
Obv: Simple two in Chinese.

Y#	Date	Mintage	VG	Fine	VF	XF
33	AH1321	—	15.00	22.00	55.00	90.00
	1322	—	15.00	22.00	55.00	90.00
	1323	—	17.50	30.00	55.00	90.00

Obv: Official two in Chinese.

33.1	AH1323	—	15.00	22.00	55.00	90.00
	1324	—	15.00	22.00	55.00	90.00
	1325	—	15.00	22.00	55.00	90.00

3 MISCALS

SILVER, 10.30 g
Obv: Simple three in Chinese.

34	AH1321	—	17.50	30.00	75.00	110.00
	1322	—	17.50	30.00	75.00	110.00
	1323	—	17.50	30.00	75.00	110.00

Obv: Official three in Chinese.

34a	AH1322	—	10.00	20.00	32.50	65.00
	1323	—	10.00	20.00	32.50	65.00
	1324	—	10.00	20.00	32.50	65.00
	1325	—	10.00	20.00	32.50	65.00

5 MISCALS

SILVER, 17.90 g
Obv: Simple five in Chinese.

Y#	Date	Mintage	VG	Fine	VF	XF
35	AH1321	—	20.00	35.00	70.00	125.00
	1322	—	20.00	35.00	70.00	125.00
	1323	—	20.00	35.00	70.00	125.00

Obv: Official five in Chinese.

35a	AH1322	—	15.00	30.00	60.00	100.00
	1323	—	20.00	40.00	70.00	125.00
	1324	—	15.00	30.00	60.00	100.00
	1325	—	15.00	30.00	60.00	100.00

Republic
SAR (TAEL)

SILVER, 35.00 g
Obv: Large characters.
Rev: Rosette at top between wheat ears.

Y#	Date	Year	VG	Fine	VF	XF
45	ND(1917)	6	10.00	12.50	17.50	35.00

Obv: Similar to Y#45 but w/small characters.
Rev: W/o rosette at top.

45.1	ND(1917)	6	10.00	12.50	17.50	35.00

Rev: Rosette at top between branches.

45.2	ND(1918)	7	12.50	20.00	30.00	60.00

Ushi (Wushih) now Wushi Mint
EMPIRE
10 CASH

 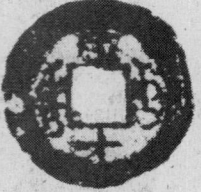

CAST COPPER
Rev: K'u (Kuche) above, Ushi in Manchu and Turki right and left.

C#	Date	Emperor	Good	VG	Fine	VF
34-4	ND(1909-11)	Hsuan T'ung	45.00	70.00	100.00	150.00

Yanghissar (Han-cheng) now Yengisar Mint
EMPIRE
1/2 MISCAL

SILVER, 1.45 g

Y#	Date	Mintage	Good	VG	Fine	VF
A7.14 (K998)	ND(1875-1908)		15.00	35.00	50.00	100.00

A7.20   ND(1875-1908)

Yarkand (Soche) now Sache Mint
EMPIRE
10 CASH

CAST COPPER

C#	Date	Emperor	Good	VG	Fine	VF
35-3	ND(1851-61)	Hsien Feng	3.50	5.00	7.50	12.50

Obv: Type A-2

35-7	ND(1862-74)	T'ung Chih	5.50	7.00	9.50	15.00

50 CASH
CAST COPPER

35-4	ND(1851-61)	Hsien Feng	100.00	135.00	175.00	250.00

100 CASH

CAST COPPER, 50-54mm
Obv: Type C

C#	Date	Emperor	Good	VG	Fine	VF
35-5.1	ND(1851-61)	Hsien Feng	110.00	150.00	300.00	600.00

45mm

| 35-5.2 | ND(1851-61) | Hsien Feng | 110.00 | 150.00 | 300.00 | 600.00 |

Hammered Coinage
1/2 MISCAL

SILVER, 1.45 g
Rev: Turki and Chinese leg.

Y#	Date	Mintage	Good	VG	Fine	VF
A7.15 (K998b)	ND (1875-1908)		5.00	7.50	12.50	22.00

Rev: Date at left.

| A7.16 (K1180) | AH1295 | — | 5.00 | 7.50 | 12.50 | 22.00 |

Rev: Date at right.

| A7.17 (K1180v) | AH1295 | — | 5.00 | 7.50 | 12.50 | 22.00 |

Rev: Turki, Chinese and Manchu leg.

| A7.18 (K1181) | ND (1875-1908) | | 5.00 | 7.50 | 12.50 | 22.00 |

Rebel Coinage
Ghazi Rashid

A rebel in Sinkiang (Xinjiang) about whom little is known. He was in power from 1862 until his death in 1867.

PUL

CAST COPPER

C#	Date	Good	VG	Fine	VF
36-7.1	ND	10.00	15.00	25.00	40.00

Obv: Incuse Turki leg. modified.

| 36-7.2 | ND | 10.00 | 15.00 | 25.00 | 40.00 |

Obv. leg: *Atalyq Ghazi*.

C#	Date	Good	VG	Fine	VF
36-8	ND	100.00	175.00	250.00	400.00

CASH

COPPER
Small legends

C#	Date	Mint	Good	VG	Fine	VF
36-1	AH1280	Kotsha	8.00	12.50	17.50	30.00

Large legends

| 36-2 | AH1280 | Kotsha | 8.00 | 12.50 | 17.50 | 30.00 |

NOTE: The date of C#36-1 and 36-2 is found at the top of the reverse. These coins are usually undated or with the date illegible. Even in clearly dated specimens, which are worth a substantial premium, the "0" never seems to be detectable.

| 36-3 | — | Aksu | — | — | — | Rare |

SZECHUAN PROVINCE
Sichuan

A province located in south central China. The largest of the Chinese provinces, Szechuan (Sichuan) is a plateau region watered by many rivers. These rivers carry much trading traffic. Agriculture or mining are the occupational choices of most of the populace. In World War II the national capitol was moved to Chungking in Szechuan (Sichuan). Chengtu was an active imperial mint that opened in 1732 and was in practically continuous operation until the advent of modern equipment. Modern minting was introduced in the province when Chengtu began milled coinage in 1898. A mint was authorized for Chungking in 1905 but it did not begin operations until 1913. The Chengtu Mint was looted by soldiers in 1925. The last republic issues from Szechuan (Sichuan) were dated 1932.

The machinery for the first Szechuan (Sichuan) Mint was produced in New Jersey and the dies were engraved in Philadelphia. The mint was opened in 1898, but closed within a few months and did not reopen until 1901. There is no doubt now that Y#234-238 (K#145-149) were the first issues of this mint, contrary to the Kann listings.

EMPIRE
CASH

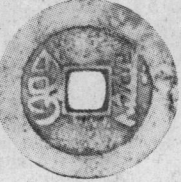

CAST BRASS
Obv: Type A

C#	Date	Emperor	Good	VG	Fine	VF
24-2	ND(1796-1820)	Chia Ch'ing	.50	1.00	1.50	2.00

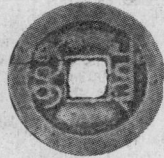

Obv: Type A

| 24-3 | ND(1821-50) | Tao Kuang | .50 | 1.00 | 2.00 | 3.00 |

C#	Date	Emperor	Good	VG	Fine	VF
24-4	ND(1851-61)	Hsien Feng	1.50	3.00	4.00	5.00

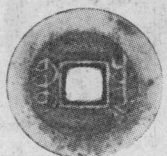

Reduced size.

| 24-4a | ND(1851-61) | Hsien Feng | 1.50 | 3.00 | 4.00 | 5.00 |

Rev: Character *Shih* (ten) above.
| 24-4.1 | ND(1851-61) | Hsien Feng | 5.00 | 8.00 | 12.50 | 20.00 |

Rev: Character *Wen* (unit) above.
| 24-4.2 | ND(1851-61) | Hsien Feng | 5.00 | 8.00 | 12.50 | 20.00 |

Rev: Character *Kung* (work) above.
| 24-4.3 | ND(1851-61) | Hsien Feng | 5.00 | 8.00 | 12.50 | 20.00 |

Rev: Character *Erh* (two) above.
| 24-4.4 | ND(1851-61) | Hsien Feng | 5.00 | 8.00 | 12.50 | 20.00 |

Rev: Circle above.
| 24-4.5 | ND(1851-61) | Hsien Feng | 5.00 | 8.00 | 12.50 | 20.00 |

Rev: Crescent standing on end above.
| 24-4.6 | ND(1851-61) | Hsien Feng | 5.00 | 8.00 | 12.50 | 20.00 |

Rev: Two horizontal and one vertical lines above.
| 24-4.7 | ND(1851-61) | Hsien Feng | 5.00 | 8.00 | 12.50 | 20.00 |

Rev: Two figures above, possibly 15.
| 24-4.8 | ND(1851-61) | Hsien Feng | 5.00 | 8.00 | 12.50 | 20.00 |

Rev: Crescent below.
| 24-4.9 | ND(1851-61) | Hsien Feng | 5.00 | 8.00 | 12.50 | 20.00 |

Obv: Type A-2
| 24-8 | ND(1862-74) | T'ung Chih | 5.00 | 8.00 | 12.50 | 20.00 |

Rev: Character *Shih* (ten) above and dot below.
| 24-8.1 | ND(1862-74) | T'ung Chih | 5.00 | 8.00 | 12.50 | 20.00 |

Rev: Character *Shih* above and crescent on edge below.
| 24-8.2 | ND(1862-74) | T'ung Chih | 5.00 | 8.00 | 12.50 | 20.00 |

Rev: Character *Shih* above and *San* below.
| 24-8.3 | ND(1862-74) | T'ung Chih | 5.00 | 8.00 | 12.50 | 20.00 |

Rev: Character *Shih* above and *Lin* below.
| 24-8.4 | ND(1862-74) | T'ung Chih | 5.00 | 8.00 | 12.50 | 20.00 |

Rev: Character *Wen* (unit) above and *Yi*.

below.

C#	Date	Emperor	Good	VG	Fine	VF
24-8.5	ND(1862-74)	T'ung Chih	5.00	8.00	12.50	20.00

Rev: Character *Wen* above and *Chi* below.

| 24-8.6 | ND(1862-74) | T'ung Chih | 5.00 | 8.00 | 12.50 | 20.00 |

Rev: Character *Wen* above and *Chuan* below.

| 24-8.7 | ND(1862-74) | T'ung Chih | 5.00 | 8.00 | 12.50 | 20.00 |

Obv: Type A

| 24-9 | ND(1875-1908) | Kuang Hsu | 7.50 | 12.50 | 17.50 | 35.00 |

NOTE: Refer to "Additional Characters" chart in the introduction to China.

10 CASH

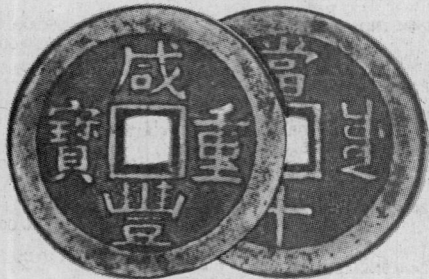

CAST BRASS
Obv: Type B-1
Rev: Type I mint mark.

| 24-5 | ND(1851-61) | Hsien Feng | 15.00 | 25.00 | 35.00 | 50.00 |

Rev: Type II mint mark.

| 24-5.1 | ND(1851-61) | Hsien Feng | 35.00 | 45.00 | 60.00 | 75.00 |

Rev: Type I mint mark.

| 24-10 | ND(1875-1908) | Kuang Hsu | — | — | Rare | — |

50 CASH

CAST BRASS
Obv: Type B-1.
Rev: Type II mint mark.

| 24-6 | ND(1851-61) | Hsien Feng | 55.00 | 75.00 | 100.00 | 125.00 |

100 CASH

CAST BRASS
Obv: Type C.
Rev: Type II mint mark.

| 24-7 | ND(1851-61) | Hsien Feng | 70.00 | 90.00 | 120.00 | 150.00 |

MILLED COINAGE
5 CASH

COPPER
Rev: Side view dragon.

Y#	Date	Mintage	VG	Fine	VF	XF
225	ND(1903-04)	.085	100.00	125.00	175.00	250.00

Rev: Flying dragon.

| 228 | ND(1903-04) | Inc. Ab. | 100.00 | 150.00 | 200.00 | 275.00 |

10 CASH

COPPER
Obv: Thick Manchu characters in center, large rosettes.

| 226 | ND(1903-05) | 95.960 | 20.00 | 40.00 | 60.00 | 100.00 |

Obv: Thin Manchu characters, small rosettes.

| 226.1 | ND(1903-05) | Inc. Ab. | 22.00 | 45.00 | 70.00 | 125.00 |

Obv: Large rosettes.

| 226.2 | ND(1903-05) | Inc. Ab. | 20.00 | 40.00 | 60.00 | 100.00 |

Obv: Two characters at bottom, 6-9mm apart.
Rev: Trident-shaped flame on dragons body under letters CHU.

| 229 | ND(1903-05) | Inc. Ab. | 4.00 | 6.50 | 10.00 | 17.50 |

Obv: Characters at bottom 4-5mm apart.

| 229.1 | ND(1903-05) | Inc. Ab. | 4.00 | 6.50 | 10.00 | 17.50 |

Obv: Manchu at 3 o'clock is lower in relation to center characters.

| 229.2 | ND(1903-05) | Inc. Ab. | 4.00 | 6.50 | 10.00 | 17.50 |

Obv: Characters 6-9mm apart.
Rev: Trident-shaped flame under letters HUE.

| 229.3 | ND(1903-05) | Inc. Ab. | 4.00 | 6.50 | 10.00 | 17.50 |

BRASS

| 229.3a | ND(1903-05) | Inc. Ab. | 4.00 | 6.50 | 10.00 | 17.50 |

Obv: Characters 4-5mm apart.

| 229.4 | ND(1903-05) | Inc. Ab. | 4.00 | 6.50 | 10.00 | 17.50 |

Obv: Bottom characters 6-9mm apart. Rev: W/o trident-shaped flame, instead a cloud pointing to the letter U.

Y#	Date	Mintage	VG	Fine	VF	XF
229.5	ND(1903-05)	Inc. Ab.	2.50	4.00	7.50	12.00

COPPER

| 229.5a | ND(1903-05) | Inc. Ab. | 3.00 | 5.00 | 10.00 | 15.00 |

BRASS
Obv: Characters 4-5mm apart.

| 229.6 | ND(1903-05) | Inc. Ab. | 4.00 | 6.00 | 10.00 | 17.50 |

COPPER

| 229.6a | ND(1903-05) | Inc. Ab. | 2.00 | 3.00 | 5.50 | 10.00 |

BRASS
Obv: Manchu at 3 o'clock is lower.

| 229.7 | ND(1903-05) | Inc. Ab. | 3.75 | 6.00 | 10.00 | 17.50 |

COPPER

| 229.7a | ND(1903-05) | Inc. Ab. | 2.00 | 3.50 | 6.00 | 9.00 |

BRASS
Obv: Characters 4-5mm apart. Rev: W/o cloud under CHU, high point of dragon's body under letter C, tail joins body over letter S in CASH.

| 229.8 | ND(1903-05) | Inc. Ab. | 4.00 | 6.00 | 9.00 | 17.50 |

COPPER

| 229.8a | ND(1903-05) | Inc. Ab. | 2.00 | 3.50 | 6.00 | 9.00 |

Rev: High point of dragons body under letter H, tail joins body over letter C in CASH.

| 229.9 | ND(1903-05) | Inc. Ab. | 2.00 | 3.50 | 6.00 | 9.00 |

| 231 | ND(1903-05) | Inc. Ab. | 150.00 | 200.00 | 225.00 | 275.00 |

Y#	Date	Mintage	VG	Fine	VF	XF
10t	CD1906	337,748	1.00	1.50	3.00	6.00

Bottom of Manchu character at 11 o'clock curls to left.
| 20t.1 | CD1909 | 231,930 | 1.00 | 1.50 | 3.00 | 6.00 |

BRASS
| 20t.1a | CD1909 | Inc. Ab. | 3.00 | 5.00 | 10.00 | 15.00 |

COPPER
Bottom of Manchu character at 11 o'clock curls to right.
| 20t.2 | CD1909 | Inc. Ab. | 5.00 | 9.00 | 12.00 | 17.50 |

20 CASH

COPPER
| 227 | ND(1903-05) | 25,319 | 100.00 | 125.00 | 175.00 | 250.00 |

Obv: Small Manchu at 3 and 9 o'clock.
Rev: Trident flame points to E of SZE.
| 230 | ND(1903-05) | Inc. Ab. | 12.00 | 20.00 | 35.00 | 60.00 |

Obv: Large Manchu at 3 and 9 o'clock. Rev: Large trident flame points to C of CHUEN.
| 230.1 | ND(1903-05) | Inc. Ab. | 12.00 | 20.00 | 35.00 | 60.00 |

Obv: Large Manchu. Rev: Trident flame under ZE.

Y#	Date	Mintage	VG	Fine	VF	XF
230.3	ND(1903-05)	Inc. Ab.	15.00	30.00	50.00	80.00

Rev: Trident flame under CHU of CHUEN, large letters.
| 230.4 | ND | — | 30.00 | 60.00 | 100.00 | 160.00 |

Rev: Trident flame points to E of CHUEN, small letters.
| 230.5 | ND(1903-05) | Inc. Ab. | — | — | | |

Obv: Different small Manchu.
Rev: Large 5 petalled rosettes, dragon differs.
| 230.6 | ND(1903-05) | Inc. Ab. | 12.00 | 20.00 | 35.00 | 60.00 |

BRASS
Obv: Small Manchu. Rev: Larger cloud under CHUEN.
| 230.7a | ND(1903-05) | Inc. Ab. | 15.00 | 25.00 | 40.00 | 70.00 |

Rev: Front view dragon.
| 232 | ND | — | — | Reported, not confirmed | | |

COPPER
| 11t | CD1906 | 51,028 | 10.00 | 17.50 | 27.50 | 50.00 |

Obv: Bottom of Manchu character at 11 o'clock curls right.
Y#	Date	Mintage	VG	Fine	VF	XF
21t.1	CD1909	33,414	15.00	27.50	40.00	70.00

Obv: Bottom of Manchu character at 11 o'clock curls left.
| 21t.2 | CD1909 | — | 15.00 | 27.50 | 40.00 | 70.00 |

BRASS
| 21t.1a | CD1909 | Inc. Ab. | 25.00 | 35.00 | 65.00 | 100.00 |

5 CENTS

1.3000 g, .820 SILVER, .0343 oz ASW
Y#	Date	Mintage	Fine	VF	XF	Unc
234	ND(1898; 1901-08)	.671	12.00	17.50	30.00	70.00

Errors in the English leg.
| 234.1 | ND(1901-08) | Inc. Ab. | 15.00 | 22.50 | 35.00 | 80.00 |

BRASS (OMS)
| 234a | ND(1898) | — | — | 250.00 | 350.00 | |

WHITE METAL, Piefort (OMS)
| 234b | ND(1898) | — | — | 250.00 | 350.00 | |

SILVER, 1.30 g
| 239 | ND(1910) | .566 | 20.00 | 30.00 | 50.00 | 110.00 |

10 CENTS

2.6000 g, .820 SILVER, .0686 oz ASW
| 235 | ND(1898; 1901-08) | 1.274 | 10.00 | 17.50 | 27.50 | 70.00 |

BRASS (OMS)
| 235a | ND(1898) | — | — | 250.00 | 350.00 | |

SILVER, 2.60 g
| 240 | ND(1909-11) | .278 | 25.00 | 30.00 | 50.00 | 110.00 |

20 CENTS

5.3000 g, .820 SILVER, .1397 oz ASW
Rev: Five flames on pearl.
| 236 | ND(1898; 1901-08) | .897 | 10.00 | 16.00 | 27.50 | 60.00 |

Rev: Six flames on pearl.
| 236.1 | ND(1898; 1901-08) | Inc. Ab. | 10.00 | 16.00 | 27.50 | 60.00 |

Rev: Seven flames on pearl.
| 236.2 | ND(1898; 1901-08) | Inc. Ab. | 10.00 | 16.00 | 27.50 | 60.00 |

Various errors in English leg.
| 236.3 | ND(1901-08) | Inc. Ab. | 15.00 | 22.50 | 35.00 | 70.00 |

BRASS (OMS)
| 236a | ND(1898) | | | | | |

5.3000 g, .820 SILVER, .1397 oz ASW
| 241 | ND(1909-11) | .041 | — | — | Rare | |

50 CENTS

13.2000 g, .860 SILVER, .3650 oz ASW
Rev: Dragon w/narrow face, small cross at
either side, large fireball.

Y#	Date	Mintage	Fine	VF	XF	Unc
237	ND(1898; 1901-08)	.474	17.50	35.00	60.00	150.00

Various errors in English leg.
237.1 ND(1901-08)
　　　Inc. Ab.　20.00　40.00　75.00　175.00

Rev: Dragon w/tapering face and small chin, small
fireball, small cross at either side of dragon.
237.2 ND(1901-08)
　　　Inc. Ab.　22.50　35.00　60.00　150.00

Rev: Dragon w/wide face and smaller fireball, thicker
spines on top of dragon's head, small cross at
either side of dragon.
237.3 ND(1901-08)
　　　Inc. Ab.　22.50　35.00　60.00　150.00

BRASS (OMS)
237a ND(1898)　—　—　—　550.00

SILVER, 13.20 g
242 ND(1909-11)
　　　.038　75.00　125.00　175.00　300.00

Rev. leg: Inverted A in place of V in PROVINCE.
242.1 ND(1909-11)
　　　Inc. Ab.　75.00　125.00　175.00　300.00

DOLLAR

26.8000 g, .900 SILVER, .7756 oz ASW
Rev: Dragon w/narrow face and large fireball, small
cross at either side of dragon.

Y#	Date	Mintage	Fine	VF	XF	Unc
238	ND(1898; 1901-08)	6.487	10.00	13.00	22.50	225.00

BRASS (OMS)
238a ND(1898)　—　—　—　850.00

SILVER
Rev. leg: Inverted A instead of V in PROVINCE.
238.1 ND(1901-08)
　　　Inc. Ab.　10.00　16.00　25.00　200.00

Rev: Dragon w/wider face and flatter pearl, small
cross at either side of dragon.
238.2 ND(1901-08)
　　　Inc. Ab.　10.00　16.00　25.00　300.00

Rev: 7 MACE and 3 CANDAREENS instead of
2 CANDAREENS.
238.3 ND(1901-08)
　　　Inc. Ab.　20.00　40.00　100.00　500.00

Rev: Large spines on dragon's body.
243 ND(1909-11)
　　　2.846　12.50　22.50　60.00　300.00

Rev: Inverted A Instead of V in PROVINCE.
243.1 ND(1909-11)
　　　Inc. Ab.　12.50　22.50　65.00　275.00

Rev: Small spines on dragon's body.
243.2 ND(1909-11)
　　　Inc. Ab.　65.00　100.00　200.00　500.00

REPUBLIC

Many coins in silver and minor metals, issued by warlords and Chinese Communists, circulated in such provinces as Kansu (Gansu), Szechuan (Sichuan) and Yunnan. These coins were struck or sometimes cast of silver or copper, but also of debased metals of cruder craftsmanship. Some coins in this category include Y#217, Y#459.3 and many pieces among Y#446 through Y#464. Y#447 through Y#450 come in differing degrees of copper: red copper, debased (yellow) copper and greenish yellow brass. To classify as copper, the color of the coin must be red to brown-red.

5 CASH

COPPER

Y#	Date	Mintage	VG	Fine	VF	XF
441	Yr.1 (1912)	.471	40.00	80.00	125.00	225.00

NOTE: Varieties exist.

BRASS
441a Yr.1 (1912) I.A.　—　—　—　—

SILVER
441b Yr.1 (1912)　—　—　—　1000.　1500.

COPPER
443 Yr.1 (1912) I.A.　35.00　70.00　110.00　150.00

446 Yr.1 (1912) I.A.　—　—　Rare　—

BRASS
446a Yr.1 (1912) I.A.　—　—　Rare　—

10 CASH

COPPER
Obv: Two rosettes
447 Yr.1 (1912)
　　　108.618　1.75　3.00　10.00　20.00
　　Yr.2 (1913) I.A.　6.00　15.00　25.00　50.00

BRASS
447a Yr.1 (1912) I.A.　.80　1.50　2.50　5.00
　　Yr.2 (1913) I.A.　1.60　4.00　8.00　20.00

Obv: Three rosettes.
447.1a Yr.2 (1913) I.A.　—　—　Rare　—

Szechuan / CHINA 381

20 CASH

COPPER
Obv: Two rosettes.

Y#	Date	Mintage	VG	Fine	VF	XF
448	Yr.1 (1912)	115.061	1.00	2.50	5.00	15.00
	Yr.2 (1913)	I.A.	—	Reported, not confirmed		

BRASS

Y#	Date	Mintage	VG	Fine	VF	XF
448a	Yr.1 (1912)	I.A.	.75	1.50	2.50	6.00
	Yr.2 (1913)	I.A.	1.00	2.00	3.50	7.00

COPPER
Obv: Three rosettes.

Y#	Date	Mintage	VG	Fine	VF	XF
448.1	Yr.2 (1913)	I.A.	350.00	500.00	650.00	800.00
	Yr.3 (1914)	I.A.	—	Reported, not confirmed		

BRASS

Y#	Date	Mintage	VG	Fine	VF	XF
448.1a	Yr.2 (1913)	I.A.	2.50	6.00	12.00	25.00
	Yr.3 (1914)	I.A.	2.50	6.00	12.00	25.00

NOTE: There are many varieties of this 20 Cash; small and large rosettes; open and closed size characters and exaggerated size character with horns.

2 CENTS

COPPER

Y#	Year	Date	VG	Fine	VF	XF
476	19	(1930)	100.00	225.00	325.00	525.00

BRASS

Y#	Year	Date	VG	Fine	VF	XF
476a	19	(1930)	—	—	—	—

50 CASH

COPPER
Rev: Small flower in center.

Y#	Date	Mintage	VG	Fine	VF	XF
449	Yr.1 (1912)	489.382	2.00	4.00	7.00	15.00

BRASS

Y#	Date	Mintage	VG	Fine	VF	XF
449a	Yr.1 (1912)	I.A.	1.50	3.50	6.00	10.00

COPPER
Rev: Larger flower in center.

Y#	Date	Mintage	VG	Fine	VF	XF
449.1	Yr.1 (1912)	I.A.	2.00	5.00	10.00	20.00

BRASS

Y#	Date	Mintage	VG	Fine	VF	XF
449.1a	Yr.1 (1912)	I.A.	2.50	6.00	12.50	25.00

COPPER
Obv: Three rosettes. Rev: Small flower in center.

Y#	Date	Mintage	VG	Fine	VF	XF
449.2	Yr.2 (1913)	I.A.	2.25	5.50	11.00	22.00

BRASS

Y#	Date	Mintage	VG	Fine	VF	XF
449.2a	Yr.2 (1913)	I.A.	2.25	5.50	11.00	22.00
	Yr.3 (1914)	I.A.	2.25	5.50	11.00	22.00

COPPER

Y#	Date	Mintage	VG	Fine	VF	XF
462	Yr.15 (1926)	.090	18.00	35.00	65.00	100.00

BRASS

Y#	Date	Mintage	VG	Fine	VF	XF
462a	Yr.15 (1926)	I.A.	16.00	32.50	55.00	80.00

100 CASH

COPPER
Obv: Two rosettes. Rev: Large flower in center.

Y#	Date	Mintage	VG	Fine	VF	XF
450	Yr.2 (1913)	399.212	2.50	6.00	8.50	17.50
	Yr.3 (1914)	—	30.00	40.00	50.00	60.00

BRASS

Y#	Date	Mintage	VG	Fine	VF	XF
450a	Yr.2 (1913)	I.A.	1.50	3.00	6.00	10.00

COPPER
Obv: Three rosettes.
Rev: Small flower in center.

Y#	Date	Mintage	VG	Fine	VF	XF
450.1	Yr.2 (1913)	I.A.	3.50	9.00	15.00	25.00
	Yr.3 (1914)	—	—	—	—	—

COPPER or BRASS
200 Cash, Y#459 cut in half.

Y#	Date	Mintage	VG	Fine	VF	XF
459x	ND	2	3.50	9.50	16.00	26.00

NOTE: It has been reported that the 200 Cash, Y#459 was cut in half and circulated locally as 100 Cash and cut in quarters for 50 Cash.

COPPER

Y#	Date	Mintage	VG	Fine	VF	XF
463	Yr.15 (1926)	7.055	3.50	9.00	14.50	25.00

BRASS

Y#	Date	Mintage	VG	Fine	VF	XF
463a	Yr.15 (1926)	Inc. Ab.	3.25	8.00	12.50	20.00

NOTE: Two reverse varieties known. Often struck over older 10 Cash coins.

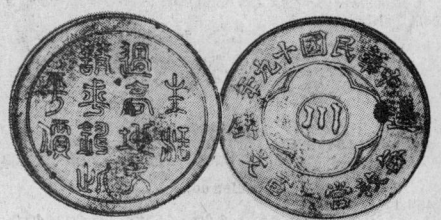

COPPER

Y#	Date	Mintage	VG	Fine	VF	XF
466	Yr.15 (1926)	Inc. Ab.	150.00	225.00	300.00	400.00
	Yr.19 (1930)	—	125.00	150.00	200.00	300.00

BRASS

Y#	Date	Mintage	VG	Fine	VF	XF
466a	Yr.19 (1930)	—	125.00	150.00	225.00	375.00

Szechuan / CHINA 382

200 CASH

COPPER

Y#	Date	Mintage	VG	Fine	VF	XF
459	Yr.2 (1913)	360.274	—	Reported, not confirmed		

BRASS

| 459a | Yr.2 (1913) | I.A. | 20.00 | 40.00 | 80.00 | 125.00 |

COPPER
Obv: Tassels draped over flag poles.

| 459.1 | Yr.2 (1913) | I.A. | 6.00 | 10.00 | 25.00 | 40.00 |

BRASS

| 459.1a | Yr.2 (1913) | — | 4.50 | 8.00 | 20.00 | 35.00 |

COPPER
Rev: Smaller stars at sides.

| 459.2 | Yr.2 (1913) | I.A. | 5.00 | 9.00 | 22.50 | 37.50 |

Plain edge.

| 464 | Yr.15 (1926) | 404.644 | 4.00 | 12.00 | 17.00 | 30.00 |

Reeded edge.

| 464.1 | Yr.15 (1926) | Inc. Ab. | 6.00 | 15.00 | 25.00 | 40.00 |

BRASS
Plain edge.

| 464a | Yr.15 (1926) | Inc. Ab. | 4.50 | 12.00 | 17.00 | 30.00 |

Reeded edge

| 464.1a | Yr.15 (1926) | I.A. | — | — | — | — |

Obv: Similar to Y#464. Rev: Dot within first 0 of 200.

Y#	Date	Mintage	VG	Fine	VF	XF
464.2	Yr.15 (1926)	I.A.				

NOTE: Many varieties: Open and closed buds; overstruck on earlier pieces and on virgin flans; different sizes and thicknesses.

10 CENTS

SILVER, 2.60 g

Y#	Date	Mintage	Fine	VF	XF	Unc
453	Yr.1 (1912)	.370	17.50	30.00	50.00	100.00

NICKEL

| 468 | ND | — | 35.00 | 90.00 | 110.00 | 160.00 |

SILVER

| 468a | ND | — | 25.00 | 60.00 | 90.00 | 125.00 |

IRON

| 468b | ND | — | 20.00 | 50.00 | 70.00 | 125.00 |

COPPER-NICKEL

| 468c | ND | — | 12.00 | 30.00 | 45.00 | 70.00 |

BRASS (OMS)

| 468d | ND | | | | | |

20 CENTS

SILVER, 5.20 g

| 454 | Yr.1 (1912) | .095 | 30.00 | 50.00 | 85.00 | 150.00 |

Tibetan War

K#	Date	Mintage	Fine	VF	XF	Unc
795	1932	—	45.00	110.00	165.00	250.00

NOTE: Authenticity not established.

50 CENTS

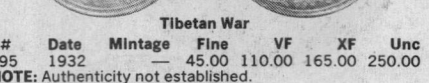

SILVER, 12.90 g

Y#	Date	Mintage	Fine	VF	XF	Unc
455	Yr.1 (1912)	37.942	10.00	20.00	40.00	115.00
	Yr.2 (1913)	I.A.			Rare	

COPPER (OMS)

| 455a | Yr.1 (1912) | | | | | |

SILVER, 10.50 g
Sun Yat-sen

Y#	Date	Mintage	Fine	VF	XF	Unc
473	Yr.17 (1928)	I.A.	100.00	300.00	475.00	750.00

DOLLAR

SILVER, 25.60 g

| 456 | Yr.1 (1912) | 55.670 | 7.00 | 10.00 | 15.00 | 70.00 |

Rev: Right hand character w/2 dots instead of horizontal stroke.

| 456.1 | Yr.1 (1912) | I.A. | — | — | — | — |
| 456.2 | Yr.3 (1914) | I.A. | — | — | Rare | — |

NOTE: Silver content ranged from 0.88 to 0.50 fine.

25.50 g
Sun Yat-sen
Similar to 50 Cents, Y#473.

| 474 | Yr.17 (1928) | I.A. | 400.00 | 600.00 | 850.00 | 1400 |

COPPER (OMS)

| 474a | Yr.17 (1928) | | | | | |

TAIWAN

For historical information refer to introductory paragraph of the Republic of China following the People's Republic of China listings.

EMPIRE
CASH

CAST BRASS
Obv: Type A

C#	Date	Emperor	Good	VG	Fine	VF
25-2	ND(1796-1820)	Chia Ch'ing	—	—	Rare	

 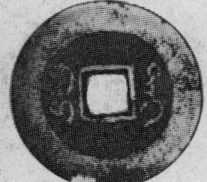

Obv: Type A

| 25-6 | ND(1851-61) | Hsien Feng | 30.00 | 40.00 | 50.00 | 60.00 |

5 CASH

CAST BRASS
Obv: Manchu *Boo* left, Chinese *Tai* right, *Wu Wen* above and below.

| 25-8 | ND(1851-61) | Hsien Feng | Reported, not confirmed | | | |

10 CASH
CAST BRASS

C#	Date	Emperor	Good	VG	Fine	VF
25-7	ND(1851-61)	Hsien Feng	Reported, not confirmed			

MILLED COINAGE

臺灣製局

Made in Taiwan

臺省製造

Made in Tai Province

5 CENTS
1.3000 g, .820 SILVER, .0343 oz ASW
Similar to 10 Cents, Y#247.

Y#	Date	Mintage	Fine	VF	XF	Unc
246	ND(1893-94)		100.00	175.00	250.00	500.00

10 CENTS

2.7000 g, .820 SILVER, .0712 oz ASW
Obv: Four Chinese characters above meaning: *Made in Taiwan*; large characters in outside circle; small characters inside.

247	ND(1893-94)		20.00	30.00	60.00	250.00

Obv: Smaller characters in outside circle, larger characters inside circle.

| 247.1 | ND(1893-94) | | 20.00 | 30.00 | 60.00 | 250.00 |

Obv: Four Chinese characters above meaning: *Made in Tai Province*.

| 247.2 | ND(1893-94) | | 25.00 | 40.00 | 100.00 | 300.00 |

20 CENTS
5.4000 g, .820 SILVER, .1424 oz ASW
Obv: Four Chinese characters above, meaning *Made in Taiwan*.

| 248 | ND(1894) | — | | — | Rare | |

Obv: Four Chinese characters above, meaning: *Made in Tai Province*.

| 248.1 | ND(1894) | — | | — | Rare | |

NOTE: These coins were minted at an arsenal in Taiwan.

DOLLAR
"Old Man"

SILVER, 26.80 g

C#	Date	Mintage	VG	Fine	VF	XF
25-3	ND(1837-1845)	150.00	225.00	400.00	2000.	

NOTE: C#25-3 normally comes w/2 chops at lower left on the reverse. Many varieties exist.

25.00 g
Obv: Chinese *Chia Yi Hsien Tsao*.

K#	Year	Date	VG	Fine	VF	XF
3	1	(1862)	1800.	3000.	4500.	6500.

NOTE: Market valuations for the dollar coins above are for specimens with a few light chops. For unchopped specimens, add 10 percent and for heavily chopped specimens deduct 20 percent.

"Military Ration"

Rev: Crossed lotus flowers.

C#	Date	Mintage	VG	Fine	VF	XF
25-4	ND(1853)	—	150.00	250.00	500.00	2700.

NOTE: C#25-4 normally comes w/2 chops (one being a Chinese numeral *six*) on the reverse.

25.30 g
Rev: Crossed brushes.

C#	Date	Mintage	VG	Fine	VF	XF
25-5	ND(1862)	—	200.00	300.00	600.00	3200.

NOTE: The market values shown for C#25-3/25-5 are for coins which have been lightly chopmarked. Attribution of C#25-4 and C#25-5 to Taiwan is not fully accepted. Other sources attribute these coins to Chihli (Hebei) Province.

YUNNAN PROVINCE

A province located in south China bordering Burma. It is very mountainous with many lakes. Yunnan was the home of various active imperial mints. A modern mint was established at Kunming in 1905 and the first struck copper coins were issued in 1906 and the first struck silver coins in 1908. General Tang Chi-Yao issued coins in gold, silver and copper with his portrait in 1919. The last Republican coins were struck here in 1949.

EMPIRE
Yunnanfu Mint
CASH

CAST BRASS
Obv: Type A

C#	Date	Emperor	Good	VG	Fine	VF
26-2	ND(1796-1820)	Chia Ch'ing	.10	.25	.50	.75

Rev: Crescent above.

| 26-2.1 | ND(1796-1820) | Chia Ch'ing | 1.00 | 2.00 | 3.00 | 5.00 |

Obv: Type A

| 26.3 | ND(1821-50) | Tao Kuang | .10 | .25 | .50 | .75 |

Rev: Crescent above.

| 26.3.1 | ND(1821-50) | Tao Kuang | 2.50 | 3.50 | 5.00 | 7.50 |

Rev: Horizontal line above.

| 26.3.2 | ND(1821-50) | Tao Kuang | 1.50 | 2.00 | 4.00 | 6.00 |

Obv: Type A

| 26.4 | ND(1851-61) | Hsien Feng | .50 | 1.00 | 1.50 | 2.50 |

Rev: Crescent above.

| 26.4.1 | ND(1851-61) | Hsien Feng | 5.00 | 7.50 | 10.00 | 15.00 |

Rev: Crescent below.

| 26.4.2 | ND(1851-61) | Hsien Feng | 5.00 | 7.50 | 10.00 | 15.00 |

Rev: Crescent standing on end above.

| 26.4.3 | ND(1851-61) | Hsien Feng | 5.00 | 7.50 | 10.00 | 15.00 |

Yunnan / CHINA

Rev: Dot within crescent above.
C#	Date	Emperor	Good	VG	Fine	VF
26-4.4	ND(1851-61)	Hsien Feng	5.00	7.50	10.00	15.00

Rev: Circle above.
26-4.5 ND(1851-61)
Hsien Feng 5.00 7.50 10.00 15.00

Rev: Circle below.
26-4.6 ND(1851-61)
Hsien Feng 5.00 7.50 10.00 15.00

Rev: Dot within circle above.
26-4.7 ND(1851-61)
Hsien Feng 5.00 7.50 10.00 15.00

Rev: Dot within circle below.
26-4.8 ND(1851-61)
Hsien Feng 5.00 7.50 10.00 15.00

Rev: An X above the center.
26-4.9 ND(1851-61)
Hsien Feng 5.00 7.50 10.00 15.00

Rev: Character *Ho* above and circle below.
26-4.10 ND(1851-61)
Hsien Feng 5.00 7.50 10.00 15.00

Rev: Character *Ho* above and dot within circle below.
26-4.11 ND(1851-61)
Hsien Feng 5.00 7.50 10.00 15.00

Rev: Character *Kung* above.
26-4.12 ND(1851-61)
Hsien Feng 5.00 7.50 10.00 15.00

Rev: Character *Yi* (one) above.
26-4.13 ND(1851-61)
Hsien Feng 5.00 7.50 10.00 15.00

Rev: Character *Erh* (two) above.
26-4.14 ND(1851-61)
Hsien Feng Reported, not confirmed

Rev: Character *San* (three) above.
26-4.15 ND(1851-61)
Hsien Feng 5.00 7.50 10.00 15.00

Rev: Character *Ssu* (four) above.
26-4.16 ND(1851-61)
Hsien Feng 5.00 7.50 10.00 15.00

Rev: Character above probably meaning "five".
26-4.17 ND(1851-61)
Hsien Feng 5.00 7.50 10.00 15.00

Rev: Character *Shih* (ten) above and a crescent below.
26-4.18 ND(1851-61)
Hsien Feng 5.00 7.50 10.00 15.00

Rev: Character *Chin* above and dot in circle below.
26-4.19 ND(1851-61)
Hsien Feng 5.00 7.50 10.00 15.00

Rev: Manchu character above.
26-4.20 ND(1851-61)
Hsien Feng 5.00 7.50 10.00 15.00

Rev: X above hole in center.
26-4.21 ND(1851-61)
Hsien Feng 5.00 7.50 10.00 15.00

 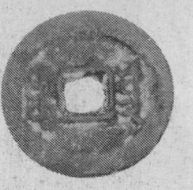

Obv: Type A-2
C#	Date	Emperor	Good	VG	Fine	VF
26-7	ND(1862-74)	T'ung Chih	1.50	3.00	4.00	6.00

Rev: Circle above.
26-7.1 ND(1862-74)
T'ung Chih 5.00 7.50 10.00 15.00

Rev: Dot within circle above.
26-7.2 ND(1862-74)
T'ung Chih 5.00 7.50 10.00 15.00

Rev: Dot within crescent above.
26-7.3 ND(1862-74)
T'ung Chih 5.00 7.50 10.00 15.00

Rev: Crescent below.
26-7.4 ND(1862-74)
T'ung Chih 5.00 7.50 10.00 15.00

Rev: Vertical line above.
26-7.5 ND(1862-74)
T'ung Chih 5.00 7.50 10.00 15.00

Rev: Vertical line below.
26-7.6 ND(1862-74)
T'ung Chih 5.00 7.50 10.00 15.00

Rev: Character *Kung* above center.
26-7.7 ND(1862-74)
T'ung Chih 5.00 7.50 10.00 15.00

Rev: Character *Ho* above.
26-7.8 ND(1862-74)
T'ung Chih 5.00 7.50 10.00 15.00

Rev: Character *Ta* above.
26-7.9 ND(1862-74)
T'ung Chih 5.00 7.50 10.00 15.00

Rev: Character *Shan* above.
26-7.10 ND(1862-74)
T'ung Chih 5.00 7.50 10.00 15.00

Rev: Character *Chuan* below.
26-7.11 ND(1862-74)
T'ung Chih 5.00 7.50 10.00 15.00

Rev: Character *Yi* (one) above.
26-7.12 ND(1862-74)
T'ung Chih 5.00 7.50 10.00 15.00

Rev: Character *Wu* (five) inverted below.
26-7.13 ND(1862-74)
T'ung Chih 5.00 7.50 10.00 15.00

Rev: Character *Liu* (six) above.
26-7.14 ND(1862-74)
T'ung Chih 5.00 7.50 10.00 15.00

Rev: Characters *Liu* (six) above, but sideways.
26-7.15 ND(1862-74)
T'ung Chih 5.00 7.50 10.00 15.00

Rev: Character *Pa* (eight) above.
26-7.16 ND(1862-74)
T'ung Chih 5.00 7.50 10.00 15.00

Rev: Character *Shih* (ten) above.
26-7.17 ND(1862-74)
T'ung Chih 5.00 7.50 10.00 15.00

Rev: Character *Shih* (ten) above, crescent below.
26-7.18 ND(1862-74)
T'ung Chih 5.00 7.50 10.00 15.00

Rev: Characters *Shih Yi* (eleven) above.
26-7.19 ND(1862-74)
T'ung Chih 5.00 7.50 10.00 15.00

Rev: Characters *Shih* (ten) above and *Yi* (one) below.
C#	Date	Emperor	Good	VG	Fine	VF
26-7.20	ND(1862-74)	T'ung Chih	5.00	7.50	10.00	15.00

Rev: Characters *Shih* (ten) above *San* (three) below.
26-7.21 ND(1862-74)
T'ung Chih 5.00 7.50 10.00 15.00

Rev: Character *Jen* above.
26-7.22 ND(1862-74)
T'ung Chih 5.00 7.50 10.00 15.00

Rev: Inverted crescent above.
26-7.23 ND(1862-74)
T'ung Chih 5.00 7.50 10.00 15.00

26-9 ND(1875-1908)
Kuang Hsu 2.00 4.00 5.00 7.00

Rev: Character *Kung* above.
26-9.1 ND(1875-1908)
Kuang Hsu 2.00 5.00 7.50 10.00

Rev: Character *Ssu* (four) above.
26-9.2 ND(1875-1908)
Kuang Hsu 2.50 5.00 7.50 10.00

Rev: Character *Chin* above.
26-9.3 ND(1875-1908)
Kuang Hsu 2.50 5.00 7.50 10.00

Rev: Crescent above, dot below.
26-9.4 ND(1875-1908)
Kuang Hsu 2.50 5.00 7.50 10.00

Rev: Dot above hole.
26-9.5 ND(1875-1908)
Kuang Hsu 2.50 5.00 7.50 10.00

Rev: Character *Wang* above hole.
26-11 ND(1909-11)
Hsuan T'ung 75.00 100.00 150.00 220.00

Refer to "Additional Characters" chart in the Introduction to China.

10 CASH

CAST BRASS
Obv: Type B-1

C#	Date	Emperor	Good	VG	Fine	VF
26-5	ND(1851-61)	Hsien Feng	2.00	5.00	7.00	13.00

37mm
| 26-8 | ND(1862-74) | T'ung Chih | 30.00 | 40.00 | 45.00 | 50.00 |

35mm
| 26-8.1 | ND(1862-74) | T'ung Chih | 30.00 | 40.00 | 45.00 | 50.00 |
| 26-10 | ND(1875-1908) | Kuang Hsu | — | — | Rare | — |

50 CASH
CAST BRASS
| 26-6 | ND(1851-61) | Hsien Feng | 50.00 | 60.00 | 70.00 | 80.00 |

Tungch'uan Mint
CASH

CAST BRASS
Obv: Type A-1
Rev: Type 1 mint mark.
| 27-1 | ND(1796-1820) | Chia Ch'ing | .75 | 1.50 | 3.50 | 6.00 |

Rev: Type 2 mint mark.
| 27-1.1 | ND(1796-1820) | Chia Ch'ing | 5.00 | 7.50 | 10.00 | 15.00 |

Obv: Type A
Rev: Type 1 mint mark.
| 27-2 | ND(1821-50) | Tao Kuang | .50 | 1.00 | 1.50 | 2.50 |

 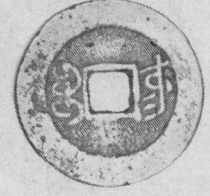

Rev: Type 3 mint mark.
| 27-2.1 | ND(1821-50) | Tao Kuang | .50 | 1.00 | 1.50 | 2.50 |

Obv: Type A
C#	Date	Emperor	Good	VG	Fine	VF
27-3	ND(1851-61)	Hsien Feng	1.50	3.00	4.00	6.00

Rev: Character *Cheng* above.
| 27-3.1 | ND(1851-61) | Hsien Feng | 5.00 | 7.50 | 10.00 | 15.00 |

Obv: Type A-2
| 27-5 | ND(1862-74) | T'ung Chih | 1.50 | 3.00 | 4.00 | 6.00 |

Rev: Character *Cheng* above and crescent below.
| 27-5.1 | ND(1862-74) | T'ung Chih | 5.00 | 7.50 | 10.00 | 15.00 |

Rev: Character *Cheng* above, dot below.
| 27-5.2 | ND(1862-74) | T'ung Chih | 5.00 | 7.50 | 10.00 | 15.00 |

Obv: Type A
| 27-6 | ND(1875-1908) | Kuang Hsu | 5.00 | 7.50 | 10.00 | 15.00 |

Rev: Character *Chin* above.
| 27-6.1 | ND(1875-1908) | Kuang Hsu | 5.00 | 7.50 | 10.00 | 15.00 |

Rev: Characters *Ts'un* below.
| 27-6.2 | ND(1875-1908) | Kuang Hsu | 5.00 | 7.50 | 10.00 | 15.00 |
| 27-7 | ND(1909-11) | Hsuan T'ung | — | — | Rare | — |

10 CASH

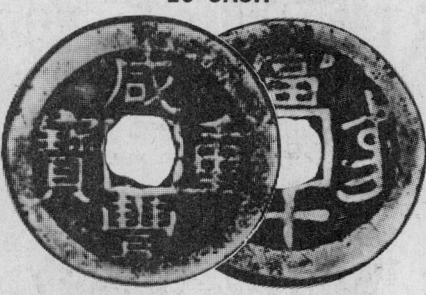

BRASS
Obv: Type B-1
| 27-4 | ND(1851-61) | Hsien Feng | 5.00 | 9.00 | 16.00 | 30.00 |

Uncertain Mint
The following coins bear a Manchu mint mark, different from Fukien (Fujian) which reads, 'FU'. though previously attributed to Fukien (Fujian), they are now believed to have been produced in Yunnan.

CASH
CAST BRASS
Obv: Type A-2
Rev: Crescent above.
KM#	Date	Emperor	Good	VG	Fine	VF
1	ND(1851-61)	Hsien Feng	10.00	15.00	20.00	25.00

Rev: Circle above.
| 2 | ND(1851-61) | Hsien Feng | 10.00 | 15.00 | 20.00 | 25.00 |

Obv: Type A-2.
Rev: W/o characters above or below center hole.
| 10 | ND(1862-74) | T'ung Chih | 10.00 | 15.00 | 20.00 | 25.00 |

Rev: Crescent above.
| 11 (1) | ND(1862-74) | T'ung Chih | 10.00 | 15.00 | 20.00 | 25.00 |

 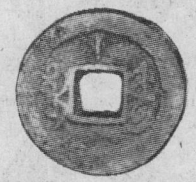

Rev: Vertical line above.
| 12 (1.2) | ND(1862-74) | T'ung Chih | 25.00 | 30.00 | 35.00 | 40.00 |

Rev: Vertical line below.
| 13 | ND(1862-74) | T'ung Chih | 25.00 | 30.00 | 35.00 | 40.00 |

Rev: Dot above.
| 14 | ND(1862-74) | T'ung Chih | 25.00 | 30.00 | 35.00 | 40.00 |

Rev: Dot below.
| 15 | ND(1862-74) | T'ung Chih | 25.00 | 30.00 | 35.00 | 40.00 |

Rev: With "X" above.
| 16 (1.12) | ND(1862-74) | T'ung Chih | 25.00 | 30.00 | 35.00 | 40.00 |

Rev: Character *Cheng* above.
| 21 (1.10) | ND(1862-74) | T'ung Chih | 25.00 | 30.00 | 35.00 | 40.00 |

Rev: Character *Cheng* above and circle below.
| 22 (1.11) | ND(1862-74) | T'ung Chih | 25.00 | 30.00 | 35.00 | 40.00 |

Rev: Character *Chih* above.
| 23 (1.6) | ND(1862-74) | T'ung Chih | 25.00 | 30.00 | 35.00 | 40.00 |

Yunnan / CHINA   386

Rev: Character Chu above. | **Rev: Character Sin above.** | **Rev: Character Shih (ten) above.**

KM#	Date	Emperor	Good	VG	Fine	VF
25 (1.13)	ND(1862-74)	T'ung Chih	25.00	30.00	35.00	40.00

KM#	Date	Emperor	Good	VG	Fine	VF
43 (1.14)	ND(1862-74)	T'ung Chih	25.00	30.00	35.00	40.00

KM#	Date	Emperor	Good	VG	Fine	VF
70 (1.14)	ND(1862-74)	T'ung Chih	25.00	30.00	35.00	40.00

NOTE: Other varieties probably exist. Refer to "Additional Characters" chart in the introduction.

MILLED COINAGE
10 CASH

Rev: Character Chuan above. | **Rev: Character Ta above.**

	Date	Emperor	Good	VG	Fine	VF
27 (1.5)	ND(1862-74)	T'ung Chih	25.00	30.00	35.00	40.00
45 (1.3)	ND(1862-74)	T'ung Chih	25.00	30.00	35.00	40.00

COPPER
Obv: Large mint mark Yun in center.

Y#	Date	Mintage	VG	Fine	VF	XF
10u	CD1906	36,701	10.00	22.00	35.00	60.00

Rev: Character Chung above. | **Rev: Character Yu above.**

| 29 (1.7) | ND(1862-74) | T'ung Chih | 25.00 | 30.00 | 35.00 | 40.00 |
| 47 (1.8) | ND(1862-74) | T'ung Chih | 25.00 | 30.00 | 35.00 | 40.00 |

Obv: Small mint mark Yun in center.
| 10u.1 | CD1906 | Inc. Ab. | 25.00 | 55.00 | 85.00 | 125.00 |

Rev: Character Feng above. | **Rev: Yun above.**

| 31 (1.15) | ND(1862-74) | T'ung Chih | 25.00 | 30.00 | 35.00 | 40.00 |
| 49 | ND(1862-74) | T'ung Chih | 25.00 | 30.00 | 35.00 | 40.00 |

Rev: Character Ho above.
| 33 (1.4) | ND(1862-74) | T'ung Chih | 25.00 | 30.00 | 35.00 | 40.00 |

Obv: Mint mark Tien in center.
| 10v | CD1906 | Inc. Ab. | 12.00 | 30.00 | 40.00 | 65.00 |

20 CASH

Rev: Jen above. | **Rev: Yi (one) above.**

| 35 | ND(1862-74) | T'ung Chih | 25.00 | 30.00 | 35.00 | 40.00 |
| 61 (1.1) | ND(1862-74) | T'ung Chih | 25.00 | 30.00 | 35.00 | 40.00 |

COPPER
Obv: Large mint mark Yun in center.
| 11u | CD1906 | .645 | 125.00 | 175.00 | 225.00 | 275.00 |

Rev: Character Kung above. | **Rev: Erh (two) above.**

| 37 (1.9) | ND(1862-74) | T'ung Chih | 25.00 | 30.00 | 35.00 | 40.00 |
| 62 | ND(1862-74) | T'ung Chih | 25.00 | 30.00 | 35.00 | 40.00 |

Rev: Shan above. | **Rev: San (three) above.**

| 39 | ND(1862-74) | T'ung Chih | 25.00 | 30.00 | 35.00 | 40.00 |
| 63 | ND(1862-74) | T'ung Chih | 25.00 | 30.00 | 35.00 | 40.00 |

Rev: Shun above. | **Rev: Wu (five) above.**

| 41 | ND(1862-74) | T'ung Chih | 25.00 | 30.00 | 35.00 | 40.00 |
| 65 | ND(1862-74) | T'ung Chih | 25.00 | 30.00 | 35.00 | 40.00 |

Obv: Small mint mark Yun in center.
| 11u.1 | CD1906 | — | 125.00 | 175.00 | 225.00 | 275.00 |

Obv: Mint mark Tien in center.

Y#	Date	Mintage	VG	Fine	VF	XF
11v.1	CD1906	Inc. Ab.	150.00	275.00	400.00	550.00

BRASS

| 11v.1a | CD1906 | Inc.Ab. | 175.00 | 350.00 | 450.00 | 600.00 |

Obv: YUN-NAN PROVINCE + TWENTY CASH in English.
Rev: Dragon in small circle.

Hsu#	Date	Mintage	VG	Fine	VF	XF
324	CD 1906	—	—	—	—	1150.

10 CENTS

SILVER, 2.60 g

Y#	Date	Mintage	Fine	VF	XF	Unc
255	ND(1911)	.902	15.00	30.00	45.00	90.00

20 CENTS

SILVER, 5.30 g

| 252 | ND(1908) | .532 | 18.00 | 35.00 | 60.00 | 100.00 |

NOTE: Many minor varieties.

Rev: Two circles beneath pearl.

| 256 | ND(1911) | I.A. | 12.50 | 17.50 | 32.50 | 65.00 |

Rev: Three circles beneath pearl.

| 256.1 | ND(1911) | I.A. | 12.50 | 22.50 | 37.50 | 65.00 |

50 CENTS

SILVER, 13.20 g

| 253 | ND(1908) | — | 6.00 | 10.00 | 18.00 | 75.00 |

COPPER (OMS)

| 253a | ND(1908) | — | — | — | — | 250.00 |

BRASS (OMS)

| 253b | ND(1908) | — | — | — | — | 250.00 |

SILVER, 13.20 g

Rev: Two circles under pearl.

Y#	Date	Mintage	Fine	VF	XF	Unc
257	ND(1911)	—	4.50	6.00	9.00	20.00

Rev: Three circles under pearl.

| 257.1 | ND(1911) | — | 4.50 | 6.00 | 9.00 | 20.00 |

Rev: Four circles under pearl.

| 257.2 | ND(1911) | — | 4.50 | 6.00 | 9.00 | 20.00 |

COPPER (OMS)

| 257a | ND(1908) | — | — | — | 200.00 | — |

NOTE: There are more than 30 varieties of Y#257. In 1949 this coin was restruck in large numbers, but in reduced fineness.

SILVER, 13.20 g
Rev: Seven flames on pearl.

| 259 | ND(1909-11) | — | 7.00 | 13.50 | 22.50 | 80.00 |

Rev: Nine flames on pearl.

| 259.1 | ND(1909-11) | — | 7.00 | 13.50 | 22.50 | 80.00 |

DOLLAR

SILVER, 26.80 g

| 254 | ND(1908) | — | 12.50 | 20.00 | 35.00 | 135.00 |

COPPER (OMS)

| 254a | ND(1908) | — | — | — | — | 350.00 |

SILVER, 26.80 g
Rev: One circle under pearl.

| 258 | ND(1911) | — | 10.00 | 13.00 | 17.50 | 135.00 |

Rev: Four circles under pearl.

| 258.1 | ND(1911) | — | 10.00 | 13.00 | 17.50 | 135.00 |

NOTE: Although reign-dated 1875-1908 it appears that Y#255-258 were not issued until 1911. Y#258.1 was restruck in 1949.

Obv: Four characters at top.

| 260 | ND(1909-11) | — | 15.00 | 25.00 | 60.00 | 140.00 |

Obv: Seven characters at top.

| 260.1 | CD1910 | — | — | — | — | 32,500. |

REPUBLIC
CENT
BRASS
Similar to 2 Cents, Y#489.

Y#	Year	Date	VG	Fine	VF	XF
488	21	(1932)	—	—	Rare	—

2 CENTS

BRASS

| 489 | 21 | (1932) | 175.00 | 325.00 | 500.00 | 750.00 |

50 CASH

BRASS

Y#	Date	Mintage	VG	Fine	VF	XF
478	ND ca.1919	—	10.00	20.00	40.00	65.00

COPPER

| 478a | ND ca.1919 | — | 20.00 | 40.00 | 80.00 | 125.00 |

5 CENTS

BRASS

Y#	Year	Date	VG	Fine	VF	XF
490	21	(1932)	125.00	175.00	250.00	350.00

COPPER-NICKEL

| 485 | 12 | (1923) | 15.00 | 25.00 | 40.00 | 75.00 |

10 CENTS

COPPER-NICKEL
Reeded edge.

| 486 | 12 | (1923) | 1.75 | 2.50 | 3.75 | 7.50 |

Unreeded edge.

| 486.1 | 12 | (1923) | 2.50 | 4.00 | 6.50 | 12.50 |

East Hopei / CHINA

20 CENTS

SILVER, 5.60 g

Y#	Year	Date	Fine	VF	XF	Unc
491	21	(1932)	4.00	7.00	11.00	20.00

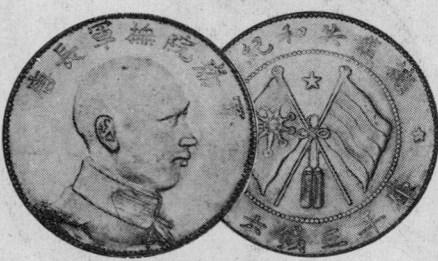

Rev: Provincial Capitol.

| 493 | 38 | (1949) | 1.00 | 3.00 | 5.00 | 35.00 |

50 CENTS

SILVER, 13.10 g
Gen. T'ang Chi-yao

Y#	Date	Mintage	Fine	VF	XF	Unc
480	ND ca.1916	—	10.00	20.00	45.00	110.00

Gen. T'ang Chi-yao

| 479 | ND ca.1919 | — | 5.00 | 7.50 | 12.50 | 30.00 |

Y#	Year	Date	Fine	VF	XF	Unc
492	21	(1932)	3.50	5.00	8.00	15.00

5 DOLLARS

GOLD, uniface
Similar to 10 Dollars, K#1520.

Y#	Date	Mintage	Fine	VF	XF	Unc
1521	ND(1917)	—	—	—	Rare	—

.750 GOLD, 4.50 g
Gen. T'ang Chi-yao
Rev: W/numeral 2 below flag tassels.

| 481 | ND (1919) | *.060 | 200.00 | 400.00 | 600.00 | 1250. |

Rev: W/o numeral 2 below flag tassels.
| 481.1 | ND (1919) | I.A. | — | Reported, not confirmed |

K#	Date	Mintage	Fine	VF	XF	Unc
1529	ND(1925)	—	300.00	500.00	800.00	1300.

10 DOLLARS

GOLD, uniface

Y#	Date	Mintage	Fine	VF	XF	Unc
1520	ND(1917)	—	—	—	Rare	—

.750 GOLD, 8.50 g
Gen. T'ang Chi-yao
Rev: W/numeral 1 below flag tassels.

| 482 | ND (1919) | .900 | 250.00 | 500.00 | 800.00 | 1500. |

Rev: W/o numeral 1 below flag tassels.

| 482.1 | ND (1919) | I.A. | 200.00 | 400.00 | 700.00 | 1250. |

K#	Date	Mintage	Fine	VF	XF	Unc
1528	ND(1925)	—	300.00	600.00	800.00	1300.

YUNNAN-SZECHUAN
Yunnan-Sichuan

These two coins have a 2 character mint mark in the center of the obverse, indicating the provinces of Yunnan and Szechuan (Sichuan).

EMPIRE
10 CASH

COPPER

Y#	Date	Mintage	VG	Fine	VF	XF
10w	CD1906	—	20.00	40.00	60.00	110.00

20 CASH

COPPER

| 11w | CD1906 | — | 100.00 | 150.00 | 200.00 | 250.00 |

CHINA-JAP. PUPPET STATES

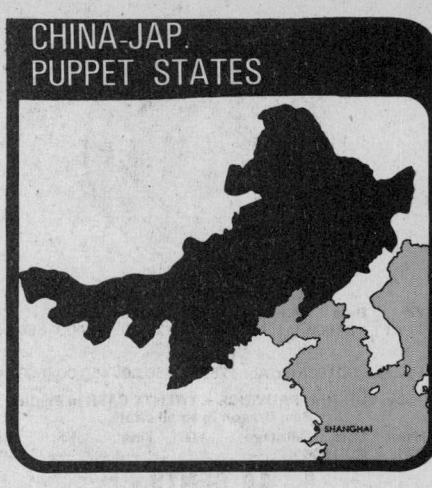

The greatest external threat to the territorial integrity of China was posed by Japan, which urgently needed room for an expanding population and raw materials for its industrial and military machines, and which recognized the necessity of controlling all of China if it was to realize its plan of dominating the rest of the Asiatic and South Sea countries. The Japanese had large investments in Manchuria (a name given by non-Chinese to the three northeastern provinces of China) which allowed them privileges that compromised Chinese sovereignty. The articulate of China remained unreconciled to Japan's growing power in Manchuria, and the resultant friction occasioned a series of vexing incidents which Japan decided to eliminate by direct action. On the night of Sept. 18-19, 1931, with a contrived incident for an excuse, Japanese forces seized the city of Mukden (Shenyang), and within a few weeks completely demolished Chinese power north of the Great Wall.

In Feb. 1932, after the Japanese occupation of Manchuria, they set up Manchukuo as an independent republic. Jehol (Rehe) was occupied by the Japanese in 1933 and added to Manchukuo. Manchukuo was established as an empire in 1934 with the deposed Manchu emperor Hsuan T'ung (the late Henry Pu Yi) as the puppet emperor K'ang Te. Lacking the means to face the Japanese armies in the field, the Chinese could only trade space for time.

Not content with confining its control of China to the areas north of the Great Wall, the Japanese launched a major campaign in 1937, and by the fall of 1938 had occupied in addition to Manchuria the provinces of Hopei (Hopeh) and Chahar (Ch'a-ha-erh), most of the port cities, and the major cities as far west as Hankow (Han-k'ou). In addition, they dominated or threatened the provinces of Suiyuan, Shansi (Shanxi) and Shantung (Shandong).

Still the Chinese did not yield. The struggle was prolonged until the advent of World War II, which brought about the defeat of Japan and the return of the puppet states to Chinese control.

As the victorious Japanese armies swept deeper into China, Japan established central banks under control of the Bank of Japan in the conquered provinces for the purpose of establishing control over banking and finance in the puppet states, and eventually in all of China. These included the Chi Tung Bank which had its main office in Tientsin (Tianjin) with branches in Peking (Beijing), Chinan (Jinan) and Tangshan; the Federal Reserve Bank of China with main office in Peking (Beijing) and branches in 37 other cities; and the Hua Hsing Bank with main office in Shanghai and two branches. The puppet states of Manchukuo, previously detailed in this introduction, and Meng Chiang, which comprised a greater part of Inner Mongolia, were also major coin-issuing entities.

EAST HOPEI
AUTONOMOUS
Chi Tung Bank

The Chi Tung Bank was the banking institution of the "East Hopei Autonomous Government" established by the Japanese in 1936 to undermine the political position of China in the northwest provinces. It issued both coins and notes between 1937 and 1939 with a restraint uncharacteristic of the puppet banks of the China-Japanese puppet states.

5 LI

COPPER

Y#	Year	Date	Fine	VF	XF	Unc
516	26	(1937)	7.50	12.50	20.00	40.00

FEN

COPPER

Y#	Year	Date	Fine	VF	XF	Unc
517	26	(1937)	3.00	6.00	9.00	25.00

5 FEN

COPPER-NICKEL

518	26	(1937)	2.50	4.50	6.50	18.00

CHIAO

COPPER-NICKEL
Obv: T'ien Ning Pagoda in Peking.

519	26	(1937)	2.50	4.50	6.50	18.00

2 CHIAO

COPPER-NICKEL

520	26	(1937)	3.00	4.00	7.00	25.00

MANCHUKUO

The former Japanese puppet state of Manchukuo (largely Manchuria), comprising the northeastern Chinese provinces of Fengtien (Liaoning), Kirin (Jilin), Heilungkiang (Heilongjiang) and Jehol (Rehe), had an area of 503,143 sq. mi. (1,303,134 sq. km.) and a population of 43.3 million. Capital: Changchun, renamed Hsinking. The area is rich in fertile soil, timber and mineral resources, including coal, iron and gold.

Until the closing years of the 19th century when Chinese influence became predominant, Manchuria was chiefly a domain of the tribal Manchus and their Mongol allies. Coincident with the rise of Chinese influence, foreign imperialistic powers began to appreciate the value of the area to their expansionist philosophy. Japan, overpopulated and poor in resources, desired it as a source of raw materials and for increased living area. Russia wanted it as the eastern terminus of the Trans-Siberian railway that was to unite its Asian empire. The inevitable conflict of Japanese, Chinese and Russian interests required that one or more of the powers be eliminated. Japan eliminated China on the night of Sept. 18, 1931, when, on the pretext of a contrived incident, it moved militarily to seize control of the Three Eastern Provinces. Early in 1932 Japan declared Manchuria independent by virtue of a voluntary separatist movement and established the state of Manchukuo. To give the puppet state an aura of legitimacy, the deposed emperor of the former Manchu dynasty was recalled from retirement and designated "chief executive". The area was restored to China at the end of World War II.

RULERS
Ta T'ung, 1932-1934
K'ang Te, 1934-1945

The puppet emperor under the assumed name of K'ang Te was previously the last emperor of China (Pu'-yi, or Hsuan T'ung, 1909-11).

MONETARY SYSTEM
10 Li = 1 Fen
10 Fen = 1 Chiao

IDENTIFICATION OF REIGN CHARACTERS

'Nien' Year   1932-1934   Ta T'ung

'Nien' Year   1934-1945   K'ang Te

DATE ABBREVIATIONS
TT - Ta T'ung
KT - K'ang Te

NOTE: Uncirculated aluminum coins without any planchet defects are worth up to twice the market valuations given.

5 LI

BRONZE

Y#	Year	Date	Fine	VF	XF	Unc
1	TT 2	(1933)	20.00	35.00	50.00	100.00
	TT 3	(1934)	4.00	9.00	15.00	30.00

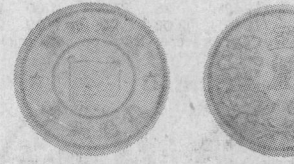

5	KT 1	(1934)	3.00	7.50	10.00	25.00
	KT 2	(1935)	3.00	7.50	10.00	25.00
	KT 3	(1936)	17.50	27.50	40.00	70.00
	KT 4	(1937)	4.00	10.00	12.50	27.50
	KT 6	(1939)	150.00	200.00	275.00	375.00

FEN

BRONZE

2	TT 2	(1933)	2.00	4.00	8.00	25.00
	TT 3	(1934)	1.50	3.00	5.00	20.00

6	KT 1	(1934)	1.00	3.00	6.00	15.00
	KT 2	(1935)	1.00	3.00	5.00	10.00
	KT 3	(1936)	1.00	3.00	5.00	10.00
	KT 4	(1937)	1.00	3.00	5.00	10.00
	KT 5	(1938)	1.00	3.00	5.00	10.00
	KT 6	(1939)	1.00	3.00	5.00	10.00

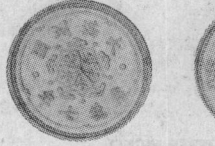

ALUMINUM

9	KT 6	(1939)	.40	.75	2.00	5.00
	KT 7	(1940)	.40	.75	2.00	5.00
	KT 8	(1941)	.40	.75	2.00	5.00
	KT 9	(1942)	.40	.75	2.00	5.00
	KT 10	(1943)	.40	.75	2.00	5.00

13	KT 10	(1943)	.75	2.00	5.00	10.00
	KT 11	(1944)	.75	2.00	5.00	10.00

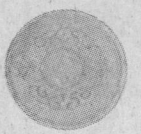

RED FIBER

Y#	Year	Date	VG	Fine	VF	XF
13a	KT 12	(1945)	.50	1.25	3.00	4.50

BROWN FIBER

13a.1	KT 12	(1945)	1.50	4.00	10.00	15.00

5 FEN

COPPER-NICKEL

Y#	Year	Date	Fine	VF	XF	Unc
3	TT 2	(1933)	.75	2.00	5.00	15.00
	TT 3	(1934)	.40	1.00	2.00	10.00

Greek rim border varieties

Narrow Design   Wide Design

7	KT 1	(1934)	.60	1.50	3.00	6.00
	KT 2	(1935)	.60	1.50	3.00	6.00
	KT 3	(1936)	narrow border design			
			.60	1.50	3.00	6.00
	KT 3	(1936)	wide border design			
			1.25	3.00	6.00	12.00
	KT 4	(1937)	1.00	2.00	4.00	7.50
	KT 6	(1939)	1.00	2.00	4.00	7.50

ALUMINUM

11	KT 7	(1940)	.60	1.50	3.00	6.00
	KT 8	(1941)	.40	.75	2.00	4.00
	KT 9	(1942)	.40	.75	2.00	4.00
	KT 10	(1943)	.40	.75	2.00	4.00

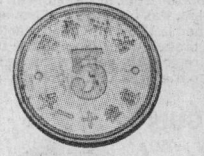

A13	KT 10	(1943)	1.00	2.50	5.00	12.50
	KT 11	(1944)	1.00	2.50	5.00	12.50

RED FIBER

Y#	Year	Date	VG	Fine	VF	XF
A13a	KT 11	(1944)	1.00	2.00	3.50	6.00

BROWN FIBER

A13a.1	KT 11	(1944)	4.00	10.00	15.00	20.00

CHIAO
(10 Fen)

Manchukuo / CHINA   390

COPPER-NICKEL

Y#	Year	Date	Fine	VF	XF	Unc
4	TT 2	(1933)	1.50	3.00	7.00	15.00
	TT 3	(1934)	.80	2.00	3.75	12.50

 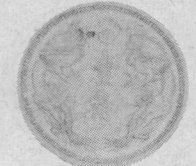

8	KT 1	(1934)	.80	2.00	3.00	7.50
	KT 2	(1935)	.80	2.00	3.00	7.50
	KT 5	(1938)	.80	2.00	3.00	7.50
	KT 6	(1939)	.80	2.00	3.00	7.50

10	KT 7	(1940)	1.00	3.00	5.00	10.00

ALUMINUM

12	KT 7	(1940)	.80	2.00	3.00	7.50
	KT 8	(1941)	.80	2.00	3.00	7.50
	KT 9	(1942)	.80	2.00	3.00	7.50
	KT 10	(1943)	200.00	300.00	400.00	500.00

14	KT 10	(1943)	1.50	3.00	5.00	12.50

MENG-CHIANG

As Japanese troops moved into North China in 1937, the political situation became fluid in several provinces bordering on Manchukuo. On September 27, 1937 the Chanan Bank was established. As the situation became more settled the Japanese effected the merger of two local banks with the Bank of Chanan under a new title. Meng Chiang (Mongolian Borderlands or Mongol Territory) Bank. The Meng Chiang Bank was organized on November 27 and opened on December 1, 1937 with headquarters in Kalgan (Zhangjiakou) and branch offices in about a dozen locations throughout the region. Its notes were declared the exclusive currency for the area. The bank closed at the end of the war.

5 CHIAO

COPPER-NICKEL

Y#	Date	Mintage	Fine	VF	XF	Unc
521	Yr.27 (1938)	10.800	2.50	5.00	9.00	25.00

PROVISIONAL GOVT. OF CHINA

In late 1937 the Japanese North China Expeditionary Army established the "Provisional Government of China" at Peking (Beijing).

FEDERAL RESERVE BANK

The Federal Reserve Bank of China was opened in 1938 by Japanese military authorities in Peking (Beijing). It was the puppet financial agency of the Japanese in northeast China. This puppet bank issued both coins and currency, but in modest amounts.

FEN

ALUMINUM

Y#	Year	Date	Fine	VF	XF	Unc
523	30	(1941)	.50	1.00	2.00	6.00
	31	(1942)	.50	1.00	2.00	6.00
	32	(1943)	3.00	6.00	10.00	30.00

5 FEN

ALUMINUM

524	30	(1941)	.75	2.00	4.00	10.00
	31	(1942)	.75	2.00	4.00	10.00
	32	(1943)	2.00	4.00	8.00	20.00

NOTE: The 5 Fen pieces were struck on both thick and thin planchets.

CHIAO

ALUMINUM

525	30	(1941)	.40	1.00	2.00	6.00
	31	(1942)	.40	1.00	2.00	6.00
	32	(1943)	1.50	3.00	6.00	15.00

NOTE: The 1 Chiao pieces were struck on both thick and thin planchets.

REFORMED GOVERNMENT REPUBLIC OF CHINA

On March 28, 1938 the Japanese Central China Expeditionary Army established the Reformed Government of the Republic of China at Nanking (Nanjing).

HUA HSING COMMERCIAL BANK

The Hua Hsing Commercial Bank was a financial agency created and established by the government of Japan and its puppet authorities in Shanghai in May 1939. Notes and coins were issued until sometime in 1941, with the quantities restricted by Chinese aversion to accepting them.

FEN

BRONZE

A522	29	(1940)	100.00	200.00	300.00	400.00

10 FEN

COPPER-NICKEL

522	29	(1940)	1.00	1.50	2.00	3.50

CHINA/People's Republic

The People's Republic of China, located in eastern Asia, has an area of 3,691,514 sq. mi. (9,560,951 sq. km.) (including Manchuria and Tibet) and a population of 1.04 billion. Capital: Peking (Beijing). The economy is based on agriculture, mining, and manufacturing. Textiles, clothing, metal ores, tea and rice are exported.

China's ancient civilization began in the Huang Ho basin about 1500 B.C. The warring feudal states comprising early China were first united under Emperor Ch'in Shih (246-210 B.C.) who gave China its name and first central government. Subsequent dynasties alternated brilliant cultural achievements with internal disorder until the Empire was brought down by the revolution of 1911, and the Republic of China installed in its place. Chinese culture attained a pre-eminence in art, literature and philosophy, but a traditional backwardness in industry and administration ill prepared China for the demands of 19th century Western expansionism which exposed it to military and political humiliations, and mandated a drastic revision of political practice in order to secure an accommodation with the modern world.

The Republic of 1911 barely survived the stress of World War I, and was subsequently all but shattered by the rise of nationalism and the emergence of the Chinese Communist movement. Moscow, which practiced a policy of cooperation between Communists and other parties in movements for national liberation, sought to establish an entente between the Chinese Communist Party and the Kuomintang ('National People's Party') of Sun Yat-sen. The ensuing cooperation was based on little more than the hope each had of using the other.

An increasingly uneasy association between the Kuomintang and the Chinese Communist Party developed and continued until April 12, 1927, when Chiang Kai-shek, Sun Yat-sen's political heir, instituted a bloody purge to stamp out the Communists within the Kuomintang and the government and virtually paralyzed their ranks throughout China. Some time after the mid-1927 purges, the Chinese Communist Party turned to armed force to resist Chiang Kai-shek and during the period of 1930-34 acquired control over large parts of Kiangsi (Jiangxi), Fukien (Fujian), Hunan and Hupeh (Hubei). The Nationalist Nanking government responded with a series of campaigns against the soviet power bases and, by October of 1934, succeeded in driving the remnants of the Communist army to a refuge in Shensi (Shaanxi) Province. There the Communists reorganized under the leadership of Mao Tse-tung, defeated the Nationalist forces, and on Sept. 21, 1949, established the People's Republic of China. Thereafter relations between Russia and Communist China steadily deteriorated until 1958, when China emerged as an independent center of Communist power.

MONETARY SYSTEM
Before 1949

10 Cash (Wen) = 1 Cent (Fen)
100 Cents (Fen) = 1 Dollar (Yuan)

SOVIET PERIOD

Prior to 1949, the People's Republic of China did not exist as such, but the Communists did control areas known as Soviets. Most of the Soviets were established on the borders of two or more provinces and were named according to the provinces involved. Thus there were such soviets as the Kiangsi-Hunan Soviet, the Hunan-Hupeh-Kiangsi Soviet, the Hupeh-Honan-Anhwei Soviet and others. In 1931 some of the soviets in the southern Kiangsi area were consolidated into the Chinese Soviet Republic, which lasted until the Long March of 1934.

CHINESE SOVIET REPUBLIC

In November, 1931, the first congress of the Chinese Soviet proclaimed and established the "Chinese Soviet Republic" under the Chairmanship of Mao Tse-Tung.

CENT

P'ing Chiang County Soviet / CHINA 391

COPPER

Y#	Date	Mintage	VG	Fine	VF	XF
506	ND	—	10.00	20.00	30.00	40.00

Y#	Date	Mintage	Fine	VF	XF	Unc
506a	ND	(restrike)	—	8.00	20.00	

5 CENTS

COPPER

Y#	Date	Mintage	VG	Fine	VF	XF
507	ND	—	20.00	30.00	50.00	70.00

Y#	Date	Mintage	Fine	VF	XF	Unc
507a	ND	(restrike)	—	—	9.00	21.50

20 CENTS

SILVER, 5.50 g

Y#	Date	Mintage	VG	Fine	VF	XF
508	1932	—	15.00	25.00	40.00	60.00
	1933	—	10.00	20.00	30.00	50.00

NOTE: Many minor varieties exist.

DOLLAR

SILVER
Obv: Crude facing portrait of Lenin, leg. above, date below. Rev: Hammer, sickle and value within wreath.

KM#	Date	Mintage	VG	Fine	VF	XF
5	1931	—	—	—	Rare	—

NOTE: For previously listed KM#6 refer to Shensi-North Soviet, KM#2.

HSIANG-O-HSI SOVIET
(Kiangsi-West Hupeh)

FEN

COPPER
Obv: Large star, leg. around.
Rev: Denomination within wreath, leg. around.

KM#	Date	Mintage	VG	Fine	VF	XF
1	ND(1931)	—	—	—	Rare	—

HUNAN SOVIET
DOLLAR

SILVER
Obv: Hammer and sickle in star, 8 characters above.
Rev: Characters within wreath and above.

1	1931	—	—	—	Rare	—
(Y502)						

HUPEH-HONAN-ANHWEI SOVIET

The Hupeh-Honan Anhwei Soviet District was a large revolutionary base. It was formerly made up of three separate special districts: East Hupeh, South Honan and West Anhwei which united until after 1930. Between 1931 and 1932 this Bank has issued a quantity of copper and silver coins as well as banknotes.

DOLLAR

SILVER, 26.80 g

Y#	Date	Mintage	VG	Fine	VF	XF
503	1932	—	250.00	575.00	750.00	1000.

27.20 g

504	1932	—	150.00	200.00	275.00	500.00

NOTE: Attribution of Y#503 to the Hupeh-Honan-Anhwei Soviet is not definite.

MIN-CHE-KAN SOVIET
(Fukien-Chekiang-Kiangsi)
DOLLAR

SILVER
Obv: Profile portrait of Lenin, leg. above.
Rev: Value in center, 9 characters above, date below.

KM#	Date	Mintage	VG	Fine	VF	XF
1	1934	—	—	—	Rare	—
(Y501)						

Obv: 15 character leg. around globe w/hammer and sickle.

2	1934	—	—	—	Rare	—

P'ING CHIANG COUNTY SOVIET
DOLLAR

SILVER
Obv: Hammer and sickle in star, 8 characters above.
Rev: Characters within wreath and above.

1	1931	—	—	—	Rare	—

SHENSI-NORTH SOVIET
DOLLAR

SILVER
Rev: Value in plain field.

KM#	Date	Year	VG	Fine	VF	XF
1	(1935)	5	1750.	2250.	2850.	—

Rev: Value within wheat stalks.

| 2 | (1935) | 5 | 2500. | 3000. | 3500. | — |

NOTE: Date is given in the 5th year of the Soviet Republic. They were issued after the Long March.

SZECHUAN-SHENSI SOVIET

The Szechuan-Shensi Soviet District was founded in 1933. Within two years and three months from January, 1933 to March, 1935, this Soviet District had issued quite a quantity of banknotes, copper and silver coins. These issues circulated rather popularly throughout the central district.

200 CASH

COPPER, 37mm.

Y#	Date	Mintage	Good	VG	Fine	VF
510	1933	—	20.00	50.00	80.00	140.00

34mm
Rev: Small 200 center.

Y#	Date	Mintage	Good	VG	Fine	VF
510.1	1933	—	20.00	50.00	800.00	1400.

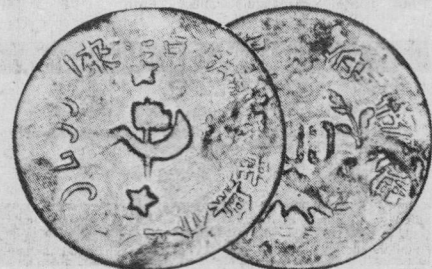

Rev: Large 200 center.

| 510.2 | 1933 | — | 20.00 | 50.00 | 800.00 | 1400. |

Rev: Square O's in 200.

| 510.3 | 1933 | — | 40.00 | 60.00 | 100.00 | 180.00 |

Rev: Value retrograde in wreath.
| 510.4 | 1933 | — | | | Rare | — |

Obv: Sickle reversed.
| 510.5 | 1933 | — | 12.50 | 30.00 | 50.00 | 85.00 |

Obv: Date w/closed 3 and backwards 4.

Y#	Date	Mintage	VG	Fine	VF	XF
511	1934	—	45.00	70.00	90.00	135.00

Obv: Date w/open 3 and backwards 4.
| 511.1 | 1934 | — | 45.00 | 70.00 | 90.00 | 135.00 |

Obv: Date w/4 corrected.
| 511.2 | 1934 | — | 45.00 | 70.00 | 90.00 | 135.00 |

Obv: Date w/4 corrected.
Well struck; usually found in choice condition.

Y#	Date	Mintage	Fine	VF	XF	Unc
511a	1934	(restrike)	—	—	12.50	22.50

NOTE: Many varieties of 200 Cash pieces exist. Unlisted varieties do not carry a premium.

500 CASH

COPPER, 35mm.
Obv: Small stars flanking date.

Y#	Date	Mintage	VG	Fine	VF	XF
512	1934	—	75.00	100.00	175.00	275.00

32.5mm
Obv: Large stars flanking date,
hammer handle across lower leg of star.
| 512.1 | 1934 | — | 50.00 | 100.00 | 160.00 | 250.00 |

33-34mm
Obv: Hammer handle extends between right legs of star.
| 512.2 | 1934 | — | 50.00 | 100.00 | 150.00 | 225.00 |

NOTE: Many varieties of 500 Cash pieces exist. Unlisted varieties do not carry a premium.

DOLLAR

SILVER, 26.30 g
Obv: Similar to Y#513.1.
Rev: Large solid stars.

| 513 | 1934 | — | 100.00 | 175.00 | 250.00 | 325.00 |

Rev: Medium solid stars.

Y#	Date	Mintage	VG	Fine	VF	XF
513.1	1934	—	100.00	175.00	250.00	325.00

Rev: Small solid stars.

513.2	1933	—	—	—	Rare	—
	1934	—	100.00	175.00	250.00	325.00

Rev: Outlined stars.

513.3	1934	—	100.00	200.00	275.00	350.00

Obv: Similar to Y#513.1.
Rev: Pentagram stars

513.4	1934	—	—	75.00	150.00	225.00	300.00

NOTE: Many minor varieties exist.

COINAGE OF UNCERTAIN ORIGIN
DOLLAR

SILVER, 26.40 g
c/m: Three Chinese characters in rectangular box, meaning SOVIET on obv. Y#329.

K#	Date	Mintage	VG	Fine	VF	XF
650k	ND	—	125.00	200.00	325.00	500.00

NOTE: For previously listed Y#501 and Y#502 refer to Min-Che-Kan Soviet KM#1 and Hunan Soviet KM#1.

WAN-HSI-PEI SOVIET
(Northwest Anhwei)
50 CASH

COPPER
Obv: Legend around globe w/hammer and sickle.
Rev: Value in star within wreath all within leg.

KM#	Date	Mintage	VG	Fine	VF	XF
1	ND(1931-32)	—	—	—	Rare	—

Rev: Value in circle, Chinese leg. above, Western leg. below.

2	ND(1931-32)	—	—	—	Rare	—

PEOPLE'S REPUBLIC
MONETARY SYSTEM

10 Fen (Cents) = 1 Jiao
10 Jiao = 1 Renminbi Yuan

MINT MARKS

(s) - Shanghai
(y) - Shengyang

FEN

ALUMINUM

Y#	Date	Mintage	Fine	VF	XF	Unc
1	1955	—	.20	.50	1.50	5.00
	1956	—	.40	1.00	2.50	7.50
	1957	—	.60	1.50	3.50	10.00
	1958	—	.10	.25	.75	2.50
	1959	—	.10	.25	.75	2.50
	1961	—	.10	.25	.75	2.50
	1963	—	.10	.25	.50	1.50
	1964	—	.10	.25	.50	1.50
	1971	—	.10	.25	.50	1.00
	1972	—	.10	.25	.50	1.00
	1973	—	—	.10	.25	.50	1.50
	1974	—	—	.10	.25	.50	1.00
	1975	.500	.10	.25	.50	1.00
	1976	—	—	.10	.25	.50
	1977	—	—	.10	.25	.50
	1978	—	—	.10	.25	.50
	1979	—	—	—	.10	.25
	1980	—	—	—	.10	.25
	1980	—	—	—	Proof	1.00
	1981	—	—	—	.10	.25
	1981	—	—	—	Proof	1.00
	1982	—	—	—	.10	.25
	1982	—	—	—	Proof	1.00
	1983	—	—	—	.10	.25
	1983	2.412	—	—	Proof	1.00
	1984	—	—	—	.10	.25
	1984	3.283	—	—	Proof	1.00
	1985	—	—	—	.10	.25
	1985	—	—	—	Proof	1.00
	1986	—	—	—	Proof	1.00
	1987	—	—	—	.10	.25

2 FEN

ALUMINUM

2	1956	—	.10	.25	.75	1.50
	1959	—	.20	.50	1.00	4.00
	1960	—	.20	.50	1.00	4.00
	1961	—	.10	.25	.75	1.50
	1962	—	.10	.25	.75	1.50
	1963	—	.10	.25	.75	1.50
	1964	—	.10	.25	.50	1.25
	1974	—	.10	.25	.50	1.50
	1975	—	.10	.25	.50	1.00
	1976	—	.10	.25	.50	1.00
	1977	.360	.10	.25	.50	.75
	1978	—	—	.10	.20	.35
	1979	—	—	.10	.20	.35
	1980	—	—	.10	.20	.35
	1980	—	—	—	Proof	1.00
	1981	—	—	.10	.20	.35
	1981	—	—	—	Proof	1.00
	1982	—	.10	.25	.50	1.00
	1982	—	—	—	Proof	1.00
	1983	—	—	.10	.20	.35
	1983	1.790	—	—	Proof	1.00
	1984	—	—	.10	.20	.35
	1984	1.963	—	—	Proof	1.00
	1985	—	—	.10	.20	.35
	1985	—	—	—	Proof	1.00
	1986	—	—	—	Proof	1.00
	1987	—	.10	.20	.35

5 FEN

ALUMINUM

3	1955	—	.30	.75	2.00	10.00
	1956	—	.15	.35	.75	2.00
	1957	—	.15	.35	.75	2.50
	1974	—	.15	.25	.50	1.50
	1975	—	.15	.25	.50	1.50
	1976	.350	.15	.25	.50	.75
	1979	—	—	—	—	—
	1980	—	—	.15	.25	.40
	1980	—	—	—	Proof	1.00
	1981	—	—	.15	.25	.40
	1981	—	—	—	Proof	1.00
	1982	—	—	.15	.25	.40
	1982	—	—	—	Proof	1.00
	1983	—	—	.15	.25	.40
	1983	.484	—	—	Proof	1.00
	1984	—	—	.15	.25	.40
	1984	.600	—	—	Proof	1.00
	1985	—	—	.15	.25	.40
	1985	—	—	—	Proof	1.00
	1986	—	—	.15	.25	.40
	1986	—	—	—	Proof	1.00
	1987	—	—	.15	.25	.40

JIAO

COPPER-ZINC

24	1980	—	—	—	—	.50

People's Republic / CHINA 394

Y#	Date	Mintage	Fine	VF	XF	Unc
(23)	1980	—	—	—	—	1.00
	1981	—	—	—	—	.50
	1981	—	—	—	Proof	1.00
	1982	—	—	—	Proof	1.00
	1983	3.100	—	—	Proof	1.00
	1984	3.500	—	—	Proof	1.00
	1985	—	—	—	Proof	1.00
	1986	—	—	—	Proof	1.00

BRASS
Sixth National Games - Gymnast

Y#	Date	Mintage	Fine	VF	XF	Unc
148	1987	—	—	—	1.00	1.50

Sixth National Games - Soccer

| 149 | 1987 | — | — | — | 1.00 | 1.50 |

Sixth National Games - Volleyball

| 150 | 1987 | — | — | — | 1.00 | 1.50 |

2 JIAO

COPPER-ZINC

Y#	Date	Mintage	Fine	VF	XF	Unc
25	1980	—	—	—	—	.60
(24)	1980	—	—	—	Proof	1.25
	1981	—	—	—	—	.60
	1981	—	—	—	Proof	1.25
	1982	—	—	—	Proof	1.25
	1983	4.200	—	—	Proof	1.25
	1984	2.500	—	—	Proof	1.25
	1985	—	—	—	Proof	1.25
	1986	—	—	—	Proof	1.25

5 JIAO

COPPER-ZINC

Y#	Date	Mintage	Fine	VF	XF	Unc
26	1980	—	—	—	—	.75
(25)	1980	—	—	—	Proof	1.50
	1981	—	—	—	—	.75
	1981	—	—	—	Proof	1.50
	1982	—	—	—	Proof	1.50
	1983	3.000	—	—	Proof	1.50
	1984	3.500	—	—	Proof	1.50
	1985	—	—	—	Proof	1.50
	1986	—	—	—	Proof	1.50

2.2000 g, .900 SILVER, .0637 oz ASW
Marco Polo

Y#	Date	Mintage	VF	XF	Unc
53	1983	7,000	—	Proof	10.00

YUAN

COPPER-NICKEL

Y#	Date	Mintage	Fine	VF	XF	Unc
27	1980	—	—	—	—	2.00
(26)	1980	—	—	—	Proof	3.00
	1981	—	—	—	—	2.00
	1981	—	—	—	Proof	3.00
	1982	—	—	—	Proof	3.00
	1983	3.100	—	—	Proof	3.00
	1984	4.100	—	—	Proof	3.00
	1985	—	—	—	Proof	3.00
	1986	—	—	—	Proof	3.00

COPPER
1980 Olympics - Archery

Y#	Date	Mintage	VF	XF	Unc
10 (9)	1980	.026	—	Proof	6.00

1980 Olympics - Wrestling

| 11 (10) | 1980 | .026 | — | Proof | 4.00 |

1980 Olympics - Equestrian
Obv: Similar to Y#14.

| 12 (11) | 1980 | .026 | — | Proof | 6.00 |

1980 Olympics - Soccer
Obv: Similar to Y#14.

| 13 (12) | 1980 | .026 | — | Proof | 4.00 |

1980 Olympics - Alpine Skiing

Y#	Date	Mintage	VF	XF	Unc
14 (13)	1980	.029	—	Proof	4.00

1980 Olympics - Speed Skating

| 15 (14) | 1980 | .029 | — | Proof | 4.00 |

1980 Olympics - Figure Skating

| 16 (15) | 1980 | .029 | — | Proof | 4.00 |

1980 Olympics - Biathlon

| 17 (16) | 1980 | .029 | — | Proof | 4.00 |

World Cup Soccer

| 34 | 1982 | — | — | — | 4.00 |
| | 1982 | — | — | Proof | 4.00 |

Panda

| 58 | 1983 | — | — | Proof | 13.50 |
| | 1984 | — | — | Proof | 13.50 |

COPPER-NICKEL
35th Anniversary of People's Republic

| 85 | 1984 | — | — | Proof | 6.00 |

5 YUAN

Y#	Date	Mintage	VF	XF	Unc
71	1984	.014	—	Proof	35.00

People's Republic / CHINA 395

35th Anniversary of People's Republic
Y#	Date	Mintage	VF	XF	Unc
86	1984	—	—	Proof	6.00

22.2200 g, .900 SILVER, .6430 oz ASW
Marco Polo

Y#	Date	Mintage	VF	XF	Unc
54	1983	6,100	—	Proof	75.00

Founders of Chinese Culture - Lao-Tse
90	1985	8,175	—	Proof	50.00

35th Anniversary of People's Republic
| 87 | 1984 | — | — | Proof | 6.00 |

8.4500 g, .800 SILVER, .2173 oz ASW
1984 Summer and Winter Olympics
| 61 | 1984 | 9,000 | — | Proof | 40.00 |

Founders of Chinese Culture - Qu Yuan
| 91 | 1985 | 8,175 | — | Proof | 50.00 |

20th Anniversary of Tibet Autonomous Region
| 96 | 1985 | 10.000 | — | — | 2.00 |
| | 1985 | .010 | — | Proof | 6.00 |

22.2200 g, .900 SILVER, .6430 oz ASW
Soldier Statues from Archeological Discovery
| 68 | 1984 | .014 | — | Proof | 35.00 |

Founders of Chinese Culture - Sun Wu
| 92 | 1985 | 8,175 | — | Proof | 50.00 |

30th Anniversary Sinkiang Autonomous Region
| 109 | 1985 | 10.000 | — | — | 2.00 |
| | 1985 | .010 | — | Proof | 10.00 |

Soldier Statues from Archeological Discovery
| 69 | 1984 | .014 | — | Proof | 35.00 |

Founders of Chinese Culture
Chen Sheng and Wu Guang
| 93 | 1985 | 8,175 | — | Proof | 50.00 |

40th Anniversary of Mongolian Autonomous Region
| 140 | 1987 | | | | |

Soldier Statues from Archeological Discovery
| 70 | 1984 | .014 | — | Proof | 35.00 |

Year of Peace
| 151 | 1986 | — | — | — | 5.00 |

Wildlife - Giant Panda
| 106 | 1986 | *.020 | — | — | 55.00 |
| | 1986 | *.025 | — | Proof | 75.00 |

People's Republic / CHINA 396

18.6100 g, .925 SILVER, .5535 oz ASW
Soccer

Y#	Date	Mintage	VF	XF	Unc
112	1986	.010	—	Proof	35.00

18.6100 g, .925 SILVER, .5535 oz ASW
Year of Peace

Y#	Date	Mintage	VF	XF	Unc
119	1986	.010	—	Proof	50.00

Poet Li Bai

Y#	Date	Mintage	VF	XF	Unc
135	1987	4,000	—	Proof	30.00

22.2200 g, .900 SILVER, .6367 oz ASW
Chinese Culture - Cai Lun - Paper Making

| 113 | 1986 | 9,675 | — | Proof | 35.00 |

22.2200 g, .900 SILVER, .6367 oz ASW
The Ship Empress of China

| 132 | 1986 | *.060 | — | — | 20.00 |

Poet Du Fu

| 136 | 1987 | 4,000 | — | Proof | 35.00 |

Chinese Culture - Zhang Heng - Chemist

| 114 | 1986 | 9,675 | — | Proof | 35.00 |

Bridge Builder Li Chun

| 137 | 1987 | 4,000 | — | Proof | 35.00 |

Chinese Culture - Zu Chang Zhi - Mathematician

| 115 | 1986 | 9,675 | — | Proof | 35.00 |

31.4700 g, .900 SILVER, .9107 oz ASW
1988 Winter Olympics - Downhill Skier

| 129 | 1988 | .020 | — | — | Proof | 30.00 |

Princess Chengwen and Song Zan Gan Bu

| 138 | 1987 | 4,000 | — | Proof | 35.00 |

22.2200 g, .900 SILVER, .6430 oz ASW
Military Hero of Song Dynasty - Yue Fei

| 160 | 1988 | *.025 | — | Proof | 50.00 |

Chinese Culture - Sima Qian - Writer

| 116 | 1986 | 9,675 | — | Proof | 35.00 |

1988 Summer Olympics - Woman Hurdler

| 130 | 1988 | .020 | — | — | Proof | 30.00 |

People's Republic / CHINA 397

Bi Sheng - Inventor of Movable-type Printing in China

Y#	Date	Mintage	VF	XF	Unc
161	1988	*.025	—	Proof	50.00

Su Shi - Song Dynasty Poet

162 1988 *.025 — Proof 50.00

Li Quingznao - Poetess of Song Dynasty

163 1988 *.025 Proof 50.00

10 YUAN

15.0000 g, .850 SILVER, .4099 oz ASW
Year of the Pig

44 1983 6,500 Proof 175.00

1.2000 g, .900 GOLD, .0347 oz AGW
Marco Polo

55 1983 .050 Proof 45.00

27.0000 g, .900 SILVER, .7813 oz ASW
Pandas

57 1983 .010 Proof 200.00

15.0000 g, .850 SILVER, .4099 oz ASW
Year of the Rat

59 1984 9,960 Proof 125.00

16.8100 g, .925 SILVER, .5000 oz ASW
Womens Decade

Y#	Date	Mintage	VF	XF	Unc
62	1984	4,000	—	Proof	35.00

Olympics - Volleyball

63 1984 9,100 Proof 35.00

Olympics - Speed Skating

64 1984 4,000 Proof 35.00

27.0000 g, .925 SILVER, .8031 oz ASW
Pandas

67 1984 .010 Proof 125.00

15.0000 g, .900 SILVER, .4341 oz ASW
Year of the Ox

78 1985 9,800 Proof 55.00

27.0000 g, .900 SILVER, .7813 oz ASW
Dr. Cheng Jiageng

Y#	Date	Mintage	VF	XF	Unc
88	1984	6,000	—	Proof	55.00

Pandas

95 1985 .010 Proof 75.00

34.5600 g, .900 SILVER, 1.0000 OZ ASW
20th Anniversary of Tibet Autonomous Region

97 1985 .010 Proof 45.00

People's Republic / CHINA 398

15.0000 g, .900 SILVER, .4341 oz ASW
Year of the Tiger

Y#	Date	Mintage	VF	XF	Unc
98	1986	.015	—	Proof	75.00

34.5600 g, .900 SILVER, 1.0000 oz ASW
30th Anniversary Sinkiang Autonomous Region

110	1985	.010	—	Proof	40.00

NOTE: For a similar 5 ounce medallic issue refer to UNUSUAL WORLD COINS, 2nd edition, Krause Publications, 1988.

27.0000 g, .999 SILVER, .8681 oz ASW
Sun Yat Sen
Obv: Portrait above horizontal legend and below arched legend. Rev: Sun Yat Sen's residence.

111	1986	.010	—	Proof	40.00

15.0000 g, .900 SILVER, .4341 oz ASW
Year of the Rabbit
Obv: Yellow Crane Pavilion above legend.
Rev: 2 rabbits above denomination.

121	1987	.010	—	Proof	75.00

Year of the Dragon

141	1988	.013	—	Proof	50.00

20 YUAN

10.3500 g, .800 SILVER, .2662 oz ASW
1980 Olympics - Wrestling
Obv: Similar to 1 Yuan, Y#14.

18 (17)	1980	.029	—	Proof	12.50

15.0000 g, .850 SILVER, .4099 oz ASW
Year of the Dog

38	1982	8,560	—	Proof	175.00

25 YUAN

19.4400 g, .800 SILVER, .5000 oz ASW
World Soccer Cup

Y#	Date	Mintage	VF	XF	Unc
35	1982	.040	—	Proof	25.00

World Soccer Cup

36	1982	.040	—	Proof	25.00

30 YUAN

15.0000 g, .800 SILVER, .3858 oz ASW
1980 Olympics - Equestrian
Obv: Similar to Y#21. Rev: Similar to 1 Yuan, Y#12.

19 (18)	1980	.029	—	Proof	15.00

1980 Olympics - Soccer
Obv: Similar to Y#21. Rev: Similar to 1 Yuan, Y#13.

20 (19)	1980	5,000	—	Proof	20.00

1980 Olympics - Speed Skating

21 (20)	1980	.020	—	Proof	15.00

15.0000 g, .850 SILVER, .4099 oz ASW
Year of the Rooster

32 (34)	1981	.010	—	Proof	725.00

35 YUAN

19.4400 g, .800 SILVER, .5000 oz ASW
UNICEF and IYC

8	1979	.012	—	—	30.00

33.5800 g, .800 SILVER, .8638 oz ASW
70th Anniversary of 1911 Revolution

Y#	Date	Mintage	VF	XF	Unc
46	1981	3,885	—	Proof	110.00

50 YUAN

155.5000 g, .999 SILVER, 5.0000 oz ASW
120th Anniversary of Sun Yat-sen's Birthday
Illustration reduced. Actual size: 70mm

KM#	Date	Mintage	VF	XF	Unc
108	1986	3,000	—	Proof	185.00

Year of the Rabbit
Similar to 150 Yuan, Y#123.

122	1987	4,000	—	Proof	200.00

Year of the Dragon
Illustration reduced. Actual size: 70mm
Obv: Similar to 10 Yuan, Y#141.

KM#	Date	Mintage	VF	XF	Unc
142	1988	5,000	—	Proof	250.00

100 YUAN

11.0000 g, .900 GOLD, .3183 oz AGW
Marco Polo

Y#	Date	Mintage	VF	XF	Unc
56	1983	950 pcs.	—	Proof	750.00

11.3180 g, .917 GOLD, .3337 oz AGW
Emperor Qin Shi Huang

| 72 | 1984 | 9,200 | — | Proof | 400.00 |

Founders of Chinese Culture - Confucius

| 94 | 1985 | 4,300 | — | Proof | 450.00 |

Wildlife - Wild Yak

| 107 | 1986 | 3,000 | — | Proof | 300.00 |

Chinese Culture - Liu-Bang - Revolutionary Soldier

| 117 | 1986 | 4,054 | — | Proof | 375.00 |

Year of Peace
Similar to 5 Yuan, Y#119.

| 120 | 1986 | 350 pcs. | — | Proof | 1500. |

373.2360 g, .999 SILVER, 12.0000 oz ASW
China's Railroad
Illustration reduced. Actual size: 80mm

Y#	Date	Mintage	VF	XF	Unc
131	1987	3,000	—	Proof	275.00

11.3180 g, .917 GOLD, .3337 oz AGW
Emperor Li Shimin
Obv: State emblem and legend.

| 139 | 1987 | 1,300 | — | Proof | 650.00 |

373.2360 g, .999 SILVER, 12.0000 oz ASW
Year of the Dragon
Illustration reduced. Actual size: 80mm
Obv: Similar to 10 Yuan, Y#141.

| 143 | 1988 | 3,000 | — | Proof | 525.00 |

11.3180 g, .917 GOLD, .3337 oz AGW

Emperor Zhao Quangying

Y#	Date	Mintage	VF	XF	Unc
164	1988	*.025	—	Proof	450.00

150 YUAN

8.0000 g, .917 GOLD, .2359 oz AGW
Year of the Pig

| 45 | 1983 | 2,125 | — | Proof | 1000. |

Year of the Rat

| 60 | 1984 | 2,100 | — | Proof | 2350. |

Year of the Ox
Obv: Similar to 10 Yuan, Y#78.

| 79 | 1985 | — | — | Proof | 400.00 |

Year of the Tiger
Obv: Qing Dynasty Palace

| 99 | 1986 | 5,049 | — | Proof | 450.00 |

Year of the Rabbit

| 123 | 1987 | 4,750 | — | Proof | 450.00 |

Year of the Dragon
Obv: Similar to 10 Yuan, Y#141.

| 144 | 1988 | 7,500 | — | Proof | 300.00 |

200 YUAN

8.4700 g, .917 GOLD, .2497 oz AGW
Chinese Bronze Age Finds
Obv: Similar to 800 Yuan, Y#31. Rev: Leopard.

| 28 (27) | 1981 | 1,000 | — | Proof | 800.00 |

People's Republic / CHINA 400

Rev: Winged creature.

Y#	Date	Mintage	VF	XF	Unc
29 (28)	1981	1,000	—	Proof	2400.

World Cup Soccer

| 37 | 1982 | 1,261 | — | Proof | 850.00 |

Year of the Dog
Obv: Temple. Rev: Dog.

| 39 | 1982 | 2,500 | — | Proof | 700.00 |

Decade for Women

| 89 | 1985 | — | — | — | — |

NOTE: Not released.

250 YUAN

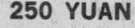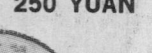

8.0000 g, .917 GOLD, .2358 oz AGW
1980 Olympics
Alpine Skiing

| 22 (21) | 1980 | .010 | — | Proof | 175.00 |

Year of the Rooster

| 33 (35) | 1981 | 4,982 | — | Proof | 850.00 |

300 YUAN

10.0000 g, .917 GOLD, .2948 oz AGW
1980 Olympics
Archery

| 23 (22) | 1980 | .015 | — | Proof | 225.00 |

400 YUAN

16.9500 g, .917 GOLD, .4997 oz AGW
30th Anniversary of Peoples' Republic
Tien An Men

| 4 | 1979 | .070 | — | Proof | 300.00 |

30th Anniversary of Peoples' Republic
People's Heroes Monument

Y#	Date	Mintage	VF	XF	Unc
5	1979	.070	—	Proof	300.00

30th Anniversary of Peoples' Republic
Chairman Mao Memorial Hall

| 6 | 1979 | .070 | — | Proof | 300.00 |

30th Anniversary of Peoples' Republic
Great Hall of the People

| 7 | 1979 | .070 | — | Proof | 300.00 |

Chinese Bronze Age Finds

| 30 (29) | 1981 | 1,000 | — | Proof | 1000. |

13.3600 g, .917 GOLD, .3939 oz AGW
70th Anniversary of 1911 Revolution

| 47 | 1981 | 1,338 | — | Proof | 1250. |

450 YUAN

17.1700 g, .900 GOLD, .4968 oz AGW
International Year of the Child

| 9 (8) | 1979 | .012 | — | Proof | 275.00 |

500 YUAN

155.5000 g, .999 GOLD, 5.0000 oz AGW
Year of the Dragon
Illustration reduced. Actual size: 60mm
Obv: Similar to 10 Yuan, Y#141.

Y#	Date	Mintage	VF	XF	Unc
145	1988	3,000	—	Proof	3800.

800 YUAN

33.2000 g, .917 GOLD, .9789 oz AGW
Chinese Bronze Age Finds

| 31 (30) | 1981 | 1,000 | — | Proof | 2000. |

1000 YUAN

373.2000 g, .999 GOLD, 12.0000 oz AGW
Year of the Dragon
Illustration reduced. Actual size: 70mm
Obv: Similar to 10 Yuan, Y#141.

| 146 | 1988 | 500 pcs. | — | Proof | 15,000. |

SILVER BULLION ISSUES
10 YUAN
(1 Ounce)

People's Republic / CHINA 401

31.1000 g, .999 SILVER, 1.0000 oz ASW

Y#	Date	Mintage	VF	XF	Unc
133	1987	.030	—	Proof	45.00

50 YUAN
(5 Ounces)

155.5000 g, .999 SILVER, 5.0000 oz ASW
Reduced in size. Actual size: 70mm.

134	1987	.025	—	Proof	230.00

GOLD BULLION ISSUES
Temple of Heaven/Panda Series

NOTE: The previously listed non-denominated series dated 1982 are now listed in UNUSUAL WORLD COINS, 2nd edition, Krause Publications, 1988.

5 YUAN
(1/20 Ounce)

1.5551 g, .999 GOLD, .0500 oz AGW

48	1983	.058	—	Proof	90.00

73	1984	.086	—	Proof	50.00

80	1985	.207	—	Proof	75.00

Y#	Date	Mintage	VF	XF	Unc
101	1986	.053	—	—	50.00
	1986P	.010	—	Proof	75.00

124	1987(s)	.099	—	—	50.00
	1987(y)	.039	—	—	50.00
	1987P	.010	—	Proof	75.00

Rev: Panda pawing bamboo.

152	1988	—	—	—	40.00

10 YUAN
(1/10 Ounce)

3.1103 g, .999 GOLD, .1000 oz AGW

49	1983	.074	—	Proof	100.00

74	1984	.085	—	Proof	65.00

81	1985	.141	—	Proof	65.00

102	1986	.045	—	—	60.00
	1986P	.010	—	Proof	175.00

125	1987(s)	.099	—	—	65.00
	1987(y)	.037	—	—	65.00
	1987P	.010	—	Proof	100.00

Rev: Panda pawing bamboo.

153	1988	—	—	—	60.00

25 YUAN
(1/4 Ounce)

7.7758 g, .999 GOLD, .2500 oz AGW

50	1983	.039	—	Proof	200.00

Y#	Date	Mintage	VF	XF	Unc
75	1984	.038	—	Proof	180.00

82	1985	:088	—	Proof	185.00

103	1986	.033	—	—	135.00
	1986P	.010	—	Proof	350.00

126	1987(s)	.073	—	—	135.00
	1987(y)	.031	—	—	145.00
	1987P	.010	—	Proof	200.00

Rev: Panda pawing bamboo.

154	1988	—	—	—	150.00

50 YUAN
(1/2 Ounce)

15.5517 g, .999 GOLD, .5000 oz AGW

51	1983	.023	—	—	450.00

76	1984	.017	—	Proof	425.00

83	1985	.068	—	Proof	260.00

People's Republic / CHINA 402

Y#	Date	Mintage	VF	XF	Unc
104	1986	.028	—	—	240.00
	1986P	.010	—	Proof	625.00

Y#	Date	Mintage	VF	XF	Unc
105	1986	.097	—	—	475.00
	1986P	.010	—	Proof	1200.

127	1987(s)	.078	—	—	245.00
	1987(y)	.017	—	—	400.00
	1987P	.010	—	Proof	500.00

128	1987(s)	.084	—	—	475.00
	1987(y)	.047	—	—	525.00
	1987P	.010	—	Proof	800.00

Rev: Panda pawing bamboo.

| 155 | 1988 | — | — | — | 300.00 |

100 YUAN
(1 Ounce)

Rev: Panda pawing bamboo.

| 156 | 1988 | — | — | — | 600.00 |

500 YUAN

373.2420 g, .999 GOLD, 12.0000 oz AGW
Reduced size, actual coin is 70mm.

Y#	Date	Mintage	VF	XF	Unc
66	1984	238 pcs.	—	Proof	27,000.

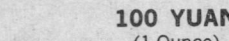

31.1035 g, .999 GOLD, 1.0000 oz AGW

| 52 | 1983 | .022 | — | Proof | 1300. |

| 77 | 1984 | .023 | — | Proof | 1300. |

| 84 | 1985 | .158 | — | Proof | 475.00 |

155.5150 g, .999 GOLD, 5.0000 oz AGW
Illustration reduced. Actual size: 60mm

| 147 | 1987 | *3,000 | — | Proof | 3900. |

1000 YUAN
(12 Ounces)

Reduced size, actual coin is 70mm.

| 118 | 1986 | 2,500 | — | Proof | 7000. |

Obv: Similar to Y#66. Rev: Mother panda and cub.

Y#	Date	Mintage	VF	XF	Unc
157	1987	—		Proof	6300.

PLATINUM BULLION ISSUES
100 YUAN
31.1030 g, .999 PLATINUM, 1.0000 oz APW
Similar to 100 Yuan, Y#128.

158	1987	—		Proof	675.00

Similar to 100 Yuan, Y#156.

| 159 | 1988 | — | | Proof | 675.00 |

MINT SETS (MS)

KM#	Date	Mintage	Identification	Issue Price	Mkt. Val.
MS1	1979(3)	—	Y1-3, medal	—	7.50
MS2	1980(7)	—	Y24-26(2),27	—	15.00
MS3	1982(4)	—	Y40-43	750.00	4300.

PROOF SETS (PS)

PS1	1979(4)	70,000	Y4-7	1695.	1200.
PS2	1980(14)	1,000	Y9-22	1750.	450.00
PS3	1980(7)	—	Y1-3,23-26	—	—
PS4	1980(4)	—	Y10-13	—	20.00
PS5	1980(4)	—	Y28-31	2950.	6250.
PS6	1980(3)	1,000	Y18-20	—	55.00
PS7	1981(7)	10,000	Y1-3,24-27	—	10.00
PS8	1982(7)	—	Y1-3,24-27	—	10.00
PS9	1983(7)	—	Y1-3,24-27	—	12.50
PS10	1984(7)	—	Y1-3,24-27	—	12.50
PS11	1985(7)	—	Y1-3,24-27	—	10.00
PS12	1985(2)	—	Y109-110	45.00	45.00
PS13	1986(7)	—	Y1-3,24-27	10.00	—
PS14	1986(5)	10,000	Y101-105	—	2400.
PS15	1987(5)	—	Y124-128	—	1100.
PS16	1987(2)	—	Y133-134	278.00	275.00
PS17	1988(4)	—	Y160-163	200.00	200.00

REPUBLIC OF CHINA

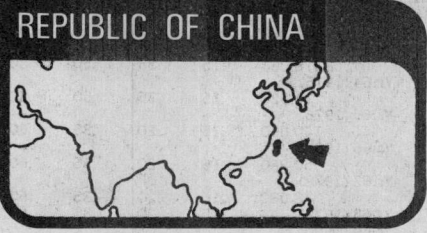

The Republic of China, comprising Taiwan (an island located 90 miles (145 km.) off the southeastern coast of mainland China), the offshore islands of Quemoy and Matsu and nearby islets of the Pescadores chain, has an area of 14,000 sq. mi. (35,981 sq. km.) and a population of 17 million. Capital: Taipei. During the past decade, manufacturing has replaced agriculture in importance. Fruits, vegetables, plywood, textile yarns and fabrics and clothing are exported.

Chinese migration to Taiwan began as early as the sixth century. The Dutch established a base on the island in 1624 and held it until 1661, when they were driven out by supporters of the Ming dynasty who used it as a base for their unsuccessful attempt to displace the ruling Manchu dynasty of mainland China. After being occupied by Manchu forces in 1683, Taiwan remained under the suzerainty of China until its cession to Japan in 1895. It was returned to China following World War II. On Dec. 8, 1949, Taiwan became the last remnant of Sun Yat-sen's Republic of China when Chiang Kai-Shek moved his army and government from mainland China to the island following his defeat by the Communist forces of Mao Tse-tung, and with American support proceeded to make it the showcase of democracy in Asia.

The coins of Nationalist China do not carry A.D. dating, but are dated according to the year of the republic, which was established in 1911. However, republican years are added to 1911 to find the western year. Thus republican year 38 plus 1911 equals Gregorian calendar year 1949AD.

MONETARY SYSTEM
10 Cents = 1 Chiao
10 Chiao = 1 Dollar (Yuan)

10 CENTS

BRONZE

Y#	Date	Mintage	Fine	VF	XF	Unc
531	Yr.38 (1949)	157.600	.10	.25	.75	2.00

ALUMINUM

| 533 | Yr.44 (1955) | 583.980 | | .10 | .15 | 1.00 |

545	Yr.56 (1967)	89.999	—	.10	.15	.40
	Yr.59 (1970)	30.000	—	.10	.25	.50
	Yr.60 (1971)	19.925		.20	.40	1.00
	Yr.61 (1972)	11.141	.10	.40	.60	1.25
	Yr.62 (1973)	111.400			.10	.40
	Yr.63 (1974)	71.930		.10	.25	.50

20 CENTS

ALUMINUM
Sun Yat-sen

| 534 | Yr.39 (1950) | 327.495 | — | .10 | .25 | 1.50 |

50 CENTS

5.0000 g, .720 SILVER, .1157 oz ASW
Sun Yat-sen

Y#	Date	Mintage	Fine	VF	XF	Unc
532	Yr.38 (1949)	—	1.50	2.00	3.50	5.00

BRASS

| 535 | Yr.43 (1954) | 279.624 | | .10 | .25 | 1.00 |

546	Yr.56 (1967)	109.999		.10	.15	.50
	Yr.59 (1970)	6.010	.15	.30	.60	1.25
	Yr.60 (1971)	4.434	.20	.40	.80	1.50
	Yr.61 (1972)	21.171		.10	.20	1.00
	Yr.62 (1973)	88.840		.10	.20	1.00
	Yr.69 (1980)	3.972		.10	.20	1.00
	Yr.70 (1981)	100.000		.10	.20	1.00

BRONZE

| 550 (549) | Yr.70 (1981) | 103.800 | — | | .10 | .40 |

DOLLAR (YUAN)

COPPER-NICKEL-ZINC

536	Yr.49 (1960)	321.717		.10	.20	.35
	Yr.59 (1970)	48.800	.10	.20	.50	1.00
	Yr.60 (1971)	41.532	.10	.20	.50	1.00
	Yr.61 (1972)	105.309		.10	.20	.35
	Yr.62 (1973)	353.924		.10	.20	.35
	Yr.63 (1974)	535.605		.10	.20	.35
	Yr.64 (1975)	456.874		.10	.20	.35
	Yr.65 (1976)	634.497		.10	.20	.35
	Yr.66 (1977)	116.900		.10	.20	.35
	Yr.67 (1978)	104.245		.10	.20	.35
	Yr.68 (1979)	—	.10	.20	.50	1.00
	Yr.69 (1980)	113.900		.10	.20	.35

ALUMINUM (OMS)

| 536a | Yr.64 (1975) | — | | | — | 100.00 |

GOLD (OMS)

| 536b | Yr.64 (1975) | — | | | — | 750.00 |

Republic / CHINA 404

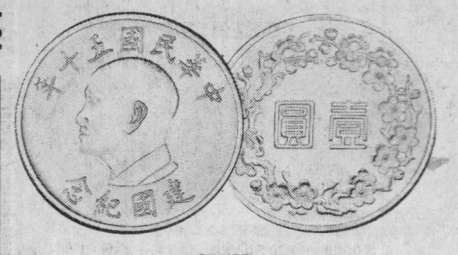

SILVER
Chiang Kai-shek

Y#	Date	Mintage	Fine	VF	XF	Unc
A537	Yr.50 (1961)	—	—	—	—	250.00

NOTE: This coin was struck to commemorate the 50th anniversary of the Republic. It was either released accidentally or was released and quickly withdrawn and is scarce today.

COPPER-NICKEL
80th Birthday of Chiang Kai-shek

543	Yr.55 (1966)	—	.15	.25	.35	.60

COPPER-NICKEL-ZINC
F.A.O. Issue

547	Yr.58 (1969)	10.000	.15	.25	.40	.75

BRONZE
Chiang Kai-shek

551 (550)	Yr.70 (1981)	1,080.000	—	—	.10	.15
	Yr.71 (1982)	780.000	—	—	.10	.15
	Yr.72 (1983)	420.000	—	—	.10	.15
	Yr.73 (1984)	110.000	—	—	.10	.15

5 DOLLARS

COPPER-NICKEL
Sun Yat-sen

537	Yr.54 (1965)	—	.25	.75	1.25	3.00

Chiang Kai-shek

548	Yr.59 (1970)	12.360	.15	.40	.80	1.50
	Yr.60 (1971)	20.575	.15	.35	.50	.80
	Yr.61 (1972)	27.998	.15	.35	.50	.75

Y#	Date	Mintage	Fine	VF	XF	Unc
548	Yr.62 (1973)	50.122	.15	.35	.50	.80
	Yr.63 (1974)	418.068	.15	.35	.50	.80
	Yr.64 (1975)	39.520	.15	.35	.50	.80
	Yr.65 (1976)	140.000	.15	.20	.35	.60
	Yr.66 (1977)	50.260	.15	.20	.35	.60
	Yr.67 (1978)	78.082	.15	.20	.35	.60
	Yr.68 (1979)	—	.15	.20	.35	.60
	Yr.69 (1980)	273.000	.15	.20	.35	.60
	Yr.70 (1981)	162.000	.15	.20	.35	.60

GOLD (OMS)

548a	Yr.62 (1973)	—	—	—	—	1100.

COPPER-NICKEL

552 (551)	Yr.70 (1981)	522.432	—	.15	.20	.50
	Yr.71 (1982)	66.000	—	.15	.20	.50
	Yr.72 (1983)	34.000	—	.15	.20	.50
	Yr.73 (1984)	280.000	—	.15	.20	.50

10 DOLLARS

COPPER-NICKEL
Sun Yat-sen

538	Yr.54 (1965)	—	.50	1.00	1.50	4.00

Chiang Kai-shek

553 (552)	Yr.70 (1981)	123.000	—	.30	.40	.65
	Yr.71 (1982)	361.000	—	.30	.40	.65
	Yr.72 (1983)	196.000	—	.30	.40	.65
	Yr.73 (1984)	220.000	—	.30	.40	.65

50 DOLLARS

17.1000 g, .750 SILVER, .4123 oz ASW
Sun Yat-sen

539	Yr.54 (1965)	—	—	—	—	12.00

100 DOLLARS

22.2100 g, .750 SILVER, .5335 oz ASW
Sun Yat-sen

Y#	Date	Mintage	Fine	VF	XF	Unc
540	Yr.54 (1965)	—	—	—	—	17.00

1000 DOLLARS

15.0000 g, .900 GOLD, .4340 oz AGW
Sun Yat-sen

541	Yr.54 (1965)	—	—	—	—	275.00

2000 DOLLARS

30.0000 g, .900 GOLD, .8681 oz AGW
Sun Yat-sen

542	Yr.54 (1965)	—	—	—	—	600.00

31.0600 g, .900 GOLD, .8988 oz AGW
80th Birthday of Chiang Kai-shek

544	Yr.55 (1966)	—	—	—	—	650.00

NOTE: For a similar medallic issue struck in silver refer to UNUSUAL WORLD COINS, 2nd edition, Krause Publications, 1988.

MINT SETS (MS)

KM#	Date	Mintage	Identification	Issue Price	Mkt. Val.
MS1	1965 (4)	—	Y537-540	—	35.00

Listings For
CHINESE TURKESTAN: refer to
China/Sinkiang (Xinjiang)

FOREIGN ENCLAVES

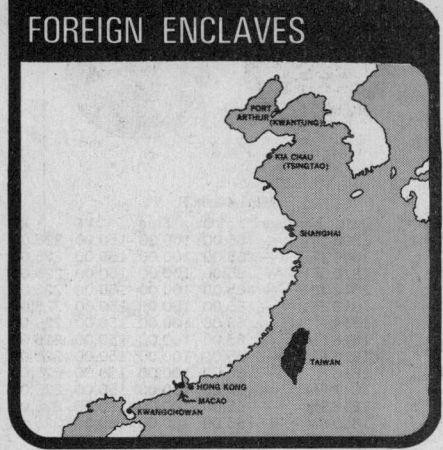

The Age of Exploration brought European traders to China as early as the 16th century. By 1560, the Portuguese were firmly in control of Macao. British, French and Dutch traders soon followed, and in 1784 the first clipper ship of the United States arrived.

Commerce, however, was severely limited by the refusal of the Chinese ruling class to treat the representatives of foreign powers as equals. By the end of the 18th century, only the port of Canton (Guangzhou) had been opened to European merchants, who were forbidden to enter Canton (Guangzhou) proper or travel inland.

The need for raw materials and expanded markets created by the Industrial Revolution brought increased pressure on China to open its doors to foreign traders. Actual military operations between 1839 and 1860, followed in the main by the threat of further attack by the western nations procured from China extensive trade concessions. Among the more notable were the cession of Hong Kong to Great Britain, and the establishment of foreign enclaves at Kiau Chau (Germany), Kwang Chowan (France), Kuantung (Russia), Shanghai and elsewhere that were virtually sovereign empires within the Chinese Empire.

Military defeats, territorial and trade concessions, and the interference by Christian missionaries in local Chinese governments and customs created mass antagonism toward foreigners, and increased the activities of secret societies who became dedicated to ousting the foreigner from China. Chief among the xenophobic organizations was the I Ho Ch'uan "Righteous Harmony Fists", a society known as the 'Boxers' because its members practiced ritual shadow-boxing to make themselves invulnerable to bullets. In the autumn of 1899, they began to murder Chinese Christians and foreigners. The Empress Dowager T'zu Hsi abetted their work by procrastination and allowing any foreigners in China to be killed. The resulting 'Boxer Uprising' was a fiasco, albeit a bloody one.

Massacring Christians and foreigners as they moved north, the Boxers entered Peking (Beijing) in June 1900. There they besieged some 1,000 foreigners and 3,000 Chinese Christians in the Legation Quarter until a seven-nation expeditionary force drove them off 55 days later. Although the nations had not declared war on China, they exacted additional concessions and heavy indemnities from the Manchu government. The United States, one of the principal recipients of the Boxer indemnities, later returned a major portion to China for educational development. Another portion was used to establish a fund to assist Chinese students in American schools.

HONG KONG

The free port of Hong Kong, a British-controlled commercial center and entrepot, is located 90 miles (145 km.) southeast of Canton (Guangzhou). For historical background and coin listings, refer to Hong Kong.

KIAU CHAU

Kiau Chau (Kiao Chau, Kiaochow, Kiautscho), a former German trading enclave, was located on the Shantung Peninsula of eastern China. Following the murder of two missionaries in Shantung in 1897, Germany occupied Kiaochow Bay, and during subsequent negotiations with the Chinese government obtained a 99-year lease on 177 sq. mi. of land. The enclave was established as a free port in 1899, and a customs house set up to collect tariffs on goods moving to and from the Chinese interior. The Japanese took the port as their first action in World War I to deprive German sea marauders of their east Asian supply and refitting base and retained possession until 1922, when it was restored to China by the Washington Conference on China and naval armaments. It fell again to Japan in 1938, but not before the Chinese had destroyed its manufacturing facilities. It is presently a part of the People's Republic of China.

RULERS
Wilhelm II, 1897-1918

MONETARY SYSTEM
100 Cents = 1 Dollar

5 CENTS

COPPER-NICKEL

Y#	Date	Mintage	Fine	VF	XF	Unc
1	1909	.610	25.00	35.00	50.00	80.00
	1909	—	—	—	Proof	300.00

10 CENTS

COPPER-NICKEL

2	1909	.670	25.00	35.00	50.00	80.00
	1909	—	—	—	Proof	300.00

KWANGCHOWWAN

Kwangchowwan (Kuang-Chou Wan), a French commercial center and free port, was located on the Luichow Peninsula which projects southward from China toward the island of Hainan. France acquired a 99-year lease to the 309 sq. mi. (800 sq. km.) enclave, with full territorial jurisdiction, in 1898. It was occupied by Japan during 1943-1945 in accordance with the Vichy-Tokyo agreement of 1941 which gave control of French Indochina to Japan. Upon relinquishment of all French claims in 1945, it became the Chinese municipality of Chankiang (Ch'an Chiang). In 1949 it was incorporated in the People's Republic of China. There are no known coins issued specifically for Kwangchowan.

KWANTUNG

Kwantung (Kuan-Tung), a name applied in the late 19th century to the southern tip of the Liaotung peninsula which projects southward into the Gulf of Chihli from present Liaoning province. The British captured Lu-Shun on the southeast tip of the peninsula in 1860 and renamed it Port Arthur. In 1898, Russia forced a 25-year lease to the 925 sq. mi. enclave from the Ch'ing dynasty, but lost it to Japan as a result of the Russo-Japanese War. Japan controlled the area until defeated in World War II. From 1945 to 1955, Port Arthur was under joint Russian-Chinese administration, following which it passed to Chinese control. During the Russian occupation, Russian copper and silver coins circulated in the area. Under the Japanese, demonitized silver yen counterstamped GIN also circulated.

MACAO

Macao, the oldest European settlement in the Far East, is 35 miles (56 km.) southwest of Hong Kong. For historical background and coin listings, refer to Macao.

SHANGHAI

The port of Shanghai was opened to foreign trade in 1842 as demanded by the foreign victors in the Opium War, and quickly grew to become the most important port in China. Several countries acquired control over certain sections of the city, and beginning in 1854 organized themselves into what was to become the International Settlement. This confederation remained virtually autonomous until the Second World War when Shanghai was occupied by the Japanese. A number of different tokens and encased postage stamps were issued for use in Shanghai.

TAIWAN

The island of Taiwan (Formosa) had been a part of the Chinese empire since the 17th century. In 1895, however, the island was ceded to Japan following the Sino-Japanese War. Japan held the island until 1945 when it was returned to China.

Prior to 1895, Chinese cash coins and dragon silver coins were issued for the island (see Taiwan Province), but under the Japanese no coins were minted specifically for Taiwan. Demonitized Japanese silver yen coins, counterstamped GIN were placed in circulation there following the occupation.

COLOMBIA

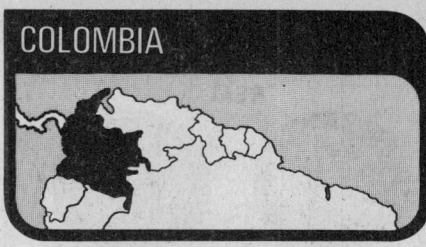

The Republic of Colombia, located in the northwestern corner of South America has an area of 439,737 sq. mi. (1,138,914 sq. km.) and a population of 27.4 million. Capital: Bogota. The economy is primarily agricultural with a mild, rich coffee the chief crop. Colombia has the world's largest platinum deposits and important reserves of coal, iron ore, petroleum and limestone; precious metals and emeralds are also mined. Coffee, crude oil, bananas and sugar are exported.

The northern coast of present Colombia was one of the first parts of the American continent to be visited by Spanish navigators, and the site, at Darien in Panama, of the first permanent European settlement on the American mainland in 1510. New Granada, as Colombia was known until 1861, stemmed from the settlement of Santa Marta in 1525. New Granada was established as a Spanish colony in 1549. Independence was declared in 1813, and secured in 1819. In 1819, Simon Bolivar united Colombia, Venezuela, Panama and Ecuador as the Republic of Gran Colombia. Venezuela withdrew from the Republic in 1829; Ecuador in 1830; and Panama in 1903.

RULERS
Spanish, until 1819

MINT MARKS
FS, NR, NoRo, SF - Nuevo Reino (Bogota)
P, PN, Pn - Popayan

MONETARY SYSTEM
8 Reales = 1 Peso
2 Pesos = 1 Escudo
8 Escudos = 1 Onza

COLONIAL MILLED COINAGE
1/4 REAL
.8462 g, .896 SILVER, .0243 oz ASW
Mint mark: NR
Obv: Castle. Rev: Lion.

KM#	Date	Mintage	VG	Fine	VF	XF
63	1801	—	5.00	10.00	15.00	50.00
	1802	—	10.00	20.00	35.00	70.00
	1803/2	—	6.00	12.00	20.00	50.00
	1803	—	7.50	15.00	25.00	50.00
	1804	—	5.00	10.00	15.00	50.00
	1805	—	6.00	12.00	20.00	50.00
	1806	—	7.50	15.00	25.00	50.00
	1807	—	12.50	25.00	40.00	65.00
	1808/6	—	20.00	40.00	65.00	110.00
	1808	—	5.00	10.00	15.00	50.00

67.1	1809	—	17.50	35.00	55.00	75.00
	1810/09/01	—	10.00	20.00	32.50	60.00
	1810/09	—	10.00	18.50	30.00	55.00
	1810/1	—	10.00	18.50	30.00	55.00
	1810	—	7.50	15.00	25.00	45.00
	1811	—	12.50	25.00	45.00	65.00
	1812	—	7.50	15.00	30.00	50.00
	1813	—	12.50	25.00	45.00	70.00
	1814	—	5.00	10.00	20.00	35.00
	1815	—	10.00	20.00	40.00	65.00
	1816	—	6.00	12.00	25.00	40.00
	1817	—	5.00	10.00	15.00	30.00
	1818/7	—	6.00	13.50	20.00	40.00
	1818	—	5.00	10.00	15.00	35.00
	1819	—	25.00	45.00	65.00	85.00

Mint mark: PN
Similar to KM#63.

67.2	1816	—	12.00	20.00	40.00	85.00
	1822	—	—	—	—	—

1/2 REAL

1.6925 g, .896 SILVER, .0487 oz ASW
Mint mark: NR
Obv. leg: FERND. VII..., bust of Charles IV.

69.1	1810 JJ	—	32.50	55.00	80.00	140.00
	1812 JF(error)	—	50.00	100.00	150.00	—
	1816 FJ	—	32.50	55.00	80.00	140.00
	1818 FJ	—	32.50	55.00	80.00	140.00
	1819 FJ	—	32.50	55.00	80.00	140.00

Mint mark: P

COLOMBIA

KM#	Date	Mintage	VG	Fine	VF	XF
69.2	1810 JF	—	12.50	25.00	45.00	100.00
	1816 FJ	—	27.50	50.00	85.00	150.00
	1819 MF	—	10.00	15.00	50.00	90.00

REAL

3.3834 g, .896 SILVER, .0974 oz ASW
Mint mark: NR
Obv: Bust of Charles IIII.

58	1801/797 JJ	—	10.00	25.00	75.00	—
	1801 JJ	—	6.00	12.50	60.00	125.00
	1802 JJ	—	6.00	12.50	60.00	125.00
	1804 JJ	—	12.50	25.00	65.00	125.00

Obv. leg: FERDND VII...., bust of Charles IV.

68.1	1809 FJ	—	Reported, not confirmed			
	1810 JF	—	6.00	12.50	35.00	80.00
	1810 JJ	—	15.00	30.00	65.00	125.00
	1812 FJ	—	7.50	15.00	40.00	85.00
	1812/4 JF	—	10.00	20.00	55.00	100.00
	1812 JF	—	8.00	20.00	40.00	85.00
	1816 FJ	—	6.00	12.50	35.00	80.00
	1817 FJ	—	7.50	15.00	40.00	85.00
	1818 FJ	—	8.00	17.50	60.00	100.00
	1819 FJ	—	7.50	17.50	40.00	85.00
	1819 FJ (inverted J)					
		—	6.00	12.50	40.00	85.00
	1819 J	—	6.00	12.50	40.00	85.00
	1820 FJ	—	25.00	50.00	90.00	150.00
	1821 FJ	—	30.00	55.00	100.00	175.00

Mint mark: P

68.2	1810 JF	—	18.00	35.00	90.00	150.00
	1813 JF	—	30.00	55.00	100.00	175.00
	1820 FM	—	18.00	35.00	90.00	150.00
	1822 FM	—	—	—	—	—

2 REALES

6.7680 g, .896 SILVER, .1949 oz ASW
Mint mark: NR
Obv. leg: FERDND VII...., bust of Charles IV.

70.1	1811 JF	—	17.50	35.00	75.00	125.00
	1816 FJ	—	17.50	35.00	75.00	125.00
	1816 JJ/FJ	—	17.50	35.00	75.00	125.00
	1817 FJ	—	17.50	35.00	75.00	125.00
	1818/7 FJ	—	45.00	85.00	150.00	225.00
	1818 FJ	—	25.00	55.00	125.00	200.00
	1819/8 FJ	—	25.00	55.00	125.00	200.00
	1819 FJ	—	25.00	55.00	125.00	200.00

Mint mark: P

70.2	1810 JF	—	12.00	20.00	40.00	100.00
	1811/0 JF	—	32.50	50.00	70.00	140.00
	1811 JF	—	27.50	45.00	60.00	120.00
	1813 JF	—	27.50	45.00	60.00	120.00
	1814/3 JF	—	60.00	125.00	225.00	450.00
	1814 JF	—	50.00	100.00	200.00	400.00
	1818 MF	—	27.50	45.00	60.00	120.00
	1819 MF	—	12.00	20.00	40.00	100.00
	1820/10 MF	—	35.00	85.00	150.00	300.00
	1820 MF	—	20.00	35.00	50.00	110.00
	1820 FM	—	20.00	35.00	50.00	110.00

Obv. leg: FERDND. 7.D.G.ET. CONST.

74	1822 O	—	25.00	50.00	100.00	200.00

8 REALES

27.0730 g, .896 SILVER, .7799 oz ASW
Mint mark: P
Obv. leg: FERDND VII...., bust of Charles IV.

KM#	Date	Mintage	VG	Fine	VF	XF
71	1810 JF	—	850.00	1500.	3000.	5000.
	1811 JF	—	700.00	1250.	2500.	4000.
	1812 JF	—	450.00	800.00	1600.	3500.
	1813/2 JF	—	800.00	1400.	2750.	4500.
	1813 JF	—	850.00	1500.	3000.	5000.
	1814/3 JF	—	450.00	800.00	1600.	3500.
	1814 JF	—	500.00	1000.	2000.	3750.
	1815 JF	—	Reported, not confirmed			
	1816 F	—	450.00	800.00	1600.	3500.
	1820 FM	—	—	—	Rare	—
	1820 MF	—	—	—	Rare	—

ESCUDO

3.3750 g, .875 GOLD, .0949 oz AGW
Mint mark: NR
Obv: Bust of Charles IIII.

KM#	Date	Mintage	VG	Fine	VF	XF
56.1	1801 JJ	—	80.00	125.00	200.00	275.00
	1802/1 JJ	—	80.00	125.00	200.00	275.00
	1802 JJ	—	50.00	100.00	150.00	225.00
	1803 JJ	—	50.00	100.00	150.00	225.00
	1804 JJ	—	50.00	100.00	150.00	225.00
	1805 JJ	—	50.00	100.00	150.00	225.00
	1806 JJ	—	80.00	125.00	175.00	275.00
	1807 JJ	—	100.00	150.00	225.00	325.00
	1808 JJ	—	50.00	100.00	150.00	225.00

Mint mark: P

56.2	1801 JF	—	60.00	90.00	130.00	200.00
	1802 JF	—	60.00	90.00	130.00	200.00
	1803 JF	—	80.00	125.00	175.00	275.00
	1804 JF	—	80.00	125.00	175.00	275.00
	1804 JT	—	100.00	150.00	225.00	350.00
	1805 JT	—	80.00	125.00	175.00	275.00
	1805 JF	—	100.00	150.00	225.00	350.00
	1806 JT	—	80.00	125.00	175.00	250.00
	1806 JF	—	80.00	125.00	175.00	250.00
	1807 JF	—	80.00	125.00	175.00	275.00
	1808 JF	—	80.00	125.00	175.00	275.00

Mint mark: NR
Obv. leg: FERDND VII...., bust of Charles IV.
Rev: Arms, order chain.

64.1	1808 JF	—	100.00	150.00	225.00	400.00
	1809 JF	—	80.00	125.00	175.00	300.00
	1810 JF	—	50.00	100.00	175.00	275.00
	1811 JJ	—	100.00	150.00	225.00	400.00
	1812 JF	—	50.00	100.00	150.00	200.00
	1813 JF	—	50.00	100.00	150.00	175.00
	1814 JF	—	50.00	100.00	150.00	175.00
	1815 JF	—	50.00	100.00	150.00	175.00
	1816 JF	—	50.00	100.00	150.00	175.00
	1817 JF	—	50.00	100.00	150.00	175.00
	1818 JF	—	50.00	100.00	150.00	175.00
	1819 JF	—	50.00	100.00	150.00	175.00
	1820 JF	—	80.00	125.00	175.00	275.00

Mint mark: P

KM#	Date	Mintage	VG	Fine	VF	XF
64.2	1808 JF	—	65.00	100.00	150.00	225.00
	1809 JF	—	65.00	100.00	150.00	225.00
	1810 JF	—	65.00	100.00	150.00	225.00
	1812 JF	—	65.00	100.00	150.00	225.00
	1813 JF	—	65.00	100.00	150.00	225.00
	1814 JF	—	65.00	100.00	150.00	225.00
	1816 FM	—	65.00	100.00	150.00	225.00
	1816 FR	—	65.00	100.00	150.00	225.00
	1816 F	—	65.00	100.00	150.00	225.00
	1817 FM	—	65.00	100.00	150.00	225.00
	1818 FM	—	65.00	100.00	150.00	225.00
	1819 FM	—	65.00	100.00	150.00	225.00

2 ESCUDOS

6.7500 g, .875 GOLD, .1899 oz AGW
Mint mark: NR
Obv: Bust right. Rev: Crowned arms, order chain.

60.1	1801 JJ	—	125.00	200.00	275.00	350.00
	1803 JJ	—	175.00	225.00	300.00	375.00
	1804 JJ	—	200.00	275.00	325.00	450.00
	1805 JJ	—	100.00	150.00	225.00	300.00
	1806 JJ	—	325.00	400.00	500.00	725.00
	1807 JJ	—	100.00	150.00	225.00	300.00
	1808 JJ	—	125.00	200.00	275.00	350.00

Mint mark: P

60.2	1802 JF	—	100.00	150.00	225.00	300.00
	1804 JF	—	125.00	200.00	275.00	350.00
	1804 SF	—	200.00	275.00	350.00	500.00
	1805 JT	—	325.00	425.00	525.00	850.00

Mint mark: NR
Obv. leg: FERDND VII...., bust of Charles IV.
Rev: Arms, order chain.

65.1	1808 JJ	—	200.00	275.00	350.00	525.00
	1809 JJ	—	125.00	200.00	275.00	450.00
	1810 JF	—	250.00	325.00	425.00	725.00
	1811 JF	—	225.00	300.00	400.00	675.00

Mint mark: P

65.2	1817 FM	—	275.00	325.00	400.00	700.00
	1818 FM	—	275.00	325.00	400.00	700.00
	1819 FM	—	275.00	325.00	400.00	700.00

4 ESCUDOS

13.5000 g, .875 GOLD, .3798 oz AGW
Mint mark: NR
Obv. leg: CAROL IIII...., bust of Charles IV.

61.1	1801 JJ	—	225.00	450.00	550.00	1100
	1803 JJ	—	225.00	450.00	550.00	1100
	1804 JJ	—	225.00	450.00	650.00	1300
	1805 JJ	—	225.00	450.00	600.00	1250
	1806 JJ	—	225.00	450.00	600.00	1250
	1807 JJ	—	350.00	650.00	1000	1650

Mint mark: P

61.2	1801 JF	—	300.00	600.00	675.00	1375
	1802 JF	—	250.00	500.00	650.00	1300
	1807 SF	—	550.00	1100	1500	2000
	1808 JF	—	650.00	1300	1800	2600

Mint mark: NR
Obv. leg: FERDND VII...., bust of Charles IV.
Rev: Arms, order chain.

72	1818 JF	—	300.00	600.00	850.00	1550
	1819 JF	—	300.00	600.00	850.00	1550

8 ESCUDOS

27.0000 g, .875 GOLD, .7596 oz AGW
Mint mark: NR
Obv. leg: CAROL IIII...., bust of Charles IV.
Rev: Crowned arms, order chain.

62.1	1801 JJ	—	375.00	425.00	650.00	900.00
	1802/1 JJ	—	375.00	425.00	650.00	900.00
	1802 JJ	—	375.00	425.00	650.00	900.00
	1803/2 JJ	—	375.00	425.00	650.00	900.00
	1803 JJ	—	375.00	425.00	650.00	900.00
	1804/3 JJ	—	375.00	425.00	650.00	900.00
	1804 JJ	—	375.00	425.00	650.00	900.00
	1805 JJ	—	375.00	425.00	650.00	900.00
	1806 JJ	—	375.00	425.00	650.00	900.00
	1807 JJ	—	375.00	425.00	650.00	900.00
	1808 JJ	—	375.00	425.00	650.00	900.00
	1808 JF	—	2000.	3500.	6000.	8500.

Mint mark: P.
Rev: Similar to KM#66.1.

KM#	Date	Mintage	VG	Fine	VF	XF
62.2	1801 JF	—	375.00	425.00	700.00	1000.
	1802 JF	—	375.00	425.00	700.00	1000.
	1803 JF	—	375.00	425.00	700.00	1000.
	1804 JJ	—	1500.	2500.	3500.	4500.
	1804 JF	—	375.00	425.00	700.00	1000.
	1805 JF	—	750.00	1500.	2000.	3000.
	1805 PJ	—	500.00	800.00	1200.	2000.
	1806 JF	—	375.00	425.00	700.00	1000.
	1807 JF	—	375.00	425.00	700.00	1000.
	1808 JF	—	550.00	900.00	1300.	2000.

Mint mark: NR
Obv. leg: FERDND. VII...., bust of Charles IV.

KM#	Date	Mintage	VG	Fine	VF	XF
66.1	1808 JJ	—	600.00	1000.	1400.	2000.
	1808 JF/JJ	—	650.00	1200.	1750.	2250.
	1808 JF	—	650.00	1200.	1750.	2250.
	1809 JF	—	375.00	425.00	650.00	1000.
	1810 JF	—	375.00	425.00	650.00	1000.
	1811/0 JF	—	375.00	425.00	650.00	1000.
	1811 JF	—	375.00	425.00	650.00	1000.
	1812 JF	—	375.00	425.00	650.00	1000.
	1813/2 JF	—	375.00	425.00	800.00	1300.
	1813 JF	—	375.00	425.00	650.00	1000.
	1814/3 JF	—	375.00	425.00	650.00	1000.
	1814 JF	—	375.00	425.00	650.00	1000.
	1815/4 JF	—	375.00	425.00	650.00	1000.
	1815 JF	—	375.00	425.00	650.00	1000.
	1816 JF	—	375.00	425.00	650.00	1000.
	1817 JF	—	375.00	425.00	650.00	1000.
	1818 JF	—	375.00	425.00	650.00	1000.
	1819 JF	—	375.00	425.00	650.00	1000.
	1820 JF	—	375.00	425.00	650.00	1000.

Mint mark: P

KM#	Date	Mintage	VG	Fine	VF	XF
66.2	1808 JF	—	375.00	425.00	650.00	900.00
	1809 JF	—	375.00	425.00	650.00	900.00
	1811/0 JF	—	375.00	425.00	650.00	900.00
	1810 JF	—	375.00	425.00	650.00	900.00
	1811 JF	—	375.00	425.00	650.00	900.00
	1812 JF	—	375.00	425.00	650.00	900.00
	1813 JF	—	375.00	425.00	650.00	900.00
	1814 JF	—	375.00	425.00	650.00	900.00
	1815 JF	—	375.00	425.00	650.00	900.00
	1815 FR	—	375.00	425.00	650.00	900.00
	1816 FM	—	375.00	425.00	800.00	1100.

KM#	Date	Mintage	VG	Fine	VF	XF
66.2	1816 JF	—	375.00	425.00	800.00	1100.
	1816 FR	—	450.00	700.00	1000.	1500.
	1816 F	—	375.00	425.00	650.00	900.00
	1817 FM	—	375.00	425.00	650.00	900.00
	1818 FM	—	375.00	425.00	650.00	900.00
	1819 FM	—	375.00	425.00	650.00	900.00
	1820 FM	—	375.00	425.00	650.00	900.00

POPAYAN
MEDIO (1/2) REAL

COPPER
Obv: P/ANO/1813. Rev: Value.

KM#	Date	Mintage	VG	Fine	VF	XF
1	1813	—	200.00	300.00	500.00	750.00

2 REALES

COPPER
Obv: NUEVO REYNO DE GRANADA, ANO/1813
Rev: PROVINCIA DE POPAYAN, value.

| 2 | 1813 | — | 17.50 | 32.50 | 45.00 | 75.00 |

8 REALES

COPPER

| 3 | 1813 | — | 60.00 | 100.00 | 175.00 | 300.00 |

SANTA MARTA

A city in Colombia on the shores of the Caribbean Sea. Founded in 1525, it is the oldest city in Colombia. Santa Marta was one of several areas in Colombia that remained longer under Spanish rule. Coins made here were crudely produced by the beseiged royalists who copied certain elements of Spanish Imperial coin designs.

1/4 REAL

COPPER

KM#	Date	Mintage	Good	VG	Fine	VF
2	1813	—	13.50	27.50	55.00	85.00

| 4 | 1820 | — | 4.00 | 8.50 | 20.00 | 42.50 |
| | 1821 | | | | | |

1/2 REAL

COPPER

| 1 | ND (1812-13) | — | 50.00 | 100.00 | 200.00 | 300.00 |

| 3 | 1813 | — | — | — | Rare | — |

2 REALES

SILVER

KM#	Date	Mintage	Good	VG	Fine	VF
5	1820	—	200.00	350.00	500.00	650.00

COUNTERMARKED COINAGE
8 REALES

27.0700 g, .903 SILVER, .7859 oz ASW
c/m: S.M. and VPB monogram on Mexico KM#110.

| 6 | 1809 TH | — | 350.00 | 500.00 | 750.00 | 1100. |

REPUBLICAN COINAGE
CARTAGENA

A port city on the northern coast of Colombia. It was a very important city in the Spanish colonies and was heavily fortified to ward off British and French privateers. Cartagena was the first major city in Colombia to declare independence from Spain -- November 11, 1811. In 1815, after a four month siege, it fell to the Spaniards. In the intervening time coins were made at Cartagena for local use. All these coins are crude in both die-work and planchets as well as striking.

1/2 REAL

COPPER

2	1812	—	6.50	14.00	22.50	32.50
	1813	—	6.50	18.50	27.50	37.50
	ND	—	5.00	8.50	18.00	30.00

DOS (2) REALES

COPPER

1	1811	—	10.00	25.00	42.50	75.00
	1812	—	10.00	25.00	42.50	75.00
	1813	—	10.00	25.00	42.50	75.00
	1814	—	6.50	18.50	27.50	50.00

CUNDINAMARCA

A province in central Colombia with Bogota as its capital, was the first to declare independence - July 16,

1813. Spain regained control in 1816 and held it until 1819. After the battle of Boyaca the province was again free. Coins made before and after the Spanish re-occupation, and through 1821, when the Gran Colombia plan was put into effect, bear the provincial disignation. Imperial Spanish types were struck during the Spanish re-occupation.

1/4 REAL
.7000 g, .583 SILVER, .0131 oz ASW
Obv: Liberty cap, date. Rev: Pomegranate.

KM#	Date	Mintage	Good	VG	Fine	VF
2	1814	—	15.00	30.00	40.00	75.00
	1815	—	20.00	35.00	45.00	85.00

1/2 REAL
SILVER
State of Cundinamarca

| 3 | 1814 JF | — | 40.00 | 85.00 | 150.00 | 275.00 |

1.3000 g, .666 SILVER, .0278 oz ASW
Province of Cundinamarca

| 8 | 1821 Ba JF | — | 8.50 | 22.50 | 50.00 | 100.00 |

REAL

2.5000 g, .583 SILVER, .0468 oz ASW
State of Cundinamarca

1	1813 JF	—	12.50	37.50	55.00	85.00
	1814 JF	—	12.50	42.00	65.00	95.00
	1815 JF	—	18.00	45.00	70.00	115.00
	1816 JF	—	12.50	42.00	65.00	95.00

2.7800 g, .666 SILVER, .0595 oz ASW
Province of Cundinamarca

| 9 | 1821 Ba JF | — | 6.00 | 16.50 | 37.50 | 75.00 |

2 REALES
4.9000 g, .583 SILVER, .0918 oz ASW
State of Cundinamarca

4	1815 JF	—	12.00	22.50	40.00	75.00
	1816/5 JF	—	15.00	27.50	45.00	80.00
	1816 JF	—	12.00	22.50	40.00	75.00

4.9800 g, .666 SILVER, .1066 oz ASW
Republica de Colombia

5	1820 JF	—	32.00	75.00	150.00	325.00
	1820 Ba JF	—	—	—	Rare	—
	1821 Ba JF	—	5.00	10.00	20.00	35.00
	1821 JF	—	27.50	65.00	150.00	300.00
	1823 JF	—	65.00	160.00	275.00	400.00

8 REALES

23.0000 g, .666 SILVER, .4924 oz ASW
Republica de Colombia

KM#	Date	Mintage	Good	VG	Fine	VF
6	1820 JF	—	10.00	30.00	50.00	100.00
	1820 Ba JF	—	50.00	75.00	125.00	250.00
	1821 JF	—	8.00	20.00	40.00	80.00
	1821 Ba JF	—	10.00	30.00	50.00	100.00

Mule. Obv: KM#6. Rev: Similar to KM#78.

| 7 | 1820 JF | — | 75.00 | 125.00 | 250.00 | 500.00 |

NATIONAL COINAGE
MINT MARKS

A - Antioquia
AM - Bogota
B, BA, BOGOTA - Santa Fe de Bogota
H - Birmingham
M - Medellin
P, PN, POPAYAN - Popayan

UNITED PROVINCES OF NUEVA GRANADA
PROVISIONAL ISSUES
1813-1821

1/4 REAL

.7000 g, .666 SILVER, .0149 oz ASW
Obv: Liberty cap. Rev: Pomegranate.

| 79.1 | 1820 | — | 12.00 | 20.00 | 40.00 | 60.00 |
| | 1821 | — | 12.00 | 20.00 | 40.00 | 60.00 |

Mint mark: BA

| 79.2 | 1821 | — | 15.00 | 30.00 | 60.00 | 120.00 |

Mint mark: Pn

| 79.3 | 1822 | — | — | — | Rare | — |

REAL
3.1500 g, .666 SILVER, .0674 oz ASW
Obv. leg: LIBERTAD AMERICANA around Indian head.
Rev. leg: NUEVA GRANADA around pomegranate.

| 75 | 1819 JF | — | 20.00 | 45.00 | 100.00 | 200.00 |

2 REALES

5.9000 g, .666 SILVER, .1263 oz ASW

| 76 | 1819 JF | — | 15.00 | 35.00 | 110.00 | 225.00 |

Rev: Pomegranate divides value.

| 77 | 1819 JF | — | 30.00 | 50.00 | 75.00 | 125.00 |
| | 1820 JF | — | 35.00 | 60.00 | 100.00 | 175.00 |

8 REALES

23.0000 g, .666 SILVER, .4924 oz ASW

KM#	Date	Mintage	Good	VG	Fine	VF
78	1819 JF	—	25.00	45.00	90.00	175.00
	1819/20 JF	—	30.00	50.00	100.00	200.00
	1820 JF	—	25.00	45.00	90.00	175.00

REPUBLIC OF COLOMBIA
1821-1837

1/4 REAL
.7000 g, .666 SILVER, .0149 oz ASW
Mint mark: B
Rev: Mint mark and initials below 1/4.

| 85.1 | 1826 TR | — | 25.00 | 45.00 | 60.00 | 80.00 |

NOTE: Counterfeits of the above type with initials RS are reported for 1825-27.

Rev: Mint mark above 1/4, initials.

85.2	1826 RS	—	10.00	17.50	30.00	45.00
	1827 RS	—	3.00	6.00	8.50	18.50
	1828 RS	—	4.50	8.50	11.00	20.00
	1829 RS	—	3.50	6.50	9.00	18.50
	1833 RS	—	5.00	9.00	12.00	22.50
	1834 RS	—	3.00	6.00	8.50	18.50
	1836 RS	—	4.50	8.50	11.00	20.00

Mint mark: P

85.3	1826 RU	—	4.50	10.00	18.00	30.00
	1832 RU	—	—	—	Rare	—
	1833 RU	—	8.50	15.00	22.50	35.00
	1834 RU	—	4.00	7.00	10.00	17.50
	1836 RU	—	7.00	12.50	20.00	32.50

1/2 REAL

1.5500 g, .666 SILVER, .0331 oz ASW
Mint mark: BA
Obv: Fasces between crossed cornucopias.
Rev: Value in wreath.

88.1	1833 RS	—	9.00	17.00	28.00	55.00
	1834 RS	—	7.00	15.00	25.00	50.00
	1835	—	10.00	20.00	30.00	60.00

Mint mark: PN

88.2	1834	—	10.00	17.50	27.50	50.00
	1835 RU	—	—	—	Rare	—
	1836 RU	—	9.00	15.00	25.00	40.00

REAL

3.1000 g, .666 SILVER, .0663 oz ASW
Mint mark: BA

87.1	1827 B RR	—	25.00	50.00	100.00	200.00
	1827 RR	—	4.50	8.00	12.50	20.00
	1828 RR	—	6.50	10.00	17.00	27.50
	1828 RS	—	4.50	8.00	12.50	20.00
	1829 RS	—	—	—	Rare	—
	1833/29 RS	—	6.00	12.00	22.00	37.50
	1833 RS	—	2.75	5.50	10.00	20.00
	1834 RS	—	22.50	45.00	75.00	—
	1835 RS	—	2.25	3.75	7.50	15.00
	1836 RS	—	2.25	3.75	7.50	12.50

Mint mark: PN

KM#	Date	Mintage	Good	VG	Fine	VF
87.2	1827 RU	—	—	—	Rare	—
	1828/7 RU	—	5.00	10.00	17.50	27.50
	1828 MF	—	3.50	6.50	12.00	20.00
	1828 RU	—	3.50	6.50	12.00	20.00
	1828 RU/MF	—	—	—	—	—
	1829 MF	—	3.50	6.50	12.00	20.00
	1829 RU	—	3.50	6.50	12.00	20.00
	1830 RU	—	2.25	5.25	9.00	15.00
	1831 RU	—	3.50	6.50	12.00	20.00
	1832 RU	—	3.50	6.50	12.00	20.00
	1833 RU	—	3.00	6.00	11.00	17.50
	1834	—	8.50	13.50	25.00	35.00
	1835	—	—	Reported, not confirmed		

8 REALES

27.0200 g, .835 SILVER, .7253 oz ASW

KM#	Date	Mintage	Good	VG	Fine	VF
89	1834 RS	—	32.50	55.00	150.00	300.00
	1835/4 RS	—	18.50	37.50	80.00	175.00
	1835 RS	—	27.50	50.00	135.00	275.00
	1836 RS	—	18.50	37.50	80.00	175.00

PESO

3.3750 gm., .875 GOLD, .0949 oz AGW
Bogota Mint

KM#	Date	Mintage	Good	VG	Fine	VF
80	1821 JF	—	100.00	200.00	350.00	500.00

KM#	Date	Mintage	VG	Fine	VF	XF
84	1825 JF	—	55.00	60.00	75.00	115.00
	1826 JF	—	55.00	60.00	75.00	115.00
	1826 PJ	—	55.00	60.00	75.00	115.00
	1827 JF	—	55.00	60.00	75.00	115.00
	1827 RR	—	55.00	60.00	75.00	115.00
	1829 RS	—	55.00	60.00	75.00	115.00
	1830 RS	—	55.00	60.00	75.00	115.00
	1833 RS	—	55.00	60.00	75.00	115.00
	1834 RS	—	55.00	60.00	75.00	115.00
	1835 RS	—	55.00	60.00	75.00	115.00
	1836 RS	—	55.00	60.00	75.00	115.00

ESCUDO

3.3750 g, .875 GOLD, .0949 oz AGW
Bogota Mint

KM#	Date	Mintage	VG	Fine	VF	XF
81.1	1822 MF	—	—	—	—	—
	1823 JF	—	55.00	75.00	125.00	200.00
	1824 JF	—	55.00	75.00	125.00	200.00
	1825 JF	—	55.00	75.00	125.00	200.00
	1826 JF	—	55.00	75.00	125.00	200.00
	1832 PR	—	55.00	75.00	125.00	200.00
	1832 EM	—	—	—	Rare	—

Popayan Mint

KM#	Date	Mintage	VG	Fine	VF	XF
81.2	1823 FM	—	55.00	65.00	115.00	175.00
	1824 FM	—	55.00	65.00	100.00	150.00
	1825 FM	—	55.00	65.00	100.00	150.00
	1826/5 FM	—	55.00	65.00	115.00	175.00
	1826 FM	—	55.00	65.00	100.00	150.00
	1826 RU	—	55.00	65.00	115.00	175.00
	1827 FM	—	55.00	65.00	100.00	150.00
	1827 RU/FM	—	—	—	Rare	—
	1827 RU	—	—	—	Rare	—
	1828 RU	—	55.00	65.00	115.00	175.00
	1829 RU	—	55.00	65.00	100.00	150.00
	1830 RU	—	55.00	65.00	115.00	175.00
	1831 RU	—	55.00	65.00	100.00	150.00
	1832 RU	—	55.00	65.00	100.00	150.00
	1833/2 RU	—	55.00	65.00	115.00	175.00
	1834 RU	—	55.00	65.00	115.00	175.00
	1835 RU	—	—	—	—	—
	1836/4 RU	—	55.00	65.00	115.00	175.00
	1836 RU	—	55.00	65.00	100.00	150.00

2 ESCUDOS

6.7500 g, .875 GOLD, .1899 oz AGW
Bogota Mint

KM#	Date	Mintage	VG	Fine	VF	XF
83	1823 JF	—	125.00	225.00	350.00	500.00
	1824 JF	—	125.00	225.00	350.00	500.00
	1825 JF	—	125.00	225.00	350.00	500.00
	1826 JF	—	125.00	225.00	350.00	500.00
	1829 RS	—	125.00	225.00	350.00	500.00
	1836 RS	—	125.00	225.00	350.00	500.00

4 ESCUDOS

13.5000 g, .875 GOLD, .3798 oz AGW
Bogota Mint

KM#	Date	Mintage	VG	Fine	VF	XF
86	1826 JF	—	—	—	Rare	—

8 ESCUDOS

27.0000 g, .875 GOLD, .7596 oz AGW
Bogota Mint

KM#	Date	Mintage	VG	Fine	VF	XF
82.1	1822 JF	—	—	—	Rare	—
	1823 JF	—	375.00	450.00	650.00	900.00
	1824 JF	—	375.00	450.00	650.00	900.00
	1825 JF	—	375.00	450.00	650.00	900.00
	1826 JF	—	375.00	450.00	650.00	900.00
	1827 JF	—	400.00	600.00	1000.	1500.
	1827 RR	—	400.00	600.00	1000.	1500.
	1828 RR	—	375.00	450.00	650.00	900.00
	1829 RS	—	375.00	450.00	650.00	900.00
	1830 RS	—	375.00	450.00	650.00	900.00
	1831 RS	—	375.00	450.00	650.00	900.00
	1832 RS	—	375.00	450.00	650.00	900.00
	1833 RS	—	375.00	450.00	650.00	900.00
	1834 RS	—	375.00	450.00	650.00	900.00
	1835 RS	—	375.00	450.00	650.00	900.00
	1836 RS	—	375.00	450.00	650.00	900.00

Popayan Mint

KM#	Date	Mintage	VG	Fine	VF	XF
82.2	1822 FM	—	—	—	Rare	—
	1823 FM	—	375.00	450.00	650.00	900.00
	1824 FM	—	375.00	450.00	650.00	900.00
	1825 FM	—	375.00	450.00	650.00	900.00
	1826 FM	—	375.00	450.00	650.00	900.00
	1827 FM	—	400.00	600.00	1000.	1500.
	1827 UR	—	400.00	600.00	1000.	1500.
	1828 FM	—	400.00	600.00	1000.	1500.
	1828 UR	—	375.00	450.00	650.00	900.00
	1829 FM	—	—	—	—	—
	1829 UR	—	375.00	450.00	650.00	900.00
	1830 FW M inverted	—	—	—	Rare	—
	1830 UR	—	375.00	450.00	650.00	900.00
	1831 UR	—	400.00	600.00	1000.	1500.
	1832 UR	—	375.00	450.00	650.00	900.00
	1833 UR	—	375.00	450.00	650.00	900.00
	1834 UR	—	375.00	450.00	650.00	900.00
	1835 UR	—	375.00	450.00	650.00	900.00
	1836 UR	—	375.00	450.00	650.00	900.00
	1837 UR	—	400.00	600.00	1000.	1500.
	1838 UR	—	—	—	Rare	—

REPUBLIC OF NUEVA GRANADA

1837-1859

1/4 REAL

.6800 g, .666 SILVER, .0145 oz ASW
Bogota Mint

KM#	Date	Mintage	Good	VG	Fine	VF
90.1	1837	—	5.00	10.00	15.00	30.00
	1838	—	5.00	10.00	15.00	30.00
	1839	—	4.00	8.00	12.50	25.00
	1840	—	5.00	10.00	15.00	30.00
	1841	—	4.00	8.00	12.50	25.00
	1842	—	5.00	10.00	15.00	30.00
	1843	—	4.00	8.00	12.50	25.00
	1844	—	4.00	8.00	12.50	25.00
	1845	—	5.00	10.00	15.00	30.00
	1846	—	3.00	6.50	12.00	20.00
	1847	—	3.75	7.00	13.50	22.50
	1848	—	18.00	30.00	55.00	115.00

Popayan Mint

KM#	Date	Mintage	Good	VG	Fine	VF
90.2	1838	—	10.00	17.50	28.00	45.00
	1841	—	4.00	7.25	12.50	22.00
	1842	—	4.00	7.25	12.50	22.00
	1843	—	4.00	7.25	12.50	22.00
	1844	—	5.00	9.00	15.00	27.50
	1845	—	4.00	7.25	12.50	22.00
	1846	—	3.00	6.00	10.00	20.00

1/2 REAL

1.2600 g, .666 SILVER, .0269 oz ASW
Bogota Mint

KM#	Date	Mintage	Good	VG	Fine	VF
96.1	1839 RS	—	2.00	3.50	8.00	16.00
	1840 RS	—	4.00	7.50	12.50	22.00
	1841 RS	—	—	Reported, not confirmed		
	1842 RS	—	4.00	7.50	12.50	22.00
	1843 RS	—	4.50	8.50	15.00	24.00
	1844 RS	—	4.00	7.50	12.50	22.00
	1845 RS	—	2.50	5.50	10.00	18.50
	1846 RS	—	3.00	6.50	12.00	20.00
	1847/6 RS	—	2.50	5.50	10.00	18.50
	1847 RS	—	2.25	4.50	7.50	15.00

Popayan Mint

KM#	Date	Mintage	Good	VG	Fine	VF
96.2	1838 RU	—	2.50	6.00	11.00	18.50
	1839 RU	—	3.50	7.00	11.00	19.00
	1840	—	6.50	12.50	17.50	30.00
	1841 RU	—	5.00	9.00	15.00	30.00
	1841 VU	—	12.50	18.50	40.00	80.00
	1842 UM	—	6.50	12.50	17.50	32.50
	1843 UM	—	8.50	13.50	22.00	45.00
	1844 UE	—	4.50	8.50	13.50	22.50
	1844 UM	—	—	—	Rare	—
	1845 UE	—	6.00	12.00	17.50	35.00
	1846 UE	—	2.00	5.00	9.00	17.50
	1846 UM	—	3.00	6.50	11.00	18.50
	1848 UE	—	20.00	35.00	45.00	85.00

NOTE: 1848 date w/star over last 8 in date has been reported.

REAL

2.7000 g, .666 SILVER, .0578 oz ASW
Bogota Mint

KM#	Date	Mintage	Good	VG	Fine	VF
91.1	1837 RS	—	2.25	5.50	11.00	16.50
	1838 RS	—	2.00	4.50	7.00	10.00
	1839 RS	—	2.25	5.50	11.00	16.50
	1840/39 RS	—	5.50	12.50	17.50	27.50
	1841 RS	—	—	Reported, not confirmed		

Nueva Granada / COLOMBIA 410

KM#	Date	Mintage	Good	VG	Fine	VF
91.1	1842 RS	—	Reported, not confirmed			
	1843 RS	—	4.00	7.00	12.50	18.50
	1844 RS	—	4.00	7.00	12.50	18.50
	1845 RS	—	2.50	5.50	10.00	15.00
	1846 RS	—	5.00	10.00	18.00	30.00
	1847	—	4.00	7.00	12.50	18.50

Popayan Mint

KM#	Date	Mintage	Good	VG	Fine	VF
91.2	1839 RU	—	5.00	10.00	15.00	25.00
	1840	—	Reported, not confirmed			
	1841	—	Reported, not confirmed			
	1844 UM	—	4.00	9.00	14.00	20.00
	1845 UM	—	5.00	10.00	15.00	25.00
	1846/4	—	5.00	10.00	15.00	25.00
	1846	—	11.50	17.50	32.50	

2 REALES
5.5000 g, .666 SILVER, .1177 oz ASW
Bogota Mint

KM#	Date	Mintage	Good	VG	Fine	VF
97.1	1839 RS	—	12.00	22.00	40.00	68.00
	1840 RS	—	2.50	6.00	11.00	22.50
	1841 RS	—	18.50	37.00	75.00	135.00
	1842 RS	—	—	—	Rare	—
	1843 RS	—	3.00	5.50	10.00	18.50
	1844/3 RS	—	5.00	10.00	15.00	30.00
	1844 RS	—	4.50	8.00	13.00	25.00
	1845 RS	—	6.50	12.00	20.00	40.00
	1846/5 RS	—	20.00	37.00	60.00	100.00

Popayan Mint

KM#	Date	Mintage	Good	VG	Fine	VF
97.2	1840 RU	—	12.50	25.00	35.00	65.00
	1841 VU	—	10.00	18.00	30.00	55.00
	1842/0/1 UM	—	22.50	42.50	85.00	160.00
	1842 VU	—	27.50	50.00	120.00	200.00
	1842 UM	—	10.00	18.00	30.00	55.00
	1843/2 UM	—	12.50	25.00	35.00	65.00
	1844 UM	—	12.50	22.00	32.00	55.00
	1846 UM	—	—	—	Rare	—

8 REALES

SILVER

KM#	Date	Mintage	VG	Fine	VF	XF
92	1837 RS	—	65.00	175.00	350.00	675.00
	1838 RS	—	—	Rare	—	—

KM#	Date	Mintage	Good	VG	Fine	VF
98	1839 RS	—	6.00	13.00	30.00	60.00
	1840 RS	—	7.00	16.00	35.00	70.00
	1841 RS	—	8.00	19.00	37.50	75.00
	1842 RS	—	10.00	20.00	45.00	85.00
	1843 RS	—	7.00	16.00	35.00	70.00
	1844 RS	—	8.00	19.00	37.50	75.00
	1845 RS	—	8.00	19.00	37.50	75.00
	1846/4 RS	—	10.00	20.00	45.00	90.00
	1846/5 RS	—	10.00	20.00	45.00	90.00
	1846 RS	—	8.00	19.00	37.50	75.00

PESO

1.6875 g, .875 GOLD, .0474 oz AGW

Bogota Mint

KM#	Date	Mintage	VG	Fine	VF	XF
93	1837 RS	—	30.00	50.00	80.00	125.00
	1838 RS	—	30.00	50.00	80.00	125.00
	1839 RS	—	30.00	50.00	80.00	125.00
	1840/39 RS	—	40.00	60.00	90.00	150.00
	1841 RS	—	40.00	60.00	90.00	150.00
	1842 RS	—	30.00	50.00	80.00	125.00
	1844 RS	—	30.00	50.00	80.00	125.00
	1846/3	—	30.00	50.00	80.00	125.00
	1846 RS	—	30.00	50.00	80.00	125.00

2 PESOS

3.3750 g, .900 GOLD, .0976 oz AGW
Popayan Mint

KM#	Date	Mintage	VG	Fine	VF	XF
95	1838 RU	—	55.00	75.00	110.00	175.00
	1842 VU	—	55.00	75.00	110.00	175.00
	1843 UM	—	55.00	75.00	110.00	175.00
	1843 VU	—	55.00	75.00	110.00	175.00
	1844 UM	—	55.00	75.00	110.00	175.00
	1845 UM	—	55.00	75.00	110.00	175.00
	1845 UE	—	55.00	75.00	110.00	175.00
	1846 UE	—	55.00	75.00	110.00	175.00
	1846 UM	—	55.00	75.00	110.00	175.00

3.2258 g, .900 GOLD, .0933 oz AGW
Bogota Mint

KM#	Date	Mintage	VG	Fine	VF	XF
99	1848	—	—	—	Rare	—
	1849	—	—	—	Rare	—
	1851	—	600.00	1200.	1800.	2700.

DIEZ I SEIS (16) PESOS

27.0000 g, .900 GOLD, .7813 oz AGW
Bogota Mint

KM#	Date	Mintage	VG	Fine	VF	XF
94.1	1837 RS	—	375.00	425.00	500.00	700.00
	1838 RS	—	375.00	425.00	500.00	700.00
	1839/8 RS	—	375.00	425.00	500.00	700.00
	1839 RS	—	375.00	425.00	500.00	700.00
	1840 RS	—	375.00	425.00	500.00	700.00
	1841 RS	—	375.00	425.00	500.00	700.00
	1842 RS	—	375.00	425.00	500.00	700.00
	1843 RS	—	375.00	425.00	500.00	700.00
	1844 RS	—	375.00	425.00	500.00	700.00
	1845 RS	—	375.00	425.00	500.00	700.00
	1846 RS	—	375.00	425.00	550.00	1100.
	1847 RS	—	375.00	425.00	500.00	700.00
	1848 RS		2 known			
	1849 RS	—	—	—	—	—

Popayan Mint

	1837 RU	—	375.00	425.00	500.00	700.00
94.2	1838 RU	—	375.00	425.00	500.00	700.00
	1839 RU	—	375.00	425.00	500.00	700.00
	1840 RU	—	375.00	425.00	600.00	1200.
	1841 RU	—	—	—	Rare	—
	1841 VU	—	375.00	425.00	500.00	700.00
	1842 VU	—	375.00	425.00	500.00	700.00
	1842 UM	—	375.00	425.00	500.00	700.00
	1843 UM	—	375.00	425.00	500.00	700.00
	1844 UM	—	375.00	425.00	500.00	700.00
	1845 UM	—	375.00	425.00	500.00	700.00
	1846 UM	—	375.00	425.00	550.00	1000.
	1846 UE	—	375.00	425.00	600.00	1200.

25.8064 g, .900 GOLD, .7468 oz AGW
Bogota Mint

KM#	Date	Mintage	VG	Fine	VF	XF
100	1848	—	400.00	450.00	600.00	1000.
	1849	—	400.00	450.00	600.00	1000.
	1850	—	400.00	450.00	600.00	1000.
	1851	—	—	Reported, not confirmed		
	1852	—	400.00	450.00	600.00	1000.
	1853	—	500.00	750.00	1000.	2000.

FIRST DECIMAL COINAGE
MONETARY SYSTEM
10 Decimos de Real = 1 Real (1847-53)
10 Reales = 1 Peso (1847-53)
10 Decimos = 1 Peso (1853-72)

1/2 DECIMO DE REAL
(1/20 Real)

COPPER

KM#	Date	Mintage	VG	Fine	VF	XF
101	1847	—	2.50	4.50	9.00	30.00
	1847	—	—	—	Proof	55.00
	1848	—	5.00	12.50	30.00	80.00

DECIMO DE REAL
(1/10 Real)

COPPER

102	1847	—	2.50	5.00	12.50	27.50
	1847	—	—	—	Proof	100.00
	1848	—	7.50	18.50	45.00	85.00

1/4 REAL
.9000 g, .900 SILVER, .0260 oz ASW
Bogota Mint

108.1	1850	—	2.50	5.00	8.50	16.00
	1851	—	3.00	7.00	14.00	25.00

Popayan Mint

108.2	1849	—	3.50	7.00	15.00	35.00
	1850	—	3.50	7.00	15.00	35.00
	1851	—	2.50	6.00	14.00	32.50
	1852	—	3.50	7.00	15.00	35.00
	1853	—	3.50	7.00	15.00	35.00
	1855	—	6.50	9.00	17.50	50.00
	1856	—	8.00	15.00	25.00	65.00
	1858	—	15.00	30.00	60.00	125.00

Bogota Mint
Obv: Similar to C#153.2. Rev: Caduceus at each side of '1/4' instead of 3 stars below.

113	1852	—	18.00	37.50	80.00	175.00
	1858	—	—	—	Rare	—

MEDIO (1/2) REAL

1.4000 g, .900 SILVER, .0405 oz ASW
Bogota Mint

110	1850	5.000	8.00	15.00	25.00	65.00
	1851	2.500	2.50	6.00	10.00	27.50

KM#	Date	Mintage	VG	Fine	VF	XF
110	1852/1	—	3.50	7.00	12.00	32.50
	1852	2.500	2.50	6.00	10.00	27.50
	1853	2.500	2.00	5.00	9.00	25.00
	1854	—	—	Reported, not confirmed		

MEDIO (1/2) DECIMO

1.5000 g, .900 SILVER, .0434 oz ASW
Bogota Mint

114	1853	—	8.00	15.00	22.50	35.00
	1854	—	4.00	8.50	16.00	28.00
	1855	—	4.00	8.50	16.00	28.00
	1856	—	6.00	11.00	18.00	32.00
	1857	—	5.00	10.00	18.00	30.00
	1858	—	5.00	10.00	18.00	30.00

UN (1) REAL

2.7000 g, .900 SILVER, .0781 oz ASW
Bogota Mint

103	1847	—	3.50	7.50	12.00	17.50

2.5000 g, .900 SILVER, .0723 oz ASW

112	1851	—	2.50	5.50	15.00	40.00
	1852	—	1.50	4.50	7.50	15.00
	1853	—	2.50	5.50	15.00	38.00

UN (1) DECIMO

2.5000 g, .900 SILVER, .0723 oz ASW
Bogota Mint

115	1853	—	3.50	5.00	8.00	25.00
	1854	—	2.50	4.25	7.00	18.50
	1855	—	2.50	4.25	7.00	18.50
	1856	—	2.00	3.75	6.50	17.50
	1857	—	2.00	3.75	6.50	17.50
	1858/7	—	3.00	4.75	7.50	22.50
	1858	—	2.25	4.00	7.00	18.00

DOS (2) REALES

5.0000 g, .900 SILVER, .1447 oz ASW
Bogota Mint
Obv: Date above shield.

| 104 | 1847 | — | — | — | Rare | — |

NOTE: Possibly a pattern.

Obv: Date below shield

105	1847	—	3.25	7.50	15.00	25.00
	1848	—	3.00	5.25	8.50	25.00
	1849	—	2.50	5.00	7.50	20.00

109	1849	—	—	—	Rare	—
	1850	—	4.00	7.00	15.00	37.50
	1851	—	4.00	7.00	15.00	37.50
	1852	—	6.00	10.00	35.00	68.00
	1853	—	5.50	9.00	20.00	52.50

DOS (2) DECIMOS

5.0000 g, .900 SILVER, .1447 oz ASW
Bogota Mint

KM#	Date	Mintage	VG	Fine	VF	XF
117	1854/3	—	7.50	20.00	60.00	150.00
	1854	—	5.00	10.00	25.00	60.00
	1855/3	—	4.50	9.00	35.00	75.00
	1855	—	3.50	7.50	16.50	30.00
	1856/5	—	5.50	12.00	38.00	75.00
	1857	—	4.00	9.00	18.50	40.00
	1858/7	—	15.00	40.00	80.00	165.00

OCHO (8) REALES

20.0000 g, .900 SILVER, .5787 oz ASW
Bogota Mint

| 106 | 1847 | — | 30.00 | 60.00 | 100.00 | 225.00 |

DIEZ (10) REALES

25.0000 g, .900 SILVER, .7234 oz ASW

107	1847	—	25.00	45.00	70.00	200.00
	1848	—	20.00	30.00	50.00	175.00
	1849/8	—	35.00	65.00	125.00	275.00
	1849	—	25.00	50.00	90.00	225.00

NOTE: Struck at Bogota and Popayan without mint marks.

Bogota Mint

111	1850	—	20.00	45.00	100.00	200.00
	1851	—	20.00	45.00	100.00	200.00

PESO

25.0000 g, .900 SILVER, .7234 oz ASW

118	1855/1	—	18.00	37.50	75.00	125.00
	1855	—	15.00	30.00	45.00	65.00
	1856/5	—	12.50	25.00	40.00	60.00

KM#	Date	Mintage	VG	Fine	VF	XF
118	1856	—	17.50	32.50	50.00	70.00
	1857/6	—	15.00	30.00	45.00	65.00
	1857	—	12.50	25.00	40.00	60.00
	1858/7	—	15.00	30.00	45.00	65.00
	1858	—	12.50	25.00	40.00	60.00
	1859/6	—	18.00	35.00	65.00	115.00

1.6875 g, .875 GOLD, .0474 oz AGW
Similar to 2 Pesos, KM#121.

119	1856	—	65.00	150.00	300.00	500.00
	1857	—	—	Reported, not confirmed		
	1858	—	65.00	150.00	300.00	500.00

2 PESOS

3.2258 g, .900 GOLD, .0933 oz AGW
Mint mark: P
Rev: Value in wreath.

121	1857	—	55.00	85.00	150.00	250.00
	1858/48	—	55.00	90.00	175.00	275.00
	1858	—	55.00	85.00	150.00	250.00

5 PESOS

8.0648 g, .900 GOLD, .2333 oz AGW
Mint mark: B

KM#	Date	Mintage	VG	Fine	VF	XF
120	1856	—	—	—	Rare	—
	1857	—	175.00	400.00	850.00	1350.
	1858	—	—	—	Rare	—

10 PESOS

16.4000 g, .900 GOLD, .4745 oz AGW
Bogota Mint

116.1	1853	—	—	—	Rare	—
	1854	—	350.00	700.00	1250.	1500.
	1855	—	350.00	700.00	1250.	1500.
	1856	—	450.00	800.00	1400.	1800.
	1857	—	450.00	800.00	1400.	1800.

Popayan Mint

116.2	1853	—	250.00	400.00	600.00	900.00
	1856	—	—	—	Rare	—
	1857	—	—	—	Rare	—

16.1290 g, .900 GOLD, .4667 oz AGW
Bogota Mint
Rev. leg: DIEZ PESOS

122.1	1857	—	275.00	500.00	900.00	1400.
	1858	—	275.00	500.00	900.00	1400.

Nueva Granada / COLOMBIA 412

Popayan Mint

KM#	Date	Mintage	VG	Fine	VF	XF
122.2	1853	—	225.00	325.00	Rare	—
	1856	—	225.00	325.00	500.00	800.00
	1857	—	225.00	325.00	500.00	800.00
	1858	—	225.00	325.00	500.00	800.00

GRANADINE CONFEDERATION
1859-1861

MONETARY SYSTEM
10 Reales = 1 Peso
10 Decimos = 1 Peso

1/4 REAL
.9000 g, .666 SILVER, .0192 oz ASW
Popayan Mint
Rev: 3 stars.

KM#	Date	Mintage	Good	VG	Fine	VF
123	1859	—	3.00	7.00	12.50	20.00
	1860	—	2.50	5.50	10.00	18.00
	1861	—	2.50	5.50	10.00	18.00
	1862	—	3.00	7.00	12.50	20.00

1/4 DECIMO

.9000 g, .666 SILVER, .0192 oz ASW
Bogota Mint
Rev: Caducei flanking fraction.

131	1860	—	—	7.50	18.00	35.00	65.00

Rev: 9 stars below fraction.

132.1	1861	—	3.50	7.50	12.50	27.50
	1862	—	4.50	9.00	15.00	40.00

Popayan Mint

132.2	1860	—	12.50	27.50	55.00	125.00

1/2 REAL

1.2500 g, .900 SILVER, .0362 oz ASW
Popayan Mint

133	1862	—	6.00	12.50	27.50	60.00
	1862/48	—	6.00	12.50	27.50	60.00

MEDIO (1/2) DECIMO

1.2500 g, .900 SILVER, .0362 oz ASW

KM#	Date	Mintage	VG	Fine	VF	XF
124	1859	—	8.00	17.50	30.00	75.00
	1860/59	—	9.00	20.00	35.00	80.00
	1860	—	6.00	14.00	25.00	50.00
	1861	—	8.00	17.50	30.00	75.00

UN (1) DECIMO

2.5000 g, .900 SILVER, .0723 oz ASW

125	1859	—	4.00	8.50	20.00	35.00
	1860	—	8.50	22.50	35.00	75.00

DOS (2) REALES

5.0000 g, .900 SILVER, .1447 oz ASW
Popayan Mint

134	1862/48/47	—	6.50	15.00	27.50	62.50
	1862/49	—	5.50	10.00	22.50	55.00
	1862/52	—	25.00	45.00	85.00	125.00
	1862	—	6.00	12.50	25.00	55.00

NOTE: These are struck from reworked dies of KM#109.

PESO

25.0000 g, .900 SILVER, .7234 oz ASW
Bogota Mint

KM#	Date	Mintage	VG	Fine	VF	XF
126	1859	—	10.00	17.50	45.00	85.00
	1860	—	10.00	17.50	45.00	85.00
	1861	—	12.50	30.00	65.00	125.00

1.6129 g, .900 GOLD, .0466 oz AGW
Mint mark: M

135	1862	—	—	—	Rare	—

2 PESOS

3.2258 g, .900 GOLD, .0933 oz AGW
Mint mark: P

127	1859	—	75.00	150.00	350.00	600.00
	1860	—	—	—	Rare	—

5 PESOS

8.0645 g, .900 GOLD, .2333 oz AGW
Mint mark: P

128	1859	—	—	—	—	4750.

Mint mark: M

136	1862	—	—	—	—	5750.

DIEZ (10) PESOS

16.1290 g, .900 GOLD, .4667 oz AGW
Bogota Mint

129.1	1859	3,481	250.00	400.00	700.00	1000.
	1860	9,687	225.00	300.00	600.00	900.00
	1861	834 pcs.	275.00	500.00	800.00	1200.

Popayan Mint

129.2	1858	—	250.00	400.00	700.00	1100.
	1859	—	225.00	400.00	600.00	950.00
	1860	—	250.00	400.00	700.00	1100.
	1861	—	250.00	400.00	700.00	1100.
	1862	—	250.00	400.00	700.00	1100.

VEINTE (20) PESOS

32.2580 g, .900 GOLD, .9335 oz AGW
Bogota Mint

KM#	Date	Mintage	VG	Fine	VF	XF
130	1859	2,002	700.00	1500.	3250.	5000.

ESTADOS UNIDOS DE NUEVA GRANADA
1861-1862

UN (1) DECIMO

2.5000 g, .900 SILVER, .0723 oz ASW
Bogota Mint

137	1861	—	18.00	42.50	90.00	160.00

PESO
25.0000 g, .900 SILVER, .7234 oz ASW
Bogota Mint

138	1861	—	60.00	135.00	250.00	450.00

ESTADOS UNIDOS DE COLOMBIA
1862-1886

1/4 DECIMO

.8500 g, .900 SILVER, .0245 oz ASW
Bogota Mint

143.1	1863	.048	4.00	6.50	9.00	17.50
	1864	.435	2.00	4.50	7.50	14.50
	1865	.206	2.00	5.00	8.00	16.00
	1866	.267	2.00	5.00	8.00	16.00
	1867	.208	2.00	5.00	8.00	16.00

.8500 g, .666 SILVER, .0182 oz ASW

143.1a	1868	.023	—	—	Rare	—
	1869	.183	3.00	5.00	7.50	13.50
	1870	.092	4.25	7.00	9.00	16.50
	1871	.413	3.25	5.50	8.00	14.00
	1873 Inc.KM169	—	—	Rare	—
	1881 Inc.KM169	8.50	17.50	25.00	50.00

.8500 g, .900 SILVER, .0245 oz ASW
Popayan Mint

143.2	1863	—	3.00	5.00	7.50	12.50
	1864	.504	3.00	5.00	7.50	12.50
	1865/3	—	10.00	18.00	27.50	45.00
	1865	.291	—	5.00	7.50	12.50
	1866	.157	6.00	12.50	18.00	30.00
	1867	.055	6.00	12.50	18.00	30.00

.8500 g, .666 SILVER, .0182 oz ASW

143.2a	1868	—	6.50	15.00	25.00	42.50
	1869	—	2.50	5.00	6.50	10.00
	1870	—	4.25	8.00	11.00	17.50
	1871	.155	3.00	6.00	7.50	12.00
	1872/1	.041	4.00	7.00	10.00	15.00
	1872 Inc. Ab.	3.00	6.00	8.00	12.00
	1873	—	2.50	5.00	7.50	12.00
	1874	—	3.75	7.00	9.00	14.00
	1875	—	2.50	5.00	6.50	10.00
	1876	—	6.00	13.00	18.00	35.00
	1877	.025	3.00	6.00	8.00	12.00
	1878	.025	4.25	8.00	11.00	18.00
	1879	—	5.00	11.00	15.00	25.00
	1880	—	2.50	5.00	7.00	12.00
	1881	—	2.50	5.00	7.00	12.00
	1883	—	—	Reported, not confirmed
	1888	—	—	—	Rare	—

NOTE: Varieties exist.

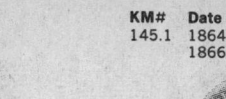

Medellin Mint

KM#	Date	Mintage	VG	Fine	VF	XF
143.3	1874	—	6.50	15.00	25.00	45.00

MEDIO (1/2) DECIMO

1.2500 g, .900 SILVER, .0362 oz ASW
Bogota Mint

144	1863	.028	10.00	20.00	40.00	75.00
	1864	Inc. Ab.	10.00	25.00	45.00	85.00
	1865	.029	13.50	27.50	55.00	100.00

1.2500 g, .666 SILVER, .0268 oz ASW

144a	1867	.363	8.00	20.00	45.00	85.00

150.1	1868					
		Inc. KM144a	3.00	7.00	9.00	15.00
	1869	.173	—	—	Rare	—
	1870	.140	5.00	11.00	15.00	27.50
	1871	.100	9.00	17.50	22.50	35.00

Medellin Mint

150.2	1868	.062	5.00	11.00	17.50	30.00
	1869	.026	8.00	15.00	30.00	45.00
	1870	—	—	Reported, not confirmed		
	1873	.014	5.50	12.50	22.00	35.00
	1874	—	5.00	12.00	30.00	42.50
	1876	—	—	Reported, not confirmed		

Popayan Mint

150.3	1869	—	4.00	12.00	22.00	35.00
	1870	.382	4.00	12.00	22.00	35.00
	1874	—	4.00	12.00	22.00	35.00
	1875	.573	4.00	12.00	22.00	35.00
	1876	—	5.00	16.50	32.00	42.50
	1878	—	—	—	Rare	—

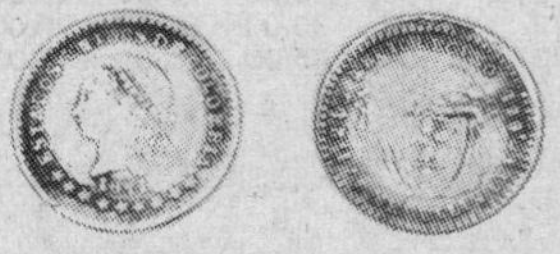

1.2500 g, .835 SILVER, .0336 oz ASW
Medellin Mint

150.2a	1870	Inc. Ab.	8.50	17.50	25.00	37.50
	1871	.061	3.50	8.00	16.00	25.00
	1872/1	Inc. Ab.	6.50	13.50	25.00	37.50
	1872	Inc. Ab.	4.00	8.50	17.50	25.00
	1873	—	5.50	12.00	22.50	32.50
	1874/61	—	6.00	13.50	25.00	40.00
	1874	—	5.00	10.00	22.50	32.50

Popayan Mint

150.3a	1875	Inc. Ab.	7.50	17.50	27.50	45.00

0,835/0,666 SILVER

150.3b	1875/65	—	12.50	25.00	40.00	75.00

UN (1) DECIMO

2.5000 g, .900 SILVER, .0723 oz ASW
Bogota Mint

KM#	Date	Mintage	VG	Fine	VF	XF
145.1	1863	.096	4.50	8.50	12.50	30.00
145.1	1864	.039	5.50	10.00	17.50	37.50
	1866	.112	3.50	7.50	10.00	25.00

Popayan Mint

145.2	1863/48	—	6.00	11.00	20.00	40.00
	1864/48	.028	4.50	9.00	17.50	37.50
	1864	—	18.00	37.50	55.00	110.00

NOTE: The overdates appear to have been struck from re-cut dies of Un Real, 1848 Popayan (pattern only).

2.5000 g, .835 SILVER, .0671 oz ASW
Bogota Mint

145.1a	1866	.606	4.00	11.00	18.50	35.00

Popayan Mint

145.2a	1866	.034	15.00	32.50	55.00	120.00

NOTE: Some, or all, appear to have been struck from re-cut dies of Un Real, 1848 Popayan (pattern only).

Bogota Mint

151.1	1868	.146	3.00	9.00	22.50	40.00
	1869	.082	3.00	8.00	18.50	35.00
	1871	.144	2.50	6.50	13.50	27.50
	1872	.133	3.00	7.00	16.50	30.00

Medellin Mint
Obv: AB below bust.

151.2	1874/3	—	20.00	52.00	85.00	175.00
	1874	—	15.00	35.00	60.00	120.00

DOS (2) REALES

5.0000 g, .835 SILVER, .1342 oz ASW
Popayan Mint

162	1880	3,000	37.50	80.00	160.00	250.00

NOTE: Some are apparently from re-cut dies of 2 Decimos, 1854-1858.

DOS (2) DECIMOS

5.0000 g, .900 SILVER, .1447 oz ASW
Bogota Mint

149	1865	—	45.00	115.00	175.00	250.00

5.0000 g, .835 SILVER, .1342 oz ASW

149a.1	1866	—	4.50	12.00	25.00	55.00
	1867	—	3.50	8.00	17.50	40.00

Rev. leg: Lei 0.835/0.900
Popayan Mint

149a.2	1867	—	7.50	20.00	40.00	80.00

.666 SILVER

149b	1867	—	10.00	25.00	50.00	90.00

Rev. leg: Lei 0.835/0.666.

KM#	Date	Mintage	VG	Fine	VF	XF
149c	1867	—	15.00	37.50	75.00	120.00

5.0000 g, .835 SILVER, .1342 oz ASW
Bogota Mint

155.1	1872	.024	8.50	17.50	37.50	75.00

Medellin Mint

155.2	1870	.015	6.00	13.50	25.00	40.00
	1871	.036	16.50	35.00	55.00	85.00
	1872	.045	4.00	9.00	18.00	35.00

NOTE: Each date of KM#155.2 has slightly different head, with 2 varieties for 1872. Varieties in legend spacings exist.

Obv: Similar to 5 Decimos, KM#153.4.
Rev: Inverted fineness.

159	1873	800 pcs.	—	—	Rare	—

Obv: Large head. Rev: Large arms.

160	1874	—	1.75	4.25	12.50	30.00

MEDIO (1/2) PESO

12.5000 g, .835 SILVER, .3356 oz ASW
Medellin Mint

152	1868	—	—	—	Rare	—

CINCO (5) DECIMOS

12.5000 g, .835 SILVER, .3356 oz ASW
Bogota Mint

153.1	1868	9,161	35.00	58.00	100.00	185.00
	1869	.187	8.00	16.50	42.50	90.00
	1870	.206	8.00	16.50	42.50	85.00
	1871	.273	10.00	22.50	50.00	115.00

Medellin Mint

153.2	1868	5 known	—	—	—	—
	1869	1,054	275.00	500.00	750.00	1000.

153.3	1872	.030	27.50	55.00	85.00	135.00
	1873	.090	7.00	18.00	35.00	75.00

COLOMBIA 414

Obv: Small round head. **Rev:** Small arms, fineness faces in (counter-clockwise).

KM#	Date	Mintage	VG	Fine	VF	XF
153.4	1873	Inc. Ab.	35.00	75.00	130.00	200.00
	1874	.185	5.00	11.00	22.50	50.00
	1875/4	.197	6.00	13.00	25.00	55.00

Rev: Fineness faces out (clockwise).

153.5	1875	Inc. Ab.	5.50	11.00	25.00	50.00
	1876/5	—	12.50	25.00	45.00	90.00
	1876	—	10.00	22.00	38.00	75.00
	1877	2 known	—	—	—	—

Popayan Mint

153.6	1869	1 known	—	—	Rare	—
	1870/9	7,774	—	Reported, not confirmed		
	1870	Inc. Ab.	115.00	185.00	300.00	475.00
	1871	—	125.00	220.00	400.00	700.00
	1873/69	7,743	—	—	Rare	—
	1873	Inc. Ab.	100.00	175.00	250.00	425.00
	1874	.011	125.00	220.00	375.00	625.00
	1878	3,158	100.00	175.00	250.00	425.00
	1880	2 known	—	—	Rare	—

Medellin Mint
Obv: Large head. **Rev:** Large arms.

161.1	1877/4	.168	15.00	20.00	40.00	75.00
	1878/4	.318	12.00	17.50	30.00	55.00
	1878/4 lg.8 I.A.		—	—	Rare	—
	1879/4 pointed tail 9					
		.379	6.00	10.00	22.50	45.00
	1879/4 ball tailed 9					
		Inc. Ab.	6.00	10.00	22.50	45.00
	1880/74	.411	30.00	60.00	115.00	225.00
	1880	Inc. Ab.	4.00	7.50	14.00	27.50
	1881	.379	5.00	10.00	20.00	40.00
	1881 square Liberty head					
		Inc. Ab.	50.00	85.00	140.00	200.00
	1882	—	3.00	6.50	11.00	22.50
	1883	1.096	3.00	6.50	11.00	22.50
	1884/3	1.429	—	—	Rare	—
	1884	Inc. Ab.	3.00	6.50	11.00	22.50
	1885	—	3.75	7.00	11.00	22.50
	1886	—	22.50	50.00	85.00	125.00
	1886 round top 3 in fineness					
			—	—	Rare	—

Similar to KM#153.3 but different head and smaller letters and numbers.

161.2	1880	1 known	—	—	Rare	—
	1882	—	—	—	Rare	—
	1883	—	—	—	Rare	—

12.2000 g, .500/.835 SILVER

161.2a	1886/4	—	65.00	140.00	250.00	400.00
	1886	—	45.00	125.00	225.00	330.00

NOTE: The above coin always shows traces of 0.835 under 0.500.

12.5000 g, .500 SILVER, .2009 oz ASW
Obv: Modified head. **Rev:** 2 stars, leg: LEV.

KM#	Date	Mintage	VG	Fine	VF	XF
164.1	1886	—	—	—	Rare	—

Rev: W/o stars, leg: LEI.

| 164.2 | 1886 | — | — | — | Rare | — |

.500/.835 SILVER
Rev: W/o stars or dots, leg: LEV.

| 164.3 | 1886 | 1 known | — | — | Rare | — |

PESO

25.0000 g, .900 SILVER, .7234 oz ASW
Bogota Mint

139.1	1862	.055	12.50	30.00	50.00	90.00
	1863	.018	9.00	22.50	40.00	60.00
	1864	.104	9.00	22.50	40.00	60.00
	1865	.122	9.00	22.50	40.00	60.00
	1866	.091	9.00	22.50	40.00	60.00
	1867	.044	12.50	30.00	50.00	90.00
	1868	.017	12.50	30.00	50.00	90.00

Popayan Mint

| 139.2 | 1863 | — | 200.00 | 500.00 | 700.00 | 1000. |

1.6129 g, .900 GOLD, .0466 oz AGW
Medellin Mint
Obv. leg: ESTADOS UNIDOS DE COLOMBIA.

| 146.1 | 1863 | .011 | 350.00 | 600.00 | 1000. | 1500. |

Obv. leg: COLOMBIA.

| 146.2 | 1864 | 1,072 | 600.00 | 1000. | 1500. | 2000. |

25.0000 g, .900 SILVER, .7234 oz ASW
Bogota Mint

KM#	Date	Mintage	VG	Fine	VF	XF
154.1	1868	—	300.00	500.00	800.00	1200.
	1869	—	—	—	Rare	—
	1870	.046	60.00	100.00	160.00	250.00
	1871	.040	40.00	85.00	150.00	250.00

Medellin Mint

154.2	1869	3,598	70.00	125.00	175.00	250.00
	1870/69	.048	80.00	140.00	200.00	275.00
	1870	Inc. Ab.	60.00	100.00	160.00	240.00
	1871	.055	30.00	60.00	90.00	180.00

1.6129 g, .900 GOLD, .0466 oz AGW
Rev: Arms.

156	1872/1	.062	45.00	75.00	115.00	175.00
	1872	Inc. Ab.	30.00	60.00	90.00	125.00
	1873	.018	45.00	75.00	115.00	175.00

Rev: Condor

157.1	1872	Inc. Ab.	30.00	45.00	65.00	100.00
	1873/2	—	80.00	140.00	250.00	400.00
	1873	—	20.00	40.00	60.00	100.00

Bogota Mint

157.2	1872	—	30.00	50.00	75.00	115.00
	1873	3,374	30.00	50.00	75.00	115.00
	1874	.014	30.00	50.00	75.00	115.00
	1875	7,002	30.00	50.00	75.00	115.00
	1878	—	75.00	150.00	250.00	350.00

NOTE: 1871 date exists but is almost certainly counterfeit.

2 PESOS

3.2258 g, .900 GOLD, .0933 oz AGW
Mint mark: M

| 147 | 1863 | 2,996 | 150.00 | 225.00 | 350.00 | 550.00 |

Medellin Mint

KM#	Date	Mintage	VG	Fine	VF	XF
A154	1871	.066	55.00	65.00	80.00	125.00
	1872	.030	65.00	80.00	120.00	175.00
	1876	—	80.00	100.00	140.00	200.00

3.2258 g, .666 GOLD, .0690 oz AGW

A154a	1885/74	—	—	—	Rare	—

5 PESOS

8.0645 g, .900 GOLD, .2333 oz AGW
Medellin Mint
Obv. leg: ESTADOS UNIDOS DE COLOMBIA.

140	1862	—	Reported, not confirmed			
	1863	.029	1500.	2500.	3500.	4500.

Obv. leg: COLOMBIA above.

148	1864	8,035	2000.	3000.	4500.	5500.

8.0645 g, .666 GOLD, .1728 oz AGW

163	1885/inverted 5	—	1000.	1500.	2000.	3000.
	1885/74	—	—	—	Rare	—

10 PESOS

16.1290 g, .900 GOLD, .4667 oz AGW
Bogota Mint

141.1	1862	.011	275.00	500.00	850.00	1300.
	1863	.017	275.00	500.00	850.00	1200.

Medellin Mint

141.2	1863	—	—	—	—	—
	1864	—	—	—	—	—
	1867	.014	—	—	Rare	—
	1868	.018	250.00	350.00	600.00	850.00
	1869	.018	250.00	350.00	650.00	900.00
	1870	7,786	250.00	375.00	650.00	900.00
	1871	6,018	250.00	375.00	650.00	900.00
	1872	.014	—	—	—	—
	1873	8,623	250.00	350.00	600.00	850.00
	1875	—	250.00	375.00	650.00	900.00
	1876/5	—	250.00	375.00	650.00	900.00
	1876	—	250.00	350.00	600.00	850.00

16.1290 g, .666 GOLD, .3453 oz AGW

141.2a	1886/74	—	—	—	Rare	—

16.1290 g, .900 GOLD, .4667 oz AGW
Popayan Mint

KM#	Date	Mintage	VG	Fine	VF	XF
141.3	1863	—	250.00	375.00	650.00	900.00
	1864	.010	250.00	350.00	600.00	850.00
	1865	8,727	250.00	350.00	600.00	850.00
	1866	.013	250.00	350.00	600.00	850.00
	1867	—	300.00	400.00	700.00	1000.
	1869	—	250.00	375.00	650.00	900.00
	1871	2,617	250.00	375.00	650.00	900.00
	1874					

20 PESOS

32.2580 g, .900 GOLD, .9335 oz AGW
Bogota Mint

142.1	1862	—	475.00	600.00	1250.	1800.
	1863	—	475.00	600.00	1250.	1800.
	1868	—	475.00	600.00	1250.	1800.
	1869	—	475.00	600.00	1250.	1800.
	1870	.017	475.00	600.00	1250.	1800.
	1871	1,641	—	Reported, not confirmed		
	1872	1,471	475.00	600.00	1250.	1800.
	1873	2,731	475.00	600.00	1250.	1800.
	1874	1,656	475.00	600.00	1250.	1800.
	1875	1,696	475.00	600.00	1250.	1800.
	1876	2,299				

1868

1869

Medellin Mint
NOTE: On 1868, arrows in shield on reverse point between zeros in 0.900. On 1869, arrows point at zeros in 0.900.

142.2	1863	—	450.00	550.00	1000.	1600.
	1868	7,984	450.00	550.00	1000.	1600.
	1869	7,313	450.00	550.00	1000.	1600.
	1870	.012	—	—	—	—
	1871	5,996	—	—	—	—

Popayan Mint

KM#	Date	Mintage	VG	Fine	VF	XF
142.3	1862	—	Reported, not confirmed			
	1863	—	475.00	550.00	1000.	1600.
	1868	—	475.00	550.00	1000.	1600.
	1869	—	475.00	550.00	1000.	1600.
	1870	8,247	475.00	550.00	1000.	1600.
	1871	5,885	475.00	550.00	1000.	1600.
	1872	—	475.00	550.00	1000.	1600.
	1873	—	475.00	550.00	1000.	1600.
	1874/3	5,352	475.00	550.00	1000.	1600.
	1874	Inc. Ab.	475.00	550.00	1000.	1600.
	1875	5,240	475.00	550.00	1000.	1600.
	1877	1,219				
	1878	2,873	475.00	550.00	1000.	1600.

Medellin Mint
Modified design

158	1872	.017	475.00	550.00	1250.	1750.
	1873	Inc. Ab.	475.00	550.00	1250.	1750.

MODERN DECIMAL SYSTEM
100 Centavos = 1 Peso

1-1/4 CENTAVOS

COPPER-NICKEL

KM#	Date	Mintage	Fine	VF	XF	Unc
173	1874	2.400	1.25	2.50	5.00	15.00

2-1/2 CENTAVOS

.9000 g, .666 SILVER, .0192 oz ASW

KM#	Date	Mintage	VG	Fine	VF	XF
169	1872	.328	2.00	4.50	8.00	14.00
	1873	.302	2.00	4.50	8.00	14.00
	1874	.075	4.00	8.00	14.00	27.50
	1875	.056	2.50	5.00	9.50	18.00
	1876	.071	4.00	8.00	14.00	27.50
	1877	.078	2.50	5.00	9.50	16.00
	1878	.347	2.00	3.25	4.75	10.00
	1879	.402	2.00	3.25	4.75	10.00
	1880	.123	2.00	3.25	4.75	10.00
	1881	.123	2.00	3.25	4.75	10.00

NOTE: Varieties exist.

COPPER-NICKEL, 14mm

KM#	Date	Mintage	Fine	VF	XF	Unc
179	1881	24.000	.10	.25	.75	4.00

18mm

180	1881	4.000	.65	1.75	3.50	9.00

COPPER
Reeded edge

181	1885	—	2.00	5.00	10.00	27.50

NOTE: Varieties exist.

COLOMBIA 416

COPPER-NICKEL

M#	Date	Mintage	Fine	VF	XF	Unc
82	1886	12.000	.35	1.00	2.75	6.00

CINCO (5) CENTAVOS

1.2500 g, .666 SILVER, .0268 oz ASW
Bogota Mint

KM#	Date	Mintage	VG	Fine	VF	XF
170	1872	—	4.00	12.50	20.00	35.00
	1873	.089	3.00	6.75	12.50	22.50
	1874	.276	2.00	4.00	9.00	17.50

1.2500 g, .835 SILVER, .0335 oz ASW
Medellin Mint

174	1874	—	13.50	27.50	42.50	85.00

1.2500 g, .666 SILVER, .0268 oz ASW
Bogota Mint

174a.1	1875	.077	1.50	3.00	5.00	12.50
	1876	.019	4.00	10.00	17.50	27.50
	1877	.094	2.50	5.50	8.50	15.00
	1878	.190	1.25	2.75	5.00	12.50
	1879/8	.177	1.25	2.75	5.00	12.50
	1879	Inc. Ab.	1.25	2.75	5.00	12.50
	1880	.044	4.00	10.00	18.00	27.50
	1881	.219	3.00	7.50	15.00	25.00
	1882	—	1.25	3.00	5.00	12.50
	1883/2	.412	1.50	4.00	7.50	15.00
	1883	Inc. Ab.	1.25	3.00	5.00	12.50
	1884	.220	2.50	5.50	8.50	14.00
	1885	—	1.50	3.50	6.50	12.50

Medellin Mint

174a.2	1875	—	6.00	12.00	18.00	25.00

10 CENTAVOS

2.5000 g, .835 SILVER, .0671 oz ASW
Bogota Mint

171	1872	Inc. Ab.	5.00	12.50	25.00	42.50
	1873	.043	5.00	12.50	25.00	42.50
	1874	Inc. Be.	2.50	5.00	12.00	17.50

175.1	1874	.179	1.00	2.50	3.50	7.00
	1875	.265	1.00	2.50	3.50	7.00
	1878	.419	1.50	3.00	6.00	12.00
	1879	Inc. Ab.	1.00	2.50	3.50	7.00
	1880/79	.134	5.00	11.50	16.50	27.50
	1880	Inc. Ab.	4.00	10.00	15.00	25.00
	1881	.020	1.50	3.00	4.00	8.00
	1882	—	2.50	4.00	6.00	12.00
	1883	.202	1.00	2.50	3.50	7.00
	1884/3	—	1.50	3.00	6.00	12.00
	1884	—	1.00	2.50	3.50	7.00
	1885	—	4.00	12.00	17.00	30.00

Medellin Mint

175.2	1885(0.835)	—	6.00	10.00	16.00	35.00
	1885(0.835/0.500)		7.00	12.50	18.00	40.00

2.5000 g, .500 SILVER, .0402 oz ASW

175.2a	1885(0.500)	—	13.50	22.50	32.50	70.00
	1885(0.500/0.835)		13.50	22.50	32.50	70.00
	1886	—	13.50	22.50	32.50	70.00

20 CENTAVOS

5.0000 g, .835 SILVER, .1342 oz ASW
Medellin Mint
Obv: Large head. Rev. leg: GRAM 5.

KM#	Date	Mintage	VG	Fine	VF	XF
176.1	1874	—	9.00	18.00	35.00	75.00

Rev. leg: GRAMOS 5.

176.2	1874	—	22.50	50.00	80.00	150.00
	1882/74	—	15.00	25.00	40.00	60.00

Bogota Mint
Obv: Small head. Rev. leg: GRAMOS 5.

176.3	1884/3	—	16.50	35.00	60.00	110.00
	1884	—	15.00	32.50	55.00	100.00

Medellin Mint
Obv: Small head. Rev. leg: GRAM 5.

178.1	1875	—	10.00	15.00	22.50	37.50
	1876	—	2.00	3.00	7.50	16.50
	1877	—	6.00	10.00	16.00	27.50
	1882	—	4.00	7.00	12.00	32.50

Obv: Small head, tiny B in O of ESTADOS.

178.2	1875	—	8.50	15.00	24.00	37.50
	1876/5	—	7.50	14.00	22.00	35.00
	1876	—	7.00	12.50	20.00	32.50

Obv: Small head. Rev. leg: GRAMOS 5

178.3	1882/1	—	3.00	6.00	10.00	15.00
	1882	—	2.00	3.25	6.50	12.50
	1884	—	2.50	5.00	10.00	15.00
	1885/4	—	—	—	Rare	—
	1885	—	17.50	35.00	55.00	80.00
	1885(0.835/0.500)					
		—	22.00	40.00	65.00	115.00

5.0000 g, .500 SILVER, .0804 oz ASW
Medellin Mint

178.3a	1886(0.500)	—	37.50	75.00	120.00	175.00
	1886(0.500/0.835)					
		—	37.50	75.00	120.00	175.00

50 CENTAVOS

12.5000 g, .835 SILVER, .3356 oz ASW
Bogota Mint
Rev: '50' in numerals
Obv. and rev: Small letters.

KM#	Date	Mintage	VG	Fine	VF	XF
172.1	1872	.027	15.00	35.00	65.00	125.00
	1873	.101	10.00	17.50	35.00	70.00

Obv. and rev: Large letters.

172.2	1874	.280	6.00	10.00	17.50	37.50
	1875	—	—	Rare	—	

NOTE: Varieties exist.

Rev: CINCUENTA for denomination.

177.1	1874	Inc. Ab.	3.75	6.00	12.50	22.50
	1875	.621	2.50	7.00	13.00	22.50
	1876	.259	4.75	9.50	20.00	45.00
	1877/6	—	8.00	15.00	27.50	55.00
	1877	.133	4.50	9.50	18.00	35.00
	1878	.264	5.50	10.00	18.00	35.00
	1879	.307	3.50	8.00	14.00	25.00
	1880	1.249	2.50	6.00	13.00	20.00
	1881	1.086	2.50	6.00	13.00	20.00
	1882/1	—	—	—	Rare	—
	1882	—	3.00	7.00	13.00	22.50
	1883	.221	2.50	7.00	13.00	22.50
	1884	.993	2.50	6.00	12.00	20.00
	1885	—	12.50	20.00	40.00	80.00

Popayan Mint

177.2	1880	—	150.00	275.00	450.00	700.00

12.5000 g, .500 SILVER, .2009 oz ASW
Bogota Mint

177a.1	1885	—	4.00	7.50	15.00	30.00
	1886/76	—	—	—	Rare	—
	1886	—	6.00	12.50	22.50	45.00

Medellin Mint

177a.2	1886	—	75.00	150.00	300.00	600.00

Obv: KM#161. Rev: KM#177a.2.

A183	1886	—	—	—	Rare	—

REPUBLIC

CENTAVO

COPPER-NICKEL

KM#	Date	Mintage	Fine	VF	XF	Unc
275	1918	.989	4.00	12.00	20.00	40.00
(197)	1919	.496	12.50	25.00	37.50	65.00
	1920	7.540	3.00	7.50	12.50	25.00
	1921	12.460	2.00	6.00	12.00	20.00
	1933	3.000	1.00	3.00	5.00	10.00
	1935	5.000	1.00	3.00	5.00	10.00
	1936	1.540	2.00	5.00	7.50	12.00
	1938	7.920	.20	.30	1.00	3.00
	1941B	1.000	.35	.75	1.50	5.00
	1946B	2.096	.30	.55	1.00	3.00
	1947B	1.835	.30	.55	1.25	4.00
	1948B	1.139	.35	.75	1.50	5.00

NICKEL-CLAD STEEL

KM#	Date	Mintage	Fine	VF	XF	Unc
275a	1952	8.697	—	Reported, not confirmed		
(197a)	1952B	Inc. Ab.	.10	.15	.25	1.00
	1954B	5.080	.10	.15	.25	1.00
	1956	1.315	.10	.15	.40	1.50
	1957	.900	.15	.25	.50	2.50
	1958	1.596	.10	.15	.40	2.00

BRONZE

KM#	Date	Mintage	Fine	VF	XF	Unc
205	1942	1.000	.20	.50	1.50	3.50
	1942B	Inc. Ab.	.25	.75	2.00	5.00
	1943B	4.515	.15	.35	1.00	3.00
	1944B	4.515	.15	.35	1.00	3.00
	1945	3.769	.15	.35	1.00	3.00
	1945B	—	.15	.35	1.00	3.00
	1948B	.585	.30	1.00	2.50	6.50
	1949B	4.255	.15	.35	1.00	3.50
	1950B	5.827	.15	.35	1.00	3.50
	1951B	Inc. Ab.	.20	.60	1.75	4.50
	1957	2.500	—	.10	.20	1.00
	1958	.590	.10	.25	.50	2.00
	1959	2.677	—	.10	.20	1.00
	1960	2.500	—	.10	.20	1.00
	1961	3.673	—	.10	.20	1.00
	1962	4.065	—	.10	.20	1.00
	1963	1.845	.10	.15	.30	2.00
	1964/44	3.165	.10	.30	.75	2.50
	1964	Inc. Ab.	—	.10	.20	.75
	1965 large date					
		5.510	—	.10	.20	.75
	1965 sm. dt.	I.A.	—	.10	.20	.75
	1966	3.910	—	.10	.20	.75

NOTE: Several date varieties exist.

COPPER-CLAD STEEL

KM#	Date	Mintage	Fine	VF	XF	Unc
205a	1967	5.730	—	.10	.15	.25
	1968	7.390	—	.10	.15	.25
	1969	6.870	—	.10	.15	.25
	1970	3.839	—	.10	.15	.25
	1971	3.020	—	.10	.20	.50
	1972	3.100	—	.10	.15	.25
	1973	—	—	—	.10	.20
	1974	2.000	—	—	.10	.20
	1975	1.000	—	—	.10	.20
	1976	1.000	—	—	.10	.20
	1977	.900	—	—	.10	.20
	1978	.224	—	.10	.20	.40

NOTE: Several date varieties exist.

BRONZE
Uprising Sesquicentennial

KM#	Date	Mintage	Fine	VF	XF	Unc
218	1960	.500	.75	1.50	3.00	5.00

NOTE: This and the other issues in the uprising commemorative series offer the usual design of the period with the dates 1810-1960 added at the bottom of the obverse.

DOS, II (2) CENTAVOS

COPPER-NICKEL

KM#	Date	Mintage	Fine	VF	XF	Unc
198	1918	.745	3.00	7.00	15.00	45.00
	1919	.930	7.00	12.00	25.00	70.00
	1920	3.855	1.25	2.25	7.50	15.00
	1921	11.145	.30	1.00	3.00	9.00
198	1922	10 pcs.	known	—	—	400.00
	1933	3.500	.35	1.00	3.00	6.00
	1935	2.500	.35	1.00	3.00	6.00
	1938	3.872	.25	.75	2.00	5.00
	1941B	.500	.50	1.50	3.00	7.00
	1942B	.500	.50	1.50	3.00	7.00
	1946B	2.593	.25	.75	2.00	5.00
	1947B	1.337	.30	1.00	2.50	6.00

BRONZE

KM#	Date	Mintage	Fine	VF	XF	Unc
210	1948B	2.648	.50	1.00	4.00	7.50
	1949B	1.278	.50	1.00	4.50	8.50
	1950B	2.285	.50	1.00	4.00	8.50

ALUMINUM-BRONZE
Obv: Divided legend

KM#	Date	Mintage	Fine	VF	XF	Unc
211	1952B	5.038	—	.10	.25	1.00
	1965/3	1.830	—	.15	.20	.35
	1965	Inc. Ab.	—	.10	.15	.25

Obv: Continuous legend

KM#	Date	Mintage	Fine	VF	XF	Unc
214	1955	2.513	.10	.20	.75	3.00
	1955B	Inc. Ab.	—	.10	.20	.85
	1959	4.609	—	.10	.15	.50

Uprising Sesquicentennial

KM#	Date	Mintage	Fine	VF	XF	Unc
219	1960	.250	.75	1.50	2.00	5.00

2-1/2 CENTAVOS

COPPER-NICKEL

KM#	Date	Mintage	Fine	VF	XF	Unc
190	1902	.400	50.00	120.00	175.00	225.00

CINCO (5) CENTAVOS

COPPER-NICKEL

KM#	Date	Mintage	Fine	VF	XF	Unc
183	1886	1.000	.15	.50	1.50	5.00
	1888	—	.15	.50	1.50	5.00

KM#	Date	Mintage	Fine	VF	XF	Unc
184	1886	Inc. Ab.	.15	.50	1.50	5.00
	1902	.400	45.00	75.00	120.00	160.00

1.2500 g, .666 SILVER, .0268 oz ASW

KM#	Date	Mintage	Fine	VF	XF	Unc
191	1902	.400	.50	1.25	2.50	6.75

COPPER-NICKEL

KM#	Date	Mintage	Fine	VF	XF	Unc
199	1918	.767	7.50	11.00	16.00	35.00
	1919	1.926	2.00	3.50	6.50	17.50
199	1920	2.062	3.50	8.50	12.50	25.00
	1921	1.574	1.50	3.00	6.00	17.50
	1922	2.623	2.00	3.50	7.00	17.50
	1922 H	—	—	—	—	—
	1924	.120	10.00	20.00	30.00	65.00
	1933	2.000	.75	1.50	2.50	5.00
	1933B	—	—	Reported, not confirmed		
	1935	11.616	.50	1.50	2.00	4.00
	1936	—	3.50	6.00	10.00	25.00
	1938B	2.000	.75	2.00	3.50	8.00
	1938	3.867	.50	1.35	2.00	5.00
	1938 large 8 in date					
		Inc. Ab.	.75	2.00	3.50	8.00
	1939/5	2.000	1.00	2.00	3.50	8.00
	1939	Inc. Ab.	.50	1.35	2.50	5.50
	1941	—	3.75	6.50	9.00	18.00
	1941B	.500	1.25	2.50	3.50	7.00
	1946 small date					
		40.000	.20	.60	1.00	2.00
	1946 large date					
		3.330	2.00	4.00	7.50	15.00
	1949B	2.750	.45	1.00	2.00	4.00
	1949	—	1.75	3.00	4.50	10.00
	1950B	3.611	.45	1.00	2.00	4.00

NOTE: Varieties exist.

BRONZE

KM#	Date	Mintage	Fine	VF	XF	Unc
206	1942	—	1.25	2.50	4.00	12.00
	1942B	.800	.50	1.25	2.00	7.00
	1943	—	1.00	1.75	3.50	10.00
	1943B	6.053	.20	.60	1.00	3.00
	1944	—	.25	.75	1.25	4.00
	1944B	9.013	.20	.60	1.00	3.00
	1945/4	—	.50	1.25	2.50	6.50
	1945	—	.50	1.25	2.50	6.50
	1945B	11.101	.25	.75	1.25	3.50
	1946/5	—	1.25	2.50	3.50	9.00
	1946	—	.50	1.25	2.00	5.00
	1952	—	1.25	2.50	3.50	9.00
	1952B	3.985	.15	.40	.75	1.25
	1953B	5.180	.10	.25	.50	1.00
	1954B	1.159	.10	.25	.50	1.00
	1955B	6.819	.10	.25	.50	1.00
	1956	8.772	.10	.25	.50	1.00
	1956B	—	.35	1.25	2.50	6.50
	1957	8.912	.10	.25	.50	1.00
	1958	15.016	.10	.25	.40	.80
	1959	14.271	.10	.25	.40	.80
	1960	11.716	.10	.25	.40	.80
	1960/660	I.A.	.25	.75	1.00	2.00
	1961	11.200	.10	.25	.40	.65
	1962	10.928	—	.10	.20	.35
	1963	15.113	—	.10	.20	.40
	1964	9.336	—	.10	.20	.35
	1965	6.460	—	.10	.20	.40
	1966	7.170	—	.10	.35	1.00

NOTE: Some coins of 1942-56 have weak "B".

COPPER-CLAD STEEL

KM#	Date	Mintage	Fine	VF	XF	Unc
206a	1967	10.280	—	—	.10	.25
	1968	8.900	—	—	.10	.25
	1969	17.800	—	—	.10	.25
	1970	14.842	—	—	.10	.25
	1971	10.730	—	—	.10	.25
	1972	10.170	—	—	.10	.25
	1973	10.525	—	—	.10	.25
	1974	5.310	—	—	.10	.20
	1975	5.631	—	—	.10	.20
	1976	3.009	—	—	.10	.20
	1977	2.000	—	—	.10	.20
	1978	.468	—	.10	.15	.30
	1979	8.087	—	—	.10	.20

NOTE: Date varieties exist for 1967, 1970 and 1973.

BRONZE
Uprising Sesquicentennial

KM#	Date	Mintage	Fine	VF	XF	Unc
220	1960	.400	1.75	3.50	7.50	25.00

Republic / COLOMBIA 418

10 CENTAVOS

2.5000 g, .666 SILVER, .0536 oz ASW

KM#	Date	Mintage	Fine	VF	XF	Unc
188	1897 (Brussels)	2.642	1.00	2.00	3.50	10.00

2.5000 g, .900 SILVER, .0723 oz ASW

KM#	Date	Mintage	Fine	VF	XF	Unc
196	1911	5.065	1.00	1.75	5.00	25.00
	1913	8.305	1.00	1.75	4.00	20.00
	1914	3.840	1.00	1.75	5.00	25.00
	1920	2.149	1.25	2.00	5.00	25.00
	1926	—	—	—	—	—
	1934B	.140	2.50	4.00	8.00	35.00
	1934/24	I.A.	—	—	—	—
	1934	Inc. Ab.	15.00	25.00	35.00	75.00
	1937	10.000	10.00	20.00	30.00	60.00
	1938	2.055	.50	1.00	2.00	6.50
	1940	.450	1.50	2.50	4.50	15.00
	1941	4.415	.50	1.00	2.00	6.50
	1942	3.140	7.00	12.00	20.00	40.00
	1942B	Inc. Ab.	.50	1.00	2.00	6.50

2.5000 g, .500 SILVER, .0401 oz ASW
Rev: Mint mark at bottom.

KM#	Date	Mintage	Fine	VF	XF	Unc
207.1	1945B	4.830	.50	1.25	2.50	6.00
	1945 B-B	—	—	—	—	—
	1946/5B	—	.60	1.50	3.00	8.00
	1946B	—	.60	1.50	3.00	8.00
	1947/5B	7.366	1.50	3.00	5.00	10.00
	1947/6B	I.A.	1.50	3.00	5.00	10.00

Rev: Mint mark at top.

KM#	Date	Mintage	Fine	VF	XF	Unc
207.2	1947/5B	I.A.	2.00	4.00	7.50	20.00
	1947B	Inc. Ab.	2.00	4.00	7.50	20.00
	1948/5B	3.629	.60	1.50	3.00	8.00
	1948B	Inc. Ab.	.50	1.00	2.25	6.00
	1949B	5.923	.50	1.00	2.00	5.00
	1950B	6.783	.50	1.00	2.25	6.00
	1951/5B	5.185	.50	1.00	2.25	6.00
	1951B	Inc. Ab.	.50	1.00	2.00	5.00
	1952B	1.060	1.00	1.50	3.00	8.00

COPPER-NICKEL 18mm

KM#	Date	Mintage	Fine	VF	XF	Unc
212.1	1952B	6.035	.10	.25	.60	2.25
	1953B	6.985	.10	.25	.60	2.25

18.5mm

KM#	Date	Mintage	Fine	VF	XF	Unc
212.2	1954B	13.006	.10	.20	.30	2.00
	1955B	9.968	.10	.20	.30	1.75
	1956	36.010	.10	.20	.30	1.00
	1958	41.695	.20	.50	1.00	3.00
	1959	36.653	.10	.20	.30	1.00
	1960	32.290	.10	.20	.30	2.00
	1961	17.780	.10	.20	.30	2.00
	1962	8.930	.10	.20	.30	1.50
	1963 wide date	37.540	.10	.20	.30	1.00
	1964	61.672	.10	.20	.30	.75
	1965	12.804	.10	.20	.30	1.50
	1966 lg. date	23.544	.10	.20	.30	.50

Uprising Sesquicentennial

KM#	Date	Mintage	Fine	VF	XF	Unc
221	1960	1.000	.75	1.25	2.50	8.00

NICKEL-CLAD STEEL

KM#	Date	Mintage	Fine	VF	XF	Unc
226	1967	26.980	—	.10	.15	.50
	1968	23.670	—	.10	.15	.50
	1969	29.450	—	.10	.15	.50

Obv. leg: Divided after REPUBLICA DE

KM#	Date	Mintage	Fine	VF	XF	Unc
236	1969	Inc. Ab.	—	.10	.15	—
	1970	—	—	.10	.15	—
	1971	—	—	.10	.15	.20

Obv. leg: Divided after REPUBLICA

KM#	Date	Mintage	Fine	VF	XF	Unc
243	1970	38.935	—	.10	.15	.20
	1971	53.314	—	.10	.15	.20

Obv. leg: Continuous

KM#	Date	Mintage	Fine	VF	XF	Unc
253	1972	58.000	—	.10	.15	.20
	1973	46.549	—	.10	.15	.20
	1974	49.740	—	.10	.15	.20
	1975	46.037	—	.10	.15	.20
	1976	46.084	—	.10	.15	.20
	1977	8.127	—	.10	.15	.20
	1978	97.081	—	.10	.15	.20

20 CENTAVOS

5.0000 g, .666 SILVER, .1072 oz ASW

KM#	Date	Mintage	Fine	VF	XF	Unc
189	1897 (Brussels)	1.441	1.25	2.50	5.00	15.00

5.0000 g, .900 SILVER, .1446 oz ASW

KM#	Date	Mintage	Fine	VF	XF	Unc
197	1911	1.206	1.50	3.50	7.50	17.50
	1913	1.630	1.50	3.50	7.50	22.50
	1914	2.560	1.50	3.50	9.00	25.00
	1920	1.242	1.50	3.50	9.00	25.00
	1921	.372	5.00	12.00	25.00	60.00
	1922	.045	15.00	35.00	65.00	—
	1933B on obv.	.330	2.00	5.00	9.00	25.00
	1933B on rev. Inc. Ab.	12.50	25.00	45.00	125.00
	1933B both sides Inc. Ab.	3.00	6.00	10.00	30.00
	1938	1.410	1.25	2.50	5.00	15.00
	1941	—	1.50	3.50	7.50	22.50
	1942	.155	12.00	22.50	35.00	65.00
	1942B	Inc. Ab.	1.50	3.50	7.50	20.00

5.0000 g, .500 SILVER, .0803 oz ASW
Rev: Mint mark in field below CENTAVOS.

KM#	Date	Mintage	Fine	VF	XF	Unc
208.1	1945B	1.675	1.00	2.50	5.00	10.00
	1945BB*	I.A.	5.00	9.00	16.00	35.00
	1946/5B	6.599	1.00	2.50	5.00	10.00
	1946B	Inc. Ab.	1.50	3.00	5.50	12.00
	1946/5(M)	—	6.00	13.50	20.00	45.00
	1946(M)	—	4.00	7.00	12.50	25.00
	1947/5B	9.708	2.50	4.50	8.00	20.00
	1947(M)	—	5.00	8.50	15.00	35.00

NOTE: 1945BB has extra B on wreath at bottom.

Rev: Mint mark on wreath at top.

KM#	Date	Mintage	Fine	VF	XF	Unc
208.2	1947/5B(M)	I.A.	5.00	10.00	20.00	50.00
	1948/5(M)	1.748	—	—	Rare	—
	1948/5B	I.A.	1.50	3.00	5.00	12.00
	1948B	Inc. Ab.	1.50	3.00	5.00	14.00
	1949/5B	.403	5.00	10.00	20.00	50.00
	1949B	Inc. Ab.	4.00	7.50	15.00	40.00
	1950/45B	1.899	4.50	8.00	18.50	55.00
	1950B	Inc. Ab.	4.00	7.50	15.00	40.00
	1951/45B	7.498	.75	2.00	4.00	9.00
	1951B	Inc. Ab.	.75	2.00	3.50	7.00

NOTE: Almost all dies for 1946-51 show at least faint traces of overdating from 1945. Coins with absolutely no underdate, and those with very bold underdate, are generally worth more to advanced specialists.

5.0000 g, .300 SILVER, .0482 oz ASW

KM#	Date	Mintage	Fine	VF	XF	Unc
213	1952B	3.887	—	—	Rare	—
	1953B	17.819	.40	.60	1.25	3.50

COPPER-NICKEL
Obv: Small date.

KM#	Date	Mintage	Fine	VF	XF	Unc
215.1	1956	39.778	.10	.15	.20	1.00
	1959	44.779	.10	.15	.20	1.00
	1961	10.740	.15	.25	.50	2.00
	1966	23.060	.10	.15	.20	1.00

Obv: Large date.

KM#	Date	Mintage	Fine	VF	XF	Unc
215.2	1963	12.035	—	.10	.20	.75
	1964	29.075	—	.10	.20	.50
	1965	19.180	.10	.20	.40	1.50

Uprising Sesquicentennial

KM#	Date	Mintage	Fine	VF	XF	Unc
222	1960	.500	.75	1.50	3.00	8.00

Jorge Eliecer Gaitan

KM#	Date	Mintage	Fine	VF	XF	Unc
224	1965	1.000	—	.10	.20	.50

NICKEL-CLAD STEEL

KM#	Date	Mintage	Fine	VF	XF	Unc
227	1967	15.720	—	.10	.20	.75
	1968	26.680	—	.10	.20	.75
	1969	22.470	—	.10	.20	.75

Obv. leg: Divided after REPUBLICA

KM#	Date	Mintage	Fine	VF	XF	Unc
237	1969	Inc.KM227	—	.10	.20	.30
	1970	44.358	—	—	.10	.20

Republic / COLOMBIA 419

Obv. leg: Divided after REPUBLICA DE

KM#	Date	Mintage	Fine	VF	XF	Unc
245	1971	77.526	—	—	.10	.20

Obv. leg: Continuous

246.1	1971	Inc. Ab.	—	—	.10	.20
	1972	41.891	—	—	.10	.20
	1973/1	41.440	—	—	.10	.20
	1973	Inc. Ab.	—	—	.10	.25
	1974	45.941	—	—	.10	.20
	1975	28.635	—	—	.10	.20
	1976	29.590	—	—	.10	.20
	1977	2.054	—	—	.10	.25
	1978	10.630	—	—	.10	.20

Rev: Dot between 20 and CENTAVOS.

246.3	1971	Inc. Ab.	—	—	.10	.20

Obv: Dot under DE.
Rev: 2 dots between 20 and CENTAVOS.

| 246.4 | 1971 | Inc. Ab. | — | — | .10 | .20 |

Rev: 3 dots between 20 and CENTAVOS.

| 246.5 | 1971 | Inc. Ab. | — | — | .10 | .20 |

Obv: Smaller letters in legend.
Rev: Wreath with larger 20 and smaller CENTAVOS.

| 246.2 | 1979 | 16.655 | — | — | .10 | .20 |

25 CENTAVOS

ALUMINUM-BRONZE

| 267 | 1979 | 88.874 | — | .10 | .15 | .25 |

CINCO (5) DECIMOS

12.5000 g, .500 SILVER, .2009 oz ASW
Obv: So-called Greek profile.

KM#	Date	Mintage	VG	Fine	VF	XF
165	1887	.084	27.50	50.00	100.00	185.00
	1888	—	45.00	100.00	225.00	375.00

Obv: Large head.

166	1888	—	20.00	47.50	75.00	150.00
	1889	—	—	—	Rare	—

Obv: Long-necked Liberty head.

KM#	Date	Mintage	VG	Fine	VF	XF
167	1888	—	—	—	Rare	—

12.5000 g, .835 SILVER, .3356 oz ASW
Obv: Large head. Rev: 2 stars and 2 dots.

| 168 | 1889 | — | — | — | Rare | — |

50 CENTAVOS

12.5000 g, .500 SILVER, .2009 oz ASW
Bogota Mint

185	1887	1.764	6.75	15.00	32.50	85.00
	1888	—	—	—	Rare	—

Similar to KM#186.1a.

| 186.1 | 1888 | — | 40.00 | 90.00 | 175.00 | 350.00 |

12.5000 g, .835 SILVER, .3356 oz ASW

186.1a	1889	.130	12.50	30.00	55.00	100.00
	1898	—	10.00	22.50	45.00	85.00
	1899	—	60.00	125.00	250.00	525.00

Obv: Incuse lettering on head band.

186.2	1906	.446	6.00	10.00	22.50	45.00
	1907	1.126	5.00	9.00	17.50	37.50
	1908/7	.871	17.50	37.50	70.00	145.00
	1908	Inc. Ab.	7.50	14.00	22.50	45.00

30.4mm
400th Anniversary of Columbus' Discovery of America
Obv: Tip of cap points to left side of A in REPUBLICA.

KM#	Date	Mintage	Fine	VF	XF	Unc
187.1	1892	4.826	6.50	15.00	30.00	75.00
	1892	—	—	Proof		1750.

Reduced size, 29.6mm.
Obv: Tip of cap points to right side of A in REPUBLICA.

| 187.2 | 1892 | Inc. Ab. | 5.50 | 12.50 | 25.00 | 60.00 |

KM#	Date	Mintage	Fine	VF	XF	Unc
192	1902	.960	9.00	17.00	30.00	65.00

12.5000 g, .900 SILVER, .3617 oz ASW
Mints: Birmingham and Bogota
Obv: Sharper featured bust.
Rev: Left wing and flags far from legend.

193.1	1912	1.207	BV	5.00	15.00	50.00
	1913	.417	4.00	7.00	20.00	55.00
1914 closed 4
		.769	BV	6.50	20.00	75.00
1915 small date
		.946	BV	6.00	15.00	40.00
	1916	1.060	BV	6.00	15.00	45.00
1917 normal 7
		.099	10.00	20.00	30.00	65.00
1917 foot on 7
		Inc. Ab.	5.00	9.00	22.50	50.00
	1918	.400	4.00	7.00	20.00	50.00
	1919	Inc. Ab.	15.00	25.00	35.00	80.00
	1922	.150	8.00	14.00	27.50	75.00
	1923	.150	8.00	14.00	27.50	75.00
	1931B	.700	BV	4.00	10.00	25.00
	1931	Inc. Ab.	40.00	75.00	120.00	350.00
	1932/12B	.300	8.00	14.00	25.00	50.00
	1932B	Inc. Ab.	BV	4.00	9.00	22.50
1932 flat top 3, w/o B
		Inc. Ab.	20.00	30.00	40.00	80.00
	1933/13B					
		1.000	3.50	5.00	10.00	25.00
	1933/23B I.A.	5.00	10.00	17.50	35.00
	1933B	Inc. Ab.	BV	4.00	9.00	22.50

Mint: Medellin
Rev: Larger letters, left wing and flags close to legend.

193.2	1914 open 4	—	5.00	9.00	22.50	75.00
	1915 lg.dt.	—	35.00	65.00	95.00	175.00
	1918	—	BV	6.00	15.00	40.00
	1919	—	6.00	11.00	25.00	70.00
	1921	.300	6.00	11.00	25.00	70.00
	1922	—	5.00	9.00	22.50	65.00
1932/22M
		1.200	8.00	14.00	25.00	50.00
	1932M	Inc. Ab.	BV	4.00	9.00	22.50
1932 round top 3, no M
		Inc. Ab.	17.50	30.00	45.00	100.00
	1933M	.800	BV	4.00	9.00	25.00
1933/23 round top 3's, no M
		Inc. Ab.	15.00	25.00	35.00	75.00

Obv: Rounded feature bust.

274	1916	1.300	BV	6.50	12.00	35.00
(196)	1917	.142	7.00	12.50	25.00	80.00
	1921	1.000	BV	5.50	10.00	25.00
	1922	3.000	BV	5.00	9.00	25.00
	1934	10.000	BV	4.00	7.00	20.00

Republic / COLOMBIA 420

12.5000 g, .500 SILVER, .2009 oz ASW

KM#	Date	Mintage	Fine	VF	XF	Unc
209	1947/6B	1.240	3.00	6.00	15.00	45.00
	1947B	Inc. Ab.	3.00	6.00	15.00	45.00
	1948/6B	.707	3.00	6.00	15.00	45.00
	1948B	Inc. Ab.	3.00	6.00	15.00	45.00

COPPER-NICKEL

217	1958	3.596	.15	.30	.50	2.00
	1959 small date					
		13.466	.15	.30	.45	1.50
	1960	4.360	.15	.30	.75	8.00
	1961	3.260	.15	.30	.75	7.00
	1962	2.336	.15	.30	.75	6.00
	1963 lg.dt.	4.098	.15	.30	.50	1.50
	1964	9.274	.10	.20	.40	1.50
	1965	5.800	.10	.15	.25	1.00
	1966	2.820	.15	.30	.50	1.50

Uprising Sesquicentennial

223	1960	.200	1.50	3.00	7.50	15.00

Jorge Eliecer Gaitan

225	1965	.600	.10	.15	.30	.60

NICKEL-CLAD STEEL

228	1967	3.460	.10	.15	.25	.65
(229)	1968	5.460	.10	.15	.25	.65
	1969	1.590	.10	.15	.25	.65

244.1	1970 small date					
		30.906	—	.10	.15	.35
	1971	32.650	—	.10	.15	.30
	1972	25.290	—	.10	.15	.30

KM#	Date	Mintage	Fine	VF	XF	Unc
244.1	1973	8.060	—	.10	.15	.30
	1974 large date					
		19.541	—	.10	.15	.25
	1975	4.325	—	.10	.15	.30
	1976	13.181	—	.10	.15	.25
	1977	10.413	—	.10	.15	.25
	1978	10.736	—	.10	.15	.25

244.2	1979	22.584	—	.10	.15	.25
	1980	26.540	—	.10	.15	.25

NOTE: Various sizes of dates exist.

PESO

25.0000 g, .900 SILVER, .7234 oz ASW
Bogota Mint

216	1956	.012	6.00	9.00	15.00	22.50

GOLD (OMS)

216a	1956	3 pcs.	—	—	—	—

COPPER-NICKEL

229	1967	4.000	.15	.30	.50	1.00

258	1974	56.020	—	.10	.15	.40
	1975	117.714	—	.10	.15	.35
	1976	98.728	—	.10	.15	.35
	1977	62.083	—	.10	.15	.35
	1978	48.624	—	.10	.15	.35
	1979	83.908	—	.10	.15	.35
	1980	93.406	—	.10	.15	.35
	1981	65.219	—	.10	.15	.35

6.7100 g, SILVER (OMS)

258a	1974	—	—	—	—	—

2 PESOS

BRONZE

263	1977	76.661	.10	.15	.25	.50
	1978	69.575	.10	.15	.25	.50
	1979	56.537	.10	.15	.25	.50
	1980	108.521	.10	.15	.25	.50
	1981	40.368	.10	.15	.25	.50
	1987	—	.10	.15	.25	.50

2-1/2 PESOS

3.9940 g, .917 GOLD, .1177 oz AGW

KM#	Date	Mintage	Fine	VF	XF	Unc
194	1913	.018	—	BV	75.00	125.00
	Obv: Bolivar, large head.					
200	1919A	—	—	BV	60.00	100.00
	1919B	—	—	Reported, not confirmed			
	1919	.034	—	BV	60.00	100.00
	1920/19A	—	—	BV	60.00	100.00
	1920	.034	—	BV	60.00	100.00
	1920A	—	—	BV	60.00	100.00

Obv: Bolivar, small head, MEDELLIN below bust.

203	1924	—	—	BV	60.00	100.00
	1925	—	—	BV	60.00	100.00
	1927	—	—	BV	60.00	100.00
	1928	.014	—	BV	60.00	100.00
	1929	—	—	BV	60.00	100.00

5 PESOS

7.9881 g, .917 GOLD, .2355 oz AGW

195	1913	.017	—	BV	110.00	150.00
	1917	.043	—	BV	110.00	150.00
	1918/3	.423	—	BV	110.00	150.00
	1918	Inc. Ab.	—	BV	110.00	150.00
	1919	2.181	—	BV	100.00	135.00

Obv: Bolivar, large head.

201	1919	Inc. Ab.	—	BV	100.00	135.00
	1919A	Inc. Ab.	—	BV	100.00	135.00
	1919B	—	—	Reported, not confirmed		
	1920	.870	—	BV	100.00	135.00
	1920A	Inc.Ab.	—	BV	100.00	135.00
	1920B	.108	—	BV	100.00	135.00
	1921A	6 known	—	—	Rare	—
	1922B	.029	—	BV	100.00	135.00
	1923B	.074	—	BV	100.00	135.00
	1924	—	—	BV	100.00	135.00
	1924B	.705	—	BV	100.00	135.00

Obv: Bolivar, small head, MEDELLIN below bust.

204	1924	.120	—	BV	100.00	125.00
	1925/4	.668	—	BV	100.00	125.00
	1925	Inc. Ab.	—	BV	100.00	125.00
	1926	.383	—	BV	100.00	125.00
	1927	.365	—	BV	100.00	125.00
	1928	.314	—	BV	100.00	125.00
	1929	.321	—	BV	100.00	125.00
	1930	.502	—	BV	100.00	125.00

NOTE: 1925 dated coins exist with an Arabic and a Spanish style 5.

Republic / COLOMBIA 421

COPPER-NICKEL
International Eucharistic Congress

KM#	Date	Mintage	Fine	VF	XF	Unc
230	1968B	.660	.25	.50	.75	1.50

NICKEL-CLAD STEEL
6th Pan-American Games

| 247 | 1971 | 2.000 | .15 | .35 | .60 | 1.25 |

BRONZE

268	1980	146.268	.15	.35	.60	1.25
	1981	9.148	.15	.35	.60	1.25
	1982	84.107	.15	.35	.60	1.25
	1984	—	.15	.35	.60	1.25
	1985	—	.15	.35	.60	1.25
	1987	—	.15	.35	.60	1.25
	1988 sm.dt.	—	.15	.35	.60	1.25
	1988 lg.dt.	—	.15	.35	.60	1.25

10 PESOS

15.9761 g, .917 GOLD, .4710 oz AGW

| 202 | 1919 | .101 | — | BV | 250.00 | 350.00 |
| | 1924B | .055 | — | BV | 250.00 | 350.00 |

COPPER-NICKEL-ZINC
Cordoba, San Andreas Island and Providencia

270	1981	20.949	—	.15	.25	1.25
	1982	83.605	—	.15	.25	1.25
	1983	104.051	—	.15	.25	1.25
	1985	—	—	.15	.25	1.25
	1988	—	—	.15	.25	1.25

20 PESOS

ALUMINUM-BRONZE

| 271 | 1982 | — | — | .15 | .20 | .30 |

KM#	Date	Mintage	Fine	VF	XF	Unc
271	1984	—	—	.15	.20	.30
	1985	—	—	.15	.20	.30
	1987	—	—	.15	.20	.30
	1988	—	—	.15	.20	.30

NOTE: 1985 and 1988 coins exist with large and small dates.

50 PESOS

COPPER-NICKEL
National Constitution

272	1986	—	—	—	—	.45
	1987	—	—	—	—	.45
	1988	—	—	—	—	.45

100 PESOS

4.3000 g, .900 GOLD, .1244 oz AGW
International Eucharistic Congress

KM#	Date	Mintage	VF	XF	Unc
231	1968	.108	—	—	65.00
	1968	8,000	—	Proof	85.00

Battle of Boyaca
Obv: Bust of Bolivar. Rev: Bust of Paris.

| 238 | 1969 | 6,000 | — | Proof | 100.00 |

Pan American Games

| 248 | 1971 | 6,000 | — | Proof | 100.00 |

200 PESOS

8.6000 g, .900 GOLD, .2488 oz AGW
International Eucharistic Congress
Rev: Arms and value.

| 232 | 1968 | .108 | — | — | 130.00 |
| | 1968 | 8,000 | — | Proof | 150.00 |

Battle of Boyaca
Obv: Bust of Bolivar. Rev: Bust of Soublette.

| 239 | 1969 | 6,000 | — | — | 175.00 |

Pan American Games

| 249 | 1971 | 6,000 | — | Proof | 175.00 |

300 PESOS

12.9000 g, .900 GOLD, .3733 oz AGW
International Eucharistic Congress

| 233 | 1968 | .062 | — | — | 185.00 |
| | 1968 | 8,000 | — | Proof | 225.00 |

Battle of Boyaca
Obv: Bust of Bolivar. Rev: Bust of Anzoategui.

KM#	Date	Mintage	VF	XF	Unc
240	1969	6,000	—	Proof	225.00

Pan American Games

| 250 | 1971 | 6,000 | — | Proof | 250.00 |

500 PESOS

21.5000 g, .900 GOLD, .6221 oz AGW
International Eucharistic Congress
Rev: Arms and value.

| 234 | 1968 | .014 | — | — | 325.00 |
| | 1968 | 8,000 | — | Proof | 350.00 |

Battle of Boyaca
Obv: Bust of Bolivar. Rev: Bust of Rondon.

| 241 | 1969 | 6,000 | — | — | 350.00 |

Pan American Games

| 251 | 1971 | 6,000 | — | Proof | 400.00 |

28.2800 g, .925 SILVER, .8411 oz ASW
Conservation Series
Rev: Orinoco crocodile.

| 264 | 1978 | 2,678 | — | — | 25.00 |
| | 1978 | 3,233 | — | Proof | 35.00 |

750 PESOS

35.0000 g, .925 SILVER, 1.0409 oz ASW
Conservation Series
Obv: Similar to 500 Pesos, KM#264.
Rev: Chestnut-bellied hummingbird.

KM#	Date	Mintage	VF	XF	Unc
265	1978	2,656	—	—	30.00
	1978	3,100	—	Proof	40.00

1000 PESOS

4.3000 g, .900 GOLD, .1244 oz AGW
Guillermo Valencia

| 254 | 1973 | 10,003 | — | Proof | 65.00 |

Foundation of Santa Marta

| 259 | 1975 | 2,500 | — | Proof | 75.00 |

Tricentennial Of Medellin

| 260 | 1975 | 4,000 | — | Proof | 75.00 |

1500 PESOS

68.5000 g, .900 GOLD, 1.9823 oz AGW
International Eucharistic Congress
Obv: Similar to 300 Pesos, KM#233.

| 235 | 1968 | 5,722 | — | — | 1000. |
| | 1968 | 8,000 | — | Proof | 1200. |

Battle of Boyaca

KM#	Date	Mintage	VF	XF	Unc
242	1969	6,000	—	Proof	1200.

Pan American Games
Obv: Similar to 300 Pesos, KM#250.

| 252 | 1971 | 6,000 | — | Proof | 1400. |

19.1000 g, .900 GOLD, .5527 oz AGW
Bank of Republic Museum

| 255 | 1973 | 4,911 | — | Proof | 275.00 |

8.6000 g, .900 GOLD, .2488 OZ AGW
Guillermo Valencia

| 256 | 1973 | 5,000 | — | Proof | 150.00 |

2000 PESOS

12.9000 g, .900 GOLD, .3733 oz AGW
Guillermo Valencia

KM#	Date	Mintage	VF	XF	Unc
257	1973	5,003	—	Proof	225.00

8.6000 g, .900 GOLD, .2488 oz AGW
Foundation of Santa Marta

| 261 | 1975 | 2,500 | — | Proof | 150.00 |

Tricentennial Of Medellin

| 262 | 1975 | 4,000 | — | Proof | 150.00 |

15000 PESOS

33.4370 g, .900 GOLD, .9676 oz AGW
Conservation Series
Rev: Ocelot.

| 266 | 1978 | 490 pcs. | — | — | 650.00 |
| | 1978 | 148 pcs. | — | Proof | 2000. |

17.2900 g, .900 GOLD, .5000 oz AGW
Jose Maria Cordova

| 275 | 1980 | 250 pcs. | — | Proof | 350.00 |

Antonio Jose De Sucre

| 276 | 1980 | 250 pcs. | — | Proof | 350.00 |

30000 PESOS

34.5800 g, .900 GOLD, 1.0007 oz AGW
Death of Bolivar

| 269 | 1980 | 500 pcs. | — | Proof | 750.00 |

35000 PESOS

8.6400 g, .900 GOLD, .2500 oz AGW
President Santos

KM#	Date	Mintage	VF	XF	Unc
273	1988	*900 pcs.	—	Proof	200.00

70000 PESOS

17.2800 g, .900 GOLD, .5000 oz AGW
President Santos

| 274 | 1988 | *600 pcs. | — | Proof | 400.00 |

INFLATIONARY COINAGE
P/M - Papel moneda

Beginning about 1886, Colombia fell victim to rampant "printing press" inflation. Deluged by paper money without solid backing the peso gradually declined in value until it was equal to 1 centavo of the old silver-based currency. The 1, 2 and 5 peso p/m coins later circulated at par with the newer 1, 2 and 5 centavo coins.

1 PESO P/M

COPPER-NICKEL

KM#	Date	Mintage	Fine	VF	XF	Unc
277	1907 AM	2.860	1.25	2.00	4.00	15.00
(271)	1907 AM	—	—	—	Proof	80.00
	1910 AM	1.205	1.75	2.75	6.00	25.00
	1911 AM	2.816	2.00	3.00	7.00	27.50
	1912 AM	6.094	1.50	2.25	5.00	20.00
	1912 H	2.000	1.50	2.25	5.00	17.50
	1913 AM	.306	3.50	7.00	12.50	30.00
	1914 AM	.552	4.00	8.00	15.00	40.00
	1916 AM	.234	5.00	9.00	17.00	47.50

SILVER (OMS)

| 277a | 1907 | — | — | Reported, not confirmed |

GOLD (OMS)

| 277b | 1907 | — | — | Reported, not confirmed |

2 PESOS P/M

COPPER-NICKEL

278	1907 AM	4.161	1.75	3.25	6.00	25.00
(272)	1907 AM	—	—	—	Proof	90.00
	1910/07 AM	.649	—	—	—	—
	1910 AM Inc. Ab.	4.00	6.50	12.50	40.00
	1911	.458	4.25	7.50	15.00	42.50
	1913	.082	—	Reported, not confirmed
	1914 AM	1.000	4.00	6.50	12.50	40.00

SILVER (OMS)

| 278a | 1907 | — | — | Reported, not confirmed |

GOLD (OMS)

| 278b | 1907 | — | — | Reported, not confirmed |

5 PESOS P/M

COPPER-NICKEL

KM#	Date	Mintage	Fine	VF	XF	Unc
279	1907 AM	6.143	1.25	2.00	4.50	17.50
(273)	1907 AM	—	—	—	Proof	110.00
	1909 AM	4.000	1.50	2.50	5.00	20.00
	1912 H	2.000	1.50	2.00	5.00	20.00
	1912 AM	1.897	2.75	5.50	12.00	35.00
	1913 AM Inc. Ab.	—	—	—	Rare	—
	1914 AM Inc. Ab.	4.00	8.00	15.00	42.50

SILVER (OMS)

| 279a | 1907 | — | — | Reported, not confirmed |

GOLD (OMS)

| 279b | 1907 | — | — | Reported, not confirmed |

CIVIL WAR COINAGE
Province Of Santander
General Ramon Gonzales Valencia

These coins were struck in Santander in 1902 by General Valencia, to pay his troops after the Battle of Palonegro. Legend has it that they were struck using the brass of expended cartridges. Because the planchets are very thin, the struck uniface surface shows through backwards when examined from the reverse.

10 CENTAVOS

BRASS, uniface

KM#	Date	Mintage	Fine	VF	XF
1	ND(1902)	—	15.00	22.50	40.00

20 CENTAVOS

BRASS, uniface
Similar to 50 Centavos, KM#3.

| 2 | 1902 | — | 13.50 | 18.50 | 35.00 |

50 CENTAVOS

BRASS, uniface

| 3 | 1902 | — | 10.00 | 15.00 | 30.00 |

PROOF SETS (PS)

KM#	Date	Mintage	Identification	Issue Price	Mkt. Val.
PS1	1968(5)	8,000	KM231-235	340.00	1950.
PS2	1969(5)	6,000	KM238-242	—	2000.
PS3	1971(5)	6,000	KM248-252	—	2300.
PS4	1973(5)	—	KM254,256,257	—	450.00
PS5	1975(2)	2,500	KM260,262	195.00	235.00
PS6	1975(2)	4,000	KM259,261	195.00	245.00
PS7	1979(2)	—	KM264a-265a	—	75.00

LEPROSARIUM TOKEN ISSUES (Tn)
BOGOTA MINT

Special coinage for use in the three government colonies of Agua de Dios, Cano de Lord, and Contratacion. The hospitals were closed in the late 1950's and patients were allowed to exchange these special coins for regular currency at any bank.

CENTAVO

COPPER-NICKEL

KM#	Date	Mintage	Good	VG	Fine	VF
Tn9	1921	.300	.50	1.00	2.75	6.50

2 CENTAVOS

COPPER-NICKEL

KM#	Date	Mintage	Good	VG	Fine	VF
Tn10	1921	.350	.50	1.00	3.50	7.50

2-1/2 CENTAVOS

BRASS

| Tn1 | 1901 | .020 | 6.00 | 12.50 | 20.00 | 42.50 |

5 CENTAVOS

BRASS

| Tn2 | 1901 | .015 | 6.00 | 12.50 | 20.00 | 42.50 |

COPPER-NICKEL

| Tn11 | 1921 | .200 | .75 | 1.50 | 3.75 | 8.00 |

10 CENTAVOS

BRASS

| Tn3 | 1901 | .010 | 10.00 | 15.00 | 25.00 | 45.00 |

COPPER-NICKEL

| Tn12 | 1921 | .200 | .75 | 1.50 | 3.75 | 8.00 |

20 CENTAVOS

BRASS

| Tn4 | 1901 | .030 | 10.00 | 15.00 | 25.00 | 45.00 |

50 CENTAVOS

BRASS

| Tn5 | 1901 | .026 | 13.50 | 20.00 | 35.00 | 60.00 |

COPPER-NICKEL

| Tn13 | 1921 | .120 | 1.75 | 3.25 | 5.50 | 14.00 |

INFLATIONARY TOKEN ISSUES (Tn)
P/M - Papel Moneda

1 Peso equaled in value to 1 Centavo of the old silver currency. It later circulated at par with the newer 1 Centavo coins.

PESO P/M

BRASS

KM#	Date	Mintage	Good	VG	Fine	VF
Tn14	1928	.050	1.50	4.25	8.00	16.00

COPPER

| Tn14a | 1928 | Inc. Ab. | — | Rare | — | — |

COPPER-NICKEL

| Tn6 | 1907 | .792 | 3.00 | 4.50 | 10.00 | 30.00 |

5 PESOS P/M
COPPER-NICKEL

| Tn7 | 1907 | .159 | 5.00 | 10.00 | 17.50 | 35.00 |

10 PESOS P/M
COPPER-NICKEL

| Tn8 | 1907 | .129 | 6.00 | 12.00 | 22.50 | 45.00 |

COMOROS

The Federal Islamic Republic of the Comoros, a volcanic archipelago located in the Mozambique Channel of the Indian Ocean 300 miles (483 km.) northwest of Madagascar, has an area of 694 sq. mi. (1,797 sq. km.) and a population of 337,949. Capital: Moroni. The economy of the islands is based on agriculture. There are practically no mineral resources. Vanilla, essence for perfumes, copra, and sisal are exported.

Ancient Phoenician traders were probably the first visitors to the Comoro Islands, but the first detailed knowledge of the area was gathered by Arab sailors. Arab dominion and culture were firmly established when the Portuguese, Dutch, and French arrived in the 16th century. In 1843 a Malagasy ruler ceded the island of Mayotte to France; the other three principal islands of the archipelago--Anjouan, Moheli, and Grand Comore-- came under French protection in 1886. The islands were joined administratively with Madagascar in 1912. The Comoros became partially autonomous, with the status of a French overseas territory, in 1946, and achieved complete internal autonomy in 1961. On Dec. 31, 1975, after 133 years of French association, the Comoro Islands became the independent Republic of the Comoros.

Mayotte retained the option of determining its future ties and in 1976 voted to remain French. Its present status is that of a French Territorial Collectivity. French currency now circulates there.

TITLES
Daulat Anjazanchiyah

دولة انجزنجية

Comor

كموز

RULERS
Said Ali ibn Said Amr, regnant, 1890
French, 1886-1975

MINT MARKS
(a) - Paris, privy marks only
A - Paris

MONETARY SYSTEM
100 Centimes = 1 Franc

ANJOUAN SULTANATE
5 CENTIMES

BRONZE   PRIVY MARK
Rev. privy mark: Fasces

KM#	Date	Mintage	Fine	VF	XF	Unc
1.1	AH1308A	.100	6.50	12.00	20.00	65.00

Rev. privy mark: Torch

| 1.2 | AH1308A | .200 | 6.50 | 12.00 | 20.00 | 65.00 |

10 CENTIMES

BRONZE   PRIVY MARK
Rev. privy mark: Fasces

| 2.1 | AH1308A | .050 | 10.00 | 16.00 | 30.00 | 75.00 |

Rev. privy mark: Torch

| 2.2 | AH1308A | .100 | 10.00 | 16.00 | 30.00 | 75.00 |

5 FRANCS

.900 SILVER

KM#	Date	Mintage	Fine	VF	XF	Unc
3	AH1308A	2,050	300.00	450.00	650.00	1000.

COLONIAL COINAGE
FRANC

ALUMINUM

| 4 | 1964(a) | .500 | .15 | .25 | .35 | .60 |

2 FRANCS

ALUMINUM

| 5 | 1964(a) | .600 | .15 | .25 | .40 | .75 |

5 FRANCS

ALUMINUM

| 6 | 1964(a) | 1.000 | .20 | .40 | .70 | 1.10 |

10 FRANCS

ALUMINUM-BRONZE

| 7 | 1964(a) | .600 | .20 | .45 | .80 | 1.50 |

20 FRANCS

ALUMINUM-BRONZE

KM#	Date	Mintage	Fine	VF	XF	Unc
8	1964(a)	.500	.30	.60	1.00	1.75

REPUBLIC
5 FRANCS

ALUMINUM
F.A.O. Issue

| 15 | 1984(a) | 1.000 | .20 | .35 | .60 | 1.20 |

25 FRANCS

NICKEL
F.A.O. Issue

| 14 | 1981(a) | 1.000 | .50 | 1.25 | 2.50 | 5.00 |
| | 1982(a) | — | .20 | .40 | .65 | 1.20 |

50 FRANCS

NICKEL
F.A.O. Issue

| 9 | 1975(a) | — | .50 | 1.00 | 1.50 | 2.50 |

100 FRANCS

NICKEL
F.A.O. Issue

| 13 | 1977(a) | .500 | .60 | 1.00 | 1.75 | 3.50 |

5000 FRANCS

44.8300 g, .925 SILVER, 1.3332 oz ASW
Obv: Similar to 20,000 Francs, KM#12.
Rev: Cluster of flowers.

| 10 | 1976 | 700 pcs. | — | — | — | 35.00 |
| | 1976 | 1,000 | — | — | Proof | 40.00 |

10000 FRANCS

3.0700 g, .900 GOLD, .0888 oz AGW
Obv: Similar to 20,000 Francs, KM#12.

| 11 | 1976 | 500 pcs. | — | — | — | 70.00 |
| | 1976 | 500 pcs. | — | — | Proof | 80.00 |

20000 FRANCS

6.1400 g, .900 GOLD, .1776 oz AGW

KM#	Date	Mintage	Fine	VF	XF	Unc
12	1976	500 pcs.	—	—	—	115.00
	1976	500 pcs.	—	—	Proof	175.00

FLEUR DE COIN SETS (SS)

KM#	Date	Mintage	Identification	Issue Price	Mkt. Val.
SS1	1964(a)	—	KM4-8	—	10.00

NOTE: This set issued with Reunion set.

MINT SETS (MS)

| MS1 | 1976(3) | 500 | KM10-12 | — | 225.00 |

PROOF SETS (PS)

| PS1 | 1976(3) | 500 | KM10-12 | 229.00 | 300.00 |

CONGO PEOPLE'S REP.

The People's Republic of the Congo (formerly the French Middle Congo overseas territory), located on the equator in west-central Africa, has an area of 132,047 sq. mi. (342,000 sq. km.) and a population of 1.6 million. Capital: Brazzaville. Agriculture, forestry, mining, and food processing are the principal industries. Timber, industrial diamonds, potash, peanuts, and cocoa beans are exported.

The Portuguese were the first Europeans to explore the Congo (Brazzaville) area, 14th century. They conducted a slave trade with the tribal kingdoms of Teke, Loango, and Kongo without attempting developmental colonization. French influence was established in 1883 when the king of Teke signed a treaty with Savorgnan de Brazza, thereby placing his kingdom under the protection of France. While a French protectorate, the area was known as Middle Congo. In 1910 Middle Congo became a part of French Equatorial Africa, which also included Gabon, Ubangi-Shari (now the Central African Republic), and Chad. Following World War II, during which it was an important center of Free French activities, the Middle Congo was given a large measure of internal autonomy, and its inhabitants were made French citizens. Upon approval of the constitution of the Fifth French Republic, 1958, it became a member of the new French Community. On Aug. 15, 1960, Middle Congo became the independent Republic of the Congo-Brazzaville. In Jan. 1970 the country's name was changed to People's Republic of the Congo. A new constitution which asserts the government's advocacy of socialism was adopted in 1973.

NOTE: For earlier and related coinage see French Equatorial Africa and the Equatorial African States.

RULERS
French

MINT MARKS
(a) - Paris, privy marks only

MONETARY SYSTEM
100 Centimes = 1 Franc

100 FRANCS

NICKEL

KM#	Date	Mintage	Fine	VF	XF	Unc
1	1971(a)	2.500	8.00	15.00	25.00	40.00
	1972(a)	—	8.00	15.00	25.00	40.00

2	1975(a)	—	5.00	10.00	17.50	30.00
	1982(a)	—	2.50	5.00	8.00	12.50
	1983(a)	—	2.50	5.00	8.00	12.50

Listings For
CONGO-BELGE: refer to Zaire
CONGO DEMOCRATIC REPUBLIC: refer to Zaire

CONGO PEOPLE'S REPUBLIC 426

COPPER-NICKEL
International Games - Handball

KM#	Date	Mintage	Fine	VF	XF	Unc
3	1984	—	—	—	Proof	25.00

500 FRANCS

COPPER-NICKEL

4	1985(a)	—	—	2.00	3.50	6.00
	1986(a)	—	—	2.00	3.50	6.00

COOK ISLANDS

Cook Islands, a political dependency of New Zealand consisting of 15 islands located in the South Pacific Ocean about 2,000 miles (3,218 km.) northeast of New Zealand, has an area of 90 sq. mi. (234 sq. km.) and a population of 15,693. Capital: Avarua. The United States claims the islands of Danger, Manahiki, Penrhyn, and Rakahanga atolls. Citrus and canned fruits and juices, copra, clothing, jewelry, and mother-of-pearl shell are exported.

The islands were first sighted by Spanish navigator Alvaro de Mendada in 1595. Portuguese navigator Pedro Fernandes de Quieros landed on Rakahanga in 1606. English navigator Capt. James Cook sailed to the islands on three occasions: 1773, 1774 and 1777. He named them Hervey Islands, in honor of Augustus John Hervey, a lord of the Admiralty. The islands were declared a British protectorate in 1888, and were annexed to New Zealand in 1901. They were granted internal self-government in 1965. New Zealand provides an annual subsidy and retains responsibility for defense and foreign affairs.

As a territory of New Zealand, Cook Islands are considered to be within the Commonwealth of Nations.

RULERS
British

MINT MARKS
FM - Franklin Mint, U.S.A. *

*NOTE: From 1975 the Franklin Mint has produced coinage in up to three different qualities. Qualities of issue are designated in () after each date and are defined as follows:

(M) MATTE - Normal circulation strike or a dull finish produced by sandblasting special uncirculated (polish finish) or proof quality dies.

(U) SPECIAL UNCIRCULATED - Polished or proof-like in appearance without any frosted features.

(P) PROOF - The highest quality obtainable having mirror-like fields and frosted features.

MONETARY SYSTEM
(Until 1967)
12 Pence = 1 Shilling
20 Shillings = 1 Pound
(Commencing 1967)
100 Cents = 1 Dollar

CENT

BRONZE

KM#	Date	Mintage	VF	XF	Unc
1	1972	.117	—	.10	.20
	1972	.017	—	Proof	.50
	1973	8,500	—	.10	.20
	1973	.013	—	Proof	.50
	1974	.300	—	.10	.20
	1974	7,300	—	Proof	.50
	1975	.429	—	.10	.20
	1975FM(M)	1,000	—	—	.50
	1975FM(U)	2,251	—	—	.20
	1975FM(P)	.021	—	Proof	.50
	1976FM(M)	1,001	—	—	.50
	1976FM(U)	1,066	—	—	.20
	1976FM(P)	.018	—	Proof	.50
	1977FM(M)	1,171	—	—	.50
	1977FM(U)	1,002	—	—	.20
	1977FM(P)	5,986	—	Proof	.50
	1979FM(M)	1,000	—	—	.50
	1979FM(U)	500 pcs.	—	—	1.00
	1979FM(P)	4,058	—	Proof	.50
	1983	—	—	.10	.20
	1983	.010	—	Proof	.50

Edge: 1728 CAPTAIN COOK 1978.

1a	1978FM(M)	1,000	—	—	1.00
	1978FM(U)	767 pcs.	—	—	1.00
	1978FM(P)	6,287	—	Proof	.50

Wedding of Prince Charles and Lady Diana
Edge: THE ROYAL WEDDING 29 JULY 1981

1b	1981FM(M)	1,000	—	—	.50
	1981FM(U)	1,100	—	—	.50
	1981FM(P)	9,205	—	Proof	.40

2 CENTS

BRONZE

KM#	Date	Mintage	VF	XF	Unc
2	1972	.063	.10	.15	.30
	1972	.017	—	Proof	.75
	1973	8,500	.15	.20	.40
	1973	.013	—	Proof	.75
	1974	.120	.10	.15	.30
	1974	7,300	—	Proof	.75
	1975	.129	.10	.15	.25
	1975FM(M)	1,000	—	—	.75
	1975FM(U)	2,251	—	—	.30
	1975FM(P)	.021	—	Proof	.75
	1976FM(M)	1,001	—	—	.75
	1976FM(U)	1,066	—	—	.30
	1976FM(P)	.018	—	Proof	.75
	1977FM(M)	1,171	—	—	.75
	1977FM(U)	1,002	—	—	.30
	1977FM(P)	5,986	—	Proof	.75
	1979FM(M)	1,000	—	—	.75
	1979FM(U)	500 pcs.	—	—	.30
	1979FM(P)	4,058	—	Proof	.75
	1983	—	.10	.15	.25
	1983	.010	—	Proof	.75

Edge: 1728 CAPTAIN COOK 1978.

2a	1978FM(M)	1,000	—	—	.75
	1978FM(U)	767 pcs.	—	—	.75
	1978FM(P)	6,287	—	Proof	.50

Wedding of Prince Charles and Lady Diana
Edge: THE ROYAL WEDDING 29 JULY 1981

2b	1981FM(M)	1,000	—	—	.75
	1981FM(U)	1,100	—	—	.75
	1981FM(P)	9,205	—	Proof	.50

5 CENTS

COPPER-NICKEL

3	1972	.032	.10	.20	.40
	1972	.017	—	Proof	1.00
	1973	8,500	.15	.25	.50
	1973	.013	—	Proof	1.00
	1974	.080	.10	.20	.40
	1974	7,300	—	Proof	1.00
	1975	.089	.10	.20	.40
	1975FM(M)	1,000	—	—	1.00
	1975FM(U)	2,251	—	—	.40
	1975FM(P)	.021	—	Proof	1.00
	1976FM(M)	1,001	—	—	1.00
	1976FM(U)	1,066	—	—	.40
	1976FM(P)	.018	—	Proof	1.00
	1977FM(M)	1,171	—	—	1.00
	1977FM(U)	1,002	—	—	.40
	1977FM(P)	5,986	—	Proof	1.00
	1979FM(M)	1,000	—	—	1.00
	1979FM(U)	500 pcs.	—	—	.40
	1979FM(P)	4,058	—	Proof	1.00
	1983	—	.10	.20	.40
	1983	.010	—	Proof	1.00

Edge: 1728 CAPTAIN COOK 1978.

3a	1978FM(M)	1,000	—	—	1.00
	1978FM(U)	767 pcs.	—	—	.75
	1978FM(P)	6,287	—	Proof	.50

Wedding of Prince Charles and Lady Diana
Edge: THE ROYAL WEDDING 29 JULY 1981

3b	1981FM(M)	1,000	—	—	1.00
	1981FM(U)	1,100	—	—	1.00
	1981FM(P)	9,205	—	Proof	.50

33	1987	—	—	.10	.20

10 CENTS

COOK ISLANDS 427

KM#	Date	Mintage	VF	XF	Unc
4	1972	.035	.10	.20	.50
	1972	.017	—	Proof	1.25
	1973	.059	.10	.20	.50
	1973	.013	—	Proof	1.25
	1974	.050	.10	.20	.50
	1974	7,300	—	Proof	1.25
	1975	.059	.10	.20	.50
	1975FM(M)	1,000	—	—	1.25
	1975FM(U)	2,251	—	—	.50
	1975FM(P)	.021	—	Proof	1.25
	1976FM(M)	1,001	—	—	1.25
	1976FM(U)	1,066	—	—	.50
	1976FM(P)	.018	—	Proof	1.25
	1977FM(M)	1,171	—	—	1.25
	1977FM(U)	1,002	—	—	.50
	1977FM(P)	5,986	—	Proof	1.25
	1983	—	.10	.20	.50
	1983	.010	—	—	1.25

Edge: 1728 CAPTAIN COOK 1978.

4a	1978FM(M)	1,000	—	—	1.25
	1978FM(U)	767 pcs.	—	—	1.25
	1978FM(P)	6,287	—	Proof	1.00

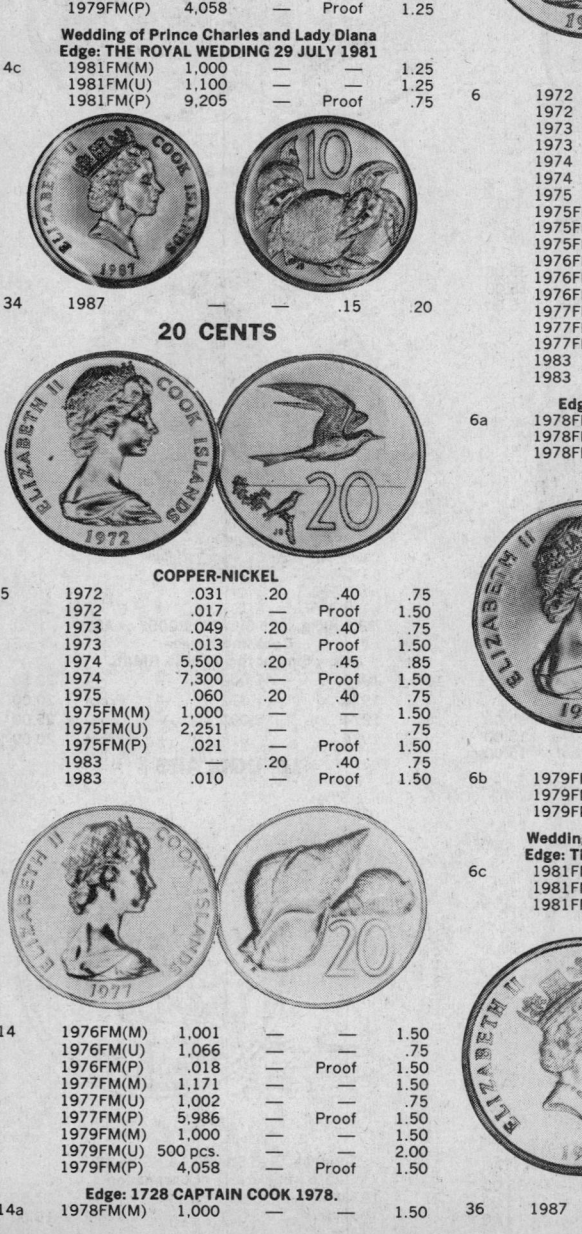

F.A.O. Issue

4b	1979FM(M)	9,000	—	—	1.00
	1979FM(U)	500 pcs.	—	—	1.50
	1979FM(P)	4,058	—	Proof	1.25

Wedding of Prince Charles and Lady Diana
Edge: THE ROYAL WEDDING 29 JULY 1981

4c	1981FM(M)	1,000	—	—	1.25
	1981FM(U)	1,100	—	—	1.25
	1981FM(P)	9,205	—	Proof	.75

| 34 | 1987 | — | — | .15 | .20 |

20 CENTS

COPPER-NICKEL

5	1972	.031	.20	.40	.75
	1972	.017	—	Proof	1.50
	1973	.049	.20	.40	.75
	1973	.013	—	Proof	1.50
	1974	5,500	.20	.45	.85
	1974	7,300	—	Proof	1.50
	1975	.060	.20	.40	.75
	1975FM(M)	1,000	—	—	1.50
	1975FM(U)	2,251	—	—	.75
	1975FM(P)	.021	—	Proof	1.50
	1983	—	.20	.40	.75
	1983	.010	—	Proof	1.50

14	1976FM(M)	1,001	—	—	1.50
	1976FM(U)	1,066	—	—	.75
	1976FM(P)	.018	—	Proof	1.50
	1977FM(M)	1,171	—	—	1.50
	1977FM(U)	1,002	—	—	.75
	1977FM(P)	5,986	—	Proof	1.50
	1979FM(M)	1,000	—	—	1.50
	1979FM(U)	500 pcs.	—	—	2.00
	1979FM(P)	4,058	—	Proof	1.50

Edge: 1728 CAPTAIN COOK 1978.

14a	1978FM(M)	1,000	—	—	1.50
	1978FM(U)	767 pcs.	—	—	2.00
	1978FM(P)	6,287	—	Proof	1.00

Wedding of Prince Charles and Lady Diana
Edge: THE ROYAL WEDDING 29 JULY 1981

14b	1981FM(M)	1,000	—	—	1.50
	1981FM(U)	1,100	—	—	1.50
	1981FM(P)	9,205	—	Proof	1.00

| 35 | 1987 | — | — | .25 | .35 |

50 CENTS

COPPER-NICKEL

6	1972	.031	.40	.75	1.25
	1972	.017	—	Proof	2.00
	1973	.019	.40	.75	1.25
	1973	.013	—	Proof	2.00
	1974	.010	.40	.75	1.25
	1974	7,300	—	Proof	2.00
	1975	.019	.40	.75	1.25
	1975FM(M)	1,000	—	—	2.00
	1975FM(U)	2,251	—	—	1.25
	1975FM(P)	.021	—	Proof	2.00
	1976FM(M)	1,001	—	—	2.00
	1976FM(U)	1,066	—	—	1.25
	1976FM(P)	.018	—	Proof	2.00
	1977FM(M)	1,171	—	—	2.00
	1977FM(U)	1,002	—	—	1.25
	1977FM(P)	5,986	—	Proof	2.00
	1983	—	.40	.75	1.25
	1983	.010	—	Proof	2.00

Edge: 1728 CAPTAIN COOK 1978.

6a	1978FM(M)	1,000	—	—	2.00
	1978FM(U)	767 pcs.	—	—	2.00
	1978FM(P)	6,287	—	Proof	2.00

F.A.O. Issue

6b	1979FM(M)	9,000	.50	1.00	1.50
	1979FM(U)	500 pcs.	—	—	2.50
	1979FM(P)	4,058	—	Proof	2.00

Wedding of Prince Charles and Lady Diana
Edge: THE ROYAL WEDDING 29 JULY 1981

6c	1981FM(M)	1,000	—	—	2.00
	1981FM(U)	1,100	—	—	2.00
	1981FM(P)	9,205	—	Proof	1.50

| 36 | 1987 | — | — | .55 | .75 |

DOLLAR

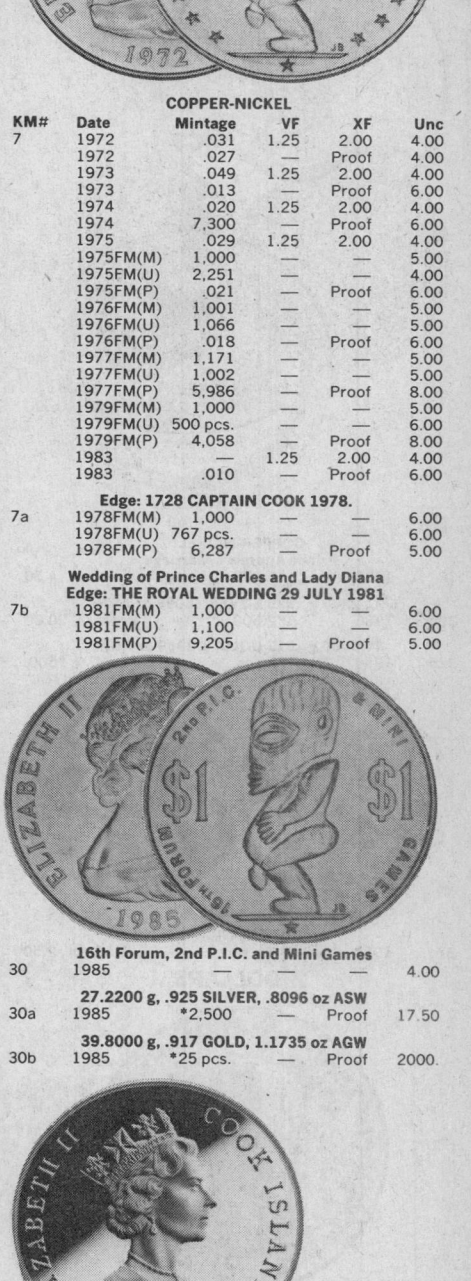

COPPER-NICKEL

KM#	Date	Mintage	VF	XF	Unc
7	1972	.031	1.25	2.00	4.00
	1972	.027	—	Proof	4.00
	1973	.049	1.25	2.00	4.00
	1973	.013	—	Proof	6.00
	1974	.020	1.25	2.00	4.00
	1974	7,300	—	Proof	6.00
	1975	.029	1.25	2.00	4.00
	1975FM(M)	1,000	—	—	5.00
	1975FM(U)	2,251	—	—	4.00
	1975FM(P)	.021	—	Proof	6.00
	1976FM(M)	1,001	—	—	5.00
	1976FM(U)	1,066	—	—	5.00
	1976FM(P)	.018	—	Proof	6.00
	1977FM(M)	1,171	—	—	5.00
	1977FM(U)	1,002	—	—	5.00
	1977FM(P)	5,986	—	Proof	8.00
	1979FM(M)	1,000	—	—	5.00
	1979FM(U)	500 pcs.	—	—	6.00
	1979FM(P)	4,058	—	Proof	8.00
	1983	—	1.25	2.00	4.00
	1983	.010	—	Proof	6.00

Edge: 1728 CAPTAIN COOK 1978.

7a	1978FM(M)	1,000	—	—	6.00
	1978FM(U)	767 pcs.	—	—	6.00
	1978FM(P)	6,287	—	Proof	5.00

Wedding of Prince Charles and Lady Diana
Edge: THE ROYAL WEDDING 29 JULY 1981

7b	1981FM(M)	1,000	—	—	6.00
	1981FM(U)	1,100	—	—	6.00
	1981FM(P)	9,205	—	Proof	5.00

16th Forum, 2nd P.I.C. and Mini Games

| 30 | 1985 | | | | 4.00 |

27.2200 g, .925 SILVER, .8096 oz ASW

| 30a | 1985 | *2,500 | — | Proof | 17.50 |

39.8000 g, .917 GOLD, 1.1735 oz AGW

| 30b | 1985 | *25 pcs. | — | Proof | 2000. |

COOK ISLANDS 428

COPPER-NICKEL
60th Birthday of Queen Elizabeth II

KM#	Date	Mintage	VF	XF	Unc
31	1986	.020	—	—	4.50

27.2200 g, .925 SILVER, .8096 oz ASW
| 31a | 1986 | *2,500 | — | Proof | 20.00 |

44.0000 g, .917 GOLD, 1.2969 oz AGW
| 31b | 1986 | *60 pcs. | — | Proof | 1500. |

COPPER-NICKEL
Prince Andrew's Marriage
| 32 | 1986 | *.020 | — | — | 4.50 |

27.2200 g, .925 SILVER, .8096 oz ASW
| 32a | 1986 | *2,500 | — | Proof | 20.00 |

44.0000 g, .917 GOLD, 1.2969 oz AGW
| 32b | 1986 | *75 pcs. | — | Proof | 1500. |

COPPER-NICKEL
| 37 | 1987 | — | — | 1.50 | 2.50 |

2 DOLLARS

25.7000 g, .925 SILVER, .7643 oz ASW
20th Anniversary of Coronation
Obv: Similar to 50 Cents, KM#6.
| 8 | 1973 | .016 | — | — | 10.00 |
| | 1973 | .046 | — | Proof | 10.00 |

COPPER-NICKEL
| 38 | 1987 | — | — | 2.25 | 3.50 |

2-1/2 DOLLARS

27.3500 g, .925 SILVER, .8133 oz ASW
Cook 2nd Voyage
Obv: Similar to 50 Cents, KM#6.
KM#	Date	Mintage	VF	XF	Unc
9	1973	6,000	—	—	15.00
	1973	.012	—	Proof	15.00
	1974	2,000	—	—	20.00
	1974	.012	—	Proof	15.00

5 DOLLARS

27.3000 g, .500 SILVER, .4388 oz ASW
Obv: Similar to 50 Cents, KM#6.
Rev: Mangara Kingfisher.
15	1976FM(M)	251 pcs.	—	—	35.00
	1976FM(U)	2,192	—	—	15.00
	1976FM(P)	.028	—	Proof	15.00

Obv: Similar to 50 Cents, KM#6.
Rev: Atiu Swiftlet.
17	1977FM(M)	252 pcs.	—	—	35.00
	1977FM(U)	4,032	—	—	15.00
	1977FM(P)	.011	—	Proof	15.00

Wildlife Conservation
Obv: Similar to 50 Cents, KM#6.
Rev: Polynesian Warbler.
20	1978FM(M)	250 pcs.	—	—	35.00
	1978FM(U)	3,659	—	—	15.00
	1978FM(P)	.011	—	Proof	15.00

Cook Island Conservation Day
Obv: Similar to 50 Cents, KM#6.
Rev: Rarotongan Fruit Dove
KM#	Date	Mintage	VF	XF	Unc
24	1979FM(U)	2,500	—	—	22.50
	1979FM(P)	8,612	—	Proof	17.50

ALUMINUM-BRONZE
| 39 | 1987 | — | — | 5.00 | 7.50 |

7-1/2 DOLLARS

33.8000 g, .925 SILVER, 1.0052 oz ASW
Cook 2nd Voyage
Obv: Similar to 50 Cents, KM#6.
10	1973	6,000	—	—	22.50
	1973	.012	—	Proof	20.00
	1974	2,000	—	—	25.00
	1974	.013	—	Proof	20.00

10 DOLLARS

27.9000 g, .925 SILVER, .8297 oz ASW
25th Anniversary of Coronation
| 21 | 1978FM(U) | 5,350 | — | — | 17.50 |
| | 1978FM(P) | .011 | — | Proof | 15.00 |

20 DOLLARS

28.2800 g, .925 SILVER, .8411 oz ASW
International Year of the Scout

KM#	Date	Mintage	VF	XF	Unc
28	1983	*.010	—	—	20.00
	1983	*.010	—	Proof	20.00

25 DOLLARS

48.8500 g, .925 SILVER, 1.4527 oz ASW
Queen's Silver Jubilee
Obv: Similar to 50 Cents, KM#6.

18	1977FM(M)	100 pcs.	—	—	75.00
	1977FM(U)	4,068	—	—	30.00
	1977FM(P)	.017	—	Proof	20.00

50 DOLLARS

97.2000 g, .925 SILVER, 2.8907 oz ASW
Winston Churchill Centenary
Obv: Similar to 50 Cents, KM#6.

11	1974	1,202	—	—	60.00
	1974	2,502	—	Proof	70.00

.925 SILVER, GILT

11a	1974	2,002	—	—	100.00

3.9400 g, .500 GOLD, .0633 oz AGW
Wedding of Prince Charles and Lady Diana

27	1981	220 pcs.	—	—	75.00
	1981	1,309	—	Proof	95.00

28.2800 g, .925 SILVER, .8411 oz ASW
1988 Olympics - Torch Bearer
Obv: Similar to 1 Dollar, KM#32.

KM#	Date	Mintage	VF	XF	Unc
40	1987P	.020	—	Proof	50.00

100 DOLLARS

16.7185 g, .917 GOLD, .4929 oz AGW
Winston Churchill Centenary

12	1974	368 pcs.	—	—	350.00
	1974	1,453	—	Proof	300.00

9.6000 g, .900 GOLD, .2778 oz AGW
Cook 2nd Voyage

13	1975FM(M)	100 pcs.	—	—	400.00
	1975FM(U)	7,447	—	—	150.00
	1975FM(P)	.017	—	Proof	250.00

U.S. Bicentennial

16	1976FM(M)	50 pcs.	—	—	350.00
	1976FM(U)	852 pcs.	—	—	175.00
	1976FM(P)	9,373	—	Proof	250.00

Queen's Silver Jubilee

19	1977FM(M)	50 pcs.	—	—	350.00
	1977FM(U)	562 pcs.	—	—	175.00
	1977FM(P)	9,364	—	Proof	250.00

Membership in Commonwealth of Nations

25	1979FM(U)	400 pcs.	—	—	175.00
	1979FM(P)	3,367	—	Proof	250.00

200 DOLLARS

16.6000 g, .900 GOLD, .4803 oz AGW
Discovery of Hawaii by Capt. Cook

KM#	Date	Mintage	VF	XF	Unc
22	1978FM(M)	26 pcs.	—	—	600.00
	1978FM(U)	621 pcs.	—	—	300.00
	1978FM(P)	3,216	—	Proof	300.00

Legacy of Captain James Cook

26	1979FM(U)	271 pcs.	—	—	325.00
	1979FM(P)	1,939	—	Proof	300.00

15.9800 g, .917 GOLD, .4712 oz AGW
Year of the Scout

29	1983		—	Proof	450.00

250 DOLLARS

17.9000 g, .900 GOLD, .5180 oz AGW
250th Anniversary Birth of James Cook

23	1978FM(M)	25 pcs.	—	—	600.00
	1978FM(U)	200 pcs.	—	—	325.00
	1978FM(P)	1,757	—	Proof	325.00

MINT SETS (MS)

KM#	Date	Mintage	Identification	Issue Price	Mkt. Val.
MS1	1972(7)	11,045	KM1-7	7.50	5.00
MS2	1973(9)	3,652	KM1-7,9,10	52.50	45.00
MS3	1973(7)	3,023	KM1-7	10.00	6.00
MS4	1973(2)	2,348	KM9,10	45.00	37.50
MS5	1974(9)	913	KM1-7,9,10	52.50	50.00
MS6	1974(7)	2,087	KM1-7	10.00	6.00
MS7	1974(2)	587	KM9,10	45.00	45.00
MS8	1975(7)	2,251	KM1-7	10.00	6.00
MS9	1976(8)	1,066	KM1-4,6,7,14,15	20.00	20.00
MS10	1977(8)	1,171	KM1-4,6,7,14,17	20.00	20.00
MS11	1978(8)	767	KM1a-4,6a,7a,14a,20	20.00	25.00
MS12	1979(8)	500	KM1-3,4b,6b,7,14,24	—	25.00
MS13	1981(7)	1,100	KM1b-3b,4c,6c,7b,14b	—	10.00
MS14	1983(7)		KM1-7	—	6.00
MS15	1987(7)		KM33-39	—	15.00

PROOF SETS (PS)

PS1	1972(7)	17,101	KM1-7	20.00	8.00
PS2	1973(9)	7,395	KM1-7,9,10	89.50	45.00
PS3	1973(7)	5,136	KM1-7	29.50	10.00
PS4	1973(2)	4,754	KM9,10	60.00	35.00
PS5	1974(9)	4,444	KM1-7,9,10	95.00	45.00
PS6	1974(7)	5,300	KM1-7	32.50	10.00
PS7	1974(2)	2,856	KM9,10	65.00	35.00
PS8	1975(7)	21,290	KM1-7	31.50	10.00
PS9	1976(8)	17,658	KM1-4,6,7,14,15	40.00	22.50
PS10	1977(8)	5,986	KM1-4,6,7,14,17	42.00	25.00
PS11	1978(8)	6,287	KM1a-4,4a,6a,7a,14a,20	42.00	25.00
PS12	1979(8)	4,058	KM1-3,4b,6b,7,14,24	44.00	25.00
PS13	1981(7)	9,205	KM1b-3b,4c,6c,7b,14b	39.50	12.50
PS14	1983(7)	10,000	KM1-7	29.95	10.00

COSTA RICA 430

The Republic of Costa Rica, located in southern Central America between Nicaragua and Panama, has an area of 19,575 sq. mi. (50,700 sq. km.) and a population of 2.2 million. Capital: San Jose. Agriculture predominates; coffee, bananas, beef and sugar contribute heavily to the country's export earnings.

Costa Rica was discovered by Christopher Columbus in 1502, during his last voyage to the new world, and was a colony of Spain from 1522 until independence in 1821. Columbus named the territory Nueva Cartago; the name Costa Rica wasn't generally employed until 1540. Bartholomew Columbus attempted to found the first settlement but was driven off by Indian attacks and the country wasn't pacified until 1530. Costa Rica was absorbed for two years (1821-23) into the Mexican Empire of Agustin de Iturbide. From 1823 to 1848, it was a constituent state of the Central American Republic (q.v.). It was established as a republic in 1848. Today, Costa Rica remains a model of orderly democracy in Latin America.

MINT MARKS
CR - San Jose 1825-1947
NOTE: Also see Central American Republic.
HEATON - Heaton
BIRMm - Birmingham 1889-1893

ISSUING BANK INITIALS - MINT
BCCR - Philadelphia 1951-1958, 1961
BICR - Philadelphia 1935
BNCR - London 1937, 1948
BNCR - San Jose 1942-1947
GCR - Philadelphia 1905-1914, 1929
GCR - San Jose 1917-1941

ASSAYER'S INITIALS
MM - 1842
JB - 1847-1864
GW - 1850-1890
CY - 1902
JCV - 1903

MONETARY SYSTEM
8 Reales = 1 Peso
16 Pesos = 8 Escudos = 1 Onza

REAL SERIES
1/2 REAL
1.5000 g, .903 SILVER, .0435 oz ASW
San Jose Mint
Obv: Radiant 6 pointed star in circle over branches.
Rev: Tobacco plant and value in circle, date below.

KM#	Date	Mintage	VG	Fine	VF	XF
32	1842MM	—	18.00	37.50	65.00	120.00

REAL

2.2600 g, .903 SILVER, .0656 oz ASW
San Jose Mint

65	1847 JB	—	6.00	10.00	15.00	32.00
	1847 JB (error) backwards B					
		—	7.00	12.50	17.50	35.00

2.5000 g, .903 SILVER, .0725 oz ASW

66	1849 JB	—	3.50	7.00	10.00	27.50
	1850 JB	—	4.50	9.00	15.00	40.00

1/2 ESCUDO

1.7000 g, .875 GOLD, .0478 oz AGW
San Jose Mint

97	1850 JB	3,388	40.00	65.00	100.00	150.00

KM#	Date	Mintage	VG	Fine	VF	XF
97	1851 JB	6,565	40.00	65.00	100.00	150.00
	1853 JB	8,491	40.00	65.00	100.00	150.00
	1854 JB	4,663	40.00	65.00	100.00	150.00
	1855 JB	8,822	40.00	65.00	100.00	150.00
	1855 GW	I.A.	40.00	65.00	100.00	150.00
	1864 JB	9,018	40.00	65.00	100.00	150.00

ESCUDO

3.3000 g, .875 GOLD, .0928 oz AGW
San Jose Mint
Rev: Denomination .1.-E.

33.1	1842 MM	.010	300.00	600.00	1200.	2000.

Rev: Denomination 1.-E.

33.2	1842 MM	I.A.	350.00	800.00	1500.	2250.

98	1850 JB	6,167	60.00	100.00	150.00	250.00
	1851 JB	4,388	60.00	100.00	150.00	250.00
	1853 JB	2,979	75.00	150.00	250.00	500.00
	1855 JB	4,095	70.00	125.00	200.00	350.00

2 ESCUDOS

6.7500 g, .875 GOLD, .1899 oz AGW
San Jose Mint

99	1850 JB	3,641	110.00	150.00	200.00	300.00
	1854 JB Inc. Ab.		110.00	150.00	200.00	300.00
	1854 GW	I.A.	110.00	150.00	200.00	300.00
	1855 JB	.060	110.00	125.00	175.00	300.00
	1855 GW	I.A.	110.00	150.00	200.00	300.00
	1858 GW	.017	110.00	125.00	175.00	300.00
	1862 GW	5,896	125.00	150.00	200.00	325.00
	1863 GW	5,632	125.00	200.00	325.00	500.00

1/2 ONZA

12.6000 g, .875 GOLD, .3545 oz AGW
San Jose Mint

100	1850 JB	.018	200.00	300.00	400.00	800.00
	1850 JB	—	—	—	Proof	4200.

COUNTERMARKED COINAGE
1841-1842

Type I
c/m: Radiant 6-pointed star in 7mm circle.
NOTE: An additional plug was cut from each coin to 'pay for the work'. Market valuations are for holed coins.

1/2 REAL
SILVER
c/m: Type I on Mexico 1/2 Real, KM#72.

KM#	Date	Good	VG	Fine	VF
1	ND(1792-1808)	—	—	Rare	

REAL
SILVER
c/m: Type I on Spanish American 1 Real.

KM#	Date	Good	VG	Fine	VF
4	ND	—	Reported, not confirmed		

2 REALES
SILVER
c/m: Type I on Bolivia (Potosi) 2 Reales, KM#53.

7	ND(1773-89)	15.00	30.00	60.00	90.00

c/m: Type I on Guatemala 2 Reales, KM#34.1.

8	ND(1772-76)	15.00	30.00	60.00	90.00

c/m: Type I on Mexico 2 Reales, KM#91.

12	ND(1800)	15.00	30.00	60.00	90.00

c/m: Type I on Mexico 2 Reales, KM#92.

9	ND(1809-12)	15.00	30.00	60.00	90.00

c/m: Type I on Mexico 2 Reales, KM#372.8.

10	ND(1825-41)	15.00	30.00	60.00	90.00

c/m: Type I on Peru 2 Reales, KM#141.1.

11	ND(1825-40)	15.00	30.00	60.00	90.00

c/m: Type I on Peru 2 Reales, KM#95.

13	ND	15.00	30.00	60.00	90.00

4 REALES
SILVER
c/m: Type I on Bolivia (Potosi) 4 Reales, KM#54.

14	ND(1773-89)	100.00	175.00	300.00	450.00

c/m: Type I on Bolivia (Potosi) 4 Reales, KM#72.

15	ND(1791-1808)	100.00	175.00	300.00	450.00

c/m: Type I on Guatemala, 4 Reales, KM#35.1.

16	ND(1772-76)	625.00	900.00	1350.	—

8 REALES
SILVER
c/m: Type I on Mexico 8 Reales, KM#106.

19	ND(1772-89)	75.00	150.00	225.00	325.00

COSTA RICA 431

c/m: Type I on Mexico 8 Reales, KM#376.

KM#	Date	Good	VG	Fine	VF
20	ND(1824)	125.00	225.00	325.00	450.00

c/m: Type I on Mexico 8 Reales, KM#377.10.
| 21 | ND(1824-41) | 75.00 | 125.00 | 175.00 | 300.00 |

c/m: Type I on Peru 8 Reales, KM#78.
| 22 | ND(1772-89) | 75.00 | 150.00 | 225.00 | 325.00 |

c/m: Type I on Peru 8 Reales, KM#142.1.
| 23 | ND(1825-28) | 75.00 | 125.00 | 175.00 | 300.00 |

c/m: Type I on Peru 8 Reales, KM#142.3.
| 24 | ND(1828-40) | 75.00 | 125.00 | 175.00 | 300.00 |

c/m: Type I on North Peru 8 Reales, KM#155.
| 25 | ND(1836-39) | 75.00 | 150.00 | 225.00 | 325.00 |

c/m: Type I on Spanish 8 Reales, C#136.
| 26 | ND(1809-30) | 75.00 | 150.00 | 225.00 | 325.00 |

c/m: Type I on Mexico 8 Reales, KM#111.
| 27 | ND(1812-22) | — | — | — | 1350. |

1841-1842

Type II
c/m: Radiant 6-pointed star in 4mm circle.

4 ESCUDOS

GOLD
c/m: Type II on Central American Republic, 4 Escudos, KM#16.

KM#	Date	Good	VG	Fine	VF
29	ND(1828-41)	—	—	—	Rare

COUNTERSTAMPED COINAGE
1845

Type III
Obv. c/s: COSTA RICA and 2 R. around female head.
Rev. c/s: HABILITADA POR EL GOB. around tree.

2 REALES

SILVER
c/s: Type III on Spanish (Seville) 2 Reales.
| 35 | ND(1732) | — | — | — | — |

c/s: Type III on Spanish (Madrid) 2 Reales, C#38.
| 36 | ND(1772-88) | 8.50 | 15.00 | 27.50 | 50.00 |

NOTE: The coin illustrated above also has the lattice c/m of the Province of Trinidad and would command a premium.

c/s: Type III on Spanish (Madrid) 2 Reales, C#69.
| 37 | ND(1788-1808) | 8.50 | 15.00 | 27.50 | 50.00 |

c/s: Type III on Spanish (Seville) 2 Reales, C#69.
| 38 | ND(1793-1808) | 8.50 | 15.00 | 27.50 | 50.00 |

c/s: Type III on Spanish 2 Reales, C#89.
| 39 | ND(1811-13) | 15.00 | 25.00 | 40.00 | 65.00 |

c/s: Type III on Spanish 4 Reales, C#90.
| 40 | ND(1808-13) | 10.00 | 15.00 | 35.00 | 85.00 |

c/s: Type III on Spanish (Madrid) 2 Reales, C#134.
| 41 | ND(1814-33) | 10.00 | 17.50 | 30.00 | 55.00 |

c/s: Type III on Spanish (Seville) 2 Reales, C#134.
KM#	Date	Good	VG	Fine	VF
42	ND(1815-33)	10.00	17.50	30.00	55.00

c/s: Type III on Spanish 4 Reales, C#135.
| 43 | ND(1811-33) | 25.00 | 50.00 | 95.00 | 150.00 |

c/s: Type III on Trinidad, Cuba c/s on Spanish (Seville) 2 Reales, KM#12.
| 44 | ND(1793-1808) | 14.00 | 18.00 | 32.50 | 55.00 |

NOTE: The coin illustrated above also has the lattice c/m of the Province of Trinidad and would command a premium.

1846

Type IV
Obv. c/s: REPUB. DE CENT. DE AMER. 1846 around sun over mountains in a 14mm circle.
Rev. c/s: HABILITADA EN COSTA RICA J.B. . . around tree, 1-R.

REAL

SILVER
c/s: Type IV on Spanish American 'cob' 1 Real.
| 47 | 1846 | 8.50 | 15.00 | 25.00 | 45.00 |

4 REALES

SILVER
c/s: Type IV with additional c/m 4 in square on Guatemala 'cob' 4 Reales, KM#5.
KM#	Date	Year	Good	VG	Fine	VF
50	1846	—	250.00	400.00	600.00	800.00

c/s: Type IV with additional c/m 4 in square on United States 50 Cents.
| 51 | 1837 | — | — | — | — | — |

1846

Type V
Obv. c/s: REPUB. DE CENT. DE AMER. 1846 around sun over mountains in a 14mm circle.
Rev. c/s: HABILITADA EN COSTA RICA J-B around tree, 2-R.

2 REALES

SILVER
c/s: Type V on Bolivia (Potosi) 'cob' 2 Reales, KM#29.

KM#	Date	Year	Good	VG	Fine	VF
54	1846	(1700-46)	20.00	35.00	60.00	90.00

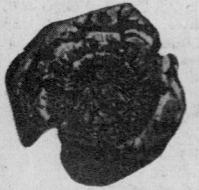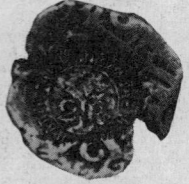

c/s: Type V on Peru (Lima) 'cob' 2 Reales, KM#30.

55	1846	(1700-46)	20.00	35.00	60.00	90.00

8 REALES

SILVER
c/s: Type V with additional c/m 8 in circle on Bolivia (Potosi) 'cob' 8 Reales, KM#31.

58	1846	(1700-46)	400.00	550.00	800.00	1000.

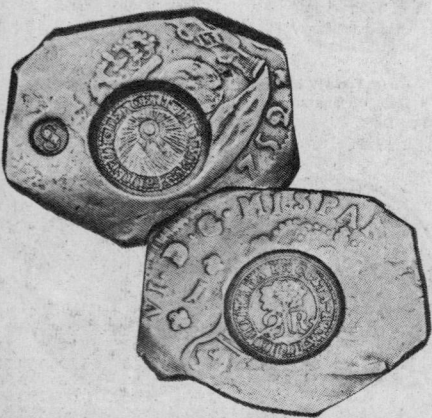

c/s: Type V on Guatemala 'cob' 8 Reales, KM#12.

59	1846	(1747-53)	400.00	550.00	800.00	1000.

c/s: Type V on Peru (Lima) 'cob' 8 Reales of Charles II.

KM#	Date	Year	Good	VG	Fine	VF
60	1846	(1665-1700)	400.00	550.00	800.00	1000.

c/s: Type V on Peru (Lima) 'cob' 8 Reales, KM#34.

61	1846	(1700-46)	400.00	550.00	800.00	1000.

c/s: Type V on Mexico City 'cob' 8 Reales, KM#48.

62	1846	(1733-34)	400.00	550.00	800.00	1000.

COUNTERMARKED COINAGE
1849-1850

Type VI
c/m: HABILITADA POR EL GOBIERNO around lion in 5mm circle.

Local Series
1/2 REAL

1.6500 g, .903 SILVER, .0479 oz ASW
c/m: Type VI on Central American Republic 1/2 Real, KM#20.

KM#	Date	Year	Good	VG	Fine	VF
67	(1849)	1831 E	5.00	9.00	15.00	22.00
		1831 F	5.00	9.00	15.00	22.00
		1843 M	4.00	6.00	11.00	20.00
		1845 B	4.00	6.00	11.00	20.00

1.6500 g, .750 SILVER, .0397 oz ASW
c/m: Type VI on Central American Republic 1/2 Real, KM#20a.

68	(1849)	1846 JB 'CRESCA'	3.50	5.00	10.00	17.50
		1846 JB 'CREZCA'	3.50	5.00	10.00	17.50
		1847 JB 'CRESCA'	3.50	5.00	10.00	17.50
		1847 JB 'CREZCA'	3.50	5.00	10.00	17.50
		1848 JB	3.50	5.00	10.00	17.50
		1849 JB	3.50	7.00	12.00	22.00

c/m: Type VI on Costa Rica 1/2 Real, KM#32.

69	(1849)	1842 MM	7.50	13.50	25.00	40.00

REAL

3.2500 g, .903 SILVER, .0943 oz ASW
c/m: Type VI on Central American Republic 1 Real, KM#21.

72	(1849)	1831 E	7.50	12.50	27.50	47.50
	(1849)	1831 F	6.00	9.50	25.00	42.50
	(1849)	1848 JB	9.00	18.00	32.50	50.00

3.2500 g, .750 SILVER, .0783 oz ASW
c/m: Type VI on Central American Republic 1 Real, KM#21a.

72a	(1849)	1848 JB	9.00	18.00	32.50	50.00
		1849 JB	5.50	10.00	25.00	42.50

c/m: Type VI on Costa Rica 1 Real, KM#65.

73	(1849)	1847 JB	12.50	22.50	40.00	62.50
		1849 JB (error) backwards B	14.00	27.50	50.00	70.00

c/m: Type VI on Costa Rica 1 Real, KM#66.

KM#	Date	Year	Good	VG	Fine	VF
74	(1849)	1849 JB	12.50	22.50	40.00	67.50
		1850 JB	15.00	27.50	45.00	75.00

2 REALES

6.5000 g, .750 SILVER, .1567 oz ASW
c/m: Type VI on Central American Republic 2 Reales, KM#24.

77	(1849)	1849 JB	5.50	11.00	18.50	32.50

4 REALES

NOTE: Half dollar size coins with Type VI c/m are modern fabrications. Refer to listings in UNUSUAL WORLD COINS, 2nd edition, Krause Publications 1988.

8 REALES

NOTE: Crown size coins with Type VI c/m are modern fabrications. Refer to listings in UNUSUAL WORLD COINS, 2nd edition, Krause Publications, 1988.

1/2 ESCUDO

1.7000 g, .875 GOLD, .0478 oz AGW
Mint mark: CR
c/m: Type VI on Central American Republic 1/2 Escudo, KM#13.

KM#	Date	Year	VG	Fine	VF	XF
80	(1857)	1828 F	50.00	100.00	150.00	225.00
		1843 M	50.00	100.00	150.00	225.00
		1846 JB	35.00	60.00	100.00	175.00
		1847 JB	35.00	60.00	100.00	175.00
		1848 JB	40.00	80.00	125.00	200.00
		1849 JB	50.00	100.00	150.00	225.00

Mint mark: NG
c/m: Type VI on Central American Republic 1/2 Escudo, KM#5.

81	(1857)	1825 M	—	—	—	—

ESCUDO

3.3000 g, .875 GOLD, .0928 oz AGW
Mint mark: CR
c/m: Type VI on Central American Republic 1 Escudo, KM#14.

84	(1857)	1833 E	90.00	175.00	275.00	375.00
		1833 F	90.00	175.00	275.00	375.00
		1844 M	55.00	125.00	225.00	325.00
		1845 JB	90.00	175.00	275.00	375.00
		1846 JB	65.00	125.00	225.00	325.00
		1847 JB	65.00	125.00	225.00	325.00
		1848 JB	65.00	125.00	225.00	325.00
		1849 JB	65.00	125.00	225.00	325.00

English Series
REAL

.925 SILVER
c/m: Type VI on Great Britain 6 Pence, KM#665.

KM#	Date	Year	Good	VG	Fine	VF
87	(1857)	1816-20	6.00	10.00	20.00	35.00

c/m: Type VI on Great Britain 6 Pence, KM#698.

88	(1857)	1826-29	7.50	16.50	30.00	50.00

c/m: Type VI on Great Britain 6 Pence, KM#712.

89	(1857)	1831,34-37	7.50	15.00	27.50	45.00

c/m: Type VI on Great Britain 6 Pence, KM#733.

90	(1857)	1838-46,48-49	5.50	10.00	20.00	35.00

2 REALES

5.6552 g, .925 SILVER, .1682 oz ASW
c/m: Type VI on Great Britain Shilling, KM#666.

KM#	Date	Year	Good	VG	Fine	VF
93	(1857)	1816-20	7.50	12.50	22.50	40.00

c/m: Type VI on Great Britain Shilling, KM#734.

94	(1857)	1838-46,49	6.50	12.00	20.00	35.00

PESO SERIES
1/16 PESO

1.4600 g, .903 SILVER, .0423 oz ASW

KM#	Date	Mintage	VG	Fine	VF	XF
101	1850 JB	—	10.00	17.50	35.00	65.00
	1855/0 JB	—	12.50	25.00	40.00	75.00
	1855 JB	—	8.00	15.00	30.00	60.00
	1862 JB	—			Rare	
	1862 GW	—	25.00	45.00	75.00	150.00

1/8 PESO

2.9500 g, .903 SILVER, .0856 oz ASW

102	1850 JB	—	6.00	12.50	20.00	45.00
	1853 JB	—	9.00	15.00	32.50	55.00
	1855 JB	—	6.00	12.50	20.00	45.00

1/4 PESO

6.4000 g, .903 SILVER, .1858 oz ASW

103	1850 JB	—	5.50	11.00	25.00	55.00
	1853 JB	—	9.00	18.00	35.00	65.00
	1855 JB	—	11.00	24.00	45.00	70.00

DECIMAL COINAGE
100 Centavos = 1 Peso (1864-1896)
1/4 CENTAVO

COPPER-NICKEL

108	ND(1865)	.020	30.00	55.00	90.00	150.00

CENTAVO

COPPER-NICKEL

109	1865	.033	4.00	10.00	22.50	37.50
	1866	.039	5.00	12.50	25.00	45.00
	1867	.044	8.50	20.00	37.50	70.00
	1868	.020	3.00	7.50	12.00	20.00

KM#	Date	Mintage	VG	Fine	VF	XF
120	1874	.031	1.50	3.25	5.50	10.00

5 CENTAVOS

1.2680 g, .750 SILVER, .0305 oz ASW

110	1865 GW	.233	2.50	6.00	15.00	30.00
	1869 GW	—	4.00	10.00	25.00	60.00
	1870 GW	.027	12.00	25.00	55.00	100.00
	1871 GW	—	6.00	15.00	40.00	75.00
	1872 GW	.328	7.00	16.50	45.00	90.00
	1875/1 GW	—	2.25	5.50	13.50	27.50
	1875 GW	—	2.00	5.00	12.00	25.00

KM#	Date	Mintage	Fine	VF	XF	Unc
125	1885 GW	.180	1.75	3.50	8.00	20.00
	1886/5 GW	.251	2.25	4.50	10.00	27.50
	1887 GW	.491	1.50	3.00	7.00	18.00

Mint mark: HEATON BIRMM

128	1889	.520	1.00	2.00	4.00	15.00
	1889	—	—	Proof		150.00
	1890	.431	1.00	2.00	4.00	15.00
	1892	.280	1.25	2.25	4.50	17.50

10 CENTAVOS

2.5360 g, .750 SILVER, .0611 oz ASW

KM#	Date	Mintage	VG	Fine	VF	XF
111	1865 GW	.185	3.50	8.00	17.50	35.00
	1868 GW	.010	50.00	95.00	175.00	—
	1870 GW	.048	15.00	30.00	55.00	100.00
	1872 GW	.018	45.00	85.00	150.00	—

121	1875 GW	.286	2.50	5.00	10.00	22.50

2.5000 g, .750 SILVER, .0602 oz ASW

KM#	Date	Mintage	Fine	VF	XF	Unc
126	1886 GW	.120	2.50	5.50	12.00	35.00
	1887 GW	.245	2.00	4.50	10.00	27.50

Mint mark: HEATON BIRMM

129	1889	.260	1.25	2.50	5.00	16.00
	1889	—	—	Proof		200.00
	1890	.215	1.25	3.00	6.00	18.00
	1892	.140	1.75	3.50	7.00	20.00

25 CENTAVOS

6.2500 g, .750 SILVER, .1507 oz ASW

KM#	Date	Mintage	VG	Fine	VF	XF
105	1864 GW	.223	6.00	17.50	55.00	130.00

106	1864 GW	I.A.	10.00	25.00	85.00	200.00
	1865 GW	.042	5.00	12.50	25.00	75.00
	1875 GW	.121	3.50	7.50	18.00	55.00

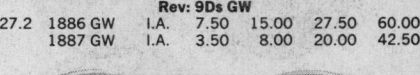

Rev: GW 9Ds

KM#	Date	Mintage	Fine	VF	XF	Unc
127.1	1886 GW	.100	5.00	9.00	17.50	40.00
	1887 GW	.200	6.50	12.50	22.50	50.00

Rev: 9Ds GW

127.2	1886 GW	I.A.	7.50	15.00	27.50	60.00
	1887 GW	I.A.	3.50	8.00	20.00	42.50

Mint mark: HEATON BIRMM.

130	1889/8	.410	2.50	6.50	12.50	32.50
	1889/99	I.A.	2.50	6.50	12.50	32.50
	1889	Inc. Ab.	2.00	4.50	10.00	27.50
	1889	—	—	Proof		250.00
	1890/80	.395	2.25	5.50	12.50	32.50
	1890	Inc. Ab.	2.00	4.50	10.00	27.50
	1892	.440	2.00	4.50	10.00	27.50
	1893	.670	1.50	3.50	7.00	25.00

50 CENTAVOS

12.5000 g, .750 SILVER, .3014 oz ASW

KM#	Date	Mintage	VG	Fine	VF	XF
112	1865 GW	.029	8.00	20.00	55.00	130.00
	1866/5 GW	.117	8.00	20.00	60.00	140.00
	1866 GW	I.A.	10.00	25.00	70.00	160.00
	1867 GW	.005	40.00	100.00	275.00	450.00
	1870 GW	.006	55.00	100.00	275.00	450.00
	1872 GW	I.A.	55.00	100.00	275.00	450.00
	1875 GW	.069	7.00	17.50	50.00	120.00

COSTA RICA 434

KM#	Date	Mintage	Fine	VF	XF	Unc
124.1	1880 GW	.389	6.00	14.00	22.50	75.00
	1885 GW	.152	6.50	15.00	25.00	80.00
	1886 GW	.097	7.00	17.50	30.00	85.00
	1887 GW	.208	7.00	17.50	30.00	85.00
	1889 GW*	.205	— Reported, not confirmed			
	1890/80 GW					
		.058	5.50	12.50	20.00	67.50
	1890	Inc. Ab.	5.50	12.50	20.00	67.50

*NOTE: Not released for circulation.

PESO

1.5253 g, .875 GOLD, .0429 oz AGW

KM#	Date	Mintage	VG	Fine	VF	XF
107	1864 GW	6,383	40.00	75.00	125.00	150.00
	1866 GW	.035	30.00	60.00	90.00	125.00
	1868 GW	—	55.00	90.00	150.00	175.00

NOTE: Several varieties exist dated 1866.

Design modified

| 116 | 1871 GW | .011 | 30.00 | 60.00 | 90.00 | 125.00 |
| | 1872 GW | .037 | 30.00 | 60.00 | 90.00 | 125.00 |

2 PESOS

2.9355 g, .875 GOLD, .0825 oz AGW

113	1866 GW	.013	50.00	85.00	125.00	200.00
	1867 GW	—	65.00	125.00	175.00	250.00
	1868 GW	—	50.00	85.00	125.00	200.00

Design modified (19mm)

| 122 | 1876 GW | 2,161 | | | | Rare |

5 PESOS

7.3387 g, .875 GOLD, 22mm, .2064 oz AGW

114	1867 GW	.039	110.00	130.00	175.00	250.00
	1868 GW	6,752	110.00	130.00	175.00	250.00
	1869 GW	.011	110.00	130.00	175.00	250.00
	1870 GW	.015	110.00	130.00	175.00	250.00

21mm

| 117 | 1873 GW | 5,167 | 200.00 | 375.00 | 700.00 | 1000. |
| | 1875 GW | I.A. | 200.00 | 375.00 | 700.00 | 1000. |

8.0645 g, .900 GOLD, .2333 oz AGW

KM#	Date	Mintage	VG	Fine	VF	XF
118	1873 GW	I.A.	1750.	2250.	2750.	3250.

10 PESOS

14.6774 g, .875 GOLD, .4129 oz AGW

115	1870 GW	.020	225.00	275.00	350.00	500.00
	1871 GW	.030	250.00	325.00	400.00	600.00
	1872 GW	4,555	250.00	350.00	425.00	650.00

| 123 | 1876 GW | 3,389 | 500.00 | 1000. | 1500. | 2000. |

20 PESOS

32.2580 g, .900 GOLD, .9334 oz AGW

KM#	Date	Mintage	Fine	VF	XF	Unc
119	1873 GW	*	—	—	Rare	

*NOTE: Stack's Hammel sale 9-82 AU realized $16,000., Pacific Coast Auction Galleries, Long Beach sale 6-86 AU realized $17,000.

COUNTERSTAMPED COINAGE
1889

Type VII
Obv. c/s: COSTA RICA above national arms.
Rev: HABILITADA POR EL GOBIERNO around lion/CR in 7mm circle.

50 CENTAVOS

12.6804 g, .835 SILVER, .3275 oz ASW
c/s: Type VII on Colombia (Bogota) 50 Centavos, KM#172.1.

KM#	Date	Year	Good	VG	Fine	VF
133	(1889)	1872	20.00	35.00	75.00	100.00
		1873	15.00	25.00	50.00	75.00
		1874	12.00	20.00	40.00	60.00

c/s: Type VII on Colombia (Bogota) Cincuenta Centavos, KM#177.1.

KM#	Date	Year	Good	VG	Fine	VF
134	(1889)	1874	17.50	30.00	45.00	65.00
		1875	17.50	30.00	45.00	65.00
		1876	17.50	30.00	45.00	65.00
		1877	17.50	30.00	45.00	65.00
		1878	17.50	30.00	45.00	65.00
		1879	15.00	25.00	40.00	60.00
		1880	15.00	25.00	40.00	60.00
		1881	15.00	25.00	40.00	60.00
		1882	15.00	25.00	40.00	60.00
		1883	15.00	25.00	40.00	60.00
		1884	15.00	25.00	40.00	60.00
		1885	30.00	50.00	80.00	125.00

c/s: Type VII on Colombia (Medellin) Cinco Decimos, KM#161.1.

135	(1889)	1874	20.00	35.00	50.00	75.00
		1875	20.00	35.00	50.00	75.00
		1876	20.00	35.00	50.00	75.00
		1877	20.00	35.00	50.00	75.00
		1878	20.00	35.00	50.00	75.00
		1879	20.00	35.00	50.00	75.00
		1880	20.00	35.00	50.00	75.00
		1881	17.50	30.00	45.00	65.00
		1882	17.50	30.00	45.00	65.00
		1883	17.50	30.00	45.00	65.00
		1884	15.00	25.00	40.00	60.00
		1885	15.00	25.00	40.00	60.00
		1886	45.00	75.00	100.00	145.00

c/s: Type VII on Colombia (Bogota) Cinco Decimos, KM#153.1.

| 136 | (1889) | 1868 | 37.50 | 75.00 | 150.00 | 300.00 |
| | | 1870 | 25.00 | 50.00 | 100.00 | 200.00 |

MONETARY REFORM
100 Centimos = 1 Colon

2 CENTIMOS

COPPER-NICKEL

KM#	Date	Mintage	Fine	VF	XF	Unc
144	1903	.360	.50	1.00	2.75	5.00

5 CENTIMOS

1.0000 g, .900 SILVER, .0289 oz ASW

145	1905	.500	BV	.75	2.00	8.00
	1910	.400	BV	.75	2.00	9.00
	1912	.540	BV	.75	1.50	5.00
	1914	.510	BV	.75	1.50	5.50

COSTA RICA 435

10 CENTIMOS

2.0000 g, .900 SILVER, .0578 oz ASW

KM#	Date	Mintage	Fine	VF	XF	Unc
146	1905	.400	BV	1.00	3.00	10.00
	1910	.400	BV	1.00	3.00	10.00
	1912	.270	BV	1.00	3.00	10.00
	1914	.150	BV	1.25	3.50	12.00

50 CENTIMOS

10.0000 g, .900 SILVER, .2893 oz ASW

143	1902CY	.120	16.50	27.50	45.00	90.00
	1903JCV	.380	12.00	20.00	35.00	70.00
	1914GCR	.200	300.00	500.00	850.00	1200.

NOTE: Most specimens were counterstamped UN COLON/1923.See KM#165.

DOS (2) COLONES

1.5560 g, .900 GOLD, .0450 oz AGW

139	1897	500 pcs.	—	—	Proof	750.00
	1900	.045	30.00	35.00	45.00	55.00
	1915	5,000	40.00	60.00	75.00	90.00
	1916	5,000	40.00	60.00	75.00	90.00
	1921	3,000	50.00	75.00	95.00	125.00
	1922	.013	30.00	40.00	60.00	75.00
	1926	.015	30.00	40.00	60.00	75.00
	1928	.025	30.00	40.00	60.00	75.00

CINCO (5) COLONES

3.8900 g, .900 GOLD, .1125 oz AGW

142	1899	.100	BV	60.00	75.00	115.00
	1900	.100	BV	60.00	75.00	115.00

DIEZ (10) COLONES

7.7800 g, .900 GOLD, .2251 oz AGW

140	1897	.060	BV	115.00	125.00	175.00
	1899	.050	BV	115.00	125.00	175.00
	1900	.140	BV	115.00	125.00	175.00

VEINTE (20) COLONES

15.5600 g, .900 GOLD, .4502 oz AGW

141	1897	.020	BV	225.00	300.00	400.00
	1899	.025	BV	225.00	300.00	400.00
	1900	5,000	BV	250.00	375.00	675.00

MONETARY REFORM

100 Centavos = 1 Colon

5 CENTAVOS

BRASS

KM#	Date	Mintage	Fine	VF	XF	Unc
147	1917	.400	2.50	5.00	12.00	35.00
	1918	1.000	1.50	4.00	10.00	30.00
	1919	.500	2.50	5.00	12.00	35.00

10 CENTAVOS

2.0000 g, .500 SILVER, .0321 oz ASW

148	1917	.100	.75	1.50	3.25	8.00

BRASS
Rev: GCR at lower right.

149.1	1917	.500	2.00	4.50	10.00	35.00

Rev: GCR at bottom center.

149.2	1917	Inc. Ab.	2.00	4.50	10.00	35.00
	1918	.900	1.50	3.50	8.00	30.00
	1919	.250	2.00	4.50	10.00	35.00

50 CENTAVOS

10.0000 g, .500 SILVER, .1607 oz ASW

150	1917GCR	9,400	—	—	800.00	1000.
	1918GCR	.030	—	—	—	—

NOTE: All but 10 examples of the 1917 issue and the complete 1918 mintage were counterstamped UN COLON/1923. See KM#165.

MONETARY REFORM

100 Centimos = 1 Colon

5 CENTIMOS

BRASS

151	1920	.500	1.75	3.50	7.50	20.00
	1921	.500	1.75	3.50	7.50	20.00
	1922	.500	2.00	4.00	8.50	22.50
	1936	1.500	.40	.75	1.50	7.00
	1938	1.000	.50	1.00	2.00	8.50
	1940	1.300	.40	.75	1.50	7.00
	1941	1.000	.40	.85	2.00	8.50

BRONZE

169	1929	1.500	.75	1.50	4.50	12.50

COPPER-NICKEL

178	1942	.270	.50	1.00	2.00	4.50

NOTE: Struck over 2 Centimos, KM#144.

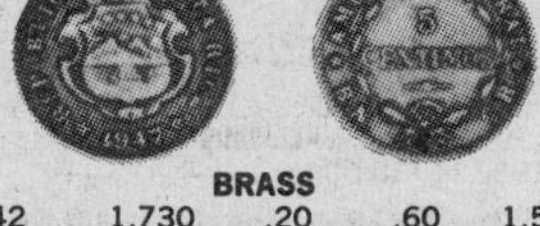

BRASS

179	1942	1.730	.20	.60	1.50	4.50
	1943	1.000	.20	.60	1.50	4.50
	1946	1.000	.35	.90	2.00	5.50
	1947	3.000	.15	.45	1.00	3.50

COPPER-NICKEL
Rev: Large lettering B.C. - C.R. divided.

KM#	Date	Mintage	Fine	VF	XF	Unc
184.1	1951	3.000	.30	.65	1.25	3.00

Obv: Small ships, 5 stars in shield.
Rev: Small lettering B.C.C.R. not divided.

184.2	1951	7.000	.10	.15	.40	1.00

STAINLESS-STEEL

184.2a	1953	9.040	—	—	.10	.25
	1958	19.940	—	—	.10	.15
	1967	6.020	—	—	.10	.20

COPPER-NICKEL
Obv: Small ships, 7 stars in shield.

184.3	1969	20.000	—	—	.10	.15
	1978	—	—	—	—	—

NOTE: Varieties exist.

Obv: Large ships, 7 stars in shield.

184.4	1972	12.550	—	—	.10	.15
	1973	20.000	—	—	.10	.15
	1976	33.270	—	—	.10	.15
	1977	30.000	—	—	.10	.15
	1978	7.520	—	—	.10	.15

NOTE: Dies vary for each date.

BRASS

184.4a	1979	3.060	—	—	.10	.15

10 CENTIMOS

BRASS

152	1920	.850	1.25	2.50	5.00	15.00
	1921	.750	1.25	2.50	5.00	15.00
	1922	.750	1.25	2.50	5.00	15.00

BRONZE

170	1929	.500	1.00	2.25	5.00	17.50

BRASS

174	1936	.750	.35	.75	1.50	10.00
	1941	.500	.35	.75	1.50	10.00

COSTA RICA 436

KM#	Date	Mintage	Fine	VF	XF	Unc
180	1942	1.000	.25	.50	1.25	6.00
	1943	.500	.30	.65	1.75	7.50
	1946	.500	.30	.65	1.75	7.50
	1947	1.500	.20	.40	1.00	5.00

COPPER-NICKEL
Obv: Small ships, 5 stars in shield.

| 185.1 | 1951 | 2.500 | .10 | .20 | .70 | 1.25 |

STAINLESS-STEEL

185.1a	1953	5.290	—	—	.10	.75
	1958	10.470	—	—	.10	.25
	1967	5.500	—	—	.10	.25
	1979	20.000	—	—	.10	.20

COPPER-NICKEL
Obv: Small ships, 7 stars in field.

185.2	1969	10.000	—	—	.10	.15
	1975	5.000	—	—	.10	.15
	1976	40.000	—	—	.10	.15

NOTE: Dies vary for each date.

STAINLESS STEEL

| 185.2b | 1979 | 10.000 | — | — | .10 | .15 |

Obv: Large ships, 7 stars in field.

185.3	1972	20.000	—	—	.10	.15
	1975	Inc. Ab.	—	—	.10	.15
	1976	Inc. Ab.	—	—	.10	.15

STAINLESS STEEL

| 185.3a | 1979 | Inc. Ab. | — | — | .10 | .15 |

ALUMINUM
Obv: Small ships, 7 stars in field.

| 185.2a | 1982 | 40.000 | — | — | .10 | .15 |

25 CENTIMOS

3.4500 g, .650 SILVER, .0721 oz ASW

| 168 | 1924 | 1.340 | 1.25 | 2.25 | 4.50 | 16.00 |

COPPER-NICKEL

| 171 | 1935 | 1.200 | .25 | .75 | 2.00 | 12.00 |

KM#	Date	Mintage	Fine	VF	XF	Unc
175	1937	1.600	.25	.75	1.75	8.00
	1937	—	—	—	Proof	100.00
	1948	9.200	.10	.20	.40	1.25
	1948	—	—	—	Proof	—

BRASS

181	1944	.800	.60	1.25	3.00	15.00
	1945	1.200	.50	1.00	2.50	12.00
	1946	1.200	.50	1.00	2.50	9.50

BRONZE

| 181a | 1945 | Inc. Ab. | 1.00 | 2.00 | 4.00 | 20.00 |

COPPER-NICKEL
Obv: Small ships, 7 stars in shield.

188.1	1967	4.000	—	—	.10	.50
	1969	4.000	—	—	.10	.50
	1970	—	—	—	.10	.30
	1974	—	—	—	.10	.30
	1976	—	—	—	.10	.30
	1978	—	—	—	.10	.30

NOTE: Dies vary for each date.

Obv: Large ships, 7 stars in shield.

188.2	1972	8.000	—	—	.10	.20
	1974	—	—	—	.10	.20
	1976	12.000	—	—	.10	.20
	1977	12.000	—	—	.10	.20
	1978	—	—	—	.10	.20

STAINLESS STEEL

| 188.2a | 1980 | 30.000 | — | — | .10 | .20 |

ALUMINUM

| 188.2b | 1982 | 30.000 | — | — | .10 | .20 |

Reeded edge. Reduced size, 17mm.

| 188.3 | 1983 | — | — | — | .10 | .20 |
| | 1986 | — | — | — | .10 | .20 |

NOTE: Dies vary for each date.

50 CENTIMOS

COPPER-NICKEL

KM#	Date	Mintage	Fine	VF	XF	Unc
172	1935	.700	.50	1.25	4.00	22.50

| 176 | 1937 | .600 | .30 | 1.00 | 3.00 | 14.00 |
| | 1937 | — | — | — | Proof | 125.00 |

| 182 | 1948 | 4.000 | .15 | .25 | .50 | 2.00 |
| | 1948 | — | — | — | Proof | — |

Obv: Small ships, 7 stars in shield.

189.1	1965	1.000	—	.10	.25	1.00
	1968	2.000	—	.10	.15	.50
	1970	4.000	—	.10	.15	.30
	1978	—	—	.10	.15	.30

NOTE: Dies vary for each date.

Obv: Large ships, 7 stars in shield.

189.2	1972	4.000	—	.10	.15	.30
	1975 lg.dt.	.524	—	.10	.15	.30
	1975 sm.dt.	I.A.	—	.10	.15	.30
	1976	6.000	—	.10	.15	.30
	1977	6.000	—	.10	.15	.30

STAINLESS STEEL

209	1982	12.000	—	—	.10	.20
	1983	—	—	—	.10	.20
	1984	—	—	—	.10	.20

COSTA RICA 437

UN (1) COLON

COPPER-NICKEL

KM#	Date	Mintage	Fine	VF	XF	Unc
173	1935	.350	.75	2.00	6.50	35.00

177	1937	.300	.50	1.25	4.50	20.00
	1937	—	—	Proof		150.00
	1948	1.350	.20	.40	.75	2.00
	1948	—	—	Proof	—	—

STAINLESS-STEEL

186.1	1954	.990	.20	.35	1.00	7.50

COPPER-NICKEL
Obv: Small ships, 5 stars in shield.

186.1a	1961	1.000	.10	.20	.50	2.00

Obv: Small ships, 7 stars in shield.

186.2	1965	1.000	.10	.20	.35	1.00
	1968	2.000	.10	.20	.25	.50
	1970	2.000	.10	.20	.25	.50
	1974	—	.10	.20	.25	.50
	1976	—	.10	.20	.25	.50
	1977	—	.10	.20	.25	.50
	1978	—	—	—	—	—

NOTE: Dies vary for each date.

Obv: Large ships, 7 stars in shield.

186.3	1972	2.000	.10	.20	.25	.50
	1975	1.028	.10	.20	.25	.50
	1976	12.000	.10	.20	.25	.50
	1977	22.000	.10	.20	.25	.50
	1978	—	.10	.20	.25	.50

STAINLESS STEEL

KM#	Date	Mintage	Fine	VF	XF	Unc
210	1982	12.000	—	—	.10	.25
	1983	—	—	—	.10	.25
	1984	—	—	—	.10	.25

NOTE: Varieties exist.

2 COLONES

COPPER-NICKEL

183	1948	1.380	.50	.75	1.25	3.00
	1948	—	—	Proof	—	—

STAINLESS-STEEL
Obv: Small ships, 5 stars in shield.

187.1	1954	1.030	.25	.50	2.00	10.00

COPPER-NICKEL

187.1a	1961	—	.15	.30	.50	1.25

Obv: Large ships, 7 stars in shield.

187.2	1961	1.000	.15	.30	.50	1.00

Obv: Small ships, 7 stars in shield.

187.3	1968	2.000	.15	.30	.40	.75
	1970	1.000	.15	.30	.50	.90
	1972	2.000	.15	.30	.40	.75
	1978	—	.15	.30	.40	.75

NOTE: Dies vary for each date.

4.3000 g, .999 SILVER, .1381 oz ASW
20th Anniversary of the Central Bank

190	1970	5,157	—	—	Proof	7.50

STAINLESS STEEL

211	1982	12.000	—	—	—	.50
	1983	—	—	—	.10	.50

5 COLONES

10.7800 g, .999 SILVER, .3463 oz ASW
400th Year of the Founding of New Carthage

KM#	Date	Mintage	Fine	VF	XF	Unc
191	1970	5,157	—	—	Proof	12.50

NICKEL
25th Anniversary of the Central Bank

203	1975	2.000	—	—	.15	.35	1.25
	1975	5,000	—	—	Proof		2.00

STAINLESS STEEL

214	1983	—	—	.10	.15	.50
	1985	—	—	—	.15	.50

10 COLONES

21.7000 g, .999 SILVER, .6976 oz ASW
Obv: Similar to 5 Colones, KM#191.

192	1970	5,157	—	—	Proof	20.00

NICKEL
25th Anniversary of the Central Bank

204	1975	.500	.25	.50	1.00	2.00
	1975	5,000	—	—	Proof	4.00

STAINLESS STEEL

215	1983	—	—	.20	.30	1.00
	1985	—	—	—	.30	1.00

COSTA RICA 438

20 COLONES

43.7000 g, .999 SILVER, 1.4050 oz ASW
Obv: Similar to 5 Colones, KM#191.

KM#	Date	Mintage	Fine	VF	XF	Unc
193	1970	7,500	—	—	Proof	40.00

NICKEL
25th Anniversary of the Central Bank

205	1975	.250	.50	1.00	2.00	4.00
	1975	5,000	—	—	Proof	9.00

STAINLESS STEEL

216	1983	—	—	.35	.60	1.50

25 COLONES

53.9000 g, .999 SILVER, 1.7312 oz ASW
25 Years of Social Legislation
Obv: Similar to 5 Colones, KM#191.

194	1970	6,800	—	—	Proof	50.00

50 COLONES

7.4500 g, .900 GOLD, .2155 oz AGW

KM#	Date	Mintage	Fine	VF	XF	Unc
195	1970	3,507	—	—	Proof	175.00

25.5500 g, .500 SILVER, .4107 oz ASW
Conservation Series
Rev: Green Turtle.

200	1974	7,599	—	—	—	17.50

28.2800 g, .925 SILVER, .8411 oz ASW

200a	1974	.011	—	—	Proof	20.00

100 COLONES

14.9000 g, .900 GOLD, .4311 oz AGW

196	1970	3,507	—	—	Proof	300.00

32.1000 g, .500 SILVER, .5160 oz ASW
Conservation Series
Obv: Similar to 1500 Colones, KM#202.
Rev: Manatee.

201	1974	7,599	—	—	—	22.50

35.0000 g, .925 SILVER, 1.0409 oz ASW

201a	1974	.011	—	—	Proof	25.00

International Year of the Child

206	1979	9,500	—	—	—	12.50
	1979	5,000	—	—	Proof	20.00

200 COLONES

NICKEL
Dr. Oscar Arias

KM#	Date	Mintage	Fine	VF	XF	Unc
224	1987	—	—	—	—	7.50

200 COLONES

29.8000 g, .900 GOLD, .8623 oz AGW
Obv: Similar to 100 Colones, KM#196.

197	1970	3,507	—	—	Proof	600.00

250 COLONES

30.3300 g, .925 SILVER, .9020 oz ASW

212	1982FM(P)					
		1,109	—	—	Proof	30.00

217	1983FM(P)					
		393 pcs.	—	—	Proof	60.00

300 COLONES

10.9700 g, .925 SILVER, .3262 oz ASW
125th Anniversary of Juan Santamaria

207	1981	.010	—	—	Proof	10.00

200th Anniversary of Founding of Alajuela

223	1981	—	—	—	Proof	10.00

500 COLONES

74.5200 g, .900 GOLD, 2.1565 oz AGW
Obv: Similar to 100 Colones, KM#196.

KM#	Date	Mintage	Fine	VF	XF	Unc
198	1970	3,507	—	—	Proof	1300.

1000 COLONES

194.0400 g, .900 GOLD, 5.6153 oz AGW
Obv: Similar to 100 Colones, KM#196.

| 199 | 1970 | 3,507 | — | — | Proof | 3250. |

10.9700 g, .925 SILVER, .3272 oz ASW
Dr. Oscar Arias

| 225 | 1987 | — | — | — | — | 30.00 |

1500 COLONES

33.4370 g, .900 GOLD, .9676 oz AGW
Conservation Series
Rev: Giant Anteater.

| 202 | 1974 | 2,418 | — | — | — | 500.00 |
| | 1974 | 726 pcs. | — | — | Proof | 750.00 |

6.9800 g, .500 GOLD, .1122 oz AGW

KM#	Date	Mintage	Fine	VF	XF	Unc
213	1982FM(P) 724 pcs.	—	—	Proof	150.00

| 218 | 1983FM(P) | — | — | — | Proof | 250.00 |

5000 COLONES

15.0000 g, .900 GOLD, .4341 oz AGW
125th Anniversary of Juan Santamaria

| 208 | 1981 | — | — | — | — | 250.00 |
| | 1981 | 2,000 | — | — | Proof | 300.00 |

COUNTERSTAMPED COINAGE
50 CENTIMOS
1923

Type VIII
Obv. c/s: 1923 in 11mm circle.
Rev. c/s: 50 CENTIMOS in 11mm circle.

6.2500 g, .900 SILVER, .1808 oz ASW
c/s: Type VIII on 25 Centavos, KM#105.

KM#	Date	Year	VG	Fine	VF	XF
155	1923	1864 GW	—	—	Rare	—

c/s: Type VIII on 25 Centavos, KM#106.

156	1923	1864 GW	—	—	Rare	—
		1865 GW	15.00	25.00	50.00	100.00
		1875 GW	15.00	25.00	50.00	100.00

c/s: Type VIII on 25 Centavos, KM#127.1.
Rev: GW 9Ds

| 157 | 1923 | 1886 GW | 3.00 | 5.00 | 8.00 | 12.00 |
| | | 1887 GW | 3.00 | 5.00 | 8.00 | 12.00 |

c/s: Type VIII on 25 Centavos, KM#127.2.
Rev: 9Ds GW

| 158 | 1923 | 1886 GW | 4.00 | 7.00 | 12.00 | 20.00 |
| | | 1887 GW | 3.00 | 5.00 | 8.00 | 12.00 |

c/s: Type VIII on 25 Centavos, KM#130.

159	1923	1889	1.50	2.75	5.00	8.50
		1890/80	2.50	3.75	7.00	10.00
		1890	1.50	2.75	5.00	8.50
		1892	1.50	2.75	5.00	8.50
		1893	1.25	2.50	4.50	7.50

NOTE: The entire mintage of 1,866,000 was created by counterstamping the above coins.

UN (1) COLON
1923

Type IX
Obv. c/s: 1923 in 14mm circle.
Rev. c/s: UN COLON in 14mm circle.

12.5000 g, .900 SILVER, .3617 oz ASW
c/s: Type IX on 50 Centavos, KM#112.

162	1923	1865 GW	15.00	25.00	35.00	100.00
		1866/5GW	17.50	30.00	40.00	120.00
		1867 GW	—	—	Rare	—
		1870 GW	—	—	Rare	—
		1872 GW	—	—	Rare	—
		1875 GW	15.00	25.00	35.00	100.00

c/s: Type IX on 50 Centavos, KM#124.

163	1923	1880 GW	3.00	6.00	9.00	14.50
		1885 GW	3.00	6.00	9.00	14.50
		1886 GW	4.00	8.00	12.00	18.00
		1887 GW	3.50	7.00	10.00	16.00
		1890 GW	4.00	8.00	11.00	17.00

c/s: Type IX on 50 Centimos, KM#143.

KM#	Date	Year	VG	Fine	VF	XF
164	1923	1902 CY	3.75	6.00	8.50	14.00
		1903 JCV	3.00	5.00	7.00	11.00
		1914 GCR	3.75	6.00	8.50	14.00

10.000 g, .500 SILVER, .1607 oz ASW
c/s: Type IX on 50 Centimos, KM#150.

| 165 | 1923 | 1917GCR | 4.50 | 8.00 | 12.00 | 17.50 |
| | | 1918GCR | 5.50 | 10.00 | 15.00 | 22.50 |

NOTE: A total of 9,390 of 50 Centimos, KM#150 dated 1917 and 29,800 dated 1918 were counterstamped. The entire mintage of 460,000 was created by counterstamping the above coins.

MINT SETS (MS)

KM#	Date	Mintage	Identification	Issue Price	Mkt. Val.
MS1	1975(3)	—	KM203-205	—	7.50

PROOF SETS (PS)

PS1	1889(4)	—	KM128-130,KM-Pn3	—	—
PS2	1937(3)	—	KM175-177	—	375.00
PS3	1970(10)	570	KM190-199	—	5780.
PS4	1970(5)	4,650	KM190-194	52.00	130.00
PS5	1970(5)	3,000	KM195-199	832.00	5650.
PS6	1974(2)	30,000	KM200a-201a	50.00	45.00
PS7	1975(3)	—	KM203-205	—	15.00
PS8	1976(5)	5,000	KM184.2a,185.1a,186.2,188.2, 189.2	—	6.00

Listings For
CRETE: refer to Greece
CROATIA: refer to Yugoslavia

CUBA

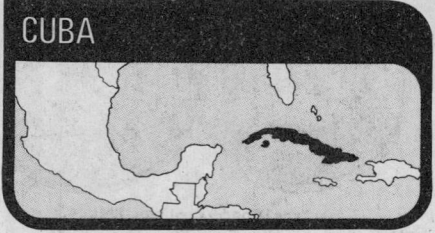

The Republic of Cuba, situated at the northern edge of the Caribbean Sea about 90 miles (145 km.) south of Florida, has an area of 44,218 sq. mi. (114,524 sq. km.) and a population of 10 million. Capital: Havana. The Cuban economy is based on the cultivation and refining of sugar, which provides 80 percent of export earnings.

Discovered by Columbus in 1492 and settled by Diego Velasquez in the early 1500s, Cuba remained a Spanish possession until 1898, except for a brief British occupancy of Havana in 1762-63. Cuban attempts to gain freedom were crushed, even while Spain was granting independence to its other American possessions. Ten years of warfare, 1868-78, between Spanish troops and Cuban rebels exacted guarantees of rights which were never implemented. The final revolt, begun in 1895, evoked American sympathy, and with the aid of U.S. troops independence was proclaimed on May 20, 1902. Fulgencio Batista seized the government in 1952 and established a dictatorship. Opposition to Batista, led by Fidel Castro, drove him into exile on Jan 1, 1959. A communist-type, 25-member collective leadership headed by Castro was inaugurated in March, 1962.

RULERS
Spanish, until 1898

MONETARY SYSTEM
100 Centavos = 1 Peso

PROVINCE OF TRINIDAD
2 REALES
.903 SILVER
c/m: Lattice on Spanish (Seville) 2 Reales, C#38.

KM#	Date	Good	VG	Fine	VF
1	ND(1772-78)	10.00	20.00	30.00	40.00

c/m: Lattice on Spanish (Madrid) 2 Reales, C#69.
| 2 | ND(1788-1808) | 10.00 | 17.50 | 25.00 | 35.00 |

c/m: Lattice on Spanish (Seville) 2 Reales, C#69.
| 3 | ND(1788-1808) | 10.00 | 17.50 | 25.00 | 35.00 |

c/m: Lattice on Spanish (Catalonia) 2 Reales, C#134.
| 4 | ND(1810-33) | 10.00 | 17.50 | 25.00 | 35.00 |

c/m: Lattice on Spanish (Madrid) 2 Reales, C#134.
| 5 | ND(1810-33) | 10.00 | 17.50 | 25.00 | 35.00 |

c/m: Lattice on Spanish (Seville) 2 Reales, C#134.
| 6 | ND(1810-33) | 10.00 | 17.50 | 25.00 | 35.00 |

c/m: Lattice on Spanish (Madrid) 4 Reales, C#90.
| 7 | ND(1808-13) | 10.00 | 17.50 | 25.00 | 35.00 |

c/m: Lattice on Spanish (Seville) 4 Reales, C#90.
| 8 | ND(1808-13) | 10.00 | 17.50 | 25.00 | 35.00 |

CUBA
KEY COUNTERMARKS
Key countermarks are found in two varieties:

A - Short & thick

B - Long & thin

It is thought that these c/m were used 1872-1877 by the Cuban revolutionary troops as a fund raising device. Most are struck on Mexican coins.

Values for these pieces vary according to the rarity of the date and type of coin on which the c/m is found. Prices listed here are for the most common.

REAL SERIES
2 REALES

.903 SILVER
c/m: Key on Mexican 2 Reales, KM#374.

KM#	Date	Good	VG	Fine	VF
1	ND	12.50	17.50	25.00	35.00

4 REALES

.903 SILVER
c/m: Key on Mexican 4 Reales, KM#375.
| 2 | ND | 15.00 | 22.50 | 27.50 | 37.50 |

8 REALES

.903 SILVER
c/m: Key on Mexican 8 Reales, KM#377.
| 3 | ND(1824-97) | 25.00 | 37.50 | 50.00 | 75.00 |

DECIMAL SERIES
25 CENTAVOS

.903 SILVER
c/m: Key on Mexican 25 Centavos, KM#406.
| 4 | ND(1869-77) | 12.50 | 17.50 | 25.00 | 35.00 |

50 CENTAVOS

.903 SILVER
c/m: Key on Mexican 50 Centavos, KM#407.
| 5 | ND(1869-77) | 15.00 | 20.00 | 30.00 | 40.00 |

PESO

.903 SILVER
c/m: Key on Mexican Peso, KM#388.

KM#	Date	Good	VG	Fine	VF
6	ND(1866-67)	35.00	70.00	115.00	200.00

c/m: Key on Mexican Peso, KM#408.
| 7 | ND(1869-77) | 25.00 | 50.00 | 75.00 | 100.00 |

REPUBLIC
CENTAVO

COPPER-NICKEL

KM#	Date	Mintage	Fine	VF	XF	Unc
9	1915	9.396	.25	1.00	2.00	15.00
	1915	—	—	—	Proof	150.00
	1916	9.318	.25	2.00	3.50	17.50
	1916	—	—	—	Proof	200.00
	1920	19.378	.10	.40	2.50	12.50
	1938	2.000	2.00	4.00	8.00	20.00

BRASS
| 9a | 1943 | 20.000 | .10 | .40 | 1.50 | 4.00 |

COPPER-NICKEL
| 9b | 1946 | 50.000 | — | .10 | .50 | .75 |
| | 1961 | 100.000 | .15 | .25 | .60 | 1.00 |

BRASS
Birth of Jose Marti Centennial
| 26 | 1953 | 50.000 | .10 | .15 | .50 | 1.25 |
| | 1953 | — | — | — | Proof | 7.50 |

COPPER-NICKEL
| 30 | 1958 | 50.000 | — | .10 | .40 | 1.00 |

ALUMINUM
33	1963	200.020	—	.10	.30	.60
	1966	50.000	—	.10	.40	.80
	1969	50.000	—	.10	.40	.80
	1970	50.000	—	.10	.40	.80
	1971	49.960	.20	.40	.80	1.50
	1972	100.000	—	.10	.40	.80
	1978	50.000	—	.10	.40	.80
	1979	100.000	—	.10	.40	.80
	1981	—	—	.10	.40	.80
	1982	—	—	.10	.40	.80
	1985	—	—	.10	.40	.80

2 CENTAVOS

COPPER-NICKEL

KM#	Date	Mintage	Fine	VF	XF	Unc
10	1915	6.090	.25	1.25	2.50	10.00
	1915	—	—	—	Proof	200.00
	1916	5.322	.25	1.25	3.50	12.50
	1916	—	—	—	Proof	250.00

ALUMINUM
Obv: Arms. Rev. leg: PATRIA O MUERTE at top.

104	1983	—	—	—	—	.10
	1985	—	—	—	—	.10

5 CENTAVOS

COPPER-NICKEL

11	1915	5.096	.10	.50	3.00	10.00
	1915	—	—	—	Proof	250.00
	1916	1.714	.25	1.00	5.00	15.00
	1916	—	—	—	Proof	300.00
	1920	10.000	.10	.50	3.00	10.00

BRASS

11a	1943	6.000	1.00	3.50	7.50	25.00

COPPER-NICKEL

11b	1946	40.000	.10	.15	.35	1.50
	1960	20.000	.10	.15	.35	1.00
	1961	70.000	.10	.15	.40	.75

ALUMINUM

34	1963	80.000	—	.10	.25	.75
	1966	50.000	—	.10	.25	.75
	1968	—	—	.10	.25	.75
	1969	—	—	.10	.25	.75
	1971	100.020	—	.10	.25	.75
	1972	100.000	—	.10	.25	.75

10 CENTAVOS

2.5000 g, .900 SILVER, .0723 oz ASW

12	1915	5.690	.75	1.50	4.00	20.00
	1915	—	—	—	Proof	300.00
	1916	.560	2.50	5.50	12.50	45.00
	1916	—	—	—	Proof	400.00
	1920	3.090	.75	1.50	3.00	15.00
	1948	5.120	—	BV	1.50	3.50
	1949	9.880	—	BV	1.50	3.25

50th Year of Republic

23	1952	10.000	—	BV	1.50	3.00

20 CENTAVOS

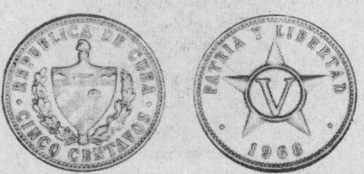

5.0000 g, .900 SILVER, .1446 oz ASW

13	1915	7.915	1.25	2.50	6.00	20.00
	1915	—	—	—	Proof	400.00
	1916	2.535	3.50	5.00	10.00	40.00

KM#	Date	Mintage	Fine	VF	XF	Unc
13	1916	—	—	—	Proof	550.00
	1920	6.130	1.25	2.50	5.00	15.00
	1932	.184	15.00	45.00	135.00	425.00
	1948	6.830	BV	2.00	3.50	7.00
	1949	13.170	BV	1.75	3.00	5.00

50th Year of Republic

24	1952	8.700	BV	1.50	2.50	5.00

COPPER-NICKEL

31	1962	83.860	.35	1.00	1.50	3.50
	1968	25.750	.35	1.00	1.50	3.50

ALUMINUM

35	1969	25.000	.35	1.00	1.50	2.50
	1970	29.560	.35	1.00	1.50	2.50
	1971	25.000	.35	1.00	1.50	2.50
	1972	—	.35	1.00	1.50	2.50

25 CENTAVOS

6.2500 g, .900 SILVER, .1808 oz ASW
Birth of Jose Marti Centennial

27	1953	19.000	—	BV	2.50	6.00
	1953	—	—	—	Proof	Rare

40 CENTAVOS

10.0000 g, .900 SILVER, .2893 oz ASW

14	1915	2.633	3.50	6.50	15.00	90.00
	1915	—	—	—	Proof	650.00
	1916	.188	15.00	35.00	125.00	450.00
	1916	—	—	—	Proof	950.00
	1920	.540	3.00	6.00	12.50	85.00
	1920	—	—	—	Proof	Rare

50th Year of Republic

25	1952	1.250	BV	3.00	6.00	12.50

COPPER-NICKEL

KM#	Date	Mintage	Fine	VF	XF	Unc
32	1962	15.250	2.00	5.00	8.00	10.00

50 CENTAVOS

12.5000 g, .900 SILVER, .3617 oz ASW
Birth of Jose Marti Centennial

28	1953	2.000	—	4.00	6.00	12.50
	1953	—	—	—	Proof	Rare

PESO

26.7295 g, .900 SILVER, .7735 oz ASW

8	1898	1.000	—	—	Proof	3750.

15	1915	1.976	7.50	12.50	22.50	90.00
	1915	—	—	—	Proof	1350.
	1916	.843	10.00	20.00	45.00	225.00
	1916	—	—	—	Proof	1750.
	1932	3.550	7.50	10.00	20.00	75.00
	1933	6.000	7.50	10.00	20.00	65.00
	1934	3.000	7.50	10.00	20.00	70.00

CUBA 442

1.6718 g, .900 GOLD, .0483 oz AGW

KM#	Date	Mintage	Fine	VF	XF	Unc
16	1915	6,850	50.00	100.00	200.00	350.00
	1915	—	—	—	Proof	1750.
	1916	.011	50.00	100.00	200.00	300.00
	1916	—	—	—	Proof	1750.

26.7295 g, .900 SILVER, .7735 oz ASW
'ABC'

22	1934	7.000	12.00	25.00	45.00	100.00
	1935	12.500	12.00	25.00	50.00	125.00
	1936	16.000	12.00	25.00	50.00	125.00
	1937	11.500	150.00	250.00	375.00	1000.
	1938	10.800	12.00	25.00	50.00	125.00
	1939	9.200	12.00	25.00	50.00	125.00

Birth of Jose Marti Centennial

29	1953	1.000	—	—	8.00	15.00
	1953	—	—	—	Proof	Rare

COPPER-NICKEL
Carlos Manuel de Cespedes

186	1977	3,000	—	—	—	4.00

Ignacio Agramonte

KM#	Date	Mintage	Fine	VF	XF	Unc
187	1977	3,000	—	—	—	4.00

Maximo Gomez

| 188 | 1977 | 3,000 | — | — | — | 4.00 |

Antonio Maceo

| 189 | 1977 | 3,000 | — | — | — | 4.00 |

Bolshevic Revolution

| 190 | 1977 | 6,000 | — | — | — | 4.00 |

Nonaligned Nations Conference

| 191 | 1979 | 3,000 | — | — | — | 4.00 |

Cuban Flower - Mariposa

| 46 | 1980 | 7,000 | — | — | — | 4.00 |

Olympics - Athletes in Frames

| 192 | 1980 | 3,000 | — | — | — | 4.00 |

Olympics - 3 Athletic Figures

KM#	Date	Mintage	Fine	VF	XF	Unc
193	1980	3,000	—	—	—	4.00

Soviet - Cuban Space Flight

| 194 | 1980 | 3,000 | — | — | — | 4.00 |

Cuban Flower - Azahar

| 53 | 1981 | 7,000 | — | — | — | 4.00 |

Cuban Flower - Orquidea

| 54 | 1981 | 7,000 | — | — | — | 4.00 |

Cuban Fauna- Crocodile
Obv: Similar to KM#58.

| 55 | 1981 | 5,000 | — | — | — | 4.00 |

Cuban Fauna - Colibri
Obv: Similar to KM#58.

| 56 | 1981 | 5,000 | — | — | — | 4.00 |

Cuban Fauna- Zunzun
Obv: Similar to KM#58.

| 57 | 1981 | 5,000 | — | — | — | 4.00 |

Soccer Games - Spain 1982

58	1981	—	—	—	—	4.00
	1981	.010	—	—	Proof	6.00

Sugar Production

59	1981	—	—	—	—	4.00
	1981	.010	—	—	Proof	6.00

CUBA 443

XIV Central American and Caribbean Games

KM#	Date	Mintage	Fine	VF	XF	Unc
60	1981	—	—	—	—	4.00
	1981	5,000	—	—	Proof	6.00

XIV Central American and Caribbean Games
Obv: Similar to KM#60.

61	1981	—	—	—	—	4.00
	1981	5,000	—	—	Proof	6.00

XIV Central American and Caribbean Games
Obv: Similar to KM#60.

62	1981	—	—	—	—	4.00
	1981	5,000	—	—	Proof	6.00

Cuban Fauna - Tocororo
Obv: Similar to KM#60.

63	1981	5,000	—	—	—	4.00

Cuban Fauna - Almiqui
Obv: Similar to KM#60.

64	1981	5,000	—	—	—	4.00

Cuban Fauna - Manjuari
Obv: Similar to KM#60.

65	1981	5,000	—	—	—	4.00

Columbus' Ship - Nina

KM#	Date	Mintage	Fine	VF	XF	Unc
66	1981	—	—	—	—	4.00

Columbus' Ship - Pinta

67	1981	—	—	—	—	4.00

Columbus' Ship - Santa Maria

68	1981	—	—	—	—	4.00

Ernest Hemingway

88	1982	7,000	—	—	—	4.00

Ernest Hemingway

89	1982	7,000	—	—	—	4.00

Ernest Hemingway

90	1982	7,000	—	—	—	4.00

Miguel De Cervantes

KM#	Date	Mintage	Fine	VF	XF	Unc
91	1982	7,000	—	—	—	4.00

Hidalgo Don Quijote

92	1982	7,000	—	—	—	4.00

Hidalgo Don Quijote

93	1982	7,000	—	—	—	4.00

F.A.O. Issue - Citrus Fruit

94	1982	6,609	—	—	—	4.00

F.A.O. Issue - Cow

95	1982	5,684	—	—	—	4.00

BRASS

105	1983	10,000	.25	.50	1.00	2.00
	1984	—	.25	.50	1.00	2.00
	1987	—	.25	.50	1.00	2.00

COPPER-NICKEL
Railroad
Similar to 5 Pesos, KM#110.

106	1983	7,000	—	—	—	4.00

World Fisheries

107	1983	—	—	—	—	4.00

CUBA 444

1984 Olympics - Runner

KM#	Date	Mintage	Fine	VF	XF	Unc
173	1983	—	—	—	—	6.50

1984 Olympics - Discus Thrower
| 174 | 1983 | — | — | — | — | 6.50 |

1984 Olympics - Judo
| 175 | 1983 | — | — | — | — | 6.50 |

Olympics - Woman Holding Torch
| 195 | 1983 | 3,000 | — | — | — | 4.00 |

Olympics - Hockey
| 196 | 1983 | 3,000 | — | — | — | 4.00 |

Olympics - Downhill Skier
| 197 | 1983 | 3,000 | — | — | — | 4.00 |

Transportation - Freighter
Similar to 5 Pesos, KM#117.
| 116 | 1984 | — | — | — | — | 4.00 |

Santisima Trinidad
Similar to 5 Pesos, KM#119.
| 118 | 1984 | — | — | — | — | 4.00 |

Transportation - Volanta Coach

KM#	Date	Mintage	Fine	VF	XF	Unc
130	1984	—	—	—	—	4.00

Castillos - El Morro La Habana
Similar to 5 Pesos, KM#141.
| 140 | 1984 | — | — | — | — | 4.00 |

Castillos - La Fuerza La Habana
Similar to 5 Pesos, KM#143.
| 142 | 1984 | — | — | — | — | 4.00 |

Castillos - El Morro Stgo. De Cuba
Similar to 5 Pesos, KM#145.
| 144 | 1984 | — | — | — | — | 4.00 |

Transportation - Hot Air Balloon
| 172 | 1984 | 10 pcs. | — | — | — | — |

International Year of Music - Bach
| 120 | 1985 | 2,000 | — | — | — | 4.00 |

Soccer
| 122 | ND(1985) | 5,000 | — | — | — | 4.00 |

Wildlife Preservation - Crocodile
| 124 | 1985 | 5,000 | — | — | — | 4.00 |

Wildlife Preservation - Crocodile (error)
| 181 | 1985 | — | — | — | — | — |

Wildlife Preservation - Iguana

KM#	Date	Mintage	Fine	VF	XF	Unc
126	1985	5,000	—	—	—	4.00

Wildlife Preservation - Iguana (error)
| 182 | 1985 | — | — | — | — | — |

Wildlife Preservation - Parrot
| 128 | 1985 | 5,000 | — | — | — | 4.00 |

Wildlife Preservation - Parrot (error)
| 183 | 1985 | — | — | — | — | — |

40th Anniversary of FAO
| 132 | ND(1985) | — | — | — | — | 4.00 |

F.A.O. - Forestry
| 133 | 1985 | — | — | — | — | 4.00 |

100th Anniversary of Automobile
Similar to 5 Pesos, KM#135.
| 134 | 1986 | — | — | — | — | 4.00 |

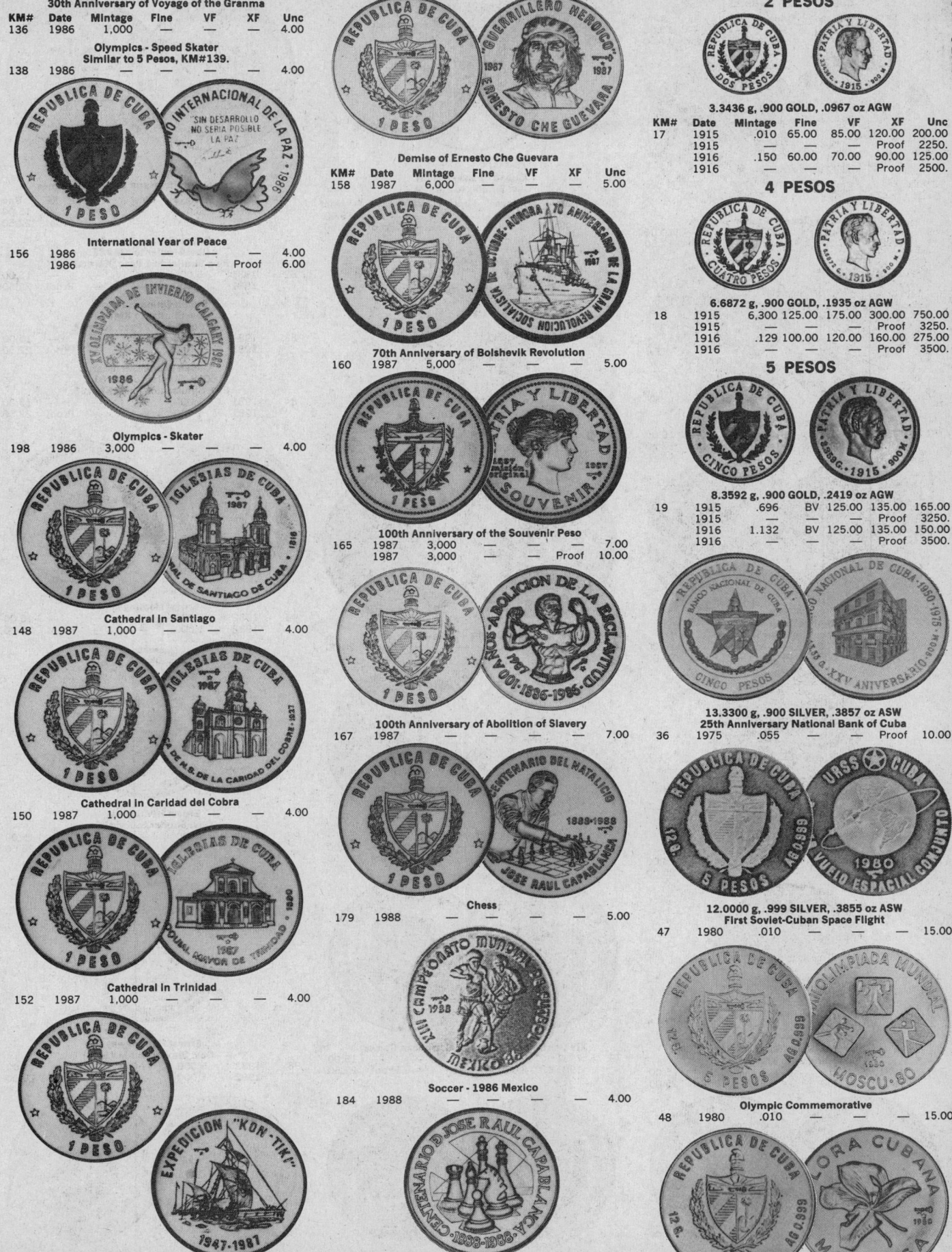

CUBA 446

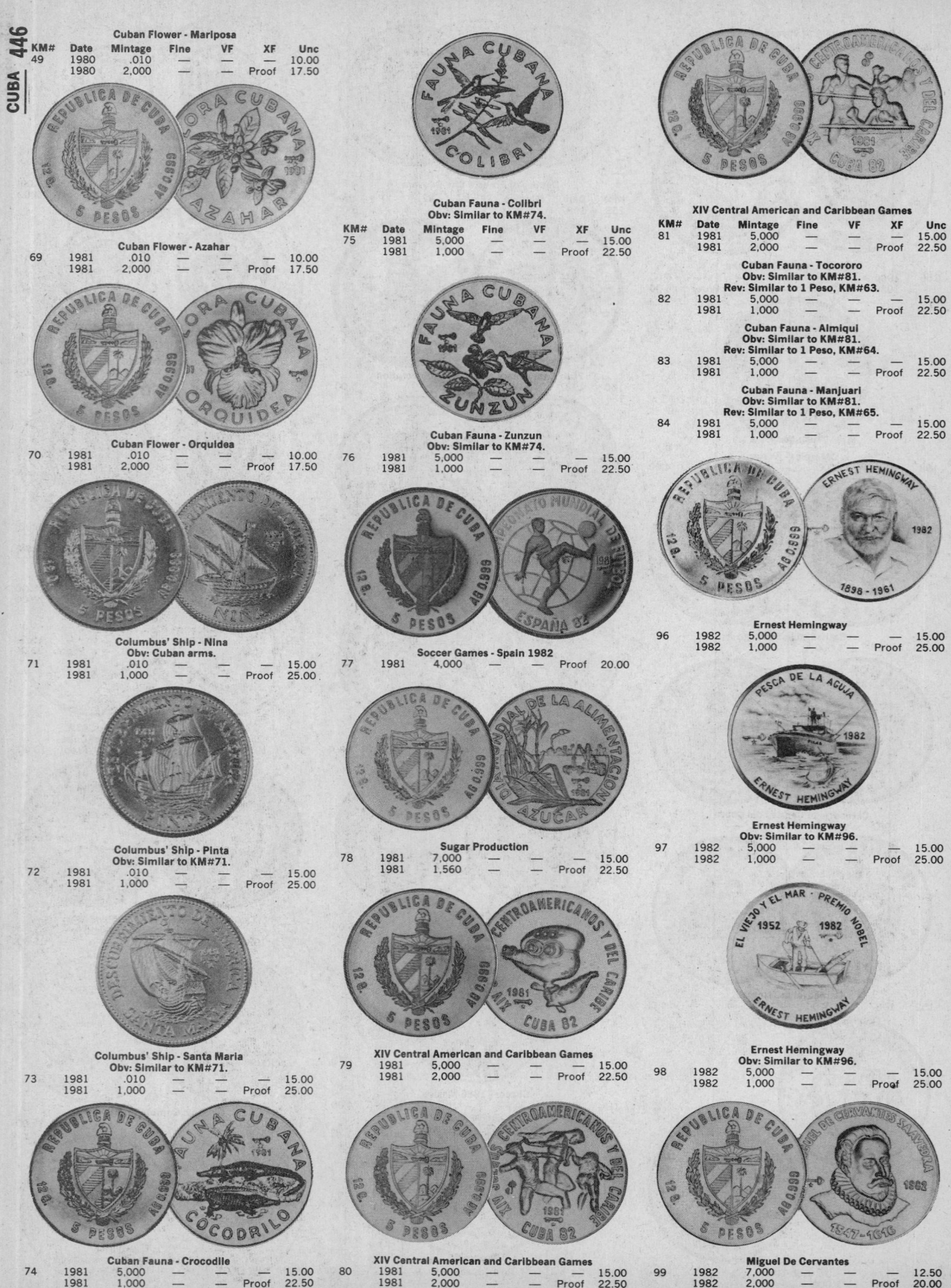

Cuban Flower - Mariposa

KM#	Date	Mintage	Fine	VF	XF	Unc
49	1980	.010	—	—	—	10.00
	1980	2,000	—	—	Proof	17.50

Cuban Flower - Azahar

69	1981	.010	—	—	—	10.00
	1981	2,000	—	—	Proof	17.50

Cuban Flower - Orquidea

70	1981	.010	—	—	—	10.00
	1981	2,000	—	—	Proof	17.50

Columbus' Ship - Nina
Obv: Cuban arms.

71	1981	.010	—	—	—	15.00
	1981	1,000	—	—	Proof	25.00

Columbus' Ship - Pinta
Obv: Similar to KM#71.

72	1981	.010	—	—	—	15.00
	1981	1,000	—	—	Proof	25.00

Columbus' Ship - Santa Maria
Obv: Similar to KM#71.

73	1981	.010	—	—	—	15.00
	1981	1,000	—	—	Proof	25.00

Cuban Fauna - Crocodile

74	1981	5,000	—	—	—	15.00
	1981	1,000	—	—	Proof	22.50

Cuban Fauna - Colibri
Obv: Similar to KM#74.

KM#	Date	Mintage	Fine	VF	XF	Unc
75	1981	5,000	—	—	—	15.00
	1981	1,000	—	—	Proof	22.50

Cuban Fauna - Zunzun
Obv: Similar to KM#74.

76	1981	5,000	—	—	—	15.00
	1981	1,000	—	—	Proof	22.50

Soccer Games - Spain 1982

77	1981	4,000	—	—	—	Proof	20.00

Sugar Production

78	1981	7,000	—	—	—	15.00
	1981	1,560	—	—	Proof	22.50

XIV Central American and Caribbean Games

79	1981	5,000	—	—	—	15.00
	1981	2,000	—	—	Proof	22.50

XIV Central American and Caribbean Games

80	1981	5,000	—	—	—	15.00
	1981	2,000	—	—	Proof	22.50

XIV Central American and Caribbean Games

KM#	Date	Mintage	Fine	VF	XF	Unc
81	1981	5,000	—	—	—	15.00
	1981	2,000	—	—	Proof	22.50

Cuban Fauna - Tocororo
Obv: Similar to KM#81.
Rev: Similar to 1 Peso, KM#63.

82	1981	5,000	—	—	—	15.00
	1981	1,000	—	—	Proof	22.50

Cuban Fauna - Almiqui
Obv: Similar to KM#81.
Rev: Similar to 1 Peso, KM#64.

83	1981	5,000	—	—	—	15.00
	1981	1,000	—	—	Proof	22.50

Cuban Fauna - Manjuari
Obv: Similar to KM#81.
Rev: Similar to 1 Peso, KM#65.

84	1981	5,000	—	—	—	15.00
	1981	1,000	—	—	Proof	22.50

Ernest Hemingway

96	1982	5,000	—	—	—	15.00
	1982	1,000	—	—	Proof	25.00

Ernest Hemingway
Obv: Similar to KM#96.

97	1982	5,000	—	—	—	15.00
	1982	1,000	—	—	Proof	25.00

Ernest Hemingway
Obv: Similar to KM#96.

98	1982	5,000	—	—	—	15.00
	1982	1,000	—	—	Proof	25.00

Miguel De Cervantes

99	1982	7,000	—	—	—	12.50
	1982	2,000	—	—	Proof	20.00

CUBA 447

Hidalgo Don Quijote
KM#	Date	Mintage	Fine	VF	XF	Unc
100	1982	7,000	—	—	—	12.50
	1982	2,000	—	—	Proof	20.00

Hidalgo Don Quijote
101	1982	7,000	—	—	—	12.50
	1982	2,000	—	—	Proof	20.00

F.A.O. Issue - Citrus Fruit
Similar to 1 Peso, KM#94.
102	1982	3,125	—	—	—	15.00
	1982	1,040	—	—	Proof	22.50

F.A.O. Issue - Cow
Similar to 1 Peos, KM#95.
103	1982	4,177	—	—	—	15.00
	1982	1,000	—	—	Proof	22.50

1984 Winter Olympics - Hockey
Obv: Similar to KM#99.
108	1983	5,000	—	—	Proof	25.00

1984 Summer Olympics - Runner
Obv: Similar to KM#99.
109	1983	5,000	—	—	Proof	25.00

Railroad
110	1983	5,000	—	—	—	20.00
	1983	2,000	—	—	Proof	25.00

World Fisheries - Saltwater Crayfish
111	1983	—	—	—	—	20.00

Winter Olympics - Woman Holding Torch
Obv: Similar to KM#114.
KM#	Date	Mintage	Fine	VF	XF	Unc
112	1983	5,000	—	—	Proof	30.00

Winter Olympics - Downhill Skier
Obv: Similar to KM#114.
113	1983	5,000	—	—	Proof	30.00

Summer Olympics - Discus Thrower
114	1983	5,000	—	—	Proof	30.00

Summer Olympics - Judo
Obv: Similar to KM#114.
115	1983	5,000	—	—	Proof	30.00

Transportation - Volanta Coach
Similar to 1 Peso, KM#130.
131	1983	—	—	—	—	20.00

Transportation - Freighter
117	1984	—	—	—	—	20.00

Santisima Trinidad
119	1984	—	—	—	—	20.00

Castle - El Morro La Habana
KM#	Date	Mintage	Fine	VF	XF	Unc
141	1984	5,000	—	—	—	20.00

Castle - La Fuerza La Habana
143	1984	5,000	—	—	—	20.00

Castle - El Morro Stgo. De Cuba
145	1984	5,000	—	—	—	20.00

International Year of Music - Bach
Similar to 1 Peso, KM#120.
121	1985	2,000	—	—	—	15.00
	1985	—	—	—	Proof	20.00

Soccer
Similar to 1 Peso, KM#122.
123	1985	5,000	—	—	—	15.00
	1985	—	—	—	Proof	20.00

Wildlife Preservation - Crocodile
125	1985	5,000	—	—	—	15.00
	1985	—	—	—	Proof	20.00

Wildlife Preservation - Iquana
127	1985	—	—	—	—	15.00
	1985	—	—	—	Proof	20.00

Wildlife Preservation - Parrot
129	1985	—	—	—	—	15.00
	1985	—	—	—	Proof	20.00

FAO Issue - Lobster
Obv: Similar to KM#129.
Rev: Lobster, palm tree & sugar cane.
146	ND(1985)	—	—	—	—	30.00

CUBA 448

FAO Issue - Forestry
Obv: Similar to KM#129. Rev: Stylized forest.

KM#	Date	Mintage	Fine	VF	XF	Unc
147	ND(1985)	—	—	—	—	30.00

100th Anniversary of the Automobile

| 135 | 1986 | 2,000 | — | — | — | 30.00 |

30th Anniversary of Voyage of the Granma

| 137 | 1986 | 2,500 | — | — | — | 30.00 |

Olympics

| 139 | 1986 | — | — | — | — | 30.00 |

Olympics - Skater
Rev: W/o rings above skater.

| 199 | 1986 | .010 | — | — | — | 30.00 |

International Year of Peace

| 157 | 1986 | — | — | — | — | 15.00 |
| | 1986 | — | — | — | Proof | 20.00 |

Cathedral in Santiago

| 149 | 1987 | 2,500 | — | — | — | 27.50 |

Cathedral in Caridad del Cobre

KM#	Date	Mintage	Fine	VF	XF	Unc
151	1987	2,500	—	—	—	27.50

Cathedral in Trinidad

| 153 | 1987 | 2,500 | — | — | — | 27.50 |

Kon-Tiki

| 155 | 1987 | 5,000 | — | — | — | 15.00 |

Demise of Ernesto Che Guevara

| 159 | 1987 | 5,000 | — | — | — | 15.00 |

70th Anniversary of Bolshevik Revolution

| 161 | 1987 | 3,000 | — | — | — | 20.00 |
| | 1987 | 1,000 | — | — | Proof | 25.00 |

100th Anniversary of Souvenir Peso

| 166 | 1987 | 3,000 | — | — | — | 20.00 |

Chess

KM#	Date	Mintage	Fine	VF	XF	Unc
180	1988	—	—	—	—	15.00

Soccer - Mexico 1986
Similar to 1 Peso, KM#184.

| 185 | 1988 | — | — | — | — | 15.00 |
| | 1988 | — | — | — | Proof | 20.00 |

Jose Capablanca
Similar to 1 Peso, KM#200.

| 201 | 1988 | — | — | — | — | 30.00 |

10 PESOS

16.7185 g, .900 GOLD, .4838 oz AGW

20	1915	.095	—	BV	275.00	350.00
	1915	—	—	—	Proof	6000.
	1916	1.169	—	BV	250.00	300.00
	1916	—	—	—	Proof	Rare

26.6600 g, .900 SILVER, .7715 oz ASW
25th Anniversary National Bank of Cuba

| 37 | 1975 | .055 | — | — | Proof | 20.00 |

18.0000 g, .999 SILVER, .5782 oz ASW

20 PESOS

CUBA 449

First Soviet-Cuban Space Flight

KM#	Date	Mintage	Fine	VF	XF	Unc
50	1980	.010	—	—	—	27.50

Olympic Commemorative
| 51 | 1980 | .010 | — | — | — | 27.50 |

31.1000 g, .999 SILVER, 1.0000 oz ASW
30th Anniversary of Castro Revolution
| 162 | 1987 | 2,000 | — | — | — | 50.00 |
| | 1988 | — | — | — | — | 50.00 |

Ernesto Che Guevara
| 163 | 1987 | 2,000 | — | — | — | 50.00 |
| | 1988 | — | — | — | — | 50.00 |

Castro Revolution March
| 164 | 1987 | 2,000 | — | — | — | 50.00 |
| | 1988 | — | — | — | — | 50.00 |

First Train in Spanish America 1837
Obv: Similar to KM#162. Rev: Train.
| 205 | 1988 | 2,000 | — | — | — | Proof 50.00 |

First Train in Spain 1848
Obv: Similar to KM#162. Rev: Train.
| 206 | 1988 | 2,000 | — | — | — | Proof 50.00 |

First Train in England 1830
Obv: Similar to KM#162. Rev: Train.
| 207 | 1988 | 2,000 | — | — | — | Proof 50.00 |

33.4370 g, .900 GOLD, .9676 oz AGW

KM#	Date	Mintage	Fine	VF	XF	Unc
21	1915	.057	BV	475.00	550.00	750.00
	1915	—	—	—	Proof	10,000.
	1916	10 pcs.	—	—	Proof	Rare

26.0000 g, .925 SILVER, .7732 oz ASW
Ignacio Agramonte
| 38 | 1977 | .075 | — | — | Proof | 35.00 |

Maximo Gomez
| 39 | 1977 | .075 | — | — | Proof | 35.00 |

Antonio Maceo
| 40 | 1977 | .075 | — | — | Proof | 35.00 |

60th Anniversary Socialist Revolution.
KM#	Date	Mintage	Fine	VF	XF	Unc
41	1977	100 pcs.	—	—	Proof	1000.

Nonaligned Nations Conference
| 44 | 1979 | .020 | — | — | — | 35.00 |
| | 1979 | — | — | — | Proof | 40.00 |

62.2000 g, .999 SILVER, 2.0000 oz ASW
Triumph of the Revolution

CUBA 450

KM#	Date	Mintage	Fine	VF	XF	Unc
169	1987	500 pcs.	—	—	Proof	90.00
	1988	—	—	—	Proof	90.00

Ernesto Che Guevara

170	1987	500 pcs.	—	—	Proof	90.00
	1988	—	—	—	Proof	90.00

March of Victory

171	1987	500 pcs.	—	—	Proof	90.00
	1988	—	—	—	Proof	90.00

100 PESOS

12.0000 g, .917 GOLD, .3538 oz AGW
Lenin

42	1977	10 pcs.	—	—	—	Proof 250.00

Carlos Manuel de Cespedes

43	1977	.025	—	—	—	Proof 200.00

Nonaligned Nations Conference

45	1979	.020	—	—	—	Proof 200.00

First Soviet-Cuban Space Flight

KM#	Date	Mintage	Fine	VF	XF	Unc
52	1980	1,000	—	—	—	250.00

Columbus' Ship - Nina
Obv: Similar to KM#45.

85	1981	2,000	—	—	—	225.00

Columbus' Ship - Pinta
Obv: Similar to KM#45.

86	1981	2,000	—	—	—	225.00

Columbus' Ship - Santa Maria
Obv: Similar to KM#45.

87	1981	2,000	—	—	—	225.00

31.1030 g, .999 GOLD, 1.0000 oz AGW
Castro Revolution - Soldiers
Obv: Similar to 10 Pesos, KM#162.
Rev: Marching soldiers.

202	1988	100 pcs.	—	—	Proof	650.00

Castro Revolution - Che Guevara
Obv: Similar to 10 Pesos, KM#162.
Rev: Portrait of Che Guevara.

203	1988	100 pcs.	—	—	Proof	650.00

Castro Revolution - Victory
Obv: Similar to 10 Pesos, KM#162.
Rev: Victory celebration scene.

204	1988	100 pcs.	—	—	Proof	650.00

PROOF SETS (PS)

KM#	Date	Mintage	Identification	Issue Price	Mkt. Val.
PS1	1915(7)	20	KM9-15	—	4500.
PS2	1915(6)	24	KM16-21	—	27,500.
PS3	1916(7)	20	KM9-15	—	5000.
PS4	1916(6)	—	KM16-21	—	45,000.
PS5	1953(4)	—	KM26-29	—	Rare
PS6	1975(2)	—	KM36,37	—	30.00
PS7	1977(4)	—	KM38-40,43	—	235.00
PS8	1979(2)	—	KM44,45	—	190.00

*NOTE: Spanish or English legends on holders.

Listings For
CURACAO: refer to Netherlands Antilles

CYPRUS

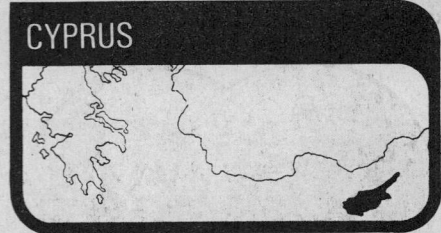

The Republic of Cyprus, a member of the British Commonwealth, lies in the eastern Mediterranean Sea 44 miles (71 km.) south of Turkey and 60 miles (97 km.) west of Syria. It is the third largest island in the Mediterranean Sea, having an area of 3,572 sq. mi. (9,251 sq. km.) and a population of 672,045. Capital: Nicosia. Agriculture and mining are the chief industries. Asbestos, copper, citrus fruit, iron pyrites and potatoes are exported.

The importance of Cyprus dates from the Bronze Age when it was desired as a principal source of copper (from which the island derived its name) and as a strategic trading center. Its role as an international marketplace made it a prime disseminator of the ten prevalent cultures, a role that still influences the civilization of Western man. Because of its fortuitous position and influential role, Cyprus was conquered by a succession of empires: the Assyrian, Egyptian, Persian, Macedonian, Ptolemaic, Roman and Byzantine. It was taken from Isaac Comnenus by Richard the Lion-Hearted in 1191, sold to the Knights Templars, conquered by Venice and Turkey, and made a crown colony of Britain in 1925. Finally, on Aug. 16, 1960, it became an independent republic.

In 1964, the ethnic Turks, who favor partition of Cyprus into separate Greek and Turkish states, withdrew from active participation in the government. Turkish forces invaded Cyprus in 1974 and gained control of 40 percent of the island. In 1975, Turkish Cypriots proclaimed their own state in northern Cyprus.

Cyprus is a member of the Commonwealth of Nations. The president is Chief of State and Head of Government.

RULERS
British, until 1960

MINT MARKS
H - Birmingham, England

MONETARY SYSTEM
9 Piastres = 1 Shilling
20 Shillings = 1 Pound

1/4 PIASTRE

BRONZE, 21.8mm

KM#	Date	Mintage	Fine	VF	XF	Unc
1.1	1879	.150	5.00	15.00	30.00	90.00
	1879	—	—	—	Proof	300.00
	1880	.072	10.00	25.00	50.00	110.00
	1880	—	—	—	Proof	365.00
	1881	.072	10.00	25.00	50.00	110.00
	1881	—	—	—	Proof	300.00
	1881H	.108	5.50	16.00	40.00	100.00
	1881H	—	—	—	Proof	300.00
	1882H	.036	15.00	30.00	90.00	150.00
	1884	.072	10.00	25.00	50.00	150.00
	1885	.036	15.00	40.00	90.00	150.00
	1887	.060	12.50	32.50	80.00	135.00
	1887	—	—	—	Proof	365.00
	1895	.072	12.00	30.00	80.00	125.00
	1898	.072	12.00	30.00	80.00	125.00
		Reduced size, 21mm				
1.2	1900	.036	10.00	25.00	55.00	125.00
	1900	—	—	—	Proof	365.00
	1901	.072	8.00	23.50	50.00	100.00

8	1902	.072	5.00	12.50	30.00	80.00
	1905	.422	4.00	12.50	25.00	60.00
	1908	.036	35.00	75.00	125.00	300.00

KM#	Date	Mintage	Fine	VF	XF	Unc
16	1922	.072	5.00	12.50	30.00	80.00
	1926	.360	3.50	7.50	15.00	65.00
	1926	—	—	—	Proof	365.00

1/2 PIASTRE

BRONZE

2	1879	.250	7.50	15.00	35.00	125.00
	1879	—	—	—	Proof	300.00
	1881	.054	10.00	20.00	55.00	140.00
	1881H	.072	10.00	20.00	55.00	140.00
	1881H	—	—	—	Proof	325.00
	1882H	.054	10.00	20.00	55.00	140.00
	1882H	—	—	—	Proof	325.00
	1884	.036	20.00	50.00	100.00	250.00
	1884	—	—	—	Proof	325.00
	1885	.054	15.00	30.00	80.00	200.00
	1886	.122	7.50	15.00	45.00	125.00
	1887	.060	10.00	20.00	60.00	150.00
	1887	—	—	—	Proof	325.00
	1889	.054	12.50	32.50	80.00	200.00
	1890	.180	20.00	50.00	100.00	250.00
	1890	—	—	—	Proof	400.00
	1891	.108	27.50	75.00	135.00	250.00
	1896	.036	35.00	100.00	175.00	300.00
	1900	.036	35.00	100.00	175.00	300.00
	1900	—	—	—	Proof	300.00

11	1908	.036	30.00	80.00	200.00	400.00

17	1922	.036	15.00	40.00	150.00	250.00
	1927	.108	3.50	10.00	35.00	80.00
	1927	—	—	—	Proof	365.00
	1930	.180	3.50	10.00	35.00	90.00
	1930	—	—	—	Proof	365.00
	1931	.090	5.00	15.00	40.00	100.00
	1931	—	—	—	Proof	365.00

COPPER-NICKEL

20	1934	1.440	.75	2.50	6.50	16.50
	1934	—	—	—	Proof	250.00

22	1938	1.080	.35	1.00	4.00	12.50
	1938	—	—	—	Proof	325.00

BRONZE

22a	1942	1.080	.25	1.00	2.50	12.50

KM#	Date	Mintage	Fine	VF	XF	Unc
22a	1942	—	—	—	Proof	200.00
	1943	1.620	.25	1.00	2.50	12.50
	1944	2.160	.25	1.00	2.50	12.50
	1945	1.080	.25	1.00	2.50	12.50
	1945	—	—	—	Proof	200.00

29	1949	1.080	.15	.35	1.00	3.50
	1949	—	—	—	Proof	200.00

PIASTRE

BRONZE
Rev: Thin '1'

3.1	1879	.250	8.00	25.00	50.00	125.00
	1879	—	—	—	Proof	375.00
	1881	.036	15.00	35.00	150.00	250.00
	1881	—	—	—	Proof	500.00
	1881H	.036	15.00	35.00	150.00	250.00
	1881H	—	—	—	Proof	500.00

Rev: Thick '1'

3.2	1881	Inc. Ab.	—	—	Proof	1000.
	1881H	Inc. Ab.	10.00	32.50	100.00	225.00
	1881H	—	—	—	Proof	800.00
	1882H	.018	135.00	200.00	350.00	1000.
	1882H	—	—	—	Proof	1500.
	1884	.018	135.00	200.00	350.00	1000.
	1884	—	—	—	Proof	1250.
	1885	.054	25.00	70.00	115.00	275.00
	1885	—	—	—	Proof	900.00
	1886	.227	10.00	30.00	85.00	175.00
	1887	.045	10.00	32.50	100.00	200.00
	1889	.027	25.00	80.00	200.00	400.00
	1890	.090	20.00	70.00	150.00	300.00
	1891	.054	25.00	80.00	200.00	400.00
	1895	.054	25.00	80.00	200.00	400.00
	1896	.054	25.00	80.00	200.00	400.00
	1900	.027	25.00	80.00	200.00	400.00
	1900	—	—	—	Proof	1100.

12	1908	.027	80.00	200.00	350.00	600.00

18	1922	.054	10.00	25.00	100.00	200.00
	1927	.127	5.00	20.00	50.00	100.00
	1927	—	—	—	Proof	400.00
	1930	.096	6.00	22.50	60.00	125.00

KM#	Date	Mintage	Fine	VF	XF	Unc
18	1930	—	—	—	Proof	400.00
	1931	.045	10.00	30.00	70.00	150.00
	1931	—	—	—	Proof	600.00

COPPER-NICKEL

21	1934	1.440	1.00	2.50	6.50	16.50
	1934	—	—	—	Proof	250.00

23	1938	2.700	.60	1.50	3.00	12.50
	1938	—	—	—	Proof	300.00

BRONZE

23a	1942	1.260	.50	1.00	2.50	10.00
	1942	—	—	—	Proof	225.00
	1943	2.520	.50	1.00	2.50	10.00
	1944	3.240	.50	1.00	2.50	10.00
	1945	1.080	.50	1.00	2.50	10.00
	1945	—	—	—	Proof	200.00
	1946	1.080	.50	1.00	2.50	10.00
	1946	—	—	—	Proof	200.00

Obv. leg: DEI GRATIA REX for REX IMPERATOR.

30	1949	1.080	.25	.60	1.50	3.50
	1949	—	—	—	Proof	225.00

3 PIASTRES

1.8851 g, .925 SILVER, .0561 oz ASW

4	1901	.300	8.00	20.00	40.00	100.00
	1901	—	—	—	Proof	375.00

4-1/2 PIASTRES

2.8276 g, .925 SILVER, .0841 oz ASW

5	1901	.400	5.00	15.00	40.00	100.00
	1901	—	—	—	Proof	450.00

15	1921	.600	3.50	10.00	30.00	60.00

24	1938	.192	2.00	4.00	12.00	30.00
	1938	—	—	—	Proof	400.00

CYPRUS 452

9 PIASTRES

5.6552 g, .925 SILVER, .1682 oz ASW

KM#	Date	Mintage	Fine	VF	XF	Unc
6	1901	.600	10.00	30.00	80.00	175.00
	1901	—	—	—	Proof	600.00

KM#	Date	Mintage	Fine	VF	XF	Unc
9	1907	.060	25.00	90.00	225.00	400.00

KM#	Date	Mintage	Fine	VF	XF	Unc
13	1913	.050	20.00	70.00	150.00	300.00
	1919	.400	2.50	10.00	27.50	85.00
	1921	.490	2.50	10.00	27.50	85.00

KM#	Date	Mintage	Fine	VF	XF	Unc
25	1938	.504	1.50	3.00	6.50	25.00
	1938	—	—	—	Proof	400.00
	1940	.800	1.50	3.00	6.50	25.00
	1940	—	—	—	Proof	400.00

SHILLING

COPPER-NICKEL

KM#	Date	Mintage	Fine	VF	XF	Unc
27	1947	1.440	.50	1.00	5.00	30.00
	1947	—	—	—	Proof	325.00

Obv. leg: ET IND IMP dropped.

KM#	Date	Mintage	Fine	VF	XF	Unc
31	1949	1.440	.50	1.00	5.00	30.00
	1949	—	—	—	Proof	325.00

18 PIASTRES

11.3104 g, .925 SILVER, .3364 oz ASW

KM#	Date	Mintage	Fine	VF	XF	Unc
7	1901	.200	25.00	100.00	250.00	500.00
	1901	—	—	—	Proof	1100.

KM#	Date	Mintage	Fine	VF	XF	Unc
10	1907	.020	40.00	165.00	375.00	1000.

KM#	Date	Mintage	Fine	VF	XF	Unc
14	1913	.025	35.00	140.00	350.00	600.00
	1921	.155	25.00	60.00	150.00	350.00

KM#	Date	Mintage	Fine	VF	XF	Unc
26	1938	.200	3.50	5.00	10.00	40.00
	1938	—	—	—	Proof	450.00
	1940	.100	3.50	5.00	10.00	40.00
	1940	—	—	—	Proof	450.00

2 SHILLINGS

COPPER-NICKEL

KM#	Date	Mintage	Fine	VF	XF	Unc
28	1947	.720	1.00	2.50	7.50	35.00
	1947	—	—	—	Proof	450.00

Obv. leg: ET IND. IMP. dropped.

KM#	Date	Mintage	Fine	VF	XF	Unc
32	1949	.720	1.00	2.50	7.50	35.00
	1949	—	—	—	Proof	450.00

45 PIASTRES

28.2759 g, .925 SILVER, .8409 oz ASW
50th Anniversary of British Rule

KM#	Date	Mintage	Fine	VF	XF	Unc
19	1928	.080	15.00	25.00	40.00	170.00
	1928	517 pcs.	—	—	Proof	600.00

DECIMAL COINAGE
50 Mils = 1 Shilling

20 Shillings = 1 Pound
1000 Mils = 1 Pound

MIL

ALUMINUM

KM#	Date	Mintage	VF	XF	Unc
38	1963	5.000	—	—	.10
	1963	.025	—	Proof	.75
	1971	.500	—	.10	.15
	1972	.500	—	.10	.15

3 MILS

BRONZE

KM#	Date	Mintage	VF	XF	Unc
33	1955	6.250	—	.10	.20
	1955	2.000	—	Proof	4.00

5 MILS

BRONZE

KM#	Date	Mintage	VF	XF	Unc
34	1955	10.000	.15	.25	.40
	1955	2.000	—	Proof	5.00
	1956	2.950	.15	.30	.50
	1956	—	—	Proof	175.00

KM#	Date	Mintage	VF	XF	Unc
39	1963	12.000	—	.10	.25
	1963	.025	—	Proof	1.00
	1970	2.500	—	.10	.25
	1971	2.500	—	.10	.25
	1972	2.500	—	.10	.25
	1973	5.000	—	.10	.25
	1974	2.500	—	.10	.25
	1976	2.000	—	.10	.25
	1977	2.000	—	.10	.25
	1978	2.000	—	.10	.25
	1979	2.000	—	.10	.25
	1980	4.000	—	.10	.25

ALUMINUM
Obv: Small date.

KM#	Date	Mintage	VF	XF	Unc
50.1	1981	12.500	—	—	.10

Obv: Large date.

KM#	Date	Mintage	VF	XF	Unc
50.2	1982	15.000	—	—	.10

25 MILS

COPPER-NICKEL

KM#	Date	Mintage	VF	XF	Unc
35	1955	2.500	.25	.35	.50
	1955	2.000	—	Proof	5.00

CYPRUS 453

KM#	Date	Mintage	VF	XF	Unc
40	1963	2.500	.10	.15	.30
	1963	.025	—	Proof	1.25
	1968	1.500	.10	.15	.30
	1971	1.000	.10	.15	.30
	1972	.500	.10	.15	.35
	1973	1.000	.10	.15	.30
	1974	1.000	.10	.15	.30
	1976	2.000	.10	.15	.30
	1977	.500	.10	.15	.30
	1978	.500	.10	.15	.30
	1979	1.000	.10	.15	.30
	1980	2.000	.10	.15	.30
	1981	3.000	.10	.15	.30
	1982	1.000	.10	.15	.30

50 MILS

COPPER-NICKEL

36	1955	4.000	.35	.50	1.00
	1955	2.000	—	Proof	5.00

41	1963	2.800	.20	.30	.60
	1963	.025	—	Proof	1.50
	1970	.500	.20	.35	.75
	1971	.500	.20	.35	.75
	1972	.750	.20	.30	.60
	1973	.750	.20	.30	.60
	1974	1.500	.20	.30	.60
	1976	1.500	.20	.30	.60
	1977	.500	.20	.30	.60
	1978	.500	.20	.30	.60
	1979	1.000	.20	.30	.60
	1980	3.000	.20	.30	.60
	1981	4.000	.20	.30	.60
	1982	2.000	.20	.30	.60

100 MILS

COPPER-NICKEL

37	1955	2.500	.50	.75	1.50
	1955	2.000	—	Proof	6.00
	1957	*.500	10.00	15.00	35.00
	1957	—	—	Proof	200.00

*NOTE: All but 10,000 of 1957 issue were melted down.

42	1963	1.750	.40	.65	1.25
	1963	.025	—	Proof	2.00
	1971	.500	.50	.75	1.50
	1973	.750	.40	.65	1.25
	1974	1.000	.50	.75	1.50
	1976	1.500	.40	.65	1.25
	1977	.500	.50	.75	1.50
	1978	1.000	.50	.75	1.50
	1979	1.000	.40	.65	1.25
	1980	1.000	.40	.65	1.25
	1981	2.000	.40	.65	1.25
	1982	2.000	.40	.65	1.25

500 MILS

COPPER-NICKEL
F.A.O. Issue

KM#	Date	Mintage	VF	XF	Unc
43	1970	.080	1.25	2.00	4.00

22.6200 g, .800 SILVER, .5818 oz ASW

43a	1970	5,000	—	Proof	110.00

COPPER-NICKEL

44	1975	.500	1.25	1.75	3.00
	1977	.300	1.25	1.75	3.00

14.1400 g, .800 SILVER, .3637 oz ASW

44a	1975	.010	—	Proof	20.00

COPPER-NICKEL
Refugee Commemorative

45	1976	.025	1.25	1.75	2.50

14.1400 g, .925 SILVER, .4205 oz ASW

45a	1976	.025	—	Proof	15.00

COPPER-NICKEL
Human Rights Commemorative

48	1978	.050	1.25	1.75	3.00

14.1400 g, .925 SILVER, .4205 oz ASW

48a	1978	5,000	—	Proof	65.00

COPPER-NICKEL
Summer Olympic Games

KM#	Date	Mintage	VF	XF	Unc
49	1980	.050	1.25	1.75	4.50

14.1400 g, .925 SILVER, .4205 oz ASW

49a	1980	7,500	—	Proof	65.00

COPPER-NICKEL
F.A.O. Issue

51	1981	.050	1.25	1.75	3.00

14.1400 g, .925 SILVER, .4205 oz ASW

51a	1981	7,500	—	Proof	35.00

POUND

COPPER-NICKEL
Refugee Commemorative

46	1976	.025	2.00	2.50	5.00

28.2800 g, .925 SILVER, .8411 oz ASW

46a	1976	.025	—	Proof	20.00

50 POUNDS

15.9800 g, .917 GOLD, .4711 oz AGW
Archbishop Makarios

47	1977	.039	—	—	300.00
	1977	.051	—	Proof	350.00

MONETARY REFORM
100 Cents = 1 Pound

CYPRUS 454

1/2 CENT

KM#	Date	Mintage	VF	XF	Unc
52	1983	10,000	—	.10	.15
	1983	6,250	—	Proof	2.00

ALUMINUM

CENT

NICKEL-BRASS

53	1983	15,000	—	.10	.20
	1983	6,250	—	Proof	2.00
	1985	5,000	—	.10	.20
	1987	5,000	—	.10	.20

2 CENTS

NICKEL-BRASS

54	1983	12,000	—	.15	.25
	1983	6,250	—	Proof	2.00
	1985	8,000	—	.15	.25

5 CENTS

NICKEL-BRASS

55	1983	15,000	—	.20	.50
	1983	6,250	—	Proof	3.00
	1985	5,000	—	.20	.50
	1987	5,000	—	.20	.50

10 CENTS

NICKEL-BRASS

56	1983	10,000	—	.35	.75
	1983	6,250	—	Proof	4.50
	1985	5,000	—	.35	.75
	1988		—	.35	.75

20 CENTS

NICKEL-BRASS

57	1983	10,000	—	.50	1.00
	1983	6,200	—	Proof	6.50
	1985	5,040	—	.50	1.00

50 CENTS

COPPER-NICKEL
Forestry - F.A.O.

KM#	Date	Mintage	VF	XF	Unc
58	1985	.033	1.25	1.75	3.50

14.1400 g, .925 SILVER, .4205 oz ASW

| 58a | 1985 | 4,000 | — | Proof | 20.00 |

COPPER-NICKEL
Olympics - Symbols

| 60 | 1988 | .014 | — | — | 5.00 |

14.1400 g, .925 SILVER, .4205 oz ASW

| 60a | 1988 | 4,000 | — | Proof | 20.00 |

POUND

COPPER-NICKEL
World Wildlife Fund

| 59 | 1986 | .039 | — | — | 4.50 |

.925 SILVER

| 59a | 1986 | .013 | — | Proof | 35.00 |

COPPER-NICKEL
Olympics - Symbols

| 61 | 1988 | .014 | — | — | 6.00 |

28.2800 g, .925 SILVER, .8411 oz ASW

| 61a | 1988 | 4,000 | — | Proof | 30.00 |

MINT SETS (MS)

KM#	Date	Mintage	Identification	Issue Price	Mkt. Val.
MS1	1955(5)	2,550	KM33-37*	2.20	6.50
MS2	1963(5)	8,050	KM38-42	1.95	5.00
MS3	1971(5)	3,000	KM38-42	1.65	5.00
MS4	1972(4)	3,000	KM39-42	2.35	5.00
MS5	1973(4)	5,000	KM39-42	2.75	5.00
MS6	1974(4)	5,000	KM39-42	3.25	5.00
MS7	1976(3)	5,000	KM39-42	1.25	4.50
MS8	1976(2)	25,000	KM45-46	6.50	6.00
MS9	1977(5)	10,000	KM39-42,44	—	6.50
MS10	1978(5)	—	KM39-42,48	5.50	6.50
MS11	1981(5)	—	KM40-42,50-51	5.00	6.50
MS12	1981(4)	—	KM40-42,50	5.00	6.50
MS13	1982(4)	5,000	KM40-42,50	5.00	6.50
MS14	1983(6)	11,400	KM52-57	15.00	10.00

*NOTE: This set consists of 3 uncirculated and 2 circulated coins.

PROOF SETS (PS)

PS1	1879(3)	—	KM1,2,3.1	—	1000.
PS2	1900(3)	—	KM1,2,3.2	—	1750.
PS3	1901(4)	—	KM4-7	—	2500.
PS4	1934(2)	—	KM20-21	—	500.00
PS5	1938(5)	—	KM22-26	—	2000.
PS6	1947(2)	—	KM27-28	—	775.00
PS7	1949(2)	—	KM31-32	—	775.00
PS8	1955(5)	2,000	KM33-37	5.50	22.50
PS9	1963(5)	24,501	KM38-42 with case	9.00	6.50
PS10	1963(5)	500	KM38-42 sealed	8.70	6.50
PS11	1976(2)	25,000	KM45a-46a	50.00	35.00
PS12	1983(6)	6,250	KM52-57	40.00	20.00

CZECHOSLOVAK SOC. REP.

The Czechoslovak Socialist Republic, located in central Europe, has an area of 49,371 sq. mi. (127,869 sq. km.) and a population of 15.4 million. Capital: Prague. Machinery is the chief export of the highly industrialized economy.

Czechoslovakia proclaimed itself a republic on Oct. 28, 1918. When Adolf Hitler became dictator of Nazi Germany he provoked Czechoslovakia's German minority in the Sudetenland to agitate for autonomy. At Munich in Sept. of 1938, France and Britain, vainly seeking to avoid World War II, forced the cession of the Sudetenland to Germany. In March, 1939, Germany invaded Czechoslovakia and established a protectorate over the provinces of Bohemia and Moravia. Bohemia is a historic province in northwest Czechoslovakia that includes the city of Prague, one of the oldest continuously occupied sites in Europe; and Moravia is an area of considerable mineral wealth in central Czechoslovakia. Slovakia, a province in southeastern Czechoslovakia that was once a separate country bounded by Poland, Hungary and Austria, was constituted as a puppet republic. World War II defeat of the Axis powers re-established the physical integrity and independence of Czechoslovakia, while bringing it within the Russian sphere of influence. On Feb. 23-25, 1948, the Communists seized control of the government in a coup d'etat, and adopted a constitution making the country a 'people's republic'. A new constitution adopted June 11, 1960, converted the country into a 'socialist republic'.

MONETARY SYSTEM
100 Haleru = 1 Koruna

PEOPLE'S REPUBLIC
HALER

ALUMINUM

KM#	Date	Mintage	Fine	VF	XF	Unc
35	1953	—	—	—	.10	.20
	1954	—	—	—	.10	.20
	1955	—	—	—	.10	.20
	1956	—	—	—	.10	.20
	1957	—	—	—	.10	.20
	1958	—	.10	.25	.35	.60
	1959	—	—	—	.10	.20
	1960	—	—	—	.10	.20

2 HALERE

ZINC

5	1923	2.700	3.00	5.00	7.50	15.00
	1924	17.300	2.25	3.50	5.00	9.00
	1925	2.000	3.00	5.00	7.50	15.00

3 HALERE

ALUMINUM

36	1953	—	—	—	.10	.15	.25
	1954	—	—	—	.10	.15	.25

5 HALERU

BRONZE

6	1923	37.800	.20	.30	.50	2.00
	1924	100 pcs.	20.00	30.00	40.00	60.00
	1925	12.000	.20	.30	.50	2.50
	1926	1.084	1.50	3.25	6.00	12.00
	1927	8.916	.25	.35	.75	2.50
	1928	5.320	.30	.45	.75	2.50
	1929	12.680	.25	.35	.75	2.50
	1930	5.000	.25	.35	.75	2.50
	1931	7.448	.25	.35	.75	2.50
	1932	3.556	.60	1.00	2.00	5.00
	1938	14.244	.25	.35	.75	2.00

ALUMINUM

KM#	Date	Mintage	Fine	VF	XF	Unc
37	1953	—	.10	.15	.25	.40
	1954	—	.10	.15	.25	.40
	1955	—	.30	.50	.75	2.00

10 HALERU

BRONZE

3	1922	6.000	.30	.45	1.00	2.75
	1923	24.000	.25	.35	.75	2.00
	1924	5.320	.30	.45	1.00	3.00
	1925	24.680	.25	.35	.60	2.25
	1926	10.000	.25	.35	.75	2.25
	1927	10.000	.25	.35	.75	2.25
	1928	14.290	.25	.35	.75	2.25
	1929	5.710	1.25	2.00	3.50	7.00
	1930	6.980	.30	.45	1.00	2.50
	1931	6.740	.30	.45	1.00	2.50
	1932	11.280	.25	.35	.75	2.00
	1933	4.190	.35	.60	1.25	5.00
	1934	13.200	.25	.35	.75	2.00
	1935	3.420	.50	.75	1.50	5.00
	1936	8.560	.25	.35	.75	2.00
	1937	20.200	.25	.35	.75	2.00
	1938	21.400	.25	.35	.75	2.00

ALUMINUM

38	1953(k)	—	—	.10	.20	.40
	1953(l)	—	.10	.15	.30	.75
	1954	—	—	.10	.20	.40
	1955	—	.50	.75	1.25	2.00
	1956	—	—	.10	.20	.40
	1958	—	—	.10	.20	.40

(k) - Kremnica-130 notches in milled edge.
(l) - Leningrad-133 notches in milled edge.

20 HALERU

COPPER-NICKEL

1	1921	40.000	.25	.35	.60	2.50
	1922	9.100	.25	.35	.60	2.50
	1924	20.931	.25	.35	.60	2.50
	1925	4.244	.60	1.00	2.00	6.00
	1926	14.825	.25	.35	.60	2.50
	1927	11.757	.25	.35	.60	2.50
	1928	14.018	.25	.35	.60	2.50
	1929	4.225	.30	.50	1.25	3.50
	1930	—	.30	.40	.75	3.00
	1931	5.000	.30	.40	.75	3.00
	1933	Inc. Ab.	2.50	3.50	7.00	14.00
	1937	8.208	.25	.35	.60	2.50
	1938	18.787	.25	.35	.60	2.50

BRONZE

20	1947	—	100.00	150.00	185.00	250.00
	1948	24.340	.10	.15	.40	1.00
	1949	25.660	.10	.15	.40	1.00
	1950	11.132	.10	.15	.40	1.00

ALUMINUM

KM#	Date	Mintage	Fine	VF	XF	Unc
31	1951	46.800	.10	.15	.25	.50
	1952	80.340	.10	.15	.25	.50

25 HALERU

COPPER-NICKEL

16	1933	22.711	.50	1.00	2.00	4.00

ALUMINUM

39	1953(k)	—	.10	.20	.30	.60
	1953(l)	—	.30	.75	.75	1.00
	1954	—	.10	.20	.30	.60

(k) - Kremnica-134 notches in milled edge.
(l) - Leningrad-145 notches in milled edge.

50 HALERU

COPPER-NICKEL

2	1921	3.000	.25	.50	1.00	3.00
	1922	37.000	.20	.40	.60	2.50
	1924	10.000	.20	.40	.60	2.50
	1925	1.415	.50	1.00	2.00	5.00
	1926	1.585	1.25	2.00	4.00	10.00
	1927	2.000	.50	1.00	2.00	6.00
	1931	6.000	.25	.50	1.00	2.50

BRONZE

21	1947	50.000	.15	.25	.40	1.00
	1948	20.000	.15	.25	.40	1.00
	1949	12.715	.15	.25	.40	1.00
	1950	17.415	.15	.25	.40	1.00

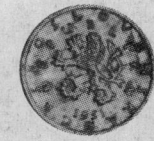

ALUMINUM

32	1951	60.000	.15	.35	.50	.75
	1952	60.000	.25	.45	.60	1.00
	1953	34.920	.60	1.00	2.00	5.00

KORUNA

COPPER-NICKEL

4	1922	50.000	.30	.50	.75	2.00
	1923	15.385	.30	.50	.75	2.00
	1924	21.041	.30	.50	.75	2.00
	1925	8.574	.40	.60	1.00	3.00
	1929	5.000	.50	.75	1.25	3.50
	1930	5.000	1.00	1.50	3.00	8.00
	1937	3.806	.40	.60	1.00	3.00
	1938	8.582	.40	.60	1.00	3.00

CZECHOSLOVAK SOC. REP. 456

KM#	Date	Mintage	Fine	VF	XF	Unc
19	1946	88.000	.15	.25	.50	1.00
	1947	12.550	1.50	2.50	3.75	6.50

ALUMINUM

22, (32)	1947	—	25.00	65.00	100.00	150.00
	1950	62.190	.20	.35	.45	.75
	1951	61.395	.20	.35	.45	.75
	1952	101.105	.20	.30	.40	.65
	1953	73.905	.40	.75	1.75	3.25

ALUMINUM-BRONZE

46	1957	—	.20	.30	.45	1.00
	1958	—	.20	.30	.45	1.00
	1959	—	.15	.25	.35	.60
	1960	—	.15	.25	.35	.60

2 KORUNY

COPPER-NICKEL

23	1947	20.000	.20	.40	.60	1.25
	1948	20.476	.20	.40	.60	1.50

5 KORUN

COPPER-NICKEL

10	1925	16.475	1.50	2.50	3.00	6.00
	1926	8.912	1.75	2.75	3.50	7.00
	1927	4.614	2.50	4.00	5.75	10.00

7.0000 g, .500 SILVER, .1125 oz ASW

11	1928	1.710	2.00	3.00	5.00	10.00
	1929	12.861	1.00	2.00	4.00	8.00
	1930	10.429	1.00	2.00	4.00	8.00
	1931	2.000	2.00	3.00	5.00	10.00
	1932	—	4.00	7.50	10.00	35.00

NOTE: Edge varieties exist.

NICKEL

KM#	Date	Mintage	Fine	VF	XF	Unc
11a	1937	—	60.00	100.00	150.00	250.00
	1938	17.200	1.25	2.50	4.00	6.50

ALUMINUM

34	1952	40.715	17.50	25.00	35.00	45.00

NOTE: Not released for circulation. Nearly all were melted.

10 KORUN

10.0000 g, .700 SILVER, .2250 oz ASW
10th Anniversary of Independence

12	1928	1.000	2.00	4.00	5.00	9.00

15	1930	4.949	2.00	3.50	6.00	10.00
	1931	6.689	2.00	5.00	9.00
	1932	11.448	1.75	2.50	4.00	8.00
	1933	.915	7.50	12.50	35.00	125.00

12.0000 g, .500 SILVER, .1929 oz ASW
10th Anniversary Slovak Uprising

40	1954	.245	BV	2.00	3.00	4.00
	1954	5,000	—	—	Proof	7.50

10th Anniversary Nazi Liberation

42	1955	.295	BV	2.50	4.00	6.00
	1955	5,000	—	—	Proof	8.00

250th Anniversary Technical College

KM#	Date	Mintage	Fine	VF	XF	Unc
47	1957	.075	BV	2.50	4.00	6.00
	1957	5,000	—	—	Proof	8.00

J. A. Komensky

48	1957	.150	BV	2.50	4.00	6.00
	1957	5,000	—	—	Proof	8.00

20 KORUN

12.0000 g, .700 SILVER, .2700 oz ASW

17	1933	2.280	BV	4.00	7.00	14.00
	1934	3.280	BV	4.00	7.00	14.00

Death of President Masaryk

18	1937	1.000	BV	3.00	6.00	9.00

25 KORUN

16.0000 g, .500 SILVER, .2572 oz ASW
10th Anniversary Slovak Uprising

41	1954	.245	—	—	5.00	8.00
	1954	5,000	—	—	Proof	12.50

CZECHOSLOVAK SOC. REP. 457

10th Anniversary Nazi Liberation

KM#	Date	Mintage	Fine	VF	XF	Unc
43	1955	.195	—	—	5.00	8.00
	1955	5,000	—	—	Proof	15.00

50 KORUN

10.0000 g, .500 SILVER, .1607 oz ASW
1944 Slovak Uprising

24	1947	1.000	BV	2.50	3.50	5.00

3rd Anniversary Prague Uprising

25	1948	1.000	BV	2.50	3.50	5.00

Stalin 70th Birthday

28	1949	1.000	BV	2.50	3.50	5.00

20.0000 g, .900 SILVER, .5787 oz ASW
10th Anniversary Nazi Liberation

44	1955	.120	BV	6.00	12.00	20.00

NOTE: 2 varieties of artist's name exist.

100 KORUN

14.0000 g, .500 SILVER, .2250 oz ASW
600th Anniversary Charles University

26	1948	1.000	BV	2.50	3.50	5.50

30th Anniversary of Independence

27	1948	1.000	BV	2.50	3.50	5.50

7th Centennial Jihlava Mining Privileges

KM#	Date	Mintage	Fine	VF	XF	Unc
29	1949	1.000	BV	2.50	3.50	5.50

Stalin 70th Birthday

30	1949	1.000	BV	2.50	3.50	5.50

30th Anniversary Communist Party

33	1951	1.000	BV	2.50	3.50	5.50

24.0000 g, .900 SILVER, .6945 oz ASW
10th Anniversary Nazi Liberation

45	1955	.075	BV	9.00	17.50	27.50

TRADE COINAGE
DUKAT

3.4900 g, .986 GOLD, .1106 oz AGW
Duke Wenceslas

KM#	Date	Mintage	VF	XF	Unc
7	1923	1,000	250.00	600.00	1000.

NOTE: The above coins are serially numbered next to date.

Similar to KM#7 but w/o serial numbers.

8	1923	.062	55.00	75.00	100.00
	1924	.033	55.00	75.00	100.00
	1925	.066	55.00	75.00	100.00
	1926	.059	55.00	75.00	100.00
	1927	.026	55.00	75.00	100.00
	1928	.019	55.00	75.00	115.00
	1929	.010	60.00	80.00	150.00
	1930	.011	60.00	80.00	150.00
	1931	.043	55.00	75.00	100.00
	1932	.027	55.00	75.00	100.00
	1933	.058	55.00	75.00	100.00
	1934	9,729	80.00	100.00	160.00
	1935	.013	55.00	75.00	115.00
	1936	.015	55.00	75.00	115.00
	1937	324 pcs.	200.00	400.00	750.00
	1938	56 pcs.	600.00	800.00	1500.
	1939	*276 pcs.	200.00	400.00	750.00
	1951	500 pcs.	150.00	300.00	750.00

*NOTE: Czech reports show mintage of 20 for Czechoslovakia and 256 for state of Slovakia.

2 DUKATY

6.9800 g, .986 GOLD, .2212 oz AGW
Duke Wenceslas

KM#	Date	Mintage	VF	XF	Unc
9	1923	4,000	150.00	225.00	350.00
	1929	3,262	150.00	225.00	350.00
	1930	Inc. Ab.	150.00	250.00	400.00
	1931	2,994	150.00	225.00	350.00
	1932	5,496	150.00	225.00	350.00
	1933	4,671	150.00	225.00	350.00
	1934	2,403	150.00	225.00	350.00
	1935	2,577	150.00	225.00	350.00
	1936	819 pcs.	300.00	400.00	500.00
	1937	8 pcs.	1500.	2000.	3500.
	1938	*186 pcs.	600.00	800.00	1000.
	1951	200 Pcs.	300.00	500.00	1000.

*NOTE: Czech reports show mintage of 14 for Czechoslovakia and 172 for state of Slovakia.

5 DUKATU

17.4500 g, .986 GOLD, .5532 oz AGW
Duke Wenceslas

13	1929	1,827	350.00	450.00	675.00
	1930	543 Pcs.	500.00	700.00	1000.
	1931	1,528	350.00	450.00	675.00
	1932	1,827	350.00	450.00	675.00
	1933	1,752	350.00	450.00	675.00
	1934	1,101	350.00	450.00	675.00
	1935	1,037	350.00	450.00	675.00
	1936	728 pcs.	500.00	700.00	1000.
	1937	4 pcs.	—	—	5000.
	1938	*56 pcs.	1000.	2000.	3000.
	1951	100 pcs.	400.00	800.00	2000.

*NOTE: Czech reports show mintage of 12 for Czechoslovakia and 44 for state of Slovakia.

10 DUKATU

34.9000 g, .986 GOLD, 1.1064 oz AGW
Duke Wenceslas

14	1929	1,564	700.00	1000.	1400.
	1930	394 pcs.	1000.	1900.	2800.
	1931	1,239	700.00	1000.	1500.
	1932	1,035	700.00	1000.	1500.
	1933	1,780	700.00	1000.	1500.
	1934	1,298	700.00	1000.	1500.
	1935	600 pcs.	750.00	1200.	1800.
	1936	633 pcs.	750.00	1200.	1800.
	1937	34 pcs.	—	—	8000.
	1938	*192 pcs.	2000.	2800.	4000.
	1951	100 pcs.	2000.	2800.	5000.

*NOTE: Czech reports show mintage of 20 for Czechoslovakia and 172 for state of Slovakia.

SOCIALIST REPUBLIC
HALER

CZECHOSLOVAK SOC. REP. 458

3 HALERE

ALUMINUM

KM#	Date	Mintage	Fine	VF	XF	Unc
51	1962	—	—	—	.10	.15
	1963	—	—	—	.10	.15
	1963	—	—	—	Proof	—
	1986	—	—	—	.10	.15

5 HALERU

ALUMINUM

52	1962	—	150.00	200.00	250.00	300.00
	1963	—	—	—	.10	.15
	1963	—	—	—	Proof	—

ALUMINUM

53	1962	—	—	.10	.15	.25
	1963	—	—	.10	.15	.25
	1966	—	—	.10	.15	.25
	1966	—	—	—	Proof	Rare
	1967	—	—	.10	.15	.25
	1968	—	—	.10	.15	.20
	1970	—	—	.10	.15	.20
	1972	—	—	.10	.15	.20
	1973	—	—	.10	.15	.20
	1974	—	—	.10	.15	.20
	1975	—	—	.10	.15	.20
	1976	—	—	.10	.15	.20

86	1977	—	—	—	.10	.25
	1978	—	—	—	.10	.25
	1979	—	—	—	.10	.25
	1980	—	—	—	.10	.25
	1981	—	—	—	.10	.25
	1981	—	—	—	Proof	—
	1982	—	—	In mint set only	—	
	1983	—	—	—	.10	.25
	1984	—	—	In mint set only	—	
	1985	—	—	In mint set only	—	
	1986	—	—	—	.10	.25
	1986	—	—	—	Proof	—
	1987	—	—	—	.10	.25
	1988	—	—	—	.10	.25

10 HALERU

ALUMINUM

49.1	1961	—	—	.10	.20	.35
	1962	—	—	.10	.20	.35
	1963	—	—	.10	.20	.35
	1964	—	—	.10	.20	.35
	1965	—	—	.10	.20	.35
	1966	—	—	.10	.20	.35
	1966	—	—	—	Proof	Rare
	1967	—	—	.10	.20	.35
	1968	—	—	.10	.20	.35
	1969	—	—	.10	.15	.35
	1970	—	—	.10	.20	.35
	1971	—	—	.10	.20	.35
	1974	—	—	.10	.20	.35

Obv: Flat top 3 in date.

KM#	Date	Mintage	Fine	VF	XF	Unc
49.2	1963	3,600 est.	12.50	25.00	37.50	65.00

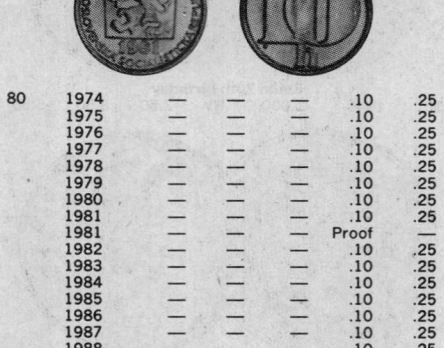

80	1974	—	—	—	.10	.25
	1975	—	—	—	.10	.25
	1976	—	—	—	.10	.25
	1977	—	—	—	.10	.25
	1978	—	—	—	.10	.25
	1979	—	—	—	.10	.25
	1980	—	—	—	.10	.25
	1981	—	—	—	.10	.25
	1981	—	—	—	Proof	—
	1982	—	—	—	.10	.25
	1983	—	—	—	.10	.25
	1984	—	—	—	.10	.25
	1985	—	—	—	.10	.25
	1986	—	—	—	.10	.25
	1987	—	—	—	.10	.25
	1988	—	—	—	.10	.25

NOTE: Varieties exist.

20 HALERU

BRASS

74	1972	—	—	.10	.20	.40
	1973	—	—	.10	.20	.40
	1974	—	—	.10	.20	.40
	1975	—	—	.10	.20	.40
	1976	—	—	.10	.20	.40
	1977	—	—	.10	.20	.40
	1978	—	—	.10	.20	.40
	1979	—	—	.10	.20	.40
	1980	—	—	.10	.15	.30
	1981	—	—	.10	.15	.30
	1981	—	—	—	Proof	—
	1982	—	—	.10	.15	.30
	1983	—	—	.10	.15	.30
	1984	—	—	.10	.15	.30
	1985	—	—	.10	.15	.30
	1986	—	—	.10	.15	.30
	1987	—	—	.10	.15	.30
	1988	—	—	.10	.15	.30

NOTE: Varieties exist.

25 HALERU

ALUMINUM

54	1962	—	.10	.15	.20	.35
	1963	—	.10	.15	.20	.35
	1964	—	.10	.15	.20	.35
	1964	—	—	—	Proof	—

NOTE: 25 Haleru ceased to be legal tender Dec. 31, 1972.

50 HALERU

BRONZE

KM#	Date	Mintage	Fine	VF	XF	Unc
55.1	1963	—	.10	.20	.30	.45
	1964	—	.10	.20	.30	.45
	1965	—	.10	.20	.30	.45
	1965	—	—	—	Proof	—
	1969	—	.10	.20	.30	.45
	1970	—	.10	.20	.30	.40
	1971	—	.10	.20	.30	.40
	1974	—	.10	.20	.30	.40

Obv: Small date, w/o dots.

55.2	1969	—	12.50	20.00	35.00	60.00

COPPER-NICKEL

89	1978	—	—	—	.10	.50
	1979	—	—	—	.10	.50
	1980	—	—	—	.10	.50
	1981	—	—	—	.10	.50
	1981	—	—	—	Proof	—
	1982	—	—	—	.10	.50
	1983	—	—	—	.10	.50
	1984	—	—	—	.10	.50
	1985	—	—	—	.10	.50
	1986	—	—	—	.10	.50
	1987	—	—	—	.10	.50
	1988	—	—	—	.10	.50

NOTE: Date varieties exist.

KORUNA

ALUMINUM-BRONZE

50	1961	—	—	.15	.30	.60
	1962	—	—	.15	.30	.60
	1963	—	—	.15	.30	.60
	1964	—	—	.15	.30	.60
	1965	—	—	.15	.30	.60
	1966	—	.40	.65	.90	1.25
	1966	—	—	—	Proof	Rare
	1967	—	—	.15	.30	.60
	1968	—	—	.15	.30	.60
	1969	—	—	.15	.30	.60
	1970	—	—	.15	.30	.60
	1971	—	—	.15	.30	.60
	1975	—	—	.15	.30	.60
	1976	—	—	.15	.30	.60
	1977	—	—	.15	.30	.75
	1979	—	—	.15	.30	.75
	1980	—	—	.15	.30	.75
	1981	—	—	.15	.30	.75
	1981	—	—	—	Proof	—
	1982	—	—	.15	.30	.75
	1983	—	—	.15	.30	.75
	1984	—	—	.15	.30	.75
	1985	—	—	.15	.30	.75
	1986	—	—	.15	.30	.75
	1987	—	—	.15	.30	.75
	1988	—	—	.15	.30	.75

NOTE: Date varieties exist.

2 KORUNY

COPPER-NICKEL

75	1972	—	—	.25	.35	.75
	1973	—	—	.25	.35	.75
	1974	—	—	.25	.35	.75
	1975	—	—	.25	.35	.75
	1976	—	—	.25	.35	.75
	1977	—	—	.25	.35	.75
	1980	—	—	.25	.35	.75
	1981	—	—	.25	.35	.75
	1981	—	—	—	Proof	—
	1982	—	—	.25	.35	.75
	1983	—	—	.25	.35	.75
	1984	—	—	.25	.35	.75
	1985	—	—	.25	.35	.75
	1986	—	—	.25	.35	.75
	1987	—	—	.25	.35	.75
	1988	—	—	.25	.35	.75

NOTE: Date and edge varieties exist.

3 KORUNY

COPPER-NICKEL

KM#	Date	Mintage	Fine	VF	XF	Unc
57	1965	—	—	.40	.60	1.00
	1966	—	—	.40	.60	1.00
	1966	—	—	—	Proof	Rare
	1968	—	—	.40	.60	1.00
	1969	—	—	.40	.60	1.00

5 KORUN

COPPER-NICKEL

60	1966	—	—	.75	1.00	2.00
	1966	—	—	—	Proof	Rare

1966 Varieties on obverse of coin
Large Date: No space between letter B in REPUBLIC and coat of arms.
Small Date: Space between letter B in REPUBLIC and coat of arms.
Plain Edge: No ornamental inscription on edge.
So far there has been no indication of any of the varieties as being scarce.

	1967	—	—	—	.75	1.50
	1968	—	—	—	.75	1.50
	1969 straight date					
		—	—	—	.75	1.50
	1969 date in semi-circle					
		—	.75	1.25	2.00	3.00
	1970	—	—	—	.75	1.50
	1973 (2 vars.)	—	—	—	.75	1.25
	1974 (3 vars.)	—	—	—	.75	1.25
	1975	—	—	—	.75	1.25
	1978	—	—	—	.75	1.25
	1979	—	—	—	.75	1.25
	1980	—	—	—	.75	1.25
	1981	—	—	—	.75	1.25
	1981	—	—	—	Proof	—
	1982	—	—	—	.75	1.25
	1983	—	—	—	.75	1.25
	1984	—	—	—	.75	1.25
	1985	—	—	—	.75	1.25
	1986	—	—	—	.75	1.25
	1987	—	—	—	.75	1.25
	1988	—	—	—	.75	1.25
	1989	—	—	—	.75	1.25

10 KORUN

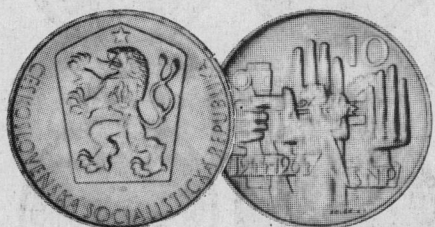

12.0000 g, .500 SILVER, .1929 oz ASW
20th Anniversary 1944 Slovak Uprising

56	1964	.120	—	—	3.00	4.00

550th Anniversary of Death of Jan Hus

58	1965	.055	—	—	5.00	7.00
	1965	5,000	—	—	Proof	9.00

1100th Anniversary of Great Moravia

KM#	Date	Mintage	Fine	VF	XF	Unc
61	1966	.115	—	—	4.00	6.00
	1966	5,000	—	—	Proof	9.00

500th Anniversary Bratislava University

62	1967	.055	—	—	9.00	12.50
	1967	5,000	—	—	Proof	17.50

Prague National Theater Centennial

63	1968	.055	—	—	15.00	20.00
	1968	5,000	—	—	Proof	40.00

20 KORUN

9.0000 g, .500 SILVER, .1446 oz ASW
Centennial Death of Andrej Sladkovic

76	1972	.055	—	—	3.00	4.00
	1972	5,000	—	—	Proof	15.00

25 KORUN

16.0000 g, .500 SILVER, .2572 oz ASW
20th Anniversary Czechoslovakian Liberation

59	1965	.145	—	—	5.00	8.00
	1965	5,000	—	—	Proof	15.00

Sesquicentennial Prague National Museum

64	1968	.055	—	—	5.00	8.00
	1968	5,000	—	—	Proof	50.00

100th Anniversary Death of J. E. Purkyne

KM#	Date	Mintage	Fine	VF	XF	Unc
66	1969	.045	—	—	5.00	8.00
	1969	5,000	—	—	Proof	10.00

NOTE: Edge varieties exist.

25th Anniversary 1944 Slovak Uprising

67	1969	.025	—	—	20.00	35.00
	1969	5,000	—	—	Proof	40.00

10.0000 g, .500 SILVER, .1607 oz ASW
50th Anniversary Slovak National Theater

68	1970	.045	—	—	4.00	7.00
	1970	5,000	—	—	Proof	45.00

25th Anniversary of Liberation

69	1970	.095	—	—	4.00	6.00
	1970	5,000	—	—	Proof	15.00

50 KORUN

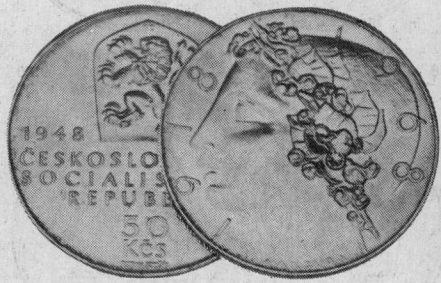

20.0000 g, .900 SILVER, .5787 oz ASW
50th Anniversary of Czechoslovakia
20th Anniversary People's Republic

65	1968	.058	—	—	25.00	45.00
	1968	2,000	—	—	Proof	175.00

CZECHOSLOVAK SOC. REP. 460

13.0000 g, .700 SILVER, .2926 oz ASW
Lenin Birth Centennial

KM#	Date	Mintage	Fine	VF	XF	Unc
70	1970	.044	—	—	6.00	9.00
	1970	6,200	—	—	Proof	30.00

50th Anniversary Czechoslovak Communist Party

71	1971	.045	—	—	6.00	9.00
	1971	5,000	—	—	Proof	40.00

50th Anniv. Death of Pavol Orsagh-Hvlezdoslav

72	1971	.045	—	—	6.00	9.00
	1971	5,000	—	—	Proof	35.00

50th Anniversary Death of J.V.Myslbek

77	1972	.045	—	—	6.00	9.00
	1972	5,000	—	—	Proof	30.00

25th Anniversary Victory of Communist Party

78	1973	.055	—	—	6.00	9.00
	1973	5,000	—	—	Proof	30.00

200th Anniversary Birth of Josef Jungmann

79	1973	.045	—	—	6.00	9.00
	1973	5,000	—	—	Proof	17.50

Janko Jesensky Birth Centennial

KM#	Date	Mintage	Fine	VF	XF	Unc
81	1974	.055	—	—	6.00	9.00
	1974	5,000	—	—	Proof	14.00

S. K. Neumann Birth Centennial

83	1975	.055	—	—	6.00	9.00
	1975	5,000	—	—	Proof	10.00

125th Anniversary of Death of Jan Kollar

87	1977	.075	—	—	6.00	9.00
	1977	5,000	—	—	Proof	12.00

Centennial of Birth of Zdenek Nejedly

90	1978	.075	—	—	6.00	9.00
	1978	5,000	—	—	Proof	12.00

650th Anniversary of Kremnica Mint

91	1978	.093	—	—	6.00	9.00
	1978	7,000	—	—	Proof	12.00

30th Anniversary of 9th Congress

98	1979	.094	—	—	6.00	9.00
	1979	6,000	—	—	Proof	12.00

7.0000 g, .500 SILVER, .1125 oz ASW
Prague

KM#	Date	Mintage	Fine	VF	XF	Unc
121	1986	.090	—	—	—	6.00
	1986	.010	—	—	Proof	9.00

Levoca

122	1986	.090	—	—	—	6.00
	1986	.010	—	—	Proof	9.00

Telc

124	1986	.090	—	—	—	6.00
	1986	.010	—	—	Proof	9.00

Bratislava

125	1986	.090	—	—	—	6.00
	1986	.010	—	—	Proof	9.00

Cesky Krumlov

126	1986	.090	—	—	—	6.00
	1986	.010	—	—	Proof	9.00

Environmental Protection - Horses

127	1987	.095	—	—	—	6.00
	1987	5,000	—	—	Proof	9.00

300th Anniversary of Birth of Juras Janosik

129	1988	.070	—	—	—	13.00
	1988	2,500	—	—	Proof	16.00

CZECHOSLOVAK SOC. REP. 461

150th Anniversary of Breslau to Brunn Railroad

KM#	Date	Mintage	Fine	VF	XF	Unc
133	1989	—	—	—	—	10.00
	1989	—	—	—	Proof	12.50

100 KORUN

15.0000 g, .700 SILVER, .3376 oz ASW
Centennial Death of Josef Manes

73	1971	.045	—	—	12.00	15.00
	1971	5,000	—	—	Proof	27.50

Bedrich Smetana Birth Sesquicentennial

82	1974	.075	—	—	12.00	15.00
	1974	5,000	—	—	Proof	25.00

Janko Kral Death Centennial

84	1976	.075	—	—	12.00	15.00
	1976	5,000	—	—	Proof	25.00

Viktor Kaplan Birth Centennial

85	1976	.075	—	—	12.00	15.00
	1976	5,000	—	—	Proof	25.00

Vaclav Hollar

88	1977	.095	—	—	12.00	15.00
	1977	5,000	—	—	Proof	25.00

75th Anniversary of Birth of Julius Fucik

KM#	Date	Mintage	Fine	VF	XF	Unc
92	1978	.075	—	—	12.00	15.00
	1978	5,000	—	—	Proof	25.00

King Karel IV

93	1978	.090	—	—	12.00	15.00
	1978	.010	—	—	Proof	25.00

150th Anniversary of Birth of Jan Botto

99	1979	.075	—	—	12.00	15.00
	1979	5,000	—	—	Proof	25.00

650th Anniversary Birth of Peter Parler

100	1980	.091	—	—	12.00	15.00
	1980	9,000	—	—	Proof	20.00

9.0000 g, .500 SILVER, .1446 oz ASW
Fifth Spartakiade Games

101	1980	.110	—	—	—	15.00
	1980	.010	—	—	Proof	20.00

Centennial of Birth of Bohumir Smeral

102	1980	.074	—	—	—	15.00
	1980	6,000	—	—	Proof	20.00

20th Anniversary of Manned Space Flight

KM#	Date	Mintage	Fine	VF	XF	Unc
103	1981	.095	—	—	—	15.00
	1981	5,000	—	—	Proof	20.00

Centennial of Birth of Prof. Otakar Spaniel

104	1981	.115	—	—	—	15.00
	1981	5,000	—	—	Proof	20.00

Centennial of Birth of Ivan Olbracht

106	1982	.076	—	—	—	15.00
	1982	4,000	—	—	Proof	20.00

150th Anniversary of Horse Drawn Railway

107	1982	.076	—	—	—	15.00
	1982	7,000	—	—	Proof	20.00

100th Anniversary of Death of Karl Marx

108	1982	.046	—	—	—	15.00
	1982	4,000	—	—	Proof	20.00

Centennial of Birth of Jaroslav Hasek

109	1983	.076	—	—	—	15.00
	1983	4,000	—	—	Proof	20.00

Centennial of Death of Samo Chalupka

KM#	Date	Mintage	Fine	VF	XF	Unc
110	1983	.076	—	—	—	15.00
	1983	4,000	—	—	Proof	20.00

1985 Ice Hockey Championships

KM#	Date	Mintage	Fine	VF	XF	Unc
117	1985	.066	—	—	—	15.00
	1985	4,000	—	—	Proof	20.00

Prague Exposition

KM#	Date	Mintage	Fine	VF	XF	Unc
130	1988	.060	—	—	—	17.50
	1988	2,500	—	—	Proof	30.00

100th Anniversary of Prague Theater

111	1983	.140	—	—	—	15.00
	1983	.010	—	—	Proof	20.00

125th Anniversary of Birth of Martin Kukucin

118	1985	.062	—	—	—	15.00
	1985	3,000	—	—	Proof	20.00

Centennial of Birth of Martin Benka

132	1988	.040	—	—	—	17.50
	1988	2,000	—	—	Proof	30.00

500 KORUN

300th Anniversary of Birth of Matej Bel

113	1984	.057	—	—	—	15.00
	1984	3,000	—	—	Proof	20.00

Helsinki Conference

119	1985	.075	—	—	—	15.00
	1985	5,000	—	—	Proof	20.00

24.0000 g, .900 SILVER, .6944 oz ASW
125th Anniversary of Death of Ludovit Stur

105	1981	.051	—	—	—	27.50
	1981	4,000	—	—	Proof	35.00

150th Anniversary of Birth of Jan Neruda

114	1984	.076	—	—	—	15.00
	1984	4,000	—	—	Proof	20.00

250th Anniversary of Death of Petr Brandl

120	1985	.071	—	—	—	15.00
	1985	4,000	—	—	Proof	20.00

100th Anniversary of Prague Theater

112	1983	.055	—	—	—	27.50
	1983	5,000	—	—	Proof	35.00

Centennial of Birth of Antonin Zapotocky

115	1984	.076	—	—	—	15.00
	1984	4,000	—	—	Proof	20.00

150th Anniversary of Death of Karel Hynek Macha

123	1986	.075	—	—	—	15.00
	1986	5,000	—	—	Proof	20.00

200th Anniversary of Birth of Jan Holly

116	1985	.062	—	—	—	15.00
	1985	3,000	—	—	Proof	20.00

13.0000 g, .500 SILVER, .2090 oz ASW
225th Anniversary of Mining Academy

128	1987	.075	—	—	—	16.50
	1987	5,000	—	—	Proof	27.50

20th Anniversary of National Federation

KM#	Date	Mintage	Fine	VF	XF	Unc
131	1988	*.040	—	—	—	20.00
	1988	*2,000	—	—	Proof	40.00

MINT SETS (MS)

KM#	Date	Mintage	Identification	Issue Price	Mkt. Val.
MS1	1980(7)	—	KM50,60,74,75,80,86,89	5.00	5.00
MS2	1981(7)	—	KM50,60,74,75,80,86,89	—	5.00
MS3	1982(7)	—	KM50,60,74,75,80,86,89	—	5.00
MS4	1983(7)	—	KM50,60,74,75,80,86,89	—	5.00
MS5	1984(7)	—	KM50,60,74,75,80,86,89	—	5.00
MS6	1985(7)	—	KM50,60,74,75,80,86,89	—	5.00
MS7	1986(7)	—	KM50,60,74,75,80,86,89	—	5.00
MS8	1987(7)	—	KM50,60,74-75,80,86,89	—	5.00
MS9	1988(7)	—	KM50,60,74,75,80,86,89	—	5.00

PROOF SETS (PS)

PS1	1981(7)	—	KM50,60,74,75,80,86,89	—	—

BOHEMIA-MORAVIA

Bohemia, a province in north-west Czechoslovakia, was combined with the majority of Moravia in central Czechoslovakia (excluding parts of north and south Moravia which were joined with Silesia in 1938) to form the German protectorate in March, 1939, after the German invasion. Toward the end of war in 1945 the protectorate was dissolved and Bohemia and Moravia once again became part of Czechoslovakia.

10 HALERU

ZINC

KM#	Date	Mintage	Fine	VF	XF	Unc
1	1940	82.114	.25	.50	.75	2.50
	1941	Inc. Ab.	.25	.50	.75	3.50
	1942	Inc. Ab.	.25	.50	.75	3.50
	1943	Inc. Ab.	.50	.75	1.50	4.50
	1944	Inc. Ab.	.75	1.50	2.50	5.50

20 HALERU

ZINC

2	1940	106.526	.25	.50	1.00	3.50
	1941	Inc. Ab.	.25	.50	1.00	3.50
	1942	Inc. Ab.	.25	.50	1.00	3.50
	1943	Inc. Ab.	.50	.75	1.50	4.50
	1944	Inc. Ab.	.50	1.00	1.75	4.00

50 HALERU

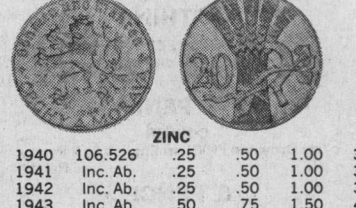

ZINC

3	1940	53.270	.35	.75	1.25	5.00
	1941	Inc. Ab.	.35	.75	1.25	5.00
	1942	Inc. Ab.	.35	.75	1.25	5.00
	1943	Inc. Ab.	.75	1.50	3.00	7.00
	1944	Inc. Ab.	.35	.75	1.25	5.00

KORUNA

ZINC

KM#	Date	Mintage	Fine	VF	XF	Unc
4	1941	102.817	.50	.75	1.50	5.00
	1942	Inc. Ab.	.50	.75	1.50	5.00
	1943	Inc. Ab.	.50	.75	1.50	5.00
	1944	Inc. Ab.	.50	.75	1.50	5.00

SLOVAKIA

Slovakia (Slovak Socialist Republic), a constituent republic of Czechoslovakia, has an area of 18,923 sq. mi. (49,011 sq. km.) and a population of 4.9 million. Capital: Bratislava. Textiles, steel, and wood products are exported.

In 1938, the Slovaks declared themselves an autonomous state within a federal Czecho-Slovak state. After the German occupation, Slovakia became nominally independent under the protection of Germany, March 16, 1939. Father Jozef Tiso was appointed President. Slovakia was liberated from German control in Oct. 1944, but in May 1945 ceased to be independent Slovak state. In 1968 it became a constituent state of Czechoslovakia.

MONETARY SYSTEM

100 Halierov = 1 Koruna

5 HALIEROV

ZINC

8	1942	1.000	1.50	2.50	4.50	8.00

10 HALIEROV

BRONZE

1	1939	15.000	1.50	2.00	4.00	8.00
	1942	7.000	1.50	2.00	4.00	8.00

20 HALIEROV

BRONZE

4	1940	10.972	1.25	2.00	3.00	6.00
	1941	4.028	1.25	2.00	3.00	6.00
	1942	6.474	1.25	3.00	5.00	9.00

ALUMINUM

4a	1942	Inc. Ab.	1.00	1.50	2.00	4.50
	1943	15.000	1.00	1.50	2.00	4.50

50 HALIEROV

COPPER-NICKEL

5	1940	—	30.00	45.00	60.00	125.00
	1941	8.000	1.00	2.00	3.00	6.00

ALUMINUM

5a	1943	4.400	1.00	1.50	2.50	5.00
	1944	2.621	1.25	2.00	4.00	7.00

KORUNA

COPPER-NICKEL

6	1940	2.350	.75	1.25	2.25	6.00
	1941	11.650	.50	1.00	2.00	5.00
	1942	6.000	.50	1.00	2.00	5.00
	1944	.884	1.50	2.50	4.50	10.00
	1945	3.321	.75	1.25	2.25	6.00

5 KORUN

NICKEL

KM#	Date	Mintage	Fine	VF	XF	Unc
2	1939	5.101	1.50	2.00	3.50	12.50

Approximately 2,000,000 pieces were melted down by the Czechoslovak National Bank in 1947.

10 KORUN

7.0000 g, .500 SILVER, .1125 oz ASW.
Rev: Variety 1 - Cross atop church held by left figure.

9.1	1944	1.381	2.00	4.00	5.00	8.00

Rev: Variety 2 - W/o cross.

9.2	1944	Inc. Ab.	2.50	5.00	7.00	10.00

20 KORUN

15.0000 g, .500 SILVER, .2411 oz ASW.

3	1939	.200	5.00	10.00	15.00	40.00

Rev: Variety 1 - Single bar cross in church at lower right.

7.1	1941	2.500	2.00	3.50	5.00	10.00

Rev: Variety 2 - Double bar cross.

7.2	1941	Inc. Ab.	4.00	6.50	9.00	15.00

50 KORUN

16.5000 g, .700 SILVER, .3713 oz ASW.
5th Anniversary of Independence

10	1944	2.000	3.00	5.00	7.50	12.50

Listings For

DAHOMEY: refer to Benin

DANISH WEST INDIES

464

The Danish West Indies (now the U.S. organized unincorporated territory of the Virgin Islands of the United States) consisted of the islands of St. Thomas, St. John, St. Croix, and 62 islets located in the Caribbean Sea 40 miles (64 km.) east of Puerto Rico. The islands have a combined area of 133 sq. mi. (344 sq. km.) and a population of 110,000. Capital: Charlotte Amalie. Tourism is the principal industry. Watch movements, costume jewelry, pharmaceuticals, and rum are exported.

The Virgin Islands were discovered by Columbus in 1493, during his second voyage to America. During the 17th century the islands, actually the peaks of a submerged mountain range, were held at various times by Spain, Holland, England, France and Denmark, and during the same period were favorite resorts of the buccaneers operating in the Caribbean and the coastal waters of eastern North America. Control of the 100-island chain finally passed to Denmark and England. The Danish islands were purchased by the United States in 1917 for $25 million, mainly because they command the Anegada Passage into the Caribbean Sea, a strategic point on the defense perimeter of the Panama Canal.

RULERS
Danish, until 1917

MINT MARKS
See Denmark

MINTMASTER'S INITIALS
See Denmark

MONEYER'S INITIALS
See Denmark

MONETARY SYSTEM
(Until 1849)
96 Skilling = 1 Daler

II SKILLING

1.2180 g, .250 SILVER, .0098 oz ASW
Obv: Crowned arms. Rev: Value and date.

KM#	Date	Mintage	VG	Fine	VF	XF
13	1816	—	6.50	12.50	25.00	45.00
	1837 flat top 3					
		*.500	6.50	11.50	22.50	35.00
	1837 round top 3					
	Inc. Ab.		7.00	13.00	25.00	42.50
18	1847	*.250	6.50	11.50	22.50	35.00
19	1848	*1.000	4.50	7.50	15.00	27.50

X SKILLING

2.4360 g, .625 SILVER, .0489 oz ASW

| 14 | 1816 | *.083 | 8.50 | 17.50 | 30.00 | 55.00 |

16	1840	*.110	7.50	15.00	28.00	45.00
	1845	*.100	7.00	13.50	25.00	40.00
	1845	—	—	—	Proof	—
	1847	*.113	7.50	15.00	28.00	45.00
20	1848	*.404	8.50	17.50	30.00	50.00
	1848	—	—	—	Proof	—
	1848 plain edge					
	Inc. Ab.		9.00	20.00	32.00	55.00

XX SKILLING

4.8720 g, .625 SILVER, .0979 oz ASW
Obv: Crowned arms. Rev: Value and date.

15	1816	*.020	15.00	32.50	80.00	135.00
17	1840	*.050	12.00	25.00	65.00	120.00
	1845	*.055	12.00	25.00	65.00	120.00
	1847	*.050	12.00	25.00	65.00	120.00
21	1848 incuse edge		12.00	25.00	65.00	120.00
	1848	*.070	—	—	Proof	315.00
	1848 plain edge					
	Inc. Ab.		20.00	35.00	80.00	150.00

COUNTERMARKED COINAGE
1849-1859

The only countermark authorized for the Danish West Indies was the crowned F R VII monogram, which was used between 1849 through 1859. Although the majority of the coins countermarked in those years were of United States origin, numerous pieces from European and Latin American countries were also employed for this purpose.

COUNTERFEITS: This series has been counterfeited extensively. A common counterfeit countermark lacks the small cross on top of the crown and small shallow striking of c/m especially in beads of crown.

U. S. SERIES
1/2 CENT
COPPER
c/m: Crowned FRVII on U.S. 1/2 Cent.

KM#	Date	Mintage	Fine	VF	XF
24	ND(1808)	—	—	Rare	—
	ND(1809)	—	—	Unique	—
	ND(1834)	—	—	Unique	—

CENT

COPPER
c/m: Crowned FRVII on U.S. large Cent.

| 25 | ND(1838) | — | — | Rare | — |

25 CENTS

SILVER
c/m: Crowned FRVII on U.S. 25 Cent.

| 26 | ND(1849) | — | — | Rare | — |

50 CENTS

SILVER
c/m: Crowned FRVII on U.S. 50 Cent.

| 27 | ND(1823) | — | — | Rare | — |

DOLLAR

SILVER
c/m: Crowned FRVII on U.S. Dollar.

| 28 | ND(1847) | — | — | Rare | — |

BRAZIL SERIES
40 REIS
COPPER
c/m: Crowned FRVII on Brazil 40 Reis.

| 31 | ND(1826) | — | — | Unique | — |

960 REIS

SILVER
c/m: Crowned FRVII on Brazil 960 Reis.

KM#	Date	Mintage	Fine	VF	XF
32	ND(1819)	—	—	Rare	—

BRITISH WEST INDIES SERIES
1/8 DOLLAR

SILVER
c/m: Crowned FRVII on 'Anchor' 1/8 Dollar.

| 35 | ND(1822) | — | 250.00 | 350.00 | 500.00 |

1/4 DOLLAR

SILVER
c/m: Crowned FRVII on 'Anchor' 1/4 Dollar.

| 36 | ND(1822) | — | 350.00 | 500.00 | 650.00 |

ENGLISH SERIES
FARTHING
COPPER
c/m: Crowned FRVII on English Farthing.

| 39 | ND | — | 45.00 | 65.00 | 100.00 |

1/2 PENNY
COPPER
c/m: Crowned FRVII on English 1/2 Penny.

| 40 | ND | — | — | Rare | — |

6 PENCE

SILVER
c/m: Crowned FRVII on English 6 Pence.

| 41 | ND | — | 100.00 | 150.00 | 225.00 |

SHILLING

SILVER
c/m: Crowned FRVII on English Shilling.

| 42 | ND | — | 125.00 | 150.00 | 225.00 |

1/2 CROWN

SILVER
c/m: Crowned FRVII on English 1/2 Crown.

KM#	Date	Mintage	Fine	VF	XF
43	ND(1818)	—	250.00	350.00	500.00

CROWN

SILVER
c/m: Crowned FRVII on English Bank Dollar.

44	ND	—	350.00	500.00	750.00

FRENCH SERIES
5 SOLS

SILVER
c/m: Crowned FRVII on French 5 Sols.

47	ND	—	65.00	100.00	150.00

1/2 FRANC

SILVER
c/m: Crowned FRVII on French 1/2 Franc.

48	ND	—	65.00	100.00	150.00

MEXICAN SERIES
8 REALES

SILVER
c/m: Crowned FRVII on Mexican 8 Reales.

51	ND	—	175.00	250.00	400.00

NETHERLANDS SERIES
25 CENTS

SILVER
c/m: Crowned FRVII on Netherlands 25 Cents.

KM#	Date	Mintage	Fine	VF	XF
54	ND(1826)	—	175.00	275.00	375.00

SPANISH SERIES
4 MARAVEDI

COPPER
c/m: Crowned FRVII on Spanish 4 Maravedi.

57	ND	—	75.00	100.00	150.00

REAL

SILVER
c/m: Crowned FRVII on Spanish or Spanish Colonial 1 Real.

58	ND(1782)	—	75.00	125.00	200.00

2 REALES

SILVER
c/m: Crowned FRVII on Mexico Mint 2 Reales.

59	ND(1761)	—	100.00	150.00	225.00

4 REALES

SILVER
c/m: Crowned FRVII on Spanish or Spanish Colonial 4 Reales.

60	ND(1806)	—	450.00	650.00	1000.

DECIMAL COINAGE
20 Cents = 1 Franc

CENT

BRONZE

KM#	Date	Mintage	VG	Fine	VF	XF
63	1859(o)	.216	1.75	3.00	7.00	12.50
	1859(o) 10 pcs.	—	—	Proof		Rare
	1860(o)	.250	2.25	4.50	8.00	18.00

| 68 | 1868(c) | .240 | 1.75 | 3.00 | 7.00 | 12.50 |
| | 1868(c) | | | | Proof | |

KM#	Date	Mintage	VG	Fine	VF	XF
68	1878(h)	.020	3.00	6.00	10.00	22.50
	1879(h)	.040	150.00	200.00	250.00	450.00
	1883(h)	.210	2.25	4.50	8.00	17.50

3 CENTS

1.0440 g, .625 SILVER, .0210 oz ASW

| 64 | 1859(c) | .291 | 2.00 | 5.00 | 10.00 | 22.50 |
| | 1859(c) 10 pcs. | — | — | Proof | | Rare |

5 CENTS

1.7400 g, .625 SILVER, .0349 oz ASW

| 65 | 1859(c) | .150 | 2.00 | 5.00 | 10.00 | 20.00 |
| | 1859(c) 10 pcs. | — | — | Proof | | Rare |

69	1878(h)	.500	6.75	14.00	27.50	50.00
	1878(h)				Proof	365.00
	1879(h) Inc. Ab.		6.75	14.00	27.50	50.00

10 CENTS

3.4850 g, .625 SILVER, .0699 oz ASW

66	1859(c)	.250	2.00	5.00	12.00	25.00
	1859(c) 10 pcs.	—	—	Proof		Rare
	1862/1(c)	.140	—	—		
	1862(c) Inc. Ab.		6.75	10.00	16.00	30.00
	1862(c)				Proof	225.00

70	1878(h)	.080	6.00	12.50	27.50	50.00
	1878(h)				Proof	
	1879(h)	.120	12.00	22.00	47.50	75.00
	1879(h)				Proof	

20 CENTS

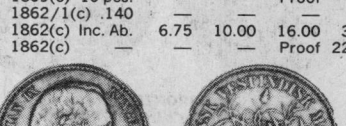

6.9610 g, .625 SILVER, .1399 oz ASW

67	1859(c)	.430	7.50	15.00	27.50	50.00
	1859(c) 10 pcs.	—	—	Proof		Rare
	1862(c)	.560	7.50	15.00	27.50	50.00
	1862(c)				Proof	375.00

71	1878(h)	.200	12.50	17.50	32.50	70.00
	1878(h)	—			Proof	425.00
	1879(h)	.300	55.00	100.00	165.00	250.00

MONETARY REFORM
5 Bit = 1 Cent
5 Francs = 1 Daler

DANISH WEST INDIES

DANISH WEST INDIES

1/2 CENT - 2 1/2 BIT

BRONZE
Mintmaster's Initials: P-GJ

KM#	Date	Mintage	VG	Fine	VF	XF
74	1905(h)	.190	2.50	5.00	8.00	15.00
	1905(h)				Proof	Rare

CENT - 5 BIT

BRONZE
Mintmaster's Initials: P-GJ

| 75 | 1905(h) | .500 | 1.50 | 3.00 | 5.00 | 10.00 |

Mintmaster's Initials: VBP-AH-GJ

| 83 | 1913(h) | .200 | 5.00 | 8.50 | 25.00 | 40.00 |

2 CENTS - 10 BIT

BRONZE
Mintmaster's Initials: P-GJ

| 76 | 1905(h) | .150 | 2.50 | 5.50 | 12.50 | 20.00 |
| | 1905(h) | 20 pcs. | | | Proof | Rare |

5 CENTS - 25 BIT

NICKEL
Mintmaster's Initials: P-GJ

| 77 | 1905(h) | .199 | 1.00 | 2.00 | 5.00 | 10.00 |
| | 1905(h) | 20 pcs. | — | — | Proof | Rare |

10 CENTS - 50 BIT

2.5000 g, .800 SILVER, .0643 oz ASW
Mintmaster's Initials: P-GJ

| 78 | 1905(h) | .175 | 1.50 | 3.50 | 7.00 | 12.50 |
| | 1905(h) | 20 pcs. | — | — | Proof | Rare |

20 CENTS - 1 FRANC

5.0000 g, .800 SILVER, .1286 oz ASW
Mintmaster's Initials: P-GJ

| 79 | 1905(h) | .150 | 7.50 | 12.50 | 30.00 | 60.00 |
| | 1905(h) | 20 pcs. | | | Proof | Rare |

Mintmaster's Initials: P-GJ

KM#	Date	Mintage	VG	Fine	VF	XF
81	1907(h)	.101	10.00	15.00	30.00	60.00
	1907(h)	10 pcs.			Proof	Rare

40 CENTS - 2 FRANCS

10.0000 g, .800 SILVER, .2572 oz ASW
Mintmaster's Initials: P-GJ

| 80 | 1905(h) | .038 | 15.00 | 30.00 | 65.00 | 125.00 |
| | 1905(h) | 20 pcs. | | | Proof | Rare |

Mintmaster's Initials: P-GJ

| 82 | 1907(h) | .025 | 20.00 | 45.00 | 100.00 | 175.00 |
| | 1907(h) | 10 pcs. | | | Proof | 1100. |

4 DALER - 20 FRANCS

6.4516 g, .900 GOLD, .1867 oz AGW
Mintmaster's Initials: P-GJ

KM#	Date	Mintage	Fine	VF	XF	Unc
72	1904(h)	.121	150.00	275.00	375.00	550.00
	1905(h)	I.A.	150.00	275.00	400.00	600.00

10 DALER - 50 FRANCS

16.1290 g, .900 GOLD, .4667 oz AGW
Mintmaster's Initials: P-GJ

| 73 | 1904(h) | 2,005 | 1250. | 2000. | 4000. | 6000. |

PROOF SETS (PS)

KM#	Date	Mintage	Identification	Issue Price	Mkt. Val.
PS1	1859(5)	10	KM63-67	—	Rare
PS2	1862(2)			—	Rare
PS3	1878			—	Rare
PS4	1905(5)	20	KM76-80	—	Rare
PS5	1907(2)	10	KM81-82	—	Rare

Listings For
DANZIG: refer to Poland

DENMARK

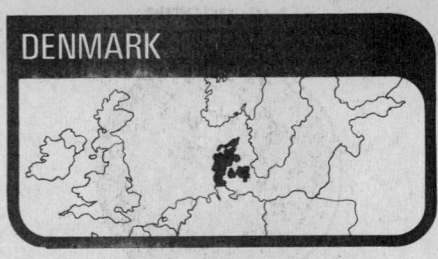

The Kingdom of Denmark, a constitutional monarchy located at the mouth of the Baltic Sea, has an area of 16,629 sq. mi. (43,069 sq. km.) and a population of 5.1 million. Capital: Copenhagen. Most of the country is arable. Agriculture, which employs the majority of the people, is conducted by small farmers served by cooperatives. The largest industries are food processing, iron and metal, and fishing. Machinery, meats (chiefly bacon), dairy products and chemicals are exported.

Denmark, a great power during the Viking period of the 9th-11th centuries, conducted raids on western Europe and England, and in the 11th century united England, Denmark and Norway under the rule of King Canute. Despite a struggle between the crown and the nobility (13th-14th centuries) which forced the King to grant a written constitution, Queen Margaret (1387-1412) succeeded in uniting Denmark, Norway, Sweden, Finland and Greenland under the Danish crown, placing all of Scandinavia under the rule of Denmark. An unwise alliance with Napoleon contributed to the dismembering of the empire and fostered a liberal movement which succeeded in making Denmark a constitutional monarchy in 1849.

The present decimal system of coinage was introduced in 1874.

RULERS

Christian VII, 1766-1808
Frederik VI, 1808-1839
Christian VIII, 1839-1848
Frederik VII, 1848-1863
Christian IX, 1863-1906
Frederik VIII, 1906-1912
Christian X, 1912-1947
Frederik IX, 1947-1972
Margrethe II, 1972-

MINT MARKS

(a) - Altona (1842 issues), apple
(c) - Copenhagen, crown
(h) - Copenhagen, heart
(o) - Altona, orb
KM - Copenhagen

MINTMASTER'S INITIALS

Altona

Letter	Date	Name
MF	1786-1816	Michael Flor
CB	1817-1819	Cajus Branth
FF, IFF	1819-1856	Johan Friedrich Freund
TA	1848-1851	Theodor Andersen
FA	1856-1863	Hans Frederik Alsing

Copenhagen

HIAB	1797-1810	Hans Jacob Arnold Branth
HIAB	1810-1821	Ole Varberg
CFG	1821-1831	Conrad Frederik Gerlach
VS, WS	1835-1861	Georg Wilhelm Svendsen
RH	1861-1869	Rasmus Hinnerup
CS	1869-1893	Diderik Christian Andreas Svendsen
P, VBP	1893-1918	Vilhelm Buchard Poulsen
HCN	1919-1927	Hans Christian Nielsen
N	1927-1955	Niels Peter Nielsen
C	1956-1971	Alfred Frederik Christiansen
S	1971-1978	Vagn Sorensen
B	1978-1981	Peter M. Bjarno
R	1982-	N. Norregaard Rasmussen

MONEYER'S INITIALS

Altona

FA	1825-1855	Hans Frederik Alsing
FK	1841-1863	Frederik Christopher Krohn
HL	1848-1851	Carl Heinrich Lorenz
PP	1852-1863	Peter Petersen

Copenhagen

PG	1800-1807	Peter Leonard Gianelli
IC, ICF	1810-1841	Johannes Conradsen
M	1813	Christian Andreas Muller
CC	1836	Christen Christensen
FK	1841-1873	Frederik Christopher Krohn
HC	1873-1901	Harald Conradsen
GI, GJ	1901-1933	Knud Gunnar Jensen
AH	1908-1924	Andreas Frederik Vilhelm Hansen
HS, S	1933-1968	Harald Salomon
B	1968	Frode Bahnsen

MONETARY SYSTEM

(Until 1813)
64 Skilling Danske = 4 Mark = 1 Krone
96 Skilling Danske = 6 Mark = 1 Speciedaler
12 Marks = 1 Ducat

(Commencing 1813)
96 Rigsbank Skilling = 1 Rigs(bank)daler
30 Schilling Courant = 1 Rigs(bank)daler
2 Rigsbankdaler = 1 Rigsdaler Species

2 Rigsbankdaler = 1 Specie(daler)
5 Species(daler) = 1 D'or

1/5 RIGSBANKSKILLING

COPPER

C#	Date	Mintage	VG	Fine	VF	XF
118	1842 FF	—	4.00	8.00	15.00	30.00

Rev. denomination: 1/5 R.B.S.

| 118a | 1842 FF | — | 1.25 | 3.00 | 6.00 | 10.00 |

1/2 RIGSBANKSKILLING

COPPER

| 100 | 1838 | — | 1.00 | 2.00 | 5.00 | 10.00 |

| 119 | 1842 VS | — | 2.00 | 4.00 | 8.00 | 15.00 |

| 131 | 1852 VS | — | 1.75 | 3.00 | 6.50 | 11.50 |

1/2 SKILLINGRIGSMONT

BRONZE

| 134 | 1857(o) | — | .75 | 1.25 | 2.75 | 5.50 |
| | 1857(c) | — | — | — | — | 250.00 |

Y#	Date	Mintage	VG	Fine	VF	XF
1	1868	—	1.00	1.50	3.50	7.00

SKILLING

.9230 g, .138 SILVER, .0041 oz ASW
Obv: Crowned FR VI monogram. Rev: Value, DANSK, date.

C#	Date	Mintage	VG	Fine	VF	XF
104	1808 MF	—	2.00	4.25	9.00	15.00
	1809 MF	—	1.50	2.75	6.00	9.00
	1810 MF	—	—	—	Unique	

COPPER, 15mm

| 87.1 | 1812 MF | — | 1.25 | 1.50 | 3.25 | 5.50 |

RIGSBANKSKILLING

COPPER

| 93 | 1813 | — | .75 | 1.50 | 5.00 | 12.00 |

Obv: Crowned oval arms
Rev: Value and date

| 101 | 1818 | — | 1.25 | 2.50 | 6.25 | 14.00 |

C#	Date	Mintage	VG	Fine	VF	XF
120	1842 FF(o)	—	1.75	4.00	8.50	16.00
	1842 VS(c)	—	1.75	4.00	8.50	16.00

Obv: Large bust.

| 132 | 1852 VS | — | 3.00 | 6.50 | 15.00 | 26.00 |

Obv: Small bust.

| 132a | 1852 VS | — | — | — | Rare | |

Obv: Medium bust.

| 132b | 1853 VS | — | 1.75 | 3.50 | 7.00 | 12.50 |

RIGSMONTSKILLING

BRONZE

135	1856(o)	—	.75	1.50	3.00	9.00
	1856(c)	—	—	—	—	175.00
	1860(o)	—	1.00	2.00	3.50	10.00
	1863(c)	—	1.25	2.25	5.00	10.00

Y#	Date	Mintage	VG	Fine	VF	XF
2	1867	—	.75	1.50	3.00	6.50
	1869	—	1.00	1.75	3.50	7.00
	1870	—	1.25	2.50	6.00	11.00
	1871	—	1.75	3.25	7.00	12.50
	1872	—	.75	1.50	3.50	7.00

2 SKILLING

1.5000 g, .250 SILVER, .0121 oz ASW

C#	Date	Mintage	VG	Fine	VF	XF
53	1801 HIAB	—	1.25	2.50	4.75	10.00
	1801 MF	—	2.25	4.00	7.00	12.00
	1805 MF	—	1.50	2.75	5.00	10.00

COPPER

Obv: Truncation in a curved line

| 88a | 1809 | — | 1.25 | 2.50 | 6.00 | 11.50 |
| | 1810 | — | 1.25 | 2.50 | 5.50 | 10.50 |

Obv: Truncation in a broken curved line.

| 88b | 1810 | — | 1.50 | 2.75 | 6.25 | 12.00 |
| | 1811 | — | 1.50 | 3.00 | 7.00 | 14.00 |

C#	Date	Mintage	VG	Fine	VF	XF
94	1815	—	1.25	2.50	6.00	12.00

2 RIGSBANKSKILLING

COPPER

| 102 | 1818 | — | 4.00 | 9.00 | 15.00 | 30.00 |

1.1120 g, .208 SILVER, .0074 oz ASW

| 106 | 1836 IFF | .152 | 2.00 | 5.00 | 7.50 | 12.50 |

COPPER

| 121 | 1842 VS | — | 15.00 | 35.00 | 75.00 | 140.00 |

3 SKILLING

COPPER

| 89 | 1812 | — | 1.00 | 2.00 | 4.50 | 8.50 |

| 95 | 1815 | — | 1.50 | 3.50 | 8.00 | 14.00 |

3 RIGSBANKSKILLING

1.5190 g, .229 SILVER, .0112 oz ASW

| 107 | 1836 IFF | .130 | 5.00 | 12.50 | 22.50 | 50.00 |

| 122 | 1842 FF | — | 1.50 | 3.00 | 7.50 | 15.00 |

Rev. denomination: 3 R.B.S.

| 122a | 1842 FF | — | 1.50 | 3.00 | 7.50 | 14.00 |

4 SKILLING

2.5980 g, .250 SILVER, .0209 oz ASW

C#	Date	Mintage	VG	Fine	VF	XF
56	1807 MF	—	3.00	5.50	10.00	20.00

		COPPER				
96	1815	—	2.50	5.00	14.00	30.00

4 RIGSBANKSKILLING

1.8560 g, .250 SILVER, .0149 oz ASW

108	1836 IFF	.073	6.00	15.00	27.50	50.00

For use in Schleswig-Holstein
Rev: 1-1/4 SCH.

123	1841(h)	—	1.50	3.50	8.50	16.00
	1842 VS(c)	—	1.50	2.75	6.50	12.50
	1842 FF(o)	—	—	—	Rare	—

4 RIGSMONTSKILLING

1.8560 g, .250 SILVER, .0149 oz ASW

136	1854 FF(o)	—	2.00	3.50	11.50	22.00
	1856 VS(c)	—	.75	2.00	5.50	13.00

Y#	Date	Mintage	VG	Fine	VF	XF
4	1867 RH	—	1.75	3.50	8.00	15.00
	1869 CS	—	2.00	4.00	9.00	17.50
	1870 CS	—	1.75	3.50	8.00	15.00
	1871 CS	—	1.75	3.50	8.00	15.00
	1872 CS	—	2.25	5.00	10.00	20.00
	1873 CS	—	2.25	5.00	10.00	20.00
	1874 CS	—	6.25	12.50	30.00	55.00

6 SKILLING

		COPPER				
C#	Date	Mintage	VG	Fine	VF	XF
97	1813	—	2.50	6.00	15.00	30.00

8 RIGSBANKSKILLING

2.8090 g, .375 SILVER, .0339 oz ASW
For use in Schleswig-Holstein
Rev: 2-1/2 SCHILL.COUR.

124	1843 FF	—	10.00	20.00	40.00	90.00

NOTE: For 8 Reichsbank Schillinge dated 1816-1819 see Schleswig-Holstein in German States listings.

12 SKILLING

COPPER
Struck over 1 Skilling, C#47.

C#	Date	Mintage	VG	Fine	VF	XF
90	1812	—	5.50	12.50	25.00	50.00

98	1813	—	2.50	6.00	15.00	30.00

1/6 RIGSDALER

5.0490 g, .406 SILVER, .0659 oz ASW
Offering for Fatherland

105	1808 MF	—	6.00	12.50	20.00	37.50

NOTE: Varieties exist.

16 SKILLING

COPPER

99	1814	—	3.50	7.50	17.50	35.00

16 RIGSBANKSKILLING

4.2140 g, .500 SILVER, .0677 oz ASW
For use in Schleswig-Holstein
Rev: 5 SCHILL.COURANT.

125	1842 VS	—	12.50	25.00	40.00	80.00
	1844 VS	—	—	—	Rare	—

16 RIGSMONTSKILLING

3.8980 g, .500 SILVER, .0626 oz ASW

137	1854 VS(c)	—	—	—	Rare	—
	1856 VS(c)	—	1.50	3.25	7.75	15.00
	1857 VS(c)	—	2.00	3.50	8.75	16.00
	1858 VS(c)	—	2.25	4.75	10.00	20.00

32 RIGSBANKSKILLING

6.1290 g, .687 SILVER, .1354 oz ASW

C#	Date	Mintage	VG	Fine	VF	XF
109	1818 CB	—	—	—	Rare	—
	1820 IFF	—	20.00	40.00	70.00	135.00

6.1290 g, .687 SILVER, .1354 oz ASW
For use in Schleswig-Holstein
Rev: 10 SCHILL.COURANT.

126	1842 FF	—	15.00	27.50	45.00	80.00
	1843 FF	—	17.50	30.00	50.00	85.00
	1843 FF/Fk	—	60.00	110.00	160.00	250.00

1/2 RIGSDALER

7.2240 g, .875 SILVER, .2032 oz ASW

138	1854 VS(c)	—	9.00	20.00	32.50	50.00
	1855 VS(c)	—	8.00	17.50	30.00	45.00

RIGSBANKDALER

14.4470 g, .875 SILVER, .4064 oz ASW

110	1813 M	—	45.00	80.00	140.00	225.00
	1813 IC	—	25.00	30.00	55.00	90.00
	1813 IC-MF	—	30.00	45.00	75.00	140.00
	1818 IC-CB	—	30.00	37.50	60.00	100.00
	1819 IC-FF	—	35.00	40.00	70.00	125.00

Obv: Small head.

110a	1826 FF	—	35.00	80.00	130.00	200.00
	1827 FF	—	40.00	95.00	135.00	210.00
	1828 FF	—	35.00	80.00	130.00	200.00
	1833 FF	—	30.00	70.00	125.00	200.00
	1833 KM	—	55.00	100.00	160.00	245.00
	1834 KM	—	55.00	100.00	160.00	245.00

Obv: Large head.

110b	1833 FF	—	40.00	80.00	130.00	210.00
	1834 FF	—	70.00	135.00	200.00	300.00
	1834 KM	—	55.00	100.00	155.00	245.00
	1835 FF	—	70.00	135.00	200.00	300.00
	1835 WS	—	80.00	150.00	220.00	335.00
	1836 FF	—	40.00	90.00	150.00	220.00
	1838 WS	—	30.00	60.00	110.00	175.00
	1839 FF	—	40.00	85.00	135.00	210.00

DENMARK 469

C#	Date	Mintage	VG	Fine	VF	XF
112	1833 KM	—	35.00	65.00	100.00	150.00
	1834 FF	—	30.00	55.00	80.00	125.00
	1834 KM	—	40.00	70.00	100.00	160.00
	1835 FF	—	30.00	55.00	80.00	125.00
	1835 WS	—	30.00	55.00	80.00	125.00
	1837 WS	—	30.00	55.00	80.00	125.00
	1838 FF	—	27.00	50.00	75.00	115.00
	1838 WS	—	27.00	50.00	75.00	115.00
	1838 SW (error)	—	—	—	—	—
	1839 FF	—	27.00	55.00	75.00	115.00
	1839 WS	—	27.00	55.00	75.00	115.00

SPECIE DALER

Christian VIII Death And Accession Of Frederik VII

C#	Date	Mintage	VG	Fine	VF	XF
141	1848 VS	.047	50.00	110.00	175.00	280.00

For use in Schleswig-Holstein.
Rev: 30 SCHILL.COURANT.

C#	Date	Mintage	VG	Fine	VF	XF
127	1842 VS(c)	—	15.00	32.00	47.50	75.00
	1843 VS(c)	—	20.00	45.00	60.00	90.00
	1844 FF(o)	—	18.00	40.00	55.00	85.00
	1845 FF(o)	—	16.00	37.50	55.00	85.00
	1846 VS(c)	—	17.00	35.00	50.00	80.00
	1847 FF(o)	—	17.00	35.00	50.00	80.00
	1847 VS(c)	—	12.50	25.00	40.00	65.00
	1848 VS(c)	—	12.50	27.50	42.50	70.00

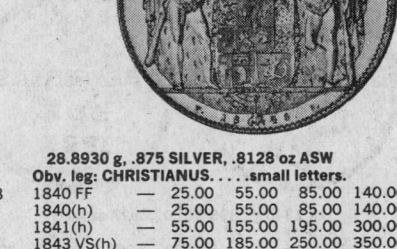

	Date	Mintage	VG	Fine	VF	XF
139	1849 VS	—	40.00	90.00	160.00	275.00
	1851 VS	—	35.00	70.00	140.00	235.00

RIGSDALER

14.4470 g, .875 SILVER, .4064 oz ASW

	Date	Mintage	VG	Fine	VF	XF
140	1854 VS(c)	—	10.00	17.50	25.00	45.00
	1855 FF(o)	—	12.50	22.50	35.00	55.00
	1855 VS(c)	—	15.00	27.50	42.50	65.00

RIGSDALER SPECIES

28.8930 g, .875 SILVER, .8128 oz ASW
Obv: Head of Frederik VI right
Rev: Crowned oval arms

	Date	Mintage	VG	Fine	VF	XF
111	1819 IFF	—	150.00	300.00	600.00	900.00

28.8930 g, .875 SILVER, .8128 oz ASW
Obv. leg: CHRISTIANUS.....small letters.

	Date	Mintage	VG	Fine	VF	XF
128	1840 FF	—	25.00	55.00	85.00	140.00
	1840(h)	—	25.00	55.00	85.00	140.00
	1841(h)	—	55.00	155.00	195.00	300.00
	1843 VS(h)	—	75.00	185.00	250.00	350.00
	1843 VS(c)	—	30.00	70.00	110.00	175.00
	1844 FF(o)	—	30.00	70.00	110.00	175.00
	1845 FF(o)	—	25.00	50.00	85.00	140.00
	1845 VS(h)	—	—	—	Rare	—
	1845 VS(c)	—	25.00	55.00	85.00	140.00
	1846 VS(c)	—	25.00	55.00	85.00	140.00
	1847 FF(o)	—	25.00	55.00	100.00	155.00

Obv. leg: CHRISTIANVS.....large letters.

	Date	Mintage	VG	Fine	VF	XF
128a	1846 VS(c)	—	40.00	60.00	100.00	170.00
	1847 VS(c)	—	40.00	60.00	100.00	170.00
	1848 VS	—	40.00	60.00	100.00	170.00

Obv: Similar to 2 Rigsdaler, C#143.

	Date	Mintage	VG	Fine	VF	XF
142	1849 VS(c)	—	35.00	60.00	100.00	160.00
	1851 FF(o)	—	—	—	Rare	—
	1853 FF(o)	—	40.00	70.00	115.00	180.00
	1853 VS(c)	—	35.00	60.00	100.00	160.00
	1854 VS(c)	—	80.00	125.00	185.00	275.00

2 RIGSDALER

28.8930 g, .875 SILVER, .8128 oz ASW

	Date	Mintage	VG	Fine	VF	XF
143	1854 FF(o)	—	30.00	45.00	80.00	125.00
	1854 VS(c)	—	32.50	55.00	100.00	150.00
	1855 FF(o)	—	30.00	50.00	90.00	140.00
	1855 VS(c)	—	30.00	47.50	85.00	135.00
	1856 FF(o)	—	—	—	Rare	—
	1863 RH(c)	.360	37.50	70.00	130.00	225.00

112	1820 FF	—	30.00	55.00	85.00	130.00
	1820 CFG	—	40.00	70.00	100.00	160.00
	1822 FF	—	30.00	55.00	85.00	130.00
	1822 CFG	—	40.00	70.00	100.00	160.00
	1824 FF	—	30.00	55.00	85.00	130.00
	1824 CFG	—	30.00	55.00	85.00	130.00
	1825 FF	—	30.00	55.00	80.00	125.00
	1825 CFG	—	30.00	55.00	85.00	130.00
	1826 FF	—	30.00	55.00	85.00	125.00
	1827 FF	—	40.00	75.00	110.00	160.00
	1828 FF	—	27.00	55.00	85.00	125.00
	1829 FF	—	30.00	55.00	85.00	130.00
	1833 FF	—	27.00	50.00	75.00	115.00

DENMARK 470

**Frederik VII Death
and Accession of Christian IX**

Y#	Date	Mintage	VG	Fine	VF	XF
3	1863 RH	.101	50.00	110.00	175.00	250.00

Rev: Similar to C#143.

5	1864 RH	.237	55.00	110.00	180.00	275.00
	1868 RH	.261	60.00	125.00	190.00	300.00
	1871 CS	.586	65.00	140.00	210.00	330.00
	1872 CS	.149	65.00	140.00	210.00	330.00

TRADE COINAGE
CHR(ISTIAN) D'OR

6.6420 g, .896 GOLD, .1913 oz AGW

C#	Date	Mintage	VG	Fine	VF	XF
129	1843 FF(o)	.038	250.00	525.00	900.00	1450.
	1844 FF(o)	I.A.	250.00	550.00	975.00	1550.
	1845 FF(o)	I.A.	250.00	550.00	975.00	1550.
	1847 FF(o)	I.A.	250.00	550.00	975.00	1550.

Y#	Date	Mintage	VG	Fine	VF	XF
6	1869 CS	539 pcs.	500.00	1125.	1800.	2600.

FR(EDERIK) D'OR

6.6420 g, .896 GOLD, .1913 oz AGW

C#	Date	Mintage	VG	Fine	VF	XF
113	1827 IFF	—	500.00	1000.	3000.	4000.

114	1828 FF	.021	400.00	900.00	1500.	2750.

C#	Date	Mintage	VG	Fine	VF	XF
114a	1829 FF	7,625	300.00	600.00	1500.	2000.
	1830	.012	—	—	Rare	
	1831 FF	—	300.00	600.00	1500.	2000.
	1833 FF	—	300.00	600.00	1500.	2000.
	1834 FF	—	—	—	Rare	
	1835 FF	—	300.00	600.00	1500.	2000.
	1837 FF	—	300.00	600.00	1500.	2000.
	1838 FF	—	300.00	600.00	1500.	2000.

144	1853 FF	678 pcs.	500.00	1100.	1600.	3500.

2 FR(EDERIK) D'OR

13.2840 g, .896 GOLD, .3827 oz AGW

115	1826 IFF	—	—	—	Unique	
	1827 IFF	—	500.00	1000.	2000.	3000.

116	1828 FF	.168	350.00	800.00	1700.	2450.
	1829 FF	.096	375.00	850.00	1800.	2600.
	1830 FF	.105	375.00	850.00	1800.	2600.
	1833 FF	—	375.00	850.00	1800.	2600.
	1834 FF	—	375.00	850.00	1800.	2600.
	1835 FF	—	400.00	875.00	1850.	2650.
	1836 FF	—	—	—	Rare	

117	1836 FF	—	350.00	850.00	1800.	2600.
	1837 FF	—	325.00	800.00	1700.	2350.
	1838 FF	—	325.00	800.00	1700.	2350.
	1838 WS	—	650.00	1300.	2300.	3250.
	1839 FF	—	325.00	800.00	1900.	2600.

145	1850 KF(c)VS	—	300.00	700.00	1700.	2550.
	1851 FF(o)	1.205	325.00	750.00	1800.	2675.
	1852 FF(o)	I.A.	325.00	750.00	1800.	2675.
	1853 FF(o)	I.A.	300.00	700.00	1700.	2550.
	1854 FF(o)	I.A.	325.00	750.00	1800.	2675.
	1855 FF(o)	I.A.	325.00	750.00	1800.	2675.
	1856 FA(o)	I.A.	325.00	800.00	1900.	2700.

C#	Date	Mintage	VG	Fine	VF	XF
145	1857 FA(o)	I.A.	300.00	700.00	1700.	2550.
	1859 FA(o)	I.A.	300.00	700.00	1700.	2550.
	1863 RH(c)	*	475.00	950.00	2000.	3000.

*Total mintage 1853VS and 1863RH .031.

2 CHR(ISTIAN) D'OR

13.2840 g, .896 GOLD, .3827 oz AGW

130	1841(h)	—	350.00	700.00	2100.	3500.
	1842 FF(o)	—	250.00	575.00	1900.	3100.
	1844 FF(o)	—	375.00	675.00	2100.	3300.
	1844 VS(c)	—	325.00	650.00	2000.	3200.
	1845 FF(o)	—	250.00	575.00	1900.	3100.
	1847 FF(o)	—	225.00	550.00	1850.	3000.

Total mintage 1841(h) and 1844 VS(c) 9,222 pcs.
Total mintage 1842-47 FF .551.

Y#	Date	Mintage	VG	Fine	VF	XF
7	1866 RH	.042	500.00	1200.	3000.	4000.
	1867 RH Inc. Ab.		—	—	Rare	
	1869 CS Inc. Ab.	500.00	1200.	3000.	4000.	
	1870 CS Inc. Ab.		—	—	Rare	

DECIMAL COINAGE
100 Ore = 1 Krone

ORE

BRONZE
Mintmaster's Initials: CS

Y#	Date	Mintage	Fine	VF	XF	Unc
8.1	1874(h)	5.540	3.00	5.00	11.00	30.00
	1875(h)	2.361	4.00	6.00	13.00	35.00
	1876(h)	1.483	225.00	300.00	450.00	675.00
	1878(h)	1.016	22.50	37.50	60.00	125.00
	1879(h)	1.491	15.00	22.50	35.00	70.00
	1880(h)	1.989	5.00	10.00	20.00	40.00
	1881(h)	.260	300.00	400.00	625.00	925.00
	1882(h)	1.782	5.00	10.00	20.00	40.00
	1883(h)	2.989	2.00	3.50	9.00	25.00
	1886(h)	.997	30.00	45.00	65.00	110.00
	1887(h)	3.007	5.00	9.00	17.50	35.00
	1888(h)	1.505	5.00	9.00	17.50	35.00
	1889(h)	2.999	2.00	3.50	8.00	22.50
	1891(h)	4.982	1.50	3.00	5.00	15.00
	1892(h)	.494	40.00	70.00	115.00	175.00

Mintmaster's Initials: VBH

8.2	1894(h)	4.982	.50	1.00	3.00	14.00
	1897/4(h)	2.988	1.75	3.00	6.50	18.00
	1897(h)	I.A.	1.75	3.00	6.00	17.00
	1899/7(h)	5.012	.55	1.10	4.00	14.00
	1899(h)	I.A.	.50	1.00	3.50	12.00
	1902/802(h)	2.977	.55	1.10	4.00	14.00
	1902(h)	I.A.	.50	1.00	3.50	12.00
	1904/804(h)	4.962	.75	1.50	5.00	16.00
	1904(h)	I.A.	.50	1.00	3.50	12.00

20	1907(h)	5.975	.50	1.00	3.50	12.00
	1909(h)	2.985	.50	1.00	3.50	12.00
	1910(h)	2.994	1.00	2.00	5.00	15.00
	1912(h)	3.006	1.00	2.00	5.00	15.00

Mintmaster's Initials: VBP-GJ

28.1	1913(h)	5.011	.25	.50	1.00	5.00
	1915(h)	4.940	.50	1.00	1.75	7.50

DENMARK 471

Y#	Date	Mintage	Fine	VF	XF	Unc
28.1	1916(h)	2.439	.50	1.00	2.50	8.50
	1917(h)	4.564	8.50	12.50	20.00	35.00

IRON

28.1a	1918(h)	6.776	1.00	2.00	6.00	17.50

BRONZE
Mintmaster's Initials: HCN-GJ

28.2	1919(h)	4.586	.25	1.00	2.00	6.00
	1920(h)	2.367	4.00	7.50	12.50	20.00
	1921(h)	3.121	.50	1.50	2.50	6.00
	1922(h)	3.267	.50	1.50	2.50	6.00
	1923(h)	2.938	.50	1.50	2.50	6.00

IRON

28.2a	1919(h)	.931	3.50	7.50	12.50	25.00

BRONZE

46.1	1926(h)	1.572	2.00	4.00	10.00	20.00
	1927(h)	Inc. Ab.	—	.20	1.00	10.00

Mintmaster's Initials: N-GJ

46.2	1927(h)	I.A.	4.00	6.00	12.00	25.00
	1928(h)	29.691	.10	.20	1.75	6.00
	1929(h)	5.172	.10	.20	1.75	6.00
	1930(h)	5.306	.10	.20	1.25	6.00
	1932(h)	5.089	.10	.20	1.25	6.00
	1933(h)	2.095	.75	1.50	3.00	10.00
	1934(h)	3.665	—	.10	.50	5.00
	1935(h)	5.668	—	.10	.40	3.50
	1936(h)	5.584	—	.10	.40	2.50
	1937(h)	6.877	—	.10	.40	2.50
	1938(h)	3.850	—	.10	.40	2.50
	1939(h)	5.662	—	.10	.30	1.75
	1940(h)	1.965	—	.10	.30	1.75

NOTE: For coins dated 1941 refer to Faeroe Islands.

ZINC
Mintmaster's Initials: N-S

51	1941(h)	21.570	.15	.30	1.50	10.00
	1942(h)	6.997	.15	.30	1.50	10.00
	1943(h)	15.082	.15	.30	1.50	10.00
	1944(h)	11.981	.15	.30	1.50	10.00
	1945(h)	.916	.75	2.00	4.00	15.00
	1946(h)	.712	2.00	4.00	8.00	20.00

56.1	1948(h)	.460	.65	1.00	2.00	7.50
	1949(h)	2.513	.15	.30	.75	5.00
	1950(h)	9.453	.15	.30	.75	5.00
	1951(h)	2.931	.25	.50	.75	5.00
	1952(h)	7.626	.15	.30	.60	3.50
	1953(h)	11.994	.10	.20	.40	3.00
	1954(h)	12.642	.10	.20	.40	3.00
	1955(h)	14.177	.10	.20	.40	3.00

Mintmaster's Initials: C-S

56.2	1956(h)	20.211	—	.10	.25	2.50
	1957(h)	20.900	—	.10	.25	2.50
	1958(h)	16.021	—	.10	.25	2.50
	1959(h)	15.929	—	.10	.25	2.00
	1960(h)	23.982	—	—	.15	1.50
	1961(h)	18.986	—	—	.15	1.00
	1962(h)	16.992	—	—	.10	.75
	1963(h)	28.986	—	—	.10	.65
	1964(h)	21.971	—	—	.10	.50
	1965(h)	29.943	—	—	.10	.30
	1966(h)	35.907	—	—	.10	.30
	1967(h)	32.959	—	—	.10	.30
	1968(h)	21.889	—	—	.10	.20
	1969(h)	29.243	—	—	.10	.20
	1970(h)	22.970	—	—	.10	.20
	1971(h)	21.983	—	—	.10	.20

Mintmaster's Initials: S-S

56.3	1972(h)	13.000	—	—	.10	.20

BRONZE
Mintmaster's Initials: C-S

66	1960(h)	8.990	—	—	.75	1.50
	1962(h)	I.A.	—	—	.75	1.50
	1963(h)	9.980	—	—	.75	1.50
	1964(h)	2.990	—	—	.75	1.50

NOTE: Only an estimated 100,000 of each date of Y#66 were sold, the balance being remelted.

2 ORE

BRONZE
Mintmaster's Initials: C-S

Y#	Date	Mintage	Fine	VF	XF	Unc
9.1	1874(h)	8.828	1.00	2.00	6.00	20.00
	1875(h)	2.817	2.00	4.00	10.00	45.00
	1876(h)	.231	60.00	100.00	150.00	300.00
	1880(h)	1.012	6.00	12.00	25.00	40.00
	1881(h)	1.484	5.00	10.00	22.00	35.00
	1883(h)	1.990	2.00	4.00	7.50	20.00
	1886(h)	1.493	4.00	7.00	12.00	25.00
	1887(h)	I.A.	25.00	40.00	60.00	115.00
	1889/7(h)	1.993	2.50	5.00	7.50	20.00
	1889(h)	I.A.	2.00	3.50	6.00	15.00
	1891(h)	1.903	2.00	3.50	6.00	15.00
	1892(h)	.573	20.00	35.00	50.00	90.00

Mintmaster's Initials: VBP

9.2	1894(h)	2.486	1.00	2.00	4.00	10.00
	1897/4(h)	2.479	1.50	3.00	6.00	15.00
	1897(h)	I.A.	1.00	2.00	4.00	10.00
	1899/7(h)	2.504	1.25	2.50	5.00	12.50
	1899(h)	I.A.	1.00	2.00	4.00	10.00
	1902/802(h)	3.502	1.50	3.00	6.00	15.00
	1902(h)	I.A.	1.00	2.00	4.00	10.00
	1906(h)	2.498	1.00	2.00	4.00	10.00

21	1907(h)	2.502	.50	1.00	3.00	7.50
	1909(h)	2.485	1.00	2.50	5.00	12.00
	1912(h)	2.480	1.00	2.50	5.00	10.00

Mintmaster's Initials: VBP-GJ

29.1	1913(h)	.822	12.00	25.00	40.00	70.00
	1914(h)	2.499	1.00	2.50	4.50	9.00
	1915(h)	2.485	1.00	2.50	4.50	9.00
	1916(h)	1.383	1.00	2.50	4.50	9.00
	1917(h)	1.837	6.00	10.00	20.00	35.00

IRON

29.1a	1918(h)	4.161	1.00	2.50	5.00	15.00

BRONZE
Mintmaster's Initials: HCN-GJ

29.2	1919(h)	5.503	2.00	4.00	6.00	12.00
	1920(h)	2.528	.50	1.00	2.00	5.00
	1921(h)	2.158	1.00	2.50	4.50	8.00
	1923(h)	2.625	1.00	2.50	4.50	8.00

IRON

29.2a	1919(h)	1.944	10.00	17.50	25.00	50.00

BRONZE

47.1	1926(h)	.301	20.00	30.00	60.00	110.00
	1927(h)	15.359	.10	.20	1.00	6.00

Mintmaster's Initials: N-GH

47.2	1927(h)	I.A.	.50	1.00	2.50	10.00
	1928(h)	5.758	.10	.20	1.50	7.00
	1929(h)	6.817	.10	.20	1.50	7.00
	1930(h)	2.327	.50	1.00	1.50	7.00
	1931(h)	5.135	.10	.20	1.50	6.00
	1932(h)	I.A.	.50	1.00	2.00	10.00
	1934(h)	.756	.25	.75	1.50	6.00
	1935(h)	1.391	.10	.20	.80	4.50
	1936(h)	2.973	.10	.20	.60	4.00
	1937(h)	3.437	.10	.20	.50	3.50
	1938(h)	2.177	—	.10	.25	2.50
	1939(h)	3.165	—	.10	.25	2.50
	1940(h)	1.582	—	.10	.25	2.50

NOTE: For coins dated 1941 refer to Faeroe Islands.

ALUMINUM
Mintmaster's Initials: N-S

Y#	Date	Mintage	Fine	VF	XF	Unc
52	1941(h)	26.205	.10	.50	1.00	6.00

ZINC

52a	1942(h)	12.934	.15	.35	1.00	7.50
	1943(h)	9.603	.15	.35	1.00	7.50
	1944(h)	6.069	.15	.35	1.00	7.50
	1945(h)	.329	2.00	4.00	6.00	20.00
	1947(h)	.589	.50	1.00	2.50	10.00

57.1	1948(h)	1.927	.25	.50	1.00	4.00
	1949(h)	1.603	2.00	4.00	6.00	15.00
	1950(h)	4.544	.25	.50	1.00	4.00
	1951(h)	3.766	.25	.50	1.00	5.00
	1952(h)	4.874	.10	.20	.75	3.50
	1953(h)	8.112	—	.10	.65	2.50
	1954(h)	6.497	—	.10	.65	2.50
	1955(h)	6.968	—	.10	.30	1.75

Mintmaster's Initials: C-S

57.2	1956(h)	10.004	—	.10	.30	1.75
	1957(h)	15.329	—	.10	.30	1.75
	1958(h)	8.120	—	.10	.20	1.50
	1959(h)	10.462	—	.10	.20	1.50
	1960(h)	16.504	—	.10	.20	1.25
	1961(h)	15.504	—	.10	.20	1.00
	1962(h)	10.980	—	.10	.20	1.00
	1963(h)	19.470	—	.10	.20	1.00
	1964(h)	15.411	—	.10	.20	1.00
	1965(h)	20.173	—	—	.10	.75
	1966(h)	21.949	—	—	.10	.40
	1967(h)	22.439	—	—	.10	.40
	1968(h)	17.632	—	—	.10	.40
	1969(h)	29.276	—	—	.10	.30
	1970(h)	23.864	—	—	.10	.20
	1971(h)	35.811	—	—	.10	.20

Mintmaster's Initials: S-S

57.3	1972(h)	6.496	—	—	.10	.40

BRONZE
Mintmaster's Initials: C-S

67	1960(h)	I.A.	—	—	.75	1.50
	1962(h)	I.A.	—	—	.75	1.50
	1963(h)	.990	—	—	.75	1.50
	1964(h)	3.990	—	—	.75	1.50
	1965(h)	11.980	—	—	.75	1.50
	1966(h)	12.000	—	—	.75	1.50

NOTE: Only an estimated 100,000 of each date of Y#67 were sold, the balance being remelted.

5 ORE

BRONZE
Mintmaster's Initials: CS

10.1	1874(h)	2.762	3.00	5.00	14.00	55.00
	1875(h)	.207	15.00	25.00	35.00	90.00
	1882(h)	.076	15.00	25.00	35.00	90.00
	1884(h)	.321	7.50	14.00	22.50	60.00
	1890(h)	.598	25.00	45.00	75.00	140.00
	1891(h)	.787	7.50	14.00	22.50	60.00

Mintmaster's Initials: VBP

10.2	1894(h)	.595	5.00	9.00	17.50	40.00
	1898(h)	.397	9.00	17.50	30.00	70.00
	1899(h)	.601	5.00	9.00	15.00	30.00
	1902(h)	.601	5.00	9.00	15.00	30.00
	1904(h)	.397	9.00	14.00	22.50	50.00
	1906(h)	1.000	5.00	9.00	15.00	30.00

DENMARK 472

Y#	Date	Mintage	Fine	VF	XF	Unc
22	1907(h)	1.000	3.00	5.00	10.00	25.00
	1908(h)	1.198	3.00	5.00	10.00	25.00
	1912(h)	.999	3.00	5.00	10.00	25.00

Mintmaster's Initials: VBP-GJ

30.1	1913(h)	.216	30.00	45.00	75.00	125.00
	1914(h)	.785	4.00	6.00	11.00	25.00
	1916(h)	.887	4.00	6.00	11.00	25.00
	1917(h)	.494	4.00	6.00	11.00	25.00

IRON

30.1a	1918(h)	1.733	3.00	6.00	12.00	30.00

BRONZE
Mintmaster's Initials: HCN-GJ

30.2	1919(h)	.624	2.00	4.00	7.00	12.50
	1920(h)	2.618	2.00	4.00	7.00	12.50
	1921(h)	3.248	2.00	4.00	7.00	12.50
	1923(h)	.369	45.00	90.00	135.00	185.00

IRON

30.2a	1919(h)	1.035	6.00	12.00	22.50	50.00

BRONZE

48.1	1926(h)	—	—	—	Unique	—
	1927(h)	4.564	.10	.20	1.00	10.00

Mintmaster's Initials: N-GJ

48.2	1927(h)	I.A.	2.50	4.50	9.00	25.00
	1928(h)	6.704	.10	.20	1.00	10.00
	1929(h)	1.116	.25	.50	2.00	12.00
	1930(h)	2.153	.25	.50	2.00	12.00
	1932(h)	1.011	.25	.50	2.00	10.00
	1934(h)	.524	.25	.50	1.50	10.00
	1935(h)	1.124	1.00	2.00	4.00	15.00
	1936(h)	1.091	.15	.35	1.00	4.50
	1937(h)	1.209	.15	.35	.75	4.50
	1938(h)	1.093	.30	.50	1.00	4.50
	1939(h)	1.402	.10	.15	.40	2.50
	1940(h)	2.735	.10	.15	.40	2.50

NOTE: For coins dated 1941 refer to Faeroe Islands.

ALUMINUM
Mintmaster's Initials: N-S

53	1941(h)	16.984	.10	.75	2.50	10.00

ZINC

53a	1942(h)	2.963	.40	1.00	2.50	10.00
	1943(h)	4.522	.40	1.00	2.50	10.00
	1944(h)	2.800	.40	1.00	2.50	10.00
	1945(h)	1.700	2.00	4.00	6.00	15.00

Y#	Date	Mintage	Fine	VF	XF	Unc
58.1	1950(h)	.657	3.00	6.00	10.00	20.00
	1951(h)	1.858	.75	1.25	2.50	10.00
	1952(h)	3.562	.50	1.00	1.75	7.00
	1953(h)	5.944	.50	1.00	1.75	7.00
	1954(h)	3.060	.35	.75	1.50	6.00
	1955(h)	2.314	.35	.75	1.50	6.00

Mintmaster's Initials: C-S

58.2	1956(h)	5.888	.25	.75	1.50	5.00
	1957(h)	8.606	.10	.20	.50	3.00
	1958(h)	9.598	.10	.20	.50	3.00
	1959(h)	6.110	.10	.20	.50	3.00
	1960(h)	11.800	—	.10	.35	1.50
	1961(h)	8.995	—	.10	.35	1.50
	1962(h)	9.729	—	.10	.35	1.50
	1963(h)	8.980	—	.10	.35	1.50
	1964(h)	6.738	—	.10	.35	1.50

BRONZE

68.1	1960(h)	3.760	.10	.20	.50	1.50
	1962(h)	5.873	.10	.20	.50	1.50
	1963(h)	23.287	—	—	.10	.60
	1964(h)	41.521	—	—	.10	.60
	1965(h)	14.229	—	—	.10	.60
	1966(h)	23.410	—	—	.10	.60
	1967(h)	15.094	—	—	.10	.45
	1968(h)	16.105	—	—	.10	.35
	1969(h)	23.594	—	—	.10	.25
	1970(h)	26.176	—	—	.10	.20
	1971(h)	10.076	—	—	.10	.20

Mintmaster's Initials: S-S

68.2	1972(h)	27.938	—	—	.10	.20

COPPER CLAD IRON
Mintmaster's Initials: S-B

78.1	1973(h)	—	—	—	—	.10
	1974(h)	71.796	—	—	—	.10
	1975(h)	45.004	—	—	—	.10
	1976(h)	73.296	—	—	—	.10
	1977(h)	74.066	—	—	—	.10
	1978(h)	52.425	—	—	—	.10

Mintmaster's Initials: B-B

78.2	1979(h)	58.953	—	—	—	.10
	1980(h)	54.362	—	—	—	.10
	1981(h)	52.201	—	—	—	.10

Mintmaster's Initials: R-B

78.3	1982(h)	74.296	—	—	—	.10
	1983(h)	70.655	—	—	—	.10
	1984(h)	27.599	—	—	—	.10
	1985(h)	56.676	—	—	—	.10
	1986(h)	62.496	—	—	—	.10
	1987(h)	71.798	—	—	—	.10
	1988(h)	—	—	—	—	.10

10 ORE

1.4500 g, .400 SILVER, .0186 oz ASW
Mintmaster's Initials: CS

11.1	1874(h)	8.975	3.00	5.00	17.50	50.00
	1875(h)	1.387	4.00	6.00	20.00	50.00
	1882(h)	1.057	17.50	25.00	50.00	90.00
	1884(h)	1.019	17.50	25.00	50.00	90.00
	1886(h)	.508	35.00	50.00	75.00	140.00
	1888(h)	.306	50.00	75.00	115.00	170.00
	1889(h)	1.030	5.00	9.00	17.50	35.00
	1891(h)	1.507	4.00	7.50	12.50	25.00

Mintmaster's Initials: VBP

11.2	1894(h)	1.521	4.00	7.50	12.50	25.00
	1897(h)	2.044	2.00	4.00	6.00	20.00
	1899(h)	2.049	2.00	4.00	6.00	20.00
	1903/803(h)	3.007	2.00	4.00	6.00	15.00
	1903(h)	I.A.	1.50	3.00	5.00	15.00
	1904(h)	2.449	9.00	17.50	27.50	50.00
	1905(h)	1.571	2.00	4.00	6.00	15.00

23	1907(h)	3.068	2.00	3.00	4.50	10.00
	1910(h)	2.530	2.00	3.00	4.50	10.00
	1911(h)	.579	15.00	22.50	35.00	60.00
	1912(h)	1.951	2.00	3.00	5.50	12.50

Mintmaster's Initials: VBP-GJ

Y#	Date	Mintage	Fine	VF	XF	Unc
36.1	1914(h)	2.128	1.25	2.00	4.00	10.00
	1915(h)	.915	3.00	6.00	9.00	15.00
	1916(h)	2.699	1.25	2.00	4.00	10.00
	1917(h)	4.014	1.25	2.00	4.00	10.00
	1918(h)	5.042	.50	1.00	2.50	5.00

Mintmaster's Initials: HCN-GJ

36.2	1919(h)	10.184	.50	1.00	2.50	5.00

COPPER-NICKEL

31	1920(h)	10.234	2.00	3.00	4.50	11.00
	1921(h)	8.064	2.00	3.00	4.50	11.00
	1922(h)	3.065	8.00	14.00	20.00	37.50
	1923(h)	1.790	125.00	200.00	275.00	350.00

49.1	1924(h)	14.661	.10	.30	1.00	7.00
	1925(h)	8.678	.15	.40	1.00	10.00
	1926(h)	4.107	.15	.40	1.00	10.00

Mintmaster's Initials: N-GJ

49.2	1929(h)	5.037	.25	.50	1.00	10.00
	1931(h)	3.054	.25	.50	1.00	10.00
	1933(h)	1.274	3.00	4.50	9.00	20.00
	1934(h)	2.013	.25	.50	1.00	10.00
	1935(h)	2.848	.25	.50	1.00	6.00
	1936(h)	3.320	.25	.50	1.00	6.00
	1937(h)	2.234	.25	.50	1.00	6.00
	1938(h)	2.991	.25	.50	1.00	6.00
	1939(h)	2.973	.25	.50	1.00	6.00
	1940(h)	2.998	.25	.50	1.00	5.00
	1941(h)	.748	1.00	2.00	5.00	10.00
	1946(h)	.460	.50	1.00	2.00	5.00
	1947(h)	1.292	60.00	90.00	125.00	175.00

NOTE: For coins dated 1941 without mint marks refer to Faeroe Islands.

ZINC

49a	1941(h)	7.706	.25	.75	2.00	10.00
	1942(h)	8.676	.25	.75	2.00	10.00
	1943(h)	2.181	.25	.75	3.00	12.00
	1944(h)	7.994	.25	.75	2.00	10.00
	1945(h)	1.280	15.00	25.00	40.00	75.00

COPPER-NICKEL
Mintmaster's Initials: N-S

59.1	1948(h)	5.317	.10	.50	2.00	5.00
	1949(h)	7.595	.10	.20	1.00	3.00
	1950(h)	6.886	.10	.20	1.00	3.00
	1951(h)	8.763	.10	.20	1.00	3.00
	1952(h)	6.810	.10	.20	1.00	3.00
	1953(h)	11.946	—	.10	.50	3.00
	1954(h)	19.739	—	.10	.50	2.50
	1955(h)	17.623	—	.10	.40	2.50

Mintmaster's Initials: C-S

59.2	1956(h)	12.323	—	.10	.40	2.50
	1957(h)	13.227	—	.10	.40	1.50
	1958(h)	10.870	—	.10	.40	1.50
	1959(h)	1.255	15.00	20.00	30.00	50.00
	1960(h)	5.107	—	.10	.30	1.00

69.1	1960(h)	I.A.	—	.10	.40	1.50
	1961(h)	20.258	—	.10	.20	2.00
	1962(h)	12.785	—	.10	.20	2.00
	1963(h)	17.171	—	.10	.15	1.50
	1964(h)	14.282	—	.10	.15	1.50
	1965(h)	21.857	—	.10	.15	1.50
	1966(h)	24.160	—	.10	.15	1.25
	1967(h)	21.544	—	—	.10	.75
	1968(h)	7.586	—	—	.10	.60
	1969(h)	31.534	—	—	.10	.40
	1970(h)	37.813	—	—	.10	.20
	1971(h)	17.719	—	—	.10	.20

Y#	Date	Mintage	Fine	VF	XF	Unc
69.2	1972(h)	46.959	—	—	.10	.20

Mintmaster's Initials: S-B

79.1	1973(h)	37.538	—	—	.10	.20
	1974(h)	38.570	—	—	.10	.20
	1975(h)	62.633	—	—	.10	.20
	1976(h)	64.359	—	—	.10	.20
	1977(h)	61.994	—	—	.10	.20
	1978(h)	30.302	—	—	.10	.20

Mintmaster's Initials: B-B

79.2	1979(h)	10.224	—	—	.10	.20
	1980(h)	37.233	—	—	.10	.20
	1981(h)	51.565	—	—	.10	.20

Mintmaster's Initials: R-B

79.3	1982(h)	40.195	—	—	.10	.20
	1983(h)	35.634	—	—	.10	.20
	1984(h)	17.828	—	—	.10	.20
	1985(h)	29.317	—	—	.10	.20
	1986(h)	46.254	—	—	.10	.20
	1987(h)	27.897	—	—	.10	.20
	1988(h)		—	—	.10	.20

25 ORE

2.4200 g, .600 SILVER, .0467 oz ASW
Mintmaster's Initials: CS

12.1	1874(h)	8.139	4.00	11.00	25.00	50.00
	1891(h)	1.214	5.00	12.00	25.00	45.00

Mintmaster's Initials: VBP

12.2	1894(h)	1.206	4.00	10.00	20.00	35.00
	1900/800(h)	1.206	4.50	11.00	22.50	40.00
	1900(h)	I.A.	4.00	10.00	20.00	35.00
	1904(h)	1.922	6.00	12.00	25.00	40.00
	1905/805(h)	1.722	4.00	7.50	11.50	30.00
	1905(h)	I.A.	3.50	7.00	11.00	27.50

24	1907(h)	2.009	2.25	5.50	11.00	22.50
	1911(h)	2.015	2.25	5.50	11.00	22.50

Mintmaster's Initials: VBP-GJ

37.1	1913(h)	2.016	2.50	4.00	8.00	17.50
	1914(h)	.347	40.00	70.00	120.00	175.00
	1915(h)	2.862	2.50	3.50	6.00	15.00
	1916(h)	.938	2.50	5.00	10.00	20.00
	1917(h)	1.354	25.00	40.00	75.00	150.00
	1918(h)	2.090	2.50	4.00	6.00	12.50

Mintmaster's Initials: HCN-GJ

37.2	1919(h)	9.295	.75	1.25	2.50	5.00

COPPER-NICKEL

32	1920(h)	12.288	2.00	4.00	6.00	12.50
	1921(h)	9.444	2.00	4.00	6.00	12.50
	1922(h)	5.701	12.00	17.50	25.00	40.00

50.1	1924(h)	8.035	.20	.50	2.00	7.00
	1925(h)	1.906	3.00	5.00	10.00	25.00
	1926(h)	2.659	.20	.50	2.00	17.50

Mintmaster's Initials: N-GJ

Y#	Date	Mintage	Fine	VF	XF	Unc
50.2	1929(h)	.886	.75	2.00	4.00	22.00
	1930(h)	3.423	.75	2.00	4.00	22.00
	1932(h)	.846	3.00	8.00	12.00	30.00
	1933(h)	.479	17.50	25.00	35.00	60.00
	1934(h)	1.660	.50	2.00	4.00	17.50
	1935(h)	1.032	6.00	11.00	17.50	32.50
	1936(h)	1.453	.50	2.00	4.00	14.00
	1937(h)	1.612	2.00	3.50	6.50	16.00
	1938(h)	1.794	.75	2.00	5.00	14.00
	1939(h)	1.972	6.00	11.00	17.50	32.50
	1940(h)	1.356	.50	.75	2.50	7.00
	1946(h)	2.323	.50	.75	2.50	5.00
	1947(h)	1.751	.50	1.25	4.50	11.00

NOTE: For coins dated 1941 refer to Faeroe Islands.

ZINC

50a	1941(h)	15.332	.50	1.25	5.00	16.00
	1942(h)	.997	.50	1.25	3.00	14.00
	1943(h)	5.784	.50	1.25	5.00	17.00
	1944(h)	10.665	.25	.50	1.00	9.00
	1945(h)	4.543	.50	1.25	4.00	15.00

COPPER-NICKEL
Mintmaster's Initials: N-S

60.1	1948(h)	1.853	1.00	2.50	4.50	12.00
	1949(h)	15.000	.10	.30	1.00	7.00
	1950(h)	13.771	.10	.30	1.00	7.00
	1951(h)	5.045	.10	.30	1.00	8.00
	1952(h)	2.018	.50	1.00	2.50	12.50
	1953(h)	9.553	.10	.25	.75	2.50
	1954(h)	11.337	.10	.25	.75	2.50
	1955(h)	6.385	.15	.25	.75	2.50

Mintmaster's Initials: C-S

60.2	1956(h)	10.228	.10	.25	.75	2.50
	1957(h)	7.421	.10	.25	.75	2.50
	1958(h)	3.600	.10	.25	.75	2.50
	1959(h)	2.211	1.50	2.00	2.50	6.00
	1960(h)	3.453	.15	.30	.75	2.50

70	1960(h)	I.A.	4.00	6.00	8.00	12.00
	1961(h)	20.860	.10	.20	.40	1.25
	1962(h)	12.563	.10	.20	.40	1.25
	1964(h)	6.175	.10	.20	.40	1.25
	1965(h)	13.492	.10	.20	.40	1.25
	1966(h)	50.220	.10	.20	.40	1.25
	1967(h)	87.468	6.00	10.00	14.00	20.00

76.1	1966(h)	I.A.	—	—	.10	.30
	1967(h)	I.A.	—	—	.10	.30
	1968(h)	39.142	—	—	.10	.30
	1969(h)	16.974	—	—	.10	.30
	1970(h)	5.393	—	—	.10	.20
	1971(h)	12.725	—	—	.10	.20

Mintmaster's Initials: S-S

76.2	1972(h)	31.422	—	—	.10	.20

Mintmaster's Initials: S-B

80.1	1973(h)	30.834	—	—	.10	.20
	1974(h)	22.178	—	—	.10	.20
	1975(h)	28.798	—	—	.10	.20
	1976(h)	48.388	—	—	.10	.20
	1977(h)	32.239	—	—	.10	.20
	1978(h)	17.444	—	—	.10	.20

Mintmaster's Initials: B-B

80.2	1979(h)	24.261	—	—	.10	.20
	1980(h)	30.448	—	—	.10	.20
	1981(h)	1.427	—	—	.10	.30

Mintmaster's Initials: R-B

80.3	1982(h)	24.671	—	—	.10	.20

DENMARK 473

Y#	Date	Mintage	Fine	VF	XF	Unc
80.3	1983(h)	32.706	—	—	.10	.20
	1984(h)	22.882	—	—	.10	.20
	1985(h)	29.048	—	—	.10	.20
	1986(h)	53.496	—	—	.10	.20
	1987(h)	30.575	—	—	.10	.20
	1988(h)		—	—	.10	.20

1/2 KRONE

ALUMINUM-BRONZE
Mintmaster's Initials: HCN-GJ

33.1	1924(h)	2.150	2.00	5.00	10.00	22.50
	1925(h)	3.432	2.00	5.00	10.00	22.50
	1926(h)	.716	7.50	12.00	20.00	32.50

Mintmaster's Initials: N-GJ

33.2	1939(h)	.226	30.00	50.00	70.00	100.00
	1940(h)	1.871	1.00	2.00	4.00	6.00	12.50

KRONE

7.5000 g, .800 SILVER, .1929 oz ASW
Mintmaster's Initials: CS

13.1	1875(h)	4.040	4.00	15.00	50.00	130.00
	1876(h)	1.284	10.00	22.50	60.00	170.00
	1892(h)	.701	10.00	14.00	25.00	55.00

Mintmaster's Initials: VBP

13.2	1898(h)	.201	27.50	40.00	60.00	95.00

38	1915(h)	1.410	3.00	4.50	7.50	15.00
	1916(h)	.992	4.00	6.00	10.00	18.00

ALUMINUM-BRONZE
Mintmaster's Initials: HCN-GJ

34.1	1924(h)	.999	100.00	150.00	275.00	550.00
	1925(h)	6.314	.75	1.50	10.00	50.00
	1926(h)	2.706	.75	1.50	10.00	50.00

Mintmaster's Initials: N-GJ

34.2	1929(h)	.501	4.00	10.00	20.00	60.00
	1930(h)	.540	10.00	20.00	35.00	90.00
	1931(h)	.540	4.00	7.00	20.00	50.00
	1934(h)	.529	2.00	4.00	15.00	40.00
	1935(h)	.505	14.00	22.50	35.00	90.00
	1936(h)	.558	2.25	4.50	12.00	40.00
	1938(h)	.407	9.00	15.00	22.00	60.00
	1939(h)	1.517	.50	1.00	2.50	14.00
	1940(h)	1.496	.50	1.00	2.50	14.00
	1941 N(h)GJ	.661	2.00	4.00	6.00	25.00

Mintmaster's Initials: N-S

54	1942(h)	3.952	.50	1.00	2.25	14.00
	1943(h)	.798	2.50	6.00	15.00	40.00
	1944(h)	1.760	.25	.75	2.00	12.50
	1945(h)	2.581	.25	.75	2.00	12.50
	1946(h)	4.321	.25	.50	1.00	4.50
	1947(h)	5.060	.25	.50	1.00	4.50

DENMARK 474

Y#	Date	Mintage	Fine	VF	XF	Unc
61.1	1947(h)	I.A.	1.00	2.25	3.75	10.00
	1948(h)	4.248	.25	.50	1.00	5.50
	1949(h)	1.300	.75	2.25	7.00	16.00
	1952(h)	2.124	.50	2.00	5.00	14.00
	1953(h)	.573	.75	2.25	7.00	16.00
	1954(h)	.584	8.00	12.00	18.00	27.50
	1955(h)	1.359	2.00	4.00	7.50	15.00

Mintmaster's Initials: C-S

61.2	1956(h)	2.858	.25	.50	1.00	4.00
	1957(h)	10.896	.20	.40	1.00	2.50
	1958(h)	1.507	.20	.40	1.00	2.50
	1959(h)	.243	6.00	8.00	12.50	20.00
	1960(h)	1.000	—	400.00	450.00	650.00

COPPER-NICKEL

71.1	1960(h)		.25	.50	1.00	2.50
	1961(h)	10.348	.20	.25	1.00	3.50
	1962(h)	27.068	.20	.25	1.00	3.50
	1963(h)	32.083	.20	.25	.50	2.00
	1964(h)	5.984	.20	.25	.50	2.00
	1965(h)	13.799	.20	.25	.50	1.50
	1966(h)	10.890	.20	.25	.50	1.50
	1967(h)	18.304	.20	.25	.50	1.00
	1968(h)	8.213	.20	.25	.50	1.00
	1969(h)	9.597	—	.20	.30	.75
	1970(h)	9.460	—	.20	.30	.75
	1971(h)	13.985	—	.20	.30	.60

Mintmaster's Initials: S-S

| 71.2 | 1972(h) | 21.019 | — | .15 | .25 | .50 |

Mintmaster's Initials: S-B

81.1	1973(h)	18.268	—	—	.20	.40
	1974(h)	17.742	—	—	.20	.40
	1975(h)	20.136	—	—	.20	.40
	1976(h)	28.049	—	—	.20	.40
	1977(h)	25.685	—	—	.20	.40
	1978(h)	11.286	—	—	.20	.40

Mintmaster's Initials: B-B

81.2	1979(h)	25.216	—	—	.20	.40
	1980(h)	25.825	—	—	.20	.40
	1981(h)	8.889	—	—	.20	.40

Mintmaster's Initials: R-B

81.3	1982(h)	5.011	—	—	.20	.40
	1983(h)	13.946	—	—	.20	.40
	1984(h)	36.439	—	—	.20	.40
	1985(h)	10.843	—	—	.20	.40
	1986(h)	12.556	—	—	.20	.40
	1987(h)	20.120	—	—	.20	.40
	1988(h)	—	—	—	.20	.40

2 KRONER

15.0000 g, .800 SILVER, .3858 oz ASW
Mintmaster's Initials: CS

14.1	1875(h)	3.396	7.00	16.00	50.00	125.00
	1876(h)	1.381	7.00	16.00	50.00	125.00

Mintmaster's Initials: VBP

14.2	1897(h)	.151	35.00	50.00	85.00	140.00
	1899(h)	.152	25.00	40.00	65.00	110.00

25th Anniversary of Reign

Y#	Date	Mintage	Fine	VF	XF	Unc
15	1888	.101	15.00	25.00	35.00	70.00

Golden Wedding Anniversary

| 16 | 1892 CS(h) | .101 | 15.00 | 25.00 | 35.00 | 70.00 |

40th Anniversary of Reign

| 17 | 1903 P(h) | .103 | 10.00 | 15.00 | 20.00 | 37.50 |

Christian IX Death and Accession of Frederik VIII

| 25 | 1906 VBP(h) | .151 | 6.00 | 12.00 | 15.00 | 27.50 |

Frederik VIII Death and Accession of Christian X

| 40 | 1912 VBP(h) | .102 | 6.00 | 12.00 | 18.00 | 35.00 |

39	1915 VBP(h)	.657	12.00	18.00	25.00	45.00
	1916 VBP(h)	.402	6.00	10.00	15.00	25.00

Silver Wedding Anniversary

Y#	Date	Mintage	Fine	VF	XF	Unc
41	1923 HCN(h)	.203	5.00	8.00	12.00	16.00

ALUMINUM-BRONZE
Mintmaster's Initials: HCN-GJ

35.1	1924(h)	1.138	15.00	30.00	85.00	250.00
	1925(h)	3.248	.75	2.00	15.00	55.00
	1926(h)	1.126	.75	2.00	15.00	55.00

Mintmaster's Initials: N-GJ

35.2	1936(h)	.400	4.00	6.00	15.00	40.00
	1938(h)	.191	12.00	18.00	30.00	60.00
	1939(h)	.723	.50	2.00	6.00	25.00
	1940(h)	.743	2.00	4.00	8.00	30.00
	1941(h)	.129	20.00	32.50	55.00	120.00

15.0000 g, .800 SILVER, .3858 oz ASW
King's 60th Birthday

| 42 | 1930 N(h) | .303 | 4.00 | 6.00 | 8.00 | 14.00 |

25th Anniversary of Reign

| 43 | 1937 N(h)S | .209 | 4.00 | 6.00 | 8.00 | 14.00 |

King's 75th Birthday

| 55 | 1945 N(h)S | .157 | 5.00 | 7.00 | 9.00 | 16.00 |

ALUMINUM-BRONZE
Mintmaster's Initials: N-S

62.1	1947(h)	1.151	.75	1.50	5.00	12.50
	1948(h)	.857	.50	1.00	2.50	8.50

DENMARK 475

Y#	Date	Mintage	Fine	VF	XF	Unc
62.1	1949(h)	.272	2.00	3.50	6.50	16.00
	1951(h)	1.576	.50	1.00	2.00	7.50
	1952(h)	1.958	.50	1.00	2.00	6.50
	1953(h)	.432	2.00	3.00	5.00	14.00
	1954(h)	.716	2.00	3.00	5.00	14.00
	1955(h)	.457	2.00	3.00	5.00	14.00

Mintmaster's Initials: C-S

62.2	1956(h)	1.444	.35	.55	1.00	7.50
	1957(h)	2.610	.35	.55	.75	3.00
	1958(h)	2.605	.35	.55	.75	3.00
	1959(h)	.192	4.00	9.00	14.00	25.00

15.0000 g, .800 SILVER, .3858 oz ASW
Greenland Commemorative

63	1953 N(h)S	.152	7.00	14.00	22.00	30.00

Princess Margrethe's 18th Birthday

64	1958 C(h)	.301	—	4.00	6.00	9.00

5 KRONER

17.0000 g, .800 SILVER, .4372 oz ASW
Silver Wedding Anniversary

65	1960 C(h)S	.410	—	—	5.00	7.00

COPPER-NICKEL
Mintmaster's Initials: C-S

72.1	1960(h)	6.418	—	—	.85	1.10	2.00
	1961(h)	9.744	—	—	.85	1.50	5.00
	1962(h)	2.074	—	—	.85	1.75	6.00
	1963(h)	.709	—	—	.85	1.75	7.00
	1964(h)	1.443	—	—	.85	1.75	6.00
	1965(h)	2.574	—	—	.85	1.25	3.50
	1966(h)	4.370	—	—	.85	1.25	3.00
	1967(h)	1.864	—	—	.85	1.10	2.50
	1968(h)	4.132	—	—	.85	1.10	2.00
	1969(h)	.072	3.00	4.00	5.00	7.50
	1970(h)	2.246	—	—	.85	1.00	1.50
	1971(h)	4.767	—	—	.85	1.00	1.50

Mintmaster's Initials: S-S

72.2	1972(h)	2.599	—	—	.75	1.00	1.50

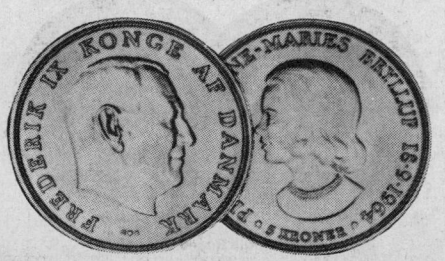

17.0000 g, .800 SILVER, .4372 oz ASW
Wedding of Princess Anne Marie

Y#	Date	Mintage	Fine	VF	XF	Unc
73	1964 C(h)S	.359	—	—	4.00	5.00

COPPER-NICKEL
Mintmaster's Initials: S-B

82.1	1973(h) narrow rim	3.774	—	—	.85	1.50
	1973(h) wide rim Inc. Ab.	—	—	.85	1.25
	1974(h)	5.239	—	—	.85	1.25
	1975(h)	5.810	—	—	.85	1.25
	1976(h)	7.651	—	—	.85	1.25
	1977(h)	6.885	—	—	.85	1.25
	1978(h)	2.984	—	—	.85	1.25

Mintmaster's Initials: B-B

82.2	1979(h)	2.861	—	—	.85	1.25
	1980(h)	3.622	—	—	.85	1.25
	1981(h)	1.057	—	—	.85	1.25

Mintmaster's Initials: R-B

82.3	1982(h)	1.002	—	—	.85	1.25
	1983(h)	1.044	—	—	.85	1.25
	1984(h)	.713	—	—	.85	1.25
	1985(h)	.621	—	—	.85	1.25
	1986(h)	1.042	—	—	.85	1.25
	1987(h)	.611	—	—	.85	1.25
	1988(h)	—	—	—	.85	1.25

10 KRONER

4.4803 g, .900 GOLD, .1296 oz AGW
Mintmaster's Initials: CS

18.1	1873(h)	.369	75.00	110.00	145.00	225.00
	1874(h)	I.A.	75.00	125.00	170.00	260.00
	1877(h)	.098	75.00	150.00	185.00	275.00
	1877(h)	—	—	—	Proof	1000.
	1890(h)	.151	75.00	115.00	140.00	210.00

Mintmaster's Initials: VBP

18.2	1898(h)	.100	75.00	120.00	150.00	220.00
	1900(h)	.204	75.00	110.00	120.00	180.00

26	1908(h)	.461	75.00	85.00	95.00	125.00
	1909(h)	I.A.	75.00	85.00	95.00	125.00

44	1913(h)	.312	75.00	85.00	95.00	125.00
	1917(h)	.132	75.00	85.00	110.00	150.00

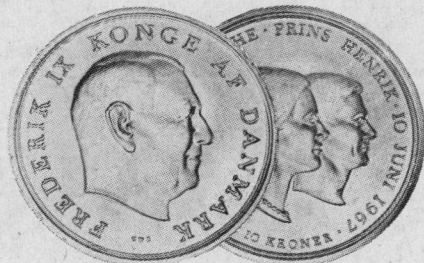

20.4000 g, .800 SILVER, .5247 oz ASW
Wedding of Princess Margrethe

74	1967 C(h)S	.498*	—	—	5.00	7.00

NOTE: 78,383 of these coins were melted.

Wedding of Princess Benedikte
Obv: Similar to Y#74.

Y#	Date	Mintage	Fine	VF	XF	Unc
75	1968 C(h)S	.297*	—	—	6.00	8.00

***NOTE:** 42,923 of these coins were melted.

Death of Frederik IX
and Accession of Margrethe II

77	1972 S(h)S	.400	—	—	5.00	7.00

COPPER-NICKEL
Mintmaster's Initials: B-B

83.1	1979(h)	76.801	—	—	1.65	2.25
	1981(h)	10.520	—	—	1.65	2.25

Mintmaster's Initials: R-B

83.2	1982(h)	1.065	—	—	1.65	2.25
	1983(h)	1.123	—	—	1.65	2.25
	1984(h)	.748	—	—	1.65	2.25
	1985(h)	.720	—	—	1.65	2.25
	1986(h)	.719	—	—	1.65	2.25
	1988(h)	—	—	—	1.65	2.25

Crown Prince's Coming of Age

84	1986 R(h)B	1.090	—	—	1.75	3.00
	1986 R(h)B	2,000	—	—	Proof	800.00

14.3000 g, .800 SILVER, .3678 oz ASW

84a	1986 R(h)B	.024	—	—	Proof	80.00

20 KRONER

8.9606 g, .900 GOLD, .2592 oz AGW
Mintmaster's Initials: CS

19.1	1873(h)	1.153	BV	135.00	150.00	200.00
	1874(h)	I.A.	400.00	800.00	1100.	1500.
	1876(h)	.351	BV	135.00	150.00	200.00
	1877(h)	I.A.	BV	135.00	175.00	225.00
	1890(h)	.102	BV	135.00	150.00	200.00

Mintmaster's Initials: VBP

19.2	1900(h)	.100	BV	135.00	150.00	200.00

DENMARK

Y#	Date	Mintage	Fine	VF	XF	Unc
27	1908(h)	.243	BV	135.00	150.00	175.00
	1909(h)	.365	BV	135.00	150.00	175.00
	1910(h)	.200	BV	135.00	150.00	175.00
	1911(h)	.183	BV	135.00	150.00	175.00
	1912(h)	.184	BV	135.00	150.00	175.00

45.1	1913(h)	.815	BV	130.00	150.00	175.00
	1914(h)	.920	BV	130.00	150.00	175.00
	1915(h)	.532	BV	130.00	150.00	175.00
	1916(h)	1.401	BV	130.00	150.00	175.00
	1917(h)	I.A.	BV	130.00	150.00	175.00

Mintmaster's Initials: HCN

45.2	1926(h)	.358	—	—	4000.	12,000.
	1927(h)	I.A.	—	—	4000.	12,000.

Mintmaster's Initials: N

45.3	1930(h)	1.285	—	—	—	12,000.
	1931(h)	I.A.	—	—	—	12,000.

NOTE: The 1926-1931 dated 20 Kroners were not released for circulation. Only two each of the 1930 and 1931 dated coins are known.

MINT SETS (MS)

KM#	Date	Mintage	Identification	Issue Price	Mkt. Val.
MS1	1956(7)	—	Y56-62	—	80.00
MS2	1957(7)	—	Y56-62	—	70.00
MS3	1958(7)	—	Y56-62	—	70.00
MS4	1959(7)	—	Y56-62	—	250.00
MS5	1960(10)	—	Y56-60,68-72	—	100.00
MS6	1961(7)	—	Y56-58,69-72	—	70.00
MS7	1962(8)	—	Y56-58,68-72	—	60.00
MS8	1963(7)	—	Y56-58,68,69,71,72	—	45.00
MS9	1964(8)	—	Y56-58,68-72	—	45.00
MS10	1965(7)	—	Y56,57,68-72	—	30.00
MS11	1966(8)	—	Y56,57,68-72,76	—	30.00
MS12	1967(8)	—	Y56,57,68-72,76	—	50.00
MS13	1968(7)	—	Y56,57,68,69,71,72,76	—	20.00
MS14	1969(7)	—	Y56,57,68,69,71,72,76	—	30.00
MS15	1970(7)	—	Y56,57,68,69,71,72,76	—	8.00
MS16	1971(7)	—	Y56,57,68,69,71,72,76	—	8.00
MS17	1972(7)	—	Y56,57,68,69,71,72,76	—	5.00
MS18	1973(5)	—	Y78-82	—	6.00
MS19	1974(7)	—	Y78-82	6.00	6.00
MS20	1975(5)	4,300	Y78-82	6.00	45.00
MS21	1976(5)	6,000	Y78-82	3.55	25.00
MS22	1977(5)	6,000	Y78-82	—	20.00
MS23	1978(5)	6,000	Y78-82	—	6.00
MS24	1979(5)	6,000	Y78-83	—	6.00
MS25	1980(5)	4,000	Y78-82	—	55.00
MS26	1981(6)	15,000	Y78-83	—	6.00
MS27	1982(6)	20,000	Y78-83	—	6.00
MS28	1983(6)	20,000	Y78-83	—	6.00
MS29	1984(6)	18,000	Y78-83	—	6.00
MS30	1985(6)	20,000	Y78-83	—	6.00
MS31	1986(6)	20,000	Y78-82,84	—	7.00
MS32	1987(6)	—	Y78.3-82.3,83.2	—	6.00
MS33	1988(6)	—	Y78.3-82.3,83.2	—	6.00

FAEROE ISLANDS

The Faeroe Islands, a self-governing community within the kingdom of Denmark, are situated in the North Atlantic between Iceland and the Shetland Islands. The 17 inhabited islands and numerous islets and reefs have an area of 540 sq. mi. (1,399 sq. km.) and a population of 43,502. Capital: Thorshavn. The principal industries are fishing and grazing. Fish and fish products are exported.

While it is thought that Irish hermits lived on the islands in the 7th and 8th centuries, the present inhabitants are descended from 6th century Norse settlers. The Faeroe Islands became a Norwegian fief in 1035 and became Danish in 1380 when Norway and Denmark were united. They have ever since remained in Danish possession and were granted self-government (except for an appointed governor-general) with their own legislature, executive and flag in 1948.

The islands were occupied by British troops during World War II, after the German occupation of Denmark. The Faeroe Island coinage was struck in London during World War II.

RULERS
Danish

MONETARY SYSTEM
100 Ore = 1 Krone

ORE

BRONZE

KM#	Date	Mintage	Fine	VF	XF	Unc
1	1941	.100	25.00	40.00	50.00	65.00
	1941	—	—	—	Proof	150.00

2 ORE

BRONZE

2	1941	.100	4.00	8.00	14.00	25.00
	1941	—	—	—	Proof	150.00

5 ORE

BRONZE

3	1941	.100	4.00	7.00	12.00	22.50
	1941	—	—	—	Proof	150.00

10 ORE

COPPER-NICKEL

4	1941	.100	5.00	9.00	15.00	32.50
	1941	—	—	—	Proof	175.00

25 ORE

COPPER-NICKEL

5	1941	.100	5.00	9.00	15.00	32.50
	1941	—	—	—	Proof	175.00

DJIBOUTI

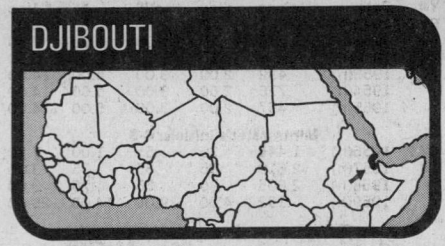

The Republic of Djibouti (formerly French Somaliland and the French Overseas Territory of Afars and Issas), located in northeast Africa at the Bab el Mandeb Strait connecting the Suez Canal and the Red Sea with the Gulf of Aden and the Indian Ocean, has an area of 8,494 sq. mi. (22,000 sq. km.) and a population of *327,000. Capital: Djibouti. The tiny nation has less than one sq. mi. of arable land, and no natural resources except salt, sand, and camels. The commercial activities of the transshipment port of Djibouti and the Addis Ababa-Djibouti railroad are the basis of the economy. Salt, fish and hides are exported.

French interest in former French Somaliland began in 1839 with concessions obtained by a French naval lieutenant from the provincial sultans. French Somaliland was made a protectorate in 1884 and its boundaries were delimited by the Franco-British and Ethiopian accords of 1887 and 1897. It became a colony in 1896 and a territory within the French Union in 1946. In 1958 it voted to join the new French Community as an overseas territory, and reaffirmed that choice by a referendum in March, 1967. Its name was changed from French Somaliland to the French Territory of Afars and Issas on July 5, 1967.

The French Tricolor, which had flown over the strategically important territory for 115 years, was lowered for the last time on June 27, 1977, when French Afars and Issas became Africa's 49th independent state, under the name of the Republic of Djibouti.

COUNTERMARKED COINAGE
RUPEE-TALER (RYAL) COINAGE SERIES

Coins privately countermarked (c/m) around 1900 with 12 scalloped square with Arabic inscription. Sometimes coins have additional c/m's on the coin showing silver fineness.

1/2 RUPEE SIZE
.917 SILVER
c/m: On India 1/2 Rupee.

KM#	Date	VG	Fine	VF	XF
1	ND	30.00	50.00	75.00	175.00

RUPEE SIZE

.917 SILVER
c/m: On India Rupee, KM#450.

2.1	ND(1835,40)	20.00	30.00	50.00	100.00

c/m: On India Rupee, KM#457.

2.2	ND(1840)	20.00	30.00	50.00	100.00

c/m: On India Rupee, KM#458.

KM#	Date	VG	Fine	VF	XF
2.3	ND(1840)	20.00	30.00	50.00	100.00

c/m: On India Rupee, KM#473.
| 2.4 | ND(1862,74-1901) | | | | |
| | | 20.00 | 30.00 | 50.00 | 100.00 |

RYAL SIZE (TALER)

.833 SILVER
c/m: On Austria Burgau M.T. Thaler, KM#T1.
| 3.1 | ND(1780) | 25.00 | 40.00 | 65.00 | 125.00 |

c/m: With additional Arabic "830".
| 3.2 | ND(1780) | 30.00 | 50.00 | 80.00 | 150.00 |

FRENCH SOMALILAND

MINT MARKS
(a) - Paris (privy marks only)
MONETARY SYSTEM
100 Centimes = 1 Franc

FRANC

ALUMINUM

KM#	Date	Mintage	Fine	VF	XF	Unc
4	1948(a)	.200	7.50	12.50	20.00	30.00
	1949(a)	Inc. Ab.	5.00	10.00	17.50	25.00

KM#	Date	Mintage	Fine	VF	XF	Unc
8	1959(a)	.500	.25	.50	1.25	2.00
	1965(a)	.200	.35	.60	1.50	2.50

2 FRANCS

ALUMINUM

| 5 | 1948(a) | .200 | 7.50 | 12.50 | 20.00 | 30.00 |
| | 1949(a) | Inc. Ab. | 5.00 | 10.00 | 17.50 | 25.00 |

| 9 | 1959(a) | .200 | .25 | .75 | 1.50 | 2.75 |
| | 1965(a) | .240 | .25 | .75 | 1.50 | 2.75 |

5 FRANCS

ALUMINUM

| 6 | 1948(a) | .500 | 1.50 | 5.00 | 8.00 | 15.00 |

| 10 | 1959(a) | .500 | .25 | .75 | 1.50 | 3.00 |
| | 1965(a) | .200 | .25 | .75 | 1.50 | 3.00 |

10 FRANCS

ALUMINUM-BRONZE

| 11 | 1965(a) | .250 | .50 | 1.00 | 1.50 | 3.00 |

20 FRANCS

ALUMINUM-BRONZE

| 7 | 1952(a) | .500 | 1.50 | 3.00 | 6.50 | 13.50 |

KM#	Date	Mintage	Fine	VF	XF	Unc
12	1965(a)	.200	.50	1.00	2.00	4.00

FLEUR DE COIN SETS (SS)

KM#	Date	Mintage	Identification	Issue Price	Mkt. Val.
SS1	1965(5)	1,898	KM8-12	—	12.50

FRENCH AFARS & ISSAS

MINT MARKS
(a) - Paris (privy marks only)
MONETARY SYSTEM
100 Centimes = 1 Franc

FRANC

ALUMINUM

KM#	Date	Mintage	VF	XF	Unc
16	1969(a)	.100	1.50	3.00	5.00
	1971(a)	.100	1.50	3.00	5.00
	1975(a)	.300	1.00	2.00	3.00

2 FRANCS

ALUMINUM

| 13 | 1968(a) | .100 | 1.50 | 3.00 | 5.00 |
| | 1975(a) | .180 | 1.00 | 2.00 | 3.00 |

5 FRANCS

ALUMINUM

| 14 | 1968(a) | .100 | 1.50 | 3.00 | 5.00 |
| | 1975(a) | .300 | 1.00 | 2.00 | 3.00 |

10 FRANCS

ALUMINUM-BRONZE

17	1969(a)	.100	2.50	5.50	8.00
	1970(a)	.300	2.00	3.50	6.00
	1975(a)	.360	1.25	2.50	4.00

20 FRANCS

ALUMINUM-BRONZE

| 15 | 1968(a) | .300 | 2.00 | 4.00 | 7.00 |
| | 1975(a) | .300 | 1.50 | 2.75 | 4.50 |

French Afars & Issas / DJIBOUTI 478

50 FRANCS

COPPER-NICKEL

KM#	Date	Mintage	VF	XF	Unc
18	1970(a)	.300	3.00	5.00	8.00
	1975(a)	.180	2.25	4.50	6.00

100 FRANCS

COPPER-NICKEL

19	1970(a)	.600	3.50	8.00	12.00
	1975(a)	.400	2.50	6.50	10.00

DJIBOUTI

FRANC

ALUMINUM

20	1977(a)	—	1.00	2.00	6.00

2 FRANCS

ALUMINUM

21	1977(a)	—	1.00	2.00	6.00

5 FRANCS

ALUMINUM

22	1977(a)	—	1.00	1.50	4.00

10 FRANCS

ALUMINUM-BRONZE

23	1977(a)	—	1.00	1.50	4.00
	1983(a)	—	.75	1.25	3.00

20 FRANCS

ALUMINUM-BRONZE

KM#	Date	Mintage	VF	XF	Unc
24	1977(a)	—	1.00	1.50	4.00
	1983(a)	—	.75	1.25	3.00

50 FRANCS
COPPER-NICKEL
Similar to 100 Francs, KM#26.

25	1977(a)	—	2.00	4.00	8.00
	1982(a)	—	1.50	3.50	6.00
	1983(a)	—	1.50	3.50	6.00

100 FRANCS

COPPER-NICKEL

26	1977(a)	—	2.50	4.50	10.00

DOMINICA

The Commonwealth of Dominica, situated in the Lesser Antilles midway between Guadeloupe to the north and Martinque to the south, has an area of 290 sq. mi. (751 sq. km.) and a population of *76,000. Capital: Roseau. Agriculture is the chief economic activity of the mountainous island. Bananas are the chief export.

Columbus discovered and named the island on Nov. 3, 1493. Spain neglected it and it was finally colonized by the French in 1632. The British drove the French from the island in 1756. Thereafter it changed hands between the French and British a dozen or more times before becoming permanently British in 1805. Throughout the greater part of its British history, Dominica was a presidency of the Leeward Islands. In 1940 its administration was transferred to the Windward Islands and it was established as a separate colony with considerable local autonomy. Dominica became a West Indies associated state with a built in option for independence in 1967. Full independence was attained on Nov. 3, 1978. Dominica, which has a republican form of government, is a member of the Commonwealth of Nations. The Queen of England is recognized as the head of the Commonwealth, but not as the Chief of State of Dominica.

RULERS
British, until 1978

MONETARY SYSTEM
100 Cents = 1 Dollar

2 BITS

SILVER
Holed Spanish or Spanish Colonial 2 Reales.

KM#	Date	Good	VG	Fine	VF
9	ND(1816)	35.00	60.00	75.00	100.00

3 BITS

SILVER
c/m: Crowned 3 on 1/2 of 23mm center plug cut from Spanish or Spanish Colonial 8 Reales.

4	ND(1813)	60.00	100.00	175.00	275.00

2 SHILLINGS 6 PENCE

SILVER
c/m: '2.6' on 1/4 segment of Spanish or Spanish Colonial 8 Reales.

10	ND(1816-18)	100.00	175.00	250.00	400.00

4 BITS

SILVER
c/m: Crowned '4' on center ring segment of Spanish or Spanish Colonial 8 Reales.

5	ND(1813)	100.00	175.00	250.00	400.00

5-1/2 BITS
(4 Shilling 1-1/2 Pence)

DOMINICA

SILVER
Crenalated center hole in San Luis Potosi
4 Reales, KM#72.

KM#	Date	Good	VG	Fine	VF
2	ND(1791-1808)	650.00	1000.	1500.	2150.

6 BITS

SILVER
c/m: Crowned 'G' on obv. or rev. of center plug
cut from Spanish or Spanish Colonial 8 Reales.

| 6 | ND(1813) | 32.50 | 65.00 | 135.00 | 250.00 |

11 BITS

SILVER
Crenalated center hole in Mexico 8 Reales, KM#109.

| 3.2 | ND(1781-1808) | 75.00 | 120.00 | 200.00 | 325.00 |

NOTE: The center plug was used for the 1-1/2 Bits, C#21.

12 BITS

SILVER
c/m: Crowned 12 with crenalated center hole on holed
Lima 8 Reales, KM#97.

| 7 | ND(1813) | 175.00 | 300.00 | 500.00 | 775.00 |

16 BITS

SILVER
c/m: Crowned '16' on obv. and rev. of
Mexico 8 Reales, KM#109.

| 8.2 | ND(1813) | 100.00 | 175.00 | 300.00 | 500.00 |

MODERN COINAGE
4 DOLLARS

COPPER-NICKEL
F.A.O. issue

KM#	Date	Mintage	VF	XF	Unc
11	1970	.013	3.00	5.00	9.00
	1970	2,000	—	Proof	25.00

10 DOLLARS

20.5000 g, .925 SILVER, .6097 oz ASW
History of Carnival

| 12 | 1978 | 1,500 | — | 7.50 | 20.00 |
| | 1978 | 2,000 | — | Proof | 32.50 |

Visit of Pope John Paul II
Obv: Similar to 300 Dollars, KM#15.

| 16 | 1979 | 1,150 | — | 7.50 | 20.00 |
| | 1979 | 3,450 | — | Proof | 27.50 |

COPPER-NICKEL
Royal Visit

KM#	Date	Mintage	VF	XF	Unc
20	1985	*.100	—	4.50	7.50

28.2800 g, .925 SILVER, .8409 oz ASW

| 20a | 1985 | *5,000 | — | Proof | 37.50 |

47.5400 g, .917 GOLD, 1.4013 oz AGW

| 20b | 1985 | *250 pcs. | — | Proof | 1200. |

20 DOLLARS

40.9100 g, .925 SILVER, 1.2167 oz ASW
50th Anniversary of Graf Zeppelin
Obv: Similar to 300 Dollars, KM#15.

| 13 | 1978 | 500 pcs. | — | 15.00 | 65.00 |
| | 1978 | 1,000 | — | Proof | 75.00 |

Israel and Egypt Peace Treaty
Obv: Similar to 300 Dollars, KM#15.

| 17 | 1979 | 200 pcs. | — | 15.00 | 75.00 |
| | 1979 | 200 pcs. | — | Proof | 90.00 |

150 DOLLARS

9.6000 g, .900 GOLD, .2778 oz AGW

| 14 | 1978 | 300 pcs. | — | — | 175.00 |
| | 1978 | 400 pcs. | — | Proof | 185.00 |

DOMINICA 480

Israel and Egypt Peace Treaty

KM#	Date	Mintage	VF	XF	Unc
18	1979	100 pcs.	—	—	300.00
	1979	100 pcs.	—	Proof	375.00

300 DOLLARS

19.2000 g, .900 GOLD, .5556 oz AGW

15	1978	500 pcs.	—	—	350.00
	1978	800 pcs.	—	Proof	350.00

Visit of Pope John Paul II

19	1979	5,000	—	—	325.00
	1979	300 pcs.	—	—	375.00

DOMINICAN REP.

The Dominican Republic, which occupies the eastern two-thirds of the island of Hispaniola, has an area of 18,816 sq. mi. (48,734 sq. km.) and a population of *7.3 million. Capital: Santo Domingo. The agricultural economy produces sugar, coffee, tobacco and cocoa.

Columbus discovered Hispaniola in 1492, and named it La Isla Espanola - 'the Spanish Island'. Santo Domingo, the oldest white settlement in the Western Hemisphere, was the base from which Spain conducted its exploration of the New World. Later, French buccaneers settled the western third of Hispaniola, a colony named St. Dominique, which in 1697 was ceded to France by Spain. In 1804, following a bloody revolt by former slaves, the French colony became the Republic of Haiti - 'mountainous country'. The Spanish called their part of Hispaniola Santo Domingo. In 1822, the Haitians conquered the entire island and held it until 1844, when Juan Pablo Duarte, the national hero of the Dominican Republic, drove them out of eastern Hispaniola and established an independent Dominican Republic. The republic returned voluntarily to Spanish dominion - after being rejected by France, Britain and the United States - from 1861 to 1865, when independence was restored.

MINT MARKS
A - Paris
(a) - Berlin
H - Birmingham, England
Mo - Mexico

RULERS
Spanish, until 1822
Haiti, 1822-1844

MONETARY SYSTEM
16 Reales = 1 Escudo

SANTO DOMINGO
1/4 REAL

COPPER

KM#	Date	Mintage	Good	VG	Fine	VF
1	ND	—	45.00	75.00	125.00	200.00

2	ND	—	12.00	20.00	32.50	50.00

NOTE: Several varieties of fraction and letter arrangement on reverse exist.

2/4 REAL
NOTE: Coin previously listed here has been moved to Venezuela, Province of Maracaibo.

REAL

SILVER

4	ND	—	50.00	90.00	150.00	250.00

2 REALES

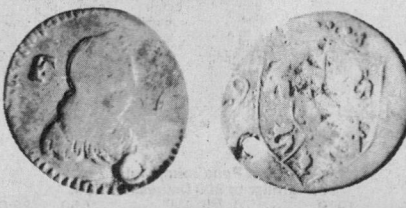

SILVER

5	ND	—	60.00	100.00	175.00	300.00

COUNTERMARKED COINAGE
REAL

.903 SILVER
c/m: Crowned F.7o on Mexico 1 Real, KM#75.

KM#	Date	Good	VG	Fine	VF
8	ND(1732-47)	40.00	65.00	100.00	175.00

8 REALES

.903 SILVER
c/m: Crowned F.7o on Mexico 8 Reales, KM#109.

11	ND(1791-1808)	750.00	1000.	—	—

DOMINICAN REPUBLIC
MONETARY SYSTEM
8 Reales = 1 Peso

1/4 REAL

BRONZE

KM#	Date	Mintage	Fine	VF	XF	Unc
1	1844	1,600	7.00	15.00	37.50	—

BRASS

2	1844	—	5.00	10.00	20.00	75.00
	1848 plain 4	—	5.00	10.00	20.00	75.00
	1848 crosslet 4	—	5.00	10.00	20.00	75.00

NOTE: Many varieties exist.

DECIMAL COINAGE
100 Centavos = 1 Peso

CENTAVO

BRASS

3	1877	1,000	1.50	2.50	5.00	15.00

1-1/4 CENTAVOS

COPPER-NICKEL

KM#	Date	Mintage	Fine	VF	XF	Unc
6	1882	.400	6.50	13.00	32.50	85.00
	1888A	.500	2.50	5.00	12.50	50.00
	1888A	—	—	—	Proof	275.00

2-1/2 CENTAVOS

COPPER-NICKEL

4	1877	.021	17.50	25.00	45.00	100.00

7	1882	—	4.50	10.00	27.50	65.00
	1888A large date					
		4.000	.75	2.00	6.00	50.00
	1888A lg. date—	—	—	—	Proof	250.00
	1888(a) small date					
		.950	1.25	3.00	7.50	50.00
	1888H	4.000	.75	2.00	6.00	50.00
	1888H	—	—	—	Proof	350.00

NOTE: 1888A w/small date was struck at the Berlin Mint.

5 CENTAVOS

COPPER-NICKEL

5	1877	.130	10.00	20.00	32.50	75.00

10 CENTAVOS

2.5000 g, .350 SILVER, .0281 oz ASW

13	1897A	.764	2.50	8.00	20.00	150.00

20 CENTAVOS

5.0000 g, .350 SILVER, .0563 oz ASW

14	1897A	1.395	2.00	6.00	17.50	150.00

1/2 PESO

12.5000 g, .350 SILVER, .1407 oz ASW

15	1897A	.917	3.50	15.00	40.00	300.00

PESO

25.0000 g, .350 SILVER, .2813 oz ASW

KM#	Date	Mintage	Fine	VF	XF	Unc
16	1897A	1.455	7.50	25.00	75.00	550.00

MONETARY REFORM
(of 1891)
100 Centesimos = 1 Franco

5 CENTESIMOS

BRONZE

8	1891A	.400	1.00	3.00	10.00	45.00
	1891A	—	—	—	Proof	200.00

10 CENTESIMOS

BRONZE

9	1891A	.300	1.00	3.00	10.00	60.00
	1891A	—	—	—	Proof	250.00

50 CENTESIMOS

2.5000 g, .835 SILVER, .0671 oz ASW

10	1891A	.150	3.50	10.00	30.00	100.00
	1891A	—	—	—	Proof	300.00

UN (1) FRANCO

5.000 g, .835 SILVER, .1342 oz ASW

11	1891A	.125	8.00	15.00	35.00	175.00
	1891A	—	—	—	Proof	450.00

CINCO (5) FRANCOS

25.0000 g, .900 SILVER, .7234 oz ASW

12	1891A	.150	45.00	85.00	145.00	600.00
	1891A	—	—	—	Proof	3000.

MONETARY REFORM
100 Centavos = 1 Peso Oro

CENTAVO

BRONZE

KM#	Date	Mintage	Fine	VF	XF	Unc
17	1937	1.000	.50	1.50	7.50	75.00
	1937	—	—	—	Proof	250.00
	1939	2.000	.50	1.25	5.00	50.00
	1941	2.000	.25	.50	3.00	12.00
	1942	2.000	.25	.50	3.00	15.00
	1944	5.000	.20	.50	1.50	10.00
	1947	3.000	.20	.50	1.00	8.00
	1949	3.000	.20	.40	1.00	8.00
	1951	3.000	.20	.35	.75	8.00
	1952	3.000	.20	.35	.75	5.00
	1955	3.000	.15	.35	.75	3.00
	1956	3.000	.15	.35	.75	3.00
	1957	5.000	.10	.25	.75	2.50
	1959	5.000	.10	.25	.75	2.50
	1961	5.000	.10	.20	1.00	1.00
	1961	10 pcs.	—	—	Proof	200.00

100th Anniversary Restoration of the Republic
Rev: HP below bust.

25	1963	13.000	—	—	.10	.40

31	1968	5.000	—	—	.10	.20
	1971	6.000	—	—	.10	.20
	1972	3.000	—	—	.10	.20
	1972	500 pcs.	—	—	Proof	20.00
	1975	.500	—	—	.10	.20

F.A.O. Issue
Rev: HP below bust.

32	1969	5.000	—	—	.10	.30

Duarte Centennial

40	1976	3.995	—	—	.10	.20
	1976	5.000	—	—	Proof	1.00

48	1978	2.995	—	—	.10	.15
	1978	5.000	—	—	Proof	2.00
	1979	2.985	—	—	.10	.15
	1979	500 pcs.	—	—	Proof	20.00
	1980	.200	—	—	.10	.15
	1980	3.000	—	—	Proof	1.00
	1981	3.000	—	—	Proof	1.00

3.5800 g, .900 SILVER, .1036 oz ASW

48a	1978	15 pcs.	—	—	Proof	100.00
	1979	15 pcs.	—	—	Proof	100.00
	1980	15 pcs.	—	—	Proof	100.00
	1981	15 pcs.	—	—	Proof	100.00

DOMINICAN REPUBLIC 482

COPPER-PLATED-ZINC
Caonabo

KM#	Date	Mintage	Fine	VF	XF	Unc
64	1984 Mo	10.000	—	—	—	.25
	1984 Mo	1,600	—	—	Proof	1.50
	1986	18.067	—	—	—	.25
	1986	1,600	—	—	Proof	1.50
	1987	15.000	—	—	—	.25
	1987	1,600	—	—	Proof	1.50

2.0000 g, .900 SILVER, .0578 oz ASW

64a	1984 Mo	100 pcs.	—	—	Proof	20.00
	1986	100 pcs.	—	—	Proof	20.00

5 CENTAVOS

COPPER-NICKEL
Rev: HP below bust.

18	1937	2.000	1.00	1.75	5.00	50.00
	1937	—	—	—	Proof	300.00
	1939	.200	3.50	8.00	40.00	250.00
	1951	2.000	.75	1.25	2.00	20.00
	1956	1.000	.20	.50	.80	3.50
	1959	1.000	.20	.50	.80	3.50
	1961	4.000	.10	.20	.35	.75
	1961	10 pcs.	—	—	Proof	550.00
	1971	.440	.10	.15	.20	.50
	1972	2.000	.10	.15	.20	.40
	1972	500 pcs.	—	—	Proof	25.00
	1974	5.000	—	—	.10	.40
	1974	500 pcs.	—	—	Proof	25.00

5.0000 g, .350 SILVER, .0563 oz ASW

18a	1944	2.000	1.50	3.50	7.50	30.00

COPPER-NICKEL
100th Anniversary Restoration of the Republic
Rev: HP below bust.

26	1963	4.000	—	.10	.15	.60

Duarte Centennial

41	1976	5.595	—	—	.10	.50
	1976	5,000	—	—	Proof	2.00

49	1978	1.996	—	—	.10	.35
	1978	5,000	—	—	Proof	1.50
	1979	2.988	—	—	.10	.35
	1979	500 pcs.	—	—	Proof	25.00
	1980	5.300	—	—	.10	.35
	1980	3,000	—	—	Proof	2.00
	1981	4.500	—	—	.10	.35
	1981	3,000	—	—	Proof	2.00

5.8600 g, .900 SILVER, .1696 oz ASW

49a	1978	15 pcs.	—	—	Proof	100.00
	1979	15 pcs.	—	—	Proof	100.00
	1980	15 pcs.	—	—	Proof	100.00
	1981	15 pcs.	—	—	Proof	100.00

COPPER-NICKEL
Human Rights

KM#	Date	Mintage	Fine	VF	XF	Unc
59	1983	3.998	—	—	.10	.20
	1983	1,600	—	—	Proof	2.00
	1984 Mo	10.000	—	—	.10	.20
	1984 Mo	1,600	—	—	Proof	2.00
	1986	12.898	—	—	.10	.20
	1986	1,600	—	—	Proof	2.00
	1987	10.000	—	—	.10	.20
	1987	1,700	—	—	Proof	2.00

5.0000 g, .900 SILVER, .1447 oz ASW

59a	1983	100 pcs.	—	—	Proof	30.00
	1984 Mo	100 pcs.	—	—	Proof	30.00
	1986	100 pcs.	—	—	Proof	30.00

10 CENTAVOS

2.5000 g, .900 SILVER, .0723 oz ASW
Rev: HP below bust.

19	1937	1.000	BV	2.00	5.00	40.00
	1937	—	—	—	Proof	350.00
	1939	.150	3.00	6.00	15.00	200.00
	1942	2.000	1.00	2.00	3.00	30.00
	1944	1.000	1.00	2.00	4.00	50.00
	1951	.500	1.00	2.00	3.00	10.00
	1952	.500	1.00	2.00	3.00	10.00
	1953	.750	1.00	2.00	3.00	8.00
	1956	1.000	.75	1.50	2.50	8.00
	1959	2.000	BV	1.25	2.25	7.00
	1961	2.000	BV	1.00	2.00	6.00

2.5000 g, .650 SILVER, .0522 oz ASW
100th Anniversary Restoration of the Republic
Rev: HP below bust.

27	1963	4.000	—	—	BV	1.00	2.00

COPPER-NICKEL
Rev: HP below bust.
Plain edge

19a	1967	10.000	—	—	.15	.50
	1973	8.000	—	—	.15	.50
	1973	500 pcs.	—	—	Proof	25.00
	1975	8.000	—	—	.15	.50

Duarte Centennial

42	1976	5.595	—	—	.10	.75
	1976	5,000	—	—	Proof	2.00

50	1978	3.000	—	—	.10	.50
	1978	5,000	—	—	Proof	2.00
	1979	4.020	—	—	.10	.50
	1979	500 pcs.	—	—	Proof	25.00
	1980	4.400	—	—	.10	.35
	1980	3,000	—	—	Proof	3.00
	1981	6.000	—	—	.10	.35
	1981	3,000	—	—	Proof	3.00

2.9500 g, .900 SILVER, .0854 oz ASW

50a	1978	15 pcs.	—	—	Proof	100.00
	1979	15 pcs.	—	—	Proof	100.00
	1980	15 pcs.	—	—	Proof	100.00
	1981	15 pcs.	—	—	Proof	100.00

COPPER-NICKEL
Human Rights
H - Tower mint mark - London

60	1983	4.998	—	—	.10	.35
	1983 H	4.000	—	—	.10	.35
	1983 H	1,600	—	—	Proof	2.50
	1984 Mo	15.000	—	—	.10	.25

KM#	Date	Mintage	Fine	VF	XF	Unc
60	1984 Mo	1,600	—	—	Proof	2.50
	1986	15.515	—	—	.10	.25
	1986	1,600	—	—	Proof	2.50
	1987	20.000	—	—	.10	.25
	1987	1,700	—	—	Proof	2.50

2.5000 g, .900 SILVER, .0723 oz ASW

60a	1983 H	100 pcs.	—	—	Proof	30.00
	1984 Mo	100 pcs.	—	—	Proof	30.00
	1986	100 pcs.	—	—	Proof	30.00

25 CENTAVOS

6.2500 g, .900 SILVER, .1808 oz ASW
Rev: HP below bust.

20	1937	.560	BV	5.00	15.00	75.00
	1937	—	—	—	Proof	400.00
	1939	.160	4.00	8.00	20.00	350.00
	1942	.560	2.00	4.00	10.00	150.00
	1944	.400	2.00	4.00	8.00	125.00
	1947	.400	2.00	4.00	8.00	125.00
	1951	.400	2.00	4.00	8.00	125.00
	1952	.400	2.00	3.00	5.00	12.50
	1956	.400	2.00	2.50	4.00	10.00
	1960	.600	2.00	2.50	4.00	10.00
	1961	.800	2.00	2.50	4.00	10.00

6.2500 g, .650 SILVER, .1306 oz ASW
100th Anniversary Restoration of the Republic

28	1963	2.400	—	—	BV	1.50	3.00

COPPER-NICKEL
Plain edge

20a.1	1967	5.000	—	—	.10	.20	.75
	1972	.800	—	—	.10	.40	1.00
	1972	500 pcs.	—	—	—	Proof	25.00

Reeded edge

20a.2	1974	2.000	—	—	.10	.40	1.00
	1974	500 pcs.	—	—	—	Proof	25.00

Duarte Centennial

43	1976	3.195	—	—	.10	.40	1.00
	1976	5,000	—	—	—	Proof	2.50

51	1978	.996	—	—	.35	.75
	1978	5,000	—	—	Proof	3.00
	1979	2.089	—	—	.15	.50
	1979	500 pcs.	—	—	Proof	30.00
	1980	2.600	—	—	.15	.50
	1980	3,000	—	—	Proof	3.00
	1981	3.200	—	—	.15	.50
	1981	3,000	—	—	Proof	3.00

7.3200 g, .900 SILVER, .2118 oz ASW

51a	1978	15 pcs.	—	—	Proof	150.00
	1979	15 pcs.	—	—	Proof	150.00
	1980	15 pcs.	—	—	Proof	150.00
	1981	15 pcs.	—	—	Proof	150.00

DOMINICAN REPUBLIC 483

COPPER-NICKEL
Human Rights

KM#	Date	Mintage	Fine	VF	XF	Unc
61	1983	.793	—	.10	.20	.50
	1983 H	5,000	—	—	—	2.50
	1983 H	1,600	—	—	Proof	8.00
	1984 Mo	6.400	—	—	.15	.40
	1984 Mo	1,600	—	—	Proof	8.00
	1986	10.132	—	—	.15	.40
	1986	1,600	—	—	Proof	8.00
	1987	20.000	—	—	.15	.40
	1987	1,700	—	—	Proof	8.00

6.2500 g, .900 SILVER, .1808 oz ASW

61a	1983 H	100 pcs.	—	—	Proof	40.00
	1984 Mo	100 pcs.	—	—	Proof	40.00
	1986	100 pcs.	—	—	Proof	40.00

1/2 PESO

12.5000 g, .900 SILVER, .3617 oz ASW
Rev: HP below bust.

21	1937	.500	BV	7.50	12.50	75.00
	1937	—	—	—	Proof	500.00
	1944	.100	BV	10.00	25.00	300.00
	1947	.200	BV	7.50	15.00	200.00
	1951	.200	BV	7.50	15.00	150.00
	1952	.140	BV	7.50	12.50	75.00
	1959	.100	BV	6.00	10.00	40.00
	1960	.100	BV	6.00	9.00	30.00
	1961	.400	BV	4.00	6.00	25.00

12.5000 g, .650 SILVER, .2612 oz ASW
100th Anniversary Restoration of the Republic
Rev: HP below bust.

| 29 | 1963 | .300 | — | BV | 4.00 | 7.50 |

COPPER-NICKEL
Rev: HP below bust.
Plain edge

| 21a.1 | 1967 | 1.500 | — | .20 | .40 | 1.50 |
| | 1968 | .600 | — | .20 | .40 | 1.50 |

Rev: HP below bust.
Reeded edge

21a.2	1973	.600	—	.20	.40	1.50
	1973	500 pcs.	—	—	Proof	35.00
	1975	.600	—	.20	.40	1.50

Duarte Centennial

| 44 | 1976 | .195 | — | .20 | .40 | 1.50 |
| | 1976 | 5,000 | — | — | Proof | 3.00 |

52	1978	.296	—	.20	.40	1.50
	1978	5,000	—	—	Proof	4.00
	1979	.967	—	.20	.40	1.50
	1979	500 pcs.	—	—	Proof	35.00
	1980	1.000	—	.20	.40	1.50

KM#	Date	Mintage	Fine	VF	XF	Unc
52	1980	3,000	—	—	Proof	5.00
	1981	1.300	—	.20	.40	1.50
	1981	3,000	—	—	Proof	5.00

14.5500 g, .900 SILVER, .4210 oz ASW

52a	1978	15 pcs.	—	—	Proof	150.00
	1979	15 pcs.	—	—	Proof	150.00
	1980	15 pcs.	—	—	Proof	150.00
	1981	15 pcs.	—	—	Proof	150.00

COPPER-NICKEL
Human Rights

62	1983	.393	—	.20	.40	1.50
	1983 H	5,000	—	—	—	4.00
	1983 H	1,600	—	—	Proof	15.00
	1984 Mo	3.200	—	.20	.40	1.50
	1984 Mo	1,600	—	—	Proof	15.00
	1986	5.225	—	.20	.40	1.50
	1986	1,600	—	—	Proof	15.00
	1987	3.000	—	.20	.40	1.50
	1987	1,700	—	—	Proof	15.00

12.5000 g, .900 SILVER, .3617 oz ASW

62a	1983 H	100 pcs.	—	—	Proof	50.00
	1984 Mo	100 pcs.	—	—	Proof	50.00
	1986	100 pcs.	—	—	Proof	50.00

PESO

26.7000 g, .900 SILVER, .7725 oz ASW
Rev: HP below bust.

22	1939	.015	15.00	20.00	45.00	750.00
	1939	—	—	—	Proof	2250.
	1952	.020	BV	7.00	10.00	15.00

25th Anniversary of Trujillo Regime

| 23 | 1955 | .050* | 7.50 | 10.00 | 15.00 | 25.00 |

*30,550 officially melted following Trujillo's assassination in 1961.

26.7000 g, .650 SILVER, .5579 oz ASW
100th Anniversary Restoration of the Republic

| 30 | 1963 | .020 | — | — | 5.00 | 7.50 |
| | 1963 | — | — | — | Proof | — |

COPPER-NICKEL
125th Anniversary of the Republic

KM#	Date	Mintage	Fine	VF	XF	Unc
33	1969	.030	—	—	1.50	3.00

26.7000 g, .900 SILVER, .7725 oz ASW
25th Anniversary Central Bank

| 34 | 1972 | .027 | — | — | — | 8.00 |
| | 1972 | 3,000 | — | — | Proof | 14.00 |

12th Central American and Caribbean Games

| 35 | 1974 | .050 | — | — | — | 8.00 |
| | 1974 | 5,000 | — | — | Proof | 14.00 |

COPPER-NICKEL
Duarte Centennial

| 45 | 1976 | .025 | — | — | 1.00 | 2.00 |
| | 1976 | 5,000 | — | — | Proof | 7.50 |

DOMINICAN REPUBLIC 484

KM#	Date	Mintage	Fine	VF	XF	Unc
53	1978	.035	—	—	1.00	2.00
	1978	5,000	—	—	Proof	7.50
	1979	.045	—	—	1.00	2.00
	1979	500 pcs.	—	—	Proof	40.00

NOTE: The above coin was counterstamped 10thAN-IV.S.N.D. 1969 1979 by the Dominican Republic's National Numismatic Society. Numbered 1-100.

	1980	.020	—	—	1.00	2.00
	1980	3,000	—	—	Proof	6.00
	1981	3,000	—	—	Proof	6.00

30.9200 g, .900 SILVER, .8947 oz ASW
53a	1978	15 pcs.	—	—	Proof	300.00
	1979	15 pcs.	—	—	Proof	300.00
	1980	15 pcs.	—	—	Proof	300.00
	1981	15 pcs.	—	—	Proof	300.00

COPPER-NICKEL
Human Rights
63	1983	.093	—	—	1.00	2.50
	1983 H	5,000	—	—	—	6.00
	1983 H	1,600	—	—	Proof	15.00
	1984 Mo	.120	—	—	1.00	2.50
	1984 Mo	1,600	—	—	Proof	15.00

17.0000 g, .900 SILVER, .4919 oz ASW
63a	1983	100 pcs.	—	—	Proof	100.00
	1984	100 pcs.	—	—	Proof	100.00

NICKEL BONDED STEEL
15th Central American and Caribbean Games
65	1986	.100	—	—	1.00	2.50
	1986	1,700	—	—	Proof	15.00

COPPER-NICKEL, 6.25 g
65a	1986	548 pcs.	—	—	—	40.00
	1986	48 pcs.	—	—	Proof	

COPPER-NICKEL, 10.00 g
65b	1986	550 pcs.	—	—	—	40.00
	1986	50 pcs.	—	—	Proof	

COPPER-NICKEL, 19.84 g
500th Anniversary of Discovery and Evangelization
| 66 | 1988 | .100 | — | — | — | 2.50 |

10 PESOS

28.0000 g, .900 SILVER, .8102 oz ASW
International Banker's Conference
KM#	Date	Mintage	Fine	VF	XF	Unc
37	1975	.026	—	—	—	10.00
	1975	4,000	—	—	Proof	14.00

30.0000 g, .900 SILVER, .8681 oz ASW
Pueblo Viejo Mine
38	1975	.045	—	—	—	10.00
	1975	5,000	—	—	Proof	14.00

23.3300 g, .925 SILVER, .6938 oz ASW
International Year of the Child
| 57 | 1982 | 8,712 | — | — | Proof | 17.50 |

25 PESOS

65.0000 g, .925 SILVER, 1.9332 oz ASW
Pope John Paul II's Visit

Rev: Similar to 250 Pesos, KM#56.
KM#	Date	Mintage	Fine	VF	XF	Unc
54	1979	3,000	—	—	—	30.00
	1979	6,000	—	—	Proof	35.00

30 PESOS

29.6220 g, .900 GOLD, .8572 oz AGW
25th Anniversary of Trujillo Regime
| 24 | 1955 | .033 | — | — | BV | 475.00 |

11.7000 g, .900 GOLD, .3385 oz AGW
12th Central American and Caribbean Games
36	1974	.025	—	—	—	175.00
	1974	5,000	—	—	Proof	200.00

78.0000 g, .925 SILVER, 2.3199 oz ASW
30th Anniversary of Central Bank
46	1977	5,000	—	—	—	50.00
	1977	2,000	—	—	Proof	65.00

100 PESOS

10.0000 g, .900 GOLD, .2893 oz AGW
Pueblo Viejo Mine
39	1975	.018	—	—	—	150.00
	1975	2,000	—	—	Proof	175.00

Pope John Paul II's Visit

KM#	Date	Mintage	Fine	VF	XF	Unc
55	1979	1,000	—	—	—	200.00
	1979	3,000	—	—	Proof	225.00

200 PESOS

31.0000 g, .800 GOLD, .7974 oz AGW
Duarte Centennial

47	1977	1,000*	—	—	—	450.00
	1977	2,000*	—	—	Proof	500.00

NOTE: Large quantity melted for bullion.

17.1700 g, .900 GOLD, .4969 oz AGW
International Year of the Child

58	1982	4,303	—	—	Proof	275.00

250 PESOS

31.1000 g, .900 GOLD, .9000 oz AGW
Pope John Paul II's Visit

56	1979	1,000	—	—	—	500.00
	1979	3,000	—	—	Proof	600.00

MINT SETS (MS)

KM#	Date	Mintage	Identification	Issue Price	Mkt. Val.
MS1	1983(5)	2,000	KM59-63	10.00	5.25
MS2	1984(6)	2,000	KM59-64	—	5.25
MS3	1986(5)	2,000	KM59-62,64	10.00	3.00
MS4	1987(5)	1,000	KM59-62,64	10.00	3.00

PROOF SETS (PS)

KM#	Date	Mintage	Identification	Issue Price	Mkt. Val.
PS1	1937(5)	—	KM17-21	—	2000.
PS2	1972(4)	500	KM18,20a.1,31,34	20.00	90.00
PS3	1973(2)	500	KM19a,21a.2	5.00	60.00
PS4	1974(2)	500	KM18,20a.2	5.00	50.00
PS5	1974(2)	500	KM35-36	120.00	220.00
PS6	1975(2)	500	KM38-39	200.00	200.00
PS7	1976(6)	5,000	KM40-45	10.00	20.00
PS8	1978(6)	5,000	KM48-53	10.00	20.00
PS9	1978(6)	15	KM48a-53a	175.00	900.00
PS10	1979(6)	500	KM48-53	15.00	175.00
PS11	1979(6)	15	KM48a-53a	255.00	900.00
PS12	1980(6)	3,000	KM48-53	15.00	20.00
PS13	1980(6)	15	KM48a-53a	255.00	900.00
PS14	1981(6)	3,000	KM48-53	15.00	20.00
PS15	1981(6)	15	KM48a-53a	300.00	900.00
PS16	1983(2)	1,600	KM59-60	15.00	15.00
PS17	1983(2)	300	Piedforts of KM59 & 60	25.00	25.00
PS18	1983(2)	100	KM59a,60a	45.00	45.00
PS19	1983(3)	1,570	KM61-63	25.00	25.00
PS20	1983(3)	270	Piedforts of KM61-63	45.00	45.00
PS21	1983(3)	70	KM61a-63a	125.00	125.00
PS22	1984(6)	1,570	KM59-64	20.00	45.00
PS23	1984(6)	270	Piedforts of KM59-64	45.00	45.00
PS24	1984(6)	70	KM59a-64a	250.00	250.00
PS25	1986(5)	1,570	KM59-62,64	30.00	30.00
PS26	1986(5)	270	Piedforts of KM59-62,64	75.00	75.00
PS27	1986(5)	70	KM59a-62a,64a	150.00	150.00
PS28	1987(5)	1,600	KM59-62,64	—	30.00
PS29	1987(5)	300	Piedforts of KM59-62,64	—	75.00

SPECIAL SETS (SS)

Contain Unc, Proofs, and Piedforts

SS1	1983(15)	30	KM61-63,61a-63a inc. all mintmarks	200.00	200.00
SS2	1984(24)	30	KM59-64	400.00	400.00
SS3	1986(20)	30	KM59-64	300.00	300.00
SS4	1986(2)	1,700	KM65, Nickel-bonded Steel, Proof & Unc	35.00	35.00
SS5	1986(3)	300	KM65, Proof, Unc & Piedfort	75.00	75.00
SS6	1986(2)	23	KM65a, Proof & Unc	—	—
SS7	1986(3)	25	KM65a, Proof, Unc & Piedfort, 20 g	—	—
SS8	1986(2)	25	KM65b, Proof & Unc	—	—
SS9	1986(3)	25	KM65b, Proof, Unc & Piedfort	—	—
SS10	1987(15)	100	KM59-62,64,Proof, Unc & Piedfort	—	—

EAST AFRICA

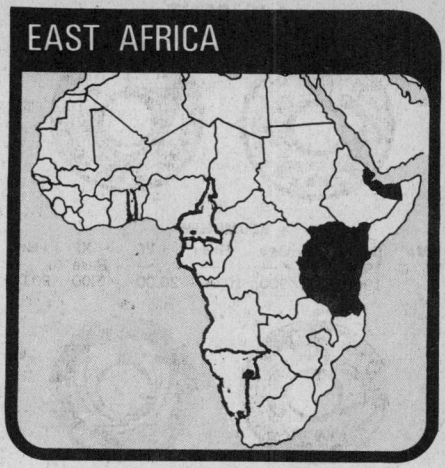

East Africa was an administrative grouping of five separate British territories: Kenya, Tanganyika (now part of Tanzania), the Sultanate of Zanzibar and Pemba (now part of Tanzania), Uganda and British Somaliland (now part of Somalia). See individual entries for specific statistics and history.

The common interest of Kenya, Tanzania and Uganda invited cooperation in economic matters and considerations of political union. The territorial governors, organized as the East Africa High Commission, met periodically to administer such common activities as taxation, industrial development and education. The authority of the Commission did not infringe upon the constitution and internal autonomy of the individual colonies. A common coinage and banknotes, which were also legal tender in Aden, was provided for use of the member colonies by the East Africa Currency Board. The coinage through 1919 had the legend "East Africa and Uganda Protectorate".

The East African coinage includes two denominations of 1936 which bear the name of Edward VIII.

NOTE: For later coinage see Kenya, Tanzania and Uganda.

RULERS
British

MINT MARKS
A - Ackroyd & Best, Morley
I - Bombay Mint
H - Heaton Mint, Birmingham, England
K,KN - King's Norton Mint
SA - Pretoria Mint

MONETARY SYSTEM
64 Pice = 1 Rupee

EAST AFRICA PROTECTORATE

PICE

BRONZE

KM#	Date	Mintage	Fine	VF	XF	Unc
1	1897	.640	5.00	10.00	25.00	85.00
	1897	—	—	—	Proof	200.00
	1898	6.400	2.50	6.00	20.00	75.00
	1898	—	—	—	Proof	200.00
	1899	3.200	2.00	5.00	15.00	50.00
	1899	—	—	—	Proof	200.00

SILVER (OMS)

1a	1897	—	—	—	Proof	500.00
	1898	—	—	—	Proof	500.00
	1899	—	—	—	Proof	500.00

GOLD (OMS)

1b	1897	—	—	—	Proof	2500.
	1899	—	—	—	Proof	2500.

EAST AFRICA & UGANDA PROTECTORATE

MONETARY SYSTEM
100 Cents = 1 Rupee

1/2 CENT

ALUMINUM

KM#	Date	Mintage	Fine	VF	XF	Unc
6	1907	—	—	—	Rare	—
	1908	.900	10.00	20.00	45.00	90.00

COPPER-NICKEL

| 6a | 1909 | .900 | 7.50 | 15.00 | 35.00 | 75.00 |

CENT

ALUMINUM

5	1906	—	—	—	Rare	—
	1907	6.948	2.00	5.00	10.00	30.00
	1907	—	—	—	Proof	200.00
	1908	2.871	3.00	7.00	20.00	40.00

COPPER-NICKEL

5a	1908	—	—	—	Unique	—
	1909	25.000	.50	1.25	3.00	7.00
	1910	6.000	.50	1.25	4.00	12.00

7	1911H	25.000	.25	1.00	2.50	15.00
	1912H	20.000	.25	1.00	2.00	8.00
	1913	4.529	.75	1.50	3.75	20.00
	1914	6.000	.75	1.75	5.00	15.00
	1914H	2.500	1.00	2.50	6.00	17.00
	1916H	1.824	.75	2.00	5.00	20.00
	1917H	3.176	.75	2.50	6.00	17.00
	1918H	10.000	.50	1.00	3.25	12.00

5 CENTS

COPPER-NICKEL

| 11.1 | 1907 | — | — | — | Rare | — |

11.2	1913H	.300	1.50	4.00	15.00	35.00
	1914K	1.240	.75	3.25	6.00	22.50
	1914K*	—	—	—	Proof	200.00
	1919H	.200	10.00	15.00	40.00	110.00

*NOTE: The 1914K was issued with British West Africa KM#8 in a double (4 pc.) Specimen Set.

10 CENTS

COPPER-NICKEL

KM#	Date	Mintage	Fine	VF	XF	Unc
2	1906	—	750.00	1500.	2000.	3000.
	1907	1.000	1.50	4.00	10.00	30.00
	1910	.500	3.00	7.00	20.00	55.00

8	1911H	1.250	1.50	4.00	7.50	40.00
	1912H	1.050	2.00	5.00	12.50	55.00
	1913	.050	50.00	90.00	150.00	400.00
	1918H	.400	7.50	20.00	40.00	135.00

25 CENTS

2.9160 g, .800 SILVER, .0750 oz ASW

3	1906	.400	2.50	4.00	20.00	50.00
	1910H	.200	4.00	8.00	30.00	80.00

10	1912	.180	4.00	8.00	25.00	75.00
	1913	.300	2.75	6.50	20.00	50.00
	1914H	.080	20.00	35.00	60.00	100.00
	1914H	—	—	—	Proof	300.00
	1918H	.040	125.00	250.00	425.00	750.00

50 CENTS

5.8319 g, .800 SILVER, .1500 oz ASW

4	1906	.200	4.50	12.50	35.00	140.00
	1909	.100	15.00	30.00	85.00	300.00
	1910	.100	10.00	25.00	65.00	225.00

9	1911	.150	6.00	12.50	30.00	140.00
	1911	—	—	—	Proof	250.00
	1912	.100	8.00	20.00	50.00	200.00
	1913	.200	5.00	12.50	30.00	125.00
	1914H	.180	5.00	12.50	30.00	125.00
	1918H	.060	60.00	150.00	250.00	500.00
	1919	.100	200.00	300.00	500.00	1200.

PROOF SETS

KM#	Date	Mintage	Identification	Mkt.Val.
101	1906-7 (4)	—	KM2-5, Pn2, Pn3	Rare

EAST AFRICA

MONETARY SYSTEM

100 Cents = 1 Florin
(Commencing May, 1921)

100 Cents = 1 Shilling

CENT

COPPER-NICKEL

KM#	Date	Mintage	Fine	VF	XF	Unc
12	1920H	*2.908	30.00	60.00	140.00	200.00
	1920H	—	—	—	Proof	300.00
	1921	**	—	—	Rare	—

*NOTE: Only about 30% of total mintage released to circulation.
**NOTE: Not released for circulation.

BRONZE

22	1922	8.250	.25	.85	4.00	10.00
	1922H	43.750	.25	.50	1.50	5.00
	1923	50.000	.25	.50	1.50	5.00
	1924	Inc. Ab.	.25	.75	3.25	10.00
	1924H	17.500	.25	.75	3.25	8.00
	1924KN	10.720	.25	.75	3.25	8.00
	1924KN	—	—	—	Proof	125.00
	1925	6.000	40.00	75.00	150.00	300.00
	1925KN	6.780	2.00	4.00	12.00	35.00
	1927	10.000	.25	.75	3.00	10.00
	1927	—	—	—	Proof	125.00
	1928H	12.000	.25	.75	3.25	8.00
	1928KN	11.764	.35	1.00	3.50	10.00
	1928KN	—	—	—	Proof	125.00
	1930	15.000	.25	.75	2.00	5.00
	1930	—	—	—	Proof	125.00
	1935	10.000	.25	.50	1.25	5.00

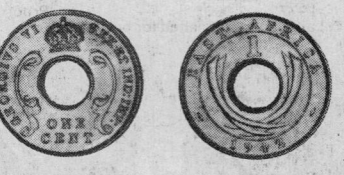

29	1942	25.000	.10	.25	.85	2.50
	1942I	15.000	.15	.30	1.00	3.00

Obv. leg: ET IND.IMP. dropped.

32	1949	4.000	—	—	.85	2.50
	1949	—	.10	—	Proof	125.00
	1950	16.000	.10	.25	.85	2.50
	1950	—	—	—	Proof	150.00
	1951H	9.000	.10	.25	.85	2.50
	1951H	—	—	—	Proof	125.00
	1951KN	11.140	.10	.25	.85	2.50
	1951KN	—	—	—	Proof	125.00
	1952	7.000	.10	.25	.85	2.50
	1952H	13.000	.10	.25	.85	2.50
	1952H	—	—	—	Proof	125.00
	1952KN	5.230	.10	.35	1.25	5.00

35	1954	8.000	.10	.25	.85	2.50
	1954	—	—	—	Proof	125.00
	1955	5.000	.10	.25	.50	1.75
	1955H	6.384	.10	.20	.65	1.75
	1955KN	4.000	.10	.20	.65	1.75
	1956H	15.616	.10	.15	.30	1.75
	1956KN	9.680	.10	.20	.45	1.75
	1957	15.000	.10	.20	.65	1.75
	1957H	5.000	1.00	2.00	5.00	10.00
	1957KN	Inc. Ab.	.10	.20	.65	1.75
	1959N	10.000	.10	.20	.45	1.75
	1959KN	10.000	.10	.20	.45	1.75
	1961	1.800	.15	.40	2.00	3.50
	1961	—	—	—	Proof	100.00
	1961H	1.800	.15	.40	2.00	3.50
	1962H	10.320	.10	.20	.40	1.25

5 CENTS

COPPER-NICKEL

KM#	Date	Mintage	Fine	VF	XF	Unc
13	1920H	*.550	65.00	125.00	175.00	350.00
	1920H	—	—	—	Proof	400.00

*NOTE: Only about 30% of total mintage released to circulation.

BRONZE

KM#	Date	Mintage	Fine	VF	XF	Unc
18	1921	1.000	2.00	4.00	10.00	35.00
	1922	2.500	.50	1.25	4.50	12.50
	1923	2.400	.50	1.25	4.50	12.50
	1923	—	—	—	Proof	175.00
	1924	4.800	.50	1.00	3.00	15.00
	1925	6.600	.50	1.00	3.00	10.00
	1928	1.200	.50	1.00	3.50	22.50
	1928	—	—	—	Proof	175.00
	1933	5.000	.50	1.00	2.50	10.00
	1934	3.910	.50	1.00	3.50	15.00
	1934	—	—	—	Proof	175.00
	1935	5.800	.50	1.00	3.00	10.00
	1935	—	—	—	Proof	175.00
	1936	1.000	1.50	5.00	7.50	60.00

KM#	Date	Mintage	Fine	VF	XF	Unc
23	1936H	3.500	.25	.50	1.00	4.00
	1936H	—	—	—	Proof	125.00
	1936KN	2.150	.25	.50	1.00	4.00
	1936KN	—	—	—	Proof	125.00

Thick flan

KM#	Date	Mintage	Fine	VF	XF	Unc
25.1	1937H	3.000	.50	1.00	2.00	4.00
	1937KN	3.000	.50	1.00	2.00	6.00
	1939H	2.000	.50	1.00	3.00	15.00
	1939KN	2.000	.50	1.00	3.00	15.00
	1941	—	2.50	6.00	14.00	40.00
	1941I	20.000	.50	1.00	2.00	5.00

Thin flan, reduced weight.

25.2	1942	16.000	.50	1.00	2.00	3.50
	1942SA	4.120	1.00	2.00	7.50	30.00
	1943SA	17.880	.50	1.00	5.00	10.00

Obv. leg: ET IND.IMP. dropped.

33	1949	4.000	.25	.50	3.00	5.00
	1949	—	—	—	Proof	175.00
	1951H	6.000	.25	.50	2.00	5.00
	1951H	—	—	—	Proof	175.00
	1952	11.200	.20	.40	1.00	3.00
	1952	—	—	—	Proof	150.00

KM#	Date	Mintage	Fine	VF	XF	Unc
37	1955	2.000	.10	.25	.75	2.00
	1955	—	—	—	Proof	150.00
	1955H	4.000	.20	.50	1.25	3.50
	1955H	—	—	—	Proof	150.00
	1955KN	2.000	.35	.80	2.50	5.00
	1956H	3.000	.15	.35	1.00	3.00
	1956KN	3.000	1.50	3.00	5.00	10.00
	1957H	5.000	.10	.25	.75	2.00
	1957KN	5.000	.10	.25	.75	2.00
	1961H	4.000	.15	.35	1.00	3.00
	1963	12.600	—	.10	.30	.85
	1963	—	—	—	Proof	100.00

Post-Independence Issue

39	1964	7.600	—	.10	.20	.50

10 CENTS

COPPER-NICKEL

KM#	Date	Mintage	Fine	VF	XF	Unc
14	1920H	*.700	150.00	200.00	250.00	400.00
	1920H	—	—	—	Proof	600.00

*NOTE: Only about 30% of total mintage released to circulation.

BRONZE

19	1921	.130	3.00	7.50	25.00	65.00
	1922	7.120	.75	2.50	5.00	17.50
	1923	1.200	1.25	4.00	15.00	45.00
	1924	4.900	.65	2.25	6.00	25.00
	1925	4.800	.65	2.25	6.00	25.00
	1927	2.000	.75	2.50	6.50	20.00
	1928	3.800	.75	2.50	6.50	30.00
	1928	—	—	—	Proof	175.00
	1933	6.260	.75	2.50	6.50	17.50
	1934	3.649	.75	2.50	6.50	30.00
	1935	7.300	.65	2.00	5.00	15.00
	1936	.500	1.50	5.00	15.00	50.00

24	1936	2.000	1.00	3.50	8.00	20.00
	1936	—	—	—	Proof	200.00
	1936H	4.330	.25	.50	1.50	5.00
	1936KN	4.142	.25	.50	1.50	5.00

NOTE: For listing of mule dated 1936H w/obv. of KM#24 and rev. of British West Africa KM#16 refer to British West Africa listings.

COPPER-NICKEL

24a	1936KN	—	—	—	—	—

Thick flan

KM#	Date	Mintage	Fine	VF	XF	Unc
26.1	1937	2.000	.25	.75	2.50	5.00
	1937	—	—	—	Proof	175.00
	1937H	2.500	.25	.75	2.50	10.00
	1937H	—	—	—	Proof	175.00
	1937KN	2.500	.25	.75	2.75	10.00
	1937KN	—	—	—	Proof	175.00
	1939H	2.000	.25	.70	3.50	15.00
	1939KN	2.030	.25	.70	3.50	12.50
	1939KN	—	—	—	Proof	175.00
	1941I	15.682	.75	2.00	5.00	17.50
	1941I	—	—	—	Proof	175.00
	1941	—	.75	2.00	5.00	17.50
	1941	—	—	—	Proof	175.00

NOTE: Many dates, including 1941I, exist w/o center hole.

Thin flan, reduced weight.

26.2	1942	12.000	.20	.50	1.75	4.00
	1942	—	—	—	Proof	175.00
	1942I	4.317	2.00	4.00	9.00	17.50
	1943SA	14.093	.25	.50	4.50	10.00
	1945SA	5.000	.25	.50	2.50	12.50

Obv. leg: ET IND.IMP. dropped.

34	1949	4.000	.20	.40	1.75	4.00
	1949	—	—	—	Proof	175.00
	1950	8.000	.20	.40	1.75	4.00
	1950	—	—	—	Proof	200.00
	1951	14.500	.20	.40	1.25	3.00
	1951	—	—	—	Proof	175.00
	1952	15.800	.20	.40	1.25	3.00
	1952H	2.000	.40	1.25	3.00	10.00

38	1956	6.001	.35	1.00	2.50	10.00
	1956	—	—	—	Proof	175.00

Post-Independence Issue

40	1964H	10.002	.10	.15	.30	1.00

25 CENTS

2.9160 g, .500 SILVER, .0469 oz ASW

15	1920H	.748	25.00	40.00	80.00	150.00
	1920H	—	—	—	Proof	250.00

EAST AFRICA 488

50 CENTS

5.8319 g, .500 SILVER, .0937 oz ASW
Fifty Cents-One Shilling

KM#	Date	Mintage	Fine	VF	XF	Unc
16	1920A	*.012	1500.	2000.	3000.	4000.
	1920H	*.062	600.00	1000.	1250.	1600.

*NOTE: Not released for circulation.

3.8879 g, .250 SILVER, .0312 oz ASW
Fifty Cents-Half Shilling

20	1921	6.200	1.00	2.00	7.50	30.00
	1922	Inc. Ab.	1.00	2.00	6.00	27.50
	1923	.396	3.00	6.00	30.00	75.00
	1924	1.000	2.00	4.00	10.00	40.00

27	1937H	4.000	.75	1.25	3.50	12.50
	1937H	—	—	—	Proof	275.00
	1942H	5.000	.75	1.25	4.00	20.00
	1943I	2.000	1.50	3.00	7.50	30.00
	1944SA	1.000	2.00	4.00	9.00	32.50

COPPER-NICKEL
Obv. leg: ET INDIA IMPERATOR dropped.

30	1948	7.290	.20	.40	1.75	5.00
	1948	—	—	—	Proof	250.00
	1949	12.960	.15	.30	1.25	4.00
	1949	—	—	—	Proof	325.00
	1952KN	2.000	.20	.40	1.75	7.50

36	1954	3.700	.15	.35	1.00	3.00
	1954	—	—	—	Proof	225.00
	1955H	1.600	.25	.50	2.50	5.00
	1955H	—	—	—	Proof	225.00
	1955KN	—	.15	.35	1.75	4.00
	1956H	2.000	.15	.25	1.25	3.00
	1956H	—	—	—	Proof	225.00
	1956KN	2.000	.15	.35	1.75	4.00
	1958H	2.600	.15	.40	2.00	5.00
	1960	4.000	.10	.25	1.25	3.25
	1962KN	4.000	.15	.35	1.75	4.00
	1963	6.000	.10	.25	1.25	3.25

FLORIN

11.6638 g, .500 SILVER, .1875 oz ASW

17	1920	1.479	15.00	35.00	100.00	300.00
	1920A	.542	200.00	300.00	600.00	2000.
	1920H	9.689	12.50	30.00	75.00	250.00
	1921	—	—	Proof	—	Rare

SHILLING

7.7759 g, .250 SILVER, .0625 oz ASW

KM#	Date	Mintage	Fine	VF	XF	Unc
21	1921	6.141	1.50	2.75	8.50	20.00
	1921H	4.240	1.75	3.00	10.00	30.00
	1922	18.858	1.25	2.25	6.50	17.50
	1922H	20.052	1.25	2.25	6.50	17.50
	1923	4.000	3.50	7.00	15.00	35.00
	1924	44.604	1.00	2.00	4.50	15.00
	1925	28.405	1.00	2.00	4.50	12.50

28	1937H	7.672	1.00	2.00	4.00	12.50
	1937H	—	—	—	Proof	325.00
	1941I	7.000	1.25	2.00	6.00	20.00
	1942H	4.430	1.25	2.00	7.50	25.00
	1942H	—	—	—	Proof	325.00
	1942I	3.9000	—	—	5.00	20.00
	1943I	*25-50 pcs.	250.00	400.00	600.00	1250.
	1944H	10.000	1.25	2.00	7.50	25.00
	1944SA	5.820	1.25	2.00	5.00	22.50
	1945SA	10.080	1.25	2.00	5.00	22.50
	1946SA	18.260	1.25	2.00	3.50	17.50

NOTE: Three varieties of reverse exist for above coin.

COPPER-NICKEL
Obv. leg: ET INDIA IMPERATOR dropped.

31	1948	19.704	.50	.90	1.50	6.50
	1949	38.318	.50	.90	1.50	6.50
	1949	—	—	—	Proof	250.00
	1949H	12.584	.50	.90	1.50	7.50
	1949KN	15.060	.50	.90	1.50	7.50
	1950	56.362	.50	.90	1.50	3.50
	1950	—	—	—	Proof	250.00
	1950H	12.416	.50	.90	2.25	6.00
	1950KN	10.040	.40	.70	2.00	5.00
	1952	55.605	.35	.60	1.25	3.25
	1952	—	—	—	Proof	175.00
	1952H	8.024	.35	.60	1.25	3.50
	1952KN	9.360	.35	.60	1.25	3.50

MINT SETS (MS)

KM#	Date	Mintage	Identification	Mkt.Val.
MS1	1921-2(5)	—	KM18-22	2000.

PROOF SETS (PS)

PS1	1949(5)	—	KM30-34	1000.
PS2	1950(3)	—	KM31,32,34	600.00

EAST CARIBBEAN STATES

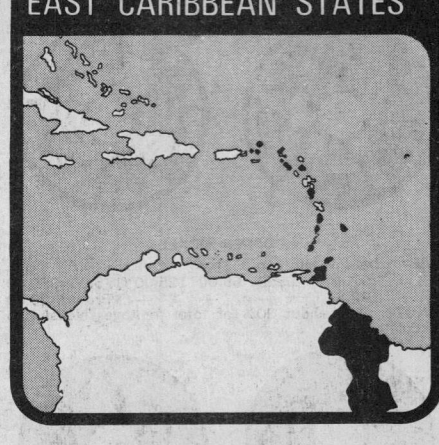

The East Caribbean States, formerly the British Caribbean Territories (Eastern group), formed a currency board in 1950 to provide the constituent territories of Trinidad & Tobago, Barbados, British Guiana (now Guyana), British Virgin Islands, Anguilla, Saba, St. Kitts, Nevis, Antigua, Dominica, St. Lucia, St. Vincent and Grenada with a common currency, thereby permitting withdrawal of the regular British Pound currency. This was dissolved in 1965 and after the breakup, the East Caribbean Territories, a grouping including Barbados, the Leeward and Windward Islands, came into being. Coinage of the dissolved 'Eastern Group' continues to circulate although paper currency of the East Caribbean Authority was first issued in 1965.

A series of 4-dollar coins tied to the FAO coinage program were released in 1970 under the name of the Caribbean Development Bank by eight loosely federated island groupings in the eastern Caribbean. These issues are listed individually in this volume under Antigua, Barbados, Dominica, Grenada, Montserrat, St. Kitts, St. Lucia and St. Vincent.

RULERS
British

BRITISH EAST CARIBBEAN TERRITORIES

MONETARY SYSTEM
100 Cents = 1 Br. W. Indies Dollar

1/2 CENT

BRONZE

KM#	Date	Mintage	Fine	VF	XF	Unc
1	1955	.500	.30	.50	.75	2.00
	1955	2,000	—	—	Proof	3.00
	1958	.200	.50	.75	1.25	2.50
	1958	20 pcs.	—	—	Proof	250.00

CENT

BRONZE

2	1955	8.000	.15	.25	.60	1.00
	1955	2,000	—	—	Proof	3.00
	1957	3.000	.15	.25	1.75	3.00
	1957	—	—	—	Proof	125.00
	1958	1.500	.35	.50	4.50	7.50
	1958	20 pcs.	—	—	Proof	275.00
	1959	.500	.40	.60	6.00	20.00
	1959	—	—	—	Proof	125.00
	1960	2.500	.15	.25	.60	1.25
	1960	—	—	—	Proof	125.00
	1961	2.280	.25	.35	.75	1.25
	1961	—	—	—	Proof	125.00
	1962	2.000	.15	.25	.50	1.25
	1962	—	—	—	Proof	125.00
	1963	.750	.45	.70	1.20	2.50
	1963	—	—	—	Proof	125.00
	1964	2.500	—	—	.20	.35
	1964	—	—	—	Proof	125.00
	1965	4.800	—	—	.20	.35
	1965	—	—	—	Proof	5.00

2 CENTS

BRONZE

KM#	Date	Mintage	Fine	VF	XF	Unc
3	1955	5.500	.15	.25	.50	.85
	1955	2,000	—	—	Proof	3.00
	1957	1.250	.15	.25	1.25	2.50
	1957	—	—	—	Proof	135.00
	1958	1.250	.15	.25	2.50	5.00
	1958	20 pcs.	—	—	Proof	300.00
	1960	.750	.15	.25	1.75	3.00
	1960	—	—	—	Proof	135.00
	1961	.788	.15	.25	1.75	3.00
	1961	—	—	—	Proof	135.00
	1962	1.060	.10	.20	.30	.75
	1962	—	—	—	Proof	135.00
	1963	.250	.50	.75	1.50	5.00
	1963	—	—	—	Proof	135.00
	1964	1.188	.10	.20	.30	.65
	1964	—	—	—	Proof	135.00
	1965	2.001	—	.10	.20	.40
	1965	—	—	—	Proof	5.00

5 CENTS

NICKEL-BRASS

KM#	Date	Mintage	Fine	VF	XF	Unc
4	1955	8.600	.15	.25	.60	1.25
	1955	2,000	—	—	Proof	4.00
	1956	2.000	.15	.25	.60	1.00
	1956	—	—	—	Proof	300.00
	1960	1.000	.20	.30	.90	1.50
	1960	—	—	—	Proof	150.00
	1962	1.300	.15	.25	.50	1.00
	1962	—	—	—	Proof	150.00
	1963	.200	.25	.35	1.20	2.00
	1963	—	—	—	Proof	150.00
	1964	1.350	—	.10	.30	.75
	1964	—	—	—	Proof	150.00
	1965	2.400	—	.10	.20	.50
	1965	—	—	—	Proof	5.00

10 CENTS

COPPER-NICKEL

KM#	Date	Mintage	Fine	VF	XF	Unc
5	1955	5.000	.15	.25	.45	.75
	1955	2,000	—	—	Proof	4.00
	1956	4.000	.15	.25	.45	.75
	1956	—	—	—	Proof	175.00
	1959	2.000	.15	.25	.60	1.00
	1959	—	—	—	Proof	175.00
	1961	1.260	.20	.30	.50	1.00
	1961	—	—	—	Proof	175.00
	1962	1.200	.15	.25	.50	1.00
	1962	—	—	—	Proof	175.00
	1964	1.400	.10	.20	.35	.65
	1965	3.200	.10	.20	.30	.50
	1965	—	—	—	Proof	5.00

25 CENTS

COPPER-NICKEL

KM#	Date	Mintage	Fine	VF	XF	Unc
6	1955	7.000	.35	.50	.70	1.00
	1955	2,000	—	—	Proof	6.00
	1957	.800	.75	1.00	2.25	4.50
	1957	—	—	—	Proof	200.00
	1959	1.000	.35	.50	1.25	2.25
	1959	—	—	—	Proof	200.00
	1961	.744	.50	.75	2.50	5.00
	1961	—	—	—	Proof	200.00
	1962	.480	.25	.50	1.25	2.50
	1962	—	—	—	Proof	200.00
	1963	.480	.25	.50	1.25	2.50
	1963	—	—	—	Proof	200.00
	1964	.480	.25	.50	1.00	1.75
	1964	—	—	—	Proof	200.00

KM#	Date	Mintage	Fine	VF	XF	Unc
6	1965	1.280	.25	.50	.75	1.00
	1965	—	—	—	Proof	7.50

50 CENTS

COPPER-NICKEL

7	1955	1.500	.75	1.25	1.75	3.00
	1955	2,000	—	—	Proof	12.00
	1965	.100	2.00	5.00	7.50	15.00
	1965	—	—	—	Proof	10.00

PROOF SETS (PS)

KM#	Date	Mintage	Identification	Issue Price	Mkt. Val.
PS1	1955(7)	2,000	KM1-7	—	30.00
PS2	1958(3)	20	KM1-3	—	800.00
PS3	1965(6)	—	KM2-7	—	35.00

EAST CARIBBEAN TERRITORIES

MONETARY SYSTEM
100 Cents = 1 Dollar

10 DOLLARS

COPPER-NICKEL
Caribbean Development Bank

KM#	Date	Mintage	VF	XF	Unc
1	1980	—	—	—	6.00

28.2800 g, .925 SILVER, .8411 oz ASW

1a	1980	.010	—	Proof	27.50

COPPER-NICKEL
Wedding of Prince Charles and Lady Diana

2	1981	.050	—	—	6.00

28.2800 g, .925 SILVER, .8411 oz ASW

2a	1981	.030	—	Proof	30.00

PROOF SETS (PS)

KM#	Date	Mintage	Identification	Issue Price	Mkt. Val.
PS1	1970(8)	2,000	4 Dollars	57.60	125.00

NOTE: These 4 dollar F.A.O. commemorative coins are listed individually under their respective names: Antigua, Barbados, Dominica, Grenada, Montserrat, St. Kitts, St. Lucia and St. Vincent.

EAST CARIBBEAN STATES

CENT

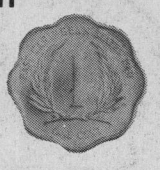

ALUMINUM

KM#	Date	Mintage	VF	XF	Unc
1	1981	—	—	—	.10
	1981	5,000	—	Proof	1.25
	1983	—	—	—	.10
	1984	—	—	—	.10
	1986	—	—	—	.10
	1986	2,500	—	Proof	1.25

2 CENTS

ALUMINUM

2	1981	—	—	.10	.15
	1981	5,000	—	Proof	1.50
	1984	—	—	.10	.15
	1986	—	—	.10	.15
	1986	2,500	—	Proof	1.50

5 CENTS

ALUMINUM

3	1981	—	—	.10	.20
	1981	5,000	—	Proof	2.25
	1984	—	—	.10	.20
	1986	—	—	.10	.20
	1986	2,500	—	Proof	2.25

10 CENTS

COPPER-NICKEL

4	1981	—	.10	.15	.25
	1981	5,000	—	Proof	3.00
	1986	—	.10	.15	.25
	1986	2,500	—	Proof	3.00

25 CENTS

COPPER-NICKEL

5	1981	—	.15	.20	.40
	1981	5,000	—	Proof	4.00
	1986	—	.15	.20	.40
	1986	2,500	—	Proof	4.00

DOLLAR

ALUMINUM-BRONZE

6	1981	—	.50	.75	1.50
	1981	5,000	—	Proof	8.00
	1986	—	.50	.75	1.50
	1986	2,500	—	Proof	8.00

EAST CARIBBEAN STATES 490

10 DOLLARS

COPPER-NICKEL
World Food Day

KM#	Date	Mintage	VF	XF	Unc
7	1981	—	—	—	6.00

28.2800 g, .500 SILVER, .4546 oz ASW

| 7a | 1981 | .010 | — | — | 10.00 |
| | 1981 | 5,000 | — | Proof | 32.50 |

50 DOLLARS

28.2800 g, .925 SILVER, .8411 oz ASW
International Year of the Scout

| 8 | 1983 | .010 | — | — | 25.00 |
| | 1983 | .010 | — | Proof | 30.00 |

International Year of the Disabled Persons

| 10 | 1983 | .010 | — | — | 25.00 |
| | 1983 | .010 | — | Proof | 30.00 |

500 DOLLARS

15.9800 g, .917 GOLD, .4712 oz AGW
International Year of the Scout
Obv: Similar to 50 Dollars, KM#8.
Rev: One scout standing, one scout kneeling.

| 9 | 1983 | 2,000 | — | — | 400.00 |
| | 1983 | 2,000 | — | Proof | 500.00 |

PROOF SETS (PS)

KM#	Date	Mintage	Identification	Issue Price	Mkt. Val.
PS1	1981(6)	5,000	KM1-6	29.00	20.00
PS2	1986(6)	2,500	KM1-6	30.75	20.00

Listings For
EAST GERMANY: refer to Germany/East

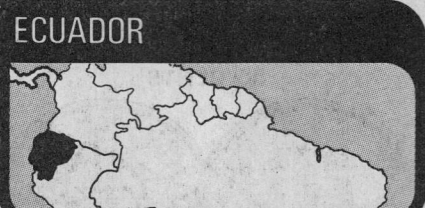

ECUADOR

The Republic of Ecuador, located astride the equator on the Pacific Coast of South America, has an area of 109,484 sq. mi. (283,561 sq. km.) and a population of *10.5 million. Capital: Quito. Agriculture is the mainstay of the economy but there are appreciable deposits of minerals and petroleum. It is the world's largest exporter of bananas and balsa wood. Coffee, cacao and sugar are also valuable exports.

Ecuador was first sighted, 1526, by Francisco Pizarro. Conquest was undertaken by Sebastian de Benalcazar, who founded Quito in 1534. Ecuador was incorporated in the Viceroyalty of New Granada through the 16th and 17th centuries. After two attempts to attain independence were crushed, 1810 and 1812, Antonio Sucre, the able lieutenant of Bolivar, won Ecuador's freedom on May 24, 1822. It then joined Venezuela, Colombia and Panama in a confederacy known as Gran Colombia, and became an independent republic when the confederacy was dissolved, 1830.

MINT MARKS
BIRMm - Birmingham
D - Denver
H - Heaton, Birmingham
HF - LeLocle (Swiss)
LIMA - Lima
Mo - Mexico
PHILA.U.S.A. - Philadelphia
QUITO - Quito
SANTIAGO - Chile

ASSAYERS INITIALS
FP - Feliciano Paredes
GJ - Guillermo Jameson
MV - Miguel Vergara
ST - Santiago Taylor

MONETARY SYSTEM
16 Reales = 1 Escudo

COUNTERMARKED COINAGE
1831
M.D.Q. - Moneda de Quito

1/4 REAL
SILVER
c/m: MDQ monogram on Colombia (Nueva Granada)
1/4 Real, KM#79.1.

KM#	Date	Mintage	Good	VG	Fine	VF
1	ND(1820)	—	—	—	Rare	—
	ND(1821)	—	—	—	Rare	—

c/m: MDQ monogram on Colombia (Nueva Granada)
1/4 Real, KM#79.2.

| 2 | ND(1821 Ba) | — | — | — | Rare | — |

1/2 REAL

SILVER
c/m: MDQ monogram on Colombia (Cundinamarca)
1/2 Real, KM#8.

| 3 | ND(1821) | — | — | — | Rare | — |

REAL
SILVER
c/m: MDQ monogram on Colombia (Nueva Granada)
Real, KM#75.

| 4 | ND(1819 JF) | — | — | — | Rare | — |

c/m: MDQ monogram on Colombia (Cundinamarca)
Real, KM#9.

| 5 | ND(1821) | — | — | — | Rare | — |

---

2 REALES

SILVER
c/m: MDQ monogram on Colombia (Nueva Granada)
2 Reales, KM#76.

KM#	Date	Mintage	Good	VG	Fine	VF
6	ND(1819 JF)	—	—	—	Rare	—

c/m: MDQ monogram on Colombia (Nueva Granada)
2 Reales, KM#77.

| 7 | ND(1819 JF) | — | — | — | Rare | — |
| | ND(1820 JF) | — | — | — | Rare | — |

c/m: MDQ monogram on Colombia (Cundinamarca)
2 Reales, KM#5.

8	ND(1820 JF)	—	—	—	Rare	—
	ND(1820 Ba JF)	—	—	—	Rare	—
	ND(1821 Ba JF)	—	—	—	Rare	—
	ND(1821 JF)	—	100.00	150.00	—	—
	ND(1823 JF)	—	—	—	Rare	—

8 REALES
SILVER
c/m: MDQ monogram on Colombia (Nueva Granada)
8 Reales, KM#78.

9	ND(1819 JF)	—	—	—	Rare	—
	ND(1820/19 JF)	—	—	—	Rare	—
	ND(1820 JF)	—	—	—	Rare	—

c/m: MDQ monogram on Colombia (Cundinamarca)
8 Reales, KM#6.

10	ND(1820 JF)	—	—	—	Rare	—
	ND(1820 Ba JF)	—	—	—	Rare	—
	ND(1821 JF)	—	150.00	185.00	225.00	—
	ND(1821 Ba JF)	—	—	—	Rare	—

c/m: MDQ monogram on Colombia (Cundinamarca)
8 Reales, KM#7.

| 11 | ND(1820 JF) | — | — | — | Rare | — |

REGULAR COINAGE
UN QUARTO (1/4) REAL
.750 SILVER, 0.72-.83 g
Obv: Fortress and 2 eliptical lines.

KM#	Date	Mintage	VG	Fine	VF	XF
25	1842 MV	—	350.00	500.00	750.00	1500.

14mm. Obv: Fortress and bird.

26	1842 MV-S	—	125.00	275.00	450.00	600.00
	1843 MV	—	100.00	200.00	350.00	475.00
	1843 MV-A	—	65.00	125.00	250.00	375.00

NOTE: The A and S above are found on the mountain below the castle.

SILVER

| 36 | 1849 GJ | — | 17.50 | 35.00 | 60.00 | 95.00 |

ECUADOR 491

KM#	Date	Mintage	VG	Fine	VF	XF
36	1850 GJ	—	30.00	50.00	75.00	135.00
	1851 GJ	—	22.50	45.00	60.00	80.00
	1852 GJ	—	5.00	20.00	35.00	45.00
	1855 GJ	—	17.50	35.00	60.00	90.00
	1856 GJ	—	17.50	35.00	60.00	90.00
	1862 GJ	—	375.00	650.00	900.00	1500.

1/2 REAL

.750 SILVER, 1.30 g
Obv. leg: EL ECUADOR EN COLOMBIA,
MoR (Medio Real).

12.1	1833 GJ	—	13.50	28.00	50.00	150.00
	1835 GJ	—	—	Reported, not confirmed		

Rev: Denomination 1/2 R

12.2	1833 GJ	—	22.50	50.00	85.00	175.00
	1835 GJ	—	—	Reported, not confirmed		

Obv. leg: REPUBLICA DEL ECUADOR.

22	1838 ST	—	8.50	18.50	45.00	100.00
	1840 MV	—	15.00	37.50	75.00	150.00
	1840 WV	W is inverted M				
		—	35.00	80.00	135.00	190.00
	1843	—	—	Reported, not confirmed		

1.55-1.85 g, 15-17mm

35	1848 GJ	—	7.50	18.00	35.00	65.00
	1849 GJ	—	12.50	27.50	45.00	100.00

REAL

.750 SILVER, 3.00-3.40 g
Obv. leg: EL ECUADOR EN COLOMBIA.

13	1833 GJ	—	15.00	40.00	65.00	135.00
	1834 GJ	—	12.50	37.50	55.00	90.00
	1835 GJ	—	17.50	42.50	70.00	125.00
	1836 GJ	—	—	—	Rare	—

3.40-3.92 g
Obv. leg: REPUBLICA DEL ECUADOR.

17	1836 GJ	—	16.50	35.00	70.00	125.00
	1836 FP	—	25.00	50.00	90.00	185.00
	1837 FP	—	—	—	Rare	—
	1838 ST	—	18.50	40.00	80.00	175.00
	1838 MV	—	50.00	135.00	225.00	400.00
	1839 MV	—	15.00	37.50	75.00	165.00
	1840 MV	—	12.50	32.50	70.00	135.00
	1841 MV	—	—	—	Rare	—

Obv. and rev. legends transposed.

20	1837 FP	—	250.00	400.00	550.00	750.00
	1838 ST	—	70.00	165.00	275.00	400.00

2 REALES

.750 SILVER, 5.17-5.60 g, 25-27mm
Obv. leg: EL ECUADOR EN COLOMBIA.

KM#	Date	Mintage	VG	Fine	VF	XF
14	1833 GJ	—	60.00	125.00	200.00	400.00
	1834 GJ	—	17.50	35.00	70.00	135.00
	1834 JG	—	—	—	Rare	—
	1835 GJ	—	17.50	30.00	65.00	150.00
	1836 GJ	—	100.00	150.00	275.00	350.00

5.80-6.10 g
Obv. leg: REPUBLICA DEL ECUADOR

18	1836 GJ	—	12.50	20.00	35.00	80.00
	1836 FP	—	15.00	32.50	50.00	110.00
	1837 FP	—	—	650.00	—	—
	1838 ST	—	17.50	32.50	60.00	130.00
	1838 MV	—	12.50	25.00	45.00	100.00
	1839 MVLA	—	17.50	30.00	45.00	100.00
	1839 MVLA	A is inverted V				
		—	27.50	40.00	70.00	150.00
	1840 MV	—	20.00	35.00	55.00	140.00
	1840 MV	V is inverted A				
		—	20.00	40.00	65.00	150.00
	1841 MV	—	30.00	55.00	80.00	150.00

Obv. and rev. legends transposed.

21	1837 FP	—	22.50	40.00	75.00	175.00
	1838 ST	—	90.00	125.00	200.00	375.00

5.50-6.05 g

33	1847 GJ	—	6.50	17.50	37.50	85.00
	1848/7 GJ	—	7.50	22.50	50.00	125.00
	1848	—	9.00	30.00	60.00	150.00
	1849 GJ	—	6.50	17.50	37.50	85.00
	1850 GJ	—	6.50	17.50	37.50	85.00
	1851 GJ	—	6.50	17.50	37.50	85.00
	1852 GJ	—	6.50	17.50	37.50	85.00

Obv: 2 R flanking arms.
Rev: Liberty head w/long hair.

38	1857 GJ	—	500.00	1000.	1800.	3250.
	1862 GJ	—	750.00	1500.	2500.	4500.

6.7600 g, .666 SILVER, .1447 oz ASW
Rev: Liberty head w/short hair.

40	1862 GJ	—	750.00	1500.	2000.	4000.

4 REALES

.750 SILVER, 12.30-12.75 g

24	1841 MV	—	12.50	30.00	55.00	130.00
	1842 MV	—	12.50	30.00	55.00	130.00
	1843 MV	—	12.50	30.00	55.00	130.00

12.30 g

KM#	Date	Mintage	VG	Fine	VF	XF
27	1844 MVA	—	250.00	400.00	—	—

NOTE: The A above is found on the breast of the condor.

11.70 g

29	1845 MVA	—	250.00	500.00	—	—

NOTE: The A above is found on the breast of the condor.

13.35 g

37	1855 GJ	—	20.00	40.00	75.00	175.00
	1857 GJ	—	15.00	37.50	65.00	155.00

13.4300 g, .666 SILVER, .2876 oz ASW

37a	1862 GJ	—	900.00	2000.	3000.	4500.

41	1862	—	40.00	125.00	250.00	500.00

8 REALES

.903 SILVER, 25.00 g

32	1846 GJ	—	600.00	900.00	1250.	2500.

ECUADOR 492

5 FRANCOS

25.0000 g, .900 SILVER, .7234 oz ASW

KM#	Date	Mintage	VG	Fine	VF	XF
39	1858 GJ	—	100.00	235.00	345.00	750.00

ESCUDO

3.3000 g, .875 GOLD, .0928 oz AGW

15	1828	—	—	—	—	—
	1833 GJ	—	90.00	300.00	350.00	525.00
	1834 GJ	—	90.00	250.00	325.00	475.00
	1835 GJ	—	115.00	325.00	400.00	575.00
	1845 GJ	—	—	—	Rare	—

NOTE: The 1828 dated coins are considered contemporary counterfeits.

DOUBLE ESCUDO

6.7666 g, .875 GOLD, .1903 oz AGW

16	1833 GJ	—	—	—	Rare	—
	1834 GJ	—	—	—	Rare	—
	1835 GJ	—	300.00	500.00	900.00	1500.
	1835 FP	2 known	—	—	Rare	—

4 ESCUDOS

13.5000 g, .875 GOLD, .3798 oz AGW

19	1836 FPA	—	275.00	500.00	800.00	1350.
	1837 FPA	—	225.00	325.00	550.00	825.00
	1838 FPA	—	700.00	1350.	2100.	2750.
	1838 STA	3 to 4 pcs. known	—	—	3500.	—
	1838 MVA	—	425.00	900.00	1350.	2250.
	1839 MVA	—	400.00	700.00	1350.	2000.
	1841 MVA	—	—	—	—	—

NOTE: Engraver's initial A near front of bust.

8 ESCUDOS

27.0640 g, .875 GOLD, .7614 oz AGW

KM#	Date	Mintage	VG	Fine	VF	XF
23	1838 STA	—	750.00	2000.	3000.	3500.
	1838 MVA	—	750.00	2000.	3500.	5000.
	1839 MVA	—	600.00	1750.	2250.	3000.
	1840 MVA	—	500.00	850.00	1700.	2500.
	1841 MVA	—	400.00	600.00	1000.	1500.
	1841 MVS	—	750.00	2000.	3000.	3500.
	1842 MVA	—	500.00	850.00	1700.	2500.
	1843 MVS	—	500.00	850.00	1800.	2750.

NOTE: Engraver's initial A near front of bust, S toward back.

28	1844 MV	—	—	—	*Rare	—
	1845 MV	—	—	—	Rare	—

*NOTE: Stack's Hammel sale 9-82 VF/G 1844 MV realized $32,000.

Obv: Flagpoles extend below arms. Rev: Bust left.

30	1845 MV	—	3000.	4500.	5500.

Obv: W/o flagpoles below arms. Rev: Bust left.

31	1845 MV	—	—	3000.	4500.	5750.

34	1847 GJ	—	—	3000.	3750.	5500.
	1848 GJ	—	—	3000.	3750.	5500.
	1849/7 GJ	—	—	Reported, not confirmed		
	1849 GJ	—	—	—	—	—
	1850 GJ	—	—	3000.	3750.	5500.
	1852/0 GJ	—	—	1000.	1500.	2000.

KM#	Date	Mintage	VG	Fine	VF	XF
34	1854 GJ	—	—	—	—	—
	1855/2 GJ	—	—	1500.	2250.	3000.
	1856 GJ	—	—	3000.	3750.	5500.

DECIMAL COINAGE
10 Centavos = 1 Decimo
10 Decimos = 1 Sucre
25 Sucres = 1 Condor

MEDIO (1/2) CENTAVO

COPPER-NICKEL

KM#	Date	Mintage	Fine	VF	XF	Unc
47	1884H	.600	7.50	15.00	27.50	50.00
	1884H	—	—	—	Proof	175.00
	1886H	.400	Reported, not confirmed			

COPPER

54	1890H	2.000	2.50	6.00	15.00	45.00

COPPER-NICKEL

57	1909H	4.000	2.00	5.00	10.00	30.00

UN (1) CENTAVO

COPPER

45	1872HEATON	17.50	25.00	50.00	100.00
	1872HEATON	—	—	Proof	250.00
	1890H	2.000	4.00	10.00	22.50	75.00

COPPER-NICKEL

48	1884	.500	7.50	20.00	45.00	100.00
	1884	—	—	—	Proof	175.00
	1886	1.000	5.00	12.50	25.00	65.00

58	1909H	3.000	2.00	5.00	11.00	30.00

BRONZE

67	1928	2.016	.30	.80	2.50	5.00

DOS (2) CENTAVOS

COPPER

KM#	Date	Mintage	Fine	VF	XF	Unc
46	1872HEATON	—	18.00	35.00	70.00	150.00
	1872HEATON	—	—	—	Proof	250.00

COPPER-NICKEL

| 59 | 1909H | 2.500 | 3.00 | 6.50 | 15.00 | 50.00 |

DOS Y MEDIO (2-1/2) CENTAVOS

COPPER-NICKEL

| 61 | 1917 | 1.600 | 3.50 | 7.50 | 20.00 | 65.00 |

NICKEL

| 68 | 1928 | 4.000 | 1.25 | 2.75 | 7.50 | 22.50 |

MEDIO (1/2) DECIMO

COPPER-NICKEL

49	1884HEATON					
		.600	6.50	15.00	32.50	75.00
	1884HEATON	—	—	—	Proof	200.00
	1886HEATON					
		.600	5.75	15.00	30.00	70.00

1.2500 g, .900 SILVER, .0361 oz ASW

55	1893LIMA rev: "G.1.250"				
		1.718	1.00	1.75	3.50	7.50
	1893LIMA rev: "G.1:250"				
	Inc. Ab.	1.00	1.75	3.50	7.50
	1894/3LIMA				
		.243	2.75	4.50	8.50	17.50
	1897LIMA	.800	1.75	2.50	4.50	9.50
	1899/87LIMA				
		.560	2.00	4.00	9.00	18.50
	1899/7LIMA I.A.	—	—	—	—
	1899LIMA	1.75	3.50	8.00	17.50
	1899LIMA obv: ECUADO.R				
	Inc. Ab.	1.50	3.00	10.00	22.00
	1902/892LIMA				
		1.000	1.00	1.75	4.50	9.50
	1902LIMA I.A.	.75	1.25	3.00	6.50
	1905/6LIMA				
		.500	2.50	5.00	10.00	25.00
	1905LIMA I.A.	.75	1.25	3.50	7.50
	1912LIMA .020	.75	1.25	3.50	6.50
	1915BIRMm				
		2.000	.50	1.00	2.00	4.50

CINCO (5) CENTAVOS

COPPER-NICKEL

KM#	Date	Mintage	Fine	VF	XF	Unc
60.1	1909H	2.000	2.50	7.50	25.00	55.00

Thin planchet

60.2	1917(PHILA.)					
		1.200	2.00	7.50	27.50	60.00
	1918(PHILA.)					
		7.980	.75	1.50	5.00	10.00

| 63 | 1919 | 12.000 | .60 | 1.25 | 3.50 | 7.50 |

NOTE: Three varieties exist.

| 65 | 1924H | 10.000 | 1.00 | 1.75 | 4.00 | 9.00 |

NICKEL

| 69 | 1928 | 16.000 | .75 | 1.00 | 2.00 | 4.50 |

| 75 | 1937HF | 15.000 | .10 | .20 | .35 | .75 |

BRASS

| 75a | 1942 | 2.000 | .50 | 1.25 | 2.50 | 5.75 |
| | 1944D | 3.000 | .50 | 1.00 | 2.00 | 3.75 |

COPPER-NICKEL

| 75b | 1946 | 40.000 | — | — | .10 | .25 |

NICKEL-CLAD STEEL

| 75c.1 | 1970 | — | — | — | .10 | .25 |

Obv. leg: ECADOR.

| 75c.2 | 1970 | — | — | — | — | — |

UN (1) DECIMO

2.5000 g, .900 SILVER, .0723 oz ASW

KM#	Date	Mintage	VG	Fine	VF	XF
50	1884HEATON					
		.050	2.00	5.00	15.00	35.00
	1884HEATON	—	—	—	Proof	300.00
	1889HEATON					
		.100	BV	3.00	15.00	35.00
	1889/789SANTIAGO				
		1.000	6.00	10.00	25.00	65.00
	1889SANTIAGO				
	I.A.	1.50	2.50	6.00	17.50
	1890HEATON				
		.150	2.00	5.00	15.00	35.00
	1892LIMA	.350	2.00	3.00	10.00	22.50
	1893LIMA	.848	BV	1.75	3.00	6.50
	1894LIMA	.206	BV	2.50	6.00	17.50
	1899/4LIMA				
		.220	2.00	3.00	10.00	22.50
	1899LIMA I.A.	—	—	—	42.50
50	1900LIMA JR				
		.480	BV	1.50	2.50	6.00
	1900LIMA I.A.	BV	3.50	5.00	10.00
	1900LIMA JF	—	—	—	—
	1900LIMA JF/TF JR				
	1900LIMA F	—	—	—	—
	1902LIMA JR				
		.519	BV	1.50	3.00	6.00
	1902LIMA I.A.	BV	1.50	2.50	8.00
	1905LIMA .250	BV	1.50	2.50	8.00
	1912LIMA .030	1.50	2.50	4.00	10.00
	1915BIRMm				
		1.000	BV	1.25	2.00	5.00
	1916PHILA				
		2.000	BV	1.25	2.00	5.00

DIEZ (10) CENTAVOS

COPPER-NICKEL

KM#	Date	Mintage	Fine	VF	XF	Unc
62	1918	1.000	5.50	11.00	18.50	37.50

| 64 | 1919 | 2.000 | 1.00 | 2.00 | 4.00 | 10.00 |

| 66 | 1924H | 5.000 | .75 | 1.50 | 3.00 | 9.00 |
| | 1924H | — | — | — | Proof | 100.00 |

NICKEL

| 70 | 1928 | 16.000 | .50 | 1.00 | 2.50 | 8.00 |

| 76 | 1937HF | 7.500 | .25 | .50 | 1.00 | 2.50 |

BRASS

| 76a | 1942 | 5.000 | .60 | 1.00 | 1.75 | 2.50 |

COPPER-NICKEL

| 76b | 1946 | 40.000 | .10 | .15 | .25 | 1.00 |

NICKEL-CLAD STEEL

76c	1964	20.000	—	—	.10	.25
	1968	15.000	—	—	.10	.25
	1972	20.000	—	—	.10	.15
	1976	10.000	—	—	.10	.15

NOTE: Varieties exist.

DOS (2) DECIMOS

5.0000 g, .900 SILVER, .1446 oz ASW

KM#	Date	Mintage	VG	Fine	VF	XF
51	1884HEATON					
		.025	4.50	7.50	10.00	22.50
	1884HEATON	—	—	—	Proof	600.00
	1889HEATON					

ECUADOR 494

KM#	Date	Mintage	VG	Fine	VF	XF
51		.050	3.75	6.75	12.50	32.50
	1889LIMA	.075	3.50	6.50	10.00	22.50
	1889SANTIAGO	1.000	BV	4.50	8.50	17.50
	1890HEATON	1.075	3.75	6.75	12.50	32.50
	1891SANTIAGO	.230	BV	5.00	7.50	12.50
	1891/89LIMA	.025	BV	5.00	7.50	12.50
	1892/89LIMA	1.138	BV	4.00	7.50	10.00
	1893/89LIMA	.390	BV	5.00	7.50	12.50
	1894/89LIMA	.409	BV	5.00	7.50	10.00
	1895/89LIMA	.160	BV	5.00	7.50	10.00
	1895PHILA.	5.000	BV	3.00	4.00	7.00
	1896/89LIMA	.109	2.00	5.00	7.50	17.50
	1912LIMA	.050	3.50	5.00	7.50	17.50
	1914LIMA	.110	2.00	5.00	7.50	12.50
	1914LIMA. I.A.		BV	3.00	5.00	9.00
	1914PHILA.	2.500	BV	3.00	4.50	6.50
	1915LIMA	.157	10.00	22.50	50.00	100.00
	1916PHILA.	1.000	BV	3.00	4.50	6.50

20 CENTAVOS

NICKEL

KM#	Date	Mintage	Fine	VF	XF	Unc
77	1937HF	7.500	.25	.50	1.00	1.50

BRASS

77a	1942	5.000	.60	1.00	2.00	4.50
	1944D	15.000	.40	.75	1.50	3.75

COPPER-NICKEL

77b	1946	30.000	—	.10	.20	.35	.50

NICKEL-CLAD STEEL

77c	1959	14.400	—	—	.10	.25
	1962	14.400	—	—	.10	.25
	1966	24.000	—	—	.10	.25
	1969	24.000	—	—	.10	.25
	1971	12.000	—	—	.10	.25
	1972	48.432	—	—	.10	.25
	1975	—	—	—	.10	.25
	1978	37.500	—	—	.10	.25

COPPER-NICKEL

77d (Y53d)	1974	72.000	—	—	.10	.25
	1975	—	—	—	.10	.25

NICKEL-COATED STEEL

77e	1980	18.000	—	—	.10	.25
	1981	21.000	—	—	.10	.25

MEDIO (1/2) SUCRE

12.5000 g, .900 SILVER, .3617 oz ASW

KM#	Date	Mintage	VG	Fine	VF	XF
52	1884HEATON	.020	10.00	24.00	50.00	120.00
	1884HEATON	—	—	—	Proof	1000.

CINQUENTA (50) CENTAVOS

2.5000 g, .720 SILVER, .0579 oz ASW

KM#	Date	Mintage	Fine	VF	XF	Unc
71	1928PHILA.	1.000	.75	1.25	2.50	7.50
	1930PHILA.	.155	2.00	4.00	6.50	14.00

NICKEL-CLAD STEEL

KM#	Date	Mintage	Fine	VF	XF	Unc
81	1963	20.000	—	.10	.15	.35
	1971	5.000	—	.10	.15	.35
	1974	—	—	.10	.15	.35
	1975	—	—	.10	.15	.35
	1977	40.000	—	.10	.15	.35
	1979	25.000	—	.10	.15	.35
	1982	20.000	—	.10	.15	.35

Obv: Modified coat of arms.

87	1985	30.000	—	.10	.15	.35

UN (1) SUCRE

25.0000 g, .900 SILVER, .7234 oz ASW

KM#	Date	Mintage	VG	Fine	VF	XF
53	1884HEATON	.250	BV	12.50	17.50	35.00
	1884HEATON	—	—	—	Proof	2000.
	1888HEATON	.100	10.00	20.00	30.00	60.00
	1888SANTIAGO	.373	BV	12.50	17.50	35.00
	1889HEATON	.150	BV	12.50	17.50	35.00
	1889SANTIAGO	.327	BV	12.50	17.50	35.00
	1890HEATON	.012	30.00	50.00	75.00	150.00
	1890LIMA	.287	BV	12.50	17.50	35.00
	1891LIMA	.143	BV	12.50	17.50	35.00
	1892HEATON	.060	20.00	30.00	45.00	90.00
	1892LIMA	.058	20.00	30.00	45.00	90.00
	1895HEATON	.102	15.00	25.00	35.00	70.00
	1895LIMA	.174	BV	12.50	17.50	35.00
	1896T.F.LIMA	.148	20.00	30.00	50.00	100.00
	1896F.LIMA I.A.	.020	20.00	30.00	40.00	80.00
	1897LIMA	.462	BV	12.50	17.50	35.00

5.0000 g, .720 SILVER, .1157 oz ASW

KM#	Date	Mintage	Fine	VF	XF	Unc
72	1928PHILA.	3.000	1.75	2.25	5.00	12.50
	1930PHILA.	.400	4.00	8.00	16.00	30.00
	1934PHILA.	2.000	1.75	2.25	5.00	12.50

NICKEL

KM#	Date	Mintage	Fine	VF	XF	Unc
78	1937HF 26.5mm	9.000	.50	.75	1.50	4.00
	1946 25.9mm	18.000	.40	.60	.80	1.25

COPPER-NICKEL

78a	1959	8.400	.25	.50	.65	1.00
	1959	—	—	—	Proof	125.00

NICKEL-CLAD STEEL

78b	1964	20.000	—	.10	.25	.50
	1970	24.000	—	.10	.25	.50
	1971	8.092	—	.10	.25	.50
	1974	40.308	—	.10	.25	.50
	1978	32.000	—	.10	.25	.50
	1979	32.000	—	.10	.25	.50
	1980	110.000	—	.10	.25	.50
	1981	70.000	—	.10	.25	.50

Obv: Modified coat of arms.

83	1974	23.100	—	.10	.20	.35
	1975	.592	—	.10	.20	.50
	1977	32.000	—	.10	.20	.35

Obv: Modified coat of arms.

85	1985	—	—	—	—	.25
	1986	—	—	—	—	.25

DOS (2) SUCRES

10.0000 g, .720 SILVER, .2315 oz ASW

73	1928PHILA.	.500	2.50	5.00	12.50	25.00
	1930PHILA.	.100	10.00	15.00	30.00	60.00

80	1944Mo	1.000	2.50	3.50	4.50	6.00

COPPER-NICKEL

82	1973	—	—	.10	.25	.60

NOTE: Not released to circulation.

CINCO (5) SUCRES

25.0000 g, .720 SILVER, .5787 oz ASW

79	1943Mo	1.000	—	BV	6.00	10.00
	1944Mo	2.600	—	BV	5.00	8.00

COPPER-NICKEL

KM#	Date	Mintage	Fine	VF	XF	Unc
84	1973	500 pcs.*	—	—	—	Rare

*NOTE: Only 7 pieces were distributed to Ecuadorian government officials. The rest are in vaults of the National Bank.

DIEZ (10) SUCRES

8.1360 g, .900 GOLD, .2354 oz AGW

56	1899BIRMm					
		.050	125.00	150.00	175.00	325.00
	1900BIRMm					
		.050	125.00	150.00	225.00	375.00

1000 SUCRES

23.3300 g, .925 SILVER, .6938 oz ASW
Obv: Coat of arms. Rev: Soccer player.

86	1986	.010	—	—	Proof	20.00

UN (1) CONDOR

8.3592 g, .900 GOLD, .2419 oz AGW

74	1928BIRMm					
		.020	125.00	175.00	250.00	375.00

GALAPAGOS ISLANDS

The Galapagos Islands, a territory of Ecuador situated in the Pacific Ocean 650 miles west of Ecuador, have an area of 3,028 sq. mi. (7,842 sq. km.) and a population of 3,100. Capital: San Cristobal, on the island of that name. The archipelago of more than 60 islands scattered over 23,000 sq. mi. of the Pacific was discovered by the Spaniards early in the 16th century, and became part of Ecuador in 1832. The islands are notable for their unique plant and animal life, including 15 species of giant tortoise which are the longest-lived animals on earth, with life spans of more than 200 years.

1/2 DECIMO

.900 SILVER
c/m: Script RA on 1/2 Decimo, KM#55.

KM#	Date	Mintage	Good	VG	Fine	VF
1	ND(1893-?)	—	15.00	30.00	40.00	60.00

UN (1) DECIMO

.900 SILVER
c/m: Script RA on Un Decimo, KM#50.

2	ND(1884-?)	—	10.00	17.50	25.00	40.00

DOS (2) DECIMOS

.900 SILVER
c/m: Script RA on Dos Decimos, KM#51.

3	ND(1884-?)	—	15.00	30.00	40.00	60.00

1/2 SUCRE

.900 SILVER
c/m: Script RA on 1/2 Sucre, KM#52.

4	ND(1884-?)	—	20.00	35.00	50.00	75.00

UN (1) SUCRE

.900 SILVER
c/m: Script RA on Un Sucre, KM#42.

KM#	Date	Mintage	Good	VG	Fine	VF
5	ND(1884-?)	—	30.00	55.00	75.00	100.00

NOTE: The script RA countermarks, initials of a well known merchant, Rogelio Alvarado, are attributed to the Galapagos Islands where it is believed the coins were used to pay prisoners in a penal colony.

EGYPT

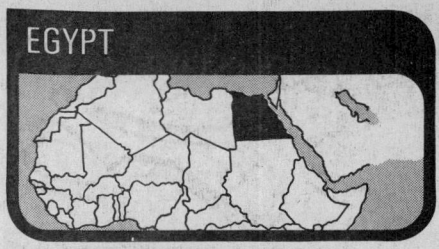

The Arab Republic of Egypt, located on the northeastern corner of Africa, has an area of 386,102 sq. mi. (1,000,000 sq. km.) and a population of *54.8 million. Capital: Cairo. Although Egypt is an almost rainless expanse of desert, its economy is predominantly agricultural. Cotton, rice and petroleum are exported. Other main sources of income are revenues from the Suez Canal, remittances of Egyptian workers abroad and tourism.

Egyptian history dates back to about 3000 B.C. when the empire was established by uniting the upper and lower kingdoms. Following its 'Golden Age' (16th to 13th centuries B.C.), Egypt was conquered by Persia (525 B.C.) and Alexander the Great (332 B.C.). The Ptolemies, descended from one of Alexander's generals, ruled until the suicide of Cleopatra (30 B.C.) when Egypt became the private domain of the Roman emperor, and subsequently part of the Byzantine world. Various Muslim dynasties ruled Egypt from 641 on, including Ayyubid Sultans to 1250 and Mamluks to 1517, when it was conquered by the Ottoman Turks, interrupted by the occupation of Napoleon (1798-1801). A semi-independent dynasty was founded by Muhammad Ali in 1805 which lasted until 1952. Turkish rule became increasingly casual, permitting Great Britain to inject its influence by purchasing shares in the Suez Canal. British troops occupied Egypt in 1882, becoming the de facto rulers. On Dec. 14, 1914, Egypt was made a protectorate of Britain. British occupation ended on Feb. 28, 1922, when Egypt became a sovereign, independent kingdom. The monarchy was abolished and a republic proclaimed on July 23, 1952.

On Feb. 1, 1958, Egypt and Syria formed the United Arab Republic. Yemen joined on March 8 in an association known as the United Arab States. Syria withdrew from the United Arab Republic on Sept. 29, 1961, and on Dec. 26 Egypt dissolved its ties with Yemen in the United Arab States. On Sept. 2, 1971, Egypt finally shed the name United Arab Republic in favor of the Arab Republic of Egypt.

RULERS
Ottoman, until 1882

Local Viceroys
Muhammad Ali, 1805-1848
Ibrahim Pasha, 1848
Abbas I Pasha, 1848-1854
Sa'id Pasha, 1854-1863

Local Kedives
Isma'il Pasha, 1863-1879
Mohammed Tewfik Pasha, 1879-
British, 1882-1922

Local Kedives
Mohammed Tewfik Pasha, 1882-
Abbas II Hilmi, 1892-1914

Local Sultans
Hussein Kamil, 1914-1917
Ahmed Fuad I, 1917-1922
Kingdom, 1922-1952
Ahmed Fuad I, 1922-1936
Farouk I, 1936-1952
Fuad II, 1952-1953
Republic, 1952-

MONETARY SYSTEM
40 Paras = 1 Qirsh (Piastre)
   (1885-1916)
10 Ochr-El-Qirsh = 1 Piastre
   (Commencing 1916)
10 Milliemes = 1 Piastre (Qirsh)
100 Piastres = 1 Pound (Gunayh)

MINT MARKS
Egyptian coins issued prior to the advent of the British Protectorate series of Sultan Hussein Kamil introduced in 1916 were very similar to Turkish coins of the same period. They can best be distinguished by the presence of the Arabic word *Misr* (Egypt) on the reverse, which generally appears immediately above the Muslim accession date of the ruler, which is presented in Arabic numerals. Each coin is individually dated according to the regnal years.

BP - Budapest, Hungary
H - Birmingham, England
KN - King's Norton, England

ENGRAVER
W - Emil Weigand, Berlin

EGYPT 496

YEAR IDENTIFICATION

'MISR'
ACCESSION DATE
DENOMINATIONS

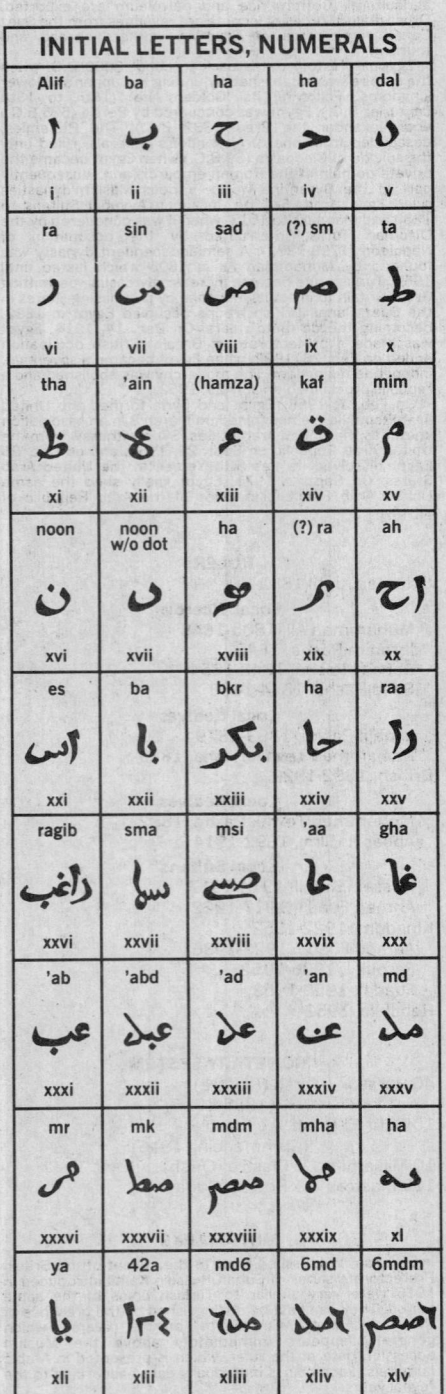

PARA   QIRSH

NOTE: The unit of value on coins of this period is generally presented on the obverse immediately below the toughra, as shown in the illustrations above.

PIASTRES 1916-1933

MILLIEMES   PIASTRES 1934 -

TITLES

المملكة المصرية

Al-Mamlaka   Al-Misriya
(The Kingdom of Egypt)

U.A.R. EGYPT

The legend illustrated is *Jumhuriyat Misr Al-'Arabiyya* which translates to 'The Arab Republic of Egypt'. Similar legends are found on the modern issues of Syria.

OTTOMAN COINAGE

MUSTAFA IV
AH1222-1223/1807-1808AD

PARA
BILLON, 14mm, 0.30-0.40 g
Accession Date: AH1222
Obv: Toughra. Rev: Mintname over date.

KM#	Year	Mintage	Good	VG	Fine	VF
155	1	—	10.00	15.00	25.00	50.00

20 PARA

BILLON
Accession Date: AH1222
Similar to Piastre, KM#157.

KM#	Year	Mintage	VG	Fine	VF	XF
156	1	—	500.00	800.00	1300.	2000.

PIASTRE

BILLON, 10.65 g
Accession Date: AH1222

157	1	—	550.00	1000.	1750.	3000.

1/2 ZERI MAHBUB
GOLD, 20mm, 1.65 g
Accession Date: AH1222

158	1	—	250.00	400.00	650.00	1000.

ZERI MAHBUB

GOLD, 2.30 g
Accession Date: AH1222

159	1	—	275.00	400.00	600.00	800.00

2 ZERI MAHBUB

GOLD, 32mm, 4.70 g
Accession Date: AH1222

160	1	—	250.00	400.00	650.00	1000.

MAHMUD II
AH1223-1255/1808-1839AD

ASPER
BRASS, uniface
Accession Date: AH1223

KM#	Year	Mintage	Good	VG	Fine	VF
		—	50.00	80.00	110.00	150.00

NOTE: The precise status of this piece is undetermined.

AKCHEH
BILLON, 11-12mm, 0.10-0.20 g
Accession Date: AH1223
Similar to 1 Para, KM#161.

KM#	Year					
A161	16	—	1.00	2.00	3.00	10.00
	17	—	1.00	2.00	3.00	10.00
	18	—	1.00	2.00	3.00	10.00
	19	—	1.00	2.00	3.00	10.00

KM#	Year	Mintage	Good	VG	Fine	VF
A161	19	—	1.00	2.00	3.00	10.00
	20	—	1.00	2.00	3.00	10.00
	21	—	1.00	2.00	3.00	10.00

PARA

BILLON, 12-13mm, 0.15-0.28 g
Accession Date: AH1223

KM#	Year	Mintage	Good	VG	Fine	VF
161	1	—	.75	1.50	4.00	8.50
	2	—	.75	1.50	4.00	8.50
	3	—	.75	1.50	4.00	8.50
	4	—	.75	1.50	4.00	8.50
	5	—	.75	1.50	4.00	8.50
	6	—	.75	1.50	4.00	8.50
	7	—	.75	1.50	4.00	8.50
	8	—	.75	1.50	4.00	8.50
	9	—	.75	1.50	4.00	8.50
	10	—	.75	1.50	4.00	8.50
	11	—	.75	1.50	4.00	8.50
	12	—	.75	1.50	4.00	8.50
	13	—	.75	1.50	4.00	8.50
	14	—	.75	1.50	4.00	8.50
	15	—	.75	1.50	4.00	8.50
	16	—	.75	1.50	4.00	8.50
	17	—	1.00	3.00	10.00	15.00
	18	—	1.00	3.00	10.00	15.00
	19	—	2.00	4.00	15.00	20.00
	21	—	—	Reported, not confirmed		

COPPER

KM#	Year	Mintage	Good	VG	Fine	VF
162	28	—	8.00	20.00	45.00	100.00
	29	—	8.00	20.00	45.00	100.00

15mm

KM#	Year	Mintage	Good	VG	Fine	VF
163	29		8.00	20.00	45.00	100.00

NOTE: KM#163 does not bear any denomination.

15-17mm

KM#	Year	Mintage	Good	VG	Fine	VF
164	29	—	8.00	20.00	45.00	100.00
	30	—	8.00	20.00	45.00	100.00
	31	—	8.00	20.00	45.00	100.00
	32	—	8.00	20.00	45.00	100.00

5 PARA

BILLON, 15-16mm., 0.50-0.70 g
Accession Date: AH1223

KM#	Year	Mintage	Good	VG	Fine	VF
165	5	—	15.00	20.00	30.00	50.00
	6	—	15.00	20.00	30.00	50.00
	7	—	15.00	20.00	30.00	50.00
	8	—	15.00	20.00	30.00	50.00
	9	—	10.00	15.00	25.00	45.00
	10	—	10.00	15.00	25.00	45.00
	12	—	10.00	15.00	25.00	45.00
	13	—	10.00	15.00	25.00	45.00
	14	—	10.00	15.00	25.00	45.00
	15	—	10.00	15.00	25.00	45.00
	16	—	10.00	15.00	25.00	45.00
	17	—	10.00	15.00	25.00	45.00
	18	—	10.00	15.00	25.00	45.00
	19	—	10.00	15.00	25.00	45.00
	20	—	10.00	15.00	25.00	45.00
	21	—	10.00	15.00	25.00	45.00

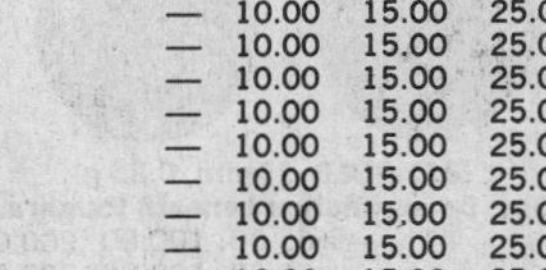

14mm., 0.40 g
Obv: Rose added to right of toughra.

KM#	Year	Mintage	Good	VG	Fine	VF
166	21	—	5.00	15.00	30.00	60.00
	22	—	4.00	10.00	22.50	40.00
	23	—	4.00	10.00	22.50	40.00
	24	—	4.00	10.00	22.50	40.00
	25	—	4.00	10.00	22.50	40.00
	26	—	5.00	15.00	30.00	60.00
	27	—	45.00	70.00	120.00	185.00
	28	—	45.00	70.00	120.00	185.00

COPPER, 22-24mm, 6.14-7.41 g
Floral designs in wreath

KM#	Year	Mintage	Good	VG	Fine	VF
167	28	—	3.00	6.00	12.50	25.00
	29	—	3.00	6.00	12.50	25.00

W/o wreath and denomination.

KM#	Year	Mintage	Good	VG	Fine	VF
168	29	—	5.00	7.00	15.00	30.00

Obv: Denomination added below toughra, *Adli* beside.

KM#	Year	Mintage	Good	VG	Fine	VF
169	29	—	2.00	5.00	10.00	20.00
	30	—	2.00	5.00	10.00	20.00
	31	—	2.00	5.00	10.00	20.00
	32	—	3.00	7.00	15.00	25.00

10 PARA

BILLON, 17-18mm., 0.90-1.40 g
Accession Date: AH1223
Plain dotted borders.

KM#	Year	Mintage	Good	VG	Fine	VF
170.1	8	—	20.00	40.00	80.00	150.00
	9	—	10.00	20.00	40.00	75.00
	12	—	10.00	20.00	40.00	75.00
	15	—	10.00	20.00	40.00	75.00
	—	—	—	—	Rare	—

Ornate borders.

KM#	Year	Mintage	Good	VG	Fine	VF
170.2	18	—	3.50	9.00	20.00	32.50
	19	—	3.50	9.00	20.00	32.50
	20	—	3.50	9.00	20.00	32.50
	21	—	5.00	12.50	25.00	45.00

0.75-0.78 g
Wavy borders

KM#	Year	Mintage	Good	VG	Fine	VF
171	21	—	6.00	15.00	25.00	50.00
	22	—	5.00	12.50	20.00	40.00
	23	—	5.00	12.50	20.00	40.00
	24	—	5.00	12.50	20.00	40.00
	25	—	5.00	12.50	20.00	40.00
	26	—	13.50	30.00	75.00	150.00
	27	—	25.00	55.00	120.00	200.00

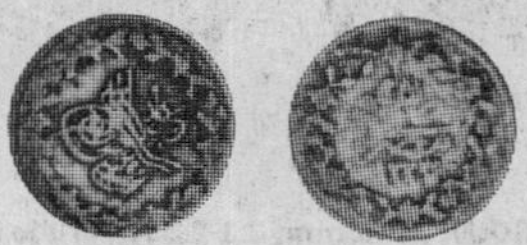

Wreath borders, 12mm, 0.30 g

KM#	Year	Mintage	Good	VG	Fine	VF
172	28	—	30.00	60.00	125.00	250.00
	29	—	15.00	30.00	60.00	125.00

.833 SILVER, 14mm, 0.35 g
Obv: Denomination below toughra.

KM#	Year	Mintage	VG	Fine	VF	XF
173	29	—	50.00	100.00	180.00	300.00
	30	—	50.00	100.00	180.00	300.00
	31	—	50.00	100.00	180.00	300.00
	32	—	50.00	100.00	180.00	300.00

20 PARA

BILLON, 22-24mm, 2.40-3.80 g
Accession Date: AH1223
Rev: Date

KM#	Year	Mintage	Good	VG	Fine	VF
174	1	—	65.00	115.00	200.00	300.00

KM#	Year	Mintage	Good	VG	Fine	VF
174	5	—	15.00	25.00	40.00	75.00
	6	—	16.50	27.50	45.00	85.00
	7	—	15.00	25.00	40.00	75.00
	8	—	15.00	25.00	40.00	75.00
	9	—	15.00	25.00	40.00	75.00
	10	—	15.00	25.00	40.00	75.00
	11	—	15.00	25.00	40.00	75.00

Obv: Mintname and date below toughra.

KM#	Year	Mintage	Good	VG	Fine	VF
175	5	—	20.00	45.00	125.00	200.00

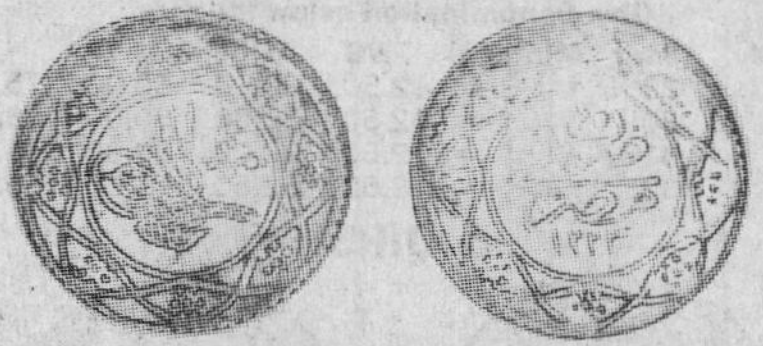

21mm, 1.38-1.62 g

KM#	Year	Mintage	Good	VG	Fine	VF
176	21	—	10.00	20.00	30.00	50.00
	22	—	7.50	15.00	25.00	40.00
	23	—	7.50	15.00	25.00	40.00
	24	—	7.50	15.00	25.00	40.00
	25	—	7.50	15.00	25.00	40.00
	27	—	40.00	60.00	100.00	150.00

15mm, 0.58-0.62 g

KM#	Year	Mintage	Good	VG	Fine	VF
177	28	—	12.00	18.00	35.00	65.00
	29	—	12.00	18.00	35.00	65.00

.833 SILVER, 15-16mm, 0.68-0.70 g
Obv: Denomination below toughra.

KM#	Year	Mintage	VG	Fine	VF	XF
178	29	—	20.00	40.00	80.00	160.00
	30	—	20.00	40.00	80.00	160.00
	31	—	20.00	40.00	80.00	160.00
	32	—	20.00	40.00	80.00	160.00

QIRSH

BILLON, 29-31mm, 7.00 g
Accession Date: AH1223

KM#	Year	Mintage	Good	VG	Fine	VF
179	1	—	25.00	50.00	100.00	150.00
	3	—	15.00	40.00	50.00	100.00
	5	—	15.00	40.00	50.00	100.00
	6	—	12.50	30.00	45.00	80.00
	7	—	12.50	30.00	45.00	80.00
	8	—	15.00	35.00	50.00	90.00

Obv: Mintname and date below toughra.

KM#	Year	Mintage	Good	VG	Fine	VF
180	5	—	40.00	65.00	135.00	225.00

(Yeni Kurus)

2.67-3.08 g
Wavy borders, 26-27mm.

KM#	Year	Mintage	Good	VG	Fine	VF
181	21	—	5.00	10.00	20.00	40.00
	22	—	3.00	7.50	15.00	30.00
	23	—	3.00	7.50	15.00	30.00
	24	—	3.00	7.50	15.00	30.00
	25	—	3.00	7.50	15.00	30.00
	26	—	5.00	10.00	20.00	40.00
	27	—	15.00	25.00	50.00	100.00

19mm, 1.00-1.31 g
Wreath borders

KM#	Year	Mintage	Good	VG	Fine	VF
182	28	—	9.00	12.00	18.00	30.00
	29	—	12.00	15.00	25.00	35.00

EGYPT

.833 SILVER, 19-20mm, 1.40 g
Obv: Denomination below toughra.

KM#	Year	Mintage	VG	Fine	VF	XF
183	29	—	12.50	30.00	50.00	75.00
	30	—	12.50	30.00	50.00	75.00
	31	—	12.50	30.00	50.00	75.00
	32	—	12.50	32.50	55.00	85.00

5 QIRSH

.833 SILVER, 24-26mm, 7.00 g
Accession Date: AH1223

184	29	—	150.00	260.00	425.00	650.00
	30	—	150.00	260.00	425.00	650.00
	31	—	150.00	260.00	425.00	650.00

10 QIRSH

.833 SILVER, 30mm, 14.00 g
Accession Date: AH1223
Similar to 5 Qirsh, KM#184.

185	29	—	—	—	Rare	—

20 QIRSH

.833 SILVER, 37mm, 27.80-28.06 g
Accession Date: AH1223

186	29	—	400.00	700.00	1050.	1450.
	30	—	425.00	750.00	1250.	1650.
	31	—	375.00	675.00	1000.	1400.
	32	—	425.00	750.00	1250.	1650.

GOLD COINAGE

NOTE: The following listings are incomplete, and any information about additional dates, years and types would be appreciated.

PRE-REFORM COINAGE
Prior to AH1251 (1834AD)

The basic unit was the 'Mahbub' or 'Zer Mahbub' (Zer = Gold), which weighed approximately 2.35 g from AH 1223 until 1247 (Yr. 15), when it was reduced to about 1.6 g. Fractional denominations were Halves (Nisfiya) and Quaters (Rubiya). The value of the Mahbub in terms of silver Piastres fluctuated according to the relative values of gold and silver, and the price of debased Egyptian silver coin.

1/4 MAHBUB
(Rubiya)

.875 GOLD, 13-14mm, 0.35-0.60 g
Accession Date: AH1223
Plain borders of dots
Rev. leg: *Azze Nasruhu Duribe Fi*......

189	—	—	150.00	225.00	300.00	450.00

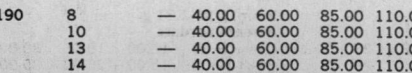

190	8	—	40.00	60.00	85.00	110.00
	10	—	40.00	60.00	85.00	110.00
	13	—	40.00	60.00	85.00	110.00
	14	—	40.00	60.00	85.00	110.00

12-13mm, 0.35-0.40 g
Plain borders of dots.

KM#	Year	Mintage	VG	Fine	VF	XF
191	15	—	25.00	40.00	60.00	85.00
	16	—	17.50	27.50	45.00	65.00
	17	—	25.00	40.00	60.00	85.00
	18	—	17.50	27.50	45.00	65.00
	21	—	—	—	—	—

(Saadiya)
Ornamental borders

192	19	—	30.00	45.00	65.00	75.00
	20	—	40.00	65.00	90.00	115.00
	21	—	60.00	90.00	115.00	140.00

(Coyrek Rumi)

Vine-like borders

193	21	—	25.00	35.00	50.00	100.00
	22	—	25.00	35.00	50.00	100.00
	23	—	25.00	35.00	50.00	100.00
	24	—	25.00	35.00	50.00	100.00
	25	—	25.00	35.00	50.00	100.00
	26	—	20.00	30.00	40.00	90.00
	27	—	30.00	40.00	70.00	150.00
	28	—	100.00	175.00	275.00	375.00

Different design and w/o year.

201	—	—	—	—	—	—

1/2 MAHBUB
(Nisfiya)

.875 GOLD, 19-20mm, 1.15-1.20 g
Accession Date: AH1223

194	1	—	85.00	140.00	300.00	450.00
	5	—	85.00	140.00	300.00	450.00
	8	—	85.00	140.00	300.00	450.00

(Khayriya)

.875 GOLD, 16mm, 0.70-0.80 g

195	21	—	20.00	30.00	75.00	150.00
	22	—	20.00	30.00	60.00	125.00
	23	—	20.00	30.00	60.00	125.00
	24	—	20.00	30.00	60.00	125.00
	25	—	20.00	30.00	60.00	125.00
	26	—	20.00	30.00	75.00	150.00
	27	—	30.00	40.00	100.00	200.00
	28	—	40.00	50.00	125.00	250.00

MAHBUB
(Altin)

.875 GOLD, 25-26mm, 2.1-2.35 g, crude flan
Accession Date: AH1223

197	1	—	90.00	175.00	350.00	600.00
	3	—	90.00	175.00	350.00	600.00
	5	—	90.00	175.00	350.00	600.00
	7	—	150.00	250.00	425.00	800.00
	8	—	150.00	250.00	425.00	800.00

10 dot next to toughra
| | | — | 150.00 | 250.00 | 425.00 | 800.00 |

10 rose branch next to toughra
		—	180.00	300.00	425.00	800.00
	11	—	90.00	175.00	350.00	600.00
	13	—	150.00	250.00	425.00	800.00
	14	—	90.00	175.00	350.00	600.00

23mm, 2.35 g, thicker & well-shaped flan
| 198 | 15 | — | 120.00 | 220.00 | 425.00 | 1000. |

W/o *Azza Nashruhu*.
| 199 | 5 | — | 100.00 | 200.00 | 375.00 | 700.00 |

2 MAHBUB

.875 GOLD, 28mm, 3.60 g
Accession Date: AH1223

KM#	Year	Mintage	VG	Fine	VF	XF
200	5	—	300.00	500.00	850.00	1750.

NOTE: The above piece may be a medal or token.

TEK RUMI

GOLD, 23mm, 2.35 g
Accession Date: AH1223
Similar to 1/4 Mahbub, KM#193.

| 202 | 11 | — | — | — | Rare | — |

GIFTE RUMI

GOLD, 28mm, 3.60 g
Accession Date: AH1223
Similar to 1/4 Mahbub, KM#193.

| 203 | 5 | — | — | — | Rare | — |

NOUSF or 1/2 MISRIYA
(10 Qirsh)

.875 GOLD, 0.70-0.75 g
Accession Date: AH1223

213	28	—	30.00	50.00	125.00	200.00
	29	—	30.00	50.00	125.00	200.00

REFORMED COINAGE
AH1251-1326/1834-1908AD

5 QIRSH
(Rubiya, or 1/4 Misriya)

.875 GOLD, 0.30-0.35 g
Accession Date: AH1223

210	28	—	85.00	140.00	215.00	325.00
	29	—	60.00	100.00	150.00	250.00

0.42 g
Obv: W/o value below toughra.

| 211 | 29 | — | 60.00 | 100.00 | 150.00 | 250.00 |

Obv: Denomination added below toughra.

212	30	—	65.00	100.00	150.00	200.00
	31	—	65.00	100.00	150.00	200.00
	32	—	65.00	100.00	150.00	200.00

10 QIRSH
(Nousf or 1/2 Misriya)

.875 GOLD, 15mm, 0.85 g
Obv: Denomination beneath toughra.

214	29	—	65.00	100.00	200.00	350.00
	30	—	65.00	100.00	200.00	350.00
	32	—	—	—	Reported, not confirmed	

20 QIRSH
(Misriya)

.875 GOLD, 18mm, 1.70 g
Accession Date: AH1223

215	29	—	60.00	100.00	150.00	300.00
	30	—	60.00	100.00	150.00	300.00
	31	—	60.00	100.00	150.00	300.00
	32	—	60.00	100.00	150.00	300.00

Obv. and rev: 4 roses around edge.

KM#	Year	Mintage	VG	Fine	VF	XF
216	32	—	75.00	125.00	200.00	400.00

100 QIRSH
(1 Pound)

.875 GOLD, 22mm, 8.40 g
Accession Date: AH1223

217	30	—	500.00	850.00	1500.	2500.
	31	—	500.00	850.00	1500.	2500.

ABDUL MEJID
AH1255-1277 / 1839-1861AD

PARA

COPPER, 16mm, 1.20 g
Accession Date: AH1255

KM#	Year	Mintage	Good	VG	Fine	VF
220	1	—	12.00	30.00	75.00	150.00
	2	—	10.00	20.00	50.00	100.00
	4	—	10.00	20.00	50.00	100.00
	5	—	10.00	20.00	50.00	100.00
	6	—	10.00	20.00	50.00	100.00

15mm. Similar to 5 Para, KM#224.

221	8	—	—	—	Rare	—

5 PARA

COPPER, 21mm, 6.40 g
Accession Date: AH1255

222	1	—	1.00	2.00	5.00	12.50
	2	—	1.00	2.00	5.00	12.50
	3	—	1.00	2.00	5.00	12.50
	4	—	1.00	2.00	5.00	12.50
	5	—	1.00	2.00	5.00	12.50
	6	—	1.00	2.00	5.00	12.50

223	6	—	2.00	3.00	7.50	17.00
	7	—	1.00	2.00	5.00	16.00
	8	—	4.50	8.50	15.00	27.50

224	8	—	4.00	7.50	12.50	25.00
	12	—	—	Reported, not confirmed		
	13	—	2.00	5.00	12.50	25.00
	14	—	1.00	2.50	10.00	20.00
	15	—	1.00	2.00	7.50	15.00
	16	—	1.00	2.00	7.50	15.00

10 PARA

.833 SILVER, 15mm, 0.37 g
Accession Date: AH1255

KM#	Year	Mintage	VG	Fine	VF	XF
225	1	—	15.00	30.00	60.00	90.00
	2	—	15.00	30.00	60.00	75.00
	3	—	12.50	25.00	50.00	75.00
	4	—	12.50	25.00	50.00	75.00
	5	—	12.50	25.00	50.00	75.00
	6	—	12.50	25.00	50.00	75.00
	7	—	12.50	25.00	50.00	75.00
	8	—	12.50	25.00	50.00	75.00
	9	—	12.50	25.00	50.00	75.00
	10	—	15.00	30.00	60.00	90.00
	11	—	15.00	30.00	60.00	90.00
	12	—	15.00	30.00	60.00	90.00
	13	—	30.00	60.00	120.00	180.00
	14	—	15.00	30.00	60.00	90.00

KM#	Year	Mintage	VG	Fine	VF	XF
225	15	—	15.00	30.00	60.00	90.00
	18	—	17.50	35.00	65.00	100.00
	19	—	17.50	35.00	65.00	100.00
	20	—	17.50	35.00	65.00	100.00
	21	—	—	Reported, not confirmed		
	22	—	17.50	35.00	65.00	100.00
	23	—	15.00	30.00	60.00	90.00

COPPER, 29mm, 12.90 g

226	15	—	4.50	8.00	15.00	45.00
	16	—	6.00	15.00	22.00	60.00

20 PARA

.833 SILVER, 16mm, 0.68 g
Accession Date: AH1255

227	1	—	15.00	30.00	50.00	75.00
	2	—	15.00	30.00	50.00	75.00
	3	—	15.00	30.00	50.00	75.00
	4/3	—	17.50	35.00	60.00	90.00
	4	—	15.00	30.00	50.00	75.00
	5	—	15.00	30.00	50.00	75.00
	6	—	15.00	30.00	50.00	75.00
	7	—	15.00	30.00	50.00	75.00
	8	—	15.00	30.00	50.00	75.00
	9	—	15.00	30.00	50.00	75.00
	10	—	15.00	30.00	50.00	75.00
	11	—	17.50	35.00	60.00	90.00
	12	—	17.50	35.00	60.00	90.00
	13	—	17.50	35.00	60.00	90.00
	14	—	17.50	35.00	60.00	90.00
	15	—	17.50	35.00	60.00	90.00
	18/6	—	20.00	40.00	70.00	110.00
	18	—	20.00	40.00	70.00	110.00
	19	—	30.00	60.00	90.00	150.00
	20	—	20.00	40.00	70.00	110.00
	21	—	20.00	40.00	70.00	110.00
	22	—	20.00	40.00	70.00	110.00
	23	—	17.50	35.00	60.00	90.00

QIRSH

.833 SILVER, 19mm, 1.42 g
Accession Date: AH1255

228	1	—	15.00	30.00	50.00	75.00
	2	—	15.00	30.00	50.00	75.00
	3	—	15.00	30.00	50.00	75.00
	4	—	17.50	35.00	60.00	90.00
	5	—	15.00	30.00	50.00	75.00
	6	—	15.00	30.00	50.00	75.00
	7	—	17.50	35.00	60.00	90.00
	8/7	—	17.50	35.00	60.00	90.00
	8	—	17.50	35.00	60.00	90.00
	9	—	17.50	35.00	60.00	90.00
	10	—	17.50	35.00	60.00	90.00
	11	—	17.50	35.00	60.00	90.00
	12	—	17.50	35.00	60.00	90.00
	13	—	17.50	35.00	60.00	90.00
	14	—	17.50	35.00	60.00	90.00
	15	—	17.50	35.00	60.00	90.00
	16	—	17.50	35.00	60.00	90.00
	17	—	22.50	45.00	75.00	115.00
	18	—	22.50	45.00	75.00	115.00
	19	—	22.50	45.00	75.00	115.00
	20	—	22.50	45.00	75.00	115.00
	21	—	—	Reported, not confirmed		
	22	—	22.50	45.00	75.00	115.00
	23	—	17.50	35.00	65.00	100.00

5 QIRSH

.833 SILVER, 25-26mm, 6.80-7.00 g

Accession Date: AH1255

KM#	Year	Mintage	VG	Fine	VF	XF
229	1	—	150.00	250.00	500.00	800.00
	2	—	150.00	250.00	500.00	800.00
	3	—	150.00	250.00	500.00	800.00
	4	—	150.00	250.00	500.00	800.00
	5	—	150.00	250.00	500.00	800.00
	6	—	150.00	250.00	500.00	800.00
	16	—	200.00	300.00	750.00	1250.
	23	—	—	Reported, not confirmed		

.875 GOLD, 0.427 g

230	1	—	17.50	30.00	50.00	85.00
	2	—	17.50	30.00	50.00	85.00
	3	—	17.50	30.00	50.00	85.00
	4	—	17.50	30.00	50.00	85.00
	5	—	17.50	30.00	50.00	85.00
	6	—	17.50	30.00	50.00	85.00
	7	—	17.50	30.00	50.00	85.00
	8	—	17.50	30.00	50.00	85.00
	9	—	17.50	30.00	50.00	85.00
	10	—	17.50	30.00	50.00	85.00
	11	—	17.50	30.00	50.00	85.00
	12	—	17.50	30.00	50.00	85.00
	13	—	22.50	37.50	60.00	125.00
	14	—	17.50	30.00	50.00	85.00
	15	—	17.50	30.00	50.00	85.00
	16	—	17.50	30.00	50.00	85.00
	18	—	17.50	30.00	50.00	85.00
	19	—	17.50	30.00	50.00	85.00
	20	—	17.50	30.00	50.00	85.00
	22	—	17.50	30.00	50.00	85.00
	23	—	17.50	30.00	50.00	85.00

10 QIRSH

.833 SILVER, 30mm, 14.00 g
Accession Date: AH1255

231	1	—	200.00	300.00	650.00	1250.
	2	—	200.00	300.00	650.00	1250.
	3	—	175.00	250.00	600.00	1250.
	4	—	175.00	250.00	550.00	1200.
	5	—	250.00	400.00	750.00	1500.
	6	—	300.00	750.00	1200.	2000.
	10	—	—	Reported, not confirmed		
	16	—	—	Reported, not confirmed		

NOTE: Has oblique and vertical milled edges.

.875 GOLD, 15mm, 0.840 g

231a	1	—	—	—	—	—

20 QIRSH

.833 SILVER, 36-38mm, 27.70-28.00 g
Accession Date: AH1255

232	1	—	350.00	600.00	1100.	1500.
	2	—	325.00	575.00	1100.	1500.
	3	—	375.00	650.00	1250.	1750.
	4	—	325.00	575.00	1100.	1500.

.875 GOLD, 1.71 g

233	1	—	400.00	650.00	1000.	1750.

50 QIRSH
(1/2 Pound)

.875 GOLD, 4.274 g
Accession Date: AH1255
Beaded border.

EGYPT 500

KM#	Year	Mintage	VG	Fine	VF	XF
234.1	1	550 pcs.	200.00	300.00	600.00	800.00
	2	—	100.00	150.00	300.00	500.00
	3	—	100.00	125.00	250.00	400.00
	4	—	75.00	100.00	200.00	300.00
	5	—	75.00	100.00	200.00	300.00

Toothed border.

234.2	6	—	75.00	125.00	250.00	400.00
	7	—	75.00	150.00	300.00	500.00
	8	—	75.00	150.00	300.00	500.00
	11	—	75.00	150.00	300.00	500.00
	15	—	BV	75.00	150.00	250.00
	16	—	—	100.00	200.00	350.00

100 QIRSH
(1 Pound)

.875 GOLD, 8.544 g, .2404 oz AGW
Accession Date: AH1255
Beaded border.

235.1	1	—	BV	200.00	300.00	500.00
	2	—	BV	150.00	250.00	400.00
	3	—	BV	125.00	200.00	350.00
	4	—	BV	115.00	175.00	275.00
	5	—	BV	115.00	175.00	275.00

Toothed border.

235.2	6	—	BV	115.00	175.00	275.00
	7	—	BV	125.00	200.00	350.00
	8	—	BV	125.00	200.00	350.00
	9	—	135.00	200.00	300.00	500.00
	10	—	135.00	200.00	300.00	500.00
	11	—	BV	125.00	200.00	350.00
	12	—	BV	125.00	200.00	350.00
	13	—	BV	125.00	200.00	350.00
	14	—	BV	125.00	200.00	350.00
	15	—	BV	115.00	150.00	250.00
	16	—	BV	125.00	175.00	275.00
	17	—	BV	150.00	200.00	350.00
	18	—	—	Reported, not confirmed		

NOTE: For crude copy of year 2 see Sudan Y#3.

ABDUL AZIZ
AH1277-1293/1861-1876AD

4 PARA

BRONZE, 22mm, 2.26 g
Accession Date: AH1277

KM#	Year	Mintage	Fine	VF	XF	Unc
240	4	—	5.00	10.00	25.00	75.00

10 PARA

BRONZE, 30mm, 6.10-6.60 g
Accession Date: AH1277
Obv: W/o flower at right of toughra.

241	4	—	1.00	2.00	10.00	30.00
	5	—	1.00	2.00	10.00	30.00
	6	—	2.00	3.00	12.00	40.00
	7	—	2.00	3.00	12.00	50.00
	9	—	1.00	2.00	10.00	30.00
	10	—	2.00	3.00	12.00	40.00

COPPER, 5.80 g
Obv: Flower added at right of toughra.

KM#	Year	Mintage	VG	Fine	VF	XF
242	8	.204	250.00	425.00	650.00	1250.
	9	—	200.00	350.00	550.00	1200.
	11	200 pcs.	—	Rare, Unc.		5000.

.833 SILVER, 16mm, 0.29-0.33 g

KM#	Year	Mintage	Fine	VF	XF	Unc
243	2	—	20.00	40.00	70.00	160.00
	3	—	15.00	25.00	50.00	125.00
	4	—	15.00	25.00	50.00	125.00
	5	—	20.00	35.00	60.00	150.00
	6	—	10.00	20.00	35.00	75.00
	7	—	7.50	15.00	30.00	60.00
	8	—	6.00	12.50	25.00	40.00
	9	—	6.00	12.50	25.00	50.00

.900 SILVER, 0.30-0.33 g

243a	10	—	7.50	12.50	25.00	50.00
	11	—	7.50	12.50	25.00	50.00
	12	—	12.50	20.00	40.00	75.00
	13	—	12.50	20.00	40.00	75.00
	14	—	15.00	25.00	60.00	125.00
	15	—	22.50	40.00	80.00	175.00
	16	—	20.00	35.00	75.00	150.00

20 PARA

BRONZE, 29.5-32mm, 12.10-12.70 g
Accession Date: AH1277
Obv: W/o flower at right of toughra.

244	3	—	2.50	5.00	20.00	50.00
	4	—	2.50	5.00	20.00	50.00
	5	—	1.50	3.00	15.00	35.00
	6	—	1.50	3.00	15.00	35.00
	8	—	2.00	4.00	17.50	45.00
	9	—	1.00	2.00	12.00	35.00
	10	—	2.00	4.00	17.50	45.00

12.50 g
Similar, but crude & thick, (struck at Cairo).

| 245 | 7 | 1.190 | 150.00 | 250.00 | 400.00 | 1250. |

COPPER, 12.50 g
Obv: Flower at right of toughra.

KM#	Year	Mintage	Fine	VF	XF	Unc
246	8	2.395	15.00	30.00	60.00	175.00
	9	3.089	10.00	25.00	50.00	135.00
	10	.966	12.00	30.00	75.00	145.00
	11	200 pcs.	—	—	Rare	2000.

.833 SILVER, 15-16mm, 0.65-0.70 g

247	1	—	50.00	100.00	175.00	350.00
	2	—	25.00	50.00	100.00	175.00
	3	—	12.50	25.00	50.00	125.00
	4	—	10.00	20.00	45.00	100.00
	5	—	12.50	30.00	60.00	125.00
	6	—	10.00	20.00	45.00	100.00
	7	—	7.50	15.00	35.00	85.00
	8	—	6.00	12.00	25.00	50.00
	9	—	6.00	12.00	20.00	50.00

.900 SILVER, 0.65-0.70 g

247a	10	—	6.00	12.00	25.00	50.00
	11	—	6.00	12.00	25.00	50.00
	12	—	6.00	12.00	25.00	50.00
	13	—	10.00	20.00	40.00	80.00
	14	—	10.00	20.00	40.00	80.00
	15	—	20.00	40.00	80.00	150.00
	16	—	—	Reported, not confirmed		

40 PARA
(1 Qirsh)

BRONZE, 37mm, 25.63 g
Accession Date: AH1277
2 Vars: Large or small toughra.

| 248 | 10 | — | 3.00 | 7.50 | 25.00 | 95.00 |

COPPER, 36mm, 24.00 g
Obv: Flower added at right of toughra.

249	9	125 pcs.	—	—	Rare	—
	10	.150	500.00	700.00	1000.	—
	11	200 pcs.	—	—	Rare	—

NOTE: An example of year 10 struck in gold is reported, not confirmed.

QIRSH

.833 SILVER, 18mm, 1.18-1.25 g
Accession Date: AH1277

250	1	—	30.00	50.00	100.00	250.00
	2	—	20.00	35.00	75.00	150.00
	3	—	15.00	25.00	50.00	100.00
	4	—	15.00	25.00	50.00	100.00
	5	—	20.00	35.00	75.00	150.00
	6	—	12.50	25.00	45.00	90.00
	7	—	10.00	20.00	40.00	80.00
	8	—	5.00	10.00	20.00	50.00
	9	—	5.00	10.00	20.00	50.00

.900 SILVER, 1.18-1.23 g

250a	10	—	5.00	10.00	20.00	60.00
	11/10	—	6.00	12.00	25.00	65.00
	11	—	5.00	10.00	20.00	50.00
	12	—	5.00	10.00	20.00	50.00
	13	—	7.50	15.00	35.00	75.00
	14	—	7.50	15.00	35.00	75.00
	15	—	5.00	10.00	20.00	50.00
	16	—	5.00	10.00	20.00	50.00

Mule. Obv: KM#250a. Rev: KM#277.
Accession Date: Error: AH1293

| 250b | 1 | — | — | — | Rare | — |

2-1/2 QIRSH

3.1500 g, .833 SILVER, .0844 oz ASW
Accession Date: AH1277
Obv: W/o flower at right of toughra.
20mm

KM#	Year	Mintage	Fine	VF	XF	Unc
251	4	3.803	40.00	85.00	125.00	300.00

3.5000 g, .833 SILVER, .0938 oz ASW
Obv: Flower at right of toughra.
22mm

252	8	—	175.00	275.00	375.00	650.00
	9	—	150.00	250.00	350.00	600.00

3.6000 g, .900 SILVER, .1013 oz ASW

252a	10	—	150.00	250.00	350.00	600.00
	11	—	300.00	450.00	900.00	1500.
	12	—	350.00	550.00	1000.	1800.
	13	—	350.00	550.00	1000.	1800.
	15	—	600.00	1000.	1800.	3000.

5 QIRSH

6.2000 g, .833 SILVER, .1661 oz ASW
Accession Date: AH1277
Obv: W/o flower at right of toughra.
25-26mm

253.1	4	4.108	35.00	75.00	110.00	350.00

Rev: Regnal year retrograde.

253.2	4	—	60.00	125.00	175.00	450.00

6.60-7.00 g
Obv: Flower at right of toughra.

254	1	—	225.00	400.00	700.00	1200.
	2	—	150.00	300.00	550.00	800.00
	3	—	150.00	300.00	550.00	800.00
	4	—	175.00	350.00	650.00	1000.
	5	—	200.00	400.00	700.00	1250.
	6	—	200.00	400.00	700.00	1250.
	7	—	200.00	400.00	700.00	1250.
	8	—	150.00	250.00	350.00	750.00
	9	—	150.00	350.00	350.00	750.00
	10	—	300.00	500.00	700.00	1500.

.900 SILVER, 6.60-7.00 g

254a	10	—	150.00	400.00	750.00	750.00
	11	—	200.00	400.00	750.00	1250.
	12	—	200.00	400.00	750.00	1250.
	13	—	200.00	400.00	750.00	1250.
	15	—	200.00	400.00	750.00	1250.

0.4272 g, .875 GOLD, .0120 oz AGW

KM#	Year	Mintage	VG	Fine	VF	XF
255	3	—	20.00	30.00	40.00	65.00
	4	—	20.00	30.00	40.00	65.00
	5	—	20.00	30.00	40.00	65.00
	6	—	20.00	30.00	40.00	65.00
	7	—	20.00	30.00	40.00	65.00
	8	—	20.00	30.00	40.00	65.00
	9	—	20.00	30.00	40.00	65.00
	10	—	20.00	30.00	40.00	65.00
	11	—	20.00	30.00	40.00	65.00
	12	—	20.00	30.00	40.00	65.00
	13	—	20.00	30.00	40.00	65.00
	14	—	20.00	30.00	40.00	65.00
	15	—	20.00	30.00	40.00	65.00

10 QIRSH

14.0000 g, .900 SILVER, .4051 oz ASW
Accession Date: AH1277
Obv: Flower at right of toughra.
29mm

256	2	—	200.00	350.00	600.00	1250.
	3	—	200.00	350.00	600.00	1250.
	4	—	200.00	350.00	600.00	1250.

12.5000 g, .833 SILVER, .3617 oz ASW
Obv: W/o flower at right of toughra.

KM#	Year	Mintage	Fine	VF	XF	Unc
257	4	3.803	50.00	100.00	175.00	450.00

14.0000 g, .900 SILVER, .4051 oz ASW
Similar to Y#10a.

KM#	Year	Mintage	VG	Fine	VF	XF
258	10	—	300.00	600.00	1000.	2000.
	11	—	—	—	Rare	—

0.8554 g, .875 GOLD, .0240 oz AGW

259	10	—	50.00	75.00	90.00	115.00
	11	—	50.00	75.00	90.00	115.00
	12	—	50.00	75.00	90.00	115.00
	14	—	50.00	75.00	90.00	115.00

20 QIRSH

28.0000 g, .833 SILVER, .7500 oz ASW
Accession Date: AH1277
37mm

260	1	—	200.00	350.00	850.00	1250.
	2	—	225.00	400.00	1000.	1500.

28.0000 g, .900 SILVER, .8103 oz ASW

260a	11	—	—	—	Rare	—

25 QIRSH
(1/4 Pound)

2.1360 g, .875 GOLD, .0601 oz AGW

Accession Date: AH1277

KM#	Year	Mintage	VG	Fine	VF	XF
261	8	—	35.00	50.00	75.00	125.00
	9	—	35.00	50.00	75.00	125.00
	10	—	35.00	50.00	75.00	125.00
	11	—	35.00	50.00	75.00	125.00
	12	—	35.00	50.00	75.00	125.00
	13	—	50.00	75.00	125.00	175.00
	14	—	50.00	75.00	125.00	175.00
	15	—	50.00	75.00	125.00	175.00

50 QIRSH
(1/2 Pound)

4.2740 g, .875 GOLD, .1202 oz AGW
Accession Date: AH1277

262	11	—	85.00	125.00	250.00	350.00
	12	—	85.00	125.00	250.00	350.00
	13	—	85.00	125.00	250.00	350.00
	14	—	85.00	125.00	250.00	350.00
	15	—	85.00	125.00	250.00	350.00
	16	—	85.00	125.00	250.00	350.00

100 QIRSH
(1 Pound)

8.5440 g, .875 GOLD, .2404 oz AGW
Accession Date: AH1277
Obv: Flower at right of toughra.

263	1	—	—	Reported, not confirmed		
	2	—	150.00	175.00	225.00	300.00
	3	—	—	Reported, not confirmed		
	4	—	BV	125.00	175.00	250.00
	5	—	BV	125.00	175.00	250.00
	6	—	BV	125.00	175.00	250.00
	7	—	BV	125.00	175.00	250.00
	8	—	BV	125.00	175.00	250.00
	9	—	BV	125.00	175.00	250.00
	10	—	BV	125.00	175.00	250.00
	11	—	BV	125.00	175.00	250.00
	12	—	BV	125.00	175.00	250.00
	13	—	BV	125.00	175.00	250.00
	14	—	150.00	200.00	265.00	350.00
	15	—	BV	125.00	175.00	250.00
	16	—	150.00	200.00	265.00	350.00

Obv: W/o flower at right of toughra.

264	4	.020	150.00	350.00	750.00	1000.

500 QIRSH
(5 Pounds)

42.7200 g, .875 GOLD, 1.2018 oz AGW
Accession Date: AH1277

KM#	Year	Mintage	Fine	VF	XF	Unc
265	8	118 pcs.	3500.	7500.	12,500.	17,500.
	9	Inc. Ab.	3000.	6000.	10,000.	15,000.
	11	200 pcs.	3000.	6000.	10,000.	15,000.
	15	56 pcs.	3000.	6000.	10,000.	15,000.

MURAD V
AH1293/1876AD

QIRSH

.900 SILVER, 18mm, 1.20 g
Accession Date: AH1293
Obv: Toughra of Murad V.

KM#	Year	Mintage	Fine	VF	XF	Unc
270	1	—	100.00	150.00	300.00	450.00

50 QIRSH
(1/2 Egyptian Pound)

4.2740 g, .875 GOLD, .1202 oz AGW
Accession Date: AH1293
Obv: Toughra of Murad V.

KM#	Year	Mintage	VG	Fine	VF	XF
271	1	—	400.00	650.00	1000.	1500.

100 QIRSH
(1 Egyptian Pound)

8.5440 g, .875 GOLD, .2402 oz AGW
Accession Date: AH1293
Obv: Toughra of Murad V.

272	1	—	250.00	750.00	1250.	1750.

ABDUL HAMID II
AH1293-1327/1876-1909AD

1/40 QIRSH

BRONZE
Accession Date: AH1293

KM#	Year	Mintage	Fine	VF	XF	Unc
287	10	1.669	.50	1.50	4.00	10.00
	12	2.476	.50	1.50	3.00	10.00
	18	—	40.00	60.00	100.00	160.00
	19	—	.75	1.50	5.00	15.00
	20	—	5.00	10.00	20.00	40.00
	24	1.601	.75	1.50	4.00	12.50
	26	1.999	.50	1.00	3.00	10.00
	27	1.200	1.00	1.50	4.00	12.50
	29	2.000	.50	1.00	3.00	10.00
	31H	2.400	.50	1.00	3.00	10.00
	32H	Inc. Be.	.50	1.00	3.00	10.00
	33H	1.200	.50	1.00	2.00	7.00
	35H	1.200	2.00	4.00	7.50	15.00

1/20 QIRSH

BRONZE
Accession Date: AH1293

KM#	Year	Mintage	Fine	VF	XF	Unc
288	10	4.105	.50	1.50	4.00	10.00
	12	4.457	.50	1.50	4.00	10.00
	18	—	10.00	20.00	30.00	75.00
	19	—	2.50	5.00	10.00	20.00
	20	—	8.00	15.00	30.00	75.00
	21	—	2.00	3.50	10.00	20.00
	24	.801	1.00	3.00	5.00	15.00
	26	1.405	.75	1.50	3.00	10.00
	27	1.402	.75	1.50	3.00	10.00
	29	3.200	.50	1.00	3.00	10.00
	31H	3.000	.50	1.00	3.00	10.00
	32H	Inc. Be.	.50	1.00	3.00	10.00
	33H	1.400	1.00	2.00	5.00	15.00
	35H	1.400	2.00	5.00	10.00	20.00

1/10 QIRSH

COPPER-NICKEL
Accession Date: AH1293

KM#	Year	Mintage	Fine	VF	XF	Unc
289	10	2.307	.50	1.00	4.00	12.50
	12	3.435	.50	1.00	4.00	12.50
	18	—	6.00	12.00	30.00	75.00
	19	—	.50	1.00	5.00	15.00

KM#	Year	Mintage	Fine	VF	XF	Unc
289	20	—	.50	1.00	5.00	15.00
	21	—	.50	1.00	5.00	15.00
	22	—	4.00	10.00	20.00	60.00
	23	—	.50	1.00	6.00	17.50
	24	1.005	.50	1.00	4.00	12.50
	25	2.000	.50	1.00	5.00	15.00
	27	3.010	.40	.75	3.00	10.00
	28	6.000	.50	1.00	3.00	10.00
	29	1.500	.75	1.50	4.00	15.00
	30	1.000	.50	1.00	3.00	12.50
	31H	3.000	.75	1.50	4.00	15.00
	32H	Inc. Be.	.50	1.00	3.00	12.50
	33H	2.000	.40	.75	2.50	8.50
	35H	2.000	1.00	3.00	6.00	20.00

2/10 QIRSH

COPPER-NICKEL
Accession Date: AH1293

290	10	3.201	1.00	3.00	6.00	20.00
	12	2.009	1.00	3.00	6.00	20.00
	20	—	8.00	15.00	30.00	75.00
	21	.500	2.00	6.00	12.00	40.00
	24	.500	1.00	3.00	6.00	20.00
	25	.250	3.00	5.00	10.00	35.00
	27	1.002	1.00	3.00	6.00	20.00
	28	2.000	1.00	3.00	6.00	20.00
	29	1.500	1.00	3.00	6.00	20.00
	30	—	3.00	6.00	12.00	40.00
	31H	1.000	1.00	2.50	6.00	20.00
	33H	1.500	1.00	2.50	6.00	20.00
	35H	.750	2.00	6.00	10.00	35.00

10 PARA

.833 SILVER
Accession Date: AH1293

275	1	—	75.00	100.00	160.00	325.00
	2	—	80.00	120.00	180.00	430.00
	3	—	75.00	100.00	160.00	325.00

20 PARA

0.5500 g, .833 SILVER, .0147 oz ASW
Accession Date: AH1293

276	1	—	75.00	135.00	175.00	425.00
	2	—	70.00	125.00	140.00	400.00
	3	—	75.00	135.00	175.00	425.00
	5	—	—	—	750.00	1000.

5/10 QIRSH

COPPER-NICKEL
Accession Date: AH1293

291	10	7.003	2.00	4.00	12.50	40.00
	11	10.005	.50	2.00	6.00	20.00
	13	5.003	.50	2.00	6.00	20.00
	20	1.002	3.00	10.00	20.00	60.00
	21	3.404	.65	2.50	7.50	25.00
	23	1.000	2.50	5.00	12.50	40.00
	24	3.605	.45	2.00	6.00	20.00
	25	1.998	.45	2.00	6.00	20.00
	27	4.999	.30	1.50	5.00	20.00
	29	12.000	.30	1.50	5.00	20.00
	30	2.000	.50	2.00	6.00	25.00
	33H	1.000	2.00	6.00	12.50	40.00
	Common date		—	—	Proof	145.00

QIRSH

.833 SILVER
Accession Date: AH1293

KM#	Year	Mintage	Fine	VF	XF	Unc
277	1	—	3.00	12.00	25.00	75.00
	2	—	3.00	12.00	20.00	60.00
277	3	—	2.50	10.00	17.50	50.00
	4	—	3.00	12.00	20.00	60.00
	5	—	4.00	15.00	25.00	75.00

1.4000 g, .833 SILVER, .0375 oz ASW

292	10 W	8.192	1.00	3.00	7.50	20.00
	17 W	.546	1.00	4.00	10.00	30.00
	27 W	.200	1.25	4.00	10.00	27.50
	29 W	.100	1.50	4.00	10.00	30.00
	29H	.100	1.25	3.00	7.50	25.00
	33H	.100	1.25	3.00	7.50	25.00
	33H	—	—	—	Proof	120.00
	Common date		—	—	Proof	120.00

COPPER-NICKEL

299	22	.200	10.00	25.00	45.00	100.00
	23	1.500	2.00	6.00	20.00	50.00
	25	.751	3.00	8.00	30.00	60.00
	27	.999	2.00	6.00	20.00	50.00
	29	3.500	2.00	5.00	15.00	40.00
	30	.500	2.50	6.00	20.00	55.00
	33H	1.000	2.00	5.00	15.00	40.00

2 QIRSH

2.8000 g, .833 SILVER, .0750 oz ASW
Accession Date: AH1293
Obv: Flower to right of toughra.

293	10 W	4.011	1.00	3.00	7.50	25.00
	11 W	.989	2.00	5.00	12.50	30.00
	17 W	.540	2.00	5.00	12.50	30.00
	19 W	—	—	Reported, not confirmed		
	20 W	1.113	2.00	5.00	12.50	35.00
	24 W	.500	2.00	5.00	12.50	45.00
	27 W	1.000	2.00	4.00	10.00	30.00
	29 W	.450	2.00	4.00	10.00	30.00
	29H	1.250	2.00	4.00	10.00	30.00
	30H	.500	3.00	6.00	15.00	35.00
	31H	Inc. Ab.	3.00	6.00	15.00	35.00
	33H	.450	2.00	4.00	10.00	30.00
	Common date		—	—	Proof	165.00

2-1/2 QIRSH

3.4600 g, .833 SILVER, .0927 oz ASW
Accession Date: AH1293

278	6	2 pcs.	—	—	—	4500.

5 QIRSH

6.9200 g, .833 SILVER, .1854 oz ASW
Accession Date: AH1293
Obv: Flower at right of toughra.

279	2	—	1000.	1400.	—	—
	6	2 pcs.	—	—	—	4000.

7.0000 g, .833 SILVER, .1875 oz ASW

KM#	Year	Mintage	Fine	VF	XF	Unc
294	10 W	4.195	3.00	7.50	15.00	50.00
	11 W	Inc. Ab.	4.00	10.00	25.00	75.00
	15 W	.600	8.00	20.00	40.00	125.00
	16 W	1.205	5.00	12.50	25.00	75.00
	17 W	.872	6.00	15.00	30.00	100.00
	19 W	—	—	Reported, not confirmed		
	20 W	.464	10.00	25.00	50.00	125.00
	21 W	.633	5.00	12.50	20.00	60.00
	22 W	1.118	5.00	12.50	20.00	60.00
	24 W	1.050	5.00	12.50	20.00	60.00
	27 W	.448	5.00	12.50	20.00	50.00
	29 W	.600	5.00	10.00	20.00	50.00
	29 H	3.465	5.00	10.00	20.00	50.00
	30 H	1.213	5.00	10.00	22.50	60.00
	31 H	1.959	5.00	10.00	22.50	60.00
	32 H	Inc.Be.	5.00	10.00	20.00	50.00
	33 H	2.800	3.00	7.50	20.00	60.00
	Common date	—	—	—	Proof	260.00

0.4200 g, .875 GOLD, .0118 oz AGW
Obv: Flower at right of toughra.

KM#	Year	Mintage	VG	Fine	VF	XF
280	1	—	—	Reported, not confirmed		
	2	—	200.00	300.00	500.00	1000.
	3	—	40.00	65.00	75.00	100.00
	4	—	—	Reported, not confirmed		
	5	—	100.00	150.00	200.00	250.00
	6	—	150.00	250.00	400.00	650.00
	7	—	40.00	65.00	75.00	100.00

Obv: Al-Ghazi right of toughra.
Rev: Wreath border.

| A298 | 15 | — | 150.00 | 250.00 | 400.00 | 650.00 |

Obv: Al-Ghazi at right of toughra.

298	7	—	—	Reported, not confirmed		
	15	—	100.00	200.00	325.00	600.00
	16	—	15.00	25.00	40.00	65.00
	18	—	15.00	25.00	40.00	65.00
	24	—	25.00	50.00	100.00	150.00
	26	—	25.00	50.00	100.00	150.00
	34	.008	20.00	30.00	40.00	75.00

NOTE: Varieties of borders exist for year 15.

10 QIRSH

14.0000 g, .833 SILVER, .3749 oz ASW
Accession Date: AH1293
Obv: Flower at right of toughra.

KM#	Year	Mintage	Fine	VF	XF	Unc
281	6	2 pcs.	—	—	—	6000.

295	10 W	4.030	5.00	10.00	30.00	100.00
	11 W	Inc. Ab.	8.00	15.00	35.00	100.00
	15 W	.300	15.00	30.00	60.00	150.00
	15 W	—	—	—	Proof	400.00
	16 W	.602	8.00	15.00	40.00	125.00
	17 W	.380	10.00	20.00	45.00	150.00
	20 W	.340	15.00	30.00	45.00	150.00
	21 W	.420	10.00	20.00	40.00	125.00
	22 W	.600	10.00	20.00	40.00	125.00
	24 W	.500	10.00	20.00	40.00	125.00
	27 W	.250	15.00	25.00	50.00	150.00
	29 W	*2.450	8.00	15.00	35.00	100.00
	29 H	2.950	8.00	15.00	30.00	100.00
	30 H	1.000	8.00	15.00	30.00	100.00
	31 H	1.250	10.00	20.00	40.00	150.00
	32 H	Inc.Be.	8.00	15.00	30.00	100.00
	33 H	2.400	8.00	12.50	30.00	100.00
	Common date	—	—	—	Proof	400.00

*Estimated.

0.8544 g, .875 GOLD, .0240 oz AGW

Obv: Al-Ghazi at right of toughra.

KM#	Year	Mintage	VG	Fine	VF	XF
282	4	—	300.00	500.00	750.00	1100.
	5	—	—	Reported, not confirmed		
	7	—	—	Reported, not confirmed		
	8	—	—	Reported, not confirmed		
	17	—	20.00	40.00	60.00	100.00
	18	—	25.00	50.00	75.00	125.00
	23	—	40.00	60.00	100.00	185.00
	34	.005	20.00	40.00	60.00	100.00

20 QIRSH

.833 SILVER, 37mm, 27.57 g
Accession Date: AH1293

283	1	—	550.00	900.00	1500.	2000.
	5	—	575.00	950.00	1600.	2225.
	6	2 pcs.	—	—	—	12,500.

28.0000 g, .833 SILVER, .7499 oz ASW

KM#	Year	Mintage	Fine	VF	XF	Unc
296	10 W	.874	12.00	25.00	60.00	350.00
	11 W	.126	15.00	40.00	80.00	425.00
	15 W	.029	17.50	40.00	125.00	500.00
	16 W	.055	15.00	40.00	80.00	425.00
	17 W	.054	17.50	50.00	125.00	500.00
	17 W	—	—	—	Proof	650.00
	20 W	.172	12.00	40.00	80.00	425.00
	21 W	.158	12.00	30.00	70.00	375.00
	22 W	.287	12.00	30.00	70.00	375.00
	24 W	.500	12.00	30.00	70.00	375.00
	27 W	.250	15.00	40.00	80.00	425.00
	29 W	.500	12.00	30.00	70.00	375.00
	29 H	.425	12.00	30.00	70.00	375.00
	30 H	.200	12.00	30.00	70.00	375.00
	31 H	.250	12.00	30.00	70.00	375.00
	32 H	Inc.Be.	12.00	30.00	70.00	375.00
	33 H	.300	12.00	30.00	70.00	375.00
	Common date	—	—	—	Proof	825.00

25 QIRSH
SILVER
Accession Date: AH1293
Obv: Flower right of toughra.

| A284 | 6 | 2 pcs. | — | — | Reported, not confirmed | |

50 QIRSH
(1/2 Pound)

4.2740 g, .875 GOLD, .1202 oz AGW
Accession Date: AH1293

KM#	Year	Mintage	VG	Fine	VF	XF
284	2	—	—	Reported, not confirmed		
	3	—	—	Reported, not confirmed		
	6	2 pcs.	—	—	—	14,300.

NOTE: Previously reported year 1 examples are those of Murad V.

100 QIRSH
(1 Pound)

8.5440 g, .875 GOLD, .2404 oz AGW
Accession Date: AH1293
Obv: Toughra of Abdul Hamid II.

KM#	Year	Mintage	Fine	VF	XF	Unc
285	1	—	400.00	800.00	1350.	2250.
	3	—	—	Reported, not confirmed		
	5	—	—	Reported, not confirmed		
	6	4 pcs.	—	—	—	14,850.
	8	—	—	—	—	Rare

8.5000 g, .875 GOLD, .2391 oz AGW
Floral border.

| 297 | 12 | .052 | 125.00 | 150.00 | 200.00 | 300.00 |

500 QIRSH
(5 Pounds)

42.7400 g, .875 GOLD, 1.2024 oz AGW
Accession Date: AH1293

286	1	—	1250.	3000.	5000.	7500.
	6	5 pcs.	—	—	—	26,400.

MUHAMMAD V
AH1327-1332/1909-1914AD

1/40 QIRSH

BRONZE
Accession Date: AH1327

300	2H	2.000	1.50	3.00	7.50	25.00
	3H	2.000	1.50	3.00	7.50	25.00
	4H	1.200	1.50	3.00	7.50	25.00
	6H	1.200	1.00	2.00	5.00	20.00

1/20 QIRSH

BRONZE
Accession Date: AH1327

301	2H	2.000	1.00	3.00	5.00	15.00
	3H	2.000	1.50	4.00	7.00	20.00
	4H	2.400	1.00	3.00	5.00	15.00
	6H	1.400	.75	2.00	5.00	15.00

1/10 QIRSH

COPPER-NICKEL
Accession Date: AH1327

302	2H	3.000	3.00	6.00	10.00	25.00
	3	1.000	5.00	12.00	20.00	50.00
	4H	3.000	1.00	2.00	4.00	12.50
	6H	3.000	.75	1.50	3.00	12.50
	Common date—	—	—	Proof	110.00

2/10 QIRSH

EGYPT 504

COPPER-NICKEL
Accession Date: AH1327

KM#	Year	Mintage	Fine	VF	XF	Unc
303	2H	1.000	2.00	4.00	7.00	25.00
	3	.500	10.00	15.00	25.00	50.00
	4H	1.000	2.00	4.00	7.00	25.00
	6H	—	1.25	3.00	7.00	25.00
	Common date—	—	—	—	Proof	120.00

5/10 QIRSH

 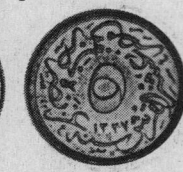

COPPER-NICKEL
Accession Date: AH1327

304	2H	2.131	2.50	6.00	15.00	50.00
	3	1.000	5.00	15.00	35.00	75.00
	4H	3.327	1.00	2.50	6.00	25.00
	6H	3.000	1.00	2.50	6.00	25.00

QIRSH

1.4000 g, .833 SILVER, .0375 oz ASW
Accession Date: AH1327

305	2H	.251	2.00	4.00	17.50	27.50
	3H	.171	2.25	4.50	17.50	35.00

COPPER-NICKEL

306	2H	1.000	2.00	6.00	15.00	40.00
	3	.300	20.00	40.00	75.00	150.00
	4H	.500	4.00	10.00	25.00	75.00
	6H	2.500	2.00	5.00	10.00	30.00

2 QIRSH

2.8000 g, .833 SILVER, .0750 oz ASW
Accession Date: AH1327

307	2H	.250	6.00	15.00	30.00	100.00
	3H	.300	6.00	15.00	30.00	100.00

5 QIRSH

7.0000 g, .833 SILVER, .1875 oz ASW
Accession Date: AH1327

308	2H	.574	10.00	30.00	60.00	150.00
	3H	2.400	5.00	12.50	30.00	65.00
	4H	1.351	6.00	15.00	35.00	85.00
	6H	7.400	4.00	10.00	20.00	55.00
	Common date—	—	—	—	Proof	375.00

10 QIRSH

14.0000 g, .833 SILVER, .3749 oz ASW
Accession Date: AH1327

KM#	Year	Mintage	Fine	VF	XF	Unc
309	2H	.300	20.00	30.00	60.00	200.00
	3H	1.300	8.00	15.00	30.00	100.00
	4H	.300	10.00	25.00	40.00	200.00
	6H	4.212	6.00	12.50	25.00	100.00
	Common date—	—	—	—	Proof	475.00

20 QIRSH

28.0000 g, .833 SILVER, .7499 oz ASW
Accession Date: AH1327

310	2H	.075	30.00	50.00	150.00	500.00
	3H	.600	15.00	30.00	75.00	300.00
	4H	.100	25.00	40.00	75.00	400.00
	6H	.875	12.50	25.00	55.00	300.00
	Common date—	—	—	—	Proof	950.00

BRITISH OCCUPATION
1914-1922

HUSSEIN KAMIL
AH1333-1336/1914-1917AD

1/2 MILLIEME

BRONZE
Accession Date: AH1333

KM#	Date	Year	Mintage	VF	XF	Unc
312	AH1335	1916	—	—	—	—
	1335	1917	4.000	3.50	7.50	25.00

MILLIEME

COPPER-NICKEL
Accession Date: AH1333

313	AH1335	1917	4.002	3.00	6.00	20.00
	1335	1917H	12.000	1.00	2.50	12.50

2 MILLIEMES

COPPER-NICKEL
Accession Date: AH1333

314	AH1335	1916H	.300	3.00	7.50	30.00
	1335	1917	3.006	2.50	6.00	20.00
	1335	1917H	9.000	1.00	3.00	12.50

5 MILLIEMES

COPPER-NICKEL
Accession Date: AH1333

315	AH1335	1916	3.000	5.00	10.00	30.00
	1335	1916H	3.000	3.00	8.00	25.00
	1335	1917	6.776	2.00	6.00	20.00
	1335	1917H	37.000	1.00	2.00	15.00

10 MILLIEMES

COPPER-NICKEL
Accession Date: AH1333

KM#	Date	Year	Mintage	VF	XF	Unc
316	AH1335	1916	1.007	5.00	10.00	40.00
	1335	1916H	1.000	4.00	8.00	30.00
	1335	1917	1.011	5.00	15.00	50.00
	1335	1917H	6.000	2.00	4.00	20.00
	1335	1917KN	4.000	3.00	6.00	25.00

2 PIASTRES

2.8000 g, .833 SILVER, .0749 oz ASW
Accession Date: AH1333

317.1	AH1335	1916	2.505	4.00	10.00	30.00
	1335	1917	4.461	2.00	5.00	20.00

W/o inner circle.

317.2	AH1335	1917H	2.180	2.00	5.00	20.00

5 PIASTRES

7.0000 g, .833 SILVER, .1874 oz ASW
Accession Date: AH1333

318.1	AH1335	1916	6.000	5.00	15.00	40.00
	1335	1917	9.218	4.00	12.50	35.00

W/o inner circle.

318.2	AH1335	1917H	5.036	4.00	12.50	45.00
	1335	1917H	—	—	Proof	300.00

10 PIASTRES

14.0000 g, .833 SILVER, .3749 oz ASW
Accession Date: AH1333

319	AH1335	1916	2.900	10.00	25.00	100.00
	1335	1917	4.859	10.00	20.00	75.00

W/o inner circle.

320	AH1335	1917H	2.000	10.00	30.00	125.00

20 PIASTRES

28.0000 g, .833 SILVER, .7499 oz ASW
Accession Date: AH1333

KM#	Date	Year	Mintage	VF	XF	Unc
321	AH1335	1916	1.500	20.00	35.00	175.00
	1335	1917	.840	20.00	35.00	200.00
	1335	1917	—	—	Proof	Rare

W/o inner circle.

| 322 | AH1335 | 1917H | .250 | 40.00 | 75.00 | 300.00 |

100 PIASTRES

8.5000 g, .875 GOLD, .2391 oz AGW
Accession Date: AH1333

| 324 | AH1335 | 1916 | .010 | 150.00 | 200.00 | 300.00 |

NOTE: Restrikes may exist.

FAUD I
Sultan, AH1336-1341/1917-1922AD

2 PIASTRES

2.8000 g, .833 SILVER, .0749 oz ASW
Accession Date: AH1335

| 325 | AH1338 | 1920H | 2.820 | 75.00 | 150.00 | 350.00 |

5 PIASTRES

7.0000 g, .833 SILVER, .1874 oz ASW
Accession Date: AH1335

| 326 | AH1338 | 1920H | 1.000 | 50.00 | 100.00 | 350.00 |

10 PIASTRES

14.0000 g, .833 SILVER, .3749 oz ASW
Accession Date: AH1335

| 327 | AH1338 | 1920H | .500 | 35.00 | 75.00 | 350.00 |

20 PIASTRES

28.0000 g, .833 SILVER, .7499 oz ASW
Accession Date: AH1335

KM#	Date	Year	Mintage	VF	XF	Unc
328	AH1338	1920H	2 known	—	Rare	—

KINGDOM
1922-1952

FAUD I
King, AH1341-1355/1922-1936AD

1/2 MILLIEME

BRONZE

| 330 | AH1342 | 1924H | 3.000 | 5.00 | 10.00 | 25.00 |

343	AH1348	1929BP	1.000	15.00	25.00	50.00
	1351	1932H	1.000	7.50	15.00	30.00
	1351	1932H	—	—	Proof	150.00

MILLIEME

BRONZE

| 331 | AH1342 | 1924H | 6.500 | 3.00 | 7.50 | 25.00 |

344	AH1348	1929BP	4.500	4.00	10.00	25.00
	1351	1932H	2.500	1.25	3.00	15.00
	1352	1933H	5.110	3.00	10.00	20.00
	1354	1935H	18.000	.50	2.00	8.00

2 MILLIEMES

COPPER-NICKEL

| 332 | AH1342 | 1924H | 4.500 | 3.00 | 10.00 | 25.00 |
| | 1342 | 1924H | — | — | Proof | 85.00 |

| 345 | AH1348 | 1929BP | 3.500? | 1.00 | 3.00 | 10.00 |

2-1/2 MILLIEMES

COPPER-NICKEL

KM#	Date	Year	Mintage	VF	XF	Unc
356	AH1352	1933	4.000	3.00	8.00	30.00

5 MILLIEMES

COPPER-NICKEL

| 333 | AH1342 | 1924 | 6.000 | 3.00 | 7.50 | 27.50 |

346	AH1348	1929BP	4.000	2.00	8.00	25.00
	1352	1933H	3.000	4.00	12.00	35.00
	1354	1935H	8.000	1.00	5.00	12.50

10 MILLIEMES

COPPER-NICKEL

| 334 | AH1342 | 1924 | 2.000 | 5.00 | 15.00 | 50.00 |

347	AH1348	1929BP	1.500	4.00	10.00	35.00
	1352	1933H	4.000	4.00	10.00	45.00
	1354	1935H	4.000	2.00	7.50	20.00

2 PIASTRES

2.8000 g, .833 SILVER, .0749 oz ASW

| 335 | AH1342 | 1923H | 2.500 | 4.00 | 10.00 | 30.00 |

| 348 | AH1348 | 1929BP | .500 | 2.00 | 4.00 | 17.50 |

NOTE: Edge varieties exist.

5 PIASTRES

7.0000 g, .833 SILVER, .1874 oz ASW

336	AH1341	1923	.800	10.00	25.00	50.00
	1341	1923H	1.800	6.00	20.00	50.00
	1341	1923H	—	—	Proof	225.00

EGYPT 506

KM#	Date	Year	Mintage	VF	XF	Unc
349	AH1348	1929BP	.800	10.00	35.00	60.00
	1352	1933	1.300	7.50	25.00	50.00
	1352	1933	—	—	Proof	250.00

10 PIASTRES

14.0000 g, .833 SILVER, .3749 oz ASW

337	AH1341	1923	.400	10.00	32.50	100.00
	1341	1923H	1.000	10.00	32.50	100.00
	1341	1923H	—	—	Proof	450.00

350	AH1348	1929BP	.400	12.50	32.50	100.00
	1352	1933	.350(?)	10.00	25.00	65.00
	1352	1933	—	—	Proof	—

20 PIASTRES

28.0000 g, .833 SILVER, .7499 oz ASW

338	AH1341	1923	.100	30.00	75.00	325.00
	1341	1923H	.050	30.00	75.00	325.00
	1341	1923H	—	—	Proof	800.00

1.7000 g, .875 GOLD, .0478 oz AGW

339	AH1341	1923	.065	50.00	65.00	150.00

Obv: Bust left.

351	AH1348	1929	—	50.00	65.00	140.00
	1348	1929	—	—	Proof	—
	1349	1930	—	50.00	65.00	140.00
	1349	1930	—	—	Proof	—

28.0000 g, .833 SILVER, .7499 oz ASW

KM#	Date	Year	Mintage	VF	XF	Unc
352	AH1348	1929BP	.050	35.00	75.00	450.00
	1352	1933	.025	22.50	45.00	250.00
	1352	1933	—	—	Proof	—

50 PIASTRES

4.2500 g, .875 GOLD, .1195 oz AGW

340	AH1341	1923	.018	75.00	100.00	200.00

353	AH1348	1929	—	90.00	120.00	200.00
	1348	1929	—	—	Proof	—
	1349	1930	—	90.00	120.00	200.00
	1349	1930	—	—	Proof	—

100 PIASTRES

8.5000 g, .875 GOLD, .2391 oz AGW

341	AH1340	1922	.025	125.00	175.00	250.00

Obv: Bust left

354	AH1348	1929	—	125.00	175.00	250.00
	1349	1930	—	125.00	175.00	250.00
	1349	1930	—	—	Proof	—

500 PIASTRES

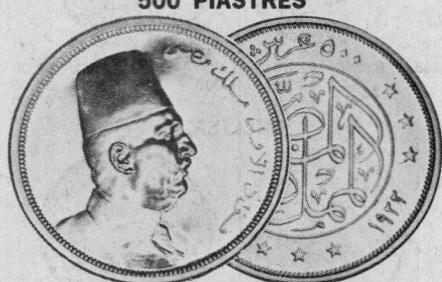

42.5000 g, .875 GOLD, 1.1957 oz AGW

342	AH1340	1922	1,800	—	2000.	2500.
	1340	1922	—	—	Proof	3500.

NOTE: Circulation coins were struck in both red and yellow gold.

355	AH1348	1929	—	—	2000.	2500.
	1349	1930	—	—	2000.	2500.
	1351	1932	—	—	2000.	2500.
	1351	1932	—	—	Proof	3500.

FAROUK I
AH1355-1372/1936-1952AD

1/2 MILLIEME

BRONZE

357	AH1357	1938	4.000	4.00	7.50	20.00
	1357	1938	—	—	Proof	100.00

MILLIEME

BRONZE

KM#	Date	Year	Mintage	VF	XF	Unc
358	AH1357	1938	26.240	.50	2.00	7.00
	1357	1938	—	—	Proof	60.00
	1364	1945	10.000	3.00	10.00	50.00
	1366	1947	—	3.00	10.00	50.00
	1369	1950	5.000	1.00	3.00	10.00
	1369	1950	—	—	Proof	65.00

COPPER-NICKEL

| 362 | AH1357 | 1938 | 3.500 | 2.50 | 5.00 | 15.00 |

2 MILLIEMES

COPPER-NICKEL

| 359 | AH1357 | 1938 | 2.500 | 4.00 | 10.00 | 25.00 |

5 MILLIEMES

BRONZE

360	AH1357	1938	—	1.00	3.00	8.00
	1357	1938	—	—	Proof	40.00
	1362	1943	—	1.00	3.00	8.00

COPPER-NICKEL

363	AH1357	1938	7.000	1.00	3.00	10.00
	1357	1938	—	—	Proof	50.00
	1360	1941	11.500	.50	2.50	8.00

10 MILLIEMES

BRONZE

361	AH1357	1938	—	1.00	3.00	10.00
	1357	1938	—	—	Proof	50.00
	1362	1943	—	.75	3.00	10.00

COPPER-NICKEL

364	AH1357	1938	3.500	1.00	3.00	12.50
	1357	1938	—	—	Proof	65.00
	1360	1941	5.322	1.00	3.00	12.50

2 PIASTRES

2.80000 g, .833 SILVER, .0749 oz ASW

KM#	Date	Year	Mintage	VF	XF	Unc
365	AH1356	1937	.500	1.00	2.50	7.50
	1356	1937	—	—	Proof	—
	1358	1939	.500	4.00	10.00	75.00
	1358	1939	—	—	Proof	—
	1361	1942	10.000	1.50	4.00	10.00
	?	1948	Reported, not confirmed			

NOTE: Rim varieties exist for AH1361 dated coins.

PLATINUM (OMS)

| 365a | AH1361 | 1942 | — | — | Rare | — |

2.8000 g, .500 SILVER, .0450 oz ASW

| 369 | AH1363 | 1944 | .032 | 1.00 | 1.50 | 4.00 |

5 PIASTRES

7.0000 g, .833 SILVER, .1874 oz ASW

366	AH1356	1937	—	3.00	6.00	15.00
	1356	1937	—	—	Proof	225.00
	1358	1939	8.000	3.00	6.00	15.00
	1358	1939	—	—	Proof	225.00

10 PIASTRES

14.0000 g, .833 SILVER, .3749 oz ASW

367	AH1356	1937	2.800	7.50	12.50	35.00
	1356	1937	—	—	Proof	—
	1358	1939	2.850	7.50	12.50	35.00
	1358	1939	—	—	Proof	100.00

20 PIASTRES

28.0000 g, .833 SILVER, .7499 oz ASW

368	AH1356	1937	—	15.00	27.50	80.00
	1356	1937	—	—	Proof	950.00
	1358	1939	—	15.00	27.50	80.00
	1358	1939	—	—	Proof	1150.

1.7000 g, .875 GOLD, .0478 oz AGW
Royal Wedding

| 370 | AH1357 | 1938 | .020 | 55.00 | 90.00 | 140.00 |
| | 1357 | 1938 | — | — | Proof | 250.00 |

50 PIASTRES

4.2500 g, .875 GOLD, .1195 oz AGW
Royal Wedding

KM#	Date	Year	Mintage	VF	XF	Unc
371	AH1357	1938	.010	100.00	125.00	250.00
	1357	1938	—	—	Proof	400.00

100 PIASTRES

8.5000 g, .875 GOLD, .2391 oz AGW
Royal Wedding

| 372 | AH1357 | 1938 | 5.000 | 150.00 | 200.00 | 300.00 |
| | 1357 | 1938 | — | — | Proof | 600.00 |

NOTE: Circulation coins were struck in both red and yellow gold.

500 PIASTRES

42.5000 g, .875 GOLD, 1.1957 oz AGW
Royal Wedding

| 373 | AH1357 | 1938 | — | — | 2000. | 3000. |
| | 1357 | 1938 | — | — | Proof | 3500. |

REPUBLIC
1953-1958

MILLIEME

ALUMINUM-BRONZE
Rev: Small sphinx w/outlined base.

375	AH1373	1954	—	50.00	100.00	200.00
	1374	1954	—	3.00	6.00	25.00
	1374	1955	—	2.00	5.00	15.00
	1375	1955	—	2.00	5.00	15.00
	1375	1956	—	2.00	5.00	15.00

Rev: Small sphinx w/o base outlined.

376	AH1374	1954	—	2.00	5.00	15.00
	1374	1955	—	1.00	2.00	6.00
	1375	1955	—	1.00	2.00	6.00
	1375	1956	—	1.50	2.50	10.00

Rev: Large sphinx.

377	AH1375	1956	—	.50	1.00	4.00
	1376	1957	—	.75	1.50	5.00
	1377	1958	—	.75	1.50	5.00

5 MILLIEMES

ALUMINUM-BRONZE
Rev: Small sphinx

378	AH1373	1954	—	5.00	10.00	35.00
	1374	1954	—	4.00	8.00	25.00
	1374	1955	—	10.00	20.00	50.00
	1375	1956	—	3.00	6.00	15.00

Rev: Large sphinx

KM#	Date	Year	Mintage	VF	XF	Unc
379	AH1376	1957	—	2.00	4.00	10.00
	1377	1957	—	2.00	4.00	10.00
	1377	1958	—	2.00	4.00	10.00

10 MILLIEMES

ALUMINUM-BRONZE
Rev: Small sphinx

380	AH1373	1954	—	5.00	10.00	25.00
	1374	1954	—	4.00	8.00	20.00
	1374	1955	—	3.00	6.00	15.00

Rev: Large sphinx

381	AH1374	1955	—	50.00	85.00	150.00
	1375	1956	—	3.00	6.00	15.00
	1376	1957	—	2.00	5.00	12.00
	1377	1958	—	2.00	5.00	12.00

5 PIASTRES

3.5000 g, .720 SILVER, .0810 oz ASW

382	1375	1956	—	1.50	3.00	6.00
	1376	1956	—	3.00	5.00	10.00
	1376	1957	—	1.50	3.00	6.00

10 PIASTRES

7.0000 g, .625 SILVER, .1406 oz ASW

| 383 | AH1374 | 1955 | 1.408 | 2.50 | 6.00 | 15.00 |

NOTE: Varieties in date sizes exist.

7.0000 g, .720 SILVER, .1620 oz ASW

| 383a | 1375 | 1956 | — | 2.50 | 6.00 | 11.00 |
| | 1376 | 1957 | — | 2.50 | 5.00 | 10.00 |

20 PIASTRES

14.0000 g, .720 SILVER, .3241 oz ASW

| 384 | AH1375 | 1956 | — | 6.00 | 10.00 | 20.00 |

EGYPT 507

25 PIASTRES

17.5000 g., .720 SILVER, .4051 oz ASW
Suez Canal Nationalization

KM#	Date	Year	Mintage	VF	XF	Unc
385	AH1375	1956	.258	7.00	10.00	20.00

National Assembly Inauguration

| 389 | AH1376 | 1957 | .246 | 7.00 | 9.00 | 15.00 |

50 PIASTRES

28.0000 g., .900 SILVER, .8102 oz ASW
Evacuation of the British

| 386 | AH1375 | 1956 | .250 | 7.50 | 15.00 | 27.50 |

POUND

8.5000 g., .875 GOLD, .2391 oz AGW
3rd and 5th Anniversaries of Revolution

| 387 | AH1374 | 1955 | .016 | — | — | 200.00 |
| | 1377 | 1957 | .010 | — | — | 225.00 |

NOTE: Struck in red and yellow gold.

5 POUNDS

42.5000 g., .875 GOLD, 1.1957 oz AGW
3rd and 5th Anniversaries of Revolution

KM#	Date	Year	Mintage	VF	XF	Unc
388	AH1374	1955	—	—	—	1400.
	1377	1957	—	—	—	1400.

NOTE: Struck in red and yellow gold.

SPECIMEN SETS (SS)

KM#	Date	Mintage	Identification	Issue Price	Mkt. Val.
SS1	1916/7(10)	—	KM315-324	—	1500.

PROOF SETS (PS)

| PS1 | 1938(4) | — | KM370-373 | — | 4750. |

UNITED ARAB REPUBLIC
1958-1971
MILLIEME

ALUMINUM-BRONZE

KM#	Date	Year	Mintage	VF	XF	Unc
393	AH1380	1960	—	.10	.15	.30
	1386	1966	—	—	Proof	3.00

2 MILLIEMES

ALUMINUM-BRONZE

| 403 | AH1381 | 1962 | — | .15 | .35 | .60 |
| | 1386 | 1966 | — | — | Proof | 3.00 |

5 MILLIEMES

ALUMINUM-BRONZE

| 394 | AH1380 | 1960 | — | .15 | .45 | .85 |
| | 1386 | 1966 | — | — | Proof | 3.00 |

ALUMINUM

| 410 | AH1386 | 1967 | — | .15 | .40 | .65 |

10 MILLIEMES

ALUMINUM-BRONZE
Obv: *Misr* above denomination.

395	AH1377	1958	—	15.00	20.00	40.00
	1380	1960	16.080	.80	1.50	2.50
	1386	1966	—	—	Proof	4.00

Obv: W/o *Misr* above denomination.

KM#	Date	Year	Mintage	VF	XF	Unc
396	AH1377	1958	—	15.00	20.00	40.00

ALUMINUM

| 411 | AH1386 | 1967 | — | .10 | .25 | .65 |

20 MILLIEMES

ALUMINUM-BRONZE
Agriculture and Industrial Fair

| 390 | AH1378 | 1958 | — | .75 | 1.50 | 8.50 |

5 PIASTRES

3.5000 g., .720 SILVER, .0810 oz ASW

| 397 | AH1380 | 1960 | — | 1.75 | 2.50 | 4.00 |
| | 1386 | 1966 | — | — | Proof | 7.50 |

2.5000 g., .720 SILVER, .0578 oz ASW
Diversion of the Nile

| 404 | AH1384 | 1964 | .500 | 1.25 | 2.00 | 3.25 |
| | 1384 | 1964 | 2,000 | — | Proof | 7.50 |

COPPER-NICKEL

| 412 | AH1387 | 1967 | 10.800 | .50 | .75 | 1.50 |

NOTE: Edge varieties exist.

International Fair

| 414 | AH1388 | 1968 | .500 | .75 | 1.00 | 2.50 |

Handicraft Fair

| 417 | AH1389 | 1969 | .500 | .75 | 1.00 | 2.50 |

10 PIASTRES

7.0000 g, .720 SILVER, .1620 oz ASW
U.A.R. Founding

KM#	Date	Year	Mintage	VF	XF	Unc
392	AH1378	1959	—	3.25	6.00	17.50

398	AH1380	1960	.500	3.00	4.50	7.50
	1386	1966	—	—	Proof	15.00

5.0000 g, .720 SILVER, .1157 oz ASW
Diversion of the Nile

405	AH1384	1964	.500	2.50	4.00	6.00
	1384	1964	2,000	—	Proof	15.00

COPPER-NICKEL

413	AH1387	1967	13.200	.60	.90	2.00

Cairo International Fair

419	AH1389	1969	1.000	.75	1.25	3.00

F.A.O. Issue

418	ND	(1970)	.500	.75	1.25	3.50

Banque Misr 50 Years

420	AH1390	1970	.500	.60	1.00	2.00

Cairo International Industrial Fair

KM#	Date	Year	Mintage	VF	XF	Unc
421.1 (421)	AH1390	1970	.500	.60	1.00	3.25

New shorter Arabic Inscriptions

421.2 (422)	AH1391	1971	.500	.60	1.00	2.75

20 PIASTRES

14.0000 g, .720 SILVER, .3241 oz ASW

399	AH1380	1960	.400	6.00	10.00	27.50
	1386	1966	—	—	Proof	40.00

25 PIASTRES

17.5000 g, .720 SILVER, .4051 oz ASW
National Assembly

400	AH1380	1960	.250	7.00	9.00	20.00

10.0000 g, .720 SILVER, .2315 oz ASW
Diversion of the Nile

406	AH1384	1964	.250	—	4.50	7.50
	1384	1964	2,000	—	Proof	27.50

6.0000 g, .720 SILVER, .1388 oz ASW
President Nasser

422	AH1390	1970	.700	2.50	4.00	6.00

50 PIASTRES

20.0000 g, .720 SILVER, .4630 oz ASW
Diversion of the Nile

KM#	Date	Year	Mintage	VF	XF	Unc
407	AH1384	1964	.250	5.00	6.00	8.00
	1384	1964	2,000	—	Proof	45.00

12.5000 g, .720 SILVER, .2893 oz ASW
President Nasser

423	AH1390	1970	.400	3.00	5.00	8.00

1/2 POUND

4.2500 g, .875 GOLD, .1195 oz AGW
U.A.R. Founding

391	AH1377	1958	.030	—	—	225.00

POUND

8.5000 g, .875 GOLD, .2391 oz AGW
Aswan Dam

401	AH1379	1960	.252	—	—	175.00

25.0000 g, .720 SILVER, .5787 oz ASW
Aswan High Dam

415	AH1387	1968	.100	5.00	6.00	8.00

EGYPT 510

Al-Azhar Mosque 1000th Anniversary

KM#	Date	Year Mintage	VF	XF	Unc
424	AH1359-1361 1970-1972	.100	6.00	7.00	9.00

President Nasser

| 425 | AH1390 | 1970 | .400 | 5.00 | 6.00 | 8.00 |

8.0000 g, .875 GOLD, .2251 oz AGW
President Nasser

| 426 | AH1390 | 1970 | .010 | — | — | 175.00 |

5 POUNDS

42.5000 g, .875 GOLD, 1.1957 oz AGW
Aswan Dam

| 402 | AH1379 | 1960 | 5,000 | — | — | 700.00 |

26.0000 g, .875 GOLD, .7315 oz AGW
Diversion of the Nile

| 408 | AH1384 | 1964 | — | — | — | 600.00 |

1400th Anniversary of the Koran

| 416 | AH1388 | 1968 | .010 | — | — | 575.00 |

Al-Azhar Mosque 1000th Anniversary

KM#	Date	Year Mintage	VF	XF	Unc
427	AH1390	1970	—	—	—	600.00

President Nasser

| 428 | AH1390 | 1970 | 3,000 | — | — | 500.00 |

10 POUNDS

52.0000 g, .875 GOLD, 1.4630 oz AGW
Diversion of the Nile

| 409 | AH1384 | 1964 | 2,000 | — | — | 1000. |

PROOF SETS (PS)

KM#	Date	Mintage	Identification	Issue Price	Mkt. Val.
PS2	1964(4)	2,000	KM404-407	18.00	95.00
PS3	1966(7)	2,500	KM393-395,397-399,403	9.00	75.00

ARAB REPUBLIC
1971-
MILLIEME

ALUMINUM

KM#	Date	Year Mintage	VF	XF	Unc
A423	AH1392	1972	—	.10	.30	.50

5 MILLIEMES

ALUMINUM
Mule. Obv: KM#A425. Rev: KM#433.

| A424 | AH1392 | 1972 | — | 10.00 | 20.00 | 45.00 |

| A425 | AH1392 | 1972 | 16.000 | .20 | .50 | 2.50 |

BRASS

| 432 | AH1393 | 1973 | — | .10 | .15 | .30 |

ALUMINUM
F.A.O. Issue

KM#	Date	Year Mintage	VF	XF	Unc
433	AH1393	1973	10.000	.10	.20	.35

Mule. Obv: KM#A425. Rev: KM#433.

| 568 | AH1393 | 1973 | — | — | — | 20.00 |

BRASS
Mule. Obv: KM#432. Rev: KM#445.

| 434 | AH1393 | 1973 | — | 5.00 | 10.00 | 20.00 |

International Women's Year

| 445 | AH1395 | 1975 | 10.000 | .10 | .15 | .30 |

F.A.O. Issue

| 462 | AH1397 | 1977 | 5.000 | .10 | .20 | .50 |

1971 Corrective Revolution

| 463 | AH1397 | 1977 | 2.500 | .10 | .20 | .50 |
| | 1399 | 1979 | 2.500 | .10 | .20 | .50 |

ALUMINUM-BRONZE
Sadat's Corrective Revolution

| 497 | AH1400 | 1980 | 2.500 | 5.00 | 8.00 | 12.00 |

10 MILLIEMES

ALUMINUM

| A426 | AH1392 | 1972 | 20.000 | .50 | 2.00 | 6.00 |

NOTE: Edge varieties exist.

BRASS

| 435 | AH1393 | 1973 | — | .10 | .25 | .50 |
| | 1396 | 1976 | — | .75 | 1.50 | 3.00 |

F.A.O. Issue

| 446 | AH1395 | 1975 | 10.000 | .10 | .20 | .35 |

EGYPT 511

F.A.O. Issue

KM#	Date	Year	Mintage	VF	XF	Unc
449	AH1396	1976	10.000	.10	.20	.30

F.A.O. Issue

| 464 | AH1397 | 1977 | 10.000 | .10 | .20 | .85 |

1971 Corrective Revolution

| 465 | AH1397 | 1977 | 2.500 | .10 | .20 | .65 |
| | 1399 | 1979 | 2.500 | .20 | .40 | 1.00 |

F.A.O. Issue

| 476 | AH1398 | 1978 | 2.000 | .10 | .20 | .80 |

International Year of the Child

| 483 | AH1399 | 1979 | 2.000 | .10 | .25 | .75 |

ALUMINUM-BRONZE
Sadat's Corrective Revolution

| 498 | AH1400 | 1980 | 2.500 | .10 | .25 | .75 |

F.A.O. Issue

| 499 | AH1400 | 1980 | 2.000 | .10 | .20 | .60 |

PIASTRE

ALUMINUM-BRONZE
Obv: Christian date left of denomination.

| 553.1 | AH1404 | 1984 | — | — | — | .10 |

Obv: Islamic date left of denomination.

| 553.2 | AH1404 | 1984 | — | — | — | .10 |

2 PIASTRES

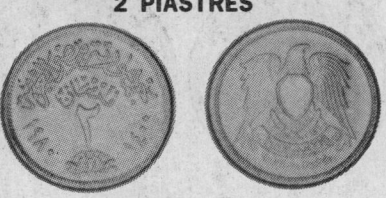

ALUMINUM-BRONZE

KM#	Date	Year	Mintage	VF	XF	Unc
500	AH1400	1980	—	.20	.30	.60

Obv: Christian date left of denomination.

| 554.1 | AH1404 | 1984 | — | — | — | .10 |

Obv: Islamic date left of denomination.

| 554.2 | AH1404 | 1984 | — | — | — | .10 |

5 PIASTRES

COPPER-NICKEL
UNICEF 25th Anniversary

| A427 | AH1392 | 1972 | .500 | .75 | 1.00 | 2.50 |

NOTE: Error in spelling "UNICFE"

Rev: Islamic falcon

| A428 | AH1392 | 1972 | — | .50 | .75 | 2.00 |

Cairo State Fair

| 436 | AH1393 | 1973 | .500 | .60 | .75 | 2.25 |

National Bank of Egypt 75th Anniversary

| 437 | AH1393 | 1973 | 1.000 | .60 | .75 | 2.00 |

1st Anniversary October War

| A441 | AH1394 | 1974 | 2.000 | .60 | .75 | 2.00 |

International Woman's Year

KM#	Date	Year	Mintage	VF	XF	Unc
447	AH1395	1975	2.000	.50	.65	1.00

Mule. Obv: KM#A428. Rev: KM#451.

| 450 | 1396 | 1976 | — | 5.00 | 10.00 | 20.00 |

1976 Cairo Trade Fair

| 451 | AH1396 | 1976 | .500 | .60 | .75 | 2.00 |

1971 Corrective Revolution

| 466 | AH1397 | 1977 | 1.000 | .50 | .60 | 1.50 |
| | 1399 | 1979 | — | .50 | .60 | 1.50 |

50th Anniversary of Textile Industry

| 467 | AH1397 | 1977 | 1.000 | .50 | .75 | 1.65 |

F.A.O. Issue

| 468 | AH1397 | 1977 | — | .50 | .75 | 1.65 |

NOTE: Edge varieties exist.

Portland Cement

| 477 | AH1398 | 1978 | .500 | .50 | .75 | 1.65 |

F.A.O. Issue

| 478 | AH1398 | 1978 | 1.000 | .50 | .75 | 1.65 |

EGYPT 512

International Year of the Child

KM#	Date	Year	Mintage	VF	XF	Unc
484	AH1399	1979	1.000	.50	.75	1.65

First Anniversary October War

KM#	Date	Year	Mintage	VF	XF	Unc
442	AH1394	1974	2.000	.60	.90	2.50

25th Anniversary of Abbasia Mint

KM#	Date	Year	Mintage	VF	XF	Unc
485	AH1399	1979	1.000	.50	.80	2.00

Applied Professions

| 501 | AH1400 | 1980 | .500 | .50 | .75 | 1.35 |

Sadat's Corrective Revolution of May 15, 1971
Similar to 1 Pound, KM#514.

| 502 | AH1400 | 1980 | 1.000 | .50 | .75 | 1.65 |

F.A.O. Issue

| 448 | AH1395 | 1975 | 2.000 | .60 | .90 | 2.25 |

National Education Day

| 486 | AH1399 | 1979 | 1.000 | .50 | .80 | 1.85 |

ALUMINUM-BRONZE
Obv: Christian date left of denomination.

| 555.1 | AH1404 | 1984 | — | — | .10 | .40 |

Reopening of the Suez Canal

| 452 | AH1396 | 1976 | 5.000 | .60 | .90 | 3.00 |

Mule. Obv: KM#452. Rev: KM#430.

| 431 | AH1392 | 1972 | — | 7.50 | 15.00 | 27.50 |

Doctor's Day

| 503 | AH1400 | 1980 | 1.000 | .50 | .80 | 2.00 |

Obv: Islamic date left of denomination.

| 555.2 | AH1404 | 1984 | — | — | .10 | .40 |

F.A.O. Issue

| 469 | AH1397 | 1977 | 1.000 | .60 | .90 | 2.00 |

Egyptian-Israeli Peace Treaty

| 504 | AH1400 | 1980 | 1.000 | 2.50 | 4.00 | 6.00 |

| 622 | AH1404 | 1984 | — | — | — | .10 |

10 PIASTRES

1971 Corrective Revolution

| 470 | AH1397 | 1977 | 1.000 | .50 | .80 | 2.25 |
| | 1399 | 1979 | 1.000 | .50 | .80 | 2.25 |

F.A.O. Issue

| 505 | AH1400 | 1980 | 1.000 | .50 | .80 | 1.85 |

COPPER-NICKEL
Cairo International Fair

| 429 | AH1392 | 1972 | .500 | .60 | 1.00 | 2.00 |

20th Anniversary Economic Union

| 471 | AH1397 | 1977 | 1.000 | .50 | .80 | 2.00 |

Sadat's Corrective Revolution of May 15, 1971

| 506 | AH1400 | 1980 | 1.000 | .50 | .80 | 2.00 |
| | 1401 | 1981 | — | .50 | .80 | 3.00 |

Rev: Islamic falcon

| 430 | AH1392 | 1972 | — | .60 | 1.00 | 2.00 |

Cairo International Fair

| 479 | AH1398 | 1978 | — | — | .50 | .80 | 2.50 |

Scientist's Day

| 520 | AH1401 | 1981 | — | — | .50 | .80 | 2.00 |

Trade Unions

KM#	Date	Year	Mintage	VF	XF	Unc
521	AH1402	1981	—	.50	.80	1.75

50th Anniversary of Egyptian Products Co.

| 599 | AH1402 | 1982 | — | .50 | .80 | 2.00 |

Circulation Coinage

| 556 | AH1404 | 1984 | — | — | .10 | .50 |

National Planning Institute

| 570 | AH1405 | 1985 | .100 | — | — | 2.00 |

Egyptian Parliament

| 573 | AH1405 | 1985 | .250 | — | — | 2.00 |

20 PIASTRES

COPPER-NICKEL

| 507 | AH1400 | 1980 | — | .75 | 1.00 | 2.35 |

Circulation Coinage

| 557 | AH1404 | 1984 | — | — | .20 | .75 |

Cairo International Airport

KM#	Date	Year	Mintage	VF	XF	Unc
596	AH1405	1985	—	—	—	3.00

Professions

| 597 | AH1406 | 1985 | — | — | — | 3.00 |

Soldiers

| 606 | AH1406 | 1986 | — | — | — | 3.00 |

Census

| 607 | AH1407 | 1986 | — | — | — | 3.00 |

25 PIASTRES

6.0000 g, .720 SILVER, .1388 oz ASW
National Bank of Egypt 75th Anniversary

| 438 | AH1393 | 1973 | .100 | 4.00 | 6.00 | 9.00 |

POUND

24.6000 g, .720 SILVER, .5695 oz ASW
F A O: Aswan Dam

| 439 | AH1393 | 1973 | .050 | — | 5.00 | 6.00 | 8.00 |

8.0000 g, .875 GOLD, .2250 oz AGW
National Bank of Egypt 75th Anniversary

| 440 | AH1393 | 1973 | 7,000 | — | — | 200.00 |

15.0000 g, .720 SILVER, .3472 oz ASW
First Anniversary October War

KM#	Date	Year	Mintage	VF	XF	Unc
443	AH1394	1974	.050	—	—	10.00

F.A.O. Issue

| 453 | AH1396 | 1976 | .050 | — | — | 10.00 |

Reopening of Suez Canal

| 454 | AH1396 | 1976 | .250 | — | — | 9.00 |

Om Kalsoum

| 455 | AH1396 | 1976 | .250 | — | — | 9.00 |

8.0000 g, .875 GOLD, .2250 oz AGW

| 456 | AH1396 | 1976 | 5,000 | — | — | 225.00 |

15.0000 g, .720 SILVER, .3472 oz ASW
King Faisal

| 457 | AH1396 | 1976 | .100 | — | — | 9.00 |

8.0000 g, .875 GOLD, .2250 oz AGW

| 458 | AH1396 | 1976 | 8,000 | — | — | 200.00 |

EGYPT

15.0000 g, .720 SILVER, .3472 oz ASW
F.A.O. Issue

KM#	Date	Year	Mintage	VF	XF	Unc
472	AH1397	1977	.050	—	—	10.00

1971 Corrective Revolution

473	AH1397	1977	.050	—	—	10.00
	1399	1979	.049	—	—	10.00
	1399	1979	1,500	—	Proof	25.00

20th Anniversary of Economic Union

474	AH1397	1977	.050	—	—	10.00

8.0000 g, .875 GOLD, .2250 oz AGW

475	AH1397	1977	5,000	—	—	200.00

15.0000 g, .720 SILVER, .3472 oz ASW
Portland Cement

480	AH1398	1978	.050	—	—	10.00

25th Anniversary of Ain Shams University

481	AH1398	1978	.050	—	—	10.00

F.A.O. Issue

KM#	Date	Year	Mintage	VF	XF	Unc
482	AH1398	1978	.050	—	—	10.00

25th Anniversary of Abbasia Mint

488	AH1399	1979	.023	—	—	10.00
	1399	1979	2,000	—	Proof	20.00

F.A.O. Issue and I.Y.C.

489	AH1399	1979	.048	—	—	10.00
	1399	1979	2,500	—	Proof	17.50

National Education Day
Rev: Similar to KM#453.

490	AH1399	1979	.098	—	—	9.00
	1399	1979	2,000	—	Proof	17.50

Land Bank

491	AH1399	1979	.098	—	—	9.00
	1399	1979	2,000	—	Proof	20.00

8.0000 g, .875 GOLD, .2250 oz AGW
Bank of Land Reform

492	AH1399	1979	4,200	—	—	175.00
	1399	1979	800 pcs.	—	Proof	400.00

15.0000 g, .720 SILVER, .3472 oz ASW
Hegira Issue

493	AH1400	1979	.097	—	—	9.00
	1400	1979	3,000	—	Proof	15.00

8.0000 g, .875 GOLD, .2250 oz AGW

494	AH1400	1979	2,000	—	—	175.00
	1400	1979	2,000	—	Proof	300.00

15.0000 g, .720 SILVER, .3472 oz ASW
Egyptian - Israeli Peace Treaty

KM#	Date	Year	Mintage	VF	XF	Unc
508	AH1400	1980	.095	—	—	9.00
	1400	1980	5,000	—	Proof	20.00

8.0000 g, .875 GOLD, .2250 oz AGW
Egyptian-Israeli Peace Treaty

509	AH1400	1980	9,500	—	—	175.00
	1400	1980	500 pcs.	—	Proof	300.00

15.0000 g, .720 SILVER, .3472 oz ASW
Applied Professions in Egypt

510	AH1400	1980	.022	—	—	10.00
	1400	1980	3,000	—	Proof	15.00

Doctor's Day

511	AH1400	1980	.097	—	—	9.00
	1400	1980	3,000	—	Proof	15.00

8.0000 g, .875 GOLD, .2250 oz AGW

512	AH1400	1980	5,000	—	—	225.00

15.0000 g, .720 SILVER, .3472 oz ASW
F.A.O. Issue

513	AH1400	1980	.097	—	—	9.00
	1400	1980	3,000	—	Proof	15.00

Sadat's Corrective Revolution of May 15, 1971

514	AH1400	1980	.047	—	—	10.00
	1400	1980	3,000	—	Proof	17.50

EGYPT 515

Cairo University Law Facility

KM#	Date	Year	Mintage	VF	XF	Unc
515	AH1400	1980	.047	—	—	10.00
	1400	1980	3,000	—	Proof	17.50

8.0000 g, .875 GOLD, .2250 oz AGW

516	AH1400	1980	2,000	—	—	175.00
	1400	1980	—	—	Proof	250.00

15.0000 g, .720 SILVER, .3472 oz ASW
Scientist's Day
| 522 | AH1401 | 1981 | .025 | — | — | 10.00 |

World Food Day
523	AH1401	1981	.050	—	—	10.00
	1401	1981	1,500	—	Proof	25.00

3rd Anniversary of Suez Canal Reopening
524	AH1401	1981	.050	—	—	10.00
	1401	1981	2,000	—	Proof	25.00

8.0000 g, .875 GOLD, .2251 oz AGW

| 525 | AH1401 | 1981 | 5,000 | — | Proof | 250.00 |

15.0000 g, .720 SILVER, .3472 oz ASW

25th Anniversary of Nationalization of Suez Canal

KM#	Date	Year	Mintage	VF	XF	Unc
528	AH1401	1981	.025	—	—	10.00
	1401	1981	1,500	—	Proof	25.00

8.0000 g, .875 GOLD, .2250 oz AGW
| 529 | AH1401 | 1981 | 3,000 | — | — | 200.00 |

15.0000 g, .720 SILVER, .3472 oz ASW
F.A.O. Issue
| 532 | AH1401 | 1981 | .050 | — | — | 10.00 |

25th Anniversary of Egyptian Industry
| 526 | AH1402 | 1981 | .025 | — | — | 10.00 |

25th Anniversary of Trade Unions
| 527 | AH1402 | 1981 | .025 | — | — | 10.00 |

100th Anniversary of Revolt by Urabi Pasha
530	AH1402	1981	.025	—	—	10.00
	1402	1981	1,500	—	Proof	25.00

8.0000 g, .875 GOLD, .2250 oz AGW
| 531 | AH1402 | 1981 | 3,000 | — | — | 250.00 |

15.0000 g, .720 SILVER, .3472 oz ASW
Egypt Air Golden Jubilee
| 539 | AH1402 | 1982 | .020 | — | — | 12.00 |

1000th Anniversary of Al Azhar Mosque
KM#	Date	Year	Mintage	VF	XF	Unc
540	AH1402	1982	.023	—	—	12.00
	1402	1982	4,000	—	Proof	17.50

8.0000 g, .875 GOLD, .2250 oz AGW
| 541 | AH1402 | 1982 | 2,000 | — | Proof | 250.00 |

15.0000 g, .720 SILVER, .3472 oz ASW
50th Anniversary of Egyptian Products Co.
544	AH1402	1982	5,000	—	—	20.00
	1402	1982	2,000	—	Proof	25.00

Return of Sinai to Egypt
545	AH1402					
		1982(1983)	.050	—	—	10.00
	1402					
		1982(1983)	2,000	—	Proof	20.00

50th Anniversary of Air Force
542	AH1403	1982	.010	—	—	15.00
	1403	1982	2,260	—	Proof	25.00

8.0000 g, .875 GOLD, .2250 oz AGW
| 543 | AH1403 | 1982 | 2,000 | — | Proof | 250.00 |

15.0000 g, .720 SILVER, .3472 oz ASW
Two Popular Poets
| 549 | AH1403 | 1983 | .025 | — | — | 12.00 |

EGYPT 516

Misr Insurance Company

KM#	Date	Year	Mintage	VF	XF	Unc
551	AH1404	1984	.020	—	—	12.00

Helwan University Faculty of Fine Arts

| 559 | AH1404 | 1984 | .025 | — | — | 12.00 |

8.0000 g, .875 GOLD, .2250 oz AGW
50th Anniversary of Egyptian Radio Broadcasting
Similar to 5 Pounds, KM#561.

| 583 | AH1404 | 1984 | 2,000 | — | — | 200.00 |

National Planning Institute
Similar to 5 Pounds, KM#572.

| 571 | AH1405 | 1985 | 200 pcs. | — | — | 300.00 |

Egyptian Parliament
Similar to 5 Pounds, KM#575.

| 574 | AH1405 | 1985 | 100 pcs. | — | — | 350.00 |

Cairo Stadium
Similar to 5 Pounds, KM#578.

| 577 | AH1405 | 1985 | 300 pcs. | — | — | 250.00 |

Egyptian Television
Similar to 5 Pounds, KM#581.

| 580 | AH1405 | 1985 | 150 pcs. | — | — | 300.00 |

Commerce Day
Obv: Arabic legends, seals and date.
Rev: Stylized depictions of commercial activity.

| 604 | AH1405 | 1985 | 2,000 | — | Proof | 200.00 |

Faculty of Economics and Political Science
Obv: Arabic legends, seals and date.
Rev: Graph within wreath, partial gear wheel.

| 605 | AH1405 | 1985 | 250 pcs. | — | Proof | 250.00 |

5 POUNDS

26.0000 g, .875 GOLD, .7315 oz AGW
National Bank of Egypt 75th Anniversary

| 441 | AH1393 | 1973 | 1,000 | — | — | 500.00 |
| | 1393 | 1973 | — | — | Proof | 650.00 |

1973 October War

| 444 | AH1394 | 1974 | 1,000 | — | — | 750.00 |

King Faisal Of Saudi Arabia

KM#	Date	Year	Mintage	VF	XF	Unc
459	AH1396	1976	2,500	—	—	650.00

Suez Canal

| 460 | AH1396 | 1976 | 2,000 | — | — | 650.00 |

Om Kalsoum

| 461 | AH1396 | 1976 | 1,000 | — | — | 900.00 |

Credit Foncier Egyptian

| 495 | AH1399 | 1979 | 1,750 | — | — | 575.00 |
| | 1399 | 1979 | 250 pcs. | — | Proof | 850.00 |

Hegira Issue

| 496 | AH1399 | 1979 | 2,000 | — | — | 700.00 |

Egyptian-Israeli Peace Treaty

| 517 | AH1400 | 1980 | 2,375 | — | — | 500.00 |
| | 1400 | 1980 | 125 pcs. | — | Proof | 900.00 |

Doctor's Day

| 518 | AH1400 | 1980 | 1,000 | — | — | 650.00 |

24.0000 g, .925 SILVER, .7138 oz ASW
International Year of the Child

| 533 | AH1401 | 1981 | .010 | — | Proof | 35.00 |

26.0000 g, .875 GOLD, .7315 oz AGW
3rd Anniversary of Suez Canal Reopening

| 534 | AH1401 | 1981 | 925 pcs. | — | — | 575.00 |
| | 1401 | 1981 | 75 pcs. | — | Proof | 1000. |

25th Anniversary of Nationalization of Suez Canal

KM#	Date	Year	Mintage	VF	XF	Unc
537	AH1401	1981	1,000	—	—	650.00

25th Anniversary of the Ministry of Industry

| 535 | AH1402 | 1981 | 1,500 | — | Proof | 650.00 |

100th Anniversary of Revolt by Arabi Pasha

| 536 | AH1402 | 1981 | 1,000 | — | — | 650.00 |

1000th Anniversary of Al Azhar Mosque

| 546 | AH1402 | 1982 | 1,500 | — | — | 650.00 |

50th Anniversary of Air Force

| 547 | AH1402 | 1982 | 1,000 | — | — | 650.00 |

17.5000 g, .720 SILVER, .4051 oz ASW
75th Anniversary of Cairo University

| 552 | AH1404 | 1983 | .025 | — | — | 15.00 |

EGYPT 517

Los Angeles Olympics
KM#	Date	Year	Mintage	VF	XF	Unc
558	AH1404	1984	.020	—	—	15.00

Academy of Arabic Languages
| 560 | AH1404 | 1984 | .025 | — | — | 15.00 |

50th Anniversary of Egyptian Radio Broadcasting
| 561 | AH1404 | 1984 | .025 | — | — | 15.00 |

Sculptor Mahmoud Mokhtar
| 565 | AH1404 | 1984 | — | — | — | 15.00 |

Golden Jubilee of Petroleum Industry
| 566 | AH1404 | 1984 | .010 | — | — | 15.00 |

Diamond Jubilee of Cooperation
KM#	Date	Year	Mintage	VF	XF	Unc
567	AH1404	1984	.010	—	—	15.00

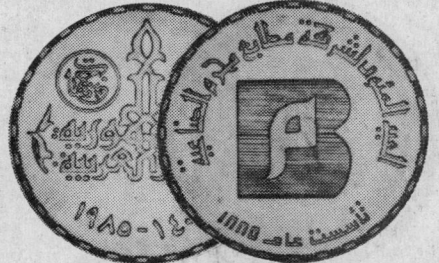

100th Anniversary of Moharram Printing Press Co.
| 563 | AH1405 | 1985 | .020 | — | — | 15.00 |

40.0000 g, .875 GOLD, 1.1253 oz AGW
| 564 | AH1405 | 1985 | 8 pcs. | — | — | 2500. |

17.5000 g, .720 SILVER, .4051 oz ASW
National Planning Institute
| 572 | AH1405 | 1985 | .015 | — | — | 15.00 |

Egyptian Parliament
| 575 | AH1405 | 1985 | .019 | — | — | 15.00 |

26.0000 g, .875 GOLD, .7315 oz AGW
| 576 | AH1405 | 1985 | 10 pcs. | — | — | 2500. |

17.5000 g, .720 SILVER, .4051 oz ASW
Cairo Stadium
KM#	Date	Year	Mintage	VF	XF	Unc
578	AH1405	1985	.025	—	—	15.00

26.0000 g, .875 GOLD, .7315 oz AGW
| 579 | AH1405 | 1985 | 10 pcs. | — | — | 2500. |

17.5000 g, .720 SILVER, .4051 oz ASW
Egyptian Television
| 581 | AH1405 | 1985 | 5,000 | — | — | 15.00 |

26.0000 g, .875 GOLD, .7315 oz AGW
| 582 | AH1405 | 1985 | 25 pcs. | — | — | 2000. |

17.5000 g, .720 SILVER, .4051 oz ASW
Cairo International Airport
| 585 | AH1405 | 1985 | .020 | — | — | 15.00 |

EGYPT 518

Tutankhamun

KM#	Date	Year	Mintage	VF	XF	Unc
592	AH1405	1985	4,000	—	—	15.00

The Prophet's Mosque

KM#	Date	Year	Mintage	VF	XF	Unc
584	AH1406	1985	1,000	—	—	15.00

17.6800 g, .720 SILVER, .4093 oz ASW
World Soccer Championships

KM#	Date	Year	Mintage	VF	XF	Unc
589	AH1406	1986	5,000	—	—	25.00

XV UIA Congress
593   AH1405   1985   .010   —   —   15.00

Professions
587   AH1406   1985   —   —   —   15.00

Faculty of Economics & Political Science
598   AH1405   1985   8,000   —   —   15.00

Faculty of Commerce
586   AH1406   1986   —   —   —   15.00

17.5000 g, .720 SILVER, .4051 oz ASW
African Soccer Championship Games
590   AH1406   1986   .015   —   Proof   20.00

Commerce Day
600   AH1405   1985   1,000   —   —   20.00

25th Anniversary of Egyptian National Bank
588   AH1406   1986   —   —   —   15.00

Ministry of Health
594   AH1406   1986   .010   —   —   15.00

EGYPT 519

KM#	Date						Mecca			
						609	AH1406	1986	—	—	—	20.00
							1406	1986	—	—	Proof	25.00

Engineer's Syndicate

KM#	Date	Year	Mintage	VF	XF	Unc
			Soldiers			
601	AH1406	1986	—	—	—	20.00
610	AH1407	1986	—	—	—	20.00

Restoration of Parliament Building
614 AH1406 1986 — — — 20.00

Egyptian Industry
616 AH1407 1986 — — — 20.00

Petroleum Industry
602 AH1406 1986 — — — 20.00

Atomic Energy
615 AH1406 1986 — — — 20.00

AIDA
611 AH1407 1987 — — — 30.00
8.0000 g, .900 GOLD, .2315 oz AGW
612 AH1407 1987 — — — 275.00

National Theater
608 AH1406 1986 — — — 20.00

Census
603 AH1407 1986 — — — 20.00

EGYPT 520

17.5000 g, .720 SILVER, .4051 oz ASW
Parliament's Museum

KM#	Date	Year	Mintage	VF	XF	Unc
617	AH1407	1987	—	—	—	20.00

Veterinarian Day
618 AH1407 1987 — — — 20.00

Petroleum Company
619 AH1407 1987 — — — 20.00

17.5000 g, .900 SILVER, .5084 oz ASW
Faculty of Fine Arts
630 AH1407 1987 — — — 20.00

17.5000 g, .720 SILVER, .4051 oz ASW
First African Subway

KM#	Date	Year	Mintage	VF	XF	Unc
620	AH1408	1987	—	—	—	20.00

Hellwan Company
623 AH1408 1987 — — — 20.00

Police Day
621 AH1408 1988 — — — 20.00

17.5000 g, .900 SILVER, .5084 oz ASW
Summer Olympics - Pharoah and Athletes

KM#	Date	Year	Mintage	VF	XF	Unc
624	AH1408	1988	8,000	—	—	25.00
	1408	1988	2,000	—	Proof	35.00

Summer Olympics - Athletes and Mythelogical Figures
| 626 | AH1408 | 1988 | 8,000 | — | — | 25.00 |
| | 1408 | 1988 | 2,000 | — | Proof | 35.00 |

Winter Olympics - Ski Jumper and Figure Skater
| 628 | AH1408 | 1988 | 8,000 | — | — | 25.00 |
| | 1408 | 1988 | 2,000 | — | Proof | 35.00 |

Air Travel
631 AH1408 1988 — — — 20.00

17.5000 g, .720 SILVER, .4051 oz ASW
Cairo Opera House

KM#	Date	Year	Mintage	VF	XF	Unc
649	AH1409	1988	—	—	—	20.00

10 POUNDS

40.0000 g, .875 GOLD, 1.1254 oz AGW
Egyptian-Israeli Peace Treaty

519	AH1400	1980	950 pcs.	—	—	900.00
	1400	1980	50 pcs.	—	Proof	1350.

25th Anniversary of Ministry of Industry

538	AH1402	1981	18 pcs.	—	—	1500.
	1402	1981	1,000	—	Proof	750.00

1000th Anniversary of Al Azhar Mosque

548	AH1402	1982	1,322	—	—	750.00

50 POUNDS
8.5000 g, .900 GOLD, .2460 oz AGW
Summer Olympics - Pharoah and Athletes
Similar to 5 Pounds, KM#624.

625	AH1408	1988	300 pcs.	—	—	250.00
	1408	1988	100 pcs.	—	Proof	300.00

Summer Olympics - Athletes and Mythological Figures
Similar to 5 Pounds, KM#626.

627	AH1408	1988	300 pcs.	—	—	250.00
	1408	1988	100 pcs.	—	Proof	300.00

Winter Olympics - Ski Jumper and Figure Skater
Similar to 5 Pounds, KM#628.

629	AH1408	1988	300 pcs.	—	—	250.00
	1408	1988	100 pcs.	—	Proof	300.00

100 POUNDS

17.1500 g, .900 GOLD, .4963 oz AGW
Queen Nefertiti

KM#	Date	Year	Mintage	VF	XF	Unc
550	AH—	1983	.016	—	Proof	1000.

Cleopatra VII

562	AH—	1984	2,121	—	Proof	1000.

The Golden Falcon

569	AH—	1985	1,800	—	Proof	800.00

Tutankhamun

591	AH—	1986	7,500	—	Proof	1000.

Mythological Golden Ram

613	AH—	1987	7,500	—	Proof	900.00

Golden Warrior

648	AH—	1988	5,500	—	Proof	650.00

PROOF SETS (PS)

KM#	Date	Mintage	Identification	Issue Price	Mkt. Val.
PS4	1980(3)	—	KM509,517,519	—	2550.

EL SALVADOR
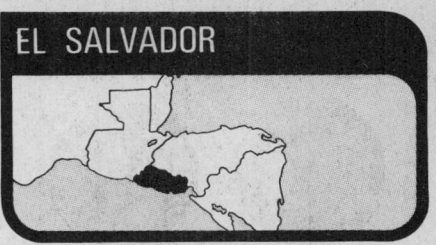

The Republic of El Salvador, a Central American country bordered by Guatemala, Honduras and the Pacific Ocean, has an area of 8,124 sq. mi. (21,041 sq. km.) and a population of *5.5 million. Capital: San Salvador. This most intensely cultivated country of Latin America produces coffee, (the major crop), cotton, sugar and balsam for export. Gold, silver and other metals are largely unexploited.

The first Spanish attempt to subjugate the area was undertaken in 1523 by Pedro de Alvarado, Cortes' lieutenant. He was forced to retreat by superior Indian forces, but returned in 1525 and succeeded in bringing the region under control of the Captaincy General of Guatemala, where it remained until 1821. In 1821, El Salvador and the other Central American provinces jointly declared their independence from Spain. In 1823 the Republic of Central America was formed by the five Central American States. When this federation was dissolved in 1839, El Salvador became an independent republic.

MINT MARKS
C.A.M. - Central American Mint, San Salvador
H - Birmingham
S - San Francisco
Mo - Mexico

PROVISIONAL COINAGE
MONETARY SYSTEM
16 Reales = 1 Escudo

1/4 REAL
SILVER

KM#	Date	Mintage	Good	VG	Fine	VF
1	—	(3 known)	—	—	Rare	

1/2 REAL

SILVER
Obv. leg: POR LA LIVERTAD DEL SAL,
star above volcano within branches.
Rev. leg: MONEDA PROVISIONAL,
halo above column within branches.

14	1833	—	100.00	175.00	275.00	400.00

Obv. leg: POR LA LIBERTAD DEL SAL.
S-volcano-S over water within circle.
Rev: Liberty cap over 1. - column - 1/2 over water.

21.1	1835	—	100.00	175.00	275.00	400.00

Obv. leg: POR LA LIBERTAD DEL SAL,
star above S - volcano - S over water.

21.2	1835	—	110.00	200.00	300.00	425.00

Obv. leg: POR LA LIBERTAD DEL SALVA,
star above S - volcano - S over water.
Rev. leg: MONEDA PROVISIONAL,
Liberty cap over column: 1 - column - M

21.3	1835	—	90.00	175.00	250.00	375.00

REAL

SILVER
Obv. leg: ESTADO DEL SALVADOR,
star above volcano within branches.
Rev. leg: MONEDA PROVISIONAL IND*,
star in wreath above 1. - column - R. within branches.

17	1833	—	75.00	150.00	250.00	350.00

EL SALVADOR 522

Obv. leg: POR LA LIVERTAD DEL SALVADOR.
Rev: 1. - (thin) column - R. within branches.

KM#	Date	Mintage	Good	VG	Fine	VF
18.1	1833	—	50.00	100.00	175.00	275.00

Obv: Similar to KM#18.1.
Rev: 1. - (thick) column - R. within branches.

18.2	1833	—	50.00	100.00	175.00	275.00

Obv. leg: POR LA LIVERTAD DEL SALVADOR*
Rev: Similar to KM#18.2.

18.3	1833	—	50.00	100.00	175.00	275.00

Obv: Star over volcano over water in half circle of stars.

18.4	1833	—	75.00	150.00	250.00	350.00

Obv. leg: POR LA LIVERTAD DE SAL, volcano within branches.
Rev. leg: MONEDA PROVISIONAL IND, column within branches.

18.5	1834	—	—	—	—	Rare

Obv. leg: POR LA LIVERTAD DEL SAL, star over S. - volcano - S. within circle.
Rev. leg: MONEDA PROVISIONAL, Liberty cap over I. - column - R., water below within circle.

18.6	1835	—	50.00	115.00	175.00	275.00

Obv. leg: POR LA LIVERTAD DEL SAL.

18.7	1835 NA	—	75.00	150.00	250.00	350.00

Obv. leg: POR LA LIBERTAD DEL SAL, star over S - volcano - S over water within circle.

18.8	1835	—	50.00	115.00	175.00	275.00

NOTE: Varieties also exist with 2 or 3 dots after SAL.

Obv. leg: POR LA LIBERTAD DEL SAL, star over S - volcano - S over water within circle of dots.

18.9	1835	—	50.00	115.00	175.00	275.00

Obv. leg: POR LA LIBERTAD DEL SA:

18.10	1835	—	50.00	115.00	200.00	300.00

Obv. leg: POR LA LIBERTAD DE SALV.

KM#	Date	Mintage	Good	VG	Fine	VF
18.11	1835	—	50.00	115.00	175.00	275.00

2 REALES

SILVER
Obv. leg: POR LA LIVERTAD. SALV, Liberty cap over 2. - column - R. over water.
Rev. leg: MONEDA PROVISIONAL, volcano.

4	1828 FP	—	30.00	55.00	100.00	165.00

Obv: Inner circle added.

5.1	1828 FP	—	30.00	55.00	100.00	165.00
	1828 F	—	35.00	65.00	125.00	200.00

Obv. leg: POR LA LIBERTAD. SALB.

5.2	1828 FP	—	30.00	55.00	100.00	165.00

Obv. leg: POR LA LIBERTAD SALVAD.
Rev. leg: MONEDA PROBISIONAL.

5.3	1829 RL	—	35.00	75.00	150.00	200.00

Obv. leg: POR LA LIBERTAD SALVAD.

5.4	1829 RL	—	35.00	65.00	125.00	175.00

Obv. leg: POR LA LIBERTAD SALVADOR.

5.5	1829	—	35.00	65.00	125.00	175.00

Obv. leg: POR LA LIBERTAD DEL SALVADR, star over S - volcano - S. over water.
Rev: Liberty cap over 2 - column - R.

11.1	1832	—	35.00	65.00	125.00	175.00

Obv. leg: POR LA LIBERTAD DEL SALVADOR
Rev: Liberty cap over 2 - column - R between sprays within dotted circle.

11.2	1832 RL	—	35.00	65.00	125.00	175.00

Rev: 2 - column - R within solid circle.

11.3	1832 RL	—	35.00	65.00	125.00	175.00

Obv. leg: POR LA LIBERTAD SALVADORE

KM#	Date	Mintage	Good	VG	Fine	VF
11.4	1832	—	35.00	65.00	125.00	175.00

Obv. leg: POR LA LIBERTAD SALVADO

11.5	1832	—	35.00	65.00	125.00	175.00

Obv. leg: POR LA LIVERTAD DEL SALV, star above retrograde S - volcano - S over water.
Rev: Liberty cap over 2. - column - R within branches.

11.6	1833	—	35.00	65.00	125.00	175.00
	1834/3T	—	40.00	80.00	150.00	200.00

Obv: Regular S' recut over retrograde S'.

11.7	1834/3	—	40.00	80.00	150.00	200.00

Obv. leg: POR LA LIBERTAD DEL SALVA, star over S - volcano - S over water.

11.8	1833 RL	—	35.00	65.00	125.00	175.00

NOTE: Varieties exist with 2 or 3 dots after SALVA.

Obv. leg: POR LA LIBERTAD DEL SALVAD

11.9	1833/2 RL	—	40.00	80.00	150.00	200.00
	1833 RL	—	35.00	65.00	125.00	175.00

Obv. leg: POR LA LIBERTAD DEL SALV

11.10	1833 L	—	35.00	65.00	125.00	175.00

Obv. leg: LIBERTAD SALVO DORENO

11.11	1833	—	35.00	65.00	125.00	175.00

Obv. leg: POR LA LIBERTAD DEL SALVADOR.

11.12	1833 RL	—	35.00	65.00	125.00	175.00

EL SALVADOR 523

Obv. leg: POR LA LIVERTAD DEL SALV.
Rev. leg: MONEDA PROVISIONAL
with retrograde "S".

KM#	Date	Mintage	Good	VG	Fine	VF
11.13	1834	—	40.00	75.00	135.00	200.00

4 REALES

SILVER
Obv. leg: POR LA LIBERTAD SALV,
Liberty cap over column between retrograde R. - 4.

| 8.1 | 1828 F | — | 3250. | 4500. | 5500. | 8000. |

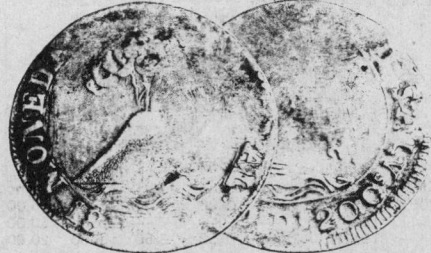

Obv. leg: POR LA LIBERTAD DEL SALV, corrected 4. - R.
Rev. leg: MONEDA PROVISIONAL.

| 8.2 | 1828 F | — | 3250. | 4500. | 5500. | 8000. |

COUNTERMARKED COINAGE
2 REALES

SILVER
c/m: SAP monogram on 2 Reales, KM#5.

| 24.1 | 1828 FP | — | — | — | — | — |
| | 1829 RL | — | — | — | — | — |

c/m: SAP monogram on Central American Republic
2 Reales, KM#9.

| 25 | 1831 F | — | 100.00 | 200.00 | 400.00 | 600.00 |

NOTE: This countermark, appearing to be a SAP monogram has previously been attributed to El Salvador, and also to various Caribbean islands. Inclusion here for reference only.

REPUBLIC
COUNTERMARKED COINAGE
1830

Type I
Volcano, 'S' on either side, '1830' below, in rectangle.

4 REALES

SILVER
c/m: Type I on Mexico 4 Reales, KM#97.

KM#	Date	Year Mintage	Good	VG	Fine
27	1830	(1772-89)	—	Rare	—

1839

Type II
Volcano, '1839' below, in rectangle.
Exists with normal 3 and retrograde 3 in date.

1/2 REAL
SILVER
c/m: Type II on Chile 1/2 Real, KM#90.

| 30 | 1839 | (1833-4) | — | Rare | — |

REAL

SILVER
c/m: Type II on Peru 1 Real, KM#145.1.

| 33 | 1839 | (1826-36) | — | — | Rare |

2 REALES

SILVER
c/m: Type II on Peru (Lima) 2 Reales, KM#141.1.

| 36 | 1839 | (1828-39) | — | 200.00 | 350.00 | 500.00 |

c/m: Type II on South Peru 2 Reales, KM#169.1.

| 37 | 1839 | (1837) | — | — | Rare |

8 REALES
SILVER
c/m: Type II on South Peru 8 Reales, KM#170.2.

| 40 | 1839 | (1837-39) | — | — | Rare |

TYPE III-A
Plain Liberty cap over shield
on draped flags within 10mm circle.

TYPE III-B
Radiant Liberty cap over shield
on draped flags within 12mm circle.

TYPE III-C
Liberty cap over shield
within branches in 12mm circle.
NOTE: Other countermark varieties are known to exist.

SPANISH 'REAL' SERIES
1/2 REAL
SILVER
c/m: Type III on Guatemala 1/2 Real, KM#2.

KM#	Date	Year	Good	VG	Fine	VF
43	ND	—	35.00	50.00	70.00	100.00

REAL

SILVER
c/m: Type III on Bolivia (Potosi) 'cob' 1 Real, KM#42.

| 46 | ND | — | 17.50 | 25.00 | 40.00 | 60.00 |

c/m: Type III on Bolivia (Potosi) 1 Real, KM#52.

| 47 | ND | (1773-89) | 12.50 | 17.50 | 27.50 | 40.00 |

c/m: Type III on Chile 1 Real, KM#65.

| 48 | ND | (1808-17) | 15.00 | 25.00 | 35.00 | 50.00 |

c/m: Type III on Colombia 1 Real, KM#91.1.

| 49 | ND | (1837-46) | 17.50 | 25.00 | 35.00 | 50.00 |

c/m: Type III on Mexico Charles and Johanna
1 Real, KM#9.

| 50 | ND | (1536-72) | 15.00 | 30.00 | 42.50 | 60.00 |

c/m: Type III on Mexico City Philip II Real, KM#27.

| 51 | ND | (1556-98) | 21.50 | 30.00 | 42.50 | 60.00 |

c/m: Type III on Spain 1 Real, C#37.

| 52 | ND | (1772-88) | 13.50 | 20.00 | 27.50 | 40.00 |

2 REALES
SILVER
c/m: Type III on Bolivia (Potosi) 2 Reales, KM#53.

| 55 | ND | (1773-89) | 13.50 | 20.00 | 27.50 | 40.00 |

c/m: Type III on Colombia 2 Reales, KM#97.

| 56 | ND | (1837-46) | 22.50 | 30.00 | 37.50 | 50.00 |

c/m: Type III on Mexico 2 Reales, KM#86.

| 57 | ND | (1747-60) | 17.50 | 25.00 | 35.00 | 50.00 |

c/m: Type III on Mexico 2 Reales, KM#89.

| 58 | ND | (1789-90) | 17.50 | 22.50 | 30.00 | 45.00 |

c/m: Type III on Mexico 2 Reales, KM#90.

| 59 | ND | (1790) | 21.50 | 27.50 | 40.00 | 55.00 |

EL SALVADOR 524

c/m: Type III on Mexico 2 Reales, KM#91.

KM#	Date	Year	Good	VG	Fine	VF
60	ND	(1792-1808)	15.00	22.50	30.00	45.00

c/m: Type III on Mexico 2 Reales, KM#93.
| 61 | ND | (1812-21) | 15.00 | 22.50 | 30.00 | 45.00 |

c/m: Type III on Peru 2 Reales, KM#53.
| 62 | ND | (1752-59) | 20.00 | 32.50 | 45.00 | 60.00 |

c/m: Type III on Peru (Lima) 2 Reales, KM#95.
| 63 | ND | (1791-1808) | 15.00 | 22.50 | 32.50 | 48.00 |

c/m: Type III on Spanish 2 Reales, C#134.
| 64 | ND | (1810-33) | 17.50 | 25.00 | 35.00 | 50.00 |

4 REALES

SILVER
c/m: Type III on Guatemala 4 Reales, KM#85.
| 67 | ND | (1747-53) | — | — | Rare | — |

c/m: Type III on Mexico Sombrerete 4 Reales, KM#175.
| 68 | ND | (1812) | — | — | Rare | — |

8 REALES
SILVER
c/m: Type III on Chile 8 Reales, KM#31.
| 71 | ND | (1773-89) | — | — | Rare | — |

ENGLISH 'STERLING' SERIES
6 PENCE
SILVER
c/m: Type III on Great Britain 6 Pence, KM#394.

KM#	Date	Year	Good	VG	Fine	VF
74	ND	(1816-20)	22.00	30.00	42.50	55.00

c/m: Type III on Great Britain 6 Pence, KM#425.
| 75 | ND | (1831-37) | 22.00 | 30.00 | 42.50 | 55.00 |

SHILLING

SILVER
c/m: Type III on Great Britain Shilling, KM#395.
| 78 | ND | (1816-20) | 25.00 | 32.50 | 45.00 | 60.00 |

c/m: Type III on Great Britain Shilling, KM#409.
| 79 | ND | (1823-25) | 25.00 | 32.50 | 45.00 | 60.00 |

c/m: Type III on Great Britain Shilling, KM#414.
| 80 | ND | (1825-29) | 25.00 | 32.50 | 45.00 | 60.00 |

Type IV
R in beaded 5mm circle.

1/2 REAL

SILVER
c/m: Type IV on Guatemala 1/2 Real, KM#131.
| 83 | ND | (1859-61) | 140.00 | 200.00 | 275.00 | 400.00 |

c/m: Type IV on Guatemala 1/2 Real, KM#138.
| 84 | ND | (1862-65) | 140.00 | 200.00 | 275.00 | 400.00 |

REAL
SILVER
c/m: Type IV on Colombia 1 Real, KM#87.
| 87 | ND | (1827-36) | 15.00 | 22.00 | 35.00 | 50.00 |

c/m: Type IV on Guatemala 1 Real, KM#132.
| 88 | ND | (1859-60) | 15.00 | 22.00 | 30.00 | 42.50 |

c/m: Type IV on Guatemala 1 Real, KM#137.
| 89 | ND | (1862-65) | 15.00 | 22.00 | 30.00 | 42.50 |

2 REALES

SILVER
c/m: Type IV on Guatemala 2 Reales, KM#134.
| 92 | ND | (1860-61) | 17.50 | 25.00 | 32.50 | 45.00 |

c/m: Type IV on Guatemala 2 Reales, KM#139.
| 93 | ND | (1861-65) | 17.50 | 25.00 | 32.50 | 45.00 |

4 REALES
SILVER
c/m: Type IV on Guatemala 4 Reales, KM#136.
| 96 | ND | (1860-61) | 100.00 | 140.00 | 200.00 | 285.00 |

8 REALES

SILVER
c/m: Type IV on Guatemala 1 Peso, KM#178.

KM#	Date	Year	Good	VG	Fine	VF
99	ND	(1859)	—	—	Rare	—

NOTE: Two copper coins of Brazil have also been reported with the Type IV c/m. A 20 Reis dated 1827 and an 80 Reis of the 1820's c/m: '40'.

TYPE V
Zig-Zag Test Mark

2 REALES

SILVER
c/m: Type V on Guatemala 2 Reales, KM#82. (Peru 2 Reales).
| 102 | ND | (1825-40) | 60.00 | 85.00 | 125.00 | 175.00 |

c/m: Type V on Peru 2 Reales, KM#141.1.
| 103 | ND | (1825-40) | 60.00 | 85.00 | 125.00 | 175.00 |

DECIMAL COINAGE
100 Centavos = 1 Peso

CENTAVO

COPPER-NICKEL

KM#	Date	Mintage	Fine	VF	XF	Unc
106	1889H	1.500	1.00	3.00	5.00	15.00
	1889H	—	—	—	Proof	150.00
	1913H	2.500	1.50	3.50	6.00	20.00

COPPER
108	1892/1	.182	45.00	80.00	120.00	225.00
	1892	Inc. Ab.	35.00	70.00	110.00	200.00
	1892	10 pcs.	—	—	Proof	750.00

COPPER-NICKEL
127	1915	5.000	.75	2.50	7.00	20.00
	1919	1.000	1.50	4.00	10.00	35.00
	1920	1.490	1.00	3.00	8.00	25.00
	1925	.200	4.00	8.00	15.00	40.00
	1926	.400	3.00	6.00	12.00	35.00
	1928S	5.000	.75	2.00	6.00	22.50
	1936	2.500	.75	2.00	6.00	22.50

3 CENTAVOS

COPPER-NICKEL

EL SALVADOR 525

KM#	Date	Mintage	Fine	VF	XF	Unc
107	1889H	.333	1.50	4.50	9.00	25.00
	1889H	—	—	—	Proof	200.00
	1913H	1.000	2.00	6.00	14.00	40.00

| 128 | 1915 | 2.700 | 2.00 | 5.00 | 15.00 | 40.00 |

1/4 REAL

BRONZE
| 120 | 1909 | — | 20.00 | 30.00 | 45.00 | 60.00 |

The decimal value of the above coin was about 3 Centavos. It was apparently struck in response to the continuing use of the real monetary system in local market places and rural areas.

5 CENTAVOS

1.2500 g, .835 SILVER, .0336 oz ASW
109	1892CAM	.080	6.00	12.50	25.00	50.00
	1892CAM	—	—	—	Proof	500.00
	1893CAMnc. Ab.	6.00	12.50	25.00	50.00

| 121 | 1911 | 1.000 | 2.00 | 4.00 | 8.00 | 30.00 |

| 124 | 1914 | 2.000 | 1.50 | 3.00 | 6.00 | 22.50 |
| | 1914 | 20 pcs. | — | — | Proof | 100.00 |

COPPER-NICKEL
129	1915	2.500	.75	2.00	6.00	25.00
	1916	1.500	1.25	3.00	8.00	32.50
	1917	1.000	1.50	4.00	10.00	40.00
	1918/7	1.000	1.25	3.00	8.00	30.00
	1918	Inc. Ab.	1.25	3.00	8.00	32.50
	1919	2.000	1.00	3.00	8.00	25.00
	1920	2.000	.75	2.00	6.00	20.00
	1921	1.780	1.00	2.50	7.00	25.00
	1925	.50	1.50	5.00	17.50

10 CENTAVOS

2.5000 g, .835 SILVER, .0671 oz ASW
| 110 | 1892CAM | .012 | 50.00 | 100.00 | 150.00 | 300.00 |
| | 1892CAM | — | — | — | Proof | 500.00 |

| 122 | 1911 | 1.000 | 2.25 | 4.00 | 8.00 | 25.00 |

KM#	Date	Mintage	Fine	VF	XF	Unc
125	1914	1.500	2.00	3.50	6.00	22.50
	1914	20 pcs.	—	—	Proof	200.00

20 CENTAVOS

5.0000 g, .835 SILVER, .1342 oz ASW
111	1892CAM	.146	10.00	25.00	65.00	125.00
	1892CAM	—	—	—	Proof	350.00
	1893CAM	—	—	Reported, not confirmed

25 CENTAVOS

6.2500 g, .835 SILVER, .1678 oz ASW
| 123 | 1911 | .600 | 4.75 | 6.00 | 10.00 | 30.00 |

126	1914 15 DE SEPT	1.400	5.50	6.50	10.00	25.00
	1914 15 SEP I.A.	5.50	6.50	10.00	25.00
	1914 15 SET DE 1821 Inc. Ab.	5.50	6.50	10.00	25.00
	1914 20 pcs.	—	—	Proof	550.00

50 CENTAVOS

12.5000 g, .900 SILVER, .3617 oz ASW
| 112 | 1892CAM | .043 | 30.00 | 65.00 | 150.00 | 275.00 |
| | 1892CAM | — | — | — | Proof | 750.00 |

113	1892CAM	.340	10.00	20.00	50.00	120.00
	1893CAM	I.A.	12.00	25.00	55.00	125.00
	1894CAM	I.A.	14.00	27.50	60.00	145.00

UN (1) PESO

25.0000 g, .900 SILVER, .7234 oz ASW
KM#	Date	Mintage	Fine	VF	XF	Unc
114	1892CAM	.041	60.00	170.00	250.00	700.00
	1892CAM	—	—	—	Proof	1000.

115.1	1892CAM	.950	25.00	50.00	100.00	200.00
	1893/2 CAM Inc. Ab.	10.00	22.50	37.50	100.00
	1893CAM	I.A.	8.00	17.50	27.50	85.00
	1894CAM	I.A.	6.50	12.00	20.00	80.00
	1895CAM	I.A.	6.50	12.00	20.00	80.00
	1896CAM	I.A.	100.00	200.00	400.00	—
	1904CAM	.600	6.50	12.00	20.00	80.00
	1908CAM	1.600	7.00	10.00	18.00	65.00
	1911CAM	.500	8.00	15.00	25.00	85.00
	1914CAM	*.700	—	Reported, not confirmed

NOTE: Struck at the Brussels mint, but then remelted for the striking of 1914 minor coinage.

Rev: Heavier portrait (wider right shoulder).
115.2	1904CAM	.400	8.00	15.00	35.00	100.00
	1909CAM	.690	6.50	12.00	20.00	80.00
	1911CAM	1.020	6.50	12.00	20.00	80.00
	1914CAM	2.100	6.50	12.00	20.00	80.00
	1914CAM	—	—	—	Proof	2250.

2-1/2 PESOS

4.0323 g, .900 GOLD, .1167 oz AGW
| 116 | 1892CAM 597 pcs. | 400.00 | 600.00 | 1000. | 1500. |
| | 1892CAM | — | — | — | Proof | 1750. |

5 PESOS

8.0645 g, .900 GOLD, .2334 oz AGW
| 117 | 1892CAM 558 pcs. | 450.00 | 700.00 | 1200. | 1750. |
| | 1892CAM | — | — | — | Proof | 2250. |

EL SALVADOR 526

10 PESOS

16.1290 g, .900 GOLD, .4667 oz AGW

KM#	Date	Mintage	Fine	VF	XF	Unc
118	1892CAM	321 pcs.	800.00	1500.	2000.	3000.
	1892CAM	—	—	—	Proof	3250.

20 PESOS

32.2580 g, .900 GOLD, .9334 oz AGW

119	1892CAM	200 pcs.	1500.	2250.	3000.	4500.
	1892CAM	—	—	—	Proof	5000.

MONETARY REFORM
100 Centavos = 1 Colon

CENTAVO

COPPER-NICKEL

133	1940	1.000	1.25	3.50	7.00	20.00

BRONZE

135	1942	5.000	.20	.50	1.00	4.50
	1943	5.000	.20	.50	1.00	4.50
	1945	5.000	.20	.40	.75	3.00
	1947	5.000	.20	.50	1.00	3.50
	1951	10.000	.10	.30	.75	2.50
	1952	10.000	.10	.20	.50	1.75
	1956	10.000	.10	.20	.40	1.25
	1966	5.000	—	—	.10	.85
	1968	5.000	—	—	.10	.60
	1969	5.000	—	—	.10	.75
	1972	20.000	—	—	.10	.50

BRASS

135a	1976	20.000	—	—	.10	.20
	1977	40.000	—	—	.10	.20

COPPER-ZINC
Obv: Smaller portrait, DH monogram at truncation.
Rev: Denomination in wreath, SM at right base of 1.

135c	1981	50.000	—	—	.10	.15

COPPER CLAD STEEL

135b	1986	30.000	—	—	.10	.15

2 CENTAVOS

NICKEL-BRASS

147	1974	10.002	—	.10	.15	.20

3 CENTAVOS

NICKEL-BRASS

KM#	Date	Mintage	Fine	VF	XF	Unc
148	1974	10.002	—	.10	.15	.20	.40

5 CENTAVOS

COPPER-NICKEL

134	1940	.800	.50	1.00	3.00	8.00
	1951	2.000	.25	.50	1.25	5.00
	1956	8.000	.10	.25	.40	1.00
	1959	6.000	.10	.15	.25	.75
	1963	10.000	.10	.15	.30	1.00
	1966	6.000	.10	.15	.25	.50
	1967	10.000	.10	.15	.25	.50
	1972	10.000	—	.10	.15	.30
	1974	10.002	—	.10	.15	.30

COPPER-NICKEL-ZINC

134a	1944	5.000	.25	.50	1.50	5.00
	1948	3.000	.25	.50	1.00	2.50
	1950	2.000	.25	.50	1.50	5.00
	1952	4.000	.20	.35	.75	4.00

NICKEL-CLAD-STEEL

149	1975	15.000	—	.10	.15	.30
	1976	15.000	—	.10	.15	.30
	1984	15.000	—	.10	.15	.30
	1986	30.000	—	.10	.15	.30

COPPER-NICKEL

149a	1977	26.000	—	.10	.15	.30

10 CENTAVOS

COPPER-NICKEL

130	1921	2.000	1.50	5.00	12.00	30.00
	1925	2.000	2.00	6.00	14.00	35.00
	1940	.500	3.50	9.00	20.00	55.00
	1951	1.000	.50	1.50	3.00	8.00
	1967	2.000	—	.10	.50	2.00
	1968	3.000	—	.10	.40	1.00
	1969	3.000	—	.10	.40	1.00
	1972	7.000	—	.10	.25	.75

COPPER-NICKEL-ZINC

130a	1952	2.000	.15	.25	.50	2.00

NICKEL-CLAD-STEEL

150	1975	15.000	—	.15	.25	.50

COPPER-NICKEL

150a	1977	24.000	—	.10	.20	.40

COPPER-ZINC-NICKEL

150b	1985	15.000	—	.10	.15	.30

25 CENTAVOS

7.5000 g, .900 SILVER, .2170 oz ASW

KM#	Date	Mintage	Fine	VF	XF	Unc
136	1943	1.000	1.50	3.00	6.00	10.00
	1944	1.000	1.50	3.00	6.00	10.00

2.5000 g, .900 SILVER, .0723 oz ASW

137	1953	14.000	.50	1.00	1.50	3.50

NICKEL

139	1970	14.000	—	.10	.20	.60
	1973	28.000	—	.10	.20	.50
	1975	20.000	—	.10	.20	.50
	1977	22.400	—	.10	.20	.50

COPPER-NICKEL

139a	1986	21.000	—	.10	.20	.40

50 CENTAVOS

5.0000 g, .900 SILVER, .1446 oz ASW

138	1953	3.000	1.00	2.00	3.50	6.00

NICKEL, 1.65mm thick

140.1	1970	3.000	—	.20	.30	.60

2.00mm thick

140.2	1977	1.500	—	.20	.30	.60

UN (1) COLON

25.0000 g, .900 SILVER, .7234 oz ASW

131	1925Mo	2,000	75.00	125.00	200.00	300.00

2.3000 g, .999 SILVER, .0738 oz ASW
150th Anniversary of Independence

KM#	Date	Mintage	VF	XF	Unc
141	1971	.021	—	Proof	7.50

COPPER-NICKEL
Cristobal Colon

KM#	Date	Mintage	Fine	VF	XF	Unc
153	1984	10.000	—	.40	.60	1.00
	1985	20.000	—	.40	.60	1.00

5 COLONES

11.5000 g, .999 SILVER, .3694 oz ASW
150th Anniversary of Independence

KM#	Date	Mintage	VF	XF	Unc
142	1971	.018	—	Proof	20.00

20 COLONES

15.5600 g, .900 GOLD, .4502 oz AGW

KM#	Date	Mintage	Fine	VF	XF	Unc
132	1925	100 pcs.	—	2250.	3250.	4250.

25 COLONES

2.9400 g, .900 GOLD, .0850 oz AGW
150th Anniversary of Independence

KM#	Date	Mintage	VF	XF	Unc
143	1971	7,650	—	Proof	150.00

25.0000 g, .900 SILVER, .7234 oz ASW
18th Annual Governors' Assembly

151	1977	2,000	—	—	20.00
	1977	.020	—	Proof	25.00

50 COLONES

5.9000 g, .900 GOLD, .1707 oz AGW
150th Anniversary of Independence

144	1971	3,530	—	Proof	150.00

100 COLONES

11.8000 g, .900 GOLD, .3414 oz AGW
150th Anniversary of Independence

KM#	Date	Mintage	VF	XF	Unc
145	1971	2,750	—	Proof	250.00

200 COLONES

23.6000 g, .900 GOLD, .6829 oz AGW
150th Anniversary of Independence

146	1971	2,245	—	Proof	450.00

250 COLONES

16.0000 g, .917 GOLD, .4717 oz AGW
18th Annual Governors' Assembly

152	1977	4,000	—	—	250.00
	1977	400 pcs.	—	Proof	350.00

PROOF SETS (PS)

KM#	Date	Mintage	Identification	Issue Price	Mkt. Val.
PS1	1889H(2)	—	KM106-107	—	350.00
PS2	1892(10)	—	KM108-112,114,116-119	—	16,000.
PS3	1971(6)	—	KM141-146	—	1025.
PS4	1971(4)	—	KM143-146	250.00	1000.
PS5	1971(2)	—	KM141-142	6.00	25.00

Listings For
EQUATORIAL AFRICAN STATES: refer to Central African Empire

EQUATORIAL GUINEA

The Republic of Equatorial Guinea (formerly Spanish Guinea) consists of Rio Muni, located on the coast of west-Central Africa between Cameroon and Gabon, and the off-shore islands of Fernando Po, Annobon, Corisco, Elobey Grande and Elobey Chico. The equatorial country has an area of 10,831 sq. mi. (28,051 sq. km.) and a population of *389,000. Capital: Malabo. The economy is based on agriculture and forestry. Cacao, wood and coffee are exported.

Fernando Po was discovered between 1474 and 1496 by Portuguese navigators charting a route to the spice islands of the Far East. Portugal retained control of it and the adjacent islands until 1778 when they, together with trading rights to the African coast between the Ogooue and Niger rivers, were ceded to Spain. Fernando Po was administered, with Spanish consent, by the British from 1827 to 1844 when it was reclaimed by Spain. Mainland Rio Muni was granted to Spain by the Berlin Conference of 1885. The name of the colony was changed from Spanish Guinea to Equatorial Guinea in Dec. of 1963. Independence was attained on Oct. 12, 1968.

NOTE: The 1969 coinage carries the actual minting date in the stars at the sides of the large date.

PESETA

ALUMINUM-BRONZE

KM#	Date	Mintage	Fine	VF	XF	Unc
1	1969(69)	—	1.50	2.50	4.00	6.00

5 PESETAS

COPPER-NICKEL

2	1969(69)	—	3.75	5.50	9.00	12.50

25 PESETAS

COPPER-NICKEL

3	1969(69)	—	5.00	8.00	12.50	17.50

5.0000 g, .999 SILVER, .1606 oz ASW
World Bank

5	1970	2,475	—	Proof	7.50

United Nations

6	1970	2,475	—	Proof	7.50

EQUATORIAL GUINEA 528

50 PESETAS

COPPER-NICKEL

KM#	Date	Mintage	Fine	VF	XF	Unc
4	1969(69)	—	6.00	10.00	15.00	25.00

10.0000 g, .999 SILVER, .3212 oz ASW
Praying Hands

| 7 | 1970 | 3,840 | — | — | Proof | 10.00 |

75 PESETAS

15.0000 g, .999 SILVER, .4818 oz ASW
Pope John XXIII
Obv: Similar to KM#10.

| 8 | 1970 | 4,000 | — | — | Proof | 20.00 |

Centennial of Birth of Vladimir Ilyich Lenin

| 9 | 1970 | 4,000 | — | — | Proof | 20.00 |

Abraham Lincoln

| 10 | 1970 | 4,390 | — | — | Proof | 20.00 |

Obv: Similar to KM#10.

KM#	Date	Mintage	Fine	VF	XF	Unc
11	1970	4,000	—	—	Proof	20.00

100 PESETAS

20.0000 g, .999 SILVER, .6430 oz ASW
Praying Hands
Obv: Similar to KM#13.1.

| 12 | 1970 | 4,000 | — | — | Proof | 20.00 |

Naked Maja

| 13.1 | 1970 | .030 | — | — | Proof | 42.50 |

Obv: Fineness stamp at base of right tusk.

| 13.2 | 1970 | Inc. Ab. | — | — | Proof | 42.50 |

Obv: Fineness stamp below base of right tusk.

| 13.3 | 1970 | Inc. Ab. | — | — | Proof | 42.50 |

Obv: Fineness stamp above letters AN.

| 13.4 | 1970 | Inc. Ab. | — | — | Proof | 42.50 |

Obv: 1000 in oval counterstamp at base of right tusk.

| 13.5 | 1970 | Inc. Ab. | — | — | Proof | 42.50 |

150 PESETAS

30.0000 g, .999 SILVER, .9636 oz ASW
Centennial of the Capital Rome, Roma

KM#	Date	Mintage	Fine	VF	XF	Unc
14	1970	3,520	—	—	Proof	35.00

Centennial of the Capital Rome, Coliseum

| 15 | 1970 | 3,520 | — | — | Proof | 35.00 |

Centennial of the Capital Rome, Athena

| 16 | 1970 | 3,520 | — | — | Proof | 35.00 |

Centennial of the Capital Rome, Mercury

| 17 | 1970 | 3,520 | — | — | Proof | 35.00 |

200 PESETAS

40.0000 g, .999 SILVER 1.2848 oz ASW
World Soccer Championship in Mexico

| 18 | 1970 | 4,280 | — | — | Proof | 50.00 |

Centennial of Birth of Mahatma Gandhi

EQUATORIAL GUINEA 529

First President Francisco Macias

KM#	Date	Mintage	Fine	VF	XF	Unc
19	1970	4,000	—	—	Proof	40.00

250 PESETAS
3.5200 g, .900 GOLD, .1018 oz AGW
Naked Maja
Similar to 100 Pesetas, KM#13.1.

20	1970	3,500	—	—	Proof	125.00

Praying Hands
Similar to 100 Pesetas, KM#12.

21	1970	2,000	—	—	Proof	100.00

500 PESETAS
7.0500 g, .900 GOLD, .2040 oz AGW
Rev: Bust of Pope John XXIII

22	1970	1,680	—	—	Proof	150.00

Vladimir Ilyich Lenin
Similar to 75 Pesetas, KM#9.

23	1970	1,680	—	—	Proof	150.00

Abraham Lincoln

24	1970	1,700	—	—	Proof	150.00

Mahatma Gandhi

25	1970	1,680	—	—	Proof	150.00

750 PESETAS
10.5700 g, .900 GOLD, .3058 oz AGW
Centennial of the Capital Rome, Roma
Similar to 150 Pesetas, KM#14.

26	1970	1,650	—	—	Proof	220.00

Centennial of the Capital Rome, Coliseum
Similar to 150 Pesetas, KM#15.

27	1970	1,550	—	—	Proof	220.00

Centennial of the Capital Rome, Athena
Similar to 150 Pesetas, KM#16.

28	1970	1,550	—	—	Proof	220.00

Centennial of the Capital Rome, Mercury
Similar to 150 Pesetas, KM#17.

29	1970	1,550	—	—	Proof	220.00

1000 PESETAS
14.1000 g, .900 GOLD, .4080 oz AGW
World Soccer Championship in Mexico
Similar to 200 Pesetas, KM#18.

30	1970	1,190	—	—	Proof	300.00

5000 PESETAS
70.5200 g, .900 GOLD, 2.0407 oz AGW
First President Francisco Macias
Similar to 200 Pesetas, KM#19.

31	1970	330 pcs.	—	—	Proof	1350.

MONETARY REFORM
EKUELE

BRASS

KM#	Date	Mintage	Fine	VF	XF	Unc
32	1975	3,000	1.00	1.50	2.50	5.00

NOTE: Withdrawn from circulation.

5 EKUELE

COPPER-NICKEL

33	1975	2.800	1.25	2.50	4.00	8.00

NOTE: Withdrawn from circulation.

10 EKUELE

COPPER-NICKEL

34	1975	1.300	2.25	3.50	6.00	10.00

NOTE: Withdrawn from circulation.

1000 EKUELE

21.4300 g, .925 SILVER, .6373 oz ASW
President Masie Nguema Biyogo

35	1978	.031	—	—	Proof	17.50

2000 EKUELE

42.8800 g, .925 SILVER, 1.2753 oz ASW

President Masie Nguema Biyogo

KM#	Date	Mintage	Fine	VF	XF	Unc
36	1978	.031	—	—	Proof	32.50

31.1000 g, .927 SILVER, .9270 oz ASW
XXII Olympics

37	ND(1979)	.011	—	—	Proof	37.50

42.8700 g, .925 SILVER, 1.2749 oz ASW
Soccer Games - Argentina 1978
Obv: Similar to KM#36.

38	ND(1979)	195 pcs.	—	—	Proof	175.00

31.0000 g, .927 SILVER, .9270 oz ASW
Zebra
Obv: Similar to KM#37.

55	1980(1983)	1,000	—	—	Proof	40.00

Impalas
Obv: Similar to KM#37.

56	1980(1983)	1,000	—	—	Proof	40.00

EQUATORIAL GUINEA

Tiger
Obv: Similar to KM#37.

KM#	Date	Mintage	Fine	VF	XF	Unc
57	1980(1983)	1,000	—	—	Proof	40.00

Cheetah
Obv: Similar to KM#37.

| 58 | 1980(1983) | 1,000 | — | — | Proof | 40.00 |

5000 EKUELE

6.9600 g, .917 GOLD, .2052 oz AGW
President Masie Nguema Biyogo

| 39 | 1978 | .031 | — | — | Proof | 150.00 |

10,000 EKUELE

13.9200 g, .917 GOLD, .4104 oz AGW
President Masie Nguema Biyogo

| 40 | 1978 | .031 | — | — | Proof | 300.00 |

Soccer Games - Argentina 1978

| 41 | ND(1979) | 121 pcs. | — | — | Proof | 450.00 |

MONETARY REFORM
EKWELE

ALUMINUM-BRONZE

				T.E. Nkogo.			
KM#	Date	Mintage	Fine	VF	XF	Unc	
50	1980	.200	—	—	—	50.00	

62.2900 g, .999 GOLD, 2.0009 oz AGW
Pope John Paul II
Obv: Coat of arms.

| 54 | 1982 | — | — | — | — | 1400. |

5 BIPKWELE

COPPER-NICKEL
Obv: T.E. Nkogo right. Rev: Value and arms.

| 51 | 1980 | .200 | — | — | — | 40.00 |

25 BIPKWELE

COPPER-NICKEL
T.E. Nkogo

| 52 | 1980 | .200 | — | — | — | 40.00 |
| | 1981 | .800 | — | — | — | — |

50 BIPKWELE

COPPER-NICKEL
Obv: T.E. Nkogo right. Rev: Value and arms.

| 53 | 1980 | .200 | — | — | — | 50.00 |
| | 1981 | .500 | — | — | — | — |

1000 BIPKWELE

12.5000 g, .925 SILVER, .3717 oz ASW
Juan Carlos I Visit
Obv: Similar to 10,000 Bipkwele, KM#48.
Rev: Similar to 2000 Bipkwele, KM#44.

| 42 | 1979 | 5,125 | — | — | — | 20.00 |
| | 1979 | 3,000 | — | — | Proof | 27.50 |

Juan Carlos I Visit
Rev: Similar to 2000 Bipkwele, KM#45.

| 43 | 1979 | 5,125 | — | — | — | 20.00 |
| | 1979 | 3,000 | — | — | Proof | 27.50 |

2000 BIPKWELE

25.0000 g, .925 SILVER, .7435 oz ASW
Juan Carlos I Visit

| 44 | 1979 | 5,125 | — | — | — | 25.00 |
| | 1979 | 3,000 | — | — | Proof | 30.00 |

Juan Carlos I Visit

KM#	Date	Mintage	Fine	VF	XF	Unc
45	1979	5,125	—	—	—	25.00
	1979	3,000	—	—	Proof	30.00

5000 BIPKWELE

4.0000 g, .917 GOLD, .1179 oz AGW
Juan Carlos I Visit

| 46 | 1979 | 4,250 | — | — | — | 75.00 |
| | 1979 | 2,000 | — | — | Proof | 100.00 |

Juan Carlos I Visit

| 47 | 1979 | 4,250 | — | — | — | 75.00 |
| | 1979 | 2,000 | — | — | Proof | 100.00 |

10,000 BIPKWELE

8.0000 g, .917 GOLD, .2358 oz AGW
Juan Carlos I Visit

| 48 | 1979 | 4,250 | — | — | — | 150.00 |
| | 1979 | 2,000 | — | — | Proof | 175.00 |

Juan Carlos I Visit

| 49 | 1979 | 4,250 | — | — | — | 150.00 |
| | 1979 | 2,000 | — | — | Proof | 175.00 |

MONETARY REFORM
100 FRANCOS

COPPER-NICKEL

| 59 | 1985(a) | — | — | .50 | .80 | 1.50 |

MINT SETS (MS)

KM#	Date	Mintage	Identification	Issue Price	Mkt. Val.
MS1	1975(3)	—	KM32-34	—	23.00

PROOF SETS (PS)

PS1	1970(27)	330	KM5-31	—	3750.
PS2	1970(15)	2,475	KM5-19	126.50	400.00
PS3	1970(12)	330	KM20-31	—	3350.

Listings For

ERITREA: refer to Ethiopia
ESSEQUIBO & DEMERARY: refer to Guyana
ESTONIA: refer to Baltic Regions

ETHIOPIA

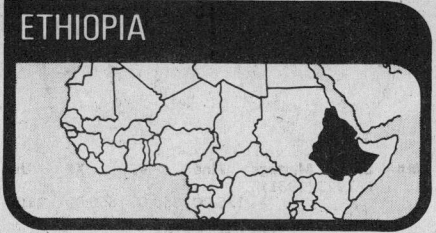

The Peoples Democratic Republic of Ethiopia, Africa's oldest independent nation, faces on the Red Sea in East-Central Africa. The country has an area of 471,778 sq. mi. (1,221,900 sq. km.) and a population of *47.7 million people who are divided among 40 tribes and speak 270 languages and dialects. Capital: Addis Ababa. The economy is predominantly agricultural and pastoral. Gold and platinum are mined and petroleum fields are being developed. Coffee, oilseeds, hides and cereals are exported.

Ethiopia was supposedly founded by Menelik I, son of Solomon and the Queen of Sheba in the 10th century B.C. Modern Ethiopian history began with the reign of Emperor Menelik II (1889-1913) under whose guidance the country emerged from medieval isolation. Ethiopia was invaded by Mussolini in 1935, and together with Italian Somaliland and Eritrea became part of Italian East Africa until liberated by British and Ethiopian troops in 1941. Haile Selassie I, 225th consecutive Solomonic ruler was deposed by a military committee on Sept. 12, 1974. As of July 1976, Ethiopia's present rule is by a military provisional government which refers to the country as Socialist Ethiopia.

No coins, patterns or presentation pieces are known bearing Emperor Lij Yasu's likeness or titles. Coins of Menelik II were struck during this period with dates frozen.

RULERS
Menelik II, 1889-1913
Lij Yasu, 1913-1916
Zauditu, Empress, 1916-1930
Haile Selassie I
 1930-36, 1941-1974

MINT MARKS
A - Paris
(a) - Paris, privy marks only

Coinage of Menelik II, 1889-1913
NOTE: The first national issue coinage, dated 1887 and 1888 E.E., carried a cornucopia, A, and fasces on the reverse. Subsequent dates have a torch substituted for the fasces, the A being dropped. All issues bearing these marks were struck at the Paris Mint. Coins without mint marks were struck in Addis Ababa.

MONETARY SYSTEM
(Until about 1903)
40 Besa = 20 Gersh = 1 Birr
(After 1903)
32 Besa = 16 Gersh = 1 Birr

DATING
Ethiopian coinage is dated by the Ethiopian Era calendar (E.E.) which commenced 7 years and 8 months after the advent of A.D. dating.

EXAMPLE
1900 (10 and 9 = 19 x 100)
  36 (Add 30 and 6)
1936 E.E.
   8 (Add)
1943/4 AD

KINGDOM OF ABYSSINIA
MAHALEKI

SILVER, 15mm
Obv: Crown. Rev: Date, denomination and script of Ethiopia.

KM#	Date	Mintage	Fine	VF	XF	Unc
1	EE1885 (1892)		75.00	150.00	250.00	350.00

NOTE: The above issue has been reported to be the last issue of the Harrar Mint following the capture of that city in 1887 by Menelik's forces.

MONETARY REFORM
1/100 BIRR
(Yaber Matawasho 'Matonya')

COPPER

KM#	Date	Mintage	Fine	VF	XF	Unc
9	EE1889A (1897)	.500	5.00	10.00	18.00	40.00

1/4 GERSH
(Ya Gersh Rub)

COPPER, 26mm

| 6 | EE1888A (1896) | 200 pcs. | 600.00 | 900.00 | 1350. | 2250. |

1/2 GERSH
(Ya Gersh Alad)

COPPER

| 7 | EE1888A (1896) | 200 pcs. | 500.00 | 800.00 | 1200. | 2000. |

1/32 BIRR
(Ya Birr 32nd)

First Issue

COPPER or BRASS
Enlargement (below lion)

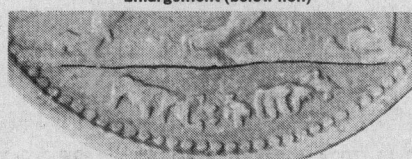

Defaced, with plain and rough edge.

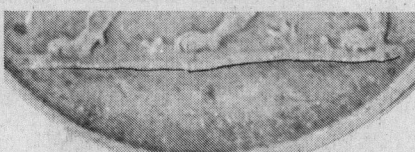

Obliterated, plain and reeded edge.

| 10 | EE1889 (1897) | | 3.50 | 7.50 | 15.00 | 50.00 |

NOTE: This issue was struck from dies intended for a silver 1/8 Birr of the die series that included KM#14 and 15. These are found with the denomination partially to almost totally effaced from beneath the lion. First struck at the Addis Ababa Mint about 1903 from dies prepared at Paris.

Second Issue

Enlargement (below lion)

| 11 | EE1889 (1897) | 3.353 | 4.00 | 10.00 | 22.50 | 60.00 |

NOTE: Struck at the Addis Ababa Mint in 1922, 1931 and 1933 from newly prepared dies having corrected denominations.

GERSH
(1/20 Birr)

COPPER

KM#	Date	Mintage	Fine	VF	XF	Unc
8	EE1888A (1896)	200 pcs.	550.00	850.00	1400.	2200.

1.4038 g, .835 SILVER, .0377 oz ASW
Rev: Lion's left leg raised.

12	EE1889A (1897)	1.000	6.00	12.50	20.00	40.00
	1891A (1898)	4.000	4.00	8.00	15.00	30.00
	1895A (1903)	*44.789	2.00	3.50	6.00	12.50

*NOTE: Struck between 1903-1928.

Rev: Lion's right leg raised.

| 13 | EE1889 (1897) | — | 50.00 | 75.00 | 150.00 | 350.00 |

GOLD (OMS)
| 13a | EE1889 (1897) | — | 700.00 | 1000. | 1500. | 2000. |

1/8 BIRR
(Ya Birr Tamun/of Birr Eighth)

3.5094 g, .835 SILVER, .0942 oz ASW
Rev: Lion's left leg raised.

| 2 | EE1887A (1894) | .025 | 15.00 | 25.00 | 50.00 | 185.00 |
| | 1888A (1896) | 200 pcs. | 300.00 | 400.00 | 500.00 | 750.00 |

1/4 BIRR
(Ya Birr Rub/of Birr Fourth)

7.0188 g, .835 SILVER, .1884 oz ASW
Rev: Lion's left leg raised.

| 3 | EE1887A (1894) | .015 | 10.00 | 20.00 | 40.00 | 120.00 |
| | 1888A (1896) | | | | | |

ETHIOPIA 532

KM#	Date	Mintage	Fine	VF	XF	Unc
3	1889A (1897)	200 pcs.	—	—	—	—
	1895A (1903)	.400	5.00	10.00	20.00	100.00
	*	.821	5.00	10.00	20.00	90.00

*NOTE: Struck between 1903 and 1925.

Rev: Lion's right leg raised.

| 14 | EE1889 (1897) | — | 15.00 | 30.00 | 60.00 | 150.00 |

GOLD (OMS)

| 14a | EE1889 (1897) | — | 500.00 | 800.00 | 1500. | 2500. |

1/2 BIRR
(Ya Birr Alad / of Birr Half)

14.0375 g, .835 SILVER, .3768 oz ASW
Rev: Lion's left leg raised.

4	EE1887A (1894)	.010	12.00	35.00	70.00	225.00
	1888A (1896)	200 pcs.	300.00	400.00	500.00	750.00
	1889A (1897)	*.420	12.00	17.50	35.00	150.00

*NOTE: Struck between 1897 and 1925.

Rev: Lion's right leg raised.

| 15 | EE1889 (1897) | — | 60.00 | 100.00 | 175.00 | 350.00 |

GOLD (OMS)

| 15a | EE1889 (1897) | — | 500.00 | 750.00 | 1200. | 1800. |

BIRR

28.0750 g, .835 SILVER, .7537 oz ASW

Rev: Lion's left fore leg raised.

KM#	Date	Mintage	Fine	VF	XF	Unc
5	EE1887A (1894)	.020	27.50	50.00	100.00	275.00
	1887A (1894)	—	—	—	Proof	425.00
	1888A (1896)	200 pcs.	—	—	—	—
	1889A (1897)	.418	15.00	25.00	65.00	200.00

Rev: Lion's right fore leg raised.

19	EE1892 (1899)	.401	12.50	25.00	60.00	175.00
	1892 (1899)	—	—	—	Proof	325.00
	1895 (1903)	*.459	12.50	25.00	60.00	175.00
	1895 (1903)	—	—	—	Proof	500.00

*NOTE: Struck in 1901, 1903 and 1904.

1/4 WERK
(Ya Werk Rub / of Werk Fourth)

1.7500 g, .900 GOLD, 16mm, .0506 oz AGW

| 16 | EE1889 (1897) | — | 50.00 | 125.00 | 200.00 | 300.00 |

1/2 WERK
(Ya Werk Alad / of Werk Half)

3.5000 g, .900 GOLD, .1012 oz AGW

| 17 | EE1889 (1897) | — | 75.00 | 150.00 | 250.00 | 375.00 |

| 20 | EE1923 (1931) | — | 125.00 | 250.00 | 425.00 | 700.00 |

WERK

7.0000 g, .900 GOLD, .2025 oz AGW

| 18 | EE1889 (1897) | — | 125.00 | 175.00 | 275.00 | 450.00 |

KM#	Date	Mintage	Fine	VF	XF	Unc
21	EE1923 (1931)	—	175.00	350.00	650.00	1100.

PROOF SETS

KM#	Date	Mintage	Identification	Issue Price	Mkt. Val.
101	1894 (4)	—	KM2-5	—	2500.

KINGDOM OF ETHIOPIA
MONETARY SYSTEM
100 Matonas = 100 Santeems
100 Santeems (Cents) = 1 Birr (Dollar)

MATONA

COPPER

KM#	Date	Mintage	Fine	VF	XF	Unc
27	EE1923 (1931)	*1.250	1.50	2.50	4.50	13.00

*NOTE: Struck by ICI in Birmingham, England. Other denominations in the Matona series were struck in Addis Ababa.

CENT
(Ano Santeem)

COPPER

| 32 | EE1936 (1944) | 20.000 | — | .10 | .20 | .50 |

NOTE: Coins in the one cent to fifty cent denominations were struck at Philadelphia and the Royal Mint, London between 1944 and 1975 with the date EE1936 frozen.

5 MATONAS

COPPER
Plain edge

| 28.1 | EE1923 (1931) | 1.363 | 2.00 | 3.50 | 6.00 | 20.00 |

Reeded edge

| 28.2 | EE1923 (1931) | Inc. Ab. | 2.00 | 3.50 | 6.00 | 20.00 |

5 CENTS
(Ammist Santeem)

COPPER

| 33 | EE1936 (1944) | *219.000 | — | .10 | .20 | .50 |

*NOTE: Struck between 1944-1966.

10 MATONAS

NICKEL

| 29 | EE1923 (1931) | .936 | 1.50 | 2.50 | 5.00 | 12.50 |

10 CENTS
(Assir Santeem)

ETHIOPIA 533

COPPER

KM#	Date	Mintage	Fine	VF	XF	Unc
34	EE1936 (1944)	*348.998	—	.10	.25	.75

*NOTE: Struck between 1945-1975.

25 MATONAS

NICKEL

KM#	Date	Mintage	Fine	VF	XF	Unc
30	EE1923 (1931)	2.742	1.25	2.00	4.00	10.00

25 CENTS
(Haya Ammist Santeem)

COPPER

KM#	Date	Mintage	Fine	VF	XF	Unc
35	EE1936 (1944)	10.000	5.00	10.00	17.50	35.00

KM#	Date	Mintage	Fine	VF	XF	Unc
36	EE1936 (1944)	*30.000	.10	.20	.35	1.75

*NOTE: Issued in 1952 and 1953. Crude and refined edges.

50 MATONAS

NICKEL

KM#	Date	Mintage	Fine	VF	XF	Unc
31	EE1923 (1931)	1.621	1.50	2.50	5.00	12.50

50 CENTS
(Amsa Santeem)

7.0307 g, .800 SILVER, .1808 oz ASW

KM#	Date	Mintage	Fine	VF	XF	Unc
37	EE1936 (1944)	*30.000	2.00	3.50	5.00	10.00

*NOTE: Struck in 1944-1945.

7.0307 g, .700 SILVER, .1582 oz ASW

37a	EE1936 (1944)	*20.434	2.00	3.50	5.00	10.00

*NOTE: Struck in 1947.

SOCIALIST ETHIOPIA
CENT

ALUMINUM
F.A.O. issue

KM#	Date	Mintage	Fine	VF	XF	Unc
43	EE1969 (1977)	35.034	.10	.20	.30	.50
	1969 (1977) FM	.012	—	—	Proof	1.00

5 CENTS

COPPER-ZINC

44	EE1969 (1977)	268.577	.15	.20	.30	.60
	1969 (1977) FM	.012	—	—	Proof	2.00

10 CENTS

COPPER-ZINC

45	EE1969 (1977)	243.338	.15	.30	.50	.75
	1969 (1977) FM	.012	—	—	Proof	3.00

25 CENTS

COPPER-NICKEL

46	EE1969 (1977)	44.983	.20	.30	.60	1.25
	1969 (1977) FM	.012	—	—	Proof	4.00

50 CENTS

COPPER-NICKEL

47	EE1969 (1977)	46.907	.40	.75	1.25	2.50
	1969 (1977) FM	.012	—	—	Proof	7.50

2 BIRR

COPPER-NICKEL
World Soccer Games 1982

KM#	Date	Mintage	Fine	VF	XF	Unc
64	1982	—	—	—	—	5.00

5 DOLLARS

20.0000 g, .925 SILVER, .5948 oz ASW
Theodros II
Rev: Similar to 10 Dollars, KM#53.

KM#	Date	Mintage	VF	XF	Unc
48	1972	—	—	Proof	50.00
	1972F	—	—	Proof	50.00

Yohannes IV
Rev: Similar to 10 Dollars, KM#53.

49	1972	—	—	Proof	50.00
	1972F	—	—	Proof	50.00

Menelik II

50	1972	—	—	Proof	50.00
	1972F	—	—	—	40.00
	1972F	—	—	Proof	50.00

ETHIOPIA 534

Zauditu
Rev: Similar to 10 Dollars, KM#53.

KM#	Date	Mintage	VF	XF	Unc
51	1972	—	—	Proof	50.00
	1972F	—	—	Proof	50.00

25.0000 g, .999 SILVER, .8030 oz ASW
Haile Selassie

| 52 | 1972HF | 3.000 | — | Proof | 12.50 |

10 DOLLARS

4.0000 g, .900 GOLD, .1157 oz AGW

| 38 | 1966 | .028 | — | Proof | 100.00 |

40.0000 g, .925 SILVER, 1.1895 oz ASW

| 53 | 1972 | — | — | Proof | 85.00 |

10 BIRR

28.2800 g, .925 SILVER, .8410 oz ASW
Conservation Series
Rev: Bearded vulture.

KM#	Date	Mintage	VF	XF	Unc
61	1979	4,002	—	—	25.00
61a	1979	3,460	—	Proof	40.00

20 DOLLARS

8.0000 g, .900 GOLD, .2315 oz AGW

| 39 | 1966 | .025 | — | Proof | 150.00 |

20 BIRR

23.3300 g, .925 SILVER, .6938 oz ASW
International Year of the Child

| 54 | EE1972(1981) | — | — | — | 25.00 |
| | 1972(1981) | .016 | — | Proof | 35.00 |

World Soccer Games 1982

KM#	Date	Mintage	VF	XF	Unc
65	1982	.010	—	Proof	27.50

Decade for Women

| 73 | 1984 | 372 pcs. | — | Proof | 45.00 |

25 BIRR

31.6500 g, .925 SILVER, .9413 oz ASW
Conservation Series
Obv: Similar to 10 Birr, KM#64.
Rev: Mountain Nyala.

| 62 | 1979 | 4,002 | — | — | 35.00 |

35.0000 g, .925 SILVER, 1.0409 oz ASW

| 62a | 1979 | 3,295 | — | Proof | 60.00 |

50 DOLLARS

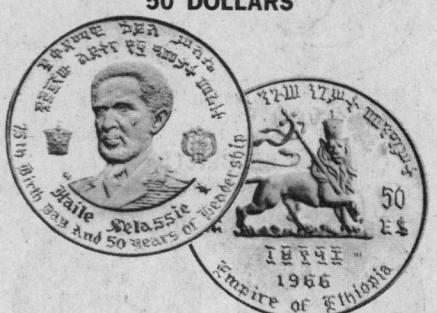

20.0000 g, .900 GOLD, .5787 oz AGW
Obv: Bust of Selassie. Rev: Arms.

| 40 | 1966 | .015 | — | Proof | 350.00 |

Obv: Bust of Theodoro II. Rev: Lion.

| 55 | 1972 | — | — | Proof | 500.00 |

Obv: Bust of Yohannes IV.

| 56 | 1972 | — | — | — | 500.00 |

Obv: Bust of Menelik II.

| 57 | 1972 | — | — | Proof | 500.00 |

Obv: Bust of Zewdith.

| 58 | 1972 | — | — | Proof | 500.00 |

50 BIRR

28.2800 g, .925 SILVER, .8411 oz ASW
International Year of Disabled Persons

KM#	Date	Mintage	VF	XF	Unc
66	1982	.011	—	—	20.00
	1982	.010	—	Proof	25.00

100 DOLLARS

40.0000 g, .900 GOLD, 1.1575 oz AGW
Obv: Bust of Selassie. Rev: Arms.

| 41 | 1966 | .011 | — | Proof | 650.00 |

Obv: Bust of Selassie. Rev: Lion.

| 59 | 1972 | — | — | Proof | 1000. |

200 DOLLARS

80.0000 g, .900 GOLD, 2.3151 oz AGW

| 42 | 1966 | 8,823 | — | Proof | 1350. |

200 BIRR

7.1300 g, .900 GOLD, .2063 oz AGW
World Soccer Games 1982

| 67 | 1982 | 1,310 | — | Proof | 250.00 |

Decade for Women

KM#	Date	Mintage	VF	XF	Unc
72	1984	298 pcs.	—	Proof	350.00

400 BIRR

17.1700 g, .900 GOLD, .4968 oz AGW
International Year of the Child

| 60 | EE1972(1980) | 8 pcs. | — | — | — |
| | EE1972(1980) | 3,387 | — | Proof | 350.00 |

500 BIRR

33.4370 g, .900 GOLD, .9676 oz AGW
Conservation Series
Obv: Similar to 10 Birr, KM#61.
Rev: Walia Ibex.

| 63 | 1979 | 547 pcs. | — | — | 600.00 |
| | 1979 | 160 pcs. | — | Proof | 1200. |

15.9800 g, .917 GOLD, .5006 oz AGW
International Year of Disabled Persons

| 68 | 1982 | 2,007 | — | — | 350.00 |
| | 1982 | 2,042 | — | Proof | 450.00 |

PROOF SETS (PS)

KM#	Date	Mintage	Identification	Issue Price	Mkt. Val.
PS1	1966(5)	8,823	KM38-42	—	2600.
PS2	1972(5)	10,000	KM48-52	46.00	215.00
PS3	1972(5)	10,000	KM55-59	—	3000.
PS4	1977(5)	11,724	KM43-47	25.00	17.50
PS5	1979(2)	—	KM61a-62a	—	100.00

ERITREA

Eritrea, an Ethiopian province fronting on the Red Sea, was an Italian colony from 1890 until its incorporation into Italian East Africa in 1936. It was under the British Military Administration from 1941 to Sept. 15, 1952, when the United Nations designated it an autonomous unit within the federation of Ethiopia and Eritrea. On Nov. 14, 1962, it was fully integrated with Ethiopia.

RULERS

Umberto I, 1889-1900
Vittorio Emanuele III, 1900-1945

MINT MARKS

M - Milan
R - Rome

MONETARY SYSTEM

100 Centesimi - 1 Lira
5 Lire - 1 Tallero

50 CENTESIMI

2.5000 g, .835 SILVER, .0671 oz ASW

KM#	Date	Mintage	Fine	VF	XF	Unc
1	1890M	1.800	22.50	45.00	80.00	150.00

LIRA

5.0000 g, .835 SILVER, .1342 oz ASW

2	1890R	.598	20.00	40.00	75.00	150.00
	1891R	2.401	20.00	40.00	75.00	150.00
	1896R	1.500	40.00	75.00	150.00	600.00

2 LIRE

10.0000 g, .835 SILVER, .2685 oz ASW

| 3 | 1890R | 1.000 | 35.00 | 70.00 | 110.00 | 250.00 |
| | 1896R | .750 | 40.00 | 75.00 | 125.00 | 325.00 |

5 LIRE/TALLERO

28.1250 g, .900 SILVER, .8139 oz ASW

| 4 | 1891 | .196 | 75.00 | 150.00 | 300.00 | 1000. |
| | 1896 | .200 | 75.00 | 150.00 | 325.00 | 1200. |

TALLERO

28.0668 g, .835 SILVER, .7535 oz ASW

| 5 | 1918R | .510 | 30.00 | 50.00 | 80.00 | 250.00 |

HARAR

Harar, a province and city located in eastern Ethiopia, was founded by Arab immigrants from Yemen in the 7th century. The sultanate conquered Ethiopia in the mid-16th century, and was in turn conquered by Egypt in 1875 and by Ethiopia in 1887.

TITLES
El-Harar الهرر

RULERS
Ahmad II,
　　　　AH1209-1236/AD1794-1821
'Abd Al-Rahman,
　　　　AH1236-1240/AD1821-1825
'Abd Al-Karim,
　　　　AH1240-1250/AD1825-1834
Abu Baker II,
　　　　AH1250-1268/AD1834-1852
Muhammad II,
　　　　AH1272-1292/AD1856-1875
'Abdallah,
　　　　AH1303-1304/AD1885-1887

MONETARY SYSTEM
Not known; 22 Mahallak were said to be equal to one Ashrafi, but it is probably that the 'Ashrafi' was a foreign coin of some sort.
The brass coins are of various sizes, but were probably all called 'Mahallak'. The denominations of the billon and silver are unknown.

MAHALLAK

BRASS, 7-9mm, 0.20 g
Anonymous, without name of ruler.

KM#	Date	Mintage	Good	VG	Fine	VF
4	AH1222	—	10.00	15.00	25.00	40.00
	1227	—	10.00	15.00	25.00	40.00

Other dates reported to exist.

BRASS, 5-7mm, 0.13 g

| 5 | ND | — | 4.00 | 7.50 | 12.50 | 18.50 |

Said to be an issue of 'Abd al-Karim.

About 10 mm, 1/2 g. Anonymous.

| 6 | AH1257 | — | 10.00 | 17.50 | 30.00 | 45.00 |
| | 1258 | — | 10.00 | 17.50 | 30.00 | 45.00 |

In the name of Muhammad II.
9-12mm.

| 7 | AH1274 | — | 6.00 | 11.50 | 17.50 | 27.50 |

Rev: Different inscription.

| 8 | AH1276 | — | Reported, not confirmed |||||
| | 1279 | — | 7.00 | 11.50 | 17.50 | 25.00 |

1276 is probably a misreading for 1279.

10-14mm

| 9 | AH1284 | — | 3.00 | 6.00 | 11.50 | 17.50 |

15-19mm
Anonymous, in name of 'THE WEAK SLAVE'.

| 11 | AH1303 | — | 3.00 | 6.00 | 11.00 | 16.00 |
| | 1304 | — | 5.00 | 10.00 | 18.00 | 25.00 |

SILVER COINS
10mm

| 10 | AH1288 | — | 20.00 | 30.00 | 55.00 | 85.00 |

Listings For
FAEROE ISLANDS: refer to Denmark

FALKLAND ISLANDS

The Colony of the Falkland Islands and Dependencies, a British colony located in the South Atlantic about 500 miles northeast of Cape Horn, has an area of 4,700 sq. mi. (12,173 sq. km.) and a population of *1,800. East Falkland, West Falkland, South Georgia, and South Sandwich are the largest of the 200 islands. Capital: Stanley. Sheep grazing is the main industry. Wool, whale oil, and seal oil are exported.

The Falklands were discovered by British navigator John Davis (Davys) in 1592, and named by Capt. John Strong - for Viscount Falkland, treasurer of the British navy - in 1690. French navigator Louis De Bougainville established the first settlement, at Port Louis, in 1764. The following year Capt. John Byron claimed the islands for Britain and left a small party at Saunders Island. Spain later forced the French and British to abandon their settlements but did not implement its claim to the islands. In 1829 the Republic of Buenos Aires, which claimed to have inherited the Spanish rights, sent Louis Vernet to develop a colony on the islands. In 1831 he seized three American sealing vessels, whereupon the men of the corvette, the U.S.S. Lexington, destroyed his settlement and proclaimed the Falklands to be 'free of all governance'. Britain, which had never renounced its claim, then re-established its settlement in 1833.

RULERS
British

MONETARY SYSTEM
100 Pence = 1 Pound

1/2 PENNY

BRONZE

KM#	Date	Mintage	VF	XF	Unc
1	1974	.140	—	.10	.25
	1974	.023	—	Proof	1.50
	1980	—	—	.10	.15
	1980	.010	—	Proof	1.50
	1982	—	—	.10	.15
	1982	—	—	Proof	1.50

PENNY

BRONZE

2	1974	.096	—	.10	.15	.35
	1974	.023	—	Proof	2.00
	1980	—	—	.10	.15	.25
	1980	.010	—	Proof	2.00
	1982	—	—	.10	.15	.25
	1982	—	—	Proof	2.00
	1983	—	—	.10	.15	.25
	1985	—	—	.10	.15	.25
	1987	.111	—	.10	.15	.25
	1987	—	—	Proof	2.00

2 PENCE

BRONZE

3	1974	.072	—	.10	.15	.50
	1974	.023	—	Proof	3.00
	1980	—	—	.10	.15	.35
	1980	.010	—	Proof	3.00
	1982	—	—	.10	.15	.35
	1982	—	—	Proof	3.00
	1983	—	—	.10	.15	.35
	1985	—	—	.10	.15	.35
	1987	.106	—	.10	.15	.35
	1987	—	—	Proof	3.00

5 PENCE

COPPER-NICKEL

KM#	Date	Mintage	VF	XF	Unc
4	1974	.067	.10	.25	.65
	1974	.023	—	Proof	4.00
	1980	—	.10	.25	.50
	1980	.010	—	Proof	4.00
	1982	—	.10	.25	.50
	1982	—	—	Proof	4.00
	1983	—	.10	.25	.50
	1985	—	.10	.25	.50
	1987	5,000	—	.25	.50
	1987	—	—	Proof	4.00

10 PENCE

COPPER-NICKEL

5	1974	.087	.20	.35	1.50
	1974	.023	—	Proof	5.00
	1980	—	.20	.35	1.00
	1980	.010	—	Proof	5.00
	1982	—	.20	.35	1.00
	1982	—	—	Proof	5.00
	1983	—	.20	.35	.75
	1985	—	.20	.35	.75
	1987	4,000	—	.35	.75
	1987	—	—	Proof	5.00

20 PENCE

COPPER-NICKEL

17	1982	—	.35	.50	1.00
	1982	—	—	Proof	5.00
	1983	—	.35	.50	1.00
	1985	—	.35	.50	1.00
	1987	4,250	—	.50	1.00
	1987	—	—	Proof	5.00

50 PENCE

COPPER-NICKEL
Queen's Silver Jubilee

| 10 | 1977 | .100 | 1.00 | 1.50 | 3.00 |

28.2800 g, .925 SILVER, .8411 oz ASW

| 10a | 1977 | .022 | — | Proof | 27.50 |

COPPER-NICKEL

| 14 | 1980 | — | 1.00 | 1.50 | 3.00 |
| | 1980 | — | — | Proof | 6.00 |

FALKLAND ISLANDS 537

KM#	Date	Mintage	VF	XF	Unc
14	1982	—	1.00	1.50	2.75
	1982	—	—	Proof	6.00
	1983	—	1.00	1.50	2.50
	1985	—	1.00	1.50	2.50
	1987	4,000	1.00	1.50	2.50
	1987	—	—	Proof	6.00

Queen Mother

15	1980		1.00	1.50	3.00

28.2800 g, .925 SILVER, .8411 oz ASW

15a	1980		—	Proof	25.00

COPPER-NICKEL
Wedding of Prince Charles and Lady Diana
Obv: Similar to KM#15.

16	1981		1.00	1.50	3.00

28.2800 g, .925 SILVER, .8411 oz ASW

16a	1981	.040	—	Proof	25.00

COPPER-NICKEL
Liberation From Argentine Forces
Obv: Similar to KM#15.

18	1982		1.00	1.50	3.00

28.2800 g, .925 SILVER, .8411 oz ASW

18a	1982	*.025	—	Proof	25.00

47.5000 g, .917 GOLD, 1.4005 oz AGW
Liberation From Argentine Forces

18b	1982	25 pcs.	—	Proof	7500.

COPPER-NICKEL
150th Anniversary of British Rule
Obv: Similar to KM#15.

KM#	Date	Mintage	VF	XF	Unc
19	1983	*.050	1.00	1.50	3.50

28.2800 g, .925 SILVER, .8411 oz ASW

| 19a | 1983 | *.010 | — | Proof | 30.00 |

47.5400 g, .917 GOLD, 1.4017 oz AGW

| 19b | 1983 | 150 pcs. | — | Proof | 3000. |

COPPER-NICKEL
Opening of Mount Pleasant Airport

21	1985		—	—	2.50

28.2750 g, .925 SILVER, .8410 oz ASW

21a	1985	*5,000	—	Proof	32.50

COPPER-NICKEL
King Penguins
Obv: Similar to KM#21.

25	1987		—	—	3.50

28.2800 g, .925 SILVER, .8411 oz ASW

25a	1987	*.025	—	Proof	30.00

1/2 POUND

3.9900 g, .917 GOLD, .1176 oz AGW

6	1974	2,673	—	Proof	300.00

POUND

7.9900 g, .917 GOLD, .2356 oz AGW

KM#	Date	Mintage	VF	XF	Unc
7	1974	2,675	—	Proof	400.00

NICKEL-BRASS

24	1987	—	—	—	3.35

9.5000 g, .925 SILVER, .2825 oz ASW

| 24a | 1987 | *5,000 | — | Proof | 30.00 |

19.6500 g, .917 GOLD, .5791 oz AGW

| 24b | 1987 | *200 pcs. | — | Proof | 700.00 |

2 POUNDS

15.9800 g, .917 GOLD, .4712 oz AGW

8	1974	2,158	—	Proof	800.00

28.2800 g, .500 SILVER, .4546 oz ASW
Commonwealth Games

22	1986	*.050	—	—	12.50

28.2800 g, .925 SILVER, .8411 oz ASW

| 22a | 1986 | *.020 | — | Proof | 27.50 |

5 POUNDS

39.9400 g, .917 GOLD, 1.1776 oz AGW
Obv: Similar to 2 Pounds, KM#8.

9	1974	2,158	—	Proof	1500.

FALKLAND ISLANDS

538

28.2800 g, .925 SILVER, .8411 oz ASW
Conservation Series
Obv: Portrait of Queen Elizabeth II.
Rev: Humpback whale.

KM#	Date	Mintage	VF	XF	Unc
11	1979	3,998	—	—	30.00
	1979	3,432	—	Proof	40.00

10 POUNDS

35.0000 g, .925 SILVER, 1.0409 oz AGW
Conservation Series
Obv: Portrait of Queen Elizabeth II.
Rev: Flightless steamer duck.

12	1979	3,996	—	—	35.00
	1979	3,247	—	Proof	45.00

25 POUNDS

150.0000 g, .925 SILVER, 4.4614 oz ASW
100 Years of Self Sufficiency
Size reduced. Actual size: 65mm

20	1985	*.020	—	Proof	190.00

Prince Andrew's Wedding
Size reduced. Actual size: 65mm

KM#	Date	Mintage	VF	XF	Unc
23	1986	*.020	—	Proof	100.00

150 POUNDS

33.4370 g, .900 GOLD, .9676 oz AGW
Conservation Series
Obv: Portrait of Queen Elizabeth II.
Rev: Falkland fur seal.

13	1979	488 pcs.	—	—	900.00
	1979	164 pcs.	—	Proof	2000.

MINT SETS (MS)

KM#	Date	Mintage	Identification	Issue Price	Mkt. Val.
MS1	1987(7)	—	KM2-5,14,17,24	10.00	9.00

PROOF SETS (PS)

PS1	1974(5)	20,000	KM1-5	12.00	15.50
PS2	1974(4)	2,000	KM6-9	1100.	3000.
PS3	1979(2)	10,000	KM11-12	—	85.00
PS4	1980(6)	10,000	KM1-5,14	35.00	21.50
PS5	1982(8)	5,000	KM1-5,14,17,18a	—	51.50
PS6	1982(7)	5,000	KM1-5,14,17	—	26.50
PS7	1987(7)	*2,500	KM2-5,14,17,24a	35.00	55.00

FIJI ISLANDS

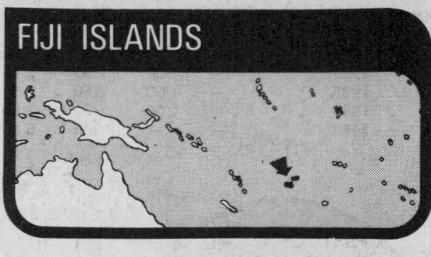

The Republic of Fiji, consists of about 320 islands located in the southwestern Pacific 1,100 miles (1,770 km.) north of New Zealand. The islands have a combined area of 7,056 sq. mi. (18,274 sq. km.) and a population of *758,000. Capital: Suva. Fiji's economy is based on agriculture and mining. Sugar, coconut products, manganese, and gold are exported.

The first European to sight Fiji was the Dutch navigator Abel Tasman in 1643 and the islands were visited by British naval captain James Cook in 1774. The first complete survey of the island was conducted by the United States in 1840. Settlement by missionaries from Tonga and traders attracted by the sandalwood trade began in 1801. Following a lengthy period of intertribal warfare, the islands were unconditionally ceded to Great Britain in 1874 by King Cakobau. Fiji became a sovereign and independent nation on Oct. 10, 1970, the 96th anniversary of the cession of the islands to Queen Victoria.

Fiji was declared a Republic in 1987 following two military coups. It left the British Commonwealth and Queen Elizabeth ceased to be the Head.

RULERS
British

MINT MARKS
S - San Francisco, U.S.A.

MONETARY SYSTEM
12 Pence = 1 Shilling
2 Shillings = 1 Florin
20 Shillings = 1 Pound

1/2 PENNY

COPPER-NICKEL

KM#	Date	Mintage	Fine	VF	XF	Unc
1	1934	.096	1.00	3.00	6.00	15.00
	1934	—	—	—	Proof	—

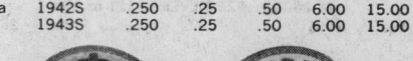

14	1940	.024	10.00	20.00	30.00	60.00
	1940	—	—	—	Proof	300.00
	1941	.096	.75	1.50	4.00	13.50
	1941	—	—	—	Proof	250.00

BRASS

14a	1942S	.250	.25	.50	6.00	15.00
	1943S	.250	.25	.50	6.00	15.00

COPPER-NICKEL
Obv. leg: EMPEROR dropped.

16	1949	.096	.50	1.00	2.00	6.00
	1949	—	—	—	Proof	200.00
	1950	.115	.25	.50	1.00	4.00
	1950	—	—	—	Proof	—
	1951	.115	.25	.50	1.00	4.00
	1951	—	—	—	Proof	190.00
	1952	.228	.15	.35	.75	3.00
	1952	—	—	—	Proof	—

20	1954	.228	.15	.25	.50	1.00
	1954	—	—	—	Proof	180.00

FIJI 539

PENNY

COPPER-NICKEL

KM#	Date	Mintage	Fine	VF	XF	Unc
2	1934	.480	.50	1.00	6.00	18.50
	1934	—	—	—	Proof	—
	1935	.240	.65	1.25	6.50	35.00
	1935	—	—	—	Proof	—
	1936	.240	.65	1.25	6.50	40.00
	1936	—	—	—	Proof	—

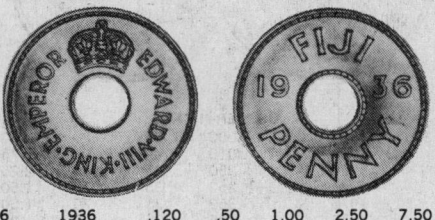

6	1936	.120	.50	1.00	2.50	7.50
	1936	—	—	—	Proof	225.00

7	1937	.360	.50	1.00	3.50	10.00
	1937	—	—	—	Proof	225.00
	1940	.144	2.00	3.00	14.00	35.00
	1940	—	—	—	Proof	225.00
	1941	.228	.50	1.00	2.50	8.00
	1941	—	—	—	Proof	225.00
	1945	.240	3.00	5.00	17.50	40.00
	1945	—	—	—	Proof	225.00

BRASS

7a	1942S	1.000	.50	1.00	6.00	20.00
	1943S	1.000	.50	1.00	6.00	25.00

COPPER-NICKEL
Obv. leg: EMPEROR dropped.

17	1949	.120	.25	.50	1.00	6.50
	1949	—	—	—	Proof	225.00
	1950	.058	2.00	5.00	15.00	85.00
	1950	—	—	—	Proof	175.00
	1952	.230	.25	.50	1.00	6.50
	1952	—	—	—	Proof	175.00

21	1954	.511	.20	.50	1.00	6.50
	1954	—	—	—	Proof	175.00
	1955	.230	.25	.50	1.50	8.00
	1955	—	—	—	Proof	175.00
	1956	.230	.25	.50	1.50	8.00
	1956	—	—	—	Proof	175.00
	1957	.360	.10	.25	.75	3.00
	1957	—	—	—	Proof	175.00
	1959	.864	.10	.20	.35	.75
	1959	—	—	—	Proof	175.00
	1961	.432	.20	.45	.75	1.50
	1961	—	—	—	Proof	175.00
	1963	.432	.20	.45	.75	1.25
	1963	—	—	—	Proof	175.00
	1964	.864	.10	.20	.35	1.00
	1964	—	—	—	Proof	150.00
	1965	1.440	.10	.15	.25	.50
	1966	.720	.10	.15	.25	.50
	1967	.720	.10	.15	.25	.50
	1968	.720	.10	.15	.25	.50

THREEPENCE

NICKEL-BRASS

KM#	Date	Mintage	Fine	VF	XF	Unc
15	1947	.450	1.00	2.00	6.00	20.00
	1947	—	—	—	Proof	250.00

Obv. leg: EMPEROR dropped.

18	1950	.450	.50	1.00	4.00	14.00
	1950	—	—	—	Proof	250.00
	1952	.400	.50	1.00	5.00	22.50
	1952	—	—	—	Proof	250.00

22	1955	.400	.50	1.00	4.25	11.00
	1955	—	—	—	Proof	200.00
	1956	.200	.50	1.00	5.00	25.00
	1956	—	—	—	Proof	200.00
	1958	.200	.50	1.00	4.25	11.00
	1958	—	—	—	Proof	185.00
	1960	.240	.25	.50	3.00	11.00
	1960	—	—	—	Proof	185.00
	1961	.240	.25	.50	1.50	10.00
	1961	—	—	—	Proof	185.00
	1963	.240	.15	.30	1.00	5.00
	1963	—	—	—	Proof	150.00
	1964	.240	.15	.30	.50	3.00
	1965	.800	.10	.20	.35	2.00
	1967	.800	.10	.20	.35	2.00

SIXPENCE

2.8276 g, .500 SILVER, .0455 oz ASW

3	1934	.160	1.50	3.00	25.00	70.00
	1934	—	—	—	Proof	600.00
	1935	.120	2.00	5.00	30.00	80.00
	1935	—	—	—	Proof	—
	1936	.040	3.00	7.50	40.00	90.00
	1936	—	—	—	Proof	—

8	1937	.040	3.00	10.00	30.00	80.00
	1937	—	—	—	Proof	400.00

Obv: Smaller head.

11	1938	.040	3.00	10.00	30.00	80.00
	1938	—	—	—	Proof	—
	1940	.040	3.00	10.00	30.00	80.00
	1940	—	—	—	Proof	—
	1941	.040	5.00	15.00	40.00	110.00
	1941	—	—	—	Proof	—

2.8276 g, .900 SILVER, .0818 oz ASW

11a	1942S	.400	BV	1.00	2.50	7.50
	1943S	.400	BV	1.00	2.50	7.50

COPPER-NICKEL

KM#	Date	Mintage	Fine	VF	XF	Unc
19	1953	.800	.15	.30	1.00	2.50
	1953	—	—	—	Proof	200.00
	1958	.400	.25	.50	1.50	7.50
	1958	—	—	—	Proof	200.00
	1961	.400	.25	.50	1.50	6.00
	1961	—	—	—	Proof	200.00
	1962	.400	.25	.50	1.00	5.00
	1962	—	—	—	Proof	200.00
	1965	.800	.15	.30	.75	4.00
	1967	.800	.15	.30	.75	3.50

SHILLING

5.6552 g, .500 SILVER, .0909 oz ASW

4	1934	.360	1.75	8.00	35.00	120.00
	1934	—	—	—	Proof	800.00
	1935	.180	1.75	8.00	37.50	155.00
	1935	—	—	—	Proof	—
	1936	.140	2.00	8.00	37.50	155.00
	1936	—	—	—	Proof	—

9	1937	.040	4.00	10.00	40.00	175.00
	1937	—	—	—	Proof	500.00

Obv: Smaller head.

12	1938	.040	2.50	10.00	45.00	175.00
	1938	—	—	—	Proof	—
	1941	.040	2.75	12.50	50.00	200.00
	1941	—	—	—	Proof	—

5.6552 g, .900 SILVER, .1636 oz ASW

12a	1942S	.500	BV	2.50	3.50	9.00
	1943S	.500	BV	2.50	3.50	9.00

COPPER-NICKEL

23	1957	.400	.50	.75	2.00	9.00
	1957	—	—	—	Proof	—
	1958	.400	.50	.75	2.25	12.50
	1958	—	—	—	Proof	—
	1961	.200	.75	1.00	2.25	12.50
	1961	—	—	—	Proof	275.00
	1962	.400	.35	.75	1.25	6.00
	1962	—	—	—	Proof	250.00
	1965	.800	.25	.50	.75	3.00

FLORIN

11.3104 g, .500 SILVER, .1818 oz ASW

5	1934	.200	2.00	10.00	40.00	225.00

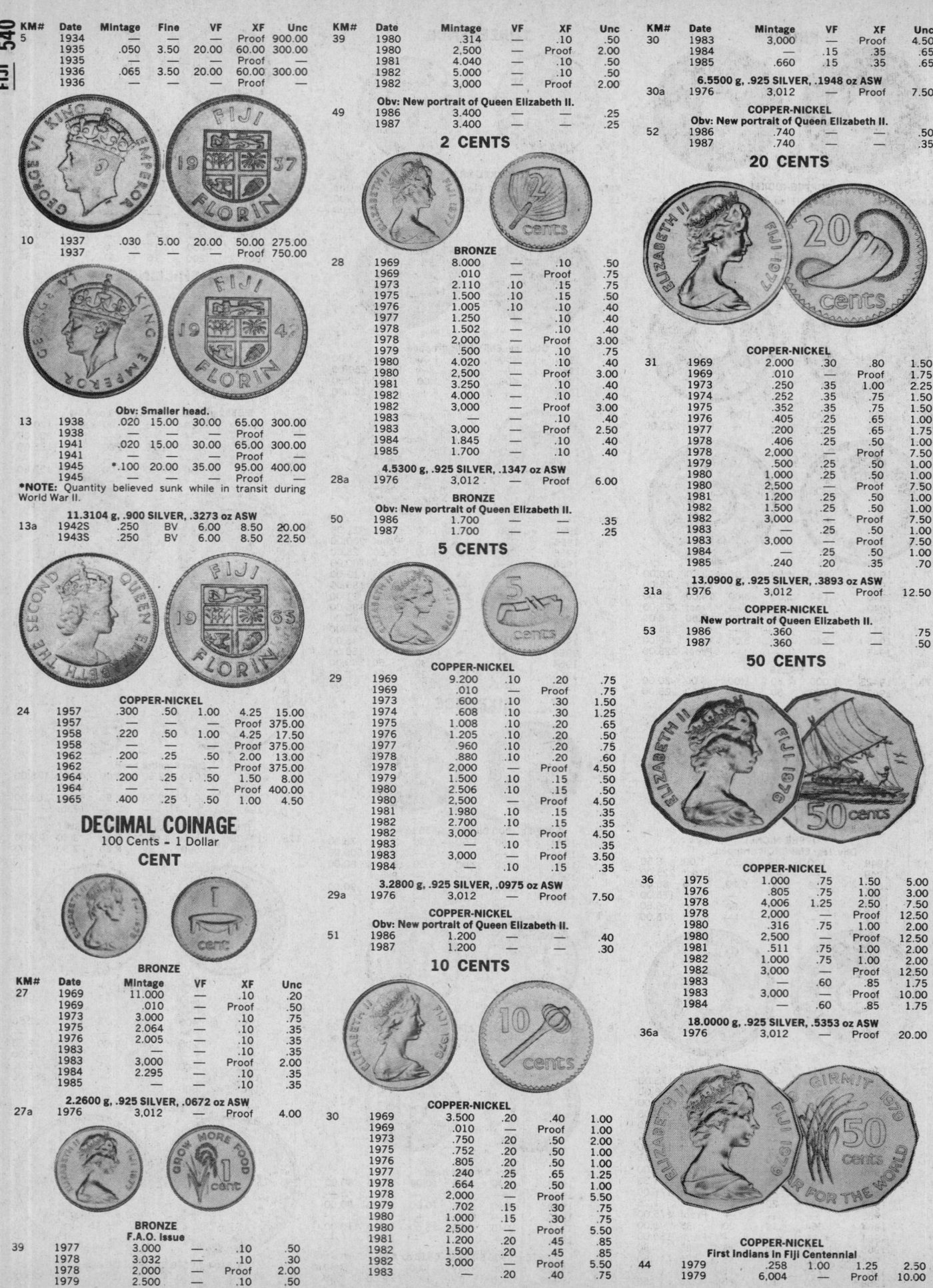

FIJI 541

Prince Charles, 10th Anniversary of Independence

KM#	Date	Mintage	VF	XF	Unc
45	1980	.010	—	—	5.00

Obv: New portrait of Queen Elizabeth II.
Rev: Similar to KM#36.

| 54 | 1986 | .160 | — | — | 1.25 |
| | 1987 | .160 | — | — | 1.00 |

DOLLAR

COPPER-NICKEL
Obv: Similar to 20 Cents, KM#31.

32	1969	.070	1.00	1.50	3.00
	1969	.010	—	Proof	3.00
	1976	5,007	1.50	3.00	6.50

28.2800 g, .925 SILVER, .8411 oz ASW

| 32a | 1976 | 3,012 | — | Proof | 30.00 |

COPPER-NICKEL
Independence Commemorative
Obv: Similar to 20 Cents, KM#31.

| 33 | 1970 | .015 | — | — | 5.00 |
| | 1970 | .015 | — | Proof | 6.00 |

28.2800 g, .925 SILVER, .8411 oz ASW

| 33a | 1970 | 1,000 | — | Proof | 110.00 |

10 DOLLARS

30.3000 g, .925 SILVER, .9012 oz ASW
Queen's Silver Jubilee
Obv: Similar to 20 Cents, KM#31.

| 40 | 1977 | 3,010 | —Proof only | 45.00 |

28.2800 g, .500 SILVER, .4547 oz ASW
Conservation Series
Obv: Similar to 20 Cents, KM#31.
Rev: Pink-billed parrot finch.

KM#	Date	Mintage	VF	XF	Unc
41	1978	3,582	—	—	25.00

28.2800 g, .925 SILVER, .8411 oz ASW

| 41a | 1978 | 4,026 | — | Proof | 30.00 |

28.4400 g, .500 SILVER, .4572 oz ASW
Prince Charles, 10th Anniversary of Independence

| 46 | 1980 | 5,001 | — | — | 22.50 |

30.4800 g, .925 SILVER, .9066 oz ASW

| 46a | 1980 | 3,001 | — | Proof | 35.00 |

30.0000 g, .925 SILVER, .8922 oz ASW
Wedding of Prince Charles and Lady Diana
Obv: Similar to 20 Cents, KM#31.

| 48 | 1981 | 5,000 | — | Proof | 30.00 |

28.2800 g, .925 SILVER, .8411 oz ASW
25th Anniversary World Wildlife Fund
Obv: Similar to 20 Cents, KM#31.
Rev: Fijian ground frog.

| 55 | 1986 | *.025 | — | Proof | 25.00 |

20 DOLLARS

35.0000 g, .500 SILVER, .5627 oz ASW
Conservation Series
Obv: Similar to 20 Cents, KM#31.
Rev: Golden cowrie.

KM#	Date	Mintage	VF	XF	Unc
42	1978	3,584	—	—	27.50

35.0000 g, .925 SILVER, 1.0409 oz ASW

| 42a | 1978 | 3,869 | — | Proof | 35.00 |

25 DOLLARS

48.6000 g, .925 SILVER, 1.4455 oz ASW
100th Anniversary of Cession to Great Britain
Obv: Similar to 20 Cents, KM#31.

| 34 | 1974 | 2,400 | — | — | 35.00 |
| | 1974 | 8,299 | — | Proof | 35.00 |

King Cakobau
Obv: Similar to 20 Cents, KM#31.

| 37 | 1975 | 836 pcs. | — | — | 50.00 |
| | 1975 | 5,157 | — | Proof | 35.00 |

100 DOLLARS

31.3600 g, .500 GOLD, .5042 oz AGW
100th Anniversary of Cession to Great Britain
Obv: Similar to 250 Dollars, KM#43.

| 35 | 1974 | 1,109 | — | — | 250.00 |
| | 1974 | 2,321 | — | Proof | 325.00 |

COPPER (OMS)

| 35a | 1974 | | — | Proof | 450.00 |

FINLAND 542

31.3000 g, .500 GOLD, .5032 oz AGW
King Cakobau
Obv: Similar to 250 Dollars, KM#43.

KM#	Date	Mintage	VF	XF	Unc
38	1975	593 pcs.	—	—	275.00
	1975	3,197	—	Proof	325.00

200 DOLLARS

15.9800 g, .917 GOLD, .4712 oz AGW
Prince Charles, 10th Anniversary of Independence

47	1980	500 pcs.	—	—	275.00
	1980	1,166	—	Proof	325.00

25th Anniversary World Wildlife Fund
Obv: Similar to 10 Cents, KM#31. Rev: Ogmodon.

56	1986	*5,000	—	Proof	475.00

250 DOLLARS

33.4370 g, .900 GOLD, .9676 oz AGW
Conservation Series
Rev: Banded Iguana.

43	1978	810 pcs.	—	—	600.00
	1978	252 pcs.	—	Proof	850.00

MINT SETS (MS)

KM#	Date	Mintage	Identification	Issue Price	Mkt. Val.
MS1	1976(7)	5,001	KM27-32,36	9.00	13.50
MS2	1978(6)	4,006	KM28-31,36,39	4.50	11.00
MS3	1978(3)	—	KM41-43	444.00	655.00
MS4	1978(2)	—	KM41-42	44.00	55.00
MS5	1983(6)	3,000	KM27-31,36	5.00	5.00
MS6	1984(6)	5,000	KM27-31,36	3.60	5.00

PROOF SETS (PS)

PS1	1969(6)	10,000	KM27-32	7.20	8.00
PS2	1976(7)	3,023	KM27a-32a36a	87.50	87.50
PS3	1978(6)	2,000	KM28-31,36,39	31.00	35.00
PS4	1978(2)	—	KM41a,42a	76.00	65.00
PS5	1978(3)	—	KM41a,42a,43	726.00	915.00
PS6	1980(5)	2,500	KM28-31,36,39	45.00	35.00
PS7	1982(6)	3,000	KM28-31,36,39	32.00	35.00
PS8	1983(6)	3,000	KM27-31,36	27.00	32.00

FINLAND

The Republic of Finland, the second most northerly state of the European continent, has an area of 130,120 sq. mi. (337,009 sq. km.) and a population of 5.0 million. Capital: Helsinki. Lumbering, shipbuilding, metal and woodworking are the leading industries. Paper, timber, woodpulp, plywood and metal products are exported.

The Finns, who probably originated in the Volga region of Russia, took Finland from the Lapps late in the 7th century. They were conquered in the 12th century by Eric IX of Sweden, and brought into contact with Western Christendom. In 1809, Sweden was conquered by Alexander I of Russia, and the peace terms gave Finland to Russia which became a grand duchy within the Russian Empire until Dec. 6, 1917, when, shortly after the Bolshevik revolution, it declared its independence. After a brief but bitter civil war between the Russian sympathizers and Finnish nationalists in which the Whites (nationalists) were victorious, a new constitution was adopted, and on Dec. 6, 1917 Finland was established as a republic.

RULERS

Alexander II, 1855-1881
Alexander III, 1881-1894
Nicholas II, 1894-1917

MONETARY SYSTEM

100 Pennia = 1 Markka

COMMENCING 1963

100 Old Markka = 1 New Markka

MINT MARKS

H - Birmingham 1921
Heart (h) - Copenhagen 1922
No mm - Helsinki

MINTMASTER INITIALS

Letter	Date	Name
H	1948-1958	Uolevi Helle
K	1976-1978	Timo Koivuranta
K-H	1977,1979	Timo Koivuranta & Heikki Haivaoja (Designer)
K-M	1983	Timo Koivuranta & Pertti Makinen
K-N	1978	Timo Koivuranta & Antti Neuvonen
K-T	1982	Timo Koivuranta & Erja Tielinen
L	1885-1912	Johan Conrad Lihr
L	1948	V. U. Liuhto
M	1987-	Tapio Makkonen
N	1983-1987	Tapio Nevalainen
P-N	1985	Reijo Paavilainen & Tapio Nevalainen
S	1864-1885	Aug. F. Soldan
S	1912-1947	Isac Sundell
S	1958-1975	Allan Soiniemi
S-H	1967-1971	Allan Soiniemi & Heikki Haivaoja (Designer)

GRAND DUCHY

PENNI

COPPER
Dotted border

KM#	Date	Mintage	Fine	VF	XF	Unc
1.1	1864	.030	1000.	1300.	2000.	3000.
	1865	.515	15.00	25.00	50.00	120.00
	1866/5	3.673	25.00	40.00	85.00	175.00
	1866	Inc. Ab.	8.00	12.00	25.00	50.00
	1867	3.843	8.00	12.00	25.00	50.00
	1869	1.575	15.00	25.00	35.00	70.00
	1870	.500	35.00	60.00	120.00	180.00
	1871	1.500	7.00	12.00	25.00	50.00

Dentilated border

1.2	1872	1.000	8.00	15.00	30.00	60.00
	1873	2.000	4.00	8.00	20.00	40.00
	1874	1.450	4.00	7.00	20.00	50.00
	1875	1.550	4.00	6.00	17.00	50.00
	1876	2.005	3.00	8.00	20.00	50.00

10	1881	.600	7.00	12.00	25.00	70.00
	1882	.100	30.00	50.00	95.00	145.00

KM#	Date	Mintage	Fine	VF	XF	Unc
10	1883	3.900	1.00	3.00	6.00	20.00
	1884	.404	30.00	60.00	110.00	165.00
	1888	2.290	1.00	3.00	5.00	15.00
	1891	1.008	2.00	5.00	10.00	20.00
	1892	1.510	1.00	2.00	5.00	11.00
	1893	2.290	.75	1.50	4.00	10.00
	1893 dot after date					
	Inc. Ab.	.75	1.50	4.00	10.00
	1894	1.810	.75	1.50	4.00	10.00

13	1895	.880	1.50	3.50	7.50	20.00
	1898	1.430	.75	1.25	3.00	10.00
	1899	1.540	.75	1.25	3.00	7.50
	1900	3.550	.50	1.00	2.00	4.00
	1901	1.520	.75	1.25	2.50	5.00
	1902	1.000	.75	1.25	2.50	7.50
	1903 sm.	31.145	.75	1.25	2.50	7.50
	1903 lg.3	I.A.	1.00	2.00	5.00	12.00
	1904	.500	2.50	5.00	10.00	20.00
	1905	1.390	.50	1.00	2.00	4.00
	1906	1.020	.50	1.00	2.00	4.00
	1907 normal 7					
	2.490	.75	1.25	2.50	7.00
	1907 w/o serif on 7 arm					
	Inc. Ab.	.30	.75	1.75	4.00
	1908	.950	.50	1.00	2.00	5.00
	1909	3.060	.25	.65	1.25	2.50
	1911	2.550	.25	.65	1.25	2.50
	1912	2.450	.25	.65	1.25	2.50
	1913	1.650	.25	.65	1.25	3.00
	1914	1.900	.25	.65	1.25	3.50
	1915	2.250	.25	.65	1.25	2.50
	1916	3.040	.25	.50	1.00	2.00

5 PENNIA

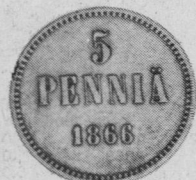

COPPER
Dotted border

4.1	1865	.480	6.00	20.00	40.00	100.00
	1866	2.490	1.00	5.00	12.00	60.00
	1867	1.660	2.00	6.00	15.00	70.00
	1870	.300	5.00	15.00	50.00	130.00

NOTE: Varieties exist.

Dentilated border

4.2	1872	.500	3.00	10.00	27.00	100.00
	1873	1.000	1.00	5.00	12.00	60.00
	1875	1.000	1.00	5.00	12.00	60.00

NOTE: Varieties exist.

11	1888	.600	2.00	7.00	12.00	70.00
	1889	1.070	1.00	5.00	10.00	60.00
	1892	.330	3.00	7.00	17.00	100.00

15	1896	.410	2.00	8.00	22.00	70.00
	1897	.590	1.00	5.00	12.00	60.00
	1898	1.150	1.00	4.00	10.00	35.00
	1899	.860	1.00	5.00	11.00	40.00
	1901	.990	1.00	4.00	10.00	35.00
	1905	.620	1.00	4.00	12.00	40.00
	1906	.960	.75	2.50	10.00	35.00
	1907	.770	.75	2.50	10.00	40.00
	1908	1.660	.75	2.50	8.00	25.00
	1910	.060	20.00	35.00	75.00	175.00
	1911	1.050	.75	2.50	6.00	20.00
	1912	.460	1.50	5.00	15.00	40.00
	1913	1.060	.65	1.25	4.00	15.00
	1914	.820	.65	1.25	3.00	15.00
	1915	2.080	.30	.75	3.00	10.00
	1916	4.470	.30	.75	3.00	10.00
	1917	4.070	.30	.75	3.00	10.00

10 PENNIA

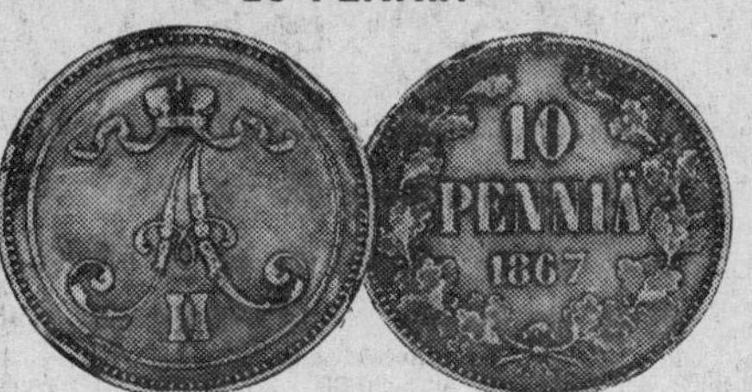

COPPER
Dotted border

KM#	Date	Mintage	Fine	VF	XF	Unc
5.1	1865	.250	3.00	12.00	30.00	125.00
	1866/5	.850	5.00	17.00	40.00	175.00
	1866	Inc. Ab.	2.00	8.00	20.00	100.00
	1867	1.440	2.00	7.00	20.00	90.00

Dentilated border

KM#	Date	Mintage	Fine	VF	XF	Unc
5.2	1875	.100	40.00	70.00	125.00	400.00
	1876	.300	3.00	10.00	35.00	115.00

NOTE: Varieties exist.

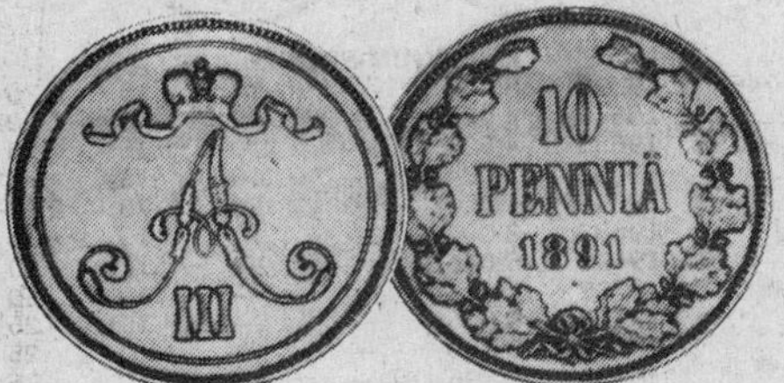

KM#	Date	Mintage	Fine	VF	XF	Unc
12	1889	.100	10.00	25.00	55.00	275.00
	1890	.106	8.00	20.00	50.00	250.00
	1891	.295	5.00	12.00	35.00	110.00

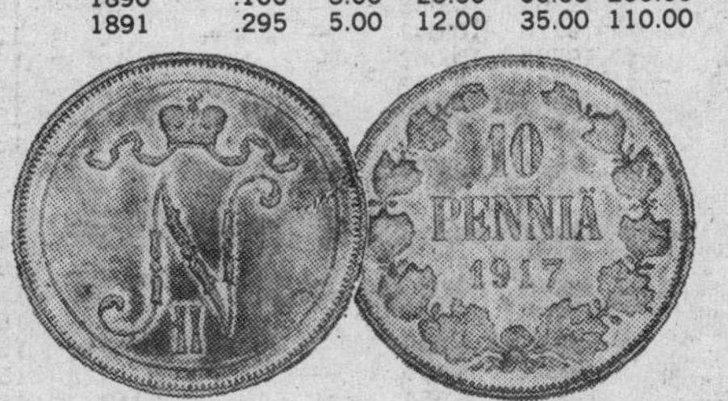

KM#	Date	Mintage	Fine	VF	XF	Unc
14	1895	.210	3.00	10.00	27.00	105.00
	1896	.294	3.00	10.00	27.00	105.00
	1897	.502	1.50	5.00	15.00	75.00
	1898	.040	25.00	45.00	125.00	350.00
	1899	.440	1.25	5.00	15.00	70.00
	1900	.524	1.25	5.00	15.00	70.00
	1905	.500	1.25	5.00	10.00	50.00
	1907	.503	1.25	5.00	10.00	50.00
	1908	.320	1.50	6.00	12.00	60.00
	1909	.180	2.00	7.50	15.00	75.00
	1910	.241	1.50	6.00	12.00	55.00
	1911	.370	1.00	3.00	10.00	40.00
	1912	.191	1.50	6.00	12.00	50.00
	1913	.150	2.50	7.00	20.00	60.00
	1914	.605	.75	1.50	5.00	15.00
	1915	.420	.50	1.00	3.00	10.00
	1916	1.952	.50	1.00	3.00	10.00
	1917	1.600	.75	1.50	4.00	12.00

25 PENNIA

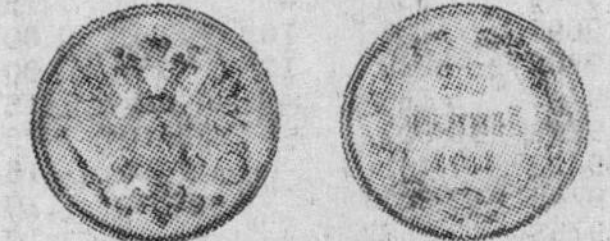

1.2747 g, .750 SILVER, .0307 oz ASW
Dotted border

KM#	Date	Mintage	Fine	VF	XF	Unc
6.1	1865S	.705	10.00	22.00	45.00	115.00
	1866S	.810	7.00	15.00	35.00	95.00
	1867S	.400	170.00	250.00	500.00	1300.
	1868S	.136	100.00	150.00	350.00	800.00
	1869S	.264	25.00	40.00	80.00	175.00
	1871S	.150	40.00	70.00	150.00	330.00

Dentilated border

KM#	Date	Mintage	Fine	VF	XF	Unc
6.2	1872S	.400	6.00	15.00	40.00	125.00
	1873S	.800	3.00	10.00	30.00	75.00
	1875S	.810	3.00	10.00	30.00	75.00
	1876S	1,200	850.00	1350.	2000.	3000.
	1889L	.404	3.00	8.00	20.00	60.00
	1890L	.800	1.50	3.00	10.00	40.00
	1891L	.280	2.50	6.00	15.00	60.00
	1894L	.820	1.50	3.00	10.00	50.00
	1897L	.450	1.50	3.00	12.00	40.00
	1898L	.444	1.50	3.00	10.00	35.00
	1898L/inverted L					
		Inc. Ab.	15.00	25.00	40.00	125.00
	1899L	.312	1.50	3.00	15.00	40.00
	1901L	.993	1.00	2.00	5.00	15.00
	1902L	.210	3.00	7.00	15.00	45.00
	1906L	.281	2.00	5.00	10.00	40.00
	1907L	.590	1.00	2.00	4.00	10.00

KM#	Date	Mintage	Fine	VF	XF	Unc
6.2	1908L	.340	1.00	2.50	5.00	12.00
	1909L	1.099	.75	1.50	3.00	10.00
	1910L	.392	2.50	5.00	10.00	30.00
	1913S	.832	.50	1.00	1.50	3.00
	1915S	2.400	.50	.75	1.00	1.50
	1916S	6.392	.50	.75	1.00	1.50
	1917S	5.820	.50	.75	1.00	1.50

50 PENNIA

2.5494 g, .750 SILVER, .0615 oz ASW
Dotted border

KM#	Date	Mintage	Fine	VF	XF	Unc
2.1	1864S	.104	5.00	15.00	50.00	150.00
	1865S	1.184	3.50	10.00	35.00	110.00
	1866S	.363	10.00	25.00	75.00	225.00
	1868S	.140	40.00	80.00	225.00	650.00
	1869S	.144	15.00	30.00	60.00	200.00
	1869S slanted 9					
		Inc. Ab.	15.00	30.00	75.00	220.00
	1871S	.320	3.00	8.00	25.00	90.00

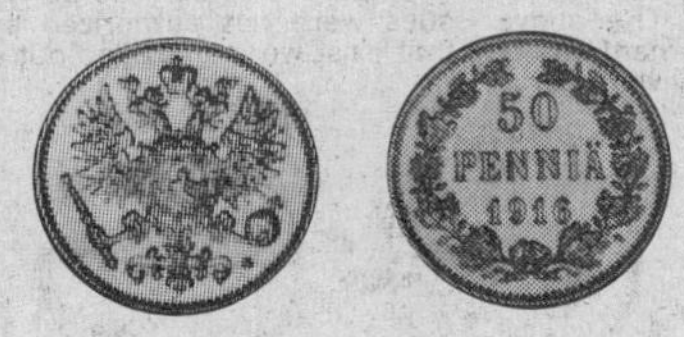

Dentilated border

KM#	Date	Mintage	Fine	VF	XF	Unc
2.2	1872S	.200	3.00	8.00	25.00	90.00
	1872S	—	—	—	Proof	200.00
	1874S	.402	2.50	5.00	20.00	80.00
	1876S	600 pcs.	3000.	4000.	5000.	7500.
	1889L	.312	2.00	4.00	22.00	90.00
	1890L	.693	1.00	2.50	12.00	45.00
	1891L	.282	1.00	3.00	15.00	60.00
	1892L	.344	1.00	2.50	12.00	50.00
	1893L	.400	1.00	2.50	12.00	50.00
	1907L	.260	1.00	3.00	15.00	60.00
	1908L	.353	.75	2.00	10.00	30.00
	1911L	.616	.75	1.25	2.50	5.00
	1914S	.600	.75	1.00	1.50	4.00
	1915S	1.000	.75	1.00	1.50	2.50
	1916S	4.752	.75	1.00	1.50	2.50
	1917S	3.972	.75	1.00	1.50	2.50

MARKKA

5.1828 g, .868 SILVER, .1446 oz ASW
Dotted border

KM#	Date	Mintage	Fine	VF	XF	Unc
3.1	1864S	.075	27.00	50.00	100.00	170.00
	1865S	1.673	2.50	5.00	20.00	85.00
	1866S	1.990	2.50	5.00	20.00	75.00
	1867S	.852	10.00	20.00	50.00	200.00
	1870S	5 known	—	—	Rare	—

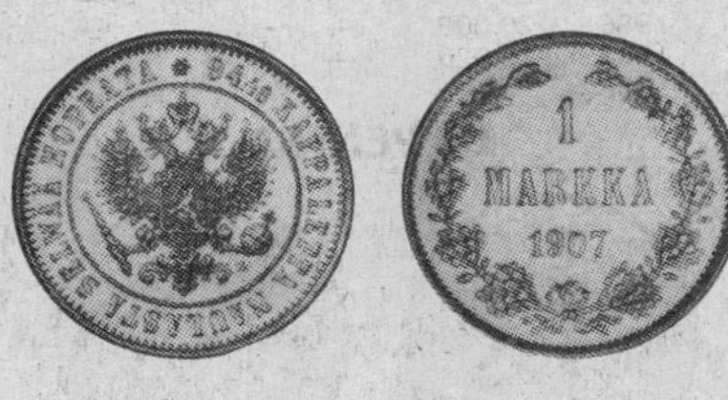

Dentilated border

KM#	Date	Mintage	Fine	VF	XF	Unc
3.2	1872S	.538	4.00	10.00	35.00	130.00
	1874S	1.002	2.50	6.00	15.00	50.00
	1890L	.841	2.50	6.00	15.00	60.00
	1892L	.484	2.50	6.00	15.00	60.00
	1893L	.254	3.00	7.50	22.00	75.00
	1907L	.350	2.00	3.00	8.00	25.00
	1908L	.153	4.00	10.00	25.00	50.00
	1915S	1.212	2.00	3.00	6.00	10.00

2 MARKKAA

10.3657 g, .868 SILVER, .2893 oz ASW
Dotted border

KM#	Date	Mintage	Fine	VF	XF	Unc
7.1	1865S	.203	5.00	12.00	30.00	120.00
	1866/5S	.820	10.00	25.00	60.00	220.00
	1866S	Inc. Ab.	10.00	25.00	55.00	200.00
	1867S	6 known	—	—	Rare	—
	1870S	.500	5.00	12.00	30.00	120.00

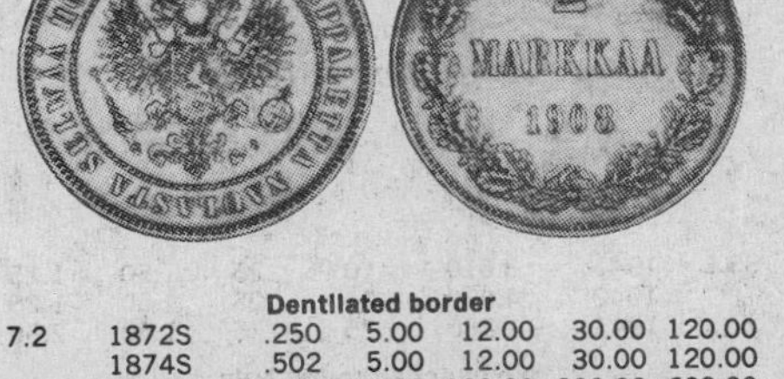

Dentilated border

KM#	Date	Mintage	Fine	VF	XF	Unc
7.2	1872S	.250	5.00	12.00	30.00	120.00
	1874S	.502	5.00	12.00	30.00	120.00
	1905L	.024	60.00	100.00	200.00	600.00
	1906L	.225	5.00	10.00	22.00	50.00
	1907L	.125	7.00	15.00	40.00	80.00
	1908L	.124	5.00	8.00	20.00	48.00

10 MARKKAA

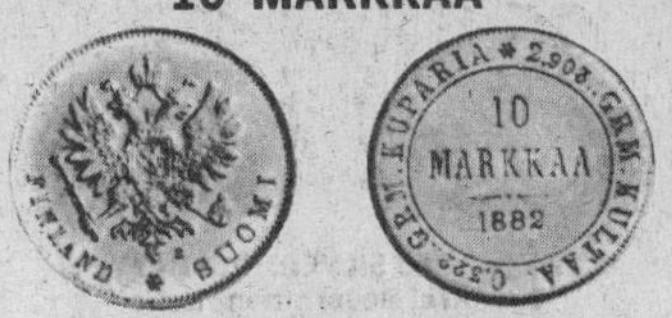

3.2258 g, .900 GOLD, .0933 oz AGW
Regal Issues

KM#	Date	Mintage	Fine	VF	XF	Unc
8	1878S	.254	60.00	100.00	150.00	185.00
	1879/0S	.200	90.00	135.00	200.00	260.00
	1879S	Inc. Ab.	60.00	100.00	140.00	185.00
	1881S	.100	125.00	160.00	210.00	285.00
	1882S	.386	60.00	100.00	140.00	185.00
	1904L	.102	275.00	450.00	650.00	950.00
	1905L	.043	1500.	2500.	3200.	4500.
	1913S	.396	55.00	100.00	145.00	185.00

20 MARKKAA

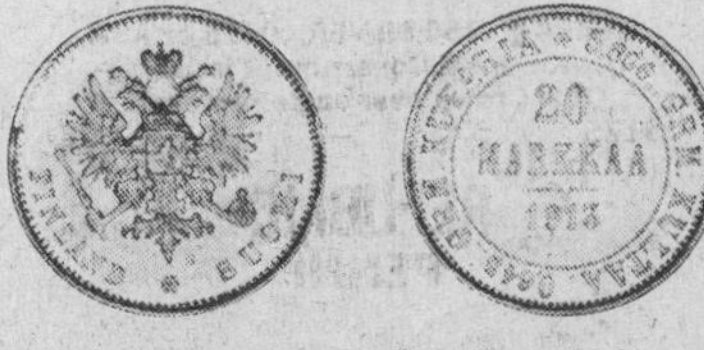

6.4516 g, .900 GOLD, .1867 oz AGW
Regal Issues

KM#	Date	Mintage	Fine	VF	XF	Unc
9	1878S	.235	250.00	320.00	400.00	550.00
	1879S	.300	100.00	130.00	155.00	230.00
	1880S	.090	600.00	800.00	1000.	1350.
	1891L	.091	110.00	175.00	240.00	330.00
	1903L	.112	100.00	130.00	180.00	260.00
	1904L	.188	100.00	130.00	155.00	250.00
	1910L	.201	100.00	130.00	155.00	260.00
	1911L	.161	125.00	175.00	240.00	300.00
	1912L	.881	500.00	750.00	1000.	1500.
	1912S	Inc. Ab.	100.00	130.00	150.00	230.00
	1913S	.214	100.00	130.00	150.00	230.00

CIVIL WAR COINAGE

PENNI

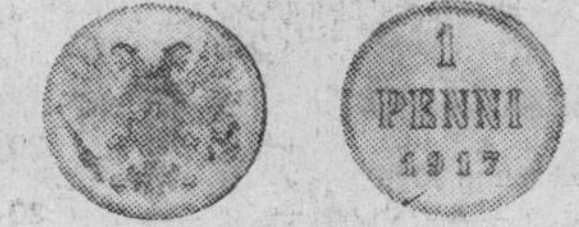

COPPER
Kerenski Government Issue

KM#	Date	Mintage	Fine	VF	XF	Unc
16	1917	1.650	.25	.75	1.00	1.50

5 PENNIA

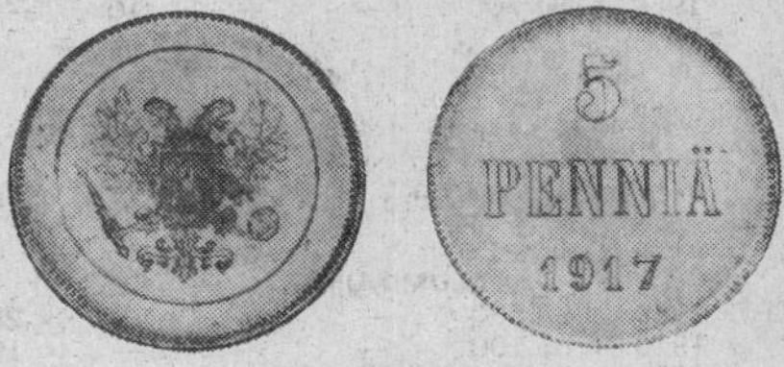

COPPER
Kerenski Government Issue

KM#	Date	Mintage	Fine	VF	XF	Unc
17	1917	Inc. Ab.	.30	.75	2.50	5.00

Finnish Liberated Government Issue
Obv: Wreath knot centered between 9 and 1 of date.

KM#	Date	Mintage	Fine	VF	XF	Unc
21.1	1918	.035	15.00	25.00	35.00	60.00

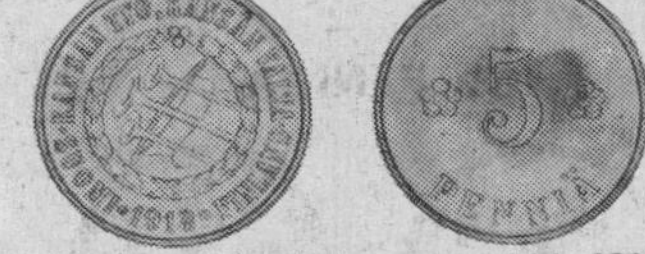

Obv: Wreath knot above second 1 in 1918.

KM#	Date	Mintage	Fine	VF	XF	Unc
21.2	1918	Inc. Ab.	40.00	60.00	100.00	150.00

NOTE: This type was unofficially struck outside of Finland in the early 1920's.

10 PENNIA

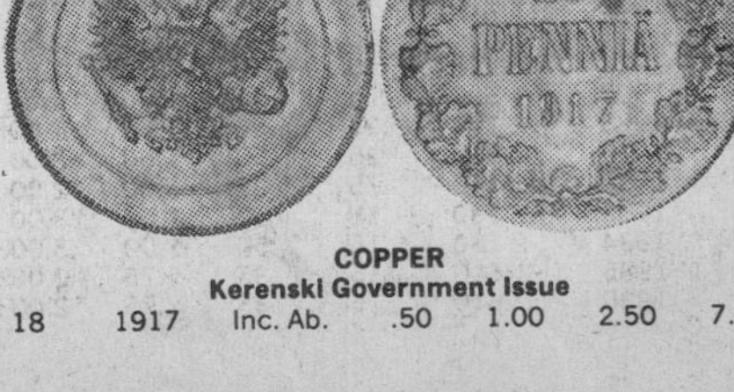

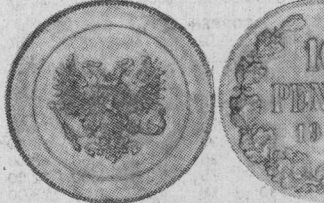

COPPER
Kerenski Government Issue

KM#	Date	Mintage	Fine	VF	XF	Unc
18	1917	Inc. Ab.	.50	1.00	2.50	7.50

FINLAND 544

25 PENNIA

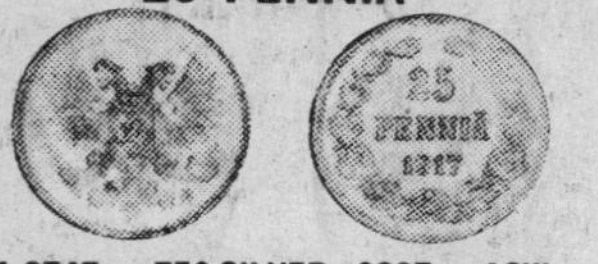

1.2747 g, .750 SILVER, .0307 oz ASW
Kerenski Government Issue
Obv: Crown over eagle removed.

KM#	Date	Mintage	Fine	VF	XF	Unc
19	1917S	2.310	—	BV	1.00	1.50

50 PENNIA

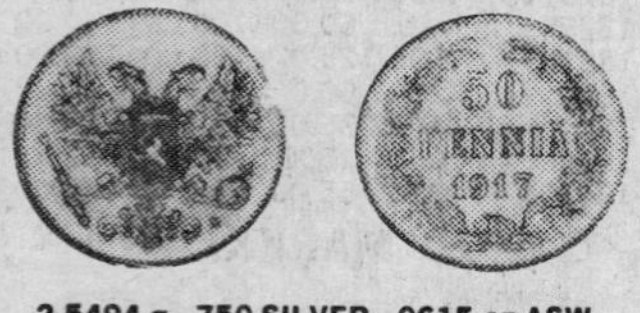

2.5494 g, .750 SILVER, .0615 oz ASW
Kerenski Government Issue
Obv: Crown over eagle removed.

KM#	Date	Mintage	Fine	VF	XF	Unc
20	1917S	.570	—	BV	1.25	2.00

REPUBLIC

PENNI

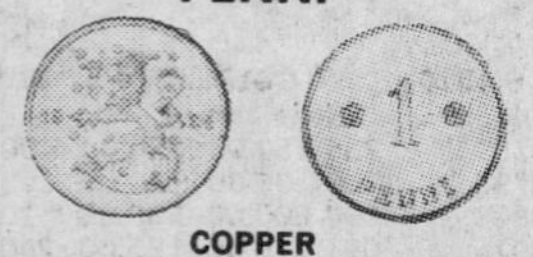

COPPER
Republic Issues

KM#	Date	Mintage	Fine	VF	XF	Unc
23	1919	1.200	.25	.65	1.75	3.00
	1920	.720	.25	.65	1.75	3.00
	1921	.510	.35	1.00	2.00	4.00
	1922	1.060	.25	.65	1.75	3.00
	1923	.990	.25	.65	1.75	3.00
	1924	2.180	.25	.65	1.75	3.00

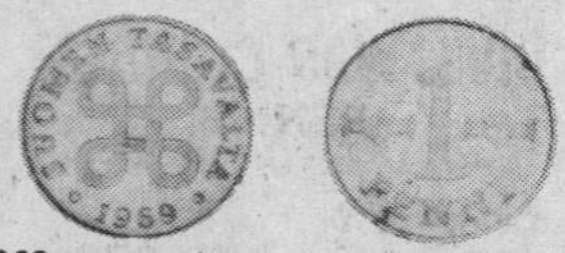

KM#	Date	Mintage	Fine	VF	XF	Unc
44	1963 square edge					
		62.460	—	.10	.20	.60
	1963 round edge					
		118.870	—	.10	.20	.60
	1964	49.300	—	.10	.30	.80
	1965	43.110	—	.10	.30	.80
	1966	36.880	—	.10	.20	.50
	1967	62.790	—	.10	.20	.50
	1968	73.400	—	—	.10	.40
	1969	51.700	—	—	.10	.40

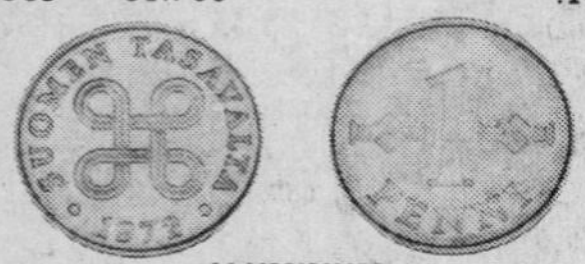

ALUMINUM

KM#	Date	Mintage	Fine	VF	XF	Unc
44a	1969	28.500	—	—	.10	.25
	1970	85.100	—	—	—	.10
	1971	70.240	—	—	—	.10
	1972	95.100	—	—	—	.10
	1973	115.500	—	—	—	.10
	1974	100.132	—	—	—	.10
	1975	111.960	—	—	—	.10
	1976	34.965	—	—	—	.10
	1977	61.393	—	—	—	.10
	1978	90.132	—	—	—	.10
	1979	33.388	—	—	—	.10

5 PENNIA

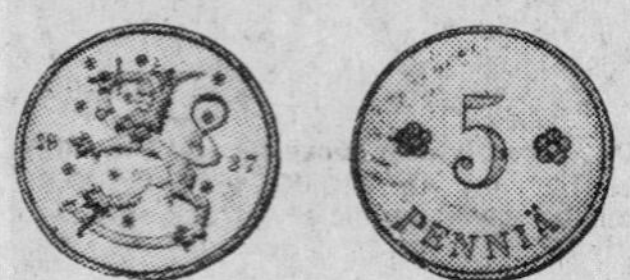

IRON

KM#	Date	Mintage	Fine	VF	XF	Unc
22	1918	.090	750.00	1000.	1500.	2000.

COPPER

KM#	Date	Mintage	Fine	VF	XF	Unc
22a	1918	4.270	.10	.25	.75	3.50
	1919	4.640	.10	.25	.75	3.50
	1920	7.710	.10	.25	.75	2.50
	1921	5.910	.10	.25	.75	2.50
	1922	8.540	.10	.25	.75	2.50
	1927	1.520	.75	1.50	3.50	15.00
	1928	2.110	.25	.50	1.50	8.00
	1929	1.500	.25	.50	1.50	8.00
	1930	2.140	.75	1.25	3.00	12.00
	1932	2.130	.15	.50	1.00	3.00
	1934	2.180	.15	.50	1.00	3.00
	1935	1.610	.15	.35	.75	2.00
	1936	2.610	.15	.35	.75	2.00
22a	1937	3.830	.10	.25	.50	2.00
	1938	4.300	.10	.25	.50	2.00
	1939	2.270	.10	.25	.50	2.00
	1940	1.610	.25	.50	1.25	4.00

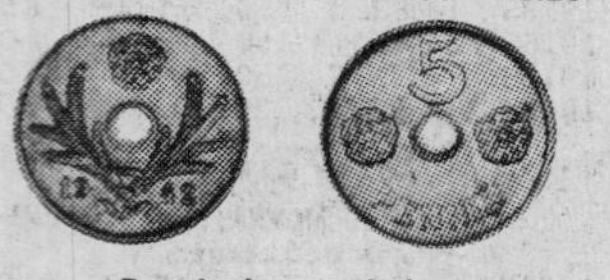

Punched center hole

KM#	Date	Mintage	Fine	VF	XF	Unc
64.1	1941	5.950	.10	.20	.50	1.25
(32.1)	1942	4.280	.10	.20	.50	1.25
	1943	1.530	.10	.50	1.25	2.50

W/o punched center hole

KM#	Date	Mintage	Fine	VF	XF	Unc
64.2	1941	Inc. Ab.	20.00	25.00	50.00	75.00
(32.2)	1942	Inc. Ab.	20.00	25.00	50.00	75.00
	1943	Inc. Ab.	40.00	60.00	80.00	110.00

NOTE: The above issues were not authorized by the government and any that exist were smuggled out of the mint by workmen.

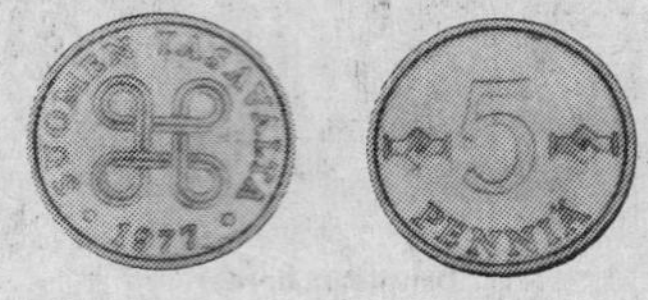

KM#	Date	Mintage	Fine	VF	XF	Unc
45	1963	60.820	—	.10	.25	1.00
	1964	4.634	.50	1.00	2.00	7.50
	1965	10.264	—	.10	.15	.50
	1966	8.064	—	.10	.15	.50
	1967	9.968	—	.10	.15	.50
	1968	6.144	—	.10	.15	.50
	1969	3.598	—	.15	.25	1.00
	1970	13.772	—	.10	.10	.20
	1971	20.010	—	—	.10	.20
	1972	24.122	—	—	.10	.20
	1973	25.644	—	—	.10	.20
	1974	21.530	—	—	.10	.20
	1975	25.010	—	—	.10	.20
	1976	25.551	—	—	.10	.20
	1977	1.489	—	.10	.20	.50

ALUMINUM

KM#	Date	Mintage	Fine	VF	XF	Unc
45a	1977	30.552	—	—	—	.10
	1978	26.112	—	—	—	.10
	1979	40.042	—	—	—	.10
	1980	60.026	—	—	—	.10
	1981	2.044	—	—	.10	.25
	1982	10.012	—	—	—	.10
	1983	33.885	—	—	—	.10
	1984	25.001	—	—	—	.10
	1985	25.000	—	—	—	.10
	1986	20.000	—	—	—	.10
	1987	20.020	—	—	—	.10
	1988	—	—	—	—	.10

10 PENNIA

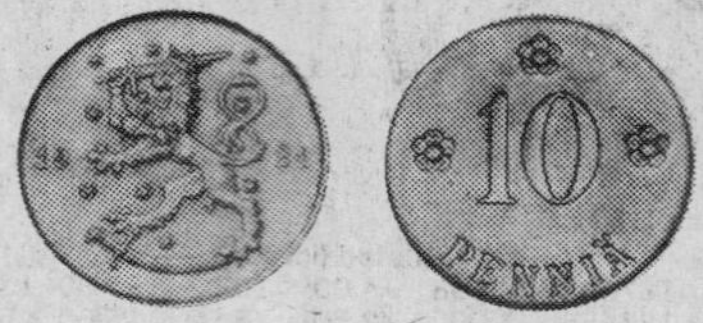

COPPER
Republic Issues

KM#	Date	Mintage	Fine	VF	XF	Unc
24	1919	3.670	.10	.25	.75	5.00
	1920	2.380	.10	.25	.75	5.00
	1921	3.970	.10	.25	.75	5.00
	1922	2.180	.10	.25	.75	5.00
	1923	.910	.75	1.50	5.00	12.00
	1924	1.350	.25	.50	1.00	6.00
	1926	1.690	.25	.50	1.00	6.00
	1927	1.330	.50	1.00	2.50	10.00
	1928	1.006	.50	1.00	2.50	10.00
	1929	1.560	.35	.85	2.00	7.00
	1930	.650	.75	1.50	5.00	12.00
	1931	1.040	1.00	2.00	6.00	15.00
	1934	1.680	.35	.85	1.50	6.00
	1935	1.690	.15	.25	.75	5.00
	1936	2.010	.15	.25	.75	5.00
	1937	2.420	.10	.25	.50	3.50
	1938	2.940	.10	.25	.50	3.50
	1939	2.100	.10	.25	.50	3.50
	1940	2.010	.25	.50	1.00	5.00

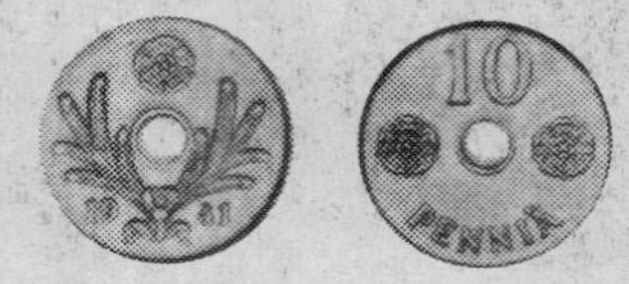

KM#	Date	Mintage	Fine	VF	XF	Unc
33.1	1941	3.610	.10	.25	.50	1.25
	1942	4.970	.10	.25	.50	1.25
	1943	1.860	.25	.75	1.50	2.50

W/o punched center hole

KM#	Date	Mintage	Fine	VF	XF	Unc
33.2	1941	Inc. Ab.	15.00	25.00	40.00	60.00
	1942	Inc. Ab.	15.00	25.00	40.00	60.00
	1943	Inc. Ab.	20.00	30.00	50.00	80.00

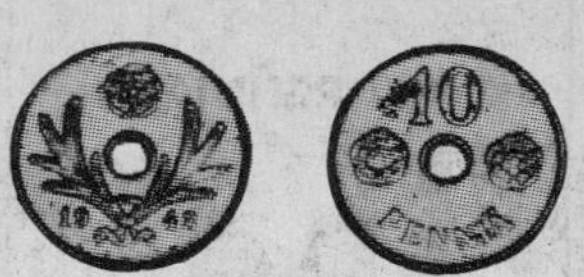

IRON
Reduced planchet size

KM#	Date	Mintage	Fine	VF	XF	Unc
34.1	1943	1.430	.10	.25	1.00	3.50
	1944	3.040	.10	.25	1.00	3.00
	1945	1.810	.25	.50	2.00	10.00

W/o punched center hole

KM#	Date	Mintage	Fine	VF	XF	Unc
34.2	1943	Inc. Ab.	20.00	25.00	50.00	75.00
	1944	Inc. Ab.	20.00	25.00	50.00	75.00
	1945	Inc. Ab.	30.00	40.00	60.00	100.00

NOTE: The above issues were not authorized by the government and any that exist were smuggled out of the mint by workmen.

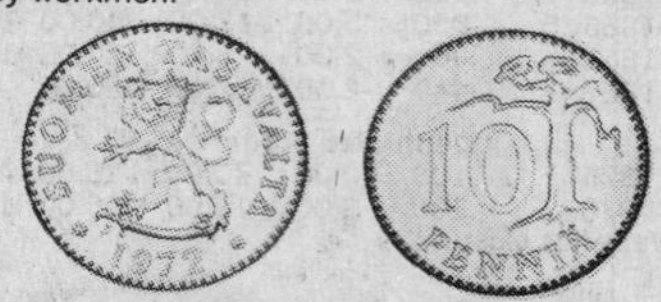

ALUMINUM-BRONZE

KM#	Date	Mintage	Fine	VF	XF	Unc
46	1963S	38.420	—	.10	.15	.75
	1964S	6.926	—	.10	.30	1.50
	1965S	4.524	—	.10	.15	.75
	1966S	3.094	—	.10	.15	.75
	1967S	1.050	.10	.20	.75	2.00
	1968S	3.004	—	.10	.15	.75
	1969S	5.046	—	—	.10	.50
	1970S	3.996	—	—	.10	.50
	1971S	15.026	—	—	.10	.25
	1972S	19.900	—	—	.10	.25
	1973S	9.196	—	—	.10	.25
	1974S	8.930	—	—	.10	.25
	1975S	15.064	—	—	.10	.15
	1976K	10.063	—	—	.10	.15
	1977K	10.042	—	—	.10	.15
	1978K	10.062	—	—	.10	.15
	1979K	13.072	—	—	.10	.15
	1980K	23.654	—	—	.10	.15
	1981K	30.036	—	—	.10	.15
	1982K	35.548	—	—	.10	.15

ALUMINUM

KM#	Date	Mintage	Fine	VF	XF	Unc
46a	1983K	6.320	—	—	.10	.15
	1983N	4.191	—	—	.10	.15
	1984N	20.061	—	—	.10	.15
	1985N	20.000	—	—	.10	.15
	1986N	15.000	—	—	.10	.15
	1987N	1.400	—	—	.10	.15
	1987M	8.654	—	—	.10	.15
	1988M	—	—	—	.10	.15

20 PENNIA

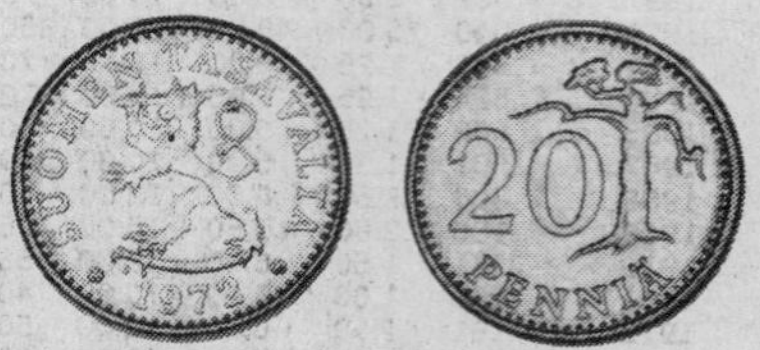

ALUMINUM-BRONZE

KM#	Date	Mintage	Fine	VF	XF	Unc
47	1963S	39.970	—	.10	.15	.75
	1964S	4.248	.10	.25	.50	2.00
	1965S	5.704	—	.10	.15	.75
	1966S	4.085	—	.10	.15	.75
	1967S	1.716	—	.10	.15	.75
	1968S	1.330	—	.10	.15	.75
	1969S	.201	.10	.25	1.00	2.00
	1970S	.230	.10	.25	1.00	2.00
	1971S	5.150	—	.10	.15	.35
	1972S	10.001	—	.10	.15	.35
	1973S	9.462	—	.10	.15	.35
	1974S	12.705	—	—	.10	.20
	1975S	12.068	—	—	.10	.20
	1976K	20.058	—	—	.10	.20
	1977K	10.063	—	—	.10	.20
	1978K	10.014	—	—	.10	.20
	1979K	7.513	—	—	.10	.20
	1980K	20.047	—	—	.10	.15
	1981K	30.002	—	—	.10	.15
	1982K	35.050	—	—	.10	.15
	1983K	7.113	—	—	.10	.15
	1983N	12.889	—	—	.10	.15
	1984N	20.029	—	—	.10	.15
	1985N	15.004	—	—	.10	.15
	1986N	20.001	—	—	.10	.15
	1987N	1.200	—	—	.10	.15
	1987M	19.954	—	—	.10	.15
	1988M	—	—	—	.10	.15

NOTE: Some coins dated 1971 are magnetic and command a higher premium.

25 PENNIA

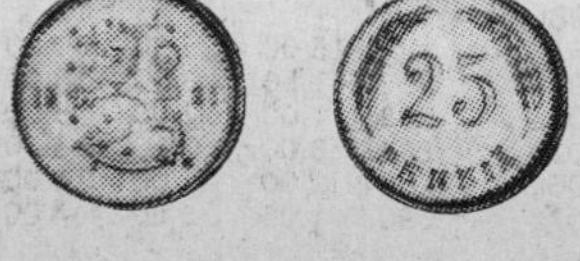

FINLAND 545

COPPER-NICKEL
Republic Issues

KM#	Date	Mintage	Fine	VF	XF	Unc
25	1921H	20.096	.10	.25	1.00	2.00
	1925S	1.250	.50	1.50	5.00	12.00
	1926S	2.820	.40	1.25	3.00	8.00
	1927S	1.120	.50	1.50	5.00	12.00
	1928S	2.920	.40	1.00	2.25	7.00
	1929S	.200	2.00	4.00	10.00	25.00
	1930S	1.090	.50	1.50	5.00	12.00
	1934S	1.260	.40	.75	2.00	7.00
	1935S	2.190	.30	.50	1.50	6.00
	1936S	2.300	.20	.40	1.00	3.00
	1937S	4.020	.20	.40	1.00	3.00
	1938S	4.500	.20	.40	1.00	3.00
	1939S	2.712	.20	.40	1.00	3.00
	1940S	4.840	.15	.30	.75	2.00

COPPER

KM#	Date	Mintage	Fine	VF	XF	Unc
25a	1940S	.072	.50	1.00	3.00	12.00
	1941S	5.980	.10	.35	1.00	3.00
	1942S	6.464	.10	.35	1.00	3.00
	1943S	4.912	.25	.50	1.50	5.00

IRON

KM#	Date	Mintage	Fine	VF	XF	Unc
25b	1943S	2.700	.15	.50	1.50	7.00
	1944S small closed 4's	5.480	.15	.50	1.25	6.00
	1944S large open 4's	Inc. Ab.	.15	.50	1.25	6.00
	1945S	6.810	.25	.75	2.00	8.00

50 PENNIA

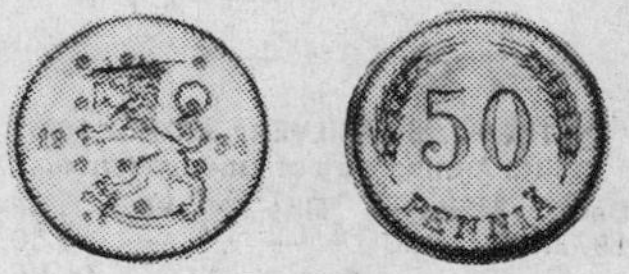

COPPER-NICKEL
Republic Issues

KM#	Date	Mintage	Fine	VF	XF	Unc
26	1921H	10.072	.15	.30	1.00	3.00
	1923S	6.000	.25	1.00	3.00	12.00
	1929S	.984	.75	1.50	5.00	20.00
	1934S	.612	1.00	2.50	7.50	22.00
	1935S	.610	1.00	2.50	7.50	22.00
	1936S	1.520	.30	.50	1.50	6.00
	1937S	2.350	.15	.25	.75	3.50
	1938S	2.330	.15	.25	.75	3.00
	1939S	1.280	.15	.25	.75	3.00
	1940S	3.152	.15	.25	.75	2.50

COPPER

KM#	Date	Mintage	Fine	VF	XF	Unc
26a	1940S	.480	1.25	2.50	5.00	12.00
	1941S	3.860	.15	.40	1.00	3.00
	1942S	5.900	.15	.40	1.00	3.00
	1943S	3.140	.25	.50	1.50	4.00

IRON

KM#	Date	Mintage	Fine	VF	XF	Unc
26b	1943S	1.580	.25	.50	1.50	15.00
	1944S	7.600	.15	.40	1.00	12.00
	1945S	4.700	.15	.40	1.00	12.00
	1946S	2.632	.30	.50	1.50	12.00
	1947S	1.748	.50	1.50	3.50	15.00
	1948L	1.112	3.00	5.00	10.00	20.00

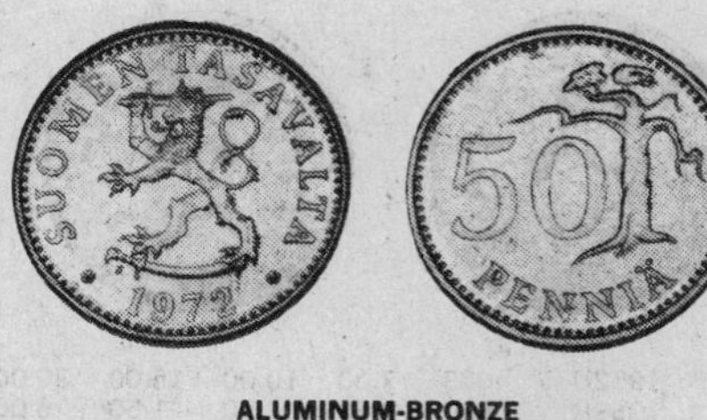

ALUMINUM-BRONZE

KM#	Date	Mintage	Fine	VF	XF	Unc
48	1963S	17.316	—	.15	.50	1.50
	1964S	3.101	—	.15	.50	2.00
	1965S	1.667	—	.15	.25	1.50
	1966S	1.051	—	.15	.25	1.00
	1967S	.400	.25	.50	1.00	2.50
	1968S	.816	—	.15	.50	2.00
	1969S	1.341	—	.15	.25	1.00
	1970S	2.250	—	.15	.25	1.00
	1971S	10.003	—	—	.15	.45
	1972S	7.892	—	—	.15	.45
	1973S	5.430	—	—	.15	.45
	1974S	5.049	—	—	.15	.25
	1975S	4.305	—	—	.15	.25
	1976K	7.022	—	—	.15	.25
	1977K	8.077	—	—	.15	.25
	1978K	8.048	—	—	.15	.25
	1979K	8.004	—	—	.15	.25
	1980K	5.349	—	—	.15	.25
	1981K	20.031	—	—	.15	.25
	1982K	5.042	—	—	.15	.25
	1983K	4.044	—	—	.15	.25
	1983N	1.016	—	—	.15	.35
	1984N	3.006	—	—	.15	.25
	1985N	10.000	—	—	.15	.25
	1986N	9.002	—	—	.15	.25
	1987N	.700	—	—	.15	.25
	1987M	4.305	—	—	.15	.25
	1988M	—	—	—	.15	.25

NOTE: Some 1971 issues are magnetic and command a premium.

MARKKA

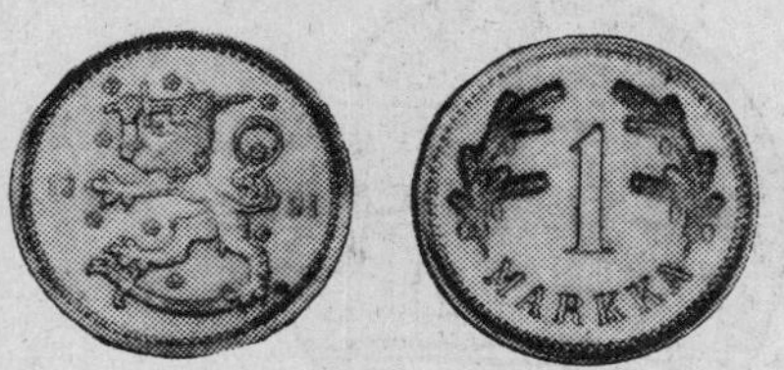

COPPER-NICKEL
Republic Issues

KM#	Date	Mintage	Fine	VF	XF	Unc
27	1921H	10.048	.50	1.00	2.50	5.00
	1922 heart	10.000	.75	1.50	3.50	10.00
	1923S	1.780	5.00	10.00	22.50	45.00
	1924S	3.270	2.50	5.00	12.00	25.00

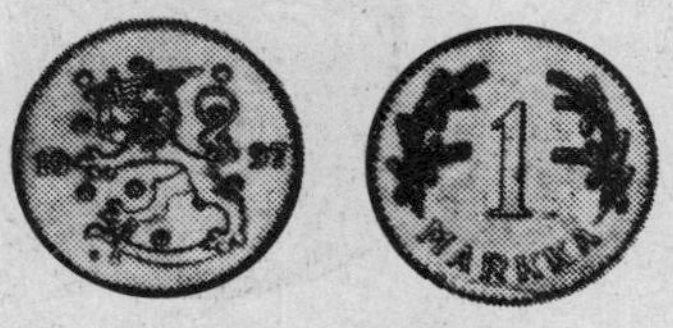

Reduced size

KM#	Date	Mintage	Fine	VF	XF	Unc
30	1928S	3.000	.15	.30	3.00	16.50
	1929S	3.862	.15	.30	3.00	16.50
	1930S	10.284	.15	.30	1.00	12.00
	1931S	2.830	.15	.30	1.00	12.00
	1932S	4.140	.15	.30	1.00	10.00
	1933S	4.032	.15	.30	1.00	10.00
	1936S	.562	.50	1.50	5.00	22.50
	1937S	4.930	.15	.30	1.00	6.00
	1938S	4.410	.15	.25	1.00	6.00
	1939S	3.070	.15	.25	1.00	6.00
	1940S	3.372	.15	.25	1.00	6.00

NOTE: Coins dated 1928S, 1929S and 1930S are known to be restruck on 1921-24, KM#27 coins. (1928S: 2 or 3 known).

COPPER

KM#	Date	Mintage	Fine	VF	XF	Unc
30a	1940S	.084	1.50	3.50	8.00	16.50
	1941S	8.970	.15	.50	1.25	6.00
	1942S	11.200	.15	.50	1.00	4.00
	1943S	7.460	.15	.50	1.25	5.00
	1949H	250 pcs.	700.00	1000.	1650.	2250.
	1950H	.320	.50	1.00	2.00	10.00
	1951H	4.630	.25	.50	1.00	6.00

IRON

KM#	Date	Mintage	Fine	VF	XF	Unc
30b	1943S	7.460	.15	.25	1.00	8.00
	1944S	12.830	.15	.25	1.00	8.00
	1945S	21.950	.15	.25	1.00	8.00
	1946S	2.630	.15	.30	1.25	9.00
	1947S	1.750	.25	.50	1.50	12.50
	1948L	20.500	.15	.25	1.00	8.00
	1949H	17.358	.15	.25	.75	7.00
	1950H	14.654	.15	.25	.75	7.00
	1951H	21.414	.15	.25	.75	7.00
	1952H	5.410	.25	.50	1.50	10.00

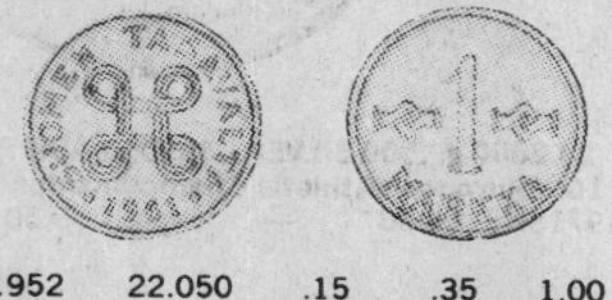

KM#	Date	Mintage	Fine	VF	XF	Unc
36	1952	22.050	.15	.35	1.00	5.50
	1953	28.618	.15	.35	1.00	5.50

NICKEL-PLATED IRON

KM#	Date	Mintage	Fine	VF	XF	Unc
36a	1953	6.000	2.00	3.00	7.00	15.00
	1954	36.400	—	.10	.25	.50
	1955	38.100	—	.10	.25	.50
	1956	35.600	—	.10	.25	.50
	1957	29.100	—	.10	.25	.50
	1958	19.940	.10	.20	.35	.70
	1959 thick letters	23.920	—	.10	.25	.50
	1959 thin letters	Inc. Ab.	—	.10	.25	.50
	1960	22.020	—	.10	.25	.50
	1961	32.220	—	.10	.25	.50
	1962	29.040	—	.10	.25	.50

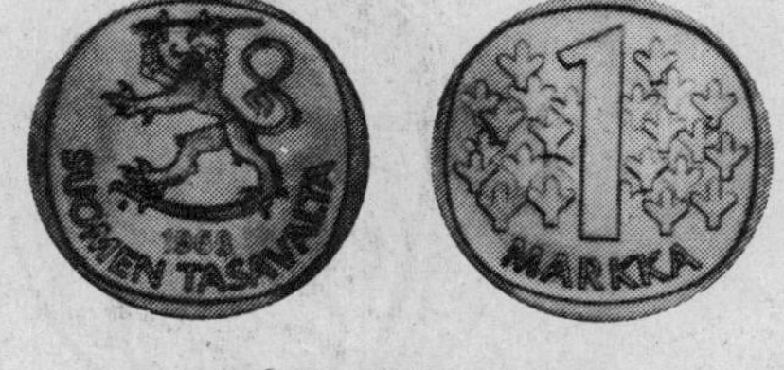

6.4000 g, .350 SILVER, .0720 oz ASW

KM#	Date	Mintage	Fine	VF	XF	Unc
49	1964S	9.999	—	BV	1.50	4.00
	1965S	15.107	—	BV	1.00	2.00
	1966S	15.183	—	BV	.75	1.50
	1967S	6.249	—	BV	.75	1.50
	1968S	3.063	—	BV	.75	1.50

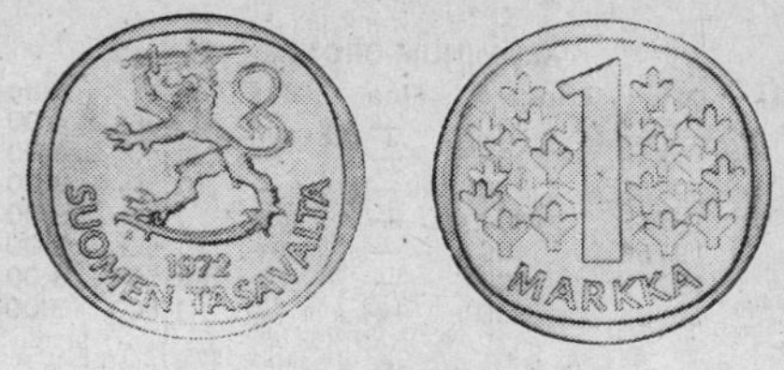

COPPER-NICKEL

KM#	Date	Mintage	Fine	VF	XF	Unc
49a	1969S	1.308	.30	.40	.50	1.00
	1970S	12.255	—	.30	.40	.60
	1971S	19.676	—	.30	.40	.60
	1972S	19.885	—	.30	.40	.60
	1973S	17.060	—	.30	.40	.60
	1974S	18.065	—	.30	.40	.60
	1975S	11.523	—	—	.30	.45
	1976K	12.048	—	—	.30	.45
	1977K	10.077	—	—	.30	.45
	1978K	10.022	—	—	.30	.45
	1979K	11.311	—	—	.30	.45
	1980K	19.306	—	—	.30	.45
	1981K	32.003	—	—	.30	.45
	1982K	30.001	—	—	.30	.45
	1983K	8.075	—	—	.30	.45
	1983N	11.927	—	—	.30	.45
	1984N	15.000	—	—	.30	.45
	1985N	19.001	—	—	.30	.45
	1986N	10.000	—	—	.30	.45
	1987N	.700	—	—	.30	.45
	1987M	9.303	—	—	.30	.45
	1988M	—	—	—	.30	.45

5 MARKKAA

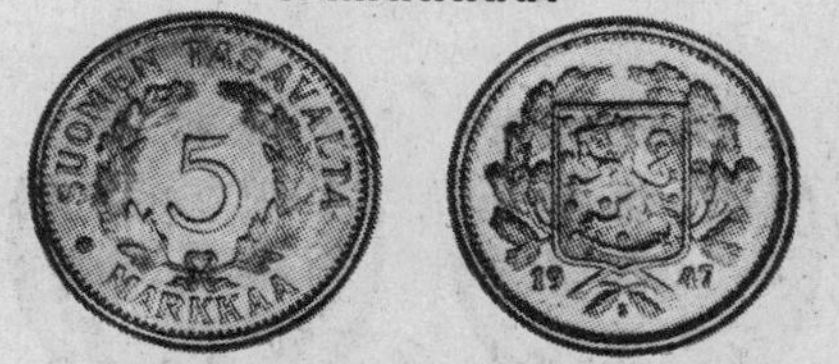

ALUMINUM-BRONZE

KM#	Date	Mintage	Fine	VF	XF	Unc
31	1928S	.580	25.00	45.00	100.00	250.00
	1929S	Inc. Ab.	25.00	40.00	90.00	220.00
	1930S	.592	.75	1.75	7.00	35.00
	1931S	3.090	.50	1.00	6.00	30.00
	1932S	.964	5.00	10.00	25.00	70.00
	1933S	1.050	.50	1.00	6.00	30.00
	1935S	.440	1.50	3.00	12.00	50.00
	1936S	.470	1.50	3.00	12.00	45.00
	1937S	1.032	.50	1.00	6.00	15.00
	1938S	.912	.50	1.00	6.00	15.00
	1939S	.752	.50	1.00	6.00	15.00
	1940S	.820	1.25	2.75	8.00	20.00
	1941S	1.452	.50	1.00	4.00	10.00
	1942S	1.390	.50	1.00	5.00	12.00
	1946S	.618	3.50	7.00	20.00	60.00

BRASS

KM#	Date	Mintage	Fine	VF	XF	Unc
31a	1946S	5.538	.20	.50	1.50	3.50
	1947S	6.550	.25	.75	2.00	6.00
	1948L	8.210	.25	.50	1.50	5.00
	1949H thin H	11.014	.20	.50	1.50	3.50
	1949H wide H	Inc. Ab.	.20	.50	1.50	3.50
	1950H	4.760	.20	.50	1.50	3.50
	1951H	7.8000	.20	.50	1.50	3.50
	1952H	1.210	2.50	6.00	12.00	25.00

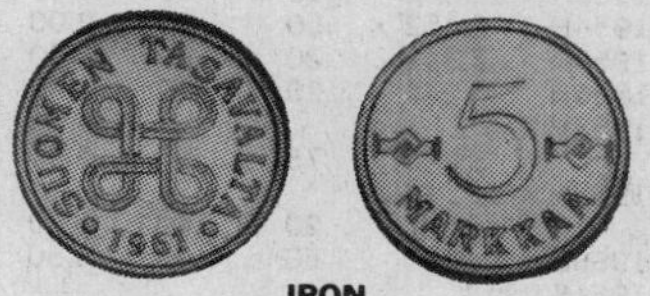

IRON

KM#	Date	Mintage	Fine	VF	XF	Unc
37	1952	10.820	.20	.35	2.00	8.00
	1953	9.772	.20	.35	3.00	10.00

NICKEL-PLATED IRON

KM#	Date	Mintage	Fine	VF	XF	Unc
37a	1953	Inc. Ab.	35.00	60.00	80.00	125.00
	1954	6.696	—	.20	.35	1.50
	1955	9.894	—	.20	.35	1.50
	1956	8.220	—	.20	.35	1.00
	1957	4.276	—	.20	.35	1.00
	1958	3.300	—	.20	.35	1.50
	1959	5.874	—	.20	.35	1.00
	1960	3.066	.10	.25	.35	1.50
	1961	7.254	.10	.25	.35	1.50
	1962	4.542	.50	1.00	3.00	6.00

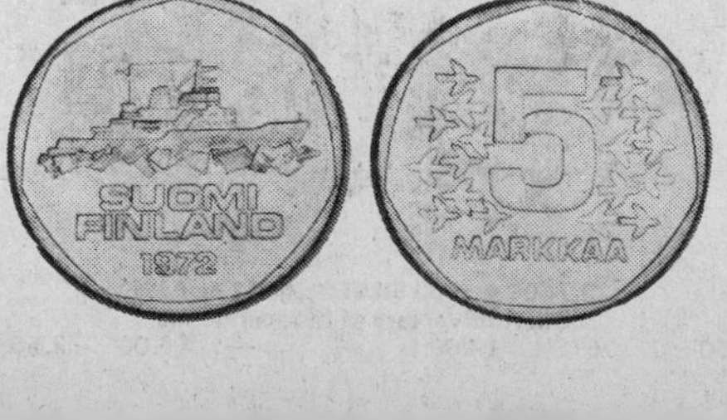

FINLAND 546

ALUMINUM-BRONZE

KM#	Date	Mintage	Fine	VF	XF	Unc
53	1972S	.400	—	—	2.00	4.00
	1973S	2.188	—	—	1.50	3.00
	1974S	.300	—	—	1.50	3.00
	1975S	.300	—	—	1.50	3.00
	1976K	.400	—	—	1.50	3.00
	1977K	.300	—	—	1.50	3.00
	1978K	.300	—	—	1.50	3.00

57	1979K	2.005	—	—	1.35	2.00
	1980K	.501	—	—	1.50	2.50
	1981K	1.009	—	—	1.35	2.00
	1982K	3.004	—	—	1.35	2.00
	1983K	8.776	—	—	1.35	2.00
	1983N	11.230	—	—	1.35	2.00
	1984N	15.001	—	—	1.35	2.00
	1985N	8.004	—	—	1.35	2.00
	1986N	5.006	—	—	1.35	2.00
	1987N	.660	—	—	1.35	2.00
	1987M	2.347	—	—	1.35	2.00
	1988M		—	—	1.35	2.00

10 MARKKAA

ALUMINUM-BRONZE

63	1928S	.730	2.50	5.00	15.00	75.00
(30)	1929S	Inc. Ab.	2.00	4.00	12.00	60.00
	1930S	.260	1.00	2.50	8.00	50.00
	1931S	1.530	1.00	2.50	8.00	50.00
	1932S	1.010	1.00	2.50	8.00	50.00
	1934S	.154	1.50	3.00	12.00	60.00
	1935S	.081	2.00	4.00	12.00	75.00
	1936S	.304	2.00	4.00	12.00	60.00
	1937S	.181	1.50	2.50	8.00	60.00
	1938S	.631	.75	1.50	5.00	30.00
	1939S	.133	4.00	8.00	15.00	60.00

38	1952H	6.390	.20	.50	1.75	5.00
	1953H	22.650	.15	.35	1.00	3.00
	1954H	2.452	.50	1.00	2.00	6.00
	1955H	2.342	.20	.50	1.50	5.00
	1956H	4.240	.20	.40	1.00	4.00
	1958H thin 1	3.292	.75	1.50	5.00	10.00
	1958H wide 1	Inc. Ab.	.20	.40	1.00	4.00
	1960S	.740	.50	1.00	3.50	8.00
	1961S thin 1	3.580	.20	.50	1.50	5.00
	1961S wide 1	Inc. Ab.	.50	1.25	3.50	8.00
	1962S	1.852	.30	.60	1.75	5.00

NOTE: The "1" in the denomination on all 1952 to 1956 issues is the thin variety. 1960 issues are the wide variety, and 1962's are thin. Varieties exist in root length of tree.

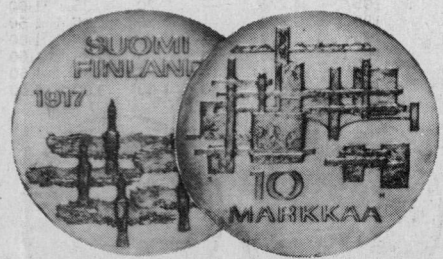

23.7500 g, .900 SILVER, .6872 oz ASW
50th Anniversary of Independence

| 50 | 1967SH | 1.000 | — | — | 5.00 | 7.50 |

22.7500 g, .500 SILVER, .3657 oz ASW
Paasikivi Birth Centennial

KM#	Date	Mintage	Fine	VF	XF	Unc
51	1970SH	.600	—	—	3.50	5.00

24.2000 g, .500 SILVER, .3890 oz ASW
10th European Athletic Championships

| 52 | 1971SH | 1.000 | — | — | 3.50 | 5.00 |

23.5000 g, .500 SILVER, .3778 oz ASW
75th Birthday of President Kekkonen

| 54 | 1975SH | 1.000 | — | — | 3.50 | 5.00 |

21.7800 g, .500 SILVER, .3501 oz ASW
60th Anniversary of Independence

KM#	Date	Mintage	Fine	VF	XF	Unc
55	1977KH	.400	—	—	3.50	5.00

20 MARKKAA

ALUMINUM-BRONZE

32	1931S	.016	30.00	40.00	60.00	90.00
	1932S	.014	30.00	40.00	65.00	95.00
	1934S	.390	2.00	5.00	17.50	60.00
	1935S	.250	2.00	5.00	17.50	60.00
	1936S	.110	3.00	5.00	17.50	70.00
	1937S	.510	.75	1.50	10.00	40.00
	1938S	.360	.75	1.50	9.00	30.00
	1939S	.960	.65	1.50	6.00	15.00

39	1952H	.083	7.00	10.00	15.00	30.00
	1953H	2.880	.25	.50	1.50	6.00
	1954H	17.034	.15	.50	1.25	5.00
	1955H	2.800	.25	.50	1.50	6.00
	1956H	2.540	.25	.50	1.50	6.00
	1957H	1.050	.50	1.00	3.00	8.00
	1958H	.515	1.00	3.00	7.00	15.00
	1959S	1.580	.25	.50	1.50	6.00
	1960S	3.850	.15	.50	1.00	4.00
	1961S	4.430	.15	.50	1.00	4.00
	1962S	2.280	.15	.50	1.50	6.00

25 MARKKAA

FINLAND 547

26.5500 g, .500 SILVER, .4268 oz ASW
Winter Games in Lahti

KM#	Date	Mintage	Fine	VF	XF	Unc
56	1978KN	.500	—	—	6.50	8.50

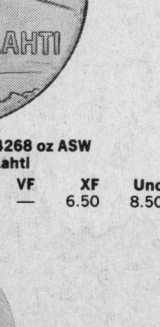

750th Anniversary of Turku
| 58 | 1979KH | .300 | — | — | 6.50 | 8.50 |

50 MARKKAA

ALUMINUM-BRONZE

40	1952H	.991	1.00	3.00	6.00	15.00
	1953H	10.300	.25	.50	2.00	7.00
	1954H	1.170	.50	1.00	3.00	8.00
	1955H	.583	.75	1.50	4.00	10.00
	1956H	.792	.75	1.50	4.00	10.00
	1958H	.242	10.00	18.00	25.00	35.00
	1960S	.110	12.00	20.00	30.00	50.00
	1961S	1.811	.50	1.00	2.00	6.00
	1962S	.405	1.00	2.00	4.00	12.00

19.9500 g, 500 SILVER, .3207 oz ASW
80th Birthday of President Kekkonen
| 59 | 1981K | .500 | — | — | 12.50 | 16.50 |

22.8500 g, .500 SILVER, .3673 oz ASW
World Ice Hockey Championship Games

KM#	Date	Mintage	Fine	VF	XF	Unc
60	1982KT	.400	—	—	12.50	16.50

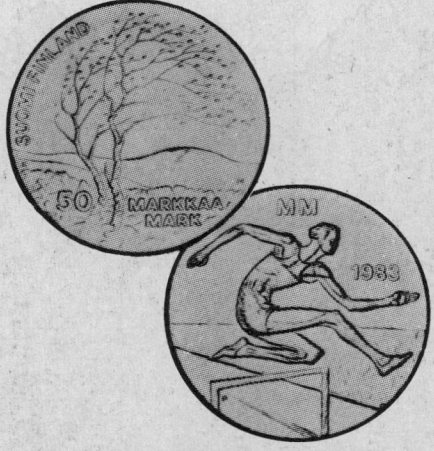

22.0000 g, .500 SILVER, .3537 oz ASW
1st World Athletics Championships
| 61 | 1983KM | .450 | — | — | 12.50 | 16.50 |

20.0000 g, .500 SILVER, .3215 oz ASW
National Epic - The Kalevala
| 62 | 1985PN | .300 | — | — | 12.50 | 18.00 |

100 MARKKAA

4.2105 g, .900 GOLD, .1218 oz AGW
| 28 | 1926S | .050 | — | 450.00 | 650.00 | 950.00 |

5.2000 g, .500 SILVER, .0836 oz ASW

41	1956H	3.012	—	BV	1.50	3.00
	1957H	3.012	—	BV	1.50	3.00
	1958H	1.704	BV	1.50	2.50	4.00
	1959S	1.270	3.00	4.00	6.00	8.00
	1960S	.290	4.00	6.00	8.00	10.00

200 MARKKAA

8.4210 g, .900 GOLD, .2436 oz AGW

KM#	Date	Mintage	Fine	VF	XF	Unc
29	1926S	.050	—	550.00	900.00	1250.00

8.3000 g, .500 SILVER, .1334 oz ASW

42	1956H	1.552	—	BV	2.50	5.00
	1957H	2.157	—	BV	2.50	5.00
	1958H	1.477	BV	2.50	4.00	7.00
	1958S	.034	200.00	250.00	300.00	400.00
	1959S	.070	20.00	25.00	30.00	55.00

500 MARKKAA

12.0000 g, .500 SILVER, .1929 oz ASW
1952 Olympic Games
| 35 | 1951H | .019 | 165.00 | 250.00 | 325.00 | 400.00 |
| | 1952H | .586 | 20.00 | 25.00 | 35.00 | 50.00 |

1000 MARKKAA

14.0000 g, .875 SILVER, .3938 oz ASW
Markka Currency System Centennial
| 43 | 1960SJ | .201 | 8.00 | — | 15.00 | 20.00 |

MINT SETS (MS)

KM#	Date	Mintage	Identification	Issue Price	Mkt. Val.
MS1	1973(7)	10,029	KM44a,45-48,49a,53 hard plastic holder	3.25	12.00
MS2	1973(7)	9,978	KM44a,45-48,49a,53 soft plastic holder	4.00	20.00
MS3	1974(7)	79,258	KM44a,45-48,49a,53	3.75	5.00
MS4	1975(7)	58,820	KM44a,45-48,49a,53	3.75	5.00
MS5	1976(7)	45,263	KM44a,45-48,49a,53	3.75	6.00
MS6	1977(7)	40,392	KM44a,45-48,49a,53	4.00	7.00
MS7	1978(7)	42,000	KM44a,45a,46-48,49a,53	4.45	6.00
MS8	1979(7)	36,000	KM44a,45a,46-48,49a,57	4.85	6.00
MS9	1980(6)	37,800	KM45a,46-48,49a,57	5.00	6.00
MS10	1981(6)	35,600	KM45a,46-48,49a,57	5.25	6.00
MS11	1982(6)	34,900	KM45a,46-48,49a,57	5.50	6.00
MS12	1983K(6)	30,100	KM45a,46a,47-48,49a,57	3.25	5.00
MS13	1983N(6)	9,250	KM45a,46a,47-48,49a,57	3.25	10.00
MS14	1984N(6)	29,400	KM45a,46a,47-48,49a,57	3.25	5.00
MS15	1984N(6)	600	KM45a,46a,47-48,49a,57 Russian text	3.75	22.00
MS16	1985N(6)	39,000	KM45a-46a,47-48,49a,57 Finnish text	3.25	5.00
MS17	1985N(6)	1,540	KM45a-46a,47-48,49a,57 Russian text	4.65	13.00
MS18	1985N(6)	1,650	KM45a-46a,47-48,49a,57 English text	3.75	6.00
MS19	1986N(6)	37,100	KM45a-46a,47-48,49a,57 Finnish text	3.25	5.00
MS20	1986N(6)	1,300	KM45a-46a,47-48,49a,57 Russian text	5.00	13.00
MS21	1986N(6)	1,800	KM45a-46a,47-48,49a,57 English text	4.25	11.00
MS22	1987N(6)	34,300	KM45a-46a,47-48,49a,57 Finnish text	—	5.00
MS23	1987N(6)	1,120	KM45a-46a,47-48,49a,57 Russian text	—	10.00
MS24	1987N(6)	1,400	KM45a-46a,47-48,49a,57 English text	—	10.00
MS25	1987M(6)	16,600	KM45a-46a,47-48,49a,57 Finnish text	—	5.00
MS26	1987M(6)	300	KM45a-46a,47-48,49a,57 Russian text	—	10.00
MS27	1987M(6)	180	KM45a-46a,47-48,49a,57 English text	—	12.00
MS28	1988M(6)	—	KM45a-46a,47-48,49a,57	—	12.50

Listings For
FORMOSA: refer to China, Republic of

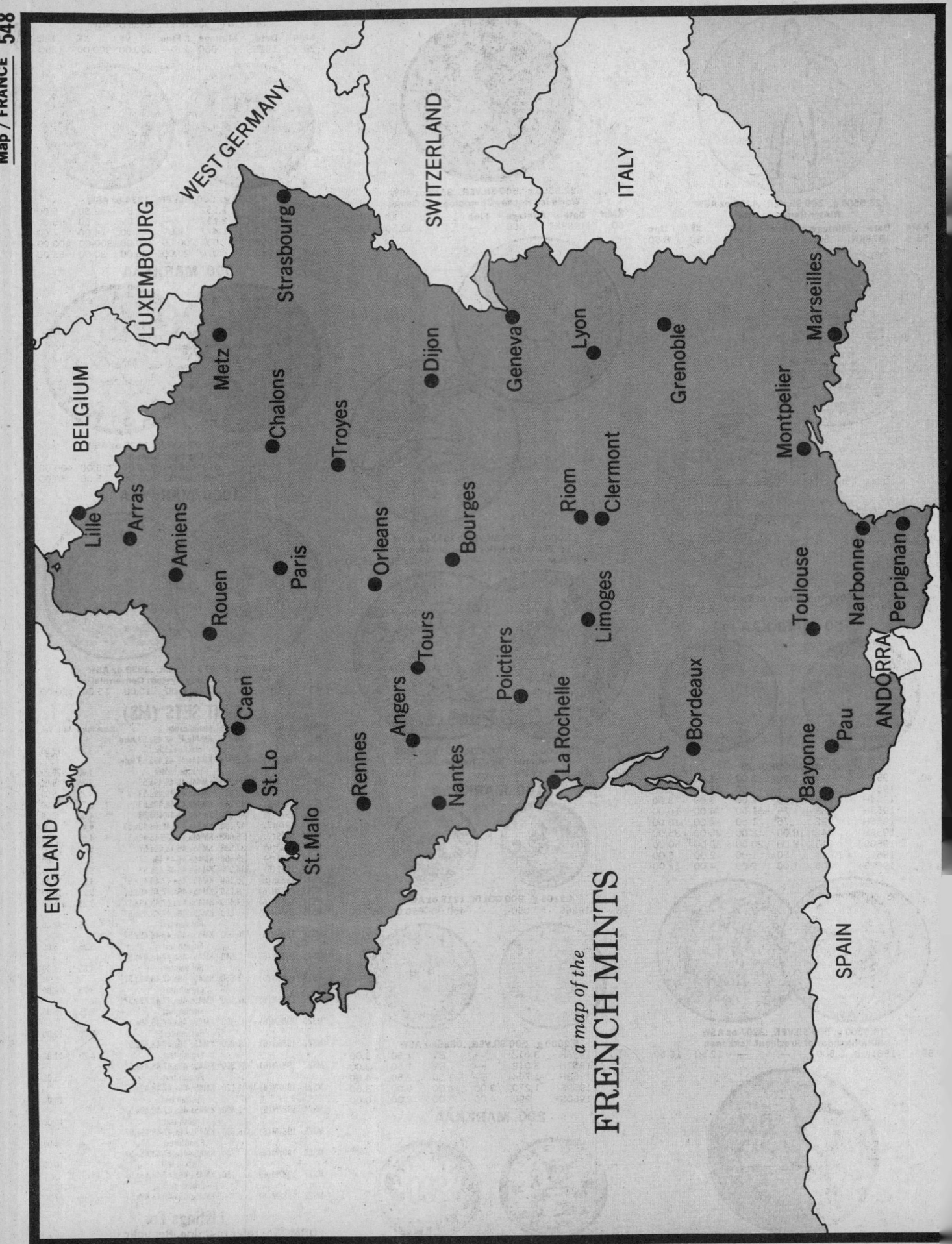

FRANCE

The French Republic, largest of the West European nations, has an area of 211,208 sq. mi. (547,026 sq. km.) and a population of *55.8 million. Capital: Paris. Agriculture, mining and manufacturing are the most important elements of France's diversified economy. Textiles and clothing, iron and steel products, machinery and transportation equipment, agricultural products and wine are exported.

France, the Gaul of ancient times, emerged from the Renaissance as a modern centralized national state which reached its zenith during the reign of Louis XIV (1643-1715) when it became an absolute monarchy and the foremost power in Europe. Although his reign marks the golden age of French culture, the domestic abuses and extravagance of Louis XIV plunged France into a series of costly wars. This, along with a system of special privileges granted the nobility and other favored groups, weakened the monarchy, brought France to bankruptcy - and laid the way for the French Revolution of 1789-94 that shook Europe and affected the whole world.

The monarchy was abolished and the First Republic formed in 1793. The new government fell in 1799 to a coup led by Napoleon Bonaparte who, after declaring himself First Consul for life, had himself proclaimed emperor of France and king of Italy. Napoleon's military victories made him master of much of Europe, but his disastrous Russian campaign of 1812 initiated a series of defeats that led to his abdication in 1814 and exile to the island of Elba. The monarchy was briefly restored under Louis XVIII. Napoleon returned to France in March 1815, but his efforts to regain power were totally crushed at the battle of Waterloo. He was exiled to the island of St. Helena where he died in 1821.

The monarchy under Louis XVIII was again restored in 1815, but the ultrareactionary regime of Charles X (1824-30) was overthrown by a liberal revolution and Louis Philippe of Orleans replaced him as monarch. The monarchy was ousted by the Revolution of 1848 and the Second Republic proclaimed. Louis Napoleon Bonaparte (nephew of Napoleon I) was elected president of the Second Republic. He was proclaimed emperor in 1852. As Napoleon III, he gave France two decades of prosperity under a stable, autocratic regime, but led it to defeat in the Franco-Prussian War of 1870, after which the Third Republic was established.

The Third Republic endured until 1940 and the capitulation of France to the swiftly maneuvering German forces. Marshal Henri Petain formed a puppet government that sued for peace and ruled unoccupied France from Vichy. Meanwhile, General Charles de Gaulle escaped to London where he formed a wartime government in exile and the Free French army. De Gaulle's provisional exile government was officially recognized by the Allies after the liberation of Paris in 1944, and De Gaulle, who had been serving as head of the provisional government, was formally elected to that position. In October 1945, the people overwhelmingly rejected a return to the prewar government, thus paving the way for the formation of the Fourth Republic.

De Gaulle was unanimously elected president of the Fourth Republic, but resigned in January 1946 when leftists withdrew their support. In actual operation, the Fourth Republic was remarkably like the Third, with the National Assembly the focus of power. The later years of the Fourth Republic were marked by a burst of industrial expansion unmatched in modern French history. The growth rate, however, was marred by a nagging inflationary trend that weakened the franc and undermined the competitive posture of France's export trade. This and the Algerian conflict led to the recall of De Gaulle to power, the adoption of a new constitution vesting strong powers in the executive, and the establishment in 1958 of the current Fifth Republic.

RULERS

Napoleon as Consul, 1799-1804
Napoleon I as Emperor, 1804-1814
 (first restoration)
Louis XVIII, 1814-1815
Napoleon I, 1815
 (second restoration)
Louis XVIII, 1815-1824
Charles X, 1824-1830
Louis Philippe, 1830-1848
Second Republic, 1848-1852
Napoleon III, 1852-1870
Government of National Defense, 1870-1871
Third Republic, 1871-1940
Vichy State, 1940-1944
De Gaulle's Provisional Govt., 1944-1947
Fourth Republic, 1947-1958
Fifth Republic, 1959-

MINT MARKS AND PRIVY MARKS

In addition to the date and mint mark which are customary on western civilization coinage, most coins manufactured by the French Mints contain two small 'Marques et Differents' as the French call them. These privy marks represent the men responsible for the dies which struck the coins. One privy mark is for the Engraver General (since 1880 the title is Chief Engraver). The other privy mark is the signature of the Mint Director of each mint. Since 1880 this privy mark has represented the office rather than the personage of the Mint Director, and a standard privy mark has been used (cornucopia).

For most dates these privy marks are unimportant minor features. During some issue dates, however, the marks changed. To be even more accurate sometimes the marks changed when the date didn't, even though it should have. These coins can be attributed to the proper mintage report only by considering the privy marks. Previous references have by and large ignored these privy marks. It is entirely possible that unattributed varieties may exist for any privy mark transition. All transition years which may have two varieties of privy marks have the known attribution indicated after the date (if it has been confirmed).

ENGRAVER GENERALS' PRIVY MARKS

Engraver Generals' privy marks may appear on coins of other mints which are dated as follows:

A - PARIS

Date	Privy Mark
AN XI-1816	Tiolier (in script) alternate
AN 13-1815	Tr (in script) signatures
1817-1824	T (in script) on Louis XVIII 1/4 F. only
1816-1824	Horse head on other Louis XVIII (h)
1824-1830	T (in script) (t)
1830-1842	Star (s)
1843-1855	Dog head (d) or D
1855-1879	Anchor (a)
1879	Anchor with bar (ab)
1880-1896	Fasces (f)
1896-1930	Torch (t)
1931-1958	Wing (w)
1958-1974	Owl (o)
1974—	Fish

MINT DIRECTOR PRIVY MARKS

Not all modern coins struck from dies produced at Paris have the 'A' mint mark. In the absence of a mint mark, the cornucopia privy mark serves to attribute a coin to Paris design.

A - PARIS

Date	Privy Mark
L'AN 6-1821	Cock
1822-42	Anchor
1843-45	Prow of ship (p)
1846-60	Hand (ha)
1860-79	Bee (b)
1871	(Commune), Trident (t)
1880-98	Cornucopia
1897-1920	None (n)
1901—	Cornucopia (c)

B - ROUEN

Date	Privy Mark
L'AN 12-1844	Sheep
1845-46	Hand
1853-57	Pick and shovel

B - BEAUMONT-LE-ROGER

1943-58	Cornucopia

(b) - BRUSSELS

1939	None

BB - STRASBOURG

L'AN 5-1825	Sheaf
1826-34	Beaver (b)
1835-60	Bee
1860-70	Cross (c)

BD - PAU

C - CASTELSARRASIN

1914, 42-46	Cornucopia

C - SAINT LO

CC, CL - GENOA

1805, 13-14	Prow of ship

CH - CHALONS

D - LYON

L'AN XI-1823	Bee (b)
1823-39	Arc (a)
1839-42	Tower
1848-57	Lion

E - TOURS

F - ANGERS

G - GENEVE

L'AN 12 - 1805	Fish

G - POITIERS

H - LA ROCHELLE

L'AN 11-1817	Monogram
1817-23	Lyre (l)
1824-37	Trident

I - LIMOGES

L'AN XI-1822	Horizontal clasped hands
1823-37	Vertical clasped hands

K - BORDEAUX

Date	Privy Mark
L'AN 13-1809	Fish (f)
1809-57	Leaf (l)
1861-68	Pick and hammer
1870-1871	M/star
1870-78	Cross

L - BAYONNE

AN XI-1828	Tulip (t)
1810	Tulip to right of date (tr)
1829-35	Rose
1836-37	Monogram

M - TOULOUSE

AN 14-1811	Hammer (h)
1811-37	Monogram (m)

MA - MARSEILLES

1787-1809	Star
1809-23	Monogram
1824-38	Palm tree
1853-57	Shell

O - CLERMONT

O - RIOM

P - DIJON

P - SEMUR

Q - NARBONNE

Q - PERPIGNAN

L'AN 4-1837	Grapes

R - LONDON

1815	Lis (no engraver signature)

R - SAINT ANDRE

S - TROYES

T - NANTES

L'AN 4-1818	Anchor
1818-20	Key
1826-35	Olive branch

U - TURIN

U, L'AN 11 - 1814	Heart

W - LILLE

L'AN 4-1840	Caduceus (c)
1841-46	Retort (r)
1853-57	Lamp

X - AMIENS

Y - BOURGES

Z - GRENOBLE

9 - RENNES

9 - SAINT MALO

- BESANCON

Flag (u)- UTRECHT

1811-14	Fish

Crowned R (R) - ROME

1811-14	Wolf

Thunderbolt (t) - POISSY

1922-24	Cornucopia

Star (s) - MADRID

1916	Cornucopia

MONETARY SYSTEM
(Commencing 1794)

10 Centimes = 1 Decime
10 Decimes = 1 Franc

UN (1) CENTIME

BRONZE
Mint mark: A
Second Republic

Y#	Date	Mintage	VF	XF	Unc	BU
1	1848	8.615	3.00	6.00	8.00	12.00
	1849	8.664	3.00	6.00	8.00	13.00
	1850	2.721	8.00	20.00	30.00	55.00
	1851	2.712	5.00	10.00	15.00	30.00

Second Empire

Y#	Date	Mintage	VF	XF	Unc	BU
14.1	1853	4.076	3.00	8.00	12.00	20.00
	1854	2.750	6.00	16.00	25.00	40.00
	1855(d)	6.034	4.00	12.00	18.00	30.00
	1855(a)	I.A.	12.00	30.00	45.00	75.00
	1855(a)	—	—	—	Proof	100.00
	1856	2.878	8.00	20.00	30.00	50.00
	1857	2.000	9.00	24.00	35.00	60.00

Mint mark: B

Y#	Date	Mintage	VF	XF	Unc	BU
14.2	1853	.824	7.00	16.00	25.00	45.00
	1854	1.709	12.00	32.00	47.50	80.00
	1855(a)	1.971	12.00	32.00	47.50	80.00
	1855(d)	I.A.	12.00	32.00	47.50	80.00
	1856	4.373	4.00	12.00	18.00	30.00
	1857	3.000	6.00	16.00	25.00	40.00

Mint mark: BB

Y#	Date	Mintage	VF	XF	Unc	BU
14.3	1853	2.558	4.00	12.00	18.00	30.00
	1854	1.447	6.00	16.00	25.00	40.00
	1855(a)	.248	24.00	60.00	90.00	150.00
	1855(d)	I.A.	24.00	60.00	90.00	150.00
	1856	1.874	7.00	18.00	27.50	45.00
	1857	—	—	Rare		—

Mint mark: D

Y#	Date	Mintage	VF	XF	Unc	BU
14.4	1853	.964	6.00	16.00	25.00	45.00
	1854	1.546	10.00	25.00	38.00	65.00
	1855(a)	2.466	10.00	25.00	38.00	65.00
	1855(d)	I.A.	16.00	40.00	60.00	100.00
	1856	.880	25.00	60.00	90.00	150.00
	1857	1.000	12.00	32.00	47.50	80.00

NOTE: The 1853 dated coins exist with large and small D's.

Mint mark: K

Y#	Date	Mintage	VF	XF	Unc	BU
14.5	1853	.405	12.00	30.00	45.00	75.00
	1854	1.150	12.00	30.00	45.00	75.00
	1855(a)	Inc. Ab.	12.00	30.00	45.00	75.00
	1855(d)	1.455	12.00	30.00	45.00	75.00
	1856	2.062	10.00	25.00	38.00	65.00
	1857	1.000	12.00	30.00	45.00	75.00

Mint mark: MA

Y#	Date	Mintage	VF	XF	Unc	BU
14.6	1853	.225	16.00	40.00	60.00	100.00
	1854	1.976	6.00	16.00	25.00	40.00
	1855(a)	2.839	12.00	32.00	47.50	80.00
	1855(d)	I.A.	8.00	20.00	30.00	50.00
	1856	.305	20.00	50.00	75.00	125.00
	1857	1.500	6.00	16.00	25.00	40.00

Mint mark: W

Y#	Date	Mintage	VF	XF	Unc	BU
14.7	1853	1.634	4.00	12.00	18.00	35.00
	1854	1.399	—	Reported, not confirmed		
	1855(d)	3.102	4.00	12.00	18.00	35.00
	1855(a)	I.A.	9.00	22.00	32.50	55.00
	1856	2.707	6.00	16.00	25.00	45.00
	1857	2.500	9.00	22.00	32.50	55.00

Mint mark: A

Y#	Date	Mintage	VF	XF	Unc	BU
18.1	1861	7.398	2.00	6.00	9.00	15.00
	1862	15.561	1.50	4.00	6.00	12.00
	1870	1.000	12.00	26.00	40.00	65.00

Mint mark: BB

Y#	Date	Mintage	VF	XF	Unc	BU
18.2	1861	3.012	2.50	7.00	10.00	18.00
	1862	4.493	2.50	7.00	10.00	18.00

Mint mark: K

Y#	Date	Mintage	VF	XF	Unc	BU
18.3	1861	1.999	4.00	12.00	18.00	30.00
	1862	7.431	2.00	5.00	8.00	14.00

Mint mark: A
Third Republic

Y#	Date	Mintage	VF	XF	Unc	BU
41.1	1872	1.250	3.50	7.00	10.00	18.00
	1874	1.000	4.00	8.00	12.00	20.00
	1875	1.000	3.50	7.00	10.00	18.00
	1877	1.000	3.50	7.00	10.00	18.00
	1878	1.500	3.00	6.00	9.00	16.00
	1879(ab)	.800	4.00	8.00	12.00	20.00
	1882	.419	7.00	16.00	25.00	40.00
	1884	.400	8.00	18.00	27.50	45.00
	1885	.400	7.00	16.00	25.00	40.00
	1886	.400	7.00	16.00	25.00	40.00
	1887	.400	7.00	16.00	25.00	40.00
	1888	.400	7.00	16.00	25.00	40.00
	1889	.400	7.00	16.00	25.00	40.00
	1890	.400	7.00	16.00	25.00	40.00
	1891	1.400	3.50	8.00	12.00	20.00
	1892	.800	5.00	10.00	15.00	25.00
	1893	.300	10.00	20.00	30.00	50.00
	1894	.500	6.00	14.00	20.00	35.00
	1895	3.000	1.50	4.00	6.00	10.00
	1896(f)	3.000	1.50	3.00	5.00	10.00
	1897	2.000	1.50	4.00	7.50	14.00

Mint mark: K

Y#	Date	Mintage	VF	XF	Unc	BU
41.2	1872	.750	7.00	18.00	27.50	45.00
	1875	2.000	4.00	10.00	15.00	25.00
	1878	.289	20.00	40.00	60.00	90.00

Mint: Paris - w/o mint mark.

Y#	Date	Mintage	VF	XF	Unc	BU
58	1898	.250	6.00	12.00	18.00	30.00
	1898	—	—	—	Proof	250.00
	1899	1.500	1.50	5.00	8.00	15.00
	1900	.221	30.00	60.00	80.00	125.00
	1900	—	—	—	Proof	150.00
	1901	1.000	2.00	5.00	8.00	16.00
	1902	1.000	2.00	5.00	8.00	16.00
	1903	2.000	2.00	4.00	7.00	13.00
	1904	1.000	2.00	5.00	8.00	16.00
	1908	4.500	2.00	5.00	8.00	30.00
	1909	1.500	2.00	5.00	8.00	30.00
	1910	1.500	20.00	40.00	50.00	65.00
	1911	5.000	1.00	2.00	3.50	7.00
	1912	2.000	1.00	3.00	4.00	8.00
	1913	1.500	1.00	4.00	6.00	12.00
	1914	1.000	2.00	4.00	7.00	14.00
	1916	1.996	1.00	3.00	4.00	8.00
	1919	2.407	1.00	2.00	3.00	4.50
	1920	2.594	1.00	2.00	3.00	5.00

NOTE: No privy marks on Y#58 of any date.

CHROME-STEEL
1 New Centime - 1 Old Franc
Fifth Republic

Y#	Date	Mintage	Fine	VF	XF	Unc
102	1962	34.200	—	—	.10	.25
	1963	16.811	—	.10	.15	.35
	1964	22.654	—	—	.10	.25
	1965	47.799	—	—	.10	.25
	1966	19.688	—	—	.10	.25
	1967	52.308	—	—	.10	.25
	1968	40.890	—	—	.10	.25
	1969	35.430	—	—	.10	.25
	1970	29.600	—	—	.10	.25
	1971	3.070	—	—	.10	.25
	1972	1.000	—	.10	.15	.35
	1973	1.727	—	.10	.15	.35
	1974	7.850	—	—	.10	.25
	1975	.720	—	.10	.25	1.00
	1976	4.450	—	—	.10	.25
	1977	6.400	—	—	.10	.25
	1978	1.318	—	.10	.15	.35
	1979	2.172	—	—	.10	.25
	1980	.060	—	—	—	1.00
	1982	.050	—	—	—	1.00
	1983	.100	—	—	—	1.00
	1984	.050	—	—	—	1.00
	1985	—	—	—	—	1.00
	1986	—	—	—	—	1.00
	1987	—	—	—	—	1.00
	1987	.015	—	—	Proof	2.00

DEUX (2) CENTIMES

Small D

Large D

BRONZE
Mint mark: A
Second Empire

Y#	Date	Mintage	VF	XF	Unc	BU
15.1	1853	.610	7.50	15.00	22.00	40.00
	1854	3.118	2.00	5.00	10.00	22.00
	1855(d)	5.417	2.00	5.00	10.00	26.00
	1855(a)	I.A.	2.00	5.00	10.00	22.00
	1856	1.738	3.00	6.00	12.00	26.00
	1857	1.250	3.00	6.00	12.00	26.00

Mint mark: B

Y#	Date	Mintage	VF	XF	Unc	BU
15.2	1853	.539	10.00	20.00	35.00	90.00
	1854	1.995	4.00	10.00	18.00	36.00
	1855(d)	1.754	4.00	10.00	18.00	36.00
	1855(a)	I.A.	4.00	10.00	18.00	32.00
	1856	4.324	2.00	5.00	10.00	22.00
	1857	2.000	4.00	10.00	18.00	38.00

Mint mark: BB

Y#	Date	Mintage	VF	XF	Unc	BU
15.3	1853	.168	12.00	30.00	45.00	85.00
	1854	2.003	3.00	6.00	10.00	22.00
	1855(d)	2.135	3.00	6.00	10.00	22.00
	1855(a)	I.A.	3.00	6.00	10.00	22.00
	1856	1.282	4.00	8.00	12.00	26.00

Mint mark: D

Y#	Date	Mintage	VF	XF	Unc	BU
15.4	1853 sm.D	—	30.00	60.00	85.00	150.00
	1853 lg.D	—	30.00	60.00	85.00	150.00
	1854 small D	2.524	12.00	30.00	50.00	90.00
	1854 lg.D	I.A.	5.00	15.00	22.00	45.00
	1855(d) small D	2.554	5.00	15.00	22.00	45.00
	1855(d) large D	Inc. Ab.	5.00	15.00	22.00	45.00
	1855(a) small D	Inc. Ab.	5.00	15.00	22.00	45.00
	1855(a) large D	Inc. Ab.	5.00	15.00	22.00	45.00
	1856	.774	—	—	—	—
	1857 small D	1.000	20.00	35.00	55.00	100.00
	1857 lg.D	I.A.	8.00	20.00	30.00	55.00

Mint mark: K

Y#	Date	Mintage	VF	XF	Unc	BU
15.5	1853	.117	16.00	35.00	65.00	125.00
	1854	1.545	4.00	8.00	16.00	35.00
	1855(d)	1.068	6.00	12.00	20.00	60.00
	1855(a)	Inc. Ab.	6.00	12.00	20.00	60.00
	1856	2.281	3.00	6.00	10.00	30.00
	1857	.750	8.00	16.00	25.00	65.00

Mint mark: MA

Y#	Date	Mintage	VF	XF	Unc	BU
15.6	1853	.163	16.00	35.00	65.00	125.00
	1854	1.312	8.00	16.00	22.00	60.00
	1855(a)	2.438	8.00	16.00	22.00	60.00
	1855(d)	I.A.	8.00	16.00	22.00	60.00
	1856	2.781	3.00	6.00	10.00	30.00
	1857	1.250	8.00	16.00	22.00	60.00

Mint mark: W

Y#	Date	Mintage	VF	XF	Unc	BU
15.7	1853	.070	35.00	75.00	110.00	175.00
	1854	3.402	3.00	6.00	10.00	30.00
	1855(a)	.939	8.00	16.00	25.00	65.00
	1855(d)	I.A.	8.00	16.00	25.00	65.00
	1856	2.581	3.00	6.00	10.00	30.00
	1857	2.250	3.00	6.00	10.00	35.00

Mint mark: A
Obv: Bust points to 1 in date.

Y#	Date	Mintage	VF	XF	Unc	BU
19.1	1861	4.054	2.00	4.00	7.00	13.00

Mint mark: BB

Y#	Date	Mintage	VF	XF	Unc	BU
19.2	1861	2.440	2.00	4.00	8.00	15.00

Mint mark: K

Y#	Date	Mintage	VF	XF	Unc	BU
19.3	1861	3.291	2.00	4.00	7.00	13.00

Mint mark: A
Obv: Recut die (r), bust points to 8 in date.

Y#	Date	Mintage	VF	XF	Unc	BU
19.4	1861(r)	I.A.	2.00	4.00	7.00	13.00
(Y19.2)	1862/1	7.515	3.00	4.00	8.00	15.00
	1862	Inc. Ab.	2.00	3.50	5.50	11.00

Mint mark: BB

Y#	Date	Mintage	VF	XF	Unc	BU
19.5	1861(r)	I.A.	2.00	4.00	8.00	15.00
	1862	2.807	2.00	4.00	8.00	15.00

Mint mark: K

Y#	Date	Mintage	VF	XF	Unc	BU
19.6	1861(r)	I.A.	2.00	4.00	7.00	13.00
	1862	13.692	2.00	3.50	5.50	11.00

Mint mark: A
Third Republic

Y#	Date	Mintage	VF	XF	Unc	BU
42.1	1877	.500	4.00	10.00	16.00	25.00
	1878	.750	3.00	7.00	12.00	20.00
	1879(ab)	.600	3.00	7.00	12.00	20.00
	1882	.290	10.00	20.00	30.00	45.00
	1883	.500	4.00	10.00	16.00	25.00
	1884	.300	6.00	14.00	20.00	35.00
	1885	.300	6.00	14.00	20.00	35.00
	1886	.300	6.00	14.00	20.00	35.00
	1887	.300	6.00	14.00	20.00	35.00
	1888	.400	6.00	14.00	20.00	30.00
	1889	.600	3.00	7.00	12.00	20.00
	1890	.300	6.00	14.00	20.00	35.00
	1891	.300	6.00	14.00	20.00	35.00
	1892	.500	4.00	10.00	16.00	25.00
	1893	.250	10.00	25.00	32.00	55.00

Y#	Date	Mintage	VF	XF	Unc	BU
42.1	1894	.150	18.00	40.00	50.00	75.00
	1895	1.000	1.50	5.00	7.50	12.00
	1896(f)	1.000	1.50	5.00	7.50	12.00
	1897	1.250	1.50	4.00	7.00	12.00

Mint mark: K

42.2	1878	.363	8.00	13.00	18.00	30.00

Mint: Paris - w/o mint mark.

59	1898	.125	7.00	12.00	16.00	25.00
	1898	—	—	—	Proof	250.00
	1899	.750	3.00	6.00	10.00	20.00
	1900	.101	65.00	135.00	175.00	225.00
	1900	—	—	—	Proof	225.00
	1901	1.000	3.00	6.00	10.00	20.00
	1902	.750	3.00	6.00	10.00	20.00
	1903	.750	3.00	6.00	10.00	20.00
	1904	.500	4.00	10.00	15.00	25.00
	1907	.250	20.00	60.00	70.00	90.00
	1908	3.500	1.00	2.50	3.75	8.00
	1909	1.750	10.00	30.00	45.00	60.00
	1910	1.750	2.00	4.00	6.00	12.00
	1911	5.000	1.00	1.50	2.50	6.00
	1912	1.500	1.00	3.00	5.00	11.00
	1913	1.750	1.00	3.00	5.00	11.00
	1914	2.000	1.00	2.00	3.50	9.00
	1916	.500	2.00	4.00	5.50	11.00
	1919	.902	2.00	3.00	5.00	8.00
	1920	.598	2.00	4.00	5.50	11.00

NOTE: No privy marks appeared on Y#59 of any date.

CINQ (5) CENTIMES

BELL METAL
Mint mark: BB

KM#	Date	Mintage	VG	Fine	VF	XF
149	1808	—	25.00	50.00	100.00	175.00

BRONZE
Mint mark: A
Second Empire

Y#	Date	Mintage	VF	XF	Unc	BU
16.1	1853	13.928	4.00	12.00	20.00	50.00
	1854	28.767	4.00	12.00	20.00	50.00
	1855(d)	26.932	4.00	12.00	20.00	50.00
	1855(a)	I.A.	4.00	12.00	20.00	50.00
	1856	25.799	4.00	12.00	20.00	50.00
	1857	5.729	5.00	15.00	25.00	65.00

Mint mark: B

16.2	1853	4.424	5.00	15.00	25.00	65.00
	1854	16.354	4.00	12.00	20.00	50.00
	1855(d)	18.290	4.00	12.00	20.00	50.00
	1855(a)	I.A.	4.00	12.00	20.00	50.00
	1856	14.813	4.00	12.00	20.00	50.00
	1857	1.843	15.00	40.00	60.00	85.00

Mint mark: BB

16.3	1853	4.148	6.00	15.00	22.00	60.00
	1854	20.380	4.00	12.00	20.00	50.00
	1855(d)		4.00	12.00	20.00	50.00
		17.108	4.00	12.00	20.00	50.00
	1855(a)	I.A.	4.00	12.00	20.00	50.00
	1856	10.372	4.00	12.00	20.00	50.00
	1857	1.662	15.00	40.00	65.00	100.00

Mint mark: D

16.4	1853	5.013	6.00	15.00	22.00	60.00
	1854	18.597	4.00	12.00	20.00	50.00
	1855(d) small D					
		14.250	4.00	12.00	20.00	50.00
	1855(d) large D					
		Inc. Ab.	4.00	12.00	20.00	50.00
	1855(a) small D					
		Inc. Ab.	4.00	12.00	20.00	50.00
	1855(a) large D					
		Inc. Ab.	4.00	12.00	20.00	50.00
	1856	7.669	4.00	12.00	20.00	50.00
	1857	1.531	15.00	40.00	65.00	100.00

Mint mark: K

Y#	Date	Mintage	VF	XF	Unc	BU
16.5	1853	1.652	11.00	25.00	45.00	75.00
	1854	13.608	4.00	12.00	20.00	50.00
	1855(d)	15.761	4.00	12.00	20.00	50.00
	1855(a)	I.A.	4.00	12.00	20.00	50.00
	1856	14.775	4.00	12.00	20.00	50.00
	1857	2.417	10.00	25.00	45.00	75.00

Mint mark: MA

16.6	1853	1.654	11.00	25.00	45.00	75.00
	1854	14.835	4.00	12.00	20.00	50.00
	1855(d)	15.417	4.00	12.00	20.00	50.00
	1855(a)	Inc. Ab.	4.00	12.00	20.00	50.00
	1856	16.997	4.00	12.00	20.00	50.00
	1857	4.188	5.00	15.00	25.00	65.00

Mint mark: W

16.7	1853	5.398	6.00	15.00	22.00	60.00
	1854	14.957	4.00	12.00	20.00	50.00
	1855(d)	17.473	4.00	12.00	20.00	50.00
	1855(a)	I.A.	4.00	12.00	20.00	50.00
	1856	15.472	4.00	12.00	20.00	50.00
	1857	1.842	15.00	40.00	65.00	100.00

Mint mark: A

20.1	1861	6.857	6.00	15.00	22.00	60.00
	1862	5.300	6.00	15.00	22.00	60.00
	1863	12.128	4.00	12.00	20.00	50.00
	1864	3.053	8.00	20.00	40.00	70.00
	1865	2.619	10.00	25.00	45.00	75.00

Mint mark: BB

20.2	1861	7.124	6.00	15.00	22.00	60.00
	1862	8.584	6.00	15.00	22.00	60.00
	1863	2.323	10.00	25.00	45.00	80.00
	1864	6.110	6.00	15.00	22.00	60.00
	1865	7.226	6.00	15.00	22.00	60.00

Mint mark: K

20.3	1861	6.582	6.00	15.00	22.00	60.00
	1862	7.065	6.00	15.00	22.00	60.00
	1863	9.437	6.00	15.00	22.00	60.00
	1864	5.831	6.00	15.00	22.00	60.00

Mint mark: A
Third Republic

43.1	1871	2.238	4.00	8.00	18.00	50.00
	1872	4.263	3.00	6.00	17.00	40.00
	1873	1.492	4.00	10.00	20.00	60.00
	1874	1.730	4.00	10.00	20.00	60.00
	1875	1.193	4.00	10.00	20.00	65.00
	1876	2.481	4.00	8.00	18.00	50.00
	1877	.766	10.00	35.00	50.00	125.00
	1878	.300	25.00	50.00	80.00	250.00
	1879(a)	1.955	4.00	8.00	18.00	50.00
	1879 anchor w/bar					
		Inc. Ab.	12.00	20.00	30.00	80.00
	1880	1.172	4.00	8.00	18.00	50.00
	1881	2.502	3.00	6.00	17.00	40.00
	1882	1.600	4.00	10.00	22.00	70.00
	1883	2.400	3.00	6.00	17.00	40.00
	1884	1.680	4.00	8.00	18.00	50.00
	1885	2.000	3.00	6.00	17.00	40.00
	1886	1.680	4.00	8.00	18.00	50.00
	1887	1.008	4.00	10.00	20.00	65.00
	1888	1.660	4.00	8.00	18.00	50.00
	1889	1.660	4.00	8.00	18.00	50.00
	1890	1.680	4.00	8.00	18.00	50.00
	1891	1.600	4.00	8.00	18.00	50.00
	1892	1.600	3.00	6.00	17.00	40.00
	1893	1.600	3.00	6.00	17.00	40.00
	1894	2.240	2.00	5.00	12.50	35.00
	1896(f)	6.695	2.00	4.00	10.00	30.00
	1896(t)	Inc. Ab.	4.00	8.00	18.00	50.00
	1897	12.600	2.00	4.00	8.00	25.00
	1898	1.200	4.00	8.00	18.00	50.00

Mint mark: K

43.2	1871	.016	60.00	125.00	250.00	500.00
	1872	4.064	4.00	8.00	18.00	50.00
	1873	1.997	6.00	12.00	25.00	75.00
	1874	1.326	6.00	12.00	25.00	75.00
	1875	.760	12.00	30.00	50.00	115.00
	1876	1.597	10.00	25.00	45.00	100.00
	1877	1.193	6.00	12.00	25.00	75.00
	1878	.166	35.00	85.00	120.00	225.00

Mint: Paris - w/o mint mark.

Y#	Date	Mintage	VF	XF	Unc	BU
60	1898	7.900	2.00	5.00	10.00	25.00
	1898	—	—	—	Proof	400.00
	1899	7.400	2.00	6.00	12.00	30.00
	1900(n)	7.400	2.00	6.00	12.00	30.00
	1900(n)	—	—	—	Proof	—
	1901(c)	6.000	4.00	8.00	18.00	50.00
	1902	7.900	2.00	6.00	12.00	30.00
	1903	2.879	4.00	8.00	16.00	40.00
	1904	8.000	2.00	6.00	12.00	30.00
	1905	2.100	10.00	25.00	35.00	90.00
	1906	8.394	2.00	6.00	12.00	30.00
	1907	7.900	2.00	6.00	12.00	30.00
	1908	6.090	2.00	6.00	12.00	30.00
	1909	8.000	2.00	6.00	12.00	30.00
	1910	4.000	2.00	6.00	12.00	30.00
	1911	15.386	1.00	2.00	5.00	10.00
	1912	20.000	1.00	2.00	5.00	10.00
	1913	12.603	1.00	2.00	5.00	10.00
	1914	7.000	1.00	3.00	6.00	12.00
	1915	6.032	1.00	3.00	6.00	12.00
	1916	41.531	.75	1.50	3.00	7.00
	1916(S)	Inc. Ab.	.75	1.50	3.00	7.00
	1917	16.963	1.00	3.00	6.00	12.00
	1920	8.152	5.00	10.00	15.00	25.00
	1921	.142	200.00	400.00	600.00	900.00

COPPER-NICKEL

71	1914	—	—	—	Rare	—
	1917	10.458	2.00	3.00	6.00	10.00
	1918	35.592	.50	1.00	2.00	5.00
	1919	43.848	.50	1.00	2.00	5.00
	1920	51.321	.50	1.00	2.00	5.00

Y#	Date	Mintage	Fine	VF	XF	Unc
72	1920	Inc. Ab.	5.00	10.00	20.00	50.00
	1921	32.908	.25	.50	1.00	4.00
	1922	31.700	.25	.50	1.00	4.00
	1922(t)	17.717	.35	.75	1.25	4.50
	1923	23.322	.50	1.00	1.50	5.50
	1923(t)	45.097	.25	.50	1.00	3.50
	1924	47.018	.25	.50	1.00	3.50
	1924(t)	21.210	.50	1.00	1.50	5.50
	1925	66.838	.25	.50	1.00	3.50
	1926	19.820	.25	.50	1.25	5.00
	1927	6.044	2.50	5.00	10.00	20.00
	1929	.022	—	—	—	—
	1930	31.902	.20	.50	1.00	3.00
	1931	34.711	.20	.50	1.00	3.00
	1932	31.112	.20	.50	1.00	3.00
	1933	12.970	.35	.75	1.50	5.50
	1934	27.144	.30	.65	1.25	5.00
	1935	57.221	.25	.50	1.00	3.00
	1936	64.341	.15	.25	.75	3.00
	1937	26.329	.15	.25	.75	3.00
	1938	21.614	.15	.25	.75	3.00

NICKEL-BRONZE

72a	.1938.	26.330	.15	.50	1.00	3.00
	.1938. star	I.A.	65.00	125.00	250.00	400.00
	.1939.	52.673	.10	.25	.75	2.00
	.1939. star	I.A.	—	—	Rare	—

CHROME-STEEL
5 New Centimes - 5 Old Francs
Fifth Republic

103	1961	39.000	.10	.20	.50	2.00
	1962	166.360	.10	.15	.20	.75
	1963	71.900	.10	.20	.40	1.00
	1964	126.480	.10	.15	.30	.75

FRANCE 552

ALUMINUM-BRONZE

Y#	Date	Mintage	Fine	VF	XF	Unc
A104	1966	502.512	—	—	—	.10
	1967	11.745	—	—	.10	.25
	1968	110.395	—	—	—	.10
	1969	94.955	—	—	—	.10
	1970	58.900	—	—	—	.10
	1971	93.190	—	—	—	.10
	1972	100.515	—	—	—	.10
	1973	100.344	—	—	—	.10
	1974	103.890	—	—	—	.10
	1975	95.835	—	—	—	.10
	1976	148.395	—	—	—	.10
	1977	115.285	—	—	—	.10
	1978	189.804	—	—	—	.10
	1979	180.000	—	—	—	.10
	1980	180.010	—	—	—	.10
	1981	.050	—	—	—	.50
	1982	138.000	—	—	—	.10
	1983	132.000	—	—	—	.10
	1984	150.000	—	—	—	.10
	1985	—	—	—	—	1.00
	1986	—	—	—	—	1.00
	1987	—	—	—	—	1.00
	1987	.015	—	—	Proof	2.00
	1988	—	—	—	—	.10

(UN) (1) DECIME
STRASBOURG PROVISIONAL ISSUES

BRONZE
Mint mark: BB

C#	Date	Mintage	VG	Fine	VF	XF
174	1814 w/o dot after DECIME					
		.544	7.50	15.00	35.00	100.00
	1814 dot after DECIME.					
	Inc. Ab.		10.00	20.00	45.00	125.00
	1814. w/o dot after DECIME					
	Inc. Ab.		12.50	25.00	50.00	150.00
	1814. dot after DECIME.					
	Inc. Ab.		12.50	25.00	50.00	150.00
	1815 w/o dot after DECIME					
	Inc. Ab.		15.00	35.00	60.00	175.00
	1815 dot after DECIME					
	Inc. Ab.		15.00	35.00	60.00	175.00
	1815. w/o dot after DECIME					
	Inc. Ab.		15.00	35.00	60.00	175.00
	1815. dot after DECIME.					
	Inc. Ab.		15.00	35.00	60.00	175.00

C#	Date	Mintage	VG	Fine	VF	XF
175	1814	1.208	10.00	20.00	45.00	125.00
	1814.	I.A.	12.50	25.00	50.00	150.00
	1815	I.A.	7.50	15.00	35.00	100.00
	1815.	I.A.	10.00	20.00	45.00	125.00

DIX (10) CENTIMES

BILLON
Mint mark: A

C#	Date	Mintage	Fine	VF	XF	Unc
150.1	1807	—	40.00	100.00	175.00	350.00
	1808	6.269	2.00	5.00	15.00	45.00
	1809	7.529	2.00	5.00	15.00	45.00
	1810	—	—	—	Unique	—

Mint mark: B

150.2	1808	.163	12.50	35.00	75.00	200.00
	1809	.831	4.00	11.00	30.00	95.00
	1810	1.231	3.00	8.00	20.00	65.00

Mint mark: BB

150.3	1808	1.425	3.00	8.00	20.00	65.00
	1809	.695	4.00	11.00	30.00	95.00
	1810	—	—	—	Unique	—

Mint mark: D

| 150.10 | 1810 | — | Reported, not confirmed | | | |

Mint mark: H

150.4	1808	.129	12.50	35.00	75.00	200.00
	1809	.631	4.00	11.00	30.00	95.00
	1810	.673	4.00	11.00	30.00	95.00

Mint mark: I

150.5	1808	1.062	3.00	8.00	20.00	75.00
	1809	3.473	2.00	5.00	15.00	60.00
	1810	3.066	2.00	5.00	15.00	60.00

Mint mark: M

| 150.6 | 1808 | .860 | 4.00 | 11.00 | 30.00 | 95.00 |
| | 1809 | 1.070 | 3.00 | 8.00 | 20.00 | 75.00 |

Mint mark: Q

150.7	1808	—	—	—	Rare	—
	1809	.555	6.00	15.00	35.00	115.00
	1810	.130	15.00	35.00	75.00	200.00

Mint mark: T

150.8	1808	.054	20.00	55.00	125.00	350.00
	1809	.134	11.00	35.00	75.00	200.00
	1810	.103	15.00	40.00	90.00	270.00

Mint mark: W

| 150.9 | 1808 | 1.576 | 3.00 | 8.00 | 20.00 | 65.00 |
| | 1809 | 1.160 | 3.00 | 8.00 | 20.00 | 65.00 |

BRONZE
Mint mark: A
Second Empire

Y#	Date	Mintage	VF	XF	Unc	BU
17.1	1852	.577	20.00	50.00	70.00	100.00
	1853	12.256	4.00	12.00	20.00	55.00
	1854	13.327	4.00	12.00	20.00	55.00
	1855(d)	14.816	4.00	12.00	20.00	55.00
	1855(a)	I.A.	4.00	12.00	20.00	55.00
	1856	19.149	4.00	12.00	20.00	55.00
	1857	3.096	8.00	20.00	45.00	100.00

Mint mark: B

17.2	1853	3.546	7.00	20.00	35.00	85.00
	1854	8.065	4.00	12.00	20.00	65.00
	1855(d)	9.960	4.00	12.00	20.00	65.00
	1855(a)	I.A.	4.00	12.00	20.00	65.00
	1856	11.637	4.00	12.00	20.00	65.00
	1857	1.620	10.00	25.00	45.00	95.00

Mint mark: BB

17.3	1853	4.582	7.00	20.00	30.00	75.00
	1854	8.433	4.00	12.00	20.00	65.00
	1855(d)	11.953	4.00	12.00	20.00	65.00
	1855(a)	I.A.	4.00	12.00	20.00	65.00
	1856	7.781	4.00	12.00	20.00	65.00
	1857	1.685	10.00	25.00	45.00	95.00

Mint mark: D

17.4	1853	3.709	7.00	20.00	35.00	85.00
	1854	8.487	4.00	12.00	20.00	65.00
	1855(d)	12.099	8.00	20.00	45.00	100.00
	1855(a)	I.A.	4.00	12.00	20.00	65.00
	1856	4.419	4.00	12.00	20.00	65.00
	1857	.699	—	—	—	—

Mint mark: K

| 17.5 | 1853 | 1.203 | 10.00 | 25.00 | 45.00 | 95.00 |

Y#	Date	Mintage	VF	XF	Unc	BU
17.5	1854	7.083	4.00	12.00	25.00	75.00
	1855(d)	11.797	4.00	12.00	20.00	65.00
	1855(a)	I.A.	4.00	12.00	20.00	65.00
	1856	8.871	4.00	12.00	20.00	65.00
	1857	1.179	10.00	25.00	50.00	100.00

Mint mark: MA

17.6	1853	.889	16.00	35.00	55.00	115.00
	1854	7.995	4.00	12.00	20.00	65.00
	1855(d)	11.309	4.00	12.00	20.00	65.00
	1855(a)	I.A.	4.00	12.00	20.00	65.00
	1856	10.937	4.00	12.00	20.00	65.00
	1857	2.052	8.00	25.00	50.00	100.00

Mint mark: W

17.7	1853	3.107	5.00	14.00	22.00	70.00
	1854	8.242	4.00	12.00	20.00	65.00
	1855(d)	9.837	4.00	12.00	20.00	65.00
	1855(a)	I.A.	4.00	12.00	20.00	65.00
	1856	11.402	4.00	12.00	20.00	65.00
	1857	1.858	10.00	25.00	45.00	95.00

Mint mark: A

21.1	1861	3.638	6.00	15.00	25.00	75.00
	1862	4.736	6.00	15.00	25.00	75.00
	1863	4.873	6.00	15.00	25.00	75.00
	1864	1.556	18.00	30.00	50.00	90.00
	1865	1.608	12.00	25.00	40.00	85.00

Mint mark: BB

21.2	1861	4.625	6.00	15.00	25.00	75.00
	1862	4.702	6.00	15.00	25.00	75.00
	1863	1.340	12.00	25.00	40.00	85.00
	1864	3.053	6.00	15.00	25.00	80.00
	1865	4.797	6.00	15.00	25.00	75.00

Mint mark: K

21.3	1861	4.363	6.00	15.00	25.00	75.00
	1862	5.244	6.00	15.00	25.00	75.00
	1863	4.521	6.00	15.00	25.00	75.00
	1864	3.075	6.00	15.00	25.00	80.00

Mint mark: A
Third Republic

44.1	1870	.889	7.00	18.00	30.00	65.00
	1871	1.840	4.00	10.00	20.00	55.00
	1872	4.399	3.00	8.00	15.00	35.00
	1873	2.096	4.00	10.00	18.00	40.00
	1874	1.194	4.00	10.00	20.00	55.00
	1875	1.434	35.00	80.00	125.00	200.00
	1876	.458	10.00	22.00	35.00	80.00
	1877	.392	10.00	22.00	35.00	80.00
	1878	.150	20.00	50.00	75.00	150.00
	1879	.823	7.00	18.00	30.00	65.00
	1880	1.414	4.00	10.00	20.00	55.00
	1881	.749	9.00	20.00	32.00	75.00
	1882	1.100	4.00	10.00	20.00	55.00
	1883	.700	10.00	22.00	35.00	80.00
	1884	1.060	5.00	11.00	20.00	60.00
	1885	.900	6.00	14.00	22.00	75.00
	1886	1.060	5.00	11.00	20.00	65.00
	1887	.874	6.00	14.00	22.00	75.00
	1888	1.050	5.00	11.00	18.00	60.00
	1889	1.010	5.00	11.00	18.00	60.00
	1890	1.060	5.00	11.00	18.00	60.00
	1891	1.000	5.00	11.00	18.00	60.00
	1892	1.020	5.00	11.00	18.00	60.00
	1893	1.120	5.00	11.00	20.00	60.00
	1894	.800	6.00	14.00	22.00	75.00
	1895	.600	8.00	16.00	25.00	80.00
	1896(f)	4.447	2.00	5.00	15.00	35.00
	1896(t)	Inc. Ab.	4.00	10.00	20.00	55.00
	1897	7.250	2.00	4.00	12.00	30.00
	1898	1.400	4.00	10.00	20.00	55.00

Mint mark: K

44.2	1871	.027	100.00	200.00	260.00	350.00
	1872	4.359	4.00	9.00	17.00	35.00
	1873	2.001	4.00	11.00	18.00	45.00
	1874	1.337	6.00	12.00	20.00	60.00
	1875	.430	16.00	35.00	50.00	100.00
	1876	.601	12.00	25.00	45.00	80.00
	1877	.403	16.00	35.00	50.00	100.00
	1878	.100	50.00	110.00	160.00	225.00

Mint: Paris - w/o mint mark.

Y#	Date	Mintage	VF	XF	Unc	BU
61	1898	4.000	3.00	6.00	17.50	30.00
	1899	4.000	3.00	6.00	17.50	30.00
	1900(n)	5.000	3.00	6.00	17.50	35.00
	1900(n)	—	—	—	Proof	—
	1901(c)	2.700	4.00	10.00	22.00	65.00
	1902	3.800	4.00	10.00	22.00	65.00
	1903	3.650	4.00	10.00	20.00	55.00
	1904	3.800	4.00	10.00	20.00	55.00
	1905	.950	50.00	90.00	135.00	225.00
	1906	3.000	4.00	10.00	22.00	65.00
	1907	4.000	3.00	6.00	12.00	35.00
	1908	3.500	3.00	6.00	12.00	50.00
	1909	2.933	3.00	6.00	12.00	50.00
	1910	3.567	3.00	6.00	12.00	35.00
	1911	7.903	1.50	3.00	7.00	25.00
	1912	9.500	1.50	3.00	7.00	22.00
	1913	9.000	1.50	3.00	7.00	22.00
	1914	6.000	1.50	3.00	7.00	22.00
	1915	4.362	1.50	3.00	7.00	22.00
	1916	22.477	1.00	2.00	5.00	18.00
	1916(s)	Inc. Ab.	1.00	2.00	5.00	16.00
	1917	11.914	1.00	2.00	5.00	16.00
	1920	4.119	6.00	12.00	20.00	55.00
	1921	1.896	15.00	30.00	45.00	70.00

NICKEL

Y#	Date	Mintage	Fine	VF	XF	Unc
73	1914 dash	3.972	350.00	700.00	950.00	1300.

COPPER-NICKEL

Y#	Date	Mintage	Fine	VF	XF	Unc
73a	1917	8.171	.75	1.50	3.50	8.00
	1918	30.605	.25	.50	1.00	4.50
	1919	33.489	.25	.50	1.00	4.50
	1920	38.845	.25	.50	1.00	4.50
	1921	42.768	.25	.50	1.00	4.50
	1922	23.033	.25	.50	1.00	4.50
	1922(T)	12.412	.65	1.00	2.25	6.00
	1923	18.701	.40	.75	1.50	5.00
	1923(T)	30.016	.25	.50	1.00	4.00
	1924	43.949	.25	.50	1.00	3.50
	1924(T)	13.591	.65	1.00	2.25	8.00
	1925	46.266	.25	.50	1.00	4.00
	1926	25.660	.25	.50	1.00	3.50
	1927	16.203	.40	.75	1.50	5.50
	1928	6.967	1.50	3.00	5.00	11.00
	1929	24.531	.25	.50	1.00	4.50
	1930	22.146	.25	.50	1.00	4.50
	1931	49.107	.25	.50	1.00	3.50
	1932	30.317	.25	.50	1.00	3.50
	1933	13.042	.35	.65	1.50	6.00
	1934	24.067	.25	.50	1.00	3.00
	1935	47.487	.25	.50	1.00	2.75
	1936	57.738	.25	.50	1.00	2.75
	1937	25.308	.25	.50	1.00	2.75
	1938	17.063	.25	.50	1.00	3.00

NICKEL-BRONZE

Y#	Date	Mintage	Fine	VF	XF	Unc
73c	.1938.	24.151	.25	.50	1.00	2.00
	1.938.	Inc. Ab.	—	—	—	—
	.1939.	62.269	.10	.20	.50	1.25

Thin flan

Y#	Date	Mintage	Fine	VF	XF	Unc
73c.1	.1939.	Inc. Ab.	.15	.30	.65	1.75

ZINC

Rev: W/o dash under MES in C MES.

Y#	Date	Mintage	Fine	VF	XF	Unc
73b.1	1941	235.875	1.00	1.75	6.00	15.00

Rev: Dash under MES in C MES.

Y#	Date	Mintage	Fine	VF	XF	Unc
73b.2	1941	Inc. Ab.	.75	1.25	2.50	10.00

Rev: Dot before and after date.

Y#	Date	Mintage	Fine	VF	XF	Unc
73b.3	.1941.	Inc. Ab.	.25	.50	1.00	6.00

Vichy French State Issues

Y#	Date	Mintage	Fine	VF	XF	Unc
V91.1	1941	70.860	.35	.65	1.50	6.00
	1942	139.598	.30	.65	1.25	4.00
	1943	21.520	.60	.90	2.00	8.00

Mint mark: B

Y#	Date	Mintage	Fine	VF	XF	Unc
V91.2	1942	—	—	—	—	—
	1943	—	—	—	—	—
	1944	—	—	—	—	—

Mint: Paris - w/o mint mark.
Thin flan

Y#	Date	Mintage	Fine	VF	XF	Unc
V91.3	1942	—	—	—	—	—
(Y-V91.1)	1943	—	—	—	—	—

Y#	Date	Mintage	Fine	VF	XF	Unc
V93	1943	22.008	.25	.75	2.25	7.00
	1944	58.463	.25	.50	2.00	5.00

Fourth Republic Issues

Y#	Date	Mintage	Fine	VF	XF	Unc
74.1	1945	38.174	1.00	2.00	4.00	12.00
	1946	—	—	—	Rare	—

Mint mark: B

Y#	Date	Mintage	Fine	VF	XF	Unc
74.2	1945	7.246	1.50	3.00	6.00	16.00
	1946	10.566	1.00	2.50	5.00	14.00

Mint mark: C

Y#	Date	Mintage	Fine	VF	XF	Unc
74.3	1945	8.379	3.00	5.00	10.00	25.00

ALUMINUM-BRONZE
Mint: Paris - w/o mint mark.
10 New Centimes = 10 Old Francs
Fifth Republic

Y#	Date	Mintage	Fine	VF	XF	Unc
104	1962	29.100	—	—	.10	.40
	1963	217.601	—	—	—	.10
	1964	93.409	—	—	.10	.20
	1965	41.220	—	—	.10	.30
	1966	16.422	—	.10	.15	.40
	1967	196.728	—	—	—	.10
	1968	111.700	—	—	—	.10
	1969	129.530	—	—	—	.10
	1970	77.020	—	—	—	.10
	1971	26.280	—	—	—	.10
	1972	45.700	—	—	—	.10
	1973	58.000	—	—	—	.10
	1974	91.990	—	—	—	.10
	1975	74.450	—	—	—	.10
	1976	137.320	—	—	—	.10
	1977	140.110	—	—	—	.10
	1978	154.360	—	—	—	.10
	1979	140.000	—	—	—	.10
	1980	140.010	—	—	—	.10
	1981	135.000	—	—	—	.10
	1982	110.000	—	—	—	.10
	1983	150.000	—	—	—	.10
	1984	200.000	—	—	—	.10
	1985	—	—	—	—	1.00
	1986	—	—	—	—	1.00
	1987	—	—	—	—	.10
	1987	.015	—	—	Proof	2.00
	1988	—	—	—	—	.10

VINGT (20) CENTIMES

1.0000 g, .900 SILVER, .0289 oz ASW
Mint mark: A
Second Republic

Y#	Date	Mintage	Fine	VF	XF	Unc
2.1	1849	4,877	75.00	175.00	350.00	650.00
	1850	6.157	5.00	12.50	25.00	55.00
	1851	3.309	8.00	20.00	35.00	70.00

Mint mark: BB

Y#	Date	Mintage	Fine	VF	XF	Unc
2.2	1850	.048	30.00	60.00	150.00	275.00

Mint mark: K

Y#	Date	Mintage	Fine	VF	XF	Unc
2.3	1850	.344	20.00	35.00	75.00	175.00

Mint mark: A
Second Empire - Napoleon III

Y#	Date	Mintage	Fine	VF	XF	Unc
22.1	1853 small head	.680	10.00	20.00	40.00	80.00
	1854	1.683	4.00	10.00	20.00	50.00
	1855(d)	.362	10.00	20.00	45.00	100.00
	1856	.603	8.00	17.50	40.00	80.00
	1857	.840	6.00	15.00	35.00	70.00
	1858	.704	8.00	17.50	40.00	80.00
	1859	3.620	3.00	6.00	15.00	45.00
	1860/50	6.536	3.00	6.00	15.00	40.00
	1860(h)	Inc. Ab.	3.00	6.00	15.00	40.00
	1862	.054	50.00	100.00	200.00	400.00

Mint mark: BB

Y#	Date	Mintage	Fine	VF	XF	Unc
22.2	1856	.013	75.00	175.00	350.00	600.00
	1860(b)	2.986	4.00	8.00	15.00	50.00
	1863	.398	17.50	35.00	65.00	150.00

Mint mark: D

Y#	Date	Mintage	Fine	VF	XF	Unc
22.3	1856	.396	12.50	25.00	50.00	125.00

1.0000 g, .835 SILVER, .0268 oz ASW
Mint mark: A

Y#	Date	Mintage	Fine	VF	XF	Unc
27.1	1864	.268	10.00	20.00	45.00	125.00
	1865	—	—	Reported, not confirmed		
	1866	1.460	3.00	6.00	15.00	40.00

Mint mark: BB

Y#	Date	Mintage	Fine	VF	XF	Unc
27.2	1864	.112	15.00	30.00	60.00	150.00
	1866	.843	5.00	12.00	25.00	60.00

Mint mark: K

Y#	Date	Mintage	Fine	VF	XF	Unc
27.3	1864	.058	30.00	60.00	120.00	225.00
	1866	.413	10.00	20.00	45.00	100.00

Mint mark: A

Y#	Date	Mintage	Fine	VF	XF	Unc
28.1	1867	5.611	2.00	4.00	7.00	17.50
	1868	.353	5.00	12.00	25.00	60.00

Mint mark: BB

Y#	Date	Mintage	Fine	VF	XF	Unc
28.2	1867	3.114	2.50	5.00	8.00	20.00
	1868	Inc. Be.	10.00	20.00	45.00	80.00
	1869	.200	—	—	—	—

Mint mark: K

Y#	Date	Mintage	Fine	VF	XF	Unc
28.3	1867	.091	20.00	40.00	80.00	175.00

1.0000 g, .900 SILVER, 15mm, .0289 oz ASW
Mint mark: A

Y#	Date	Mintage	Fine	VF	XF	Unc
47	1878	30 pcs.	—	—	1500.	2000.

16mm

Y#	Date	Mintage	Fine	VF	XF	Unc
—	1889	100 pcs.	—	—	1000.	1250.

NOTE: Considered an Essai.

ZINC
Vichy French State Issues

Y#	Date	Mintage	Fine	VF	XF	Unc
V90	1941	54.044	.75	1.00	4.00	10.00

Thick flan, 3.50 g

Y#	Date	Mintage	Fine	VF	XF	Unc
V92.1	1941	31.397	.50	.75	3.00	10.00
	1942	112.868	.50	.75	2.00	7.00
	1943	64.138	.50	.75	3.00	8.00

Mint mark: B

V92.2	1942	—	—	—	—	—

Mint: Paris - w/o mint mark.
Thin flan, 3.00 g

Y#	Date	Mintage	Fine	VF	XF	Unc
V92.3	1941		.50	.75	3.00	10.00
(Y-V92.1)	1943	Inc. Ab.	.50	.75	3.00	7.00
	1944	5.250	5.00	10.00	20.00	35.00

IRON

Y#	Date	Mintage	Fine	VF	XF	Unc
V92a	1944	.695	20.00	40.00	70.00	125.00

ZINC
Fourth Republic Issues

75.1	1945	6.003	2.00	5.00	10.00	20.00
	1946	2.662	4.00	8.00	15.00	30.00

Mint mark: B

75.2	1945	.100	35.00	70.00	125.00	200.00
	1946	5.525	75.00	150.00	300.00	—

Mint mark: C

75.3	1945	.299	15.00	35.00	60.00	120.00

ALUMINUM-BRONZE
Mint: Paris - w/o mint mark.
Fifth Republic

105	1962	48.200	—	—	.10	.40
	1963	190.330	—	—	.10	.30
	1964	127.521	—	—	.10	.30
	1965	27.024	—	.10	.20	.40
	1966	21.755	—	.10	.20	.40
	1967	138.780	—	—	.10	.15
	1968	77.408	—	—	.10	.20
	1969	50.570	—	—	.10	.20
	1970	70.040	—	—	.10	.15
	1971	31.080	—	—	.10	.15
	1972	39.740	—	—	.10	.15
	1973	45.240	—	—	.10	.15
	1974	54.250	—	—	.10	.15
	1975	40.570	—	—	.10	.15
	1976	117.610	—	—	—	.10
	1977	100.340	—	—	—	.10
	1978	125.015	—	—	—	.10
	1979	70.000	—	—	—	.10
	1980	20.010	—	—	.10	.15
	1981	125.000	—	—	—	.10
	1982	150.000	—	—	—	.10
	1983	110.000	—	—	—	.10
	1984	200.000	—	—	—	.10
	1985	—	—	—	—	1.00
	1986	—	—	—	—	1.00
	1987	—	—	—	—	.10
	1987	.015	—	—	Proof	2.00

QUART (1/4) FRANC

1.2500 g, .900 SILVER, .0362 oz ASW
Mint mark: A
Obv: BONAPARTE PR. CONSUL.

C#	Date	Mintage	VG	Fine	VF	XF
141.1	AN12	.171	12.50	22.50	55.00	110.00

Mint mark: BB

141.2	AN12	1,565	45.00	90.00	200.00	400.00

Mint mark: D

141.3	AN12	—	35.00	75.00	175.00	375.00

Mint mark: I

C#	Date	Mintage	VG	Fine	VF	XF
141.4	AN12	.041	15.00	30.00	70.00	200.00

Mint mark: L

141.5	AN12	.019	20.00	40.00	75.00	225.00

Mint mark: M

141.6	AN12	.039	15.00	30.00	70.00	200.00

Mint mark: MA

141.7	AN12	9,080	25.00	50.00	125.00	275.00

Mint mark: Q

141.8	AN12	.028	20.00	40.00	75.00	225.00

Mint mark: T

141.9	AN12	.010	25.00	50.00	100.00	250.00
	Common date				Unc.	275.00

Mint mark: A
Obv: NAPOLEON EMPEREUR.

151.1	AN12	.019	20.00	40.00	75.00	175.00
	AN13	.128	10.00	20.00	40.00	100.00
	AN14	—	—	Reported, not confirmed		

Mint mark: BB

151.8	AN13	2,194	50.00	100.00	200.00	400.00

Mint mark: D

151.2	AN12	5,156	35.00	70.00	135.00	275.00

Mint mark: H

151.3	AN12	.012	25.00	50.00	100.00	200.00
	AN13/12	—	40.00	80.00	200.00	400.00
	AN13	2,744	40.00	80.00	200.00	400.00

Mint mark: I

151.4	AN12	.032	17.50	35.00	75.00	175.00
	AN13	.118	12.50	27.50	65.00	150.00

Mint mark: K

151.5	AN12	8,122	35.00	65.00	110.00	225.00
	AN13	.018	20.00	40.00	90.00	175.00
	AN14	1,757	50.00	100.00	200.00	400.00

Mint mark: L

151.9	AN13	.025	20.00	40.00	75.00	175.00
	AN14	—	50.00	80.00	120.00	300.00

Mint mark: M

151.6	AN12	.016	20.00	40.00	75.00	175.00
	AN13	.039	17.50	35.00	70.00	160.00

Mint mark: MA

151.10	AN13	8,114	25.00	50.00	100.00	200.00

Mint mark: T

151.7	AN12	3,606	50.00	100.00	175.00	375.00
	AN13	6,801	30.00	60.00	125.00	250.00

Mint mark: U

151.11	AN13	.014	50.00	100.00	200.00	400.00
	AN14	100 pcs.	275.00	425.00	750.00	2000.
	Common date				Unc.	300.00

Mint mark: A

151.12	1806	.031	20.00	45.00	80.00	175.00
(Y151.2)	1807	—	—	—	—	—

Mint mark: I

151.13	1806	4,583	30.00	70.00	110.00	225.00
	1807	8,356	25.00	50.00	100.00	200.00

Mint mark: K

151.14	1806	4,359	30.00	75.00	120.00	250.00
	1807	5,538	30.00	75.00	120.00	250.00

Mint mark: L

151.15	1806	.018	20.00	45.00	80.00	175.00
	1807	7,618	25.00	50.00	100.00	200.00

Mint mark: M

151.18	1807	1,626	125.00	—	—	—

Mint mark: Q

151.16	1806	8,948	25.00	50.00	100.00	200.00
	1807	9,713	25.00	50.00	100.00	200.00

Mint mark: U

151.17	1806	1,361	50.00	100.00	200.00	400.00
	1807	.013	25.00	75.00	150.00	300.00

Mint mark: A
Negro head.

151a	1807	.041	45.00	80.00	135.00	250.00

Laureate head.

C#	Date	Mintage	VG	Fine	VF	XF
151b.1	1807	.017	30.00	60.00	125.00	250.00
	1808	—	40.00	75.00	140.00	325.00

Mint mark: I

151b.2	1808	1,466	50.00	125.00	225.00	400.00

Mint mark: L

151b.3	1808	4,393	30.00	85.00	175.00	325.00

Mint mark: A

161	1809	.034	30.00	55.00	110.00	225.00

Mint mark: A

C#	Date	Mintage	Fine	VF	XF	Unc
177.1	1817	.100	10.00	25.00	50.00	150.00
	1818	.028	20.00	50.00	100.00	325.00
	1819	.011	25.00	60.00	120.00	350.00
	1820	.012	25.00	60.00	120.00	350.00
	1821	.022	20.00	50.00	100.00	325.00
	1822	.036	20.00	50.00	100.00	225.00
	1823	.044	20.00	50.00	100.00	225.00
	1824	.083	15.00	30.00	75.00	175.00

Mint mark: B

177.2	1817	.021	22.50	50.00	85.00	275.00
	1818	.016	25.00	60.00	110.00	350.00
	1819	.015	25.00	60.00	110.00	350.00
	1822	.030	22.50	50.00	100.00	325.00
	1823	.013	25.00	60.00	120.00	350.00
	1824	.018	25.00	60.00	110.00	350.00

Mint mark: BB

177.3	1817	3,772	—	—	—	—

Mint mark: D

177.4	1817	.012	25.00	60.00	100.00	350.00

Mint mark: I

177.5	1817	.016	25.00	60.00	100.00	350.00
	1823	1,870	—	—	—	—

Mint mark: L

177.6	1817	.014	25.00	60.00	100.00	350.00
	1823	.012	25.00	60.00	110.00	350.00
	1824	.031	22.50	50.00	100.00	325.00

Mint mark: M

177.7	1817	4,314	35.00	90.00	170.00	475.00
	1823	3,994	40.00	100.00	200.00	500.00
	1824	7,774	35.00	75.00	175.00	425.00

Mint mark: MA

177.8	1817	2,132	—	—	—	—

Mint mark: Q

177.9	1817	.013	25.00	60.00	100.00	350.00
	1823	.011	25.00	60.00	110.00	350.00

Mint mark: T

177.10	1817	7,606	35.00	75.00	140.00	500.00

Mint mark: W

177.11	1817	.014	25.00	50.00	100.00	350.00
	1818	3,294	40.00	100.00	200.00	550.00
	1819	3,170	40.00	100.00	200.00	550.00
	1820	5,894	35.00	75.00	145.00	475.00
	1822	4,486	40.00	100.00	175.00	525.00
	1823	.016	25.00	50.00	120.00	350.00
	1824	.011	25.00	50.00	120.00	350.00

Mint mark: A

185.1	1825	9,448	35.00	75.00	150.00	350.00
	1826	.083	15.00	30.00	60.00	150.00
	1827	.322	6.00	15.00	35.00	100.00
	1828	.446	6.00	15.00	35.00	100.00
	1829	.154	7.00	17.50	50.00	150.00
	1830	.659	6.00	15.00	35.00	100.00
	1830 reeded edge	Inc.Ab.	—	—	Rare	—

Mint mark: B

185.2	1826	.023	20.00	35.00	75.00	275.00
	1827	.017	20.00	35.00	75.00	275.00
	1828	.023	20.00	35.00	75.00	250.00
	1829	.032	15.00	25.00	50.00	200.00

Mint mark: BB

185.9	1827	1,567	60.00	175.00	300.00	650.00
	1828	.013	20.00	35.00	75.00	275.00
	1829	.014	20.00	35.00	75.00	275.00

C#	Date	Mintage	Fine	VF	XF	Unc
		Mint mark: D				
185.3	1826	.013	20.00	35.00	75.00	275.00
	1827	7,820	35.00	75.00	175.00	350.00
	1828	.013	20.00	35.00	75.00	275.00
	1829	.052	15.00	25.00	50.00	200.00
		Mint mark: H				
185.11	1828	.016	20.00	35.00	75.00	275.00
		Mint mark: I				
185.10	1827	828	—	—	—	—
	1828	2,226	45.00	125.00	250.00	450.00
	1829	.010	20.00	35.00	75.00	275.00
		Mint mark: K				
185.12	1829	.027	20.00	35.00	75.00	250.00
	1830	.021	20.00	35.00	75.00	250.00
		Mint mark: L				
185.4	1826	.011	20.00	35.00	75.00	275.00
	1827	7,582	35.00	85.00	175.00	350.00
	1828	.015	20.00	35.00	75.00	275.00
	1829	6,486	35.00	85.00	175.00	350.00
	1830	.015	20.00	35.00	75.00	275.00
		Mint mark: M				
185.5	1826	4,861	40.00	100.00	175.00	400.00
	1827	4,292	40.00	100.00	175.00	400.00
	1828	.048	20.00	35.00	75.00	250.00
	1829	.014	20.00	35.00	75.00	275.00
		Mint mark: Q				
185.6	1826	7,534	35.00	85.00	150.00	375.00
	1828	.013	20.00	35.00	75.00	275.00
		Mint mark: T				
185.7	1826	1,753	—	—	—	—
	1828	6,316	25.00	50.00	150.00	350.00
	1829	6,481	25.00	50.00	150.00	350.00
		Mint mark: W				
185.8	1826	.015	20.00	35.00	75.00	275.00
	1827	.022	20.00	35.00	75.00	250.00
	1828	.047	20.00	35.00	60.00	200.00
	1829	.108	10.00	20.00	50.00	150.00
	1830	.074	15.00	30.00	50.00	150.00
		Mint mark: A				
196.1	1831	.075	6.00	12.00	25.00	85.00
	1832	.286	5.00	10.00	20.00	65.00
	1833	.155	5.00	10.00	20.00	65.00
	1834	.770	4.00	7.00	17.50	50.00
	1835	.801	4.00	7.00	17.50	50.00
	1836	.898	4.00	7.00	17.50	50.00
	1837	.830	4.00	7.00	17.50	50.00
	1838	.922	4.00	7.00	17.50	50.00
	1839	1.180	4.00	7.00	17.50	50.00
	1840	1.246	4.00	7.00	17.50	50.00
	1841	1.303	4.00	7.00	17.50	50.00
	1842	.647	4.00	7.00	17.50	50.00
	1843	.478	4.00	7.00	17.50	50.00
	1844	.816	4.00	7.00	17.50	50.00
	1845	.396	4.00	7.00	17.50	50.00
		Mint mark: B				
196.2	1831	.052	6.00	12.00	27.50	85.00
	1832	.135	5.00	10.00	20.00	65.00
	1833	.080	5.00	10.00	20.00	75.00
	1834	.070	5.00	10.00	20.00	75.00
	1835	—	—	—	Rare	—
	1835 (error: PRANCAIS)					
		Inc. Ab.	—	—	Rare	—
	1836	8,413	15.00	30.00	60.00	225.00
	1837	.094	5.00	10.00	20.00	65.00
	1838	.049	10.00	20.00	40.00	100.00
	1839	.053	10.00	20.00	40.00	100.00
	1840/30	.053		1 known		
	1840	Inc. Ab.	10.00	20.00	40.00	100.00
	1841	.289	4.00	8.00	20.00	65.00
	1842	.642	4.00	8.00	17.50	60.00
	1843	.762	4.00	8.00	17.50	60.00
	1844	.018	10.00	20.00	40.00	100.00
	1845	4,603	6.00	10.00	17.50	55.00
		Mint mark: BB				
196.3	1831	3,629	—	—	—	—
	1832	.011	10.00	20.00	40.00	100.00
	1833	7,890	15.00	35.00	75.00	225.00
	1834	6,063	15.00	35.00	75.00	225.00
	1835	.010	10.00	20.00	40.00	100.00
	1836	.011	10.00	20.00	40.00	110.00
	1837	9,762	12.00	30.00	55.00	225.00
	1838	6,561	55.00	125.00	350.00	750.00
	1839	.013	10.00	20.00	45.00	120.00
	1844	.036	6.00	12.00	27.50	85.00
	1845	.051	6.00	12.00	27.50	85.00
		Mint mark: D				
196.4	1831	.034	6.00	12.00	27.50	85.00
	1832	.141	5.00	10.00	20.00	65.00
	1833	.016	10.00	20.00	40.00	110.00
	1834	.030	6.00	12.00	27.50	85.00
	1835	.028	6.00	12.00	27.50	85.00
	1837	8,352	15.00	30.00	60.00	225.00
	1838	6,199	—	—	—	—
	1839	5,163	—	—	—	—
	1840	.015	10.00	20.00	40.00	115.00

C#	Date	Mintage	Fine	VF	XF	Unc
		Mint mark: H				
196.5	1831	.026	10.00	20.00	40.00	110.00
	1832	.040	6.00	12.00	27.50	85.00
	1833	.014	10.00	20.00	40.00	110.00
	1834	.046	6.00	12.00	27.50	85.00
	1835	9,989	15.00	30.00	60.00	225.00
		Mint mark: I				
196.6	1831	967 pcs.	—	—	—	—
	1832	.034	6.00	12.00	27.50	90.00
	1833	.024	10.00	20.00	40.00	110.00
	1834	.040	6.00	12.00	27.50	85.00
	1835	.044	6.00	12.00	27.50	85.00
		Mint mark: K				
196.7	1831	.036	6.00	12.00	27.50	85.00
	1832	.020	6.00	12.00	27.50	85.00
	1833	.022	10.00	20.00	40.00	110.00
	1834	.036	6.00	12.00	27.50	85.00
	1835	.041	6.00	12.00	27.50	85.00
	1836	9,500	15.00	30.00	60.00	225.00
	1837	.011	10.00	20.00	40.00	110.00
	1838	.016	10.00	20.00	40.00	115.00
	1839	.016	10.00	20.00	40.00	115.00
	1840	.030	6.00	12.00	27.50	85.00
	1841	.092	6.00	12.00	25.00	75.00
	1842	.023	10.00	20.00	40.00	110.00
	1843	.027	10.00	20.00	40.00	110.00
	1844	.023	10.00	20.00	40.00	110.00
	1845	.016				
		Mint mark: L				
196.8	1831	6,182	15.00	30.00	60.00	225.00
	1832	.022	7.00	15.00	35.00	100.00
	1833	8,927	15.00	30.00	60.00	225.00
	1834	8,789	15.00	30.00	60.00	225.00
		Mint mark: M				
196.9	1831	6,831	20.00	40.00	80.00	275.00
	1832	.035	6.00	12.00	27.50	85.00
	1833	.017	10.00	20.00	40.00	110.00
	1834	8,218	15.00	30.00	60.00	225.00
	1835	.011	10.00	20.00	40.00	110.00
		Mint mark: MA				
196.13	1832	Inc. Be.	—	—	Rare	—
	1833	3,452				
		Mint mark: Q				
196.10	1831	.011	10.00	20.00	40.00	110.00
	1832	.018	10.00	20.00	40.00	110.00
	1834	.014	10.00	20.00	40.00	115.00
		Mint mark: T				
196.12	1832	8,486	15.00	30.00	60.00	225.00
	1833	.018	10.00	20.00	40.00	110.00
	1834	.034	7.00	15.00	30.00	90.00
		Mint mark: W				
196.11	1831	.160	5.00	10.00	20.00	60.00
	1832	.218	5.00	10.00	20.00	70.00
	1833	.141	5.00	10.00	20.00	70.00
	1834	.404	5.00	10.00	20.00	65.00
	1835	.133	5.00	10.00	20.00	65.00
	1836	.089	5.00	10.00	25.00	80.00
	1837	.168	5.00	10.00	20.00	65.00
	1838	.100	5.00	10.00	20.00	65.00
	1839	.114	5.00	10.00	20.00	65.00
	1840	.042	5.00	10.00	20.00	85.00
	1841	.168	5.00	10.00	20.00	65.00
	1842	.091	5.00	10.00	20.00	65.00
	1843	.073	5.00	10.00	20.00	65.00
	1844	.367	4.00	8.00	17.50	60.00
	1845	.330	4.00	8.00	17.50	60.00

25 CENTIMES

1.2500 g, .900 SILVER, .0362 oz ASW

Mint mark: A

C#	Date	Mintage	Fine	VF	XF	Unc
197.1	1845	Inc. Ab.	4.00	8.00	25.00	85.00
	1846	1,748	3.00	6.00	15.00	55.00
	1847	3,000	3.00	6.00	15.00	45.00
	1848	.142	5.00	10.00	20.00	70.00
		Mint mark: B				
197.2	1845	Inc. Ab.	3.00	6.00	12.50	45.00
		Mint mark: BB				
197.3	1845	Inc. Ab.	5.00	10.00	35.00	125.00
	1846	7,922	12.00	30.00	65.00	225.00
	1847	9,939	12.00	30.00	65.00	225.00
	1848	5,886	15.00	50.00	150.00	300.00
		Mint mark: K				
197.4	1845	Inc. Ab.	8.00	20.00	50.00	150.00
	1846	.012	10.00	25.00	60.00	275.00
	1847	3,905	25.00	65.00	175.00	350.00
		Mint mark: W				
197.5	1845	Inc. Ab.	5.00	10.00	20.00	65.00
	1846	.039	7.50	15.00	35.00	125.00

NICKEL
Mint: Paris - w/o mint mark.
Third Republic

Y#	Date	Mintage	Fine	VF	XF	Unc
69	1903	16.000	.25	.75	1.50	9.00
70	1904	16.000	.25	.75	1.50	8.00
	1905	8.000	.25	.75	1.50	9.00
76	1914(-)	.941	3.00	6.00	10.00	16.00
	1915(-)	.535	4.00	7.00	12.00	20.00
	1916(-)	.100	10.00	20.00	40.00	60.00
	1917(-)	.065	25.00	50.00	75.00	125.00

COPPER-NICKEL

76a	1917	3.085	1.00	1.50	2.00	6.00
	1918	18.330	.15	.35	.75	3.00
	1919	5.106	.50	.75	1.25	4.50
	1920	18.108	.15	.35	.75	3.00
	1921	18.531	.15	.35	.75	3.00
	1922	17.766	.15	.35	.75	3.00
	1923	19.718	.15	.35	.75	3.00
	1924	24.535	.15	.35	.75	3.00
	1925	17.807	.15	.35	.75	3.00
	1926	13.226	.15	.35	.75	3.00
	1927	13.465	.15	.35	.75	3.00
	1928	9.960	.25	.50	1.00	4.00
	1929	12.887	.15	.35	.75	3.00
	1930	28.363	.15	.35	.75	2.00
	1931	22.121	.15	.35	.75	2.00
	1932	30.364	.15	.35	.75	2.00
	1933	28.562	.15	.35	.75	2.00
	1936	4.657	2.00	4.00	8.00	15.00
	1937	7.780	.25	.50	1.00	3.00

NICKEL-BRONZE

76b	.1938.	5.170	.25	.50	1.00	3.00
	.1939. thick flan (1.55mm)					
		42.964	.15	.35	.75	1.75
	.1939. thin flan (1.35mm)					
		Inc. Ab.	.15	.35	.75	1.75
	.1940.	3.446	6.00	12.00	18.00	35.00

DEMI (1/2) FRANC

2.5000 g, .900 SILVER, .0723 oz ASW
Mint mark: A
Obv: BONAPARTE PREMIER CONSUL.

C#	Date	Mintage	VG	Fine	VF	XF
142.1	ANXI	.031	10.00	50.00	100.00	225.00
	AN12	.280	10.00	20.00	50.00	150.00
		Mint mark: BB				
142.2	AN12	2,125	75.00	175.00	325.00	650.00
		Mint mark: D				
142.3	AN12	.015	12.50	30.00	70.00	150.00
		Mint mark: G				
142.4	AN12	7,407	75.00	175.00	350.00	750.00

FRANCE 555

FRANCE 556

Mint mark: H
C#	Date	Mintage	VG	Fine	VF	XF
142.5	AN12	1,988	75.00	150.00	325.00	650.00

Mint mark: I
| 142.6 | AN12 | .416 | 7.50 | 15.00 | 40.00 | 125.00 |

Mint mark: K
| 142.7 | AN12 | .012 | 15.00 | 35.00 | 80.00 | 175.00 |

Mint mark: L
| 142.8 | AN12 | .067 | 10.00 | 20.00 | 50.00 | 150.00 |

Mint mark: M
| 142.9 | AN12 | .136 | 10.00 | 20.00 | 50.00 | 140.00 |

Mint mark: MA
| 142.10 | AN12 | .026 | 10.00 | 20.00 | 50.00 | 160.00 |

Mint mark: Q
| 142.11 | AN12 | .054 | 10.00 | 20.00 | 50.00 | 150.00 |

Mint mark: T
| 142.12 | AN12 | .017 | 12.50 | 30.00 | 70.00 | 175.00 |

Mint mark: U
| 142.13 | AN12 | 3,150 | 60.00 | 135.00 | 250.00 | 500.00 |
| Common date | | | | | Unc. | 275.00 |

Obv: NAPOLEON EMPEREUR.
Mint mark: A
C#	Date	Mintage	VG	Fine	VF	XF
152.1	AN12	.039	12.00	25.00	60.00	125.00
	AN13	.427	7.50	15.00	35.00	100.00
	AN14	.020	25.00	50.00	100.00	200.00

Mint mark: BB
| 152.2 | AN12 | 1,825 | 35.00 | 75.00 | 150.00 | 300.00 |
| | AN13 | 895 pcs. | 75.00 | 125.00 | 200.00 | 500.00 |

Mint mark: D
| 152.8 | AN13 | 2,402 | 35.00 | 70.00 | 140.00 | 275.00 |

Mint mark: G
| 152.9 | AN13 | 1,181 | — | — | Rare | — |

Mint mark: H
| 152.3 | AN12 | 7,286 | 25.00 | 50.00 | 100.00 | 225.00 |
| | AN13 | 5,036 | 25.00 | 50.00 | 100.00 | 225.00 |

Mint mark: I
| 152.4 | AN12 | .022 | 15.00 | 30.00 | 75.00 | 150.00 |
| | AN13 | .206 | 7.50 | 15.00 | 35.00 | 125.00 |

Mint mark: K
152.5	AN12	.019	17.50	35.00	80.00	175.00
	AN13	.037	12.00	25.00	60.00	150.00
	AN14	1,757	—	—	Rare	—

Mint mark: L
| 152.10 | AN13 | .046 | 10.00 | 20.00 | 55.00 | 140.00 |
| | AN14 | 3,889 | 35.00 | 75.00 | 150.00 | 300.00 |

Mint mark: M
| 152.6 | AN12 | .099 | 7.50 | 15.00 | 40.00 | 125.00 |
| | AN13 | .212 | 7.50 | 15.00 | 35.00 | 125.00 |

Mint mark: MA
| 152.11 | AN13 | 6,103 | 25.00 | 50.00 | 100.00 | 225.00 |

Mint mark: Q
| 152.12 | AN13 | .034 | 12.00 | 25.00 | 60.00 | 150.00 |

Mint mark: T
| 152.7 | AN12 | 3,735 | 30.00 | 65.00 | 130.00 | 250.00 |
| | AN13 | 6,140 | 25.00 | 50.00 | 100.00 | 225.00 |

Mint mark: U
152.13	AN13	1,662	35.00	75.00	150.00	300.00
	AN14	—	45.00	90.00	200.00	350.00
Common date					Unc.	275.00

Mint mark: A
| 152.14 (C152.2) | 1806 | .156 | 7.50 | 15.00 | 40.00 | 125.00 |

Mint mark: I
| 152.15 | 1806 | 7,027 | 17.50 | 35.00 | 90.00 | 225.00 |
| | 1807 | 3,848 | 20.00 | 40.00 | 100.00 | 275.00 |

Mint mark: K
| 152.16 | 1806 | 1,673 | 30.00 | 60.00 | 140.00 | 300.00 |
| | 1807 | 2,983 | 25.00 | 50.00 | 110.00 | 275.00 |

Mint mark: L
152.17	1806	.042	10.00	20.00	65.00	170.00
	1807/6	.017	40.00	100.00	125.00	225.00
	1807	Inc. Ab.	15.00	30.00	80.00	200.00

Mint mark: M
| 152.20 | 1807 | 1,791 | — | Reported, not confirmed | | |

Mint mark: Q
| 152.18 | 1806 | .015 | 15.00 | 30.00 | 80.00 | 200.00 |
| | 1807 | .014 | 3 known | Rare | — | — |

Mint mark: U
152.19	1806	9,592	17.50	35.00	90.00	225.00
	1807	4,448	20.00	40.00	100.00	275.00
Common date					Unc.	325.00

Mint mark: A
Negro head.
C#	Date	Mintage	VG	Fine	VF	XF
152a	1807	.058	50.00	100.00	250.00	600.00

Laureate head.
| 152b.1 | 1807 | .046 | 40.00 | 80.00 | 150.00 | 350.00 |
| | 1808 | 6.606 | 5.00 | 10.00 | 20.00 | 45.00 |

Mint mark: B
| 152b.2 | 1808 | .559 | 6.00 | 12.00 | 25.00 | 70.00 |

Mint mark: BB
| 152b.3 | 1808 | 1.596 | 5.00 | 10.00 | 20.00 | 60.00 |

Mint mark: D
| 152b.4 | 1808 | .871 | 6.00 | 12.00 | 25.00 | 70.00 |

Mint mark: H
| 152b.5 | 1808 | .336 | 7.00 | 15.00 | 30.00 | 80.00 |

Mint mark: I
| 152b.6 | 1808 | .298 | 10.00 | 20.00 | 40.00 | 90.00 |

Mint mark: K
| 152b.7 | 1808 | .363 | 7.00 | 15.00 | 30.00 | 80.00 |

Mint mark: L
| 152b.8 | 1808 | 3,394 | 50.00 | 100.00 | 200.00 | 375.00 |

Mint mark: M
| 152b.9 | 1808 | .054 | 20.00 | 40.00 | 80.00 | 150.00 |

Mint mark: MA
C#	Date	Mintage	VG	Fine	VF	XF
152b.10	1808	.028	20.00	40.00	80.00	175.00

Mint mark: Q
| 152b.11 | 1808 | .289 | 10.00 | 20.00 | 40.00 | 90.00 |

Mint mark: T
| 152b.12 | 1808 | .128 | 12.00 | 25.00 | 40.00 | 90.00 |

Mint mark: U
| 152b.13 | 1808 | 3,339 | 50.00 | 100.00 | 200.00 | 375.00 |

Mint mark: W
| 152b.14 | 1808 | 1.069 | 5.00 | 10.00 | 20.00 | 50.00 |
| Common date | | | | | Unc. | 150.00 |

Mint mark: A
C#	Date	Mintage	VG	Fine	VF	XF
162.1	1809	1.680	5.00	10.00	20.00	60.00
	1810	1.362	5.00	10.00	20.00	60.00
	1811	1.860	5.00	10.00	20.00	60.00
	1812	1.720	5.00	10.00	20.00	60.00
	1813	.627	5.00	10.00	20.00	60.00
	1814	.107	10.00	20.00	50.00	100.00

Mint mark: B
162.2	1809	.014	15.00	27.50	75.00	175.00
	1810	.285	6.00	12.00	27.50	85.00
	1811	.252	6.00	12.00	27.50	85.00
	1812	.192	6.00	12.00	30.00	90.00

Mint mark: BB
| 162.10 | 1810 | .011 | 17.50 | 35.00 | 80.00 | 200.00 |
| | 1811 | .037 | 10.00 | 22.00 | 55.00 | 140.00 |

Mint mark: CL
| 162.16 | 1813 | 8,385 | — | — | Rare | — |

Mint mark: D
162.3	1809	.043	12.00	22.00	55.00	140.00
	1810	.071	10.00	20.00	50.00	130.00
	1811	.221	6.00	12.00	27.50	85.00
	1812	.155	6.00	12.00	30.00	90.00
	1813	.110	8.00	17.50	40.00	110.00

Mint mark: H
162.11	1810	3,563	30.00	60.00	110.00	250.00
	1811	.120	7.50	15.00	30.00	100.00
	1812	.270	6.00	12.00	27.50	85.00
	1813	.138	7.50	15.00	35.00	100.00

Mint mark: I
162.13	1811	.134	7.50	15.00	35.00	100.00
	1812	.137	6.00	12.00	27.50	85.00
	1813	.097	8.00	17.50	40.00	100.00

Mint mark: K
162.4	1809	.043	12.00	22.00	55.00	140.00
	1810	.041	12.00	22.00	55.00	140.00
162.4	1811	.016	15.00	30.00	75.00	175.00
	1812	.034	12.00	25.00	60.00	150.00
	1813	.058	10.00	20.00	50.00	125.00

Mint mark: L
162.12	1810	.055	10.00	22.00	50.00	125.00
	1810(Tr)	I.A.	—	Reported, not confirmed		
	1811	.095	8.00	17.50	40.00	100.00
	1812	.052	10.00	20.00	50.00	125.00
	1813	.044	10.00	22.00	55.00	140.00

Mint mark: M
162.5	1809	.021	12.00	25.00	70.00	160.00
	1810	.033	12.00	25.00	60.00	150.00
	1811	.049	10.00	22.00	55.00	140.00
	1812	.105	8.00	17.50	40.00	110.00
	1813	.159	6.00	12.00	30.00	90.00
	1814	.036	30.00	60.00	100.00	300.00

Mint mark: MA
162.6	1809	3,176	30.00	65.00	120.00	275.00
	1810	.011	15.00	30.00	80.00	200.00
	1811	.069	10.00	20.00	50.00	125.00
	1812	.052	10.00	20.00	50.00	125.00
	1813	.070	8.00	17.50	45.00	120.00

Mint mark: Q
162.7	1809	.070	10.00	20.00	50.00	125.00
	1811	.126	7.50	15.00	35.00	100.00
	1812	.106	8.00	17.50	40.00	110.00
	1813	.044	10.00	22.00	50.00	140.00
	1814	—	—	Reported, not confirmed		

Mint mark: T
162.14	1811	.114	8.00	17.50	40.00	100.00
	1812	.081	6.00	12.00	45.00	120.00
	1813	.053	10.00	20.00	50.00	125.00

Mint mark: U
| 162.8 | 1809 | 5,853 | 25.00 | 55.00 | 100.00 | 225.00 |
| | 1811 | .039 | 10.00 | 22.00 | 55.00 | 140.00 |

Mint mark: W
162.9	1809	.314	6.00	12.00	25.00	80.00
	1810	.240	6.00	12.00	27.50	85.00
	1811	.246	6.00	12.00	27.50	85.00
	1812	.337	6.00	12.00	25.00	80.00
	1813	.058	6.00	12.00	30.00	90.00

Mint mark: Flag
162.15	1812	5,084	35.00	70.00	150.00	375.00
	1813	6,894	30.00	60.00	125.00	300.00
Common date					Unc.	200.00

Mint mark: A
178.1	1816	.261	6.00	12.00	30.00	90.00
	1817	.236	6.00	12.00	30.00	90.00
	1818	.050	10.00	20.00	45.00	120.00
	1819	.047	10.00	22.00	50.00	130.00
	1820	.043	10.00	22.00	50.00	130.00
	1821	.082	8.00	17.50	40.00	100.00
	1822	.584	6.00	12.00	30.00	85.00
	1823	.500	6.00	12.00	30.00	85.00
	1824	.613	6.00	12.00	30.00	85.00

Mint mark: B
178.2	1816	.019	12.00	25.00	60.00	150.00
	1817	8,759	15.00	30.00	70.00	175.00
	1818	7,803	15.00	30.00	70.00	175.00
	1822	.034	12.00	25.00	55.00	140.00
	1823	.018	12.00	25.00	60.00	150.00
	1824	.042	10.00	22.00	50.00	125.00

Mint mark: D
| 178.11 | 1824 | .018 | 12.00 | 25.00 | 60.00 | 150.00 |

Mint mark: H
178.9	1817	.086	8.00	17.50	40.00	110.00
	1818	.014	12.00	25.00	60.00	150.00
	1819	2,463	22.00	45.00	100.00	250.00
	1822	1,332	35.00	75.00	125.00	300.00
	1823	3,558	20.00	40.00	90.00	225.00
	1824	.020	12.00	25.00	60.00	150.00

Mint mark: I
178.3	1816	2,692	22.00	45.00	100.00	250.00
	1823	3,113	20.00	40.00	90.00	225.00
	1824	.011	12.00	25.00	65.00	150.00

Mint mark: K
178.10	1817	.213	6.00	12.00	30.00	90.00
	1820	7,794	15.00	30.00	70.00	160.00
	1823	8,136	15.00	30.00	70.00	160.00
	1824	.053	10.00	20.00	45.00	120.00

Mint mark: L
178.4	1816	3,273	20.00	40.00	90.00	225.00
	1817	8,767	15.00	30.00	70.00	160.00
	1818	2,816	22.00	45.00	100.00	250.00
	1823	.036	12.00	25.00	55.00	140.00
	1824	.056	12.00	25.00	60.00	150.00

Mint mark: M
178.5	1816	4,682	17.50	35.00	80.00	175.00
	1823	8,632	15.00	30.00	70.00	160.00
	1824	.011	12.00	25.00	65.00	150.00

Mint mark: Q
| 178.6 | 1816 | .012 | 12.00 | 25.00 | 65.00 | 150.00 |

FRANCE 557

C#	Date	Mintage	VG	Fine	VF	XF
178.6	1819	4,488	17.50	35.00	80.00	175.00
	1820	.017	12.00	25.00	60.00	150.00
	1823	.101	7.50	15.00	35.00	100.00
	1824	.170	6.00	12.00	30.00	90.00

Mint mark: T

C#	Date	Mintage	VG	Fine	VF	XF
178.7	1816	5,964	17.50	35.00	80.00	175.00
	1819	1,741	25.00	55.00	110.00	275.00

Mint mark: W

C#	Date	Mintage	VG	Fine	VF	XF
178.8	1816	8,728	15.00	30.00	70.00	160.00
	1817	.025	10.00	22.00	55.00	140.00
	1818	7,811	15.00	30.00	70.00	160.00
	1819	5,166	17.50	35.00	80.00	175.00
	1821	.037	12.00	25.00	55.00	140.00
	1822	.015	12.00	25.00	60.00	150.00
	1823	.070	8.00	17.50	40.00	110.00
	1824	.102	7.50	15.00	35.00	100.00
	Common date				Unc.	175.00

Mint mark: A

C#	Date	Mintage	VG	Fine	VF	XF
186.1	1825	.011	20.00	50.00	100.00	200.00
	1826	.361	5.00	10.00	25.00	60.00
	1827	.786	5.00	10.00	20.00	60.00
	1828	.508	5.00	10.00	20.00	60.00
	1829	.538	5.00	10.00	20.00	60.00
	1830	.377	5.00	10.00	25.00	60.00

Mint mark: B

C#	Date	Mintage	VG	Fine	VF	XF
186.2	1826	6,019	20.00	45.00	80.00	200.00
	1827	.019	12.00	25.00	50.00	125.00
	1828	.056	7.50	15.00	35.00	100.00
	1829	.116	5.00	10.00	35.00	90.00

Mint mark: BB

C#	Date	Mintage	VG	Fine	VF	XF
186.3	1826	.011	15.00	30.00	60.00	150.00
	1827	2,476	25.00	50.00	120.00	250.00
	1828	.023	10.00	20.00	45.00	100.00
	1829	.022	10.00	20.00	45.00	100.00

Mint mark: D

C#	Date	Mintage	VG	Fine	VF	XF
186.4	1826	.020	12.00	25.00	50.00	125.00
	1827	5,629	22.00	45.00	90.00	200.00
	1828	.083	7.50	15.00	35.00	100.00
	1829	.028	10.00	20.00	45.00	120.00

Mint mark: H

C#	Date	Mintage	VG	Fine	VF	XF
186.5	1826	.023	10.00	20.00	45.00	120.00
	1827	.014	15.00	30.00	60.00	150.00
	1828	.026	10.00	20.00	45.00	120.00
	1829	.058	7.50	15.00	35.00	100.00

Mint mark: I

C#	Date	Mintage	VG	Fine	VF	XF
186.6	1826	1,435	25.00	55.00	125.00	275.00
	1827	1,520	25.00	55.00	125.00	275.00
	1828	2,526	25.00	50.00	125.00	250.00
	1829	.015	12.00	25.00	50.00	125.00

Mint mark: K

C#	Date	Mintage	VG	Fine	VF	XF
186.7	1826	.017	12.00	25.00	50.00	125.00
	1827	9,597	22.00	45.00	70.00	200.00
	1828	.027	10.00	20.00	45.00	120.00
	1829	.037	8.00	17.50	40.00	100.00
	1830	.022	10.00	20.00	45.00	120.00

Mint mark: L

C#	Date	Mintage	VG	Fine	VF	XF
186.8	1826	.036	8.00	17.50	40.00	100.00
	1827	.031	8.00	17.50	40.00	100.00
	1828	.027	10.00	20.00	45.00	120.00
	1829	.016	12.00	25.00	50.00	125.00
	1830	.018	12.00	25.00	50.00	125.00

Mint mark: M

C#	Date	Mintage	VG	Fine	VF	XF
186.9	1826	9,192	17.50	35.00	70.00	175.00
	1827	7,288	22.00	45.00	70.00	200.00
	1828	.072	7.50	15.00	35.00	100.00
	1829	.016	12.00	25.00	50.00	125.00
	1830	7,826	20.00	40.00	70.00	175.00

Mint mark: MA

C#	Date	Mintage	VG	Fine	VF	XF
186.13	1829	.032	10.00	22.00	50.00	125.00

Mint mark: Q

C#	Date	Mintage	VG	Fine	VF	XF
186.10	1826	.063	7.50	15.00	35.00	100.00
	1827	.011	15.00	30.00	60.00	150.00
	1828	.030	8.00	17.50	40.00	100.00
	1829	.019	10.00	20.00	50.00	125.00

Mint mark: T

C#	Date	Mintage	VG	Fine	VF	XF
186.12	1827	8,815	20.00	40.00	70.00	175.00
	1828	.018	12.00	25.00	50.00	125.00
	1829	3,609	25.00	50.00	100.00	250.00

Mint mark: W

C#	Date	Mintage	VG	Fine	VF	XF
186.11	1826	.038	8.00	17.50	40.00	100.00
	1827	.030	8.00	17.50	40.00	100.00
	1828	.170	6.00	12.00	30.00	90.00
	1829	.126	6.00	12.00	30.00	90.00
	1830	.131	6.00	12.00	30.00	90.00
	Common date				Unc.	175.00

Mint mark: A

C#	Date	Mintage	Fine	VF	XF	Unc
198.1	1831	.110	7.50	15.00	35.00	100.00
	1832	.345	6.00	12.00	30.00	90.00
	1833	.272	6.00	12.00	30.00	90.00
	1834	.419	6.00	12.00	30.00	90.00
	1835	.831	6.00	12.00	30.00	75.00
	1836	.432	6.00	12.00	30.00	90.00
	1837	.137	7.50	15.00	35.00	90.00
	1838	.385	6.00	12.00	30.00	90.00
	1839	.636	6.00	12.00	30.00	90.00
	1840	1.107	5.00	10.00	25.00	90.00
	1841	1.119	5.00	10.00	25.00	90.00
	1842	.338	7.50	15.00	35.00	90.00
	1843	.152	7.50	15.00	35.00	90.00
	1844	.196	7.50	15.00	35.00	90.00
	1845	.494	7.50	15.00	35.00	90.00

Mint mark: B

C#	Date	Mintage	Fine	VF	XF	Unc
198.2	1831	.136	7.50	15.00	35.00	90.00
	1832	.256	6.00	12.00	30.00	90.00
	1833	.093	7.50	15.00	35.00	90.00
	1834	.086	9.00	17.50	35.00	90.00
	1835	.054	10.00	20.00	45.00	120.00
	1836	.043	10.00	20.00	45.00	120.00
	1837	.158	7.50	15.00	35.00	90.00
	1838	.084	9.00	17.50	35.00	90.00
	1839	.116	9.00	17.50	35.00	90.00
	1840	.117	9.00	17.50	35.00	90.00
	1841	.831	6.00	12.00	30.00	90.00
	1842	.250	7.50	15.00	35.00	90.00
	1843	.213	7.50	15.00	35.00	90.00
	1844	.046	7.50	15.00	35.00	90.00
	1845	2.501	5.00	10.00	25.00	75.00

Mint mark: BB

C#	Date	Mintage	Fine	VF	XF	Unc
198.3	1831	2,767	—	—	—	—
	1832	.010	12.00	25.00	50.00	120.00
	1833	.029	7.50	15.00	30.00	90.00
	1834	.020	10.00	20.00	40.00	100.00
	1835	5,346	—	—	—	—
	1836	.022	9.00	17.50	35.00	100.00
	1837	5,952	20.00	35.00	75.00	200.00
	1838	5,820	—	—	—	—
	1839	6,896	20.00	35.00	75.00	200.00
	1840	770 pcs.	—	—	—	—
	1841	.010	10.00	20.00	40.00	110.00
	1842	.308	7.50	15.00	30.00	90.00
	1844	.025	7.50	15.00	30.00	90.00
	1845	.044	—	—	—	—

Mint mark: D

C#	Date	Mintage	Fine	VF	XF	Unc
198.4	1831	.016	7.50	15.00	30.00	90.00
	1832	.206	7.50	15.00	30.00	90.00
	1833	.032	7.50	15.00	30.00	90.00
	1834	.064	7.50	15.00	30.00	90.00
	1835	.015	10.00	20.00	40.00	110.00
	1836	8,706	17.50	35.00	75.00	200.00
	1837	7,556	17.50	35.00	75.00	200.00
	1838	2,432	—	—	—	—
	1840	.019	9.00	17.50	35.00	100.00

Mint mark: H

C#	Date	Mintage	Fine	VF	XF	Unc
198.5	1831	.018	7.50	15.00	30.00	90.00
	1832	.077	7.50	15.00	30.00	90.00
	1833	.043	7.50	15.00	30.00	90.00
	1834	.086	7.50	15.00	30.00	90.00

Mint mark: I

C#	Date	Mintage	Fine	VF	XF	Unc
198.6	1831	.013	10.00	20.00	40.00	110.00
	1832	.026	7.50	15.00	30.00	90.00
	1833	.049	7.50	15.00	30.00	90.00
	1834	.025	7.50	15.00	30.00	90.00
	1835	.045	7.50	15.00	30.00	90.00

Mint mark: K

C#	Date	Mintage	Fine	VF	XF	Unc
198.7	1831	.035	7.50	15.00	30.00	90.00
	1832	.040	7.50	15.00	30.00	90.00
	1833	.029	7.50	15.00	30.00	90.00
	1834	.069	7.50	15.00	30.00	90.00
	1835	.050	7.50	15.00	30.00	90.00
	1836	.015	10.00	20.00	40.00	110.00
	1837	.026	10.00	20.00	40.00	110.00
	1838	.017	10.00	20.00	40.00	110.00
	1839	.018	10.00	20.00	40.00	110.00
	1840	.043	7.50	15.00	30.00	90.00
	1841	.026	7.50	15.00	30.00	90.00
	1842	.035	7.50	15.00	30.00	90.00
	1843	.034	7.50	15.00	30.00	90.00
	1844	.023	7.50	15.00	30.00	90.00
	1845	.022	—	—	—	—

Mint mark: L

C#	Date	Mintage	Fine	VF	XF	Unc
198.8	1831	4,723	25.00	50.00	125.00	300.00
	1832	.034	7.50	15.00	30.00	90.00
	1833	.016	10.00	20.00	40.00	110.00
	1834	.010	10.00	20.00	40.00	110.00

Mint mark: M

C#	Date	Mintage	Fine	VF	XF	Unc
198.9	1831	8,289	20.00	35.00	75.00	200.00
	1832	.092	6.00	15.00	30.00	90.00
	1833	.026	6.00	15.00	30.00	90.00
	1834	.019	7.00	15.00	30.00	90.00
	1835	.023	7.00	15.00	30.00	90.00
	1836	6,173	—	—	—	—

Mint mark: MA

C#	Date	Mintage	Fine	VF	XF	Unc
198.10	1831	— 400.00		—	—	—
	1832	.052	6.00	15.00	30.00	90.00
	1835	.029	7.00	15.00	30.00	90.00

Mint mark: Q

C#	Date	Mintage	Fine	VF	XF	Unc
198.11	1831	.012	10.00	20.00	40.00	120.00
	1832	.021	10.00	20.00	40.00	120.00
	1833	.055	7.50	15.00	30.00	90.00
	1834	1,824	400.00	—	—	—

Mint mark: T

C#	Date	Mintage	Fine	VF	XF	Unc
198.12	1831	5,573	20.00	35.00	75.00	200.00
	1832	.033	6.00	12.00	25.00	90.00
	1833	.014	7.00	15.00	35.00	100.00
	1834	.055	6.00	12.00	25.00	90.00

Mint mark: W

C#	Date	Mintage	Fine	VF	XF	Unc
198.13	1831	.125	6.00	12.00	25.00	90.00
	1832	.427	6.00	12.00	25.00	90.00
	1833	.151	6.00	12.00	25.00	90.00
	1834	.683	6.00	12.00	25.00	90.00
	1835	.183	6.00	12.00	25.00	90.00
	1836	.087	6.00	12.00	25.00	90.00
	1837	.267	6.00	12.00	25.00	90.00
	1838	.132	6.00	12.00	25.00	90.00
	1839	.119	6.00	12.00	25.00	90.00
	1840	.079	6.00	12.00	25.00	90.00
	1841	.234	6.00	12.00	25.00	90.00
	1842	.215	6.00	12.00	25.00	90.00
	1843	.233	6.00	12.00	25.00	90.00
	1844	.408	6.00	12.00	25.00	90.00
	1845	.525	6.00	12.00	25.00	75.00

50 CENTIMES

2.5000 g, .900 SILVER, .0723 oz ASW

Mint mark: A

C#	Date	Mintage	Fine	VF	XF	Unc
199.1	1845	.494	7.50	15.00	30.00	75.00
	1846	3.165	7.50	15.00	30.00	70.00
	1847	3.437	6.00	12.00	25.00	70.00
	1848	.218	7.50	15.00	30.00	80.00

Mint mark: B

C#	Date	Mintage	Fine	VF	XF	Unc
199.2	1845	Inc. C198.2	7.50	15.00	30.00	70.00
	1846	1.000	7.50	15.00	30.00	70.00

Mint mark: BB

C#	Date	Mintage	Fine	VF	XF	Unc
199.3	1845	Inc. C198.3	12.00	25.00	50.00	125.00
	1846	.017	12.00	25.00	50.00	125.00
	1847	.044	10.00	22.00	40.00	100.00
	1848	.018	12.00	25.00	50.00	125.00

Mint mark: K

C#	Date	Mintage	Fine	VF	XF	Unc
199.4	1845	Inc. C198.7	—	—	—	—
	1846	.022	9.00	17.50	35.00	70.00
	1847	8,915	20.00	40.00	90.00	200.00

Mint mark: W

C#	Date	Mintage	Fine	VF	XF	Unc
199.5	1845	Inc. C198.13	—	—	—	—
	1846	.070	7.50	15.00	30.00	70.00

Mint mark: A
Second Republic

Y#	Date	Mintage	Fine	VF	XF	Unc
3.1	1849	2,655	150.00	200.00	450.00	700.00
	1850	2.165	6.00	12.00	30.00	85.00
	1851	.850	10.00	22.50	45.00	115.00

Mint mark: BB

Y#	Date	Mintage	Fine	VF	XF	Unc
3.2	1850	.040	25.00	60.00	125.00	300.00

Mint mark: K

Y#	Date	Mintage	Fine	VF	XF	Unc
3.3	1850	.031	35.00	80.00	175.00	350.00

Mint mark: A
President Louis-Napoleon

Y#	Date	Mintage	Fine	VF	XF	Unc
11	1852	1.010	30.00	60.00	150.00	350.00

Second Empire

Y#	Date	Mintage	Fine	VF	XF	Unc
23.1	1853	.154	25.00	50.00	120.00	250.00
	1854	1.080	10.00	25.00	55.00	125.00
	1855	.400	15.00	35.00	80.00	175.00
	1856	1.436	8.00	20.00	50.00	100.00
	1857	1.632	8.00	20.00	50.00	110.00
	1858	5.559	4.00	15.00	30.00	75.00
	1859	3.880	5.00	20.00	35.00	80.00
	1860(h)	2.657	5.00	20.00	40.00	85.00
	1862	1.549	10.00	25.00	60.00	125.00

FRANCE 558

Mint mark: BB

Y#	Date	Mintage	Fine	VF	XF	Unc
23.2	1856	1.196	10.00	25.00	50.00	110.00
	1859	1.112	10.00	25.00	50.00	110.00
	1860(c)	1.555	8.00	20.00	45.00	100.00
	1861(c)	.355	25.00	60.00	125.00	250.00
	1862	1.007	20.00	50.00	125.00	250.00
	1863	.137	45.00	110.00	200.00	350.00

Mint mark: D

| 23.3 | 1856 | 1.246 | 10.00 | 25.00 | 50.00 | 110.00 |

2.5000 g, .835 SILVER, .0671 oz ASW
Mint mark: A

29.1	1864	7.598	3.00	6.00	15.00	55.00
	1865	7.398	3.00	6.00	15.00	60.00
	1866	5.921	3.00	6.00	15.00	60.00
	1867	14.528	3.00	6.00	15.00	40.00
	1868	2.789	5.00	10.00	25.00	85.00

Mint mark: BB

29.2	1864	4.626	3.00	6.00	15.00	60.00
	1865	5.175	3.00	6.00	15.00	60.00
	1866	5.256	3.00	6.00	15.00	60.00
	1867	9.992	3.00	6.00	15.00	60.00
	1868	Inc. Be.	30.00	60.00	120.00	200.00
	1869	1.800	12.00	25.00	50.00	90.00

Mint mark: K

29.3	1864	1.828	10.00	20.00	40.00	90.00
	1865	4.901	3.00	6.00	15.00	60.00
	1866	3.500	4.00	8.00	18.00	65.00
	1867	4.692	3.00	6.00	15.00	60.00

Mint mark: A
Third Republic

48.1	1871	.236	8.00	15.00	60.00	125.00
	1872	4.243	2.00	4.00	15.00	40.00
	1873	.926	5.00	10.00	35.00	70.00
	1874	1.228	4.00	8.00	30.00	65.00
	1878	30 pcs.	—	—	Proof	2250.
	1881	5.391	2.00	4.00	12.00	35.00
	1882	2.320	3.00	6.00	15.00	45.00
	1886	.309	10.00	25.00	70.00	125.00
	1887	1.866	3.00	6.00	10.00	50.00
	1888	4.517	1.50	3.00	10.00	30.00
	1889	100 pcs.	—	—	Proof	2000.
	1894	3.600	1.50	3.00	7.00	25.00
	1895	7.200	1.50	3.00	6.00	20.00

Mint mark: K

48.2	1871	.723	5.00	10.00	40.00	85.00
	1872	1.643	3.00	6.00	18.00	70.00
	1873	.166	30.00	60.00	125.00	250.00

Mint: Paris - w/o mint mark.

62	1897	.088	30.00	60.00	90.00	150.00
	1897	—	—	—	Proof	300.00
	1898	30.000	1.00	2.00	5.00	14.00
	1898	—	—	—	Proof	275.00
	1899	18.000	1.50	3.00	6.00	20.00
	1900	9.195	3.00	6.00	12.00	40.00
	1900	—	—	—	Proof	250.00
	1901	4.960	3.00	6.00	12.00	50.00
	1902	3.778	3.00	6.00	12.00	55.00
	1903	2.222	10.00	20.00	40.00	125.00
	1904	4.000	3.00	6.00	12.00	40.00
	1905	2.381	5.00	10.00	20.00	75.00
	1906	2.679	4.00	8.00	16.00	50.00
	1907	7.332	1.50	3.00	6.00	25.00
	1908	14.304	1.00	2.00	5.00	20.00
	1909	9.900	1.00	2.00	5.00	20.00
	1910	15.923	.75	1.50	4.00	15.00
	1911	1.330	10.00	20.00	40.00	125.00
	1912	16.000	.50	1.00	2.00	8.00
	1913	14.000	.50	1.00	2.00	8.00
	1914	9.657	.50	1.00	2.00	9.00
	1915	20.893	.50	1.00	1.50	5.00
	1916	52.963	.50	1.00	1.50	4.00
	1917	48.629	.50	1.00	1.50	4.00
	1918	36.492	.50	1.00	1.50	4.00
	1919	24.299	.50	1.00	1.50	4.00
	1920	8.509	.50	1.00	2.00	7.00

ALUMINUM-BRONZE

Y#	Date	Mintage	Fine	VF	XF	Unc
77	1921	8.692	1.50	3.00	6.00	15.00
	1922	86.226	.15	.25	.75	3.00
	1923	119.584	.15	.25	.75	2.00
	1924	97.036	.15	.25	.75	3.00
	1925	48.017	.15	.25	.75	3.00
	1926	46.447	.15	.25	.75	3.00
	1927	23.703	.25	.50	1.50	5.00
	1928	10.329	.35	.75	2.00	6.00
	1929	6.669	1.50	3.00	8.00	16.00

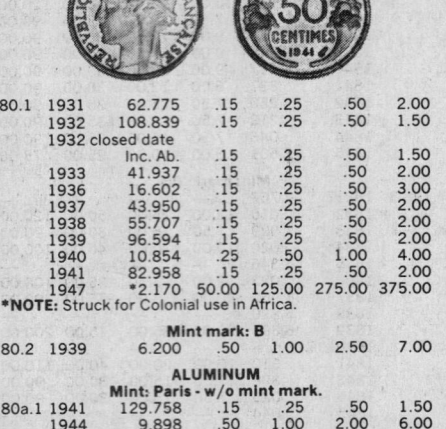

80.1	1931	62.775	.15	.25	.50	2.00
	1932	108.839	.15	.25	.50	1.50
	1932 closed date					
		Inc. Ab.	.15	.25	.50	1.50
	1933	41.937	.15	.25	.50	2.00
	1936	16.602	.15	.25	.50	3.00
	1937	43.950	.15	.25	.50	2.00
	1938	55.707	.15	.25	.50	2.00
	1939	96.594	.15	.25	.50	2.00
	1940	10.854	.25	.50	1.00	4.00
	1941	82.958	.15	.25	.50	2.00
	1947	*2.170	50.00	125.00	275.00	375.00

*NOTE: Struck for Colonial use in Africa.

Mint mark: B

| 80.2 | 1939 | 6.200 | .50 | 1.00 | 2.50 | 7.00 |

ALUMINUM
Mint: Paris - w/o mint mark.

80a.1	1941	129.758	.15	.25	.50	1.50
	1944	9.898	.50	1.00	2.00	6.00
	1945	26.224	.15	.25	.50	1.50
	1946	21.764	.15	.25	.50	1.50
	1947	51.744	.15	.25	.60	1.25

Mint mark: B

80a.2	1944	.020	—	—	—	—
	1945	6.357	.50	1.00	2.00	6.00
	1946	29.344	.15	.25	.50	2.00
	1947	18.504	.25	.50	1.00	4.00

Mint mark: C

80a.3	1944	17.220	—	—	—	—
	1945	2.968	2.50	5.00	9.00	16.00
	1946	2.841				

Mint: Paris - w/o mint mark.
Vichy French State Issues

V94.1	1942	50.134	.15	.25	.50	1.50
	1943	84.462	.15	.25	.50	1.50
	1944	57.410	.25	.75	1.25	5.00

Mint mark: B

V94.2	1943	21.916	10.00	20.00	30.00	60.00
	1944	27.334	.60	1.25	2.50	10.00

Mint mark: C

V94.3	1943	.040	—	—	—	—
	1944 small C					
		27.173	.40	1.00	1.75	7.50
	1944 large C					
		Inc. Ab.	—	—	—	—

Mint: Paris - w/o mint mark.
Thin flan.

Y#	Date	Mintage	Fine	VF	XF	Unc
V94.4	1942	—	.15	.25	.50	1.50
(Y-V94.1)	1943	—	.15	.25	.50	1.50

ALUMINUM-BRONZE
50 New Centimes = 50 Old Francs
Obv: 3 folds in collar.

Y#	Date	Mintage	Fine	VF	XF	Unc
106.1	1962	37.560	.30	.60	1.25	2.50
	1963	62.482	.20	.40	.90	2.00
	1964	41.446	.45	.90	1.50	3.50

Obv: 4 folds in collar.

Y#	Date	Mintage	Fine	VF	XF	Unc
106.2	1962	Inc. Ab.	50.00	90.00	130.00	175.00
	1963	Inc. Ab.	.20	.40	1.00	2.00

1/2 FRANC

NICKEL
Mint: Paris - w/o mint mark.

107	1965 small legends					
		184.834	—	—	.15	.30
	1965 large legends					
		Inc. Ab.	—	—	.15	.30
	1966	88.890	—	—	.15	.30
	1967	28.392	—	—	.15	.40
	1968	57.548	—	—	.15	.30
	1969	47.144	—	—	.15	.30
	1970	42.298	—	—	.15	.30
	1971	36.068	—	—	.15	.30
	1972	42.302	—	—	.15	.30
	1972 w/o O.ROTY					
		Inc. Ab.	25.00	50.00	100.00	150.00
	1973	48.372	—	—	.15	.30
	1974	37.072	—	—	.15	.30
	1975	22.752	—	—	.15	.40
	1976	115.314	—	—	.15	.30
	1977	131.644	—	—	.15	.30
	1978	63.360	—	—	.15	.30
	1979	.050	—	—	—	.50
	1980	.060	—	—	—	.50
	1981	.050	—	—	—	.50
	1982	.050	—	—	—	.50
	1983	50.000	—	—	.15	.30
	1984	80.000	—	—	.15	.30
	1985	—	—	—	—	1.50
	1986	—	—	—	—	1.50
	1987	—	—	—	—	.30
	1987	.015	—	—	Proof	4.00

FRANC

5.0000 g, .900 SILVER, .1446 oz ASW
Mint mark: A
Obv: BONAPARTE PREMIER CONSUL.

C#	Date	Mintage	VG	Fine	VF	XF
143.1	ANXI	.232	15.00	40.00	90.00	225.00
	AN12	1.311	10.00	25.00	80.00	175.00

Mint mark: BB

| 143.8 | AN12 | 5.737 | 125.00 | 300.00 | 500.00 | 850.00 |

Mint mark: D

143.2	ANXI	.012	30.00	60.00	140.00	275.00
	AN12	.053	15.00	35.00	90.00	225.00

Mint mark: G

143.3	ANXI	.013	125.00	300.00	600.00	1000.
	AN12	7.397	125.00	300.00	600.00	1000.

Mint mark: H

| 143.9 | AN12 | .057 | 15.00 | 35.00 | 90.00 | 225.00 |

Mint mark: I

| 143.10 | AN12 | .279 | 10.00 | 20.00 | 60.00 | 175.00 |

Mint mark: K

| 143.11 | AN12 | .102 | 15.00 | 30.00 | 80.00 | 200.00 |

Mint mark: L

143.4	ANXI	.022	25.00	55.00	130.00	275.00
	AN12	.125	12.00	25.00	70.00	190.00

Mint mark: M

| 143.12 | AN12 | .285 | 10.00 | 20.00 | 60.00 | 175.00 |

Mint mark: MA

143.5	ANXI	.012	30.00	60.00	140.00	275.00
	AN12	.141	15.00	35.00	80.00	200.00

Mint mark: Q

143.6	ANXI	.034	25.00	50.00	120.00	250.00
	AN12	.140	15.00	35.00	80.00	200.00

Mint mark: T

| 143.13 | AN12 | .046 | 20.00 | 40.00 | 100.00 | 225.00 |

Mint mark: U

| 143.14 | AN12 | 5.580 | 75.00 | 150.00 | 300.00 | 600.00 |

Mint mark: W

143.7	ANXI	5.756	75.00	150.00	300.00	600.00
	AN12	.028	25.00	50.00	100.00	250.00
	Common date				Unc.	400.00

FRANCE 559

Mint mark: A
Obv: NAPOLEON EMPEREUR.

C#	Date	Mintage	VG	Fine	VF	XF
153.1	AN12	.326	15.00	35.00	85.00	175.00
	AN13	2.454	12.00	25.00	65.00	150.00
	AN14	.298	20.00	45.00	100.00	200.00
	Mint mark: B					
153.2	AN12	.030	20.00	45.00	110.00	225.00
	AN13	2,906	35.00	70.00	150.00	300.00
	Mint mark: BB					
153.13	AN13	3,410	35.00	70.00	150.00	300.00
	AN14					
		491 pcs.	325.00	750.00	1250.	1750.
	Mint mark: D					
153.3	AN12	3,968	35.00	70.00	150.00	300.00
	AN13	.010	30.00	60.00	150.00	275.00
	AN14	2,450	40.00	85.00	175.00	350.00
	Mint mark: G					
153.14	AN13	.011	125.00	300.00	500.00	850.00
	Mint mark: H					
153.4	AN12	4,398	30.00	65.00	150.00	275.00
	AN13	.043	20.00	40.00	100.00	225.00
	AN14	7,164	35.00	75.00	150.00	300.00
	Mint mark: I					
153.5	AN12	.043	20.00	40.00	100.00	225.00
	AN13	.390	12.00	25.00	75.00	175.00
	AN14	2,847	40.00	85.00	175.00	350.00
	Mint mark: K					
153.6	AN12	.024	25.00	50.00	125.00	250.00
	AN13	.061	20.00	35.00	90.00	200.00
	AN14	1,526	50.00	100.00	200.00	400.00
	Mint mark: L					
153.7	AN12	4,253	30.00	65.00	150.00	275.00
	AN13	.073	20.00	35.00	90.00	200.00
	AN14	4,107	—	—	Rare	—
	Mint mark: M					
153.8	AN12	.300	15.00	30.00	80.00	175.00
	AN13	.651	12.00	25.00	70.00	160.00
	AN14	1,096	50.00	100.00	200.00	400.00
	Mint mark: MA					
153.9	AN12	5,582	30.00	65.00	150.00	300.00
	AN13	.028	20.00	50.00	125.00	250.00
	AN14	6,910	35.00	75.00	150.00	300.00
	Mint mark: Q					
153.10	AN12	.025	25.00	50.00	125.00	250.00
	AN13	.117	15.00	30.00	85.00	175.00
	Mint mark: T					
153.11	AN12	3,462	35.00	75.00	150.00	300.00
	AN13	.013	30.00	60.00	150.00	275.00
	Mint mark: U					
153.12	AN12	1,166	—	—	Rare	—
	AN13	.015	200.00	400.00	800.00	1200.
	AN14	4,667		3 known	Rare	—
	Mint mark: W					
153.15	AN13	.017	27.50	55.00	125.00	250.00
	AN14	4,667	50.00	100.00	200.00	400.00
	Common date				Unc.	350.00
	Mint mark: A					
153.16 (C153.2)	1806	.828	10.00	20.00	75.00	175.00
	Mint mark: B					
153.26	1807	3,465	35.00	75.00	175.00	350.00
	Mint mark: H					
153.17	1806	8,472	30.00	65.00	150.00	300.00
	1807	4,728	35.00	75.00	160.00	325.00
	Mint mark: I					
153.18	1806	.034	25.00	50.00	125.00	250.00
	1807	.011	30.00	60.00	150.00	275.00
	Mint mark: K					
153.19	1806	3,173	35.00	75.00	175.00	350.00
	1807	2,362	40.00	85.00	200.00	375.00
	Mint mark: L					
153.20	1806	.253	17.50	35.00	90.00	200.00
	1807	.177	20.00	40.00	100.00	225.00
	Mint mark: M					
153.21	1806	1,066	50.00	100.00	200.00	400.00
	1807	.023	25.00	50.00	125.00	250.00
	Mint mark: MA					
153.22	1806	1,010	50.00	100.00	200.00	400.00
	1807	1,493	50.00	100.00	200.00	400.00
	Mint mark: Q					
153.23	1806	.016	25.00	50.00	125.00	275.00
	1807	9,659	30.00	65.00	150.00	300.00
	Mint mark: U					
153.24	1806	.015	50.00	100.00	200.00	400.00
	1807	.011	100.00	200.00	300.00	600.00

Mint mark: W

C#	Date	Mintage	VG	Fine	VF	XF
153.25	1806	.028	25.00	50.00	125.00	250.00
	1807	.015	25.00	50.00	125.00	275.00
	Common date				Unc.	350.00

Mint mark: A
Negro head.

153a	1807	.100	100.00	200.00	400.00	800.00

Laureate head.

153b.1	1807	.050	50.00	100.00	250.00	600.00
	1808	4.599	6.00	12.00	40.00	100.00
	Mint mark: B					
153b.2	1808	.765	7.50	15.00	50.00	150.00
	Mint mark: BB					
153b.3	1808	2.126	6.00	12.00	40.00	125.00
	Mint mark: D					
153b.4	1808	.752	7.50	15.00	50.00	150.00
	Mint mark: H					
153b.5	1808	.316	8.00	17.50	55.00	150.00
	Mint mark: I					
153b.6	1808	.256	10.00	20.00	60.00	150.00
	Mint mark: K					
153b.7	1808	.228	10.00	20.00	60.00	150.00
	Mint mark: L					
153b.8	1808	.016	30.00	60.00	125.00	275.00
	Mint mark: M					
153b.9	1808	.130	12.00	25.00	75.00	175.00
	Mint mark: MA					
153b.10	1808	.029	20.00	40.00	100.00	250.00
	Mint mark: Q					
153b.11	1808	.064	17.50	35.00	90.00	225.00
	Mint mark: T					
153b.12	1808	.106	12.00	25.00	80.00	200.00
	Mint mark: U					
153b.13	1808	.013	100.00	200.00	400.00	900.00
	Mint mark: W					
153b.14	1808	2.422	6.00	12.00	40.00	125.00
	Common date				Unc.	300.00

Mint mark: A

163.1	1809	.980	6.00	12.00	40.00	125.00
	1810	1.676	6.00	12.00	40.00	125.00
	1811	1.347	6.00	12.00	40.00	125.00
	1812	.563	7.50	15.00	45.00	140.00
	1813	.446	7.50	15.00	45.00	140.00
	1814	.042	20.00	40.00	125.00	250.00
	Mint mark: B					
163.2	1809	.202	10.00	20.00	50.00	150.00
	1810	.167	12.00	22.50	60.00	160.00
	1811	.253	10.00	20.00	50.00	150.00
	1812	.118	12.00	25.00	65.00	175.00
	1813	.061	12.00	27.50	70.00	175.00
	Mint mark: BB					
163.12	1810	4,336	30.00	60.00	125.00	325.00
	1811	.012	20.00	45.00	90.00	225.00
	1812	5,571	25.00	50.00	120.00	300.00
	Mint mark: CL					
163.17	1813	7,229	40.00	80.00	200.00	400.00
	Mint mark: D					
163.3	1809	.047	15.00	30.00	80.00	200.00
	1810	.039	15.00	30.00	80.00	200.00
	1811	.242	10.00	20.00	50.00	150.00
	1812	.147	12.00	22.50	60.00	160.00
	1813	.078	12.00	25.00	65.00	175.00
	Mint mark: H					
163.4	1809	.034	17.50	35.00	90.00	225.00
	1810	.016	20.00	40.00	100.00	250.00
	1811	.105	12.00	25.00	65.00	175.00
	1812	.165	10.00	22.00	60.00	160.00
	1813	.096	12.00	25.00	65.00	175.00

Mint mark: I

C#	Date	Mintage	VG	Fine	VF	XF
163.13	1810	.018	20.00	40.00	100.00	250.00
	1811	.085	12.00	25.00	65.00	175.00
	1812	.091	12.00	25.00	65.00	175.00
	1813	.076	15.00	27.50	75.00	175.00
	Mint mark: K					
163.5	1809	.074	12.00	25.00	65.00	175.00
	1810	.093	12.00	25.00	65.00	175.00
	1811	.048	15.00	30.00	80.00	200.00
	1812	.041	15.00	30.00	80.00	200.00
	1813	.068	12.00	25.00	70.00	175.00
	Mint mark: L					
163.6	1809	.028	17.50	35.00	90.00	225.00
	1810	.047	15.00	30.00	80.00	200.00
	1810(TR)	I.A.	—	—	Unique	—
	1811	.188	10.00	22.00	60.00	160.00
	1812	.047	15.00	30.00	80.00	200.00
	1813	.033	17.50	35.00	90.00	225.00
	Mint mark: M					
163.7	1809	8,855	25.00	50.00	125.00	300.00
	1810	.035	15.00	30.00	80.00	200.00
	1811	.081	12.00	25.00	65.00	175.00
	1812	.125	10.00	22.00	60.00	160.00
	1813	.181	10.00	22.00	60.00	160.00
	1814	.029	25.00	50.00	125.00	275.00
	Mint mark: MA					
163.8	1809	.020	20.00	40.00	100.00	250.00
	1810	.028	17.50	35.00	90.00	225.00
	1811	.044	15.00	30.00	80.00	200.00
	1812	.036	15.00	30.00	80.00	200.00
	1813	.044	15.00	30.00	80.00	200.00
	Mint mark: Q					
163.9	1809	.163	10.00	22.00	60.00	160.00
	1810	.073	12.00	25.00	65.00	175.00
	1811	.161	10.00	22.00	60.00	160.00
	1812	.034	17.50	35.00	90.00	225.00
	1813	.075	12.00	25.00	70.00	175.00
	Mint mark: R					
163.15	1812	.012	75.00	150.00	350.00	650.00
	1813	779 pcs.	175.00	300.00	500.00	1000.
	Mint mark: T					
163.14	1811	.042	15.00	30.00	80.00	200.00
	1812	.041	15.00	30.00	80.00	200.00
	1813	.020	15.00	30.00	80.00	200.00
	Mint mark: U					
163.10	1809	5,549	50.00	100.00	175.00	350.00
	1810	10,200	200.00	—	—	—
	1812	.021	100.00	200.00	450.00	800.00
	1813	6,065	—	—	Rare	—
	Mint mark: W					
163.11	1809	.196	10.00	22.00	60.00	160.00
	1810	.187	10.00	22.00	60.00	160.00
	1811	.265	10.00	20.00	50.00	150.00
	1812	.143	10.00	22.00	60.00	160.00
	1813	.093	12.00	25.00	65.00	175.00
	Mint mark: Flag					
163.16	1812	.012	100.00	175.00	350.00	700.00
	1813	.069	60.00	125.00	250.00	500.00
	Common date				Unc.	300.00

Mint mark: A

179.1	1816	.253	7.50	15.00	50.00	125.00
	1817	.178	9.00	17.50	55.00	140.00
	1818	.060	10.00	22.00	65.00	160.00
	1819	.027	15.00	27.50	75.00	175.00
	1820	.028	15.00	27.50	75.00	175.00
	1821	.100	10.00	20.00	60.00	150.00
	1822	.635	6.00	12.00	45.00	125.00
	1823	.360	7.50	15.00	50.00	125.00
	1824	.417	6.00	12.00	45.00	125.00
	Mint mark: B					
179.2	1816	.016	17.50	35.00	90.00	225.00
	1817	.031	15.00	27.50	75.00	175.00
	1818	3,866	25.00	50.00	125.00	300.00
	1819	.010	25.00	40.00	100.00	250.00
	1820	.016	17.50	35.00	90.00	225.00
	1822	.031	15.00	27.50	75.00	175.00
	1823	7,577	20.00	40.00	100.00	250.00
	1824	.066	10.00	22.00	65.00	160.00
	Mint mark: D					
179.9	1817	5,362	22.00	45.00	100.00	250.00
	1823	3,485	25.00	50.00	125.00	300.00
	1824	.030	15.00	27.50	75.00	175.00
	Mint mark: H					
179.10	1817	.048	12.00	25.00	70.00	150.00
	1818	8,477	20.00	40.00	100.00	250.00
	1819	8,141	20.00	40.00	100.00	250.00
	1820	6,709	22.00	45.00	100.00	250.00
	1821	5,083	22.00	45.00	100.00	250.00
	1822	.016	17.50	35.00	90.00	200.00
	1823	.014	17.50	35.00	90.00	200.00
	1824	.033	15.00	27.50	75.00	175.00

FRANCE 560

Mint mark: I

C#	Date	Mintage	VG	Fine	VF	XF
179.3	1816	5,041	22.00	45.00	100.00	250.00
	1823	5,273	22.00	45.00	100.00	250.00
	1824	.033	15.00	27.50	75.00	175.00

Mint mark: K

C#	Date	Mintage	VG	Fine	VF	XF
179.11	1817	.307	7.50	15.00	50.00	125.00
	1820	.020	15.00	30.00	80.00	200.00
	1823	5,173	22.00	45.00	100.00	250.00
	1824	.123	10.00	17.50	55.00	140.00

Mint mark: L

C#	Date	Mintage	VG	Fine	VF	XF
179.4	1816	5,770	22.00	45.00	100.00	250.00
	1817	5,059	22.00	45.00	100.00	250.00
	1818	1,450	35.00	70.00	150.00	350.00
	1823	.036	12.00	25.00	70.00	150.00
	1824	.054	10.00	22.00	65.00	150.00

Mint mark: M

C#	Date	Mintage	VG	Fine	VF	XF
179.5	1816	.070	10.00	20.00	60.00	150.00
	1817	.021	15.00	30.00	80.00	200.00
	1823	.036	12.00	25.00	70.00	150.00
	1824	.059	10.00	22.00	65.00	150.00

Mint mark: MA

C#	Date	Mintage	VG	Fine	VF	XF
179.12	1824	7,209	20.00	40.00	100.00	250.00

Mint mark: Q

C#	Date	Mintage	VG	Fine	VF	XF
179.6	1816	.025	15.00	27.50	75.00	175.00
	1817	5,045	22.00	45.00	100.00	250.00
	1819	.013	17.50	35.00	90.00	200.00
	1820	.022	15.00	30.00	80.00	200.00
	1821	4,942	25.00	50.00	125.00	300.00
	1822	3,838	25.00	50.00	125.00	300.00
	1823	.033	15.00	27.50	75.00	175.00
	1824	.052	10.00	22.00	65.00	150.00

Mint mark: T

C#	Date	Mintage	VG	Fine	VF	XF
179.7	1816	2,240	30.00	60.00	150.00	325.00
	1818	1,728	30.00	60.00	150.00	325.00
	1819	4,094	25.00	50.00	125.00	300.00

Mint mark: W

C#	Date	Mintage	VG	Fine	VF	XF
179.8	1816	.015	17.50	35.00	90.00	200.00
	1817	.019	15.00	30.00	80.00	200.00
	1818	.016	17.50	35.00	90.00	200.00
	1819	.024	15.00	30.00	80.00	200.00
	1820	.013	17.50	35.00	90.00	225.00
	1821	.200	10.00	20.00	55.00	140.00
	1822	.061	10.00	22.00	65.00	150.00
	1823	.277	7.50	15.00	50.00	125.00
	1824	.388	7.50	15.00	50.00	125.00
	Common date				Unc.	300.00

Mint mark: A

C#	Date	Mintage	VG	Fine	VF	XF
187.1	1825	.335	7.50	15.00	50.00	125.00
	1826	.326	7.50	15.00	50.00	125.00
	1827	.431	6.00	12.00	45.00	120.00
	1828	.517	6.00	12.00	45.00	120.00
	1829	.290	7.50	15.00	50.00	125.00
	1830	.234	7.50	15.00	50.00	125.00
	1830 reeded edge	—	—	—	Rare	—

Mint mark: B

C#	Date	Mintage	VG	Fine	VF	XF
187.2	1825	.017	15.00	30.00	80.00	200.00
	1826	.020	15.00	30.00	80.00	200.00
	1827	.096	10.00	20.00	60.00	150.00
	1828	.070	10.00	22.00	65.00	160.00
	1829	.124	8.00	17.50	55.00	140.00
	1830	.075	10.00	20.00	60.00	150.00

Mint mark: BB

C#	Date	Mintage	VG	Fine	VF	XF
187.3	1825	9,256	20.00	40.00	100.00	250.00
	1826	.012	20.00	40.00	100.00	250.00
	1827	.013	17.50	35.00	90.00	225.00
	1828	.024	15.00	30.00	80.00	200.00
	1829	.021	15.00	30.00	80.00	200.00

Mint mark: D

C#	Date	Mintage	VG	Fine	VF	XF
187.4	1825	.040	12.00	25.00	70.00	170.00
	1826	.028	15.00	27.50	75.00	175.00
	1827	.036	12.00	25.00	70.00	170.00
	1828	.076	10.00	20.00	60.00	150.00
	1829	.031	15.00	27.50	75.00	175.00

Mint mark: H

C#	Date	Mintage	VG	Fine	VF	XF
187.5	1825	.023	15.00	30.00	80.00	200.00
	1826	.028	15.00	27.50	75.00	175.00
	1827	5,444	22.00	45.00	100.00	250.00
	1828	.027	15.00	27.50	75.00	175.00
	1829	.051	10.00	22.00	65.00	150.00

Mint mark: I

C#	Date	Mintage	VG	Fine	VF	XF
187.6	1825	6,663	22.00	45.00	100.00	250.00
	1826	4,206	25.00	50.00	125.00	300.00
	1827	6,850	22.00	45.00	100.00	250.00
	1828	5,236	22.00	45.00	100.00	250.00
	1829	.020	15.00	30.00	80.00	200.00
	1830	1,025	35.00	75.00	150.00	350.00

Mint mark: K

C#	Date	Mintage	VG	Fine	VF	XF
187.7	1825	.024	15.00	30.00	80.00	200.00
	1826	.038	12.00	25.00	70.00	170.00
	1827	.044	12.00	25.00	70.00	170.00
187.7	1828	.132	8.00	17.50	55.00	140.00
	1829	.050	12.00	25.00	70.00	170.00
	1830	.021	15.00	30.00	80.00	200.00

Mint mark: L

C#	Date	Mintage	VG	Fine	VF	XF
187.8	1825	3,830	25.00	50.00	125.00	300.00
	1826	.028	15.00	27.50	75.00	175.00
	1827	.047	12.00	25.00	70.00	170.00
	1828	.044	12.00	25.00	70.00	170.00
	1829	.033	15.00	27.50	75.00	175.00
	1830	.013	17.50	35.00	90.00	225.00

Mint mark: M

C#	Date	Mintage	VG	Fine	VF	XF
187.9	1825	6,069	22.00	45.00	100.00	250.00
	1826	.031	15.00	27.50	75.00	175.00
	1827	.024	15.00	30.00	80.00	200.00
	1828	.072	10.00	20.00	60.00	150.00
	1829	.046	12.00	25.00	70.00	170.00
	1830	.021	15.00	30.00	80.00	200.00

Mint mark: MA

C#	Date	Mintage	VG	Fine	VF	XF
187.13	1829	.066	10.00	22.00	65.00	160.00

Mint mark: Q

C#	Date	Mintage	VG	Fine	VF	XF
187.10	1825	5,653	22.00	45.00	100.00	250.00
	1826	.025	15.00	27.50	75.00	175.00
	1827	.020	17.50	35.00	90.00	225.00
	1828	.018	15.00	30.00	80.00	200.00
	1829	.013	17.50	35.00	90.00	225.00

Mint mark: T

C#	Date	Mintage	VG	Fine	VF	XF
187.12	1826	5,930	22.00	45.00	100.00	250.00
	1827	.014	17.50	35.00	90.00	225.00
	1828	.036	12.00	25.00	70.00	170.00
	1829	.014	17.50	35.00	90.00	225.00
	1830	8,871	20.00	40.00	100.00	250.00

Mint mark: W

C#	Date	Mintage	VG	Fine	VF	XF
187.11	1825	.078	10.00	20.00	60.00	150.00
	1826	.130	8.00	17.50	55.00	140.00
	1827	.519	6.00	12.00	40.00	120.00
	1828	.418	6.00	12.00	45.00	120.00
	1829	.149	8.00	17.50	55.00	140.00
	1830	.078	10.00	20.00	60.00	150.00
	Common date				Unc.	275.00

C#	Date	Mintage	VG	Fine	VF	XF
	Mint mark: A					
200.1	1831	.202	20.00	45.00	90.00	250.00
	Mint mark: B					
200.2	1831	.400	20.00	45.00	90.00	250.00
	Mint mark: BB					
200.3	1831	.018	35.00	75.00	200.00	400.00
	Mint mark: D					
200.4	1831	.127	27.50	55.00	125.00	300.00
	Mint mark: H					
200.5	1831	.027	30.00	70.00	150.00	350.00
	Mint mark: I					
200.6	1831	.021	35.00	75.00	175.00	375.00
	Mint mark: K					
200.7	1831	.053	25.00	60.00	125.00	300.00
	Mint mark: L					
200.8	1831	2,406	60.00	125.00	250.00	500.00
	Mint mark: M					
200.9	1831	.038	30.00	65.00	150.00	325.00
	Mint mark: Q					
200.10	1831	.018	35.00	75.00	200.00	400.00
	Mint mark: T					
200.11	1831	.043	40.00	65.00	150.00	325.00
	Mint mark: W					
200.12	1831	.453	20.00	45.00	100.00	250.00
	Common date				Unc.	450.00

Mint mark: A
Laureate head

C#	Date	Mintage	Fine	VF	XF	Unc
201.1	1832	.379	10.00	25.00	50.00	150.00
	1833	.114	10.00	25.00	50.00	160.00
	1834	.330	10.00	25.00	50.00	160.00
	1835	.483	10.00	25.00	50.00	160.00
	1836	.138	10.00	25.00	50.00	175.00
	1837	.241	12.00	30.00	60.00	160.00
	1838	.183	12.00	30.00	60.00	175.00
	1839	.243	12.00	30.00	60.00	160.00
	1840	.481	10.00	25.00	50.00	160.00
	1841	.623	10.00	25.00	50.00	160.00
	1842	.130	12.00	30.00	60.00	175.00
201.1	1843	.074	12.00	35.00	70.00	185.00
	1844	.072	12.00	35.00	70.00	185.00
	1845	.215	12.00	30.00	60.00	175.00
	1846	1.225	10.00	25.00	50.00	160.00
	1847	2.401	10.00	25.00	50.00	160.00
	1848	.228	12.00	35.00	70.00	185.00

Mint mark: B

C#	Date	Mintage	Fine	VF	XF	Unc
201.2	1832	.197	15.00	45.00	90.00	160.00
	1833	.098	12.00	35.00	70.00	175.00
	1834	.146	10.00	25.00	50.00	160.00
	1835	.103	12.00	30.00	60.00	175.00
	1836	.093	12.00	35.00	70.00	185.00
	1837	.212	12.00	30.00	60.00	160.00
	1838	.145	12.00	30.00	60.00	175.00
	1839	.184	12.00	30.00	60.00	175.00
	1840	.148	10.00	25.00	50.00	160.00
	1841	.663	10.00	25.00	50.00	160.00
	1842	.158	12.00	30.00	60.00	175.00
	1843	.130	12.00	30.00	60.00	175.00
	1844	.045	15.00	45.00	90.00	200.00
	1845	.882	10.00	25.00	50.00	160.00
	1846	.818	10.00	25.00	50.00	160.00

Mint mark: BB

C#	Date	Mintage	Fine	VF	XF	Unc
201.3	1832	.042	15.00	40.00	90.00	185.00
	1833	.079	12.00	35.00	70.00	175.00
	1834	.068	12.00	35.00	70.00	175.00
	1835	.046	12.00	35.00	70.00	185.00
	1836	.050	12.00	35.00	70.00	185.00
	1837	.013	20.00	50.00	100.00	200.00
	1838	.024	15.00	40.00	80.00	160.00
	1839	.043	12.00	35.00	70.00	185.00
	1840	.017	20.00	50.00	100.00	200.00
	1841	.053	12.00	35.00	70.00	185.00
	1842	.244	12.00	30.00	60.00	175.00
	1843	.072	12.00	35.00	70.00	185.00
	1844	.076	12.00	35.00	70.00	185.00
	1845	.083	12.00	35.00	70.00	185.00
	1846	.024	20.00	50.00	100.00	200.00
	1847	.068	12.00	35.00	70.00	185.00
	1848	.021	25.00	60.00	125.00	250.00

Mint mark: D

C#	Date	Mintage	Fine	VF	XF	Unc
201.4	1832	.127	10.00	25.00	50.00	160.00
	1833	.024	15.00	40.00	80.00	185.00
	1834	.059	12.00	35.00	70.00	175.00
	1835	.052	12.00	35.00	70.00	175.00
	1836	.019	20.00	50.00	100.00	200.00
	1837	2,531	—	—	—	—
	1838	.012	22.50	45.00	90.00	185.00
	1839	.011	22.50	50.00	100.00	200.00
	1840	7,130	40.00	80.00	150.00	300.00

Mint mark: H

C#	Date	Mintage	Fine	VF	XF	Unc
201.5	1832	.080	12.00	30.00	60.00	175.00
	1833	.026	15.00	40.00	80.00	185.00
	1834	.079	12.00	30.00	60.00	175.00
	1835	.017	15.00	40.00	80.00	185.00

Mint mark: I

C#	Date	Mintage	Fine	VF	XF	Unc
201.6	1832	.037	15.00	40.00	80.00	185.00
	1833	.034	15.00	40.00	80.00	185.00
	1834	.045	12.00	30.00	60.00	175.00
	1835	.048	12.00	30.00	60.00	175.00

Mint mark: K

C#	Date	Mintage	Fine	VF	XF	Unc
201.7	1832	.035	15.00	40.00	80.00	185.00
	1833	.030	15.00	40.00	80.00	185.00
	1834	.070	12.00	30.00	60.00	175.00
	1835	.058	12.00	30.00	60.00	175.00
	1836	.040	12.00	30.00	60.00	175.00
	1837	.034	15.00	40.00	80.00	185.00
	1838	.017	20.00	50.00	100.00	200.00
	1839	.048	12.00	30.00	60.00	175.00
	1840	.048	12.00	30.00	60.00	175.00
	1841	.042	12.00	30.00	60.00	175.00
	1842	.032	15.00	40.00	80.00	185.00
	1843	.039	15.00	40.00	80.00	185.00
	1844	.023	20.00	50.00	100.00	200.00
	1845	.023	20.00	50.00	100.00	200.00
	1846	.023	20.00	50.00	100.00	200.00
	1847	*6,787	—	300.00	—	—

***NOTE:** One piece extant.

Mint mark: L

C#	Date	Mintage	Fine	VF	XF	Unc
201.8	1832	.031	15.00	30.00	60.00	175.00
	1833	.018	20.00	40.00	80.00	185.00
	1834	.012	22.50	45.00	90.00	200.00
	1835	3,647	80.00	180.00	350.00	—

Mint mark: M

C#	Date	Mintage	Fine	VF	XF	Unc
201.9	1832	.051	15.00	40.00	80.00	185.00
	1833	.049	12.00	30.00	60.00	175.00
	1834	.037	15.00	40.00	80.00	185.00
	1835	.025	15.00	40.00	80.00	185.00

Mint mark: MA

C#	Date	Mintage	Fine	VF	XF	Unc
201.10	1832	.078	12.00	30.00	60.00	175.00
	1833	.057	12.00	30.00	60.00	175.00
	1834	.018	20.00	50.00	100.00	200.00
	1835	.012	22.50	60.00	120.00	225.00
	1837	—	—	—	Rare	—
	1838	.020	20.00	50.00	100.00	200.00

Mint mark: Q

C#	Date	Mintage	Fine	VF	XF	Unc
201.11	1832	—	—	—	Rare	—
	1833	.019	20.00	50.00	100.00	200.00
	1834	.057	12.00	30.00	60.00	175.00

Mint mark: T

C#	Date	Mintage	Fine	VF	XF	Unc
201.12	1832	.034	15.00	40.00	80.00	185.00
	1833	.031	15.00	40.00	80.00	185.00
	1834	.102	12.00	30.00	60.00	175.00
	1835	.051	10.00	30.00	60.00	175.00

FRANCE 561

Mint mark: W

C#	Date	Mintage	Fine	VF	XF	Unc
201.13	1832	.155	10.00	25.00	50.00	160.00
	1833	.213	10.00	25.00	50.00	160.00
	1834	.608	10.00	25.00	50.00	160.00
	1835	.206	10.00	25.00	50.00	160.00
	1836	.049	10.00	30.00	60.00	175.00
	1837	.266	12.00	30.00	60.00	175.00
	1838	.162	12.00	30.00	60.00	175.00
	1839	.120	10.00	30.00	60.00	160.00
	1840	.079	12.00	30.00	60.00	175.00
	1841	.321	10.00	25.00	50.00	160.00
	1842	.195	12.00	30.00	60.00	175.00
	1843	.271	12.00	30.00	60.00	175.00
	1844	.381	10.00	25.00	50.00	160.00
	1845	.478	10.00	25.00	50.00	160.00
	1846	.074	12.00	30.00	60.00	175.00

Mint mark: A
Second Republic

Y#	Date	Mintage	Fine	VF	XF	Unc
4.1	1849	1.289	12.50	25.00	60.00	120.00
	1850	1.041	20.00	40.00	75.00	150.00
	1851	.638	20.00	40.00	75.00	150.00

Mint mark: BB

| 4.2 | 1849 | .015 | 80.00 | 200.00 | 375.00 | 800.00 |
| | 1850 | .213 | 40.00 | 80.00 | 175.00 | 400.00 |

Mint mark: K

| 4.3 | 1849 | .019 | 80.00 | 200.00 | 375.00 | 850.00 |
| | 1850 | .035 | 50.00 | 100.00 | 300.00 | 600.00 |

Mint mark: A
President Louis-Napoleon

| 12 | 1852 | 1.015 | 35.00 | 70.00 | 150.00 | 325.00 |

Second Empire - Napoleon III

24.1	1853 lg. head					
		.183	50.00	125.00	250.00	400.00
	1853 lg. head	—	—	—	Proof	325.00
	1853 sm. head					
	Inc. Ab.	75.00	150.00	300.00	600.00
	1854	.764	25.00	50.00	150.00	350.00
	1855(d)	.757	25.00	50.00	150.00	350.00
	1855(a)	I.A.	25.00	50.00	150.00	350.00
	1856	1.196	20.00	40.00	100.00	250.00
	1857	1.681	20.00	40.00	100.00	250.00
	1858	5.607	10.00	20.00	50.00	200.00
	1859	3.830	12.50	25.00	70.00	200.00
	1860(h)	2.740	12.50	25.00	70.00	200.00
	1860(b)	I.A.	12.50	25.00	70.00	200.00
	1861	2.012	50.00	125.00	250.00	500.00
	1863	.019	—	—	—	—
	1864	.022	—	—	—	—

Mint mark: BB

24.2	1856	1.635	15.00	40.00	100.00	250.00
	1859	1.333	15.00	40.00	100.00	250.00
	1860	I.A.	15.00	40.00	125.00	300.00
	1861	.218	75.00	175.00	400.00	800.00
	1862	1.124	60.00	140.00	275.00	550.00
	1863	.054	80.00	200.00	450.00	900.00

Mint mark: D

| 24.3 | 1856 | 1.227 | 15.00 | 40.00 | 100.00 | 250.00 |

5.0000 g, .835 SILVER, .1342 oz ASW
Mint mark: A
Laureate head.

| 30.1 | 1866 | 14.638 | 4.00 | 8.00 | 15.00 | 60.00 |
| | 1867 | 12.131 | 4.00 | 8.00 | 15.00 | 60.00 |

Y#	Date	Mintage	Fine	VF	XF	Unc
30.1	1868	14.942	4.00	8.00	15.00	60.00
	1869	2.935	6.00	12.00	30.00	100.00
	1870	.788	—	—	—	—

Mint mark: BB

30.2	1866	7.204	4.00	8.00	15.00	60.00
	1867	7.295	4.00	8.00	15.00	60.00
	1868	10.230	4.00	8.00	15.00	60.00
	1869	3.094	6.00	12.00	30.00	100.00
	1870	1.992	10.00	17.50	50.00	150.00

Mint mark: K

30.3	1866	1.402	8.00	15.00	35.00	100.00
	1867	6.092	5.00	10.00	20.00	75.00
	1868	.022	100.00	250.00	375.00	750.00

Mint mark: A
Third Republic

49.1	1871 small A					
		2.980	2.00	3.50	12.00	50.00
	1871 large A					
	Inc. Ab.	2.00	3.50	12.00	50.00
	1872 small A					
		10.129	2.00	3.50	12.00	45.00
	1872 large A					
	Inc. Ab.	2.00	3.50	12.00	45.00
	1878	30 pcs.	—	—	Proof	3000.
	1881	2.010	2.00	3.50	12.00	55.00
	1887	3.292	2.00	3.50	12.00	45.00
	1888	3.244	2.00	3.50	12.00	45.00
	1889	100 pcs.	—	—	Proof	3500.
	1894	1.600	2.00	3.50	12.00	60.00
	1895	3.200	2.00	3.50	10.00	45.00

Mint mark: K

49.2	1871 small K					
		1.252	2.00	4.00	15.00	75.00
	1871 large K					
	Inc. Ab.	2.00	4.00	15.00	75.00
	1872 large K					
		5.779	2.00	3.50	12.00	50.00
	1872 small K					
	Inc. Ab.	2.00	3.50	12.00	50.00
	1873	.019	80.00	200.00	350.00	700.00

Mint: Paris - w/o mint mark.

63.1	1898	15.000	2.00	3.00	6.00	25.00
	1898	—	—	—	Proof	400.00
	1899	11.000	2.00	4.00	8.00	30.00
	1900	.099	75.00	150.00	350.00	700.00
	1900	—	—	—	Proof	300.00
	1901	6.200	3.00	6.00	12.00	65.00
	1902	6.000	3.00	6.00	12.00	70.00
	1903	.472	25.00	50.00	175.00	400.00
	1904	7.000	3.00	6.00	12.00	65.00
	1905	6.004	3.00	6.00	12.00	70.00
	1906	1.908	7.50	15.00	40.00	125.00
	1907	2.563	4.00	8.00	16.00	75.00
	1908	3.961	3.00	6.00	12.00	60.00
	1909	10.924	2.00	3.00	7.50	30.00
	1910	7.725	2.00	3.00	7.50	35.00
	1911	5.542	2.00	3.00	7.50	35.00
	1912	10.001	2.00	3.00	6.00	25.00
	1913	13.654	1.00	2.00	4.00	15.00
	1914	14.361	1.00	2.00	4.00	14.00
	1915	47.955	1.00	1.25	1.75	6.00
	1916	92.029	1.00	1.25	1.75	5.00
	1917	57.153	1.00	1.25	1.75	5.00
	1918	50.112	1.00	1.25	1.75	5.00
	1919	46.112	1.00	1.25	1.75	5.00
	1920	19.322	1.00	1.50	2.25	7.00

Mint mark: C

| 63.2 | 1914 | .043 | 100.00 | 225.00 | 450.00 | 700.00 |

ALUMINUM-BRONZE
Mint: Paris - w/o mint mark.
Chamber of Commerce

78	1920	.590	1.50	3.00	8.00	25.00
	1921	54.572	.15	.25	1.00	6.00
	1922	111.343	.15	.25	1.00	6.00
	1923	140.138	.15	.25	1.00	5.00

Y#	Date	Mintage	Fine	VF	XF	Unc
78	1924	87.715	.15	.25	1.00	6.00
	1925	36.523	.15	.25	1.00	6.00
	1926	1.580	1.50	3.00	8.00	25.00
	1927	11.330	.25	.50	2.00	8.00
	1928	.405	—	—	—	—

81	1931	15.504	.15	.25	1.00	4.00
	1932	29.768	.15	.25	1.00	4.00
	1933	15.356	.15	.25	1.00	4.00
	1934	17.286	.15	.25	1.00	4.00
	1935	1.166	7.50	15.00	30.00	60.00
	1936	23.817	.15	.25	1.00	3.00
	1937	30.940	.15	.25	1.00	3.00
	1938	66.165	.15	.25	1.00	3.00
	1939	48.434	.15	.25	1.00	3.00
	1940	25.525	.15	.25	1.00	3.00
	1941	34.705	.15	.25	1.00	3.00

ALUMINUM

81a.1	1941	60.877	.10	.20	.50	4.00
	1943	4.400	—	—	Rare	—
	1944	22.608	.10	.20	.50	4.00
	1945	61.780	.10	.15	.25	2.50
	1946	52.516	.10	.15	.25	2.50
	1947	110.448	.10	.15	.25	2.50
	1948	96.092	.10	.15	.25	2.50
	1949	41.090	.10	.15	.25	2.50
	1950	27.882	.10	.15	.25	2.50
	1957	16.497	.10	.15	.25	1.50
	1958	21.197	.10	.15	.25	1.50
	1959	41.985	.10	.15	.25	1.50

Mint mark: B

81a.2	1944	1.725				
	1945	4.251	.50	1.50	3.00	10.00
	1946	26.493	.10	.20	.50	2.50
	1947	51.562	.10	.20	.50	2.50
	1948	45.481	.10	.20	.50	2.50
	1949	35.840	.10	.20	.50	2.50
	1950	18.800	.10	.20	.50	2.50
	1957	63.976	.10	.20	.50	1.50
	1958	13.412	.10	.20	.50	1.50

Mint mark: C

81a.3	1944	33.600	.25	.50	1.50	10.00
	1945	5.220	.35	.75	2.00	10.00
	1946	9.669				

ZINC
Mint mark: A

| 81b | 1943 | *.017 | 150.00 | 300.00 | 500.00 | 900.00 |

*NOTE: Struck for Colonial use in Africa.

ALUMINUM
Mint: Paris - w/o mint mark.
Vichy French State Issues

V95.1	1942 LB	102.972	.10	.15	.25	2.00
	1942	Inc. Ab.	—	—	—	—
	1943	175.886	.10	.15	.25	2.00
	1943 thin flan					
		Inc. Ab.	.10	.15	.25	2.00
	1944	50.605	.10	.15	.25	2.50

Mint mark: B

| V95.2 | 1943 | 68.082 | 10.00 | 20.00 | 40.00 | 60.00 |
| | 1944 | 13.622 | .50 | 1.50 | 5.00 | 15.00 |

Mint mark: C

| V95.3 | 1943 | 29.678 | — | — | — | — |
| | 1944 | 74.859 | .15 | .25 | 1.50 | 7.50 |

NOTE: Mint mark varieties exist.

NICKEL
Mint: Paris - w/o mint mark.
1 New Franc = 100 Old Francs
Fifth Republic

108	1960	406.375	—	—	.20	.40
	1961	119.611	—	—	.20	.40
	1962	14.015	—	—	.20	.50
	1964	77.425	—	—	.20	.40
	1965	44.252	—	—	.20	.40
	1966	38.038	—	—	.20	.40

FRANCE 562

Y#	Date	Mintage	Fine	VF	XF	Unc
108	1967	11.320	—	—	.20	.50
	1968	51.550	—	—	.20	.40
	1969	70.595	—	—	.20	.40
	1970	42.560	—	—	.20	.40
	1971	42.475	—	—	.20	.40
	1972	48.250	—	—	.20	.40
	1973	70.000	—	—	.20	.40
	1974	82.235	—	—	.20	.40
	1975	101.685	—	—	.20	.40
	1976	192.520	—	—	.20	.40
	1977	230.085	—	—	.20	.40
	1978	136.580	—	—	.20	.40
	1979	.050	—	—	—	.60
	1980	.060	—	—	—	.60
	1981	.050	—	—	—	.60
	1982	.050	—	—	—	.60
	1983	.100	—	—	—	.60
	1984	.050	—	—	—	.60
	1985	—	—	—	—	2.00
	1986	—	—	—	—	2.00
	1987	—	—	—	—	.40
	1987	.015	—	—	Proof	4.50

30th Anniversary of Fifth Republic

Y#	Date	Mintage				Unc
129	1988	50.000				.20

22.2000 g, .900 SILVER, .6424 oz ASW
30th Anniversary of Fifth Republic
Similar to KM#129.

130	1988	.060			Proof	60.00

9.0000 g, .920 GOLD, .2662 oz AGW
30th Anniversary of Fifth Republic
Similar to KM#129.

131	1988	.020			Proof	265.00

2 FRANCS

10.0000 g, .900 SILVER, .2893 oz ASW
Mint mark: A
Obv: BONAPARTE PREMIER CONSUL.

C#	Date	Mintage	VG	Fine	VF	XF
144.1	AN12	.187	40.00	70.00	140.00	400.00
	AN12	—	—	—	Proof	2250.

Mint mark: BB

144.2	AN12	1,965	75.00	125.00	250.00	750.00

Mint mark: D

144.3	AN12	2,672	—	Reported, not confirmed		

Mint mark: G

144.4	AN12	2,859	60.00	120.00	250.00	650.00

Mint mark: H

144.5	AN12	.012	40.00	85.00	175.00	600.00

Mint mark: I

144.6	AN12	.102	40.00	75.00	150.00	475.00

Mint mark: K

144.7	AN12	.026	40.00	85.00	175.00	525.00

Mint mark: L

144.8	AN12	.015	40.00	85.00	175.00	575.00

Mint mark: M

144.9	AN12	.066	40.00	80.00	160.00	500.00

Mint mark: MA

144.10	AN12	6,804	50.00	100.00	200.00	600.00

Mint mark: Q

144.11	AN12	.021	40.00	80.00	170.00	500.00

Mint mark: T

144.12	AN12	4,484	—	Reported, not confirmed		

Mint mark: U

144.13	AN12	—	—	Unique	—	

Mint mark: W

144.14	AN12	5,850	55.00	110.00	225.00	625.00

Mint mark: A
Obv: NAPOLEON EMPEREUR.

C#	Date	Mintage	VG	Fine	VF	XF
154.1	AN12	.060	40.00	75.00	150.00	475.00
	AN13/2	—	30.00	50.00	100.00	375.00
	AN13	.742	30.00	50.00	100.00	375.00
	AN14	.232	60.00	90.00	175.00	475.00
	1806	.169	60.00	90.00	175.00	450.00

Mint mark: B

154.2	AN12	.014	35.00	75.00	200.00	500.00
	1807	563	—	Reported, not confirmed		

Mint mark: BB

154.3	AN12	1,798	—	—	—	—
	AN13	4,341	150.00	—	—	—
	1806	1,477	—	Reported, not confirmed		

Mint mark: D

154.11	AN13	2,560	—	Reported, not confirmed		
	AN14	204	—	Reported, not confirmed		
	1806	530	—	Reported, not confirmed		

Mint mark: G

154.12	AN13	.013	350.00	750.00	1500.	—

Mint mark: H

154.4	AN12	2,800	—	Reported, not confirmed		
	AN13	3,727	55.00	110.00	210.00	500.00
	AN14	1,063	60.00	120.00	250.00	800.00

Mint mark: I

154.5	AN12	3,561	—	Reported, not confirmed		
	AN13/2	.124	20.00	40.00	150.00	450.00
	AN13	Inc. Ab.	20.00	40.00	150.00	450.00
	AN14	6,299	—	Reported, not confirmed		
	1806	.021	35.00	70.00	175.00	425.00
	1807	.082	30.00	65.00	150.00	375.00

Mint mark: K

154.6	AN12	.010	30.00	65.00	175.00	450.00
	AN13	.036	25.00	50.00	160.00	400.00
	AN14	1,210	—	—	Rare	—
	1806	754	—	Reported, not confirmed		
	1807	3,665	50.00	100.00	250.00	500.00

Mint mark: L

154.7	AN12	1,247	75.00	150.00	300.00	600.00
	AN13	.022	30.00	60.00	175.00	500.00
	AN14	5,183	—	Reported, not confirmed		
	1806	.072	30.00	65.00	150.00	375.00
	1807	.054	30.00	65.00	160.00	400.00

Mint mark: M

154.8	AN12	.016	35.00	75.00	180.00	500.00
	AN13	.334	30.00	60.00	170.00	500.00
	1807	8,878	40.00	90.00	200.00	550.00

Mint mark: MA

154.9	AN12	5,249	—	Reported, not confirmed		
	AN13	.011	30.00	65.00	180.00	525.00
	AN14	—	—	—	Rare	—
	1806	2,289	—	Reported, not confirmed		

Mint mark: Q

154.13	AN13	.052	20.00	40.00	150.00	475.00
	1806	.042	35.00	70.00	150.00	400.00
	1807	.033	35.00	70.00	175.00	425.00

Mint mark: T

154.10	AN12	1,444	60.00	120.00	250.00	800.00
	AN13	4,600	—	Reported, not confirmed		

Mint mark: U

154.14	AN13	7,221	—	—	Rare	—
	AN14	—	—	—	Rare	—
	1806	.010	—	—	Rare	—
	1807	.010	250.00	—	—	—

Mint mark: W

154.15	AN13	.011	30.00	60.00	150.00	400.00
	AN14	—	50.00	100.00	250.00	700.00
	1806	.010	40.00	80.00	200.00	450.00
	1807	4,114	50.00	100.00	250.00	500.00

Mint mark: A
Obv: Negro head.

154a	1807	—	275.00	425.00	850.00	2000.

Laureate head.

154b.1	1807	.043	175.00	275.00	475.00	950.00
	1808	1.100	25.00	50.00	125.00	325.00

Mint mark: B

C#	Date	Mintage	VG	Fine	VF	XF
154b.2	1808	.161	30.00	65.00	140.00	350.00

Mint mark: I

154b.3	1808	.106	35.00	70.00	150.00	375.00

Mint mark: K

154b.4	1808	.038	40.00	80.00	175.00	400.00

Mint mark: L

154b.5	1808	.019	45.00	90.00	175.00	425.00

Mint mark: M

154b.6	1808	.028	40.00	80.00	170.00	400.00

Mint mark: MA

154b.7	1808	7,676	50.00	100.00	200.00	500.00

Mint mark: Q

154b.8	1808	4,965	60.00	100.00	225.00	500.00

Mint mark: U

154b.9	1808	2,297	100.00	175.00	450.00	1000.

Mint mark: W

154b.10	1808	.040	40.00	80.00	175.00	400.00
	Common date				Unc.	650.00

Mint mark: A

164.1	1809	.469	20.00	40.00	90.00	275.00
	1810	.771	17.50	35.00	80.00	250.00
	1811	2.509	12.50	25.00	50.00	200.00
	1812	.308	22.00	45.00	100.00	275.00
	1813	.442	20.00	40.00	90.00	275.00
	1814	.095	40.00	80.00	175.00	400.00

Mint mark: B

164.2	1809	.136	30.00	60.00	125.00	300.00
	1810	.072	30.00	65.00	135.00	325.00
	1811	.290	22.00	45.00	100.00	275.00
	1812	.057	30.00	60.00	140.00	350.00
	1813	.031	35.00	70.00	160.00	375.00

Mint mark: BB

164.10	1810	1,389	—	Reported, not confirmed		
	1811	.012	40.00	80.00	175.00	400.00
	1812	2,835	—	Reported, not confirmed		

Mint mark: CL

164.16	1813	906	175.00	250.00	400.00	1000.

Mint mark: D

164.11	1810	.018	35.00	75.00	175.00	375.00
	1811	.037	30.00	65.00	150.00	350.00
	1812	.061	25.00	50.00	125.00	275.00
	1813	.033	35.00	70.00	160.00	350.00

Mint mark: H

164.3	1809	4,534	50.00	100.00	225.00	450.00
	1810	5,710	50.00	100.00	225.00	450.00
	1811	.044	30.00	65.00	150.00	350.00
	1812	.081	25.00	55.00	125.00	300.00
	1813	.080	25.00	55.00	125.00	300.00

Mint mark: I

164.12	1810	.029	30.00	65.00	150.00	350.00
	1811	.137	25.00	50.00	120.00	300.00
	1812	.209	22.00	45.00	100.00	275.00
	1813	.098	25.00	55.00	125.00	325.00

Mint mark: K

164.4	1809	3,451	60.00	125.00	225.00	475.00
	1810	3,518	60.00	125.00	225.00	475.00
	1811	.028	30.00	60.00	125.00	325.00
	1812	.021	30.00	60.00	125.00	325.00
	1813	.027	30.00	60.00	125.00	325.00

Mint mark: L

164.5	1809	.027	35.00	70.00	160.00	375.00
	1810	.032	35.00	70.00	160.00	375.00
	1811	.099	25.00	55.00	125.00	325.00
	1812	.042	30.00	65.00	150.00	350.00
	1813	.033	35.00	70.00	160.00	375.00

Mint mark: M

164.13	1810	.011	45.00	90.00	200.00	425.00
	1811	.124	25.00	50.00	125.00	300.00
	1812	.145	25.00	50.00	125.00	300.00
	1813	.221	22.00	45.00	100.00	275.00
	1814	.046	30.00	65.00	150.00	350.00

Mint mark: MA

164.6	1809	.027	35.00	70.00	150.00	350.00
	1810	8,843	40.00	80.00	175.00	375.00
	1811	.039	30.00	60.00	125.00	300.00
	1812	.016	35.00	70.00	150.00	350.00
	1813	.018	35.00	70.00	150.00	350.00

Mint mark: Q

164.7	1809	.020	35.00	70.00	160.00	375.00
	1810	4,857	50.00	100.00	225.00	450.00
	1811	.075	25.00	55.00	125.00	325.00
	1812	.086	25.00	55.00	125.00	325.00
	1813	.253	22.00	45.00	100.00	275.00
	1814	.016	45.00	90.00	200.00	425.00

FRANCE 563

C#	Date	Mintage	VG	Fine	VF	XF
	Mint mark: T					
164.14	1811	.035	30.00	65.00	150.00	350.00
	1812	.019	35.00	75.00	150.00	375.00
	1813	.011	45.00	90.00	200.00	425.00
	Mint mark: U					
164.8	1809	3,149	—	—	Rare	—
	1810	3,077	—	—	Rare	—
	1811	3,893	—	—	Rare	—
	Mint mark: W					
164.9	1809	.062	30.00	60.00	135.00	325.00
	1810	.048	30.00	60.00	135.00	325.00
	1811	.118	20.00	45.00	100.00	250.00
	1812	.108	20.00	45.00	100.00	250.00
	1813	.088	20.00	45.00	100.00	250.00
	Mint mark: Flag					
164.15	1812	9,493	85.00	140.00	275.00	650.00
	1813/2	.041	—	—	—	—
	1813	Inc. Ab.	75.00	125.00	250.00	500.00
	Common date				Unc.	550.00

C#	Date	Mintage	VG	Fine	VF	XF
	Mint mark: A					
171	1815	6,783	150.00	250.00	500.00	1000.

C#	Date	Mintage	VG	Fine	VF	XF
	Mint mark: A					
180.1	1816	.061	25.00	55.00	150.00	375.00
	1817	.214	20.00	40.00	100.00	350.00
	1818	.013	35.00	75.00	175.00	450.00
	1819	2,334	—	—	—	—
	1820	.053	25.00	55.00	140.00	375.00
	1821	.139	22.00	45.00	125.00	350.00
	1822	.421	20.00	30.00	75.00	200.00
	1823	.268	20.00	40.00	100.00	250.00
	1824	.284	20.00	40.00	100.00	250.00
	Mint mark: B					
180.2	1816	4,398	40.00	85.00	200.00	475.00
	1817	.015	35.00	75.00	175.00	450.00
	1818	3,039	45.00	90.00	225.00	500.00
	1819	.012	35.00	75.00	175.00	450.00
	1822	.030	30.00	65.00	150.00	400.00
	1824	.071	25.00	50.00	125.00	375.00
	Mint mark: D					
180.11	1820	2,282	—	—	—	—
	1822	2,181	—	—	—	—
	1823	7,251	40.00	80.00	175.00	450.00
	1824	.108	22.00	45.00	120.00	350.00
	Mint mark: H					
180.3	1816	7,037	40.00	80.00	175.00	450.00
	1817	.037	30.00	60.00	150.00	400.00
	1818	8,530	40.00	80.00	175.00	450.00
	1819	5,309	40.00	85.00	200.00	475.00
	1820	2,801	—	—	—	—
	1821	2,897	—	—	—	—
	1822	9,806	40.00	80.00	175.00	450.00
	1823	.020	35.00	70.00	170.00	425.00
	1824	.027	30.00	65.00	160.00	400.00
	Mint mark: I					
180.4	1816	3,956	40.00	85.00	200.00	475.00
	1823	.010	35.00	75.00	175.00	450.00
	1824	.053	25.00	55.00	140.00	375.00
	Mint mark: K					
180.8	1817	.213	20.00	40.00	100.00	350.00
	1820	.011	35.00	75.00	175.00	450.00
	1823	2,545	—	—	—	—
	1824	.038	30.00	60.00	150.00	400.00
	Mint mark: L					
180.5	1816	1,068	—	—	—	—
	1817	3,026	—	—	—	—
	1818	444 pcs.	—	—	—	—
	1823	.027	30.00	65.00	150.00	400.00
	1824	.048	30.00	65.00	150.00	400.00
	Mint mark: M					
180.6	1816	1,699	—	—	—	—
	1817	.030	30.00	65.00	150.00	400.00
	1822	1,496	—	—	—	—
	1823	.094	25.00	50.00	125.00	350.00
	1824	.132	22.00	45.00	100.00	300.00
	Mint mark: MA					
180.12	1824	7,455	40.00	80.00	175.00	450.00

C#	Date	Mintage	VG	Fine	VF	XF
	Mint mark: Q					
180.7	1816	.013	35.00	75.00	175.00	450.00
	1817	.047	30.00	60.00	150.00	400.00
	1818	.052	25.00	55.00	140.00	375.00
	1819	.064	25.00	55.00	140.00	375.00
	1820	.047	30.00	60.00	150.00	400.00
	1821	.028	30.00	60.00	150.00	400.00
	1822	.011	35.00	75.00	175.00	450.00
	1823	3,399	—	—	—	—
	1824	.053	25.00	55.00	140.00	375.00
	Mint mark: T					
180.9	1817	1,456	—	—	—	—
	Mint mark: W					
180.10	1817	8,504	40.00	80.00	175.00	450.00
	1818	3,208	—	—	—	—
	1821	.022	35.00	70.00	150.00	425.00
	1822	.102	22.00	45.00	120.00	350.00
	1823	.265	20.00	30.00	75.00	225.00
	1824	.460	20.00	30.00	75.00	200.00
	Common date				Unc.	600.00

C#	Date	Mintage	VG	Fine	VF	XF
	Mint mark: A					
188.1	1825	.034	30.00	60.00	140.00	375.00
	1826	.122	20.00	40.00	100.00	300.00
	1827	.268	17.50	35.00	90.00	275.00
	1828	.235	17.50	35.00	90.00	275.00
	1829	.145	20.00	40.00	100.00	300.00
	1830	.044	25.00	55.00	125.00	375.00
	1830 reeded edge	Inc. Ab.	—	—	Rare	—
	Mint mark: B					
188.2	1825	.017	35.00	70.00	150.00	400.00
	1826	.024	35.00	70.00	150.00	400.00
	1827	.138	20.00	40.00	100.00	325.00
	1828	.059	25.00	50.00	120.00	350.00
	1829	.102	20.00	40.00	100.00	325.00
	1830	.064	25.00	50.00	120.00	350.00
	Mint mark: BB					
188.3	1825	5,856	40.00	80.00	175.00	450.00
	1826	.019	35.00	70.00	150.00	400.00
	1827	.019	35.00	70.00	150.00	400.00
	1828	.025	35.00	70.00	150.00	400.00
	1829	.018	35.00	70.00	150.00	400.00
	Mint mark: D					
188.4	1825	.027	30.00	60.00	140.00	375.00
	1826	.072	22.00	45.00	100.00	350.00
	1827	.116	20.00	40.00	100.00	325.00
	1828	.108	20.00	40.00	100.00	325.00
	1829	.096	20.00	40.00	100.00	325.00
	Mint mark: H					
188.5	1825	3,215	—	—	—	—
	1826	.019	35.00	70.00	150.00	400.00
	1827	.019	35.00	70.00	150.00	400.00
	1828	.016	35.00	70.00	150.00	400.00
	1829	.049	25.00	55.00	125.00	375.00
	Mint mark: I					
188.6	1825	6,239	40.00	80.00	175.00	450.00
	1826	.032	30.00	60.00	140.00	375.00
	1827	.022	35.00	70.00	150.00	400.00
	1828	4,863	40.00	80.00	175.00	450.00
	1829	.016	35.00	70.00	150.00	400.00
	1830	5,635	40.00	80.00	175.00	450.00
	Mint mark: K					
188.7	1825	.011	35.00	70.00	150.00	400.00
	1826	.011	35.00	70.00	150.00	400.00
	1827	.033	30.00	60.00	140.00	375.00
	1828	.081	22.00	45.00	100.00	350.00
	1829	.033	30.00	60.00	140.00	375.00
	1830	.014	35.00	70.00	160.00	400.00
	Mint mark: L					
188.8	1825	4,397	40.00	80.00	175.00	450.00
	1826	.025	35.00	70.00	150.00	400.00
	1827	.052	25.00	50.00	100.00	350.00
	1828	.046	25.00	55.00	125.00	375.00
	1829	.021	30.00	65.00	150.00	400.00
	1830	.013	30.00	65.00	150.00	400.00
	Mint mark: M					
188.9	1825	6,770	40.00	80.00	175.00	450.00
	1826	.040	25.00	55.00	125.00	375.00
	1827	.031	30.00	60.00	140.00	375.00
	1828	.120	20.00	40.00	100.00	325.00
	1829	.049	25.00	55.00	125.00	375.00
	1830	.016	35.00	70.00	150.00	400.00
	Mint mark: MA					
188.13	1829	.041	25.00	55.00	125.00	375.00
	Mint mark: Q					
188.10	1825	4,956	40.00	80.00	175.00	450.00
	1826	.021	30.00	65.00	150.00	400.00
	1827	.014	35.00	70.00	160.00	425.00
	1828	.024	35.00	70.00	160.00	425.00
	1829	.011	35.00	70.00	160.00	425.00
	1830	6,688	40.00	80.00	175.00	450.00

C#	Date	Mintage	VG	Fine	VF	XF
	Mint mark: T					
188.12	1826	9,189	35.00	75.00	175.00	425.00
	1827	.043	25.00	55.00	125.00	375.00
	1828	.031	30.00	60.00	140.00	375.00
	1829	.050	25.00	50.00	120.00	350.00
	1830	.012	35.00	70.00	150.00	400.00
	Mint mark: W					
188.11	1825	.015	35.00	70.00	150.00	400.00
	1826	.155	20.00	40.00	100.00	300.00
	1827	.481	15.00	30.00	75.00	250.00
	1828	.358	15.00	30.00	75.00	275.00
	1829	.105	20.00	40.00	100.00	300.00
	1830	.109	20.00	40.00	100.00	300.00
	Common date				Unc.	650.00

C#	Date	Mintage	Fine	VF	XF	Unc
	Mint mark: A					
202.1	1831	.010	35.00	75.00	225.00	600.00
	1832	.688	25.00	50.00	100.00	300.00
	1833	.194	25.00	60.00	125.00	400.00
	1834	.493	25.00	50.00	100.00	300.00
	1835	.452	25.00	50.00	100.00	300.00
	1836	.112	25.00	60.00	125.00	400.00
	1837	.104	25.00	60.00	125.00	400.00
	1838	.093	25.00	60.00	150.00	450.00
	1839	.036	35.00	75.00	225.00	600.00
	1840	.042	35.00	75.00	175.00	475.00
	1841	.068	35.00	75.00	175.00	475.00
	1842	.017	35.00	75.00	225.00	575.00
	1843	.068	35.00	75.00	175.00	475.00
	1844	.030	35.00	75.00	225.00	550.00
	1845 prow	.019	35.00	75.00	225.00	575.00
	1845 hand	I.A.	35.00	75.00	225.00	575.00
	1846	.305	25.00	50.00	100.00	300.00
	1847	.784	25.00	50.00	100.00	300.00
	1848	.098	35.00	75.00	175.00	475.00
	Mint mark: B					
202.2	1831	.049	35.00	75.00	175.00	475.00
	1832	.384	25.00	50.00	125.00	400.00
	1833	.105	25.00	60.00	150.00	450.00
	1834	.296	25.00	50.00	125.00	400.00
	1835	.066	35.00	75.00	175.00	475.00
	1836	.113	25.00	60.00	150.00	450.00
	1837	.256	25.00	50.00	125.00	400.00
	1838	.156	25.00	50.00	125.00	400.00
	1839	.102	25.00	60.00	150.00	450.00
	1840	.121	25.00	60.00	150.00	450.00
	1841	.022	35.00	75.00	225.00	600.00
	1842	.147	25.00	60.00	150.00	450.00
	1843	.067	35.00	75.00	175.00	475.00
	1844	.013	35.00	75.00	225.00	600.00
	1845	.155	25.00	50.00	125.00	400.00
	1846	.046	35.00	75.00	175.00	475.00
	Mint mark: BB					
202.5	1832	.055	35.00	75.00	175.00	475.00
	1833	.074	35.00	75.00	175.00	475.00
	1834	.077	35.00	75.00	175.00	475.00
	1834(b)	I.A.	35.00	75.00	175.00	475.00
	1835	.038	35.00	75.00	175.00	475.00
	1836	.073	35.00	75.00	175.00	475.00
	1837	.022	40.00	80.00	225.00	600.00
	1838	.082	35.00	75.00	175.00	475.00
	1839	.047	35.00	75.00	175.00	475.00
	1840	.064	35.00	75.00	175.00	475.00
	1841	.061	35.00	75.00	175.00	475.00
	1842	.026	35.00	75.00	225.00	575.00
	1843	.059	35.00	75.00	175.00	475.00
	1844	.086	35.00	75.00	175.00	475.00
	1845	.076	35.00	75.00	175.00	475.00
	1846	.044	35.00	75.00	175.00	475.00
	1847	.060	35.00	75.00	175.00	475.00
	1848	.027	35.00	75.00	225.00	600.00
	Mint mark: D					
202.6	1832	.239	25.00	50.00	125.00	400.00
	1833	.098	35.00	75.00	175.00	475.00
	1834	.098	35.00	75.00	175.00	475.00
	1835	.040	35.00	75.00	175.00	475.00
	1836	5,519	45.00	90.00	300.00	800.00
	1837	6,306	45.00	90.00	300.00	650.00
	1838	3,478	—	—	—	—
	1839 arc	7,299	50.00	110.00	300.00	750.00
	1839 tower	I.A.	50.00	110.00	300.00	750.00
	1840	.010	35.00	75.00	225.00	600.00
	1848	.012	35.00	75.00	225.00	600.00
	Mint mark: H					
202.7	1832	.186	25.00	60.00	150.00	450.00
	1833	.022	30.00	65.00	200.00	550.00
	1834	.072	35.00	75.00	175.00	475.00
	1835	.023	40.00	80.00	225.00	600.00
	Mint mark: I					
202.3	1831	.038	35.00	75.00	175.00	475.00
	1832	.034	35.00	75.00	175.00	475.00
	1833	.034	30.00	65.00	200.00	550.00
	1834	.048	35.00	75.00	175.00	475.00
	1835	.048	35.00	75.00	175.00	475.00

FRANCE 564

C# 202.8 — Mint mark: K

Date	Mintage	Fine	VF	XF	Unc
1832	.076	35.00	75.00	175.00	475.00
1833	.023	30.00	65.00	200.00	550.00
1834	.057	35.00	75.00	175.00	475.00
1835	.042	35.00	75.00	175.00	475.00
1836	.020	30.00	65.00	200.00	550.00
1837	.036	40.00	80.00	225.00	600.00
1838	.019	35.00	75.00	225.00	600.00
1839	.031	35.00	75.00	225.00	575.00
1840	.039	35.00	75.00	175.00	475.00
1841	.029	35.00	75.00	225.00	550.00
1842	.033	35.00	75.00	225.00	550.00
1843	.037	35.00	75.00	225.00	575.00
1844	.031	35.00	75.00	225.00	550.00
1845	.018	35.00	75.00	225.00	525.00
1846	.018	35.00	75.00	225.00	600.00
1847	6,504	60.00	125.00	375.00	800.00

202.9 — Mint mark: L

Date	Mintage	Fine	VF	XF	Unc
1832	.024	30.00	65.00	200.00	550.00
1833	.014	40.00	80.00	225.00	600.00
1834	.015	40.00	80.00	225.00	600.00
1835	2,669				

202.10 — Mint mark: M

Date	Mintage	Fine	VF	XF	Unc
1832	.069	35.00	75.00	175.00	475.00
1833	.050	30.00	65.00	200.00	550.00
1834	.078	35.00	75.00	175.00	475.00
1835	.041	35.00	75.00	175.00	475.00
1836	6,733	45.00	90.00	300.00	750.00

202.11 — Mint mark: MA

Date	Mintage	Fine	VF	XF	Unc
1832	.064	35.00	75.00	175.00	475.00
1833	.021	30.00	65.00	200.00	550.00
1834	.019	40.00	80.00	225.00	600.00
1835	.015	40.00	80.00	225.00	600.00
1837	—	—	—	Rare	—
1838	.025	35.00	75.00	225.00	600.00

202.12 — Mint mark: Q

Date	Mintage	Fine	VF	XF	Unc
1832	.022	30.00	65.00	200.00	550.00
1833	.037	30.00	65.00	200.00	550.00
1834	.069	35.00	75.00	175.00	475.00

202.13 — Mint mark: T

Date	Mintage	Fine	VF	XF	Unc
1832	.104	25.00	60.00	150.00	450.00
1833	.028	30.00	65.00	200.00	550.00
1834	.104	25.00	60.00	150.00	475.00
1835	.017	40.00	80.00	225.00	600.00

202.4 — Mint mark: W

Date	Mintage	Fine	VF	XF	Unc
1831	.033	35.00	75.00	175.00	475.00
1832	.427	25.00	50.00	100.00	300.00
1833	.168	25.00	50.00	125.00	400.00
1834	.583	25.00	50.00	100.00	300.00
1835	.147	25.00	50.00	125.00	400.00
1836	.060	35.00	75.00	175.00	475.00
1837	.230	25.00	50.00	100.00	300.00
1838	.170	25.00	50.00	125.00	400.00
1839	.105	25.00	60.00	150.00	450.00
1840(c)	.063	25.00	75.00	175.00	475.00
1840(r)	I.A.	35.00	75.00	175.00	475.00
1841	.290	25.00	50.00	100.00	300.00
1842	.190	25.00	50.00	100.00	300.00
1843	.296	25.00	50.00	100.00	300.00
1844	.290	25.00	50.00	100.00	300.00
1845	.353	25.00	50.00	100.00	300.00
1846	.049	35.00	75.00	175.00	475.00

Mint mark: A — Second Republic

Y#	Date	Mintage	Fine	VF	XF	Unc
5.1	1849	.665	65.00	200.00	450.00	850.00
	1850	.857	50.00	150.00	350.00	750.00
	1851	.351	65.00	200.00	450.00	850.00

Mint mark: BB

Y#	Date	Mintage	Fine	VF	XF	Unc
5.2	1849	.014	125.00	300.00	500.00	1200.
	1850	.202	75.00	175.00	400.00	850.00

Mint mark: K

Y#	Date	Mintage	Fine	VF	XF	Unc
5.3	1849	.017	100.00	200.00	500.00	1000.
	1850	9,914	200.00	400.00	700.00	1800.

Mint mark: A — Second Empire

Y#	Date	Mintage	Fine	VF	XF	Unc
25.1	1853	.049	300.00	500.00	800.00	1250.
	1854	.215	150.00	250.00	450.00	850.00
	1855(d)	.082	175.00	350.00	600.00	1000.
	1856	.241	150.00	250.00	450.00	850.00
	1857	.389	150.00	250.00	450.00	850.00
25.1	1858	1,288	—	—	VF Rare	—
	1859	894 pcs.	—	—	Rare	—

Mint mark: BB

Y#	Date	Mintage	Fine	VF	XF	Unc
25.2	1856	.693	150.00	—	500.00	1000.

Mint mark: D

Y#	Date	Mintage	Fine	VF	XF	Unc
25.3	1856	.289	150.00	300.00	550.00	1100.

10.0000 g, .835 SILVER, .2684 oz ASW — Mint mark: A

Y#	Date	Mintage	Fine	VF	XF	Unc
31.1	1866	3.226	5.00	15.00	30.00	90.00
	1867	3.695	5.00	15.00	30.00	90.00
	1868	3.762	5.00	15.00	30.00	90.00
	1869	1.104	12.00	30.00	60.00	150.00
	1870	3.187	5.00	15.00	30.00	90.00

Mint mark: BB

Y#	Date	Mintage	Fine	VF	XF	Unc
31.2	1866	3.090	5.00	15.00	30.00	90.00
	1867	3.471	5.00	15.00	30.00	90.00
	1868	.733	10.00	25.00	70.00	250.00
	1869	.367	15.00	35.00	70.00	175.00
	1870	1.001	—	—	—	—

Mint mark: K

Y#	Date	Mintage	Fine	VF	XF	Unc
31.3	1866	.437	20.00	40.00	80.00	250.00
	1867	1.744	7.50	20.00	40.00	150.00
	1868	.087	40.00	90.00	250.00	500.00

Mint mark: A — Third Republic

Y#	Date	Mintage	Fine	VF	XF	Unc
45.1	1870	.239	25.00	70.00	175.00	400.00

Mint mark: K

Y#	Date	Mintage	Fine	VF	XF	Unc
45.2	1870(a)	.560	35.00	75.00	200.00	500.00
	1870(s)	I.A.	35.00	75.00	200.00	500.00
	1871	1.256	25.00	50.00	150.00	350.00

Mint mark: A

Y#	Date	Mintage	Fine	VF	XF	Unc
50.1	1870 lg.A	1.324	5.00	10.00	30.00	100.00
	1873 sm.a	I.A.	5.00	10.00	30.00	100.00
	1871 lg.A	4.757	5.00	10.00	30.00	75.00
	1871 sm.a	I.A.	5.00	10.00	30.00	100.00
	1872	2.306	5.00	10.00	30.00	80.00
	1873	.528	15.00	40.00	90.00	250.00
	1878	30 pcs.	—	—	Proof	6000.
	1881	1.014	10.00	20.00	50.00	150.00
	1887	2.343	5.00	15.00	30.00	85.00
	1888	.131	30.00	60.00	125.00	300.00
	1889	100 pcs.	—	—	Proof	5000.
	1894	.300	10.00	30.00	70.00	200.00
	1895	.600	8.00	20.00	45.00	135.00

Mint mark: K

Y#	Date	Mintage	Fine	VF	XF	Unc
50.2	1871 lg. K	1.215	5.00	10.00	30.00	100.00
	1871 sm. k	I.A.	5.00	10.00	30.00	100.00
	1872	1.467	5.00	10.00	30.00	100.00

Mint: Paris - w/o mint mark.

Y#	Date	Mintage	Fine	VF	XF	Unc
64.1	1898(a)	5.000	3.00	5.00	10.00	30.00
	1898(a)				Proof	350.00
	1899(a)	3.500	3.00	6.00	12.00	40.00
	1900(a)	.500	25.00	50.00	150.00	300.00
	1900(a)	—			Proof	400.00
	1901(a)	1.860	5.00	10.00	25.00	125.00
	1902(a)	2.000	5.00	10.00	25.00	125.00
	1904(a)	1.500	8.00	17.50	35.00	160.00
	1905(a)	2.000	5.00	10.00	25.00	115.00
64.1	1908(a)	2.502	4.00	8.00	15.00	75.00
	1909(a)	1.000	5.00	10.00	20.00	110.00
	1910(a)	2.190	3.00	7.50	15.00	75.00
	1912(a)	1.000	5.00	10.00	20.00	100.00
	1913(a)	.500	10.00	25.00	50.00	125.00
	1914(a)	5.719	2.00	4.00	7.00	20.00
	1915(a)	13.963	2.00	3.00	5.00	13.00
	1916(a)	17.887	2.00	3.00	5.00	10.00
	1917(a)	16.555	2.00	3.00	5.00	10.00
	1918(a)	12.026	2.00	3.00	5.00	10.00
	1919(a)	9.261	2.00	3.00	5.00	14.00
	1920(a)	3.014	2.00	4.00	7.00	20.00

Mint mark: C

Y#	Date	Mintage	Fine	VF	XF	Unc
64.2	1914	.462	10.00	17.50	35.00	45.00
	1914	—	—	Matte Proof		500.00

ALUMINUM-BRONZE
Mint: Paris - w/o mint mark.
French Chamber of Commerce Series

Y#	Date	Mintage	Fine	VF	XF	Unc
79	1920(a)	14.363	2.00	4.00	8.00	30.00
	1921(a)	Inc. Ab.	.50	1.00	2.50	10.00
	1922(a)	29.463	.25	.50	1.50	7.50
	1923(a)	43.960	.25	.50	1.25	5.00
	1924(a)	29.631	.25	.50	1.50	7.50
	1925(a)	31.607	.25	.50	1.50	7.50
	1926(a)	2.962	3.00	5.00	10.00	30.00
	1927(a)	1.678	75.00	150.00	300.00	450.00

Y#	Date	Mintage	Fine	VF	XF	Unc
82	1931(a)	1.717	1.50	3.00	7.00	20.00
	1932(a)	8.943	.50	1.00	1.50	6.00
	1933(a)	8.413	.50	1.00	1.50	6.00
	1934(a)	6.896	.50	1.00	1.50	6.00
	1935(a)	.298	12.50	25.00	50.00	100.00
	1936(a)	12.394	.25	.50	1.00	4.50
	1937(a)	11.055	.25	.50	1.00	4.50
	1938(a)	28.072	.20	.35	.75	3.50
	1939(a)	25.403	.20	.35	.75	3.50
	1940(a)	9.716	.25	.50	1.00	4.50
	1941(a)	16.684	.20	.35	.75	3.50

ALUMINUM

Y#	Date	Mintage	Fine	VF	XF	Unc
82a.1	1941(a)		.20	.30	.60	2.50
	1944(a)	7.224	.20	.30	.60	4.50
	1945(a)	16.636	.20	.30	.60	2.50
	1946(a)	34.930	.20	.30	.60	2.50
	1947(a)	78.984	.20	.30	.60	2.50
	1948(a)	32.354	.20	.30	.60	2.50
	1949(a)	13.683	.20	.30	.60	2.50
	1950(a)	12.191	.20	.30	.60	2.50
	1958(o)	9.906	.20	.30	.60	2.50
	1959(a)	17.774	.20	.30	.60	2.50

Mint mark: B

Y#	Date	Mintage	Fine	VF	XF	Unc
82a.2	1944	.170	—	—	—	—
	1945	1.726	2.00	4.00	10.00	30.00
	1946	6.018	.50	1.00	2.50	12.50
	1947	26.220	.25	.50	1.00	6.00
	1948	39.090	.25	.50	1.00	6.00
	1949	23.955	.25	.50	1.00	6.00
	1950	18.185	.25	.50	1.00	6.00

Mint mark: C

Y#	Date	Mintage	Fine	VF	XF	Unc
82a.3	1944	9.828	—	—	—	—
	1945	1.165	3.00	6.00	12.00	35.00
	1946	1.533	—	—	—	—

Mint: Paris - w/o mint mark.
Vichy French State Issues

Y#	Date	Mintage	Fine	VF	XF	Unc
V96.1	1943(a)	106.997	.20	.35	.75	3.00
	1944(a)	25.546	.20	.35	.75	3.50

Mint mark: B

Y#	Date	Mintage	Fine	VF	XF	Unc
V96.2	1943	34.131	6.00	12.00	17.50	40.00
	1944	10.298	1.50	3.00	6.00	15.00

Mint mark: C

FRANCE 565

Y#	Date	Mintage	Fine	VF	XF	Unc
V96.3	1943	7.575	—	—	—	—
	1944	19.470	1.50	3.00	6.00	15.00

BRASS
Mint: Philadelphia, U.S.A., w/o mint mark.
Allied Occupation Issue

89	1944	50.000	1.00	1.50	3.00	8.00

NICKEL

109	1979	130.000	—	—	.40	.65
	1980	100.010	—	—	.40	.65
	1981	120.000	—	—	.40	.65
	1982	90.000	—	—	.40	.65
	1983	90.000	—	—	.40	.65
	1984	.050	—	—	—	.75
	1985	—	—	—	—	2.00
	1986	—	—	—	—	2.00
	1987	—	—	—	—	.75
	1987	.015	—	—	Proof	5.00

5 FRANCS

25.0000 g, .900 SILVER, .7234 oz ASW
Mint mark: A

C#	Date	Mintage	VG	Fine	VF	XF
138.1	L'AN10	.561	35.00	60.00	120.00	425.00
	L'AN11	1.558	15.00	30.00	90.00	350.00
	Mint mark: G					
138.9	L'AN10	4,447	200.00	500.00	1200.	1500.
	Mint mark: K					
138.3	L'AN10	.060	25.00	55.00	130.00	700.00
	L'AN11	.029	40.00	70.00	225.00	700.00
	Mint mark: L					
138.4	L'AN10	.165	22.00	45.00	120.00	475.00
	L'AN11	.170	35.00	60.00	140.00	500.00
	Mint mark: MA					
138.10	L'AN9	2,201	—	Reported, not confirmed		
138.10	L'AN10	.039	30.00	60.00	150.00	700.00
	L'AN11	.160	22.00	45.00	120.00	500.00
	Mint mark: Q					
138.5	L'AN10	.134	22.00	45.00	120.00	550.00
	L'AN11	.360	20.00	40.00	110.00	425.00
	Mint mark: T					
138.6	L'AN10	5,232	—	Reported, not confirmed		
	L'AN11	9,950	60.00	120.00	325.00	1100.
	Common date					800.00

Mint mark: A
Obv. leg: BONAPARTE PREMIER CONSUL.

C#	Date	Mintage	VG	Fine	VF	XF
145.1	ANXI	3.878	20.00	40.00	100.00	300.00
	ANXI w/o dots flanking privy mark					
	Inc. Ab.	150.00	300.00	700.00		
145.2	ANXI	5,547	125.00	250.00	500.00	900.00
	Mint mark: K					
145.3	ANXI	.031	45.00	100.00	225.00	475.00
	Mint mark: L					
145.4	ANXI	.119	35.00	70.00	175.00	350.00
	Mint mark: MA					
145.5	ANXI	.206	30.00	60.00	150.00	325.00
	Mint mark: Q					
145.6	ANXI	.309	30.00	60.00	150.00	325.00
	Mint mark: T					
145.7	ANXI	.018	75.00	150.00	250.00	500.00

Mint mark: A

C#	Date	Mintage	VG	Fine	VF	XF
145.8 (C145.2)	AN12	3.454	20.00	40.00	100.00	300.00
	Mint mark: B					
145.9	AN12	.035	40.00	80.00	200.00	450.00
	Mint mark: BB					
145.10	AN12	.018	40.00	80.00	200.00	450.00
	Mint mark: D					
145.11	AN12	.116	40.00	90.00	190.00	350.00
	Mint mark: G					
145.12	AN12	.014	300.00	600.00	1200.	1800.
	Mint mark: H					
145.13	AN12	.070	40.00	90.00	190.00	350.00
	Mint mark: I					
145.14	AN12	.422	35.00	70.00	175.00	350.00
	Mint mark: K					
145.15	AN12	.462	40.00	90.00	175.00	350.00
	Mint mark: L					
145.16	AN12	.311	35.00	70.00	175.00	350.00
	Mint mark: M					
145.17	AN12	1.199	20.00	40.00	100.00	300.00
	Mint mark: MA					
145.18	AN12	.148	40.00	90.00	175.00	350.00
	Mint mark: Q					
145.19	AN12	.578	35.00	70.00	175.00	350.00
	Mint mark: T					
145.20	AN12	.113	40.00	90.00	175.00	350.00
	Mint mark: U					
145.21	AN12	9,953	80.00	175.00	400.00	800.00
	Mint mark: W					
145.22	AN12	.028	35.00	55.00	135.00	350.00

Mint mark: A
Obv. leg: NAPOLEON EMPEREUR.
Rev: Similar to C#155a.1.

C#	Date	Mintage	VG	Fine	VF	XF
155.1	AN12	.767	27.50	55.00	140.00	300.00
	Mint mark: B					
155.2	AN12	.010	40.00	90.00	250.00	550.00
	Mint mark: D					
155.3	AN12	.014	40.00	90.00	225.00	525.00
	Mint mark: H					
155.4	AN12	.015	40.00	90.00	200.00	475.00
	Mint mark: I					
155.5	AN12	.090	35.00	70.00	160.00	450.00
	Mint mark: K					
155.6	AN12	.071	30.00	60.00	150.00	500.00
	Mint mark: L					
155.7	AN12	.016	40.00	70.00	200.00	500.00
	Mint mark: M					
155.8	AN12	.427	25.00	50.00	125.00	400.00
	Mint mark: MA					
155.9	AN12	2,030	—	Reported, not confirmed		
	Mint mark: Q					
155.10	AN12	.055	35.00	70.00	160.00	400.00
	Mint mark: T					
155.11	AN12	.011	40.00	90.00	200.00	500.00
	Mint mark: W					
155.12	AN12	4,366	80.00	125.00	300.00	650.00

Mint mark: A
Obv: Monogram below bust.

155a.1	AN13	5.121	25.00	50.00	125.00	300.00
	AN14	1.855	25.00	50.00	125.00	300.00
	Mint mark: B					
155a.2	AN13	4,901	—	Reported, not confirmed		
	Mint mark: BB					
155a.3	AN13	7,510	—	—	—	—
	AN14	.831	—	—	—	—
	Mint mark: D					
155a.4	AN13	.024	35.00	70.00	180.00	325.00
	AN14	3,890	90.00	150.00	250.00	600.00
	Mint mark: G					
155a.5	AN13	6,487	200.00	500.00	1200.	1500.
	Mint mark: H					
155a.6	AN13	.035	40.00	90.00	175.00	325.00
	AN14	3,780	90.00	150.00	250.00	600.00
	Mint mark: I					
155a.7	AN13	.333	30.00	60.00	125.00	300.00
	AN14	.012	—	—	—	—
	Mint mark: K					
155a.8	AN13	.161	35.00	70.00	140.00	300.00
	AN14	2,113	110.00	175.00	300.00	750.00
	Mint mark: L					
155a.9	AN13	.207	30.00	60.00	125.00	300.00
	AN14	.015	35.00	75.00	150.00	450.00
	Mint mark: M					
155a.10	AN13	1.547	30.00	60.00	125.00	300.00
	AN14	.040	40.00	90.00	165.00	350.00
	Mint mark: MA					
155a.11	AN13	.064	35.00	70.00	150.00	325.00

C#	Date	Mintage	VG	Fine	VF	XF
		Mint mark: Q				
155a.12	AN13	.245	30.00	60.00	125.00	300.00
		Mint mark: T				
155a.13	AN13	.025	40.00	90.00	160.00	350.00
	AN14	632	—	Reported, not confirmed		
		Mint mark: U				
155a.14	AN13	.021	100.00	200.00	400.00	800.00
	AN14	.014	125.00	250.00	500.00	1000.
		Mint mark: W				
155a.15	AN13	.034	40.00	75.00	150.00	325.00
	AN14	.014	40.00	75.00	150.00	450.00

Mint mark: A
Obv: Similar to C#155a.1.

C#	Date	Mintage	VG	Fine	VF	XF
155a.16 (C155a.2)	1806	.826	25.00	50.00	100.00	200.00
		Mint mark: B				
155a.17	1806	.025	90.00	135.00	225.00	425.00
	1807	.044	40.00	90.00	175.00	325.00
		Mint mark: BB				
155a.18	1806	.660	25.00	50.00	100.00	200.00
	1807	1,296	—	—	—	—
		Mint mark: D				
155a.19	1806	2,771	—	—	—	—
	1807	2,423	—	—	—	—
		Mint mark: H				
155a.20	1806	.028	—	Reported, not confirmed		
	1807	4,847	80.00	225.00	325.00	750.00
		Mint mark: I				
155a.21	1806	.239	35.00	70.00	150.00	325.00
	1807	.091	35.00	70.00	160.00	325.00
		Mint mark: K				
155a.22	1806	.029	35.00	70.00	160.00	325.00
	1807	.010	40.00	80.00	200.00	475.00
		Mint mark: L				
155a.23	1806	.551	25.00	50.00	100.00	200.00
	1807	.375	35.00	70.00	150.00	325.00
		Mint mark: M				
155a.24	1806	.022	35.00	70.00	160.00	350.00
	1807	.101	35.00	70.00	175.00	325.00
		Mint mark: Q				
155a.25	1806	.078	35.00	70.00	150.00	350.00
	1807	.025	40.00	75.00	175.00	350.00
		Mint mark: T				
155a.26	1806	706 pcs.	—	Reported, not confirmed		
	1807	—	—	—	Rare	—
		Mint mark: U				
155a.27	1806	.031	90.00	150.00	300.00	600.00
	1807	.030	90.00	150.00	300.00	600.00
		Mint mark: W				
155a.28	1806	.032	40.00	90.00	190.00	500.00
	1807	.029	40.00	100.00	175.00	350.00

Mint mark: A
Obv: Similar to C#155a.1. Rev: Similar to C#155c.

| 155b | 1807 | .049 | 300.00 | 500.00 | 800.00 | 1400. |

Rev. leg: REPUBLIQUE FRANCAISE.

C#	Date	Mintage	VG	Fine	VF	XF
155c.1	1807	.041	200.00	300.00	600.00	1000.
	1808	6.462	20.00	35.00	55.00	120.00
		Mint mark: B				
155c.2	1808	1.542	20.00	35.00	55.00	120.00
		Mint mark: BB				
155c.3	1808	.068	30.00	50.00	150.00	250.00
		Mint mark: D				
155c.4	1808	.065	30.00	50.00	150.00	250.00
		Mint mark: H				
155c.5	1808	7,204	50.00	100.00	175.00	350.00
		Mint mark: I				
155c.6	1808	.107	30.00	50.00	110.00	200.00
		Mint mark: K				
155c.7	1808	.054	40.00	90.00	190.00	275.00
		Mint mark: L				
155c.8	1808	.144	20.00	35.00	75.00	150.00
		Mint mark: M				
155c.9	1808	.351	20.00	35.00	55.00	100.00
		Mint mark: MA				
155c.10	1808	2,681	100.00	200.00	400.00	700.00
		Mint mark: Q				
155c.11	1808	.012	55.00	95.00	180.00	350.00
		Mint mark: T				
155c.12	1808	2,682	50.00	100.00	200.00	400.00
		Mint mark: U				
155c.13	1808	.014	55.00	125.00	300.00	450.00
		Mint mark: W				
155c.14	1808	.550	20.00	35.00	55.00	100.00
Common date					Unc.	400.00

Mint mark: A
Obv: Similar to C#155c.1.
Rev. leg: EMPIRE FRANCAIS.

C#	Date	Mintage	VG	Fine	VF	XF
165.1	1809	3.254	15.00	25.00	40.00	85.00
	1810	8.797	12.50	17.50	40.00	85.00
	1811	31.050	12.50	17.50	40.00	85.00
	1812	9.311	12.50	17.50	40.00	85.00
	1813	9.757	12.50	17.50	40.00	85.00
	1814	1.329	20.00	35.00	85.00	175.00
		Mint mark: B				
165.2	1809	3.036	15.00	25.00	40.00	85.00
	1810	.632	20.00	30.00	60.00	150.00
	1811	3.772	17.50	25.00	50.00	110.00
	1812	3.039	17.50	25.00	50.00	110.00
	1813	.728	20.00	30.00	55.00	120.00
	1814	.020	25.00	40.00	80.00	160.00
		Mint mark: BB				
165.3	1809	2,856	—	Reported, not confirmed		
	1810	.028	30.00	45.00	110.00	200.00
	1811	.327	25.00	35.00	70.00	190.00
	1812	.139	30.00	50.00	120.00	175.00
	1813	.025	30.00	55.00	135.00	275.00
	1814	5,382	—	Reported, not confirmed		
		Mint mark: CL				
165.18	1813	.014	150.00	375.00	500.00	850.00
	1814	1,191	—	—	—	—
		Mint mark: D				
165.4	1809	.011	35.00	60.00	175.00	325.00
	1810	.043	30.00	45.00	110.00	200.00
	1811	1.568	15.00	25.00	40.00	85.00
	1812	2.295	15.00	30.00	50.00	100.00
	1813	.917	15.00	25.00	40.00	95.00
		Mint mark: H				
165.5	1809	9,006	35.00	65.00	175.00	325.00

C#	Date	Mintage	VG	Fine	VF	XF
165.5	1811	1.029	25.00	30.00	50.00	110.00
	1812	1.824	15.00	25.00	40.00	85.00
	1813	1.795	15.00	25.00	40.00	85.00
	1814	.169	20.00	35.00	75.00	150.00
		Mint mark: I				
165.6	1809	.065	30.00	50.00	110.00	275.00
	1810	.026	30.00	45.00	110.00	225.00
	1811	1.830	15.00	25.00	40.00	85.00
	1812	2.672	20.00	30.00	50.00	100.00
	1813	2.555	15.00	25.00	40.00	85.00
	1814	.027	30.00	60.00	125.00	200.00
		Mint mark: K				
165.7	1809	.105	30.00	60.00	125.00	225.00
	1810	.120	20.00	35.00	75.00	150.00
	1811	1.081	15.00	25.00	40.00	85.00
	1812	1.664	20.00	30.00	45.00	100.00
	1813	1.281	20.00	30.00	45.00	100.00
		Mint mark: L				
165.8	1809	.217	17.50	25.00	60.00	150.00
1810 mint mark at right						
		.185	30.00	45.00	110.00	250.00
1810 mint mark at left						
		Inc. Ab.	30.00	45.00	110.00	250.00
	1811	1.123	22.50	30.00	50.00	115.00
	1812	.936	15.00	25.00	40.00	100.00
	1813	1.161	15.00	25.00	40.00	100.00
		Mint mark: M				
165.9	1809	.034	30.00	50.00	110.00	250.00
	1810	.072	30.00	40.00	90.00	200.00
	1811	1.101	15.00	25.00	40.00	95.00
	1812	1.617	15.00	25.00	40.00	85.00
	1813	2.213	15.00	25.00	40.00	85.00
	1814	.369	25.00	35.00	70.00	200.00
		Mint mark: MA				
165.10	1809	.012	35.00	70.00	175.00	325.00
	1810	.012	35.00	70.00	125.00	225.00
	1811	.671	22.50	35.00	60.00	125.00
	1812	.612	15.00	25.00	40.00	95.00
	1813	.834	22.50	30.00	50.00	110.00
	1814	.016	35.00	60.00	190.00	300.00
		Mint mark: Q				
165.14	1810	.118	30.00	40.00	90.00	200.00
	1811	1.213	22.50	30.00	50.00	115.00
	1812	1.460	22.50	30.00	50.00	110.00
	1813	1.826	15.00	20.00	40.00	85.00
	1814	.367	17.50	30.00	60.00	150.00
		Mint mark: R				
165.16	1812R/cr	.049	150.00	300.00	600.00	900.00
	1813R/cr	.017	100.00	225.00	450.00	700.00
		Mint mark: T				
165.11	1809	2.218	40.00	90.00	200.00	300.00
	1811	.724	15.00	25.00	40.00	100.00
	1812	.926	15.00	25.00	40.00	100.00
	1813	.564	15.00	25.00	40.00	100.00
	1814	8,745	55.00	90.00	225.00	325.00
		Mint mark: U				
165.12	1809	.016	150.00	300.00	450.00	650.00
	1810	.014	150.00	300.00	450.00	650.00
	1811	.169	75.00	150.00	250.00	500.00
	1812/1	—	75.00	150.00	250.00	500.00
	1812	.105	60.00	125.00	250.00	500.00
	1813	.060	100.00	200.00	300.00	550.00
		Mint mark: W				
165.13	1809	1.221	25.00	35.00	55.00	125.00
	1810	.297	17.50	30.00	60.00	150.00
	1811	3.290	15.00	25.00	50.00	110.00
	1812	4.342	15.00	25.00	40.00	85.00
	1813	1.824	15.00	25.00	40.00	85.00
	1814	.033	30.00	60.00	125.00	275.00
		Mint mark: WA				
165.15	1811	Inc. Ab.	—	—	Rare	—
		Mint mark: Flag				
165.17	1812	.055	100.00	225.00	350.00	575.00
	1813	.362	75.00	150.00	300.00	500.00
Common date					Unc.	300.00

Mint mark: A
First Restoration

C#	Date	Mintage	VG	Fine	VF	XF
168.1	1814	1.466	15.00	25.00	50.00	110.00
	1815	.413	20.00	35.00	75.00	150.00

Mint mark: B
168.2	1814	.634	15.00	25.00	50.00	110.00
	1815	.254	20.00	35.00	75.00	150.00

Mint mark: BB
168.3	1814	4.913	40.00	95.00	200.00	325.00
	1815	1.551	—	—	Rare	—

Mint mark: D
168.4	1814	.082	25.00	50.00	100.00	175.00
	1815	7.482	45.00	115.00	200.00	350.00

Mint mark: H
168.5	1814	.046	30.00	60.00	150.00	275.00
	1815	.034	35.00	75.00	200.00	325.00

Mint mark: I
168.6	1814	1.554	15.00	25.00	50.00	110.00
	1815	1.739	15.00	25.00	50.00	110.00

Mint mark: K
168.7	1814	.355	20.00	35.00	75.00	150.00
	1815	.108	20.00	35.00	75.00	175.00

Mint mark: L
168.8	1814	1.902	15.00	25.00	50.00	110.00
	1815	1.130	15.00	25.00	50.00	110.00

Mint mark: M
168.9	1814	2.377	15.00	25.00	50.00	110.00
	1815	1.406	22.50	35.00	60.00	120.00

Mint mark: MA
168.10	1814	.099	35.00	60.00	120.00	250.00
	1815	7.461	—	—	100.00	175.00

Mint mark: Q
168.11	1814	1.182	15.00	25.00	50.00	110.00
	1815/4	.925	30.00	50.00	75.00	200.00
	1815	Inc. Ab.	20.00	30.00	50.00	125.00

Mint mark: T
168.12	1814	5.235	55.00	125.00	250.00	375.00
	1815	8.006	25.00	50.00	100.00	175.00

Mint mark: W
168.13	1814	.104	30.00	50.00	120.00	250.00
	1815	.114	32.50	55.00	150.00	250.00
Common date					Unc.	350.00

Mint mark: A
"The Hundred Days"
172.1	1815	.473	50.00	100.00	200.00	350.00

Mint mark: B
172.2	1815	.093	75.00	150.00	300.00	600.00

Mint mark: BB
172.3	1815	3.723	400.00	800.00	1200.	2000.

Mint mark: I
172.4	1815	.596	50.00	100.00	200.00	350.00

Mint mark: L
172.5	1815	.097	75.00	125.00	300.00	600.00

Mint mark: M
C#	Date	Mintage	VG	Fine	VF	XF
172.6	1815	.080	85.00	160.00	325.00	725.00

Mint mark: Q
172.7	1815	.021	90.00	175.00	375.00	750.00

Mint mark: W
172.8	1815	.021	90.00	175.00	375.00	750.00
Common date					Unc.	1000.

Mint mark: A
Second Restoration
181.1	1816	3.210	12.00	20.00	30.00	65.00
	1817	3.778	12.00	20.00	30.00	65.00
	1818	.086	25.00	50.00	80.00	175.00
	1819	.658	17.50	25.00	37.50	80.00
	1820	3.226	12.00	20.00	30.00	65.00
	1821	9.526	12.00	17.50	25.00	65.00
	1822	13.453	12.00	17.50	25.00	65.00
	1823	6.536	12.00	17.50	25.00	65.00
	1824	9.066	12.00	17.50	25.00	65.00

Mint mark: B
181.2	1816	.922	12.00	20.00	30.00	65.00
	1817	1.580	25.00	40.00	75.00	150.00
	1818	2.190	12.00	20.00	30.00	65.00
	1819	3.437	12.00	17.50	25.00	65.00
	1820	.210	35.00	60.00	90.00	150.00
	1821	.123	25.00	35.00	65.00	150.00
	1822	.897	12.00	20.00	30.00	65.00
	1823	.393	25.00	35.00	65.00	125.00
	1824	1.246	12.00	20.00	30.00	65.00

Mint mark: BB
181.3	1816	8.115	25.00	50.00	100.00	200.00
	1817	3.510	—	—	—	—
	1818	1.119	35.00	80.00	150.00	250.00
	1819	2.469	35.00	80.00	150.00	250.00
	1820	1.976	35.00	70.00	150.00	250.00
	1821	1.527	40.00	85.00	175.00	300.00
	1823	3.712	35.00	75.00	150.00	250.00

Mint mark: D
181.4	1816	6.446	25.00	50.00	100.00	200.00
	1817	3.605	30.00	60.00	110.00	225.00
	1820	.017	25.00	40.00	65.00	160.00
	1823	.994	12.00	20.00	30.00	65.00
	1824	2.448	12.00	17.50	25.00	65.00
	1824 inverted D					
	Inc. Ab.	—	—	—	Rare	—

Mint mark: H
181.5	1816	6.575	30.00	50.00	90.00	200.00
	1817	.110	30.00	60.00	110.00	225.00
	1818	.012	25.00	40.00	65.00	150.00
	1819	.033	30.00	60.00	110.00	200.00
	1820	.018	25.00	40.00	65.00	165.00
	1821	.018	25.00	40.00	70.00	165.00
	1822	.077	20.00	30.00	45.00	110.00
	1823	.329	15.00	22.50	30.00	65.00
	1824	.771	12.00	20.00	30.00	65.00

Mint mark: I
181.6	1816	.306	15.00	22.50	30.00	65.00
	1817	4.204	30.00	40.00	80.00	225.00
	1818	1.568	40.00	80.00	160.00	275.00
	1819	1.104	45.00	85.00	175.00	300.00
	1820	639	90.00	135.00	275.00	450.00
	1821	6.320	35.00	65.00	100.00	200.00
	1822	8.712	35.00	55.00	100.00	210.00
	1823	.269	15.00	22.50	30.00	65.00
	1824	1.039	12.00	20.00	30.00	65.00

Mint mark: K
181.7	1816	.034	30.00	55.00	125.00	275.00
	1817	.386	15.00	22.50	30.00	65.00
	1818	.017	25.00	35.00	60.00	150.00
	1820	.018	25.00	35.00	65.00	160.00
	1822	.393	15.00	25.00	40.00	100.00
	1823	.800	12.00	20.00	30.00	65.00
	1824	1.010	12.00	20.00	30.00	65.00

Mint mark: L
181.8	1816	1.001	12.00	20.00	30.00	65.00
	1817	.377	15.00	22.50	30.00	65.00
	1818	.010	30.00	40.00	65.00	150.00
	1823	.898	12.00	20.00	30.00	65.00
	1824	1.068	22.50	35.00	55.00	110.00

Mint mark: M

C#	Date	Mintage	VG	Fine	VF	XF
181.9	1816	.651	12.00	20.00	30.00	65.00
	1817	.188	25.00	30.00	50.00	125.00
	1818	2.920	40.00	80.00	175.00	275.00
	1823	.958	12.00	20.00	30.00	65.00
	1824	1.589	12.00	20.00	30.00	65.00

Mint mark: MA
181.10	1816	.018	30.00	50.00	90.00	200.00
	1817	.010	30.00	40.00	65.00	160.00
	1818	7.805	40.00	80.00	160.00	275.00
	1819	1.186	45.00	85.00	175.00	300.00
	1820	440 pcs.	90.00	175.00	300.00	500.00
	1821	198	125.00	200.00	400.00	800.00
	1823	3.847	35.00	80.00	160.00	275.00
	1824	1.422	15.00	25.00	35.00	90.00

Mint mark: Q
181.11	1816	.591	12.00	20.00	30.00	65.00
	1817	.105	15.00	25.00	40.00	100.00
	1819	1.618	50.00	85.00	175.00	300.00
	1820	2.770	45.00	75.00	160.00	275.00
	1821	5.626	27.50	65.00	125.00	250.00
	1822	.020	25.00	35.00	65.00	175.00
	1823	.715	12.00	20.00	30.00	65.00
	1824	1.006	12.00	20.00	30.00	65.00

Mint mark: T
181.12	1816	.011	35.00	65.00	125.00	250.00
	1817	.025	30.00	40.00	65.00	175.00
	1818	.024	25.00	35.00	60.00	140.00
	1819	.020	22.50	30.00	55.00	125.00
	1820	.011	35.00	65.00	95.00	250.00

Mint mark: W
181.13	1816	.072	30.00	50.00	90.00	200.00
	1817	.438	15.00	25.00	40.00	100.00
	1818	.066	25.00	45.00	75.00	200.00
	1819	.034	27.50	40.00	80.00	175.00
	1820	.106	25.00	35.00	60.00	150.00
	1821	3.674	12.00	17.50	25.00	65.00
	1822	4.839	12.00	17.50	25.00	65.00
	1823	4.168	12.00	17.50	25.00	65.00
	1824	9.807	12.00	17.50	25.00	65.00
Common date					Unc.	225.00

Mint mark: A
Rev: Similar to C#181.

189.1	1824	.408	20.00	35.00	60.00	150.00
	1825	2.492	10.00	15.00	25.00	45.00
	1826	7.171	10.00	15.00	25.00	45.00
	1827	6.822	10.00	15.00	25.00	45.00
	1828	8.803	10.00	15.00	25.00	45.00
	1829	4.827	10.00	15.00	25.00	45.00
	1830	6.333	10.00	15.00	25.00	45.00

Mint mark: B
189.2	1825	.113	25.00	40.00	60.00	135.00
	1826	.595	10.00	15.00	25.00	45.00
	1827	2.792	10.00	15.00	25.00	45.00
	1828	1.898	10.00	15.00	25.00	45.00
	1829	2.834	10.00	15.00	25.00	45.00
	1830	2.910	10.00	15.00	25.00	45.00

Mint mark: BB
189.3	1825	.157	20.00	35.00	55.00	135.00
	1826	.411	10.00	15.00	25.00	45.00
	1827	.393	10.00	15.00	25.00	45.00
	1828	.699	10.00	15.00	25.00	45.00
	1829	.548	10.00	15.00	25.00	45.00
	1830	.112	20.00	35.00	60.00	150.00

Mint mark: D
189.4	1825	.185	25.00	40.00	65.00	135.00
	1826	1.437	10.00	15.00	25.00	45.00
	1827	1.651	10.00	15.00	25.00	45.00
	1828	2.743	10.00	15.00	25.00	45.00
	1829	1.608	10.00	15.00	25.00	45.00
	1830	.631	20.00	35.00	55.00	125.00

Mint mark: H
189.5	1825	.157	30.00	40.00	65.00	135.00
	1826	.573	10.00	15.00	25.00	45.00
	1827	.419	10.00	15.00	25.00	45.00
	1828	.490	10.00	15.00	25.00	45.00
	1829	1.155	10.00	15.00	25.00	45.00
	1830	.574	10.00	15.00	25.00	45.00

Mint mark: I
189.6	1825	.155	25.00	40.00	65.00	135.00
	1826	.536	10.00	15.00	25.00	45.00
	1827	.335	20.00	35.00	55.00	125.00
	1828	.124	10.00	15.00	25.00	45.00
	1829	.475	20.00	35.00	55.00	125.00
	1830	.067	35.00	65.00	115.00	200.00

Mint mark: K
189.7	1825	.326	10.00	15.00	25.00	45.00
	1826	.429	10.00	15.00	25.00	45.00

FRANCE 568

C#	Date	Mintage	VG	Fine	VF	XF
189.7	1827	1.147	10.00	15.00	25.00	45.00
	1828	1.632	10.00	15.00	25.00	45.00
	1829	1.011	10.00	15.00	25.00	45.00
	1830	.713	10.00	15.00	25.00	45.00

Mint mark: L

C#	Date	Mintage	VG	Fine	VF	XF
189.8	1825	.227	17.50	30.00	50.00	125.00
	1826	.720	10.00	15.00	25.00	45.00
	1827	1.144	20.00	35.00	55.00	125.00
	1828	1.083	10.00	15.00	25.00	45.00
	1829	.857	10.00	15.00	25.00	45.00
	1830	.399	20.00	35.00	55.00	125.00

Mint mark: M

C#	Date	Mintage	VG	Fine	VF	XF
189.9	1825	.154	25.00	40.00	65.00	135.00
	1826	.670	10.00	15.00	25.00	45.00
	1827	.806	10.00	15.00	25.00	45.00
	1828	1.818	10.00	15.00	25.00	45.00
	1829	.873	10.00	15.00	25.00	45.00
	1830	.496	10.00	15.00	25.00	45.00

Mint mark: MA

C#	Date	Mintage	VG	Fine	VF	XF
189.10	1825	.176	17.50	30.00	55.00	125.00
	1826	1.072	10.00	15.00	25.00	45.00
	1827	1.531	10.00	15.00	25.00	45.00
	1828	1.201	10.00	15.00	25.00	45.00
	1829	1.258	10.00	15.00	25.00	45.00
	1830	1.803	20.00	35.00	65.00	125.00

Mint mark: Q

C#	Date	Mintage	VG	Fine	VF	XF
189.11	1825	.163	25.00	40.00	65.00	135.00
	1826	.346	10.00	15.00	25.00	45.00
	1827	.484	10.00	15.00	25.00	45.00
	1828	.394	20.00	35.00	60.00	150.00
	1829	.360	10.00	15.00	25.00	45.00
	1830	.151	20.00	32.50	60.00	150.00

Mint mark: W

C#	Date	Mintage	VG	Fine	VF	XF
189.12	1825	1.104	10.00	15.00	25.00	45.00
	1826	3.583	10.00	15.00	25.00	45.00
	1827	11.525	10.00	15.00	25.00	45.00
	1828	9.610	10.00	15.00	25.00	45.00
	1829	3.235	10.00	15.00	25.00	45.00
	1830	4.134	10.00	15.00	25.00	45.00

Mint mark: T

C#	Date	Mintage	VG	Fine	VF	XF
189.13	1826	.203	20.00	35.00	55.00	125.00
	1827	.865	10.00	15.00	25.00	45.00
	1828	.933	10.00	15.00	25.00	45.00
	1829	.888	10.00	15.00	25.00	45.00
	1830	.137	20.00	32.50	60.00	150.00
Common date—		—	—	—	Unc.	200.00

Edge inscription in relief.

C#	Date	Mintage	VG	Fine	VF	XF
189a	1827A	Inc. C189.1	50.00	100.00	200.00	350.00
	1830A	Inc. C189.1	50.00	100.00	200.00	350.00

Mint mark: A
Incused edge lettering.
Obv. leg: LOUIS PHILIPPE I ROI....

C#	Date	Mintage	VG	Fine	VF	XF
203.1	1830	2.421	12.00	20.00	32.50	75.00
	1831	11.785	12.00	20.00	30.00	65.00

Mint mark: B

C#	Date	Mintage	VG	Fine	VF	XF
203.2	1830	1.025	15.00	25.00	40.00	100.00
	1831	7.889	12.00	20.00	32.50	75.00

Mint mark: BB

C#	Date	Mintage	VG	Fine	VF	XF
203.3	1830	5.125	35.00	75.00	150.00	250.00
	1831	.983	12.00	20.00	32.50	75.00

Mint mark: D

C#	Date	Mintage	VG	Fine	VF	XF
203.4	1830	.368	25.00	35.00	60.00	125.00
	1831	3.460	12.00	20.00	32.50	75.00

Mint mark: H

C#	Date	Mintage	VG	Fine	VF	XF
203.5	1830	.030	25.00	50.00	100.00	200.00
	1831	.843	12.00	20.00	32.50	75.00

Mint mark: I

C#	Date	Mintage	VG	Fine	VF	XF
203.6	1830	.028	25.00	50.00	100.00	200.00
	1831	.502	12.00	20.00	32.50	75.00

Mint mark: K

C#	Date	Mintage	VG	Fine	VF	XF
203.7	1830	.123	15.00	30.00	60.00	150.00
	1831	1.523	12.00	20.00	32.50	75.00

Mint mark: L

C#	Date	Mintage	VG	Fine	VF	XF
203.8	1830	8.931	35.00	75.00	160.00	300.00
	1831	.430	12.00	20.00	32.50	75.00

Mint mark: M

C#	Date	Mintage	VG	Fine	VF	XF
203.9	1830	.050	30.00	50.00	75.00	175.00
	1831	1.337	12.00	20.00	32.50	75.00

Mint mark: MA

C#	Date	Mintage	VG	Fine	VF	XF
203.10	1830	.065	30.00	50.00	75.00	175.00
	1831	2.062	12.00	20.00	32.50	75.00

Mint mark: Q

C#	Date	Mintage	VG	Fine	VF	XF
203.11	1830	.012	30.00	60.00	125.00	225.00
	1831	.357	15.00	25.00	50.00	100.00

Mint mark: T

C#	Date	Mintage	VG	Fine	VF	XF
203.12	1830	.125	25.00	35.00	60.00	150.00
	1831	1.261	12.00	20.00	32.50	75.00

Mint mark: W

C#	Date	Mintage	VG	Fine	VF	XF
203.13	1830	1.020	12.00	20.00	32.50	75.00
	1831	8.226	12.00	20.00	30.00	65.00
Common date					Unc.	250.00

Mint mark: A
Raised edge lettering.

C#	Date	Mintage	VG	Fine	VF	XF
203.14 (C203.2)	1830	Inc. Ab.	12.00	20.00	32.50	75.00
	1831	Inc. Ab.	12.00	20.00	30.00	65.00

Mint mark: B

C#	Date	Mintage	VG	Fine	VF	XF
203.16	1831	Inc. Ab.	12.00	20.00	32.50	75.00

Mint mark: W

C#	Date	Mintage	VG	Fine	VF	XF
203.15	1830	1 known	—	—	Rare	—
	1831	Inc. Ab.	12.00	20.00	30.00	65.00

Mint mark: A
Incused edge lettering.
Obv. leg: LOUIS PHILIPPE ROI....

C#	Date	Mintage	VG	Fine	VF	XF
203a.1	1830	Inc. Ab.	15.00	30.00	80.00	250.00

Mint mark: B

| 203a.2 | 1830 | Inc. Ab. | 17.50 | 35.00 | 100.00 | 275.00 |

Mint mark: D

| 203a.3 | 1830 | Inc. Ab. | 22.50 | 45.00 | 125.00 | 325.00 |

Mint mark: W

| 203a.4 | 1830 | Inc. Ab. | 17.50 | 35.00 | 100.00 | 275.00 |

Mint mark: A
Raised edge lettering.

| 203a.5 (C203a.2) | 1830 | Inc. Ab. | 30.00 | 60.00 | 150.00 | 400.00 |

Mint mark: A
Incused edge lettering.

C#	Date	Mintage	VG	Fine	VF	XF
A204.1	1831	Inc. Ab.	20.00	40.00	75.00	175.00

Mint mark: B

| A204.2 | 1831 | Inc. Ab. | 20.00 | 40.00 | 75.00 | 175.00 |

Mint mark: BB

| A204.3 | 1831 | Inc. Ab. | 15.00 | 25.00 | 40.00 | 100.00 |

Mint mark: D

| A204.4 | 1831 | Inc. Ab. | 15.00 | 25.00 | 40.00 | 100.00 |

Mint mark: I

| A204.5 | 1831 | Inc. Ab. | 15.00 | 25.00 | 40.00 | 100.00 |

Mint mark: K

| A204.6 | 1831 | Inc. Ab. | 15.00 | 25.00 | 40.00 | 100.00 |

Mint mark: M

| A204.7 (C-A204.6) | 1831 | Inc. Ab. | 15.00 | 25.00 | 40.00 | 100.00 |

C#	Date	Mintage	VG	Fine	VF	XF
A204.8	1831	Inc. Ab.	15.00	25.00	40.00	100.00

Mint mark: Q

| A204.9 (C-A204.7) | 1831 | Inc. Ab. | 17.50 | 30.00 | 60.00 | 125.00 |

Mint mark: A
Raised edge lettering.

| B204.1 (C-A204.8) | 1831 | Inc. Ab. | 12.00 | 20.00 | 30.00 | 65.00 |

Mint mark: B

| B204.2 (C-A204.9) | 1831 | Inc. Ab. | 12.00 | 20.00 | 32.50 | 75.00 |

Mint mark: BB

| B204.3 (C-A204.10) | 1831 | Inc. Ab. | 12.00 | 20.00 | 32.50 | 75.00 |

Mint mark: D

| B-204.4 (C-A204.11) | 1831 | Inc. Ab. | 12.00 | 20.00 | 32.50 | 75.00 |

Mint mark: H

| B204.5 (C-A204.12) | 1831 | Inc. Ab. | 12.00 | 20.00 | 32.50 | 75.00 |

Mint mark: K

| B204.6 (C-A204.13) | 1831 | Inc. Ab. | 12.00 | 20.00 | 32.50 | 75.00 |

Mint mark: L

| B204.7 (C-A204.14) | 1831 | Inc. Ab. | 20.00 | 32.50 | 60.00 | 125.00 |

Mint mark: M

| B204.8 (C-A204.15) | 1831 | Inc. Ab. | 12.00 | 20.00 | 32.50 | 75.00 |

Mint mark: MA

| B204.9 (C-A204.16) | 1831 | Inc. Ab. | 12.00 | 20.00 | 32.50 | 75.00 |

Mint mark: T

| B204.10 (C-A204.17) | 1831 | Inc. Ab. | 12.00 | 20.00 | 32.50 | 75.00 |

Mint mark: W

| B204.11 (C-A204.18) | 1831 | Inc. Ab. | 12.00 | 20.00 | 30.00 | 65.00 |

Mint mark: A
Rev: Mint marks at edge outside wreath.

C#	Date	Mintage	Fine	VF	XF	Unc
204.1 (C204)	1832	7.800	9.00	15.00	35.00	150.00
	1833	8.211	9.00	15.00	35.00	150.00
	1834	11.307	9.00	15.00	35.00	150.00
	1835	5.807	9.00	15.00	35.00	150.00
	1836	1.940	9.00	15.00	35.00	150.00
	1837	6.884	9.00	15.00	35.00	150.00
	1838	4.805	9.00	15.00	35.00	150.00
	1839	5.071	9.00	15.00	35.00	150.00
	1840	4.769	9.00	15.00	35.00	150.00
	1841	1.005	9.00	15.00	35.00	150.00
	1842	.755	15.00	30.00	60.00	250.00
	1843	1.838	9.00	15.00	35.00	150.00
	1844	1.971	9.00	15.00	35.00	150.00
	1845(d)	3.096	9.00	15.00	35.00	150.00
	1845(p)	I.A.	9.00	15.00	35.00	150.00
	1846	5.434	9.00	15.00	35.00	150.00
	1847	12.578	9.00	15.00	35.00	150.00
	1848	3.196	9.00	15.00	35.00	150.00
	1848	—	—	—	Proof	1500.

Mint mark: B

204.2	1832	2.852	9.00	15.00	35.00	150.00
	1833	3.791	9.00	15.00	35.00	150.00
	1834	4.453	9.00	15.00	35.00	150.00
	1835	2.793	9.00	15.00	35.00	150.00
	1836	2.631	9.00	15.00	35.00	150.00
	1837	6.075	9.00	15.00	35.00	150.00
	1838	4.002	9.00	15.00	35.00	150.00
	1839	3.467	9.00	15.00	35.00	150.00
	1840	3.337	9.00	15.00	35.00	150.00
	1841	1.652	9.00	15.00	35.00	150.00
	1842	3.489	9.00	15.00	35.00	150.00
	1843	2.472	9.00	15.00	35.00	150.00
	1844	.361	15.00	30.00	60.00	250.00

Mint mark: BB

204.3	1832	1.725	9.00	15.00	35.00	150.00
	1833	1.799	9.00	15.00	35.00	150.00
	1834 bee	1.621	15.00	30.00	60.00	250.00
	1834(b)	I.A.	9.00	15.00	35.00	150.00
	1835	1.286	9.00	15.00	35.00	150.00
	1836	1.188	9.00	15.00	35.00	150.00
	1837	.600	15.00	30.00	60.00	250.00
	1838	1.535	9.00	15.00	35.00	150.00

C#	Date	Mintage	Fine	VF	XF	Unc
204.3	1839	1.064	9.00	15.00	35.00	150.00
	1840	1.186	9.00	15.00	35.00	150.00
	1841	2.082	9.00	15.00	35.00	150.00
	1842	2.471	9.00	15.00	35.00	150.00
	1843	1.422	9.00	15.00	35.00	150.00
	1844	1.890	9.00	15.00	35.00	150.00
	1845	2.041	9.00	15.00	35.00	150.00
	1846	.840	9.00	15.00	35.00	150.00
	1847	1.577	9.00	15.00	35.00	150.00
	1848	.935	9.00	15.00	35.00	150.00

Mint mark: D

204.4	1832	3.007	9.00	15.00	35.00	150.00
	1833	1.487	9.00	15.00	35.00	150.00
	1834	2.119	9.00	15.00	35.00	150.00
	1835	1.084	9.00	15.00	35.00	150.00
	1836	.200	15.00	30.00	60.00	250.00
	1837	.093	25.00	50.00	125.00	400.00
	1838	.149	15.00	30.00	60.00	250.00
	1839(b)	.519	15.00	30.00	60.00	250.00
	1839(a)	I.A.	15.00	30.00	60.00	250.00
	1840	.070	30.00	60.00	125.00	400.00

Mint mark: H

204.5	1832	.900	9.00	15.00	35.00	150.00
	1833/2	.844	15.00	30.00	60.00	250.00
	1833	Inc. Ab.	9.00	15.00	35.00	150.00
	1834	2.184	9.00	15.00	35.00	150.00
	1835	.467	15.00	30.00	50.00	225.00

Mint mark: I

204.6	1832	.703	15.00	30.00	50.00	225.00
	1833	1.014	15.00	30.00	60.00	250.00
	1834	1.933	9.00	15.00	35.00	150.00
	1835	.598	15.00	30.00	50.00	225.00

Mint mark: K

204.7	1832	.602	15.00	30.00	60.00	250.00
	1833	.749	9.00	15.00	35.00	150.00
	1834	2.157	9.00	15.00	35.00	150.00
	1835	.928	9.00	15.00	35.00	150.00
	1836	.296	15.00	30.00	60.00	250.00
	1837	.813	9.00	15.00	35.00	150.00
	1838	.450	9.00	15.00	35.00	150.00
	1839	.897	9.00	15.00	35.00	150.00
	1840	1.186	9.00	15.00	35.00	150.00
	1841	.995	9.00	15.00	35.00	150.00
	1842	1.026	9.00	15.00	35.00	150.00
	1843	.794	9.00	15.00	35.00	150.00
	1844	.398	9.00	15.00	35.00	150.00
	1845	.537	9.00	15.00	35.00	150.00
	1846	.511	9.00	15.00	35.00	150.00
	1847	.167	15.00	30.00	60.00	250.00
	1848	.166	25.00	50.00	125.00	400.00

Mint mark: L

204.8	1832	.567	9.00	15.00	35.00	150.00
	1833	.378	15.00	30.00	50.00	225.00
	1834	.359	15.00	30.00	50.00	225.00
	1835	.064	30.00	60.00	125.00	400.00

Mint mark: M

204.9	1832	.729	15.00	30.00	60.00	250.00
	1833	.669	15.00	30.00	60.00	250.00
	1834	.889	10.00	20.00	40.00	175.00
	1835	.412	15.00	30.00	60.00	250.00
	1836	.072	30.00	60.00	150.00	400.00

Mint mark: MA

204.10	1832	1.184	9.00	15.00	35.00	150.00
	1833	.872	15.00	30.00	60.00	250.00
	1834	.489	9.00	15.00	35.00	150.00
	1835	.373	12.50	25.00	50.00	225.00
	1836	.362	12.50	25.00	50.00	225.00
	1837	.724	9.00	15.00	35.00	150.00
	1838	2.116	9.00	15.00	35.00	150.00
	1839	.020	50.00	100.00	200.00	550.00

Mint mark: Q

204.11	1832	.716	9.00	15.00	35.00	150.00
	1833	.663	9.00	15.00	35.00	150.00
	1834	.942	9.00	15.00	35.00	150.00
	1835	.040	30.00	60.00	150.00	400.00

Mint mark: T

204.12	1832	1.592	9.00	15.00	35.00	150.00
	1833	1.437	9.00	15.00	35.00	150.00
	1834	2.119	9.00	15.00	35.00	150.00
	1835	.294	20.00	35.00	60.00	250.00

Mint mark: W

204.13	1832	4.483	9.00	15.00	35.00	150.00
	1833	9.270	9.00	15.00	35.00	150.00
	1834	11.733	9.00	15.00	35.00	150.00
	1835	5.016	9.00	15.00	35.00	150.00
	1836	1.614	9.00	15.00	35.00	150.00
	1837	6.652	9.00	15.00	35.00	150.00
	1838	4.190	9.00	15.00	35.00	150.00
	1839	3.269	9.00	15.00	35.00	150.00
	1840(c)	1.714	9.00	15.00	35.00	150.00
	1840(r)	I.A.	15.00	30.00	60.00	250.00
	1841	8.926	9.00	15.00	35.00	150.00
	1842	5.436	9.00	15.00	35.00	150.00
	1843	7.846	9.00	15.00	35.00	150.00
	1844	8.775	9.00	15.00	35.00	150.00
	1845W	11.107	9.00	15.00	35.00	150.00
	1846	1.658	9.00	15.00	35.00	150.00

Mint mark: A
Second Republic

Y#	Date	Mintage	Fine	VF	XF	Unc
7.1	1848	16.648	8.00	12.50	25.00	100.00
	1849	29.338	8.00	12.50	25.00	100.00
	1849	—	—	—	Proof	1750.

Mint mark: BB

7.2	1848	2.300	12.00	20.00	40.00	175.00
	1849	2.594	12.00	20.00	40.00	175.00

Mint mark: D

7.3	1848	.136	45.00	90.00	175.00	500.00
	1849	9.711	90.00	200.00	350.00	1000.

Mint mark: K

7.4	1848	.428	25.00	50.00	100.00	375.00
	1849	.471	30.00	55.00	125.00	375.00

Mint mark: A

6.1	1849	7.437	12.00	18.00	45.00	175.00
	1850	14.619	12.00	18.00	35.00	150.00
	1851	13.223	12.00	18.00	35.00	150.00

Mint mark: BB

6.2	1849	.916	15.00	25.00	65.00	250.00
	1850	1.169	35.00	70.00	150.00	350.00

Mint mark: K

6.3	1850	.332	40.00	80.00	175.00	450.00

Mint mark: A

13.1	1852	16.117	12.50	25.00	75.00	250.00
1852 sign. J.J.Barre	Inc. Ab.	100.00	200.00	400.00	700.00

Mint mark: BB

13.2	1852	.041	100.00	200.00	400.00	1250.

Mint mark: A
Second Empire

26.1	1854	.011	175.00	300.00	500.00	1500.
	1855	4.075	25.00	50.00	100.00	400.00
	1856	4.683	25.00	50.00	100.00	400.00
	1857	.093	150.00	325.00	650.00	1750.
	1858	.027	150.00	325.00	600.00	1600.
	1859	3.365	250.00	500.00	1000.	2000.

Mint mark: BB

Y#	Date	Mintage	Fine	VF	XF	Unc
26.2	1855	.786	30.00	55.00	200.00	600.00
	1856	2.223	25.00	45.00	200.00	600.00

Mint mark: D

26.3	1855	—	60.00	125.00	250.00	800.00
	1856	2.249	25.00	45.00	200.00	600.00

1.6129 g, .900 GOLD, .0467 oz AGW
Mint mark: A
Bare head, 14.4mm.

33	1854	3.562	35.00	65.00	100.00	275.00
1854 plain edge	Inc. Ab.	50.00	100.00	150.00	300.00
	1855	.938	65.00	110.00	200.00	400.00

16.7mm.

33a.1	1856	2.960	30.00	40.00	65.00	175.00
	1857	3.479	30.00	40.00	65.00	175.00
	1858	2.983	30.00	40.00	65.00	175.00
	1859	5.660	30.00	40.00	65.00	175.00
	1860	4.798	30.00	40.00	65.00	175.00

Mint mark: BB

33a.2	1858	—	65.00	125.00	200.00	450.00
	1859	2.279	30.00	40.00	65.00	175.00
	1860	2.022	30.00	40.00	65.00	175.00

25.0000 g, .900 SILVER, .7234 oz ASW
Mint mark: A

32.1	1861	.022	125.00	250.00	500.00	1000.
	1862	.021	125.00	250.00	500.00	1000.
	1863	.022	125.00	250.00	500.00	1000.
	1864	.032	125.00	250.00	500.00	1000.
	1865	.025	125.00	250.00	500.00	1000.
	1866	.038	125.00	250.00	500.00	1000.
	1867	6.586	8.00	12.00	25.00	125.00
	1868	6.634	8.00	12.00	25.00	125.00
	1869	2.056	8.00	12.00	25.00	175.00
	1870	6.620	8.00	12.00	25.00	125.00

Mint mark: BB

32.2	1865	.073	125.00	250.00	500.00	1000.
	1867	4.224	8.00	12.00	25.00	125.00
	1868	12.090	8.00	12.00	25.00	125.00
	1869	9.597	8.00	12.00	25.00	125.00
	1870	2.055	8.00	12.00	25.00	175.00

1.6129 g, .900 GOLD, .0467 oz AGW
Mint mark: A
Laureate head

38.1	1862	1.101	30.00	35.00	65.00	175.00
	1863	1.591	30.00	35.00	65.00	175.00
	1864	2.240	30.00	35.00	65.00	175.00
	1865	.824	30.00	35.00	65.00	175.00
	1866	1.949	30.00	35.00	65.00	175.00
	1867	1.006	30.00	35.00	65.00	175.00
	1868	1.864	30.00	35.00	65.00	175.00

FRANCE 570

Mint mark: BB

Y#	Date	Mintage	Fine	VF	XF	Unc
38.2	1862	.882	30.00	35.00	65.00	175.00
	1863	1.104	30.00	35.00	65.00	175.00
	1864	1.000	30.00	35.00	65.00	175.00
	1865	.828	30.00	35.00	65.00	175.00
	1866	1.388	30.00	35.00	65.00	175.00
	1867	1.504	30.00	35.00	65.00	175.00
	1868	.439	30.00	35.00	70.00	200.00
	1869	.288	30.00	35.00	75.00	225.00

25.0000 g, .900 SILVER, .7234 oz ASW
Mint mark: A
Obv: E.A.OUDINE F. below truncation.

| 46.1 | 1870(a) | .064 | 45.00 | 100.00 | 350.00 | 600.00 |

Mint mark: K

46.2	1870(a)	.544	50.00	80.00	175.00	500.00
	1870 M/star	I.A.	40.00	80.00	175.00	500.00
	1871 M/star	.630	35.00	80.00	175.00	500.00

Obv: A.E.OUDINE F. (error) below truncation.

| 46.3 | 1870 M/star | I.A. | 100.00 | 250.00 | 500.00 | 1000. |

Obv: E.A.OUDINE F. (error) below truncation.

| 46.4 | 1870 M/star | I.A. | 100.00 | 250.00 | 500.00 | 1000. |

Mint mark: A
Third Republic

| 51 | 1870 | 1.185 | 20.00 | 40.00 | 100.00 | 350.00 |

52.1	1870	.261	35.00	70.00	175.00	400.00
	1871	.238	35.00	70.00	175.00	400.00
	1872	.057	30.00	55.00	125.00	250.00
	1873	27.077	7.00	9.00	14.00	30.00
	1874	7.999	8.00	10.00	18.00	45.00
	1875	13.339	8.00	10.00	18.00	40.00
	1876	8.800	8.00	10.00	18.00	60.00
	1877	2.632	15.00	15.00	25.00	90.00
	1878	1.154	600.00	1200.	2000.	3500.
	1878	30 pcs.	—	—	Proof	6000.

Mint mark: K

52.2	1871	.075	70.00	160.00	300.00	650.00
	1872	.021	300.00	450.00	750.00	1500.
	1873	3.853	8.00	11.00	22.50	50.00
	1874	4.000	8.00	11.00	22.50	50.00
	1875	1.661	12.00	16.00	35.00	120.00
	1876	1.732	12.00	16.00	35.00	120.00
	1877	.661	20.00	30.00	80.00	200.00
	1878	.263	30.00	60.00	120.00	300.00

Trident

Mint mark: A
Edge inscription: DIEU PROTEGE LA FRANCE.
Trident symbol-issued by Commune.

Y#	Date	Mintage	Fine	VF	XF	Unc
52a (53)	1871	.075	125.00	200.00	350.00	650.00

Edge inscription: TRAVAIL-GARANTIE-NATIONALE.

| 52b (53a) | 1871 | .010 | | | | |

1.6129 g, .900 GOLD, .0467 oz AGW

| A54 | 1878 | 30 pcs. | — | — | Proof | 6000. |
| | 1889 | 40 pcs. | — | — | Proof | 6000. |

NICKEL
Mint: Paris - w/o mint mark.

| 83 | 1933(a) | 160.078 | 1.00 | 1.50 | 3.00 | 5.00 |

84	1933(a)	56.686	.50	1.00	2.00	4.00
	1935(a)	54.164	.50	1.00	2.00	4.00
	1936(a)	.117	300.00	600.00	1000.	1500.
	1937(a)	.157	30.00	60.00	100.00	150.00
	1938(a)	4.977	10.00	20.00	40.00	60.00

ALUMINUM-BRONZE
For Colonial use in Algeria.

84a.1	1938(a)	10.144	6.00	12.00	25.00	60.00
(Y84a)	1939(a)	Inc. Ab.	2.50	5.00	10.00	17.50
	1940(a)	38.758	1.00	1.50	2.50	7.50

For Colonial use in Africa.

84a.2	1945(a)	13.044	1.50	3.00	5.00	10.00
(Y84a.1)	1946(a)	21.790	1.50	3.00	5.00	10.00
	1947(a)	2.662	125.00	250.00	350.00	500.00

Mint mark: C

| 84a.3 | 1945 | Inc. Ab. | 2.50 | 5.00 | 10.00 | 20.00 |
| | 1946 | Inc. Ab. | 5.00 | 10.00 | 15.00 | 30.00 |

ALUMINUM
Mint: Paris - w/o mint mark.

84b.1	1945(a)	95.399	.20	.35	.75	2.75
	1946(a)	61.332	.20	.35	.75	2.75
	1947(a)	46.576	.20	.35	.75	2.75
	1948(a)	104.473	.20	.35	.75	2.25
	1949(a)	203.252	.20	.35	.75	2.25
	1950(a)	128.372	.20	.35	.75	2.25
	1952(a)	4.000	7.50	15.00	30.00	100.00

NOTE: Exist with open and closed "9"s.

Mint mark: B

Y#	Date	Mintage	Fine	VF	XF	Unc
84b.2	1945	6.043	.25	.50	1.00	4.00
	1946	13.360	.20	.35	.75	3.00
	1947	30.839	.20	.35	.75	3.00
	1948	28.047	15.00	35.00	60.00	100.00
	1949	48.414	.20	.35	.75	3.00
	1950	28.952	.20	.35	.75	3.00

NOTE: Exist with open and closed "9"s.

Mint mark: C

| 84b.3 | 1945 | 2.208 | 2.00 | 4.00 | 8.00 | 20.00 |
| | 1946 | 1.269 | 5.00 | 10.00 | 20.00 | 50.00 |

COPPER-NICKEL
Mint: Paris - w/o mint mark.

| V97 | 1941(a) | 13.782 | 65.00 | 100.00 | 140.00 | 200.00 |

NOTE: Never released for circulation.

12.0000 g, .835 SILVER, .3221 oz ASW
5 New Francs = 500 Old Francs
Fifth Republic

110	1960	55.182	—	BV	2.50	4.00
	1961	15.630	—	BV	2.50	4.00
	1962	42.500	—	BV	2.50	4.00
	1963	37.936	—	BV	2.50	4.00
	1964	32.378	—	BV	2.50	4.00
	1965	5.121	—	BV	2.50	4.50
	1966	5.010	—	BV	2.50	4.50
	1967	.500	—	BV	3.50	7.00
	1968	.550	—	BV	3.50	7.00
	1969	.498	—	BV	3.50	7.00

NICKEL-CLAD COPPER-NICKEL

110a	1970	57.890	—	—	.90	1.25
	1971	142.204	—	—	.90	1.25
	1972	45.492	—	—	.90	1.25
	1973	45.000	—	—	.90	1.25
	1974	26.888	—	—	.90	1.25
	1975	16.712	—	—	.90	1.25
	1976	1.630	—	.90	1.25	2.00
	1977	.460	—	.90	1.50	2.25
	1978	30.022	—	—	.90	1.25
	1979	.050	—	—	—	1.65
	1980	.060	—	—	—	1.65
	1981	.050	—	—	—	1.65
	1982	.050	—	—	—	1.65
	1983	.100	—	—	—	1.65
	1984	.050	—	—	—	1.65
	1985	—	—	—	—	3.00
	1986	—	—	—	—	3.00
	1987	—	—	—	—	1.65
	1987	.015	—	—	Proof	5.00

10 FRANCS

3.2258 g, .900 GOLD, .0933 oz AGW
Mint mark: A

9	1850	.592	55.00	100.00	200.00	600.00
	1850	—	—	—	Proof	4000.
	1851	3.115	BV	65.00	150.00	450.00

Bare head, 17.2mm

| 34.1 | 1854 | 3.900 | BV | 75.00 | 200.00 | 450.00 |
| | 1855 | 6.117 | BV | 75.00 | 200.00 | 450.00 |

Plain edge

| 34.2 | 1854 | Inc. Ab. | 60.00 | 125.00 | 300.00 | 500.00 |
| | 1854 | — | — | — | Proof | 1250. |

19mm

34.3	1855	6.117	BV	55.00	75.00	175.00
	1856	10.778	BV	55.00	75.00	175.00
	1857	14.498	BV	55.00	75.00	175.00
	1858	7.534	BV	55.00	75.00	175.00

FRANCE 571

Y#	Date	Mintage	Fine	VF	XF	Unc
34.3	1858	7.534	BV	55.00	75.00	175.00
	1859	10.111	BV	55.00	75.00	175.00
	1860	6.000	BV	55.00	75.00	175.00

Mint mark: BB

34.4	1855	32,188	BV	100.00	150.00	500.00
	1858	.677	BV	55.00	75.00	200.00
	1859	2.279	BV	55.00	75.00	175.00
	1860	3.104	BV	55.00	75.00	175.00

Mint mark: A
Laureate head

39.1	1861	.363	BV	75.00	125.00	250.00
	1862	2.844	BV	55.00	75.00	175.00
	1863	2.346	BV	55.00	75.00	175.00
	1864	3.339	BV	55.00	75.00	175.00
	1865	1.673	BV	55.00	75.00	175.00
	1866	3.720	BV	55.00	75.00	175.00
	1867	1.205	BV	55.00	75.00	175.00
	1868	3.416	BV	55.00	75.00	175.00

Mint mark: BB

39.2	1861	.044	75.00	100.00	150.00	300.00
	1862	1.462	BV	55.00	75.00	175.00
	1863	1.905	BV	55.00	75.00	175.00
	1864	1.449	BV	55.00	75.00	175.00
	1865	1.576	BV	55.00	75.00	175.00
	1866	2.776	BV	55.00	75.00	175.00
	1867	2.346	BV	55.00	75.00	175.00
	1868	1.117	BV	55.00	75.00	175.00
	1869	.109	50.00	75.00	125.00	175.00

Mint mark: A

54	1889	—	—	—	Proof	8000.
	1895	.214	BV	55.00	65.00	200.00
	1896	.585	BV	55.00	65.00	175.00
	1899	1.600	BV	55.00	65.00	175.00

65	1899	.699	BV	55.00	70.00	125.00
	1900	1.570	BV	55.00	60.00	100.00
	1900	—	—	—	Proof	—
	1901	2.100	BV	55.00	60.00	100.00
	1905	1.426	BV	55.00	60.00	100.00
	1906	3.665	BV	55.00	60.00	100.00
	1907	3.364	BV	55.00	60.00	100.00
	1908	1.650	BV	55.00	60.00	100.00
	1909	.599	BV	55.00	65.00	125.00
	1910	2.110	BV	55.00	60.00	100.00
	1911	1.881	BV	55.00	60.00	100.00
	1912	1.756	BV	55.00	60.00	100.00
	1914	3.041	BV	55.00	60.00	100.00

10.0000 g, .680 SILVER, .2186 oz ASW
Mint: Paris - w/o mint mark.

86	1929	16.292	BV	—	3.00	5.00	9.00
	1930	36.986	BV	—	3.00	5.00	9.00
	1931	35.468	BV	—	3.00	5.00	9.00
	1932	40.288	BV	—	3.00	5.00	9.00
	1933	31.146	BV	—	3.00	5.00	9.00
	1934	52.001	BV	—	3.00	5.00	9.00
	1937	.052	75.00	100.00	150.00	250.00
	1938	14.090	BV	—	3.00	5.00	11.00
	1939	8.299	BV	—	3.00	5.00	11.00

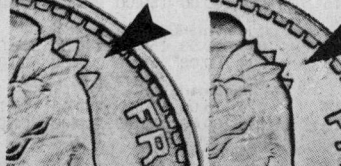

Long Leaves   Short Leaves

COPPER-NICKEL

Y#	Date	Mintage	Fine	VF	XF	Unc
86a.1	1945(ll)	6.557	.25	.75	2.00	6.00
	1945(sl)	Inc. Ab.	7.50	15.00	30.00	50.00
	1946(ll)	24.409	—	—	Rare	—
	1946(sl)	Inc. Ab.	.25	.50	1.25	4.00
	1947	41.627	.25	.50	1.00	3.00

Mint mark: B

86a.2	1946(ll)	8.452	5.00	10.00	20.00	60.00
	1946(sl)	I.A.	.25	.75	1.75	4.00
	1947	17.188	.25	.50	1.00	3.00

Mint: Paris - w/o mint mark.
Obv: Small head.

86b.1	1947	Inc. Ab.	.30	.75	1.25	4.00
	1948	155.945	.20	.35	.75	1.50
	1949	118.149	.20	.35	.75	1.50

Mint mark: B

86b.2	1947	Inc. Ab.	1.50	3.50	7.50	20.00
	1948	40.500	.25	.50	1.00	2.50
	1949	29.518	.35	.75	1.50	4.00

ALUMINUM-BRONZE
Mint: Paris w/o mint mark.

98.1	1950	13.534	.35	.65	1.00	4.00
	1951	153.689	.20	.35	.75	2.00
	1952	76.810	.20	.35	.75	2.00
	1953	46.272	.25	.50	.75	3.00
	1954	2.207	.75	1.50	4.00	12.00
	1955	47.466	.20	.35	.75	2.00
	1956	2.570	—	Reported, not confirmed		
	1957	26.351	.20	.35	.75	2.00
	1958(w)	27.213	.20	.35	.75	2.00
	1959	.125	—	Reported, not confirmed		

Mint mark: B

98.2	1950	4.808	.50	1.00	2.50	10.00
	1951	106.866	.20	.35	.75	2.00
	1952	72.346	.20	.35	.75	2.00
	1953	36.466	.25	.50	1.00	3.00
	1954	21.634	.50	.75	1.25	4.00
	1958	1.500	—	Reported, not confirmed		

25.0000 g, .900 SILVER, .7234 oz ASW
Mint: Paris - w/o mint mark.
10 New Francs = 1000 Old Francs
Fifth Republic

Y#	Date	Mintage	Fine	VF	XF	Unc
111	1965	8.051	—	BV	6.00	9.00
	1966	9.800	—	BV	6.00	9.00
	1967	10.100	—	BV	6.00	9.00
	1968	3.884	—	BV	6.00	9.00
	1969	.755	—	BV	6.00	9.00
	1970	4.799	—	BV	6.00	9.00
	1971	.501	—	BV	6.00	9.00
	1972	.900	—	BV	6.00	9.00
	1973	.128	—	BV	6.00	10.00

NICKEL-BRASS

A112	1974	22.348	—	—	1.75	2.25
	1975	59.013	—	—	1.75	2.25
	1976	104.093	—	—	1.75	2.25
	1977	100.028	—	—	1.75	2.25
	1978	97.590	—	—	1.75	2.25
	1979	110.000	—	—	1.75	2.25
	1980	80.010	—	—	1.75	2.25
	1981	.050	—	—	—	2.50
	1982	.050	—	—	—	2.50
	1983	.084	—	—	—	2.50
	1984	39.988	—	—	1.75	2.25
	1985		—	—	1.75	2.25
	1986		—	—	—	4.00
	1987		—	—	—	2.25
	1987	.015	—	—	Proof	7.50

COPPER-NICKEL
Leon Gambetta Balloon Flight

113	1982	3.000	—	—	2.00	3.50

NICKEL-BRONZE
200th Anniversary of Montgolfier Balloon

115	1983	2.984	—	—	2.00	3.50

200th Anniversary of Birth of Stendhal

116	1983	2.984	—	—	2.00	3.00

FRANCE 572

Francois Rude

Y#	Date	Mintage	Fine	VF	XF	Unc
118	1984	9,988	—	—	1.75	2.25

Centennial of Victor Hugo's Death

| 119 | 1985 | 10,000 | — | — | 1.75 | 2.25 |

12.0000 g, .900 SILVER, .3472 oz ASW

| 119a | 1985 | .020 | — | — | — | 27.50 |

12.0000 g, .999 SILVER, .3854 oz ASW

| 119b | 1985 | 8,000 | — | — | Proof | 50.00 |

7.0000 g, .900 SILVER, .2025 oz ASW
Robert Schuman

| 122a | 1986 | .020 | — | — | — | 22.50 |

7.0000 g, .950 SILVER, .2138 oz ASW

| 122b | 1986 | 6,000 | — | — | Proof | 90.00 |

7.0000 g, .920 GOLD, .2071 oz AGW

| 122c | 1986 | 5,000 | — | — | Proof | 250.00 |

NICKEL

| 123 | 1986 | — | — | — | 1.75 | 2.50 |

12.0000 g, .900 SILVER, .3473 oz ASW
French Millenium

| 125 | 1987 | .020 | — | — | — | 22.50 |

12.0000 g, .950 SILVER, .3665 oz ASW

| 125a | 1987 | .010 | — | — | Proof | 50.00 |

12.0000 g, .920 GOLD, .3549 oz AGW

| 125b | 1987 | 6,000 | — | — | Proof | 325.00 |

14.0000 g, .999 PLATINUM, .4497 oz APW

| 125c | 1987 | 1,000 | — | — | Proof | 625.00 |

ALUMINUM-BRONZE RING STEEL CENTER
Spirit of Bastille

| 127 | 1988 | — | — | — | 1.75 | 3.00 |

GOLD RING-GOLD, PALLADIUM & SILVER CENTER

| 127a | 1988 | 5,000 | — | — | Proof | 375.00 |

ALUMINUM-BRONZE
Roland Garros

Y#	Date	Mintage	Fine	VF	XF	Unc
128	1988	*30,000	—	—	1.75	3.00

12.0000 g, .900 SILVER, .3665 oz ASW

| 128a | 1988 | .010 | — | — | — | 22.50 |
| | 1988 | .010 | — | — | Proof | 55.00 |

12.0000 g, .920 GOLD, .3550 oz AGW

| 128b | 1988 | 3,000 | — | — | Proof | 400.00 |

20 FRANCS

6.4516 g, .900 GOLD, .1867 oz AGW
Mint mark: A
Bare head

C#	Date	Mintage	Fine	VF	XF	Unc
146	ANXI	.058	150.00	225.00	450.00	1400.
	AN12	.988	125.00	150.00	300.00	900.00
	AN12	—	—	—	Proof	5500.

Obv. leg: NAPOLEON EMPEREUR.

| 156 | AN12 | .428 | 100.00 | 125.00 | 350.00 | 1000. |

Redesigned head.

| 156a.1 | AN13 | .519 | 125.00 | 150.00 | 300.00 | 900.00 |
| | AN14 | .148 | 125.00 | 175.00 | 400.00 | 900.00 |

Mint mark: I

| 156a.2 | AN13 | — | — | — | — | — |
| | AN14 | 1,646 | 750.00 | 1250. | 2500. | 3500. |

Mint mark: Q

| 156a.3 | AN13 | 522 pcs. | 1000. | 1500. | 3000. | 4000. |
| | AN14 | 2,710 | 375.00 | 625.00 | 1250. | 2250. |

Mint mark: T

| 156a.4 | AN13 | 918 pcs. | 875.00 | 1400. | 2750. | 3750. |

Mint mark: U

| 156a.5 | AN14 | 1,755 | 500.00 | 800.00 | 1500. | 2500. |

Mint mark: W

| 156a.6 | AN14 | — | — | — | — | — |

Mint mark: A

| 156a.7 | 1806 | .964 | 100.00 | 125.00 | 225.00 | 800.00 |
| | 1807 | .826 | 100.00 | 125.00 | 225.00 | 800.00 |

Mint mark: I

| 156a.8 | 1806 | 8,143 | 200.00 | 400.00 | 800.00 | 1500. |

Mint mark: M

| 156a.12 | 1807 | 5,296 | 225.00 | 450.00 | 850.00 | 1500. |

Mint mark: Q

| 156a.9 | 1806 | 3,973 | 300.00 | 600.00 | 1000. | 1750. |

Mint mark: U

| 156a.10 | 1806 | .017 | 150.00 | 300.00 | 600.00 | 1250. |
| | 1807 | 2,557 | 400.00 | 800.00 | 1250. | 2000. |

Mint mark: W

| 156a.11 | 1806 | 4,242 | 200.00 | 400.00 | 800.00 | 1500. |
| | 1807 | 5,181 | 200.00 | 400.00 | 850.00 | 1500. |

Mint mark: A
Laureate head

C#	Date	Mintage	Fine	VF	XF	Unc
156b.1	1807	Inc. Ab.	100.00	125.00	175.00	500.00
	1808	1.450	100.00	125.00	175.00	500.00

Mint mark: K

| 156b.2 | 1808 | 281 pcs. | — | — | Rare | — |

Mint mark: M

| 156b.3 | 1808 | .022 | 150.00 | 250.00 | 500.00 | 1000. |

Mint mark: Q

| 156b.4 | 1808 | 646 pcs. | — | — | Rare | — |

Mint mark: U

| 156b.5 | 1808 | 1,505 | 375.00 | 625.00 | 1250. | 1750. |

Mint mark: W

| 156b.6 | 1808 | 8,489 | 200.00 | 350.00 | 750.00 | 1250. |

C#	Date	Mintage	Fine	VF	XF	Unc
166.1	1809	.688	100.00	125.00	200.00	550.00
	1810	1,936	100.00	125.00	150.00	400.00
	1811	3,705	100.00	125.00	150.00	400.00
	1812	3,072	100.00	125.00	150.00	400.00
	1813	2,798	100.00	125.00	150.00	400.00
	1814	.328	100.00	150.00	225.00	600.00

Mint mark: CL

| 166.10 | 1813 | 4,380 | 500.00 | 1000. | 2000. | 4000. |
| | 1814 | 887 pcs. | 750.00 | 1500. | 3000. | 6000. |

Mint mark: H

166.2	1809	501 pcs.	750.00	1500.	3000.	4500.
	1810	2,454	500.00	1000.	2000.	3000.
	1811	1,278	625.00	1250.	2500.	5000.

Mint mark: K

166.3	1809	3,614	250.00	500.00	1000.	1500.
	1810	.015	225.00	450.00	900.00	1750.
	1811	.011	225.00	450.00	900.00	1750.
	1812	2,650	375.00	750.00	1500.	3000.
	1813	869 pcs.	625.00	1250.	2500.	5000.

Mint mark: L

166.4	1809	2,383	325.00	650.00	1250.	2500.
	1812	.018	125.00	175.00	300.00	800.00
	1813	.019	125.00	175.00	300.00	800.00

Mint mark: M

166.5	1809	5,007	225.00	450.00	900.00	1750.
	1810	1,983	300.00	600.00	1200.	2500.
	1811	4,971	250.00	400.00	850.00	1750.
	1812	6,498	175.00	300.00	650.00	1400.

Mint mark: Q

166.8	1810	2,343	450.00	875.00	1750.	3500.
	1812	5,470	250.00	500.00	1000.	2000.
	1813	.013	175.00	350.00	700.00	1400.
	1814	3,289	300.00	600.00	1200.	2400.

Mint mark: R

| 166.9 | 1812(c) | .014 | 250.00 | 500.00 | 750.00 | 2000. |
| | 1813 | 5,532 | 300.00 | 600.00 | 1000. | 2500. |

Mint mark: U

166.6	1809	3,400	375.00	750.00	1500.	3000.
	1810	5,891	225.00	450.00	900.00	2000.
	1811	.020	150.00	250.00	450.00	1100.
	1812	7,339	175.00	300.00	550.00	1500.
	1813	925 pcs.	750.00	1500.	3000.	4500.

Mint mark: W

166.7	1809	.017	125.00	200.00	400.00	1000.
	1810	.223	100.00	125.00	175.00	550.00
	1811	.328	100.00	125.00	175.00	550.00
	1812	.346	100.00	125.00	175.00	550.00
	1813	.104	100.00	125.00	175.00	600.00
	1814	.016	125.00	200.00	350.00	1000.

Mint mark: Flag

| 166.11 | 1813 | .090 | 150.00 | 250.00 | 350.00 | 1100. |

Mint mark: A
The Hundred Days

| 166.12 (C166.1) | 1815 | .436 | 120.00 | 200.00 | 300.00 | 900.00 |

Mint mark: L

| 166.13 | 1815 | .018 | 150.00 | 200.00 | 400.00 | 1000. |

Mint mark: W

| 166.14 | 1815 | 9,369 | 200.00 | 350.00 | 700.00 | 1500. |

Mint mark: A
Engraver: Tiolier

| 170.1 | 1814 | 2,684 | 100.00 | 125.00 | 150.00 | 375.00 |
| | 1815 | 2,113 | 100.00 | 125.00 | 150.00 | 375.00 |

Mint mark: B

| 170.6 | 1815 | 1,539 | 300.00 | 600.00 | 1200. | 1500. |

Mint mark: K

| 170.2 | 1814 | .063 | 100.00 | 150.00 | 200.00 | 600.00 |
| | 1815 | .030 | 100.00 | 150.00 | 200.00 | 600.00 |

Mint mark: L

| 170.3 | 1814 | .045 | 100.00 | 150.00 | 200.00 | 600.00 |
| | 1815 | .034 | 100.00 | 150.00 | 200.00 | 600.00 |

Mint mark: Q

| 170.4 | 1814 | .029 | 100.00 | 175.00 | 250.00 | 700.00 |
| | 1815 | .039 | 100.00 | 150.00 | 200.00 | 600.00 |

Mint mark: W

| 170.5 | 1814 | .060 | 100.00 | 150.00 | 200.00 | 600.00 |
| | 1815 | .088 | 100.00 | 150.00 | 200.00 | 600.00 |

FRANCE 573

Mint mark: R
Engraver: T. Wyon, Jr.

C#	Date	Mintage	Fine	VF	XF	Unc
182	1815	.872	100.00	125.00	175.00	450.00

Mint mark: A

183.1	1816	.522	100.00	125.00	150.00	325.00
	1817	2.135	100.00	125.00	150.00	325.00
	1818	2.681	100.00	125.00	150.00	325.00
	1819	2.350	100.00	125.00	150.00	325.00
	1820	1.317	100.00	125.00	150.00	325.00
	1821	.012	125.00	200.00	300.00	650.00
	1822	.213	100.00	125.00	150.00	325.00
	1823	.012	125.00	200.00	300.00	650.00
	1824	1.510	100.00	125.00	150.00	325.00

Mint mark: B

183.2	1816	.022	—	—	—	—

Mint mark: H

183.8	1822	1,253	500.00	1000.	1250.	2000.

Mint mark: K

183.3	1816	4,947	—	—	—	—
	1817	4,803	175.00	275.00	475.00	1000.

Mint mark: L

183.4	1816	.022	—	—	—	—
	1817	.036	125.00	200.00	300.00	650.00
	1818	5,394	150.00	225.00	350.00	850.00

Mint mark: MA

183.9	1824	2,001	625.00	1250.	1500.	1750.

Mint mark: Q

183.5	1816	.016	100.00	150.00	225.00	550.00
	1817	.097	100.00	125.00	200.00	500.00
	1818	.025	100.00	150.00	200.00	500.00
	1819	.034	100.00	125.00	225.00	550.00
	1820	.060	100.00	125.00	225.00	550.00
	1824	.012	100.00	150.00	275.00	650.00

Mint mark: T

183.7	1818	.016	100.00	125.00	200.00	550.00
	1819	8,734	100.00	150.00	250.00	625.00
	1820	5,749	100.00	150.00	250.00	625.00

Mint mark: W

183.6	1816	.054	100.00	125.00	200.00	600.00
	1817	.156	100.00	125.00	150.00	500.00
	1818	1.315	100.00	125.00	150.00	500.00
	1819	.219	100.00	125.00	150.00	500.00
	1820	.044	100.00	125.00	200.00	600.00
	1821	8,446	100.00	150.00	250.00	700.00
	1822	.020	100.00	125.00	200.00	600.00
	1823	7,655	100.00	150.00	250.00	700.00
	1824	.253	100.00	125.00	150.00	500.00

Mint mark: A

190.1	1825	.664	100.00	125.00	200.00	900.00
	1826	.035	150.00	225.00	375.00	1400.
	1827	.154	100.00	150.00	250.00	1200.
	1828	.279	100.00	150.00	250.00	900.00
	1829	7,783	150.00	250.00	425.00	1700.
	1830	.431	100.00	150.00	250.00	1200.

Mint mark: Q

190.3	1826	4,574	500.00	1000.	1250.	2500.

Mint mark: T

190.4	1828	3,175	500.00	1000.	1250.	2500.

Mint mark: W

190.2	1825	.062	125.00	200.00	350.00	1200.
	1826	6,436	200.00	275.00	450.00	1400.
	1827	3,431	225.00	350.00	550.00	1600.
	1828	.015	150.00	250.00	350.00	1200.
	1829	5,946	200.00	275.00	450.00	1400.
	1830	.015	150.00	250.00	350.00	1200.

Mint mark: A
Incuse edge lettering.

C#	Date	Mintage	Fine	VF	XF	Unc
205.1	1830	.018	125.00	200.00	300.00	1200.
	1831	2.162	100.00	125.00	150.00	1000.

Mint mark: B

205.2	1831	.088	150.00	300.00	550.00	1500.

Mint mark: W

205.3	1831	.107	110.00	150.00	200.00	1200.

Mint mark: A
Raised edge lettering.

205.4	1831	Inc. Ab.	110.00	150.00	200.00	1000.

Mint mark: B

205.5	1831	—	125.00	175.00	250.00	1000.

Mint mark: T

205.6	1831	—	500.00	800.00	1250.	2000.

Mint mark: W

205.7	1831	Inc. Ab.	110.00	150.00	250.00	1500.

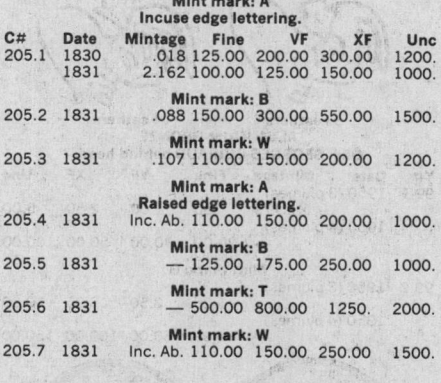

Mint mark: A

206.1	1832	6,360	175.00	350.00	700.00	1500.
	1832	—	—	—	Proof	6000.
	1833	.207	100.00	125.00	175.00	900.00
	1834	.744	100.00	125.00	175.00	900.00
	1835	.097	100.00	125.00	175.00	900.00
	1836	.139	100.00	125.00	175.00	900.00
	1837	.034	100.00	150.00	200.00	900.00
	1838	.173	100.00	125.00	175.00	900.00
	1839	1.012	100.00	125.00	150.00	900.00
	1840	2.045	100.00	125.00	150.00	900.00
	1841	.610	100.00	125.00	175.00	900.00
	1842	.071	125.00	150.00	200.00	900.00
	1843	.106	100.00	125.00	175.00	900.00
	1844	.103	100.00	125.00	175.00	900.00
	1845	939 pcs.	625.00	1250.	1750.	3000.
	1846	.103	100.00	125.00	175.00	900.00
	1847	.385	100.00	125.00	175.00	900.00
	1848	.442	100.00	125.00	150.00	900.00

Mint mark: B

206.2	1832	.015	100.00	150.00	200.00	900.00
	1833	.155	100.00	125.00	175.00	900.00
	1834	.077	100.00	125.00	175.00	900.00
	1835	.026	100.00	150.00	225.00	900.00

Mint mark: L

206.5	1834	.021	100.00	150.00	200.00	900.00
	1835	856 pcs.	625.00	1250.	2000.	3250.

Mint mark: T

206.3	1832	868 pcs.	750.00	1500.	2500.	3500.

Mint mark: W

206.4	1832	.027	100.00	150.00	200.00	900.00
	1833	.032	100.00	150.00	200.00	900.00
	1834	.041	100.00	150.00	200.00	900.00
	1835	.030	100.00	150.00	200.00	900.00
	1836	.010	100.00	150.00	225.00	900.00
	1837	.011	100.00	150.00	225.00	900.00
	1838	.012	100.00	150.00	225.00	900.00
	1839	.022	100.00	125.00	200.00	900.00
	1840	4,550	150.00	300.00	425.00	1500.
	1841	8,524	125.00	275.00	400.00	1200.
	1842	.022	100.00	125.00	200.00	900.00
	1843	.035	100.00	125.00	200.00	900.00
	1844	.034	100.00	125.00	200.00	900.00
	1845	5,018	125.00	250.00	375.00	1200.
	1846	1,408	375.00	750.00	1250.	1200.

Mint mark: A

Y#	Date	Mintage	Fine	VF	XF	Unc
8	1848	1.543	100.00	125.00	175.00	500.00
	1848	—	—	—	Proof	6000.
	1849	1.303	100.00	125.00	175.00	500.00

Y#	Date	Mintage	Fine	VF	XF	Unc
10	1849	.053	100.00	125.00	200.00	750.00
	1850	3.964	BV	100.00	125.00	450.00
	1850	—	—	—	Proof	6000.
	1851	12.704	BV	100.00	125.00	400.00

A13	1852	10.494	BV	100.00	125.00	600.00
	1852	—	—	—	Proof	5000.

35.1	1853	5.729	BV	100.00	115.00	175.00
	1853	—	—	—	Proof	5000.
	1854	23.486	BV	100.00	115.00	175.00
	1854	—	—	—	Proof	4000.
	1855(d)	16.595	BV	100.00	115.00	175.00
	1855(a)	Inc. Ab.	BV	100.00	115.00	175.00
	1856	17.303	BV	100.00	115.00	175.00
	1857	19.193	BV	100.00	115.00	175.00
	1858	16.861	BV	100.00	115.00	175.00
	1859	20.295	BV	100.00	115.00	175.00
	1860	10.220	BV	100.00	115.00	175.00

Mint mark: BB

35.2	1855	1.760	BV	100.00	125.00	200.00
	1856	1.125	BV	100.00	125.00	200.00
	1858	2.017	BV	100.00	125.00	200.00
	1859	5.871	BV	100.00	115.00	175.00
	1860	5.727	BV	100.00	115.00	175.00

Mint mark: D

35.3	1855	.045	100.00	125.00	200.00	450.00

Mint mark: A

40.1	1861	2.607	BV	100.00	110.00	175.00
	1861	—	—	—	Proof	5000.
	1862	4.826	BV	100.00	110.00	175.00
	1863	3.920	BV	100.00	110.00	175.00
	1864	7.059	BV	100.00	110.00	175.00
	1865	2.951	BV	100.00	110.00	175.00
	1866	6.992	BV	100.00	110.00	175.00
	1867	2.923	BV	100.00	110.00	175.00
	1868	9.281	BV	100.00	110.00	175.00
	1869	4.046	BV	100.00	110.00	175.00
	1870	.865	BV	100.00	110.00	200.00

Mint mark: BB

40.2	1861	1.423	BV	100.00	110.00	175.00
	1862	2.907	BV	100.00	110.00	175.00
	1863	4.753	BV	100.00	110.00	175.00
	1864	3.323	BV	100.00	110.00	175.00
	1865	3.088	BV	100.00	110.00	175.00
	1866	6.979	BV	100.00	110.00	175.00
	1867	4.516	BV	100.00	110.00	175.00
	1868	4.829	BV	100.00	110.00	175.00
	1869	7.317	BV	100.00	110.00	175.00
	1870	1.853	BV	100.00	110.00	200.00

Mint mark: A

55	1871	2.508	BV	100.00	110.00	175.00
	1874	1.216	BV	100.00	110.00	125.00
	1875	11.746	BV	100.00	110.00	125.00
	1876	8.825	BV	100.00	110.00	125.00
	1877	12.759	BV	100.00	110.00	125.00
	1878	9.189	BV	100.00	110.00	125.00
	1878	30 pcs.	—	—	Proof	6000.

FRANCE 574

Y#	Date	Mintage	Fine	VF	XF	Unc
55	1879	1.038	BV	100.00	110.00	125.00
	1886	.985	BV	100.00	110.00	125.00
	1887	1.231	BV	100.00	110.00	125.00
	1887	—	—	—	Proof	5000.
	1888	.028	100.00	125.00	175.00	300.00
	1889	.873	BV	100.00	110.00	125.00
	1889	100 pcs.	—	—	Proof	7000.
	1890	1.030	BV	100.00	110.00	125.00
	1891	.871	BV	100.00	110.00	125.00
	1892	.226	BV	100.00	110.00	125.00
	1893	2.517	BV	100.00	110.00	125.00
	1894	.491	BV	100.00	110.00	125.00
	1895	5.293	BV	100.00	110.00	125.00
	1896	5.330	BV	100.00	110.00	125.00
	1897	11.069	BV	100.00	110.00	125.00
	1898	8.866	BV	100.00	110.00	125.00

Edge inscription: DIEU PROTEGE LA FRANCE.

66	1899	1.500	BV	100.00	110.00	125.00
	1900	.615	BV	100.00	110.00	150.00
	1900	Inc. Ab.	—	—	Proof	2000.
	1901	2.643	BV	100.00	110.00	125.00
	1902	2.394	BV	100.00	110.00	125.00
	1903	4.405	BV	100.00	110.00	125.00
	1904	7.706	BV	100.00	110.00	125.00
	1905	9.158	BV	100.00	110.00	125.00
	1906	14.613	BV	100.00	110.00	125.00

Edge inscription: LIBERTE EGALITE FRATERNITE.

66a	1906	—	BV	95.00	100.00	115.00
	1907	17.716	BV	95.00	100.00	115.00
	1908	6.721	BV	95.00	100.00	115.00
	1909	9.637	BV	95.00	100.00	115.00
	1910	5.779	BV	95.00	100.00	115.00
	1911	5.346	BV	95.00	100.00	115.00
	1912	10.332	BV	95.00	100.00	115.00
	1913	12.163	BV	95.00	100.00	115.00
	1914	6.518	BV	95.00	100.00	115.00

NOTE: Some dates from 1907-1914 have been officially restruck.

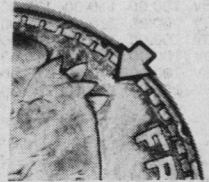 
Long Leaves — Short Leaves
Mint: Paris - w/o mint mark.
20.0000 g, .680 SILVER, .4372 oz ASW

87	1929(sl)	3.234	BV	5.00	10.00	30.00
	1933(sl)	24.447*	BV	5.00	6.00	20.00
	1933(ll)	Inc. Ab.	BV	5.00	6.00	20.00
	1934(sl)	11.785	BV	5.00	6.00	20.00
	1936(sl)	.048	150.00	250.00	450.00	650.00
	1937(sl)	1.189	7.50	10.00	20.00	40.00
	1938(sl)	10.910	BV	5.00	6.00	20.00
	1939(sl)	3.918	500.00	900.00	1200.	2000.

*NOTE: Counterfeits exist in bronze-aluminum with thin silver sheath.

3 Feathers — 4 Feathers
ALUMINUM-BRONZE
Obv: GEORGES GUIRAUD behind head.

Y#	Date	Mintage	Fine	VF	XF	Unc
99.1	1950 (3 plumes)	5.779	.50	1.00	2.50	5.00
	1950 (4 plumes)	—	20.00	30.00	50.00	100.00

Mint mark: B

99.2	1950 (3 plumes)	—	1.25	2.50	6.25	30.00
	1950 (4 plumes)	—	30.00	60.00	100.00	150.00

Mint: Paris - w/o mint mark.
Obv: G. GUIRAUD behind head.

99a.1	1950 (3 plumes)	120.656	1.00	2.00	4.00	10.00
	1950 (4 plumes)	Inc. Ab.	.25	.40	1.00	2.50
	1951 (4 plumes)	97.922	.25	.40	1.00	2.50
	1952 (4 plumes)	130.281	.25	.40	1.00	2.50
	1953 (4 plumes)	58.522	.30	.50	1.25	3.00
	1954 (4 plumes)	1.573	—	—	—	—
	1957 (4 plumes)	.063	—	—	—	—

Mint mark: B

99a.2	1950 (3 plumes)	43.355	20.00	30.00	45.00	100.00
	1950 (4 plumes)	Inc. Ab.	.30	.50	1.00	2.50
	1951 (4 plumes)	46.815	.30	.50	1.25	3.00
	1952 (4 plumes)	54.381	.30	.50	1.25	3.00
	1953 (4 plumes)	42.410	.30	.50	1.25	3.00
	1954 (4 plumes)	1.573	125.00	250.00	500.00	700.00

40 FRANCS

12.9039 g, .900 GOLD, .3734 oz AGW
Mint mark: A

C#	Date	Mintage	Fine	VF	XF	Unc
147	ANXI	.226	200.00	225.00	350.00	1500.
	AN12	.253	200.00	225.00	350.00	1500.

157.1	AN13	.252	200.00	225.00	350.00	1200.
	AN13	—	—	—	Proof	15,000.
	AN14	.121	200.00	225.00	350.00	1200.

Mint mark: U

| 157.2 | AN14 | — | — | — | Rare | — |

Mint mark: W

C#	Date	Mintage	Fine	VF	XF	Unc
157.3	AN14	—	—	—	Rare	—

Mint mark: A

157.4	1806	.196	200.00	225.00	400.00	1200.
	1807	.017	200.00	400.00	800.00	1600.

Mint mark: CL

| 157.5 | 1806 | — | — | — | Rare | — |

Mint mark: I

157.6	1806	7,103	250.00	500.00	1250.	2500.
	1807	1,859	350.00	750.00	2000.	3500.

Mint mark: M

157.7	1806	—	—	—	—	—
	1807	4,994	300.00	600.00	1250.	3000.

Mint mark: U

157.8	1806	.059	225.00	325.00	650.00	1500.
	1807	619 pcs.	1000.	2000.	3500.	—

Mint mark: W

157.9	1806	4,336	300.00	650.00	1250.	3000.
	1807	6,043	300.00	650.00	1250.	3000.

Mint mark: A
Laureate head

157a.1	1807	*.253	200.00	225.00	350.00	1000.
	1808	.044	200.00	225.00	350.00	1000.

Mint mark: H

| 157a.2 | 1808 | .012 | 225.00 | 450.00 | 900.00 | 2250. |

Mint mark: M

| 157a.3 | 1808 | 4,226 | 300.00 | 500.00 | 1000. | 2750. |

Mint mark: U

| 157a.4 | 1808 | 346 pcs. | — | — | Rare | — |

Mint mark: W

| 157a.5 | 1808 | 6,356 | 225.00 | 450.00 | 950.00 | 2750. |

Mint mark: A

167.1	1809	.013	225.00	375.00	700.00	1800.
	1809	—	—	—	Proof	6800.
	1811	1.262	200.00	225.00	300.00	750.00
	1812	.693	200.00	225.00	325.00	1100.
	1813	.045	200.00	300.00	600.00	1500.
	1813	—	—	—	Proof	12,000.

Mint mark: CL

| 167.6 | 1813 | 3,070 | 500.00 | 1000. | 2000. | 3500. |

Mint mark: K

167.5	1810	886 pcs.	—	—	Rare	—
	1811	6,333	300.00	625.00	1250.	2500.

Mint mark: M

| 167.2 | 1809 | 1,402 | 500.00 | 1000. | 1750. | 3250. |

Mint mark: U

| 167.3 | 1809 | — | — | — | Rare | — |

Mint mark: W

167.4	1809	5,925	300.00	600.00	1200.	2400.
	1810	.057	200.00	250.00	450.00	1500.
	1812	.014	200.00	275.00	550.00	1700.

Mint mark: A

C#	Date	Mintage	Fine	VF	XF	Unc
184.1	1816	.041	200.00	300.00	600.00	1200.
	1817	.090	200.00	300.00	500.00	850.00
	1818	.011	200.00	350.00	750.00	1250.
	1820	5,480	250.00	500.00	1000.	2250.
	1822	373 pcs.	—	—	Rare	—
	1823	161 pcs.	—	—	Rare	—
	1824	.015	200.00	275.00	450.00	900.00

Mint mark: B

184.2	1816	767 pcs.	1000.	2000.	3500.	5000.

Mint mark: H

184.6	1822	611 pcs.	1000.	2000.	3500.	5000.

Mint mark: L

184.3	1816	2,923	375.00	675.00	1000.	2750.
	1817	377 pcs.	—	—	Rare	—

Mint mark: Q

184.4	1816	.011	200.00	300.00	450.00	1250.

Mint mark: W

184.5	1816	3,210	200.00	300.00	600.00	1200.
	1818	.353	200.00	225.00	300.00	700.00
	1819	4,610	200.00	300.00	600.00	1200.

Mint mark: A

191.1	1824	.050	225.00	275.00	450.00	2000.
	1826	62 pcs.	—	—	Rare	—
	1827	106 pcs.	—	—	Rare	—
	1828	.052	225.00	275.00	450.00	2000.
	1829	.021	225.00	300.00	500.00	2000.
	1830	.354	225.00	250.00	325.00	1750.

Mint mark: MA

191.2	1830	1,026	—	—	Rare	—

Mint mark: A

207.1	1831	.063	200.00	250.00	500.00	1200.
	1832	.022	200.00	275.00	500.00	1200.
	1832	—	—	—	Proof	9000.
	1833	.221	200.00	250.00	450.00	1200.
	1834	.303	200.00	225.00	400.00	1000.
	1835	.036	200.00	275.00	500.00	1200.
	1836	.053	200.00	275.00	500.00	1200.
	1837	.028	200.00	275.00	500.00	1200.
	1838	.031	200.00	275.00	500.00	1200.
	1839	23 pcs.	—	—	Rare	—

Mint mark: B

207.2	1832	3,947	300.00	450.00	900.00	2200.
	1833	1,392	450.00	900.00	1750.	3500.

Mint mark: L

207.3	1834	.012	225.00	325.00	600.00	1800.
	1835	856 pcs.	600.00	1200.	2000.	4500.

50 FRANCS

16.1290 g, .900 GOLD, .4667 oz AGW
Mint mark: A
Bare head

Y#	Date	Mintage	Fine	VF	XF	Unc
36.1	1855	.152	250.00	275.00	350.00	500.00
	1856	.097	250.00	275.00	350.00	500.00
	1857	.320	250.00	275.00	350.00	500.00
	1858	.085	250.00	275.00	350.00	500.00
	1859	.034	250.00	275.00	350.00	500.00

Mint mark: BB

36.2	1855	3,051	250.00	350.00	600.00	1000.
	1856	3,803	250.00	375.00	600.00	1000.
	1858	9,135	250.00	350.00	550.00	1000.
	1859	.032	250.00	275.00	400.00	600.00
	1860	.029				

Mint mark: A
Laureate head

Y#	Date	Mintage	Fine	VF	XF	Unc
A40.1	1862	.024	250.00	275.00	375.00	600.00
	1862	—	—	—	Proof	7500.
	1864	.029	250.00	275.00	375.00	600.00
	1865	3,740	250.00	400.00	600.00	1000.
	1866	.039	250.00	275.00	375.00	600.00
	1867	2,000	250.00	400.00	600.00	1000.
	1868	.016	250.00	275.00	375.00	650.00

Mint mark: BB

A40.2	1862	7,310	250.00	300.00	400.00	750.00
	1863	8,251	250.00	300.00	400.00	750.00
	1866	.017	250.00	275.00	375.00	650.00
	1867	.020	250.00	275.00	375.00	650.00
	1868	—	350.00	450.00	650.00	1250.
	1869	1,795	350.00	450.00	650.00	1250.

Mint mark: A

56	1878	5,294	350.00	700.00	1200.	2000.
	1887	301 pcs.	550.00	1250.	2250.	4500.
	1889	100 pcs.	—	—	Proof	6500.
	1896	800 pcs.	450.00	900.00	1800.	3500.
	1900	200 pcs.	650.00	1500.	2500.	5000.
	1904	.020	300.00	600.00	900.00	1900.

ALUMINUM-BRONZE
Mint: Paris - w/o mint mark.

100.1	1950	.600	40.00	70.00	150.00	350.00
	1951	68.630	.25	.50	1.00	3.50
	1952	74.212	.25	.50	1.00	3.50
	1953	63.172	.25	.50	1.00	3.50
	1954	.997	15.00	25.00	50.00	75.00
	1958(w)	.501	25.00	50.00	75.00	135.00

Mint mark: B

100.2	1951	11.829	.50	1.00	2.00	7.00
	1952	13.432	.50	1.00	2.00	7.00
	1953	23.376	.35	.75	1.25	5.00
	1954	6.531	4.00	8.00	15.00	30.00

30.0000 g, .900 SILVER, .8682 oz ASW
Mint: Paris - w/o mint mark.
5000 Old Francs = 50 New Francs

Y#	Date	Mintage	Fine	VF	XF	Unc
112	1974	4.200	—	BV	6.50	9.00
	1975	4.500	—	BV	6.50	9.00
	1976	7.509	—	BV	6.50	9.00
	1977	7.859	—	BV	6.50	9.00
	1978	12.006	—	BV	6.50	9.00
	1979	12.000	—	BV	6.50	9.00
	1980	.060	—	BV	10.00	50.00

100 FRANCS

32.2581 g, .900 GOLD, .9335 oz AGW
Mint mark: A

37.1	1855	.051	450.00	500.00	550.00	900.00
	1856	.057	450.00	500.00	550.00	900.00
	1857	.103	450.00	500.00	550.00	900.00
	1858	.092	450.00	500.00	550.00	900.00
	1859	.022	450.00	500.00	550.00	900.00

Mint mark: BB

37.2	1855	4,173	450.00	500.00	550.00	1100.
	1856	876 pcs.	600.00	1000.	1500.	3000.
	1858	1,928	475.00	525.00	625.00	1300.
	1859	9,305	450.00	500.00	550.00	1100.
	1860	5,405	450.00	500.00	550.00	1100.

Mint mark: A

B40.1	1861	—	—	—	Proof	8000.
	1862	6,650	450.00	550.00	800.00	1400.
	1864	5,536	450.00	550.00	800.00	1400.
	1865	1,517	475.00	600.00	1000.	1800.
	1866	9,041	450.00	500.00	750.00	1200.
	1867	4,309	450.00	550.00	800.00	1400.
	1868	2,315	450.00	550.00	1000.	1800.
	1869	.029	450.00	500.00	700.00	1100.
	1870	.010	3000.	6000.	12,000.	20,000.

Mint mark: BB

B40.2	1862	3,078	450.00	600.00	800.00	1400.
	1863	3,745	450.00	600.00	800.00	1400.
	1864	1,333	475.00	600.00	850.00	1800.
	1866	3,075	450.00	600.00	850.00	1600.
	1867	2,807	450.00	600.00	850.00	1600.
	1868	789 pcs.	525.00	800.00	1200.	2600.
	1869	.014	450.00	550.00	750.00	1100.

FRANCE 576

15.0000 g, .900 SILVER, .4340 oz ASW
Mint: Paris - w/o mint mark.
Pantheon

Y#	Date	Mintage	Fine	VF	XF	Unc
114	1982	3.000	—	—	—	22.50
	1982	.025	—	—	Proof	65.00
	1983	4.984	—	—	—	22.50
	1983	.017	—	—	Proof	65.00
	1984	4.997	—	—	—	22.50
	1985	.987	—	—	—	25.00
	1985	.013	—	—	Proof	65.00
	1986	—	—	—	—	45.00
	1987	—	—	—	—	45.00
	1987	.015	—	—	Proof	65.00

Marie Curie's Two Nobel Prizes
117 1984 3.886 — — — 35.00

15.0000 g, .999 SILVER, .4818 oz ASW
117a 1984 1,000 — — Proof 150.00

17.0000 g, .920 GOLD, .5029 oz AGW
117b 1984 5,000 — — Proof 450.00

15.0000 g, .900 SILVER, .4340 oz ASW
Centennial of Emile Zola's Novel, Germinal
120 1985 4.001 — — — 30.00
     1985 .013 — — Proof 65.00

15.0000 g, .999 SILVER, .4818 oz ASW
120a 1985 5,000 — — Proof 125.00

17.0000 g, .920 GOLD, .5028 oz AGW
120b 1985 2,500 — — Proof 450.00

15.0000 g, .900 SILVER, .4340 oz ASW
Statue of Liberty
121 1986 .020 — — — 27.50

15.0000 g, .999 SILVER, .4818 oz ASW
121a 1986 .018 — — Proof 110.00

17.0000 g, .920 GOLD, .5029 oz AGW
121b 1986 .013 — — — 400.00
      1986 .017 — — Proof 450.00

20.0000 g, .999 PLATINUM, .6430 oz APW
121c 1986 9,500 — — Proof 750.00

15.0000 g, .900 SILVER, .4340 oz ASW
General Lafayette

Y#	Date	Mintage	Fine	VF	XF	Unc
124	1987	.025	—	—	—	35.00

15.0000 g, .999 SILVER, .4818 oz ASW
124a 1987 .030 — — Proof 75.00

17.0000 g, .920 GOLD, .5029 oz AGW
124b 1987 .010 — — — 400.00
      1987 .020 — — Proof 450.00

20.0000 g, .999 PLATINUM, .6430 oz APW
124c 1987 8,500 — — Proof 750.00

17.0000 g, .900 PALLADIUM, .4920 oz APW
124d 1987 7,000 — — Proof 225.00

15.0000 g, .900 SILVER, .4340 oz ASW
Fraternity
126 1988 4.853 — — — 30.00

15.0000 g, .950 SILVER, .4582 oz ASW
126a 1988 .020 — — Proof 70.00

17.0000 g, .920 GOLD, .5029 oz AGW
126b 1988 3,000 — — — 450.00
      1988 .012 — — Proof 450.00

20.0000 g, .999 PLATINUM, .6430 oz APW
126c 1988 5,000 — — Proof 750.00

17.0000 g, .900 PALLADIUM, .4920 oz APW
126d 1988 7,000 — — Proof 225.00

15.0000 g, .900 SILVER, .4340 oz ASW
Human Rights
132 1989 — — — — 25.00

15.0000 g, .950 SILVER, .4582 oz ASW
132a 1989 .010 — — Proof 60.00

17.0000 g, .920 GOLD, .5029 oz AGW
132b 1989 1,000 — — — 400.00
      1989 .020 — — Proof 430.00

20.0000 g, .999 PLATINUM, .6430 oz APW
132c 1989 — — — Proof 950.00

17.0000 g, .900 PALLADIUM, .4920 oz APW
132d 1989 — — — Proof 225.00

SPECIMEN 'FDC' SETS (SS)
(Fleur de Coin)

KM#	Date	Mintage	Identification	Issue Price	Mkt. Val.
SS1	1964(7)	25,600	Y102-108,110	4.00	9.00
SS2	1965(7)	35,000	Y102,104,105, 107,108,110,111	7.60	16.00
SS3	1966(8)	7,171	Y102,A104,104,105, 107,108,110,111	9.00	65.00
SS4	1967(8)	2,305	Same as S3	10.00	300.00
SS5	1968(8)	3,000	Same as S3 w/box	10.00	400.00
SS5A	1968(8)	Inc. Ab.	Same as S3 w/o box	—	150.00
SS6	1969(8)	6,050	Same as S3	10.00	80.00
SS7	1970(8)	10,000	Y102,A104,104,105, 107,108,110a,111	9.00	35.00
SS8	1971(8)	12,000	Same as S7	9.00	35.00
SS9	1972(8)	15,000	Same as S7	9.00	40.00
SS10	1973(8)	79,000	Same as S7	12.00	20.00
SS11	1974(9)	98,800	Y102,A104,104,105,107, 108,110a,A112,113	31.00	20.00
SS12	1975(9)	52,000	Same as S11	32.00	20.00
SS13	1976(9)	35,700	Same as S11	35.00	25.00
SS14	1977(9)	25,000	Same as S11	36.00	30.00
SS15	1978(9)	24,000	Same as S11	39.00	30.00
SS16	1979(10)	40,500	Y102,A104,104,105,107-109, 110a,A112,112	55.00	50.00
SS17	1980(10)	60,000	Same as S16	90.00	55.00
SS18	1981(9)	26,000	Y102,A104,104,105,107-109, 110a,A112	—	50.00
SS19	1982(11)	27,500	Y102,A104,104,105,107-109, 110a,A112,113,114	—	85.00
SS20	1983(12)	16,561	Y102,A104,104,105,107-109, 110a,A112,114-116	—	95.00
SS21	1984(12)	13,388	Y102,A104,104,105,107-109, 110a,A112,114,117-118	—	110.00
SS22	1985(12)	12,224	Y102,A104,104,105,107-109, 110a,A112,114,119-120	—	125.00
SS23	1986(12)	13,000	Y102,A104,104,105,107-109, 110a,A112,114,121-122	—	125.00

6.5500 g, .900 GOLD, .1895 oz AGW
Mint: Paris - w/o mint mark.

88	1929	50 pcs.	—	—	3000.	6000.
	1932	50 pcs.	—	—	4000.	7000.
	1933	300 pcs.	—	—	2000.	3000.
	1934	10 pcs.	—	—	10,000.	15,000.
	1935	6.102	—	—	500.00	950.00
	1936	7.689	—	—	500.00	950.00

COPPER-NICKEL

101.1	1954	97.285	.35	.75	1.50	4.00
	1955	152.517	.25	.65	1.25	3.50
	1956	7.578	2.50	5.00	15.00	40.00
	1957	11.312	.50	1.00	2.00	6.00
	1958(w)	3.256	.50	1.00	2.50	10.00
	1958(o)	Inc. Ab.	20.00	40.00	60.00	120.00

Mint mark: B

101.2	1954	86.261	.35	.75	1.50	4.00
	1955	136.585	.25	.65	1.25	3.00
	1956	19.154	.50	1.00	2.00	6.00
	1957	25.702	.75	1.25	1.75	5.00
	1958	54.072	.75	1.50	3.00	8.00

Mint mark: A
Edge inscription: DIEU PROTEGE LA FRANCE.

Y#	Date	Mintage	Fine	VF	XF	Unc
57.1	1878	.013	450.00	475.00	500.00	850.00
	1878	30 pcs.	—	—	Proof	16,000.
	1879	.039	450.00	475.00	500.00	800.00
	1881	.022	450.00	475.00	550.00	850.00
	1882	.037	450.00	475.00	550.00	850.00
	1885	2.894	450.00	650.00	850.00	1250.
	1886	.039	450.00	475.00	550.00	850.00
	1887	234 pcs.	750.00	1750.	3500.	7500.
	1889	100 pcs.	—	—	Proof	13,000.
	1894	143 pcs.	1250.	2750.	5500.	10,000.
	1896	400 pcs.	500.00	1000.	2500.	6000.
	1899	.010	450.00	475.00	550.00	800.00
	1900	.020	450.00	475.00	550.00	800.00
	1901	.010	450.00	475.00	550.00	800.00
	1902	.010	450.00	475.00	550.00	800.00
	1903	.010	450.00	475.00	550.00	800.00
	1904	.020	450.00	475.00	550.00	800.00
	1905	.010	450.00	475.00	550.00	800.00
	1906	.030	450.00	475.00	550.00	800.00

Edge inscription: LIBERTE EGALITE FRATERNITE.

57.2	1907	.020	450.00	475.00	500.00	700.00
	1908	.023	450.00	475.00	500.00	700.00
	1909	.020	450.00	475.00	500.00	700.00
	1910	.020	450.00	475.00	500.00	700.00
	1911	.030	450.00	475.00	500.00	700.00
	1912	.020	450.00	475.00	500.00	700.00
	1913	.030	450.00	475.00	500.00	700.00
	1914	1,281	2000.	4500.	7000.	10,000.

KM#	Date	Mintage	Identification	Issue Price	Mkt. Val.
SS24	1987(10)	15,000	Y102,A104,104-105,107-109, 110a,A112,114	68.00	125.00

PROOF SETS (PS)

PS1	1830(7)	—	C185-191	—	Rare
PS2	1878(5)	30	Y41-44,48	—	Rare
PS3	1889(4)	20	Y41-44	—	Rare
PS4	1897(5)	—	Y41-44,62	—	Rare
PS5	1900(9)	100	Y58-62,63.1-64.1,65-66	—	Rare
PS6	1987(12)	15,000	Y102,A104,104-105,107-109, 110a,A112,114,124-125	151.50	160.00

ANTWERP
ANVERS

Antwerp, the largest town in Belgium, grew from a tiny walled marquisate under Godfrey of Bouillon one of the leaders of the First Crusade in the 11th century to the chief port and commercial center of 15th-century western Europe. Not only was it an acknowledged leader in trade and commerce, but also in the arts. The following centuries carried as much tragedy as triumph. Antwerp was plundered by Spain and its Protestant citizens murdered during the religious troubles of the 16th century. It served as the chief military harbor of Napoleon during the fall of the First Empire. It was the scene of the most famous siege of World War I, and was repeatedly battered by V-bombs during World War II. The French-auspice Antwerp coins of 1814-15 were a necessity money issued while Antwerp, under General Carnot, was besieged by the Allies.

SIEGE COINAGE

The following coins were minted by the French while besieged in Antwerp, Belgium. Some have the monogram N for Napoleon, others have a double L monogram for Louis XVIII of France.

5 CENTIMES
COPPER, 34mm
Obv: N in wreath, date below. Rev: Value.

KM#	Date	Mintage	VG	Fine	VF	XF
1 (C1.1)	1814	180 pcs.	50.00	150.00	350.00	600.00

29mm
| 2.1 (C1.2) | 1814 | — | 6.00 | 15.00 | 35.00 | 75.00 |

Obv: V above ribbon.
| 2.2 (C1.3) | 1814 | .011 | 4.00 | 10.00 | 30.00 | 60.00 |

Obv: V below ribbon bow.
| 2.3 (C1.4) | 1814 | 2,820 | 8.00 | 18.00 | 50.00 | 90.00 |

Obv: JLGN on ribbon
| 2.4 (C1.5) | 1814 | .017 | 5.00 | 12.00 | 40.00 | 75.00 |

Obv: Type I, ornate LL monogram.
| 3.1 (C3.1) | 1814 | .010 | 4.00 | 10.00 | 30.00 | 50.00 |

Obv: V below ribbon bow.
| 3.2 (C3.2) | 1814 | — | 12.00 | 25.00 | 60.00 | 120.00 |

Obv: JLGP on ribbon
| 3.3 (C3.3) | 1814 | .031 | 6.00 | 15.00 | 40.00 | 80.00 |

Obv: Type II, plain LL monogram, JLGP on ribbon.
| 4.1 (C3.4) | 1814 | — | 6.00 | 15.00 | 40.00 | 80.00 |

Obv: V below ribbon
| 4.2 (C3.5) | 1814 | — | 6.00 | 15.00 | 40.00 | 80.00 |

10 CENTIMES

COPPER
Obv: JEAN LOUIS GAGNEPAIN on ribbon, pearls on N.

KM#	Date	Mintage	VG	Fine	VF	XF
5.1 (C2.1)	1814	.018	7.50	20.00	70.00	140.00

Obv: Shading on N. Rev: Similar to KM#7.2.
| 5.2 (C2.2) | 1814 | 7,500 | 10.00 | 20.00 | 45.00 | 125.00 |

Obv: R below ribbon bow.
| 5.3 (C2.3) | 1814 | .066 | 5.00 | 12.50 | 30.00 | 70.00 |

Obv: W above ribbon bow. Rev: Similar to KM#7.2.
| 5.4 (C2.4) | 1814 | .029 | 4.00 | 8.00 | 25.00 | 60.00 |

Obv: Type I, ornate LL monogram.
| 6 (C4.1) | 1814 | .020 | 7.50 | 15.00 | 40.00 | 90.00 |

Obv: Type II, plain LL monogram.
| 7.1 (C4.2) | 1814 | — | 7.50 | 15.00 | 40.00 | 90.00 |

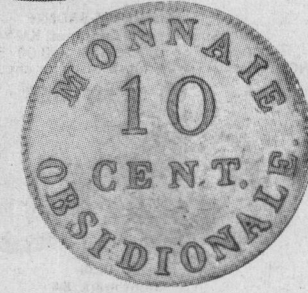

Obv: R below ribbon bow.
| 7.2 (C4.3) | 1814 | .053 | 5.00 | 12.50 | 30.00 | 75.00 |

Obv: JEAN LOUIS GAGNEPAIN on ribbon, R below bow.
| 7.3 (C4.4) | 1814 | .035 | 9.00 | 22.50 | 60.00 | 110.00 |

Listings For
FRENCH AFARS & ISSAS: refer to Dijibouti
FRENCH COCHIN CHINA: refer to Vietnam

FRENCH COLONIES

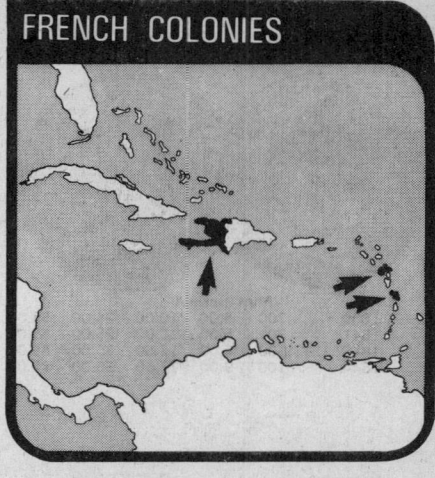

The coins catalogued under this heading were not issued for use in any particular colony but were intended for general use in the West Indies, particularly Martinique, Guadeloupe, and Saint-Dominique (western Hispaniola) until it attained independence as Haiti in 1804.

RULERS
French

MINT MARKS
A - Paris
AA - Metz
B - Rouen
D - Lyons
H - LaRochelle
Q - Perpignan

MONETARY SYSTEM
12 Deniers = 1 Sol (Sou)
100 Centimes = 1 Franc

5 CENTIMES

BRONZE
Mint mark: A

KM#	Date	Mintage	VG	Fine	VF	XF
10.1	1825	.607	2.50	6.00	12.50	35.00
	1828	.501	3.00	7.50	15.00	40.00
	1829	.299	5.00	10.00	25.00	55.00
	1830	.402	4.50	9.00	20.00	50.00

Mint mark: H
| 10.2 | 1827 | .600 | 2.50 | 6.00 | 12.50 | 35.00 |

Mint mark: A
12	1839	.300	4.50	9.00	20.00	50.00
	1841	.607	2.50	6.00	12.50	35.00
	1843	.202	7.50	15.00	30.00	60.00
	1844	.201	7.50	15.00	30.00	60.00

10 CENTIMES

BRONZE
Mint mark: A
11.1	1825	.301	5.00	10.00	25.00	55.00
	1828	.235	7.50	15.00	30.00	60.00
	1829	.152	9.00	17.50	35.00	85.00

FRENCH COLONIES

FRENCH COLONIES

Mint mark: H

KM#	Date	Mintage	VG	Fine	VF	XF
11.2	1827	.300	5.00	10.00	25.00	55.00

Mint mark: A

13	1839	.300	5.00	10.00	25.00	55.00
	1841	.301	5.00	10.00	25.00	55.00
	1843	.100	9.00	17.50	35.00	85.00
	1844	.100	9.00	17.50	35.00	85.00

FRENCH EQ. AFRICA

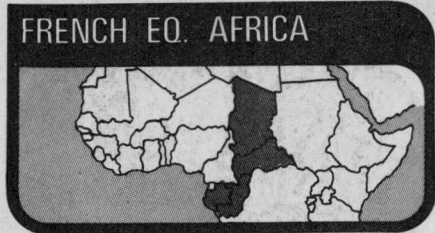

French Equatorial Africa, an area consisting of four self governing dependencies (Middle Congo, Ubangi-Shari, Chad and Gabon) in West-Central Africa, had an area of 969,111 sq. mi. (2,509,987 sq. km.). Capital: Brazzaville. The area, rich in natural resources, exported cotton, timber, coffee, cacao, diamonds and gold.

Little is known of the history of these parts of Africa prior to French occupation - which began with no thought of territorial acquisition. France's initial intent was simply to establish a few supply stations along the west coast of Africa to service the warships assigned to combat the slave trade in the early part of the 19th century. French settlement began in 1839. Gabon (then Gabun) and the Middle Congo were secured between 1885 and 1891; Chad and Ubangi-Shari between 1894 and 1897. The four colonies were joined to form French Equatorial Africa in 1910. The dependencies were changed from colonies to territories within the French Union in 1946, and all the inhabitants were made French citizens. In 1958 they voted to become autonomous republics within the new French Community, and attained full independence in 1960.

For later coinage see Central African States, Congo People's Republic, Gabon and Chad.

RULERS
French, until 1960

MINT MARKS
(a) - Paris, privy marks only
(t) - Poissy, privy marks only, thunderbolt
SA - Pretoria (1942-1943)

ENGRAVERS INITIALS
GLS - Steynberg

MONETARY SYSTEM
100 Centimes = 1 Franc

5 CENTIMES
ALUMINUM-BRONZE
Similar to 10 Centimes, KM#4.

KM#	Date	Mintage	Fine	VF	XF	Unc
3	1943	*44.000	90.00	150.00	250.00	450.00

10 CENTIMES

ALUMINUM-BRONZE

4	1943	*13.000	75.00	100.00	150.00	300.00

25 CENTIMES
ALUMINUM-BRONZE
Similar to 10 Centimes, KM#4.

5	1943	*4.160	200.00	350.00	500.00	750.00

*NOTE: KM#3-5 were not released for circulation.

50 CENTIMES

BRASS
Mint mark: SA

1	1942	8.000	1.50	3.00	7.50	17.50

BRONZE

1a	1943	16.000	1.00	2.00	5.00	12.50

FRANC

BRASS
Mint mark: SA

2	1942	3.000	2.00	3.50	8.00	25.00

BRONZE

KM#	Date	Mintage	Fine	VF	XF	Unc
2a	1943	6.000	1.50	2.50	6.00	20.00

ALUMINUM

6	1948(a)	15.000	.15	.25	.50	2.00

2 FRANCS

ALUMINUM

7	1948(a)	5.040	.25	.50	1.50	4.00

5 FRANCS

ALUMINUM-BRONZE

8	1958(a)	30.000	.25	.50	1.00	3.00

10 FRANCS

ALUMINUM-BRONZE

9	1958(a)	25.000	.25	.50	1.50	4.00

25 FRANCS

ALUMINUM-BRONZE

10	1958(a)	12.000	.50	1.00	2.00	6.00

FRENCH GUIANA

The French Overseas Department of French Guiana, located on the northeast coast of South America, bordered by Surinam and Brazil, has an area of 35,135 sq. mi. (91,000 sq. km.) and a population of 92,038. Capital: Cayenne. Placer gold mining and shrimp processing are the chief industries. Shrimp, lumber, gold, cocoa, and bananas are exported.

The coast of Guiana was sighted by Columbus in 1498 and explored by Amerigo Vespucci in 1499. The French established the first successful trading stations and settlements, and placed the area under direct control of the French Crown in 1674. Portuguese and British forces occupied French Guiana for five years during the Napoleonic Wars. Devil's Island, the notorious penal colony in French Guiana where Capt. Alfred Dreyfus was imprisoned, was established in 1852 - and finally closed in 1947. When France adopted a new constitution in 1946, French Guiana voted to remain within the French Union as an Overseas Department.

In the late eighteenth century, a series of 2 sous coins was struck for the colony. It is possible that the contemporary imitations of this issue outnumber the originals. These are the host coin for many of the West Indies counterstamp items. As an Overseas Department, Guiana now uses the coins of metropolitan France, however, the franc used in the former colony was always distinct in value from that of the homeland as well as that used in the islands of the French West Indies.

RULERS
French

MINT MARKS
A - Paris

MONETARY SYSTEM
100 Centimes = 10 Decimes = 1 Franc

COLONY OF CAYENNE
2 SOUS

BILLON
Mint mark: A

KM#	Date	Mintage	VG	Fine	VF	XF
3	1816	—	30.00	65.00	110.00	250.00

FRENCH GUIANA
10 CENTIMES

BILLON, 2.50 g
Mint mark: A

| | 1818 | 2.000 | 7.00 | 15.00 | 30.00 | 75.00 |

| 2 | 1846 | 1.400 | 7.00 | 15.00 | 25.00 | 65.00 |

FRENCH INDO-CHINA

French Indo-China, made up of the protectorates of Annam, Tonkin, Cambodia and Laos and the colony of Cochin-China was located on the Indo-Chinese peninsula of Southeast Asia. The colony had an area of 286,194 sq. mi. (741,242 sq. km.). Principal cities: Saigon, Haiphong, Vientiane, Pnom-Penh and Hanoi.

The forebears of the modern Indo-Chinese peoples originated in the Yellow River Valley of northern China, from whence they were driven into the Indo-Chinese peninsula by the Han Chinese. The Chinese followed southward in the second century B.C., conquering the peninsula and ruling it until 938, leaving a lingering heritage of Chinese learning and culture. Indo-Chinese independence was basically maintained until the arrival of the French in the mid-19th century who established control over all of Vietnam, Laos and Cambodia. Activities directed toward obtaining self-determination accelerated during the Japanese occupation of World War II.

In Aug. of 1945, an uprising erupted involving the French and Vietnamese Nationalists, culminated in the French military disaster at Dien Bien Phu (May, 1954) and the subsequent Geneva Conference that brought an end to French colonial rule in Indo-China.

For later coinage see Kampuchia, Laos and Vietnam.

RULERS
French, until 1954

MINT MARKS
A - Paris
(a) - Paris, privy marks only
B - Beaumont-le-Roger
C - Castlesarrasin
H - Heaton, Birmingham
(p) - Thunderbolt - Poissy
S - San Francisco, U.S.A.
None - Osaka, Japan
None - Hanoi, Tonkin

MONETARY SYSTEM
5 Sapeques = 1 Cent
100 Cents = 1 Piastre

SAPEQUE

BRONZE
Mint mark: A

KM#	Date	Mintage	Fine	VF	XF	Unc
6	1887	5.000	1.50	4.00	15.00	50.00
	1888	5.000	3.00	7.00	20.00	70.00
	1889	100 pcs.	—	—	Proof	500.00
	1892	1.636	15.00	35.00	100.00	300.00
	1893	.864	75.00	150.00	325.00	500.00
	1894	2.500	7.50	20.00	40.00	125.00
	1897	2.829	7.50	20.00	40.00	125.00
	1898	2.171	10.00	35.00	75.00	250.00
	1899	5.000	2.50	7.50	15.00	50.00
	1900	2.657	7.50	25.00	50.00	150.00
	1900	100 pcs.	—	—	Proof	500.00
	1901	4.843	3.00	7.50	20.00	75.00
	1902	2.500	7.50	20.00	40.00	100.00

1/4 CENT

ZINC

25	1942	221.800	7.50	17.50	35.00	80.00
	1943	279.450	18.00	40.00	65.00	150.00
	1944	46.122	150.00	250.00	400.00	1000.

NOTE: Lead counterfeits dated 1941 and 1942 are known.

1/2 CENT

BRONZE

KM#	Date	Mintage	Fine	VF	XF	Unc
20	1935(a)	26.365	.25	.50	1.75	6.00
	1936(a)	23.635	.25	.50	1.75	6.00
	1937(a)	10.244	.50	1.25	3.50	10.00
	1938(a)	16.665	.25	.75	2.00	8.00
	1939(a)	17.305	.25	.75	2.00	8.00
	1940(a)	11.218	4.00	8.00	20.00	40.00

ZINC

| 20a | 1939(a) | .185 | 100.00 | 200.00 | 300.00 | 600.00 |
| | 1940(a) | — | 200.00 | 300.00 | 400.00 | 700.00 |

CENT

BRONZE
Mint mark: A

1	1885	3.673	1.25	4.00	10.00	35.00
	1885	—	—	—	Proof	450.00
	1886	1.883	2.00	6.00	20.00	60.00
	1887	2.362	1.50	5.00	15.00	40.00
	1888	2.564	1.50	5.00	15.00	40.00
	1889	1.573	2.00	6.00	20.00	55.00
	1889	100 pcs.	—	—	Proof	400.00
	1892	2.648	1.50	4.00	20.00	50.00
	1893	1.852	5.00	10.00	35.00	100.00
	1894	.465	10.00	17.50	70.00	175.00

Rev. leg: UN CENTIEME DE PIASTRE

| 7 | 1895 | .290 | 30.00 | 60.00 | 150.00 | 325.00 |

8	1896	5.690	2.00	3.00	7.50	25.00
	1897	11.055	1.00	2.00	5.00	20.00
	1898	5.000	5.00	7.50	25.00	85.00
	1899	8.000	1.00	2.00	4.00	20.00
	1900	3.000	3.00	5.00	10.00	40.00
	1900	100 pcs.	—	—	Proof	450.00
	1901	9.750	2.00	3.00	7.50	25.00
	1902	5.050	3.00	5.00	10.00	40.00
	1903	8.000	4.00	7.50	10.00	35.00
	1906	2.000	5.00	10.00	25.00	75.00

12.1	1908	3.000	10.00	25.00	45.00	200.00
	1909	5.000	25.00	45.00	80.00	250.00
	1910	7.703	1.00	4.00	10.00	30.00
	1911	15.234	.75	3.00	10.00	20.00
	1912	17.027	.75	3.00	10.00	20.00
	1913	3.945	2.00	7.00	20.00	50.00
	1914	11.027	.75	3.00	15.00	30.00
	1916	1.312	8.00	15.00	30.00	60.00
	1917	9.762	1.00	4.00	10.00	20.00
	1918	2.372	6.00	12.50	25.00	50.00
	1919	9.148	1.00	4.00	7.50	15.00
	1920	18.305	.75	3.00	5.00	12.50
	1921	14.722	.75	2.00	3.00	8.00
	1922	8.850	.75	2.00	3.00	10.00
	1923	1.079	20.00	35.00	60.00	150.00
	1926	11.672	.75	2.00	4.00	10.00
	1927	3.328	5.00	10.00	25.00	50.00
	1930	4.682	1.25	2.75	5.00	10.00

1931 torch privy mark
| | | 5.318 | 35.00 | 50.00 | 125.00 | 375.00 |

1931 wing privy mark

580 FRENCH INDO-CHINA

KM#	Date	Mintage	Fine	VF	XF	Unc
12.1		Inc. Ab.	45.00	85.00	175.00	500.00
	1937	8.902	.25	.50	1.00	5.00
	1938	15.499	.25	.50	.75	4.00
	1939	15.599	.25	.50	.75	4.00

Mint: San Francisco - w/o mint mark.

12.2	1920	13.290	1.00	2.50	5.00	17.50
	1921	1.610	30.00	60.00	150.00	350.00

Mint mark: Thunderbolt

12.3	1922	9.476	1.00	1.75	3.50	9.00
	1923	27.891	.50	1.00	2.00	6.00

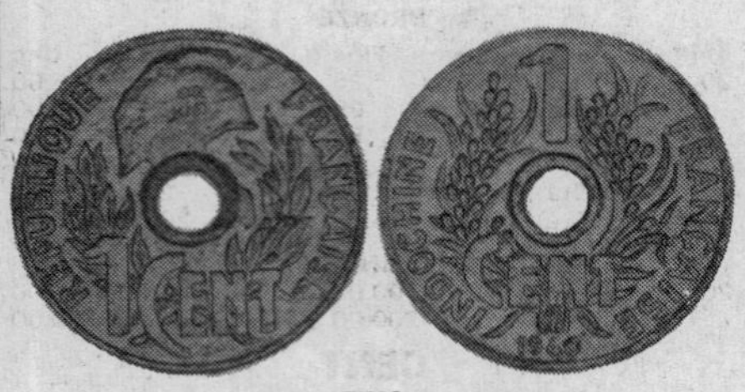

ZINC
Vichy Government Issues

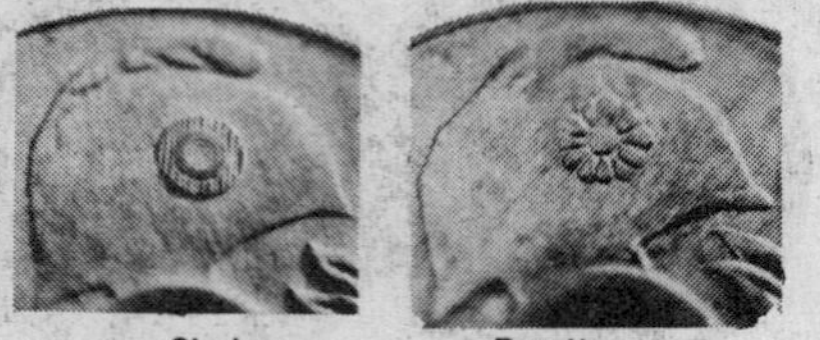

Circles **Rosette**

Type 1, circles on Phrygian cap.

24.1	1940 T1	1.990	5.00	10.00	25.00	50.00

Type 2, rosette on Phrygian cap.
Variety 1, 12 petals - Variety 2, 11 petals.

24.2	1940 T2 V1	—	5.00	10.00	25.00	50.00

Type 2, rosette on Phrygian cap.

24.3	1940 T2 V2	—	5.00	10.00	25.00	60.00
	1941 T2 V2	—	2.00	5.00	15.00	40.00

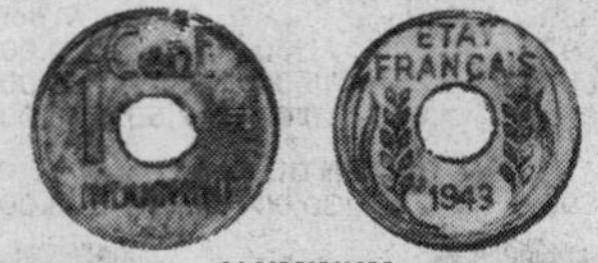

ALUMINUM

26	1943	—	.25	.50	1.00	2.50

NOTE: Edge varieties exist - plain, grooved and partially grooved.

5 CENTS

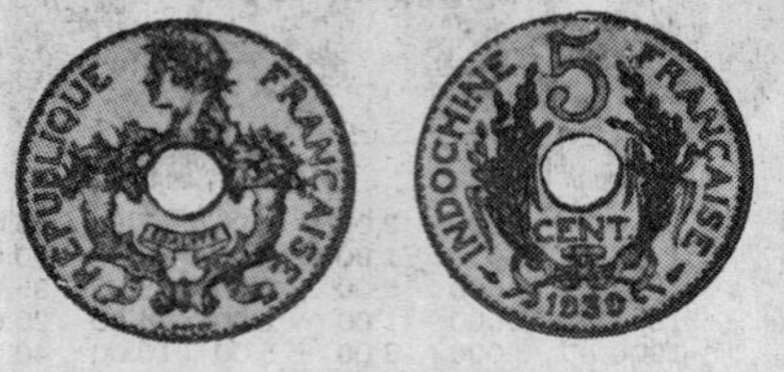

5.0000 g, COPPER-NICKEL, 1.6mm thick

18.1	1923(a)	1.611	3.00	5.00	15.00	40.00
	1924(a)	3.389	1.00	3.00	12.00	30.00
	1925(a)	6.000	1.00	1.75	7.00	20.00
	1930(a)	4.000	1.00	2.00	8.00	25.00
	1937(a)	10.000	.50	1.00	4.00	15.00
	1938(a)	—	—	—	Proof	250.00

Mint mark: A

18.2	1938	1.480	30.00	65.00	100.00	300.00

4.0000 g, NICKEL-BRASS, 1.3mm thick

18.1a	1938(a)	50.569	.25	.50	1.00	5.00
	1939(a)	38.501	.25	.50	1.00	5.00

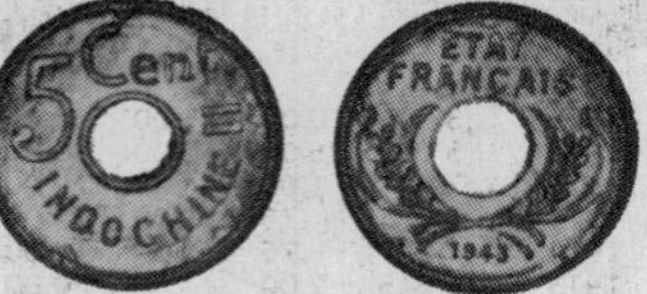

ALUMINUM
Vichy Government Issue

27	1943(a)	—	.25	.50	1.00	3.00

NOTE: Edge varieties exist - reeded - rare, plain, grooved and partially grooved.

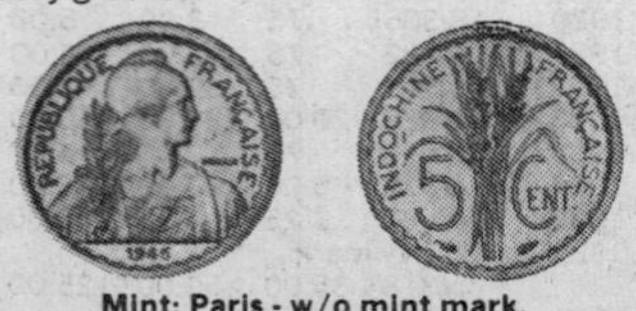

Mint: Paris - w/o mint mark.

Postwar Issues

KM#	Date	Mintage	Fine	VF	XF	Unc
30.1	1946(a)	28.000	.25	.60	1.00	4.00

Mint mark: B

30.2	1946	22.000	.25	.60	1.00	4.00

10 CENTS

2.7210 g, .900 SILVER, .0787 oz ASW
Mint mark: A
Rev. leg: TITRE 0.900. POIDS 2.721

2	1885	2.040	5.00	10.00	25.00	75.00
	1888	1.000	5.00	10.00	30.00	100.00
	1889	100 pcs.	—		Proof	600.00
	1892	.200	40.00	75.00	125.00	300.00
	1893	.600	15.00	25.00	50.00	125.00
	1894	.500	20.00	40.00	75.00	150.00
	1895	.600	20.00	40.00	75.00	150.00

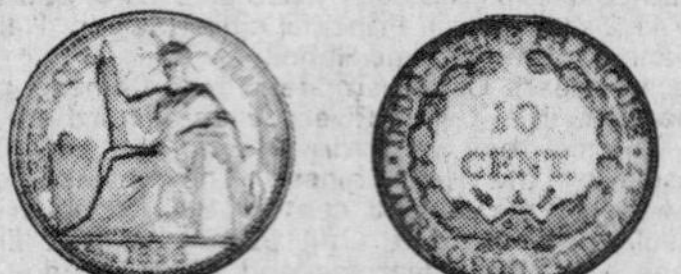

2.7000 g, .900 SILVER, .0781 oz ASW
Rev. leg: TITRE 0.900. POIDS 2 GR. 7

2a	1895	.300	225.00	350.00	500.00	1000.
	1896 fasces	.650	20.00	60.00	100.00	200.00
	1896 torch	Inc. Ab.	50.00	75.00	125.00	250.00
	1897	.900	20.00	60.00	100.00	175.00

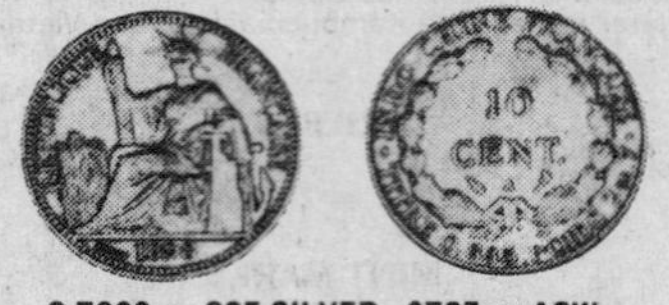

2.7000 g, .835 SILVER, .0725 oz ASW
Rev. leg: TITRE 0,835. POIDS 2 GR. 7

9	1898	.500	50.00	100.00	200.00	500.00
	1899	4.100	4.00	10.00	25.00	80.00
	1900	3.600	4.00	10.00	30.00	80.00
	1900	100 pcs.	—	—	Proof	650.00
	1901	2.950	9.00	30.00	75.00	175.00
	1902	7.050	5.00	15.00	35.00	100.00
	1903	1.300	15.00	40.00	100.00	300.00
	1908	1.000	50.00	100.00	200.00	450.00
	1909	1.000	40.00	90.00	175.00	400.00
	1910	2.689	30.00	75.00	125.00	300.00
	1911	2.311	30.00	45.00	90.00	200.00
	1912	2.500	30.00	45.00	90.00	200.00
	1913	4.847	7.50	12.50	35.00	75.00
	1914	2.667	12.00	35.00	50.00	125.00
	1916	2.000	12.00	35.00	60.00	150.00
	1917	1.500	30.00	40.00	70.00	160.00
	1919	1.500	40.00	75.00	125.00	250.00

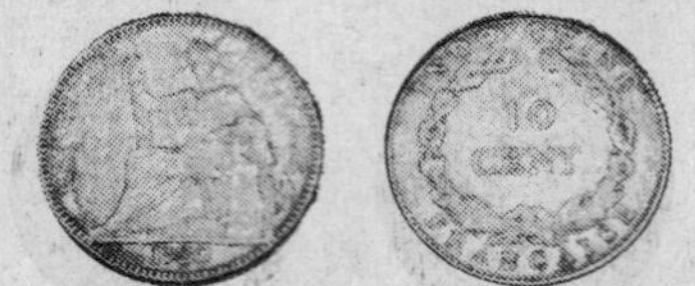

3.0000 g, .400 SILVER, .0386 oz ASW
Mint: San Francisco - w/o mint mark.
Rev: W/o fineness indicated.

14	1920	10.000	10.00	15.00	40.00	100.00

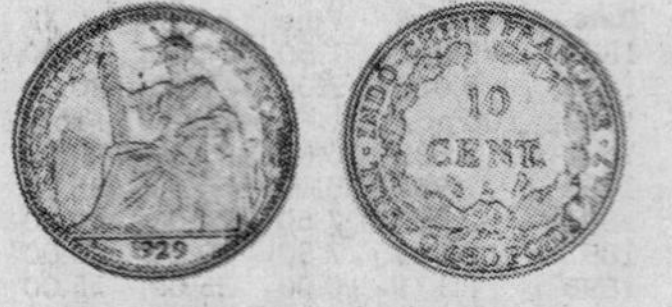

2.7000 g, .680 SILVER, .0590 oz ASW
Mint mark: A
Rev. leg: TITRE 0,680 POIDS 2 GR. 7

16.1	1921	12.516	1.50	3.00	8.00	17.50
	1922	22.381	1.50	3.00	8.00	17.50
	1923	21.755	1.50	3.00	8.00	20.00
	1924	2.816	2.00	5.00	12.50	35.00
	1925	4.909	1.75	3.50	10.00	25.00
	1927	6.471	2.50	7.00	17.50	40.00
	1928	1.593	35.00	75.00	125.00	450.00
	1929	5.831	1.50	3.00	10.00	30.00
	1930	6.608	1.50	3.00	10.00	30.00
	1931	100 pcs.	—	—	Proof	300.00
16.2	1937(a)	25.000	1.00	1.50	3.00	8.00

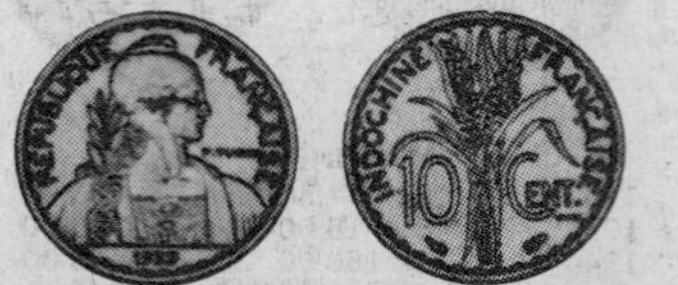

NICKEL

KM#	Date	Mintage	Fine	VF	XF	Unc
21	1939(a)	16.841	.25	.50	1.00	4.00
	1940(a)	25.505	.25	.50	1.25	5.00

NOTE: The coins above have no dots left and right of date and are magnetic.

COPPER-NICKEL

21a.1	1939(a)	2.237	8.00	15.00	30.00	75.00

Mint mark: S

21a.2	1941	50.000	.20	.40	.60	3.00

NOTE: Coins dated 1939 have small dots left and right of date and both are non-magnetic.

Mule. Obv: KM#21. Rev: KM#21a.1.

22	1939(a)	Inc.KM21a.1	35.00	60.00	100.00	175.00

NOTE: W/o dots left and right of date and non-magnetic.

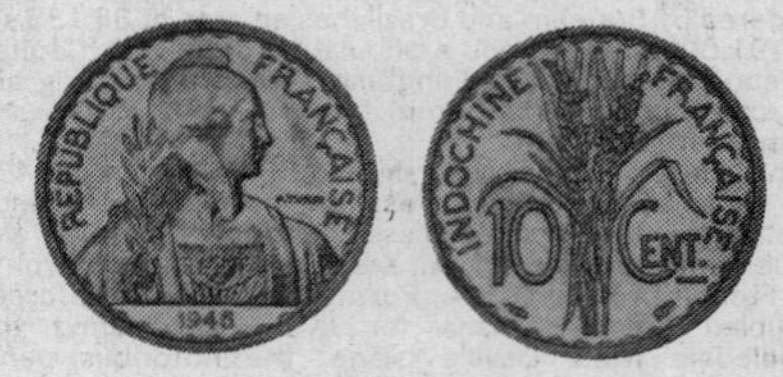

ALUMINUM

28.1	1945(a)	40.170	.25	.50	1.00	5.00

Mint mark: B

28.2	1945	9.830	.50	1.50	3.50	11.00

20 CENTS

5.4430 g, .900 SILVER, .1575 oz ASW
Mint mark: A
Rev. leg: TITRE 0.900. POIDS 5.443

3	1885	1.280	10.00	30.00	75.00	250.00
	1887	.250	40.00	100.00	175.00	375.00
	1887	—	—	—	Proof	500.00
	1889	100 pcs.	—	—	Proof	1000.
	1892	.200	50.00	100.00	225.00	500.00
	1893	.200	35.00	100.00	200.00	400.00
	1894	.250	30.00	70.00	150.00	400.00
	1895	.300	25.00	55.00	110.00	300.00

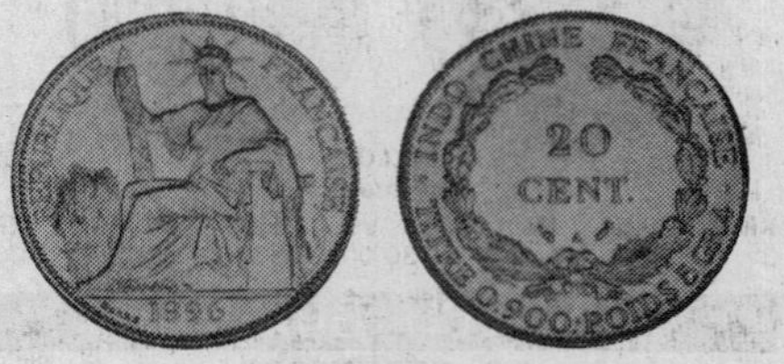

5.4000 g, .900 SILVER, .1562 oz ASW
Rev. leg: TITRE 0.900. POIDS 5 GR. 4

3a	1895	.250	50.00	100.00	250.00	700.00
	1896 torch	.300	50.00	100.00	350.00	750.00
	1896 fasces	I.A.	60.00	150.00	400.00	900.00
	1897	.300	50.00	100.00	350.00	700.00

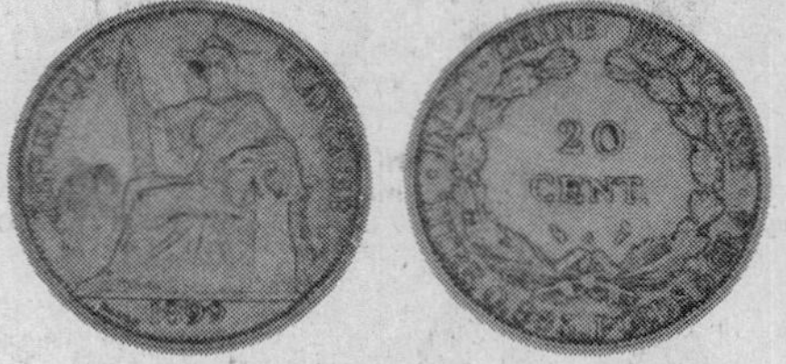

5.4000 g, .835 SILVER, .1450 oz ASW

10	1898	.250	50.00	120.00	275.00	550.00
	1899	2.050	7.50	20.00	60.00	175.00
	1900	1.750	10.00	35.00	100.00	275.00
	1900	100 pcs.	—	—	Proof	1000.
	1901	1.375	20.00	50.00	110.00	300.00
	1902	3.525	7.50	20.00	60.00	175.00
	1903	.675	50.00	100.00	200.00	600.00
	1908	.500	100.00	250.00	450.00	1000.
	1909	.200	100.00	200.00	300.00	1000.
	1911	2.340	7.50	20.00	50.00	100.00
	1912	.160	80.00	150.00	400.00	1250.
	1913	1.252	50.00	100.00	200.00	400.00
	1914	2.500	7.50	15.00	25.00	125.00
	1916	1.000	12.50	35.00	100.00	225.00

.835 SILVER
Mule. Obv: KM#10 . Rev: KM#3a.

13	1909	Inc. Y15	100.00	225.00	550.00	1000.

6.0000 g, .400 SILVER, .0772 oz ASW
Mint: San Francisco - w/o mint mark.
Rev: W/o fineness indicated.

15	1920	4.000	12.50	25.00	50.00	125.00

5.4000 g, .680 SILVER, .1181 oz ASW
Mint mark: A
Rev. leg: TITRE 0.680 POIDS 5 GR. 4

KM#	Date	Mintage	Fine	VF	XF	Unc
17.1	1921	3.663	2.00	4.00	10.00	30.00
	1922	5.812	2.00	4.00	8.00	20.00
	1923	7.109	2.00	4.00	8.00	20.00
	1924	1.400	6.00	12.50	30.00	75.00
	1925	2.556	4.00	10.00	22.50	60.00
	1927	3.245	3.00	7.50	15.00	30.00
	1928	.794	12.50	30.00	60.00	225.00
	1929	.644	15.00	30.00	80.00	250.00
	1930	5.576	1.50	3.00	5.00	10.00
17.2	1937(a)	17.500	1.00	1.50	2.50	8.00

NICKEL
Security edge

| 23 | 1939(a) | .318 | 15.00 | 30.00 | 70.00 | 125.00 |

COPPER-NICKEL
Reeded edge

| 23a.1 | 1939(a) | 14.676 | .25 | .50 | 1.00 | 5.00 |

Mint mark: S

| 23a.2 | 1941 | 25.000 | .25 | .50 | 1.00 | 4.00 |

ALUMINUM

| 29.1 | 1945(a) | 15.412 | .50 | 1.00 | 2.50 | 7.50 |

Mint mark: B

| 29.2 | 1945 | 6.665 | 2.00 | 4.00 | 8.00 | 22.50 |

Mint mark: C

| 29.3 | 1945 | 22.423 | | 1.00 | 3.00 | 9.00 |

50 CENTS

13.6070 g, .900 SILVER, .3937 oz ASW
Mint mark: A
Rev. leg: TITRE 0.900. POIDS 13.607 GR.

4	1885	.040	75.00	100.00	250.00	750.00
	1885	—	—	—	Proof	—
	1889	100 pcs.	—	—	Proof	1350.
	1894	.100	25.00	50.00	125.00	500.00
	1895	.100	35.00	85.00	175.00	600.00

13.5000 g, .900 SILVER, .3906 oz ASW
Rev. leg: TITRE 0.900. POIDS 13 GR. 5

4a.1	1896	.110	20.00	40.00	75.00	400.00
	1900	—	—	—	—	—
	1900	100 pcs.	—	—	Proof	1350.

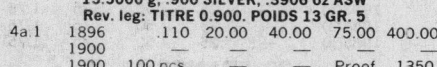

| 4a.2 | 1936(a) | 4.000 | 3.00 | 4.00 | 6.00 | 15.00 |

COPPER-NICKEL
Rev. leg: BRONZE DE NICKEL

KM#	Date	Mintage	Fine	VF	XF	Unc
31	1946(a)	32.292	2.00	4.00	7.00	20.00

PIASTRE

27.2150 g, .900 SILVER, .7875 oz ASW
Mint mark: A
Rev. leg: TITRE 0.900 POIDS 27.215 GR.

5	1885	.800	25.00	50.00	125.00	350.00
	1885	—	—	—	Proof	—
	1886	3.216	10.00	15.00	50.00	175.00
	1886	—	—	—	Proof	4000.
	1887	3.076	10.00	15.00	50.00	175.00
	1888	.948	20.00	40.00	100.00	325.00
	1889	1.240	15.00	25.00	75.00	275.00
	1889	100 pcs.	—	—	Proof	1750.
	1890	6.108	1200.	2000.	2800.	
	1893	.795	25.00	80.00	125.00	400.00
	1894	1.308	15.00	30.00	100.00	300.00
	1895	1.782	10.00	20.00	50.00	150.00

27.0000 g, .900 SILVER, .7812 oz ASW
Rev. leg: TITRE 0.900. POIDS 27 GR.

5a.1	1895	3.798	8.00	12.50	25.00	135.00
	1896	11.858	8.00	10.00	17.50	115.00
	1897	2.511	8.00	12.50	25.00	125.00
	1898	4.304	8.00	12.50	25.00	125.00
	1899	4.681	8.00	12.50	25.00	125.00
	1900	13.319	8.00	10.00	17.50	110.00
	1900	100 pcs.	—	—	Proof	1800.
	1901	3.150	8.00	12.50	25.00	125.00
	1902	3.327	8.00	12.50	25.00	125.00
	1903	10.077	8.00	10.00	17.50	100.00
	1904	5.751	8.00	10.00	17.50	115.00
	1905	3.561	8.00	10.00	17.50	125.00
	1906	10.194	8.00	10.00	17.50	95.00
	1907	14.062	8.00	10.00	17.50	95.00
	1908	13.986	8.00	10.00	17.50	100.00
	1909	9.201	8.00	10.00	17.50	110.00
	1910	.761	30.00	70.00	150.00	300.00
	1913	3.244	8.00	12.50	25.00	125.00
	1924	2.831	8.00	12.50	25.00	125.00
	1925	2.882	8.00	12.50	25.00	125.00
	1926	6.383	8.00	10.00	17.50	100.00
	1927	8.184	8.00	10.00	17.50	95.00
	1928	5.290	8.00	10.00	17.50	95.00

Mint: San Francisco - w/o mint mark.

KM#	Date	Mintage	Fine	VF	XF	Unc
5a.2	1921	4.850	8.00	12.50	25.00	140.00
	1922	1.150	10.00	20.00	40.00	200.00

Mint mark: H

| 5a.3 | 1921 | 8.430 | 8.00 | 10.00 | 17.50 | 125.00 |
| | 1922 | 8.570 | 8.00 | 10.00 | 17.50 | 100.00 |

Mule. Obv: KM#5a.1. Rev: KM#5.

| 11 | 1905(a) | Inc.Y9a | 100.00 | 150.00 | 200.00 | 400.00 |

20.0000 g, .900 SILVER, .5787 oz ASW

| 19 | 1931(a) | 16.000 | 5.00 | 10.00 | 15.00 | 40.00 |

COPPER-NICKEL
Security edge

| 32.1 | 1946(a) | 2.520 | 7.50 | 12.50 | 20.00 | 100.00 |
| | 1947(a) | .261 | 10.00 | 17.50 | 30.00 | 125.00 |

Reeded edge.

| 32.2 | 1947(a) | 41.958 | .50 | .75 | 1.25 | 4.50 |

PROOF SETS (PS)

KM#	Date	Mintage	Identification	Issue Price	Mkt. Val.
PS1	1889(6)	100	KM1-6	—	6500.
PS2	1900(6)	100	KM4a.1-5a.1,6,8-10	—	6500.

FRENCH OCEANIA

The Colony of French Oceania (now the Territory of French Polynesia), comprising 130 basalt and coral islands scattered among five archipelagoes in the South Pacific, had an area of 1,544 sq. mi. (3,999 sq. km.). Capital: Papeete. The colony produced phosphates, copra and vanilla.

Tahiti of the Society Islands, the hub of French Oceania, was visited by Capt. Cook in 1769 and by Capt. Bligh in the Bounty 1788-89. The Society Islands were claimed by France in 1768, and in 1903 grouped with the Marquesas Islands, the Tuamotu Archipelago, the Gambier Islands and the Austral Islands under a single administrative head located at Papeete, Tahiti, to form the colony of French Oceania.

RULERS
French

MINT MARKS
(a) - Paris, privy marks only

MONETARY SYSTEM
100 Centimes = 1 Franc

50 CENTIMES

ALUMINUM

KM#	Date	Mintage	Fine	VF	XF	Unc
1	1949(a)	.795	.50	1.00	2.00	6.00

FRANC

ALUMINUM

2	1949(a)	2.000	.20	.35	.75	3.00

2 FRANCS

ALUMINUM

3	1949(a)	1.000	.40	.60	1.75	6.00

5 FRANCS

ALUMINUM

4	1952(a)	2.000	.50	1.00	2.00	7.00

FRENCH POLYNESIA

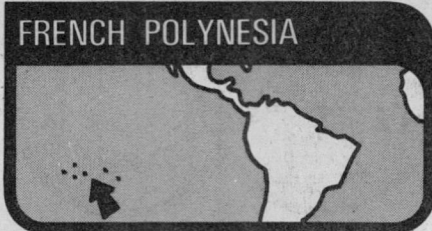

The Territory of French Polynesia (formerly French Oceania has an area of 1,544 sq. mi. (4,000 sq. km.) and a population of *185,000. It is comprised of the same five archipelagoes that were grouped administratively to form French Oceania.

The colony of French Oceania became the Territory of French Polynesia by act of the French National Assembly in March, 1957. In Sept. of 1958 it voted in favor of the new constitution of the Fifth Republic, thereby electing to remain within the new French Community.

Picturesque, mountainous Tahiti, the setting of many tales of adventure and romance, is one of the most inspiringly beautiful islands in the world. Robert Louis Stevenson called it 'God's sweetest works'. It was there that Paul Gaugin, one of the pioneers of the Impressionist movement, painted the brilliant, exotic pictures that later made him famous. The arid coral atolls of Tuamotu comprise the most economically valuable area of French Polynesia. Pearl oysters thrive in the warm, limpid lagoons, and extensive portions of the atolls are valuable phosphate rock.

RULERS
French

MINT MARKS
(a) - Paris, privy marks only

MONETARY SYSTEM
100 Centimes = 1 Franc

50 CENTIMES

ALUMINUM

KM#	Date	Mintage	Fine	VF	XF	Unc
1	1965(a)	.895	.10	.25	.50	1.50

FRANC

ALUMINUM

2	1965(a)	5.300	—	.10	.20	.75

Obv. leg: I.E.O.M. added

11	1975(a)	2.000	—	.10	.15	.50
	1977(a)	1.000	—	.10	.15	.50
	1979(a)	1.500	—	.10	.15	.50
	1981(a)	1.000	—	.10	.15	.50
	1982(a)	2.000	—	.10	.15	.50
	1983(a)	—	—	.10	.15	.50
	1984(a)	—	—	.10	.15	.50
	1985(a)	—	—	.10	.15	.50

2 FRANCS

ALUMINUM

3	1965(a)	2.250	—	.10	.25	1.00

Obv. leg: I.E.O.M. added

KM#	Date	Mintage	Fine	VF	XF	Unc
10	1973(a)	.400	—	.10	.25	1.00
	1975(a)	1.000	—	.10	.25	1.00
	1977(a)	1.000	—	.10	.25	1.00
	1979(a)	2.000	—	.10	.25	1.00
	1982(a)	1.000	—	.10	.25	1.00
	1983(a)	—	—	.10	.25	1.00

5 FRANCS

ALUMINUM

4	1965(a)	1.520	.10	.25	.50	1.75

Obv. leg: I.E.O.M. added

12	1975(a)	.500	.10	.25	.50	1.75
	1977(a)	.500	.10	.25	.50	1.75
	1979(a)	—	.10	.25	.50	1.75
	1982(a)	.500	.10	.25	.50	1.75
	1983(a)	—	.10	.25	.50	1.75

10 FRANCS

NICKEL

5	1967(a)	1.000	.25	.50	.75	2.00

Obv: I.E.O.M. below head

8	1972(a)	.300	.25	.50	.75	2.75
	1973(a)	.400	.25	.50	.75	2.75
	1975(a)	1.000	.25	.50	.75	1.75
	1979(a)	.500	.25	.50	.75	1.75
	1982(a)	.500	.25	.50	.75	1.75
	1983(a)	—	.25	.50	.75	1.75
	1984(a)	—	.25	.50	.75	1.75
	1985(a)	—	.25	.50	.75	1.75

20 FRANCS

NICKEL

KM#	Date	Mintage	Fine	VF	XF	Unc
6	1967(a)	.750	.35	.75	1.25	4.00
	1969(a)	.250	.35	1.00	2.00	7.00
	1970(a)	.500	.35	.75	1.25	5.00

Obv: I.E.O.M. below head

9	1972(a)	.300	.25	.50	1.00	3.00
	1973(a)	.300	.25	.50	1.00	3.00
	1975(a)	.700	.25	.50	1.00	2.50
	1977(a)	.150	.25	.50	1.00	3.00
	1979(a)	.500	.25	.50	1.00	2.50
	1983(a)	—	.25	.50	1.00	2.50
	1986(a)		.25	.50	1.00	2.50

50 FRANCS

NICKEL

| 7 | 1967(a) | .600 | .50 | 1.00 | 2.00 | 5.00 |

Obv: I.E.O.M. below head.

13	1975(a)	.500	.50	.75	1.25	4.00
	1979(a)	—	.50	.75	1.25	4.00
	1982(a)	.500	.50	.75	1.25	4.00

100 FRANCS

NICKEL-BRONZE

14	1976(a)	2.000	1.00	1.50	2.00	4.00
	1979(a)	—	1.00	1.50	2.25	5.00
	1982(a)	1.000	1.00	1.50	2.25	5.00
	1984(a)	—	1.00	1.50	2.25	5.00

FLEUR DE COIN SETS (SS)

KM#	Date	Mintage	Identification	Issue Price	Mkt. Val.
SS1	1965(4)	2,200	KM1-4	—	6.00
SS2	1967(3)	2,200	KM5-7	10.00	10.00

NOTE: KM#SS1 was issued with French Somaliland.
KM#SS1: refer to Djibouti.

NOTE: KM#SS2 was issued with New Caledonia and New Hebrides.

Listings For

FRENCH SOMALILAND: refer to Djibouti

FRENCH WEST AFRICA

French West Africa (Afrique Occidentale Francaise), a former federation of French colonial territories on the northwest coast of Africa, has an area of 1,831,079 sq. mi. (4,742,495 sq. km.) and a population of about 17 million. Capital: Dakar. The constituent territories were Mauritania, Senegal, Dahomey, French Sudan, Ivory Coast, Upper Volta, Niger, French Guinea, and later on the mandated area of Togo. Peanuts, palm kernels, cacao, coffee and bananas were exported.

Prior to the mid-19th century, France, as the other European states, maintained establishments on the west coast of Africa for the purpose of trading in slaves and gum, but made no serious attempt at colonization. From 1854 onward, the coastal settlements were gradually extended into the interior until, by the opening of the 20th century, acquisition ended and organization and development began. French West Africa was formed in 1895 by grouping the several colonies under one administration (at Dakar) while retaining a large measure of autonomy to each of the constituent territories. The inhabitants of French West Africa were made French citizens in 1946. With the exception of French Guinea, all of the colonies voted in 1958 to become autonomous members of the new French Community. French Guinea voted to become the fully independent Republic of Guinea. The present-day independent states are members of the "Union Monetaire Ouest-Africaine".

For later coinage see West African States.

RULERS
French

MINT MARKS
(a) - Paris, privy marks only

MONETARY SYSTEM
100 Centimes = 1 Franc
5 Francs = 1 Unit

50 CENTIMES

ALUMINUM-BRONZE

KM#	Date	Mintage	Fine	VF	XF	Unc
1	1944(a)	10.000	2.00	4.00	12.00	20.00
	1944(a)	—	—	—	Proof	

FRANC

ALUMINUM-BRONZE

2	1944(a)	15.000	—	3.00	5.00	15.00
	1944(a)	—	—	—	Proof	

ALUMINUM

3	1948(a)	30.110	.15	.20	.35	1.00
	1955(a)	5.200	.20	.35	.50	1.25

2 FRANCS

ALUMINUM

KM#	Date	Mintage	Fine	VF	XF	Unc
4	1948(a)	12.665	.20	.30	.50	1.50
	1955(a)	1.400	.25	.40	.75	2.00

5 FRANCS

ALUMINUM-BRONZE

| 5 | 1956(a) | 85.000 | .30 | .60 | 1.00 | 2.00 |

10 FRANCS

ALUMINUM-BRONZE

| 6 | 1956(a) | 64.133 | .50 | 1.00 | 1.50 | 3.00 |

For French West Africa and Togo

| 8 | 1957(a) | 30.000 | .50 | 1.00 | 1.50 | 2.75 |

25 FRANCS

ALUMINUM-BRONZE

| 7 | 1956(a) | 37.877 | .50 | 1.00 | 2.00 | 3.75 |

For French West Africa and Togo

| 9 | 1957(a) | 30.000 | .50 | 1.00 | 2.00 | 3.75 |

Listings For

FUJAIRAH: refer to United Arab Emirates

GABON

The Gabonese Republic, a member of the French Community, straddles the equator on the west coast of Africa. The hot and humid rain forest country has an area of 103,347 sq. mi. (267,667 sq. km.) and a population of *1.11 million, almost all of Bantu origin. Capital: Libreville. Extravagantly rich in resources, Gabon exports crude oil, manganese ore, gold and timbers.

Gabon was first visited by Portuguese navigator Diego Cam in the 15th century. Dutch, French and British traders, lured by the rich stands of hard woods and oil palms, quickly followed. The French founded their first settlement on the left bank of the Gabon River in 1839 and established their presence by signing treaties with the tribal chiefs. After gradually extending their influence into the interior during the last half of the 19th century, France occupied Gabon in 1885 and, in 1910, organized it as one of the four territories of French Equatorial Africa. It became an autonomous republic within the French Union in 1946, and on Aug. 17, 1960, became a completely independent republic within the new French Community.

For earlier coinage see French Equatorial Africa, Central African States and the Equatorial African States.

MINT MARKS
(a) - Paris, privy marks only
(t) - Poissy, privy marks only, thunderbolt

10 FRANCS
3.2000 g, .900 GOLD, .0926 oz AGW
Independence - President Mba
Similar to 25 Francs, KM#2.

KM#	Date	Mintage	Fine	VF	XF	Unc
1	1960	500 pcs.	—	—	Proof	75.00

25 FRANCS

8.0000 g, .900 GOLD, .2315 oz AGW
Independence - President Mba

2	1960	.010				125.00
	1960	500 pcs.	—	—	Proof	160.00

50 FRANCS
16.0000 g, .900 GOLD, .4630 oz AGW
Independence - President Mba
Similar to 25 Francs, KM#2.

3	1960	500 pcs.	—	—	Proof	320.00

100 FRANCS
32.0000 g, .900 GOLD, .9260 oz AGW
Independence - President Mba
Similar to 25 Francs, KM#2.

4	1960	500 pcs.	—	—	Proof	640.00

NICKEL

12	1971(a)	1.300	5.00	10.00	15.00	25.00
	1972(a)	2.000	5.00	10.00	15.00	25.00
13	1975(a)	—	4.00	7.00	10.00	15.00
	1977(a)	—	4.00	7.00	10.00	15.00
	1978(a)	—	4.00	7.00	10.00	15.00
	1982(a)	—	1.50	2.50	4.00	7.50
	1983(a)	—	1.50	2.50	4.00	7.50
	1984(a)	—	1.50	2.50	4.00	7.50

500 FRANCS

COPPER-NICKEL

14	1985(a)	—	2.00	3.50	5.00	7.50

1000 FRANCS

3.5000 g, .900 GOLD, .1012 oz AGW

KM#	Date	Mintage	Fine	VF	XF	Unc
6	1969	4,000	—	—	Proof	75.00

3000 FRANCS

10.5000 g, .900 GOLD, .3038 oz AGW

7	1969	4,000	—	—	Proof	200.00

5000 FRANCS

17.5000 g, .900 GOLD, .5064 oz AGW

8	1969	4,000	—	—	Proof	325.00

Visit of President Georges Pompidou

11	1971(a)	—	—	—	Proof	450.00

10000 FRANCS

35.0000 g, .900 GOLD, 1.0128 oz AGW

9	1969	4,000	—	—	Proof	675.00

20000 FRANCS
70.0000 g, .900 GOLD, 2.0257 oz AGW
Rev: Apollo XI at launching pad.

10	1969	4,000	—	—	Proof	1600.

PROOF SETS (PS)

KM#	Date	Mintage	Identification	Issue Price	Mkt. Val.
PS1	1960(4)	500	KM1-4	—	1200.
PS2	1969(5)	4,000	KM6-10	—	2875.

GAMBIA, THE

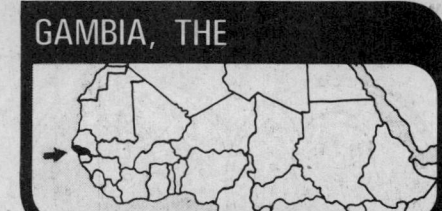

The Republic of The Gambia, an independent member of the British Commonwealth, occupies a strip of land 7 miles (11 km.) to 20 miles (32 km.) wide and 200 miles (322 km.) long encompassing both sides of West Africa's Gambia River, and completely surrounded by Senegal. The republic, one of Africa's smallest countries, has an area of 4,361 sq. mi. (11,295 sq. km.) and a population of *840,000. Capital: Banjul. Agriculture and tourism are the principal industries. Peanuts constitute 95 per cent of export earnings.

The Gambia was once part of the great empires of Ghana and Songhay. When Portuguese gold seekers and slave traders visited The Gambia in the 15th century, it was part of the Kingdom of Mali. In 1588 the territory became, through purchase, the first British colony in Africa. English slavers established Fort James, the first settlement, on a small island a dozen miles up the Gambia River in 1664. After alternate periods of union with Sierra Leone and existence as a seperate colony The Gambia became a British colony in 1888. On Feb. 18, 1965, The Gambia achieved independence as a constitutional monarchy within the Commonwealth of Nations, with the Queen of England as Chief of State. It became a republic on April 24, 1970, remaining a member of the Commonwealth, but with the president as Chief of State and Head of Government.

Gambia's 8 Shillings coin is a unique denomination in world coinage.

For earlier coinage see British West Africa.

RULERS
Elizabeth II, 1952-1970

MONETARY SYSTEM
12 Pence = 1 Shilling
4 Shillings = 1 Dirham
20 Shillings = 1 Pound

PENNY

BRONZE

KM#	Date	Mintage	VF	XF	Unc
1	1966	3.600	.20	.40	.75
	1966	6,600	—	Proof	1.00

3 PENCE

NICKEL-BRASS

2	1966	2.000	.25	.50	1.00
	1966	6,600	—	Proof	1.00

6 PENCE

COPPER-NICKEL

3	1966	1.500	.30	.50	1.00
	1966	6,600	—	Proof	1.25

SHILLING

COPPER-NICKEL

4	1966	2.500	.40	.70	1.25
	1966	6,600	—	Proof	1.50

THE GAMBIA 585

2 SHILLINGS

COPPER-NICKEL

KM#	Date	Mintage	VF	XF	Unc
5	1966	1.600	.60	1.00	2.00
	1966	6.600	—	Proof	2.25

4 SHILLINGS

COPPER-NICKEL

6	1966	.800	1.25	2.50	5.00
	1966	6.600	—	Proof	3.50

8 SHILLINGS

COPPER-NICKEL

7	1970	.025	2.00	4.00	8.00

32.4000 g, .925 SILVER, .9635 oz ASW

7a	1970	4,500	—	Proof	30.00

NOTE: VIP issued proofs have a frosted relief, value: $175.00.

DECIMAL COINAGE
100 Bututs = 1 Dalasi

BUTUT

BRONZE

KM#	Date	Mintage	VF	XF	Unc
8	1971	12.449	—	.10	.15
	1971	.032	—	Proof	.50
	1973	3.000	—	.10	.20
	1974	—	—	.35	.50
	1975	—	—	.10	.20

F.A.O. Issue

14	1974	26.062	—	.10	.15

5 BUTUTS

BRONZE

9	1971	5.400	—	.10	.35
	1971	.032	—	Proof	.50
	1977	1.506	—	.10	.35

10 BUTUTS

NICKEL-BRASS

10	1971	3.000	.10	.15	.50
	1971	.032	—	Proof	1.00
	1977	.750	.10	.15	.50

25 BUTUTS

COPPER-NICKEL

11	1971	3.040	.15	.30	.75
	1971	.032	—	Proof	1.00

50 BUTUTS

COPPER-NICKEL

12	1971	1.700	.25	.50	1.25
	1971	.032	—	Proof	1.50

DALASI

COPPER-NICKEL
Obv: Similar to 50 Bututs, KM#12.

13	1971	1.300	1.25	2.00	3.50
	1971	.032	—	Proof	3.50

10 DALASIS

28.2800 g, .500 SILVER, .4546 oz ASW
10th Anniversary of Independence

KM#	Date	Mintage	VF	XF	Unc
16	1975	.050	—	—	8.00

28.2800 g, .925 SILVER, .8411 oz ASW

16a	1975	.020	—	Proof	15.00

28.2800 g, .500 SILVER, .4546 oz ASW
Commonwealth Games

23	1986	*.050	—	—	15.00

28.2800 g, .925 SILVER, .8411 oz ASW

23a	1986	*.020	—	Proof	30.00

20 DALASIS

THE GAMBIA

20 DALASIS

28.6300 g, .925 SILVER, .8514 oz ASW
Conservation Series
Rev: Spur-Winged Goose.

KM#	Date	Mintage	VF	XF	Unc
17	1977	4,302	—	—	25.00

28.2800 g, .925 SILVER, .8411 oz ASW

| 17a | 1977 | 4,404 | — | Proof | 35.00 |

World Food Day
Obv: Similar to 500 Dalasis, KM#19.

| 20 | 1981 | .010 | — | — | 22.50 |
| | 1981 | 5,000 | — | Proof | 27.50 |

Year of the Scout

| 21 | 1983 | *.010 | — | — | 22.50 |
| | 1983 | Inc. Ab. | — | Proof | 27.50 |

World Wildlife Fund - Monkey
Obv: Similar to KM#17.

| 24 | 1987 | *.025 | — | Proof | 35.00 |

40 DALASIS

35.2900 g, .925 SILVER, 1.0495 oz ASW
Conservation Series
Rev: Aardvark.

KM#	Date	Mintage	VF	XF	Unc
18	1977	4,304	—	—	30.00

35.0000 g, .925 SILVER, 1.0409 oz ASW

| 18a | 1977 | 4,183 | — | Proof | 45.00 |

250 DALASIS

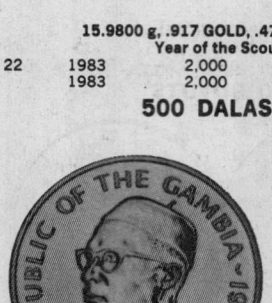

15.9800 g, .917 GOLD, .4712 oz AGW
Year of the Scout

| 22 | 1983 | 2,000 | — | — | 350.00 |
| | 1983 | 2,000 | — | Proof | 500.00 |

500 DALASIS

33.4370 g, .900 GOLD, .9676 oz AGW
Conservation Series
Rev: Sitatunga.

| 19 | 1977 | 699 pcs. | — | — | 650.00 |
| | 1977 | 285 pcs. | — | Proof | 850.00 |

1000 DALASIS

10.0000 g, .917 GOLD, .2948 oz AGW
World Wildlife Fund - Bird

KM#	Date	Mintage	VF	XF	Unc
25	1987	*5,000	—	Proof	450.00

PROOF SETS (PS)

KM#	Date	Mintage	Identification	Issue Price	Mkt. Val.
PS1	1966(6)	5,100	KM1-6	13.00	10.50
PS2	1970/66(7)	1,500	KM1-6,7a	25.00	50.00
PS3	1971(6)	26,249	KM8-13	—	8.00
PS4	1977(2)	—	KM17a,18a	60.00	80.00

Listings For
GERMAN EAST AFRICA: refer to Tanzania
GERMAN NEW GUINEA: refer to Papua-New Guinea

GERMAN STATES

Although the origin of the German Empire can be traced to the Treaty of Verdun, 843, that ceded Charlemagne's lands east of the Rhine to German Prince Louis, it was for centuries little more than a geographic expression, consisting of hundreds of effectively autonomous big and little states. Nominally the states owed their allegiance to the Holy Roman Emperor, who was also a German king, but as the Emperors exhibited less and less concern for Germany the actual power devolved on the lords of the individual states. The fragmentation of the empire climaxed with the tragic denouement of the Thirty Years War, 1618-48, which devastated much of Germany, destroyed its agriculture and medieval commercial eminence and ended the attempt of the Hapsburgs to unify Germany. Deprived of administrative capacity by a lack of resources, the imperial authority became utterly powerless. At this time Germany contained an estimated 1,800 individual states, some with a population of as little as 300. The German Empire of recent history (the creation of Bismarck) was formed on April 14, 1871, when the king of Prussia became Emperor William I of Germany. The new empire comprised 4 kingdoms, 5 grand duchies, 13 duchies and principalities, 3 free cities and the nonautonomous province of Alsace-Lorraine. The states had the right to issue gold and silver coins of higher value than 1 mark; coins of 1 mark and under were general issues of the empire.

MINT MARKS

A - Berlin, 1850-date
A - Clausthal (Hannover) 1832-1849
B - Bayreuth, Franconia (Prussia) 1796-1804
B - Breslau (Prussia, Silesia) 1750-1826
B - Brunswick (Brunswick) 1850-1860
B - Brunswick (Westphalia) 1809-1813
B - Dresden (Saxony) 1861-1872
B - Hannover (Brunswick) 1860-1871
B - Hannover (East Friesland) 1823-1825
B - Hannover (Germany) 1866-1878
B - Hannover (Hannover) 1821-1866
B - Regensburg (Regensburg) 1809
B.H. Frankfurt (Free City of Frankfurt) 1808
B (rosette) H - Regensburg (Rhenish Confederation) 1802-1812
C - Cassel (Westphalia) 1810-1813
C - Clausthal (Brunswick)
C - Clausthal (Hannover) 1813-1834
C - Clausthal (Westphalia) 1810-1811
C - Frankfurt (Germany) 1866-1879
D - Aurich (East Friesland under Prussia) 1750-1806
D - Dusseldorf, Rhineland (Prussia) 1816-1848
D - Munich (Germany) 1872-date
E - Dresden (Germany) 1872-1887
E - Muldenhutte (Germany) 1887-1953
F - Dresden (Saxony) 1845-1858
F - Magdeburg (Prussia) 1750-1806
F - Cassel (Hesse-Cassel) 1803-1807
F - Stuttgart (Germany) 1872-date
G - Dresden (Saxony) 1833-1844, 1850-1854
G - Glatz (Prussian Silesia) 1807-1809
G - Karlsruhe (Germany) 1872-date
G - Stettin in Pomerania (Prussia) 1750-1806
GN-BW - Bamberg (Bamberg)
H - Darmstadt (Germany) 1872-1882
H - Dresden (Saxony) 1804-1812
H.K. - Rostock (Rostock) 1862-1864
I - Hamburg (Germany)
J - Hamburg (Germany) 1873-date
J - Paris (Westphalia) 1808-1809
M.C. - Brunswick (Brunswick) 1813-14, 1820
P.R. - Dusseldorf (Julich-Berg) 1783-1804
S - Dresden (Saxony) 1813-1832
S - Hannover (Hannover) 1839-1844

MONETARY SYSTEM

Until 1871 the Mark (Marck) was a measure of weight.

North German States until 1837
2 Heller = 1 Pfennig
8 Pfennig = 1 Mariengroschen
12 Pfennige = 1 Groschen
24 Groschen = 1 Thaler
2 Gulden = 1-1/3 Reichsthaler
1 Speciesthaler (before 1753)
1 Convention Thaler (after 1753)

North German States after 1837
12 Pfennige = 1 Groschen
30 Groschen = 1 Thaler
1 Vereinsthaler (after 1857)

South German States until 1837
8 Heller = 4 Pfennige = 1 Kreuzer
24 Kreuzer Landmunze = 20 Kreuzer Convention Munze
120 Convention Kreuzer = 2 Convention Gulden = 1 Convention Thaler

South German States after 1837
8 Heller = 4 Pfennige = 1 Kreuzer

German States 1857-1871
As a result of the Monetary Convention of 1857, all the German States adopted a Vereinsthaler of uniform weight being 1/30 fine pound silver. They did continue to use their regional minor coin units to divide the Vereinsthaler for small change purposes.
After the German unification in 1871 when the old Thaler system was abandoned in favor of the mark system (100 pfennig = 1 mark) the Vereinsthaler continued to circulate as a legal tender 3 Mark coin, and the double Thaler as a 6 Mark coin until 1908. In 1908 the Vereinsthalers were officially demonetized and the Thaler coinage was replaced by the new 3 Mark coin which had the same specifications as the old Vereinsthaler. The double Thaler coinage was not replaced as there was no great demand for a 6 Mark coin. Until the 1930's the German public continued to refer to the 3 Mark piece as a "Thaler".

Commencing 1871
100 Pfennig = 1 Mark

ANHALT-BERNBURG

Located in north-central Germany. Appeared as part of the patrimony of Albrecht the Bear of Brandenburg in 1170. Bracteates were first made in the 12th century. It was originally in the inheritance of Heinrich the Fat in 1252 and became extinct in 1468. The division of 1603, among the sons of Joachim Ernst, revitalized Anhalt-Bernburg. Bernburg passed to Dessau after the death of Alexander Carl in 1863.

RULERS
Alexius Friedrich Christian, 1796-1834
Alexander Carl, 1834-1863

MINTMASTER'S INITIALS
Letter	Date	Name
HS	1795-1821	Hans Schluter
Z	1821-1848	Johann Carl Ludwig Zincken

PFENNIG
COPPER
Similar to KM#76 but 3 lines on reverse.

KM#	Date	Mintage	Fine	VF	XF	Unc
74 (C57)	1807	—	3.00	5.00	8.00	45.00

Rev. leg: SCHEIDE MUNTZ

| 76 (C57a) | 1808 | — | 2.00 | 5.00 | 10.00 | 65.00 |

Rev. leg: SCHEIDEMUNZE

77.1 (C58)	1822	—	2.00	5.00	7.00	35.00
	1823	—	2.00	5.00	7.00	35.00
	1827	—	2.00	5.00	7.00	35.00

Rev. leg: SCHEIDEMUNZE HZL ANHALT

| 77.2 (C58a) | 1831 Z | — | 2.00 | 5.00 | 7.00 | 35.00 |

4 PFENNIG

COPPER

| 78.1 (C59) | 1822 | — | 2.00 | 8.00 | 15.00 | 50.00 |
| | 1823 | — | 2.00 | 8.00 | 15.00 | 50.00 |

Rev. value: 4 PFENNIGE

| 78.2 (C59a) | 1831 Z | — | 2.00 | 8.00 | 15.00 | 75.00 |

1/48 THALER
.9700 g, .250 SILVER, .0077 oz ASW
Obv: Crowned arms in branches. Rev: Value.

KM#	Date	Mintage	Fine	VF	XF	Unc
75 (C60)	1807	—	3.00	6.00	20.00	80.00

1/24 THALER
1.9800 g, .350 SILVER, .0234 oz ASW
Rev. leg: HANH BERNB . . . . .

79 (C61)	1822	—	2.00	4.00	10.00	40.00
	1823	—	2.00	4.00	10.00	40.00
	1827	—	2.00	4.00	10.00	40.00

Rev. leg: HZL. ANHALT . . . . .

| 81 (C61a) | 1831 Z | — | 2.00 | 4.00 | 10.00 | 50.00 |

1/6 THALER

5.3400 g, .520 SILVER, .0892 oz ASW

| 85 (C73) | 1856A | .060 | 8.00 | 12.00 | 20.00 | 60.00 |

| 87 (C74) | 1861A | .062 | 5.00 | 8.00 | 12.00 | 50.00 |
| | 1862A | .060 | 5.00 | 8.00 | 12.00 | 50.00 |

2/3 THALER

14.0300 g, .833 SILVER, .3757 oz ASW
Rev. leg: HERZOG ZU ANHALT . . . . . ,
value: XX EINE FEINE MARK

72 (C62)	1806 HS	—	25.00	40.00	60.00	125.00
	1808 HS	—	25.00	40.00	60.00	125.00
	1809 HS	—	25.00	40.00	60.00	125.00

THALER
(Convention)

Anhalt - Cothen / GERMAN STATES 589

28.0600 g, .833 SILVER, .7515 oz ASW

KM#	Date	Mintage	Fine	VF	XF	Unc
73	1806 HS	—	225.00	400.00	1000.	3500.
(C63)	1809 HS	—	400.00	800.00	2000.	5000.

(Mining)

22.2700 g, .750 SILVER, .5370 oz ASW

82	1834	.015	35.00	75.00	175.00	400.00
(C75)						

84	1846A	.010	20.00	35.00	65.00	140.00
(C76)	1852A	.010	20.00	35.00	65.00	140.00
	1855A	.020	20.00	35.00	65.00	140.00

(Vereins)

18.5200 g, .900 SILVER, .5358 oz ASW

86	1859A	.024	40.00	65.00	150.00	325.00
(C77)						

(Mining)

88	1861A	.010	20.00	40.00	70.00	150.00
(C78)	1862A	.020	20.00	35.00	65.00	135.00

2 THALER
(3-1/2 Gulden)

37.1200 g, .900 SILVER, 1.0741 oz ASW

KM#	Date	Mintage	Fine	VF	XF	Unc
83	1840A	3,600	300.00	450.00	600.00	1500.
(C79)	1845A	7,200	300.00	450.00	600.00	1500.
	1855A	5,000	300.00	450.00	600.00	1500.

TRADE COINAGE
DUCAT

3.5000 g, .986 GOLD, .1109 oz AGW
Obv. leg: EX AURO ANHALTINO.
Rev. leg: ALEXIUS FRIED CHRIST. . . .

80	1825 Z	116 pcs.	850.00	1400.	2400.	3500.
(C64)						

JOINT COINAGE
UNDER ALEXANDER CARL
FOR ANHALT-COTHEN
AND ANHALT-DESSAU

PFENNIG

COPPER
Rev. leg: 288 EINEN THALER.

91	1839	.589	2.00	4.00	8.00	35.00
(C65)	1840	.654	2.00	4.00	8.00	35.00

96	1856A	.360	2.00	4.00	8.00	35.00
(C66)	1862A	.360	2.00	4.00	8.00	35.00
	1864A	.300	2.00	4.00	8.00	35.00
	1867B	.180	2.00	4.00	8.00	35.00

3 PFENNIGE

COPPER

92	1839	.386	2.00	4.00	8.00	35.00
(C67)	1840	.292	2.00	4.00	8.00	35.00

KM#	Date	Mintage	Fine	VF	XF	Unc
98	1861A	.240	2.00	4.00	8.00	35.00
(C68)	1864A	.200	2.00	4.00	8.00	35.00
	1867B	.240	2.00	4.00	8.00	35.00

6 PFENNIGE

.8100 g, .375 SILVER, .0097 oz ASW

94	1840	.322	2.00	4.00	10.00	50.00
(C69)						

GROSCHEN

1.6200 g, .375 SILVER, .0195 oz ASW
Obv: Crowned shield. Rev. leg: 24 EINEN THALER

93	1839	.319	1.00	3.00	6.00	30.00
(C70)	1840	Inc. Ab.	1.00	3.00	6.00	30.00

SILBERGROSCHEN

2.1900 g, .222 SILVER, .0156 oz ASW

95	1851A	.176	1.00	3.00	6.00	30.00
(C71)	1852A	.197	1.00	3.00	6.00	30.00
	1855A	.303	1.00	3.00	6.00	30.00
	1859A	.150	1.00	3.00	6.00	30.00
	1862A	.300	1.00	3.00	6.00	30.00

2-1/2 SILBERGROSCHEN

3.2400 g, .375 SILVER, .0390 oz ASW

97	1856A	.120	1.00	3.00	7.00	45.00
(C72)	1859A	.060	1.00	3.00	7.00	45.00
	1861A	.120	1.00	3.00	7.00	45.00
	1862A	.240	1.00	3.00	7.00	45.00
	1864A	.120	1.00	3.00	7.00	45.00

ANHALT - COTHEN

Cothen has a checkered history after the patrimony of Heinrich the Fat in 1252. It was often ruled with other segments of the House of Anhalt. Founded as a separate line in 1603, became extinct in 1665 and passed to Plotzkau which changed the name to Cothen. It passed to Dessau after the death of Heinrich in 1847.

RULERS
Heinrich, 1830-1847

2 THALER
(3-1/2 Gulden)

37.1200 g, .900 SILVER, 1.0743 oz ASW

KM#	Date	Mintage	Fine	VF	XF	Unc
39 (C115)	1840A	3,100	400.00	800.00	2500.	6000.

ANHALT - DESSAU

Dessau was part of the 1252 division that included Zerbst and Cothen. In 1396 Zerbst divided into Zerbst and Dessau. In 1508 Zerbst was absorbed into Dessau. Dessau was given to the eldest son of Joachim Ernst in the division of 1603. As other lines became extinct, they fell to Dessau, which united all branches in 1863.

RULERS
Leopold Friedrich Franz, 1751-1817
Leopold Friedrich, 1817-1871
Friedrich I, 1871-1904
Friedrich II, 1904-1918

VI EINEN (1/6) THALER

5.3400 g, .520 SILVER, .0892 oz ASW

KM#	Date	Mintage	Fine	VF	XF	Unc
19 (C123)	1865A	.120	12.50	25.00	50.00	150.00

EIN (1) THALER
(Vereins)

18.5200 g, .900 SILVER, .5359 oz ASW

KM#	Date	Mintage	Fine	VF	XF	Unc
14 (C124)	1858A	.027	30.00	60.00	100.00	350.00

Separation of Anhalt Duchies - 1603
Reunion of Anhalt Duchies - 1863

15 (C125)	1863A	.050	30.00	60.00	100.00	175.00

20 (C126)	1866A	.031	30.00	60.00	100.00	250.00
	1869A	.032	30.00	60.00	100.00	250.00

2 THALER
(3-1/2 Gulden)

37.1200 g, .900 SILVER, 1.0741 oz ASW

KM#	Date	Mintage	Fine	VF	XF	Unc
13 (C127)	1839A	4,700	250.00	500.00	800.00	1500.
	1843A	4,700	250.00	500.00	800.00	1500.
	1846A	4,700	250.00	500.00	800.00	1500.

MONETARY REFORM
2 MARK

11.1110 g, .900 SILVER, .3215 oz ASW

22 (Y1)	1876A	.200	100.00	200.00	500.00	1000.

23 (Y3)	1896A	.050	150.00	300.00	500.00	750.00
	1896A	—	—	—	Proof	850.00

27 (Y7)	1904A	.050	125.00	275.00	425.00	700.00
	1904A	150 pcs.	—	—	Proof	800.00

3 MARK

16.6670 g, .900 SILVER, .4823 oz ASW

29	1909A	.100	40.00	75.00	115.00	165.00

KM#	Date	Mintage	Fine	VF	XF	Unc
(Y8)	1911A	.100	40.00	75.00	115.00	165.00
	Common date	—	—	—	Proof	250.00

Silver Wedding Anniversary

30	1914A	.200	25.00	45.00	65.00	100.00
(Y10)	1914A	1,000	—	—	Proof	150.00

5 MARK

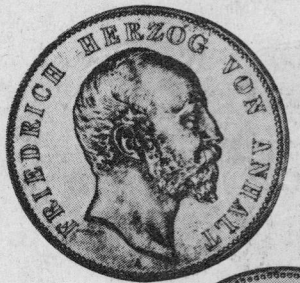

27.7770 g, .900 SILVER, .8038 oz ASW

24	1896A	.010	500.00	800.00	1500.	2000.
(Y4)	1896A	—	—	—	Proof	2500.

Silver Wedding Anniversary
Rev: Similar to 3 Mark, KM#30.

31	1914A	.030	60.00	175.00	200.00	300.00
(Y11)	1914A	1,000	—	—	Proof	450.00

10 MARK

3.9820 g, .900 GOLD, .1152 oz AGW

25	1896A	.020	450.00	750.00	1000.	1500.
(Y5)	1896A	200 pcs.	—	—	Proof	1600.
	1901A	.020	450.00	750.00	1000.	1500.
	1901A	200 pcs.	—	—	Proof	1600.

20 MARK

7.9650 g, .900 GOLD, .2304 oz AGW

21	1875A	.025	450.00	800.00	1200.	1700.
(Y2)	1875A	—	—	—	Proof	3500.

KM#	Date	Mintage	Fine	VF	XF	Unc
26	1896A	.015	450.00	750.00	1100.	1500.
(Y6)	1896A	200 pcs.	—	—	Proof	2000.
	1901A	.015	450.00	750.00	1100.	1400.
	1901A	200 pcs.	—	—	Proof	2000.

28	1904A	.025	450.00	750.00	1000.	1500.
(Y9)	1904A	200 pcs.	—	—	Proof	2500.

AUGSBURG
FREE CITY

Founded as a Roman colony in the reign of Augustus it was declared a Free City in 1276. The mint rights were granted in 1521 but the first coins are dated somewhat earlier. Augsburg was given to Bavaria in 1806.

HELLER
COPPER
Obv: Crowned arms. Rev: Value, date.

KM#	Date	Mintage	VG	Fine	VF	XF
188	1801	—	2.00	3.00	4.00	10.00
(C2)						

Obv: State arms in oval shield.
Rev: Value and date.

KM#	Date	Mintage	Fine	VF	XF	Unc
190	1801	—	1.00	3.00	8.00	50.00
(C2a)	1803	—	1.00	3.00	8.00	50.00
	1804	—	1.00	3.00	8.00	50.00
	1805	—	1.00	3.00	8.00	50.00

PFENNING
COPPER
Obv: Arms in shield.
Rev: inscription: STADTMYNZ.

KM#	Date	Mintage	VG	Fine	VF	XF
189	1801	—	2.00	4.00	6.00	10.00
(C3b)	1802	—	2.00	4.00	6.00	10.00
	1803	—	2.00	4.00	6.00	10.00

Rev. inscription: STADT MUNZ.

KM#	Date	Mintage	Fine	VF	XF	Unc
191	1803	—	1.00	4.00	10.00	50.00
(C3d)	1804	—	1.00	4.00	10.00	50.00
	1805	—	1.00	4.00	10.00	50.00

BADEN

Located in southwest Germany. The ruling house of Baden began in 1112. Various branches developed and religious wars between the branches were settled in 1648. The branches unified under Baden-Durlach after the extinction of the Baden-Baden line in 1771. The last ruler abdicated at the end of World War I. The first coins were issued in the late 1300s.

BADEN-DURLACH
RULERS

Carl Friedrich,
   Margrave in all Baden, 1771-1803
   As Elector, 1803-1806
   As Grand Duke, 1806-1811
Carl Ludwig Friedrich, 1811-1818
Ludwig I, 1818-1830
Leopold I, 1830-1852
Ludwig II, 1852-1856, Insane and deposed
Friedrich I as Prince Regent, 1852-1856
   As Grand Duke, 1856-1907
Friedrich II, 1907-1918

MINTMASTER'S INITIALS

Letter	Date	Name
B	1778-1808	Johann Martin Buckle
B.HB	1790-1812	Johann Heinrich Boltschauser, die-cutter and mint warden
CS.S	1761-1811	Ernst Christoph Steinhauser, mint warden
FE	1802	Franz Eberle, mint warden

1/4 KREUZER

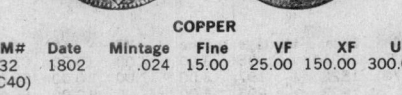

COPPER

KM#	Date	Mintage	Fine	VF	XF	Unc
132	1802	.024	15.00	25.00	150.00	300.00
(C40)						

Obv: Crowned shield. Rev: Value, date within wreath.

153	1810	—	—	—	Rare	—
(C49)						

181	1821	—	3.00	8.00	20.00	65.00
(C76)	1824	.128	3.00	8.00	20.00	65.00

1/2 KREUZER

COPPER

133	1803	.027	8.00	15.00	40.00	225.00
(C41)	1804	.104	8.00	15.00	25.00	175.00
	1805	.157	8.00	15.00	25.00	175.00

139	1806	—	3.00	7.00	15.00	125.00
(C50)	1808	—	3.00	7.00	15.00	125.00
	1809	.877	3.00	7.00	15.00	100.00
	1810	.129	3.00	7.00	15.00	125.00
(C64)	1812	.105	3.00	7.00	15.00	100.00

Obv: Crowned draped arms. Rev: Similar to KM#165.

164	1814	.078	3.00	7.00	20.00	100.00
(C67)	1815	.062	3.00	7.00	20.00	100.00
	1816	.039	3.00	7.00	20.00	100.00
	1817	.102	3.00	7.00	20.00	100.00

Obv: Smaller crowned draped arms.

165	1814	Inc. Ab.	3.00	7.00	15.00	80.00
(C67b)						

Rev. value: 1/2 KREU/ZER

171	1817	—	3.00	7.00	15.00	80.00
(C67a)						

182	1821	.127	3.00	7.00	15.00	70.00
(C74)						

186	1822	.109	3.00	7.00	12.00	65.00
(C77)	1823	.035	3.00	7.00	15.00	110.00
	1824	.066	3.00	7.00	15.00	80.00
	1825	.053	3.00	7.00	15.00	90.00
	1826	.191	3.00	7.00	12.00	60.00

KM#	Date	Mintage	Fine	VF	XF	Unc
188	1827	—	3.00	7.00	15.00	75.00
(C79)	1828	.137	3.00	7.00	15.00	75.00
	1829	.204	3.00	7.00	15.00	75.00
	1830	Inc. Ab.	3.00	7.00	15.00	75.00

Obv: D on truncation.

194	1830	.024	3.00	7.00	15.00	85.00
(C100)	1834	.076	3.00	7.00	12.00	60.00
	1835	.028	3.00	7.00	15.00	90.00

213	1842	.101	1.00	4.00	10.00	55.00
(C100a)	1844	.052	1.00	4.00	10.00	65.00
	1845	.074	1.00	4.00	10.00	60.00
	1846	.090	1.00	4.00	10.00	60.00
	1847	.256	1.00	4.00	10.00	50.00
	1848	.089	1.00	4.00	10.00	60.00
	1849	.102	1.00	4.00	10.00	55.00
	1850	.074	1.00	4.00	10.00	60.00
	1851/0	.087	1.00	4.00	10.00	65.00
	1851	Inc. Ab.	1.00	4.00	10.00	60.00
	1852	.227	1.00	4.00	10.00	50.00

230	1856	.195	1.00	4.00	10.00	45.00
(C138)						

241	1859	.219	1.00	2.00	10.00	35.00
(C141)	1860	.120	1.00	2.00	10.00	45.00
	1861	.109	1.00	2.00	10.00	45.00
	1862	.117	1.00	2.00	10.00	45.00
	1863	.298	1.00	2.00	10.00	35.00
	1864	.094	2.00	4.00	12.00	50.00
	1865	.349	1.00	2.00	10.00	35.00
	1866	.239	1.00	2.00	10.00	35.00
	1867	—	1.00	2.00	10.00	35.00
	1870	.038	5.00	10.00	25.00	125.00
	1871	—	1.75	6.00	15.00	35.00

EIN (1) KREUZER

COPPER

134	1803	.146	10.00	20.00	35.00	200.00
(C42)	1805	.096	10.00	20.00	35.00	200.00
	1806	—	—	—	Rare	—

141	1807	.096	6.00	14.00	30.00	125.00
(C51)	1808	1.704	3.00	7.00	15.00	65.00

Baden-Durlach / GERMAN STATES 592

KM#	Date	Mintage	Fine	VF	XF	Unc
147 (C52)	1809	1.263	3.00	7.00	10.00	75.00
	1810	.639	3.00	7.00	10.00	75.00
	1811	.125	3.00	7.00	10.00	75.00

Obv: Crowned arms. Rev: Value, date within wreath.

| 154 (C65) | 1812 | .285 | 3.00 | 10.00 | 50.00 | 125.00 |

Obv: Leg., crowned arms. Rev: value: 1 KREUZ/ER, date.

| 157 (C66) | 1813 | — | 3.00 | 6.00 | 15.00 | 100.00 |

Rev. value: 1/KREUZER/1813 within circle of dots.

| 158 (C66a) | 1813 | .320 | 3.00 | 6.00 | 15.00 | 100.00 |

| 159 (C66b) | 1813 | — | 3.00 | 6.00 | 15.00 | 100.00 |

| 160 (C68.1) | 1813 | — | 3.00 | 6.00 | 15.00 | 100.00 |

Obv: Date between dots.

| 166.1 (C68.2) | 1814 | .489 | 3.00 | 6.00 | 15.00 | 100.00 |

Obv: Date between stars.

166.2 (C68.3)	1814	Inc. Ab.	3.00	7.00	10.00	65.00
	1815	.490	3.00	7.00	10.00	65.00
	1816	.464	3.00	7.00	10.00	65.00
	1817	.327	3.00	7.00	10.00	65.00

Obv: Date between crosses.

| 166.3 (C68.4) | 1815 | — | 3.00 | 7.00 | 10.00 | 65.00 |

Rev. value: 1 KREU-/ZER

167 (C68.5)	1814	—	3.00	7.00	10.00	65.00
	1815	.490	3.00	7.00	10.00	65.00
	1816	.464	3.00	7.00	10.00	65.00
	1817	Inc. Ab.	3.00	7.00	10.00	65.00
	1820	—	3.00	7.00	10.00	65.00

KM#	Date	Mintage	Fine	VF	XF	Unc
183 (C78)	1821	.055	3.00	7.00	10.00	65.00
	1822	.197	3.00	7.00	10.00	65.00
	1823	.205	3.00	7.00	10.00	65.00
	1824	.253	3.00	7.00	10.00	65.00
	1825	.335	3.00	7.00	10.00	65.00
	1826	—	3.00	7.00	10.00	65.00

189 (C80)	1827	.515	2.00	7.00	10.00	50.00
	1828	1.206	2.00	7.00	10.00	50.00
	1829	.603	2.00	7.00	10.00	50.00
	1830	.149	2.00	7.00	10.00	50.00

Obv. leg: Period after BADEN.

| 197.1 (C102.1) | 1831 | .227 | 1.00 | 4.00 | 10.00 | 50.00 |

Obv. leg: W/o period after BADEN.

197.2 (C102.2)	1831	Inc. Ab.	1.00	3.00	6.00	40.00
	1832	.172	1.00	3.00	6.00	40.00
	1833	.181	1.00	3.00	6.00	40.00
	1834	.250	1.00	3.00	6.00	40.00
	1835	.294	1.00	3.00	6.00	40.00
	1836	.163	1.00	3.00	6.00	40.00
	1837	—	1.00	3.00	6.00	40.00

Obv: W/o D on truncation.

203 (C102.3)	1836	.321	1.00	3.00	6.00	40.00
	1837	Inc. Ab.	1.00	3.00	6.00	40.00
	1838	.642	1.00	3.00	6.00	40.00
	1839	.254	1.00	3.00	6.00	40.00
	1840	.573	1.00	3.00	6.00	40.00
	1841	.423	1.00	3.00	6.00	40.00
	1842	.865	1.00	3.00	6.00	40.00
	1843	.527	1.00	3.00	6.00	40.00
	1844	.663	1.00	3.00	6.00	40.00
	1845	1.442	1.00	3.00	6.00	40.00

Erection of Carl Friedrich's Statue

| 216 (C104) | 1844 | .054 | 15.00 | 25.00 | 50.00 | 125.00 |

218 (C102a)	1845	Inc. Ab.	1.00	3.00	7.00	40.00
	1846	.452	1.00	3.00	7.00	40.00
	1847	.639	1.00	3.00	7.00	40.00
	1848	.232	1.00	3.00	7.00	40.00
	1849	.872	1.00	3.00	7.00	40.00
	1850	.238	1.00	3.00	7.00	40.00
	1851	1.208	1.00	3.00	7.00	40.00
	1852	.821	1.00	3.00	7.00	40.00

Titles as Prince Regent

| 231 (C130) | 1856 | .707 | 20.00 | 35.00 | 65.00 | 140.00 |

Titles as Grand Duke

KM#	Date	Mintage	Fine	VF	XF	Unc
232 (C139)	1856	.660	4.00	10.00	—	40.00

Birth of Heir

| 238 (C140) | 1857 | — | 3.00 | 6.00 | 15.00 | 60.00 |

242 (C142)	1859	.898	1.00	2.00	6.00	25.00
	1860	.655	1.00	2.00	6.00	25.00
	1861	.726	1.00	2.00	6.00	25.00
	1862	.623	1.00	2.00	6.00	25.00
	1863	.765	1.00	2.00	6.00	25.00
	1864	.724	1.00	2.00	6.00	25.00
	1865	.778	1.00	2.00	6.00	25.00
	1866	.732	1.00	2.00	6.00	25.00
	1867	.698	1.00	2.00	6.00	25.00
	1868	.885	1.00	2.00	6.00	25.00
	1869	.858	1.00	2.00	6.00	25.00
	1870	.918	1.00	2.00	6.00	25.00
	1871	—	1.00	2.00	6.00	25.00

Leopold Memorial

| 244 (C143) | 1861 | — | 18.00 | 30.00 | 50.00 | 75.00 |

50th Anniversary Baden's Constitution

| 250 (C144) | 1868 | .025 | 18.00 | 30.00 | 50.00 | 75.00 |

Church at Seckenheim

| 251 (C146) | 1869 | 1.000 | 45.00 | 75.00 | 125.00 | 200.00 |

Victory over France in Franco-Prussian War

| 252 (C145) | 1871 | — | 2.00 | 4.00 | 8.00 | 25.00 |

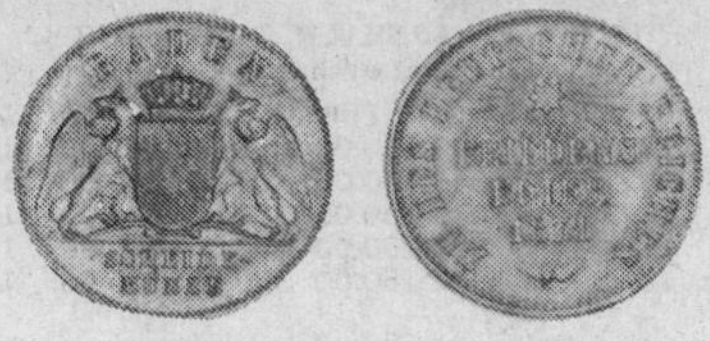

Obv: SCHEIDE MUNZE under shield.

KM#	Date	Mintage	Fine	VF	XF	Unc
253 (C145a)	1871	—	32.50	45.00	60.00	80.00

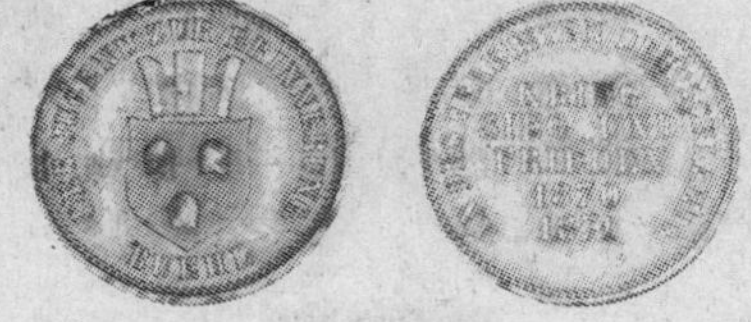

Buehl Victory

KM#	Date	Mintage	Fine	VF	XF	Unc
254 (C147)	1871	—	45.00	75.00	125.00	200.00

Karlsruhe Victory
Obv: Arms. Rev: Legend.

KM#	Date	Mintage	Fine	VF	XF	Unc
255 (C148)	1871	—	18.00	30.00	45.00	75.00

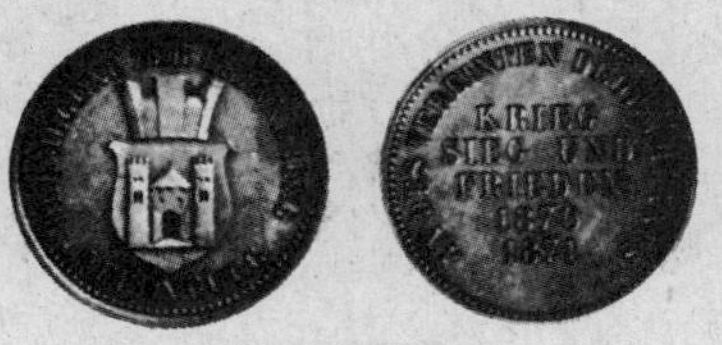

Offenburg Victory

KM#	Date	Mintage	Fine	VF	XF	Unc
256 (C149)	1871	—	35.00	60.00	90.00	150.00

DREI (3) KREUZER

(1 Groschen)

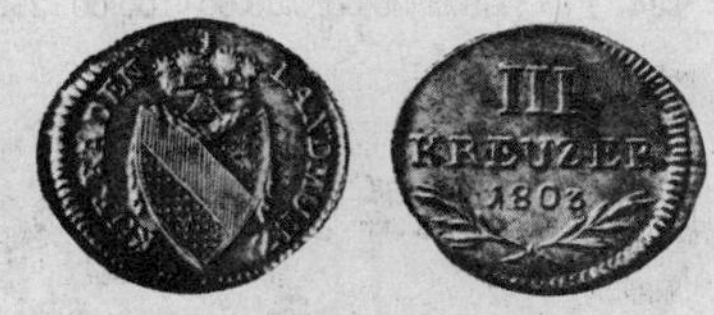

1.4230 g, .313 SILVER, .0143 oz ASW

KM#	Date	Mintage	Fine	VF	XF	Unc
135	1803	.189	10.00	35.00	125.00	350.00
(C43)	1805	.445	10.00	25.00	75.00	200.00
	1806	.126	10.00	25.00	100.00	300.00

Obv: Lion in shield faces left.

KM#	Date	Mintage	Fine	VF	XF	Unc
144 (C53)	1808	.410	10.00	25.00	100.00	300.00

Obv: Lion in shield faces right.

KM#	Date	Mintage	Fine	VF	XF	Unc
148	1809	.208	8.00	20.00	65.00	300.00
(C54)	1810	.262	8.00	20.00	65.00	300.00
	1811	.316	8.00	20.00	65.00	300.00

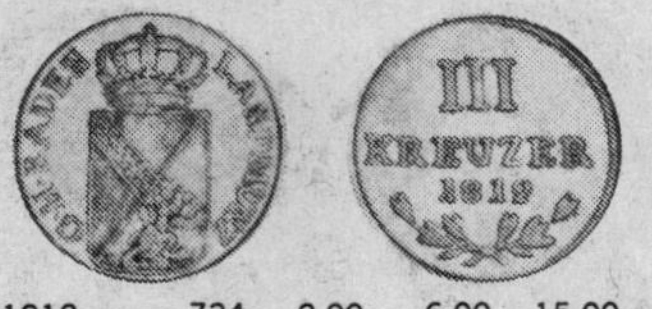

KM#	Date	Mintage	Fine	VF	XF	Unc
155.1	1812	.734	2.00	6.00	15.00	65.00
(C69)	1813	.273	2.00	6.00	15.00	65.00

Rev: Z backwards in KREUZER

KM#	Date	Mintage	Fine	VF	XF	Unc
155.2 (C69a)	1812	Inc. Ab.	7.50	18.50	50.00	125.00

1.2470 g, .313 SILVER, .0125 oz ASW
Rev. value: 3 KREUTZER within branches

KM#	Date	Mintage	Fine	VF	XF	Unc
161	1813	—	2.00	7.00	15.00	65.00
(C71)	1814	.280	2.00	7.00	15.00	65.00
	1815	.214	2.00	7.00	15.00	65.00
	1816	.243	2.00	7.00	15.00	65.00

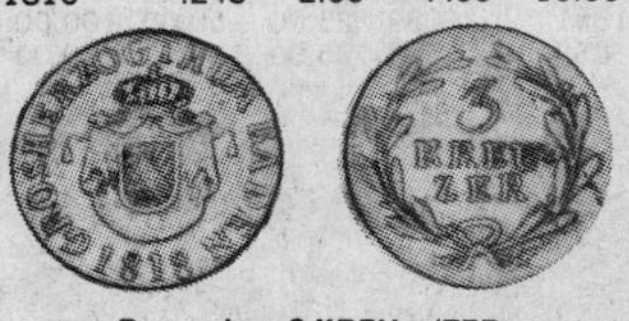

Rev. value: 3 KREU - /ZER.

KM#	Date	Mintage	Fine	VF	XF	Unc
172	1817	.371	2.00	7.00	15.00	65.00
(C71a)	1818	.593	2.00	7.00	15.00	65.00
	1819	.815	2.00	7.00	15.00	65.00
	1820	Inc. Ab.	2.00	7.00	15.00	65.00

Obv: Larger shield, w/o drape.

KM#	Date	Mintage	Fine	VF	XF	Unc
178	1820	Inc. Ab.	2.00	7.00	15.00	65.00
(C82)	1821	.065	2.00	7.00	15.00	65.00
	1824	.096	2.00	7.00	15.00	65.00
	1825	.073	2.00	7.00	15.00	65.00

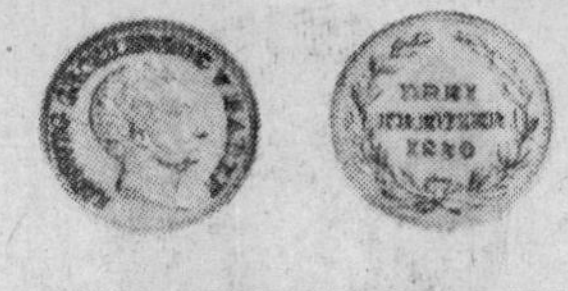

1.1400 g, .375 SILVER, .0134 oz ASW
Rev. value: DREI KREUZER

KM#	Date	Mintage	Fine	VF	XF	Unc
191	1829	1.277	2.00	7.00	10.00	40.00
(C83)	1830	1.009	2.00	7.00	10.00	40.00

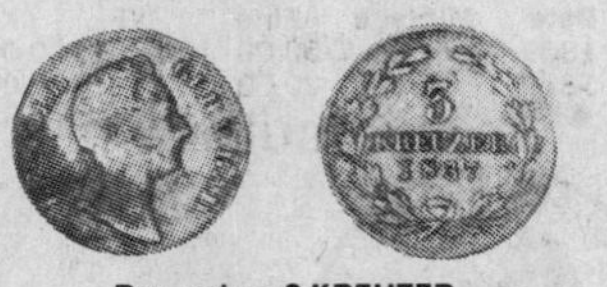

Rev. value: 3 KREUZER

KM#	Date	Mintage	Fine	VF	XF	Unc
199	1832	.729	2.00	7.00	10.00	50.00
(C106)	1833	.846	2.00	7.00	10.00	50.00
	1834	.549	2.00	7.00	10.00	50.00
	1835	.476	1.00	4.00	10.00	50.00
	1836	.723	1.00	4.00	10.00	50.00
	1837	—	1.00	4.00	10.00	50.00

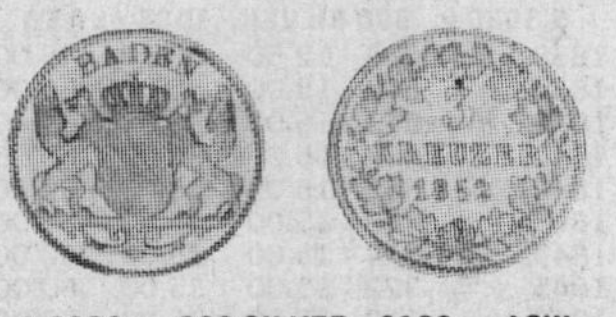

1.2990 g, .333 SILVER, .0139 oz ASW

KM#	Date	Mintage	Fine	VF	XF	Unc
211	1841	.328	1.00	4.00	10.00	40.00
(C107)	1842	.420	1.00	4.00	10.00	40.00
	1843	.168	1.00	4.00	10.00	40.00
	1844	.361	1.00	4.00	10.00	40.00
	1845	.385	1.00	4.00	10.00	40.00
	1846	.219	1.00	4.00	10.00	40.00
	1847	.392	1.00	4.00	10.00	40.00
	1848	.195	1.00	4.00	10.00	40.00
	1849	.397	1.00	4.00	10.00	40.00
	1850	.212	1.00	4.00	10.00	40.00
	1851	.196	1.00	4.00	10.00	40.00
	1852	.192	1.00	4.00	10.00	40.00

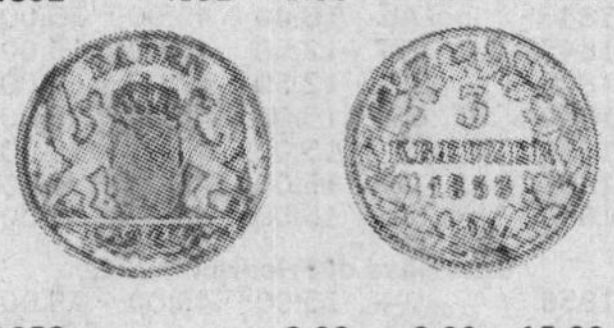

KM#	Date	Mintage	Fine	VF	XF	Unc
226	1853	—	3.00	8.00	15.00	60.00
(C131)	1854	—	3.00	8.00	15.00	60.00
	1855	—	3.00	8.00	15.00	60.00
	1856	—	3.00	8.00	15.00	60.00

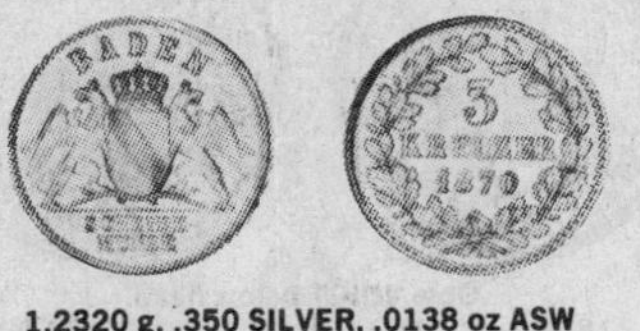

1.2320 g, .350 SILVER, .0138 oz ASW
Obv: SCHEIDE/MUNZE under arms.

KM#	Date	Mintage	Fine	VF	XF	Unc
246	1866	.240	1.00	3.00	7.00	40.00
(C150)	1867	.389	1.00	3.00	7.00	40.00
	1868	.315	1.00	3.00	7.00	40.00
	1869	.285	1.00	3.00	7.00	40.00
	1870	.259	1.00	3.00	7.00	40.00
	1871	—	1.00	3.00	7.00	40.00

6 KREUZER

(1/15 Thaler)

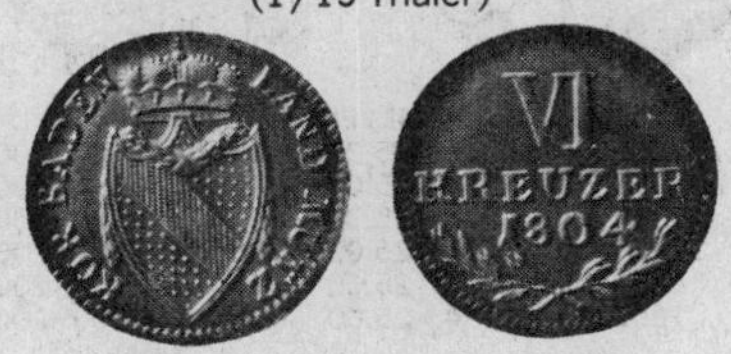

2.3530 g, .375 SILVER, .0283 oz ASW

KM#	Date	Mintage	Fine	VF	XF	Unc
137 (C45)	1804	.055	15.00	50.00	150.00	400.00

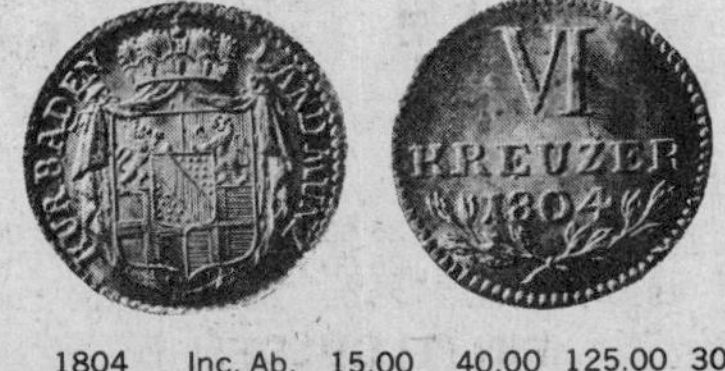

KM#	Date	Mintage	Fine	VF	XF	Unc
138	1804	Inc. Ab.	15.00	40.00	125.00	300.00
(C46)	1805	.461	15.00	40.00	125.00	300.00

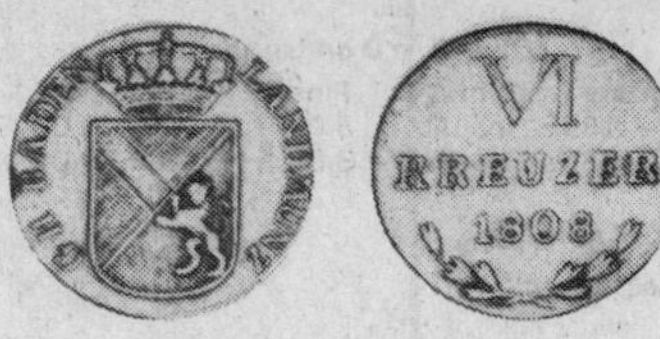

Obv: Lion in arms facing left.

KM#	Date	Mintage	Fine	VF	XF	Unc
140	1806	.131	7.00	20.00	60.00	250.00
(C55)	1807	.371	7.00	20.00	60.00	250.00
	1808	1.118	6.00	15.00	45.00	200.00

Obv: Lion in arms facing right.

KM#	Date	Mintage	Fine	VF	XF	Unc
149 (C56)	1809	.539	10.00	25.00	75.00	200.00

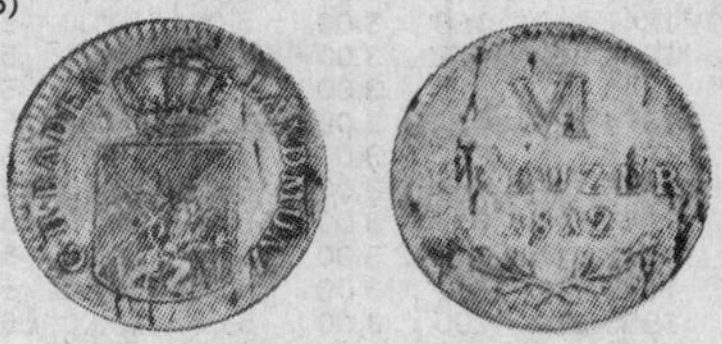

Obv. leg: G.H.BADEN. . . .

KM#	Date	Mintage	Fine	VF	XF	Unc
156	1812	.339	5.00	10.00	35.00	125.00
(C70)	1813	.559	5.00	10.00	35.00	125.00

Obv. leg: G H BADEN. . . . . Rev: VI KREUTZER, date within wreath

KM#	Date	Mintage	Fine	VF	XF	Unc
162 (C70a)	1813	Inc. Ab.	5.00	10.00	45.00	100.00

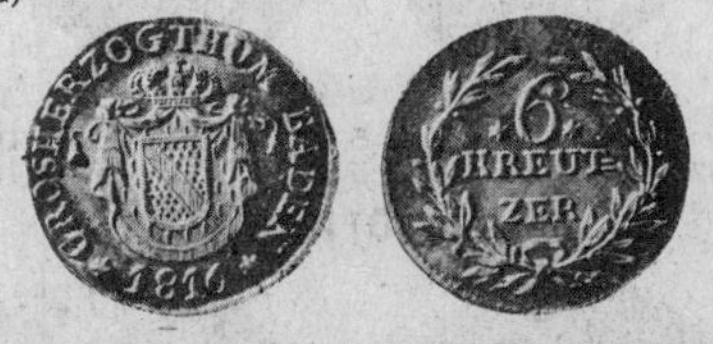

2.2270 g, .375 SILVER, .0268 oz ASW
Rev. value: 6 KREUT - /ZER within olive wreath.

KM#	Date	Mintage	Fine	VF	XF	Unc
168	1814	.115	5.00	10.00	50.00	125.00
(C72)	1815	.244	5.00	10.00	50.00	125.00
	1816	1.603	5.00	10.00	50.00	125.00
	1817	.563	5.00	10.00	50.00	125.00

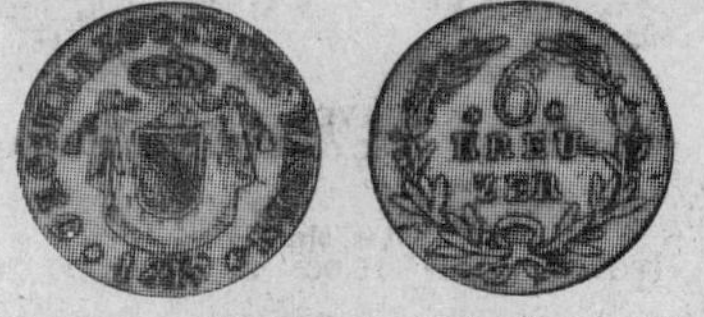

Rev. value: 6 KREU - /ZER within olive wreath.

KM#	Date	Mintage	Fine	VF	XF	Unc
170	1816	Inc. Ab.	4.00	10.00	25.00	75.00
(C72a)	1817	Inc. Ab.	4.00	10.00	25.00	75.00
	1818	.112	4.00	10.00	25.00	75.00

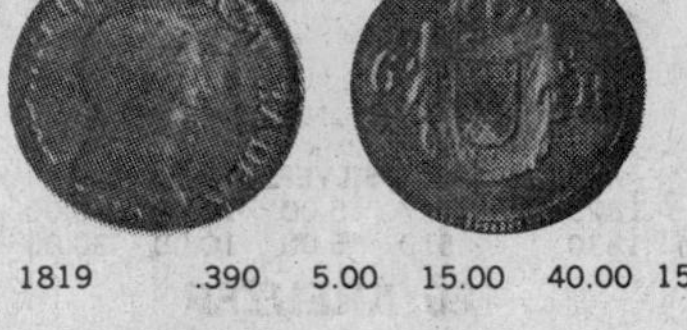

KM#	Date	Mintage	Fine	VF	XF	Unc
173 (C84)	1819	.390	5.00	15.00	40.00	150.00

Obv: Larger head right, hair combed forward.
Rev: Crowned shield

KM#	Date	Mintage	Fine	VF	XF	Unc
179 (C85)	1820	.095	5.00	15.00	40.00	150.00

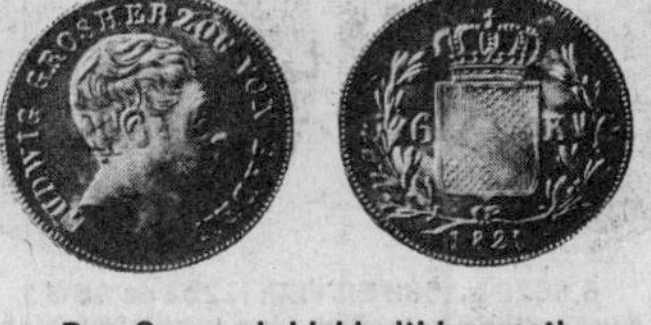

Rev: Crowned shield within wreath.

KM#	Date	Mintage	Fine	VF	XF	Unc
180	1820	Inc. Ab.	5.00	15.00	30.00	125.00
(C86)	1821	.186	5.00	15.00	30.00	125.00

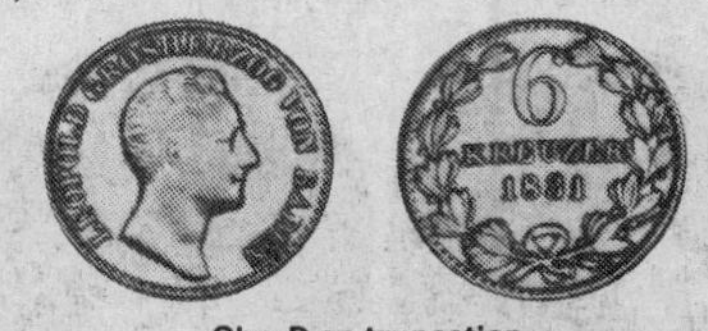

Obv: D on truncation.

KM#	Date	Mintage	Fine	VF	XF	Unc
198.1	1831	.862	3.00	7.00	15.00	75.00
(C108.1)	1832	.929	3.00	7.00	15.00	75.00
	1833	1.003	3.00	7.00	15.00	75.00
	1834	.898	3.00	7.00	15.00	75.00
	1835	1.025	3.00	7.00	15.00	75.00
	1836	.917	3.00	7.00	15.00	75.00

Baden-Durlach / GERMAN STATES 594

Obv: W/o D on truncation.

KM#	Date	Mintage	Fine	VF	XF	Unc
198.2	1835	Inc. Ab.	3.00	8.00	20.00	125.00
(C108.2)	1837	.415	3.00	8.00	20.00	125.00

2.5980 g, .333 SILVER, .0278 oz ASW

210	1840	1.317	3.00	5.00	10.00	50.00
(C109)	1841	.168	3.00	5.00	10.00	50.00
	1842	.612	3.00	5.00	10.00	50.00
	1843	.615	3.00	5.00	10.00	50.00
	1844	.757	3.00	5.00	10.00	50.00
	1845	.262	3.00	5.00	10.00	50.00
	1846	.368	3.00	5.00	10.00	50.00
	1847	.857	3.00	5.00	10.00	50.00
	1848	.377	3.00	5.00	10.00	50.00
	1849	.371	3.00	5.00	10.00	50.00
	1850	.200	3.00	5.00	10.00	50.00

228	1855	—	5.00	10.00	25.00	100.00
(C132)	1856	—	5.00	10.00	25.00	100.00

ZEHN (10) KREUZER

3.8980 g, .500 SILVER, .0626 oz ASW

145	1808	.068	50.00	175.00	250.00	450.00
(C57)						

Obv: Bust w/short hair.

150	1809	Inc. Ab.	15.00	25.00	75.00	250.00
(C58)						

2.7840 g, .500 SILVER, .0447 oz ASW

192	1829	.527	5.00	10.00	30.00	125.00
(C87)	1830	.510	5.00	10.00	30.00	125.00

20 KREUZER

6.6820 g, .583 SILVER, .1252 oz ASW
Obv: Bust w/long hair. Rev: Lion in shield facing left.

142	1807 B	.015	65.00	140.00	275.00	600.00
(C59)						

Rev: Lion in shield facing right.

146	1808	—	45.00	100.00	180.00	350.00
(C60)	1808 B	—	60.00	150.00	250.00	500.00

Obv: Bust w/short hair.

KM#	Date	Mintage	Fine	VF	XF	Unc
151	1809	—	50.00	100.00	200.00	350.00
(C61)	1810	.170	20.00	—	100.00	225.00

1/2 GULDEN

5.3030 g, .900 SILVER, .1534 oz ASW

209	1838	1.044	12.50	30.00	45.00	125.00
(C110)	1839	.500	15.00	35.00	60.00	140.00
	1840	.511	15.00	35.00	60.00	140.00
	1841	.417	15.00	35.00	60.00	140.00
	1842	.362	15.00	35.00	60.00	140.00
	1843	.469	15.00	35.00	60.00	140.00
	1844	.274	15.00	35.00	60.00	140.00
	1845	.322	15.00	35.00	60.00	140.00
	1846	.118	15.00	35.00	60.00	140.00

Obv: W/o D on truncation, larger head.

221	1846	Inc. Ab.	15.00	45.00	75.00	180.00
(C110a)	1847	.537	12.50	40.00	65.00	150.00
	1848	.332	12.50	40.00	65.00	150.00
	1849	.069	15.00	45.00	75.00	180.00
	1850	—	15.00	45.00	75.00	180.00
	1851	.122	15.00	45.00	75.00	180.00
	1852	.026	15.00	45.00	75.00	180.00

Obv: Head of Friedrich right.

233	1856	—	15.00	45.00	75.00	180.00
(C133)						

Obv: VOIGT below head.

234	1856	.150	25.00	50.00	100.00	250.00
(C151)	1860	.342	25.00	50.00	100.00	250.00

5.2910 g, .900 SILVER, .0850 oz ASW

243	1860	Inc. Ab.	25.00	50.00	75.00	200.00
(C151a)	1861	.264	25.00	50.00	75.00	200.00
	1862	.233	25.00	50.00	75.00	200.00
	1863	.227	25.00	50.00	75.00	200.00
	1864	.117	25.00	50.00	75.00	200.00
	1865	.184	25.00	50.00	75.00	200.00

248	1867	.155	25.00	50.00	75.00	200.00
(C152)	1868	.070	25.00	50.00	75.00	200.00
	1869	.073	25.00	50.00	75.00	200.00

EIN (1) GULDEN
(2/3 Thaler)

12.7270 g, .750 SILVER, .3069 oz ASW
Obv: Bust w/short hair.

KM#	Date	Mintage	Fine	VF	XF	Unc
184	1821	.090	150.00	300.00	600.00	1000.
(C88)	1822	.045	150.00	300.00	600.00	1000.
	1823	.039	150.00	300.00	600.00	1000.
	1824	.050	150.00	300.00	600.00	1000.
	1825	.022	150.00	300.00	600.00	1000.

Obv: Curly hair.

187	1826	.094	700.00	1200.	1800.	3000.
(C88a)						

10.6060 g, .900 SILVER, .3069 oz ASW
Obv: W/o period after BADEN.

207	1837	.629	25.00	50.00	100.00	250.00
(C112)	1838	.210	25.00	50.00	100.00	250.00
	1839	.485	25.00	50.00	100.00	250.00
	1840	.468	25.00	50.00	100.00	250.00
	1841	.387	25.00	50.00	100.00	250.00

Obv: Period after BADEN.

214	1842	.390	25.00	50.00	100.00	250.00
(C112a)	1843	.444	25.00	50.00	100.00	250.00
	1844	.585	25.00	50.00	100.00	250.00
	1845	.439	25.00	50.00	100.00	250.00

219	1845	Inc. Ab.	25.00	50.00	100.00	250.00
(C112b)	1846	—	25.00	50.00	100.00	250.00
	1847	.397	25.00	50.00	100.00	250.00
	1848	.116	25.00	50.00	100.00	250.00
	1849	.021	25.00	50.00	100.00	250.00
	1850	8.652	25.00	50.00	100.00	250.00
	1851	.089	25.00	50.00	100.00	250.00
	1852	.033	75.00	125.00	200.00	300.00

Blessing on the Baden Mines

224	1852	Inc. Ab.	75.00	125.00	200.00	300.00
(C114)						

Baden-Durlach / GERMAN STATES — 595

10.5820 g, .900 SILVER, .3062 oz ASW
Obv. leg: FRIEDRICH PRINZ.....

KM#	Date	Mintage	Fine	VF	XF	Unc
235 (C134)	1856	.149	100.00	225.00	375.00	675.00

Obv. leg: FRIEDRICH GROSHERZOG.....
Rev: Similar to KM#235.

236 (C153)	1856	.342	50.00	75.00	100.00	250.00
	1859	.195	50.00	75.00	100.00	250.00
	1860	.044	50.00	75.00	100.00	250.00

Mint Visit

239 (C154)	1857	776 pcs.	225.00	375.00	500.00	900.00

First Shooting Festival at Mannheim

247 (C155)	1863	.012	60.00	90.00	125.00	200.00

Second Shooting Festival at Karlsruhe

249 (C156)	1867	.014	45.00	90.00	175.00	250.00

ZWEI (2) GULDEN

25.4540 g, .750 SILVER, .6138 oz ASW

185 (C90)	1821	.030	150.00	250.00	500.00	1500.
	1822	.020	150.00	250.00	500.00	1500.
	1823	7,040	150.00	250.00	500.00	1500.
	1824	.017	150.00	250.00	500.00	1500.
	1825	6,642	150.00	250.00	500.00	1500.

21.2100 g, .900 SILVER, .6138 oz ASW

KM#	Date	Mintage	Fine	VF	XF	Unc
222 (C120)	1846	.592	50.00	75.00	150.00	400.00
	1847	.232	50.00	75.00	150.00	400.00
	1848	.273	50.00	75.00	150.00	400.00
	1849	.041	50.00	100.00	200.00	500.00
	1850	.140	50.00	75.00	150.00	400.00
	1851	.124	50.00	75.00	150.00	400.00
	1852	.142	50.00	75.00	150.00	400.00

Rev: Similar to KM#222.

237 (C135)	1856	.084	125.00	250.00	400.00	750.00

5 GULDEN

3.4390 g, .903 GOLD, .0998 oz AGW

176.1 (C94.1)	1819 PH	3,000	500.00	1000.	1500.	2000.

Obv: W/o engraver's initials below head.

176.2 (C94.2)	1819	695 pcs.	650.00	1000.	1500.	2000.
	1821	465 pcs.	675.00	1125.	1750.	2400.
	1822	1,718	525.00	875.00	1500.	2000.
	1823	1,854	525.00	875.00	1500.	2000.
	1824	2,763	525.00	750.00	1350.	1750.
	1825	1,508	525.00	875.00	1500.	2000.
	1826	887 pcs.	600.00	1000.	1650.	2250.

Obv: Curly hair.

190 (C94a)	1827	2,877	450.00	850.00	2250.	3000.
	1828	2,317	450.00	850.00	2250.	3000.

10 GULDEN

6.8780 g, .903 GOLD, .1997 oz AGW

KM#	Date	Mintage	Fine	VF	XF	Unc
177.1 (C95.1)	1819 PH	4,332	950.00	1500.	2500.	3250.

Obv: W/o engraver's initials below head.

177.2 (C95.2)	1821	812 pcs.	1150.	1850.	3000.	3750.
	1823	373 pcs.	1250.	2000.	3250.	4000.
	1824	328 pcs.	1400.	2250.	3500.	4250.
	1825	Inc. Ab.	1400.	2250.	3500.	4250.

EIN (1) THALER

28.0600 g, .833 SILVER, .7515 oz ASW

136 (C48)	1803 FE HB	675 pcs.	500.00	900.00	2100.	4000.

152 (C62)	1809 B E	6,219	300.00	550.00	1100.	2200.
	1810 B	2,815	250.00	450.00	900.00	2000.
	1811 B E	3,885	225.00	400.00	850.00	1800.

Baden-Durlach / GERMAN STATES 596

(Krone)

29.5160 g, .871 SILVER, .8266 oz ASW

KM#	Date	Mintage	Fine	VF	XF	Unc
163	1813 D	—	150.00	275.00	600.00	1200.
(C73)	1814 D	.036	150.00	275.00	600.00	1200.

Rev: W/o mintmaster's initial.

169	1814	Inc. Ab.	150.00	225.00	475.00	1000.
(C73a)	1815	.038	125.00	185.00	375.00	800.00
	1816	.036	100.00	165.00	325.00	700.00
	1817	.052	100.00	165.00	325.00	700.00
	1818	.039	100.00	165.00	365.00	800.00
(C91)	1819	—	125.00	200.00	500.00	1200.

Obv: WD monogram below bust.

175.1	1819	—	175.00	325.00	800.00	1750.
(C92)						

Obv: DOELL on truncation.

175.2	1819	—	150.00	325.00	700.00	1500.
(C92a)	1820	.038	150.00	350.00	800.00	1600.
	1821	.019	150.00	375.00	875.00	1800.

18.1480 g, .875 SILVER, .5105 oz ASW

KM#	Date	Mintage	Fine	VF	XF	Unc
193	1829	.168	50.00	100.00	175.00	400.00
(C93)	1830	.101	50.00	100.00	175.00	400.00

Obv. leg: W/o dot after BADEN.

195.1	1830	.238	85.00	175.00	250.00	650.00
(C115)	1831	.168	85.00	115.00	200.00	450.00
	1832	.176	85.00	115.00	200.00	450.00
	1832 star	I.A.	85.00	125.00	200.00	475.00

Obv. leg: Dot after BADEN.

195.2	1832 star	I.A.	85.00	125.00	200.00	475.00
(C115)	1833 star	.115	85.00	125.00	200.00	475.00
	1833	Inc. ab.	75.00	100.00	200.00	450.00
	1834	.036	75.00	100.00	200.00	450.00
	1835	.075	75.00	100.00	200.00	450.00
	1836 lg.6	.085	85.00	135.00	200.00	475.00
	1837	—	75.00	100.00	200.00	450.00

Rev. leg: Hyphen between KRONEN-THALER.

195.3	1834	Inc. Ab.	75.00	100.00	200.00	450.00
(C115)	1836	Inc. Ab.	100.00	125.00	225.00	700.00

Mint Visit

KM#	Date	Mintage	Fine	VF	XF	Unc
200	1832	—	600.00	850.00	1100.	2000.
(C116)						

Blessings on the Baden Mines

202	1834	6,517	200.00	300.00	500.00	1300.
(C117)						

204	1836	8,250	175.00	250.00	500.00	1150.
(C118)						

Mule. Obv: KM#195.2 rev. Rev: KM#204.

205	1836	—	—	—	Rare	—
(C115/8)						

Rev: Arms of Ten Customs Union States.

206	1836	.018	65.00	90.00	150.00	300.00
(C119)						

(Vereins)

18.5190 g, .900 SILVER, .5359 oz ASW

240	1857	.019	50.00	80.00	150.00	350.00
(C157)	1858	.232	35.00	65.00	125.00	225.00
	1859	.289	35.00	65.00	125.00	225.00
	1860	.174	35.00	65.00	125.00	225.00
	1861	.358	35.00	65.00	125.00	225.00
	1862	.400	35.00	65.00	125.00	225.00
	1863	.326	35.00	65.00	125.00	225.00

KM#	Date	Mintage	Fine	VF	XF	Unc
(C157)	1864	.322	35.00	65.00	125.00	225.00
	1865	.265	35.00	65.00	125.00	225.00

245	1865	Inc. Ab.	35.00	65.00	135.00	275.00
(C158)	1866	.149	35.00	65.00	135.00	275.00
	1867	.096	35.00	65.00	135.00	275.00
	1868	.102	35.00	65.00	135.00	275.00
	1869	.062	35.00	65.00	135.00	275.00
	1870	.022	35.00	65.00	135.00	275.00
	1871	—	35.00	65.00	135.00	275.00

2 THALER
(3-1/2 Gulden)

37.1200 g, .900 SILVER, 1.0743 oz ASW

212	1841	.231	125.00	175.00	400.00	1000.
(C121)	1842	.033	150.00	200.00	550.00	1150.
	1843	.035	150.00	200.00	600.00	1250.

Carl Friedrich
Obv: Similar to KM#212.

217.1	1844	4,323	125.00	200.00	350.00	750.00
(C122)						

Plain edge.

217.2	1844	—	—	—	—	Rare
(C122a)						

KM#	Date	Mintage	Fine	VF	XF	Unc
220	1845	.057	150.00	200.00	425.00	800.00
(C123)	1846	1,130	300.00	400.00	900.00	1500.
	1847	.031	150.00	200.00	400.00	700.00
	1852	.060	135.00	185.00	350.00	625.00

Obv: BALBACH below truncation.
Rev: Similar to KM#220.

225	1852	9 pcs.	—	—	Rare	—
(C136)	1854	.085	450.00	800.00	2000.	4000.

Obv: Different head, w/o engraver's name.

229	1855	2 pcs.	—	—	Rare	—
(C136a)						

FUNF (5) THALER
(500 Kreuzer)

5.7320 g, .903 GOLD, .1664 oz AGW

196	1830	1,788	800.00	1250.	2000.	2500.
(C97)						

MONETARY REFORM
2 MARK

11.1110 g, .900 SILVER, .3215 oz ASW

KM#	Date	Mintage	Fine	VF	XF	Unc
265	1876G	1.740	35.00	100.00	800.00	1600.
(Y12)	1877G	.760	35.00	100.00	700.00	1800.
	1880G	.070	60.00	160.00	900.00	2000.
	1883G	.050	65.00	160.00	750.00	2000.
	1888G	.080	70.00	140.00	1000.	2000.

269	1892G	.110	35.00	90.00	320.00	600.00
(Y12a)	1894G	.110	35.00	90.00	320.00	600.00
	1896G	.210	25.00	75.00	320.00	700.00
	1898G	.090	30.00	90.00	325.00	1100.
	1899G	.330	30.00	70.00	300.00	650.00
	1900G	.220	25.00	75.00	300.00	600.00
	1901G	.400	25.00	75.00	250.00	500.00
	1902G	5,368	250.00	750.00	1400.	2500.
	1902G	—	—	—	Proof	2250.

50th Year of Reign

271	1902G	.380	15.00	25.00	35.00	45.00
(Y20)						

272	1902G	.200	25.00	60.00	120.00	300.00
(Y17)	1903G	.490	20.00	45.00	110.00	180.00
	1904G	1.120	20.00	40.00	70.00	140.00
	1905G	.610	20.00	45.00	60.00	160.00
	1906G	.110	45.00	90.00	180.00	350.00
	1907G	.910	20.00	40.00	55.00	120.00

Golden Wedding Anniversary

276	1906	.350	15.00	30.00	35.00	50.00
(Y22)						

Baden-Durlach / GERMAN STATES 598

Friedrich Death

KM#	Date	Mintage	Fine	VF	XF	Unc
278	1907	.350	20.00	40.00	50.00	75.00
(Y24)	1907	—	—	—	Proof	150.00

283	1911G	.080	125.00	300.00	425.00	750.00
(Y26)	1913G	.140	100.00	225.00	375.00	650.00
	Common date	—	—	—	Proof	1000.

3 MARK

16.6670 g, .900 SILVER, .4823 oz ASW

280	1908G	.300	10.00	20.00	30.00	65.00
(Y27)	1909G	.760	10.00	20.00	30.00	65.00
	1910G	.670	10.00	20.00	30.00	65.00
	1911G	.380	10.00	20.00	35.00	60.00
	1912G	.840	10.00	20.00	30.00	50.00
	1914G	.410	10.00	20.00	25.00	45.00
	1915G	.170	20.00	60.00	80.00	125.00
	Common date	—	—	—	Proof	175.00

5 MARK

27.7770 g, .900 SILVER, .8038 oz ASW

263.1	1875G	.310	35.00	70.00	800.00	3250.
(Y13.1)	1876G	.470	35.00	70.00	950.00	2750.
	1888G	.030	300.00	625.00	1650.	4500.

Obv: W/o cross bar in 'A' of BADEN.

263.2	1875G	Inc. Ab.	35.00	70.00	700.00	2400.
(Y13.2)	1876G	Inc. Ab.	35.00	70.00	1000.	2500.
	1888G	Inc. Ab.	45.00	100.00	650.00	2000.
	Common date	—	—	—	Proof	4500.

1.9910 g, .900 GOLD, .0576 oz AGW

266	1877G	.350	150.00	250.00	400.00	600.00
(Y14)	1877G	—	—	—	Proof	1500.

27.7770 g, .900 SILVER, .8038 oz ASW
Obv: W/o cross bar in 'A' of BADEN.
Rev: Large eagle.

268.1	1891	.040	225.00	450.00	1500.	6000.
(Y13a.1)						

Obv: Normal 'A' in BADEN.

KM#	Date	Mintage	Fine	VF	XF	Unc
268.2	1891	Inc. Ab.	30.00	90.00	375.00	1250.
(Y13a.2)	1893	.040	25.00	65.00	325.00	1000.
	1894	.060	25.00	60.00	225.00	950.00
	1895	.070	25.00	60.00	250.00	950.00
	1898	.130	25.00	60.00	250.00	1000.
	1899	.060	27.50	70.00	375.00	750.00
	1900	.130	27.50	70.00	375.00	900.00
	1901	.130	25.00	70.00	275.00	900.00
	1902	.040	35.00	85.00	250.00	900.00
	Common date	—	—	—	Proof	900.00

50th Year of Reign
Rev: Similar to KM#268.2.

273	1902G	.050	40.00	90.00	150.00	200.00
(Y21)	1902G	—	—	—	Proof	625.00

Rev: Similar to KM#268.2.

274	1902G	.130	35.00	65.00	225.00	475.00
(Y18)	1903G	.440	20.00	45.00	175.00	450.00
	1904G	.240	20.00	45.00	175.00	450.00
	1907G	.240	20.00	45.00	175.00	450.00
	Common date	—	—	—	Proof	400.00

Golden Wedding Anniversary

277	1906	.060	50.00	100.00	150.00	200.00
(Y23)	1906	—	—	—	Proof	275.00

Death of Friedrich
Rev: Similar to KM#268.2.

KM#	Date	Mintage	Fine	VF	XF	Unc
279	1907	.060	65.00	125.00	160.00	225.00
(Y25)	1907	—	—	—	Proof	275.00

Rev: Similar to KM#268.2.

281	1908G	.180	35.00	55.00	150.00	600.00
(Y28)	1913G	.240	30.00	50.00	140.00	425.00
	Common date	—	—	—	Proof	525.00

10 MARK

3.9820 g, .900 GOLD, .1152 oz AGW
Rev: Type I.

260	1872G	.270	65.00	125.00	200.00	325.00
(Y15)	1873G	.470	65.00	125.00	200.00	325.00
	1873G	—	—	—	Proof	1750.

Rev: Type II.

264	1875G	.340	75.00	150.00	200.00	325.00
(Y15a)	1876G	1.390	65.00	125.00	225.00	350.00
	1877G	.160	65.00	125.00	200.00	325.00
	1878G	.240	65.00	125.00	200.00	325.00
	1878G	—	—	—	Proof	1300.
	1879G	.098	100.00	200.00	275.00	400.00
	1880G	1.169	6000.00	10,000.	15,000.	30,000.
	1881G	.190	75.00	150.00	250.00	375.00
	1881G	—	—	—	Proof	1300.
	1888G	.120	65.00	125.00	200.00	325.00

Rev: Type III.

267	1890G	.073	125.00	225.00	325.00	500.00
(Y15b)	1891G	.110	125.00	175.00	250.00	350.00
	1893G	.180	125.00	175.00	250.00	325.00
	1896G	.052	125.00	200.00	300.00	450.00
	1897G	.070	125.00	225.00	275.00	400.00
	1898G	.260	115.00	165.00	250.00	325.00
	1898G	—	—	—	Proof	1300.
	1900G	.031	150.00	400.00	500.00	800.00
	1901G	.091	125.00	165.00	225.00	325.00
	1901G	—	—	—	Proof	1300.

275	1902G	.030	175.00	300.00	450.00	650.00

KM#	Date	Mintage	Fine	VF	XF	Unc
(Y19)	1903G	.110	125.00	200.00	250.00	350.00
	1903G	—	—	—	Proof	1000.
	1904G	.150	110.00	150.00	225.00	325.00
	1905G	.096	125.00	200.00	250.00	350.00
	1905G	—	—	—	Proof	1000.
	1906G	.120	125.00	150.00	225.00	325.00
	1906G	—	—	—	Proof	1000.
	1907G	.120	110.00	150.00	225.00	325.00
	1907G	—	—	—	Proof	1000.

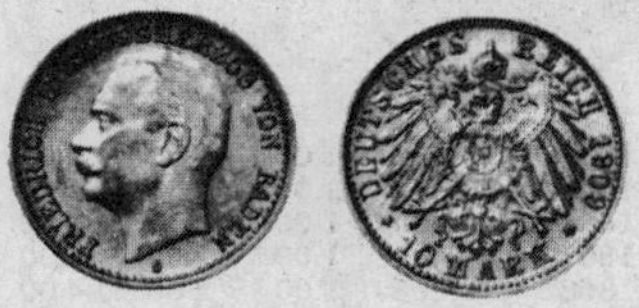

KM#	Date	Mintage	Fine	VF	XF	Unc
282	1909G	.086	225.00	500.00	650.00	850.00
(Y29)	1909G	—	—	—	Proof	2000.
	1910G	.061	225.00	500.00	650.00	850.00
	1910G	—	—	—	Proof	2000.
	1911G	.029	2000.	4500.	6500.	8000.
	1912G	.026	700.00	1200.	2200.	3000.
	1913G	.042	500.00	800.00	1100.	1900.
	1913G	—	—	—	Proof	2000.

20 MARK

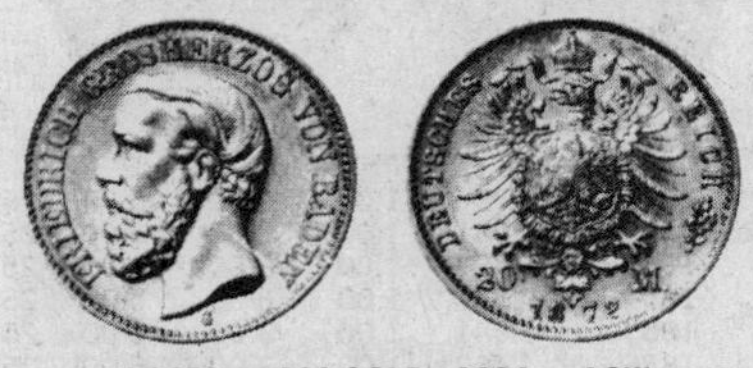

7.9650 g, .900 GOLD, .2304 oz AGW
Rev: Type I.

KM#	Date	Mintage	Fine	VF	XF	Unc
261	1872G	.400	125.00	150.00	225.00	325.00
(Y16)	1872G	—	—	—	Proof	2250.
	1873G	.520	125.00	160.00	300.00	350.00
	1873G	—	—	—	Proof	2250.

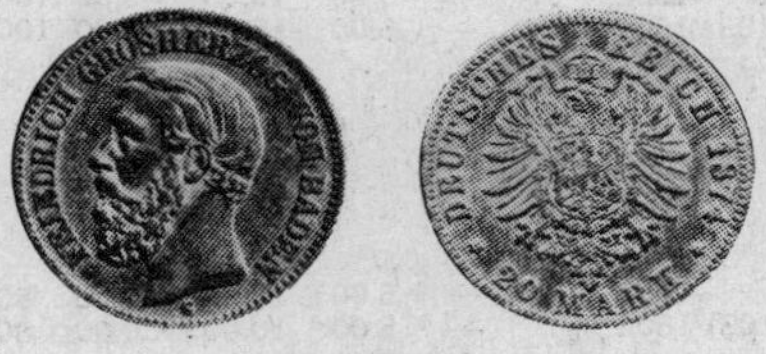

Rev: Type II.

KM#	Date	Mintage	Fine	VF	XF	Unc
262	1874G	.150	225.00	400.00	600.00	900.00
(Y16a)	1874G	—	—	—	Proof	3000.

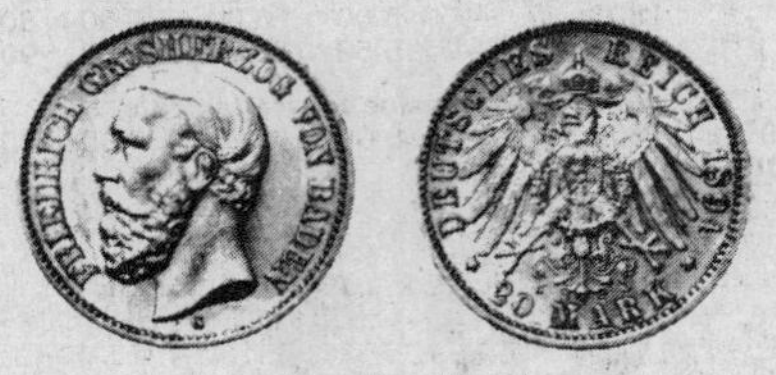

Rev: Type III.

KM#	Date	Mintage	Fine	VF	XF	Unc
270	1894G sm. 4					
(Y16b)		.400	135.00	160.00	250.00	400.00
	1894G lg.4	.400	135.00	160.00	250.00	400.00
	1894G	—	—	—	Proof	1300.
	1895G	.100	135.00	225.00	300.00	450.00
	1895G	—	—	—	Proof	1300.

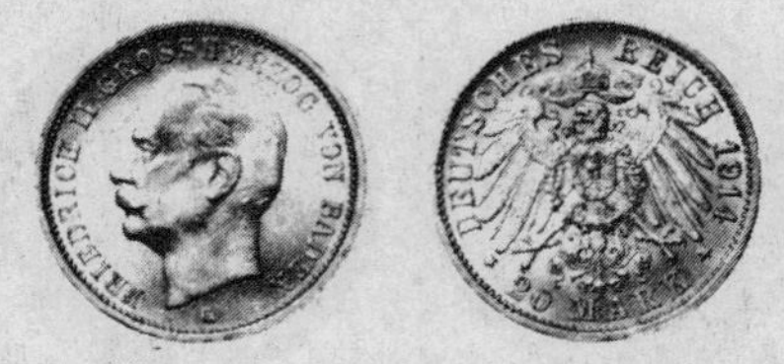

KM#	Date	Mintage	Fine	VF	XF	Unc
284	1911G	.190	125.00	150.00	200.00	300.00
(Y30)	1911G	—	—	—	Proof	800.00
	1912G	.310	125.00	140.00	200.00	300.00
	1913G	.085	125.00	150.00	225.00	325.00
	1914G	.280	125.00	150.00	200.00	300.00
	1914G	—	—	—	Proof	800.00

TRADE COINAGE

DUCAT

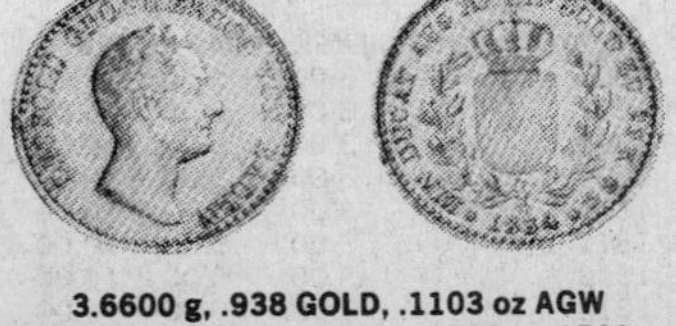

3.6600 g, .938 GOLD, .1103 oz AGW

KM#	Date	Mintage	Fine	VF	XF	Unc
201	1832	6,631	—	1000.	1500.	2000.

KM#	Date	Mintage	Fine	VF	XF	Unc
(C124)	1833	2,496	—	1100.	1600.	2100.
	1834	1,992	—	1150.	1650.	2200.
	1835	2,470	—	1100.	1600.	2100.
	1836	1,777	—	1150.	1650.	2200.

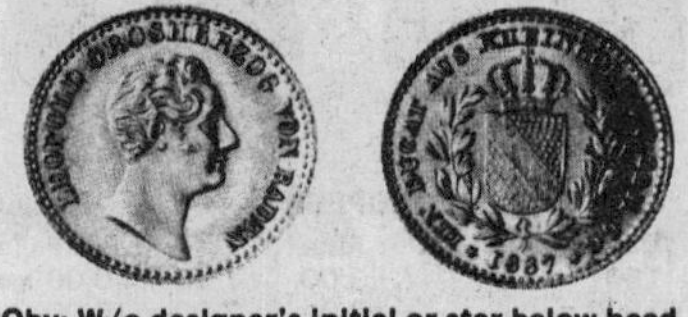

Obv: W/o designer's initial or star below head.

KM#	Date	Mintage	Fine	VF	XF	Unc
208	1837	1,467	—	1125.	1650.	2200.
(C124.1)	1838	2,095	—	1125.	1650.	2200.
	1839	2,448	—	1100.	1600.	2100.
	1840	2,044	—	1125.	1650.	2200.
	1841	2,145	—	1125.	1650.	2200.
	1842	2,130	—	1125.	1650.	2200.

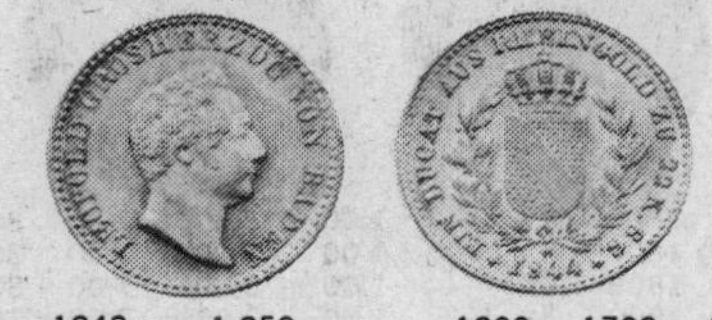

KM#	Date	Mintage	Fine	VF	XF	Unc
215	1843	1,350	—	1300.	1700.	2200.
(C124a)	1844	850 pcs.	—	1500.	2000.	2500.
	1845	2,097	—	1200.	1600.	2000.
	1846	1,950	—	1200.	1600.	2000.

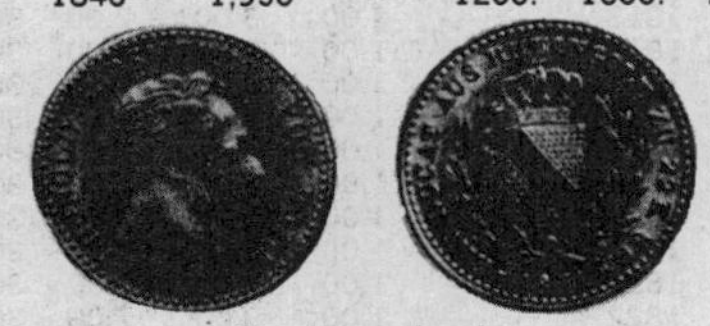

Obv: Larger head.

KM#	Date	Mintage	Fine	VF	XF	Unc
223.1	1847	1,870	—	1200.	1600.	2100.
(C124b)	1848	1,590	—	1200.	1600.	2100.
	1849	1,420	—	1200.	1600.	2100.
	1850	1,390	—	1200.	1600.	2100.
	1851	1,280	—	1200.	1600.	2100.
	1852	1,450	—	1350.	1750.	2250.

Obv: Star below head.

KM#	Date	Mintage	Fine	VF	XF	Unc
223.2 (C124c)	1852	Inc. Ab.	—	1350.	1750.	2250.

NOTE: Posthumous issue.

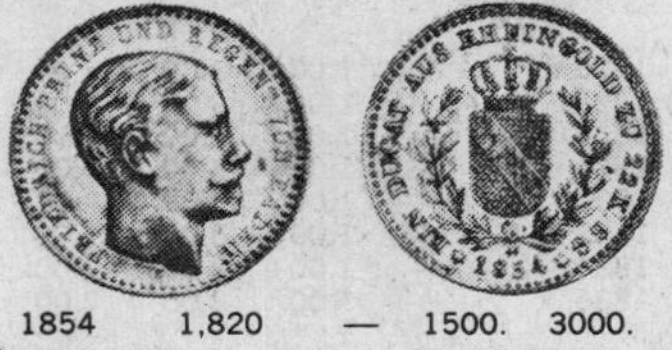

KM#	Date	Mintage	Fine	VF	XF	Unc
227 (C137)	1854	1,820	—	1500.	3000.	4000.

BAMBERG

Bishopric in northern Bavaria. The see was founded in 1007 and the first coinage appeared soon after. The bishops were made princes of the empire in the mid-1200s. It was annexed to Bavaria in 1802.

RULERS

Christoph Franz, Freiherr von Buseck, Bishop, 1795-1802
Georg Karl, von Fechenbach, 1802-1803

DUCAT

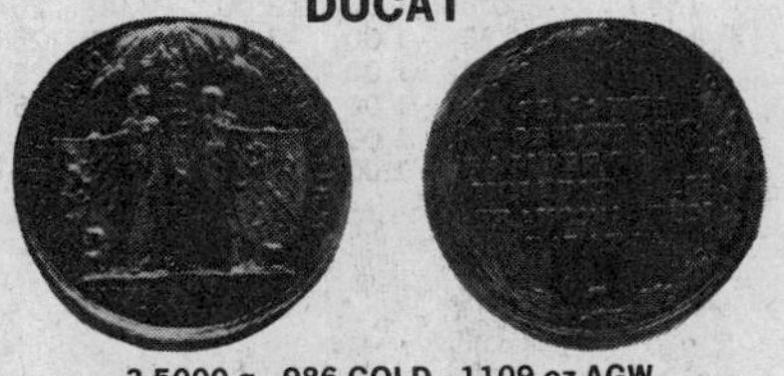

3.5000 g, .986 GOLD, .1109 oz AGW
Union of Bamberg with Bavaria

KM#	Date	Mintage	Fine	VF	XF	Unc
154 (C60)	1802	—	400.00	800.00	1350.	1900.

BAVARIA

Located in south Germany. In 1180 the Duchy of Bavaria was given to the Count of Wittelsbach by the emperor. He is the ancestor of all who ruled in Bavaria until 1918. Primogeniture was proclaimed in 1506 and in 1623 the dukes of Bavaria were given the electoral right. Bavaria, which had been divided for the various heirs, was reunited in 1799. The title of king was granted to Bavaria in 1805.

RULERS

Maximilian IV, Joseph as Elector, 1799-1805
Maximilian IV,
As King Maximilian I, Joseph, 1806-1825
Ludwig I, 1825-1848
Maximilian II, 1848-1864
Ludwig II, 1864-1886
Otto, 1886-1913
Prince Regent Luitpold, 1886-1912
Ludwig III, 1913-1918

HELLER

COPPER
Obv: Shield and date in diamond.
Rev. value: 1/HEL/LER in diamond.

KM#	Date	Mintage	Fine	VF	XF	Unc
305	1801	—	5.00	10.00	15.00	50.00
(C100)	1802	—	5.00	10.00	15.00	50.00
	1803	—	5.00	10.00	15.00	50.00
	1804	—	5.00	10.00	15.00	50.00
	1805	—	5.00	10.00	15.00	50.00

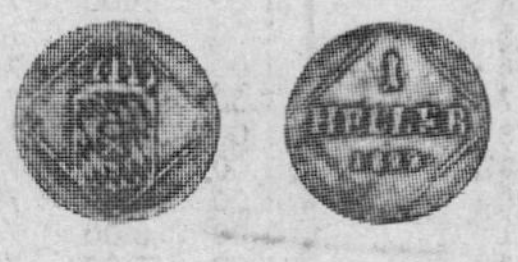

KM#	Date	Mintage	Fine	VF	XF	Unc
340	1806	—	3.00	5.00	10.00	35.00
(C134)	1807	—	3.00	5.00	10.00	35.00
	1808	—	3.00	5.00	10.00	35.00
	1809	—	3.00	5.00	10.00	35.00
	1810	—	3.00	5.00	10.00	35.00
	1811	—	3.00	5.00	10.00	35.00
	1812	—	3.00	5.00	10.00	35.00
	1813	—	3.00	5.00	10.00	35.00
	1814	—	3.00	5.00	10.00	35.00
	1815	—	3.00	5.00	10.00	35.00
	1816	—	3.00	5.00	10.00	35.00
	1817	—	3.00	5.00	10.00	35.00
	1818	—	3.00	5.00	10.00	35.00
	1819	—	3.00	5.00	10.00	35.00
	1820	—	3.00	5.00	10.00	35.00
	1821	—	3.00	5.00	10.00	35.00
	1822	—	3.00	5.00	10.00	35.00
	1823	—	3.00	5.00	10.00	35.00
	1824	—	3.00	5.00	10.00	35.00
	1825	—	3.00	5.00	10.00	35.00

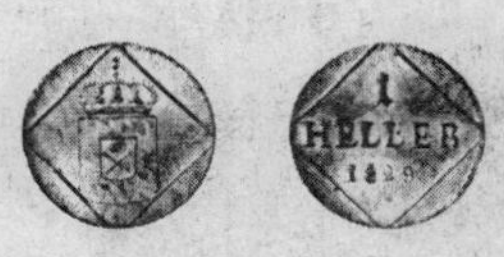

KM#	Date	Mintage	Fine	VF	XF	Unc
383	1828	—	3.00	5.00	10.00	35.00
(C155)	1829	—	3.00	5.00	10.00	35.00
	1830	—	3.00	5.00	10.00	35.00
	1831	—	3.00	5.00	10.00	35.00
	1832	—	3.00	5.00	10.00	35.00
	1833	—	3.00	5.00	10.00	35.00
	1834	—	3.00	5.00	10.00	35.00
	1835	—	3.00	5.00	10.00	35.00

KM#	Date	Mintage	Fine	VF	XF	Unc
419	1839	.256	1.00	2.00	5.00	25.00
(C158)	1840	.169	1.00	2.00	5.00	25.00
	1841	—	1.00	2.00	5.00	25.00
	1842	—	1.00	2.00	5.00	25.00
	1843	—	1.00	2.00	5.00	25.00
	1844	.190	1.00	2.00	5.00	25.00
	1845	.434	1.00	2.00	5.00	25.00
	1846	—	1.00	2.00	5.00	25.00
	1847	.074	1.00	2.00	5.00	25.00
	1848	.514	1.00	2.00	5.00	25.00

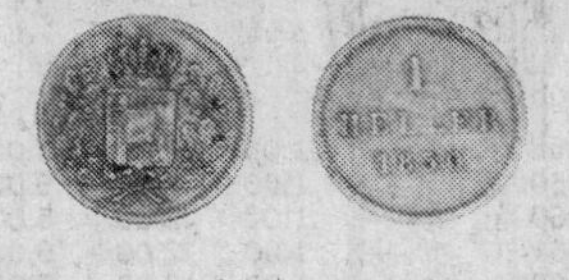

KM#	Date	Mintage	Fine	VF	XF	Unc
449	1849	.346	1.00	2.00	5.00	20.00
(C220)	1850	.306	1.00	2.00	5.00	20.00
	1851	.437	1.00	2.00	5.00	20.00
	1852	.206	1.00	2.00	5.00	20.00
	1853	.279	1.00	2.00	5.00	20.00
	1854	.193	1.00	2.00	5.00	20.00
	1855	.132	1.00	2.00	5.00	20.00
	1856	.034	1.00	2.00	5.00	20.00

PFENNIG

COPPER
Obv: Bavaria shield in ornamental cartouche.
Rev: Value above date.

KM#	Date	Mintage	Fine	VF	XF	Unc
306	1801	—	2.00	7.00	15.00	40.00
(C101)	1802	—	2.00	7.00	15.00	40.00
	1803	—	2.00	7.00	15.00	40.00
	1804	—	2.00	7.00	15.00	40.00
	1805	—	2.00	7.00	15.00	40.00

Bavaria / GERMAN STATES 600

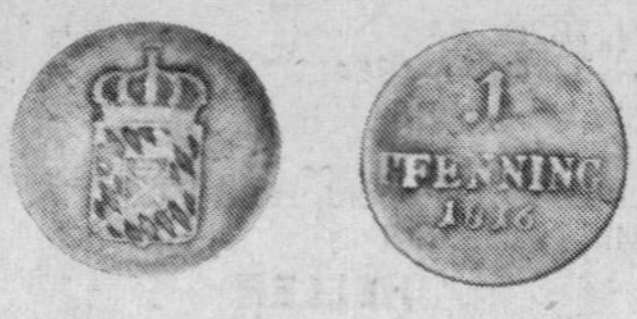

KM#	Date	Mintage	Fine	VF	XF	Unc
341	1806	—	1.00	3.00	7.00	25.00
(C135)	1807	—	1.00	3.00	7.00	25.00
	1808	—	1.00	3.00	7.00	25.00
	1809	—	1.00	3.00	7.00	25.00
	1810	—	1.00	3.00	7.00	25.00
	1811	—	1.00	3.00	7.00	25.00
	1812	—	1.00	3.00	7.00	25.00
	1813	—	1.00	3.00	7.00	25.00
	1814	—	1.00	3.00	7.00	25.00
	1815	—	1.00	3.00	7.00	25.00
	1816	—	1.00	3.00	7.00	25.00
	1817	—	1.00	3.00	7.00	25.00
	1818	—	1.00	3.00	7.00	25.00
	1819	—	1.00	3.00	7.00	25.00
	1820	—	1.00	3.00	7.00	25.00
	1821	—	1.00	3.00	7.00	25.00
	1822	—	1.00	3.00	7.00	25.00
	1823	—	1.00	3.00	7.00	25.00
	1824	—	1.00	3.00	7.00	25.00
	1825	—	1.00	3.00	7.00	25.00

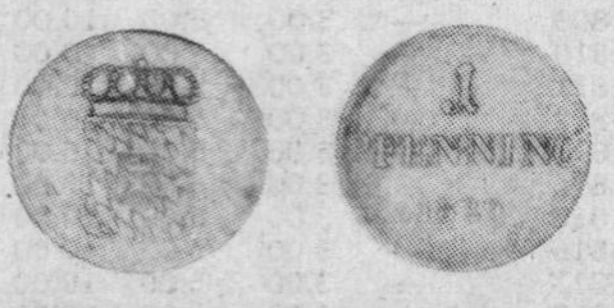

384	1828	—	1.00	3.00	7.00	20.00
(C156)	1829	—	1.00	3.00	7.00	20.00
	1830	—	1.00	3.00	7.00	20.00
	1831	—	1.00	3.00	7.00	20.00
	1832	—	1.00	3.00	7.00	20.00
	1833	—	1.00	3.00	7.00	20.00
	1834	—	1.00	3.00	7.00	20.00
	1835	—	1.00	3.00	7.00	20.00

420	1839	.801	1.00	2.00	5.00	15.00
(C159)	1840	.732	1.00	2.00	5.00	15.00
	1841	.970	1.00	2.00	5.00	15.00
	1842	.817	1.00	2.00	5.00	15.00
	1843	.892	1.00	2.00	5.00	15.00
	1844	.645	1.00	2.00	5.00	15.00
	1845	1.037	1.00	2.00	5.00	15.00
	1846	1.487	1.00	2.00	5.00	15.00
	1847	1.808	1.00	2.00	5.00	15.00
	1848	1.815	1.00	2.00	5.00	15.00

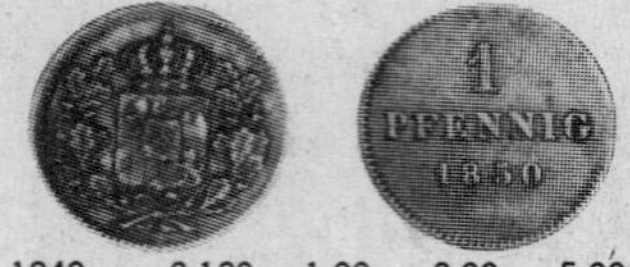

450	1849	2.120	1.00	2.00	5.00	15.00
(C221)	1850	2.494	1.00	2.00	5.00	15.00
	1851	2.162	1.00	2.00	5.00	15.00
	1852	2.634	1.00	2.00	5.00	15.00
	1853	1.950	1.00	2.00	5.00	15.00
	1854	1.842	1.00	2.00	5.00	15.00
	1855	1.576	1.00	2.00	5.00	15.00
	1856	1.530	1.00	2.00	5.00	15.00

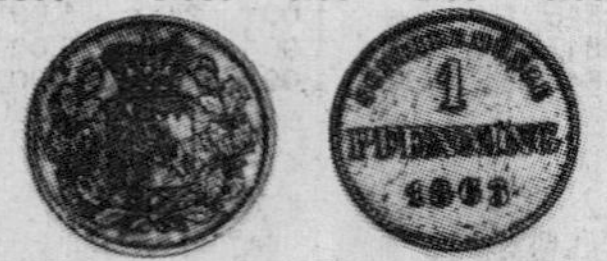

471	1858	—	1.00	2.00	5.00	15.00
(C224)	1859	—	1.00	2.00	5.00	15.00
	1860	—	1.00	2.00	5.00	15.00
	1861	—	1.00	2.00	5.00	15.00
	1862	—	1.00	2.00	5.00	15.00
	1863	2.284	1.00	2.00	5.00	15.00
	1864	2.304	1.00	2.00	5.00	15.00

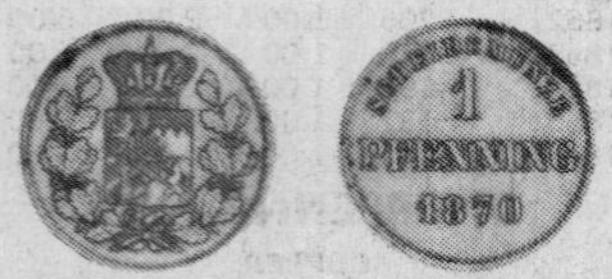

486	1865	1.401	1.00	2.00	5.00	15.00
(C250)	1866	1.485	1.00	2.00	5.00	15.00
	1867	1.633	1.00	2.00	5.00	15.00
	1868	1.394	1.00	2.00	5.00	15.00
	1869	1.474	1.00	2.00	5.00	15.00
	1870	1.608	1.00	2.00	5.00	15.00
	1871	1.534	1.00	2.00	5.00	15.00

2 PFENNIG

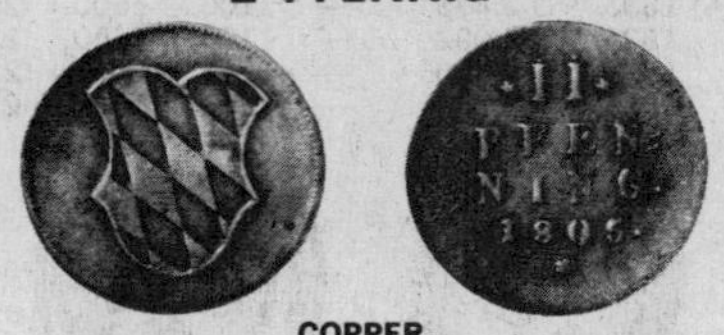

COPPER

KM#	Date	Mintage	Fine	VF	XF	Unc
307	1801	—	3.00	7.00	10.00	40.00
(C102)	1802	—	3.00	7.00	10.00	40.00
	1803	—	3.00	7.00	10.00	40.00
	1804	—	3.00	7.00	10.00	40.00
	1805	—	3.00	7.00	10.00	40.00

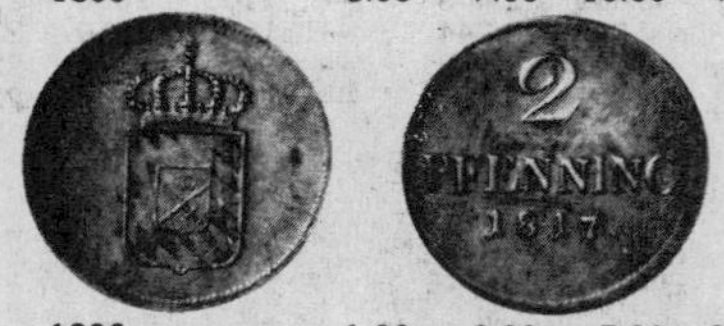

342	1806	—	1.00	3.00	7.00	30.00
(C136)	1807	—	1.00	3.00	7.00	30.00
	1808	—	1.00	3.00	7.00	30.00
	1809	—	1.00	3.00	7.00	30.00
	1810	—	1.00	3.00	7.00	30.00
	1811	—	1.00	3.00	7.00	30.00
	1812	—	1.00	3.00	7.00	30.00
	1813	—	1.00	3.00	7.00	30.00
	1814	—	1.00	3.00	7.00	30.00
	1815	—	1.00	3.00	7.00	30.00
	1816	—	1.00	3.00	7.00	30.00
	1817	—	1.00	3.00	7.00	30.00
	1818	—	1.00	3.00	7.00	30.00
	1819	—	1.00	3.00	7.00	30.00
	1820	—	1.00	3.00	7.00	30.00
	1821	—	1.00	3.00	7.00	30.00
	1822	—	1.00	3.00	7.00	30.00
	1823	—	1.00	3.00	7.00	30.00
	1824	—	1.00	3.00	7.00	30.00
	1825	—	1.00	3.00	7.00	30.00

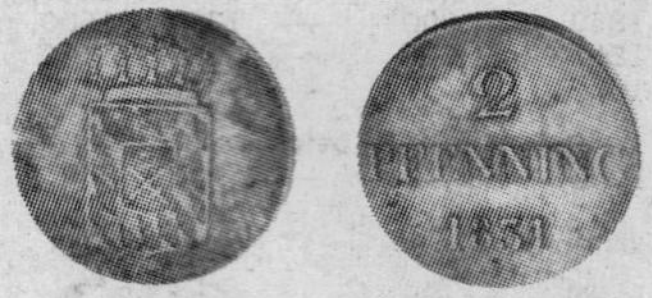

385	1828	—	1.00	3.00	7.00	30.00
(C157)	1829	—	1.00	3.00	7.00	30.00
	1830	—	1.00	3.00	7.00	30.00
	1831	—	1.00	3.00	7.00	30.00
	1832	—	1.00	3.00	7.00	30.00
	1833	—	1.00	3.00	7.00	30.00
	1834	—	1.00	3.00	7.00	30.00
	1835	—	1.00	3.00	7.00	30.00

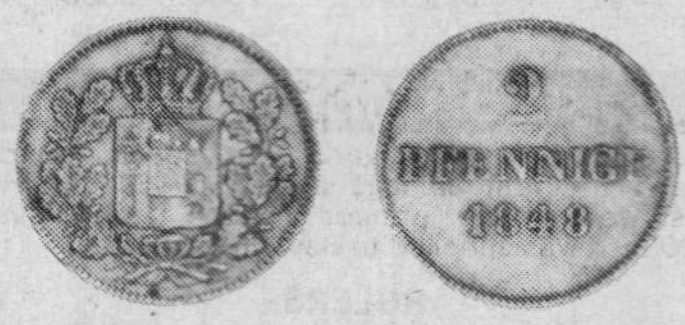

421	1839	.320	1.00	3.00	7.00	25.00
(C160)	1840	.320	1.00	3.00	7.00	25.00
	1841	.442	1.00	3.00	7.00	25.00
	1842	.353	1.00	3.00	7.00	25.00
	1843	.203	1.00	3.00	7.00	25.00
	1844	.226	1.00	3.00	7.00	25.00
	1845	.242	1.00	3.00	7.00	25.00
	1846	.232	1.00	3.00	7.00	25.00
	1847	.663	1.00	3.00	7.00	25.00
	1848	.776	1.00	3.00	7.00	25.00

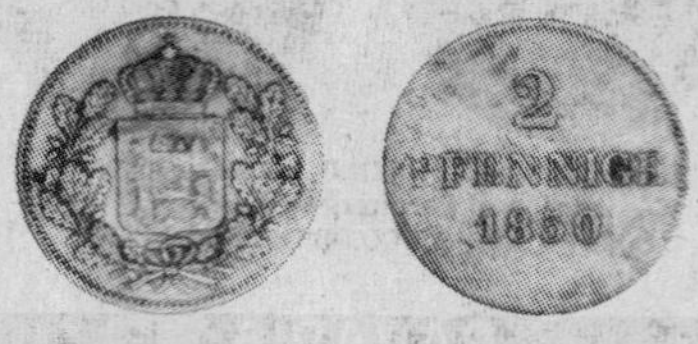

451	1849	.454	1.00	3.00	7.00	25.00
(C222)	1850	1.477	1.00	3.00	7.00	25.00

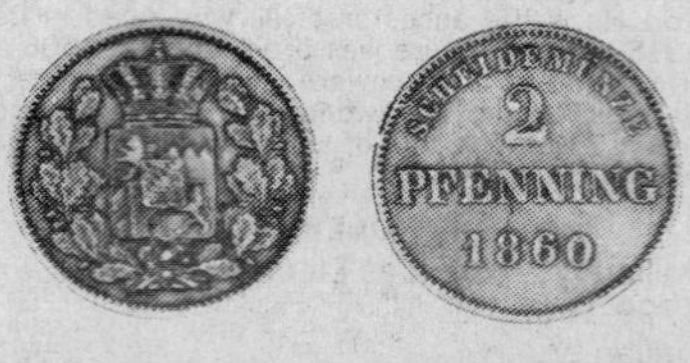

472	1858	—	1.00	2.00	4.00	20.00
(C225)	1859	—	1.00	2.00	4.00	20.00
	1860	—	1.00	2.00	4.00	20.00

KM#	Date	Mintage	Fine	VF	XF	Unc
(C225)	1861	—	1.00	2.00	4.00	20.00
	1862	—	1.00	2.00	4.00	20.00
	1863	.228	1.00	2.00	4.00	20.00

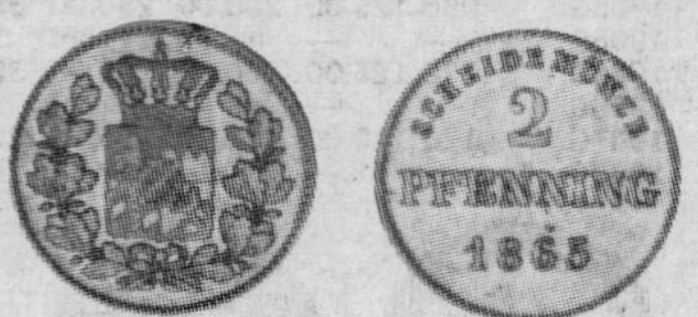

478	1864	.589	1.00	2.00	4.00	20.00
(C251)	1865	.358	1.00	2.00	4.00	20.00
	1866	.234	1.00	2.00	4.00	20.00
	1867	.481	1.00	2.00	4.00	20.00
	1868	.208	1.00	2.00	4.00	20.00
	1869	.466	1.00	2.00	4.00	20.00
	1870	.476	1.00	2.00	4.00	20.00
	1871	.466	1.00	2.00	4.00	20.00

1/2 KREUZER

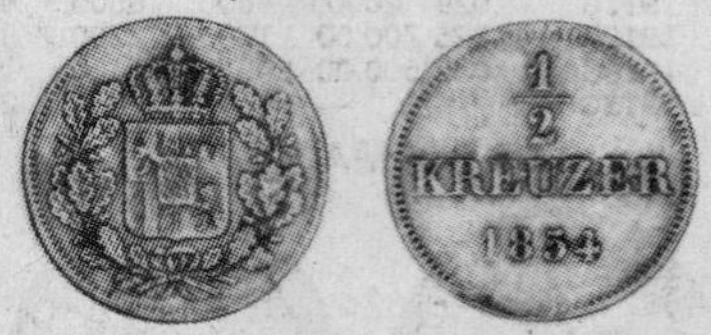

COPPER

463	1851	.796	1.00	3.00	5.00	25.00
(C223)	1852	.981	1.00	3.00	5.00	25.00
	1853	.797	1.00	3.00	5.00	25.00
	1854	.528	1.00	3.00	5.00	25.00
	1855	.641	1.00	3.00	5.00	25.00
	1856	.462	1.00	3.00	5.00	25.00

KREUZER

.7700 g, .187 SILVER, .0046 oz ASW
Obv: Head right, MAX. IOS.
Rev: Crowned shield within palm branches.

308	1802	—	5.00	15.00	40.00	100.00
(C103a)	1803	—	5.00	15.00	40.00	100.00

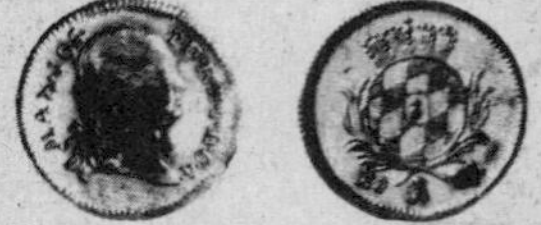

317	1801	—	5.00	10.00	30.00	80.00
(C103)	1802	—	5.00	10.00	30.00	80.00

Obv. leg: MAX. IOS. H.I.B.C. Rev: W/o numeric value.

315	1801	—	5.00	10.00	30.00	80.00
(C103.1)	1802	—	5.00	10.00	30.00	80.00
	1803	—	5.00	10.00	30.00	80.00
	1806/0	—	5.50	11.00	32.50	90.00

Rev: Numeral value separating date.

329 (C103.1a)	1804	—	5.00	10.00	30.00	80.00

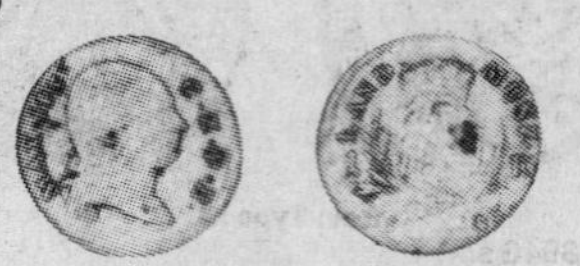

Obv. leg: MAX. IOS. C.Z.P.B.
Rev: LAND MUNZ, oval arms separating value.

330	1804	—	5.00	10.00	30.00	80.00
(C103.2)	1805	—	5.00	10.00	30.00	80.00

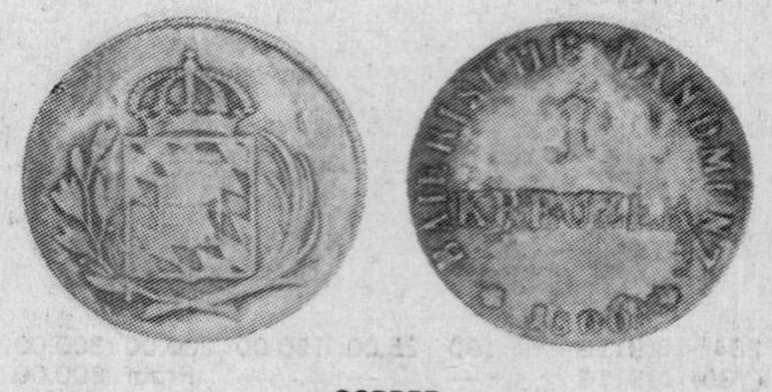

COPPER

343 (C130)	1806	.145	25.00	50.00	125.00	250.00

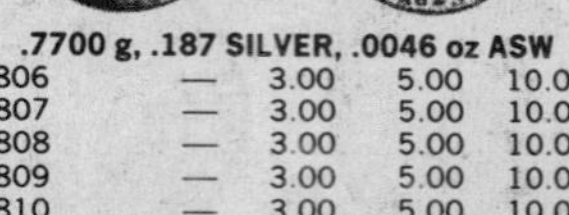

.7700 g, .187 SILVER, .0046 oz ASW

344	1806	—	3.00	5.00	10.00	65.00
(C137)	1807	—	3.00	5.00	10.00	65.00
	1808	—	3.00	5.00	10.00	65.00
	1809	—	3.00	5.00	10.00	65.00
	1810	—	3.00	5.00	10.00	65.00
	1811	—	3.00	5.00	10.00	65.00
	1812	—	3.00	5.00	10.00	65.00
	1813	—	3.00	5.00	10.00	65.00
	1814	—	3.00	5.00	10.00	65.00

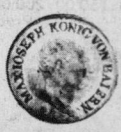

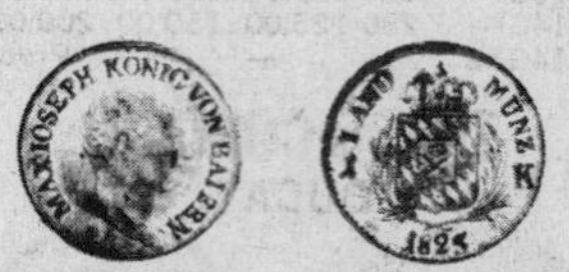

KM#	Date	Mintage	Fine	VF	XF	Unc
(C137)	1815	—	3.00	5.00	10.00	65.00
	1816	—	3.00	5.00	10.00	65.00
	1817	—	3.00	5.00	10.00	65.00
	1818	—	3.00	5.00	10.00	65.00
	1819	—	3.00	5.00	10.00	65.00
	1820	—	3.00	5.00	10.00	65.00
	1821	—	3.00	5.00	10.00	65.00
	1822	—	3.00	5.00	10.00	65.00
	1823	—	3.00	5.00	10.00	65.00
	1824	—	3.00	5.00	10.00	65.00
	1825	—	3.00	5.00	10.00	65.00

Obv. leg: LUDWIG KOENIG.....

KM#	Date	Mintage	Fine	VF	XF	Unc
376	1827	—	3.00	5.00	10.00	75.00
(C161)	1828	—	3.00	5.00	10.00	75.00
	1829	—	3.00	5.00	10.00	75.00
	1830	—	3.00	5.00	10.00	75.00

Obv. leg: LUDWIG I KOENIG.....

KM#	Date	Mintage	Fine	VF	XF	Unc
390	1830	—	3.00	5.00	10.00	60.00
(C161a)	1831	—	3.00	5.00	10.00	60.00
	1832	—	3.00	5.00	10.00	60.00
	1833	—	3.00	5.00	10.00	60.00
	1834	—	3.00	5.00	10.00	60.00
	1835	—	3.00	5.00	10.00	60.00

.8400 g, .166 SILVER, .0044 oz ASW

KM#	Date	Mintage	Fine	VF	XF	Unc
422	1839	1.474	1.00	2.00	5.00	20.00
(C189)	1840	1.769	1.00	2.00	5.00	20.00
	1841	1.591	1.00	2.00	5.00	20.00
	1842	1.855	1.00	2.00	5.00	20.00
	1843	1.373	1.00	2.00	5.00	20.00
	1844	1.324	1.00	2.00	5.00	20.00
	1845	1.660	1.00	2.00	5.00	20.00
	1846	1.849	1.00	2.00	5.00	20.00
	1847	1.519	1.00	2.00	5.00	20.00
	1848	1.746	1.00	2.00	5.00	20.00

KM#	Date	Mintage	Fine	VF	XF	Unc
452	1849	1.971	1.00	2.00	5.00	20.00
(C226)	1850	3.135	1.00	2.00	5.00	20.00
	1851	2.084	1.00	2.00	5.00	20.00
	1852	1.915	1.00	2.00	5.00	20.00
	1853	1.528	1.00	2.00	5.00	20.00
	1854	1.650	1.00	2.00	5.00	20.00
	1855	1.510	1.00	2.00	5.00	20.00
	1856	1.335	1.00	2.00	5.00	20.00

KM#	Date	Mintage	Fine	VF	XF	Unc
473	1858	2.400	1.00	2.50	4.50	10.00
(C229)	1859	—	1.00	2.50	4.50	10.00
	1860	.231	1.00	2.50	4.50	10.00
	1861	3.276	1.00	2.50	4.50	10.00
	1862	3.358	1.00	2.50	4.50	10.00
	1863	3.356	1.00	2.50	4.50	10.00
	1864	3.293	1.00	2.50	4.50	10.00

KM#	Date	Mintage	Fine	VF	XF	Unc
487	1865	1.837	1.00	2.50	4.50	10.00
(C252)	1866	2.542	1.00	2.50	4.50	10.00
	1867	2.305	1.00	2.50	4.50	10.00
	1868	2.526	1.00	2.50	4.50	10.00
	1869	2.774	1.00	2.50	4.50	10.00
	1870	2.199	1.00	2.50	4.50	10.00
	1871	2.634	1.00	2.50	4.50	10.00

3 KREUZER
(1 Groschen)

1.3500 g, .333 SILVER, .0144 oz ASW
Obv: Head right, MAX. IOS. P. B.
Rev: Crowned oval arms separating value.

KM#	Date	Mintage	Fine	VF	XF	Unc
309	1801	—	5.00	15.00	50.00	125.00
(C104)	1802	—	5.00	15.00	50.00	125.00

Obv. leg: MAX. IOS. H.I.B.C. &

KM#	Date	Mintage	Fine	VF	XF	Unc
322	1803	—	5.00	15.00	50.00	125.00
(C104a)	1804	—	5.00	15.00	50.00	125.00

Obv. leg: MAX. IOS. C.Z.P.B.

KM#	Date	Mintage	Fine	VF	XF	Unc
331	1804	—	5.00	15.00	50.00	125.00
(C104b)	1805	—	5.00	15.00	50.00	125.00

Obv: Head right. Rev: Shield w/crown above crossed scepter and sword.

KM#	Date	Mintage	Fine	VF	XF	Unc
352	1807	—	5.00	15.00	50.00	125.00
(C138)	1808	—	5.00	15.00	50.00	125.00
	1809	—	5.00	15.00	50.00	125.00
	1810	—	5.00	15.00	50.00	125.00
	1811	—	5.00	15.00	50.00	125.00
	1812	—	5.00	15.00	50.00	125.00
	1813	—	5.00	15.00	50.00	125.00
	1814	—	5.00	15.00	50.00	125.00
	1815	—	5.00	15.00	50.00	125.00
	1816	—	5.00	15.00	50.00	125.00
	1817	—	5.00	15.00	50.00	125.00
	1818	—	5.00	15.00	50.00	125.00
	1819	—	5.00	15.00	50.00	125.00
	1820	—	5.00	15.00	50.00	125.00
	1821	—	5.00	15.00	50.00	125.00
	1822	—	5.00	15.00	50.00	125.00
	1823	—	5.00	15.00	50.00	125.00
	1824	—	5.00	15.00	50.00	125.00
	1825	—	5.00	15.00	50.00	125.00

1.3000 g, .333 SILVER, .0139 oz ASW
Obv. leg: LUDWIG KOENIG.....

KM#	Date	Mintage	Fine	VF	XF	Unc
377	1827	—	5.00	15.00	50.00	125.00
(C162)	1828	—	5.00	15.00	50.00	125.00
	1829	—	5.00	15.00	50.00	125.00
	1830	—	5.00	15.00	50.00	125.00

Obv. leg: LUDWIG I KOENIG.....

KM#	Date	Mintage	Fine	VF	XF	Unc
391	1830	—	5.00	10.00	25.00	75.00
(C162a)	1831	—	5.00	10.00	25.00	75.00
	1832	—	5.00	10.00	25.00	75.00
	1833	—	5.00	10.00	25.00	75.00
	1834	—	5.00	10.00	25.00	75.00
	1835	—	5.00	10.00	25.00	75.00
	1836	—	5.00	10.00	25.00	75.00

KM#	Date	Mintage	Fine	VF	XF	Unc
423	1839	.456	2.00	5.00	7.00	25.00
(C190)	1840	.235	2.00	5.00	7.00	30.00
	1841	.337	2.00	5.00	7.00	30.00
	1842	.370	2.00	5.00	7.00	30.00
	1843	.337	2.00	5.00	7.00	30.00
	1844	.269	2.00	5.00	7.00	30.00
	1845	.361	2.00	5.00	7.00	30.00
	1846	.463	2.00	5.00	7.00	30.00
	1847	.563	2.00	5.00	7.00	30.00
	1848	.447	2.00	5.00	7.00	30.00

KM#	Date	Mintage	Fine	VF	XF	Unc
453	1849	.373	2.00	5.00	7.00	30.00
(C227)	1850	.615	2.00	5.00	7.00	30.00
	1851	.582	2.00	5.00	7.00	30.00
	1852	.282	2.00	5.00	7.00	30.00
	1853	.280	2.00	5.00	7.00	30.00
	1854	.388	2.00	5.00	7.00	30.00
	1855	.285	2.00	5.00	7.00	30.00
	1856	.091	2.00	5.00	7.00	30.00

1.2300 g, .350 SILVER, .0138 oz ASW

KM#	Date	Mintage	Fine	VF	XF	Unc
488	1865	.832	2.00	5.00	7.00	30.00
(C253)	1866	.566	2.00	5.00	7.00	30.00
	1867	.099	2.00	5.00	7.00	30.00
	1868	.065	2.00	5.00	7.00	30.00

6 KREUZER

2.7000 g, .333 SILVER, .0289 oz ASW
Obv: Head right, leg: MAX. IOS. P. B.

Rev: Crowned arms, date below.

KM#	Date	Mintage	Fine	VF	XF	Unc
310	1802	—	10.00	25.00	50.00	200.00
(C105)	1803	—	10.00	25.00	50.00	200.00

Obv. leg: MAX. IOS. H.I.B.C. &

KM#	Date	Mintage	Fine	VF	XF	Unc
318	1801	—	10.00	20.00	40.00	125.00
(C105a)	1803	—	10.00	20.00	40.00	125.00
	1804	—	10.00	20.00	40.00	125.00

Obv. leg: MAX. IOS. C.Z.P.B.

KM#	Date	Mintage	Fine	VF	XF	Unc
332	1804	—	20.00	40.00	80.00	200.00
(C105b)	1805	—	20.00	40.00	80.00	200.00

Obv: Head right.
Rev: Crowned arms w/shield divided.

KM#	Date	Mintage	Fine	VF	XF	Unc
345	1806	—	25.00	50.00	100.00	250.00
(C131)						

KM#	Date	Mintage	Fine	VF	XF	Unc
346	1806	—	5.00	20.00	50.00	125.00
(C139)	1807	—	5.00	20.00	50.00	125.00
	1808	—	5.00	20.00	50.00	125.00
	1809	—	5.00	20.00	50.00	125.00
	1810	—	5.00	20.00	50.00	125.00
	1811	—	5.00	20.00	50.00	125.00
	1812	—	5.00	20.00	50.00	125.00
	1813	—	5.00	20.00	50.00	125.00
	1814	—	5.00	20.00	50.00	125.00
	1815	—	5.00	20.00	50.00	125.00
	1816	—	5.00	20.00	50.00	125.00
	1817	—	5.00	20.00	50.00	125.00
	1818	—	5.00	20.00	50.00	125.00
	1819	—	5.00	20.00	50.00	125.00
	1820	—	5.00	20.00	50.00	125.00
	1821/0	—	5.00	20.00	50.00	125.00
	1821	—	5.00	20.00	50.00	125.00
	1822	—	5.00	20.00	50.00	125.00
	1823	—	5.00	20.00	50.00	125.00
	1824	—	5.00	20.00	50.00	125.00
	1825	—	5.00	20.00	50.00	125.00

2.6000 g, .333 SILVER, .0278 oz ASW
Obv. leg: LUDWIG KOENIG.....

KM#	Date	Mintage	Fine	VF	XF	Unc
378	1827	—	5.00	25.00	65.00	125.00
(C163)	1828	—	5.00	25.00	65.00	125.00
	1829	—	5.00	25.00	65.00	125.00

Obv. leg: LUDWIG I KOENIG.....

KM#	Date	Mintage	Fine	VF	XF	Unc
392	1830	—	5.00	15.00	50.00	100.00
(C163a)	1831	—	5.00	15.00	50.00	100.00
	1832	—	5.00	15.00	50.00	100.00
	1833	—	5.00	15.00	50.00	100.00
	1834	—	5.00	15.00	50.00	100.00
	1835	—	5.00	15.00	50.00	100.00

KM#	Date	Mintage	Fine	VF	XF	Unc
424	1839	.800	4.00	7.00	20.00	60.00
(C191)	1840	—	4.00	7.00	20.00	60.00
	1841	—	4.00	7.00	20.00	60.00
	1842	—	4.00	7.00	20.00	60.00
	1843	—	4.00	7.00	20.00	60.00
	1844	—	4.00	7.00	20.00	60.00

Bavaria / GERMAN STATES 602

KM#	Date	Mintage	Fine	VF	XF	Unc
(C191)	1845	—	4.00	7.00	20.00	60.00
	1846	—	4.00	7.00	20.00	60.00
	1847	—	4.00	7.00	20.00	60.00
	1848	—	4.00	7.00	20.00	60.00

KM#	Date	Mintage	Fine	VF	XF	Unc
454	1849	—	4.00	7.00	20.00	60.00
(C228)	1850	—	4.00	7.00	20.00	60.00
	1851	—	4.00	7.00	20.00	60.00
	1852	—	4.00	7.00	20.00	60.00
	1853	—	4.00	7.00	20.00	60.00
	1854	—	4.00	7.00	20.00	60.00
	1855	—	4.00	7.00	20.00	60.00
	1856	—	4.00	7.00	20.00	60.00

2.4600 g, .350 SILVER, .0276 oz ASW
Obv. leg: SCHEIDE MUNZE added.

491	1866	.087	7.50	15.00	50.00	175.00
(C254)	1867	.024	10.00	25.00	75.00	200.00

10 KREUZER
3.9000 g, .500 SILVER, .0626 oz ASW
Obv: Head right in wreath. Rev: Crowned 3 fold oval arms.

316	1801	—	30.00	50.00	125.00	275.00
(C108)						

Rev. leg: POPOLO

319	1801	—	40.00	60.00	150.00	375.00
(C108.1)						

20 KREUZER
6.6800 g, .583 SILVER, .1252 oz ASW
Obv: Head right within wreath. Rev: Crowned arms within crossed branches, date and value below.

311	1801	—	55.00	90.00	150.00	275.00
(C112)	1802	—	75.00	130.00	225.00	400.00
	1803	—	55.00	90.00	150.00	275.00

333	1804	—	55.00	100.00	200.00	475.00
(C114)	1805	—	55.00	100.00	200.00	475.00

347	1806	—	25.00	60.00	125.00	225.00
(C140)	1807	—	25.00	60.00	125.00	225.00
	1808	—	25.00	60.00	125.00	225.00
	1809	—	25.00	60.00	125.00	225.00
	1810	—	25.00	60.00	125.00	225.00
	1811	—	25.00	60.00	125.00	225.00
	1812	—	25.00	60.00	125.00	225.00
	1813	—	25.00	60.00	125.00	225.00
	1814	—	25.00	60.00	125.00	225.00
	1815	—	25.00	60.00	125.00	225.00
	1816	—	25.00	60.00	125.00	225.00
	1817	—	25.00	60.00	125.00	225.00
	1818	—	25.00	60.00	125.00	225.00
	1819	—	25.00	60.00	125.00	225.00
	1820	—	25.00	60.00	125.00	225.00
	1821	—	25.00	60.00	125.00	225.00
	1822	—	25.00	60.00	125.00	225.00
	1823	—	25.00	60.00	125.00	225.00
	1824	—	25.00	60.00	125.00	225.00
	1825	—	25.00	60.00	125.00	225.00

1/2 GULDEN

5.3000 g, .900 SILVER, .1533 oz ASW

KM#	Date	Mintage	Fine	VF	XF	Unc
417	1838	1.750	15.00	25.00	50.00	100.00
(C192)	1839	.474	15.00	25.00	50.00	100.00
	1840	.233	15.00	25.00	50.00	125.00
	1841	.243	15.00	25.00	50.00	100.00
	1842	.508	15.00	25.00	50.00	100.00
	1843	.337	15.00	25.00	50.00	125.00
	1844	1.452	15.00	25.00	50.00	100.00
	1845	1.869	15.00	25.00	50.00	100.00
	1846	1.181	15.00	25.00	50.00	125.00
	1847	.241	15.00	25.00	50.00	125.00
	1848	.407	15.00	25.00	50.00	125.00

444	1848	Inc. Ab.	20.00	30.00	50.00	125.00
(C230)	1849	.218	20.00	30.00	50.00	125.00
	1850	.189	20.00	30.00	50.00	125.00
	1851	.171	20.00	30.00	50.00	125.00
	1852	.120	20.00	30.00	50.00	125.00
	1853	.206	20.00	30.00	50.00	125.00
	1854	.146	20.00	30.00	50.00	125.00
	1855	.060	20.00	30.00	50.00	100.00
	1856	.074	20.00	30.00	50.00	100.00
	1857	.020	25.00	40.00	65.00	150.00
	1858	.183	20.00	30.00	50.00	100.00
	1859	.405	20.00	30.00	50.00	100.00
	1860	.292	20.00	30.00	50.00	100.00
	1861	.254	20.00	30.00	50.00	100.00
	1862	.141	20.00	30.00	50.00	100.00
	1863	.190	20.00	30.00	50.00	100.00
	1864	.160	20.00	30.00	50.00	100.00

Obv: Head w/part in hair.

479	1864	Inc. Ab.	40.00	75.00	125.00	250.00
(C255a)	1865	.227	35.00	60.00	100.00	200.00
	1866	.101	40.00	75.00	125.00	250.00

Obv: Head w/o part in hair.

492	1866	Inc. Ab.	40.00	75.00	125.00	250.00
(C255b)	1867	.100	35.00	60.00	100.00	200.00
	1868	.121	35.00	60.00	100.00	200.00
	1869	.133	35.00	75.00	100.00	200.00
	1870	.111	35.00	60.00	100.00	200.00
	1871	.051	40.00	75.00	125.00	225.00

GULDEN

10.6000 g, .900 SILVER, .3067 oz ASW

414	1837	2.057	15.00	25.00	75.00	125.00
(C193)	1838	2.045	15.00	25.00	75.00	125.00
	1839	2.320	15.00	25.00	75.00	125.00
	1840	3.591	15.00	25.00	75.00	125.00

KM#	Date	Mintage	Fine	VF	XF	Unc
(C193)	1841	4.362	15.00	25.00	75.00	125.00
	1842	1.449	15.00	25.00	75.00	125.00
	1843	4.832	15.00	25.00	75.00	125.00
	1844	3.491	15.00	25.00	75.00	125.00
	1845	1.115	15.00	25.00	75.00	125.00
	1846	.686	15.00	25.00	85.00	150.00
	1847	.387	15.00	25.00	85.00	150.00
	1848	.437	15.00	25.00	85.00	150.00

445	1848	Inc. Ab.	20.00	40.00	75.00	125.00
(C231)	1849	.366	20.00	40.00	75.00	125.00
	1850	.343	20.00	40.00	75.00	125.00
	1851	.224	20.00	40.00	75.00	125.00
	1852	.453	20.00	40.00	75.00	125.00
	1853	.257	20.00	40.00	75.00	125.00
	1854	.513	20.00	40.00	75.00	125.00
	1855	1.076	20.00	40.00	75.00	125.00
	1856	.455	20.00	40.00	75.00	125.00
	1857	.032	25.00	60.00	100.00	150.00
	1858	.144	25.00	60.00	100.00	150.00
	1859	.529	25.00	60.00	100.00	150.00
	1860	.452	25.00	60.00	100.00	150.00
	1861	.358	25.00	60.00	100.00	150.00
	1862	.266	25.00	60.00	100.00	150.00
	1863	.234	25.00	60.00	100.00	150.00
	1864	.414	25.00	60.00	100.00	150.00

Obv: Head w/part in hair.

480	1864	Inc. Ab.	50.00	100.00	150.00	250.00
(C256)	1865	.167	50.00	100.00	150.00	250.00
	1866	.122	50.00	100.00	150.00	250.00

Obv: Head w/o part in hair.

493	1866	Inc. Ab.	50.00	100.00	150.00	250.00
(C256a)	1867	.086	50.00	100.00	150.00	250.00
	1868	.122	50.00	100.00	150.00	250.00
	1869	.122	50.00	100.00	150.00	250.00
	1870	.072	50.00	100.00	150.00	250.00
	1871	.035	60.00	120.00	175.00	275.00

ZWEY (2) GULDEN

21.2100 g, .900 SILVER, .6138 oz ASW

Bavaria / GERMAN STATES 603

Obv. leg: LUDWIG I KOENIG V. BAYERN.

KM#	Date	Mintage	Fine	VF	XF	Unc
438	1845	.883	30.00	50.00	125.00	275.00
(C194)	1846	1.523	30.00	50.00	125.00	275.00
	1847	1.491	30.00	50.00	125.00	275.00
	1848	.950	30.00	50.00	125.00	275.00

Obv. leg: MAXIMILIAN II KOENIG V. BAYERN.
Rev: Similar to KM#438.

446	1848	Inc. Ab.	27.50	50.00	120.00	250.00
(C232)	1849	.741	27.50	50.00	120.00	250.00
	1850	.915	27.50	50.00	120.00	250.00
	1851	1.157	27.50	50.00	120.00	250.00
	1852	1.356	27.50	50.00	120.00	250.00
	1853	.634	27.50	50.00	120.00	250.00
	1854	.430	27.50	50.00	120.00	250.00
	1855	.585	30.00	60.00	150.00	300.00
	1856	.510	30.00	60.00	150.00	300.00

Restoration of Madonna Column in Munich
Obv: Similar to KM#446.

465	1855	1.000	20.00	30.00	50.00	125.00
(C233)						

1/2 THALER
14.0300 g, .833 SILVER, .3757 oz ASW
Similar to 1 Thaler, KM#313.

312	1801	—	150.00	275.00	500.00	1000.
(C115)	1802	—	150.00	275.00	500.00	1000.
	1803	—	185.00	325.00	575.00	1100.

323	1803	—	185.00	325.00	575.00	1100.
(C116)	1804	—	185.00	325.00	575.00	1100.
	1805	—	185.00	325.00	575.00	1100.

(Without denomination)

324	ND (1799-1805)					
(C123)		—	65.00	165.00	250.00	450.00

KM#	Date	Mintage	Fine	VF	XF	Unc
348	ND (1806-08)					
(C146)		*1,500	100.00	250.00	400.00	750.00

Obv: Head, script legends.

353	ND (1807-08)	—	100.00	200.00	400.00	800.00
(C147)						

Obv: Legends in block letters.

357	ND (1808-37)					
(C148)		.025	95.00	200.00	300.00	625.00

THALER

28.0000 g, .833 SILVER, .7500 oz ASW

313	1801	—	100.00	175.00	400.00	900.00
(C118)	1802	—	120.00	200.00	475.00	1000.

Obv. leg: D.G. MAXIM. IOSEPH

320.1	1802	—	1000.	1500.	3500.	5000.
(C118a)						

Obv. leg: D.G. MAX. IOSEPH

KM#	Date	Mintage	Fine	VF	XF	Unc
320.2	1802	—	650.00	1250.	1750.	3000.
(C118c)	1803	—	650.00	1250.	1750.	3000.

Obv: Uniformed bust right, MAXIMILIAN

321	1802	—	350.00	700.00	1500.	3000.
(C118b)						

325	1803	—	125.00	200.00	450.00	1000.
(C120)						

Obv. leg. ends: . . . .ZU PFALZBAIERN.

326	1803	—	175.00	400.00	1000.	2200.
(C121)	1804	—	175.00	400.00	1000.	2200.
	1805	—	175.00	400.00	1000.	2200.

Obv: Similar to KM#326.

334	1804	—	1500.	3000.	4000.	6000.
(C122)	1805	—	125.00	200.00	450.00	1000.

Bavaria / GERMAN STATES 604

KM#	Date	Mintage	Fine	VF	XF	Unc
349 (C132)	1806	—	100.00	250.00	600.00	1750.

Rev: Crowned lions facing outward.

| 350 (C132a) | 1806 | — | 200.00 | 400.00 | 1000. | 2000. |

Obv: Bust w/pigtail.

| 354 (C141) | 1807 | .100 | 1500. | 3000. | 5000. | 7500. |

355 (C142)	1807	Inc. Ab.	75.00	150.00	250.00	700.00
	1808	.055	75.00	150.00	250.00	700.00
	1809	8,932	85.00	150.00	275.00	750.00
	1810	6,721	90.00	160.00	300.00	900.00
	1811	.011	90.00	160.00	300.00	900.00
	1812	8,432	90.00	160.00	300.00	900.00
	1813	5,888	90.00	160.00	300.00	900.00
	1814	4,579	90.00	160.00	300.00	900.00
	1815	6,913	90.00	160.00	300.00	900.00
	1816	.011	90.00	160.00	300.00	900.00
	1817	4,638	90.00	160.00	300.00	900.00
	1818	—	90.00	160.00	300.00	900.00
	1819	—	90.00	160.00	300.00	900.00
	1820	3,974	90.00	160.00	300.00	900.00
	1821	3,826	90.00	160.00	300.00	900.00
	1822	—	90.00	160.00	300.00	900.00

(Krone)

Obv: Error: JOEPHUS in legend.

KM#	Date	Mintage	Fine	VF	XF	Unc
358.2 (C143a)	1813	Inc. Ab.	100.00	225.00	625.00	1250.

(Convention)

28.0600 g, .833 SILVER, .7515 oz ASW
Granting of Bavarian Constitution

| 361 (C144) | 1818 | .040 | 30.00 | 60.00 | 100.00 | 175.00 |

Rev: Similar to KM#355.

367 (C145)	1822	.051	100.00	200.00	450.00	1000.
	1823	.047	150.00	350.00	750.00	1800.
	1824	3,907	100.00	225.00	500.00	1200.
	1825	1,932	100.00	200.00	450.00	1000.

Coronation of Ludwig I

| 370 (C165) | 1825 | — | 150.00 | 200.00 | 300.00 | 500.00 |

Death of Reichenbach and Fraunhofer
Obv: Similar to KM#370.

KM#	Date	Mintage	Fine	VF	XF	Unc
371 (C166)	1826	—	150.00	200.00	275.00	450.00

Removal of University From Landshut to Munich
Obv: Similar to KM#370.

| 372 (C167) | 1826 | — | 150.00 | 200.00 | 275.00 | 450.00 |

(Krone)

29.5400 g, .871 SILVER, .8272 oz ASW

373 (C164)	1826	.051	100.00	150.00	250.00	500.00
	1827	.066	130.00	200.00	300.00	750.00
	1828	.079	100.00	150.00	300.00	500.00
	1829	.094	130.00	200.00	300.00	750.00

(Convention)

29.3400 g, .868 SILVER, .8188 oz ASW

358.1 (C143)	1809	.063	40.00	75.00	175.00	325.00
	1810	.924	40.00	75.00	175.00	325.00
	1811	.196	40.00	75.00	200.00	425.00
	1812	.618	40.00	75.00	125.00	325.00
	1813	.656	40.00	75.00	125.00	325.00
	1814	.975	40.00	75.00	125.00	325.00
	1815	.769	40.00	75.00	125.00	325.00
	1816	2.453	40.00	75.00	125.00	325.00
	1817	.399	40.00	75.00	125.00	325.00
	1818	.119	40.00	100.00	200.00	425.00
	1819	.292	40.00	100.00	200.00	425.00
	1820	.132	40.00	100.00	200.00	425.00
	1821	.260	40.00	75.00	185.00	350.00
	1822	.052	40.00	100.00	200.00	425.00
	1823	.016	40.00	100.00	200.00	425.00
	1824	.031	40.00	100.00	200.00	425.00
	1825	.081	40.00	75.00	185.00	350.00

28.0600 g, .833 SILVER, .7515 oz ASW
Bavaria-Wurttemberg Customs Treaty Signing
Obv: Similar to KM#370.

| 379 (C168) | 1827 | — | 150.00 | 200.00 | 275.00 | 500.00 |

Bavaria / GERMAN STATES 605

Founding of Order of Ludwig
Obv: Similar to KM#370.

KM#	Date	Mintage	Fine	VF	XF	Unc
380 (C169)	1827	—	150.00	200.00	275.00	500.00

Loyalty of Bavarians to Royal Family
Obv: Similar to KM#370.

KM#	Date	Mintage	Fine	VF	XF	Unc
393 (C174)	1830	—	150.00	200.00	250.00	450.00

Formation of Customs Union With Prussia, Saxony, Hesse and Thuringia
Obv: Similar to KM#370.

KM#	Date	Mintage	Fine	VF	XF	Unc
403 (C177)	1833	—	150.00	200.00	250.00	500.00

Founding of Theresien Order
Obv: Similar to KM#370.

381 (C170)	1827	—	150.00	200.00	275.00	500.00

(Krone)

29.5400 g, .871 SILVER, .8272 oz ASW

394 (C164a)	1830	.061	75.00	150.00	300.00	650.00
	1831	.064	75.00	150.00	300.00	650.00
	1832	.070	75.00	150.00	300.00	650.00
	1833	.040	75.00	200.00	400.00	900.00
	1834	.017	90.00	150.00	300.00	650.00
	1835	7,502	100.00	200.00	400.00	900.00
	1836	7,816	100.00	150.00	300.00	650.00
	1837	.212	75.00	150.00	300.00	600.00

(Convention)

Monument For Bavarians Who Fell In Russia
Obv: Similar to KM#370.

404 (C178)	1833	—	150.00	200.00	250.00	500.00

Blessings of Heaven On Royal Family
Obv: Similar to KM#370.

386 (C171)	1828	—	100.00	125.00	175.00	375.00

Provincial Legislature
Obv: Similar to KM#370.

405 (C179)	1834	—	150.00	200.00	275.00	500.00

Constitution Monument Erection
Obv: Similar to KM#370.

387 (C172)	1828	—	150.00	200.00	275.00	450.00

28.0600 g, .833 SILVER, .7515 oz ASW
Opening of the Legislature
Similar to KM#370.

401 (C175)	1831	—	150.00	225.00	450.00	650.00

Erection of Monument at Oberwittelsbach
Obv: Similar to KM#370.

406 (C180)	1834	—	150.00	200.00	300.00	550.00

Commercial Treaty Between Bavaria, Prussia, Hesse and Wurttemberg
Obv: Similar to KM#370.

389 (C173)	1829	—	150.00	200.00	275.00	500.00

Prince Otto of Bavaria First King of Greece
Obv: Similar to KM#370.

402 (C176)	1832	—	150.00	200.00	250.00	500.00

Entry of Baden to German Customs Union
Obv: Similar to KM#370.

407 (C181)	1835	—	150.00	200.00	250.00	550.00

Bavaria / GERMAN STATES   606

Establishment of Bavarian Mortgage Bank
Obv: Similar to KM#370.

KM#	Date	Mintage	Fine	VF	XF	Unc
408 (C182)	1835	—	150.00	225.00	300.00	575.00

Monument for King Otto Leaving His Mother
Obv: Similar to KM#370.

409 (C183)	1835	—	150.00	200.00	250.00	450.00

Construction of First Steam Railway
Obv: Similar to KM#370.

410 (C184)	1835	—	150.00	200.00	275.00	500.00

Monument in Munich to King Maximilian Joseph
Obv: Similar to KM#370.

411.1 (C185)	1835	—	150.00	200.00	300.00	500.00

Rev: Sceptre not beyond shoulder.

411.2 (C185a)	1835	—	175.00	300.00	450.00	750.00

School Given To Benedictine Order
Obv: Similar to KM#370.

KM#	Date	Mintage	Fine	VF	XF	Unc
412 (C186)	1835	—	150.00	225.00	350.00	550.00

Erection of Otto Chapel at Kiefersfelden
Obv: Similar to KM#370.

413 (C187)	1836	—	150.00	200.00	275.00	500.00

Order of St. Michael as Order of Merit
Obv: Similar to KM#370.

415 (C188)	1837	—	150.00	200.00	300.00	575.00

(Vereins)

18.5200 g, .900 SILVER, .5360 oz ASW

468 (C234)	1857	1.560	20.00	40.00	80.00	150.00
	1858	2.283	20.00	40.00	80.00	150.00
	1859	2.661	20.00	40.00	80.00	150.00
	1860	2.471	20.00	40.00	80.00	150.00
	1861	2.682	20.00	40.00	80.00	150.00
	1862	2.587	20.00	40.00	80.00	150.00
	1863	2.587	20.00	40.00	80.00	150.00
	1864	1.458	20.00	40.00	80.00	150.00

Obv: Head w/part in hair.

KM#	Date	Mintage	Fine	VF	XF	Unc
481 (C257.1)	1864	Inc. Ab.	60.00	135.00	250.00	500.00
	1865	1.144	35.00	75.00	150.00	400.00
	1866	1.075	40.00	80.00	175.00	450.00

Obv: Head w/o part in hair. Rev: Arms.

494.1 (C257.2)	1866	Inc. Ab.	35.00	50.00	150.00	175.00
	1867	.595	35.00	55.00	160.00	190.00
	1868	.312	35.00	60.00	160.00	325.00
	1869	.277	35.00	75.00	180.00	375.00
	1870	.264	35.00	60.00	160.00	325.00
	1871	.718	35.00	55.00	150.00	300.00

New arabesques under arms.

494.2 (C257.3)	1871	—	300.00	600.00	1100.	1800.

Obv: J. REIS below truncation.

495 (C257.4)	1871	Inc. Ab.	125.00	250.00	400.00	600.00

489 (C258)	ND(1865)	.110	20.00	35.00	75.00	115.00
	1866	Inc. Ab.	20.00	35.00	60.00	100.00
	1867	Inc. Ab.	20.00	35.00	60.00	100.00
	1868	Inc. Ab.	20.00	35.00	60.00	100.00
	1869	Inc. Ab.	20.00	35.00	60.00	100.00
	1870	Inc. Ab.	20.00	35.00	60.00	100.00
	1871	Inc. Ab.	20.00	35.00	60.00	100.00

Bavaria / GERMAN STATES 607

German Victory in Franco-Prussian War

KM#	Date	Mintage	Fine	VF	XF	Unc
496 (C259)	1871	.150	30.00	45.00	70.00	130.00
	1871	—	—	—	Proof	375.00

ZWEI (2) THALERS
(3-1/2 Gulden)

37.1200 g, .900 SILVER, 1.0743 oz ASW
Monetary Union of Six South German States

416 (C197)	1837	—	150.00	200.00	275.00	450.00

Reapportionment of Bavaria
Obv: Similar to KM#416.

418 (C198)	1838	—	150.00	300.00	450.00	750.00

Maximilian I, Elector of Bavaria

Obv: Similar to KM#416.

KM#	Date	Mintage	Fine	VF	XF	Unc
425 (C199)	1839	—	150.00	200.00	375.00	575.00

Obv: Similar to KM#416.

426 (C195)	1839	.113	150.00	250.00	500.00	1400.
	1840	.193	125.00	200.00	400.00	1200.
	1841	.450	150.00	250.00	500.00	1400.

Albrecht Durer
Obv: Similar to KM#416.

427 (C200)	1840	—	150.00	200.00	300.00	550.00

Jean Paul Friedrich Richter
Obv: Similar to KM#416.

429 (C201)	1841	—	150.00	200.00	300.00	550.00

Walhalla Commemorative
Obv: Similar to KM#416.

430 (C202)	1842	—	150.00	200.00	250.00	450.00

Marriage of Crown Prince of Bavaria and Marie,
Royal Princess of Prussia
Obv: Similar to KM#416.

431.1 (C203)	1842	—	150.00	200.00	250.00	450.00

Obv: (Error date) 1 OCTB. 1842

KM#	Date	Mintage	Fine	VF	XF	Unc
431.2 (C203a)	1842	—	150.00	200.00	250.00	450.00

Obv: Similar to KM#416.

432 (C196)	1842	.085	100.00	250.00	400.00	1200.
	1843	.277	100.00	150.00	250.00	700.00
	1844	.122	100.00	175.00	300.00	800.00
	1845	.167	100.00	175.00	300.00	800.00
	1846	.132	100.00	225.00	400.00	1000.
	1847	.012	100.00	225.00	400.00	1000.
	1848	.192	100.00	150.00	250.00	700.00

100th Anniversary Academy of Erlangen
Obv: Similar to KM#416.

434 (C204)	1843	—	150.00	200.00	300.00	550.00

Completion of the General's Hall in Munich
Obv: Similar to KM#416.

437 (C205)	1844	—	150.00	200.00	325.00	600.00

Bavaria / GERMAN STATES 608

Chancellor Baron von Kreittmayr
Obv: Similar to KM#416.

KM#	Date	Mintage	Fine	VF	XF	Unc
439 (C206)	1845	—	200.00	325.00	550.00	1000.

Birth of Two Grandsons
Obv: Similar to KM#416.

| 440 (C207) | 1845 | — | 150.00 | 275.00 | 400.00 | 650.00 |

Completion of Canal Between Danube and Main Rivers
Obv: Similar to KM#416.

| 441 (C208) | 1846 | — | 200.00 | 325.00 | 450.00 | 725.00 |

Bishop Julius Echter von Mespelbrunn
Obv: Similar to KM#416.

| 442 (C209) | 1847 | — | 200.00 | 400.00 | 600.00 | 1300. |

Abdication of Ludwig I for Maximilian
Obv: Similar to KM#416.

| 443 (C210) | 1848 | — | 400.00 | 900.00 | 1600. | 3200. |

New Constitution
Edge: VEREINSMUNZE

KM#	Date	Mintage	Fine	VF	XF	Unc
447.1 (C237)	1848	—	175.00	225.00	400.00	700.00

Edge: CONVENTION-VOM

| 447.2 (C237a) | 1848 | — | 175.00 | 325.00 | 500.00 | 775.00 |
| | (restrike post 1857) | | | | | |

Edge: DREY EIN HALB GULDEN

| 447.3 (C237b) | 1848 | — | 225.00 | 425.00 | 700.00 | 1100. |
| | (restrike post 1857) | | | | | |

Johann Christoph von Gluck
Obv: Similar to KM#447.1. Edge: VEREINSMUNZE.

| 448.1 (C238) | 1848 | — | 500.00 | 750.00 | 1500. | 3000. |

Edge: DREY EIN HALB GULDEN

| 448.2 (C238a) | 1848 | — | 500.00 | 750.00 | 1500. | 3000. |

Orlando Di Lasso
Obv: Similar to KM#447.1. Edge: VEREINSMUNZE.

| 455.1 (C239) | 1849 | — | 700.00 | 1250. | 1750. | 3500. |

Edge: DREY EIN HALB GULDEN

| 455.2 (C239a) | 1849 | — | 700.00 | 1250. | 1750. | 3500. |

| 456 (C235) | 1849 | — | 125.00 | 250.00 | 500.00 | 1200. |
| | 1850 | — | 100.00 | 200.00 | 400.00 | 900.00 |

KM#	Date	Mintage	Fine	VF	XF	Unc
(C235)	1851	—	100.00	175.00	350.00	700.00
	1852	—	100.00	200.00	400.00	900.00
	1853	—	100.00	175.00	350.00	700.00
	1854	—	100.00	150.00	250.00	550.00
	1855	.417	100.00	150.00	250.00	550.00
	1856	.142	100.00	150.00	250.00	550.00

Exhibition of German Products in Crystal Palace
Obv: Similar to KM#447.1. Edge: VEREINS MUNZE.

| 464.1 (C240) | 1854 | — | 175.00 | 250.00 | 350.00 | 550.00 |

Edge: CONVENTION-VOM

| 464.2 (C240a) | 1854 | — | 175.00 | 250.00 | 350.00 | 550.00 |

Erection of Monument to King Maximilian II
Obv: Similar to KM#447.1.

| 467 (C241) | 1856 | 1,152 | 300.00 | 425.00 | 750.00 | 1400. |

(Vereins)

37.0400 g, .900 SILVER, 1.0717 oz ASW
Obv: Similar to KM#447.1.

| 474 (C236.1) | 1859 | .028 | 350.00 | 500.00 | 1350. | 2700. |
| | 1860 | .069 | 200.00 | 375.00 | 600.00 | 1250. |

Obv: Different hair style.

475 (C236.2)	1861	.029	300.00	450.00	800.00	1600.
	1862	8,727	400.00	550.00	1000.	2000.
	1863	.011	350.00	500.00	800.00	1800.
	1864	8,201	350.00	550.00	1000.	2000.

Bavaria / GERMAN STATES 609

Rev: Similar to KM#474.

KM#	Date	Mintage	Fine	VF	XF	Unc
490	1865	2,490	2750.	4500.	6000.	8500.
(C260)	1867	1,760	3750.	6500.	8500.	14,000.
	1869	—	3750.	6500.	8500.	14,000.

1/2 KRONE

5.0000 g, .900 GOLD, .1446 oz AGW

469	1857	1,749	1000.	1800.	2800.	3600.
(C248)	1858	1,020	1200.	2000.	3000.	3800.
	1859	1,200	1000.	1800.	3000.	4000.
	1860	—	1600.	2400.	3600.	4300.
	1861	32 pcs.	1600.	2400.	3600.	4300.
	1863	—	1600.	2400.	3600.	4300.
	1863	—	—	—	Proof	*
	1864	—	1800.	2600.	4000.	5000.

*NOTE: Stack's Hammel sale 9/82 Proof realized $13,000.

482	1864	—	2600.	3400.	5200.	6400.
(C261)	1865	—	1600.	2400.	3600.	5200.
	1866	—	2000.	2800.	4000.	5600.
	1867	12 pcs.	1600.	2400.	3600.	5200.
	1868	—	2600.	3400.	5000.	6400.
	1869	—	2000.	2800.	4000.	5600.
	1869	—	—	—	Proof	*

*NOTE: Stack's Hammel sale 9/82 Proof realized $17,000.

KRONE

10.0000 g, .900 GOLD, .2892 oz AGW

470	1857	771 pcs.	1600.	2400.	4400.	6400.
(C249)	1858	753 pcs.	2000.	2800.	5200.	6800.
	1859	200 pcs.	2200.	3000.	5400.	7200.
	1860	45 pcs.	2500.	3500.	6500.	9000.
	1861	65 pcs.	2500.	3500.	6500.	9000.
	1863	—	2500.	3500.	6500.	9000.
	1864	—	2500.	3500.	6500.	9000.

483	1864	—	3250.	4500.	7250.	9750.
(C262)	1865	—	2500.	3500.	6500.	9000.
	1865	12 pcs.	—	—	Proof	*
	1866	—	2500.	3500.	6500.	9000.
	1867	12 pcs.	2500.	3500.	6500.	9000.
	1868	—	3250.	4500.	7250.	9750.
	1869	—	3250.	4500.	7250.	9750.

*NOTE: Stack's Hammel sale 9/82 Proof realized $29,000.

MONETARY REFORM
2 MARK

11.1110 g, .900 SILVER, .3215 oz ASW

KM#	Date	Mintage	Fine	VF	XF	Unc
505	1876D	5.370	30.00	60.00	225.00	550.00
(Y31)	1877D	1.512	30.00	60.00	250.00	700.00
	1880D	.169	75.00	150.00	600.00	1200.
	1883D	.104	60.00	150.00	325.00	800.00

507	1888D	.172	150.00	300.00	700.00	1200.
(Y36)						

511	1891D	.246	12.00	32.50	90.00	240.00
(Y36a)	1893D	.246	20.00	37.50	90.00	200.00
	1896D	.492	10.00	25.00	55.00	150.00
	1898D	.201	50.00	100.00	225.00	500.00
	1899D	.753	10.00	25.00	50.00	140.00
	1900D	.722	14.00	25.00	45.00	110.00
	1901D	.829	14.00	25.00	45.00	125.00
	1902D	1.341	10.00	22.00	35.00	110.00
	1903D	1.406	10.00	22.00	35.00	100.00
	1904D	2.320	10.00	22.00	35.00	100.00
	1905D	1.406	10.00	22.00	35.00	85.00
	1906D	1.055	10.00	22.00	45.00	95.00
	1907D	2.106	10.00	22.00	35.00	75.00
	1908D	.633	10.00	22.00	35.00	85.00
	1912D	.214	10.00	22.00	35.00	100.00
	1913D	.098	35.00	70.00	140.00	210.00

90th Birthday

516	1911D	.640	10.00	17.50	25.00	40.00
(Y41)	1911D	—	—	—	Proof	100.00

519	1914D	.574	30.00	60.00	90.00	120.00
(Y44)						

3 MARK

16.6670 g, .900 SILVER, .4823 oz ASW

KM#	Date	Mintage	Fine	VF	XF	Unc
515	1908D	.681	10.00	15.00	25.00	60.00
(Y37)	1909D	.827	10.00	15.00	25.00	60.00
	1910D	1.497	10.00	15.00	25.00	60.00
	1911D	.843	10.00	15.00	25.00	60.00
	1912D	1.014	10.00	15.00	25.00	60.00
	1913D	.713	10.00	15.00	25.00	60.00

90th Birthday

517	1911D	.640	12.50	20.00	30.00	60.00
(Y42)	1911D	—	—	—	Proof	90.00

520	1914D	.717	15.00	30.00	45.00	60.00
(Y45)	1914D	—	—	—	Proof	125.00

Golden Wedding Anniversary

523	1918D	130 pcs.	—	12,500.	20,000.	25,000.
(Y48)						

5 MARK

27.7770 g, .900 SILVER, .8038 oz ASW
Rev: Similar to KM#508.

502	1874D	.085	40.00	70.00	350.00	800.00
(Y32)	1875D	.657	40.00	70.00	325.00	700.00
	1876D	1.130	35.00	60.00	250.00	600.00

Bavaria / GERMAN STATES

1.9910 g, .900 GOLD, .0576 oz AGW

KM#	Date	Mintage	Fine	VF	XF	Unc
506	1877D	.635	125.00	200.00	275.00	400.00
(Y33)	1877D	—	—	—	Proof	1500.
	1878D	.128	350.00	800.00	1000.	1400.

27.7770 g, .900 SILVER, .8038 oz ASW

508	1888D	.069	175.00	275.00	900.00	1500.
(Y38)						

Obv: Similar to KM#508.

512	1891D	.098	17.50	35.00	100.00	300.00
(Y38a)	1893D	.098	25.00	50.00	120.00	300.00
	1894D	.141	17.50	35.00	120.00	300.00
	1895D	.141	22.50	45.00	110.00	300.00
	1896D	.028	55.00	125.00	600.00	1000.
	1898D	.303	15.00	30.00	60.00	175.00
	1899D	.141	25.00	50.00	90.00	225.00
	1900D	.295	15.00	30.00	90.00	200.00
	1901D	.295	15.00	30.00	90.00	200.00
	1902D	.506	15.00	30.00	65.00	175.00
	1903D	1.012	15.00	30.00	65.00	175.00
	1904D	.548	20.00	40.00	60.00	175.00
	1906D	.070	35.00	75.00	200.00	400.00
	1907D	.753	15.00	25.00	55.00	125.00
	1908D	.577	15.00	25.00	50.00	125.00
	1913D	.520	17.50	25.00	45.00	100.00

Regents 90th Birthday
Rev: Similar to KM#512.

518	1911D	.160	25.00	70.00	100.00	135.00
(Y43)	1911D	—	—	—	Proof	175.00

Rev: Similar to KM#512.

521	1914D	.142	35.00	80.00	130.00	175.00
(Y46)						

10 MARK

3.9820 g, .900 GOLD, .1152 oz AGW
Obv: J. REIS under truncation. Rev: Type I.

KM#	Date	Mintage	Fine	VF	XF	Unc
500	1872D	.626	65.00	125.00	175.00	350.00
(Y34)	1872D	—	—	—	Proof	1600.
	1873D	1.198	65.00	125.00	175.00	300.00
	1873D	—	—	—	Proof	1600.

Rev: Type II.

503	1874D	.407	65.00	120.00	160.00	250.00
(Y34a)	1874D	—	—	—	Proof	1300.
	1875D	.816	65.00	120.00	160.00	250.00
	1876D	.684	65.00	120.00	160.00	250.00
	1877D	.283	65.00	120.00	160.00	250.00
	1878D	.638	65.00	120.00	160.00	250.00
	1879D	.224	65.00	120.00	160.00	250.00
	1880D	.229	65.00	120.00	160.00	250.00
	1881D	.157	65.00	120.00	160.00	250.00
	1881D	—	—	—	Proof	1300.

Obv. leg: ....VON BAYERN. Rev: Type II.

509	1888D	.281	100.00	200.00	275.00	450.00
(Y39)	1888D	—	—	—	Proof	1300.

Rev: Type III.

510	1890D	.422	65.00	130.00	150.00	200.00
(Y39a)	1893D	.422	65.00	130.00	150.00	200.00
	1896D	.281	65.00	120.00	170.00	225.00
	1898D	.590	65.00	130.00	150.00	200.00
	1900D	.141	125.00	150.00	225.00	300.00
	1900D	—	—	—	Proof	700.00

Obv. leg: ....V. BAYERN

514	1900D	Inc. Ab.	65.00	140.00	225.00	325.00
(Y39b)	1901D	.141	65.00	140.00	200.00	300.00
	1902D	.070	65.00	125.00	200.00	300.00
	1903D	.534	65.00	120.00	180.00	250.00
	1904D	.210	65.00	120.00	180.00	250.00
	1905D	.281	65.00	120.00	180.00	250.00
	1906D	.141	65.00	120.00	190.00	250.00
	1907D	.211	65.00	120.00	190.00	250.00
	1909D	.209	65.00	120.00	190.00	250.00
	1910D	.141	65.00	120.00	190.00	250.00
	1911D	.072	65.00	125.00	200.00	300.00
	1912D	.141	65.00	120.00	190.00	250.00
Common date	—	—	—	—	Proof	800.00

20 MARK

7.9650 g, .900 GOLD, .2304 oz AGW
Rev: Type I.

501	1872D	1.554	125.00	150.00	250.00	500.00
(Y35)	1872D	—	—	—	Proof	1600.
	1873D	2.770	125.00	150.00	250.00	400.00
	1873D	—	—	—	Proof	1600.

Rev: Type II.

KM#	Date	Mintage	Fine	VF	XF	Unc
504	1874D	.615	125.00	150.00	200.00	300.00
(Y35a)	1875D	—	725.00	1400.	2000.	2500.
	1875D	—	—	—	Proof	1500.
	1876D	.482	125.00	150.00	200.00	350.00
	1878D	.050	300.00	625.00	850.00	1400.
	1878D	—	—	—	Proof	1500.

Rev: Type III.

513	1895D	.501	125.00	140.00	160.00	250.00
(Y40)	1895D	—	—	—	Proof	800.00
	1900D	.501	125.00	140.00	160.00	250.00
	1905D	.501	125.00	140.00	160.00	250.00
	1905D	—	—	—	Proof	800.00
	1913D	*.311	—	17,500.	22,500.	25,000.
	1913D	—	—	—	Proof	35,000.

522	1914D	*.533	—	2000.	2500.	3000.
(Y47)	1914D	—	—	—	Proof	3600.

*NOTE: Never officially released.

TRADE COINAGE
EIN (1) GOLDGULDEN

3.2500 g, .770 GOLD, .0805 oz AGW

327	1803	—	—	1500.	2250.	3250.
(C126)						

Rev. leg: SENATUS-POPULUS/QUE WIRCE-BURGENSIS.

328	1803	—	—	7000.	10,000.	14,000.

359	1815	—	—	1500.	2250.	3250.
(C150)						

360	ND(1817)	—	—	1250.	1750.	2750.
(C150a)	1817	—	—	1250.	1750.	2750.

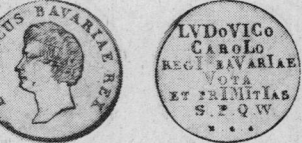

Date in chronogram.

374	1826	—	—	1000.	1500.	1850.
(C216)						

Rev: Landscape.

382	ND(1827-36)	—	—	1100.	1600.	2150.
(C217)						

Obv: Head right. Rev: Wurzburg city view.

435	ND(1843)	—	—	1100.	1600.	2150.
(C218)						

Bavaria / GERMAN STATES 611

Rev: Wurzburg shield.

KM#	Date	Mintage	Fine	VF	XF	Unc
436 (C219)	ND(1843)	—		1100.	1600.	2150.

Rev: Wurzburg city view.

| 458 (C244) | ND(1850) | — | | 1500. | 2000. | 3000. |

Rev: Wurzburg shield.

| 459 (C245) | ND(1850) | — | | 1500. | 2000. | 3000. |

**Mule. Obv: Head left of DUCAT.
Rev: Wurzburg city view.**

| 460 (C245a) | ND | | | | | |

Rev: Wurzburg city view.

| 484 (C263) | ND(1864) | — | | 800.00 | 1200. | 1650. |

Rev: Wurzburg shield.

| 485 (C264) | ND(1864) | — | | 800.00 | 1200. | 1650. |

DUCAT

**3.4900 g, .937 GOLD, .1051 oz AGW
Obv. leg: D.G. MAX. IOS. . . .**

| 314.1 (C124) | 1801 | — | 750.00 | 1250. | 2250. | 2850. |
| | 1802 | — | 1000. | 1500. | 2500. | 3100. |

Obv. leg: D.G. MAXIM. IOSEPH

314.2 (C124a)	1801	—	1000.	1500.	2500.	3000.
	1802	—	1000.	1500.	2500.	3000.
	1803	—	1250.	1750.	2750.	3250.

Obv. leg: MAXIMILIAN IOSEPH. . . .

| 335 (C128) | 1804 | — | 1750. | 2250. | 3000. | 3750. |
| | 1805 | — | 1250. | 1750. | 2500. | 3250. |

| 351 (C133) | 1806 | 3,937 | 1750. | 2250. | 3250. | 4250. |

3.4900 g, .937 GOLD, .1051 oz AGW

356 (C149)	1807	2,260	650.00	1125.	1750.	2500.
	1808	1,465	500.00	1050.	1600.	2250.
	1809	3,263	750.00	1250.	2000.	2750.
	1810	3,124	850.00	1350.	2250.	3000.
	1811	—	600.00	1100.	1750.	2500.

KM#	Date	Mintage	Fine	VF	XF	Unc
(C149)	1812	—	850.00	1350.	2250.	3000.
	1813	—	600.00	1100.	1750.	2500.
	1814	—	600.00	1100.	1750.	2500.
	1815	—	750.00	1250.	2000.	2750.
	1816	—	600.00	1000.	1600.	2250.
	1817	—	600.00	1100.	1750.	2500.
	1818	—	600.00	1100.	1750.	2500.
	1819	—	750.00	1250.	2000.	2750.
	1820	—	600.00	1100.	1750.	2500.
	1821	—	500.00	1050.	1600.	2250.
	1822	—	600.00	1100.	1750.	2500.

Obv. leg: BAEIRN. . . . .

| 362 | 1821 | — | 1250. | 1950. | 3000. | 4200. |
| (C149a) | 1822 | — | 750.00 | 1250. | 1850. | 2650. |

Rev. leg: EX AURO DANUBII around river god.

| 363 (C151) | 1821 | — | 2250. | 3250. | 4250. | 5500. |

Rev. leg: EX AURO OENI around river god.

| 364 (C152) | 1821 | — | 2500. | 3500. | 5500. | 8500. |

Isar - Gold Ducat

| 365 (C153) | 1821 | — | 1750. | 2750. | 5000. | 7750. |

Rhine - Gold Ducat

| 366 (C154) | 1821 | — | 1000. | 1750. | 3500. | 4750. |

Obv: Older head.

368 (C149b)	1823	4,400	600.00	1000.	1600.	2250.
	1824	.019	750.00	1250.	2000.	2750.
	1825	3,000	600.00	1000.	1650.	2300.

375 (C211)	1826	696 pcs.	1250.	1850.	2375.	2850.
	1827	4,200	1750.	2500.	3250.	3850.
	1828	3,090	1750.	2000.	2500.	3000.

Obv. leg: LUDWIG I

388.1 (C211a)	1828	1,351	800.00	1300.	1800.	2350.
	1829	1,143	600.00	1000.	1500.	2100.
	1830	1,731	600.00	1000.	1500.	2100.
	1831	3,907	1000.	1500.	2100.	2600.
	1832	1,884	600.00	1000.	1500.	2100.
	1833	1,230	1000.	1500.	2100.	2600.
	1834	1,711	1200.	1800.	2600.	3250.

Struck in collared dies.

| 388.2 (C211b) | 1835 | 2,048 | 600.00 | 1000. | 1500. | 2100. |

KM#	Date	Mintage	Fine	VF	XF	Unc
428 (C211c)	1840	5,000	600.00	1000.	1500.	2100.
	1841	2,309	650.00	1150.	1800.	2350.
	1842	810 pcs.	650.00	1150.	1800.	2350.
	1843	2,358	650.00	1150.	1800.	2350.
	1844	4,259	850.00	1500.	2350.	3150.
	1845	2,470	600.00	1000.	1500.	2100.
	1846	3,642	650.00	1150.	1800.	2350.
	1847	5,122	600.00	1000.	1500.	2100.
	1848	1,470	600.00	1000.	1500.	2100.

Rev. leg: EX AURO DANUBII above River God.

| 395.1 (C212) | 1830 | — | 1500. | 3000. | 4500. | 6250. |

Rev: Inverted "C" in date.

| 395.2 (C212b) | 1830 | — | 1500. | 3250. | 4750. | 6500. |

Obv. leg: LUDWIG I. . . .

| 396 (C212a) | 1830 | — | 1500. | 3000. | 4500. | 6250. |

Inn - Gold Ducat

| 397 (C213) | 1830 | — | 1500. | 3000. | 4500. | 6250. |

Isar - Gold Ducat

| 398 (C214) | 1830 | — | 1750. | 3600. | 5350. | 7500. |

Rhine - Gold Ducat

| 399 (C215) | 1830 | — | 1000. | 2500. | 4000. | 5750. |

Obv. leg: LUDWIG I. . . .

| 400 (C215a) | 1830 | — | 1000. | 2500. | 4000. | 5750. |

Rhine - Gold Ducat

| 433 (C215b) | 1842 | — | 500.00 | 1250. | 2250. | 3250. |
| | 1846 | — | 400.00 | 1000. | 2000. | 3000. |

Bavaria / GERMAN STATES 612

Obv. leg: .....KOENIG V BAYERN

KM#	Date	Mintage	Fine	VF	XF	Unc
457 (C242)	1849	1,470	750.00	1250.	1750.	2250.
	1850	1,519	500.00	1000.	1250.	1750.
	1851	3,815	400.00	600.00	900.00	1200.
	1852	4,396	400.00	600.00	900.00	1200.
	1853	5,603	400.00	600.00	900.00	1200.
	1854	5,707	400.00	600.00	900.00	1200.
	1855	1,540	500.00	1000.	1250.	1750.
	1856	3,782	400.00	600.00	900.00	1200.

Obv. leg: .....BAVARIAE REX

| 461 (C242a) | 1850 | 100 pcs. | 1750. | 2250. | 3500. | 5250. |

Rev. leg: AUS DEM BERGBAU BEI GOLDKRONACH

| 466 (C243) | 1855 | — | 12,500. | 17,500. | 25,000. | 35,000. |

Rhine - Gold Ducat

462 (C246)	1850	—	500.00	1000.	1700.	2000.
	1851	—	550.00	1200.	2000.	2250.
	1852	—	500.00	1000.	1700.	2000.
	1853	—	500.00	1000.	1700.	2000.
	1854	—	425.00	900.00	1500.	1800.
	1855	—	600.00	1400.	2500.	3000.
	1856	—	425.00	900.00	1500.	1800.

Reduced size

| 477 (C246a) | 1863 | — | 1500. | 2500. | 4000. | 4950. |

BERG

Located in western Germany. The first Count of Berg took his title in 1101 and the first coins appeared c. 1135. Not until 1380, did a duke rule in Berg. In 1801 Berg was absorbed by France but in 1806, along with Cleves and Julich, became the Grand Duchy of Berg. It was transferred to Westphalia in 1808 and given to Prussia in 1814.

RULERS
Maximilian IV, Joseph (of Bavaria) 1799-1806
Joachim Murat, 1806-1808

MINTMASTER'S INITIALS

Letter	Date	Name
PR,R.,.R	1783-1804	Peter Rudesheim
TS,S,S..,T:s,Sr	1805-1818	Theodor Stockmar

1/2 STUBER

COPPER

KM#	Date	Mintage	Fine	VF	XF	Unc
2 (C1)	1802.R.	—	5.00	10.00	20.00	80.00
	1803.R.	—	5.00	10.00	20.00	80.00
	1804.R.	—	5.00	10.00	20.00	80.00
5 (C1a)	1805 S	—	5.00	10.00	20.00	80.00

Obv: Monogram w/o rosettes.

| 6 (C1b) | 1805 s | — | 5.00 | 10.00 | 20.00 | 80.00 |

3 STUBER

1.8500 g, .220 SILVER, .0130 oz ASW

1 (C2)	1801.R.	—	5.00	10.00	20.00	80.00
	1802.R.	—	5.00	10.00	20.00	80.00
	1803.R.	—	5.00	10.00	20.00	80.00
	1804.R.	—	5.00	10.00	20.00	80.00

KM#	Date	Mintage	Fine	VF	XF	Unc
(C2)	1805.R.	—	5.00	10.00	20.00	80.00
	1806.R.	—	5.00	10.00	20.00	80.00

7 (C2b)	1805 S	—	7.50	15.00	30.00	90.00
	1805 T.S.	—	7.50	15.00	30.00	90.00
	1806 S	—	7.50	15.00	30.00	90.00

Obv: Royal crown.

| 9 (C2a) | 1806 S | — | 10.00 | 20.00 | 40.00 | 125.00 |

10 (C5)	1806 S	—	6.00	12.50	25.00	90.00
	1806 Sr	—	6.00	12.50	25.00	90.00
	1807 S	—	6.00	12.50	25.00	90.00
	1807 Sr	—	6.00	12.50	25.00	90.00

NOTE: KM#1, 9 and 10 were restruck officially in 1808-1809 for circulation and were equal to 10 Centimes.

1/2 THALER
(Reichs)

9.7440 g, .750 SILVER, .2349 oz ASW

| 4 (C3) | 1803 PR | — | 125.00 | 250.00 | 500.00 | 1000. |
| | 1804 PR | — | 125.00 | 250.00 | 500.00 | 1000. |

THALER
(Reichs)

19.4880 g, .750 SILVER, .4690 oz ASW

3 (C4)	1802 PR	—	225.00	450.00	850.00	2000.
	1803 PR	—	250.00	500.00	900.00	2250.
	1804 PR	—	275.00	550.00	950.00	2500.
	1805 PR	—	300.00	600.00	1000.	2750.

Obv: T. S. below larger head.

KM#	Date	Mintage	Fine	VF	XF	Unc
8 (C4a)	1805 TS	9,396	350.00	550.00	1000.	2500.
	1806 TS	7,044	400.00	600.00	1200.	2750.

| 11 (C6) | 1806 TS | 8,356 | 450.00 | 650.00 | 1300. | 2750. |

(Cassa)

17.3230 g, .751 SILVER, .4177 oz ASW

| 12 (C7) | 1807 TS | — | 1000. | 2000. | 3000. | 5000. |

Obv: Similar to KM#12.

| 13 (C7a) | 1807 TS | — | 1500. | 2500. | 5000. | 10,000. |

BIBERACH

Located in Wurttemberg 22 miles to the southwest of Ulm, Biberach became a free imperial city in 1312. The city came under the control of Baden in 1803 and then of Wurttemberg in 1806.

TRADE COINAGE
DUCAT
3.5000 g, .986 GOLD, .1109 oz AGW

Peace of Luneville
Obv: City god kneeling at altar, eye of God w/rays above.
Rev: 9-line inscription w/Roman numeral date.

KM#	Date	Mintage	VG	Fine	VF	XF
20	1801	—	—	850.00	1500.	2250.

BIRKENFELD

Located in southwest Germany. For most of the time prior to 1801, Birkenfeld was in the possession of the Counts Palatine. It was a part of France from 1801-1814, Prussia from 1814-1817 and was made a principality in 1817.

RULERS
Paul Friedrich August (of Oldenburg), 1829-1853
Nikolaus Friedrich Peter (of Oldenburg), 1853-1900

MINT MARKS
B - Hannover

PFENNIG

COPPER

KM#	Date	Mintage	Fine	VF	XF	Unc
6 (C1)	1848	.158	3.00	7.00	10.00	40.00

20 (C6)	1859B	.072	4.00	8.00	15.00	50.00

2 PFENNIGE

COPPER

7 (C2)	1848	.117	3.00	7.00	10.00	50.00

15 (C7)	1858B	.072	3.00	7.00	10.00	50.00

3 PFENNIGE

COPPER

8 (C3)	1848	.121	3.00	7.00	15.00	60.00

Obv: Crowned NFP monogram.

16 (C8)	1858B	.072	3.00	7.00	15.00	60.00

1/2 SILBER GROSCHEN

1.0900 g, .220 SILVER, .0077 oz ASW

17 (C9)	1858B	.060	7.00	10.00	20.00	80.00

SILBER GROSCHEN

2.1900 g, .220 SILVER, .0154 oz ASW
Obv: Crowned arms. Rev: Value.

KM#	Date	Mintage	Fine	VF	XF	Unc
9 (C4)	1848	.063	5.00	10.00	15.00	80.00

Obv: Different arms.

18 (C10)	1858B	.060	5.00	10.00	15.00	80.00

2-1/2 SILBER GROSCHEN
(1/12 Thaler)

3.2200 g, .375 SILVER, .0388 oz ASW
Obv: Crowned arms. Rev: Value.

10 (C5)	1848	.023	25.00	50.00	100.00	200.00

Obv: Different arms.

19 (C11)	1858B	.036	25.00	50.00	100.00	200.00

BRANDENBURG-ANSBACH-BAYREUTH

Held by Prussia from 1791 to 1805 and then given to Bavaria.

RULERS
Friedrich Wilhelm III of Prussia, 1797-1805

PFENNIG

.2600 g, .111 SILVER, .0009 oz ASW
Obv: Crowned FWR monogram. Rev: Value.

17 (C9)	1801B	.616	3.00	7.00	15.00	40.00
	1803B	.984	3.00	7.00	15.00	40.00

KREUZER

.7200 g, .163 SILVER, .0037 oz ASW

18 (C12)	1802B	.324	3.00	7.00	20.00	50.00
	1803B	.533	3.00	7.00	20.00	50.00
	1804B	1.243	3.00	7.00	20.00	50.00

3 KREUZER

1.0500 g, .336 SILVER, .0113 oz ASW

15 (C13)	1801B	1.335	7.00	15.00	30.00	100.00
	1802B	1.330	7.00	15.00	30.00	100.00

6 KREUZER

2.4400 g, .375 SILVER, .0294 oz ASW

16 (C14)	1801B	.340	10.00	20.00	60.00	125.00
	1802B	.249	10.00	20.00	60.00	125.00

TRADE COINAGE
DUCAT

3.5000 g, .986 GOLD, .1109 oz AGW

19 (C15)	1803B	—	—	Rare	—

BREMEN

Located in northwest Germany. The city was founded c. 787 but was nominally under control of the archbishops until 1646 when it became a Free Imperial City. Bremen was granted the mint right in 1369 and there was practically continuous coinage until 1907.

FREE CITY
MINTMASTER'S INITIALS

Letter	Date	Name
OHK	1761-1805	Otto Heinrich Knorre

SCHWAREN

COPPER

KM#	Date	Mintage	VG	Fine	VF	XF
241 (C1.3)	1859	.069	2.00	4.00	8.00	16.00

2-1/2 SCHWAREN

COPPER
Rev: D.B. in exergue.

KM#	Date	Mintage	Fine	VF	XF	Unc
220 (C2.1)	1802	.196	2.50	5.00	10.00	30.00

SILVER (OMS)

220a (C2.1a)	1802					

COPPER

225 (C2.2)	1820	.183	2.50	5.00	10.00	30.00

234 (C2a)	1841	.131	7.50	15.00	30.00	60.00
	1853	.177	2.00	4.00	8.00	25.00
	1861	.072	2.00	4.00	8.00	25.00
	1866	.162	2.00	4.00	8.00	25.00

235 (C-A3)	1841	Inc. Ab.				

1/2 GROTEN

COPPER

236 (C3)	1841	Inc.KM234	5.00	10.00	25.00	60.00

GROTEN

.7700 g, .281 SILVER, .0069 oz ASW

230 (C11)	1840	.262	2.00	5.00	10.00	35.00

Bremen / GERMAN STATES 614

1.9440 g, .740 SILVER, .0462 oz ASW

KM#	Date	Mintage	Fine	VF	XF	Unc
231 (C15)	1840	.079	5.00	15.00	30.00	75.00

2.9200 g, .494 SILVER, .0463 oz ASW

KM#	Date	Mintage	Fine	VF	XF	Unc
240 (C15a)	1857	.311	4.00	8.00	17.50	45.00

| 245 (C15b) | 1861 | .127 | 4.00 | 8.00 | 17.50 | 45.00 |

12 GROTE

3.8890 g, .740 SILVER, .0925 oz ASW

KM#	Date	Mintage	Fine	VF	XF	Unc
232 (C19)	1840	.193	7.00	12.00	30.00	100.00
	1841	.112	7.00	12.00	30.00	110.00
	1845	.063	7.00	12.00	30.00	125.00
	1846	.056	7.00	12.00	30.00	125.00

Obv: Crowned cornered arms.

| 242 (C19a) | 1859 | .450 | 3.00 | 6.00 | 15.00 | 50.00 |
| | 1860 | .150 | 4.00 | 8.00 | 20.00 | 60.00 |

36 GROTE
(= 1/2 Thaler)

8.7700 g, .986 SILVER, .2780 oz ASW

KM#	Date	Mintage	Fine	VF	XF	Unc
233 (C21)	1840	.170	17.50	30.00	55.00	150.00
	1841	.044	20.00	35.00	60.00	150.00
	1845	.084	20.00	35.00	60.00	150.00
	1846	.085	20.00	35.00	60.00	150.00
	1859	.121	20.00	35.00	60.00	150.00

| 243 (C22) | 1859 | .050 | 20.00 | 35.00 | 60.00 | 150.00 |
| | 1864 | .100 | 20.00 | 35.00 | 60.00 | 150.00 |

EIN (1) THALER

17.5390 g, .986 SILVER, .5560 oz ASW
50th Anniversary of Liberation of Germany

KM#	Date	Mintage	Fine	VF	XF	Unc
246 (C26)	1863	.020	35.00	55.00	85.00	150.00

Opening of New Business Exchange

| 247 (C27) | 1864 | 5,000 | 60.00 | 100.00 | 150.00 | 225.00 |

2nd German Shooting Festival

| 248 (C28) | 1865 | .050 | 35.00 | 55.00 | 85.00 | 125.00 |

Victory Over France

| 249 (C29) | 1871B | .061 | 30.00 | 50.00 | 80.00 | 125.00 |

MONETARY REFORM
2 MARK

11.1110 g, .900 SILVER, .3215 oz ASW

KM#	Date	Mintage	Fine	VF	XF	Unc
250	1904J	.100	17.50	35.00	80.00	120.00
(Y49)	1904J	200 pcs.	—	—	Proof	300.00

5 MARK

27.7770 g, .900 SILVER, .8038 oz ASW

251	1904	—	2250.	4500.	5500.	9500.
(Y50)	1906J	.041	55.00	135.00	210.00	285.00
	1906J	—	—	—	Proof	600.00

10 MARK

3.9820 g, .900 GOLD, .1152 oz AGW

| 253 | 1907J | .020 | 400.00 | 500.00 | 700.00 | 1000. |
| (Y51) | 1907J | — | — | — | Proof | 1700. |

20 MARK

7.9650 g, .900 GOLD, .2304 oz AGW

| 252 | 1906J | .020 | 350.00 | 500.00 | 750.00 | 1200. |
| (Y52) | 1906J | — | — | — | Proof | 2500. |

BRUNSWICK-LUNEBURG-CALENBERG-HANNOVER

Located in north-central Germany. The first duke began his rule in 1235. The first coinage appeared c. 1175. There was considerable shuffling of territory until 1692 when Ernst August became the elector of Hannover. Georg Ludwig became George I of England in 1714. There was separate coinage for Luneburg until during the reign of George III. The name was changed to Hannover in 1814.

RULERS
Georg III, (King of Great Britain), 1760-1814
After 1814 see Kingdom of Hannover

BRUNSWICK MINTS AND MINTMASTERS
Clausthal Mint

Letter	Date	Name
A	1833-1849	Vacant Mintmastership
C	1751-1753,1790-1792,1800-1802	Commission
GM,GFM	1802-1807	Georg Friedrich Michaelis
IWL	1807-1819	Johann Wilhelm Lunde
WAJA	1821-1838	Wilhelm August Julius Albert

Hannover Mint
| C | 1800-1806 | Commission |

PFENNING
COPPER

Obv: Wildman holding staff. Rev: Value and date.

KM#	Date	Mintage	Fine	VF	XF	Unc
330	1803 GFM	—	6.00	12.00	18.00	50.00
(C106)	1804 GFM	—	6.00	12.00	18.00	50.00

Obv: Crowned GR monogram.

	Rev: Denomination: PFENN					
KM#	Date	Mintage	Fine	VF	XF	Unc
360	1801 .C.	—	4.00	7.00	10.00	40.00
(C100.2)	1802 .C.	—	4.00	7.00	10.00	40.00
	1802 GFM	—	4.00	7.00	10.00	40.00
	1803 GFM	—	4.00	7.00	10.00	40.00
	1804 GFM	—	4.00	7.00	10.00	40.00
	1806 GFM	—	4.00	7.00	10.00	40.00

2 PFENNING

COPPER

402	1801 .C.	—	3.00	7.00	10.00	70.00
(C102)	1802 GFM	—	3.00	7.00	10.00	70.00
	1803 GFM	—	3.00	7.00	10.00	70.00
	1804 GFM	—	3.00	7.00	10.00	70.00
	1807 GFM	—	3.00	7.00	10.00	70.00

4 PFENNING

BILLON
Obv: Crowned GR monogram. Rev: Value, date.

344	1802 .C.	—	3.00	7.00	15.00	40.00
(C109b)	1804 GFM	—	3.00	7.00	15.00	40.00

MARIENGROSCHEN
Obv: Crowned GR monogram.
Rev: Value, date.

345	1802 .C.	—	3.00	7.00	15.00	40.00
(C117b)	1803 GFM	—	3.00	7.00	15.00	40.00

12 EINEN (1/12)THALER
(2 Groschen)

SILVER

336	1801 PLM	—	3.00	7.00	15.00	60.00
(C126a.1)	1801 EC	—	3.00	7.00	15.00	60.00
	1801 .C.	8,780	3.00	7.00	15.00	60.00
	1802 .C.	—	3.00	7.00	15.00	60.00
	1802 GFM	—	3.00	7.00	15.00	60.00
	1803 GFM	—	3.00	7.00	15.00	60.00
	1804 GFM	—	3.00	7.00	15.00	60.00
	1805 GFM	—	3.00	7.00	15.00	60.00
	1806 GFM	—	3.00	7.00	15.00	60.00
	1807 GFM	—	3.00	7.00	15.00	60.00

1/6 THALER

SILVER
W/o French arms or titles.

415	1802 C.	—	20.00	30.00	60.00	175.00
(C138a)	1802 GFM	—	20.00	30.00	60.00	175.00
	1803 GFM	—	20.00	30.00	60.00	175.00
	1804/3 GFM	—	37.50	65.00	120.00	250.00
	1804 GFM	—	—	—	—	—

KM#	Date	Mintage	Fine	VF	XF	Unc
419	1804 GFM	—	15.00	25.00	75.00	200.00
(C130a)						

420	1804 GFM	—	15.00	25.00	75.00	200.00
(132c)						

423	1807 GM	—	15.00	20.00	40.00	125.00
(C138b)						

1/3 THALER

SILVER

417	1803 GFM	—	30.00	50.00	100.00	225.00
(C147d)	1804 GFM	—	30.00	50.00	100.00	225.00

421	1804 GFM	—	40.00	85.00	125.00	300.00
(C143a)						

1/2 THALER
(Cassen)

SILVER
Rev. value: CASSEN GELD

410	1801 C	372 pcs.	—	—	Rare	—
(C150)						

Rev. value: CASSEN-GELD

KM#	Date	Mintage	Fine	VF	XF
411	1801 C	—	—	—	Rare
(C150a)					

2/3 THALER

SILVER

412	1801 .C.	—	30.00	50.00	100.00	200.00
(C160)	1802 .C.	—	30.00	50.00	100.00	200.00

413	1801 .C.	—	30.00	50.00	100.00	200.00
(C162)	1802	—	30.00	50.00	100.00	200.00
	1802 .C.	—	30.00	50.00	100.00	200.00
	1802 GFM	—	30.00	50.00	100.00	200.00
	1803 GFM	—	30.00	50.00	100.00	200.00
	1804 GFM	—	30.00	50.00	100.00	200.00
	1805 GFM	—	30.00	50.00	100.00	200.00

422	1805 GFM	—	30.00	50.00	100.00	200.00
(C162a)	1806 GFM	—	30.00	50.00	100.00	200.00
	1807 GFM	—	30.00	50.00	100.00	200.00

THALER
(Cassengeld)

SILVER

KM#	Date	Mintage	Fine	VF	XF	Unc
414 (C171)	1801 C	126 pcs.	450.00	850.00	1250.	2000.

TRADE COINAGE
DUCAT
3.5000 g, .986 GOLD, .1109 oz AGW
Obv: Square arms.

416	1802 C	—	350.00	525.00	900.00	1400.
(C172b)	1802 GFM	—	400.00	600.00	1000.	1600.
	1804 GFM	—	300.00	525.00	800.00	1200.

PISTOLE

6.6500 g, .900 GOLD, .1924 oz AGW

418 (C174)	1803 C	—	350.00	650.00	1100.	2000.

BRUNSWICK-WOLFENBUTTEL

Located in north-central Germany. Wolfenbuttel was annexed to Brunswick in 1257. The Wolfenbuttel line of the Brunswick house was founded in 1318 and was a fairly constant line until 1884 when Prussia installed a government that lasted until 1913. Brunswick was given to the Kaiser's son-in-law, who was the previous duke's grandson, in 1913 and he was forced to abdicate in 1918.

RULERS
Karl Wilhelm Ferdinand, 1780-1806
Friedrich Wilhelm, 1806-1815
Karl II (under regency of George III of Great Britain), 1815-1820
Karl II (under regency of George IV of Great Britain), 1820-1823
Karl II, 1823-1830
Wilhelm, 1831-1884
Prussian rule, 1884-1913
Ernst August, 1913-1918

MINTMASTER'S INITIALS

Letter	Date	Name
B,LB	1844-1866	Theodor Wilhelm Bruel, in Hannover
B	1850-1859	Johann W. Chr. Brumleu, in Brunswick
CvC	1820-1850	Cramer von Clausbruch, in Brunswick
FR	1814-1820	Friedrich Ritter, in Brunswick
K	1776-1802	Christian Friedrich Krull,
MC	1779-1806,1820	Munz - Commission at Brunswick

PFENNIG
COPPER
Obv: Horse left. Rev: Value, date.

KM#	Date	Mintage	Fine	VF	XF	Unc
995	1801 MC	—	2.00	4.00	7.00	40.00
(C113)	1802 MC	—	2.00	4.00	7.00	40.00
	1803 MC	—	2.00	4.00	7.00	40.00
	1804 MC	—	2.00	4.00	7.00	40.00
	1805 MC	—	2.00	4.00	7.00	40.00
	1806 MC	—	2.00	4.00	7.00	40.00

Obv: M.C. below horse.

KM#	Date	Mintage	Fine	VF	XF	Unc
1050.1	1813 MC	—	2.00	3.00	6.00	40.00
(C164.1)	1814 MC	—	2.00	3.00	6.00	40.00

Obv: F.R. below horse.

1050.2	1814 FR	—	1.00	2.00	5.00	35.00
(C164.2)	1815 FR	—	1.00	2.00	5.00	35.00

Obv: F.R. below horse, GEORG P.R.T.N.

1068	1816 FR	—	3.00	5.00	10.00	60.00
(C175)	1818 FR	—	3.00	5.00	10.00	60.00

1069	1816 FR	—	2.00	3.00	6.00	40.00
(C175a)	1817 FR	—	2.00	3.00	6.00	40.00
	1818 FR	—	2.00	3.00	6.00	40.00
	1819 FR	—	2.00	3.00	6.00	40.00
	1820 FR	—	2.00	3.00	6.00	40.00

Obv. leg: FRIEDRICH WILHELM......

1075 (C164a)	1818	—	15.00	30.00	60.00	140.00

Obv. leg: GEORG D.G.

1076 (C175b)	1818 FR	—	2.00	4.00	7.00	50.00

Obv. leg: GEORG T.N. begins at upper left.

1077	1818 FR	—	2.00	4.00	7.00	50.00
(C175d)	1819 FR	—	2.00	4.00	7.00	50.00
	1820 FR	—	2.00	4.00	7.00	50.00

Obv. leg: GEORG T.N. begins at lower left.

1078 (C175c)	1819 FR	—	2.00	4.00	7.00	50.00

Obv: W/o F.R., leg: GEORG IV. R.TVT....
Rev: MC below date.

1079	1819 MC	—	2.00	4.00	7.00	50.00
(C184)	1820 MC	—	2.00	4.00	7.00	50.00

Obv. leg: GEORGE IV D.G.R.TVT.....

1085	1820 MC	—	2.00	4.00	7.00	50.00
(C184a)	1822 MC	—	2.00	4.00	7.00	50.00
	1823 MC	—	2.00	4.00	7.00	50.00

Obv. leg: GEORGE IV D.G.R.T.N....ET.L.

1094	1822 CvC	—	2.00	4.00	7.00	50.00
(C184b)	1823 CvC	—	2.00	4.00	7.00	50.00

Obv. leg. ends: BR. U.LUEN. Rev: Value.

KM#	Date	Mintage	Fine	VF	XF	Unc
1098	1823 CvC	—	1.00	2.00	3.00	30.00
(C194)	1824 CvC	—	1.00	2.00	3.00	30.00
	1825 CvC	—	1.00	2.00	3.00	30.00
	1826 CvC	—	1.00	2.00	3.00	30.00
	1828 CvC	—	1.00	2.00	3.00	30.00
	1829/8 CvC	—	3.00	6.00	12.50	32.50
	1829 CvC	—	1.00	2.00	3.00	30.00
	1830 CvC	—	1.00	2.00	3.00	30.00

Obv. leg. ends: BR.U.L.

1107 (C194a)	1824 CvC	—	1.00	2.00	3.00	30.00

Obv. leg. ends: BR. U. LUEN. Rev. value: PFENNING.

1120	1831 CvC	—	1.00	3.00	4.00	35.00
(C206)	1832 CvC	—	1.00	3.00	4.00	35.00
	1833 CvC	—	1.00	3.00	4.00	35.00
	1834 CvC	—	1.00	3.00	4.00	35.00

Rev. value: PFENNIG

1127 (C206a)	1834 CvC	—	1.00	—	5.00	40.00

1142	1851 B	—	1.00	2.00	4.00	30.00
(C207)	1852 B	.270	1.00	2.00	4.00	30.00
	1853 B	.139	1.00	2.00	4.00	30.00
	1855 B	.079	1.00	2.00	4.00	30.00
	1856 B	.514	1.00	2.00	4.00	30.00

Rev: W/o B under date.

1148	1854	.126	3.00	5.00	10.00	90.00
(C207a)	1856	Inc.Ab.	3.00	5.00	10.00	90.00

Obv. leg: HERZOGTH.BRAUNSCHWEIG.

1154	1859	.103	1.00	2.00	3.50	20.00
(C208)	1860	.307	1.00	2.00	3.50	20.00

2 PFENNIGE

COPPER

1056	1814 FR	—	2.00	3.00	5.00	40.00
(C165.1)	1815 FR	—	2.00	3.00	5.00	40.00

Obv: W/o F.R. below monogram.

1064 (C165.2)	1815	—	2.00	3.00	5.00	40.00

Rev: M.C. below date.

1086 (C185.1)	1820 MC	—	2.00	3.00	5.00	45.00

Rev: C.v.C. below date.

1099 (C185.2)	1823 CvC	—	2.00	3.00	5.00	45.00

1108	1824 CvC	—	2.00	3.00	5.00	45.00
(C195)	1826 CvC	—	2.00	3.00	5.00	45.00
	1827 CvC	—	2.00	3.00	5.00	45.00

KM#	Date	Mintage	Fine	VF	XF	Unc
(C195)	1828 CvC	—	2.00	3.00	5.00	45.00
	1829 CvC	—	2.00	3.00	5.00	45.00
	1830 CvC	—	2.00	3.00	5.00	45.00

Obv. leg: WILHELM.....

1123	1832 CvC	—	2.00	3.00	5.00	60.00
(C209)	1833 CvC	—	2.00	3.00	5.00	60.00
	1834 CvC	—	2.00	3.00	5.00	60.00

Rev. value: PFENNIG.

1128	1834 CvC	—	2.00	5.00	10.00	70.00
(C209a)						

1143	1851 B	—	.75	1.25	2.50	25.00
(C210)	1852 B	.135	.75	1.25	2.50	25.00
	1853 B	.124	.75	1.25	2.50	25.00
	1854 B	.063	.75	1.25	2.50	25.00
	1855 B	.189	.75	1.25	2.50	25.00
	1855	—	—	—	—	—
	1856 B	.253	.75	1.25	2.50	25.00

1155	1859	.062	.75	1.25	2.50	25.00
(C211)	1860	.147	.75	1.25	2.50	25.00

4 PFENNIGE
BILLON
Obv: Horse. Rev: Value

997	1801 MC	—	3.00	6.00	12.00	35.00
(C117)	1802 MC	—	3.00	6.00	12.00	35.00
	1803 MC	—	3.00	6.00	12.00	35.00
	1804 MC	—	3.00	6.00	12.00	35.00

1.2300 g, .187 SILVER, .0073 oz ASW
Obv: Prancing horse left, 'F.R.' below, leg. ends: BRIETL. Rev: Value.

1087	1820 FR	.035	5.00	15.00	35.00	150.00
(C176)						

Obv: W/o F.R. Rev: C.V.C. below date.

1100	1823 CvC	.063	3.00	10.00	15.00	85.00
(C186)						

6 PFENNIGE
BILLON
Obv: Horse. Rev: Value.

1019	1802 MC	—	4.00	8.00	15.00	40.00
(C119)	1804 MC	—	4.00	8.00	15.00	40.00

1.3900 g, .250 SILVER, .0111 oz ASW
Obv: M.C. below horse.

1057	1814 MC	—	3.00	6.00	15.00	40.00
(C166)						

Obv: B. instead of BR in legend.

1058	1814 MC	—	3.00	6.00	15.00	40.00
(C166a.1)						

Obv: F.R. below mound.

1059	1814 FR	—	3.00	7.00	20.00	60.00
(C166a.2)	1815 FR	.133	3.00	7.00	20.00	60.00

BILLON
Obv. leg. ends: GEORG T.N. CAROLI D. BR

1070	1816 FR	.036	5.00	10.00	25.00	100.00
(C177)	1819 FR	.030	5.00	10.00	25.00	100.00

Obv. leg: GEORG IV. Rev: C.V.C. below date.

1101	1823 CvC	.060	3.00	7.00	20.00	80.00
(C187)						

Obv. leg. ends: BR U L

KM#	Date	Mintage	Fine	VF	XF	Unc
1116	1828 CvC	—	3.00	7.00	15.00	40.00
(C196)						

1/2 GROSCHEN
(1/60 Thaler)
(Vereins)

1.0900 g, .220 SILVER, .0077 oz ASW

1151	1858	.576	1.50	3.00	6.00	25.00
(C212)	1859	.131	2.00	4.00	8.00	30.00
	1860	.313	1.50	3.00	6.00	25.00

MARIENGROSCHEN
BILLON
Obv: Horse left. Rev: Value, date.

1031	1802 MC	—	4.00	8.00	15.00	40.00
(C121)	1803 MC	—	4.00	8.00	15.00	40.00
	1804 MC	—	4.00	8.00	15.00	40.00
	1805 MC	—	4.00	8.00	15.00	40.00
	1806 MC	—	4.00	8.00	15.00	40.00

GROSCHEN

SILVER

KM#	Date	Mintage	VG	Fine	VF	XF
1137	1847 CVC	—	—	—	Rare	—

(1/30 Thaler)
(Vereins)

2.1900 g, .220 SILVER, .0154 oz ASW

KM#	Date	Mintage	Fine	VF	XF	Unc
1150	1857	.039	4.00	8.00	12.00	45.00
(C213)	1858	.713	2.00	4.00	8.00	35.00
	1859	.594	2.00	4.00	8.00	35.00
	1860	.095	2.00	4.00	10.00	35.00

2 MARIENGROSCHEN

BILLON

1045	1804 M.C.	—	5.00	10.00	20.00	50.00
(C127)						

4 GUTE GROSCHEN

5.3500 g, .521 SILVER, .0896 oz ASW

1135	1840 CvC	.060	15.00	30.00	60.00	200.00
(C214)						

8 GUTE GROSCHEN

SILVER
Obv: Revised arms.

1026	1801 MC	—	15.00	30.00	60.00	150.00
(C145a)	1803 MC	—	15.00	30.00	60.00	150.00
	1804 MC	—	15.00	30.00	60.00	150.00
	1805 MC	—	15.00	30.00	60.00	150.00

16 GUTE GROSCHEN
SILVER
Obv: Arms. Rev: Value.

KM#	Date	Mintage	Fine	VF	XF	Unc
1020	1801 MC	—	18.00	40.00	90.00	200.00
(C149a)	1802 MC	—	18.00	40.00	90.00	200.00
	1803 MC	—	18.00	40.00	90.00	200.00
	1804 MC	—	18.00	40.00	90.00	200.00
	1805 MC	—	18.00	40.00	90.00	200.00

24 MARIENGROSCHEN
(= 2/3 Thaler)
SILVER
Similar to KM#1065.

1034	1801 MC	—	25.00	60.00	140.00	325.00
(C155)	1802 MC	—	25.00	60.00	140.00	325.00
	1803 MC	—	25.00	60.00	140.00	325.00
	1804 MC	—	25.00	60.00	140.00	325.00
	1805 MC	—	25.00	60.00	140.00	325.00
	1806 MC	—	25.00	60.00	140.00	325.00

13.0800 g, .993 SILVER, .4176 oz ASW
Obv. leg: FRIDERICVS.....

1060	1814 FR	—	100.00	175.00	300.00	525.00
(C170)	1815 FR	.036	100.00	175.00	300.00	525.00

1065	1815 FR	—	90.00	150.00	250.00	450.00
(C180)	1816 FR	.027	90.00	150.00	250.00	450.00
	1817 FR	.019	90.00	150.00	250.00	450.00
	1818 FR	.017	90.00	150.00	250.00	450.00

Obv. leg: REX BRITANNIAR.

1088	1820 MC	.024	100.00	180.00	300.00	550.00
(C190.1)						

Rev: CvC below date.

1091	1821 CvC	.029	85.00	145.00	250.00	450.00
(C190.2)	1823 CvC	.030	85.00	145.00	250.00	450.00

Obv. leg: ZU BRAUNS.

1102	1823 CvC	—	75.00	125.00	200.00	375.00
(C199)	1824 CvC	—	75.00	125.00	200.00	375.00
	1825 CvC	—	75.00	125.00	200.00	375.00
	1826 CvC	.040	75.00	125.00	200.00	375.00
	1828 CvC	—	75.00	125.00	200.00	375.00
	1829 CvC	.034	75.00	125.00	200.00	375.00

Brunswick-Wolfenbuttel / GERMAN STATES 618

Obv. leg: ZU BRAUNSCHW.

KM#	Date	Mintage	Fine	VF	XF	Unc
1109	1824 CvC	.032	50.00	100.00	150.00	250.00
(C199a)	1825 CvC	.032	50.00	100.00	150.00	250.00
	1826 CvC	—	50.00	100.00	150.00	250.00
	1828 CvC	—	50.00	100.00	150.00	250.00
	1829 CvC	—	50.00	100.00	150.00	250.00

1124	1832 CvC	.032	40.00	80.00	125.00	225.00
(C215)	1833 CvC	.027	40.00	80.00	125.00	225.00
	1834 CvC	.030	40.00	80.00	125.00	225.00

24 EINEN (1/24) THALER
BILLON
Obv: Horse. Rev: Value.

999	1802 MC	—	3.00	7.00	15.00	45.00
(C123)						

1.9400 g, .375 SILVER, .0233 oz ASW
Rev: F.R. under date.

1061	1814 FR	—	3.00	6.00	10.00	50.00
(C167)	1815 FR	.066	3.00	6.00	10.00	50.00

Obv. leg: GEORG T.N.CAROLI D.BR:. Rev: Value.

1080	1819 FR	.058	4.00	10.00	40.00	150.00
(C178)						

Obv. leg: GEORG IV. Rev: Value, M.C. below date.

1089	1820 MC	—	3.00	7.00	15.00	60.00
(C188.1)						

Rev: C.v.C. below date.

1103	1823 CvC	—	3.00	7.00	20.00	80.00
(C188.2)						

Obv. leg: BRAUNSCHW. U. LUEN.

1112	1825 CvC	—	5.00	15.00	25.00	100.00
(C197)						

1/12 THALER
BILLON
Similar to KM#1051.3.

1000	1801 MC	—	4.00	8.00	15.00	50.00
(C131)	1802 MC	—	4.00	8.00	15.00	50.00
	1803 MC	—	4.00	8.00	15.00	50.00
	1804 MC	—	4.00	8.00	15.00	50.00

KM#	Date	Mintage	Fine	VF	XF	Unc
(C131)	1805 MC	—	4.00	8.00	15.00	50.00
	1806 MC	—	4.00	8.00	15.00	50.00

3.3400 g, .437 SILVER, .0469 oz ASW
Obv: Prancing horse left, MC below. Rev: Value.

1051.1	1813 MC	—	4.00	8.00	15.00	50.00
(C168)	1814 MC	—	4.00	8.00	15.00	50.00

Obv: FR below horse.

1051.2	1815 FR	—	3.00	5.00	10.00	45.00
(C168a)						

Obv: W/o initials below horse. Rev: FR below date.

1051.3	1815 FR	—	3.00	5.00	10.00	45.00
(C168c)						

Obv. leg: GEORG D.

1071	1816 FR	—	3.00	8.00	20.00	80.00
(C179)	1817 FR	—	3.00	8.00	20.00	80.00
	1818 FR	—	3.00	8.00	20.00	80.00
	1819 FR	—	3.00	8.00	20.00	80.00

Obv. leg: GEORG IV.

1090	1820 MC	—	3.00	7.00	15.00	60.00
(C189.1)						

Rev: CvC below date.

1092	1821 CvC	—	3.00	5.00	10.00	50.00
(C189.2)	1822 CvC	—	3.00	5.00	10.00	50.00
	1823 CvC	—	3.00	5.00	10.00	50.00

Obv. leg: BRAUNSCHW. U. LUEN.

1104	1823 CvC	—	3.00	5.00	10.00	50.00
(C198)	1824 CvC	—	3.00	5.00	10.00	50.00
	1825 CvC	—	3.00	5.00	10.00	50.00
	1826 CvC	—	3.00	5.00	10.00	50.00
	1827 CvC	—	3.00	5.00	10.00	50.00
	1828 CvC	—	3.00	5.00	10.00	50.00
	1829 CvC	—	3.00	5.00	10.00	50.00
	1830 CvC	—	3.00	5.00	10.00	50.00

Obv. leg: BRAUNSCH. U.L.

1105	1823 CvC	—	7.50	15.00	30.00	125.00
(C198a)	1824 CvC	—	7.50	15.00	30.00	125.00
	1825 CvC	—	7.50	15.00	30.00	125.00
	1826 CvC	—	7.50	15.00	30.00	125.00

Obv. leg: BRAUNS. U. LUEN.

1106	1823 CvC	—	3.00	5.00	10.00	50.00
(C198b)	1824 CvC	—	3.00	5.00	10.00	50.00
	1828 CvC	—	3.00	5.00	10.00	50.00
	1829 CvC	—	3.00	5.00	10.00	50.00

1/6 THALER

SILVER

KM#	Date	Mintage	Fine	VF	XF	Unc
1001	1801 MC	—	6.00	12.00	30.00	90.00
(C139)	1802 MC	—	6.00	12.00	30.00	90.00
	1803 MC	—	6.00	12.00	30.00	90.00
	1804 MC	—	6.00	12.00	30.00	90.00

5.2000 g, .563 SILVER, .0941 oz ASW
Obv: Prancing horse left, M.C. below. Rev: Value.

KM#	Date	Mintage	Fine	VF	XF	Unc
1052	1813 MC	—	7.50	15.00	40.00	125.00
(C169-	1814 MC	—	7.50	15.00	40.00	125.00
C169a)						

THALER
SILVER
Obv: Small arms. Rev: Value, date.

1030	1801 MC	—	—	—	Rare	—
(C156a)						

28.0600 g, .833 SILVER, .7516 oz ASW

1093	1821 CvC	1,480	400.00	800.00	1500.	3000.
(C190.5)						

(Convention)

22.2700 g, .750 SILVER, .5371 oz ASW
Obv: FRITZ.F. at truncation.

1129	1837 CvC	2,788	75.00	150.00	400.00	900.00
(C216)	1838 CvC	.033	50.00	100.00	300.00	600.00

Obv: Smaller head.

1130	1839 CvC	.041	35.00	70.00	200.00	500.00
(C216.1)						

Obv: Smaller head, w/o name at truncation.
Rev: Similar to KM#1129.

KM#	Date	Mintage	Fine	VF	XF	Unc
1131	1839 CvC	I.A.	25.00	50.00	150.00	400.00
(C216a)	1840 CvC	.086	25.00	50.00	150.00	400.00
	1841 CvC	.304	20.00	40.00	125.00	350.00
	1842 CvC	.117	20.00	40.00	125.00	350.00
	1848 CvC	.011	30.00	60.00	200.00	550.00
	1850 CvC	5,671	35.00	80.00	250.00	700.00

Obv. leg. ends: U.L.
Rev: Similar to KM#1129.

1144	1851 B	5,742	50.00	135.00	325.00	850.00
(C216b)						

Obv. leg. ends: LUN.
Rev: Similar to KM#1129.

1146	1853 B	.024	35.00	125.00	285.00	750.00
(C217)	1854 B	.097	25.00	45.00	160.00	425.00
	1855 B	.010	40.00	135.00	315.00	825.00

(Vereins)

18.5200 g, .900 SILVER, .5360 oz ASW

1152	1858 B	.049	30.00	55.00	125.00	250.00
(C219)	1859 B	.030	35.00	65.00	150.00	330.00
	1865 B	.020	30.00	55.00	125.00	250.00
	1866 B	.010	25.00	45.00	110.00	215.00
	1867 B	.010	30.00	55.00	125.00	250.00
	1870 B	.107	30.00	55.00	125.00	250.00
	1871 B	.048	25.00	45.00	110.00	215.00

2 THALER
(3-1/2 Gulden)

37.1200 g, .900 SILVER, 1.0743 oz ASW
Obv: FRITZ F. at truncation, CvC below.
Rev: Crowned draped arms.

KM#	Date	Mintage	Fine	VF	XF	Unc
1136	1842 CvC	.052	100.00	200.00	500.00	1200.
(C220)	1843 CvC	.068	100.00	200.00	500.00	1200.
	1844 CvC	.015	125.00	275.00	650.00	1800.
	1845 CvC	.011	125.00	275.00	650.00	1800.
	1846 CvC	.015	125.00	275.00	650.00	1800.
	1847 CvC	.015	125.00	240.00	550.00	1400.
	1848 CvC	.011	125.00	240.00	550.00	1400.
	1849 CvC	.013	125.00	275.00	650.00	1800.
	1850 CvC	.077	125.00	275.00	650.00	1800.

Obv: Similar to KM#1136 but B below truncation.

1140	1850	—	—	—	—	—
(C220a)	1850 B	Inc.Ab.	100.00	150.00	400.00	850.00
	1851 B	.010	125.00	200.00	625.00	1450.
	1852 B	.011	125.00	200.00	625.00	1450.
	1854 B	.253	90.00	125.00	150.00	400.00
	1855 B	.620	90.00	125.00	150.00	400.00

25th Anniversary of Reign
Obv: Similar to KM#1136 but B below truncation.

1149	1856 B	.017	90.00	125.00	175.00	300.00
(C221)						

2 1/2 THALER

3.3200 g, .900 GOLD, .0961 oz AGW
Similar to KM#1072.

1032	1801 MC	—	375.00	750.00	1350.	2000.
(C160a)	1802 MC	—	300.00	625.00	1150.	1750.
	1806 MC	—	300.00	625.00	1150.	1750.

Obv: Crowned many quartered arms w/garlands.
Rev: Value, F.R. below.

1066	1815 FR	—	600.00	1000.	1650.	2500.
(C172)						

Rev. leg: BR. . . . .

1072	1816 FR	—	575.00	800.00	1125.	1650.
(C181)	1818 FR	—	825.00	1150.	1350.	2000.
	1819 FR	—	700.00	950.00	1250.	1750.

1095	1822 CvC	—	550.00	900.00	1500.	2000.
(C191)						

Rev: W/o legend around border.

1113	1825 CvC	—	350.00	500.00	875.00	1500.
(C201)	1828 CvC	—	425.00	625.00	1000.	1650.

1117	1829 CvC	—	400.00	600.00	900.00	1500.
(C204)						

KM#	Date	Mintage	Fine	VF	XF	Unc
1125	1832 CvC	—	450.00	650.00	1000.	1500.
(C223)						

1145	1851 B	4,138	350.00	500.00	750.00	1100.
(C226)						

5 THALERS

6.6500 g, .900 GOLD, .1924 oz AGW
Obv: Similar to KM#1110. Rev: Similar to KM#1062.

1025	1801 MC	—	575.00	875.00	1250.	1750.
(C161a)	1802 MC	—	425.00	625.00	1000.	1500.
	1804 MC	—	575.00	875.00	1250.	1750.
	1805 MC	—	500.00	750.00	1150.	1650.
	1806 MC	—	500.00	750.00	1150.	1650.

Obv. leg: FRIDERICVS. . . . .

1081	1814 FR	—	—	—	—	—

1062	1814 FR	—	600.00	925.00	1350.	2000.
(C173)	1815 FR	—	525.00	800.00	1200.	1750.

Rev. leg: BR. ET LUN.

1073	1816 FR	—	675.00	1000.	1650.	2250.
(C182)	1817 FR	—	575.00	875.00	1500.	2150.
	1818 FR	—	675.00	1000.	1650.	2250.
	1819 FR	—	675.00	1000.	1650.	2250.
1096	1822 CvC	—	675.00	1000.	1650.	2250.
(C192)	1823 CvC	—	850.00	1250.	1850.	2750.

1110	1824 CvC	—	425.00	625.00	950.00	1500.
(C202)	1825 CvC	—	445.00	675.00	1000.	1650.
	1828 CvC	—	445.00	675.00	1000.	1650.
	1830 CvC	—	500.00	775.00	1150.	1750.

1126	1832 CvC	—	525.00	800.00	1250.	1850.
(C224)	1834 CvC	—	575.00	900.00	1500.	2150.

10 THALERS

13.3000 g, .900 GOLD, .3848 oz AGW
Similar to KM#1054.

1041	1801 MC	—	675.00	1150.	2000.	3000.
(C162a)	1804 MC	—	750.00	1250.	2000.	3000.
	1805 MC	—	550.00	875.00	1500.	2500.
	1806 MC	—	750.00	1250.	1850.	2750.

Brunswick-Wolfenbuttel / GERMAN STATES 620

KM#	Date	Mintage	Fine	VF	XF	Unc
1054 (C174)	1813 MC	—	750.00	1250.	1850.	2750.
	1814 MC	—	675.00	1150.	1750.	2350.
1055 (C174a)	1814 FR	—	750.00	1250.	1850.	2750.

1074 (C183)	1817 FR	—	675.00	1150.	1750.	2350.
	1818 FR	—	550.00	875.00	1500.	2200.
	1819 FR	—	675.00	1150.	1750.	2350.
1097 (C193)	1822 CvC	—	750.00	1250.	1850.	2750.

1111 (C203)	1824 CvC	—	750.00	1250.	1850.	2500.
	1825 CvC	—	600.00	1000.	1650.	2250.
	1829 CvC	—	825.00	1350.	2000.	2750.
	1830 CvC	—	750.00	1250.	1850.	2500.

1115 (C205)	1827 CvC	—	900.00	1500.	2250.	3150.
	1828 CvC	—	900.00	1500.	2250.	3150.
	1829 CvC	—	825.00	1350.	2000.	2750.
	1829 CvC	—	—	—	Proof	5250.

1121 (C222)	1831 CvC	—	750.00	1250.	1850.	2500.

1122 (C225)	1831 CvC	—	525.00	875.00	1350.	2250.
	1832 CvC	—	525.00	875.00	1350.	2250.
	1833 CvC	—	600.00	1000.	1500.	2000.
	1834 CvC	—	450.00	750.00	1250.	2000.

Obv. leg. ends: U.L.

KM#	Date	Mintage	Fine	VF	XF	Unc
1141 (C227)	1850 B	9,763	975.00	1650.	2150.	2750.

Obv. leg. ends: LUN.

1147 (C227a)	1853 B	.150	400.00	650.00	1000.	2000.
	1854 B	.163	400.00	650.00	1000.	2000.
	1855 B	.020	750.00	1250.	1750.	2500.
	1856 B	.057	400.00	650.00	1000.	2000.
	1857 B	.054	400.00	650.00	1100.	2250.

KRONE

11.1110 g, .900 GOLD, .3215 oz AGW

1153 (C228)	1858 B	.032	500.00	900.00	1350.	2350.
	1859 B	.013	600.00	1100.	1750.	2750.

MONETARY REFORM
3 MARK

16.6670 g, .900 SILVER, .4823 oz ASW
Ernst August Wedding and Accession

1161 (Y54)	1915A	1,700	500.00	1000.	1500.	2500.
	1915A	—	—	—	Proof	2500.

Obv. leg: U.LUNEB added.

1162 (Y54a)	1915A	.032	45.00	100.00	150.00	200.00
	1915A	—	—	—	Proof	250.00

5 MARK

27.7770 g, .900 SILVER, .8038 oz ASW
Ernst August Wedding and Accession

KM#	Date	Mintage	Fine	VF	XF	Unc
1163 (Y55)	1915A	1,400	500.00	1000.	1500.	2500.
	1915A	—	—	—	Proof	2500.

Obv. leg: U.LUNEB added.
Rev: Similar to KM#1163.

1164 (Y55a)	1915A	8,600	150.00	325.00	500.00	750.00
	1915A	—	—	—	Proof	750.00

20 MARK

7.9650 g, .900 GOLD, .2304 oz AGW
Rev: Type II.

1160 (Y53)	1875A	.100	250.00	500.00	1000.	1500.
	1876A	—	—	—	—	3600.

TRADE COINAGE
DUCAT

3.5000 g, .986 GOLD, .1109 oz AGW
Similar to KM#1067.

1023 (C159a)	1801 MC	—	450.00	750.00	1250.	1600.

Obv: Crowned many quartered arms w/garlands.
Rev: Value, EX AVRO HERCINIA.

1063 (C171.1)	1814 HC	376 pcs.	575.00	1000.	1750.	2350.

1067 (C171.2)	1815 FR	220 pcs.	725.00	1250.	2000.	2750.
1114 (C200)	1825 CvC	530 pcs.	750.00	1250.	2100.	2850.

EAST FRIESLAND

A county located on the North Sea coast between the Ems and Weser Rivers in North Germany. The count was raised to rank of prince in 1654. At the death of the last prince in 1744, East Friesland passed to Prussia. From 1815 to 1866 East Friesland was part of Hannover until Hannover was absorbed by Prussia in 1866.

RULERS

Friedrich Wilhelm III (of Prussia),
  1797-1807
George IV (of Great Britain),
  1815-1820

MINT MARKS

A - Berlin
B - Breslau
D - Aurich

F - Magdeburg
Star - Dresden

MONETARY SYSTEM
Witte = 4 Hohlpfennig = 1/3 Schilling =
1/20 Schaf = 1/10 Stuber
Ciffert = 6 Witten
Stuber = 10 Witten = 1/30 Reichstaler
Schaf = 20 Witten = 2 Stuber
Flindrich = 3 Stuber
Schilling = 6 Stuber
288 Pfennige = 54 Stuber =
36 Mariengroschen = 1 Reichsthaler

1/4 STUBER
COPPER
Obv: Crowned FW monogram. Rev: Value, date.

KM#	Date	Mintage	Fine	VF	XF	Unc
272 (C35)	1802 A	1.296	2.00	3.00	5.00	30.00
	1803 A	Inc. Ab.	2.00	3.00	5.00	30.00
	1804 A	.216	2.00	3.00	5.00	30.00

290 (C40)	1823	.710	3.00	6.00	10.00	75.00
	1824	Inc. Ab.	3.00	6.00	10.00	75.00
	1825	Inc. Ab.	3.00	6.00	10.00	75.00

STUBER

BILLON

280 (C37)	1804 A	.378	20.00	32.50	55.00	90.00

291 (C41)	1823 B	.161	12.00	20.00	45.00	75.00

2 STUBER
BILLON
Obv: Bust. Rev: Value.

281 (C38)	1804 A	.216	30.00	60.00	120.00	225.00

Obv: Crowned monogram GR. Rev: Value.

292 (C42)	1823 B	.081	15.00	30.00	60.00	115.00

ERFURT

A city in central Germany. It was a mint for the archbishops of Mainz in the 11th, 12th and 13th centuries. It also served as an Imperial Mint in the 12th century. Independence was granted in 1255 and the mint right was obtained in 1341 and 1354. Erfurt was occupied by Swedish force from 1631 until 1648, during the Thirty Years War. A local coinage was produced until 1802 when Erfurt fell to Prussia.

RULERS
Friedrich Carl Joseph, Freiherr von und zu Erthal, Archbishop, 1774-1802

MINTMASTER'S INITIALS
Letter	Date	Name
C	1779-1804	Julianus Eberhard Volkmar Claus, Mint director
S	1801-1802	Johann Blasius Siegling, Mint director

6 PFENNIG
BILLON
Obv: Wheel in crowned shield. Rev: Value.

KM#	Date	Mintage	Fine	VF	XF	Unc
122 (C7)	1801 S	—	3.00	6.00	10.00	50.00

COPPER (OMS)

122a (C7a)	1801 S					

GROSCHEN
(1/24 Taler)

BILLON

KM#	Date	Mintage	Fine	VF	XF	Unc
123 (C9)	1801 S	—	4.00	10.00	30.00	75.00

Obv: Shield within branches.

124 (C9a)	1802 S	—	4.00	10.00	30.00	75.00

FRANKFURT

A free city in west-central Germany, founded as a Roman settlement in the 1st century and for several centuries the site of the election of the Holy Roman Emperors. It housed the Imperial Mint from early times and obtained the mint right in 1428 with almost continuous coinage until 1866. Frankfurt am Main was merged into the Confederation of the Rhine in 1806 and was made the Grand Duchy of Frankfurt in 1810. The Congress of Vienna restored its freedom in 1815 but when the city sided with the Austrians in the Austro-Prussian War, victorious Prussia absorbed it in 1866.

MINTMASTER'S INITIALS
Frankfurt Mint
Letter	Date	Name
G.B., I.G.B.	1790-1825	Johann Georg Bunsen
S.T.	1836-1837	Samuel Tomschutz
Z	1843-1856	Johann Philipp Zollman

WARDEN'S INITIALS
Frankfurt Mint
GH	1798-1816	Georg Hille

ENGRAVERS
Frankfurt Mint
A.V. NORDHEIM
1857-1866

Wiesbaden Mint
ZOLLMANN
1818-1843   Johann Philipp Zollman

In some instances old dies were used later with initials beyond the date range of the man that held the position.

HELLER

COPPER

KM#	Date	Mintage	Fine	VF	XF	Unc
300 (C2)	1814 G.B.	.332	8.00	15.00	30.00	65.00

Transition Issue

304	1814	—				

301 (C2a)	1814 G(F)B	—	2.00	4.00	8.00	40.00
	1815 G(F)B	.166	2.00	4.00	8.00	40.00
	1816 G(F)B	—	2.00	4.00	8.00	40.00
	1817 G(F)B	—	2.00	4.00	8.00	40.00
	1818 G(F)B	—	2.00	4.00	8.00	40.00
	1819 G(F)B	—	2.00	4.00	8.00	40.00
	1820/02 G(F)B	—	2.00	4.00	8.00	45.00
	1820 G(F)B	—	2.00	4.00	8.00	40.00
	1821 G(F)B	—	2.00	4.00	8.00	40.00
	1822 G(F)B	—	2.00	4.00	8.00	40.00
	1824 G(F)B	—	2.00	4.00	8.00	40.00
	1825 G(F)B	—	2.00	4.00	8.00	40.00

NOTE: Varieties exist.

310 (C2b)	1836 S(F)T	.120	2.00	4.00	8.00	50.00
	1837 S(F)T	.144	2.00	4.00	8.00	50.00

KM#	Date	Mintage	Fine	VF	XF	Unc
311 (C3)	1838	—	2.00	4.00	8.00	50.00

327 (C3a)	1841	.173	2.00	4.00	8.00	40.00
	1842	.328	2.00	4.00	8.00	40.00
	1843	—	2.00	4.00	8.00	40.00
	1844	.162	2.00	4.00	8.00	40.00
	1845	.169	2.00	4.00	8.00	40.00
	1846	.205	2.00	4.00	8.00	40.00
	1847	.453	2.00	4.00	8.00	40.00
	1849	.396	2.00	4.00	8.00	40.00
	1850	.669	2.00	4.00	8.00	40.00
	1851	.275	2.00	4.00	8.00	40.00
	1852	.325	2.00	4.00	8.00	40.00

Obv. leg: FREIE STADT.

332 (C3b)	1843	.038	12.50	25.00	50.00	100.00

 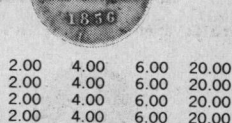

351 (C4)	1853	.411	2.00	4.00	6.00	20.00
	1854	.271	2.00	4.00	6.00	20.00
	1855	.430	2.00	4.00	6.00	20.00
	1856	.484	2.00	4.00	6.00	20.00
	1857	.723	2.00	4.00	6.00	20.00
	1858	.377	2.00	4.00	6.00	20.00

356 (C5)	1859	.377	2.00	4.00	6.00	20.00
	1860	.353	2.00	4.00	6.00	20.00
	1861	.378	2.00	4.00	6.00	30.00
	1862	.391	2.00	4.00	6.00	20.00
	1863	.370	2.00	4.00	6.00	20.00
	1864	.390	2.00	4.00	6.00	20.00
	1865	.384	2.00	4.00	6.00	20.00

PFENNIG
COPPER
Obv: Displayed eagle. Rev: Value, date.

268 (C6)	1801 G(F)B	—	2.00	4.00	10.00	35.00
	1802 G(F)B	—	2.00	4.00	10.00	35.00
	1803 P(F)B	—	2.00	4.00	10.00	35.00
	1803 G(F)B	—	2.00	4.00	10.00	35.00
	1804 G(F)B	—	2.00	4.00	10.00	35.00
	1805 G(F)B	—	2.00	4.00	10.00	35.00
	1806 G(F)B	—	2.00	4.00	10.00	35.00

NOTE: Varieties exist.

KREUZER
(Convention)

BILLON

KM#	Date	Mintage	VG	Fine	VF	XF
295 (C21)	1803 GB GH	—	5.00	15.00	30.00	60.00
	1804 GB GH	—	5.00	15.00	30.00	60.00
	1805 GB GH	—	5.00	15.00	30.00	60.00

Rev: Rosettes at sides of "1".

296 (C21a)	1804 GB GH	—	5.00	15.00	30.00	60.00
	1805 GN GH	—	5.00	15.00	30.00	60.00

Rev: Dot at sides of "1".

297 (C21b)	1804 GB GH	—	5.00	15.00	30.00	60.00
	1805 GB GH	—	5.00	15.00	30.00	60.00

Obv: Rosette below date.

298	1808 GB GH	—	5.00	15.00	30.00	60.00

Frankfurt / GERMAN STATES 621

Frankfurt / GERMAN STATES 622

.8350 g, .167 SILVER, .0044 oz ASW

KM#	Date	Mintage	Fine	VF	XF	Unc
312	1838	.078	2.00	4.00	10.00	30.00
(C24)	1841	.123	2.00	4.00	10.00	22.50
	1842	.402	2.00	4.00	10.00	22.50
	1843	.169	2.00	4.00	10.00	22.50
	1844	.215	2.00	4.00	10.00	22.50
	1845	.205	2.00	4.00	10.00	22.50
	1846	.101	2.00	4.00	10.00	22.50
	1847	.553	2.00	4.00	10.00	22.50
	1848	.482	2.00	4.00	10.00	22.50
	1849	.627	2.00	4.00	10.00	22.50
	1850	.612	2.00	4.00	10.00	22.50
	1851	.543	2.00	4.00	10.00	22.50
	1852	.889	2.00	4.00	10.00	22.50
	1853	.526	2.00	4.00	10.00	22.50
	1854	.589	2.00	4.00	10.00	22.50
	1855	.677	2.00	4.00	10.00	22.50
	1856	1.227	2.00	4.00	10.00	22.50
	1857	.774	2.00	4.00	10.00	22.50

BILLON

317	ND (1839)	—	1.00	3.00	10.00	30.00
(M1)						

NOTE: Varieties exist.

.8330 g, .167 SILVER, .0044 oz ASW
Obv: Eagle w/long body.

357	1859	.358	2.00	4.00	10.00	25.00
(C25)	1860	.640	2.00	4.00	10.00	25.00
	1861	.313	2.00	4.00	10.00	25.00
	1862	—	25.00	52.50	80.00	125.00

Obv: Eagle w/heart-shaped body.

367	1862	.645	2.00	4.00	8.00	20.00
(C25.1)	1863	.611	2.00	4.00	8.00	20.00
	1864	.344	2.00	4.00	8.00	20.00
	1865	.366	2.00	4.00	8.00	20.00
	1866	.151	2.00	5.00	10.00	25.00

3 KREUZER

1.2990 g, .333 SILVER, .0139 oz ASW

313	1838	.080	3.00	7.00	18.00	40.00
(C29)	1841	.085	3.00	7.00	18.00	40.00
	1842	.109	3.00	7.00	18.00	40.00
	1843	.089	3.00	7.00	18.00	40.00
	1846	.154	3.00	7.00	18.00	40.00

BILLON
Obv: Crowned eagle. Rev: View of city.

318	ND (1839)	—	1.00	3.00	10.00	30.00
(M2)						

1.2990 g, .333 SILVER, .0139 oz ASW

334	1846	Inc. Ab.	2.00	5.00	12.50	35.00
(C29a)	1848	.038	2.00	5.00	12.50	35.00
	1849/6	.950	2.00	5.00	12.50	40.00
	1849	Inc. Ab.	2.00	5.00	12.50	35.00
	1850	.182	2.00	5.00	12.50	35.00
	1851	.158	2.00	5.00	12.50	35.00
	1852	.129	2.00	5.00	12.50	35.00
	1853	.069	2.00	5.00	12.50	35.00
	1854	.154	2.00	5.00	12.50	35.00
	1855	.148	2.00	5.00	12.50	35.00
	1856	.084	2.00	5.00	12.50	35.00

1.2900 g, .350 SILVER, .0145 oz ASW

KM#	Date	Mintage	Fine	VF	XF	Unc
373	1866	.096	5.00	10.00	20.00	60.00
(C30)						

6 KREUZER

2.5900 g, .333 SILVER, .0277 oz ASW

314	1838	.110	2.00	6.00	15.00	60.00
(C37)	1841	.123	2.00	6.00	15.00	60.00
	1842	.161	2.00	6.00	15.00	60.00
	1843	.260	2.00	6.00	15.00	60.00
	1844	.370	2.00	6.00	15.00	60.00
	1845	.105	2.00	6.00	15.00	60.00
	1846	.211	2.00	6.00	15.00	60.00

.333 SILVER
Obv: Crowned eagle. Rev: View of city.

319	ND (1839)	—	6.50	12.50	22.50	50.00
(M3)						

335	1846	Inc. Ab.	2.00	6.00	15.00	50.00
(C37a)	1848	.291	2.00	6.00	15.00	50.00
	1849	.171	2.00	6.00	15.00	50.00
	1850	.152	2.00	6.00	15.00	50.00
	1851	.159	2.00	6.00	15.00	50.00
	1852	.221	2.00	6.00	15.00	50.00
	1853	.106	2.00	6.00	15.00	50.00
	1855	.181	2.00	6.00	15.00	50.00
	1856	.166	2.00	6.00	15.00	50.00

350	1852	Inc. Ab.	3.50	10.00	25.00	65.00
(C38)	1853	Inc. Ab.	3.50	10.00	25.00	65.00
	1854	.212	3.50	10.00	25.00	65.00
	1856	Inc. Ab.	3.50	10.00	25.00	65.00

2.4600 g, .350 SILVER, .0276 oz ASW

374	1866	.038	5.00	10.00	20.00	70.00
(C39)						

1/2 GULDEN

5.3000 g, .900 SILVER, .1533 oz ASW

315	1838	.120	25.00	40.00	90.00	200.00
(C64)	1838	—	—	—	Proof	225.00
	1840	.391	15.00	30.00	70.00	150.00
	1841	.161	25.00	40.00	90.00	200.00

KM#	Date	Mintage	Fine	VF	XF	Unc
330	1842	.075	25.00	40.00	90.00	200.00
(C64a)	1843	.056	25.00	40.00	90.00	200.00
	1844	.049	25.00	40.00	90.00	200.00
	1845	.072	25.00	40.00	90.00	200.00
	1846	.047	25.00	40.00	90.00	200.00
	1847	.051	25.00	40.00	90.00	200.00
	1849	.055	25.00	40.00	90.00	200.00

368	1862	.014	60.00	100.00	200.00	500.00
(C64b)						

GULDEN

10.6000 g, .900 SILVER, .3067 oz ASW

316	1838	.120	35.00	70.00	140.00	250.00
(C70)	1838	—	—	—	Proof	—
	1839	—	—	—	—	2500.
	1840	.391	35.00	70.00	140.00	250.00
	1841	.161	35.00	70.00	140.00	250.00

Obv: Eagle w/large arabesques.

331	1842	.123	22.00	45.00	90.00	200.00
(C70a)	1843	.172	22.00	45.00	90.00	200.00
	1844	.122	22.00	45.00	90.00	200.00
	1845	.101	22.00	45.00	90.00	200.00
	1846	.120	22.00	45.00	90.00	200.00
	1847	.121	22.00	45.00	90.00	200.00
	1848	.078	22.00	45.00	90.00	225.00
	1849	.090	22.00	45.00	90.00	225.00
	1850	.030	35.00	65.00	125.00	250.00
	1851	.064	35.00	65.00	125.00	250.00
	1852	.064	35.00	65.00	125.00	250.00
	1853	.029	35.00	65.00	125.00	250.00
	1854	.034	35.00	65.00	125.00	250.00
	1855	.038	35.00	65.00	125.00	250.00

Obv: Eagle w/small arabesques.

358	1859	.059	30.00	60.00	125.00	250.00
(C70b)	1861	.211	25.00	50.00	100.00	200.00

Obv: Eagle w/o arabesques.

KM#	Date	Mintage	Fine	VF	XF	Unc
369	1862	.011	100.00	200.00	400.00	800.00
(C70c)	1863	.056	50.00	100.00	200.00	300.00

ZWEY (2) GULDEN

21.2200 g, .900 SILVER, .6138 oz ASW

333	1845	.114	50.00	75.00	150.00	275.00
(C82)	1846	.281	50.00	75.00	150.00	275.00
	1847	.215	50.00	75.00	150.00	275.00
	1848	.147	50.00	75.00	150.00	275.00
	1849	.023	75.00	100.00	200.00	400.00
	1850	.031	100.00	200.00	400.00	800.00
	1851	.032	75.00	100.00	200.00	400.00
	1852	.026	100.00	150.00	250.00	500.00
	1853	.056	75.00	100.00	200.00	400.00
	1854	6.028	100.00	150.00	250.00	500.00
	1856	.036	75.00	100.00	200.00	400.00

Constitutional Convention, May 1, 1848

336	1848	—	—	—	Rare	—
(C83a)						

Constitutional Convention, May 18, 1848

337	1848	8,600	60.00	120.00	180.00	250.00
(C83)						

NOTE: Coins were struck in anticipation of the Constitutional Convention scheduled to take place May 1, 1848. When the convention was delayed till May 18, 1848 the coins were recalled and the dies were altered to reflect this new date.

Archduke Johann of Austria elected as Vicar

KM#	Date	Mintage	Fine	VF	XF	Unc
338	1848	.036	30.00	50.00	75.00	150.00
(C84)	1848	—	—	—	Proof	200.00

339	1848	—	2000.	3500.	5000.	7500.
(C84a)						

Opening of German Parliament
Obv: KM#337 rev. Rev: KM#333.

340	1848	—	2000.	3500.	5000.	7500.
(C-A83)						

Friedrich Wilhelm IV of Prussia elected as Emperor of Germany

341.1	1849	200 pcs.	2000.	3500.	5000.	7500.
(C85)						

Plain edge.

341.2	1849 (1890)	(restrike)	—	—	—	—
(C85a)						

Obv: Similar to KM#333.

342	1849	—	—	—	—	8300.
(C85b)						

Centenary of Goethe's Birth

343	1849	8,500	60.00	90.00	150.00	220.00
(C86)	1849	—	—	—	Proof	250.00

300th Anniversary of Religious Peace

KM#	Date	Mintage	Fine	VF	XF	Unc
353	1855	.032	50.00	70.00	110.00	175.00
(C87)						

EIN (1) THALER
(Vereins)

18.5200 g, .900 SILVER, .5360 oz ASW

354	1857	1,350	200.00	400.00	800.00	1600.

Obv: House roofs visible around tower at left.

355	1857	—	150.00	300.00	600.00	1200.
(C77.1)	1858	.012	50.00	100.00	200.00	400.00

(Gedenk)

Schiller Centennial

359	1859	.025	25.00	50.00	—	75.00	125.00
(C79)	1859	—	—	—	—	Proof	150.00

(Vereins)

360	1859	.283	20.00	40.00	60.00	120.00
(C78)	1860	1.700	17.50	35.00	50.00	100.00
	1861	—	75.00	150.00	300.00	600.00

Obv: Different hair-knot.

366	1861	.016	100.00	200.00	450.00	1000.
(C78a)						

Frankfurt / GERMAN STATES 624

Obv: Different dress.

KM#	Date	Mintage	Fine	VF	XF	Unc
370 (C78b)	1862	.312	17.50	35.00	60.00	125.00
	1863	.021	25.00	50.00	100.00	200.00
	1864	.105	17.50	35.00	60.00	125.00
	1865	.207	17.50	35.00	60.00	125.00

(Gedenk)

German Shooting Festival
Obv: Similar to KM#359.

371 (C80)	1862	.044	25.00	50.00	70.00	100.00
	1862	—	—	—	Proof	225.00

Assembly of Princes

372 (C81)	1863	.020	50.00	75.00	125.00	200.00
	1863	—	—	—	Proof	250.00

ZWEI (2) THALER
(3-1/2 Gulden)

37.1000 g, .900 SILVER, 1.0743 oz ASW

New Mint Opening in 1840

KM#	Date	Mintage	Fine	VF	XF	Unc
325 (C88)	1840	649 pcs.	500.00	1250.	1500.	3000.

326 (C89)	1840 Inc. KM329	75.00	150.00	250.00	500.00
	1841 Inc. KM329	75.00	150.00	250.00	450.00
	1842 Inc. KM329	—	—	Rare	—
	1843 Inc. KM329	85.00	150.00	325.00	600.00
	1844 Inc. KM329	85.00	150.00	325.00	600.00

Mule. Obv: KM#326. Rev: Obv. of KM#329.

328 (C89a)	ND(1838)	—	—	—	7500.

Rev: Value.

329 (C90)	1841	.121	60.00	100.00	225.00	450.00
	1841	—	—	—	Proof	450.00
	1842	.287	60.00	100.00	225.00	450.00
	1843	.123	60.00	100.00	225.00	450.00
	1844	.196	60.00	100.00	225.00	450.00
	1845	.036	100.00	150.00	300.00	600.00
	1846	.072	75.00	125.00	275.00	550.00
	1847	.071	75.00	125.00	275.00	550.00

KM#	Date	Mintage	Fine	VF	XF	Unc
(C90)	1851	8,354	100.00	175.00	300.00	600.00
	1854	.107	60.00	100.00	225.00	450.00
	1855	.072	75.00	125.00	275.00	550.00

37.0400 g, .900 SILVER, 1.0717 oz ASW

365 (C91)	1860	.341	35.00	65.00	85.00	150.00
	1861	1.787	35.00	65.00	85.00	150.00
	1862	.344	35.00	65.00	85.00	150.00
	1866	.637	35.00	65.00	85.00	150.00

TRADE COINAGE
DUCAT

3.5000 g, .986 GOLD, .1109 oz AGW

352 (C95)	1853	1,121	300.00	500.00	1000.	1500.
	1856	665 pcs.	350.00	600.00	1100.	1600.

FRIEDBERG
IMPERIAL CITY

The fortified town of Friedberg, located in Hesse about 14 miles north of Frankfurt am Main, dates from Roman times. It attained free status in 1211 and was the site of an imperial mint until the mid-13th century. In 1349 Friedberg passed to the countship of Schwarzburg, loosing its free status shortly thereafter. Local nobles began electing one among themselves to the office of burgrave-for-life. The burgraves obtained the mint right in 1541 and recognized only the emperor as overlord. In 1802 Friedberg passed in fief to Hesse-Darmstadt and was mediatized in 1818.

RULERS
Johann Maria Rudolph von Waldbott-Bassenheim, 1777-1805
Clemens August von Westphalen, 1805-1818

MINTMASTERS INITIALS
Letter	Date	Name
GB(F)GH	1790-1833	Johann Georg Bunsen, in Frankfurt
	1798-1816	Georg Hille, warden in Frankfurt

EIN (1) THALER
(Convention)

SILVER

KM#	Date	Mintage	Fine	VF	XF	Unc
75 (C4)	1804 GB(F)GH	—	175.00	300.00	600.00	1300.

FURSTENBERG

A noble family with holdings in Baden and Wurttemberg. The lord of Furstenberg assumed the title of Count in the 13th century which was raised to the rank of Prince in 1664. The Furstenberg possessions were mediatized in 1806.

FURSTENBERG-STUHLINGEN

Karl Joachim, 1796-1804
Carl Egon, 1804-1854

MINT MARKS
G - Gunzburg

MINTMASTER'S INITIALS

Letter	Date	Name
CH	1784-1808	Christian Heugelin, warden in Stuttgart
ILW,W	1798-1845	Johann Ludwig Wagner, die-cutter in Stuttgart in Nuremberg

EIN (1) KREUZER

COPPER

KM#	Date	Mintage	Fine	VF	XF	Unc
35 (C13)	1804 W.	.040	30.00	70.00	150.00	275.00

3 KREUZER

1.4200 g, .312 SILVER, .0142 oz ASW

| 36 (C14) | 1804 W. | .012 | 65.00 | 135.00 | 250.00 | 425.00 |

6 KREUZER

2.3500 g, .375 SILVER, .0283 oz ASW

| 37 (C15) | 1804 W. | 6,720 | 75.00 | 155.00 | 275.00 | 500.00 |

10 KREUZER

3.8900 g, .500 SILVER, .0625 oz ASW

| 38 (C16) | 1804 W. | 6,075 | 100.00 | 175.00 | 300.00 | 550.00 |

20 KREUZER

6.6800 g, .583 SILVER, .1252 oz ASW
Obv: Bust right, leg. ends: PRINC. IN FURSTENBERG.
Rev: Crowned arms.

KM#	Date	Mintage	Fine	VF	XF	Unc
39 (C17)	1804 W.	3,011	135.00	225.00	325.00	600.00

Obv. leg. ends: PRINC FURSTENBERG.

| 40 (C17a) | 1804 | Inc. Ab. | 135.00 | 225.00 | 325.00 | 600.00 |

EIN (1) THALER
(Convention)

28.0600 g, .833 SILVER, .7515 oz ASW

| 41 (C18) | 1804 ILW-CH | 388 pcs. | 500.00 | 1000. | 1600. | 3000. |

FURTHER AUSTRIA
Vorderoesterreich

Name given to imperial lands in South Swabia in the 18th century. In 1805 it was divided by Baden and Bavaria.

RULERS
Franz II (Austria), 1792-1805

MINT MARKS
A - Wien
F - Hall
G - Baia Mare (Nagybanya)
H - Gunzburg

HELLER

COPPER

| 21 (C12) | 1801H | — | 4.00 | 7.00 | 20.00 | 125.00 |
| | 1803H | — | 4.00 | 7.00 | 20.00 | 125.00 |

1/4 KREUZER

COPPER, 1.40 g

25 (C13a)	1801H	—	—	—	—	Rare
	1802H	—	10.00	25.00	50.00	100.00
	1803H	—	6.50	20.00	40.00	80.00

1/2 KREUTZER

COPPER, 2.80 g

26 (C14b)	1801H	—	—	—	—	Rare
	1802H	—	15.00	85.00	125.00	185.00
(C14b)	1803H	—	8.50	20.00	40.00	75.00
	1804H	—	—	—	Rare	
31 (C14a)	1805H	—	—	—	Rare	

EIN (1) KREUZER

COPPER, 5.70 g
Rev: Small lettering.

27 (C15b)	1801H	—	3.00	10.00	25.00	50.00
	1802H	—	3.00	10.00	25.00	50.00
	1803H	—	3.00	10.00	25.00	50.00
	1804H	—	3.00	10.00	25.00	50.00

| 30 (C15a) | 1804H | — | — | — | Rare | |
| | 1805H | — | 3.00 | 10.00 | 25.00 | 50.00 |

3 KREUZER

1.4100 g, .312 SILVER, .0141 oz ASW

28 (C16a)	1802A	—	—	—	—	Rare
	1802G	—	—	—	—	Rare
	1802H	—	—	—	—	Rare
	1803H	—	—	—	—	Rare
	1804H	—	—	—	—	Rare
	1805H	—	—	—	—	Rare

6 KREUZER

2.3500 g, .375 SILVER, .0283 oz ASW

29 (C17a)	1802A	—	—	—	Rare	—
	1802G	—	—	—	Rare	—
	1802H	—	3.00	10.00	30.00	65.00
	1803H	—	3.00	10.00	30.00	65.00
	1804H	—	3.00	10.00	30.00	65.00
	1805A	—	3.00	10.00	30.00	65.00
	1805H	—	3.00	10.00	30.00	65.00

HAMBURG

The city of Hamburg is located on the Elbe River about 75 miles from the North Sea. It was founded by Charlemagne in the 9th century. In 1241 it joined Lubeck to form the Hanseatic League. The mint right was leased to the citizens in 1292, however the first local hohlpfennings had been struck almost 50 years earlier. In 1510 Hamburg was formally made a Free City, though in fact it had been free for about 250 years. It was occupied by the French during the Napoleonic period. In 1866 it joined the North German Confederation and became a part of the German Empire in 1871. The Hamburg coinage is almost continuous up to the time of World War I.

MINTMASTER'S INITIALS

Letter	Date	Name
CAIG, CAJG	1813	C.A.J. Ginquembre, French director of mint
HL	1673-1692	Hermann Luders
HSK	1805-1842	Hans Schierven Knoph
IHL	1725-1759	Johann Hinrich Lowe
IR	1692-1724	Jochim Rustmeyer
MF	1635-1668	Matthias Freude der Alter
MF	1668-1673	Matthias Freude der Jungere
OHK	1761-1805	Otto Heinrich Knorre

City arms - a triple-turreted gate

DREILING
(3 Pfennig - 1/4 Schilling - 1/128 Thaler)

.5100 g, .187 SILVER, .0030 oz ASW
Obv: Castle w/O.H.K. below. Rev: 'I' between rosettes.

KM#	Date	Mintage	Fine	VF	XF	Unc
220 (C1a.1)	1803 OHK	.355	2.00	4.00	10.00	30.00

Obv: Castle w/H.S.K. below.

| 235 (C1a.2) | 1807 HSK | .384 | 1.00 | 3.00 | 6.00 | 20.00 |
| | 1809 HSK | .768 | 1.00 | 3.00 | 6.00 | 20.00 |

Rev: 'I' between dots.

| 250 | 1823 HSK | .021 | 1.00 | 3.00 | 6.00 | 20.00 |

KM#	Date	Mintage	Fine	VF	XF	Unc
(C1a.3)	1832 HSK	.036	1.00	3.00	6.00	20.00
	1833 HSK	.303	1.00	3.00	6.00	20.00
	1836 HSK	.293	1.00	3.00	6.00	20.00
	1839 HSK	.299	1.00	3.00	6.00	20.00

Obv: Redesigned castle. Rev: 'I' between rosettes.

| 260 (C1a.4) | 1841 HSK | .554 | 1.00 | 3.00 | 6.00 | 20.00 |

Obv: W/o initials below castle. Rev: 'I' between 5-pointed stars.

| 264 (C1a.5) | 1846 | .574 | 1.00 | 3.00 | 6.00 | 20.00 |

Rev: 'I' between 6-pointed stars.

| 270 (C1a.6) | 1851 | .578 | 1.00 | 3.00 | 6.00 | 20.00 |

Beaded borders.

| 275 (C1a.7) | 1855A | .320 | 1.00 | 2.50 | 5.00 | 20.00 |
| | 1855 | 2.613 | 1.00 | 2.00 | 4.00 | 15.00 |

SECHSLING
(6 Pfennig - 1/2 Schilling - 1/64 Thaler)
.7600 g, .250 SILVER, .0061 oz ASW

Obv: Castle w/O.H.K. below. Rev: 'I' between rosettes.

| 213 (C3a.1) | 1803 OHK | .182 | 1.00 | 3.00 | 6.00 | 40.00 |

Obv: Castle w/H.S.K. below.

236 (C3a.2)	1807 HSK	.096	2.00	4.00	8.00	50.00
	1809 HSK	.192	1.00	3.00	6.00	40.00
	1817 HSK	.048	2.00	4.00	8.00	50.00
	1823 HSK	.030	2.00	4.00	8.00	50.00
	1833 HSK	.135	1.00	3.00	6.00	40.00
	1836 HSK	.155	1.00	3.00	6.00	40.00
	1839 HSK	.354	1.00	3.00	6.00	40.00

Rev: 'I' between dots.

| 255 (C3a.3) | 1832 HSK | .066 | 2.00 | 4.00 | 8.00 | 45.00 |

Obv: Redesigned castle. Rev: 'I' between rosettes.

| 261 (C3a.4) | 1841 HSK | .293 | 1.00 | 3.00 | 6.00 | 40.00 |

Obv: W/o initials below castle. Rev: 'I' between 5-pointed stars.

| 265 (C3a.5) | 1846 | .480 | 1.00 | 3.00 | 6.00 | 20.00 |

Rev: 'I' between 6-pointed stars.

| 271 (C3a.6) | 1851 | .480 | 1.00 | 3.00 | 6.00 | 20.00 |

Beaded borders.

| 276 (C3a.7) | 1855A | .098 | 2.00 | 4.00 | 8.00 | 35.00 |
| | 1855 | 1.841 | 1.00 | 3.00 | 6.00 | 20.00 |

SCHILLING
(12 Pfennig - 1/32 Thaler)

1.0800 g, .375 SILVER, .0130 oz ASW
Obv: Castle w/H.S.K. below.

246 (C6.2)	1817 HSK	.019	2.00	6.00	10.00	60.00
	1818 HSK	.029	2.00	6.00	10.00	60.00
	1819 HSK	.149	2.00	6.00	10.00	60.00

Rev. leg: HAMB. COVR., 'I' between dots.

KM#	Date	Mintage	Fine	VF	XF	Unc
251.1 (C6a.1)	1823 HSK	.138	1.00	3.00	6.00	35.00
	1828 HSK	.142	1.00	3.00	6.00	35.00
	1832 HSK	.142	1.00	3.00	6.00	35.00

Rev: 'I' between rosettes.

| 251.2 (C6a.2) | 1837 HSK | .153 | 1.00 | 3.00 | 6.00 | 35.00 |
| | 1840 HSK | .144 | 1.00 | 3.00 | 6.00 | 35.00 |

Obv: Redesigned castle.

| 262 (C6a.3) | 1841 HSK | .149 | 1.00 | 3.00 | 6.00 | 35.00 |

Rev: 'I' between 5-pointed stars.

| 266 (C6a.4) | 1846 | .240 | 1.00 | 3.00 | 6.00 | 35.00 |

Rev: 'I' between 6-pointed stars.

| 272 (C6a.5) | 1851 | .240 | 1.00 | 3.00 | 6.00 | 35.00 |

Beaded borders.

| 277 (C6a.6) | 1855A | .112 | 1.00 | 2.00 | 5.00 | 25.00 |
| | 1855 | 1.841 | 1.00 | 2.00 | 5.00 | 20.00 |

32 SCHILLING

18.3200 g, .750 SILVER, .4417 oz ASW

| 238 (C39) | 1808 HSK | .210 | 30.00 | 60.00 | 100.00 | 300.00 |

14.1700 g, .968 SILVER, .4410 oz ASW

| 241 (C39a) | 1809 HSK | .880 | 25.00 | 50.00 | 90.00 | 175.00 |
| 242 (C39b) | 1809 CAIG | 3.058 | 20.00 | 40.00 | 80.00 | 150.00 |

MONETARY REFORM
2 MARK

11.1110 g, .900 SILVER, .3215 oz ASW

KM#	Date	Mintage	Fine	VF	XF	Unc
290 (Y57)	1876J	2.325	20.00	45.00	250.00	450.00
	1877J	.500	25.00	50.00	275.00	550.00
	1878J	.350	25.00	50.00	325.00	625.00
	1880J	.099	40.00	100.00	350.00	750.00
	1883J	.060	40.00	100.00	350.00	675.00
	1888J	.100	30.00	60.00	300.00	575.00

294 (Y57a)	1892J	.141	15.00	25.00	75.00	325.00
	1893J	.146	15.00	25.00	75.00	275.00
	1896J	.286	15.00	20.00	50.00	175.00
	1898J	.118	25.00	60.00	160.00	400.00
	1899J	.286	15.00	20.00	60.00	175.00
	1900J	.501	12.50	25.00	60.00	175.00
	1901J	.482	12.50	20.00	50.00	150.00
	1902J	.779	12.50	20.00	50.00	125.00
	1903J	.817	12.50	20.00	40.00	125.00
	1904J	1.248	12.50	20.00	40.00	125.00
	1905J	.204	25.00	40.00	75.00	225.00
	1906J	1.225	12.50	20.00	40.00	125.00
	1907J	1.226	12.50	20.00	40.00	100.00
	1908J	.368	12.50	25.00	40.00	125.00
	1911J	.204	12.50	25.00	60.00	125.00
	1912J	.079	15.00	40.00	95.00	250.00
	1913J	.105	12.50	25.00	60.00	125.00
	1914J	.328	10.00	20.00	40.00	100.00
Common date	—	—	—	Proof	275.00

3 MARK

16.6670 g, .900 SILVER, .4823 oz ASW

296 (Y58)	1908J	.408	12.50	20.00	25.00	50.00
	1909J	1.389	12.50	20.00	25.00	50.00
	1910J	.526	12.50	20.00	25.00	50.00
	1911J	.922	12.50	20.00	25.00	50.00
	1912J	.491	12.50	20.00	25.00	50.00
	1913J	.344	12.50	20.00	25.00	50.00
	1914J	.575	12.50	20.00	25.00	50.00
Common date	—	—	—	Proof	200.00

5 MARK

27.7770 g, .900 SILVER, .8038 oz ASW
Rev: Type I.

287 (Y59)	1875J	.286	30.00	75.00	400.00	1250.
	1876J	.930	30.00	50.00	350.00	1000.
	1888J	.040	50.00	150.00	400.00	1250.

1.9910 g, .900 GOLD, .0576 oz AGW

KM#	Date	Mintage	Fine	VF	XF	Unc
291 (Y60)	1877J	.441	125.00	200.00	275.00	450.00
	1877J	—	—	—	Proof	Rare

27.7770 g, .900 SILVER, .8038 oz ASW
Rev: Type II.

KM#	Date	Mintage	Fine	VF	XF	Unc
293 (Y59a)	1891J	.059	20.00	65.00	125.00	450.00
	1893J	.055	20.00	50.00	125.00	400.00
	1894J	.082	20.00	50.00	125.00	350.00
	1895J	.082	25.00	50.00	125.00	350.00
	1896J	.016	100.00	250.00	600.00	1200.
	1898J	.176	20.00	50.00	125.00	350.00
	1899J	.082	20.00	50.00	125.00	350.00
	1900J	.172	17.50	40.00	95.00	300.00
	1901J	.172	17.50	40.00	95.00	300.00
	1902J	.294	17.50	35.00	75.00	250.00
	1903J	.588	17.50	35.00	70.00	150.00
	1904J	.319	15.00	30.00	70.00	175.00
	1907J	.326	15.00	30.00	70.00	175.00
	1908J	.458	15.00	30.00	70.00	150.00
	1913J	.327	15.00	30.00	50.00	125.00

10 MARK

3.9820 g, .900 GOLD, .1152 oz AGW
Rev: Type I.

KM#	Date	Mintage	Fine	VF	XF	Unc
285 (Y56)	1873B	.025	600.00	900.00	1400.	2500.
	1873B	—	—	—	Proof	Rare

Rev: Type II.

KM#	Date	Mintage	Fine	VF	XF	Unc
286 (Y56a)	1874B	.050	400.00	650.00	1000.	1400.

KM#	Date	Mintage	Fine	VF	XF	Unc
288 (Y61)	1875J	.565	65.00	110.00	160.00	250.00
	1875J	—	—	—	Proof	1000.
	1876J	—	700.00	1000.	1500.	1900.
	1877J	.220	65.00	110.00	160.00	250.00
	1878J	.316	65.00	110.00	160.00	250.00
	1879J	.255	65.00	110.00	160.00	250.00
	1880J	.139	65.00	110.00	160.00	250.00
	1888J	.163	65.00	110.00	160.00	250.00

KM#	Date	Mintage	Fine	VF	XF	Unc
292 (Y61a)	1890J	.245	65.00	110.00	160.00	250.00
	1893J	.246	65.00	110.00	160.00	250.00
	1896J	.164	65.00	110.00	160.00	250.00
	1898J	.344	65.00	110.00	160.00	225.00
	1900J	.082	65.00	110.00	160.00	250.00
	1901J	.082	70.00	110.00	160.00	300.00
	1902J	.041	150.00	250.00	350.00	450.00
	1903J	.230	65.00	110.00	160.00	250.00
	1905J	.164	65.00	110.00	160.00	250.00

KM#	Date	Mintage	Fine	VF	XF	Unc
(Y61a)	1906J	.163	65.00	110.00	160.00	250.00
	1907J	.111	65.00	110.00	160.00	250.00
	1908J	.032	150.00	250.00	350.00	450.00
	1909J	.122	65.00	110.00	160.00	250.00
	1909J	—	—	—	Proof	600.00
	1910J	.041	150.00	250.00	350.00	450.00
	1911J	.075	70.00	150.00	200.00	350.00
	1911J	—	—	—	Proof	600.00
	1912J	.048	150.00	250.00	350.00	450.00
	1912J	—	—	—	Proof	600.00
	1913J	.041	150.00	200.00	300.00	400.00
	1913J	—	—	—	Proof	600.00

20 MARK

7.9650 g, .900 GOLD, .2304 oz AGW
Rev: Type II.

KM#	Date	Mintage	Fine	VF	XF	Unc
289 (Y62)	1875J	.313	115.00	165.00	200.00	300.00
	1876J	1.723	115.00	135.00	150.00	225.00
	1877J	1.324	115.00	135.00	150.00	225.00
	1878J	2.080	115.00	135.00	150.00	225.00
	1879J	.104	250.00	425.00	750.00	1250.
	1880J	.120	115.00	150.00	275.00	400.00
	1881J	500 pcs.	15,000.	20,000.	25,000.	30,000.
	1883J	.125	115.00	140.00	180.00	350.00
	1884J	.639	115.00	140.00	180.00	350.00
	1887J	.251	115.00	140.00	180.00	350.00
	1889J	.014	500.00	1000.	1250.	1750.

Rev: Type III.

KM#	Date	Mintage	Fine	VF	XF	Unc
295 (Y62a)	1893J	.815	115.00	135.00	160.00	225.00
	1894J	.501	115.00	135.00	160.00	225.00
	1895J	.501	115.00	135.00	160.00	225.00
	1897J	.500	115.00	135.00	160.00	225.00
	1899J	1.002	115.00	135.00	160.00	225.00
	1900J	.501	115.00	135.00	160.00	225.00
	1908J	—	—	—	Rare	—
	1913J	.491	115.00	130.00	150.00	200.00
	1913J	—	—	—	Proof	900.00

TRADE COINAGE

DUCAT

3.4900 g, .979 GOLD, .1099 oz AGW

KM#	Date	Mintage	Fine	VF	XF	Unc
227.1 (C49)	1801	7,236	375.00	625.00	1150.	1500.
	1802	9,199	375.00	625.00	1150.	1500.
	1803	6,365	375.00	625.00	1150.	1500.
	1804	7,284	375.00	625.00	1150.	1500.
	1805	9,466	375.00	625.00	1150.	1500.
227.2 (C49.1)	1806	7,521	375.00	625.00	1150.	1500.

KM#	Date	Mintage	Fine	VF	XF	Unc
237 (C52)	1807	6,000	250.00	500.00	800.00	1500.

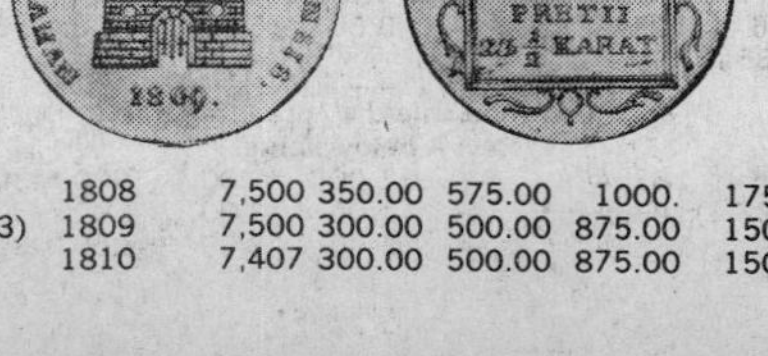

KM#	Date	Mintage	Fine	VF	XF	Unc
239 (C53)	1808	7,500	350.00	575.00	1000.	1750.
	1809	7,500	300.00	500.00	875.00	1500.
	1810	7,407	300.00	500.00	875.00	1500.

KM#	Date	Mintage	Fine	VF	XF	Unc
245 (C55)	1811	.011	300.00	500.00	875.00	1250.
	1815	9,965	300.00	500.00	875.00	1250.
	1817	5,000	325.00	550.00	975.00	1350.
	1818	7,000	325.00	550.00	975.00	1350.
	1819	8,901	300.00	500.00	875.00	1250.
	1820	7,000	300.00	500.00	875.00	1250.
	1821	9,900	300.00	500.00	875.00	1250.
	1822	.013	300.00	500.00	875.00	1250.
	1823	8,700	300.00	500.00	875.00	1250.
	1824	6,970	300.00	500.00	875.00	1250.
	1825	.010	300.00	500.00	875.00	1250.
	1826	.012	300.00	500.00	875.00	1250.
	1827	.011	300.00	500.00	875.00	1250.
	1828	8,601	300.00	500.00	875.00	1250.
	1829	9,606	300.00	500.00	875.00	1250.
	1830	.012	300.00	500.00	875.00	1250.
	1831	9,200	300.00	500.00	875.00	1250.
	1832	9,500	300.00	500.00	875.00	1250.
	1833	9,440	300.00	500.00	875.00	1250.
	1834	.010	250.00	400.00	750.00	1000.

KM#	Date	Mintage	Fine	VF	XF	Unc
256 (C56.1)	1835	.010	250.00	425.00	750.00	1150.
	1836	8,067	250.00	425.00	750.00	1150.
	1837	8,156	250.00	425.00	750.00	1150.
	1838	9,000	250.00	425.00	750.00	1150.
	1839	9,045	250.00	425.00	750.00	1150.
	1840	9,882	250.00	425.00	750.00	1150.
	1841	.010	250.00	425.00	750.00	1150.
	1842	.012	225.00	375.00	625.00	1000.

Struck in a collar.

KM#	Date	Mintage	Fine	VF	XF	Unc
263 (C56.2)	1843	.012	225.00	375.00	625.00	1000.
	1844	9,768	250.00	425.00	750.00	1150.
	1845	.012	200.00	325.00	550.00	875.00
	1846	.011	200.00	325.00	550.00	875.00
	1847	.010	200.00	325.00	550.00	875.00
	1848	.013	200.00	325.00	550.00	875.00
	1849	.010	200.00	325.00	550.00	875.00
	1850	.011	200.00	325.00	550.00	875.00

Obv: Knights shield redesigned.

KM#	Date	Mintage	Fine	VF	XF	Unc
273 (C56.3)	1851	8,497	225.00	375.00	750.00	1000.
	1852	9,476	225.00	375.00	750.00	1000.
	1853	.010	225.00	375.00	750.00	1000.

Rev. leg. ends: 979 MILLES

KM#	Date	Mintage	Fine	VF	XF	Unc
274 (C56a.1)	1854	.012	175.00	250.00	400.00	750.00
	1855	.011	175.00	250.00	400.00	750.00
	1856	.011	175.00	250.00	400.00	750.00
	1857	.012	175.00	250.00	400.00	750.00
	1858	.010	175.00	250.00	400.00	750.00
	1859	.014	175.00	250.00	400.00	750.00
	1860	.015	175.00	250.00	400.00	750.00
	1861	.015	175.00	250.00	400.00	750.00
	1862	.017	150.00	200.00	350.00	700.00
	1863	.020	150.00	200.00	350.00	700.00
	1864	.024	150.00	200.00	350.00	700.00
	1865	.017	150.00	200.00	350.00	700.00
	1866	.024	150.00	200.00	350.00	700.00
	1867	.026	150.00	200.00	350.00	700.00

Rev: Mintmark B below shell.

KM#	Date	Mintage	Fine	VF	XF	Unc
280 (C56a.2)	1868B	.025	135.00	175.00	300.00	600.00
	1869B	.026	135.00	175.00	300.00	600.00
	1870B	.030	135.00	175.00	300.00	600.00
	1871B	.030	135.00	175.00	300.00	600.00
	1872B	.030	135.00	175.00	300.00	600.00

2 DUCATS

6.9800 g, .979 GOLD, .2197 oz AGW

KM#	Date	Mintage	Fine	VF	XF	Unc
228.1 (C50)	1801	1,273	650.00	1250.	1750.	2350.
	1802	1,256	650.00	1250.	1750.	2350.
	1803	837 pcs.	650.00	1350.	2350.	3000.
	1804	—	650.00	1300.	2000.	2500.
	1805	Inc. C49	650.00	1250.	1750.	2350.

Hamburg / GERMAN STATES   628

Rev. leg: . . . .D.G.R.IMP. . .

KM#	Date	Mintage	Fine	VF	XF	Unc
228.2	1804	1,072	650.00	1250.	1750.	2350.
(C50a)	1806	1,201	650.00	1250.	1750.	2350.

240	1808	1,250	500.00	1000.	1500.	2000.
(C54)	1809	1,250	500.00	1000.	1500.	2000.
	1810	1,050	500.00	1000.	1500.	2000.

5 DUCATS
(1/2 Portugaloser)

17.5000 g, .986 GOLD, .5548 oz AGW

234	1801	—	700.00	1000.	1500.

HANNOVER
KINGDOM

A state located in northwest Germany which became Hannover when Ernst August of Brunswick-Luneberg chose the title of Elector of Hannover after his capital city. During the Napoleonic wars it was first occupied by Prussia and then incorporated into the Kingdom of Westphalia. In 1814 it was raised to the status of a Kingdom. Hannover was absorbed by Prussia in 1866.

RULERS
George III, 1760-1820
Georg IV, 1820-1830
Wilhelm IV, 1830-1837
Ernst August, 1837-1851
Georg V, 1851-1866

MINT MARKS
A - Clausthal, 1832-1849
C - Clausthal, 1814-1833

MINTMASTER'S INITIALS
Letter	Date	Name
B	1817-1838	Ludwig August Bruel
B	1844-1868	Theodor Wilhelm Bruel
CHH,H	1802-1817	Christian Heinrich Haase
LAB,LB	1817-1838	Ludwig August Bruel
S	1839-1844	Carl Schulter

PFENNIG

 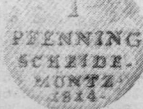

COPPER
Obv: H below crowned GR monogram.

KM#	Date	Mintage	Fine	VF	XF	Unc
103.1 (C1)	1814H	—	3.00	5.00	15.00	50.00

Obv: C below crowned monogram.

103.2 (C1b)	1814C	—	3.00	5.00	15.00	50.00

104 (C1a)	1814C	—	1.00	3.00	7.00	40.00
	1817C	—	1.00	3.00	7.00	40.00
	1818C	—	1.00	3.00	7.00	40.00
	1819C	—	1.00	3.00	7.00	40.00
	1820C	—	1.00	3.00	7.00	40.00

125.1 (C17)	1821C	—	1.00	3.00	7.00	25.00
	1822C	—	1.00	3.00	7.00	25.00
	1823C	—	1.00	3.00	7.00	25.00
	1824C	—	1.00	3.00	7.00	25.00
	1825C	—	1.00	3.00	7.00	25.00
	1826C	—	1.00	3.00	7.00	25.00
	1827 w/o mint mark	—	1.00	3.00	7.00	25.00
	1827C	—	1.00	3.00	7.00	25.00
	1828C	—	1.00	3.00	7.00	25.00
	1829C	—	1.00	3.00	7.00	25.00
	1830C	—	1.00	3.00	7.00	25.00

Rev: B below value.

125.2 (C17a)	1826B	—	1.00	3.00	7.00	25.00
	1828B	—	1.00	3.00	7.00	25.00
	1829B	—	1.00	3.00	7.00	25.00
	1830B	—	1.00	3.00	7.00	25.00

Obv: Date below crowned WR monogram.
Rev: A below value.

150.1 (C35.1)	1832A	—	1.00	3.00	7.00	30.00
	1833A	—	1.00	3.00	7.00	30.00
	1834A	—	1.00	3.00	7.00	30.00

Rev: B below value.

150.2 (C35.2)	1832B	—	1.00	3.00	7.00	30.00
	1833B	—	1.00	3.00	7.00	30.00
	1834B	—	1.00	3.00	7.00	30.00
	1835B	—	1.00	3.00	7.00	30.00

Rev: C below value.

150.3 (C35.3)	1831/30C	—	1.50	4.00	8.50	35.00
	1831C	—	1.00	3.00	7.00	30.00
	1832C	—	1.00	3.00	7.00	30.00
	1833C	—	1.00	3.00	7.00	30.00

Obv: IV below WR monogram.

156 (C35a)	1834A	—	3.00	5.00	15.00	75.00

Obv: Crowned shield w/prancing horse.
Rev: A below value.

166.1 (C36.1)	1835A	—	1.00	3.00	7.00	30.00
	1836A	—	1.00	3.00	7.00	30.00
	1837A	—	1.00	3.00	7.00	30.00

Rev: B below value.

KM#	Date	Mintage	Fine	VF	XF	Unc
166.2 (C36.2)	1835B	—	1.00	3.00	7.00	30.00
	1836B	—	1.00	3.00	7.00	30.00
	1837B	—	1.00	3.00	7.00	30.00

Obv: Crowned EAR monogram. Rev: A below value.

173.1 (C56.1)	1837A	—	1.00	3.00	7.00	30.00
	1838A	—	1.00	3.00	7.00	30.00
	1839A	—	1.00	3.00	7.00	30.00
	1840A	—	1.00	3.00	7.00	30.00
	1841A	—	1.00	3.00	7.00	30.00
	1842A	—	1.00	3.00	7.00	30.00
	1843A	—	1.00	3.00	7.00	30.00
	1844A	—	1.00	3.00	7.00	30.00
	1845A	—	1.00	3.00	7.00	30.00
	1846A	—	1.00	3.00	7.00	30.00

Rev: B below value.

173.2 (C56.2)	1838B	—	2.00	7.00	20.00	75.00

Rev: S below value.

173.3 (C56.3)	1839S	—	2.00	7.00	20.00	75.00
	1841S	—	2.00	7.00	20.00	75.00
	1842S	—	2.00	7.00	20.00	75.00

Obv: Date below monogram. Rev: SCHEIDEMUNZE below value, B mint mark.

176 (C56a)	1838B	—	20.00	40.00	75.00	150.00

King's Visit to Clausthal Mint

183 (C58)	ND(1839)	—	35.00	70.00	140.00	225.00

Rev: B below value.

201.1 (C59.1)	1845B	—	1.00	2.00	4.00	20.00
	1846B	—	1.00	2.00	4.00	20.00
	1847B	—	1.00	2.00	4.00	20.00
	1848B	—	1.00	2.00	4.00	20.00
	1849B	—	1.00	2.00	4.00	20.00
	1850B	—	1.00	2.00	4.00	20.00
	1851B	—	1.00	2.00	4.00	20.00

Rev: A below value.

201.2 (C59.2)	1846A	—	1.00	2.00	4.00	20.00
	1847A	—	1.00	2.00	4.00	20.00
	1848A	—	1.00	2.00	4.00	20.00
	1849A	—	1.00	2.00	4.00	20.00

Obv: V below monogram.

216 (C83)	1852B	—	15.00	30.00	60.00	125.00

221 (C84)	1853B	—	1.00	2.00	3.00	30.00
	1854B	—	1.00	2.00	3.00	30.00
	1855B	—	1.00	2.00	3.00	30.00
	1856B	—	1.00	2.00	3.00	20.00

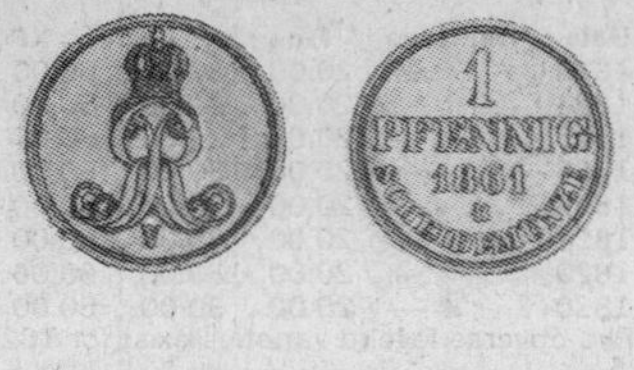

KM#	Date	Mintage	Fine	VF	XF	Unc
233 (C85)	1858B	—	1.00	2.00	3.00	20.00
	1859B	—	1.00	2.00	3.00	20.00
	1860B	—	1.00	2.00	3.00	20.00
	1861B	—	1.00	2.00	3.00	20.00
	1862B	—	1.00	2.00	3.00	20.00
	1863B	2.324	1.00	2.00	3.00	20.00
	1864B	—	1.00	2.00	3.00	20.00

2 PFENNIG

COPPER

Obv: Crowned GR monogram, date below. Rev: Value.

115 (C2)	1817C	—	5.00	10.00	25.00	100.00
	1818C	—	5.00	10.00	25.00	100.00
126.1 (C18)	1821C	—	2.00	4.00	7.00	50.00
	1822C	—	2.00	4.00	7.00	50.00
	1823C	—	2.00	4.00	7.00	50.00
	1824C	—	2.00	4.00	7.00	50.00
	1825C	—	2.00	4.00	7.00	50.00
	1826C	—	2.00	4.00	7.00	50.00
	1827C	—	2.00	4.00	7.00	50.00
	1828C	—	2.00	4.00	7.00	50.00
	1829C	—	2.00	4.00	7.00	50.00
	1830C	—	2.00	4.00	7.00	50.00

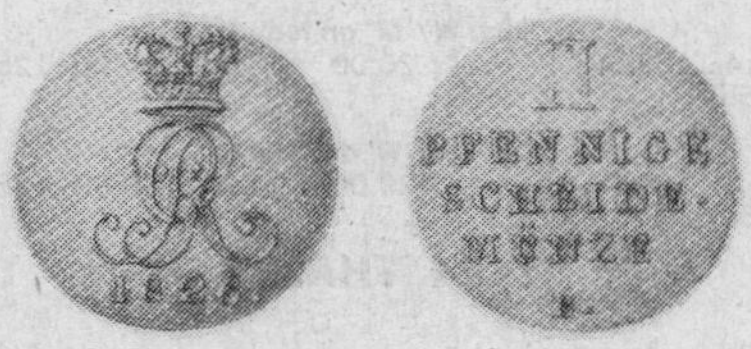

Rev: B below value.

126.2 (C18a)	1826B	.154	2.00	5.00	10.00	70.00

Obv: Crowned WR monogram above date. Rev: C below value.

147.1 (C37.1)	1831C	—	2.00	4.00	7.00	70.00
	1833C	—	2.00	4.00	7.00	70.00
	1834C	—	2.00	4.00	7.00	70.00

Rev: A below value.

147.2 (C37.2)	1834A	—	3.00	7.00	20.00	70.00

Obv: IV below monogram. Rev: Date.

157 (C37a)	1834A	—	3.00	7.00	20.00	70.00

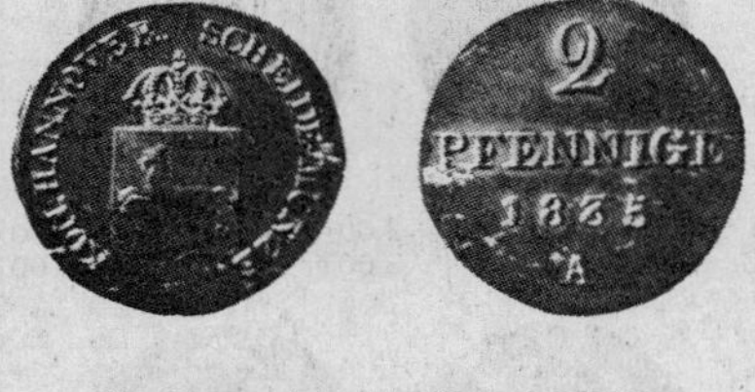

Obv: Crowned shield w/prancing horse.

167.1 (C38)	1835A	—	2.00	5.00	7.00	70.00
	1836A	—	2.00	5.00	7.00	70.00
	1837A	—	2.00	5.00	10.00	70.00

Pearl border

167.2 (C38a)	1837A	—	3.00	7.00	20.00	100.00

Obv: Crowned EAR monogram. Rev: Value, A below date.

174.1 (C60.1)	1837A	—	1.00	3.00	7.00	40.00
	1838A	—	1.00	3.00	7.00	40.00
	1839A	—	1.00	3.00	7.00	40.00
	1840A	—	1.00	3.00	7.00	40.00
	1841A	—	1.00	3.00	7.00	40.00
	1842A	—	1.00	3.00	7.00	40.00
	1843A	—	1.00	3.00	7.00	40.00
	1844A	—	1.00	3.00	7.00	40.00
	1845A	—	1.00	3.00	7.00	40.00
	1846A	—	1.00	3.00	7.00	40.00

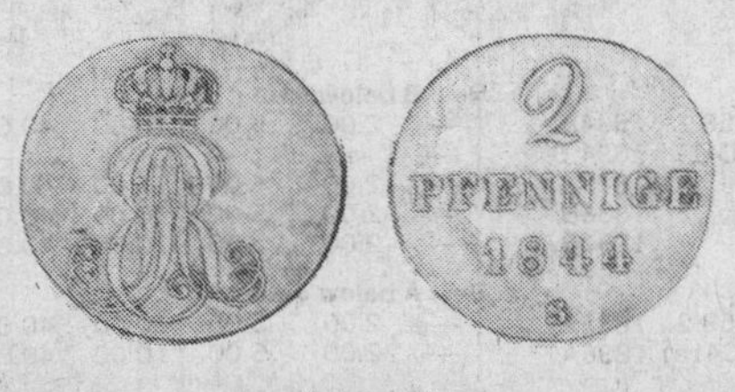

Rev: S below date.

174.2 (C60.2)	1842S	—	2.00	6.00	15.00	65.00
	1844S	—	2.00	6.00	15.00	65.00

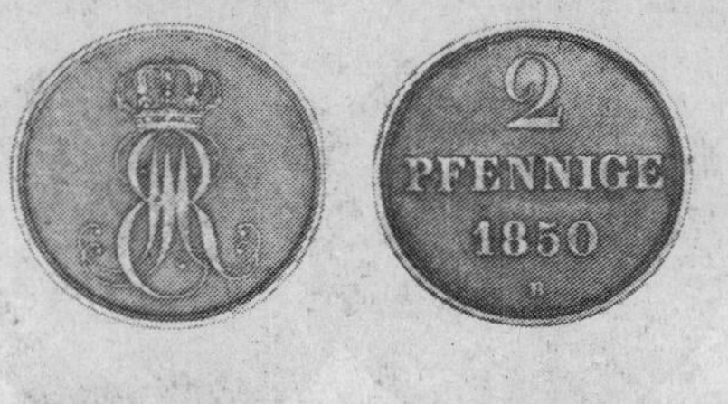

Rev: B below date, struck in a ring.

KM#	Date	Mintage	Fine	VF	XF	Unc
202.1 (C61.1)	1845B	—	1.00	2.00	5.00	30.00
	1846B	—	1.00	2.00	5.00	30.00
	1847B	—	1.00	2.00	5.00	30.00
	1848B	—	1.00	2.00	5.00	30.00
	1849B	—	1.00	2.00	5.00	30.00
	1850B	—	1.00	2.00	5.00	30.00
	1851B	—	1.00	2.00	5.00	30.00

Rev: A below date.

202.2 (C61.2)	1846A	—	1.00	2.00	5.00	30.00
	1847A	—	1.00	2.00	5.00	30.00
	1848A	—	1.00	2.00	5.00	30.00
	1849A	—	1.00	2.00	5.00	30.00

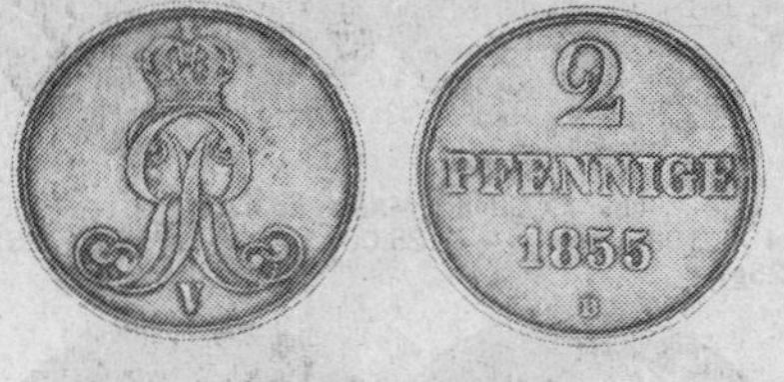

Rev: B below date.

217 (C86)	1852B	—	1.00	2.00	4.00	30.00
	1853B	—	1.00	2.00	4.00	30.00
	1854B	—	1.00	2.00	4.00	30.00
	1855B	—	1.00	2.00	4.00	30.00
	1856B	—	1.00	2.00	4.00	30.00

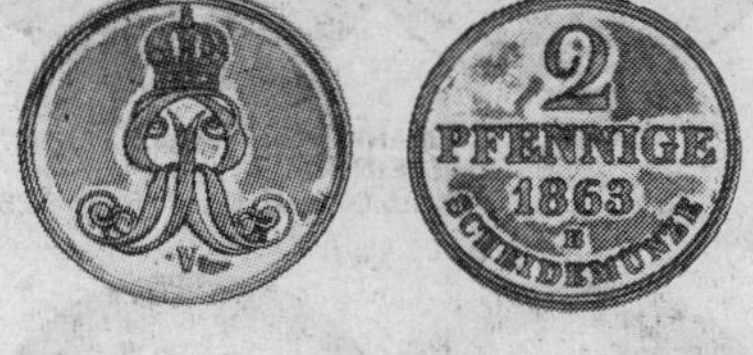

234 (C87)	1858B	—	1.00	2.00	4.00	30.00
	1859B	—	1.00	2.00	4.00	30.00
	1860B	—	1.00	2.00	4.00	30.00
	1861B	—	1.00	2.00	4.00	30.00
	1862B	—	1.00	2.00	4.00	30.00
	1863B	.607	1.00	2.00	4.00	30.00
	1864B	—	1.00	2.00	4.00	30.00

4 PFENNIG

(1/2 Mariengroschen)

1.2300 g, .187 SILVER, .0073 oz ASW
Obv. C below crowned GR monogram.
Rev. leg: NACH DEM REICHS FUSS

105.1 (C3.1)	1814C	—	7.50	15.00	30.00	75.00
	1815C	—	7.50	15.00	30.00	75.00

Obv: H below monogram.

105.2 (C3.2)	1815H.	—	7.50	15.00	30.00	75.00
	1816H.	—	7.50	15.00	30.00	75.00

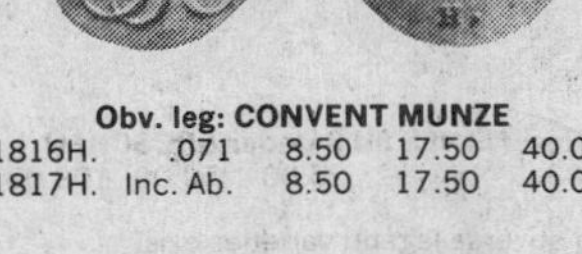

Obv. leg: CONVENT MUNZE

112 (C3a)	1816H.	.071	8.50	17.50	40.00	100.00
	1817H.	Inc. Ab.	8.50	17.50	40.00	100.00

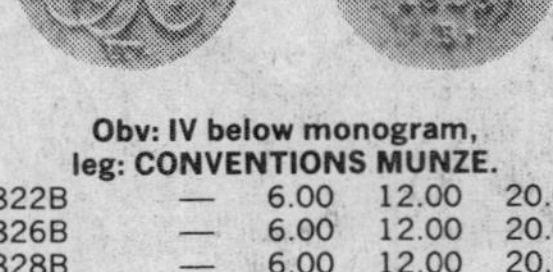

Obv: IV below monogram,
leg: CONVENTIONS MUNZE.

135 (C20)	1822B	—	6.00	12.00	20.00	50.00
	1826B	—	6.00	12.00	20.00	50.00
	1828B	—	6.00	12.00	20.00	50.00
	1830B	—	6.00	12.00	20.00	50.00

COPPER
Obv: Date below monogram.
Rev: C below SCHEIDEMUNZE.

143 (C19)	1827C	—	50.00	90.00	150.00	350.00

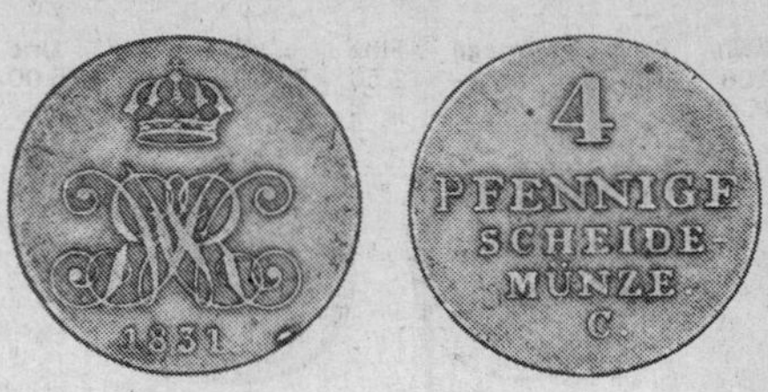

KM#	Date	Mintage	Fine	VF	XF	Unc
148 (C39)	1831C	—	50.00	85.00	140.00	325.00

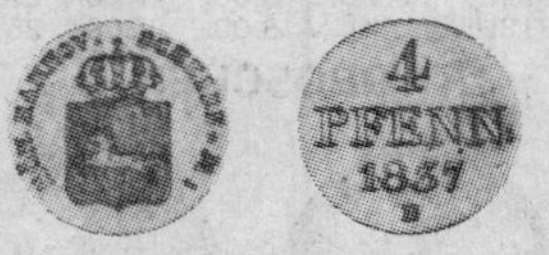

.9200 g, .218 SILVER, .0064 oz ASW
Rev: B below date.

168 (C40)	1835B	—	2.00	3.00	7.00	30.00
	1836B	—	2.00	3.00	7.00	30.00
	1837B	—	2.00	3.00	7.00	30.00
177.1 (C62.1)	1838B	—	2.00	3.00	7.00	30.00

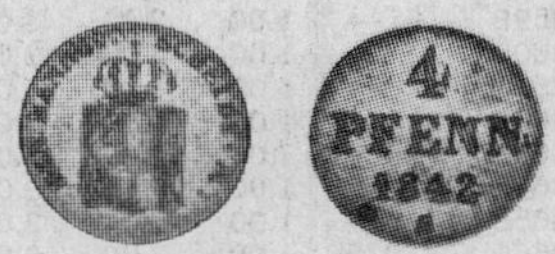

Rev: S below date.

177.2 (C62.2)	1840S	—	2.00	3.00	7.00	30.00
	1841S	—	2.00	3.00	7.00	30.00
	1842S	—	2.00	3.00	7.00	30.00

6 PFENNIG

1.3900 g, .218 SILVER, .0097 oz ASW
Obv: Crowned shield w/prancing horse.
Rev: S below value.

198.1 (C63.1)	1843S	—	3.00	7.00	15.00	50.00
	1844S	—	3.00	7.00	15.00	50.00

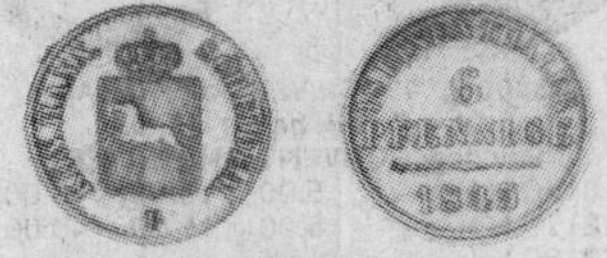

Rev: B below shield.

198.2 (C63.2)	1844B	—	3.00	7.00	15.00	40.00
	1845B	—	3.00	7.00	15.00	40.00
	1846B	—	3.00	7.00	15.00	40.00

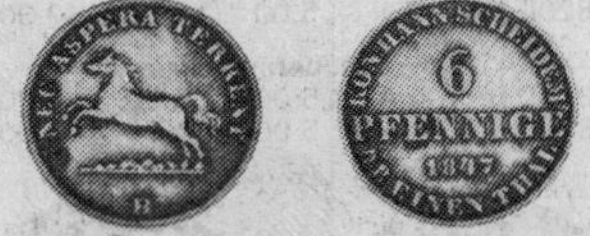

205 (C64)	1846B	—	1.00	3.00	5.00	25.00
	1847B	—	1.00	3.00	5.00	25.00
	1848B	—	1.00	3.00	5.00	25.00
	1849B	—	1.00	3.00	5.00	25.00
	1850B	—	1.00	3.00	5.00	25.00
	1851B	—	1.00	3.00	5.00	25.00

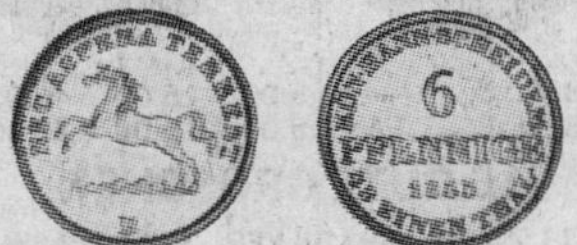

218 (C88)	1852B	—	1.00	3.00	6.00	30.00
	1853B	—	1.00	3.00	6.00	30.00
	1854B	—	1.00	3.00	6.00	30.00
	1855B	—	1.00	3.00	6.00	30.00

1/2 GROSCHEN

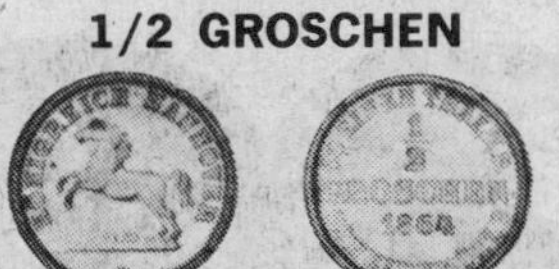

1.0900 g, .220 SILVER, .0077 oz ASW

235 (C89)	1858B	—	1.00	2.00	4.00	25.00
	1859B	—	1.00	2.00	4.00	25.00
	1861B	—	1.00	2.00	4.00	25.00
	1862B	—	1.00	2.00	4.00	25.00
	1863B	.047	1.00	2.00	4.00	25.00
	1864B	—	1.00	2.00	4.00	25.00
	1865B	—	1.00	2.00	4.00	25.00

MARIENGROSCHEN

(1/36 Thaler)

1.4800 g, .312 SILVER, .0148 oz ASW
Obv: C below crowned GR monogram.
Rev: Value, leg: NACH DEM REICHFUSS.

KM#	Date	Mintage	Fine	VF	XF	Unc
106 (C4)	1814C	—	12.50	30.00	70.00	175.00

Rev: H below date.

113 (C4a)	1816H	.443	3.00	7.00	25.00	75.00
	1817H	Inc. Ab.	3.00	7.00	25.00	75.00
	1818H	Inc. Ab.	3.00	7.00	25.00	75.00

GROSCHEN

2.1900 g, .220 SILVER, .0154 oz ASW

236 (C91)	1858B	—	1.00	2.00	3.00	25.00
	1859B	—	1.00	2.00	3.00	25.00
	1860B	—	1.00	2.00	3.00	25.00
	1861B	—	1.00	2.00	3.00	25.00
	1862B	—	1.00	2.00	3.00	25.00
	1863B	.069	1.00	2.00	3.00	25.00
	1864B	—	1.00	2.00	3.00	25.00
	1865B	—	1.00	2.00	3.00	25.00
	1866B	.076	1.00	2.00	3.00	25.00

3 MARIENGROSCHEN

3.3400 g, .437 SILVER, .0469 oz ASW
Obv: C.H.H. below ledge.
Rev. leg: CONVENTIONSMUNZE

114.1 (C8.1)	1816C.H.H.	—	5.00	15.00	40.00	100.00
	1817C.H.H.	—	5.00	15.00	40.00	100.00
	1818C.H.H.	12.000	5.00	15.00	40.00	100.00

Obv: .L.A.B. below ledge.

114.2 (C8.2)	1819L.A.B.	—	5.00	15.00	40.00	100.00
	1820L.A.B.	I.A.	5.00	15.00	40.00	100.00

Obv: L.B. below ledge.

114.3 (C8.3)	1819L.B.	I.A.	5.00	15.00	40.00	100.00
	1820L.B.	—	5.00	15.00	40.00	100.00

120 (C22)	1820L.B.	—	5.00	15.00	40.00	100.00
	1821L.B.	I.A.	5.00	15.00	40.00	100.00

16 GUTE GROSCHEN

11.7700 g, .993 SILVER, .3758 oz ASW
Obv: Prancing horse w/M on ledge,
leg: GEORGIUS.III.D.G.BRITAN.&.HANNOV.REX.

121.1 (C11)	1820	—	90.00	150.00	250.00	425.00

Obv. leg: GEORGIUS.III.D.G.BRITANNIARUM.

121.2 (C11a)	1820	—	90.00	150.00	250.00	425.00

Obv: Prancing horse, M on ledge XX.EINE.F.MARK. below,
leg: GEORGIUS.IV.D.G.BRITAN.& HANNOV.REX.
Rev: Value, CONVENTIONS-MUNZE. below.

122 (C25)	1820	—	30.00	60.00	100.00	165.00

Obv: XX.E.F. MARK below ledge.
Rev. leg: CONV-MUNZE FEIN SILBER.

KM#	Date	Mintage	Fine	VF	XF	Unc
123 (C25b)	1820	—	30.00	55.00	90.00	150.00

Obv: XX.EINE.F.MARK. below ledge.

124 (C25g)	1820	—	25.00	45.00	75.00	125.00

Obv: XX.E.F.MARK. below ledge.
Rev: FEIN SILB.

127 (C25c)	1821	—	25.00	45.00	75.00	125.00

Rev: CONV MUNZE FEIN SILB around bottom.

128 (C25d)	1821	—	25.00	50.00	100.00	175.00

NOTE: Seven obverse legend varieties exist.

Rev: FEINES SILB under GROSCHEN.

136 (C25a)	1822	—	25.00	50.00	100.00	175.00

NOTE: Two obverse legend varieties exist.

137 (C25e)	1822	—	25.00	50.00	100.00	175.00

NOTE: Two obverse legend varieties exist.

138	1822	—	20.00	30.00	60.00	125.00

KM#	Date	Mintage	Fine	VF	XF	Unc
(C25f)	1823	—	20.00	30.00	60.00	125.00
	1824	—	20.00	30.00	60.00	125.00
	1825	—	20.00	30.00	60.00	125.00
	1826	—	20.00	30.00	60.00	125.00
	1827	—	20.00	30.00	60.00	125.00
	1828	—	20.00	30.00	60.00	125.00
	1829	—	20.00	30.00	60.00	125.00
	1830	—	20.00	30.00	60.00	125.00

NOTE: Two obverse legend varieties exist for 1822, 1823 and 1825.

145.1 (C45)	1830	—	20.00	30.00	60.00	125.00

145.2 (C45)	1831	—	20.00	30.00	60.00	125.00
	1832	—	20.00	30.00	60.00	125.00
	1832A	—	20.00	30.00	60.00	125.00

Obv: W/'L' on ledge.

145.3 (C45a)	1832A	—	20.00	30.00	60.00	125.00
	1833A	—	20.00	30.00	60.00	125.00
	1834A	—	20.00	30.00	60.00	125.00

Obv: W/'M' on ledge.

145.4 (C45b)	1832A	—	20.00	30.00	60.00	125.00

Obv: W/'W' on ledge.

145.5 (C45c)	1834A	—	20.00	30.00	60.00	125.00

1/24 THALER

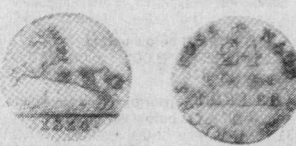

1.9400 g, .312 SILVER, .0194 oz ASW
Obv: Date below prancing horse.
Rev. value, leg: NACH DEM REICHFUSS.

107 (C5)	1814C	—	3.00	7.00	20.00	100.00

116 (C6)	1817H	.946	3.00	7.00	20.00	100.00
	1818	—	3.00	7.00	20.00	100.00

Obv: IV below monogram.

141 (C21)	1826B	.139	3.00	6.00	15.00	60.00
	1827B	.328	3.00	6.00	15.00	60.00
	1828B	.904	3.00	6.00	15.00	60.00

Rev: B below date.

158.1 (C41)	1834B	—	2.00	5.00	10.00	40.00
	1834.B.	—	—	—	—	—
	1835B	—	2.00	5.00	10.00	40.00
	1836B	—	2.00	5.00	10.00	40.00
	1837B	—	2.00	5.00	10.00	40.00

Rev: A below date.

158.2 (C41a)	1835A	—	2.00	5.00	10.00	40.00
	1836A	—	2.00	5.00	10.00	40.00

Rev: B below date.

178.1 (C65.1)	1838B	—	2.00	5.00	10.00	40.00

Rev: S below date.

KM#	Date	Mintage	Fine	VF	XF	Unc
178.2	1839S	—	2.00	4.00	10.00	40.00
(C65.2)	1841S	—	2.00	4.00	10.00	40.00
	1842S	—	2.00	4.00	10.00	40.00

Rev: A below date.

178.3	1839A	—	2.00	4.00	10.00	40.00
(C65.3)	1840A	—	2.00	4.00	10.00	40.00
	1841A	—	2.00	4.00	10.00	40.00
	1842A	—	2.00	4.00	10.00	40.00
	1843A	—	2.00	4.00	10.00	40.00
	1844A	—	2.00	4.00	10.00	40.00
	1845A	—	2.00	4.00	10.00	40.00
	1846A	—	2.00	4.00	10.00	40.00

Obv: B below prancing horse. Rev: Value, SCHEIDEMUNZE.

203	1845B	—	1.00	3.00	7.00	40.00
(C65.4)	1846B	—	1.00	3.00	7.00	40.00

Obv. leg: NEC ASPERA TERRENT.

227	1854B	—	1.00	3.00	7.00	40.00
(C90)	1855B	—	1.00	3.00	7.00	40.00
	1856B	—	1.00	3.00	7.00	40.00

1/12 THALER
(3 Mariengroschen)

3.2400 g, .437 SILVER, .0455 oz ASW
Obv: Prancing horse, S on ledge.
Rev: Value, leg: NACH DEM REICHS FUSS.

108	1814C	—	5.00	15.00	40.00	100.00
(C7)	1815C	—	5.00	15.00	40.00	100.00
	1816C	—	5.00	15.00	40.00	100.00

139	1822L.B.	1.908	5.00	15.00	40.00	100.00
(C23)	1823L.B.	1.900	5.00	15.00	40.00	100.00
	1823LB Inc. Ab.		5.00	15.00	40.00	100.00
	1824L.B.	.502	5.00	15.00	40.00	100.00

2.6700 g, .520 SILVER, .0446 oz ASW
Obv: B below head.

159	1834B	—	5.00	15.00	40.00	100.00
(C43)	1835B	—	5.00	15.00	40.00	100.00
	1836B	—	5.00	15.00	40.00	100.00
	1837B	—	5.00	15.00	40.00	100.00
179.1	1838B	—	5.00	15.00	40.00	100.00
(C66.1)						

Obv: S below head.

179.2	1839S	—	5.00	15.00	40.00	100.00
(C66.2)	1840S	—	5.00	15.00	40.00	100.00

194.1	1841S	—	3.00	5.00	15.00	60.00
(C66a)	1842S	—	3.00	5.00	15.00	60.00
	1843S	—	3.00	5.00	15.00	60.00
	1844S	—	3.00	5.00	15.00	60.00

Obv: B below head.

KM#	Date	Mintage	Fine	VF	XF	Unc
194.2	1844B	—	3.00	5.00	15.00	40.00
(C66b)	1845B	—	3.00	5.00	15.00	40.00
	1846B	—	3.00	5.00	15.00	40.00
	1847B	—	3.00	5.00	15.00	40.00

Obv: Larger head.

206	1848B	—	3.00	5.00	15.00	40.00
(C66c)	1849B	—	3.00	5.00	15.00	40.00
	1850B	—	3.00	5.00	15.00	40.00
	1851B	—	3.00	5.00	15.00	40.00

Obv: BREHMER F at truncation.

219	1852B	—	3.00	5.00	15.00	40.00
(C92)	1853B	—	3.00	5.00	15.00	40.00

3.2200 g, .375 SILVER, .0388 oz ASW
Obv: W/o name at truncation.
Rev: value: SCHEIDEMUNZE.

237	1859B	—	3.00	5.00	15.00	40.00
(C93)	1860B	—	3.00	5.00	15.00	40.00
	1862B	—	3.00	5.00	15.00	40.00

1/6 THALER

5.8500 g, .500 SILVER, .0940 oz ASW
Obv: B below ledge.

129	1821B	.150	15.00	30.00	75.00	225.00
(C24)						

5.3500 g, .520 SILVER, .0895 oz ASW

160	1834	.360	20.00	40.00	75.00	200.00
(C44)						

Obv: S below larger head.
Rev: Crowned arms on cartouche.

190	1840S	.457	20.00	40.00	75.00	225.00
(C67)						

Rev: Shield w/square corners.

195	1841S Inc. Ab.	20.00	40.00	75.00	200.00
(C67a)					

199	1844B Inc. Ab.	20.00	40.00	75.00	250.00
(C67b)	1845B Inc. Ab.	20.00	40.00	75.00	250.00
	1847B Inc. Ab.	20.00	40.00	75.00	250.00

5.3400 g, .520 SILVER, .0893 oz ASW

238	1859B	—	12.00	20.00	35.00	65.00
(C94)	1860B	—	12.00	20.00	35.00	65.00
	1862B	—	12.00	20.00	35.00	65.00
	1863B	.087	12.00	20.00	35.00	65.00
	1866B	5,904	30.00	50.00	90.00	165.00

2/3 THALER

13.0800 g, .993 SILVER, .4176 oz ASW

KM#	Date	Mintage	Fine	VF	XF	Unc
100.1	1813C	—	45.00	100.00	150.00	250.00
(C10)	1814C	—	45.00	100.00	150.00	250.00

Obv: M below truncation.

100.2	1814	—	50.00	110.00	175.00	275.00
(C10a)						

140	1822C	—	40.00	80.00	120.00	250.00
(C26)	1823C	—	40.00	80.00	120.00	250.00
	1824C	—	40.00	80.00	120.00	250.00
	1825C	—	40.00	80.00	120.00	250.00
	1826C	—	40.00	80.00	120.00	250.00
	1827C	—	40.00	80.00	120.00	250.00
	1828C	—	40.00	80.00	120.00	250.00
	1829C	—	40.00	80.00	120.00	250.00

NOTE: Several varieties exist.

17.3200 g, .750 SILVER, .4177 oz ASW
Rev. value: 18 STUCK EINE MARK FEIN.

142	1826B	—	55.00	125.00	250.00	450.00
(C26a)	1827B	—	55.00	125.00	250.00	450.00
	1828B	—	55.00	125.00	250.00	450.00

13.0800 g, .993 SILVER, .4176 oz ASW
Obv: Ribbon inscribed
HONI SOIT QUI MAL Y PENSE.

151	1832	—	37.50	80.00	135.00	225.00
(C46)	1833	—	37.50	80.00	135.00	225.00

Rev: Similar to KM#151.

154	1833A	.050	140.00	250.00	400.00	650.00
(C46.5)						

Hannover / GERMAN STATES

KM#	Date	Mintage	Fine	VF	XF	Unc
161.1 (C47)	1834A	Inc. Ab.	135.00	250.00	375.00	575.00

Obv. and rev: Raised edge and circle of dots around legend. Struck in collar.

| 161.2 (C47a) | 1834A | Inc. Ab. | — | — | — | — |

Obv: Similar to KM#161.1.

| 162 (C47b) | 1834A | Inc. Ab. | 650.00 | 900.00 | 1250. | 1750. |

Rev: AUSBEUTE DER GRUBE

| 163 (C48) | 1834A | Inc. Ab. | 1350. | 2000. | 3000. | 4500. |

Obv: Different head right, A below.

| 180 (C68a) | 1838A | — | 50.00 | 110.00 | 250.00 | 375.00 |
| | 1839A | — | 50.00 | 110.00 | 250.00 | 375.00 |

THALER

23.5400 g, .993 SILVER, .7516 oz ASW

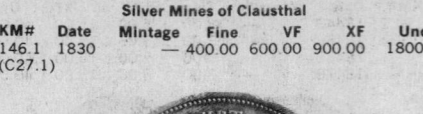

Silver Mines of Clausthal

KM#	Date	Mintage	Fine	VF	XF	Unc
146.1 (C27.1)	1830	—	400.00	600.00	900.00	1800.

Rev: Flat 3 in date.

| 146.2 (C27.2) | 1830 | — | 400.00 | 600.00 | 900.00 | 1800. |

22.2700 g, .750 SILVER, .5370 oz ASW

| 164 (C49) | 1834B | .044 | 40.00 | 115.00 | 350.00 | 1000. |

16.8200 g, .993 SILVER, .5370 oz ASW
Obv: Similar to KM#164, A below head.

| 165 (C50) | 1834A | — | 45.00 | 100.00 | 325.00 | 850.00 |
| | 1835A | — | 45.00 | 90.00 | 250.00 | 700.00 |

Obv: Similar to KM#164.

169 (C49a)	1835A	—	70.00	100.00	375.00	900.00
	1836A	—	30.00	50.00	150.00	450.00
	1837A	—	30.00	50.00	150.00	450.00

22.2700 g, .750 SILVER, .5370 oz ASW
Rev: Similar to KM#169.

| 172 (C49b) | 1836B | — | 70.00 | 100.00 | 300.00 | 800.00 |

16.8200 g, .993 SILVER, .5370 oz ASW

KM#	Date	Mintage	Fine	VF	XF	Unc
181 (C69)	1838A	—	35.00	75.00	185.00	475.00
	1839A	—	35.00	75.00	185.00	475.00

Rev: Similar to KM#181.

182 (C69a)	1838A	—	35.00	75.00	185.00	475.00
	1839A	—	35.00	75.00	185.00	475.00
	1840A	—	45.00	90.00	225.00	600.00

King's Visit to Clausthal Mint
Obv: Similar to KM#182.

| 184 (C70) | 1839A | — | 125.00 | 225.00 | 375.00 | 600.00 |

Obv: Similar to KM#182.
Rev. leg: FEINES---SILBER

| 191 (C71) | 1840A | — | — | — | — | Rare |

Obv: Similar to KM#182.

| 192 (C71a) | 1840A | — | 40.00 | 70.00 | 175.00 | 400.00 |
| | 1841A | — | 40.00 | 70.00 | 175.00 | 400.00 |

Obv: S below truncation.

Hannover / GERMAN STATES 633

Rev: Similar to KM#192.

KM#	Date	Mintage	Fine	VF	XF	Unc
193 (C71b)	1840S	—	75.00	150.00	500.00	1300.

Obv: BRANDT F. at truncation.
Rev: Similar to KM#192.

| 196 (C71c) | 1841S | — | 40.00 | 80.00 | 200.00 | 625.00 |

Obv: A below head.
Rev: Similar to KM#192.

197.1 (C71d)	1842A	.620	20.00	40.00	135.00	325.00
	1843A	.638	25.00	50.00	175.00	400.00
	1844A	.622	25.00	50.00	175.00	400.00
	1845A	.656	25.00	50.00	175.00	400.00
	1846A	.650	25.00	50.00	175.00	400.00
	1847A	.625	20.00	40.00	135.00	325.00
	1848A	.661	20.00	40.00	135.00	325.00
	1849A	.357	25.00	50.00	175.00	400.00

Obv: B below head.

197.2 (C71e)	1844B	—	45.00	85.00	200.00	550.00
	1845B	—	25.00	50.00	135.00	350.00
	1846B	—	45.00	85.00	200.00	550.00
	1847B	—	45.00	85.00	200.00	550.00

Wedding of Crown Prince Georg of Hannover and
Duchess Marie of Sachsen-Altenburg

| 207 (C73) | 1843S | 1,010 | 150.00 | 300.00 | 500.00 | 900.00 |

Obv: BREHMER F. at truncation.

| 208 (C72) | 1848B | — | 25.00 | 50.00 | 150.00 | 300.00 |
| | 1849B | — | 25.00 | 50.00 | 150.00 | 300.00 |

Rev: HARZ SEGEN above crown.

KM#	Date	Mintage	Fine	VF	XF	Unc
209.1 (C74)	1849	—	50.00	125.00	300.00	850.00

Rev: BERGSEGEN DES HARZES above crown.

| 209.2 (C74a) | 1850B | .712 | 25.00 | 50.00 | 100.00 | 200.00 |
| | 1851B | .453 | 25.00 | 50.00 | 100.00 | 200.00 |

Rev: Similar to KM#209.2.

220 (C95)	1852B	.170	25.00	50.00	100.00	200.00
	1853B	.180	25.00	50.00	100.00	200.00
	1854/3B	—	—	—	—	—
	1854B	.951	25.00	50.00	100.00	200.00
	1855B	.974	25.00	50.00	100.00	200.00
	1856B	.077	25.00	50.00	100.00	200.00

Visit of Royal Family to Mint
Obv: Similar to KM#220.

| 222 (C96) | 1853B | — | 1500. | 2500. | 3500. | 4800. |

18.5200 g, .900 SILVER, .5360 oz ASW
Obv: Similar to KM#220.

230 (C97)	1857B	.274	20.00	40.00	70.00	140.00
	1858B	.432	20.00	40.00	70.00	140.00
	1859B	.554	20.00	40.00	65.00	120.00
	1860B	.790	20.00	40.00	65.00	120.00
	1861B	.736	20.00	40.00	65.00	120.00
	1862B	.133	20.00	40.00	65.00	120.00
	1863B	.233	20.00	40.00	65.00	120.00
	1864B	.158	20.00	40.00	65.00	120.00
	1865B	—	20.00	35.00	55.00	120.00
	1866B	.159	20.00	35.00	50.00	100.00

50th Anniversary of Battle of Waterloo
Obv: Similar to KM#220.

KM#	Date	Mintage	Fine	VF	XF	Unc
241 (C98)	1865B	.015	30.00	50.00	80.00	135.00

50th Anniversary of Union of East Friesia and Hannover
Obv: Similar to KM#220.

| 242 (C99) | 1865B | 1,000 | 150.00 | 225.00 | 375.00 | 600.00 |
| | 1865B | — | — | — | Proof | 550.00 |

Frisian Oath Commemorative
Obv: Similar to KM#220.

| 243 (C100) | 1865B | 2,000 | 125.00 | 200.00 | 300.00 | 500.00 |

2 THALER
(3-1/2 Gulden)

37.1200 g, .900 SILVER, 1.0742 oz ASW
Visit of Royal Family to Mint

| 228 (C101) | 1854B | — | 1250. | 2250. | 3500. | 5000. |
| | 1854B | — | — | — | Proof | 8000. |

634 Hannover / GERMAN STATES

Obv: Similar to KM#228.

KM#	Date	Mintage	Fine	VF	XF	Unc
229	1854B	.102	100.00	150.00	200.00	350.00
(C102)	1855B	.842	90.00	125.00	175.00	325.00

37.0400 g, .900 SILVER, 1.0719 oz ASW
Obv: Similar to KM#228.

240	1862B	.133	100.00	150.00	200.00	350.00
(C103)	1866B	.038	90.00	125.00	175.00	325.00

2-1/2 THALER

3.3400 g, .903 GOLD, .0970 oz AGW

109	1814C.H.H.	—	325.00	500.00	750.00	1150.
(C13)						

130	1821B	—	225.00	450.00	675.00	1100.
(C29)	1827B	—	225.00	450.00	675.00	1100.
	1830B	—	225.00	450.00	675.00	1100.

152	1832B	—	200.00	400.00	600.00	1000.
(C52)	1833B	—	200.00	400.00	600.00	1000.
	1835B	—	200.00	400.00	600.00	1000.

3.3200 g, .896 GOLD, .0956 oz AGW

152a	1836B	—	150.00	300.00	550.00	900.00
(C52a)	1837B	—	150.00	300.00	550.00	900.00

185.1	1839S	—	225.00	400.00	600.00	1000.
(C76.1)	1840S	—	225.00	400.00	600.00	1000.
	1843S	—	225.00	400.00	600.00	1000.

KM#	Date	Mintage	Fine	VF	XF	Unc
185.2	1845B	—	225.00	400.00	600.00	1000.
(C76.2)	1846B	—	225.00	400.00	600.00	1000.
	1847B	—	225.00	400.00	600.00	1000.
	1848B	—	225.00	400.00	600.00	1000.

215	1850B	—	200.00	300.00	500.00	900.00
(C77)						

Obv: BREHMER F. at truncation, B below.

223	1853B	—	250.00	500.00	1000.	1500.
(C104)	1855B	—	175.00	350.00	700.00	1000.

5 THALER

6.6500 g, .896 GOLD, .1916 oz AGW

101	1813TW	—	250.00	425.00	750.00	1500.
(C14)	1814TW	—	250.00	425.00	750.00	1500.
	1815TW	—	275.00	500.00	875.00	1750.

6.6800 g, .903 GOLD, .1940 oz AGW

110	1814C	—	825.00	1350.	2250.	3250.
(C15)	1815C	—			Rare	

131	1821C	185 pcs.	1500.	2500.	4000.	6000.
(C30)						

132	1821B	—	250.00	450.00	700.00	1000.
(C31)	1825B	—	250.00	450.00	700.00	1000.
	1828B	—	250.00	450.00	700.00	1000.
	1829B	—	250.00	450.00	700.00	1000.
	1830B	—	250.00	450.00	700.00	1000.

6.6500 g, .896 GOLD, .1916 oz AGW

170	1835B	—	350.00	500.00	900.00	1500.
(C53)						

KM#	Date	Mintage	Fine	VF	XF	Unc
186	1839S	—	400.00	700.00	1200.	1800.
(C78)						

Obv: B below head.

204	1845B	—	300.00	500.00	800.00	1350.
(C79)	1846B	—	375.00	650.00	1100.	1600.
	1848B	—	375.00	650.00	1100.	1600.

210	1849B	—	325.00	525.00	800.00	1350.
(C80.1)	1851B	—	325.00	525.00	800.00	1350.

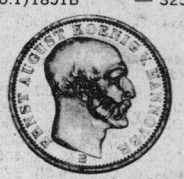

Rev. leg: HARZ GOLD added.

211	1849B	—	350.00	600.00	900.00	1400.
(C80.2)	1850B	—	325.00	525.00	800.00	1300.

Obv: BREHMER F. at truncation, B below.

224	1853B	—	300.00	500.00	800.00	1200.
(C105)	1855B	—	300.00	500.00	800.00	1200.
	1856B	—	400.00	800.00	1250.	2000.

Rev. leg: HARZ GOLD added.

225	1853B	—	500.00	875.00	1500.	2250.
(C106)	1856B	—	550.00	1150.	1850.	2650.

10 THALER

13.3600 g, .903 GOLD, .3879 oz AGW

102	1813 C.H.H.	—	1000.	1500.	2250.	3250.
(C16)	1814 C.H.H.	—	750.00	1100.	1650.	2500.

133	1821B	—	600.00	1000.	1600.	2200.
(C32)	1822B	—	475.00	800.00	1300.	1800.

KM#	Date	Mintage	Fine	VF	XF	Unc
(C32)	1823B	—	475.00	800.00	1300.	1800.
	1824B	—	475.00	800.00	1300.	1800.
	1825B	—	325.00	550.00	1100.	1600.
	1827B	—	325.00	550.00	1100.	1600.
	1828B	—	325.00	550.00	1100.	1600.
	1829B	—	325.00	550.00	1100.	1600.
	1830B	—	325.00	550.00	1100.	1600.

153	1832	—	550.00	900.00	1500.	2500.
(C54)						

155	1833	—	550.00	900.00	1500.	2500.
(C55)						

13.3000 g, .896 GOLD, .3832 oz AGW
Obv: B under head.

171	1835B	—	675.00	1150.	1900.	2650.
(C55a)	1836B	—	650.00	1125.	1875.	2600.
	1837B	—	550.00	900.00	1500.	2250.

175	1837B	—	—	—	10,000.	15,000.
(C81)	1838B	—	500.00	900.00	1500.	2250.

Obv: S below head.

187	1839S	—	400.00	600.00	1200.	2000.
(C81a)						

Obv: BRANDT F. on truncation.

200.1	1844S	—	600.00	1000.	1650.	2250.
(C82)						

Obv: B below head.

200.2	1844B	—	675.00	1150.	1850.	2500.
(C82a)						

Obv: W/o markings on truncation, leg: V. HANNOVER.

KM#	Date	Mintage	Fine	VF	XF	Unc
200.3	1846B	—	400.00	800.00	1200.	1800.
(C82b)	1847B	—	400.00	800.00	1200.	1800.
	1848B	—	300.00	600.00	900.00	1500.

Obv. leg: VON HANNOVER

212	1849B	—	500.00	1000.	1500.	2250.
(C82c)	1850B	—	350.00	600.00	1000.	1500.
	1851B	—	500.00	1000.	1500.	2250.

226	1853B	—	450.00	750.00	1250.	1750.
(C107)	1854B	—	300.00	500.00	900.00	1250.
	1855B	—	450.00	750.00	1250.	1750.
	1856B	—	500.00	900.00	1500.	2150.

TRADE COINAGE
DUCAT

3.5000 g, .986 GOLD, .1109 oz AGW

111	1815C	—	525.00	875.00	1400.	2000.
(C12)	1818C	—	600.00	1000.	1650.	2250.
134	1821C	252 pcs.	975.00	1650.	2400.	3250.
(C28)	1824C	749 pcs.	900.00	1500.	2250.	3000.
	1827C	1,300	825.00	1400.	2000.	2750.

149	1831C	1,550	750.00	1250.	1900.	2500.
(C51)						

1/2 KRONE

5.5500 g, .900 GOLD, .1606 oz AGW

231	1857B	4,105	300.00	600.00	1000.	1500.
(C108)	1858B	116 pcs.	900.00	1500.	2150.	2750.
	1859B	790 pcs.	400.00	800.00	1200.	1750.
	1862B	96 pcs.	1500.	2000.	3000.	4000.
	1864B	.013	300.00	600.00	1000.	1500.
	1866B	2,909	300.00	600.00	1000.	1500.

KRONE

11.1100 g, .900 GOLD, .3215 oz AGW

232	1857B	.145	350.00	600.00	900.00	1400.
(C109)	1858B	.047	450.00	800.00	1200.	1800.
	1859B	.020	500.00	850.00	1300.	1900.
	1860B	.015	550.00	1000.	1500.	2250.
	1861B	780 pcs.	1000.	1500.	2000.	3000.
	1862B	.020	525.00	875.00	1400.	1900.
	1863B	.126	350.00	500.00	900.00	1400.
	1864B	.014	450.00	800.00	1100.	1700.
	1866B	.383	350.00	500.00	900.00	1400.

HESSE-CASSEL
(Hessen-Kassel)

The Hesse principalities were located for the most part north of the Main River, bounded by Westphalia on the west, the Brunswick duchies on the north, the Saxon duchies on the east and Rhine Palatinate and the bishoprics of Mainz and Fulda on the south. The rule of the landgraves of Hesse began in the second half of the 13th century, the dignity of Prince of the Empire being acquired in 1292. In 1567 the patrimony was divided by four surviving sons, only those of Cassel and Darmstadt surviving for more than a generation. In Hesse-Cassel the landgrave was raised to the rank of elector in 1803. The electorate formed part of the Kingdom of Westphalia from 1806 to 1813. In 1866 Hesse-Cassel fell to Prussia.

RULERS
Wilhelm IX, 1785-1803
Wilhelm I, As Elector, 1803-1821
Wilhelm II, 1821-1847
Friedrich Wilhelm, 1847-1866

MINT MARKS
C - Cassel
(.L.) - Lippoldsberg

MINTMASTER'S INITIALS

Letter	Date	Name
CP	1820-1861	Christoph Pfeuffer, die-cutter
D.F., F.	1774-1831	Dietrich Flalda
FH	1786-1821	Friedrich Heenwagen
H	1775-1820	Carl Ludwig Holzemer, die-cutter
K	1804-1833	Wilhelm Korner medalleur, possibly

HELLER
COPPER
Similar to KM#553 but 19mm.

KM#	Date	Mintage	Fine	VF	XF	Unc
543	1801	—	2.00	4.00	10.00	55.00
(C89)	1802	—	2.00	4.00	10.00	55.00
	1803	—	2.00	4.00	10.00	55.00

553	1803	—	2.00	4.00	10.00	60.00
(C111)	1805	—	2.00	4.00	10.00	60.00
	1806	—	2.00	4.00	10.00	60.00
	1814	—	2.00	4.00	10.00	60.00

Obv: Crowned WK monogram w/1 ring at bottom of W.

565	1817	—	2.00	4.00	10.00	60.00
(C111.5)	1818	—	2.00	4.00	10.00	60.00
	1819	—	2.00	4.00	10.00	60.00
	1820	—	2.00	4.00	10.00	60.00

575	1822	—	2.00	4.00	7.00	40.00
(C121)	1823	—	2.00	4.00	7.00	40.00
	1824	—	2.00	4.00	7.00	40.00
	1825	—	2.00	4.00	7.00	40.00
	1827	—	2.00	4.00	7.00	40.00

Obv: Crowned WK monogram w/2 rings at bottom of W.

576	1822	—	2.00	4.00	7.00	40.00
(C121a)	1825	—	2.00	4.00	7.00	40.00
	1827	—	2.00	4.00	7.00	40.00
	1828	—	2.00	4.00	7.00	40.00
	1829	—	2.00	4.00	7.00	40.00
	1831	—	2.00	4.00	7.00	40.00

Obv: Crowned arms, leg: KURHESSEN.
Rev. value: SCHEIDE MUNZE.

602	1842	.037	5.00	10.00	25.00	100.00
(C135)						

Obv. leg: 360 EINEN THALER.

605	1843	—	1.00	2.00	5.00	30.00
(C138)	1845	—	1.00	2.00	5.00	30.00
	1847	—	1.00	2.00	5.00	30.00

613	1849	—	1.00	2.00	3.00	30.00
(C153)	1852	—	1.00	2.00	3.00	30.00
	1854	—	1.00	2.00	3.00	30.00
	1856	—	1.00	2.00	3.00	30.00
	1858	—	1.00	2.00	3.00	30.00
	1859	—	1.00	2.00	3.00	30.00
	1860	—	1.00	2.00	3.00	30.00
	1861	—	1.00	2.00	3.00	30.00
	1862	—	1.00	2.00	3.00	30.00
	1863	—	1.00	2.00	3.00	30.00

636 Hesse-Cassel / GERMAN STATES

KM#	Date	Mintage	Fine	VF	XF	Unc
(C153)	1864	—	1.00	2.00	3.00	30.00
	1865	—	1.00	2.00	3.00	30.00
	1866	—	1.00	2.00	3.00	30.00

2 HELLER

COPPER

Obv: WK monogram w/elector's cap. Rev: Value.

561 (C112)	1814	—	5.00	10.00	20.00	100.00

Obv: Crowned WK monogram w/1 ring at bottom of W.

564	1816	—	3.00	7.00	15.00	75.00
(C112.5)	1818	—	3.00	7.00	15.00	75.00
	1820	—	3.00	7.00	15.00	75.00
585 (C122)	1831	—	2.00	4.00	7.00	25.00

Obv: Crowned WK monogram w/2 rings at bottom of W.

589 (C134)	1833	—	2.00	4.00	7.00	25.00

606 (C139)	1843	—	2.00	4.00	7.00	25.00

3 HELLER

COPPER

607	1843	—	2.00	4.00	8.00	35.00
(C140)	1844	—	2.00	4.00	8.00	35.00
	1845	—	2.00	4.00	8.00	35.00
	1846	—	2.00	4.00	8.00	35.00

612	1848	—	1.50	3.00	6.00	30.00
(C154)	1849	—	1.50	3.00	6.00	30.00
	1850	—	1.50	3.00	6.00	30.00
	1851	—	1.50	3.00	6.00	30.00
	1852	—	1.50	3.00	6.00	30.00
	1853	—	1.50	3.00	6.00	30.00
	1854	—	1.50	3.00	6.00	30.00
	1856	—	1.50	3.00	6.00	30.00
	1858	—	1.50	3.00	6.00	30.00
	1859	—	1.50	3.00	6.00	30.00
	1860	—	1.50	3.00	6.00	30.00
	1861	—	1.50	3.00	6.00	30.00
	1862	—	1.50	3.00	6.00	30.00
	1863	—	1.50	3.00	6.00	30.00
	1864	—	1.50	3.00	6.00	30.00
	1865	—	1.50	3.00	6.00	30.00
	1866	—	1.50	3.00	6.00	30.00

4 HELLER

COPPER

Obv: Crowned WK monogram w/1 ring at bottom of W.

562	1815	—	3.00	7.00	20.00	125.00
(C113)	1816	—	3.00	7.00	20.00	125.00
	1817	—	3.00	7.00	20.00	125.00
	1818	—	3.00	7.00	20.00	125.00
	1819	—	3.00	7.00	20.00	125.00
	1820	—	3.00	7.00	20.00	125.00
	1821	—	3.00	7.00	20.00	125.00

Obv: Crowned WK monogram w/2 rings at bottom of W.

KM#	Date	Mintage	Fine	VF	XF	Unc
571	1821	—	2.00	4.00	10.00	65.00
(C123)	1822	—	2.00	4.00	10.00	65.00
	1824	—	2.00	4.00	10.00	65.00
	1826	—	2.00	4.00	10.00	65.00
	1827	—	2.00	4.00	10.00	65.00
	1828	—	2.00	4.00	10.00	65.00
	1829	—	2.00	4.00	10.00	65.00
	1830	—	2.00	4.00	10.00	65.00
	1831	—	2.00	4.00	10.00	65.00

1/2 SILBER GROSCHEN

.9700 g, .250 SILVER, .0077 oz ASW

Obv: Crowned arms. Rev. value: SILBER GROSCHEN.

603 (C141)	1842	1.491	2.00	4.00	10.00	65.00

SILBER GROSCHEN

1.5600 g, .312 SILVER, .0156 oz ASW

601	1841	5.925	1.00	3.00	7.00	40.00
(C142)	1845	.062	2.00	4.00	8.00	45.00
	1847	.456	2.00	4.00	8.00	45.00

615	1851	.262	1.00	3.00	7.00	30.00
(C155)	1852	.147	1.00	3.00	7.00	30.00
	1853	.125	1.00	3.00	7.00	30.00
	1854	.098	1.00	3.00	7.00	30.00
	1855	.054	1.00	3.00	7.00	30.00
	1856	.234	1.00	3.00	7.00	30.00
	1857	.119	1.00	3.00	7.00	30.00
	1858	.058	1.00	3.00	7.00	30.00
	1859	.235	1.00	3.00	7.00	30.00
	1860	.156	1.00	3.00	7.00	30.00
	1861	.165	1.00	3.00	7.00	30.00
	1862	—	1.00	3.00	7.00	30.00
	1863	—	1.00	3.00	7.00	30.00
	1864	.122	1.00	3.00	7.00	30.00
	1865	.192	1.00	3.00	7.00	30.00
	1866	.182	1.00	3.00	7.00	30.00

2 SILBER GROSCHEN

2.6000 g, .375 SILVER, .0313 oz ASW

604 (C143)	1842	2.414	10.00	20.00	45.00	90.00

2-1/2 SILBER GROSCHEN

3.2500 g, .375 SILVER, .0391 oz ASW

620	1852 CP	.034	3.00	7.00	20.00	75.00
(C156)	1853 CP	.049	3.00	7.00	20.00	75.00
	1856 CP	.039	3.00	7.00	20.00	75.00
	1859 CP	.069	3.00	7.00	20.00	75.00
	1860 CP	.042	3.00	7.00	20.00	75.00
	1861 CP	.034	3.00	7.00	20.00	75.00
	1862 CP	.031	3.00	7.00	20.00	75.00
	1865 CP	.023	3.00	7.00	20.00	75.00

24 EINEN (1/24) THALER

BILLON

529	1801	—	3.00	7.00	20.00	100.00
(C96)	1802	—	3.00	7.00	20.00	100.00

KM#	Date	Mintage	Fine	VF	XF	Unc
554.1	1803 F	.526	3.00	7.00	20.00	100.00
(C115.1)	1804 F	—	3.00	7.00	20.00	100.00
	1805 F	—	3.00	7.00	20.00	100.00
	1806 F	—	3.00	7.00	20.00	100.00
	1807 F	.997	3.00	7.00	20.00	100.00

Obv: Rampant lion left.
Rev: Value, w/o mintmark below date.

554.2	1814	—	3.00	7.00	20.00	100.00
(C115.2)	1815	—	3.00	7.00	20.00	100.00
	1816	—	3.00	7.00	20.00	100.00
	1817	—	3.00	7.00	20.00	100.00
	1818	—	3.00	7.00	20.00	100.00
	1819	—	3.00	7.00	20.00	100.00
	1820	—	3.00	7.00	20.00	100.00
	1821	—	3.00	7.00	20.00	100.00
577 (C124)	1822	—	17.50	35.00	70.00	165.00

VI EINEN (1/6) THALER

SILVER

546	1801 F	—	10.00	20.00	40.00	150.00
(C99)	1802 F	—	10.00	20.00	40.00	150.00

.625 SILVER

Obv: Crowned arms within laurel branches. Rev: Value.

555 (C116)	1803 F	—	10.00	20.00	45.00	165.00

556	1803 F	—	10.00	20.00	45.00	165.00
(C116a)	1804 F	—	10.00	20.00	45.00	165.00
	1805 F	—	10.00	20.00	45.00	165.00
	1806 F	—	10.00	20.00	45.00	165.00
	1807 F	.040	10.00	20.00	45.00	165.00

Obv: Lion in oval shield. Rev: Value, date.

572	1821	.038	15.00	30.00	100.00	275.00
(C125)	1822	.056	15.00	30.00	100.00	250.00

5.3200 g, .500 SILVER, .0855 oz ASW

Obv. leg: KURF S.L.V. HESSEN.

579.1	1823	.182	10.00	20.00	40.00	150.00
(C126)	1824	.276	10.00	20.00	40.00	150.00
	1825	.306	10.00	20.00	40.00	150.00
	1826	.147	10.00	20.00	40.00	150.00
	1827	.280	10.00	20.00	40.00	150.00
	1828	.395	10.00	20.00	40.00	150.00
	1829	.590	10.00	20.00	40.00	150.00
	1830	.524	10.00	20.00	40.00	150.00
	1831	.201	10.00	20.00	40.00	150.00

Obv. leg: KURF. V. HESSEN

579.2 (C126a)	1831	.022	75.00	140.00	250.00	475.00

Rev: THAELR (error)

579.3 (C126b)	1828	—	50.00	115.00	200.00	325.00

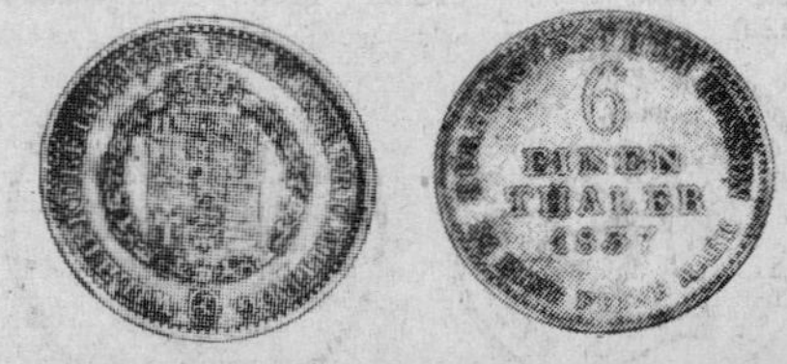

Obv. leg: . . . . . KURPR.U.MITREG.

590	1833	.046	5.00	15.00	35.00	145.00

KM#	Date	Mintage	Fine	VF	XF	Unc
(C144)	1834	.599	5.00	10.00	25.00	85.00
	1835	.810	5.00	10.00	25.00	85.00
	1836	.528	5.00	10.00	25.00	85.00
	1837	.624	5.00	10.00	25.00	85.00
	1838	.558	5.00	10.00	25.00	85.00
	1839	.228	5.00	10.00	25.00	100.00
	1840	6,000	5.00	20.00	50.00	225.00
	1841	.192	5.00	10.00	20.00	100.00
	1842	1.404	5.00	10.00	20.00	85.00
	1843	—	5.00	10.00	25.00	100.00
	1844	6,132	5.00	20.00	50.00	225.00
	1845	.095	5.00	10.00	25.00	115.00
	1846	.045	5.00	15.00	35.00	145.00

Obv. leg: ......KURPR. – MITREG
| 609 | 1846 | Inc.Ab. | 75.00 | 145.00 | 250.00 | 475.00 |
| (C144a) | 1847 | .103 | 65.00 | 125.00 | 225.00 | 400.00 |

5.3500 g, .520 SILVER, .0894 oz ASW
Obv: C.P. at truncation.
616	1851 CP	.030	10.00	20.00	30.00	125.00
(C157)	1852 CP	.033	10.00	20.00	30.00	125.00
	1854 CP	.013	10.00	20.00	30.00	125.00
	1855 CP	.022	10.00	20.00	30.00	125.00
	1856 CP	—	10.00	20.00	30.00	125.00

1/3 THALER

8.5000 g, .625 SILVER, .1708 oz ASW
578	1822	.105	10.00	40.00	75.00	175.00
(C127)	1823	.125	10.00	40.00	75.00	175.00
	1824	.099	10.00	40.00	75.00	175.00
	1825	.162	10.00	40.00	75.00	175.00
	1826	.280	10.00	40.00	75.00	175.00
	1827	.278	10.00	40.00	75.00	175.00
	1828	—	10.00	40.00	75.00	175.00
	1829	.219	10.00	40.00	75.00	175.00

1/2 THALER

11.1200 g, .750 SILVER, .2681 oz ASW
| 567 | 1819 | — | 25.00 | 50.00 | 100.00 | 250.00 |
| (C117) | 1820 | — | 25.00 | 50.00 | 100.00 | 250.00 |

THALER
SILVER
Obv: Small bust right.
Rev: Crowned oval arms w/griffon supporters.
| 552 | 1802 FH | — | — | — | Rare | — |
| (C106b) | | | | | | |

| 560 | 1813 K | — | 600.00 | 1500. | 3000. | 4500. |
| (C106.5) | | | | | | |

NOTE: Possibly a pattern.

22.2700 g, .750 SILVER, .5371 oz ASW
Obv. leg: KURF. SOUV.
KM#	Date	Mintage	Fine	VF	XF	Unc
568	1819	—	60.00	100.00	425.00	1000.
(C118)	1820	—	75.00	140.00	575.00	1200.

Obv. leg: SOUV.LANDGR.Z.HESSEN.
| 573.1 | 1821 | 2,385 | 85.00 | 200.00 | 700.00 | 1500. |
| (C128.1) | 1822 | 3,456 | 100.00 | 260.00 | 900.00 | 1900. |

Obv: W/o period after HESSEN.
| 573.2 | 1821 | Inc. Ab. | 85.00 | 200.00 | 700.00 | 1500. |
| (C128.2) | | | | | | |

587	1832	.020	25.00	50.00	150.00	450.00
(C145)	1833	.017	25.00	50.00	150.00	450.00
	1834	.037	25.00	50.00	150.00	450.00
	1835	.014	25.00	50.00	150.00	450.00
	1836	.040	30.00	60.00	175.00	575.00
	1837	.026	25.00	50.00	175.00	450.00
	1838	4,041	40.00	70.00	200.00	800.00
	1839	2,574	25.00	50.00	150.00	450.00
	1841	.025	25.00	50.00	150.00	450.00
	1842	.031	25.00	60.00	175.00	575.00

Obv: C.PFEUFFER F. at truncation.
617	1851	3,963	75.00	150.00	500.00	1500.
(C158)	1854	7,338	60.00	100.00	325.00	1250.
	1855	.028	35.00	65.00	275.00	800.00

18.5200 g, .900 SILVER, .5360 oz ASW
Obv: Similar to KM#617 but w/C.P. at truncation.
621.1	1858 CP	.062	30.00	60.00	150.00	500.00
(C159)	1859 CP	.037	30.00	60.00	150.00	500.00
	1860 CP	.031	30.00	60.00	150.00	500.00
	1862 CP	.032	30.00	60.00	150.00	500.00
	1864 CP	.032	30.00	60.00	150.00	500.00
	1865 CP	.031	30.00	60.00	150.00	500.00

Obv: W/o C.P. at truncation.
KM#	Date	Mintage	Fine	VF	XF	Unc
621.2	1858	Inc. Ab.	30.00	60.00	150.00	500.00
(C159a)	1859	Inc. Ab.	30.00	60.00	150.00	500.00
	1860	Inc. Ab.	30.00	65.00	150.00	500.00
	1861	.032	30.00	65.00	150.00	500.00
	1862	—	30.00	65.00	150.00	500.00
	1863	.032	30.00	65.00	150.00	500.00
	1864	Inc. Ab.	30.00	65.00	150.00	500.00
	1865	Inc. Ab.	30.00	65.00	150.00	500.00

2 THALERS

37.1200 g, .900 SILVER, 1.0742 oz ASW
600	1840	.019	90.00	150.00	375.00	1200.
(C146)	1841	.019	100.00	175.00	425.00	1350.
	1842	.019	100.00	175.00	425.00	1350.
	1843	.018	115.00	185.00	460.00	1425.
	1844	.059	130.00	200.00	500.00	1600.
	1845	—	130.00	200.00	500.00	1600.

Obv: Larger letters.
| 608 | 1844 | Inc. Ab. | 90.00 | 150.00 | 375.00 | 1200. |
| (C146b) | 1845 | — | 130.00 | 210.00 | 500.00 | 1600. |

Obv. leg: KURPRINZ-MITREGENT.
| 610 | 1847 | .010 | 400.00 | 750.00 | 1700. | 3800. |
| (C146a) | | | | | | |

Hesse-Cassel / GERMAN STATES 638

Obv: CP on truncation.

KM#	Date	Mintage	Fine	VF	XF	Unc
618	1851 CP	3,996	150.00	300.00	500.00	1100.
(C160)	1854 CP	.141	100.00	150.00	325.00	800.00
	1855 CP	.357	85.00	125.00	275.00	600.00

5 THALER
6.6500 g, .900 GOLD, .1924 oz AGW
Obv: Bust right. Rev: Similar to KM#557.

545	1801 F	—	300.00	650.00	1000.	1750.
(C110)						

557	1803 F	1,659	650.00	1250.	2250.	3250.
(C119)	1805 F	1,941	775.00	1500.	2500.	3750.
	1806 F	875 pcs.	900.00	1750.	3000.	4250.

563	1815	2,226	900.00	1500.	2500.	3750.
(C120)						

Obv. leg: WILHELMUS I.ELECT.HASS.

566	1817	2,352	900.00	1500.	2500.	3750.
(C120a)	1819	1,548	1050.	1750.	3000.	4250.

Obv. leg: WILHELM I KURF.....

570	1820	534 pcs.	1000.	1850.	3500.	5250.
(C120b)						

Obv. leg: S.L. Z. HESSEN

574.1	1821	1,142	500.00	1200.	2250.	4500.
(C129)	1823	1,140	500.00	1200.	2250.	4500.

Obv. leg: S.L.V.HESSEN

KM#	Date	Mintage	Fine	VF	XF	Unc
574.2	1823	518 pcs.	750.00	1500.	2500.	4500.
(C129a)	1825	409 pcs.	750.00	1500.	2500.	4500.
	1828	952 pcs.	675.00	1250.	2250.	4000.
	1829	502 pcs.	750.00	1500.	2500.	4500.

591	1834	1,025	500.00	875.00	1500.	2000.
(C147)	1836	2,002	500.00	875.00	1500.	2000.
	1837	256 pcs.	575.00	1000.	1750.	2250.
	1839	1,996	500.00	875.00	1500.	2000.
	1840	.017	425.00	750.00	1250.	1750.
	1841	.016	425.00	750.00	1250.	1750.
	1842	6,909	425.00	750.00	1250.	1750.
	1843	1,657	500.00	875.00	1500.	2000.
	1844	1,495	500.00	875.00	1500.	2000.
	1845	1,364	500.00	875.00	1500.	2000.

Obv. leg: KURPR.-MITREG

611	1847	1,438	750.00	1250.	2000.	3000.
(C147a)						

Obv: CP at truncation.

619	1851 CP	596 pcs.	800.00	1300.	2250.	3000.
(C161)						

10 THALER

13.3000 g, .900 GOLD, .3848 oz AGW

594	1838	126 pcs.	1400.	2000.	3000.	4000.
(C148)	1840 Inc. KM591	1000.	1500.	2500.	3500.
	1841 Inc. KM591	1000.	1500.	2500.	3500.

OBER-HESSEN
1/4 KREUZER

COPPER
Obv: Arms, HESSEN CASSEL. Rev: Value.

550	1801	—	5.00	7.00	15.00	75.00
(C93)	1802	—	5.00	7.00	15.00	75.00

Obv: Crowned arms. Rev: Value within rosettes.

580	1824	—	2.00	4.00	8.00	40.00
(C130)	1825	—	2.00	4.00	8.00	40.00
	1827	—	2.00	4.00	8.00	40.00
	1829	—	2.00	4.00	8.00	40.00
	1830	—	2.00	4.00	8.00	40.00

Similar to KM#580.

592	1834	—	2.00	4.00	8.00	40.00
(C149)	1835	—	2.00	4.00	8.00	40.00

1/2 KREUZER
COPPER
Obv: Arms, HESSEN CASSEL. Rev: Value.

551	1801	—	3.00	6.00	15.00	75.00
(C94)	1802	—	3.00	6.00	15.00	75.00
	1803	—	3.00	6.00	15.00	75.00

Obv: Elector's cap above arms. Rev: Value.

KM#	Date	Mintage	Fine	VF	XF	Unc
558	1803F	—	3.00	6.00	15.00	75.00
(C114)	1804F	—	3.00	6.00	15.00	75.00

581	1824	—	2.00	4.00	8.00	40.00
(C131)	1825	—	2.00	4.00	8.00	40.00
	1826	—	2.00	4.00	8.00	40.00
	1827	—	2.00	4.00	8.00	40.00
	1828	—	2.00	4.00	8.00	40.00
	1829	—	2.00	4.00	8.00	40.00
	1830	—	2.00	4.00	8.00	40.00

Similar to KM#581.

593	1834	—	2.00	4.00	8.00	40.00
(C150)						

KREUZER
COPPER
Obv: Crowned arms. Rev: Value within rosettes.

582	1825	—	2.00	4.00	8.00	40.00
(C132)	1828	—	2.00	4.00	8.00	40.00
	1829	—	2.00	4.00	8.00	40.00

Similar to KM#582.

588	1832	—	2.00	4.00	8.00	40.00
(C151)	1833	—	2.00	4.00	8.00	40.00
	1835	—	2.00	4.00	8.00	40.00

6 KREUZER
BILLON
Obv: Crowned arms. Rev: Value within rosettes.

583	1826	—	5.00	10.00	40.00	90.00
(C133)	1827	—	5.00	10.00	40.00	90.00
	1828	—	5.00	10.00	40.00	90.00

Rev: W/o rosettes.

586	1831	—	3.00	7.00	30.00	75.00
(C152)	1832	—	3.00	7.00	30.00	75.00
	1833	—	3.00	7.00	30.00	75.00
	1834	—	3.00	7.00	30.00	75.00

HESSE-DARMSTADT

A state located in southwest Germany was founded in 1567. The Landgrave was elevated to the status of Grand Duke in 1806. In 1815 the Congress of Vienna awarded Hesse-Darmstadt the cities of Mainz and Worms which were relinquished along with the newly acquired Hesse-Homburg, to the Prussians in 1866. It became part of the German Empire in 1871 and endured until the abdication of the Grand Duke in 1918.

RULERS
Ludwig X, 1790-1806
 As Grand Duke Ludwig I,
 1806-1830
Ludwig II, 1830-1848
Ludwig III, 1848-1877
Ludwig IV, 1877-1892
Ernst Ludwig, 1892-1918

MINTMASTER'S INITIALS

Letter	Date	Name
HR	1817—	Hector Roessler
RF	1772-1809	Remigius Fehr

HELLER
COPPER
Obv: Crowned pointed arms, G.H.-K.M. Rev: Value.

KM#	Date	Mintage	Fine	VF	XF	Unc
291	1824	—	1.00	2.00	7.00	40.00
(C108)						

302	1837	—	1.00	2.00	7.00	35.00
(C127)	1840	—	1.00	2.00	7.00	35.00
	1841	—	1.00	2.00	7.00	35.00
	1842	.103	1.00	2.00	7.00	35.00
	1843	.175	1.00	2.00	7.00	35.00
	1844	.241	1.00	2.00	7.00	35.00
	1845	—	1.00	2.00	7.00	35.00
	1846	—	1.00	2.00	7.00	35.00
	1847	—	1.00	2.00	7.00	35.00

Obv: Crowned square arms.

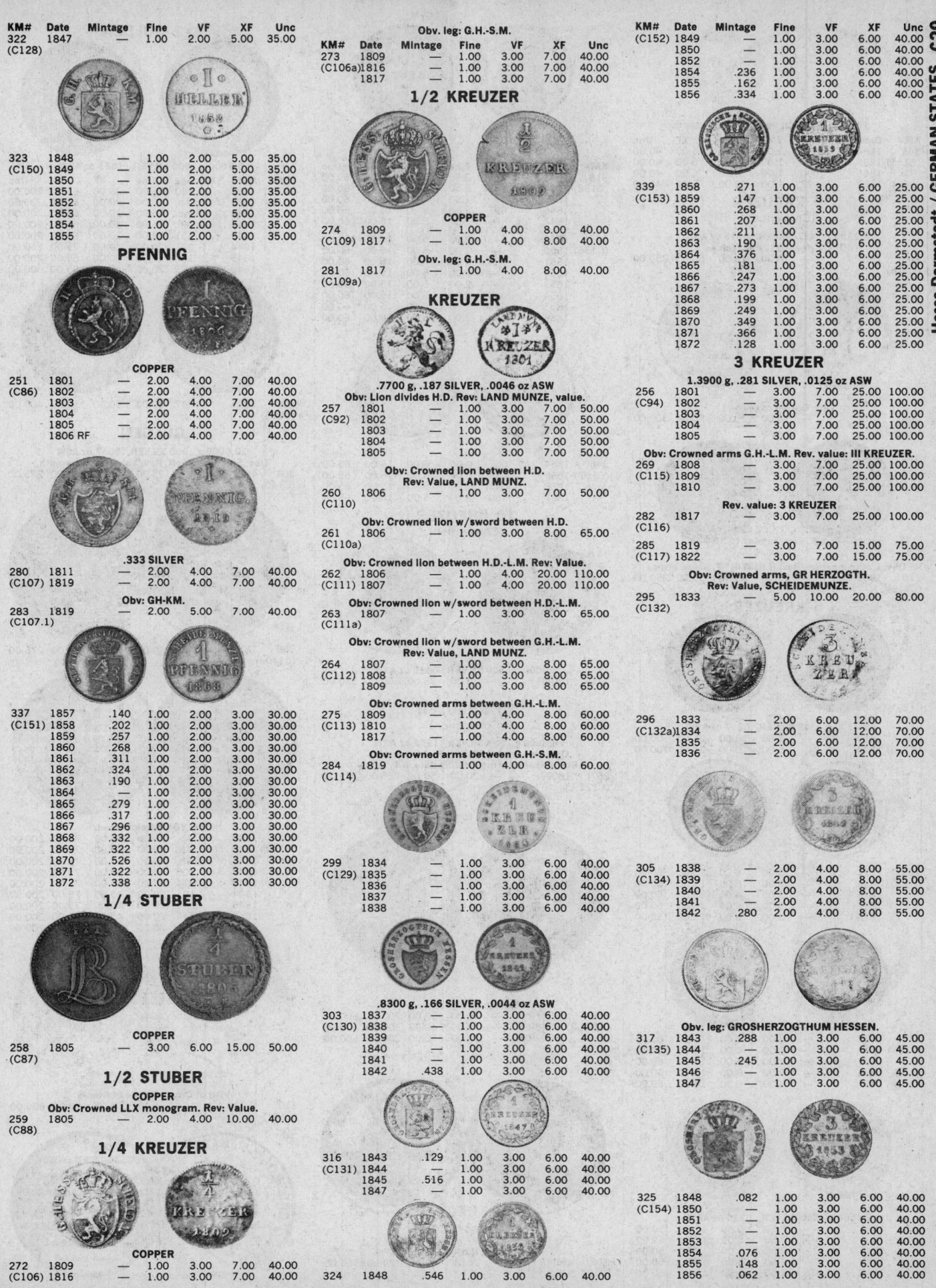

1.2300 g, .250 SILVER, .0138 oz ASW

KM#	Date	Mintage	Fine	VF	XF	Unc
345	1864	.095	1.00	3.00	6.00	40.00
(C155)	1865	.087	1.00	3.00	6.00	40.00
	1866	.090	1.00	3.00	6.00	40.00
	1867	.077	1.00	3.00	6.00	40.00

5 KREUZER
(Convention)

2.2300 g, .437 SILVER, .0313 oz ASW
Obv: Crowned L. Rev: Value.

265	1807	—	10.00	25.00	50.00	250.00
(C118)						

Obv: Curled edges on L

266	1807	—	10.00	30.00	60.00	300.00
(C118a)						

Obv: L at truncation. Rev: R.IUSTIRT F. below arms.

270	1808	—	10.00	25.00	50.00	250.00
(C119)						

6 KREUZER

2.4300 g, .343 SILVER, .0267 oz ASW

286	1819	—	5.00	10.00	25.00	100.00
(C120)	1820	—	5.00	10.00	25.00	100.00

290	1821	—	3.00	6.00	15.00	60.00
(C120a)	1824	—	3.00	6.00	15.00	60.00
	1826	—	3.00	6.00	15.00	60.00
	1827	—	3.00	6.00	15.00	60.00
	1828	—	3.00	6.00	15.00	60.00

297	1833	—	3.00	6.00	15.00	60.00
(C136)	1834	—	3.00	6.00	15.00	60.00
	1835	—	3.00	6.00	15.00	60.00
	1836	—	3.00	6.00	15.00	60.00
	1837	—	3.00	6.00	15.00	60.00

2.4600 g, .350 SILVER, .0276 oz ASW

306	1838	—	2.50	5.00	12.50	50.00
(C137)	1839	—	2.50	5.00	12.50	50.00
	1840	—	2.50	5.00	12.50	50.00
	1841	—	2.50	5.00	12.50	50.00
	1842	.816	2.50	5.00	12.50	50.00

KM#	Date	Mintage	Fine	VF	XF	Unc
318	1843	.775	2.50	5.00	15.00	60.00
(C138)	1844	.331	2.50	5.00	15.00	60.00
	1845	.235	2.50	5.00	15.00	60.00
	1846	.897	2.50	5.00	15.00	60.00
	1847	—	2.50	5.00	15.00	60.00
326	1848	.243	2.00	5.00	15.00	60.00
(C156)	1850	—	2.00	5.00	15.00	60.00
	1851	—	2.00	5.00	15.00	60.00
	1852	—	2.00	5.00	15.00	60.00
	1853	—	2.00	5.00	15.00	60.00
	1854	.033	2.00	5.00	15.00	60.00
	1855	.072	2.00	5.00	15.00	60.00
	1856	.044	2.00	5.00	15.00	60.00

346	1864	.052	2.00	5.00	15.00	65.00
(C157)	1865	.039	2.00	5.00	15.00	65.00
	1866	.043	2.00	5.00	15.00	65.00
	1867	.060	2.00	5.00	15.00	65.00

10 KREUZER
(Convention)

3.9000 g, .500 SILVER, .0626 oz ASW

271	1808R.F.	—	15.00	35.00	200.00	350.00
(C121)						

20 KREUZER
(Convention)

6.6800 g, .583 SILVER, .1252 oz ASW
Obv: Head right, FRISCH F. at truncation.
Rev: Crowned arms dividing date, R.F. below.

267	1807	—	20.00	50.00	225.00	575.00
(C122.1)						

Obv. leg: LUDEWIG.....

268	1807R.F.	—	20.00	50.00	200.00	500.00
(C122.2)	1808R.F.	—	20.00	50.00	200.00	500.00
	1809R.F.	—	20.00	50.00	200.00	500.00

Obv. leg: LUDWIG.....

276	1809R.F.	—	20.00	50.00	200.00	500.00
(C122.2a)						

1/2 GULDEN

5.3000 g, .900 SILVER, .1533 oz ASW

KM#	Date	Mintage	Fine	VF	XF	Unc
307	1838	1.080	15.00	30.00	65.00	200.00
(C139)	1839	Inc. Ab.	15.00	30.00	65.00	200.00
	1840	Inc. Ab.	15.00	30.00	65.00	200.00
	1841	Inc. Ab.	15.00	30.00	65.00	200.00
	1843	.151	15.00	30.00	65.00	200.00
	1844	.081	15.00	40.00	75.00	250.00
	1845	.167	15.00	30.00	65.00	200.00
	1846	.033	20.00	40.00	85.00	300.00

336	1855	.047	30.00	60.00	150.00	400.00
(C158)						

GULDEN

10.6000 g, .900 SILVER, .3067 oz ASW
Obv: Small head left. Rev: Value within wreath.

304	1837	1.122	25.00	40.00	85.00	225.00
(C140)						

308	1838	Inc. Ab.	30.00	50.00	100.00	275.00
(C140a)						

Obv: VOIGT below head.

309	1839	Inc. Ab.	20.00	40.00	75.00	200.00
(C140b)	1840	Inc. Ab.	20.00	40.00	75.00	200.00
	1841	Inc. Ab.	20.00	40.00	75.00	200.00
	1842	.605	20.00	40.00	75.00	200.00
	1843	.314	20.00	40.00	75.00	200.00
	1844	.191	20.00	40.00	75.00	200.00
	1845	.176	20.00	40.00	75.00	200.00
	1846	.144	20.00	40.00	75.00	200.00
	1847	.251	20.00	40.00	75.00	200.00

Visit of Crown Prince of Russia

319	1843	—	125.00	250.00	400.00	850.00
(C141)						

Public Freedom Through German Parliament

KM#	Date	Mintage	Fine	VF	XF	Unc
327 (C142)	1848	—	125.00	175.00	275.00	600.00

10.5800 g, .900 SILVER, .3061 oz ASW

328 (C159)	1848	.090	40.00	75.00	200.00	400.00
	1854	.044	40.00	75.00	200.00	400.00
	1855	.090	40.00	75.00	200.00	400.00
	1856	.153	20.00	40.00	125.00	300.00

ZWEY (2) GULDEN

28.0600 g, .833 SILVER, .7516 oz ASW

KM#	Date	Mintage	Fine	VF	XF	Unc
277 (C123)	1809 L	—	200.00	350.00	700.00	1600.

(Krone)

KM#	Date	Mintage	Fine	VF	XF	Unc
298 (C143)	1833 HR	.124	75.00	150.00	300.00	800.00
	1835 HR	.558	100.00	175.00	375.00	1100.
	1836 HR Inc. Ab.		75.00	150.00	300.00	800.00
	1837 HR Inc. Ab.		100.00	175.00	375.00	1100.

(Vereins)

21.2100 g, .900 SILVER, .6138 oz ASW

321 (C144)	1845	.044	50.00	100.00	225.00	550.00
	1846	.270	45.00	100.00	210.00	500.00
	1847	.030	55.00	115.00	275.00	700.00

29.5100 g, .871 SILVER, .8264 oz ASW

| 287 (C124) | 1819 HR | .019 | 275.00 | 400.00 | 850.00 | 1800. |

18.5200 g, .900 SILVER, .5360 oz ASW

338 (C160)	1857	.091	35.00	70.00	150.00	350.00
	1858	.537	35.00	70.00	150.00	300.00
	1859	.594	35.00	70.00	150.00	300.00
	1860	.608	35.00	70.00	150.00	300.00
	1861	.414	35.00	70.00	150.00	300.00
	1862	.242	35.00	70.00	150.00	300.00
	1863	.215	35.00	70.00	150.00	300.00
	1864	.073	35.00	70.00	175.00	350.00
	1865	.078	35.00	70.00	175.00	350.00
	1866	.059	35.00	70.00	175.00	350.00
	1867	.024	35.00	70.00	175.00	350.00
	1868	.048	35.00	70.00	185.00	425.00
	1869	.034	35.00	70.00	185.00	425.00
	1870	.039	35.00	70.00	175.00	350.00
	1871	.033	35.00	70.00	175.00	350.00

2 THALER
(3-1/2 Gulden)

329 (C161)	1848	.252	70.00	150.00	350.00	900.00
	1849	Inc. Ab.	70.00	150.00	350.00	900.00
	1853	Inc. Ab.	50.00	100.00	270.00	650.00
	1854	.127	40.00	80.00	215.00	500.00
	1855	.149	40.00	80.00	215.00	500.00
	1856	.064	40.00	80.00	215.00	500.00

EIN (1) THALER

| 292 (C125) | 1825 HR | .171 | 100.00 | 165.00 | 350.00 | 950.00 |

37.1200 g, .900 SILVER, 1.0742 oz ASW

310 (C145)	1839	.024	100.00	175.00	350.00	800.00
	1840	.368	85.00	140.00	275.00	600.00
	1841	.688	75.00	125.00	200.00	525.00
	1842	.286	90.00	150.00	315.00	700.00

Hesse-Darmstadt / GERMAN STATES

Obv: Similar to KM#310.

KM#	Date	Mintage	Fine	VF	XF	Unc
320 (C146)	1844	.377	90.00	150.00	300.00	700.00

Rev: Similar to KM#320.

335 (C162)	1854	.043	300.00	500.00	1000.	2200.

5 GULDEN
3.4250 g, .904 GOLD, .0995 oz AGW
Obv: Head left, C.V. below. Rev: Crowned draped arms, value 5G, leg: AUS HESS. RHEINGOLD.

300 (C147)	1835 HR	60 pcs.	2000.	4000.	7500.	10,000.

301 (C148)	1835 HR	.022	700.00	1500.	2000.	3250.
	1840 HR	Inc. Ab.	300.00	600.00	850.00	1350.
	1841 HR	Inc. Ab.	350.00	750.00	1000.	1650.
	1842 HR	Inc. Ab.	350.00	750.00	1000.	1650.

10 GULDEN

6.8500 g, .904 GOLD, .1991 oz AGW

293 (C126)	1826 HR	1,700	600.00	1500.	2500.	4000.
	1827 HR	1,705	600.00	1500.	2500.	3500.

315 (C149)	1840 HR	.017	300.00	750.00	1250.	2000.
	1841 HR	Inc. Ab.	300.00	750.00	1250.	2000.
	1842 HR	Inc. Ab.	300.00	750.00	1250.	2000.

MONETARY REFORM
2 MARK

11.1110 g, .900 SILVER, .3215 oz ASW

KM#	Date	Mintage	Fine	VF	XF	Unc
355 (Y63)	1876H	.202	125.00	300.00	2100.	4200.
	1877H	.338	125.00	325.00	2250.	4500.

359 (Y68)	1888A	.022	450.00	1250.	2000.	3500.
	1888A	500 pcs.	—	—	Proof	5200.

Rev: Type III.

363 (Y68a)	1891A	.063	275.00	625.00	1000.	2250.
	1891A	—	—	—	Proof	2750.

368 (Y75)	1895A	.054	150.00	300.00	600.00	1000.
	1896A	8,950	300.00	600.00	900.00	1400.
	1896A	200 pcs.	—	—	Proof	2000.
	1898A	.034	175.00	325.00	650.00	1100.
	1898A	360 pcs.	—	—	Proof	1500.
	1899A	.053	175.00	325.00	650.00	1100.
	1899A	128 pcs.	—	—	Proof	1600.
	1900A	8,950	350.00	625.00	950.00	1500.
	1900A	200 pcs.	—	—	Proof	2100.

400th Birthday of Philipp The Magnanimous

372 (Y80)	1904	.100	20.00	40.00	65.00	85.00
	1904	2,250	—	—	Proof	135.00

3 MARK

16.6670 g, .900 SILVER, .4823 oz ASW

375 (Y79)	1910A	.200	30.00	60.00	95.00	140.00
	1910A	—	—	—	Proof	250.00

25 Year Jubilee

KM#	Date	Mintage	Fine	VF	XF	Unc
376 (Y82)	1917A	1,333	—	1750.	2500.	3000.
	1917A	Inc. Ab.	—	—	Proof	3500.

5 MARK

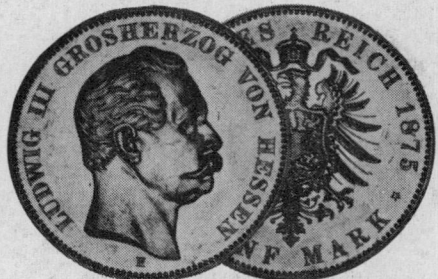

27.7770 g, .900 SILVER, .8038 oz ASW
Rev: Type II.

353 (Y64)	1875H	.148	45.00	125.00	1700.	4200.
	1876H	.290	45.00	125.00	1500.	3500.

1.9910 g, .900 GOLD, .0576 oz AGW

356 (Y65)	1877H	.103	175.00	400.00	700.00	1200.
	1877H	—	—	—	Proof	Rare

Rev: Type II.

357 (Y70)	1877H	.079	300.00	—	800.00	1200.
	1877H	—	—	—	Proof	2000.

27.7770 g, .900 SILVER, .8038 oz ASW
Rev: Type II.

360 (Y69)	1888A	8,940	425.00	1200.	2250.	4000.
	1888A	400 pcs.	—	—	Proof	4000.

Rev: Type III.

364 (Y69a)	1891A	.025	225.00	400.00	1500.	3000.
	1891A	—	—	—	Proof	4000.

369 (Y76)	1895A	.039	90.00	200.00	750.00	1750.
	1898A	.037	90.00	200.00	750.00	1750.
	1899A	4,475	110.00	225.00	800.00	2000.

KM#	Date	Mintage	Fine	VF	XF	Unc
(Y76)	1900A	.018	200.00	350.00	1000.	2500.
	1900A	*200 pcs.	—	—	Proof	2500.

400th Birthday of Philipp The Magnanimous

373	1904	.040	40.00	90.00	135.00	240.00
(Y81)	1904	700 pcs.	—	—	Proof	350.00

10 MARK

3.9820 g, .900 GOLD, .1152 oz AGW

350	1872H	.030	120.00	175.00	425.00	700.00
(Y66)	1872H	—	—	—	Proof	Rare
	1873H	.423	110.00	150.00	325.00	600.00
	1873H	—	—	—	Proof	Rare

Rev: Type II.

354	1875H	.191	100.00	170.00	250.00	400.00
(Y66a)	1876H	.513	120.00	150.00	225.00	350.00
	1877H	.094	140.00	180.00	300.00	500.00

358	1878H	.132	140.00	275.00	425.00	750.00
(Y71)	1878H	—	—	—	Proof	2000.
	1879H	.056	200.00	300.00	600.00	1000.
	1879H	—	—	—	Proof	2000.
	1880H	.109	220.00	325.00	625.00	1100.
	1880H	—	—	—	Proof	2000.
361	1888A	.036	220.00	325.00	625.00	1000.
	1888A	500 pcs.	—	—	Proof	2750.

Edge: Vines and stars.

362	1890A	.054	275.00	400.00	750.00	1100.
(Y71a)						

Rev: Type III.

366	1893A	.054	275.00	400.00	750.00	1100.
(Y73)	1893A	450 pcs.	—	—	Proof	2700.

370	1896A	.036	200.00	450.00	800.00	1200.
(Y77)	1896A	230 pcs.	—	—	Proof	2250.
	1898A	.075	175.00	325.00	600.00	1000.
	1898A	500 pcs.	—	—	Proof	2250.

20 MARK

7.9650 g, .900 GOLD, .2304 oz AGW
Rev: Type I.

KM#	Date	Mintage	Fine	VF	XF	Unc
351	1872H	.183	125.00	225.00	400.00	650.00
(Y67)	1872H	—	—	—	Proof	Rare
	1873H	.521	120.00	175.00	350.00	600.00

Rev: Type II.

352	1874H	.134	175.00	300.00	700.00	1000.
(Y67a)						

365	1892A	.025	500.00	750.00	1100.	1800.
(Y72)	1892A	—	—	—	Proof	4500.

Rev: Type III.

367	1893A	.025	500.00	750.00	1000.	1400.
(Y74)	1893A	—	—	—	Proof	2500.

371	1896A	.015	300.00	500.00	900.00	1500.
(Y78)	1896A	230 pcs.	—	—	Proof	1500.
	1897A	.045	125.00	175.00	350.00	650.00
	1897A	400 pcs.	—	—	Proof	1300.
	1898A	.070	125.00	175.00	350.00	550.00
	1898A	500 pcs.	—	—	Proof	1300.
	1899A	.040	125.00	175.00	400.00	750.00
	1899A	600 pcs.	—	—	Proof	1300.
	1900A	.040	125.00	175.00	350.00	600.00
	1900A	500 pcs.	—	—	Proof	1300.
	1901A	.080	125.00	175.00	325.00	500.00
	1901A	600 pcs.	—	—	Proof	1300.
	1903A	.040	125.00	175.00	350.00	750.00
	1903A	100 pcs.	—	—	Proof	1500.
374	1905A	.045	125.00	200.00	300.00	500.00
(Y78a)	1905A	200 pcs.	—	—	Proof	1500.
	1906A	.085	125.00	175.00	275.00	425.00
	1906A	199 pcs.	—	—	Proof	1500.
	1908A	.040	125.00	175.00	275.00	450.00
	1911A	.150	125.00	175.00	300.00	450.00

HESSE-HOMBURG

Hesse-Homburg, located in southwest Germany was created from part of Hesse-Darmstadt in 1596 and was mediatized to Darmstadt 1801-1815. In 1815 it was restored to independence and added the Lordships of Meisenheim and Kreuznach. The Homburg line became extinct in 1866, passed to Darmstadt and was almost immediately annexed to Prussia.

RULERS
Friedrich V Ludwig, 1751-1820
Friedrich VI Josef, 1820-1829
Ludwig Wilhelm, 1829-1839
Philipp August, 1839-1846
Gustav Adolph, 1846-1848
Ferdinand Heinrich, 1848-1866

MINTMASTERS INITIALS

Letter	Date	Name
RS	1817-1845	Rudolph Stadelmann, die-cutter in Darmstadt and Homburg
C.SCHNITZSPAHN	d.1877	Christian Schnitzspahn, chief die-cutter and medalleur in Darmstadt
C.VOIGT, VOIGT	1829-?	Carl F. Voigt, chief die-cutter and medalleur in Munich

KREUZER

.8300 g, .166 SILVER, .0044 oz ASW

KM#	Date	Mintage	Fine	VF	XF	Unc
13	1840	.048	30.00	60.00	100.00	250.00
(C3)						

3 KREUZER

1.3800 g, .281 SILVER, .0124 oz ASW

14	1840	.015	35.00	75.00	150.00	300.00
(C4)						

SILVER
Obv: Hessian lion in shield, leg: LANDGRAFTHUM HESSEN. Rev: 3/KREUZER/date in oak wreath.

19	1856					

6 KREUZER

2.4300 g, .343 SILVER, .0267 oz ASW
Obv: Crowned arms. Rev: Value within wreath.

15	1840	.057	30.00	75.00	150.00	350.00
(C5)						

1/2 GULDEN

5.3000 g, .900 SILVER, .1533 oz ASW

11	1838 VOIGHT					
(C1)		.011	75.00	150.00	225.00	375.00
	1839		—	—	Proof	475.00

Obv: RS at truncation.

16	1840 RS	.010	60.00	120.00	200.00	400.00
(C6)	1841 RS	6,560	60.00	120.00	200.00	400.00
	1843 RS	6,900	60.00	120.00	200.00	400.00
	1844 RS	.018	60.00	120.00	200.00	400.00
	1845	Inc. Ab.	60.00	120.00	200.00	400.00
	1846 RS	4,300	60.00	120.00	200.00	400.00

GULDEN

10.6000 g, .900 SILVER, .3067 oz ASW

12	1838 VOIGT					
(C2)		.011	60.00	140.00	300.00	725.00
	1839		—	—	Proof	875.00

Hesse-Homburg / GERMAN STATES 644

KM#	Date	Mintage	Fine	VF	XF	Unc
17	1841 RS	.014	60.00	140.00	300.00	700.00
(C7)	1843 RS	6,800	60.00	140.00	300.00	700.00
	1844 RS	.014	60.00	140.00	300.00	700.00
	1845 RS	8,100	60.00	140.00	300.00	700.00
	1846 RS	8,100	60.00	140.00	300.00	700.00

ZWEY (2) GULDEN

21.2100 g, .900 SILVER, .6317 oz ASW

18	1846 C.VOIGT					
(C8)		.011	300.00	600.00	1200.	3000.

EIN (1) THALER
(Vereins)

18.5200 g, .900 SILVER, .5358 oz ASW

20	1858	5,000	50.00	100.00	200.00	500.00
(C9)	1859	6,579	50.00	100.00	200.00	500.00
	1860	6,593	50.00	100.00	200.00	500.00
	1861	6,588	50.00	100.00	200.00	500.00
	1862	6,592	50.00	100.00	200.00	500.00
	1863	6,575	50.00	100.00	200.00	500.00

HOHENLOHE

This south German family traces its ancestry to the 900's. In 1209 the house divided but one of the lines became extinct in 1390. Thereafter there were numerous divisions with the last major one being in 1600.

HOHENLOHE-KIRCHBERG

This principality was located in southern Germany. The Kirchberg line was founded in 1701. The first ruler to be made prince of the empire was in 1764 and the last prince died in 1819.

RULERS
Christian Friedrich Carl, 1767-1806

1/2 THALER
(Convention)

C#	Date	Mintage	Fine	VF	XF	Unc
13b	1804 D	—	250.00	450.00	750.00	1250.

HOHENLOHE-NEUENSTEIN-OEHRINGEN

This principality was located in southern Germany. The Neuenstein-Oehringen line was founded in 1610 and the first prince of the empire from this line was proclaimed in 1764. The line became extinct in 1805 and the lands passed to Ingelfingen.

RULERS
Ludwig Friedrich Carl, 1765-1805

10 KREUZER
(Convention)

SILVER

C#	Date	Mintage	VG	Fine	VF	XF
53	1803 ICE	—	15.00	30.00	75.00	200.00

TRADE COINAGE
DUCAT

3.5000 g, .986 GOLD, .1109 oz AGW
81st Birthday

C#	Date	Mintage	Fine	VF	XF	Unc
65	1804 D	—	750.00	1750.	2800.	4500.

2 DUCATS

7.0000 g, .986 GOLD, .2219 oz AGW
81st Birthday
Obv: Bust right. Rev: Crowned arms.

66	1804 D	—	800.00	1600.	3000.	4250.

HOHENZOLLERN-HECHINGEN

Located in southern Germany, the Hechingen line was founded in 1576. They obtained the mint right c. 1622 and were named prince of the empire in 1623. As a result of the 1848 revolutions the princes abdicated in favor of Prussia in 1849.

RULERS
Hermann Friedrich Otto, 1798 - 1810
Friedrich Hermann Otto, 1810 - 1838
Friedrich Wilhelm Constantin, 1838-1849

MINTMASTER'S INITIALS
Letter	Date	Name
CH, ICH	1783-1808	Johann Christian Heuglin
C.VOIGT	1829-1873	Carl Friedrich Voigt, medalist
ILW, W	1798-1845	Johann Ludwig Wagner, die-cutter

3 KREUZER

1.2900 g, .333 SILVER, .0138 oz ASW
Obv: Crowned arms. Rev: Value within wreath.

C#	Date	Mintage	Fine	VF	XF	Unc
3	1845	.030	10.00	25.00	50.00	160.00
3	1846	.030	10.00	25.00	50.00	160.00
	1847	8,000	15.00	30.00	60.00	200.00

6 KREUZER

2.5900 g, .333 SILVER, .0277 oz ASW
Obv: Crowned arms. Rev: Value within wreath.

4	1841	.024	15.00	35.00	60.00	175.00
	1842	.026	15.00	35.00	60.00	175.00
	1845	.025	15.00	35.00	60.00	175.00
	1846	.025	15.00	35.00	60.00	175.00
	1847	.026	15.00	35.00	60.00	175.00

1/2 GULDEN

5.3000 g, .900 SILVER, .1533 oz ASW

5	1839	.015	35.00	75.00	150.00	300.00
	1841	6,000	35.00	75.00	150.00	325.00
	1842	5,540	35.00	75.00	150.00	325.00
	1843	6,000	35.00	75.00	150.00	325.00
	1844	6,000	35.00	75.00	150.00	325.00
	1845	6,000	35.00	75.00	150.00	325.00
	1846	6,000	35.00	75.00	150.00	325.00
	1847	6,000	35.00	75.00	150.00	325.00

GULDEN

10.6000 g, .900 SILVER, .3067 oz ASW

6	1839	.015	50.00	125.00	200.00	450.00
	1841	6,000	50.00	125.00	200.00	500.00
	1842	6,000	50.00	125.00	200.00	500.00
	1843	8,280	50.00	125.00	200.00	500.00
	1844	6,000	50.00	125.00	200.00	500.00
	1845	5,465	50.00	125.00	200.00	500.00
	1846	5,718	50.00	125.00	200.00	500.00
	1847	6,324	50.00	125.00	200.00	500.00

ZWEY (2) GULDEN

21.2100 g, .900 SILVER, .6138 oz ASW

7	1846	4,300	175.00	450.00	1000.	1500.
	1847	4,300	175.00	450.00	800.00	1400.

EIN (1) THALER

28.0600 g, .833 SILVER, .7516 oz ASW

C#	Date	Mintage	Fine	VF	XF	Unc
2.1	1804 W-CH	2,000	400.00	800.00	1400.	3000.

Obv: ILH below shoulder.

| 2.2 | 1804 ILH-CH | — | 400.00 | 800.00 | 1400. | 3000. |

2 THALER
(3-1/2 Gulden)

37.1200 g, .900 SILVER, 1.0742 oz ASW

8	1844	2,346	400.00	800.00	1600.	2800.
	1845	1,000	425.00	925.00	1800.	3200.
	1846	570 pcs.	500.00	1000.	2000.	3600.

HOHENZOLLERN-SIGMARINGEN

Located in southern Germany, the Sigmaringen line was founded in 1576. They obtained the mint right c. 1622 and were named Prince of the Empire in 1623. As a result of the 1848 revolutions the princes abdicated in favor of Prussia in 1849.

RULERS
Carl, 1831-1848
Carl Anton, 1848-1849

MINTMASTER'S INITIALS
Letter	Date	Name
D	1828-1848	Carl Wilhelm Doell
BALBACH	1848-1856	Othemar Balbach, medalist

EIN (1) KREUZER

COPPER
Obv: Crowned arms. Rev: EIN KREUZER within wreath.

C#	Date	Mintage	Fine	VF	XF	Unc
1	1842	.180	3.00	7.00	20.00	80.00
	1846	.055	3.00	7.00	20.00	100.00

.6200 g, .250 SILVER, .0049 oz ASW
Rev: 1 KREUZER within wreath

2	1842	.120	3.00	7.00	20.00	100.00
	1846	.060	3.00	7.00	20.00	100.00

3 KREUZER

1.2900 g, .333 SILVER, .0138 oz ASW

3	1839	.052	5.00	10.00	25.00	125.00
	1841	.068	5.00	10.00	25.00	125.00
	1842	.072	5.00	10.00	25.00	125.00
	1844	.170	5.00	10.00	25.00	125.00
	1845	.126	5.00	10.00	25.00	125.00
	1846	.126	5.00	10.00	25.00	125.00
	1847	.060	5.00	10.00	25.00	125.00

6 KREUZER

2.5900 g, .333 SILVER, .0277 oz ASW
Obv: Crowned arms. Rev: Value within wreath.

4	1839	.075	7.00	15.00	40.00	135.00
	1840	.075	7.00	15.00	40.00	135.00
	1841	.075	7.00	15.00	40.00	135.00
	1842	.074	7.00	15.00	40.00	135.00
	1844	.140	7.00	15.00	40.00	135.00
	1845	.208	7.00	15.00	40.00	135.00
	1846	.208	7.00	15.00	40.00	135.00
	1847	—	7.00	15.00	40.00	135.00

1/2 GULDEN

5.3000 g, .900 SILVER, .1533 oz ASW

5	1838	.012	50.00	75.00	135.00	225.00
	1839	.012	50.00	75.00	135.00	225.00
	1840	.012	50.00	75.00	135.00	225.00
	1841	.012	50.00	75.00	135.00	225.00
	1842	.012	50.00	75.00	135.00	225.00
	1843	.012	50.00	75.00	135.00	225.00
	1844	.012	50.00	75.00	135.00	225.00
	1845	.012	50.00	75.00	135.00	225.00
	1846	.012	50.00	75.00	135.00	225.00
	1847	3,068	70.00	110.00	150.00	300.00
	1848	—	50.00	75.00	135.00	225.00

GULDEN
10.6000 g, .900 SILVER, .3067 oz ASW
Obv: Head left, D below. Rev: Value within wreath.

| 6 | 1838 D | — | 65.00 | 125.00 | 200.00 | 350.00 |

Obv: DOELL below head.

C#	Date	Mintage	Fine	VF	XF	Unc
6a	1838	.018	65.00	120.00	200.00	350.00
	1839	.012	65.00	120.00	200.00	350.00
	1840	.012	65.00	120.00	200.00	350.00
	1841	.012	65.00	120.00	200.00	350.00
	1842	.012	65.00	120.00	200.00	350.00
	1843	.012	65.00	120.00	200.00	350.00
	1844	.012	65.00	120.00	200.00	350.00
	1845	.012	65.00	120.00	200.00	350.00
	1846	.012	65.00	120.00	200.00	350.00
	1847	.012	65.00	120.00	200.00	350.00
	1848	3,068	90.00	150.00	250.00	425.00

Obv: BALBACH below head

| 10a | 1849 | 5,000 | 150.00 | 250.00 | 450.00 | 675.00 |

ZWEI (2) GULDEN

21.2100 g, .900 SILVER, .6138 oz ASW

7	1845 D	9,206	125.00	250.00	650.00	1200.
	1846 D	9,206	125.00	250.00	650.00	1200.
	1847 D	9,206	125.00	250.00	650.00	1200.
	1848 D	6,905	125.00	250.00	700.00	1300.

Obv: BALBACH below bust.

| 11a | 1849 | 1,213 | 325.00 | 600.00 | 900.00 | 1800. |

2 THALER
(3-1/2 Gulden)

Hohenzollern-Sigmaringen / GERMAN STATES 646

37.1200 g, .900 SILVER, 1.0742 oz ASW

C#	Date	Mintage	Fine	VF	XF	Unc
8	1841	2,857	325.00	600.00	1200.	2400.
	1842	2,857	325.00	600.00	1200.	2400.
	1843	2,877	325.00	600.00	1200.	2400.

Obv: Similar to C#8.

9	1844	3,300	325.00	600.00	1100.	2000.
	1846	6,600	300.00	550.00	1100.	2200.
	1847	2,000	350.00	650.00	1200.	2200.

HOHENZOLLERN UNDER PRUSSIA

In 1849, Prussia obtained the Hohenzollern lands due to the 1848 revolutions and political unrest. One series of coins was issued by Prussia for their Hohenzollern holdings.

RULERS
Friedrich Wilhelm IV (of Prussia), 1849-1861

KREUZER

COPPER

| 1 | 1852A | .030 | 15.00 | 30.00 | 60.00 | 100.00 |

3 KREUZER

1.2900 g, .333 SILVER, .0138 oz ASW

2	1852A	.022	15.00	30.00	75.00	150.00
	1852A	—	—	—	Proof	150.00

6 KREUZER

2.5900 g, .333 SILVER, .0277 oz ASW

C#	Date	Mintage	Fine	VF	XF	Unc
3	1852A	.027	20.00	40.00	100.00	200.00
	1852A	—	—	—	Proof	200.00

1/2 GULDEN

5.3000 g, .900 SILVER, .1537 oz ASW

| 4 | 1852A | .053 | 65.00 | 100.00 | 150.00 | 225.00 |

GULDEN

10.6000 g, .900 SILVER, .3067 oz ASW

5	1852A	.050	65.00	100.00	150.00	275.00
	1852A	—	—	—	Proof	350.00

ISENBURG

Located in western Germany. The first coins for the Isenburg line appeared c. 1600. The territories of the Isenburg family were consolidated in 1806 and the ruler was made a sovereign prince of the Rhine Confederation. The 1815 Congress of Vienna placed the principality under Austrian rule. It was mediatized to Hesse-Darmstadt in 1815 and eventually went to Prussia.

RULERS
Carl, 1806-1813

6 KREUZER

BILLON

| 1 | 1811 | 1.000 | 30.00 | 60.00 | 125.00 | 275.00 |

12 KREUZER

SILVER
Obv: J. LAROQUE F. at truncation.

| 2 | 1811 | .500 | 60.00 | 125.00 | 250.00 | 450.00 |

EIN (1) THALER
(Reichs)

SILVER

C#	Date	Mintage	Fine	VF	XF	Unc
3	1811	—	500.00	1000.	1750.	3000.

NOTE: Also struck as pieforts. Very rare.

TRADE COINAGE
DUCAT

3.5000 g, .986 GOLD, .1109 oz AGW

| 4 | 1811 | — | — | — | Reported, not confirmed |

2 DUCATS

7.0000 g, .986 GOLD, .2218 oz AGW

| 5 | 1811 | — | 1400. | 3000. | 5000. | 8000. |

NOTE: Struck w/1 Ducat dies, C#4.

KNYPHAUSEN

The district of Knyphausen was located in northwestern Germany in East Friesland. Local nobility ruled from the 14th century and until 1623 when it was sold to Oldenburg. It became autonomous in 1653 and was acquired through marriage to the Bentinck family in 1733. Coins were struck c. 1800. It was claimed by both Anhalt and Oldenburg and the arms of Knyphausen appear on coins of both places.

RULERS
Wilhelm Gustav Friedrich, 1774-1835

1/8 THALER
(9 Grote)

SILVER
Obv: Arms.
Rev: Crowned double-headed eagle dividing value.

| 2 | 1807 | — | 275.00 | 550.00 | 1000. | 1450. |

| 1 | 1807 | .016 | 125.00 | 250.00 | 500.00 | 725.00 |

LAUENBURG

The duchy, located in northern Germany was established in 1260. The ruling line became extinct in 1689 and the lands were inherited by Hannover in 1705. After the Napoleonic Wars, the 1815 Congress of Vienna assigned the property to Prussia who traded it to Denmark for Swedish Pomerania. Prussia regained Lauenburg in 1864.

RULERS
Frederick VI (of Denmark), 1816-1839

MINTMASTER'S INITIALS		
Letter	Date	Name
FF	—	Johann Friedrich Freund

2/3 THALER

17.3200 g, .750 SILVER, .4177 oz ASW

C#	Date	Mintage	Fine	VF	XF	Unc
1	1830 FF	—	150.00	250.00	400.00	800.00

LEININGEN

Scattered lands located in southwestern Germany. It was founded c. 1110. First coins were struck in the 13th century. Leiningen was annexed to France in 1801. The lands were mediatized in 1806 and were absorbed by Baden, Bavaria, Hesse and Nassau.

RULERS
Ludwig, 1597-1622
Karl Friedrich Wilhelm, 1756-1807

PFENNIG

BILLON
Obv: Eagles below crown within branches. Rev: Value.

| 1 | 1805 | — | 35.00 | 75.00 | 150.00 | 300.00 |

2 PFENNIG
BILLON
Obv: Crowned arms. Rev: Value, branch below.

| 2 | 1805 | — | 50.00 | 100.00 | 200.00 | 400.00 |

3 KREUZER

BILLON
Obv: Crowned arms within branches.
Rev: Value, branch below.

| 3 | 1804 | — | 40.00 | 90.00 | 200.00 | 400.00 |

| 3a | 1805 | — | 35.00 | 75.00 | 175.00 | 350.00 |

6 KREUZER

BILLON
Obv: Crowned arms within branches.
Rev: Value, branch below.

| 5 | 1804 | — | 50.00 | 125.00 | 300.00 | 600.00 |

| 5a | 1805 | — | 40.00 | 90.00 | 200.00 | 400.00 |

LIPPE-DETMOLD

A state located in northwestern Germany was founded c. 1120. The first coinage was struck c. 1225. The rulers were elevated to the rank of count in 1528 and given the title of prince in 1720, but it wasn't confirmed until 1789. The principality joined the German Empire 1871 and remained until abdicated in 1918.

RULERS
Friedrich Wilhelm Leopold

Alone, 1789-1802
Paul Alexander Leopold II
under Regency of Pauline of
Anhalt-Bernburg, 1802-1820
As Independent Prince, 1820-1851
Paul Friedrich Emil Leopold III,
1851-1875
Woldemar, 1875 - 1895
Alexander, 1895 - 1905
Leopold IV, 1905-1918

HELLER

COPPER

C#	Date	Mintage	Fine	VF	XF	Unc
70	1802 T	.166	9.00	15.00	30.00	55.00
	1802	Inc. Ab.	2.00	4.00	10.00	40.00
	1809 T	.108	2.00	4.00	10.00	40.00
	1812 T	—	2.00	4.00	10.00	40.00
	1814 T	—	2.00	4.00	10.00	40.00
	1816 T	—	2.00	4.00	10.00	40.00
	1816	—	2.00	4.00	10.00	40.00

Obv: Blooming rose. Rev: value: I HELLER, date.

74	1821ST	—	2.00	4.00	10.00	40.00
	1822ST	—	2.00	4.00	10.00	40.00
	1825ST	—	2.00	4.00	10.00	.40.00
	1826ST	—	2.00	4.00	10.00	40.00
	1828ST	—	2.00	4.00	10.00	40.00
	1835ST	—	2.00	4.00	10.00	40.00
	1836ST	—	2.00	4.00	10.00	40.00
	1840ST	—	2.00	4.00	10.00	40.00

Rev. value: 1 HELLER, date.

| 74a | 1826 ST | — | 2.00 | 4.00 | 10.00 | 40.00 |

PFENNING

COPPER

| 71.1 | 1802 | .120 | 3.00 | 7.00 | 20.00 | 100.00 |

Rev: T under date.

| 71.2 | 1818 T | — | 3.00 | 7.00 | 15.00 | 90.00 |

Rev: W/o T.

| 71.3 | 1818 | — | 3.00 | 7.00 | 15.00 | 90.00 |

Rev: ST below date.

75	1820ST	—	3.00	7.00	15.00	60.00
	1821ST	—	3.00	7.00	15.00	60.00
	1824ST	—	3.00	7.00	15.00	60.00
	1825ST	—	3.00	7.00	15.00	60.00

Rev: value: PFENNING

| 75a | 1821ST | — | — | — | — | — |
| | 1824ST | — | 3.00 | 7.00 | 20.00 | 75.00 |

75b	1828ST	—	1.00	3.00	7.00	50.00
	1829ST	—	1.00	3.00	7.00	50.00
	1830ST	—	1.00	3.00	7.00	50.00
	1836ST	—	1.00	3.00	7.00	50.00
	1840ST	—	1.00	3.00	7.00	50.00

| 77 | 1847 A | .972 | 1.00 | 3.00 | 7.00 | 40.00 |

| 83 | 1851 A | 1.080 | 1.00 | 3.00 | 7.00 | 35.00 |
| | 1858 A | .900 | 1.00 | 3.00 | 7.00 | 35.00 |

1-1/2 PFENNING

COPPER

C#	Date	Mintage	Fine	VF	XF	Unc
76	1821 T	—	3.00	5.00	10.00	65.00
	1823 T	—	3.00	5.00	10.00	65.00
	1824 T	—	3.00	5.00	10.00	65.00
	1825 T	—	3.00	5.00	10.00	65.00

2 PFENNING
COPPER
Obv: Blooming rose.
Rev: Value, rosette under date.

| 72 | 1802 | .127 | 3.00 | 7.00 | 20.00 | 100.00 |

3 PFENNINGE
COPPER
Obv: Crowned shield w/blooming rose. Rev: Value.

| 78 | 1847A | 1.020 | 2.00 | 5.00 | 10.00 | 60.00 |

| 84 | 1858A | .060 | 3.00 | 7.00 | 15.00 | 75.00 |

1/2 SILBER GROSCHEN
.9700 g, .250 SILVER, .0077 oz ASW
Obv: Head right. Rev: Value.

| 79 | 1847A | .321 | 3.00 | 7.00 | 20.00 | 85.00 |

MARIENGROSCHEN
BILLON
Obv: Arms. Rev: Value and date.

C#	Date	Mintage	VG	Fine	VF	XF
73	1802	—	1.00	3.00	5.00	10.00
	1803	—	1.00	3.00	5.00	10.00

| 73a | 1804 | — | 1.00 | 3.00 | 5.00 | 10.00 |

SILBER GROSCHEN

1.5500 g, .312 SILVER, .0155 oz ASW

C#	Date	Mintage	Fine	VF	XF	Unc
80	1847A	.750	3.00	7.00	20.00	60.00

2.1900 g, .220 SILVER, .0154 oz ASW

| 85 | 1860A | .432 | 2.00 | 5.00 | 10.00 | 50.00 |

2-1/2 SILBER GROSCHEN
3.2400 g, .375 SILVER, .0390 oz ASW
Obv: Head right. Rev: Value.

| 81 | 1847A | .363 | 3.00 | 7.00 | 20.00 | 75.00 |

3.2200 g, .375 SILVER, .0388 oz ASW

| 86 | 1860A | .120 | 3.00 | 7.00 | 20.00 | 75.00 |

EIN (1) THALER
(Vereins)

Lippe-Detmold / GERMAN STATES

18.5200 g, .900 SILVER, .5360 oz ASW

C#	Date	Mintage	Fine	VF	XF	Unc
87	1860A	.026	40.00	75.00	135.00	285.00
	1866A	.018	45.00	80.00	150.00	315.00

2 THALER
(3-1/2 Gulden)

37.1200 g, .900 SILVER, 1.0742 oz ASW

	Date	Mintage	Fine	VF	XF	Unc
82	1843A	.017	200.00	400.00	700.00	1400.

MONETARY REFORM
2 MARK

11.1110 g, .900 SILVER, .3215 oz ASW

Y#	Date	Mintage	Fine	VF	XF	Unc
83	1906A	.020	100.00	200.00	300.00	450.00
	1906A	1,100	—	—	Proof	450.00

3 MARK

16.6670 g, .900 SILVER, .4823 oz ASW

Y#	Date	Mintage	Fine	VF	XF	Unc
84	1913A	.015	125.00	250.00	325.00	475.00
	1913A	100 pcs.	—	—	Proof	550.00

LOWENSTEIN-WERTHEIM
ROCHEFORT

The Catholic line of Rochefort was founded in 1635. Rochefort counts were made princes of the empire in 1711. Lowenstein-Wertheim was mediatized in 1806 after which other counts were made Bavarian princes in 1812.

RULERS
Constantin, 1789-1806

PFENNING

COPPER

C#	Date	Mintage	Fine	VF	XF	Unc
115a	1801	—	2.00	5.00	10.00	65.00
	1802	—	2.00	5.00	10.00	65.00

VIRNEBURG & ROCHEFORT JOINT COINAGE
PFENNING

COPPER

	Date		Fine	VF	XF	Unc
133	1802	—	2.00	4.00	10.00	50.00
	1804	—	2.00	4.00	10.00	50.00

Obv: Spade shield

| 133a | 1804 | — | 2.00 | 3.00 | 8.00 | 40.00 |

Obv: (error) L.M. above shield.

| 133b | 1804 | — | 4.00 | 7.00 | 15.00 | 100.00 |

BILLON
Obv: Eagle over 3 roses, 1 PF above. Rev: Blank.

138	1801	—	3.00	7.00	15.00	60.00
	1802	—	3.00	7.00	15.00	60.00
	1803	—	3.00	7.00	15.00	60.00
	1804	—	3.00	7.00	15.00	60.00

KREUZER

BILLON

140	1801	—	3.00	6.00	10.00	50.00
	1802	—	3.00	6.00	10.00	50.00
	1803	—	3.00	6.00	10.00	50.00
	1804	—	3.00	6.00	10.00	50.00
	1805	—	3.00	6.00	10.00	50.00
	1806	—	3.00	6.00	10.00	50.00

NOTE: Varieties exist.

3 KREUZER

BILLON
Obv: Arms. Rev: Value

142	1801	—	6.00	15.00	40.00	150.00
	1802	—	6.00	15.00	40.00	150.00
	1803	—	6.00	15.00	40.00	150.00
	1804	—	6.00	15.00	40.00	150.00
	1805	—	6.00	15.00	40.00	150.00

NOTE: 3 varieties exist.

LUBECK
FREE CITY

Lubeck became a free city of the empire in 1188 and from c. 1190 into the 13th century an imperial mint existed in the town. It was granted the mint right in 1188, 1226 and 1340, but actually began its first civic coinage c. 1350. Occupied by the French during the Napoleonic Wars, it was restored as a free city in 1813 and became part of the German Empire in 1871.

MINTMASTER'S INITIALS

Letter	Date	Name
HDF	1773-1801	Hermann David Friederichsen

2 MARK

11.1110 g, .900 SILVER, .3215 oz ASW

Y#	Date	Mintage	Fine	VF	XF	Unc
85	1901A	.025	100.00	175.00	225.00	350.00
	1901A	—	—	—	Proof	450.00

85a	1904A	.025	45.00	75.00	130.00	185.00
	1904A	200 pcs.	—	—	Proof	275.00
	1905A	.025	45.00	75.00	130.00	225.00
	1905A	178 pcs.	—	—	Proof	275.00
	1906A	.025	45.00	75.00	130.00	225.00
	1906A	200 pcs.	—	—	Proof	275.00
	1907A	.025	45.00	75.00	130.00	225.00
	1911A	.025	45.00	75.00	130.00	225.00
	1912A	.025	45.00	75.00	130.00	225.00

3 MARK

16.6670 g, .900 SILVER, .4823 oz ASW

86	1908A	.033	25.00	70.00	125.00	190.00
	1909A	.033	25.00	70.00	125.00	190.00
	1910A	.033	25.00	70.00	125.00	190.00
	1911A	.033	25.00	70.00	125.00	190.00
	1912A	.034	25.00	70.00	125.00	190.00
	1913A	.030	25.00	70.00	125.00	190.00
	1914A	.010	35.00	85.00	150.00	225.00
	Common date		—	—	Proof	250.00

5 MARK

27.7770 g, .900 SILVER, .8038 oz ASW

87	1904A	.010	100.00	250.00	375.00	500.00
	1904A	200 pcs.	—	—	Proof	800.00
	1907A	.010	100.00	250.00	375.00	500.00
	1908A	.010	100.00	275.00	400.00	550.00
	1913A	6,000	100.00	275.00	400.00	600.00

10 MARK

3.9820 g, .900 GOLD, .1152 oz AGW

Y#	Date	Mintage	Fine	VF	XF	Unc
88	1901A	.010	300.00	500.00	800.00	1100.
	1901A	200 pcs.	—	—	Proof	1800.
	1904A	.010	300.00	500.00	800.00	1100.
	1904A	130 pcs.	—	—	Proof	1800.

88a	1905A	.010	300.00	500.00	800.00	1100.
	1905A	247 pcs.	—	—	Proof	2250.
	1906A	.010	300.00	500.00	800.00	1100.
	1906A	216 pcs.	—	—	Proof	2250.
	1909A	.010	300.00	500.00	800.00	1100.
	1910A	.010	300.00	500.00	800.00	1100.

TRADE COINAGE

DUCAT

3.5000 g, .986 GOLD, .1109 oz AGW

C#	Date	Mintage	Fine	VF	XF	Unc
24	1801 HDF	—	400.00	750.00	1250.	1650.

MECKLENBURG-SCHWERIN

The duchy of Mecklenburg was located along the Baltic coast between Holstein and Pomerania. Schwerin was annexed to Mecklenburg in 1357. In 1658 the Mecklenburg dynasty was divided into two lines. The 1815 Congress of Vienna elevated the duchy to the status of grand duchy and it became a part of the German Empire in 1871 until 1918 when the last grand duke abdicated.

RULERS

Friedrich Franz I, 1785-1837
Paul Friedrich, 1837-1842
Friedrich Franz II, 1842-1883
Friedrich Franz III, 1883-1897
Friedrich Franz IV, 1897-1918

MINT MARKS

A - Berlin
B - Hannover

PFENNIG

COPPER

C#	Date	Mintage	Fine	VF	XF	Unc
73	1831	.514	2.50	5.00	10.00	40.00

102	1872B	2.335	1.00	2.00	4.00	15.00

2 PFENNIG

COPPER

74	1831	.257	2.50	5.00	10.00	60.00

103	1872B	1.155	1.50	3.00	6.00	30.00

3 PFENNIG

(1 Dreiling)

.5000 g, .187 SILVER, .0030 oz ASW
Rev. leg: MECK. SCHWERIN: SCHEID

C#	Date	Mintage	Fine	VF	XF	Unc
57	1801	.204	2.00	4.00	10.00	65.00
	1803	.117	2.00	4.00	10.00	65.00
	1804	.113	2.00	4.00	10.00	65.00
	1805	.414	2.00	4.00	10.00	65.00
	1810	.117	2.00	4.00	10.00	65.00
	1811	.273	2.00	4.00	10.00	65.00
	1813	—	2.00	4.00	10.00	80.00
	1814	.060	2.00	4.00	10.00	80.00
	1815	.081	2.00	4.00	10.00	80.00

BILLON
Obv: Crowned FF monogram.
Rev: Value 3 PFEN.

75	1816	.199	2.00	4.00	10.00	70.00
	1817	.083	2.00	4.00	10.00	80.00
	1818	.077	2.00	4.00	10.00	80.00
	1819	.251	2.00	4.00	10.00	70.00

Rev. value: I DREILING, date.

76	1819	.596	2.00	4.00	7.00	40.00
	1820	.845	2.00	4.00	7.00	40.00
	1821	.516	2.00	4.00	7.00	40.00
	1822	1.021	2.00	4.00	7.00	40.00
	1824	.235	2.00	4.00	7.00	40.00

.4500 g, .125 SILVER, .0018 oz ASW

76.4	1828	.684	2.00	4.00	7.00	40.00
	1829	.207	2.00	4.00	7.00	40.00
	1830	.793	2.00	4.00	7.00	40.00

76.7	1831	.064	3.00	5.00	10.00	50.00
	1832	.308	3.00	5.00	7.00	40.00
	1833	.048	3.00	5.00	10.00	50.00
	1836	.452	3.00	5.00	7.00	40.00

94	1838	—	3.00	5.00	10.00	60.00
	1839	.172	3.00	5.00	10.00	60.00
	1840	.112	3.00	5.00	10.00	60.00
	1841	.100	3.00	5.00	10.00	60.00
	1842	.157	3.00	5.00	10.00	60.00

105	1842	.203	3.00	5.00	10.00	55.00
	1843	.230	3.00	5.00	10.00	55.00
	1844	.125	3.00	5.00	10.00	55.00
	1845	.170	3.00	5.00	10.00	55.00
	1846	.077	3.00	5.00	10.00	55.00

COPPER

101	1843	.089	1.50	3.00	6.00	40.00
	1845	.151	1.50	3.00	6.00	40.00
	1846	.073	1.50	3.00	6.00	40.00
	1848	—	1.50	3.00	6.00	40.00

101a	1852A	—	1.00	2.00	4.00	25.00
	1853A	—	1.00	2.00	4.00	25.00
	1854A	—	1.00	2.00	4.00	25.00
	1855A	1.135	1.00	2.00	4.00	25.00
	1858A	—	1.00	2.00	4.00	25.00
	1859A	—	1.00	2.00	4.00	25.00
	1860A	—	1.00	2.00	4.00	25.00
	1861A	—	1.00	2.00	4.00	25.00
	1863A	—	1.00	2.00	4.00	25.00
	1864A	1.076	1.00	2.00	4.00	25.00

5 PFENNIG

COPPER

C#	Date	Mintage	Fine	VF	XF	Unc
104	1872B	.459	4.00	8.00	17.50	40.00

6 PFENNIG

.7600 g, .250 SILVER, .0061 oz ASW

59	1801	.080	3.00	5.00	10.00	40.00
	1802	.141	3.00	5.00	10.00	40.00
	1803	.060	3.00	5.00	10.00	40.00
	1804	.062	3.00	5.00	10.00	40.00
	1805	.321	3.00	5.00	10.00	40.00
	1809	.084	3.00	5.00	10.00	40.00
	1810	.081	3.00	5.00	10.00	40.00
	1811	.222	3.00	5.00	10.00	40.00
	1813	.254	3.00	5.00	10.00	40.00
	1815	.199	3.00	5.00	10.00	40.00

Obv: Crowned FF monogram. Rev: Value 6 PFEN.

77	1816	.255	3.00	5.00	10.00	40.00
	1817	.300	3.00	5.00	10.00	40.00

.9000 g, .125 SILVER, .0036 oz ASW
W/o legends

79	1831	.128	2.00	7.00	15.00	75.00

SECHSLING

.7600 g, .250 SILVER, .0061 oz ASW

78	1820	.150	2.00	4.00	10.00	55.00
	1821	.249	2.00	4.00	10.00	55.00
	1822	.272	2.00	4.00	10.00	55.00
	1823	.320	2.00	4.00	10.00	55.00
	1824	.419	2.00	4.00	10.00	55.00

.9000 g, .125 SILVER, .0036 oz ASW

78.4	1828	—	2.00	4.00	10.00	75.00
	1829	.190	2.00	4.00	10.00	75.00

SCHILLING

1.0800 g, .375 SILVER, .0130 oz ASW

61	1801	1.301	3.00	7.00	15.00	60.00
	1802	2.431	3.00	7.00	15.00	60.00
	1803	2.348	3.00	7.00	15.00	60.00
	1804	2.603	3.00	7.00	15.00	60.00
	1805	2.501	3.00	7.00	15.00	60.00
	1806	1.766	3.00	7.00	15.00	60.00
	1807	.585	3.00	7.00	15.00	60.00
	1808	.243	3.00	7.00	15.00	60.00
	1809	.342	3.00	7.00	15.00	60.00
	1810	.250	3.00	7.00	15.00	60.00

Rev: Value.

80	1817	.031	10.00	20.00	50.00	250.00

1.1100 g, .312 SILVER, .0111 oz ASW
Obv. leg: GR. HZ. U.M.S.

81	1826	.159	3.00	7.00	20.00	80.00
	1827	.342	3.00	7.00	20.00	80.00

Obv. leg: GR. HERZOG V. Rev: Value, legend.

81.4	1829	.054	4.00	8.00	15.00	90.00
	1830	.501	3.00	6.00	10.00	55.00
	1831	.528	3.00	6.00	10.00	55.00
	1832	.119	3.00	6.00	10.00	75.00
	1833	.091	3.00	6.00	10.00	75.00
	1834	.118	3.00	6.00	10.00	75.00
	1835	.109	3.00	6.00	10.00	75.00
	1836	.163	3.00	6.00	10.00	70.00
	1837	.082	3.00	6.00	10.00	75.00

Obv: Crowned PF monogram

95	1838	.021	4.00	7.00	15.00	115.00
	1839	.125	4.00	7.00	15.00	70.00
	1840	.052	4.00	7.00	15.00	90.00
	1841	.046	4.00	7.00	15.00	90.00
	1842	.030	4.00	7.00	15.00	100.00

Mecklenburg-Schwerin / GERMAN STATES 650

	BILLON				
C# Date	Mintage	Fine	VF	XF	Unc
106 1842	.108	2.00	4.00	8.00	45.00
1843	.139	2.00	4.00	8.00	45.00
1844	.116	2.00	4.00	8.00	45.00
1845	.246	2.00	4.00	8.00	45.00
1846	.154	2.00	4.00	8.00	45.00

4 SCHILLINGE

3.0600 g, .562 SILVER, .0553 oz ASW

| 63 | 1809 | 1,408 | 40.00 | 60.00 | 100.00 | 450.00 |

3.3000 g, .437 SILVER, .0464 oz ASW

| 82 | 1826 | .621 | 10.00 | 15.00 | 35.00 | 130.00 |

3.0600 g, .500 SILVER, .0492 oz ASW
Obv: Head left, leg: GR. HERZOG. . . .

| 83 | 1828 | .070 | 15.00 | 25.00 | 50.00 | 185.00 |

Obv. leg: GROSSHERZOG. . . .

83a	1829	.200	10.00	15.00	35.00	115.00
	1830	1.793	10.00	15.00	35.00	115.00
	1831	.476	10.00	15.00	35.00	115.00
	1832	.121	10.00	15.00	35.00	115.00
	1833	.049	10.00	20.00	40.00	135.00

Obv: Crowned arms within 2 crossed branches.

| 96 | 1838 | .015 | 10.00 | 20.00 | 40.00 | 120.00 |
| | 1839 | .039 | 10.00 | 20.00 | 40.00 | 120.00 |

8 SCHILLINGE

6.6000 g, .437 SILVER, .0927 oz ASW

| 84 | 1827 | .025 | 15.00 | 30.00 | 100.00 | 250.00 |

1/48 THALER

1.3000 g, .208 SILVER, .0086 oz ASW

| 107 | 1848 | — | 2.00 | 4.00 | 8.00 | 45.00 |

| 107a | 1852A | — | 1.50 | 3.00 | 6.00 | 40.00 |
| | 1853A | — | 1.50 | 3.00 | 6.00 | 40.00 |

C#	Date	Mintage	Fine	VF	XF	Unc
107a	1855A	2.819	1.50	3.00	6.00	40.00
	1858A	—	1.50	3.00	6.00	40.00
	1860A	—	1.50	3.00	6.00	40.00
	1861A	—	1.50	3.00	6.00	40.00
	1862A	—	1.50	3.00	6.00	40.00
	1863A	—	1.50	3.00	6.00	40.00
	1864A	—	1.50	3.00	6.00	40.00
	1866A	2.034	1.50	3.00	6.00	40.00

1/12 THALER

2.4400 g, .500 SILVER, .0392 oz ASW

| 108 | 1848 | 2.047 | 5.00 | 10.00 | 25.00 | 75.00 |

NOTE: Varieties exist.

1/6 THALER

5.3500 g, .520 SILVER, .0894 oz ASW

| 109 | 1848A | .137 | 10.00 | 35.00 | 80.00 | 150.00 |

2/3 THALER

17.3200 g, .750 SILVER, .4177 oz ASW

70	1801	.169	25.00	60.00	100.00	250.00
	1808	.655	25.00	60.00	100.00	250.00
	1810	.338	25.00	60.00	100.00	250.00

| 71 | 1813 | 9,918 | 100.00 | 165.00 | 275.00 | 450.00 |

Obv. leg: G.G. HERZOG. Rev: Date below value.

| 85 | 1817 | 6,783 | 275.00 | 450.00 | 750.00 | 1250. |

Obv. leg: G.G. GR. HERZ.

| 85a | 1825 | .035 | 85.00 | 175.00 | 325.00 | 600.00 |

	Obv. leg: SCHW.				
C# Date	Mintage	Fine	VF	XF	Unc
86 1825	.043	100.00	180.00	300.00	600.00
1826	—	100.00	180.00	300.00	600.00

Obv. leg: SCHWERIN

| 86a | 1826 | .103 | 100.00 | 180.00 | 300.00 | 600.00 |

| 87 | 1828 | .057 | 100.00 | 165.00 | 330.00 | 600.00 |
| 87a | 1829 | — | — | — | Rare | — |

13.1700 g, .986 SILVER, .4175 oz ASW

97	1839	.291	30.00	60.00	125.00	250.00
	1840	.856	25.00	50.00	100.00	200.00
	1841	.118	35.00	70.00	150.00	300.00

| 110 | 1845 | 1,563 | 375.00 | 550.00 | 825.00 | 1250. |

EIN (1) THALER

22.2700 g, .750 SILVER, .5370 oz ASW

| 111 | 1848A | .528 | 30.00 | 60.00 | 120.00 | 225.00 |

18.5200 g, .900 SILVER, .5360 oz ASW

| 112 | 1864A | .100 | 30.00 | 60.00 | 140.00 | 275.00 |

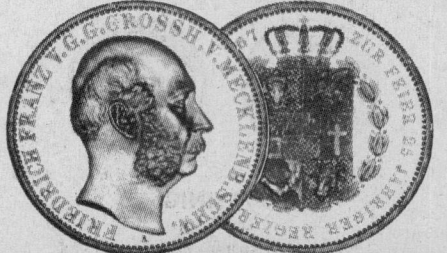

25th Anniversary of Reign

| 113 | 1867A | .010 | 30.00 | 60.00 | 140.00 | 225.00 |

ZWEI EIN HALB (2-1/2) THALER

3.3300 g, .896 GOLD, .0959 oz AGW

C#	Date	Mintage	Fine	VF	XF	Unc
90	1831	7,755	375.00	750.00	1250.	2500.
	1833	124 pcs.	600.00	1000.	1750.	2500.
	1835	195 pcs.	600.00	1000.	1750.	2500.

| 98 | 1840 | 2,910 | 300.00 | 500.00 | 750.00 | 1100. |

FUNF (5) THALER

6.6600 g, .896 GOLD, .1919 oz AGW

92	1828	1,753	600.00	1200.	1800.	2750.
	1831	3,878	600.00	1200.	1800.	2750.
	1832	3,334	600.00	1200.	1800.	2750.
	1833	125 pcs.	1000.	1200.	3000.	3750.
	1835	100 pcs.	1000.	1200.	3000.	3750.

| 99 | 1840 | 1,454 | 650.00 | 1250. | 1750. | 3000. |

ZEHN (10) THALER

13.3200 g, .896 GOLD, .3837 oz AGW

93	1828	876 pcs.	1250.	2500.	3750.	5000.
	1831	1,938	1000.	2000.	3250.	4250.
	1832	1,667	1000.	2000.	3250.	4250.
	1833	128 pcs.	1500.	3000.	4500.	6000.

| 100 | 1839 | .092 | 500.00 | 1100. | 1500. | 2000. |

MONETARY REFORM
2 MARK

11.1110 g, .900 SILVER, .3215 oz ASW

Y#	Date	Mintage	Fine	VF	XF	Unc
89	1876A	.300	100.00	250.00	750.00	1500.

Y#	Date	Mintage	Fine	VF	XF	Unc
89	1876A	—	—	—	Proof	2000.

93	1901A	.050	125.00	300.00	450.00	1000.
	1901A	1,000	—	—	Proof	1000.

Friedrich Franz IV Wedding

96	1904A	.100	15.00	35.00	65.00	90.00
	1904A	6,000	—	—	Proof	150.00

3 MARK

16.6670 g, .900 SILVER, .4823 oz ASW
100 Years as Grand Duchy

98	1915A	.033	40.00	90.00	150.00	200.00
	1915A	—	—	—	Proof	350.00

5 MARK

27.7770 g, .900 SILVER, .8038 oz ASW
Friedrich Franz IV Wedding

97	1904A	.040	35.00	100.00	175.00	225.00
	1904A	2,500	—	—	Proof	450.00

100 Years as Grand Duchy

99	1915A	.010	125.00	250.00	425.00	700.00
	1915A	—	—	—	Proof	800.00

10 MARK

3.9820 g, .900 GOLD, .1152 oz AGW
Rev: Type I.

Y#	Date	Mintage	Fine	VF	XF	Unc
90	1872A	.016	700.00	1000.	1750.	2750.
	1872A	—	—	—	Proof	Rare

Rev: Type II.

90a	1878A	.050	300.00	500.00	700.00	1000.
	1878A	—	—	—	Proof	2500.

92	1890A	.100	150.00	300.00	500.00	900.00
	1890A	—	—	—	Proof	1800.

Rev: Type III.

94	1901A	.010	450.00	800.00	1400.	1750.
	1901A	200 pcs.	—	—	Proof	1950.

20 MARK

7.9650 g, .900 GOLD, .2304 oz AGW
Rev: Type I.

91	1872A	.069	375.00	650.00	1000.	1750.
	1872A	200 pcs.	—	—	Proof	Rare

Rev: Type III.

95	1901A	5,000	900.00	1750.	2750.	4000.
	1901A	200 pcs.	—	—	Proof	3250.

MECKLENBURG-STRELITZ

The duchy of Mecklenburg was located along the Baltic Coast between Holstein and Pomerania. The Strelitz line was founded in 1658 when the Mecklenburg line was divided into two lines. The 1815 Congress of Vienna elevated the duchy to the status of grand duchy. It became a part of the German Empire in 1871 until 1918 when the last grand duke died.

RULERS

Karl II, 1794-1816
Georg, 1816-1860
Friedrich Wilhelm, 1860-1904
Adolph Friedrich V, 1904-1914
Adolph Friedrich VI, 1914-1918

PFENNIG
COPPER
Obv: Crowned G. Rev: Value.

C#	Date	Mintage	Fine	VF	XF	Unc
40	1838	.058	5.00	10.00	25.00	125.00

| 46 | 1872 | .118 | 1.50 | 3.00 | 6.00 | 30.00 |

Mecklenburg-Strelitz / GERMAN STATES 652

1-1/2 PFENNIG

COPPER

C#	Date	Mintage	Fine	VF	XF	Unc
41	1838	.040	5.00	10.00	25.00	125.00

2 PFENNIG

COPPER

| 47 | 1872 | .203 | 1.50 | 3.00 | 6.00 | 35.00 |

3 PFENNIG

COPPER

42	1832	.290	1.50	3.00	6.00	35.00
	1843	.283	1.50	3.00	6.00	35.00
	1845/3	—	1.50	3.00	6.00	35.00
	1845	.193	1.50	3.00	6.00	35.00
	1847	—	1.50	3.00	6.00	35.00

| 42a | 1855A | 1.501 | 1.50 | 3.00 | 6.00 | 35.00 |
| | 1859A | .580 | 1.50 | 3.00 | 6.00 | 35.00 |

| 45 | 1862A | Inc. Ab. | 1.50 | 3.00 | 6.00 | 35.00 |
| | 1864A | Inc. Ab. | 1.50 | 3.00 | 6.00 | 35.00 |

5 PFENNIG

COPPER

| 48 | 1872 | .118 | 1.50 | 3.00 | 6.00 | 35.00 |

4 SCHILLINGE

3.2500 g, .375 SILVER, .0392 oz ASW

44	1846	.165	5.00	15.00	30.00	100.00
	1847	.170	5.00	15.00	30.00	100.00
	1849	.135	5.00	15.00	30.00	100.00

1/48 THALER

1.3000 g, .208 SILVER, .0086 oz ASW

43	1838	.145	2.00	4.00	10.00	40.00
	1841	.055	3.00	6.00	12.50	50.00
	1845	.097	2.00	4.00	10.00	40.00
	1847	.231	2.00	4.00	10.00	40.00

C#	Date	Mintage	Fine	VF	XF	Unc
43a	1855A	.634	1.50	3.00	6.00	30.00
	1859A	.720	1.50	3.00	6.00	30.00

| 49 | 1862A | Inc. Ab. | 1.50 | 3.00 | 6.00 | 30.00 |
| | 1864A | Inc. Ab. | 1.50 | 3.00 | 6.00 | 30.00 |

EIN (1) THALER

18.5200 g, .900 SILVER, .5360 oz ASW

| 50 | 1870A | .050 | 25.00 | 40.00 | 85.00 | 175.00 |

MONETARY REFORM
2 MARK

11.1110 g, .900 SILVER, .3215 oz ASW

Y#	Date	Mintage	Fine	VF	XF	Unc
100	1877A	.100	125.00	250.00	1400.	2750.
	1877A	—	—	—	Proof	3000.

| 103 | 1905A | .010 | 135.00 | 300.00 | 575.00 | 750.00 |
| | 1905A | 2,500 | — | — | Proof | 750.00 |

3 MARK

16.6670 g, .900 SILVER, .4823 oz ASW

| 106 | 1913A | 7,000 | 200.00 | 400.00 | 800.00 | 1200. |
| | 1913A | — | — | — | Proof | 1200. |

10 MARK

3.9820 g, .900 GOLD, .1152 oz AGW
Rev: Type I.

| 101 | 1873A | 1,500 | 3500. | 5000. | 6500. | 7500. |
| | 1873A | — | — | — | Proof | 13,000. |

Y#	Date	Mintage	Fine	VF	XF	Unc
101a	1874A	3,000	2000.	4000.	5000.	7000.
	1880A	4,000	1500.	3250.	4000.	5000.

| 104 | 1905A | 1,000 | 1500. | 2250. | 3000. | 4500. |
| | 1905A | 160 pcs. | — | — | Proof | 3750. |

20 MARK

7.9650 g, .900 GOLD, .2304 oz AGW

| 102 | 1873A | 6,750 | 1500. | 2750. | 4000. | 6500. |

Rev: Type II.

| 102a | 1874A | 6,000 | 1500. | 2750. | 4000. | 6500. |

Rev: Type III.

| 105 | 1905A | 1,000 | 2000. | 3000. | 5000. | 6000. |
| | 1905A | 150 pcs. | — | — | Proof | 5500. |

MUNSTER

BISHOPRIC

A Bishopric, located in Westphalia, was established c. 802. The first Munster coinage was struck c. 1228. In 1802 the bishopric was secularized and divided. From 1806-1810 most of Munster belonged to Berg, from 1810-1814 to France and from 1814 onward, to Prussia.

During the 16th and 17th centuries treasury tokens, mostly counterstamped with the arms or initials of the current treasurer were issued. These were replaced in the middle of the 17th century by Cathedral coins, showing St. Paul with a sword. They last appeared at the end of the 18th century.

RULERS

Maximilian Franz of Austria,
 1784-1801
Sede Vacante, 1801
Anton Victor of Prussia, 1801-1802

1/24 THALER
(Reichs)

BILLON
Obv: Value. Rev: Date.

C#	Date	Mintage	Fine	VF	XF	Unc
40	1801	—	37.50	60.00	100.00	175.00

1/3 THALER
(Reichs)

SILVER

C#	Date	Mintage	Fine	VF	XF	Unc
41	1801	—	90.00	140.00	200.00	325.00

2/3 THALER

SILVER

42	1801	—	135.00	210.00	300.00	475.00

EIN (1) THALER

SILVER

43	1801	200 pcs.	750.00	1200.	2200.	4500.

NASSAU

The duchy of Nassau, located on both sides of the River Lahn in the Middle Rhineland was established in 1158. The lands were frequently divided and combined. The first coins were struck c. 1260. The Weilburg line was founded in 1355 and the Usingen line in 1642. In 1806 they united under a common administration. The Usingen line became extinct in 1816 leaving a fully united duchy under the Weilburg rulers. The house ended with the ouster of the duke in 1866 by Prussia.

JOINT COINAGE
Nassau-Weilburg & Nassau-Usingen

RULERS
Friedrich August, 1803-1816
Friedrich Wilhelm, 1788-1816

MINTMASTER'S INITIALS

Letter	Date	Name
CT	—	Christian Teichmann

1/4 KREUZER

COPPER
Obv: Crowned arms, leg: HERZOGL NASS.
Rev: L below date.

C#	Date	Mintage	Fine	VF	XF	Unc
1	1808	.449	1.00	3.00	6.00	40.00

1a	1808	Inc. Ab.	1.00	3.00	6.00	40.00
	1809	—	1.00	3.00	6.00	40.00
	1810	—	1.00	3.00	6.00	40.00
	1811	—	1.00	3.00	6.00	40.00
	1812	1.470	1.00	3.00	6.00	40.00
	1813	.280	1.00	3.00	6.00	40.00
	1814	.278	1.00	3.00	6.00	40.00

NOTE: Several varieties exist.

1/2 KREUZER

COPPER

2	1813	.445	2.00	4.00	10.00	65.00

KREUZER

COPPER

3	1808	.799	15.00	40.00	85.00	275.00
	1809	—	1.00	3.00	7.00	50.00

Rev: L below wreath.

3a	1808	Inc. Ab.	15.00	40.00	85.00	275.00

Obv. leg: HERZ:

3b	1809	—	5.00	10.00	25.00	100.00
	1810	—	3.00	5.00	15.00	50.00
	1813	.131	3.00	5.00	15.00	50.00

3 KREUZER
(1 Groschen)

1.3800 g, .281 SILVER, .0124 oz ASW
Obv. leg: HERZ. NASS. SCHEIDE.M.
Rev: Value.

4a	1809	.010	10.00	25.00	80.00	200.00

Obv. leg: HERZ. NASSAU. SCHEIDEMUNZ.

4	1810	.750	7.00	20.00	40.00	125.00
	1811	—	10.00	30.00	60.00	150.00

Obv. leg: HERZ. NASSAU. SCHEIDE. M.

C#	Date	Mintage	Fine	VF	XF	Unc
4b	1811	.270	7.00	15.00	25.00	125.00
	1812	.480	5.00	10.00	20.00	100.00
	1813	.506	5.00	10.00	20.00	90.00
	1814	.844	2.50	5.00	10.00	40.00
	1815	.675	2.50	5.00	10.00	40.00
	1816	.091	2.50	5.00	10.00	40.00
	1817	.259	2.50	5.00	10.00	40.00
	1818	.675	2.50	5.00	10.00	40.00
	1819	.928	2.50	5.00	10.00	40.00

5 KREUZER

2.2200 g, .437 SILVER, .0311 oz ASW
Obv. leg: HERZ. NASSAU.....

5	1808	4,000	150.00	300.00	600.00	1000.
	1809	—	10.00	20.00	50.00	125.00

Obv. leg: HERZOGL. NASS....

5a	1808	Inc. Ab.	10.00	20.00	50.00	140.00

Obv. leg: HERZ. NASSAUISCHE.
Rev: Value, L below.

5b	1808	—	10.00	20.00	50.00	140.00
	1809	—	10.00	20.00	50.00	140.00

10 KREUZER

3.8900 g, .500 SILVER, .0625 oz ASW
Obv. leg: HERZ. NASSAUISCHE CONVENTIONS MUNZ.
Rev: L below value.

6	1809	—	200.00	400.00	750.00	1250.

Obv. leg: HERZ. NASSAU. CONVENT. MUNZ.

6a	1809	—	20.00	45.00	90.00	150.00

Obv. leg: HERZ. NASSAUISCHE.....

6b	1809	—	20.00	45.00	90.00	150.00

Obv. leg: HERZ. NASSAU. Rev: W/o L.

6c	1809	—	20.00	45.00	90.00	150.00

20 KREUZER

6.6800 g, .583 SILVER, .1252 oz ASW
Obv. leg: HERZ. NASSAUISCHE CONVENTIONS MUNZ.

7	1809	—	100.00	200.00	400.00	750.00

Obv. leg: HERZ. NASSAUISCHE CONVENT. MUNZ.

7a	1809	—	20.00	40.00	60.00	125.00

GERMAN STATES — Nassau-Weilburg

Rev: Wreath w/o bow, running horse below.

C#	Date	Mintage	Fine	VF	XF	Unc
7b	1809	—	20.00	40.00	60.00	125.00

Rev: 60 between rosettes

| 7c | 1809 | — | 20.00 | 40.00 | 60.00 | 125.00 |

Obv. leg: . . . . . CONVENTIONS. Rev: Value within branches.

| 7d | 1809 | — | 20.00 | 40.00 | 60.00 | 125.00 |

Obv. leg: . . . . . CONVENT. Rev: L below wreath.

| 7e | 1809 | — | 20.00 | 40.00 | 60.00 | 125.00 |

Rev: W/o bow on wreath, prancing horse below.

| 7f | 1809 | — | 20.00 | 40.00 | 60.00 | 125.00 |

Obv. leg: HERZ: NASS: CONV: MUNZ:

| 7g | 1809 | — | 20.00 | 40.00 | 60.00 | 125.00 |

TRADE COINAGE
DUCAT

3.5000 g, .986 GOLD, .1109 oz AGW

| 8 | 1809 | 3,543 | 500.00 | 1000. | 1600. | 2250. |

SEPARATE COINAGE
Nassau-Usingen
RULERS
Friedrich August, 1803-1816

10 KREUZER

3.8900 g, .500 SILVER, .0625 oz ASW

| 9.1 | 1809 | — | 200.00 | 375.00 | 700.00 | 1200. |

Obv: L at truncation

| 9.2 | 1809 L | — | 200.00 | 375.00 | 700.00 | 1200. |

20 KREUZER

6.6800 g, .583 SILVER, .1252 oz ASW
Obv: Head right, L at truncation. Rev: Crowned arms.

| 10 | 1809 L | — | 20.00 | 45.00 | 90.00 | 250.00 |

C#	Date	Mintage	Fine	VF	XF	Unc
10a	1809 L	—	20.00	45.00	90.00	250.00

1/2 THALER
(Convention)

14.0300 g, .833 SILVER, .3757 oz ASW

| 11 | 1809 L | — | 50.00 | 110.00 | 200.00 | 400.00 |

EIN (1) THALER
(Convention)

28.0600 g, .833 SILVER, .7515 oz ASW
Obv: Head right, L at truncation.
Rev: Similar to C#12c.

| 12 | 1809 L | — | 350.00 | 550.00 | 1200. | 2400. |

Rev: Date dividing C.T.

12c	1810 CT	—	200.00	350.00	800.00	1600.
	1811 CT	—	200.00	275.00	600.00	1200.
	1812 CT	—	200.00	300.00	725.00	1500.
	1813 CT	.042	200.00	300.00	725.00	1500.
	1815 CT	—	200.00	300.00	725.00	1500.

Patriot Nicolaus Fischer

Obv: Similar to C#12.

C#	Date	Mintage	Fine	VF	XF	Unc
12a	1812	—	—	—	—	—

Nassau-Weilburg
RULERS
Friedrich Wilhelm II, 1788-1816

10 KREUZER

3.8900 g, .500 SILVER, .0625 oz ASW

| 30 | 1809 | — | 25.00 | 50.00 | 150.00 | 250.00 |

Obv: L at truncation

| 30a | 1809 | — | 25.00 | 50.00 | 150.00 | 250.00 |

20 KREUZER

6.6800 g, .583 SILVER, .1252 oz ASW

| 31 | 1809 | — | 25.00 | 50.00 | 150.00 | 250.00 |
| | 1810 | — | 25.00 | 50.00 | 150.00 | 250.00 |

1/2 THALER
(Convention)

14.0300 g, .833 SILVER, .3757 oz ASW
Obv: L on truncation.

| 32 | 1809 L | — | 80.00 | 160.00 | 250.00 | 350.00 |

EIN (1) THALER
(Convention)

28.0600 g, .833 SILVER, .7515 oz ASW
Obv: Similar to 1/2 Thaler, C#32.

| 33 | 1809 L | — | 450.00 | 850.00 | 1700. | 3400. |

Rev: Arms between laurel and palm branches.

| 33a | 1809 L | — | 450.00 | 850.00 | 1700. | 3400. |

**Obv: Similar to 1/2 Thaler, C#32.
Rev: Date dividing C.T.**

C#	Date	Mintage	Fine	VF	XF	Unc
33b	1810 CT	—	175.00	375.00	900.00	1900.
	1811 CT	—	175.00	275.00	700.00	1500.
	1812 CT	—	175.00	375.00	900.00	1900.

33c	1813 CT	.042	275.00	450.00	1000.	2000.
	1815 CT	—	300.00	560.00	1150.	2400.

United Nassau

RULERS
Duke Wilhelm, 1816-1839
Duke Adolph, 1839-1866

MINTMASTER'S INITIALS

Letter	Date	Name
CT	—	Christian Teichmann

HELLER
**COPPER
Obv: Crowned arms. Rev: Value.**

C#	Date	Mintage	Fine	VF	XF	Unc
51	1842	.182	2.00	4.00	8.00	35.00

PFENNIG

COPPER

52	1859	.220	2.00	4.00	8.00	35.00
	1860	.580	2.00	4.00	8.00	35.00
	1862	.490	2.00	4.00	8.00	35.00

1/4 KREUZER

COPPER

35	1817	.433	1.00	2.00	4.00	20.00
	1818	.894	1.00	2.00	4.00	20.00
	1819	4.932	1.00	2.00	4.00	20.00

Rev: W/o period after date.

35a	1817	Inc. Ab.	1.00	2.00	4.00	20.00
	1818	—	1.00	2.00	4.00	20.00
	1819	Inc. Ab.	1.00	2.00	4.00	20.00
	1822	4.210	1.00	2.00	4.00	20.00

NOTE: Several varieties exist.

EIN (1) KREUZER
**COPPER, 22-24mm
Obv: Crowned spade-shaped arms. Rev: Value in wreath.**

36	1817	.203	1.00	3.00	6.00	30.00
	1818	.084	1.00	3.00	6.00	30.00

**.5300 g, .229 SILVER, .0039 oz ASW
Rev: W/o wreath.**

C#	Date	Mintage	Fine	VF	XF	Unc
38	1817	.079	1.00	3.00	6.00	30.00
	1823	.545	1.00	3.00	6.00	30.00
	1824	.564	1.00	3.00	6.00	30.00
	1828	—	1.00	3.00	6.00	30.00

COPPER, 22-24mm

37	1830	.265	1.00	3.00	6.00	30.00
	1832	.517	1.00	3.00	6.00	30.00
	1834	.326	1.00	3.00	6.00	30.00
	1836	.200	1.00	3.00	6.00	30.00
	1838	.269	1.00	3.00	6.00	30.00

.5300 g, .229 SILVER, .0039 oz ASW

39	1832	.144	1.00	3.00	6.00	30.00
	1833	1.037	1.00	3.00	6.00	30.00
	1835	.408	1.00	3.00	6.00	30.00

COPPER

53	1842	.480	1.00	3.00	6.00	30.00
	1844	.188	1.00	3.00	6.00	30.00
	1848	.249	1.00	3.00	6.00	30.00
	1854	.274	1.00	3.00	6.00	30.00
	1855	—	1.00	3.00	6.00	30.00
	1856	.357	1.00	3.00	6.00	30.00

54	1859	.836	1.00	3.00	6.00	30.00
	1860	.610	1.00	3.00	6.00	30.00
	1861	.556	1.00	3.00	6.00	30.00
	1862	.610	1.00	3.00	6.00	30.00
	1863	.576	1.00	3.00	6.00	30.00

.5300 g, .229 SILVER, .0039 oz ASW

55	1861	.664	1.00	3.00	6.00	30.00

3 KREUZER
**1.3800 g, .281 SILVER, .0124 oz ASW
Obv: Crowned spade-shaped arms, NASSAU. Rev: Value.**

40	1817	.259	2.50	5.00	10.00	40.00
	1818	.675	2.50	5.00	10.00	40.00
	1819	.928	2.50	5.00	10.00	40.00

40a	1822	.671	2.50	5.00	10.00	40.00
	1823	.671	2.50	5.00	10.00	40.00
	1824	—	2.50	5.00	10.00	40.00
	1825	.192	2.50	5.00	10.00	40.00
	1826	.352	2.50	5.00	10.00	40.00
	1827	.308	2.50	5.00	10.00	40.00
	1828	.308	2.50	5.00	10.00	40.00

1.2900 g, .281 SILVER, .0116 oz ASW

41	1831	.509	2.50	5.00	10.00	40.00
	1832	.388	2.50	5.00	10.00	40.00
	1833	.042	2.50	5.00	10.00	40.00
	1834	.292	2.50	5.00	10.00	40.00
	1836	.340	2.50	5.00	10.00	40.00

1.2900 g, .333 SILVER, .0138 oz ASW

C#	Date	Mintage	Fine	VF	XF	Unc
56	1841	—	60.00	100.00	150.00	225.00
	1842	.112	2.00	4.00	8.00	35.00
	1844	.056	2.00	4.00	8.00	35.00
	1845	—	2.00	4.00	8.00	35.00
	1847	.210	2.00	4.00	8.00	35.00
	1848	.541	2.00	4.00	8.00	35.00
	1853	.091	2.00	4.00	8.00	35.00
	1855	.179	2.00	4.00	8.00	35.00

6 KREUZER
**2.2200 g, .375 SILVER, .0267 oz ASW
Obv: Crowned square arms, leg: NASSAUISCHE.
Rev: Value in wreath.**

42	1817	.109	3.00	6.00	12.00	40.00
	1818	.263	3.00	6.00	12.00	40.00
	1819	.378	3.00	6.00	12.00	40.00

Obv. leg: NASSAU.

42a	1822	.306	3.00	6.00	12.00	40.00
	1823	.306	3.00	6.00	12.00	40.00
	1824	.083	4.00	8.00	15.00	50.00
	1825	.176	3.00	6.00	12.00	40.00
	1826	.314	3.00	6.00	12.00	40.00
	1827	.302	3.00	6.00	12.00	40.00
	1828	.303	3.00	6.00	12.00	40.00

43	1831	1.100	3.00	6.00	12.00	40.00
	1832	.377	3.00	6.00	12.00	40.00
	1833	.641	3.00	6.00	12.00	40.00
	1834	.565	3.00	6.00	12.00	40.00
	1835	.832	3.00	6.00	12.00	40.00
	1836	.452	3.00	6.00	12.00	40.00
	1837	.314	3.00	6.00	12.00	40.00

2.5900 g, .333 SILVER, .0277 oz ASW

43a	1838	.201	3.00	6.00	12.00	40.00
	1839	.109	3.00	6.00	12.00	40.00

57	1840	.094	4.00	8.00	15.00	50.00
	1841	.321	3.00	6.00	12.00	40.00
	1844	.073	4.00	8.00	15.00	50.00
	1846	—	3.00	6.00	12.00	40.00
	1847	—	3.00	6.00	12.00	40.00
	1848	.198	3.00	6.00	12.00	40.00
	1855	.190	3.00	6.00	12.00	40.00

1/2 GULDEN

5.3000 g, .900 SILVER, .1533 oz ASW

44	1838	.108	20.00	40.00	75.00	150.00
	1839	.108	20.00	40.00	75.00	150.00

Nassau / GERMAN STATES 656

C#	Date	Mintage	Fine	VF	XF	Unc
58	1840	.095	20.00	40.00	75.00	150.00
	1841	.125	20.00	40.00	75.00	150.00
	1842	.031	20.00	40.00	75.00	150.00
	1843	.104	20.00	40.00	75.00	150.00
	1844	.117	20.00	40.00	75.00	150.00
	1845	.072	20.00	40.00	75.00	150.00

Obv: Head left.

59	1856	.313	20.00	40.00	75.00	150.00
	1860	.104	20.00	40.00	75.00	150.00

GULDEN

10.6000 g, .900 SILVER, .3067 oz ASW

45	1838	.190	25.00	50.00	100.00	250.00
	1839	.108	25.00	50.00	100.00	250.00

Obv: ZOLLMANN on truncation.

60	1840	.117	25.00	50.00	100.00	175.00
	1841	.124	25.00	50.00	100.00	175.00
	1842	.020	25.00	50.00	100.00	175.00
	1843	.236	25.00	50.00	100.00	175.00
	1844	.093	25.00	50.00	100.00	175.00
	1845	.138	25.00	50.00	100.00	175.00
	1846	.048	25.00	50.00	100.00	175.00
	1847	.231	25.00	50.00	100.00	175.00
	1855	.188	25.00	50.00	100.00	175.00

61	1855	Inc. Ab.	25.00	50.00	100.00	200.00
	1856	.040	25.00	50.00	100.00	200.00

ZWEY (2) GULDEN

21.2100 g, .900 SILVER, .6138 oz ASW
Obv: ZOLLMANN on truncation.

C#	Date	Mintage	Fine	VF	XF	Unc
65	1846	.177	50.00	125.00	300.00	800.00
	1847	.088	60.00	150.00	350.00	875.00

EIN (1) THALER
(Krone)

29.5300 g, .871 SILVER, .8270 oz ASW
Obv: Head right, L below. Rev: Crowned draped arms, date below dividing C.T.

46	1816 CT	—	—	—	Rare	—

47	1817 CT	.013	250.00	500.00	1200.	2500.

Obv: Similar to C#49 w/P.Z. on truncation.

48	1818 CT	4,500	250.00	500.00	1200.	2400.
	1825 CT	2,000	300.00	600.00	1400.	2800.

Obv: Deep ZOLLMANN. F on truncation.

49	1831	—	200.00	350.00	500.00	1400.
	1832	567 pcs.	125.00	225.00	350.00	800.00
	1833	—	125.00	225.00	350.00	800.00
	1836	—	125.00	225.00	350.00	800.00
	1837	2,683	125.00	225.00	350.00	800.00

Visit of Duke to the Mint
Obv: Similar to C#49.

C#	Date	Mintage	Fine	VF	XF	Unc
49a	1831	—	500.00	900.00	1600.	2400.

(Vereins)

18.5200 g, .900 SILVER, .5360 oz ASW
Obv: Z on truncation.

62	1859 Z	.050	45.00	80.00	175.00	400.00
	1860 Z	.030	45.00	80.00	175.00	400.00

Obv: F. KORN on truncation.

62a	1863	.145	45.00	80.00	200.00	500.00

Visit of Grand Duke to Mint

63	1861	3 pcs.	—	—	Proof	12,000.

25th Anniversary of Reign

64	1864	6,162	35.00	55.00	115.00	190.00

ZWEI (2) THALER
(3-1/2 Gulden)

37.1200 g, .900 SILVER, 1.0742 oz ASW
Obv: Similar to C#67a, ZOLLMANN on truncation.

C#	Date	Mintage	Fine	VF	XF	Unc
66	1840	.056	250.00	450.00	1000.	2000.

| 67a | 1844 | .021 | 175.00 | 300.00 | 650.00 | 1400. |
| | 1847 | — | — | — | Rare | — |

Obv: Truncation bare.

| 67 | 1844 | Inc. Ab. | 175.00 | 300.00 | 650.00 | 1400. |
| | 1854 | .072 | 175.00 | 300.00 | 600.00 | 1250. |

37.0400 g, .900 SILVER, 1.0719 oz ASW
Obv: C ZOLLMANN on truncation.

| 68 | 1860 | .130 | 125.00 | 225.00 | 400.00 | 1000. |

TRADE COINAGE
DUCAT
3.5000 g, .986 GOLD, .1109 oz AGW
Obv: Head right. Rev: Crowned draped arms.

C#	Date	Mintage	Fine	VF	XF	Unc
50	1818 CT	501 pcs.	650.00	1100.	2000.	3500.

NURNBERG

Nurnberg, in Franconia, was made a Free City in 1219. In that same year an Imperial mint was established there and continued throughout the rest of the century. The mint right was obtained in 1376 and again in 1422. City coins were struck from c. 1390 to 1806 when the city was made part of Bavaria.

PFENNIG
BILLON
State shield between branches over value and date. Uniface.

| 10 | 1806 | — | 3.00 | 7.00 | 15.00 | 40.00 |

Oval state shield w/garland draped over urn, value below date. Uniface.

| 10a | 1806 | — | 3.00 | 7.00 | 15.00 | 40.00 |

Oval state shield, garland w/loop over value and date. Uniface.

| 10b | 1806 | — | 3.00 | 7.00 | 15.00 | 40.00 |

Garland hanging from urn on pedestal above state shield, value and date below. Uniface.

| 11 | 1806 | — | 3.00 | 7.00 | 15.00 | 40.00 |
| | 1807 | — | 3.00 | 7.00 | 15.00 | 40.00 |

State shield in front of altar, value and date below. Uniface.

| 11a | 1806 | — | 3.00 | 7.00 | 15.00 | 40.00 |
| | 1807 | — | 3.00 | 7.00 | 15.00 | 40.00 |

KREUZER

BILLON
Obv: Pyramid w/city arms; date below. Rev: City view.

C#	Date	Mintage	VG	Fine	VF	XF
36	1806	—	2.50	—	9.00	20.00

Rev: Rose bush.

| 36a | 1806 | — | 2.25 | 3.00 | 7.50 | 20.00 |

Obv: Spade arms w/mural crown and garlands. Rev: Value and date.

| 37 | 1806 | — | 2.25 | 3.00 | 7.50 | 20.00 |
| | 1807 | — | 2.25 | 3.00 | 7.50 | 20.00 |

Obv: Pryamid w/city arms; date below. Rev: City view.

| 38 | 1807 | — | 4.00 | 6.50 | 10.00 | 20.00 |

3 KREUZER
BILLON
Obv: Crowned shield w/garland. Rev: Value within wreath, date below.

C#	Date	Mintage	Fine	VF	XF	Unc
44	1806	—	2.00	6.00	15.00	50.00

Rev. leg: NURNB: SCHEIDE MUNZ.

| 44a | 1806 | — | 2.00 | 6.00 | 15.00 | 50.00 |
| | 1807 | — | 2.00 | 6.00 | 15.00 | 50.00 |

6 KREUZER

BILLON

| 51 | 1806 | — | 4.00 | 8.00 | 15.00 | 50.00 |
| | 1807 | — | 4.00 | 8.00 | 15.00 | 50.00 |

TRADE COINAGE
DUCAT

3.5000 g, .986 GOLD, .1109 oz AGW

| 89 | 1806 | — | 200.00 | 400.00 | 650.00 | 1000. |

2 DUCATS
7.0000 g, .986 GOLD, .2219 oz AGW

Obv: City view. Rev: Lamb w/flag.

C#	Date	Mintage	Fine	VF	XF	Unc
90	1806	—	450.00	1000.	1900.	3200.

3 DUCATS
10.5000 g, .986 GOLD, .3329 oz AGW
Obv: City view. Rev: Lamb w/flag.

| | 1806 | — | 1000. | 2100. | 3600. | 6000. |

OLDENBURG

The county of Oldenburg, located on the North Sea, near Friesland was established in 1180. The first coins were struck c. 1290. It was ruled by Denmark from 1667 to 1773 and was raised to the status of duchy in 1777. The Bishopric of Lubeck was joined to it in 1803 and the territory was annexed to France in 1810. The 1815 Congress of Vienna elevated Oldenburg to grand duchy. They entered the German Empire in 1871 and remained there until the grand duke abdicated in 1918.

RULERS
Peter Friedrich Wilhelm, 1785-1823
Peter Friedrich Ludwig, 1823-1829
Paul Friedrich August, 1829-1853
Nicolaus Friedrich Peter, 1853-1900
Friedrich August, 1900-1918

MINTMASTER'S INITIALS
I.H.M. - Johann Heinrich Macelung
N - Samuel Mathias Neudorf
B - Johann Ephraim Bauert

SCHWAREN

COPPER

| 43 | 1846 | .126 | 2.50 | 5.00 | 10.00 | 45.00 |

Rev: B below date.

| 43a | 1852 B | .144 | 1.50 | 3.00 | 6.00 | 40.00 |

| 54 | 1854 B | .072 | 2.00 | 4.00 | 8.00 | 45.00 |
| | 1856 B | .072 | 2.00 | 4.00 | 8.00 | 45.00 |

55	1858 B	1.084	1.00	3.00	5.00	35.00
	1859 B	.108	1.00	3.00	5.00	35.00
	1860 B	.288	1.00	3.00	5.00	35.00
	1862 B	.180	1.00	3.00	5.00	35.00
	1864 B	.180	1.00	3.00	5.00	35.00
	1865 B	.108	1.00	3.00	5.00	35.00
	1866 B	.144	1.00	3.00	5.00	35.00
	1869 B	.180	1.00	3.00	5.00	35.00

3 SCHWAREN
(3 Pfennig)

COPPER

57	1858 B	.372	1.00	3.00	6.00	35.00
	1859 B	.432	1.00	3.00	6.00	35.00
	1860 B	.060	2.00	4.00	8.00	45.00
	1862 B	.012	2.00	4.00	8.00	45.00
	1864 B	.060	2.00	4.00	8.00	45.00
	1865 B	.060	2.00	4.00	8.00	45.00
	1866 B	.036	2.00	4.00	8.00	45.00
	1869 B	.096	2.00	4.00	8.00	45.00

1/4 GROTE
(1 Pfennig)

Oldenburg / GERMAN STATES 658

	COPPER				
C#	Date	Mintage	Fine	VF	XF	Unc
44	1846	.090	2.50	5.00	10.00	50.00

1/2 GROTE

COPPER
25	1802	.078	3.00	7.00	15.00	70.00
	1816	.149	3.00	7.00	15.00	60.00

45	1831	.072	2.00	5.00	10.00	50.00
	1835	.075	2.00	5.00	10.00	50.00

| 45a | 1840 | .122 | 2.00 | 5.00 | 10.00 | 50.00 |

| 46 | 1846 | .088 | 2.00 | 5.00 | 10.00 | 55.00 |

56	1853 B	.072	2.00	4.00	7.00	45.00
	1856 B	.072	2.00	4.00	7.00	45.00

GROTE
.9700 g, .208 SILVER, .0064 oz ASW
Obv: Crowned arms w/garland, N.D.C.F. Rev: Value.
| 28 | 1817 | .391 | 4.00 | 7.00 | 25.00 | 85.00 |

.9200 g, .218 SILVER, .0064 oz ASW
Obv. leg: SCHEIDE-M.
| 47 | 1836 B | .361 | 3.00 | 6.00 | 20.00 | 75.00 |

48	1849 B	.043	2.00	5.00	15.00	60.00
	1850 B	.081	2.00	4.00	10.00	50.00

58	1853 B	.057	2.00	4.00	10.00	45.00
	1856 B	.072	2.00	4.00	10.00	45.00
	1857 B	.027	2.00	4.00	10.00	45.00

2 GROTE
(1/36 Thaler)

1.3900 g, .291 SILVER, .0130 oz ASW
Obv. leg: N.D.C.F.
C#	Date	Mintage	Fine	VF	XF	Unc
33	1815	1.080	5.00	15.00	30.00	150.00

3 GROTE
(1/24 Thaler)

1.9400 g, .312 SILVER, .0194 oz ASW
| 49 | 1840 S | .486 | 3.00 | 6.00 | 20.00 | 80.00 |

| 61 | 1856 B | .156 | 3.00 | 6.00 | 15.00 | 75.00 |

4 GROTE
(1/18 Thaler)
2.3900 g, .340 SILVER, .0261 oz ASW
Obv: Crowned arms w/garlands, N.D.C.F. Rev: Value.
35	1816	.393	3.00	5.00	10.00	50.00
	1818	.126	3.00	5.00	10.00	50.00

| 50 | 1840 S | .380 | 3.00 | 5.00 | 10.00 | 50.00 |

6 GROTE
(1/12 Thaler)

3.5700 g, .340 SILVER, .0390 oz ASW
37	1816	.309	3.00	7.00	20.00	75.00
	1818	.060	3.00	7.00	20.00	75.00

GOLD (OMS)
| 37a | 1816 | — | — | — | Proof | — |

12 GROTE
(1/6 Thaler)

4.8700 g, .520 SILVER, .0783 oz ASW
39	1816	.036	6.00	15.00	25.00	100.00
	1818	.066	6.00	15.00	25.00	100.00

1/2 GROSCHEN

1.0900 g, .220 SILVER, .0077 oz ASW
59	1858 B	1.020	1.50	3.50	10.00	30.00
	1864 B	.060	2.00	5.00	12.00	40.00
	1865 B	.048	2.00	5.00	12.00	40.00
	1866 B	.168	2.00	5.00	12.00	35.00
	1869 B	.120	2.00	5.00	12.00	35.00

GROSCHEN

2.1900 g, .220 SILVER, .0154 oz ASW
C#	Date	Mintage	Fine	VF	XF	Unc
60	1858 B	.720	3.00	5.00	10.00	60.00

60a	1858 B	1.080	3.00	5.00	10.00	50.00
	1864 B	.030	3.00	5.00	10.00	60.00
	1865 B	.030	3.00	5.00	10.00	60.00
	1866 B	.120	3.00	5.00	10.00	60.00
	1869 B	.090	3.00	5.00	10.00	60.00

2-1/2 GROSCHEN
(1/12 Thaler)

3.2200 g, .375 SILVER, .0388 oz ASW
| 62 | 1858 B | .600 | 3.00 | 7.00 | 20.00 | 80.00 |

1/6 THALER

5.3500 g, .520 SILVER, .0894 oz ASW
| 51 | 1846 B | .164 | 25.00 | 50.00 | 100.00 | 225.00 |

1/3 THALER

7.7900 g, .625 SILVER, .1565 oz ASW
41	1816	.018	60.00	100.00	300.00	450.00
	1818	.033	50.00	80.00	250.00	400.00

EIN (1) THALER

22.2700 g, .750 SILVER, .5370 oz ASW
| 52 | 1846 B | .042 | 75.00 | 150.00 | 500.00 | 1250. |

18.5200 g, .900 SILVER, .5360 oz ASW
| 63 | 1858 | .017 | 70.00 | 130.00 | 225.00 | 450.00 |

C#	Date	Mintage	Fine	VF	XF	Unc
63	1860	.047	60.00	120.00	180.00	375.00
	1866	.072	50.00	100.00	150.00	300.00

2 THALER
(3-1/2 Gulden)

37.1200 g, .900 SILVER, 1.0742 oz ASW

53	1840	.019	700.00	1250.	2500.	4750.
	1840	—	—	—	Proof	4500.

MONETARY REFORM
2 MARK

11.1110 g, .900 SILVER, .3215 oz ASW

Y#	Date	Mintage	Fine	VF	XF	Unc
108	1891A	.100	125.00	250.00	400.00	650.00
	1891A	—	—	—	Proof	650.00

109	1900A	.050	100.00	200.00	450.00	850.00
	1900A	—	—	—	Proof	900.00
	1901A	.075	85.00	200.00	450.00	850.00
	1901A	—	—	—	Proof	900.00

5 MARK

27.7770 g, .900 SILVER, .8038 oz ASW

110	1900A	.020	225.00	500.00	1500.	2500.
	1900A	—	—	—	Proof	3000.
	1901A	.010	250.00	700.00	1600.	3250.
	1901A	—	—	—	Proof	3500.

10 MARK

3.9820 g, .900 GOLD, .1152 oz AGW

Y#	Date	Mintage	Fine	VF	XF	Unc
107	1874B	.015	750.00	1250.	2000.	3750.
	1874B	—	—	—	Proof	Rare

OSNABRUCK

The city of Osnabruck is located northeast of Munster. Although the city owed its original growth to the bishopric it achieved considerable independence from the bishops and joined the Hanseatic League. It had its own local coinage from the early 16th century until 1805. It was absorbed by Hannover in 1803.

CITY
HELLER
COPPER
Obv: Wheel. Rev: Value, date below.

C#	Date	Mintage	Fine	VF	XF	Unc
1a	1801	—	2.00	4.00	7.00	75.00

1-1/2 PFENNING

COPPER

5	1805	—	2.00	4.00	7.00	75.00

2 PFENNING
COPPER
Similar to 3 Pfennig, C#11.

7	1801	—	3.00	6.00	15.00	100.00
	1802	—	3.00	6.00	15.00	100.00
	1803	—	3.00	6.00	15.00	100.00
	1804	—	3.00	6.00	15.00	100.00
	1805	—	3.00	6.00	15.00	100.00

3 PFENNING

COPPER

11	1805	—	5.00	10.00	25.00	100.00

PFALZ
(Rhenish Palatinate, Rheinpfalz)

The office of count palatine of the Rhine is first mentioned in the 10th century and the first coins were struck in the 11th century. There were many divisions. The lines of Neuburg, Sulzbach, Zweibrucken and Birkenfeld were founded in 1569 and were culminated in Maximilian Josef of Zweibrucken who became king and elector of Bavaria by 1805.

Rhein Pfalz
RULERS
Maximilian Joseph,
Elector of Pfalz-Bayern,
1799-1805

1/2 KREUZER
COPPER
Obv: Crowned shield w/lion, dividing RP.
Rev: Value and date within wreath.

1	1802	—	6.00	12.00	30.00	135.00

KREUZER
COPPER
Obv: Crowned shield w/lion, dividing RP.
Rev: Value and date within wreath.

2	1802	—	7.00	15.00	30.00	160.00

EIN (1) THALER
(Convention)
SILVER
Obv: Head right.
Rev: Crowned shield within branches.

3	1802	—	2500	4000	6500.	10,000.

POMERANIA

A duchy on the Baltic Sea, near modern day Poland, was founded in the late 11th century. After many divisions, Pomerania was annexed to Sweden in 1637. Brandenburg-Prussia had an interest in the area and slowly acquired bits until in 1815 all of Pomerania belonged to Prussia. The arms of Pomerania appear on coins of Brandenburg-Prussia from the 17th century onward.

RULERS
Gustav IV Adolf of Sweden, 1792-1809

3 PFENNINGE
COPPER
Obv: Griffon left w/sceptor, K.S.P.L.M. above.
Rev: Value date.

C#	Date	Mintage	VG	Fine	VF	XF
29	1806	.384	3.00	6.00	10.00	25.00
	1808	.258	3.00	6.00	10.00	25.00

Obv. leg: "K. SCHWED. POM. LANDES M".

30	1806	—	—	—	—	Rare

Obv. leg: "K.S.P. LANDESM".

31	1808	—	—	—	—	Rare

PRUSSIA

The Kingdom of Prussia, located in north central Germany, came into being in 1701. The ruler received the title of King in Prussia in exchange for his support during the War of the Spanish Succession. During the Napoleonic Wars, Prussia allied itself with Saxony. When they were defeated in 1806 they were forced to cede a large portion of their territory. In 1813 the French were expelled and their territories were returned to them plus additional territories. After defeating Denmark and Austria, in 1864 and 1866 they acquired more territory. Prussia was the pivotal state of unification of Germany in 1871 and their King was proclaimed emperor of all Germany. World War I brought an end to the Empire and the Kingdom of Prussia in 1918.

RULERS
Friedrich Wilhelm III, 1797-1840
Friedrich Wilhelm IV, 1840-1861
Wilhelm I, 1861-1888
Friedrich III, March 1888-June 1888
Wilhelm II, 1888-1918

MINT MARKS
A - Berlin = Prussia, East Friesland, East Prussia, Posen
B - Bayreuth = Brandenburg-Ansbach-Bayreuth
B - Breslau = Silesia, Posen, South Prussia
C - = Cleve
D - Aurich = East Friesland, Prussia
E - Konigsberg = East Prussia
F - Magdeburg
G - Stettin
G - Schwerin, Plon-Rethwisch Mint, 1763 only
S - Schwabach = Brandenburg-Ansbach-Bayreuth
Star - Dresden

PFENNIG

COPPER

95	1801	—	1.50	3.00	5.00	10.00
	1804	—	1.50	3.00	5.00	10.00
	1806	—	1.50	3.00	5.00	10.00

BILLON
Obv: Crowned FRW monogram.

100	1801	—	1.50	3.00	5.00	10.00
	1802	—	1.50	3.00	5.00	10.00
	1803	—	1.50	3.00	5.00	10.00
	1804	—	1.50	3.00	5.00	10.00

Obv: Smaller W in crowned FRW monogram.

100a	1804	—	1.50	3.00	5.00	10.00
	1806	—	1.50	3.00	5.00	10.00

COPPER

C#	Date	Mintage	Fine	VF	XF	Unc
97	1810	—	2.50	5.00	10.00	40.00
	1811	—	2.50	5.00	10.00	40.00
	1814	—	2.50	5.00	10.00	40.00
	1816	—	2.50	5.00	10.00	40.00

Prussia / GERMAN STATES 660

C#	Date	Mintage	Fine	VF	XF	Unc
123	1821	—	1.50	3.00	6.00	35.00
	1822	—	1.50	3.00	6.00	35.00
	1825	—	1.50	3.00	6.00	35.00
	1826	—	1.50	3.00	6.00	35.00
	1827	—	1.50	3.00	6.00	35.00
	1828	—	1.50	3.00	6.00	35.00
	1832	—	1.50	3.00	6.00	35.00
	1833	—	1.50	3.00	6.00	35.00
	1835	—	1.50	3.00	6.00	35.00
	1836	—	1.50	3.00	6.00	35.00
	1837	—	1.50	3.00	6.00	35.00
	1838	—	1.50	3.00	6.00	35.00
	1839	—	1.50	3.00	6.00	35.00
	1840	—	1.50	3.00	6.00	35.00

Mint mark: B
Rev: B below date.

123a	1821	—	2.00	4.00	8.00	40.00
	1822	—	2.00	4.00	8.00	40.00
123b	1826	—	2.00	4.00	8.00	40.00

Mint mark: D
Rev: D below date.

123c	1821	—	1.50	3.00	6.00	40.00
	1822	—	1.50	3.00	6.00	40.00
	1823	—	1.50	3.00	6.00	40.00
	1824	—	1.50	3.00	6.00	40.00
	1825	—	1.50	3.00	6.00	40.00
	1826	—	1.50	3.00	6.00	40.00
	1827	—	1.50	3.00	6.00	40.00
	1828	—	1.50	3.00	6.00	40.00
	1829	—	1.50	3.00	6.00	40.00
	1830	—	1.50	3.00	6.00	40.00
	1831	—	1.50	3.00	6.00	40.00
	1832	—	1.50	3.00	6.00	40.00
	1833	—	1.50	3.00	6.00	40.00
	1834	—	1.50	3.00	6.00	40.00
	1835	—	1.50	3.00	6.00	40.00
	1836	—	1.50	3.00	6.00	40.00
	1837	—	1.50	3.00	6.00	40.00
	1838	—	1.50	3.00	6.00	40.00
	1839	—	1.50	3.00	6.00	40.00
	1840	—	1.50	3.00	6.00	40.00

Mint mark: A
Rev: A below date.

136	1841	—	.75	1.50	4.00	35.00
	1842	—	.75	1.50	4.00	35.00

Mint mark: D
Rev: D below date.

136a	1841	—	.75	1.50	4.00	35.00
	1842	—	.75	1.50	4.00	35.00

Mint mark: A

140	1843	—	.75	1.50	4.00	35.00
	1844	—	.75	1.50	4.00	35.00
	1845	—	.75	1.50	4.00	35.00

Mint mark: D
Rev: D below date.

140a	1844	—	.75	1.50	4.00	35.00
	1845	—	.75	1.50	4.00	35.00

Mint mark: A

140b	1846	—	.75	1.50	4.00	30.00
	1847	—	.75	1.50	4.00	30.00
	1848	—	.75	1.50	4.00	30.00
	1849	—	.75	1.50	4.00	30.00
	1850	—	.75	1.50	4.00	30.00
	1851	—	.75	1.50	4.00	30.00
	1852	—	.75	1.50	4.00	30.00
	1853	—	.75	1.50	4.00	30.00
	1854	—	.75	1.50	4.00	30.00
	1855	—	.75	1.50	4.00	30.00
	1856	—	.75	1.50	4.00	30.00
	1857	—	.75	1.50	4.00	30.00
	1858	—	.75	1.50	4.00	30.00
	1859	—	.75	1.50	4.00	30.00
	1860	—	.75	1.50	4.00	30.00

Mint mark: D
Rev: D below date.

140c	1846	—	1.00	2.00	5.00	35.00
	1847	—	1.00	2.00	5.00	35.00
	1848	—	1.00	2.00	5.00	35.00

Mint mark: A

C#	Date	Mintage	Fine	VF	XF	Unc
161	1861	—	.50	1.00	2.50	20.00
	1862	—	.50	1.00	2.50	20.00
	1863	—	.50	1.00	2.50	20.00
	1864	—	.50	1.00	2.50	20.00
	1865	—	.50	1.00	2.50	20.00
	1866	—	.50	1.00	2.50	20.00
	1867	—	.50	1.00	2.50	20.00
	1868	—	.50	1.00	2.50	20.00
	1869	—	.50	1.00	2.50	20.00
	1870	—	.50	1.00	2.50	20.00
	1871	—	.50	1.00	2.50	20.00
	1872	—	.50	1.00	2.50	20.00
	1873	—	.50	1.00	2.50	20.00

Mint mark: B
Rev: B below date.

161a	1867	—	.50	1.00	2.50	20.00
	1868	—	.50	1.00	2.50	20.00
	1869	—	.50	1.00	2.50	20.00
	1870	—	.50	1.00	2.50	20.00
	1871	—	.50	1.00	2.50	20.00
	1872	—	.50	1.00	2.50	20.00
	1873	—	.50	1.00	2.50	20.00

Mint mark: C
Rev: C below date.

161b	1867	—	.50	1.00	2.50	20.00
	1868	—	.50	1.00	2.50	20.00
	1870	—	.50	1.00	2.50	20.00
	1871	—	.50	1.00	2.50	20.00
	1872	—	.50	1.00	2.50	20.00
	1873	—	.50	1.00	2.50	20.00

2 PFENNIG

COPPER
Mint mark: A

98	1810	—	2.50	5.00	10.00	50.00
	1814	—	2.50	5.00	10.00	50.00
	1816	—	2.50	5.00	10.00	50.00

124	1821	—	2.00	4.00	8.00	45.00
	1822	—	2.00	4.00	8.00	45.00
	1825	—	2.00	4.00	8.00	45.00
	1826	—	2.00	4.00	8.00	45.00
	1827	—	2.00	4.00	8.00	45.00
	1828	—	2.00	4.00	8.00	45.00
	1830	—	2.00	4.00	8.00	45.00
	1832	—	2.00	4.00	8.00	45.00
	1833	—	2.00	4.00	8.00	45.00
	1835	—	2.00	4.00	8.00	45.00
	1836	—	2.00	4.00	8.00	45.00
	1837	—	2.00	4.00	8.00	45.00
	1838	—	2.00	4.00	8.00	45.00
	1839	—	2.00	4.00	8.00	45.00
	1840	—	2.00	4.00	8.00	45.00

Mint mark: B
Rev: B below date.

124a	1821	—	3.00	5.00	10.00	50.00
	1822	—	3.00	5.00	10.00	50.00

Mint mark: D
Rev: D below date.

124b	1823	—	2.00	4.00	8.00	40.00
	1824	—	2.00	4.00	8.00	40.00
	1825	—	2.00	4.00	8.00	40.00
	1826	—	2.00	4.00	8.00	40.00
	1827	—	2.00	4.00	8.00	40.00
	1828	—	2.00	4.00	8.00	40.00
	1829	—	2.00	4.00	8.00	40.00
	1830	—	2.00	4.00	8.00	40.00
	1831	—	2.00	4.00	8.00	40.00
	1832	—	2.00	4.00	8.00	40.00
	1833	—	2.00	4.00	8.00	40.00
	1834	—	2.00	4.00	8.00	40.00
	1835	—	2.00	4.00	8.00	40.00
	1836	—	2.00	4.00	8.00	40.00
	1837	—	2.00	4.00	8.00	40.00
	1838	—	2.00	4.00	8.00	40.00
	1839	—	2.00	4.00	8.00	40.00

Mint mark: A

C#	Date	Mintage	Fine	VF	XF	Unc
137	1841	—	1.00	2.00	5.00	40.00
	1842	—	1.00	2.00	5.00	40.00

Mint mark: D
Rev: D below date.

137a	1841	—	1.00	2.00	5.00	40.00
	1842	—	1.00	2.00	5.00	40.00

Mint mark: A

141	1843	—	1.00	2.00	5.00	40.00
	1844	—	1.00	2.00	5.00	40.00
	1845	—	1.00	2.00	5.00	40.00

Mint mark: D
Rev: D below date.

141a	1844	—	1.00	2.00	5.00	40.00
	1845	—	1.00	2.00	5.00	40.00

Mint mark: A

141b	1846	—	.75	1.50	3.00	30.00
	1847	—	.75	1.50	3.00	30.00
	1848	—	.75	1.50	3.00	30.00
	1849	—	.75	1.50	3.00	30.00
	1850	—	.75	1.50	3.00	30.00
	1851	—	.75	1.50	3.00	30.00
	1852	—	.75	1.50	3.00	30.00
	1853	—	.75	1.50	3.00	30.00
	1854	—	.75	1.50	3.00	30.00
	1855	—	.75	1.50	3.00	30.00
	1856	—	.75	1.50	3.00	30.00
	1857	—	.75	1.50	3.00	30.00
	1858	—	.75	1.50	3.00	30.00
	1859	—	.75	1.50	3.00	30.00
	1860	—	.75	1.50	3.00	30.00

Mint mark: D
Rev: D below date.

141c	1846	—	1.00	2.00	4.00	35.00
	1847	—	1.00	2.00	4.00	35.00
	1848	—	1.00	2.00	4.00	35.00

Mint mark: A

162	1861	—	.50	1.25	2.50	20.00
	1862	—	.50	1.25	2.50	20.00
	1863	—	.50	1.25	2.50	20.00
	1864	—	.50	1.25	2.50	20.00
	1865	—	.50	1.25	2.50	20.00
	1866	—	.50	1.25	2.50	20.00
	1867	—	.50	1.25	2.50	20.00
	1868	—	.50	1.25	2.50	20.00
	1869	—	.50	1.25	2.50	20.00
	1870	—	.50	1.25	2.50	20.00
	1871	—	.50	1.25	2.50	20.00

Mint mark: B
Rev: B below date.

162a	1867	—	.50	1.25	2.50	20.00
	1868	—	.50	1.25	2.50	20.00
	1869	—	.50	1.25	2.50	20.00
	1870	—	.50	1.25	2.50	20.00
	1871	—	.50	1.25	2.50	20.00
	1873	—	.50	1.25	2.50	20.00

Mint mark: C
Rev: C below date.

162b	1867	—	.50	1.25	2.50	20.00
	1868	—	.50	1.25	2.50	20.00
	1871	—	.50	1.25	2.50	20.00
	1872	—	.50	1.25	2.50	20.00
	1873	—	.50	1.25	2.50	20.00

3 PFENNIG

.7000 g, .250 SILVER, .0056 oz ASW

C#	Date	Mintage	VG	Fine	VF	XF
102	1801	—	1.50	3.00	6.00	15.00
	1802	—	1.50	3.00	6.00	15.00
	1803	—	1.50	3.00	6.00	15.00
	1804	—	1.50	3.00	6.00	15.00
	1806	—	1.50	3.00	6.00	15.00

Obv: Smaller crown.
| 102a | 1804 | — | 3.00 | 7.00 | 25.00 | 40.00 |
| | 1806 | — | — | Reported, not confirmed | | |

COPPER

C#	Date	Mintage	Fine	VF	XF	Unc
125	1821	—	2.00	4.00	8.00	50.00
	1822	—	2.00	4.00	8.00	50.00
	1823	—	—	Reported, not confirmed		
	1824	—	—	Reported, not confirmed		
	1825	—	2.00	4.00	8.00	50.00
	1826	—	2.00	4.00	8.00	50.00
	1827	—	2.00	4.00	8.00	50.00
	1828	—	2.00	4.00	8.00	50.00
	1829	—	2.00	4.00	8.00	50.00
	1830	—	2.00	4.00	8.00	50.00
	1831	—	2.00	4.00	8.00	50.00
	1832	—	2.00	4.00	8.00	50.00
	1833	—	2.00	4.00	8.00	50.00
	1835	—	2.00	4.00	8.00	50.00
	1836	—	2.00	4.00	8.00	50.00
	1837	—	2.00	4.00	8.00	50.00
	1838	—	2.00	4.00	8.00	50.00
	1839	—	2.00	4.00	8.00	50.00
	1840	—	2.00	4.00	8.00	50.00

Mint mark: B
Rev: B below date.
| 125a | 1821 | — | 3.00 | 6.00 | 12.00 | 65.00 |
| | 1822 | — | 3.00 | 6.00 | 12.00 | 65.00 |

Mint mark: D
Rev: D below date.
125b	1823	—	2.00	4.00	8.00	50.00
	1824	—	2.00	4.00	8.00	50.00
	1825	—	2.00	4.00	8.00	50.00
	1826	—	2.00	4.00	8.00	50.00
	1827	—	2.00	4.00	8.00	50.00
	1828	—	2.00	4.00	8.00	50.00
	1829	—	2.00	4.00	8.00	50.00
	1830	—	2.00	4.00	8.00	50.00
	1831	—	2.00	4.00	8.00	50.00
	1832	—	2.00	4.00	8.00	50.00
	1833	—	2.00	4.00	8.00	50.00
	1834	—	2.00	4.00	8.00	50.00
	1835	—	2.00	4.00	8.00	50.00
	1836	—	2.00	4.00	8.00	50.00
	1837	—	2.00	4.00	8.00	50.00
	1838	—	2.00	4.00	8.00	50.00
	1839	—	2.00	4.00	8.00	50.00
	1840	—	2.00	4.00	8.00	50.00

Mint mark: A
| 138 | 1841 | — | 1.50 | 3.00 | 6.00 | 40.00 |
| | 1842 | — | 1.50 | 3.00 | 6.00 | 40.00 |

Mint mark: D
Rev: D below date.
| 138a | 1841 | — | 3.00 | 6.00 | 12.00 | 65.00 |
| | 1842 | — | 3.00 | 6.00 | 12.00 | 65.00 |

Mint mark: A

C#	Date	Mintage	Fine	VF	XF	Unc
143	1843	—	1.50	3.00	6.00	40.00
	1844	—	1.50	3.00	6.00	40.00
	1845	—	1.50	3.00	6.00	40.00

Mint mark: D
Rev: D below date.
| 143a | 1843 | — | 2.00 | 4.00 | 8.00 | 50.00 |
| | 1844 | — | 2.00 | 4.00 | 8.00 | 50.00 |

Mint mark: A
Struck in collared dies.
143b	1846	—	1.00	2.00	5.00	30.00
	1847	—	1.00	2.00	5.00	30.00
	1848	—	1.00	2.00	5.00	30.00
	1849	—	1.00	2.00	5.00	30.00
	1850	—	1.00	2.00	5.00	30.00
	1851	—	1.00	2.00	5.00	30.00
	1852	—	1.00	2.00	5.00	30.00
	1853	—	1.00	2.00	5.00	30.00
	1854	—	1.00	2.00	5.00	30.00
	1855	—	1.00	2.00	5.00	30.00
	1856	—	1.00	2.00	5.00	30.00
	1857	—	1.00	2.00	5.00	30.00
	1858	—	1.00	2.00	5.00	30.00
	1859	—	1.00	2.00	5.00	30.00
	1860	—	1.00	2.00	5.00	30.00

Mint mark: D
Struck in collared dies. Rev: D below date.
143c	1846	—	2.00	4.00	8.00	45.00
	1847	—	2.00	4.00	8.00	45.00
	1848	—	2.00	4.00	8.00	45.00

Mint mark: A
Mule. Rev: Reuss-Schleiz 3 PFENNIGE.
| 143d | 1850 | — | 15.00 | 40.00 | 75.00 | 150.00 |

163	1861	—	.75	1.50	3.00	20.00
	1862	—	.75	1.50	3.00	20.00
	1863	—	.75	1.50	3.00	20.00
	1864	—	.75	1.50	3.00	20.00
	1865	—	.75	1.50	3.00	20.00
	1866	—	.75	1.50	3.00	20.00
	1867	—	.75	1.50	3.00	20.00
	1868	—	.75	1.50	3.00	20.00
	1869	—	.75	1.50	3.00	20.00
	1870	—	.75	1.50	3.00	20.00
	1871	—	.75	1.50	3.00	20.00
	1872	—	.75	1.50	3.00	20.00
	1873	—	.75	1.50	3.00	20.00

Mint mark: B
Rev: B below date.
163a	1867	—	.75	1.50	3.00	20.00
	1868	—	.75	1.50	3.00	20.00
	1869	—	.75	1.50	3.00	20.00
	1870	—	.75	1.50	3.00	20.00
	1871	—	.75	1.50	3.00	20.00
	1872	—	.75	1.50	3.00	20.00
	1873	—	.75	1.50	3.00	20.00

Mint mark: C
Rev: C below date.
163b	1867	—	.75	1.50	3.00	20.00
	1868	—	.75	1.50	3.00	20.00
	1869	—	.75	1.50	3.00	20.00
	1870	—	.75	1.50	3.00	20.00
	1871	—	.75	1.50	3.00	20.00
	1872	—	.75	1.50	3.00	20.00
	1873	—	.75	1.50	3.00	20.00

4 PFENNIG

COPPER
Mint mark: A
Similar to C#126b but A below date.

C#	Date	Mintage	Fine	VF	XF	Unc
126	1821	—	3.00	6.00	12.00	60.00
	1822	—	3.00	6.00	12.00	60.00
	1825	—	3.00	6.00	12.00	60.00
	1826	—	3.00	6.00	12.00	60.00
	1827	—	3.00	6.00	12.00	60.00
	1829	—	3.00	6.00	12.00	60.00
	1830	—	3.00	6.00	12.00	60.00
	1832	—	3.00	6.00	12.00	60.00
	1834	—	—	Reported, not confirmed		
	1836	—	3.00	6.00	12.00	60.00
	1837	—	3.00	6.00	12.00	60.00
	1838	—	3.00	6.00	12.00	60.00
	1839	—	3.00	6.00	12.00	60.00
	1840	—	3.00	6.00	12.00	60.00

Mint mark: B
Rev: B below date.
126a	1821	—	4.00	8.00	15.00	70.00
	1822	—	4.00	8.00	15.00	70.00
	1825	—	4.00	8.00	15.00	70.00

Mint mark: D
126b	1823	—	3.00	6.00	12.00	60.00
	1824	—	3.00	6.00	12.00	60.00
	1825	—	3.00	6.00	12.00	60.00
	1826	—	3.00	6.00	12.00	60.00
	1828	—	3.00	6.00	12.00	60.00
	1829	—	3.00	6.00	12.00	60.00
	1831	—	3.00	6.00	12.00	60.00
	1832	—	3.00	6.00	12.00	60.00
	1833	—	3.00	6.00	12.00	60.00
	1834	—	3.00	6.00	12.00	60.00
	1836	—	3.00	6.00	12.00	60.00
	1837	—	3.00	6.00	12.00	60.00
	1838	—	3.00	6.00	12.00	60.00
	1839	—	3.00	6.00	12.00	60.00
	1840	—	—	Reported, not confirmed		

Mint mark: A
| 139 | 1841 | — | 2.50 | 5.00 | 10.00 | 45.00 |
| | 1842 | — | 2.50 | 5.00 | 10.00 | 45.00 |

Mint mark: D
Rev: D below date.
| 139a | 1841 | — | 3.00 | 6.00 | 12.00 | 50.00 |
| | 1842 | — | 3.00 | 6.00 | 12.00 | 50.00 |

Mint mark: A
144	1843	—	2.50	5.00	10.00	45.00
	1844	—	2.50	5.00	10.00	45.00
	1845	—	2.50	5.00	10.00	45.00

Mint mark: D
Rev: D below date.
| 144a | 1844 | — | 3.00 | 6.00 | 12.00 | 50.00 |

Mint mark: A
Struck in collared dies.

662 Prussia / GERMAN STATES

C#	Date	Mintage	Fine	VF	XF	Unc
144b	1846	—	2.50	5.00	10.00	40.00
	1847	—	2.50	5.00	10.00	40.00
	1848	—	2.50	5.00	10.00	40.00
	1849	—	— Reported, not confirmed			
	1850	—	2.50	5.00	10.00	40.00
	1851	—	2.50	5.00	10.00	40.00
	1852	—	2.50	5.00	10.00	40.00
	1853	—	2.50	5.00	10.00	40.00
	1854	—	2.50	5.00	10.00	40.00
	1855	—	2.50	5.00	10.00	40.00
	1856	—	2.50	5.00	10.00	40.00
	1857	—	2.50	5.00	10.00	40.00
	1858	—	2.50	5.00	10.00	40.00
	1860	—	2.50	5.00	10.00	40.00

Mint mark: D
Struck in collared dies.

C#	Date	Mintage	Fine	VF	XF	Unc
144c	1846	—	3.00	6.00	12.00	50.00
	1847	—	3.00	6.00	12.00	50.00
	1848	—	3.00	6.00	12.00	50.00

Mint mark: A

C#	Date	Mintage	Fine	VF	XF	Unc
164	1861	—	2.00	4.00	8.00	40.00
	1862	—	2.00	4.00	8.00	40.00
	1863	—	2.00	4.00	8.00	40.00
	1864	—	2.00	4.00	8.00	40.00
	1865	—	2.00	4.00	8.00	40.00
	1866	—	2.00	4.00	8.00	40.00
	1867	—	2.00	4.00	8.00	40.00
	1868	—	2.00	4.00	8.00	40.00
	1869	—	2.00	4.00	8.00	40.00
	1870	—	2.00	4.00	8.00	40.00
	1871	—	2.00	4.00	8.00	40.00

Mint mark: C
Rev: C below date.

C#	Date	Mintage	Fine	VF	XF	Unc
164a	1867	—	2.00	4.00	8.00	40.00
	1868	—	2.00	4.00	8.00	40.00
	1871	—	2.00	4.00	8.00	40.00

1/2 SILBER GROSCHEN

1.0900 g, .222 SILVER, .0077 oz ASW
Mint mark: A

C#	Date	Mintage	Fine	VF	XF	Unc
127	1821	—	3.00	6.00	12.00	50.00
	1822	—	3.00	6.00	12.00	50.00
	1823	—	3.00	6.00	12.00	50.00
	1824	—	3.00	6.00	12.00	50.00
	1825	—	3.00	6.00	12.00	50.00
	1826	—	3.00	6.00	12.00	50.00
	1827	—	3.00	6.00	12.00	50.00
	1828	—	3.00	6.00	12.00	50.00
	1829	—	3.00	6.00	12.00	50.00
	1830	—	3.00	6.00	12.00	50.00
	1831	—	3.00	6.00	12.00	50.00
	1832	—	3.00	6.00	12.00	50.00
	1833	—	3.00	6.00	12.00	50.00
	1834	—	3.00	6.00	12.00	50.00
	1835	—	3.00	6.00	12.00	50.00
	1836	—	3.00	6.00	12.00	50.00
	1837	—	3.00	6.00	12.00	50.00
	1838	—	3.00	6.00	12.00	50.00
	1839	—	3.00	6.00	12.00	50.00
	1840	—	3.00	6.00	12.00	50.00

Mint mark: D
Rev: D below date.

C#	Date	Mintage	Fine	VF	XF	Unc
127a	1824	—	4.00	8.00	15.00	60.00
	1825	—	4.00	8.00	15.00	60.00
	1826	—	4.00	8.00	15.00	60.00
	1828	—	4.00	8.00	15.00	60.00

Mint mark: A

C#	Date	Mintage	Fine	VF	XF	Unc
145	1841	—	2.50	5.00	10.00	40.00
	1842	—	2.50	5.00	10.00	40.00
	1843	—	2.50	5.00	10.00	40.00
	1844	—	2.50	5.00	10.00	40.00
	1845	—	2.50	5.00	10.00	40.00
	1846	—	2.50	5.00	10.00	40.00
	1847	—	2.50	5.00	10.00	40.00
	1848	—	2.50	5.00	10.00	40.00
	1849	—	2.50	5.00	10.00	40.00
	1850	—	2.50	5.00	10.00	40.00
	1851	—	2.50	5.00	10.00	40.00
	1852	—	2.50	5.00	10.00	40.00

Obv: Older head.

C#	Date	Mintage	Fine	VF	XF	Unc
145a	1853	—	2.50	5.00	10.00	40.00
	1854	—	2.50	5.00	10.00	40.00
	1855	—	2.50	5.00	10.00	40.00
	1856	—	2.50	5.00	10.00	40.00
	1857	—	— Reported, not confirmed			
	1858	—	2.50	5.00	10.00	40.00
	1859	—	— Reported, not confirmed			
	1860	—	2.50	5.00	10.00	40.00

C#	Date	Mintage	Fine	VF	XF	Unc
165	1861	—	1.00	2.00	5.00	20.00
	1862	—	1.00	2.00	5.00	20.00
	1863	—	1.00	2.00	5.00	20.00
	1864	—	1.00	2.00	5.00	20.00
	1865	—	1.00	2.00	5.00	20.00
	1866	—	1.00	2.00	5.00	20.00
	1867	—	1.00	2.00	5.00	20.00
	1868	—	1.00	2.00	5.00	20.00
	1869	—	1.00	2.00	5.00	20.00
	1870	—	1.00	2.00	5.00	20.00
	1871	—	1.00	2.00	5.00	20.00
	1872	—	1.00	2.00	5.00	20.00

Mint mark: B
Rev: B below date.

C#	Date	Mintage	Fine	VF	XF	Unc
165a	1866	—	1.00	2.00	5.00	20.00
	1867	—	1.00	2.00	5.00	20.00
	1868	—	1.00	2.00	5.00	20.00
	1869	—	1.00	2.00	5.00	20.00
	1870	—	1.00	2.00	5.00	20.00
	1871	—	1.00	2.00	5.00	20.00
	1872	—	1.00	2.00	5.00	20.00
	1873	—	1.00	2.00	5.00	20.00

Mint mark: C
Rev: C below date.

C#	Date	Mintage	Fine	VF	XF	Unc
165b	1867	—	1.25	2.50	7.50	25.00
	1868	—	1.25	2.50	7.50	25.00
	1872	—	1.25	2.50	7.50	25.00

SILBER GROSCHEN

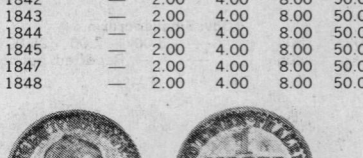

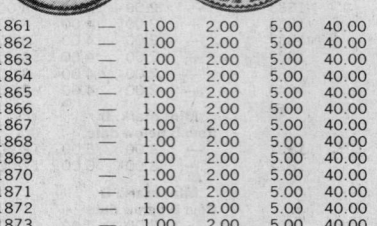

2.1900 g, .222 SILVER, .0156 oz ASW
Mint mark: A

C#	Date	Mintage	Fine	VF	XF	Unc
128	1821	—	3.00	6.00	12.00	50.00
	1822	—	3.00	6.00	12.00	50.00
	1823	—	3.00	6.00	12.00	50.00
	1824	—	3.00	6.00	12.00	50.00
	1825	—	3.00	6.00	12.00	50.00
	1826	—	3.00	6.00	12.00	50.00
	1827	—	3.00	6.00	12.00	50.00
	1828	—	3.00	6.00	12.00	50.00
	1829	—	3.00	6.00	12.00	50.00
	1830	—	3.00	6.00	12.00	50.00
	1831	—	3.00	6.00	12.00	50.00
	1832	—	3.00	6.00	12.00	50.00
	1833	—	3.00	6.00	12.00	50.00
	1834	—	3.00	6.00	12.00	50.00
	1835	—	3.00	6.00	12.00	50.00
	1836	—	3.00	6.00	12.00	50.00
	1837	—	3.00	6.00	12.00	50.00
	1838	—	3.00	6.00	12.00	50.00
	1839	—	3.00	6.00	12.00	50.00
	1840	—	3.00	6.00	12.00	50.00

Mint mark: D
Rev: D below date.

C#	Date	Mintage	Fine	VF	XF	Unc
128a	1821	—	3.00	6.00	12.00	50.00
	1822	—	3.00	6.00	12.00	50.00
	1823	—	3.00	6.00	12.00	50.00
	1824	—	3.00	6.00	12.00	50.00
	1825	—	3.00	6.00	12.00	50.00
	1826	—	3.00	6.00	12.00	50.00
	1827	—	3.00	6.00	12.00	50.00
	1828	—	3.00	6.00	12.00	50.00
	1830	—	3.00	6.00	12.00	50.00
	1832	—	3.00	6.00	12.00	50.00
	1833	—	3.00	6.00	12.00	50.00
	1834	—	3.00	6.00	12.00	50.00
	1837	—	3.00	6.00	12.00	50.00
	1839	—	3.00	6.00	12.00	50.00
	1840	—	3.00	6.00	12.00	50.00

Mint mark: A

C#	Date	Mintage	Fine	VF	XF	Unc
146	1841	—	2.00	4.00	8.00	35.00
	1842	—	2.00	4.00	8.00	35.00
	1843	—	2.00	4.00	8.00	35.00
	1844	—	2.00	4.00	8.00	35.00
	1845	—	2.00	4.00	8.00	35.00
	1846	—	2.00	4.00	8.00	35.00
	1847	—	2.00	4.00	8.00	35.00
	1848	—	2.00	4.00	8.00	35.00
	1849	—	2.00	4.00	8.00	35.00
	1850	—	2.00	4.00	8.00	35.00
	1851	—	2.00	4.00	8.00	35.00
	1852	—	2.00	4.00	8.00	35.00

Mint mark: D
Rev: D below date.

C#	Date	Mintage	Fine	VF	XF	Unc
146a	1841	—	2.00	4.00	8.00	50.00
	1842	—	2.00	4.00	8.00	50.00
	1843	—	2.00	4.00	8.00	50.00
	1844	—	2.00	4.00	8.00	50.00
	1845	—	2.00	4.00	8.00	50.00
	1847	—	2.00	4.00	8.00	50.00
	1848	—	2.00	4.00	8.00	50.00

Mint mark: A
Obv: Older head.

C#	Date	Mintage	Fine	VF	XF	Unc
146b	1853	—	2.00	4.00	8.00	50.00
	1854	—	2.00	4.00	8.00	50.00
	1855	—	2.00	4.00	8.00	50.00
	1856	—	2.00	4.00	8.00	50.00
	1857	—	2.00	4.00	8.00	50.00
	1858	—	2.00	4.00	8.00	50.00
	1859	—	2.00	4.00	8.00	50.00
	1860	—	2.00	4.00	8.00	50.00

C#	Date	Mintage	Fine	VF	XF	Unc
166	1861	—	1.00	2.00	5.00	40.00
	1862	—	1.00	2.00	5.00	40.00
	1863	—	1.00	2.00	5.00	40.00
	1864	—	1.00	2.00	5.00	40.00
	1865	—	1.00	2.00	5.00	40.00
	1866	—	1.00	2.00	5.00	40.00
	1867	—	1.00	2.00	5.00	40.00
	1868	—	1.00	2.00	5.00	40.00
	1869	—	1.00	2.00	5.00	40.00
	1870	—	1.00	2.00	5.00	40.00
	1871	—	1.00	2.00	5.00	40.00
	1872	—	1.00	2.00	5.00	40.00
	1873	—	1.00	2.00	5.00	40.00

Mint mark: B
Rev: B below date.

C#	Date	Mintage	Fine	VF	XF	Unc
166a	1866	—	1.00	2.00	5.00	40.00
	1867	—	1.00	2.00	5.00	40.00
	1868	—	1.00	2.00	5.00	40.00
	1869	—	1.00	2.00	5.00	40.00
	1870	—	1.00	2.00	5.00	40.00
	1871	—	1.00	2.00	5.00	40.00
	1872	—	1.00	2.00	5.00	40.00
	1873	—	1.00	2.00	5.00	40.00

Mint mark: C
Rev: C below head.

C#	Date	Mintage	Fine	VF	XF	Unc
166b	1867	—	1.00	2.00	5.00	40.00
	1868	—	1.00	2.00	5.00	40.00
	1869	—	1.00	2.00	5.00	40.00
	1870	—	1.00	2.00	5.00	40.00
	1871	—	1.00	2.00	5.00	40.00
	1872	—	1.00	2.00	5.00	40.00
	1873	—	1.00	2.00	5.00	40.00

2-1/2 SILBER GROSCHEN

3.2400 g, .375 SILVER, .0390 oz ASW
Mint mark: A

C#	Date	Mintage	Fine	VF	XF	Unc
147	1842	—	3.00	6.00	12.00	55.00
	1843	—	3.00	6.00	12.00	55.00
	1844	—	3.00	6.00	12.00	55.00
	1848	—	3.00	6.00	12.00	55.00

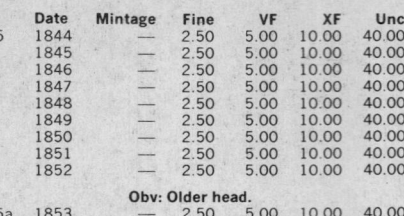

C#	Date	Mintage	Fine	VF	XF	Unc
147	1849	—	3.00	6.00	12.00	55.00
	1850	—	3.00	6.00	12.00	55.00
	1851	—	3.00	6.00	12.00	55.00
	1852	—	3.00	6.00	12.00	55.00

147a	1853	—	3.00	6.00	12.00	55.00
	1854	—	3.00	6.00	12.00	55.00
	1855	—	3.00	6.00	12.00	55.00
	1856	—	3.00	6.00	12.00	55.00
	1857	—	3.00	6.00	12.00	55.00
	1858	—	3.00	6.00	12.00	55.00
	1859	—	3.00	6.00	12.00	55.00
	1860	—	3.00	6.00	12.00	55.00

167	1861	—	2.00	4.00	8.00	50.00
	1862	—	2.00	4.00	8.00	50.00
	1863	—	2.00	4.00	8.00	50.00
	1864	—	2.00	4.00	8.00	50.00
	1865	—	2.00	4.00	8.00	50.00
	1866	—	2.00	4.00	8.00	50.00
	1867	—	2.00	4.00	8.00	50.00
	1868	—	1.50	3.00	6.00	35.00
	1869	—	1.50	3.00	6.00	35.00
	1870	—	1.50	3.00	6.00	35.00
	1871	—	1.50	3.00	6.00	35.00
	1872	—	1.50	3.00	6.00	35.00
	1873	—	1.50	3.00	6.00	35.00

Mint mark: B
Rev: B below date.

167a	1869	—	1.50	3.00	6.00	40.00
	1870	—	1.50	3.00	6.00	40.00
	1871	—	1.50	3.00	6.00	40.00
	1872	—	1.50	3.00	6.00	40.00
	1873	—	1.50	3.00	6.00	40.00

Mint mark: C
Rev: C below date.

167b	1867	—	1.50	3.00	6.00	35.00
	1868	—	1.50	3.00	6.00	35.00
	1869	—	1.50	3.00	6.00	35.00
	1870	—	1.50	3.00	6.00	35.00
	1871	—	1.50	3.00	6.00	35.00
	1872	—	1.50	3.00	6.00	35.00
	1873	—	1.50	3.00	6.00	35.00

4 GROSCHEN

5.3450 g, .521 SILVER, .0895 oz ASW
Mint mark: A

104	1801	—	8.00	15.00	50.00	175.00
	1802	—	8.00	15.00	50.00	175.00
	1803	—	8.00	15.00	50.00	175.00
	1804	—	8.00	15.00	50.00	175.00
	1805	—	8.00	15.00	50.00	175.00
	1806	—	12.00	20.00	100.00	225.00
	1807	—	12.00	20.00	100.00	225.00
	1808	—	12.00	20.00	100.00	225.00
	1809	—	12.00	20.00	100.00	225.00

Mint mark: B
Rev: B below date.

104b	1802	—	10.00	20.00	50.00	150.00
	1803	—	10.00	20.00	50.00	150.00
	1804	—	10.00	20.00	50.00	150.00
	1805	—	10.00	20.00	50.00	150.00

Mint mark: G
Rev: G below value.

104a	1808	—	15.00	20.00	100.00	225.00
	1809	—	15.00	20.00	100.00	225.00

Mint mark: A

C#	Date	Mintage	Fine	VF	XF	Unc
106	1816	11.652	10.00	25.00	65.00	250.00
	1817	14.484	10.00	25.00	65.00	250.00
	1818	—	10.00	25.00	65.00	250.00

Mint mark: D

106a	1818	—	25.00	50.00	200.00	275.00

1/6 THALER

5.3450 g, .521 SILVER, .0895 oz ASW
Mint mark: A

105	1809	—	10.00	20.00	50.00	200.00
	1810	—	10.00	20.00	50.00	200.00
	1811	—	10.00	20.00	50.00	200.00
	1812	—	10.00	20.00	50.00	200.00
	1813	—	10.00	20.00	50.00	200.00
	1814	—	10.00	20.00	50.00	200.00
	1815	—	10.00	20.00	50.00	200.00
	1816	—	10.00	20.00	50.00	200.00

Mint mark: B
Rev: B below date.

105a	1812	—	10.00	20.00	50.00	200.00
	1813	—	10.00	20.00	50.00	200.00
	1814	—	10.00	20.00	50.00	200.00
	1815	—	10.00	20.00	50.00	200.00
	1816	—	10.00	20.00	50.00	200.00
	1817	—	10.00	20.00	50.00	200.00

Mint mark: D
Rev: D below date.

105b	1817	—	15.00	30.00	70.00	225.00
	1818	—	15.00	30.00	70.00	225.00

5.3450 g, .521 SILVER, .0895 oz ASW
Mint mark: A

129	1822	3.264	4.00	10.00	40.00	100.00
	1823	8.550	4.00	10.00	40.00	100.00
	1824	3.504	4.00	10.00	40.00	100.00
	1825	4.662	4.00	10.00	40.00	100.00
	1826	3.300	4.00	10.00	40.00	100.00
	1827	.972	4.00	10.00	40.00	100.00
	1835	.060	10.00	20.00	70.00	150.00
	1837	.042	10.00	20.00	70.00	150.00
	1838	.048	10.00	20.00	70.00	150.00
	1839	.576	4.00	10.00	40.00	100.00
	1840	.954	4.00	10.00	40.00	100.00

Mint mark: D
Obv: D below head.

129a	1823	.066	10.00	20.00	70.00	150.00
	1826	.636	4.00	10.00	45.00	125.00
	1827	.924	4.00	10.00	45.00	125.00
	1828	—	4.00	10.00	45.00	125.00
	1835	—	4.00	10.00	45.00	125.00
	1840	.762	4.00	10.00	45.00	125.00

Mint mark: A

148	1841	.786	4.00	10.00	35.00	125.00
	1842	3.046	4.00	10.00	35.00	125.00
	1843	1.566	4.00	10.00	35.00	125.00
	1844	.948	4.00	10.00	35.00	125.00
	1845	.312	4.00	10.00	35.00	125.00
	1846	.270	4.00	10.00	35.00	125.00
	1847	.240	4.00	10.00	35.00	125.00
	1848	.912	4.00	10.00	35.00	125.00
	1849	2.556	4.00	10.00	35.00	125.00
	1850	.078	5.00	15.00	45.00	150.00
	1851	—	4.00	10.00	35.00	125.00
	1852	.372	4.00	10.00	35.00	125.00

Mint mark: D
Obv: D below head.

148a	1841	.678	4.00	10.00	35.00	125.00
	1842	.576	4.00	10.00	35.00	125.00
	1843	.426	4.00	10.00	35.00	125.00
	1844	.270	4.00	10.00	35.00	125.00
	1845	.096	5.00	15.00	40.00	150.00

Mint mark: A
Obv: A below older head.

C#	Date	Mintage	Fine	VF	XF	Unc
148b	1853	.216	4.00	10.00	35.00	125.00
	1854	.116	4.00	10.00	35.00	125.00
	1855	.030	5.00	15.00	40.00	150.00
	1856	.051	5.00	15.00	40.00	150.00

Rev: Crowned eagle w/sceptre and orb.

149	1858	.096	10.00	25.00	50.00	150.00
	1859	.032	10.00	25.00	50.00	150.00
	1860	.128	10.00	25.00	50.00	150.00

168	1861	.249	20.00	40.00	75.00	150.00
	1862	1.180	20.00	40.00	75.00	150.00
	1863	.413	20.00	40.00	75.00	150.00
	1864	.441	20.00	40.00	75.00	150.00

Rev: Eagle w/larger head.

168a	1865	.194	40.00	75.00	100.00	250.00
	1867	.148	40.00	75.00	100.00	250.00
	1868	.128	40.00	75.00	100.00	250.00

1/3 THALER

8.3520 g, .666 SILVER, .1788 oz ASW
Mint mark: A

108	1801	—	15.00	30.00	75.00	225.00
	1802	—	15.00	30.00	75.00	225.00
	1804	—	15.00	30.00	75.00	225.00
	1807	—	15.00	30.00	75.00	225.00

Mint mark: G
Rev: G below bow on branches.

108a	1809	—	25.00	50.00	175.00	400.00

Mint mark: A

109	1809	—	65.00	125.00	300.00	500.00

Mint mark: G
Rev: G below date.

109a	1809	—	50.00	100.00	250.00	400.00

2/3 THALER

17.3230 g, .750 SILVER, .4177 oz ASW
Mint mark: A

Obv: Crowned arms in branches. Rev: Value, date.

C#	Date	Mintage	Fine	VF	XF	Unc
111	1810	—	50.00	100.00	200.00	350.00

THALER
(Reichs)

22.2720 g, .750 SILVER, .5371 oz ASW
Mint mark: A
Rev: Crowned, supported arms above value, date.

C#	Date	Mintage	Fine	VF	XF	Unc
113	1801	—	30.00	80.00	200.00	700.00
	1802	—	30.00	80.00	200.00	700.00
	1803	—	30.00	80.00	200.00	700.00
	1804	—	50.00	80.00	275.00	800.00
	1805	—	50.00	80.00	275.00	800.00
	1806	—	50.00	80.00	275.00	800.00
	1807	—	50.00	80.00	275.00	800.00
	1809	—	50.00	80.00	275.00	800.00

Mint mark: B
Rev: B below date.

113b	1801	—	35.00	125.00	300.00	900.00
	1802	—	35.00	125.00	300.00	900.00
	1803	—	40.00	180.00	400.00	1000.

Mint mark: G
Rev: G below date.

113a	1808	.033	200.00	350.00	1400.	3200.
	1809	—	200.00	350.00	7500.	13,000.

Mint mark: A
Obv. leg: PRUSSEN (error).

113c	1803	—	—	—	—	—

114	1809	—	25.00	50.00	175.00	500.00
	1810	—	25.00	50.00	175.00	500.00
	1810 THAELR (error)					
	1811	—	25.00	50.00	175.00	600.00
	1812	—	25.00	50.00	175.00	600.00

C#	Date	Mintage	Fine	VF	XF	Unc
114	1813	—	25.00	50.00	150.00	325.00
	1814	—	25.00	50.00	125.00	275.00
	1815	—	25.00	50.00	150.00	325.00
	1816	—	25.00	50.00	150.00	325.00

Mint mark: B
Rev: B below date.

114a	1812	—	35.00	75.00	300.00	800.00
	1813	—	35.00	75.00	300.00	800.00
	1815	—	50.00	100.00	400.00	1000.
	1816	—	35.00	75.00	300.00	800.00

Visit Of Friedrich Wilhelm IV To Berlin Mint
Mint mark: A

115	1812	—	1500.	3000.	6000.	10,000.

Obv: Uniformed bust left, legend FR. WILH....
Rev: Crowned eagle on cannon, flags
and drums, A below date.

116	1816	—	200.00	375.00	1400.	4000.
	1817	—	250.00	550.00	1900.	4800.

Obv. leg: FRIEDR. WILHELM........

116a	1816	—	30.00	100.00	300.00	800.00
	1817	—	30.00	50.00	160.00	400.00
	1818	—	30.00	50.00	160.00	400.00
	1819	—	30.00	50.00	160.00	750.00
	1820	—	30.00	50.00	160.00	750.00
	1821	—	30.00	50.00	160.00	750.00
	1822	—	30.00	100.00	300.00	800.00

Mint mark: D
Rev: D below date.

116b	1818	—	30.00	60.00	275.00	800.00
	1819	—	30.00	60.00	275.00	800.00
	1820	—	30.00	60.00	275.00	800.00
	1821	—	—	—	Rare	
	1822	—	30.00	65.00	300.00	850.00

Mint mark: A

130	1823	.761	25.00	50.00	110.00	400.00
	1824	1.144	25.00	50.00	110.00	400.00
	1825	.405	25.00	50.00	110.00	400.00
	1826	.687	25.00	50.00	110.00	400.00

Mint mark: D
Obv: D below head.

130a	1823	.013	75.00	125.00	500.00	1200.
	1824	.016	40.00	80.00	300.00	800.00
	1825	.036	50.00	120.00	350.00	950.00

Mint mark: A
Obv: A below head. Rev: Arms of different design.

C#	Date	Mintage	Fine	VF	XF	Unc
130b	1827	.078	65.00	150.00	500.00	1200.
	1828	1.578	30.00	60.00	185.00	600.00

Obv: D below head. Rev: Arms of different design.

130c	1828	.012	75.00	200.00	650.00	1600

Mint mark: A
Obv: A below older head.

130d	1828	1.578	—	—	Rare	
	1829	4.002	20.00	50.00	90.00	200.00
	1830	6.888	20.00	50.00	90.00	200.00
	1831	4.595	20.00	50.00	90.00	200.00
	1832	.267	25.00	50.00	100.00	300.00
	1833	.448	25.00	50.00	100.00	300.00
	1834	1.299	20.00	50.00	90.00	200.00
	1835	.449	25.00	50.00	100.00	300.00
	1835	—	—	—	Proof	600.00
	1836	.526	25.00	50.00	100.00	300.00
	1837	.466	25.00	50.00	100.00	300.00
	1838	.314	25.00	50.00	100.00	300.00
	1839	.247	25.00	50.00	100.00	300.00
	1840	1.630	20.00	50.00	90.00	200.00
Common date	—	—	—	Proof	—	

Mint mark: D
Obv: D below older head.

130e	1829	.277	30.00	50.00	225.00	650.00
	1830	.651	30.00	50.00	175.00	550.00
	1831	.045	30.00	50.00	175.00	550.00
	1832	.029	30.00	60.00	225.00	800.00
	1833	.019	30.00	60.00	225.00	800.00
	1834	.021	30.00	60.00	225.00	800.00
	1835	.016	30.00	60.00	225.00	800.00
	1836	.021	30.00	60.00	225.00	800.00
	1837	.015	30.00	60.00	225.00	800.00
	1838	.025	30.00	60.00	225.00	800.00
	1839	.012	30.00	60.00	225.00	800.00
	1840	.011	30.00	60.00	225.00	800.00

(Mining)

Mint mark: A

131	1826	.050	35.00	80.00	200.00	600.00
	1827	.050	35.00	80.00	200.00	600.00
	1828	.050	35.00	80.00	200.00	600.00

Obv: A below older head.

131a	1829	—	25.00	60.00	110.00	250.00
	1830	—	25.00	60.00	110.00	250.00
	1831	—	25.00	60.00	110.00	250.00
	1832	—	25.00	60.00	110.00	325.00
	1833	—	25.00	60.00	110.00	325.00
	1834	—	25.00	60.00	110.00	300.00
	1835	—	25.00	60.00	110.00	325.00
	1836	—	25.00	60.00	110.00	325.00
	1837	—	25.00	60.00	110.00	325.00
	1838	—	25.00	60.00	110.00	325.00
	1839	—	25.00	60.00	110.00	325.00
	1840	—	25.00	60.00	100.00	225.00

Prussia / GERMAN STATES 665

C#	Date	Mintage	Fine	VF	XF	Unc
150	1841	2.280	35.00	85.00	275.00	800.00

(Reichs)

C#	Date	Mintage	Fine	VF	XF	Unc
150b	1842	.518	30.00	60.00	160.00	400.00
	1843	.600	25.00	50.00	100.00	225.00
	1844	.918	25.00	50.00	100.00	225.00
	1845	.720	25.00	50.00	100.00	225.00
	1846	1.115	25.00	50.00	100.00	225.00
	1847	1.283	25.00	50.00	100.00	225.00
	1848	3.743	25.00	50.00	100.00	225.00
	1849	.892	25.00	50.00	100.00	225.00
	1850	.350	25.00	50.00	100.00	225.00
	1851	.731	30.00	60.00	160.00	400.00
	1852	.329	30.00	60.00	160.00	400.00
	Common date	—	—	—	Proof	

C#	Date	Mintage	Fine	VF	XF	Unc
150a	1853	.300	30.00	60.00	125.00	250.00
	1854	3.500	25.00	50.00	100.00	200.00
	1855	7.300	25.00	50.00	100.00	200.00
	1856	.940	25.00	50.00	100.00	200.00

(Mining)

C#	Date	Mintage	Fine	VF	XF	Unc
151	1841	.050	50.00	110.00	300.00	950.00

Obv: A below larger head. Rev: Dot after THALER.

151b	1842	.050	30.00	65.00	150.00	350.00
	1843	.050	30.00	65.00	150.00	350.00
	1844	.050	30.00	65.00	150.00	350.00
	1845	.050	30.00	65.00	150.00	350.00
	1846	.050	30.00	65.00	150.00	350.00

Rev: W/o dot after THALER.

151c	1847	.050	30.00	65.00	150.00	350.00
	1848	.050	30.00	65.00	150.00	350.00
	1849	.050	30.00	65.00	150.00	350.00
	1850	.050	30.00	65.00	150.00	350.00
	1851	.050	30.00	65.00	150.00	350.00
	1852	.050	30.00	65.00	150.00	350.00

C#	Date	Mintage	Fine	VF	XF	Unc
151a	1853	.050	30.00	65.00	150.00	350.00
	1854	.050	30.00	65.00	150.00	350.00
	1855	.050	30.00	65.00	150.00	350.00
	1856	.050	30.00	65.00	150.00	350.00
	Common date	—	—	—	Proof	

(Vereins)

18.5200 g, .900 SILVER, .5360 oz ASW

152	1857	.836	20.00	30.00	60.00	175.00
	1858	1.120	20.00	30.00	60.00	175.00
	1859	17.600	17.50	25.00	50.00	125.00
	1860	17.429	17.50	25.00	50.00	125.00
	1861	.010	40.00	80.00	125.00	250.00
	1861	—	—	—	Proof	250.00

(Mining)

Obv: Similar to C#152.

153	1857	.047	30.00	65.00	150.00	350.00
	1858	.095	30.00	65.00	150.00	350.00
	1859	.094	30.00	65.00	150.00	350.00
	1860	.298	30.00	65.00	150.00	350.00
	Common date	—	—	—	Proof	

(Vereins)

Coronation of Wilhelm and Augusta

| 169 | 1861 | 1.000 | 17.50 | 25.00 | 40.00 | 60.00 |
| | 1861 | — | — | — | Proof | |

Obv: A below head right. Rev: Eagle.

170	1861	13.716	20.00	35.00	65.00	125.00
	1862	6.057	20.00	40.00	75.00	140.00
	1863	1.668	20.00	45.00	90.00	200.00

C#	Date	Mintage	Fine	VF	XF	Unc
170a	1864	1.379	25.00	35.00	75.00	150.00
	1865	2.584	20.00	35.00	65.00	140.00
	1866	24.409	20.00	35.00	65.00	140.00
	1867	31.390	20.00	35.00	65.00	140.00
	1868	6.286	20.00	35.00	65.00	140.00
	1869	3.630	20.00	35.00	65.00	140.00
	1870	3.140	20.00	35.00	65.00	140.00
	1871	7.600	20.00	35.00	65.00	140.00
	Common date	—	—	—	Proof	

Mint mark: B
Obv: B under bust.

170b	1866	.034	25.00	55.00	150.00	350.00
	1867	.593	25.00	55.00	150.00	350.00
	1868	.048	30.00	75.00	175.00	450.00
	1869	.370	30.00	75.00	175.00	450.00
	1870	.611	25.00	55.00	150.00	350.00
	1871	.245	25.00	55.00	150.00	350.00

Mint mark: C
Obv: C under bust.

170c	1867	.179	50.00	125.00	300.00	700.00
	1868	5.139	75.00	165.00	600.00	1250.
	1869	.044	50.00	125.00	300.00	700.00
	1870	.190	50.00	125.00	300.00	700.00
	1871	.028	50.00	125.00	300.00	700.00
	Common date	—	—	—	Proof	

(Mining)

Mint mark: A

| 171 | 1861 | .070 | 35.00 | 55.00 | 100.00 | 300.00 |
| | 1862 | .145 | 30.00 | 50.00 | 90.00 | 250.00 |

(Vereins)

Victory over Austria

| 172 | 1866 | .500 | 30.00 | 55.00 | 80.00 | 125.00 |

Victory over France

| 173 | 1871 | .880 | 17.50 | 25.00 | 40.00 | 60.00 |
| | 1871 | — | — | — | Proof | 150.00 |

2 THALER
(3-1/2 Gulden)

Prussia / GERMAN STATES 666

37.1190 g, .900 SILVER, 1.0742 oz ASW
Mint mark: A

C#	Date	Mintage	Fine	VF	XF	Unc
132	1839	.172	100.00	150.00	300.00	800.00
	1840	.789	75.00	125.00	225.00	600.00
132a	1841	—	—	—	Rare	—

154	1841	4.307	55.00	85.00	185.00	400.00
	1842	1.249	55.00	85.00	200.00	475.00
	1843	.193	55.00	85.00	200.00	475.00
	1844	1.069	55.00	85.00	200.00	475.00
	1845	.961	55.00	85.00	200.00	475.00
	1846	1.472	55.00	85.00	200.00	475.00
	1847	.232	—	—	Rare	—
	1848	4.147	—	—	Rare	—
	1850	.221	55.00	85.00	200.00	475.00
	1851	.379	55.00	85.00	200.00	475.00
	Common date	—	—	—	Proof	—

Rev: Similar to C#154.

154a	1853	2.500	200.00	450.00	1200.	2000.
	1854	.147	90.00	125.00	275.00	500.00
	1855	.100	75.00	110.00	225.00	425.00
	1856	.627	60.00	90.00	160.00	375.00

37.0370 g, .900 SILVER, 1.0718 oz ASW
Obv: Similar to C#154a.

155	1858	.017	200.00	375.00	1000.	1600.
	1859	.174	150.00	300.00	750.00	1325.
	Common date	—	—	—	Proof	—

Rev: Similar to C#155.

C#	Date	Mintage	Fine	VF	XF	Unc
174	1861	9,490	500.00	1000.	1800.	3200.
	1862	.058	250.00	460.00	1200.	2000.
	1863	337 pcs.	—	—	Rare	—
	1863	—	—	—	Proof	3000.

Similar to C#174b.

174a	1865	.023	175.00	350.00	1000.	1500.
	1866	5,110	225.00	425.00	1100.	2000.
	1867	1,195	250.00	550.00	1500.	3200.
	1868	1,584	250.00	550.00	1500.	3200.
	1869	1,901	250.00	550.00	1500.	3200.
	1870	3,155	250.00	550.00	1500.	3200.
	1871	1,134	235.00	350.00	1100.	1750.
	Common date	—	—	—	Proof	1800.

Mint mark: C

174b	1866	.226	150.00	260.00	425.00	800.00
	1867	1.049	100.00	200.00	350.00	700.00

1/2 KRONE

5.5550 g, .900 GOLD, .1607 oz AGW
Mint mark: A

159	1858	2.036	800.00	1500.	2000.	3250.

175	1862	6.365	500.00	1000.	1500.	2000.
	1863	3.642	500.00	1000.	1500.	2000.
	1864	4.840	500.00	1000.	1500.	2000.
	1866	.014	500.00	1000.	1500.	2000.
	1867	5,711	500.00	1000.	1500.	2000.
	1868	.092	400.00	800.00	1200.	1600.
	1869	—	800.00	1600.	2600.	3200.

Mint mark: B
Obv: B below head.

175a	1868	3,718	800.00	1500.	2000.	3750.

KRONE

11.1110 g, .916 GOLD, .3272 oz AGW
Mint mark: A

160	1858	6.320	600.00	1400.	1800.	3000.
	1859	.034	550.00	1200.	1600.	2600.
	1860	.016	650.00	1500.	2000.	3250.

Obv: A below head.

C#	Date	Mintage	Fine	VF	XF	Unc
176	1861	2,488	650.00	1200.	1600.	3000.
	1862	5,558	650.00	1200.	1600.	3000.
	1863	2,653	650.00	1200.	1600.	3000.
	1864	792 pcs.	800.00	1400.	2000.	3250.
	1866	720 pcs.	800.00	1400.	2000.	3250.
	1867	4,087	400.00	800.00	1200.	2000.
	1867	—	—	—	Proof	2500.
	1868	.097	400.00	800.00	1200.	2000.
	1869	—	1000.	1400.	2000.	3600.
	1870	1,764	800.00	1400.	2000.	3250.

Mint mark: B
Obv: B below head.

176a	1867	.015	500.00	1250.	2000.	3000.
	1868	.040	500.00	1250.	2000.	3000.

MONETARY REFORM
2 MARK

11.1110 g, .900 SILVER, .3215 oz ASW
Mint mark: A

Y#	Date	Mintage	Fine	VF	XF	Unc
111	1876	13.370	10.00	40.00	200.00	425.00
	1877	3.634	10.00	35.00	175.00	475.00
	1879	.029	100.00	200.00	1000.	1900.
	1880	.665	25.00	75.00	550.00	1200.
	1883	.164	35.00	115.00	400.00	800.00
	1884	.140	40.00	140.00	450.00	1000.

Mint mark: B

111.1	1876	3.985	10.00	40.00	225.00	475.00
	1877	1.301	15.00	50.00	320.00	625.00

Mint mark: C

111.2	1876	5.233	10.00	40.00	275.00	500.00
	1877	1.307	15.00	50.00	320.00	625.00

Mint mark: A

116	1888	.500	12.50	20.00	40.00	75.00
	1888	—	—	—	Proof	175.00

120	1888	.141	100.00	250.00	400.00	600.00
	1888	—	—	—	Proof	750.00

120a	1891	.544	10.00	20.00	40.00	150.00
	1891	—	—	—	Proof	500.00
	1892	.182	100.00	200.00	400.00	800.00
	1892	—	—	—	Proof	2000.
	1893	.948	10.00	20.00	40.00	140.00
	1896	1.772	10.00	20.00	40.00	140.00
	1898	1.042	12.50	30.00	60.00	175.00

Y#	Date	Mintage	Fine	VF	XF	Unc
120a	1901	.398	40.00	85.00	175.00	350.00
	1902	3.948	8.00	14.00	40.00	115.00
	1903	4.079	8.00	14.00	40.00	115.00
	1904	9.981	8.00	14.00	40.00	115.00
	1905	6.423	8.00	14.00	35.00	80.00
	1905	620 pcs.	—	—	Proof	175.00
	1906	4.000	8.00	14.00	30.00	70.00
	1906	85 pcs.	—	—	Proof	175.00
	1907	8.085	8.00	14.00	25.00	60.00
	1908	2.389	8.00	14.00	30.00	95.00
	1911	1.181	9.00	17.50	30.00	100.00
	1912	.733	9.00	17.50	30.00	100.00

200 Years Kingdom of Prussia

128	1901	2.600	5.00	10.00	15.00	30.00
	1901	—	—	—	Proof	70.00

100 Years Defeat of Napoleon

132	1913	1.500	10.00	12.50	17.50	30.00
	1913	—	—	—	Proof	60.00

25th Year of Reign

134	1913	1.500	10.00	12.50	17.50	30.00
	1913	—	—	—	Proof	75.00

3 MARK

16.6670 g, .900 SILVER, .4823 oz ASW
Mint mark: A

121	1908	2.859	10.00	15.00	22.50	45.00
	1909	6.344	10.00	15.00	22.50	45.00
	1910	5.791	10.00	15.00	22.50	45.00
	1911	3.242	10.00	15.00	22.50	45.00
	1912	4.626	10.00	15.00	22.50	45.00
	Common date	—	—	—	Proof	150.00

Berlin University

130	1910	.200	17.50	35.00	70.00	95.00
	1910	—	—	—	Proof	300.00

Breslau University

Y#	Date	Mintage	Fine	VF	XF	Unc
131	1911	.400	12.50	27.50	55.00	80.00
	1911	—	—	—	Proof	250.00

100 Years Defeat of Napoleon

133	1913	1.000	12.50	15.00	20.00	30.00
	1913	—	—	—	Proof	100.00

25th Year of Reign

135	1913	1.000	12.50	15.00	20.00	30.00
	1913	—	—	—	Proof	90.00

125	1914	2.020	12.50	15.00	20.00	35.00
	1914	—	—	—	Proof	100.00

Centenary Absorption of Mansfeld
Rev: Similar to Y#131.

136	1915	.030	75.00	250.00	400.00	550.00
	1915	—	—	—	Proof	700.00

5 MARK

27.7770 g, .900 SILVER, .8038 oz ASW
Mint mark: A

Y#	Date	Mintage	Fine	VF	XF	Unc
112	1874	.838	17.50	45.00	275.00	575.00
	1875	.853	17.50	50.00	350.00	1000.
	1876	2.041	15.00	40.00	225.00	525.00
	Common date	—	—	—	Proof	1750.

Mint mark: B

112.1	1875	.919	17.50	45.00	350.00	1000.
	1876	2.098	15.00	45.00	225.00	475.00

Mint mark: C

| 112.2 | 1876 | .812 | 17.50 | 45.00 | 225.00 | 1000. |

1.9910 g, .900 GOLD, .0576 oz AGW
Mint mark: A

113	1877	1.217	100.00	150.00	200.00	300.00
	1877	—	—	—	Proof	1300.
	1878	.502	100.00	150.00	200.00	300.00
	1878	—	—	—	Proof	1300.

Mint mark: B

113.1	1877	.517	100.00	150.00	200.00	350.00
	1877	—	—	—	Proof	1100.

Mint mark: C

| 113.2 | 1877 | .688 | 100.00 | 150.00 | 200.00 | 325.00 |

27.7770 g, .900 SILVER, .8038 oz ASW
Mint mark: A

117	1888	.200	40.00	75.00	125.00	175.00
	1888	—	—	—	Proof	500.00

Rev: Type II.

122	1888	.056	175.00	425.00	800.00	1100.
	1888	—	—	—	Proof	1750.

Prussia / GERMAN STATES 668

Y#	Date	Mintage	Fine	VF	XF	Unc
122a	1891	.130	15.00	35.00	130.00	625.00
	1892	.224	15.00	35.00	130.00	625.00
	1893	.215	15.00	35.00	150.00	625.00
	1894	.440	15.00	40.00	110.00	525.00
	1895	.831	15.00	40.00	130.00	525.00
	1896	.046	95.00	175.00	750.00	1800.
	1898	1.134	15.00	30.00	100.00	450.00
	1899	.529	15.00	35.00	140.00	450.00
	1900	1.080	15.00	30.00	100.00	325.00
	1901	.668	15.00	30.00	100.00	325.00
	1902	1.951	15.00	25.00	70.00	225.00
	1903	3.856	15.00	22.50	65.00	225.00
	1904	2.060	15.00	22.50	65.00	200.00
	1906	.231	20.00	35.00	100.00	300.00
	1907	2.102	15.00	22.50	50.00	175.00
	1908	2.231	15.00	22.50	50.00	200.00
	Common date	—	—	—	Proof	550.00

200 Years Kingdom of Prussia

| 129 | 1901 | .460 | 25.00 | 45.00 | 65.00 | 100.00 |
| | 1901 | — | — | — | Proof | 175.00 |

126	1913	1.962	20.00	25.00	35.00	85.00
	1914	1.587	20.00	25.00	35.00	85.00
	Common date	—	—	—	Proof	350.00

10 MARK

3.9820 g, .900 GOLD, .1152 oz AGW
Mint mark: A

114	1872	3.123	60.00	100.00	135.00	200.00
	1872	—	—	—	Proof	1600.
	1873	3.016	60.00	100.00	135.00	200.00
	1873	—	—	—	Proof	1600.

Mint mark: B
Obv: B below head.

| 114b | 1872 | 1.418 | 60.00 | 100.00 | 135.00 | 275.00 |
| | 1873 | 2.273 | 60.00 | 100.00 | 135.00 | 275.00 |

Mint mark: C
Obv: C below head.

| 114c | 1872 | 1.747 | 60.00 | 100.00 | 135.00 | 275.00 |
| | 1873 | 2.295 | 60.00 | 100.00 | 135.00 | 275.00 |

Mint mark: A.
Obv: A below head. Rev: Type II.

Y#	Date	Mintage	Fine	VF	XF	Unc
114a	1874	.833	60.00	100.00	150.00	250.00
	1874	—	—	—	Proof	1100.
	1875	2.430	60.00	100.00	150.00	250.00
	1877	.851	60.00	100.00	150.00	250.00
	1878	1.126	60.00	100.00	150.00	250.00
	1879	1.012	60.00	100.00	150.00	200.00
	1879	—	—	—	Proof	550.00
	1880	1.762	60.00	100.00	150.00	200.00
	1882	8.382	1500.	3300.	4500.	7000.
	1883	.013	1200.	1800.	2200.	3000.
	1883	—	—	—	Proof	10,000.
	1886	.014	1500.	2200.	3200.	5000.
	1888	.189	—	100.00	150.00	250.00
	1888	—	—	—	Proof	1300.

Mint mark: B
Obv: B below head.

114d	1874	1.028	60.00	100.00	150.00	300.00
	1875	.456	60.00	100.00	150.00	300.00
	1876	2.800	1000.	1600.	2200.	3000.
	1876	—	—	—	Proof	10,000.
	1877	.247	60.00	100.00	150.00	350.00
	1878	.015	—	—	Rare	—

Mint mark: C
Obv: C below head.

114e	1874	.321	60.00	100.00	150.00	250.00
	1874	—	—	—	Proof	1300.
	1875	1.532	60.00	100.00	150.00	250.00
	1876	.027	500.00	1200.	1500.	2500.
	1877	.328	60.00	100.00	150.00	300.00
	1878	.516	60.00	100.00	150.00	300.00
	1879	.282	60.00	100.00	150.00	250.00

Mint mark: A

| 118 | 1888 | .876 | 60.00 | 90.00 | 125.00 | 175.00 |
| | 1888 | — | — | — | Proof | 600.00 |

Rev: Type II.

| 123 | 1889 | .024 | 1400. | 2000. | 2500. | 3500. |
| | 1889 | — | — | — | Proof | 6000. |

Rev: Type III.

123a	1890	1.512	BV	100.00	135.00	200.00
	1890	—	—	—	Proof	500.00
	1892	.035	400.00	700.00	1000.	1500.
	1893	.368	BV	100.00	135.00	200.00
	1894	.018	600.00	1200.	1500.	2000.
	1895	.029	400.00	750.00	1350.	1900.
	1896	1.081	BV	100.00	135.00	200.00
	1897	.114	BV	125.00	250.00	400.00
	1898	2.280	BV	100.00	135.00	200.00
	1899	.300	BV	100.00	165.00	225.00
	1900	.742	BV	100.00	135.00	200.00
	1900	—	—	—	Proof	500.00
	1901	.702	BV	100.00	135.00	200.00
	1901	—	—	—	Proof	500.00
	1902	.271	BV	100.00	135.00	200.00
	1902	—	—	—	Proof	500.00
	1903	1.685	BV	100.00	135.00	200.00
	1903	—	—	—	Proof	500.00
	1904	1.178	BV	100.00	135.00	200.00
	1905	1.073	BV	100.00	135.00	200.00
	1905	117 pcs.	—	—	Proof	500.00
	1906	.542	BV	100.00	135.00	175.00
	1906	150 pcs.	—	—	Proof	500.00
	1907	.813	BV	100.00	135.00	175.00
	1907	—	—	—	Proof	500.00
	1909	.532	BV	100.00	135.00	175.00
	1909	—	—	—	Proof	500.00
	1910	.803	BV	100.00	135.00	175.00
	1911	.271	BV	100.00	135.00	200.00
	1911	—	—	—	Proof	500.00
	1912	.542	BV	100.00	135.00	175.00
	1912	—	—	—	Proof	500.00

20 MARK

7.9650 g, .900 GOLD, .2304 oz AGW
Mint mark: A

Y#	Date	Mintage	Fine	VF	XF	Unc
115	1871	.502	BV	135.00	150.00	300.00
	1871	—	—	—	Proof	1800.
	1872	7.717	BV	135.00	150.00	225.00
	1872	2.491	—	—	Proof	1800.
	1873	9.063	BV	135.00	150.00	225.00
	1873	—	—	—	Proof	1800.

Mint mark: B
Obv: B below head.

| 115b | 1872 | 1.918 | BV | 135.00 | 150.00 | 225.00 |
| | 1873 | 3.441 | BV | 135.00 | 150.00 | 225.00 |

Mint mark: C
Obv: C below head.

115c	1872	3.056	BV	135.00	150.00	225.00
	1873	5.228	BV	135.00	150.00	225.00
	1873	—	—	—	Proof	1800.

Mint mark: A
Rev: Type II.

115a	1874	.762	BV	115.00	140.00	200.00
	1874	—	—	—	Proof	1300.
	1875	4.203	BV	115.00	140.00	200.00
	1876	2.673	BV	115.00	140.00	200.00
	1877	1.250	BV	115.00	140.00	200.00
	1878	2.175	BV	115.00	140.00	200.00
	1879	1.023	BV	115.00	140.00	200.00
	1881	.428	BV	115.00	140.00	200.00
	1882	.655	BV	115.00	140.00	200.00
	1882	—	—	—	Proof	1300.
	1883	4.283	BV	115.00	140.00	200.00
	1884	.224	BV	115.00	140.00	200.00
	1885	.407	BV	115.00	140.00	200.00
	1886	.176	BV	115.00	140.00	200.00
	1887	5.645	BV	115.00	140.00	200.00
	1887	—	—	—	Proof	1300.
	1888	.534	BV	115.00	140.00	200.00
	1888	—	—	—	Proof	1300.

Mint mark: B
Obv: B below head.

115d	1874	.824	BV	115.00	150.00	225.00
	1875	*1,500	165.00	400.00	650.00	1200.
	1877	.501	BV	200.00	200.00	350.00

Mint mark: C
Obv: C below head.

115e	1874	.088	115.00	135.00	165.00	250.00
	1876	.423	135.00	275.00	400.00	550.00
	1877	6.384	1000.	1650.	2200.	2750.
	1878	.082	120.00	250.00	400.00	600.00

Mint mark: A

| 119 | 1888 | 5.364 | BV | 115.00 | 135.00 | 175.00 |
| | 1888 | — | — | — | Proof | 700.00 |

124	1888	.756	BV	115.00	135.00	225.00
	1888	—	—	—	Proof	1000.
	1889	10.885	BV	115.00	135.00	175.00
	1889	—	—	—	Proof	1000.

Rev: Type III.

Y#	Date	Mintage	Fine	VF	XF	Unc
124a	1890	3.695	BV	115.00	125.00	150.00
	1891	2.752	BV	115.00	125.00	150.00
	1891	—	—	—	Proof	600.00
	1892	1.815	BV	115.00	125.00	150.00
	1893	3.172	BV	115.00	125.00	150.00
	1894	5.815	BV	115.00	125.00	150.00
	1895	4.135	BV	115.00	125.00	150.00
	1896	4.239	BV	115.00	125.00	150.00
	1896	—	—	—	Proof	600.00
	1897	5.394	BV	115.00	125.00	150.00
	1898	6.592	BV	115.00	125.00	150.00
	1899	5.873	BV	115.00	125.00	150.00
	1899	—	—	—	Proof	600.00
	1900	5.163	BV	115.00	125.00	140.00
	1901	5.188	BV	115.00	125.00	140.00
	1901	—	—	—	Proof	600.00
	1902	4.138	BV	115.00	125.00	140.00
	1903	2.870	BV	115.00	125.00	140.00
	1904	3.453	BV	115.00	125.00	140.00
	1905	4.221	BV	115.00	125.00	140.00
	1905	—	—	—	Proof	600.00
	1906	7.788	BV	115.00	125.00	140.00
	1906	124 pcs.	—	—	Proof	600.00
	1907	2.576	BV	115.00	125.00	140.00
	1908	3.274	BV	115.00	125.00	140.00
	1909	5.213	BV	115.00	125.00	140.00
	1910	8.646	BV	115.00	125.00	140.00
	1911	4.746	BV	115.00	125.00	140.00
	1912	5.569	BV	115.00	125.00	140.00
	1913	6.102	BV	115.00	125.00	140.00
	1913	—	—	—	Proof	600.00

Mint mark: J
Obv: J below head.

124b	1905	.921	BV	115.00	150.00	200.00
	1906	.082	125.00	200.00	300.00	450.00
	1909	.350	115.00	150.00	175.00	—
	1909	—	—	—	Proof	800.00
	1910	.753	BV	115.00	150.00	200.00
	1912	.503	BV	115.00	150.00	200.00

Mint mark: A

127	1913	6.102	BV	115.00	135.00	175.00
	1913	—	—	—	Proof	1200.
	1914	2.137	BV	115.00	135.00	175.00
	1914	—	—	—	Proof	1200.
	1915	1.268	750.00	1250.	2500.	3000.

TRADE COINAGE
1/2 FREDERICK D'OR

3.3410 g, .903 GOLD, .0970 oz AGW
Obv: L at truncation.

C#	Date	Mintage	Fine	VF	XF	Unc
118	1802	—	275.00	350.00	800.00	1500.
	1803	—	550.00	800.00	1200.	2000.
	1804	—	300.00	500.00	900.00	1625.
	1806	—	275.00	400.00	800.00	1500.
	1814	—	300.00	500.00	900.00	1625.
	1816	—	350.00	600.00	1000.	1750.

| 121 | 1817 | — | 300.00 | 500.00 | 700.00 | 1250. |

C#	Date	Mintage	Fine	VF	XF	Unc
133	1825	—	300.00	500.00	750.00	1000.
	1827	—	375.00	650.00	875.00	1125.
	1828	—	600.00	1000.	1250.	1500.
	1829	—	500.00	875.00	1125.	1375.
	1830	—	350.00	625.00	875.00	1125.
	1831	—	350.00	625.00	875.00	1125.
	1832	—	350.00	625.00	875.00	1125.
	1833	—	350.00	625.00	875.00	1125.
	1834	—	350.00	625.00	875.00	1125.
	1838	—	350.00	625.00	875.00	1125.
	1839	—	400.00	750.00	1000.	1250.
	1840	—	500.00	875.00	1125.	1375.

156	1841	—	300.00	500.00	750.00	1000.
	1842	—	300.00	500.00	750.00	1000.
	1843	—	400.00	750.00	1000.	1250.
	1844	—	400.00	750.00	1000.	1250.
	1845	—	400.00	750.00	1000.	1250.
	1846	—	400.00	750.00	1000.	1250.
	1849	—	400.00	750.00	1000.	1250.

| 156a | 1853 | — | 400.00 | 750.00 | 1000. | 1250. |

FREDERICK D'OR

6.6820 g, .903 GOLD, .1940 oz AGW
Mint mark: A

119	1801	—	400.00	600.00	950.00	1400.
	1802	—	450.00	600.00	950.00	1400.
	1803	—	400.00	475.00	800.00	1200.
	1804	—	450.00	600.00	950.00	1400.
	1805	—	350.00	525.00	950.00	1200.
	1806	—	350.00	525.00	950.00	1200.
	1807	—	350.00	525.00	950.00	1200.
	1808	—	550.00	800.00	1200.	1600.
	1809	—	350.00	475.00	800.00	1200.
	1810	—	450.00	600.00	950.00	1400.
	1811	—	450.00	600.00	950.00	1400.
	1812	—	350.00	475.00	800.00	1200.
	1813	—	400.00	525.00	875.00	1300.
	1816	—	450.00	600.00	950.00	1400.

Mint mark: B

119a	1800	—	450.00	600.00	1000.	1400.
	1801	—	450.00	600.00	1000.	1400.
	1802	—	450.00	600.00	1000.	1400.
	1803	—	550.00	800.00	1200.	1800.
	1804	—	550.00	800.00	1200.	1800.
	1805	—	550.00	800.00	1200.	1800.

Mint mark: A

122	1817	—	500.00	800.00	1200.	1800.
	1818	—	400.00	550.00	1000.	1500.
	1819	—	650.00	1000.	1500.	2000.
	1822	—	400.00	550.00	1000.	1500.

134	1825	—	300.00	400.00	800.00	1250.
	1827	—	400.00	600.00	1000.	1500.
	1828	—	300.00	550.00	800.00	1400.
	1829	—	400.00	550.00	1000.	1500.
	1830	—	400.00	550.00	1000.	1500.
	1831	—	300.00	550.00	900.00	1400.
	1832	—	400.00	550.00	900.00	1400.
	1833	—	300.00	550.00	900.00	1400.
	1834	—	300.00	550.00	1000.	1500.
	1836	—	300.00	550.00	1000.	1500.

C#	Date	Mintage	Fine	VF	XF	Unc
134	1837	—	300.00	550.00	800.00	1400.
	1838	—	300.00	550.00	800.00	1500.
	1839	—	300.00	550.00	800.00	1400.
	1840	—	300.00	550.00	800.00	1250.

157	1841	—	300.00	550.00	800.00	1250.
	1842	—	300.00	550.00	800.00	1250.
	1843	—	300.00	550.00	800.00	1400.
	1844	—	300.00	550.00	800.00	1250.
	1845	—	300.00	550.00	800.00	1250.
	1846	—	300.00	550.00	800.00	1250.
	1847	—	300.00	550.00	800.00	1400.
	1848	—	300.00	550.00	800.00	1250.
	1849	—	300.00	550.00	800.00	1250.
	1850	—	300.00	550.00	800.00	1400.
	1851	—	300.00	550.00	800.00	1500.
	1852	—	300.00	550.00	800.00	1400.

157a	1853	—	300.00	550.00	800.00	1250.
	1854	—	300.00	550.00	800.00	1250.
	1855	—	300.00	550.00	800.00	1250.

2 FREDERICK D'OR

13.3630 g, .903 GOLD, .3880 oz AGW
Obv: L at truncation.

120	1800	—	600.00	875.00	1600.	2400.
	1801	—	700.00	975.00	1800.	2600.
	1802	—	800.00	1250.	2200.	3000.
	1806	—	800.00	1250.	2200.	3000.
	1811	—	700.00	975.00	1800.	2600.
	1813	—	725.00	1000.	2000.	2800.
	1814	—	800.00	1250.	2200.	3000.

135	1825	—	800.00	1200.	1600.	2000.
	1826	—	700.00	1100.	1500.	1800.
	1827	—	600.00	1000.	1400.	1600.
	1828	—	600.00	1000.	1400.	1600.
	1829	—	700.00	1100.	1500.	1800.
	1830	—	550.00	900.00	1300.	1500.
	1831	—	550.00	900.00	1300.	1500.
	1832	—	700.00	1100.	1500.	1800.
	1836	—	800.00	1200.	1600.	2000.
	1837	—	550.00	900.00	1300.	1500.
	1838	—	600.00	1000.	1400.	1600.
	1839	—	500.00	800.00	1200.	1400.
	1840	—	500.00	800.00	1200.	1400.

158	1841	—	500.00	800.00	1200.	1500.
	1842	—	500.00	800.00	1200.	1500.
	1843	—	600.00	1250.	1750.	2000.
	1844	—	800.00	1500.	2000.	2250.
	1845	—	800.00	1500.	2000.	2250.
	1846	—	500.00	800.00	1200.	1500.
	1848	—	500.00	800.00	1200.	1500.
	1849	—	500.00	800.00	1200.	1500.
	1852	—	500.00	800.00	1200.	1500.

C#	Date	Mintage	Fine	VF	XF	Unc
158a	1853	—	500.00	800.00	1200.	2000.
	1854	—	500.00	800.00	1200.	2000.
	1855	—	750.00	1500.	2000.	2500.

PYRMONT

A county, southwest of Hannover, was established c. 1160. Their first coins were struck in the 13th century. In 1625 Pyrmont was incorporated with Waldeck. Occasional issues of special coins for Pyrmont were struck in the 18th and 19th centuries.

RULERS
Georg, Prince, 1805-1812

MINTMASTER'S INITIALS
Letter	Date	Name
FW	1807-1829	Friedrich Welle

24 EINEN (1/24) THALER

1.9900 g, .368 SILVER, .0235 oz ASW
Obv: Crowned and mantled 2 shields of arms.
Rev: Value over date.

C#	Date	Mintage	VG	Fine	VF	XF
6	1806 FW	—	25.00	50.00	100.00	175.00
	1807 FW	—	25.00	50.00	100.00	175.00

EIN (1) THALER
(Convention)

28.0600 g, .833 SILVER, .7515 oz ASW

C#	Date	Mintage	Fine	VF	XF	Unc
7	1811 FW	—	850.00	1500.	3250.	6000.

REGENSBURG
Ratisbon

The Bishopric, located in central Bavaria, was established in 470. Regular episcopal coins appeared in the 11th century. Regensburg became a Free City in 1180 and in 1230 received the right to mint its own coins. The dated city coinage extends from c. 1511 to 1802. In 1803 the city was given to the bishop and the city and Bishopric were united with Bavaria.

FREE CITY
MINTMASTER'S INITIALS
Letter	Date	Name
B.BF,G.C.B.	1773-1803	Georg Christoph Busch
GZ,Z	1791-1802	Johann Leonhard Zollner
K, Kornlein	1773-1802	Johann Nikolaus Kornlein

HELLER
COPPER, uniface
Crossed keys.

C#	Date	Mintage	VG	Fine	VF	XF
2	1801	—	2.50	4.50	7.50	15.00
	1802	—	2.50	4.50	7.50	15.00
	1803	—	2.50	4.50	7.50	15.00

EIN (1) THALER

SILVER

C#	Date	Mintage	Fine	VF	XF	Unc
57	1801 Z	—	1000.	2000.	2800.	4800.
	1802 Z	—	1000.	2000.	2800.	4800.

TRADE COINAGE
DUCAT

3.5000 g, .986 GOLD, .1109 oz AGW
Obv: Crowned imperial eagle.

C#	Date	Mintage	VG	Fine	VF	XF
103	ND (1792-1803)	150.00	350.00	650.00	1000.

REUSS

The Reuss family, whose lands were located in Thuringia, was founded c. 1035. Greiz was founded in 1303. Upper and Lower Greiz lines were founded in 1535 and the territories were divided until 1768. In 1778 the ruler was made a prince of the Holy Roman Empire. The principality endured until 1918.

MINT MARKS
A - Berlin
B - Hannover

MINTMASTER'S INITIALS
Letter	Date	Name
DF, DOELL(d. 1835)		Johann Veit Doll, die-cutter
FA	1785-1790	Facius, die-cutter
	1790-1835	mintmaster in Eisenach
L	1803-1833	Georg Christoph Lowel, mintmaster in Saalfeld
S, ST	1785-1790	Johann Leonhard Stockmar, die-cutter
	1790-1835	mintmaster in Eisenach

REUSS-GREIZ
OBER (Upper) - GREIZ
RULERS
Heinrich XIII, 1800-1817
Heinrich XIX, 1817-1836
Heinrich XX, 1836-1859
Heinrich XXII, 1859-1902
Heinrich XXIV, 1902-1918

HELLER
COPPER
Obv: Crowned lion on crowned oval shield. Rev: Value.

C#	Date	Mintage	Fine	VF	XF	Unc
37	1812	.045	2.50	5.00	10.00	60.00
37	1815	.045	2.50	5.00	10.00	60.00

Obv: Crowned lion on crowned oval shield. Rev: Value.

C#	Date	Mintage	Fine	VF	XF	Unc
52	1817	.040	2.50	5.00	10.00	60.00
	1819	.048	2.50	5.00	10.00	60.00

PFENNIG

COPPER

C#	Date	Mintage	Fine	VF	XF	Unc
38	1806	.187	2.50	5.00	10.00	60.00
	1808	.273	2.50	5.00	10.00	60.00

Obv: Crowned lion on crowned oval shield.

C#	Date	Mintage	Fine	VF	XF	Unc
39	1808	—	2.50	5.00	10.00	60.00
	1810	.443	2.50	5.00	10.00	60.00
	1812	—	2.50	5.00	10.00	60.00
	1813	—	2.50	5.00	10.00	60.00
	1814	—	2.50	5.00	10.00	60.00
	1815	—	2.50	5.00	10.00	60.00
	1816	—	2.50	5.00	10.00	60.00

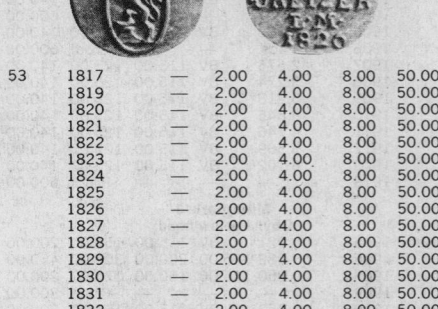

C#	Date	Mintage	Fine	VF	XF	Unc
53	1817	—	2.00	4.00	8.00	50.00
	1819	—	2.00	4.00	8.00	50.00
	1820	—	2.00	4.00	8.00	50.00
	1821	—	2.00	4.00	8.00	50.00
	1822	—	2.00	4.00	8.00	50.00
	1823	—	2.00	4.00	8.00	50.00
	1824	—	2.00	4.00	8.00	50.00
	1825	—	2.00	4.00	8.00	50.00
	1826	—	2.00	4.00	8.00	50.00
	1827	—	2.00	4.00	8.00	50.00
	1828	—	2.00	4.00	8.00	50.00
	1829	—	2.00	4.00	8.00	50.00
	1830	—	2.00	4.00	8.00	50.00
	1831	—	2.00	4.00	8.00	50.00
	1832	—	2.00	4.00	8.00	50.00

Obv: King's crown.

C#	Date	Mintage	Fine	VF	XF	Unc
57	1864 A	.360	1.50	3.00	6.00	40.00

Obv: Prince's crown.

C#	Date	Mintage	Fine	VF	XF	Unc
57a	1868 A	.360	1.50	3.00	6.00	35.00

3 PFENNIG

COPPER

C#	Date	Mintage	Fine	VF	XF	Unc
40	1805	.092	2.50	5.00	10.00	60.00
	1806	—	2.50	5.00	10.00	60.00
	1808	.256	2.50	5.00	10.00	60.00
	1810	.415	2.50	5.00	10.00	60.00
	1812	.296	2.50	5.00	10.00	60.00
	1813	—	2.50	5.00	10.00	60.00
	1814	—	2.50	5.00	10.00	60.00
	1815	—	2.50	5.00	10.00	60.00
	1816	—	2.50	5.00	10.00	60.00

C#	Date	Mintage	Fine	VF	XF	Unc
54	1817	.144	2.00	4.00	8.00	50.00
	1819	—	2.00	4.00	8.00	50.00
	1820	—	2.00	4.00	8.00	50.00
	1821	—	2.00	4.00	8.00	50.00
	1822	—	2.00	4.00	8.00	50.00

C#	Date	Mintage	Fine	VF	XF	Unc
54	1823	—	2.00	4.00	8.00	50.00
	1824	—	2.00	4.00	8.00	50.00
	1825	—	2.00	4.00	8.00	50.00
	1826	—	2.00	4.00	8.00	50.00
	1827	—	2.00	4.00	8.00	50.00
	1828	—	2.00	4.00	8.00	50.00
	1829	—	2.00	4.00	8.00	50.00
	1830	—	2.00	4.00	8.00	50.00
	1831	—	2.00	4.00	8.00	50.00
	1832	—	2.00	4.00	8.00	50.00
	1833 L	—	2.00	4.00	8.00	50.00

Obv: King's crown.

| 58 | 1864 A | .360 | 1.50 | 3.00 | 6.00 | 40.00 |

Obv: Prince's crown.

| 58a | 1868 A | .240 | 1.50 | 3.00 | 6.00 | 40.00 |

GROSCHEN

1.7600 g, .368 SILVER, .0208 oz ASW

| 42 | 1805 | .251 | 2.50 | 5.00 | 10.00 | 50.00 |
| | 1812 | .110 | 2.50 | 5.00 | 10.00 | 50.00 |

2.1900 g, .220 SILVER, .0154 oz ASW

| 59 | 1868 A | .090 | 2.50 | 5.00 | 10.00 | 50.00 |

1/6 THALER

5.3600 g, .541 SILVER, .0932 oz ASW

| 45 | 1808 L | 9,006 | 100.00 | 175.00 | 325.00 | 500.00 |

1/3 THALER

7.0100 g, .833 SILVER, .1877 oz ASW

| 47 | 1809 L | 1,500 | 200.00 | 400.00 | 800.00 | 1200. |

EIN (1) THALER
(Convention)

28.0600 g, .833 SILVER, .7515 oz ASW
Obv. leg: D.G. HENR. XIII . . . . .

C#	Date	Mintage	Fine	VF	XF	Unc
49	1806 DOELL-L					
	345 pcs.	750.00	1400.	3200.	7500.
	1807 DOELL-L					
	200 pcs.	750.00	1400.	3200.	7500.

Obv. leg: V.G.G. HEINRICH . . . . .
Rev: Similar to C#49.

50	1807 DF-L					
	300 pcs.	1000.	1600.	3500.	7500.
	1812 DF-L	2,275	900.00	1500.	2750.	6500.

| 51 | 1812 DF-L | I.A. | 350.00 | 700.00 | 1250. | 3000. |

18.5200 g, .900 SILVER, .5360 oz ASW

C#	Date	Mintage	Fine	VF	XF	Unc
55	1858 A	9,500	60.00	100.00	200.00	450.00

| 60 | 1868 A | 7,100 | 60.00 | 100.00 | 200.00 | 450.00 |

2 THALER
(3-1/2 Gulden)

37.1200 g, .900 SILVER, 1.0742 oz ASW

56	1841 A	2,400	200.00	375.00	750.00	1600.
	1844 A	2,400	200.00	375.00	750.00	1600.
	1848 A	2,400	200.00	375.00	750.00	1600.
	1851 A	2,400	200.00	375.00	750.00	1600.

MONETARY REFORM
2 MARK

11.1110 g, .900 SILVER, .3215 oz ASW
Rev: Type II.

Y#	Date	Mintage	Fine	VF	XF	Unc
137	1877B	.020	150.00	300.00	1500.	2750.
	1877B	—			Proof	3000.

Reuss-Greiz / GERMAN STATES 672

Rev: Type III.

Y#	Date	Mintage	Fine	VF	XF	Unc
137a	1892A	.010	125.00	325.00	650.00	950.00
	1892A	—	—	—	Proof	1200.

	1899A	.010	100.00	200.00	400.00	550.00
139	1899A	120 pcs.	—	—	Proof	600.00
	1901A	.010	100.00	200.00	400.00	550.00
	1901A	—	—	—	Proof	600.00

3 MARK

16.6670 g, .900 SILVER, .4823 oz ASW

140	1909A	.010	100.00	250.00	400.00	550.00
	1909A	—	—	—	Proof	1000.

20 MARK

7.9650 g, .900 GOLD, .2304 oz AGW
Rev: Type II.

138	1875B	1,510	5000.	8000.	11,000.	14,000.
	1875B	—	—	—	Proof	Rare

REUSS-EBERSDORF

The Reuss family, whose lands were located in Thuringia, was founded c. 1035. The Ebersdorf line was founded in 1671 from the Lobenstein branch. The county became a principality in 1806. They inherited Lobenstein in 1824 and were forced to abdicate in 1849 and Lobenstein-Ebersdorf went to Schleiz.

RULERS
Heinrich LI, 1779-1822
Heinrich LXXII, 1822-1824

PFENNIG
COPPER
Obv: Crowned shield w/hound's head. Rev: Value.

C#	Date	Mintage	Fine	VF	XF	Unc
20	1812	.035	5.00	10.00	20.00	90.00

2 PFENNIG
COPPER
Obv: Crowned shield w/hound's head. Rev: Value.

21	1812	.029	5.00	10.00	25.00	100.00

3 PFENNIG

COPPER
Obv: Crowned shield w/hound's head. Rev: Value.

22	1812	.018	5.00	15.00	60.00	150.00

4 PFENNIG
COPPER
Obv: Crowned shield w/hound's head. Rev: Value.

23	1812	.023	7.00	15.00	30.00	100.00

6 PFENNIG

.9500 g, .250 SILVER, .0076 oz ASW

C#	Date	Mintage	Fine	VF	XF	Unc
27	1812	7,376	7.00	15.00	30.00	100.00

8 PFENNIG
 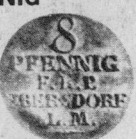
1.3000 g, .250 SILVER, .0104 oz ASW

29	1812	.011	10.00	20.00	40.00	150.00

GROSCHEN

1.7600 g, .368 SILVER, .0208 oz ASW

31	1812	8,962	7.00	15.00	35.00	125.00
	1814	.087	7.00	15.00	35.00	125.00

EIN (1) THALER
(Species)

28.0600 g, .833 SILVER, .7515 oz ASW

33	1812 L	1,574	350.00	700.00	1400.	3000.

REUSS-LOBENSTEIN

The Reuss family, whose lands were located in Thuringia, was founded c. 1035. The Lobenstein line was founded in 1635. The county became a principality in 1790. In 1824 Lobenstein was given to Ebersdorf.

RULERS
Heinrich XXXV, 1782-1805
Heinrich LIV, 1805-1824

3 PFENNIG

BILLON
Obv: Crowned lion.

C#	Date	Mintage	Fine	VF	XF	Unc
10	1804	.110	3.00	6.00	10.00	60.00
	1807	.054	3.00	6.00	10.00	60.00

Obv: Uncrowned lion.

15	1807	—	3.00	6.00	10.00	60.00

1/48 THALER

.9700 g, .250 SILVER, .0077 oz ASW
Obv: Crowned lion. Rev: Value.

12	1805	.033	6.00	12.00	25.00	75.00

REUSS-LOBENSTEIN-EBERSDORF

This line was formed by the merger between Ebersdorf and Lobenstein in 1824. The prince abdicated during political troubles in 1848 and the lands went to Schleiz in 1849.

RULERS
Heinrich LXXII (as Prince of Reuss-Ebersdorf) 1822-1824
(as Prince of Reuss-Lobenstein-Ebersdorf), 1824-1849

PFENNIG

COPPER

C#	Date	Mintage	Fine	VF	XF	Unc
1	1841A	.316	4.00	8.00	15.00	45.00
	1844A	.381	4.00	8.00	15.00	45.00

3 PFENNIG

COPPER

2	1841A	.107	5.00	10.00	20.00	50.00
	1844A	.180	5.00	10.00	20.00	50.00

1/2 SILBER GROSCHEN
1.0900 g, .222 SILVER, .0077 oz ASW
Obv: Crowned shield w/crowned lion. Rev: Value.

3	1841A	.070	5.00	10.00	20.00	60.00

SILBER GROSCHEN
2.1900 g, .222 SILVER, .0156 oz ASW
Obv: Crowned shield w/crowned lion. Rev: Value.

4	1841A	.059	5.00	10.00	20.00	60.00
	1844A	.087	5.00	10.00	20.00	60.00

2 THALER
(3-1/2 Gulden)

37.1200 g, .900 SILVER, 1.0742 oz ASW

5	1840A	2,750	200.00	400.00	750.00	1700.
	1847A	2,750	200.00	400.00	750.00	1700.

25th Anniversary of Reign
Obv: Similar to C#5.

C#	Date	Mintage	Fine	VF	XF	Unc
6	1847A	500 pcs.	400.00	700.00	1500.	2750.

REUSS-SCHLEIZ

The Reuss family, whose lands were located in Thuringia, was founded c. 1035. The Schleiz line originated as Saalburg in 1635 until 1666. The county of Schleiz became a principality in 1806 and lasted until 1918 when the last prince abdicated.

RULERS
Heinrich XLII, 1784-1818
Heinrich LXII, 1818-1854
Heinrich LXVII, 1854-1867
Heinrich XIV, 1867-1913
Heinrich XXVII, 1913-1918

1/2 PFENNIG
(1 Heller)

COPPER

C#	Date	Mintage	Fine	VF	XF	Unc
25	1841A	—	15.00	25.00	50.00	150.00

PFENNIG

COPPER

26	1841A	.751	4.00	7.00	20.00	75.00
	1847A	1.138	4.00	7.00	20.00	75.00

27	1850A	.540	2.00	4.00	8.00	40.00

35	1855A	.362	2.00	4.00	8.00	40.00
	1858A	.360	2.00	4.00	8.00	40.00
	1862A	.202	2.00	4.00	8.00	40.00
	1864A	.540	2.00	4.00	8.00	40.00

40	1868A	.360	2.00	4.00	8.00	40.00

3 PFENNIG
COPPER
Obv: Oval crowned shield w/crowned lion. Rev: Value.

20	1815	.076	5.00	10.00	20.00	75.00
	1816	Inc. Ab.	5.00	10.00	20.00	75.00

C#	Date	Mintage	Fine	VF	XF	Unc
28	1841A	.250	4.00	8.00	15.00	55.00
	1844A	.379	3.00	6.00	12.50	50.00

29	1850A	.311	3.00	6.00	12.50	50.00

36	1855A	.242	3.00	6.00	12.50	50.00
	1858A	.360	3.00	6.00	12.50	50.00
	1862A	.125	3.00	6.00	12.50	50.00
	1864A	.240	3.00	6.00	12.50	50.00

41	1868A	.120	3.00	6.00	12.50	50.00

SILBER GROSCHEN
1.7600 g, .368 SILVER, .0208 oz ASW
Obv: Oval crowned arms, crowned lion w/1 tail.
Rev: Value.

22	1815	—	4.00	8.00	15.00	100.00

Obv: Uncrowned lion w/1 tail.
22a	1816S	.033	4.00	8.00	15.00	100.00

Obv: Crowned lion w/2 tails.
22b	1816S	Inc. Ab.	4.00	8.00	15.00	100.00

2.1900 g, .222 SILVER, .0156 oz ASW
30	1841A	.064	3.00	6.00	12.50	80.00
	1844A	.092	3.00	6.00	12.50	80.00
	1846A	.062	3.00	6.00	12.50	80.00

Obv. leg: JUNGERER LINIE
31	1850A	.062	4.00	8.00	15.00	100.00

37	1855A	.031	4.00	8.00	15.00	100.00

2 SILBER GROSCHEN
3.1100 g, .312 SILVER, .0311 oz ASW
Obv: Crowned shield w/crowned lion. Rev: Value.

32	1850A	.064	4.00	8.00	15.00	100.00

38	1855A	.031	10.00	20.00	40.00	100.00

EIN (1) THALER
(Vereins)

18.5200 g, .900 SILVER, .5360 oz ASW

C#	Date	Mintage	Fine	VF	XF	Unc
39	1858A	10,000	40.00	65.00	125.00	325.00
	1862A	10,000	40.00	65.00	125.00	325.00

Rev: Similar to C#39.
42	1868A	.014	40.00	65.00	125.00	325.00

2 THALER
(3-1/2 Gulden)

37.1200 g, .900 SILVER, 1.0742 oz ASW
33	1840A	2,650	250.00	400.00	800.00	1500.
	1844A	3,000	250.00	400.00	800.00	1500.
	1846A	2,650	250.00	400.00	800.00	1500.
	1853A	2,700	250.00	400.00	800.00	1500.
	1854A	2,700	225.00	450.00	1000.	1600.

25th Anniversary of Reign
Obv: Similar to C#33.
34	1843A	500 pcs.	350.00	700.00	1500.	3000.

MONETARY REFORM
2 MARK

11.1110 g, .900 SILVER, .3215 oz ASW

Y#	Date	Mintage	Fine	VF	XF	Unc
141	1884A	.100	150.00	300.00	850.00	1500.
	1884A		—	—	Proof	2500.

10 MARK

3.9820 g, .900 GOLD, .1152 oz AGW

142	1882A	4,800	1250.	2500.	4000.	5000.
	1882A	200 pcs.	—	—	Proof	10,000.

20 MARK

7.9650 g, .900 GOLD, .2304 oz AGW

143	1881A	.012	1000.	1500.	2500.	3250.
	1881A	500 pcs.	—	—	Proof	6000.

RHENISH CONFEDERATION
Issues for Carl von Dahlberg, 1804-1817

MINTMASTER'S INITIALS

Letter	Date	Name
B, CB	1773-1811	Christoph Busch, Regensburg
BH	1790-1825	Johann Georg Bunsen, mint-master in Frankfurt
	1798-1816	Johann Georg Hille, mintwarden in Frankfurt

HELLER

COPPER
Obv. leg: FURST PRIM SCHEIDE MUNZ.

C#	Date	Mintage	Fine	VF	XF	Unc
1	1808 BH	.033	10.00	30.00	70.00	150.00
	1810 BH	—	10.00	30.00	70.00	150.00
	1812 BH	—	10.00	30.00	70.00	150.00

Obv. leg: GROSH FRANKF SCHEIDE MUNZ.

2	1810 BH	—	10.00	30.00	70.00	150.00
	1812 BH	—	10.00	30.00	70.00	150.00

KREUZER

BILLON
Obv. leg: SCHEID.MUNZ.

3.1	1808 BH	—	8.00	25.00	50.00	150.00
	1809 BH	—	8.00	25.00	50.00	150.00
	1810 BH	—	8.00	25.00	50.00	150.00

Obv. leg: SCHEIDMUNZ.

3.2	1809 BH	—	8.00	25.00	60.00	150.00

1/2 THALER
(Convention)

.833 SILVER

C#	Date	Mintage	Fine	VF	XF	Unc
5	1809 B	—	65.00	100.00	175.00	300.00

EIN (1) THALER
(Convention)

28.0600 g, .833 SILVER, .7516 oz ASW

4	1808 BH	—	175.00	375.00	650.00	1200.

6	1809 B	—	150.00	325.00	1100.	2500.

C#	Date	Mintage	Fine	VF	XF	Unc
7	1809 CB	—	150.00	325.00	800.00	2200.

TRADE COINAGE
DUCAT

3.5000 g, .986 GOLD, .1109 oz AGW

8	1809 BH	—	500.00	1000.	1750.	2750.

ROSTOCK

A city, near the Baltic Sea in Mecklenburg, has a history from the 12th century. The first municipal charter dates from 1218. In 1325 Rostock obtained the mint right and not long after, joined the Hanseatic League. The city coinage extends to 1864.

MINTMASTER'S INITIALS

Letter	Date	Name
AIB	1805-1825	Andreas Joachim Brand

PFENNIG
COPPER
Obv: Griffin shield within ring. Rev: Value.

C#	Date	Mintage	Fine	VF	XF	Unc
2a	1801 FL	—	3.00	6.00	15.00	60.00
	1802 FL	—	3.00	6.00	15.00	60.00

Obv. leg: ROSTOCKER begins at 8 o'clock.

4	1802	—	3.00	6.00	15.00	60.00
	1805	—	3.00	6.00	15.00	60.00

Obv: W/o circle between griffin and legend.

4a	1815	—	2.00	4.00	7.00	60.00
	1824	—	2.00	4.00	7.00	60.00

5	1848	—	3.00	6.00	15.00	60.00

3 PFENNIG

COPPER

10	1815 A.S.	—	3.00	6.00	15.00	65.00
	1824 A.S.	—	3.00	6.00	15.00	65.00
10a	1843 B.S.	.192	3.00	6.00	15.00	65.00

C#	Date	Mintage	Fine	VF	XF	Unc
11	1855	—	3.00	6.00	15.00	65.00

| 12 | 1859 | — | 3.00 | 6.00 | 15.00 | 65.00 |

| 12a | 1862H.K. | — | 3.00 | 6.00 | 15.00 | 65.00 |
| | 1864H.K. | — | 3.00 | 6.00 | 15.00 | 65.00 |

SAXE-ALTENBURG

A duchy, located in Thuringia in northwest Germany. It came into being in 1826 when Saxe-Gotha-Altenburg became extinct. The duke of Saxe-Hildburghausen ceded Hildburghausen to Meiningen in exchange for Saxe-Altenburg. The last duke abdicated in 1918.

RULERS
Joseph, 1834-1848
Georg, 1848-1853
Ernst I, 1853-1908
Ernst II, 1908-1918

MINTMASTER'S INITIALS
B - Gustav Julius Buschick
F - Gustav Theodor Fischer
G - Johann Georg Grohmann

PFENNIG
COPPER
Obv: Crowned arms. Rev: Value.

| 1 | 1841 G | .220 | 1.50 | 3.00 | 6.00 | 40.00 |

Obv: Crowned heart shaped arms.

| 2 | 1843 G | .089 | 2.00 | 4.00 | 8.00 | 45.00 |

Rev: F below date.

| 11 | 1852 F | .120 | 1.50 | 3.00 | 6.00 | 40.00 |

Rev: F below date.

| 14 | 1856 F | .041 | 2.00 | 4.00 | 8.00 | 45.00 |
| | 1858 F | .129 | 1.50 | 3.00 | 6.00 | 40.00 |

Rev: W/o mintmaster's initial.

| 14a | 1857 | — | 1.50 | 3.00 | 6.00 | 40.00 |

Rev: B below date.

14b	1861 B	.163	1.50	3.00	6.00	40.00
	1863 B	.302	1.50	3.00	6.00	40.00
	1865 B	.150	1.50	3.00	6.00	40.00

2 PFENNIG
COPPER
Obv: Crowned arms. Rev: Value.

| 3 | 1841 G | .150 | 2.00 | 4.00 | 8.00 | 45.00 |

Obv: Crowned heart shaped arms.

C#	Date	Mintage	Fine	VF	XF	Unc
4	1843 G	.046	2.50	5.00	10.00	50.00

| 12 | 1852 F | .060 | 2.50 | 5.00 | 10.00 | 50.00 |
| 15 | 1856 F | .029 | 2.50 | 5.00 | 10.00 | 50.00 |

5 PFENNIG
(1/2 Neugroschen)
1.0600 g, .229 SILVER, .0078 oz ASW
Obv: Crowned arms. Rev: Value.

| 5 | 1841 G | .097 | 4.00 | 8.00 | 20.00 | 75.00 |
| | 1842 G | .130 | 4.00 | 8.00 | 20.00 | 75.00 |

10 PFENNIG
(1 Neugroschen)
2.1200 g, .229 SILVER, .0156 oz ASW
Obv: Crowned arms. Rev: Value.

| 6 | 1841 G | .146 | 4.00 | 8.00 | 20.00 | 75.00 |
| | 1842 G | .065 | 4.00 | 8.00 | 20.00 | 75.00 |

20 PFENNIG
(2 Neugroschen)
3.1100 g, .312 SILVER, .0311 oz ASW

| 7 | ND | — | 5.00 | 10.00 | 20.00 | 60.00 |
| 7a | 1841 G | .231 | 6.00 | 12.00 | 25.00 | 80.00 |

1/6 THALER

5.3450 g, .520 SILVER, .0894 oz ASW

| 8 | 1841 G | .060 | 10.00 | 25.00 | 100.00 | 250.00 |
| | 1842 G | .060 | 10.00 | 25.00 | 100.00 | 250.00 |

EIN (1) THALER

22.2720 g, .750 SILVER, .5371 oz ASW

| 9 | 1841 G | .020 | 75.00 | 150.00 | 325.00 | 1000. |

(Vereins)

18.5200 g, .900 SILVER, .5360 oz ASW

16	1858 F	.032	40.00	75.00	150.00	325.00
	1858 F	—	—	—	Proof	450.00
	1864 B	.022	30.00	60.00	125.00	300.00
	1869 B	.023	30.00	60.00	125.00	300.00

2 THALER
(3-1/2 Gulden)

37.1190 g, .900 SILVER, 1.0742 oz ASW

C#	Date	Mintage	Fine	VF	XF	Unc
10	1841 G	9,400	200.00	375.00	800.00	1600.
	1842 G	4,700	250.00	500.00	1000.	2000.
	1843 G	4,700	225.00	450.00	900.00	1900.
	1847 F	9,400	200.00	375.00	850.00	1800.

Rev: Similar to Thaler, C#16.

| 13 | 1852 F | 9,400 | 250.00 | 450.00 | 900.00 | 1900. |

MONETARY REFORM

2 MARK

11.1110 g, .900 SILVER, .3215 oz ASW
Ernst 75th Birthday

Y#	Date	Mintage	Fine	VF	XF	Unc
144	1901A	.050	100.00	200.00	400.00	600.00
	1901A	500 pcs.	—	—	Proof	700.00

5 MARK

27.7770 g, .900 SILVER, .8038 oz ASW
Ernst 75th Birthday

| 145 | 1901A | .020 | 200.00 | 425.00 | 800.00 | 1200. |
| | 1901A | 500 pcs. | — | — | Proof | 1250. |

Saxe-Altenburg / GERMAN STATES 676

Ernst 50th Year of Reign

Y#	Date	Mintage	Fine	VF	XF	Unc
147	1903A	.020	100.00	200.00	300.00	425.00
	1903A	300 pcs.	—	—	Proof	500.00

20 MARK

7.9650 g, .900 GOLD, .2304 oz AGW

146	1887A	.015	800.00	1000.	1500.	2000.
	1887A	—	—	—	Proof	3750.

SAXE-COBURG-SAALFELD

A duchy, located in northwest Germany, was founded in 1680 as Saxe-Saalfeld. They obtained Coburg in 1735. In 1826, Saalfeld was given to Meiningen and the ruler became the first duke of Saxe-Coburg-Gotha.

RULERS

Franz, 1800-1806
Ernst I, 1806-1826

MINTMASTER'S INITIALS

Letter	Date	Name
L	1803-1816	Georg Christoph Loewel
S	1816-1826	Laurentius Theodor Sommer, warden

HELLER

COPPER

C#	Date	Mintage	Fine	VF	XF	Unc
63	1808	—	2.00	4.00	10.00	50.00
	1809	.112	2.00	4.00	10.00	50.00
	1810	.071	2.00	4.00	10.00	50.00
	1814	.050	2.00	4.00	10.00	50.00
	1815	Inc. Ab.	2.00	4.00	10.00	50.00
	1817	—	2.00	4.00	10.00	50.00
	1818	—	2.00	4.00	10.00	50.00
	1819	—	2.00	4.00	10.00	50.00
	1824	—	2.00	4.00	10.00	50.00
	1826	—	2.00	4.00	10.00	50.00

68	1809	—	3.00	5.00	10.00	50.00

PFENNIG

COPPER

47	1804	—	1.50	3.00	6.00	50.00
	1805	—	1.50	3.00	6.00	50.00
	1808	.083	1.50	3.00	6.00	50.00
	1809	.055	1.50	3.00	6.00	50.00
	1814	.043	1.50	3.00	6.00	50.00
	1815	Inc. Ab.	1.50	3.00	6.00	50.00
	1817	—	1.50	3.00	6.00	50.00
	1819	—	1.50	3.00	6.00	50.00
	1820	—	1.50	3.00	6.00	50.00
	1821	—	1.50	3.00	6.00	50.00
	1822	—	1.50	3.00	6.00	50.00
	1823	—	1.50	3.00	6.00	50.00
	1824	—	1.50	3.00	6.00	50.00
	1826	—	1.50	3.00	6.00	50.00

Rev: W/o rosettes on sides of 'I'.

47a	1805	—	1.50	3.00	6.00	50.00

BILLON

C#	Date	Mintage	Fine	VF	XF	Unc
56	1805	—	1.50	3.00	6.00	50.00
73	1808	.962	4.00	7.00	15.00	70.00

COPPER

69	1809	—	3.00	5.00	10.00	60.00

2 PFENNIG

COPPER

70	1810	.124	3.00	10.00	20.00	60.00
	1817	—	3.00	10.00	20.00	60.00
	1818	—	3.00	10.00	20.00	60.00

Rev: W/o rosettes on sides of 2.

70a	1810	Inc. Ab.	3.00	10.00	20.00	60.00

3 PFENNIG

.7900 g, .125 SILVER, .0031 oz ASW

49	1804	—	3.00	7.00	15.00	50.00
	1805	—	3.00	7.00	15.00	50.00
	1806	—	3.00	7.00	15.00	50.00

COPPER
Obv: Arms on crowned cartouche w/festoons.

48	1806	—	3.00	5.00	10.00	45.00

Rev. value: III PFENNIG

65	1807	—	4.00	8.00	20.00	60.00
	1808	.063	4.00	8.00	20.00	60.00

65a	1821	—	2.00	6.00	15.00	50.00
	1822	—	2.00	6.00	15.00	50.00
	1823	—	2.00	6.00	15.00	50.00
	1824	—	2.00	6.00	15.00	50.00
	1825	—	2.00	6.00	15.00	50.00
	1826	—	2.00	6.00	15.00	50.00

4 PFENNIG

COPPER
Obv: Crowned E within two crossed branches. Rev: Value.

71	1809	.027	4.00	8.00	20.00	75.00
	1810	8,106	4.00	8.00	20.00	75.00
	1818	—	4.00	8.00	20.00	75.00
	1820	—	4.00	8.00	20.00	75.00

KREUZER

.7900 g, .125 SILVER, .0031 oz ASW

57	1805	—	3.00	8.00	15.00	70.00

Obv: Crowned E within two crossed branches.
Rev: Value, leg: H.S.C.

C#	Date	Mintage	Fine	VF	XF	Unc
74	1808	.068	3.00	7.00	15.00	60.00
	1812	.018	3.00	7.00	15.00	60.00
	1813	.018	3.00	7.00	15.00	60.00
	1815	.021	3.00	7.00	15.00	60.00
	1817	—	3.00	7.00	15.00	60.00
	1818	—	3.00	7.00	15.00	60.00
	1820	—	3.00	7.00	15.00	60.00

Rev. leg: H.S.C.S.

74a	1824 S	—	3.00	5.00	10.00	60.00
	1825 S	—	3.00	5.00	10.00	60.00
	1826 S	—	3.00	5.00	10.00	60.00

6 PFENNIG

1.2900 g, .229 SILVER, .0094 oz ASW

66	1808	.047	4.00	8.00	20.00	75.00
	1810	—	4.00	8.00	20.00	75.00
	1818 S	—	4.00	8.00	20.00	75.00
	1820 S	—	4.00	8.00	20.00	75.00

3 KREUZER

1.5000 g, .243 SILVER, .0117 oz ASW
Obv: Crowned oval arms. Rev: Value.

58	1804	—	2.00	6.00	15.00	60.00

Obv: Pointed arms.

58a	1805	—	2.00	6.00	15.00	60.00

Rev. leg: H.S. COBURG. L.M.

59	1805	—	2.00	6.00	15.00	65.00

Rev. leg: H.S. COBURG LAND. M.

59a	1805	—	2.00	6.00	15.00	65.00

Obv: Crowned E within, L below crossed branches.
Rev: Value, leg: H.S.C.

75b	1808	—	3.00	7.00	15.00	65.00
75	1808 L	.137	3.00	7.00	15.00	65.00
	1810 L	.151	3.00	7.00	15.00	65.00
	1812 L	.196	3.00	7.00	15.00	65.00
	1813 L	.143	3.00	7.00	15.00	65.00
	1814 L	.116	3.00	7.00	15.00	65.00
	1815 L	.026	3.00	7.00	15.00	65.00

Obv: S below crossed branches.

75c	1816 S	—	3.00	7.00	15.00	65.00
	1817 S	—	3.00	7.00	15.00	65.00
	1818 S	—	3.00	7.00	15.00	65.00
	1819 S	—	3.00	7.00	15.00	65.00
	1820 S	—	3.00	7.00	15.00	65.00

Rev. leg: H.S.C.S.

75a	1821 S	—	4.00	8.00	20.00	70.00
	1822 S	—	4.00	8.00	20.00	70.00
	1823 S	—	4.00	8.00	20.00	70.00
	1824 S	—	4.00	8.00	20.00	70.00
	1825 S	—	4.00	8.00	20.00	70.00
	1826 S	—	4.00	8.00	20.00	70.00

Obv: G below crossed branches.

75d	1826 G	—	4.00	8.00	20.00	70.00

6 KREUZER

2.7200 g, .305 SILVER, .0266 oz ASW
Obv: Crowned shield. Rev: Value.

60	1804	—	3.00	7.00	20.00	100.00
	1805	—	3.00	7.00	20.00	100.00

C#	Date	Mintage	Fine	VF	XF	Unc
61	1805	—	3.00	7.00	20.00	100.00

Obv: Crowned E within, L below crossed branches.
Rev. leg: H.S.C.

76	1808 L	.075	3.00	7.00	15.00	65.00
	1810 L	.056	3.00	7.00	15.00	65.00
	1812 L	.089	3.00	7.00	15.00	65.00
	1813 L	.042	3.00	7.00	15.00	65.00
	1814 L	.050	3.00	7.00	15.00	65.00
	1815 L	.011	3.00	7.00	15.00	65.00

Obv: S below crossed branches.

76b	1816 S	—	3.00	7.00	15.00	65.00
	1817 S	—	3.00	7.00	15.00	65.00
	1818 S	—	3.00	7.00	15.00	65.00
	1819 S	—	3.00	7.00	15.00	65.00
	1820 S	—	3.00	7.00	15.00	65.00

Rev. leg: H.S.C.S.

76a	1821 S	—	4.00	8.00	25.00	65.00
	1822 S	—	4.00	8.00	25.00	100.00
	1823 S	—	4.00	8.00	25.00	100.00
	1824 S	—	4.00	8.00	25.00	100.00
	1825 S	—	4.00	8.00	25.00	100.00
	1826 S	—	4.00	8.00	25.00	100.00

10 KREUZER

3.8900 g, .500 SILVER, .0625 oz ASW
Obv: Crowned arms, leg: SACHS. SOUV.
Rev: Value within bound branches.

77	1820 S	—	25.00	50.00	150.00	350.00

Obv. leg: SACHS. COBURG.

77a	1824 S	—	50.00	75.00	175.00	400.00

20 KREUZER

6.6800 g, .583 SILVER, .1252 oz ASW

79	1807 L	—	25.00	65.00	150.00	400.00

Rev: Date below wreath.

79a	1807	—	30.00	75.00	175.00	450.00

80	1812 L	.030	15.00	50.00	125.00	375.00
	1813 L	.046	15.00	50.00	125.00	375.00
	1819 S	—	15.00	50.00	125.00	375.00
	1820 S	—	15.00	50.00	125.00	375.00

80a	1823 S	—	15.00	50.00	125.00	375.00
	1824 S	—	15.00	50.00	125.00	375.00
	1825 S	—	15.00	50.00	125.00	375.00
	1826 S	—	15.00	50.00	125.00	375.00

GROSCHEN

1.9800 g, .368 SILVER, .0234 oz ASW
Obv: Crowned E within two crossed branches.

67	1808	.026	2.00	4.00	10.00	60.00

C#	Date	Mintage	Fine	VF	XF	Unc
67	1810	—	2.00	4.00	10.00	60.00
	1818 S	—	2.00	4.00	10.00	60.00

48 EINEN (1/48) THALER

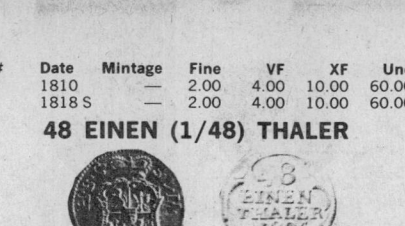

.9700 g, .250 SILVER, .0077 oz ASW

52	1804	—	4.00	8.00	20.00	125.00

52a	1804	—	—	—	Rare	—
	1805	—	3.00	7.00	15.00	125.00
	1806	—	—	—	Rare	—

24 EINEN (1/24) THALER

1.9800 g, .368 SILVER, .0234 oz ASW

54	1805	—	3.00	8.00	20.00	100.00

EIN (1) THALER

28.0600 g, .833 SILVER, .7521 oz ASW

62	1805 L	600 pcs.	300.00	600.00	1000.	2000.

81	1817	—	150.00	300.00	600.00	1200.

Edge: E IN SPECIESTHALER

81a	1817	—	150.00	300.00	700.00	1500.

(Krone)

29.3800 g, .871 SILVER, .8228 oz ASW

C#	Date	Mintage	Fine	VF	XF	Unc
82	1825	—	1000.	2000.	3500.	6000.
	1825	—	—	—	Proof	12,000.

SAXE-COBURG-GOTHA

Located in northwest Germany, Saxe-Coburg-Gotha was created for the duke of Saxe-Coburg-Saalfeld after the dispersal of Saalfeld and the acquisition of Gotha in 1826. The last duke abdicated in 1918.

RULERS
Ernst I, 1826-1844
Ernst II, 1844-1893
Alfred, 1893-1900
Carl Eduard, 1900-1918

MINTMASTER'S INITIALS

Letter	Date	Name
B	1860-1887	Gustav Julius Buschick
EK	1828-38	Ernst Kleinsteuber
F	1845-60	Gustav Theodor Fischer
G	1826-28	Graupner
G	1838-44	Johann Georg Grohmann
ST	1826-1828	Strebel

PFENNIG

COPPER

C#	Date	Mintage	Fine	VF	XF	Unc
83	1833	—	2.00	4.00	8.00	50.00
	1834	—	2.00	4.00	8.00	50.00
	1835	—	2.00	4.00	8.00	50.00
	1836	—	2.00	4.00	8.00	50.00
	1837	—	2.00	4.00	8.00	50.00

Obv: Crowned arms within branches.

100	1841 G	.333	2.00	4.00	8.00	50.00

Obv: F above crowned arms.

109	1847 F	.207	1.50	3.00	6.00	50.00
	1851 F	.059	1.50	3.00	6.00	50.00
	1852 F	.201	1.50	3.00	6.00	50.00
	1856 F	.600	1.50	3.00	6.00	50.00

Obv: B above arms.

109a	1865 B	.150	1.50	3.00	6.00	50.00

109b	1868 B	.200	1.50	3.00	6.00	50.00
	1870 B	.096	1.50	3.00	6.00	50.00

1-1/2 PFENNIG

COPPER

84	1834	—	2.00	4.00	8.00	50.00
	1835	—	2.00	4.00	8.00	50.00

2 PFENNIG

COPPER

85	1834	—	2.00	4.00	8.00	50.00
	1835	—	2.00	4.00	8.00	50.00

Saxe-Coburg-Gotha / GERMAN STATES 678

C#	Date	Mintage	Fine	VF	XF	Unc
101	1841 G	.333	2.00	4.00	8.00	50.00

Obv: F and date below bow.

C#	Date	Mintage	Fine	VF	XF	Unc
110	1847 F	.130	1.50	3.00	6.00	50.00
	1851 F	.125	1.50	3.00	6.00	50.00
	1852 F	.146	1.50	3.00	6.00	50.00
	1856 F	.600	1.50	3.00	6.00	50.00

Obv: B and date below bow.

C#	Date	Mintage	Fine	VF	XF	Unc
110a	1868 B	.136	1.50	3.00	6.00	50.00
	1870 B	.118	1.50	3.00	6.00	50.00

3 PFENNIG

COPPER

C#	Date	Mintage	Fine	VF	XF	Unc
86	1834	—	4.00	8.00	17.50	65.00

KREUZER

.7900 g, .125 SILVER, .0031 oz ASW
Obv: ST below crowned E. Rev: Value in script.

C#	Date	Mintage	Fine	VF	XF	Unc
86.5	1827 ST	—	5.00	12.00	30.00	120.00

C#	Date	Mintage	Fine	VF	XF	Unc
87	1827 ST	—	5.00	12.00	30.00	120.00
	1828 ST	—	5.00	12.00	30.00	120.00

Obv: EK below crowned E.

C#	Date	Mintage	Fine	VF	XF	Unc
87a	1829 EK	—	5.00	12.00	30.00	120.00
	1830 EK	—	5.00	12.00	30.00	120.00

Rev: KREUZER around bottom rim.

C#	Date	Mintage	Fine	VF	XF	Unc
88	1831	—	2.00	6.00	10.00	60.00
	1832	—	2.00	6.00	10.00	60.00
	1833	—	2.00	6.00	10.00	60.00
	1834	—	2.00	6.00	10.00	60.00
	1836	—	2.00	6.00	10.00	60.00
	1837	—	2.00	6.00	10.00	60.00

3 KREUZER

1.5000 g, .243 SILVER, .0117 oz ASW
Obv: Crowned E within branches, ST below.
Rev: Value in script.

C#	Date	Mintage	Fine	VF	XF	Unc
89.5	1827 ST	—	10.00	30.00	50.00	200.00

C#	Date	Mintage	Fine	VF	XF	Unc
90	1827 ST	—	8.00	20.00	40.00	175.00
	1828 ST	—	8.00	20.00	40.00	175.00
	1829 S	—	8.00	20.00	40.00	175.00
	1829 ST	—	8.00	20.00	40.00	175.00

Obv: EK below crowned E.

C#	Date	Mintage	Fine	VF	XF	Unc
90a	1828 EK	—	8.00	20.00	40.00	175.00
	1830 EK	—	8.00	20.00	40.00	175.00
	1831 EK	—	8.00	20.00	40.00	175.00

C#	Date	Mintage	Fine	VF	XF	Unc
91	1831	—	2.00	5.00	15.00	80.00
	1832	—	2.00	5.00	15.00	80.00
	1833	—	2.00	5.00	15.00	80.00
	1834	—	2.00	5.00	15.00	80.00
	1835	—	2.00	5.00	15.00	80.00
	1836	—	2.00	5.00	15.00	80.00
	1837	—	2.00	5.00	15.00	80.00

Obv: Crowned arms. Rev: Value within branches.

C#	Date	Mintage	Fine	VF	XF	Unc
101.3	1838	.358	2.00	5.00	15.00	80.00

6 KREUZER

2.7300 g, .305 SILVER, .0267 oz ASW
Obv: G below crowned E within branches.

C#	Date	Mintage	Fine	VF	XF	Unc
92	1827 G	—	7.00	15.00	50.00	150.00

Obv: ST below crowned E.

C#	Date	Mintage	Fine	VF	XF	Unc
92a	1827 ST	—	7.00	15.00	50.00	150.00
	1828 ST	—	7.00	15.00	50.00	150.00

Obv: EK below crowned E.

C#	Date	Mintage	Fine	VF	XF	Unc
92b	1828 EK	—	7.00	15.00	50.00	150.00
	1829 EK	—	7.00	15.00	50.00	150.00
	1830 EK	—	7.00	15.00	50.00	150.00

C#	Date	Mintage	Fine	VF	XF	Unc
93	1831	—	3.00	5.00	20.00	100.00
	1832	—	3.00	5.00	20.00	100.00
	1833	—	3.00	5.00	20.00	100.00
	1834	—	3.00	5.00	20.00	100.00
	1835	—	3.00	5.00	20.00	100.00
	1836	—	3.00	5.00	20.00	100.00
	1837	—	3.00	5.00	20.00	100.00

C#	Date	Mintage	Fine	VF	XF	Unc
101.6	1838	.209	3.00	5.00	20.00	100.00

10 KREUZER

3.8900 g, .500 SILVER, .0625 oz ASW
Similar to C#94b.

C#	Date	Mintage	Fine	VF	XF	Unc
94	1831	—	20.00	35.00	70.00	250.00
	1832	—	20.00	35.00	70.00	250.00
	1833	—	20.00	35.00	70.00	250.00
	1834	—	20.00	35.00	70.00	250.00

C#	Date	Mintage	Fine	VF	XF	Unc
94b	1835	—	15.00	30.00	60.00	200.00
	1836	—	15.00	30.00	60.00	200.00
	1837	—	15.00	30.00	60.00	200.00

20 KREUZER

6.6800 g, .583 SILVER, .1252 oz ASW
Obv. leg: COBURG & GOTHA, crowned arms.
Rev: ST below value.

C#	Date	Mintage	Fine	VF	XF	Unc
95	1827 ST	—	20.00	50.00	125.00	300.00

Obv. leg: COBURG UND GOTHA

C#	Date	Mintage	Fine	VF	XF	Unc
95a	1827 ST	—	20.00	50.00	125.00	300.00
	1828 ST	—	20.00	50.00	125.00	300.00

Rev: E.K. below branches.

C#	Date	Mintage	Fine	VF	XF	Unc
95b	1828 EK	—	20.00	50.00	125.00	300.00
	1830 EK	—	20.00	50.00	125.00	300.00

Similar to C#96a.

C#	Date	Mintage	Fine	VF	XF	Unc
96	1831	—	20.00	50.00	125.00	300.00
	1834	—	20.00	50.00	125.00	300.00

Obv. leg: ZU SACHSEN COBURG-GOTHA

C#	Date	Mintage	Fine	VF	XF	Unc
96a	1835	—	15.00	35.00	60.00	200.00
	1836	—	15.00	35.00	60.00	200.00

1/2 GROSCHEN

1.0600 g, .229 SILVER, .0078 oz ASW

C#	Date	Mintage	Fine	VF	XF	Unc
102	1841 G	.247	5.00	10.00	35.00	125.00
	1844 G	.065	5.00	10.00	35.00	125.00

C#	Date	Mintage	Fine	VF	XF	Unc
111	1851 F	.032	2.00	4.00	8.00	50.00
	1855 F	.130	2.00	4.00	8.00	50.00
	1858 F	.060	2.00	4.00	8.00	50.00

Obv: B below arms.

C#	Date	Mintage	Fine	VF	XF	Unc
114	1868 B	.032	2.00	4.00	8.00	50.00
	1870 B	.052	2.00	4.00	8.00	50.00

GROSCHEN

1.9800 g, .368 SILVER, .0234 oz ASW

C#	Date	Mintage	Fine	VF	XF	Unc
89	1837	—	5.00	10.00	30.00	125.00

2.1200 g, .229 SILVER, .0156 oz ASW

C#	Date	Mintage	Fine	VF	XF	Unc
103	1841 G	.355	8.00	15.00	40.00	175.00

C#	Date	Mintage	Fine	VF	XF	Unc
112	1847 F	.130	2.00	4.00	8.00	50.00
	1851 F	.049	2.00	4.00	8.00	50.00
	1855 F	.130	2.00	4.00	8.00	50.00
	1858 F	.033	2.00	4.00	8.00	50.00

115	1865 B	.070	2.00	4.00	8.00	50.00
	1868 B	.031	2.00	4.00	8.00	50.00
	1870 B	.030	2.00	4.00	8.00	50.00

2 GROSCHEN
3.1100 g, .312 SILVER, .0311 oz ASW
Obv: Crowned arms within branches. Rev: Value.

104	1841 G	.214	8.00	20.00	40.00	150.00
	1844 G	.032	8.00	20.00	40.00	150.00

113	1847 F	.097	5.00	10.00	25.00	75.00
	1851 F	.032	5.00	10.00	25.00	75.00
	1855 F	.081	5.00	10.00	25.00	75.00
	1858 F	.055	5.00	10.00	25.00	75.00

3.2200 g, .300 SILVER, .0310 oz ASW

116	1865 B	.070	5.00	10.00	20.00	65.00
	1868 B	.030	5.00	10.00	20.00	65.00
	1870 B	.031	5.00	10.00	20.00	65.00

1/6 THALER

5.3450 g, .521 SILVER, .0895 oz ASW

105	1841 G	.048	15.00	40.00	75.00	225.00
	1842 G	.048	15.00	40.00	75.00	225.00
	1843 G	.048	15.00	40.00	75.00	225.00

Obv: Different head.

117	1845 F	.123	15.00	35.00	75.00	225.00

117a	1848 F	.130	10.00	30.00	60.00	200.00

Obv: Head w/beard.

117b	1852 F	.048	15.00	35.00	75.00	225.00
	1855 F	.060	15.00	35.00	75.00	225.00

5.3400 g, .520 SILVER, .0892 oz ASW

C#	Date	Mintage	Fine	VF	XF	Unc
118	1864 B	.060	10.00	30.00	60.00	200.00

25th Anniversary of Reign

119	1869 B	.012	10.00	30.00	50.00	150.00

1/2 THALER
(Convention)
(1 Gulden)

14.0300 g, .833 SILVER, .3757 oz ASW

97	1830 EK	—	65.00	135.00	300.00	650.00
	1831	—	65.00	135.00	300.00	650.00
	1832	—	65.00	135.00	300.00	650.00
	1834	—	65.00	135.00	300.00	650.00
	1835 HF	—	65.00	135.00	300.00	650.00
97a	1834 HF	—	65.00	135.00	300.00	650.00

EIN (1) THALER
(Krone)

29.3800 g, .871 SILVER, .8228 oz ASW

98	1827	—	350.00	700.00	1000.	2000.

(Convention)

28.0600 g, .833 SILVER, .7514 oz ASW

C#	Date	Mintage	Fine	VF	XF	Unc
99	1828	31 pcs.	—	—	Rare	—
	1828	—	—	—	Proof	10,000

99a	1829 EK	1,095	400.00	800.00	1500.	2750.

Rev: W/o mintmaster's initials.

99b	1832	304 pcs.	—	—	Rare	—
	1833	Inc. Ab.	—	—	Rare	—
99c	1835	—	800.00	1700.	3000.	5000.

22.2700 g, .750 SILVER, .5371 oz ASW
Rev: Crowned draped arms within wreath.

106	1841 G	.016	75.00	150.00	400.00	1000.
	1842 G	.016	75.00	150.00	400.00	1000.

120	1846 F	.032	75.00	150.00	400.00	1000.

Saxe-Coburg-Gotha / GERMAN STATES 680

C#	Date	Mintage	Fine	VF	XF	Unc
120a	1848 F	.016	75.00	150.00	400.00	1000.

| 120b | 1851 F | 8,000 | 75.00 | 150.00 | 400.00 | 1000. |
| | 1852 F | 8,000 | 75.00 | 150.00 | 400.00 | 1000. |

(Vereins)

18.5200 g, .900 SILVER, .5360 oz ASW

121	1862 B	.040	45.00	90.00	200.00	450.00
	1864 B	.040	45.00	90.00	200.00	450.00
	1870 B	.022	60.00	100.00	225.00	500.00

25th Anniversary of Reign

| 122 | 1869 B | 6.000 | 45.00 | 85.00 | 150.00 | 300.00 |

2 THALER
(3-1/2 Gulden)

37.1200 g, .900 SILVER, 1.0743 oz ASW

107	1841 G	.011	250.00	500.00	1000.	2200.
	1842 G	5,350	300.00	600.00	1100.	2400.
	1843 G	5,350	300.00	600.00	1100.	2400.

Rev: Similar to C#123a.

C#	Date	Mintage	Fine	VF	XF	Unc
123	1847 F	.011	350.00	625.00	1400.	2800.

| 123a | 1854 F | .016 | 225.00 | 425.00 | 1000. | 2000. |

MONETARY REFORM
2 MARK

11.1110 g, .900 SILVER, .3215 oz ASW

Y#	Date	Mintage	Fine	VF	XF	Unc
149	1895A	.015	250.00	650.00	900.00	1250.

152	1905A	8,000	125.00	275.00	600.00	950.00
	1905A	2,000	—	—	Proof	850.00
	1911A	100 pcs.	4000.	6000.	8000.	10,000.
	1911A	—	—	—	Proof	6000.

5 MARK

27.7770 g, .900 SILVER, .8038 oz ASW

Y#	Date	Mintage	Fine	VF	XF	Unc
150	1895A	4,000	750.00	1500.	2000.	3000.
	1895A	—	—	—	Proof	3250.

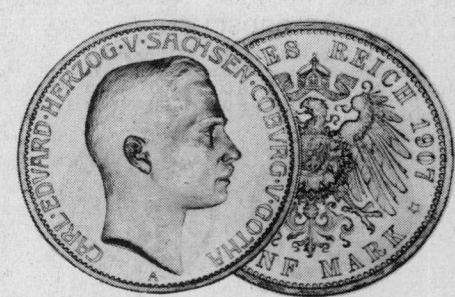

Rev: Similar to Y#150.

| 153 | 1907A | .010 | 300.00 | 600.00 | 1000. | 1500. |
| | 1907A | — | — | — | Proof | 1800. |

10 MARK

3.9820 g, .900 GOLD, .1152 oz AGW

| 154 | 1905A | 9,511 | 400.00 | 600.00 | 1000. | 1400. |
| | 1905A | 489 pcs. | — | — | Proof | 3500. |

20 MARK

7.9650 g, .900 GOLD, .2304 oz AGW
Rev: Type I.

| 148 | 1872E | 1,000 | 7000. | 11,000. | 15,000. | 19,000. |
| | 1872E | — | — | — | Proof | Rare |

| 148a | 1886A | .020 | 500.00 | 900.00 | 1400. | 1800. |
| | 1886A | — | — | — | Proof | 3750. |

| 151 | 1895A | 775 pcs. | 500.00 | — | 1200. | 2000. | 2750. |
| | 1895A | 225 pcs. | — | — | Proof | 4500. |

Y#	Date	Mintage	Fine	VF	XF	Unc
155	1905A	9.516	400.00	750.00	1200.	1800.
	1905A	484 pcs.	—	—	Proof	3750.

TRADE COINAGE
DUCAT

3.5000 g, .986 GOLD, .1109 oz AGW
Obv: Head left, Z.S. Rev: Crowned arms within bound branches.

C#	Date	Mintage	Fine	VF	XF	Unc
108	1831 EK	600 pcs.	900.00	2000.	3250.	4250.

| 108a | 1836 | 1.600 | 600.00 | 1250. | 2500. | 3250. |
| | 1842 | 508 pcs. | 600.00 | 1500. | 3000. | 3750. |

SAXE-HILDBURGHAUSEN
Saxe-Hildburghausen was founded in 1680. During the 1826 reshuffle, it was exchanged for Altenburg.

RULERS
Joseph Friedrich, Prince Regent, 1780-1784
  Joint Regent, 1784-87
  Alone, 1786-1826

HELLER

COPPER
65a	1804	—	3.00	5.00	15.00	50.00
	1805	—	3.00	5.00	15.00	50.00
	1806	—	3.00	5.00	15.00	50.00

66	1808	—	1.50	4.00	7.00	40.00
	1809	—	1.50	4.00	7.00	40.00
	1811	—	1.50	4.00	7.00	40.00
	1812	—	1.50	4.00	7.00	40.00
	1816	—	1.50	4.00	7.00	40.00
	1817	—	1.50	4.00	7.00	40.00
	1818	—	1.50	4.00	7.00	40.00

67	1820	—	1.50	4.00	7.00	40.00
	1821	—	1.50	4.00	7.00	40.00
	1822	—	1.50	4.00	7.00	40.00
	1823	—	1.50	4.00	7.00	40.00
	1824	—	1.50	4.00	7.00	40.00
	1825	—	1.50	4.00	7.00	40.00

PFENNIG

COPPER

C#	Date	Mintage	Fine	VF	XF	Unc
69	1823	—	3.00	5.00	15.00	50.00
	1825	—	3.00	5.00	15.00	50.00
	1826	—	3.00	5.00	15.00	50.00

Obv: Crowned rectangular arms.
| 69.5 | 1826 | — | 4.00 | 7.00 | 20.00 | 75.00 |

1/8 KREUZER

COPPER
Obv: Crowned F within crossed branches.
Rev: Value, leg: KREUZER LANDMUNZE.
| 67a | 1825 | — | 2.00 | 10.00 | 10.00 | 50.00 |

1/4 KREUZER

COPPER
| 70 | 1825 | — | 3.00 | 10.00 | 15.00 | 50.00 |

Obv: Crowned heart shaped arms, H.S.H.H.
| 71 | 1825 | — | 3.00 | 10.00 | 15.00 | 50.00 |

1/2 KREUZER
COPPER
Obv: Crowned arms. Rev: Value in script.
| 72 | 1808 | — | 3.00 | 7.00 | 20.00 | 60.00 |
| | 1809 | — | 3.00 | 7.00 | 20.00 | 60.00 |

Obv: Crowned heart-shaped arms, leg: HERZ.Z.S.
Rev: Value
| 73 | 1823 | — | 3.00 | 8.00 | 25.00 | 75.00 |

Obv. leg: HERZOGTHUM
| 73b | 1823 | — | 3.00 | 8.00 | 25.00 | 75.00 |

Rev: Value, leg: KREUZER LANDMUNZE.
| 73a | 1823 | — | 3.00 | 10.00 | 30.00 | 75.00 |

KREUZER
BILLON
| 74a | 1804 | — | 7.00 | 15.00 | 30.00 | 125.00 |
| | 1805 | — | 7.00 | 15.00 | 30.00 | 125.00 |

Obv: Crowned oval arms within branches. Rev: Value.
| 76 | 1806 | — | 6.00 | 15.00 | 20.00 | 100.00 |
| | 1811 | — | 6.00 | 15.00 | 20.00 | 100.00 |

3 KREUZER
BILLON
Obv: Crowned F within wreath.
Rev: Value within ring.
83	1808	—	3.00	8.00	20.00	100.00
	1810	—	3.00	8.00	20.00	100.00
	1811	—	3.00	8.00	20.00	100.00
	1812	—	3.00	8.00	20.00	100.00
	1815	—	3.00	8.00	20.00	100.00
	1816	—	3.00	8.00	20.00	100.00
	1817	—	3.00	8.00	20.00	100.00
	1818	—	3.00	8.00	20.00	100.00
	1820	—	3.00	8.00	20.00	100.00

6 KREUZER

BILLON
86	1808	—	6.00	12.00	30.00	125.00
	1811	—	6.00	12.00	30.00	125.00
	1812	—	6.00	12.00	30.00	125.00
	1815	—	6.00	12.00	30.00	125.00
	1816	—	6.00	12.00	30.00	125.00
	1817	—	6.00	12.00	30.00	125.00
	1818	—	6.00	12.00	30.00	125.00

Obv: Crowned F within crossed branches. Rev: Value.
88	1820	—	6.00	10.00	25.00	110.00
	1821	—	6.00	10.00	25.00	110.00
	1823	—	6.00	10.00	25.00	110.00
	1824	—	6.00	10.00	25.00	110.00
	1825	—	6.00	10.00	25.00	110.00

SAXE-MEININGEN
Saxe-Meiningen was founded in 1680. It was called Saxe-Coburg-Meiningen until 1826 when it exchanged Coburg for Hildburghausen.

RULERS
Bernhard II Under Regency of Luise
  Eleonore, 1803-1821
Bernhard II, 1821-1866
Georg II, 1866-1914
Bernhard III, 1914-1918

MINTMASTER'S INITIALS
Letter	Date	Name
F.HELFRICHT	d.1892	Ferdinand Helfricht, die-cutter and chief medaileur
K	1835-1837	Georg Krell, warden then mintmaster
L	1803-1833	Georg Christoph Loewel
VOIGT		J.C. Voigt, die-cutter and medaileur

HELLER
COPPER
Obv: Crowned heart-shaped arms, leg: H. Rev: Value.

C#	Date	Mintage	Fine	VF	XF	Unc
21	1814	—	2.00	4.00	8.00	50.00

Obv. leg: HERZ.
| 21a | 1814 | — | 2.00 | 4.00 | 8.00 | 50.00 |

PFENNIG

COPPER
Obv. leg: HERZ.
| 23 | 1818 | .090 | 3.00 | 7.00 | 15.00 | 75.00 |

34	1832	.275	2.00	4.00	8.00	45.00
	1833	.093	2.00	4.00	8.00	45.00
	1835	.034	2.00	4.00	8.00	45.00

Obv: Crowned arms within branches.
| 35 | 1839 | .079 | 2.00 | 4.00 | 8.00 | 45.00 |
| | 1842 | .132 | 2.00 | 4.00 | 8.00 | 45.00 |

37	1860	.240	1.50	3.00	6.00	40.00
	1862	.243	1.50	3.00	6.00	40.00
	1863	.240	1.50	3.00	6.00	40.00
	1865	.240	1.50	3.00	6.00	40.00
	1866	.480	1.50	3.00	6.00	40.00

| 65 | 1867 | .240 | 1.50 | 3.00 | 6.00 | 40.00 |
| | 1868 | .480 | 1.50 | 3.00 | 6.00 | 40.00 |

2 PFENNIG

COPPER
39	1832	.202	1.50	3.00	6.00	40.00
	1833	.101	1.50	3.00	6.00	40.00
	1835	.036	1.50	3.00	6.00	40.00

| 40 | 1839 | .075 | 1.50 | 3.00 | 6.00 | 40.00 |
| | 1842 | .184 | 1.50 | 3.00 | 6.00 | 40.00 |

Saxe-Meiningen / GERMAN STATES 682

C#	Date	Mintage	Fine	VF	XF	Unc
42	1860	.361	1.50	3.00	6.00	40.00
	1862	.357	1.50	3.00	6.00	40.00
	1863	.120	1.50	3.00	6.00	40.00
	1864	.480	1.50	3.00	6.00	40.00
	1865	.240	1.50	3.00	6.00	40.00
	1866	.480	1.50	3.00	6.00	40.00

66	1867	.480	1.50	3.00	6.00	40.00
	1868	.240	1.50	3.00	6.00	40.00
	1869	.240	1.50	3.00	6.00	40.00
	1870	.720	1.50	3.00	6.00	40.00

1/8 KREUZER

COPPER

30	1828	—	2.50	5.00	10.00	50.00

1/4 KREUZER

COPPER
Obv: Crowned heart shaped arms, leg: HERZ.
Rev: Value.

22	1812	—	2.50	5.00	10.00	50.00
	1814	—	2.50	5.00	10.00	50.00
	1818	.066	2.50	5.00	10.00	50.00

Obv: Crowned heart shaped arms, leg. HERZ.
Rev: Value, leg: LANDMUNZE.

31	1823	—	4.00	8.00	15.00	60.00

33	1828	—	1.50	3.00	6.00	50.00
	1829	.168	1.50	3.00	6.00	40.00
	1830	.161	1.50	3.00	6.00	40.00
	1831	.321	1.50	3.00	6.00	40.00
	1832	.063	1.50	3.00	6.00	40.00

NOTE: Many varieties in legend size exist.

Obv. leg: MEINIGEN

33a	1829	Inc. Ab.	1.50	3.00	6.00	40.00

Rev. value: KREUZER.

36	1854	.240	1.50	3.00	6.00	40.00

1/2 KREUZER

COPPER

24	1812	—	2.50	5.00	10.00	50.00
	1814	—	2.50	5.00	10.00	50.00
	1818	.102	2.50	5.00	10.00	50.00

38	1828	—	2.00	4.00	8.00	45.00
	1831	—	2.00	4.00	8.00	45.00

C#	Date	Mintage	Fine	VF	XF	Unc
38.1	1829	.121	1.50	3.00	6.00	40.00
	1830L	.144	1.50	3.00	6.00	40.00
	1831L	.341	1.50	3.00	6.00	40.00
	1832L	.045	1.50	3.00	6.00	40.00

41	1854	.240	1.50	3.00	6.00	40.00

KREUZER
(Convention)

.7300 g, .166 SILVER, .0038 oz ASW
Obv: Crowned draped arms, H.S.C.M. Rev: Value.

26	1808	—	2.50	5.00	10.00	60.00

Obv: Drape extends beneath crown.

26a	1812	.307	4.00	8.00	15.00	80.00

COPPER

25	1814	—	4.00	8.00	15.00	60.00
	1818	.090	4.00	8.00	15.00	60.00

Obv: Crowned rectangular arms, leg: HERZ.

43	1828	—	2.50	5.00	10.00	50.00
	1829	.144	2.50	5.00	10.00	50.00
	1830	.118	2.50	5.00	10.00	50.00

.7300 g, .166 SILVER, .0038 oz ASW
Obv: Crowned arms dividing S.M.

47	1828	.211	2.50	5.00	10.00	50.00
	1829	—	2.50	5.00	10.00	50.00
	1829 L	.255	2.50	5.00	10.00	50.00
	1830 L	.092	2.50	5.00	10.00	50.00

COPPER

43a	1831	.166	2.00	4.00	8.00	40.00
	1832	.032	2.00	4.00	8.00	40.00
	1833	.104	2.00	4.00	8.00	40.00
	1834	.177	2.00	4.00	8.00	40.00
	1835	.035	2.00	4.00	8.00	40.00

.7300 g, .166 SILVER, .0038 oz ASW
Obv: Crowned arms within bound branches, L initial.

48	1831 L	.212	2.00	4.00	8.00	50.00
	1832 L	.348	2.00	4.00	8.00	50.00
	1833 L	.272	2.00	4.00	8.00	50.00
	1834 L	.162	2.00	4.00	8.00	50.00

Obv: K mintmaster initial.

48a	1835 K	.059	2.00	4.00	8.00	50.00
	1836 K	.055	2.00	4.00	8.00	50.00
	1837 K	.049	2.00	4.00	8.00	50.00

.8300 g, .166 SILVER, .0044 oz ASW

49	1839	.348	2.00	4.00	8.00	45.00

COPPER
Obv: Crowned arms within branches. Rev: Value.

44	1842	.180	2.00	4.00	8.00	40.00

Obv: Rosette below crowned arms.

C#	Date	Mintage	Fine	VF	XF	Unc
45	1854	.202	2.00	4.00	8.00	40.00

.8400 g, .165 SILVER, .0044 oz ASW

50	1864	.240	2.00	4.00	8.00	45.00
	1866	.240	2.00	4.00	8.00	45.00

3 KREUZER

1.3600 g, .305 SILVER, .0133 oz ASW
Obv: Crowned draped arms. Rev: Value within wreath.

27	1808	—	6.00	10.00	30.00	125.00

Obv: Drape extends beneath crown.

27a	1812	.263	3.00	6.00	20.00	100.00
	1813	Inc. Ab.	3.00	6.00	20.00	100.00

Obv: Crowned arms dividing S.M. Rev: Value.

51	1827	.171	2.00	4.00	8.00	50.00
	1828	.077	2.00	4.00	8.00	50.00
	1829	—	2.00	4.00	8.00	50.00

Obv: L mintmaster initial.

51a	1829 L	1.263	2.00	4.00	8.00	50.00
	1830 L	.533	2.00	4.00	8.00	50.00

52	1831 L	.540	2.00	4.00	8.00	50.00
	1832 L	.918	2.00	4.00	8.00	50.00
	1833 L	1.284	2.00	4.00	8.00	50.00
	1834 L	.187	2.00	4.00	8.00	50.00
	1835 L	—	2.00	4.00	8.00	50.00
52a	1835 K	.800	2.00	4.00	8.00	50.00
	1836 K	.399	2.00	4.00	8.00	50.00
	1837 K	.246	2.00	4.00	8.00	50.00

1.2900 g, .333 SILVER, .0138 oz ASW
Obv: Crowned arms, leg: HERZOGTHUM.
Rev: Value within branches.

53	1840	.207	2.00	4.00	8.00	50.00

6 KREUZER

2.4300 g, .333 SILVER, .0260 oz ASW
Obv: Crowned, draped arms, leg: S.COB.
Rev: Value within wreath.

28	1808	—	15.00	25.00	50.00	150.00
	1812	—	15.00	25.00	50.00	150.00
	1813	—	15.00	25.00	50.00	150.00

Obv: Drape extends beneath crown.

28a	1812	.087	10.00	20.00	40.00	150.00
	1813	Inc. Ab.	10.00	20.00	40.00	150.00

2.4400 g, .347 SILVER, .0272 oz ASW

54	1826	—	5.00	15.00	25.00	80.00
	1827	.486	5.00	15.00	25.00	80.00
	1828	.179	5.00	15.00	25.00	80.00
	1829	—	5.00	15.00	25.00	80.00

Obv: W/L mintmaster initial.

54a	1828 L	—	5.00	15.00	25.00	80.00
	1829 L	1.513	5.00	15.00	25.00	80.00
	1830 L	.747	5.00	15.00	25.00	80.00

C#	Date	Mintage	Fine	VF	XF	Unc
55	1831 L	.684	3.00	5.00	10.00	60.00
	1832 L	.658	3.00	5.00	10.00	60.00
	1833 L	.723	3.00	5.00	10.00	60.00
	1834 L	.409	3.00	5.00	10.00	60.00
	1835 L	—	3.00	5.00	10.00	60.00

Obv: W/K mintmaster initial.

55a	1835K	.512	3.00	5.00	10.00	60.00
	1836 K	.432	3.00	5.00	10.00	60.00
	1837 K	.253	3.00	5.00	10.00	60.00

2.5900 g, .333 SILVER, .0277 oz ASW
Obv: Crowned arms, leg: HERZOGTHUM.
Rev: Value within branches.

56	1840	.097	4.00	7.00	15.00	75.00

20 KREUZER

.583 SILVER
Obv: Bust right.
Rev: Value within square entwined w/flowers.

29	1812	5 pcs. known	—	Rare	—

1/2 GULDEN

5.3000 g, .900 SILVER, .1533 oz ASW

57	1838	.071	20.00	50.00	100.00	250.00
	1839	.045	20.00	50.00	100.00	250.00
	1840	.032	20.00	50.00	100.00	250.00
	1841	.057	20.00	50.00	100.00	250.00

Obv: Different head w/HELFRICHT below.

57a	1843	.133	20.00	50.00	100.00	225.00
	1846	.106	20.00	50.00	100.00	225.00

57b	1854	.108	20.00	50.00	100.00	250.00

GULDEN

11.8000 g, .989 SILVER, .3752 oz ASW

58	1829	2,000	125.00	200.00	325.00	700.00

12.8300 g, .750 SILVER, .3093 oz ASW

C#	Date	Mintage	Fine	VF	XF	Unc
59	1830 L	9,118	65.00	125.00	200.00	350.00
	1831 L	5,511	50.00	100.00	150.00	300.00
	1832 L	4,688	50.00	100.00	150.00	300.00
	1833 L	.010	35.00	75.00	120.00	250.00

59a	1835 K	2,015	75.00	150.00	200.00	400.00
	1836 K	2,028	75.00	150.00	200.00	400.00
	1837 K	2,148	75.00	150.00	200.00	400.00

10.6000 g, .900 SILVER, .3067 oz ASW

60	1838	.071	40.00	80.00	160.00	250.00
	1839	.071	40.00	80.00	160.00	250.00
	1840	.032	40.00	80.00	160.00	250.00
	1841	.031	40.00	80.00	160.00	250.00

Obv: HELFRICHT below bust.

60a	1843	.133	40.00	80.00	160.00	250.00
	1846	.149	40.00	80.00	160.00	250.00

60b	1854	.108	45.00	90.00	175.00	275.00

2 GULDEN

21.2100 g, .900 SILVER, .6138 oz ASW

C#	Date	Mintage	Fine	VF	XF	Unc
62	1854	.167	50.00	90.00	185.00	375.00

EIN (1) THALER
(Convention)

28.0600 g, .833 SILVER, .7514 oz ASW
Death of Georg I

19	ND(1803)L	—	300.00	600.00	1200.	2000.

18.5200 g, .900 SILVER, .5360 oz ASW
Obv: HELFRICHT on truncation.

61	1859	.040	35.00	75.00	135.00	325.00
	1860	.040	35.00	75.00	135.00	325.00
	1861	.040	35.00	75.00	135.00	325.00
	1862	.040	35.00	75.00	135.00	325.00
	1863	.040	35.00	75.00	135.00	325.00
	1866	.040	35.00	75.00	135.00	325.00

Obv: HELFRICHT on truncation.

67	1867	6,644	90.00	175.00	450.00	900.00

2 THALER
(3-1/2 Gulden)

Saxe-Meiningen / GERMAN STATES 684

37.1200 g, .900 SILVER, 1.0743 oz ASW
Obv: VOIGT below bust.

C#	Date	Mintage	Fine	VF	XF	Unc
63	1841	.012	300.00	525.00	1400.	2600.

Obv: Similar to C#63.

64	1843	.011	200.00	400.00	800.00	1600.
	1846	.015	200.00	350.00	700.00	1500.

Obv: HELFRICHT below bust. Rev: Similar to C#64.

64a	1853	.014	200.00	350.00	700.00	1500.
	1854	.014	200.00	350.00	700.00	1500.

MONETARY REFORM
2 MARK

11.1110 g, .900 SILVER, .3215 oz ASW

Y#	Date	Mintage	Fine	VF	XF	Unc
159	1901D	.020	100.00	250.00	400.00	650.00

Obv: Long beard.

Y#	Date	Mintage	Fine	VF	XF	Unc
161.1	1902D	.020	225.00	750.00	1200.	2000.

Obv: Short beard.

161.2	1902D	.020	100.00	200.00	350.00	700.00
	1913D	5,000	150.00	250.00	450.00	650.00

Death of Georg II

166	1915	.030	35.00	60.00	140.00	200.00

3 MARK

16.6670 g, .900 SILVER, .4823 oz ASW

162	1908D	.035	35.00	100.00	140.00	200.00
	1908D	—	—	—	Proof	200.00
	1913D	.030	35.00	100.00	140.00	200.00

Death of Georg II

167	1915	.030	30.00	75.00	150.00	200.00
	1915	—	—	—	Proof	225.00

5 MARK

27.7770 g, .900 SILVER, .8038 oz ASW

160	1901D	.020	85.00	225.00	425.00	725.00
	1901D	—	—	—	Proof	700.00

Obv: Long beard.

163.1	1902D	.020	60.00	175.00	325.00	500.00

Obv: Short beard.

Y#	Date	Mintage	Fine	VF	XF	Unc
163.2	1902D	.020	60.00	150.00	325.00	650.00
	1908D	.060	50.00	150.00	275.00	450.00

10 MARK

3.9820 g, .900 GOLD, .1152 oz AGW

157	1890D	2,000	1250.	2000.	2500.	3700.
	1890D	—	—	—	Proof	7000.
	1898D	2,000	1000.	1500.	1850.	2750.
	1898D	—	—	—	Proof	7000.

164	1902D	2,000	800.00	1400.	2000.	3000.
	1902D	—	—	—	Proof	4250.
	1909D	2,000	800.00	1400.	2000.	3000.
	1909D	—	—	—	Proof	4250.
	1914D	1,002	1000.	1600.	2000.	3000.
	1914D	—	—	—	Proof	4250.

20 MARK

7.9650 g, .900 GOLD, .2304 oz AGW
Rev: Type I.

156	1872D	3,000	4000.	6000.	8000.	10,000.
	1872D	—	—	—	Proof	16,000.

Rev: Type II.

156a	1881D	—	4000.	6000.	8000.	12,000.
	1882D	3,061	2000.	3500.	4000.	6500.
	1882D	—	—	—	Proof	11,000.

158	1889D	4,032	1750.	3000.	4500.	6000.
	1889D	—	—	—	Proof	9000.

Rev: Type III.

Y#	Date	Mintage	Fine	VF	XF	Unc
158a	1900D	1,005	1500.	3000.	3500.	5500.
	1900D	—	—	—	Proof	11,000.
	1905D	1,000	1500.	3000.	3500.	5500.
	1905D	—	—	—	Proof	11,000.

165	1910D	1,004	1500.	3000.	3500.	5000.
	1910D	—	—	—	Proof	7000.
	1914D	1,001	1500.	3000.	3500.	5000.
	1914D	—	—	—	Proof	7000.

SAXE-WEIMAR-EISENACH

Saxe-Weimar-Eisenach was founded in 1644. It was raised to the status of a grand duchy in 1814. The last grand duke abdicated in 1918.

RULERS
Carl August, 1775-1828
Carl Friedrich, 1828-1853
Carl Alexander, 1853-1901
Wilhelm Ernst, 1901-1918

MINTMASTER'S INITIALS

Letter	Date	Name
JLST, LS, ST	1785-1790	Johann Leonhard Stockmar, die-cutter
	1793-1835	mintmaster

HELLER

COPPER

C#	Date	Mintage	Fine	VF	XF	Unc
55c	1801	—	2.00	4.00	8.00	65.00
	1813	—	2.00	4.00	8.00	65.00

PFENNIG

COPPER
Rev: Value and date; line below date.

56c	1801	—	3.00	7.00	15.00	60.00
	1803	—	3.00	7.00	15.00	60.00
	1807	.030	3.00	7.00	15.00	60.00

Rev: Value and date; 1's in date reversed; line below date.

56d	1810	.080	3.00	7.00	15.00	60.00
	1813	—	3.00	7.00	15.00	60.00

Rev: Value and date; line below date.

61	1821	.100	2.00	4.00	8.00	40.00
	1824	—	2.00	4.00	8.00	40.00
	1826	—	2.00	4.00	8.00	40.00
77	1830	—	2.50	5.00	10.00	50.00

81	1840A	.760	2.00	4.00	8.00	45.00
	1841A	.760	2.00	4.00	8.00	45.00
	1844A	.361	2.00	4.00	8.00	45.00
	1851A	.360	2.00	4.00	8.00	45.00

Denticled border

89	1858A	.720	1.50	3.00	6.00	40.00
	1865A	.720	1.50	3.00	6.00	40.00

1-1/2 PFENNIG

COPPER

57	1807	.034	10.00	20.00	35.00	125.00

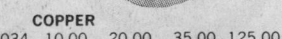

C#	Date	Mintage	Fine	VF	XF	Unc
62	1824	—	3.00	5.00	10.00	50.00
78	1830	—	3.00	5.00	10.00	50.00

2 PFENNIG

COPPER

58c	1803	—	4.00	7.00	20.00	125.00
	1807	.036	3.00	6.00	15.00	80.00

Milled edge

58d	1803	—	4.00	7.00	20.00	125.00
	1807	.036	3.00	6.00	15.00	80.00

Rev: Similar to C#58c but w/rosette below date.

58e	1813	—	3.00	6.00	15.00	80.00

Rev: Value over date; rosette below date.

63	1821	.068	2.00	5.00	8.00	60.00
	1826	—	2.00	5.00	8.00	60.00

Rev: Line below date.

79	1830	—	2.00	5.00	8.00	60.00

Denticled border

90	1858A	—	1.50	3.00	6.00	25.00
	1865A	—	1.50	3.00	6.00	25.00

3 PFENNIG

COPPER
Leaf edge

59c	1807	.049	5.00	10.00	25.00	100.00

Reeded edge

59d	1807	Inc. Ab.	4.00	7.00	17.00	60.00

Rev: Rosette under date.

59e	1804	—	2.00	4.00	8.00	40.00

Leaf edge

64	1824	—	2.00	4.00	8.00	40.00

Reeded edge

64a	1824	—	2.00	4.00	8.00	40.00

80	1830	—	2.00	4.00	8.00	40.00

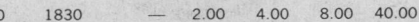

Straight date

C#	Date	Mintage	Fine	VF	XF	Unc
80.1	1830	—	2.00	4.00	8.00	40.00

Obv: Crowned Saxon arms in circular legend.
Rev: Value over date; SCHEIDE MUNZE above.

82	1840A	—	2.00	4.00	8.00	40.00

4 PFENNIG

COPPER
Obv: Saxon arms; S.W.u.E. above.
Rev: Value over date; w/o line under date.

60	1810	.146	5.00	10.00	25.00	125.00

Rev: Line under date.

60a	1810	Inc. Ab.	5.00	10.00	25.00	125.00
	1812	—	5.00	10.00	25.00	125.00

Rev: Rosette under date.

60b	1813	—	5.00	10.00	25.00	125.00

Reeded edge

65	1821	.092	4.00	7.00	15.00	100.00
	1826	—	4.00	7.00	15.00	100.00

Leaf edge

65a	1821	Inc. Ab.	4.00	7.00	15.00	100.00

1/2 GROSCHEN

1.0900 g, .222 SILVER, .0077 oz ASW
Obv: Crowned arms. Rev: Value.

85	1840A	2.400	2.00	4.00	8.00	40.00
91	1858A	.300	2.00	4.00	8.00	40.00

GROSCHEN

2.1900 g, .222 SILVER, .0156 oz ASW
Obv: Crowned arms. Rev: Value.

86	1840A	2.408	2.00	4.00	8.00	40.00

92	1858A	.300	2.00	4.00	8.00	40.00

1/48 THALER

1.0600 g, .229 SILVER, .0078 oz ASW

C#	Date	Mintage	Fine	VF	XF	Unc
67	1801	—	2.00	4.00	8.00	45.00
	1804	—	2.00	4.00	8.00	45.00
	1808	.286	2.00	4.00	8.00	45.00
	1810	.327	2.00	4.00	8.00	45.00
	1813	—	2.00	4.00	8.00	45.00
	1814	—	2.00	4.00	8.00	45.00

Obv: G.H.S.W.E. above arms.
| 38 | 1815 | — | 2.00 | 4.00 | 8.00 | 45.00 |

Obv: S.W.E. above arms.
69	1821	.243	3.00	6.00	20.00	80.00
	1824	—	3.00	6.00	20.00	80.00
	1826	—	3.00	6.00	20.00	80.00

Obv: Saxon arms w/S.W.E. above.
| 83 | 1831 | — | 3.00 | 6.00 | 15.00 | 70.00 |

Rev: Reversed 1's in date.
| 83a | 1831 | — | 3.00 | 6.00 | 15.00 | 70.00 |

1/24 THALER

2.1200 g, .229 SILVER, .0156 oz ASW
Obv: S.W.U.E. above arms. Rev: Value.

70	1801	—	3.00	7.00	20.00	90.00
	1804	—	3.00	7.00	20.00	90.00
	1808	.199	3.00	7.00	20.00	90.00
	1810	.452	3.00	7.00	20.00	90.00
	1813	—	3.00	7.00	20.00	90.00
	1814 small letters					
		—	3.00	7.00	20.00	90.00

Obv: G.H.S.W.E. above arms.
| 71 | 1815 | — | 8.00 | 15.00 | 50.00 | 175.00 |

Obv: S.W.E. above arms.
72	1821	.493	5.00	10.00	25.00	90.00
	1824	—	5.00	10.00	25.00	90.00
	1826	—	5.00	10.00	25.00	90.00

Rev. value: ENIEN
| 72a | 1821 | Inc. Ab. | — | — | — | — |

Rev. value: EINEN
| 84 | 1830 | — | 3.00 | 6.00 | 20.00 | 80.00 |

1/2 THALER
(Species)

14.0300 g, .833 SILVER, .3757 oz ASW
| 74 | 1813 LS | — | 35.00 | 75.00 | 125.00 | 300.00 |

EIN (1) THALER
(Convention)

28.0600 g, .833 SILVER, .7514 oz ASW
C#	Date	Mintage	Fine	VF	XF	Unc
75	1813 LS	—	125.00	275.00	600.00	1000.

| 76 | 1815 | 5,273 | 250.00 | 450.00 | 900.00 | 2000. |

22.2700 g, .750 SILVER, .5370 oz ASW
| 87 | 1841A | .203 | 40.00 | 75.00 | 180.00 | 475.00 |

(Vereins)

18.5200 g, .900 SILVER, .5360 oz ASW
93	1858A	.063	40.00	75.00	140.00	300.00
	1866A	.044	40.00	75.00	140.00	300.00
	1870A	.045	40.00	75.00	140.00	300.00

2 THALER
(3-1/2 Gulden)

37.1200 g, .900 SILVER, 1.0742 oz ASW
C#	Date	Mintage	Fine	VF	XF	Unc
88	1840A	.019	150.00	300.00	600.00	1300.
	1842A	.038	150.00	300.00	600.00	1300.
	1843A	Inc. Ab.	200.00	350.00	700.00	1600.
	1848A	.019	150.00	300.00	600.00	1300.

Rev: Similar to C#88.
| 94 | 1855A | .019 | 225.00 | 400.00 | 900.00 | 1750. |

MONETARY REFORM
2 MARK

11.1110 g, .900 SILVER, .3215 oz ASW
Y#	Date	Mintage	Fine	VF	XF	Unc
168	1892A	.050	75.00	150.00	350.00	550.00
	1898A	.100	50.00	125.00	325.00	525.00
	1898A	—	—	—	Proof	650.00

| 170 | 1901A | .100 | 100.00 | 300.00 | 400.00 | 750.00 |
| | 1901A | — | — | — | Proof | 800.00 |

Grand Duke's 1st Marriage
| 172 | 1903A | .040 | 35.00 | 60.00 | 100.00 | 140.00 |
| | 1903A | 1,000 | — | — | Proof | 200.00 |

Jena University 350th Anniversary

Y#	Date	Mintage	Fine	VF	XF	Unc
174	1908A	.050	25.00	50.00	100.00	125.00

3 MARK

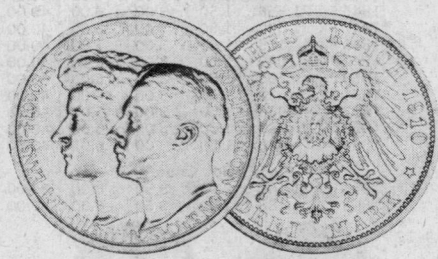

16.6670 g, .900 SILVER, .4823 oz ASW
Grand Duke's 2nd Marriage

176	1910A	.133	15.00	35.00	70.00	85.00
	1910A	—	—	—	Proof	125.00

Centenary of Grand Duchy

177	1915A	.050	25.00	75.00	125.00	175.00
	1915A	200 pcs.	—	—	Proof	400.00

5 MARK

27.7770 g, .900 SILVER, .8038 oz ASW
Grand Duke's 1st Marriage

173	1903A	.024	50.00	100.00	225.00	300.00
	1903A	*1,000	—	—	Proof	425.00

Jena University 350th Anniversary

175	1908A	.040	75.00	125.00	200.00	250.00
	1908A	—	—	—	Proof	625.00

20 MARK

7.9650 g, .900 GOLD, .2304 oz AGW

169	1892A	5,000	600.00	1000.	1500.	2000.
	1892A	—	—	—	Proof	5000.
	1896A	.015	650.00	1250.	1750.	2250.
	1896A	380 pcs.	—	—	Proof	5000.

Y#	Date	Mintage	Fine	VF	XF	Unc
171	1901A	5,000	750.00	1500.	2000.	2750.
	1901A	—	—	—	Proof	4500.

SAXONY

Saxony, located in southeast Germany was founded in 850. The first coinage was struck c. 990. It was divided into two lines in 1464. The electoral right was obtained by the elder line in 1547. During the time of the Reformation. Saxony was one of the more powerful states in central Europe. It became a kingdom in 1806. At the Congress of Vienna in 1815, they were forced to cede half its territories to Prussia.

RULERS
Friedrich August III, 1763-1806
 Later Friedrich August I, 1806-1827
Anton, 1827-1836
Friedrich August II, 1836-1854
Johann, 1854-1873
Albert, 1873-1902
Georg, 1902-1904
Friedrich August III, 1904-1918

MINT MARKS
L - Leipzig

MINTMASTER'S INITIALS
Dresden Mint

Letter	Date	Name
B	1860-1887	Gustav Julius Buschick
C,IC,IEC		
F	1845-1860	Gustav Theodor Fischer
G	1833-1844	Johann Georg Grohmann
GS,IGS,S		
	1812-1832	Johann Gotthelf Studer
H,SGH	1804-1813	Samuel Gottlieb Helbig
	1779-1804	Johann Ernst Croll

HELLER
COPPER
Obv: Crowned arms. Rev: Value above date.

C#	Date	Mintage	Fine	VF	XF	Unc
90	1801 C	—	1.50	4.00	8.00	40.00
	1805/705 H	—	1.50	4.00	8.00	40.00
	1805 H	—	1.50	4.00	8.00	40.00

Obv: Crowned arms within branches.
Rev: Value, w/o legends.

157	1813 H	.562	3.00	5.00	10.00	60.00
	1813 S	Inc. Ab.	3.00	5.00	10.00	60.00

PFENNIG
COPPER
Obv: Crowned arms. Rev: Value above date.

91	1801 C	—	2.00	4.00	10.00	50.00
	1804/799 C	—	2.00	4.00	10.00	50.00
	1804 C	—	2.00	4.00	10.00	50.00
	1805 H/C	—	2.00	4.00	10.00	50.00
	1805 H	—	2.00	4.00	10.00	50.00
	1806 H/795 C	—				
		—	2.00	4.00	10.00	50.00
	1806 H	—	2.00	4.00	10.00	50.00

Obv: Crowned arms within branches.
Rev: Value, w/o legends, pearl borders both sides.

158	1807 H	.691	3.00	7.00	20.00	75.00
	1807 H/799 C					
		—	4.00	8.00	25.00	85.00
	1807/86 H	—	4.00	8.00	25.00	85.00

Obv: Trefoil border.

158a	1808 H	.014	4.00	8.00	15.00	75.00

GOLD (OMS)

158c	1808 H	—	—	—	—	—

COPPER

158b	1811 H	1.267	2.00	4.00	10.00	75.00
	1815 S	—	2.00	4.00	10.00	75.00
	1816 S	—	2.00	4.00	10.00	75.00
	1822 S	—	2.00	4.00	10.00	75.00
	1825 S	.230	2.00	4.00	10.00	75.00

C#	Date	Mintage	Fine	VF	XF	Unc
201	1831 S	1.154	2.00	4.00	8.00	45.00
	1832 S	.527	2.00	4.00	8.00	45.00
	1833 G	1.152	2.00	4.00	8.00	45.00

220	1836 G	.226	1.50	3.00	6.00	40.00
	1837 G	.940	1.50	3.00	6.00	40.00
	1838 G	1.473	1.50	3.00	6.00	40.00

221	1841 G	.492	1.50	3.00	6.00	30.00
	1842 G	.323	1.50	3.00	6.00	30.00
	1843 G	1.115	1.50	3.00	6.00	30.00
	1846 F	.450	1.50	3.00	6.00	30.00
	1847 F	.546	1.50	3.00	6.00	30.00
	1848 F	1.447	1.50	3.00	6.00	30.00
	1849 F	.783	1.50	3.00	6.00	30.00
	1850 F	.815	1.50	3.00	6.00	30.00
	1851 F	1.556	1.50	3.00	6.00	30.00
	1852 F	.918	1.50	3.00	6.00	30.00
	1853 F	1.164	1.50	3.00	6.00	30.00
	1854 F	.548	1.50	3.00	6.00	30.00

248	1855 F	.657	1.50	3.00	6.00	30.00
	1856 F	3.457	1.50	3.00	6.00	30.00
	1859 F	2.341	1.50	3.00	6.00	30.00

248a	1861 B	.338	1.50	3.00	6.00	30.00

250	1862 B	1.094	1.50	3.00	6.00	30.00
	1863 B	4.484	1.50	3.00	6.00	30.00
	1865 B	3.877	1.50	3.00	6.00	30.00
	1866 B	1.129	1.50	3.00	6.00	30.00
	1868 B	2.084	1.50	3.00	6.00	30.00
	1871 B	.331	1.50	3.00	6.00	30.00
	1872 B	.591	1.50	3.00	6.00	30.00
	1873 B	.549	1.50	3.00	6.00	30.00

2 PFENNIG

COPPER

222	1841 G	1.263	2.00	4.00	8.00	40.00

222a	1841 G	Inc. Ab.	1.50	3.00	6.00	40.00
	1843 F	.112	1.50	3.00	6.00	40.00
	1846 F	.090	1.50	3.00	6.00	40.00
	1847 F	.401	1.50	3.00	6.00	40.00
	1848 F	.518	1.50	3.00	6.00	40.00

688 Saxony / GERMAN STATES

C#	Date	Mintage	Fine	VF	XF	Unc
222a	1849 F	.365	1.50	3.00	6.00	40.00
	1850 F	.647	1.50	3.00	6.00	40.00
	1851 F	.271	1.50	3.00	6.00	40.00
	1852 F	.361	1.50	3.00	6.00	40.00
	1853 F	.576	1.50	3.00	6.00	40.00
	1854 F	.056	2.00	4.00	8.00	45.00

249	1855 F	.536	1.50	3.00	6.00	40.00
	1856 F	2.182	1.50	3.00	6.00	40.00
	1859 F	1.103	1.50	3.00	6.00	40.00

249a	1861 B	.163	2.00	4.00	8.00	45.00

251	1862 B	.739	1.25	2.50	5.00	30.00
	1863 B	.456	1.25	2.50	5.00	30.00
	1864 B	3.139	1.25	2.50	5.00	30.00
	1866 B	.551	1.25	2.50	5.00	30.00
	1869 B	2.220	1.25	2.50	5.00	30.00
	1873 B	.262	1.50	3.00	6.00	35.00

3 PFENNIG

COPPER

92	1801 C	—	3.00	6.00	15.00	50.00
	1802 C	—	3.00	6.00	15.00	50.00
	1803 C	—	3.00	6.00	15.00	50.00
	1804 H	—	3.00	6.00	15.00	50.00
	1806 H	—	3.00	6.00	15.00	50.00

160	1807 H	.317	4.00	8.00	20.00	70.00
	1808 H	.295	4.00	8.00	20.00	70.00
	1809 H	4,800	15.00	30.00	60.00	125.00
	1811 H	.128	4.00	8.00	20.00	70.00
	1812 H	.096	4.00	8.00	20.00	70.00
	1814 S	.211	4.00	8.00	20.00	70.00
	1815 S	.432	4.00	8.00	20.00	70.00
	1822 S	—	4.00	8.00	20.00	70.00
	1823 S	.019	4.00	8.00	20.00	70.00
	1824 S	.123	4.00	8.00	20.00	70.00

Obv: Crowned arched arms. Rev: 3 PFENNIGE.

161	1825 S	.168	4.00	8.00	20.00	70.00
	1826 S	.031	5.00	10.00	25.00	80.00
202	1831 S	.077	5.00	10.00	15.00	60.00
	1832 S	.226	3.00	6.00	12.00	50.00

Rev: G below date.

202b	1833 G	.069	4.00	8.00	15.00	60.00

Rev: G below date.

202a	1834 G	.500	3.00	6.00	12.00	40.00

C#	Date	Mintage	Fine	VF	XF	Unc
223	1836 G	.039	4.00	8.00	15.00	60.00
	1837 G	.542	3.00	6.00	12.00	50.00

4 PFENNIG

COPPER

162	1808 H	1.548	6.00	12.50	30.00	100.00
	1809/6 H	1.059	6.00	12.50	30.00	100.00
	1809/8 H	I.A.	6.00	12.50	30.00	100.00
	1809 H	Inc. Ab.	6.00	12.50	30.00	100.00
	1810 H	.886	6.00	12.50	30.00	100.00

5 PFENNIG

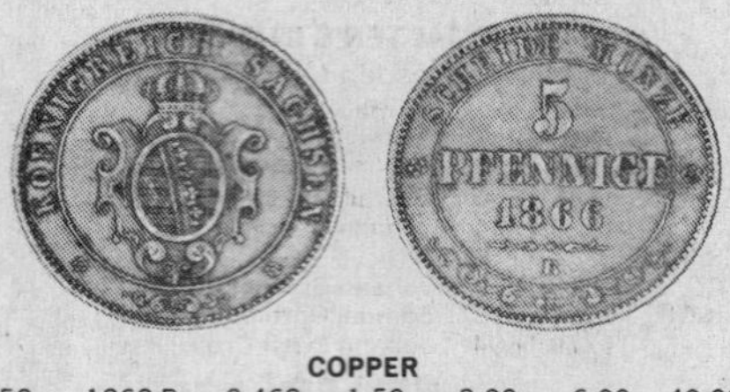

COPPER

252	1862 B	2.468	1.50	3.00	6.00	40.00
	1863 B	.693	1.50	3.00	6.00	40.00
	1864 B	1.090	1.50	3.00	6.00	40.00
	1866 B	.141	1.50	3.00	6.00	40.00
	1867 B	.444	1.50	3.00	6.00	40.00
	1869 B	.860	1.50	3.00	6.00	40.00

8 PFENNIG

1.2900 g, .250 SILVER, .0103 oz ASW

165	1808 H	2.594	4.00	8.00	20.00	60.00
	1809 H	4.722	4.00	8.00	20.00	60.00

1/2 NEU-GROSCHEN

(5 Pfennig)

1.0600 g, .229 SILVER, .0078 oz ASW

224	1841 G	2.248	1.50	3.00	5.00	25.00
	1842 G	2.845	1.50	3.00	5.00	25.00
	1843 G	3.552	1.50	3.00	5.00	25.00
	1844 G	1.354	1.50	3.00	5.00	25.00
	1848 F	.500	1.50	3.00	5.00	25.00
	1849 F	.579	1.50	3.00	5.00	25.00
	1851 F	.506	1.50	3.00	5.00	25.00
	1852 F	.497	1.50	3.00	5.00	25.00
	1853 F	.256	2.00	4.00	6.00	35.00
	1854 F	.107	2.00	4.00	6.00	35.00

253	1855 F	.444	2.00	3.00	5.00	45.00
	1856 F	.713	2.00	3.00	5.00	45.00

NEU-GROSCHEN

(10 Pfennig)

2.1200 g, .229 SILVER, .0156 oz ASW

C#	Date	Mintage	Fine	VF	XF	Unc
225	1841 G	4.500	1.50	3.00	6.00	40.00
	1842 G	2.463	1.50	3.00	6.00	40.00
	1845 F	.457	1.50	3.00	6.00	40.00
	1846 F	1.656	1.50	3.00	6.00	40.00
	1847 F	1.532	1.50	3.00	6.00	40.00
	1848 F	.105	1.50	3.00	6.00	40.00
	1849 F	1.049	1.50	3.00	6.00	40.00
	1850 F	.505	1.50	3.00	6.00	40.00
	1851 F	.676	1.50	3.00	6.00	40.00
	1852 F	.949	1.50	3.00	6.00	40.00
	1853 F	.798	1.50	3.00	6.00	40.00
	1854 F	.443	1.50	3.00	6.00	40.00

Rev: F below value.

254	1855 F	1.106	2.00	3.50	6.00	35.00
	1856 F	1.188	2.00	3.50	6.00	35.00

2.1000 g, .230 SILVER, .0155 oz ASW
Rev: B below value.

254a	1861 B	.395	2.50	5.00	7.50	45.00

255	1863 B	1.514	1.50	3.00	5.00	30.00
	1865 B	.557	2.00	4.00	6.00	35.00
	1867 B	.296	2.00	4.00	6.00	35.00

256	1867 B	.897	2.00	4.00	8.00	40.00
	1868 B	.608	2.00	4.00	8.00	40.00
	1870 B	.908	2.00	4.00	8.00	40.00
	1871 B	.293	2.00	4.00	8.00	40.00
	1873 B	.420	2.00	4.00	8.00	40.00

2 NEU-GROSCHEN

(20 Pfennig)

3.1100 g, .312 SILVER, .0311 oz ASW

226	1841 G	3.125	1.50	3.00	6.00	40.00
	1842 G	1.413	1.50	3.00	6.00	40.00
	1844 G	1.477	1.50	3.00	6.00	40.00
	1846 F	.516	1.50	3.00	6.00	40.00
	1847 F	.425	1.50	3.00	6.00	40.00
	1848 F	1.062	1.50	3.00	6.00	40.00
	1849 F	.656	1.50	3.00	6.00	40.00
	1850 F	.380	1.50	3.00	6.00	40.00
	1851 F	.588	1.50	3.00	6.00	40.00
	1852 F	.974	1.50	3.00	6.00	40.00
	1853 F	.604	1.50	3.00	6.00	40.00
	1854 F	.790	1.50	3.00	6.00	40.00

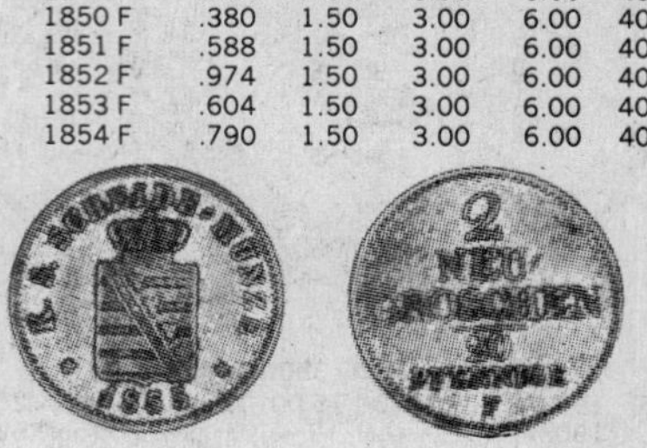

257	1855 F	.921	2.50	5.00	10.00	60.00
	1856 F	2.207	2.50	5.00	10.00	60.00

3.2200 g, .300 SILVER, .0310 oz ASW

258	1863 B	.557	2.50	5.00	10.00	50.00
	1864 B	.447	2.50	5.00	10.00	50.00
	1865 B	.371	2.50	5.00	10.00	50.00
	1866 B	.448	2.50	5.00	10.00	50.00

C#	Date	Mintage	Fine	VF	XF	Unc
259	1868 B	.419	4.00	8.00	15.00	55.00
	1869 B	.599	4.00	8.00	15.00	55.00
	1871 B	.245	4.00	8.00	15.00	55.00
	1873 B	.468	4.00	8.00	15.00	55.00

1/48 THALER

.9700 g, .250 SILVER, .0077 oz ASW
Obv: Crowned shield between crossed laurel branches.
Rev: Value, date below.

C#	Date	Mintage	Fine	VF	XF	Unc
97	1802 C	—	3.00	5.00	10.00	75.00
	1803 C	—	3.00	5.00	10.00	75.00
	1805 H	—	3.00	5.00	10.00	75.00
	1806 H	—	3.00	5.00	10.00	75.00

C#	Date	Mintage	Fine	VF	XF	Unc
163	1806 H	—	3.00	5.00	10.00	75.00
	1806/797 H	—	4.00	7.00	13.50	100.00
	1807 H	2.990	3.00	5.00	10.00	75.00
	1808 H	1.816	3.00	5.00	10.00	75.00
	1811/01 H	4.242	4.00	7.00	13.50	100.00
	1811 H	Inc. Ab.	3.00	5.00	10.00	75.00
	1812 H	5.382	3.00	5.00	10.00	75.00
	1812 S	Inc. Ab.	3.00	5.00	10.00	75.00
	1813 H	.730	3.00	5.00	10.00	75.00
	1813 S	Inc. Ab.	3.00	5.00	10.00	75.00
	1814 S	2.871	3.00	5.00	10.00	75.00
	1815 S	1.059	3.00	5.00	10.00	75.00

1/24 THALER

1.9800 g, .368 SILVER, .0234 oz ASW
Obv: Crowned shield between crossed laurel branches, leg: FRID.AVG. . . . . Rev: Value, date below.

C#	Date	Mintage	Fine	VF	XF	Unc
98	1801 EDC	—	2.50	5.00	10.00	50.00
	1802 EDC	—	2.50	5.00	10.00	50.00
	1806 SGH	—	—	—	—	—

C#	Date	Mintage	Fine	VF	XF	Unc
166	1816 IGS	.146	2.50	5.00	10.00	50.00
	1817 IGS	.252	2.50	5.00	10.00	50.00
	1818 IGS	.166	2.50	5.00	10.00	50.00

Obv. leg: FRIED. . . . . .

C#	Date	Mintage	Fine	VF	XF	Unc
167	1819 IGS	.337	3.00	7.00	15.00	60.00
	1820 IGS	.268	3.00	7.00	15.00	60.00
	1821 IGS	.321	3.00	7.00	15.00	60.00
	1822 IGS	.439	3.00	7.00	15.00	60.00

Obv. leg: FRIEDR. . . . .

C#	Date	Mintage	Fine	VF	XF	Unc
167a	1823 IGS	.368	3.00	7.00	15.00	60.00

Obv: Crowned arched arms.

C#	Date	Mintage	Fine	VF	XF	Unc
168	1824 S	.332	2.50	5.00	10.00	50.00
	1825 S	.262	2.50	5.00	10.00	50.00
	1826 S	.311	2.50	5.00	10.00	50.00
	1827 S	.067	3.00	6.00	12.00	60.00

Obv: Crowned arched arms within crossed branches.

C#	Date	Mintage	Fine	VF	XF	Unc
203	1827 S	.066	5.00	10.00	20.00	85.00
	1828 S	.100	5.00	10.00	20.00	85.00

1/12 THALER

3.3400 g, .437 SILVER, .0469 oz ASW
Obv: Crowned large oval arms. Rev: Value above date.

C#	Date	Mintage	Fine	VF	XF	Unc
100	1801 EDC	—	2.50	5.00	10.00	65.00
	1802 EDC	—	2.50	5.00	10.00	65.00

C#	Date	Mintage	Fine	VF	XF	Unc
169	1806 SGH	.037	5.00	10.00	20.00	90.00
	1807 SGH	.038	5.00	10.00	20.00	90.00
	1808 SGH	.140	4.00	7.00	15.00	75.00
	1809 SGH	1.071	4.00	7.00	15.00	75.00
	1810 SGH	.515	4.00	7.00	15.00	75.00
	1811 SGH	—	4.00	7.00	15.00	75.00
	1812 IGS	5.172	4.00	7.00	15.00	75.00
	1812 SGH	I.A.	4.00	7.00	15.00	75.00
	1813 IGS	2.055	4.00	7.00	15.00	75.00
	1813 SGH	I.A.	4.00	7.00	15.00	75.00
	1814 IGS	.063	5.00	10.00	20.00	90.00
	1816 IGS	—	4.00	7.00	15.00	75.00
	1817 IGS	—	4.00	7.00	15.00	75.00
	1818 IGS	—	4.00	7.00	15.00	75.00

Obv. leg: VGVST. . . .

C#	Date	Mintage	Fine	VF	XF	Unc
169a	1809 SGH	I.A.	4.00	7.00	15.00	75.00

Obv. leg: FRIED. . . .

C#	Date	Mintage	Fine	VF	XF	Unc
170	1819 IGS	—	3.00	6.00	12.00	65.00
	1820 IGS	—	3.00	6.00	12.00	65.00
	1821 IGS	—	3.00	6.00	12.00	65.00
	1822 IGS	—	3.00	6.00	12.00	65.00
	1823 IGS	1.624	3.00	6.00	12.00	65.00

Obv. leg: FRIEDR. . . . .

C#	Date	Mintage	Fine	VF	XF	Unc
170a	1823 IGS	I.A.	3.00	6.00	12.00	65.00

Obv: Crowned arched arms.

C#	Date	Mintage	Fine	VF	XF	Unc
171	1824 S	2.470	2.50	5.00	10.00	50.00
	1825 S	1.721	2.50	5.00	10.00	50.00
	1826 S	.763	2.50	5.00	10.00	50.00
	1827 S	.564	2.50	5.00	10.00	50.00

Obv: Crowned arched arms within crossed branches.

C#	Date	Mintage	Fine	VF	XF	Unc
204	1827 S	.060	4.00	8.00	15.00	65.00
	1828 S	.256	2.50	5.00	10.00	50.00

C#	Date	Mintage	Fine	VF	XF	Unc
204a	1829 S	1.431	2.50	5.00	10.00	50.00
	1830 S	1.684	2.50	5.00	10.00	50.00
	1831 S	.206	2.50	5.00	10.00	50.00
	1832 S	.882	2.50	5.00	10.00	50.00

C#	Date	Mintage	Fine	VF	XF	Unc
227	1836 G	.690	3.00	6.00	12.00	60.00

1/6 THALER

(Reichs)

5.3900 g, .541 SILVER, .0937 oz ASW

C#	Date	Mintage	Fine	VF	XF	Unc
108	1803 IEC	—	7.50	15.00	35.00	110.00
	1804 IEC	—	7.50	15.00	35.00	110.00
	1804 SGH	—	7.50	15.00	35.00	110.00
	1805 SGH	—	7.50	15.00	35.00	110.00
	1806 SGH	—	7.50	15.00	35.00	110.00

C#	Date	Mintage	Fine	VF	XF	Unc
172	1806 SGH	.018	15.00	25.00	50.00	150.00
	1807 SGH	.317	7.50	15.00	35.00	110.00
	1808 SGH	2.421	7.50	15.00	35.00	110.00
	1809 SGH	3.608	7.50	15.00	35.00	110.00
	1810 SGH	2.405	7.50	15.00	35.00	110.00
	1813 SGH	.229	7.50	15.00	35.00	110.00
172a	1813 IGS	—	7.50	15.00	35.00	110.00
	1817 IGS	.119	7.50	15.00	35.00	110.00

5.3400 g, .521 SILVER, .0894 oz ASW

C#	Date	Mintage	Fine	VF	XF	Unc
173	1825 GS	.068	15.00	30.00	60.00	150.00

Death of King Friedrich August

C#	Date	Mintage	Fine	VF	XF	Unc
174	1827 S	.048	7.50	15.00	30.00	60.00

Rev: Crowned arched arms within crossed branches.

C#	Date	Mintage	Fine	VF	XF	Unc
205	1827 S	.019	25.00	50.00	100.00	200.00
	1828 S	.018	25.00	50.00	100.00	200.00

Obv: Older head.

C#	Date	Mintage	Fine	VF	XF	Unc
205a	1829 S	.124	20.00	40.00	80.00	200.00

Death of King Anton

C#	Date	Mintage	Fine	VF	XF	Unc
206	1836 G	.046	15.00	30.00	60.00	125.00

C#	Date	Mintage	Fine	VF	XF	Unc
228	1841 G	.450	6.00	12.00	30.00	90.00
	1842 G	1.322	6.00	12.00	30.00	90.00
	1843 G	.655	6.00	12.00	30.00	90.00
	1846 F	.601	6.00	12.00	30.00	90.00
	1847 F	.366	6.00	12.00	30.00	90.00
	1848 F	.270	6.00	12.00	30.00	90.00
	1849 F	.449	6.00	12.00	30.00	90.00
	1850 F	.134	6.00	12.00	30.00	90.00

C#	Date	Mintage	Fine	VF	XF	Unc
228a	1851 F	.228	6.00	12.00	30.00	90.00
	1852 F	.340	6.00	12.00	30.00	90.00

Saxony / GERMAN STATES 690

Death of King Friedrich August II
Obv. leg: D.9.AUG. 1854 below head.
Rev. leg: ER SAEETE.

C#	Date	Mintage	Fine	VF	XF	Unc
229	1854 F	.521	5.00	10.00	25.00	85.00

260	1855 F	.476	5.00	10.00	25.00	100.00
	1856 F	1.529	5.00	10.00	25.00	100.00

5.3420 g, .520 SILVER, .0893 oz ASW

261	1860 B	.871	4.00	8.00	17.50	60.00
	1860 F	.052	6.00	12.50	25.00	100.00
	1861 B	1.099	4.00	8.00	17.50	60.00
	1863 B	.589	4.00	8.00	17.50	60.00
	1864 B	.161	4.00	8.00	17.50	60.00
	1865 B	.683	4.00	8.00	17.50	60.00
	1866/5 B	.475	4.00	8.00	17.50	65.00
	1866 B	Inc. Ab.	4.00	8.00	15.00	60.00
	1869 B	.626	4.00	8.00	15.00	60.00
	1870 B	.280	4.00	8.00	15.00	60.00
	1871 B	.293	4.00	8.00	15.00	60.00

1/3 THALER
(Reichs)

7.0160 g, .833 SILVER, .1880 oz ASW
Obv: Head right.
Rev: Crowned oval arms within crossed branches.

113	1801 IEC	—	17.50	30.00	60.00	125.00
	1802 IEC	—	17.50	30.00	60.00	125.00

Obv. leg: FEID, head right.

175	1806 SGH	.027	40.00	80.00	125.00	225.00
	1808 SGH	.277	20.00	45.00	75.00	135.00
	1809 SGH	.303	20.00	45.00	75.00	135.00
	1810 SGH	.295	20.00	45.00	75.00	135.00
	1811 SGH	.278	20.00	45.00	75.00	135.00
	1812 SGH	.080	30.00	60.00	100.00	175.00

Obv: I.G.S. mintmasters initial.

175.1	1815 IGS	5.740	60.00	120.00	200.00	325.00
	1816 IGS	9.049	50.00	100.00	160.00	275.00
	1817 IGS	8.929	50.00	100.00	160.00	275.00

Obv. leg: FEIN.

175a	1808	Inc. Ab.	30.00	60.00	90.00	175.00

Obv. leg: ACHTZIG

175b	1808	Inc. Ab.	40.00	85.00	135.00	225.00

176	1818 IGS	.019	40.00	80.00	150.00	250.00
	1821 IGS	—	40.00	80.00	150.00	250.00

8.2540 g, .708 SILVER, .1880 oz ASW
Obv: Head right.
Rev: Crowned arched arms within crossed branches.

207	1827 S	8.700	50.00	100.00	200.00	350.00
	1828 S	.010	50.00	100.00	200.00	350.00
	1829 S	.021	35.00	70.00	150.00	300.00
	1830 S	.097	35.00	70.00	150.00	300.00

8.3520 g, .667 SILVER, .1790 oz ASW

C#	Date	Mintage	Fine	VF	XF	Unc
230	1852 F	.194	15.00	30.00	60.00	125.00
	1853 F	.403	15.00	30.00	60.00	125.00
	1854 F	1.156	15.00	30.00	60.00	125.00

Death of King Friedrich August II

231	1854 F	.029	20.00	40.00	80.00	125.00

Obv: Mint mark below head left.
Rev: Crowned draped rectangular arms.

262	1856 F	.308	25.00	50.00	100.00	175.00

8.3200 g, .667 SILVER, .1784 oz ASW

263	1858 F	.326	20.00	40.00	80.00	150.00
	1859 F	.617	20.00	40.00	80.00	150.00

264	1860 B	.345	17.50	35.00	70.00	125.00

2/3 THALER
(Reichs)

14.0310 g, .833 SILVER, .3760 oz ASW

121	1801 IEC	—	25.00	40.00	75.00	150.00
	1802 IEC	—	25.00	40.00	75.00	150.00
	1805 SGH	—	25.00	40.00	75.00	150.00
	1806 SGH	—	25.00	40.00	75.00	150.00

177	1806 SGH	.084	25.00	35.00	60.00	200.00
	1807 SGH	.075	25.00	35.00	60.00	200.00
	1808 SGH	.171	25.00	35.00	60.00	200.00
	1809 SGH	.165	25.00	35.00	60.00	200.00
	1810 SGH	.165	25.00	35.00	60.00	200.00
	1811 SGH	.161	25.00	35.00	60.00	200.00
	1812 SGH	.086	25.00	35.00	60.00	200.00

C#	Date	Mintage	Fine	VF	XF	Unc
177	1813 IGS	—	25.00	35.00	60.00	200.00
	1814 IGS	.025	25.00	35.00	60.00	200.00
	1815 IGS	.048	25.00	35.00	60.00	200.00
	1816 IGS	.055	25.00	35.00	60.00	200.00
	1817 IGS	.060	25.00	35.00	60.00	200.00

178a	1822 IGS	.023	60.00	125.00	250.00	450.00

208	1827 S	.011	50.00	100.00	200.00	400.00
	1828 S	.012	50.00	100.00	200.00	400.00

Obv: Different head right.

208a	1829 S	.013	60.00	125.00	250.00	450.00

EIN (1) THALER
(Mining)

28.0630 g, .833 SILVER, .7520 oz ASW
Obv: Head right. Rev: Crowned oval arms,
leg: DER SEEGEN DES BERGBAVES.

136a	1801 IEC	—	75.00	150.00	300.00	600.00
	1802 IEC	—	75.00	150.00	300.00	600.00
	1803 IEC	—	75.00	150.00	300.00	600.00
	1804 IEC	—	75.00	150.00	300.00	600.00
	1804 SGH	—	75.00	150.00	300.00	600.00
	1805 SGH	—	75.00	150.00	300.00	600.00
	1806 SGH	—	75.00	150.00	300.00	600.00

(Convention)
Rev. leg: X.EINE.FEINE.MARK, date.

135	1801 IEC	—	35.00	65.00	100.00	300.00
	1802 IEC	—	35.00	65.00	100.00	300.00
	1803 IEC	—	35.00	65.00	100.00	300.00
	1804 IEC	—	35.00	65.00	100.00	300.00
	1804 SGH	—	35.00	65.00	100.00	300.00
	1805 SGH	—	35.00	65.00	100.00	300.00
	1806 SGH	—	35.00	65.00	100.00	300.00

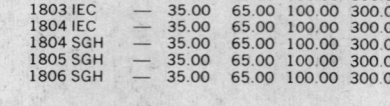

180	1806 SGH	.663	750.00	1250.	2500.	5000.
	1807 SGH	—	750.00	1250.	2500.	5000.

Saxony / GERMAN STATES 691

Obv: Small bust. Rev: Crowned arms.

C#	Date	Mintage	Fine	VF	XF	Unc
180b	1807 SGH	.461	35.00	60.00	100.00	225.00
	1808 SGH	1.534	35.00	60.00	100.00	225.00
	1809 SGH	.563	35.00	60.00	100.00	225.00
	1810 SGH	.368	35.00	60.00	100.00	225.00
	1811 SGH	.395	35.00	60.00	100.00	225.00
	1812 SGH	.134	35.00	60.00	100.00	225.00
	1813 IGS	.773	35.00	60.00	100.00	225.00
	1813 I.A.		35.00	60.00	100.00	225.00
	1815 IGS	.510	35.00	60.00	150.00	225.00
	1816 IGS	—	35.00	60.00	100.00	225.00
	1817 IGS	—	35.00	60.00	100.00	225.00

Edge inscription: GOTT SEGNE SACHSEN

| 180a | 1816 IGS | | 50.00 | 75.00 | 125.00 | 250.00 |

(Mining)

| 179 | 1807 SGH | — | 75.00 | 175.00 | 400.00 | 800.00 |

(Convention)

Mining Academy at Freiberg

C#	Date	Mintage	Fine	VF	XF	Unc
182	1815	—	1000.	1500.	3000.	4500.

(Convention)

| 183 | 1816 IGS | — | 600.00 | 800.00 | 1500. | 2500. |

Obv: Similar to C#180b.

181	1807 SGH	—	75.00	150.00	400.00	800.00
	1808 SGH	—	75.00	150.00	400.00	800.00
	1809 SGH	—	75.00	150.00	400.00	800.00
	1810 SGH	—	75.00	150.00	400.00	800.00
	1811 SGH	—	75.00	150.00	400.00	800.00
	1812 SGH	—	75.00	150.00	400.00	800.00
	1813 SGH	—	75.00	150.00	400.00	800.00
	1813 IGS	—	40.00	80.00	150.00	300.00
	1815 IGS	—	40.00	80.00	150.00	300.00
	1816 IGS	—	40.00	80.00	150.00	300.00
	1817 IGS	—	200.00	300.00	600.00	1250.

Legend right to left.

181a	1811 SGH	—	75.00	150.00	400.00	800.00
	1813 SGH	—	75.00	150.00	400.00	800.00
	1811 IGS	—	75.00	150.00	400.00	800.00
	1813 IGS	—	75.00	150.00	400.00	800.00
	1815 IGS	—	75.00	150.00	400.00	800.00
	1816 IGS	—	75.00	150.00	400.00	800.00

184	1817 IGS	—	35.00	60.00	125.00	250.00
	1818 IGS	—	35.00	60.00	125.00	250.00
	1819 IGS	—	35.00	60.00	125.00	250.00
	1820 IGS	—	35.00	60.00	125.00	250.00
	1821 IGS	—	35.00	60.00	125.00	250.00

(Mining)

Rev. leg: DER SEGEN.

C#	Date	Mintage	Fine	VF	XF	Unc
185	1817 IGS	—	75.00	150.00	300.00	600.00
	1818 IGS	—	75.00	150.00	300.00	600.00
	1819 IGS	—	75.00	150.00	300.00	600.00
	1820 IGS	—	75.00	150.00	300.00	600.00
	1821 IGS	—	75.00	150.00	300.00	600.00

(Convention)

Obv: Different bust. Rev. leg: W/o DER SEGEN.

| 186 | 1822 IGS | — | 40.00 | 60.00 | 150.00 | 300.00 |
| | 1823 IGS | .512 | 40.00 | 60.00 | 150.00 | 300.00 |

(Mining)

Obv. leg: W/DER SEGEN added.

| 187 | 1822 IGS | — | 50.00 | 125.00 | 350.00 | 625.00 |
| | 1823 IGS | — | 50.00 | 125.00 | 350.00 | 625.00 |

(Convention)

188	1824 S	.546	35.00	60.00	125.00	275.00
	1825 S	.546	35.00	60.00	125.00	250.00
	1826 S	.546	35.00	60.00	125.00	250.00
	1827 S	.423	35.00	60.00	125.00	275.00

Saxony / GERMAN STATES 692

(Mining)

C#	Date	Mintage	Fine	VF	XF	Unc
189	1824 S	—	60.00	125.00	225.00	475.00
	1825 S	—	60.00	125.00	225.00	475.00
	1826 S	—	60.00	125.00	225.00	475.00
	1827 S	.018	60.00	125.00	225.00	475.00

C#	Date	Mintage	Fine	VF	XF	Unc
209	1827 S	.107	45.00	80.00	150.00	375.00
	1828 S	.609	40.00	60.00	125.00	300.00

Forstin University

C#	Date	Mintage	Fine	VF	XF	Unc
212	1830	25 pcs.	—	—	Rare	—

209a	1829 S	.534	30.00	60.00	100.00	200.00
	1830 S	.620	30.00	60.00	100.00	200.00
	1831 S	.697	30.00	60.00	100.00	200.00
	1832 S	.979	30.00	60.00	100.00	200.00
	1833 G	.190	30.00	60.00	100.00	200.00
	1834 G	.486	30.00	60.00	100.00	200.00
	1835 G	.458	30.00	60.00	100.00	200.00
	1836 G	.585	30.00	60.00	100.00	200.00

Agriculture Educational Establishment at Tharant
Rev: LANDWIRTSCHAFTL

| 213 | 1830 | 25 pcs. | — | — | Rare | — |

| 189a | 1824 GS | — | 150.00 | 450.00 | 1200. | 2000. |
(Convention)

(Mining)
Rev. leg: SEGEN DES BERGBAUS.

| 210 | 1828 S | .018 | 150.00 | 300.00 | 750.00 | 1900. |

Obv: Older head.

210a	1829 S	.019	65.00	175.00	450.00	1000.
	1830 S	.019	65.00	200.00	500.00	1200.
	1831 S	.019	65.00	175.00	450.00	1000.
	1832 S	.013	65.00	175.00	450.00	1000.
	1833 G	3,000	65.00	200.00	500.00	1200.
	1834 G	5,500	65.00	175.00	450.00	1000.
	1835 G	4,986	65.00	175.00	450.00	1000.
	1836 G	4,836	65.00	200.00	500.00	1200.

(Convention)

New Constitution

| 214 | 1831 S | .014 | 40.00 | 80.00 | 125.00 | 250.00 |

Death of King Friedrich August

| 190 | 1827 S | .014 | 60.00 | 100.00 | 150.00 | 250.00 |

(Mining)
Edge inscription: SEGEN DES BERGBAUS

| 190a | 1827 S | 4,357 | 75.00 | 150.00 | 200.00 | 400.00 |

(Convention)

Mining Academy at Freiberg
Obv: Similar to C#209.

| 211 | 1829 | 200 pcs. | 1000. | 2000. | 4000. | 6000. |

Saxony / GERMAN STATES 693

Death of King Anton

C#	Date	Mintage	Fine	VF	XF	Unc
215	1836 G	.012	40.00	80.00	125.00	250.00

(Mining)

Edge inscription: SEGEN DES BERGBAUS

| 215a | 1836 G | 2.500 | 100.00 | 250.00 | 500.00 | 1000. |

(Convention)

| 232 | 1836 G | .034 | 100.00 | 200.00 | 600.00 | 1200. |
| | 1837 G | .031 | 125.00 | 275.00 | 700.00 | 1400. |

Obv. legend continuous.

232a	1836 G	3,260	450.00	1000.	2200.	4000.
	1837 G	.094	50.00	90.00	225.00	475.00
	1838 G	.139	40.00	75.00	200.00	400.00

(Mining)

Obv. leg: KOENIG. Rev. leg: SEGEN DES, etc.

233	1836 G	3.262	450.00	1000.	2200.	4000.
	1837 G	5.770	135.00	275.00	700.00	1400.
	1838 G	.036	90.00	175.00	475.00	875.00

(Convention)

22.2720 g, .750 SILVER, .5371 oz ASW
Visit to Dresden Mint
Lettered edge

| 234 | 1839 G | — | 900.00 | 1800. | 3000. | 4500. |

Plain edge

| 234a | 1839 | | | | Rare | |

C#	Date	Mintage	Fine	VF	XF	Unc
235	1839 G	.643	25.00	50.00	100.00	250.00
	1840 G	1.406	25.00	50.00	100.00	250.00
	1841 G	2.505	25.00	50.00	100.00	250.00
	1842 G	.974	25.00	50.00	100.00	250.00
	1843 G	1.251	25.00	50.00	100.00	250.00
	1844 G	1.026	25.00	50.00	100.00	250.00

Obv: F below head.

235a	1845 F	.973	25.00	50.00	100.00	250.00
	1846 F	.860	25.00	50.00	100.00	250.00
	1847 F	.677	25.00	50.00	100.00	250.00
	1848 F	1.592	25.00	50.00	100.00	250.00
	1849 F	1.368	25.00	50.00	100.00	250.00

235b	1850 F	1.074	25.00	50.00	125.00	325.00
	1851 F	1.351	25.00	50.00	125.00	325.00
	1852 F	1.105	25.00	50.00	125.00	325.00
	1853 F	1.171	25.00	50.00	125.00	325.00
	1854 F	1.075	25.00	50.00	125.00	325.00

(Mining)

Obv: G below head.

236	1841 G	.011	75.00	150.00	450.00	1000.
	1842 G	.017	75.00	150.00	450.00	1000.
	1843 G	.017	75.00	150.00	450.00	1000.
	1844 G	.011	75.00	150.00	450.00	1000.

Obv: F below head.

236b	1845 F	.019	60.00	150.00	300.00	600.00
	1846 F	.022	60.00	150.00	300.00	600.00
	1847 F	.040	60.00	125.00	250.00	500.00
	1848 F	.021	60.00	150.00	300.00	600.00
	1849 F	.038	60.00	150.00	300.00	600.00

236a	1850 F	.034	50.00	125.00	250.00	500.00
	1851 F	.033	50.00	100.00	225.00	400.00
	1852 F	.047	50.00	125.00	250.00	500.00
	1853 F	.055	50.00	100.00	200.00	400.00
	1854 F	.037	50.00	100.00	200.00	400.00

Death of King Friedrich August II

C#	Date	Mintage	Fine	VF	XF	Unc
237	1854 F	.016	30.00	60.00	100.00	200.00

(Mining)

Edge: SEGEN DES BERGBAUS and crossed hammers.

| 237a | 1854 F | 8,829 | 40.00 | 75.00 | 125.00 | 250.00 |

(Convention)

| 265 | 1854 F | .525 | 30.00 | 60.00 | 150.00 | 450.00 |

(Mining)

Rev: Similar to C#269.

| 266 | 1854 F | .027 | 90.00 | 175.00 | 425.00 | 1000. |

(Convention)

Visit to Mint by King Johann

| 267 | 1855 F | 5,250 | 35.00 | 65.00 | 125.00 | 300.00 |
| | 1855 F | — | — | — | Proof | 400.00 |

Rev: Similar to C#265.

| 268 | 1855 F | .863 | 25.00 | 40.00 | 125.00 | 300.00 |
| | 1856 F | 1.089 | 25.00 | 40.00 | 100.00 | 250.00 |

(Mining)

Saxony / GERMAN STATES 694

C#	Date	Mintage	Fine	VF	XF	Unc
269	1855F	.056	65.00	125.00	350.00	800.00
	1856F	.056	65.00	125.00	350.00	800.00

(Vereins)

C#	Date	Mintage	Fine	VF	XF	Unc
272b	1868 B	.181	25.00	50.00	70.00	150.00
	1869 B	.190	25.00	50.00	70.00	150.00
	1870 B	.236	25.00	50.00	70.00	150.00
	1871 B	.203	25.00	50.00	70.00	150.00

(Vereins)

37.1200 g, .900 SILVER, 1.0742 oz ASW

C#	Date	Mintage	Fine	VF	XF	Unc
238	1839 G	.020	90.00	125.00	300.00	600.00
	1840 G	.068	90.00	125.00	300.00	600.00
	1841 G	.039	90.00	125.00	300.00	600.00
	1842 G	.071	70.00	100.00	250.00	450.00
	1843 G	.059	70.00	100.00	250.00	450.00

Similar to C#238 w/F below head.

238a	1847 F	.147	50.00	85.00	185.00	400.00
	1848 F	.078	65.00	125.00	225.00	550.00
	1849 F	.015	65.00	125.00	225.00	550.00
	1850 F	.113	50.00	85.00	185.00	400.00
	1851 F	.246	50.00	85.00	185.00	400.00
	1852 F	.209	50.00	85.00	185.00	400.00
	1853 F	.303	50.00	85.00	185.00	400.00
	1854 F	.886	50.00	85.00	185.00	400.00

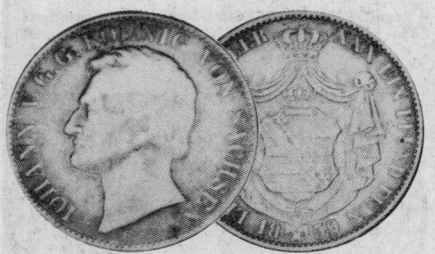

18.5200 g, .900 SILVER, .5360 oz ASW

270	1857 F	.969	25.00	45.00	100.00	250.00
	1858 F	.200	25.00	45.00	100.00	250.00
	1859 F	2.490	20.00	35.00	90.00	225.00

(Mining)

273	1860 B	2.669	25.00	50.00	90.00	200.00
	1861 B	1.409	25.00	50.00	90.00	200.00

Obv: Similar to C#269.

271	1857 F	.035	75.00	150.00	400.00	800.00
	1858 F	.034	75.00	150.00	400.00	800.00

273a	1861 B	1.070	25.00	50.00	70.00	150.00
	1862 B	2.134	25.00	50.00	70.00	150.00
	1863 B	1.471	25.00	50.00	70.00	150.00
	1864 B	1.904	25.00	50.00	70.00	150.00
	1865 B	1.335	25.00	50.00	70.00	150.00
	1866 B	1.181	25.00	50.00	70.00	150.00
	1867 B	2.020	25.00	50.00	70.00	150.00
	1868 B	1.683	25.00	50.00	70.00	150.00
	1869 B	1.622	25.00	50.00	70.00	150.00
	1870 B	1.693	25.00	50.00	70.00	150.00
	1871 B	1.687	25.00	50.00	70.00	150.00

Mining Academy at Freiberg
Obv: Similar to C#238.

239	1841 G	200 pcs.	750.00	1500.	3000.	4500.

Rev. leg: SEGEN DES BERGBAUS.

272	1858 F	.061	35.00	65.00	135.00	325.00
	1859 F	.094	35.00	65.00	135.00	325.00
	1860 B	.298	25.00	50.00	100.00	250.00
	1861 B large letters					
		.016	40.00	75.00	150.00	350.00
	1861 B small letters					
		.130	75.00	150.00	450.00	1000.

Victory Over France

274	1871 B	.045	35.00	50.00	100.00	200.00

2 THALER
(3-1/2 Gulden)

Forest and Agriculture Education Establishment
Obv: Similar to C#238.

240	1847 F	50 pcs.	3000.	6000.	8500.	12,000.

Rev. leg: SEGEN DES BERGBAUS.

272a	1861 B	.130	25.00	50.00	70.00	150.00
	1862 B	.145	25.00	50.00	70.00	150.00
	1863 B	.135	25.00	50.00	70.00	150.00
	1864 B	.120	25.00	50.00	70.00	150.00
	1865 B	.221	25.00	50.00	70.00	150.00
	1866 B	.185	25.00	50.00	70.00	150.00
	1867 B	.175	25.00	50.00	70.00	150.00

Saxony / GERMAN STATES 695

Death of King Friedrich August II

C#	Date	Mintage	Fine	VF	XF	Unc
241	1854 F	6,148	100.00	200.00	300.00	500.00
	1854 F	—	—	—	Proof	800.00

Rev: Similar to C#238.

275	1855 F	.462	50.00	90.00	190.00	350.00
	1856 F	.091	75.00	110.00	210.00	400.00

Mining Academy at Freiberg
Obv: Similar to C#275 w/F below head.

276	1857 F	100 pcs.	750.00	1500.	3000.	4500.

Obv: B below head.

276a	1857 B	206 pcs.	700.00	1400.	2500.	4000.

37.0370 g, .900 SILVER, 1.0718 oz ASW
Obv: Similar to C#275.

277	1857 F	.351	50.00	80.00	180.00	365.00
	1858 F	.454	50.00	80.00	180.00	365.00
	1859 F	.323	50.00	80.00	180.00	365.00

Rev. value: VEREINSTHAELR

277a	1858	Inc. Ab.	35.00	90.00	175.00	375.00

Obv: Similar to C#275.

C#	Date	Mintage	Fine	VF	XF	Unc
278	1861 B	.730	65.00	100.00	200.00	400.00

Golden Wedding Anniversary

279	1872 B	.049	50.00	75.00	125.00	200.00

Obv: W/o legend on rim.

279a	1872 B	Inc. Ab.	100.00	250.00	350.00	500.00

2-1/2 THALER

3.3410 g, .902 GOLD, .0970 oz AGW

245	1842 G	560 pcs.	300.00	600.00	1300.	2250.
	1845 F	420 pcs.	300.00	600.00	1300.	2250.
	1848 F	2,445	250.00	500.00	1000.	2000.
	1854 F	308 pcs.	400.00	700.00	1500.	2500.

5 THALER

6.6820 g, .902 GOLD, .1940 oz AGW
Similar to C#150a.

150	1801 IEC	—	400.00	1000.	2000.	3750.
	1802 IEC	—	400.00	1000.	2000.	3750.

150a	1805 SGH	—	—	—	—	—
	1806 SGH	—	500.00	1000.	2000.	4000.

C#	Date	Mintage	Fine	VF	XF	Unc
195	1806 SGH	.044	500.00	1000.	2500.	5000.
	1807 SGH	.152	500.00	1000.	1800.	3500.
	1808 SGH	.135	300.00	600.00	1250.	2750.
	1809 SGH	.054	300.00	600.00	1250.	2750.
	1810 SGH	.235	300.00	600.00	1250.	2750.
	1812 SGH	.098	300.00	600.00	1250.	2750.
	1813 SGH	.118	300.00	600.00	1250.	2750.

Rev: IGS below branches.

195a	1815 IGS	.020	250.00	500.00	1250.	2500.
	1816 IGS	—	400.00	1000.	1750.	3250.
	1817 IGS	—	250.00	500.00	1250.	2500.

Obv: Uniformed bust left.

196	1818 IGS	—	800.00	2000.	5000.	7500.

197	1825 S	.060	250.00	600.00	1500.	3000.
	1826 S	2,590	400.00	1000.	2500.	4000.
	1827 S	700 pcs.	500.00	1000.	2500.	4000.

218	1827 S	405 pcs.	500.00	1000.	2500.	4000.
	1828 S	855 pcs.	500.00	1000.	2500.	4000.

Obv: Older head.

218a	1829 S	385 pcs.	500.00	1000.	2500.	4000.
	1830 S	2,800	550.00	1100.	2750.	4250.
	1831 S	245 pcs.	700.00	1500.	3500.	5000.
	1832 S	175 pcs.	700.00	1250.	3000.	4500.
	1834 G	490 pcs.	700.00	1250.	3000.	4500.
	1835 G	380 pcs.	700.00	1250.	3000.	4500.
	1836 G	455 pcs.	700.00	1500.	3500.	5000.

243	1837 G	490 pcs.	400.00	750.00	2000.	3250.
	1838 G	175 pcs.	500.00	750.00	2000.	3250.
	1839 G	210 pcs.	500.00	850.00	2250.	3500.

246	1842 G	4,455	250.00	400.00	1000.	2000.
	1845 F	1,483	300.00	500.00	1200.	2250.
	1848 F	1,964	300.00	500.00	1200.	2250.
	1849 F	1,110	300.00	500.00	1200.	2250.
	1853 F	511 pcs.	450.00	800.00	1500.	2500.
	1854 F	4,570	300.00	500.00	1200.	2250.

10 THALER

13.3640 g, .902 GOLD, .3880 oz AGW

156	1801 IEC	—	800.00	2000.	3500.	4750.
	1802 IEC	—	800.00	2000.	3500.	4750.
	1803 IEC	—	800.00	2000.	3500.	4750.
	1804 IEC	—	600.00	1500.	2750.	3750.

Saxony / GERMAN STATES

C#	Date	Mintage	Fine	VF	XF	Unc
156	1804 SGH	—	500.00	1100.	2250.	3250.
	1805 SGH	—	600.00	1500.	2750.	3750.
	1806 SGH	—	500.00	1100.	2250.	3250.

198	1806 SGH	—	600.00	1250.	2500.	3500.
	1807 SGH	—	600.00	1250.	2500.	3500.
	1808 SGH	—	500.00	1000.	2000.	3000.
	1809 SGH	—	600.00	1250.	2500.	3500.
	1810 SGH	—	500.00	1000.	2000.	3000.
	1811 SGH	—	500.00	1000.	2000.	3000.
	1812 SGH	—	500.00	1000.	2000.	3000.
	1813 SGH	—	450.00	850.00	1750.	2750.
	1813 IGS	—	500.00	1000.	2000.	3000.
	1815 IGS	—	450.00	850.00	1750.	2750.
	1816 IGS	—	600.00	1250.	2500.	3500.
	1817 IGS	—	450.00	850.00	1750.	2750.

199	1818 IGS	—	2000.	4000.	7500.	9000.

200	1825 S	—	800.00	2000.	4000.	5000.
	1826 S	—	700.00	1500.	3000.	4000.
	1827 S	9,250	700.00	1500.	3000.	4000.

Obv: Head right.
Rev: Crowned arched arms within crossed branches.

219	1827 S	875 pcs.	1200.	3000.	6000.	7500.
	1828 S	5,530	800.00	2250.	5000.	6000.

Obv: Older head.

219a	1829 S	3,010	800.00	2000.	4000.	5000.
	1830 S	.018	650.00	1600.	3250.	4500.
	1831 S	3,255	1250.	2500.	5000.	7000.
	1832 S	2,625	800.00	2000.	4000.	5000.
	1833 G	—	1250.	2500.	5000.	7000.
	1834 G	3,080	1250.	2500.	5000.	7000.
	1835 G	2,715	1250.	2500.	5000.	7000.
	1836 G	4,655	1250.	2500.	5000.	7000.

Obv: Different head.
Rev: Crowned rectangular arms within crossed branches.

244	1836 G	1,110	600.00	1250.	2500.	3250.
	1837 G	2,400	600.00	1250.	2500.	3250.
	1838 G	1,750	700.00	1500.	3000.	3750.
	1839 G	1,855	700.00	1500.	3000.	3750.

247	1839 G	1,855	800.00	2000.	4000.	5000.
	1845 F	2,100	600.00	1250.	2500.	3250.
	1848 F	4,761	700.00	1500.	3000.	4000.
	1849 F	1,928	700.00	1500.	3000.	4000.
	1853 F	1,038	700.00	1500.	3000.	4000.
	1854 F	1,620	800.00	2000.	4000.	5000.

1/2 KRONE

5.5560 g, .900 GOLD, .1608 oz AGW

C#	Date	Mintage	Fine	VF	XF	Unc
280	1857 F	4,831	475.00	1000.	2000.	2750.
	1858 F	2,455	475.00	1000.	2000.	2750.
	1862 B	2,177	550.00	1200.	2250.	3000.
	1866 B	1,559	550.00	1200.	2250.	3000.
	1868 B	1,516	550.00	1200.	2500.	3250.
	1870 B	1,740	550.00	1200.	2500.	3250.

KRONE

11.1110 g, .900 GOLD, .3215 oz AGW

281	1857 F	3,580	525.00	1350.	2500.	3000.
	1858 F	4,610	525.00	1350.	2500.	3000.
	1859 F	9,040	525.00	1350.	2500.	3000.
	1860 B	5,067	525.00	1350.	2750.	3500.
	1861 B	3,908	525.00	1350.	2500.	3000.
	1862 B	3,229	525.00	1350.	2750.	3500.
	1863 B	3,538	525.00	1350.	2500.	3500.
	1865 B	4,371	525.00	1350.	2500.	3000.
	1867 B	2,155	525.00	1350.	2750.	3500.
	1868 B	5,262	525.00	1350.	2500.	3000.
	1870 B	2,700	525.00	1350.	2500.	3000.
	1871 B	2,140	525.00	1350.	2750.	3500.

MONETARY REFORM
2 MARK

11.1110 g, .900 SILVER, .3215 oz ASW

Y#	Date	Mintage	Fine	VF	XF	Unc
180	1876 E	1.613	30.00	80.00	500.00	1200.
	1877 E	.796	30.00	80.00	450.00	1100.
	1877 E	—	—	—	Proof	1000.
	1879 E	.036	70.00	175.00	700.00	1900.
	1880 E	.058	70.00	125.00	550.00	1900.
	1883 E	.056	70.00	125.00	550.00	2000.
	1888 E	.091	40.00	100.00	450.00	1700.

180a	1891 E	.130	25.00	65.00	125.00	300.00
	1893 E	.130	25.00	85.00	175.00	325.00
	1895 E	.117	30.00	115.00	200.00	375.00
	1896 E	.144	25.00	85.00	175.00	350.00
	1898 E	.107	25.00	85.00	175.00	400.00
	1899 E	.401	15.00	60.00	110.00	225.00
	1900 E	.384	15.00	60.00	110.00	200.00
	1901 E	.440	12.50	55.00	100.00	200.00
	1902 E	.543	10.00	55.00	100.00	175.00

Death of Albert

185	1902 E	.168	15.00	40.00	65.00	90.00
	1902 E	—	—	—	Proof	200.00

Y#	Date	Mintage	Fine	VF	XF	Unc
187	1903 E	.746	30.00	60.00	140.00	275.00
	1904 E	1.266	17.50	50.00	100.00	200.00

Death of Georg

191	1904 E	.150	15.00	35.00	60.00	90.00
	1904 E	55 pcs.	—	—	Proof	225.00

193	1905 E	.559	20.00	40.00	80.00	150.00
	1905 E	100 pcs.	—	—	Proof	200.00
	1906 E	.559	20.00	40.00	80.00	150.00
	1907 E	1.118	20.00	40.00	80.00	150.00
	1908 E	.336	20.00	45.00	75.00	150.00
	1911 E	.186	20.00	45.00	75.00	150.00
	1912 E	.168	20.00	45.00	75.00	150.00
	1914 E	.298	20.00	40.00	70.00	150.00
	Common date	—	—	—	Proof	225.00

500th Anniversary Leipzig University

198	1909	.125	15.00	30.00	65.00	90.00

3 MARK

16.6670 g, .900 SILVER, .4823 oz ASW

194	1908 E	.276	10.00	25.00	40.00	60.00
	1909 E	1.197	10.00	25.00	30.00	50.00
	1910 E	.745	10.00	25.00	30.00	50.00
	1911 E	.581	10.00	25.00	30.00	50.00
	1912 E	.379	10.00	25.00	30.00	50.00
	1913 E	.307	10.00	25.00	30.00	50.00
	Common date	—	—	—	Proof	150.00

Battle of Leipzig Centennial

Y#	Date	Mintage	Fine	VF	XF	Unc
200	1913 E	1.000	15.00	20.00	30.00	35.00
	1913 E	.017	—	—	Proof	125.00

Jubilee of Reformation

Y#	Date	Mintage	Fine	VF	XF	Unc
201	1917 E	100 pcs.	—	—	Proof 27,500.	40,000.

5 MARK

27.7770 g, .900 SILVER, .8038 oz ASW

Y#	Date	Mintage	Fine	VF	XF	Unc
181	1875 E	.494	30.00	60.00	750.00	2200.
	1876 E	.635	25.00	50.00	650.00	1900.
	1889 E	.036	40.00	100.00	750.00	2700.

1.9910 g, .900 GOLD, .0576 oz AGW

Y#	Date	Mintage	Fine	VF	XF	Unc
182	1877 E	.402	100.00	175.00	250.00	400.00
	1877 E	—	—	—	Proof	1000.

27.7770 g, .900 SILVER, .8038 oz ASW

Y#	Date	Mintage	Fine	VF	XF	Unc
181a	1891 E	.052	30.00	60.00	600.00	1100.
	1893 E	.052	30.00	60.00	600.00	1100.
	1894 E	.075	30.00	60.00	600.00	1100.
	1895 E	.089	30.00	60.00	600.00	1100.
	1898 E	.160	25.00	50.00	450.00	800.00
	1899 E	.074	25.00	50.00	450.00	900.00
	1900 E	.157	25.00	50.00	400.00	800.00
	1901 E	.156	25.00	50.00	300.00	700.00
	1902 E	.168	20.00	35.00	250.00	500.00

Death of Albert

Y#	Date	Mintage	Fine	VF	XF	Unc
186	1902 E	.100	30.00	60.00	125.00	165.00
	1902 E	—	—	—	Proof	425.00

Y#	Date	Mintage	Fine	VF	XF	Unc
188	1903 E	.536	20.00	40.00	125.00	450.00
	1904 E	.291	25.00	50.00	160.00	600.00
Common date		—	—	—	Proof	750.00

Death of Georg

Y#	Date	Mintage	Fine	VF	XF	Unc
192	1904 E	.037	40.00	125.00	225.00	275.00
	1904 E	70 pcs.	—	—	Proof	400.00

Y#	Date	Mintage	Fine	VF	XF	Unc
195	1907 E	.398	20.00	40.00	90.00	150.00
	1908 E	.317	20.00	40.00	90.00	175.00
	1914 E	.298	17.50	35.00	80.00	150.00

500th Anniversary Leipzig University

Y#	Date	Mintage	Fine	VF	XF	Unc
199	1909	.050	40.00	90.00	175.00	225.00
	1909	—	—	—	Proof	525.00

10 MARK

3.9820 g, .900 GOLD, .1152 oz AGW
Obv: E below head. Rev: Type I.

Y#	Date	Mintage	Fine	VF	XF	Unc
178	1872 E	.339	65.00	100.00	150.00	325.00
	1873 E	.715	65.00	100.00	150.00	300.00

Rev: Type II.

Y#	Date	Mintage	Fine	VF	XF	Unc
183	1874 E	.048	450.00	750.00	1200.	2500.
	1875 E	.528	70.00	100.00	150.00	250.00
	1877 E	.201	70.00	100.00	150.00	300.00
	1878 E	.225	70.00	100.00	150.00	300.00
	1879 E	.182	70.00	100.00	150.00	300.00
	1881 E	.240	70.00	100.00	150.00	300.00
	1888 E	.149	70.00	100.00	150.00	300.00

Rev: Type III.

Y#	Date	Mintage	Fine	VF	XF	Unc
183a	1891 E	.224	80.00	125.00	150.00	275.00
	1893 E	.224	80.00	125.00	150.00	275.00
	1896 E	.150	80.00	125.00	150.00	275.00
	1898 E	.313	80.00	125.00	150.00	275.00
	1900 E	.074	80.00	125.00	150.00	275.00
	1900 E	—	—	—	Proof	1500.
	1901 E	.075	80.00	125.00	150.00	275.00
	1902 E	.037	80.00	125.00	150.00	325.00

Y#	Date	Mintage	Fine	VF	XF	Unc
189	1903 E	.284	80.00	125.00	200.00	300.00
	1903 E	100 pcs.	—	—	Proof	1100.
	1904 E	.149	80.00	125.00	200.00	300.00

Y#	Date	Mintage	Fine	VF	XF	Unc
196	1905 E	.112	70.00	125.00	150.00	275.00
	1906 E	.075	70.00	125.00	150.00	275.00
	1907 E	.112	70.00	125.00	150.00	275.00
	1909 E	.112	70.00	125.00	150.00	275.00
	1910 E	.075	70.00	125.00	150.00	275.00
	1910 E	—	—	—	Proof	850.00
	1911 E	.038	70.00	125.00	150.00	325.00
	1912 E	.075	70.00	125.00	150.00	300.00
Common Date		—	—	—	Proof	800.00

20 MARK

7.9650 g, .900 GOLD, .2304 oz AGW
Rev: Type I.

Y#	Date	Mintage	Fine	VF	XF	Unc
179	1872 E	.890	115.00	130.00	150.00	250.00
	1872 E	—	—	—	Proof	Rare
	1873 E	1.085	115.00	130.00	150.00	250.00

Rev: Type II.

Y#	Date	Mintage	Fine	VF	XF	Unc
184	1874 E	.153	115.00	135.00	150.00	350.00
	1876 E	.482	115.00	135.00	150.00	350.00
	1876 E	—	—	—	Proof	1800.
	1877 E	1,181	9000.	17,000.	25,000.	35,000.
	1878 E	1,564	11,000.	22,000.	38,000.	45,000.

Rev: Type III.

Y#	Date	Mintage	Fine	VF	XF	Unc
184a	1894 E	.639	115.00	125.00	150.00	325.00
	1895 E	.113	115.00	125.00	225.00	375.00

Saxony / GERMAN STATES 698

Y#	Date	Mintage	Fine	VF	XF	Unc
190	1903 E	.250	115.00	150.00	225.00	350.00
	1903 E	—	—	—	Proof	1800.

Y#	Date	Mintage	Fine	VF	XF	Unc
197	1905 E	.500	115.00	125.00	150.00	250.00
	1913 E	.121	115.00	140.00	200.00	325.00
	1914 E	.325	115.00	165.00	225.00	425.00
	Common date	—	—	—	Proof	1100.

TRADE COINAGE
DUCAT

3.5000 g, .986 GOLD, .1109 oz AGW

C#	Date	Mintage	Fine	VF	XF	Unc
145	1801 IEC	—	300.00	600.00	1250.	3000.
	1802 IEC	—	200.00	400.00	750.00	2000.
	1803 IEC	—	300.00	600.00	1250.	3000.
	1804 IEC	—	250.00	500.00	1000.	2500.
145a	1804 SGH	—	300.00	700.00	1250.	2500.
	1805 SGH	—	350.00	800.00	1500.	3000.
	1806 SGH	—	300.00	700.00	1250.	2500.

C#	Date	Mintage	Fine	VF	XF	Unc
192	1806 SGH	3,207	200.00	400.00	1000.	2000.
	1807 SGH	2,660	300.00	800.00	1500.	2500.
	1808 SGH	2,010	300.00	800.00	1500.	2500.
	1809 SGH	1,608	300.00	800.00	1500.	2500.
	1810 SGH	1,072	300.00	800.00	1500.	2500.
	1811 SGH	268 pcs.	350.00	800.00	1750.	3000.
	1812 SGH	67 pcs.	400.00	800.00	1750.	3000.
	1813 SGH	—	300.00	600.00	1500.	2500.

C#	Date	Mintage	Fine	VF	XF	Unc
192a	1813 IGS	—	300.00	600.00	1500	2500.
	1814 IGS	134 pcs.	500.00	1000.	2000.	3500.
	1815 IGS	804 pcs.	350.00	800.00	1750.	3000.
	1816 IGS	2,243	300.00	600.00	1300.	2500.
	1817 IGS	1,812	300.00	600.00	1300.	2500.
	1818 IGS	1,466	300.00	600.00	1300.	2500.
	1819 IGS	1,466	300.00	600.00	1300.	2500.
	1820 IGS	2,502	300.00	600.00	1300.	2500.
	1821 IGS	1,948	300.00	600.00	1300.	2500.
	1822 IGS	1,898	300.00	600.00	1300.	2500.

400th Jubilee of Leipzig University
Obv: Bust in coronet and cape right.
Rev. leg: SALVA SIT.

Fr#	Date	Mintage	Fine	VF	XF	Unc
2586	1809	—	300.00	600.00	1200.	2000.

Obv: Uniformed bust left, leg: FRIEDR.AUGUST. . . . .
Rev: Crowned oval arms within crossed branches.

C#	Date	Mintage	Fine	VF	XF	Unc
193	1823 IGS	1,380	300.00	600.00	1200.	2000.

Obv. leg: FRIEDR.AUG.KOEN. . . .

C#	Date	Mintage	Fine	VF	XF	Unc
194	1824 IGS	2,847	300.00	600.00	1000.	1800.

C#	Date	Mintage	Fine	VF	XF	Unc
194a	1825 IGS	1,725	300.00	600.00	1200.	2000.
	1826 IGS	2,415	300.00	600.00	1200.	2000.
	1827 IGS	1,639	300.00	600.00	1200.	2000.

Rev: S below shield.

C#	Date	Mintage	Fine	VF	XF	Unc
217	1827 S	587 pcs.	400.00	900.00	1500.	2500.
	1828 S	771 pcs.	400.00	900.00	1500.	2500.

C#	Date	Mintage	Fine	VF	XF	Unc
217a	1829 S	2,070	300.00	600.00	1200.	2000.
	1830 S	1,898	300.00	600.00	1200.	2000.
	1831 S	862 pcs.	400.00	900.00	1500.	2500.
	1832 S	776 pcs.	400.00	900.00	1500.	2500.

Rev: G below shield.

C#	Date	Mintage	Fine	VF	XF	Unc
217b	1833 G	2,156	400.00	900.00	1500.	2500.
	1834 G	1,582	400.00	900.00	1500.	2500.
	1835 G	119 pcs.	600.00	1250.	2000.	3000.
	1836 G	804 pcs.	600.00	1250.	2000.	3000.

Obv: Different head.

C#	Date	Mintage	Fine	VF	XF	Unc
242	1836 G	100 pcs.	600.00	1250.	2250.	3250.
	1837 G	168 pcs.	600.00	1250.	2250.	3250.
	1838 G	637 pcs.	400.00	1100.	2250.	3250.

SCHAUMBURG-HESSEN

Located in northwest Germany, Schaumburg-Hessen was founded in 1640 when Schaumburg-Gehmen was divided between Hesse-Cassel and Lippe-Alverdissen. The two became known as Schaumburg-Hessen and Schaumburg-Lippe. Cassel struck coins for its half as late as 1832.

RULERS

Wilhelm (of Hesse-Cassel), 1785-1821
Wilhelm II, (of Hesse-Cassel), 1821-1847

MONETARY SYSTEM

12 Gute Pfennig = 1 Groschen

PFENNIG
(Guter)

COPPER
Obv: Crowned shield separating WL. Rev: Value.

C#	Date	Mintage	Fine	VF	XF	Unc
3	1801	—	2.50	5.00	10.00	50.00
	1802	—	2.50	5.00	10.00	50.00
	1803	—	2.50	5.00	10.00	50.00

Obv: Elector's cap over arms dividing W.K.
Rev: Value, F below.

C#	Date	Mintage	Fine	VF	XF	Unc
4	1804F	—	3.00	6.00	12.00	60.00
	1805F	—	3.00	6.00	12.00	60.00
	1806F	—	3.00	6.00	12.00	60.00
	1807F	—	3.00	6.00	12.00	60.00
	1814F	—	3.00	6.00	12.00	60.00

Rev: Rosette under value and date.

C#	Date	Mintage	Fine	VF	XF	Unc
4b	1815	—	3.00	6.00	12.00	60.00

C#	Date	Mintage	Fine	VF	XF	Unc
4a	1816	—	2.00	4.00	8.00	45.00
	1818	—	2.00	4.00	8.00	45.00
	1819	—	2.00	4.00	8.00	45.00
	1820	—	2.00	4.00	8.00	45.00
	1821	—	2.00	4.00	8.00	45.00
5	1824	—	2.00	4.00	8.00	45.00
	1826	—	2.00	4.00	8.00	45.00
	1827	—	2.00	4.00	8.00	45.00
	1828	—	2.00	4.00	8.00	45.00
	1829	—	2.00	4.00	8.00	45.00
	1830	—	2.00	4.00	8.00	45.00
6	1832	—	2.00	4.00	8.00	45.00

SCHAUMBURG-LIPPE

Located in northwest Germany, Schaumburg-Lippe was founded in 1640 when Schaumburg-Gehmen was divided between Hesse-Cassel and Lippe-Alverdissen. The two became known as Schaumburg-Hessen and Schaumburg-Lippe. They were elevated into a county independent of Lippe. Schaumburg-Lippe minted currency into the 20th century. The last prince died in 1911.

RULERS

Georg Wilhelm, 1787-1860
Adolph Georg, 1860-1893
Albrecht Georg, 1893-1911

PFENNIG
(Guter)

COPPER
Obv: Crowned arms. Rev: Value.

C#	Date	Mintage	Fine	VF	XF	Unc
36	1824	—	1.50	3.00	6.00	30.00
	1826	—	1.50	3.00	6.00	30.00

C#	Date	Mintage	Fine	VF	XF	Unc
37	1858 A	1.440	2.00	4.00	8.00	35.00

2 PFENNIG

COPPER

C#	Date	Mintage	Fine	VF	XF	Unc
38	1858 A	.360	3.00	6.00	10.00	40.00

3 PFENNIG

COPPER

C#	Date	Mintage	Fine	VF	XF	Unc
39	1858 A	.360	3.00	6.00	10.00	40.00

4 PFENNIG

COPPER
Obv: Crowned arms, garlands and roses. Rev: Value.

C#	Date	Mintage	Fine	VF	XF	Unc
30	1802	.288	12.00	25.00	45.00	90.00

.7500 g, .186 SILVER, .0044 oz ASW

Obv: Crowned arms.

C#	Date	Mintage	Fine	VF	XF	Unc
41	1821	.491	7.50	17.50	35.00	60.00

| 41a | 1828 | — | 7.50 | 17.50 | 35.00 | 60.00 |

COPPER

| 40 | 1858 A | .180 | 6.00 | 12.50 | 25.00 | 50.00 |

1/2 SILBER GROSCHEN

1.0900 g, .220 SILVER, .0077 oz ASW

| 45 | 1858 A | .120 | 6.00 | 12.50 | 25.00 | 50.00 |

MARIENGROSCHEN

1.5500 g, .388 SILVER, .0193 oz ASW
Obv: Crowned arms, garlands and roses. Rev: Value.

| 32 | 1802 | .144 | 20.00 | 45.00 | 75.00 | 125.00 |

| 42 | 1821 | .143 | 7.50 | 17.50 | 35.00 | 60.00 |
| | 1828 | — | 7.50 | 17.50 | 35.00 | 60.00 |

SILBER GROSCHEN

2.1900 g, .220 SILVER, .0154 oz ASW

| 46 | 1858 A | .210 | 6.00 | 12.50 | 22.50 | 45.00 |

2-1/2 SILBER GROSCHEN

3.2200 g, .375 SILVER, .0388 oz ASW

| 47 | 1858 A | .061 | 10.00 | 20.00 | 50.00 | 100.00 |

1/24 THALER

1.9900 g, .368 SILVER, .0235 oz ASW

| 43 | 1821 | .195 | 12.00 | 25.00 | 45.00 | 90.00 |
| | 1826 | — | 12.00 | 25.00 | 45.00 | 90.00 |

1/2 THALER

14.0310 g, .833 SILVER, .3760 oz ASW

| 44 | 1821 | 5.400 | 75.00 | 150.00 | 300.00 | 450.00 |

THALER

28.0630 g, .833 SILVER, .7520 oz ASW

C#	Date	Mintage	Fine	VF	XF	Unc
34	1802	4,000	175.00	300.00	700.00	1300.

18.5200 g, .900 SILVER, .5360 oz ASW

| 48 | 1860 B | 8,356 | 60.00 | 100.00 | 250.00 | 550.00 |

| 51 | 1865 B | 7,000 | 40.00 | 75.00 | 175.00 | 325.00 |

2 THALER

37.0370 g, .900 SILVER, 1.0718 oz ASW
50th Anniversary of Reign as Prince
Obv: Similar to 1 Thaler, C#48.

| 49 | 1857 B | 2,000 | 150.00 | 250.00 | 450.00 | 750.00 |

10 THALER

13.2840 g, .900 GOLD, .3826 oz AGW

C#	Date	Mintage	Fine	VF	XF	Unc
50	1829 FF					
	874 pcs.	4000.	9500.	18,500.*	25,000.
	1829 w/o FF					
	179 pcs.	4250.	10,000.	20,000.	27,500.

*NOTE: Stack's Hammel sale 9/82 AU realized $20,000.

MONETARY REFORM
2 MARK

11.1110 g, .900 SILVER, .3215 oz ASW

Y#	Date	Mintage	Fine	VF	XF	Unc
203	1898 A	5,000	200.00	400.00	700.00	1000.
	1898 A	162 pcs.	—	—	Proof	1000.
	1904 A	5,000	175.00	350.00	600.00	900.00
	1904 A	200 pcs.	—	—	—	900.00

3 MARK

16.6670 g, .900 SILVER, .4823 oz ASW
Death of Prince George

| 206 | 1911 A | .050 | 30.00 | 75.00 | 100.00 | 140.00 |
| | 1911 A | — | — | — | Proof | 200.00 |

5 MARK

27.7770 g, .900 SILVER, .8038 oz ASW

204	1898 A	3,000	350.00	800.00	1100.	1750.
	1898 A	90 pcs.	—	—	Proof	2500.
	1904 A	3,000	350.00	800.00	1100.	1750.
	1904 A	250 pcs.	—	—	Proof	1800.

20 MARK

7.9650 g, .900 GOLD, .2304 oz AGW

| 202 | 1874 B | 3,000 | 2000. | 4000. | 6000. | 8000. |
| | 1874 B | — | — | — | Proof | Rare |

205	1898 A	5,000	600.00	1000.	1400.	2000.
	1898 A	250 pcs.	—	—	Proof	4000.
	1904 A	5,500	600.00	1000.	1400.	2000.
	1904 A	132 pcs.	—	—	Proof	4000.

SCHLESWIG-HOLSTEIN

Schleswig-Holstein is the border area between Denmark and Germany. The duchy of Schleswig was Danish while Holstein was German. The 1773 Treaty of Zarskoje Selo

transferred Holstein to the Danes in exchange for Oldenburg. There was a great deal of trouble in the area during the 19th century. It was settled when Prussia annexed the territory in 1866.

RULERS
Christian VII (of Denmark), 1784-1808
Friedrich VI (of Denmark), 1808-1839
Christian VIII (of Denmark), 1839-1848

PROVISIONAL GOVERNMENT
1848-1851

ALTONA MINTMASTER'S INITIALS
C.B. - Calus Branth
I.F.F., F.F - Johann Friedrich Freund
MF, M.F, M.F. - Michael Flor
T.A. - Theodor C.W. Andersen
V.S. - Georg Vilhelm Svendsen

MONETARY SYSTEM
4 Dreiling = 2 Sechsling = 1 Schilling
60 Schilling = 1 Speciesdaler

DREILING

COPPER

C#	Date	Mintage	Fine	VF	XF	Unc
23	1850 TA	.200	3.00	6.00	15.00	50.00

SECHSLING

COPPER

24	1850 TA	.203	5.00	10.00	25.00	85.00
	1851 TA	.163	5.00	10.00	25.00	85.00

SCHILLING
1.4620 g, .250 SILVER, .0117 oz ASW
Obv: Crowned arms in sprays. Rev: Denomination.

25	1851 TA	—	—	—	Rare	—

2-1/2 SCHILLING
(1/24 Speciesthaler)
2.8090 g, .375 SILVER, .0339 oz ASW
Obv: Crowned CR monogram. Rev: Value above date.

4	1801 MF	.211	3.00	7.00	20.00	75.00

20	1809 MF	.960	5.00	10.00	30.00	100.00
	1812 MF	.528	5.00	10.00	30.00	100.00

5 SCHILLING
(1/12 Speciesthaler)
4.2140 g, .500 SILVER, .0677 oz ASW
Obv: Crowned interlaced CR monogram, VII within.
Rev: Value.

5	1801 MF	.103	5.00	10.00	30.00	100.00

8 SCHILLING

2.8090 g, .375 SILVER, .0339 oz ASW

21	1816 MF	.056	7.00	15.00	40.00	150.00
	1818 CB	.243	7.00	15.00	40.00	150.00
	1819 IFF	.925	7.00	15.00	40.00	150.00

16 SCHILLING

4.2140 g, .500 SILVER, .0677 oz ASW

C#	Date	Mintage	Fine	VF	XF	Unc
22	1816 MF	.031	8.00	20.00	50.00	150.00
	1818 CB	.125	8.00	20.00	50.00	150.00

Rev: 1/12 SP added.

22a	1831 IFF	.198	8.00	20.00	50.00	150.00
	1839 IFF	.063	8.00	20.00	50.00	150.00

20 SCHILLING
(1/3 Speciesthaler)

9.6310 g, .875 SILVER, .2709 oz ASW

7	1808 MF	.124	65.00	125.00	200.00

40 SCHILLING
(2/3 Speciesthaler)
19.2630 g, .875 SILVER, .5419 oz ASW
Similar to 20 Schilling, C#7.

8	1808 MF	—	85.00	150.00	225.00	500.00

60 SCHILLING
(Speciesthaler)
28.8930 g, .875 SILVER, .8128 oz ASW
Similar to 20 Schilling, C#7.

9	1801 MF	.312	65.00	125.00	300.00	500.00
	1804 MF	.106	65.00	125.00	300.00	500.00
	1807 MF	.102	65.00	125.00	300.00	500.00
	1808 MF	1.304	100.00	225.00	600.00	1000

NOTE: Many die varieties exist.

SCHWARZBURG-RUDOLSTADT

The Schwarzburg family held territory in central and northern Thuringia. After many divisions, two lines, Sondershausen and Rudolstadt were founded in 1552. The count of Rudolstadt was raised to the rank of prince in 1710. The last prince abdicated in 1918.

RULERS
Ludwig Friedrich II, 1793-1807
Friedrich Gunther, 1807-1867
Albert, 1867-1869
George, 1869-1890
Gunther Viktor, 1890-1918

PFENNIG
COPPER
Obv: SCHWARZB/RUD-LM. Rev: Value: 1 PF in script.

50	1801	—	3.00	7.00	15.00	60.00
	1802	—	3.00	7.00	15.00	60.00

63	1825	—	2.50	6.00	10.00	40.00

Obv: Crowned arms. Rev: value: SCHEIDE MUNZE.

65	1842A	—	2.00	6.00	10.00	35.00

2 PFENNIG
COPPER
Obv: Crowned FG monogram within crossed branches.
Rev: Value.

57	1812	—	3.00	7.00	15.00	70.00

Obv: Crowned arms

66	1842A	—	3.00	6.00	10.00	45.00

3 PFENNIG

COPPER
Obv. leg: SCHWARZB/RUD-LM. Rev: Value, 3 PF in script.

C#	Date	Mintage	Fine	VF	XF	Unc
51	1804	—	3.00	5.00	8.00	45.00

Obv: Monogram FG within crossed branches. Rev: Value.

58	1813	—	3.00	5.00	8.00	45.00

Obv: Crown above monogram.

64	1825	—	3.00	5.00	10.00	50.00

Obv: Crowned arms. Rev. leg: SCHEIDEMUNZE.

67	1842A	—	3.00	5.00	8.00	45.00

4 PFENNIG
COPPER
Obv: Monogram FG within crossed branches. Rev: Value.

59	1812	—	5.00	8.00	20.00	90.00
	1813	—	5.00	8.00	20.00	90.00

6 PFENNIG

1.3300 g, .250 SILVER, .0106 oz ASW

53	1800	—	5.00	8.00	20.00	85.00
	1801	—	5.00	8.00	20.00	85.00
60	1808	—	5.00	8.00	20.00	85.00

Obv: Rosette above & ledge below SCHWARZB/RUD-LM.

60a	1812	—	5.00	8.00	20.00	85.00
	1813	—	5.00	8.00	20.00	85.00

1/8 KREUZER

COPPER
Obv: Crowned arms within branches. Rev: Value.

73	1840	.024	3.00	7.00	15.00	40.00
	1855	—	3.00	7.00	15.00	40.00

1/4 KREUZER

COPPER

74	1840	.972	2.00	4.00	8.00	30.00
	1852	—	2.00	4.00	8.00	30.00
	1853	—	2.00	4.00	8.00	30.00
	1855	—	2.00	4.00	8.00	30.00
	1856	—	2.00	4.00	8.00	30.00

74a	1857	—	2.00	4.00	8.00	25.00
	1859	—	2.00	4.00	8.00	25.00
	1860	—	2.00	4.00	8.00	25.00
	1861	—	2.00	4.00	8.00	25.00
	1863	—	2.00	4.00	8.00	25.00
	1865	—	2.00	4.00	8.00	25.00
	1866	—	2.00	4.00	8.00	25.00
82	1868	.096	3.00	6.00	12.00	45.00

KREUZER

COPPER

C#	Date	Mintage	Fine	VF	XF	Unc
76	1840	.480	3.00	6.00	12.00	40.00

76a	1864	—	2.00	4.00	8.00	30.00
	1865	—	2.00	4.00	8.00	30.00
	1866	—	2.00	4.00	8.00	30.00

83	1868	.037	4.00	8.00	15.00	40.00

3 KREUZER

1.2900 g, .333 SILVER, .0138 oz ASW

77	1839	.155	5.00	10.00	20.00	100.00
	1840	Inc. Ab.	5.00	10.00	20.00	100.00
	1841	Inc. Ab.	5.00	10.00	20.00	100.00
	1842	Inc. Ab.	5.00	10.00	20.00	100.00
	1846	Inc. Ab.	5.00	10.00	20.00	100.00

1.2300 g, .350 SILVER, .0138 oz ASW
Obv. leg: SCHEIDE MUNZE added.

77a	1866	.010	10.00	15.00	30.00	125.00

6 KREUZER

2.5900 g, .333 SILVER, .0277 oz ASW

78	1840	.165	5.00	10.00	20.00	125.00
	1842	Inc. Ab.	5.00	10.00	20.00	125.00
	1846	Inc. Ab.	5.00	10.00	20.00	125.00

2.4600 g, .350 SILVER, .0276 oz ASW
Obv. leg: SCHEIDE MUNZE added.

78a	1866	.010	12.00	20.00	40.00	150.00

1/2 GROSCHEN

1.0900 g, .222 SILVER, .0077 oz ASW
Obv: Crowned arms. Rev: Value.

68	1841A	—	3.00	10.00	20.00	100.00

GROSCHEN

BILLON
Obv. leg: SCHWARZB. RUD-LM. Rev: Value.

61	1803	—	3.00	7.00	15.00	70.00
	1808	—	3.00	7.00	15.00	70.00

Obv: Rosette above, legend below.
Rev: Value with rosettes.

61a	1812	—	4.00	8.00	17.00	90.00

2.1900 g, .222 SILVER, .0156 oz ASW
Obv: Crowned arms. Rev: Value.

69	1841A	—	3.00	7.00	15.00	70.00

1/2 GULDEN

5.3030 g, .900 SILVER, .1535 oz ASW

C#	Date	Mintage	Fine	VF	XF	Unc
79	1841	.157	15.00	30.00	75.00	200.00
	1842	Inc. Ab.	15.00	30.00	75.00	200.00
	1843	Inc. Ab.	15.00	30.00	75.00	200.00
	1846	Inc. Ab.	15.00	30.00	75.00	200.00

GULDEN

10.6060 g, .900 SILVER, .3069 oz ASW
Obv: Similar to 1/2 Gulden, C#79.

80	1841	.163	25.00	50.00	100.00	250.00
	1842	Inc. Ab.	25.00	50.00	100.00	250.00
	1843	Inc. Ab.	25.00	50.00	100.00	250.00
	1846	Inc. Ab.	25.00	50.00	100.00	250.00

ZWEY (2) GULDEN

21.2110 g, .900 SILVER, .6138 oz ASW
Obv: Similar to 1/2 Gulden, C#79.

81	1846	500 pcs.	250.00	450.00	800.00	1800.

THALER
(Species)

28.0630 g, .833 SILVER, .7520 oz ASW

62	1812 L	—	90.00	150.00	275.00	600.00
	1813 L	—	100.00	175.00	300.00	650.00

(Vereins)

Schwarzburg-Rudolstadt / GERMAN STATES

18.5200 g, .900 SILVER, .5360 oz ASW

C#	Date	Mintage	Fine	VF	XF	Unc
70	1858	.016	40.00	65.00	130.00	275.00
	1859	6,000	50.00	75.00	150.00	300.00

70a	1862	.048	40.00	65.00	130.00	275.00
	1863	.017	40.00	65.00	130.00	275.00

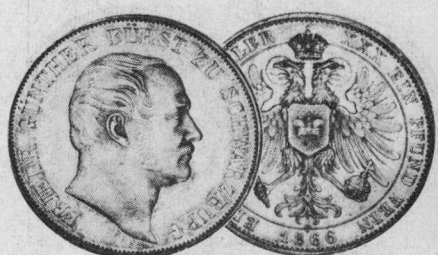

70b	1866	.027	40.00	65.00	130.00	275.00

50th Anniversary of Reign
Rev. leg: ZUR FEIER 50 JAEHRIGER REGIERUNG....

71	1864	4,500	50.00	75.00	150.00	300.00
	1864	—	—	—	Proof	500.00

84	1867	.013	50.00	80.00	175.00	450.00

2 THALER
(3-1/2 Gulden)

Schwarzburg-Rudolstadt / GERMAN STATES

37.1200 g, .900 SILVER, 1.0742 oz ASW

C#	Date	Mintage	Fine	VF	XF	Unc
72	1841 A	.010	100.00	200.00	450.00	1000.
	1845 A	5.100	100.00	200.00	450.00	1000.

MONETARY REFORM
2 MARK

11.1110 g, .900 SILVER, .3215 oz ASW

Y#	Date	Mintage	Fine	VF	XF	Unc
207	1898 A	.100	125.00	250.00	500.00	600.00
	1898 A	375 pcs.	—	—	Proof	900.00

10 MARK

3.9820 g, .900 GOLD, .1152 oz AGW

208	1898 A	.010	600.00	1100.	1500.	2000.
	1898 A	700 pcs.	—	—	Proof	3500.

TRADE COINAGE
DUCAT

3.5000 g, .986 GOLD, .1109 oz AGW

C#	Date	Mintage	Fine	VF	XF	Unc
55	1803	311 pcs.	600.00	1300.	2500.	4000.

SCHWARZBURG-SONDERSHAUSEN

The Schwarzburg family held territory in central and northern Thuringia. After many divisions, two lines, Sondershausen and Rudolstadt were founded in 1552. The count of Sondershausen was raised to the rank of prince in 1709. The last prince died in 1909 and the lands passed to Rudolstadt.

RULERS
Gunther Friedrich Carl I, 1794-1835
Gunther Friedrich Carl II, 1835-1880
Karl Gunther, 1880-1909

PFENNIG

COPPER

C#	Date	Mintage	Fine	VF	XF	Unc
18	1846 A	1.613	1.50	3.00	6.00	35.00
	1858 A	.360	2.00	4.00	8.00	40.00

3 PFENNIG

COPPER

19	1846 A	.682	3.00	6.00	12.00	50.00
	1858 A	.360	3.00	6.00	12.00	50.00
	1870 A	.120	3.00	6.00	12.00	50.00

1/2 SILBER GROSCHEN

1.0900 g, .222 SILVER, .0077 oz ASW

20	1846 A	.657	3.00	6.00	12.00	50.00
	1851 A	Inc. Ab.	3.00	6.00	12.00	50.00
	1858 A	.180	3.00	6.00	12.00	50.00

SILBER GROSCHEN

2.1900 g, .222 SILVER, .0156 oz ASW

21	1846 A	.584	3.00	6.00	12.00	60.00
	1851 A	Inc. Ab.	3.00	6.00	12.00	60.00
	1858 A	.150	3.00	6.00	12.00	60.00
	1870 A	.120	3.00	6.00	12.00	60.00

THALER
(Vereins)

18.5200 g, .900 SILVER, .5360 oz ASW

22	1859 A	.015	50.00	75.00	150.00	400.00
	1865 A	.010	50.00	75.00	150.00	400.00
	1870 A	.011	50.00	75.00	150.00	400.00

2 THALER
(3-1/2 Gulden)

37.1200 g, .900 SILVER, 1.0741 oz ASW

C#	Date	Mintage	Fine	VF	XF	Unc
23	1841 A	4.300	125.00	225.00	500.00	1100.
	1845 A	8.600	100.00	200.00	425.00	950.00
	1854 A	8.600	100.00	200.00	425.00	950.00

MONETARY REFORM
2 MARK

11.1110 g, .900 SILVER, .3215 oz ASW

Y#	Date	Mintage	Fine	VF	XF	Unc
209	1896 A	.050	100.00	250.00	450.00	600.00
	1896 A	190 pcs.	—	—	Proof	800.00

25th Year of Reign
Struck w/thick rim.

211	1905 A	.013	45.00	80.00	175.00	200.00
	1905 A	5.000	—	—	Proof	250.00

Struck w/thin rim.

211a	1905 A	.062	25.00	40.00	95.00	125.00
	1905 A	5.000	—	—	Proof	150.00

3 MARK

16.6670 g, .900 SILVER, .4823 oz ASW
Death of Karl Gunther

212	1909 A	.070	25.00	70.00	90.00	130.00
	1909 A	—	—	—	Proof	175.00

20 MARK

7.9650 g, .900 GOLD, .2304 oz AGW

210	1896 A	5.000	750.00	1250.	2000.	2500.
	1896 A	—	—	—	Proof	5500.

SILESIA

A duchy, located in northeastern Germany, was separated into many segments. They were greatly influenced by Bohemia and Austria. The first coins were struck c. 1169. Special coins for Silesian possessions were struck by Bohemia from 1327. From 1526, when Bohemia and its Silesian possessions fell to Austria, a special series of coins were struck by Austria for the area. After the Prussian invasion, in 1740, they also minted coins from

1743 through 1797.

RULERS
Friedrich Wilhelm III, 1797-1840

MINT MARKS
B, Breslau
W, Wratislawia (i.e. Breslau)

1/2 KREUZER
COPPER
Obv: Crowned FW monogram. Rev: Value.

C#	Date	Mintage	Fine	VF	XF	Unc
53	1806A	—	12.00	25.00	40.00	70.00

KREUZER
BILLON
Obv: Uniformed bust left. Rev: Crowned arms w/eagle.

57	1806A	—	17.50	40.00	90.00	200.00
	1808G	—	17.50	40.00	90.00	200.00

Obv: Crowned arms w/eagle within crossed branches.
Rev: Value.

| 54 | 1810A | .055 | 15.00 | 30.00 | 60.00 | 125.00 |

9 KREUZER

BILLON

| 60 | 1808G | — | 55.00 | 100.00 | 175.00 | 300.00 |

18 KREUZER
.563 SILVER
Obv: Uniformed bust left.
Rev: Crowned eagle w/scepter and orb.

| 61 | 1808G | — | 100.00 | 200.00 | 375.00 | 750.00 |

GROSCHEL
BILLON
Obv: Crowned FWR monogram. Rev: Value.

56	1805 A	—	20.00	40.00	75.00	150.00
	1806A	—	20.00	40.00	75.00	150.00
	1808G	—	20.00	40.00	75.00	150.00
	1809G	—	20.00	40.00	75.00	150.00

STOLBERG-ROSSLA

Stolberg, a county located in the Harz mountains of central Germany, had its own coinage from the 11th century. The Rossla line was founded in 1704.

RULERS
Johann Wilhelm Christof, 1776-1826

MINTMASTER'S INITIALS

Letter	Date	Name
EHAZ,Z	1792-1807	Ernst Hermann Agathus Ziegler

PFENNIG
COPPER
Obv: Stag left before column.
Rev: Value over date.

C#	Date	Mintage	VG	Fine	VF	XF
47	1801 Z	—	5.00	10.00	15.00	30.00

STOLBERG-WERNIGERODE

Stolberg, a county located in the Harz mountains of central Germany, had its own coinage from the 11th century. The lines of Wernigerode and Stolberg were established in 1641. A division of the lands occurred in 1645 but only the Wernigerode branch issued coins after 1800. Although administered by Prussia from 1714, the country retained a certain amount of sovereignty until 1876.

RULERS
Christian Friedrich, 1778-1824
Henrich XII, 1824-1854

TRADE COINAGE
DUCAT

3.5000 g, .986 GOLD, .1109 oz AGW
Golden Wedding Anniversary of the Count

C#	Date	Mintage	Fine	VF	XF	Unc
25	1818	308 pcs.	500.00	1100.	1800.	3500.

C#	Date	Mintage	Fine	VF	XF	Unc
26	1824	—	500.00	1000.	2000.	3500.

TEUTONIC ORDER

The Order of Knights was founded during the Third Crusade in 1198. They acquired considerable territory by conquest from the heathen Prussians in the late 13th and early 14th centuries. The seat of the Grand Master moved from Acre to Venice and in 1309 to Marienburg, Prussia. The Teutonic Order began striking coins in the late 13th century. In 1355 permission was granted to strike hellers at Mergentheim. However, the bulk of the Order's coinage until 1525 was schillings and half schoters minted in and for Prussia. In 1809 the Order was suppressed and Mergentheim was annexed to Wurttemberg.

RULERS
Max Franz, 1780-1801
Carl Ludwig, 1801-1804
Anton Victor, 1804-1809

30 KREUZER

SILVER
Death of Grand Master Max Franz

C#	Date	Mintage	VG	Fine	VF	XF
26	1801	—	30.00	60.00	125.00	250.00

WALDECK

The county of Waldeck was located on the border of Hesse. Their first coinage appeared c. 1250. Pyrmont was united with Waldeck in 1625 but was ruled separately for a while in the 19th century. They were reunited in 1812. The rulers gained the status of prince in 1712. The administration was turned over to Prussia in 1867 but the princes retained some sovereignty until 1918.

WALDECK-PYRMONT

RULERS
Friedrich Karl August in Waldeck, 1763-1812
Georg (In Pyrmont), 1805-1812
 (Refer to Pyrmont for listings)
 (In Waldeck-Pyrmont), 1812-1813
Georg Heinrich, 1813-1845
Emma, As Regent For Georg Victor, 1845-1852
Georg Victor, 1852-1893
Friedrich, 1893-1918

MINTMASTER'S INITIALS
A.W. - Albert Welle
F.W., F*w, W, .W. - Friedrich Welle

PFENNIG
COPPER
Obv: Crowned F monogram. Rev: Value.

C#	Date	Mintage	Fine	VF	XF	Unc
42b	1809 FW	—	3.00	7.00	15.00	80.00
	1810 FW	—	3.00	7.00	15.00	80.00

Obv: Crowned arms.

| 43a | 1809 FW | — | 3.00 | 6.00 | 15.00 | 75.00 |

Rev. value: 1 PFENNIG.

| 43b | 1810 FW | — | 3.00 | 6.00 | 15.00 | 75.00 |

Obv: Crowned GH monogram.

| 65 | 1816 FW | — | 3.00 | 6.00 | 12.00 | 65.00 |
| | 1817 FW | — | 3.00 | 6.00 | 12.00 | 65.00 |

C#	Date	Mintage	Fine	VF	XF	Unc
66	1816 FW	—	3.00	6.00	12.00	65.00
	1817 W	—	3.00	6.00	12.00	65.00

Obv: Crowned Waldeck-Pyrmont arms.

| 67 | 1821 FW | — | 2.50 | 5.00 | 10.00 | 50.00 |

Obv: Arms in beaded border.

| 67a | 1821 FW | — | 2.50 | 5.00 | 10.00 | 50.00 |

Obv: Crowned draped arms.

| 68 | 1825 FW | — | 3.00 | 6.00 | 15.00 | 75.00 |

69	1842A	.352	2.00	4.00	8.00	40.00
	1843A	.220	2.00	4.00	8.00	40.00
	1845A	.384	2.00	4.00	8.00	40.00

| 85 | 1855A | .366 | 1.50 | 3.00 | 6.00 | 35.00 |

| 85a | 1867B | .540 | 1.50 | 3.00 | 6.00 | 35.00 |

3 PFENNIG
COPPER
Obv: Crowned F monogram, leg: FURSTL. WALDECK SCH. MUNZ. Rev. value: III PFENNIGE.

| 44a | 1809 FW | — | 4.00 | 8.00 | 20.00 | 125.00 |
| | 1810 FW | — | 4.00 | 8.00 | 20.00 | 125.00 |

Obv: Crowned star arms.

| 45 | 1809 FW | — | 4.00 | 8.00 | 25.00 | 125.00 |

Obv: Arms within pearl circle.

| 45a | 1810 FW | — | 7.00 | 10.00 | 30.00 | 150.00 |

| 70 | 1819 FW | — | 3.00 | 6.00 | 15.00 | 75.00 |

Rev. value: PFENNIG

| 70b | 1819 FW | — | 3.00 | 6.00 | 15.00 | 75.00 |

| 70a | 1819 FW | — | 3.00 | 6.00 | 15.00 | 75.00 |

| 71 | 1824 FW | — | 3.00 | 6.00 | 12.00 | 65.00 |
| | 1825 FW | — | 3.00 | 6.00 | 12.00 | 65.00 |

Waldeck-Pyrmont / GERMAN STATES 704

C#	Date	Mintage	Fine	VF	XF	Unc
72	1842A	.247	2.50	5.00	10.00	50.00
	1843A	.114	2.50	5.00	10.00	50.00
	1845A	.249	2.50	5.00	10.00	50.00

| 86 | 1855A | .243 | 2.00 | 4.00 | 8.00 | 40.00 |

| 86.1 | 1867B | .420 | 2.00 | 4.00 | 8.00 | 40.00 |

1/2 GROSCHEN

COPPER

| 46 | 1809 FW | — | 20.00 | 45.00 | 90.00 | 175.00 |

Obv: Crowned draped arms.

| 73 | 1825 FW | — | 20.00 | 40.00 | 80.00 | 150.00 |

GROSCHEN
(Marien)

1.3900 g, .312 SILVER, .0139 oz ASW

| 74 | 1814 FW | — | 6.00 | 12.00 | 25.00 | 100.00 |
| | 1820 FW | — | 6.00 | 12.00 | 25.00 | 100.00 |

| 74a | 1820 FW | — | — | Rare | — |

Obv: Crowned draped arms.

| 74b | 1820 FW | — | 6.00 | 12.00 | 25.00 | 100.00 |
| | 1823 FW | — | 6.00 | 12.00 | 25.00 | 100.00 |

(Silber)

Obv: Inscription WALDECK U.P.

C#	Date	Mintage	Fine	VF	XF	Unc
76	1836 AW	.164	6.00	12.00	25.00	100.00
	1839 AW	.046	6.00	12.00	25.00	100.00

Obv: Inscription WALDECK U. PYRMONT

77	1842A	.310	4.00	8.00	17.50	75.00
	1843A	.191	4.00	8.00	17.50	75.00
	1845A	.182	4.00	8.00	17.50	75.00

Rev: A below value and date.

| 87 | 1855A | .156 | 5.00 | 10.00 | 20.00 | 80.00 |

| 87a | 1867B | .180 | 4.00 | 8.00 | 17.50 | 65.00 |

2 MARIENGROSCHEN

2.3900 g, .375 SILVER, .0288 oz ASW

78	1820 FW	—	5.00	10.00	30.00	150.00
	1822 FW	—	5.00	10.00	30.00	150.00
	1823 FW	—	5.00	10.00	30.00	150.00
	1824 FW	—	5.00	10.00	30.00	150.00
	1825 FW	—	5.00	10.00	30.00	150.00

Rev: A.W. below value.

| 78a | 1827 AW | — | 5.00 | 10.00 | 30.00 | 150.00 |
| | 1828 AW | — | 5.00 | 10.00 | 30.00 | 150.00 |

24 EINEN (1/24) THALER

1.9800 g, .368 SILVER, .0234 oz ASW

| 75 | 1818 FW | — | 5.00 | 10.00 | 30.00 | 150.00 |
| | 1819 FW | — | 5.00 | 10.00 | 30.00 | 150.00 |

1/6 THALER

5.3400 g, .520 SILVER, .0892 oz ASW

| 79 | 1837 AW | .034 | 15.00 | 30.00 | 75.00 | 200.00 |

| 79a | 1843A | .038 | 15.00 | 30.00 | 75.00 | 200.00 |
| | 1845A | .038 | 15.00 | 30.00 | 75.00 | 200.00 |

IV EINEN (1/4) THALER

7.0000 g, .620 SILVER, .1395 oz ASW

C#	Date	Mintage	Fine	VF	XF	Unc
53	1810 FW	—	100.00	200.00	375.00	700.00

Rev: Date and value in larger letters.

| 53a | 1810 FW | — | 75.00 | 150.00 | 300.00 | 600.00 |

Obv. leg. ends: PYRMONT &.

| 62 | 1812 FW | — | 600.00 | 1250. | 1750. | 2250. |

Obv. leg. ends: PYRMONT EC

| 62a | 1813 FW | — | 600.00 | 1250. | 1750. | 2250. |

3 EINEN (1/3) THALER

8.8000 g, .620 SILVER, .1754 oz ASW

| 80 | 1824 FW | — | 60.00 | 120.00 | 250.00 | 375.00 |

| 80a | 1824 FW | — | 60.00 | 120.00 | 250.00 | 375.00 |

| 81 | 1824 FW | — | 60.00 | 120.00 | 250.00 | 375.00 |

THALER

28.0600 g, .833 SILVER, .7515 oz ASW
Obv. leg: FRIDERICUS PR. ....

C#	Date	Mintage	Fine	VF	XF	Unc
59	1810 FW	—	400.00	700.00	1500.	3500.

2 THALER
(3-1/2 Gulden)

MONETARY REFORM
5 MARK

27.7770 g, .900 SILVER, .8038 oz ASW

C#	Date	Mintage	Fine	VF	XF	Unc
213	1903A	2,000	600.00	1300.	2500.	3250.
	1903A	300 pcs.	—	—	Proof	3750.

20 MARK

7.9650 g, .900 GOLD, .2304 oz AGW

214	1903A	2,000	1000.	2000.	2500.	3250.
	1903A	150 pcs.	—	—	Proof	6500.

WALLMODEN-GIMBORN

The town of Gimborn, located in Westphalia, was purchased from Schwarzenberg in 1782. The following year it was raised to the rank of county. In 1806, Wallmoden-Gimborn was annexed to Berg. In 1815, the land went to Prussia.

RULERS
Johann Ludwig, 1782-1806

1/24 THALER

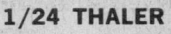

1.9900 g, .368 SILVER, .0235 oz ASW

1	1802	—	45.00	100.00	175.00	325.00

1/2 THALER

Obv. leg: FRIDERICUS D.G. PR. . . . .

59a	1810 FW	—	600.00	1100.	2500.	5200.

14.0300 g, .833 SILVER, .3757 oz ASW

2	1802	—	150.00	300.00	500.00	900.00

TRADE COINAGE
DUCAT

3.5000 g, .986 GOLD, .1109 oz AGW

3	1802	400 pcs.	900.00	2000.	3500.	5000.

WESTPHALIA

A kingdom, located in western Germany, created by Napoleon for his brother. It was comprised of parts of Hesse-Cassel, Brunswick, Hildesheim, Paderborn, Halberstadt, Osnabruck, Minden, etc. In 1813 and 1814, Westphalia was divided and returned to its former owners.

RULERS
Jerome (Hieronymus) Napoleon, 1807-1813

MINT MARKS

63	1813 FW	—	600.00	1100.	2500.	5000.

29.5170 g, .868 SILVER, .8237 oz ASW
Similar to C#63.
Edge inscription: KRONEN THALER

64	1813 FW	—	600.00	1100.	2500.	5000.

Similar to C#63.
Edge inscription: WALDECKISCHER

64a	1813 FW	—	600.00	1100.	2500.	5000.

Edge: Stars

64b	1813 FW	—	600.00	1100.	2500.	5000.

37.1200 g, .900 SILVER, 1.0742 oz ASW

C#	Date	Mintage	Fine	VF	XF	Unc
83	1842A	4,500	350.00	700.00	1200.	2000.
	1845A	4,500	350.00	700.00	1200.	2000.

Rev: Similar to C#83.

84	1847A	1,000	650.00	1100.	1900.	3250.

29.4500 g, .868 SILVER, .8218 oz ASW

82	1824 FW	—	200.00	350.00	700.00	1400.

18.5200 g, .900 SILVER, .5358 oz ASW

88	1859A	.014	40.00	85.00	165.00	325.00
	1867A	.019	40.00	85.00	165.00	325.00

89	1856A	.011	300.00	500.00	1000.	1700.

Westphalia / GERMAN STATES

B - Brunswick
C.C. - Cassel, mm on rev.
C.C. - Clausthal, mm on obv.
C & eagle head - Cassel
F - Cassel
J & horse head - Cassel
J & horse head - Paris

MINTMASTER'S INITIALS

Letter	Date	Name
F	1783-1831	Dietrich Heinrich Fulda in Cassel

GERMAN STANDARD

PFENNIG

COPPER

C#	Date	Mintage	Fine	VF	XF	Unc
1	1808C	—	5.00	12.00	22.00	50.00

2 PFENNIG

COPPER
Obv: Crowned HN monogram. Rev: Value.

2	1808C	—	5.00	10.00	20.00	65.00
	1810C	—	5.00	12.00	25.00	75.00

4 PFENNIG

BILLON SILVER

3	1808C	—	15.00	25.00	40.00	110.00
3a	1809C	—	10.00	15.00	30.00	70.00

MARIENGROSCHEN

BILLON SILVER

4	1808C	—	6.00	12.00	25.00	90.00
	1810C	—	6.00	12.00	35.00	100.00

24 MARIENGROSCHEN

17.3200 g, .750 SILVER, .4177 oz ASW

12	1810B	—	50.00	135.00	265.00	425.00

24 EINEN (1/24) THALER

1.9900 g, .368 SILVER, .0235 oz ASW
Obv: Crowned HN monogram w/ribbons. Rev: Value.

17	1807 F	—	12.00	25.00	50.00	125.00
	1808/7 F	—	10.00	25.00	45.00	125.00
	1808 F	—	10.00	20.00	40.00	100.00
	1809 F	—	15.00	25.00	55.00	140.00

Obv: Crown w/o ribbons.

17a	1809C	—	10.00	20.00	40.00	150.00

12 EINEN (1/12) THALER

3.3400 g, .437 SILVER, .0469 oz ASW

5	1808C	—	10.00	25.00	60.00	175.00
	1809C	—	10.00	25.00	60.00	175.00
	1810C	—	10.00	25.00	60.00	175.00

1/6 THALER
(Reichs)

3.1800 g, .994 SILVER, .1016 oz ASW

C#	Date	Mintage	Fine	VF	XF	Unc
6	1808C	—	15.00	30.00	75.00	150.00
	1812C	—	15.00	30.00	75.00	150.00
6a	1810C	—	30.00	75.00	175.00	325.00

5.8500 g, .500 SILVER, .0939 oz ASW

11	1808B	—	12.50	30.00	65.00	125.00
	1809B	—	12.50	30.00	65.00	125.00
	1810B	—	12.50	30.00	65.00	125.00
	1812B	—	12.50	30.00	65.00	125.00
	1813B	—	12.50	30.00	65.00	125.00

18	1808 F	—	10.00	20.00	50.00	110.00
	1809 C	—	10.00	20.00	50.00	110.00
	1809 F	—	10.00	20.00	50.00	110.00
	1810 C	—	10.00	20.00	50.00	110.00
	1810 F	—	10.00	20.00	50.00	110.00
	1813 C	—	10.00	20.00	50.00	110.00

2/3 THALER
(Reichs)

13.0800 g, .994 SILVER, .4180 oz ASW

7	1808C	—	40.00	80.00	150.00	300.00
	1810C	—	40.00	80.00	150.00	300.00

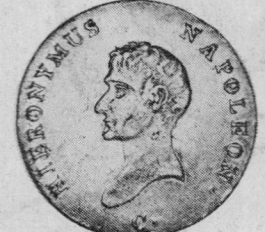

Rev: Similar to C#7.

7a	1809C	—	75.00	150.00	250.00	400.00
	1810C	—	75.00	125.00	225.00	325.00

8	1811C	—	50.00	100.00	200.00	400.00

C#	Date	Mintage	Fine	VF	XF	Unc
9	1811C	—	50.00	100.00	150.00	300.00
	1812C	—	60.00	125.00	175.00	350.00
	1813C	—	50.00	100.00	150.00	300.00

THALER

28.0600 g, .833 SILVER, .7515 oz ASW

19	1810C	5 pcs.	—	—	20,000.	30,000.

20	1810C	—	125.00	225.00	400.00	975.00
	1811C	—	125.00	225.00	400.00	975.00
	1812C	—	125.00	225.00	400.00	975.00

20a	1811C	—	125.00	225.00	400.00	975.00
	1812C	—	125.00	225.00	400.00	975.00
	1813C	—	125.00	225.00	400.00	975.00

(Mining)

Obv: Similar to C#20a, but top of head closer to rim.

C#	Date	Mintage	Fine	VF	XF	Unc
10	1811C	—	250.00	500.00	1000.	2000.

Obv: Similar to C#10 but small bust.

| 10a | 1811C | — | 275.00 | 550.00 | 1100. | 2200. |

V (5) THALER

6.6500 g, .900 GOLD, .1924 oz AGW

| 13 | 1810B | — | 1000. | 2400. | 3750. | 8500. |

Obv: Bust left w/o laurel wreath.

| 14 | 1811B | — | — | — | — | — |

14a	1811B	—	900.00	2000.	4000.	6000.
	1812B	—	800.00	1750.	3500.	5000.
	1813B	—	900.00	2000.	4000.	6000.

X (10) THALER

13.3000 g, .900 GOLD, .3848 oz AGW

| 15 | 1810B | — | 1000. | 2000. | 4000. | 6000. |

Obv: Bust left, w/o laurel wreath.

| 16 | 1811B | — | — | — | — | — |

16a	1811B	—	550.00	1650.	3000.	4500.
	1812B	—	550.00	1650.	3000.	4500.
	1813B	—	475.00	1650.	2500.	4000.

FRENCH STANDARD
CENTIME

COPPER

| 21 | 1809C | — | 2.50 | 7.50 | 20.00 | 50.00 |
| | 1812C | — | 2.50 | 7.50 | 20.00 | 50.00 |

2 CENTIMES

COPPER

C#	Date	Mintage	Fine	VF	XF	Unc
22	1808C	—	2.50	5.00	17.50	55.00
	1809C	—	2.50	5.00	17.50	55.00
	1810C	—	2.50	5.00	17.50	55.00
	1812C	—	2.50	5.00	17.50	55.00
22a	1808J	—	25.00	50.00	100.00	225.00

3 CENTIMES

COPPER

23	1808C	—	2.50	5.00	20.00	55.00
	1809C	—	2.50	5.00	20.00	55.00
	1810C	—	2.50	5.00	17.50	55.00
	1812C	—	2.50	5.00	17.50	55.00
23a	1808J	—	25.00	50.00	100.00	225.00

5 CENTIMES

COPPER

24	1808C	—	2.50	5.00	25.00	65.00
	1809C	—	2.50	5.00	20.00	65.00
	1812C	—	2.50	5.00	20.00	65.00
24a	1808J	—	25.00	50.00	100.00	225.00
	1809J	—	—	—	Rare	

10 CENTIMES

1.9700 g, .200 SILVER, .0126 oz ASW

25	1808C	—	3.00	12.50	35.00	80.00
	1809C	—	3.00	12.50	35.00	80.00
	1810C	—	3.00	12.50	35.00	80.00
	1812C	—	3.00	12.50	35.00	80.00

20 CENTIMES

3.8700 g, .200 SILVER, .0248 oz ASW

26	1808C	—	4.00	17.50	40.00	110.00
	1810C	—	4.00	17.50	40.00	110.00
	1812C	—	4.00	17.50	40.00	110.00

1/2 FRANK

2.5000 g, .900 SILVER, .0723 oz ASW

| 27a | 1808J | — | 100.00 | 225.00 | 450.00 | 650.00 |

FRANK

5.0000 g, .900 SILVER, .1447 oz ASW

C#	Date	Mintage	Fine	VF	XF	Unc
28	1808J	—	150.00	325.00	625.00	1000.

2 FRANKEN

10.0000 g, .900 SILVER, .2894 oz ASW

| 29 | 1808J | — | 225.00 | 450.00 | 750.00 | 1250. |

5 FRANKEN

25.0000 g, .900 SILVER, .7235 oz ASW

| 30 | 1808J | — | 500.00 | 1000. | 2000. | 3500. |
| 30a | 1809J | — | 500.00 | 1000. | 2000. | 3500. |

1.6200 g, .900 GOLD, .0469 oz AGW

| 31 | 1813C | — | 150.00 | 350.00 | 500.00 | 950.00 |

10 FRANKEN

3.2300 g, .900 GOLD, .0936 oz AGW

| 32 | 1813C | — | 250.00 | 600.00 | 900.00 | 1250. |

20 FRANKEN

6.4500 g, .900 GOLD, .1868 oz AGW

33	1808J	—	225.00	400.00	800.00	1500.
	1809J	—	225.00	400.00	800.00	1500.
33a	1808C	.013	225.00	350.00	800.00	1500.
	1809C	9,104	225.00	350.00	800.00	1500.
	1811C	.019	225.00	350.00	800.00	1500.
	1813C	—	500.00	1000.	1500.	4000.

Mint mark: Horse's head

| 33b | 1809C | — | — | — | — | 500.00 |

W/o inscription (restrikes ca. 1867).

| 33c | — | — | — | — | — | — |

40 FRANKEN

12.9000 g, .900 GOLD, .3733 oz AGW

C#	Date	Mintage	Fine	VF	XF	Unc
34	1813C	80 pcs.	2000.	4000.	7500.	12,000.

W/o edge inscription (restrikes ca. 1867).

| 34a | 1813C | 5,385 | — | — | 2200. | 4000. |

WISMAR

A seaport on the Baltic, the city of Wismar is said to have obtained municipal rights from Mecklenburg in 1229. It was an important member of the Hanseatic League in the 13th and 14th centuries. Their coinage began at the end of the 13th century and terminated in 1854. They belonged to Sweden from 1648 to 1803. A special plate money was struck by the Swedes in 1715 when the town was under siege. In 1803, Sweden sold Wismar to Mecklenburg-Schwerin. The transaction was confirmed in 1815.

RULERS
Swedish, 1648-1803
Friedrich Franz I, 1785-1837
Paul Friedrich, 1837-1842
Friedrich Franz II, 1842-1883

MINTMASTER'S INITIALS
FL - F. Lautersack
FS - Friedrich Schmidt
HM - Joachim Heinrich Meese
ICM - Carl Johann Joachim Mau
IZ - Johann Joachim Zeller
S - Heinrich Schroeder

UNDER MECKLENBURG-SCHWERIN
3 PFENING

COPPER

C#	Date	Mintage	Fine	VF	XF	Unc
3	1824 FL	—	—	—	—	—
	1824 IZ	—	2.50	5.00	10.00	55.00
	1825 IZ	—	2.50	5.00	10.00	55.00

Obv: MONETA.

3b	1829 HM	—	2.50	5.00	10.00	55.00
	1830 HM	—	2.50	5.00	10.00	55.00
3d	1840 FS	—	2.50	5.00	10.00	55.00
3e	1845 S	—	2.50	5.00	10.00	55.00

| 3a | 1835 ICM | — | 2.50 | 5.00 | 10.00 | 55.00 |

| 3c | 1840 FS | — | 2.50 | 5.00 | 10.00 | 55.00 |

C#	Date	Mintage	Fine	VF	XF	Unc
4	1854 S	—	2.50	5.00	10.00	55.00

WÜRTTEMBERG

Located in South Germany, between Baden and Bavaria, Württemberg obtained the mint right in 1374. In 1495 the rulers became dukes. In 1802 the duke exchanged some of his land on the Rhine with France for territories nearer his capital city. Napoleon elevated the duke to the status of elector in 1803 and made him a king in 1806. The kingdom joined the German Empire in 1871 and endured until the king abdicated in 1918.

RULERS
Friedrich, as Duke Friedrich II, 1797-1803
  As Elector Friedrich I, 1803-1806
  As King Friedrich I, 1806-1816
Wilhelm I, 1816-1864
Karl I, 1864-1891
Wilhelm II, 1891-1918

MINTMASTER'S INITIALS
AD - Gottlob August Doell
CH,ICH - Johann Christian Heuglin
CS,C,Sch F - Christian Schnitzspahn
C VOIGT - Carl Friedrich Voigt
DFH,DH,FH - Daniel Friedrich Heuglin
IPR,PR,R - Johann Peter Rasp
PB - Peter Bruckman
S,VS - Veit Schrempf
SS - Simon Schnell
W,LW,ILW - Johann Ludwig Wagner

1/4 KREUZER

COPPER

C#	Date	Mintage	Fine	VF	XF	Unc
158	1842	.198	2.00	4.00	8.00	45.00
	1843	.118	2.00	4.00	8.00	45.00
	1852	—	2.00	4.00	8.00	45.00
	1853	—	2.00	4.00	8.00	45.00
	1854	—	2.00	4.00	8.00	45.00
	1855	—	2.00	4.00	8.00	45.00
	1856	—	2.00	4.00	8.00	45.00

159	1858	—	2.00	4.00	8.00	45.00
	1860	—	2.00	4.00	8.00	45.00
	1861	—	2.00	4.00	8.00	45.00
	1862	—	2.00	4.00	8.00	45.00
	1863	—	2.00	4.00	8.00	45.00
	1864	—	2.00	4.00	8.00	45.00

203	1865	—	2.00	4.00	8.00	40.00
	1866	—	2.00	4.00	8.00	40.00
	1867	—	2.00	4.00	8.00	40.00
	1868	—	2.00	4.00	8.00	40.00
	1869	—	2.00	4.00	8.00	40.00
	1871	—	2.00	4.00	8.00	40.00
	1872	—	2.00	4.00	8.00	40.00

1/2 KREUZER

BILLON

138	1812	—	3.00	6.00	15.00	75.00
	1813	.470	3.00	6.00	15.00	75.00
	1816	.126	3.00	6.00	15.00	75.00
	ND	—	3.00	6.00	15.00	75.00

Obv: Crowned W.

| 162 | ND | — | 10.00 | — | 30.00 | 175.00 |

Obv: Crowned W dividing date.

| A163 | 1818 | — | 7.00 | 10.00 | 20.00 | 120.00 |

C#	Date	Mintage	Fine	VF	XF	Unc
163	1824	.840	2.50	5.00	10.00	50.00
	1828	—	2.50	5.00	10.00	50.00
	1829	.780	2.50	5.00	10.00	50.00
	1831	.620	2.50	5.00	10.00	50.00
	1833	Inc. 1831	2.50	5.00	10.00	50.00
	1834	Inc. 1831	2.50	5.00	10.00	50.00
	1835	Inc. 1831	2.50	5.00	10.00	50.00
	1836	Inc. 1831	2.50	5.00	10.00	50.00
	1837	Inc. 1831	2.50	5.00	10.00	50.00

COPPER

160	1840	—	1.50	3.00	6.00	30.00
	1841	—	1.50	3.00	6.00	30.00
	1842	.452	1.50	3.00	6.00	30.00
	1844	—	1.50	3.00	6.00	30.00
	1845	—	1.50	3.00	6.00	30.00
	1846	—	1.50	3.00	6.00	30.00
	1847	—	1.50	3.00	6.00	30.00
	1848	—	1.50	3.00	6.00	30.00
	1849	—	1.50	3.00	6.00	30.00
	1850	—	1.50	3.00	6.00	30.00
	1851	—	1.50	3.00	6.00	30.00
	1852	—	1.50	3.00	6.00	30.00
	1853	—	1.50	3.00	6.00	30.00
	1854	—	1.50	3.00	6.00	30.00
	1855	—	1.50	3.00	6.00	30.00
	1856	—	1.50	3.00	6.00	30.00

161	1858	—	1.50	3.00	6.00	30.00
	1859	—	1.50	3.00	6.00	30.00
	1860	—	1.50	3.00	6.00	30.00
	1861	—	1.50	3.00	6.00	30.00
	1862	—	1.50	3.00	6.00	30.00
	1863	—	1.50	3.00	6.00	30.00
	1864	—	1.50	3.00	6.00	30.00

204	1865	—	1.50	3.00	6.00	30.00
	1866	—	1.50	3.00	6.00	30.00
	1867	—	1.50	3.00	6.00	30.00
	1868	—	1.50	3.00	6.00	30.00
	1869	—	1.50	3.00	6.00	30.00
	1870	.147	1.50	3.00	6.00	30.00
	1871	.290	1.50	3.00	6.00	30.00
	1872	.177	1.50	3.00	6.00	30.00

EIN (1) KREUZER

BILLON
Obv: Crowned FII. Rev: Value, branches reach middle of coin.

| 108a | 1801 | — | 7.00 | 15.00 | 30.00 | 125.00 |
| | 1802 | — | 7.00 | 15.00 | 30.00 | 125.00 |

Obv: Legends. Rev: Crowned arms.

| 122 | 1803 | — | 6.00 | 12.50 | 25.00 | 80.00 |
| | 1804 | — | 6.00 | 12.50 | 25.00 | 80.00 |

Obv: Crowned F II monogram, w/o leg.
Rev: Value above branches.

| 122a | 1805 | — | 6.00 | 12.50 | 25.00 | 80.00 |

Obv: Crowned FR monogram.

139	1807	—	5.00	10.00	20.00	60.00
	1808	—	5.00	10.00	20.00	60.00
	1809	—	5.00	10.00	20.00	60.00
	1810	—	5.00	10.00	20.00	60.00
	1811	—	5.00	10.00	20.00	60.00
	1812	—	5.00	10.00	20.00	60.00
	1813	.530	5.00	10.00	20.00	60.00
	1814	—	5.00	10.00	20.00	60.00
	1816	.630	5.00	10.00	20.00	60.00

Obv: Crowned W within wreath.

| 164 | 1818 | — | 7.50 | 15.00 | 30.00 | 100.00 |

C#	Date	Mintage	Fine	VF	XF	Unc
165	1824 W	.780	4.00	8.00	20.00	60.00
	1825 W	.300	4.00	8.00	20.00	60.00
	1826 W	—	4.00	8.00	20.00	60.00
	1827 W	—	4.00	8.00	20.00	60.00
	1828 W	—	4.00	8.00	20.00	60.00
	1829 W	—	4.00	8.00	20.00	60.00
	1830 W	—	4.00	8.00	20.00	60.00
	1831 W	—	4.00	8.00	20.00	60.00
	1832 W	—	4.00	8.00	20.00	60.00
	1833 W	—	4.00	8.00	20.00	60.00
	1834 W	—	4.00	8.00	20.00	60.00
	1835 W	—	4.00	8.00	20.00	60.00
	1836 W	—	4.00	8.00	20.00	60.00
	1837 W	—	4.00	8.00	20.00	60.00
	1838 W	—	4.00	8.00	20.00	60.00

.6200 g, .250 SILVER, .0049 oz ASW
Obv: Crowned arms, leg: WURTTEMBERG.
Rev: Value within wreath.

C#	Date	Mintage	Fine	VF	XF	Unc
166	1839	—	3.00	6.00	15.00	50.00
	1840	—	3.00	6.00	15.00	50.00
	1841	—	3.00	6.00	15.00	50.00
	1842	—	3.00	6.00	15.00	50.00

C#	Date	Mintage	Fine	VF	XF	Unc
166a	1842	—	1.50	3.00	6.00	40.00
	1843	—	1.50	3.00	6.00	40.00
	1844	—	1.50	3.00	6.00	40.00
	1845	—	1.50	3.00	6.00	40.00
	1846	—	1.50	3.00	6.00	40.00
	1847	—	1.50	3.00	6.00	40.00
	1848	—	1.50	3.00	6.00	40.00
	1849	—	1.50	3.00	6.00	40.00
	1850	—	1.50	3.00	6.00	40.00
	1851	—	1.50	3.00	6.00	40.00
	1852	—	1.50	3.00	6.00	40.00
	1853	—	1.50	3.00	6.00	40.00
	1854	—	1.50	3.00	6.00	40.00
	1855	—	1.50	3.00	6.00	40.00
	1856	—	1.50	3.00	6.00	40.00
	1857	—	1.50	3.00	6.00	40.00

.8300 g, .166 SILVER, .0044 oz ASW

C#	Date	Mintage	Fine	VF	XF	Unc
166b	1857	.095	1.50	3.00	6.00	30.00
	1858	.072	1.50	3.00	6.00	30.00
	1859	.050	1.50	3.00	6.00	30.00
	1860	.049	1.50	3.00	6.00	30.00
	1861	.097	1.50	3.00	6.00	30.00
	1862	.056	1.50	3.00	6.00	30.00
	1863	.098	1.50	3.00	6.00	30.00
	1864	.151	1.50	3.00	6.00	30.00

C#	Date	Mintage	Fine	VF	XF	Unc
205	1865/3	.086	1.50	3.00	6.00	30.00
	1865	.086	1.50	3.00	6.00	30.00
	1866	.078	1.50	3.00	6.00	30.00
	1867	.119	1.50	3.00	6.00	30.00
	1868	.119	1.50	3.00	6.00	30.00
	1869	.120	1.50	3.00	6.00	30.00
	1870	.126	1.50	3.00	6.00	30.00
	1871	—	1.50	3.00	6.00	30.00
	1872	.100	1.50	3.00	6.00	30.00
	1873	.080	1.50	3.00	6.00	30.00

3 KREUZER

1.3500 g, .333 SILVER, .0144 oz ASW
Obv: 3 in oval border. Rev: Date divided by W.

C#	Date	Mintage	Fine	VF	XF	Unc
110d	1801	—	10.00	20.00	50.00	100.00
	1802	—	10.00	20.00	50.00	100.00

Obv: F. II. monogram, W below inscription.
Rev: Crowned oval arms.

C#	Date	Mintage	Fine	VF	XF	Unc
124	1803	—	10.00	20.00	50.00	100.00

Rev: Crowned rectangular arms.

C#	Date	Mintage	Fine	VF	XF	Unc
124a	1804	—	5.00	10.00	20.00	100.00
	1805	—	5.00	10.00	20.00	100.00
	1806	—	5.00	10.00	20.00	100.00
	1086(error)	—	6.00	12.50	25.00	125.00

Obv: FR monogram. Rev: Crowned electoral arms.

C#	Date	Mintage	Fine	VF	XF	Unc
140	1806	—	10.00	35.00	75.00	275.00

C#	Date	Mintage	Fine	VF	XF	Unc
141	1807	—	5.00	10.00	20.00	100.00
	1808	—	5.00	10.00	20.00	100.00
	1809	—	5.00	10.00	20.00	100.00
	1810	—	5.00	10.00	20.00	100.00
	1811	—	5.00	10.00	20.00	100.00
	1812	—	5.00	10.00	20.00	100.00
	1813	—	5.00	10.00	20.00	100.00
	1814	.160	5.00	10.00	20.00	100.00

Obv: Crowned W within wreath. Rev: Value.

C#	Date	Mintage	Fine	VF	XF	Unc
167	1818	—	6.00	12.00	25.00	125.00

C#	Date	Mintage	Fine	VF	XF	Unc
168	1823	—	6.00	12.00	25.00	125.00

Obv: Date and W below head.

C#	Date	Mintage	Fine	VF	XF	Unc
168.1	1823 W	—	6.00	12.00	25.00	125.00
	1824 W	—	6.00	12.00	25.00	125.00
	1825 W	.380	6.00	12.00	25.00	125.00

C#	Date	Mintage	Fine	VF	XF	Unc
168a	1826	—	5.00	10.00	25.00	100.00
	1827	—	5.00	10.00	25.00	100.00
	1828	—	5.00	10.00	25.00	100.00
	1829	—	5.00	10.00	25.00	100.00
	1830	—	5.00	10.00	25.00	100.00
	1831	—	5.00	10.00	25.00	100.00
	1832	—	5.00	10.00	25.00	100.00
	1834	—	5.00	10.00	25.00	100.00
	1835	—	5.00	10.00	25.00	100.00
	1836	—	5.00	10.00	25.00	100.00
	1837	—	5.00	10.00	25.00	100.00

1.2900 g, .333 SILVER, .0138 oz ASW
Obv: Crowned rectangular arms, leg: WURTTEMBERG.
Rev: Value within wreath.

C#	Date	Mintage	Fine	VF	XF	Unc
169	1839	—	5.00	10.00	25.00	100.00
	1840	—	5.00	10.00	25.00	100.00
	1841	—	5.00	10.00	25.00	100.00
	1842	—	5.00	10.00	25.00	100.00

C#	Date	Mintage	Fine	VF	XF	Unc
169a	1842	—	1.50	3.00	6.00	40.00
	1843	—	1.50	3.00	6.00	40.00
	1844	—	1.50	3.00	6.00	40.00
	1845	—	1.50	3.00	6.00	40.00
	1846	—	1.50	3.00	6.00	40.00
	1847	—	1.50	3.00	6.00	40.00
	1848	—	1.50	3.00	6.00	40.00
	1849	—	1.50	3.00	6.00	40.00
	1850	—	1.50	3.00	6.00	40.00
	1851	—	1.50	3.00	6.00	40.00
	1852	—	1.50	3.00	6.00	40.00
	1853	—	1.50	3.00	6.00	40.00
	1854	—	1.50	3.00	6.00	40.00
	1855	—	1.50	3.00	6.00	40.00
	1856	—	1.50	3.00	6.00	40.00

6 KREUZER

2.7000 g, .333 SILVER, .0289 oz ASW

C#	Date	Mintage	Fine	VF	XF	Unc
126	1803W	—	15.00	40.00	100.00	225.00
	1804W	—	15.00	40.00	100.00	225.00

Obv: W/o W below monogram.

C#	Date	Mintage	Fine	VF	XF	Unc
126a	1804	—	15.00	40.00	100.00	225.00
	1805	—	15.00	40.00	100.00	225.00

Rev: Electoral arms.

C#	Date	Mintage	Fine	VF	XF	Unc
142	1806	—	15.00	40.00	100.00	200.00

Rev: Crowned arms w/flags in left half of shield.

C#	Date	Mintage	Fine	VF	XF	Unc
142a	1806	—	15.00	40.00	100.00	200.00

Rev: Arms dividing date.

C#	Date	Mintage	Fine	VF	XF	Unc
142b	1806	—	15.00	40.00	100.00	200.00

C#	Date	Mintage	Fine	VF	XF	Unc
143	1806	—	4.00	8.00	15.00	60.00
	1807	—	4.00	8.00	15.00	60.00
	1808	—	4.00	8.00	15.00	60.00
	1809	—	4.00	8.00	15.00	60.00
	1810	—	4.00	8.00	15.00	60.00
	1811	—	4.00	8.00	15.00	60.00
	1812	—	4.00	8.00	15.00	60.00
	1814	—	4.00	8.00	15.00	60.00

Obv: Crowned W within wreath. Rev: Value.

C#	Date	Mintage	Fine	VF	XF	Unc
170	1817	—	7.50	15.00	30.00	75.00
	1818	—	7.50	15.00	30.00	75.00
170a	1819	—	7.50	15.00	30.00	75.00
	1821	—	7.50	15.00	30.00	75.00

Obv: Head right, date below.
Rev: Crowned circular arms within wreath.

C#	Date	Mintage	Fine	VF	XF	Unc
171.1	1823	—	10.00	20.00	60.00	200.00

Obv: Narrower head.

C#	Date	Mintage	Fine	VF	XF	Unc
171.2	1823	—	10.00	20.00	60.00	200.00

Obv: WILHELM KON. . . .

C#	Date	Mintage	Fine	VF	XF	Unc
171.3	1823	—	10.00	20.00	60.00	200.00
	1825	—	10.00	20.00	60.00	200.00

Rev: Crowned tapered arms within branches.

C#	Date	Mintage	Fine	VF	XF	Unc
171a	1825	—	10.00	20.00	50.00	175.00
	1826	—	10.00	20.00	50.00	175.00
	1827	—	10.00	20.00	50.00	175.00
	1828	—	10.00	20.00	50.00	175.00
	1829	—	10.00	20.00	50.00	175.00
	1830	—	10.00	20.00	50.00	175.00
	1831	—	10.00	20.00	50.00	175.00
	1832	—	10.00	20.00	50.00	175.00
	1833	—	10.00	20.00	50.00	175.00
	1834	—	10.00	20.00	50.00	175.00
	1835	—	10.00	20.00	50.00	175.00
	1836	—	10.00	20.00	50.00	175.00
	1837	—	10.00	20.00	50.00	175.00

2.5900 g, .333 SILVER, .0277 oz ASW

C#	Date	Mintage	Fine	VF	XF	Unc
172	1838	—	5.00	10.00	20.00	85.00
	1839	—	5.00	10.00	20.00	85.00
	1840	—	5.00	10.00	20.00	85.00
	1841	—	5.00	10.00	20.00	85.00
	1842	—	5.00	10.00	20.00	85.00

C#	Date	Mintage	Fine	VF	XF	Unc
172a	1842	—	2.50	5.00	10.00	50.00
	1843	—	2.50	5.00	10.00	50.00
	1844	—	2.50	5.00	10.00	50.00
	1845	—	2.50	5.00	10.00	50.00
	1846	—	2.50	5.00	10.00	50.00
	1847	—	2.50	5.00	10.00	50.00
	1848	—	2.50	5.00	10.00	50.00
	1849	—	2.50	5.00	10.00	50.00
	1850	—	2.50	5.00	10.00	50.00
	1851	—	2.50	5.00	10.00	50.00
	1852	—	2.50	5.00	10.00	50.00
	1853	—	2.50	5.00	10.00	50.00
	1854	—	2.50	5.00	10.00	50.00
	1855	—	2.50	5.00	10.00	50.00
	1856	—	2.50	5.00	10.00	50.00

10 KREUZER
(Convention)

BILLON

| 128 | 1805 ILW | — | 80.00 | 150.00 | 300.00 | 550.00 |

Rev. leg: AD NORMAN.

| 144 | 1808 ILW | .025 | 80.00 | 150.00 | 300.00 | 550.00 |
| | 1809 ILW | .010 | 90.00 | 175.00 | 325.00 | 575.00 |

Obv. leg: FRIEDRICH KOENIG......
Rev. leg: NACH DEM.

| 145 | 1812 ILW | .026 | 90.00 | 175.00 | 325.00 | 575.00 |

Obv. leg: FRID. KOENIG......

| 145.1 | 1812 ILW | — | 90.00 | 175.00 | 325.00 | 575.00 |

| 173 | 1818 W | .152 | 80.00 | 150.00 | 300.00 | 550.00 |

| 174 | 1823 | .011 | 80.00 | 150.00 | 300.00 | 550.00 |

12 KREUZER

3.9000 g, .500 SILVER, .0627 oz ASW

C#	Date	Mintage	Fine	VF	XF	Unc
175	1824 W	.045	15.00	30.00	60.00	125.00

| 175a | 1825 W | .025 | 15.00 | 30.00 | 60.00 | 125.00 |

20 KREUZER
(Convention)

6.6800 g, .583 SILVER, .1251 oz ASW
Obv: Different bust left, leg: .... ELECTOR.
Rev: Crowned oval arms.

| 130 | 1805 W | — | 17.50 | 35.00 | 60.00 | 125.00 |

Obv. leg: WURTTEMB

146	1807 ILW	—	12.50	25.00	40.00	100.00
	1808 ILW	—	12.50	25.00	40.00	100.00
	1809 ILW	—	12.50	25.00	40.00	100.00
	1810 ILW	—	12.50	25.00	40.00	100.00

| 147 | 1810 ILW | — | 17.50 | 35.00 | 70.00 | 125.00 |
| | 1812 ILW | — | 17.50 | 35.00 | 70.00 | 125.00 |

Obv: Larger head.

| 147a | 1810 | — | 17.50 | 35.00 | 60.00 | 125.00 |

| 148 | 1812 ILW | .105 | 12.50 | 25.00 | 50.00 | 100.00 |

| 176 | 1818 W | .180 | 50.00 | 100.00 | 225.00 | 375.00 |

| 177 | 1823 W | .033 | 50.00 | 100.00 | 225.00 | 375.00 |

24 KREUZER

6.6800 g, .583 SILVER, .1251 oz ASW

C#	Date	Mintage	Fine	VF	XF	Unc
178	1824 W	—	50.00	100.00	225.00	375.00
	1825 W	—	50.00	100.00	225.00	375.00
	1825	—	50.00	100.00	225.00	375.00

1/2 GULDEN

5.2900 g, .900 SILVER, .1530 oz ASW
Obv: VOIGT under head.

179	1838	.824	15.00	50.00	100.00	200.00
	1839	.464	80.00	175.00	500.00	900.00
	1840	.516	15.00	35.00	75.00	150.00
	1841	.412	15.00	35.00	75.00	150.00
	1844	.154	100.00	200.00	400.00	800.00
	1845	.280	15.00	35.00	75.00	150.00
	1846	.338	15.00	35.00	75.00	150.00
	1847	.682	15.00	35.00	70.00	140.00
	1848	.498	15.00	35.00	70.00	140.00
	1849	.312	15.00	35.00	75.00	150.00
	1850	.286	15.00	35.00	75.00	150.00
	1852	.228	15.00	35.00	75.00	150.00
	1853	.192	15.00	35.00	75.00	150.00
	1854	.140	15.00	35.00	75.00	150.00
	1855	.112	15.00	35.00	75.00	150.00
	1856	.108	15.00	35.00	75.00	150.00
	1858	—	15.00	35.00	75.00	150.00

Obv: W/o VOIGT under head.

179a	1858	.219	15.00	90.00	150.00	250.00
	1859	.072	15.00	90.00	150.00	250.00
	1860	.299	15.00	40.00	80.00	160.00
	1861	.693	15.00	40.00	80.00	160.00
	1862	.149	15.00	50.00	100.00	200.00
	1863	—	15.00	50.00	100.00	200.00
	1864	.161	15.00	37.50	75.00	140.00

Obv: Head right w/C.S. on truncation.

206	1865 CS	.166	15.00	50.00	100.00	250.00
	1866 CS	.276	15.00	50.00	100.00	250.00
	1867 CS	.071	15.00	50.00	100.00	250.00
	1868 CS	.105	15.00	50.00	100.00	250.00

Obv: W/o C.S. on truncation.

206a	1868	Inc. Ab.	15.00	50.00	100.00	200.00
	1869	.072	15.00	50.00	100.00	200.00
	1870	.044	15.00	60.00	100.00	200.00
	1871	.041	15.00	60.00	100.00	200.00

GULDEN

12.7200 g, .750 SILVER, .3067 oz ASW

| 180 | 1824 W | .021 | 80.00 | 175.00 | 500.00 | 900.00 |

Wurttemberg / GERMAN STATES 711

C#	Date	Mintage	Fine	VF	XF	Unc
181	1825 W	—	150.00	300.00	600.00	1000.

10.6000 g, .900 SILVER, .3067 oz ASW
Obv: VOIGT under head.
Obv: WAGNER F at truncation, leg.: WURTTEMB.

182	1838	.712	15.00	50.00	100.00	200.00
	1839	.365	15.00	50.00	100.00	200.00
	1840	2.561	15.00	50.00	100.00	200.00
	1841	—	25.00	100.00	200.00	400.00
	1842	2.493	15.00	50.00	100.00	200.00
	1843	1.983	15.00	50.00	100.00	200.00
	1844	.379	15.00	50.00	100.00	200.00
	1845	.044	15.00	50.00	100.00	200.00
	1846	.042	15.00	50.00	100.00	200.00
	1847	.056	15.00	50.00	100.00	200.00
	1848/6	.058	17.50	60.00	125.00	250.00
	1848	Inc. Ab.	15.00	50.00	100.00	200.00
	1849	.129	15.00	50.00	100.00	200.00
	1850	.114	15.00	50.00	100.00	200.00
	1851	.096	15.00	50.00	100.00	200.00
	1852	.032	15.00	50.00	100.00	200.00
	1853	.235	15.00	50.00	100.00	200.00
	1854	.090	15.00	50.00	100.00	200.00
	1855	.223	15.00	50.00	100.00	200.00
	1856	—	15.00	50.00	100.00	200.00

Obv: A.D. below head.

182a	1837 AD	.443	25.00	100.00	150.00	300.00
	1838 AD	Inc.Ab.	25.00	100.00	150.00	300.00

Obv: W/o VOIGT below head.

182b	1839	—	35.00	75.00	150.00
	1840	—	15.00	35.00	75.00	150.00
	1841	—	25.00	75.00	125.00	250.00
182c	1848	Inc.Ab.	25.00	75.00	125.00	250.00

25th Anniversary of Reign

183	1841	—	20.00	35.00	60.00	100.00

Visit of King to New Mint

184	1844	—	650.00	1250.	2000.	3000.

NOTE: Restrikes exist.

Visit of Queen to Mint

C#	Date	Mintage	Fine	VF	XF	Unc
185	1845	17 pcs.	—	—	Rare	—

2 GULDEN

25.4500 gm., .750 SILVER, .6138 oz ASW

187	1824 W	.015	200.00	350.00	900.00	1800.

Obv: Larger head right.
Rev. leg. ends: SC.

187a	1824 ILW					
		Inc. Ab.	—	—	Rare	—

Obv: WAGNER F at truncation, leg: WURTTEMB.
Rev: Crowned pointed arms within branches.

188	1825 W	9,934	300.00	500.00	1200.	2600.

Obv: W/o name at bottom, leg: WURTTEMBERG.

188a	1825 W	Inc Ab	—	—	Rare	—

21.2100 g, .900 SILVER, .6138 oz ASW

C#	Date	Mintage	Fine	VF	XF	Unc
189	1845	.562	45.00	75.00	150.00	350.00
	1846	.621	45.00	75.00	150.00	350.00
	1847	1.160	45.00	75.00	150.00	350.00
	1848	.336	45.00	75.00	150.00	350.00
	1849	.486	45.00	75.00	150.00	350.00
	1850	.280	45.00	75.00	150.00	350.00
	1851	.140	45.00	75.00	150.00	350.00
	1852	.225	45.00	75.00	150.00	350.00
	1853	.175	45.00	75.00	150.00	350.00
	1854	.074	45.00	75.00	150.00	350.00
	1855	.133	45.00	75.00	150.00	350.00
	1856	.267	45.00	75.00	150.00	350.00

5 GULDEN

3.4250 g, .904 GOLD, .0997 oz AGW

198	1825 W	5.956	350.00	650.00	1000.	1800.

198a	1824 W	2.282	500.00	1100.	1800.	2500.
	1835 W	1.443	600.00	1400.	2200.	3000.

198b	1839 W	822 pcs.	800.00	1600.	2500.	3250.

10 GULDEN

6.8500 g, .904 GOLD, .1990 oz AGW

199	1824 W	1.896	900.00	1800.	2500.	4000.
	1825 W	1.240	900.00	1800.	2500.	4000.

Visit of King to Mint

200	1825 W	8 pcs.	—	—	—	15,000.

SILVER (OMS)

200a	1825 W	—	—	—	800.00

1/2 THALER

14.0300 g, .833 SILVER, .3759 oz ASW

132	1805 ILW	—	350.00	750.00	1500.	2000.

THALER
(Convention)

Wurttemberg / GERMAN STATES 712

28.0600 g, .833 SILVER, .7515 oz ASW

C#	Date	Mintage	Fine	VF	XF	Unc
134	1803	—	750.00	1200.	2500.	4500.

Obv. leg: D G REX WURT. S.R.I.AR.VEXILL.ET ELECT.

| 149 | 1806 | — | — | — | Rare | — |

C#	Date	Mintage	Fine	VF	XF	Unc
150	1809	—	—	—	Rare	—

Obv: Large head.

C#	Date	Mintage	Fine	VF	XF	Unc
A153	1810 ILW	—	300.00	800.00	2000.	4500.

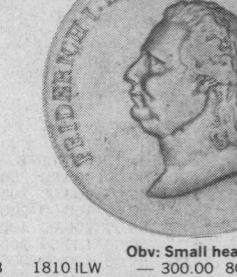

Obv: I.L.W. below bust, leg: WURTTEMBERGIAE.

| 150a | 1809 ILW | — | — | — | Rare | — |

(Kronen)

29.4900 g, .868 SILVER, .8230 oz ASW
Obv: Military bust; leg: . . . . .D.G.REX . . . .
Rev: Crowned arms between lion and stag.

| 151 | 1810 ILW | — | — | — | Rare | — |

Obv: Small head.

| 153 | 1810 ILW | — | 300.00 | 800.00 | 1750. | 4000. |

Obv. leg: D.G.REX WURTEMBERGIAE.

| 149a | 1806 | — | — | — | Rare | — |

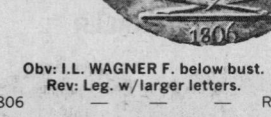

Obv: Military bust; leg: . . . . . I KOENIG . . . .

| 152 | 1810 ILW | — | — | — | Rare | — |

| 153a | 1811 ILW | 2,000 | 400.00 | 800.00 | 2000. | 4500. |

Obv: I.L. WAGNER F. below bust.
Rev: Leg. w/larger letters.

| 149b | 1806 | — | — | — | Rare | — |

| 154 | 1812 ILW | .015 | 300.00 | 600.00 | 1200. | 2500 |

(Convention)
28.0600 g, .833 SILVER, .7515 oz ASW
Obv: Head left, WAGNER F below.
Rev: Value within wreath.

C#	Date	Mintage	Fine	VF	XF	Unc
190	1817				Rare	—

| 190a | 1818 | — | 500.00 | 1000. | 2000. | 4500. |

(Kronen)

29.4900 g, .868 SILVER, .8230 oz ASW

| 191 | 1817 | .044 | 400.00 | 600.00 | 1500. | 3000. |

Rev: Similar to C#191.

| 191a | 1818 | Inc. Ab. | 300.00 | 550.00 | 1200. | 2500. |
| | 1818/7 | Inc. Ab. | — | — | — | — |

29.4900 g, .868 SILVER, .8231 oz ASW

C#	Date	Mintage	Fine	VF	XF	Unc
192	1825	.226	85.00	135.00	300.00	600.00
	1826	—	100.00	150.00	375.00	800.00
	1827	—	100.00	150.00	375.00	800.00
	1828	—	100.00	150.00	375.00	800.00
	1829	—	100.00	150.00	375.00	800.00
	1830 W under bust					
		6,695	100.00	150.00	375.00	800.00
	1831	9,074	100.00	150.00	375.00	800.00
	1832 W under bust					
		—	100.00	150.00	375.00	800.00
	1833	—	100.00	150.00	375.00	800.00

NOTE: Varieties exist.

Obv: W below truncation.

192a	1834 W	—	100.00	150.00	375.00	800.00
	1835 W	—	100.00	150.00	375.00	800.00
	1837 W	.170	85.00	135.00	300.00	600.00

Free Trade
Obv: Similar to C#192a.

| 193 | 1833 W | — | 75.00 | 125.00 | 225.00 | 450.00 |
| | 1833 LW | — | — | — | — | — |

(Vereins)

18.5200 g, .900 SILVER, .5360 oz ASW

186	1857	.452	25.00	55.00	135.00	275.00
	1858	.644	25.00	55.00	135.00	275.00
	1859	1.333	25.00	55.00	135.00	275.00
	1860	.645	25.00	55.00	135.00	275.00

C#	Date	Mintage	Fine	VF	XF	Unc
186	1861	.754	25.00	55.00	135.00	275.00
	1862	.648	25.00	55.00	135.00	275.00
	1863	.621	25.00	55.00	135.00	275.00
	1864	.533	25.00	55.00	135.00	275.00

| 207 | 1865 | .276 | 125.00 | 225.00 | 650.00 | 1500. |

Rev: Antlers extend into leg.

207a	1865	Inc. Ab.	40.00	75.00	200.00	475.00
	1866	.346	40.00	75.00	200.00	475.00
	1867	.165	40.00	75.00	200.00	475.00
207b	1868	.078	45.00	90.00	220.00	525.00
	1869	.031	50.00	100.00	240.00	550.00
	1870	.044	50.00	100.00	240.00	550.00

Victorious Conclusion of Franco-Prussian War
| 208 | 1871 C. SCH.F. | | | | | |
| | | .114 | 25.00 | 45.00 | 85.00 | 150.00 |

2 THALER
(3-1/2 Gulden)

37.1200 g, .900 SILVER, 1.0742 oz ASW

194	1840	.162	125.00	225.00	450.00	1000.
	1842	.051	175.00	300.00	600.00	1200.
	1843	.245	125.00	225.00	450.00	1000.
	1854	.168	125.00	225.00	450.00	1000.
	1855	Inc.Ab.	125.00	225.00	450.00	1000.

Wurttemberg / GERMAN STATES 714

Marriage of Crown Prince Carl to Olga, Grand Duchess of Russia
Rev: Similar to C#194.

C#	Date	Mintage	Fine	VF	XF	Unc
195	1846	5,808	100.00	200.00	375.00	750.00

GOLD (OMS)

195a 1846

37.0400 g, .900 SILVER, 1.0717 oz ASW
Restoration of Ulm Cathedral

209	1869	—	125.00	200.00	425.00	800.00
	1871	4,031	100.00	200.00	400.00	600.00

MONETARY REFORM
2 MARK

11.1110 g, .900 SILVER, .3215 oz ASW

Y#	Date	Mintage	Fine	VF	XF	Unc
215	1876F	1.550	30.00	75.00	525.00	1400.
	1877F	1.107	30.00	125.00	600.00	1700.
	1880F	.129	60.00	175.00	700.00	2300.
	1883F	.074	60.00	150.00	675.00	2000.
	1888F	.123	30.00	120.00	575.00	1600.
	1888F	—	—	—	Proof	1600.

220	1892	.177	16.00	45.00	95.00	200.00
	1893	.174	16.00	45.00	75.00	175.00
	1896	.351	12.00	28.00	50.00	125.00
	1898	.144	20.00	45.00	90.00	195.00
	1899	.538	12.00	19.00	35.00	125.00
	1900	.516	10.00	16.00	40.00	100.00
	1901	.592	12.00	19.00	40.00	100.00

Y#	Date	Mintage	Fine	VF	XF	Unc
220	1902	.816	10.00	17.00	45.00	100.00
	1903	.811	12.00	19.00	40.00	100.00
	1904	1.988	10.00	17.00	35.00	90.00
	1905	.610	12.00	21.00	35.00	90.00
	1906	1.505	12.00	21.00	50.00	90.00
	1907	1.504	10.00	15.00	30.00	90.00
	1908	.451	10.00	22.00	40.00	100.00
	1912	.251	10.00	16.00	35.00	90.00
	1913	.226	10.00	17.00	40.00	100.00
	1914	.316	10.00	17.00	45.00	100.00
Common date	—	—	—	—	Proof	175.00

3 MARK

16.6670 g, .900 SILVER, .4823 oz ASW

221	1908F	.300	10.00	17.50	25.00	55.00
	1909F	1.907	10.00	17.50	25.00	50.00
	1910F	.837	10.00	17.50	25.00	50.00
	1911F	.425	10.00	17.50	25.00	50.00
	1912F	.849	10.00	17.50	25.00	45.00
	1913F	.267	10.00	17.50	25.00	65.00
	1914F	.733	10.00	17.50	25.00	45.00
Common date	—	—	—	—	Proof	175.00

Silver Wedding Anniversary
Obv: Normal bar in H of CHARLOTTE.

225	1911F	.493	12.50	20.00	50.00	60.00
	1911F	—	—	—	Proof	125.00

Obv: High bar in H of CHARLOTTE.

225a	1911F	7,000	100.00	250.00	450.00	600.00

25th Year of Reign

226	1916F	1,000	—	—	Proof	4000.

NOTE: 650 pieces have been melted.

5 MARK

27.7770 g, .900 SILVER, .8038 oz ASW

216	1874F	.113	30.00	60.00	900.00	2400.
	1875F	.318	30.00	60.00	900.00	2000.
	1876F	.897	30.00	60.00	600.00	1700.
	1888F	.049	40.00	100.00	900.00	2100.

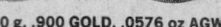

1.9910 g, .900 GOLD, .0576 oz AGW

Y#	Date	Mintage	Fine	VF	XF	Unc
217	1877F	.488	100.00	200.00	250.00	425.00
	1877 F	—	—	—	Proof	1300.
	1878F	.050	325.00	650.00	1250.	2000.

27.7770 g, .900 SILVER, .8038 oz ASW

222	1892F	.069	20.00	70.00	200.00	400.00
	1893F	.071	20.00	70.00	200.00	400.00
	1894F	.020	150.00	400.00	1250.	2000.
	1895F	.201	20.00	40.00	175.00	350.00
	1898F	.216	15.00	30.00	175.00	350.00
	1899F	.112	15.00	30.00	175.00	350.00
	1900F	.211	15.00	30.00	85.00	275.00
	1901F	.211	15.00	30.00	85.00	275.00
	1902F	.361	15.00	30.00	85.00	275.00
	1903F	.722	15.00	30.00	70.00	250.00
	1904F	.391	15.00	30.00	70.00	250.00
	1906F	.045	25.00	60.00	200.00	400.00
	1907F	.436	15.00	30.00	70.00	150.00
	1908F	.522	15.00	30.00	60.00	150.00
	1913F	.341	15.00	30.00	55.00	150.00
Common date	—	—	—	—	Proof	300.00

10 MARK

3.9820 g, .900 GOLD, .1152 oz AGW
Rev: Type I.

218	1872F	.271	65.00	100.00	200.00	300.00
	1872F	—	—	—	Proof	1300.
	1873F	.675	65.00	100.00	200.00	300.00
	1873F	—	—	—	Proof	1300.

Rev: Type II.

218a	1874F	.205	65.00	120.00	170.00	300.00
	1875F	.532	65.00	120.00	150.00	250.00
	1876F	.933	65.00	120.00	160.00	300.00
	1876F	—	—	—	Proof	1300.
	1877F	.271	65.00	120.00	170.00	300.00
	1878F	.337	65.00	120.00	160.00	300.00
	1879F	.211	65.00	120.00	160.00	275.00
	1880F	.245	65.00	120.00	170.00	300.00
	1881F	.079	75.00	150.00	200.00	325.00
	1888F	.200	65.00	120.00	160.00	275.00
	1888F	—	—	—	Proof	1300.

Rev: Type III.

218b	1890F	.220	90.00	130.00	190.00	275.00
	1891F	.080	100.00	150.00	225.00	400.00

223	1893F	.300	65.00	100.00	165.00	225.00
	1896F	.200	65.00	100.00	165.00	225.00
	1898F	.420	65.00	100.00	165.00	225.00
	1900F	.090	80.00	125.00	175.00	225.00
	1901F	.110	65.00	125.00	175.00	225.00
	1902F	.050	125.00	150.00	200.00	250.00
	1903F	.180	65.00	100.00	165.00	225.00
	1904F	.350	65.00	100.00	150.00	225.00
	1904F	—	—	—	Proof	800.00
	1905F	.200	65.00	100.00	150.00	225.00
	1905F	—	—	—	Proof	800.00
	1906F	.100	65.00	100.00	165.00	225.00

Y#	Date	Mintage	Fine	VF	XF	Unc
223	1906F	50 pcs.	—	—	Proof	800.00
	1907F	.150	65.00	100.00	150.00	225.00
	1907F	—	—	—	Proof	800.00
	1909F	.100	65.00	125.00	150.00	225.00
	1909F	—	—	—	Proof	800.00
	1910F	.150	65.00	125.00	175.00	225.00
	1910F	—	—	—	Proof	800.00
	1911F	.050	140.00	275.00	425.00	550.00
	1911F	—	—	—	Proof	800.00
	1912F	.049	140.00	275.00	425.00	650.00
	1912F	—	—	—	Proof	800.00
	1913F	.050	140.00	275.00	425.00	550.00
	1913F	—	—	—	Proof	800.00

20 MARK

7.9650 g, .900 GOLD, .2304 oz AGW
Rev: Type I.

219	1872F	.662	115.00	125.00	175.00	425.00
	1872F	—	—	—	Proof	1900
	1873F	1.352	115.00	125.00	175.00	425.00
	1873F	—	—	—	Proof	1900

Rev: Type II.

219a	1874F	.322	115.00	125.00	200.00	450.00
	1876F	.359	115.00	125.00	200.00	450.00

Rev: Type III.

224	1894F	.501	BV	115.00	140.00	250.00
	1897F	.400	BV	115.00	140.00	250.00
	1897F	—	—	—	Proof	700.00
	1898F	.106	BV	115.00	165.00	275.00
	1900F	.500	BV	115.00	140.00	250.00
	1900F	—	—	—	Proof	700.00
	1905F	.501	BV	115.00	140.00	250.00
	1905F	—	—	—	Proof	500.00
	1913F	.043	4000.	7500.	12,000.	18,000.
	1913F	—	—	—	Proof	60,000.
	1914F	.558	3800.	7500.	12,000.	18,000.
	1914F	—	—	—	Proof	60,000.

TRADE COINAGE
DUCAT

3.5000 g, .986 GOLD, .1109 oz AGW
Visit of Duke to Mint
Obv: Bust right. Rev: IN HOCHST..... within wreath.

C#	Date	Mintage	Fine	VF	XF	Unc
136	1803 ILW	—	—	—	—	Rare

Rev. leg. DEN 9. IAN 1804 added.

| 136a | 1804 ILW | — | — | — | — | Rare |

Rev: Crowned circular arms within branches.

| 137 | 1804 CH | — | 500.00 | 1000. | 2000. | 3500. |

C#	Date	Mintage	Fine	VF	XF	Unc
155	1808 CH	—	500.00	1000.	2000.	3500.

| 156 | 1813 ILW | — | 600.00 | 1250. | 2500. | 4000. |

| 196 | 1818 W | — | 600.00 | 1250. | 2500. | 3500. |

197	1840	.081	175.00	350.00	525.00	850.00
	1841/0	.232	150.00	300.00	425.00	750.00
	1841	Inc. Ab.	150.00	300.00	425.00	750.00
	1842	.025	175.00	350.00	525.00	850.00
	1848	.062	175.00	350.00	525.00	850.00

4 DUCATS

14.0000 g, .986 GOLD, .4438 oz AGW
25th Anniversary of Reign

| 201 | 1841 | 6,236 | 500.00 | 1000. | 1500. | 2500. |

Visit of King to Mint

| 202 | 1844 | 17 pcs. | 2500. | 4000. | 7500. | 10,000. |

FREDERICK D'OR = 1 KAROLIN

6.6500 g, .900 GOLD, .1924 oz AGW

| 157 | 1810 ILW | — | 1500. | 3000. | 6000. | 9000. |

WURZBURG
BISHOPRIC

A Bishopric, located in Franconia, was established in 741. The mint right was obtained in the 11th century. The first coins were struck c. 1040. In 1441 the bishops were confirmed as dukes. In 1803 the area was secularized and granted to Bavaria. It was made a grand duchy in 1806 but the 1815 Congress of Vienna returned it to Bavaria.

RULERS

Georg Carl, Freiherr von Fechenbach
Bishop, 1795-1803
Ferdinand, Grand Duke, 1806-1814

MONETARY SYSTEM
3 Drier (Kortling) = 1 Shillinger
7 Shillinger = 15 Kreuzer
28 Shillinger = 1 Guter Gulden
44-4/5 Shillinger = 1 Convention Thaler

VIERTEL (1/4) KREUZER

COPPER

C#	Date	Mintage	Fine	VF	XF	Unc
151	1811	—	4.00	8.00	35.00	150.00

1/2 KREUZER

COPPER

152	1810	—	5.00	10.00	40.00	150.00
	1811	—	5.00	10.00	40.00	150.00

KREUZER

SILVER
Obv: Crowned arms, dividing G.W.L.M. above. Rev: Value.

| 153 | 1808 | — | 4.00 | 7.00 | 25.00 | 120.00 |

Obv: W/o legend.

| 153a | 1808 | — | 4.00 | 7.00 | 25.00 | 120.00 |

Rev: Value and G.W.L.M.

| 153b | 1808 | — | 4.00 | 7.00 | 25.00 | 120.00 |

3 KREUZER

SILVER

154	1807	—	4.00	8.00	30.00	120.00
	1808	—	4.00	8.00	30.00	120.00
	1809	—	4.00	8.00	30.00	120.00

6 KREUZER

SILVER
Obv: Large crown.

155	1807	—	7.00	15.00	50.00	150.00
	1808	—	7.00	15.00	50.00	150.00

Obv: Small crown.

| 155a | 1809 | — | 7.00 | 15.00 | 50.00 | 150.00 |

TRADE COINAGE
GOLDGULDEN

3.2500 g, .770 GOLD, .0805 oz AGW
Obv: Head of Ferdinand right.
Rev: Palm tree, arms, value and date.

159	1807	—	1000.	1800.	2800.	3500.
	1809	—	1000.	1800.	2800.	3500.

Wurzburg / GERMAN STATES 716

C#	Date	Mintage	Fine	VF	XF	Unc
160	1812R	—	1000.	1800.	2800.	3500.

Rev: Crowned battle flag; value and date.

| 161 | 1813R | — | 4000. | 7000. | 10,000. | 12,500. |

| 162 | 1814R | — | 3000. | 5000. | 8000. | 10,000. |

Germany, a nation of north-central Europe which from 1871 to 1945 was, successively, an empire, a republic and a totalitarian state, attained its territorial peak as an empire when it comprised a 208,780 sq. mi. (540,740 sq. km.) homeland and an overseas colonial empire.

As the power of the Roman Empire waned, several war like tribes residing in northern Germany moved south and west, invading France, Belgium, England, Italy and Spain. In 800 A.D. the Frankish king Charlemagne, who ruled most of France and Germany, was crowned Emperor of the Holy Roman Empire, a loose federation of an estimated 1,800 German States that lasted until 1806. Modern Germany was formed from the eastern part of Charlemagne's empire.

After 1812, the German States were reduced to a federation of 32, of which Prussia was the strongest. In 1871, Prussian chancellor Otto von Bismarck united the German states into an empire ruled by William I, the Prussian king. The empire initiated a colonial endeavor and became one of the world's greatest powers. Germany disintegrated as a result of World War I, and was reestablished as the Weimar Republic. The humiliation of defeat, economic depression, poverty and discontent gave rise to Adolf Hitler, 1933, who reconstituted Germany as the Third Reich and after initial diplomatic and military triumphs, led it to disaster in World War II. For subsequent history, see East and West Germany.

RULERS
Wilhelm I, 1871-1888
Friedrich III, 1888
Wilhelm II, 1888-1918

MINT MARKS
A - Berlin
B - Hannover (1866-1878)
B - Vienna (1938-1944)
C - Frankfurt (1866-1879)
D - Munich
E - Dresden (1872-1887)
E - Muldenhutten (1887-1953)
F - Stuttgart
G - Karlsruhe
H - Darmstadt (1872-1882)
J - Hamburg

MONETARY SYSTEM
(Until 1923)
100 Pfennig = 1 Mark
(During 1923-1924)
100 Rentenpfennig = 1 Rentenmark
(Commencing 1924)
100 Reichspfennig = 1 Reichsmark
(Commencing 1945)
100 Pfennig = 1 Mark

EMPIRE
1871-1918

PFENNIG

COPPER

KM#	Date	Mintage	Fine	VF	XF	Unc
1	1873A	.184	100.00	175.00	375.00	650.00
	1873B	.095	225.00	350.00	550.00	850.00
	1873D	.052	175.00	300.00	450.00	800.00
	1874A	26.760	.75	4.00	10.00	25.00
	1874B	8.743	2.50	10.00	20.00	65.00
	1874C	15.744	2.50	10.00	20.00	65.00
	1874D	7.074	5.00	15.00	20.00	75.00
	1874E	4.522	10.00	15.00	30.00	75.00
	1874F	3.985	2.50	7.50	17.50	60.00
	1874G	4.768	7.50	30.00	60.00	100.00
	1874H	2.013	30.00	50.00	100.00	160.00

KM#	Date	Mintage	Fine	VF	XF	Unc
1	1875A	64.669	.75	1.50	7.50	20.00
	1875B	27.618	1.00	2.50	10.00	40.00
	1875C	22.654	1.00	2.50	15.00	40.00
	1875D	13.342	1.00	2.50	10.00	25.00
	1875E	7.779	5.00	15.00	30.00	60.00
	1875F	15.271	1.00	3.00	12.50	35.00
	1875G	12.021	5.00	10.00	20.00	60.00
	1875H	3.516	30.00	60.00	100.00	200.00
	1875J	7.242	2.50	10.00	20.00	50.00
	1876A	34.542	.75	1.50	7.50	20.00
	1876B	5.995	3.00	5.00	10.00	25.00
	1876C	11.044	3.00	5.00	10.00	25.00
	1876D	12.651	3.00	5.00	10.00	25.00
	1876E	6.532	2.50	7.50	20.00	50.00
	1876F	11.404	3.00	6.00	10.00	25.00
	1876G	3.331	7.50	20.00	35.00	70.00
	1876H	2.998	30.00	60.00	100.00	160.00
	1876J	1.165	50.00	100.00	150.00	250.00
	1877A	.472	60.00	120.00	200.00	250.00
	1877B	.088	325.00	550.00	800.00	1000.
	1885A	5.448	1.50	6.00	15.00	30.00
	1885E	.430	35.00	75.00	115.00	200.00
	1885G	1.100	20.00	50.00	80.00	125.00
	1885J	1.696	10.00	20.00	40.00	65.00
	1886A	14.114	1.00	2.50	7.50	15.00
	1886D	2.873	1.00	2.50	10.00	30.00
	1886E	2.060	3.00	6.00	20.00	50.00
	1886F	1.726	2.50	5.00	17.50	45.00
	1886G	.814	25.00	45.00	85.00	115.00
	1886J	1.593	7.50	15.00	30.00	50.00
	1887A	15.923	1.00	1.50	10.00	25.00
	1887D	5.177	2.50	4.00	10.00	25.00
	1887E	2.315	3.00	6.00	20.00	50.00
1887E dot after PFENNIG						
	25 pcs.	—	—	—	—	
	1887F	6.345	2.50	5.00	15.00	30.00
	1887G	1.888	3.00	7.50	20.00	35.00
	1887J	2.082	1.50	3.00	10.00	25.00
	1888A	19.936	1.00	2.50	10.00	20.00
	1888D	3.277	6.00	9.00	12.50	25.00
	1888E	1.310	5.00	10.00	20.00	40.00
	1888F	.584	20.00	30.00	60.00	80.00
	1888G	1.385	5.00	10.00	20.00	30.00
	1888J	2.803	4.00	7.50	12.50	25.00
	1889A	20.750	1.00	2.50	10.00	20.00
	1889D	8.454	2.00	3.00	15.00	30.00
	1889E	4.330	1.00	2.50	12.50	25.00
	1889F	5.010	1.00	2.50	12.50	30.00
	1889G	3.411	1.50	3.00	15.00	25.00
	1889J	3.308	2.50	5.00	10.00	30.00
Common date		—	—	Proof	175.00	

KM#	Date	Mintage	Fine	VF	XF	Unc
10	1890A	17.295	.50	1.50	3.50	10.00
	1890D	7.030	1.00	2.50	5.00	12.50
	1890E	3.730	.50	2.00	6.50	12.50
	1890F	4.189	.50	2.00	6.50	15.00
	1890G	3.050	2.00	4.00	6.50	15.00
	1890J	2.247	2.00	4.00	6.50	15.00
	1891A	12.040	2.00	4.00	5.00	10.00
	1891D	.876	10.00	25.00	40.00	65.00
	1891E	.528	20.00	45.00	55.00	70.00
	1891F	1.263	5.00	10.00	20.00	25.00
	1891G	.360	40.00	70.00	115.00	150.00
	1891J	1.837	7.50	15.00	25.00	45.00
	1892A	22.341	.25	.50	1.50	5.00
	1892D	6.139	2.00	3.50	8.50	15.00
	1892E	3.195	2.00	3.50	7.50	15.00
	1892F	5.013	1.00	2.00	5.00	10.00
	1892G	2.689	1.50	2.50	6.00	12.50
	1892J	3.980	.50	1.50	4.00	7.50
	1893A	18.966	.25	.50	2.00	5.00
	1893D	7.027	.25	1.00	4.00	7.50
	1893E	1.218	7.50	15.00	25.00	35.00
	1893F	1.460	1.00	2.00	6.00	12.50
	1893G	.700	12.50	25.00	35.00	50.00
	1893J	1.825	.50	5.00	15.00	30.00
	1894A	17.592	.25	.50	2.00	5.00
	1894D	5.530	.25	1.00	4.00	10.00
	1894E	5.040	.50	1.50	5.00	12.50
	1894F	4.206	.20	1.00	4.00	15.00
	1894G	2.351	.50	1.50	5.00	10.00
	1894J	2.619	.50	2.00	6.00	12.50
	1895A	20.152	.25	1.00	2.50	5.00
	1895D	1.496	10.00	25.00	35.00	50.00
	1895E	1.191	5.00	15.00	25.00	35.00
	1895F	4.366	.25	2.50	6.50	12.50
	1895G	3.051	1.00	3.00	7.50	15.00
	1895J	3.839	2.00	5.00	12.50	20.00
	1896A	27.094	.10	.25	1.50	5.00
	1896D	7.025	.10	.25	1.50	5.00
	1896E	3.725	.25	2.50	5.00	10.00
	1896F	3.450	.10	.20	1.50	5.00
	1896G	3.028	.25	4.00	7.50	10.00
	1897A	8.534	.25	1.00	3.50	7.50
	1897D	2.600	1.00	2.50	6.00	10.00
	1897E	1.294	3.50	7.50	12.50	17.50
	1897F	2.390	2.50	6.50	15.00	25.00
	1897G	1.122	6.00	15.00	20.00	30.00
	1897J	4.941	1.00	2.00	5.00	10.00
	1898A	18.564	.10	.25	1.00	5.00
	1898D	4.430	.25	2.00	5.00	15.00
	1898E	2.432	.50	5.00	10.00	17.50
	1898F	4.193	.20	1.00	2.50	6.00

KM#	Date	Mintage	Fine	VF	XF	Unc
10	1898G	1.951	.25	5.00	7.50	12.50
	1898J	3.231	.25	2.50	5.00	10.00
	1899A	22.009	.10	.25	2.00	4.00
	1899D	4.590	.10	.25	2.00	4.00
	1899E	3.725	.25	2.50	5.00	12.50
	1899F	4.300	.10	.20	1.00	3.50
	1899G	2.550	.20	1.50	5.00	15.00
	1899J	2.416	.20	1.00	4.00	7.50
	1900A	51.804	.10	.25	1.00	3.50
	1900D	14.635	.10	.25	1.00	3.50
	1900E	7.887	.20	1.00	3.50	7.50
	1900F	10.312	.10	.50	1.50	5.00
	1900G	6.138	.20	1.00	3.50	7.50
	1900J	9.917	.20	1.00	3.50	7.50
	1901A	21.045	.10	.25	1.00	3.50
	1901D	5.337	.25	1.00	3.50	7.50
	1901E	1.397	1.00	6.00	9.00	14.00
	1901F	2.925	.25	2.50	5.00	10.00
	1901G	1.977	2.50	5.00	10.00	20.00
	1901J	2.011	3.00	10.00	15.00	30.00
	1902A	7.474	.50	5.00	10.00	15.00
	1902D	2.811	5.00	10.00	15.00	20.00
	1902E	1.183	5.00	10.00	15.00	20.00
	1902F	1.250	2.50	7.50	12.50	17.50
	1902G	.881	7.50	12.50	17.50	30.00
	1902J	.012	300.00	550.00	750.00	1000.
	1903A	12.690	.10	.50	1.50	5.00
	1903D	3.140	2.00	4.00	7.50	12.50
	1903E	1.956	2.00	4.00	7.50	12.50
	1903F	2.945	1.50	3.00	6.00	10.00
	1903G	1.377	2.50	10.00	15.00	25.00
	1903J	2.832	.10	.50	2.00	6.00
	1904A	28.625	.10	.25	1.00	3.50
	1904D	4.118	.10	.50	1.50	4.00
	1904E	2.778	.25	2.50	5.00	15.00
	1904F	4.520	.25	2.00	4.00	10.00
	1904G	3.232	.20	3.00	6.00	12.50
	1904J	4.467	.10	.50	1.50	4.00
	1905A	19.631	.10	.25	1.00	3.50
	1905D	6.084	.10	.25	1.00	3.50
	1905E	3.564	.10	.50	1.50	4.00
	1905F	4.153	.10	.20	1.00	3.50
	1905G	3.051	.20	1.00	3.00	6.00
	1905J	4.085	.10	.20	1.00	3.50
	1906A	46.921	.10	.50	1.50	4.00
	1906D	5.633	.10	.50	1.50	4.00
	1906E	7.278	.10	.50	1.50	4.00
	1906F	7.173	.10	.50	1.50	4.00
	1906G	5.194	.10	.50	1.50	4.00
	1906J	3.622	.10	.50	1.50	4.00
	1907A	33.711	.10	.50	1.50	4.00
	1907D	14.691	.10	.50	1.50	4.00
	1907E	3.719	.10	.50	1.50	4.00
	1907F	7.026	.10	.20	1.50	4.00
	1907G	3.052	.10	.50	1.50	4.00
	1907J	6.722	.10	.50	1.50	4.00
	1908A	21.922	.10	.50	1.50	4.00
	1908D	10.629	.10	.50	1.50	4.00
	1908E	3.400	.10	.50	1.50	4.00
	1908F	6.112	.10	.20	1.50	4.00
	1908G	3.663	.10	.50	1.50	4.00
	1908J	5.581	.10	.50	1.50	4.00
	1909A	21.430	.10	.25	1.00	2.50
	1909D	2.814	.20	1.00	2.50	7.50
	1909E	2.562	1.50	4.00	6.00	10.00
	1909F	2.425	1.50	4.00	6.00	10.00
	1909G	1.220	1.50	4.00	7.50	15.00
	1909J	1.634	1.50	4.00	6.50	12.50
	1910A	10.761	.10	.50	1.50	4.00
	1910D	4.221	.10	.25	1.00	2.50
	1910E	1.600	.25	1.50	5.00	10.00
	1910F	3.009	.20	1.50	5.00	7.50
	1910G	1.834	.25	4.00	6.00	10.00
	1910J	2.450	.25	5.00	7.50	15.00
	1911A	38.172	.10	.50	1.50	4.00
	1911D	8.657	.10	.50	1.50	4.00
	1911E	5.236	.10	.50	1.50	4.00
	1911F	5.780	.10	.50	1.50	4.00
	1911G	2.075	.10	.50	1.50	4.00
	1911J	5.594	.10	.50	1.50	4.00
	1912A	42.693	.10	.50	1.50	4.00
	1912D	10.173	.10	.50	1.50	4.00
	1912E	5.689	.10	.50	1.50	4.00
	1912F	7.441	.10	.50	1.50	4.00
	1912G	5.526	.10	.50	1.50	4.00
	1912J	5.615	.10	.50	1.50	4.00
	1913A	32.671	.10	.50	1.50	4.00
	1913D	8.161	.10	.50	1.50	4.00
	1913E	2.258	1.50	4.00	7.50	10.00
	1913F	6.620	.10	.20	1.00	2.50
	1913G	3.209	.10	.50	1.50	4.00
	1913J	1.456	.50	5.00	10.00	15.00
	1914A	9.976	.10	.50	1.50	4.00
	1914D	1.842	.10	.50	1.50	4.00
	1914E	2.926	.20	1.00	2.00	5.00
	1914F	3.316	.10	.50	1.50	4.00
	1914G	2.100	.20	1.00	2.00	5.00
	1914J	4.368	.10	.50	1.50	4.00
	1915A	14.738	.10	.50	1.50	4.00
	1915D	1.771	.10	.25	2.50	5.00
	1915E	2.779	.20	1.50	3.50	7.50
	1915F	1.411	.20	1.50	3.50	10.00
	1915G	2.041	.20	1.50	4.00	9.00
	1915J	2.981	.20	1.50	3.50	7.50
	1916A	5.960	.10	.50	1.50	4.00
	1916D	5.401	.20	1.00	3.00	6.00
	1916E	.818	1.00	5.00	7.50	10.00
	1916F	1.104	.50	2.00	5.00	9.00
	1916G	.671	1.50	7.50	10.00	12.50
	1916J	.898	1.50	6.00	9.00	12.50
	Common date	—	—	—	Proof	30.00

ALUMINUM

KM#	Date	Mintage	Fine	VF	XF	Unc
24	1916G	—	125.00	250.00	350.00	550.00
	1917A	27.159	.15	.50	2.00	5.00
	1917A	—	—	—	Proof	40.00
	1917D	6.940	.15	.50	2.00	6.00
	1917E	3.862	.50	2.00	4.50	8.00
	1917E	—	—	—	Proof	40.00
	1917F	5.125	.25	2.00	4.00	7.00
	1917G	3.139	.25	2.00	4.50	8.00
	1917G	—	—	—	Proof	40.00
	1917J	4.182	.25	2.00	4.00	8.00
	1917J	—	—	—	Proof	40.00
	1918A	—	—	250.00	500.00	750.00
	1918D	.318	10.00	20.00	27.50	40.00
	1918F	—	—	—	600.00	—
	Common date		—	—	Proof	40.00

NOTE: The 1918-F is a pattern from burned out ruins of the Stuttgart Mint destroyed in World War II.

2 PFENNIG

COPPER

KM#	Date	Mintage	Fine	VF	XF	Unc
2	1873A	.877	2.50	7.50	35.00	75.00
	1873B	.290	25.00	50.00	75.00	125.00
	1873C	.161	25.00	50.00	75.00	125.00
	1873D	2.358	5.00	12.50	40.00	85.00
	1873F	.022	75.00	175.00	325.00	500.00
	1873G	.118	50.00	125.00	200.00	275.00
	1874A	37.360	.50	2.50	10.00	25.00
	1874B	10.310	1.50	7.50	17.50	35.00
	1874C	17.474	1.00	5.00	15.00	30.00
	1874D	2.943	3.50	10.00	25.00	40.00
	1874E	5.090	2.50	12.50	25.00	40.00
	1874F	6.405	1.00	7.50	20.00	35.00
	1874G	6.128	1.00	7.50	20.00	35.00
	1874H	2.706	10.00	20.00	40.00	55.00
	1875A	28.963	.50	1.00	12.50	25.00
	1875B	15.844	1.00	3.50	20.00	35.00
	1875C	35.541	.50	1.00	12.50	25.00
	1875D	11.160	.50	1.00	10.00	25.00
	1875E	7.872	1.00	1.50	15.00	30.00
	1875F	9.827	.50	1.00	12.50	30.00
	1875G	11.903	.50	1.00	12.50	30.00
	1875H	3.309	3.50	7.50	20.00	40.00
	1875J	14.210	.50	1.00	12.50	30.00
	1876A	18.906	.50	1.00	12.50	30.00
	1876B	7.097	.50	1.00	15.00	30.00
	1876C	12.280	.50	1.00	15.00	30.00
	1876D	10.296	.50	1.00	15.00	30.00
	1876E	4.988	1.00	1.50	15.00	30.00
	1876F	7.207	.50	1.50	15.00	30.00
	1876G	3.502	1.00	2.50	15.00	35.00
	1876H	3.630	1.00	3.00	20.00	40.00
	1876J	1.995	4.00	7.50	17.50	40.00
	1877A	9.827	.50	1.00	15.00	30.00
	1877B	.060	150.00	200.00	325.00	550.00
	Common date		—	—	Proof	175.00

KM#	Date	Mintage	Fine	VF	XF	Unc
16	1904A	5.414	.10	.25	1.00	6.00
	1904D	1.404	.10	.50	2.00	7.50
	1904E	.744	2.00	6.00	12.50	25.00
	1904F	1.002	.10	1.00	4.00	10.00
	1904G	.495	2.00	6.00	12.50	25.00
	1904J	.044	4.00	10.00	25.00	45.00
	1905A	5.172	.10	.25	1.00	6.00
	1905D	1.570	.10	.50	2.00	7.50
	1905E	.924	.10	1.00	3.50	10.00
	1905F	1.115	.10	1.00	2.50	7.50
	1905G	1.030	.10	1.00	3.00	10.00
	1905J	1.609	.10	1.00	3.00	10.00
	1906A	8.459	.10	.25	1.00	6.00
	1906D	3.539	.10	.25	1.00	6.00
	1906E	2.055	.10	.25	1.00	6.00
	1906F	2.840	.10	.25	1.00	6.00
	1906G	1.527	.10	.25	1.00	6.00
	1906J	1.908	.10	.25	1.00	6.00
	1907A	13.468	.10	.25	1.00	6.00
	1907D	1.921	.10	.25	1.00	6.00
	1907E	.744	.25	2.00	6.00	10.00
	1907F	1.059	.10	.50	1.50	6.00
	1907G	.610	.25	1.00	3.00	6.00
	1907J	.952	.10	.50	1.50	6.00
	1908A	5.421	.10	.25	1.00	6.00
	1908D	1.407	.10	.50	1.50	6.00
	1908E	.745	1.00	5.00	7.50	10.00

KM#	Date	Mintage	Fine	VF	XF	Unc
16	1908F	1.003	.10	.50	2.00	7.50
	1908G	.610	.25	1.00	4.00	7.50
	1908J	.817	.10	.50	2.50	12.50
	1910A	5.421	.10	.25	1.00	6.00
	1910D	1.407	.10	.50	1.50	6.00
	1910E	.745	.25	4.00	6.50	10.00
	1910F	1.003	.25	1.50	4.00	7.50
	1910G	.517	.25	1.50	5.00	7.50
	1910J	.568	.25	1.00	3.50	7.50
	1911A	8.187	.10	1.00	2.50	6.00
	1911D	2.100	.10	.50	2.50	6.00
	1911E	1.133	.10	.50	3.00	6.00
	1911F	1.490	.10	.50	3.00	6.00
	1911G	1.313	.10	.50	3.00	6.00
	1911J	1.883	.10	.50	2.50	6.00
	1912A	13.580	.10	.25	1.00	6.00
	1912D	3.109	.10	.50	2.00	6.00
	1912E	1.808	.10	1.00	3.00	6.00
	1912F	2.366	.10	.50	2.00	6.00
	1912G	1.395	.10	.50	2.50	6.00
	1912J	1.605	.10	.50	2.50	6.00
	1913A	4.212	.10	.25	1.00	6.00
	1913D	2.525	.10	.50	1.50	6.00
	1913E	.413	3.00	15.00	20.00	30.00
	1913F	1.602	.10	.50	2.00	6.00
	1913G	.741	.25	1.00	3.00	6.00
	1913J	1.254	.10	.50	1.50	6.00
	1914A	5.350	.10	.25	1.00	6.00
	1914E	1.201	1.00	3.50	7.50	12.50
	1914F	.158	25.00	45.00	75.00	150.00
	1914G	.610	2.00	6.00	15.00	25.00
	1914J	.817	.10	1.00	3.00	7.50
	1915A	3.897	.10	1.00	3.00	6.00
	1915D	1.407	.10	1.00	2.00	6.00
	1915E	.288	5.00	15.00	25.00	45.00
	1915F	.904	.10	.25	1.00	6.00
	1916A	3.524	.10	1.00	3.00	6.00
	1916D	.915	.25	1.00	2.00	6.00
	1916E	.484	1.00	2.50	6.00	12.50
	1916F	.651	.25	1.00	4.00	7.50
	1916G	.397	.50	2.50	6.00	15.00
	1916J	.531	.50	2.50	6.00	15.00
	Common date		—	—	Proof	30.00

5 PFENNIG

COPPER-NICKEL

KM#	Date	Mintage	Fine	VF	XF	Unc
3	1874A	10.003	.25	1.00	12.50	25.00
	1874B	5.054	.50	2.50	15.00	45.00
	1874C	3.707	.50	2.50	15.00	45.00
	1874D	2.447	.50	2.50	15.00	45.00
	1874E	5.465	.50	2.50	15.00	45.00
	1874F	3.562	1.50	4.00	17.50	50.00
	1874G	2.721	1.50	4.00	17.50	50.00
	1875A	30.844	.25	1.00	12.50	30.00
	1875B	11.658	.50	2.50	15.00	45.00
	1875C	18.082	.50	2.50	15.00	45.00
	1875D	12.380	.50	2.50	15.00	45.00
	1875E	6.745	.50	2.50	15.00	45.00
	1875F	9.758	.50	2.50	15.00	45.00
	1875G	10.220	.50	2.50	15.00	45.00
	1875H	.703	20.00	45.00	75.00	125.00
	1875J	9.781	.50	2.50	15.00	50.00
	1876A	22.342	.25	1.00	12.50	30.00
	1876B	8.925	.50	2.50	15.00	45.00
	1876C	8.680	.50	2.50	15.00	45.00
	1876D	14.467	.50	2.50	15.00	30.00
	1876E	6.899	.50	2.50	15.00	30.00
	1876F	6.826	.50	2.50	15.00	30.00
	1876G	6.942	.50	2.50	15.00	30.00
	1876H	3.027	3.00	6.00	25.00	55.00
	1876J	11.920	.50	2.50	15.00	30.00
	1888A	7.366	.25	1.00	15.00	30.00
	1888/78D	1.967	3.00	6.00	25.00	50.00
	1888D	Inc. Ab.	2.50	5.00	20.00	45.00
	1888E	1.016	3.00	4.00	17.50	40.00
	1888F	1.412	1.00	2.00	12.50	30.00
	1888G	.853	6.00	8.00	22.50	45.00
	1888J	1.130	6.00	8.00	22.50	45.00
	1889A	10.804	.25	1.00	9.00	22.50
	1889D	2.816	1.00	2.50	10.00	30.00
	1889E	1.492	2.00	3.50	12.50	35.00
	1889F	2.010	1.00	2.50	10.00	30.00
	1889G	1.221	2.00	4.00	15.00	35.00
	1889J	1.636	2.50	4.00	17.50	35.00
	Common date		—	—	Proof	125.00

KM#	Date	Mintage	Fine	VF	XF	Unc
11	1890A	4.548	.10	.50	4.00	12.50
	1890D	2.813	.25	1.00	5.00	15.00
	1890E	1.318	.25	1.00	6.00	17.50
	1890F	1.068	.25	1.00	5.00	15.00
	1890G	.948	.25	1.00	6.00	17.50
	1890J	1.629	.20	1.00	5.00	15.00
	1891A	6.313	.10	.50	4.00	12.50
	1891E	.173	12.50	35.00	50.00	80.00

718 GERMANY

KM#	Date	Mintage	Fine	VF	XF	Unc
11	1891F	.942	.25	1.00	5.00	15.00
	1891G	.271	5.00	17.50	30.00	55.00
	1892A	2.279	.10	1.00	4.00	12.50
	1892D	.920	.25	1.00	5.00	15.00
	1892E	.346	2.50	12.50	20.00	35.00
	1892F	.464	4.00	15.00	25.00	45.00
	1892G	.800	3.00	15.00	22.50	35.00
	1892J	.093	50.00	100.00	150.00	225.00
	1893A	8.572	.10	.50	4.00	12.50
	1893D	1.892	.25	1.00	5.00	15.00
	1893E	1.149	.25	1.00	6.00	17.50
	1893F	1.546	.15	1.00	5.00	15.00
	1893G	.422	4.00	15.00	20.00	40.00
	1893J	1.544	.20	1.00	5.00	15.00
	1894A	10.830	.10	.50	4.00	12.50
	1894D	2.812	.25	1.00	5.00	15.00
	1894E	.802	.25	1.50	6.00	17.50
	1894F	.300	1.00	4.00	10.00	30.00
	1894G	.280	1.00	5.00	12.50	35.00
	1894J	1.634	.20	1.00	5.00	15.00
	1895E	.686	.25	2.50	7.50	22.50
	1895F	1.705	.15	1.50	5.00	15.00
	1895G	.940	.25	2.00	6.00	17.50
	1896A	1.459	.25	1.00	5.00	15.00
	1896E	.658	.25	2.50	7.50	17.50
	1896F	2.009	.10	1.00	5.00	15.00
	1896G	1.221	800.00	1200.	1600.	2000.
	1896J	1.634	.20	1.00	5.00	15.00
	1897A	9.390	.10	.50	3.00	10.00
	1897D	2.812	.25	1.00	3.00	10.00
	1897E	.833	.25	2.00	5.00	15.00
	1897G	Inc. Ab.	.10	1.00	4.50	15.00
	1898A	10.836	.10	.30	2.00	7.50
	1898D	2.812	.10	.50	2.00	8.00
	1898E	1.492	.10	.50	2.00	8.00
	1898F	2.007	.10	.50	2.50	8.00
	1898G	1.220	.10	.50	1.50	12.50
	1898J	1.635	.20	1.00	2.00	8.00
	1899A	10.884	.10	.30	1.00	6.50
	1899D	2.812	.10	.50	2.00	8.00
	1899E	1.488	.10	.50	3.00	10.00
	1899F	2.006	.10	.50	2.00	7.50
	1899G	1.222	.10	.50	2.00	7.50
	1899J	1.634	.10	.50	2.00	7.50
	1900A	18.941	.10	.30	1.00	6.50
	1900D	4.254	.10	.50	1.50	8.00
	1900E	2.236	.10	.50	2.00	7.50
	1900F	3.209	.10	.25	1.50	8.00
	1900G	2.136	.10	.50	2.00	7.50
	1900J	2.859	.10	.50	2.00	7.50
	1901A	8.155	.10	.30	1.00	6.50
	1901D	2.779	.10	.20	.50	6.50
	1901E	1.492	.10	.50	2.00	8.00
	1901F	1.810	.10	.25	1.00	6.50
	1901G	.915	.10	.50	2.00	8.00
	1901J	1.226	.10	.25	1.00	6.50
	1902A	8.949	.10	.30	1.00	6.50
	1902D	2.812	.10	.20	.50	6.50
	1902E	1.120	.10	.50	2.00	10.00
	1902F	1.800	.10	.50	2.00	10.00
	1902G	1.220	.10	.50	3.50	10.00
	1902J	1.636	.10	.25	1.50	6.50
	1903A	5.932	.10	.30	1.00	6.50
	1903D	1.406	.10	.50	2.50	7.50
	1903E	1.114	.10	1.00	4.00	12.00
	1903F	1.209	.10	.50	4.00	12.00
	1903G	.610	.10	1.50	5.00	15.00
	1903J	.817	.10	1.00	4.00	12.00
	1904A	6.791	.10	.30	1.50	6.50
	1904D	1.408	.10	.50	2.00	7.50
	1904E	.746	.10	1.50	4.00	12.00
	1904F	1.006	.10	.50	2.50	8.00
	1904G	.610	.10	1.00	3.00	9.00
	1904J	.818	.10	.50	2.50	8.00
	1905A	8.129	.10	.20	.50	8.00
	1905D	2.109	.10	.20	.50	8.00
	1905E	1.117	.10	.20	.50	8.00
	1905F	1.505	.10	.20	.50	8.00
	1905G	.915	.10	.50	2.50	10.00
	1905J	1.226	.10	.20	.50	8.00
	1906A	18.970	.10	.20	.50	6.50
	1906D	4.922	.10	.20	.50	6.50
	1906E	2.605	.10	.20	.50	6.50
	1906F	3.512	.10	.20	.50	6.50
	1906G	2.136	.10	.25	1.00	8.00
	1906J	2.859	.10	.20	.50	6.50
	1907A	11.930	.10	.20	.50	6.50
	1907D	2.113	.10	.20	.50	6.50
	1907E	1.517	.10	.25	1.00	8.00
	1907F	1.845	.10	.20	.50	6.50
	1907G	.915	.10	.50	1.00	8.00
	1907J	1.636	.10	.20	.50	6.50
	1908A	22.114	.10	.20	.50	6.50
	1908D	4.991	.10	.20	.50	6.50
	1908E	2.919	.10	.20	.50	8.00
	1908/7F	5.124	30.00	60.00	80.00	150.00
	1908F	Inc. Ab.	.10	.20	.50	6.50
	1908/1108G	3.357	—	—	—	—
	1908G	Inc. Ab.	.10	.15	.50	6.50
	1908J	3.264	.10	.20	.50	4.00
	1909A	5.797	.10	.30	2.00	8.00
	1909D	2.753	.10	.50	2.50	8.00
	1909E	.984	.25	2.50	5.00	15.00
	1909F	.252	2.00	5.00	7.50	17.50
	1909/8J	1.632	1.00	5.00	15.00	45.00
	1909J	Inc. Ab.	.10	2.50	5.00	10.00
	1910A	7.344	.10	.20	1.00	6.50
	1910D	2.814	.10	.20	.50	6.50
	1910E	1.290	.10	.50	1.50	8.00
	1910F	1.721	.10	.20	.50	6.50

KM#	Date	Mintage	Fine	VF	XF	Unc
11	1910G	1.222	.10	.20	.50	6.50
	1910J	.152	10.00	40.00	65.00	130.00
	1911A	15.660	.10	.15	.50	6.50
	1911D	2.221	.10	.20	.50	6.50
	1911E	1.770	.10	.20	.50	6.50
	1911F	2.714	.10	.20	.50	6.50
	1911G	1.833	.10	.20	1.00	6.50
	1911J	3.116	.10	.15	.50	6.50
	1912A	19.320	.10	.15	.50	6.50
	1912D	4.015	.10	.20	.50	6.50
	1912E	2.568	.10	.20	.50	6.50
	1912F	3.679	.10	.15	.50	6.50
	1912G	2.440	.10	.20	.50	6.50
	1912J	3.020	.10	.15	.50	6.50
	1913A	15.506	.10	.15	.50	6.50
	1913D	5.519	.10	.20	.50	6.50
	1913E	2.373	.10	.20	.50	7.50
	1913F	2.054	.10	.20	.50	6.00
	1913G	1.221	.10	.20	.50	6.00
	1913J	.253	5.00	12.50	17.50	30.00
	1914A	23.605	.10	.15	.50	6.00
	1914D	3.014	.10	.20	.50	6.00
	1914E	1.710	.10	.20	.50	6.00
	1914F	2.206	.10	.20	.50	6.00
	1914G	1.218	.10	.20	.50	6.00
	1914J	3.235	.10	.15	.50	6.00
	1915D	3.516	.10	.50	2.00	7.00
	1915E	.834	1.00	6.00	8.00	15.00
	1915F	1.894	.10	.50	2.00	6.00
	1915G	.894	.50	5.00	6.50	10.00
	1915J	1.669	.10	.50	3.50	10.00
	1915	—	1.00	5.00	12.50	25.00
	Common date		—	—	Proof	40.00

IRON

KM#	Date	Mintage	Fine	VF	XF	Unc
19	1915A	34.631	.10	.25	2.00	7.50
	1915D	2.021	.50	7.50	12.50	20.00
	1915E	4.670	.50	5.00	10.00	20.00
	1915F	3.500	.25	2.50	7.50	15.00
	1915G	3.676	.25	2.00	5.00	12.50
	1915J	2.100	.25	2.00	5.00	12.50
	1916A	51.003	.10	.25	1.50	8.50
	1916D	19.590	.10	.50	1.50	8.50
	1916E	2.271	1.00	10.00	15.00	22.50
	1916F	10.479	.15	1.00	2.00	8.50
	1916G	5.599	.25	1.50	3.50	12.00
	1916J	10.253	.25	3.00	7.50	15.00
	1917A	87.315	.10	.50	1.00	7.50
	1917D	19.581	.10	.50	1.00	7.50
	1917E	11.092	.50	5.00	7.50	10.00
	1917F	10.930	.10	.50	2.00	8.50
	1917F mule w/Polish rev. of Y#5, see Poland					
	1917G	6.720	.25	3.00	6.00	10.00
	1917J	11.686	.25	2.00	5.00	10.00
	1918A	223.516	.10	.50	1.00	6.50
	1918D	29.130	.10	.50	1.00	6.50
	1918E	23.600	.25	1.00	6.00	12.50
	1918F	24.598	.10	.25	1.00	6.50
	1918G	12.697	.10	.50	1.00	6.50
	1918J	20.240	.10	.50	1.00	6.50
	1919A	112.102	.10	.20	.50	6.00
	1919D	41.163	.10	.25	1.00	6.50
	1919E	20.608	.25	3.00	6.00	12.50
	1919F	32.700	.10	.25	1.00	6.50
	1919G	13.925	.10	.50	2.50	10.00
	1919J	16.249	.15	1.00	2.00	7.50
	1920A	80.300	.10	.20	.50	6.00
	1920D	25.502	.10	.50	1.00	6.50
	1920E	11.646	.25	2.50	10.00	22.50
	1920F	24.300	.10	.25	1.00	6.50
	1920G	10.244	.20	2.00	3.50	12.50
	1920J	16.857	.10	.20	1.00	6.50
	1921A	143.418	.10	.20	.50	6.00
	1921D	38.133	.10	.25	1.00	6.50
	1921E	21.104	2.50	5.00	10.00	17.50
	1921F	24.800	.10	.25	1.00	6.50
	1921G	21.289	.10	.25	1.00	6.50
	1921J	28.928	.15	1.00	3.00	10.00
	1922A	89.062	—	—	Rare	—
	1922D	31.240	.10	.25	1.00	6.50
	1922E	19.156	5.00	7.50	12.50	20.00
	1922F	16.436	.10	.25	1.00	6.50
	1922G	19.708	.10	.25	1.00	6.50
	1922J	16.820	.25	2.50	6.00	12.50
	Common date		—	—	Proof	40.00

10 PFENNIG

COPPER-NICKEL

KM#	Date	Mintage	Fine	VF	XF	Unc
4	1873A	.931	6.00	10.00	22.50	70.00
	1873B	.333	17.50	25.00	40.00	100.00
	1873C	.522	15.00	20.00	35.00	100.00
	1873D	.472	5.00	10.00	25.00	75.00
	1873F	.476	20.00	30.00	50.00	100.00
4	1873G	.519	15.00	20.00	35.00	100.00
	1873H	.044	100.00	150.00	225.00	350.00
	1874A	7.664	.25	2.00	12.50	40.00
	1874B	2.669	2.50	5.00	17.50	50.00
	1874C	12.029	.25	2.00	12.50	40.00
	1874D	3.586	10.00	17.50	35.00	100.00
	1874E	3.157	10.00	17.50	30.00	60.00
	1874F	7.309	1.00	2.50	12.50	45.00
	1874G	5.552	1.00	2.50	12.50	45.00
	1874H	3.323	12.50	20.00	40.00	100.00
	1875A	15.523	.25	2.00	10.00	40.00
	1875B	4.120	1.00	2.50	12.50	45.00
	1875C	8.304	1.00	2.50	12.00	40.00
	1875D	13.365	1.00	2.50	12.00	40.00
	1875E	9.833	1.00	2.50	12.50	40.00
	1875F	7.975	1.00	2.50	12.50	40.00
	1875G	5.390	2.50	5.00	15.00	45.00
	1875H	4.268	12.50	20.00	40.00	80.00
	1875J	9.407	1.00	2.50	12.00	40.00
	1876A	34.175	.25	2.00	10.00	35.00
	1876B	10.120	1.00	2.50	12.00	35.00
	1876C	13.214	.25	2.00	10.00	35.00
	1876D	16.787	.25	2.00	10.00	35.00
	1876E	6.161	1.00	2.50	12.50	35.00
	1876F	7.034	1.00	2.50	12.50	35.00
	1876G	6.222	1.00	2.50	12.50	35.00
	1876H	3.227	17.50	30.00	40.00	75.00
	1876J	11.315	1.00	2.50	12.00	40.00
	1888A	8.519	.25	2.00	10.00	30.00
	1888D	2.493	.50	2.50	12.00	30.00
	1888E	1.268	1.00	7.50	20.00	40.00
	1888F	1.340	1.00	7.50	20.00	40.00
	1888G	1.081	1.00	7.50	20.00	35.00
	1888J	1.436	.50	2.50	12.00	30.00
	1889A	11.542	.25	2.00	10.00	30.00
	1889D	2.813	.50	2.00	10.00	30.00
	1889E	1.493	.50	2.50	12.00	30.00
	1889F	2.432	.50	2.50	12.00	30.00
	1889G	1.223	.50	5.00	20.00	40.00
	1889J	1.638	.50	2.50	12.00	30.00
	Common date		—	—	Proof	125.00

GOLD (OMS)

KM#	Date	Mintage	Fine	VF	XF	Unc
4a	1873G	—	—	—	—	—

COPPER-NICKEL

KM#	Date	Mintage	Fine	VF	XF	Unc
12	1890A	6.878	.10	.25	1.00	7.50
	1890F	.784	.25	1.50	3.50	10.00
	1890G	.976	.25	2.00	4.00	12.50
	1890J	1.637	.25	1.00	2.50	10.00
	1891A	4.239	.10	.25	1.00	10.00
	1891D	2.812	.10	.30	1.50	10.00
	1891E	1.489	.20	1.00	2.50	15.00
	1891F	1.226	.25	2.50	5.00	15.00
	1891G	.247	7.00	20.00	30.00	50.00
	1892A	2.413	.15	.50	2.00	9.00
	1892D	2.812	.10	.30	2.00	9.00
	1892E	.870	.25	2.50	5.00	15.00
	1892F	.663	.25	2.50	5.00	15.00
	1892G	.300	6.00	15.00	25.00	40.00
	1892J	—	1000.	1500.	2000.	2500.
	1893A	8.435	.10	.25	2.00	9.00
	1893E	.362	.50	6.00	12.50	35.00
	1893F	1.345	.15	.50	1.50	9.00
	1893G	.921	.25	1.50	3.50	10.00
	1893J	1.636	.10	.30	1.50	9.00
	1894E	.260	7.50	25.00	40.00	65.00
	1896A	4.996	.10	1.00	1.50	9.00
	1896D	2.812	.20	1.00	1.50	9.00
	1896E	1.495	.20	1.00	2.50	9.00
	1896F	2.009	.15	1.00	1.50	9.00
	1896G	.200	6.00	15.00	25.00	40.00
	1896J	1.632	.10	.30	1.50	9.00
	1897A	5.842	.10	.25	1.50	9.00
	1897G	1.020	.25	1.50	2.50	10.00
	1898A	10.833	.10	.25	1.00	7.50
	1898D	2.814	.10	.25	1.00	7.50
	1898E	.805	.20	.50	2.00	10.00
	1898F	2.007	.15	.50	2.00	10.00
	1898G	.480	.50	3.00	6.00	17.50
	1898J	1.635	.10	.30	1.50	8.00
	1899A	10.838	.10	.25	1.00	7.50
	1899D	3.813	.10	.25	1.00	7.50
	1899E	2.175	.10	.30	1.50	7.50
	1899F	2.008	.10	.25	1.00	7.50
	1899G	1.382	.10	.25	1.00	7.50
	1899J	1.635	.10	.25	1.00	7.50
	1900A	34.559	.10	.25	1.00	6.00
	1900D	8.694	.10	.25	1.00	6.00
	1900E	4.490	.10	.30	1.50	7.50
	1900F	5.933	.10	.25	1.00	6.00
	1900G	4.239	.10	.25	1.50	7.50
	1900J	5.720	.10	.25	1.00	6.00
	1901A	10.200	.10	.25	1.00	6.00
	1901D	3.259	.10	.25	1.00	6.00
	1901E	1.863	.10	.30	1.00	6.00
	1901F	2.594	.10	.25	1.00	6.00
	1901G	1.527	.10	.25	1.00	4.50
	1901J	1.225	.10	.25	1.00	6.00
	1902A	5.878	.10	.25	1.00	6.00
	1902D	1.406	.10	.25	1.00	6.00
	1902E	.502	.25	3.00	6.00	15.00

GERMANY 719

KM#	Date	Mintage	Fine	VF	XF	Unc
12	1902F	1.003	.10	.25	1.00	7.50
	1902G	.610	.25	1.50	3.50	9.00
	1902J	.815	.25	1.50	3.00	9.00
	1903A	5.131	.10	.25	1.00	6.00
	1903D	1.406	.10	.30	1.50	6.00
	1903E	.988	.15	.30	1.00	6.00
	1903F	1.003	.10	.25	1.00	6.00
	1903G	.610	.25	.50	1.50	7.50
	1903J	.816	.20	.40	1.50	12.50
	1904A	5.189	.10	.25	1.00	5.00
	1904D	1.056	.10	.30	1.00	6.00
	1904E	.559	.25	1.00	2.50	7.50
	1904F	.753	.10	.25	1.00	6.00
	1904G	.457	1.00	5.00	7.50	15.00
	1904J	.612	.25	1.50	3.50	9.00
	1905A	8.650	.10	.25	1.00	6.00
	1905A	250 pcs.	—	—	Proof	100.00
	1905D	1.846	.10	.25	1.00	6.00
	1905E	.980	.15	.30	1.00	6.00
	1905F	1.310	.10	.25	1.00	6.00
	1905G	.642	.25	1.00	2.00	8.00
	1905J	1.430	.10	.25	1.00	6.00
	1906A	14.470	.10	.25	1.00	6.50
	1906D	4.132	.10	.25	1.00	6.50
	1906E	2.189	.10	.25	1.00	6.50
	1906F	2.953	.10	.25	1.00	6.50
	1906G	1.952	.10	.25	1.00	6.50
	1906J	2.042	.10	.25	1.00	6.00
	1907A	17.971	.10	.25	1.00	6.00
	1907D	2.813	.10	.25	1.00	6.00
	1907E	2.291	.10	.25	1.00	6.00
	1907F	3.206	.10	.25	1.00	6.00
	1907G	1.889	.10	.25	1.00	6.00
	1907J	2.750	.10	.25	1.00	6.00
	1908A	20.410	.10	.25	1.00	6.00
	1908D	6.773	.10	.25	1.00	6.00
	1908E	2.490	.10	.25	1.00	6.00
	1908F	3.535	.10	.25	1.00	6.00
	1908G	1.708	.10	.25	1.00	6.00
	1908J	2.649	.10	.25	1.00	6.00
	1909A	2.270	.25	1.00	2.50	9.00
	1909D	.966	.25	1.50	3.00	9.00
	1909E	.806	.50	3.00	6.00	15.00
	1909F	.780	.50	3.00	6.00	15.00
	1909G	.980	.25	2.50	5.00	15.00
	1909J	.725	.25	2.50	5.00	15.00
	1910A	3.734	.10	.20	.50	5.00
	1910D	1.406	.25	.50	1.00	6.00
	1910E	.300	3.50	10.00	15.00	25.00
	1910F	1.003	.25	.50	1.00	6.00
	1910G	.610	.25	.50	1.00	6.00
	1911A	13.554	.10	.15	.50	6.00
	1911D	2.508	.10	.15	.50	6.00
	1911E	2.246	.10	.15	.50	6.00
	1911F	2.235	.10	.15	.50	6.00
	1911G	1.678	.10	.15	.50	6.00
	1911J	3.062	.10	.15	.50	6.00
	1912A	21.312	.10	.15	.50	6.00
	1912D	6.988	.10	.15	.50	6.00
	1912E	2.649	.10	.15	.50	6.00
	1912F	3.787	.10	.15	.50	6.00
	1912G	2.441	.10	.15	.50	6.00
	1912J	2.730	.10	.15	.50	6.00
	1913A	13.466	.10	.15	.50	6.00
	1913D	3.164	.10	.15	.50	6.00
	1913E	1.478	.10	.15	.50	6.00
	1913F	1.991	.10	.15	.50	6.00
	1913G	1.373	.10	.15	.50	6.00
	1913J	1.550	.10	.15	.50	6.00
	1914A	18.570	.10	.15	.50	6.00
	1914D	2.301	.10	.15	.50	6.00
	1914E	3.478	.10	.15	.50	6.00
	1914F	4.515	.10	.15	.50	6.00
	1914G	2.689	.10	.15	.50	6.00
	1914J	1.589	.10	.15	.50	6.00
	1915A	10.639	.10	.15	.50	6.00
	1915D	2.277	.10	.15	.50	6.00
	1915E	1.027	.25	2.50	5.00	15.00
	1915F	1.508	.10	.15	.50	6.00
	1915G	.363	15.00	50.00	75.00	150.00
	1915J	2.677	.20	1.00	2.50	7.50
	1916D	1.128	.15	1.00	2.50	9.00
	Common date		—	—	Proof	45.00

IRON

KM#	Date	Mintage	Fine	VF	XF	Unc
20	1915A	—	125.00	275.00	350.00	475.00
	1916A	69.143	.10	.35	1.50	6.00
	1916D	11.609	.10	.30	1.50	6.50
	1916E	8.280	.15	.50	3.50	7.50
	1916F	7.473	.15	.50	3.00	7.50
	1916G	5.878	.15	.50	3.50	7.50
	1916J	11.683	.15	.50	3.50	6.50
	1916	—	—	—	Rare	—
	1917A	53.198	.10	.20	1.00	2.00
	1917D	16.370	.10	.30	1.50	2.50
	1917E	9.182	.15	.50	2.50	5.00
	1917F	11.341	.15	.50	2.50	5.00
	1917F mule w/Polish rev. of Y#6, see Poland					
	1917G	7.088	.15	.50	3.00	7.50
	1917J	9.205	.15	.50	3.50	7.50
	1918D	.042	300.00	550.00	850.00	1150.
	1921A	16.265	1.00	4.00	6.00	12.50
20	1922D	—	2.00	7.50	12.50	20.00
	1922E	2.235	17.50	35.00	50.00	100.00
	1922F	1.928	.50	3.00	5.00	10.00
	1922G	1.358	15.00	30.00	40.00	85.00
	1922J	2.420	1.00	4.00	6.00	12.50
	1922	—	100.00	175.00	250.00	450.00
	Common date		—	—	Proof	60.00

ZINC

Eagle and beaded border similar to KM#20.1.

KM#	Date	Mintage	Fine	VF	XF	Unc
25	1916F	—	150.00	400.00	600.00	900.00
	1917A	—	75.00	150.00	225.00	325.00
	1917	—	60.00	120.00	160.00	275.00
	1922J	—	—	—	Rare	—

W/o mint mark.
3.10-3.33 g

KM#	Date	Mintage	Fine	VF	XF	Unc
26.1	1917	75.073	.10	.20	1.00	5.50
	1918	202.008	.10	.20	1.00	5.50
	1918	28 pcs.	—	—	Proof	—
	1919	147.800	.10	.20	1.00	5.50
	1919	50 pcs.	—	—	Proof	—
	1920	223.019	.10	.20	1.00	5.50
	1920	40 pcs.	—	—	Proof	—
	1921	319.334	.10	.20	1.00	5.50
	1921	24 pcs.	—	—	Proof	—
	1922	274.499	.10	.20	1.00	5.50
	1922	12 pcs.	—	—	Proof	—
	Common date		—	—	Proof	80.00

Thinner planchet

KM#	Date	Mintage	Fine	VF	XF	Unc
26.2	1918	Inc. Ab.	—	—	—	—
	1920	Inc. Ab.	—	—	—	—
	1921	Inc. Ab.	—	—	—	—

20 PFENNIG

1.1110 g, .900 SILVER, .0321 oz ASW

KM#	Date	Mintage	Fine	VF	XF	Unc
5	1873A	2.159	5.00	12.50	25.00	50.00
	1873B	.664	15.00	25.00	50.00	80.00
	1873C	.904	17.50	25.00	50.00	75.00
	1873D	1.201	10.00	15.00	30.00	50.00
	1873E	100 pcs.	300.00	550.00	1000.	1500.
	1873F	.450	15.00	20.00	40.00	65.00
	1873G	.763	12.50	17.50	35.00	50.00
	1873H	.054	150.00	300.00	450.00	650.00
	1874A	8.830	6.00	9.00	12.50	27.50
	1874B	9.222	6.00	9.00	12.50	27.50
	1874C	1.303	9.00	14.00	20.00	37.50
	1874D	10.087	7.50	10.00	15.00	27.50
	1874E	2.281	7.50	12.50	20.00	40.00
	1874F	7.222	6.50	10.00	14.00	45.00
	1874G	3.281	10.00	15.00	20.00	50.00
	1874H	1.842	12.50	17.50	25.00	50.00
	1875A	9.034	5.00	7.50	10.00	25.00
	1875B	2.768	10.00	15.00	20.00	40.00
	1875C	5.938	6.00	9.00	12.50	27.50
	1875D	15.032	6.00	9.00	12.50	25.00
	1875E	1.486	17.50	27.50	37.50	125.00
	1875F	7.668	6.00	9.00	12.50	30.00
	1875G	3.940	10.00	15.00	20.00	35.00
	1875H	1.340	17.50	25.00	35.00	50.00
	1875J	3.502	12.50	17.50	22.50	50.00
	1876A	6.959	6.00	10.00	15.00	30.00
	1876B	5.089	6.00	10.00	15.00	32.50
	1876C	5.911	6.00	10.00	15.00	32.50
	1876D	14.152	5.00	9.00	12.50	27.50
	1876E	11.648	7.50	12.50	17.50	30.00
	1876F	13.635	5.00	9.00	10.00	27.50
	1876G	7.820	5.00	9.00	10.00	27.50
	1876H	1.433	17.50	35.00	45.00	80.00
	1876J	10.272	6.00	10.00	17.50	25.00
	1877	.700	125.00	225.00	325.00	550.00
	Common date		—	—	Proof	300.00

COPPER-NICKEL

KM#	Date	Mintage	Fine	VF	XF	Unc
9	1887A	2.712	7.50	20.00	27.50	45.00
	1887D	.704	7.50	27.50	40.00	70.00
	1887E	.373	15.00	35.00	50.00	90.00
	1887E	50 pcs.	—	—	Proof	4500.
	1887E star under value					
		50 pcs.	—	—	—	4500.
	1887F	.503	15.00	30.00	45.00	70.00
	1887G	.306	15.00	30.00	50.00	85.00
	1887J	.408	15.00	30.00	50.00	85.00
	1888A	5.426	7.50	25.00	30.00	55.00
	1888D	1.406	10.00	25.00	35.00	60.00
9	1888E	.744	10.00	25.00	35.00	70.00
	1888F	1.005	10.00	25.00	35.00	65.00
	1888G	.611	10.00	25.00	35.00	70.00
	1888/7J	.818	25.00	45.00	60.00	100.00
	1888J	Inc. Ab.	10.00	25.00	35.00	70.00
	Common date		—	—	Proof	150.00

KM#	Date	Mintage	Fine	VF	XF	Unc
13	1890A	2.716	15.00	27.50	45.00	110.00
	1890/80D	.703	15.00	30.00	50.00	125.00
	1890D	Inc. Ab.	15.00	30.00	50.00	125.00
	1890E	.373	17.50	45.00	100.00	165.00
	1890F	.503	15.00	30.00	50.00	125.00
	1890G	.306	17.50	40.00	80.00	150.00
	1890J	.410	15.00	30.00	50.00	125.00
	1892A	2.712	10.00	25.00	40.00	90.00
	1892D	.703	15.00	35.00	45.00	110.00
	1892E	.372	15.00	40.00	70.00	135.00
	1892F	.502	15.00	35.00	60.00	125.00
	1892G	.304	15.00	45.00	70.00	135.00
	1892J	.409	15.00	35.00	70.00	135.00
	Common date		—	—	Proof	200.00

25 PFENNIG

NICKEL

KM#	Date	Mintage	Fine	VF	XF	Unc
18	1909A	.962	2.50	6.00	10.00	16.00
	1909D	1.406	2.50	6.00	10.00	16.00
	1909E	.250	15.00	27.50	40.00	60.00
	1909F	.400	2.50	7.50	12.50	20.00
	1909G	.610	2.50	7.50	12.50	20.00
	1909J	.010	400.00	600.00	900.00	1500.
	1910A	9.522	3.00	8.00	12.00	17.50
	1910D	1.408	3.00	8.00	12.00	17.50
	1910E	1.242	3.00	8.00	12.00	17.50
	1910F	1.605	3.00	8.00	12.00	19.50
	1910G	.330	3.00	8.00	12.00	17.50
	1910J	1.561	3.00	8.00	12.00	16.00
	1911A	3.179	3.00	8.00	12.00	16.00
	1911D	.506	3.00	8.00	15.00	20.00
	1911E	.747	3.00	8.00	17.50	25.00
	1911G	.892	3.00	8.00	17.50	25.00
	1911J	.516	3.00	8.00	17.50	25.00
	1912A	2.590	3.00	8.00	12.00	17.50
	1912D	.900	3.00	8.00	17.50	25.00
	1912F	1.003	3.00	8.00	17.50	22.50
	1912J	.362	12.50	25.00	35.00	60.00
	Common date		—	—	Proof	100.00

50 PFENNIG

2.7770 g, .900 SILVER, .0803 oz ASW

KM#	Date	Mintage	Fine	VF	XF	Unc
6	1875A	7.095	7.50	15.00	30.00	70.00
	1875B	2.799	8.00	16.00	50.00	80.00
	1875C	2.047	8.00	16.00	32.50	70.00
	1875D	4.668	8.00	16.00	32.50	80.00
	1875E	.353	125.00	250.00	400.00	650.00
	1875F	.874	22.50	50.00	80.00	140.00
	1875G	2.034	15.00	17.50	37.50	90.00
	1875H	.175	150.00	300.00	400.00	650.00
	1875J	2.411	12.50	20.00	50.00	95.00
	1876A	34.475	8.00	15.00	30.00	55.00
	1876B	11.016	8.00	15.00	30.00	70.00
	1876C	10.945	8.00	15.00	30.00	70.00
	1876D	3.641	12.50	25.00	45.00	75.00
	1876E	4.127	8.00	15.00	30.00	70.00
	1876F	4.448	12.50	20.00	40.00	70.00
	1876G	1.797	12.50	20.00	40.00	100.00
	1876H	1.877	12.50	25.00	45.00	120.00
	1876J	3.589	8.00	17.50	35.00	70.00
	1877A	3.249	8.00	17.50	35.00	70.00
	1877B	3.691	8.00	17.50	35.00	70.00
	1877C	2.388	15.00	32.50	45.00	95.00
	1877D	3.004	12.50	20.00	40.00	70.00
	1877E	1.121	22.50	45.00	85.00	160.00
	1877F	1.311	25.00	37.50	70.00	100.00
	1877H	.622	75.00	100.00	170.00	220.00
	1877J	1.526	40.00	65.00	125.00	200.00
	Common date		—	—	Proof	200.00

GERMANY 720

KM#	Date	Mintage	Fine	VF	XF	Unc
8	1877A	6.746	20.00	35.00	80.00	125.00
	1877B	3.097	22.50	40.00	85.00	150.00
	1877C	2.820	20.00	40.00	85.00	150.00
	1877D	5.315	18.00	30.00	80.00	135.00
	1877E	2.296	20.00	35.00	85.00	150.00
	1877F	2.145	20.00	35.00	85.00	150.00
	1877G	2.061	22.50	40.00	85.00	175.00
	1877H	1.510	30.00	60.00	120.00	220.00
	1877J	1.337	22.50	40.00	85.00	175.00
	1878E	.364	200.00	325.00	475.00	950.00
	Common Date	—	—	Proof	300.00	

KM#	Date	Mintage	Fine	VF	XF	Unc
15	1896A	.389	90.00	180.00	275.00	350.00
	1898A	.387	90.00	180.00	275.00	350.00
	1900J	.192	100.00	200.00	300.00	400.00
	1900J	—	—	—	Proof	500.00
	1901A	.194	100.00	225.00	325.00	425.00
	1902F	.095	150.00	250.00	350.00	500.00
	1902F	—	—	—	Proof	500.00
	1903A	.384	125.00	200.00	250.00	325.00
	Common date		—	—	Proof	350.00

1/2 MARK

2.7770 g, .900 SILVER, .0803 oz ASW

KM#	Date	Mintage	Fine	VF	XF	Unc
17	1905A	37.766	.75	1.00	5.00	12.00
	1905D	7.636	.75	1.50	5.00	12.00
	1905E	4.908	.75	1.50	5.00	12.00
	1905F	6.310	.75	1.50	5.00	12.00
	1905G	3.886	.75	1.50	5.00	15.00
	1905J	6.316	.75	1.50	5.00	12.00
	1906A	29.754	.75	1.50	5.00	12.00
	1906D	11.977	.75	1.50	5.00	12.00
	1906E	5.821	.75	1.50	5.00	15.00
	1906F	8.036	.75	1.50	5.00	12.00
	1906G	4.273	.75	1.50	5.00	18.00
	1906J	2.179	.75	2.50	7.50	22.50
	1907A	14.168	.75	1.50	5.00	12.00
	1907D	2.884	.75	1.50	5.00	12.00
	1907E	.600	2.50	7.50	12.50	25.00
	1907F	1.202	.75	1.50	5.00	12.00
	1907G	.927	2.50	7.50	12.50	22.50
	1907J	3.268	.75	1.50	5.00	17.50
	1908A	5.018	.75	1.50	5.00	12.00
	1908D	.400	7.50	17.50	22.50	37.50
	1908E	.591	1.75	7.50	17.50	30.00
	1908F	1.000	650.00	1250.	1800.	2400.
	1908G	.675	1.25	5.00	10.00	22.50
	1908/7J	1.309	1.25	5.00	10.00	22.50
	1908J	Inc. Ab.	1.25	5.00	10.00	22.50
	1909A	5.404	.75	1.50	5.00	12.00
	1909/5D	1.001	.75	1.50	5.00	12.00
	1909D	Inc. Ab.	.75	1.50	5.00	12.00
	1909E	.745	1.25	5.00	10.00	20.00
	1909F	.999	.75	2.50	7.50	12.00
	1909G	.607	1.25	5.00	10.00	17.50
	1909J	.816	1.25	5.00	10.00	17.50
	1911A	2.710	1.25	5.00	7.50	20.00
	1911/05D	.703	1.25	5.00	7.50	20.00
	1911D	Inc. Ab.	1.25	5.00	7.50	20.00
	1911E	.376	5.00	17.50	25.00	35.00
	1911F	.502	2.50	7.50	15.00	25.00
	1911G	.610	2.50	7.50	15.00	25.00
	1911J	.418	5.00	17.50	27.50	37.50
	1912A	2.709	1.25	5.00	7.50	20.00
	1912/5D	.703	1.50	10.00	15.00	25.00
	1912D	Inc. Ab.	1.50	10.00	15.00	25.00
	1912E	.369	5.00	17.50	25.00	32.50
	1912F	.501	2.50	7.50	12.50	25.00
	1912J	.399	5.00	17.50	27.50	37.50
	1913A	5.419	.75	1.50	5.00	12.00
	1913/05D	1.406	.75	1.50	5.00	12.00
	1913D	Inc. Ab.	.75	1.50	5.00	12.00
	1913E	.745	2.50	5.00	7.50	12.50
	1913F	1.003	.75	1.50	5.00	12.00
	1913G	.610	1.25	5.00	10.00	17.50
	1913J	.817	1.25	5.00	10.00	22.50
	1914A	13.525	.75	1.50	4.00	9.00
	1914/05D	.328	2.50	10.00	15.00	27.50
	1914D	Inc. Ab.	2.50	10.00	15.00	27.50
	1914J	2.292	.75	3.00	5.00	12.00
	1915A	13.015	.75	1.50	3.50	8.00
	1915/05D	5.117	.75	1.50	3.50	8.00
	1915D	Inc. Ab.	.75	1.50	3.50	8.00
17	1915E	3.308	.75	1.50	3.50	8.00
	1915F	5.309	.75	1.50	3.50	8.00
	1915G	2.730	.75	1.50	3.50	8.00
	1915J	2.285	.75	1.50	3.50	8.00
	1916A	9.750	.75	1.50	3.50	8.00
	1916/616D	4.397	.75	1.50	3.50	8.00
	1916/05D	I.A.	.75	1.50	3.50	8.00
	1916/5D	I.A.	.75	1.50	3.50	8.00
	1916D	Inc. Ab.	.75	1.50	3.50	8.00
	1916E	1.640	.75	1.50	3.50	8.00
	1916F	2.410	.75	1.50	3.50	8.00
	1916G	1.779	.75	1.50	3.50	8.00
	1916J	1.464	.75	1.50	3.50	8.00
	1917A	14.692	.75	1.50	3.50	8.00
	1917/05D	.979	.75	1.50	3.50	8.00
	1917D	Inc. Ab.	.75	1.50	3.50	8.00
	1917E	1.561	.75	1.50	3.50	8.00
	1917F	.450	2.50	10.00	15.00	30.00
	1917G	.619	2.50	10.00	15.00	30.00
	1917J	1.039	1.50	4.00	6.00	12.50
	1918A*	14.622	.75	1.50	3.50	8.00
	1918/05D	3.670	.75	1.50	3.50	8.00
	1918D*	Inc. Ab.	.75	1.50	3.50	8.00
	1918E*	2.807	2.50	7.50	10.00	15.00
	1918E	19 pcs.	—	—	Proof	—
	1918F*	4.010	.75	1.50	4.00	8.00
	1918G*	1.032	1.50	6.00	10.00	12.50
	1918J*	3.452	.75	1.50	5.00	12.00
	1919A*	9.124	.75	1.50	5.00	12.00
	1919/1619D	2.195	.75	1.50	5.00	12.00
	1919/05D	I.A.	.75	1.50	5.00	12.00
	1919D*	Inc. Ab.	.75	1.50	5.00	12.00
	1919E*	1.767	2.50	7.50	12.50	18.00
	1919F*	1.559	2.00	6.00	12.00	22.50
	1919J*	1.875	1.00	3.00	5.00	12.50
	Common date		—	—	Proof	75.00

***NOTE:** Some were issued with a black finish to prevent hoarding.

MARK

5.5500 g, .900 SILVER, .1606 oz ASW

KM#	Date	Mintage	Fine	VF	XF	Unc
7	1873A	.930	2.50	5.00	25.00	75.00
	1873B	.089	12.50	25.00	100.00	150.00
	1873C	.018	65.00	140.00	225.00	350.00
	1873D	.244	5.00	12.50	65.00	100.00
	1873F	.109	10.00	20.00	80.00	125.00
	1874A	6.310	2.50	6.00	30.00	60.00
	1874B	2.672	6.00	15.00	65.00	90.00
	1874C	.840	6.00	15.00	70.00	95.00
	1874D	7.079	2.50	6.00	30.00	75.00
	1874E	3.240	4.00	15.00	50.00	80.00
	1874F	6.155	2.50	6.00	30.00	75.00
	1874G	4.210	2.50	12.50	25.00	90.00
	1874H	1.893	4.00	7.50	55.00	135.00
	1875A	30.340	2.50	7.50	27.50	55.00
	1875B	7.690	2.50	7.50	70.00	90.00
	1875C	6.209	2.50	7.50	55.00	85.00
	1875D	7.538	2.50	5.00	30.00	70.00
	1875E	4.646	2.50	7.50	50.00	80.00
	1875F	7.074	2.50	5.00	20.00	65.00
	1875G	6.072	2.50	7.50	40.00	80.00
	1875H	2.300	2.50	7.50	45.00	85.00
	1875J	7.728	2.50	7.50	20.00	65.00
	1876A	17.297	2.50	5.00	30.00	70.00
	1876C	4.790	2.50	7.50	45.00	85.00
	1876D	2.956	2.50	7.50	45.00	85.00
	1876F	4.161	2.50	7.50	45.00	85.00
	1876G	2.333	2.50	7.50	40.00	80.00
	1876H	2.481	2.50	7.50	40.00	80.00
	1876J	1.109	2.50	7.50	50.00	90.00
	1877A	.697	4.00	7.50	40.00	80.00
	1877B	.048	35.00	45.00	130.00	250.00
	1878A	1.527	2.50	7.50	50.00	80.00
	1878B	.582	5.00	12.50	60.00	150.00
	1878C	.600	10.00	25.00	120.00	225.00
	1878E	.318	7.50	20.00	100.00	175.00
	1878F	1.039	5.00	12.50	60.00	90.00
	1878G	.525	5.00	12.50	50.00	80.00
	1878J	.895	5.00	12.50	50.00	80.00
	1879A	.156	45.00	80.00	160.00	225.00
	1880A	1.071	5.00	12.50	60.00	90.00
	1880D	.338	5.00	12.50	75.00	135.00
	1880E	.173	10.00	20.00	100.00	165.00
	1880F	.223	10.00	20.00	100.00	165.00
	1880G	.146	50.00	75.00	150.00	250.00
	1880H	.164	25.00	50.00	150.00	275.00
	1880J	.197	10.00	22.50	110.00	175.00
	1881A	6.386	2.50	5.00	30.00	70.00
	1881D	2.040	2.50	5.00	30.00	60.00
	1881E	1.081	5.00	10.00	70.00	115.00
	1881F	1.455	4.00	10.00	45.00	90.00
	1881G	.426	7.50	12.50	75.00	125.00
	1881H	.387	7.50	12.50	75.00	125.00
	1881J	.790	5.00	10.00	45.00	90.00
	1882A	1.474	2.50	12.50	55.00	115.00
	1882G	.459	7.50	12.50	60.00	120.00
	1882H	.109	35.00	70.00	200.00	350.00
	1882J	.098	7.50	12.50	60.00	120.00
	1883A	.809	5.00	10.00	45.00	80.00
7	1883D	.208	30.00	50.00	100.00	180.00
	1883E	.112	30.00	60.00	200.00	325.00
	1883F	.148	17.50	30.00	125.00	200.00
	1883G	.091	65.00	100.00	250.00	375.00
	1883J	.121	25.00	40.00	150.00	235.00
	1885A	1.467	2.50	5.00	35.00	75.00
	1885G	.468	5.00	15.00	75.00	125.00
	1885J	.413	7.50	15.00	90.00	135.00
	1886A	1.101	3.00	7.50	35.00	65.00
	1886D	1.445	3.00	7.50	40.00	80.00
	1886E	.764	7.50	15.00	60.00	100.00
	1886F	1.031	2.50	6.00	40.00	70.00
	1886G	.161	15.00	45.00	135.00	200.00
	1886J	.427	7.50	15.00	75.00	125.00
	1887A	3.006	2.50	7.50	40.00	80.00
	Common date		—	—	Proof	350.00

KM#	Date	Mintage	Fine	VF	XF	Unc
14	1891A	.711	7.50	12.50	20.00	60.00
	1891D	Inc.Be.	200.00	300.00	500.00	900.00
	1892A	.909	5.00	12.50	20.00	60.00
	1892D	.418	5.00	12.50	20.00	60.00
	1892E	.223	10.00	16.00	25.00	90.00
	1892F	.302	5.00	12.50	20.00	60.00
	1892G	.183	12.00	18.00	35.00	85.00
	1892J	.237	15.00	35.00	65.00	100.00
	1893A	1.633	2.50	5.00	10.00	50.00
	1893D	.425	2.50	5.00	17.50	50.00
	1893E	.224	7.50	17.50	25.00	80.00
	1893F	.300	7.50	15.00	20.00	75.00
	1893J	.254	5.00	12.50	22.50	90.00
	1894G	.184	20.00	40.00	60.00	145.00
	1896A	2.160	2.50	5.00	12.50	45.00
	1896D	.562	2.50	6.00	15.00	55.00
	1896E	.297	5.00	15.00	30.00	80.00
	1896F	.401	2.50	6.00	15.00	75.00
	1896G	.243	7.50	20.00	40.00	90.00
	1896J	.326	5.00	15.00	30.00	85.00
	1898A	1.000	5.00	12.50	20.00	65.00
	1899A	1.439	2.50	5.00	12.50	50.00
	1899D	.633	2.50	5.00	12.50	50.00
	1899E	.335	5.00	12.50	17.50	60.00
	1899F	.393	2.50	5.00	12.50	50.00
	1899G	.274	4.00	10.00	25.00	75.00
	1899J	.368	4.00	10.00	25.00	75.00
	1900A	1.625	2.50	5.00	10.00	30.00
	1900/800D	.421	2.50	5.00	10.00	50.00
	1900/801D	.915	2.50	5.00	10.00	50.00
	1900D	Inc. Ab.	2.50	5.00	10.00	50.00
	1900E	.223	5.00	15.00	20.00	55.00
	1900F	.301	5.00	15.00	20.00	60.00
	1900G	.183	7.50	17.50	25.00	90.00
	1900J	.246	10.00	20.00	30.00	80.00
	1901A	3.821	2.50	5.00	10.00	15.00
	1901D	Inc. Ab.	2.50	5.00	12.00	20.00
	1901E	.484	2.50	6.00	17.50	27.50
	1901F	.802	2.50	5.00	10.00	15.00
	1901G	.579	2.50	5.00	12.50	25.00
	1901J	.531	2.50	5.00	12.50	25.00
	1902A	5.222	1.50	4.00	8.00	15.00
	1902D	1.546	1.50	4.00	8.00	15.00
	1902E	.819	1.50	4.00	8.00	17.50
	1902F	.953	1.50	4.00	8.00	15.00
	1902G	.270	6.00	25.00	35.00	55.00
	1902J	.898	2.50	5.00	10.00	20.00
	1903A	3.965	1.25	2.00	5.00	12.50
	1903/803D	.914	1.25	2.50	6.00	12.50
	1903D	Inc. Ab.	1.25	2.50	6.00	12.50
	1903E	.485	5.00	10.00	15.00	25.00
	1903F	.652	5.00	7.50	12.00	22.50
	1903G	.614	2.50	5.00	12.00	22.50
	1903J	.531	5.00	12.00	20.00	30.00
	1904A	3.243	1.25	2.00	5.00	12.50
	1904D	1.761	1.25	2.00	6.00	15.00
	1904E	.931	2.50	5.00	10.00	15.00
	1904F	1.255	2.50	4.00	7.50	15.00
	1904G	.664	2.50	5.00	10.00	15.00
	1904J	1.021	2.50	5.00	10.00	15.00
	1905A	10.303	1.25	2.00	5.00	10.00
	1905D	1.759	2.50	4.00	7.50	15.00
	1905E	.931	2.50	4.00	10.00	15.00
	1905F	Inc.Ab.	800.00	1400.	1750.	2000.
	1905G	.860	2.50	5.00	10.00	15.00
	1905J	1.021	1.50	5.00	6.00	17.50
	1906A	5.414	1.25	2.50	5.00	12.00
	1906D	1.412	1.25	2.50	7.50	12.50
	1906E	.745	1.50	5.00	10.00	15.00
	1906F	2.257	1.25	2.50	5.00	15.00
	1906G	.609	2.50	5.00	10.00	15.00
	1906G	10-30 pcs.	—	—	Proof	—
	1906J	.372	2.50	6.00	12.50	20.00
	1907A	9.201	1.25	2.50	5.00	12.00
	1907D	2.387	1.25	2.50	5.00	12.50
	1907E	1.265	1.25	2.50	6.00	15.00
	1907F	1.704	1.25	2.50	6.00	15.00
	1907G	1.035	1.25	2.50	6.00	15.00
	1907J	1.833	1.25	2.50	6.00	15.00
	1908A	4.338	1.25	2.50	5.00	10.00
	1908D	1.126	1.25	2.50	5.00	12.50
	1908E	.596	2.50	5.00	10.00	25.00

KM#	Date	Mintage	Fine	VF	XF	Unc
14	1908F	.802	1.25	2.50	5.00	12.50
	1908G	.488	2.50	5.00	10.00	15.00
	1908J	.653	2.50	5.00	10.00	15.00
	1909A	4.151	1.25	2.50	5.00	10.00
	1909D	1.968	1.25	3.00	5.00	12.50
	1909E	Inc.Be.	25.00	75.00	125.00	200.00
	1909G	.854	5.00	20.00	30.00	45.00
	1909J	.053	75.00	150.00	200.00	300.00
	1910A	5.870	1.25	1.50	4.00	10.00
	1910D	1.406	1.25	2.50	5.00	12.00
	1910E	1.050	2.50	5.00	7.50	17.50
	1910F	1.631	2.50	5.00	7.50	17.50
	1910G	.610	2.50	5.00	12.00	16.00
	1910J	1.094	2.50	5.00	12.00	17.50
	1911A	5.693	1.25	2.50	5.00	10.00
	1911D	.126	10.00	20.00	30.00	45.00
	1911E	.738	4.00	6.00	12.50	20.00
	1911F	.773	2.50	6.00	12.50	20.00
	1911G	.305	4.00	6.00	12.50	20.00
	1911J	.812	4.00	6.00	12.50	20.00
	1912A	2.439	1.25	2.50	5.00	10.00
	1912D	.632	1.25	2.50	5.00	12.00
	1912E	.708	2.50	5.00	12.00	16.00
	1912F	.502	2.50	5.00	12.00	16.00
	1912J	.409	2.50	6.00	12.00	20.00
	1913F	.450	10.00	27.50	45.00	60.00
	1913G	.275	20.00	40.00	60.00	90.00
	1913J	.368	15.00	30.00	45.00	65.00
	1914A	11.304	1.25	1.50	3.00	9.00
	1914/9D	3.515	1.25	1.50	3.00	9.00
	1914D	Inc. Ab.	1.25	1.50	3.00	9.00
	1914E	2.235	1.25	1.50	3.00	9.00
	1914F	2.300	1.25	1.50	3.00	9.00
	1914G	1.911	1.25	1.50	3.00	9.00
	1914J	2.978	1.25	1.50	3.00	9.00
	1915A	13.817	1.25	1.50	3.00	9.00
	1915D	4.218	1.25	1.50	3.00	9.00
	1915E	2.235	1.25	1.50	3.00	9.00
	1915F	2.911	1.25	1.50	3.00	9.00
	1915G	1.749	1.25	1.50	3.00	9.00
	1915J	1.634	1.25	1.50	3.00	9.00
	1916F	.306	12.00	22.50	35.00	50.00
	Common date		—	—	Proof	100.00

WW I OCCUPATION COINAGE

Issued by authority of the German Military Commander of the East for use in the Baltic States, Poland, and Northwest Russia.

KOPEK

IRON

KM#	Date	Mintage	Fine	VF	XF	Unc
21	1916A	11.942	2.50	5.00	10.00	15.00
	1916A	—	—	—	Proof	75.00
	1916J	8.000	2.50	5.00	10.00	15.00
	1916J	—	—	—	Proof	75.00

2 KOPEKS

IRON

KM#	Date	Mintage	Fine	VF	XF	Unc
22	1916A	6.973	2.50	5.00	12.50	17.50
	1916A	—	—	—	Proof	75.00
	1916J	8.000	2.50	5.00	12.50	17.50
	1916J	—	—	—	Proof	75.00

3 KOPEKS

IRON

KM#	Date	Mintage	Fine	VF	XF	Unc
23	1916A	8.670	2.50	5.00	12.50	20.00
	1916A	—	—	—	Proof	75.00
	1916J	8.000	2.50	5.00	12.50	20.00
	1916J	—	—	—	Proof	75.00

WEIMAR REPUBLIC

1919-1933

RENTENPFENNIG

BRONZE

KM#	Date	Mintage	Fine	VF	XF	Unc
30	1923A	12.629	.15	.50	1.50	5.00
	1923D	*2.314	.25	2.00	5.00	18.00
	1923E	2.200	1.50	4.00	7.50	20.00
	1923F	.160	1.50	4.00	7.50	20.00
	1923G	1.004	.25	1.50	4.00	16.00
	1923J	1.470	.25	1.50	6.00	20.00
	1924A	55.273	.15	.50	2.50	7.50
	1924D	17.540	.20	1.50	5.00	10.00
	1924E	6.838	.20	1.50	6.00	12.50
	1924F	10.347	.20	1.50	5.00	10.00
	1924G	7.366	.25	1.50	6.00	12.50
	1924J	11.024	.20	1.50	5.00	10.00
	1925A	—	300.00	500.00	650.00	800.00
	1929F	—	125.00	225.00	350.00	500.00
	Common date		—	—	Proof	40.00

REICHSPFENNIG

BRONZE

KM#	Date	Mintage	Fine	VF	XF	Unc
37	1924A	13.496	.10	.25	1.00	6.00
	1924D	6.206	.10	.25	1.00	6.00
	1924E	1.100	100.00	175.00	225.00	300.00
	1924F	2.650	.15	.30	1.00	6.00
	1924G	5.100	.15	.50	2.00	8.50
	1924J	24.400	.10	.25	1.00	6.00
	1925A	40.925	.10	.25	1.00	5.00
	1925D	1.558	5.00	12.50	22.50	40.00
	1925E	10.460	.10	.25	1.00	6.00
	1925F	5.673	.10	.25	1.00	6.00
	1925G	13.502	.10	.25	1.00	6.00
	1925J	30.300	.10	.25	1.00	6.00
	1927A	4.671	.10	.25	1.00	6.00
	1927D	4.203	.15	.50	2.00	8.50
	1927E	8.000	.15	.50	3.50	12.00
	1927F	2.350	.25	1.00	2.00	8.50
	1927G	3.236	.15	.50	3.50	12.00
	1928A	19.300	.10	.25	1.00	3.50
	1928D	10.200	.10	.25	1.00	3.50
	1928F	8.672	.10	.25	1.00	3.50
	1928G	3.764	.15	.50	2.00	6.00
	1929A	37.170	.10	.25	1.00	3.50
	1929D	9.337	.10	.25	1.00	3.50
	1929E	6.600	.15	.30	1.00	5.00
	1929F	3.150	.10	.25	1.50	6.00
	1929G	1.986	.15	.50	2.00	6.00
	1930A	40.997	.10	.25	1.00	3.50
	1930D	6.441	.10	.25	1.00	3.50
	1930E	1.412	6.00	12.00	25.00	60.00
	1930F	6.415	.10	.50	1.50	6.00
	1930G	5.017	.10	.25	1.00	3.50
	1931A	38.481	.10	.25	1.00	3.50
	1931D	5.998	.10	.25	1.00	3.50
	1931E	12.800	.15	.50	2.00	6.00
	1931F	12.591	.10	.25	1.00	3.50
	1931G	2.622	.15	.50	2.50	7.50
	1932A	17.096	.10	.25	1.00	3.50
	1933A	37.846	.10	.25	1.00	3.50
	1933E	2.945	.35	2.00	4.50	9.00
	1933F	5.023	.10	.50	1.00	5.00
	1934A	51.214	.10	.25	1.00	5.00
	1934D	7.408	.10	.25	1.00	5.00
	1934E	4.628	.50	3.50	9.00	15.00
	1934F	5.667	.10	.25	1.00	5.00
	1934G	2.450	.15	.30	1.00	5.00
	1934J	4.271	.15	.50	3.00	8.50
	1935A	35.894	.10	.25	1.00	5.00
	1935D	15.489	.10	.25	1.00	5.00
	1935E	8.351	.15	.50	2.50	7.50
	1935F	12.094	.10	.25	1.00	5.00
	1935G	7.454	.10	.25	1.00	5.00
	1935J	8.505	.10	.25	1.00	5.00
	1936A	*50.949	.10	.25	1.00	5.00
	1936D	12.262	.10	.25	1.00	5.00
	1936E	2.576	.50	3.00	10.00	15.00
	1936F	6.915	.10	.25	1.00	5.00
	1936G	*2.940	.15	.30	1.00	5.00
	1936J	*5.421	.15	.50	2.00	7.50
	Common date		—	—	Proof	50.00

2 RENTENPFENNIG

BRONZE

KM#	Date	Mintage	Fine	VF	XF	Unc
31	1923A	8.587	.15	.50	2.50	10.00
	1923D	1.490	.15	.50	3.00	8.50
	1923F	Inc.Ab.	.50	5.00	15.00	25.00
	1923G	Inc.Ab.	.25	1.00	6.50	12.50
	1923J	Inc.Ab.	.50	5.00	12.50	20.00
	1924A	80.864	.10	.25	2.50	7.50
	1924D	19.899	.10	.25	2.50	7.50
	1924E	6.595	.15	.50	3.00	9.00
	1924F	14.969	.15	.50	3.00	7.50
	1924G	10.349	.15	.50	3.00	7.50
	1924J	21.196	.25	1.00	5.00	7.50
	Common date		—	—	Proof	80.00

2 REICHSPFENNIG

BRONZE

KM#	Date	Mintage	Fine	VF	XF	Unc
38	1923F	—	400.00	600.00	750.00	1000.
	1924A	19.620	.10	.25	1.00	6.00
	1924D	3.482	.10	.30	1.50	10.00
	1924E	4.253	.15	1.50	7.50	15.00
	1924F	4.567	.10	.20	1.00	7.50
	1924G	7.560	.10	.20	1.00	7.50
	1924J	7.489	.10	.25	1.00	7.50
	1925A	22.433	.10	.25	1.00	6.00
	1925D	2.412	.15	.60	2.50	10.00
	1925E	5.414	.10	.30	1.50	7.50
	1925F	4.851	.10	.30	1.50	7.50
	1925G	2.456	.25	1.50	7.50	17.50
	1936A	3.220	.25	2.00	7.50	15.00
	1936D	6.525	.10	.30	1.50	7.50
	1936E	.573	5.00	15.00	22.50	40.00
	1936F	3.100	.15	.50	1.00	6.00
	Common date		—	—	Proof	70.00

4 REICHSPFENNIG

BRONZE

KM#	Date	Mintage	Fine	VF	XF	Unc
75	1932A	27.101	2.50	6.50	10.00	18.00
	1932A	—	—	—	Proof	125.00
	1932D	7.055	2.50	5.00	12.50	22.50
	1932D	—	—	—	Proof	125.00
	1932E	3.729	2.50	7.50	15.00	40.00
	1932E	—	—	—	Proof	125.00
	1932F	5.022	2.50	7.50	15.00	40.00
	1932F	—	—	—	Proof	125.00
	1932G	3.050	5.00	15.00	25.00	50.00
	1932G	—	—	—	Proof	125.00
	1932J	4.094	2.50	10.00	20.00	40.00
	1932J	—	—	—	Proof	125.00

5 RENTENPFENNIG

ALUMINUM-BRONZE

KM#	Date	Mintage	Fine	VF	XF	Unc
32	1923A	3.083	.20	1.00	2.50	10.00
	1923D	Inc.Be.	.30	1.50	3.00	17.50
	1923F	Inc.Be.	50.00	100.00	125.00	175.00
	1923G	Inc.Be.	25.00	45.00	85.00	120.00
	1924A	171.966	.10	.50	2.00	7.50
	1924D	31.163	.20	.50	1.00	6.00
	1924E	12.206	.20	.50	1.00	7.50
	1924F	29.032	.20	.50	1.00	7.50
	1924G	19.217	.20	.50	1.00	7.50
	1924J	32.332	.20	.50	1.00	7.50
	1925F	—	500.00	750.00	1000.	1500.
	Common date		—	—	Proof	80.00

5 REICHSPFENNIG

ALUMINUM-BRONZE

KM#	Date	Mintage	Fine	VF	XF	Unc
39	1924A	14.469	.20	.50	2.50	12.50
	1924D	8.139	.20	.50	2.50	7.50
	1924E	5.976	.20	1.00	5.00	12.50
	1924F	3.134	.20	1.00	5.00	12.50
	1924G	4.790	.20	1.00	7.50	12.50
	1924J	2.200	.25	1.00	3.50	10.00
	1925A	85.239	.15	.40	2.00	6.00
	1925D	39.750	.15	.35	2.00	6.00

GERMANY 722

KM#	Date	Mintage	Fine	VF	XF	Unc
39	1925E	17.554	.20	1.00	5.00	10.00
	1925F large 5					
		20.990	.15	.35	2.50	5.00
	1925F small 5					
		Inc. Ab.	.15	.35	2.50	5.00
	1925G	10.232	.20	1.00	5.00	10.00
	1925J	10.950	.20	1.00	5.00	12.50
	1926A	22.377	.15	.40	2.00	10.00
	1926E	5.990	10.00	20.00	35.00	45.00
	1926F	2.871	5.00	12.50	25.00	35.00
	1930A	7.418	.20	.50	3.00	10.00
	1935A	19.178	.15	.25	.50	5.00
	1935D	5.480	.15	.35	1.00	7.00
	1935E	2.384	.20	.50	3.00	9.00
	1935F	4.585	.15	.40	1.50	7.00
	1935G	2.652	.20	.50	3.00	9.00
	1935J	2.614	.20	.50	3.00	9.00
	1936A	36.992	.15	.25	.50	6.00
	1936D	8.108	.15	.35	1.00	7.00
	1936E	2.981	.20	.50	3.00	9.00
	1936F	6.643	.15	.30	1.00	6.00
	1936G	2.274	.20	.35	1.00	7.00
	1936J	4.470	.20	.50	3.00	9.00
	Common date		—	—	Proof	60.00

10 RENTENPFENNIG

ALUMINUM-BRONZE

KM#	Date	Mintage	Fine	VF	XF	Unc
33	1923A	Inc.Be.	.25	2.50	6.00	17.50
	1923D	Inc.Be.	.50	5.00	10.00	25.00
	1923F	Inc. Be.	50.00	90.00	150.00	250.00
	1923G	Inc. Be.	2.50	15.00	25.00	50.00
	1924A	169.956	.20	.40	2.50	7.50
	1924D	33.894	.15	.50	1.00	10.00
	1924E	18.679	.20	1.00	1.50	7.50
	1924F	42.237	.15	.50	1.00	7.50
	1924F	—	—	—	Proof	75.00
	1924G	18.758	.20	.50	1.00	10.00
	1924J	33.928	.15	.50	1.00	10.00
	1925F	.013	250.00	500.00	750.00	1000.

10 REICHSPFENNIG

ALUMINUM-BRONZE

KM#	Date	Mintage	Fine	VF	XF	Unc
40	1924A	20.883	.15	.25	1.00	10.00
	1924D	9.639	.15	.50	1.50	12.00
	1924E	5.185	.20	1.00	1.50	15.00
	1924F	2.758	1.00	7.50	15.00	37.50
	1924G	4.363	.20	1.00	1.50	15.00
	1924J	3.993	.15	.50	1.00	12.00
	1925A	102.319	.10	.15	.50	7.50
	1925D	36.853	.10	.15	.50	7.50
	1925E	18.700	.15	.50	1.00	12.00
	1925F	12.516	.10	.15	.50	10.00
	1925G	10.360	.10	.50	1.00	10.00
	1925J	8.755	4.00	12.50	25.00	37.50
	1926A	14.390	.20	2.00	4.00	12.50
	1926G	1.481	2.50	10.00	20.00	37.50
	1928A	2.308	2.00	6.00	9.00	15.00
	1928G	Inc. Be.	40.00	80.00	130.00	180.00
	1929A	25.712	.15	.50	1.50	10.00
	1929D	7.049	.15	.50	1.50	10.00
	1929E	3.138	.20	1.00	2.50	15.00
	1929F	3.740	.20	1.00	2.50	15.00
	1929G	2.729	.30	3.50	6.00	18.00
	1929J	4.086	.20	2.50	5.00	16.00
	1930A	7.540	.20	2.00	2.50	10.00
	1930D	2.148	.25	3.50	5.00	12.50
	1930E	2.090	1.00	5.00	12.50	20.00
	1930F	2.006	1.00	5.00	10.00	27.50
	1930G	1.542	5.00	15.00	30.00	50.00
	1930J	1.637	2.50	5.00	12.50	25.00
	1931A	9.661	.20	2.50	5.00	12.50
	1931D	.664	15.00	35.00	60.00	100.00
	1931F	1.482	2.50	10.00	12.50	27.50
	1931G	.038	175.00	300.00	450.00	600.00
	1932A	4.528	.25	3.50	6.00	15.00
	1932D	2.812	.50	5.00	7.50	15.00
	1932E	1.491	6.00	12.50	17.50	30.00
	1932F	1.806	6.00	12.50	17.50	30.00
	1932G	.137	375.00	625.00	900.00	1100.
	1933A	1.349	20.00	35.00	50.00	100.00
	1933G	1.046	5.00	10.00	15.00	35.00
	1933J	1.634	1.00	8.50	14.00	30.00
	1934A	3.200	.20	1.00	6.00	15.00
	1934D	1.252	1.00	7.50	10.00	20.00
	1934E	Inc. Be.	22.50	45.00	65.00	100.00
	1934F	.100	20.00	40.00	60.00	90.00
	1934G	.150	20.00	40.00	65.00	125.00
	1935A	35.890	.10	.15	1.00	7.00
	1935D	8.960	.10	.25	1.50	10.00
	1935E	5.966	.15	.35	2.00	12.00

KM#	Date	Mintage	Fine	VF	XF	Unc
40	1935F	7.944	.10	.30	1.50	10.00
	1935G	4.847	.10	.50	3.00	12.50
	1935J	8.995	.10	.30	1.50	10.00
	1936A	24.527	.10	.15	.50	6.00
	1936D	8.092	.10	.20	1.00	10.00
	1936E	2.441	.20	.50	2.50	12.00
	1936F	4.889	.10	.30	1.50	10.00
	1936G	1.715	.15	.60	2.50	12.00
	1936J	1.632	.25	3.00	5.00	15.00
	Common date		—	—	Proof	60.00

50 PFENNIG

ALUMINUM

KM#	Date	Mintage	Fine	VF	XF	Unc
27	1919A	7.173	.25	1.50	4.00	6.00
	1919D	.791	.50	1.50	3.50	10.00
	1919E	.930	1.50	6.00	10.00	20.00
	1919E	35 pcs.	—	—	Proof	—
	1919F	.160	5.00	10.00	18.00	40.00
	1919G	.660	.75	5.00	7.50	12.50
	1919J	.800	3.00	7.50	12.00	30.00
	1920A	119.793	.10	.15	.25	1.00
	1920D	28.306	.10	.15	.25	1.00
	1920E	14.400	.25	1.50	4.00	10.00
	1920E	226 pcs.	—	—	Proof	35.00
	1920F	10.932	.10	.15	.25	1.00
	1920G	5.040	.20	1.50	2.50	5.00
	1920J	15.423	.10	.25	1.00	4.00
	1921A	184.468	.10	.15	.25	1.00
	1921D	48.729	.10	.15	.25	1.00
	1921E	31.210	.15	1.50	2.50	5.00
	1921E	332 pcs.	—	—	Proof	35.00
	1921F	46.950	.10	.15	.25	1.00
	1921G	19.107	.10	.20	.50	1.00
	1921J	28.013	.10	.25	1.00	4.00
	1922A	145.215	.10	.15	.25	1.00
	1922D	58.019	.10	.15	.25	1.00
	1922E	33.930	.15	1.50	2.50	5.00
	1922E	333 pcs.	—	—	Proof	35.00
	1922F	33.000	.10	.15	.25	1.00
	1922G	36.745	.10	.20	.50	1.00
	1922J	36.202	.25	2.50	4.50	9.00

50 RENTENPFENNIG

ALUMINUM-BRONZE

KM#	Date	Mintage	Fine	VF	XF	Unc
34	1923A	.451	5.00	17.50	30.00	50.00
	1923D	.192	12.50	20.00	35.00	55.00
	1923F	.120	45.00	90.00	120.00	175.00
	1923G	.120	15.00	30.00	55.00	90.00
	1923J	4,000	600.00	1200.	1600.	2000.
	1924A	117.365	5.00	10.00	15.00	35.00
	1924D	30.971	5.00	10.00	15.00	40.00
	1924E	14.668	5.00	10.00	20.00	45.00
	1924F	21.968	5.00	10.00	15.00	40.00
	1924G	13.349	7.50	15.00	22.50	40.00
	1924J	17.252	5.00	10.00	15.00	40.00
	Common date		—	—	Proof	125.00

50 REICHSPFENNIG

ALUMINUM-BRONZE

KM#	Date	Mintage	Fine	VF	XF	Unc
41	1924A	.801	325.00	850.00	1100.	1400.
	1924A	—	—	—	Proof	1500.
	1924E	Inc.Be.	900.00	1900.	2800.	4250.
	1924F	.055	1250.	2500.	4000.	6500.
	1924G	.011	1500.	3250.	5500.	7000.
	1924G	—	—	—	Proof	3000.
	1925E	1.805	500.00	800.00	1000.	1250.
	1925E	196 pcs.	—	—	Proof	3000.

NICKEL

KM#	Date	Mintage	Fine	VF	XF	Unc
49	1927A	16.309	2.00	3.50	5.00	10.00
	1927D	2.228	2.50	5.00	7.50	12.50
	1927E	1.070	5.00	10.00	15.00	20.00
	1927F	1.940	2.50	5.00	7.50	12.50
	1927G	1.756	4.00	7.50	10.00	15.00
	1927J	4.056	2.50	5.00	7.50	12.50
	1928A	43.864	.25	1.50	3.50	7.50
	1928D	14.088	.50	2.50	5.00	10.00
	1928E	8.618	.50	3.50	6.00	12.50
	1928F	9.954	.50	2.50	5.00	10.00
	1928G	6.177	.50	4.50	7.50	15.00
	1928J	6.565	.50	2.50	5.00	10.00
	1929A	10.298	.50	2.00	4.00	7.50
	1929D	1.965	.50	3.50	6.00	12.50
	1929E	—	—	Reported, not confirmed		
	1929F	1.162	5.00	12.50	20.00	32.50
	1930A	4.128	.50	4.50	7.50	12.50
	1930D	1.406	1.00	10.00	15.00	27.50
	1930E	.745	5.00	17.50	25.00	45.00
	1930F	.320	20.00	60.00	85.00	100.00
	1930G	.610	5.00	20.00	40.00	50.00
	1930J	.526	3.00	20.00	35.00	45.00
	1930	—	—	—	—	—
	1931A	5.624	.50	4.00	7.50	10.00
	1931D	1.125	1.50	12.50	17.50	30.00
	1931F	1.484	1.50	12.00	16.00	25.00
	1931G	.060	45.00	90.00	135.00	200.00
	1931J	.291	25.00	50.00	65.00	100.00
	1932E	.598	20.00	50.00	70.00	16.00
	1932G	.096	875.00	1500.	1750.	2250.
	1933G	.333	40.00	80.00	125.00	185.00
	1933J	.654	35.00	65.00	110.00	140.00
	1935A	6.390	.50	4.00	6.00	8.50
	1935D	2.812	2.50	7.50	15.00	20.00
	1935E	.745	7.50	30.00	40.00	50.00
	1935F	2.006	2.50	7.50	10.00	15.00
	1935G	.650	12.50	37.50	50.00	70.00
	1935J	1.635	2.00	15.00	20.00	27.50
	1935	—	1.00	6.00	12.50	25.00
	1936A	7.696	2.50	5.00	7.50	12.50
	1936D	.844	4.00	22.50	50.00	70.00
	1936E	1.190	7.50	27.50	35.00	75.00
	1936F	.602	15.00	40.00	65.00	80.00
	1936G	.936	5.00	15.00	30.00	40.00
	1936J	.490	25.00	75.00	100.00	160.00
	1937A	10.842	.25	2.50	5.00	7.50
	1937D	2.814	.50	4.00	7.50	10.00
	1937F	1.700	.50	2.50	10.00	12.50
	1937J	.300	45.00	95.00	125.00	175.00
	1938E	1.200	7.50	12.50	22.50	30.00
	1938G	1.299	7.50	12.50	25.00	35.00
	1938J	1.333	7.50	15.00	25.00	35.00
	Common date		—	—	Proof	75.00

MARK

5.0000 g, .500 SILVER, .0803 oz ASW

KM#	Date	Mintage	Fine	VF	XF	Unc
42	1924A	75.536	5.00	10.00	15.00	30.00
	1924D	17.099	6.00	12.50	25.00	50.00
	1924E	12.293	6.00	12.50	25.00	50.00
	1924E	115 pcs.	—	—	Proof	225.00
	1924F	16.550	7.50	17.50	20.00	40.00
	1924G	10.065	7.50	17.50	25.00	45.00
	1924J	13.481	7.50	17.50	20.00	40.00
	1925A	13.878	8.00	30.00	50.00	90.00
	1925D	6.100	8.00	15.00	35.00	60.00
	Common date		—	—	Proof	125.00

REICHSMARK

5.0000 g, .500 SILVER, .0803 oz ASW

KM#	Date	Mintage	Fine	VF	XF	Unc
44	1925A	34.527	3.00	10.00	20.00	32.00
	1925A	600 pcs.	—	—	Proof	175.00
	1925D	13.854	3.00	12.50	22.50	35.00
	1925E	6.460	7.50	20.00	32.00	50.00
	1925F	8.035	7.50	17.50	27.50	50.00
	1925G	4.520	7.50	20.00	32.00	50.00
	1925J	6.800	7.50	17.50	27.50	50.00
	1926A	35.555	7.50	12.50	22.50	45.00

GERMANY 723

KM#	Date	Mintage	Fine	VF	XF	Unc
44	1926D	4.424	7.50	15.00	27.50	50.00
	1926E	3.225	7.50	15.00	45.00	60.00
	1926E	31 pcs.	—	—	Proof	125.00
	1926F	3.045	7.50	20.00	27.50	50.00
	1926G	3.410	7.50	27.50	45.00	60.00
	1926J	1.290	25.00	90.00	135.00	200.00
	1927A	.364	125.00	275.00	475.00	750.00
	1927F	1.959	15.00	45.00	85.00	125.00
	1927J	2.451	10.00	30.00	60.00	100.00

2 REICHSMARK

10.0000 g, .500 SILVER, .1608 oz ASW

KM#	Date	Mintage	Fine	VF	XF	Unc
45	1925A	16.145	10.00	15.00	20.00	45.00
	1925D	2.272	10.00	35.00	50.00	
	1925E	1.971	10.00	17.50	40.00	85.00
	1925E	101 pcs.	—	—	Proof	200.00
	1925F	2.414	10.00	17.50	35.00	65.00
	1925G	.929	10.00	20.00	45.00	90.00
	1925J	2.326	10.00	17.50	35.00	65.00
	1926A	31.645	5.00	10.00	17.50	35.00
	1926D	11.322	5.00	10.00	20.00	45.00
	1926E	5.107	7.50	15.00	25.00	55.00
	1926E	30 pcs.	—	—	Proof	—
	1926F	7.115	7.50	15.00	25.00	50.00
	1926G	5.171	7.50	15.00	25.00	55.00
	1926J	5.305	7.50	15.00	25.00	55.00
	1927A	6.399	7.50	15.00	25.00	50.00
	1927D	.466	400.00	850.00	1200.	1850.
	1927E	.373	125.00	400.00	600.00	1100.
	1927E	53 pcs.	—	—	Proof	2150.
	1927F	.502	65.00	125.00	200.00	300.00
	1927J	.540	50.00	100.00	150.00	220.00
	1931D	2.109	22.50	40.00	60.00	115.00
	1931E	1.118	25.00	45.00	65.00	135.00
	1931F	1.505	22.50	45.00	65.00	135.00
	1931G	.915	35.00	75.00	115.00	200.00
	1931J	1.226	22.50	40.00	65.00	135.00
Common date					Proof	150.00

3 MARK

ALUMINUM
Reeded edge

28.1	1922A	15.497	.25	2.50	5.00	10.00
	1922A	—	—	—	Proof	50.00
	1922E	2,000	90.00	175.00	300.00	500.00
	1922E	1,000	—	—	Proof	650.00

Lettered edge

| 28.2 | 1922F | — | — | — | 175.00 |

NOTE: The market values for KM#28.2 are for fire damaged coins. Only 1 pc. is known in perfect condition.

3rd Anniversary Weimar Constitution

29	1922A	32.514	.25	1.00	1.50	2.50
	1922D	8.441	175.00	250.00	350.00	550.00
	1922D	—	—	—	Proof	500.00
	1922E	2.440	.50	5.00	7.50	15.00
	1922E	.022	—	—	Proof	25.00
	1922F	6.023	2.50	12.50	20.00	30.00
	1922G	3.655	.25	2.50	5.00	12.50
	1922J	4.896	.25	1.50	4.00	7.50
	1923E	2.030	17.50	40.00	60.00	85.00
	1923E	2,291	—	—	Proof	80.00
	1923F*	—	—	325.00		

*Fire damaged.

KM#	Date	Mintage	Fine	VF	XF	Unc
43	1924A	24.386	17.50	35.00	45.00	85.00
	1924D	3.769	12.50	35.00	60.00	110.00
	1924E	3.353	20.00	40.00	65.00	110.00
	1924E	115 pcs.	—	—	Proof	400.00
	1924F	4.518	20.00	40.00	65.00	110.00
	1924G	2.745	20.00	40.00	65.00	110.00
	1924J	3.677	20.00	40.00	65.00	110.00
	1925D	2.558	35.00	85.00	110.00	175.00
Common date					Proof	300.00

3 REICHSMARK

15.0000 g, .500 SILVER, .2411 oz ASW
Rhineland - 1000 Years

46	1925A	3.052	17.50	35.00	45.00	60.00
	1925A	—	—	—	Proof	125.00
	1925D	1.123	17.50	35.00	45.00	60.00
	1925D	—	—	—	Proof	150.00
	1925E	.441	20.00	40.00	50.00	70.00
	1925E	229 pcs.	—	—	Proof	175.00
	1925F	.173	20.00	40.00	55.00	75.00
	1925F	—	—	—	Proof	250.00
	1925G	.300	20.00	40.00	55.00	75.00
	1925G	—	—	—	Proof	200.00
	1925J	.492	20.00	40.00	50.00	70.00
	1925J	—	—	—	Proof	250.00

Lubeck - 700 Years

48	1926A	.200	65.00	125.00	165.00	225.00
	1926A	—	—	—	Proof	400.00

100th Year Bremerhaven

50	1927A	.150	65.00	125.00	150.00	200.00
	1927A	—	—	—	Proof	425.00

Nordhausen 1000th Anniversary

52	1927A	.100	65.00	120.00	140.00	215.00
	1927A	—	—	—	Proof	425.00

Marburg University 400th Year

KM#	Date	Mintage	Fine	VF	XF	Unc
53	1927A	.130	65.00	120.00	135.00	200.00
	1927A	—	—	—	Proof	250.00

Tubingen University 450th Year

54	1927F	.050	160.00	300.00	350.00	450.00
	1927F	—	—	—	Proof	600.00

Founding of Naumburg

57	1928A	.100	60.00	100.00	140.00	225.00
	1928A	—	—	—	Proof	350.00

400th Year Durer's Death

58	1928D	.050	150.00	300.00	350.00	400.00
	1928D	—	—	—	Proof	750.00

Dinkelsbuhl's 1000th Anniversary

59	1928D	.040	250.00	450.00	525.00	650.00
	1928D	—	—	—	Proof	1050.

Lessing's 200th Anniversary

60	1929A	.217	17.50	30.00	40.00	80.00
	1929A	—	—	—	Proof	125.00
	1929D	.056	20.00	35.00	50.00	100.00
	1929D	—	—	—	Proof	250.00
	1929E	.030	20.00	35.00	60.00	115.00
	1929E	—	—	—	Proof	275.00
	1929F	.040	20.00	35.00	50.00	100.00
	1929F	—	—	—	Proof	250.00
	1929G	.024	20.00	35.00	60.00	115.00
	1929G	—	—	—	Proof	325.00

KM#	Date	Mintage	Fine	VF	XF	Unc
60	1929J	.033	20.00	35.00	65.00	125.00
	1929J	—	—	—	Proof	325.00

			Waldeck-Prussia Union			
62	1929A	.170	60.00	100.00	140.00	170.00
	1929A	—	—	—	Proof	325.00

			Constitution 10th Year			
63	1929A	1.421	17.50	35.00	40.00	75.00
	1929A	—	—	—	Proof	200.00
	1929D	.499	17.50	35.00	45.00	75.00
	1929D	—	—	—	Proof	200.00
	1929E	.122	22.50	45.00	65.00	85.00
	1929E	—	—	—	Proof	300.00
	1929F	.370	17.50	35.00	45.00	75.00
	1929F	—	—	—	Proof	200.00
	1929G	.256	22.50	45.00	65.00	85.00
	1929G	—	—	—	Proof	200.00
	1929J	.342	17.50	35.00	45.00	85.00
	1929J	—	—	—	Proof	200.00

			Meissen 1000th Anniversary			
65	1929E	.200	25.00	45.00	65.00	90.00
	1929E	—	—	—	Proof	275.00

			Graf Zeppelin Flight			
67	1930A	.542	35.00	60.00	80.00	100.00
	1930A	—	—	—	Proof	300.00
	1930D	.141	37.50	65.00	85.00	110.00
	1930D	—	—	—	Proof	275.00
	1930E	.075	37.50	65.00	90.00	125.00
	1930E	—	—	—	Proof	350.00
	1930F	.100	37.50	65.00	90.00	125.00
	1930F	—	—	—	Proof	275.00
	1930G	.061	40.00	70.00	110.00	170.00
	1930G	—	—	—	Proof	350.00
	1930J	.082	45.00	75.00	100.00	170.00
	1930J	—	—	—	Proof	300.00

			700th Year Death of Von Der Vogelweide			
69	1930A	.163	35.00	60.00	80.00	120.00
	1930A	—	—	—	Proof	275.00
	1930D	.042	35.00	60.00	80.00	120.00
	1930D	—	—	—	Proof	225.00
	1930E	.022	37.50	75.00	100.00	135.00

KM#	Date	Mintage	Fine	VF	XF	Unc
69	1930E	—	—	—	Proof	275.00
	1930F	.030	40.00	80.00	110.00	145.00
	1930F	—	—	—	Proof	325.00
	1930G	.018	45.00	85.00	125.00	150.00
	1930G	—	—	—	Proof	275.00
	1930J	.025	37.50	75.00	100.00	135.00
	1930J	—	—	—	Proof	275.00

			Liberation of Rhineland			
70	1930A	1.734	22.50	35.00	45.00	60.00
	1930A	—	—	—	Proof	200.00
	1930D	.450	22.50	35.00	50.00	70.00
	1930D	—	—	—	Proof	200.00
	1930E	.038	65.00	125.00	200.00	325.00
	1930E	—	—	—	Proof	500.00
	1930F	.321	25.00	40.00	65.00	85.00
	1930F	—	—	—	Proof	200.00
	1930G	.195	25.00	40.00	65.00	85.00
	1930G	—	—	—	Proof	200.00
	1930J	.261	25.00	40.00	65.00	85.00
	1930J	—	—	—	Proof	200.00

			300th Anniversary Magdeburg Rebuilding			
72	1931A	.100	100.00	175.00	225.00	300.00
	1931A	—	—	—	Proof	350.00

			Centenary Von Stein Death			
73	1931A	.150	70.00	125.00	150.00	250.00
	1931A	—	—	—	Proof	375.00

74	1931A	13.324	125.00	225.00	300.00	400.00
	1931D	2.232	150.00	250.00	350.00	450.00
	1931E	2.235	150.00	250.00	350.00	450.00
	1931F	2.357	150.00	250.00	350.00	450.00
	1931G	1.468	150.00	250.00	350.00	525.00
	1931J	1.115	150.00	250.00	350.00	525.00
	1932A	2.933	125.00	235.00	300.00	450.00
	1932D	1.986	150.00	250.00	350.00	500.00
	1932F	.653	250.00	500.00	675.00	900.00
	1932G	.210	500.00	1000.	1500.	2000.
	1932J	1.336	150.00	250.00	350.00	525.00
	1933G	.152	1000.	1500.	2000.	2750.
	Common date	—	—	—	Proof	1250.

Centenary Goethe's Death

KM#	Date	Mintage	Fine	VF	XF	Unc
76	1932A	.217	35.00	65.00	100.00	150.00
	1932A	—	—	—	Proof	250.00
	1932D	.056	40.00	70.00	100.00	150.00
	1932D	—	—	—	Proof	325.00
	1932E	.030	50.00	100.00	125.00	200.00
	1932E	—	—	—	Proof	300.00
	1932F	.040	40.00	70.00	100.00	150.00
	1932F	—	—	—	Proof	250.00
	1932G	.024	40.00	70.00	100.00	175.00
	1932G	—	—	—	Proof	300.00
	1932J	.033	40.00	70.00	100.00	175.00
	1932J	—	—	—	Proof	300.00

5 REICHSMARK

25.0000 g, .500 SILVER, .4019 oz ASW
Rhineland-1000 Years

47	1925A	.684	40.00	80.00	100.00	150.00
	1925A	—	—	—	Proof	250.00
	1925D	.452	45.00	90.00	115.00	150.00
	1925D	—	—	—	Proof	275.00
	1925E	.204	50.00	100.00	125.00	175.00
	1925E	226 pcs.	—	—	Proof	275.00
	1925F	.212	45.00	90.00	115.00	150.00
	1925F	—	—	—	Proof	250.00
	1925G	.089	50.00	100.00	125.00	175.00
	1925G	—	—	—	Proof	400.00
	1925J	.043	70.00	140.00	175.00	275.00
	1925J	—	—	—	Proof	450.00

100th Year Bremerhaven

51	1927A	.050	200.00	350.00	450.00	600.00
	1927A	—	—	—	Proof	800.00

450th Year University of Tubingen

55	1927F	.040	200.00	350.00	450.00	600.00
	1927F	—	—	—	Proof	800.00

56	1927A	7.926	30.00	90.00	120.00	175.00
	1927D	1.471	35.00	120.00	150.00	225.00
	1927E	1.100	40.00	125.00	200.00	300.00
	1927F	.700	30.00	100.00	140.00	200.00
	1927G	.759	60.00	135.00	200.00	300.00
	1927J	1.006	35.00	120.00	170.00	250.00
	1928A	15.466	30.00	90.00	115.00	200.00
	1928D	4.613	30.00	100.00	120.00	210.00
	1928E	2.310	30.00	120.00	170.00	250.00

KM#	Date	Mintage	Fine	VF	XF	Unc
56	1928F	3.771	30.00	100.00	120.00	210.00
	1928G	1.923	35.00	100.00	150.00	250.00
	1928J	2.450	35.00	100.00	150.00	275.00
	1929A	6.730	30.00	90.00	115.00	210.00
	1929D	2.020	30.00	100.00	140.00	250.00
	1929E	.860	50.00	160.00	225.00	350.00
	1929F	.814	50.00	160.00	225.00	400.00
	1929G	.950	50.00	160.00	225.00	350.00
	1929J	.779	50.00	160.00	225.00	350.00
	1930A	3.790	35.00	120.00	150.00	300.00
	1930D	.606	120.00	375.00	500.00	725.00
	1930E	.354	135.00	375.00	600.00	1100.
	1930F	.630	135.00	325.00	500.00	850.00
	1930G	.367	175.00	425.00	700.00	1100.
	1930J	.740	135.00	325.00	450.00	750.00
	1931A	14.651	30.00	90.00	110.00	200.00
	1931D	3.254	35.00	90.00	125.00	225.00
	1931E	2.245	40.00	120.00	150.00	275.00
	1931F	4.152	35.00	100.00	135.00	225.00
	1931G	1.620	100.00	150.00	200.00	500.00
	1931J	3.092	35.00	100.00	135.00	250.00
	1932A	32.303	40.00	85.00	100.00	175.00
	1932D	8.556	35.00	80.00	120.00	225.00
	1932E	4.013	40.00	110.00	140.00	275.00
	1932F	5.019	35.00	80.00	120.00	250.00
	1932G	3.504	35.00	80.00	120.00	250.00
	1932J	3.752	40.00	120.00	150.00	300.00
	1933J	.423	550.00	1000.	1800.	2250.
	1933J	—	—	—	Proof	3000.
	Common date	—	—	—	Proof	700.00

Graf Zeppelin Flight

KM#	Date	Mintage	Fine	VF	XF	Unc
68	1930A	.217	60.00	100.00	165.00	225.00
	1930A	—	—	—	Proof	650.00
	1930D	.056	70.00	115.00	175.00	250.00
	1930D	—	—	—	Proof	550.00
	1930E	.030	75.00	120.00	175.00	350.00
	1930E	—	—	—	Proof	1300.
	1930F	.040	75.00	115.00	175.00	250.00
	1930F	—	—	—	Proof	450.00
	1930G	.024	80.00	120.00	175.00	350.00
	1930G	—	—	—	Proof	600.00
	1930J	.033	70.00	115.00	175.00	300.00
	1930J	—	—	—	Proof	550.00

KM#	Date	Mintage	Fine	VF	XF	Unc
35	1923F	—	—	—	Proof	50.00
	1923D	24.923	.20	.50	1.00	2.00
	1923G	—	—	—	Proof	50.00
	1923J	16.258	.25	1.50	2.50	6.00
	1923J	—	—	—	Proof	50.00

500 MARK

ALUMINUM

36	1923A	59.278	.20	1.00	1.50	2.00
	1923A	—	—	—	Proof	45.00
	1923D	13.683	.25	1.00	1.50	3.00
	1923D	—	—	—	Proof	45.00
	1923E	2.128	1.00	7.50	12.50	15.00
	1923E	—	—	—	Proof	45.00
	1923F	7.963	.25	1.50	2.00	5.00
	1923F	—	—	—	Proof	45.00
	1923G	4.404	.25	2.50	5.00	7.50
	1923G	—	—	—	Proof	45.00
	1923J	1.008	15.00	30.00	40.00	65.00
	1923J	—	—	—	Proof	250.00

THIRD REICH
1933-1945
REICHSPFENNIG

BRONZE

89	1936A Inc.KM37	1.50	—	4.00	7.50	15.00
	1936E	.150	25.00	50.00	80.00	135.00
	1936F	4.600	22.50	50.00	75.00	130.00
	1936G Inc.KM37	15.00	—	30.00	60.00	80.00
	1936J Inc.KM37	10.00	—	30.00	50.00	70.00
	1937A	67.180	.10	.25	.50	2.50
	1937D	14.060	.10	.25	.50	2.50
	1937E	10.700	.15	.35	1.00	5.00
	1937F	11.058	.15	.35	1.00	5.00
	1937G	4.250	.15	.35	1.00	5.00
	1937J	6.714	.15	.35	1.00	5.00
	1938A	75.707	.10	.25	.50	5.00
	1938B	2.378	.50	6.00	9.00	12.50
	1938D	13.930	.10	.25	.50	5.00
	1938E	14.503	.10	.25	.50	5.00
	1938F	11.714	.10	.25	.50	5.00
	1938G	8.390	.10	.25	.50	5.00
	1938J	15.458	.10	.25	.50	6.00
	1939A	97.541	.10	.25	.50	5.00
	1939B	22.732	.15	.35	1.00	7.50
	1939D	20.760	.10	.25	.50	5.00
	1939E	12.478	.10	.25	.50	7.50
	1939F	12.482	.10	.25	.50	5.00
	1939G	12.250	.10	.25	.50	5.00
	1939J	8.368	.10	.25	.50	7.50
	1940A	27.094	.10	.25	.50	6.00
	1940F	7.850	.15	.35	1.00	6.00
	1940G	3.875	1.00	10.00	15.00	20.00
	1940J	7.450	.50	4.00	5.00	8.00
	Common date	—	—	—	Proof	60.00

Lessing's 200th Anniversary

61	1929A	.087	50.00	100.00	125.00	200.00
	1929A	—	—	—	Proof	375.00
	1929D	.022	55.00	110.00	130.00	225.00
	1929D	—	—	—	Proof	450.00
	1929E	.012	55.00	110.00	130.00	250.00
	1929E	—	—	—	Proof	450.00
	1929F	.016	50.00	100.00	125.00	200.00
	1929F	—	—	—	Proof	400.00
	1929G	9.760	55.00	110.00	130.00	225.00
	1929G	—	—	—	Proof	450.00
	1929J	.013	55.00	110.00	170.00	300.00
	1929J	—	—	—	Proof	400.00

Liberation of Rhineland

71	1930A	.325	65.00	125.00	175.00	225.00
	1930A	—	—	—	Proof	450.00
	1930D	.084	65.00	125.00	175.00	275.00
	1930D	—	—	—	Proof	550.00
	1930E	.045	75.00	150.00	200.00	325.00
	1930E	—	—	—	Proof	475.00
	1930F	.060	65.00	125.00	175.00	275.00
	1930F	—	—	—	Proof	450.00
	1930G	.037	90.00	175.00	225.00	350.00
	1930G	—	—	—	Proof	550.00
	1930J	.049	75.00	150.00	200.00	325.00
	1930J	—	—	—	Proof	575.00

Constitution 10th Year

64	1929A	.325	45.00	90.00	125.00	180.00
	1929A	—	—	—	Proof	450.00
	1929D	.084	50.00	100.00	150.00	200.00
	1929D	—	—	—	Proof	400.00
	1929E	.045	50.00	100.00	150.00	200.00
	1929E	—	—	—	Proof	650.00
	1929F	.060	60.00	110.00	160.00	225.00
	1929F	—	—	—	Proof	400.00
	1929G	.037	60.00	110.00	160.00	225.00
	1929G	—	—	—	Proof	500.00
	1929J	.049	50.00	100.00	150.00	200.00
	1929J	—	—	—	Proof	450.00

Centenary Goethe's Death

77	1932A	.011	550.00	1250.	2000.	2800.
	1932A	—	—	—	Proof	2750.
	1932D	2,812	650.00	1350.	1850.	3000.
	1932D	—	—	—	Proof	3750.
	1932E	1,490	750.00	1500.	2000.	3500.
	1932E	—	—	—	Proof	3750.
	1932F	2,006	750.00	1500.	2000.	3500.
	1932F	—	—	—	Proof	3500.
	1932G	1,220	950.00	1750.	2250.	3500.
	1932G	—	—	—	Proof	3500.
	1932J	1,634	950.00	1750.	2250.	3500.
	1932J	—	—	—	Proof	3750.

200 MARK

ALUMINUM

35	1923A	174.900	.15	.50	1.50	2.00
	1923A	—	—	—	Proof	50.00
	1923D	35.189	.20	1.00	1.50	2.00
	1923D	—	—	—	Proof	50.00
	1923E	11.250	.25	2.00	3.50	6.50
	1923E	—	—	—	Proof	50.00
	1923F	20.090	.20	1.00	2.00	5.00

Meissen 1000th Anniversary

66	1929E	.120	150.00	225.00	400.00	600.00
	1929E	—	—	—	Proof	1200.

ZINC

97	1940A	223.948	.10	.20	1.00	5.00
	1940B	62.198	.10	.20	1.00	2.50
	1940D	43.951	.10	.20	1.00	5.00
	1940E	20.749	.20	1.00	5.00	7.50
	1940F	33.854	.10	.20	1.00	5.00
	1940G	20.165	.10	.20	1.00	5.00
	1940J	24.459	.10	.20	1.00	5.00
	1941A	281.618	.10	.15	.50	4.00
	1941B	62.285	.20	1.00	1.50	7.50
	1941D	73.745	.10	.15	.50	5.00
	1941E	49.041	.10	.50	1.50	7.50
	1941F	51.017	.10	.15	.50	5.00
	1941G	44.810	.10	.50	1.50	7.50
	1941J	57.625	.10	.15	.50	5.00
	1942A	558.877	.10	.15	.50	6.00
	1942B	124.740	.10	.20	1.00	6.00
	1942D	134.145	.10	.15	.50	6.00
	1942E	84.674	.15	1.50	2.50	8.50
	1942F	90.788	.10	.15	.50	6.00
	1942G	59.858	.10	.15	.50	6.00
	1942J	122.934	.10	.50	1.00	6.00
	1943A	372.401	.10	.15	.50	6.00
	1943B	79.315	.10	.50	1.00	6.00

GERMANY 726

KM#	Date	Mintage	Fine	VF	XF	Unc
97	1943D	91.629	.10	.15	.50	6.00
	1943E	34.191	.50	2.50	7.50	10.00
	1943F	70.269	.10	.50	1.00	6.00
	1943G	24.688	.15	1.50	2.50	7.50
	1943J	37.695	.15	1.50	2.50	7.50
	1944A	124.421	.10	.50	2.00	5.00
	1944B	87.850	.20	1.00	2.00	5.00
	1944D	56.755	.20	1.00	2.50	7.00
	1944E	41.729	.20	2.00	5.00	10.00
	1944F	15.580	.50	4.00	6.00	12.00
	1944G	34.967	.10	.50	1.00	4.00
	1945A	17.145	.25	2.50	7.50	15.00
	1945E	6.800	30.00	50.00	70.00	130.00
	Common date		—	—	Proof	80.00

2 REICHSPFENNIG

BRONZE

KM#	Date	Mintage	Fine	VF	XF	Unc
90	1936A	Inc.Be.	.50	3.00	7.50	15.00
	1936D	Inc.Be.	.50	3.00	7.50	15.00
	1936F	3.100	4.50	17.50	30.00	45.00
	1937A	34.404	.10	.50	1.50	7.00
	1937D	9.016	.10	.50	1.50	7.00
	1937E	Inc.Be.	10.00	18.00	30.00	60.00
	1937F	7.487	.10	.50	1.50	7.00
	1937G	.490	2.00	8.50	15.00	30.00
	1937J	.450	2.00	8.50	15.00	25.00
	1938A	27.264	.10	.15	.50	6.00
	1938B	2.714	1.50	4.00	7.50	15.00
	1938D	8.770	.10	.25	1.00	6.00
	1938E	5.450	.25	1.00	2.00	6.00
	1938F	10.090	.10	.25	1.00	6.00
	1938G	3.685	.10	.25	1.00	6.00
	1938J	7.243	.10	.25	1.00	6.00
	1939A	37.348	.10	.25	1.00	6.00
	1939B	9.361	.10	.25	1.00	6.00
	1939D	7.555	.10	.25	1.00	6.00
	1939E	6.650	.25	1.00	4.50	10.00
	1939F	7.019	.10	.25	1.00	6.00
	1939G	4.885	.10	.25	1.00	6.00
	1939J	6.996	.10	.25	1.00	6.00
	1940A	22.681	.10	.25	1.00	6.00
	1940D	3.855	.50	3.00	6.50	12.50
	1940E	3.412	2.50	10.00	15.00	25.00
	1940G	1.161	40.00	70.00	100.00	150.00
	1940J	2.357	1.50	7.50	12.50	20.00
	Common date		—	—	Proof	60.00

5 REICHSPFENNIG

ALUMINUM-BRONZE

KM#	Date	Mintage	Fine	VF	XF	Unc
91	1936A	Inc.Be.	12.50	22.50	45.00	90.00
	1936D	Inc.Be.	15.00	30.00	45.00	70.00
	1936G	Inc.Be.	40.00	90.00	125.00	175.00
	1937A	29.700	.10	.20	1.00	6.00
	1937D	4.992	.10	.20	1.00	7.50
	1937E	4.474	.20	1.00	3.00	10.00
	1937F	2.092	.10	.20	1.00	8.00
	1937G	2.749	2.50	7.50	15.00	20.00
	1937J	6.991	.25	2.50	5.00	12.50
	1938A	54.012	.25	2.50	5.00	7.50
	1938B	3.447	.25	1.50	5.00	10.00
	1938D	17.708	.10	.25	1.50	6.00
	1938E	8.602	.10	.40	4.00	8.00
	1938F	8.147	.10	.25	1.50	7.00
	1938G	7.323	.10	.25	1.50	7.00
	1938J	7.646	.10	.25	1.50	7.00
	1939A	35.337	.10	.25	1.50	7.00
	1939B	8.313	.10	.20	1.00	7.50
	1939D	8.304	.20	1.00	2.00	7.50
	1939E	5.138	.20	1.00	2.00	7.50
	1939F	10.339	.10	.20	1.00	6.00
	1939G	4.266	.25	2.50	7.50	12.50
	1939J	4.177	.20	2.00	7.50	10.00
	Common date		—	—	Proof	75.00

ZINC
Military Issue

KM#	Date	Mintage	Fine	VF	XF	Unc
98	1940A	—	5.00	10.00	20.00	30.00
	1940B	3.020	50.00	100.00	135.00	200.00
	1940D	—	15.00	30.00	60.00	90.00
	1940E	2.445	50.00	100.00	135.00	275.00
	1940F	—	40.00	80.00	165.00	275.00
	1940G	—	40.00	80.00	250.00	325.00
	1940J	—	40.00	80.00	250.00	325.00
	1941A	—	25.00	50.00	100.00	150.00

KM#	Date	Mintage	Fine	VF	XF	Unc
98	1941F	—	40.00	80.00	250.00	325.00
	Common date		—	—	Proof	200.00

NOTE: Circulated only in occupied territories.

KM#	Date	Mintage	Fine	VF	XF	Unc
100	1940A	174.684	.10	.20	1.00	5.00
	1940B	63.469	.20	1.00	1.50	6.00
	1940D	44.364	.20	1.00	1.50	6.00
	1940E	25.800	.30	2.00	4.00	6.00
	1940F	31.381	.20	1.00	2.00	6.00
	1940G	24.148	.20	1.00	2.50	6.00
	1940J	30.518	.20	1.00	2.00	6.00
	1941A	246.216	.10	.20	1.00	5.00
	1941B	60.297	.10	.30	2.00	7.50
	1941D	51.100	.10	.30	2.00	7.50
	1941E	26.354	.10	.30	2.00	7.50
	1941F	36.725	.10	.30	2.00	7.50
	1941G	21.276	.10	.30	2.00	7.50
	1941J	52.872	.10	.30	2.00	7.50
	1942A	161.042	.10	.20	1.00	5.00
	1942B	12.405	.25	1.50	5.00	7.50
	1942D	15.486	.10	.35	2.50	5.00
	1942E	8.800	7.50	17.50	22.50	35.00
	1942F	24.662	.10	.25	1.50	5.00
	1942G	12.749	.10	.35	2.50	7.50
	1943A	46.830	.15	.50	2.00	7.50
	1943B	.833	12.50	35.00	60.00	100.00
	1943D	13.650	.15	.50	4.00	10.00
	1943E	16.581	2.50	7.50	12.50	17.50
	1943F	9.891	.20	1.00	2.50	6.00
	1943G	7.237	.15	.50	2.00	6.00
	1944A	23.699	3.50	15.00	27.50	37.50
	1944D	26.340	.25	1.50	3.00	5.00
	1944E	19.720	.50	4.00	9.00	15.00
	1944F	6.853	.25	1.50	3.00	7.50
	1944G	3.540	65.00	115.00	180.00	250.00
	Common date		—	—	Proof	75.00

10 REICHSPFENNIG

ALUMINUM-BRONZE

KM#	Date	Mintage	Fine	VF	XF	Unc
92	1936A	Inc. Be.	2.50	12.50	20.00	40.00
	1936E	.245	65.00	135.00	175.00	275.00
	1936G	.129	100.00	225.00	300.00	500.00
	1937A	36.830	.10	.50	2.00	7.50
	1937D	6.882	.25	1.50	3.00	10.00
	1937E	3.786	2.50	12.50	20.00	35.00
	1937F	5.934	.50	2.50	5.00	12.50
	1937G	2.131	1.00	5.00	7.50	17.50
	1937J	4.439	.50	2.50	5.00	15.00
	1938A	70.068	.10	.20	1.00	5.00
	1938B	7.852	.50	2.50	5.00	12.50
	1938D	16.990	.10	.50	2.00	8.00
	1938E	10.739	.20	1.00	2.50	8.00
	1938F	12.307	.20	1.00	2.50	8.00
	1938G	8.584	.20	1.00	2.50	8.00
	1938J	10.389	.20	1.00	2.50	8.00
	1939A	40.171	.20	1.00	2.00	8.00
	1939B	7.814	.20	1.00	2.00	8.00
	1939D	11.307	.20	1.00	2.00	8.00
	1939E	5.079	.35	2.50	7.50	12.50
	1939F	6.993	.25	1.50	3.00	10.00
	1939G	5.532	.50	5.00	10.00	20.00
	1939J	5.557	.20	1.00	2.00	6.00
	Common date		—	—	Proof	75.00

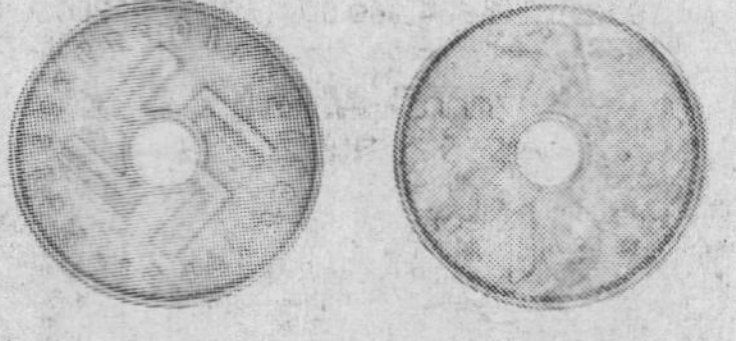

ZINC
Military Issue

KM#	Date	Mintage	Fine	VF	XF	Unc
99	1940A	—	6.00	12.50	22.50	35.00
	1940B	.840	50.00	100.00	200.00	300.00
	1940D	—	40.00	75.00	225.00	300.00
	1940E	5.100	50.00	100.00	200.00	300.00
	1940F	—	50.00	100.00	200.00	300.00
	1940G	.150	40.00	75.00	225.00	300.00
	1940J	—	50.00	100.00	200.00	300.00
	1941A	—	50.00	100.00	175.00	250.00
	1941F	—	50.00	100.00	175.00	250.00

NOTE: Circulated only in occupied territories.

KM#	Date	Mintage	Fine	VF	XF	Unc
101	1940A	212.948	.10	.35	1.50	6.00
	1940B	76.274	.15	.50	2.50	7.50
	1940D	45.434	.15	.50	2.00	6.50
	1940E	34.350	.15	.50	2.00	6.50
	1940F	27.603	.15	.50	2.00	6.50
	1940G	27.308	.15	.50	2.00	6.50
	1940J	41.678	.15	.50	2.00	6.50
	1941A	240.284	.10	.35	1.50	6.00
	1941B	70.747	.15	.50	2.50	7.50
	1941D	77.560	.15	.50	2.00	6.50
	1941E	36.548	.15	.50	2.00	6.50
	1941F	42.834	.15	.50	2.00	6.50
	1941G	28.765	.15	.50	2.00	6.50
	1941J	30.525	.15	.50	2.00	6.50
	1942A	184.545	.10	.20	.50	2.00
	1942B	16.329	.25	2.50	3.50	10.00
	1942D	40.852	.20	1.00	2.50	7.50
	1942E	18.334	.25	1.50	3.00	7.50
	1942F	32.690	.10	.35	1.50	6.00
	1942G	20.295	.25	1.50	2.50	6.00
	1942J	29.957	.25	1.50	2.50	7.50
	1943A	157.357	.15	1.50	2.50	7.50
	1943B	11.940	2.50	7.50	15.00	30.00
	1943D	17.304	.25	2.00	3.00	7.50
	1943E	10.445	5.00	10.00	17.50	30.00
	1943F	24.804	.25	2.50	5.00	7.50
	1943G	3.618	.25	2.50	6.00	12.50
	1943J	1.821	15.00	35.00	50.00	85.00
	1944A	84.164	.15	1.00	2.50	7.50
	1944B	40.781	.50	1.50	3.00	8.00
	1944D	30.369	.35	1.50	3.00	8.00
	1944E	29.963	.50	2.00	4.00	8.00
	1944F	19.639	.50	2.00	4.00	8.00
	1944G	13.023	.50	2.00	4.00	8.00
	1945A	7.112	5.00	12.50	17.50	27.50
	1945E	4.897	12.50	20.00	35.00	70.00
	Common date		—	—	Proof	80.00

50 REICHSPFENNIG

ALUMINUM

KM#	Date	Mintage	Fine	VF	XF	Unc
87	1935A	75.912	.25	2.50	6.00	17.50
	1935A	—	—	—	Proof	75.00
	1935D	19.688	.25	1.00	2.50	15.00
	1935D	—	—	—	Proof	75.00
	1935E	10.418	.50	5.00	7.50	20.00
	1935E	—	—	—	Proof	75.00
	1935F	14.061	.25	1.00	3.00	20.00
	1935F	—	—	—	Proof	75.00
	1935G	8.540	.50	4.00	9.00	22.50
	1935G	—	—	—	Proof	75.00
	1935J	11.438	.35	3.50	7.50	25.00
	1935J	—	—	—	Proof	75.00

NICKEL

KM#	Date	Mintage	Fine	VF	XF	Unc
95	1938A	5.051	10.00	20.00	30.00	50.00
	1938B	1.124	15.00	30.00	40.00	75.00
	1938D	1.260	15.00	30.00	40.00	75.00
	1938E	.949	20.00	40.00	50.00	80.00
	1938F	1.210	7.50	20.00	40.00	80.00
	1938G	.460	20.00	40.00	75.00	140.00
	1938J	.730	12.50	27.50	65.00	125.00
	1939A	15.037	12.50	22.00	30.00	40.00
	1939B	2.826	12.50	22.00	32.50	45.00
	1939D	3.648	10.00	22.00	32.50	45.00
	1939E	1.924	10.00	25.00	35.00	60.00
	1939F	2.602	10.00	25.00	35.00	60.00
	1939G	1.565	20.00	35.00	60.00	100.00
	1939J	2.114	10.00	25.00	45.00	75.00
	Common date		—	—	Proof	150.00

ALUMINUM

KM#	Date	Mintage	VF	XF	Unc
105	1981F	274.010	—	.10	.25
	1981F	.091	—	Proof	.40
	1981G	178.010	—	.10	.25
	1981G	.091	—	Proof	.40
	1981J	189.090	—	.10	.25
	1981J	.091	—	Proof	.40
	1982D	130.090	—	.10	.20
	1982D	.091	—	Proof	.40
	1982F	108.390	—	.10	.20
	1982F	.091	—	Proof	.40
	1982G	77.740	—	.10	.20
	1982G	.091	—	Proof	.40
	1982J	124.720	—	.10	.20
	1982J	.091	—	Proof	.40
	1983D	46.800	—	.10	.20
	1983D	.091	—	Proof	.40
	1983F	54.000	—	.10	.20
	1983F	.091	—	Proof	.40
	1983G	31.140	—	.10	.20
	1983G	.091	—	Proof	.40
	1983J	48.060	—	.10	.20
	1983J	.091	—	Proof	.40
	1984D	—	—	.10	.20
	1984D	.079	—	Proof	.40
	1984F	—	—	.10	.20
	1984F	.079	—	Proof	.40
	1984G	—	—	.10	.20
	1984G	.079	—	Proof	.40
	1984J	—	—	.10	.20
	1984J	.079	—	Proof	.40
	1985D	—	—	.10	.20
	1985D	—	—	Proof	.40
	1985F	—	—	.10	.20
	1985F	—	—	Proof	.40
	1985G	—	—	—	.10
	1985G	—	—	Proof	.40
	1985J	—	—	—	.10
	1985J	—	—	Proof	.40
	1986D	—	—	—	.10
	1986D	—	—	Proof	.40
	1986F	—	—	—	.10
	1986F	—	—	Proof	.40
	1986G	—	—	—	.10
	1986G	—	—	Proof	.40
	1986J	—	—	—	.10
	1986J	—	—	Proof	.40
	1987D	—	—	—	.10
	1987D	—	—	Proof	.40
	1987F	—	—	—	.10
	1987F	—	—	Proof	.40
	1987G	—	—	—	.10
	1987G	—	—	Proof	.40
	1987J	—	—	—	.10
	1987J	—	—	Proof	.40
	1988D	—	—	—	.10
	1988D	—	—	Proof	.40
	1988F	—	—	—	.10
	1988F	—	—	Proof	.40
	1988G	—	—	—	.10
	1988G	—	—	Proof	.40
	1988J	—	—	—	.10
	1988J	—	—	Proof	.40

2 PFENNIG

BRONZE
Federal Republic

KM#	Date	Mintage	VF	XF	Unc
106	1950D	26.263	.10	1.00	7.50
	1950F	30.278	.10	1.00	7.50
	1950F	200 pcs.	—	Proof	—
	1950G	17.151	.10	3.00	30.00
	1950J	27.216	.10	1.00	7.50
	1950J	—	—	Proof	17.50
	1958D	19.440	.10	1.00	7.50
	1958F	24.122	.10	1.00	7.50
	1958F	100 pcs.	—	Proof	—
	1958G	15.255	.10	1.00	7.50
	1958J	21.250	.10	1.00	7.50
	1959D	19.690	—	.25	7.50
	1959F	25.017	—	.25	7.50
	1959F	75 pcs.	—	Proof	—
	1959J	12.899	—	.25	7.50
	1959J	25.482	—	.25	7.50
	1960D	21.979	—	.25	5.00
	1960F	13.060	—	.25	5.00
	1960F	75 pcs.	—	Proof	—
	1960G	5.657	.10	.25	5.00
	1960J	17.799	—	.25	5.00
	1961D	26.662	—	.25	5.00
	1961F	24.990	—	.25	5.00
	1961G	18.060	—	.25	5.00
	1961J	22.147	—	.25	5.00
	1962D	21.297	—	.25	5.00
	1962F	42.189	—	.25	3.00
	1962G	17.297	—	.25	3.00
	1962J	30.706	—	.25	3.00
	1963D	7.648	—	.25	5.00
	1963F	18.299	—	.25	2.00
	1963G	35.838	—	.25	2.00
	1963G	—	—	Proof	—
	1963J	42.884	—	.25	2.00
	1964D	20.336	—	.25	3.00
	1964F	31.400	—	.10	1.00

KM#	Date	Mintage	VF	XF	Unc
106	1964G	18.431	—	.10	1.00
	1964G	*600	—	Proof	12.00
	1964J	13.370	—	.10	1.00
	1965D	48.541	—	.10	1.00
	1965F	27.000	—	.10	1.00
	1965F	300 pcs.	—	Proof	42.50
	1965G	13.584	—	.10	1.00
	1965G	1,200	—	Proof	2.00
	1965J	33.397	—	.10	1.00
	1966D	65.077	—	.10	.25
	1966F	52.543	—	.10	.25
	1966F	100 pcs.	—	Proof	45.00
	1966G	40.804	—	.10	.25
	1966G	3,070	—	Proof	5.50
	1966J	46.754	—	.10	.25
	1966J	1,000	—	Proof	12.50
	1967D	25.997	—	.10	2.00
	1967F	30.004	—	.10	1.00
	1967F	1,500	—	Proof	7.00
	1967G	6.280	—	1.00	3.00
	1967G	4,500	—	Proof	4.50
	1967J	26.725	—	.10	2.00
	1967J	1,500	—	Proof	10.00
	1968D	19.523	—	1.00	3.00
	1968G	15.357	—	.10	1.00
	1968G	3,651	—	Proof	4.00
	1968J	—	150.00	200.00	325.00
	1969J	—	150.00	200.00	325.00

BRONZE CLAD STEEL

KM#	Date	Mintage	VF	XF	Unc
106a	1967G	520 pcs.	—	Proof	650.00
	1968D	19.523	—	.10	.25
	1968F	30.000	—	.10	.25
	1968F	3,000	—	Proof	6.00
	1968G	13.004	—	.10	.25
	1968G	2,372	—	Proof	4.00
	1968J	20.026	—	.10	.25
	1968J	2,000	—	Proof	7.50
	1969D	39.012	—	.10	.25
	1969D	—	—	Proof	1.25
	1969F	45.029	—	.10	.25
	1969F	5,100	—	Proof	1.25
	1969G	32.157	—	.10	.25
	1969G	8.700	—	Proof	1.25
	1969J	40.102	—	.10	.25
	1969J	5,000	—	Proof	2.50
	1970D	45.525	—	.10	.25
	1970F	73.851	—	.10	.25
	1970F	5,140	—	Proof	1.25
	1970G	30.330	—	.10	.25
	1970G	10,200	—	Proof	1.25
	1970 sm.J	46.730	—	.10	.25
	1970 lg.J	Inc. Ab.	—	.10	.25
	1970J	5,000	—	Proof	1.75
	1971D	71.755	—	.10	.25
	1971D	8,000	—	Proof	1.25
	1971F	82.765	—	.10	.25
	1971F	8,000	—	Proof	1.25
	1971G	47.850	—	.10	.25
	1971G	.010	—	Proof	1.25
	1971J	73.641	—	.10	.25
	1971J	8,000	—	Proof	1.25
	1972D	52.403	—	.10	.25
	1972D	8,000	—	Proof	1.00
	1972F	60.272	—	.10	.25
	1972F	8,000	—	Proof	1.00
	1972G	34.864	—	.10	.25
	1972G	.010	—	Proof	1.00
	1972J	53.673	—	.10	.25
	1972J	8,000	—	Proof	1.00
	1973D	26.190	—	.10	.25
	1973D	9,000	—	Proof	1.00
	1973F	30.160	—	.10	.25
	1973F	9,000	—	Proof	1.00
	1973G	17.379	—	.10	.25
	1973G	9,000	—	Proof	1.00
	1973J	26.830	—	.10	.25
	1973J	9,000	—	Proof	1.00
	1974D	58.667	—	.10	.25
	1974D	.035	—	Proof	.50
	1974F	67.596	—	.10	.25
	1974F	.035	—	Proof	.50
	1974G	39.007	—	.10	.25
	1974G	.035	—	Proof	.50
	1974J	60.195	—	.10	.25
	1974J	.035	—	Proof	.50
	1975D	58.634	—	.10	.25
	1975D	.043	—	Proof	.50
	1975F	67.685	—	.10	.25
	1975F	.043	—	Proof	.50
	1975G	39.391	—	.10	.25
	1975G	.043	—	Proof	.50
	1975J	60.207	—	.10	.25
	1975J	.043	—	Proof	.50
	1976D	78.074	—	.10	.25
	1976D	.043	—	Proof	.50
	1976F	90.130	—	.10	.25
	1976F	.043	—	Proof	.50
	1976G	51.988	—	.10	.25
	1976G	.043	—	Proof	.50
	1976J	80.145	—	.10	.25
	1976J	.043	—	Proof	.50
	1977D	84.516	—	.10	.20
	1977D	.051	—	Proof	.40
	1977F	97.504	—	.10	.20
	1977F	.051	—	Proof	.40
	1977G	56.270	—	.10	.20
	1977G	.051	—	Proof	.40
	1977J	86.888	—	.10	.20
	1977J	.051	—	Proof	.40
	1978D	84.500	—	.10	.20

KM#	Date	Mintage	VF	XF	Unc
106a	1978D	.054	—	Proof	.40
	1978F	97.500	—	.10	.20
	1978F	.054	—	Proof	.40
	1978G	56.225	—	.10	.20
	1978G	.054	—	Proof	.40
	1978J	86.775	—	.10	.20
	1978J	.054	—	Proof	.40
	1979D	91.000	—	.10	.20
	1979D	.089	—	Proof	.40
	1979F	105.000	—	.10	.20
	1979F	.089	—	Proof	.40
	1979G	60.550	—	.10	.20
	1979G	.089	—	Proof	.40
	1979J	93.480	—	.10	.20
	1979J	.089	—	Proof	.40
	1980D	93.360	—	.10	.20
	1980D	.110	—	Proof	.40
	1980F	120.360	—	.10	.20
	1980F	.110	—	Proof	.40
	1980G	50.830	—	.10	.20
	1980G	.110	—	Proof	.40
	1980J	102.260	—	.10	.20
	1980J	.110	—	Proof	.40
	1981D	93.910	—	.10	.20
	1981D	.091	—	Proof	.40
	1981F	83.710	—	.10	.20
	1981F	.091	—	Proof	.40
	1981G	89.850	—	.10	.20
	1981G	.091	—	Proof	.40
	1981J	87.250	—	.10	.20
	1981J	.091	—	Proof	.40
	1982D	64.390	—	.10	.20
	1982D	.091	—	Proof	.40
	1982F	36.870	—	.10	.20
	1982F	.091	—	Proof	.40
	1982G	58.590	—	.10	.20
	1982G	.091	—	Proof	.40
	1982J	57.690	—	.10	.20
	1982J	.091	—	Proof	.40
	1983D	71.500	—	.10	.20
	1983D	.091	—	Proof	.40
	1983F	82.500	—	.10	.20
	1983F	.091	—	Proof	.40
	1983G	47.575	—	.10	.20
	1983G	.091	—	Proof	.40
	1983J	73.425	—	.10	.20
	1983J	.091	—	Proof	.40
	1984D	—	—	.10	.20
	1984D	.079	—	Proof	.40
	1984F	—	—	.10	.20
	1984F	.079	—	Proof	.40
	1984G	—	—	.10	.20
	1984G	.079	—	Proof	.40
	1984J	—	—	.10	.20
	1984J	.079	—	Proof	.40
	1985D	—	—	—	.10
	1985D	—	—	Proof	.40
	1985F	—	—	—	.10
	1985F	—	—	Proof	.40
	1985G	—	—	—	.10
	1985G	—	—	Proof	.40
	1985J	—	—	—	.10
	1985J	—	—	Proof	.40
	1986D	—	—	—	.10
	1986D	—	—	Proof	.40
	1986F	—	—	—	.10
	1986F	—	—	Proof	.40
	1986G	—	—	—	.10
	1986G	—	—	Proof	.40
	1986J	—	—	—	.10
	1986J	—	—	Proof	.40
	1987D	—	—	—	.10
	1987D	—	—	Proof	.40
	1987F	—	—	—	.10
	1987F	—	—	Proof	.40
	1987G	—	—	—	.10
	1987G	—	—	Proof	.40
	1987J	—	—	—	.10
	1987J	—	—	Proof	.40
	1988D	—	—	—	.10
	1988D	—	—	Proof	.40
	1988F	—	—	—	.10
	1988F	—	—	Proof	.40
	1988G	—	—	—	.10
	1988G	—	—	Proof	.40
	1988J	—	—	—	.10
	1988J	—	—	Proof	.40

5 PFENNIG

BRASS-CLAD STEEL
Currency Reform

KM#	Date	Mintage	VF	XF	Unc
102	1949D	60.026	.10	7.50	35.00
	1949F	66.082	.10	7.50	25.00
	1949F	250 pcs.	—	Proof	50.00
	1949G	57.356	.10	7.50	45.00
	1949J	68.977	.10	7.50	35.00
	1949J	—	—	Proof	50.00

West / GERMANY 730

BRASS PLATED STEEL
Federal Republic

KM#	Date	Mintage	VF	XF	Unc
107	1950D	271.962	—	1.00	4.00
	1950F	362.880	—	1.00	4.00
	1950F	500 pcs.	—	Proof	55.00
	1950G	180.492	—	1.00	4.00
	1950G	1,800	—	Proof	3.00
	1950J	285.283	—	1.00	4.00
	1950J	—	—	Proof	12.00
	1966D	26.036	—	1.00	7.50
	1966F	30.047	—	1.00	7.50
	1966F	100 pcs.	—	Proof	50.00
	1966G	17.333	—	1.00	7.50
	1966G	3,070	—	Proof	6.50
	1966J	26.741	—	1.00	7.50
	1966J	1,000	—	Proof	15.00
	1967D	10.418	—	1.00	7.50
	1967F	12.012	—	1.00	7.50
	1967F	1,500	—	Proof	12.50
	1967G	1.736	2.50	5.00	30.00
	1967G	4,500	—	Proof	6.00
	1967J	10.706	—	1.00	7.50
	1967J	1,500	—	Proof	15.00
	1968D	13.047	—	.25	4.00
	1968F	15.026	—	.25	4.00
	1968F	3,000	—	Proof	8.00
	1968G	13.855	—	.25	4.00
	1968G	6,023	—	Proof	5.00
	1968J	13.362	—	.25	4.00
	1968J	2,000	—	Proof	12.50
	1969D	23.488	—	.10	1.00
	1969F	27.046	—	.10	1.00
	1969F	5,000	—	Proof	2.00
	1969G	15.631	—	.10	1.00
	1969G	8,700	—	Proof	1.50
	1969J	24.120	—	.10	1.00
	1969J	5,000	—	Proof	2.00
	1970D	39.940	—	.10	.25
	1970F	45.517	—	.10	.25
	1970F	5,140	—	Proof	2.00
	1970G	27.638	—	.10	.25
	1970G	10,200	—	Proof	1.50
	1970J	40.873	—	.10	.25
	1970J	5,000	—	Proof	2.00
	1971D	57.345	—	.10	.25
	1971D	8,000	—	Proof	1.50
	1971F	66.426	—	.10	.25
	1971F	8,000	—	Proof	1.50
	1971G	38.284	—	.10	.25
	1971G	10,000	—	Proof	1.50
	1971J	58.566	—	.10	.25
	1971J	8,000	—	Proof	1.50
	1972D	52.325	—	.10	.25
	1972D	8,000	—	Proof	1.50
	1972F	60.292	—	.10	.25
	1972F	8,000	—	Proof	1.50
	1972G	34.719	—	.10	.25
	1972G	10,000	—	Proof	1.50
	1972J	54.218	—	.10	.25
	1972J	8,000	—	Proof	1.50
	1973D	15.596	—	.10	.25
	1973D	9,000	—	Proof	1.50
	1973F	18.039	—	.10	.25
	1973F	9,000	—	Proof	1.50
	1973G	10.391	—	.10	.25
	1973G	9,000	—	Proof	1.50
	1973J	16.035	—	.10	.25
	1973J	9,000	—	Proof	1.50
	1974D	15.769	—	.10	.25
	1974D	.035	—	Proof	.50
	1974F	18.143	—	.10	.25
	1974F	.035	—	Proof	.50
	1974G	10.508	—	.10	.25
	1974G	.035	—	Proof	.50
	1974J	16.055	—	.10	.25
	1974J	.035	—	Proof	.50
	1975D	15.715	—	.10	.25
	1975D	.043	—	Proof	.50
	1975F	18.013	—	.10	.25
	1975F	.043	—	Proof	.50
	1975G	10.466	—	.10	.25
	1975G	.043	—	Proof	.50
	1975J	16.201	—	.10	.25
	1975J	.043	—	Proof	.50
	1976D	47.091	—	.10	.25
	1976D	.043	—	Proof	.50
	1976F	54.370	—	.10	.25
	1976F	.043	—	Proof	.50
	1976G	31.367	—	.10	.25
	1976G	.043	—	Proof	.50
	1976J	48.321	—	.10	.25
	1976J	.043	—	Proof	.50
	1977D	52.159	—	.10	.20
	1977D	.051	—	Proof	.40
	1977F	60.124	—	.10	.20
	1977F	.051	—	Proof	.40
	1977G	34.600	—	.10	.20
	1977G	.051	—	Proof	.40
	1977J	53.481	—	.10	.20
	1977J	.051	—	Proof	.40
	1978D	41.600	—	.10	.20
	1978D	.054	—	Proof	.40
107	1978F	48.000	—	.10	.20
	1978F	.054	—	Proof	.40
	1978G	27.680	—	.10	.20
	1978G	.054	—	Proof	.40
	1978J	42.720	—	.10	.20
	1978J	.054	—	Proof	.40
	1979D	41.600	—	.10	.20
	1979D	.089	—	Proof	.40
	1979F	48.000	—	.10	.20
	1979F	.089	—	Proof	.40
	1979G	27.680	—	.10	.20
	1979G	.089	—	Proof	.40
	1979J	42.711	—	.10	.20
	1979J	.089	—	Proof	.40
	1980D	39.880	—	.10	.20
	1980D	.110	—	Proof	.40
	1980F	53.270	—	.10	.20
	1980F	.110	—	Proof	.40
	1980G	43.070	—	.10	.20
	1980G	.110	—	Proof	.40
	1980J	59.130	—	.10	.20
	1980J	.110	—	Proof	.40
	1981D	82.250	—	.10	.20
	1981D	.091	—	Proof	.40
	1981F	84.910	—	.10	.20
	1981F	.091	—	Proof	.40
	1981G	41.910	—	.10	.20
	1981G	.091	—	Proof	.40
	1981J	49.290	—	.10	.20
	1981J	.091	—	Proof	.40
	1982D	57.500	—	.10	.20
	1982D	.091	—	Proof	.40
	1982F	53.290	—	.10	.20
	1982F	.091	—	Proof	.40
	1982G	23.750	—	.10	.20
	1982G	.091	—	Proof	.40
	1982J	62.000	—	.10	.20
	1982J	.091	—	Proof	.40
	1983D	46.800	—	.10	.20
	1983D	.091	—	Proof	.40
	1983F	54.000	—	.10	.20
	1983F	.091	—	Proof	.40
	1983G	31.140	—	.10	.20
	1983G	.091	—	Proof	.40
	1983J	48.060	—	.10	.20
	1983J	.091	—	Proof	.40
	1984D	—	—	.10	.20
	1984D	.079	—	Proof	.40
	1984F	—	—	.10	.20
	1984F	.079	—	Proof	.40
	1984G	—	—	.10	.20
	1984G	.079	—	Proof	.40
	1984J	—	—	.10	.20
	1984J	.079	—	Proof	.40
	1985D	—	—	—	.10
	1985D	—	—	Proof	.40
	1985F	—	—	—	.10
	1985F	—	—	Proof	.40
	1985G	—	—	—	.10
	1985G	—	—	Proof	.40
	1985J	—	—	—	.10
	1985J	—	—	Proof	.40
	1986D	—	—	—	.10
	1986D	—	—	Proof	.40
	1986F	—	—	—	.10
	1986F	—	—	Proof	.40
	1986G	—	—	—	.10
	1986G	—	—	Proof	.40
	1986J	—	—	—	.10
	1986J	—	—	Proof	.40
	1987D	—	—	—	.10
	1987D	—	—	Proof	.40
	1987F	—	—	—	.10
	1987F	—	—	Proof	.40
	1987G	—	—	—	.10
	1987G	—	—	Proof	.40
	1987J	—	—	—	.10
	1987J	—	—	Proof	.40
	1988D	—	—	—	.10
	1988D	—	—	Proof	.40
	1988F	—	—	—	.10
	1988F	—	—	Proof	.40
	1988G	—	—	—	.10
	1988G	—	—	Proof	.40
	1988J	—	—	—	.10
	1988J	—	—	Proof	.40

10 PFENNIG

BRASS-CLAD STEEL
Currency Reform

KM#	Date	Mintage	VF	XF	Unc
103	1949D	140.558	.50	7.50	22.50
	1949D	—	—	Proof	100.00
	1949F	120.932	.50	7.50	22.50
	1949F	250 pcs.	—	Proof	50.00
	1949G	82.933	1.00	7.50	30.00
	1949 lg.J	154.095	.50	7.50	22.50
	1949J	—	—	Proof	50.00
	1949 sm.J	Inc. Ab.	.50	7.50	22.50
	1949J	—	—	Proof	50.00

BRASS PLATED STEEL
Federal Republic

KM#	Date	Mintage	VF	XF	Unc
108	1950D	393.209	—	.10	3.00
	1950F	584.340	—	.10	3.00
	1950F	500 pcs.	—	Proof	42.50
	1950G	309.045	—	.10	3.00
	1950G	1,800	—	Proof	3.00
	1950J	402.452	—	.10	3.00
	1950J	—	—	Proof	17.50
	1966D	31.220	—	.10	3.00
	1966F	36.097	—	.10	3.00
	1966F	100 pcs.	—	Proof	60.00
	1966G	25.338	—	.10	3.00
	1966G	3,070	—	Proof	8.50
	1966J	32.116	—	.10	3.00
	1966J	1,000	—	Proof	12.50
	1967D	15.632	—	.10	4.00
	1967F	18.049	—	.10	4.00
	1967F	1,500	—	Proof	15.00
	1967G	1.518	1.00	4.00	15.00
	1967G	4,500	—	Proof	7.50
	1967J	16.051	—	.10	4.00
	1967J	1,500	—	Proof	12.50
	1968D	5.207	—	.10	3.00
	1968F	6.010	—	.10	3.00
	1968F	3,000	—	Proof	10.00
	1968G	12.384	.10	.50	3.00
	1968G	6,023	—	Proof	5.00
	1968J	5.422	—	.10	3.50
	1968J	2,000	—	Proof	10.00
	1969D	41.693	—	.10	2.00
	1969F	48.084	—	.10	.25
	1969F	5,000	—	Proof	3.00
	1969G	48.760	—	.10	.25
	1969G	8,700	—	Proof	2.50
	1969J	42.756	—	.10	.25
	1969J	5,000	—	Proof	2.50
	1970D	54.085	—	.10	.25
	1970F	60.086	—	.10	.25
	1970F	5,140	—	Proof	3.00
	1970G	35.900	—	.10	.25
	1970G	10,200	—	Proof	2.00
	1970J	40.115	—	.10	.25
	1970J	5,000	—	Proof	2.50
	1971D	54.022	—	.10	.25
	1971D	8,000	—	Proof	2.50
	1971F	92.534	—	.10	.25
	1971F	8,000	—	Proof	2.50
	1971G	88.614	—	.10	.25
	1971G	.010	—	Proof	2.00
	1971 sm.J	65.622	—	.10	.25
	1971 lg.J	Inc. Ab.	—	.10	.25
	1971J	8,000	—	Proof	1.50
	1972D	104.345	—	.10	.25
	1972D	8,000	—	Proof	1.50
	1972F	110.177	—	.10	.25
	1972F	8,000	—	Proof	1.50
	1972G	71.766	—	.10	.25
	1972G	10,000	—	Proof	1.50
	1972J	96.991	—	.10	.25
	1972J	8,000	—	Proof	1.50
	1973D	26.052	—	.10	.25
	1973D	9,000	—	Proof	1.50
	1973F	30.070	—	.10	.25
	1973F	9,000	—	Proof	1.50
	1973G	17.294	—	.10	.25
	1973G	9,000	—	Proof	1.50
	1973J	26.774	—	.10	.25
	1973J	9,000	—	Proof	1.50
	1974D	15.707	—	.10	.25
	1974D	.035	—	Proof	.75
	1974F	18.135	—	.10	.25
	1974F	.035	—	Proof	.75
	1974G	10.450	—	.10	.25
	1974G	.035	—	Proof	.75
	1974J	16.056	—	.10	.25
	1974J	.035	—	Proof	.75
	1975D	15.654	—	.10	.25
	1975D	.043	—	Proof	.75
	1975F	18.043	—	.10	.25
	1975F	.043	—	Proof	.75
	1975G	10.403	—	.10	.25
	1975G	.043	—	Proof	.75
	1975J	16.111	—	.10	.25
	1975J	.043	—	Proof	.75
	1976D	65.200	—	.10	.25
	1976D	.043	—	Proof	.75
	1976F	75.282	—	.10	.25
	1976F	.043	—	Proof	.75
	1976G	43.372	—	.10	.25
	1976G	.043	—	Proof	.75
	1976J	66.930	—	.10	.25
	1976J	.043	—	Proof	.75
	1977D	64.989	—	.10	.20
	1977D	.051	—	Proof	.50
	1977F	75.052	—	.10	.20
	1977F	.051	—	Proof	.50
	1977G	43.300	—	.10	.20
	1977G	.051	—	Proof	.50
	1977J	66.800	—	.10	.20

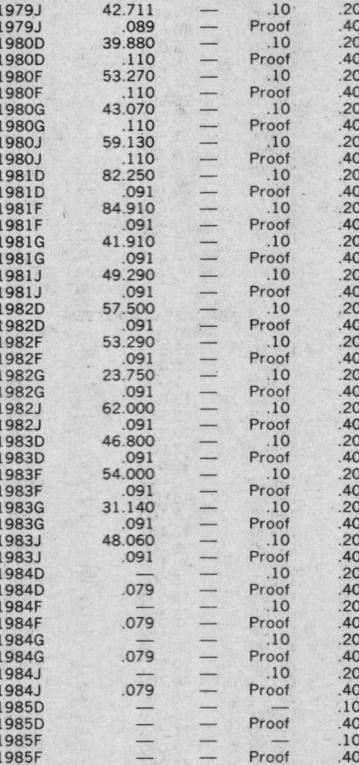

West / GERMANY 731

KM#	Date	Mintage	VF	XF	Unc
108	1977J	.051	—	Proof	.50
	1978D	91.000	—	.10	.20
	1978D	.054	—	Proof	.50
	1978F	105.000	—	.10	.20
	1978F	.054	—	Proof	.50
	1978G	60.590	—	.10	.20
	1978G	.054	—	Proof	.50
	1978J	93.490	—	.10	.20
	1978J	.054	—	Proof	.50
	1979D	104.000	—	.10	.20
	1979D	.089	—	Proof	.50
	1979F	120.000	—	.10	.20
	1979F	.089	—	Proof	.50
	1979G	69.200	—	.10	.20
	1979G	.089	—	Proof	.50
	1979J	106.800	—	.10	.20
	1979J	.089	—	Proof	.50
	1980D	65.450	—	.10	.20
	1980D	.110	—	Proof	.50
	1980F	122.780	—	.10	.20
	1980F	.110	—	Proof	.50
	1980G	75.410	—	.10	.20
	1980G	.110	—	Proof	.50
	1980J	70.960	—	.10	.20
	1980J	.110	—	Proof	.50
	1981D	135.200	—	.10	.20
	1981D	.091	—	Proof	.50
	1981F	117.410	—	.10	.20
	1981F	.091	—	Proof	.50
	1981G	69.440	—	.10	.20
	1981G	.091	—	Proof	.50
	1981J	138.360	—	.10	.20
	1981J	.091	—	Proof	.50
	1982D	74.690	—	.10	.20
	1982D	.091	—	Proof	.50
	1982F	85.140	—	.10	.20
	1982F	.091	—	Proof	.50
	1982G	50.840	—	.10	.20
	1982G	.091	—	Proof	.50
	1982J	80.620	—	.10	.20
	1982J	.091	—	Proof	.50
	1983D	33.800	—	.10	.20
	1983D	.091	—	Proof	.50
	1983F	39.000	—	.10	.20
	1983F	.091	—	Proof	.50
	1983G	22.490	—	.10	.20
	1983G	.091	—	Proof	.50
	1983J	34.710	—	.10	.20
	1983J	.091	—	Proof	.50
	1984D	—	—	.10	.20
	1984D	.079	—	Proof	.50
	1984F	—	—	.10	.20
	1984F	.079	—	Proof	.50
	1984G	—	—	.10	.20
	1984G	.079	—	Proof	.50
	1984J	—	—	.10	.20
	1984J	.079	—	Proof	.50
	1985D	—	—	—	.10
	1985D	—	—	Proof	.50
	1985F	—	—	—	.10
	1985F	—	—	Proof	.50
	1985G	—	—	—	.10
	1985G	—	—	Proof	.50
	1985J	—	—	—	.10
	1985J	—	—	Proof	.50
	1986D	—	—	—	.10
	1986D	—	—	Proof	.50
	1986F	—	—	—	.10
	1986F	—	—	Proof	.50
	1986G	—	—	—	.10
	1986G	—	—	Proof	.50
	1986J	—	—	—	.10
	1986J	—	—	Proof	.50
	1987D	—	—	—	.10
	1987D	—	—	Proof	.50
	1987F	—	—	—	.10
	1987F	—	—	Proof	.50
	1987G	—	—	—	.10
	1987G	—	—	Proof	.50
	1987J	—	—	—	.10
	1987J	—	—	Proof	.50
	1988D	—	—	—	.10
	1988D	—	—	Proof	.50
	1988F	—	—	—	.10
	1988F	—	—	Proof	.50
	1988G	—	—	—	.10
	1988G	—	—	Proof	.50
	1988J	—	—	—	.10
	1988J	—	—	Proof	.50

50 PFENNIG

COPPER-NICKEL
Currency Reform

KM#	Date	Mintage	VF	XF	Unc
104	1949D	39.108	.75	3.50	35.00
	1949F	45.118	.75	3.50	35.00
	1949F	200 pcs.	—	Proof	50.00
	1949G	25.924	.75	4.00	45.00
	1949J	42.303	.75	3.50	45.00
	1949J	—	—	Proof	50.00
	1950G	.030	100.00	150.00	225.00

NOTE: The 1950 dated coin was restruck without authorization by a mint official using genuine dies - quantity unknown.

Federal Republic
Reeded edge

KM#	Date	Mintage	VF	XF	Unc
109.1	1950D	100.735	.30	.50	7.50
	1950F	143.510	.30	.50	7.50
	1950F	450 pcs.	—	Proof	52.50
	1950G	66.421	.30	.50	7.50
	1950G	1,800	—	Proof	3.50
	1950J	102.736	.30	.50	7.50
	1950J	—	—	Proof	22.50
	1966D	8.328	.30	.35	12.50
	1966F	9.605	.30	.35	12.50
	1966F	100 pcs.	—	Proof	80.00
	1966G	5.543	.30	.35	12.50
	1966G	3,070	—	Proof	8.50
	1966J	8.569	.30	.35	12.50
	1966J	1,000	—	Proof	18.00
	1967D	5.207	.30	.35	12.50
	1967F	6.005	.30	.35	12.50
	1967F	1,500	—	Proof	15.00
	1967G	1.843	.30	1.00	17.50
	1967G	4,500	—	Proof	10.00
	1967J	10.684	.30	.35	12.50
	1967J	1,500	—	Proof	15.00
	1968D	7.809	.30	.35	10.00
	1968F	3.000	.30	.35	10.00
	1968F	3,000	—	Proof	12.00
	1968G	6.818	.30	.35	10.00
	1968G	6,023	—	Proof	6.50
	1968J	2.672	.30	.50	15.00
	1968J	2,000	—	Proof	12.50
	1969D	14.561	.30	.35	2.00
	1969F	16.804	.30	.35	2.00
	1969F	5,000	—	Proof	3.50
	1969G	9.704	.30	.35	2.00
	1969G	8,700	—	Proof	3.00
	1969J	14.969	.30	.35	2.00
	1969J	5,000	—	Proof	3.50
	1970D	25.294	.30	.35	1.00
	1970F	26.455	.30	.35	1.00
	1970F	5,140	—	Proof	3.50
	1970G	11.955	.30	.35	1.00
	1970G	10,200	—	Proof	3.00
	1970J	10.683	.30	.35	1.00
	1970J	5,000	—	Proof	3.50
	1971D	23.393	.30	.35	.50
	1971D	8,000	—	Proof	3.00
	1971F	29.746	.30	.35	.50
	1971F	8,000	—	Proof	3.00
	1971G	15.556	.30	.35	.50
	1971G	.010	—	Proof	3.00
	1971 lg.J	24.044	.30	.35	.50
	1971 sm.J	Inc. Ab.	.30	.35	.50
	1971J	8,000	—	Proof	3.00

Plain edge

KM#	Date	Mintage	VF	XF	Unc
109.2	1972D	26.008	—	.30	.50
	1972D	8,000	—	Proof	2.00
	1972F	30.043	—	.30	.50
	1972F	8,000	—	Proof	2.00
	1972G	17.337	—	.30	.50
	1972G	10,000	—	Proof	2.00
	1972J	26.707	—	.30	.50
	1972J	8,000	—	Proof	2.00
	1973D	7.810	—	.30	1.00
	1973D	9,000	—	Proof	2.00
	1973F	8.994	—	.30	.50
	1973F	9,000	—	Proof	2.00
	1973G	5.201	—	.30	.50
	1973G	9,000	—	Proof	2.00
	1973J	8.011	—	.30	.50
	1973J	9,000	—	Proof	2.00
	1974D	18.264	—	.30	1.00
	1974D	.035	—	Proof	1.00
	1974 lg.F	21.036	—	.30	.50
	1974 sm.F	Inc. Ab.	—	.30	1.00
	1974F	.035	—	Proof	1.00
	1974G	12.159	—	.30	.50
	1974G	.035	—	Proof	1.00
	1974J	18.752	—	.30	.50
	1974J	.035	—	Proof	1.00
	1975D	13.055	—	.30	1.00
	1975D	.043	—	Proof	1.00
	1975F	15.003	—	.30	.50
	1975F	.043	—	Proof	1.00
	1975G	8.675	—	.30	.50
	1975G	.043	—	Proof	1.00
	1975J	13.379	—	.30	.50
	1975J	.043	—	Proof	1.00
	1976D	10.411	—	.30	1.00
	1976D	.043	—	Proof	1.00
	1976F	12.048	—	.30	.50
	1976F	.043	—	Proof	1.00
	1976G	6.653	—	.30	.50
	1976G	.043	—	Proof	1.00
	1976J	10.716	—	.30	.50
	1976J	.043	—	Proof	1.00
	1977D	10.400	—	.30	1.00
	1977D	.051	—	Proof	.75
	1977F	12.000	—	.30	.50
	1977F	.051	—	Proof	.75
109.2	1977G	6.921	—	.30	.50
	1977G	.051	—	Proof	.75
	1977J	10.708	—	.30	.50
	1977J	.051	—	Proof	.75
	1978D	10.400	—	.30	.50
	1978D	.054	—	Proof	.75
	1978F	12.000	—	.30	.50
	1978F	.054	—	Proof	.75
	1978G	6.640	—	.30	.50
	1978G	.054	—	Proof	.75
	1978J	10.680	—	.30	.50
	1978J	.054	—	Proof	.75
	1979D	10.400	—	.30	.50
	1979D	.089	—	Proof	.75
	1979F	12.000	—	.30	.50
	1979F	.089	—	Proof	.75
	1979G	6.920	—	.30	.50
	1979G	.089	—	Proof	.75
	1979J	10.680	—	.30	.50
	1979J	.089	—	Proof	.75
	1980D	23.250	—	.30	.50
	1980D	.110	—	Proof	.75
	1980F	17.440	—	.30	.50
	1980F	.110	—	Proof	.75
	1980G	22.460	—	.30	.50
	1980G	.110	—	Proof	.75
	1980J	24.030	—	.30	.50
	1980J	.110	—	Proof	.75
	1981D	17.900	—	.30	.50
	1981D	.091	—	Proof	.75
	1981F	29.810	—	.30	.50
	1981F	.091	—	Proof	.75
	1981G	10.880	—	.30	.50
	1981G	.091	—	Proof	.75
	1981J	24.140	—	.30	.50
	1981J	.091	—	Proof	.75
	1982D	21.540	—	.30	.50
	1982D	.091	—	Proof	.75
	1982F	28.900	—	.30	.50
	1982F	.091	—	Proof	.75
	1982G	19.710	—	.30	.50
	1982G	.091	—	Proof	.75
	1982J	17.210	—	.30	.50
	1982J	.091	—	Proof	.75
	1983D	20.800	—	.30	.50
	1983D	.091	—	Proof	.75
	1983F	24.000	—	.30	.50
	1983F	.091	—	Proof	.75
	1983G	13.840	—	.30	.50
	1983G	.091	—	Proof	.75
	1983J	21.360	—	.30	.50
	1983J	.091	—	Proof	.75
	1984D	—	—	.30	.50
	1984D	.079	—	Proof	.75
	1984F	—	—	.30	.50
	1984F	.079	—	Proof	.75
	1984G	—	—	.30	.50
	1984G	.079	—	Proof	.75
	1984J	—	—	.30	.50
	1984J	.079	—	Proof	.75
	1985D	—	—	—	.35
	1985D	—	—	Proof	.75
	1985F	—	—	—	.35
	1985F	—	—	Proof	.75
	1985G	—	—	—	.35
	1985G	—	—	Proof	.75
	1985J	—	—	—	.35
	1985J	—	—	Proof	.75
	1986D	—	—	—	.35
	1986D	—	—	Proof	.75
	1986F	—	—	—	.35
	1986F	—	—	Proof	.75
	1986G	—	—	—	.35
	1986G	—	—	Proof	.75
	1986J	—	—	—	.35
	1986J	—	—	Proof	.75
	1987D	—	—	—	.35
	1987D	—	—	Proof	.75
	1987F	—	—	—	.35
	1987F	—	—	Proof	.75
	1987G	—	—	—	.35
	1987G	—	—	Proof	.75
	1987J	—	—	—	.35
	1987J	—	—	Proof	.75
	1988D	—	—	—	.35
	1988D	—	—	Proof	.75
	1988F	—	—	—	.35
	1988F	—	—	Proof	.75
	1988G	—	—	—	.35
	1988G	—	—	Proof	.75
	1988J	—	—	—	.35
	1988J	—	—	Proof	.75

MARK

COPPER-NICKEL
Federal Republic

KM#	Date	Mintage	VF	XF	Unc
110	1950D	60.467	.75	2.50	40.00
	1950D	—	—	Proof	150.00
	1950F	69.183	.75	2.50	40.00
	1950F	150 pcs.	—	Proof	—

West / GERMANY

KM# 110

Date	Mintage	VF	XF	Unc
1950G	39.826	.75	2.50	45.00
1950J	61.483	.75	2.50	45.00
1950J	—	—	Proof	100.00
1954D	5.202	1.00	7.50	80.00
1954F	6.000	1.00	7.50	80.00
1954F	175 pcs.	—	Proof	—
1954G	3.459	1.00	40.00	350.00
1954G	15 pcs.	—	Proof	1150.
1954J	5.341	1.00	7.50	80.00
1954J	—	—	Proof	175.00
1955D	3.093	1.00	7.50	80.00
1955F	4.909	1.00	7.50	80.00
1955F	100 pcs.	—	Proof	—
1955G	2.500	2.50	40.00	350.00
1955J	5.294	1.00	7.50	80.00
1956D	13.231	1.00	5.00	60.00
1956F	14.700	1.00	5.00	60.00
1956F	100 pcs.	—	Proof	—
1956G	8.362	1.00	5.00	50.00
1956J	11.478	1.00	5.00	60.00
1957D	6.820	1.00	7.50	60.00
1957D	—	—	Proof	125.00
1957F	6.390	1.00	7.50	60.00
1957F	100 pcs.	—	Proof	—
1957G	3.841	1.00	7.50	50.00
1957J	6.632	1.00	7.50	60.00
1957J	—	—	Proof	—
1958D	4.150	1.00	5.00	60.00
1958D	—	—	Proof	125.00
1958F	4.109	1.00	5.00	60.00
1958F	100 pcs.	—	Proof	—
1958G	3.460	1.00	5.00	90.00
1958J	4.656	1.00	5.00	80.00
1959D	10.409	.75	2.50	40.00
1959F	11.972	.75	2.50	40.00
1959F	100 pcs.	—	Proof	—
1959G	6.921	.75	2.50	50.00
1959J	10.691	.75	2.50	40.00
1960D	5.453	.75	2.50	40.00
1960F	5.709	.75	2.50	40.00
1960F	100 pcs.	—	Proof	—
1960G	3.632	.75	2.50	40.00
1960J	5.612	.75	2.50	40.00
1961D	7.536	.75	2.50	35.00
1961F	6.029	.75	2.50	35.00
1961G	4.843	.75	2.50	35.00
1961J	7.483	.75	2.50	35.00
1962D	10.327	.75	2.50	25.00
1962F	11.122	.75	2.50	25.00
1962G	6.054	.75	2.50	25.00
1962J	10.822	.75	2.50	25.00
1963D	12.624	.75	2.50	25.00
1963F	18.292	.75	2.50	25.00
1963G	11.253	.75	2.50	25.00
1963G	*600 pcs.	—	Proof	—
1963J	15.906	.75	2.50	25.00
1964D	8.048	.75	2.50	25.00
1964F	12.796	.75	2.50	25.00
1964G	3.465	.75	2.50	25.00
1964G	*600 pcs.	—	Proof	40.00
1964J	6.958	.75	2.50	25.00
1965D	9.388	.60	2.00	20.00
1965F	9.013	.60	2.00	20.00
1965F	300 pcs.	—	Proof	140.00
1965G	6.232	.60	2.00	20.00
1965G	1.200	—	Proof	5.00
1965J	8.024	.60	2.00	20.00
1966D	11.717	.60	2.00	15.00
1966F	11.368	.60	2.00	15.00
1966F	100 pcs.	—	Proof	120.00
1966G	7.799	.60	2.00	15.00
1966G	3.070	—	Proof	12.50
1966J	12.030	.60	2.00	15.00
1966J	1.000	—	Proof	25.00
1967D	13.017	.60	2.00	12.50
1967F	7.500	.60	2.00	12.50
1967F	1.500	—	Proof	20.00
1967G	4.324	.60	2.00	12.50
1967G	4.500	—	Proof	15.00
1967J	13.357	.60	2.00	12.50
1967J	1.500	—	Proof	20.00
1968D	1.303	.60	4.00	20.00
1968F	1.500	.60	4.00	20.00
1968F	3.000	—	Proof	15.00
1968G	5.198	.60	3.00	20.00
1968G	6.023	—	Proof	7.50
1968J	1.338	.60	4.00	25.00
1968J	2.000	—	Proof	15.00
1969D	13.025	.60	1.00	10.00
1969F	15.021	.60	1.00	10.00
1969F	5.000	—	Proof	6.00
1969G	8.665	.60	1.00	10.00
1969G	8.700	—	Proof	5.00
1969J	13.370	.60	1.00	10.00
1969J	5.000	—	Proof	5.00
1970D	17.928	.60	.75	8.00
1970F	19.408	.60	.75	8.00
1970F	5.140	—	Proof	6.00
1970G	20.386	.60	.75	8.00
1970G	10.200	—	Proof	5.00
1970J	10.707	.60	.75	8.00
1970J	5.000	—	Proof	5.00
1971D	24.513	.60	.75	3.00
1971D	8.000	—	Proof	5.00
1971F	28.275	.60	.75	3.00
1971F	8.000	—	Proof	5.00
1971G	16.375	.60	.75	3.00
1971G	.010	—	Proof	5.00
1971J	25.214	.60	.75	3.00
1971J	8.000	—	Proof	5.00
1972D	20.904	.60	.75	1.50

KM# 110 (continued)

Date	Mintage	VF	XF	Unc
1972D	8.000	—	Proof	4.00
1972F	24.086	.60	.75	1.50
1972F	8.000	—	Proof	4.00
1972G	13.868	.60	.75	1.50
1972G	.010	—	Proof	4.00
1972J	21.360	.60	.75	1.50
1972J	8.000	—	Proof	4.00
1973D	14.327	.60	.75	1.50
1973D	9.000	—	Proof	4.00
1973F	16.592	.60	.75	1.50
1973F	9.000	—	Proof	4.00
1973G	10.409	.60	.75	1.50
1973G	9.000	—	Proof	4.00
1973J	14.704	.60	.75	1.50
1973J	9.000	—	Proof	4.00
1974D	20.876	.60	.75	1.50
1974D	.035	—	Proof	1.50
1974F	24.057	.60	.75	1.50
1974F	.035	—	Proof	1.50
1974G	13.931	.60	.75	1.50
1974G	.035	—	Proof	1.50
1974J	21.440	.60	.75	1.50
1974J	.035	—	Proof	1.50
1975D	18.241	.60	.75	1.00
1975D	.043	—	Proof	1.50
1975F	21.059	.60	.75	1.00
1975F	.043	—	Proof	1.50
1975G	12.142	.60	.75	1.00
1975G	.043	—	Proof	1.50
1975J	18.770	.60	.75	1.00
1975J	.043	—	Proof	1.50
1976D	15.670	.60	.75	1.00
1976D	.043	—	Proof	1.50
1976F	18.105	.60	.75	1.00
1976F	.043	—	Proof	1.50
1976G	10.382	.60	.75	1.00
1976G	.043	—	Proof	1.50
1976J	16.046	.60	.75	1.00
1976J	.043	—	Proof	1.50
1977D	20.801	.60	.70	.85
1977D	.051	—	Proof	1.00
1977F	24.026	.60	.70	.85
1977F	.051	—	Proof	1.00
1977G	13.849	.60	.70	.85
1977G	.051	—	Proof	1.00
1977J	21.416	.60	.70	.85
1977J	.051	—	Proof	1.00
1978D	15.600	.60	.70	.85
1978D	.054	—	Proof	1.00
1978F	18.000	.60	.70	.85
1978F	.054	—	Proof	1.00
1978G	10.380	.60	.70	.85
1978G	.054	—	Proof	1.00
1978J	16.020	.60	.70	.85
1978J	.054	—	Proof	1.00
1979D	18.200	.60	.70	.85
1979D	.089	—	Proof	1.00
1979F	21.000	.60	.70	.85
1979F	.089	—	Proof	1.00
1979G	12.110	.60	.70	.85
1979G	.089	—	Proof	1.00
1979J	18.690	.60	.70	.85
1979J	.089	—	Proof	1.00
1980D	24.330	—	.60	.75
1980D	.110	—	Proof	1.00
1980F	9.670	—	.60	.75
1980F	.110	—	Proof	1.00
1980G	8.540	—	.60	.75
1980G	.110	—	Proof	1.00
1980J	16.010	—	.60	.75
1980J	.110	—	Proof	1.00
1981D	21.150	—	.60	.75
1981D	.091	—	Proof	1.00
1981F	25.910	—	.60	.75
1981F	.091	—	Proof	1.00
1981G	14.090	—	.60	.75
1981G	.091	—	Proof	1.00
1981J	18.800	—	.60	.75
1981J	.091	—	Proof	1.00
1982D	20.590	—	.60	.75
1982D	.091	—	Proof	1.00
1982F	22.990	—	.60	.75
1982F	.091	—	Proof	1.00
1982G	14.900	—	.60	.75
1982G	.091	—	Proof	1.00
1982J	11.520	—	.50	—
1982J	.091	—	Proof	1.00
1983D	18.200	—	.60	.75
1983D	.091	—	Proof	1.00
1983F	21.000	—	.60	.75
1983F	.091	—	Proof	1.00
1983G	12.100	—	.60	.75
1983G	.091	—	Proof	1.00
1983J	18.690	—	.60	.75
1983J	.091	—	Proof	1.00
1984D	—	—	.60	.75
1984D	.079	—	Proof	1.50
1984F	—	—	.60	.75
1984F	.079	—	Proof	1.50
1984G	—	—	.60	.75
1984G	.079	—	Proof	1.50
1984J	—	—	.60	.75
1984J	.079	—	Proof	1.50
1985D	—	—	—	.60
1985D	—	—	Proof	1.50
1985F	—	—	—	.60
1985F	—	—	Proof	1.50
1985G	—	—	—	.60
1985G	—	—	Proof	1.50
1985J	—	—	—	.60
1985J	—	—	Proof	1.50

KM# 110 (continued)

Date	Mintage	VF	XF	Unc
1986D	—	—	—	.60
1986D	—	—	Proof	1.50
1986F	—	—	—	.60
1986F	—	—	Proof	1.50
1986G	—	—	—	.60
1986G	—	—	Proof	1.50
1986J	—	—	—	.60
1986J	—	—	Proof	1.50
1987D	—	—	—	.60
1987D	—	—	Proof	1.50
1987F	—	—	—	.60
1987F	—	—	Proof	1.50
1987G	—	—	—	.60
1987G	—	—	Proof	1.50
1987J	—	—	—	.60
1987J	—	—	Proof	1.50
1988D	—	—	—	.60
1988D	—	—	Proof	1.50
1988F	—	—	—	.60
1988F	—	—	Proof	1.50
1988G	—	—	—	.60
1988G	—	—	Proof	1.50
1988J	—	—	—	.60
1988J	—	—	Proof	1.50

2 MARK

COPPER-NICKEL
Federal Republic

KM# 111

Date	Mintage	VF	XF	Unc
1951D	19.564	12.00	20.00	50.00
1951D	—	—	Proof	275.00
1951F	22.609	12.00	17.50	40.00
1951F	150 pcs.	—	Proof	250.00
1951G*	13.012	20.00	35.00	110.00
1951G	—	—	Proof	300.00
1951J	20.104	10.00	17.50	50.00
1951J	—	—	Proof	275.00

*NOTE: This coin was restruck without authorization by a mint official using genuine dies - quantity unknown.

Max Planck

KM# 116

Date	Mintage	VF	XF	Unc
1957D	7.452	2.00	5.00	17.50
1957D	—	—	Proof	75.00
1957F	6.337	2.00	5.00	17.50
1957F	100 pcs.	—	Proof	—
1957G	2.598	3.00	7.50	80.00
1957J	11.210	2.00	5.00	17.50
1957J	—	—	Proof	80.00
1958D	12.623	1.50	4.00	17.50
1958D	—	—	Proof	75.00
1958F	16.825	1.50	4.00	17.50
1958F	300 pcs.	—	Proof	—
1958G	10.744	1.50	4.00	22.50
1958J	9.408	1.50	4.00	17.50
1959D	1.020	4.00	10.00	125.00
1959F	.203	15.00	45.00	175.00
1960D	3.535	1.50	4.00	17.50
1960F	3.692	1.50	4.00	17.50
1960F	50 pcs.	—	Proof	—
1960G	2.695	2.00	4.00	22.50
1960J	4.676	1.50	4.00	17.50
1961D	3.918	1.50	4.00	17.50
1961F	3.872	1.50	4.00	17.50
1961G	2.776	2.00	4.00	22.50
1961J	2.940	1.50	4.00	17.50
1962D	4.105	1.50	6.00	17.50
1962F	3.344	2.00	6.00	17.50
1962G	1.800	2.00	6.00	22.50
1962G	—	—	Proof	60.00
1962J	3.609	2.00	6.00	17.50
1963D	4.411	1.50	4.00	17.50
1963F	3.752	1.50	4.00	17.50
1963G	3.448	1.50	4.00	17.50
1963G	*600 pcs.	—	Proof	—
1963J	7.348	1.50	4.00	17.50
1964D	5.205	1.50	4.00	12.50
1964F	4.834	1.50	4.00	12.50
1964G	3.044	1.50	4.00	12.50
1964G	600 pcs.	—	Proof	55.00
1964J	2.681	1.50	4.00	12.50
1965D	3.903	1.50	2.50	10.00
1965F	4.045	1.50	2.50	10.00
1965F	300 pcs.	—	Proof	190.00
1965G	2.599	1.50	2.50	10.00
1965G	1.200	—	Proof	5.00
1965J	4.007	1.50	2.50	10.00
1966D	5.855	1.50	2.50	6.00
1966F	3.750	1.50	2.50	6.00

KM#	Date	Mintage	VF	XF	Unc
116	1966F	100 pcs.	—	Proof	160.00
	1966G	3.895	1.50	2.50	6.00
	1966G	3,070	—	Proof	12.50
	1966J	6.014	1.50	2.50	6.00
	1966J	1,000	—	Proof	25.00
	1967D	3.254	1.50	2.50	6.00
	1967F	3.758	1.50	2.50	6.00
	1967F	1,500	—	Proof	20.00
	1967G	1.878	1.50	4.00	20.00
	1967G	4,500	—	Proof	15.00
	1967J	6.684	1.25	2.50	6.00
	1967J	1,500	—	Proof	22.00
	1968D	4.166	1.50	2.50	10.00
	1968F	1.050	2.00	5.00	15.00
	1968F	3,000	—	Proof	15.00
	1968G	3.060	2.00	2.50	8.00
	1968G	6.023	—	Proof	10.00
	1968J	.939	2.00	4.00	20.00
	1968J	2,000	—	Proof	18.00
	1969D	2.602	2.00	2.50	8.00
	1969F	3.005	2.00	2.50	8.00
	1969F	5,100	—	Proof	6.00
	1969G	1.754	2.00	2.50	12.50
	1969G	8,700	—	Proof	6.00
	1969J	2.680	2.00	2.50	8.00
	1969J	5,000	—	Proof	6.00
	1970D	5.203	1.50	2.00	4.00
	1970F	6.018	1.50	2.00	4.00
	1970F	5,140	—	Proof	7.50
	1970G	3.461	1.50	2.00	4.00
	1970G	.010	—	Proof	6.00
	1970J	5.691	1.50	2.00	4.00
	1970J	5,000	—	Proof	6.00
	1971D	8.451	1.00	1.25	3.00
	1971D	8,000	—	Proof	5.00
	1971F	10.017	1.00	1.25	3.00
	1971F	8,000	—	Proof	5.00
	1971G	5.631	1.00	1.25	3.00
	1971G	.010	—	Proof	5.00
	1971J	8.786	1.00	1.25	3.00
	1971J	8,000	—	Proof	5.00

COPPER-NICKEL CLAD NICKEL
Konrad Adenauer

KM#	Date	Mintage	VF	XF	Unc
124	1969D	7.001	—	1.25	3.00
	1969F	7.006	—	1.25	3.00
	1969G	7.010	—	1.25	3.00
	1969J	7.000	—	1.25	3.00
	1970D	7.318	—	1.25	3.00
	1970F	8.422	—	1.25	3.00
	1970G	4.844	—	1.25	3.00
	1970J	7.476	—	1.25	3.00
	1971D	7.287	—	1.25	3.00
	1971F	8.400	—	1.25	3.00
	1971G	4.848	—	1.25	3.00
	1971J	7.476	—	1.25	3.00
	1972D	7.286	—	1.25	3.00
	1972D	8,000	—	Proof	4.50
	1972F	8.392	—	1.25	3.00
	1972F	8,000	—	Proof	4.50
	1972G	4.848	—	1.25	3.00
	1972G	.010	—	Proof	4.50
	1972J	7.476	—	1.25	3.00
	1972J	8,000	—	Proof	4.50
	1973D	10.393	—	1.25	3.00
	1973D	9,000	—	Proof	4.50
	1973F	11.015	—	1.25	3.00
	1973F	9,000	—	Proof	4.50
	1973G	9.022	—	1.25	3.00
	1973G	9,000	—	Proof	4.50
	1973J	12.272	—	1.25	3.00
	1973J	9,000	—	Proof	4.50
	1974D	5.151	—	1.25	3.00
	1974D	.035	—	Proof	2.00
	1974F	5.894	—	1.25	3.00
	1974F	.035	—	Proof	2.00
	1974G	3.790	—	1.25	3.00
	1974G	.035	—	Proof	2.00
	1974J	5.282	—	1.25	3.00
	1974J	.035	—	Proof	2.00
	1975D	4.553	—	1.25	2.50
	1975D	.043	—	Proof	2.00
	1975F	5.270	—	1.25	2.50
	1975F	.043	—	Proof	2.00
	1975G	3.035	—	1.25	2.50
	1975G	.043	—	Proof	2.00
	1975J	4.673	—	1.25	2.50
	1975J	.043	—	Proof	2.00
	1976D	4.576	—	1.25	2.50
	1976D	.043	—	Proof	2.00
	1976F	5.257	—	1.25	2.50
	1976F	.043	—	Proof	2.00
	1976G	3.028	—	1.25	2.50
	1976G	.043	—	Proof	2.00
	1976J	4.673	—	1.25	2.50
	1976J	.043	—	Proof	2.00
	1977D	5.906	—	1.25	2.50
	1977D	.051	—	Proof	1.50
	1977F	6.765	—	1.25	2.50

KM#	Date	Mintage	VF	XF	Unc
124	1977F	.051	—	Proof	1.50
	1977G	3.892	—	1.25	2.50
	1977G	.051	—	Proof	1.50
	1977J	6.007	—	1.25	2.50
	1977J	.051	—	Proof	1.50
	1978D	3.304	—	1.25	2.50
	1978D	.054	—	Proof	1.50
	1978F	3.804	—	1.25	2.50
	1978F	.054	—	Proof	1.50
	1978G	2.217	—	1.25	2.50
	1978G	.054	—	Proof	1.50
	1978J	3.392	—	1.25	2.50
	1978J	.054	—	Proof	1.50
	1979D	3.209	—	1.25	2.50
	1979D	.089	—	Proof	1.50
	1979F	3.689	—	1.25	2.50
	1979F	.089	—	Proof	1.50
	1979G	2.165	—	1.25	2.50
	1979G	.089	—	Proof	1.50
	1979J	3.293	—	1.25	2.50
	1979J	.089	—	Proof	1.50
	1980D	10.810	—	1.25	1.50
	1980D	.110	—	Proof	1.50
	1980F	8.910	—	1.25	1.50
	1980F	.110	—	Proof	1.50
	1980G	1.170	—	1.25	1.50
	1980G	.110	—	Proof	1.50
	1980J	4.670	—	1.25	1.50
	1980J	.110	—	Proof	1.50
	1981D	8.180	—	1.25	1.50
	1981D	.091	—	Proof	1.50
	1981F	7.690	—	1.25	1.50
	1981F	.091	—	Proof	1.50
	1981G	7.070	—	1.25	1.50
	1981G	.091	—	Proof	1.50
	1981J	8.290	—	1.25	1.50
	1981J	.091	—	Proof	1.50
	1982D	9.220	—	1.25	1.50
	1982D	.091	—	Proof	1.50
	1982F	11.260	—	1.25	1.50
	1982F	.091	—	Proof	1.50
	1982G	6.640	—	1.25	1.50
	1982G	.091	—	Proof	1.50
	1982J	9.790	—	1.25	1.50
	1982J	.091	—	Proof	1.50
	1983D	1.560	—	1.25	1.50
	1983D	.091	—	Proof	1.50
	1983F	1.800	—	1.25	1.50
	1983F	.091	—	Proof	1.50
	1983G	1.030	—	1.25	1.50
	1983G	.091	—	Proof	1.50
	1983J	1.600	—	1.25	1.50
	1983J	.091	—	Proof	1.50
	1984D	—	—	1.25	1.50
	1984D	.079	—	Proof	1.75
	1984F	—	—	1.25	1.50
	1984F	.079	—	Proof	1.75
	1984G	—	—	1.25	1.50
	1984G	.079	—	Proof	1.75
	1984J	—	—	1.25	1.50
	1984J	.079	—	Proof	1.75
	1985D	—	—	—	1.50
	1985D	—	—	Proof	2.25
	1985F	—	—	—	1.50
	1985F	—	—	Proof	2.25
	1985G	—	—	—	1.50
	1985G	—	—	Proof	2.25
	1985J	—	—	—	1.50
	1985J	—	—	Proof	2.25
	1986D	—	—	—	1.50
	1986D	—	—	Proof	2.25
	1986F	—	—	—	1.50
	1986F	—	—	Proof	2.25
	1986G	—	—	—	1.50
	1986G	—	—	Proof	2.25
	1986J	—	—	—	1.50
	1986J	—	—	Proof	2.25
	1987D	—	—	—	1.50
	1987D	—	—	Proof	2.25
	1987F	—	—	—	1.50
	1987F	—	—	Proof	2.25
	1987G	—	—	—	1.50
	1987G	—	—	Proof	2.25
	1987J	—	—	—	1.50
	1987J	—	—	Proof	2.25

Theodor Heuss

KM#	Date	Mintage	VF	XF	Unc
A127	1970D	7.317	—	1.25	3.00
(127)	1970F	8.426	—	1.25	3.00
	1970G	4.844	—	1.25	3.00
	1970J	7.476	—	1.25	3.00
	1971D	7.280	—	1.25	3.00
	1971F	8.403	—	1.25	3.00
	1971G	4.841	—	1.25	3.00
	1971J	7.476	—	1.25	3.00
	1972D	7.288	—	1.25	3.00
	1972D	8,000	—	Proof	4.50
	1972F	8.401	—	1.25	3.00
	1972F	8,000	—	Proof	4.50
	1972G	4.859	—	1.25	3.00

KM#	Date	Mintage	VF	XF	Unc
(127)	1972G	.010	—	Proof	4.50
	1972J	7.476	—	1.25	3.00
	1972J	8,000	—	Proof	4.50
	1973D	10.379	—	1.25	3.00
	1973D	9,000	—	Proof	4.50
	1973F	11.018	—	1.25	3.00
	1973F	9,000	—	Proof	4.50
	1973G	8.975	—	1.25	3.00
	1973G	9,000	—	Proof	4.50
	1973J	12.360	—	1.25	3.00
	1973J	9,000	—	Proof	4.50
	1974D	5.147	—	1.25	3.00
	1974D	.035	—	Proof	2.00
	1974F	5.899	—	1.25	3.00
	1974F	.035	—	Proof	2.00
	1974G	3.820	—	1.25	3.00
	1974G	.035	—	Proof	2.00
	1974J	5.280	—	1.25	3.00
	1974J	.035	—	Proof	2.00
	1975D	4.623	—	1.25	2.00
	1975D	.043	—	Proof	2.00
	1975F	5.251	—	1.25	2.00
	1975F	.043	—	Proof	2.00
	1975G	3.034	—	1.25	2.00
	1975G	.043	—	Proof	2.00
	1975J	4.675	—	1.25	2.00
	1975J	.043	—	Proof	2.00
	1976D	4.546	—	1.25	2.00
	1976D	.043	—	Proof	2.00
	1976F	5.259	—	1.25	2.00
	1976F	.043	—	Proof	2.00
	1976G	3.028	—	1.25	2.00
	1976G	.043	—	Proof	2.00
	1976J	4.681	—	1.25	2.00
	1976J	.043	—	Proof	2.00
	1977D	5.857	—	1.25	2.00
	1977D	.051	—	Proof	1.50
	1977F	6.752	—	1.25	2.00
	1977F	.051	—	Proof	1.50
	1977G	3.892	—	1.25	2.00
	1977G	.051	—	Proof	1.50
	1977J	6.009	—	1.25	2.00
	1977J	.051	—	Proof	1.50
	1978D	3.804	—	1.25	2.00
	1978D	.054	—	Proof	1.50
	1978F	3.804	—	1.25	2.00
	1978F	.054	—	Proof	1.50
	1978G	2.217	—	1.25	2.00
	1978G	.054	—	Proof	1.50
	1978J	3.392	—	1.25	2.00
	1978J	.054	—	Proof	1.50
	1979D	3.209	—	1.25	2.00
	1979D	.089	—	Proof	1.50
	1979F	3.689	—	1.25	2.00
	1979F	.089	—	Proof	1.50
	1979G	2.165	—	1.25	2.00
	1979G	.089	—	Proof	1.50
	1979J	3.293	—	1.25	2.00
	1979J	.089	—	Proof	1.50
	1980D	2.000	—	1.25	1.50
	1980D	.110	—	Proof	1.50
	1980F	2.300	—	1.25	1.50
	1980F	.110	—	Proof	1.50
	1980G	1.300	—	1.25	1.50
	1980G	.110	—	Proof	1.50
	1980J	2.000	—	1.25	1.50
	1980J	.110	—	Proof	1.50
	1981D	2.000	—	1.25	1.50
	1981D	.091	—	Proof	1.50
	1981F	2.300	—	1.25	1.50
	1981F	.091	—	Proof	1.50
	1981G	1.300	—	1.25	1.50
	1981G	.091	—	Proof	1.50
	1981J	2.000	—	1.25	1.50
	1981J	.091	—	Proof	1.50
	1982D	3.100	—	1.25	1.50
	1982D	.091	—	Proof	1.50
	1982F	3.600	—	1.25	1.50
	1982F	.091	—	Proof	1.50
	1982G	2.100	—	1.25	1.50
	1982G	.091	—	Proof	1.50
	1982J	3.200	—	1.25	1.50
	1982J	.091	—	Proof	1.50
	1983D	1.560	—	1.25	1.50
	1983D	.091	—	Proof	1.50
	1983F	1.800	—	1.25	1.50
	1983F	.091	—	Proof	1.50
	1983G	1.030	—	1.25	1.50
	1983G	.091	—	Proof	1.50
	1983J	1.600	—	1.25	1.50
	1983J	.091	—	Proof	1.50
	1984D	—	—	1.25	1.50
	1984D	.079	—	Proof	1.75
	1984F	—	—	1.25	1.50
	1984F	.079	—	Proof	1.75
	1984G	—	—	1.25	1.50
	1984G	.079	—	Proof	1.75
	1984J	—	—	1.25	1.50
	1984J	.079	—	Proof	1.75
	1985D	—	—	—	1.50
	1985D	—	—	Proof	2.25
	1985F	—	—	—	1.50
	1985F	—	—	Proof	2.25
	1985G	—	—	—	1.50
	1985G	—	—	Proof	2.25
	1985J	—	—	—	1.50
	1985J	—	—	Proof	2.25
	1986D	—	—	—	1.50
	1986D	—	—	Proof	2.25
	1986F	—	—	—	1.50
	1986F	—	—	Proof	2.25

West / GERMANY 734

KM#	Date	Mintage	VF	XF	Unc
(127)	1986G	—	—	—	1.50
	1986G	—	—	Proof	2.25
	1986J	—	—	—	1.50
	1986J	—	—	Proof	2.25
	1987D	—	—	—	1.50
	1987D	—	—	Proof	2.25
	1987F	—	—	—	1.50
	1987F	—	—	Proof	2.25
	1987G	—	—	—	1.50
	1987G	—	—	Proof	2.25
	1987J	—	—	—	1.50
	1987J	—	—	Proof	2.25

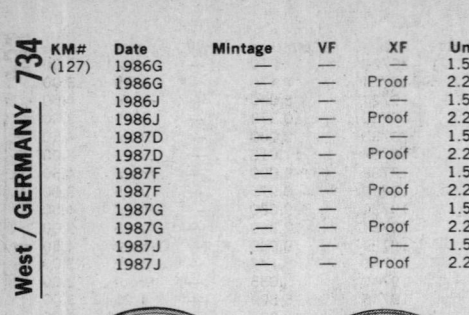

40th Anniversary of West German Mark

KM#	Date	Mintage	VF	XF	Unc
170	1988D	—	—	—	1.25
	1988D	—	—	Proof	2.00
	1988F	—	—	—	1.25
	1988F	—	—	Proof	2.00
	1988G	—	—	—	1.25
	1988G	—	—	Proof	2.00
	1988J	—	—	—	1.25
	1988J	—	—	Proof	2.00

Dr. Kurt Schumacher

KM#	Date	Mintage	VF	XF	Unc
149	1979D	3.209	—	1.25	2.00
	1979D	.089	—	Proof	1.50
	1979F	3.689	—	1.25	2.00
	1979F	.089	—	Proof	1.50
	1979G	2.165	—	1.25	2.00
	1979G	.089	—	Proof	1.50
	1979J	3.293	—	1.25	2.00
	1979J	.089	—	Proof	1.50
	1980D	2.000	—	1.25	2.00
	1980D	.110	—	Proof	1.50
	1980F	2.300	—	1.25	2.00
	1980F	.110	—	Proof	1.50
	1980G	1.300	—	1.25	2.00
	1980G	.110	—	Proof	1.50
	1980J	2.000	—	1.25	2.00
	1980J	.110	—	Proof	1.50
	1981D	2.000	—	1.25	2.00
	1981D	.091	—	Proof	1.50
	1981F	2.000	—	1.25	2.00
	1981F	.091	—	Proof	1.50
	1981G	1.300	—	1.25	2.00
	1981G	.091	—	Proof	1.50
	1981J	2.000	—	1.25	2.00
	1981J	.091	—	Proof	1.50
	1982D	3.100	—	1.25	2.00
	1982D	.091	—	Proof	1.50
	1982F	3.600	—	1.25	2.00
	1982F	.091	—	Proof	1.50
	1982G	2.100	—	1.25	2.00
	1982G	.091	—	Proof	1.50
	1982J	3.200	—	1.25	2.00
	1982J	.091	—	Proof	1.50
	1983D	1.560	—	1.25	2.00
	1983D	.091	—	Proof	1.50
	1983F	1.800	—	1.25	2.00
	1983F	.091	—	Proof	1.50
	1983G	1.030	—	1.25	2.00
	1983G	.091	—	Proof	1.50
	1983J	1.600	—	1.25	2.00
	1983J	.091	—	Proof	1.50
	1984D	—	—	1.25	2.00
	1984D	.079	—	Proof	1.75
	1984F	—	—	1.25	2.00
	1984F	.079	—	Proof	1.75
	1984G	—	—	1.25	2.00
	1984G	.079	—	Proof	1.75
	1984J	—	—	1.25	2.00
	1984J	.079	—	Proof	1.75
	1985D	—	—	—	1.50
	1985D	—	—	Proof	2.25
	1985F	—	—	—	1.50
	1985F	—	—	Proof	2.25
	1985G	—	—	—	1.50
	1985G	—	—	Proof	2.25
	1985J	—	—	—	1.50
	1985J	—	—	Proof	2.25
	1986D	—	—	—	1.50
	1986D	—	—	Proof	2.25
	1986F	—	—	—	1.50
	1986F	—	—	Proof	2.25
	1986G	—	—	—	1.50
	1986G	—	—	Proof	2.25
	1986J	—	—	—	1.50
	1986J	—	—	Proof	2.25
	1987D	—	—	—	1.50
	1987D	—	—	Proof	2.25
	1987F	—	—	—	1.50
	1987F	—	—	Proof	2.25
	1987G	—	—	—	1.50
	1987G	—	—	Proof	2.25
	1987J	—	—	—	1.50
	1987J	—	—	Proof	2.25
	1988D	—	—	—	1.50
	1988D	—	—	Proof	2.25
	1988F	—	—	—	1.50
	1988F	—	—	Proof	2.25
	1988G	—	—	—	1.50
	1988G	—	—	Proof	2.25
	1988J	—	—	—	1.50
	1988J	—	—	Proof	2.25

5 MARK

11.2000 g, .625 SILVER, .2250 oz ASW
Federal Republic

KM#	Date	Mintage	VF	XF	Unc
112.1	1951D	20.600	3.00	7.50	35.00
	1951D	—	—	Proof	250.00
	1951F	24.000	3.00	7.50	40.00
	1951F	280 pcs.	—	Proof	250.00
	1951G	13.840	3.00	7.50	40.00
	1951G	—	—	Proof	450.00
	1951J	21.360	3.00	7.50	35.00
	1951J	—	—	Proof	250.00
	1956D	1.092	10.00	35.00	100.00
	1956D	—	—	Proof	400.00
	1956F	1.200	10.00	35.00	100.00
	1956F	23 pcs.	—	Proof	900.00
	1956J	1.068	10.00	35.00	100.00
	1956J	—	—	Proof	400.00
	1957D	.566	10.00	40.00	125.00
	1957D	—	—	Proof	275.00
	1957F	2.100	7.50	35.00	110.00
	1957F	—	—	Proof	500.00
	1957G	.692	10.00	35.00	125.00
	1957G	—	—	Proof	300.00
	1957J	1.630	6.00	20.00	80.00
	1957J	—	—	Proof	250.00
	1958D	1.226	7.50	20.00	75.00
	1958D	—	—	Proof	300.00
	1958F	.600	15.00	90.00	350.00
	1958F	100 pcs.	—	Proof	750.00
	1958G	1.557	7.50	20.00	75.00
	1958G	—	—	Proof	400.00
	1958J	.060	300.00	600.00	2250.
	1958J	—	—	Proof	2000.
	1959D	.496	10.00	35.00	120.00
	1959D	—	—	Proof	400.00
	1959G	.692	12.50	35.00	120.00
	1959G	—	—	Proof	500.00
	1959J	.713	8.00	25.00	100.00
	1959J	—	—	Proof	375.00
	1960D	1.040	7.00	15.00	40.00
	1960D	—	—	Proof	300.00
	1960F	1.576	7.00	15.00	45.00
	1960F	50 pcs.	—	Proof	300.00
	1960G	.692	7.00	15.00	45.00
	1960G	—	—	Proof	250.00
	1960J	1.618	7.00	15.00	40.00
	1960J	—	—	Proof	400.00
	1961D	1.040	4.00	10.00	40.00
	1961D	—	—	Proof	225.00
	1961F	.824	4.00	15.00	45.00
	1961F	—	—	Proof	450.00
	1961J	.518	6.00	25.00	70.00
	1961J	—	—	Proof	550.00
	1963D	2.080	4.00	10.00	30.00
	1963D	—	—	Proof	350.00
	1963F	1.254	4.00	12.50	30.00
	1963F	—	—	Proof	350.00
	1963G	.600	4.00	15.00	45.00
	1963G	—	—	Proof	350.00
	1963J	2.136	4.00	15.00	40.00
	1963J	—	—	Proof	350.00
	1964D	.456	8.00	20.00	90.00
	1964D	—	—	Proof	375.00
	1964F	2.646	4.00	12.50	25.00
	1964F	—	—	Proof	350.00
	1964G	1.649	4.00	12.50	25.00
	1964G	*600 pcs.	—	Proof	80.00
	1964J	1.335	3.50	12.50	25.00
	1964J	—	—	Proof	200.00
	1965D	4.354	3.50	7.50	12.50
	1965D	—	—	Proof	175.00
	1965F	4.050	3.50	7.50	12.50
	1965F	300 pcs.	—	Proof	350.00
	1965G	2.335	3.50	7.50	12.50
	1965G	8.233	—	Proof	20.00

KM#	Date	Mintage	VF	XF	Unc
112.1	1965J	3.605	3.50	7.50	20.00
	1965J	—	—	Proof	250.00
	1966D	5.200	3.50	7.50	15.00
	1966D	—	—	Proof	250.00
	1966F	6.000	3.50	7.50	15.00
	1966F	100 pcs.	—	Proof	350.00
	1966G	3.460	3.50	7.50	12.50
	1966G	3.070	—	Proof	40.00
	1966J	5.340	3.50	7.50	15.00
	1966J	1.000	—	Proof	110.00
	1967D	3.120	3.50	7.50	20.00
	1967D	—	—	Proof	200.00
	1967F	3.598	3.50	7.50	30.00
	1967F	1.500	—	Proof	75.00
	1967G	1.406	3.50	7.50	35.00
	1967G	4.500	—	Proof	35.00
	1967J	3.204	3.50	7.50	15.00
	1967J	1.500	—	Proof	90.00
	1968D	1.300	3.50	7.50	15.00
	1968D	—	—	Proof	60.00
	1968F	1.497	3.50	7.50	15.00
	1968F	3.000	—	Proof	40.00
	1968G	1.535	3.50	7.50	12.50
	1968G	6.023	—	Proof	35.00
	1968J	1.335	3.50	7.50	12.50
	1968J	2.000	—	Proof	85.00
	1969D	2.080	3.50	7.50	12.50
	1969D	—	—	Proof	20.00
	1969F	2.395	3.50	7.50	17.50
	1969F	5.000	—	Proof	18.00
	1969G	3.484	3.50	7.50	12.50
	1969G	8.700	—	Proof	15.00
	1969J	2.136	3.50	7.50	12.50
	1969J	5.000	—	Proof	18.00
	1970D	2.000	3.50	6.00	12.50
	1970D	—	—	Proof	15.00
	1970F	1.995	3.50	6.00	12.50
	1970F	5.140	—	Proof	15.00
	1970G	6.000	3.50	6.00	12.50
	1970G	10.200	—	Proof	15.00
	1970J	4.000	3.50	6.00	12.50
	1970J	5.000	—	Proof	18.00
	1971D	4.000	3.00	4.00	7.50
	1971D	8.000	—	Proof	15.00
	1971F	3.993	3.00	4.00	7.50
	1971F	8.000	—	Proof	15.00
	1971G	6.010	3.00	4.00	7.50
	1971G	.010	—	Proof	15.00
	1971J	6.000	3.00	4.00	7.50
	1971J	8.000	—	Proof	18.00
	1972D	3.000	3.00	4.00	7.50
	1972D	8.000	—	Proof	15.00
	1972F	8.992	3.00	4.00	7.50
	1972F	8.100	—	Proof	15.00
	1972G	4.999	3.00	4.00	7.50
	1972G	.010	—	Proof	15.00
	1972J	6.000	3.00	4.00	7.50
	1972J	8.000	—	Proof	15.00
	1973D	3.380	3.00	4.00	7.50
	1973D	9.000	—	Proof	15.00
	1973F	3.891	3.00	4.00	7.50
	1973F	9.100	—	Proof	15.00
	1973G	2.240	3.00	4.00	7.50
	1973G	9.000	—	Proof	15.00
	1973J	5.571	3.00	4.00	7.50
	1973J	9.000	—	Proof	15.00
	1974D	4.594	3.00	4.00	7.50
	1974D	.035	—	Proof	12.00
	1974F	6.514	3.00	4.00	7.50
	1974F	.035	—	Proof	12.00
	1974G	3.708	3.00	4.00	7.50
	1974G	.035	—	Proof	12.00
	1974J	2.968	3.00	4.00	7.50
	1974J	.035	—	Proof	12.00

Uninscribed- plain edge errors

KM#	Date	Mintage	VF	XF	Unc
112.2	1959D	Inc. Ab.	25.00	55.00	75.00
	1959J	Inc. Ab.	25.00	55.00	75.00
	1963J	Inc. Ab.	25.00	55.00	75.00
	1964F	Inc. Ab.	25.00	55.00	75.00
	1965F	Inc. Ab.	25.00	55.00	75.00
	1965G	Inc. Ab.	25.00	55.00	75.00
	1966G	Inc. Ab.	25.00	55.00	75.00
	1967G	Inc. Ab.	25.00	55.00	75.00

Error. Edge lettering "GRUSS DICH DEUTSCHLAND AUS HERZENSGRUND"

KM#	Date	Mintage	VF	XF	Unc
112.3	1957	Inc. Ab.	800.00	1000.	1400.

COPPER-NICKEL CLAD NICKEL, 10.00 g

KM#	Date	Mintage	VF	XF	Unc
140.1	1975D	65.663	—	3.00	3.50
	1975D	.043	—	Proof	7.00
	1975F	75.002	—	3.00	3.50
	1975F	.043	—	Proof	7.00
	1975G	43.297	—	3.00	3.50
	1975G	.043	—	Proof	7.00
	1975J	67.372	—	3.00	3.50
	1975J	.043	—	Proof	7.00
	1976D	7.821	—	3.00	4.00

West / GERMANY 735

KM#	Date	Mintage	VF	XF	Unc
140.1	1976D	.043	—	Proof	7.00
	1976F	9.072	—	3.00	4.00
	1976F	.043	—	Proof	7.00
	1976G	5.784	—	3.00	4.00
	1976G	.043	—	Proof	7.00
	1976J	8.068	—	3.00	4.00
	1976J	.043	—	Proof	7.00
	1977D	8.321	—	3.00	4.00
	1977D	.051	—	Proof	5.00
	1977F	9.612	—	3.00	4.00
	1977F	.051	—	Proof	5.00
	1977G	5.746	—	3.00	4.00
	1977G	.051	—	Proof	5.00
	1977J	8.577	—	3.00	4.00
	1977J	.051	—	Proof	5.00
	1978D	7.854	—	3.00	4.00
	1978D	.054	—	Proof	5.00
	1978F	9.054	—	3.00	4.00
	1978F	.054	—	Proof	5.00
	1978G	5.244	—	3.00	4.00
	1978G	.054	—	Proof	5.00
	1978J	8.064	—	3.00	4.00
	1978J	.054	—	Proof	5.00
	1979D	7.889	—	3.00	4.00
	1979D	.089	—	Proof	5.00
	1979F	9.089	—	3.00	4.00
	1979F	.089	—	Proof	5.00
	1979G	5.279	—	3.00	4.00
	1979G	.089	—	Proof	5.00
	1979J	8.099	—	3.00	4.00
	1979J	.089	—	Proof	5.00
	1980D	8.300	—	3.00	4.00
	1980D	.110	—	Proof	5.00
	1980F	9.640	—	3.00	4.00
	1980F	.110	—	Proof	5.00
	1980G	5.500	—	3.00	4.00
	1980G	.110	—	Proof	5.00
	1980J	8.500	—	3.00	4.00
	1980J	.110	—	Proof	5.00
	1981D	8.300	—	3.00	4.00
	1981D	.091	—	Proof	5.00
	1981F	9.600	—	3.00	4.00
	1981F	.091	—	Proof	5.00
	1981G	5.500	—	3.00	4.00
	1981G	.091	—	Proof	5.00
	1981J	8.500	—	3.00	4.00
	1981J	.091	—	Proof	5.00
	1982D	8.900	—	3.00	4.00
	1982D	.091	—	Proof	5.00
	1982F	10.300	—	3.00	4.00
	1982F	.091	—	Proof	5.00
	1982G	5.990	—	3.00	4.00
	1982G	.091	—	Proof	5.00
	1982J	9.100	—	3.00	4.00
	1982J	.091	—	Proof	5.00
	1983D	6.240	—	3.00	4.00
	1983D	.091	—	Proof	5.00
	1983F	7.200	—	3.00	4.00
	1983F	.091	—	Proof	5.00
	1983G	4.152	—	3.00	4.00
	1983G	.091	—	Proof	5.00
	1983J	6.408	—	3.00	4.00
	1983J	.091	—	Proof	5.00
	1984D	—	—	3.00	4.00
	1984D	.079	—	Proof	5.00
	1984F	—	—	3.00	4.00
	1984F	.079	—	Proof	5.00
	1984G	—	—	3.00	4.00
	1984G	.079	—	Proof	5.00
	1984J	—	—	3.00	4.00
	1984J	.079	—	Proof	5.00
	1985D	—	—	3.00	4.00
	1985D	—	—	Proof	5.00
	1985F	—	—	3.00	4.00
	1985F	—	—	Proof	5.00
	1985G	—	—	3.00	4.00
	1985G	—	—	Proof	5.00
	1985J	—	—	3.00	4.00
	1985J	—	—	Proof	5.00
	1986D	—	—	3.00	4.00
	1986D	—	—	Proof	5.00
	1986F	—	—	3.00	4.00
	1986F	—	—	Proof	5.00
	1986G	—	—	3.00	4.00
	1986G	—	—	Proof	5.00
	1986J	—	—	3.00	4.00
	1986J	—	—	Proof	5.00
	1987D	—	—	3.00	4.00
	1987D	—	—	Proof	5.00
	1987F	—	—	3.00	4.00
	1987F	—	—	Proof	5.00
	1987G	—	—	3.00	4.00
	1987G	—	—	Proof	5.00
	1987J	—	—	3.00	4.00
	1987J	—	—	Proof	5.00
	1988D	—	—	—	3.00
	1988D	—	—	Proof	4.00
	1988F	—	—	—	3.00
	1988F	—	—	Proof	4.00
	1988G	—	—	—	3.00
	1988G	—	—	Proof	4.00
	1988J	—	—	—	3.00
	1988J	—	—	Proof	4.00

5.00 g, thin variety

| 140.2 | 1975 | — | — | 3.00 | 4.00 |

NOTE: Illegally produced by a German Mint official.

COMMEMORATIVE 5 MARK

11.2000 g, .625 SILVER, .2250 oz ASW
Nurnberg Museum

KM#	Date	Mintage	VF	XF	Unc
113	1952D	.199	375.00	700.00	900.00
	1952D	1,345	—	Proof	2500.

Friedrich von Schiller

| 114 | 1955F | .199 | 300.00 | 500.00 | 800.00 |
| | 1955F | 1,217 | — | Proof | 1750. |

Ludwig von Baden

| 115 | 1955G | .198 | 300.00 | 500.00 | 700.00 |
| | 1955G | *2,000 | — | Proof | 1500. |

NOTE: This coin was restruck without authorization by a German mint official using genuine dies. Quantity unknown.

Joseph Freiherr von Eichendorff

| 117 | 1957J | .198 | 300.00 | 500.00 | 700.00 |
| | 1957J | *2,000 | — | Proof | 1500. |

Johann Gottlieb Fichte

| 118 | 1964J | .495 | 100.00 | 175.00 | 250.00 |
| | 1964J | 5,000 | — | Proof | 650.00 |

Gottfried Wilhelm Leibniz

| 119 | 1966D | 1.940 | 15.00 | 30.00 | 45.00 |
| | 1966D | .060 | — | Proof | 75.00 |

Wilhelm & Alexander von Humboldt

KM#	Date	Mintage	VF	XF	Unc
120	1967F	2.000	12.50	30.00	50.00
	1967F	.060	—	Proof	165.00

Friedrich Wilhelm Raiffeisen

| 121 | 1968J | 3.860 | 3.00 | — | 10.00 |
| | 1968J | .140 | — | Proof | 32.50 |

Johannes Gutenberg

| 122 | 1968G | 2.900 | 5.00 | 15.00 | 20.00 |
| | 1968G | .100 | — | Proof | 80.00 |

Max von Pettenkoffer

| 123 | 1968D | 2.900 | 5.00 | 12.50 | 17.50 |
| | 1968D | .100 | — | Proof | 45.00 |

Varieties with frosted and unfrosted finishes. Unfrosted variety scarcer.

Theodor Fontane

| 125 | 1969G | 2.830 | 8.00 | 15.00 | 20.00 |
| | 1969G | .170 | — | Proof | 30.00 |

Gerhard Mercator

| 126 | 1969F | 5.004 | 3.00 | 4.00 | 5.00 |
| | 1969F | .200 | — | Proof | 17.50 |

West / GERMANY 736

Ludwig van Beethoven

KM#	Date	Mintage	VF	XF	Unc
127	1970F	5.000	3.00	4.00	6.00
	1970F	.200	—	Proof	17.50

Immanuel Kant

KM#	Date	Mintage	VF	XF	Unc
139	1974D	8.000	3.00	3.50	4.50
	1974D	.250	—	Proof	20.00

Heinrich von Kleist

KM#	Date	Mintage	VF	XF	Unc
146	1977G	8.000	3.00	3.50	4.50
	1977G	.250	—	Proof	17.50

German Unification

128	1971G	5.000	3.00	3.50	5.00
	1971G	.200	—	Proof	17.50

Friedrich Ebert

141	1975J	8.000	3.00	3.50	4.50
	1975J	.250	—	Proof	12.50

Gustav Stresemann

147	1978D	8.000	3.00	3.50	4.50
	1978D	.250	—	Proof	12.50

Albrecht Durer

129	1971D	8.000	3.00	4.00	5.00
	1971D	.200	—	Proof	30.00

European Monument Protection Year
11.2 g, 2.1mm thick

142.1	1975F	8.000	3.00	3.50	4.50
	1975F	.250	—	Proof	8.00

5.3 g, 1.4mm thick

142.2	1975F	Inc. Ab.	3.00	3.50	4.50

Balthasar Neumann

148	1978F	8.000	3.00	3.50	4.50
	1978F	.259	—	Proof	10.00

Nicholas Copernicus

136	1973J	8.000	3.00	3.50	4.50
	1973J	.250	—	Proof	12.50

Albert Schweitzer

143	1975G	8.000	3.00	3.50	4.50
	1975G	.250	—	Proof	15.00

150th Anniversary of German Archeological Institute

150	1979J	8.000	3.00	3.50	4.50
	1979J	.250	—	Proof	15.00

125th Anniversary Frankfurt Parliament

137	1973G	8.000	3.00	3.50	4.50
	1973G	.250	—	Proof	10.00

Jacob Christophe von Grimmelshausen

144	1976D	8.000	3.00	3.50	4.50
	1976D	.250	—	Proof	25.00

COPPER-NICKEL CLAD NICKEL
Otto Hahn

151	1979G	5.000	3.00	3.50	5.00
(151.2)	1979G	.350	—	Proof	9.00

11.2000 g, .625 SILVER, .2250 oz ASW

151a	1979G	18 pcs.	—	—	22,500.
(151.1)					

25th Anniversary Constitution

138	1974F	8.000	3.00	3.50	4.50
	1974F	.250	—	Proof	10.00

Carl Friedrich Gauss

145	1977J	8.000	3.00	3.50	4.50
	1977J	.250	—	Proof	25.00

COPPER-NICKEL CLAD NICKEL
750th Anniversary of Death of von der Vogelweide

152	1980D	5.000	3.00	3.50	5.00
	1980D	.350	—	Proof	9.00

West/GERMANY 737

100th Anniversary of Cologne Cathedral

KM#	Date	Mintage	VF	XF	Unc
153	1980F	5.000	3.00	3.50	6.50
	1980F	.350	—	Proof	10.00

Martin Luther

KM#	Date	Mintage	VF	XF	Unc
159	1983G	8.000	—	3.00	3.50
	1983G	.350	—	Proof	15.00

Frederick the Great

KM#	Date	Mintage	VF	XF	Unc
165	1986F	8.000	—	3.00	3.50
	1986F	.350	—	Proof	10.00

COMMEMORATIVE 10 MARK

200th Anniversary of Death of Gotthold Ephraim Lessing

154	1981J	6.500	—	3.00	3.50
	1981J	.350	—	Proof	9.00

150th Anniversary of German Customs Union

160	1984D	8.000	—	3.00	3.50
	1984D	.350	—	Proof	8.00

15.5000 g, .625 SILVER, .3115 oz ASW
Munich Olympics - 'In Deutschland'

130	1972D	2.500	—	6.00	9.50
	1972D	.125	—	Proof	25.00
	1972F	2.375	—	6.00	9.50
	1972F	.125	—	Proof	25.00
	1972G	2.500	—	6.00	9.50
	1972G	.125	—	Proof	25.00
	1972J	2.500	—	6.00	9.50
	1972J	.125	—	Proof	25.00

150th Anniversary of Death of Carl Reichsfreiherr vom Stein

155	1981G	6.500	—	3.00	3.50
	1981G	.350	—	Proof	9.00

Felix Mendelssohn Bartholdy

161	1984J	8.000	—	3.00	3.50
	1984J	.350	—	Proof	11.00

Munich Olympics Symbol: 'Schleife' (knot).

131	1972D	5.000	—	6.00	6.50
	1972D	.125	—	Proof	12.50
	1972F	4.875	—	6.00	6.50
	1972F	.125	—	Proof	12.50
	1972G	5.000	—	6.00	6.50
	1972G	.125	—	Proof	12.50
	1972J	5.000	—	6.00	6.50
	1972J	.125	—	Proof	12.50

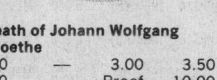

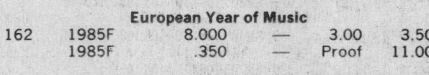

150th Anniversary of Death of Johann Wolfgang von Goethe

156	1982D	8.000	—	3.00	3.50
	1982D	.350	—	Proof	10.00

European Year of Music

162	1985F	8.000	—	3.00	3.50
	1985F	.350	—	Proof	11.00

10th Anniversary of U.N. Environmental Conference

157	1982F	8.000	—	3.00	3.50
	1982F	.350	—	Proof	9.00

German Railroad

163	1985G	8.000	—	3.00	3.50
	1985G	.350	—	Proof	9.00

Munich Olympics - 'Athletes'

132	1972D	5.000	—	6.00	6.50
	1972D	.150	—	Proof	12.50
	1972F	4.850	—	6.00	6.50
	1972F	.150	—	Proof	12.50
	1972G	5.000	—	6.00	6.50
	1972G	.150	—	Proof	12.50
	1972J	5.000	—	6.00	6.50
	1972J	.150	—	Proof	12.50

Karl Marx

158	1983J	8.000	—	3.00	3.50
	1983J	.350	—	Proof	9.00

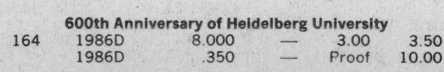

600th Anniversary of Heidelberg University

164	1986D	8.000	—	3.00	3.50
	1986D	.350	—	Proof	10.00

Munich Olympics - 'Stadium'

133	1972D	5.000	—	6.00	6.50
	1972D	.150	—	Proof	12.50

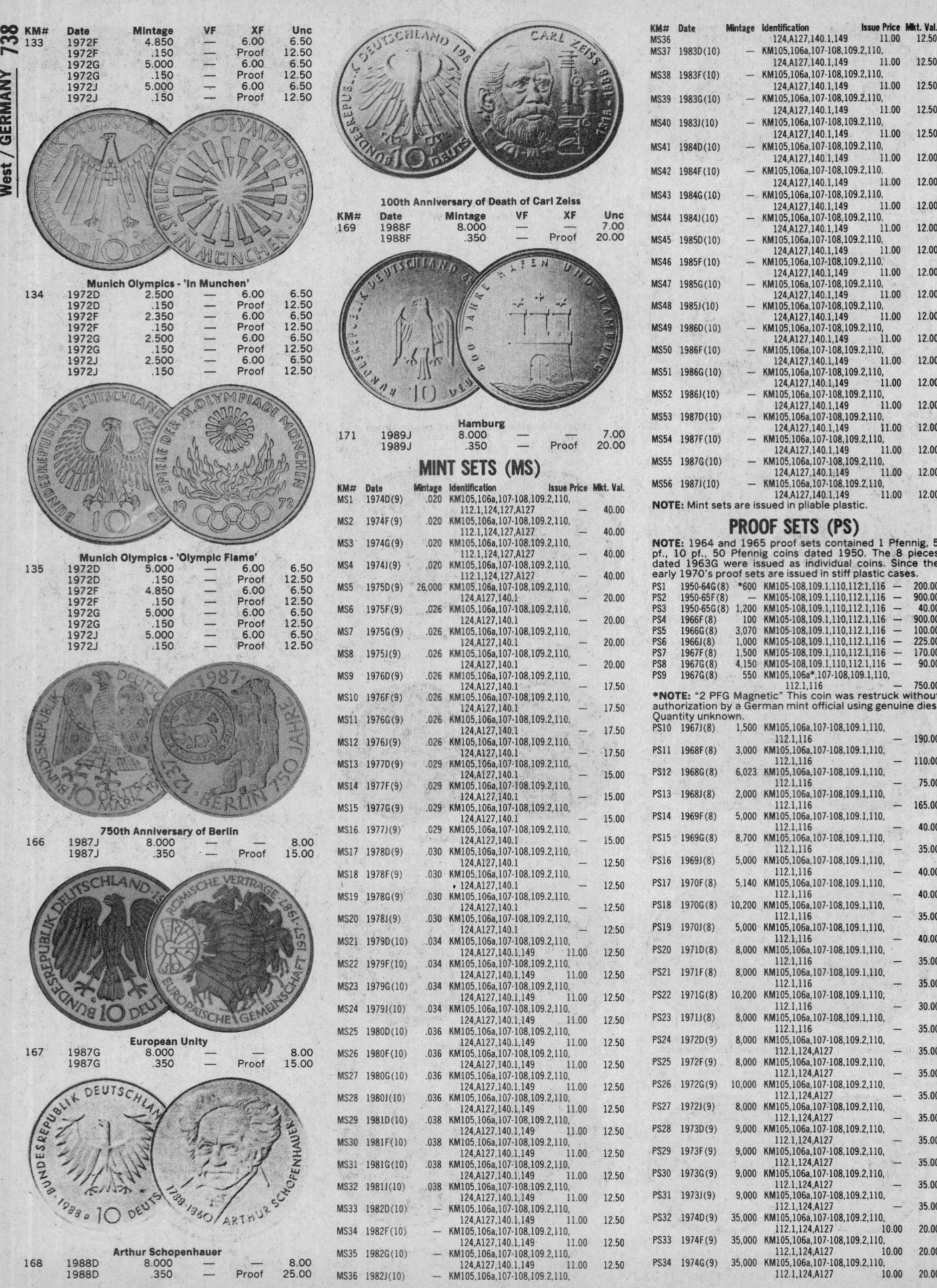

KM#	Date	Mintage	Identification	Issue Price	Mkt. Val.
PS35	1974J(9)	35,000	KM105,106a,107-108,109.2,110, 112.1,124,A127	10.00	20.00
PS36	1975D(9)	43,120	KM105,106a,107-108,109.2,110, 124,A127,140.1	10.00	15.00
PS37	1975F(9)	43,100	KM105,106a,107-108,109.2,110, 124,A127,140.1	10.00	15.00
PS38	1975G(9)	43,100	KM105,106a,107-108,109.2,110, 124,A127,140.1	10.00	15.00
PS39	1975J(9)	43,120	KM105,106a,107-108,109.2,110, 124,A127,140.1	10.00	15.00
PS40	1976D(9)	43,100	KM105,106a,107-108,109.2,110, 124,A127,140.1	10.00	14.00
PS41	1976F(9)	43,100	KM105,106a,107-108,109.2,110, 124,A127,140.1	10.00	14.00
PS42	1976G(9)	43,100	KM105,106a,107-108,109.2,110, 124,A127,140.1	10.00	14.00
PS43	1976J(9)	43,120	KM105,106a,107-108,109.2,110, 124,A127,140.1	10.00	14.00
PS44	1977D(9)	50,620	KM105,106a,107-108,109.2,110, 124,A127,140.1	12.50	10.00
PS45	1977F(9)	50,600	KM105,106a,107-108,109.2,110, 124,A127,140.1	12.50	10.00
PS46	1977G(9)	50,600	KM105,106a,107-108,109.2,110, 124,A127,140.1	12.50	10.00
PS47	1977J(9)	50,620	KM105,106a,107-108,109.2,110, 124,A127,140.1	12.50	10.00
PS48	1978D(9)	.054	KM105,106a,107-108,109.2,110, 124,A127,140.1	13.00	10.00
PS49	1978F(9)	.054	KM105,106a,107-108,109.2,110, 124,A127,140.1	13.00	10.00
PS50	1978G(9)	.054	KM105,106a,107-108,109.2,110, 124,A127,140.1	13.00	10.00
PS51	1978J(9)	.054	KM105,106a,107-108,109.2,110, 124,A127,140.1	13.00	10.00
PS52	1979D(10)	.089	KM105,106a,107-108,109.2,110, 124,A127,140.1,149	15.00	11.50
PS53	1979F(10)	.089	KM105,106a,107-108,109.2,110, 124,A127,140.1,149	15.00	11.50
PS54	1979G(10)	.089	KM105,106a,107-108,109.2,110, 124,A127,140.1,149	15.00	11.50
PS55	1979J(10)	.089	KM105,106a,107-108,109.2,110, 124,A127,140.1,149	15.00	11.50
PS56	1980D(10)	.060	KM105,106a,107-108,109.2,110, 124,A127,140.1,149	15.00	11.50
PS57	1980F(10)	.060	KM105,106a,107-108,109.2,110, 124,A127,140.1,149	15.00	11.50
PS58	1980G(10)	.060	KM105,106a,107-108,109.2,110, 124,A127,140.1,149	15.00	11.50
PS59	1980J(10)	.060	KM105,106a,107-108,109.2,110, 124,A127,140.1,149	15.00	11.50
PS60	1981D(10)	.091	KM105,106a,107-108,109.2,110, 124,A127,140.1,149	15.00	11.50
PS61	1981F(10)	.091	KM105,106a,107-108,109.2,110, 124,A127,140.1,149	15.00	11.50
PS62	1981G(10)	.091	KM105,106a,107-108,109.2,110, 124,A127,140.1,149	15.00	11.50
PS63	1981J(10)	.091	KM105,106a,107-108,109.2,110, 124,A127,140.1,149	15.00	11.50
PS64	1982D(10)	.091	KM105,106a,107-108,109.2,110, 124,A127,140.1,149	15.00	11.50
PS65	1982F(10)	.091	KM105,106a,107-108,109.2,110, 124,A127,140.1,149	15.00	11.50
PS66	1982G(10)	.091	KM105,106a,107-108,109.2,110, 124,A127,140.1,149	15.00	11.50
PS67	1982J(10)	.091	KM105,106a,107-108,109.2,110, 124,A127,140.1,149	15.00	11.50
PS68	1983D(10)	.091	KM105,106a,107-108,109.2,110, 124,A127,140.1,149	15.00	11.50
PS69	1983F(10)	.091	KM105,106a,107-108,109.2,110, 124,A127,140.1,149	15.00	11.50
PS70	1983G(10)	.091	KM105,106a,107-108,109.2,110, 124,A127,140.1,149	15.00	11.50
PS71	1983J(10)	.091	KM105,106a,107-108,109.2,110, 124,A127,140.1,149	15.00	11.50
PS72	1984D(10)	.079	KM105,106a,107-108,109.2,110, 124,A127,140.1,149	15.00	14.50
PS73	1984F(10)	.079	KM105,106a,107-108,109.2,110, 124,A127,140.1,149	15.00	14.50
PS74	1984G(10)	.079	KM105,106a,107-108,109.2,110, 124,A127,140.1,149	15.00	14.50
PS75	1984J(10)	.079	KM105,106a,107-108,109.2,110, 124,A127,140.1,149	15.00	14.50
PS76	1985D(10)	—	KM105,106a,107-108,109.2,110, 124,A127,140.1,149	15.00	16.50
PS77	1985F(10)	—	KM105,106a,107-108,109.2,110, 124,A127,140.1,149	15.00	16.50
PS78	1985G(10)	—	KM105,106a,107-108,109.2,110, 124,A127,140.1,149	15.00	16.50
PS79	1985J(10)	—	KM105,106a,107-108,109.2,110, 124,A127,140.1,149	15.00	16.50
PS80	1986D(10)	—	KM105,106a,107-108,109.2,110, 124,A127,140.1,149	15.00	16.50
PS81	1986F(10)	—	KM105,106a,107-108,109.2,110, 124,A127,140.1,149	15.00	16.50
PS82	1986G(10)	—	KM105,106a,107-108,109.2,110, 124,A127,140.1,149	15.00	16.50
PS83	1986J(10)	—	KM105,106a,107-108,109.2,110, 124,A127,140.1,149	15.00	16.50
PS84	1987D(10)	—	KM105,106a,107-108,109.2,110, 124,A127,140.1,149	15.00	16.50
PS85	1987F(10)	—	KM105,106a,107-108,109.2,110, 124,A127,140.1,149	15.00	16.50
PS86	1987G(10)	—	KM105,106a,107-108,109.2,110, 124,A127,140.1,149	15.00	16.50
PS87	1987J(10)	—	KM105,106a,107-108,109.2,110, 124,A127,140.1,149	15.00	16.50
PS88	1988D(9)	—	KM105,106a,107-108,109.2,110, 140.1,149,170	—	13.50
PS89	1988F(9)	—	KM105,106a,107-108,109.2,110, 140.1,149,170	—	13.50
PS90	1988G(9)	—	KM105,106a,107-108,109.2,110, 140.1,149,170	—	13.50
PS91	1988J(9)	—	KM105,106a,107-108,109.2,110, 140.1,149,170	—	13.50

SAARLAND

The Saar, the 10th state of the German Federal Republic, is located in the coal-rich Saar basin on the Franco-German frontier, and has an area of 991 sq. mi. and a population of 1.2 million. Capital: Saarbrucken. It is an important center of mining and heavy industry.

MINT MARKS
(a) - Paris - privy marks only

10 FRANKEN

ALUMINUM-BRONZE

KM#	Date	Mintage	Fine	VF	XF	Unc
1	1954(a)	11.000	.75	1.50	2.50	5.00

20 FRANKEN

ALUMINUM-BRONZE

| 2 | 1954(a) | 12.950 | .75 | 1.50 | 3.00 | 8.00 |

50 FRANKEN

ALUMINUM-BRONZE

| 3 | 1954(a) | 5.300 | 3.00 | 5.00 | 10.00 | 20.00 |

100 FRANKEN

COPPER-NICKEL

| 4 | 1955(a) | 11.000 | 2.50 | 4.00 | 7.50 | 15.00 |

GERMANY-EAST

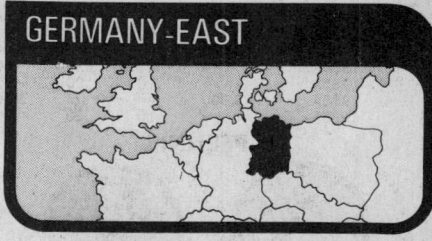

The German Democratic Republic (East Germany), located on the great north European plain, has an area of 41,768 sq. mi. (108,178 sq. km.) and a population of 16.7 million. The figures include East Berlin which has been incorporated into the G.D.R. Capital: East Berlin. The economy is highly industrialized. Machinery, transport equipment, chemicals, and lignite are exported.

During the closing days of World War II in Europe, Soviet troops advancing into Germany from the east occupied the German provinces of Mecklenburg, Brandenburg, Lusatia, Saxony and Thuringia. These five provinces comprised the occupation zone administered by the Soviet Union after the cessation of hostilities. The other three zones were administered by the U.S., Great Britain and France. Under the Potsdam agreement, questions affecting Germany as a whole were to be settled by the commanders in chief of the occupation zones acting jointly and by unanimous decision. When Soviet intransigence rendered the quadripartite commission inoperable, the three western zones were united to form the Federal Republic of Germany, May 23, 1949. Thereupon the Soviet Union dissolved its occupation zone and established it as the Democratic Republic of Germany, Oct. 7, 1949.

MINT MARKS
A - Berlin
E - Muldenhutten

MONETARY SYSTEM
100 Pfennig = 1 Mark

PFENNIG

ALUMINUM

KM#	Date	Mintage	VF	XF	Unc
1	1948A	243.000	.20	.60	3.00
	1949A	Inc. Ab.	.20	.60	3.00
	1949E	55.200	5.00	7.50	12.50
	1950A	Inc. Ab.	.20	.60	3.00
	1950E	Inc. Ab.	1.00	2.25	5.00

5	1952A	297.213	.30	.50	2.00
	1952E	49.296	.40	1.00	3.00
	1953A	114.002	.30	.75	2.00
	1953E	50.876	.40	1.25	6.00

8.1	1960A	—	.10	.25	.50
	1961A	—	.10	.25	.50
	1962A	—	.10	.25	.50
	1963A	—	.10	.25	.50
	1964A	—	.10	.25	.50
	1965A	—	1.50	3.50	7.50
	1968A	—	.10	.25	.50
	1972A	—	.10	.25	.50
	1973A	—	.10	.25	.50
	1975A	—	.10	.25	.50
	1977A	—	.10	.25	.50

Rev: Larger design features.

8.2	1978A	—	.10	.20	.50
	1979A	—	.10	.20	.50
	1979A	—	—	Proof	1.00
	1980A	—	.10	.20	.50
	1980A	—	—	Proof	1.00
	1981A	—	.10	.20	.50
	1981A	—	—	Proof	1.00
	1982A	—	.10	.20	.50
	1982A	2,500	—	Proof	1.00

East / GERMANY 740

KM#	Date	Mintage	VF	XF	Unc
8.2	1983A	—	.10	.20	.50
	1983A	2,500	—	Proof	1.00
	1984A	—	.10	.20	.50
	1985A	—	.10	.20	.50
	1985A	3,000	—	Proof	1.00
	1986A	—	.10	.20	.50

5 PFENNIG

ALUMINUM

KM#	Date	Mintage	VF	XF	Unc
2	1948A	205.072	.50	1.00	3.00
	1949A	Inc. Ab.	.50	1.00	3.00
	1950A	Inc. Ab.	.50	1.25	3.00
6	1952A	113.397	.30	.75	1.00
	1952E	24.024	.50	1.00	5.00
	1953A	40.994	.40	.60	1.00
	1953E	28.665	.50	1.00	5.00
9.1	1968A	—	.25	.35	.75
	1972A	—	.25	.35	.75
	1975A	—	.25	.35	.75

Rev: Larger design features.

9.2	1978A	—	.15	.25	.50
	1979A	—	.15	.25	.50
	1979A	—	—	Proof	1.00
	1980A	—	.15	.25	.50
	1980A	—	—	Proof	1.00
	1981A	—	.15	.25	.50
	1981A	—	—	Proof	1.00
	1982A	—	.15	.25	.50
	1982A	2,500	—	Proof	1.00
	1983A	—	.15	.25	.50
	1983A	2,500	—	Proof	1.00
	1985A	—	.15	.25	.50
	1985A	3,000	—	Proof	1.00

10 PFENNIG

ALUMINUM

3	1948A	216.537	.50	1.00	3.00
	1949A	Inc. Ab.	.50	1.00	3.00
	1950A	Inc. Ab.	.50	1.00	3.00
	1950E	16.000	1.00	3.00	6.00
7	1952A	70.427	.25	.50	1.50
	1952E	21.498	.50	1.00	3.00
	1953A	18.611	.50	.75	2.50
	1953E	11.500	.75	2.00	5.00
10.1	1963A	—	1.00	2.50	8.00
	1965A	—	.15	.25	.75
	1967A	—	.15	.25	.75
	1968A	—	.15	.25	.75
	1970A	—	.15	.25	.75
	1971A	—	.15	.25	.75
	1972A	—	.15	.25	.75
	1973A	—	.15	.25	.75

Rev: Larger design features.

KM#	Date	Mintage	VF	XF	Unc
10.2	1978A	—	.15	.25	.50
	1979A	—	.15	.25	.50
	1979A	—	—	Proof	1.00
	1980A	—	.15	.25	.50
	1980A	—	—	Proof	1.00
	1981A	—	.15	.25	.50
	1981A	—	—	Proof	1.00
	1982A	—	.15	.25	.50
	1982A	2,500	—	Proof	1.00
	1983A	—	.15	.25	.50
	1983A	2,500	—	Proof	1.00
	1985A	—	.15	.25	.50
	1985A	3,000	—	Proof	1.00

20 PFENNIG

BRASS

11	1969A	—	.20	.35	.75
	1969 w/o mm	—	.20	.35	.75
	1971A	—	.20	.35	.75
	1972A	—	.20	.35	.75
	1973A	—	.20	.35	.75
	1974A	—	.20	.35	.75
	1979A	—	.20	.35	.75
	1979A	—	—	Proof	1.50
	1980A	—	.20	.35	.75
	1980A	—	—	Proof	1.50
	1981A	—	.20	.35	.75
	1981A	—	—	Proof	1.50
	1982A	—	.20	.35	.75
	1982A	2,500	—	Proof	1.50
	1983A	—	.20	.35	.75
	1983A	2,500	—	Proof	1.50
	1984A	—	.20	.35	.75
	1985A	—	.20	.35	.75
	1985A	3,000	—	Proof	1.50

50 PFENNIG

ALUMINUM-BRONZE

4	1949A	Inc. Be.	—	Rare	—
	1950A	67.703	2.00	3.00	5.00

NOTE: Some authorities believe the 1949 dated piece is a pattern.

ALUMINUM

12	1958A	—	.25	.45	1.00
	1968A	—	.25	.45	1.00
	1971A	—	.25	.45	1.00
	1972A	—	.25	.45	1.00
	1973A	—	.25	.45	1.00
	1979A	—	.25	.45	1.00
	1979A	—	—	Proof	2.00
	1980A	—	.25	.45	1.00
	1980A	—	—	Proof	2.00
	1981A	—	.25	.45	1.00
	1981A	—	—	Proof	2.00
	1982A	—	.25	.45	1.00
	1982A	2,500	—	Proof	2.00
	1983A	—	.25	.45	1.00
	1983A	2,500	—	Proof	2.00
	1985A	—	.25	.45	1.00
	1985A	3,000	—	Proof	2.00

MARK

ALUMINUM

13	1956A	112.108	.50	1.00	2.00
	1962A	45.920	.50	1.00	2.00
	1963A	31.910	.50	1.00	2.00

KM#	Date	Mintage	VF	XF	Unc
35	1972A	—	.50	1.00	2.50
	1973A	—	.50	.75	1.50
	1975A	—	.50	.75	1.50
	1977A	—	.50	.75	1.25
	1978A	—	.50	.75	1.25
	1979A	—	.50	.75	1.25
	1979A	—	—	Proof	2.50
	1980A	—	.50	.75	1.25
	1980A	—	—	Proof	2.50
	1981A	—	.50	.75	1.25
	1981A	—	—	Proof	2.50
	1982A	—	.50	.75	1.25
	1982A	2,500	—	Proof	2.50
	1983A	—	.50	.75	1.25
	1983A	2,500	—	Proof	2.50
	1985A	—	—	.75	1.25
	1985A	3,000	—	Proof	2.50

2 MARK

ALUMINUM

14	1957A	77.961	.90	1.25	2.00
48	1974A	—	.90	1.00	2.00
	1975A	—	.90	1.00	2.00
	1977A	—	.90	1.00	1.50
	1978A	—	.90	1.00	1.50
	1979A	—	.90	1.00	1.50
	1979A	—	—	Proof	3.00
	1980A	—	.90	1.00	1.50
	1980A	—	—	Proof	3.00
	1981A	—	.90	1.00	1.50
	1981A	—	—	Proof	3.00
	1982A	—	.90	1.00	1.50
	1982A	2,500	—	Proof	3.00
	1983A	—	.90	1.00	1.50
	1983A	2,500	—	Proof	3.00
	1985A	—	.90	1.00	1.50
	1985A	3,000	—	Proof	3.00

5 MARK

COPPER-NICKEL
Robert Koch

19	1968A	.100	—	—	18.00

20th Anniversary D.D.R.

22	1969A	10.000	—	—	3.00

NOTE: Edge varieties exist.

22a	1969A	.013	—	—	45.00

East / GERMANY 741

NOTE: KM#22 was struck in .900 Cu .100 Ni and is reddish brown in color. KM#22a was struck in .750 Cu .250 Ni and is whitish in color.

Heinrich Hertz
KM#	Date	Mintage	VF	XF	Unc
23	1969A	.100	—	—	8.50

Wilhelm Conrad Rontgen
| 26 | 1970A | .100 | — | — | 8.50 |

Brandenburg Gate
29	1971A	4.000	—	—	3.00
	1979A	.030	—	—	9.00
	1979A	2,500	—	Proof	18.00
	1980A	.028	—	—	9.00
	1980A	2,500	—	Proof	18.00
	1981A	.028	—	—	9.00
	1981A	2,500	—	Proof	18.00
	1982A	.028	—	—	9.00
	1982A	2,500	—	Proof	18.00
	1987A	.271	—	—	4.00
	1987A	4,200	—	Proof	25.00

Johannes Kepler
| 30 | 1971A | .100 | — | — | 9.50 |

Johannes Brahms
| 36 | 1972A | .055 | — | — | 13.50 |

City of Meissen
37	1972A	3.500	—	—	3.00
	1983A	—	—	—	4.00
	1983A	—	—	Proof	25.00

Otto Lilienthal
KM#	Date	Mintage	VF	XF	Unc
43	1973A	.100	—	—	8.50

Philipp Reis
| 49 | 1974A | .100 | — | — | 8.50 |

Thomas Mann
| 54 | 1975A | .100 | — | — | 9.50 |

International Women's Year
| 55 | 1975A | .250 | — | — | 8.50 |
| | 1975A | — | — | Proof | 25.00 |

Ferdinand von Schill
| 60 | 1976A | .100 | — | — | 9.50 |

Friedrich Ludwig Jahn
| 64 | 1977A | .090 | — | — | 10.00 |
| | 1977A | .010 | — | Proof | 22.50 |

Friedrich Gottlieb Klopstock
KM#	Date	Mintage	VF	XF	Unc
67	1978A	.096	—	—	12.50
	1978A	4,500	—	Proof	50.00

Anti-Apartheid Year
| 68 | 1978A | .196 | — | — | 12.50 |
| | 1978A | 4,000 | — | Proof | 50.00 |

Albert Einstein
| 72 | 1979A | .056 | — | — | 12.50 |
| | 1979A | 4,500 | — | Proof | 50.00 |

Adolph von Menzel
| 76 | 1980A | .055 | — | — | 12.50 |
| | 1980A | 5,500 | — | Proof | 35.00 |

Tilman Riemenschneider
| 79 | 1981A | .055 | — | — | 12.50 |
| | 1981A | 5,500 | — | Proof | 40.00 |

Friedrich Frobel
| 84 | 1982A | .055 | — | — | 12.50 |
| | 1982A | 5,500 | — | Proof | 40.00 |

COPPER-NICKEL-ZINC
Goethe's Weimar Cottage
| 85 | 1982A | .245 | — | — | 10.00 |
| | 1982A | 5,500 | — | Proof | 47.50 |

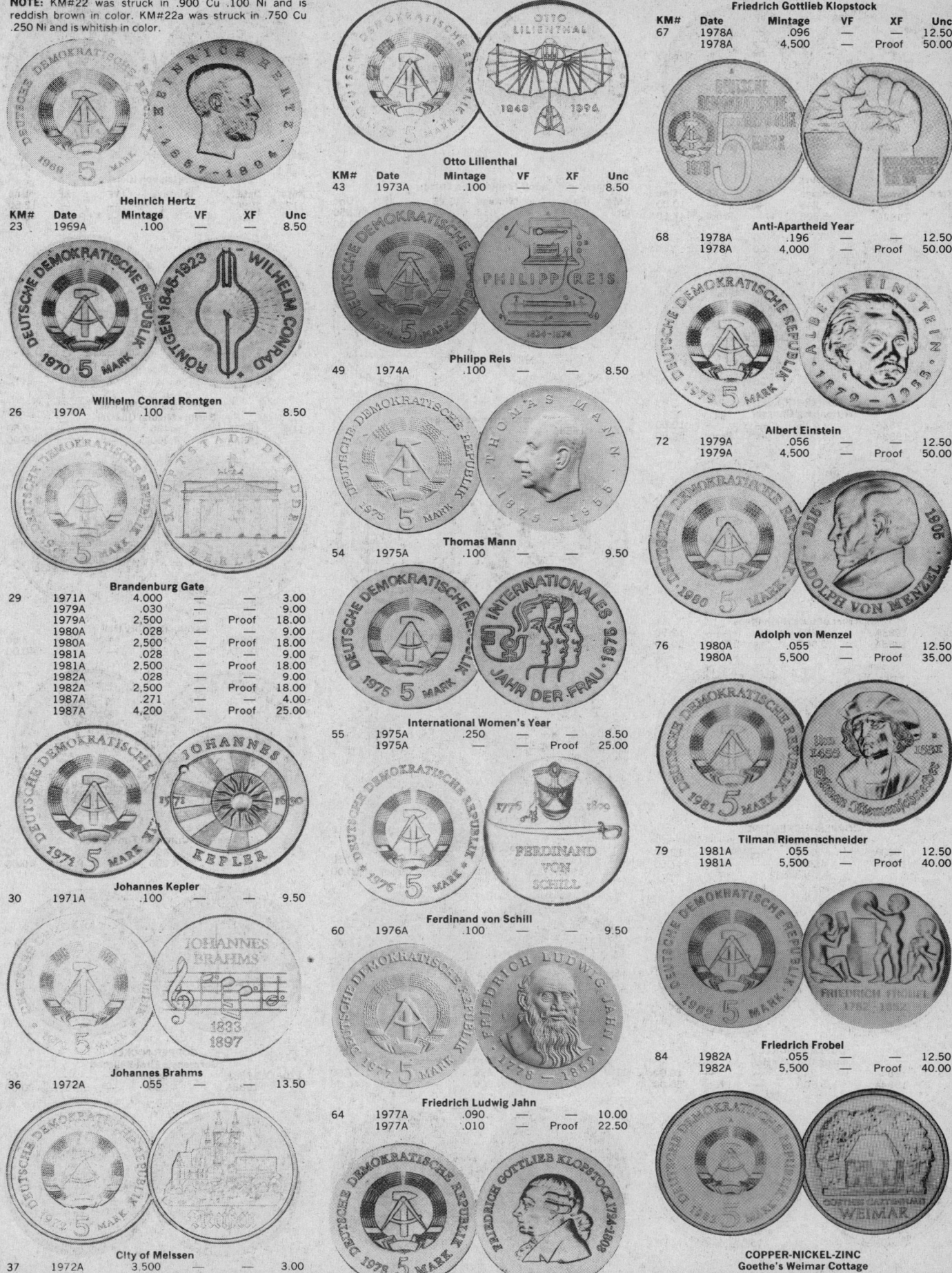

East / GERMANY 742

Wartburg Castle
KM#	Date	Mintage	VF	XF	Unc
86	1982A	.245	—	—	10.00
	1982A	5,500	—	Proof	47.50

Adolf Freiherr von Lutzow
KM#	Date	Mintage	VF	XF	Unc
98	1984A	.055	—	—	12.50
	1984A	5,000	—	Proof	50.00

Heinrich von Kleist
KM#	Date	Mintage	VF	XF	Unc
112	1986A	—	—	—	12.50
	1986A	—	—	Proof	40.00

COPPER-NICKEL
Wittenberg Church
89	1983A	.245	—	—	10.00
	1983A	5,000	—	Proof	52.50

Restoration of Dresden
102	1984A	.245	—	—	7.50
	1985A	3,000	—	Proof	40.00

COPPER-ZINC-NICKEL
Berlin - Nikolai Quarter
114	1987A	.496	—	—	7.50
	1987A	4,200	—	Proof	40.00

Martin Luther's Birth Place
90	1983A	.250	—	—	12.50
	1983A	5,000	—	Proof	50.00

Restoration of Dresden
103	1985A	.245	—	—	7.50
	1985A	5,500	—	Proof	40.00

Berlin - Red City Hall
115	1987A	.496	—	—	7.50
	1987A	4,200	—	Proof	40.00

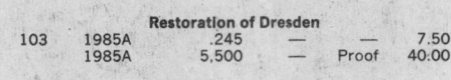

COPPER-NICKEL-ZINC
Max Planck
91	1983A	.056	—	—	12.50
	1983A	4,200	—	Proof	47.50

Caroline Neuber
104	1985A	.056	—	—	12.50
	1985A	4,000	—	Proof	50.00

Berlin - Universal Time Clock
116	1987A	.496	—	—	7.50
	1987A	4,200	—	Proof	40.00

COPPER-NICKEL
Leipzig Old City Hall
96	1984A	.245	—	—	10.00
	1984A	5,500	—	Proof	50.00

Potsdam - Sanssouci Palace
110	1986A	.296	—	—	7.50
	1986A	4,200	—	Proof	40.00

COPPER-NICKEL
Germany's First Railroad
120	1988A	.496	—	—	5.00
	1988A	4,200	—	Proof	30.00

Thomas Church of Leipzig
97	1984A	.245	—	—	10.00
	1984A	5,500	—	Proof	50.00

Potsdam - New Palace
111	1986A	.296	—	—	7.50
	1986A	4,200	—	Proof	40.00

Port City of Rostock
121	1988A	.496	—	—	5.00
	1988A	4,200	—	Proof	30.00

East / GERMANY 743

		Ernst Barlach			
KM#	Date	Mintage	VF	XF	Unc
122	1988A	.056	—	—	5.00
	1988A	4,200	—	Proof	30.00

		Albrecht Durer			
KM#	Date	Mintage	VF	XF	Unc
31	1971A	.100	—	—	22.50

17.0000 g, .625 SILVER, .3416 oz ASW
25th Anniversary D.D.R.

KM#	Date	Mintage	VF	XF	Unc
51	1974A	.070	—	—	24.00
	1974A	200 pcs.	—	Proof	1250.

10 MARK

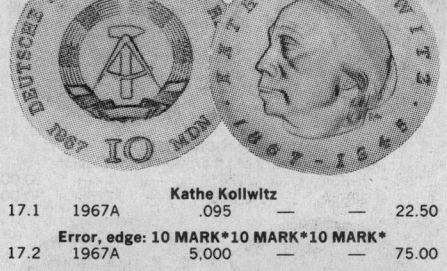

17.0000 g, .800 SILVER, .4373 oz ASW
Karl Friedrich Schinkel
Edge: 10 MARK DER DEUTSCHEN NOTEN BANK

15.1	1966A	.100	—	—	50.00
		Plain edge			
15.2	1966A	—	—	—	—

		Kathe Kollwitz			
17.1	1967A	.095	—	—	22.50
	Error, edge: 10 MARK*10 MARK*10 MARK*				
17.2	1967A	5,000	—	—	75.00

17.0000 g, .625 SILVER, .3416 oz ASW
Johann Gutenberg

20	1968A	.100	—	—	20.00

		Johann Friedrich Bottger			
24	1969A	.100	—	—	22.50

COPPER-NICKEL
Buchenwald Memorial

38	1972A	2.500	—	—	5.50

17.0000 g, .625 SILVER, .3416 oz ASW
Heinrich Heine

39	1972A	.100	—	—	21.50

COPPER-NICKEL
10th Youth Festival Games

44	1973A	1.500	—	—	5.50

17.0000 g, .625 SILVER, .3416 oz ASW
Bertolt Brecht

45	1973A	.100	—	—	22.50

COPPER-NICKEL
25th Anniversary, with state motto

50	1974A	3.000	—	—	5.50

17.0000 g, .500 SILVER, .2733 oz ASW

50a	1974A	1.500	—	Proof	850.00

		Caspar David Friedrich			
52	1974A	.075	—	—	24.00
	1974A	100 pcs.	—	Proof	1550.

		Albert Schweitzer			
56	1975A	.099	—	—	21.50
	1975A	1,040	—	Proof	75.00

17.0000 g, .500 SILVER, .2733 oz ASW
Plain edge
Mule. Obv: KM#58. Rev: KM#56.

57	1975A	6,700	—	—	40.00

COPPER-NICKEL
20th Anniversary Warsaw Pact

58	1975A	2.500	—	—	5.50

		National People's Army			
61	1976A	.750	—	—	10.00

East / GERMANY 744

17.0000 g, .500 SILVER, .2733 oz ASW
Carl Maria von Weber

KM#	Date	Mintage	VF	XF	Unc
62	1976A	.094	—	—	27.50
	1976A	6,037	—	Proof	75.00

Otto von Guericke

65	1977A	.069	—	—	27.50
	1977A	6,000	—	Proof	75.00

Justus von Liebig

69	1978A	.071	—	—	27.50
	1978A	4,500	—	Proof	75.00

COPPER-NICKEL
Joint USSR-DDR Orbital Flight

70	1978A	.748	—	—	10.00
	1978A	2,000	—	Proof	300.00

17.0000 g, .500 SILVER, .2733 oz ASW
Ludwig Feuerbach

73	1979A	.051	—	—	32.50
	1979A	4,500	—	Proof	75.00

225th Anniversary of Birth of Gerhard von Scharnhorst

77	1980A	.055	—	—	30.00
	1980A	5,500	—	Proof	75.00

COPPER-NICKEL
25th Anniversary of National People's Army

KM#	Date	Mintage	VF	XF	Unc
80	1981A	.745	—	—	10.00
	1981A	—	—	Proof	60.00

17.0000 g, .500 SILVER, .2733 oz ASW
150th Anniversary of Death of Georg Hegel

81	1981A	.050	—	—	30.00
	1981A	5,500	—	Proof	65.00

COPPER-NICKEL
700th Anniversary of Berlin Mint

82	1981A	.055	—	—	20.00
	1981A	5,500	—	Proof	70.00

17.0000 g, .500 SILVER, .2733 oz ASW
Leipzig Gewandhaus

87	1982A	.050	—	—	32.50
	1982A	5,500	—	Proof	70.00

17.1100 g, .500 SILVER, .2751 oz ASW
Richard Wagner

92	1983A	.044	—	—	32.50
	1983A	5,500	—	Proof	75.00

COPPER-NICKEL-ZINC
30th Anniversary of Workers Militia

93	1983A	.500	—	—	10.00
	1983A	Inc. Ab.	—	Proof	25.00

17.0000 g, .500 SILVER, .2733 oz ASW
Alfred Brehm

KM#	Date	Mintage	VF	XF	Unc
99	1984A	.050	—	—	35.00
	1984A	5,000	—	Proof	75.00

Restoration of Semper Opera in Dresden

101	1985A	.050	—	—	35.00
	1985A	5,000	—	Proof	65.00

COPPER-NICKEL-ZINC
40th Anniversary of Liberation from Fascism

106	1985A	.745	—	—	10.00
	1985A	5,500	—	Proof	30.00

17.0000 g, .500 SILVER, .2733 oz ASW
175th Anniversary of Humboldt University

107	1985A	.051	—	—	35.00
	1985A	4,000	—	Proof	65.00

COPPER-NICKEL
Ernst Thalmann

109	1986A	.746	—	—	10.00
	1986A	4,000	—	Proof	30.00

17.0000 g, .500 SILVER, .2733 oz ASW
Charite - Berlin

113	1986A	.046	—	—	35.00
	1986A	4,000	—	Proof	75.00

East / GERMANY 745

KM#	Date	Mintage	VF	XF	Unc
118	1987A	.051	—	—	35.00
	1987A	4,000	—	Proof	75.00

Berlin - Theater

| 123 | 1988A | .052 | — | — | 30.00 |
| | 1988A | 3,500 | — | Proof | 70.00 |

Ulrich von Hutten

| 125 | 1988A | .747 | — | — | 10.00 |
| | 1988A | 3,200 | — | Proof | 30.00 |

East German Sports — COPPER-NICKEL

| 126 | 1989A | .096 | — | — | 10.00 |
| | 1989A | 4,000 | — | Proof | 30.00 |

Council of Mutual Economic Aid

20 MARK

20.9000 g, .800 SILVER, .5376 oz ASW
Gottfried Wilhelm Leibniz
Edge: 20 MARK DER DEUTSCHEN NOTEN BANK

| 16 | 1966A | .100 | — | — | 50.00 |

Wilhelm von Humboldt

| 18.1 | 1967A | .095 | — | — | 45.00 |

Error. Edge: 20 MARK*20 MARK*20 MARK*20 MARK*

| 18.2 | 1967A | 5,000 | — | — | 100.00 |

KM#	Date	Mintage	VF	XF	Unc
21	1968A	.100	—	—	40.00

Karl Marx

20.9000 g, .625 SILVER, .4200 oz ASW
Johann Wolfgang von Goethe

| 25 | 1969A | .100 | — | — | 40.00 |

Friedrich Engels

| 28 | 1970A | .100 | — | — | 35.00 |

Karl Liebknecht-Rosa Luxemburg

| 32 | 1971A | .100 | — | — | 40.00 |
| | 1971A | — | — | Proof | — |

Heinrich Mann — COPPER-NICKEL

| 33 | 1971A | 2.000 | — | — | 7.50 |

Ernst Thälmann

| 34 | 1971A | 2.500 | — | — | 7.50 |

NOTE: Edge varieties exist.

KM#	Date	Mintage	VF	XF	Unc
40	1972A	3.000	—	—	7.50

Friedrich von Schiller

20.9000 g, .625 SILVER, .4200 oz ASW
Lucas Cranach

| 41 | 1972A | .100 | — | — | 35.00 |

Wilhelm Pieck — COPPER-NICKEL

| 42 | 1972A | 2.500 | — | — | 7.50 |

20.9000 g, .625 SILVER, .4200 oz ASW
August Bebel

| 46 | 1973A | .100 | — | — | 35.00 |

Otto Grotewohl — COPPER-NICKEL

| 47 | 1973A | 2.500 | — | — | 7.50 |

20.9000 g, .625 SILVER, .4200 oz ASW
Immanuel Kant

| 53 | 1974A | .096 | — | — | 35.00 |
| | 1974A | 4,221 | — | Proof | 70.00 |

East / GERMANY 746

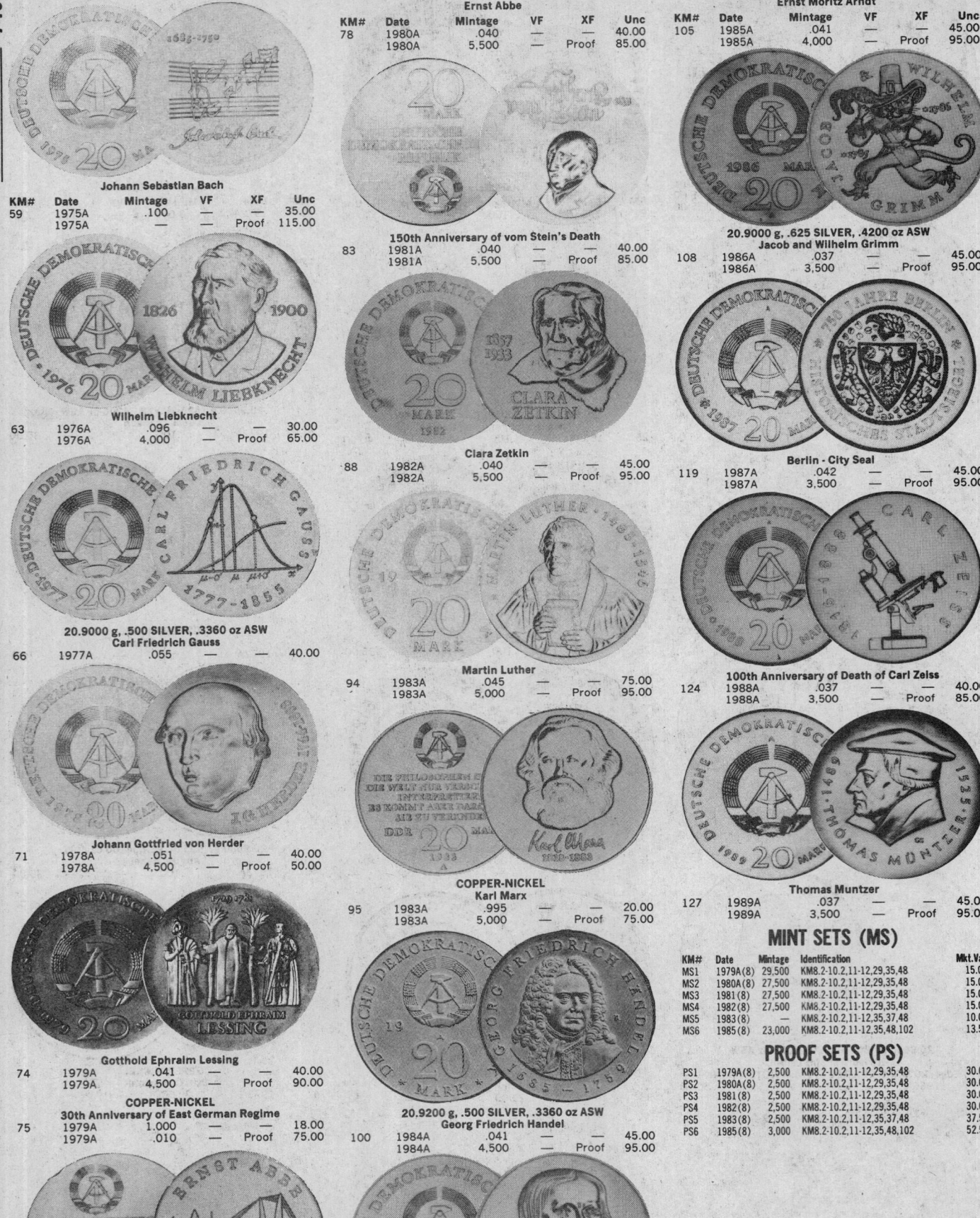

Johann Sebastian Bach

KM#	Date	Mintage	VF	XF	Unc
59	1975A	.100	—	—	35.00
	1975A	—	—	Proof	115.00

Wilhelm Liebknecht

63	1976A	.096	—	—	30.00
	1976A	4,000	—	Proof	65.00

20.9000 g, .500 SILVER, .3360 oz ASW

Carl Friedrich Gauss

66	1977A	.055	—	—	40.00

Johann Gottfried von Herder

71	1978A	.051	—	—	40.00
	1978A	4,500	—	Proof	50.00

Gotthold Ephraim Lessing

74	1979A	.041	—	—	40.00
	1979A	4,500	—	Proof	90.00

COPPER-NICKEL
30th Anniversary of East German Regime

75	1979A	1.000	—	—	18.00
	1979A	.010	—	Proof	75.00

20.9200 g, .500 SILVER, .3360 oz ASW

Ernst Abbe

KM#	Date	Mintage	VF	XF	Unc
78	1980A	.040	—	—	40.00
	1980A	5,500	—	Proof	85.00

150th Anniversary of vom Stein's Death

83	1981A	.040	—	—	40.00
	1981A	5,500	—	Proof	85.00

Clara Zetkin

88	1982A	.040	—	—	45.00
	1982A	5,500	—	Proof	95.00

Martin Luther

94	1983A	.045	—	—	75.00
	1983A	5,000	—	Proof	95.00

COPPER-NICKEL
Karl Marx

95	1983A	.995	—	—	20.00
	1983A	5,000	—	Proof	75.00

20.9200 g, .500 SILVER, .3360 oz ASW
Georg Friedrich Handel

100	1984A	.041	—	—	45.00
	1984A	4,500	—	Proof	95.00

Ernst Moritz Arndt

KM#	Date	Mintage	VF	XF	Unc
105	1985A	.041	—	—	45.00
	1985A	4,000	—	Proof	95.00

20.9000 g, .625 SILVER, .4200 oz ASW
Jacob and Wilhelm Grimm

108	1986A	.037	—	—	45.00
	1986A	3,500	—	Proof	95.00

Berlin - City Seal

119	1987A	.042	—	—	45.00
	1987A	3,500	—	Proof	95.00

100th Anniversary of Death of Carl Zeiss

124	1988A	.037	—	—	40.00
	1988A	3,500	—	Proof	85.00

Thomas Muntzer

127	1989A	.037	—	—	45.00
	1989A	3,500	—	Proof	95.00

MINT SETS (MS)

KM#	Date	Mintage	Identification	Mkt.Val.
MS1	1979A(8)	29,500	KM8.2-10.2,11-12,29,35,48	15.00
MS2	1980A(8)	27,500	KM8.2-10.2,11-12,29,35,48	15.00
MS3	1981(8)	27,500	KM8.2-10.2,11-12,29,35,48	15.00
MS4	1982(8)	27,500	KM8.2-10.2,11-12,29,35,48	15.00
MS5	1983(8)	—	KM8.2-10.2,11-12,35,37,48	10.00
MS6	1985(8)	23,000	KM8.2-10.2,11-12,35,48,102	13.50

PROOF SETS (PS)

PS1	1979A(8)	2,500	KM8.2-10.2,11-12,29,35,48	30.00
PS2	1980A(8)	2,500	KM8.2-10.2,11-12,29,35,48	30.00
PS3	1981(8)	2,500	KM8.2-10.2,11-12,29,35,48	30.00
PS4	1982(8)	2,500	KM8.2-10.2,11-12,29,35,48	30.00
PS5	1983(8)	2,500	KM8.2-10.2,11-12,35,37,48	37.50
PS6	1985(8)	3,000	KM8.2-10.2,11-12,35,48,102	52.50

GHANA

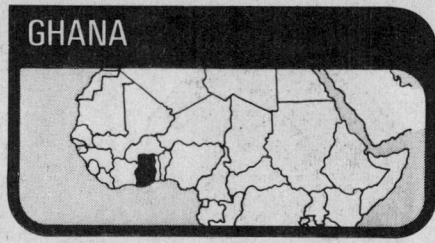

The Republic of Ghana, a member of the British Commonwealth situated on the West Coast of Africa between Ivory Coast and Togo, has an area of 92,100 sq. mi. (238,537 sq. km.) and a population of *14.8 million, almost entirely African. Capital: Accra. Cocoa (the major crop), coconuts, palm kernels and coffee are exported. Mining, second in importance to agriculture, is concentrated on gold, manganese and industrial diamonds.

First visited by Portuguese traders in 1470, and through the 17th century was used by various European powers -- England, Denmark, Holland, Germany -- as a center for their slave trade. Britain achieved control of the Gold Coast in 1821, and established the colony of Gold Coast in 1874. In 1901 Britain annexed the neighboring Ashanti Kingdom in the same year a northern region known as the Northern Territories became a British protectorate. Part of the former German colony of Togoland was mandated to Britain by the League of Nations and administered as part of the Gold Coast. The state of Ghana, comprising the Gold Coast and British Togoland, obtained independence on March 6, 1957, becoming the first Negro African colony to do so. On July 1, 1960, Ghana adopted a republican constitution, changing from a ministerial to a presidential form of government. The government was overthrown, the constitution suspended and the National Assembly dissolved by the Ghanaian army and police on Feb. 24, 1966. The government was returned to civilian authority in Oct. 1969, but was again seized by military officers in a bloodless coup on Jan. 13, 1972. Ghana remains a member of the Commonwealth of Nations, with executive authority vested in the Supreme Military council.

Ghana's monetary denomination of 'Cedi' is derived from the word 'sedie' meaning cowrie, a shell money commonly employed by coastal tribes.

GOLD COAST

RULERS
British

MONETARY SYSTEM
8 Tackoe = 1 Ackey

1/2 ACKEY

7.0900 g, .925 SILVER, .2108 oz ASW

KM#	Date	Mintage	Fine	VF	XF	Unc
8	1818	*2,170	50.00	125.00	200.00	—
	1818	—	—	—	Proof	250.00

BRONZED-COPPER (OMS)

| 8a | 1818 | — | — | — | Proof | Rare |

PEWTER (OMS)

| 8b | 1818 | — | — | — | Proof | Rare |

ACKEY

14.1300 g, .925 SILVER, .4202 oz ASW

| 9 | 1818 | *1,085 | 150.00 | 300.00 | 450.00 | — |
| | 1818 | — | — | — | Proof | 750.00 |

BRONZED-COPPER (OMS)

| 9a | 1818 | — | — | — | Proof | Rare |

PEWTER (OMS)
Plain edge.

| 9b | 1818 | — | — | — | Proof | Rare |

NOTE: For later issues see British West Africa.

GHANA

MONETARY SYSTEM
12 Pence = 1 Shilling

1/2 PENNY

BRONZE

KM#	Date	Mintage	VF	XF	Unc
1	1958	32.200	—	.10	.30
	1958	.020	—	Proof	.50

PENNY

BRONZE

| 2 | 1958 | 60.000 | — | .10 | .30 |
| | 1958 | .020 | — | Proof | .50 |

3 PENCE

COPPER-NICKEL

| 3 | 1958 | 25.200 | .10 | .15 | .35 |
| | 1958 | .020 | — | Proof | .50 |

6 PENCE

COPPER-NICKEL

| 4 | 1958 | 15.200 | — | .15 | .50 |
| | 1958 | — | — | Proof | .50 |

SHILLING

COPPER-NICKEL

| 5 | 1958 | 34.400 | .15 | .25 | 1.00 |
| | 1958 | .020 | — | Proof | 1.00 |

2 SHILLINGS

COPPER-NICKEL

| 6 | 1958 | 72.700 | .25 | .50 | 1.50 |
| | 1958 | .020 | — | Proof | 1.50 |

10 SHILLINGS

28.2800 g, .925 SILVER, .8411 oz ASW

KM#	Date	Mintage	VF	XF	Unc
7	1958	.011	—	Proof	12.00

DECIMAL COINAGE
100 Pesewas = 1 Cedi

1/2 PESEWA

BRONZE

| 12 | 1967 | 30.000 | — | .10 | .20 |
| | 1967 | 2,000 | — | Proof | .75 |

PESEWA

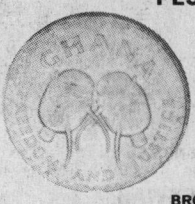 

BRONZE

13	1967	30.000	—	.10	.20
	1967	2,000	—	Proof	1.00
	1975	50.250	—	.10	.15
	1979	5.000	—	.10	.15

2-1/2 PESEWAS

COPPER-NICKEL

| 14 | 1967 | 6.000 | — | .10 | .30 |
| | 1967 | 2,000 | — | Proof | 1.25 |

5 PESEWAS

COPPER-NICKEL

| 8 | 1965 | 30.000 | .10 | .15 | .40 |

15	1967	30.000	.10	.15	.35
	1967	2,000	—	Proof	1.50
	1973	8.000	.10	.15	.25
	1975	20.000	.10	.15	.25

10 PESEWAS

COPPER-NICKEL

| 9 | 1965 | 50.000 | .10 | .20 | .50 |

GHANA

KM#	Date	Mintage	VF	XF	Unc
16	1967	13.200	.10	.20	.65
	1967	2,000	—	Proof	2.00
	1975	20.000	.10	.20	.40
	1979	5.500	.10	.20	.40

20 PESEWAS

COPPER-NICKEL

17	1967	25.800	.15	.25	1.00
	1967	2,000	—	Proof	2.50
	1975		.15	.25	.75
	1979	5.000	.15	.25	.75

25 PESEWAS

COPPER-NICKEL

| 10 | 1965 | 60.100 | .25 | .50 | 1.00 |

50 PESEWAS

COPPER-NICKEL

| 11 | 1965 | 18.200 | .50 | 1.00 | 2.00 |

BRASS

| 18 | 1979 | 60.000 | .35 | .50 | 1.00 |

| 24 | 1984 | 10.000 | — | .10 | .25 |

CEDI

BRASS

KM#	Date	Mintage	VF	XF	Unc
19	1979	160.000	.35	.75	1.35

| 25 | 1984 | 40.000 | — | .10 | .25 |

5 CEDIS

BRASS

| 26 | 1984 | 88.920 | — | .10 | .20 |

50 CEDIS

28.2800 g, .925 SILVER, .8411 oz ASW
International Year of Disabled Persons

20	1981	.010	—	—	22.50
	1981	.010	—	Proof	30.00

COPPER-NICKEL
FAO World Fisheries Conference

| 21 | ND(1984) | *.100 | — | — | 6.00 |

28.2800 g, .925 SILVER, .8411 oz ASW

| 21a | ND(1984) | *.021 | — | — | 35.00 |

47.5400 g, .917 GOLD, 1.4017 oz AGW

| 21b | ND(1984) | *105 pcs. | — | Proof | 3000. |

28.2800 g, .925 SILVER, .8411 oz ASW
Year of the Scout

| 22 | ND(1984) | *.010 | — | — | 20.00 |
| | ND(1984) | Inc. Ab. | — | Proof | 30.00 |

100 CEDIS

28.2800 g, .500 SILVER, .4546 oz ASW
Commonwealth Games

KM#	Date	Mintage	VF	XF	Unc
27	1986	*.050	—	—	15.00

28.2800 g, .925 SILVER, .8411 oz ASW

| 27a | 1986 | *.020 | — | Proof | 25.00 |

500 CEDIS

15.9800 g, .917 GOLD, .4711 oz AGW
Year of the Scout

| 23 | ND(1984) | 2,000 | — | — | 400.00 |
| | ND(1984) | 2,000 | — | Proof | 500.00 |

PROOF SETS (PS)

KM#	Date	Mintage	Identification	Issue Price	Mkt. Val.
PS1	1958(7)	6,431	KM1-7	—	16.50
PS2	1967(6)	100	KM12-17	8.53	9.00

Listings For

GHURFAH: refer to Yemen Democratic Republic

GIBRALTAR 749

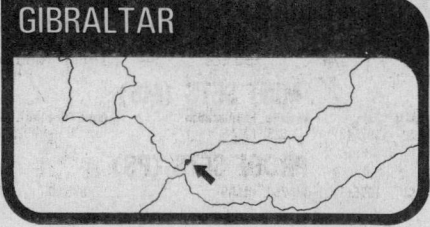

The British Colony of Gibraltar, located at the southernmost point of the Iberian Peninsula, has an area of 2.25 sq. mi. (5.8 sq. km.) and a population of *29,048. Capital (and only town): Gibraltar. Aside from its strategic importance as guardian of the western entrance to the Mediterranean Sea, Gibraltar is also a free port, British naval base, and coaling station.

Gibraltar, rooted in Greek mythology as one of the Pillars of Hercules, has long been a coveted stronghold. Moslems took it from Spain and fortified it in 711. Spain retook it in 1309, lost it again to the Moors in 1333 and retook it in 1462. After 1540 Spain strengthened its defenses and held it until the War of the Spanish Succession when it was captured by a combined British and Dutch force in 1704. Britain held it against the Franco-Spanish attacks of 1704-05 and through the historic 'Great Siege' of 1779-83. Recently Spain has attempted to discourage British occupancy by harassment and economic devices. In 1967, Gibraltar's inhabitants voted 12,138 to 44 to remain under British rule.

Gibraltar's celebrated Barbary Ape, the last monkey to be found in a wild state in Europe, is featured on the colony's first decimal crown, released in 1972.

RULERS
British

MONETARY SYSTEM
24 Quarts (Quartos) = 1 Real

1/2 QUART

COPPER

KM#	Date	Mintage	Fine	VF	XF	Unc
1	ND(1841)	—	—	—	—	Proof 600.00
	1842	.387	4.50	12.50	32.50	80.00
	1861	—	—	—	—	Proof 700.00

BRONZED COPPER (OMS)

| 1a | 1842 | — | — | — | — | Proof 225.00 |

QUART

COPPER

2	1842/0	.097	9.00	30.00	80.00	160.00
	1842/0	—	—	—	—	Proof 275.00
	1860	—	—	—	—	Proof Rare
	1861	—	—	—	—	Proof 700.00

BRONZED COPPER (OMS)

| 2a | 1841/0 | — | — | — | — | Proof 600.00 |

2 QUARTS

COPPER

3	1841	—	—	—	Proof	Rare
	1842/1	.048	15.00	40.00	80.00	175.00
	1842/1	—	—	—	Proof	325.00
	1860	—	—	—	Proof	Rare
	1861	—	—	—	Proof	700.00

MONETARY REFORM
4 Farthings = 1 Penny
12 Pence = 1 Shilling
2 Shillings = 1 Florin
5 Shillings = 1 Crown
20 Shillings = 1 Pound

CROWN

COPPER-NICKEL

KM#	Date	Mintage	VF	XF	Unc
4	1967	.125	.50	.85	1.50
	1968	.040	.65	1.00	2.00
	1969	.040	.65	1.00	2.00
	1970	.045	.65	1.00	2.00

28.2800 g, .500 SILVER, .4546 oz ASW

4a	1967	.010	—	Proof	12.00
	1967	50 pcs.	Frosted Proof		200.00

DECIMAL COINAGE
5 New Pence = 1 Shilling
25 New Pence = 1 Crown
100 New Pence = 1 Pound

PENNY

BRONZE
Barbary Partridge

| 20 | 1988 | — | — | — | .50 |

2 PENCE

BRONZE

| 21 | 1988 | — | — | — | .75 |

5 PENCE

COPPER-NICKEL
Barbary Ape

| 22 | 1988 | — | — | — | 1.00 |

10 PENCE

COPPER-NICKEL

Moorish Castle

KM#	Date	Mintage	VF	XF	Unc
23	1988	—	—	—	1.50

20 PENCE

COPPER-NICKEL

| 16 | 1988 | — | — | — | 2.00 |

25 NEW PENCE

COPPER-NICKEL

| 5 | 1971 | .075 | — | 1.00 | 2.00 |

28.2800 g, .500 SILVER, .4546 oz ASW

5a	1971	.020	—	Proof	12.00
	1971	50 pcs.	Frosted Proof		200.00

COPPER-NICKEL
25th Wedding Anniversary

| 6 | 1972 | .070 | — | 1.00 | 2.00 |

28.2800 g, .925 SILVER, .8411 oz ASW

| 6a | 1972 | .015 | — | Proof | 12.50 |

COPPER-NICKEL
Queen's Silver Jubilee

| 10 | 1977 | .065 | — | 1.00 | 2.00 |

28.2800 g, .925 SILVER, .8411 oz ASW

| 10a | 1977 | .024 | — | Proof | 12.50 |

GIBRALTAR 750

50 PENCE

COPPER-NICKEL

KM#	Date	Mintage	VF	XF	Unc
17	1988	—	—	—	2.00

Christmas
| 19 | 1988 | — | — | — | 2.50 |
| | 1988 | — | — | Proof | 15.00 |

15.5000 g, .925 SILVER, .4610 oz ASW
| 19a | 1988 | — | — | Proof | 15.00 |

26.0000 g, .917 GOLD, .7666 oz AGW
| 19b | 1988 | — | — | Proof | 450.00 |

30.4000 g, .950 PLATINUM, .9286 oz APW
| 19c | 1988 | — | — | Proof | 700.00 |

CROWN

COPPER-NICKEL
80th Birthday of Queen Mother
| 11 | 1980 | — | — | 1.00 | 2.00 |

28.2800 g, .925 SILVER, .8411 oz ASW
| 11a | 1980 | .025 | — | Proof | 15.00 |

COPPER-NICKEL
175th Anniversary of Death of Nelson
Obv: Similar to 25 New Pence, KM#6.
| 12 | 1980 | .100 | — | 1.00 | 2.00 |

28.2800 g, .925 SILVER, .8411 oz ASW
| 12a | 1980 | .015 | — | Proof | 15.00 |

COPPER-NICKEL

Wedding of Prince Charles and Lady Diana
Obv: Similar to 25 New Pence, KM#6.
KM#	Date	Mintage	VF	XF	Unc
14	1981	—	—	1.00	2.50

28.2800 g, .925 SILVER, .8411 oz ASW
| 14a | 1981 | .030 | — | Proof | 20.00 |

POUND

VIRENIUM
| 18 | 1988 | — | — | — | 2.50 |

25 POUNDS

7.7700 g, .917 GOLD, .2291 oz AGW
250th Anniversary Introduction of British Sterling
| 7 | 1975 | 2,395 | — | — | 150.00 |
| | 1975 | 750 pcs. | — | Proof | 225.00 |

50 POUNDS

15.5500 g, .917 GOLD, .4585 oz AGW
250th Anniversary Introduction of British Sterling
Obv: Similar to 25 Pounds, KM#7.
| 8 | 1975 | 1,625 | — | — | 275.00 |
| | 1975 | 750 pcs. | — | Proof | 300.00 |

15.9760 g, .917 GOLD, .4711 oz AGW
175th Anniversary of Death of Nelson
| 13 | 1980 | 7,500 | — | — | 235.00 |
| | 1980 | 5,000 | — | Proof | 275.00 |

Wedding of Prince Charles and Lady Diana
| 15 | 1981 | — | — | — | 250.00 |
| | 1981 | 2,500 | — | Proof | 300.00 |

100 POUNDS

31.1000 g, .917 GOLD, .9170 oz AGW
250th Anniversary Introduction of British Sterling
Obv: Similar to 25 Pounds, KM#7.
KM#	Date	Mintage	VF	XF	Unc
9	1975	1,625	—	—	500.00
	1975	750 pcs.	—	Proof	600.00

MINT SETS (MS)
KM#	Date	Mintage	Identification	Issue Price	Mkt. Val.
MS1	1975(3)	1,625	KM7-9	—	925.00

PROOF SETS (PS)
| PS1 | 1975(3) | 750 | KM7-9 | 875.00 | 1125. |

Listings For
GOLD COAST: refer to Ghana

GREAT BRITAIN

The United Kingdom of Great Britain and Northern Ireland, located off the northwest coast of the European continent, has an area of 94,227 sq. mi. (244,046 sq. km.) and a population of *56.7 million. Capital: London. The economy is based on industrial activity and trading. Machinery, motor vehicles, chemicals, and textile yarns and fabrics are exported.

After the departure of the Romans, who brought Britain into a more active relationship with Europe, Britain fell prey to invaders from Scandinavia and the Low Countries who drove the original Britons into Scotland and Wales, and established a profusion of kingdoms that finally united in the 11th century under the Danish King Canute. Norman rule, following the conquest of 1066, stimulated the development of those institutions which have since distinguished British life. Henry VIII (1509-47) turned Britain from continental adventuring and faced it to the sea - a decision that made Britain a world power during the reign of Elizabeth I (1558-1603). Strengthened by the Industrial Revolution and the defeat of Napoleon, 19th century Britain turned to the remote parts of the world and established a colonial empire of such extent and prosperity that the world has never seen its like. World Wars I and II sealed the fate of the Empire and relegated Britain to a lesser role in world affairs by draining her resources and inaugurating a world-wide movement toward national self-determination in her former colonies.

By the mid-20th century, most of the territories formerly comprising the British Empire had gained independence, and the empire had evolved into the Commonwealth of Nations, an association of equal and autonomous states which enjoy special trade interests. The Commonwealth is presently composed of 42 member nations, including the United Kingdom. All recognize the British monarch as head of the Commonwealth. Fourteen continue to recognize the British monarch as Chief of State. They are: United Kingdom, Australia, Bahamas, Barbados, Canada, Fiji, Jamaica, Kiribati, Mauritius, New Zealand, Papua New Guinea, St. Lucia, Solomon Islands, and Tuvalu.

RULERS

George III, 1760-1820
George IV, 1820-1830
William IV, 1830-1837
Victoria, 1837-1901
Edward VII, 1901-1910
George V, 1910-1936
Edward VIII, 1936
George VI, 1936-1952
Elizabeth II, 1952-

MINT MARKS

Commencing 1837

H - Heaton
KN - King's Norton

MONETARY SYSTEM

4 Farthings = 1 Penny
12 Pence = 1 Shilling
2 Shillings = 1 Florin
5 Shillings = 1 Crown
20 Shillings = 1 Pound (Sovereign)
21 Shillings = 1 Guinea

NOTE: Proofs exist for virtually all British coins since 1926. Those not specifically listed herein are extremely rare.

1/4 FARTHING

COPPER

KM#	Date	Mintage	Fine	VF	XF	Unc
737	1839	3.840	10.00	20.00	60.00	100.00
	1839	—	—	—	Proof	—
	1851	2.215	10.00	20.00	65.00	125.00
	1851	—	—	—	Proof	—
	1852	Inc. Ab.	10.00	20.00	60.00	115.00
	1853	Inc. Ab.	10.00	20.00	65.00	125.00
	1853	—	—	—	Proof	450.00

BRONZED COPPER (OMS)

KM#	Date	Mintage	Fine	VF	XF	Unc
737a	1852	—	—	—	Proof	450.00
	1853	*10-15	—	—	Proof	450.00

BRONZE (OMS)

KM#	Date	Mintage	Fine	VF	XF	Unc
737b	1868	—	—	—	Proof	450.00

COPPER-NICKEL (OMS)

KM#	Date	Mintage	Fine	VF	XF	Unc
737c	1868	—	—	—	Proof	350.00

***NOTE:** Although the design of the above series is of the homeland type, the issues were struck for Ceylon.

1/3 FARTHING

COPPER

KM#	Date	Mintage	Fine	VF	XF	Unc
703	1827	—	5.00	10.00	25.00	100.00
	1827	—	—	—	Proof	350.00

KM#	Date	Mintage	Fine	VF	XF	Unc
721	1835	—	5.00	10.00	25.00	100.00
	1835	—	—	—	Proof	350.00

KM#	Date	Mintage	Fine	VF	XF	Unc
743	1844	1.301	10.00	20.00	50.00	100.00
	1844 (error) RE for REG.	Inc. Ab.	15.00	35.00	65.00	125.00

BRONZE

KM#	Date	Mintage	Fine	VF	XF	Unc
750	1866	.576	1.75	4.00	12.00	35.00
	1866	—	—	—	Proof	350.00
	1868	.144	2.00	4.00	12.00	35.00
	1868	—	—	—	Proof	200.00
	1876	.162	2.50	5.00	15.00	50.00
	1878	.288	2.50	4.00	12.50	40.00
	1878	—	—	—	Proof	—
	1881	.144	2.50	4.00	12.50	45.00
	1881	—	—	—	Proof	200.00
	1884	.144	2.00	4.00	12.00	35.00
	1885	.288	1.50	3.50	10.00	30.00

COPPER-NICKEL (OMS)

KM#	Date	Mintage	Fine	VF	XF	Unc
750a	1868	—	—	—	Proof	450.00

ALUMINUM (OMS)

KM#	Date	Mintage	Fine	VF	XF	Unc
750b	1868	—	—	—	Proof	—

BRONZE

KM#	Date	Mintage	Fine	VF	XF	Unc
791	1902	.288	1.50	2.50	4.00	12.00

KM#	Date	Mintage	Fine	VF	XF	Unc
823	1913	.288	1.50	2.50	5.00	13.00

***NOTE:** Although the designs of the above types are in the homeland style, the issues were struck for Malta.

1/2 FARTHING

COPPER

Rev: Britannia's head breaks legend.

KM#	Date	Mintage	Fine	VF	XF	Unc
704.1	1828	7.680	7.00	15.00	45.00	180.00
	1828	—	—	—	Proof	350.00
	1830	—	—	—	Proof	350.00

Rev: Britannia's head below legend.

KM#	Date	Mintage	Fine	VF	XF	Unc
704.2	1828	Inc. Ab.	8.00	18.00	50.00	180.00
	1830 large date	8.776	7.00	15.00	45.00	170.00
	1830 small date	Inc. Ab.	9.00	20.00	60.00	190.00
	1830	—	—	—	Proof	350.00

BRONZED COPPER

KM#	Date	Mintage	Fine	VF	XF	Unc
704.1a	1828	—	—	—	Proof	300.00

COPPER

KM#	Date	Mintage	Fine	VF	XF	Unc
724	1837	1.935	20.00	70.00	200.00	550.00

KM#	Date	Mintage	Fine	VF	XF	Unc
738	1839	2.043	4.00	10.00	25.00	70.00
	1842	—	3.00	7.00	20.00	50.00
	1843	3.441	2.50	5.00	10.00	35.00
	1844	6.451	2.50	5.00	10.00	30.00
	1844 E of REGINA over N	Inc. Ab.	7.00	18.00	80.00	200.00
	1847	3.011	4.00	8.00	20.00	70.00
	1851/5851	—	4.00	10.00	32.50	85.00
	1851	—	4.00	10.00	25.00	75.00
	1852	.989	5.00	12.00	30.00	75.00
	1853	.955	6.50	15.00	40.00	100.00
	1853	—	—	—	Proof	300.00
	1854	.677	6.50	15.00	40.00	120.00
	1856 small date	.914	8.00	18.00	45.00	130.00
	1856 large date	Inc. Ab.	17.00	40.00	80.00	150.00

BRONZED COPPER (OMS)

KM#	Date	Mintage	Fine	VF	XF	Unc
738a	1839	*300	—	—	Proof	Rare
	1853	*10-15	—	—	Proof	Rare

BRONZE (OMS)

KM#	Date	Mintage	Fine	VF	XF	Unc
738b	1868	—	—	—	Proof	275.00

COPPER-NICKEL (OMS)

KM#	Date	Mintage	Fine	VF	XF	Unc
738c	1868	—	—	—	Proof	450.00

***NOTE:** Although the design of the above series is of the homeland type, the issues were originally struck for Ceylon. The issue was made current also in the United Kingdom by proclamation in 1842.

FARTHING

COPPER

KM#	Date	Mintage	Fine	VF	XF	Unc
661	1806	—	2.00	3.50	18.00	65.00
	1806	—	—	—	Proof	125.00
	1807	—	3.00	6.00	25.00	70.00

GILT COPPER (OMS)

KM#	Date	Mintage	Fine	VF	XF	Unc
661a	1806	—	—	—	Proof	150.00

BRONZED COPPER (OMS)

KM#	Date	Mintage	Fine	VF	XF	Unc
661b	1806	—	—	—	Proof	—

SILVER (OMS)

KM#	Date	Mintage	Fine	VF	XF	Unc
661c	1806	—	—	—	Proof	—

GOLD (OMS)

KM#	Date	Mintage	Fine	VF	XF	Unc
661d	1806	—	—	—	Proof	—

COPPER

KM#	Date	Mintage	Fine	VF	XF	Unc
677	1821	2.688	1.75	4.00	25.00	85.00
	1821	—	—	—	Proof	150.00
	1822	5.924	1.75	4.00	20.00	70.00
	1822	—	—	—	Proof	200.00
	1823	2.365	2.00	5.00	22.00	75.00
	1823 letter I for 1 in date	Inc. Ab.	5.00	12.00	30.00	125.00
	1825	4.300	1.75	4.00	22.00	75.00
	1826	6.666	2.00	5.00	22.00	75.00

KM#	Date	Mintage	Fine	VF	XF	Unc
697	1826	Inc. Ab.	1.75	4.00	25.00	80.00
	1826	—	—	—	Proof	200.00
	1827	2.365	3.00	8.00	30.00	85.00
	1828	2.365	2.50	5.50	30.00	100.00

GREAT BRITAIN 752

KM#	Date	Mintage	Fine	VF	XF	Unc
697	1829	1.505	4.00	9.00	35.00	125.00
	1830	2.365	2.50	6.00	25.00	80.00
	1831	—	—	—	Proof	200.00

BRONZED COPPER (OMS)

KM#	Date	Mintage	Fine	VF	XF	Unc
697a	1826	*150 pcs.	—	—	Proof	185.00

COPPER

KM#	Date	Mintage	Fine	VF	XF	Unc
705	1831	2.688	3.00	7.50	30.00	120.00
	1831	—	—	—	Proof	200.00
	1834	1.935	3.00	7.50	30.00	120.00
	1835	1.720	3.00	7.50	35.00	125.00
	1836	1.290	3.00	7.50	35.00	125.00
	1837	3.011	3.00	7.50	30.00	120.00

KM#	Date	Mintage	Fine	VF	XF	Unc
725	1838	.591	3.00	7.50	17.50	55.00
	1839	4.301	1.50	4.00	15.00	45.00
	1839	—	—	—	Proof	200.00
	1840	3.011	1.75	5.00	17.50	55.00
	1841	1.720	1.50	4.50	17.50	45.00
	1841*	—	—	—	Proof	175.00
	1842	1.290	3.75	12.50	30.00	70.00
	1842 4 over inverted 4					
		—	—	—	Rare	—
	1843	4.086	1.25	3.50	15.00	45.00
	1843 letter I for 1 in date					
		Inc. Ab.	3.50	8.50	32.50	125.00
	1844	.430	30.00	60.00	225.00	475.00
	1845	3.226	2.00	7.00	18.00	60.00
	1846	2.580	4.50	15.00	35.00	90.00
	1847	3.880	1.75	5.00	15.00	55.00
	1848	1.290	2.25	8.00	22.50	65.00
	1849	.645	8.00	25.00	65.00	250.00
	1850/70	.430	10.00	30.00	60.00	175.00
	1850	Inc. Ab.	2.50	6.00	15.00	60.00
	1851	1.935	6.00	15.00	40.00	130.00
	1851 D of DEI/tipped D					
		Inc. Ab.	50.00	150.00	400.00	700.00
	1852	.823	6.00	17.50	40.00	135.00
	1853/2	1.028	75.00	125.00	200.00	350.00
	1853 WW designer's initials raised					
		Inc. Ab.	1.50	4.00	12.50	35.00
	1853	—	—	—	Proof	350.00
	1853 WW designer's initials incuse					
		Inc. Ab.	7.50	12.00	27.50	50.00
	1853	—	—	—	Proof	350.00
	1854	4.946	1.25	4.00	14.00	40.00
	1855 WW designer's initials raised					
		3.441	4.00	15.00	30.00	75.00
	1855 WW designer's initials incuse					
		Inc. Ab.	3.00	12.50	27.50	70.00
	1856	1.771	3.00	10.00	32.50	80.00
	1856 R of Victoria over E					
		Inc. Ab.	25.00	60.00	150.00	300.00
	1857	1.075	1.25	3.50	12.50	35.00
	1858	1.720	1.25	3.50	12.50	35.00
	1859	1.290	10.00	20.00	60.00	120.00
	1860/59	—	—	—	—	—
	1860	—	350.00	900.00	1500.	3000.
	1864	—	—	—	Rare	—

NOTE: Proofs dated 1841 were probably restruck at a later date.

BRONZED COPPER (OMS)

KM#	Date	Mintage	Fine	VF	XF	Unc
725a	1839	*300 pcs.	—	—	Proof	Rare
	1853					
		*10-15 pcs.	—	—	Proof	Rare

SILVER (OMS)

KM#	Date	Mintage	Fine	VF	XF	Unc
725b	1839		—	—	Proof	Rare

BRONZE
Beaded border.

KM#	Date	Mintage	Fine	VF	XF	Unc
747.1	1860	2.867	2.00	4.00	10.00	30.00
	1860	—	—	—	Proof	400.00

Toothed border.

KM#	Date	Mintage	Fine	VF	XF	Unc
747.2	1860	Inc. Ab.	1.00	2.50	8.00	27.50
	1860 toothed/beaded border					
		Inc. Ab.	70.00	150.00	250.00	650.00
	1861	8.602	1.00	2.00	6.00	27.50
	1861	—	—	—	Proof	350.00
	1862 small 8					
747.2		14.336	1.00	2.00	5.00	25.00
	1862 lg.8	I.A.	1.50	3.75	9.00	30.00
	1862	—	—	—	Proof	350.00
	1863	1.434	17.00	30.00	80.00	220.00
	1863	—	—	—	Proof	700.00
	1864	2.509	1.00	2.50	12.00	35.00
	1865/2	4.659	1.50	4.00	12.00	35.00
	1865/3	Inc. Ab.	1.15	3.00	15.00	40.00
	1865 lg.8	I.A.	1.00	2.00	7.00	30.00
	1865 sm.8	I.A.	1.00	2.00	6.00	30.00
	1866	3.584	1.00	2.00	6.00	30.00
	1866	—	—	—	Proof	350.00
	1867	5.018	1.50	3.00	10.00	30.00
	1867	—	—	—	Proof	350.00
	1868	4.851	1.50	3.00	10.00	30.00
	1868	—	—	—	Proof	200.00
	1869	3.226	2.25	7.50	25.00	60.00
	1872	2.150	1.50	3.50	9.00	35.00
	1873	3.226	1.25	2.75	7.00	27.50

COPPER NICKEL (OMS)

KM#	Date	Mintage	Fine	VF	XF	Unc
747.2a	1868	—	—	—	Proof	500.00

SILVER (OMS)

KM#	Date	Mintage	Fine	VF	XF	Unc
747.2b	1861	—	—	—	Proof	1200.

GOLD (OMS)

KM#	Date	Mintage	Fine	VF	XF	Unc
747.2c	1861	—	—	—	Proof	—

BRONZE
Obv: Mature bust.

KM#	Date	Mintage	Fine	VF	XF	Unc
753	1874H	3.584	1.00	2.50	8.00	27.50
	1874H	—	—	—	Proof	200.00
	1874H normal G's over horizontal G's					
		Inc. Ab.	75.00	175.00	300.00	—
	1875 large date					
		.713	9.00	20.00	40.00	120.00
	1875 small date					
		Inc. Ab.	15.00	25.00	50.00	175.00
	1875H	6.093	1.00	2.00	5.00	17.50
	1875H	—	—	—	Proof	200.00
	1876H	1.075	6.00	15.00	30.00	75.00
	1877	—	—	—	Proof	2500.
	1878	4.009	1.00	2.00	5.00	25.00
	1878	—	—	—	Proof	350.00
	1879	3.977	1.00	2.00	5.00	25.00
	1879 large 9					
		Inc. Ab.	1.50	3.00	8.00	35.00
	1880 3 berries in wreath					
		1.843	3.75	7.50	17.50	55.00
	1880 4 berries in wreath					
		Inc. Ab.	1.15	2.50	5.00	25.00
	1881 3 berries in wreath					
		3.495	1.50	3.00	6.00	25.00
	1881 4 berries in wreath					
		Inc. Ab.	3.50	7.50	20.00	55.00
	1881 shield heraldically colored					
		—	—	—	Proof	800.00
	1881H	1.792	1.50	3.50	6.00	25.00
	1882H	1.792	1.50	3.50	6.00	25.00
	1882H	—	—	—	Proof	400.00
	1883	1.129	1.75	7.50	20.00	45.00
	1883	—	—	—	Proof	400.00
	1884	5.782	.75	1.50	3.50	15.00
	1884	—	—	—	Proof	400.00
	1885	5.442	1.00	2.00	3.50	15.00
	1885	—	—	—	Proof	400.00
	1886	7.708	.75	1.50	3.00	12.00
	1886	—	—	—	Proof	400.00
	1887	1.341	2.00	4.00	9.00	30.00
	1888	1.887	1.50	3.00	5.00	20.00
	1889	—	—	—	—	—
	1890	2.133	1.00	2.00	3.50	17.50
	1890	—	—	—	Proof	400.00
	1891	4.960	.75	1.50	3.00	15.00
	1891	—	—	—	Proof	350.00
	1892	.887	3.00	7.50	15.00	40.00
	1892	—	—	—	Proof	400.00
	1893	3.904	.75	1.50	3.00	15.00
	1894	2.397	.75	1.50	3.00	15.00
	1895	2.853	8.00	18.00	45.00	120.00
788.1	1895	Inc. Ab.	.50	1.25	3.50	9.50
	1896	3.669	.35	1.00	3.00	9.00
	1896	—	—	—	Proof	300.00
	1897	4.580	.75	2.00	5.00	17.50

Blackened finish

KM#	Date	Mintage	Fine	VF	XF	Unc
788.2	1897	Inc. Ab.	.45	1.25	3.00	9.00
	1898	4.010	.60	1.50	3.50	12.50
	1899	3.865	.35	.75	2.00	9.00
	1900	5.969	.35	.75	1.75	8.50
	1901	8.016	.30	.65	1.50	8.50

KM#	Date	Mintage	Fine	VF	XF	Unc
792	1902	5.125	.50	1.50	3.00	10.00
	1903	5.331	.60	1.75	4.00	17.00
	1903 shield heraldically colored					
		—	—	—	Proof	675.00
	1904	3.629	1.50	3.00	6.50	18.50
	1905	4.077	.60	1.75	4.00	17.00
	1906	5.340	.50	1.50	3.50	15.00
	1907	4.399	.75	1.50	4.00	16.00
	1908	4.265	.75	1.50	4.00	16.00
	1909	8.852	.50	1.50	3.50	15.00
	1910	2.598	1.50	3.50	7.50	20.00

KM#	Date	Mintage	Fine	VF	XF	Unc
808.1	1911	5.197	.50	.75	2.50	7.00
	1912	7.670	.35	.75	2.50	7.00
	1913	4.184	.50	.75	2.50	7.00
	1914	6.127	.35	.75	2.50	7.00
	1915	7.129	.50	.75	2.50	7.00
	1916	10.993	.35	.75	1.50	6.00
	1917	21.435	.15	.35	1.50	6.00
	1918	19.363	.75	1.50	4.00	12.00

Bright finish

KM#	Date	Mintage	Fine	VF	XF	Unc
808.2	1918	Inc. Ab.	.20	.40	1.00	4.00
	1919	15.089	.20	.40	1.00	4.00
	1920	11.481	.20	.40	1.00	4.00
	1921	9.469	.20	.40	1.00	4.00
	1922	9.957	.20	.40	1.00	4.00
	1923	8.034	.20	.40	1.00	4.00
	1924	8.733	.20	.40	1.00	4.00
	1925	12.635	.20	.40	1.00	4.00

Obv: Smaller head.

KM#	Date	Mintage	Fine	VF	XF	Unc
825	1926	9.792	.15	.35	.75	3.50
	1926	—	—	—	Proof	125.00
	1927	7.868	.15	.35	.75	3.50
	1927	—	—	—	Proof	125.00
	1928	11.626	.15	.35	.75	3.50
	1928	—	—	—	Proof	125.00
	1929	8.419	.15	.35	.75	3.50
	1929	—	—	—	Proof	125.00
	1930	4.195	.15	.35	.75	3.50
	1930	—	—	—	Proof	125.00
	1931	6.595	.15	.35	.75	3.50
	1931	—	—	—	Proof	125.00
	1932	9.293	.15	.35	.75	3.50
	1932	—	—	—	Proof	125.00
	1933	4.560	.15	.35	.75	3.50
	1933	—	—	—	Proof	125.00
	1934	3.053	.35	.75	1.75	6.00
	1934	—	—	—	Proof	125.00
	1935	2.227	1.00	2.00	3.50	9.00
	1935	—	—	—	Proof	150.00
	1936	9.734	.15	.35	.75	3.00
	1936	—	—	—	Proof	150.00

KM#	Date	Mintage	Fine	VF	XF	Unc
843	1937	8.131	.15	.25	.40	1.50
	1937	.026	—	—	Proof	4.00
	1938	7.450	.15	.30	.60	3.50
	1938	—	—	—	Proof	—
	1939	31.440	.10	.25	.40	1.50
	1939	—	—	—	Proof	—
	1940	18.360	.10	.25	.50	3.50
	1940	—	—	—	Proof	—
	1941	27.312	.10	.25	.40	1.50
	1941	—	—	—	Proof	—
	1942	28.858	.10	.20	.35	1.50
	1942	—	—	—	Proof	—
	1943	33.346	.10	.15	.30	1.50
	1943	—	—	—	Proof	—
	1944	25.138	.10	.15	.30	1.50
	1944	—	—	—	Proof	—
	1945	23.736	.10	.20	.35	1.50
	1945	—	—	—	Proof	—
	1946	24.365	.10	.20	.35	1.50
	1946	—	—	—	Proof	—
	1947	14.746	.10	.20	.35	1.50
	1947	—	—	—	Proof	—
	1948	16.622	.10	.20	.35	1.50
	1948	—	—	—	Proof	—

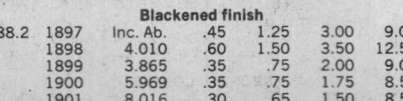

Obv. leg: W/o IND IMP.

KM#	Date	Mintage	Fine	VF	XF	Unc
867	1949	8.424	.10	.20	.35	1.50
	1949	—	—	—	Proof	—
	1950	10.325	.10	.20	.35	1.50
	1950	.018	—	—	Proof	3.00
	1951	14.016	.10	.20	.35	1.75
	1951	.020	—	—	Proof	3.00
	1952	5.251	.10	.20	.35	1.75
	1952	—	—	—	Proof	—

881	1953	6.131	.15	.25	.35	1.00
	1953	.040	—	—	Proof	2.00

Obv. leg: W/o BRITT OMN.

895	1954	6.566	.10	.15	.30	.60
	1954	—	—	—	Proof	—
	1955	5.779	.10	.15	.30	.60
	1955	—	—	—	Proof	—
	1956	1.997	.25	.50	.75	2.00
	1956	—	—	—	Proof	—

1/2 PENNY

COPPER

662	1806 w/o berries	—	2.00	4.50	18.00	90.00
	1806 3 berries	—	2.00	4.50	18.00	90.00
	1806 w/o berries	—	—	—	Proof	250.00
	1806 2 berries	—	—	—	Proof	250.00
	1806 3 berries	—	—	—	Proof	250.00
	1807	—	2.50	5.50	20.00	100.00

692	1825	.215	3.50	8.50	45.00	110.00
	1825	—	—	—	Proof	275.00
	1826/5	9.032	2.50	10.00	50.00	150.00
	1826	Inc. Ab.	2.00	7.00	35.00	100.00
	1826	—	—	—	Proof	175.00
	1827	5.376	2.50	7.50	45.00	135.00

BRONZED COPPER

692a	1826	*150	—	—	Proof	250.00

COPPER

706	1831	.806	4.50	9.00	45.00	170.00
	1834	.538	5.00	10.00	50.00	175.00
	1837	.349	4.00	8.00	40.00	160.00

BRONZED COPPER

KM#	Date	Mintage	Fine	VF	XF	Unc
706a	1831	—	—	—	Proof	200.00

COPPER

726	1838	.457	2.00	4.00	17.50	85.00
	1841	1.075	2.00	4.00	17.50	85.00
	1843	.968	6.00	15.00	45.00	150.00
	1844	1.075	4.00	10.00	35.00	100.00
	1845	1.075	30.00	70.00	275.00	750.00
	1846	.860	6.00	10.00	30.00	95.00
	1847	.725	6.00	10.00	30.00	95.00
	1848/7	.323	2.50	5.00	17.50	90.00
	1848	Inc. Ab.	2.50	6.00	22.50	95.00
	1851	.215	2.00	5.00	15.00	85.00
	1852	.637	2.00	5.50	16.00	90.00
	1853/2	1.559	6.00	15.00	45.00	110.00
	1853	Inc. Ab.	1.25	3.00	12.00	70.00
	1853	—	—	—	Proof	175.00
	1854	12.257	1.25	3.00	10.00	70.00
	1855	7.456	1.25	3.00	10.00	70.00
	1856	1.942	2.00	5.00	20.00	80.00
	1857	1.183	1.25	4.00	15.00	75.00
	1857 dots on shield	Inc. Ab.	1.25	4.00	12.00	75.00
	1858/6	2.473	5.00	12.00	37.50	110.00
	1858/7	Inc. Ab.	2.00	6.00	18.00	75.00
	1858	Inc. Ab.	1.50	4.50	15.00	70.00
	1858 sm.dt.	I.A.	2.00	5.50	18.00	70.00
	1859/8	1.290	4.50	12.00	40.00	115.00
	1859	Inc. Ab.	2.00	5.00	18.00	70.00
	1860	—	200.00	500.00	2250.	4500.

BRONZED COPPER

726a	1839 normal alignment	*300 pcs.	—	—	Proof	250.00
	1839 coin alignment	Inc. Ab.	—	—	Proof	300.00
	1841	—	—	—	Proof	—
	1853	*10-15 pcs.	—	—	Proof	Rare

SILVER (OMS)

726b	1841	—	—	—	Proof	—

BRONZE
Beaded border

748.1	1860	6.630	1.50	4.00	12.00	50.00
	1860	—	—	—	Proof	400.00

Toothed border

KM#	Date	Mintage	Fine	VF	XF	Unc
748.2	1860	Inc. Ab.	1.50	4.00	12.00	50.00
	1860 toothed/beaded border	—	—	—	—	—
	1860 w/7 berries in wreath	Inc. Ab.	1.50	4.00	12.00	45.00
	1860 w/7 berries in wreath	—	—	—	Proof	400.00
	1860 w/7 berries in wreath; rd.top lighthouse	Inc. Ab.	4.25	15.00	70.00	225.00
	1860 w/5 berries in wreath	Inc. Ab.	2.00	7.25	35.00	70.00
	1860 w/4 berries in wreath	Inc. Ab.	1.50	4.00	12.00	45.00
	1860 w/4 berries in wreath; rd.top lighthouse	Inc. Ab.	2.25	7.25	40.00	70.00
	1861/8154.118		—	—	Rare	—
	1861	Inc. Ab.	1.50	4.00	10.00	40.00
	1861	—	—	—	Proof	300.00
	1861 w/5 berries in wreath L.C.W. on rock	Inc. Ab.	10.00	25.00	75.00	300.00
	1861 w/4 berries in wreath L.C.W. on rock	Inc. Ab.	2.00	3.00	12.50	90.00
	1861 w/4 berries in wreath L.C.W. on rock	—	—	—	Proof	550.00
	1861 w/4 berries in wreath	Inc. Ab.	2.00	4.00	10.00	40.00
	1861 L.C.W. on rock	Inc. Ab.	2.50	7.00	15.00	45.00
	1861 HALF over HALP	Inc. Ab.	20.00	60.00	175.00	450.00
	1862 L.C.W. on rock, B to left of lighthouse	61.107	50.00	150.00	600.00	1200.
	1862 C to left of lighthouse	Inc. Ab.	50.00	150.00	600.00	1200.
	1862 A to left of lighthouse	Inc. Ab.	50.00	150.00	600.00	1200.
	1862	—	—	—	Proof	300.00
	1862	Inc. Ab.	1.25	3.00	12.00	45.00
	1862L.C.W.	I.A.	7.00	15.00	40.00	90.00
	1863 sm.3	15.949	1.50	5.00	20.00	50.00
	1863 sm.3	—	—	—	Proof	300.00
	1863 lg.3	I.A.	1.50	5.00	20.00	50.00
	1864	.538	3.50	8.00	25.00	85.00
	1865/3	8.064	30.00	85.00	270.00	600.00
	1865	Inc. Ab.	3.00	12.00	30.00	75.00
	1866	2.509	2.50	7.50	20.00	50.00
	1866	—	—	—	Proof	300.00
	1867	2.509	4.00	10.00	27.50	70.00
	1867	—	—	—	Proof	300.00
	1868	3.046	2.50	7.50	20.00	65.00
	1868	—	—	—	Proof	250.00
	1869	3.226	6.50	25.00	75.00	175.00
	1870	4.351	2.50	7.50	20.00	65.00
	1871	1.075	22.50	60.00	150.00	450.00
	1872	4.659	3.00	7.50	20.00	50.00
	1873	3.405	4.50	10.00	25.00	70.00
	1874 w/5 berries in wreath	Inc. Ab.	5.00	15.00	40.00	100.00

SILVER (OMS)

748.2a	1861	—	—	—	Proof	1250.

COPPER NICKEL (OMS)

748.2b	1861	—	—	—	Proof	650.00
	1868	—	—	—	Proof	375.00

ALUMINUM BRONZE (OMS)

748.2c	1861	—	—	—	Proof	750.00

GOLD (OMS)

748.2d	1861	Unique	—	—	Proof	—

BRASS (OMS)

748.2e	1872	Unique	—	—	Proof	—

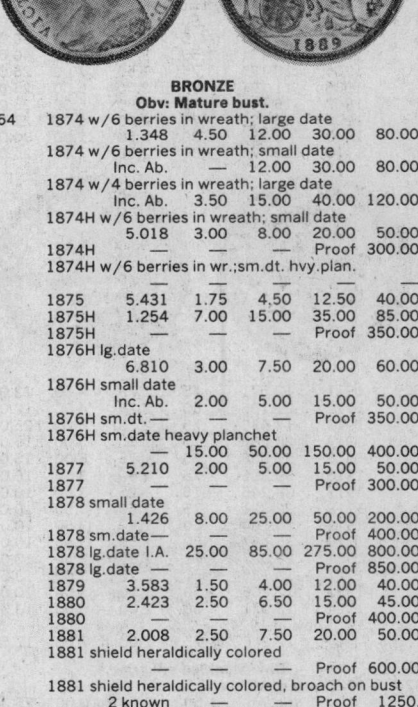

BRONZE
Obv: Mature bust.

754	1874 w/6 berries in wreath; large date	1.348	4.50	12.00	30.00	80.00
	1874 w/6 berries in wreath; small date	Inc. Ab.	—	12.00	30.00	80.00
	1874 w/4 berries in wreath; large date	Inc. Ab.	3.50	15.00	40.00	120.00
	1874H w/6 berries in wreath; small date	5.018	3.00	8.00	20.00	50.00
	1874H	—	—	—	Proof	300.00
	1874H w/6 berries in wr.;sm.dt. hvy.plan.	—	—	—	—	—
	1875	5.431	1.75	4.50	12.50	40.00
	1875H	1.254	7.00	15.00	35.00	85.00
	1875H	—	—	—	Proof	350.00
	1876H lg.date	6.810	3.00	7.50	20.00	60.00
	1876H small date	Inc. Ab.	2.00	5.00	15.00	50.00
	1876H sm.dt.	—	—	—	Proof	350.00
	1876H sm.date heavy planchet	—	15.00	50.00	150.00	400.00
	1877	5.210	2.00	5.00	15.00	50.00
	1877	—	—	—	Proof	300.00
	1878 small date	1.426	8.00	25.00	50.00	200.00
	1878 sm.date	—	—	—	Proof	400.00
	1878 lg.date	I.A.	25.00	85.00	275.00	800.00
	1878 lg.date	—	—	—	Proof	850.00
	1879	3.583	1.50	4.00	12.00	40.00
	1880	2.423	2.50	6.50	15.00	45.00
	1880	—	—	—	Proof	400.00
	1881	2.008	2.50	7.50	20.00	50.00
	1881 shield heraldically colored	—	—	—	Proof	600.00
	1881 shield heraldically colored, broach on bust	2 known	—	—	Proof	1250.
	1881H	1.792	2.50	7.50	20.00	50.00
	1882H	4.480	1.15	4.50	15.00	45.00
	1882H different dies		—	—	Proof	700.00
	1883 rose on front of dress	3.001	5.00	10.00	20.00	50.00
	1883 rose on front of dress	—	—	—	Proof	400.00
	1883 broach on front of dress	Inc. Ab.	3.50	6.00	15.00	40.00
	1884	6.990	1.15	3.00	12.50	40.00
	1884	—	—	—	Proof	350.00
	1885	8.601	1.15	3.00	12.50	40.00
	1885	—	—	—	Proof	350.00
	1886	8.586	1.00	2.75	12.50	40.00
	1886	—	—	—	Proof	175.00
	1887	10.701	1.00	2.75	10.00	35.00
	1888	6.815	1.25	3.25	11.50	37.50
	1889/8	7.748	35.00	60.00	120.00	275.00
	1889/8	1 known	—	—	Proof	—
	1889	Inc. Ab.	1.00	2.75	11.50	35.00
	1890	11.254	1.00	2.75	9.00	35.00
	1890	—	—	—	Proof	400.00
	1891	13.192	1.00	2.50	9.00	35.00
	1891	—	—	—	Proof	400.00
	1892	2.478	1.15	2.75	9.00	35.00
	1892	—	—	—	Proof	400.00

GREAT BRITAIN

KM#	Date	Mintage	Fine	VF	XF	Unc
754	1893	7.229	.80	2.25	9.00	35.00
	1894	1.768	3.00	7.00	25.00	60.00
789	1895	3.032	.75	1.50	4.00	18.00
	1895	—	—	—	Proof	400.00
	1896	9.143	.75	1.50	3.50	15.00
	1896	—	—	—	Proof	400.00
	1897	8.690	.50	1.25	4.50	20.00
	1897 high sea level					
		Inc. Ab.	.60	1.50	3.50	15.00
	1898	8.595	1.00	3.00	7.50	20.00
	1899	12.108	.75	2.00	4.50	15.00
	1900	13.805	.50	1.00	2.75	9.00
	1901	11.127	.40	.75	2.00	8.00
	1901	—	—	—	Proof	400.00

Rev: Low horizon.

793.1	1902	13.673	8.00	22.50	60.00	120.00

Rev: High horizon.

793.2	1902	Inc. Ab.	.50	2.00	5.00	15.00
	1903	11.451	.75	2.50	7.50	30.00
	1904	8.131	1.50	3.50	12.00	40.00
	1905	10.125	.75	2.50	7.00	25.00
	1906	11.101	.75	2.00	6.00	25.00
	1907	16.849	.75	2.00	6.00	25.00
	1908	16.621	.75	2.00	6.00	25.00
	1909	8.279	1.00	2.50	7.00	30.00
	1910	10.770	1.00	2.50	7.00	25.00
809	1911	12.571	.75	1.75	4.50	12.00
	1912	21.186	.50	1.25	4.00	12.00
	1913	17.476	.75	2.25	8.00	25.00
	1914	20.289	.75	1.75	5.00	15.00
	1915	21.563	.75	1.75	5.00	15.00
	1916	39.386	.75	1.50	3.50	10.00
	1917	38.245	.75	1.25	3.50	10.00
	1918	22.321	.75	1.50	3.50	10.00
	1919	28.104	.50	1.50	3.50	10.00
	1920	35.147	.50	1.50	3.50	10.00
	1921	28.027	.75	1.50	3.50	10.00
	1922	10.735	.50	2.25	5.00	13.50
	1923	12.266	.50	1.50	3.50	10.00
	1924	13.971	.50	2.00	5.00	13.50
	1925 obv. of 1924					
		12.216	.75	2.00	7.00	17.50

Obv: Modified effigy.

824	1925 obv. of 1926					
	Inc. Ab.	1.50	5.00	10.00	25.00	
	1926	6.712	1.50	3.00	6.00	15.00
	1926	—	—	—	Proof	175.00
	1927	15.590	.75	1.25	3.50	11.50
	1927	—	—	—	Proof	175.00

Obv: Smaller head.

837	1928	20.935	.25	—	2.50	9.00
	1928	—	—	—	Proof	150.00
	1929	25.680	.25	—	2.50	9.00
	1929	—	—	—	Proof	150.00
	1930	12.533	.25	.75	2.50	9.00
	1930	—	—	—	Proof	150.00
	1931	16.138	.25	.75	2.50	9.00
	1931	—	—	—	Proof	150.00

KM#	Date	Mintage	Fine	VF	XF	Unc
837	1932	14.448	.25	.75	3.50	10.00
	1932	—	—	—	Proof	85.00
	1933	10.560	.25	.75	2.75	10.00
	1933	—	—	—	Proof	150.00
	1934	7.704	.50	1.00	3.50	11.50
	1934	—	—	—	Proof	85.00
	1935	12.180	.25	.75	2.50	9.00
	1935	—	—	—	Proof	150.00
	1936	23.009	.25	.65	1.50	4.50
	1936	—	—	—	Proof	150.00

844	1937	24.504	.25	.35	.50	1.50
	1937	.026	—	—	Proof	5.00
	1938	40.320	.25	.50	1.25	3.75
	1938	—	—	—	Proof	125.00
	1939	28.925	.25	.50	1.25	3.50
	1939	—	—	—	Proof	125.00
	1940	32.162	.25	.50	2.00	5.00
	1940	—	—	—	Proof	125.00
	1941	45.120	.20	.50	1.50	5.00
	1941	—	—	—	Proof	125.00
	1942	71.909	.10	.20	.60	2.25
	1942	—	—	—	Proof	125.00
	1943	76.200	.10	.25	1.00	2.25
	1943	—	—	—	Proof	125.00
	1944	81.840	.10	.25	1.00	3.00
	1944	—	—	—	Proof	125.00
	1945	57.000	.10	.25	.90	2.00
	1945	—	—	—	Proof	125.00
	1946	22.726	.20	.50	2.75	7.00
	1946	—	—	—	Proof	125.00
	1947	21.266	.10	.25	2.00	5.00
	1947	—	—	—	Proof	125.00
	1948	26.947	.10	.25	.90	2.25
	1948	—	—	—	Proof	125.00

Obv. leg: W/o IND IMP.

868	1949	24.744	.10	.25	1.25	4.00
	1949	—	—	—	Proof	125.00
	1950	24.154	.10	.25	1.50	4.50
	1950	.018	—	—	Proof	5.00
	1951	14.868	.25	.50	1.50	6.00
	1951	.020	—	—	Proof	6.00
	1952	33.278	.10	.25	1.00	2.25
	1952	—	—	—	Proof	125.00

882	1953	8.926	.20	.40	1.00	2.25
	1953	.040	—	—	Proof	4.50

Obv. leg: W/o BRITT OMN.

896	1954	19.375	.10	.25	2.00	4.50
	1954	—	—	—	Proof	125.00
	1955	18.799	.10	.25	1.50	5.00
	1955	—	—	—	Proof	125.00
	1956	21.799	.15	.50	1.50	5.00
	1956	—	—	—	Proof	125.00
	1957	43.684	.10	—	.50	1.50
	1957	—	—	—	Proof	125.00
	1958	62.318	—	—	.10	.75
	1958	—	—	—	Proof	125.00
	1959	79.176	—	—	.10	.40
	1959	—	—	—	Proof	125.00
	1960	41.340	—	—	.10	.30

KM#	Date	Mintage	Fine	VF	XF	Unc
896	1960	—	—	—	Proof	125.00
	1961	—	—	—	Proof	125.00
	1962	41.779	—	—	.10	.20
	1962	—	—	—	Proof	125.00
	1963	45.036	—	—	.10	.20
	1963	—	—	—	Proof	125.00
	1964	78.583	—	—	.10	.15
	1964	—	—	—	Proof	125.00
	1965	98.083	—	—	—	.10
	1966	95.289	—	—	—	.10
	1967	146.491	—	—	—	.10
	1970	.731	—	—	Proof	1.50

PENNY

COPPER

663	1806	—	5.00	10.00	50.00	165.00
	1806	—	—	—	Proof	300.00
	1807	—	6.00	12.00	55.00	180.00
	1808	Unique	—	—	—	—

.4713 g, .925 SILVER, .0140 oz ASW

668	1817	—	5.00	8.00	15.00	30.00
	1817	.010	—	—	P/L	35.00
	1818	—	5.00	8.00	15.00	30.00
	1818	9,504	—	—	P/L	35.00
	1820	—	5.00	8.00	15.00	30.00
	1820	7,920	—	—	P/L	35.00

683	1822	.012	—	—	P/L	35.00
	1823	.013	—	—	P/L	30.00
	1824	9,504	—	—	P/L	35.00
	1825	8,712	—	—	P/L	30.00
	1826	8,712	—	—	P/L	30.00
	1827	7,920	—	—	P/L	30.00
	1828	7,920	—	—	P/L	30.00
	1829	7,920	—	—	P/L	30.00
	1830	7,920	—	—	P/L	30.00

COPPER

693	1825	1.075	6.00	15.00	80.00	235.00
	1825	—	—	—	Proof	500.00
	1826	5.914	4.50	12.50	60.00	200.00
	1826	—	—	—	Proof	400.00
	1827	1.452	75.00	250.00	1600.	2500.

BRONZED COPPER (OMS)

693a	1826	—	—	—	Proof	300.00

COPPER

707	1831	.806	6.00	25.00	120.00	425.00
	1831 .W.W incuse on truncation					
	Inc. Ab.	7.50	30.00	130.00	460.00	
	1831 W.W incuse on truncation					
	Inc. Ab.	8.00	32.50	140.00	500.00	
	1834	.323	8.00	35.00	140.00	500.00
	1837	.175	12.50	50.00	150.00	575.00

BRONZED COPPER (OMS)

707a	1831	—	—	—	Proof	400.00

.4713 g, .925 SILVER, .0140 oz ASW

KM#	Date	Mintage	Fine	VF	XF	Unc
708	1831	.010	—	—	P/L	22.50
	1832	8,712	—	—	P/L	22.50
	1833	8,712	—	—	P/L	22.50
	1834	8,712	—	—	P/L	22.50
	1835	8,712	—	—	P/L	22.50
	1836	8,712	—	—	P/L	22.50
	1837	8,712	—	—	P/L	22.50

KM#	Date	Mintage	Fine	VF	XF	Unc
727	1838	8,976	—	—	P/L	15.00
	1839	8,976	—	—	P/L	15.00
	1840	8,976	—	—	P/L	15.00
	1841	7,920	—	—	P/L	15.00
	1842	8,896	—	—	P/L	15.00
	1843	7,920	—	—	P/L	15.00
	1844	7,920	—	—	P/L	15.00
	1845	7,920	—	—	P/L	15.00
	1846	7,920	—	—	P/L	15.00
	1847	7,920	—	—	P/L	15.00
	1848	7,920	—	—	P/L	15.00
	1849	7,920	—	—	P/L	15.00
	1850	7,920	—	—	P/L	15.00
	1851	7,128	—	—	P/L	15.00
	1852	7,920	—	—	P/L	15.00
	1853	7,920	—	—	P/L	15.00
	1854	7,920	—	—	P/L	15.00
	1855	7,920	—	—	P/L	15.00
	1856	7,920	—	—	P/L	15.00
	1857	7,920	—	—	P/L	15.00
	1858	7,920	—	—	P/L	15.00
	1859	7,920	—	—	P/L	15.00
	1860	7,920	—	—	P/L	15.00
	1861	7,920	—	—	P/L	15.00
	1862	7,920	—	—	P/L	15.00
	1863	7,920	—	—	P/L	15.00
	1864	7,920	—	—	P/L	15.00
	1865	7,920	—	—	P/L	15.00
	1866	7,920	—	—	P/L	15.00
	1867	7,920	—	—	P/L	15.00
	1868	7,920	—	—	P/L	15.00
	1869	7,920	—	—	P/L	15.00
	1870	9,002	—	—	P/L	15.00
	1871	9,286	—	—	P/L	15.00
	1872	8,956	—	—	P/L	15.00
	1873	7,932	—	—	P/L	15.00
	1874	8,741	—	—	P/L	15.00
	1875	8,459	—	—	P/L	15.00
	1876	.010	—	—	P/L	15.00
	1877	8,936	—	—	P/L	15.00
	1878	9,903	—	—	P/L	15.00
	1879	.011	—	—	P/L	15.00
	1880	.011	—	—	P/L	15.00
	1881	9,017	—	—	P/L	15.00
	1882	.011	—	—	P/L	15.00
	1883	.012	—	—	P/L	15.00
	1884	.014	—	—	P/L	15.00
	1885	.012	—	—	P/L	15.00
	1886	.016	—	—	P/L	15.00
	1887	.018	—	—	P/L	20.00

COPPER

KM#	Date	Mintage	Fine	VF	XF	Unc
739	1841 REG:	.914	9.00	25.00	90.00	285.00
	1841	—	—	—	Proof	850.00
	1841 w/o colon after REG					
		Inc. Ab.	3.50	10.00	40.00	145.00
	1843 REG:	.484	20.00	80.00	250.00	650.00
	1843 w/o colon after REG					
		Inc. Ab.	25.00	90.00	300.00	700.00
	1844	.215	3.25	8.50	40.00	145.00
	1844	—	—	—	Proof	—
	1845	.323	5.00	15.00	65.00	195.00
	1846 near colon					
		.484	3.50	12.50	50.00	165.00
	1846 far colon					
		Inc. Ab.	3.00	10.00	45.00	145.00
	1847 near colon					
		.430	4.00	10.00	45.00	160.00
	1847 far colon					
		Inc. Ab.	3.50	10.00	45.00	165.00
	1848/6	.161	10.00	25.00	80.00	250.00
	1848/7	Inc. Ab.	5.00	10.00	35.00	145.00
	1848	Inc. Ab.	5.00	10.00	35.00	145.00
	1849	.269	50.00	135.00	450.00	900.00
	1851 far colon					
		.269	4.00	10.00	45.00	165.00
739	1851 near colon					
		Inc. Ab.	4.50	12.50	50.00	175.00
	1853 ornamental trident					
		1.021	3.00	10.00	30.00	125.00
	1853	—	—	—	Proof	500.00
	1853 plain trident					
		Inc. Ab.	3.00	10.00	30.00	125.00
	1854/3	6.559	20.00	60.00	120.00	240.00
	1854 ornamental trident					
		Inc. Ab.	2.50	6.00	25.00	100.00
	1854 plain trident					
		Inc. Ab.	2.50	6.00	25.00	100.00
	1855 ornamental trident					
		5.274	2.50	6.00	25.00	100.00
	1855 plain trident					
		Inc. Ab.	2.50	6.00	25.00	100.00
	1856 ornamental trident					
		1.212	25.00	60.00	175.00	450.00
	1856	—	—	—	Proof	1000.
	1856 plain trident					
		Inc. Ab.	30.00	75.00	225.00	550.00
	1857 large date					
		.753	2.75	6.50	30.00	125.00
	1857 small date					
		Inc. Ab.	2.75	6.50	30.00	125.00
	1858/3	Inc. Ab.	8.00	22.00	60.00	175.00
	1858/6	Inc. Ab.	12.00	30.00	100.00	300.00
	1858/7	Inc. Ab.	2.50	5.50	25.00	100.00
	1858 large date					
		Inc. Ab.	2.50	5.50	25.00	100.00
	1858 small date					
		Inc. Ab.	3.50	8.00	27.50	120.00
	1859/8	1.075	10.00	22.50	55.00	160.00
	1859	Inc. Ab.	4.00	10.00	45.00	150.00
	1859	—	—	—	Proof	—
	1860/59	.032	125.00	350.00	1000.	1500.

NOTE: 1853-1857 occur w/plain and ornamental trident.

BRONZED COPPER

KM#	Date	Mintage	Fine	VF	XF	Unc
739a	1839	*300 pcs.	—	—	Proof	500.00
	1841	—	—	—	Proof	1000.
	1853					
		*10-15 pcs.	—	—	Proof	700.00

SILVER (OMS)

KM#	Date	Mintage	Fine	VF	XF	Unc
739b	1841	—	—	—	Proof	—

BRONZE
Beaded border.

KM#	Date	Mintage	Fine	VF	XF	Unc
749.1	1860 raised lines on shield					
		5.053	5.00	10.00	45.00	100.00
	1860 raised lines on shield					
		—	—	—	Proof	400.00
	1860 raised lines on shield, extra thick flan					
		—	—	—	Proof	900.00
	1860 incuse lines on shield					
		Inc. Ab.	3.00	7.00	35.00	90.00
	1860 incuse lines on shield					
		—	—	—	Proof	800.00

Toothed border.

KM#	Date	Mintage	Fine	VF	XF	Unc
749.2	1860 beaded border/toothed border					
		Inc. Ab.	55.00	145.00	630.00	2700.
	1860 toothed border/beaded border					
		Inc. Ab.	50.00	120.00	550.00	—
	1860 L.C.W. below foot, L.C.WYON on shoulder					
		Inc. Ab.	15.00	45.00	100.00	250.00
	1860 L.C.W. below shield, L.C.WYON below					
	shoulder	I.A.	3.00	7.50	30.00	75.00
	1860 L.C.WYON on shoulder, L.C.W. below shield					
		Inc. Ab.	3.00	7.50	30.00	100.00
	1860 L.C.WYON on shoulder, L.C.W. below					
	shield	—	—	—	Proof	400.00
	1860 w/o obv. sign., 15 leaves					
		Inc. Ab.	4.50	10.00	45.00	100.00
	1860 w/o obv. sign., 16 leaves					
		Inc. Ab.	8.00	20.00	65.00	175.00
	1861 L.C.WYON on trunc.; L.C.W. below shield					
		36.449	2.00	5.00	25.00	75.00
	1861 L.C.WYON on trunc., w/o sign. on rev.					
		Inc. Ab.	3.00	12.00	30.00	80.00
	1861 L.C.WYON below trunc. L.C.W. below shield					
		Inc. Ab.	3.00	10.00	30.00	75.00
	1861 L.C.WYON below trunc., w/o sign. on rev.					
		Inc. Ab.	20.00	45.00	120.00	350.00
	1861 w/o obv. sign., 15 lvs. L.C.W. below shield					
		Inc. Ab.	4.00	12.00	30.00	75.00
	1861 w/o obv. sign., 15 leaves w/o rev. sign.					
		Inc. Ab.	50.00	150.00	300.00	1000.
	1861 w/o obv. sign., 16 lvs. L.C.W. below shield					
		Inc. Ab.	3.00	5.00	27.50	75.00
	1861 w/o obv. sign., 16 lvs. L.C.W. below shield					
		—	—	—	Proof	425.00
	1861/81 w/o obv. sign., 16 lvs. L.C.W. below					
	shield	Inc. Ab.	50.00	150.00	300.00	1000.
	1861 w/o obv. sign., 16 leaves, w/o rev. sign.					
		Inc. Ab.	2.50	8.00	20.00	75.00
	1861 w/o obv. sign., 16 leaves, w/o rev. sign.					
749.2		—	—	—	Proof	375.00
	1862/1662					
		50.534	22.50	75.00	175.00	600.00
	1862	—	—	—	Proof	500.00
	1862 L.C.WYON on shoulder w/o rev. sign.					
		Inc. Ab.	300.00	750.00	1750.	4000.
	1862 w/o sign. on obv.					
		Inc. Ab.	1.50	4.50	18.00	60.00
	1862 date numerals small, from 1/2 Penny Die					
		Inc. Ab.	12.00	30.00	75.00	175.00
	1863	28.063	1.50	4.50	18.00	55.00
	1863	—	—	—	Proof	425.00
	1863 w/small die number 2, 3, or 4 below date					
		Inc. Ab.	100.00	180.00	450.00	1200.
	1863 w/small die number 5 below date					
		Inc. Ab.	—	—	Rare	—
	1864 plain 4 in date					
		3.441	15.00	40.00	170.00	540.00
	1864 crosslet 4 in date					
		Inc. Ab.	20.00	65.00	200.00	625.00
	1865/3	8.602	30.00	90.00	250.00	775.00
	1865	Inc. Ab.	3.50	12.50	35.00	80.00
	1866	9.999	2.50	8.50	27.00	70.00
	1867	5.484	3.50	10.00	37.50	90.00
	1867	—	—	—	Proof	700.00
	1868	1.183	10.00	30.00	120.00	355.00
	1868	—	—	—	Proof	500.00
	1869	2.580	50.00	200.00	500.00	1350.
	1870	5.695	5.00	25.00	120.00	355.00
	1871	1.290	25.00	75.00	250.00	700.00
	1872	8.495	2.75	9.00	25.00	90.00
	1872 rev. upside down					
		Unique	—	—	Proof	—
	1873	8.494	2.75	9.00	25.00	90.00
	1874	5.622	3.00	10.00	25.00	100.00
	1874 16 leaves, small date					
		Inc. Ab.	7.50	17.50	37.50	110.00
	1874H	6.666	3.50	11.00	30.00	100.00
	1874H 16 leaves, large date					
		Inc. Ab.	3.00	7.50	35.00	100.00

COPPER, heavy planchet (OMS)

KM#	Date	Mintage	Fine	VF	XF	Unc
749.2a	1860 toothed border, L.C.W. on truncation					
		—	—	—	Proof	300.00
	1861 L.C.WYON below truncation, L.C.W. below					
	shield	—	—	—	Proof	375.00

COPPER-NICKEL (OMS)

KM#	Date	Mintage	Fine	VF	XF	Unc
749.2b	1868	—	—	—	Proof	600.00
	1875	—	—	—	Proof	1600.
	1877	—	—	—	Proof	1750.

SILVER (OMS)

KM#	Date	Mintage	Fine	VF	XF	Unc
749.2c	1860	—	—	—	Proof	3000.
	1861	—	—	—	Proof	3000.

GOLD (OMS)

KM#	Date	Mintage	Fine	VF	XF	Unc
749.2d	1860	Unique	—	—	Proof	—
	1861	Unique	—	—	Proof	—

BRONZE
Obv: Mature bust.

KM#	Date	Mintage	Fine	VF	XF	Unc
755	1874 17 leaves, thin ribbons					
		Inc. Ab.	3.00	10.00	30.00	100.00
	1874 17 leaves, thin ribbons, small date					
		Inc. Ab.	3.00	10.00	30.00	100.00
	1874 17 leaves, thick ribbons					
		Inc. Ab.	7.50	30.00	100.00	300.00
	1874 17 leaves, thick ribbons, small date					
		Inc. Ab.	3.00	10.00	30.00	100.00
	1874H 17 leaves, thin ribbons					
		Inc. Ab.	4.00	12.00	30.00	75.00
	1874H 17 leaves, thin ribbons, small date					
		Inc. Ab.	4.00	12.00	30.00	75.00
	1874H 17 leaves, thin ribbons, small date					
		—	—	—	Proof	300.00
	1874H 17 leaves, thin ribbons, large date					
		Inc. Ab.	15.00	50.00	250.00	700.00
	1875	10.691	3.00	9.00	22.50	65.00
	1875 small date					
		Inc. Ab.	3.00	9.00	22.50	65.00
	1875 large date					
		Inc. Ab.	3.00	9.00	22.50	65.00
	1875 large date, heavy planchet					
		Unique	—	—	Proof	—
	1875H small date					
		.753	150.00	300.00	900.00	2500.
	1875H large date					
		Inc. Ab.	25.00	90.00	250.00	650.00
	1875H large date					
		—	—	—	Proof	800.00
	1876H large date					
		11.075	3.00	8.50	17.50	50.00
	1876H large date					
		Inc. Ab.	—	—	Proof	500.00
	1876H small date					
		Inc. Ab.	3.00	8.50	17.50	50.00
	1877 small date					
		9.625	100.00	300.00	1000.	2000.
	1877 large date					

GREAT BRITAIN 756

KM#	Date	Mintage	Fine	VF	XF	Unc
755		Inc. Ab.	3.25	9.50	20.00	55.00
	1877 large date					
	1878	2.764	4.00	12.00	30.00	65.00
	1878	—	—	—	Proof	500.00
	1879 large date; raised lines on wreath					
		7.666	15.00	40.00	125.00	250.00
	1879 large date; incuse lines in wreath					
		Inc. Ab.	2.50	8.50	18.00	55.00
	1879 large date; incuse lines in wreath					
		Unique	—	—	Proof	—
	1879 sm.dt. I.A.	7.50	25.00	100.00	300.00
	1880	3.001	5.00	13.50	35.00	100.00
	1880	—	—	—	Proof	500.00
	1880 rock to left of lighthouse					
		Inc. Ab.	5.00	13.50	35.00	100.00
	1880 obv. 15 leaves as 1881					
		—	—	—	Proof	Rare
	1881	2.302	4.00	12.00	30.00	70.00
	1881	—	—	—	Proof	150.00
	1881 obv. as 1880; shield heraldically					
	colored	I.A.	100.00	300.00	750.00	2250.
	1881 obv. as 1880; shield heraldically					
	colored	I.A.	—	—	Proof	—
	1881 obv. and rev. as 1880					
		Inc. Ab.	6.00	18.00	50.00	100.00
	1881 shield heraldically colored					
		—	—	—	Proof	1100.
	1881H obv: 15 leaves in wreath					
		3.763	2.50	7.00	17.50	55.00
	1881H obv: 15 leaves in wreath					
		—	—	—	Proof	600.00
	1882H convex shield					
		7.526	2.75	10.00	50.00	100.00
	1882H flat shield					
		Inc. Ab.	2.75	8.00	20.00	55.00
	1882H	—	—	—	Proof	1000.
	1882	Inc. Ab.	75.00	225.00	725.00	1750.
	1883	6.237	2.00	6.50	17.50	70.00
	1883	—	—	—	Proof	450.00
	1884	11.703	1.50	5.00	15.00	55.00
	1884	—	—	—	Proof	500.00
	1885	7.146	1.50	5.00	15.00	55.00
	1885	—	—	—	Proof	500.00
	1886	6.088	1.25	4.00	12.50	50.00
	1886	—	—	—	Proof	700.00
	1887	5.315	1.25	4.00	15.00	50.00
	1888	5.125	1.25	4.00	15.00	50.00
	1889	12.560	1.25	4.50	15.00	55.00
	1889 14 leaves in wreath					
		Inc. Ab.	1.25	4.50	15.00	55.00
	1889 14 leaves in wreath					
		—	—	—	Proof	500.00
	1890	15.331	1.00	3.00	12.00	40.00
	1890	—	—	—	Proof	450.00
	1891	17.886	1.00	3.00	12.00	40.00
	1891	—	—	—	Proof	450.00
	1892	10.502	1.00	3.00	12.00	45.00
	1892	—	—	—	Proof	450.00
	1893	8.162	1.00	3.00	12.00	45.00
	1893	—	—	—	Proof	500.00
	1894	3.883	3.00	8.00	20.00	65.00

.4713 g, .925 SILVER, .0140 oz ASW

KM#	Date	Mintage	Fine	VF	XF	Unc
770	1888	.014	—	—	P/L	15.00
	1889	.014	—	—	P/L	15.00
	1890	.013	—	—	P/L	15.00
	1891	.022	—	—	P/L	15.00
	1892	.016	—	—	P/L	15.00

775	1893	.022	—	—	P/L	12.50
	1894	.018	—	—	P/L	12.50
	1895	.017	—	—	P/L	12.50
	1896	.017	—	—	P/L	12.50
	1897	.016	—	—	P/L	12.50
	1898	.017	—	—	P/L	12.50
	1899	.017	—	—	P/L	12.50
	1900	.017	—	—	P/L	12.50
	1901	.018	—	—	P/L	12.50

BRONZE

790	1895 P 2mm. from trident					
		5.396	15.00	40.00	120.00	275.00
	1895 P 2mm. from trident					
		Inc. Ab.	—	—	Proof	450.00
	1895 P 1mm. from trident					
		Inc. Ab.	.50	1.75	7.50	25.00
	1895 P 1mm. from trident					
		—	—	—	Proof	350.00

KM#	Date	Mintage	Fine	VF	XF	Unc
790	1896	24.147	.40	1.25	4.50	20.00
	1896	—	—	—	Proof	325.00
	1897 normal sea level					
		20.757	.35	1.00	3.75	14.00
	1897 normal sea level					
		—	—	—	Proof	375.00
	1897 high sea level					
		Inc. Ab.	15.00	40.00	120.00	275.00
	1898	14.297	1.00	3.00	10.00	25.00
	1899	26.441	.40	1.50	5.25	15.00
	1900	31.778	.35	1.00	3.75	14.00
	1901	22.206	.30	.75	2.00	10.00
	1901	—	—	—	Proof	250.00

794	1902 low sea level					
		26.977	4.00	9.00	20.00	65.00
	1902 high sea level					
		Inc. Ab.	.50	2.00	4.50	15.00
	1903	21.415	.65	2.50	6.50	22.50
	1904	12.913	1.00	3.00	10.00	35.00
	1905	17.784	.70	2.50	9.00	30.00
	1906	37.990	.60	2.00	6.00	25.00
	1907	47.322	.60	2.00	7.00	25.00
	1908	31.506	.75	2.50	7.50	35.00
	1908	—	—	—	Proof	Rare
	1909	19.617	.65	2.25	7.00	35.00
	1910	29.549	.50	1.75	5.00	25.00

.4713 g, .925 SILVER, .0140 oz ASW

795	1902	.021	—	—	P/L	12.50
	1903	.017	—	—	P/L	12.50
	1904	.019	—	—	P/L	12.50
	1905	.018	—	—	P/L	12.50
	1906	.019	—	—	P/L	12.50
	1907	.018	—	—	P/L	12.50
	1908	.018	—	—	P/L	12.50
	1909	2.948	—	—	P/L	15.00
	1910	3.392	—	—	P/L	20.00

BRONZE

810	1911	23.079	.35	1.00	4.50	18.00
	1912	48.306	.35	1.00	4.50	18.00
	1912H	16.800	1.00	5.00	25.00	85.00
	1913	65.497	.40	1.25	8.00	35.00
	1914	50.821	.35	1.00	4.50	20.00
	1915	47.311	.35	1.00	5.50	22.00
	1916	86.411	.35	1.00	4.00	20.00
	1917	107.905	.35	1.00	4.00	20.00
	1918	84.227	.35	1.00	4.00	20.00
	1918H	2.573	2.00	20.00	100.00	200.00
	1918KN	Inc. Ab.	3.25	30.00	125.00	300.00
	1919	113.761	.35	1.00	4.00	22.00
	1919H	4.526	1.25	6.50	60.00	200.00
	1919KN	Inc. Ab.	5.00	35.00	150.00	425.00
	1920	124.693	.35	1.00	4.00	16.50
	1921	129.718	.30	.75	3.00	12.00
	1922	16.347	.75	2.50	10.00	25.00
	1926	4.499	1.00	3.50	15.00	35.00
	1926	—	—	—	Proof	175.00

.4713 g, .925 SILVER, .0140 oz ASW

811	1911	1.913	—	—	P/L	15.00
	1912	1.616	—	—	P/L	15.00
	1913	1.590	—	—	P/L	15.00
	1914	1.818	—	—	P/L	15.00
	1915	2.072	—	—	P/L	15.00
	1916	1.647	—	—	P/L	15.00
	1917	1.820	—	—	P/L	15.00
	1918	1.911	—	—	P/L	15.00
	1919	1.699	—	—	P/L	15.00
	1920	1.715	—	—	P/L	15.00

.4713 g, .500 SILVER, .0076 oz ASW

| 811a | 1921 | 1.847 | — | — | P/L | 15.00 |
| | 1922 | 1.758 | — | — | P/L | 15.00 |

KM#	Date	Mintage	Fine	VF	XF	Unc
811a	1923	1.840	—	—	P/L	15.00
	1924	1.619	—	—	P/L	15.00
	1925	1.890	—	—	P/L	15.00
	1926	2.180	—	—	P/L	15.00
	1927	1.647	—	—	P/L	15.00

BRONZE
Obv: Modified head.

826	1926	Inc. Ab.	10.00	35.00	250.00	850.00
	1926	—	—	—	Proof	—
	1927	60.990	.35	1.00	4.50	10.00
	1927	—	—	—	Proof	175.00

Obv: Smaller head.

838	1928	50.178	.25	—	.50	2.25	7.00
	1928	—	—	—	Proof	165.00
	1929	49.133	.25	—	.50	2.25	8.00
	1929	—	—	—	Proof	165.00
	1930	29.098	.35	1.00	4.50	14.00
	1930	—	—	—	Proof	165.00
	1931	19.843	.35	1.00	4.50	14.00
	1931	—	—	—	Proof	165.00
	1932	8.278	1.50	3.50	15.00	40.00
	1932	—	—	—	Proof	165.00
	1933	—	—	—	Rare	—
	1934	13.966	.50	2.00	9.00	27.50
	1934	—	—	—	Proof	165.00
	1935	56.070	.25	.50	1.75	4.50
	1935	—	—	—	Proof	165.00
	1936	154.296	.20	.35	1.00	3.50
	1936	—	—	—	Proof	165.00

.4713 g, .500 SILVER, .0076 oz ASW
Obv: Modified effigy.

839	1928	1.846	—	—	P/L	15.00
	1929	1.837	—	—	P/L	15.00
	1930	1.724	—	—	P/L	15.00
	1931	1.759	—	—	P/L	15.00
	1932	1.835	—	—	P/L	15.00
	1933	1.872	—	—	P/L	15.00
	1934	1.919	—	—	P/L	15.00
	1935	1.975	—	—	P/L	15.00
	1936	1.329	—	—	P/L	15.00

BRONZE

845	1937	88.896	.20	—	.35	1.25	2.25
	1937	.026	—	—	Proof	9.00
	1938	121.560	.20	.35	1.25	2.25
	1938	—	—	—	Proof	—
	1939	55.560	.20	.35	1.25	3.50
	1939	—	—	—	Proof	—
	1940	42.284	.25	.50	2.25	8.00
	1940	—	—	—	Proof	—
	1944	42.600	.25	.50	2.25	7.00
	1944	—	—	—	Proof	—
	1945	79.531	.20	.35	1.50	5.00
	1945	—	—	—	Proof	—
	1946	66.856	.15	.25	.75	3.00
	1946	—	—	—	Proof	—
	1947	52.220	.15	.25	.75	2.25
	1947	—	—	Proof	Unique	
	1948	63.961	.15	.25	.75	3.00
	1948	—	—	—	Proof	—

.4713 g, .500 SILVER, .0076 oz ASW

| 846 | 1937 | 1.329 | — | — | P/L | 15.00 |

KM#	Date	Mintage	Fine	VF	XF	Unc
846	1938	1,275	—	—	P/L	15.00
	1939	1,253	—	—	P/L	15.00
	1940	1,375	—	—	P/L	15.00
	1941	1,255	—	—	P/L	15.00
	1942	1,243	—	—	P/L	15.00
	1943	1,347	—	—	P/L	15.00
	1944	1,259	—	—	P/L	15.00
	1945	1,367	—	—	P/L	15.00
	1946	1,479	—	—	P/L	15.00

.4713 g, .925 SILVER, .0140 oz ASW

KM#	Date	Mintage	Fine	VF	XF	Unc
846a	1947	1,387	—	—	P/L	15.00
	1948	1,397	—	—	P/L	15.00

BRONZE
Obv. leg: W/o IND IMP.

KM#	Date	Mintage	Fine	VF	XF	Unc
869	1949	14.324	.15	.25	.75	3.00
	1949	—	—	—	Proof	—
	1950	.240	2.50	8.00	15.00	30.00
	1950	.018	—	—	Proof	30.00
	1951	.120	3.50	9.00	15.00	30.00
	1951	.020	—	—	Proof	30.00

.4713 g, .925 SILVER, .0140 oz ASW

KM#	Date	Mintage	Fine	VF	XF	Unc
870	1949	1,407	—	—	P/L	15.00
	1950	1,527	—	—	P/L	15.00
	1951	1,480	—	—	P/L	15.00
	1952	1,024	—	—	P/L	15.00

BRONZE

KM#	Date	Mintage	Fine	VF	XF	Unc
883	1953	1.308	.75	1.50	2.50	4.50
	1953	.040	—	—	Proof	9.00

.4713 g, .925 SILVER, .0140 oz ASW

KM#	Date	Mintage	Fine	VF	XF	Unc
884	1953	1,050	—	—	P/L	95.00

BRONZE
Obv. leg: W/o BRITT OMN.

KM#	Date	Mintage	Fine	VF	XF	Unc
897	1954	Unique	—	—	—	—
	1961	48.313	—	.10	.15	.80
	1961	—	—	—	Proof	—
	1962	143.309	—	—	.10	.15
	1962	—	—	—	Proof	—
	1963	125.236	—	—	.10	.15
	1963	—	—	—	Proof	—
	1964	153.294	—	—	—	.10
	1964	—	—	—	Proof	—
	1965	121.310	—	—	—	.10
	1966	165.739	—	—	—	.10
	1967	654.564	—	—	—	.10
	1970	.731	—	—	Proof	2.50

.4713 g, .925 SILVER, .0140 oz ASW

KM#	Date	Mintage	Fine	VF	XF	Unc
898	1954	1,088	—	—	P/L	15.00
	1955	1,036	—	—	P/L	15.00
	1956	1,100	—	—	P/L	15.00
	1957	1,168	—	—	P/L	15.00
	1958	1,112	—	—	P/L	15.00
	1959	1,118	—	—	P/L	15.00
	1960	1,124	—	—	P/L	15.00
	1961	1,200	—	—	P/L	15.00
	1962	1,127	—	—	P/L	15.00
	1963	1,133	—	—	P/L	15.00
	1964	1,215	—	—	P/L	15.00
	1965	1,143	—	—	P/L	15.00
	1966	1,206	—	—	P/L	15.00
	1967	1,068	—	—	P/L	15.00

KM#	Date	Mintage	Fine	VF	XF	Unc
898	1968	964 pcs.	—	—	P/L	15.00
	1969	1,002	—	—	P/L	15.00
	1970	980 pcs.	—	—	P/L	15.00
	1971	1,108	—	—	P/L	15.00
	1972	1,026	—	—	P/L	15.00
	1973	1,004	—	—	P/L	15.00
	1974	1,138	—	—	P/L	15.00
	1975	1,050	—	—	P/L	15.00
	1976	1,158	—	—	P/L	15.00
	1977	1,240	—	—	P/L	17.50
	1978	1,178	—	—	P/L	17.50
	1979	1,188	—	—	P/L	17.50
	1980	1,198	—	—	P/L	17.50
	1981	1,288	—	—	P/L	17.50
	1982	1,218	—	—	P/L	17.50
	1983	1,228	—	—	P/L	17.50
	1984	1,354	—	—	P/L	17.50
	1985	1,248	—	—	P/L	17.50
	1986	—	—	—	P/L	17.50
	1987	—	—	—	P/L	17.50
	1988	—	—	—	P/L	17.50
	1989	—	—	—	P/L	17.50

1-1/2 PENCE

.7069 g, .925 SILVER, .0210 oz ASW

KM#	Date	Mintage	Fine	VF	XF	Unc
719	1834	.800	2.75	6.25	22.00	60.00
	1835/4	.634	12.00	30.00	45.00	150.00
	1835	Inc. Ab.	2.75	6.25	22.00	60.00
	1836	.158	2.75	6.25	22.00	60.00
	1837	.031	12.00	25.00	60.00	175.00

KM#	Date	Mintage	Fine	VF	XF	Unc
728	1838	.539	2.75	6.00	15.00	40.00
	1839	.760	2.50	6.00	17.50	40.00
	1840	.095	4.50	15.00	30.00	70.00
	1841	.158	3.00	7.00	20.00	40.00
	1842	1.869	3.00	7.00	20.00	40.00
	1843/34	.475	8.00	20.00	35.00	90.00
	1843	Inc. Ab.	2.00	5.00	15.00	35.00
	1860	.160	3.50	10.00	25.00	50.00
	1862	.256	3.50	10.00	25.00	50.00
	1870	—	—	—	Proof	900.00

*NOTE: Although the design of the above series is of the homeland type, the issues were struck for Ceylon and Jamaica.

2 PENCE

.9426 g, .925 SILVER, .0280 oz ASW

KM#	Date	Mintage	Fine	VF	XF	Unc
669	1817	—	6.00	11.00	20.00	45.00
	1817	2,376	—	—	P/L	30.00
	1818	—	6.00	11.00	20.00	45.00
	1818	2,376	—	—	P/L	30.00
	1820	—	6.00	11.00	20.00	45.00
	1820	1,584	—	—	P/L	30.00

KM#	Date	Mintage	Fine	VF	XF	Unc
684	1822	5,940	—	—	P/L	30.00
	1823	3,960	—	—	P/L	35.00
	1824	3,168	—	—	P/L	40.00
	1825	3,960	—	—	P/L	35.00
	1826	3,960	—	—	P/L	35.00
	1827	3,960	—	—	P/L	35.00
	1828	3,960	—	—	P/L	35.00
	1829	3,960	—	—	P/L	35.00
	1830	3,960	—	—	P/L	35.00

KM#	Date	Mintage	Fine	VF	XF	Unc
709	1831	4,752	—	—	P/L	22.50
	1832	3,564	—	—	P/L	22.50
	1833	3,564	—	—	P/L	22.50
	1834	3,564	—	—	P/L	22.50
	1835	3,564	—	—	P/L	22.50
	1836	3,564	—	—	P/L	22.50
	1837	3,564	—	—	P/L	22.50

KM#	Date	Mintage	Fine	VF	XF	Unc
729	1838	*1.045	2.00	4.00	8.00	15.00
	1838	4,488	—	—	P/L	15.00

KM#	Date	Mintage	Fine	VF	XF	Unc
729	1839	4,488	—	—	P/L	15.00
	1840	4,488	—	—	P/L	15.00
	1841	3,960	—	—	P/L	15.00
	1842	4,488	—	—	P/L	15.00
	1843	*.903	2.00	4.00	8.00	15.00
	1843	4,752	—	—	P/L	15.00
	1844	4,752	—	—	P/L	15.00
	1845	4,752	—	—	P/L	15.00
	1846	4,752	—	—	P/L	15.00
	1847	4,752	—	—	P/L	15.00
	1848	*.261	2.00	4.00	8.00	15.00
	1848	4,752	—	—	P/L	15.00
	1849	4,752	—	—	P/L	15.00
	1850	4,752	—	—	P/L	15.00
	1851	4,752	—	—	P/L	15.00
	1852	4,752	—	—	P/L	15.00
	1853	4,752	—	—	P/L	15.00
	1854	4,752	—	—	P/L	15.00
	1855	4,752	—	—	P/L	15.00
	1856	4,752	—	—	P/L	15.00
	1857	4,752	—	—	P/L	15.00
	1858	4,752	—	—	P/L	15.00
	1859	4,752	—	—	P/L	15.00
	1860	4,752	—	—	P/L	15.00
	1861	4,752	—	—	P/L	15.00
	1862	4,752	—	—	P/L	15.00
	1863	4,752	—	—	P/L	15.00
	1864	4,752	—	—	P/L	15.00
	1865	4,752	—	—	P/L	15.00
	1866	4,752	—	—	P/L	15.00
	1867	4,752	—	—	P/L	15.00
	1868	4,752	—	—	P/L	15.00
	1869	4,752	—	—	P/L	15.00
	1870	5,347	—	—	P/L	15.00
	1871	4,753	—	—	P/L	15.00
	1872	4,719	—	—	P/L	15.00
	1873	4,756	—	—	P/L	15.00
	1874	5,578	—	—	P/L	15.00
	1875	5,745	—	—	P/L	15.00
	1876	6,655	—	—	P/L	15.00
	1877	7,189	—	—	P/L	15.00
	1878	6,709	—	—	P/L	15.00
	1879	6,925	—	—	P/L	15.00
	1880	6,247	—	—	P/L	15.00
	1881	6,001	—	—	P/L	15.00
	1882	7,264	—	—	P/L	15.00
	1883	7,232	—	—	P/L	15.00
	1884	6,042	—	—	P/L	15.00
	1885	5,958	—	—	P/L	15.00
	1886	9,167	—	—	P/L	15.00
	1887	8,296	—	—	P/L	20.00

*NOTE: Struck for use in British Guyana and the West Indies. Other dates included in Maundy sets.

KM#	Date	Mintage	Fine	VF	XF	Unc
771	1888	9,528	—	—	P/L	15.00
	1889	6,727	—	—	P/L	15.00
	1890	8,613	—	—	P/L	15.00
	1891	.010	—	—	P/L	15.00
	1892	.012	—	—	P/L	15.00

KM#	Date	Mintage	Fine	VF	XF	Unc
776	1893	.014	—	—	P/L	12.50
	1894	.012	—	—	P/L	12.50
	1895	.011	—	—	P/L	12.50
	1896	.011	—	—	P/L	12.50
	1897	.011	—	—	P/L	12.50
	1898	.012	—	—	P/L	12.50
	1899	.015	—	—	P/L	12.50
	1900	.011	—	—	P/L	12.50
	1901	.014	—	—	P/L	12.50

KM#	Date	Mintage	Fine	VF	XF	Unc
796	1902	.014	—	—	P/L	12.50
	1903	.013	—	—	P/L	12.50
	1904	.014	—	—	P/L	12.50
	1905	.011	—	—	P/L	12.50
	1906	.011	—	—	P/L	12.50
	1907	8,760	—	—	P/L	12.50
	1908	.015	—	—	P/L	12.50
	1909	2,695	—	—	P/L	15.00
	1910	2,998	—	—	P/L	20.00

KM#	Date	Mintage	Fine	VF	XF	Unc
812	1911	1,635	—	—	P/L	17.50
	1912	1,678	—	—	P/L	17.50
	1913	1,880	—	—	P/L	17.50
	1914	1,659	—	—	P/L	17.50
	1915	1,465	—	—	P/L	17.50
	1916	1,509	—	—	P/L	17.50
	1917	1,506	—	—	P/L	17.50
	1918	1,547	—	—	P/L	17.50
	1919	1,567	—	—	P/L	17.50
	1920	1,630	—	—	P/L	17.50

GREAT BRITAIN 757

GREAT BRITAIN 758

.9426 g, .500 SILVER, .0152 oz ASW

KM#	Date	Mintage	Fine	VF	XF	Unc
812a	1921	1,794	—	—	P/L	20.00
	1922	3,074	—	—	P/L	20.00
	1923	1,527	—	—	P/L	20.00
	1924	1,602	—	—	P/L	20.00
	1925	1,670	—	—	P/L	20.00
	1926	1,902	—	—	P/L	20.00
	1927	1,766	—	—	P/L	20.00

Obv: Modified effigy.

KM#	Date	Mintage	Fine	VF	XF	Unc
840	1928	1,706	—	—	P/L	17.50
	1929	1,862	—	—	P/L	17.50
	1930	1,901	—	—	P/L	17.50
	1931	1,897	—	—	P/L	17.50
	1932	1,960	—	—	P/L	17.50
	1933	2,066	—	—	P/L	17.50
	1934	1,927	—	—	P/L	17.50
	1935	1,928	—	—	P/L	17.50
	1936	1,365	—	—	P/L	20.00

KM#	Date	Mintage	Fine	VF	XF	Unc
847	1937	1,472	—	—	P/L	17.50
	1938	1,374	—	—	P/L	17.50
	1939	1,436	—	—	P/L	17.50
	1940	1,277	—	—	P/L	17.50
	1941	1,345	—	—	P/L	17.50
	1942	1,231	—	—	P/L	17.50
	1943	1,239	—	—	P/L	17.50
	1944	1,345	—	—	P/L	17.50
	1945	1,355	—	—	P/L	17.50
	1946	1,365	—	—	P/L	17.50

.9426 g, .925 SILVER, .0280 oz ASW

KM#	Date	Mintage	Fine	VF	XF	Unc
847a	1947	1,479	—	—	P/L	17.50
	1948	1,385	—	—	P/L	17.50

Obv. leg: W/o IND IMP.

KM#	Date	Mintage	Fine	VF	XF	Unc
871	1949	1,395	—	—	P/L	17.50
	1950	1,405	—	—	P/L	17.50
	1951	1,580	—	—	P/L	17.50
	1952	1,064	—	—	P/L	17.50
885	1953	1,025	—	—	P/L	85.00

Obv. leg: W/o BRITT OMN.

KM#	Date	Mintage	Fine	VF	XF	Unc
899	1954	1,020	—	—	P/L	17.50
	1955	1,082	—	—	P/L	17.50
	1956	1,088	—	—	P/L	17.50
	1957	1,094	—	—	P/L	17.50
	1958	1,164	—	—	P/L	17.50
	1959	1,106	—	—	P/L	17.50
	1960	1,112	—	—	P/L	17.50
	1961	1,118	—	—	P/L	17.50
	1962	1,197	—	—	P/L	17.50
	1963	1,131	—	—	P/L	17.50
	1964	1,137	—	—	P/L	17.50
	1965	1,221	—	—	P/L	17.50
	1966	1,206	—	—	P/L	17.50
	1967	986 pcs.	—	—	P/L	17.50
	1968	1,048	—	—	P/L	17.50
	1969	1,002	—	—	P/L	17.50
	1970	980 pcs.	—	—	P/L	17.50
	1971	1,018	—	—	P/L	17.50
	1972	1,026	—	—	P/L	17.50
	1973	1,004	—	—	P/L	17.50
	1974	1,042	—	—	P/L	19.00
	1975	1,148	—	—	P/L	19.00
	1976	1,158	—	—	P/L	19.00
	1977	1,138	—	—	P/L	20.00
	1978	1,282	—	—	P/L	20.00
	1979	1,188	—	—	P/L	20.00
	1980	1,198	—	—	P/L	20.00
	1981	1,178	—	—	P/L	20.00
	1982	1,330	—	—	P/L	20.00
	1983	1,228	—	—	P/L	20.00
	1984	1,238	—	—	P/L	20.00
	1985	1,366	—	—	P/L	20.00
	1986	—	—	—	P/L	20.00
	1987	—	—	—	P/L	20.00
	1988	—	—	—	P/L	20.00
	1989	—	—	—	P/L	20.00

3 PENCE

1.4138 g, .925 SILVER, .0420 oz ASW
Obv: George III bust right. Rev: Value.

KM#	Date	Mintage	Fine	VF	XF	Unc
670	1817	—	7.00	15.00	30.00	70.00
	1817	1,584	—	—	P/L	70.00
	1818	—	7.00	15.00	30.00	70.00
	1818	1,584	—	—	P/L	70.00
	1820	—	7.00	15.00	30.00	70.00
	1820	1,320	—	—	P/L	70.00

Obv: Small head.

KM#	Date	Mintage	Fine	VF	XF	Unc
685.1	1822	3,960	—	—	P/L	80.00
	1822	—	—	—	Proof	—

Obv: Large head.

KM#	Date	Mintage	Fine	VF	XF	Unc
685.2	1823	2,640	—	—	P/L	55.00
	1824	2,112	—	—	P/L	65.00
	1825	3,432	—	—	P/L	55.00
	1826	3,432	—	—	P/L	55.00
	1827	3,168	—	—	P/L	55.00
	1828	3,168	—	—	P/L	55.00
	1829	3,168	—	—	P/L	55.00
	1830	3,168	—	—	P/L	55.00

KM#	Date	Mintage	Fine	VF	XF	Unc
710	1831	3,960	—	—	P/L	80.00
	1832	2,904	—	—	P/L	70.00
	1833	2,904	—	—	P/L	70.00
	1834	.400	3.00	8.00	25.00	110.00
	1834	2,904	—	—	P/L	70.00
	1835	.491	3.00	8.00	25.00	110.00
	1835	2,904	—	—	P/L	70.00
	1836	.411	3.00	8.00	25.00	90.00
	1836	2,904	—	—	P/L	70.00
	1837	.430	4.00	10.00	30.00	118.00
	1837	2,904	—	—	P/L	70.00

KM#	Date	Mintage	Fine	VF	XF	Unc
730	1838	1.200	2.50	6.00	30.00	72.00
	1838	4,312	—	—	P/L	40.00
	1839	.570	6.00	12.00	45.00	110.00
	1839	4,356	—	—	P/L	40.00
	1840	.630	2.50	7.50	36.00	80.00
	1840	4,356	—	—	P/L	40.00
	1841	.440	3.00	7.50	36.00	80.00
	1841	2,904	—	—	P/L	45.00
	1842	—	4.00	10.00	40.00	80.00
	1842	4,356	—	—	P/L	45.00
	1843	2,030	2.50	7.50	30.00	65.00
	1843	4,488	—	—	P/L	45.00
	1844	1,050	2.50	9.00	45.00	90.00
	1844	4,488	—	—	P/L	45.00
	1845	1,319	2.50	5.00	20.00	50.00
	1845	4,488	—	—	P/L	45.00
	1846	.052	5.00	12.50	45.00	95.00
	1846	4,488	—	—	P/L	45.00
	1847	4,488	—	—	P/L	45.00
	1848	4,488	—	—	P/L	45.00
	1849	.131	7.50	17.50	50.00	100.00
	1849	4,488	—	—	P/L	45.00
	1850	.955	2.50	5.00	30.00	60.00
	1850	4,488	—	—	P/L	45.00
	1851	.484	2.50	5.00	30.00	60.00
	1851	4,488	—	—	P/L	45.00
	1852	4,488	—	—	P/L	45.00
	1853	.036	7.50	15.00	55.00	120.00
	1853	4,488	—	—	P/L	45.00
	1854	1,472	2.50	5.00	30.00	60.00
	1854	4,488	—	—	P/L	45.00
	1855	.388	3.00	8.00	32.00	65.00
	1855	4,488	—	—	P/L	45.00
	1856	1,018	2.50	4.50	25.00	50.00
	1856	4,488	—	—	P/L	45.00
	1857	1,767	2.75	7.50	30.00	60.00
	1857	4,488	—	—	P/L	45.00
	1858	1,446	2.50	5.00	25.00	55.00
	1858	4,488	—	—	P/L	45.00
	1859	3,584	2.50	5.00	20.00	40.00
	1859	4,488	—	—	P/L	45.00
	1860	3,410	2.50	5.00	20.00	40.00
	1860	4,488	—	—	P/L	45.00
	1861	3,299	2.50	5.00	20.00	40.00
	1861	4,488	—	—	P/L	45.00
	1862	1,161	2.50	5.00	25.00	50.00
	1862	4,488	—	—	P/L	45.00
	1863	.954	4.00	9.00	40.00	75.00
	1863	4,488	—	—	P/L	45.00
	1864	1,335	2.50	5.00	30.00	60.00
	1864	4,488	—	—	P/L	45.00
	1865	1,747	2.50	9.00	40.00	70.00
	1865	4,488	—	—	P/L	45.00
	1866	1,905	2.50	5.00	20.00	65.00
	1866	4,488	—	—	P/L	45.00
	1867	.717	2.50	5.00	40.00	75.00
	1867	4,488	—	—	P/L	45.00
	1868	1,462	2.50	5.00	30.00	65.00

KM#	Date	Mintage	Fine	VF	XF	Unc
730	1868	4,488	—	—	P/L	45.00
	1868 (error) RRITANIAR					
	Inc. Ab.	22.50	55.00	225.00	450.00
	1869	—	40.00	100.00	225.00	450.00
	1869	4,488	—	—	P/L	45.00
	1870	1.288	1.75	4.00	25.00	50.00
	1870	4,488	—	—	P/L	45.00
	1871	1.004	2.00	4.00	25.00	50.00
	1871	4,488	—	—	P/L	45.00
	1872	1.298	1.75	4.00	22.50	45.00
	1872	4,488	—	—	P/L	45.00
	1873	4.060	1.60	3.25	20.00	40.00
	1873	4,488	—	—	P/L	45.00
	1874	4.432	1.60	3.25	20.00	40.00
	1874	4,488	—	—	P/L	45.00
	1875	3.311	1.60	3.25	18.00	35.00
	1875	4,488	—	—	P/L	45.00
	1876	1.839	1.60	3.25	18.00	35.00
	1876	4,488	—	—	P/L	45.00
	1877	2.627	1.60	3.25	18.00	35.00
	1877	4,488	—	—	P/L	45.00
	1878	2.424	1.60	3.25	18.00	35.00
	1878	4,488	—	—	P/L	45.00
	1879	3.145	1.60	3.25	18.00	35.00
	1879	4,488	—	—	P/L	45.00
	1879	—	—	—	Proof	150.00
	1880	1.615	1.50	3.00	18.00	35.00
	1880	4,488	—	—	P/L	45.00
	1881	3.253	1.40	2.75	15.00	30.00
	1881	4,488	—	—	P/L	45.00
	1882	.447	3.00	6.00	22.50	50.00
	1882	4,488	—	—	P/L	45.00
	1883	4.374	1.45	2.75	15.00	30.00
	1883	4,488	—	—	P/L	45.00
	1884	3.327	1.45	2.75	15.00	30.00
	1884	4,488	—	—	P/L	45.00
	1885	5.188	1.45	2.75	15.00	30.00
	1885	4,488	—	—	P/L	45.00
	1886	6.157	1.45	2.75	15.00	30.00
	1886	4,488	—	—	P/L	45.00
	1887	2.785	3.50	8.50	25.00	55.00
	1887	4,488	—	—	P/L	45.00
	1887	—	—	—	Proof	100.00

KM#	Date	Mintage	Fine	VF	XF	Unc
758	1887	Inc. Ab.	1.25	2.25	4.50	12.00
	1887	Inc. Ab.	—	—	Proof	70.00
	1888	.523	3.00	6.00	15.00	30.00
	1888	4,488	—	—	P/L	40.00
	1889	4.591	1.50	2.75	12.50	25.00
	1889	4,488	—	—	P/L	40.00
	1890	4.470	1.50	2.75	12.50	25.00
	1890	4,488	—	—	P/L	40.00
	1891	6.328	1.50	2.75	12.50	25.00
	1891	4,488	—	—	P/L	40.00
	1892	2.583	3.00	6.00	15.00	27.50
	1892	4,488	—	—	P/L	40.00
	1893 open 3					
		3.076	20.00	40.00	120.00	225.00
	1893 closed 3					
	Inc. Ab.	18.00	35.00	95.00	200.00

KM#	Date	Mintage	Fine	VF	XF	Unc
777	1893	Inc. Ab.	1.00	2.00	5.00	20.00
	1893	8,976	—	—	P/L	30.00
	1893	1,312	—	—	Proof	75.00
	1894	1.618	1.00	2.00	8.00	25.00
	1894	8,976	—	—	P/L	30.00
	1895	4.798	.75	2.00	8.00	25.00
	1895	8,976	—	—	P/L	30.00
	1896	4.607	.75	1.75	7.00	20.00
	1896	8,976	—	—	P/L	30.00
	1897	4.350	.75	1.75	5.00	20.00
	1897	8,976	—	—	P/L	30.00
	1898	4.576	.75	1.75	5.00	20.00
	1898	8,976	—	—	P/L	30.00
	1899	6.253	.75	1.75	5.00	20.00
	1899	8,976	—	—	P/L	30.00
	1900	10.661	.75	1.50	4.50	20.00
	1900	8,976	—	—	P/L	30.00
	1901	6.100	.75	1.50	4.50	20.00
	1901	8,976	—	—	P/L	30.00

KM#	Date	Mintage	Fine	VF	XF	Unc
797.1	1902	8.287	1.00	2.00	6.00	15.00
	1902	8,976	—	—	P/L	22.50
	1902	.015	—	—	Proof	20.00
	1903	5.235	1.00	3.00	10.00	30.00
	1903	8,976	—	—	P/L	22.50
	1904 type of 1903 w/small ball on 3					
		3.630	6.00	12.50	35.00	70.00
	1904	8,876	—	—	P/L	22.50

GREAT BRITAIN 759

KM#	Date	Mintage	Fine	VF	XF	Unc
797.2	1904 type of 1905 w/large ball on 3					
		Inc. Ab.	4.50	10.00	30.00	60.00
	1905	3.563	4.50	9.00	25.00	50.00
	1905	8,976	—	—	P/L	22.50
	1906	3.174	4.00	8.00	20.00	40.00
	1906	8,800	—	—	P/L	22.50
	1907	4.841	.75	2.50	9.00	25.00
	1907	.011	—	—	P/L	22.50
	1908	8.176	.75	2.25	9.00	30.00
	1908	8,760	—	—	P/L	22.50
	1909	4.055	2.00	5.00	10.00	30.00
	1909	1,983	—	—	P/L	22.50
	1910	4.565	.75	2.00	7.50	25.00
	1910	1,140	—	—	P/L	25.00

KM#	Date	Mintage	Fine	VF	XF	Unc
813	1911	5.843	.75	1.50	4.00	16.50
	1911	1,991	—	—	P/L	27.50
	1911	6,007	—	—	Proof	35.00
	1912	8.934	.60	1.00	4.00	16.50
	1912	1,246	—	—	P/L	27.50
	1913	7.144	.60	1.00	5.00	18.00
	1913	1,228	—	—	P/L	27.50
	1914	6.735	.50	.85	3.50	14.00
	1914	982 pcs.	—	—	P/L	27.50
	1915	5.452	.75	1.25	3.50	14.00
	1915	1,293	—	—	P/L	27.50
	1916	18.556	.50	.75	3.00	10.00
	1916	1,128	—	—	P/L	27.50
	1917	21.664	.50	.75	3.00	10.00
	1917	1,237	—	—	P/L	27.50
	1918	20.632	.50	.75	3.00	10.00
	1918	1,375	—	—	P/L	27.50
	1919	16.846	.50	.75	3.00	10.00
	1919	1,258	—	—	P/L	27.50
	1920	16.705	.50	.75	3.50	10.00
	1920	1,399	—	—	P/L	27.50

1.4138 g, .500 SILVER, .0227 oz ASW

KM#	Date	Mintage	Fine	VF	XF	Unc
813a	1920	Inc. Ab.	BV	.65	3.00	10.00
	1921	8.751	BV	1.50	3.00	14.00
	1921	1,386	—	—	P/L	25.00
	1922	7.981	BV	1.50	3.00	14.00
	1922	1,373	—	—	P/L	25.00
	1923	1,430	—	—	P/L	25.00
	1924	1,515	—	—	P/L	25.00
	1925	3.733	1.25	2.50	9.00	20.00
	1925	1,438	—	—	P/L	25.00
	1926	4.109	2.50	6.00	16.50	35.00
	1926	1,504	—	—	P/L	25.00
	1927	1,690	—	—	P/L	25.00

Obv: Modified effigy.

KM#	Date	Mintage	Fine	VF	XF	Unc
827	1926	Inc. Ab.	1.00	2.50	10.00	25.00
	1928	1,835	—	—	P/L	22.50
	1929	1,761	—	—	P/L	22.50
	1930	1,948	—	—	P/L	22.50
	1931	1,818	—	—	P/L	22.50
	1932	2,042	—	—	P/L	22.50
	1933	1,920	—	—	P/L	22.50
	1934	1,887	—	—	P/L	22.50
	1935	2,007	—	—	P/L	22.50
	1936	1,307	—	—	P/L	25.00

Rev: Oak sprigs w/acorns.

KM#	Date	Mintage	Fine	VF	XF	Unc
831	1927	.015	—	—	Proof	60.00
	1928	1.302	2.50	5.00	10.00	25.00
	1928	—	—	—	Proof	190.00
	1930	1.319	1.50	3.00	7.50	15.00
	1930	—	—	—	Proof	—
	1931	6.252	BV	.50	1.50	7.50
	1931	—	—	—	Proof	—
	1932	5.887	BV	.50	1.50	7.50
	1932	—	—	—	Proof	150.00
	1933	5.579	BV	.50	1.50	7.50
	1933	—	—	—	Proof	150.00
	1934	7.406	BV	.50	1.50	7.50
	1934	—	—	—	Proof	—
	1935	7.028	BV	.50	1.50	7.50
	1935	—	—	—	Proof	—
	1936	3.239	BV	.50	1.50	7.50
	1936	—	—	—	Proof	150.00

KM#	Date	Mintage	Fine	VF	XF	Unc
848	1937	8.148	BV	.50	.75	3.00
	1937	.026	—	—	Proof	10.00
	1938	6.402	BV	.50	1.00	3.50
	1938	—	—	—	Proof	125.00
	1939	1.356	.75	1.25	2.50	8.00
	1939	—	—	—	Proof	125.00
	1940	7.914	BV	.50	1.00	3.50
	1940	—	—	—	Proof	—
	1941	7.979	BV	.50	1.00	3.50
	1941	—	—	—	Proof	—
	1942	4.144	1.00	2.00	4.00	12.50
	1943	1.379	2.00	4.50	8.00	15.00
	1944	2.006	3.25	8.50	17.50	35.00
	1945	.320*	—	—	—	—

***NOTE:** Issue melted, one known.

NICKEL-BRASS

KM#	Date	Mintage	Fine	VF	XF	Unc
849	1937	45.708	.25	.40	1.00	3.00
	1937	.026	—	—	Proof	7.50
	1938	14.532	.40	.80	4.00	12.00
	1938	—	—	—	Proof	—
	1939	5.603	.70	2.00	6.00	27.50
	1939	—	—	—	Proof	—
	1940	12.636	.25	.80	2.50	7.00
	1940	—	—	—	Proof	—
	1941	60.239	.25	.40	1.00	5.00
	1941	—	—	—	Proof	—
	1942	103.214	.20	.30	1.00	3.00
	1942	—	—	—	Proof	—
	1943	101.702	.20	.30	1.00	3.00
	1943	—	—	—	Proof	—
	1944	69.760	.25	.40	1.00	4.00
	1944	—	—	—	Proof	—
	1945	33.942	.25	.50	1.50	4.50
	1945	—	—	—	Proof	—
	1946	.621	3.50	8.00	45.00	225.00
	1946	—	—	—	Proof	350.00
	1948	4.230	.60	1.50	5.50	15.00
	1948	—	—	—	Proof	—

1.4138 g, .500 SILVER, .0227 oz ASW

KM#	Date	Mintage	Fine	VF	XF	Unc
850	1937	1,351	—	—	P/L	20.00
	1938	1,350	—	—	P/L	20.00
	1939	1,234	—	—	P/L	20.00
	1940	1,290	—	—	P/L	20.00
	1941	1,253	—	—	P/L	20.00
	1942	1,325	—	—	P/L	20.00
	1943	1,335	—	—	P/L	20.00
	1944	1,345	—	—	P/L	20.00
	1945	1,355	—	—	P/L	20.00
	1946	1,365	—	—	P/L	20.00

1.4138 g, .925 SILVER, .0420 oz ASW

KM#	Date	Mintage	Fine	VF	XF	Unc
850a	1947	1,375	—	—	P/L	20.00
	1948	1,491	—	—	P/L	20.00

Obv. leg: W/o IND IMP.

KM#	Date	Mintage	Fine	VF	XF	Unc
872	1949	1,395	—	—	P/L	20.00
	1950	1,405	—	—	P/L	20.00
	1951	1,468	—	—	P/L	20.00
	1952	1,012	—	—	P/L	22.50

NICKEL-BRASS
Obv. leg: W/o IND IMP.

KM#	Date	Mintage	Fine	VF	XF	Unc
873	1949	.464	5.00	15.00	60.00	165.00
	1949	—	—	—	Proof	—
	1950	1.600	1.00	3.00	12.50	30.00
	1950	.018	—	—	Proof	22.50
	1951	1.184	1.50	3.50	12.50	30.00
	1951	.020	—	—	Proof	15.00
	1952	25.494	.25	.75	1.25	3.00
	1952	—	—	—	Proof	100.00

KM#	Date	Mintage	Fine	VF	XF	Unc
886	1953	30.618	.15	.25	.50	1.50
	1953	.040	—	—	Proof	4.50

1.4138 g, .925 SILVER, .0420 oz ASW

KM#	Date	Mintage	Fine	VF	XF	Unc
887	1953	1,078	—	—	P/L	85.00

NICKEL-BRASS
Obv. leg: W/o BRITT OMN.

KM#	Date	Mintage	Fine	VF	XF	Unc
900	1954	41.720	—	.15	.50	4.00
	1954	—	—	—	Proof	100.00
	1955	41.075	—	.15	1.00	6.00
	1955	—	—	—	Proof	—
	1956	36.902	—	.15	1.00	6.00
	1956	—	—	—	Proof	—
	1957	24.294	—	.15	.50	4.00
	1957	—	—	—	Proof	—
	1958	20.504	—	.25	1.00	6.00
	1958	—	—	—	Proof	300.00
	1959	28.499	—	.15	.50	3.50
	1959	—	—	—	Proof	—
	1960	83.078	—	.15	.40	2.00
	1960	—	—	—	Proof	—
	1961	41.102	—	.10	.20	.60
	1961	—	—	—	Proof	—
	1962	47.242	—	.10	.20	.40
	1962	—	—	—	Proof	—
	1963	35.280	—	.10	.15	.25
	1963	—	—	—	Proof	—
	1964	47.440	—	.10	.15	.25
	1964	—	—	—	Proof	—
	1965	23.907	—	.10	.15	.25
	1966	55.320	—	.10	.15	.25
	1967	49.000	—	.10	.15	.25
	1970	.731	—	—	Proof	2.50

1.4138 g, .925 SILVER, .0420 oz ASW
Obv. leg: W/o BRITT OMN.

KM#	Date	Mintage	Fine	VF	XF	Unc
901	1954	1,076	—	—	P/L	17.50
	1955	1,082	—	—	P/L	17.50
	1956	1,088	—	—	P/L	17.50
	1957	1,094	—	—	P/L	17.50
	1958	1,100	—	—	P/L	17.50
	1959	1,172	—	—	P/L	17.50
	1960	1,112	—	—	P/L	17.50
	1961	1,118	—	—	P/L	17.50
	1962	1,125	—	—	P/L	17.50
	1963	1,205	—	—	P/L	17.50
	1964	1,213	—	—	P/L	17.50
	1965	1,221	—	—	P/L	17.50
	1966	1,206	—	—	P/L	17.50
	1967	986 pcs.	—	—	P/L	17.50
	1968	964 pcs.	—	—	P/L	17.50
	1969	1,088	—	—	P/L	17.50
	1970	980 pcs.	—	—	P/L	17.50
	1971	1,018	—	—	P/L	17.50
	1972	1,026	—	—	P/L	17.50
	1973	1,098	—	—	P/L	17.50
	1974	1,138	—	—	P/L	19.00
	1975	1,148	—	—	P/L	19.00
	1976	1,158	—	—	P/L	19.00
	1977	1,138	—	—	P/L	20.00
	1978	1,178	—	—	P/L	20.00
	1979	1,294	—	—	P/L	20.00
	1980	1,198	—	—	P/L	20.00
	1981	1,178	—	—	P/L	20.00
	1982	1,218	—	—	P/L	20.00
	1983	1,342	—	—	P/L	20.00
	1984	1,354	—	—	P/L	20.00
	1985	1,366	—	—	P/L	20.00
	1986	—	—	—	P/L	20.00
	1987	—	—	—	P/L	20.00
	1988	—	—	—	P/L	20.00
	1989	—	—	—	P/L	20.00

4 PENCE (GROAT)

1.8851 g, .925 SILVER, .0561 oz ASW
Obv: Old head of George III. Rev: Value.

KM#	Date	Mintage	Fine	VF	XF	Unc
671	1817	—	10.00	22.50	40.00	90.00
	1817	1,386	—	—	P/L	70.00
	1818	—	10.00	22.50	40.00	90.00
	1818	1,188	—	—	P/L	70.00
	1820	—	10.00	22.50	40.00	90.00
	1820	990 pcs.	—	—	P/L	70.00

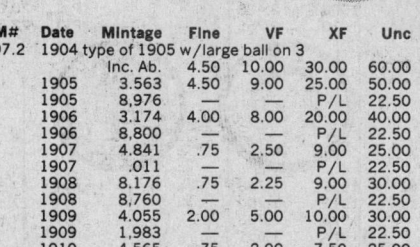

KM#	Date	Mintage	Fine	VF	XF	Unc
686	1822	—	9.00	15.00	25.00	50.00
	1822	2,970	—	—	P/L	70.00
	1823	—	9.00	15.00	25.00	50.00
	1823	1,980	—	—	P/L	60.00
	1824	—	9.00	15.00	25.00	50.00
	1824	1,584	—	—	P/L	65.00
	1825	—	9.00	15.00	25.00	50.00
	1825	2,376	—	—	P/L	60.00
	1826	—	9.00	15.00	25.00	50.00
	1826	2,376	—	—	P/L	60.00
	1827	—	9.00	15.00	25.00	50.00
	1827	2,772	—	—	P/L	60.00
	1828	—	9.00	15.00	25.00	50.00
	1828	2,772	—	—	P/L	60.00
	1829	—	9.00	15.00	25.00	50.00
	1829	2,772	—	—	P/L	60.00
	1830	—	9.00	15.00	25.00	50.00
	1830	2,772	—	—	P/L	60.00

KM#	Date	Mintage	Fine	VF	XF	Unc
711	1831	—	5.00	12.00	22.50	45.00
	1831	3,564	—	—	P/L	55.00
	1832	—	5.00	12.00	22.50	45.00
	1832	2,574	—	—	P/L	40.00
	1833	—	5.00	12.00	22.50	45.00
	1833	2,574	—	—	P/L	40.00
	1834	—	5.00	12.00	22.50	45.00
	1834	2,574	—	—	P/L	40.00
	1835	—	5.00	12.00	22.50	45.00
	1835	2,574	—	—	P/L	40.00
	1836	—	5.00	12.00	22.50	45.00
	1836	2,574	—	—	P/L	40.00
	1837	—	6.00	12.00	22.50	45.00
	1837	2,574	—	—	P/L	40.00

KM#	Date	Mintage	Fine	VF	XF	Unc
723	1836	4,253	2.25	4.50	17.50	45.00
	1836 reeded edge		—	—	Proof	600.00
	1836 plain edge		—	—	Proof	300.00
	1837	.962	4.00	8.00	20.00	60.00
	1837	—	—	—	Proof	225.00

***NOTE:** Although the design of the above coin is of the homeland type, the issues were struck for British Guiana.

GOLD (OMS)

KM#	Date	Mintage	Fine	VF	XF	Unc
723a	1836	—	—	—	Proof	4000.

1.8851 g, .925 SILVER, .0561 oz ASW

KM#	Date	Mintage	Fine	VF	XF	Unc
731.1	1838	2.150	2.25	4.50	17.50	40.00
	1838/8 second 8 over horizontal 8	Inc. Ab.	6.00	12.50	45.00	100.00
	1839	1.461	3.00	8.00	25.00	60.00
	1840	1.497	2.75	6.00	22.50	50.00
	1841	.345	4.50	13.00	35.00	75.00
	1842/1	.725	6.00	15.00	37.50	90.00
	1842	Inc. Ab.	4.00	8.00	27.50	70.00
	1842	—	—	—	Proof	500.00
	1843	1.818	3.00	8.00	27.50	70.00
	1844	.855	5.00	13.00	35.00	70.00
	1845	.915	3.00	8.00	27.50	60.00
	1846	1.366	3.00	8.00	27.50	60.00
	1847/6	.226	30.00	55.00	120.00	220.00
	1848/6	.713	3.50	10.00	32.50	70.00
	1848/7	Inc. Ab.	3.50	10.00	32.50	70.00
	1848	Inc. Ab.	3.00	6.00	22.50	50.00
	1849/8	.380	6.00	15.00	55.00	125.00
	1849	Inc. Ab.	3.50	10.00	32.50	70.00
	1851	.031	6.00	15.00	55.00	125.00
	1852	—	60.00	120.00	300.00	450.00
	1853	.012	65.00	130.00	325.00	650.00
	1854	1.097	2.75	6.00	22.50	50.00
	1855	.646	3.50	8.00	22.50	50.00
	1857	—	—	—	Proof	1250.
	1862	—	—	—	Proof	800.00

NOTE: The above issue was produced for circulation in both Great Britain and British Guiana.

Plain edge.

KM#	Date	Mintage	Fine	VF	XF	Unc
731.2	1838	—	—	—	Proof	200.00
	1839	—	—	—	Proof	200.00
	1853	*10-15 pcs.	—	—	Proof	Rare

KM#	Date	Mintage	Fine	VF	XF	Unc
732	1838	4,158	—	—	P/L	17.50
	1839	4,125	—	—	P/L	17.50
	1840	4,125	—	—	P/L	17.50
	1841	2,574	—	—	P/L	20.00
	1842	4,125	—	—	P/L	17.50
	1843	4,158	—	—	P/L	17.50
	1844	4,158	—	—	P/L	17.50
	1845	4,158	—	—	P/L	17.50
	1846	4,158	—	—	P/L	17.50
	1847	4,158	—	—	P/L	17.50
	1848	4,158	—	—	P/L	17.50
	1849	4,158	—	—	P/L	17.50
	1850	4,158	—	—	P/L	17.50
	1851	4,158	—	—	P/L	17.50
	1852	4,158	—	—	P/L	17.50
	1853	4,158	—	—	P/L	17.50
	1854	4,158	—	—	P/L	17.50
	1855	4,158	—	—	P/L	17.50
	1856	4,158	—	—	P/L	17.50
	1857	4,158	—	—	P/L	17.50
	1858	4,158	—	—	P/L	17.50
	1859	4,158	—	—	P/L	17.50
	1860	4,158	—	—	P/L	17.50
	1861	4,158	—	—	P/L	17.50
	1862	4,158	—	—	P/L	17.50
	1863	4,158	—	—	P/L	17.50
	1864	4,158	—	—	P/L	17.50
	1865	4,158	—	—	P/L	17.50
	1866	4,158	—	—	P/L	17.50
	1867	4,158	—	—	P/L	17.50
	1868	4,158	—	—	P/L	17.50
	1869	4,158	—	—	P/L	17.50
	1870	4,569	—	—	P/L	17.50
	1871	4,627	—	—	P/L	17.50
	1872	4,328	—	—	P/L	17.50
	1873	4,162	—	—	P/L	17.50
	1874	5,937	—	—	P/L	17.50
	1875	4,154	—	—	P/L	17.50
	1876	4,862	—	—	P/L	17.50
	1877	4,850	—	—	P/L	17.50
	1878	5,735	—	—	P/L	17.50
	1879	5,202	—	—	P/L	17.50
	1880	5,199	—	—	P/L	17.50
	1881	6,203	—	—	P/L	17.50
	1882	4,146	—	—	P/L	17.50
	1883	5,096	—	—	P/L	17.50
	1884	5,353	—	—	P/L	17.50
	1885	5,791	—	—	P/L	17.50
	1886	6,785	—	—	P/L	17.50
	1887	5,292	—	—	P/L	17.50

KM#	Date	Mintage	Fine	VF	XF	Unc
772	1888	.120	4.00	10.00	25.00	55.00
	1888		—	—	Proof	125.00

NOTE: The above piece was exclusively for use in British Guiana and the West Indies.

KM#	Date	Mintage	Fine	VF	XF	Unc
773	1888	9,583	—	—	P/L	20.00
	1889	6,088	—	—	P/L	20.00
	1890	9,087	—	—	P/L	20.00
	1891	.011	—	—	P/L	20.00
	1892	8,524	—	—	P/L	20.00

KM#	Date	Mintage	Fine	VF	XF	Unc
778	1893	.011	—	—	P/L	15.00
	1894	9,385	—	—	P/L	15.00
	1895	8,877	—	—	P/L	15.00
	1896	8,476	—	—	P/L	15.00
	1897	9,388	—	—	P/L	15.00
	1898	9,147	—	—	P/L	15.00
	1899	.014	—	—	P/L	15.00
	1900	9,571	—	—	P/L	15.00
	1901	.012	—	—	P/L	15.00

KM#	Date	Mintage	Fine	VF	XF	Unc
798	1902	.010	—	—	P/L	15.00
798	1903	9,729	—	—	P/L	15.00
	1904	.012	—	—	P/L	15.00
	1905	.011	—	—	P/L	15.00
	1906	.011	—	—	P/L	15.00
	1907	.011	—	—	P/L	15.00
	1908	9,929	—	—	P/L	15.00
	1909	2,428	—	—	P/L	20.00
	1910	2,755	—	—	P/L	22.50

KM#	Date	Mintage	Fine	VF	XF	Unc
814	1911	1,768	—	—	P/L	17.50
	1912	1,700	—	—	P/L	17.50
	1913	1,798	—	—	P/L	17.50
	1914	1,651	—	—	P/L	17.50
	1915	1,441	—	—	P/L	17.50
	1916	1,499	—	—	P/L	17.50
	1917	1,478	—	—	P/L	17.50
	1918	1,479	—	—	P/L	17.50
	1919	1,524	—	—	P/L	17.50
	1920	1,460	—	—	P/L	17.50

1.8851 g, .500 SILVER, .0303 oz ASW

KM#	Date	Mintage	Fine	VF	XF	Unc
814a	1921	1,542	—	—	P/L	17.50
	1922	1,609	—	—	P/L	17.50
	1923	1,635	—	—	P/L	17.50
	1924	1,665	—	—	P/L	17.50
	1925	1,786	—	—	P/L	17.50
	1926	1,762	—	—	P/L	17.50
	1927	1,681	—	—	P/L	17.50

Obv: Modified effigy.

KM#	Date	Mintage	Fine	VF	XF	Unc
841	1928	1,642	—	—	P/L	20.00
	1929	1,969	—	—	P/L	20.00
	1930	1,744	—	—	P/L	20.00
	1931	1,915	—	—	P/L	20.00
	1932	1,937	—	—	P/L	20.00
	1933	1,931	—	—	P/L	20.00
	1934	1,893	—	—	P/L	20.00
	1935	1,995	—	—	P/L	20.00
	1936	1,323	—	—	P/L	22.50
851	1937	1,325	—	—	P/L	20.00
	1938	1,424	—	—	P/L	20.00
	1939	1,332	—	—	P/L	20.00
	1940	1,367	—	—	P/L	20.00
	1941	1,345	—	—	P/L	20.00
	1942	1,325	—	—	P/L	20.00
	1943	1,335	—	—	P/L	20.00
	1944	1,345	—	—	P/L	20.00
	1945	1,355	—	—	P/L	20.00
	1946	1,365	—	—	P/L	20.00

1.8851 g, .925 SILVER, .0561 oz ASW

KM#	Date	Mintage	Fine	VF	XF	Unc
851a	1947	1,375	—	—	P/L	20.00
	1948	1,385	—	—	P/L	20.00

Obv. leg: W/o IND IMP.

KM#	Date	Mintage	Fine	VF	XF	Unc
874	1949	1,503	—	—	P/L	20.00
	1950	1,515	—	—	P/L	20.00
	1951	1,580	—	—	P/L	20.00
	1952	1,064	—	—	P/L	22.50
888	1953	1,078	—	—	P/L	85.00

Obv. leg: W/o BRITT OMN.

KM#	Date	Mintage	Fine	VF	XF	Unc
902	1954	1,076	—	—	P/L	17.50
	1955	1,082	—	—	P/L	17.50
	1956	1,088	—	—	P/L	17.50
	1957	1,094	—	—	P/L	17.50
	1958	1,100	—	—	P/L	17.50
	1959	1,106	—	—	P/L	17.50
	1960	1,180	—	—	P/L	17.50
	1961	1,118	—	—	P/L	17.50
	1962	1,197	—	—	P/L	17.50
	1963	1,205	—	—	P/L	17.50
	1964	1,213	—	—	P/L	17.50
	1965	1,221	—	—	P/L	17.50
	1966	1,206	—	—	P/L	17.50
	1967	986 pcs.	—	—	P/L	17.50
	1968	964 pcs.	—	—	P/L	17.50
	1969	1,002	—	—	P/L	17.50
	1970	1,068	—	—	P/L	17.50
	1971	1,108	—	—	P/L	17.50
	1972	1,118	—	—	P/L	17.50
	1973	1,098	—	—	P/L	17.50
	1974	1,138	—	—	P/L	19.00
	1975	1,148	—	—	P/L	19.00
	1976	1,158	—	—	P/L	19.00
	1977	1,138	—	—	P/L	20.00
	1978	1,178	—	—	P/L	20.00
	1979	1,188	—	—	P/L	20.00
	1980	1,306	—	—	P/L	20.00

KM#	Date	Mintage	Fine	VF	XF	Unc
902	1981	1,288	—	—	P/L	20.00
	1982	1,330	—	—	P/L	20.00
	1983	1,342	—	—	P/L	20.00
	1984	1,354	—	—	P/L	20.00
	1985	1,366	—	—	P/L	20.00
	1986	—	—	—	P/L	20.00
	1987	—	—	—	P/L	20.00
	1988	—	—	—	P/L	20.00
	1989	—	—	—	P/L	20.00

6 PENCE

2.8276 g, .925 SILVER, .0841 oz ASW

KM#	Date	Mintage	Fine	VF	XF	Unc
665	1816	—	3.50	8.50	30.00	75.00
	1817	10.922	3.00	8.00	30.00	75.00
	1817	—	—	—	Proof	500.00
	1817 plain edge	—	—	—	Proof	500.00
	1818	4.285	8.00	17.50	60.00	150.00
	1818	—	—	—	Proof	700.00
	1819/8	—	6.00	15.00	50.00	160.00
	1819	4.712	4.00	9.00	32.00	75.00
	1819	—	—	—	Proof	1000.
	1820	1.489	4.00	9.00	32.00	80.00
	1820	—	—	—	Proof	—

GOLD (OMS)

| 665a | 1816 | — | — | — | Proof | — |

2.8276 g, .925 SILVER, .0841 oz ASW

678	1821	.863	6.00	15.00	70.00	200.00
	1821	—	—	—	Proof	500.00
	1821 (error) BBITANNIAR					
		—	45.00	120.00	450.00	900.00

691	1824	.634	6.50	16.00	75.00	200.00
	1824	—	—	—	Proof	750.00
	1825	.483	5.50	13.00	60.00	160.00
	1825	—	—	—	Proof	300.00
	1826	.689	20.00	60.00	220.00	500.00
	1826	—	—	—	Proof	400.00

698	1826	Inc. Ab.	5.00	12.00	55.00	145.00
	1826	Inc. Ab.	—	—	Proof	250.00
	1827	.166	15.00	45.00	115.00	300.00
	1828	.016	8.00	25.00	85.00	225.00
	1829	.404	6.00	20.00	75.00	175.00
	1829	—	—	—	Proof	—

712	1831	1.340	4.50	17.50	65.00	155.00
	1831	Inc. Ab.	—	—	Proof	250.00
	1831 plain edge	—	—	—	Proof	250.00
	1834	5.892	4.50	15.00	55.00	135.00
	1834	—	—	—	Proof	—
	1834 round-topped 3					
		Inc. Ab.	—	—	—	—
	1835	1.555	6.00	20.00	60.00	140.00
	1835 round-topped 3					
		Inc. Ab.	—	—	Proof	—
	1836	1.988	11.00	37.50	120.00	240.00
	1836 round-topped 3					
		Inc. Ab.	—	—	Proof	—
	1837	.507	6.00	20.00	115.00	200.00
	1837	—	—	—	Proof	—

PALLADIUM

| 712a | 1831 | — | — | — | Proof | — |

3.0100 g, .925 SILVER, .0895 oz ASW
Rev: W/o die numbers.

KM#	Date	Mintage	Fine	VF	XF	Unc
733.1	1838	1.608	3.50	12.00	50.00	125.00
	1838	—	—	—	Proof	200.00
	1839	3.311	3.50	12.00	50.00	125.00
	1839	Inc. Ab.	—	—	Proof	300.00
	1840	2.099	4.00	12.00	65.00	140.00
	1841	1.386	4.00	14.00	70.00	145.00
	1842	.602	5.00	15.00	80.00	180.00
	1843	3.160	3.50	12.00	65.00	150.00
	1844	3.976	3.50	12.00	50.00	130.00
	1844 large 44					
		Inc. Ab.	4.00	15.00	60.00	150.00
	1845	3.714	3.50	12.00	50.00	120.00
	1846	4.267	3.50	12.00	50.00	120.00
	1848/6	.586	15.00	60.00	220.00	450.00
	1848/7	Inc. Ab.	15.00	60.00	220.00	450.00
	1848	Inc. Ab.	15.00	60.00	220.00	450.00
	1849	.210	—	None reported	—	—
	1850/30	.499	7.50	25.00	90.00	—
	1850	Inc. Ab.	5.00	20.00	75.00	180.00
	1851	2.288	4.00	15.00	50.00	125.00
	1852	.905	4.00	15.00	50.00	130.00
	1853	3.838	3.50	12.00	45.00	120.00
	1853	*40 pcs.	—	—	Proof	450.00
	1854	.840	35.00	65.00	225.00	450.00
	1855	1.129	3.50	12.00	50.00	125.00
	1855	—	—	—	Proof	—
	1856	2.780	3.50	12.00	50.00	125.00
	1857	2.233	4.00	12.00	65.00	135.00
	1858	1.932	4.00	12.00	65.00	135.00
	1858	—	—	—	Proof	600.00
	1859/8	4.689	4.00	15.00	60.00	145.00
	1859	Inc. Ab.	4.00	12.00	50.00	135.00
	1860	1.101	4.00	12.00	60.00	145.00
	1861	.600	—	Reported, not confirmed		
	1862	.990	15.00	35.00	185.00	400.00
	1863	.491	10.00	30.00	120.00	240.00
	1866	5.140	22.50	45.00	100.00	220.00

Rev: W/die numbers.

733.2	1864	4.253	3.50	12.00	50.00	125.00
	1865	1.632	3.50	12.00	50.00	125.00
	1866	Inc.Ab.	3.50	12.00	50.00	125.00

Obv: New portrait. Rev: W/die numbers.

751.1	1867	1.362	6.00	20.00	70.00	175.00
	1867	—	—	—	Proof	—
	1868	1.069	6.00	20.00	70.00	175.00
	1869	.388	6.00	22.50	75.00	200.00
	1869	—	—	—	Proof	—
	1870	.080	8.00	20.00	75.00	200.00
	1870	—	—	—	Proof	—
	1870 plain edge	—	—	—	Proof	—
	1871	3.663	3.50	12.50	45.00	100.00
	1871	—	—	—	Proof	—
	1871 plain edge	—	—	—	Proof	—
	1872	3.382	3.50	12.50	45.00	100.00
	1873	4.595	3.00	11.00	40.00	90.00
	1874	4.226	2.75	9.00	40.00	90.00
	1875	3.257	2.75	9.00	40.00	90.00
	1876	.841	8.00	20.00	65.00	150.00
	1877	4.066	3.00	11.00	40.00	95.00
	1878/7	2.625	25.00	75.00	175.00	350.00
	1878	—	—	—	Proof	—
	1878 (error) DRITANNIAR					
		Inc. Ab.	22.50	60.00	350.00	900.00
	1879	3.326	6.75	20.00	70.00	175.00
	1879	—	—	—	Proof	—

Rev: W/o die numbers.

751.2	1871	Inc. Ab.	8.00	20.00	50.00	125.00
	1877	Inc. Ab.	3.00	11.00	40.00	90.00
	1878	Inc. Ab.	3.00	11.00	40.00	90.00
	1879	Inc. Ab.	4.00	12.00	40.00	90.00
	1880 obverse of 1879					
		3.892	4.00	12.00	40.00	90.00

Obv: New portrait, longer hair waves.

757	1880	Inc. Ab.	2.50	10.00	30.00	70.00
	1880	—	—	—	Proof	—
	1881	6.239	2.25	8.00	25.00	50.00
	1881	—	—	—	Proof	—
	1881 plain edge	—	—	—	Proof	—
	1882	.760	5.00	20.00	60.00	130.00
	1883	4.987	2.25	8.00	25.00	50.00

KM#	Date	Mintage	Fine	VF	XF	Unc
757	1884	3.423	2.25	8.00	25.00	50.00
	1885	4.653	2.25	8.00	25.00	50.00
	1885	—	—	—	Proof	325.00
	1886	2.728	2.25	8.00	25.00	50.00
	1886	—	—	—	Proof	325.00
	1887	3.676	2.25	7.00	22.50	50.00
	1887	—	—	—	Proof	100.00

759	1887	Inc.KM757	1.50	3.00	6.00	12.00
	1887	—	—	—	Proof	225.00

760	1887	Inc.KM757	2.00	3.50	6.00	15.00
	1887	Inc.KM757	—	—	Proof	225.00
	1888	4.198	2.00	—	17.50	45.00
	1888	—	—	—	Proof	1500.
	1889	8.739	2.00	5.00	15.00	45.00
	1890	9.387	2.00	6.00	17.50	45.00
	1890	—	—	—	Proof	—
	1891	7.023	2.00	6.00	17.50	45.00
	1892	6.246	2.00	6.00	17.50	45.00
	1893	7.351	100.00	300.00	750.00	2250.

779	1893	Inc. Ab.	1.50	3.75	15.00	35.00
	1893	1,312	—	—	Proof	150.00
	1894	3.468	1.75	4.50	17.50	45.00
	1895	7.025	1.50	3.75	15.00	35.00
	1896	6.652	1.50	3.75	15.00	35.00
	1897	5.031	1.50	3.50	12.50	35.00
	1898	5.914	1.50	3.50	12.50	35.00
	1899	7.997	1.50	3.75	15.00	37.50
	1900	8.980	1.50	3.50	12.50	35.00
	1901	5.109	1.50	3.50	12.50	35.00

799	1902	6.356	2.00	4.00	15.00	35.00
	1902	.015	—	—	Proof	35.00
	1903	5.411	2.75	9.00	30.00	70.00
	1904	4.487	3.50	10.00	32.50	90.00
	1905	4.236	3.50	10.00	32.50	80.00
	1906	7.641	2.50	5.00	20.00	60.00
	1907	8.734	2.50	8.00	20.00	60.00
	1908	6.739	3.50	12.00	30.00	85.00
	1909	6.584	2.75	7.50	25.00	70.00
	1910	12.491	2.25	7.00	16.00	40.00

815	1911	9,165	1.00	2.00	7.50	25.00
	1911	6,007	—	—	Proof	50.00
	1912	10.984	1.00	3.00	15.00	50.00
	1913	7.500	1.50	4.50	20.00	55.00
	1914	22.715	1.00	2.00	5.00	17.50
	1915	15.695	1.00	2.00	5.00	17.50
	1916	22.207	1.00	2.00	5.00	17.50
	1917	7.725	1.50	3.00	12.50	40.00
	1918	27.559	1.00	1.75	6.00	17.50
	1919	13.375	1.00	2.00	12.00	35.00
	1920	14.136	1.00	2.00	12.00	35.00

2.8276 g, .500 SILVER, .0455 oz ASW
Narrow rim

815a.1	1920	Inc. Ab.	.75	2.00	12.50	35.00
	1921	30.340	.75	2.00	9.00	30.00
	1922	16.879	.75	2.00	9.00	30.00
	1923	6.383	1.25	3.00	11.50	45.00
	1924	17.444	.75	1.50	9.00	32.50
	1925	12.721	.75	2.50	10.00	35.00

Wide rim

815a.2	1925	Inc. Ab.	.75	1.50	9.00	22.50
	1926	21.810	.75	1.50	9.00	22.50

Obv: Modified effigy, slightly smaller bust.

| 828 | 1926 | Inc. Ab. | BV | 1.50 | 7.50 | 22.50 |

KM#	Date	Mintage	Fine	VF	XF	Unc
828	1927	8.925	BV	1.50	7.50	25.00
	1927	—	—	—	Proof	150.00

Rev: Oak sprigs w/acorns.

KM#	Date	Mintage	Fine	VF	XF	Unc
832	1927	.015	—	—	Proof	30.00
	1928	23.123	BV	.75	2.75	12.00
	1928	—	—	—	Proof	—
	1929	28.319	BV	.75	2.75	12.00
	1929	—	—	—	Proof	—
	1930	16.990	BV	.75	3.00	13.00
	1930	—	—	—	Proof	—
	1931	16.873	BV	.75	3.00	13.00
	1931	—	—	—	Proof	—
	1932	9.406	.75	1.50	4.50	22.50
	1932	—	—	—	Proof	—
	1933	22.185	BV	.75	2.75	12.00
	1933	—	—	—	Proof	150.00
	1934	9.304	.75	1.50	4.50	17.50
	1934	—	—	—	Proof	—
	1935	13.996	BV	.75	2.25	12.00
	1935	—	—	—	Proof	—
	1936	24.380	BV	.75	2.25	10.00
	1936	—	—	—	Proof	160.00

NOTE: Varieties in edge milling exist.

KM#	Date	Mintage	Fine	VF	XF	Unc
852	1937	22.303	—	BV	1.00	3.00
	1937	.026	—	—	Proof	9.00
	1938	13.403	.75	1.00	3.00	9.00
	1938	—	—	—	Proof	100.00
	1939	28.670	BV	.75	1.50	4.50
	1939	—	—	—	Proof	100.00
	1940	20.875	BV	.75	1.50	4.50
	1940	—	—	—	Proof	—
	1941	23.087	BV	.75	1.50	4.50
	1941	—	—	—	Proof	—
	1942	44.943	BV	.75	1.50	2.50
	1943	46.927	—	BV	1.00	2.50
	1943	—	—	—	Proof	—
	1944	36.953	—	BV	1.00	2.00
	1944	—	—	—	Proof	—
	1945	39.939	—	BV	1.00	2.00
	1945	—	—	—	Proof	—
	1946	43.466	—	BV	1.00	2.00
	1946	—	—	—	Proof	—

COPPER-NICKEL

862	1947	29.993	—	.15	.50	2.00
	1947	—	—	—	Proof	100.00
	1948	88.324	—	.15	.50	2.00
	1948	—	—	—	Proof	100.00

Rev. leg: W/o IND IMP.

875	1949	41.336	—	.15	.50	3.50
	1949	—	—	—	Proof	—
	1950	32.742	—	.15	.50	3.50
	1950	.018	—	—	Proof	6.00
	1951	40.399	—	.15	.50	3.50
	1951	.020	—	—	Proof	6.00
	1952	1.013	1.00	2.75	12.50	32.50
	1952	—	—	—	Proof	—

889	1953	70.324	—	.10	.40	1.50
	1953	.040	—	—	Proof	3.50

Obv. leg: W/o BRITT OMN.

903	1954	105.241	—	.10	.50	3.50
	1954	—	—	—	Proof	100.00
	1955	109.930	—	.10	.15	1.00
	1955	—	—	—	Proof	—
	1956	109.842	—	.10	.15	1.00

KM#	Date	Mintage	Fine	VF	XF	Unc
903	1956	—	—	—	Proof	—
	1957	105.654	—	.10	.15	.50
	1957	—	—	—	Proof	—
	1958	123.519	—	.10	.50	3.50
	1958	—	—	—	Proof	—
	1959	93.089	—	.10	.15	.35
	1959	—	—	—	Proof	—
	1960	103.283	—	.10	.30	2.50
	1960	—	—	—	Proof	—
	1961	115.052	—	.10	.30	2.50
	1961	—	—	—	Proof	—
	1962	166.484	—	.10	.15	.40
	1962	—	—	—	Proof	—
	1963	120.056	—	.10	.15	.25
	1963	—	—	—	Proof	—
	1964	152.336	—	.10	.15	.25
	1964	—	—	—	Proof	—
	1965	129.644	—	—	.10	.20
	1966	175.676	—	—	.10	.20
	1967	148.544	—	—	.10	.20
	1970	.731	—	—	Proof	2.00

SHILLING

5.6552 g, .925 SILVER, .1682 oz ASW

666	1816	—	3.50	8.50	30.00	90.00
	1816	—	—	—	Proof	750.00
	1816 plain edge	—	—	—	Proof	750.00
	1817	23.031	3.50	8.50	30.00	90.00
	1817 plain edge	—	—	—	Proof	650.00
	1818	1.342	10.00	30.00	75.00	175.00
	1818 (error) GEOR(IE)GE					
	Inc. Ab.	—	—	—	—	—
	1819/8	7.595	9.00	25.00	100.00	300.00
	1819	Inc. Ab.	4.00	10.00	45.00	100.00
	1820	7.975	4.00	10.00	45.00	100.00
	1820	—	—	—	Proof	650.00

GOLD (OMS)

666a	1816	—	—	—	Proof	—

5.6552 g, .925 SILVER, .1682 oz ASW

679	1821	2.463	6.00	12.50	100.00	200.00
	1821	—	—	—	Proof	650.00

687	1823	.693	10.00	30.00	120.00	260.00
	1823	—	—	—	Proof	1000.
	1824	4.158	5.50	15.00	75.00	175.00
	1824	—	—	—	Proof	1000.
	1825/3	2.459	5.50	15.00	90.00	200.00
	1825	Inc. Ab.	5.50	15.00	90.00	200.00
	1825	—	—	—	Proof	750.00

694	1825	Inc. Ab.	5.00	10.00	90.00	200.00
	1825	—	—	—	Proof	275.00
	1825 plain edge	—	—	—	Proof	325.00
	1826/2	6.352	—	—	—	—
	1826	Inc.Ab.	5.00	10.00	90.00	200.00
	1826	—	—	—	Proof	275.00
	1827	.574	10.00	30.00	150.00	300.00
	1828	—	10.00	30.00	150.00	300.00
	1829	.879	8.00	22.50	110.00	240.00
	1829	—	—	—	Proof	750.00

KM#	Date	Mintage	Fine	VF	XF	Unc
713	1831 plain edge	—	—	—	Proof	675.00
	1831 milled edge	—	—	—	Proof	750.00
	1834	3.223	5.00	22.50	90.00	200.00
	1834	—	—	—	Proof	1200.
	1835	1.449	6.75	30.00	110.00	240.00
	1835	—	—	—	Proof	1200.
	1836	3.568	5.00	20.00	90.00	200.00
	1836	—	—	—	Proof	1400.
	1837	.479	7.50	27.50	125.00	300.00
	1837	—	—	—	Proof	1400.

COPPER (OMS)

713a	1837	—	—	—	Proof	—

5.6552 g, .925 SILVER, .1682 oz ASW
High relief. W/o die numbers.

734.1	1838WW	1.956	6.00	20.00	50.00	160.00
	1838	Inc. Ab.	—	—	Proof	700.00
	1839WW	5.667	6.00	20.00	50.00	160.00
	1839WW	—	—	—	Proof	325.00
	1839	Inc. Ab.	6.00	17.50	45.00	150.00
	1839	Inc. Ab.	—	—	Proof	325.00
	1840	1.639	20.00	60.00	150.00	350.00
	1840	—	—	—	Proof	500.00
	1841	.875	7.50	30.00	80.00	270.00
	1842	2.095	4.50	17.50	50.00	150.00
	1842	—	—	—	Proof	—
	1843	1.465	9.00	30.00	80.00	240.00
	1844	4.467	4.50	17.50	50.00	150.00
	1845	4.083	6.00	20.00	65.00	175.00
	1846	4.031	4.50	17.50	60.00	175.00
	1848/6	1.041	25.00	75.00	200.00	350.00
	1849	.645	7.50	20.00	70.00	170.00
	1850/46	.685	175.00	525.00	1600.	3600.
	1850	Inc. Ab.	175.00	525.00	1600.	3600.
	1851	.470	60.00	145.00	550.00	1600.
	1851	—	—	—	Proof	—
	1852	1.307	4.50	17.50	50.00	145.00
	1853	4.256	4.50	17.50	50.00	145.00
	1853	—	—	—	Proof	600.00
	1854	.552	40.00	150.00	450.00	1100.
	1855	1.368	4.50	17.50	60.00	150.00
	1856	3.168	4.50	17.50	60.00	150.00
	1857	2.562	4.50	17.50	60.00	150.00
	1858	3.109	4.50	17.50	60.00	150.00
	1858	—	—	—	Proof	—
	1859	4.562	4.50	17.50	60.00	150.00
	1860	1.671	6.00	22.50	85.00	200.00
	1861	1.382	6.00	22.50	85.00	200.00
	1862	.954	20.00	70.00	125.00	300.00
	1863	.859	20.00	75.00	150.00	375.00

With die numbers.

734.3	1864	4.519	4.50	15.00	50.00	135.00
	1865	5.619	4.50	15.00	50.00	135.00
	1866	4.990	4.50	15.00	50.00	135.00
	1867	2.166	5.00	17.50	60.00	165.00
	1867 (error) 'BBITANNIAR'					
	1867	—	—	—	Proof	1000.
	1867 plain edge	—	—	—	Proof	—

Low relief, with die numbers.

734.2	1867	—	—	—	—	—
	1868	3.330	5.00	18.00	65.00	165.00
	1869	.737	7.00	25.00	85.00	190.00
	1870	1.467	6.00	20.00	80.00	175.00
	1871	4.910	4.00	12.50	45.00	110.00
	1871	—	—	—	Proof	—
	1871 plain edge	—	—	—	Proof	1000.
	1872	8.898	4.00	12.50	45.00	110.00
	1873	6.590	4.00	12.50	45.00	110.00
	1874	5.504	4.00	12.50	45.00	110.00
	1875	4.354	4.00	12.50	45.00	110.00
	1876	1.057	6.00	15.00	65.00	160.00
	1877	2.981	3.50	12.00	40.00	90.00
	1878	3.127	3.50	12.00	40.00	90.00
	1878	—	—	—	Proof	—
	1879	3.611	5.00	20.00	90.00	175.00

W/o die numbers.

734.4	1879	Inc. Ab.	4.00	15.00	65.00	160.00
	1880	4.843	3.00	9.00	35.00	85.00
	1880	—	—	—	Proof	—
	1880 plain edge	—	—	—	Proof	—
	1881	5.255	3.00	9.00	35.00	85.00
	1881	—	—	—	Proof	—
	1881 plain edge	—	—	—	Proof	—
	1882	1.612	7.50	20.00	75.00	190.00
	1883	7.281	3.00	8.00	30.00	85.00

KM#	Date	Mintage	Fine	VF	XF	Unc
734.4	1884	3.924	3.00	8.00	30.00	85.00
	1884	—	—	—	Proof	—
	1885	3.337	3.00	8.00	30.00	85.00
	1885	—	—	—	Proof	—
	1886	2.087	3.00	8.00	30.00	85.00
	1886	—	—	—	Proof	—
	1887	4.034	3.00	8.00	50.00	165.00
	1887	—	—	—	Proof	—

Small bust

KM#	Date	Mintage	Fine	VF	XF	Unc
761	1887	Inc. Ab.	2.00	3.00	6.00	17.50
	1887	1,084	—	—	Proof	125.00
	1888/7	4.527	3.00	6.00	20.00	55.00
	1888	Inc. Ab.	3.00	6.00	20.00	55.00
	1889	7.040	20.00	50.00	300.00	700.00
	1889	—	—	—	Proof	—

Large bust

KM#	Date	Mintage	Fine	VF	XF	Unc
774	1889	—	2.50	5.00	15.00	50.00
	1890	8.794	3.00	7.50	22.50	70.00
	1891	5.665	3.00	7.50	25.00	75.00
	1891	—	—	—	Proof	—
	1892	4.592	3.50	7.50	25.00	80.00

KM#	Date	Mintage	Fine	VF	XF	Unc
780	1893	7.039	2.00	4.00	20.00	45.00
	1893	1,312	—	—	Proof	125.00
	1894	5.953	2.50	6.00	20.00	60.00
	1895	8.800	2.00	5.00	20.00	50.00
	1896	9.265	2.00	5.00	20.00	50.00
	1897	6.270	2.00	5.00	20.00	50.00
	1898	9.769	2.00	5.00	20.00	50.00
	1899	10.965	2.00	5.00	20.00	50.00
	1900	10.938	2.00	5.00	20.00	50.00
	1901	3.426	3.00	6.00	20.00	50.00

KM#	Date	Mintage	Fine	VF	XF	Unc
800	1902	7.890	2.50	5.00	20.00	50.00
	1902	.015	—	—	Proof	50.00
	1903	2.062	4.00	15.00	60.00	110.00
	1904	2.040	4.00	15.00	60.00	115.00
	1905	.488	30.00	60.00	350.00	900.00
	1906	10.791	2.75	6.50	25.00	60.00
	1907	14.083	3.00	9.00	30.00	70.00
	1908	3.807	7.00	20.00	65.00	150.00
	1909	5.665	4.00	15.00	65.00	130.00
	1910	26.547	2.00	5.00	20.00	50.00

KM#	Date	Mintage	Fine	VF	XF	Unc
816	1911	20.066	2.00	3.00	10.00	35.00
	1911	6,007	—	—	Proof	65.00
	1912	15.594	2.00	2.50	8.50	55.00
	1913	9.002	2.50	6.00	30.00	75.00
	1914	23.416	2.00	2.50	5.00	25.00
	1915	39.279	2.00	2.50	5.00	25.00
	1916	35.862	2.00	2.50	5.00	25.00
	1917	22.203	2.00	2.50	5.00	30.00
	1918	34.916	2.00	2.50	5.00	30.00
	1919	10.824	2.25	3.50	9.00	35.00

5.6552 g, .500 SILVER, .0909 oz ASW

KM#	Date	Mintage	Fine	VF	XF	Unc
816a	1920	22.825	BV	2.50	10.00	32.50
	1921	22.649	BV	2.50	10.00	45.00
	1922	27.216	BV	3.00	15.00	42.50
	1923	14.575	BV	2.50	10.00	42.50
	1924	9.250	BV	2.50	10.00	45.00
	1925	5.419	2.50	7.50	18.00	70.00
	1926	22.516	BV	5.00	12.00	45.00

Obv: Modified effigy, slightly smaller bust.

KM#	Date	Mintage	Fine	VF	XF	Unc
829	1926	Inc. Ab.	BV	2.00	6.00	35.00
	1927	9.262	BV	2.00	7.50	40.00

Rev: Larger lion and crown.

KM#	Date	Mintage	Fine	VF	XF	Unc
833	1927	Inc. Ab.	BV	2.00	6.00	40.00
	1927	.015	—	—	Proof	35.00
	1928	18.137	—	BV	3.00	12.00
	1928	—	—	—	Proof	—
	1929	19.343	—	BV	3.00	15.00
	1929	—	—	—	Proof	—
	1930	3.137	1.50	3.50	12.00	42.50
	1930	—	—	—	Proof	—
	1931	6.994	BV	2.00	4.50	15.00
	1931	—	—	—	Proof	—
	1932	12.168	BV	2.00	4.50	15.00
	1932	—	—	—	Proof	—
	1933	11.512	BV	2.00	4.50	15.00
	1933	—	—	—	Proof	300.00
	1934	6.138	BV	3.00	10.00	35.00
	1934	—	—	—	Proof	—
	1935	9.183	—	BV	2.25	10.00
	1935	—	—	—	Proof	—
	1936	11.911	—	BV	2.25	10.00
	1936	—	—	—	Proof	300.00

Rev: English crest.

KM#	Date	Mintage	Fine	VF	XF	Unc
853	1937	8.359	—	BV	2.00	7.50
	1937	.026	—	—	Proof	11.00
	1938	4.833	—	BV	3.00	19.00
	1938	—	—	—	Proof	200.00
	1939	11.053	—	BV	2.00	6.00
	1939	—	—	—	Proof	200.00
	1940	11.099	—	BV	2.00	6.00
	1940	—	—	—	Proof	—
	1941	11.392	—	BV	2.00	6.00
	1941	—	—	—	Proof	—
	1942	17.454	—	BV	2.00	4.50
	1943	11.404	—	BV	2.00	4.50
	1944	11.587	—	BV	2.00	4.50
	1945	15.143	—	BV	2.00	4.50
	1945	—	—	—	Proof	—
	1946	18.664	—	BV	1.50	3.50
	1946	—	—	—	Proof	—

Rev: Scottish crest.

KM#	Date	Mintage	Fine	VF	XF	Unc
854	1937	6.749	—	BV	2.00	7.50
	1937	.026	—	—	Proof	9.00
	1938	4.798	—	BV	4.00	15.00
	1938	—	—	—	Proof	200.00
	1939	10.264	—	BV	2.50	6.00
	1939	—	—	—	Proof	200.00
	1940	9.913	—	BV	2.50	6.00
	1940	—	—	—	Proof	—
	1941	8.086	—	.10	3.00	1.75
	1941	—	—	—	Proof	—
	1942	13.677	—	BV	2.50	6.00
	1943	9.824	—	BV	2.50	6.00
	1944	10.990	—	BV	2.50	7.50
	1945	15.106	—	BV	1.50	3.50
	1945	—	—	—	Proof	—
	1946	16.382	—	BV	1.50	3.50
	1946	—	—	—	Proof	—

COPPER-NICKEL

Rev: English crest.

KM#	Date	Mintage	Fine	VF	XF	Unc
863	1947	12.121	.10	.25	1.00	6.00
	1947	—	—	—	Proof	—
	1948	45.577	.10	.15	.50	4.00
	1948	—	—	—	Proof	200.00

Rev: Scottish crest.

KM#	Date	Mintage	Fine	VF	XF	Unc
864	1947	12.283	.10	.25	1.00	6.00
	1947	—	—	—	Proof	—
	1948	45.352	.10	.15	.50	4.00
	1948	—	—	—	Proof	200.00

Rev: English crest, leg: W/o IND IMP.

KM#	Date	Mintage	Fine	VF	XF	Unc
876	1949	19.328	.10	.25	1.25	6.50
	1949	—	—	—	Proof	—
	1950	19.244	.10	.25	1.50	8.00
	1950	.018	—	—	Proof	9.00
	1951	9.957	.10	.25	1.50	8.00
	1951	.020	—	—	Proof	9.00

Rev: Scottish crest.

KM#	Date	Mintage	Fine	VF	XF	Unc
877	1949	21.243	.10	.25	1.25	6.50
	1949	—	—	—	Proof	—
	1950	14.300	.10	.25	1.50	8.00
	1950	.018	—	—	Proof	9.00
	1951	10.961	.10	.25	1.50	8.00
	1951	.020	—	—	Proof	9.00

Rev: English arms.

KM#	Date	Mintage	Fine	VF	XF	Unc
890	1953	41.943	—	.10	.25	1.75
	1953	.040	—	—	Proof	7.50

Rev: Scottish arms.

KM#	Date	Mintage	Fine	VF	XF	Unc
891	1953	20.664	—	.10	.25	1.75
	1953	.040	—	—	Proof	7.50

Obv. leg: W/o BRITT OMN. Rev: English arms.

KM#	Date	Mintage	Fine	VF	XF	Unc
904	1954	30.162	—	.10	.25	1.75
	1954	—	—	—	Proof	200.00
	1955	45.260	—	.10	.25	1.75
	1955	—	—	—	Proof	—
	1956	44.970	—	.10	.50	5.00
	1956	—	—	—	Proof	—
	1957	42.774	—	.10	.25	1.50
	1957	—	—	—	Proof	—
	1958	14.392	.25	.75	2.50	10.00
	1958	—	—	—	Proof	—
	1959	19.443	—	.10	.25	1.50
	1959	—	—	—	Proof	—
	1960	27.028	—	.10	.25	1.50
	1960	—	—	—	Proof	—
	1961	39.817	—	.10	.25	1.25
	1961	—	—	—	Proof	—
	1962	36.704	—	.10	.15	.50
	1962	—	—	—	Proof	—

GREAT BRITAIN 764

KM#	Date	Mintage	Fine	VF	XF	Unc
904	1963	49.434	—	—	.10	.25
	1963	—	—	—	Proof	—
	1964	8.591	—	—	.10	.25
	1964	—	—	—	Proof	—
	1965	9.216	—	—	.10	.25
	1966	15.002	—	—	.10	.25
	1970	.731	—	—	Proof	3.00

Rev: Scottish arms.

905	1954	26.772	—	.10	.25	1.75
	1954	—	—	—	Proof	150.00
	1955	27.951	—	.10	.25	1.75
	1955	—	—	—	Proof	—
	1956	42.854	—	.10	1.00	10.00
	1956	—	—	—	Proof	—
	1957	17.960	—	.10	1.00	10.00
	1957	—	—	—	Proof	—
	1958	40.823	—	.10	.25	1.75
	1958	—	—	—	Proof	—
	1959	1.013	1.00	3.00	6.00	20.00
	1959	—	—	—	Proof	—
	1960	14.376	—	.10	.50	3.50
	1960	—	—	—	Proof	—
	1961	2.763	.25	.50	1.25	6.00
	1961	—	—	—	Proof	—
	1962	17.475	—	.10	.15	.50
	1962	—	—	—	Proof	—
	1963	32.300	—	—	.10	.25
	1963	—	—	—	Proof	—
	1964	5.239	—	—	.10	.25
	1965	2.774	—	—	.10	.25
	1966	15.604	—	—	.10	.25
	1970	.731	—	—	Proof	2.50

FLORIN

11.3104 g, .925 SILVER, .3364 oz ASW

745	1848	—	—	—	Proof	3500.
	1848 plain edge	—	—	—	Proof	1500.
	1849	.414	12.50	27.50	75.00	275.00

GOLD (OMS)

| 745a | 1848 | — | — | — | Proof | 10,000. |

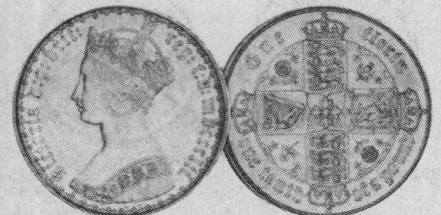

11.3104 g, .925 SILVER, .3364 oz ASW
Gothic type. Obv. leg: BRIT. . . .
W/o die numbers.

746.1	1851	1.540	—	—	—	—
	1851	—	—	—	Proof	8000.
	1852	1.015	8.50	30.00	90.00	240.00
	1852	—	—	—	Proof	1500.
	1853	3.920	8.75	35.00	100.00	300.00
	1853	—	—	—	Proof	1500.
	1854	.550	400.00	750.00	1500.	—
	1855	.831	8.50	30.00	110.00	350.00
	1856	2.202	8.75	35.00	110.00	325.00
	1857	1.671	8.00	30.00	110.00	300.00
	1857	—	—	—	Proof	2000.
	1858	2.239	8.00	30.00	110.00	300.00
	1858	—	—	—	Proof	3000.
	1859	2.568	8.00	30.00	110.00	300.00
	1860	1.475	13.00	40.00	150.00	450.00
	1862	.594	25.00	100.00	400.00	900.00
	1862 plain edge	—	—	—	Proof	4000.
	1863	.939	25.00	100.00	400.00	900.00
	1863 plain edge	—	—	—	Proof	3000.

With die numbers.

746.3	1864	1.861	8.00	30.00	110.00	350.00
	1864	—	—	—	Proof	3000.
	1865	1.580	8.50	30.00	110.00	325.00
	1866	.915	8.50	30.00	110.00	325.00
	1867	.424	20.00	60.00	250.00	700.00
	1867 plain edge	—	—	—	Proof	4000.

Obv. leg: BRITT. . . . with die number.

KM#	Date	Mintage	Fine	VF	XF	Unc
746.2	1868	.870	8.50	30.00	110.00	400.00
	1869	.297	8.50	30.00	95.00	275.00
	1869	—	—	—	Proof	2000.
	1870	1.081	8.00	30.00	110.00	325.00
	1871	3.426	8.00	30.00	110.00	325.00
	1871	—	—	—	Proof	3000.
	1871 plain edge	—	—	—	Proof	3000.
	1872	7.200	7.50	25.00	90.00	240.00
	1873	5.922	8.50	30.00	90.00	240.00
	1873	—	—	—	Proof	4000.
	1874	1.643	8.00	30.00	95.00	275.00
	1875	1.117	8.50	30.00	95.00	275.00
	1876	.580	8.50	30.00	100.00	300.00
	1877	.682	8.50	30.00	100.00	300.00
	1879	1.512	8.00	40.00	150.00	375.00

W/o die numbers.

746.4	1877	Inc. Ab.	25.00	70.00	300.00	650.00
	1878	1.787	8.00	30.00	100.00	325.00
	1878	—	—	—	Proof	4500.
	1879	Inc. Ab.	8.50	30.00	100.00	300.00
	1879	—	—	—	Proof	4000.
	1880	2.161	7.50	25.00	85.00	275.00
	1880	—	—	—	Proof	4000.
	1881	2.576	7.50	25.00	85.00	275.00
	1881	—	—	—	Proof	4500.
	1881 plain edge	—	—	—	Proof	4000.
	1881 (error) MDCCCLXXRI					
		Inc. Ab.	12.00	35.00	120.00	300.00
	1883	3.556	7.50	25.00	90.00	240.00
	1884	1.447	7.50	25.00	90.00	275.00
	1885	1.758	7.50	25.00	80.00	240.00
	1885	—	—	—	Proof	4500.
	1886	.592	8.50	30.00	100.00	300.00
	1886	—	—	—	Proof	4500.
	1887	1.777	8.50	30.00	120.00	375.00
	1887	—	—	—	Proof	4500.

NOTE: Varieties exist.

762	1887	Inc. Ab.	3.00	6.00	16.00	38.00
	1887	1.084	—	—	Proof	150.00
	1888	1.548	4.00	8.00	25.00	65.00
	1889	2.974	4.00	8.00	25.00	65.00
	1890	1.685	6.50	30.00	95.00	200.00
	1891	.836	15.00	55.00	165.00	300.00
	1892	.283	17.50	60.00	200.00	400.00
	1892	—	—	—	Proof	900.00

781	1893	1.666	3.50	10.00	25.00	65.00
	1893	1,312	—	—	Proof	150.00
	1894	1.953	3.50	10.00	35.00	75.00
	1895	2.183	3.50	10.00	30.00	70.00
	1896	2.944	3.50	10.00	35.00	75.00
	1897	1.700	3.50	10.00	30.00	70.00
	1898	3.061	3.50	10.00	35.00	70.00
	1899	3.970	3.50	10.00	30.00	70.00
	1900	5.529	3.50	10.00	30.00	70.00
	1901	2.649	3.50	10.00	25.00	65.00

KM#	Date	Mintage	Fine	VF	XF	Unc
801	1902	2.190	7.50	15.00	30.00	70.00
	1902	.015	—	—	Proof	75.00
	1903	.995	12.00	45.00	100.00	120.00
	1904	2.770	10.00	40.00	100.00	200.00
	1905	1.188	20.00	75.00	175.00	475.00
	1906	6.910	8.00	25.00	55.00	130.00
	1907	5.948	8.00	25.00	70.00	175.00
	1908	3.280	9.00	27.50	110.00	240.00
	1909	3.483	10.00	37.50	125.00	275.00
	1910	5.651	6.00	14.00	40.00	90.00

817	1911	5.951	4.00	7.50	30.00	75.00
	1911	6.007	—	—	Proof	90.00
	1912	8.572	4.50	9.00	45.00	90.00
	1913	4.545	4.50	9.00	45.00	90.00
	1914	21.253	3.00	5.00	15.00	40.00
	1915	12.358	3.00	4.00	10.00	40.00
	1916	21.064	3.00	4.00	10.00	40.00
	1917	11.182	3.00	6.00	12.50	60.00
	1918	29.212	3.00	4.00	10.00	40.00
	1919	9.469	3.00	5.00	10.00	50.00

11.3104 g, .500 SILVER, .1818 oz ASW

817a	1920	15.388	1.75	4.50	13.50	55.00
	1921	34.864	1.75	3.00	12.00	37.50
	1922	23.861	1.75	3.00	13.50	50.00
	1923	21.547	1.75	3.00	13.50	37.50
	1924	4.582	2.00	5.00	15.00	65.00
	1925	1.404	7.50	40.00	95.00	200.00
	1926	5.125	3.50	8.00	30.00	90.00

834	1927	.015	—	—	Proof	65.00
	1928	11.088	1.50	2.50	5.00	22.50
	1928	—	—	—	Proof	—
	1929	16.397	1.50	2.50	5.00	22.50
	1929	—	—	—	Proof	—
	1930	5.734	1.75	3.00	8.00	30.00
	1930	—	—	—	Proof	—
	1931	6.556	1.75	3.00	8.00	30.00
	1931	—	—	—	Proof	—
	1932	.717	12.50	35.00	120.00	240.00
	1932	—	—	—	Proof	1750.
	1933	8.685	1.50	2.50	6.00	22.50
	1933	—	—	—	Proof	300.00
	1935	7.541	1.50	2.50	6.00	22.50
	1935	—	—	—	Proof	—
	1936	9.897	1.50	2.25	4.50	17.50
	1936	—	—	—	Proof	300.00

855	1937	13.007	—	—	BV	2.50	6.50
	1937	.026	—	—	Proof	15.00	
	1938	7.909	BV	2.25	5.00	16.00	
	1938	—	—	—	Proof	200.00	
	1939	20.851	—	—	BV	2.50	5.50
	1939	—	—	—	Proof	200.00	
	1940	18.700	—	—	BV	2.50	5.50
	1940	—	—	—	Proof	—	
	1941	24.451	—	—	BV	2.25	5.00
	1941	—	—	—	Proof	—	

KM#	Date	Mintage	Fine	VF	XF	Unc
855	1942	39.895	—	BV	2.25	5.00
	1942	—	—	—	Proof	—
	1943	26.712	—	BV	2.25	5.00
	1944	27.560	—	BV	2.25	5.00
	1944	—	—	—	Proof	—
	1945	25.858	—	BV	2.25	5.00
	1945	—	—	—	Proof	—
	1946	22.300	—	BV	2.25	5.00
	1946	—	—	—	Proof	—

COPPER-NICKEL

KM#	Date	Mintage	Fine	VF	XF	Unc
865	1947	22.910	.20	.35	1.00	3.50
	1947	—	—	—	Proof	—
	1948	67.554	.20	.35	.65	2.50
	1948	—	—	—	Proof	175.00

Rev. leg: W/o IND IMP.

878	1949	28.615	.20	.35	1.50	8.00
	1949	—	—	—	Proof	—
	1950	24.357	.20	.35	1.50	8.00
	1950	.018	—	—	Proof	11.00
	1951	27.412	.20	.35	1.50	5.00
	1951	.020	—	—	Proof	13.00

892	1953	11.959	.20	.30	.60	3.50
	1953	.040	—	—	Proof	8.00

Obv. leg: W/o BRITT OMN.

906	1954	13.085	.20	.50	3.50	18.00
	1954	—	—	—	Proof	250.00
	1955	25.887	.20	.30	.50	1.75
	1955	—	—	—	Proof	—
	1956	47.824	.20	.30	.50	2.50
	1956	—	—	—	Proof	200.00
	1957	33.071	.20	.35	1.75	16.00
	1957	—	—	—	Proof	—
	1958	9.565	.25	.50	.75	8.00
	1958	—	—	—	Proof	—
	1959	14.080	.25	.50	3.50	20.00
	1959	—	—	—	Proof	—
	1960	13.832	—	.20	.30	1.75
	1960	—	—	—	Proof	—
	1961	37.735	—	.20	.40	2.00
	1961	—	—	—	Proof	—
	1962	35.148	—	.20	.30	1.50
	1962	—	—	—	Proof	—
	1963	26.471	—	.20	.25	1.00
	1963	—	—	—	Proof	—
	1964	16.539	—	.20	.25	1.00
	1965	48.163	—	.20	.25	.75
	1966	83.999	—	.20	.25	.75
	1967	39.718	—	.20	.25	.75
	1970	.731	—	—	Proof	3.00

1/2 CROWN

14.1380 g, .925 SILVER, .4205 oz ASW
Obv: Large bust.

KM#	Date	Mintage	Fine	VF	XF	Unc
667	1816	—	12.00	40.00	175.00	550.00
667	1816 reeded edge	—	—	—	Proof	1250.
	1816 plain edge	—	—	—	Proof	1250.
	1817	8.093	10.00	35.00	130.00	225.00
	1817 reeded edge	—	—	—	Proof	1250.
	1817 plain edge	—	—	—	Proof	1250.

Obv: Small head.

672	1817	Inc. Ab.	10.00	35.00	130.00	225.00
	1817	—	—	—	Proof	1250.
	1817 plain edge	—	—	—	Proof	—
	1818	2.905	15.00	40.00	150.00	350.00
	1818	—	—	—	Proof	1000.
	1819	4.790	10.00	35.00	135.00	325.00
	1819	—	—	—	Proof	1000.
	1820	2.397	15.00	50.00	175.00	375.00
	1820	—	—	—	Proof	1000.
	1820 plain edge	—	—	—	Proof	1000.

676	1820	Inc. Ab.	10.00	27.50	100.00	275.00
	1820	—	—	—	Proof	900.00
	1820 plain edge	—	—	—	Proof	900.00
	1821	1.435	12.00	30.00	145.00	275.00
	1821	—	—	—	Proof	950.00
	1823	2.004	225.00	675.00	3250.	5500.

688	1823	Inc. Ab.	12.00	30.00	160.00	400.00
	1823	—	—	—	Proof	1250.
	1824	.466	15.00	40.00	190.00	600.00
	1824	—	—	—	Proof	1250.

695	1825	2.259	12.00	37.50	135.00	300.00
	1825	—	—	—	Proof	1000.
	1825 plain edge	—	—	—	Proof	1000.
	1826	2.189	10.00	30.00	115.00	250.00
	1826	—	—	—	Proof	725.00
	1828	.050	17.50	55.00	250.00	600.00
	1829	.508	15.00	55.00	160.00	425.00

714	1831	—	—	—	Proof	1000.
	1831 plain edge	—	—	—	Proof	750.00

GREAT BRITAIN 765

KM#	Date	Mintage	Fine	VF	XF	Unc
714	1834 W.W. in caps	.993	20.00	60.00	200.00	350.00
	1834	—	—	—	Proof	—
	1834 W.W. in script					
		Inc. Ab.	15.00	40.00	150.00	300.00
	1834	—	—	—	Proof	—
	1834 plain edge	—	—	—	—	—
	1835	.282	20.00	60.00	200.00	400.00
	1836/5	1.589	30.00	65.00	225.00	500.00
	1836	Inc. Ab.	15.00	40.00	150.00	300.00
	1836 plain edge	—	—	—	Proof	—
	1837	.151	20.00	60.00	200.00	400.00

740	1839 W.W. in relief	—	200.00	750.00	2750.	4250.
	1839 plain edge	—	—	—	Proof	1100.
	1840 W.W. incuse	.386	15.00	65.00	185.00	400.00
	1841	.043	20.00	85.00	450.00	1100.
	1842	.486	10.00	35.00	150.00	350.00
	1843	.455	10.00	65.00	300.00	650.00
	1844	1.999	10.00	35.00	150.00	350.00
	1845/3	2.232	—	—	—	—
	1845	Inc. Ab.	7.50	35.00	130.00	300.00
	1846	1.540	10.00	40.00	140.00	300.00
	1848/6	.367	32.50	100.00	320.00	750.00
	1848	Inc. Ab.	40.00	120.00	400.00	900.00
	1849 large date	.261	12.50	37.50	300.00	650.00
	1849 small date	Inc. Ab.	15.00	50.00	300.00	675.00
	1850	.485	15.00	35.00	300.00	700.00
	1850	—	—	—	Proof	—
	1851	—	—	—	Proof	—
	1853	—	—	—	Proof	2500.
	1862	—	—	—	Proof	3750.
	1864	—	—	—	Proof	—

Obv: Second young head.

756	1874	2.189	10.00	25.00	80.00	250.00
	1874	—	—	—	Proof	—
	1874 plain edge	—	—	—	Proof	—
	1875	1.113	10.00	30.00	90.00	275.00
	1875	—	—	—	Proof	—
	1875 plain edge	—	—	—	—	—
	1876/5	.633	—	200.00	400.00	950.00
	1876	Inc. Ab.	10.00	30.00	90.00	275.00
	1877	.447	10.00	30.00	90.00	240.00
	1878	1.466	10.00	30.00	90.00	240.00
	1878	—	—	—	Proof	—
	1879	.901	12.00	35.00	120.00	300.00
	1879	—	—	—	Proof	—
	1880	1.346	10.00	25.00	80.00	240.00
	1880	—	—	—	Proof	—
	1881	2.301	9.00	25.00	75.00	240.00
	1881	—	—	—	Proof	1500.
	1881 plain edge	—	—	—	Proof	—
	1882	.808	12.00	32.50	85.00	240.00
	1883	2.983	9.00	27.50	75.00	240.00
	1884	1.569	9.00	27.50	75.00	240.00
	1885	1.628	9.00	27.50	75.00	240.00
	1885	—	—	—	Proof	—
	1886	.892	9.00	27.50	75.00	240.00
	1886	—	—	—	Proof	—
	1887	1.438	10.00	40.00	100.00	250.00
	1887	—	—	—	Proof	—

.916 GOLD (OMS)

756a	1874	—	—	—	Proof	Rare

GREAT BRITAIN

14.1380 g, .925 SILVER, .4205 oz ASW

KM#	Date	Mintage	Fine	VF	XF	Unc
764	1887	Inc. Ab.	4.00	8.00	12.50	40.00
	1887	1,084	—	—	Proof	175.00
	1888	1,429	6.00	12.00	35.00	90.00
	1889	4,812	6.00	12.00	30.00	75.00
	1890	3,228	6.00	12.00	40.00	90.00
	1891	2,285	6.00	12.00	40.00	90.00
	1892	1,711	7.50	15.00	45.00	110.00

KM#	Date	Mintage	Fine	VF	XF	Unc
782	1893	1,793	5.00	13.00	35.00	95.00
	1893	1,312	—	—	Proof	175.00
	1894	1,525	6.00	16.00	45.00	120.00
	1895	1,773	5.00	13.00	35.00	95.00
	1896	2,149	5.00	13.00	35.00	95.00
	1897	1,679	5.00	13.00	35.00	95.00
	1898	1,870	5.00	13.00	35.00	95.00
	1899	2,866	5.00	13.00	35.00	95.00
	1900	4,479	5.00	13.00	35.00	95.00
	1901	1,577	5.00	13.00	35.00	95.00

KM#	Date	Mintage	Fine	VF	XF	Unc
802	1902	1,316	10.00	20.00	40.00	100.00
	1902	.015	—	—	Proof	100.00
	1903	.275	17.50	75.00	300.00	850.00
	1904	.710	12.00	45.00	175.00	500.00
	1905	.166	100.00	300.00	1000.	1750.
	1906	2,886	9.00	25.00	55.00	200.00
	1907	3,694	10.00	27.50	55.00	210.00
	1908	1,759	12.00	30.00	80.00	265.00
	1909	3,052	10.00	22.50	60.00	175.00
	1910	2,558	8.50	15.00	40.00	120.00

KM#	Date	Mintage	Fine	VF	XF	Unc
818.1	1911	2,915	5.00	12.00	45.00	120.00
	1911	6,007	—	—	Proof	130.00
	1912	4,701	5.00	12.00	45.00	100.00
	1913	4,090	5.00	15.00	50.00	140.00
	1914	18,333	4.00	7.00	12.50	40.00
	1915	32,433	4.00	6.00	12.50	35.00
	1916	29,530	4.00	6.00	12.50	35.00
	1917	11,172	4.50	7.00	15.00	45.00
	1918	29,080	4.00	6.00	12.50	35.00
	1919	10,267	4.50	8.00	17.50	50.00

14.1380 g, .500 SILVER, .2273 oz ASW
Rev: Crown touches shield.

818.1a	1920	17,983	2.25	5.00	17.50	65.00
	1921	23,678	2.25	5.00	20.00	65.00
	1922	16,397	2.25	5.00	20.00	65.00

Rev: Groove between crown and shield.

818.2	1922	Inc. Ab.	—	5.00	17.50	60.00
	1923	26,309	1.75	4.50	12.50	35.00
	1924	5,866	3.00	7.50	20.00	70.00
	1925	1,413	8.00	30.00	150.00	350.00
	1926	4,474	3.00	10.00	35.00	95.00

Obv: Modified effigy; larger beads.

830	1926	Inc. Ab.	3.00	10.00	50.00	135.00
	1927	6,838	2.50	6.00	15.00	50.00

KM#	Date	Mintage	Fine	VF	XF	Unc
835	1927	.015	—	—	Proof	50.00
	1928	18,763	2.00	3.00	7.50	22.50
	1928	—	—	—	Proof	—
	1929	17,633	2.00	3.00	7.50	22.50
	1929	—	—	—	Proof	—
	1930	.810	7.50	25.00	125.00	275.00
	1930	—	—	—	Proof	—
	1931	11,264	2.00	4.00	8.00	22.50
	1931	—	—	—	Proof	—
	1932	4,794	3.50	8.00	17.50	45.00
	1932	—	—	—	Proof	—
	1933	10,311	2.00	4.00	8.00	22.50
	1933	—	—	—	Proof	500.00
	1934	2,422	3.25	7.00	25.00	85.00
	1934	—	—	—	Proof	—
	1935	7,022	2.00	3.00	6.50	20.00
	1935	—	—	—	Proof	—
	1936	7,039	2.00	3.00	6.00	17.50
	1936	—	—	—	Proof	500.00

856	1937	9,106	BV	2.00	3.50	11.00
	1937	.026	—	—	Proof	16.00
	1938	6,426	BV	2.50	7.50	25.00
	1938	—	—	—	Proof	400.00
	1939	15,479	BV	2.00	3.50	11.00
	1939	—	—	—	Proof	400.00
	1940	17,948	BV	2.00	3.00	8.00
	1940	—	—	—	Proof	—
	1941	15,774	BV	1.75	2.75	6.50
	1941	—	—	—	Proof	—
	1942	31,220	BV	1.75	2.75	6.25
	1943	15,463	BV	1.75	2.75	6.25
	1943	—	—	—	Proof	—
	1944	15,255	BV	1.75	2.75	6.25
	1945	19,849	BV	1.75	2.75	6.25
	1945	—	—	—	Proof	—
	1946	22,725	BV	1.75	2.75	6.25
	1946	—	—	—	Proof	—

COPPER-NICKEL

866	1947	21,910	.25	.50	1.25	5.00
	1947	—	—	—	Proof	400.00
	1948	71,165	.25	.50	1.25	5.00
	1948	—	—	—	Proof	350.00

Rev. leg: W/o IND IMP.

879	1949	28,273	.25	.50	1.25	10.00
	1949	—	—	—	Proof	—
	1950	28,336	.25	.50	1.50	10.00
	1950	.018	—	—	Proof	12.50
	1951	9,004	.50	.75	1.50	10.00
	1951	.020	—	—	Proof	12.50
	1952	—	—	—	Rare	—

KM#	Date	Mintage	Fine	VF	XF	Unc
893	1953	4,333	.50	.75	1.50	3.50
	1953	.040	—	—	Proof	12.00

Obv. leg: W/o BRITT OMN.

907	1954	11,615	.50	1.00	5.00	20.00
	1954	—	—	—	Proof	400.00
	1955	23,629	.25	.50	1.00	5.00
	1955	—	—	—	Proof	—
	1956	33,935	.25	.50	1.00	5.00
	1956	—	—	—	Proof	—
	1957	34,201	.25	.50	.75	3.50
	1957	—	—	—	Proof	—
	1958	15,746	.25	.75	4.00	12.50
	1958	—	—	—	Proof	—
	1959	9,029	1.00	1.50	6.50	28.00
	1959	—	—	—	Proof	—
	1960	19,929	.25	.50	.75	5.00
	1960	—	—	—	—	—
	1961	25,888	.25	.50	.75	1.75
	1961	—	—	—	P/L	10.00
	1961	—	—	—	—	—
	1962	24,013	.25	.50	.75	1.75
	1962	—	—	—	—	—
	1963	17,625	.25	.50	.75	1.75
	1963	—	—	—	Proof	—
	1964	5,974	.25	.50	.75	2.50
	1965	9,778	.15	.25	.50	1.00
	1966	13,375	.10	.20	.30	.75
	1967	33,058	.10	.20	.30	.60
	1970	.731	—	—	Proof	3.00

DOUBLE FLORIN

22.6207 g, .925 SILVER, .6727 oz ASW

763	1887 Roman I	—	10.00	15.00	35.00	90.00
	1887 Roman I	.483				
		1,084	—	—	Proof	275.00
	1887 Arabic 1	Inc. Ab.	10.00	15.00	35.00	90.00
	1887 Arabic 1	*2,916	—	—	Proof	300.00
	1888	.243	10.00	20.00	55.00	180.00
	1888 2nd I in VICTORIA, inverted 1	Inc. Ab.	20.00	35.00	120.00	325.00
	1889	1,185	9.00	15.00	40.00	100.00
	1889 2nd I in VICTORIA, inverted 1	Inc. Ab.	20.00	35.00	150.00	600.00
	1890	.782	10.00	17.50	50.00	175.00

CROWN

28.2759 g, .925 SILVER, .8409 oz ASW

675	1818 LVIII	.155	20.00	55.00	220.00	600.00
	1818 LIX	I.A.	20.00	55.00	220.00	575.00
	1819/8 LIX	.683	32.50	100.00	350.00	850.00
	1819 LIX	I.A.	20.00	55.00	220.00	650.00
	1819 LX	I.A.	20.00	55.00	220.00	600.00
	1819 plain edge	—	—	—	Proof	—
	1820/19 LX	—	17.50	50.00	275.00	700.00
	1820 LX	.448	17.50	50.00	200.00	600.00

GREAT BRITAIN 767

KM#	Date	Mintage	Fine	VF	XF	Unc
680.1	1821	.438	20.00	50.00	325.00	950.00
	1821	—	—	—	Proof	2500.
	1822	.125	22.50	65.00	500.00	1200.
	1822	—	—	—	Proof	3000.

COPPER (OMS)

680.1a	1821				Proof	1100.
	1821 SECUNDO on edge				Proof	—

WHITE METAL (OMS)

| 680.1b | 1823 | | | | Proof | — |

28.2759 g, .925 SILVER, .8409 oz ASW
TERTIO on edge

680.2	1821	—	—	—	Proof	3500.
	1822	—	20.00	55.00	450.00	1100.
	1822	—	—	—	Proof	5000.

699	1826 plain edge				Proof	—
	1826 SEPTIMO on edge					
		150 pcs.	—	—	Proof	3000.
	1826LVIII	—	—	—	Proof	—

KM#	Date	Mintage	Fine	VF	XF	Unc
715	1831	100 pcs.	—	—	Proof	8000.

741	1839	—	—	—	Proof	4500.
	1844	.094	25.00	75.00	450.00	2250.
	1844	—	—	—	Proof	—
	1845	.159	25.00	75.00	450.00	2250.
	1845	—	—	—	Proof	—
	1847	.141	30.00	90.00	550.00	2500.
	1847	—	—	—	Proof	—

GOLD (OMS)

| 741a | 1847 plain edge | — | — | — | Proof | Rare |

28.2759 g, .925 SILVER, .8409 oz ASW

744	1847 UNDECIMO on edge					
		8,000	—	—	Proof	2500.
	Impaired Proof	300.00	475.00	700.00	—	
	1847 SEPTIMO on edge					
			—	—	Proof	9000.
	1847 plain edge				Proof	2400.
	Impaired Proof	300.00	575.00	900.00	—	
	1853 SEPTIMO on edge					
		460 pcs.	—	—	Proof	7000.
	1853 plain edge	—	—	—	Proof	8000.

KM#	Date	Mintage	Fine	VF	XF	Unc
765	1887	.173	12.50	22.50	45.00	110.00
	1887	1,084	—	—	Proof	450.00
	1888	.132	15.00	32.50	65.00	250.00
	1889	1.807	12.50	22.50	45.00	150.00
	1890	.998	12.50	22.50	45.00	220.00
	1891	.566	15.00	27.50	55.00	225.00
	1892	.451	15.00	27.50	55.00	250.00

783	1893LVI	.498	15.00	35.00	95.00	240.00
	1893LVI	1,312	—	—	Proof	650.00
	1893LVII	I.A.	20.00	110.00	300.00	600.00
	1894LVII	.145	15.00	50.00	140.00	280.00
	1894LVIII	I.A.	15.00	35.00	125.00	275.00
	1895LVIII	.253	15.00	35.00	125.00	275.00
	1895LIX	I.A.	15.00	35.00	120.00	260.00
	1896LIX	.318	25.00	50.00	250.00	500.00
	1896LX	I.A.	15.00	35.00	120.00	260.00
	1897LX	.262	15.00	35.00	120.00	260.00
	1897LXI	I.A.	15.00	35.00	120.00	260.00
	1898LXI	.161	25.00	50.00	250.00	400.00
	1898LXII	I.A.	15.00	40.00	125.00	275.00
	1899LXII	.166	15.00	35.00	125.00	275.00
	1899LXIII	I.A.	15.00	35.00	125.00	275.00
	1900LXIII	.353	15.00	35.00	120.00	260.00
	1900LXIV	I.A.	15.00	35.00	120.00	260.00

803	1902	.256	35.00	75.00	110.00	250.00
	1902	.015	—	—	Proof	250.00

GREAT BRITAIN 768

28.2759 g, .500 SILVER, .4546 oz ASW

KM#	Date	Mintage	Fine	VF	XF	Unc
836	1927	.015	—	—	Proof	170.00
	1928	9,034	60.00	90.00	150.00	325.00
	1928	—	—	—	Proof	1200.
	1929	4,994	65.00	95.00	165.00	350.00
	1929	—	—	—	Proof	1500.
	1930	4,847	60.00	90.00	150.00	325.00
	1930	—	—	—	Proof	1500.
	1931	4,056	60.00	90.00	150.00	325.00
	1931	—	—	—	Proof	—
	1932	2,395	85.00	175.00	250.00	600.00
	1932	—	—	—	Proof	2500.
	1933	7,132	60.00	90.00	150.00	325.00
	1933	—	—	—	Proof	—
	1934	932 pcs.	450.00	750.00	1500.	2500.
	1934	—	—	—	Proof	3200.
	1936	2,473	110.00	135.00	250.00	500.00
	1936	—	—	—	Proof	1500.

George V Silver Jubilee
842 1935 incused edge lettering
.715 6.00 8.00 12.50 25.00
1935 specimen in box of issue
— — — — 70.00
1935 (error) edge lettering: MEN.ANNO-REGNI
XXV. Inc. Ab. — — Proof 900.00
.925 SILVER
842a 1935 raised edge lettering
2,500 — — Proof 400.00
GOLD (OMS)
842b 1935 30 pcs. — — Proof 10,000.

28.2759 g, .500 SILVER, .4546 oz ASW

KM#	Date	Mintage	Fine	VF	XF	Unc
857	1937	.419	8.00	12.00	18.50	35.00
	1937	.026	—	—	Proof	60.00

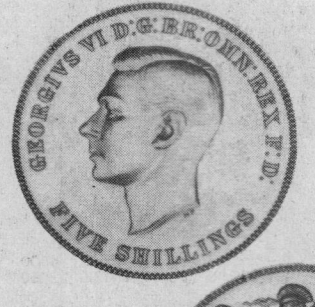

COPPER-NICKEL
Festival of Britain
880 1951 2.004 — — P/L 10.00
1951 30-50 pcs. — — V.I.P. Proof 300.00

Coronation
894 1953 5.963 — — 2.25 3.50
1953 .040 — — Proof 25.00

British Exhibition in New York

KM#	Date	Mintage	Fine	VF	XF	Unc
909	1960	1.024	—	—	4.50	6.00
	1960	.070	—	—	P/L	12.50
	1960	—	—	—	V.I.P. Proof	300.00

Winston Churchill
910 1965 9.640 — — .60 .80
1965 — Satin finish specimen 300.00

1/3 GUINEA

2.7834 g, .917 GOLD, .0820 oz AGW
648 1801 — 60.00 90.00 175.00 325.00
1802 — 60.00 90.00 175.00 325.00
1803 — 60.00 90.00 175.00 325.00

650 1804 — 60.00 90.00 175.00 350.00
1806 — 60.00 90.00 175.00 350.00
1808 — 60.00 90.00 175.00 350.00
1809 — 60.00 90.00 175.00 350.00
1810 — 60.00 90.00 175.00 350.00
1811 — 125.00 300.00 800.00 1100.
1813 — 65.00 100.00 350.00 750.00
1813 — — — Proof 1200.

1/2 GUINEA

4.1750 g, .917 GOLD, .1230 oz AGW

KM#	Date	Mintage	Fine	VF	XF	Unc
649	1801	—	100.00	125.00	200.00	525.00
	1802	—	100.00	125.00	200.00	525.00
	1803	—	100.00	125.00	200.00	525.00

KM#	Date	Mintage	Fine	VF	XF	Unc
651	1804	—	100.00	125.00	200.00	525.00
	1806	—	100.00	125.00	200.00	525.00
	1808	—	100.00	125.00	200.00	525.00
	1809	—	100.00	125.00	200.00	525.00
	1810	—	100.00	125.00	200.00	525.00
	1811	—	100.00	150.00	300.00	650.00
	1813	—	100.00	125.00	275.00	600.00

GUINEA

8.3500 g, .917 GOLD, .2461 oz AGW

KM#	Date	Mintage	Fine	VF	XF	Unc
664	1813	—	350.00	700.00	1200.	2250.
	1813	—	—	—	Proof	3500.

SOVEREIGN SERIES

1/2 SOVEREIGN

MINT MARKS

C - Ottawa, Canada
I - Bombay, India
M - Melbourne, Australia
P - Perth, Australia
S - Sydney, Australia
SA - Pretoria, South Africa

1/2 Sovereigns were struck at various foreign mints. The mint mark on the St. George/dragon type is usually found on the base under the right rear hoof of the horse. On shield type reverse the mint mark is found under the shield. Refer to appropriate country listings elsewhere in this catalog for coins having mint marks.

3.9940 g, .917 GOLD, .1177 oz AGW

KM#	Date	Mintage	Fine	VF	XF	Unc
673	1817	2.080	70.00	150.00	325.00	550.00
	1817	—	—	—	Proof	3500.
	1818/7	1.030	—	—	Rare	—
	1818	Inc. Ab.	75.00	150.00	350.00	650.00
	1818	—	—	—	Proof	5000.
	1820	.035	90.00	175.00	400.00	700.00

KM#	Date	Mintage	Fine	VF	XF	Unc
681	1821	.231	225.00	600.00	1700.	2700.
	1821	—	—	—	Proof	5000.

KM#	Date	Mintage	Fine	VF	XF	Unc
689	1823	.224	100.00	225.00	525.00	800.00
	1823	—	—	—	Proof	5500.
	1824	.592	90.00	200.00	450.00	800.00
	1825	.761	90.00	200.00	450.00	800.00
	1825	—	—	—	Proof	1500.

Obv: Bare head.

KM#	Date	Mintage	Fine	VF	XF	Unc
700	1826	.345	80.00	180.00	450.00	800.00
	1826	—	—	—	Proof	2500.
	1827	.492	85.00	200.00	475.00	1000.
	1828	1.225	80.00	190.00	450.00	900.00

KM#	Date	Mintage	Fine	VF	XF	Unc
716	1831	—	—	—	Proof	2500.

18mm

KM#	Date	Mintage	Fine	VF	XF	Unc
720	1834	.134	115.00	250.00	600.00	1400.

19mm

KM#	Date	Mintage	Fine	VF	XF	Unc
722	1835	.773	95.00	225.00	600.00	1200.
	1836	.147	275.00	900.00	3000.	9000.
	1837	.160	95.00	250.00	550.00	1000.

KM#	Date	Mintage	Fine	VF	XF	Unc
735.1	1838	.273	75.00	90.00	225.00	625.00
	1839	1,230	—	—	Proof	3000.
	1841	.509	75.00	90.00	225.00	625.00
	1842	2.223	75.00	90.00	200.00	550.00
	1843	1.252	75.00	90.00	200.00	625.00
	1844	1.127	75.00	90.00	200.00	550.00
	1845	.888	75.00	220.00	325.00	750.00
	1846	1.064	75.00	100.00	225.00	625.00
	1847	.983	75.00	90.00	200.00	550.00
	1848	.411	75.00	150.00	250.00	800.00
	1849	.845	75.00	100.00	200.00	550.00
	1850	.180	180.00	275.00	900.00	1625.
	1851	.774	70.00	100.00	225.00	625.00
	1852	1.378	70.00	100.00	200.00	550.00
	1853	2.709	70.00	100.00	200.00	550.00
	1853	—	—	—	Proof	5000.
	1854	1.125	225.00	350.00	650.00	1500.
	1855	1.120	70.00	100.00	200.00	550.00
	1856	2.392	70.00	100.00	200.00	550.00
	1857	.728	70.00	100.00	150.00	450.00
	1858	.856	70.00	100.00	175.00	495.00
	1859	2.204	70.00	90.00	175.00	495.00
	1860	1.132	70.00	90.00	175.00	495.00
	1861	1.131	70.00	100.00	200.00	575.00
	1862	—	350.00	600.00	2700.	6500.
	1863	1.572	70.00	90.00	150.00	450.00

NOTE: 1854 is much rarer than the mintage figure indicates.

Rev: With die number.

KM#	Date	Mintage	Fine	VF	XF	Unc
735.2	1863	Inc. Ab.	60.00	85.00	180.00	400.00
	1864	1.758	60.00	85.00	180.00	400.00
	1865	1.835	60.00	85.00	180.00	400.00
	1866	2.059	60.00	85.00	180.00	400.00
	1867	.993	60.00	85.00	180.00	400.00
	1869	1.862	60.00	85.00	200.00	400.00
	1870	.160	60.00	85.00	200.00	400.00
	1871	2.063	60.00	85.00	200.00	400.00
	1871 plain edge		—	—	Proof	2750.
	1872	3.249	60.00	85.00	150.00	400.00
	1873	1.927	60.00	85.00	150.00	400.00
	1874	1.884	60.00	85.00	150.00	400.00
	1875	.516	60.00	85.00	150.00	400.00
	1876	2.785	60.00	85.00	150.00	400.00
	1877	2.197	60.00	75.00	125.00	325.00
	1878	2.082	60.00	75.00	125.00	325.00
	1879	.035	75.00	125.00	200.00	300.00
	1880	1.009	60.00	75.00	125.00	325.00
	1883	2.870	60.00	90.00	150.00	325.00
	1884	1.114	60.00	90.00	150.00	325.00
	1885/3	4.469	80.00	110.00	180.00	375.00
	1885	Inc. Ab.	60.00	90.00	100.00	290.00

KM#	Date	Mintage	Fine	VF	XF	Unc
766	1887	.872	BV	65.00	100.00	125.00
	1887	797 pcs.	—	—	Proof	750.00
	1890	2.266	BV	65.00	100.00	150.00
	1891	1.079	BV	65.00	100.00	150.00
	1892	13.680	BV	65.00	100.00	150.00
	1893	4.427	BV	65.00	100.00	150.00

KM#	Date	Mintage	Fine	VF	XF	Unc
784	1893	Inc. Ab.	BV	65.00	85.00	115.00
	1893	773 pcs.	—	—	Proof	750.00
	1894	3.795	BV	60.00	75.00	125.00
	1895	2.869	BV	60.00	75.00	125.00
	1896	2.947	BV	60.00	75.00	125.00
	1897	3.568	BV	60.00	75.00	125.00
	1898	2.869	BV	60.00	75.00	125.00
	1899	3.362	BV	60.00	75.00	125.00
	1900	4.307	BV	60.00	75.00	125.00
	1901	2.038	BV	60.00	75.00	125.00

KM#	Date	Mintage	Fine	VF	XF	Unc
804	1902	4.244	BV	60.00	75.00	100.00
	1902	.015	—	—	Proof	225.00
	1903	2.522	BV	60.00	70.00	100.00
	1904	1.717	BV	60.00	70.00	100.00
	1905	3.024	BV	60.00	70.00	100.00
	1906	4.245	BV	60.00	70.00	100.00
	1907	4.233	BV	60.00	70.00	100.00
	1908	3.997	BV	60.00	70.00	100.00
	1909	4.011	BV	60.00	70.00	100.00
	1910	5.024	BV	60.00	70.00	100.00

KM#	Date	Mintage	Fine	VF	XF	Unc
819	1911	6.104	BV	60.00	70.00	100.00
	1911	3,764	—	—	Proof	325.00
	1912	6.224	BV	60.00	70.00	100.00
	1913	6.094	BV	60.00	70.00	100.00
	1914	7.251	BV	60.00	70.00	100.00
	1915	2.043	BV	60.00	70.00	100.00

KM#	Date	Mintage	Fine	VF	XF	Unc
858	1937	5,501	—	—	Proof	275.00

3.9900 g, .917 GOLD, .1176 oz AGW

KM#	Date	Mintage	Fine	VF	XF	Unc
922	1980	.010	—	—	Proof	110.00
	1982	2.500	—	—	—	70.00
	1982	.023	—	—	Proof	110.00
	1983	.022	—	—	Proof	110.00
	1984	.022	—	—	Proof	110.00

Obv: New portrait of Elizabeth II.

KM#	Date	Mintage	Fine	VF	XF	Unc
942	1985	.025	—	—	Proof	110.00
	1986	.025	—	—	Proof	125.00
	1987	.023	—	—	Proof	125.00
	1988	*.023	—	—	Proof	125.00

GREAT BRITAIN 770

500th Anniversary of the Gold Sovereign

KM#	Date	Mintage	Fine	VF	XF	Unc
955	1989	*.025	—	—	Proof	125.00

SOVEREIGN

MINT MARKS

C - Ottawa, Canada
I - Bombay, India
M - Melbourne, Australia
P - Perth, Australia
S - Sydney, Australia
SA - Pretoria, South Africa

Sovereigns were struck at various foreign mints. The mint mark on the St. George/dragon type is usually found on the base under the right rear hoof of the horse. On shield type reverse the mint mark is found under the shield. Refer to appropriate country listings elsewhere in this catalog for coins having mint marks.

7.9881 g, .917 GOLD, .2354 oz AGW

KM#	Date	Mintage	Fine	VF	XF	Unc
674	1817	3.235	150.00	225.00	525.00	1000.
	1817	—	—	—	Proof	8000.
	1818	2.347	150.00	275.00	625.00	1200.
	1819	3,574	—	—	Rare	—
	1820	.932	150.00	225.00	525.00	1000.
	1820	—	—	—	Proof	—

KM#	Date	Mintage	Fine	VF	XF	Unc
682	1821	9.405	150.00	225.00	675.00	1250.
	1821	—	—	—	Proof	4500.
	1822	5.357	160.00	225.00	725.00	1100.
	1823	.617	225.00	500.00	1400.	—
	1824	3.768	175.00	225.00	800.00	1200.
	1825	4.200	225.00	525.00	1800.	—

KM#	Date	Mintage	Fine	VF	XF	Unc
696	1825	Inc. Ab.	125.00	225.00	675.00	1200.
	1825	—	—	—	Proof	3500.
	1825 plain edge		—	—	Proof	3000.
	1826	5.724	125.00	200.00	675.00	1100.
	1826	—	—	—	Proof	3500.
	1827	2.267	125.00	225.00	725.00	1200.
	1828 only 6 or 7 known					
		.386	800.00	2500.	6500.	—
	1829	2.445	125.00	225.00	675.00	1200.
	1830	2.388	125.00	225.00	675.00	1200.
	1830	—	—	—	Proof	—
	1830 plain edge		—	—	Proof	10,000.

KM#	Date	Mintage	Fine	VF	XF	Unc
717	1831	.599	150.00	300.00	800.00	1500.
	1831	—	—	—	Proof	5500.
	1832	3.737	125.00	200.00	625.00	1200.
	1833	1.225	125.00	225.00	725.00	1300.
	1835	.723	125.00	225.00	725.00	1300.
	1836	1.714	125.00	225.00	725.00	1300.
	1837	1.173	125.00	225.00	725.00	1300.

Rev: W/o die number.

KM#	Date	Mintage	Fine	VF	XF	Unc
736.1	1838	2.719	BV	160.00	275.00	725.00
736.1	1838	—	—	—	Proof	4000.
	1839	.504	175.00	350.00	1000.	2000.
	1839	—	—	—	Proof	3500.
	1841	.124	1100.	1800.	5500.	—
	1842	4.865	—	BV	275.00	725.00
	1843/2	—	500.00	—	—	—
	1843 broad shield					
		5.982	—	BV	225.00	625.00
	1843 narrow shield					
		Inc. Ab.	725.00	1300.	3500.	—
	1844	3.000	—	BV	225.00	525.00
	1845	3.801	—	BV	225.00	475.00
	1846	3.803	—	BV	200.00	525.00
	1847	4.667	—	BV	200.00	525.00
	1848	2.247	—	BV	225.00	525.00
	1849	1.755	—	BV	225.00	575.00
	1850	1.402	—	BV	175.00	475.00
	1851	4.014	—	BV	175.00	475.00
	1852	8.053	—	BV	175.00	475.00
	1853	—	—	—	Proof	7200.
	1853 WW raised					
		10.598	—	BV	175.00	475.00
	1853 WW incuse					
		Inc. Ab.	—	BV	175.00	475.00
	1854 WW raised					
		3.590	—	BV	175.00	525.00
	1854 WW incuse					
		Inc. Ab.	—	BV	175.00	525.00
	1855 WW raised				175.00	450.00
		8.448	—	BV	175.00	450.00
	1855 WW incuse					
		Inc. Ab.	—	BV	175.00	450.00
	1856	4.806	—	BV	175.00	450.00
	1856 sm.dt.	I.A.	—	BV	175.00	450.00
	1857	4.496	—	BV	175.00	450.00
	1858	.803	BV	125.00	200.00	1000.
	1859	1.548	—	BV	175.00	525.00
	1859 sm.dt.	I.A.	—	BV	175.00	525.00
	1860	2.556	—	BV	350.00	900.00
	1861	7.623	—	BV	200.00	450.00
	1862/1	—	—	—	—	—
	1862	7.836	—	BV	175.00	400.00
	1863	5.922	—	BV	150.00	450.00
	1872	13.487	—	BV	150.00	300.00

Rev: Die number under wreath.

KM#	Date	Mintage	Fine	VF	XF	Unc
736.2	1863	Inc. Ab.	—	BV	150.00	400.00
	1864	8.656	—	BV	150.00	400.00
	1865	1.450	—	BV	150.00	400.00
	1866	4.047	—	BV	150.00	400.00
	1868	1.653	—	BV	150.00	400.00
	1869	6.441	—	BV	150.00	400.00
	1869	—	—	—	Proof	1500.
	1870	2.190	—	BV	150.00	400.00
	1871	8.767	—	BV	150.00	275.00
	1872	Inc. Ab.	—	BV	150.00	300.00
	1873	2.368	—	BV	150.00	300.00
	1874	.521	800.00	1800.	—	—

Ansell Variety
Obv: Additional line on lower edge of ribbon.

KM#	Date	Mintage	Fine	VF	XF	Unc
736.3	1859	.168	900.00	1600.	2500.	—

KM#	Date	Mintage	Fine	VF	XF	Unc
752	1871	Inc. Ab.	—	BV	150.00	350.00
	1871	—	—	—	Proof	3500.
	1872	Inc. Ab.	—	BV	120.00	290.00
	1873	Inc. Ab.	—	BV	160.00	350.00
	1874	Inc. Ab.	125.00	150.00	350.00	550.00
	1876	3.319	—	BV	135.00	350.00
	1876	Inc. Ab.	—	—	Proof	—
	1878	1.091	—	BV	135.00	350.00
	1879	.020	180.00	450.00	1350.	4000.
	1880	3.650	—	BV	135.00	350.00
	1880 w/o designers initials on rev.					
		—	—	BV	135.00	350.00
	1884	1.770	—	BV	135.00	300.00
	1885	.718	—	BV	135.00	300.00

KM#	Date	Mintage	Fine	VF	XF	Unc
767	1887	1.111	—	BV	120.00	150.00
	1887	797 pcs.	—	—	Proof	1000.
	1888	2.777	—	BV	120.00	150.00
	1889	7.257	—	BV	120.00	175.00
	1890	6.530	—	BV	120.00	175.00
767	1891	6.329	—	BV	120.00	175.00
	1892	7.105	—	BV	120.00	175.00

KM#	Date	Mintage	Fine	VF	XF	Unc
785	1893	6.898	—	BV	120.00	150.00
	1893	773 pcs.	—	—	Proof	1000.
	1894	3.783	—	BV	120.00	160.00
	1895	2.285	—	BV	120.00	160.00
	1896	3.334	—	BV	120.00	160.00
	1898	4.361	—	BV	120.00	160.00
	1899	7.516	—	BV	120.00	150.00
	1900	10.847	—	BV	120.00	150.00
	1901	1.579	—	BV	120.00	150.00

KM#	Date	Mintage	Fine	VF	XF	Unc
805	1902	4.738	—	—	BV	150.00
	1902	.015	—	—	Proof	275.00
	1903	8.889	—	—	BV	150.00
	1904	10.041	—	—	BV	150.00
	1905	5.910	—	—	BV	150.00
	1906	10.467	—	—	BV	150.00
	1907	18.459	—	—	BV	150.00
	1908	11.729	—	—	BV	150.00
	1909	12.157	—	—	BV	150.00
	1910	22.380	—	—	BV	150.00

KM#	Date	Mintage	Fine	VF	XF	Unc
820	1911	30.044	—	—	BV	135.00
	1911	3,764	—	—	Proof	500.00
	1912	30.318	—	—	BV	135.00
	1913	24.540	—	—	BV	135.00
	1914	11.501	—	—	BV	135.00
	1915	20.295	—	—	BV	135.00
	1916	1.554	—	BV	125.00	150.00
	1917	1.015	—	—	Rare	—
	1925	4.406	—	—	BV	135.00

KM#	Date	Mintage	Fine	VF	XF	Unc
859	1937	5,501	—	—	Proof	650.00

KM#	Date	Mintage	Fine	VF	XF	Unc
908	1957	2.072	—	—	BV	150.00
	1957	—	—	—	Proof	—
	1958*	8.700	—	—	BV	130.00
	1958	—	—	—	Proof	—
	1959	1.358	—	—	BV	135.00
	1959	—	—	—	Proof	—
	1962	3.000	—	—	BV	130.00
	1962	—	—	—	Proof	—
	1963	7.400	—	—	BV	130.00
	1963	—	—	—	Proof	—
	1964	3.000	—	—	BV	130.00
	1965	3.800	—	—	BV	130.00
	1966	7.050	—	—	BV	130.00
	1967	5.000	—	—	BV	130.00
	1968	4.203	—	—	BV	130.00

KM#	Date	Mintage	Fine	VF	XF	Unc
919	1974	5.003	—	—	BV	130.00
	1976	4.150	—	—	BV	130.00
	1978	7.500	—	—	BV	130.00
	1979	9.100	—	—	BV	130.00
	1979	.050	—	—	Proof	150.00
	1980	5.100	—	—	BV	130.00
	1980	.100	—	—	Proof	150.00
	1981	5.000	—	—	BV	130.00
	1981	.055	—	—	Proof	155.00
	1982	2.950	—	—	BV	130.00
	1982	.023	—	—	Proof	190.00
	1983	.022	—	—	Proof	200.00
	1984	.022	—	—	Proof	200.00

Obv: New portrait of Elizabeth II.

943	1985	.025	—	—	Proof	350.00
	1986	.025	—	—	Proof	350.00
	1987	.023	—	—	Proof	350.00
	1988	*.025	—	—	Proof	350.00

500th Anniversary of the Gold Sovereign

956	1989	*.028	—	—	Proof	250.00

2 POUNDS

15.9761 g, .917 GOLD, .4708 oz AGW

690	1823	—	300.00	500.00	1000.	1800.

701	1826	450 pcs.	—	—	Proof	6000.

718	1831	225 pcs.	—	—	Proof	9000.

768	1887	.091	250.00	300.00	500.00	600.00
	1887	797 pcs.	—	—	Proof	1600.

NOTE: Proof issues with mint mark S under right rear hoof of horse were struck at Sydney, refer to Australia listings.

KM#	Date	Mintage	Fine	VF	XF	Unc
786	1893	.052	250.00	325.00	675.00	900.00
	1893	773 pcs.	—	—	Proof	2200.

806	1902	.046	250.00	300.00	475.00	575.00
	1902	8,066	—	—	Proof	650.00

NOTE: Proof issues with mint mark S under right rear hoof of horse were struck at Sydney, refer to Australia listings.

821	1911	2,812	—	—	Proof	1300.

860	1937	5,501	—	—	Proof	750.00

15.9200 g, .917 GOLD, .4694 oz AGW

923	1980	.010	—	—	Proof	400.00
	1982	2,500	—	—	Proof	550.00
	1983	.013	—	—	Proof	550.00

Obv: New portrait of Elizabeth II.

944	1985	.013	—	—	Proof	325.00
	1987	.015	—	—	Proof	425.00
	1988	*.015	—	—	Proof	425.00

15.9800 g, .917 GOLD, .4708 oz AGW
500th Anniversary of the Gold Sovereign

KM#	Date	Mintage	Fine	VF	XF	Unc
957	1989	*.017	—	—	Proof	420.00

5 POUNDS

39.9403 g, .917 GOLD, 1.1773 oz AGW

702	1826	150 pcs.	—	—	Proof	15,000.

742	1839	400 pcs.	—	—	Proof	28,000.

769	1887	.054	625.00	725.00	1000.	1500.
	1887	797 pcs.	—	—	Proof	3600.

NOTE: Proof issues with mint mark S under right rear hoof of horse were struck at Sydney, refer to Australia listings.

787	1893	.020	675.00	750.00	1200.	2000.
	1893	773 pcs.	—	—	Proof	2750.

807	1902	*.035	625.00	700.00	850.00	1100.
	1902	8,066	—	—	Proof	1250.

NOTE: Proof issues with mint mark S under right rear hoof of horse were struck at Sydney, refer to Australia listings.
*NOTE: 27,000 pieces were remelted.

GREAT BRITAIN 772

KM#	Date	Mintage	Fine	VF	XF	Unc
822	1911	2,812	—	—	Proof	2700.

| 861 | 1937 | 5,501 | — | — | Proof | 1250. |

39.9400 g, .917 GOLD, 1.1775 oz AGW

924	1980	.010	—	—	Proof	700.00
	1981	5,400	—	—	Proof	700.00
	1982	2,500	—	—	Proof	700.00
	1984 U	.025	—	—	—	600.00
	1984	8,000	—	—	Proof	700.00

945	1985 U	.025	—	—	—	575.00
	1985	.013	—	—	Proof	700.00
	1986 U	.018	—	—	—	650.00

Obv: Draped bust.

| 949 | 1987 U | .010 | — | — | — | 800.00 |
| | 1988 U | *.010 | — | — | — | 800.00 |

500th Anniversary of the Gold Sovereign

KM#	Date	Mintage	Fine	VF	XF	Unc
958	1989	*5,000	—	—	Proof	800.00

DECIMAL COINAGE
5 New Pence = 1 Shilling
25 New Pence = 1 Crown
100 New Pence = 1 Pound

1/2 NEW PENNY

BRONZE

914	1971	1,394.188	—	—	.10	.20
	1971	.191	—	—	Proof	1.00
	1972	.127	—	—	Proof	3.00
	1973	365.680	—	—	.10	.40
	1973	.102	—	—	Proof	1.00
	1974	365.448	—	—	.10	.35
	1974	.104	—	—	Proof	1.00
	1975	197.600	—	—	.10	.45
	1975	.100	—	—	Proof	1.00
	1976	412.172	—	—	.10	.35
	1976	.108	—	—	Proof	1.00
	1977	66.368	—	—	.10	.20
	1977	.252	—	—	Proof	1.00
	1978	59.532	—	—	.10	2.00
	1978	.118	—	—	Proof	1.00
	1979	219.132	—	—	.10	.20
	1979	—	—	—	Proof	1.00
	1980	202.788	—	—	.10	.20
	1980	—	—	—	Proof	1.00
	1981	32.484	—	—	.10	.45
	1981	—	—	—	Proof	1.00

1/2 PENNY

BRONZE
Rev: HALF PENNY above crown and fraction.

926	1982	190.752	—	—	.10	.15
	1982	—	—	—	Proof	1.00
	1983	7.600	—	—	.10	.50
	1983	—	—	—	Proof	1.00
	1984	—	—	—	In Sets	2.50
	1984	—	—	—	Proof	2.00

NEW PENNY

BRONZE

915	1971	1,521.666	—	—	.10	.20
	1971	.191	—	—	Proof	1.25
	1972	.127	—	—	Proof	3.00
	1973	280.196	—	—	.10	.55
	1973	.102	—	—	Proof	1.25
	1974	330.892	—	—	.10	.55
	1974	.104	—	—	Proof	1.25
	1975	221.604	—	—	.10	.55
	1975	.100	—	—	Proof	1.25
	1976	300.160	—	—	—	.25
	1976	.108	—	—	Proof	1.25
	1977	285.430	—	—	.10	.25
	1977	.252	—	—	Proof	1.25
	1978	292.770	—	—	.10	.60
	1978	.118	—	—	Proof	1.25

KM#	Date	Mintage	Fine	VF	XF	Unc
915	1979	459.000	—	—	.10	.20
	1979	—	—	—	Proof	1.25
	1980	416.304	—	—	.10	.20
	1980	—	—	—	Proof	1.25
	1981	283.663	—	—	.10	.20
	1981	—	—	—	Proof	1.25

PENNY
BRONZE
Rev: ONE PENNY above portcullis and chains and 1.

927	1982	121.429	—	—	.10	.40
	1982	—	—	—	Proof	1.25
	1983	243.002	—	—	.10	.30
	1983	—	—	—	Proof	1.25
	1984	68.946	—	—	.10	.15
	1984	—	—	—	Proof	1.25

935	1985	—	—	—	.10	.15
	1985	—	—	—	Proof	1.25
	1986	—	—	—	.10	.30
	1986	—	—	—	Proof	1.25
	1987	—	—	—	.10	.15
	1987	—	—	—	Proof	1.25
	1988	—	—	—	.10	.15
	1988	*.125	—	—	Proof	1.25
	1989	—	—	—	.10	.15
	1989	—	—	—	Proof	1.25

2 NEW PENCE

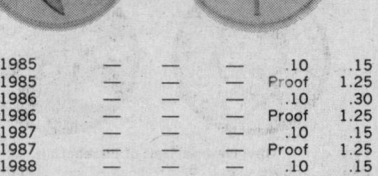

BRONZE

916	1971	1,454.856	—	—	.10	.20
	1971	.191	—	—	Proof	1.50
	1972	.127	—	—	Proof	3.50
	1973	.102	—	—	Proof	3.50
	1974	.104	—	—	Proof	3.50
	1975	145.545	—	—	.10	.40
	1975	.100	—	—	Proof	1.50
	1976	181.379	—	—	.10	.30
	1976	.108	—	—	Proof	1.50
	1977	109.281	—	—	.10	.30
	1977	.252	—	—	Proof	1.50
	1978	189.658	—	—	.10	.40
	1978	.118	—	—	Proof	1.50
	1979	268.300	—	—	.10	.20
	1979	—	—	—	Proof	1.50
	1980	408.527	—	—	.10	.20
	1980	—	—	—	Proof	1.50
	1981	277.111	—	—	.10	.15
	1981	—	—	—	Proof	1.50

2 PENCE
BRONZE
Rev: TWO PENCE above plumes of Prince of Wales and 2.

928	1982	*	—	—	In Sets	1.00
	1982	*	—	—	Proof	1.50
	1983	*	—	—	In Sets	1.00
	1983	*	—	—	Proof	1.50
	1984	*	—	—	In Sets	.75
	1984	*	—	—	Proof	1.50

936	1985	—	—	—	.10	.20
	1985	*.125	—	—	Proof	1.50
	1986	—	—	—	.10	.50
	1986	*	—	—	Proof	1.50
	1987	—	—	—	.10	.20
	1987	—	—	—	Proof	1.50
	1988	—	—	—	.10	.20
	1988	*.125	—	—	Proof	1.50
	1989	—	—	—	.10	.20
	1989	—	—	—	Proof	1.50

*Issued in sets only.

GREAT BRITAIN

5 NEW PENCE

COPPER-NICKEL

KM#	Date	Mintage	Fine	VF	XF	Unc
911	1968	98.868	—	—	.10	.30
	1969	119.270	—	—	.10	.40
	1970	225.948	—	—	.10	.40
	1971	81.783	—	—	.10	.50
	1971	.191	—	—	Proof	1.50
	1972	.231	—	—	Proof	3.50
	1973	.102	—	—	Proof	3.50
	1974	.104	—	—	Proof	3.50
	1975	116.906	—	—	.10	.30
	1975	.100	—	—	Proof	1.50
	1976	.108	—	—	Proof	3.50
	1977	24.308	—	—	.10	.35
	1977	.252	—	—	Proof	1.50
	1978	61.094	—	—	.10	.30
	1978	.118	—	—	Proof	1.50
	1979	155.456	—	—	.10	.25
	1979	—	—	—	Proof	1.50
	1980	203.020	—	—	.10	.25
	1980	—	—	—	Proof	1.50

5 PENCE
COPPER-NICKEL
Rev: FIVE PENCE above Scottish thistle and 5.

KM#	Date	Mintage	Fine	VF	XF	Unc
929	1982	*	—	—	In Sets	2.25
	1982	*	—	—	Proof	1.50
	1983	*	—	—	In Sets	1.25
	1983	*	—	—	Proof	1.50
	1984	*	—	—	In Sets	1.00
	1984	*	—	—	Proof	1.50

KM#	Date	Mintage	Fine	VF	XF	Unc
937	1985	*	—	—	.10	2.00
	1985	*.125	—	—	Proof	1.50
	1986	*	—	—	.10	1.00
	1986	*	—	—	Proof	1.50
	1987	*	—	—	.10	.25
	1987	*	—	—	Proof	1.50
	1988	*	—	—	.10	.25
	1988	*.125	—	—	Proof	1.50
	1989	—	—	—	.10	.25
	1989	—	—	—	Proof	1.50

*Issued in sets only.

10 NEW PENCE

COPPER-NICKEL

KM#	Date	Mintage	Fine	VF	XF	Unc
912	1968	336.143	—	—	.20	.40
	1969	314.008	—	—	.20	.60
	1970	133.571	—	—	.20	1.00
	1971	63.205	—	—	.20	1.00
	1971	.191	—	—	Proof	1.75
	1972	.065	—	—	Proof	3.75
	1973	152.174	—	—	.20	.50
	1973	.042	—	—	Proof	1.75
	1974	92.741	—	—	.20	.50
	1974	.041	—	—	Proof	1.75
	1975	181.559	—	—	.20	.50
	1975	.037	—	—	Proof	1.75
	1976	228.220	—	—	.20	.50
	1976	.047	—	—	Proof	1.75
	1977	59.323	—	—	.20	.60
	1977	.252	—	—	Proof	1.75
	1978	.118	—	—	Proof	1.75
	1979	115.457	—	—	.20	.60
	1979	—	—	—	Proof	1.75
	1980	88.650	—	—	.20	.60
	1980	—	—	—	Proof	1.75
	1981	3.433	—	—	.20	.50
	1981	—	—	—	Proof	1.75

10 PENCE
COPPER-NICKEL
Rev: TEN PENCE above crowned lion and 10.

KM#	Date	Mintage	Fine	VF	XF	Unc
930	1982	*	—	—	In Sets	2.00
	1982	*	—	—	Proof	1.75
	1983	*	—	—	In Sets	2.00
	1983	*	—	—	Proof	1.75
	1984	*	—	—	In Sets	1.25
	1984	*	—	—	Proof	1.75

KM#	Date	Mintage	Fine	VF	XF	Unc
938	1985	*	—	—	.20	1.00
	1985	*.125	—	—	Proof	1.75
	1986	*	—	—	.20	.80
	1986	*	—	—	Proof	1.75
	1987	*	—	—	.20	.50
	1987	*	—	—	Proof	1.75
	1988	*	—	—	.20	.50
	1988	*.125	—	—	Proof	1.75
	1989	—	—	—	.20	.50
	1989	—	—	—	Proof	1.75

*Issued in sets only.

20 PENCE

COPPER-NICKEL

KM#	Date	Mintage	Fine	VF	XF	Unc
931	1982	—	—	—	.40	.65
	1982	—	—	—	Proof	5.00
	1983	—	—	—	.40	.65
	1983	—	—	—	Proof	5.00
	1984	—	—	—	.40	.65
	1984	—	—	—	Proof	5.00

10.0000 g, .925 SILVER, .2974 oz ASW

| 931a | 1982 | .025 | — | — | Proof | 90.00 |

KM#	Date	Mintage	Fine	VF	XF	Unc
939	1985	—	—	—	.40	.75
	1985	.125	—	—	Proof	5.00
	1986	—	—	—	In Sets	.55
	1986	—	—	—	Proof	5.00
	1987	—	—	—	.40	.75
	1987	—	—	—	Proof	5.00
	1988	—	—	—	.40	.75
	1988	*.125	—	—	Proof	5.00
	1989	—	—	—	.40	.75
	1989	—	—	—	Proof	5.00

25 NEW PENCE

COPPER-NICKEL
Royal Silver Wedding Anniversary

| 917 | 1972 | 7.452 | — | — | .50 | 1.50 |
| | 1972 | .107 | — | — | Proof | 7.50 |

28.2759 g, .925 SILVER, .8409 oz ASW

| 917a | 1972 | .185 | — | — | Proof | 22.50 |

COPPER-NICKEL
Silver Jubilee of Reign

KM#	Date	Mintage	Fine	VF	XF	Unc
920	1977	37.061	—	—	.50	1.25
	1977	.172	—	—	Proof	6.00
	1977(RMF)*	—	—	—	—	4.00

NOTE: Sealed in Royal Mint Folder.

28.2759 g, .925 SILVER, .8409 oz ASW

| 920a | 1977 | .473 | — | — | Proof | 20.00 |

COPPER-NICKEL
80th Birthday of Queen Mother

| 921 | 1980 | 9.306 | — | — | .50 | 1.25 |

28.2759 g, .925 SILVER, .8409 oz ASW

| 921a | 1980 | — | — | — | Proof | 27.00 |

CROWN

COPPER-NICKEL
Wedding of Prince Charles and Lady Diana
Obv: Similar to 25 New Pence, KM#917.

| 925 | 1981 | 26.774 | — | — | .50 | 1.25 |

28.2759 g, .925 SILVER, .8409 oz ASW

| 925a | 1981 | .250 | — | — | Proof | 35.00 |

50 NEW PENCE

COPPER-NICKEL

KM#	Date	Mintage	Fine	VF	XF	Unc
913	1969	188.400	—	—	.90	2.25
	1970	19.461	—	—	.90	3.25
	1971	.191	—	—	Proof	3.00
	1972	.065	—	—	Proof	4.00
	1974	.041	—	—	Proof	3.00
	1975	.037	—	—	Proof	3.00
	1976	43.747	—	—	.90	2.00
	1976	.047	—	—	Proof	2.50
	1977	49.536	—	—	.90	2.25
	1977	.252	—	—	Proof	2.5
	1978	72.005	—	—	.90	2.0
	1978	.118	—	—	Proof	2.
	1979	58.680	—	—	.90	1
	1979	—	—	—	Proof	
	1980	89.086	—	—	.90	
	1980	—	—	—		

GREAT BRITAIN

KM#	Date	Mintage	Fine	VF	XF	Unc
913	1981	74.003	—	—	.90	2.00
	1981	—	—	—	Proof	2.50

50 PENCE
COPPER-NICKEL
Entry Into E.E.C.

918	1973	89.775	—	—	.90	2.00
	1973	.029	—	—	Proof	6.00

Rev: FIFTY PENCE above seated Britannia and 50.

932	1982	51.312	—	—	.90	1.50
	1982	—	—	—	Proof	2.50
	1983	23.436	—	—	.90	1.75
	1983	.125	—	—	Proof	2.50
	1984	—	—	—	In Sets	2.25
	1984	.125	—	—	Proof	2.50

940	1985	—	—	—	.90	1.35
	1985	.125	—	—	Proof	2.50
	1986	—	—	—	In Sets	1.35
	1986	.125	—	—	Proof	2.50
	1987	—	—	—	.90	1.35
	1987	.125	—	—	Proof	2.50
	1988	—	—	—	.90	1.35
	1988	*.125	—	—	Proof	2.50
	1989	—	—	—	.90	1.35
	1989	—	—	—	Proof	2.50

POUND

933	1983	171.400	—	—	1.80	2.50
	1983	.125	—	—	Proof	6.00

9.5000 g, .925 SILVER, .2825 oz ASW
| 933a | 1983 | .050 | — | — | Proof | 75.00 |

19.0000 g, .925 SILVER, .5651 oz ASW
| 933b | 1983 | .010 | — | — | Proof | 300.00 |

NICKEL-BRASS
Rev: Scottish thistle.

934	1984	41.445	—	—	1.80	2.50
	1984	.125	—	—	Proof	6.00

9.5000 g, .925 SILVER, .2825 oz ASW
| 934a | 1984 | .050 | — | — | Proof | 40.00 |

19.0000 g, .925 SILVER, .5651 oz ASW
| 934b | 1984 | .015 | — | — | Proof | 150.00 |

NICKEL-BRASS
Rev: Welch leek.

	1985	78.979	—	—	1.80	2.50
	1985	.125	—	—	Proof	6.00

9.5000 g, .925 SILVER, .2825 oz ASW
KM#	Date	Mintage	Fine	VF	XF	Unc
941a	1985	.050	—	—	Proof	40.00

19.0000 g, .925 SILVER, .5651 oz ASW
| 941b | 1985 | .015 | — | — | Proof | 125.00 |

NICKEL-BRASS
Northern Ireland - Blooming Flax

946	1986	—	—	—	1.80	2.50
	1986	.125	—	—	Proof	6.00

9.5000 g, .925 SILVER, .2825 oz ASW
| 946a | 1986 | .050 | — | — | Proof | 40.00 |

19.0000 g, .925 SILVER, .5651 oz ASW
| 946b | 1986 | .015 | — | — | Proof | 100.00 |

NICKEL-BRASS
Oak Tree

948	1987	—	—	—	—	2.50
	1987	.125	—	—	Proof	6.00

9.5000 g, .925 SILVER, .2825 oz ASW
| 948a | 1987 | .050 | — | — | Proof | 45.00 |

19.0000 g, .925 SILVER, .5651 oz ASW
| 948b | 1987 | .015 | — | — | Proof | 120.00 |

COPPER-ZINC-NICKEL

954	1988	—	—	—	—	2.50
	1988	*.125	—	—	Proof	6.00

9.5000 g, .925 SILVER, .2826 oz ASW
| 954a | 1988 | *.050 | — | — | Proof | 35.00 |

19.0000 g, .925 SILVER, .5651 oz ASW
| 954b | 1988 | — | — | — | Proof | 100.00 |

NICKEL
Scottish Flora
Obv: Queen's portrait. Rev: Scottish thistle.

959	1989	—	—	—	—	2.50
	1989	—	—	—	Proof	6.00

2 POUNDS

NICKEL-BRASS
Commonwealth Games

947	1986	—	—	—	3.50	5.00
	1986	.125	—	—	Proof	10.00

15.9800 g, .500 SILVER, .2569 oz ASW
| 947a | 1986 | .125 | — | — | — | 25.00 |

15.9800 g, .925 SILVER, .4752 oz ASW
| 947b | 1986 | .075 | — | — | — | 42.50 |

15.9800 g, .917 GOLD, .4710 oz AGW
| 947c | 1986 | .018 | — | — | Proof | 425.00 |

NICKEL-BRASS
Tercentenary of Bill of Rights

KM#	Date	Mintage	Fine	VF	XF	Unc
960	1989	—	—	—	—	5.50
	1989	—	—	—	Proof	8.00

Tercentenary of Claim of Right
961	1989	—	—	—	—	5.50
	1989	—	—	—	Proof	8.00

BULLION ISSUES
10 POUNDS
1/10 Ounce

3.4120 g, .917 GOLD, .1000 oz AGW
950	1987	.026	—	—	Proof	125.00
	1988	—	—	—	BV + 16%	
	1988	*.019	—	—	Proof	125.00

25 POUNDS
1/4 Ounce

8.5130 g, .917 GOLD, .2500 oz AGW
951	1987	.026	—	—	Proof	275.00
	1988	—	—	—	BV + 8%	
	1988	*.014	—	—	Proof	275.00

50 POUNDS
1/2 Ounce

17.0250 g, .917 GOLD, .5000 oz AGW
952	1987	.013	—	—	Proof	500.00
	1988	—	—	—	BV + 6%	
	1988	*6,500	—	—	Proof	500.00

100 POUNDS
1 Ounce

34.0500 g, .917 GOLD, 1.0000 oz AGW
953	1987	.013	—	—	Proof	900.00
	1988	—	—	—	BV + 4%	
	1988	*8,500	—	—	Proof	900.00

COUNTERMARKED COINAGE
BANK OF ENGLAND

Emergency issue foreign silver coins, usually Spanish Colonial, having a bust of George III within an oval (1797) or octagonal (1804) frame. Countermarked 8 Reales circulated at 4 Shillings 9 Pence in 1797 and 5 Shillings in 1804. The puncheons used for countermarking foreign coins for this series were available for many years afterward, especially the oval die and apparently a number of foreign coins other than Spanish or Spanish Colonial 8 Reales were countermarked for collectors.

Type II

1804
Head of George III in octagon.
NOTE: Coins other than 8 Reales bearing this cmk. are considered spurious by some authorities.

DOLLAR

c/m: Type II on Bolivia (Potosi) 8 Reales, KM#55.

KM#	Date	Year Mintage	Fine	VF	XF
652	ND	(1773-89)	— 125.00	250.00	400.00

c/m: Type II on Bolivia (Potosi) 8 Reales, KM#73.1.
| 653 | ND | (1791-1808) | — 125.00 | 250.00 | 400.00 |

c/m: Type II on France 1 Ecu, C#78.
| 654 | ND | (1774-92) | — | Rare | — |

c/m: Type II on Mexico 8 Reales, KM#106.
| 655 | ND | (1772-89) | — 100.00 | 175.00 | 300.00 |

c/m: Type II on Mexico 8 Reales, KM#109.
| 656 | ND | (1791-1808) | — 100.00 | 175.00 | 300.00 |

c/m: Type II on Peru (Lima) 8 Reales, KM#78.
| 657 | ND | (1772-89) | — | Rare | — |

c/m: Type II on Peru (Lima) 8 Reales, KM#97.
| 658 | ND | (1791-1808) | — | Rare | — |

c/m: Type II on Spanish (Seville) 8 Reales, C#71.
| 659 | ND | (1788-1808) | — | Rare | — |

c/m: Type II on United States 1 Dollar, C#34.
| 660 | ND | (1795-98) | — | Rare | — |

c/m: Type II on United States 1 Dollar, C#34a.
| 660a | ND | (1798-1803) | — | Rare | — |

TRADE COINAGE

This issue was struck at the Bombay (B) and Calcutta (C) Mints in India, except for 1925 and 1930 issues which were struck at London, although through error the mint marks did not appear on some early issues as indicated.

KINGDOM
Britannia Series

Issued to facilitate British trade in the Orient, the reverse design incorporates the statement of denomination in Chinese characters and Malay script.

DOLLAR

26.9568 g, .900 SILVER, .7800 oz ASW

KM#	Date	Mintage	Fine	VF	XF	Unc
T5	1895B	3.316	40.00	65.00	90.00	200.00
(T2)	1895B	Inc. Ab.	—	—	Proof	850.00
	1895	Inc. Ab.	40.00	70.00	100.00	250.00
	1895	Inc. Ab.	—	—	Proof	800.00
	1896B	6.136	60.00	90.00	150.00	350.00
	1896B	Inc. Ab.	—	—	Proof	800.00
	1897/6B	21.286	50.00	75.00	100.00	150.00
	1897B	Inc. Ab.	10.00	17.50	25.00	50.00
	1897B	Inc. Ab.	—	—	Proof	800.00
	1897	Inc. Ab.	10.00	17.50	25.00	50.00
	1897	Inc. Ab.	—	—	Proof	800.00
	1898B	21.546	10.00	17.50	25.00	50.00
	1898B	Inc. Ab.	—	—	Proof	800.00
	1898	Inc. Ab.	10.00	17.50	25.00	50.00
	1899B	30.743	10.00	17.50	25.00	50.00
	1899B	Inc. Ab.	—	—	Proof	800.00
	1900/1000B	9.107	40.00	60.00	100.00	150.00
	1900/890B I.A.	40.00	60.00	100.00	150.00
	1900	—	200.00	350.00	450.00	750.00
	1900B	Inc. Ab.	10.00	17.50	25.00	60.00
	1900B	Inc. Ab.	—	—	Proof	800.00
	1900B (restrike) 25 known	—	—	Proof	1000.
	1901/0B	.363	150.00	250.00	350.00	600.00
	1901	25.680	40.00	60.00	100.00	200.00
	1901B	Inc. Ab.	10.00	17.50	25.00	50.00
	1901B	Inc. Ab.	—	—	Proof	800.00
	1901C	1.514	25.00	40.00	60.00	175.00
	1902B	30.404	10.00	17.50	25.00	50.00
	1902B	Inc. Ab.	—	—	Proof	800.00
	1902C	1.267	25.00	40.00	60.00	175.00
	1902C	Inc. Ab.	—	—	Proof	800.00
	1903/2B	3.956	20.00	25.00	35.00	75.00
	1903B	Inc. Ab.	10.00	17.50	25.00	50.00
	1903B	Inc. Ab.	—	—	Proof	800.00
	1904/898B	.649	60.00	100.00	170.00	250.00
	1904/3B	I.A.	40.00	70.00	100.00	225.00
	1904/0B	Inc. Ab.	80.00	125.00	175.00	300.00
	1904B	Inc. Ab.	35.00	55.00	80.00	200.00
	1904B	Inc. Ab.	—	—	Proof	700.00
	1907B	1.946	10.00	17.50	25.00	50.00
	1908/3B	6.871	40.00	70.00	100.00	175.00
	1908/7B	I.A.	35.00	55.00	90.00	125.00
	1908B	Inc. Ab.	10.00	17.50	25.00	50.00
	1908B	Inc. Ab.	—	—	Proof	700.00
	1909/8B	5.954	35.00	55.00	90.00	125.00
	1909B	Inc. Ab.	10.00	17.50	25.00	50.00
	1910/0B	5.553	50.00	75.00	110.00	175.00
	1910B	Inc. Ab.	12.50	20.00	25.00	60.00
	1911/00 B	—	40.00	55.00	100.00	150.00
	1911B	37.471	10.00	17.50	25.00	50.00
	1912B	5.672	10.00	17.50	25.00	50.00
	1912B	Inc. Ab.	—	—	Proof	800.00
	1913/2 B	—	100.00	175.00	300.00	700.00
	1913B	1.567	50.00	80.00	125.00	300.00
	1913B	—	—	—	Proof	800.00
	1921B *5 known	—	—	—	15,000.
	1921B (restrike)	—	—	Proof	4500.
	1925	6.870	10.00	17.50	25.00	60.00
	1929/1B	5.100	40.00	75.00	110.00	150.00
	1929B	Inc. Ab.	10.00	17.50	25.00	50.00
	1929B	Inc. Ab.	—	—	Proof	800.00
	1930B	Inc. Ab.	10.00	17.50	25.00	50.00
	1930B	Inc. Ab.	—	—	Proof	800.00
	1930	6.660	10.00	17.50	25.00	50.00
	1934B	17.335	75.00	125.00	175.00	400.00
	1934B	Inc. Ab.	—	—	Proof	3500.
	1934B (restrike) 20 known	—	—	Proof	3000.
	1935B	15 known	1000.	2000.	3000.	6000.
	1935B	—	—	—	Proof	7500.
	1935B (restrike) 20 known	—	—	Proof	4000.

*NOTE: Original mintage 50,211.

GOLD, (OMS)

T5a	1895B (restrike)	—	—	Proof	3500.
(T2a)	1895 (restrike)	—	—	Proof	3500.
	1896B (restrike)	—	—	Proof	3500.
	1897B (restrike)	—	—	Proof	3000.
	1897 (restrike)	—	—	Proof	3000.
	1898B (restrike)	—	—	Proof	3000.
	1899B (restrike)	—	—	Proof	3000.
	1900B (restrike)	—	—	Proof	3000.
	1901B (restrike)	—	—	Proof	3000.
	1902B (restrike)	—	—	Proof	3000.

TOKEN ISSUES (Tn)
Bank of England
18 PENCE
(1 Shilling 6 Pence)

.925 SILVER

Tn2	1811	—	3.50	12.50	25.00	60.00
(Tn1)	1811	—	—	—	Proof	800.00
	1812	—	3.50	12.50	35.00	70.00
	1812	—	—	—	Proof	800.00

Tn3	1812	—	3.50	12.50	35.00	70.00
(Tn2)	1813	—	4.50	13.50	37.50	75.00
	1814	—	3.50	12.50	35.00	70.00
	1815	—	3.50	12.50	35.00	70.00
	1816	—	4.50	13.50	37.50	75.00

3 SHILLINGS

.925 SILVER

Tn4	1811	—	5.00	18.00	60.00	130.00
(Tn3)	1811	—	—	—	Proof	1000.
	1812	—	5.00	18.00	60.00	130.00

Tn5	1812	—	5.00	18.00	60.00	130.00
(Tn4)	1812	—	—	—	Proof	1000.
	1813	—	5.00	18.00	60.00	135.00
	1814	—	5.00	18.00	60.00	140.00
	1815	—	5.00	18.00	60.00	140.00
	1816	—	150.00	275.00	500.00	1000.

GREAT BRITAIN 776

DOLLAR

.903 SILVER
Bank of England

KM#	Date	Mintage	Fine	VF	XF	Unc
Tn1	1804	—	35.00	110.00	320.00	600.00
(T1)	1804	—	—	—	Proof	1500.

COPPER (OMS)

KM#	Date	Mintage	Fine	VF	XF	Unc
Tn1a (T1a)	1804	—	—	—	Proof	900.00

NOTE: The silver proofs were struck on specially prepared flans while circulation strikes were struck over Spanish and Spanish Colonial 8 Reales.

MAUNDY SETS (MDS)

These small silver coins are a special ceremonial issue struck each year for use at the traditional ceremony on Maundy Thursday when the reigning monarch (or a representative) distributes them to a selected group of elderly men and women. The amount distributed to each person (in pence) is equal to the present age of the monarch. The issue has consisted of silver 1, 2, 3 and 4 penny pieces since the reign of Charles II.

KM#	Date	Mintage	Identification	Mkt.Val.
MDS63	1817	1,584	KM668-671	230.00
MDS64	1818	1,188	KM668-671	230.00
MDS65	1820	1,584	KM668-671	230.00
MDS66	1822	2,970	KM683,684,685.1,686	240.00
MDS67	1822	—	KM683,684,685.1,686	*Proof* 345.00
MDS68	1823	1,980	KM683,684,685.2,686	200.00
MDS69	1824	1,584	KM683,684,685.2,686	230.00
MDS70	1825	2,376	KM683,684,685.2,686	200.00
MDS71	1826	2,376	KM683,684,685.2,686	200.00
MDS72	1826	—	KM683,684,685.2,686	*Proof* 345.00
MDS73	1827	2,772	KM683,684,685.2,686	200.00
MDS74	1828	2,772	KM683,684,685.2,686	200.00
MDS75	1828	—	KM683,684,685.2,686	*Proof* 345.00
MDS76	1829	2,772	KM683,684,685.2,686	200.00
MDS77	1830	2,772	KM683,684,685.2,686	200.00
MDS78	1831	3,564	KM708-711	225.00
MDS79	1831	—	KM708-711	300.00
MDS80	1832	2,574	KM708-711	175.00
MDS81	1833	2,574	KM708-711	175.00
MDS82	1834	2,574	KM708-711	175.00
MDS83	1835	2,574	KM708-711	175.00
MDS84	1836	2,574	KM708-711	175.00
MDS85	1837	2,574	KM708-711	175.00
MDS86	1838	4,158	KM727,729-730,732	100.00
MDS87	1838	—	KM727,729-730,732	200.00
MDS88	1839	4,125	KM727,729-730,732	100.00
MDS89	1839	300	KM727,729-730,732	200.00
MDS90	1840	4,125	KM727,729-730,732	100.00
MDS91	1841	2,574	KM727,729-730,732	110.00
MDS92	1842	4,125	KM727,729-730,732	100.00
MDS93	1843	4,158	KM727,729-730,732	100.00
MDS94	1844	4,158	KM727,729-730,732	100.00
MDS95	1845	4,158	KM727,729-730,732	100.00
MDS96	1846	4,158	KM727,729-730,732	100.00
MDS97	1847	4,158	KM727,729-730,732	100.00
MDS98	1848	4,158	KM727,729-730,732	100.00
MDS99	1849	4,158	KM727,729-730,732	100.00
MDS100	1850	4,158	KM727,729-730,732	100.00
MDS101	1851	4,158	KM727,729-730,732	100.00
MDS102	1852	4,158	KM727,729-730,732	100.00
MDS103	1853	4,158	KM727,729-730,732	100.00
MDS104	1853	—	KM727,729-730,732	*Proof* 350.00
MDS105	1854	4,158	KM727,729-730,732	100.00
MDS106	1855	4,158	KM727,729-730,732	85.00
MDS107	1856	4,158	KM727,729-730,732	100.00
MDS108	1857	4,158	KM727,729-730,732	100.00
MDS109	1858	4,158	KM727,729-730,732	100.00
MDS110	1859	4,158	KM727,729-730,732	100.00
MDS111	1860	4,158	KM727,729-730,732	100.00
MDS112	1861	4,158	KM727,729-730,732	100.00
MDS113	1862	4,158	KM727,729-730,732	100.00
MDS114	1863	4,158	KM727,729-730,732	100.00
MDS115	1864	4,158	KM727,729-730,732	100.00
MDS116	1865	4,158	KM727,729-730,732	100.00
MDS117	1866	4,158	KM727,729-730,732	100.00
MDS118	1867	4,158	KM727,729-730,732	100.00
MDS119	1867	—	KM727,729-730,732	*Proof* 200.00
MDS120	1868	4,158	KM727,729-730,732	100.00
MDS121	1869	4,158	KM727,729-730,732	135.00
MDS122	1870	4,488	KM727,729-730,732	100.00
MDS123	1871	4,488	KM727,729-730,732	100.00
MDS124	1871	—	KM727,729-730,732	*Proof* 200.00
MDS125	1872	4,328	KM727,729-730,732	100.00
MDS126	1873	4,162	KM727,729-730,732	100.00
MDS127	1874	4,488	KM727,729-730,732	100.00
MDS128	1875	4,154	KM727,729-730,732	100.00
MDS129	1876	4,488	KM727,729-730,732	100.00
MDS130	1877	4,488	KM727,729-730,732	100.00
MDS131	1878	4,488	KM727,729-730,732	100.00
MDS132	1878	—	KM727,729-730,732	*Proof* 200.00
MDS133	1879	4,488	KM727,729-730,732	100.00
MDS134	1880	4,488	KM727,729-730,732	100.00
MDS135	1881	4,488	KM727,729-730,732	100.00
MDS136	1881	—	KM727,729-730,732	*Proof* 250.00
MDS137	1882	4,488	KM727,729-730,732	100.00
MDS138	1883	4,488	KM727,729-730,732	100.00
MDS139	1884	4,488	KM727,729-730,732	100.00
MDS140	1885	4,488	KM727,729-730,732	100.00
MDS141	1886	4,488	KM727,729-730,732	100.00
MDS142	1887	4,488	KM727,729-730,732	100.00
MDS143	1888	4,488	KM758,770-771,773	105.00
MDS144	1889	4,488	KM758,770-771,773	105.00
MDS145	1888	—	KM758,770-771,773	*Proof* 150.00
MDS146	1890	4,488	KM758,770-771,773	105.00
MDS147	1891	4,488	KM758,770-771,773	105.00
MDS148	1892	4,488	KM758,770-771,773	105.00
MDS149	1893	8,976	KM775-778	80.00
MDS150	1894	8,976	KM775-778	80.00
MDS151	1895	8,877	KM775-778	80.00
MDS152	1896	8,476	KM775-778	80.00
MDS153	1897	9,388	KM775-778	80.00
MDS154	1898	9,147	KM775-778	80.00
MDS155	1899	8,976	KM775-778	80.00
MDS156	1900	8,976	KM775-778	80.00
MDS157	1901	8,976	KM775-778	80.00
MDS158	1902	8,976	KM795-798	70.00
MDS159	1902	—	KM795-798	*Proof* 85.00
MDS160	1903	8,976	KM795-798	70.00
MDS161	1904	8,976	KM795-798	70.00
MDS162	1905	8,976	KM795-798	70.00
MDS163	1906	8,800	KM795-798	70.00
MDS164	1907	8,760	KM795-798	70.00
MDS165	1908	8,760	KM795-798	70.00
MDS166	1909	1,983	KM795-798	85.00
MDS167	1910	1,440	KM795-798	100.00
MDS168	1911	1,768	KM811-814	90.00
MDS169	1911	6,007	KM811-814	*Proof* 100.00
MDS170	1912	1,246	KM811-814	90.00
MDS171	1913	1,228	KM811-814	90.00
MDS172	1914	982	KM811-814	90.00
MDS173	1915	1,293	KM811-814	90.00
MDS174	1916	1,128	KM811-814	90.00
MDS175	1917	1,237	KM811-814	90.00
MDS176	1918	1,375	KM811-814	90.00
MDS177	1919	1,258	KM811-814	90.00
MDS178	1920	1,399	KM811-814	90.00
MDS179	1921	1,386	KM811a-814a	90.00
MDS180	1922	1,373	KM811a-814a	90.00
MDS181	1923	1,430	KM811a-814a	90.00
MDS182	1924	1,515	KM811a-814a	90.00
MDS183	1925	1,438	KM811a-814a	90.00
MDS184	1926	1,504	KM811a-814a	90.00
MDS185	1927	1,647	KM811a-814a	90.00
MDS186	1928	1,642	KM827,839-841	90.00
MDS187	1929	1,761	KM827,839-841	90.00
MDS188	1930	1,724	KM827,839-841	90.00
MDS189	1931	1,759	KM827,839-841	90.00
MDS190	1932	1,835	KM827,839-841	90.00
MDS191	1933	1,872	KM827,839-841	90.00
MDS192	1934	1,887	KM827,839-841	90.00
MDS193	1935	1,926	KM827,839-841	90.00
MDS194	1936	1,323	KM827,839-841	100.00
MDS195	1937	1,325	KM846-847,850-851	80.00
MDS196	1937	.026	KM846-847,850-851	*Proof* 80.00
MDS197	1938	1,275	KM846-847,850-851	80.00
MDS198	1939	1,234	KM846-847,850-851	80.00
MDS199	1940	1,277	KM846-847,850-851	80.00
MDS200	1941	1,253	KM846-847,850-851	80.00
MDS201	1942	1,231	KM846-847,850-851	80.00
MDS202	1943	1,239	KM846-847,850-851	80.00
MDS203	1944	1,259	KM846-847,850-851	80.00
MDS204	1945	1,355	KM846-847,850-851	80.00
MDS205	1946	1,365	KM846-847,850-851	80.00
MDS206	1947	1,375	KM846a-847a,850a-851a	80.00
MDS207	1948	1,385	KM846a-847a,850a-851a	80.00
MDS208	1949	1,395	KM870-872,874	80.00
MDS209	1950	1,405	KM870-872,874	80.00
MDS210	1951	1,468	KM870-872,874	80.00
MDS211	1952	1,012	KM870-872,874	85.00
MDS212	1953	1,025	KM884-885,887-888	400.00
MDS213	1954	1,020	KM898-899,901-902	70.00
MDS214	1955	1,036	KM898-899,901-902	70.00
MDS215	1956	1,088	KM898-899,901-902	70.00
MDS216	1957	1,094	KM898-899,901-902	70.00
MDS217	1958	1,100	KM898-899,901-902	70.00
MDS218	1959	1,106	KM898-899,901-902	70.00
MDS219	1960	1,112	KM898-899,901-902	70.00
MDS220	1961	1,118	KM898-899,901-902	70.00
MDS221	1962	1,125	KM898-899,901-902	70.00
MDS222	1963	1,131	KM898-899,901-902	70.00
MDS223	1964	1,137	KM898-899,901-902	70.00
MDS224	1965	1,143	KM898-899,901-902	70.00
MDS225	1966	1,206	KM898-899,901-902	70.00
MDS226	1967	986	KM898-899,901-902	70.00
MDS227	1968	964	KM898-899,901-902	70.00
MDS228	1969	1,002	KM898-899,901-902	70.00
MDS229	1970	980	KM898-899,901-902	70.00
MDS230	1971	1,018	KM898-899,901-902	70.00
MDS231	1972	1,026	KM898-899,901-902	70.00
MDS232	1973	1,004	KM898-899,901-902	70.00
MDS233	1974	1,042	KM898-899,901-902	75.00
MDS234	1975	1,050	KM898-899,901-902	75.00
MDS235	1976	1,257	KM898-899,901-902	75.00
MDS236	1977	1,248	KM898-899,901-902	80.00
MDS237	1978	1,179	KM898-899,901-902	80.00
MDS238	1979	1,180	KM898-899,901-902	80.00
MDS239	1980	1,148	KM898-899,901-902	80.00
MDS240	1981	1,398	KM898-899,901-902	80.00
MDS241	1982	1,220	KM898-899,901-902	80.00
MDS242	1983	1,210	KM898-899,901-902	80.00
MDS243	1984	—	KM898-899,901-902	80.00
MDS244	1985	—	KM898-899,901-902	80.00
MDS245	1986	—	KM898-899,901-902	80.00
MDS246	1987	—	KM898-899,901-902	80.00
MDS247	1988	—	KM898-899,901-902	80.00
MDS248	1989	—	KM898-899,901-902	80.00

NOTE: The mintage figures above represent the maximum number of complete sets.

MINT SETS (MS)

KM#	Date	Mintage	Identification	Issue Price	Mkt. Val.
MS101	1953(9)	—	KM881-883,886,889-893	1.25	12.00
MS102	1968/71(5)	—	KM911-912,914-916. 10P and 5P dated 1968. 2P, 1P, 1/2P dated 1971. Blue wallet.	.50	2.00
MS103	1982(7)	—	KM926-932	6.00	6.50
MS104	1983(8)	—	KM926-933	8.75	8.50
MS105	1984(8)	—	KM926-932,934	8.75	7.00
MS106	1985(7)	—	KM935-941	8.75	7.50
MS107	1986(8)	—	KM935-940,946-947	9.75	10.00
MS108	1987(7)	—	KM935-940,948	9.00	10.00
MS109	1988(7)	—	KM935-940,954	9.00	10.00
MS110	1989(7)	—	KM935-940,959	10.00	10.00
MS111	1989(2)	—	KM960-961	11.00	11.00

PROOF SETS (PS)

KM#	Date	Mintage	Identification	Issue Price	Mkt. Val.
PS4	1831(14)	*225	KM705,706a-707a,709-714, 716-718,720,835	—	25,000.
PS5	1839(15)	300	KM725a-726a,727,729-730, 731.2,732-736,739a,740-742	—	45,000.
PS6	1839/48(16)	Inc. Ab.	KM725a-726a,727,729-730,731.2, 732-736,739a,740-742,745	—	45,000.
PS7	1853(17)	—	KM725a-726a,727,729-730,731.2, 732-736,737a-739a,740,744, 746	—	35,000.
PS8	1853(16)	Inc. Ab.	KM725a-726a,727,729-730,731.2 732-736,738a-739a,740a,744, 746	—	35,000.
PS9	1887(11)	797	KM758-759,761-769	—	9000.
PS10	1887(11)	Inc. Ab.	KM758-762,764-769	—	9000.
PS11	1887(7)	287	KM758-759,761-765	—	1500.
PS12	1887(7)	Inc. Ab.	KM758-762,764-765	—	1500.
PS13	1893(10)	773	KM777,779,787	—	10,000.
PS14	1893(6)	556	KM777,779-783	—	1800.
PS15	1902(13)	8,066	KM795-807	—	2500.
PS16	1902(11)	7,057	KM795-805	—	600.00
PS17	1911(12)	2,812	KM811-822	—	4600.
PS18	1911(10)	952	KM811-820	—	1100.
PS19	1911(8)	2,241	KM811-818	—	425.00
PS20	1927(6)	15,030	KM831-836	—	350.00
PS21	1937(15)	26,402	KM843-857	—	175.00
PS22	1937(4)	5,501	KM858-861	—	2700.
PS23	1950(9)	17,513	KM867-869,873,875-879	2.50	60.00
PS24	1951(10)	20,000	KM867-869,873,875-880	2.80	80.00
PS25	1953(10)	40,000	KM881-883,886,889-894	3.50	50.00
PS26	1970(8)	750,000	KM896-897,900,903-907 (Issued 1971)	8.75	12.50
PS27	1971(6)	350,000	KM911-916 (Issued 1973)	8.85	12.50
PS28	1972(7)	150,000	KM911-917 (Issued 1976)	13.00	12.50
PS29	1973(6)	100,000	KM911-916,918 (Issued 1976)	13.00	10.00
PS30	1974(6)	100,000	KM911-916 (Issued 1976)	13.00	10.00
PS31	1975(6)	100,000	KM911-916 (Issued 1976)	13.00	10.00
PS32	1976(6)	100,000	KM911-916	13.00	10.00
PS33	1977(7)	193,800	KM911-916,920	17.00	12.50
PS34	1978(6)	88,100	KM911-916	15.00	15.00
PS35	1979(6)	81,000	KM911-916	15.00	15.00
PS36	1980(6)	143,400	KM911-916	23.00	12.50
PS37	1980(4)	10,000	KM919,922-924	2650.	1400.
PS38	1981(2)	2,500	KM919,925a	—	160.00
PS39	1981(6)	—	KM911-916	26.00	12.50
PS40	1981(9)	5,000	KM911-916,919,924,925a	—	1000.
PS41	1982(7)	—	KM926-932	21.60	17.50
PS42	1982(4)	2,500	KM919,922-924	—	1600.
PS43	1983(8)	125,000	KM926-933	29.95	20.00
PS44	1983(3)	—	KM919,922-923	775.00	600.00
PS45	1984(8)	125,000	KM926-932,934	29.95	20.00
PS46	1984(3)	—	KM919,922,924	1275.	1100.
PS47	1985(7)	125,000	KM935-941	29.75	30.00
PS48	1985(4)	12,500	KM942-945	1395.	1500.
PS49	1986(8)	125,000	KM935-940,946-947	29.75	30.00
PS50	1986(3)	12,500	KM942-943,947c	675.00	675.00
PS51	1987(7)	125,000	KM935-940,948	29.75	30.00
PS52	1987(4)	10,000	KM950-953	1595.	1800.
PS53	1987(3)	12,500	KM942-944	675.00	775.00
PS54	1987(2)	12,500	KM950-951	325.00	400.00
PS55	1988(7)	*125,000	KM935-940,954	29.75	30.00
PS56	1988(4)	6,500	KM950-953	1595.	1800.
PS57	1988(3)	—	KM942-944	775.00	900.00
PS58	1988(2)	7,500	KM950-951	340.00	400.00
PS59	1989(9)	*100,000	KM935-940,959-961	34.95	35.00
PS60	1989(4)	—	KM950-953	—	1800.
PS61	1989(4)	*5,000	KM955-958	1595.	1600.
PS62	1989(3)	*15,000	KM955-957	775.00	795.00

***NOTE:** Estimated mintage figures.

GREECE

The Hellenic Republic of Greece is situated in southeastern Europe on the southern tip of the Balkan Peninsula. The republic includes many islands, the most important of which are Crete and the Ionian Islands. Greece (including islands) has an area of 50,944 sq. mi. (131,944 sq. km.) and a population of *10 million. Capital: Athens. Greece is still largely agricultural. Tobacco, cotton, fruit and wool are exported.

Greece, the Mother of Western civilization, attained the peak of its culture in the 5th century B.C., when it contributed more to government, drama, art and architecture than any other people to this time. Greece fell under Roman domination in the 2nd and 1st centuries B.C., becoming part of the Byzantine Empire until Constantinople fell to the Crusaders in 1202. With the fall of Constantinople to the Turks in 1453, Greece became part of the Ottoman Empire. Independence from Turkey was won with the revolution of 1821-27. In 1833, Greece was established as a monarchy, with sovereignty guaranteed by Britain, France and Russia. After a lengthy power struggle between the monarchist forces and democratic factions, Greece was proclaimed a republic in 1925. The monarchy was restored in 1935 and reconfirmed by a plebiscite in 1946. On April 21, 1967, a military junta took control of the government and suspended the constitution. King Constantine II made an unsuccessful attempt against the junta in the fall on 1968 and consequently fled to Italy. The monarchy was formally abolished by plebiscite, Dec. 8, 1974, and Greece established as the 'Hellenic Republic,' the third republic in Greek history.

RULERS
John Capodistrias, 1828-1831
King Otto, 1832-1862
George I, 1863-1913
Constantine I, 1913-1917, 1920-1922
Alexander I, 1917-1920
George II, 1922-1923, 1935-1947
Paul I, 1947-1964
Constantine II, 1964-1973

MINT MARKS
(a) - Paris, privy marks only
A - Paris
B - Vienna
BB - Strassburg
H - Heaton, Birmingham
K - Bordeaux
KN - King's Norton
(1) - London
(o) - Aegina (1828-1832), Owl
(o) - Athens (1838-1855), Owl
(p) - Poissy - Thunderbolt

MONETARY SYSTEM
Until 1831
100 Lepta = 1 Phoenix
Commencing 1831
100 Lepta = 1 Drachma

LEPTON

COPPER, 17mm
Obv: Phoenix in solid circle.

KM#	Date	Mintage	Fine	VF	XF	Unc
1	1828	.480	45.00	65.00	100.00	175.00
	1830	.026	50.00	100.00	150.00	350.00

Obv: Phoenix in pearl circle, 17mm.
| 5 | 1830 | .400 | 40.00 | 80.00 | 125.00 | 275.00 |

Obv: W/o circle, 16mm.
| 9 | 1831 | .612 | 40.00 | 70.00 | 110.00 | 240.00 |

Type 1 — ΒΑΣΙΛΕΙΑ

KM#	Date	Mintage	Fine	VF	XF	Unc
13	1832	2.200	20.00	40.00	80.00	200.00
	1833	Inc. Ab.	15.00	25.00	50.00	80.00
	1834	Inc. Ab.	60.00	100.00	200.00	600.00
	1837	.160	20.00	40.00	80.00	200.00
	1838	.270	20.00	40.00	80.00	200.00
	1839	.150	20.00	40.00	80.00	200.00
	1840	.700	20.00	40.00	80.00	200.00
	1841	.370	20.00	40.00	100.00	250.00
	1842	.120	20.00	40.00	100.00	250.00
	1843	.630	20.00	40.00	80.00	200.00

Type 2 — ΒΑΣΙΛΕΙΟΝ
22	1844	.151	25.00	70.00	175.00	350.00
	1845	.160	20.00	65.00	150.00	300.00
	1846	.141	20.00	60.00	125.00	275.00

Obv: Smaller crowned arms.
Rev: Redesigned wreath.
26	1847	.273	40.00	80.00	200.00	500.00
	1848	.084	20.00	40.00	80.00	250.00
	1849	.090	20.00	40.00	80.00	250.00

Size reduced to 15mm
| 30 | 1851 | .400 | 20.00 | 40.00 | 80.00 | 150.00 |
| | 1857 | .243 | 25.00 | 50.00 | 85.00 | 175.00 |

| 40 | 1869BB | 14.976 | 2.00 | 4.00 | 12.50 | 40.00 |
| | 1870BB | Inc. Ab. | 10.00 | 25.00 | 70.00 | 150.00 |

| 52 | 1878K | 7.132 | 2.00 | 4.00 | 10.00 | 40.00 |
| | 1879A | .398 | 3.50 | 6.00 | 25.00 | 85.00 |

2 LEPTA

COPPER
Type 1 — ΒΑΣΙΛΕΙΑ

KM#	Date	Mintage	Fine	VF	XF	Unc
14	1832	2.475	20.00	40.00	80.00	200.00
	1833	Inc. Ab.	12.50	20.00	40.00	80.00
	1834	Inc. Ab.	40.00	80.00	125.00	250.00
	1836	.049	75.00	125.00	175.00	400.00
	1837	.222	20.00	40.00	80.00	200.00
	1838	.701	20.00	40.00	80.00	175.00
	1839	.661	20.00	40.00	80.00	175.00
	1840	.520	20.00	40.00	80.00	200.00
	1842	.470	20.00	40.00	80.00	175.00

Type 2 — ΒΑΣΙΛΕΙΟΝ
| 23 | 1844 | .206 | 40.00 | 80.00 | 125.00 | 250.00 |
| | 1845 | .242 | 40.00 | 80.00 | 125.00 | 250.00 |

Obv: Smaller crowned arms.
Rev: Redesigned wreath.
27	1847	.082	40.00	100.00	175.00	375.00
	1848	.258	20.00	40.00	80.00	200.00
	1849	.146	20.00	40.00	80.00	200.00

Size reduced to 17mm.
| 31 | 1851 | .388 | 25.00 | 45.00 | 85.00 | 200.00 |
| | 1857 | .544 | 20.00 | 40.00 | 80.00 | 200.00 |

| 41 | 1869BB | 7.482 | 2.00 | 4.00 | 10.00 | 60.00 |
| | 1869BB | — | — | — | Proof | 200.00 |

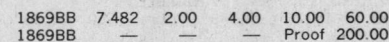

53	1878K large anchor	3.750	1.00	3.00	7.50	50.00
	1878K small anchor	Inc. Ab.	10.00	25.00	40.00	75.00
	1878K	—	—	—	Proof	200.00

5 LEPTA

COPPER, 28mm
Obv: Phoenix in solid circle.

KM#	Date	Mintage	Fine	VF	XF	Unc
2	1828	.400	40.00	60.00	100.00	250.00
	1830	.022	40.00	100.00	175.00	450.00

NOTE: Varieties exist.

Obv: Phoenix in pearl circle.
| 6 | 1828 | — | — | — | — | — |
| | 1830 | .150 | 40.00 | 80.00 | 150.00 | 350.00 |

NOTE: Varieties exist.

Obv: W/o circle.
| 10 | 1831 | .230 | 40.00 | 60.00 | 100.00 | 250.00 |

NOTE: Varieties exist.

Type 1 — ΒΑΣΙΛΕΙΑ

16	1833	2.500	20.00	40.00	80.00	150.00
	1834	Inc. Ab.	40.00	80.00	150.00	300.00
	1836	1,000	200.00	400.00	1000.	2000.
	1837	.116	40.00	60.00	125.00	250.00
	1838/7	1.472	20.00	40.00	80.00	175.00
	1838	Inc. Ab.	20.00	40.00	80.00	175.00
	1839	1.186	20.00	40.00	80.00	175.00
	1840	.417	20.00	40.00	80.00	175.00
	1841	.864	20.00	40.00	80.00	175.00
	1842	.682	20.00	40.00	80.00	175.00

Type 2 — ΒΑΣΙΛΕΙΟΝ
24	1844	.089	40.00	80.00	150.00	300.00
	1845	.316	40.00	80.00	150.00	300.00
	1846	.190	40.00	60.00	125.00	250.00

28	1847	.270	40.00	80.00	150.00	300.00
	1848	.394	40.00	80.00	150.00	275.00
	1849	.374	40.00	60.00	125.00	225.00

| 32 | 1851 | .620 | 20.00 | 40.00 | 80.00 | 175.00 |
| | 1857 | .350 | 22.00 | 45.00 | 85.00 | 190.00 |

| 42 | 1869BB | 23.945 | 1.00 | 3.50 | 8.00 | 40.00 |
| | 1870BB | Inc. Ab. | 15.00 | 30.00 | 60.00 | 200.00 |

GREECE 778

KM#	Date	Mintage	Fine	VF	XF	Unc
54	1878K	11.528	1.00	3.00	8.00	55.00
	1879A	.470	15.00	30.00	70.00	275.00
	1882A	14.400	2.00	5.00	12.50	55.00

COPPER-NICKEL

58	1894A	4.000	1.00	2.50	6.00	25.00
	1895A	4.000	1.00	2.50	6.00	25.00

NICKEL

62	1912(a)	25.053	.50	1.00	2.00	12.00

ALUMINUM

77	1954	15.000	—	.10	.50	1.50
	1971	1.002	.20	.50	1.00	6.00

10 LEPTA

COPPER, 35mm.
Obv: Phoenix in solid circle.

3	1828	.450	40.00	60.00	125.00	300.00
	1830	.034	50.00	100.00	200.00	500.00

Obv: Phoenix in pearl circle, 33mm.

8	1830	1.200	40.00	80.00	150.00	350.00

Obv: Phoenix w/o circle.

12	1831	1.223	40.00	60.00	100.00	225.00

Type 1 — ΒΑΣΙΛΕΙΑ

17	1833	.520	20.00	40.00	50.00	120.00
	1836	.919	35.00	70.00	120.00	220.00
	1837	2.660	40.00	80.00	125.00	200.00
	1838	.918	40.00	80.00	125.00	200.00

KM#	Date	Mintage	Fine	VF	XF	Unc
17	1843	.700	40.00	80.00	125.00	250.00
	1844	1.064	75.00	125.00	250.00	550.00

Type 2 — ΒΑΣΙΛΕΙΟΝ

25	1844	Inc. Ab.	40.00	80.00	125.00	250.00
	1845	.985	40.00	80.00	200.00	325.00
	1846/45	1.275	40.00	80.00	125.00	200.00
	1846	Inc. Ab.	40.00	80.00	125.00	200.00

29	1847	.740	40.00	80.00	125.00	250.00
	1848	1.174	40.00	80.00	125.00	250.00
	1849/8 small crown					
		1.160	40.00	80.00	125.00	200.00
	1849 small crown					
		Inc. Ab.	40.00	80.00	125.00	200.00
	1849 large crown					
		Inc. Ab.	200.00	400.00	600.00	1000.
	1850	1.282	40.00	80.00	125.00	200.00
	1851	.587	40.00	80.00	125.00	200.00
	1857	.883	40.00	80.00	125.00	200.00

43	1869BB	14.994	2.00	4.00	8.00	40.00
	1869BB	—	—	Proof	250.00	
	1870BB	Inc. Ab.	15.00	30.00	60.00	200.00

55	1878K	7.140	1.00	3.00	7.50	50.00
	1879A	.358	15.00	30.00	70.00	285.00
	1882A	16.000	1.00	3.00	7.00	45.00

COPPER-NICKEL

59	1894A	3.000	1.00	2.50	5.50	25.00
	1895A	3.000	1.00	2.50	5.50	25.00

NICKEL

63	1912(a)	28.973	.25	.50	2.50	14.00

1.5200 g, ALUMINUM
1.7mm thick

66.1	1922	120.00	1.00	2.00	4.00	20.00

1.6500 g, 2.2mm thick

66.2	1922	—	—	—	—	—

KM#	Date	Mintage	Fine	VF	XF	Unc
78	1954	48.000	—	.10	.35	2.00
	1959	20.000	—	.10	.35	2.00
	1964	12.000	—	.10	.35	2.00
	1965*	—	—	—	—	5.00
	1966	20.000	—	.10	.35	2.00
	1969	20.000	—	.10	.35	2.00
	1971	5.922	—	.20	1.00	7.50

*NOTE: Only sold in mint sets.

Obv: Soldier and Phoenix.

102	1973	2.742	—	—	1.00	4.00

Obv: Modified design; soldier omitted.

103	1973	4.110	—	.10	.50	2.00

113	1976	2.043	—	.10	.30	1.50
	1978	.797	.50	1.00	6.00	16.00

20 LEPTA

COPPER

11	1831	2.273	25.00	50.00	125.00	375.00

1.0000 g, .835 SILVER, .0268 oz ASW

44	1874A	2.223	3.00	—	13.50	30.00
	1874A	—	—	—	Proof	500.00
	1883A	1.000	3.50	7.00	27.50	75.00

COPPER-NICKEL

57	1893A	.248	5.00	25.00	75.00	400.00
	1894A	4.752	1.00	2.00	5.00	30.00
	1895A	5.000	1.00	2.00	5.00	30.00

GREECE

NICKEL

KM#	Date	Mintage	Fine	VF	XF	Unc
64	1912(a)	10.145	.50	1.00	3.50	14.00

COPPER-NICKEL

67	1926	20.000	—	.50	2.50	8.00

ALUMINUM

79	1954	24.000	—	.10	.50	2.00
	1959	20.000	—	.10	.50	2.00
	1964	8.000	—	.10	.50	2.00
	1966	15.000	—	.10	.50	2.00
	1969	20.000	—	.10	.50	2.00
	1971	4.108	—	.20	1.00	2.50

104	1973	2.718	—	.20	.60	4.00

105	1973	5.246	—	.20	.50	3.50

114	1976	2.506	—	.20	.40	3.00
	1978	.803	—	1.00	3.00	12.50

1/4 DRACHMA
1.2500 g, .900 SILVER, .0361 oz ASW
Obv: Young head.

18	1833	.780	25.00	50.00	100.00	150.00
	1834A	—	25.00	50.00	125.00	200.00
	1845	—	300.00	500.00	1500.	3000.
	1846	—	250.00	500.00	1500.	4000.

Obv: Old head, 15mm.

33	1851	—	200.00	500.00	1000.	2000.
	1855	—	100.00	250.00	500.00	1000.

1/2 DRACHMA

2.5000 g, .900 SILVER, .0723 oz ASW

KM#	Date	Mintage	Fine	VF	XF	Unc
19	1833	.900	25.00	50.00	75.00	175.00
	1834A	—	30.00	80.00	120.00	240.00
	1842 Owl	—	150.00	350.00	750.00	2000.
	1843 Owl	—	200.00	500.00	1000.	2500.
	1846	—	100.00	250.00	500.00	1000.
	1847	—	200.00	500.00	1000.	2000.

34	1851	—	200.00	500.00	1000.	2000.
	1855	—	100.00	250.00	500.00	1000.

50 LEPTA
2.5000 g, .835 SILVER, .0671 oz ASW
Obv: Young head.

37	1868A	60 pcs.	300.00	500.00	1000.	2500.

Obv: Old head.

45	1874A	4.501	2.50	5.50	15.00	35.00
	1874A	—	—	—	Proof	400.00
	1883A	.600	4.00	10.00	30.00	90.00

COPPER-NICKEL

65	1921H	1.000	250.00	500.00	750.00	1500.
	1921KN	1.524	400.00	750.00	1000.	2000.

68	1926	20.000	.20	.50	1.00	5.00
	1926B (1930)	20.000	.20	.50	1.00	5.00

80	1954	37.228	.15	.25	.75	1.50
	1954	—	—	—	Proof	75.00
	1957	5.108	.15	.50	2.00	10.00
	1957	—	—	—	Proof	150.00
	1959	10.160	.15	.25	.75	1.50
	1962 plain edge	20.500	.15	.25	.75	1.50
	1962 serrated edge Inc. Ab.	.15	.25	.75	1.50
	1964	20.000	.15	.25	.75	1.50
	1965*	—	—	—	—	3.00

*NOTE: Only sold in mint sets.

88	1966	30.000	.20	.50	1.00	3.50
	1970	10.160	.30	.60	1.50	4.50

97	1971	10.999	—	.10	.15	1.00
	1973	9.342	—	.20	.50	2.00

NICKEL-BRASS

KM#	Date	Mintage	Fine	VF	XF	Unc
106	1973	19.512	—	.10	.15	1.00

Markos Botsaris

115	1976	55.646	—	.10	.15	1.00
	1978	12.010	—	.10	.15	1.00
	1980	6.682	—	.10	.15	1.00
	1982	3.365	—	.10	.15	1.00
	1984	1.208	—	.10	.15	1.00
	1986	—	—	.10	.15	1.00

PHOENIX

3.8700 g, .943 SILVER, .1173 oz ASW

4	1828	.012	150.00	300.00	650.00	1300.

DRACHMA

4.5000 g, .900 SILVER, .1446 oz ASW
Obv: Young head.

15	1832	1.125	30.00	60.00	120.00	300.00
	1833	Inc. Ab.	25.00	50.00	75.00	200.00
	1833	—	—	—	Proof	1000.
	1833A	—	30.00	65.00	140.00	400.00
	1833A	—	—	—	Proof	1000.
	1834A	—	50.00	100.00	300.00	750.00
	1845(o)	—	350.00	900.00	1800.	3500.
	1846	—	125.00	250.00	500.00	1000.
	1847	—	300.00	600.00	1250.	2500.

Obv: Old head.

35	1851	—	220.00	450.00	900.00	1950.

5.0000 g, .835 SILVER, .1342 oz ASW

38	1868A	.480	25.00	50.00	100.00	250.00
	1873A	1.802	10.00	20.00	60.00	125.00
	1873A	—	—	—	Proof	500.00
	1874A	2.249	30.00	60.00	120.00	300.00
	1883A	.800	50.00	100.00	200.00	400.00

60	1910(a)	4.570	5.00	10.00	25.00	50.00
	1911(a)	1.881	5.00	15.00	25.00	75.00

COPPER-NICKEL

69	1926	15.000	.15	.25	1.25	5.00

GREECE 780

KM#	Date	Mintage	Fine	VF	XF	Unc
69	1926B (1930) 20.000		.15	.25	1.25	5.00

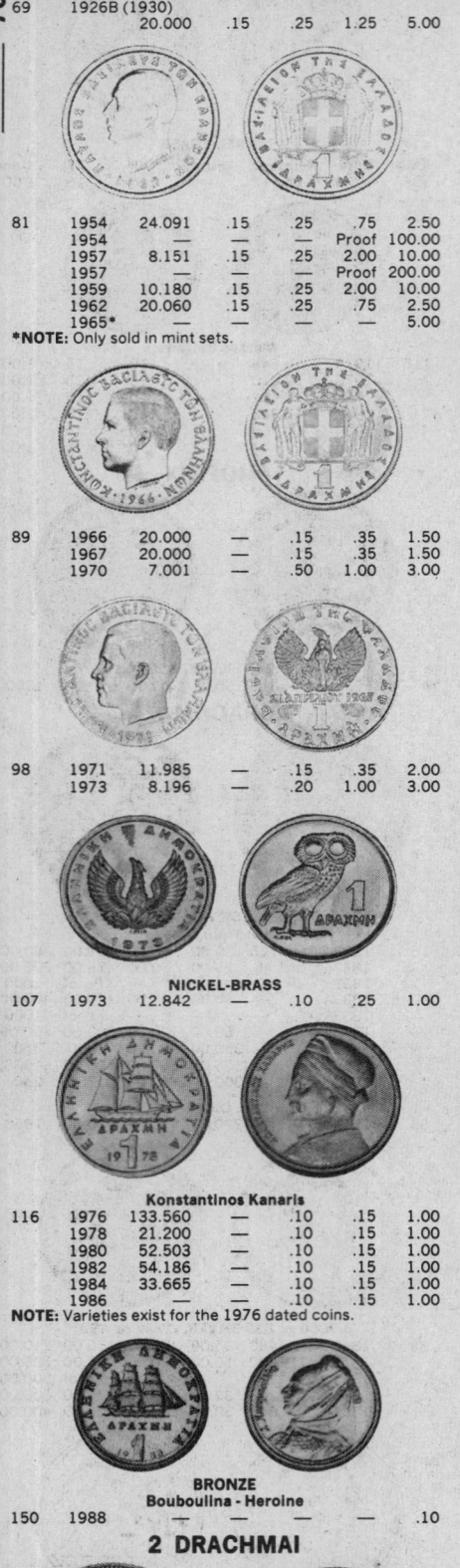

81	1954	24.091	.15	.25	.75	2.50
	1954	—	—	—	Proof	100.00
	1957	8.151	.15	.25	2.00	10.00
	1957	—	—	—	Proof	200.00
	1959	10.180	.15	.25	2.00	10.00
	1962	20.060	.15	.25	.75	2.50
	1965*	—	—	—	—	5.00

*NOTE: Only sold in mint sets.

89	1966	20.000	—	.15	.35	1.50
	1967	20.000	—	.15	.35	1.50
	1970	7.001	—	.50	1.00	3.00

98	1971	11.985	—	.15	.35	2.00
	1973	8.196	—	.20	1.00	3.00

NICKEL-BRASS

| 107 | 1973 | 12.842 | — | .10 | .25 | 1.00 |

Konstantinos Kanaris

116	1976	133.560	—	.10	.15	1.00
	1978	21.200	—	.10	.15	1.00
	1980	52.503	—	.10	.15	1.00
	1982	54.186	—	.10	.15	1.00
	1984	33.665	—	.10	.15	1.00
	1986	—	—	.10	.15	1.00

NOTE: Varieties exist for the 1976 dated coins.

BRONZE
Bouboulina - Heroine

| 150 | 1988 | — | — | — | — | .10 |

2 DRACHMAI

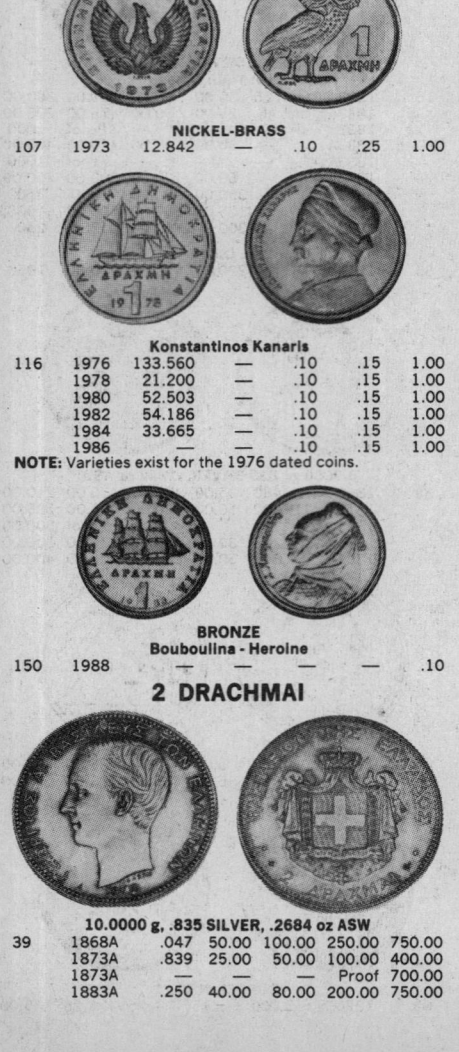

10.0000 g, .835 SILVER, .2684 oz ASW

39	1868A	.047	50.00	100.00	250.00	750.00
	1873A	.839	25.00	50.00	100.00	400.00
	1873A	—	—	—	Proof	700.00
	1883A	.250	40.00	80.00	200.00	750.00

KM#	Date	Mintage	Fine	VF	XF	Unc
61	1911(a)	1.500	5.00	20.00	50.00	100.00

COPPER-NICKEL

| 70 | 1926 | 22.000 | .50 | .75 | 2.00 | 10.00 |

82	1954	12.609	.50	.75	1.50	5.00
	1954	—	—	—	Proof	150.00
	1957	10.171	.50	.75	2.50	10.00
	1957	—	—	—	Proof	300.00
	1959	5.000	.50	.75	2.50	10.00
	1962	10.096	.50	.75	1.50	5.00
	1965*	—	—	—	—	3.00

*NOTE: Only sold in mint sets.

90	1966	10.000	.15	.25	.50	1.50
	1967	10.000	.15	.25	.50	1.50
	1970	7.000	.50	1.00	2.00	4.00

99	1971	9.998	.15	.25	.75	2.00
	1973	7.972	.20	.50	1.50	3.50

NICKEL-BRASS

| 108 | 1973 | 10.935 | .10 | .20 | .40 | 1.50 |

Georgios Karaiskakis

117	1976	115.801	—	.15	.25	1.25
	1978	16.772	—	.15	.25	1.25
	1980	45.955	—	.15	.25	1.25

KM#	Date	Mintage	Fine	VF	XF	Unc
130	1982	64.414	—	.10	.20	1.00
	1984	31.861	—	.10	.20	1.00
	1986	—	—	.10	.20	1.00

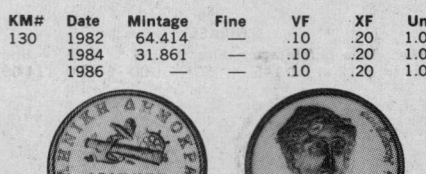

BRONZE
Manto Mavrogenous

| 151 | 1988 | — | — | — | — | .20 |

5 DRACHMAI

22.5000 g, .900 SILVER, .6511 oz ASW

20	1833	.378	100.00	200.00	500.00	1000.
	1833	—	—	—	Proof	
	1833A	—	100.00	200.00	500.00	1000.
	1833A	—	—	—	Proof	
	1833(o)	—	1200.	2400.	6000.	10,000.
	1833(o)	—	—	—	Proof	
	1844(o)	—	300.00	600.00	1200.	2400.
	1845	—	3000.	4800.	6500.	10,500.

Rev: Similar to KM#20.

36	1851	—	500.00	800.00	2000.	5000.
	1851	—	—	—	Proof	

GREECE

25.0000 g, .900 SILVER, .7234 oz ASW

KM#	Date	Mintage	Fine	VF	XF	Unc
46	1875A	1.000	25.00	60.00	175.00	400.00
	1875A reversed anchor	—	150.00	200.00	500.00	1500.
	1875A	—	—	—	Proof	1500.
	1876A	2.092	25.00	60.00	175.00	400.00
	1976A	—	—	—	Proof	2000.

1.6129 g, .900 GOLD, .0467 oz AGW

| 47 | 1876A | 9.294 | 250.00 | 400.00 | 1000. | 2000. |

NICKEL
LONDON MINT: In second set of berries on left only one berry will have a dot on it.

| 71.1 | 1930 | 23.500 | .50 | 1.00 | 2.50 | 20.00 |
| | 1930 | — | — | — | Proof | — |

BRUSSELS MINT: Two berries will have dots.

| 71.2 | 1930 | 1.500 | 1.00 | 3.00 | 7.50 | 40.00 |

COPPER-NICKEL

83	1954	21.000	.25	.50	1.00	5.00
	1954	—	—	—	Proof	200.00
	1965*	—	—	—	—	6.00

*NOTE: Only sold in mint sets.

| 91 | 1966 | 12.000 | .15 | .25 | 1.00 | 5.00 |
| | 1970 | 5.000 | .50 | 1.00 | 3.00 | 6.00 |

| 100 | 1971 | 4.014 | .15 | .25 | 1.00 | 5.00 |
| | 1973 | 3.166 | .25 | .50 | 1.50 | 3.00 |

Denomination spelling ends with I.

KM#	Date	Mintage	Fine	VF	XF	Unc
109.1	1973	13.931	.25	.50	1.00	1.75

Denomination spelling ends with A.

| 109.2 | 1973 | Inc. Ab. | 1.00 | 2.00 | 4.00 | 10.00 |

Aristotle

118	1976	104.133	.10	.20	.35	1.00
	1978	17.404	.10	.20	.35	1.00
	1980	33.701	.10	.20	.35	1.00

131	1982	42.647	.10	.20	.35	1.00
	1984	29.778	.10	.20	.35	1.00
	1986	—	.10	.20	.35	1.00

10 DRACHMAI

 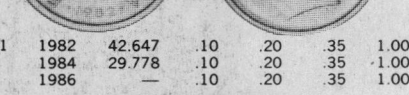

3.2258 g, .900 GOLD, .0933 oz AGW

| 48 | 1876A | .019 | 200.00 | 350.00 | 550.00 | 1500. |

7.0000 g, .500 SILVER, .1125 oz ASW

| 72 | 1930 | 7.500 | 2.50 | 5.00 | 12.50 | 50.00 |
| | 1930 | — | — | — | Proof | — |

NICKEL

84	1959	20.000	.30	.50	1.00	5.00
	1959	—	—	—	Proof	200.00
	1965*	—	—	—	—	6.00

*NOTE: Only sold in mint sets.

COPPER-NICKEL

| 96 | 1968 | 40.000 | .25 | .50 | .75 | 3.50 |

Rev. Phoenix

| 101 | 1971 | .502 | .25 | .50 | 1.00 | 5.00 |
| | 1973 | .541 | .50 | 1.00 | 2.50 | 5.00 |

KM#	Date	Mintage	Fine	VF	XF	Unc
110	1973	8.456	.25	.50	1.00	2.50

Democritus

119	1976	83.445	.15	.25	.50	1.00
	1978	14.637	.15	.25	.50	1.00
	1980	28.733	.15	.25	.50	1.00

132	1982	33.539	.15	.25	.50	1.00
	1984	23.802	.15	.25	.50	1.00
	1986	—	.15	.25	.50	1.00

20 DRACHMAI

5.7760 g, .900 GOLD, .1672 oz AGW

| 21 | 1833 | .018 | 250.00 | 650.00 | 1200. | 2000. |

6.4516 g, .900 GOLD, .1867 oz AGW

| 49 | 1876A | .037 | 125.00 | 225.00 | 350.00 | 650.00 |
| | 1876A | — | — | — | Proof | 1800. |

| 56 | 1884A | .550 | 90.00 | 125.00 | 175.00 | 250.00 |

11.3100 g, .500 SILVER, .1818 oz ASW

| 73 | 1930 | 11.500 | 4.00 | 6.00 | 12.50 | 40.00 |
| | 1930 | — | — | — | Proof | — |

6.4516 g, .900 GOLD, .1867 oz AGW

GREECE 782

5th Anniversary Restoration of Monarchy

KM#	Date	Mintage	Fine	VF	XF	Unc
74	ND(1940)	200 pcs.	—	—	Proof	3750.

7.5000 g, .835 SILVER, .2013 oz ASW

85	1960	20.000	—	BV	2.50	4.00
	1960	—	—	—	Proof	350.00
	1965*	—	—	—	—	5.00

*NOTE: Only sold in mint sets.

6.4516 g, .900 GOLD, .1867 oz AGW
1967 Revolution

92	1967	.020	—	—	—	350.00

COPPER-NICKEL

111.1	1973	3.092	.25	.50	1.00	5.00

Wide rim

111.2	1973	Inc. Ab.	.25	.50	1.50	6.00

112	1973	10.079	.20	.30	.50	1.50

Pericles

120	1976	65.353	.20	.30	.50	1.25
	1978	8.808	.20	.30	.50	1.25
	1980	17.562	.20	.30	.50	1.25

KM#	Date	Mintage	Fine	VF	XF	Unc
133	1982	24.299	.20	.30	.50	1.00
	1984	13.412	.20	.30	.50	1.00
	1986	—	.20	.30	.50	1.00

30 DRACHMAI

18.0000 g, .835 SILVER, .4832 oz ASW
Centennial of Royal Greek Dynasty

86	1963	3.000	—	BV	4.00	7.00

12.0000 g, .835 SILVER, .3221 oz ASW
Constantine and Anne-Marie Wedding

87	1964 Berne, thin letters on edge					
	1.000	—	—	BV	3.50	5.00
	1964 Konigsberg, thick letters on edge					
	1.000	—	—	BV	3.50	5.00

50 DRACHMAI

16.1290 g, .900 GOLD, .4667 oz AGW

50	1876A	182 pcs.	2000.	3000.	4000.	8500.

12.5000 g, .835 SILVER, .3355 oz ASW
1967 Revolution

93	1967(1970)	.100	—	—	25.00	30.00

COPPER-NICKEL
Solon the Archon of Athens

KM#	Date	Mintage	Fine	VF	XF	Unc
124	1980	32.251	.40	.60	1.00	2.50

Obv: Denomination in modern Greek.

134	1982	18.899	.40	.60	1.00	1.50
	1984	11.411	.40	.60	1.00	1.50

NICKEL-BRASS
Homer

147	1986	—	—	.50	1.00	3.00

100 DRACHMAI

32.2580 g, .900 GOLD, .9335 oz AGW

51	1876A	76 pcs.	5000.	8000.	13,000.	20,000.
	1876A	—	—	—	Proof	25,000.

.900 SILVER
5th Anniversary Restoration of Monarchy

75	ND(1940)					
	500 pcs.	—	—	—	Proof	750.00

GREECE 783

32.2580 g, .900 GOLD, .9335 oz AGW

KM#	Date	Mintage	Fine	VF	XF	Unc
76	ND(1940)	140 pcs.	—	—	Proof	9500.

25.0000 g, .835 SILVER, .6712 oz ASW
1967 Revolution
| 94 | 1967(1970) | .030 | — | — | 35.00 | 60.00 |

32.2580 g, .900 GOLD, .9335 oz AGW
1967 Revolution
| 95 | 1967(1970) | .010 | — | — | — | 1200. |

13.0000 g, .650 SILVER, .2717 oz ASW
50th Anniversary of Bank of Greece
| 121 | 1978 | .020 | — | — | Proof | 100.00 |

5.7800 g, .900 SILVER, .1672 oz ASW
13th European Games
| 125 | 1981 | .150 | — | — | — | 6.00 |
| | 1981 | .150 | — | — | Proof | 9.00 |

Pan-European Games
| 135 | 1982 | .150 | — | — | — | 6.00 |
| | 1982 | Inc. Ab. | — | — | Proof | 9.00 |

Pan-European Games
KM#	Date	Mintage	Fine	VF	XF	Unc
136	1982	.150	—	—	—	6.00
	1982	Inc. Ab.	—	—	Proof	9.00

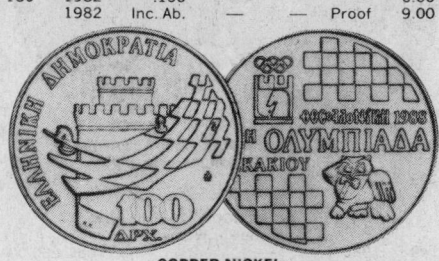

COPPER-NICKEL
28th Chess Olympics
| 152 | 1988 | — | — | — | — | 6.00 |

250 DRACHMAI

14.4400 g, .900 SILVER, .4178 oz ASW
13th European Games
| 126 | 1981 | .150 | — | — | — | 12.00 |
| | 1981 | .150 | — | — | Proof | 14.00 |

Pan-European Games
| 137 | 1982 | .150 | — | — | — | 12.00 |
| | 1982 | Inc. Ab. | — | — | Proof | 14.00 |

Pan-European Games
| 138 | 1982 | .150 | — | — | — | 12.00 |
| | 1982 | Inc. Ab. | — | — | Proof | 14.00 |

500 DRACHMAI

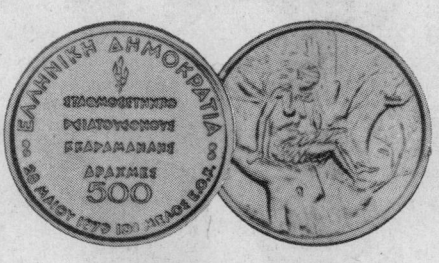

13.0000 g, .900 SILVER, .3762 oz ASW
Common Market Membership
| 122 | 1979 | — | — | — | — | 70.00 |
| | 1979 | .018 | — | — | Proof | 90.00 |

28.8800 g, .900 SILVER, .8357 oz ASW
13th European Games
KM#	Date	Mintage	Fine	VF	XF	Unc
127	1981	.150	—	—	—	22.00
	1981	.150	—	—	Proof	24.00

Pan-European Games
| 139 | 1982 | .150 | — | — | — | 22.00 |
| | 1982 | Inc. Ab. | — | — | Proof | 24.00 |

Pan-European Games
| 140 | 1982 | .150 | — | — | — | 22.00 |
| | 1982 | Inc. Ab. | — | — | Proof | 24.00 |

18.0000 g, .900 SILVER, .5209 oz ASW
Olympics - Torch
| 145 | 1984 | .025 | — | — | — | 40.00 |
| | 1984 | .025 | — | — | Proof | 55.00 |

18.1100 g, .900 SILVER, .5240 oz ASW
28th Chess Olympics
| 153 | 1988 | — | — | — | — | 35.00 |

GREECE 784

1000 DRACHMAI

23.3300 g, .925 SILVER, .6939 oz ASW
Decade For Women

KM#	Date	Mintage	Fine	VF	XF	Unc
148	1985	.020	—	—	Proof	45.00

2500 DRACHMAI

6.4500 g, .900 GOLD, .1866 oz AGW
13th European Games
Obv: Similar to 5000 Drachmal, KM#129.

| 128 | 1981 | .075 | — | — | Proof | 150.00 |

Pan-European Games
Obv: Similar to 5000 Drachmal, KM#129.

| 141 | 1982 | .050 | — | — | Proof | 150.00 |

Pan-European Games
Obv: Similar to 5000 Drachmal, KM#129.

| 142 | 1982 | .050 | — | — | Proof | 150.00 |

5000 DRACHMAI

12.5000 g, .900 GOLD, .3617 oz AGW
13th European Games

| 129 | 1981 | .075 | — | — | Proof | 275.00 |

Pan-European Games
Obv: Arms at left, torch at right.

| 143 | 1982 | .050 | — | — | Proof | 275.00 |

Pan-European Games
Obv: Similar to KM#143.

| 144 | 1982 | .050 | — | — | Proof | 275.00 |

8.0000 g, .900 GOLD, .2315 oz AGW
Olympics - Apollo
Obv: Similar to 500 Drachmal, KM#145. Rev: Apollo.

KM#	Date	Mintage	Fine	VF	XF	Unc
146	1984	.015	—	—	Proof	200.00

10,000 DRACHMAI

20.0000 g, .900 GOLD, .5787 oz AGW
Common Market Membership

| 123 | 1979 | — | — | — | — | 500.00 |

7.1300 g, .900 GOLD, .2063 oz AGW
Decade For Women

| 149 | 1985 | — | — | — | Proof | 260.00 |

MINT SETS (MS)

KM#	Date	Mintage	Identification	Issue Price	Mkt. Val.
MS1	1965(7)	—	KM78,80-85	—	18.00

NOTE: These coins were sold at the mint in Greece as a set; they have never been released for circulation. Mintages of the various coins vary from 170,000 to 190,000 pieces.

| MS2 | 1978 | 50,000 | — | — | 12.00 |

PROOF SETS (PS)

| PS1 | 1965(7) | 4,987 | KM78,80-85 | 10.25 | 20.00 |
| PS2 | 1978 | 20,000 | — | — | 20.00 |

CRETE

The island of Crete (Kreti), located 60 miles southeast of the Peloponnesus, was the center of a brilliant civilization that flourished before the advent of Greek culture. After being conquered by the Romans, Byzantines, Moslems and Venetians, Crete became part of the Turkish Empire in 1669. As a consequence of the Greek Revolution of the 1820s, it was ceded to Egypt. Egypt returned the island to the Turks in 1840, and they ceded it to Greece in 1913, after the Second Balkan War.

RULERS
Prince George, 1898-1906

MINT MARKS
A - Paris
(a) - Paris (privy marks only)

LEPTON

BRONZE, 15mm

KM#	Date	Mintage	Fine	VF	XF	Unc
1.1	1900A	.289	3.00	7.00	15.00	30.00
	1901A	1.711	2.00	5.00	12.00	25.00

16mm

| 1.2 | 1901A | Inc. Ab. | 3.00 | 6.00 | 12.00 | 30.00 |

2 LEPTA

BRONZE

| 2 | 1900A | .793 | 3.00 | 6.00 | 12.00 | 30.00 |
| | 1901A | .707 | 4.00 | 8.00 | 15.00 | 35.00 |

5 LEPTA

COPPER-NICKEL

| 3 | 1900A | 4.000 | 2.00 | 4.00 | 12.00 | 60.00 |

---

10 LEPTA

COPPER-NICKEL

KM#	Date	Mintage	Fine	VF	XF	Unc
4.1	1900A	2.000	2.00	6.00	15.00	70.00

Medal strike

| 4.2 | 1900A | — | 7.50 | 20.00 | 50.00 | 200.00 |

20 LEPTA

COPPER-NICKEL

| 5 | 1900A | 1.250 | 3.00 | 6.00 | 20.00 | 80.00 |

NOTE: For coins similar to the five listings above, but dated 1893-95, see Greece.

50 LEPTA

2.5000 g, .835 SILVER, .0671 oz ASW

| 6 | 1901(a) | .600 | 12.00 | 50.00 | 100.00 | 250.00 |

DRACHMA

5.0000 g, .835 SILVER, .1342 oz ASW

| 7 | 1901(a) | .500 | 25.00 | 50.00 | 150.00 | 400.00 |

2 DRACHMAI

10.0000 g, .835 SILVER, .2685 oz ASW

| 8 | 1901(a) | .175 | 30.00 | 75.00 | 250.00 | 600.00 |

5 DRACHMAI

25.0000 g, .900 SILVER, .7234 oz ASW

| 9 | 1901(a) | .150 | 35.00 | 100.00 | 500.00 | 1250. |

IONIAN ISLANDS

The Ionian Islands, situated in the Ionian Sea to the west of Greece, is the collective name for the islands of Corfu, Cephalonia, Zante, Santa Maura, Ithaca, Cythera and Paxo, with their minor dependencies. Before Britain acquired the islands, 1809-14, they were at various times subject to the authority of Venice, France, Russia and Turkey. They remained under British control until their cession to Greece on March 29, 1864.

Under Russia/Turkey
(1799-1807)

MONETARY SYSTEM
2 Soldi = 1 Gazetta

GAZETTA

COPPER
Similar to 5 Gazettae, KM#2.

KM#	Date	Mintage	VG	Fine	VF	XF
1	1801	—	75.00	150.00	350.00	750.00

5 GAZETTAE

COPPER
Rev: Denomination in Greek.

| 2 | 1801 | — | 100.00 | 250.00 | 500.00 | 1000. |

Rev: Denomination in Italian.

| 3 | 1801 | — | 100.00 | 250.00 | 500.00 | 1000. |

10 GAZETTAE

COPPER
Obv. leg: ΕΠΤΑΝΗΣΟΣ ΠΟΛΙΤΕΙΑ
Rev: Denomination in Greek.

| 4 | 1801 | — | 125.00 | 300.00 | 600.00 | 1200. |

Obv. leg: ΣΠΤΑΝΗΣΟΣ ΠΟΛΙΤΕΙΑ
Rev: Denomination in Italian.

| 5 | 1801 | — | — | — | — | Rare |

Under British Rule
(1809-1863)

MONETARY SYSTEM
40 Paras = 1 Piastre
220 Paras = 1 Dollar

25 PARAS

SILVER
Two countermarks, 25 and 25 with poorly drawn portrait of George III, on 3 Tari or 20 Grani coins of Sicily.

KM#	Date	Mintage	Good	VG	Fine	VF
16	(1814)	—	125.00	200.00	350.00	550.00

30 PARAS

SILVER
Two countermarks, 30 and 30 with poorly drawn portrait of George III, on 1 Real of Spain.

| 17 | (1814) | — | — | — | Rare | — |

NOTE: One piece exists with only reverse countermark on French coin of Louis XIV, but it is considered by some experts a contemporary counterfeit, since the authorization for these coins mentions only Spanish and Sicilian coins. However, it may be that the islanders were permitted to present any silver coins for countermarking.

50 PARAS

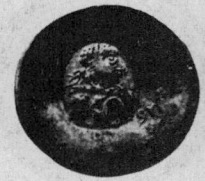 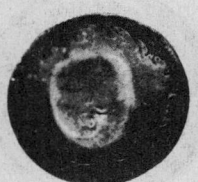

SILVER
Two countermarks, 50 and 50 with poorly drawn portrait of George III, on 6 Tari or 30 Grani coins of Sicily.

| 18 | (1814) | — | 120.00 | 165.00 | 275.00 | 450.00 |

NOTE: At least one coin exists with only 50 countermark.

60 PARAS

SILVER
Two countermarks, 60 and 60 with poorly drawn portrait of George III in oval, on 20 Grani of Naples and Sicily.

| 19 | (1814) | — | 275.00 | 400.00 | 650.00 | 1000. |

DECIMAL COINAGE

MONETARY SYSTEM
(Until 1835)
4 Lepta = Obol
100 Oboli = 1 Dollar
(Commencing 1835)
5 Lepta = Obol
100 Oboli = 1 Dollar

LEPTON

COPPER
Obv: Winged lion above date.
Rev: Seated Britannia above 4 (= 1/4 Obol).

KM#	Date	Mintage	Fine	VF	XF	Unc
30	1821	—	100.00	200.00	400.00	1000.

NOTE: Most of these coins are overstruck on Venetian coins by native craftsmen, and are very crude.

KM#	Date	Mintage	Fine	VF	XF	Unc
24	1834	—	1.00	5.00	10.00	35.00
	1834.	—	—	—	Proof	125.00
	1835.	—	1.00	5.00	10.00	35.00
	1835	—	1.00	5.00	10.00	35.00
	1848.	13.483	3.00	10.00	25.00	75.00
	1848	Inc. Ab.	3.00	10.00	25.00	75.00
	1849.	Inc. Ab.	1.00	5.00	10.00	35.00
	1849	—	—	—	Proof	125.00
	1851.	Inc. Ab.	1.00	5.00	10.00	35.00
	1851.	—	—	—	Proof	125.00
	1853.	1.344	1.00	5.00	10.00	35.00
	1853	—	—	—	Proof	125.00
	1857.	Inc. Ab.	1.00	5.00	10.00	35.00
	1857.	Inc. Ab.	1.00	5.00	10.00	35.00
	1862.	Inc. Ab.	1.00	5.00	10.00	35.00
	1862	—	—	—	Proof	125.00

2 LEPTA

COPPER

31	1819.	9.462	10.00	25.00	50.00	100.00
	1819	—	—	—	Proof	200.00
	1820.	Inc. Ab.	10.00	25.00	50.00	100.00
	1820	—	—	—	Proof	200.00

OBOL

COPPER

32	1819.	8.279	25.00	50.00	75.00	150.00
	1819	—	—	—	Proof	300.00
	1819 medal strike	—	—	—	Proof	500.00

SILVER (OMS)

| 32a | 1819 | — | — | — | Proof | 3500. |

2 OBOLI

COPPER

33	1819.	4.140	25.00	50.00	100.00	200.00
	1819	—	—	—	Proof	400.00
	1819 medal strike	—	—	—	Proof	600.00

30 LEPTA

1.4100 g, .925 SILVER, .0419 oz ASW

35	1834	—	25.00	50.00	75.00	150.00
	1834	—	—	—	Proof	350.00
	1834.	—	25.00	50.00	75.00	200.00
	1848.	.331	50.00	100.00	300.00	700.00
	1849.	Inc. Ab.	25.00	50.00	75.00	200.00
	1849	—	—	—	Proof	350.00
	1849.	Inc. Ab.	25.00	50.00	75.00	200.00
	1851.	Inc. Ab.	25.00	50.00	75.00	200.00
	1851	—	—	—	Proof	350.00
	1852.	Inc. Ab.	25.00	50.00	75.00	200.00
	1852	—	—	—	Proof	350.00
	1857.	Inc. Ab.	25.00	50.00	75.00	200.00
	1857.	Inc. Ab.	25.00	50.00	75.00	200.00
	1862	Inc. Ab.	10.00	25.00	50.00	100.00

GREENLAND

Greenland, an integral part of the Danish realm, is a huge island situated between the North Atlantic Ocean and the Polar Sea, almost entirely within the Arctic Circle. It has an area of 840,000 sq. mi. (2,175,600 sq. km.) and a population of 55,000. Capital: Godthaab. Greenland is the world's only source of natural cryolite, a fluoride of sodium and aluminum important in making aluminum. Fish products and minerals are exported.

Eric the Red discovered Greenland in 982 and established the first settlement in 986. Greenland was a republic until 1261, when the sovereignty of Norway was extended to the island. The original colony was abandoned about 1400 when increasing cold interfered with the breeding of cattle. Successful recolonization was undertaken by Denmark in 1721. In 1921 Denmark extended its claim to include the entire island, and made it a colony of the crown in 1924. The island's colonial status was abolished by amendment to the Danish constitution on June 5, 1953, and Greenland became an integral part of the Kingdom of Denmark. It has been an autonomous state since May 1, 1979.

RULERS
Danish

MINT MARKS
Heart (h) Copenhagen

MINTMASTER'S INITIALS
HCN - Hans Christian Nielsen, 1919-1927
C - Alfred Frederik Christiansen, 1956-1971

MONEYERS INITIALS
GI, GJ - Knud Gunnar Jensen, 1901-1933
HS, S - Harald Salomon, 1933-1968

MONETARY SYSTEM
100 Ore = 1 Krone

25 ORE

COPPER-NICKEL

KM#	Date	Mintage	Fine	VF	XF	Unc
5	1926HCN(h)GJ	.310	1.50	3.00	5.00	9.00

Center hole added to KM#5.

| 6 | 1926HCN(h)GJ | .060 | 9.00 | 15.00 | 30.00 | — |

NOTE: KM#5 was withdrawn from circulation and hole added in the USA.

50 ORE

ALUMINUM-BRONZE

KM#	Date	Mintage	Fine	VF	XF	Unc
7	1926HCN(h)GJ	.196	2.50	5.00	7.50	12.50

KRONE

ALUMINUM-BRONZE

| 8 | 1926HCN(h)GJ | .287 | 2.00 | 4.00 | 8.50 | 22.50 |

| 10 | 1957C(h)S | .100 | 3.50 | 6.50 | 10.00 | 18.00 |

COPPER-NICKEL

| 10a | 1960C(h)S | .109 | 2.00 | 4.00 | 5.50 | 8.50 |
| | 1964C(h)S | .110 | 2.25 | 4.50 | 5.50 | 7.00 |

5 KRONER

BRASS

| 9 | 1944 | .100 | 20.00 | 40.00 | 60.00 | 100.00 |

GRENADA

Grenada, located in the Windward Islands of the Caribbean Sea 90 miles (145 km.) north of Trinidad, has (with Carriacou and Petit Martinique) an area of 133 sq. mi. (344 sq. km.) and a population of *87,000. Capital: St. George's. Grenada is the smallest independent nation in the Western Hemisphere. The economy is based on agriculture and tourism. Sugar, coconuts, nutmeg, cocoa, and bananas are exported.

Columbus discovered Grenada in 1498 during his third voyage to the Americas. Spain failed to colonize the island, and in 1627 granted it to the British who sold it to the French who colonized it in 1650. Grenada was captured by the British in 1763, retaken by the French in 1779, and finally ceded to the British in 1783. In 1958 Grenada joined the Federation of the West Indies, which was dissolved in 1962. In 1967 it became an internally self-governing British associated state. Full independence was attained on Feb. 4, 1974. Grenada is a member of the Commonwealth of Nations. The prime minister is the Head of Government.

The early coinage of Grenada consists of cut and counterstamped pieces of Spanish or Spanish Colonial Reales, which were valued at 11 Bits. In 1787 8 Reales coins were cut into 11 triangular pieces and counterstamped with an incuse G. Later in 1814 large denomination cut pieces were issued being 1/2, 1/3 or 1/6 cuts and counterstamped with a 'TR', incuse 'G' and a number 6, 4, 2, or 1 indicating the value in bitts.

RULERS
British

MONETARY SYSTEM
1798-1840
12 Bits = 9 Shillings = 1 Dollar

NECESSITY COINAGE
BIT
(9 Pence)

SILVER
c/m: 'TR', 'G', '1' on 1/3 cut of Spanish or Spanish Colonial 2 Reales.

KM#	Date	Mintage	Good	VG	Fine	VF
11	ND(1818)	—	45.00	75.00	125.00	150.00

c/m: 'GS', 'G', '1' on 1/3 cut of Spanish or Spanish Colonial 2 Reales.

| 12 | ND(1818) | — | 45.00 | 75.00 | 125.00 | 150.00 |

2 BITS
(1 Shilling 6 Pence)

SILVER
c/m: 'TR', 'G', '2' on 1/6 cut of Spanish or Spanish Colonial 8 Reales.

| 5 | ND(1814) | *9,000 | 45.00 | 75.00 | 125.00 | 150.00 |

c/m: 'GS', 'G', '2' on 1/6 cut of Spanish or Spanish Colonial 8 Reales.

| 6 | ND(1814) | — | 45.00 | 75.00 | 125.00 | 150.00 |

4 BITS
(3 Shillings)

SILVER
c/m: 'TR', 'G', '4' on 1/3 cut of Spanish or Spanish Colonial 8 Reales.

| 7 | ND(1814) | *9,000 | 75.00 | 125.00 | 175.00 | 250.00 |

c/m: 'GS', 'G', '4' on 1/3 cut of Spanish or Spanish Colonial 8 Reales.

| 8 | ND(1814) | — | 75.00 | 125.00 | 175.00 | 250.00 |

6 BITS
(4 Shillings 6 Pence)

GUADELOUPE

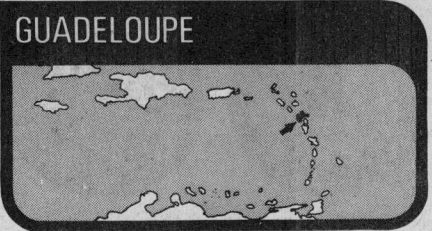

The French Overseas Department of Guadeloupe, located in the Leeward Islands of the West Indies about 300 miles (493 km.) southeast of Puerto Rico, has an area of 687 sq. mi. (1,779 sq. km.) and a population of *335,000. Actually it is two islands separated by a narrow salt water stream: volcanic Basse-Terre to the west and the flatter limestone formation of Grande-Terre to the east. Capital: Basse-Terre, on the island of that name. The principal industries are agriculture, the distillation of liquors, and tourism. Sugar, bananas, and rum are exported.

Guadeloupe was discovered by Columbus in 1493 and settled in 1635 by two Frenchmen, L'Olive and Duplessis, who took possession in the name of the French Company of the Islands of America. When repeated efforts by private companies to colonize the island failed, it was relinquished to the French crown in 1674, and established as a dependency of Martinique. The British occupied the island on two occasions, 1759-63 and 1810-16, before it passed permanently to France. A colony until 1946 Guadeloupe was then made an overseas territory of the French Union. In 1958 it voted to become an Overseas Department within the new French Community.

The well known R.F. in garland oval countermark of the French Government is only legitimate if on a French Colonies 12 deniers 1767 C#4. Two other similar but incuse RF countermarks are on cut pieces in the values of 1 and 4 escalins.

RULERS
French, until 1759, 1763-1810, 1816 -
British, 1759-1763, 1810-1816

MONETARY SYSTEM
3 Deniers = 1 Liard
4 Liards = 1 Sol (Sous)
20 Sols = 1 Livre
6 Livres = 1 Ecu
NOTE: During the British Occupation period the Spanish 8 Reales equalled 10 Livres.

CUT & COUNTERMARKED COINAGE
French Occupation
Until 1810
ESCALIN

SILVER
c/m: 'R.F.' on cut from outside ring of a center cut Spanish or Spanish Colonial 8 Reales.

KM#	Date	Year	Good	VG	Fine	VF
2	ND(1802)		25.00	42.50	70.00	140.00

4 E (ESCALINS)

SILVER
c/m: '4E RF' on center plug of Spanish or Spanish Colonial 8 Reales.

3	ND(1802)	—	150.00	250.00	400.00	1000.

20 LIVRES
.917 GOLD
c/m: '20' or '20 w/small animal head' on Brazil 6400 Reis, KM#172.

4	ND(1803)					
	(1751-77)	—			Rare	—

22 LIVRES

c/m: '22 w/small bearded human face' on Brazil 6400 Reis, KM#199.

KM#	Date	Year	Good	VG	Fine	VF
5	ND(1803)					
	(1777-86)	—		—	Rare	—

NOTE: The previously listed Brazil 6400 Reis with large 'G' in 15 pointed sunburst indent countermark are considered incorrectly attributed and possibly spurious by some authorities. Refer to "Unusual World Coins" 2nd edition c.1988.

British Occupation
1810-1816
10 SOUS

SILVER
c/m: Crowned 'G' on France 6 Sols, C#38.

13	ND(1811)					
	(1726-40)	30.00	55.00	90.00	175.00	

c/m: Crowned 'G' on France 6 Sols, C#43.

14	ND(1811)					
	(1743-70)	30.00	55.00	90.00	175.00	

c/m: Crowned 'G' on Great Britain 3 Pence, KM#591.

12	ND(1811)					
	(1762-86)	30.00	55.00	90.00	175.00	

c/m: Crowned 'G' on Spanish or Spanish Colonial 1/2 Real.

11	ND(1811)	—	30.00	55.00	90.00	175.00

20 SOUS
Livre

SILVER
c/m: Radiant 'G' on center plug of Spanish or Spanish Colonial 8 Reales.

19	ND(1811)	—	35.00	60.00	85.00	135.00

c/m: Crowned 'G' on France 12 Sols, C#39.

18	ND(1811)					
	(1726-32)	40.00	70.00	100.00	185.00	

SILVER
c/m: 'TR', 'G', '6' on 1/2 cut of Spanish or Spanish Colonial 8 Reales.

KM#	Date	Mintage	Good	VG	Fine	VF
9	ND(1814)	*.012	125.00	200.00	275.00	375.00

c/m: 'GS', 'G', '6' on 1/2 cut of Spanish or Spanish Colonial 8 Reales.

10	ND(1814)	—	125.00	200.00	275.00	375.00

4 DOLLARS

COPPER-NICKEL
F.A.O. Issue

KM#	Date	Mintage	VF	XF	Unc
15	1970	.013	—	5.00	10.00
	1970	2,000	—	Proof	25.00

10 DOLLARS

COPPER-NICKEL
Royal Visit

16	1985	*.100	—	2.50	3.50
	28.2800 g, .925 SILVER, .8411 oz ASW				
16a	1985	*5,000	—	Proof	30.00
	47.5400 g, .917 GOLD, 1.4013 oz AGW				
16b	1985	*250 pcs.	—	Proof	1200.

GUADELOUPE 788

c/m: Crowned 'G' on France 12 Sols, C#44.

KM#	Date	Year	Good	VG	Fine	VF
16	ND(1811)	(1743-70)	40.00	70.00	100.00	185.00

c/m: Crowned 'G' on France 12 Sols, C#75.

| 31 | ND(1811) | (1775-89) | 40.00 | 70.00 | 100.00 | 185.00 |

c/m: Crowned 'G' on Great Britain 6 Pence, KM#582.

| 17 | ND(1811) | (1743-58) | 40.00 | 70.00 | 100.00 | 185.00 |

c/m: Crowned 'G' on Spanish or Spanish Colonial 1 Real.

| 15 | ND(1811) | — | 40.00 | 70.00 | 100.00 | 185.00 |

40 SOUS
2 Livres

SILVER
c/m: Crowned 'G' on France 1/3 Ecu, C#30.

| 20 | ND(1811) | (1720-23) | 45.00 | 85.00 | 120.00 | 200.00 |

c/m: Crowned 'G' on France 24 Sols, C#40.

| 23 | ND(1811) | (1726-37) | 45.50 | 85.00 | 120.50 | 200.00 |

c/m: Crowned 'G' on France 24 Sols, C#45.

| 32 | ND(1811) | (1741-70) | 50.00 | 90.00 | 120.00 | 200.00 |

c/m: Crowned 'G' on France 24 Sols, C#45a.

| 33 | ND(1811) | (1771-74) | 55.00 | 100.00 | 130.00 | 225.00 |

c/m: Crowned 'G' on France 24 Sols, C#76.

KM#	Date	Year	Good	VG	Fine	VF
21	ND(1811)	(1774-90)	45.00	85.00	120.00	200.00

c/m: Crowned 'G' on Great Britain 1 Shilling, KM#607.

| 22 | ND(1811)(1787) | 40.00 | 80.00 | 110.00 | 190.00 |

2 LIVRES 5 SOUS

c/m: Crowned 'G' on quarter segment of 9 Livres, KM#24-26.

| 34 | ND(1811) | — | — | — | — | — |

NOTE: The authenticity of KM#35 has been questioned by leading authorities.

2 LIVRES 10 SOUS

SILVER
c/m: Crowned 'G' on quarter segment of Spanish or Spanish Colonial 8 Reales.

| 30 | ND(1813) | — | 20.00 | 30.00 | 40.00 | 65.00 |

9 LIVRES

SILVER
c/m: Crowned 'G' on obv. and rev. of Mexico 8 Reales, KM#106 w/crenelated square hole.

| 24 | ND(1811) | (1772-89) | 200.00 | 250.00 | 350.00 | 550.00 |

c/m: Crowned 'G' on obv. and rev. of Mexico 8 Reales, KM#109 w/crenelated square hole.

KM#	Date	Year	Good	VG	Fine	VF
25	ND(1811)	(1791-1808)	200.00	250.00	350.00	550.00

c/m: Crowned 'G' on obv. and rev. of Mexico 8 Reales, KM#110 w/crenelated square hole.

| 26 | ND(1811) | (1808-10) | 200.00 | 250.00 | 350.00 | 550.00 |

c/m: Crowned 'G' on obv. and rev. of Peru 8 Reales,
KM#97 w/crenelated square hole.

KM#	Date	Year	Good	VG	Fine	VF
35	ND(1811)					
		(1791-1808)	225.00	275.00	375.00	600.00

c/m: Crowned 'G' on obv. and rev. of Peru 8 Reales,
KM#106.2 w/crenelated square hole.

36	ND(1811)					
		(1809-11)	250.00	350.00	650.00	950.00

NOTE: The square plug was used in making 20 Sous, KM#19.

82 LIVRES, 10 SOLS

.917 GOLD
c/m: Crowned 'G' and 82.10 on Brazil 6400 Reis, KM#172.

27	ND(1811)					
		(1751-77)	2150.	3250.	5000.	8500.

c/m: Crowned 'G' and 82.10 on Brazil 6400 Reis, KM#199.

28	ND(1811)					
		(1777-86)	1250.	2000.	3000.	5000.

c/m: Crowned 'G' and 82.10 on Brazil 6400 Reis, KM#226.

29	ND(1811)					
		(1789-1805)	2000.	3000.	4500.	7500.

NOTE: Spurious countermarks on KM#27-29 lack the raised decimal point between "82" and "10".

MODERN COINAGE
MONETARY SYSTEM
100 Centimes = 1 Franc

50 CENTIMES

COPPER-NICKEL

KM#	Date	Mintage	Fine	VF	XF	Unc
45	1903	.600	5.00	9.00	25.00	100.00
(35)	1921	.600	2.00	8.00	20.00	65.00

FRANC

COPPER-NICKEL

46	1903	.700	6.00	12.00	35.00	125.00
(36)	1921	.700	5.00	10.00	30.00	90.00

GUATEMALA

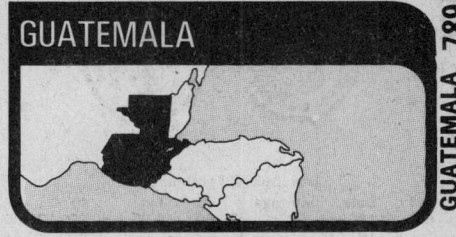

The Republic of Guatemala, the northernmost of the five Central American republics, has an area of 42,042 sq. mi. (108,889 sq. km.) and a population of *9.4 million. Capital: Guatemala City. The economy of Guatemala is heavily dependent on agriculture. The country is, however, rich in nickel resources which are being developed. Coffee, cotton and bananas are exported.

Guatemala, once the site of an ancient Mayan civilization, was conquered by Pedro de Alvarado, the resourceful lieutenant of Cortes who undertook the conquest from Mexico. Cruel but strategically skillful, he progressed rapidly along the Pacific coastal lowlands to the highland plain of Quetzaltenango where the decisive battle for Guatemala was fought. After routing the Indian forces, he established the city of Guatemala, 1524. The Spanish Captaincy-General of Guatemala included all Central America but Panama. Guatemala declared its independence of Spain in 1821 and was absorbed into the Mexican empire of Agustin Iturbide, 1822-23. From 1823 to 1839 Guatemala was a constituent state of the Central American Republic. Upon dissolution of the federation, Guatemala became an independent republic.

RULERS
Spanish until 1821

MINT MARKS
H - Heaton, Birmingham
NG - Nueva Guatemala - 1777 onward

ASSAYER'S INITIALS
Letter	Date	Name
M	1785-1822	Manuel Eusebio Sanchez

COLONIAL MILLED COINAGE
1/4 REAL
.8500 g, .903 SILVER, .0246 oz ASW
Mint mark: G
Obv: Castle. Rev: Lion.

KM#	Date	Mintage	VG	Fine	VF	XF
59	1801	—	4.00	9.00	15.00	50.00
	1802	—	4.00	9.00	15.00	50.00
	1803	—	4.00	9.00	15.00	50.00
	1804	—	4.00	9.00	15.00	50.00
	1805	—	12.50	25.00	35.00	100.00
	1806	—	10.00	20.00	30.00	90.00
	1807	—	4.00	9.00	15.00	50.00
	1808	—	4.00	9.00	15.00	50.00

72	1809	—	4.00	9.00	25.00	60.00
	1810	—	4.00	9.00	20.00	50.00
	1811	—	12.50	25.00	40.00	100.00
	1812	—	12.50	25.00	40.00	100.00
	1813	—	4.00	9.00	20.00	60.00
	1814	—	4.00	9.00	20.00	60.00
	1815	—	4.00	9.00	20.00	60.00
	1816	—	4.00	9.00	20.00	50.00
	1817	—	4.00	9.00	20.00	60.00
	1818	—	4.00	9.00	20.00	60.00
	1819	—	4.00	9.00	20.00	60.00
	1820	—	4.00	9.00	20.00	50.00
	1821	—	3.00	7.00	12.50	35.00
	1822	—	300.00	600.00	1000.	2000.

1/2 REAL
1.6900 g, .903 SILVER, .0490 oz ASW
Obv: Bust of Charles IV, leg: CAROLUS IIII. . . . .
Rev: Arms, pillar.

50	1801 M	—	6.00	10.00	18.00	55.00
	1802 M	—	6.00	10.00	18.00	55.00
	1803 M	—	6.00	12.00	25.00	65.00
	1804 M	—	6.00	12.00	25.00	65.00
	1805 M	—	6.00	12.00	25.00	65.00
	1806 M	—	6.00	12.00	25.00	65.00
	1807 M	—	6.00	12.00	25.00	65.00
	1808 M	—	15.00	30.00	60.00	125.00

Obv. leg: FERDIND VII. . . ., bust of Charles IV.

60	1808 M	—	5.00	10.00	17.50	40.00
	1809 M	—	4.50	9.00	20.00	40.00
	1810 M	—	5.00	10.00	20.00	45.00

GUATEMALA 790

Obv: Bust of Ferdinand VII.

KM#	Date	Mintage	VG	Fine	VF	XF
65	1808 M	—	20.00	40.00	80.00	125.00
	1811 M	—	—	—	Rare	—
	1812 M	—	10.00	18.00	35.00	90.00
	1813 M	—	10.00	18.00	35.00	100.00
	1814 M	—	4.00	7.00	15.00	40.00
	1815 M	—	4.00	7.00	15.00	40.00
	1816 M	—	3.00	5.00	10.00	25.00
	1817 M	—	5.00	10.00	25.00	65.00
	1818 M	—	6.00	12.00	25.00	65.00
	1819 M	—	5.00	10.00	25.00	65.00
	1820 M	—	3.00	5.00	10.00	20.00
	1821 M	—	5.00	12.00	20.00	60.00

REAL
3.3800 g, .903 SILVER, .0981 oz ASW
Rev: Arms, pillars.

54	1801 M	—	6.00	12.00	30.00	70.00
	1802/1 M	—	6.00	12.00	30.00	70.00
	1802 M	—	6.00	12.00	30.00	70.00
	1803 M	—	6.00	12.00	30.00	70.00
	1804 M	—	6.00	12.00	30.00	70.00
	1805 M	—	6.00	12.00	30.00	70.00
	1806 M	—	6.00	12.00	30.00	70.00
	1807 M	—	6.00	12.00	30.00	70.00

Obv. leg: FERDIND VII..., bust of Charles IV.

61	1808 M	—	5.00	9.00	17.50	50.00
	1809 M	—	4.00	8.50	15.00	30.00
	1810 M	—	6.00	12.00	20.00	45.00

Obv: Bust of Ferdinand VII.

66	1808 M	—	—	—	Rare	—
	1811 M	—	4.00	8.00	15.00	30.00
	1812 M	—	4.00	8.00	15.00	30.00
	1813 M	—	10.00	17.50	35.00	60.00
	1814 M	—	4.00	9.00	17.50	35.00
	1815 M	—	3.00	6.00	12.00	25.00
	1816 M	—	4.00	7.50	15.00	27.50
	1817 M	—	3.00	6.00	12.00	25.00
	1818 M	—	3.00	6.00	10.00	22.50
	1819 M	—	4.00	7.50	15.00	35.00
	1820 M	—	3.00	6.00	10.00	22.50
	1821 M	—	3.00	6.00	10.00	22.50

2 REALES
6.7700 g, .903 SILVER, .1965 oz ASW
Rev: Arms, pillars.

51	1801 M	—	4.00	7.00	15.00	55.00
	1802 M	—	6.00	12.00	30.00	65.00
	1803 M	—	12.00	25.00	55.00	100.00
	1804 M	—	4.00	7.00	15.00	55.00
	1805 M	—	4.00	7.00	15.00	55.00
	1806 M	—	18.00	35.00	65.00	125.00
	1807 M	—	18.00	35.00	65.00	125.00
	1808 M	—	10.00	20.00	40.00	90.00

Obv. leg: FERDIND VII..., bust of Charles IV.

62	1808 M	—	7.00	15.00	30.00	65.00
	1809 M	—	5.00	10.00	25.00	55.00
	1810 M	—	4.00	8.00	22.50	48.00

Obv: Bust of Ferdinand VII.

67	1808 M	—	12.00	25.00	80.00	160.00
	1811 M	—	12.00	18.00	30.00	60.00
	1812 M	—	5.00	9.00	22.50	50.00
	1813 M	—	12.00	25.00	80.00	160.00
	1814 M	—	12.00	25.00	80.00	160.00
	1815 M	—	5.00	9.00	22.50	50.00
	1816 M	—	6.00	10.00	25.00	60.00
	1817 M	—	5.00	9.00	22.50	50.00
	1818 M	—	5.00	9.00	22.50	50.00
	1819 M	—	5.00	9.00	22.50	50.00
	1820 M	—	5.00	9.00	22.50	50.00
	1821 M	—	4.00	7.00	20.00	45.00
	1822 M	—	27.50	55.00	110.00	225.00

4 REALES

13.5400 g, .903 SILVER, .3931 oz ASW

KM#	Date	Mintage	VG	Fine	VF	XF
52	1801 M	—	35.00	75.00	150.00	250.00
	1802 M	—	50.00	100.00	175.00	250.00
	1803 M	—	50.00	100.00	175.00	275.00
	1804 M	—	50.00	100.00	175.00	300.00
	1805 M	—	50.00	100.00	175.00	250.00
	1806/5 M	—	40.00	85.00	165.00	275.00
	1806 M	—	35.00	75.00	150.00	250.00
	1807 M	—	35.00	75.00	125.00	200.00

Obv. leg: FERDIND VII..., bust of Charles IV.

63	1808 M	—	100.00	200.00	350.00	550.00
	1809 M	—	75.00	150.00	275.00	450.00
	1810 M	—	75.00	150.00	275.00	450.00

Obv: Bust of Ferdinand VII.

68	1808 M	—	150.00	300.00	500.00	800.00
	1811 M	—	50.00	100.00	200.00	325.00
	1812 M	—	50.00	100.00	200.00	325.00
	1813 M	—	50.00	100.00	200.00	325.00
	1814 M	—	30.00	75.00	125.00	200.00
	1815/4 M	—	40.00	85.00	150.00	275.00
	1815 M	—	35.00	85.00	125.00	200.00
	1816 M	—	50.00	100.00	175.00	250.00
	1817 M	—	50.00	100.00	175.00	250.00
	1818 M	—	35.00	85.00	150.00	225.00
	1819 M	—	35.00	85.00	150.00	225.00
	1820 M	—	50.00	100.00	175.00	365.00
	1821 M	—	35.00	85.00	150.00	225.00

8 REALES
27.0700 g, .903 SILVER, .7859 oz ASW
Obv: Bust of Charles IIII right. Rev: Arms, pillars.

53	1801 M	—	55.00	100.00	200.00	350.00
	1802 M	—	75.00	150.00	225.00	350.00
	1803 M	—	55.00	100.00	200.00	350.00
	1804 M	—	55.00	100.00	200.00	350.00
	1805 M	—	55.00	100.00	200.00	350.00
	1806/5 M	—	75.00	200.00	325.00	425.00
	1806 M	—	55.00	100.00	200.00	350.00
	1807 M	—	55.00	100.00	200.00	350.00
	1808 M	—	110.00	260.00	450.00	825.00

Obv. leg: FERDIND VII...., bust of Charles IV.
Rev: Similar to KM#69.

64	1808 M	—	75.00	175.00	250.00	600.00
	1809/8 M	—	85.00	200.00	350.00	675.00

KM#	Date	Mintage	VG	Fine	VF	XF
64	1809 M	—	75.00	175.00	250.00	600.00
	1810 M	—	75.00	175.00	250.00	550.00
	1811 M	—	75.00	200.00	300.00	600.00

69	1808 M	—	250.00	625.00	1100.	1750.
	1811 M	—	100.00	200.00	400.00	750.00
	1812 M	—	25.00	40.00	65.00	125.00
	1813 M	—	25.00	40.00	65.00	125.00
	1814 M	—	25.00	40.00	65.00	125.00
	1815 M	—	25.00	40.00	65.00	125.00
	1816 M	—	25.00	40.00	65.00	125.00
	1817 M	—	25.00	40.00	65.00	125.00
	1818 M	—	25.00	40.00	65.00	125.00
	1819 M	—	25.00	40.00	65.00	125.00
	1820 M	—	25.00	40.00	65.00	125.00
	1821 M	—	25.00	40.00	65.00	125.00
	1822 M	—	—	Reported, not confirmed		

ESCUDO

3.3750 g, .875 GOLD, .0949 oz AGW
Obv: Bust of Charles IIII.

55	1801 M	—	300.00	625.00	1250.	2000.

74	1817 M	—	500.00	1000.	1500.	2000.

2 ESCUDOS

6.7500 g, .875 GOLD, .1899 oz AGW

70	1808 M	—	600.00	1250.	2000.	3250.
	1811 M	—	600.00	1250.	2000.	3250.
	1817 M	—	300.00	600.00	1000.	1500.

4 ESCUDOS

13.5000 g, .875 GOLD, .3798 oz AGW
Obv: Bust of Charles IIII.

57	1801 M	—	—	—	Rare	—

Obv: Bust of Ferdinand VII.

KM#	Date	Mintage	VG	Fine	VF	XF
73	1813 M	—	1750.	3500.	6000.	9000.
	1817 M	—	1000.	2000.	3500.	5000.

8 ESCUDOS

27.0000 g, .916 GOLD, .7951 oz AGW
Obv: Bust of Charles IIII.

| 58 | 1801 M | — | 2000. | 4000. | 8000. | 12,000. |

71	1808 M	—	—	—	Unique	—
	1811 M	—	2500.	4500.	8000.	15,000.
	1817 M	—	1500.	2500.	4000.	8000.

PROVISIONAL COINAGE
REAL

.903 SILVER
Mint mark: NG
Obv. leg: ESTADO DE GUATEMALA

| 75 | 1829 M | — | 60.00 | 150.00 | 275.00 | 450.00 |

COUNTERMARKED COINAGE
1838-1841

Type I
Sun over a row of volcanos in 6.5mm circle.

NOTE: A c/m of a sun over a volcano has been reported (c.f. KM#127) but has not yet been confirmed.

REAL
SILVER
c/m: Type I on Spanish Colonial 'cob' 1 Real.

KM#	Date	Good	VG	Fine	VF
78	ND	—	—	Rare	—

2 REALES
SILVER
c/m: Type I on Bolivia 2 Soles, KM#95.

| 81 | ND(1827-30) | 35.00 | 65.00 | 90.00 | 140.00 |

c/m: Type I on Peru 2 Reales, KM#141.1.

| 82 | ND(1825-40) | 35.00 | 65.00 | 90.00 | 140.00 |

4 REALES

SILVER
c/m: Type I on Bolivia (Potosi) 'cob' 4 Reales, KM#39.

| 85 | ND(1746-59) | 70.00 | 120.00 | 165.00 | 225.00 |

c/m: Type I on Bolivia (Potosi) 'cob' 4 Reales, KM#44.

| 86 | ND(1759-88) | 70.00 | 120.00 | 165.00 | 225.00 |

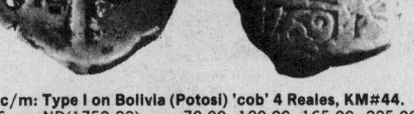

c/m: Type I on Bolivia 4 Soles, KM#96.

| 92 | ND(1827-30) | | | | |

c/m: Type I on Guatemala 'cob' 4 Reales, KM#5.

| 87 | ND(1700-46) | 90.00 | 150.00 | 225.00 | 300.00 |

c/m: Type I on Guatemala 'cob' 4 Reales, KM#11.

| 88 | ND(1747-53) | 90.00 | 150.00 | 225.00 | 300.00 |

c/m: Type I on Mexico 'cob' 4 Reales of Philip II.

KM#	Date	Good	VG	Fine	VF
89	ND(1556-98)	90.00	150.00	225.00	300.00

c/m: Type I on Peru (Lima) 'cob' 4 Reales of Charles II.

| 90 | ND(1665-1700) | — | 75.00 | 125.00 | 175.00 |

c/m: Type I on Peru (Lima) 'cob' 4 Reales of Philip V.

| 91 | ND(1700-46) | 70.00 | 120.00 | 165.00 | 225.00 |

NOTE: Market valuations are for pierced, holed or specimens without a visible date. Undamaged and/or specimens with a visible date command a premium.

8 REALES
SILVER
c/m: Type I on Bolivia (Potosi) 'cob' 8 Reales, KM#5.

| 94 | ND(1556-98) | 40.00 | 65.00 | 100.00 | 175.00 |

c/m: Type I on Bolivia (Potosi) 'cob' 8 Reales, KM#19.

| 95 | ND(1621-65) | 40.00 | 65.00 | 100.00 | 175.00 |

c/m: Type I on Bolivia (Potosi) 'Royal' 8 Reales, KM#26.

| 96 | ND(1665-1700) | — | — | Rare | — |

c/m: Type I on Bolivia (Potosi) 'cob' 8 Reales, KM#26.

| 97 | ND(1665-1700) | 40.00 | 65.00 | 100.00 | 175.00 |

GUATEMALA 792

c/m: Type I on Bolivia (Potosi) 'cob' 8 Reales, KM#31.

KM#	Date	Good	VG	Fine	VF
98	ND(1700-46)	40.00	65.00	100.00	175.00

c/m: Type I on Bolivia (Potosi) 'cob' 8 Reales, KM#40.

99	ND(1746-59)	50.00	90.00	125.00	200.00

c/m: Type I on Bolivia (Potosi) 'cob' 8 Reales, KM#45.

100	ND(1759-88)	40.00	65.00	100.00	175.00

c/m: Type I on Bolivia 8 Soles, KM#97.

112	ND(1838-41)	100.00	150.00	200.00	300.00

c/m: Type I on Guatemala 'cob' 8 Reales, KM#6.

101	ND(1733-46)	125.00	175.00	225.00	300.00

c/m: Type I on Guatemala 'cob' 8 Reales, KM#12.

102	ND(1747-53)	125.00	150.00	200.00	275.00

c/m: Type I on Mexico 'cob' 8 Reales, KM#43.

103	ND(1556-98)	— Reported, not confirmed			

c/m: Type I on Mexico 'cob' 8 Reales, KM#44.

KM#	Date	Good	VG	Fine	VF
104	ND(1621-67)	75.00	125.00	150.00	200.00

c/m: Type I on Mexico 'Royal' 8 Reales, KM#47.

105	ND(1701-28)	—	—	Rare	—

c/m: Type I on Mexico 'cob' 8 Reales, KM#47a.

106	ND(1729-33)	50.00	70.00	100.00	175.00

c/m: Type I on Mexico 'Klippe' 8 Reales, KM#48.

107	ND(1733-34)	125.00	200.00	300.00	450.00
	Date off flan	50.00	75.00	110.00	165.00

c/m: Type I on Peru (Lima) 'Royal' 8 Reales of Philip II.

KM#	Date	Good	VG	Fine	VF
108	ND(1556-98)	—	—	Rare	—

c/m: Type I on Peru (Lima) 'cob' 8 Reales of Philip IV.

109.1	ND(1621-65)	75.00	100.00	150.00	225.00

c/m: Type I on Peru (Star of Lima) 'cob' 8 Reales of Philip IV.

A109.2	ND(1659)	—	—	Rare	—

c/m: Type I on Peru (Lima) 'cob' 8 Reales of Charles II.

110.1	ND(1665-1700)	50.00	75.00	125.00	200.00

GUATEMALA 793

c/m: Type I on Peru (Lima) 'Royal' 8 Reales of Charles II.

KM#	Date	Good	VG	Fine	VF
110.2	ND(1665-1700)	300.00	600.00	1000.	1600.

c/m: Type I on Peru (Lima) 'cob' 8 Reales of Philip V.

| 111 | ND(1700-46) | 50.00 | 75.00 | 125.00 | 200.00 |

NOTE: Market valuations are for pierced, holed or specimens without a visible date. Undamaged and/or specimens with a visible date and partial legends command a premium.

Type II
Obv: Sun over 3 volcanos in 6.5mm circle.
Rev: Star, bow and arrow in 7mm circle.

8 REALES

.900 SILVER
c/m: Type II on Bolivia 8 Soles, KM#97.

KM#	Date	Good	VG	Fine	VF
114	ND(1827-40)	100.00	150.00	200.00	300.00

c/m: Type II on Chile 8 Reales, KM#96.1.
| 115 | ND(1837-40) | 125.00 | 175.00 | 225.00 | 325.00 |

c/m: Type II on Peru 8 Reales, KM#136.
| 116 | ND(1822-23) | 60.00 | 85.00 | 120.00 | 200.00 |

c/m: Type II on Peru 8 Reales, KM#142.1.
| 117 | ND(1825-28) | 60.00 | 85.00 | 120.00 | 200.00 |

c/m: Type II on Peru 8 Reales, KM#142.3.
| 118 | ND(1828-40) | 60.00 | 85.00 | 120.00 | 200.00 |

c/m: Type II on Peru (Cuzco) 8 Reales, KM#142.2.
| 119 | ND(1826-36) | 60.00 | 85.00 | 120.00 | 200.00 |

c/m: Type II on Peru (South) 8 Reales, KM#170.2.
| 120 | ND(1837-39) | 75.00 | 120.00 | 170.00 | 250.00 |

c/m: Type II on Peru (North) 8 Reales, KM#155.
| 121 | ND(1836-39) | 60.00 | 85.00 | 120.00 | 200.00 |

NOTE: Coins dated after 1840 with the Type II c/m are believed to be counterfeit by some authorities.

TYPE III
Sun behind volcano.

4 REALES

SILVER
c/m: Type III on "cob" 4 Reales, KM#11.
| 124 | ND | — | — | — | — |

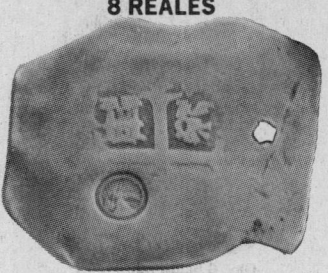

8 REALES

SILVER
c/m: Type III on "cob" 8 Reales, KM#12.
KM#	Date	Good	VG	Fine	VF
127	ND	—	—	—	—

REPUBLIC
MONETARY SYSTEM
8 Reales = 1 Peso

1/4 REAL

.7600 g, .903 SILVER, .0220 oz ASW

KM#	Date	Mintage	Fine	VF	XF	Unc
130	1859	—	—	—	Rare	—
	1860	.116	6.00	10.00	20.00	35.00
	1861	—	7.00	12.50	17.50	27.50
	1862	—	6.50	10.00	15.00	25.00
	1863	—	7.00	12.50	17.50	30.00
	1864	—	7.00	12.50	17.50	30.00
	1865	.023	22.50	45.00	75.00	150.00
	1866	.205	5.00	8.50	12.50	22.50
	1867	.169	5.00	8.50	12.50	22.50
	1868	.148	5.00	8.50	12.50	22.50
	1869	.242	5.00	8.50	12.50	22.50

.7700 g, .900 SILVER, .0222 oz ASW
Rev: 0.900 below wreath.

146	1872 P	—	2.00	3.50	5.50	8.50
	1873/2 P	.308	—	—	—	—
	1873 P	Inc. Ab.	1.00	1.75	3.00	5.00
	1874 P	—	7.50	12.50	20.00	35.00
	1875/3 P	—	—	—	—	—
	1875 P	—	1.00	1.75	3.00	12.50
	1878 F	.680	1.00	1.75	3.00	8.00

NOTE: Varieties exist.

.7700 g, .835 SILVER, .0206 oz ASW
Rev: 0.835 below small wreath.

| 146a.1 | 1878 | Inc.KM146 | 2.00 | 3.50 | 6.50 | 12.50 |

Rev: 0.835 below large wreath.
| 146a.2 | 1878 | Inc.KM146 | 1.50 | 2.50 | 3.75 | 6.00 |
| | 1879 | .171 | 1.50 | 2.50 | 3.75 | 6.00 |

Rev: W/o fineness.
146a.3	1878 large G					
	Inc. KM146	2.75	4.50	9.00	15.00
	1878 medium G					
	Inc. KM146	2.25	3.50	7.50	14.00
	1878 small G					
	Inc. KM146	2.00	3.75	7.50	14.00
	1879 large G					
	inc. KM146a.2	5.50	9.00	15.00	25.00

Obv: Long rayed sun.

151	1879					
	Inc. KM146a.2	1.50	2.00	3.00	5.00
	1880	.115	1.00	1.75	3.00	5.00
	1881	.073	3.00	4.50	8.00	13.50
	1882	—	1.00	1.75	2.50	4.00
	1883	.195	15.00	25.00	40.00	70.00
	1884	.100	1.00	1.50	2.50	4.00
	1885	—	7.50	12.50	20.00	35.00
	1886	—	1.25	2.00	3.50	5.50

GUATEMALA 794

Obv: Mountains with short rayed sun.

KM#	Date	Mintage	Fine	VF	XF	Unc
156	1887	—	1.50	2.50	4.00	6.00
	1888	—	1.00	1.50	2.25	3.50

NOTE: Varieties exist.

Obv: G below mountains.

157	1889	.870	2.00	3.00	5.00	15.00

Rev: Five stars below wreath.

158	1889	Inc.KM157	1.00	1.50	2.50	4.50
	1890	—	1.00	1.50	2.50	4.50
	1891	—	1.50	2.50	4.00	6.50
	1893/1	—	2.00	3.50	6.00	9.50
	1893/2	—	2.00	3.50	6.00	9.50

NOTE: Varieties exist.

Obv: Mountains with long rayed sun.

159	1892	.512	20.00	35.00	90.00	180.00
	1893/2	.749	2.00	4.00	8.00	15.00
	1893	Inc. Ab.	1.00	1.50	2.00	3.00

Rev: Three stars below thin wreath.

161	1893	Inc.KM159	1.00	1.50	2.00	3.00
	1894	.059	6.50	10.00	15.00	25.00

Rev: Five stars below full wreath.

162	1893	Inc.KM159	1.00	1.50	2.00	3.50
	1894	Inc.KM161	1.00	1.50	2.00	3.50
	1894H	.800	.50	.75	1.50	2.50
	1894H	—	—	—	Proof	100.00
	1895	1.482	.50	.75	1.25	2.00
	1896	2.071	.50	.75	1.25	2.00
	1897	.989	.50	.75	1.50	2.25
	1898	.384	.50	1.00	1.75	3.00
	1899	.080	1.50	2.50	4.00	6.00

COPPER-NICKEL

175	1900H	2.944	.15	.35	1.00	2.50
	1901H	5.056	.15	.35	.75	2.00

MEDIO (1/2) REAL

1.5500 g, .903 SILVER, .0449 oz ASW
Rev: MED: REAL

131	1859	—	15.00	25.00	40.00	75.00
	1860 R	.191	6.00	10.00	17.50	25.00
	1861	—	6.00	10.00	17.50	25.00

Obv. leg: RAFAEL CARRERA PTE.
Rev: MED. RL

138	1862 R	—	3.50	6.00	10.00	15.00
	1863/2 R	—	7.50	11.50	17.50	27.50
	1863 R	—	6.00	10.00	15.00	22.50
	1865/3 R	.057	5.00	9.00	15.00	22.50
	1865 R	Inc. Ab.	4.00	7.50	11.50	17.50
	1865 R	Inc. Ab.	4.00	7.50	11.50	17.50

Obv. leg: R. CARRERA FUNDADOR

KM#	Date	Mintage	Fine	VF	XF	Unc
143	1867 R	.092	3.00	5.50	8.50	22.50
	1868 R	.102	3.00	5.50	8.50	22.50
	1869	.117	3.00	5.50	8.50	22.50

1.5000 g, .900 SILVER, .0435 oz ASW

147	1872 P	—	3.50	5.00	8.00	20.00
	1873 P	.035	4.00	6.00	10.00	27.50

1.5000 g, .835 SILVER, .0402 oz ASW

147a.1	1878	—	2.75	4.50	6.50	10.00
	1879	Inc.KM152	2.00	5.00	8.00	15.00

NOTE: Wide and narrow dates exist for 1879. Large and small dates and letters exist for 1878.

Rev: W/o fineness.

147a.2	1878	—	2.75	4.50	6.50	9.50
	1893	Inc.KM163	5.00	7.50	10.00	15.00

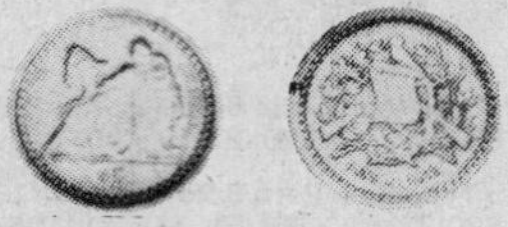

Obv: 1/2 RL.

152	1879 D	1.683	1.25	2.00	3.00	5.50
	1880/79 D	2.715	3.00	6.00	9.00	17.50
	1880 D	Inc. Ab.	.75	1.25	2.50	5.00
	1880 E	Inc. Ab.	6.00	10.00	15.00	22.50

NOTE: Varieties exist.

Obv: MEDIO REAL.

155.1	1880/770 E	Inc. KM152	3.00	4.50	7.50	12.50
	1880 E	Inc. KM152	.75	1.50	2.50	4.00
	1881 E	—	.75	2.00	3.00	4.50
	1883/1 E	.046	12.50	20.00	30.00	45.00
	1883 E	Inc. Ab.	6.00	10.00	15.00	22.50

NOTE: Varieties exist.

Rev: Star between fineness and date.

155.2	1889	.481	1.00	1.50	2.25	4.00
	1890/89	—	2.00	3.00	7.50	12.50
	1890	—	1.00	1.50	2.25	4.00

Rev: W/o fineness, small wreath.

163	1893/2	.360	20.00	35.00	75.00	125.00
	1893	Inc. Ab.	18.50	27.50	55.00	100.00

Rev: Large wreath.

164	1893 large date, blundered flat top 3	Inc. KM163	6.00	10.00	17.50	30.00
	1893 small date, round top 3	Inc. KM163	6.00	10.00	17.50	30.00

165	1894	.619	1.00	1.50	2.25	4.00
	1894H	.900	1.00	1.50	2.00	3.00
	1894H	—	—	—	Proof	100.00
	1895	.819	1.00	1.50	2.00	3.00
	1895H	.300	1.50	2.50	3.75	6.00
	1896	1.062	1.00	1.50	2.00	3.00
	1897	.528	1.00	1.50	2.00	3.00

NOTE: Varieties exist.

1.5500 g, .600 SILVER, .0299 oz ASW

KM#	Date	Mintage	Fine	VF	XF	Unc
170	1899	.486	.75	1.25	2.50	3.50

COPPER-NICKEL

176	1900	5.348	.25	.50	.60	1.75
	1901	6.652	.25	.50	.60	1.75

UN (1) REAL

3.0000 g, .903 SILVER, .0870 oz ASW
Rev: UN REAL.

132	1859	—	50.00	80.00	—	—
	1859 R	—	7.50	15.00	22.50	35.00
	1860 R	.177	3.50	6.00	10.00	17.50

Obv. leg: RAFAEL CARRERA PTE. . . .
Rev: UN RL.

137	1861 R	—	3.00	5.00	7.50	12.50
	1862 R	—	2.50	3.50	6.00	10.00
	1863 R	—	3.00	5.00	7.50	12.50
	1864 R	—	2.50	3.50	6.00	10.00
	1865 R w/Frener F below bust	—	4.00	7.00	10.00	15.00
	1865 R w/o Frener F	—	3.00	3.50	6.00	10.00

NOTE: Varieties exist.

Obv. leg: R. CARRERA FUNDADOR. . . .
Rev: 1 RL.

141	1866 R	.385	2.50	4.00	7.50	20.00
	1867 R	.199	2.50	4.00	7.50	20.00

Rev: UN REAL.

145	1868 R	.335	2.50	4.00	7.50	20.00
	1869 R	.131	2.50	4.00	7.50	20.00

3.1500 g, .900 SILVER, .0911 oz ASW

148.1	1872 P	3.816	9.00	15.00	30.00	50.00
	1874 P	—	4.50	7.50	15.00	30.00
	1878 F	.159	5.00	8.50	17.50	35.00

Obv: W/o fineness.

148.2	1878	Inc. Ab.	7.50	12.50	27.50	55.00

GUATEMALA

NOTE: Wide and narrow dates exist.

KM#	Date	Mintage	Fine	VF	XF	Unc
153	1879 D	.037	12.50	22.50	37.50	65.00

3.2500 g, .835 SILVER, .0872 oz ASW

153a.1	1883	.046	3.00	5.00	8.00	15.00

Rev: Star between fineness and date.

153a.2	1889	.332	1.50	2.75	3.50	5.00
	1890/89	—	2.50	4.50	6.50	10.00
	1890	—	1.50	2.75	3.50	5.00
	1891	—	1.50	2.75	3.50	5.00
	1893	.293	2.00	4.00	5.00	7.00

NOTE: Wide and narrow dates exist for 1893 dated coins.

166	1894	.326	2.00	2.75	3.75	5.50
	1894H	.600	2.00	2.75	3.25	4.50
	1894H	—	—	—	Proof	100.00
	1895H	.200	2.75	5.00	8.50	12.50
	1896	.203	2.00	2.75	3.75	5.50
	1897	.701	2.00	2.75	3.25	4.50
	1898	.040	6.50	10.00	17.50	27.50

Rev: W/o fineness.

171	1899	—	6.00	10.00	17.50	27.50

3.1500 g, .750 SILVER, .0759 oz ASW

172	1899	—	75.00	125.00	200.00	—

3.1000 g, .600 SILVER, .0598 oz ASW

173	1899	—	2.00	2.50	5.00	12.50

3.1500 g, .500 SILVER, .0506 oz ASW

174	1899	—	1.25	2.75	6.00	12.50
	1900	1.874	1.25	2.75	7.00	15.00

NOTE: Varieties exist for 1900 dated coins.

COPPER-NICKEL

177	1900	4.612	—	.30	.75	1.50
	1901	7.388	—	.25	.75	1.25

KM#	Date	Mintage	Fine	VF	XF	Unc
177	1910	4.000	—	.30	.75	1.50
	1911	2.000	—	.35	1.00	1.75
	1912	8.000	—	.25	.75	1.25

DOS (2) REALES

6.3000 g, .903 SILVER, .1829 oz ASW, 27.5mm
Obv. leg: RAFAEL CARRERA PE., thick letters.

133	1859	—	200.00	300.00	500.00	—

6.2000 g, .903 SILVER, .1800 oz ASW, 26mm
Obv: Thin letters.

134	1860 R	—	8.50	12.50	35.00	—
	1861 R	—	10.00	17.50	40.00	—

6.1000 g, .903 SILVER, .1770 oz ASW, 24mm
Rev: Narrower shield.

139	1862 R	—	4.00	6.50	8.50	40.00
	1863 R	—	4.00	6.50	8.50	40.00
	1864 R	—	4.00	6.50	8.50	40.00
	1865 R	.410	4.00	6.50	8.50	40.00
	1865 R w/o period after date					
	Inc. Ab.	4.50	6.50	8.50	40.00	

NOTE: Wide and narrow dates exist for 1863 dated coins.

Obv. leg: R. CARRERA FUNDADOR....

142	1866 R	.334	5.00	7.50	10.00	22.50
	1867 R	.293	5.00	7.50	10.00	22.50
	1868 R	.267	6.00	7.50	10.00	22.50
	1869 R	.124	6.75	12.00	17.50	30.00

6.1000 g, .900 SILVER, .1765 oz ASW

149	1872 P	—	6.00	10.00	15.00	—
	1873 P	.610	4.00	6.50	8.50	—

154	1879 D	.101	6.50	12.00	18.00	50.00

0.835/0.900 SILVER

KM#	Date	Mintage	Fine	VF	XF	Unc
154a (154a.1)	1881 E	2.975	7.50	10.00	12.50	15.00

6.2000 g, .835 SILVER, .1664 oz ASW
Rev: Star between fineness and date.

154b.1 (154a.2)	1892	—	170.00	280.00	400.00	—

Rev: W/o star.

154b.2 (154a.3)	1892	—	170.00	280.00	400.00	—

167	1894	1.094	2.50	4.50	7.00	12.00
	1894H	.900	2.50	4.50	7.00	12.00
	1894H	—	—	—	Proof	300.00
	1895	2.783	2.50	4.50	7.00	12.00
	1895H	.300	4.50	6.00	9.00	15.00
	1896	.605	2.50	5.00	7.00	12.00
	1897	1.041	2.50	5.00	7.00	12.00
	1898	5.172	2.25	4.00	6.50	12.00
	1899	.040	10.00	17.50	25.00	45.00

CUATRO (4) REALES

0.8065 g, .875 GOLD, .0226 oz AGW

135	1860 R	—	17.50	30.00	40.00	75.00
	1861 R	.277	17.50	30.00	40.00	75.00
	1862 R	—	17.50	30.00	40.00	75.00
	1863 R	—	17.50	30.00	40.00	75.00
	1864 R	—	25.00	60.00	100.00	150.00

12.5000 g, .903 SILVER, .3629 oz ASW
Obv. leg: RAFAEL CARRERA PTE....

KM#	Date	Mintage	VG	Fine	VF	XF
136	1860 R	4.760	—	18.00	30.00	50.00
	1861 R	—	5.00	18.00	30.00	50.00

Rev: Shield narrowed.

KM#	Date	Mintage	Fine	VF	XF	Unc
140	1863 R	—	10.00	17.50	25.00	200.00
	1865/3 R	.082	18.00	30.00	45.00	350.00
	1865 R Inc. Ab.		10.00	16.50	22.50	200.00

GUATEMALA 796

Obv. leg: R. CARRERA FUNDADOR....

KM#	Date	Mintage	Fine	VF	XF	Unc
144	1867 R	.054	15.00	18.00	25.00	—
	1868 R	.036	15.00	20.00	30.00	—
	1869 R	—	—	—	Rare	—

12.5000 g, .900 SILVER, .3617 oz ASW

150	1873 P	.024	22.50	50.00	100.00	200.00
	1878 D	.010	35.00	65.00	100.00	200.00
	1879 D	7.664	40.00	65.00	100.00	200.00
	1879 P	—	45.00	85.00	135.00	190.00
	1892 R.G.	—	60.00	135.00	275.00	550.00
	1893	—	100.00	225.00	550.00	875.00
	1893 R.G.	—	100.00	225.00	550.00	875.00

12.5000 g, .835 SILVER, .3356 oz ASW

160	1892	2.600	250.00	350.00	500.00	800.00

12.5000 g, .900 SILVER, .3617 oz ASW

168.1	1894H	.500	7.00	12.00	17.50	30.00
	1894H	—	—	—	Proof	400.00

Obv. and rev: H mint mark.

168.2	1894H	Inc. Ab.	100.00	150.00	250.00	500.00

DECIMAL COINAGE
100 Centavos (Centimos) = 1 Peso

CENTAVO

BRONZE

196	1871	—	2.50	5.00	10.00	20.00

202.1	1881	—	4.00	8.00	12.00	45.00

Die breaks in 1881 have the appearance of 1884.

202.2	1881	—	5.00	9.00	14.00	50.00

5 CENTAVOS

1.2500 g, .835 SILVER, .0335 oz ASW

KM#	Date	Mintage	Fine	VF	XF	Unc
203	1881	.118	10.00	25.00	37.50	75.00

10 CENTAVOS

2.5000 g, .835 SILVER, .0671 oz ASW

204	1881	.056	17.50	32.50	50.00	115.00

25 CENTIMOS

6.2500 g, .900 SILVER, .1808 oz ASW

189	1869 R	.181	6.00	13.50	25.00	70.00
	1870 R	.180	4.50	9.00	20.00	60.00

25 CENTAVOS

6.2500 g, .835 SILVER, .1677 oz ASW

205.1	1881 E	5.044	2.50	4.50	6.00	10.00
	1882 E	—	2.50	4.50	6.00	10.00
	1885 E	—	2.50	4.50	6.00	10.00
	1888 E	—	4.00	6.00	8.50	12.00
	1888	—	7.00	12.00	20.00	30.00
	1888 G	—	2.50	4.50	6.00	10.00
	1889 G	.496	2.50	4.50	6.00	10.00

NOTE: Varieties exist.

Star replaces assayer's initial

205.2	1889	Inc. Ab.	2.50	4.50	6.00	10.00
	1890	—	2.75	5.00	7.50	10.00
	1891	—	6.00	12.00	20.00	30.00

206	1882	—	200.00	300.00	450.00	—

Rev: W/o star.

209.1 (207.1)	1892	—	30.00	50.00	75.00	100.00

Rev: Star between fineness and date.

209.2 (207.2)	1890	—	6.00	12.00	20.00	30.00
	1892	—	2.50	4.50	6.00	10.00
	1893	—	2.25	3.75	5.00	8.50

NOTE: Varieties exist.

50 CENTAVOS

12.5000 g., .835 SILVER, .3356 oz ASW

KM#	Date	Mintage	VG	Fine	VF	XF
195	1870 R	.140	5.00	10.00	18.50	50.00

PESO

25.0000 g, .903 SILVER, .7258 oz ASW

178	1859	—	40.00	200.00	300.00	500.00
	1859 R	—	60.00	300.00	500.00	800.00

1.6129 g, .875 GOLD, .0454 oz AGW

179	1859 R	—	25.00	35.00	50.00	75.00
	1860 R	.037	25.00	35.00	50.00	75.00

27.0000 g, .903 SILVER, .7839 oz ASW

182	1862 R	—	15.00	25.00	80.00	125.00
	1863 R	—	12.00	20.00	40.00	80.00
	1864 R	—	6.00	10.00	15.00	35.00
	1864.R	—	6.00	10.00	15.00	35.00
	1865 R sm. R	.119	6.00	10.00	20.00	40.00
	1865 R lg. R I.A.	—	15.00	25.00	80.00	125.00

Rev: L10D.20G

186.1	1866 R	.109	6.00	10.00	15.00	35.00
	1867 R	.173	6.00	10.00	15.00	35.00
	1868 R	.060	6.00	10.00	15.00	35.00

GUATEMALA 797

Rev: W/o 'L' before 10Ds.20Gs.

KM#	Date	Mintage	VG	Fine	VF	XF
186.2	1869 R	.186	50.00	90.00	150.00	275.00

25.0000 g, .900 SILVER, .7234 oz ASW
Rev: L0.900

KM#	Date	Mintage	VG	Fine	VF	XF
190.1	1869/99 R	Inc. KM186	10.00	17.50	25.00	75.00
	1869 R	Inc.KM186	6.00	10.00	15.00	35.00
	1870 R	.283	6.00	10.00	15.00	30.00
	1871 R		6.00	10.00	15.00	25.00

Rev: W/o 'L' before 0.900.

| 190.2 | 1869 R | Inc.KM186 | 8.00 | 15.00 | 20.00 | 30.00 |

Rev: Date and fineness at bottom.

KM#	Date	Mintage	Fine	VF	XF	Unc
197.1	1872 P	.014	30.00	60.00	100.00	500.00
	1872 R		—	Rare	—	—
	1873 P	.078	20.00	35.00	75.00	300.00
	1873 P (error fineness 0900)					
		—	30.00	50.00	90.00	250.00

Rev: Quetzal w/ short tail.

| 197.2 | 1873 P | — | 30.00 | 50.00 | 90.00 | 250.00 |

Rev: Date and fineness at top.

| 200 | 1878 D | 1,076 | 600.00 | 1100. | 2000. | — |
| | 1879 D | .010 | 200.00 | 300.00 | 600.00 | — |

Rev: Full spray design.

KM#	Date	Mintage	VG	Fine	VF	XF
201	1879 D	Inc. KM200	150.00	300.00	400.00	550.00
	1893 G		—	—	Rare	—
	1893 RG	1,119	—	—	Rare	—

Obv: Modified Liberty design.

KM#	Date	Mintage	Fine	VF	XF	Unc
207	1882/1 E	—	—	—	Rare	—
	1888 G	—	350.00	600.00	1100.	2000.
	1889 G	—	350.00	600.00	1100.	2000.

KM#	Date	Mintage	VG	Fine	VF	XF
208	1882 A.E.	—	15.00	25.00	60.00	150.00
	1889 MG	6,794	125.00	200.00	300.00	500.00

KM#	Date	Mintage	Fine	VF	XF	Unc
210	1894	1.696	7.00	12.50	17.50	45.00
	1894H	.875	7.00	12.50	17.50	55.00
	1894H	—	—	—	Proof	800.00
	1895	1.415	7.00	12.50	17.50	50.00
	1895H	.375	7.00	12.50	17.50	55.00
	1895H	—	—	—	Proof	—
	1896/5	1.403	10.00	17.50	25.00	65.00
	1896	Inc. Ab.	7.00	12.50	17.50	50.00
	1897	—	12.00	17.50	25.00	85.00

2 PESOS

3.2258 g, .875 GOLD, .0907 oz AGW

KM#	Date	Mintage	VG	Fine	VF	XF
180	1859 R	—	50.00	65.00	125.00	200.00

4 PESOS

6.4516 g, .875 GOLD, .1815 oz AGW

| 181 | 1861 R | — | 175.00 | 250.00 | 400.00 | 550.00 |
| | 1862 R | — | 175.00 | 250.00 | 400.00 | 550.00 |

KM#	Date	Mintage	VG	Fine	VF	XF
187	1866 R	561 pcs.	250.00	500.00	700.00	950.00
	1868 R	778 pcs.	250.00	500.00	700.00	950.00
	1869 R	.020	100.00	175.00	250.00	375.00

5 PESOS

8.0645 g, .900 GOLD, .2333 oz AGW

| 191 | 1869 R | .049 | 110.00 | 125.00 | 175.00 | 250.00 |

198	1872 P	—	125.00	200.00	350.00	550.00
	1873 P	—	—	—	Rare	—
	1874 P	—	125.00	200.00	350.00	550.00
	1875 P	—	—	—	Rare	—
	1876 F	—	—	—	Rare	—
	1877 F	—	125.00	200.00	350.00	550.00
	1878 D	—	125.00	200.00	350.00	550.00

8 PESOS

12.9039 g, .875 GOLD, .3630 oz AGW

| 184 | 1864 R | — | 300.00 | 450.00 | 750.00 | 1200. |

Similar to 4 Pesos, KM#187.

| 192 | 1869 R | — | 500.00 | 650.00 | 2000. | 3000. |

10 PESOS

16.1290 g, .900 GOLD, .4667 oz AGW

| 193 | 1869 R | .020 | 225.00 | 300.00 | 450.00 | 600.00 |

16 PESOS

25.8078 g, .875 GOLD, .7259 oz AGW

183	1863 R	—	1500.	2500.	5000.	7500.
	1864 R	—	—	—	Rare	—
	1865 R	—	—	—	Rare	—

Reduced size

| 185 | 1865 R | 190 pcs. | 1000. | 1500. | 3750. | 5000. |

GUATEMALA 798

KM#	Date	Mintage	VG	Fine	VF	XF
188	1867 R	467 pcs.	—	—	—	Rare
	1869 R	3,465	400.00	600.00	800.00	1500.

20 PESOS

32.2580 g, .900 GOLD, .9334 oz AGW

| 194 | 1869 R | .016 | 450.00 | 550.00 | 700.00 | 950.00 |

| 199 | 1877 F | — | 1000. | 2000. | 5000. | 8000. |
| | 1878 F | — | 1000. | 2000. | 5000. | 8000. |

COUNTERSTAMPED COINAGE

By 1894, foreign coins had become so prevalent that on August 10 the government granted permission to counterstamp foreign 'dollars' with local 1/2 Real dies of 1894 to legitimize them.

(PESO)

.917 SILVER
c/s: On Brazil 2000 Reis, KM#475.

KM#	Date	Year	Mintage	Fine	VF	XF
213	1894	1875	—	—	Rare	—

25.0000 g, .900 SILVER, .7234 oz ASW
c/s: On Chile 8 Reales, KM#96.2.

| 214 | 1894 | 1848 JM | — | — | Rare | — |
| | 1894 | 1849 ML | — | Reported, not confirmed | | |

c/s: On Chile Peso, KM#129.

| 215 | 1894 | 1855 | — | — | Rare | — |

c/s: On Chile Peso, KM#142.1.

| 216 | 1894 | 1867 | — | 125.00 | 200.00 | 300.00 |
| | | 1868 | — | 125.00 | 200.00 | 300.00 |

KM#	Date	Year	Mintage	Fine	VF	XF
216		1869	—	50.00	75.00	125.00
		1870/69	—	50.00	75.00	125.00
		1870	—	50.00	75.00	125.00
		1871	—	75.00	125.00	200.00
		1872	—	20.00	30.00	50.00
		1873/2	—	20.00	30.00	50.00
		1873	—	20.00	30.00	50.00
		1874	—	20.00	30.00	50.00
		1875	—	20.00	30.00	50.00
		1876	—	20.00	30.00	50.00
		1877	—	20.00	30.00	50.00
		1878	—	20.00	30.00	50.00
		1879	—	20.00	30.00	50.00
		1880	—	20.00	30.00	50.00
		1881	—	20.00	30.00	50.00
		1882/1	—	20.00	30.00	50.00
		1882	—	20.00	30.00	50.00
		1883	—	20.00	30.00	50.00
		1884	—	20.00	30.00	50.00
		1885/3	—	20.00	30.00	50.00
		1885	—	20.00	30.00	50.00
		1886	—	20.00	30.00	50.00
		1887	—	Reported, not confirmed		
		1889	—	50.00	75.00	125.00
		1890/89	—	150.00	225.00	300.00
		1890	—	150.00	225.00	300.00
		1891	—	Reported, not confirmed		

c/s: Off center.

| 217 | 1894 | 1880 | — | — | — | — |

.903 SILVER
c/s: On Guatemala Peso, KM#178.

| 218 | 1894 | 1859 | — | Reported, not confirmed | | |

c/s: On Guatemala Peso, KM#190.1.

| 219 | 1894 | 1869 | — | — | Rare | — |

c/s: On Guatemala Peso, KM#208.

| 220 | 1894 | 1882 A.E. | — | — | Rare | — |

c/s: On Guatemala Peso, KM#210.

| 221 | 1894 | 1894 | — | Reported, not confirmed | | |
| | | 1894 H | — | — | Rare | — |

c/s: On Honduras Peso, KM#47.

| 222 | 1894 | 1882 | — | — | Rare | — |

c/s: On Honduras Peso, KM#52.

| 223 | 1894 | 1890 | — | 850.00 | 1350. | — |
| | | 1891 | — | 850.00 | 1350. | — |

c/s: On Peru Un Sol, KM#196.

KM#	Date	Year	Mintage	Fine	VF	XF
224	1894	1864 Y.B.	—	15.00	25.00	35.00
		1864 Y.B. Deteano	—	—	Rare	—
		1865 Y.B.	—	50.00	100.00	175.00
		1866 Y.B.	—	20.00	30.00	40.00
		1867 Y.B.	—	20.00	30.00	40.00
		1868 Y.B.	—	20.00	30.00	40.00
		1869 Y.B.	—	20.00	30.00	40.00
		1870 Y.J.	—	20.00	30.00	40.00
		1871 Y.J.	—	20.00	30.00	40.00
		1872 Y.J.	—	20.00	30.00	40.00
		1873 Y.J.	—	50.00	100.00	175.00
		1873 L.D.	—	50.00	100.00	175.00
		1874 Y.J.	—	20.00	30.00	40.00
		1875 Y.J.	—	20.00	30.00	40.00
		1879 Y.J.	—	20.00	30.00	40.00
		1880 Y.J.	—	30.00	50.00	75.00
		1881 B.F.	—	30.00	50.00	75.00
		1882 B.F.	—	40.00	60.00	100.00
		1882 F.N.	—	50.00	100.00	175.00
		1883 F.N.	—	100.00	165.00	250.00
		1884 B.D.	—	40.00	60.00	100.00
		1884 R.D.	—	20.00	30.00	40.00
		1885 R.D.	—	20.00	30.00	40.00
		1885 T.D.	—	20.00	30.00	40.00
		1886 R.D.	—	100.00	165.00	250.00
		1886 T.F.	—	25.00	45.00	65.00
		1887 T.F.	—	15.00	22.50	30.00
		1888 T.F.	—	15.00	22.50	30.00
		1889 T.F.	—	15.00	22.50	30.00
		1890/80 T.F.	—	30.00	50.00	75.00
		1890 T.F.	—	15.00	22.50	30.00
		1891 T.F.	—	15.00	22.50	30.00
		1892 T.F.	—	15.00	22.50	30.00
		1893 T.F.	—	15.00	22.50	30.00
		1393 T.F. (error)	—	450.00	600.00	900.00
		1894 T.F.	—	20.00	30.00	40.00

c/s: On Peru 5 Pesetas, KM#201.1.

225	1894	1880	B.F. with B under wreath w/o dot			
			—	80.00	110.00	160.00
		1880	B.F. with B. under wreath			
			—	80.00	110.00	160.00

c/s: On Peru 5 Pesetas, KM#201.3.

| 226 | 1894 | 1881 B | — | Reported, not confirmed | | |
| | | 1882 LM | — | 300.00 | 500.00 | 800.00 |

c/s: On Salvador Peso, KM#115.1.

227	1894	1892	—	1000.	1400.	2000.
		1893	—	1000.	1400.	2000.
		1894	—	Reported, not confirmed		

PROVISIONAL COINAGE
12-1/2 CENTAVOS

BRONZE

KM#	Date	Mintage	Fine	VF	XF	Unc
230	1915	6.000	.50	1.25	3.00	6.50

25 CENTAVOS

BRONZE

231	1915	4.000	.65	1.25	2.50	5.00

50 CENTAVOS

ALUMINUM-BRONZE

232	1922	3.803	.50	1.00	3.00	8.50

PESO

ALUMINUM-BRONZE

233	1923	1.477	.75	1.50	3.50	10.00

5 PESOS

ALUMINUM-BRONZE

234	1923	.440	1.00	2.00	6.00	20.00

MONETARY REFORM
100 Centavos = 1 Quetzal

MEDIO (1/2) CENTAVO

BRASS

248	1932	6.000	.15	.50	.75	2.50
	1932	—	—	—	Proof	—
	1946	.640	.50	1.00	2.25	6.00

UN (1) CENTAVO

COPPER

237	1925	.357	2.50	4.50	8.50	25.00

BRONZE

237a	1925	Inc. Ab.	5.00	9.00	17.00	50.00

KM#	Date	Mintage	Fine	VF	XF	Unc
247	1929	.500	1.25	2.50	4.50	20.00
	1929	—	—	—	Proof	—

BRASS

249	1932	3.000	.40	1.00	3.00	10.00
	1932	—	—	—	Proof	—
	1933	1.500	.60	1.50	4.50	12.00
	1933	—	—	—	Proof	—
	1934	1.000	.50	1.25	4.50	12.00
	1934	—	—	—	Proof	—
	1936	1.500	.40	1.00	4.50	12.00
	1936	—	—	—	Proof	—
	1938	1.000	.40	1.00	4.50	12.00
	1938	—	—	—	Proof	—
	1939	1.500	.50	1.25	4.75	9.50
	1939	—	—	—	Proof	—
	1946	.539	—	.10	.50	4.50
	1947	1.121	—	.10	.25	2.50
	1948	1.651	—	.10	.25	3.50
	1949	1.022	—	.10	.35	3.50

251	1943	.450	3.00	6.00	10.00	20.00
	1944	2.050	.50	1.25	2.50	8.00

254	1949	1.091	—	.10	.25	3.50
	1950	3.663	—	.10	.20	1.75
	1951	3.586	—	.10	.40	1.00
	1952	1.445	—	.10	.20	1.00
	1953	2.214	—	.10	.20	1.00
	1954	1.455	—	.10	.25	2.25

NICKEL-BRASS

259	1954	10.000	—	—	.10	.50
	1957	1.600	—	.10	.15	.75
	1958	2.000	—	.10	.15	.60

BRASS

260	1958	10.001	—	—	.10	.20
	1961	1.826	—	—	.10	.15
	1963	4.926	—	—	.10	.15
	1964	4.280	—	—	.10	.15

265	1965	3.845	—	—	.10	.15
	1966	6.100	—	—	.10	.15
	1967	6.400	—	—	.10	.15
	1968	2.590	—	—	.10	.15
	1969	13.780	—	—	.10	.15
	1970	10.511	—	—	.10	.15

KM#	Date	Mintage	Fine	VF	XF	Unc
273	1972	11.500	—	—	.10	.15
	1973	12.000	—	—	.10	.15

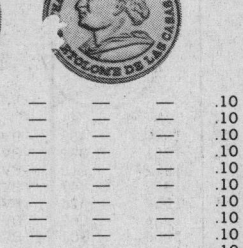

275	1974	10.000	—	—	—	.10
	1975	15.000	—	—	—	.10
	1976	15.230	—	—	—	.10
	1977	30.000	—	—	—	.10
	1978	30.000	—	—	—	.10
	1979	30.000	—	—	—	.10
	1980	20.000	—	—	—	.10
	1981	30.000	—	—	—	.10
	1982	30.000	—	—	—	.10
	1984	20.000	—	—	—	.10
	1985	—	—	—	—	.10
	1986	—	—	—	—	.10
	1987	—	—	—	—	.10
	1988	—	—	—	—	.10

NOTE: Varieties exist.

DOS (2) CENTAVOS

BRASS

250	1932	3.000	.50	1.25	3.50	17.50
	1932	—	—	—	Proof	—

252	1943	.150	3.00	7.50	12.00	30.00
	1944	1.100	.60	2.00	3.75	10.00

5 CENTAVOS

1.6667 g, .720 SILVER, .0386 oz ASW
Obv: Long-tailed quetzal.

238.1	1925	.573	2.25	4.50	8.50	22.50
	1944	1.026	BV	1.00	2.00	10.00
	1945	4.026	BV	.75	1.50	7.50
	1947	1.834	BV	1.00	1.50	4.50
	1948	1.103	BV	1.00	1.50	9.00
	1949	.551	.50	1.50	2.50	11.00

2.5000 g, .900 GOLD, .0723 oz AGW

238.1a	1925	8 pcs.	—	—	Rare	—

1.6667 g, .720 SILVER, .0386 oz ASW
Obv: Short-tailed quetzal.

238.2	1928	1.000	BV	1.00	2.00	7.50
	1928	—	—	—	Proof	—
	1929	1.000	BV	1.00	2.00	7.50
	1929	—	—	—	Proof	—
	1932	2.000	BV	1.00	1.50	6.50
	1932	—	—	—	Proof	—
	1933	.600	BV	1.00	2.50	9.00
	1933	—	—	—	Proof	—
	1934	1.200	BV	1.00	2.00	7.50
	1934	—	—	—	Proof	—
	1937	.400	BV	1.00	1.50	7.50
	1937	—	—	—	Proof	—
	1938	.300	.50	1.50	2.50	9.00
	1938	—	—	—	Proof	—
	1943	.900	BV	.75	1.50	5.00

GUATEMALA 800

Mule. Obv: KM238.2. Rev: KM255.

KM#	Date	Mintage	Fine	VF	XF	Unc
A255	1949	Inc.KM255	65.00	125.00	200.00	375.00

| 255 | 1949 | .305 | .50 | 1.50 | 3.50 | 12.50 |

NOTE: Varieties exist.

257.1	1950	.453	BV	1.00	2.00	9.00
	1951	1.032	BV	1.00	1.50	5.00
	1952	.913	BV	1.00	1.50	4.00
	1953	.447	BV	1.00	2.50	4.00
	1954	.520	BV	1.00	1.50	8.00
	1955	2.062	BV	1.00	1.50	3.00
	1956	1.301	BV	1.00	1.50	3.00
	1957	2.941	BV	1.00	1.50	2.50

2.7300 g, .620 GOLD, .0544 oz AGW

| 257.1a | 1953 | 25 pcs. | — | — | — | Rare |

NOTE: Distributed amongst delegates.

1.6667 g, .720 SILVER, .0386 oz ASW

	Small crude date		Large crude date			
257.2	1958 small date					
		3.025	BV	.75	1.00	1.50
	1958 large date					
		Inc. Ab.	BV	1.00	1.50	3.00
	1959	.232	BV	1.00	1.50	2.00

NOTE: Varieties exist.

Rev: Level ground at tree.

261	1960	4.770	—	BV	.50	1.00
	1961	6.756	—	BV	.50	1.00
	1964	1.529	—	BV	.50	1.00

COPPER-NICKEL

266	1965	1.642	—	.10	.50	2.00
	1966	3.600	—	—	.10	.25
	1967	2.800	—	—	.10	.25
	1968	4.030	—	—	.10	.25
	1969	7.210	—	—	.10	.25
	1970	8.121	—	—	.10	.25

270	1971	8.270	—	—	.10	.20
	1974	10.575	—	—	.10	.20
	1975	10.000	—	—	.10	.20
	1976	6.000	—	—	.10	.20
	1977	20.000	—	—	.10	.20

276	1977	Inc. Ab.	—	—	.10	.15
	1978	15.000	—	—	.10	.15
	1979	12.000	—	—	.10	.15
	1980	8.000	—	—	.10	.15
	1981	8.000	—	—	.10	.15
	1985	—	—	—	.10	.15
	1986	—	—	—	.10	.15
	1987	—	—	—	.10	.15
	1988	—	—	—	.10	.15

NOTE: Varieties exist.

10 CENTAVOS

3.3333 g, .720 SILVER, .0772 oz ASW
Obv: Long-tailed quetzal.

KM#	Date	Mintage	Fine	VF	XF	Unc
239.1	1925	.573	2.00	4.50	8.50	25.00
	1944	.155	1.00	2.75	5.75	15.00
	1945	1.499	BV	1.25	2.00	4.00
	1947	.471	BV	1.50	2.50	7.50
	1948	.324	BV	1.50	2.50	4.50
	1949	.145	BV	2.00	3.50	10.00

NOTE: Varieties exist.

.900 GOLD

| 239.1a | 1925 | 8 pcs. | — | — | — | Rare |

3.3333 g, .720 SILVER, .0772 oz ASW
Obv: Short-tailed quetzal.

239.2	1928	.500	BV	2.50	5.00	10.00
	1928	—	—	—	—	Proof
	1929	.500	BV	2.00	3.50	12.50
	1929	—	—	—	—	Proof
	1932	.500	BV	2.00	3.50	10.00
	1932	—	—	—	—	Proof
	1933	.650	BV	1.75	3.00	10.00
	1933	—	—	—	—	Proof
	1934	.300	BV	1.75	3.00	15.00
	1934	—	—	—	—	Proof
	1936	.200	BV	2.50	4.50	15.00
	1936	—	—	—	—	Proof
	1938	.150	1.00	3.00	5.00	12.50
	1938	—	—	—	—	Proof
	1943	.600	BV	1.25	2.50	7.50
	1947	Inc.KM239.1	BV	2.50	3.00	7.50

Rev: Small monolith.

256.1	1949	.281	BV	2.50	3.50	8.00
	1950	.550	BV	1.50	2.50	3.50
	1951	.263	BV	2.00	3.00	7.50
	1952	.307	BV	1.50	2.50	3.50
	1953	.388	BV	1.50	2.50	5.00
	1955	.896	BV	1.50	2.50	5.00
	1956	.501	BV	1.50	2.50	7.50
	1958	1.528	BV	1.50	2.50	6.00

Rev: Larger monolith.

256.2	1957	1.123	BV	1.25	2.00	3.00
	1957 (medal) I.A.	6.00	12.00	20.00	37.50	
	1958	Inc. Ab.	BV	1.50	2.50	5.00
	1958 (medal) I.A.	6.00	12.00	22.50	40.00	

Obv: Long-tailed quetzal. Rev: Small monolith.

256.3	1958	Inc. Ab.	BV	1.25	2.00	3.00
	1959	.461	BV	1.25	2.00	3.00

262	1960	1.743	BV	1.50	2.00	2.50
	1961	2.647	BV	1.50	2.00	2.50
	1964	.965	BV	1.50	2.00	2.50

COPPER-NICKEL

KM#	Date	Mintage	Fine	VF	XF	Unc
267	1965	2.227	—	.10	.20	.50
	1966	1.550	—	.10	.20	.60
	1967	3.120	—	.10	.20	.40
	1968	3.220	—	.10	.20	.40
	1969	3.530	—	.10	.20	.40
	1970	4.153	—	.10	.20	.40

| 271 | 1971 | 4.580 | — | .10 | .20 | .40 |

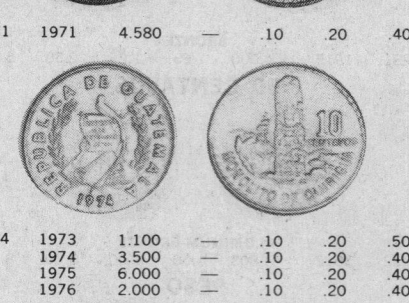

274	1973	1.100	—	.10	.20	.50
	1974	3.500	—	.10	.20	.40
	1975	6.000	—	.10	.20	.40
	1976	2.000	—	.10	.20	.40

277	1977	5.000	—	.10	.20	.25
	1978	8.500	—	.10	.20	.25
	1979	11.000	—	.10	.20	.25
	1980	5.000	—	.10	.20	.25
	1981	4.000	—	.10	.20	.25
	1983	20.000	—	.10	.20	.25
	1986	—	—	.10	.20	.25
	1987	—	—	.10	.20	.25
	1988	—	—	.10	.20	.25

NOTE: Varieties exist.

1/4 QUETZAL

8.3333 g, .720 SILVER, .1929 oz ASW
Lettered edge

| 240.1 | 1925 | 1.160 | 4.00 | 8.50 | 20.00 | 45.00 |

Obv: W/o NOBLE under scroll.

| 240.2 | 1925 | Inc. Ab. | 37.50 | 75.00 | 185.00 | 425.00 |

.900 GOLD

| 240a | 1925 | 8 pcs. | — | — | — | Rare | — |

8.3333 g, .720 SILVER, .1929 oz ASW
Rev: Larger design.

243.1	1926	2.000	2.00	4.00	10.00	30.00
	1928	.400	2.50	4.50	10.00	32.50
	1928	—	—	—	—	Proof
	1929	.400	2.50	5.00	12.50	35.00
	1929	—	—	—	—	Proof

GUATEMALA 801

Reeded edge

KM#	Date	Mintage	Fine	VF	XF	Unc
243.2	1946	.203	2.50	5.50	10.00	17.50
	1947	.134	2.50	5.50	9.00	15.00
	1948	.129	2.50	5.50	9.00	15.00
	1949/8	.025	2.50	5.50	10.00	17.50
	1949	Inc. Ab.	20.00	50.00	100.00	175.00

25 CENTAVOS

8.3333 g, .720 SILVER, .1929 oz ASW

| 253 | 1943 | .900 | 3.00 | 6.00 | 12.50 | 40.00 |
| A258 | 1949 | — | 60.00 | 120.00 | 200.00 | 375.00 |

Rev: Redesigned bust.

258	1950	.081	2.00	4.00	8.00	17.50
	1951	.011	6.00	15.00	25.00	75.00
	1952	.112	BV	2.50	5.00	8.00
	1954	.246	BV	2.50	5.00	8.00
	1955	.409	BV	2.50	5.00	8.00
	1956	.342	BV	2.50	5.00	8.00
	1957	.257	BV	2.50	5.00	8.00
	1958	.394	BV	2.50	5.00	8.00
	1959	.277	BV	2.50	5.00	8.00

263	1960	.560	BV	2.25	3.25	6.00
	1960 (medal)I.A.	20.00	50.00	100.00	175.00
	1961	.750	BV	2.25	3.25	6.00
	1963	1.100	BV	2.25	3.25	6.00
	1964	.299	BV	2.25	3.25	6.00

COPPER-NICKEL

| 268 | 1965 | 1.178 | .10 | .15 | .50 | 1.75 |
| | 1966 | .910 | .10 | .15 | .50 | 1.75 |

Rev: Modified design.

269	1967	1.140	.10	.15	.50	1.75
	1968	1.540	.10	.15	.50	1.50
	1969	2.070	.10	.15	.50	1.50
	1970	2.501	.10	.15	.50	1.50

KM#	Date	Mintage	Fine	VF	XF	Unc
272	1971	2.850	.10	.15	.40	.75
	1975	1.592	.10	.15	.30	.75
	1976	2.000	.10	.15	.30	.75

278	1977	2.000	.10	.15	.30	.75
	1978	4.400	.10	.15	.30	.65
	1979	5.400	.10	.15	.30	.65
	1981	1.600	.10	.15	.30	.75
	1982	2.000	.10	.15	.30	.65
	1984	2.000	.10	.15	.30	.65
	1987	—	.10	.15	.30	.65

NOTE: Varieties exist.

1/2 QUETZAL

16.6667 g, .720 SILVER, .3858 oz ASW

| 241.1 | 1925 | .400 | 17.50 | 27.50 | 50.00 | 185.00 |

Obv: W/o NOBLE under scroll.

| 241.2 | 1925 | Inc. Ab. | 70.00 | 100.00 | 200.00 | 700.00 |

50 CENTAVOS

12.0000 g, .720 SILVER, .2777 oz ASW

264	1962	1.983	—	BV	2.50	3.50
	1963/2	.350	3.50	7.50	12.50	20.00
	1963	Inc. Ab.	—	BV	2.50	3.50

QUETZAL

33.3333 g, .720 SILVER, .7716 oz ASW

| 242 | 1925 | *.010 | 475.00 | 625.00 | 950.00 | 1800. |

*NOTE: 7,000 pcs. were withdrawn and remelted soon after issue and more met with the same fate in 1932.

5 QUETZALES

8.3592 g, .900 GOLD, .2419 oz AGW

KM#	Date	Mintage	Fine	VF	XF	Unc
244	1926	.048	150.00	200.00	250.00	350.00

10 QUETZALES

16.7185 g, .900 GOLD, .4838 oz AGW

| 245 | 1926 | .018 | 275.00 | 350.00 | 425.00 | 650.00 |

20 QUETZALES

33.4370 g, .900 GOLD, .9676 oz AGW

| 246 | 1926 | .049 | 475.00 | 575.00 | 775.00 | 1250. |

PROOF SETS (PS)

KM#	Date	Mintage	Identification	Issue Price	Mkt. Val.
PS1	1894H(6)	—	KM162,165-167,168.1,210	—	1800.
PS2	1895/1896(6)	—	KM162,165-167,210, 4 Reales 1895 Pn8	—	Rare

GUERNSEY

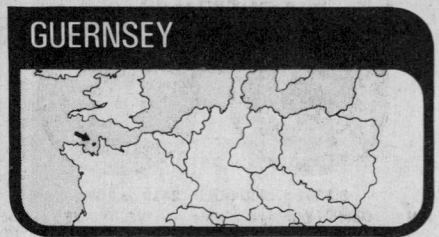

The Bailiwick of Guernsey, a British crown dependency located in the English Channel 30 miles (48 km.) west of Normandy, France, has an area of 30 sq. mi. (78 sq. km.) (including the isles of Alderney, Jethou, Herm, Brechou, and Sark), and a population of 53,794. Capital: St. Peter Port. Agriculture and cattle breeding are the main occupations.

Militant monks from the duchy of Normandy established the first permanent settlements on Guernsey prior to the Norman invasion of England, but the prevalence of prehistoric monuments suggests an earlier occupancy. The island, the only part of the duchy of Normandy belonging to the British crown, has been a possession of Britain since the Norman Conquest of 1066. During the Anglo-French wars, the harbors of Guernsey were employed in the building and outfitting of ships for the English privateers preying on French shipping. Guernsey is administered by its own laws and customs. Acts passed by the British Parliament are not applicable to Guernsey unless the island is specifically mentioned. During World War II, German troops occupied the island from June 30, 1940 till May 9, 1945.

RULERS
British

MINT MARKS
H - Heaton, Birmingham

MONETARY SYSTEM
8 Doubles = 1 Penny
12 Pence = 1 Shilling
5 Shillings = 1 Crown
20 Shillings = 1 Pound

TOKEN ISSUES (Tn)
Bank of Guernsey
5 SHILLINGS

.892 SILVER

KM#	Date	Mintage	VG	Fine	VF	XF
Tn1	1809	*10 known	2000.	4000.	8500.	13,500.

NOTE: The above issue was struck over Spanish 8 Reales. They were forbidden by the Guernsey legislation to circulate in 1809.

1 Stem   3 Stems

DOUBLE

COPPER

KM#	Date	Mintage	Fine	VF	XF	Unc
1	1830	1.649	1.00	3.00	8.50	25.00
	.1830	Inc. Ab.	5.00	15.00	30.00	45.00
	1868/30	.064	1.50	4.50	12.50	30.00
	1868	Inc. Ab.	2.00	6.00	18.00	37.50

BRONZED COPPER

| 1a | 1830 | — | — | — | Proof | 200.00 |

BRONZE

10	1885H	.056	.50	1.50	4.50	12.50
	1885H	—	—	—	Proof	200.00
	1889H	.112	.30	.85	3.00	7.50
	1889H	—	—	—	Proof	200.00
	1893H	.056	.50	1.50	4.50	12.50
	1899H	.056	.25	.75	3.00	8.50
	1902H	.084	.20	.60	2.25	4.00
	1902H	—	—	—	Proof	200.00
	1903H	.112	.15	.30	1.25	2.50
	1911H	.045	.50	1.50	4.00	12.00

BRONZED COPPER

| 10a | 1885H | — | — | — | Proof | 300.00 |

BRONZE

11	1911H	.090	.30	1.20	3.00	6.00
	1914H	.045	1.50	3.00	6.00	12.00
	1929H	.079	.30	.85	2.50	5.50
	1933H	.096	.30	.85	2.50	5.50
	1938H	.096	.30	.85	2.50	5.50

2 DOUBLES

COPPER

| 4 | 1858 | .056 | 6.00 | 18.00 | 55.00 | 125.00 |

BRONZE
Obv: Leaves w/1 stem.

8	1868	.035	7.50	13.50	35.00	70.00
	1874	.045	4.50	9.00	25.00	50.00
	1885H	.071	1.25	2.75	6.00	12.00
	1885H	—	—	—	Proof	200.00
	1889H	.036	.85	3.00	8.00	15.00
	1889H	—	—	—	Proof	200.00
	1899H	.036	.85	3.00	9.00	18.50
	1902H	.018	4.50	9.00	21.00	32.50
	1902H	—	—	—	Proof	200.00
	1903H	.018	6.00	12.50	25.00	37.50
	1906H	.018	6.00	12.50	25.00	37.50
	1908H	.018	6.00	12.50	25.00	37.50
	1911H	.029	4.50	9.00	15.00	27.50

BRONZED COPPER

| 8a | 1885H | — | — | — | Proof | 300.00 |

BRONZE
Obv: Leaves w/3 stems.

| 9 | 1868 | Inc. KM8 | 7.50 | 13.50 | 35.00 | 70.00 |

KM#	Date	Mintage	Fine	VF	XF	Unc
12	1914H	.029	4.50	9.00	18.50	27.50
	1917H	.015	20.00	40.00	80.00	175.00
	1918H	.057	1.25	2.50	9.00	15.00
	1920H	.057	1.25	2.50	9.00	15.00
	1929H	.079	.35	1.25	6.00	10.00

4 DOUBLES

COPPER

2	1830	.655	2.25	7.50	30.00	60.00
	1830	—	—	—	Proof	275.00
	1858	.114	3.00	15.00	30.00	60.00

NOTE: A rare mule restrike exists of the St. Helena obv. 1/2 Penny 1821 and rev. of Guernsey 4 Doubles dated 1830. Market valuation $600.00 (VF).

BRONZE
Obv: Leaves w/3 stems.

5	1864/54	.213	.85	1.75	9.00	18.50
	1868	.058	2.25	4.00	12.50	25.00
	1874	.069	1.50	3.00	11.50	22.50
	1885H	.070	1.25	2.25	7.50	20.00
	1885H	—	—	—	Proof	200.00
	1889H	.104	.75	1.25	6.00	15.00
	1889H	—	—	—	Proof	200.00
	1893H	.052	1.50	3.00	7.50	20.00
	1902H	.105	.85	1.75	3.00	7.50
	1902H	—	—	—	Proof	200.00
	1903H	.052	1.50	3.00	9.00	25.00
	1906H	.052	1.50	3.00	9.00	25.00
	1908H	.026	3.00	7.50	15.00	30.00
	1910H	.052	1.50	3.00	9.00	25.00
	1910H	—	—	—	Proof	200.00
	1911H	.052	2.25	4.50	13.50	27.50

NOTE: Varieties exist.

BRONZED COPPER

| 5a | 1885H | — | — | — | Proof | 300.00 |

BRONZE
Obv: Leaves w/1 stem.

| 6 | 1864 | Inc. KM5 | 1.25 | 2.25 | 9.00 | 18.50 |

13	1914H	.209	.75	1.50	4.50	12.50
	1918H	.157	.75	1.50	6.00	17.50
	1920H	.157	.45	1.25	4.50	10.00
	1945H	.096	.45	1.25	4.50	10.00
	1949H	.019	1.50	3.00	12.00	20.00

15	1956	.240	.25	.50	.75	2.25
	1956	2,100	—	—	Proof	5.00
	1966	.010	—	—	Proof	2.00

8 DOUBLES

COPPER

KM#	Date	Mintage	Fine	VF	XF	Unc
3	1834	.222	4.00	10.00	25.00	75.00
	1834	—	—	—	Proof	350.00
	1858	.111	5.00	12.50	25.00	65.00
	1858	—	—	—	Proof	375.00

BRONZE

7	1864	.280	1.25	3.00	9.00	27.50
	1864	—	—	—	Proof	175.00
	1868	.060	4.00	9.00	27.50	55.00
	1874	.070	2.25	4.50	9.00	20.00
	1885H	.070	1.50	3.00	9.00	20.00
	1885H	—	—	—	Proof	225.00
	1889H	.222	.75	2.25	6.00	12.50
	1889H	—	—	—	Proof	175.00
	1893H	.118	1.50	3.00	6.00	15.00
	1893H large date and denomination					
	Inc. Ab.	1.50	3.00	6.00	15.00
	1902H	.235	1.25	2.25	6.00	12.50
	1902H	—	—	—	Proof	200.00
	1903H	.118	.50	1.75	4.50	10.00
	1910H	.091	1.25	2.50	12.50	25.00
	1910H	—	—	—	Proof	200.00
	1911H	.078	3.00	8.50	15.00	30.00

BRONZED COPPER

| 7a | 1885H | — | — | — | Proof | 350.00 |

BRONZE

14	1914H	.157	.65	1.75	4.50	10.00
	1918H	.157	.65	1.75	4.50	10.00
	1920H	.157	.50	1.50	4.00	9.00
	1934H	.124	.50	1.50	4.00	9.00
	1934H	500 pcs.	—	—	Proof	150.00
	1938H	.120	.50	1.50	4.00	9.00
	1938H	—	—	—	Proof	200.00
	1945H	.192	.40	.85	2.00	5.50
	1947H	.240	.30	.60	2.25	5.00
	1949H	.230	.30	.60	2.25	5.00

16	1956	.500	.10	.20	.50	1.50
	1956	2,100	—	—	Proof	5.00
	1959	.500	.10	.20	.50	1.50
	1959	—	—	—	Proof	—
	1966	.010	—	—	Proof	2.00

3 PENCE

COPPER-NICKEL
Thin flan

KM#	Date	Mintage	Fine	VF	XF	Unc
17	1956	.500	.10	.20	.50	1.25
	1956	2,100	—	—	Proof	5.00

Thick flan

18	1959	.500	.10	.20	.50	1.00
	1959	—	—	—	Proof	200.00
	1966	.010	—	—	Proof	2.00

10 SHILLINGS

COPPER-NICKEL
900th Anniversary Norman Conquest

19	1966	.300	—	1.00	1.25	1.75
	1966	.010	—	—	Proof	4.00

DECIMAL COINAGE
100 Pence = 1 Pound

1/2 NEW PENNY

BRONZE

20	1971	2.294	—	—	.10	.25
	1971	.010	—	—	Proof	1.00

1/2 PENNY

BRONZE

33	1979	.020	—	—	Proof	1.00
	1981	.010	—	—	Proof	2.00

NEW PENNY

BRONZE

21	1971	1.386	—	—	.10	.20
	1971	.010	—	—	Proof	1.00

PENNY

BRONZE

27	1977	.640	—	—	.10	.20
	1979	2.400	—	—	.10	.20
	1979	.020	—	—	Proof	1.00
	1981	.010	—	—	Proof	2.00

KM#	Date	Mintage	Fine	VF	XF	Unc
40	1985	—	—	—	.10	.20
	1985	2,500	—	—	Proof	2.00
	1986	—	—	—	.10	.20
	1986	—	—	—	Proof	2.00
	1987	—	—	—	.10	.20
	1987	*2,500	—	—	Proof	2.00
	1988	—	—	—	.10	.20
	1988	—	—	—	Proof	2.00

2 NEW PENCE

BRONZE

22	1971	.654	—	—	.10	.30
	1971	.010	—	—	Proof	1.00

2 PENCE

BRONZE

28	1977	.700	—	—	.10	.20
	1979	2.400	—	—	.10	.25
	1979	.020	—	—	Proof	1.00
	1981	.010	—	—	Proof	2.00

41	1985	—	—	—	.10	.20
	1985	2,500	—	—	Proof	2.00
	1986	—	—	—	.10	.20
	1986	—	—	—	Proof	2.00
	1987	—	—	—	.10	.20
	1987	*2,500	—	—	Proof	2.00
	1988	—	—	—	.10	.20
	1988	—	—	—	Proof	2.00

5 NEW PENCE

COPPER-NICKEL

23	1968	.800	—	.10	.15	.30
	1971	.010	—	—	Proof	2.00

5 PENCE

COPPER-NICKEL

29	1977	.250	—	—	.10	.30
	1979	.200	—	—	.10	.25
	1979	.020	—	—	Proof	2.00
	1981	.010	—	—	Proof	3.00
	1982	.200	—	—	.10	.25

GUERNSEY 804

KM#	Date	Mintage	Fine	VF	XF	Unc
42	1985	—	—	—	.10	.25
	1985	2,500	—	—	Proof	2.50
	1986	—	—	—	.10	.25
	1986	—	—	—	Proof	2.50
	1987	—	—	—	.10	.25
	1987	*2,500	—	—	Proof	2.50
	1988	—	—	—	.10	.25
	1988	—	—	—	Proof	2.50

10 NEW PENCE

COPPER-NICKEL

24	1968	.600	—	.20	.30	.50
	1970	.300	—	.20	.30	.50
	1971	.010	—	—	Proof	2.00

10 PENCE

COPPER-NICKEL

30	1977	.530	—	—	.20	.40
	1979	.659	—	—	.20	.40
	1979	.020	—	—	Proof	3.00
	1981	.010	—	—	Proof	3.00
	1982	.020	—	—	.20	.50
	1984	—	—	—	.20	.50

43	1985	—	—	—	.20	.35
	1985	2,500	—	—	Proof	2.50
	1986	—	—	—	.20	.35
	1986	—	—	—	Proof	2.50
	1987	—	—	—	.20	.35
	1987	*2,500	—	—	Proof	2.50
	1988	—	—	—	.20	.35
	1988	—	—	—	Proof	2.50

20 PENCE

COPPER-NICKEL

38	1982	.500	—	—	.40	.75
	1983	—	—	—	.40	.75

44	1985	—	—	—	.40	.75
	1985	2,500	—	—	Proof	3.00
	1986	—	—	—	.40	.75
	1986	—	—	—	Proof	3.00

KM#	Date	Mintage	Fine	VF	XF	Unc
44	1987	—	—	—	.40	.75
	1987	*2,500	—	—	Proof	3.00
	1988	—	—	—	.40	.75
	1988	—	—	—	Proof	3.00

25 PENCE

COPPER-NICKEL
25th Wedding Anniversary

26	1972	.056	—	—	3.00	6.50

28.2759 g, .925 SILVER, .8410 oz ASW

26a	1972	.015	—	—	Proof	17.50

COPPER-NICKEL
Queen's Silver Jubilee

31	1977	.208	—	—	1.00	2.00

28.2759 g, .925 SILVER, .8410 oz ASW

31a	1977	.025	—	—	Proof	12.50

COPPER-NICKEL
Royal Visit

32	1978	.105	—	—	1.00	2.00

28.2759 g, .925 SILVER, .8410 oz ASW

32a	1978	.025	—	—	Proof	12.50

COPPER-NICKEL
80th Birthday of Queen Mother

KM#	Date	Mintage	Fine	VF	XF	Unc
35	1980	.150	—	—	1.00	2.00

28.2759 g, .925 SILVER, .8410 oz ASW

35a	1980	.025	—	—	Proof	15.00

COPPER-NICKEL
Wedding of Prince Charles and Lady Diana
Obv: Similar to 25 New Pence, Y#25.

36	1981	.114	—	—	1.25	2.75

28.2759 g, .925 SILVER, .8410 oz ASW

36a	1981	.012	—	—	Proof	27.50

50 NEW PENCE

COPPER-NICKEL

25	1969	.200	—	1.00	1.25	1.75
	1970	.200	—	1.00	1.25	1.75
	1971	.010	—	—	Proof	3.00

50 PENCE

COPPER-NICKEL

34	1979	.020	—	—	Proof	4.50
	1981	.200	—	.90	1.10	1.50
	1981	.010	—	—	Proof	5.50
	1982	.150	—	.90	1.10	1.50
	1983	.200	—	.90	1.10	1.50
	1984	.200	—	.90	1.10	1.50

45	1985	—	—	.90	1.10	1.50
	1985	2,500	—	—	Proof	4.00
	1986	—	—	.90	1.10	1.50
	1986	—	—	—	Proof	4.00
	1987	—	—	.90	1.10	1.50
	1987	*2,500	—	—	Proof	4.00
	1988	—	—	.90	1.10	1.50
	1988	—	—	—	Proof	4.00

POUND

COPPER-NICKEL-ZINC

KM#	Date	Mintage	Fine	VF	XF	Unc
37	1981	.200	—	1.80	2.00	2.75
	1981	.010	—	—	Proof	4.50

8.0000 g, .917 GOLD, .2358 oz AGW

| 37a | 1981 | 4,500 | — | — | Proof | 175.00 |

ALUMINUM-BRONZE

| 39 | 1983 | .269 | — | 1.80 | 2.00 | 2.75 |

COPPER-NICKEL-ZINC

46	1985	—	—	—	1.75	2.50
	1985	2,500	—	—	Proof	6.00
	1986	—	—	—	1.75	2.50
	1986	—	—	—	Proof	6.00
	1987	—	—	—	1.75	2.50
	1987	*2,500	—	—	Proof	6.00
	1988	—	—	—	1.75	2.50
	1988	—	—	—	Proof	6.00

2 POUNDS

COPPER-NICKEL
40th Anniversary of Liberation from Germans

| 47 | 1985 | 7,500 | — | — | 3.50 | 5.50 |
| | 1985 | Inc. Ab. | — | — | Proof | 8.00 |

28.2800 g, .925 SILVER, .8411 oz ASW

| 47a | 1985 | 2,407 | — | — | Proof | 35.00 |

COPPER-NICKEL

Commonwealth Games

KM#	Date	Mintage	Fine	VF	XF	Unc
48	1986	—	—	—	—	5.50
	1986	—	—	—	—	Proof	10.00

28.2800 g, .500 SILVER, .4547 oz ASW

| 48a | 1986 | *.050 | — | — | — | 15.00 |

28.2800 g, .925 SILVER, .8411 oz ASW

| 48b | 1986 | *.020 | — | — | Proof | 30.00 |

COPPER-NICKEL
William The Conqueror

| 49 | 1987 | *5,000 | — | — | — | 7.00 |
| | 1987 | *2,500 | — | — | Proof | 10.00 |

28.2800 g, .925 SILVER, .8411 oz ASW

| 49a | 1987 | 2,500 | — | — | Proof | 40.00 |

47.5400 g, .917 GOLD, 1.4012 oz AGW

| 49b | 1987 | 90 pcs. | — | — | Proof | 2000. |

COPPER-NICKEL
William II

| 50 | 1988 | 5,000 | — | — | — | 8.00 |
| | 1988 | 5,000 | — | — | Proof | 10.00 |

28.2800 g, .925 SILVER, .8411 oz ASW

| 50a | 1988 | 2,500 | — | — | Proof | 40.00 |

MINT SETS (MS)

KM#	Date	Mintage	Identification	Issue Price	Mkt. Val.
MS1	1985(8)	—	KM40-47	8.75	11.25
MS2	1986(7)	—	KM40-46	—	5.75
MS3	1987(7)	*5,000	KM40-46	11.00	5.75
MS4	1988(8)	—	KM40-46,50	13.00	14.00

PROOF SETS (PS)

PS1	1885H(4)	—	KM5,7,8,10	—	850.00
PS2	1885H(4)	—	KM5a,7a,8a,10a	—	1250.
PS3	1902H(4)	—	KM5,7-8,10	—	1000.
PS4	1910H(2)	—	KM5,7	—	500.00
PS5	1956(2)	1,050	KM15-17 double set	—	27.50
PS6	1966(4)	10,000	KM15-16,18,19	—	10.00
PS7	1971(6)	10,000	KM20-25	16.00	10.00
PS8	1979(6)	20,000	KM27-30,33-34	25.00	12.50
PS9	1981(6)	10,000	KM27-30,34,37	29.00	20.00
PS10	1985(6)	2,500	KM40-47	29.75	30.00
PS11	1986(8)	—	KM40-46,48	—	32.00
PS12	1987(8)	*2,500	KM40-46,49	33.00	32.00
PS13	1988(8)	—	KM40-46,50	—	32.00

GUINEA

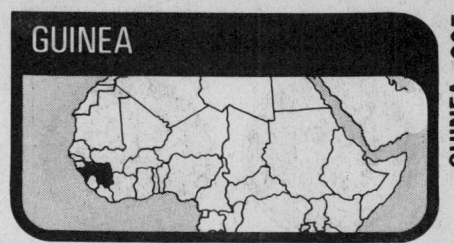

The Republic of Guinea, situated on the Atlantic Coast of Africa between Sierra Leone and Guinea-Bissau, has an area of 94,964 sq. mi. (245,957 sq. km.) and a population of *6.1 million. Capital: Conakry. Although Guinea contains one-third of the world's reserves of bauxite and significant deposits of iron ore, gold and diamonds, the economy is still dependent on argiculture. Aluminum, bananas, copra and coffee are exported.

The coast of Guinea was known to Portuguese navigators of the 15th century but was seldom visited by European traders of the 16th-18th centuries because of its dangerous coastal waters. French penetration of the area began in the mid-19th century with the entering into of protectorate treaties with several of the coastal chiefs. After a long struggle with Guinea's native leader Samory Toure, France secured the area and until 1890 administered it as a part of Senegal. In 1895 the colony (Guinee Francais) became an autonomous part of the federation of French West Africa. The inhabitants were extended French citizenship in 1946 when the colony became an overseas territory of the French Union. Guinea became an independent republic on Oct. 2, 1958, when it declined to enter the new French Community.

MONETARY SYSTEM
100 Centimes = 1 Franc

FRANC

COPPER-NICKEL

KM#	Date	Mintage	VF	XF	Unc
4	1962	—	1.75	3.00	6.00
	1962	—	—	Proof	50.00

BRASS CLAD STEEL

| 56 | 1985 | — | — | — | — |

5 FRANCS

ALUMINUM-BRONZE

| 1 | 1959 | — | 4.00 | 8.00 | 20.00 |

COPPER-NICKEL

| 5 | 1962 | — | 1.75 | 3.50 | 6.00 |
| | 1962 | — | — | Proof | 70.00 |

BRASS CLAD STEEL

| 53 | 1985 | — | .25 | .50 | 1.25 |

GUINEA 806

10 FRANCS

ALUMINUM-BRONZE

KM#	Date	Mintage	VF	XF	Unc
2	1959	—	7.50	15.00	25.00

COPPER-NICKEL

6	1962	—	3.00	6.00	10.00
	1962	—	—	Proof	85.00

BRASS CLAD STEEL

52	1985	—	.50	1.00	2.50

25 FRANCS

ALUMINUM-BRONZE

3	1959	—	15.00	25.00	65.00

COPPER-NICKEL

7	1962	—	4.00	7.50	14.00
	1962	—	—	Proof	120.00

50 FRANCS

COPPER-NICKEL

8	1969	4.000	20.00	30.00	45.00

NOTE: Not released into circulation.

100 FRANCS

5.6500 g, .999 SILVER, .1816 oz ASW
Rev: Arms over value.

9	1969	9.700	—	Proof	9.00
	1970	Inc. Ab.	—	Proof	9.00

COPPER-NICKEL

KM#	Date	Mintage	VF	XF	Unc
41	1971	2.585	25.00	35.00	50.00

NOTE: Not released into circulation.

200 FRANCS

11.7000 g, .999 SILVER, .3761 oz ASW

10	1969	.010	—	Proof	12.00
	1970	Inc. Ab.	—	Proof	12.00

Almany Samory Toure

11	1969	6.100	—	Proof	15.00
	1970	Inc. Ab.	—	Proof	15.00

250 FRANCS

14.5300 g, .999 SILVER, .4671 oz ASW

12	1969	.026	—	Proof	15.00
	1970	Inc. Ab.	—	Proof	15.00

Alpha Yaya Diallo

13	1969	6.100	—	Proof	17.50
	1970	Inc. Ab.	—	Proof	17.50

Apollo XIII

KM#	Date	Mintage	VF	XF	Unc
14	1969	4.450	—	Proof	17.50
	1970	Inc. Ab.	—	Proof	17.50

Spacecraft Sojuz

21	1970	3.500	—	Proof	20.00

500 FRANCS

29.0800 g, .999 SILVER, .9349 oz ASW
Munich Olympics

15	1969	7.200	—	Proof	25.00
	1970	1.900	—	Proof	30.00

Oiseaux Dancers
Rev: Similar to KM#15.

16	1969	7.150	—	Proof	25.00
	1970	—	—	Proof	30.00

Ekhnaton
Rev: Similar to KM#15.

KM#	Date	Mintage	VF	XF	Unc
22	1970	4,180	—	Proof	30.00

Tutankhamen
Rev: Similar to KM#15.

KM#	Date	Mintage	VF	XF	Unc
27	1970	4,280	—	Proof	35.00

20.0000 g, .900 GOLD, .5787 oz AGW

KM#	Date	Mintage	VF	XF	Unc
19	1970	4,000	—	Proof	385.00

32	1970	3,535	—	Proof	385.00

Obv: Similar to 500 Francs, KM#22.
| 33 | 1970 | 685 pcs. | — | Proof | 500.00 |

Obv: Similar to 500 Francs, KM#23.
| 34 | 1970 | 675 pcs. | — | Proof | 500.00 |

Obv: Similar to 500 Francs, KM#24.
| 35 | 1970 | 789 pcs. | — | Proof | 500.00 |

Obv: Similar to 500 Francs, KM#25.
| 36 | 1970 | 774 pcs. | — | Proof | 500.00 |

Obv: Similar to 500 Francs, KM#26.
| 37 | 1970 | 695 pcs. | — | Proof | 500.00 |

Obv: Similar to 500 Francs, KM#27.
| 38 | 1970 | 675 pcs. | — | Proof | 500.00 |

Obv: Similar to 500 Francs, KM#28.
| 39 | 1970 | 685 pcs. | — | Proof | 500.00 |

Obv: Similar to 500 Francs, KM#29.
| 40 | 1970 | 185 pcs. | — | Proof | 600.00 |

10,000 FRANCS

40.0000 g, .900 GOLD, 1.1575 oz AGW
Sekou Toure
Rev: Similar to 5000 Francs, KM#19.

20	1969	2,300	—	Proof	775.00

DECIMAL COINAGE
100 Cauris = 1 Syli

50 CAURIS

ALUMINUM

42	1971	—	10.00	15.00	25.00

SYLI

Chephren
Rev: Similar to KM#15.

| 23 | 1970 | 4,150 | — | Proof | 40.00 |

Tiyi
Rev: Similar to KM#15.

| 28 | 1970 | 4,120 | — | Proof | 35.00 |

Cleopatra
Rev: Similar to KM#15.

| 24 | 1970 | 5,250 | — | Proof | 40.00 |

Gamal Abdel Nasser
Rev: Similar to KM#15.

| 29 | 1970 | 950 | — | Proof | 55.00 |

1000 FRANCS

4.0000 g, .900 GOLD, .1157 oz AGW
Obv: Similar to 200 Francs, KM#10.
Rev: Similar to 250 Francs, KM#12.

17	1969	6,600	—	Proof	100.00
	1970	Inc. Ab.	—	Proof	100.00

2000 FRANCS

8.0000 g., .900 GOLD, .2315 oz AGW

18	1969	.015	—	Proof	150.00

Obv: Similar to 250 Francs, KM#14.
| 30 | 1970 | 1,775 | — | Proof | 200.00 |

Obv: Similar to 250 Francs, KM#21.
| 31 | 1970 | 2,840 | — | Proof | 175.00 |

5000 FRANCS

Nefertiti
Rev: Similar to KM#15.

| 25 | 1970 | 4,610 | — | Proof | 40.00 |

Rameses III
Rev: Similar to KM#15.

| 26 | 1970 | 4,330 | — | Proof | 40.00 |

43	1971	—	5.00	8.00	15.00

2 SYLIS

GUINEA 808

5 SYLIS

KM#	Date	Mintage	VF	XF	Unc
44	1971	—	6.00	9.00	15.00

ALUMINUM

200 SYLIS

| 45 | 1971 | — | 7.50 | 12.50 | 25.00 |

ALUMINUM

COPPER-NICKEL
International Games - Walk Racing

| 54 | 1984 | — | — | Proof | 25.00 |

500 SYLIS

40.0000 g, .925 SILVER, 1.1897 oz ASW
Makeba

| 46 | 1977 | 500 pcs. | — | — | 75.00 |
| | 1977 | 500 pcs. | — | Proof | 75.00 |

Lumumba
Rev: Similar to KM#46.

| 47 | 1977 | 250 pcs. | — | — | 90.00 |
| | 1977 | 150 pcs. | — | Proof | 110.00 |

30.9400 g, SILVER
International Games - Walk Racing

KM#	Date	Mintage	VF	XF	Unc
55	1984	—	—	Proof	30.00

1000 SYLIS

2.9300 g, .900 GOLD, .0847 oz AGW
Makeba
Rev: Similar to 2000 Sylis, KM#50.

| 48 | 1977 | 300 pcs. | — | — | 100.00 |
| | 1977 | 250 pcs. | — | Proof | 100.00 |

Nkrumah
Rev: Similar to 2000 Sylis, KM#50.

| 49 | 1977 | 150 pcs. | — | — | 150.00 |
| | 1977 | 150 pcs. | — | Proof | 150.00 |

2000 SYLIS

5.8700 g, .900 GOLD, .1698 oz AGW
Mao Tse Tung

| 50 | 1977 | 200 pcs. | — | — | 200.00 |
| | 1977 | 200 pcs. | — | Proof | 200.00 |

Sekou Toure

| 51 | 1977 | 100 pcs. | — | — | 175.00 |
| | 1977 | 50 pcs. | — | Proof | 225.00 |

MINT SETS (MS)

KM#	Date	Mintage	Identification	Issue Price	Mkt. Val.
MS1	1977(6)	—	KM46-51	—	760.00

PROOF SETS (PS)

PS1	1962(7)	—	KM4-7	—	325.00
PS2	1969(4)	—	KM9-13,15-16	62.50	120.00
PS3	1969(4)	—	KM17-20	236.50	1410.
PS4	1970(7)	—	KM9-13,15-16	62.50	130.00
PS5	1970(7)	—	KM22-28	85.00	255.00
PS6	1970(7)	—	KM33-39	440.00	3150.
PS7	1970(3)	—	KM12,14,21	29.95	52.50
PS8	1977(6)	—	KM46-51	—	825.00

NOTE: Coins were issued in sets made per order containing from 1 to 11 different coins.

GUINEA-BISSAU

The Republic of Guinea-Bissau, a former Portuguese overseas province on the west coast of Africa between Senegal and Guinea, has an area of 13,948 sq. mi. (36,125 sq. km.) and a population of *929,000. Capital: Bissau. The country has undeveloped deposits of oil and bauxite. Peanuts, oil-palm kernels and hides are exported.

Portuguese Guinea was discovered by Portuguese navigator Nuno Tristao in 1446. Trading rights in the area were granted to Cape Verde islanders but few prominent posts were established before 1851, and they were principally coastal installations. The chief export of this colony's early period was slaves for South America, a practice that adversely affected trade with the native people and retarded subjection of the interior. Territorial disputes with France delayed final demarcation of the colony's frontiers until 1905.

The African Party for the Independence of Guinea-Bissau was founded in 1956, and several years later began a guerrilla warfare that grew in effectiveness until 1974, when the rebels controlled most of the colony. Portugal's costly overseas wars in her African territories resulted in a military coup in Portugal in April 1974, that appreciably brightened the prospects for freedom for Guinea-Bissau. In August, 1974, the Lisbon government signed an agreement granting independence to Portuguese Guinea effective Sept. 10, 1974. The new republic took the name of Guinea-Bissau.

PORTUGUESE GUINEA

MONETARY SYSTEM
100 Centavos = 1 Escudo

5 CENTAVOS

BRONZE

KM#	Date	Mintage	Fine	VF	XF	Unc
1	1933	.100	2.00	3.50	7.50	12.50

10 CENTAVOS

BRONZE

| 2 | 1933 | .250 | 1.00 | 3.50 | 7.50 | 15.00 |

ALUMINUM

| 12 | 1973 | .100 | 1.00 | 2.00 | 3.50 | 7.00 |

20 CENTAVOS

BRONZE

| 3 | 1933 | .350 | 1.00 | 3.50 | 8.50 | 17.50 |

| 13 | 1973 | .100 | 1.00 | 2.00 | 3.50 | 7.00 |

50 CENTAVOS

NICKEL-BRONZE

KM#	Date	Mintage	Fine	VF	XF	Unc
4	1933	.600	2.00	5.00	10.00	150.00

BRONZE
500th Anniversary of Discovery

| 6 | 1946 | 2.000 | 1.00 | 2.00 | 3.50 | 7.00 |

| 8 | 1952 | 10.000 | .10 | .35 | .75 | 1.50 |

ESCUDO

NICKEL-BRONZE

| 5 | 1933 | .800 | 8.00 | 20.00 | 50.00 | 200.00 |

BRONZE
500th Anniversary of Discovery

| 7 | 1946 | 2.000 | 1.00 | 1.25 | 2.50 | 5.00 |

| 14 | 1973 | .250 | 1.00 | 2.00 | 3.50 | 7.50 |

2-1/2 ESCUDOS

COPPER-NICKEL

| 9 | 1952 | 6.000 | .50 | 1.00 | 1.75 | 4.00 |

5 ESCUDOS

COPPER-NICKEL

KM#	Date	Mintage	Fine	VF	XF	Unc
15	1973	.800	1.00	1.50	2.50	7.50

10 ESCUDOS

5.0000 g, .720 SILVER, .1157 oz ASW

| 10 | 1952 | 1.200 | BV | 2.50 | 6.00 | 10.00 |

COPPER-NICKEL

| 16 | 1973 | 1.700 | 1.00 | 1.50 | 2.50 | 7.50 |

20 ESCUDOS

10.0000 g, .720 SILVER, .2315 oz ASW

| 11 | 1952 | .750 | BV | 4.00 | 8.50 | 15.00 |

GUINEA-BISSAU

MONETARY SYSTEM
100 Centavos = 1 Peso

50 CENTAVOS

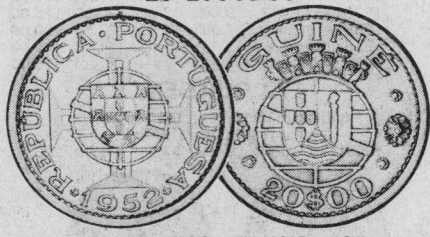

ALUMINUM
F.A.O. Issue

KM#	Date	Mintage	VF	XF	Unc
17	1977	.500	.75	1.50	3.00
	1978	5.500	.75	1.50	3.00

PESO

ALUMINUM-BRONZE
F.A.O. Issue

| 18 | 1977 | .500 | .75 | 1.50 | 3.00 |
| | 1978 | 6.500 | .75 | 1.50 | 3.00 |

2-1/2 PESOS

ALUMINUM-BRONZE
F.A.O. Issue

| 19 | 1977 | .500 | 1.00 | 2.00 | 4.00 |
| | 1978 | 3.500 | 1.00 | 2.00 | 4.00 |

5 PESOS

COPPER-NICKEL
F.A.O. Issue

KM#	Date	Mintage	VF	XF	Unc
20	1977	.580	2.00	4.00	10.00
	1978	5.420	2.00	4.00	10.00

20 PESOS

COPPER-NICKEL
F.A.O. Issue

| 21 | 1977 | .244 | 4.50 | 8.50 | 15.00 |
| | 1978 | 2.256 | 4.50 | 8.50 | 15.00 |

GUYANA

The Cooperative Republic of Guyana, an independent member of the British Commonwealth situated on the northeast coast of South America, has an area of 83,000 sq. mi. (214,969 sq. km.) and a population of 779,000. Capital: Georgetown. The economy is basically agrarian. Sugar, rice and bauxite are exported.

The original area of Essequibo and Demerary, which included present-day Surinam, French Guiana, and parts of Brazil and Venezuela, was sighted by Columbus in 1498. The first European settlement was made late in the 16th century by the Dutch, however, the region was claimed for the British by Sir Walter Raleigh during the reign of Elizabeth I. For the next 150 years, possession alternated between the Dutch and the British, with a short interval of French control. The British exercised de facto control after 1796, although the area, which included the Dutch colonies of Essequibo, Demerary and Berbice, wasn't ceded to them by the Dutch until 1814. From 1803 to 1831, Essequibo and Demerary were administered separately from Berbice. The three colonies were united in the British Crown Colony of British Guiana in 1831. British Guiana won internal self—government in 1952 and full independence, under the traditional name of Guyana, on May 26, 1966. Guyana became a republic on Feb. 23, 1970. It is a member of the Commonwealth of Nations. The president is the Chief of State. The prime minister is the Head of Government.

RULERS
British, until 1966

MONETARY SYSTEM
(Until 1839)
20 Stiver = 1 Guilder (Gulden)
3 Guilders = 12 Bits = 5 Shillings = 1 Dollar

(Commencing 1839)
3-1/8 Guilders = 50 Pence

ESSEQUIBO & DEMERARY

COLONIAL COINAGE
1/2 STIVER

COPPER

KM#	Date	Mintage	Fine	VF	XF	Unc
9	1813	.215	1.50	5.50	45.00	100.00
	1813	—	—	—	Proof	325.00

COPPER-GILT (OMS)

| 9a | 1813 | — | — | — | Proof | 600.00 |

STIVER

COPPER

| 10 | 1813 | .215 | 2.25 | 7.50 | 50.00 | 100.00 |
| | 1813 | — | — | — | Proof | 250.00 |

COPPER-GILT (OMS)

| 10a | 1813 | — | — | — | Proof | 500.00 |

1/8 GUILDER

0.9700 g, .816 SILVER, .0255 oz ASW

KM#	Date	Mintage	Fine	VF	XF	Unc
16	1832	.098	6.00	12.00	35.00	75.00
	1832	—	—	—	Proof	200.00
	1835/1	.071	10.00	19.00	37.50	95.00
	1835/3	I.A.	10.00	19.00	37.50	95.00
	1835	Inc. Ab.	7.50	17.00	30.00	70.00
	1835 plain edge	—	—	—	Proof	200.00
	1835 reeded edge	—	—	—	Proof	300.00

1/4 GUILDER

1.9400 g, .816 SILVER, .0510 oz ASW
Similar to 2 Guilders, KM#7.

| 4 | 1809 | .124 | 12.50 | 22.50 | 50.00 | 150.00 |

NOTE: Flan size varies.

Similar to 1 Guilder, KM#13.

| 11 | 1816 | .043 | 12.50 | 22.50 | 50.00 | 150.00 |
| | 1816 | — | — | — | Proof | 275.00 |

17	1832	.039	12.50	22.50	50.00	150.00
	1833	.097	9.00	17.50	40.00	125.00
	1833	—	—	—	Proof	300.00
	1835/3	.073	9.00	17.50	40.00	125.00
	1835	Inc. Ab.	7.00	12.00	27.50	100.00
	1835 plain edge	—	—	—	Proof	400.00
	1835 reeded edge	—	—	—	Proof	450.00

1/2 GUILDER

3.8800 g, .816 SILVER, .1020 oz ASW
Similar to 2 Guilders, KM#7.

| 5 | 1809 | .064 | 15.00 | 37.50 | 95.00 | 225.00 |

| 12 | 1816 | .034 | 12.50 | 27.50 | 100.00 | 200.00 |
| | 1816 | — | — | — | Proof | 300.00 |

18	1832	.087	11.00	22.50	95.00	200.00
	1832	—	—	—	Proof	300.00
	1835/3	.036	12.50	25.00	95.00	200.00
	1835	Inc. Ab.	19.00	27.50	50.00	125.00
	1835 plain edge	—	—	—	Proof	350.00
	1835 reeded edge	—	—	—	Proof	450.00

GUILDER

7.7700 g, .816 SILVER, .2040 oz ASW

| 6 | 1809 | .032 | 20.00 | 40.00 | 125.00 | 275.00 |

| 13 | 1816 | .034 | 15.00 | 30.00 | 95.00 | 225.00 |
| | 1816 | — | — | — | Proof | 350.00 |

KM#	Date	Mintage	Fine	VF	XF	Unc
19	1832	.047	10.00	25.00	60.00	200.00
	1832	—	—	—	Proof	300.00
	1835	.022	15.00	30.00	75.00	250.00
	1835 plain edge	—	—	—	Proof	425.00
	1835 reeded edge	—	—	—	Proof	500.00

2 GUILDERS

15.5500 g, .816 SILVER, .4079 oz ASW

| 7 | 1809 | .016 | 75.00 | 175.00 | 600.00 | 2000. |

| 14 | 1816 | .015 | 50.00 | 125.00 | 250.00 | 700.00 |
| | 1816 | — | — | — | Proof | Rare |

| 20 | 1832 | .014 | 60.00 | 150.00 | 650.00 | 1500 |
| | 1832 | — | — | — | Proof | Rare |

3 GUILDERS

23.3200 g, .816 SILVER, .6118 oz ASW

| 8 | 1809 | .021 | 175.00 | 300.00 | 750.00 | 2750. |

| 15 | 1816 | .010 | 100.00 | 250.00 | 500.00 | 1500. |
| | 1816 | — | — | — | Proof | Rare |

Rev: Similar to 2 Guilders, KM#20.

KM#	Date	Mintage	Fine	VF	XF	Unc
21	1832	7,156	300.00	650.00	1750.	4500.
	1832	—	—	—	Proof	Rare

BRITISH GUIANA

In October, 1835, the minting of currency two pence pieces was approved by the Treasury. These coins, identical to those in the Maundy sets, were circulated in British Guiana with dates of 1838, 1843 and 1848. Groats of the Victorian era and the seated Britannia type were also circulated in this colony. See homeland types in Great Britain.

1/8 GUILDER

0.9700 g, .816 SILVER, .0127 oz ASW

22	1836	.180	8.50	15.00	40.00	90.00
	1836	—	—	—	Proof	150.00

1/4 GUILDER

1.9400 g, .816 SILVER, .0255 oz ASW

23	1836	.216	12.50	25.00	50.00	125.00
	1836	—	—	—	Proof	300.00

1/2 GUILDER

3.8800 g, .816 SILVER, .0510 oz ASW

24	1836	.118	12.50	30.00	70.00	150.00
	1836	—	—	—	Proof	350.00

GUILDER

7.7700 g, .816 SILVER, .1020 oz ASW

25	1836	.057	15.00	35.00	95.00	200.00
	1836 plain edge	—	—	—	Proof	400.00
	1836 reeded edge	—	—	—	Proof	600.00

BRITISH GUIANA AND WEST INDIES

From 1836 through 1888 regular issue 4 Pence (Groats) as well as general issue strikes of the Maundy type 2 Pence (1838, 1843 & 1848). of Great Britain were circulated in British Guiana and the West Indies. These are listed under Great Britain.

MONETARY SYSTEM

12 Pence = 1 Shilling
4 Shillings 2 Pence = 1 Dollar

4 PENCE

1.8851 g, .925 SILVER, .0560 oz ASW

26	1891	.336	1.75	4.50	8.00	30.00
	1894	.120	2.75	6.50	12.50	45.00
	1900	.045	3.25	10.00	20.00	70.00
	1901	.060	3.00	7.50	12.50	50.00

KM#	Date	Mintage	Fine	VF	XF	Unc
27	1903	.060	3.00	7.50	17.50	50.00
	1908	.030	5.00	12.50	25.00	85.00
	1909	.036	5.00	12.50	25.00	85.00
	1910	.066	3.00	10.00	22.50	75.00

28	1911	.030	5.00	12.50	30.00	90.00
	1913	.030	5.00	12.50	30.00	90.00
	1916	.030	5.00	12.50	30.00	90.00

BRITISH GUIANA

4 PENCE

1.8851 g, .925 SILVER, .0560 oz ASW

29	1917	.072	3.00	7.50	20.00	70.00
	1918	.210	1.25	3.50	12.50	45.00
	1921	.090	3.00	7.50	15.00	55.00
	1923	.012	12.50	35.00	65.00	120.00
	1925	.030	3.50	8.50	30.00	75.00
	1926	.030	3.50	8.50	22.50	55.00
	1931	.015	10.00	25.00	55.00	100.00
	1931	—	—	—	Proof	225.00
	1935	.036	3.00	7.50	18.50	45.00
	1935	—	—	—	Proof	225.00
	1936	.063	1.75	2.50	10.00	25.00
	1936	—	—	—	Proof	225.00

30	1938	.030	1.75	2.25	5.00	15.00
	1938	—	—	—	Proof	175.00
	1939	.048	1.75	2.25	3.50	12.50
	1939	—	—	—	Proof	175.00
	1940	.090	1.25	1.75	2.50	12.00
	1940	—	—	—	Proof	175.00
	1941	.120	1.25	1.75	2.50	8.50
	1941	—	—	—	Proof	175.00
	1942	.180	1.25	1.75	2.50	8.50
	1942	—	—	—	Proof	175.00
	1943	.240	1.25	1.75	2.50	6.00
	1943	—	—	—	Proof	400.00

1.8851 g, .500 SILVER, .0303 oz ASW

30a	1944	.090	.75	1.25	2.50	6.00
	1945	.120	.50	1.00	2.00	5.00
	1945	—	—	—	Proof	200.00

GUYANA

MONETARY SYSTEM

100 Cents = 1 Dollar

MINT MARKS

FM - Franklin Mint, U.S.A.*

NOTE: From 1975 the Franklin Mint has produced coinage in up to 3 different qualities. Qualities of issue are designated in ( ) after each date and are defined as follows:

(M) MATTE - Normal circulation strike or a dull finish produced by sandblasting special uncirculated (polish finish) or proof quality dies.

(U) SPECIAL UNCIRCULATED - Polished or proof-like in appearance without any frosted features.

(P) PROOF - The highest quality obtainable having mirror-like fields and frosted features.

CENT

NICKEL-BRASS

KM#	Date	Mintage	VF	XF	Unc
31	1967	6.000	—	.10	.15
	1967	5,100	—	Proof	2.00
	1969	4.000	—	.10	.25
	1970	6.000	—	.10	.25
	1971	4.000	—	.10	.25
31	1972	4.000	—	.10	.25
	1973	4.000	—	.10	.25
	1974	11.000	—	.10	.20
	1975	—	—	.10	.25
	1976	—	—	.10	.25
	1977	16.000	—	.10	.20
	1978	10.450	—	.10	.20
	1979	—	—	.10	.20
	1980	12.000	—	.10	.20
	1981	10.000	—	.10	.20
	1982	8.000	—	.10	.20
	1983	12.000	—	.10	.20
	1985	—	—	.10	.20
	1987	—	—	.10	.20

BRONZE

37	1976FM(M)	.015	—	.10	.30
	1976FM(U)	50 pcs.	—	—	—
	1976FM(P)	.028	—	Proof	.50
	1977FM(U)	.015	—	.10	.30
	1977FM(P)	7,215	—	Proof	.50
	1978FM(U)	.015	—	.10	.30
	1978FM(P)	5,044	—	Proof	.50
	1979FM(U)	.015	—	.10	.30
	1979FM(P)	3,547	—	Proof	.50
	1980FM(U)	.030	—	.10	.30
	1980FM(P)	863 pcs.	—	Proof	.60

5 CENTS

NICKEL-BRASS

32	1967	4.600	—	.10	.25
	1967	5,100	—	Proof	2.25
	1972	1.200	—	.10	.30
	1974	3.000	—	.10	.30
	1975	—	—	.10	.30
	1976	—	—	.10	.30
	1977	1.500	—	.10	.20
	1978	2,000	—	.50	4.00
	1980	1.000	—	.10	.20
	1981	1.000	—	.10	.20
	1982	2.000	—	.10	.20
	1985	—	—	.10	.20
	1986	—	—	.10	.20
	1987	—	—	.10	.20

SILVER (OMS)

32a	1967	—	—	—	—

BRASS

38	1976FM(M)	.015	—	.10	.40
	1976FM(U)	50 pcs.	—	—	—
	1976FM(P)	.028	—	Proof	.75
	1977FM(U)	.015	—	.10	.40
	1977FM(P)	7,215	—	Proof	.75
	1978FM(U)	.015	—	.10	.40
	1978FM(P)	5,044	—	Proof	.75
	1979FM(U)	.015	—	.10	.40
	1979FM(P)	3,547	—	Proof	.75
	1980FM(U)	.030	—	.10	.40
	1980FM(P)	863 pcs.	—	Proof	.90

10 CENTS

COPPER-NICKEL

33	1967	4.000	.10	.20	.40
	1967	5,100	—	Proof	2.50
	1973	1.500	.10	.20	.35
	1974	1.700	.10	.20	.35
	1976	—	.10	.20	.35
	1977	4.000	.10	.20	.35
	1978	2.010	.10	.20	.35
	1979	—	.10	.20	.35
	1980	1.000	.10	.20	.35
	1981	1.000	.10	.20	.35
	1982	2.000	.10	.20	.35
	1985	—	.10	.20	.35
	1986	—	.10	.20	.35
	1987	—	.10	.20	.35

GUYANA 812

KM#	Date	Mintage	VF	XF	Unc
39	1976	2.006	—	.15	.50
	1976FM(M)	.010	—	.15	.60
	1976FM(U)	50 pcs.	—	—	—
	1976FM(P)	.028	—	Proof	1.00
	1977	1.500	—	.15	.50
	1977FM(U)	.010	—	.15	.60
	1977FM(P)	7.215	—	Proof	1.00
	1978FM(U)	.010	—	.15	.60
	1978FM(P)	5.044	—	Proof	1.00
	1979FM(U)	.010	—	.15	.60
	1979FM(P)	3.547	—	Proof	1.00
	1980FM(U)	.020	—	.15	.60
	1980FM(P)	863 pcs.	—	Proof	1.25

25 CENTS

COPPER-NICKEL

KM#	Date	Mintage	VF	XF	Unc
34	1967	3.500	.15	.25	.65
	1967	5,100	—	Proof	3.00
	1972	1.000	.15	.25	.65
	1974	4.000	.15	.25	.65
	1975	—	.15	.25	.65
	1976	—	.15	.25	.65
	1977	4.000	.15	.25	.65
	1978	2.006	.15	.25	.65
	1981	1.000	.15	.25	.65
	1982	1.500	.15	.25	.65
	1984	1.000	.15	.25	.65
	1985	—	.15	.25	.65
	1986	—	.15	.25	.65
	1987	—	.15	.25	.65
	1988	—	.15	.25	.65

KM#	Date	Mintage	VF	XF	Unc
40	1976FM(M)	4,000	—	.30	2.00
	1976FM(U)	50 pcs.	—	—	—
	1976FM(P)	.028	—	Proof	1.50
	1977	2.000	.15	.25	1.00
	1977FM(U)	4,000	—	.30	4.00
	1977FM(P)	7,215	—	Proof	1.50
	1978FM(U)	4,000	—	.30	4.00
	1978FM(P)	5,044	—	Proof	1.50
	1979FM(U)	4,000	—	.30	4.00
	1979FM(P)	3,547	—	Proof	1.50
	1980FM(U)	8,437	—	.30	4.00
	1980FM(P)	863 pcs.	—	Proof	1.75

50 CENTS

COPPER-NICKEL

KM#	Date	Mintage	VF	XF	Unc
35	1967	1.000	.25	.35	.75
	1967	5,100	—	Proof	3.50

KM#	Date	Mintage	VF	XF	Unc
41	1976FM(M)	2,000	—	.40	5.00
	1976FM(U)	50 pcs.	—	—	—
	1976FM(P)	.028	—	Proof	2.00
	1977FM(U)	2,000	—	.40	5.00
	1977FM(P)	7,215	—	Proof	2.00
	1978FM(U)	2,000	—	.40	5.00
	1978FM(P)	5,044	—	Proof	2.00
	1979FM(U)	2,000	—	.40	5.00
	1979FM(P)	3,547	—	Proof	2.00

KM#	Date	Mintage	VF	XF	Unc
41	1980FM(U)	4,437	—	.40	3.50
	1980FM(P)	863 pcs.	—	Proof	2.50

DOLLAR

COPPER-NICKEL
F.A.O. Issue

KM#	Date	Mintage	VF	XF	Unc
36	1970	.500	.50	1.00	2.50
	1970	5,000	—	Proof	4.00

KM#	Date	Mintage	VF	XF	Unc
42	1976FM(M)	600 pcs.	—	.50	4.00
	1976FM(U)	50 pcs.	—	—	—
	1976FM(P)	.028	—	Proof	5.00
	1977FM(U)	500 pcs.	—	.50	4.00
	1977FM(P)	7,215	—	Proof	5.00
	1978FM(U)	500 pcs.	—	.50	4.00
	1978FM(P)	5,044	—	Proof	5.00
	1979FM(U)	500 pcs.	—	.50	4.00
	1979FM(P)	3,547	—	Proof	5.00
	1980FM(U)	1,437	—	.50	4.00
	1980FM(P)	863 pcs.	—	Proof	6.00

5 DOLLARS

COPPER-NICKEL
Obv: Similar to 1 Dollar, KM#42.

KM#	Date	Mintage	VF	XF	Unc
43	1976FM(M)	400 pcs.	—	—	12.50
	1976FM(U)	150 pcs.	—	—	17.50
	1977FM(U)	100 pcs.	—	—	25.00
	1978FM(U)	100 pcs.	—	—	25.00
	1979FM(U)	100 pcs.	—	—	25.00
	1980FM(U)	547 pcs.	—	—	15.00

37.3000 g, .500 SILVER, .5996 oz ASW

KM#	Date	Mintage	VF	XF	Unc
43a	1976FM(P)	.018	—	Proof	10.00
	1977FM(P)	5,685	—	Proof	12.50
	1978FM(P)	3,825	—	Proof	15.00
	1979FM(P)	2,665	—	Proof	15.00
	1980FM(P)	347 pcs.	—	Proof	20.00

10 DOLLARS

COPPER-NICKEL
Obv: Similar to 1 Dollar, KM#42.

KM#	Date	Mintage	VF	XF	Unc
44	1976FM(M)	300 pcs.	—	—	35.00
	1976FM(U)	300 pcs.	—	—	35.00
	1977FM(U)	100 pcs.	—	—	50.00
	1978FM(U)	100 pcs.	—	—	50.00
	1979FM(U)	100 pcs.	—	—	50.00
	1980FM(U)	247 pcs.	—	—	40.00

43.2300 g, .925 SILVER, 1.2856 oz ASW

KM#	Date	Mintage	VF	XF	Unc
44a	1976FM(P)	.018	—	Proof	15.00
	1977FM(P)	5,685	—	Proof	20.00
	1978FM(P)	3,825	—	Proof	25.00
	1979FM(P)	2,665	—	Proof	25.00
	1980FM(P)	347 pcs.	—	Proof	30.00

50 DOLLARS

48.3000 g, .925 SILVER, 1.4365 oz ASW
Enmore Martyrs

KM#	Date	Mintage	VF	XF	Unc
45	1976FM(U)	100 pcs.	—	—	125.00
	1976FM	1,001	—	Proof	100.00

100 DOLLARS

5.7400 g, .500 GOLD, .0923 oz AGW

KM#	Date	Mintage	VF	XF	Unc
46	1976FM(U)	100 pcs.	—	—	110.00
	1976FM(P)	.021	—	Proof	100.00

5.5800 g, .500 GOLD, .0897 oz AGW

KM#	Date	Mintage	VF	XF	Unc
47	1977FM(U)	100 pcs.	—	—	110.00
	1977FM(P)	7,635	—	Proof	100.00

PROOF SETS (PS)

KM#	Date	Mintage	Identification	Issue Price	Mkt. Val.
PS1	1967(5)	5,100	KM31-35	10.50	10.00
PS2	1976FM(8)	17,536	KM37-42,43a,44a	45.00	35.00
PS3	1976FM(6)	10,302	KM37-42	15.00	10.00
PS4	1977FM(8)	5,685	KM37-42,43a,44a	45.00	40.00
PS5	1977FM(6)	1,530	KM37-42	15.00	15.00
PS6	1978FM(8)	3,825	KM37-42,43a,44a	47.50	40.00
PS7	1978FM(6)	1,219	KM37-42	16.00	15.00
PS8	1979FM(8)	2,665	KM37-42,43a,44a	47.50	45.00
PS9	1979FM(6)	882	KM37-42	16.00	15.00
PS10	1980FM(8)	1,900	KM37-42,43a,44a	100.00	55.00
PS11	1980FM(6)	863	KM37-42	19.00	15.00

HAITI

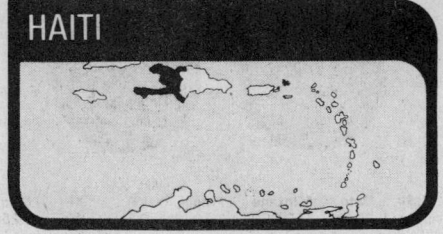

The Republic of Haiti, which occupies the western one-third of the island of Santo Domingo (Hispaniola) in the Caribbean Sea between Puerto Rico and Cuba, has an area of 10,714 sq. mi.(27,750 sq. km.) and a population of *6.2 million. Capital: Port-au-Prince. The economy is based on agriculture; light manufacturing and tourism are becoming increasingly important. Coffee, bauxite, sugar, essential oils and handicrafts are exported.

Columbus discovered Hispaniola in 1492. Spain colonized the island, making Santo Domingo the base for exploration of the Western Hemisphere. The area that is now Haiti was ceded to France by Spain in 1697. Slaves brought over from Africa to work the coffee and sugar cane plantations made it one of the richest colonies of the French Empire. One outcome of the slave revolt of the 1790's was the establishment of the Republic of Haiti in 1804, making it the oldest black republic in the world and the second oldest republic (after the United States) in the Western Hemisphere.

The French language is used on Haitian coins although that language is spoken by only about 10 percent of the populace. A form of Creole serves as the language of the majority of the inhabitants.

Two dating systems are used on Haiti's 19th century coins. One is Christian, the other is Revolutionary -- dating from 1803 when the French were finally permanently ousted by a native revolt. Thus, a date of AN30 is the equivalent of 1833 A.D. Some coins carry both date forms, and in the date listing which follows only those coins which are exclusively dated according to the revolutionary period are enumerated by AN dates in the date column.

RULERS
French, until 1804

MINT MARKS
A - Paris
(a) - Paris, privy marks only
HEATON - Birmingham

MONETARY SYSTEM
12 Deniers = 1 Sol
20 Sols = 1 Livre
100 Centimes = 1 Gourde

HISPANIOLA

TOWN OF LE CAP
(Old Cap Francois)

Port city on the northern coast of Haiti.
Under a French edict of July 13, 1781 various Spanish-American and other circulating silver coins were to be counterstamped with a crowned anchor and C for the island. These were made at the capitoli and the pieces given values of 1 Escalin and 1/2 Escalin. Copper coins were counterstamped L.C. and S.D.

MONETARY SYSTEM
15 Sols = 1 Escalin (1 Real)

COUNTERMARKED COINAGE
SOL

BRONZE
c/m: L.C. in rectangle on English 1/2 Penny token of 1792.

KM#	Date	Mintage	Good	VG	Fine	VF
5 (3)	ND(1802-09)	—	17.50	30.00	45.00	85.00

SILVER
Ring substituted for crown on anchor.

| 6 (4) | ND | — | 30.00 | 50.00 | 75.00 | 115.00 |

1/2 ESCALIN

SILVER
c/m: C and anchor on Potosi 1/2 Real cob.

KM#	Date	Mintage	Good	VG	Fine	VF
7	ND(1780-1802)	30.00	50.00	75.00	115.00

ESCALIN

SILVER
c/m: C and anchor on Angola 2 Macutas.

| 8 (10) | ND(1780-1802) | 30.00 | 50.00 | 75.00 | 115.00 |

FRENCH OCCUPATION COINAGE
SOL

BRONZE
c/m: S D in rectangle on French Sol, C#73.

| 13 (3) | ND(1802-09) | — | 45.00 | 75.00 | 120.00 | 185.00 |

c/m: ND over SD on French copper coin.

| 14 (4) | ND(1802-09) | — | 30.00 | 50.00 | 75.00 | 115.00 |

c/m: Crowned N on English 1/2 Penny, KM#392.

| 15 (5) | ND(1802-09) | — | 40.00 | 65.00 | 110.00 | 165.00 |

REPUBLICAN COINAGE
RULERS
Toussaint L'Ouverture, 1798-1802

MONETARY SYSTEM
15 Sols (Sous) = 1 Escalin (Real)

DEMY (1/2) ESCALIN
SILVER
Similar to 1 Escalin, KM#2.

| 21 (1) | ND(1802) | — | 75.00 | 150.00 | 300.00 | 600.00 |

UN (1) ESCALIN

SILVER

| 22 (2) | ND(1802) | — | 37.50 | 75.00 | 150.00 | 300.00 |

DEUX (2) ESCALIN

SILVER

| 23 (3) | ND(1802) | — | 75.00 | 150.00 | 300.00 | 600.00 |

HAITI
7 SOLS 6 DENIERS
SILVER
Similar to 15 Sols, KM#6.

3	1807	—	35.00	75.00	150.00	300.00
	1808	—	35.00	75.00	150.00	300.00
	1809	—	35.00	75.00	150.00	300.00

15 SOLS

SILVER

KM#	Date	Mintage	Good	VG	Fine	VF
6	1807	—	20.00	35.00	65.00	125.00
	1808	—	35.00	75.00	150.00	300.00
	1809	—	35.00	75.00	150.00	300.00

30 SOLS

SILVER

| 8 | 1807 | — | — | — | — | 7150. |

DECIMAL COINAGE
100 Centimes = 1 Gourde

UNE (1) CENTIME

COPPER

KM#	Date	Year	VG	Fine	VF	XF
21	1828	AN 25	12.00	28.00	50.00	85.00
	1829	AN 26	4.00	8.00	20.00	40.00
	1830	AN 27	4.00	6.50	12.50	30.00
	1830	AN 28	18.00	30.00	60.00	115.00
	1831	AN 28	2.50	5.00	7.00	12.50
	1831	AN 29	8.00	17.50	32.50	65.00
	1832	AN 28	22.50	32.50	75.00	150.00
	1832	AN 29	1.75	3.50	5.50	11.00
	1834	AN 31	2.00	4.00	5.50	11.00
	1840	AN 37	2.00	4.25	5.50	11.00
	1841	AN 38	2.50	6.00	7.50	15.00
	1842	AN 39	1.75	3.25	5.50	11.00

NOTE: Die varieties exist and diework becomes progressively cruder throughout this series.

22mm

| 24 | 1846 | AN 43 | .75 | 2.25 | 5.00 | 11.00 |

Reduced size, 21mm
Obv: Leaves point inward.
Rev: W/large star after legend.

| 25.1 | 1846 | AN 43 | .65 | 2.00 | 3.00 | 7.50 |

Rev: Large Phrygian cap.

| 25.2 | 1846 | AN 43 | 1.00 | 2.50 | 4.00 | 10.00 |

Similar to KM#25.2 but stop after legend.

| 30 | 1849 | AN 46 | 75.00 | 125.00 | 200.00 | 325.00 |

Similar to KM#25.2 but leg: EMPIRE D'HAITI.

| 33 | 1850 | AN 47 | 50.00 | 80.00 | 120.00 | 225.00 |

| 34 | 1850 | — | 3.00 | 5.00 | 8.00 | 20.00 |

HAITI

BRONZE

KM#	Date	Mintage	Fine	VF	XF	Unc
42	1881	.830	2.00	3.50	5.50	15.00
	1881	—	—	—	Proof	200.00

KM#	Date	Mintage	Fine	VF	XF	Unc
57	1949	10.000	.10	.20	.40	1.25

NICKEL-SILVER					
59	1953	3.000	—	.10	.20	.75

48	1886A	2.500	1.75	3.00	5.00	12.50
	1894A	2.070	1.75	3.00	5.00	12.50
	1895A	5.420	1.75	3.00	5.00	12.50

DEUX (2) CENTIMES

KM#	Date	Mintage	VG	Fine	VF	XF
36	1850	—	2.25	4.75	10.00	20.00

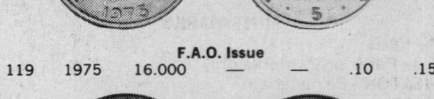

COPPER-NICKEL

62	1958	15.000	—	—	.10	.20
	1970	—	—	—	.10	.15

BRONZE

KM#	Date	Mintage	Fine	VF	XF	Unc
43	1881	.830	2.75	4.25	6.75	12.50
	1881	—	—	—	Proof	150.00

F.A.O. Issue

119	1975	16.000	—	—	.10	.15

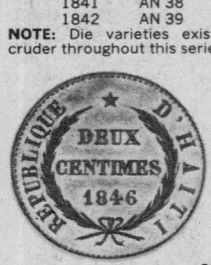

COPPER

KM#	Date	Year	VG	Fine	VF	XF
22	1828	AN 25	12.00	25.00	40.00	75.00
	1828	AN 26	10.00	20.00	35.00	60.00
	1829	AN 26	2.75	4.00	5.50	11.00
	1830	AN 26	13.50	32.50	70.00	120.00
	1830	AN 27	3.00	4.50	6.00	13.00
	1831	AN 28	2.50	4.00	5.50	11.00
	1840	AN 37	2.50	4.00	5.50	10.00
	1840 backwards 4					
		AN 37	4.00	6.50	8.00	20.00
	1841	AN 38	3.00	4.50	6.00	12.00
	1842	AN 39	3.00	4.50	6.00	12.00

NOTE: Die varieties exist and became progressively cruder throughout this series.

49	1886A	1.250	1.50	2.50	5.00	9.00
	1894A	3.750	1.50	2.50	5.00	12.00

CINQ (5) CENTIMES

39	1863HEATON					
		1.000	2.00	4.50	9.50	15.00
	1863HEATON	—	—	—	Proof	75.00

F.A.O. Issue

145	1981	.015	—	.10	.25	1.00

6 CENTIMES
.835 SILVER
Obv: Arms type.

KM#	Date	Year	VG	Fine	VF	XF
10	1813	AN 10	80.00	150.00	250.00	400.00

Rev: Petion bust.

16	1818	AN 15	80.00	150.00	250.00	400.00

Rev: Boyer bust.

17	1818	AN 15	12.50	20.00	30.00	60.00

26mm

26	1846	AN 43	1.25	3.00	4.75	8.75
	1846	AN 43	—	—	Proof	300.00
	1846	AN 43/2	2.50	4.50	5.75	11.00

COPPER-NICKEL

50	1889	.120	20.00	30.00	50.00	100.00

Reduced size, 24mm
Obv: Leaves point inward.
Rev: W/large star after legend.

27.1	1846	AN 43	1.75	3.50	5.00	9.50

NOTE: Varieties exist w/o accents on E's, date as AN 43.

Rev: Large Phrygian cap.

27.2	1846	AN 43	2.50	4.00	—	5.00	10.00
(27.1)							

52	1904 (a)	—	2.75	5.00	12.50	32.50
	1904 (a)	—	—	—	Proof	120.00

NOTE: Struck at Waterbury, Connecticut by the Scovill Mfg. Co. Design incorporates Paris privy and mint director's marks.

COPPER
Similar to 1 Centime, KM#25.2.

28	1846	AN 43	5.00	7.50	10.00	20.00

31	1849	AN 46	30.00	45.00	80.00	150.00

Obv. leg: EMPIRE D'HAITI.

35	1850	AN 47	45.00	60.00	90.00	175.00

53	1904	2.000	.50	1.00	4.00	15.00
	1904	—	—	—	Proof	90.00
	1905	20.000	—	.30	.75	2.50	10.00
	1905	—	—	—	Proof	100.00
	1906	10.000	—	Reported, not confirmed		

32	1849	AN 46	27.50	40.00	50.00	100.00

KM#	Date	Year	VG	Fine	VF	XF
37	1850	AN 47	60.00	100.00	200.00	350.00

6-1/4 CENTIMES

COPPER

KM#	Date	Year	VG	Fine	VF	XF
29	1846	AN 43	5.00	9.00	15.00	25.00

KM#	Date	Mintage	VG	Fine	VF	XF
38	1850	—	3.00	5.00	7.50	20.00

DIX (10) CENTIMES

BRONZE

KM#	Date	Mintage	Fine	VF	XF	Unc
40	1863HEATON	1.000	2.75	4.50	7.50	20.00
	1863HEATON	—			Proof	80.00

2.5000 g, .835 SILVER, .0671 oz ASW

44	1881(a)	1.500	1.25	2.00	4.00	20.00
	1881(a)	—	—	—	Proof	250.00
	1882(a)	1.800	1.25	2.00	4.00	20.00
	1882(a)	—	—	—	Proof	150.00
	1886(a)	1.500	2.00	3.50	6.00	27.50
	1886(a)	—	—	—	Proof	175.00
	1887(a)	1.050	1.50	2.75	4.00	20.00
	1887(a)	—	—	—	Proof	150.00
	1890(a)	1.000	2.00	3.50	6.00	22.50
	1890(a)	—	—	—	Proof	175.00
	1894(a)	3.720	1.25	2.00	4.00	20.00
	1894(a)	—	—	—	Proof	150.00

COPPER-NICKEL

54	1906	10.000	.50	1.00	3.00	10.00
	1906	—	—	—	Proof	100.00

KM#	Date	Mintage	Fine	VF	XF	Unc
58	1949	5.000	.15	.25	.50	1.50

NICKEL-SILVER

| 60 | 1953 | 1.500 | — | .10 | .25 | 1.25 |

COPPER-NICKEL

63	1958	7.500	—	—	.15	.30
	1970	—	—	—	.10	.20

F.A.O. Issue

120	1975	12.000	—	—	.10	.15
	1983	2.000	—	—	.10	.30

F.A.O. Issue

| 146 | 1981 | .015 | — | .10 | .25 | 1.00 |

12 CENTIMES

SILVER
Obv: Arms type.

KM#	Date	Year	Good	VG	Fine	VF
11	(1813)	AN 10	6.50	12.00	20.00	42.50
	(1814)	AN XI	4.00	8.50	15.00	30.00
	(1815)	AN 12	7.50	13.50	27.50	50.00

Rev: Petion type, large head.

| 13 | (1817) | AN 14 | 5.00 | 10.00 | 16.50 | 32.50 |

Rev: Petion type, small head.

| 14 | (1817) | AN 14 | 5.00 | 10.00 | 16.50 | 32.50 |

Rev: Boyer type.

KM#	Date	Year	Good	VG	Fine	VF
19	(1827)	AN 24	5.00	10.00	20.00	50.00
	(1828)	AN 25	10.00	20.00	40.00	85.00
	(1829)	AN 26	12.50	25.00	52.00	125.00

VINGT (20) CENTIMES

BRONZE

KM#	Date	Mintage	Fine	VF	XF	Unc
41	1863HEATON	1.000	3.50	5.00	9.50	25.00
	1863HEATON	—	—	—	Proof	60.00

NICKEL (OMS)

| 41a | 1863HEATON | — | | | | |

5.0000 g, .835 SILVER, .1342 oz ASW

45	1881(a)	1.250	2.50	4.25	7.50	25.00
	1881(a)	—	—	—	Proof	175.00
	1882(a)	1.250	2.50	4.25	7.50	25.00
	1882(a)	—	—	—	Proof	175.00
	1887(a)	.350	3.00	5.00	9.00	30.00
	1887(a)	—	—	—	Proof	200.00
	1890(a)	.070	4.50	9.00	20.00	50.00
	1890(a)	—	—	—	Proof	200.00
	1894(a)	1.850	2.50	4.25	7.50	25.00
	1894(a)	—	—	—	Proof	175.00
	1895(a)	1.270	2.50	4.25	7.50	25.00
	1895(a)	—	—	—	Proof	175.00

COPPER-NICKEL

55	1907	5.000	1.00	2.00	4.50	12.50
	1907	—	—	—	Proof	125.00

NICKEL-SILVER

| 61 | 1956 | 2.500 | .20 | .35 | .75 | 2.50 |

| 77 | 1970 | — | — | — | .10 | .50 |

COPPER-NICKEL
F.A.O. Issue

| 100 | 1972 | 1.500 | — | .10 | .25 | 1.00 |

HAITI 816

KM#	Date	Mintage	Fine	VF	XF	Unc
100	1975	4.000	—	—	.10	.50
	1983	1.500	—	—	.10	.50

F.A.O. Issue

| 147 | 1981 | .015 | — | .10 | .25 | 1.25 |

| 152 | 1986 | 2.500 | — | — | .10 | .50 |

25 CENTIMES

SILVER, 22mm
Arms type

KM#	Date	Year	Good	VG	Fine	VF
12.1	(1813)	AN 10	6.00	12.00	25.00	50.00

20mm

12.2	(1814)	AN XI	5.00	8.00	12.50	25.00
	(1815)	AN 12	4.00	6.00	10.00	20.00
	(1816)	AN 13	4.50	7.00	11.50	22.50

NOTE: The above coins exist with solid and dotted spear shafts.

Rev: Petion type.

15	(1817)	AN 14	3.00	5.00	8.00	17.50
	(1817)	AN 14P	15.00	25.00	50.00	100.00
	(1818)	AN 15	6.00	10.00	20.00	40.00

Rev: Boyer type.

18	(1825)	AN 22	—	Reported, not confirmed		
	(1827)	AN 24	3.00	5.00	12.50	25.00
	(1828)	AN 25	2.00	4.50	9.00	17.50
	(1829)	AN 26	4.00	8.00	17.50	40.00
	(1831)	AN 28	2.25	5.00	12.50	25.00
	(1833)	AN 30	7.00	15.00	25.00	50.00
	(1834)	AN 31	5.00	9.00	17.50	40.00

50 CENTIMES

SILVER

20	(1827)	AN 24	15.00	25.00	50.00	75.00
	(1828)	AN 25	3.00	7.00	12.50	22.50
	(1829)	AN 26	7.50	15.00	30.00	
	(1830)	AN 27	5.00	12.50	25.00	40.00
	(1831)	AN 28	3.00	6.00	12.00	20.00
	(1832)	AN 29	3.00	7.00	12.50	22.50
	(1833)	AN 30	7.50	17.50	40.00	85.00

BRASS

| 20a | (1828) | AN 25 | — | — | — | — |

12.5000 g, .835 SILVER, .3356 oz ASW

KM#	Date	Mintage	Fine	VF	XF	Unc
47	1882(a)	.440	6.00	11.00	15.00	40.00
	1882(a)	—	—	—	Proof	250.00
	1883(a)	.400	6.00	11.00	15.00	40.00
	1883(a)	—	—	—	Proof	200.00
	1887(a)	.250	6.00	11.00	17.50	50.00
	1887(a)	—	—	—	Proof	200.00
	1890(a)	.100	8.50	13.00	20.00	65.00
	1890(a)	—	—	—	Proof	200.00
	1895(a)	.900	6.00	11.00	15.00	40.00
	1895(a)	—	—	—	Proof	200.00

COPPER-NICKEL

56	1907	2.000	.90	1.75	5.50	15.00
	1907	—	—	—	Proof	175.00
	1908	.800	1.00	2.50	8.50	20.00
	1908	—	—	—	Proof	200.00

F.A.O. Issue

101	1972	.600	—	.10	.25	1.25
	1975	1.200	—	.10	.15	.80
	1979	—	—	.10	.15	.80
	1983	1.000	—	.10	.15	.80
	1985	—	—	—	—	.75

F.A.O. Issue

| 148 | 1981 | .015 | — | .10 | .50 | 2.00 |

Similar to 20 Centimes, KM#152.

| 153 | 1986 | 2.000 | — | .10 | .15 | .80 |

100 CENTIMES

SILVER

KM#	Date	Year	Good	VG	Fine	VF	XF
23	(1829)	AN 26	6.00	12.00	22.50	50.00	
	(1830)	AN 27	7.00	14.50	27.50	55.00	
	(1833)	AN 30	12.50	25.00	37.50	85.00	

GOURDE

25.0000 g, .900 SILVER, .7234 oz ASW

KM#	Date	Mintage	Fine	VF	XF	Unc
46	1881(a)	.200	20.00	35.00	60.00	150.00
	1881(a)	—	—	—	Proof	1300.
	1882(a)	.500	15.00	25.00	50.00	140.00
	1882(a)	—	—	—	Proof	1250.
	1887(a)	.200	15.00	25.00	50.00	140.00
	1887(a)	—	—	—	Proof	1250.
	1895(a)	.100	20.00	35.00	75.00	160.00
	1895(a)	—	—	—	Proof	1250.

BRONZE, uniface
Insurrection Issue
c/m: B.P.1G/GiH

| 51 | ND(1889) | .100 | 100.00 | 200.00 | 300.00 | 600.00 |

5 GOURDES

23.5200 g, .999 SILVER, .7555 oz ASW
Columbus Discovers America

KM#	Date	Mintage	VF	XF	Unc
64	1967	4,650	—	Proof	12.50
	1968	5,750	—	Proof	12.50
	1969	1,175	—	Proof	17.50
	1970	2,060	—	Proof	17.50

Rev: Similar to KM#64.

| 78 | 1971 | 1,585 | — | Proof | 25.00 |

10 GOURDES

47.0500 g, .999 SILVER, 1.5113 oz ASW
General Toussaint Louverture

KM#	Date	Mintage	VF	XF	Unc
65	1967	6,750	—	Proof	25.00
	1968	5,725	—	Proof	25.00
	1969	1,100	—	Proof	35.00
	1970	1,500	—	Proof	35.00

Seminole Indian Chief - Billy Bowlegs
Rev: Similar to KM#65.

KM#	Date	Mintage	VF	XF	Unc
83	1971	3,735	—	Proof	40.00

20 GOURDES

3.9500 g, .900 GOLD, .1143 oz AGW

KM#	Date	Mintage	VF	XF	Unc
66	1967	10,351	—	Proof	75.00
	1968	Inc. Ab.	—	Proof	85.00
	1969	Inc. Ab.	—	Proof	95.00
	1970	Inc. Ab.	—	Proof	100.00

25 GOURDES

Seminole Indian Chief - Osceola
Rev: Similar to KM#65.

79	1971	3,535	—	Proof	40.00

Nez Perce Indian Chief - Joseph
Rev: Similar to KM#65.

84	1971	3,235	—	Proof	40.00

117.6000 g, .999 SILVER, 3.7809 oz ASW
Actual size 60mm.
Rev: Similar to 5 Gourdes, KM#64.

67	1967	4,650	—	Proof	90.00
	1968	5,810	—	Proof	90.00
	1969	1,115	—	Proof	100.00
	1970	1,000	—	Proof	100.00

Sioux Indian Chief - Sitting Bull
Rev: Similar to KM#65.

80	1971	3,185	—	Proof	40.00

Yankton Sioux Indian Chief - War Eagle
Rev: Similar to KM#65.

85	1971	3,135	—	Proof	40.00

Fox Indian Chief - Playing Fox
Rev: Similar to KM#65.

81	1971	3,035	—	Proof	40.00

Oglala Sioux Indian Chief - Red Cloud
Rev: Similar to KM#65.

86	1971	3,235	—	Proof	40.00

Rev: Similar to 5 Gourdes, KM#64. Actual size 60mm.

88	1971	1,935	—	—	175.00

8.4800 g, .925 SILVER, .2521 oz ASW

102	1973	6,100	—	—	7.50
	1973	5,470	—	Proof	10.00
	1974	—	—	Proof	30.00

Chiricahua Indian Chief - Geronimo
Rev: Similar to KM#65.

82	1971	3,285	—	Proof	40.00

Cherokee Indian Chief - Stalking Turkey
Rev: Similar to KM#65.

87	1971	3,185	—	Proof	40.00

10.0000 g, .925 SILVER, .2973 oz ASW

HAITI

KM#	Date	Mintage	VF	XF	Unc
103	1973	.057	—	—	5.00
	1973	6,430	—	Proof	10.00

8.3750 g, .925 SILVER, .2491 oz ASW
United States Bicentennial

112	1974	.025	—	—	6.00
	1974	600 pcs.	—	Proof	20.00
	1976	—	—	—	—

International Women's Year
Rev: Similar to KM#67.

121	1975	7,180	—	—	7.50
	1975	1,440	—	Proof	12.50
122	1975	—	—	Proof	12.50

30 GOURDES

9.1100 g, .585 GOLD, .1713 oz AGW

72	1969	1,185	—	Proof	125.00
	1970	Inc. Ab.	—	Proof	150.00

40 GOURDES

12.1500 g, .585 GOLD, .2285 oz AGW

73	1969	1,005	—	Proof	175.00
	1970	Inc. Ab.	—	Proof	200.00

50 GOURDES

9.8700 g, .900 GOLD, .2856 oz AGW

68	1967	8,681	—	Proof	200.00
	1968	Inc. Ab.	—	Proof	225.00
	1969	Inc. Ab.	—	Proof	250.00
	1970	Inc. Ab.	—	Proof	275.00

Rev: Similar to KM#68.

89	1971	485 pcs.	—	Proof	300.00

20.1000 g, .925 SILVER, .5978 oz ASW

KM#	Date	Mintage	VF	XF	Unc
104	1973	8,685	—	—	12.50
	1973	5,973	—	Proof	15.00
	1974	—	—	Proof	45.00

105	1973	7,300	—	—	12.50
	1973	5,853	—	Proof	15.00
	1974	—	—	—	35.00
	1974	—	—	Proof	45.00

16.9000 g, .925 SILVER, .5026 oz ASW
Soccer Championship

106	1973	.012	—	Proof	12.50

1976 Montreal Olympiad

113	1974	.021	—	—	12.50
	1974	2,358	—	Proof	16.00
	1976	8,000	—	—	12.50

Rev: Smaller 4 in date.

114	1974	—	—	Proof	16.00

KM#	Date	Mintage	VF	XF	Unc
123	1974	960 pcs.	—	Proof	20.00
	1976	—	—	—	—

Holy Year

21.3000 g, .925 SILVER, .6334 oz ASW
Soccer Championship
Rev: Similar to KM#104.

127	1977	.011	—	—	20.00
	1977	9,000	—	Proof	25.00

Human Rights
Rev: Similar to KM#104.

128	1977	800 pcs.	—	—	25.00
	1977	545 pcs.	—	Proof	30.00

1980 Moscow Olympics

129	1977	3,969	—	—	20.00
	1977	3,720	—	Proof	27.50
	1978	—	—	Proof	35.00

20th Anniversary of European Market

130.1	1977	421 pcs.	—	—	25.00
	1977	364 pcs.	—	Proof	40.00

HAITI 819

Obv: Entire area within circle frosted.
Rev: Date added below arms.

KM#	Date	Mintage	VF	XF	Unc
130.2	1978	—	—	Proof	40.00

Reine Mondiale du Sucre
Rev: Similar to KM#104.

| 131 | 1977 | 321 pcs. | — | — | 25.00 |
| | 1977 | 602 pcs. | — | Proof | 35.00 |

20.0000 g, .925 SILVER, .5948 oz ASW
F.A.O. Issue

| 149 | 1981 | .014 | — | — | 20.00 |

Papal Visit

| 150 | 1983 | 1,000 | — | Proof | 30.00 |

60 GOURDES

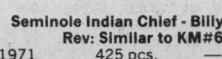

18.2200 g, .585 GOLD, .3427 oz AGW
Alexandre Petion

| 74 | 1969 | 935 pcs. | — | Proof | 300.00 |
| | 1970 | Inc. Ab. | — | Proof | 400.00 |

100 GOURDES

19.7500 g, .900 GOLD, .5715 oz AGW
Marie Jeanne

KM#	Date	Mintage	VF	XF	Unc
69	1967	8,682	—	Proof	325.00
	1968	Inc. Ab.	—	Proof	350.00
	1969	Inc. Ab.	—	Proof	350.00
	1970	Inc. Ab.	—	Proof	375.00

Seminole Indian Chief - Osceola
Rev: Similar to KM#69.

| 90 | 1971 | 435 pcs. | — | Proof | 400.00 |

Sioux Indian Chief - Sitting Bull
Rev: Similar to KM#69.

| 91 | 1971 | 475 pcs. | — | Proof | 400.00 |

Fox Indian Chief - Playing Fox
Rev: Similar to KM#69.

| 92 | 1971 | 425 pcs. | — | Proof | 400.00 |

Chiricahua Indian Chief - Geronimo
Rev: Similar to KM#69.

| 93 | 1971 | 520 pcs. | — | Proof | 400.00 |

Seminole Indian Chief - Billy Bowlegs
Rev: Similar to KM#69.

| 94 | 1971 | 425 pcs. | — | Proof | 400.00 |

Nez Perce Indian Chief - Joseph
Rev: Similar to KM#69.

KM#	Date	Mintage	VF	XF	Unc
95	1971	455 pcs.	—	Proof	400.00

Yankton Sioux Indian Chief - War Eagle
Rev: Similar to KM#69.

| 96 | 1971 | 455 pcs. | — | Proof | 400.00 |

Oglala Sioux Indian Chief - Red Cloud
Rev: Similar to KM#69.

| 97 | 1971 | 455 pcs. | — | Proof | 400.00 |

Cherokee Indian Chief - Stalking Turkey
Rev: Similar to KM#69.

| 98 | 1971 | 425 pcs. | — | Proof | 400.00 |

1.4500 g, .900 GOLD, .0419 oz AGW
Christopher Colombus

| 107 | 1973 | 3,233 | — | — | 40.00 |
| | 1973 | 915 pcs. | — | Proof | 75.00 |

43.0000 g, .925 SILVER, 1.2789 oz ASW
Sadat and Begin
Rev: Similar to KM#69.

| 132 | 1977 | 550 pcs. | — | — | 60.00 |
| | 1977 | 500 pcs. | — | Proof | 80.00 |

HAITI 820

Rev: Similar to KM#69.

KM#	Date	Mintage	VF	XF	Unc
133	1977	321 pcs.	—	—	85.00
	1977	214 pcs.	—	Proof	115.00

Charles A. Lindbergh
Rev: Similar to KM#69.

134	1977	321 pcs.	—	—	85.00
	1977	214 pcs.	—	Proof	115.00

Statue of Liberty
Rev: Similar to KM#69.

135	1977	321 pcs.	—	—	85.00
	1977	214 pcs.	—	Proof	115.00

200 GOURDES

39.4900 g, .900 GOLD, 1.1427oz AGW

70	1967	4,199	—	Proof	650.00
	1968	Inc. Ab.	—	Proof	675.00
	1969	Inc. Ab.	—	Proof	675.00
	1970	Inc. Ab.	—	Proof	675.00

Rev: Similar to 100 Gourdes, KM#69.

KM#	Date	Mintage	VF	XF	Unc
99	1971	235 pcs.	—	—	900.00

2.9100 g, .900 GOLD, .0842 oz AGW

108	1973	5,167	—	—	60.00
	1973	915 pcs.	—	Proof	100.00

Holy Year
Rev: Fineness stamped on hexagonal mound, spears w/spearheads.

115	1974	4,965	—	—	60.00
	1974	660 pcs.	—	Proof	80.00

Holy Year
Rev: Fineness stamped on oval mound, spears w/arrowheads.

124	1975	—	—	Proof	80.00

International Women's Year
Rev: Similar to KM#124.

125	1975	2,260	—	—	60.00
	1975	840 pcs.	—	Proof	125.00

250 GOURDES

75.9500 g, .585 GOLD, 1.4286oz AGW
King H. Christophe
Rev: Similar to KM#136.

75	1969	470 pcs.	—	Proof	1200.

4.2500 g, .900 GOLD, .1229oz AGW
Human Rights

136	1977	282 pcs.	—	—	150.00
	1977	288 pcs.	—	Proof	150.00

Sadat and Begin

KM#	Date	Mintage	VF	XF	Unc
137	1977	270 pcs.	—	—	125.00
	1977	520 pcs.	—	Proof	125.00

138	1977	107 pcs.	—	—	200.00
	1977	107 pcs.	—	Proof	200.00

Obv: Portrait of Lindbergh in flier's cap above Spirit of St. Louis. Rev: Similar to KM#137.

139	1977	107 pcs.	—	—	200.00
	1977	107 pcs.	—	Proof	200.00

500 GOURDES

151.9000 g, .585 GOLD, 2.8572 oz AGW
Haitian Native Art
Illustration is reduced, 68mm actual size.
Rev: Similar to KM#141.

76	1969	435 pcs.	—	Proof	2000.

7.2800 g, .900 GOLD, .2106 oz AGW

109	1973	2,380	—	—	125.00
	1973	915 pcs.	—	Proof	150.00

110	1973	2,265	—	—	125.00
	1973	915 pcs.	—	Proof	150.00

Obv: Same as 1000 Gourdes, KM#118.
Rev: Similar to KM#141.

116	1974	—	—	Proof	150.00

6.4600 g, .900 GOLD, .1869 oz AGW
1976 Montreal Olymplad
Rev: Fineness stamped on hexagonal mound, spears w/spearheads.

KM#	Date	Mintage	VF	XF	Unc
117	1974	3,489	—	—	125.00
	1974	1,140	—	Proof	150.00

1976 Montreal Olymplad
Rev: Fineness stamped on hexagonal mound, spears w/arrowheads.

KM#	Date	Mintage	VF	XF	Unc
126	1975	120 pcs.	—	—	350.00

8.5000 g, .900 GOLD, .2459 oz AGW
Soccer Championship
Rev: Similar to KM#141.

| 140 | 1977 | 450 pcs. | — | — | 225.00 |
| | 1977 | 200 pcs. | — | Proof | 275.00 |

1980 Moscow Olympics

141	1977	695 pcs.	—	—	225.00
	1977	504 pcs.	—	Proof	250.00
	1978	—	—	Proof	275.00

20th Anniversary of European Common Market
Obv: Map of Europe. Rev: Similar to KM#141.

142	1977	207 pcs.	—	—	200.00
	1977	257 pcs.	—	Proof	225.00
	1978	—	—	—	200.00
	1978	—	—	Proof	300.00

Rev: Similar to KM#141.

| 143 | 1977 | 107 pcs. | — | — | 250.00 |
| | 1977 | 107 pcs. | — | Proof | 300.00 |

Duvalier
Rev: Similar to KM#141.

| 144 | 1977 | 107 pcs. | — | — | 250.00 |
| | 1977 | 328 pcs. | — | Proof | 250.00 |

10.5000 g, .900 GOLD, .3038 oz AGW
Papal Visit

| 151 | 1983 | 1,000 | — | Proof | 200.00 |

1000 GOURDES

197.4800 g, .900 GOLD, 5.7148 oz AGW
Dr. Francois Duvalier
Rev: Similar to KM#118.

KM#	Date	Mintage	VF	XF	Unc
71	1967	2,950	—	Proof	3000.
	1968	Inc. Ab.	—	Proof	3200.
	1969	Inc. Ab.	—	Proof	3400.
	1970	Inc. Ab.	—	Proof	3600.

14.5600 g, .900 GOLD, .4213 oz AGW
Jean Claude Duvalier

| 111 | 1973 | — | — | — | 300.00 |
| | 1973 | 915 pcs. | — | Proof | 300.00 |

United States Bicentennial

| 118 | 1974 | 3,040 | — | — | 275.00 |
| | 1974 | 480 pcs. | — | Proof | 325.00 |

MINT SETS (MS)

KM#	Date	Mintage	Identification	Issue Price	Mkt. Val.
MS1	1973(9)	8,000	KM102-105,107-109(2),111	490.00	625.00
MS2	1973(4)	—	KM102-105	60.00	37.50
MS3	1975(2)	—	KM121,125	50.25	65.00
MS4	1976(3)	—	KM112-113,123	—	—

PROOF SETS (PS)

PS1	1967(5)	2,525	KM66,68-71	722.00	4250.
PS2	1967(3)	4,650	KM64,65,67	47.00	125.00
PS3	1968(5)	475	KM66,68-71	823.00	4535.
PS4	1968(3)	5,725	KM64,65,67	53.50	125.00
PS5	1969(5)	435	KM72-76	475.00	3800.
PS6	1969(5)	140	KM66,68-71	823.00	4770.
PS7	1969(3)	1,100	KM64,65,67	53.50	150.00
PS8	1970(5)	—	KM66,68-71	823.00	5025.
PS9	1970(3)	1,000	KM64,65,67	53.50	150.00
PS10	1971(9)	—	KM79-87	135.00	360.00
PS11	1971(9)	—	KM90-98	—	3600.
PS12	1973(8)	1,250	KM102-105,107-109,111	830.00	575.00
PS13	1973(4)	3,500	KM102-105	60.00	50.00
PS14	1975(2)	—	KM121,125	67.25	85.00
PS15	1975(2)	—	KM122-123	75.50	32.50

Listings For
HAWAII: refer to United States
HEJAZ: refer to Saudi Arabia

HONDURAS

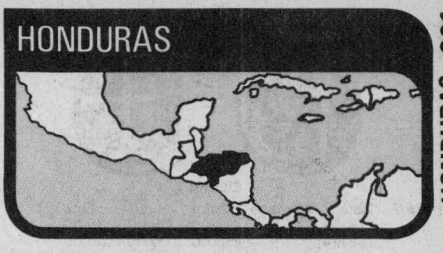

The Republic of Honduras, situated in Central America between Nicaragua and Guatemala, has an area of 43,277 sq. mi. (112,088 sq. km.) and a population of *5.1 million. Capital: Tegucigalpa. Agriculture, mining (gold and silver), and logging are the chief industries. Bananas, timber and coffee are exported.

Honduras, part of the ancient Mayan and Inca Empires, was claimed for Spain by Columbus in 1502, during his last voyage to the Americas. The first settlement was made by Cristobal de Olid under orders of Hernan Cortes, then in Mexico. The area, regarded as one of the most promising sources of gold and silver in the new world, was a part of the Captaincy General of Guatemala throughout the colonial period. After declaring its independence from Spain in 1821, Honduras fell briefly to the Mexican empire of Agustin de Iturbide, and then joined the Central American Federation (1823-39). Upon dissolution of the federation, Honduras became an independent republic.

RULERS
Spanish, until 1821
Agustin Iturbide (Emperor of Mexico), 1822-1823

MINT MARKS
A - Paris, 1869-1871
T - Tegucigalpa, 1825-1862

NOTE: Extensive die varieties exist for coins struck in Honduras with almost endless date and overdate varieties especially in the silver series. Federation style coinage continued to be issued until 1861. (See Central American Republic listings.)

MONETARY SYSTEM
16 Reales = 1 Escudo

COLONIAL COINAGE
8 REALES
SILVER, crude
Obv: Bust of Fernando VII.
Rev: Arms within legends.

KM#	Date	Mintage	Good	VG	Fine	VF
3	1813	—	—	Reported, not confirmed		

EMPIRE OF MEXICO
2 REALES

SILVER
Obv: Iturbide. Rev: Eagle on cactus.

| 6 | 1823 | — | — | — | — | Rare |

PROVISIONAL GOVERNMENT
(1823)
1/2 REAL
SILVER
Obv: T.L./1823. Rev: Similar to KM#10.

| 9 | 1823 | — | — | — | — | Rare |

| 10 | 1823 | — | — | — | — | Rare |

| 7.1 | 1823 | — | 150.00 | 250.00 | 350.00 | — |
| | (18)24 | — | 125.00 | 225.00 | 325.00 | — |

Rev: Plain fields.

| 7.2 | (18)24 | — | 175.00 | 300.00 | 425.00 | — |

HONDURAS 822

REAL

SILVER

KM#	Date	Mintage	Good	VG	Fine	VF
8	(18)23	—	25.00	55.00	85.00	—
	(18)24	—	50.00	100.00	150.00	—

2 REALES

SILVER

| 11 | 1823 | — | — | — | Rare | — |

| 12 | 1823 | — | — | — | Rare | — |

14	1823	—	—	—	Rare	—
15	(1)823	—	—	—	Rare	—
	(1)824	—	—	—	Rare	—

4 REALES

SILVER

| 16.1 | (18)23 | — | 100.00 | 200.00 | 300.00 | 500.00 |
| | (18)24 | — | 100.00 | 200.00 | 300.00 | 500.00 |

Rev: Retrograde 4.

| 16.2 | (18)24 | — | 100.00 | 200.00 | 300.00 | 500.00 |

STATE OF HONDURAS
1/2 REAL
.333 SILVER

17	1832T F	—	9.00	15.00	30.00	65.00
	1833T F	—	11.50	17.50	35.00	75.00
	1837T F	10 pcs.	—	—	—	—

.250 SILVER

| 17a | 1844T F | — | 20.00 | 40.00 | 70.00 | 110.00 |
| | 1845T G | — | 17.50 | 37.50 | 60.00 | 100.00 |

REAL
.333 SILVER

| 18 | 1832T F | — | 4.50 | 10.00 | 20.00 | 32.50 |
| | 1839T F | — | 5.00 | 12.00 | 22.50 | 40.00 |

.200 SILVER

| 18a | 1840T F | — | 5.00 | 12.00 | 22.50 | 40.00 |
| | 1844T G | — | 4.50 | 10.00 | 20.00 | 32.50 |

.172 SILVER

KM#	Date	Mintage	Good	VG	Fine	VF
18b	1845T G	—	5.00	12.00	22.50	40.00
	1846T G	—	7.50	17.50	30.00	45.00
	1849T G	—	4.50	10.00	20.00	32.50

.100 SILVER

| 18c | 1851T G | — | 4.50 | 10.00 | 20.00 | 32.50 |
| | 1852T G | — | 7.50 | 17.50 | 30.00 | 45.00 |

.0400 SILVER

| 18d | 1853T G | — | — | Reported, not confirmed | | |

COPPER

| 18e | 1856T G | — | — | Reported, not confirmed | | |

2 REALES

.333 SILVER

19	1832T F	—	4.00	7.50	15.00	25.00
	1833T F	—	3.00	6.00	10.00	15.00
	1839T F	—	6.00	12.50	22.50	35.00

NOTE: Coins dated 1833 struck in copper, with or without silvering, are very common early counterfeits.

.200 SILVER

19a	1840T F	—	7.50	15.00	30.00	45.00
	1842T G CRESCA	—	6.50	15.00	25.00	40.00
	1842T G CREZCA	—	6.50	15.00	25.00	40.00
	1844T F	—	5.00	12.50	22.50	35.00
	1844T G	—	3.50	8.50	17.50	27.50
	1845T G	—	3.50	7.50	15.00	25.00
	1846T G	—	—	—	Rare	—
	1847T G	—	4.50	10.00	20.00	30.00

.172 SILVER

| 19b | 1848T G | — | 3.50 | 7.50 | 15.00 | 25.00 |

.100 SILVER

| 19c | 1851T G | — | 6.50 | 15.00 | 25.00 | 40.00 |

.0625 SILVER

| 19d | 1852T G | — | 6.50 | 15.00 | 25.00 | 40.00 |

.0400 SILVER

| 19e | 1853T G | — | 3.50 | 8.50 | 17.50 | 27.50 |
| | 1855T G | — | — | Reported, not confirmed | | |

4 REALES

.172 SILVER

| 20 | 1849T G | — | 4.50 | 10.00 | 17.50 | 27.50 |
| | 1850T G | — | 3.50 | 7.00 | 12.50 | 22.50 |

.100 SILVER

| 20a | 1851T G | — | 2.50 | 5.50 | 9.00 | 16.50 |

.0625 SILVER

| 20b | 1852T G | — | 2.50 | 5.50 | 9.00 | 16.50 |

.0400 SILVER

20c	1853T G	—	2.50	5.50	9.00	16.50
	1854T G	—	2.50	5.50	9.00	16.50
	1855T G HOND	2.50	6.00	10.00	18.50	
	1855T G HON	3.00	6.50	12.00	22.50	

COPPER

20d	1855T G HOND	—	—	—	—	—
	1856T G	—	2.50	5.00	9.00	17.50
	1856T F	—	—	—	Rare	—

COPPER-LEAD ALLOY

| 20e | 1857T F | — | — | — | Rare | — |
| | 1857/2T F/G | — | — | — | — | — |

8 REALES

COPPER

KM#	Date	Mintage	Good	VG	Fine	VF
21	1856T G	—	6.50	12.50	25.00	40.00

COPPER-LEAD ALLOY

21a	1857T FL	—	4.50	7.50	12.50	25.00
	1858T FL	—	6.00	12.00	20.00	35.00
	1859T FL	—	8.50	15.00	25.00	42.50
	1861T FL	—	8.50	15.00	25.00	42.50

PROVISIONAL COINAGE

NOTE: The following coins with rosettes instead of dots separating legends are patterns or trial strikes which were struck in England.

PESO

COPPER
Rev: Dots separate legends.

KM#	Date	Mintage	VG	Fine	VF	XF
24	1862T A	—	3.00	7.50	15.00	27.50

2 PESOS

COPPER
Rev: Dots separate legends.

| 25 | 1862T A | — | 3.00 | 7.50 | 17.50 | 37.50 |

4 PESOS

COPPER
Rev: Dots separate legends.

| 26 | 1862T A | — | 4.50 | 12.50 | 30.00 | 60.00 |

8 PESOS

COPPER
Rev: Dots separate legends; curved base 2 in date.

KM#	Date	Mintage	VG	Fine	VF	XF
27	1862T A	—	9.00	25.00	45.00	90.00

REPUBLIC

1/8 REAL

COPPER-NICKEL

KM#	Date	Mintage	Fine	VF	XF	Unc
30	1869A	—	3.50	8.00	12.50	25.00
	1870A	—	3.00	7.00	10.00	17.50

1/4 REAL

COPPER-NICKEL

31	1869A	—	1.25	2.75	7.00	14.00
	1870A	—	2.50	5.50	10.00	20.00

1/2 REAL

COPPER-NICKEL

32	1869A	—	1.25	3.00	7.00	17.50
	1870A	—	10.00	22.50	35.00	60.00
	1871A	—	22.50	45.00	90.00	175.00

REAL

COPPER-NICKEL

33	1869A	—	7.50	18.00	32.50	70.00
	1870A	—	5.00	12.00	17.50	40.00

NOTE: Varieties exist.

PESO SERIES

100 Centavos = 1 Peso

1/2 CENTAVO

BRONZE

KM#	Date	Mintage	VG	Fine	VF	XF
45	1881	—	15.00	27.50	45.00	85.00
	1883	—	15.00	27.50	42.50	80.00
	1885	—	12.50	22.50	30.00	50.00
	1886	—	12.50	22.50	30.00	60.00
	1889	—	15.00	27.50	40.00	70.00
	1891	—	—	—	Rare	—

UN (1) CENTAVO

BRONZE

KM#	Date	Mintage	VG	Fine	VF	XF
40	1878	.346	22.50	55.00	87.50	120.00
	1879	Inc. Ab.	13.50	27.50	47.50	75.00
	1880	Inc. Ab.	12.00	22.50	42.50	65.00

Plain and reeded edges

46	1881	.132	5.00	12.50	22.50	45.00
	1884	.022	2.50	7.00	14.00	30.00
	1885	—	2.00	6.00	12.00	25.00
	1886	—	3.00	7.50	15.00	30.00
	1889/5	—	7.00	15.00	27.50	45.00
	1889	—	7.00	15.00	27.50	45.00
	1890	—	2.50	7.00	14.00	30.00
	1896	.061	5.00	12.50	22.00	40.00
	1898/88	.054	8.00	20.00	35.00	55.00
	1898	Inc. Ab.	5.00	12.50	22.00	40.00
	1899 sm.99	.180	6.00	14.00	25.00	40.00
	1899 lg.99	I.A.	6.00	14.00	25.00	40.00
	1900	.029	5.00	12.50	22.00	40.00
	1901/0	.098	7.00	12.50	22.00	32.50
	1901	Inc. Ab.	7.00	12.50	22.00	32.50
	1902	—	4.00	8.00	15.00	30.00
	1903/2/0	—	7.00	15.00	25.00	45.00
	1903/2/1	—	7.00	15.00	25.00	45.00
	1904	—	5.00	12.50	22.00	40.00
	1907/4	.234	5.00	12.50	22.00	40.00
	1907	Inc. Ab.	5.00	12.50	22.00	40.00

NOTE: Varieties exist.

Obv: KM#46. Rev: Altered KM#49.

59	1890	—	8.00	20.00	35.00	55.00
	1893	—	12.50	25.00	45.00	75.00
	1895	.045	6.00	14.00	25.00	40.00
	1907 large UN	Inc. KM46	1.50	3.50	7.00	14.50
	1907 small UN	Inc. KM46	1.50	3.50	7.00	14.50
	1908	.263	5.00	12.50	22.50	40.00

NOTE: Varieties exist.

Mule. Obv: KM#46. Rev: KM#40.

60	Undated	—	150.00	250.00	375.00	500.00

Obv: KM#49. Rev: Altered KM#49.

61	1890	—	12.00	25.00	45.00	75.00
	1891*	—	2.00	5.00	10.00	22.50
	1892	—	—	—	Rare	—
	1893*	—	2.00	5.00	10.00	22.50
	1895	—	10.00	20.00	35.00	55.00
	1908*	Inc. KM59	5.00	10.00	20.00	30.00

***NOTE:** These dates found with die-cutting error or broken die that reads REPLBLICA.
NOTE: Varieties exist.

Mule. Obv: KM#35. Rev: KM#40.

63	1895	—	200.00	300.00	450.00	600.00

Obv: KM#45. Rev: Altered KM#45.

65	1910	.410	10.00	20.00	32.50	50.00
	1911	.062	6.00	15.00	25.00	40.00

NOTE: Varieties exist.

Obv: KM#48. Rev: Altered KM#45.

KM#	Date	Mintage	VG	Fine	VF	XF
66	1910	Inc. Ab.	10.00	22.50	37.50	60.00
	1610 (error) inverted 9	Inc. Ab.	20.00	40.00	65.00	90.00
	1910 (error) second 1 inverted	Inc. Ab.	15.00	25.00	40.00	65.00
	1911	Inc. Ab.	—	—	Rare	—

Obv: KM#48. Rev: Altered KM#48.

67	1910	Inc. Ab.	4.00	8.00	15.00	25.00
	1911	Inc. Ab.	—	Reported, not confirmed		

Obv: KM#45. Rev: Altered KM#48.

68	1910	Inc. Ab.	20.00	40.00	65.00	90.00

Similar to KM#65, CENTAVO omitted.

70	1919	.168	1.50	3.50	6.00	12.50
	1920	.030	2.50	5.00	9.50	17.50

2 CENTAVOS

BRONZE
Rev: Altered KM#49.

64	1907	Inc. Be.	—	—	Rare	—
	1908	Inc. Be.	30.00	55.00	90.00	150.00

Obv: KM#46. Rev: Altered KM#46.

69	1910	.435	1.00	2.50	4.50	7.50
	1911	.068	2.25	5.00	8.00	12.50
	1912 CENTAVOS	.088	1.00	2.50	4.00	7.00
	1912 CENTAVO	Inc. Ab.	2.00	3.75	7.00	12.00
	1913	.258	1.00	2.50	4.50	9.00

NOTE: Reverse dies often very crudely recut, especially 1910 and 1911. Some coins of 1910 are struck over earlier 1 or 2 Centavos, probably 1907 or 1908.

Rev: CENTAVOS omitted.

71	1919	.117	1.50	3.00	5.00	9.00
	1920	.283	.75	1.25	2.75	5.00
	1920 dot	I.A.	.75	1.50	3.00	5.00

NOTE: Varieties exist.

5 CENTAVOS

1.2500 g, .835 SILVER, .0336 oz ASW
Obv: Arms. Rev: Tree.

34	1871	2,056	200.00	325.00	475.00	950.00
	1871	—	—	—	Proof	—

NOTE: The above coin reads "0.900" but is actually 0.835 fine.

Obv: Eagle. Rev: Standing Liberty.

43	1879	—	—	—	Rare	—

HONDURAS 824

KM#	Date	Mintage	VG	Fine	VF	XF
48	1883	—	—	Reported, not confirmed		
	1884	—	10.00	22.50	37.50	65.00
	1885	—	12.50	25.00	40.00	75.00
	1886	—	12.50	25.00	40.00	75.00
	1890	—	—	Reported, not confirmed		
	1902	—	27.50	70.00	100.00	150.00

54	1886	—	5.00	12.00	18.00	35.00
	6188 (error)					
	2 known	—	—	Rare	—	
	1895	—	—	—	Rare	—
	1896/85	.035	3.75	9.00	18.00	25.00
	1896/86 I.A.	3.75	9.00	18.00	25.00	
	1896 Inc. Ab.	3.75	9.00	18.00	25.00	

NOTE: Varieties exist.

10 CENTAVOS

2.5000 g, .835 SILVER, .0671 oz ASW

| 35 | 1871 | .017 | 12.00 | 25.00 | 45.00 | 85.00 |

NOTE: The above coin reads "0.900" but is actually 0.835 fine.

Obv: Eagle. Rev: Standing Liberty.

41	1878	—	—	—	Rare	—
	1879	—	—	—	Rare	—

49	1883	—	—	Reported, not confirmed		
	1884	—	7.50	22.50	35.00	60.00
	1885	—	6.00	17.50	27.50	50.00
	1886	—	7.50	22.50	35.00	60.00
	1889	—	27.50	60.00	100.00	155.00
	1891	—	—	Reported, not confirmed		
	1893*	—	7.50	22.50	37.50	65.00
	1895*	.053	6.00	18.50	32.50	55.00
	1900*	5.300	32.50	75.00	115.00	180.00

*NOTE: These dates found with die-cutting error or broken die that reads REPLBLICA.

Mule. Obv: KM#41. Rev: KM#49.

| 42 | 1878 | — | — | — | — | — |

Mule. Obv: KM#35. Rev: KM#49. P on reverse.

55.1	1886	—	22.50	37.50	70.00	—
	1895	—	18.00	30.00	55.00	—

1-P replaces date.

| 55.2 | ND | — | 35.00 | 70.00 | 115.00 | — |

Rev: Without P.

| 55.3 | 1895 lg. dt. | | | | | |
| | 1895 sm. dt. | | | | | |

25 CENTAVOS

6.2500 g, .900 SILVER, .1808 oz ASW

| 36 | 1871 | .177 | 2.75 | 6.75 | 15.00 | 37.50 |

KM#	Date	Mintage	VG	Fine	VF	XF
50	1883	—	2.75	6.75	11.00	23.50
	1884	—	2.00	5.00	9.00	20.00
	1885/4	—				
	1885	—	2.25	6.00	10.00	22.50
	1886/1	—	2.75	6.75	11.00	23.50
	1887	—	—	Reported, not confirmed		
	1888/7	—	5.00	12.00	22.50	42.50
	1888	—	2.25	5.00	10.00	22.50
	1890/85	—	3.50	7.50	15.00	27.50
	1890/88	—	3.50	7.50	15.00	27.50
	1890/89	—	3.50	7.50	15.00	27.50
	1891/181	—	3.50	7.50	15.00	27.50
	1891/81	—	3.50	7.50	15.00	27.50
	1891	—	3.00	6.75	12.50	25.00
	1892/81	—	—	—	—	—
	1892/1	—	2.25	5.00	10.00	20.00
	1893/83	—	2.75	6.00	11.00	22.50
	1893/88	—	2.75	6.00	11.00	22.50
	1895/83	.012	3.50	7.50	15.00	27.50
	1895 Inc. Ab.	2.25	5.00	10.00	20.00	
	1896	.274	3.50	7.00	12.50	22.50
	1898	.190	—	Reported, not confirmed		

NOTE: Varieties exist.

6.2500 g, .835 SILVER, .1678 oz ASW

50a	1899/88	.030	5.00	11.00	17.50	30.00
	1899 I.A.	5.00	11.00	17.50	30.00	
	1900/800	.039	2.25	5.00	11.00	22.50
	1900/891 I.A.	2.25	5.00	11.00	22.50	
	1900 Inc. Ab.	2.25	5.00	11.00	22.50	
	1901	.054	2.25	5.00	10.00	20.00
	1902/812	—				
	1902/891	—	3.00	6.00	11.00	22.50
	1902/1F	—	2.25	5.00	10.00	20.00
	1902F	—	3.75	7.50	15.00	27.50
	1904	—	11.00	22.50	37.50	67.50
	1907/4	.014	3.50	7.00	12.50	25.00
	1907 Inc. Ab.	6.00	12.00	22.50	37.50	
	1910	745 pcs.	—	Reported, not confirmed		
	1912	7,168	10.00	17.50	35.00	60.00
	1913	.052	5.00	10.00	17.50	32.50

NOTE: Varieties exist.

50 CENTAVOS

12.5000 g, .900 SILVER, .3617 oz ASW

| 37 | 1871 | .040 | 4.50 | 11.50 | 18.50 | 45.00 |

| 44 | 1879 | — | — | — | Rare | — |

51	1883	—	5.00	10.00	22.50	45.00
	1883P	—	8.00	15.00	27.50	55.00
	1884	—	5.00	10.00	20.00	40.00
	1885	—	5.00	10.00	22.50	45.00
	1886	—	5.50	12.50	27.50	55.00
	1887/5	—	7.00	16.00	30.00	60.00
	1887	—	7.00	16.00	30.00	60.00
	1896/86	—	50.00	100.00	185.00	—
	1897	.037	37.50	67.50	110.00	—
	1910	602 pcs.	—	—	Rare	—

12.5000 g, .835 SILVER, .3355 oz ASW

51a	1908/897	447 pcs.	45.00	90.00	150.00	225.00
	1908 Inc. Ab.	45.00	90.00	150.00	225.00	
	1911	90 pcs.	—	Reported, not confirmed		

PESO

1.6120 g, .900 GOLD, .0467 oz AGW

KM#	Date	Mintage	Fine	VF	XF	Unc
38	1871	—	325.00	550.00	825.00	1700.

Mule. Obv: KM#38. Rev: KM#56.

| 39 | 1871 | — | — | — | Rare | — |

25.0000 g, .900 SILVER, .7234 oz ASW
Rev: Small CENTRO-AMERICA.

KM#	Date	Mintage	VG	Fine	VF	XF
47	1881	.026	15.00	32.50	55.00	120.00
	1882	.076	15.00	27.50	45.00	100.00
	1883	—	15.00	30.00	50.00	110.00

Rev: Large CENTRO-AMERICA.

52	1883/1	—	75.00	175.00	300.00	475.00
	1884	—	12.50	27.50	45.00	85.00
	1885	—	12.50	25.00	40.00	75.00
	1886	—	12.50	27.50	45.00	85.00
	1887	—	12.50	27.50	45.00	85.00
	1888	—	12.50	25.00	40.00	75.00
	1889/8	—	12.50	25.00	40.00	75.00
	1889	—	12.50	25.00	40.00	75.00
	1890	—	12.50	25.00	40.00	75.00
	1891/88	—	12.50	25.00	40.00	75.00
	1891/89	—	12.50	25.00	40.00	75.00
	1892/0	—	12.50	25.00	40.00	75.00
	1892/1	—	12.50	25.00	40.00	75.00
	1893/1	—	125.00	250.00	375.00	600.00
	1895/0	—	15.00	30.00	60.00	110.00
	1895	—	15.00	30.00	60.00	110.00
	1899/87P	400.00	800.00	1500.	—	
	1902	—	17.50	40.00	70.00	120.00

KM#	Date	Mintage	VG	Fine	VF	XF
52	1903 flat top 3					
		—	17.50	35.00	60.00	100.00
	1903 round top 3					
		—	22.50	45.00	85.00	150.00
	1904	—	22.50	45.00	85.00	150.00
	1914	—	175.00	350.00	700.00	1250.

NOTE: Overdates and recut dies are prevalent.

Mule. Obv: KM#47, w/o 25 GMOS above UN PESO. Rev: KM#52.

62	1894/82	—	15.00	30.00	50.00	100.00
	1894/2 closed 4	—	20.00	37.50	60.00	125.00
	1894/2 open 4	—	20.00	37.50	60.00	125.00
	1895/85	—	15.00	30.00	50.00	100.00
	1895/3	—	15.00	30.00	50.00	100.00
	1895/4	—	15.00	30.00	50.00	100.00
	1896/4	—	25.00	55.00	90.00	—

1.6120 g, .900 GOLD, .0467 oz AGW

KM#	Date	Mintage	Fine	VF	XF	Unc
56	1887	—	—	Reported, not confirmed		
	1888	—	175.00	300.00	450.00	650.00
	1889	—	—	Reported, not confirmed		
	1890	—	—	Reported, not confirmed		
	1895	43 pcs.	175.00	300.00	450.00	650.00
	1896	—	175.00	300.00	450.00	650.00
	1899	—	—	Reported, not confirmed		
	1901	—	275.00	450.00	650.00	900.00
	1902	—	225.00	375.00	550.00	800.00
	1907	—	175.00	300.00	500.00	750.00
	1912	350 pcs.	—	Reported, not confirmed		
	1913	6,000	—	Reported, not confirmed		
	1914/882	—	275.00	450.00	600.00	900.00
	1914/03	—	275.00	450.00	600.00	900.00
	1919	—	225.00	375.00	550.00	800.00
	1920	—	225.00	375.00	550.00	800.00
	1922	—	175.00	300.00	450.00	650.00
	ND					

5 PESOS

8.0645 g, .900 GOLD, .2333 oz AGW

53	1883	—	450.00	650.00	1000.	1500.
	1888/3	—	450.00	650.00	1000.	1500.
	1889	—	—	Reported, not confirmed		
	1890	—	600.00	750.00	1100.	1750.
	1895	20 pcs.	450.00	650.00	1000.	1500.
	1896	55 pcs.	600.00	900.00	1350.	2000.
	1897	—	450.00	650.00	1000.	1500.
	1900	—	450.00	650.00	1000.	1500.
	1902	—	450.00	650.00	1000.	1500.
	1908/888	—	450.00	650.00	1000.	1500.
	1913	1,200	450.00	650.00	1000.	1500.

10 PESOS

16.1290 g, .900 GOLD, .4667 oz AGW

58	1889	—	5000.	6000.	7500.	10,000.
	1895	10 pcs.	—	Reported, not confirmed		

20 PESOS

32.2580 g, .900 GOLD, .9335 oz AGW

KM#	Date	Mintage	Fine	VF	XF	Unc
57	1888	—	3500.	4500.	5500.	7500.
	1895	—	—	—	Rare	
	1908/888	—	3500.	4500.	5500.	7500.
	1908/897	—	—	—	Rare*	
	1908	—	3500.	4500.	5500.	7500.

*NOTE: Stack's Hammel sale 9-82 VF realized $12,000.

MONETARY REFORM
100 Centavos = 1 Lempira
CENTAVO

BRONZE, thick planchet, 2.00 g

77.1	1935	2.000	.25	.75	2.00	7.50
	1939	2.000	.25	.50	1.50	6.00
	1949	4.000	.10	.30	.75	2.50

Thin planchet, 1.50 g

77.2	1954	3.500	.10	.15	.25	1.00
	1956	2.000	.10	.15	.25	.50
	1957/6	28.000	—	—	—	—
	1957	Inc. Ab.	—	.10	.15	.35

BRONZE-CLAD STEEL

77a	1974	—	—	.10	.15	.25
	1985	—	—	.10	.15	.25

2 CENTAVOS

BRONZE

78	1939	2.000	.25	.50	1.50	6.00
	1949	3.000	.10	.25	1.00	4.00
	1954	2.000	.10	.25	1.00	3.00
	1956	20.000	—	.10	.15	.50

BRONZE-CLAD STEEL

| 78a | 1974 | — | — | .10 | .15 | .25 |

5 CENTAVOS

COPPER-NICKEL
Dentilated border.

72.1	1931	2.000	.50	1.50	2.50	10.00
	1932	1.000	.35	.75	1.50	6.00
	1949	2.000	.20	.50	1.00	4.00
	1954	1.400	.15	.25	.60	4.00
	1956	10.070	—	.10	.15	.50
	1972	5.000	—	.10	.15	.25
	1980	20.000	—	.10	.15	.25
	1981	20.000	—	.10	.15	.25

BRASS

| 72.1a | 1975 | 20.000 | — | .10 | .15 | .25 |

COPPER-NICKEL
Beaded border.

| 72.2 | 1980 | Inc. Ab. | — | .10 | .15 | .25 |

10 CENTAVOS

COPPER-NICKEL
Dentilated border.

76.1	1932	1.500	.75	1.50	4.00	12.50
	1951	1.000	.25	.75	1.50	4.00
	1954	1.200	.10	.20	.35	1.00
	1956	7.560	.10	.15	.25	.75

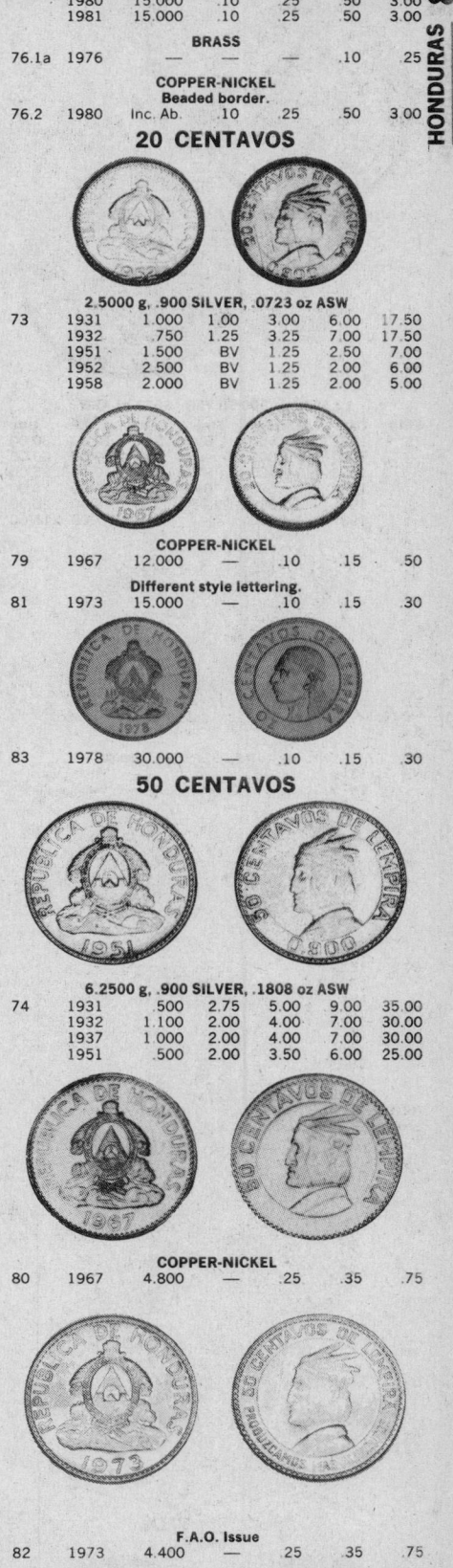

HONDURAS 826

LEMPIRA

12.5000 g, .900 SILVER, .3617 oz ASW

KM#	Date	Mintage	Fine	VF	XF	Unc
75	1931	.550	BV	5.00	10.00	30.00
	1932	1.000	—	BV	9.00	20.00
	1933	.400	BV	5.00	10.00	25.00
	1934	.600	BV	4.50	9.00	20.00
	1935	1.000	—	BV	8.00	20.00
	1937	4.000	—	BV	7.00	15.00

HONG KONG

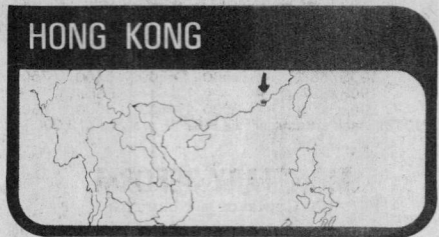

The colony of Hong Kong, a British colony situated at the mouth of the Canton or Pearl River 90 miles (145 km.) southeast of Canton, has an area of 403 sq. mi. (1,045 sq. km.) and a population of *5.6 million. Capital: Victoria. The free port of Hong Kong, the commercial center of the Far East, is a trans-shipment point for goods destined for China and the countries of the Western Pacific. Light manufacturing and tourism are important components of the economy.

Long a haven for fishermen-pirates and opium smugglers, the island of Hong Kong was ceded to Britain at the conclusion of the first Opium War, 1839-1842. At the time, the acquisition of a 'barren rock' was ridiculed by both London and English merchants operating in the Far East. The Kowloon Peninsula and Stonecutter's Island were ceded in 1860, and the so-called New Territories, comprising most of the mainland of the colony, were leased to Britain for 99 years in 1898.

The legends on Hong Kong coinage are bilingual: English and Chinese. The rare 1941 cent was dispatched to Hong Kong in several shipments. One fell into Japanese hands while another was melted down by the British and a third was sunk during enemy action.

RULERS
British

MINT MARKS
H - Heaton
KN - King's Norton

MONETARY SYSTEM
10 Mils (Wen, Ch'ien) = 1 Cent (Hsien)
10 Cents = 1 Chiao
100 Cents = 10 Chiao = 1 Dollar (Yuan)

MIL

BRONZE
Obv: Chinese value: 1 Wen.

KM#	Date	Mintage	Fine	VF	XF	Unc
1	1863	19.000	1.00	2.00	3.00	12.50
	1863	—	—	—	Proof	250.00
	1864	—	500.00	600.00	800.00	1600.
	1864	—	—	—	Proof	—
	1865	40.000	—	—	1000.	1500.

Rev: W/o Hyphen between HONG KONG.

| 2 | 1865 | Inc. Ab. | 1.00 | 2.00 | 3.50 | 15.00 |

GILT BRONZE (OMS)

| 1a | 1863 | — | — | — | Proof | 200.00 |

SILVER (OMS)

| 1b | 1863 | — | — | — | Proof | 400.00 |

BRONZE
Obv: Chinese value: 1 Ch'ien.

| 3 | 1866 | 20.000 | 1.00 | 2.00 | 4.00 | 15.00 |

CENT

BRONZE
Obv: 14 pearls in left arch of crown.

4.1	1863	1.000	1.00	2.50	6.00	32.50
	1863	—	—	—	Proof	270.00
	1863 dot on reverse	—	—	—	Proof	350.00
	1865/3	1.000	1.00	5.00	12.00	40.00
	1865	Inc. Ab.	1.00	2.50	6.00	30.00
	1865	—	—	—	Proof	270.00
	1866	1.000	1.00	2.50	6.00	30.00
	1866	—	—	—	Proof	275.00
	1875	1.000	1.00	2.50	6.00	30.00
	1875	—	—	—	Proof	275.00

KM#	Date	Mintage	Fine	VF	XF	Unc
4.1	1876	1.000	1.00	2.50	6.00	30.00
	1876	—	—	—	Proof	275.00
	1877	2.000	1.50	3.00	7.50	35.00
	1877	—	—	—	Proof	275.00

Obv: 15 pearls in left arch of crown.

4.2	1877	2.000	1.00	2.50	6.00	30.00
	1877	—	—	—	Proof	275.00
	1879	Inc. Be.	1.00	2.50	6.00	30.00
	1879	—	—	—	Proof	275.00

NICKEL (OMS)

| 4.2a | 1877 | — | — | — | Proof | 500.00 |

BRONZE
Obv: 5 pearls in center of crown.

4.3	1879	1.000	1.50	4.00	12.00	45.00
	1879	—	—	—	Proof	275.00
	1880	1.000	1.00	2.50	10.00	40.00
	1880	—	—	—	Proof	275.00
	1881	1.000	1.00	2.50	10.00	40.00
	1881	—	—	—	Proof	250.00
	1899	1.000	1.00	2.00	6.00	30.00
	1899	—	—	—	Proof	200.00
	1900H	1.000	1.00	1.50	4.00	20.00
	1900H	—	—	—	Proof	200.00
	1901	5.000	.50	1.00	3.00	17.50
	1901H	10.000	.50	1.00	2.25	12.50

11	1902	5.000	.75	1.25	2.50	20.00
	1903	5.000	.75	1.25	2.50	20.00
	1904H	10.000	.75	1.25	2.50	17.50
	1905	2.500	1.00	1.50	3.00	25.00
	1905H	12.500	.75	1.25	2.50	15.00

16	1919H	2.500	.50	1.00	2.00	10.00
	1923	2.500	.50	1.00	2.00	12.00
	1924	5.000	.50	1.00	2.00	7.50
	1925	2.500	.50	1.00	2.00	9.00
	1926	2.500	.50	1.00	2.00	9.00
	1926	—	—	—	Proof	140.00

17	1931	5.000	.20	.35	.75	2.00
	1931	—	—	—	Proof	90.00
	1933	6.500	.20	.35	.75	2.00
	1933	—	—	—	Proof	90.00
	1934	5.000	.20	.35	.75	2.00
	1934	—	—	—	Proof	90.00

| 24 | 1941 | 5.000 | 400.00 | 1000. | 1500. | 2000. |
| | 1941 | — | — | — | Proof | 4500. |

5 CENTS

1.3577 g, .800 SILVER, .0349 oz ASW

5	1866	1.313	1.50	3.00	6.00	45.00
	1866 milled edge	—	—	—	Proof	250.00
	1866 plain edge	—	—	—	Proof	275.00
	1867	Inc. Ab.	1.50	3.00	6.00	45.00
	1867	—	—	—	Proof	250.00
	1868	Inc. Ab.	1.50	3.00	6.00	35.00
	1872/68H	.136	1.50	3.00	12.00	60.00

KM#	Date	Mintage	Fine	VF	XF	Unc
5	1872H Arabic 1		1.50	3.00	10.00	45.00
	Inc. Ab.		1.50	3.00	10.00	45.00
	1872H Roman I					
	Inc. Ab.		2.25	6.00	12.50	60.00
	1873/63	.387	1.50	4.50	10.00	45.00
	1873/63H	.256	1.00	2.25	4.00	30.00
	1873H round top 3					
	Inc. Ab.		1.50	4.50	12.50	50.00
	1873 flat top 3					
	Inc. Ab.		1.50	4.50	12.50	50.00
	1873		—	—	Proof	250.00
	1873 plain edge	—	—	—	Proof	600.00
	1874H	.280	2.00	6.00	15.00	60.00
	1875H	.280	1.50	3.75	10.00	50.00
	1875H	—	—	—	Proof	275.00
	1876H	.480	1.50	3.75	10.00	50.00
	1877H	.240	1.50	3.75	10.00	50.00
	1879	.288	1.50	3.75	10.00	50.00
	1880H	.300	1.50	2.50	7.50	35.00
	1881/71	.300	1.50	3.00	10.00	50.00
	1881	Inc. Ab.	1.50	2.50	10.00	35.00
	1881	—	—	—	Proof	275.00
	1882H	.600	1.50	2.50	7.50	35.00
	1883	.550	1.50	2.50	7.50	40.00
	1883	—	—	—	Proof	275.00
	1883H	.250	3.50	7.50	18.00	50.00
	1883H	—	—	—	Proof	250.00
	1884	.960	1.50	3.00	6.00	25.00
	1884	—	—	—	Proof	250.00
	1885	3.120	.75	1.75	5.00	20.00
	1885	—	—	—	Proof	400.00
	1886	2.100	.75	1.75	5.00	20.00
	1887	2.448	.75	1.75	5.00	20.00
	1888/78	5.952	.50	1.50	4.00	18.00
	1888	Inc. Ab.	.50	1.00	2.50	20.00
	1889	5.169	.50	1.00	2.50	20.00
	1889	—	—	—	Proof	—
	1889H	2.100	.50	1.00	2.50	20.00
	1890	1.500	.50	1.00	2.50	20.00
	1890	—	—	—	Proof	250.00
	1890H	5.400	.50	1.00	2.50	18.00
	1891	6.900	.50	1.00	2.50	18.00
	1891H	2.100	.50	1.00	2.50	18.00
	1892	4.200	.50	1.00	2.50	18.00
	1892H	1.200	.50	1.00	2.50	20.00
	1892H	—	—	—	Proof	300.00
	1893	3.000	.50	1.00	2.25	15.00
	1894	4.600	.50	1.00	2.25	15.00
	1894	—	—	—	Proof	275.00
	1895	4.000	.50	1.00	2.25	12.00
	1897	4.000	.50	1.00	2.25	12.00
	1898	3.500	.50	1.00	2.25	12.00
	1899	9.377	.50	1.00	2.25	8.00
	1900	1.623	.50	1.00	2.25	10.00
	1900H	7.000	.50	1.00	2.25	8.00
	1901	10.000	.50	.75	1.50	6.00

COPPER (OMS)

KM#	Date	Mintage	Fine	VF	XF	Unc
5a	1866	—	—	—	Proof	400.00

1.3577 g, .800 SILVER, .0349 oz ASW

KM#	Date	Mintage	Fine	VF	XF	Unc
12	1903	6.000	.50	1.00	2.00	6.00
	1903	—	—	—	Proof	200.00
	1904	8.000	.50	1.00	2.00	6.00
	1904	—	—	—	Proof	175.00
	1905	1.000	.50	1.00	2.00	4.50
	1905H	7.000	.50	1.00	2.00	4.00

KM#	Date	Mintage	Fine	VF	XF	Unc
18	1932	3.000	.40	.60	1.75	3.00
	1932	—	—	—	Proof	150.00
	1933	2.000	.40	.60	1.75	3.00
	1933	—	—	—	Proof	150.00

COPPER-NICKEL

KM#	Date	Mintage	Fine	VF	XF	Unc
18a	1935	1.000	.75	1.50	2.00	5.00
	1935	—	—	—	Proof	100.00

NICKEL

KM#	Date	Mintage	Fine	VF	XF	Unc
20	1937	3.000	.50	1.00	1.50	3.00
	1937	—	—	—	Proof	60.00

KM#	Date	Mintage	Fine	VF	XF	Unc
22	1938	3.000	.20	.35	.85	2.00
	1938	—	—	—	Proof	125.00
	1939H	3.090	.20	.35	.85	2.00
	1939H	—	—	—	Proof	125.00
	1939KN	4.710	.20	.35	.65	2.00
	1941H	.777	150.00	200.00	275.00	400.00
	1941KN	1.075	75.00	100.00	150.00	300.00

NICKEL-BRASS

KM#	Date	Mintage	Fine	VF	XF	Unc
26	1949	15.000	.10	.15	.25	2.00
	1949	—	—	—	Proof	125.00
	1950	20.400	.10	.15	.25	2.00
	1950	—	—	—	Proof	—

Reeded, security edges.

KM#	Date	Mintage	Fine	VF	XF	Unc
29.1	1958H	5.000	—	.10	.15	.20
	1960	5.000	—	.10	.15	.20
	1960	—	—	—	Proof	40.00
	1963	7.000	—	.10	.15	.20
	1963	—	—	—	Proof	40.00
	1964H	—	1.50	4.00	8.00	25.00
	1965H	6.000	—	—	.10	.20
	1967	10.000	—	—	.10	.20
	1968	15.000	—	—	.10	.20

Error: Reeded, w/o security edge.

KM#	Date	Mintage	Fine	VF	XF	Unc
29.2	1958	Inc. Ab.	1.50	3.50	6.50	15.00
	1960	Inc. Ab.	1.50	3.50	6.50	15.00

Reeded edges

KM#	Date	Mintage	Fine	VF	XF	Unc
32	1971KN	14.000	—	—	.10	.15
	1971H	6.000	—	—	.10	.15
	1972H	14.000	—	—	.10	.15
	1977	6.000	—	—	.10	.15
	1978	10.000	—	—	.10	.15
	1979	4.000	—	—	.10	.15

Obv: Queen's portrait. Rev: Legend around inscription.

KM#	Date	Mintage	Fine	VF	XF	Unc
61	1988	*.050	—	—	.10	.15
	1988	*.025	—	—	Proof	1.00

10 CENTS

2.7154 g, .800 SILVER, .0698 oz ASW

KM#	Date	Mintage	Fine	VF	XF	Unc
6.1	1863	.100	3.50	8.00	15.00	60.00
	1863 reeded edge	—	—	—	Proof	250.00
	1863 plain edge	—	—	—	Proof	275.00
	1864	.200	200.00	275.00	400.00	800.00
	1864	—	—	—	Proof	1000.
	1865	.550	3.50	8.00	15.00	60.00
	1865	—	—	—	Proof	200.00

Obv: 10 pearls on right arch of crown.

KM#	Date	Mintage	Fine	VF	XF	Unc
6.2	1866	.300	1.50	3.00	10.00	45.00
	1866	—	—	—	Proof	200.00

Obv: 11 pearls on right arch of crown.

KM#	Date	Mintage	Fine	VF	XF	Unc
6.3	1866	2.479	1.50	3.00	10.00	40.00
	1867	Inc. Ab.	1.50	3.00	12.00	50.00
	1867	—	—	—	Proof	250.00
	1868	Inc. Ab.	1.50	3.00	10.00	40.00
	1869	—	—	—	Proof	450.00
	1872H	.088	8.00	20.00	40.00	225.00
	1872H	—	—	—	Proof	350.00
	1873 round top 3					
		.197	1.50	3.00	10.00	40.00
	1873	—	—	—	Proof	300.00
	1873 plain edge	—	—	—	Proof	800.00
	1873H flat top 3					
		.128	2.50	4.50	12.50	50.00
	1874H	.200	1.50	3.00	10.00	45.00
	1875H	.200	1.50	3.00	10.00	50.00
	1875H	—	—	—	Proof	300.00
	1876H	.480	1.50	3.00	10.00	50.00
	1877H	.240	1.50	3.00	10.00	50.00
	1877H	—	—	—	Proof	350.00
	1879	.288	1.50	3.00	10.00	50.00
	1879	—	—	—	Proof	300.00
	1880H	.300	1.50	3.00	10.00	50.00
	1880H	—	—	—	Proof	300.00
	1881	.300	1.50	3.00	10.00	50.00
	1881	—	—	—	Proof	300.00
	1882H	.500	1.50	3.00	10.00	50.00
	1882H	—	—	—	Proof	400.00
	1883 flat top 3					

KM#	Date	Mintage	Fine	VF	XF	Unc
6.3	1883	.550	1.50	3.00	10.00	40.00
	1883	—	—	—	Proof	300.00
	1883H round top 3					
		.250	3.00	6.00	15.00	65.00
	1883H	—	—	—	Proof	300.00
	1884	.960	1.25	2.50	4.00	25.00
	1884	—	—	—	Proof	250.00
	1885	3.120	.75	1.50	3.00	20.00
	1885	—	—	—	Proof	700.00
	1886	2.100	.75	1.50	3.00	20.00
	1886	—	—	—	Proof	200.00
	1887	2.441	.75	1.50	3.00	20.00
	1888	7.027	.75	1.50	3.00	20.00
	1888	—	—	—	Proof	200.00
	1889	4.027	.75	1.50	3.00	20.00
	1889	—	—	—	Proof	200.00
	1889H	2.100	.75	1.50	3.00	20.00
	1890	1.500	.75	2.00	4.00	35.00
	1890	—	—	—	Proof	250.00
	1890H	5.400	.75	1.50	3.00	20.00
	1891	6.150	.75	1.50	3.00	20.00
	1891H	1.750	.75	1.50	3.00	35.00
	1892	5.500	.75	1.50	3.00	20.00
	1892	—	—	—	Proof	200.00
	1892H	1.100	1.25	2.50	5.00	40.00
	1892H	—	—	—	Proof	200.00
	1893	11.250	.75	1.50	3.00	20.00
	1894	16.750	.75	1.50	3.00	20.00
	1894	—	—	—	Proof	225.00
	1895	19.000	.75	1.50	3.00	20.00
	1896	16.500	.75	1.50	3.00	20.00
	1897	23.500	.75	1.50	3.00	18.00
	1897H	10.500	.75	1.50	3.00	18.00
	1897H	—	—	—	Proof	400.00
	1898	29.500	.75	1.50	3.00	18.00
	1899	33.842	.75	1.50	3.00	18.00
	1900	7.758	.75	1.50	3.00	18.00
	1900H	41.500	.75	1.50	3.00	18.00
	1901	25.000	.75	1.50	3.00	18.00

COPPER (OMS)

KM#	Date	Mintage	Fine	VF	XF	Unc
6.1a	1863	—	—	—	Proof	150.00
	1866	—	—	—	Proof	150.00
	1869	—	—	—	Proof	150.00
	1873	—	—	—	Proof	150.00

2.7154 g, .800 SILVER, .0698 oz ASW

KM#	Date	Mintage	Fine	VF	XF	Unc
13	1902	18.000	.75	1.50	3.00	12.50
	1902	—	—	—	Proof	150.00
	1903	25.000	.75	1.50	3.00	12.50
	1903	—	—	—	Proof	150.00
	1904	30.000	.75	1.50	3.00	12.50
	1904	—	—	—	Proof	150.00
	1905	33.487	300.00	400.00	500.00	700.00
	1905	—	—	—	Proof	1100.

COPPER-NICKEL

KM#	Date	Mintage	Fine	VF	XF	Unc
19	1935	10.000	.25	.50	1.00	2.00
	1935	—	—	—	Proof	60.00
	1936	5.000	.25	.50	1.00	2.00
	1936	—	—	—	Proof	60.00

NICKEL

KM#	Date	Mintage	Fine	VF	XF	Unc
21	1937	17.500	.40	.70	1.00	2.00
	1937	—	—	—	Proof	60.00

KM#	Date	Mintage	Fine	VF	XF	Unc
23	1938	7.500	.20	.40	.60	2.00
	1938	—	—	—	Proof	50.00
	1939H	5.000	.25	.50	.75	2.00
	1939KN	5.000	.15	.30	.50	2.00
	1939KN	—	—	—	Proof	50.00

HONG KONG 828

20 CENTS

1/2 DOLLAR

NICKEL-BRASS
Reeded, security edge.

KM#	Date	Mintage	Fine	VF	XF	Unc
25	1948	30.000	.15	.25	.40	2.00
	1948	—	—	—	Proof	50.00
	1949	35.000	.15	.25	.40	2.00
	1949	—	—	—	Proof	50.00
	1950	20.000	.15	.25	.35	2.00
	1950	—	—	—	Proof	50.00
	1951	5.000	.15	.25	.40	4.00
	1951	—	—	—	Proof	50.00

Error: Reeded, w/o security edge.

| 25a | 1950 | Inc. Ab. | 2.00 | 3.75 | 5.50 | 15.00 |

5.4308 g, .800 SILVER, .1397 oz ASW

KM#	Date	Mintage	Fine	VF	XF	Unc
7	1866	.445	5.00	10.00	25.00	180.00
	1866 reeded edge	—	—	—	Proof	450.00
	1866 plain edge	—	—	—	Proof	475.00
	1867	Inc. Ab.	5.00	10.00	25.00	180.00
	1867	—	—	—	Proof	450.00
	1868	Inc. Ab.	5.00	10.00	25.00	180.00
	1868	—	—	—	Proof	450.00
	1872/68H	.064	6.50	12.00	30.00	225.00
	1872H	Inc. Ab.	5.00	10.00	25.00	180.00
	1872H	—	—	—	Proof	500.00
	1873	.096	5.00	10.00	25.00	180.00
	1873 plain edge	—	—	—	Proof	1200.
	1873H	.064	5.00	10.00	25.00	180.00
	1874H	.070	5.00	10.00	25.00	180.00
	1875H	.070	5.00	10.00	25.00	180.00
	1875H	—	—	—	Proof	450.00
	1876H	.120	5.00	10.00	25.00	180.00
	1877H	.060	5.00	10.00	25.00	200.00
	1879	.020	180.00	300.00	500.00	1200.
	1879	—	—	—	—	2000.
	1880H	.025	50.00	75.00	150.00	400.00
	1881	.030	110.00	150.00	275.00	900.00
	1881	—	—	—	Proof	1200.
	1882H	.100	5.00	10.00	25.00	180.00
	1882H	—	—	—	Proof	550.00
	1883	.138	5.00	10.00	25.00	180.00
	1883	—	—	—	Proof	400.00
	1883H	.063	5.00	10.00	25.00	180.00
	1883H	—	—	—	Proof	400.00
	1884	.080	5.00	10.00	25.00	180.00
	1884	—	—	—	Proof	400.00
	1885	.260	4.00	8.00	15.00	140.00
	1885	—	—	—	Proof	1000.
	1886	.175	4.00	8.00	15.00	175.00
	1887	.200	4.00	8.00	15.00	140.00
	1888	.500	4.00	8.00	15.00	140.00
	1888	—	—	—	Proof	500.00
	1889	.440	4.00	8.00	15.00	140.00
	1889	—	—	—	Proof	500.00
	1889H	.175	4.00	8.00	15.00	180.00
	1890	.125	4.00	8.00	15.00	140.00
	1890H	.450	4.00	8.00	15.00	140.00
	1891	.575	4.00	8.00	15.00	140.00
	1891H	.175	6.00	10.00	18.00	200.00
	1892	.450	4.00	8.00	15.00	125.00
	1892H	.100	6.00	10.00	25.00	250.00
	1893	.750	4.00	8.00	15.00	125.00
	1894	.650	4.00	8.00	15.00	125.00
	1894	—	—	—	Proof	500.00
	1895	.500	4.00	8.00	15.00	125.00
	1896	.250	4.00	8.00	15.00	125.00
	1898	.125	4.00	8.00	15.00	140.00

Reeded, w/security edges.

28.1	1955	10.000	.10	.15	.35	.75
	1955	—	—	—	Proof	40.00
	1956	3.110	.10	.20	.50	2.00
	1956	—	—	—	Proof	40.00
	1956H	4.488	.10	.15	.35	1.00
	1956KN	2.500	.25	.50	2.00	10.00
	1957H	5.250	.10	.15	.30	.90
	1957KN	2.800	.10	.15	.30	1.00
	1958KN	10.000	.10	.15	.25	.70
	1959H	20.000	.10	.15	.20	.25
	1960	12.500	.10	.15	.20	.50
	1960	—	—	—	Proof	40.00
	1960H	10.000	—	.15	.20	.40
	1961	20.000	.10	.15	.20	.25
	1961	—	—	—	Proof	40.00
	1961H	5.000	.10	.15	.20	4.00
	1961KN	5.000	.10	.15	.20	.40
	1962H	—	.10	.15	.20	.40
	1963	27.000	.10	.15	.20	4.00
	1963	—	—	—	Proof	40.00
	1963H	3.000	.20	.30	.50	1.00
	1963KN	Inc. Ab.	.10	.15	.20	.25
	1964	9.000	.10	.15	.20	.25
	1964H	21.000	.10	.15	.20	.25
	1965	40.000	.10	.15	.20	.25
	1965H	8.000	.10	.15	.20	.25
	1965KN	Inc. Ab.	.10	.15	.20	.25
	1967	10.000	.10	.15	.20	.25
	1968H	15.000	.10	.15	.20	.25

Error: Reeded, w/o security edge.

| 28.2 | 1956H | Inc. Ab. | 2.25 | 4.50 | 8.50 | 17.50 |

Reeded edges

33	1971KN	—	.30	.75	2.00	4.00
	1971H	22.000	—	.10	.15	.25
	1972KN	20.000	—	.10	.15	.25
	1973	2.250	.10	.20	.50	1.00
	1974	4.600	—	.10	.15	.25
	1975	44.840	—	.10	.15	.25
	1978	57.500	—	.10	.15	.25
	1979	101.500	—	.10	.15	.25
	1980	24.000	—	.10	.15	.25

14	1902	.250	8.00	12.00	25.00	145.00
	1902	—	—	—	Proof	500.00
	1904	.250	8.00	12.00	25.00	145.00
	1905	.750	400.00	600.00	725.00	1150.
	1905	—	—	—	Proof	1600.

49	1981	200.400	—	.10	.15	.25
	1982	—	—	.10	.15	.25
	1983	110.016	—	.10	.15	.25
	1984	30.016	—	.10	.15	.25

NICKEL-BRASS

36	1975	71.000	—	.10	.15	.25
	1976	42.000	—	.10	.15	.25
	1977	Inc. Ab.	—	.10	.15	.25
	1978	86.000	—	.10	.15	.25
	1979	94.500	—	.10	.15	.25
	1980	65.000	—	.10	.15	.25
	1982	30.000	—	.10	.15	.25
	1983	15.000	—	.10	.15	.25

BRASS
Obv: New portrait.

59	1985	—	—	—	.15	.25
	1988	—	—	—	.15	.25
	1988	—	—	—	Proof	2.00

55	1985	—	—	—	.10	.15
	1986	—	—	—	.10	.15
	1987	—	—	—	.10	.15
	1988	—	—	—	.10	.15
	1988	—	—	—	Proof	1.00

13.478 g, .900 SILVER, .3900 oz ASW

KM#	Date	Mintage	Fine	VF	XF	Unc
8	1866	.059	150.00	250.00	450.00	1250.
	1866 reeded edge	—	—	—	Proof	2250.
	1866 plain edge	—	—	—	Proof	Rare
	1867	Inc. Ab.	225.00	400.00	800.00	2400.
	1867	—	—	—	Proof	3000.
	1868	—	—	—	Proof	3000.

50 CENTS

13.5769 g, .800 SILVER, .3492 oz ASW

9	1890	.050	12.00	20.00	40.00	200.00
	1890	—	—	—	Proof	600.00
	1891	.150	8.00	15.00	30.00	200.00
	1891	—	—	—	Proof	600.00
	1891H	.070	8.00	15.00	30.00	200.00
	1892	.090	8.00	15.00	30.00	200.00
	1892	—	—	—	Proof	600.00
	1892H	.020	15.00	40.00	80.00	300.00
	1892H	—	—	—	Proof	600.00
	1893	.150	8.00	15.00	30.00	200.00
	1894	.130	8.00	15.00	30.00	200.00
	1894	—	—	—	Proof	600.00

15	1902	.100	6.50	12.00	20.00	50.00
	1902	—	—	—	Proof	500.00
	1904	.100	6.50	12.00	20.00	50.00
	1904	—	—	—	Proof	500.00
	1905	.300	5.00	10.00	15.00	35.00
	1905	—	—	—	Proof	500.00

COPPER-NICKEL
Reeded, security edge.

| 27.1 | 1951 | 15.000 | .25 | .50 | 1.00 | 5.00 |
| | 1951 | — | — | — | Proof | 125.00 |

Error: Reeded, w/o security edge.

| 27.2 | 1951 | Inc. Ab. | 2.00 | 4.00 | 8.00 | 20.00 |

Reeded, security edge.

30.1	1958H	4.000	—	.10	.20	.50
	1960	4.000	—	.10	.20	.50
	1960	—	—	—	Proof	—
	1961	6.000	—	.10	.20	.50
	1961	—	—	—	Proof	—
	1963H	10.000	—	.10	.20	.50
	1964	5.000	—	.10	.20	.50
	1965KN	8.000	—	.10	.20	.50

HONG KONG 829

KM#	Date	Mintage	Fine	VF	XF	Unc
30.1	1966	5.000	—	.10	.20	.50
	1967	12.000	—	.10	.20	.50
	1968H	12.000	—	.10	.20	.50
	1970H	4.600	—	.10	.20	.50

Error: Reeded, w/o security edge.

| 30.2 | 1958H | Inc. Ab. | 2.00 | 4.00 | 8.00 | 20.00 |

Reeded edge

34	1971KN	—	—	.10	.20	.40
	1971H	—	.10	.25	.75	2.00
	1972	30.000	—	.10	.20	.40
	1972KN	Inc. Ab.	.10	.25	.75	2.00
	1973	36.800	—	.10	.20	.40
	1974	6.000	—	.10	.20	.40
	1975	8.000	—	.10	.20	.40

NICKEL-BRASS

41	1977	60.001	—	.10	.15	.30
	1978	70.000	—	.10	.15	.30
	1979	60.640	—	.10	.15	.30
	1980	120.000	—	.10	.15	.30

BRASS
Obv: Mature Queen's portrait.
Rev: Legend around inscription.

| 62 | 1988 | *.050 | — | .10 | .15 | .30 |
| | 1988 | *.025 | — | — | Proof | 2.50 |

DOLLAR

26.9568 g, .900 SILVER, .7800 oz ASW

10	1866	2.109	40.00	70.00	100.00	400.00
	1866 reeded edge	—	—	Proof	1000.	
	1866 plain edge	—	—	Proof	2500.	
	1867/6	Inc. Ab.	50.00	75.00	110.00	400.00
	1867	Inc. Ab.	40.00	70.00	100.00	400.00
	1867	—	—	—	Proof	3000.
	1868	Inc. Ab.	40.00	70.00	100.00	400.00

COPPER (OMS)
| 10a | 1866 | — | — | — | Proof | 850.00 |

COPPER-NICKEL
Reeded, security edge.

31.1	1960H	40.000	—	.20	.30	.50
	1960KN	40.000	—	.20	.30	.50
	1970H	15.000	—	.20	.30	.50

NOTE: Mint mark is below "LL" of "DOLLAR".

Error: Reeded, w/o security edge.
| 31.2 | 1960H | Inc. Ab. | 3.00 | 6.00 | 11.50 | 22.50 |

Reeded edge
35	1971H	8.000	—	.20	.35	.75
	1972	20.000	—	.20	.35	.60
	1973	8.125	—	.20	.35	.75
	1974	26.000	—	.20	.35	.60
	1975	22.500	—	.20	.35	.60

KM#	Date	Mintage	Fine	VF	XF	Unc
43	1978	120.000	—	.20	.30	.50
	1979	104.908	—	.20	.30	.50
	1980	100.000	—	.20	.30	.50

Obv: Mature Queen's portrait. Rev: Lion within legend.
63	1987	—	—	.20	.30	.50
	1988	*.050	—	.20	.30	.50
	1988	*.025	—	—	Proof	5.00

2 DOLLARS

COPPER-NICKEL
37	1975	60.000	—	.30	.50	1.00
	1978	.504	—	.30	.60	1.25
	1979	9.032	—	.30	.50	1.00
	1980	30.000	—	.30	.50	1.00
	1981	30.000	—	.30	.50	1.00
	1982	30.000	—	.30	.50	1.00
	1983	7.002	—	.30	.50	1.00
	1984	22.002	—	.30	.50	1.00

Obv: Mature Queen's portrait.
60	1985	—	—	—	.35	.75
	1986	—	—	—	.35	.75
	1987	—	—	—	.35	.75
	1988	*.050	—	—	.35	.75
	1988	*.025	—	—	Proof	7.50

5 DOLLARS

COPPER-NICKEL
39	1976	30.000	—	.75	1.00	1.50
	1978	10.000	—	.75	1.00	1.50
	1979	12.000	—	.75	1.00	1.50

46	1980	40.000	—	.75	1.00	1.50
	1981	20.000	—	.75	1.00	1.50
	1982	10.000	—	.75	1.00	1.50
	1983	4.000	—	.75	1.00	1.50
	1984	4.500	—	.75	1.00	1.50

56	1985	—	—	—	.75	1.25
	1986	—	—	—	.75	1.25
	1987	—	—	—	.75	1.25
	1988	—	—	—	.75	1.25
	1988	—	—	—	Proof	10.00

1000 DOLLARS

15.9700 g, .917 GOLD, .4708 oz AGW
Visit of Queen Elizabeth

KM#	Date	Mintage	Fine	VF	XF	Unc
38	1975	.015	—	—	—	300.00
	1975	5.005	—	—	Proof	2200.

Year of the Dragon
| 40 | 1976 | .020 | — | — | — | 625.00 |
| | 1976 | 6.911 | — | — | Proof | 2100. |

Year of the Snake
| 42 | 1977 | .020 | — | — | — | 375.00 |
| | 1977 | .010 | — | — | Proof | 650.00 |

Year of the Horse
| 44 | 1978 | .020 | — | — | — | 350.00 |
| | 1978 | .010 | — | — | Proof | 675.00 |

Year of the Goat
| 45 | 1979 | .030 | — | — | — | 300.00 |
| | 1979 | .015 | — | — | Proof | 425.00 |

Year of the Monkey
| 47 | 1980 | .031 | — | — | — | 300.00 |
| | 1980 | .018 | — | — | Proof | 400.00 |

HONG KONG 830

Year of the Cockerel

KM#	Date	Mintage	Fine	VF	XF	Unc
48	1981	.033	—	—	—	300.00
	1981	.022	—	—	Proof	400.00

Year of the Dog

50	1982	.033	—	—	—	300.00
	1982	.022	—	—	Proof	425.00

Year of the Pig

51	1983	.033	—	—	—	700.00
	1983	.022	—	—	Proof	1250.

Year of the Rat

52	1984	.020	—	—	—	375.00
	1984	.010	—	—	Proof	550.00

Year of the Ox

53	1985	.030	—	—	—	500.00
	1985	.010	—	—	Proof	775.00

Year of the Tiger

54	1986	.020	—	—	—	500.00
	1986	.010	—	—	Proof	700.00

Royal Visit of Queen Elizabeth II

KM#	Date	Mintage	Fine	VF	XF	Unc
57	1986	.020	—	—	—	300.00
	1986	.012	—	—	Proof	525.00

Year of the Rabbit

58	1987	.020	—	—	—	375.00
	1987	.012	—	—	Proof	550.00

MINT SETS (MS)

KM#	Date	Mintage	Identification	Issue Price	Mkt. Val.
MS1	1988 (7)	—	KM55-56,59-63	13.00	12.50

PROOF SETS (PS)

PS1	1866(5)	—	KM5,6,1,7-8,10	—	3000.
PS2	1873(3)	1 known	KM5,6,3,7	—	4500.
PS3	1885(3)	1 known	KM5,6,3,7	—	3000.
PS4	1988(7)	*25,000	KM55-56,59-63	39.75	30.00

HUNGARY

The Hungarian People's Republic, located in central Europe, has an area of 35,929 sq. mi. (93,030 sq. km.) and a population of *10.6 million. Capital: Budapest. The economy is based on agriculture, bauxite and a rapidly expanding industrial sector. Machinery, chemicals, iron and steel, and fruits and vegetables are exported.

The ancient kingdom of Hungary, founded by the Magyars in the 9th century, achieved its greatest extension in the mid-14th century when its dominions touched the Baltic, Black and Mediterranean seas. After suffering repeated Turkish invasions, Hungary accepted Hapsburg rule to escape Turkish occupation, regaining independence in 1867 with the Emperor of Austria as king of a dual Austro-Hungarian Empire. In World War I, Hungary lost the greater part of its territory and population and underwent a period of drastic political revision. The short-lived republic of 1918 was followed by a chaotic interval of communist rule, 1919, and the restoration of the monarchy in 1920 with Admiral Horthy as regent of a kingdom without a king. Although a German ally in World War II, Hungary was occupied by German troops who imposed a pro-Nazi dictatorship, 1944. Soviet armies drove out the Germans in 1945 and assisted the communist minority in seizing power. A revised constitution published on Aug. 20, 1949, established Hungary as a 'People's Republic' of the Soviet type.

NOTE: Many coins of Hungary through 1948, especially 1925-1945, have been restruck in recent times. These may be identified by a rosette in the vicinity of the mintmark. Restrike mintages for Y#1 to Y#30 are usually about 1000 pieces, later date mintages are not known.

RULERS
Austrian until 1918

MINT MARKS
A, CA, WI - Vienna
B, K, KB - Kremnitz
BP - Budapest
CH - Pressburg
G, GN, NB - Nagybanya
GYF - Karlsburg
HA - Hall
S - Schmollnitz

KREMNITZ MINTMASTER'S INITIALS
D, PD - Paschal Josef V. Damiani
EvM - Edler V. Munzburg
K, SK - Sigmund Klemmer V. Klemmerberg

NAGYBANYA MINTMASTER'S INITIALS
B, IB - Josef Brunner
FL, L - Franz Anton Lochner
IV, V - Josef Vischer

MONETARY SYSTEM
Until 1857
2 Poltura = 3 Krajczar
60 Krajczar = 1 Forint (Gulden)
2 Forint = 1 Convention Thaler
1857-1891
100 Krajczar = 1 Forint
1892-1921
100 Filler = 1 Korona
Commencing 1946
100 Filler = 1 Forint

5/10 KRAJCZAR

COPPER
Mint mark: KB

KM#	Date	Mintage	Fine	VF	XF	Unc
468	1882	2.400	2.50	4.00	5.50	7.50
(Y3)	1882 (restrike)	—	—	Proof	7.00

KRAJCZAR

COPPER
Mint mark: KB

KM#	Date	Mintage	Fine	VF	XF	Unc
441.1	1868	12.530	.50	1.00	2.00	3.50
(Y1.1)	1868	(restrike)	—	—	Proof	7.50
	1869	5.070	.50	1.25	3.00	6.50
	1872	—	.50	1.50	3.00	5.50
	1873	—	35.00	65.00	100.00	150.00

Mint mark: GYF

441.2	1868	—	—	—	Rare	—
(Y1.2)						

Mint mark: KB

458	1878	4.480	12.00	18.00	30.00	45.00
(Y4.1)	1879	10.101	3.00	7.50	12.00	17.50
	1881	12.233	3.00	7.50	12.00	17.50
	1882	19.800	5.00	11.00	17.50	27.50
	1883	8.535	9.00	15.00	27.50	35.00
	1885	26.606	1.25	3.50	7.50	12.00
	1886	17.671	2.00	5.50	9.00	15.00
	1887	11.989	2.50	6.00	12.00	18.00
	1888	10.334	3.50	7.00	12.00	18.00

Mule. Obv: KM#441. Rev: KM#458.

459	1878	—	25.00	35.00	60.00	85.00
(Y4.2)						

478	1891*	16.272	2.50	5.00	8.00	12.50
(Y4a)	1892	5.871	7.00	15.00	22.50	32.50

*NOTE: Variations in thickness of planchet exist.

4 KRAJCZAR

COPPER
Mint mark: KB

442	1868	3.100	3.00	7.50	15.00	25.00
(Y2)	1868	(restrike)	—	—	Proof	15.00

NOTE: Wreath varieties exist.

10 KRAJCZAR

3.8900 g, .500 SILVER, .0625 oz ASW

421	1837	—	100.00	175.00	300.00	475.00
(C60)	1838	—	50.00	90.00	140.00	240.00
	1839	—	4.00	10.00	20.00	35.00
	1840	—	5.00	12.00	24.00	50.00
	1841	—	4.50	10.00	20.00	35.00
	1842	—	4.50	10.00	20.00	35.00
	1843	—	5.00	12.00	24.00	50.00
	1844	—	5.00	9.00	17.50	32.50
	1845	—	5.00	9.00	17.50	32.50
	1846	—	4.00	8.00	15.00	27.00
	1847	—	2.50	4.00	9.00	18.00
	1848	—	2.50	5.00	9.00	18.00

2.0000 g, .500 SILVER, .0321 oz ASW
Mint mark: KB
Obv. leg: ....AP.KIRALYA. Rev. leg: VALTO PENZ.

440	1867	c.1,000	—	—	—	—
(Y6)	1868	—	15.00	35.00	60.00	120.00
	1868	(restrike)	—	—	Proof	20.00

1.6600 g, .400 SILVER, .0213 oz ASW
Rev. leg: MAGYAR KIRALYI VALTO PENZ.

KM#	Date	Mintage	Fine	VF	XF	Unc
443.1	1868	3.250	12.00	25.00	40.00	65.00
(Y7.1)	1868	(restrike)	—	—	Proof	22.50
	1869	12.747	6.00	22.50	40.00	65.00

Mint mark: GYF

443.2	1868	1.012	20.00	40.00	85.00	175.00
(Y7.2)	1869	2.747	12.00	25.00	40.00	70.00

NOTE: Varieties exist.

Mint mark: KB
Obv. leg: AP.KIR. Rev. leg: VALTO PENZ.

451.1	1870	21.933	3.50	7.50	18.00	35.00
(Y10.1)	1870	(restrike)	—	—	Proof	17.50
	1871	(restrike from 1885)	—	Rare	—	—
	1872	1.154	7.50	15.00	30.00	50.00
	1873	1.066	7.50	15.00	30.00	50.00
	1874	1.324	9.00	18.00	35.00	55.00
	1875	.425	18.00	27.50	55.00	80.00
	1876	.518	10.00	27.50	55.00	80.00
	1877	.460	15.00	32.00	58.00	85.00
	1887	.025	80.00	135.00	190.00	275.00
	1888	.358	9.00	18.00	35.00	65.00
	1889	—	—	Reported, not confirmed		

Mint mark: GYF

451.2	1870	3.032	7.50	15.00	30.00	50.00
(Y10.2)	1871	3.383	7.50	15.00	30.00	50.00

Mint mark: KB
Mule. Obv: KM#451.1. Rev: KM#440.

444	1868	(restrike)	—	—	Rare	Proof 20.00
(Y10a)						

20 KRAJCZAR

SILVER
Mint mark: A
Obv: Ribbons on wreath forward across neck.
Rev: Madonna with child.

415.1	1830	—	55.00	110.00	220.00	400.00
(C56)						

Obv: Left ribbon on wreath behind neck

415.2	1830	—	100.00	200.00	350.00	600.00
(C56b)	1831	—	Reported, not confirmed			

Mint mark: B
Obv: Both ribbons on wreath behind neck

415.3	1832	—	40.00	80.00	160.00	325.00
(C56a)	1833	—	12.50	25.00	50.00	100.00
	1834	—	5.00	10.00	20.00	40.00
	1835	—	10.00	20.00	40.00	80.00

6.6800 g, .583 SILVER, .1252 oz ASW
Obv. leg: FERD. I. Rev. leg: S. MARIA...

422	1837	—	4.00	7.50	15.00	35.00
(C61)	1838	—	4.00	7.50	15.00	35.00
	1839	—	3.50	5.00	7.50	20.00
	1840	—	3.50	5.00	7.50	20.00
	1841	—	3.50	5.00	7.50	20.00
	1842	—	4.00	7.50	15.00	30.00
	1843	—	3.50	5.00	7.50	20.00
	1844	—	3.50	5.00	7.50	20.00

HUNGARY 831

KM#	Date	Mintage	Fine	VF	XF	Unc
(C61)	1845	—	3.50	5.00	7.50	20.00
	1846	—	3.50	5.00	7.50	20.00
	1847	—	3.50	5.00	7.50	20.00
	1848	—	3.50	5.00	7.50	20.00

2.6600 g, .500 SILVER, .0427 oz ASW
Mint mark: KB
Obv. leg: ....AP.KIRALYA. Rev. leg: VALTO PENZ.

445.1	1868	—	15.00	40.00	70.00	150.00
(Y8.1)	1868	(restrike)	—	—	Proof	20.00

Mint mark: GYF

445.2	1868	—	35.00	80.00	120.00	170.00
(Y8.2)						

Mint mark: KB
Rev. leg: MAGYAR KIRALYI VALTO PENZ.

446.1	1868	3.224	7.50	17.50	32.50	60.00
(Y9.1)	1868	(restrike)	—	—	Proof	20.00
	1869	9.487	5.00	14.00	24.00	50.00

NOTE: Varieties exist.

Mint mark: GYF

446.2	1868	1.039	9.50	20.00	42.00	80.00
(Y9.2)	1869	2.299	9.00	17.50	35.00	65.00

NOTE: Varieties exist.

Mint mark: KB
Rev. leg: VALTO PENZ.

452.1	1870	4.427	12.50	27.50	65.00	110.00
(Y11.1)	1870	(restrike)	—	—	Proof	20.00
	1871	25 pcs. (restrike from 1855)	Proof	—		
	1872	1.286	27.50	55.00	110.00	160.00

Mint mark: GYF

452.2	1870	7.213	30.00	65.00	110.00	150.00
(Y11.2)						

Mint mark: KB
Mule. Obv: KM#452.1. Rev: KM#445.1.

447	1868	(restrike)	—	—	Rare	Proof 20.00
(Y11a)						

FORINT

12.3457 g, .900 SILVER, .3572 oz ASW
Mint mark: KB

449.1	1868	.570	11.00	17.50	35.00	70.00
(Y12.1)	1868	(restrike)	—	—	Proof	40.00
	1869	.490	10.00	20.00	27.50	45.00
	1869 plain edge					

Mint mark: GYF

449.2	1868	.270	11.00	22.50	30.00	60.00
(Y12.2)	1869	.360	7.50	15.00	30.00	45.00

HUNGARY 832

Mint mark: KB

KM#	Date	Mintage	Fine	VF	XF	Unc
453.1	1870	1.250	15.00	32.50	62.50	110.00
(Y13.1)	1871	2.440	12.00	25.00	45.00	90.00
	1872	3.456	7.00	15.00	30.00	60.00
	1873	2.338	12.00	25.00	50.00	90.00
	1874	2.082	12.00	25.00	50.00	90.00
	1875	2.074	8.00	16.00	32.50	55.00
	1876	4.136	5.00	8.00	12.50	22.50
	1877	2.241	5.00	8.00	12.50	22.50
	1878	5.717	5.00	8.00	12.50	22.50
	1879	25.756	5.00	8.00	12.50	22.50

Mint mark: GYF

453.2	1870	.570	80.00	150.00	225.00	500.00
(Y13.2)	1871	.240	300.00	425.00	625.00	1100.

Mint mark: KB
Obv: Larger head and legends.

465	1880	3.815	5.00	8.00	12.00	22.50
(Y13a)	1881	15.495	4.50	6.00	9.00	15.00

NOTE: Varieties exist.

469	1882	1.897	7.00	12.50	25.00	50.00
(Y14)	1883	7.041	5.00	8.00	12.50	22.50
	1884	1.722	5.00	10.00	20.00	40.00
	1885	1.672	5.00	10.00	20.00	40.00
	1886	1.566	7.00	12.50	25.00	50.00
	1887	2.022	5.00	10.00	20.00	40.00
	1888	1.841	5.00	10.00	18.00	35.00
	1889	1.974	5.00	10.00	18.00	35.00
	1890	2.022	6.50	12.50	25.00	50.00

NOTE: Variety exists for 1882 date w/larger mint mark.

475	1890	Inc. Ab.	10.00	20.00	35.00	55.00
(Y15)	1891	1.470	7.50	15.00	22.50	45.00
	1892	1.607	7.00	15.00	22.50	45.00
	1892	(restrike)	—	—	Proof	25.00

1/2 THALER

14.0300 g, .833 SILVER, .3757 oz ASW
Mint mark: A

416	1830	—	100.00	170.00	250.00	400.00
(C57)						

Mint mark: B

KM#	Date	Mintage	Fine	VF	XF	Unc
420	1831	*	125.00	225.00	475.00	725.00
(C57a)	1833	*	70.00	180.00	320.00	550.00
	1834	—	275.00	450.00	600.00	1000.

*Restruck in 1841.

423	1837	—	300.00	550.00	900.00	1250.
(C62)	1839	—	450.00	800.00	1350.	1800.

THALER

.833 SILVER
Obv: Head right, ribbons on wreath forward across neck. Rev: Madonna w/child.

417.1	1830	—	65.00	140.00	275.00	525.00
(C58.1)						

Mint mark: B

417.2	1830	—	275.00	550.00	900.00	1350.
(C58.2)						

Obv: Ribbons on wreath behind neck.

418	1830	—	Reported, not confirmed			
(C58a)	1831	—	95.00	160.00	400.00	725.00
	1833	—	80.00	120.00	325.00	475.00

NOTE: 1831 and 1833 dated coins are restrikes from 1841.

Obv: Head right, leg: FERD I. D.G. . . . . .

424	1837	—	400.00	700.00	1000.	1400.
(C63)	1839	—	—	—	Rare	

REVOLUTIONARY COINAGE
WAR OF INDEPENDENCE
1848-1849
EGY (1) KRAJCZAR

COPPER
Kremnitz Mint

KM#	Date	Mintage	Fine	VF	XF	Unc
430.1	1848	—	2.00	6.00	12.50	25.00
(C65.1)						

Mint mark: NB

430.2	1849	—	20.00	40.00	60.00	100.00
(C65.2)						

HAROM (3) KRAJCZAR

COPPER
Mint mark: NB

434	1849	—	10.00	20.00	35.00	65.00
(C66)						

NOTE: Varieties exist overstruck w/figure of the Madonna.

HAT (6) KRAJCZAR

.220 SILVER
Mint mark: NB

435	1849	—	4.00	8.00	15.00	25.00
(C67)						

10 KRAJCZAR

3.8900 g, .500 SILVER, .0625 oz ASW
Mint mark: KB

431	1848	—	15.00	30.00	65.00	125.00
(C68)						

20 KRAJCZAR

6.6800 g, .583 SILVER, .1252 oz ASW
Mint mark: KB
Rev. leg: SZ. MARIA. . .

432	1848	—	2.50	5.00	10.00	22.50
(C69)						

MONETARY REFORM
1892-1921
100 Filler = 1 Korona

HUNGARY 833

FILLER

BRONZE
Mint mark: KB

KM#	Date	Mintage	Fine	VF	XF	Unc
480	1892	8.153	17.50	32.50	60.00	95.00
(Y23)	1892	(restrike w/rosette)				
					Proof	10.00
	1893	Inc. Ab.	1.75	3.00	5.50	16.00
	1894	8.642	.50	1.00	1.75	6.00
	1895	9.121	.50	1.00	1.75	6.00
	1896	5.397	1.25	3.00	6.00	15.00
	1897	5.157	4.50	7.50	15.00	30.00
	1898	1.419	5.00	10.00	20.00	40.00
	1899	5.066	1.75	3.50	7.00	17.50
	1900	10.461	1.00	2.00	4.00	11.50
	1901	5.994	4.00	8.00	17.00	32.50
	1902	16.299	.20	.50	1.25	4.00
	1903	2.291	9.00	20.00	35.00	55.00
	1906	.061	65.00	120.00	180.00	275.00
	1914	—	65.00	90.00	135.00	210.00
	1914	—	—	—	Proof	400.00

2 FILLER

BRONZE
Mint mark: KB

KM#	Date	Mintage	Fine	VF	XF	Unc
481	1892	17.176	40.00	60.00	95.00	150.00
(Y24)	1893	Inc. Ab.	1.75	4.00	6.50	9.00
	1894	39.150	.25	.50	1.50	3.00
	1895	65.017	.25	.50	1.50	3.00
	1896	53.716	.25	.50	1.50	3.00
	1897	37.297	.25	.50	1.50	3.00
	1898	14.073	2.25	4.50	8.50	12.50
	1899	21.570	2.25	4.50	8.50	12.50
	1900	.584	70.00	125.00	200.00	250.00
	1901	25.805	.25	.50	1.50	3.00
	1902	6.936	3.50	8.50	13.50	20.00
	1903	4.052	17.50	25.00	35.00	50.00
	1904	4.203	6.00	12.00	27.50	40.00
	1905	9.335	.50	1.00	1.75	3.00
	1906	3.140	1.75	2.50	5.00	7.50
	1907	9.443	5.50	9.00	12.00	17.50
	1908	16.486	.35	.50	1.25	3.00
	1909	19.075	.35	.50	1.25	3.00
	1910	6.025	4.50	7.50	10.00	15.00
	1910	(restrike w/rosette)				
		—	—	—	Proof	10.00
	1914	—	.35	.50	1.00	3.00
	1915	1.294	1.00	1.50	3.00	5.00

IRON

KM#	Date	Mintage	Fine	VF	XF	Unc
497	1916	—	4.50	9.00	13.00	18.00
(Y28)	1917	—	1.00	2.50	6.00	9.00
	1918	—	2.00	4.50	9.00	12.00

NOTE: Varieties in planchet thickness exist for 1917.

10 FILLER

NICKEL
Mint mark: KB

KM#	Date	Mintage	Fine	VF	XF	Unc
482	1892	15.733	3.00	6.00	17.50	27.50
(Y25)	1893	Inc. Ab.	.25	.50	1.50	3.50
	1894	39.463	.25	.50	1.50	3.50
	1895	16.804	.25	.50	1.50	3.50
	1896	—	Reported, not confirmed			
	1906	.056	75.00	175.00	250.00	325.00
	1908	6.819	.25	.50	1.50	3.50
	1909	17.204	.30	.60	1.75	3.50
	1914	—	175.00	275.00	550.00	900.00

NOTE: Edge varieties exist.

COPPER-NICKEL-ZINC

494	1914	—	200.00	300.00	500.00	900.00
(Y26)	1915	4.400	.25	.50	1.00	3.00
	1915	(restrike w/rosette)				
		—	—	—	Proof	4.00
	1916	—	.50	1.25	2.50	5.00

IRON

KM#	Date	Mintage	Fine	VF	XF	Unc
496	1915	—	9.00	20.00	32.50	55.00
(Y29)	1918	—	15.00	30.00	55.00	85.00
	1918	(restrike)	—	—	Proof	12.00
	1920	3.000	2.50	5.00	10.00	18.00
	1920	(restrike)	—	—	Proof	12.00

NOTE: Varieties exist.

20 FILLER

NICKEL
Mint mark: KB

483	1892	.696	2.00	4.00	8.00	12.00
(Y27)	1893	27.187	.50	1.25	2.50	5.00
	1894	26.117	.50	1.25	2.50	5.00
	1906	.067	275.00	400.00	600.00	1250.
	1907	1.248	2.50	5.00	8.00	11.00
	1908	10.770	.75	1.75	3.75	7.50
	1914	—	3.75	6.50	9.00	13.50
	1914	(restrike)	—	—	Proof	12.50

NOTE: Edge varieties exist.

IRON

498	1916	—	.50	1.25	2.50	7.00
(Y30)	1917	—	.75	1.75	3.50	8.00
	1918	—	.75	1.75	3.50	8.00
	1918	(restrike)	—	—	Proof	7.00
	1920	12.000	2.25	4.50	8.00	15.00
	1921	Inc. Ab.	18.00	32.50	45.00	70.00
	1921	(restrike)	—	—	Proof	10.00
	1922	—	—	—	Rare	—

NOTE: Edge varieties exist.

BRASS

498a	1922	(restrike)	—	—	—	—
(Y30a)						

KORONA

5.0000 g, .835 SILVER, .1342 oz ASW
Mint mark: KB

484	1892	.015	2.50	6.00	12.50	45.00
(Y32)	1893	24.386	BV	3.50	5.00	12.50
	1894	12.077	BV	3.25	4.50	10.00
	1895	18.544	BV	3.25	4.50	10.00
	1896	3.983	3.50	6.00	8.50	13.50
	1906	.024	160.00	240.00	325.00	450.00

NOTE: Obverse varieties exist.

Millennium Commemorative

487	1896	1.000	2.25	3.25	5.50	12.00
(Y31)	1896	(restrike)	—	—	Proof	15.00

NOTE: The above issue has been restruck in proof several times, both with and without edge inscriptions.

KM#	Date	Mintage	Fine	VF	XF	Unc
492	1912	4.004	2.50	5.00	10.00	15.00
(Y32a)	1913	5.214	50.00	80.00	140.00	190.00
	1914	—	BV	3.75	7.00	11.00
	1915	3.934	BV	3.00	4.50	6.00
	1916	—	BV	3.50	6.00	8.00

2 KORONA

10.0000 g, .835 SILVER, .2685 oz ASW
Mint mark: KB

493	1912	4.000	BV	4.50	6.50	12.50
(Y33)	1913	3.000	BV	4.50	6.50	12.50
	1914	—	20.00	30.00	50.00	80.00

5 KORONA

24.0000 g, .900 SILVER, .6944 oz ASW
Mint mark: KB

488	1900	3.840	10.00	17.00	30.00	80.00
(Y34)	1900	(restrike w/rosette)	—	Proof	40.00	
	1900	(restrike w/o rosette)	—	Proof	40.00	
	1906	1.263	1000.	1500.	2000.	2500.
	1907	.500	12.00	18.00	35.00	85.00
	1908	1.742	10.00	17.00	30.00	70.00
	1909	1.299	10.00	17.00	40.00	90.00
	1909 U.P.	(restrike)	—	—	Proof	30.00

40th Anniversary Coronation of Franz Josef

489	1907	.300	15.00	22.00	32.00	50.00
(Y35)	1907	(restrike)	—	—	Proof	30.00
	1907 U.P.	(restrike)	—	—	Proof	30.00

10 KORONA

3.3875 g, .900 GOLD, .0980 oz AGW
Mint mark: KB

KM#	Date	Mintage	Fine	VF	XF	Unc
485	1892	1.087	BV	50.00	60.00	75.00
(Y36)	1892	(restrike)	—	—	Proof	50.00
	1893	Inc. Ab.	BV	50.00	60.00	75.00
	1894	.099	BV	50.00	60.00	75.00
	1895	—	1500.	2500.	3500.	4500.
	1895	(restrike)	—	—	Proof	55.00
	1896	.032	60.00	85.00	100.00	125.00
	1897	.259	BV	50.00	60.00	75.00
	1898	.218	BV	50.00	60.00	75.00
	1899	.231	BV	50.00	60.00	75.00
	1900	.228	BV	50.00	60.00	75.00
	1901	.230	BV	50.00	60.00	75.00
	1902	.243	BV	50.00	60.00	75.00
	1903	.228	BV	50.00	60.00	75.00
	1904	1.531	BV	50.00	60.00	75.00
	1905	.869	BV	50.00	60.00	75.00
	1906	.748	BV	50.00	60.00	75.00
	1907	.752	BV	50.00	60.00	75.00
	1908	.509	BV	50.00	60.00	75.00
	1909	.574	BV	50.00	60.00	75.00
	1910	—	BV	50.00	60.00	75.00
	1911	—	BV	50.00	60.00	75.00
	1912	—	50.00	60.00	70.00	85.00
	1913	—	50.00	75.00	100.00	125.00
	1914	—	50.00	80.00	135.00	160.00
	1915	—	1000.	2000.	3000.	4000.

20 KORONA

6.7750 g, .900 GOLD, .1960 oz AGW
Mint mark: KB

KM#	Date	Mintage	Fine	VF	XF	Unc
486	1892	1.779	BV	100.00	110.00	135.00
(Y-A36)	1892	(restrike)	—	—	Proof	100.00
	1893	5.089	BV	100.00	110.00	135.00
	1894	2.526	BV	100.00	110.00	135.00
	1895	1.935	BV	100.00	110.00	135.00
	1895	(restrike)	—	—	Proof	100.00
	1896	1.023	BV	100.00	110.00	135.00
	1897	1.819	BV	100.00	110.00	135.00
	1898	1.281	BV	100.00	110.00	135.00
	1899	.712	BV	100.00	110.00	135.00
	1900	.435	BV	100.00	110.00	135.00
	1901	.510	BV	100.00	110.00	135.00
	1902	.523	BV	100.00	110.00	135.00
	1903	.505	BV	100.00	110.00	135.00
	1904	.572	BV	100.00	110.00	135.00
	1905	.526	BV	100.00	110.00	135.00
	1906	.353	BV	100.00	110.00	135.00
	1907	.194	100.00	150.00	175.00	200.00
	1908	.138	BV	100.00	110.00	135.00
	1909	.459	BV	100.00	110.00	135.00
	1910	—	125.00	175.00	250.00	300.00
	1911	—	BV	100.00	110.00	135.00
	1912	—	BV	100.00	110.00	135.00
	1913	—	110.00	140.00	165.00	200.00
	1914	—	BV	100.00	110.00	135.00
	1915	—	110.00	140.00	165.00	200.00

Rev: Bosnian arms added.

495	1914	—	BV	100.00	115.00	150.00
(Y-B36)	1916	—	125.00	175.00	275.00	400.00

Obv. leg: KAROLY.....

500	1918	—	—	—	Rare	—
(Y-F36)						

100 KORONA

33.8753 g, .900 GOLD, .9802 oz AGW
Mint mark: KB
40th Anniversary of Coronation

KM#	Date	Mintage	Fine	VF	XF	Unc
490	1907	.011	500.00	650.00	900.00	1100.
(Y-C36)	1907	(restrike)	—	—	Proof	800.00
	1907 U.P.	(restrike)	—	—	Proof	800.00

491	1907	1.088	600.00	1200.	1500.	1800.
(Y-D36)	1908	4.038	550.00	850.00	1250.	1750.
	1908	(restrike)	—	—	Proof	450.00

REGENCY
(1920-1945)

MONETARY SYSTEM
100 Filler = 1 Pengo

FILLER

BRONZE
Mint mark: BP

KM#	Date	Mintage	VF	XF	Unc
505	1926	6.471	.30	1.00	3.50
(Y37)	1927	16.529	.20	.50	2.50
	1928	7.000	.25	.60	3.00
	1929	.418	2.00	3.50	12.00
	1930	3.734	.30	1.00	4.00
	1931	10.849	.20	.60	2.50
	1932	5.000	.25	.60	2.50
	1932	(restrike)	—	Proof	3.50
	1933	5.000	.25	.60	2.50
	1934	3.111	.30	1.00	3.50
	1935	6.889	.25	.60	2.50
	1936	10.000	.20	.60	2.50
	1938	10.575	.20	.60	2.50
	1939	10.425	.20	.60	2.50

2 FILLER

BRONZE
Mint mark: BP

KM#	Date	Mintage	VF	XF	Unc
506	1926	17.777	.20	.40	2.50
(Y38)	1927	44.836	.20	.40	2.50
	1928	11.448	.20	.40	2.50
	1929	8.995	.25	.50	2.50
	1930	6.943	.25	.50	2.50
	1931	.826	.90	2.50	6.00
	1932	4.174	.25	.50	2.50
	1933	.501	1.00	3.00	6.00
	1934	9.499	.20	.40	2.00
	1935	10.000	.20	.40	2.00
	1936	2.049	.30	.60	2.00
	1937	7.951	.25	.50	2.00
	1938	14.125	.20	.40	2.00
	1939	16.875	.20	.40	2.00
	1940	7.000	.25	.50	2.00

STEEL

518.1	1940	64.500	1.25	3.00	6.00
(Y50)					

518.2	1940	78.000	.20	.75	3.50
(Y50a)	1941	22.500	.20	.75	50.00
	1942	20.000	.20	.75	3.50
	1942	(restrike)	—	Proof	7.50

ZINC

519	1943	37.000	.20	.50	3.50
(Y51)	1943	(restrike)	—	Proof	7.50
	1944	55.159	.20	.50	3.00

NOTE: Variations in planchets exist.

10 FILLER

COPPER-NICKEL
Mint mark: BP

507	1926	20.001	.40	1.00	2.50
(Y39)	1927	12.255	.40	1.00	2.50
	1935	4.740	.40	1.00	2.50
	1936	3.005	.40	1.00	2.50
	1938	6.700	.40	1.00	2.50
	1939	4.460	.40	1.00	2.50
	1940	.960	.80	3.50	4.50

STEEL

507a	1940	45.927	.15	.75	3.00
(Y52)	1941	24.963	.15	.75	3.00
	1942	44.110	.15	.75	3.00

20 FILLER

COPPER-NICKEL
Mint mark: BP

KM#	Date	Mintage	VF	XF	Unc
508	1926	25.000	.25	1.00	2.50
(Y40)	1927	.830	1.00	3.50	6.00
	1938	20.150	.25	1.00	2.50
	1939	2.020	.50	1.50	3.50
	1940	2.470	.50	1.50	3.50

STEEL

520	1941	75.007	.20	.90	3.00
(Y53)	1943	7.500	.20	.90	3.00
	1944	25.000	.20	.90	3.00
	1944	(restrike)	—	Proof	7.50

50 FILLER

COPPER-NICKEL
Mint mark: BP

509	1926	14.921	.40	1.00	3.50
(Y41)	1938	20.079	.40	1.00	3.50
	1939	2.770	.65	1.50	5.50
	1939	(restrike)	—	Proof	12.00
	1940	6.230	.45	1.25	3.50

PENGO

5.0000 g, .640 SILVER, .1029 oz ASW
Mint mark: BP

510	1926	15.000	BV	2.00	5.00
(Y42)	1927	18.000	BV	2.00	5.00
	1937	4.000	1.50	2.50	5.50
	1938	5.000	1.50	2.50	5.50
	1939	13.000	BV	2.00	5.00

ALUMINUM

521	1941	80.000	.20	.50	.80
(Y54)	1942	19.000	.20	.50	.80
	1943	—	20.00	30.00	50.00
	1944	20.650	.20	.50	.80

2 PENGO

10.0000 g, .640 SILVER, .2058 oz ASW
Mint mark: BP

511	1929	5.000	3.00	4.75	8.50
(Y43)	1931	.110	35.00	50.00	90.00
	1932	.602	3.00	4.75	8.50
	1933	1.051	3.00	4.75	8.50

KM# (Y43)	Date	Mintage	VF	XF	Unc
	1935	.050	15.00	25.00	35.00
	1936	.711	3.00	4.75	8.50
	1937	1.500	3.00	4.75	8.50
	1938	6.417	3.00	4.75	8.50
	1939	2.103	3.00	4.75	8.50

Pazmany University Tercentenary

513	1935	.050	5.00	7.00	12.50
(Y45)	1935	(restrike not marked)		Proof	22.50

Rakozi Bicentennial

514	1935	.100	5.00	6.00	11.00
(Y46)	1935	(restrike not marked)		Proof	27.50

50th Anniversary Death of Liszt

515	1936	.200	4.00	5.00	8.00
(Y47)	1936	(restrike not marked)		Proof	18.00

ALUMINUM

522.1	1941	24.000	.30	.50	.80
(Y55.1)	1942	8.000	.30	.50	.80
	1943	10.000	.30	.50	.80

Rev: Base of 2 is wavy.

522.2	1941	.040	6.25	9.50	16.00
(Y55.2)					

5 PENGO

24.9300 g, .640 SILVER, .5130 oz ASW
Mint mark: BP
Admiral Horthy
Raised, sharp edge reeding.

512.1	1930	3.650	9.00	12.00	17.50
(Y44)					

HUNGARY

25.3300 g, 36.1mm

KM#	Date	Mintage	VF	XF	Unc
512.2 (Y44a)	1930	(restrike)	—	Proof	18.50

St. Stephan

516	1938	.600	9.00	14.00	20.00
(Y48)	1938	(restrike not marked)		Proof	25.00

Horthy Government
Smooth, ornamented edge.

517	1939	.408	9.00	14.00	20.00
(Y49)					

ALUMINUM
75th Birthday of Admiral Horthy

523	1943	2.000	1.25	2.50	5.00
(Y57)	1943	(restrike)	—	Proof	5.00

PROVISIONAL GOVERNMENT
1944-1946

5 PENGO

ALUMINUM
Mint mark: BP

525	1945	5.002	1.00	2.00	3.50
(Y56)	1945	PROBAVERET			
		(restrike)	—	Proof	4.00

REPUBLIC
MONETARY SYSTEM
100 Filler = 1 Forint

HUNGARY 836

2 FILLER

BRONZE
Mint mark: BP

KM#	Date	Mintage	VF	XF	Unc
529	1946	13.665	.15	.30	.50
(Y58)	1947	23.865	.15	.30	.50
	1947	(restrike)	—	Proof	3.00

5 FILLER

ALUMINUM
Mint mark: BP

| 535 | 1948 | 24.000 | .25 | .40 | .60 |
| (Y59) | 1951 | 15.000 | .10 | .15 | .30 |

10 FILLER

ALUMINUM-BRONZE
Mint mark: BP

530	1946	23.565	.10	.25	.50
(Y60)	1947	29.580	.10	.25	.50
	1947	(restrike)	—	Proof	3.00
	1948	4.855	.20	.35	.60
	1950	8.000	.25	.50	.80

ALUMINUM

| 530a | 1950 | 2.000 | .25 | .50 | 15.00 |
| (Y60a) | | | | | |

20 FILLER

ALUMINUM-BRONZE
Mint mark: BP

531	1946	16.560	.30	.50	.75
(Y61)	1946	(restrike)	—	Proof	5.00
	1947	18.260	.25	.50	.75
	1948	5.180	.30	.50	.85
	1950	5.000	—	—	.85

50 FILLER

ALUMINUM
Mint mark: BP

| 536 | 1948 | 15.000 | .80 | 1.50 | 2.25 |
| (Y62) | 1948 | (restrike) | — | Proof | 6.50 |

FORINT

ALUMINUM
Mint mark: BP

532	1946	38.900	.50	.75	1.50
(Y63)	1947	2.600	.60	1.00	2.00
	1949	17.000	.50	.75	1.50

2 FORINT

ALUMINUM
Mint mark: BP

KM#	Date	Mintage	VF	XF	Unc
533	1946	10.000	1.00	1.75	2.50
(Y64)	1947	3.500	1.00	2.00	3.00

5 FORINT

20.0000 g, .835 SILVER, .5369 oz ASW
Mint mark: BP
Lajos Kossuth
Thick planchet

| 534 | 1946 | .040 | 6.25 | 12.50 | 20.00 |
| (Y65) | | | | | |

12.0000 g, .500 SILVER, .1929 oz ASW
1.7mm thin planchet

| 534a | 1947 | 10.004 | 2.00 | 4.00 | 6.00 |
| (Y66) | 1947 | (restrike) | — | Proof | 7.50 |

13.0000 g, .835 SILVER, .3490 oz ASW

| 534b | 1966 | 5.000 | — | Proof | 9.00 |
| (Y66a) | 1967 | 5.000 | — | Proof | 9.00 |

12.0000 g, .500 SILVER, .1929 oz ASW
Petofi 1848 Revolution

| 537 | 1948 | .100 | 2.50 | 5.00 | 8.00 |
| (Y67) | 1948 | (restrike) | — | Proof | 20.00 |

10 FORINT

20.0000 g, .500 SILVER, .3215 oz ASW
Mint mark: BP
Szechenyi 1848 Revolution

| 538 | 1948 | .100 | 4.50 | 9.00 | 15.00 |
| (Y68) | 1948 | (restrike) | — | Proof | 30.00 |

20 FORINT

28.0000 g, .500 SILVER, .4501 oz ASW
Mint mark: BP
Tancsics 1848 Revolution

KM#	Date	Mintage	VF	XF	Unc
539	1948	.050	10.00	15.00	20.00
(Y69)	1948	(restrike)	—	Proof	50.00

PEOPLE'S REPUBLIC

MONETARY SYSTEM
100 Filler = 1 Forint

2 FILLER

ALUMINUM
Mint mark: BP

546	1950	24.990	—	—	.10
(Y70)	1952	5.600	—	.10	.20
	1953	9.400	—	—	.10
	1954	10.000	—	—	.10
	1955	6.029	—	—	.15
	1956	4.000	—	—	.15
	1957	5.000	—	—	.10
	1960	3.000	—	—	.10
	1961	2.000	—	—	.10
	1962	3.000	—	—	.10
	1963	2.082	—	—	.10
	1965	.540	.10	.25	6.00
	1966		—	—	.10
	1967		—	—	.10
	1971	1.035	—	—	.10
	1972	1.000	—	—	.10
	1973	2.826	—	—	.10
	1974	.050	—	—	.10
	1975	.050	—	—	.10
	1976	.050	—	—	.10
	1977	.060	—	—	.10
	1978	.050	—	—	.10
	1979	.030	—	—	.10
	1980	—	—	—	.10
	1981	.030	—	—	.10
	1982	.030	—	—	.10
	1983	—	—	—	.10
	1984	—	—	—	.10

COPPER-NICKEL

| 546a | 1966 | 5.000 | — | Proof | 1.10 |
| (Y70a) | 1967 | 5.000 | — | Proof | 1.10 |

5 FILLER

ALUMINUM
Mint mark: BP

549	1953	10.000	—	.10	.15
(Y71)	1955	6.005	—	.10	.20
	1956	6.012	—	.10	.15
	1957	5.000	—	.10	.15
	1959	8.000	—	.10	.15

HUNGARY 837

KM#	Date	Mintage	VF	XF	Unc
(Y71)	1960	7.000	—	.10	.15
	1961	4.410	—	.10	.15
	1962	5.590	—	.10	.15
	1963	4.020	—	.10	.15
	1964	3.600	—	.10	.15
	1965	6.000	—	.10	.15
	1966	—	—	.10	.15
	1967	—	—	.10	.15
	1970	3.900	.10	.20	4.00
	1971	.100	—	.10	.15
	1972	.050	—	.10	.15
	1973	.105	—	.10	.15
	1974	.060	—	.10	.15
	1975	.060	—	.10	.15
	1976	.050	—	.10	.15
	1977	.060	—	.10	.15
	1978	.050	—	.10	.15
	1979	.030	—	.10	.15
	1980	—	—	.10	.15
	1981	.030	—	.10	.15
	1982	.030	—	.10	.15
	1983	—	—	.10	.15
	1984	—	—	.10	.15

COPPER-NICKEL

549a	1966	5.000	—	Proof	1.25
(Y71a)	1967	5.000	—	Proof	1.25

10 FILLER

ALUMINUM
Mint mark: BP

547	1950	5.040	.10	.25	15.00
(Y72)	1951	80.950	—	.10	.20
	1955	10.019	—	.10	.20
	1957	13.000	—	.10	.20
	1958	12.015	—	.10	.20
	1959	15.000	—	.10	.20
	1960	5.000	—	.10	.20
	1961	13.000	—	.10	.20
	1962	4.000	—	.10	.20
	1963	8.000	—	.10	.20
	1964	17.000	—	.10	.20
	1965	21.880	—	.10	.20
	1966	8.120	—	.10	.20

COPPER-NICKEL

547a	1966	5.000	—	Proof	1.50
(Y72b)	1967	5.000	—	Proof	1.50

ALUMINUM, reduced size

572	1967	5.000	.10	.25	15.00
(Y72a)	1968	16.086	—	.10	.15
	1969	50.760	—	.10	.15
	1970	28.399	—	.10	.15
	1971	28.800	—	.10	.15
	1972	17.220	—	.10	.15
	1973	33.720	—	.10	.15
	1974	24.930	—	.10	.15
	1975	30.000	—	.10	.15
	1976	20.025	—	.10	.15
	1977	30.075	—	.10	.15
	1978	36.005	—	.10	.15
	1979	36.060	—	.10	.15
	1980	—	—	.10	.15
	1981	36.000	—	.10	.15
	1982	45.015	—	.10	.15
	1983	—	—	.10	.15
	1984	—	—	.10	.15
	1987	—	—	.10	.15
	1988	—	—	.10	.15

20 FILLER

ALUMINUM
Mint mark: BP

550	1953	45.000	—	.10	.25
(Y73)	1955	10.023	—	.10	.25
	1957	5.000	—	.10	.25
	1958	10.000	—	.10	.25
	1959	13.000	—	.10	.25
	1961	9.000	—	.10	.25
	1963	7.000	—	.10	.25
	1964	10.400	—	.10	.20
	1965	15.000	—	.10	.25
	1966	5.000	—	.10	.25

COPPER-NICKEL

KM#	Date	Mintage	VF	XF	Unc
550a	1966	5.000	—	Proof	1.75
(Y73b)	1967	5.000	—	Proof	1.75

ALUMINUM
Reduced size

573	1967	10.000	—	.10	.20
(Y73a)	1968	57.990	—	.10	.20
	1969	25.510	—	.10	.20
	1970	16.960	—	.10	.20
	1971	20.120	—	.10	.20
	1972	29.610	—	.10	.20
	1973	25.400	—	.10	.20
	1974	35.010	—	.10	.20
	1975	30.010	—	.10	.20
	1976	30.010	—	.10	.20
	1977	30.050	—	.10	.20
	1978	30.140	—	.10	.20
	1979	32.010	—	.10	.20
	1980	—	—	.10	.20
	1981	34.030	—	.10	.20
	1982	35.010	—	.10	.20
	1983	—	—	.10	.20
	1984	—	—	.10	.20
	1987	—	—	.10	.20

627	1983	.050	.10	.20	.50
(Y149)					

50 FILLER

ALUMINUM
Mint mark: BP

551	1953	10.017	.10	.15	.40
(Y74)	1965	3.005	.10	.15	.35
	1966	1.500	.10	.15	.35
	1967	20.000	.10	.15	.35

COPPER-NICKEL

551a	1966	5.000	—	Proof	2.00
(Y74a)	1967	5.000	—	Proof	2.00

ALUMINUM

574	1967	20.000	—	.10	.25
(Y97)	1968	13.830	—	.10	.25
	1969	10.085	—	.10	.25
	1971	.050	—	.10	.25
	1972	.520	—	.10	.20
	1973	7.600	—	.10	.20
	1974	5.000	—	.10	.20
	1975	10.160	—	.10	.20
	1976	15.130	—	.10	.20
	1977	10.050	—	.10	.20
	1978	10.110	—	.10	.20
	1979	10.060	—	.10	.20
	1980	—	—	.10	.20
	1981	10.030	—	.10	.20
	1982	10.000	—	.10	.20
	1983	—	—	.10	.20
	1984	—	—	.10	.20
	1985	—	—	.10	.20
	1986	—	—	.10	.20
	1987	—	—	.10	.20
	1988	—	—	.10	.20

FORINT

ALUMINUM
Mint mark: BP

KM#	Date	Mintage	VF	XF	Unc
545	1949	19.440	.10	.25	.75
(Y75)	1950	39.060	.10	.25	.75
	1951	—	.10	.25	.75
	1952	63.018	.10	.25	.75

555	1957	7.500	.10	.25	.40
(Y80)	1958	5.070	.10	.25	.40
	1960	5.000	.10	.25	.40
	1961	5.000	.10	.25	.40
	1962	—	.10	.25	.40
	1963	3.000	.10	.25	.40
	1964	6.080	.10	.25	.40
	1965	9.810	.10	.25	.40
	1966	5.680	.10	.25	.40

5.8500 g, .835 SILVER, .1570 oz ASW

555a	1966	5.000	—	Proof	5.00
(Y80b)	1967	5.000	—	Proof	5.00

ALUMINUM
Reduced size, 22.8mm

575	1967	60.000	.10	.20	.30
(Y80a)	1968	51.430	.10	.20	.30
	1969	26.120	.10	.20	.30
	1970	10.000	.10	.20	.30
	1971	1.390	.10	.20	.30
	1972	.110	.10	.20	.40
	1973	1.990	.10	.20	.40
	1974	4.990	.10	.20	.40
	1975	10.000	.10	.20	.40
	1976	15.000	.10	.20	.40
	1977	10.050	.10	.20	.40
	1978	.050	.10	.20	.40
	1979	10.070	.10	.20	.40
	1980	—	.10	.20	.40
	1981	25.040	.10	.20	.40
	1982	10.000	.10	.20	.40
	1983	—	.10	.20	.40
	1984	—	.10	.20	.40
	1987	—	.10	.20	.40
	1988	—	.10	.20	.40

2 FORINT

COPPER-NICKEL
Mint mark: BP

548	1950	18.500	.15	.50	1.00
(Y76)	1951	4.000	.20	.50	1.00
	1952	4.540	.20	.50	1.00
	1956	—	.20	.50	1.00

556	1957	5.000	.20	.50	1.00
(Y81)	1958	1.033	—	—	1.00
	1960	4.000	.20	.50	1.00
	1961	.690	.25	.60	1.25
	1962	1.190	.20	.50	1.00

COPPER-NICKEL-ZINC

556a	1962	1.210	.15	.35	.75
(Y81a)	1963	3.100	.15	.35	.75
	1964	3.250	.15	.35	.75
	1965	4.395	.15	.35	.75
	1966	6.630	.15	.35	.75
	1967	—	.15	.35	.75

HUNGARY 838

6.1200 g, .835 SILVER, .1643 oz ASW

KM#	Date	Mintage	VF	XF	Unc
556b	1966	5,000	—	Proof	8.50
(Y81b)	1967	5,000	—	Proof	8.50

BRASS

591	1970	50.000	.15	.35	.75
(Y115)	1971	10.025	.15	.35	.75
	1972	10.015	.15	.35	.75
	1973	.820	.15	.35	.75
	1974	10.000	.15	.35	.75
	1975	20.030	.15	.35	.75
	1976	15.000	.15	.35	.75
	1977	10.115	.15	.35	.75
	1978	12.000	.15	.35	.75
	1979	10.005	.15	.35	.75
	1980	—	.15	.35	.75
	1981	10.010	.15	.35	.75
	1982	10.000	.15	.35	.75
	1983	—	.15	.35	.75
	1984	—	.15	.35	.75
	1985	—	.15	.35	.75
	1987	—	.15	.35	.75

5 FORINT

COPPER-NICKEL
Mint mark: BP

576	1967	20.000	.50	.75	1.25
(Y98)	1968	.029	25.00	35.00	45.00

NICKEL

594	1971	20.004	.30	.50	.80
(Y116)	1972	5.000	.30	.50	.80
	1973	.100	.30	.50	.80
	1974	.050	.30	.50	.80
	1975	.050	.30	.50	.80
	1976	5.090	.30	.50	.80
	1977	.050	.30	.50	.80
	1978	6.000	.30	.50	.80
	1979	10.000	.30	.50	.80
	1980	—	.30	.50	.80
	1981	5.002	.30	.50	.80
	1982	.936	.30	.50	.80
	1983	—	.30	.50	.80

F.A.O. Issue

628	1983	.050	.20	.50	1.25
(Y150)					

COPPER-NICKEL
Kossuth - Circulation Coinage

635	1983	—	.15	.25	.50
(Y116a)	1984	—	.15	.25	.50
	1985	—	.15	.25	.50
	1988	—	.15	.25	.50

10 FORINT

12.5000 g, .800 SILVER, .3215 oz ASW
Mint mark: BP
10th Anniversary of Revision
of Monetary and Economic System

KM#	Date	Mintage	VF	XF	Unc
552	1956	.022	5.00	8.00	16.00
(Y77)					

NICKEL

595	1971	24.998	.50	.80	1.50
(Y117)	1972	25.000	.50	.80	1.50
	1973	.078	.50	.80	1.50
	1974	.050	.50	.80	1.50
	1975	.050	.50	.80	1.50
	1976	3.568	.50	.80	1.50
	1977	4.618	.50	.80	1.50
	1978	.050	.50	.80	1.50
	1979	5.000	.50	.80	1.50
	1982	.030	.50	.80	1.50

NICKEL-BRONZE

595a	1983	—	.50	.75	1.25

NICKEL
F.A.O. Issue

620	1981	.060	—	1.25	2.50
(Y142)					

F.A.O. Issue

629	1983	.050	—	1.25	2.50
(Y151)					

ALUMINUM-BRONZE
Circulation Coinage

636	1983	—	.25	.40	1.00
(Y117a)	1984	—	.25	.40	1.00
	1985	—	.25	.40	1.00
	1986	—	.25	.40	1.00
	1987	—	.25	.40	1.00

20 FORINT

17.5000 g, .800 SILVER, .4501 oz ASW
Mint mark: BP
10th Anniversary of Revision
of Monetary and Economic System

KM#	Date	Mintage	VF	XF	Unc
553	1956	.022	8.00	12.00	20.00
(Y78)					

COPPER-NICKEL
Dozsa - Circulation Coinage

630	1982	12.814	.50	.75	1.25
(Y160)	1983	—	.50	.75	1.25
	1984	—	.50	.75	1.25
	1985	—	.50	.75	1.25

Forestry

637	1984	.020	—	—	3.00
(Y161)	1984	5,000	—	Proof	7.50

F.A.O. Issue

653	1985	.025	—	—	2.00
	1985	—	—	Proof	6.00

25 (HUSZONOT) FORINT

20.0000 g, .800 SILVER, .5144 oz ASW
Mint mark: BP
10th Anniversary of Revision
of Monetary and Economic System

554	1956	.022	10.00	15.00	22.50
(Y79)					

HUNGARY 839

17.5000 g, .750 SILVER, .4220 oz ASW
150th Anniversary of Birth of Liszt

KM#	Date	Mintage	VF	XF	Unc
557 (Y82)	1961	.015	—	Proof	20.00

80th Anniversary of Birth of Bartok

| 558 (Y87) | 1961 | .015 | — | Proof | 20.00 |

12.0000 g, .640 SILVER, .2469 oz ASW
400th Anniversary of Death of Zrinyi

| 567 (Y92) | 1966 | .011 | — | Proof | 20.00 |

12.0000 g, .750 SILVER, .2893 oz ASW
Kodaly 85th Birthday

| 577 (Y99) | 1967 | 3.00 | 6.00 | 10.00 | |
| | 1967 | .015 | — | Proof | 12.50 |

50 (OTVEN) FORINT

20.0000 g, .750 SILVER, .4822 oz ASW
Mint mark: BP
150th Anniversary of Birth of Liszt

| 559 (Y83) | 1961 | .015 | — | Proof | 20.00 |

3.8380 g, .986 GOLD, .1217 oz AGW
150th Anniversary of Birth of Liszt

| 560 (Y84) | 1961 | 2,500 | — | Proof | 125.00 |

20.0000 g, .750 SILVER, .4822 oz ASW
80th Anniversary of Birth of Bartok

KM#	Date	Mintage	VF	XF	Unc
561 (Y88)	1961	.015	—	Proof	20.00

3.8380 g, .986 GOLD, .1217 oz AGW
80th Anniversary of Birth of Bartok

| 562 (Y89) | 1961 | 2,500 | — | Proof | 125.00 |

20.0000 g, .640 SILVER, .4115 oz ASW
400th Anniversary of Death of Zrinyi

| 568 (Y93) | 1966 | .011 | — | Proof | 25.00 |

20.0000 g, .750 SILVER, .4822 oz ASW
Kodaly 85th Birthday

| 578 (Y100) | 1967 | — | — | — | 10.00 |
| | 1967 | .015 | — | Proof | 12.50 |

20.0000 g, .640 SILVER, .4115 oz ASW
150th Anniversary of Birth of Semmelweis

| 582 (Y104) | 1968 | .020 | — | — | 10.00 |
| | 1968 | 4,750 | — | Proof | 12.50 |

4.2050 g, .900 GOLD, .1217 oz AGW
150th Anniversary of Birth of Semmelweis

KM#	Date	Mintage	VF	XF	Unc
583 (Y106)	1968	5,105	—	Proof	125.00

16.0000 g, .640 SILVER, .3292 oz ASW
50th Year of Republic

| 589 (Y111) | 1969 | .012 | — | — | 10.00 |
| | 1969 | 3,000 | — | Proof | 12.50 |

25th Anniversary of Liberation

| 592 (Y113) | 1970 | .020 | — | — | 9.00 |
| | 1970 | 5,000 | — | Proof | 12.00 |

St. Stephen

| 596 (Y118) | 1972 | .024 | — | — | 12.00 |
| | 1972 | 6,000 | — | Proof | 15.00 |

Sandor Petofi

| 599 (Y121) | 1973 | .024 | — | — | 8.00 |
| | 1973 | 6,000 | — | Proof | 10.00 |

HUNGARY 840

50th Anniversary National Bank

KM#	Date	Mintage	VF	XF	Unc
601	1974	.024	—	—	8.00
(Y124)	1974	6,000	—	Proof	10.00

COPPER-NICKEL
25th Anniversary of World Wildlife Foundation

663	1988	—	—	—	2.00

100 (SZAZ) FORINT

7.6760 g, .986 GOLD, .2431 oz AGW
Mint mark: BP
150th Anniversary of Birth of Liszt

563	1961	2,500	—	Proof	175.00
(Y85)					

80th Anniversary of Birth of Bartok

564	1961	2,500	—	Proof	175.00
(Y90)					

8.4100 g, .900 GOLD, .2433 oz AGW
400th Anniversary of Death of Zrinyi

569	1966	3,300	—	Proof	175.00
(Y94)					

28.0000 g, .750 SILVER, .6752 oz ASW
Kodaly 85th Birthday

KM#	Date	Mintage	VF	XF	Unc
579	1967	.010	—	—	35.00
(Y101)	1967		—	Proof	40.00

28.0000 g, .640 SILVER, .5762 oz ASW
150th Anniversary of Birth of Semmelweis

584	1968	.020	—	—	10.00
(Y105)	1968	4,750	—	Proof	17.50

8.4100 g, .900 GOLD, .2433 oz AGW
150th Anniversary of Birth of Semmelweis

585	1968	4,243	—	Proof	175.00
(Y107)					

22.0000 g, .640 SILVER, .4527 oz ASW

50th Year of Republic

KM#	Date	Mintage	VF	XF	Unc
590	1969	.012	—	—	12.00
(Y112)	1969	3,000	—	Proof	15.00

25th Anniversary of Liberation

593	1970	.020	—	—	10.00
(Y114)	1970	5,000	—	Proof	12.00

St. Stephen

597	1972	.024	—	—	14.00
(Y119)	1972	6,000	—	Proof	18.00

Budapest Centennial

598	1972	.025	—	—	10.00
(Y120)	1972	6,000	—	Proof	16.00

HUNGARY 841

Sandor Petofi
KM#	Date	Mintage	VF	XF	Unc
600	1973	.024	—	—	10.00
(Y122)	1973	6,000	—	Proof	16.00

NICKEL
1st Soviet-Hungarian Space Flight
KM#	Date	Mintage	VF	XF	Unc
617	1980	.180	—	—	4.00
(Y139)	1980	.020	—	Proof	8.00

World Food Day
621	1981	.080	—	—	4.00
(Y143)	1981	.020	—	Proof	8.00

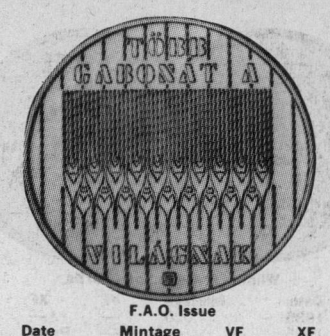

F.A.O. Issue
KM#	Date	Mintage	VF	XF	Unc
631	1983	.050	—	—	3.50
(Y152)	1983	.010	—	Proof	10.00

Simon Bolivar
632	1983	.020	—	—	5.00
(Y153)	1983	.010	—	Proof	10.00

COPPER-NICKEL
1300th Anniversary of Bulgarian Statehood
622	1981	—	—	—	4.00
(Y147)	1981	5,000	—	Proof	8.00

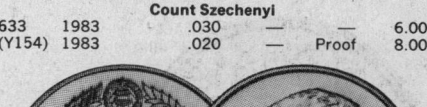

Count Szechenyi
633	1983	.030	—	—	6.00
(Y154)	1983	.020	—	Proof	8.00

CMEA Anniversary
602	1974	.020	—	—	10.00
(Y123)	1974	5,000	—	Proof	16.00

Czobel - Painter
634	1983	.020	—	—	6.00
(Y155)	1983	.010	—	Proof	10.00

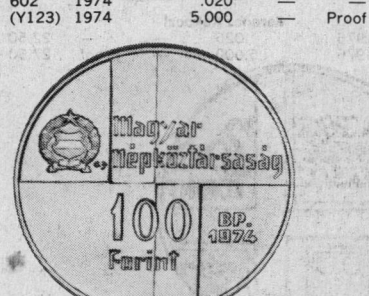

Soccer Games
626	1982	.150	—	—	2.50
(Y148)	1982	—	—	Proof	7.50

Korosi Csoma Sandor
638	1984	.020	—	—	6.00
(Y156)	1984	.010	—	Proof	10.00

50th Anniversary National Bank
603	1974	.024	—	—	10.00
(Y125)	1974	6,000	—	Proof	16.00

Forestry
639	1984	.020	—	—	6.00
(Y162)	1984	5,000	—	Proof	12.00

HUNGARY 842

Wildlife Preservation - Turtle

KM#	Date	Mintage	VF	XF	Unc
644	1985	.020	—	—	8.00
	1985	—	—	Proof	12.00

Budapest Cultural Forum

KM#	Date	Mintage	VF	XF	Unc
651	1985	.040	—	—	7.00
	1985	—	—	Proof	8.00

KM#	Date	Mintage	VF	XF	Unc
604	1975	.020	—	—	20.00
(Y126)	1975	.010	—	Proof	25.00

Wildlife Preservation - Otter

645	1985	.020	—	—	8.00
	1985	—	—	Proof	12.00

F.A.O. Issue

654	1985	.020	—	—	7.00
	1985	5,000	—	Proof	8.00

150th Anniversary Academy of Science

605	1975	.020	—	—	20.00
(Y127)	1975	.010	—	Proof	25.00

Wildlife Preservation - Wildcat

646	1985	.020	—	—	8.00
	1985	—	—	Proof	12.00

Andras Fay

655	1986	.042	—	—	7.00
	1986	8,000	—	Proof	8.00

200 (KETSZAZ) FORINT

16.8210 g, .900 GOLD, .4867 oz AGW
Mint mark: BP
150th Anniversary of Birth of Semmelweis

586	1968	2,845	—	Proof	300.00
(Y108)					

Ferencz Rakoczi

606	1976	.025	—	—	22.50
(Y128)	1976	5,000	—	Proof	27.50

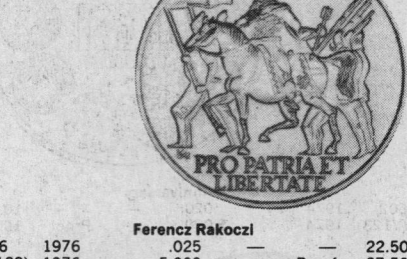

Soccer - Map of Mexico

647	1985	.030	—	—	8.00
	1985	7,500	—	Proof	12.00

28.0000 g, .640 SILVER, .5762 oz ASW
30th Anniversary of Liberation

Soccer - Indian Artifacts

648	1985	.030	—	—	9.00
	1985	7,500	—	Proof	12.50

Mihaly Munkacsy

607	1976	.025	—	—	16.50
(Y129)	1976	5,000	—	Proof	22.50

HUNGARY 843

Pal Szinyei Merse

KM#	Date	Mintage	VF	XF	Unc
608	1976	.025	—	—	16.50
(Y130)	1976	5,000	—	Proof	22.50

Gyula Derkovits

609	1976	.025	—	—	16.50
(Y131)	1976	5,000	—	Proof	22.50

Adam Manyoki

610	1977	.025	—	—	16.50
(Y132)	1977	5,000	—	Proof	22.50

Tivadar C. Kosztka

611	1977	.025	—	—	16.50
(Y133)	1977	5,000	—	Proof	22.50

Jozsef Rippl-Ronal

612	1977	.025	—	—	16.50
(Y134)	1977	5,000	—	Proof	20.00

175th Anniversary of National Museum

KM#	Date	Mintage	VF	XF	Unc
613	1977	.025	—	—	18.00
(Y135)	1977	5,000	—	Proof	22.00

First Gold Forint

614	1978	.025	—	—	18.00
(Y136)	1978	5,000	—	Proof	22.00

International Year of the Child

615	1979	9,000	—	—	18.00
(Y137)	1979	.021	—	Proof	22.00

22.0000 g, .640 SILVER, .4527 oz ASW
350th Anniversary of Death of Gabor Bethlen

KM#	Date	Mintage	VF	XF	Unc
616	1979	.015	—	—	18.00
(Y138)	1979	5,000	—	Proof	25.00

16.0000 g, .640 SILVER, .3292 oz ASW
XIII Winter Olympics

618	1980	.015	—	Proof	16.00
(Y140)					

28.0000 g, .640 SILVER, .5762 oz ASW
Wildlife Preservation - Otter

643	1985	.013	—	—	22.00
(Y163)	1985	2,000	—	Proof	35.00

HUNGARY 844

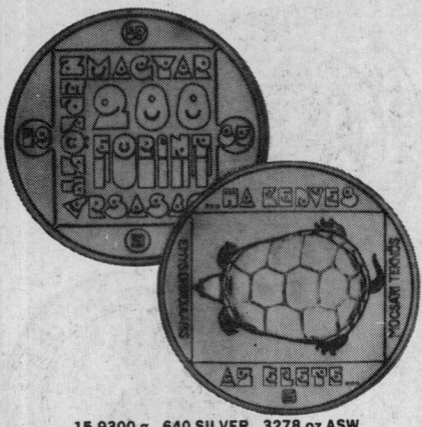

15.9300 g, .640 SILVER, .3278 oz ASW
Wildlife Preservation - Turtle

KM#	Date	Mintage	VF	XF	Unc
649	1985	.013	—	—	22.00
	1985	2,000	—	Proof	35.00

Wildlife Preservation - Wildcat
650	1985	.013	—	—	22.00
	1985	2,000	—	Proof	35.00

500 (OTSZAZ) FORINT

38.3800 g, .986 GOLD, 1.2168 oz AGW
Mint mark: BP
150th Anniversary of Birth of Liszt

565	1961	1,000	—	P/L	750.00
(Y86)					

80th Anniversary of Birth of Bartok

KM#	Date	Mintage	VF	XF	Unc
566	1961	1,000	—	P/L	750.00
(Y91)					

42.0500 g, .900 GOLD, 1.2168 oz AGW
400th Anniversary of Death of Zrinyi

570	1966	1,100	—	Proof	750.00
(Y95)					

Kodaly 85th Birthday
580	1967	—	—	—	625.00
(Y102)	1967	1,000	—	Proof	750.00

42.0000 g, .900 GOLD, 1.2154 oz AGW
150th Anniversary of Birth of Semmelweis
Rev: Similar to 50 Forint, KM#583.

KM#	Date	Mintage	VF	XF	Unc
587	1968	1,855	—	Proof	750.00
(Y109)					

39.0000 g, .640 SILVER, .8025 oz ASW
XIII Winter Olympics
Rev: Similar to 200 Forint, KM#618.

619	1980	.013	—	Proof	32.00
(Y141)					

25.0000 g, .640 SILVER, .5144 oz ASW
Centennial of Birth of Bela Bartok

623	1981	.013	—	—	27.50
(Y144)	1981	.013	—	Proof	32.50

HUNGARY 845

Budapest Cultural Forum

KM#	Date	Mintage	VF	XF	Unc
652	1985	.015	—	—	18.00
	1985	.010	—	Proof	20.00

28.0000 g, .640 SILVER, .5762 oz ASW
World Cup Soccer

KM#	Date	Mintage	VF	XF	Unc
624	1981	6,000	—	—	25.00
(Y145)	1981	.040	—	Proof	30.00

Winter Olympics - Cross Country Skiers

KM#	Date	Mintage	VF	XF	Unc
641	1984	8,000	—	—	23.00
(Y158)	1984	.012	—	Proof	28.00

Soccer - Players

	1986	8,000	—	—	23.00
656	1986	.017	—	Proof	28.00

World Cup Soccer

625	1981	6,000	—	—	25.00
(Y146)	1981	.040	—	Proof	30.00

Los Angeles Olympics - Gymnast

642	1984	8,000	—	—	23.00
(Y159)	1984	.012	—	Proof	28.00

Soccer - Stadium
Obv: Similar to KM#656.

657	1986	8,000	—	—	23.00
	1986	.017	—	Proof	28.00

Decade for Women

640	1984	8,000	—	Proof	23.00
(Y157)	1984	.020	—	Proof	28.00

HUNGARY 846

28.0000 g, .900 SILVER, .8102 oz ASW
Liberation of Budapest from the Turks

KM#	Date	Mintage	VF	XF	Unc
658	1986	.020	—	XF	23.00
	1986	.010	—	Proof	28.00

Winter Olympics - Speed Skating

659	1986	.015	—	—	23.00
	1986	.015	—	Proof	28.00

Seoul Olympics - Wrestlers

660	1987	.015	—	—	23.00
	1987	.015	—	Proof	28.00

World Wildlife Fund - Bird of Prey

KM#	Date	Mintage	VF	XF	Unc
661	1988	.025	—	Proof	28.00

St. Stephan

662	1988	.015	—	Proof	28.00

1000 (EZER) FORINT

84.1000 g, .900 GOLD, 2.4337 oz AGW
Mint mark: BP
400th Anniversary of Death of Zrinyi
Obv: Similar to 500 Forint, KM#570.

571 (Y96)	1966	330 pcs.	—	Proof	1750.

Kodaly 85th Birthday
Obv: Similar to 500 Forint, KM#580.

KM#	Date	Mintage	VF	XF	Unc
581 (Y103)	1967	500 pcs.	—	Proof	1500.

84.0000 g, .900 GOLD, 2.4308 oz AGW
150th Anniversary of Birth of Semmelweis
Rev: Similar to 500 Forint, KM#587.

588 (Y110)	1968	1,570	—	Proof	1500.

TRADE COINAGE
DUCAT

3.4900 g, .986 GOLD, .1106 oz AGW
Obv. leg: FRANC I.D.G. . . .

KM#	Date	Mintage	Fine	VF	XF	Unc
419 (C59)	1830	—	175.00	250.00	325.00	500.00
	1832	—	200.00	300.00	400.00	550.00
	1833	—	150.00	225.00	300.00	450.00
	1834	—	150.00	225.00	300.00	450.00
	1835	—	150.00	225.00	300.00	450.00

Obv. leg: FERDI. D.G. . . .

425 (C64)	1837	—	175.00	350.00	500.00	750.00
	1838	—	175.00	350.00	500.00	750.00
	1839	—	150.00	225.00	300.00	500.00
	1840	—	150.00	225.00	300.00	500.00
	1841	—	150.00	225.00	300.00	500.00
	1842	—	150.00	225.00	300.00	500.00
	1843	—	175.00	350.00	450.00	650.00
	1844	—	150.00	225.00	300.00	500.00
	1845	—	175.00	300.00	450.00	650.00
	1846	—	150.00	225.00	300.00	500.00
	1847	—	150.00	225.00	300.00	500.00
	1848	—	150.00	225.00	300.00	500.00

Rev. leg: SZ. MARIA. . . .

KM#	Date	Mintage	Fine	VF	XF	Unc
433 (C70)	1848	—	100.00	175.00	250.00	350.00

Mint mark: KB

| 448.1 (Y21.1) | 1868 | .128 | 100.00 | 200.00 | 275.00 | 400.00 |
| | 1869 | .090 | 90.00 | 150.00 | 200.00 | 300.00 |

Mint mark: GYF

| 448.2 (Y21.2) | 1868 | .400 | 85.00 | 140.00 | 200.00 | 300.00 |
| | 1869 | .270 | 90.00 | 150.00 | 200.00 | 300.00 |

Mint mark: KB
Obv: Similar to KM#448.1.
Rev: Similar to 8 Forint, KM#477.

| 456 (Y22a.1) | 1870 | .017 | | | | |
| | 1870(restrike) | | | | Proof | 100.00 |

Similar to 4 Forint, KM#454.1.

457 (Y22a.2)	1877	456 pcs.	800.00	1250.	1500.	2000.
	1879	3,651	500.00	900.00	1500.	2000.
	1880	5,075	600.00	1000.	1500.	1750.
	1880(restrike)	—			Proof	
	1881	*43 pcs.	1250.	2000.	2500.	3000.

4 FORINT/10 FRANCS

3.2258 g, .900 GOLD, .0934 oz AGW

Mint mark: GYF

| 454.1 (Y17.1) | 1870 | .049 | 55.00 | 70.00 | 90.00 | 125.00 |

Mint mark: KB

454.2 (Y17.2)	1870	.102	55.00	70.00	90.00	125.00
	1870 UP (restrike)				Proof	65.00
	1871	.090	55.00	80.00	100.00	130.00
	1872	.053	55.00	65.00	85.00	125.00
	1873	.013	80.00	115.00	175.00	200.00
	1874	8,228	80.00	115.00	175.00	210.00
	1875	.011	85.00	125.00	175.00	225.00
	1876	.024	55.00	80.00	110.00	130.00
	1877	.024	55.00	75.00	100.00	125.00
	1878	.015	55.00	80.00	110.00	130.00
	1879	.012	55.00	80.00	110.00	130.00

NOTE: Semi official restrikes have the letters UP below the bust.

Older head

466 (Y17.3)	1880	.013	55.00	80.00	110.00	130.00
	1881	.012	55.00	80.00	110.00	130.00
	1882	.013	55.00	80.00	110.00	125.00
	1883	.012	55.00	80.00	110.00	125.00
	1884	.054	55.00	65.00	95.00	125.00
	1885	.064	55.00	70.00	100.00	125.00
	1886	.039	55.00	65.00	80.00	125.00
	1887	.039	55.00	65.00	95.00	125.00
	1888	.049	55.00	65.00	95.00	125.00
	1889	.019	100.00	150.00	225.00	300.00
	1890	Inc.Y19	95.00	140.00	200.00	275.00

Rev: Fiume arms.

| 476.1 (Y19.1) | 1890 | .029 | 200.00 | 300.00 | 375.00 | 500.00 |
| | 1891 | .032 | 60.00 | 75.00 | 100.00 | 150.00 |

Mint Unknown

| 476.2 (Y19.2) | 1892 | 20 pcs. | 800.00 | 1100. | 1800. | 3000. |

8 FORINT/20 FRANCS

6.4516 g, .900 GOLD, .1867 oz AGW

455.1 (Y18.1)	1870	.046	BV	110.00	135.00	165.00
	1871	.076	BV	100.00	120.00	140.00
	1872	.273	BV	100.00	120.00	140.00
	1873	.245	BV	100.00	120.00	140.00
	1874	.237	BV	100.00	120.00	160.00
	1875	.261	BV	100.00	120.00	160.00
	1876	.314	BV	100.00	120.00	140.00
	1877	.303	BV	100.00	120.00	140.00
	1878	.308	BV	110.00	130.00	160.00
	1879	.306	BV	100.00	120.00	140.00
	1880	.301	90.00	120.00	150.00	200.00

Mint mark: GYF

| 455.2 (Y18.2) | 1870 | .125 | BV | 100.00 | 130.00 | 150.00 |
| | 1871 | .177 | BV | 100.00 | 120.00 | 140.00 |

Mint mark: KB
Obv: Larger head.

KM#	Date	Mintage	Fine	VF	XF	Unc
467 (Y18.3)	1880	Inc. Ab.	BV	100.00	110.00	140.00
	1881	.309	BV	100.00	120.00	140.00
	1882	.304	BV	100.00	120.00	140.00
	1883	.300	BV	100.00	120.00	140.00
	1884	.284	BV	100.00	120.00	140.00
	1885	.267	BV	100.00	120.00	140.00
	1886	.313	BV	100.00	120.00	140.00
	1887	.294	BV	100.00	120.00	140.00
	1888	.296	BV	100.00	120.00	140.00
	1889	.351	BV	100.00	120.00	140.00
	1890	Inc. Be.	BV	100.00	110.00	140.00

Rev: Fiume arms.

477 (Y20)	1890	.329	BV	100.00	125.00	175.00
	1891	.378	BV	100.00	130.00	160.00
	1892	.231	BV	120.00	160.00	200.00

SPECIMEN SETS (SS)

KM#	Date	Mintage	Identification	Issue Price	Mkt. Val.
SS1	1977(9)	—	Y70,71,72a,73a,80a,97,115-117	—	5.00
SS2	1978(9)	—	Y70,71,72a,73a,80a,97,115-117	—	5.00
SS3	1979(9)	—	Y70,71,72a,73a,80a,97,115-117	—	5.00
SS4	1981(9)	—	Y70,71,72a,73a,80a,97,115,116,142	—	5.00

PROOF SETS (PS)

PS1	1961(6)	2,500	Y84-86,89-91	—	2100.
PS2	1961(4)	—	Y82,83,87,88	—	120.00
PS3	1966(8)	2,000	Y66a,70a,71a,72b,73b,74a,80b,81b	15.00	30.00
PS4	1966(3)	330	Y94-96	430.00	2675.
PS5	1966(2)	11,000	Y92,93	7.50	55.00
PS6	1967(8)	5,000	Same as KM103	15.00	30.00
PS7	1967(2)	500	Y102,103	—	2250.
PS8	1968(5)	—	Y106-110	—	2850.
PS9	1968(2)	4,750	Y104,105	35.00	27.50
PS10	1969(2)	3,000	Y111,112	35.00	27.50
PS11	1970(2)	4,000	Y113,114	25.00	25.00
PS12	1972(2)	6,000	Y118,119	25.00	37.50
PS13	1973(2)	6,000	Y121,122	—	27.50
PS14	1974(2)	—	Y124,125	—	27.50
PS15	1976(3)	5,000	Y129-131	—	90.00

ICELAND 847

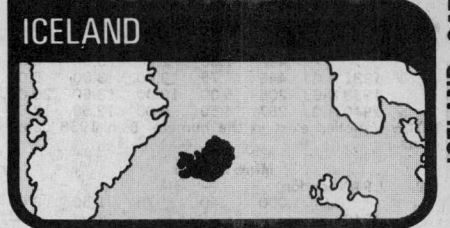

The Republic of Iceland, an island of recent volcanic origin in the North Atlantic east of Greenland and immediately south of the Arctic Circle, has an area of 39,768 sq. mi. (103,000 sq. km.) and a population of 247,357. Capital: Reykjavik. Fishing is the chief industry and accounts for more than 70 percent of the exports.

Iceland was settled by Norwegians in the 9th century and established as an independent republic in 930. The Icelandic assembly called the 'Althing', also established in 930, is the oldest parliament in the world. Iceland came under Norwegian sovereignty in 1262, and passed to Denmark when Norway and Denmark were united under the Danish crown in 1380. In 1918 it was established as a virtually independent kingdom in union with Denmark. On June 17, 1944, while Denmark was still under occupation by troops of the Third Reich, Iceland was established by plebiscite as an independent republic.

RULERS
Christian X, 1912-1944

MINT MARKS
L - London
Heart (h) - Copenhagen

MINTMASTER'S INITIALS
HCN - Hans Christian Nielsen, 1919-1927
N - Niels Peter Nielsen, 1927-1955

MONEYERS INITIALS
GI, GJ - Knud Gunnar Jensen, 1901-1933

MONETARY SYSTEM
100 Aurar = 1 Krona (Commencing 1981)
100 Old Kronur = 1 New Krona

EYRIR

BRONZE
Mint mark: Heart

KM#	Date	Mintage	Fine	VF	XF	Unc
5.1	1926 HCN-GJ	.405	1.00	2.25	4.00	6.00
	1931 N-GJ	.462	.75	1.75	2.75	5.50
	1937 N-GJ wide date	.211	2.00	4.00	5.50	9.00
	1937 N-GJ narrow date	Inc. Ab.	2.00	4.00	5.50	9.00
	1938 N-GJ	.279	.75	2.00	3.00	5.00
	1939 N-GJ large 3	.305	.75	2.00	3.00	5.00
	1939 N-GJ small 3	Inc. Ab.	.75	2.00	3.00	5.00

Mint: London

5.2	1940	1.000	.25	.50	1.00	2.50
	1940	—	—	—	Proof	
	1942	2.000	.25	.40	.75	2.00

Republic

8	1946	4.000	.10	.15	.50	1.00
	1953	4.000	.10	.15	.40	.75
	1953	—	—	—	Proof	
	1956	2.000	.10	.15	.40	.75
	1956	—	—	—	Proof	
	1957	2.000	.10	.15	.40	.75
	1957	—	—	—	Proof	
	1958	2.000	.10	.15	.40	.75
	1958	—	—	—	Proof	
	1959	1.600	.10	.15	.40	.75
	1959	—	—	—	Proof	
	1966	1.000	.10	.15	.40	.75
	1966	.015	—	—	Proof	3.25

2 AURAR

BRONZE

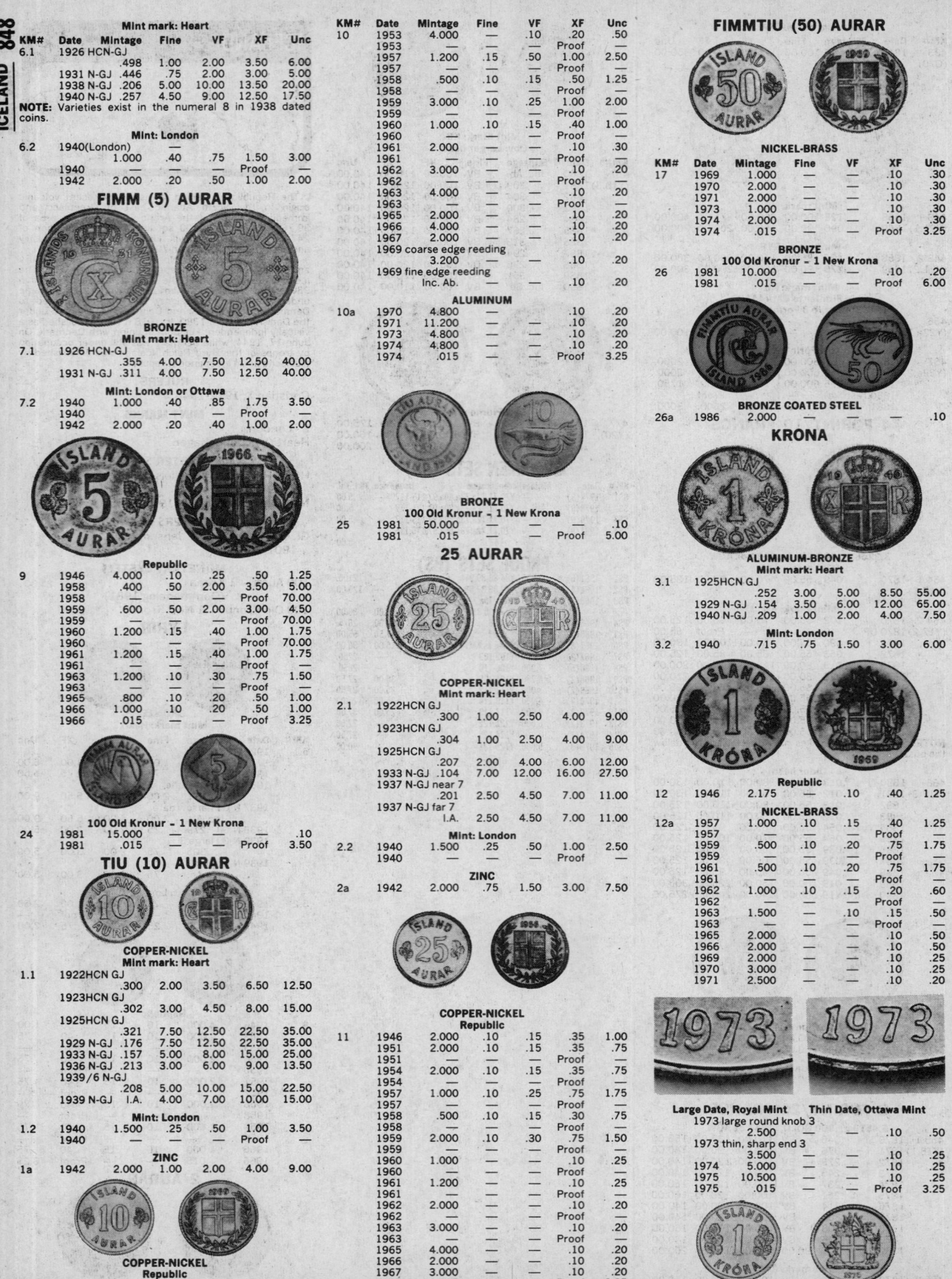

ALUMINUM

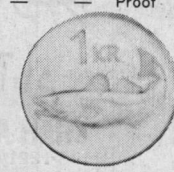

KM#	Date	Mintage	Fine	VF	XF	Unc
23	1976	10.000	—	—	.10	.20
	1977	10.000	—	—	.10	.20
	1978	13.000	—	—	.10	.20
	1980	7.225	—	—	.10	.20
	1980	.015	—	—	Proof	3.25

COPPER-NICKEL
100 Old Kronur = 1 New Krona

27	1981	18.000	—	—	.10	.30
	1981	.015	—	—	Proof	8.00
	1984	7.000	—	—	.10	.50
	1987	7.500	—	—	.10	.50

2 KRONUR

ALUMINUM-BRONZE
Mint mark: Heart

4.1	1925HCN GJ	.126	4.00	7.00	15.00	75.00
	1929 N-GJ	.077	6.50	12.50	30.00	125.00

Mint: London

4.2	1940	.546	.75	1.50	3.00	6.00

Republic

13	1946	1.086	.15	.35	.75	2.00

NICKEL-BRASS

13a.1	1958	.500	.20	.50	1.00	2.50
	1958	—	—	—	Proof	—
	1962	.500	.20	.50	1.00	2.50
	1962	—	—	—	Proof	—
	1963	.750	.15	.30	.60	1.50
	1963	—	—	—	Proof	—
	1966	1.000	.10	.20	.40	1.00
	1966	.015	—	—	Proof	3.25

Thick planchet, 11.50 g

13a.2	1966	300 pcs.	25.00	50.00	100.00	135.00

FIMM (5) KRONUR

COPPER-NICKEL

18	1969	2.000	—	.10	.20	.40
	1970	1.000	—	.10	.20	.40
	1971	.500	—	.10	.30	.60
	1973	1.100	—	.10	.15	.30
	1974	1.200	—	.10	.15	.20
	1975	1.500	—	.10	.15	.20
	1976	.500	—	.10	.15	.20
	1977	1.000	—	.10	.15	.20
	1978	4.672	—	.10	.15	.20
	1980	2.400	—	.10	.15	.20
	1980	.015	—	.10	Proof	3.25

100 Old Kronur = 1 New Krona

28	1981	4.350	—	—	.15	.50
	1981	.015	—	—	Proof	10.00
	1984	1.000	—	—	.15	.50
	1987	3.000	—	—	.15	.50

10 KRONUR

COPPER-NICKEL

KM#	Date	Mintage	Fine	VF	XF	Unc
15	1967	1.000	.10	.20	.40	1.00
	1969	.500	.10	.25	.50	1.25
	1970	1.000	—	.10	.25	.50
	1971	1.500	—	.10	.25	.50
	1973	1.500	—	.10	.25	.50
	1974	2.000	—	.10	.25	.40
	1975	2.500	—	.10	.25	.40
	1976	2.500	—	.10	.25	.40
	1977	2.000	—	.10	.25	.40
	1978	10.500	—	.10	.25	.40
	1980	4.600	—	.10	.25	.40
	1980	.015	—	.10	Proof	3.25

100 Old Kronur = 1 New Krona

29	1984	10.000	—	—	.25	1.00
	1987	7.500	—	—	.25	1.00

50 KRONUR

NICKEL
50th Anniversary of Sovereignty

16	1968	.100	.50	1.50	3.00	4.00

COPPER-NICKEL

19	1970	.800	.25	.50	.75	1.75
	1971	.500	.25	.50	.75	2.00
	1973	.050	1.00	1.50	2.50	4.00
	1974	.200	.25	.50	.75	1.50
	1975	.500	.20	.35	.50	1.00
	1976	.500	.20	.35	.50	1.00
	1977	.200	.20	.35	.50	1.00
	1978	2.040	.20	.35	.50	1.00
	1980	1.500	.20	.35	.50	1.00
	1980	.015	.20	.35	Proof	3.25

COPPER-NICKEL-ZINC

31	1987	4.000	—	—	—	2.00

500 KRONUR

8.9604 g, .900 GOLD, .2593 oz AGW
Jon Sigurdsson Sesquicentennial

KM#	Date	Mintage	Fine	VF	XF	Unc
14	1961	.010	—	—	—	225.00

20.0000 g, .925 SILVER, .5968 oz ASW
1100th Anniversary 1st Settlement

20	1974	.070	—	—	—	8.00
	1974	*.058	—	—	Proof	12.50

NOTE: 17,000 proof coins were remelted.

20.0000 g, .500 SILVER, .3215 oz ASW
100th Anniversary of Icelandic Banknotes

30	1986	*.015	—	—	—	15.00

20.0000 g, .925 SILVER, .5968 oz ASW

30a	1986	*5,000	—	—	Proof	25.00

1000 KRONUR

30.0000 g, .925 SILVER, .8923 oz ASW
1100th Anniversary 1st Settlement

21	1974	.070	—	—	—	12.00
	1974	*.058	—	—	Proof	17.50

NOTE: 17,000 proof coins were remelted.

10,000 KRONUR

15.5000 g, .900 GOLD, .4485 oz AGW
1100th Anniversary 1st Settlement

22	1974	.012	—	—	—	250.00
	1974	8,000	—	—	Proof	300.00

ICELAND 849

ICELAND 850

MINT SETS (MS)

KM#	Date	Mintage	Identification	Issue Price	Mkt. Val.
MS1	1930(3)	10,000	KM-M1-M3	—	295.00
MS2	1973(6)	—	KM10a,12a,15,17-19	3.25	5.25
MS3	1974(6)	—	KM10a,12a,15,17-19	3.25	3.50
MS4	1974(2)	70,000	KM20,21	30.00	20.00
MS5	1975(4)	—	KM12a,15,18,19	—	3.50
MS6	1976(4)	—	KM15,18,19,23	—	3.50
MS7	1977(4)	—	KM15,18,19,23	—	3.50
MS8	1978(4)	—	KM15,18,19,23	—	3.50
MS9	1980(4)	—	KM15,18,19,23	—	3.50

PROOF SETS (PS)

KM#	Date	Mintage	Identification	Issue Price	Mkt. Val.
PS1	1974(3)	8,000	KM20-22	272.00	280.00
PS2	1974(2)	58,000	KM20,21	38.00	30.00
PS3	1980(11)	15,000	(Mixed dates) 1966: KM8-9,13a.1; 1967: KM11; 1974: KM10a,17; 1975: KM12a; 1980: KM15,18,19,23	40.00	35.00
PS4	1981(5)	15,000	KM24-28	32.00	32.50
PS5	1984(6)	—	KM24-29	—	35.00

INDIA/Mughal Empire

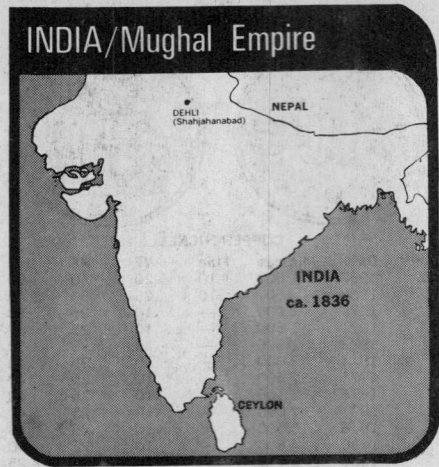

INDIA ca. 1836

The Lodi Sultanate of Delhi was conquered by Zahir-ud-din Muhammad Babur, a Chagatai Mongol descended from Tamerlane, in 1525AD. His son, Nasir-ud-din Muhammad Humayun, lost the new empire in a series of battles with the Bihari Afghan Sher Shah, who founded the short-lived Suri dynasty. Humayun, with the assistance of the Emperor of Persia, recovered his kingdom from Sher Shah's successors in 1555AD. He did not long enjoy the fruits of victory, for his fatal fall down his library steps brought his teenage son Jalal-ud-din Muhammad Akbar to the throne in the following year. During Akbar's long reign of a half century, the Mughal Empire was firmly established throughout most of North India. Under Akbar's son and grandson, the emperors Nur-ud-din Muhammad Jahangir and Shihab-ud-din Muhammad Shah Jahan, the state reached its apogee and art, culture and commerce flourished.

One of the major achievements of the Mughal government was the establishment of a universal silver currency, based on the rupee, a coin of 11.6 grams and as close to pure silver content as the metallurgy of the time was capable of attaining. Supplementary coins were the gold mohur and copper dam. The values of these coin denominations were nominally fixed at 8 rupees to 1 mohur, and 40 dams to 1 rupee, but market forces determined actual exchange rates which were different.

The maximum expansion of the geographical area under direct Mughal rule was achieved during the reign of Aurangzeb Alamgir. By his death in 1707AD, the whole peninsula, indeed the whole subcontinent of India, with minor exceptions owed fealty to the Mughal emperor.

Aurangzeb's wars, lasting decades, upset the stability and prosperity of the kingdom. The internal dissention and rebellion which resulted brought the eclipse of the empire in succeeding reigns. The Mughal monetary system, especially the silver rupee, supplanted most local currencies throughout India. The number of Mughal mints rose sharply, and direct central control declined, so that by the time of the emperor Shah Alam II, many nominally Mughal mints served independent states. The common element in all these coinage issues was the presence of the Mughal emperor's name and titles on the obverse. In the following catalog no attempt has been made to solve the problem of separating Mughal from Princely State coins by historical criteria: all Mughal-style coins are considered products of the Mughal empire until the death of Muhammad Shah in 1748AD; thereafter all coins are considered Princely State issues unless there is evidence of the mint being under ever-diminishing Imperial control.

EMPERORS

شاه عالم

Shah Alam II,
AH1174-1221/1759-1806AD

محمد اکبر

Muhammad Akbar II,
AH1221-1253/1806-1837AD

سراج الدین محمد بهادر شاه

Bahadur Shah II, Suraj-ud-din Muhammad
AH1253-1273/1837-1858AD

MINTNAMES

احمد اباد Ahmadabad

اکبر آباد Akbarabad (Agra)

چھچرولی Chhachrauli

گوکل گڑہ Gokulgarh

سہارنپور Saharanpur

شاہ جہان آباد Shahjahanabad (Dehli)

SHAH ALAM II
AH1173-1221/1759-1806AD

Except for the Delhi Mint, most of the later coins struck in the name of this Emperor were Princely State issues, and can be found in their appropriate place under the States. Earlier issues come from nearly 100 mints, and it is always a problem to determine in what year coins of a particular mint cease to be Mughal and become State issues.

The following mints, for the most part in the Delhi (Shahjahanabad) area, may be considered the nucleus of Mughal mints during Shah Alam's reign. They were located in provinces governed by Mughal functionaries, whose increasing independence is reflected in the growing eccentricity of coin design.

In some cases the distinctive geometric designs and floral devices found on the coins were true mint marks, representative of a single mint. In other instances the 'mint marks' listed below were temporary privy marks or simply decoration.

Shah Alam II legends were used in some states long after his death, until AH1314/1879AD at Ujjain, for example. This is not the case with true Mughal issues.

Akbarabad Mint

The city and fort of Agra or Akbarabad fell to the Jats of Bharatpur after the battle of Panipat in 1761AD. For issues dated AH1175-1186/1761-1773AD see Indian Princely States, Bharatpur. A succession of governors from 1770AD controlled Agra nominally as officers of the Mughal emperor.

MUGHAL GOVERNOR ISSUES
Daulat Rao Sindhia
AH1209-1218/1794-1803AD

PAISA

COPPER

KM#	Date	Year	Good	VG	Fine	VF
549	AH1216	4x	8.00	15.00	30.00	40.00

NOTE: J.W.H. - John William Hessing, Governor of Agra.

Rev: Pistol.

| 550 | AH1217 | 44 | 5.00 | 8.00 | 12.00 | 17.50 |

RUPEE

SILVER, 10.70-11.60 g
Rev: Fish.

KM#	Date	Year	VG	Fine	VF	XF
554	AH1217	44	7.50	11.50	16.00	25.00
	—	45	7.50	11.50	16.00	25.00

EAST INDIA COMPANY
RUPEE

SILVER, 10.70-11.60 g
Rev: Fish.

| 560 | AH1219 | 47 | 12.00 | 18.00 | 25.00 | 35.00 |
| | 1220 | 47 | 12.00 | 18.00 | 25.00 | 35.00 |

Chhachrauli Mint

A mint of the Mughal governor of Saharanpur.

PAISA
COPPER
Obv: Daggar mint mark. Rev: Quatrefoil and sword.

KM#	Date	Year	Good	VG	Fine	VF
610	AH1218	44	5.00	10.00	15.00	25.00

Gokulgarh Mint

Mint mark:

Sindhia Governor

RUPEE

SILVER, 10.70-11.60 g

KM#	Date	Year	VG	Fine	VF	XF
624	AH1216	44	8.50	15.00	23.50	30.00
	1217	45	8.50	15.00	23.50	30.00
	1218	46	8.50	15.00	23.50	30.00

Saharanpur Mint
LOCAL GOVERNOR ISSUES
General Perron (for Sindhia)
AH1215-1218/1800-1803

Mint mark:
stylized dagger

PAISA

COPPER
Rev: Additional symbols chakra and hexfoil.

KM#	Date	Year	Good	VG	Fine	VF
673	AH1217	44	5.00	7.00	10.00	15.00
	1218	45	5.00	7.00	10.00	15.00

RUPEE

SILVER, 10.70-11.60 g

KM#	Date	Year	VG	Fine	VF	XF
675	AH1216	43	10.00	18.00	30.00	40.00
	1218	45	10.00	18.00	30.00	40.00

Rev: Circled dot additional symbol.

676	AH1216	43	12.00	22.00	35.00	50.00
	1217	44	12.00	22.00	35.00	50.00

EAST INDIA COMPANY
PAISA

COPPER
Rev: St. Stephen's cross.

KM#	Date	Year	Good	VG	Fine	VF
690	AH1218	45	5.00	10.00	15.00	20.00

RUPEE

SILVER, 10.70-11.60 g
Rev: St. Stephen's cross.

KM#	Date	Year	VG	Fine	VF	XF
692	AH1218	45	15.00	25.00	40.00	60.00

Rev: Vertical spray.

693	AH1219	46	10.00	18.00	30.00	40.00

Rev: W/o symbol.

694	AH1220	47	10.00	18.00	30.00	40.00
	1220	49	10.00	18.00	30.00	40.00

Shahjahanabad Mint

Mint marks:

Obverse of silver and gold coins.

PAISA

COPPER

KM#	Date	Year	Good	VG	Fine	VF
700	AH1219	46	2.00	3.00	4.50	6.00
	1219	47	2.00	3.00	4.50	6.00
	1220	48	2.00	3.00	4.50	6.00

1/4 RUPEE

SILVER, 14mm, 2.68-2.90 g
Obv: Cinqfoil additional symbol.

KM#	Date	Year	VG	Fine	VF	XF
704	AH1220	48	12.00	25.00	45.00	60.00

1/2 RUPEE
SILVER, 18mm
Obv: Cinqfoil additional symbol.

707	AH1220	47	20.00	40.00	60.00	80.00

RUPEE

NOTE: The size of the Shahjahanabad rupees of Shah Alam II was subject to a wide variance. The early issues tended to be normal size for the hammered coinage (about 22mm). As the power of the emperor waned, the flan size of the Shahjahanabad rupees waxed, reflecting the increasingly ceremonial role of the coinage. The later coins should not be confused with the Nazarana (presentation) coins, which always show a full border design around the legend.

Additional Mint mark:
obv.

SILVER, 10.70-11.60 g

KM#	Date	Year	VG	Fine	VF	XF
711	AH1216	44	15.00	22.50	30.00	45.00
	1217	44	15.00	22.50	30.00	45.00
	1217	45	15.00	22.50	30.00	45.00
	1218	45	15.00	22.50	30.00	45.00

Additional Mint mark:
obv.

712	AH1218	46	25.00	40.00	75.00	125.00

Additional Mint mark:
obv.

713	AH1218	46	30.00	60.00	100.00	150.00
	1221	49	30.00	60.00	100.00	150.00

Obv. and rev. leg: Within wreath of roses, thistles and shamrocks.

714	AH1219	47	25.00	40.00	75.00	125.00
	1220	47	25.00	40.00	75.00	125.00
	1220	48	25.00	40.00	75.00	125.00
	1221	48	25.00	40.00	75.00	125.00

NAZARANA RUPEE

SILVER

718	AH1218	46	60.00	100.00	140.00	175.00

Mughal Empire / INDIA 851

NAZARANA MOHUR

GOLD, 10.70-11.40 g

KM#	Date	Year	Fine	VF	XF	Unc
721	AH1217	45	250.00	300.00	400.00	600.00
	1218	46	250.00	300.00	400.00	600.00

Obv. and rev. leg: Within wreath of roses, thistles and shamrocks.

722	AH1219	47	275.00	400.00	600.00	750.00
	1221	48	275.00	400.00	600.00	750.00

Saharanpur Mint

Mint mark: ك

RUPEE

SILVER, 10.70-11.60 g

KM#	Date	Year	VG	Fine	VF	XF
760	AH1203	1	750.00	1000.	1250.	1500.

MUHAMMAD AKBAR II
AH1221-1253/1806-1837AD

Shahjahanabad Mint

The mint of the walled city of Delhi produced a limited number of coins each year with which the East India Company's resident paid a pension to the Mughal Emperor. KM#777 was struck for this purpose until 1818, when the mint was closed for regular coinage. Thereafter, only a few presentation coins (KM#779.1) were struck annually on the occasion of the king's accession.

PAISA

COPPER

KM#	Date	Year	Good	VG	Fine	VF
770	AH1222	1	2.00	3.00	4.50	6.00
	1222	2	2.00	3.00	4.50	6.00

Rev: Letter "S" by regnal year.

771	AH1225	4	2.00	3.00	4.50	6.00
	1225	5	2.00	3.00	4.50	6.00
	1226	5	2.00	3.00	4.50	6.00
	1230	9	—	—	—	—
	1231	10	2.00	3.00	4.50	6.00
	1233	12	2.00	3.00	4.50	6.00

1/4 RUPEE
SILVER, 2.68-2.90 g

KM#	Date	Year	VG	Fine	VF	XF
773	AH—	7	15.00	25.00	40.00	60.00

1/2 RUPEE
SILVER, 5.35-5.80 g

KM#	Date	Year	VG	Fine	VF	XF
775	AH1221	1	25.00	45.00	75.00	100.00
	1225	4	25.00	45.00	75.00	100.00

RUPEE

SILVER, 10.70-11.60 g

776	AH1202	1	—	—	—	—

777	AH1221	1	14.00	20.00	35.00	50.00
	1222	1	14.00	20.00	35.00	50.00
	1222	2	14.00	20.00	35.00	50.00
	1223	2	14.00	20.00	35.00	50.00
	1223	3	14.00	20.00	35.00	50.00
	1224	3	14.00	20.00	35.00	50.00
	1225	4	14.00	20.00	35.00	50.00
	1226	5	14.00	20.00	35.00	50.00
	1227	6	14.00	20.00	35.00	50.00
	1227	7	14.00	20.00	35.00	50.00
	1228	7	14.00	20.00	35.00	50.00
	1228	8	14.00	20.00	35.00	50.00
	1229	9	14.00	20.00	35.00	50.00
	12xx	11	14.00	20.00	35.00	50.00

NAZARANA RUPEE

SILVER

779.1	AH1223	3	600.00	800.00	1000.	1200.
	1224	3	600.00	800.00	1000.	1200.
	1225	4	600.00	800.00	1000.	1200.
	1226	5	600.00	800.00	1000.	1200.
	1227	7	600.00	800.00	1000.	1200.
	1235	15	600.00	800.00	1000.	1200.
	1237	17	600.00	800.00	1000.	1200.
	1239	19	600.00	800.00	1000.	1200.
	1240	20	600.00	800.00	1000.	1200.
	1241	21	600.00	800.00	1000.	1200.
	1242	22	600.00	800.00	1000.	1200.
	1248	28	600.00	800.00	1000.	1200.
	1249	29	600.00	800.00	1000.	1200.

SILVER, 10.70-11.40 g

779.2	AH1251	31	—	—	Rare	—
	1252	32	—	—	Rare	—

MOHUR

GOLD, 10.70-11.40 g

781	AH122x	2	200.00	400.00	470.00	600.00
	12xx	6	200.00	400.00	470.00	600.00

NAZARANA MOHUR

GOLD, 10.70-11.40 g

783	AH1221	1	—	—	Rare	—
	1234	12	—	—	Rare	—

SURAJ-UD-DIN MUHAMMAD BAHADUR SHAH II
AH1253-1273/1837-1857AD

Shahjahanabad Mint
NAZARANA RUPEE

SILVER, 10.70-11.40 g

KM#	Date	Year	VG	Fine	VF	XF
790	AH1253	1	250.00	600.00	1000.	1400.
	1254	2	250.00	600.00	1000.	1400.
	1255	3	250.00	600.00	1000.	1400.
	1256	4	250.00	600.00	1000.	1400.
	1257	5	250.00	600.00	1000.	1400.
	1258	6	250.00	600.00	1000.	1400.

ASSAM

AHOM KINGDOM

It was in the 13th century that a tribal leader called Sukapha, with about 9,000 followers, left their traditional home in the Shan States of Northern Burma, and carved out the Ahom Kingdom in upper Assam.

The Ahom Kingdom gradually increased in power and extent over the following centuries, particularly during the reign of King Suhungmung (1497-1539). This king also took on a Hindu title, Svarga Narayan, which shows the increasing influence of the Brahmins over the court. Although several of the other Hindu states in north-east India started a silver coinage during the 16th century, it was not until the mid-17th century that the Ahoms first struck coin.

From the time of Kusain Shah's invasion of Cooch Behar in 1494AD the Muslims had cast acquisitive eyes towards the valley of the Brahmaputra, but the Ahoms managed to preserve their independence. In 1661 Aurangzeb's governor in Bengal, Mir Jumla, made a determined effort to bring Assam under Mughal rule. Cooch Behar was annexed without difficulty, and in March 1662 Mir Jumla occupied Gargaon, the Ahom capital, without opposition. However, during the rainy season the Muslim forces suffered severely from disease, lack of food and from the occasional attacks from the Ahom forces, who had tactically withdrawn from the capital together with the king. After the end of the monsoon a supply line was opened with Bengal again, but morale in the Muslim army was low, so Mir Jumla was forced to agree to peace terms somewhat less onerous than the Mughals liked to impose on subjugated states. The Ahoms agreed to pay tribute, but the Ahom kingdom remained entirely independent of Mughal control, and never again did a Muslim army venture into upper Assam.

During the eighteenth century the Kingdom became weakened with civil war, culminating in the expulsion of Gaurinatha Simha from his capital in 1787 by the Moamarias. The British helped Gaurinatha regain his kingdom in 1794, but otherwise took little interest in the affairs of Assam. The end of the Ahom Kingdom was not due to intervention from Bengal, but from Burma. After initial invasions commencing in 1816, the Burmese conquered the whole of Assam in 1821/2, and seemed bent on expanding their Kingdom even further. The British in Bengal were quick to retaliate and drove the Burmese from Assam in 1824, and from then on Assam became firmly under British control with no further independent coinage.

RULERS

Ruler's names, where present on the coins, usually appear on the obverse (dated) side, starting either at the end of the first line, after Shri, or in the second line. Most of the Ahom rulers after the adoption of Hinduism in about 1500AD had both an Ahom and a Hindu name.

HINDU NAME	AHOM NAME
Kamalesvara Simha	Suklingpha

কমলেশ্বৰসিংহ
SE1717-1733/1795-1811AD
Chandrakanta Simha **Sudingpha**

চন্দ্ৰকান্তসিংহ
SE1733-1740/1811-1818AD
Brajanatha Simha

ব্ৰজনাথসিংহ
SE1740-1741/1818-1819AD
Chandrakanta Simha **Sudingpha**

চন্দ্ৰকান্তসিংহ
SE1741-1743/1819-1821AD
Jogesvara Simha

জোগেশ্বৰসিংহ
SE1743-1746/1821-1824AD

Coinage

It is frequently stated that coins were first struck in Assam during the reign of King Suklenmung (1539-1552), but this is merely due to a misreading of the Ahom legend on the coins of King Supungmung (1663-70). The earliest Ahom coins known, therefore, were struck during the reign of King Jayadhvaja Simha (1648-1663).

Although the inscription and general design of these first coins of the Ahom Kingdom were copied from the coins of Cooch Behar, the octagonal shape was entirely Ahom, and according to tradition was chosen because of the belief that the Ahom country was eight sided. Apart from the unique shape, the coins were of similar fabric and weight standard to the Moghul rupee.

The earliest coins had inscriptions in Sanskrit using the Bengali script, but the retreat of the Moghul army under Mir Jumla in 1663 seems to have led to a revival of Ahom nationalism that may account for the fact that most of the coins struck between 1663 and 1696 had inscriptions in the old Ahom script, with invocations to Ahom deities.

Up to this time all the coins, following normal practice in North-East India, were merely dated to the coronation year of the ruler, but Rudra Simha (1696-1714) instituted the practice of dating coins to the year of issue. This ruler was a fervent Hindu, and reinstated Sanskrit inscriptions on the coins. After this the Ahom script was used on a few rare ceremonial issues.

The majority of coins issued were of silver, with binary subdivions down to a fraction of 1/32nd rupee. Cowrie shells were used for small change. Gold coins were struck throughout the period, often using the same dies as were used for the silver coins. A few copper coins were struck during the reign of Brajanatha Simha (1818-19), but these are very rare.

CHANDRAKANTA SIMHA
SE1732-39,41,42/1810-17,19,20AD

1/32 RUPEE
SILVER, oval, 0.34-0.36 g

KM#	Date	Year	VG	Fine	VF	XF
245	ND	—	15.00	20.00	26.50	35.00

1/16 RUPEE
SILVER, 7mm, octagonal, 0.67-0.72 g

| 246 | ND | — | 15.00 | 20.00 | 26.50 | 35.00 |

1/8 RUPEE

SILVER, 1.34-1.45 g

| 247 | ND | — | 15.00 | 20.00 | 26.50 | 35.00 |

1/4 RUPEE

SILVER, 2.68-2.90 g

| 248 | SE1741 | (1819) | 25.00 | 35.00 | 45.00 | 60.00 |
| | 1742 | (1820) | 25.00 | 35.00 | 45.00 | 60.00 |

1/2 RUPEE

SILVER, 5.35-5.80 g

| 249 | ND | — | 25.00 | 35.00 | 45.00 | 60.00 |

RUPEE

SILVER, 10.70-11.60 g

| 250 | SE1741 | (1819) | 30.00 | 40.00 | 50.00 | 70.00 |
| | 1742 | (1820) | 30.00 | 40.00 | 50.00 | 70.00 |

| 251 | SE1742 | (1820) | 30.00 | 40.00 | 50.00 | 70.00 |

1/32 MOHUR
GOLD

| 252 | ND | — | 20.00 | 35.00 | 50.00 | 75.00 |

1/16 MOHUR
GOLD

| 253 | ND | — | 30.00 | 45.00 | 70.00 | 100.00 |

MOHUR
GOLD, 10.70-11.40 g

| 257 | SE1741 | (1819) | 225.00 | 260.00 | 300.00 | 375.00 |

BRAJANATHA SIMHA
SE1739-1740/1818-1819AD

PANA

COPPER, 5.60 g

| 258 | ND | — | 12.50 | 21.50 | 35.00 | 50.00 |

Assam / INDEPENDENT KINGDOM 854

2 PANA
COPPER, 11.00 g

KM#	Date	Year	VG	Fine	VF	XF
259	ND	—	16.50	27.50	45.00	65.00

1/32 RUPEE
SILVER, 6mm, round, 0.34-0.36 g

| 260 | ND | — | 15.00 | 20.00 | 26.50 | 35.00 |

1/16 RUPEE
SILVER, 0.67-0.72 g

| 261 | ND | — | 15.00 | 20.00 | 26.50 | 35.00 |

1/8 RUPEE
SILVER, 1.34-1.45 g

| 262 | ND | — | 15.00 | 20.00 | 26.50 | 35.00 |

1/4 RUPEE
SILVER, 2.68-2.90 g

| 263 | SE1739 | (1817) | 16.50 | 27.50 | 40.00 | 55.00 |
| | 1740 | (1818) | 16.50 | 27.50 | 40.00 | 55.00 |

1/2 RUPEE
SILVER, 5.35-5.80 g

| 264 | ND | 7 | 16.50 | 27.50 | 40.00 | 55.00 |

RUPEE
SILVER, 10.70-11.60 g

| 265 | SE1739 | (1817) | 18.50 | 30.00 | 50.00 | 70.00 |
| | 1740 | (1818) | 18.50 | 30.00 | 50.00 | 70.00 |

1/32 MOHUR
GOLD

| 266 | ND | — | 20.00 | 30.00 | 50.00 | 75.00 |

1/8 MOHUR
GOLD, octagonal, 1.34-1.42 g

| 268 | ND | — | 35.00 | 50.00 | 75.00 | 100.00 |

1/4 MOHUR
GOLD, octagonal, 2.68-2.85 g

| 269 | SE1739 | (1817) | 50.00 | 65.00 | 85.00 | 125.00 |

MOHUR

GOLD, 10.70-11.40 g

| 271 | SE1739 | (1817) | 225.00 | 250.00 | 285.00 | 325.00 |
| | 1740 | (1818) | 225.00 | 250.00 | 285.00 | 325.00 |

JOGESVARA SIMHA
SE1743/1821AD

1/8 RUPEE

SILVER, 1.34-1.45 g

KM#	Date	Year	VG	Fine	VF	XF
274	ND	—	17.50	25.00	32.50	45.00

1/4 RUPEE
SILVER, octagonal, 2.68-2.90 g

| 275 | SE1743 | (1821) | 20.00 | 27.50 | 37.50 | 50.00 |

1/2 RUPEE

SILVER, 5.35-5.80 g

| 276 | ND | — | 30.00 | 40.00 | 50.00 | 70.00 |

RUPEE

SILVER, 10.70-11.60 g

| 277 | SE1743 | (1821) | 40.00 | 60.00 | 75.00 | 100.00 |

1/4 MOHUR
GOLD, octagonal, 2.68-2.85 g

| 281 | SE1743 | (1821) | 250.00 | 300.00 | 350.00 | 400.00 |

COOCH BEHAR

During the 15th century, the area that was to become Cooch Behar was ruled by the powerful Hindu kings of Kamata, who were defeated by Sultan 'Ala al din Husain Shah of Bengal in 1494AD. In 1511AD the kingdom of Cooch Behar was established by Chandan, a chieftain of the Koch tribe.

Chandan was succeeded about 1522 by Visvasimha, who consolidated the kingdom, and set up his capital at the present town of Cooch Behar. It was he who laid the foundations of the prosperity of the area by developing the Tibetan trade routes through Bhutan. Visvasimha is said to have abdicated about 1555AD to become an ascetic, and was succeeded by his son Nara Narayan, under whose reign the state reached the zenith of its power.

From the solid basis set up by his father, Nara Narayan set out, assisted by his brother Sukladhvaja, to extend the borders of his kingdom. Over the next quarter century he proceeded to subdue part of the Assam Valley, Kachar, Manipur, the Khasi and Jaintia Hills and part of Tripura and Sylhet. Nara Narayan was the first king of Cooch Behar to strike coins, and the varied style may indicate that he set up several mints over his empire. The style of one piece is very similar to that of later pieces struck by the Rajas of Jaintiapur, which suggests Jaintiapur as the mint for this variety, but no other varieties have been assigned to specific mints.

After the death of Sukladhvaja, who was a great general, the military strength of the kingdom waned. Nara Narayan quarrelled with Sukladhvaja's son Raghu Deva, and the latter set himself up as ruler of the eastern part of the kingdom in 1581, initially under the suzerainty of his uncle, but after Nara Narayan's death, as full independent ruler.

Nara Narayan's son, Lakshmi Narayan inherited the western part of the kingdom, but no attempt was made to consolidate the conquests made by his father, and Kachar, Tripura and other states reverted to their former fully independent state. Lakshmi Narayan was a weak, peaceloving king, who preferred to declare himself a vassal of the Mughal Emperor in 1596, rather than make any attempt to preserve his independence. In accepting Mughal suzerainty, he gravely offended his subjects, who rose in revolt. The Mughals assisted Lakshmi Narayan quell the rebellion, and in 1603 a treaty was signed under which Lakshmi Narayan agreed never again to strike full rupees and to abandon certain other royal prerogatives. The Eastern Kingdom under Raghu Deva and his son Parikshit refused to bow to Mughal domination in the same way, and in 1612 the Mughals invaded and destroyed their kingdom.

After Lakshmi Narayan's death in 1627, the new ruler Vira Narayan exhibited a certain degree of independence by striking full rupees and retaking the former Eastern Cooch Behar Kingdom from the Mughals. By this time, however, a powerful leader had emerged in Bhutan, and trade was disrupted by wars between Bhutan and Tibet, causing a reduction in the number of coins struck.

The Mughals soon recaptured the eastern territories, but the next ruler, Prana Narayan, was able to reopen trade links with Tibet through Bhutan. In 1661 Prana Narayan was expelled from his capital by the Mughal governor of Bengal, Mir Jumla, and sought refuge in Bhutan. At this time Mir Jumla struck coins in Cooch Behar in the name of the Mughal Emperor Aurangzeb, but while Mir Jumla was stuck in Assam during the monsoon of 1663, Prana Narayan managed to regain control of his kingdom, paying tribute to the Mughal Emperor.

For the next century Cooch Behar was relatively peaceful until there was a dispute over the succession in 1772. After a confusing period during which the Bhutanese installed their own nominated ruler and captured Dhairyendra Narandra, the Chief Minister appealed to the British for assistance. With an eye on the potentially lucrative Tibetan trade, which had increased somewhat in volume since Prithvi Narayan's rise to power in Nepal, the British agreed to support Darendra Narayan, so long as British suzerainty was acknowledged.

Over the following decades the British gradually increased their control over the state. After large numbers of debased silver half, or "Narainy" rupees had been struck, the British decided to close the mint, and after that a few coins only were struck at the coronation of each ruler, although it was only in 1866 that the local coins ceased to be legal tender.

Bhutanese copies: Until the 1780's the Bhutanese used to periodically send surplus silver to the mint in Cooch Behar to strike into coin for local use, as Cooch Behar coins circulated widely in Bhutan. After the Cooch Behar mint was closed in 1788 the Bhutanese established their own mints, striking copies of the 1/2 rupees - initially of fine silver with slight differences in design from the original Cooch Behar coins, but later the silver content reduced until they were of pure copper or brass. For these issues see Bhutan listing.

RULERS
Harendra Narayan, CB273-329/
   SE1705-1761/1783-1839AD
Shivendra Narayan, CB329-337/
   SE1761-1769/1839-1847AD
Narendra Narayan, CB337-353/
   SE1769-1785/1847-1863AD
Nripendra Narayan, CB353-401/
   SE1785-1833/1863-1911AD
Raja Rajendra Narayan, CB401-403/
   SE1833-1835/1911-1913AD
Jitendra Narayan, CB403-412/
   SE1835-1844/1913-1922AD
Jagaddipendra Narayan, CB412-439/
   SE1844-1871/1922-1949AD

DATING
The coins are dated in either the Saka era (Saka yr. + 78 = AD year) or the Cooch Behar era (CB yr. + 1510 = AD year) calculated from the year of the founding of the kingdom by Chandan in 1511AD. Some coins have dates in both eras, but as the Saka always refers back to the accession year, and the Cooch Behar year seems to show the actual date of striking, the two years do not necessarily correspond to the same AD year.

Unfortunately the dies for the half rupees were usually rather broader than the flans, so the year is only rarely visible.

HARENDRA NARAYAN
CB273-329/SE1705-1761/1783-1839AD
These names usually cannot be differentiated.

'rendra' center left on obverse

1/2 RUPEE
SILVER, 4.70 g

KM#	Date	Year	VG	Fine	VF	XF
141	ND	—	5.00	8.00	11.00	15.00

KACHAR

The Kacharis are probably the original inhabitants of the Assam Valley, and in the 13th century ruled much of the south bank of the Brahmaputra from their capital at Dimapur.

Around 1530 the Ahoms inflicted several crushing defeats on the Kacharis, Dimapur was sacked, and the Kacharis were forced to retreat further south and set up a new capital at Maibong.

Very little is known about this obscure state, and the only time that coins were struck in any quantity was during the late 16th and early 17th centuries. One coin, indeed, proudly announces the conquest of Sylhet, but this military prowess seems to have been short lived, and the small kingdom was only saved from Muslim domination by its isolation and lack of economic worth.

A few coins were struck during the 18th and 19th centuries, but this was probably merely as a demonstration of independence, rather than for any economic reason.

In 1819, the last Kachari ruler, Govind Chandra was ousted by the Manipuri ruler Chaurajit Simha, and during the Burmese occupation of Manipur and Assam, the Manipuris remained in control of Kachar. In 1824, Govind Chandra was restored to his throne by the British, and ruled under British suzerainty. By all accounts his administration was not a success, and in 1832, soon after Govind Chandra had been murdered, the British took over the administration of the State in "compliance with the frequent and earnestly expressed wishes of the people".

The earliest coins of Kachar were clearly copied from the contemporary coins of Cooch Behar, with weight standard also copied from the Bengali standard. The flans are, however, even broader than those of the Cooch Behar coins, making the coins very distinctive.

A number of spectacular gold and silver coins,

purporting to come from Kachar, appeared in Calcutta during the 1960's, but as their authenticity has been doubted, they have been omitted from this listing.

RULERS

A list of the Kings of Kachar has been preserved in local traditions, but is rather unreliable. The following list has been compiled from this traditional list, together with names and dates obtained from other sources, but may not be completely accurate.

Krishna Chandra Narayan,
 SE1712-1735/c.1790-1813AD
Govinda Chandra,
 SE1735-1741/1814-1819AD
Chaurajit Singh, (of Manipur),
 SE1741-1745/1819-1823AD
Gambhir Singh, (of Manipur),
 SE1745-1746/1823-1824AD
Govinda Chandra,
 SE1746-1752/1824-1830AD

GOVINDA CHANDRA
SE1735-1752/1813-1830AD

RUPEE

SILVER, 25mm, 10.70-11.60 g

KM#	Date	Year	VG	Fine	VF	XF
150	SE1736	(1814)	80.00	130.00	225.00	325.00

MANIPUR

Although the Manipuri traditions preserve a long list of kings which purports to go back to the early years of the Christian era, the first ruler whose existence can be verified from more tangible sources was a Naga called Panheiba, who adopted the Hindu religion and took the name of Gharib Niwaz about 1714AD.

Gharib Niwaz seems to have been a powerful ruler, who was successful in the frequent wars with Burma, and hence raised the country from obscurity. He was murdered in 1750, together with his eldest son, and it was during the reign of the latter's son, Gaura Singh, that the British first came into contact with Manipur. After the death of Gharib Niwaz the Burmese had more success with their incursions into Manipur, and by 1761 there was a danger that the capital would be captured, so the Manipuris appealed to the British for military assistance. This was granted, and in 1762 British troops helped the Manipuris drive out the Burmese, and a treaty of alliance was signed. On this occasion 500 meklee gold rupees were sent to the British as part payment for the expenses of this assistance.

Gaura Singh died in 1764 and from then until 1798 his brother Jai Singh heroically defended his country against the Burmese. In the early years of his reign he suffered many setbacks, but for the last ten years of his reign his position was fairly secure. In 1798 Jai Singh abdicated and died the following year. The next 35 years were to see five of his eight sons on the throne, plotting against each other and enlisting Burmese support for their internecine rivalry. After 1812 the Manipuri King was little more than a puppet in the hands of the Burmese, and when the Kings tried to assert their independence they were ousted to become Kings of Kachar.

In 1824, after the 1st Burma war, the Burmese were finally driven out of Manipur and Gambhir Singh, one of the younger sons of Jai Singh, asked for British assistance to regain control of his kingdom. This was granted, and from 1825 until his death in 1834 Gambhir Singh ruled well and restored an element of prosperity to his kingdom. A British resident was stationed in Manipur, but the King ruled his country independently. The British stayed aloof from several palace intrigues and revolutions, and it was only in 1891, after several British Officials had been killed, that the administration was brought under the control of a British Political Agent.

RULERS

Madhu Chandra, SE1723-1728/
 1801-1806AD
Chaurajit Singh, SE1728-1734/
 1806-1812AD
Marjit Singh, under Burmese suzerainty,
 SE1734-1741/1812-1819AD
Huidromba Subol, SE1741-1742/
 1819-1820AD
Gambhir Singh, SE1742-1743/
 1820-1821AD
Jadu Singh, SE1743-1745/
 1821-1823AD
Raghab Singh, SE1745-1746/
 1823-1824AD
Bhadra Singh, SE1746-1747/
 1824-1825AD
Gambhir Singh, restored by the British,
 SE1747-1756/1825-1834AD
Chandra Kirti, SE1756-1765/
 1834-1843AD
Nar Singh, SE1765-1771/
 1843-1849AD
Chandra Kirti, SE1771-1808/
 1849-1886AD
Sura Chandra Singh, SE1808-1812/
 1886-1890AD
Kula Chandra Singh, SE1812-1813/
 1890-1891AD
Chura Chandra, SE1813-1862/
 1891-1941AD
Bodh Chandra, SE1862-1870/
 1941-1949AD

COINAGE

The only coins struck in quantity for circulation in Manipur were small bell-metal (circa 74 percent copper, 23 percent tin, 3 percent zinc) coins called "sel". According to local tradition these coins were first struck in the 17th century, but this is doubtful, and it seems likely that the sels were first struck in the second half of the 18th century. Unfortunately few of the sels can be attributed to any particular ruler, as they merely bear a Nagari letter deemed auspicious for the particular reign, and it has not been recorded which letter was deemed auspicious for which ruler.

The value of the sel functioned relative to the rupees which also circulated in Manipur for making large purchases, although Government accounts were kept in sel until 1891. Prior to 1838 the sel was valued at about 900 to the rupee, but after that date it fell in value to around 480 to the rupee, although there were occasional fluctuations. About 1878, speculative hoarding of sel forced the value up to 240 to the rupee, but large numbers of sel were struck at this time, and from then until 1891, when the sel were withdrawn from circulation, their value remained fairly stable at about 400 to the rupee.

During the years after 1714AD some square gold and silver coins were struck, but as few have survived, they were probably only struck in small quantities for ceremonial rather than monetary use.

Apart from the coins mentioned above, some larger bell-metal coins have been attributed to Manipur, but the attribution is still somewhat tentative. Also several other gold coins, two with an image of Krishna playing the flute, have been discovered in Calcutta in recent years, but as their authenticity has been queried, they have not been included in the following listing.

DATING

Most of the silver and gold coins of Manipur are dated in the Saka era (Sake date + 78 = AD date), but at least one coin is dated in the Manipuri "Chandrabda" era, which may be converted to the AD year by adding 788 to the Chandrabda date.

MONETARY SYSTEM
(Until 1838AD)
880 to 960 Sel = 1 Rupee
 (Commencing 1838AD)
420-480 Sel = 1 Rupee

CHAURAJIT SINGH
SE1725-1734/1803-1812AD

1/4 RUPEE

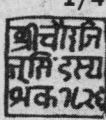 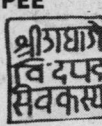

SILVER, 2.68-2.90 g

C#	Date	Year	VG	Fine	VF	XF
55	SE1726	(1804)	50.00	75.00	110.00	130.00
	1729	(1807)	50.00	75.00	110.00	130.00

1/2 RUPEE

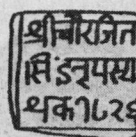 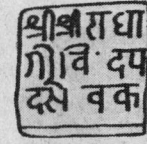

SILVER, 5.35-5.80 g

| 56 | SE1726 | (1804) | 55.00 | 90.00 | 125.00 | 160.00 |

RUPEE

SILVER, 10.70-11.60 g

57	SE1728	(1806)	80.00	130.00	190.00	250.00
	1729	(1807)	80.00	130.00	190.00	250.00
	1732	(1810)	80.00	130.00	190.00	250.00
	1734	(1812)	55.00	90.00	125.00	160.00

MOHUR

GOLD, 11.20-12.50 g

C#	Date	Year	VG	Fine	VF	XF
61	SE1731	(1809)	225.00	375.00	625.00	875.00

MARJIT SINGH
SE1734-1741/1812-1819AD

RUPEE

SILVER, 11.50 g

| 71 | SE1736 | (1814) | 45.00 | 80.00 | 130.00 | 190.00 |

MOHUR

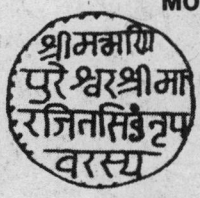 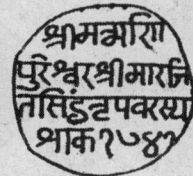

GOLD, 10.70-11.40 g

| 75 | SE1741 | (1819) | 375.00 | 625.00 | 875.00 | 1150. |

GAMBHIR SINGH
SE1748-1756/1826-1834AD

MOHUR

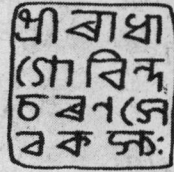 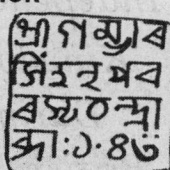

GOLD, 10.70-11.40 g

| 85 | 1043* | (1831) | 375.00 | 625.00 | 875.00 | 1150. |

*NOTE: Chandrabdah 1043 (a local date system).

ANONYMOUS ISSUES

These bear a single Bengali character, of uncertain significance, and cannot be assigned to particular rulers. All are uniface.

SEL

BRONZE BELL-METAL, uniface
Sri

C#	Date		Good	VG	Fine	VF
1	ND			3.50	6.00	10.00

NOTE: Many variations in style exist, 2 varieties are illustrated above.

Ma

| 2 | ND | 5.00 | 8.00 | 11.50 | 15.00 |

Ra

| 3 | ND | 6.00 | 10.00 | 15.00 | 20.00 |

(Said to be on issue of Nara Singh, 1843-50)

Ka

| 4 | ND | 6.00 | 10.00 | 15.00 | 20.00 |

(Struck before 1820)

La

| 5 | ND | 6.00 | 10.00 | 15.00 | 20.00 |

(Perhaps an issue of Sura Chandra, 1886-90)

Ku

| 6 | ND | 6.00 | 10.00 | 15.00 | 20.00 |

(Probably an issue of Kula Chandra Singh, 1890-91)

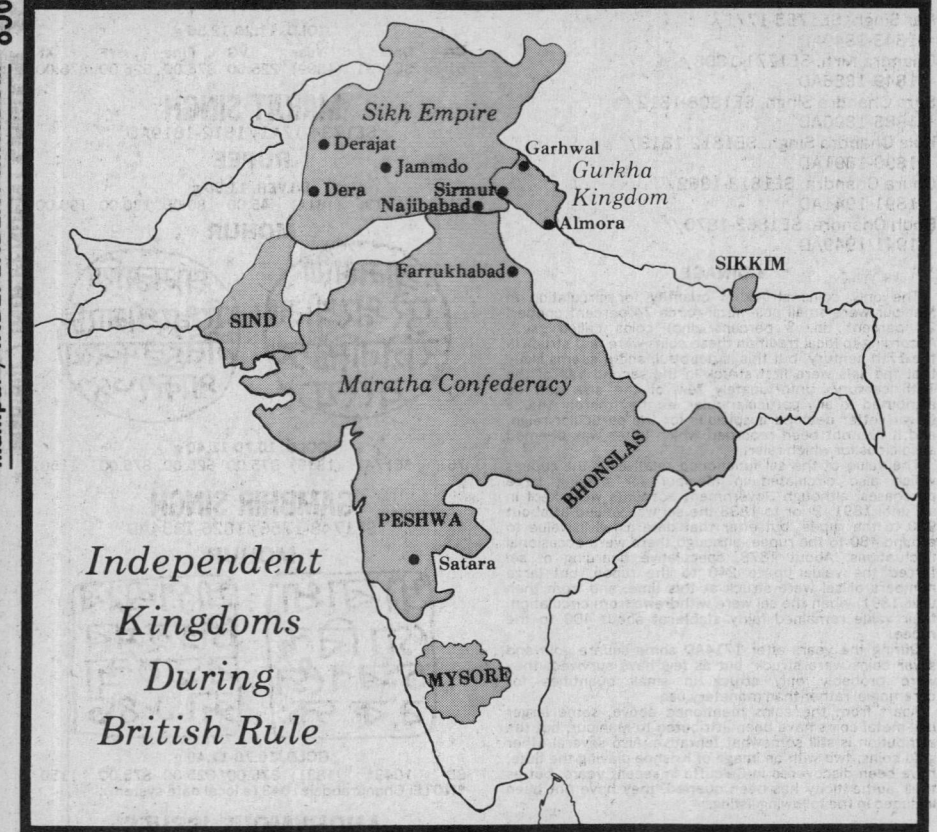

Independent Kingdoms During British Rule

C#	Date	Year	VG	Fine	VF	XF
86.2a	AH1228	39	35.00	65.00	100.00	150.00

SILVER, 10.70-11.60 g

GURKHA KINGDOM

GARHWAL
RULERS
Girvan Yuddha, of Nepal
VS1860-1872 / 1803-1815AD

Srinagar Mint
In the names of Shah Alam II
and Girvan Yuddha, of Nepal
VS1860-1863 / 1803-1806AD

TIMASHA

SILVER

C#	Date		Good	VG	Fine	VF
35	VS(18)65	(1808)	6.50	10.00	15.00	22.50
	(18)66	(1809)	6.50	10.00	15.00	22.50
	ND		4.00	6.50	10.00	15.00

In the names of Muhammad Akbar II
and Girvan Yuddha, of Nepal
VS1863-1870 / 1806-1813AD

TIMASHA

SILVER

C#	Date		Good	VG	Fine	VF
36	VS(18)66	(1809)	6.50	10.00	15.00	20.00
	(18)67	(1810)	6.50	10.00	15.00	20.00
	(18)68	(1811)	6.50	10.00	15.00	20.00
	(18)69	(1812)	6.50	10.00	15.00	20.00
	(18)70	(1813)	6.50	10.00	15.00	20.00

In the name of Girvan Yuddha
VS1860-1873 / 1803-1816AD

PAISA

COPPER

C#	Date		Good	VG	Fine	VF
30	VS1859	(1802)	4.00	6.00	8.00	12.50
	1872	(1815)	3.00	4.50	7.00	10.00
	1873	(1816)	4.00	6.00	8.00	12.50

TIMASHA

SILVER

C#	Date	Year	VG	Fine	VF	XF
37	ND	—	6.00	10.00	15.00	20.00

KUMAON
RULER
Girvan Yuddha, of Nepal
VS1860-1873 / 1803-1816AD

FARRUKHABAD

Farrukhabad a district in north India was founded early in the eighteenth century by the Afghan, Mohammed Khan (d.1743), who was governor first of Allahabad and later of Malwa. The subsequent struggles of his sons with Awadh, with the Rohillas and with the Marathas, culminated in Farrukhabad becoming a tributary to Awadh, by which state Farrukhabad was entirely surrounded. In 1801 Farrukhabad was ceded to the British by the Nawab Vizier of Awadh.

For similar coins struck in the name of Ahmad Shah (Durrani) dated AH1174, 1176 refer to Afghanistan, Durrani listings. For later issues with fixed regnal year 45 refer to India-British / Bengal Presidency listings.

MINTNAME
Commencing AH1167

احمدنکر فرخ اباد

Ahmadnagar-Farrukhabad
NOTE: Catalog numbers refer to Craig's Mughal listing.

Ahmadnagar - Farrukhabad Mint
In the name of Shah Alam II
AH1173-1221 / 1759-1806AD

FALUS

COPPER

C#	Date	Year	Good	VG	Fine	VF
71.5	AH1219	39	4.50	8.50	13.50	20.00

In the name of Muhammad Akbar II
AH1221-1253 / 1806-1837AD

1/2 ANNA

COPPER

C#	Date	Year	Good	VG	Fine	VF
123.5	AH1226	6	5.00	10.00	15.00	22.50
	1233	12	4.50	8.50	13.50	20.00

In the name of Shah Alam II
AH1173-1221 / 1759-1806AD

RUPEE

SILVER, 10.70-11.60 g

C#	Date	Year	VG	Fine	VF	XF
86.2	AH1216	39	8.50	13.50	20.00	35.00
	1217	39	8.50	13.50	20.00	35.00
	1218	39	8.50	13.50	20.00	35.00
	1219	39	8.50	13.50	20.00	35.00
	1220	39	8.50	13.50	20.00	35.00
	1224	39	8.50	13.50	20.00	35.00
	1225	39	8.50	13.50	20.00	35.00
	1227	39	8.50	13.50	20.00	35.00
	1228	39	8.50	13.50	20.00	35.00

NAZARANA RUPEE
Issued after cession to the British

Almora Mint
PAISA

COPPER

C#	Date	Year	Good	VG	Fine	VF
10	VS(18)66 (1809)		3.00	5.00	8.00	11.50

MARATHA CONFEDERACY

The origins of the Marathas are lost in the early history of the remote hill country of the Western Ghats in present-day Maharashtra. By the fifteenth century they had come into occasional prominence for their resistance to Muslim incursions into their homelands. They were a rugged wiry people who, by the seventeenth century, had accomodated themselves to the political realities of their times by becoming feudatories, as mercenaries, to the sultans of Bijapur. It is not clear exactly what happened to suddenly thrust the Marathas into the limelight of Indian history in the seventeenth century. The most likely explanation seems to be that the broad sweep of Aurangzeb's campaigns across the Deccan, his insensitivity towards Hindu sentiment, and the pre-eminence he gave to Islam, all served to politicize a hitherto politically quiescent people. And just as Aurangzeb supplied the occasion, the Marathas found in Sivaji the man.

In the seventeenth century Shahji, the father of Sivaji, was holder of a small fiefdom under the Bijapur sultans. His son, taking advantage of the declining authority of his overlords, seized some of the surrounding territory. Bijapur proved incapable of quelling his insurrection. Drawing encouragement from this experience, Sivaji's forces sacked and plundered the Mughal port of Surat in 1664. From this point until his death in 1680 Sivaji maintained a sort of running guerilla war with Aurangzeb. There were no decisive victories for either side but Sivaji left behind him a cohesive and well organized regional alliance in the Western Deccan, a small isolated kingdom in Tanjore and a few pockets of territory on the west coast.

After Sivaji's death the struggle was renewed as Aurangzeb advanced into the Deccan. It was the years after Aurangzeb's death, in 1707 which really saw revival as the Maratha confederacy gained a new cohesiveness and its military successes began to make it look as if the Marathas might even become the new masters of India. The revenues of much of the Deccan now flowed into (finished up in) Maratha pockets. Baji Rao I, the Peshwa, pressed as far north as the gates of Delhi and in 1738 he gained control of Malwa. Parts of Gujarat also were in confederacy hands. Bengal was invaded, Orissa annexed (1751), and the territories of the Nizam of Hyderabad and the Carnatic appeared at risk. It was during this period that some of the great Maratha families gained prominence - the Holkars, the Sindhias, the Gaekwars and the Bhonslas - families who later, as the confederacy began to disintegrate and give way to rivalry, would assert their own regional interests at the expense of the alliance.

The turning point for Maratha fortunes was the battle of Panipat on January 14th 1761. Intending to stop the Afghan, Ahmad Shah Abdali (Durrani), in his tracks, the Marathas assembled the greatest army in their history and placed it under the unified command of the Peshwa of Poona. By nightfall the Peshwa's son and heir, Bhao Sahib, and all the leading chiefs, were dead. Maratha losses were said to have been in excess of a hundred thousand men. The Marathas would still remain a force to be reckoned with, they would again cross the Chambel (1767), and they would still give the Nizam's forces a thrashing (1795), but from 1761 onwards internal dissension grew rife and the Maratha Confederacy would never again exhibit sufficient cohesion to be considered a serious contender for the crown of India.

This powerful alliance of Marathi warriors owed nominal allegiance to the Rajas of Satara (descendents of Shivaji) and drew their unity from the leadership of the Peshwa, the hereditary prime minister of the confederation. In the mid-eighteenth century the Marathas were at the apogee of their influence, having hastened the end of effective Mughal power in the Deccan and western India. They successfully checked the intrusions of the Durranis into north India, although the experience left them so militarily exhausted that the dominance in Hindustan passed to other hands.

The great families of the lieutenants of the Peshwa gradually carved out regional power bases and became progressively less responsive to the authority of their formal superiors. The Maratha power as such was broken in a series of wars with the East India Company, bitterly fought and very close contests which settled the fate of large sections of India. Broadly speaking the Marathas may for convenience sake be listed in two categories, the lines which became extinct through British action and those which accomodated the English after defeat and survived to become Princely States. The latter will be found elsewhere in the catalogue; the non-surviving political units are catalogued below.

BHONSLAS
RULERS

Raghoji II, 1788-1816AD
Raghoji III, 1816-1853AD

MINTS

Cuttack

Most coins are imitations of Mughal coins of Ahmad Shah (1748-54AD), more or less barbarized. The Bhonsla mints were closed when the state was abolished in 1854.

CUTTACK MINT

Rev. symbols and

"Zareepathka" flag added after 1825.

1/16 RUPEE
SILVER, 0.61-0.72 g

KM#	Date	Year	VG	Fine	VF	XF
11 (8)	ND	—	10.00	15.00	22.50	35.00

1/8 RUPEE

SILVER, 1.33-1.45 g

| 12 (9) | ND | — | 10.00 | 15.00 | 22.50 | 35.00 |

1/4 RUPEE
SILVER, 2.67-2.90 g
Rev: Flag only.

| 13 (10.1) | ND | — | 9.00 | 14.00 | 20.00 | 30.00 |

Rev: Both symbols.

| 14 (10.2) | ND | — | 9.00 | 14.00 | 20.00 | 30.00 |

1/2 RUPEE
SILVER, 5.35-5.80 g
Rev: Both symbols.

| 15 (11) | ND | — | 12.00 | 16.00 | 22.50 | 35.00 |

RUPEE

SILVER, 10.70-11.60 g
W/o mint marks. Mintname: Katak
Pseudo regnal year

| 16 (12.1) | ND | 52 | 16.00 | 22.50 | 35.00 | 50.00 |

Rev: Flag only, pseudo regnal years.

17 (12.2)	ND	5	15.00	20.00	30.00	40.00
		51	15.00	20.00	30.00	40.00
		52	15.00	20.00	30.00	40.00
		511	15.00	20.00	30.00	40.00
		512	15.00	20.00	30.00	40.00
		521	15.00	20.00	30.00	40.00

Rev: Both symbols.

| 18 (12.3) | ND | 5 | 16.00 | 22.50 | 35.00 | 50.00 |

NAZARANA RUPEE

SILVER

KM#	Date	Year	VG	Fine	VF	XF
19 (17)	—	22				

PESHWAS
RULERS

Baji Rao, 1796-1818AD

MINTS

Ahmadabad احمد اباد

Gulshanabad (Nasik) گلشن اباد

Jalaun جلون

Jhansi بلونت نگر
Mintname: Balwantnagar

Kunch کونچ

Poona پونه

Saugor روشن نگر ساگر
Mintname: Ravishnagar Saugar

AHMADABAD MINT

One of Maratha Mints from 1757-1800AD, it was leased to Baroda from 1800-1804AD, returned during 1804-1806AD, released to Baroda in 1806AD, and ceded to Baroda in 1817AD. Later, in 1818AD, it was annexed by the East India Company and finally closed in 1835AD.

MINT MARKS

Obverse: Ankus  Ankus w/pennant

Mint symbol on reverse at lower left.

NOTE: Baroda coins of this mint have the Nagari initial of the ruler; British coins have the following mark on reverse:

In the name of Muhammad Akbar II
AH1221-1253/1806-1837AD

PAISA
COPPER

| 53 (33) | AH1232 | 10 | 3.00 | 4.00 | 6.50 | 9.00 |

1/2 RUPEE
SILVER, 18mm, 5.35-5.80 g
Mint mark: Ankus.

| 54 (34) | AH— | | 6.00 | 9.00 | 14.00 | 20.00 |

Mint mark: Ankus w/pennant.

| 55 (38) | AHxxxx | | 6.00 | 9.00 | 14.00 | 20.00 |

RUPEE

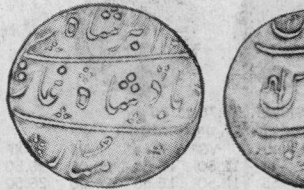

SILVER, 10.70-11.60 g
Mint mark: Ankus and scissors.

| 56 (36) | AH1230 | 8 | 13.50 | 18.50 | 25.00 | 35.00 |

Maratha Confederacy / INDEPENDENT KINGDOM 858

Mint mark: Ankus.

KM#	Date	Year	VG	Fine	VF	XF
57 (37)	AH122x	8	7.50	12.50	18.50	25.00
		9	7.50	12.50	18.50	25.00

Mint mark: Ankus w/pennant.

| 58 (39) | AH1231 | 9 | 8.50 | 13.50 | 20.00 | 30.00 |

GULSHANABAD MINT
Nasik

In the name of Shah Alam II
AH1173-1221/1759-1806AD

Rev: symbols
Symbol: on rev.

1/4 RUPEE
SILVER, 2.68-2.90 g

| 107 (98) | AH1236 | — | 10.00 | 12.50 | 16.50 | 21.50 |

1/2 RUPEE

SILVER, 5.35-5.80 g

| 108 (99) | AH1229 | — | 10.00 | 15.00 | 20.00 | 30.00 |
| | 1235 | — | 10.00 | 15.00 | 20.00 | 30.00 |

RUPEE

SILVER, 10.70-11.60 g

KM#	Date	Year	Mintage	VG	Fine	VF
109 (100)	AH1219	—	14.00	18.50	22.50	30.00
	1227	—	14.00	18.50	22.50	30.00
	1229	—	14.00	18.50	22.50	30.00
	1232	—	14.00	18.50	22.50	30.00
	1234	—	14.00	18.50	22.50	30.00
	1235	—	14.00	18.50	22.50	30.00
	1236	—	14.00	18.50	22.50	30.00
	1251	—	14.00	18.50	22.50	30.00

JALAUN MINT

Obv. symbols: and
Rev: or

In the name of Shah Alam II
AH1173-1221/1759-1806AD

RUPEE

Mintname:

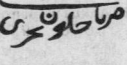

Zarb ba Jalaun Hijri

SILVER, 10.70-11.60 g
Crude fabric, narrow flan.

KM#	Date	Year	VG	Fine	VF	XF
124 (65.1)	AH1224	49	12.50	16.50	20.00	26.50
	1222	55	12.50	16.50	20.00	26.50

Mintname:

Zarb Ku(nch), Kuna(r), Jalaun

Fine fabric, normal flan.

KM#	Date	Year	VG	Fine	VF	XF
125 (66)	AH—	49	18.50	22.50	30.00	45.00

Crude fabric, narrow flan.

126 (66.1)	AH1222	17 (error)				
			8.50	12.50	15.00	20.00
	1223	17 (error)				
			8.50	12.50	15.00	20.00
	—	21	8.50	12.50	15.00	20.00
	1222	51	8.50	12.50	15.00	20.00
	1222	52	8.50	12.50	15.00	20.00
	1222	53	8.50	12.50	15.00	20.00
	1222	55	8.50	12.50	15.00	20.00
	1222	57	8.50	12.50	15.00	20.00

In the names of Shah Alam II and Latif Khan
AH1173-1221/1759-1806AD

| 128 (66.2) | AH— | 53 | 35.00 | 40.00 | 50.00 | 75.00 |

JHANSI MINT

Mint mark:

 on reverse

Mintname:

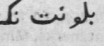

Balwantnagar

In the name of Shah Alam II
AH1173-1221/1759-1806AD

RUPEE

SILVER, 10.70-11.60 g
Obv: 99111 added.

144 (78.5)	AH1220	47	11.50	15.00	20.00	27.50
	1221	48	11.50	15.00	20.00	27.50
	1224	52	11.50	15.00	20.00	27.50
	1234	—	11.50	15.00	20.00	27.50

Rev: Lily.

| 145 (79) | AH— | 3 | 12.50 | 17.50 | 22.50 | 30.00 |
| | — | 4 | 12.50 | 17.50 | 22.50 | 30.00 |

KUNCH MINT

Mint marks:

 rev. all coins
#1 obv.

 #2, obv.

 #3, obv.

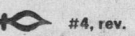 #4, rev. 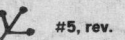 #5, rev.

Mintname:

Kunch Hijri

East India Company
As administrator of Kunch for Holkar from AH1220-R.Y.47/1805AD.

RUPEE
SILVER, 10.70-11.60 g
Obv: Symbols #1, #2, #3.
Rev: Symbol #4.

KM#	Date	Year	VG	Fine	VF	XF
178 (7)	AH1220	47	15.00	25.00	35.00	50.00
	1221	47	15.00	25.00	35.00	50.00

POONA MINT

"Muhiabad Poona" Mint opened in 1750 and closed between 1834-1835.

In the name of Ali Gauhar, the name of Shah Alam II before his accession

NOTE: On Feb. 10, 1818AD (AH1233, Falsi Era 1128) the British East India Company took over Poona, so all coins of that date or later are British Colonial issues.

Mint marks:

| 1 | 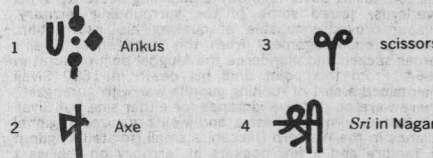 Ankus | 3 | scissors |
| 2 | Axe | 4 | Sri in Nagari |

1/8 RUPEE

SILVER, 1.34-1.45 g
Rev: Mint mark #1.

| 207 (112) | — | — | 7.50 | 12.50 | 20.00 | 30.00 |

1/4 RUPEE
SILVER, 2.68-2.90 g
Rev: Mint mark #1 w/regnal year in Persian numerals.

| 208 (113) | — | — | — | — | Reported, not confirmed |

Rev: Mint mark #1 w/Fasli date in Nagari numerals.

| 209 (114) | FE1238 | (1828) | 7.50 | 10.00 | 16.50 | 25.00 |

Rev: Mint mark: #2.

| 210 (115) | FE1242 | — | 12.50 | 20.00 | 30.00 | 50.00 |

1/2 RUPEE

SILVER, 5.35-5.80 g
Rev: Mint mark #1 w/regnal year in Persian numerals.

| 211 (116) | — | — | — | — | — | — |

Rev: Mint mark #1 w/Fasli date in Nagari numerals.

212 (117)	FE1233	(1823)	10.00	15.00	20.00	30.00
	1236	(1826)	10.00	15.00	20.00	30.00
	1240	(1830)	10.00	15.00	20.00	30.00

RUPEE

SILVER, 10.70-11.60 g
Ankusi Rupee
Rev: Mint mark #1 w/regnal year in Persian numerals.

KM#	Date	Year	Fine	VF	XF
213 (120)	—	11	10.00	12.50	16.50	25.00
	—	12	10.00	12.50	16.50	25.00
	—	15	10.00	12.50	16.50	25.00

KM#	Date	Year	VG	Fine	VF	XF
(120)	AH1225	—	10.00	14.00	20.00	27.50
	1229	—	10.00	14.00	20.00	27.50

NOTE: This coin was copied by the local rulers at Alibagh, Wai and Wadgaon.

Rev: Mint mark #1, Fasli date in Nagari numerals

KM#	Date	Year	VG	Fine	VF	XF
214	FE1232	(1822)	11.50	13.50	15.00	20.00
(122)	1233	(1823)	11.50	13.50	15.00	20.00
	1234	(1824)	11.50	13.50	15.00	20.00
	1235	(1825)	11.50	13.50	15.00	20.00
	1236	(1826)	11.50	13.50	15.00	20.00
	1237	(1827)	11.50	13.50	15.00	20.00
	1238	(1828)	11.50	13.50	15.00	20.00
	1239	(1829)	11.50	13.50	15.00	20.00
	1240	(1830)	11.50	13.50	15.00	20.00
	1241	(1831)	11.50	13.50	15.00	20.00
	1242	(1832)	11.50	13.50	15.00	20.00
	1243	(1833)	11.50	13.50	15.00	20.00
	1244	(1834)	11.50	13.50	15.00	20.00

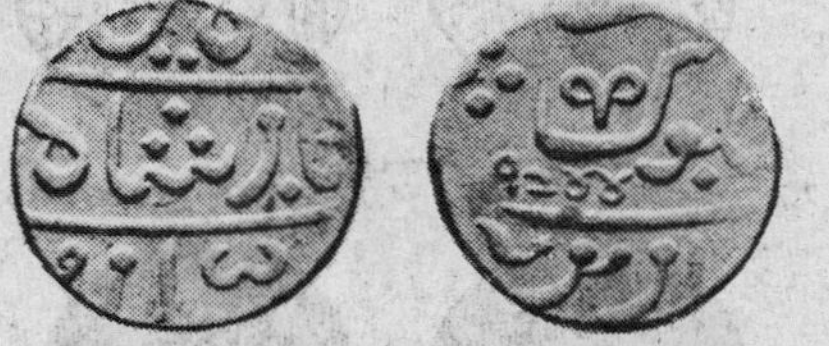

Rev: Mint mark #3, Fasli date in Nagari numerals.

KM#	Date	Year	VG	Fine	VF	XF
217	AH1230	(1820)	11.50	16.50	22.50	30.00
(126)	1231	(1821)	11.50	16.50	22.50	30.00
	1232	(1822)	11.50	16.50	22.50	30.00
	1234	(1824)	11.50	16.50	22.50	30.00
	1236	(1826)	11.50	16.50	22.50	30.00
	1238	(1828)	11.50	16.50	22.50	30.00
	1239	(1829)	11.50	16.50	22.50	30.00
	1240	(1830)	11.50	16.50	22.50	30.00
	1241	(1831)	11.50	16.50	22.50	30.00
	1242	(1832)	11.50	16.50	22.50	30.00
	1243	(1833)	11.50	16.50	22.50	30.00
	1244	(1834)	11.50	16.50	22.50	30.00
	ND	30	12.50	17.50	23.50	32.00

SAUGOR MINT

In the name of Shah Alam II

AH1173-1221/1759-1806AD

RUPEE

Mintmarks:

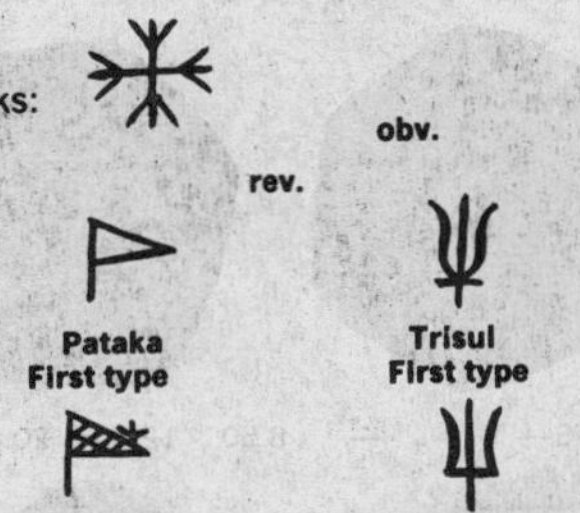
obv.
rev.
Pataka
First type
Trisul
First type
Second type
Second type

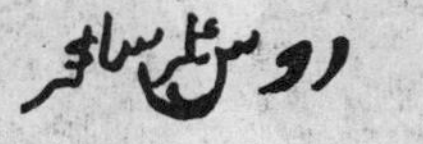

Mintname: Ravishnagar Sagar

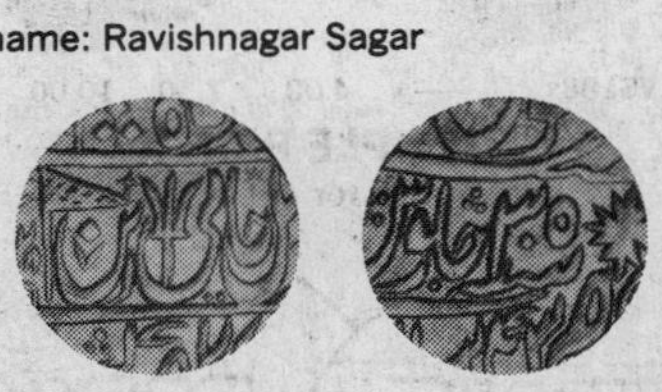

KM#	Date	Year	VG	Fine	VF	XF
240	AH1216	42	10.00	12.50	15.00	20.00
(167.3)	1218	43	10.00	12.50	15.00	20.00
	1218	44	10.00	12.50	15.00	20.00
	1219	44	10.00	12.50	15.00	20.00
	1220	45	10.00	12.50	15.00	20.00
	1222	47	10.00	12.50	15.00	20.00
	—	48	10.00	12.50	15.00	20.00
	1224	49	10.00	12.50	15.00	20.00

East India Company

Local issues post 1818-1819AD

PAISA

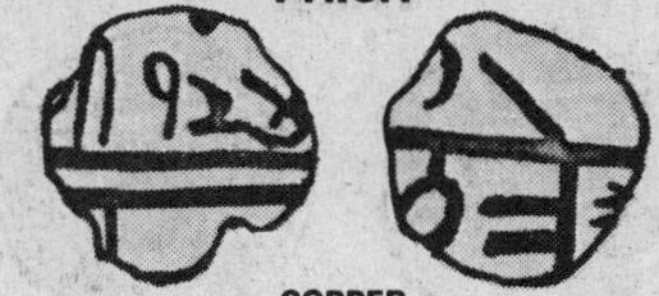

COPPER

KM#	Date	Year	Good	VG	Fine	VF
270	FE1230	(1820)	3.50	5.00	7.00	10.00
(192)	1231	(1821)	3.50	5.00	7.00	10.00
	1232	(1822)	3.50	5.00	7.00	10.00
	1233	(1823)	3.50	5.00	7.00	10.00
	1234	(1824)	3.50	5.00	7.00	10.00
	1235	(1825)	3.50	5.00	7.00	10.00
	1237	(1827)	3.50	5.00	7.00	10.00
	1238	(1828)	3.50	5.00	7.00	10.00
	1240	(1830)	3.50	5.00	7.00	10.00

Mintname: Bagalkot Mint بگلکوت

RUPEE

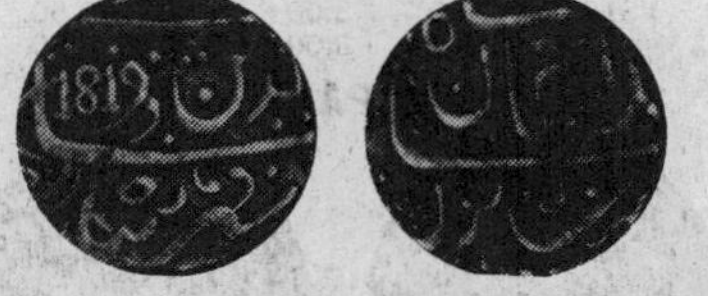

SILVER, 10.70-11.60 g

KM#	Date	Year	VG	Fine	VF	XF
271 (195)	1819	—	25.00	33.50	50.00	70.00

PUDUKKOTTAI

Pudukota

Pudukkottai was founded by Raghunatha Raya Tondaiman in 1686 when he defeated the Pallavaraya chiefs of the area. The family came from Tondaimandalam, a small village near Tirupathi, and belonged to the Kallen (or robber) caste. In the late eighteenth century the Tondaimans aided the British in their struggles against the French in the Carnatic. With British ascendancy, the Pudukkottai rulers were confirmed in their control of the region. This was regularized in 1806 when, subject to a yearly tribute of one elephant, the rajas of Pudukkottai were guaranteed their position. In 1948 the State was merged into Trichinopoly District.

RULERS

Martanda Bhairava, 1886-1928AD
Rajagopala, 1928-1947AD

1/20 ANNA

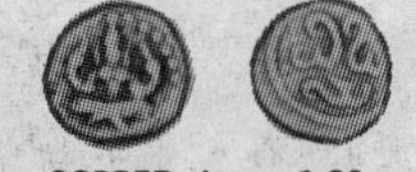

COPPER, dump, 1.30 g

Y#	Date	VG	Fine	VF	XF
A1	ND	.90	1.50	2.00	3.00

1/16 ANNA

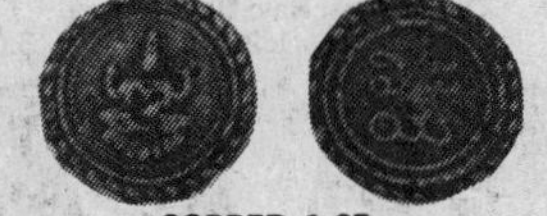

COPPER, 1.65 g

KM#	Date	Year	Good	VG	Fine	VF
1	ND	—	—	—	Rare	—

Milled Coinage

1/20 ANNA

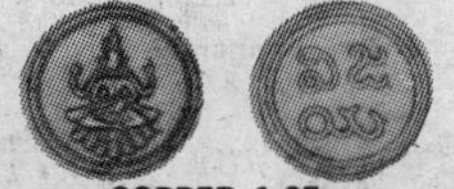

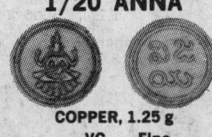

COPPER, 1.25 g

Y#	Date	VG	Fine	VF	XF
1	ND	.25	.50	.75	1.25

ROHILKHAND

The nawabs of Rohilkhand were Rohillas who traced their origins to Sardar Daud Khan (d. 1749), an Afghan adventurer. Daud Khan's adopted son, Ali Muhammed, annexed a huge tract of land north of the Ganges between Itawa and the Himalayas, and received the title of nawab from the Mughal emperor.

In 1754 this territory was partitioned among his many sons, who thereafter formed a loose confederacy, alternately given to feuding internally and uniting to meet aggression by the Marathas, Awadh, and Imperial forces in turn. By the end of the century Rohilla power had been crushed by the combined forces of Awadh and the British, leaving only Rampur in Rohilla hands under the sovereignty of Nawab Faizullah Khan. In 1801 Rampur was ceded to the East India Company and in 1950 it was absorbed into Uttar Pradesh.

MINTS

Mintname: Bareli بريلي

BARELI MINT
REVOLT OF 1857

The Mutiny

During the mutiny of 1857-58AD, Khan Bahadur Khan, a descendent of Hafiz Rahmat Khan, declared himself Subahdar of Rohilkhand under the Mughal Emperor Bahadur Shah Zafar. The independent government sat at Bareli, issuing rupees on the Mughal pattern of Shah Alam II, with current Hijri year and a regnal year dating from AH1202/1788AD, the year Rohilla power ended with the death of Ghulam Qadir.

RUPEE

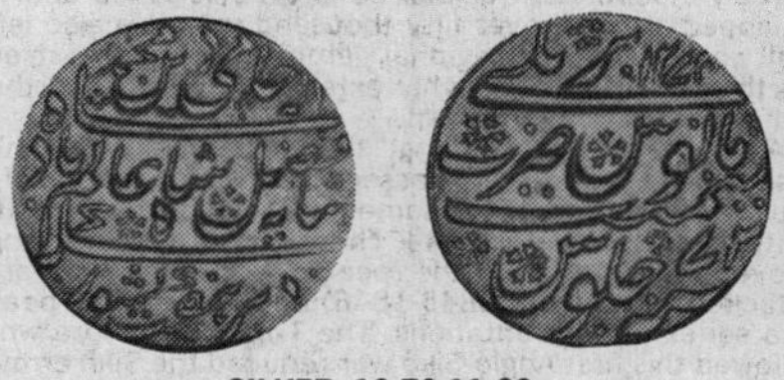

SILVER, 10.70-11.60 g

KM#	Date	Year	VG	Fine	VF	XF
46	AH1274	72	—	—	Rare	—

SIKH EMPIRE

The father of Sikhism, Guru Nanak (1469-1539), was distinguished from almost all others who founded states or empires in India by being a purely religious teacher. Deeply Indian in the basic premises which underlay even those aspects of his theology which differed from the mainstream, he stressed the unity of God and the universal brotherhood of man. He was totally opposed to the divisions of the caste system and his teaching struggled to attain a practical balance between Hinduism and Islam. His message was a message of reconciliation, first with God, then with man. He exhibited no political ambition.

Guru Nanak was succeeded by nine other gurus of Sikhism. Together they laid the foundations of a religious community in the Punjab which would, much later, transform itself into the Sikh Empire. Gradually this gentle religion of reconciliation became transformed into a formidable, aggressive military power. It was a metamorphosis which was, at least partly, thrust upon the Sikh community by Mughal oppression. The fifth guru of Sikhism, Arjun, was executed in 1606 on the order of Jahangir. His successor, Hargobind, was to spend his years in constant struggle against the Mughals, first against Jahangir and later against Shah Jahan. The ninth guru, Tegh Bahadur, was executed by Aurangzeb for failing to embrace Islam. The stage had been set for a full confrontation with Mughal authority. It was against such a background that Sikhism's tenth guru, Guru Govind Singh (1675-1708), set about organizing the Sikhs into a military power. He gave new discipline to Sikhism. Its adherents were forbidden wine and tobacco and they were required to conform to the five outward signs of allegiance - to keep their hair unshaven and to wear short drawers (kuchcha), a comb (kungha), an iron bangle (kara) and a dagger (kirpan).

With Govind Singh's death the Khalsa, the Sikh brotherhood, emerged as the controlling body of Sikhism and the Granth, the official compilation of Govind Singh's teaching, became the "Bible" of Sikhism. At this point the Sikhs took to the hills. It was here, constantly harassed by Mughal forces, that Sikh militarism was forged into an effective weapon and tempered by fire. Gradually the Sikhs emerged from their safe forts in the hills and made their presence felt in the plains of the Punjab. As Nadir Shah retired from Delhi laden with the prizes of war in 1739, the stragglers of his Persian army were cut down by the Sikhs. Similarly, Ahmad Shah Durrani's first intrusion into India (1747-1748) was made the more lively by Sikh sorties into his rearguard. Gradually the Sikhs became both more confident and more effective, and their quite frequent military reversals served only to strengthen their determination and to deepen their sense of identity. Their first notable success came about 1756 when the Sikhs temporarily occupied Lahore and used the Mughal mint to strike their own rupee bearing the inscription, *"Coined by the grace of the Khalsa in the country of Ahmad, conquered by Jessa the Kalal"*. But the Sikhs were, as yet, most effective as guerilla bands operating out of the hill country. On Ahmad Shah's fifth expedition into India (1759-1761) the Sikhs reverted to their well-tried role of forming tight mobile units which could choose both the time and the place of their attacks on the Durrani army. In spite of a serious reverse at Ludhiana in 1762 at the hands of Ahmad Shah, the Sikhs once again regrouped. In December 1763 they decisively defeated the Durrani governor of Sirhind and occupied the area.

The Sikhs now swept all before them, recapturing Lahore in 1764. The whole tract of land between the Jhelum and the Sutlej was now divided among the Sikh chieftains. At Amritsar the Govind Shahi rupee, proclaiming that Guru Govind Singh had received *Deg, Tegh and Fath"* (Grace, Power and Victory) from Nanak, was struck. The name of the Mughal emperor was pointedly omitted. The Sikhs now subdivided into twelve "equals", each responsible for its own fate and each conducting its own military adventures into surrounding areas. By 1792 the most prominent chief in the Punjab was Mahan Singh of the Sukerchakia misl. His death that same year left the boy destined to become Sikhism's best-known statesman, Ranjit Singh, as his successor. A year later Shah Zaman, King of Kabul, recognized

Sikh Empire / INDEPENDENT KINGDOM

(confirmed) him as the possessor of Lahore.

For the next forty years Ranjit Singh dominated Sikh affairs. In 1802 he seized Amritsar and followed this by capturing Ludhiana (1806), Multan (1818), Kashmir (1819), Ladakh (1833) and Peshawar (1834). By the time of his death in June 1839 Ranjit was the only leader in India capable of offering a serious challenge to the East India Company.

By a treaty concluded in 1809 with the British, Ranjit had been confirmed as ruler of the tracts he had occupied south of the Sutlej, but the agreement had restricted him from seeking any further expansion to the north or west of the river. In spite of the terms of the treaty, the British remained suspicious of Ranjit's ultimate intentions. His steady policy of expansion frequently left apprehensions in the minds of the British - with whose interests Ranjit's own often clashed - that the Sikhs had secret ambitions against Company controlled territory. But it was to Ranjit's credit that he welded the Sikhs of the Punjab into an effective and unified fighting force, capable of resisting both the Afghans and the Marathas and able to stand up to British pressures. He inherited a loose alliance of fiercely independent chiefs, he left a disciplined and well equipped army of over fifty thousand men. He also left a well consolidated regional empire in the extreme north-west of India, roughly extending over the northern half of present-day Pakistan.

After the death of Ranjit the Sikh empire began to disintegrate as power passed from chief to chief in murderous rivalry. At the same time relationships with the British began to deteriorate. The treaty of 1809 no longer proved able to hold the peace, and the Sikh army attacked the British (1845-1846) only to be badly beaten in a series of confrontations. The Treaty of Lahore which followed this first Anglo-Sikh war reduced the Sikh army to a maximum of twenty thousand men and twelve thousand cavalry. It obliged the Sikhs to cede the Jallandar Doab and Kashmir to the British, and required them to pay an indemnity of fifty thousand pounds and accept a British resident at their court. In 1848 the Sikhs again revolted, and were again crushed. In 1849 the Punjab was annexed and from that time onward they came under British rule.

RULERS

Ranjit Singh
  VS1856-1896/1799-1839AD
Kurruk Singh
  VS1896-1897/1839-1840AD
Sher Singh
  VS1897-1900/1840-1843AD
Dulip Singh
  VS1900-1906/1843-1849AD

MINTS

Amritsar   امرتسر

Kashmir   ਕਸ਼ਮੀਰ or كشمير

Lahore   لاهور

Multan   ملتان

Nimak

Pathankot

Peshawar   بشاور

NOTE: Most coins struck after the accession of Ranjit Singh bear a large pipal leaf on one side, and have Persian or Gurmukhi (Punjabi) legends in the name of Gobind Singh, the tenth and last Guru of the Sikhs, 1675-1708AD. Earlier pieces are similar, but lack the pipal leaf. There is a great variety of coppers, and only representative types are catalogued here; many crude pieces were struck at the official and at unofficial mints, and bear illegible or semi-literate inscriptions. None of the coins bear the name of the Sikh ruler.

AMRITSAR MINT

First Copper Series
Persian legends. Various types.

1/2 PAISA

COPPER

KM#	Date	Year	Good	VG	Fine	VF
3	VS1897	(1840)	3.25	5.00	8.50	12.50

PAISA

COPPER

KM#	Date	Year	Good	VG	Fine	VF
4.1	VS1880	(1823)	2.00	3.25	5.00	8.50
	1881	(1824)	2.00	3.25	5.00	8.50
	1882	(1825)	2.00	3.25	5.00	8.50

4.2	VS1896	(1839)	3.00	5.00	8.50	12.50
	1897	(1840)	3.00	5.00	8.50	12.50

2 PAISE

COPPER

6	VS1880	(1823)	4.00	7.50	12.50	20.00

Second Copper Series
Gurmukhi legends. Obv: Pipal leaf in center.

PAISA

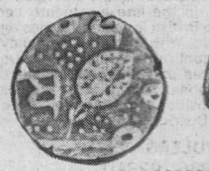

COPPER

7.1	—	—	1.25	2.50	3.00	5.00

NOTE: Full flan specimen strikes show date VS1885 or 1886. Date always off flan on normal strikes.

Obv: Cross. Rev: Double line.

7.10	—	—	1.25	2.00	3.00	5.00

Rev: Banner, end down.

7.2	—	—	1.25	2.00	4.00	6.00

Rev: Banner, end up.

7.9	—	—	2.00	3.50	—	7.50

Rev: Flower.

7.3	—	—	1.25	2.00	3.00	5.00

Rev: Cross.

7.4	VS188x	—	1.50	2.75	4.00	6.00

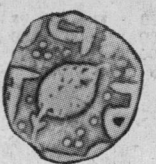 

Rev: Trident.

KM#	Date	Year	Good	VG	Fine	VF
7.5	—	—	1.40	2.50	3.50	5.50

Rev: Katar.

7.6	—	—	2.00	3.25	5.00	7.50

Rev: Lion.

7.7	—	—	4.00	6.50	10.00	15.00

Rev: Pipal leaf spray.

7.8	—	—	2.75	4.00	5.50	8.00

2 PAISE

COPPER

8.1	VS1xxx	—	4.00	7.50	10.00	15.00

8.2	VS—	—	8.50	12.50	20.00	30.00

8.3	VS188x	—	4.00	7.50	10.00	15.00

MULTIPLE PAISAS
(Not struck for circulation)

COPPER

9.1	VS1885	(1828)	—	—	Rare	—

Sikh Empire / INDEPENDENT KINGDOM 861

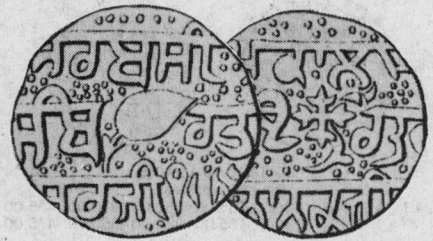

Rev: Banner.

KM#	Date	Year	Good	VG	Fine	VF
9.2	—	—	—	—	Rare	—

Rev: Cross.

| 9.3 | — | — | — | — | Rare | — |

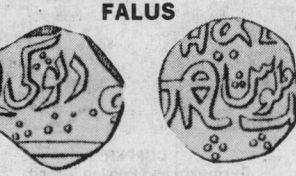

Rev: Banner ?

| 9.4 | — | — | — | — | Rare | — |

Third Copper Series
Persian and Gurmukhi legends.

FALUS

COPPER

| 10.1 | — | — | 6.00 | 10.00 | 15.00 | 25.00 |

10.2	VS1900	—	2.75	5.00	7.50	12.50
	1901	—	2.75	5.00	7.50	12.50
	ND	—	2.75	5.00	7.50	12.50

| 10.3 | — | — | 6.00 | 10.00 | 15.00 | 25.00 |

| 10.4 | — | — | 6.00 | 10.00 | 15.00 | 25.00 |

Silver Series

1/8 RUPEE

SILVER, 1.34-1.45 g
Obv: Dated VS1884.

KM#	Date	Year	VG	Fine	VF	XF
17.1	VS(18)95	(1838)	9.00	15.00	22.50	30.00

Obv: Dated VS1885.

17.2	VS(18)99	(1842)	9.00	15.00	22.50	30.00
	1900	(1843)	9.00	15.00	22.50	30.00
	1903	(1846)	9.00	15.00	22.50	30.00

1/4 RUPEE

SILVER, 15mm, 2.68-2.90 g

| 18.1 | VS(18)80 | (1823) | 10.00 | 16.00 | 22.50 | 30.00 |

Rev: Dated VS1884.

18.2	VS(18)85	(1828)	8.50	14.00	20.00	27.50
	(18)86	(1829)	8.50	14.00	20.00	27.50
	(18)89	(1832)	8.50	14.00	20.00	27.50
	(18)95	(1838)	8.50	14.00	20.00	27.50

Obv: Dated VS1885.

18.3	VS(18)93	(1836)	8.50	14.00	20.00	27.50
	(18)94	(1837)	8.50	14.00	20.00	27.50
	(18)97	(1840)	8.50	14.00	20.00	27.50
	(18)98	(1841)	8.50	14.00	20.00	27.50
	(18)99	(1842)	8.50	14.00	20.00	27.50
	1900	(1843)	8.50	14.00	20.00	27.50
	1901	—	8.50	14.00	20.00	27.50
	1902	—	8.50	14.00	20.00	27.50
	1903	—	8.50	14.00	20.00	27.50

18.4	—	—	8.50	14.00	20.00	27.50
	—	—	8.50	14.00	20.00	27.50
	VS1904	(1847)	8.50	14.00	20.00	27.50

1/2 RUPEE

SILVER, 5.35-5.80 g
Obv: Actual date.

| 19.1 | VS1880 | (1823) | 8.50 | 11.50 | 15.00 | 22.50 |

Obv: Dated VS1884.

19.2	VS(18)85	(1828)	8.50	11.50	15.00	22.50
	(18)92	(1835)	8.50	11.50	15.00	22.50
	(18)93	(1836)	8.50	11.50	15.00	22.50
	(18)95	(1838)	8.50	11.50	15.00	22.50
	(18)99	(1842)	8.50	11.50	15.00	22.50

Obv: Dated VS1885.

19.3	VS(18)93	(1836)	8.50	11.50	15.00	22.50
	(18)97	(1840)	8.50	11.50	15.00	22.50
	(18)98	(1841)	8.50	11.50	15.00	22.50
	(18)99	(1842)	8.50	11.50	15.00	22.50
	1900	(1843)	8.50	11.50	15.00	22.50
	1901	(1844)	8.50	11.50	15.00	22.50
	1902	(1845)	8.50	11.50	15.00	22.50
	1903	(1846)	8.50	11.50	15.00	22.50
	1904	(1847)	8.50	11.50	15.00	22.50
	1905	(1848)	8.50	11.50	15.00	22.50

NOTE: Some specimens dated 1903 have SATE.

| 19.4 | VS(18)97 | — | 8.50 | 14.00 | 20.00 | 27.50 |

KM#	Date	Year	VG	Fine	VF	XF
19.5	VS1902	—	9.00	15.00	22.50	30.00

RUPEE

SILVER, 10.70-11.60 g
Obv: Second legend arrangement.
Rev: Katar.

A20.2	VS1859	(1802)	16.50	22.50	30.00	45.00
	1862	(1805)	16.50	22.50	30.00	45.00
	1863	(1806)	16.50	22.50	30.00	45.00
	1864	(1807)	16.50	22.50	30.00	45.00
	1865	(1808)	16.50	22.50	30.00	45.00

Rev: Pipal leaf, date above. Early fabric, small dies.

Late fabric, large dies.

20.1	VS1858	(1801)	10.00	15.00	20.00	27.50
	1859	(1802)	10.00	15.00	20.00	27.50
	1860	(1803)	8.50	12.50	16.50	25.00
	1861	(1804)	8.50	12.50	16.50	25.00
	1863	(1806)	8.50	12.50	16.50	25.00
	1864	(1807)	8.50	12.50	16.50	25.00
	1865	(1808)	7.50	9.00	12.50	18.50
	1866	(1809)	7.50	9.00	12.50	18.50
	1867	(1810)	7.50	9.00	12.50	18.50
	1868	(1811)	7.50	9.00	12.50	18.50
	1869	(1812)	7.50	9.00	12.50	18.50
	1870	(1813)	7.50	9.00	12.50	18.50
	1871	(1814)	7.50	9.00	12.50	18.50
	1872	(1815)	7.50	9.00	12.50	18.50
	1873	(1816)	7.50	9.00	12.50	18.50
	1874	(1817)	7.50	9.00	12.50	18.50
	1875	(1818)	7.50	9.00	12.50	18.50
	1876	(1819)	7.50	9.00	12.50	18.50
	1877	(1820)	7.50	9.00	12.50	18.50
	1878	(1821)	7.50	9.00	12.50	18.50
	1879	(1822)	7.50	9.00	12.50	18.50

Larger flan

20.5	VS1880	(1823)	7.50	9.00	12.50	18.50
	1881	(1824)	7.50	9.00	12.50	18.50
	1882	(1825)	7.50	9.00	12.50	18.50
	1883	(1826)	7.50	9.00	12.50	18.50
	1884	(1827)	7.50	9.00	12.50	18.50
	1888	(1831)	—	—	Rare	—
	1889	(1832)	—	—	Rare	—

NOTE: The mint symbols appear to change frequently in the above series.

Obv: Hand. Rev: Dotted leaf.

| 20.2 | VS1859 | (1802) | 13.50 | 17.50 | 22.50 | 32.50 |

862 Sikh Empire / INDEPENDENT KINGDOM

Obv: Double oval. Rev: Dotted leaf.

KM#	Date	Year	VG	Fine	VF	XF
20.3	VS1858	(1801)	11.50	15.00	20.00	27.50
	1859	(1802)	11.50	15.00	20.00	27.50

The "Mora" Rupee
Rev: Branches w/berries.

B20	VS1858	(1801)	21.50	27.50	37.50	50.00
	1860	(1803)	21.50	27.50	37.50	50.00
	1861	(1804)	21.50	27.50	37.50	50.00

D20	VS1863	(1806)	21.50	27.50	37.50	50.00
	1862	(1805)	21.50	27.50	37.50	50.00

The "Arisi" Rupee
Rev: Symbol said to be mirror.

C20	VS1862	(1805)	21.50	27.50	37.50	50.00
	1863	(1806)	21.50	27.50	37.50	50.00

Obv: Partial or full actual dates.
Rev: VS1884 fixed.

21	VS(18)85	(1828)	6.50	8.50	11.50	20.00
	(18)86	(1829)	6.50	8.50	11.50	20.00
	(18)87	(1830)	6.50	8.50	11.50	20.00
	(18)88	(1831)	6.50	8.50	11.50	20.00
	(18)89	(1832)	6.50	8.50	11.50	20.00
	(18)90	(1833)	6.50	8.50	11.50	20.00
	(18)91	(1834)	6.50	8.50	11.50	20.00
	(18)92	(1835)	6.50	8.50	11.50	20.00
	(18)93	(1836)	6.50	8.50	11.50	20.00
	(18)95	(1838)	8.00	11.50	15.00	22.50
	(18)96	(1839)	8.00	11.50	15.00	22.50
	(18)97	(1840)	10.00	12.50	17.50	25.00
	(18)98/7					
		(1841)	10.00	12.50	17.50	25.00
	(18)98	(1841)	10.00	12.50	17.50	25.00
	(18)99	(1842)	8.00	11.50	15.00	22.50
	1900	(1843)	10.00	13.50	17.50	25.00
	1901	(1844)	10.00	13.50	17.50	25.00
	1903	(1846)	10.00	13.50	17.50	25.00
	1904	(1847)	10.00	13.50	17.50	25.00

Obv: Partial actual dates.
Rev: VS1885 fixed.

22.1	VS(18)93	(1836)	10.00	15.00	20.00	27.50
	(18)94	(1837)	10.00	15.00	20.00	27.50

Rev: Katar.

22.2	VS(18)94	(1837)	11.50	16.50	21.50	28.50

Obv: Dot cluster.

KM#	Date	Year	VG	Fine	VF	XF
22.3	VS(18)94	(1837)	6.50	8.50	11.50	17.50
	(18)95	(1838)	6.50	8.50	11.50	17.50
	(18)96	(1839)	6.50	8.50	11.50	17.50
	(18)97	(1840)	6.50	8.50	11.50	17.50
	(18)98	(1841)	6.50	8.50	11.50	17.50

Obv. Nagari: *Om.*

22.4	VS(18)97	(1840)	14.00	17.50	22.50	30.00

Obv: Trisul (trident).

22.5	VS(18)98	(1841)	14.00	17.50	22.50	30.00
	(18)99	(1842)	14.00	17.50	22.50	30.00

Obv: Chhatra (umbrella).

22.6	VS(18)99	(1842)	9.00	11.50	15.00	20.00
	1900	(1843)	9.00	11.50	15.00	20.00
	1901	(1844)	11.50	13.00	15.00	20.00

Obv: Three-lobed leaf.
Similar to 1/2 Rupee, KM#19.5.

22.7	VS1902	(1845)	11.50	15.00	20.00	27.50

Obv: Pataka (banner).

22.8	VS1902	(1845)	13.50	17.50	22.50	30.00
	1903	(1846)	13.50	17.50	22.50	30.00

Obv: Gurmukhi Sate beneath chhatra.

22.9	VS1903	(1846)	14.00	17.50	22.50	30.00
	1904	(1847)	14.00	17.50	22.50	30.00

Obv: Lazy W beneath chhatra.

22.10	VS1905	(1848)	10.00	13.50	18.50	26.50
	1906	(1849)	10.00	13.50	18.50	26.50

Obv: Nagari *Shiva.*

KM#	Date	Year	VG	Fine	VF	XF
22.11	VS1905	(1848)	13.50	17.50	22.50	30.00

MOHUR

GOLD, 10.70-11.40 g
Rev: W/pipal leaf.

24.1	VS1858	(1801)	185.00	250.00	350.00	475.00
	1861	(1804)	185.00	250.00	350.00	475.00

Rev: W/o pipal leaf.

24.2	VS1868	(1811)	185.00	250.00	350.00	475.00
	1901	(1844)	185.00	250.00	350.00	475.00

"Mora" type similar to 1 Rupee, KM#B20.

23	VS1862	(1805)	—	—	Rare	—

"Arisi" type similar to 1 Rupee, KM#C20.

26	VS1862	(1805)	—	—	Rare	—
	1863	(1806)	—	—	Rare	—

DOUBLE MOHUR

GOLD

25	VS1884	(18)85	—	Extremely Rare	—

KASHMIR MINT

PAISA

COPPER
Gurmukhi and Persian legends

KM#	Date	Year	Good	VG	Fine	VF
40.1	VS2078 (imaginary)					
		—	4.50	7.50	12.50	20.00

Persian and Gurmukhi legends.

40.2	ND	—	4.00	6.00	10.00	16.50

Persian legends, sword.

41.1	VS1894	(1837)	3.00	5.00	8.00	15.00

Persian legends, rosette.

41.2	ND	—	3.50	5.50	9.00	15.00

1/4 RUPEE

SILVER, 2.75 g

43	VS1898	(1841)	—	—	Rare	—

1/2 RUPEE

SILVER, 5.50 g

44	ND	—	—	—	Rare	—

RUPEE

SILVER, 7.60 g
Gurmukhi legends

KM#	Date	Year	VG	Fine	VF	XF
45	VS1892	—	—	—	—	Rare

NOTE: KM#45 is of light weight.

SILVER, 10.70-11.60 g
Obv: Flower spray. Rev: Date to right.

| 46.1 | VS1876 | — | 11.50 | 13.50 | 18.50 | 26.50 |

Obv: Flower spray. Rev: Legend divided horizontally.

| 46.2 | VS1876 | (1819) | 11.50 | 13.50 | 18.50 | 26.50 |

Obv: Flower spray. Rev: Legend divided vertically.

| 46.3 | VS1877 | (1820) | 11.50 | 13.50 | 18.50 | 26.50 |
| | 1878 | (1821) | 11.50 | 13.50 | 18.50 | 26.50 |

Obv: Gurmukhi *Hara.*

| 46.4 | VS1878 | (1821) | 11.50 | 13.50 | 18.50 | 26.50 |
| | 1879 | (1822) | 11.50 | 13.50 | 18.50 | 26.50 |

Obv: Nagari *Om Sri.*

| 46.5 | VS1879 | (1822) | 12.50 | 16.50 | 21.50 | 30.00 |

Obv: Nagari *Haraji* or *Hara.*

| 46.6 | VS1879 | (1822) | 12.50 | 16.50 | 21.50 | 30.00 |

Rev: Sword across leaf stem.

| 46.14 | VS1880 | (1823) | — | — | Rare | — |

Obv: Floral symbol

| 46.7 | VS1881 | (1824) | 11.50 | 13.50 | 18.50 | 26.50 |

Obv: Banner.

KM#	Date	Year	VG	Fine	VF	XF
46.8	VS1881	(1824)	11.50	13.50	18.50	26.50
	1882	(1825)	11.50	13.50	18.50	26.50
	1883	(1826)	11.50	13.50	18.50	26.50

Obv: Dotted chakra.

| 46.9 | VS1883 | (1826) | 11.50 | 13.50 | 18.50 | 26.50 |

NOTE: Some also have Persian *Kaf.*

Obv: Persian *Ram* and *Kaf.*

| 46.10 | VS— | — | 11.50 | 13.50 | 18.50 | 26.50 |

Obv: Persian letter.

| 46.11 | VS1885 | (1828) | 11.50 | 13.50 | 18.50 | 26.50 |
| | 1887 | (1830) | 11.50 | 13.50 | 18.50 | 26.50 |

Rev: Cross and letter form "I".

| 46.12 | VS188x | — | 11.50 | 13.50 | 18.50 | 26.50 |

Rev: Letter in field, *Bha.*

| 46.13 | VS1887 | (1830) | 11.50 | 13.50 | 18.50 | 26.50 |
| | 1888 | (1831) | 11.50 | 13.50 | 18.50 | 26.50 |

Rev: Circled date.

| 48 | VS1884 | (1827) | 15.00 | 22.50 | 30.00 | 40.00 |

Obv: Date.

| 49 | VS1889 | (1832) | 12.50 | 16.50 | 21.50 | 30.00 |
| | 1890 | (1833) | 12.50 | 16.50 | 21.50 | 30.00 |

Rev: Lion to right of leaf.

| A50 | VS1890 | (1833) | — | — | Rare | — |

Rev: Date at top.

| B50 | VS1891 | (1834) | 20.00 | 27.50 | 35.00 | 50.00 |

Obv: Circled sword.

KM#	Date	Year	VG	Fine	VF	XF
50	VS1893	(1836)	12.50	16.50	21.50	27.50
	1894	(1837)	12.50	16.50	21.50	27.50
	1895	(1838)	12.50	16.50	21.50	27.50
	1896	(1839)	12.50	16.50	21.50	27.50
	1897	(1840)	12.50	16.50	21.50	27.50
	1898	(1841)	12.50	16.50	21.50	27.50

Rev: Outlined leaf.

| 51 | VS1894 | (1837) | 12.50 | 16.50 | 21.50 | 27.50 |
| | 1897 | (1840) | 12.50 | 16.50 | 21.50 | 27.50 |

19mm
Obv: Persian letter *Sin.*

52	VS1898	(1841)	12.50	17.50	25.00	35.00
	1899	(1842)	12.50	17.50	25.00	35.00
	1900	(1843)	12.50	17.50	25.00	35.00
	1901	(1844)	12.50	17.50	25.00	35.00
	1902	(1845)	12.50	17.50	25.00	35.00
	1903	(1846)	12.50	17.50	25.00	35.00

LAHORE MINT
Dar-us-Sultanat

PAISA

COPPER

KM#	Date	Year	Good	VG	Fine	VF
60	VS1880	(1823)	3.75	6.50	10.00	15.00
	1881	(1824)	3.75	6.50	10.00	15.00
	1888	(1831)	3.75	6.50	10.00	15.00

1/2 RUPEE

SILVER, 18mm, 5.35-5.80 g

KM#	Date	Year	VG	Fine	VF	XF
62	VS1864	(1807)	13.50	20.00	30.00	45.00
	1889	(1832)	13.50	20.00	30.00	45.00

In the name of Guru Gobind Singh

RUPEE

SILVER, 10.70-11.60 g
Actual VS years.

66.1	VS1858	(1801)	12.50	17.50	22.50	30.00
	1859	(1802)	12.50	17.50	22.50	30.00
	1860	(1803)	12.50	17.50	22.50	30.00
	1861	(1804)	12.50	17.50	22.50	30.00
	1862	(1805)	12.50	17.50	22.50	30.00
	1863	(1806)	12.50	17.50	22.50	30.00
	1864	(1807)	12.50	17.50	22.50	30.00
	1865	(1808)	12.50	17.50	22.50	30.00
	1866	(1809)	12.50	17.50	22.50	30.00
	1867	(1810)	12.50	17.50	22.50	30.00
	1868	(1811)	12.50	17.50	22.50	30.00
	1869	(1812)	12.50	17.50	22.50	30.00
	1870	(1813)	12.50	17.50	22.50	30.00
	1871	(1814)	12.50	17.50	22.50	30.00
	1872	(1815)	12.50	17.50	22.50	30.00
	1873	(1816)	12.50	17.50	22.50	30.00
	1874	(1817)	12.50	17.50	22.50	30.00
	1875	(1818)	12.50	17.50	22.50	30.00
	1877	(1820)	12.50	17.50	22.50	30.00

KM#	Date	Year	VG	Fine	VF	XF
66.1	1878	(1821)	12.50	17.50	22.50	30.00
	1879	(1822)	12.50	17.50	22.50	30.00
	1880	(1823)	12.50	17.50	22.50	30.00
	1881	(1824)	12.50	17.50	22.50	30.00
	1882	(1825)	12.50	17.50	22.50	30.00
	1883	(1826)	12.50	17.50	22.50	30.00
	1884	(1827)	12.50	17.50	22.50	30.00
	1887	(1830)	12.50	17.50	22.50	30.00

Obv: Actual date. Rev: VS1884.

66.2	VS18(87)	(1831)	12.50	17.50	22.50	30.00
	18(88)	(1831)	12.50	17.50	22.50	30.00
	(18)89	(1832)	12.50	17.50	22.50	30.00
	(18)90	(1833)	12.50	17.50	22.50	30.00
	(18)91	(1834)	12.50	17.50	22.50	30.00
	(18)92	(1835)	12.50	17.50	22.50	30.00

Rev: VS1885

67	VS(18)94	(1837)	12.50	17.50	22.50	30.00
	(18)95	(1838)	12.50	17.50	22.50	30.00
	(18)96	(1839)	12.50	17.50	22.50	30.00
	1902	(1845)	12.50	17.50	22.50	30.00
	1903	(1846)	12.50	17.50	22.50	30.00

Rev: Two seated figures and VS1885.

| 68 | VS(18)93 | (1836) | — | — | Rare | — |

MOHUR
GOLD, 10.85 g

| 69 | VS1884 | (1827) | — | — | Rare | — |

MULTAN MINT
PAISA

COPPER

KM#	Date	Year	Good	VG	Fine	VF
77	VS1875	(1818)	3.50	6.00	10.00	17.50
	1878	(1821)	3.50	6.00	10.00	17.50

NOTE: Also found with botched or fictitious dates.

DOUBLE PAISA

COPPER

| 78 | VS1904 | (1847) | 50.00 | 65.00 | 80.00 | 100.00 |

1/2 RUPEE

SILVER

KM#	Date	Year	VG	Fine	VF	XF
81	VS1880	(1823)	—	—	—	—

RUPEE

SILVER, 10.70-11.60 g
Obv: Plain. Rev: Pipal leaf.

84	VS1875	(1818)	12.50	20.00	27.50	40.00
	1876	(1819)	12.50	20.00	27.50	40.00
	1877	(1820)	12.50	20.00	27.50	40.00
	1878	(1821)	12.50	20.00	27.50	40.00
	1879	(1822)	12.50	20.00	27.50	40.00

Obv: Trident. Rev: Pipal leaf.

KM#	Date	Year	VG	Fine	VF	XF
85	VS1880	(1823)	12.50	20.00	27.50	40.00
	1881	(1824)	12.50	20.00	27.50	40.00
	1882	(1825)	12.50	20.00	27.50	40.00
	1883	(1826)	12.50	20.00	27.50	40.00
	1884	(1827)	12.50	20.00	27.50	40.00

Obv: Flower. Rev: Pipal leaf.

86.1	VS1885	(1828)	10.00	17.50	25.00	35.00
	1886	(1829)	10.00	17.50	25.00	35.00
	1887	(1830)	10.00	17.50	25.00	35.00
	1888	(1831)	10.00	17.50	25.00	35.00
	1890	(1832)	10.00	17.50	25.00	35.00
	1891	(1834)	10.00	17.50	25.00	35.00
	1892	(1835)	10.00	17.50	25.00	35.00
	1893	(1836)	10.00	17.50	25.00	35.00
	1894	(1837)	10.00	17.50	25.00	35.00
	1895	(1838)	10.00	17.50	25.00	35.00
	1896	(1839)	10.00	17.50	25.00	35.00
	1897	(1840)	10.00	17.50	25.00	35.00
	1898	(1841)	10.00	17.50	25.00	35.00
	1899	(1842)	10.00	17.50	25.00	35.00
	1900	(1843)	10.00	17.50	25.00	35.00
	1901	(1844)	10.00	17.50	25.00	35.00
	1902	(1845)	10.00	17.50	25.00	35.00
	1904	(1847)	10.00	17.50	25.00	35.00
	1905	(1848)	10.00	17.50	25.00	35.00

NAZARANA RUPEE

SILVER, 10.70-11.60 g

| 86.2 | VS1896 | (1839) | 35.00 | 65.00 | 100.00 | 150.00 |

1/20 MOHUR

GOLD, 0.57 g

| 87 | VS1905 | (1848) | 17.50 | 25.00 | 32.50 | 50.00 |

NOTE: Struck by Diwan Mulraj (April 1848-Jan. 1849/VS1905).

NIMAK MINT
(Pind Dadan Khan)
RUPEE

SILVER, 10.70-11.60 g

88	VS1904	(1847)	25.00	50.00	80.00	120.00
	1905	(1848)	25.00	50.00	80.00	120.00

Obv: Nagari *Ram Jim*.

| 89 | VS1905 | (1848) | — | — | Rare | — |

PATHANKOT MINT
PAISA

COPPER

KM#	Date	Year	Good	VG	Fine	VF
90	VS1894	(1837)	7.50	12.50	20.00	35.00

PESHAWAR MINT
FALUS

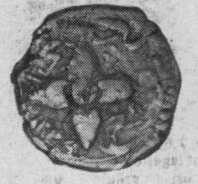 

COPPER
Rev: Persian leg.

KM#	Date	Year	Good	VG	Fine	VF
93	AH1248	—	3.00	5.00	7.50	12.50
	1249	—	3.00	5.00	7.50	12.50

Rev: Gurmukhi leg. & Nagari date.

| 94 | VS1891 | (1834) | 6.00 | 10.00 | 15.00 | 22.50 |

| 95 | ND or date off flan | — | 3.00 | 5.00 | 7.50 | 12.50 |

 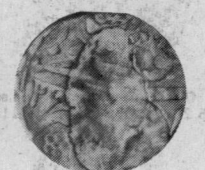

| 96 | AH126x | — | 3.00 | 5.00 | 7.50 | 12.50 |

23mm

| 97 | VS1892 | (1835) | 7.50 | 11.50 | 16.50 | 25.00 |

RUPEE

SILVER, 8.50 g
Rev: Plain pipal leaf.

KM#	Date	Year	VG	Fine	VF	XF
98.1	VS1891	(1834)	22.50	27.50	32.50	45.00

Rev: Dotted pipal leaf.

98.2	VS1892	(1835)	15.00	22.50	30.00	42.50
	1893	(1836)	15.00	22.50	30.00	42.50
	1894	(1837)	15.00	22.50	30.00	42.50

NOTE: Some specimens dated VS1894 weigh 10.50-11.00 g.

UNCERTAIN MINTS
RUPEE

SILVER, 10.70-11.60 g
Obv: Trident. Rev: Lion.
Bearing name of "Fateh Singh Ahluwalia"

| 99 | VS1862 | (1805) | 100.00 | 150.00 | 200.00 | 275.00 |

KM#	Date	Year	VG	Fine	VF	XF
72	VS1880	(1823)	—	—	Rare	—

SIKH FEUDATORY STATES

DERA

Sikh Protectorate, 1819-1847AD

Dera is known more fully as Dera Ghazi Khan, as distinguished from Dera Ismail Khan (Derajat).

PAISA

COPPER

KM#	Date	Year	Good	VG	Fine	VF
101	VS1896	(1839)	3.00	5.00	7.50	11.50
	1898	(1841)	3.00	5.00	7.50	11.50
	ND	—	2.75	4.00	5.50	8.00

RUPEE

SILVER, 10.70-11.60 g

102	VS1884/904	—	—	—	Rare	—

DERAJAT

Sikh Protectorate, 1819-1847AD

Derajat was the region centered about Dera Ismail Khan where the mint was presumably located.

NOTE: There are many varieties of copper coins, only a sample of which are listed below.

PAISA

COPPER

Obv: *Rayij*. **Mint name:** *Derajat*.

105	AH1241	—	3.25	5.00	8.50	13.50
	1242	—	3.25	5.00	8.50	13.50

Obv: *Rayij*. **Rev:** *Samadi* **monogram.**

106	AH124x	—	4.00	6.25	10.00	16.50

Obv: *Sahih*. **Rev: Mint name & date.**

108	AH1252	—	3.50	5.50	9.00	15.00

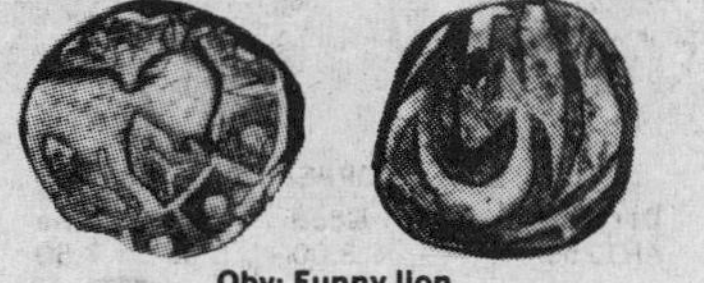

Obv: Funny lion.

110	AH1252	—	—	—	—	—

Obv: Lion left, AH date.

111	AH1246	—	2.25	4.00	6.50	10.00
	1247	—	2.25	4.00	6.50	10.00
	1249	—	2.25	4.00	6.50	10.00
	1254	—	2.25	4.00	6.50	10.00
	1261	—	2.25	4.00	6.50	10.00
	1262	—	2.25	4.00	6.50	10.00
	1265	—	2.25	4.00	6.50	10.00
	1267	—	2.25	4.00	6.50	10.00
	1276	—	2.25	4.00	6.50	10.00

Obv: *Fath*. **Rev: Leaf.**

112	—	—	2.75	4.50	7.50	11.50

Obv: Lion right.

KM#	Date	Year	Good	VG	Fine	VF
113	VS1793 (error, for 1893)	(1836)	3.25	5.00	8.00	13.50

Similar to 1 Rupee, KM#120.

114	VS189x	—	4.00	6.00	10.00	15.00

RUPEE

SILVER, 10.70-11.60 g
Obv: Date below Gurmukhi letter.
Rev: Neat leaf.

KM#	Date	Year	VG	Fine	VF	XF
119	VS1892	(1835)	30.00	40.00	50.00	70.00
	1893	(1836)	30.00	40.00	50.00	70.00

Obv: Date above Gurmukhi letter.
Rev: Crude leaf.

120	VS1892	(1835)	25.00	32.50	42.50	60.00
	1893	(1836)	25.00	32.50	42.50	60.00
	1894	(1837)	25.00	32.50	42.50	60.00
	1895	(1838)	25.00	32.50	42.50	60.00
	1896	(1839)	25.00	32.50	42.50	60.00
	1897	(1840)	25.00	32.50	42.50	60.00
	1898	(1841)	25.00	32.50	42.50	60.00
	1899	(1842)	25.00	32.50	42.50	60.00
	1900	(1843)	25.00	32.50	42.50	60.00
	1901	(1844)	25.00	32.50	42.50	60.00
	1902	(1845)	25.00	32.50	42.50	60.00
	1905	(1848)	25.00	32.50	42.50	60.00

NAJIBABAD

Symbols: 

on obv. and **on rev.**

PAISA

COPPER
Obv: Date.

KM#	Date	Year	Good	VG	Fine	VF
131	—	40	4.00	7.50	12.50	20.00

Legend of Shah Alam II

Obv:  Rev: 

132	AH1221	47	5.00	8.50	15.00	25.00

SIKKIM

A Kingdom located above northeast India between China, Bhutan and Nepal. In 1890 it became a British protectorate and later in 1949 it became a protectorate of India and in 1975, a state.

The Kingdom of Sikkim covers an area of some 2,800 sq. mi., and is situated on the southern slopes of the Himalayas, sandwiched between India to the south, Tibet to the north, Nepal to the west and Bhutan to the east. On its border with Nepal is the third highest mountain in the world, Kanchenjunga.

The Kingdom was founded in 1642 when Phuntsog Namgyal was proclaimed Chogyal or King. His ancestors had come to the Sikkim area about 150 years earlier from Eastern Tibet and, over the years had gained the confidence and respect of the indigenous inhabitants, the Lapchas. The descendents of Phuntsog Namgyal have ruled Sikkim ever since.

In the latter part of the eighteenth century Sikkim was subject to a number of Gurkha incursions, the impact of which was to place Sikkim on the British side in the Nepal War of 1815-1816. At the conclusion of this campaign Sikkim received certain tracts of land relinquished by Nepal and, in return, was obliged to accept British protection and control.

Initially Sikkim covered an area at least twice as large as it is now, but annexations by neighbouring powers reduced its size until in 1835 it reached its present area after the Chogyal "presented" the hills of Darjeeling to the British "out of friendship". In 1861 Sikkim became a protectorate of British India with the British exercising complete control over foreign affairs and defense and the Chogyal being in charge of all other internal matters.

India's independence brought little change to this situation until April 1973 when there was an uprising during which the Chogyal asked for the assistance of the Indian Government. An agreement has now been reached under which the Chogyal's powers are to be greatly reduced and the administration of Sikkim is to be headed by a "chief nomination of the Government of India."

For practically the entire period of its history, Sikkim had no coinage of its own and until the last century, trade was carried out by barter with taxes paid in kind. On the few occasions when inhabitants needed money, Tibetan coins, silver or gold bullion, or later, Indian coins were used. For only three or four years in the 1800's coins struck in Sikkim, and then they were struck by Nepalese immigrants. Since the beginning of the twentieth century Indian currency has circulated widely and exclusively.

Since the late 18th century the Nepalese have exhibited a strong urge to leave the overcrowded hills of Nepal and seek their fortunes elsewhere. Sikkim, being so close, was an obvious target for settlement and in order to prevent this, the seventh ruler of Sikkim, Tsugphud Namgyal (1793-1864) prohibited the settlement of Nepalese in Sikkim. This ban was effective until the early years of the reign of Thutob Namgyal (1874-1914) when certain powerful landowners realized that it was profitable to allow Nepalese to settle and work the land. Foremost of these were the brothers Kangsa Dewan and Phodong Lama. These two brothers struck a deal with two rich Nepalese traders, the brothers Lachmidas and Chandrabir Pradhan, under which a large tract of land which had recently been confiscated from a Sikkimese nobleman who had been convicted of embezzlement, was made over to the Nepalese brothers. This deal was strongly criticized by the Sikkimese people, but was supported by the British and finally the Kangsa brothers persuaded the Chogyal in 1878 to allow Nepalese settlement in "uninhabited and waste lands of Sikkim". Since then Nepalese immigrants have flooded into Sikkim and now comprise a majority of the population of the country.

It was the Pradhan brothers who were responsible for the Sikkim coinage. Soon after acquiring their lands they obtained licences to mine copper in a number of places, most important of which were Tuk Khani, Bhotan Khani near Rangpo and Pachay Khani. Some of this copper was sold in Nepal and Darjeeling, but some remained unsold, so in 1882 the brothers sought and obtained the permission of the Chogyal to strike copper coins. The minting was done in two places near the mines of Tuk Khani and Pachay Khani. Unfortunately for the Pradhan brothers, the Deputy Commissioner of Darjeeling forbade circulation of the Sikkim coins in the Darjeeling district and this made the coins unpopular among the people. The minting was not profitable and was discontinued in 1885.

The coins themselves are, except for the inscription, exact copies of the Nepalese paisa of Surendra Vira Vikrama Shah. They are very poorly struck and very few specimens have all the details of the design visible. The date is only very rarely legible. Three major types are known, but there is no indication of the mint of origin and die-links exist between the types. The coins are all intended to be the same denomination, one paisa, although the weights of individual specimens vary within the range 6.00 g to 4.00 g around a mean of about 5.20 g.

RULERS

Thutab Namgyel
VS1931-1968/1874-1911AD

THUTAB NAMGYEL

VS1931-1968/1874-1911AD

PAISA

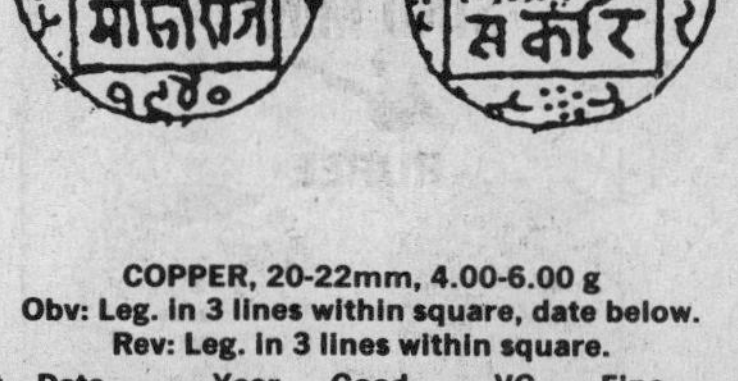

COPPER, 20-22mm, 4.00-6.00 g
Obv: Leg. in 3 lines within square, date below.
Rev: Leg. in 3 lines within square.

KM#	Date	Year	Good	VG	Fine	VF
1	VS1940	(1883)	7.50	12.50	18.50	30.00
	1941	(1884)	3.00	5.00	7.50	11.50

Obv: Leg. in 4 lines within square, date below.

KM#	Date	Year	Good	VG	Fine	VF
2	VS1941	(1884)	7.50	12.50	18.50	30.00

Obv: Leg. in 3 lines within square, date below, w/Ti of Sikimpati on third line.

3.1	VS1941	(1884)	3.00	5.00	7.50	11.50
	1942	(1885)	3.00	5.00	7.50	11.50

Rev. leg: Sarkar spelled incorrectly Sakar.

3.2	VS1941	(1884)	3.00	5.00	7.50	11.50
	1942	(1885)	3.00	5.00	7.50	11.50

Rev. leg: Sarkar spelled incorrectly Sikar.

3.3	VS1941	(1884)	3.00	5.00	7.50	11.50
	1942	(1885)	3.00	5.00	7.50	11.50

SIND

Sind has an extremely ancient historical record having been successively occupied and governed by the Indus Valley civilization (ca. 1500 BC), Alexander the Great (325BC), Chandragupta Maurya (ca.305BC), Asoka (274-232BC) and others until the first Muslim inroads into Sind after 712AD. For almost the next three hundred years Sind was subject to Arab caliphs, after which it was conquered by Sultan Mahmud of Ghazni who conducted annual raids into India after 1000AD. Even then it remained semi-independent under local dynasties until, under Akbar (who was himself born at Umarkot in Sind), Sind became part of the Mughal empire.

The amirs of Hyderabad and Khairpur came into existence after the Mughal empire had started to disintegrate. Khairpur had been governed by the Kalhoras but in the 1780s they were overthrown by the Talpurs, a Baluchi family. Khairpur State was founded by Mir Sohrab Khan Talpur. In 1813 Khairpur ceased to pay tribute to Afghanistan and, in 1832, it was recognized by the British as a separate state within Sind. In 1843, when the rest of Sind was annexed by the British in the aftermath of the Anglo-Sikh War, Khairpur remained separate and was only merged into the neighboring territory by its accession in 1947 to Pakistan.

AMIRS of HYDERABAD

In the name of Taimur Shah Durrani

HYDERABAD SIND MINT

RUPEE
SILVER, 10.70-11.60 g

KM#	Date	Year	VG	Fine	VF	XF
18	ND	—	16.50	25.00	35.00	50.00

SIND MINT

RUPEE

SILVER, 11.00-11.50 g

KM#	Date	Year	VG	Fine	VF	XF
19	AH1239	—	15.00	20.00	27.50	37.50
	1240	—	15.00	20.00	27.50	37.50
	1242	—	15.00	20.00	27.50	37.50
	1245	—	15.00	20.00	27.50	37.50

Rev. mint mark: Star below Sana.

19.2	ND	—	10.00	13.00	16.50	21.50

Mint mark: Group of 6 dots.

19.1	ND	—	10.00	13.00	16.50	21.50

7.50-7.80 g

20	AH1252	—	12.50	16.50	21.50	30.00
	1255	—	12.50	16.50	21.50	30.00
	1256	—	12.50	16.50	21.50	30.00
	1257	—	12.50	16.50	21.50	30.00

Mint mark: 6-petal flower.

20.1	ND	—	9.00	12.50	16.50	21.50

Mint mark: Rosette of 6 dots.

20.2	ND	—	9.00	12.50	16.50	21.50

Mint mark: Cross.

20.3	ND	—	11.50	15.00	20.00	30.00

Mint mark: Sprig w/3 berries.

20.4	ND	—	11.50	15.00	20.00	30.00

Rev: W/o mark, w/Fath (Victory).

21	ND	—	12.50	17.50	25.00	40.00

It is not known to which victory the reference is made.

AMIRS of KHAIRPUR
Formally independent After AH1248/1832AD

BHAKKAR MINT
In the name of Mahmud Shah Durrani

NOTE: These Rupees bear 2 mint marks, one on the obverse at the top of the central cartouche, one on the reverse, usually to the upper right of the J of Julus.

RUPEE

SILVER, 11.00-11.50 g
Obv. and rev: W/o mint marks.

C#	Date	Year	VG	Fine	VF	XF
10	AH1240	—	15.00	20.00	27.50	40.00
	1245	—	10.00	14.50	18.50	25.00

Obv. and rev: Star.

10.1	AH1252	—	10.00	14.50	18.50	25.00
	1254	—	10.00	14.50	18.50	25.00
	1255	—	10.00	14.50	18.50	25.00

Obv: Star. Rev: Branch.

10.2	AH1255	—	10.00	14.50	18.50	25.00

Obv. and rev: Branch.

10.3	AH1256	—	10.00	14.50	18.50	25.00
	1258	—	10.00	14.50	18.50	25.00

Obv: Pigeon. Rev: Plume.

10.4	AH1256	—	10.00	17.50	18.50	25.00

Obv: Pigeon. Rev: Peacock.

10.5	AH1258	—	12.50	17.50	22.50	30.00

Obv: Hare. Rev: Peacock.

10.6	AH1258	—	12.50	17.50	22.50	30.00

Rev: Date in S of Jalus.

C#	Date	Year	VG	Fine	VF	XF
10.7	AH1259	—	12.50	17.50	22.50	30.00

British Occupation
After AH1259/1843AD

RUPEE

SILVER
Obv: Hare. Rev: British lion.

11	AH1259	—	13.50	20.00	27.50	40.00
	1261	—	13.50	20.00	27.50	40.00

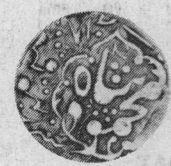 

Obv: Hare.
Obv. and rev: Floral mint marks of various kinds.

12	AH1262	—	11.50	15.00	20.00	28.50
	1264	—	11.50	15.00	20.00	28.50
	1265	—	11.50	15.00	20.00	28.50
	1266	—	11.50	15.00	20.00	28.50
	1267	—	11.50	15.00	20.00	28.50
	1268	—	11.50	15.00	20.00	28.50
	1269	—	11.50	15.00	20.00	28.50

Local Issues
SHIKARPUR MINT

Mintname: Shikarpur
Anonymous

FALUS

 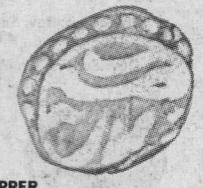

COPPER

C#	Date	Year	Good	VG	Fine	VF
30.1	AH1255	—	3.00	5.00	7.50	12.50

Rev: Star at top.

30.2	AH1255	—	3.00	5.00	7.50	12.50

TATTA MINT
In the name of Taimur Shah Durrani

RUPEE

SILVER, 10.70-11.60 g

C#	Date	Year	VG	Fine	VF	XF
45	ND	—	12.50	17.50	25.00	37.50

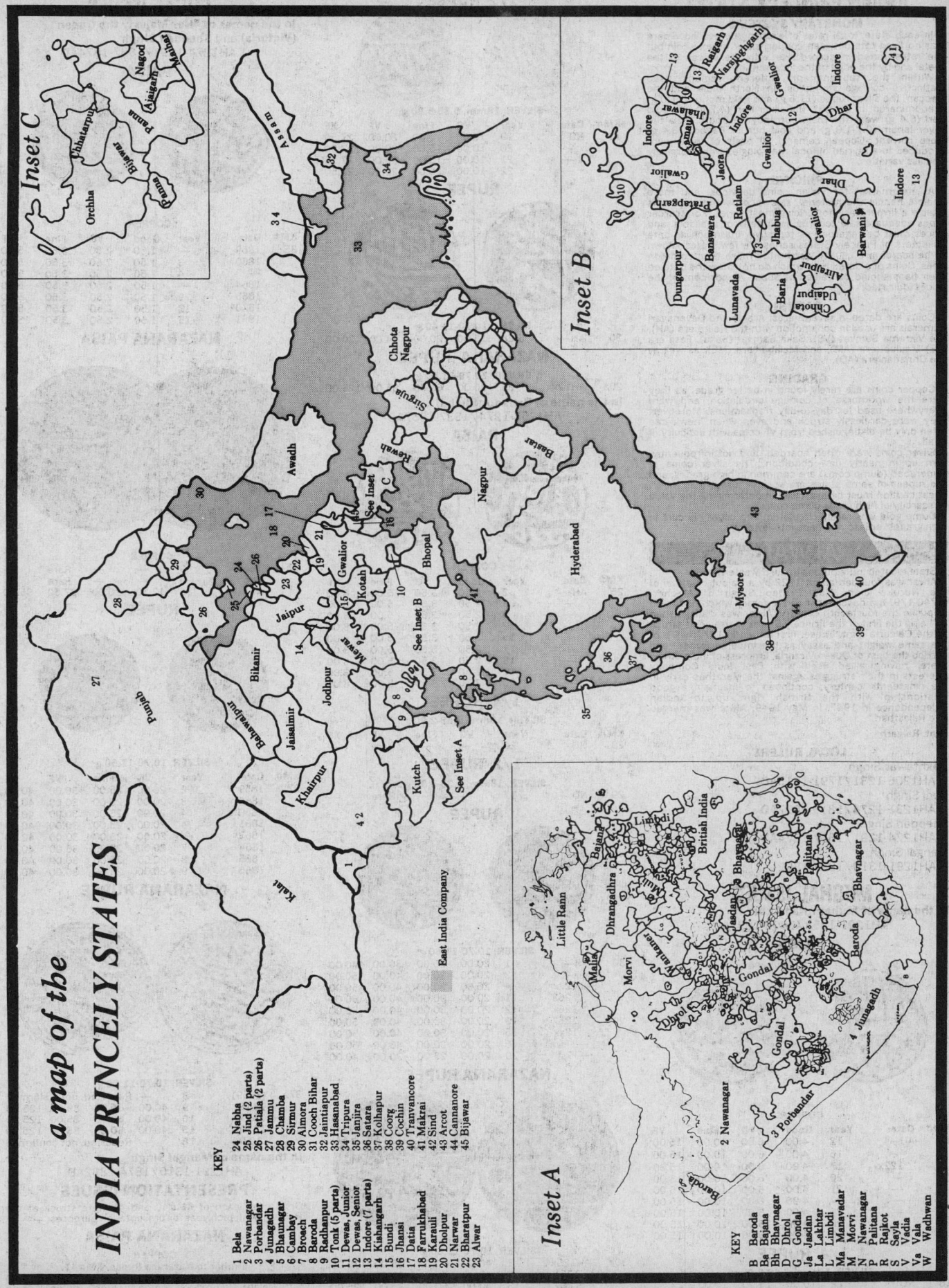

INDIAN PRINCELY STATES

MONETARY SYSTEMS

In each state, local rates of exchange prevailed. There was no fixed rate between copper, silver or gold coin but the rates varied in accordance with the values of the metal and by the edict of the local authority.

Within the subcontinent, different regions used distinctive coinage standards. In North India and the Deccan, the silver rupee (11.6 g) and gold mohur (11.0 g) predominated. In Gujarat, the silver kori (4.7 g) and gold kori (6.4 g) were the main currency. In South India the silver fanam (0.7-1.0 g) and gold hun or Pagoda (3.4 g) were current. Copper coins in all parts of India were produced to a myriad of local metrologies with seemingly endless varieties.

PRICING

As the market for Indian coins develops, and more dealers handle the material, sale records and price lists enable a firmer basis for pricing most series. For scarcer types adequate sale records are often not available, and prices must be regarded as tentative. Inasmuch as date collectors of Princely States series are few, dates known to be scarce are usually worth little more than common ones. Coins of a dated type which do not show the date on their flans should be valued at about 70 per cent of the prices indicated.

DATING

Coins are dated in several eras. Arabic and Devanagari numerals are used in conjunction with the Hejira era (AH), the Vikrama Samvat (VS), Saka Samvat (Saka), Fasli era (FE) Mauludi era (AM), and Malabar era (ME), as well as the Christian era (AD).

GRADING

Copper coins are rarely found in better grade, as they were the workhorse of coinage circulation, and were everywhere used for day-to-day transactions. Moreover, they were carelessly struck and even when 'new', can often only be distinguished from VF coins with difficulty, if at all.

Silver coins were often hoarded, and not infrequently, turn up in nearly new condition. The silver coins of Hyderabad (dump coins) are common in high grades, and the rupees of some states are scarcer 'used' than 'new'. Great caution must be exercised in determining the value or scarcity of high grade dump coins.

Dump gold was rarely circulated, and usually occurs in high grades, or is found made into jewelry.

ALWAR

State located in Rajputana in northwestern India.

Alwar was founded about 1722 by a Rajput chieftain of the Naruka clan, Rao Pratap Singh of Macheri (1740-1791), a descendant of the family which had ruled Jaipur in the fourteenth century. Alwar was distinguished by being the first of the Princely States to use coins struck at the Calcutta Mint. These, first issued in 1877, were of the same weight and assay as the Imperial Rupee, and carried the bust of Queen Victoria, Empress of India. Alwar State, having allied itself with East India Company interests in their struggles against the Marathas early in the nineteenth century, continued to maintain a good relationship with the British right up to Indian Independence in 1947. In May 1949, Alwar was merged into Rajasthan.

Mint: Rajgarh.

LOCAL RULERS

Bakhtawar Singh
  AH1206-1231/1791-1815AD
Bani Singh
  AH1231-1274/1815-1857AD
Sheodan Singh
  AH1274-1291/1857-1874AD
Mangal Singh
  AH1291-1310/1874-1892

MUGHAL ISSUES
In the name of Muhammad Akbar II
AH1221-1253/1806-1837AD

PAISA

KM#	Date	Year	COPPER Good	VG	Fine	VF
15	AH—	12	4.00	6.00	10.00	15.00
	—	16	4.00	6.00	10.00	15.00
	122x	17	4.00	6.00	10.00	15.00
	—	20	4.00	6.00	10.00	15.00
	—	21	4.00	6.00	10.00	15.00
	—	24	4.00	6.00	10.00	15.00
	—	25	4.00	6.00	10.00	15.00
	—	26	4.00	6.00	10.00	15.00
	—	28	4.00	6.00	10.00	15.00

1/4 RUPEE
SILVER, 13mm, 2.68-2.90 g

KM#	Date	Year	VG	Fine	VF	XF
18	ND	22	10.00	15.00	20.00	27.50

1/2 RUPEE

SILVER, 18mm, 5.35-5.80 g

KM#	Date	Year	VG	Fine	VF	XF
19	ND	19	10.00	15.00	20.00	27.50
	—	20	10.00	15.00	20.00	27.50
	—	21	10.00	15.00	20.00	27.50
	—	22	10.00	15.00	20.00	27.50

RUPEE

SILVER, 10.70-11.40 g

KM#	Date	Year	VG	Fine	VF	XF
20	AH—	6-28	15.00	20.00	24.00	30.00

NAZARANA RUPEE
SILVER, 10.70-11.60 g

| 20a | AH12xx | 26 | 40.00 | 60.00 | 85.00 | 125.00 |

In the name of Bahadur Shah II
AH1253-1274/1837-1857AD

PAISA

KM#	Date	Year	COPPER Good	VG	Fine	VF
25	AH—	2	2.50	3.50	5.00	8.00
	—	6	2.50	3.50	5.00	8.00
	—	9	2.50	3.50	5.00	8.00
	—	12	2.50	3.50	5.00	8.00
	—	15	2.50	3.50	5.00	8.00
	—	17	2.50	3.50	5.00	8.00
	—	18	2.50	3.50	5.00	8.00
	—	19	2.50	3.50	5.00	8.00
	—	20	2.50	3.50	5.00	8.00

1/4 RUPEE
SILVER, 16mm, 2.68-2.90 g

KM#	Date	Year	VG	Fine	VF	XF
28	ND	20	—	—	Rare	—

1/2 RUPEE
SILVER, 18mm, 5.35-5.80 g

| 29 | ND | 17 | — | — | Rare | — |

RUPEE

SILVER, 10.70-11.60 g

KM#	Date	Year	VG	Fine	VF	XF
30	AH—	1	20.00	25.00	30.00	40.00
	—	2	20.00	30.00	40.00	50.00
	12xx	4	20.00	30.00	40.00	50.00
	1263	11	20.00	30.00	40.00	50.00
	126x	12	20.00	30.00	40.00	50.00
	1267	13	20.00	30.00	40.00	50.00
	12xx	15	20.00	30.00	40.00	50.00
	—	16	20.00	30.00	40.00	50.00
	—	20	20.00	25.00	30.00	40.00

NAZARANA RUPEE

SILVER, 10.70-11.60 g

30a	AH125x	1	40.00	60.00	85.00	125.00
	1261	8	40.00	60.00	85.00	125.00
	1267	13	40.00	60.00	85.00	125.00

LOCAL ISSUES
In the names of "Her Majesty the Queen" (Victoria) and Sheodan Singh
AH1274-1291/1857-1874AD

PAISA

KM#	Date	Year	COPPER Good	VG	Fine	VF
35	1859	—	1.50	2.50	3.50	5.00
	1860	3	1.50	2.50	3.50	5.00
	—	4	1.50	2.50	3.50	5.00
	1864	—	1.50	2.50	3.50	5.00
	1865	9	1.50	2.50	3.50	5.00
	1870	13	1.50	2.50	3.50	5.00
	1871	15	1.50	2.50	3.50	5.00

NAZARANA PAISA

KM#	Date	Year	COPPER Good	VG	Fine	VF
35a	1865	9	—	—	Rare	—
	1866	9	—	—	Rare	—
	1871	15	12.50	20.00	27.50	35.00

RUPEE

SILVER, 10.70-11.60 g

KM#	Date	Year	VG	Fine	VF	XF
37	1859	2	20.00	25.00	30.00	40.00
	1860	3	20.00	25.00	30.00	40.00
	1860	4	20.00	25.00	30.00	40.00
	1861	4	20.00	25.00	30.00	40.00
	1863	—	20.00	25.00	30.00	40.00
	1864	7	20.00	25.00	30.00	40.00
	1865	8	20.00	25.00	30.00	40.00
	1865	9	20.00	25.00	30.00	40.00

NAZARANA RUPEE

SILVER, 10.70-11.60 g

KM#	Date	Year	VG	Fine	VF	XF
37a	(1859)	3	—	Reported, not confirmed		
	1865	9	40.00	60.00	85.00	125.00
	1867	10	40.00	60.00	85.00	125.00
	1870	15	40.00	60.00	85.00	125.00
	(1874)	18	—	Reported, not confirmed		

In the name of Mangal Singh
AH1291-1310/1874-1892AD

PRESENTATION ISSUES

Only a few each of KM#40 and 41 were struck at the Rajgarh Mint each year for presentation purposes.

NAZARANA PAISA
COPPER
Similar to Nazarana Rupee, KM#41.

| 40 | 1874 | — | 8.50 | 15.00 | 25.00 | 40.00 |
| | 1891 | — | 8.50 | 15.00 | 25.00 | 40.00 |

NAZARANA RUPEE

SILVER, 10.70-11.60 g

KM#	Date	Year	VG	Fine	VF	XF
41	1859	—	35.00	55.00	75.00	100.00
	1876	3	35.00	55.00	75.00	100.00
	1877	4	35.00	55.00	75.00	100.00
	188x		35.00	55.00	75.00	100.00

MILLED COINAGE
RUPEE

11.6600 g, .917 SILVER, .3438 oz ASW

KM#	Date	Mintage	Fine	VF	XF	Unc
45	1788(error)	.200	12.00	17.50	22.50	30.00
	1877	.200	10.00	12.50	16.50	25.00
	1877	—	—	—	Proof	250.00
	1878	.206	10.00	14.00	20.00	30.00
	1880	.196	10.00	12.50	16.50	25.00
	1882	.206	10.00	12.50	16.50	25.00
	1882	—	—	—	Proof	250.00

46	1891	.160	10.00	12.50	15.00	22.50
	1891	—	—	—	Proof	250.00

GOLD (OMS)

46a	1891	(restrike)	—	—	Proof	750.00

AWADH
Oudh

Kingdom located in northeastern India. The Nawabs of Awadh traced their origins to Muhammed Amin, a Persian adventurer who had attached himself to the court of Muhammed Shah, the Mughal Emperor, early in the eighteenth century. In 1720 Muhammed Amin was appointed Mughal Subahdar of Awadh, in which capacity he soon exhibited a considerable measure of independence. Until 1819, after Ghazi-ud-din had been encouraged by the Governor-General, Lord Hastings, to accept the title of King, Muhammed Amin's successors were known simply as the Nawabs of Awadh. The British offer, and Ghazi-ud-din's acceptance of it, provided a clear indication of just how far Mughal decline had proceeded. For the Mughal Emperor was now little more than a pensioner of the East India Company. Yet the coinage of Ghazi-ud-din immediately after 1819 marks also the hesitation he felt in taking so dramatic, and in the eyes of some of the princes of India, so ungrateful a step.

In 1856 Awadh was annexed by the British on the grounds of internal misrule. The king makers were now also seen as the king breakers. In setting aside the royal house of Awadh, the Muslim princes of India were added to that growing list of those who had come to fear the outcome of British hegemony. And it was here, in Awadh, that the Great Revolt of 1857 found its most fertile soil.

In 1877, Awadh along with Agra was placed under one administrator. It was made part of the United Provinces in 1902.

RULERS

Sa'adat Ali,
  AH1213-1230/1798-1814AD
Ghazi-ud-Din Haidar, as Nawab,
  AH1230-1234/1814-1819AD
  as King, AH1234-1243/1819-1827AD
Nasir-ud-Din Haider,
  AH1243-1253/1827-1837AD
Muhammad Ali Shah,
  AH1253-1258/1837-1842AD
Amjad Ali Shah,
  AH1258-1263/1842-1847AD
Wajid Ali Shah,
  AH1263-1272/1847-1856AD
Brijis Qadr,
  AH1273-1274/1857-1858AD

MINTS

Allahabad	الله اباد
Asafabad (Bareli)	آصف اباد
Asafnagar	آصف نگر
Awadh	اوده
Banaras	بنارس
Bareli	بريلي
Hathras	هاتهرسا
Itawa	اتاوا
Kanauj	قنوج
Kora	كورا
Lucknow	لكهنو
Muhammadabad (Banaras)	محمد اباد بنارس
Muradabad	مراد اباد
Najibabad	نجيب اباد
Shahabad	شاجهان اباد
Tanda	تاندة

BARELI MINT
EAST INDIA COMPANY

In the name of Shah Alam II
AH1173-1221/1759-1806AD

RUPEE

SILVER, 10.70-11.60 g
Obv. leg: *Sahib Qirani*, cross.
Rev: Fish, star-shaped flower, Persian letter *Alif*.

KM#	Date	Year	VG	Fine	VF	XF
52.1	AH1216	37	14.00	20.00	27.50	40.00

Rev: Fish, star-shaped flower, Persian letter *He*.

52.2	AH1216	37	14.00	20.00	27.50	40.00

Rev: Fish, star-shaped flower, Persian letter *Wa*.

KM#	Date	Year	VG	Fine	VF	XF
52.3	AH1216	37	12.50	17.50	25.00	32.50
	1217	37	12.50	17.50	25.00	32.50
	1218	37	12.50	17.50	25.00	32.50
	1219	37	12.50	17.50	25.00	32.50
	1220	37	12.50	17.50	25.00	32.50

NOTE: The letter *Wa* on East India Company issues was reputedly the initial of the surname of the new settlement officer for Bareli, Henry Wellesley. The earlier issue, with letter *He*, may have been a less majestic initial of his personal name.

LUCKNOW MINT
Mintname: Muhammadabad Banaras

The issues of the Nawab-Wazir in this mintname are distinguished from East India Company issues on the basis of distinctive fabric and fixed regnal year: 26 for Awadh, 17 for East India Company.

In the name of Shah Alam II
AH1173-1221/1759-1806AD

FALUS

COPPER, irregular flan

KM#	Date	Year	Good	VG	Fine	VF
97	AH1217	26	.75	1.50	2.25	3.50
(C1.1)	1218	26	.75	1.50	2.25	3.50
	1219	26	.75	1.50	2.25	3.50
	1222	26	.75	1.50	2.25	3.50
	1224	26	.75	1.50	2.25	3.50
	1230	—	.75	1.50	2.25	3.50
	1231	—	.75	1.50	2.25	3.50
	1232	—	.75	1.50	2.25	3.50
	1233	—	.75	1.50	2.25	3.50

Round flan

98	AH1222	—	1.75	3.00	4.50	7.00
(C1.2)	1223	—	1.75	3.00	4.50	7.00
	1229	29	1.75	3.00	4.50	7.00
	1233	—	1.75	3.00	4.50	7.00

1/8 RUPEE

SILVER, 1.34-1.45 g
Rev: Frozen regnal year, flag and star.

KM#	Date	Year	VG	Fine	VF	XF
100.2	AH1215	26	6.00	7.50	10.00	13.50
(C3.2)	1218	26	6.00	7.50	10.00	13.50
	1222	26	6.00	7.50	10.00	13.50
	1226	26	6.00	7.50	10.00	13.50
	1229	26	6.00	7.50	10.00	13.50
	1232	26	6.00	7.50	10.00	13.50
	1233	26	6.00	7.50	10.00	13.50

1/4 RUPEE

SILVER, 2.68-2.90 g
Rev: Frozen regnal year, flag and star.

101.2	AH1225	26	6.00	7.50	10.00	13.50
(C4.2)	1231	26	6.00	7.50	10.00	13.50
	1233	26	6.00	7.50	10.00	13.50

1/2 RUPEE

SILVER, 5.38-5.80 g

Awadh / INDIAN PRINCELY STATES

KM#	Date	Year	VG	Fine	VF	XF
102.2 (C5.2)	AH1223	26	7.50	10.00	13.50	20.00

RUPEE

SILVER, 10.70-11.60 g
Rev: Frozen regnal year, flag and star.

KM#	Date	Year	VG	Fine	VF	XF
103.2 (C6.2)	AH1216	26	12.50	14.50	17.50	22.50
	1217	26	12.50	14.50	17.50	22.50
	1218	26	12.50	14.50	17.50	22.50
	1219	26	12.50	14.50	17.50	22.50
	1220	26	12.50	14.50	17.50	22.50
	1221	26	11.50	13.50	16.50	20.00
	1222	26	11.50	13.50	16.50	20.00
	1223	26	11.50	13.50	16.50	20.00
	1224	26	11.50	13.50	16.50	20.00
	1225	26	11.50	13.50	16.50	20.00
	1226	26	11.50	13.50	16.50	20.00
	1227	26	11.50	13.50	16.50	20.00
	1228	26	11.50	13.50	16.50	20.00
	1229	26	11.50	13.50	16.50	20.00
	1230	26	11.50	13.50	16.50	20.00
	1231	26	11.50	13.50	16.50	20.00
	1232	26	11.50	13.50	16.50	20.00
	1233	26	11.50	13.50	16.50	20.00
	1234	26	11.50	13.50	16.50	20.00

NOTE: For similar coins also dated AH1229/Yr. 26, see KM#386.

Rev: W/o AH date.

103.3	ND	26	—	Rare	—

NAZARANA RUPEE

SILVER, 10.70-11.60 g
Similar to 1 Rupee, C#6, broad flan, 28mm.
Rev: Frozen regnal year.

104 (C6a)	AH1216	26	35.00	45.00	60.00	85.00

MOHUR

GOLD, 10.70-11.40 g
Rev: Frozen regnal year.

105 (C10)	AH1218	26	220.00	240.00	265.00	300.00
	1222	26	220.00	240.00	265.00	300.00
	1229	26	220.00	240.00	265.00	300.00
	1230	26	220.00	240.00	265.00	300.00

NAJIBABAD MINT

To Awadh in 1774AD. For issues before AH1188/R.Y. 15, see Rohilkhand.

In the name of Shah Alam II
AH1173-1221/1759-1806AD

PAISA
Various weight standards
COPPER
Obv: Crescent. Rev: Vertical fish.

KM#	Date	Year	Good	VG	Fine	VF
111	AH1216	43	3.00	4.00	6.00	8.50
	1218	47	3.00	4.00	6.00	8.50
	1219	—	3.00	4.00	6.00	8.50

Rev: Horizontal fish.

113	AH1216	43	5.00	7.00	10.00	15.00
	1217	44	5.00	7.00	10.00	15.00

INDEPENDENT KINGS
GHAZI-UD-DIN HAIDAR
King, AH1234-1243/1819-1827AD

In the name of Shah Alam II
AH1173-1221/1759-1806AD

FALUS

COPPER

KM#	Date	Year	Good	VG	Fine	VF
140 (C13)	AH1234	26	1.50	2.25	2.75	3.75
	1235	26	1.50	2.25	2.75	3.75

1/8 RUPEE

SILVER, 1.34-2.45 g

KM#	Date	Year	VG	Fine	VF	XF
142 (C19)	AH1234	26	10.00	13.50	18.50	25.00

1/4 RUPEE

SILVER, 2.68-2.90 g

144 (C20)	AH1234	26	10.00	13.50	18.50	25.00

1/2 RUPEE
SILVER

145	AH1234	26	20.00	30.00	60.00	100.00

RUPEE

SILVER, 10.70-11.60 g

146 (C22)	AH1234	26	12.50	14.00	18.50	35.00

1/2 MOHUR
GOLD, 5.35-5.70 g

148 (C25)	AH1234	26	110.00	120.00	135.00	150.00

MOHUR

GOLD, 10.70-11.40 g

150 (C26)	AH1234	26	225.00	250.00	285.00	325.00

In his own name
NOTE: Coins dated AH1234 have regnal year 5 for Haidar as Nawab; coins dated AH1235 and later have his regnal year as King AH1235 Yr. 1.

NOTE: The mint name comes with 2 different epithets:
VARIETY I: AH1234-1235; *Dar ul-Amaret Lakhnau Suba Awadh*
VARIETY II: AH1236-1243 *Dar us-Sultanat Lakhnau Suba Awadh*

FALUS

COPPER

Mintname: Variety I

KM#	Date	Year	Good	VG	Fine	VF
155.1 (C33.1)	AH1234	5	1.50	2.50	3.50	5.00
	1235	1	1.25	2.00	2.50	3.50

Mintname: Variety II

155.2 (C33.2)	AH1236	2	.85	1.50	2.00	3.00
	1237	3	.85	1.50	2.00	3.00
	1238	4	1.25	2.00	2.50	3.50
	1239	5	.85	1.50	2.00	3.00
	1240	6	.85	1.50	2.00	3.00

1/16 RUPEE
(Anna)

SILVER, 0.67-0.72 g

KM#	Date	Year	VG	Fine	VF	XF
157 (C35)	AH1235	1	10.00	15.00	25.00	40.00

1/8 RUPEE
(2 Annas)

SILVER, 12-14mm, 1.34-1.45 g

159 (C36)	AH1235	1	6.50	8.50	11.50	16.50
	1236	—	6.50	8.50	11.50	16.50
	—	5	6.50	8.50	11.50	16.50

1/4 RUPEE

SILVER, 15-17mm, 2.68-2.90 g

161 (C37)	AH1236	2	6.50	8.50	11.50	16.50
	—	4	6.50	8.50	11.50	16.50
	124x	8	6.50	8.50	11.50	16.50

1/2 RUPEE

SILVER, 5.35-5.80 g

163 (C38)	AH1235	1	10.00	15.00	25.00	40.00
	1236	2	15.00	20.00	30.00	50.00
	1237	3	15.00	20.00	30.00	50.00
	1238	4	7.50	10.00	13.50	18.50
	1239	5	7.50	10.00	13.50	18.50
	1240	6	7.50	10.00	13.50	18.50
	1242	8	7.50	10.00	13.50	18.50

RUPEE

SILVER, 10.70-11.60 g
Mintname: Variety I

165.1 (C39.1)	AH1234	5	12.50	14.50	17.50	27.50
	1235	1	12.50	14.50	17.50	27.50

Mintname: Variety II

165.2 (C39.2)	AH1236	2	12.50	14.50	17.50	27.50
	1237	3	12.50	14.50	17.50	27.50
	1238	4	12.50	14.50	17.50	27.50
	1239	5	12.50	14.50	17.50	27.50
	1240	6	11.50	13.50	17.50	27.50
	1241	7	11.50	13.50	17.50	27.50
	1242	8	11.50	13.50	17.50	27.50
	1243	9	11.50	13.50	17.50	27.50

1/4 ASHRAFI

GOLD, 2.68-2.85 g

KM#	Date	Year	VG	Fine	VF	XF
168	AH1236	—	65.00	85.00	110.00	135.00
(C43)	1243	—	65.00	85.00	110.00	135.00

ASHRAFI

GOLD, 10.70-11.40 g
Mintname: Variety I

170.1	AH1234	5	250.00	285.00	325.00	400.00
(C45.1)						

Mintname: Variety II

170.2	AH1235	1	250.00	285.00	325.00	400.00
(C45.2)	1236	1	250.00	285.00	325.00	400.00
	1236	2	250.00	285.00	325.00	400.00
	1239	5	250.00	285.00	325.00	400.00
	1240	6	250.00	285.00	325.00	400.00
	1241	7	250.00	285.00	325.00	400.00
	1242	8	250.00	285.00	325.00	400.00

NASIR-UD-DIN HAIDAR
AH1243-1253 / 1827-1837AD

In the name of Sulayman Jah

FALUS

COPPER

KM#	Date	Year	Good	VG	Fine	VF
175	AH1243	1	1.25	2.00	2.75	4.00
(C47)	1244	1	1.25	2.00	2.75	4.00
	1244	2	1.25	2.00	2.75	4.00

1/8 RUPEE

SILVER, 13mm, 1.34-1.45 g

KM#	Date	Year	VG	Fine	VF	XF
180	AH1244	2	5.00	7.00	10.00	14.00
(C49)						

1/4 RUPEE

SILVER, 2.68-2.90 g

182	AH1244	2	6.50	8.50	11.50	16.50
(C50)						

1/2 RUPEE

SILVER, 5.35-5.80 g

184	AH1243	1	10.00	15.00	25.00	40.00
(C51)	1244	2	7.00	9.00	12.50	17.50

RUPEE

SILVER, 10.70-11.60 g

KM#	Date	Year	VG	Fine	VF	XF
186	AH1243	1	12.50	14.50	17.50	27.50
(C52)	1244	1	12.50	14.50	17.50	27.50
	1244	2	12.50	14.50	17.50	27.50
	1245	1	12.50	14.50	17.50	27.50
	1245	2	15.00	20.00	27.50	40.00

ASHRAFI

GOLD, 10.70-11.40 g

190	AH1243	1	185.00	235.00	300.00	400.00
(C54)						

In the name of Nasir al-Din Haidar
NOTE: This series comes in 2 major varieties, the difference being in the coat of arms and position of regnal year.
Variety I: Katar (knife) above fish, regnal year within fish.
Variety II: Katar within fish, regnal year in marginal inscription.

FALUS

COPPER
Mint mark: Variety I

KM#	Date	Year	Good	VG	Fine	VF
195.1	AH1245	3	.85	1.50	2.00	2.75
(C56.1)	1246	3	.85	1.50	2.00	2.75
	1246	4	.85	1.50	2.00	2.75
	1247	4	.85	1.50	2.00	2.75
	1247	5	.85	1.50	2.00	2.75
	1248	5	.85	1.50	2.00	2.75
	1249	6	.85	1.50	2.00	2.75

Mint mark: Variety II

195.2	AH1249	6	.85	1.50	2.00	2.75
(C56.2)	1250	7	1.50	2.50	3.00	5.00

1/16 RUPEE
(Anna)

SILVER, 9-13mm, 0.67-0.72 g
Mint mark: Variety II

KM#	Date	Year	VG	Fine	VF	XF
197	AH1250	—	2.50	4.00	6.50	8.50
(C58a)	1252	—	2.50	4.00	6.50	8.50

1/8 RUPEE

SILVER, 14mm, 1.34-1.45 g
Mint mark: Variety I

199.1	AH1246	3	2.75	4.50	7.50	10.00
(C59)	1248	5	2.75	4.50	7.50	10.00

Mint mark: Variety II

199.2	AH1250	—	2.75	4.50	7.50	10.00

1/4 RUPEE

SILVER, 2.68-2.90 g
Mint mark: Variety I

KM#	Date	Year	VG	Fine	VF	XF
201.1	AH1245	3	3.50	6.00	11.00	15.00
(C60.1)	124x	4	3.50	6.00	11.00	15.00
	1247	5	3.50	6.00	11.00	15.00
	1248	5	3.50	6.00	11.00	15.00
	—	6	3.50	6.00	11.00	15.00

Mint mark: Variety II

201.2	AH1250	—	6.50	9.00	12.00	16.50
(C60.2)	1251	8	6.50	9.00	12.00	16.50

1/2 RUPEE

SILVER, 5.35-5.80 g
Mint mark: Variety I

203	AH1243	1	6.50	9.00	12.00	16.50
(C61)	1247	5	6.50	9.00	12.00	16.50
	1248	5	6.50	9.00	12.00	16.50
	1250	7	6.50	9.00	12.00	16.50

RUPEE

SILVER, 10.70-11.60 g
Mint mark: Variety I

205.1	AH1245	3	11.50	13.50	16.50	20.00
(C62.1)	1246	3	11.50	13.50	16.50	20.00
	1246	4	11.50	13.50	16.50	20.00
	1247	4	11.50	13.50	16.50	20.00
	1247	5	11.50	13.50	16.50	20.00
	1248	5	11.50	13.50	16.50	20.00
	1248	6	11.50	13.50	16.50	20.00
	1249	6	11.50	13.50	16.50	20.00

Mint mark: Variety II

205.2	AH1249	7	12.50	14.00	18.50	27.50
(C62.2)	1250	7	12.50	14.00	18.50	27.50
	1250	8	12.50	14.00	18.50	27.50
	1251	7	12.50	14.00	18.50	27.50
	1251	8	12.50	14.00	18.50	27.50
	1252	7	12.50	14.00	18.50	27.50
	1252	8	12.50	14.00	18.50	27.50
	1252	9	12.50	14.00	18.50	27.50
	1253	9	12.50	14.00	20.00	27.50
	1253	10	12.50	14.00	20.00	27.50

ASHRAFI

GOLD, 25mm, 10.70-11.40 g
Mint mark: Variety I

300	AH1245	3	185.00	235.00	300.00	400.00
(C69)	1246	3	185.00	235.00	300.00	400.00
	1252	9	185.00	235.00	300.00	400.00

872 Awadh / INDIAN PRINCELY STATES

MUHAMMAD ALI SHAH
AH1253-1258/1837-1842AD

NOTE: Mint name comes in 2 varieties.
VARIETY III. *Suba Awadh Baitu-s-Sultanat Lakhnau*, on all coins through 1256/Yr. 3.
VARIETY IV. *Mulk Awadh Baitu-s-Sultanat Lakhnau*, on all coins beginning 1256/Yr. 3.

FALUS

COPPER

KM#	Date	Year	Good	VG	Fine	VF
305	AH1253	1	1.25	2.25	3.00	4.00
(C72)	1253	—	1.25	2.25	3.00	4.00
	1254	2	1.25	2.25	3.00	4.00
	1255	—	1.25	2.25	3.00	4.00

1/8 RUPEE

SILVER, 10mm, 1.34-1.45 g

KM#	Date	Year	VG	Fine	VF	XF
310	AH1253	1	4.50	6.50	9.00	13.50
(C76)	1256	(3)	4.50	6.50	9.00	13.50

1/4 RUPEE

SILVER, 2.68-2.90 g

KM#	Date	Year	VG	Fine	VF	XF
312	AH1253	—	6.00	8.00	11.00	15.00
(C77)	1254	—	6.00	8.00	11.00	15.00
	1255	—	6.00	8.00	11.00	15.00
	1256	—	6.00	8.00	11.00	15.00

1/2 RUPEE

SILVER, 5.35-5.80 g
Mintname: Variety III.

KM#	Date	Year	VG	Fine	VF	XF
314.1	AH1254	—	7.00	9.00	12.00	16.50
(C78.1)						

Mintname: Variety IV.

KM#	Date	Year	VG	Fine	VF	XF
314.2	AH1256	3	7.00	9.00	12.00	16.50
(C78.2)	1258	—	7.00	9.00	12.00	16.50

RUPEE

SILVER, 10.70-11.60 g
Mintname: Variety III.

KM#	Date	Year	VG	Fine	VF	XF
316.1	AH1253	1	12.50	14.50	17.50	25.00
(C79.1)	1254	1	12.50	14.50	17.50	25.00
	1254	2	12.50	14.50	17.50	25.00
	1255	2	12.50	14.50	17.50	25.00
	1255	3	12.50	14.50	17.50	25.00
	1256	3	12.50	14.50	17.50	25.00

Mintname: Variety IV.

KM#	Date	Year	VG	Fine	VF	XF
316.2	AH1256	3	12.50	14.50	17.50	25.00
(C79.2)	1256	4	12.50	14.50	17.50	25.00
	1257	4	12.50	14.50	17.50	25.00
	1257	5	12.50	14.50	17.50	25.00
	1258	5	12.50	14.50	17.50	25.00

1/2 ASHRAFI

GOLD, 5.35-5.70 g

KM#	Date	Year	VG	Fine	VF	XF
320	AH1253	1	125.00	150.00	185.00	225.00
(C85)						

ASHRAFI

GOLD, 10.70-11.40 g
Mintname: Variety III.

KM#	Date	Year	VG	Fine	VF	XF
322.1	AH1253	—	175.00	225.00	275.00	325.00
(C86.1)	1255	3	175.00	225.00	275.00	325.00

Mintname: Variety IV.

KM#	Date	Year	VG	Fine	VF	XF
322.2	1258	—	175.00	225.00	275.00	325.00
(C86.2)						

AMJAD ALI SHAH
AH1258-1263/1842-1847AD

FALUS

COPPER

KM#	Date	Year	Good	VG	Fine	VF
325	AH1258	1	1.50	2.50	3.50	5.00
(C95)	1259	1	1.50	2.50	3.50	5.00
	1262	—	1.50	2.50	3.50	5.00

Finer style, 27mm

KM#	Date	Year	Good	VG	Fine	VF
326	AH1258	1	5.00	10.00	15.00	21.50
(C95a)						

1/16 RUPEE

SILVER, 0.67-0.72 g

KM#	Date	Year	VG	Fine	VF	XF
328	AH1262	—	5.00	6.50	8.50	11.50
(C97)						

1/8 RUPEE

SILVER, 1.34-1.45 g

KM#	Date	Year	VG	Fine	VF	XF
330	AH1258	—	6.00	8.00	11.00	15.00
(C98)	1259	—	6.00	8.00	11.00	15.00
	1262	—	6.00	8.00	11.00	15.00

1/4 RUPEE

SILVER, 2.68-2.90 g

KM#	Date	Year	VG	Fine	VF	XF
332	AH1259	2	12.50	16.50	21.50	27.50
(C99)	1260	3	6.00	7.50	9.00	12.50

1/2 RUPEE

SILVER, 18-20mm, 5.35-5.80 g

KM#	Date	Year	VG	Fine	VF	XF
334	AH1259	2	6.50	8.00	10.00	14.00
(C100)	1260	3	6.50	8.00	10.00	14.00
	1261	—	6.50	8.00	10.00	14.00

RUPEE

SILVER, 10.70-11.60 g

KM#	Date	Year	VG	Fine	VF	XF
336	AH1258	1	12.50	14.50	17.50	27.50
(C101)	1259	1	12.50	14.50	17.50	27.50
	1259	2	12.50	14.50	17.50	27.50
	1260	2	12.50	14.50	17.50	27.50
	1260	3	12.50	14.50	17.50	27.50
	1261	3	12.50	14.50	17.50	27.50
	1261	4	12.50	14.50	17.50	27.50
	1262	4	12.50	14.50	17.50	27.50
	1262	5	12.50	14.50	17.50	27.50
	1263	5	12.50	14.50	17.50	27.50

1/2 ASHRAFI

GOLD, 5.35-5.70 g

KM#	Date	Year	VG	Fine	VF	XF
340	AH1258	—	125.00	150.00	185.00	225.00
(C107)	1263	—	125.00	150.00	185.00	225.00

ASHRAFI

GOLD, 10.70-11.40 g

KM#	Date	Year	VG	Fine	VF	XF
342	AH1258	—	175.00	225.00	275.00	325.00
(C108)	1259	2	175.00	225.00	275.00	325.00
	1261	4	175.00	225.00	275.00	325.00
	1263	—	175.00	225.00	275.00	325.00

WAJID ALI SHAH
AH1263-1272/1847-1856AD

NOTE: Wajid Alis coins come in 3 varieties, depending on form of mint name:
VARIETY IV: *Mulk Awadh Baitu-s-Sultanat Lakhnau*, AH1263-1267/Yr.4.
VARIETY V: *Mulk Awadh Akhtarnagar*, AH1267/5 reported so far only for Rupees dated 1267/Yr. 5. The same date/year combination is also found in Var. VI.
VARIETY VI: *Baitus-s-Sultanat Lakhnau Mulk Awadh Akhtar-Nagar*, 1267/Yr. 5-1272.

1/8 FALUS

COPPER

KM#	Date	Year	Good	VG	Fine	VF
345	AH1270	8	3.50	6.00	8.00	11.50
(C109)	1271	—	3.00	5.00	7.00	10.00

1/4 FALUS

COPPER

KM#	Date	Year	Good	VG	Fine	VF
347	AH1270	7	3.00	5.00	7.00	10.00
(C110)	1270	8	3.50	6.00	8.50	12.00
	1272	9	3.00	5.00	7.00	10.00

1/2 FALUS

COPPER

KM#	Date	Year	Good	VG	Fine	VF
349	AH1269	—	2.75	4.50	6.00	8.50
(C111)	1270	7	2.75	4.50	6.00	8.50
	1270	8	2.75	4.50	6.00	8.50
	1271	—	2.75	4.50	6.00	8.50
	1272	—	2.75	4.50	6.00	8.50

FALUS

COPPER
Mintname: Variety IV.

KM#	Date	Year	Good	VG	Fine	VF
351.1	AH—	1	1.50	2.50	3.00	4.50
(C112.1)	1263	—	2.00	3.50	5.00	7.00
	1264	2	2.00	3.50	5.00	7.00

Mintname: Variety VI.

KM#	Date	Year	Good	VG	Fine	VF
351.2	AH1270	8	2.00	3.50	5.00	7.00
(C112.2)	1270	9	2.00	3.50	5.00	7.00
	1271?	—	2.00	3.50	5.00	7.00
	1272	—	2.00	3.50	5.00	7.00

Rectangular, 14x18mm

KM#	Date	Year	Good	VG	Fine	VF
351.3 (C112.3)	AH1271	—	2.00	3.50	5.00	7.00

NOTE: Barbarous versions of C#112, without legible date or year, are common and worth half of what a legible specimen commands.

1/16 RUPEE

SILVER, 0.67-0.72 g

KM#	Date	Year	VG	Fine	VF	XF
355	AH126x	—	4.50	6.50	8.50	13.50
(C114)	1270	8	4.50	6.50	8.50	13.50
	1270	2(sic)	4.50	6.50	8.50	13.50
	1271	—	4.50	6.50	8.50	13.50
	1272	—	4.50	6.50	8.50	13.50

1/8 RUPEE

SILVER, 1.34-1.45 g
Mintname: Variety IV.

KM#	Date	Year	VG	Fine	VF	XF
357.1	AH1264	1	5.00	6.50	8.50	13.50
(C115.1)	1264	2	5.00	6.50	8.50	13.50
	1265	2	5.00	6.50	8.50	11.50
	1266	—	5.00	6.50	8.50	13.50
	126x	5	5.00	6.50	8.50	13.50
	1268	—	5.00	6.50	8.50	13.50

Mintname: Variety VI.

KM#	Date	Year	VG	Fine	VF	XF
357.2	AH1268	—	5.00	6.50	8.50	13.50
(C115.2)	1269	—	5.00	6.50	8.50	13.50
	1270	8	5.00	6.50	8.50	13.50
	1271	9	5.00	6.50	8.50	13.50

1/4 RUPEE

SILVER, 2.68-2.90 g
Mintname: Variety IV.

KM#	Date	Year	VG	Fine	VF	XF
361.1	AH1263	1	5.00	6.50	8.50	11.50
(C116.1)	1265	—	5.00	6.50	8.50	11.50

Mintname: Variety VI.

KM#	Date	Year	VG	Fine	VF	XF
361.2	AH1267	5	5.00	6.50	8.50	11.50
(C116.2)	1268	—	5.00	6.50	8.50	11.50
	1269	6	5.00	6.50	8.50	11.50
	1271	9	5.00	6.50	8.50	11.50

1/2 RUPEE

SILVER, 5.35-5.80 g
Mintname: Variety IV.

KM#	Date	Year	VG	Fine	VF	XF
363.1	AH1263	2	6.50	8.50	11.00	15.00
(C117.1)	1265	2	6.50	8.50	11.00	15.00
	1266	3	6.50	8.50	11.00	15.00

Mintname: Variety VI.

KM#	Date	Year	VG	Fine	VF	XF
363.2	AH1268	5	6.50	8.50	11.00	15.00
(C117.3)	1269	6	6.50	8.50	11.00	15.00
	1271	8	6.50	8.50	11.00	15.00
	1271	9	6.50	8.50	11.00	15.00

RUPEE

SILVER, 10.70-11.60 g
Mintname: Variety IV.

KM#	Date	Year	VG	Fine	VF	XF
365.1	AH1263	1	11.50	13.50	16.50	25.00
(C118.1)	1264	1	11.50	13.50	16.50	25.00
	1264	2	11.50	13.50	16.50	25.00
	1265	1	11.50	13.50	16.50	25.00
	1265	2	11.50	13.50	16.50	25.00
	1265	3	11.50	13.50	16.50	25.00
	1266	3	11.50	13.50	16.50	25.00
	1266	4	11.50	13.50	16.50	25.00
	1267	3	11.50	13.50	16.50	25.00
	1267	4	11.50	13.50	16.50	25.00
	1268	4	11.50	13.50	16.50	25.00

Mintname: Variety V.

KM#	Date	Year	VG	Fine	VF	XF
365.2 (C118.2)	AH1267	5	17.50	25.00	35.00	50.00

Mintname: Variety VI.

KM#	Date	Year	VG	Fine	VF	XF
365.3	AH1267	5	11.50	13.50	16.50	25.00
(C118.3)	1268	5	11.50	13.50	16.50	25.00
	1268	6	11.50	13.50	16.50	25.00
	1269	6	11.50	13.50	16.50	25.00
	1269	2	(sic - 2 is a backwards 6)			
			11.50	13.50	16.50	25.00
	1269	7	11.50	13.50	16.50	25.00
	1270	7	11.50	13.50	16.50	25.00
	1270	8	11.50	13.50	16.50	25.00
	1271	8	11.50	13.50	16.50	25.00
	1271	9	11.50	13.50	16.50	25.00
	1272	9	11.50	13.50	16.50	25.00
	1272	10	11.50	13.50	16.50	25.00

1/16 ASHRAFI

GOLD, 10mm, 0.67-0.71 g

KM#	Date	Year	VG	Fine	VF	XF
370 (C120)	AH1270	—	35.00	45.00	55.00	70.00

1/8 ASHRAFI

GOLD, 1.34-1.42 g

KM#	Date	Year	VG	Fine	VF	XF
372 (C121)	AH1263-72	1-10	40.00	50.00	60.00	80.00

1/4 ASHRAFI

GOLD, 2.68-2.85 g

KM#	Date	Year	VG	Fine	VF	XF
374 (C122)	AH1263-72	1-10	60.00	75.00	90.00	120.00

1/2 ASHRAFI

GOLD, 5.35-5.70 g
Mintname: Variety IV.

KM#	Date	Year	VG	Fine	VF	XF
376 (C123)	AH1267	4	110.00	125.00	150.00	175.00

ASHRAFI

GOLD, 10.70-11.40 g
Mintname: Variety IV.

KM#	Date	Year	VG	Fine	VF	XF
378.1	AH1263	1	165.00	200.00	250.00	300.00
(C124)	1264	2	165.00	200.00	250.00	300.00
	1265	2	165.00	200.00	250.00	300.00
	1265	3	165.00	200.00	250.00	300.00
	1266	3	165.00	200.00	250.00	300.00
	1267	4	165.00	200.00	250.00	300.00

Mintname: Variety VI.

KM#	Date	Year	VG	Fine	VF	XF
378.3	AH1268	5	165.00	200.00	250.00	300.00
	1272	—	165.00	200.00	250.00	300.00

BRIJIS QADR

1857-1858AD

Nawab-Wazir during the Indian Mutiny

FALUS

COPPER

KM#	Date	Year	Good	VG	Fine	VF
380 (C125)	AH1229	26	3.00	5.00	7.50	10.00

1/8 RUPEE

SILVER, 13-14mm, 1.34-1.45 g

KM#	Date	Year	VG	Fine	VF	XF
382 (C127)	AH1229	26	7.00	10.00	14.00	20.00

NOTE: Fictitious dating in imitation of coinage before AH1234/1819. Identifiable only by style and mint name, *Awadh* at top of reverse, dated only AH1229/Yr.26.

1/2 RUPEE

SILVER, 2.68-2.90 g

KM#	Date	Year	VG	Fine	VF	XF
384 (C129)	AH1229	26	9.00	13.50	18.50	26.50

RUPEE

SILVER, 10.70-11.60 g

KM#	Date	Year	VG	Fine	VF	XF
386 (C130)	AH1229	26	30.00	50.00	75.00	100.00

ASHRAFI

GOLD, 10.70-11.40 g

KM#	Date	Year	VG	Fine	VF	XF
390 (C135)	AH1229	26	185.00	235.00	300.00	400.00

BAHAWALPUR

The Amirs of Bahawalpur established their independence from Afghan control towards the close of the eighteenth century. In the 1830's the state's independence under British suzerainty became guaranteed by treaty. With the creation of Pakistan in 1947 Bahawalpur, with an area of almost 17,500 square miles, became its premier Princely State. Bahawalpur State, named after its capital, stretched for almost three hundred miles along the left bank of the Sutlej, Panjnad and Indus rivers.

For earlier issues in the names of the Durrani rulers, see Afghanistan.

Bahawalpur / INDIAN PRINCELY STATES 874

RULERS
Amirs
Muhammad Bahawal Khan II
  AH1186-1224/1772-1809AD
Sadiq Muhammad Khan II
  AH1224-1241/1809-1825AD
Muhammad Bahawal Khan III
  AH1241-1269/1825-1852AD
Sadiq Muhammad Khan III
  AH1269-1270/1852-1853AD
Fateh Khan
  AH1270-1275/1853-1858AD
Muhammad Bahawal Khan IV
  AH1275-1283/1858-1866AD
Sir Sadiq Muhammad Khan IV
  AH1283-1317/1866-1899AD
Alhaj Muhammad Bahawal Khan V
  AH1317-1325/1899-1907AD
Sir Sadiq Muhammad Khan V
  AH1325-1365/1907-1947AD

MINTS

Ahmadpur — احمد پور

Dar al-Islam — دار الالسلام

Bahawalpur — بلھولبور

Khanpur — خانپور

AHMADPUR MINT
In the name of Mahmud Shah
AH1216-1218/1801-1803AD

RUPEE

SILVER, 10.70-11.60 g

C#	Date	Year	VG	Fine	VF	XF
18	AH1217	48	13.50	17.50	23.50	30.00
		49	13.50	17.50	23.50	30.00

Anonymous

Y#	Date	Year	VG	Fine	VF	XF
3.1	AH1246	—	8.00	15.00	25.00	37.50
	1253	—	8.00	15.00	25.00	37.50
	1254	—	8.00	15.00	25.00	37.50
	1256	—	8.00	15.00	25.00	37.50
	1257	—	8.00	15.00	25.00	37.50
	1258	—	8.00	15.00	25.00	37.50
	1259	—	8.00	15.00	25.00	37.50
	1261	—	8.00	15.00	25.00	37.50
	1262	—	8.00	15.00	25.00	37.50
	1264	—	8.00	15.00	25.00	37.50
	1265	—	8.00	15.00	25.00	37.50
	1268	—	8.00	15.00	25.00	37.50
	1275	—	8.00	15.00	25.00	37.50
	1276	—	8.00	15.00	25.00	37.50
	1277	—	8.00	15.00	25.00	37.50
	1278	—	8.00	15.00	25.00	37.50
	1279	—	8.00	15.00	25.00	37.50

Dated on obverse and reverse.

3.2	AH1258	—	8.00	15.00	25.00	37.50
	1259	—	8.00	15.00	25.00	37.50
	1259/60	—	8.00	15.00	25.00	37.50

Obv: Date in oval.

Y#	Date	Year	VG	Fine	VF	XF
3.3	AH1270	—	15.00	30.00	50.00	75.00

7.80 g

3.4	AH1278	—	8.00	15.00	25.00	37.50
	1280	—	8.00	15.00	25.00	37.50
	1281	—	8.00	15.00	25.00	37.50
	1282	—	8.00	15.00	25.00	37.50
	1283	—	8.00	15.00	25.00	37.50
	1284	—	8.00	15.00	25.00	37.50

BAHAWALPUR MINT
Anonymous

FALUS

COPPER
Square or round

Y#	Date	Year	Good	VG	Fine	VF
1	AH1225	—	3.00	5.00	7.00	10.00
	1237	13	3.00	5.00	7.00	10.00
	1248	—	3.00	5.00	7.00	10.00
	1249	—	3.00	5.00	7.00	10.00
	1254	—	3.00	5.00	7.00	10.00
	1259	—	3.00	5.00	7.00	10.00
	1261	—	3.00	5.00	7.00	10.00
	1269	—	3.00	5.00	7.00	10.00
	1270	—	3.00	5.00	7.00	10.00
	1276	—	3.00	5.00	7.00	10.00
	1277	—	3.00	5.00	7.00	10.00
	1281	—	3.00	5.00	7.00	10.00

PAISA

COPPER

2.1	AH1302	—	3.50	6.00	8.50	12.00
	1304	—	3.50	6.00	8.50	12.00
	1311	—	3.50	6.00	8.50	12.00
	1312	—	3.50	6.00	8.50	12.00
	1313	—	3.50	6.00	8.50	12.00
	1315	—	3.50	6.00	8.50	12.00
	1317	—	3.50	6.00	8.50	12.00
	1321	—	3.50	6.00	8.50	12.00
	1325	—	3.50	6.00	8.50	12.00

| 2.2 | ND | — | — | — | — | — |

RUPEE

SILVER, 11.00 g
Obv: Lily.

Y#	Date	Year	VG	Fine	VF	XF
4.1	AH1254	—	10.00	20.00	35.00	50.00
	1255	—	10.00	20.00	35.00	50.00
	1256	—	8.00	15.00	25.00	37.50
	1258	—	8.00	15.00	25.00	37.50
	1272	—	8.00	15.00	25.00	37.50
	1273	—	8.00	15.00	25.00	37.50
	1275	—	8.00	15.00	25.00	37.50
	1278	—	8.00	15.00	25.00	37.50
	1279	—	8.00	15.00	25.00	37.50

Obv: Date in rectangle, cinqfoil.

Y#	Date	Year	VG	Fine	VF	XF
4.2	AH1272	—	8.00	15.00	25.00	37.50
	1274	—	8.00	15.00	25.00	37.50

8.00-8.90 g
Obv: Flower divides date.

4a	AH1275	—	8.00	15.00	25.00	37.50
	1280	—	8.00	15.00	25.00	37.50
	1281	—	8.00	15.00	25.00	37.50

MUHAMMAD BAHAWAL KHAN V
AH1317-1325/1899-1907AD

PAISA

COPPER

Y#	Date	Year	Good	VG	Fine	VF
6	AH1324	—	3.50	6.00	9.00	12.50
	1325	—	3.50	6.00	9.00	12.50

NOTE: For anonymous Paisas struck during the years of his reign, see Y#2.

SADIQ MUHAMMAD KHAN V
AH1325-1365/1907-47AD

PAISA

COPPER, square

7.1	AH1326	—	3.50	6.00	9.00	12.50
(7)	1327	—	3.50	6.00	9.00	12.50

Rev: W/o date.

| 7.2 | ND | — | 4.00 | 7.50 | 12.50 | 20.00 |

Rev: W/o date or star.

| 7.3 | ND | — | 5.50 | 9.00 | 13.50 | 20.00 |
| (7.1) | | | | | | |

8	AH1342	—	7.50	11.00	15.00	20.00
	1343	—	7.50	11.00	15.00	20.00

Milled Coinage
1/2 PICE

COPPER

Y#	Date	Year	Fine	VF	XF	Unc
12	AH1359	1940	.35	.75	1.25	2.00

PAISA
(1/4 Anna)

COPPER

Y#	Date	Year	Fine	VF	XF	Unc
9	AH1343	—	11.50	17.50	25.00	40.00

13	AH1359	1940	.75	1.25	2.00	3.00

ANONYMOUS ISSUES
Khanpur Mint
FALUS

COPPER

C#	Date	Year	Good	VG	Fine	VF
7	ND	—	4.25	7.50	12.50	18.50

RUPEE

SILVER, 8.70 g
Dated on obverse and reverse.

Y#	Date	Year	VG	Fine	VF	XF
5.1	AH1255	—	20.00	30.00	42.50	60.00
	1258	—	20.00	30.00	42.50	60.00
	1259	—	20.00	30.00	42.50	60.00
	1261	—	20.00	30.00	42.50	60.00
	1263	—	20.00	30.00	42.50	60.00

5.2	AH1264	—	15.00	20.00	27.50	35.00
	1265	—	15.00	20.00	22.50	35.00
	1266	—	15.00	20.00	22.50	35.00
	1267	—	15.00	20.00	22.50	35.00
	1268/7	—	15.00	20.00	27.50	35.00
	1269	—	15.00	20.00	22.50	35.00
	1277	—	15.00	20.00	27.50	35.00
	1280	—	15.00	20.00	27.50	35.00
	1282	—	15.00	20.00	27.50	35.00

BANSWARA

The origins of this state in northwest India reached back into the early sixteenth century. The rulers, known as Maharawals, were Sissodia Rajputs of the Dungarpur family. Constantly harassed by the Marathas, the state concluded an alliance with the British in 1818 by which the British received a percentage of the state's revenues in return for protection against external enemies.

RULERS
Lakshaman Singh, 1862-1905AD
Shambu Singh, 1905-1920's AD

ANONYMOUS ISSUES
1/2 PAISA

COPPER

Y#	Date	Year	Good	VG	Fine	VF
1	ND	—	2.50	3.75	5.00	7.00

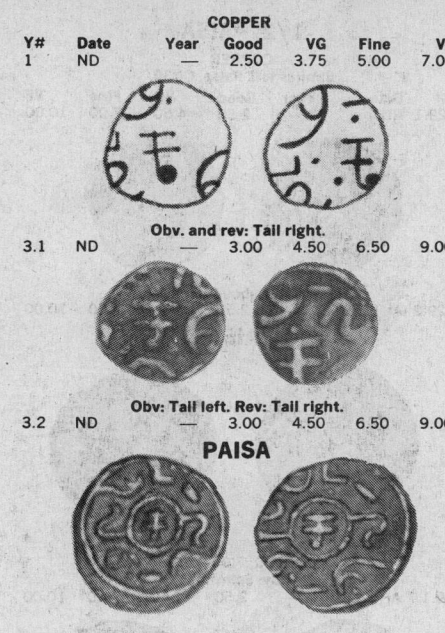

Obv. and rev: Tail right.

3.1	ND	—	3.00	4.50	6.50	9.00

Obv: Tail left. Rev: Tail right.

3.2	ND	—	3.00	4.50	6.50	9.00

PAISA

COPPER

2.1	ND	—	1.50	3.00	4.50	6.50

Obv. and rev: Dots within 2 circles.

| 2.2 | ND |

Thick and thin flans.
Obv. & rev: Tail of symbol turned right.

4.1	ND	—	1.50	3.00	4.00	5.50

Obv. & rev: Tail of symbol turned left.

4.2	ND	—	1.50	3.00	4.00	5.50

Obv: Tail left. Rev: Tail right.

4.3	ND	—	1.75	3.50	4.50	6.50

Mule: Obv. of Y#2. Rev. of Y#4.1.

4.4	ND	—	2.75	4.50	6.00	8.50

Larger symbols

5	ND	—	3.00	4.50	6.50	9.00

1/8 RUPEE

SILVER, 1.00 g

Y#	Date	Year	VG	Fine	VF	XF
6	ND	—	11.50	15.00	18.50	25.00

1/4 RUPEE

SILVER, 2.00 g

7	ND	—	11.50	15.00	18.50	25.00

1/2 RUPEE

SILVER, 4.00 g

Y#	Date	Year	VG	Fine	VF	XF
8	ND	—	12.50	16.50	20.00	26.50

RUPEE

SILVER, 8.10 g
Thick, dumpy flan, 18-20mm

9.1	ND	—	13.50	20.00	27.50	35.00

Thin, broad flan, 21-23mm

9.2	ND	—	15.00	18.50	25.00

NOTE: The authenticity of Y#6 and Y#9.2 has been questioned.

MOHUR

GOLD, 12.00 g
Similar to 1 Rupee, Y#9.1.

10.1	ND	—	225.00	250.00	285.00	325.00

Similar to 1 Rupee, Y#9.2.

10.2	ND	—	225.00	250.00	285.00	325.00

BARODA

Maratha state located in western India. The ruling line was descended from Damaji, a Maratha soldier, who received the title of "Distinguished Swordsman" in 1721AD (hence the scimitar on most Baroda coins). The Baroda title "Gaikwara" comes from "gaikwar" or cow herd, Damaji's father's occupation.

The Maratha rulers of Baroda, the Gaekwar family, rose to prominence in the mid-eighteenth century by carving out for themselves a dominion from territories which were previously under the control of the Poona Marathas, and to a lesser extent, of the Raja of Jodhpur. Chronic internal disputes regarding the succession to the masnad culminated in the intervention of British troops in support of one candidate, Anand Rao Gaekwar, in 1800. Then, in 1802, an agreement with the East India Company released the Baroda princes from their fear of domination by the Maratha Peshwa of Poona but subordinated them to Company interests. Nevertheless, for almost the next century and a half Baroda maintained a good relationship with the British and continued as a major Princely State right up to 1947, when it acceded to the Indian Union.

RULERS
Gaekwars

Anand Rao
  AH1215-1235/1800-1819AD
Sayaji Rao II
  AH1235-1264/1819-1847AD
Ganpat Rao
  AH1264-1273/1847-1856AD
Khande Rao
  AH1273-1287/1856-1870AD
Malhar Rao
  AH1287-1292/1870-1875AD
Sayaji Rao III
  AH1292-1357/Vs1932-1995/1875-1938AD
Pratap Singh
  VS1995-2008/1938-1951AD

MINTS
Ahmedabad
Amreli
Baroda
Petlad

MINT MARKS

Ahmedabad Mint

Ankus, Maratha mark.

Nagari letters denoting Baroda ruler:
Ga - Anand Rao's Shah Alam II coins, Ahmedabad Mint (with two verticle stems).

A - Anand Rao's Shah Alam II coins, Petlad Mint.

Ma - Anand Rao's Shah Alam II coins, Baroda Mint.

Baroda / INDIAN PRINCELY STATES 876

आ
A - Anand Rao's Muhammad Akbar II coins, Baroda Mint.

गा
Ga - Anand Rao's Muhammad Akbar II coins, Ahmedabad Mint (with three verticle stems).

सा
Sa - Sayaji Rao II, Baroda Mint.

सा गा or साञा
(Sri) Sa Ga - Sayaji Rao II, Amreli Mint.

ग गा
Ga Ga - Ganpat Rao, Amreli Mint.

गा
Ga - Ganpat Rao, Baroda Mint.

श्री ग गा
Sri Ga Ga - Ganpat Rao, Amreli Mint.

रवा
Kha - Khande Rao, Muhammad Akbar II coins, Baroda Mint.

रव·गा
Kha Ga - Khande Rao, coins in own name, Baroda Mint.

श्री रव गा
Sri Kha Ga - Khande Rao, Amreli Mint.

मा गा
Ma Ga - Malhar Rao.

सा गा
Sa Ga - Sayaji Rao III, Amreli Mint

सा गा
Sa Ga - Sayaji Rao III, Baroda Mint.

NOTE: The first two marks are found only on the coins of Ahmedabad Mint, and serve to identify it. The remaining 14 marks are used to indicate the ruler under whom the coin was struck; when no mint name is given after the ruler's name in the above list, that shows that the symbol was used at all his mints. Note the various forms of '*G*' and '*Ga*' used above.

AHMEDABAD MINT
A Maratha mint from 1757-1800AD, Ahmedabad was leased to Baroda 1800-1804 and 1806-1817, when it was ceded to Baroda. However, in 1818 it was annexed by the British East India Company.

In the name of Muhammad Akbar II
AH1221-1253/1806-1837AD
Nagari *Ga* and ankus

RUPEE

SILVER, 10.70-11.60 g

C#	Date	Year	VG	Fine	VF	XF
28	AH1225	—	8.50	13.50	18.50	25.00
	—	6	8.50	13.50	18.50	25.00
	AH1229	7	8.50	13.50	18.50	25.00
	1229	8	8.50	13.50	18.50	25.00
	1231	9	8.50	13.50	18.50	25.00
	1232	10	8.50	13.50	18.50	25.00
	1233	11	8.50	13.50	18.50	25.00

NOTE: The Ahmedabad Mint was acquired by the British in 1818AD (AH1233). Refer to British India, Bombay Presidency, C#42 to 45.

AMRELI MINT
SAYAJI RAO II
AH1235-1264/1819-1847AD
Nagari *Sa Ga*

1/2 PAISA
COPPER
Similar to 1 Paisa, C#30.

C#	Date	Year	Good	VG	Fine	VF
A29.1	ND	—	2.50	4.50	7.00	10.00

Obv: Katar above scimatar.

| A29.2 | AH125x | — | 2.50 | 4.50 | 7.00 | 10.00 |

PAISA

COPPER, 7.00-8.00 g
Obv: Scimitar.

| 29.1 | AH1253 | — | 2.50 | 4.50 | 7.00 | 10.00 |

Obv: Elephant left w/flag right.

| 29.2 | AH1256 | — | 3.00 | 5.50 | 8.50 | 11.50 |

Obv: Elephant and flag left.

| 29.3 | AH1256 | — | 2.50 | 4.50 | 7.00 | 10.00 |

Obv: Katar above scimitar.

29.4	AH1245	—	2.50	4.50	7.00	10.00
	1256	—	2.50	4.50	7.00	10.00
	1257	—	2.50	4.50	7.00	10.00

Obv: Elephant w/flag right. Rev: Similar to 29.4.

| 29.5 | ND | — | 5.00 | 6.50 | 10.00 | 15.00 |

Obv: Scimitar.

| 29.6 | AH1257 | — | 2.50 | 4.50 | 7.00 | 10.00 |

Obv: Crescent.

| 29.7 | AH1262 | — | 3.00 | 5.50 | 8.50 | 11.50 |

Obv: Crescent. Rev: Trident.

C#	Date	Year	Good	VG	Fine	VF
29.8	AH—	—	3.00	5.50	8.50	11.50

Obv: Large *Sa*.

| 30.1 | ND | — | 1.50 | 2.50 | 4.00 | 5.50 |

| 30.2 | ND | — | 1.50 | 2.50 | 4.00 | 5.50 |

GANPAT RAO
AH1264-1273/1847-1856AD
Nagari *Ga Ga*

1/2 PAISA
COPPER, 14mm

| A39 | AH1266 | — | 2.50 | 4.50 | 6.00 | 8.50 |

PAISA

COPPER
Obv: Lotus at left, scimitar at right.

39.1	ND	—	3.00	5.50	7.00	9.00
	AH1266	3	3.00	5.50	7.00	9.00
	1272	—	3.00	5.50	7.00	9.00

Obv: Scimitar at left, lotus at right.

| 39.2 | AH1266 | — | 3.00 | 5.50 | 7.00 | 9.00 |

KHANDE RAO
AH1273-1287/1856-1870AD
Nagari *Sri Kha Ga*

PAISA

COPPER, 7.00 g
Thin flan

Y#	Date	Year	Good	VG	Fine	VF
1.1	AH1277	—	2.00	3.50	5.50	8.00

Obv: Scimitar at upper left.

| 1.2 | AH— | 13 | 2.00 | 3.50 | 5.50 | 8.00 |

Thick flan, cruder types.

Y#	Date	Year	Good	VG	Fine	VF
1a	ND	—	2.00	3.50	5.50	8.00

1b	ND	—	2.00	3.50	5.50	8.00

SAYAJI RAO III
AH1292-1357/1875-1939AD
Nagari *Sa Ja*

1/4 PAISA

COPPER

A2	AH1312(retrograde)	5.00	8.00	12.00	18.00

1/2 PAISA
COPPER, 16mm

2	AH1312	—	1.75	3.25	4.50	6.00

PAISA

COPPER

3	AH1312(retrograde)	3.00	5.00	7.50	10.00
	1313(retrograde)	3.00	5.00	7.50	10.00

Rev: English S with serifs to left of *Sa Ga* and sword in S of *Julus*.

3a	ND	—	6.00	10.00	14.00	18.50

NOTE: These coins may have been issued by Sayaji Rao II w/blundered dates.

BARODA MINT
Mughal Issues
ANAND RAO
AH1215-1235/1800-1819AD
In the name of Muhammad Akbar II
AH1221-1253/1806-1837AD
Nagari *A* and scimitar

1/2 PAISA

COPPER, 14mm

C#	Date	Year	Good	VG	Fine	VF
20	AH1232	11	2.00	3.00	4.00	5.00
	—	14	2.00	3.00	4.00	5.00

PAISA

COPPER, 9.80 g

21	AH1226	6	1.25	2.50	3.50	5.00
	1227	7	1.25	2.50	3.50	5.00
	—	8	1.25	2.50	3.50	5.00
	—	9	1.25	2.50	3.50	5.00
	1231	11	1.25	2.50	3.50	5.00
	1234	14	1.25	2.50	3.50	5.00
	1236	16	1.25	2.50	3.50	5.00

1/8 RUPEE

SILVER, 1.34-1.45 g

C#	Date	Year	VG	Fine	VF	XF
24	AH122x	—	3.50	4.50	6.00	8.00
	1234	—	4.00	6.00	8.00	11.00

1/4 RUPEE

SILVER, 2.68-2.90 g

25	AH1228	—	4.00	6.00	8.50	12.00

1/2 RUPEE

SILVER, 5.35-5.80 g

26	AH1222	2	7.00	9.00	11.50	15.00
	1226	6	7.00	9.00	11.50	15.00
	1228	8	7.00	9.00	11.50	15.00
	1234	14	7.00	9.00	11.50	15.00

RUPEE

SILVER, 10.70-11.60 g

27	AH1222	2	8.50	13.50	18.50	25.00
	1224	4	8.50	13.50	18.50	25.00
	1225	5	8.50	13.50	18.50	25.00
	1226	6	8.50	13.50	18.50	25.00
	1227	7	8.50	13.50	18.50	25.00
	1228	8	8.50	13.50	18.50	25.00
	1229	9	8.50	13.50	18.50	25.00
	1232	12	8.50	13.50	18.50	25.00
	1233	13	8.50	13.50	18.50	25.00
	1234	14	8.50	13.50	18.50	25.00

SAYAJI RAO II
AH1235-1264/1819-1847AD
In the name of Muhammad Akbar II
AH1221-1253/1806-1837AD
Nagari *Sa* or *Sa Ga* and other symbols.

1/2 PAISA

COPPER, 14-15mm, 4.30 g
Rev: W/o symbols.

C#	Date	Year	Good	VG	Fine	VF
31.1	AH123x	—	1.25	2.50	4.00	6.00

Rev: Cross.

31.2	ND	—	1.25	2.50	4.00	6.00

Rev: Sun.

31.4	ND	—	1.25	2.50	4.00	6.00

Rev: Shaded ball.

31.8	AH1260	40	1.25	2.50	4.00	6.00

PAISA

COPPER, 18-24mm, 10.20 g
Rev: W/o symbol.

33.1	AH1236	16	1.25	2.00	3.00	4.50

Rev: Outlined cross.

C#	Date	Year	Good	VG	Fine	VF
33.2	AH1240	20	1.25	2.25	3.50	5.00

Rev: Lotus.

33.3	AH1243	23	1.25	2.25	3.50	5.00
	1244	—	1.25	2.25	3.50	5.00

Rev: Rayed sun.

33.4	AH1247	27	1.25	2.25	3.50	5.00

Rev: Flag.

33.5	AH12xx	28	1.25	2.25	3.50	5.00
	1249	29	1.25	2.25	3.50	5.00
	—	30	1.25	2.25	3.50	5.00
	1250	—	1.25	2.25	3.50	5.00
	1253	—	1.25	2.25	3.50	5.00

Rev: Upright cross.

33.6	AH1255	35	1.25	2.25	3.50	5.00

Rev: Tulip.

33.9	AH1255	36	1.25	2.25	3.50	5.00

Rev: Five-petal flower.

33.7	AH—	35	1.25	2.25	3.50	5.00
	1255	36	1.25	2.25	3.50	5.00
	1256	36	1.25	2.25	3.50	5.00
	1263	—	1.25	2.25	3.50	5.00

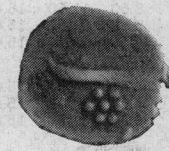 

Rev: Shaded ball.

33.8	AH1260	40	1.00	2.00	3.00	4.00
	1261	41	1.00	2.00	3.00	4.00
	1262	—	1.00	2.00	3.00	4.00
	1263	43	1.00	2.00	3.00	4.00
	—	44	1.00	2.00	3.00	4.00

Rev: Hoof.

33.10	AH1260	—	2.50	4.00	7.50	12.00

Rev: Flag and branch.

33.11	ND	—	2.00	3.50	6.00	10.00

Baroda / INDIAN PRINCELY STATES

Baroda / INDIAN PRINCELY STATES — 878

Rev: Flower

C#	Date	Year	Good	VG	Fine	VF
33.12	AH12xx	—	2.00	3.50	6.00	10.00

1/8 RUPEE
SILVER, 11-14mm, 1.34-1.45 g
Rev: Scimitar to left of *Julus.*

C#	Date	Year	VG	Fine	VF	XF
35.1	AH—	17	3.00	4.50	6.50	10.00

Rev: Scimitar above *Julus.*

| 35.2 | — | 26 | 3.00 | 4.50 | 6.50 | 10.00 |

Rev: Scimitar to right of *Julus.*

| 35.3 | AH12xx | — | 3.00 | 4.50 | 6.50 | 10.00 |

1/4 RUPEE

SILVER, 2.68-2.90 g
Rev: Scimitar to left of *Julus.*

| 36.1 | AH1238 | 18 | 5.00 | 7.00 | 10.00 | 13.50 |

Rev: Scimitar above *Julus.*

| 36.2 | AH— | 24 | 5.00 | 7.00 | 10.00 | 13.50 |

Rev: Scimitar to right of *Julus.*

36.3	AH1249	29	5.00	7.00	10.00	13.50
	1250	29	5.00	7.00	10.00	13.50
	1257	37	5.00	7.00	10.00	13.50

1/2 RUPEE

SILVER, 5.35-5.80 g

37.1	AH1238	18	7.00	8.50	11.50	15.00
	1239	19	7.00	8.50	11.50	15.00
	—	20	7.00	8.50	11.50	15.00
	1241	21	7.00	8.50	11.50	15.00
	—	27	7.00	8.50	11.50	15.00

Rev: Scimitar above *Julus.*

37.2	AH124x	24	7.00	8.50	11.50	15.00
	—	26	7.00	8.50	11.50	15.00
	—	27	7.00	8.50	11.50	15.00

Rev: Scimitar to right of *Julus.*

37.3	AH1254	33	7.00	8.50	11.50	15.00
	—	35	7.00	8.50	11.50	15.00
	—	37	7.00	8.50	11.50	15.00
	—	38	7.00	8.50	11.50	15.00
	125x	39	7.00	8.50	11.50	15.00
	1260	40	7.00	8.50	11.50	15.00
	—	42	7.00	8.50	11.50	15.00

RUPEE

SILVER, 10.70-11.60 g
Rev: Scimitar to left of *Julus.*

38.1	AH1237	17	7.50	11.50	18.50	25.00
	1238	18	7.50	11.50	18.50	25.00
	1239	19	7.50	11.50	18.50	25.00
	1240	19	7.50	11.50	18.50	25.00
	1240	20	7.50	11.50	18.50	25.00
	1241	21	7.50	11.50	18.50	25.00
	1242	22	7.50	11.50	18.50	25.00

Rev: Scimitar above *Julus.*

38.2	AH1244	24	7.50	11.50	18.50	25.00
	124x	25	7.50	11.50	18.50	25.00
	1248	27	7.50	11.50	18.50	25.00

Rev: Scimitar to right of *Julus.*

38.3	AH1247	—	7.50	11.50	18.50	25.00
	1249	29	7.50	11.50	18.50	25.00
	1250	30	7.50	11.50	18.50	25.00
	1253	33	7.50	11.50	18.50	25.00
	1255	35	7.50	11.50	18.50	25.00
	1256	36	7.50	11.50	18.50	25.00
	1258	38	7.50	11.50	18.50	25.00
	1259	39	7.50	11.50	18.50	25.00
	1260	40	7.50	11.50	18.50	25.00

GANPAT RAO
AH1264-1273/1847-1856AD
In the name of Muhammad Akbar II
AH1221-1253/1806-1837AD
Nagari *Ga* and scimitar.

1/2 PAISA
COPPER, 15mm, 5.00 g
Obv: Shaded ball in center.

C#	Date	Year	Good	VG	Fine	VF
41	AH1264-1272	—	1.00	2.00	3.00	4.50

PAISA

COPPER, 10.00 g

42	AH1263	43	2.00	3.00	4.00	5.50
	1264	44	2.00	3.00	4.00	5.50
	1265	45	2.00	3.00	4.00	5.50
	1266	46	2.00	3.00	4.00	5.50
	1272	52	2.00	3.00	4.00	5.50

Obv: Shaded ball in center.

| 43 | AH1264 | 4x | 2.00 | 3.00 | 4.00 | 5.50 |
| | 1266 | 4x | 2.00 | 3.00 | 4.00 | 5.50 |

1/8 RUPEE

SILVER, 11mm, 1.34-1.45 g

C#	Date	Year	VG	Fine	VF	XF
44	AH126x	—	2.50	4.00	6.00	9.00
	1269	—	2.50	4.00	6.00	9.00

1/4 RUPEE

SILVER, 2.68-2.90 g

| 45 | AH126x | — | 5.00 | 7.00 | 9.00 | 12.00 |
| | 1272 | 52 | 7.00 | 10.00 | 15.00 | 22.50 |

1/2 RUPEE

SILVER, 5.35-5.80 g

C#	Date	Year	VG	Fine	VF	XF
46	AH126x	43	6.00	8.00	11.50	15.00
	—	45	6.00	8.00	11.50	15.00
	1267	46	6.00	8.00	11.50	15.00
	1268	47	6.00	8.00	11.50	15.00
	—	49	6.00	8.00	11.50	15.00
	1271	—	6.00	8.00	11.50	15.00
	—	51	6.00	8.00	11.50	15.00
	1272	52	6.00	8.00	11.50	15.00

RUPEE

SILVER, 10.70-11.60 g

47	AH1264	43	7.50	13.50	18.50	25.00
	1265	43	7.50	13.50	18.50	25.00
	1265	44	7.50	13.50	18.50	25.00
	—	45	7.50	13.50	18.50	25.00
	126x	46	7.50	13.50	18.50	25.00
	1268	47	7.50	13.50	18.50	25.00
	1271	50	7.50	13.50	18.50	25.00
	1272	51	7.50	13.50	18.50	25.00
	1272	52	7.50	13.50	18.50	25.00

KHANDE RAO
AH1273-1287/1856-1870AD
In the name of Muhammad Akbar II
AH1221-1253/1806-1837AD
Nagari *Kha* and scimitar.

1/2 PAISA
COPPER, 15mm, 4.20 g
Rev: Pomegranate.

Y#	Date	Year	Good	VG	Fine	VF
1	ND	—	1.25	2.00	3.00	4.00

PAISA

COPPER, 8.40 g
Rev: Pomegranate.

| 2 | AH1273 | 52 | 1.50 | 2.50 | 3.50 | 5.00 |

1/4 RUPEE

SILVER, 2.68-2.90 g

Y#	Date	Year	VG	Fine	VF	XF
3	AH1273	—	5.00	7.00	9.00	12.00
	1278	—	5.00	7.00	9.00	12.00

1/2 RUPEE

SILVER, 5.35-5.80 g

4	AH1267	—	6.50	8.00	10.00	13.50
	1275	—	6.50	8.00	10.00	13.50
	—	52	6.50	8.00	10.00	13.50

RUPEE

SILVER, 10.70-11.60 g

5	AH1274	53	8.50	13.50	18.50	25.00
	1275	—	8.50	13.50	18.50	25.00
	128x	—	8.50	13.50	18.50	25.00

In the name of the Commander of the

Baroda / INDIAN PRINCELY STATES 879

Sovereign Band (a title of the Gaekwar, ruler of Baroda).
From AH1274 (1857AD)
Nagari *Kha Ga* and scimitar.

1/2 PAISA

COPPER, 3.40 g
Rev: Scimitar.

Y#	Date	Year	Good	VG	Fine	VF
6	AH1275	—	2.00	3.00	4.00	5.50
	1276	—	2.00	3.00	4.00	5.50
	1277	—	3.00	5.00	7.50	12.00

Rev: Scimitar and hoof.

| 6a | AH128x | — | 5.00 | 7.50 | 10.00 | 15.00 |

PAISA

COPPER, 7.00-8.00 g
Rev: Scimitar.

7	AH1274	—	2.00	3.00	4.00	5.50
	1275	—	1.25	2.25	3.25	4.00
	1276	—	1.25	2.25	3.25	4.00
	1277	—	2.00	3.00	4.00	5.50

Rev: Scimitar and hoof.

7a	AH1281	—	3.50	4.50	6.00	8.00
	1282	—	3.50	4.50	6.00	8.00
	1283	—	3.50	4.50	6.00	8.00
	1284	—	3.50	4.50	6.00	8.00
	1285	—	3.50	4.50	6.00	8.00

2 PAISA

COPPER, 15.00 g
Rev: Scimitar and hoof.

8	AH1281	—	2.50	4.00	5.50	7.50
	1284	—	2.50	4.00	5.50	7.50
	1285	—	2.50	4.00	5.50	7.50

1/8 RUPEE

SILVER, 1.34-1.45 g

Y#	Date	Year	VG	Fine	VF	XF
9	AH1282	—	3.50	5.50	7.50	10.00

1/4 RUPEE

SILVER, 2.68-2.90 g

10	AH1274	—	4.50	6.50	9.00	12.00
	1286	—	4.50	6.50	9.00	12.00

1/2 RUPEE

SILVER, 5.35-5.80 g

Y#	Date	Year	VG	Fine	VF	XF
11	AH1276	—	6.50	8.00	10.00	12.50
	1278	—	6.50	8.00	10.00	12.50
	1280	—	6.50	8.00	10.00	12.50
	1282	—	6.50	8.00	10.00	12.50
	1285	—	6.50	8.00	10.00	12.50
	1286	—	6.50	8.00	10.00	12.50

RUPEE

SILVER, 10.70-11.60 g

12	AH1274	—	7.50	12.50	16.50	22.50
	1275	—	7.50	12.50	16.50	22.50
	1276	—	7.50	12.50	16.50	22.50
	1277	—	7.50	12.50	16.50	22.50
	1278	—	7.50	12.50	16.50	22.50
	1280	—	7.50	12.50	16.50	22.50
	1281	—	7.50	12.50	16.50	22.50
	1282	—	7.50	12.50	16.50	22.50
	1283	—	7.50	12.50	16.50	22.50
	1284	—	7.50	12.50	16.50	22.50
	1285	—	7.50	12.50	16.50	22.50
	1286	—	7.50	12.50	16.50	22.50
	1287	—	7.50	12.50	16.50	22.50
	(12)87	—	7.50	12.50	16.50	22.50

NAZARANA 2 RUPEES

SILVER, 18.10 g

| A13 | AH1275 | — | — | — | Rare | — |

Milled Coinage
NAZARANA 1/2 RUPEE

SILVER, 5.65 g

| 13 | AH1287 | — | 60.00 | 90.00 | 120.00 | 160.00 |

NAZARANA RUPEE

SILVER, 11.30 g
Obv. Persian leg: *Kahnde Rao*.

| 14.1 | AH1287 | — | 35.00 | 65.00 | 90.00 | 125.00 |

Obv. Persian leg: *Khande Rao*.

| 14.2 | AH1287 | — | 50.00 | 85.00 | 125.00 | 200.00 |

Dump Coinage
MALHAR RAO
AH1287-1292/1870-1875AD

Nagari *Ma Ga* and scimitar.

1/2 PAISA

COPPER, 4.00 g

Y#	Date	Year	Good	VG	Fine	VF
15	AH1288	—	2.00	3.00	4.00	5.50
	1290	—	2.00	3.00	4.00	5.50

PAISA

COPPER, 7.60-8.60 g

16	AH1288	—	1.25	2.50	3.50	5.00
	1289	—	1.25	2.50	3.50	5.00
	1290	—	1.25	2.50	3.50	5.00
	ND	—	1.25	2.50	3.50	5.00

2 PAISA

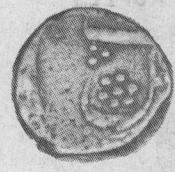 

COPPER, 16.10 g

17	AH1288	—	2.00	3.00	4.00	5.50
	1289	—	2.00	3.00	4.00	5.50

NAZARANA 2 PAISA

COPPER

| A17 | AH1289 | — | — | — | Rare | — |

1/8 RUPEE

SILVER, 11mm, 1.34-1.45 g

Y#	Date	Year	VG	Fine	VF	XF
18	AH129x	—	3.50	5.50	7.50	10.00

1/4 RUPEE

SILVER, 13mm, 2.68-2.90 g

| 19 | AH1290 | — | 4.00 | 6.00 | 8.50 | 11.50 |

1/2 RUPEE

SILVER, 5.35-5.80 g

20	AH1287	—	6.50	8.00	10.00	12.50
	1288	—	6.50	8.00	10.00	12.50
	1289	—	6.50	8.00	10.00	12.50
	1290	—	6.50	8.00	10.00	12.50

RUPEE

SILVER, 10.70-11.60 g

Y#	Date	Year	VG	Fine	VF	XF
21	AH1287	—	11.50	13.50	16.50	20.00
	1288	—	11.50	13.50	16.50	20.00
	1290	—	11.50	13.50	16.50	20.00
	—	122	11.50	13.50	16.50	20.00

NAZARANA RUPEE

SILVER, 10.70-11.60 g

Y#	Date	Year	VG	Fine	VF	XF
21a	AH1288	—	60.00	90.00	120.00	160.00

NAZARANA 2 RUPEES

SILVER, 21.40-23.20 g

Y#	Date	Year	VG	Fine	VF	XF
22	AH1288	—	—	—	Rare	—

SAYAJI RAO III
AH1292-1357/VS1932-1995/1875-1938AD
Nagari *Sa Ga* and scimitar.

1/4 PAISA
COPPER

Y#	Date	Year	Good	VG	Fine	VF
A23	VS194x	—	2.50	5.00	8.50	12.50

1/2 PAISA

COPPER

23	VS1937	(1880)	1.50	2.50	4.00	5.50
	1948	(1891)	1.50	2.50	4.00	5.50

PAISA

COPPER

24	VS1937	(1880)	1.50	2.50	4.00	5.50
	1947	(1890)	1.50	2.50	4.00	5.50
	1948	(1891)	1.50	2.50	4.00	5.50

Machine-punched planchets.

24a	VS1949	(1892)	2.00	3.50	5.00	7.00

2 PAISA

COPPER

Y#	Date	Year	Good	VG	Fine	VF
25	VS1937	(1880)	3.50	5.00	6.50	8.50
	1947	(1890)	3.50	5.00	6.50	8.50
	1948	(1891)	3.50	5.00	6.50	8.50

17.00 g
Machine-punched planchets.

25a	VS1949	(1892)	3.75	5.50	7.50	10.00

1/8 RUPEE

SILVER, 1.34-1.45 g

Y#	Date	Year	VG	Fine	VF	XF
26	AH1294	—	3.50	5.00	6.50	8.00
	1295	—	3.50	5.00	6.50	8.00
	1297	—	3.50	5.00	6.50	8.00
	1299	—	3.50	5.00	6.50	8.00

1/4 RUPEE

SILVER, 13mm, 2.68-2.90 g

27	AH1292	—	4.00	6.00	8.00	11.00
	1299	—	4.00	6.00	8.00	11.00

1/2 RUPEE

SILVER, 5.35-5.80 g

28	AH1292	—	6.50	8.00	10.00	13.00
	1293	—	6.50	8.00	10.00	13.00
	1294	—	6.50	8.00	10.00	13.00
	1295	—	6.50	8.00	10.00	13.00
	1297	—	6.50	8.00	10.00	13.00
	1298	—	6.50	8.00	10.00	13.00
	1299	—	6.50	8.00	10.00	13.00
	1300	—	6.50	8.00	10.00	13.00
	1301	—	6.50	8.00	10.00	13.00
	1302	—	6.50	8.00	10.00	13.00

RUPEE

SILVER, 10.70-11.60 g

29	AH1292	—	11.50	13.50	16.50	20.00
	1293	—	11.50	13.50	16.50	20.00
	1294	—	11.50	13.50	16.50	20.00
	1295	—	11.50	13.50	16.50	20.00
	1298	—	11.50	13.50	16.50	20.00
	1299	—	11.50	13.50	16.50	20.00
	1300	—	11.50	13.50	16.50	20.00
	1301	—	11.50	13.50	16.50	20.00
	1302	—	11.50	13.50	16.50	20.00

Milled Coinage
PAI

COPPER
Obv: Annulets between letters.

Y#	Date	Year	VG	Fine	VF	XF
30.1	VS1944	(1887)	.50	1.00	1.50	2.00

Obv: Pellets between letters.

30.1a	VS1944	(1887)	2.50	5.00	8.00	12.00

Obv: W/o annulets.
Thick planchet

30.2	VS1944	(1887)	.75	1.50	2.00	2.50
	1945	(1888)	.35	.75	1.00	1.50
	1946	(1889)	.75	1.50	2.00	2.50
	1947	(1890)	.75	1.50	2.00	2.50

Thin planchet. Obv: Large legends.

30.2a	VS1948	(1891)	.75	1.50	2.00	2.50
	1949	(1892)	.35	.75	1.00	1.50
	1950/49					
		(1893)	.75	1.25	1.75	2.25

Obv: Small legends.

30.3	VS1950	(1893)	.35	.75	1.00	1.50

PAISA

COPPER
Obv: Inner leg. curved, long hoof.

31.1	VS1940	(1883)	1.00	2.00	2.50	3.00
	1941	(1884)	1.00	2.00	2.50	3.00
	1942	(1885)	1.75	2.50	3.75	5.00

Obv: Inner leg. straight, short hoof.
Thick planchet

31.2	VS1941	(1884)	.75	1.50	2.00	2.75
	1942	(1885)	.35	.75	1.25	1.75
	1943	(1886)	.35	.75	1.25	1.75
	1944	(1887)	.35	.75	1.25	1.75
	1945	(1888)	.50	1.00	1.50	2.00
	1946/3	—	—	—	—	
	1946	(1889)	.50	1.00	1.50	2.00

Obv. & rev: Smaller inner circle.
Thin planchet

31.2a	VS1947	(1890)	.35	.75	1.25	1.75
	1948	(1891)	.30	.60	1.00	1.50
	1949	(1892)	.30	.60	1.00	1.50
	1950	(1893)	.30	.60	1.00	1.50

2 PAISA

COPPER
Obv: Inner leg. curved.
Rev: Large inner leg. and date.

Y#	Date	Year	VG	Fine	VF	XF
32.1	VS1940	(1883)	2.00	3.50	5.00	6.50
	1941	(1884)	2.00	3.50	5.00	6.50

Obv: Inner leg. straight.
Rev: Small inner leg. and date.
Thick planchet

32.2	VS1941	(1884)	1.00	2.00	3.00	4.50
	1942	(1885)	1.00	2.00	3.00	4.50
	1943	(1886)	.75	1.50	2.25	3.00
	1944/3	(1887)	.75	1.50	2.25	3.00
	1944	(1887)	.75	1.50	2.25	3.00
	1945/2	—	—	—	—	—
	1945	(1888)	.75	1.50	2.25	3.00
	1946	(1889)	1.25	2.50	4.00	6.00
	1947	(1890)	.75	1.50	2.25	3.00
	1948	(1891)	2.50	4.00	6.00	8.50
	1949	(1892)	2.50	4.00	6.00	8.50

Thin planchet

32.2a	VS1948	(1891)	.50	1.00	1.50	2.25
	1949/4 (1892)		.50	1.00	1.50	2.25
	1949/8 (1892)		.75	1.50	2.25	3.00
	1949	(1892)	.75	1.50	2.25	3.00
	1950	(1893)	.65	1.25	1.75	2.50

2 ANNAS

SILVER

Y#	Date	Year	Fine	VF	XF	Unc
33	VS1949	(1892)	5.50	8.50	13.50	20.00

33a	VS1951	(1894)	5.00	8.00	12.50	18.50
	1952	(1895)	5.00	8.00	12.50	18.50

4 ANNAS

SILVER

34	VS1949	(1892)	5.50	8.50	13.50	20.00

34a	VS1951	(1894)	5.00	7.50	11.50	17.50
	1952	(1895)	5.00	7.50	11.50	17.50

1/2 RUPEE

SILVER

Y#	Date	Year	Fine	VF	XF	Unc
35	VS1948	(1891)	30.00	40.00	55.00	75.00
	1949	(1892)	30.00	40.00	55.00	75.00

35a	VS1951	(1894)	12.50	15.00	20.00	30.00
	1952	(1895)	12.50	15.00	20.00	30.00

RUPEE

SILVER

36	VS1948	(1891)	12.50	15.00	18.50	27.50
	1949	(1892)	12.50	15.00	18.50	27.50

36a	VS1951	(1894)	11.50	13.50	16.50	23.50
	1952	(1895)	11.50	13.50	16.50	23.50
	1953	(1896)	11.50	13.50	16.50	23.50
	1954	(1897)	11.50	13.50	16.50	23.50
	1955	(1898)	11.50	13.50	16.50	23.50
	1956	(1899)	11.50	13.50	16.50	23.50

1/6 MOHUR

GOLD, 1.04-1.06 g

A37	VS1943	(1886)	165.00	225.00	275.00	350.00
37	1951	(1894)	165.00	225.00	275.00	350.00
	1953	(1896)	165.00	225.00	275.00	350.00
	1959	(1902)	165.00	225.00	275.00	350.00

1/3 MOHUR

GOLD, 16mm, 2.07-2.13 g

A38	VS1942	(1885)	185.00	250.00	325.00	400.00
38	1959	(1902)	185.00	250.00	325.00	400.00

MOHUR

GOLD, 6.20-6.40 g

A39	VS1942	(1885)	250.00	325.00	425.00	500.00

Y#	Date	Year	Fine	VF	XF	Unc
39	VS1945	(1888)	250.00	325.00	425.00	500.00
	1952	(1895)	250.00	325.00	425.00	500.00
	1953	(1896)	250.00	325.00	425.00	500.00
	1959	(1902)	250.00	325.00	425.00	500.00

PRATAP SINGH
VS1995-2008/1938-1951AD

1/3 MOHUR

GOLD, 2.07-2.13 g

40	VS1995	(1939)	—	225.00	300.00	400.00

SILVER (OMS)

40a	VS1995	(1939)				
	(restrike)		—	—	28.50	40.00

MOHUR

GOLD, 21mm, 6.20-6.40 g

41	VS1995	(1939)	—	250.00	350.00	500.00

SILVER (OMS)

41a	VS1995	(1939)				
	(restrike)		—	—	42.50	60.00

BELA

Las Bela, Beylah
State located in Baluchistan.
Of very ancient origins, the later history of Las Bela was intimately associated with that of Kalat to which State it became subject in 1758. Thereafter, however, the Arab chieftains of Las Bela, known as Jams, proved capable of demonstrating a very considerable degree of independence. The State continued up to 1947, at which time it acceded to Pakistan.

RULERS
Mir Khan Jam
  AH1256-1294/1840-1877AD
Mahmud Khan (of Kalat)
  AH- /-AD

MIR KHAN JAM
AH1256-1294/1840-1877AD

FALUS

COPPER

C#	Date	Year	Good	VG	Fine	VF
5	AH1271	—	3.50	5.50	8.50	12.50
	1276	—	3.50	5.50	8.50	12.50
	1285	—	3.50	5.50	8.50	12.50
	1286	—	3.50	5.50	8.50	12.50

MAHMUD KHAN

FALUS

COPPER

10	ND	—	3.50	5.50	8.50	12.50

BHARATPUR

State located in Rajputana in northwest India.
Bharatpur was founded by Balchand, a Jat chieftain who took advantage of Mughal confusion and weakness after the death of Aurangzeb to seize the area. In 1756 the ruler at that time, Suraj Mal, received the title of Raja. Bharatpur became increasingly associated with Maratha ambitions and, in spite of treaty ties to the East India Company, assisted the Maratha Confederacy in their struggles against the British. This gained them few friends in British circles, but the early attempts by the British to force the submission of Bharatpur fortress proved abortive. In 1826 however, the British took the opportunity offered by a bitter internal feud concerning the succession finally to reduce the stronghold. The rival claimant was exiled to Allahabad and Balwant Singh, then a child of seven, was placed on the throne under the supervision of a British Political Agent. From that time onwards Bharatpur came under British control until it acceded to the Indian Union at Independence.

RULERS
Ranjit Singh

Bharatpur / INDIAN PRINCELY STATES 882

AH1191-1220/1777-1805AD
Randhir Singh
AH1220-1239/1805-1823AD
Baldeo Singh
AH1239-1241/1823-1825AD
Durjan Singh
AH1241-1242/1825-1826AD
Balwant Singh
AH1242-1269/1826-1852AD
Jaswant Singh
AH1269-1311/1852-1893AD

MINTS
Bharatpur

Braj Indrapur

Mahe Indrapur

BHARATPUR MINT
Mintname: Bharatpur or Braj Indrapur

Mint marks:

In the name of Shah Alam II
AH1173-1221/1759-1806AD

RUPEE

SILVER, 10.70-11.60 g
Mintname: Braj Indrapur

KM#	Date	Year	VG	Fine	VF	XF
26	AH1216	44	11.50	13.50	16.50	20.00
	1217	45	11.50	13.50	16.50	20.00
	1218	46	11.50	13.50	16.50	20.00
	1219	47	11.50	13.50	16.50	20.00

In the name of Muhammad Akbar II
AH1221-1253/1806-1837AD

PAISA

COPPER

KM#	Date	Year	Good	VG	Fine	VF
101	AH1276	42	2.50	4.00	6.50	10.00
	1279	49	2.50	4.00	6.50	10.00

NOTE: This date is posthumous.

1/4 RUPEE
SILVER, 15mm, 2.68-2.90 g

KM#	Date	Year	VG	Fine	VF	XF
104	AH—	—	6.00	8.00	11.00	15.00

1/2 RUPEE

SILVER, 5.35-5.80 g

105	AH—	22	6.50	8.50	11.50	16.50
	12xx	34	6.50	8.50	11.50	16.50
	—	35	6.50	8.50	11.50	16.50

RUPEE

SILVER, 10.70-11.60 g
Narrow flan. Rev: Tiger knife.

KM#	Date	Year	VG	Fine	VF	XF
106	AH1221	—	15.00	20.00	25.00	31.50
	1222	2	11.50	13.50	16.50	20.00
	1224	4	11.50	13.50	16.50	20.00
	1225	4	20.00	25.00	30.00	37.50
	1225	5	11.50	13.50	16.50	20.00
	1226	6	11.50	13.50	16.50	20.00
	1227	7	11.50	13.50	16.50	20.00
	1228	8	11.50	13.50	16.50	20.00
	1229	9	11.50	13.50	16.50	21.50
	1230	10	11.50	13.50	16.50	20.00
	1231	11	11.50	13.50	16.50	20.00
	1232	12	11.50	13.50	16.50	20.00
	123x	13	11.50	13.50	16.50	21.50
	1234	14	11.50	13.50	16.50	20.00
	1238	18	11.50	13.50	16.50	20.00
	1239	19	11.50	13.50	16.50	21.50
	1243	22	11.50	13.50	16.50	21.50
	1244	23	11.50	13.50	16.50	21.50
	124x	24	11.50	13.50	16.50	21.50
	124x	25	11.50	13.50	16.50	21.50
	12xx	26	11.50	13.50	16.50	21.50
	1247	27	11.50	13.50	16.50	20.00
	1248	28	11.50	13.50	16.50	20.00
	1249	29	11.50	13.50	16.50	20.00
	12xx	30	11.50	13.50	16.50	21.50
	1251	31	11.50	13.50	16.50	20.00
	1252	32	11.50	13.50	16.50	20.00
	1253	34	11.50	13.50	16.50	21.50
	12xx	36	11.50	13.50	16.50	21.50
	125x	38	11.50	13.50	16.50	21.50
	1270	40	11.50	13.50	16.50	21.50
	—	46	11.50	13.50	16.50	21.50
	—	48	11.50	13.50	16.50	21.50

NOTE: Regnal years 34-48 (AH1253-1278) were posthumous, being struck during the reign of the Mughal emperor Bahadur Shah Zafar.

Wide flan

106a	AH1233	13	25.00	32.50	40.00	50.00
	1234	14	25.00	32.50	40.00	50.00
	1235	15	25.00	32.50	40.00	50.00
	1236	16	25.00	32.50	40.00	50.00
	1237	17	25.00	32.50	40.00	50.00
	1238	18	25.00	32.50	40.00	50.00

NAZARANA RUPEE

SILVER, 10.70-11.60 g

107	AH1235	15	40.00	55.00	75.00	100.00

MOHUR

GOLD, 10.70-11.40 g

110	AH—	1	220.00	240.00	265.00	300.00
	123x	11	220.00	240.00	265.00	300.00

In the name of Bahadur Shah II
AH1253-1274/1837-1858AD
Mintname: Braj Indrapur

Mint marks:

RUPEE

SILVER, 10.70-11.60 g

146	AH127x/VS1911					
		17	15.00	20.00	26.50	33.50
	127x/VS1912	18	15.00	20.00	26.50	33.50
	1273/VS1913	19	15.00	20.00	26.50	33.50
	—/VS1914	20	15.00	20.00	26.50	33.50

In the names of Queen Victoria and Jaswant Singh

Mintnames: Bharatpur and Braj Indrapur

Mint marks:

RUPEE

SILVER, 10.70-11.60 g
Rev: Katar and star.

156	VS1910	1858	27.50	40.00	55.00	80.00

Rev: Katar only.

157	VS1910	1858	27.50	40.00	55.00	80.00

MOHUR

GOLD, 10.70-11.40 g

160	VS1910	1858	250.00	300.00	400.00	500.00

With titles of Queen Victoria

RUPEE

SILVER, 10.70-11.60 g

166	VS1914	1858	32.50	45.00	60.00	90.00
	1915	1858	32.50	45.00	60.00	90.00
	1916	1859	32.50	45.00	60.00	90.00
	1917	1861	32.50	45.00	60.00	90.00
	1917	1851	(error)			
			32.50	45.00	60.00	90.00
	1922	1865	32.50	45.00	60.00	90.00

MOHUR

GOLD, 10.70-11.40 g

170	VS1915	1858	250.00	300.00	400.00	500.00
	1919	1862	250.00	300.00	400.00	500.00

NOTE: For similar coins with dagger at left and sword at right of Queen's bust, see Bindraban State.

DIG MINT
Mintnames: Mahe Indrapur
In the name of Muhammad Akbar II
AH1221-1253/1806-1837AD
Mintname: Mahe Indrapur
First Series: w/o mint marks

RUPEE

Mint marks: * ·|·

SILVER, 10.70-11.60 g
Narrow flan

KM#	Date	Year	VG	Fine	VF	XF
126	AH—	1	11.50	13.50	16.50	23.50
	—	3	11.50	13.50	16.50	23.50
	12xx	7	11.50	13.50	16.50	23.50
	1229	9	11.50	13.50	16.50	21.50
	—	10	11.50	13.50	16.50	21.50
	1231	11	11.50	13.50	16.50	21.50
	1232	12	11.50	13.50	16.50	20.00
	123x	13	11.50	13.50	16.50	21.50
	AH1237	18	11.50	13.50	16.50	21.50
	12xx	19	11.50	13.50	16.50	23.50
	12xx	24	11.50	13.50	16.50	21.50
	—	26	11.50	13.50	16.50	23.50
	1246	27	11.50	13.50	16.50	21.50
	12xx	28	11.50	13.50	16.50	20.00
	12xx	29	11.50	13.50	16.50	23.50
	12xx	31	11.50	13.50	16.50	23.50
	—	32	11.50	13.50	16.50	23.50
	—	36	11.50	13.50	16.50	23.50
	—	42	11.50	13.50	16.50	23.50
	—	47	11.50	13.50	16.50	23.50

NOTE: Issues with regnal years 32-47 are posthumous.

Wide flan

126a	AH1234	14	25.00	35.00	45.00	60.00
	12xx	15	25.00	35.00	45.00	60.00
	123x	16	25.00	35.00	45.00	60.00
	—	17	25.00	35.00	45.00	60.00

With titles of Queen Victoria
Mintnames: Dig and Mahe Indrapur

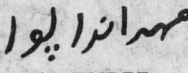

Mint marks:

1/4 RUPEE

SILVER

| 174 | VS1910 | 1858 | | | | |

RUPEE

SILVER, 10.70-11.60 g

| 176 | VS1910 | 1858 | 37.50 | 55.00 | 75.00 | 110.00 |

KUMBER MINT
RUPEE

Mint marks: ·|· *

SILVER, 10.70-11.60 g
Mintname: Mahe Indrapur

66	AH1206	34	11.50	13.50	16.50	20.00
	12xx	40	11.50	13.50	16.50	20.00
	121x	41	11.50	13.50	16.50	20.00

KM#	Date	Year	VG	Fine	VF	XF
66	121x	42	11.50	13.50	16.50	20.00
	121x	46	11.50	13.50	16.50	20.00

Narrow flan

116	AH1222	3	11.50	13.50	16.50	21.50
	12xx	5	11.50	13.50	16.50	20.00
	12xx	6	11.50	13.50	16.50	21.50
	12xx	7	11.50	13.50	16.50	21.50
	122x	8	11.50	13.50	16.50	20.00
	1229	9	11.50	13.50	16.50	20.00
	1229	10	11.50	13.50	16.50	20.00
	—	11	11.50	13.50	16.50	20.00
	1233	13	11.50	13.50	16.50	20.00
	12xx	21	11.50	13.50	16.50	20.00
	1243	22	11.50	13.50	16.50	20.00
	12xx	23	11.50	13.50	16.50	20.00
	—	24	11.50	13.50	16.50	20.00
	124x	25	11.50	13.50	16.50	20.00
	124x	26	11.50	13.50	16.50	20.00
	12xx	27	11.50	13.50	16.50	21.50
	1248	28	11.50	13.50	16.50	21.50
	1249	29	11.50	13.50	16.50	21.50
	1262	48	11.50	13.50	16.50	21.50

NOTE: The issue of regnal year 48 is posthumous.

Wide flan

116a	AH1234	14	25.00	32.50	40.00	50.00
	1235	15	25.00	32.50	40.00	50.00
	1238	16	25.00	32.50	40.00	50.00

UNCERTAIN MINT
Possibly the fortress of Ver or Wair

Mint marks: +Arabic Wa – ver?

In the name of Muhammad Akbar II
AH1221-1253/1806-1837AD

RUPEE

SILVER, 10.70-11.60 g

136	AH12xx	3	11.50	13.50	16.50	21.50
	12xx	5	11.50	13.50	16.50	23.50
	12xx	6	11.50	13.50	16.50	20.00
	122x	7	11.50	13.50	16.50	20.00
	12xx	8	11.50	13.50	16.50	20.00
	12xx	9	11.50	13.50	16.50	21.50
	123x	11	11.50	13.50	16.50	23.50
	123x	12	11.50	13.50	16.50	23.50
	1238	16	11.50	13.50	16.50	23.50
	—	19	11.50	13.50	16.50	23.50
	124x	21	11.50	13.50	16.50	23.50
	—	23	11.50	13.50	16.50	23.50
	124x	25	11.50	13.50	16.50	20.00
	12xx	26	11.50	13.50	16.50	21.50
	124x	28	11.50	13.50	16.50	20.00
	—	31	11.50	13.50	16.50	20.00
	1252	32	11.50	13.50	16.50	20.00

BHAUNAGAR

State located in northwest India on the west shore of the Gulf of Cambay.

The Thakurs of Bhaunagar, as the rulers were titled, were Gohel Rajputs. They traced their control of the area back to the thirteenth century. Under the umbrella of British paramountcy, the Thakurs of Bhaunagar were regarded as relatively enlightened rulers. The State was absorbed into Saurashtra in February 1948.

Anonymous Types: Bearing the distinguishing Nagari legend *Bahadur* in addition to the Mughal legends.

MONETARY SYSTEM

2 Trambiyo = 1 Dokda
1-1/2 Dokda = 1 Dhingla

Mughal Issues
In the name of Shah Jahan III

DOKDO

COPPER
Rev: 1825 incuse in panel.

C#	Date	Year	Good	VG	Fine	VF
15b	1825	—	3.50	5.50	7.50	9.00

NOTE: Actual date of striking unknown.

In the name of Muhammad Akbar II
AH1221-1253/1806-1837AD

DHINGLO

COPPER

| 30 | ND | — | 2.75 | 4.50 | 6.00 | 8.00 |

Anonymous Issues
DOKDA

COPPER

KM#	Date	Year	Good	VG	Fine	VF
1	VS2004	(1947)	3.00	5.00	8.00	12.50

BHOPAL

Bhopal was the second largest Muslim state located in central India. It was founded in 1723 by Dost Muhammed Khan, an Afghan adventurer of the Mirazi Khel clan, who was in the service of Aurangzeb. After the Emperor's death in 1707 Dost Muhammed asserted his independence. Early in the following century his successors, threatened by the Marathas and subjected to Pindari raids into their territory, sought to cultivate a good relationship with the British. In 1817, at the time of the Maratha and Pindari War, Bhopal signed a treaty with the British East India Company which placed them squarely under imperial protection and control. After 1897 the British rupee was recognized as the only legal tender.

RULERS

Kudsia Begam
AH1235-1253/1819-1837AD
Jahangir Muhammad Khan
AH1253-1261/1837-1844AD
Sikandar Begam
AH1261-1285/1844-1868AD
Shah Jahan Begam
AH1285-1319/1868-1901AD

Mint
Bhopal

Mughal Issues
In the name of Muhammad Akbar II
AH1221-1253/1806-1837AD

1/8 RUPEE

SILVER, 12mm, 1.34-1.45 g

C#	Date	Year	VG	Fine	VF	XF
24	AH—	16	3.50	4.50	6.00	8.00
	—	29	3.50	4.50	6.00	8.00

1/4 RUPEE

SILVER, 13mm, 2.68-2.90 g

25	AH—	16	3.50	4.50	6.00	8.00
	—	26	3.50	4.50	6.00	8.00
	—	29	3.50	4.50	6.00	8.00

1/2 RUPEE

SILVER, 15mm, 5.35-5.80 g

26	AH—	16	6.50	8.50	11.00	14.00
	—	29	6.50	8.50	11.00	14.00

Bhopal / INDIAN PRINCELY STATES 884

RUPEE

SILVER, 10.70-11.60 g

C#	Date	Year	VG	Fine	VF	XF
27	AH—	1	8.50	13.50	16.50	20.00
	—	4	8.50	13.50	16.50	20.00
	—	5	8.50	13.50	16.50	20.00
	—	6	8.50	13.50	16.50	20.00
	—	7	8.50	13.50	16.50	20.00
	—	8	8.50	13.50	16.50	20.00
	—	11	8.50	13.50	16.50	20.00
	—	13	8.50	13.50	16.50	20.00
	—	14	8.50	13.50	16.50	20.00
	—	15	8.50	13.50	16.50	20.00
	—	16	8.50	13.50	16.50	20.00
	—	17	8.50	13.50	16.50	20.00
	—	18	8.50	13.50	16.50	20.00
	—	19	8.50	13.50	16.50	20.00
	—	20	8.50	13.50	16.50	20.00
	—	21	8.50	13.50	16.50	20.00
	—	22	8.50	13.50	16.50	20.00
	—	25	8.50	13.50	16.50	20.00
	—	26	8.50	13.50	16.50	20.00
	—	27	8.50	13.50	16.50	20.00
	—	30	8.50	13.50	16.50	20.00
	—	32	8.50	13.50	16.50	20.00
	—	33	8.50	13.50	16.50	20.00
	—	34	8.50	13.50	16.50	20.00

Anonymous Issues
PAISA

COPPER, 21-22mm
Obv: *Bhopal.* Rev: Year in circle.

C#	Date	Year	Good	VG	Fine	VF
20	—	25	1.50	2.50	4.00	5.50
	—	29	1.50	2.50	4.00	5.50

Rev: Whisk

| 21 | — | 28 | 2.50 | 3.50 | 5.00 | 6.50 |

UNIFACE PAISA

COPPER
Persian *Bhopal* in circular depressed area.

| 20a | ND | — | 1.75 | 2.75 | 4.00 | 6.00 |

Persian *Sikka Bhopal* and date.

| 21a | AH1255 | — | 2.50 | 3.50 | 5.00 | 7.00 |

Fly whisk and scimitar

21b	—	13	1.50	2.50	4.00	6.00
	ND	—	1.50	2.50	4.00	6.00
	ND	26	1.50	2.50	4.00	6.00

Persian *Fateh* and scimitar.

| 21c | ND | 8 | 1.50 | 2.50 | 4.00 | 6.00 |

Persian *Jim* and year

21d	ND	5	1.50	2.50	4.00	6.00
		10	1.50	2.50	4.00	6.00
		11	1.50	2.50	4.00	6.00
		12	1.50	2.50	4.00	6.00
		47	1.75	2.75	4.50	6.50

1/4 ANNA

COPPER
Rev: Denomination.

Y#	Date	Year	Good	VG	Fine	VF
1	AH1266	—	1.00	1.75	2.50	3.50
	1269	—	1.00	1.75	2.50	3.50
	1272	—	1.00	1.75	2.50	3.50
	1273	—	1.00	1.75	2.50	3.50
	1276	—	1.00	1.75	2.50	3.50
	1279	—	1.00	1.75	2.50	3.50

Rev: Date and denomination.

| 4.1 | AH1285 | — | .75 | 1.25 | 2.00 | 3.00 |

4.2	AH1286	—	.65	1.25	1.75	2.50
	1287	—	.65	1.25	1.75	2.50
	1288	—	.65	1.25	1.75	2.50
	1289	—	.65	1.25	1.75	2.50
	1292	—	.65	1.25	1.75	2.50
	1293	—	.65	1.25	1.75	2.50
	1299	—	.75	1.25	2.00	3.00

1/2 ANNA

COPPER, 20-21mm
Rev: Denomination

| 2 | AH1276 | — | 1.50 | 2.50 | 3.50 | 5.00 |
| | 1278 | — | 1.50 | 2.50 | 3.50 | 5.00 |

Rev: Date and denomination.

5	AH1286	—	1.00	1.75	2.50	3.50
	1289	—	1.25	2.00	3.00	4.50
	1299	—	1.25	2.00	3.00	4.50
	1300	—	1.00	1.75	2.50	3.50

ANNA

COPPER
Rev: Denomination.

| 3 | AH1276 | — | 2.25 | 4.00 | 6.00 | 9.00 |

27-30mm
Rev: Date and denomination.

6	AH1286	—	2.50	4.00	6.00	8.50
	1289	—	2.50	4.00	6.00	8.50
	1300	—	2.50	4.00	6.00	8.50

1/8 RUPEE

SILVER, 1.34-1.45 g
Obv: *Zarb* above *Bhopal.*

Y#	Date	Year	VG	Fine	VF	XF
7	AH1275	—	2.00	3.00	4.50	6.50
	1288	7	2.00	3.00	4.50	6.50
	1289	8	2.00	3.00	4.50	6.50
	1291	8	2.00	3.00	4.50	6.50

Obv: *Zarb* below *Bhopal.*

11	AH129x	8	3.00	4.50	6.00	8.00
	1294	9	3.00	4.50	6.00	8.00
	1303	15	3.00	4.50	6.00	8.00
	1306	17	3.00	4.50	6.00	8.00

1/4 RUPEE

SILVER, 2.68-2.90 g
Obv: *Zarb* above *Bhopal.*

8	AH1275	—	3.50	4.50	6.00	8.00
	1282	2	3.50	4.50	6.00	8.00
	1284	8	3.50	4.50	6.00	8.00
	1287	8	3.50	4.50	6.00	8.00
	1288	8	3.50	4.50	6.00	8.00

Obv: *Zarb* below *Bhopal.*

12	AH1293	8	4.00	5.50	7.50	10.00
	1294	9	4.00	5.50	7.50	10.00
	1295	10	4.00	5.50	7.50	10.00
	1297	12	4.00	5.50	7.50	10.00
	1303	15	4.00	5.50	7.50	10.00
	1305	16	4.00	5.50	7.50	10.00

1/2 RUPEE

SILVER, 5.35-5.80 g
Obv: *Zarb* above *Bhopal.*

9	AH1275	—	6.50	8.00	10.00	13.00
	1278	—	6.50	8.00	10.00	13.00
	1279	5	6.50	8.00	10.00	13.00
	1280	—	6.50	8.00	10.00	13.00
	1281	—	6.50	8.00	10.00	13.00
	1282	2	6.50	8.00	10.00	13.00
	1283	8	6.50	8.00	10.00	13.00
	1285	5	6.50	8.00	10.00	13.00
	1287	8	6.50	8.00	10.00	13.00
	1288	7	6.50	8.00	10.00	13.00
	1288	8	6.50	8.00	10.00	13.00
	1289	8	6.50	8.00	10.00	13.00
	1291	8	6.50	8.00	10.00	13.00
	1292	—	6.50	8.00	10.00	13.00

Obv: *Zarb* below *Bhopal.*

13	AH1294	9	6.50	7.50	9.00	12.00
	1295	—	6.50	8.00	10.00	13.00
	1296	11	6.50	8.00	10.00	13.00
	130(2)	14	6.50	7.50	9.00	12.00
	1303	15	6.50	8.00	10.00	13.00
	1306	17	6.50	7.50	9.00	12.00
	130(5)	16	6.50	7.50	9.00	12.00
	1307	19	6.50	7.50	9.00	12.00
	1308	20	6.50	7.50	9.00	12.00

RUPEE

SILVER, 10.70-11.60 g
Obv: *Zarb* above *Bhopal.*

10	AH1271	—	8.50	13.50	16.50	20.00
	1271	5	8.50	13.50	16.50	20.00
	1272	—	8.50	13.50	16.50	20.00

Y#	Date	Year	VG	Fine	VF	XF
10	1275	—	8.50	13.50	16.50	20.00
	1276	—	8.50	13.50	16.50	20.00
	1277	—	8.50	13.50	16.50	20.00
	1278	2	8.50	13.50	16.50	20.00
	1279	3	8.50	13.50	16.50	20.00
	1279	4	8.50	13.50	16.50	20.00
	1279	5	8.50	13.50	16.50	20.00
	1280	5	8.50	13.50	16.50	20.00
	1281	8	8.50	13.50	16.50	20.00
	1282	2	8.50	13.50	16.50	20.00
	1282	6	8.50	13.50	16.50	20.00
	1282	8	8.50	13.50	16.50	20.00
	1283	7	8.50	13.50	16.50	20.00
	1283	8	8.50	13.50	16.50	20.00
	1284	8	8.50	13.50	16.50	20.00
	1285	5	8.50	13.50	16.50	20.00
	1285	8	8.50	13.50	16.50	20.00
	1288	7	8.50	13.50	16.50	20.00
	1288	8	8.50	13.50	16.50	20.00
	1289	8	8.50	13.50	16.50	20.00
	1289	9	8.50	13.50	16.50	20.00
	1291	8	8.50	13.50	16.50	20.00
	1292	8	8.50	13.50	16.50	20.00
	1293	—	8.50	13.50	16.50	20.00

Obv: *Zarb below Bhopal.*

14	AH1293	8	8.50	13.50	16.50	20.00
	1294	9	8.50	13.50	16.50	20.00
	1295	10	8.50	13.50	16.50	20.00
	1295	11	8.50	13.50	16.50	20.00
	1296	11	8.50	13.50	16.50	20.00
	1297	12	8.50	13.50	16.50	20.00
	1298	9	8.50	13.50	16.50	20.00
	1298	10	8.50	13.50	16.50	20.00
	1298	13	8.50	13.50	16.50	20.00
	1298	15	8.50	13.50	16.50	20.00
	1302	14	8.50	13.50	16.50	20.00
	1304	15	8.50	13.50	16.50	20.00
	1305	16	8.50	13.50	16.50	20.00
	1306	17	8.50	13.50	16.50	20.00
	1308	14	8.50	13.50	16.50	20.00

NAZARANA RUPEE

SILVER, 10.95 g

| B14 | ND | | | | | |

NAZARANA 2 RUPEES

SILVER, 21.40-23.20 g

Y#	Date	Year	Fine	VF	XF	Unc
A14	AH1286	2	100.00	150.00	250.00	400.00

SHAH JAHAN BEGAM
AH1285-1319/1868-1901AD

PIE (or 1/2 Paisa)

COPPER

Y#	Date	Year	Good	VG	Fine	VF
15	AH1305	—	1.50	2.25	3.25	4.50

1/4 ANNA

COPPER

Y#	Date	Year	Good	VG	Fine	VF
16	AH1302	—	.50	1.00	1.50	2.25
	1303	—	.50	1.00	1.50	2.25
	1305	—	.50	1.00	1.50	2.25
	1306	—	.50	1.00	1.50	2.25

1/2 ANNA

COPPER

17.1	AH1302	—	.75	1.50	2.50	4.00
	1303	—	.75	1.50	2.50	4.00
	1304	—	.75	1.50	2.50	4.00
	1306	—	.75	1.50	2.50	4.00

Large flan.

| 17.2 | AH1309 | | 2.00 | 3.00 | 4.50 | 6.00 |

ANNA

COPPER

18	AH1302	—	3.00	5.00	7.50	10.00
	1303	—	3.00	5.00	7.50	10.00
	1304	—	3.00	5.00	7.50	10.00
	1305	—	3.00	5.00	7.50	10.00
	1306	—	3.00	5.00	7.50	10.00

Struck from 1/2 Anna dies

| 18a | | | 3.00 | 5.00 | 7.00 | 10.00 |

BHOPAL FEUDATORY
NARSINGHGARH

The Rajput rulers of this feudatory traced their origins back into the fourteenth century when their ancestors migrated from Malwa through Sind before settling at Narsinghgarh.

PAISA

COPPER

| 91 | ND | | 3.00 | 5.00 | 7.00 | 10.00 |

BIKANIR

Bikanir, located in Rajputana was established as a state sometime between 1465 and 1504 by Jodhpur Rathor Rajput named Rao Bikaji. During the period of the Great Mughals Bikanir was intimately linked to Delhi by ties of both loyalty and marriage. Both Akbar and Jahangir contracted marriages with princesses of the Bikanir Rajputs, and the Bikanir nobility rendered outstanding service in the Mughal armies. Bikanir came under British influence in 1817 and after 1947 was incorporated into Rajasthan.

RULERS

Surat Singh
  AH1202-1244/1787-1828AD
Ratan Singh
  AH1244-1268/1828-1851AD
Sardar Singh
  AH1268-1289/1851-1872AD
Dungar Singh
  AH1289-1305/1872-1887AD
Ganga Singhji
  VS1944-1999/1887-1942AD

MINT

Bikanir

MINT MARKS

1. Gaj Singh, AH1159-1202

2. (")

3. Surat Singh, AH1202-1244

4. (")

5. (")

6. Ratan Singh, AH1244-1268 (2 Vars.)

7. Sardar Singh, AH1268-1289

8. Dungar Singh, AH1289-1305

9. Ganga Singh, VS1949-1999

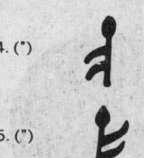

NOTE: The above symbols normally occur in groups on the obverse or reverse of the coins; the various combinations are shown for each series.

Rupees and their fractions were probably struck in every year, but only a small representation of regnal years is listed; unlisted years are probably no rarer than the listed ones; and are worth no premium.

Mughal Issues
SURAT SINGH
AH1202-1244/1787-1828AD

Regnal years of Shah Alam II
Years 28-52

RUPEE

SILVER, 10.70-11.60 g
Obv: Mark #1. Rev: Mark #3.

KM#	Date	Year	VG	Fine	VF	XF
17	AH1217	41	8.50	13.50	16.50	20.00
	1217	43	8.50	13.50	16.50	20.00
	1227	47	8.50	13.50	16.50	20.00
	1229	51	8.50	13.50	16.50	20.00
	1229	52	8.50	13.50	16.50	20.00

In the name of Shah Alam II
AH1173-1221/1759-1806AD

RATAN SINGH
AH1244-1268/1828-1851AD

UNIFACE PAISA
COPPER, round or square, 12-18mm

Bikanir / INDIAN PRINCELY STATES

Symbol of Ratan Singh

KM#	Date	Year	Good	VG	Fine	VF
20	ND	—	1.25	2.25	3.50	5.00

In the name of Alamgir II
AH1167-1173/1754-1759AD

1/2 PAISA

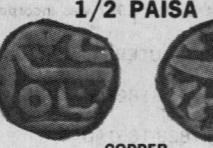

COPPER
Rev: Mark #6.

KM#	Date	Year	Good	VG	Fine	VF
22	ND	25	.75	1.25	2.00	3.00
	—	41	.75	1.25	2.00	3.00

PAISA

COPPER
Rev: Mark #6.

KM#	Date	Year	Good	VG	Fine	VF
23	ND	41	.75	1.25	2.00	3.00

NOTE: So called year 21 is debased copy of year 41.

Regnal years of Muhammad Akbar II
Years 21-52

RUPEE

SILVER, 10.70-11.60 g
Obv: Mark #1. Rev: Marks #3 and 6.

KM#	Date	Year	VG	Fine	VF	XF
32	AH1229	21	8.50	13.50	16.50	20.00
	1229	25	8.50	13.50	16.50	20.00
	1229	31	8.50	13.50	16.50	20.00
	1229	32	8.50	13.50	16.50	20.00
	1229	41	8.50	13.50	16.50	20.00
	1229	47	8.50	13.50	16.50	20.00
	1229	52	8.50	13.50	16.50	20.00

In the name of Shah Alam II
AH1173-1221/1759-1806AD

NAZARANA RUPEE

SILVER, 10.70-11.60 g

KM#	Date	Year	VG	Fine	VF	XF
32a	AH1229	25	30.00	40.00	50.00	65.00

SARDAR SINGH
AH1268-1289/1851-1872AD

In the Name of Alamgir II
AH1167-1173/1754-1759AD

1/2 PAISA

COPPER, 17mm

KM#	Date	Year	Good	VG	Fine	VF
34	AH1229	18	2.00	3.00	4.50	6.50

1/4 RUPEE

SILVER, 16mm, 2.68-2.90 g

KM#	Date	Year	VG	Fine	VF	XF
35	AH—	—	5.50	7.50	10.00	13.50

1/2 RUPEE

SILVER, 18mm, 5.35-5.80 g

KM#	Date	Year	VG	Fine	VF	XF
36	AH—	—	—	7.50	10.00	13.50	17.50

Regnal years of Bahadur Shah II
Years 18-21

RUPEE

SILVER, 10.70-11.60 g
Rev: Marks #1, 4 (or 5), 6, and 7.
Years of Bahadur Shah II

KM#	Date	Year	VG	Fine	VF	XF
37	AH1229	18	11.50	13.50	16.50	20.00
	1229	21	11.50	13.50	16.50	20.00

NAZARANA RUPEE

SILVER, 29mm, 10.70-11.60 g

KM#	Date	Year	VG	Fine	VF	XF
37a	AH1229	21	30.00	40.00	65.00	85.00

Regal Issues
In the Name of Queen Victoria
Beginning 1859AD
Reverse marks from left to right: #6, 7, 2, 5.

PAISA

COPPER

KM#	Date	Year	Good	VG	Fine	VF
41	VS1916	1859	.75	1.25	2.00	3.00

1/8 RUPEE

SILVER, 11-12mm, 1.34-1.45 g

KM#	Date	Year	VG	Fine	VF	XF
42	VS1916	1859	5.50	7.50	10.00	13.50

1/4 RUPEE

SILVER, 15mm, 2.68-2.90 g

KM#	Date	Year	VG	Fine	VF	XF
43	VS1916	1859	6.50	8.50	11.50	15.00

1/2 RUPEE

SILVER, 18mm, 5.35-5.80 g

KM#	Date	Year	VG	Fine	VF	XF
44	VS1916	1859	7.50	9.00	12.50	16.50

RUPEE

SILVER, 10.70-11.60 g

KM#	Date	Year	VG	Fine	VF	XF
45	VS1916	1859	11.50	13.50	16.50	20.00

NAZARANA RUPEE

SILVER, 30mm, 10.70-11.60 g

KM#	Date	Year	VG	Fine	VF	XF
46	VS1916	1859	40.00	60.00	80.00	100.00

Local Issues
DUNGAR SINGH
AH1289-1305/1872-1887AD
Reverse marks, left to right: #6, 7, 8, 2, 5.
All coins w/frozen date VS1916/1859AD.

PAISA

COPPER

KM#	Date	Year	Good	VG	Fine	VF
50	VS1916	1859	.75	1.25	2.00	3.00

1/8 RUPEE

SILVER, 12mm, 1.34-1.45 g

KM#	Date	Year	VG	Fine	VF	XF
51	VS1916	1859	6.00	8.00	10.00	13.50

1/4 RUPEE

SILVER, 14mm, 2.68-2.90 g

KM#	Date	Year	VG	Fine	VF	XF
52	VS1916	1859	7.50	9.00	12.50	16.50

1/2 RUPEE

SILVER, 17mm, 5.35-5.80 g

KM#	Date	Year	VG	Fine	VF	XF
53	VS1916	1859	7.50	9.00	12.50	16.50

RUPEE

SILVER, 10.70-11.60 g

KM#	Date	Year	VG	Fine	VF	XF
54	VS1916	1859	11.50	13.50	16.50	20.00

NAZARANA RUPEE

SILVER, 30mm, 10.70-11.60 g

KM#	Date	Year	VG	Fine	VF	XF
54a	VS1916	1859	40.00	60.00	80.00	100.00

GANGA SINGH
VS1944-1999/SE1965-2020/1887-1942AD
Reverse marks, left to right: #6, 7, 9, 8, 2, 5.
All dump coins w/frozen date VS1916/1859AD
and actual VS date.

PAISA

COPPER, 18mm

KM#	Date	Year	Good	VG	Fine	VF
61	VS1946	(1889)	1.75	2.50	3.50	5.00

1/8 RUPEE

SILVER, 12mm, 1.34-1.45 g

KM#	Date	Year	VG	Fine	VF	XF
62	VS1944	(1887)	6.00	8.00	10.00	13.50

1/4 RUPEE

SILVER, 2.68-2.90 g

KM#	Date	Year	VG	Fine	VF	XF
63	VS1944	(1887)	6.00	8.00	10.00	13.50

1/2 RUPEE

SILVER, 5.35-5.80 g

KM#	Date	Year	VG	Fine	VF	XF
64	VS1944	(1887)	6.50	8.50	11.00	15.00

RUPEE

SILVER, 10.70-11.60 g

KM#	Date	Year	VG	Fine	VF	XF
65	VS1944	(1887)	11.50	13.50	16.50	20.00

NAZARANA RUPEE

SILVER, 30mm, 10.70-11.60 g

KM#	Date	Year	VG	Fine	VF	XF
65a	VS1944	(1887)	40.00	60.00	80.00	100.00
	1966	(1909)	40.00	60.00	80.00	100.00

Milled Coinage
1/2 PICE

COPPER

KM#	Date	Mintage	Fine	VF	XF	Unc
70	1894	.500	6.00	12.00	17.50	25.00
	1894	—	—	—	Proof	100.00

SILVER (OMS)

70a	1894	(restrike)	—	—	Proof	125.00

GOLD (OMS)

70b	1894	(restrike)	—	—	Proof	450.00

1/4 ANNA

COPPER

71	1895	6.156	5.00	8.00	12.50	20.00
	1895	—	—	—	Proof	125.00

SILVER (OMS)

71a	1895	(restrike)	—	—	Proof	125.00

GOLD (OMS)

71b	1895	(restrike)	—	—	Proof	650.00

RUPEE

SILVER, 11.66 g

72	1892	.596	8.00	12.50	17.50	22.50
	1892	—	—	—	Proof	200.00
	1897	.111	15.00	25.00	40.00	60.00
	1897	—	—	—	Proof	200.00

BINDRABAN

This city, the modern Vrindavan, was not a princely state. The area surrounding the city, including the neighboring city of Mathura, was under Jat control in the mid-eighteenth century, although nominally subject to Awadh. After varying fortunes the area passed to the East India Company in 1803-05. The coins below display symbols of Awadh, Mughals, Delhi and Bhartpur, although it is clear that they were not mints of any of those authorities, especially in the British period.

MINTS

Bindraban — بندر(ابن)

Gokul — گوکل

Mathura — متهره

BINDRABAN MINT MINTNAMES

Mominabad — معمين اباد

Mominabad Bindraban — معمين اباد بندر(ابن)

Shahjahanabad — شاهجهان اباد

Local Issues
In the name of Queen Victoria

1/4 RUPEE

SILVER, 2.68-2.90 g

Y#	Date	Year	VG	Fine	VF	XF
1	VS1915	1858	15.00	25.00	40.00	60.00
	1916	1859	15.00	25.00	40.00	60.00
	1924	1867	15.00	25.00	40.00	60.00

1/2 RUPEE

SILVER, 5.35-5.80 g

2	VS1915	1858	20.00	35.00	50.00	65.00
	1916	1859	20.00	35.00	50.00	65.00
	1924	1867	20.00	35.00	50.00	65.00

RUPEE

SILVER, 10.70-11.60 g

3	VS1915	1858	35.00	45.00	70.00	90.00

BUNDI

State in Rajputana in northwest India.
Bundi was founded in 1342 by a Chauhan Rajput, Rao Dewa (Deoraj). Almost three hundred years later it was subdivided into three separate states, Bundi, Kotah and Jhalawar. Until the Maratha defeat early in the nineteenth century, Bundi was greatly harassed by the forces of Holkar and Sindhia. In 1818 it came under British protection and control and remained so until 1947. In 1948 the State was absorbed into Rajasthan.

RULERS
Bishen Singh
  VS1861-1878/1804-1821AD
Ram Singh
  VS1878-1946/1824-1889AD
Raghubir Singh
  VS1946-1984/1889-1927AD
Ishwari Singh
  VS1984-2004/1927-1947AD

MINT
Bundi

Mintname: Bundi   Bundish

All of the coins of Bundi struck prior to the Mutiny (1857) are in the name of the Mughal emperor and bear the following 2 marks on the reverse, to the left and right of the regnal year, respectively:

On all Mughal issues:

Only on Muhammad Akbar and Muhammad Bahadur issues:

The same symbols appear on the coins of Kotah, but the difference is that the Kotah pieces have the mint name *Kotahurf Nandgaon* and later issues only have *Nandgaon*.

Mughal Issues
In the name of Muhammad Akbar II
AH1221-1253/1806-1837AD

PAISA

COPPER, 17.30-17.75 g, round
W/leg: *Bad Shah Ghazi.*

C#	Date	Year	Good	VG	Fine	VF
15	AH—	2	2.50	3.50	4.50	6.00
(C17)	—	3	2.50	3.50	4.50	6.00
	—	4	2.50	3.50	4.50	6.00
	—	6	2.50	3.50	4.50	6.00

W/leg: *Sahib Qiran Sani.*

C#	Date	Year	Good	VG	Fine	VF
17	AH—	11	1.25	2.00	3.00	4.50
(C17a)	—	12	1.25	2.00	3.00	4.50
	—	13	1.25	2.00	3.00	4.50
	—	14	1.25	2.00	3.00	4.50
	—	15	1.50	2.50	3.50	5.00
	—	16	1.50	2.50	3.50	5.00

COPPER, 17.30-17.75 g, square
W/leg: *Sahib Qiran Sani.*

17a	AH—	24	1.50	2.50	3.50	5.00
	—	25	1.25	2.00	3.00	4.50
	—	26	1.25	2.00	3.00	4.50

1/2 RUPEE

SILVER, 15mm, 5.35-5.80 g
W/leg: *Bad Shah Ghazi.*

C#	Date	Year	VG	Fine	VF	XF
25	AH—	1	6.50	7.50	8.50	10.00

RUPEE

SILVER, 10.70-11.60 g
W/leg: *Bad Shah Ghazi.*

29	AH—	1	11.50	13.50	16.50	20.00
(C30)	—	2	11.50	13.50	16.50	20.00
	—	3	11.50	13.50	16.50	20.00

W/leg: *Sahib Qiran Sani.*

30	AH—	5	11.50	13.50	16.50	20.00
	—	6	11.50	13.50	16.50	20.00
	—	9	11.50	13.50	16.50	20.00
	—	10	11.50	13.50	16.50	20.00
	—	11	11.50	13.50	16.50	20.00
	—	12	11.50	13.50	16.50	20.00
	—	13	11.50	13.50	16.50	20.00
	—	15	11.50	13.50	16.50	20.00
	—	16	11.50	13.50	16.50	20.00
	—	18	11.50	13.50	16.50	20.00
	—	19	11.50	13.50	16.50	20.00
	—	20	11.50	13.50	16.50	20.00
	—	21	11.50	13.50	16.50	20.00
	—	22	11.50	13.50	16.50	20.00
	—	27	11.50	13.50	16.50	20.00
	—	30	11.50	13.50	16.50	20.00
	—	31	11.50	13.50	16.50	20.00
	—	32	11.50	13.50	16.50	20.00

MOHUR

GOLD, 10.70-11.40 g

33	AH—	15	220.00	240.00	265.00	300.00

In the name of Bahadur Shah II
AH1253-1274/1837-1858AD

PAISA

COPPER, 20mm

C#	Date	Year	Good	VG	Fine	VF
35	AH—	9	4.50	6.50	8.50	12.50
	—	11	4.50	6.50	8.50	12.50
	—	14	4.50	6.50	8.50	12.50
	—	19	4.50	6.50	8.50	12.50

RUPEE

SILVER, 19mm, 10.70-11.60 g

C#	Date	Year	VG	Fine	VF	XF
40	AH—	1	11.50	13.50	16.50	20.00
	—	2	11.50	13.50	16.50	20.00
	—	3	11.50	13.50	16.50	20.00
	—	4	11.50	13.50	16.50	20.00
	—	5	11.50	13.50	16.50	20.00
	—	6	11.50	13.50	16.50	20.00
	—	7	11.50	13.50	16.50	20.00
	—	8	11.50	13.50	16.50	20.00
	—	9	11.50	13.50	16.50	20.00
	—	10	11.50	13.50	16.50	20.00
	—	12	11.50	13.50	16.50	20.00
	—	13	11.50	13.50	16.50	20.00
	—	14	11.50	13.50	16.50	20.00
	—	15	11.50	13.50	16.50	20.00
	—	16	11.50	13.50	16.50	20.00
	—	18	11.50	13.50	16.50	20.00
	—	19	11.50	13.50	16.50	20.00
	—	21	11.50	13.50	16.50	20.00

Regal Issues
In the name of Queen Victoria
Obv: AD date. Rev: VS date.

Bundi / INDIAN PRINCELY STATES 888

1/4 PAISA
COPPER, 9-11mm, 5.50 g
Obv. leg: VICTORIA QUEEN. Rev: Date.

Y#	Date	Year	Good	VG	Fine	VF
1	VS1924	1867	.75	1.25	2.25	3.50

5.00-5.10 g

Y#	Date	Year	Good	VG	Fine	VF
Y-A2	VS1963	1906	.75	1.25	2.25	3.50
	1965	1908	.75	1.25	2.25	3.50
	1966	1909	.75	1.25	2.25	3.50
	1967	1910	.75	1.25	2.25	3.50

1/2 PAISA

COPPER, 10.60 g

Y#	Date	Year	Good	VG	Fine	VF
2	VS1915	1858	.35	.65	1.00	1.50
	1924	1867	.25	.50	.85	1.25
	1934	1877	.25	.50	.85	1.25
	1935	1878	.25	.50	.85	1.25
	1936	1879	.25	.50	.85	1.25
	1940	1883	.25	.50	.85	1.25
	1942	1885	.25	.50	.85	1.25
	1943	1886	.25	.50	.85	1.25
	1944	1887	.25	.50	.85	1.25
	1945	1888	.25	.50	.85	1.25
	1946	1889	.25	.50	.85	1.25
	1947	—	.25	.50	.85	1.25
	1955	1898	.25	.50	.85	1.25

PAISA

COPPER

Y#	Date	Year	Good	VG	Fine	VF
3	VS1915	1858	.35	.85	1.25	1.75
	1919	1862	.35	.85	1.25	1.75
	1921	1864	.35	.85	1.25	1.75
	1922	1864	.35	.85	1.25	1.75
	1922	1865	.35	.85	1.25	1.75
	1923	1866	.35	.85	1.25	1.75
	1924	1867	.35	.85	1.25	1.75
	1926	1869	.35	.85	1.25	1.75
	1928	1871	.35	.85	1.25	1.75
	1929	1872	.35	.85	1.25	1.75
	1932	1875	.35	.85	1.25	1.75
	1934	1877	.25	.50	.85	1.25
	1935	1878	.25	.50	.85	1.25
	1936	1879	.25	.50	.85	1.25
	1939	1882	.25	.50	.85	1.25
	1940	1883	.25	.50	.85	1.25
	1942	1885	.25	.50	.85	1.25
	1943	1886	.25	.50	.85	1.25
	1944	1887	.25	.50	.85	1.25
	1945	1888	.25	.50	.85	1.25
	1946	1889	.25	.50	.85	1.25
	1955	1898	.85	1.25	2.00	3.00
	1956	1894	.85	1.25	2.00	3.00
	1956	1899	1.25	2.25	3.50	5.00
	Date off flan		.65	1.10	1.75	2.50

1/4 RUPEE

SILVER, 2.60-2.80 g

Y#	Date	Year	VG	Fine	VF	XF
4	VS1915	1858	3.50	4.00	5.00	6.00
	1935	1888	3.50	4.00	5.00	6.00
	1936	1879	3.50	4.00	5.00	6.00
	Date off flan		1.75	2.00	2.50	3.00

Y#	Date	Year	VG	Fine	VF	XF
7	VS1944	(1887)	5.00	6.00	7.00	8.50
	1947	(1890)	3.50	4.00	5.00	6.00
	1953	(1896)	3.50	4.00	5.00	6.00
	1955	(1898)	3.50	4.00	5.00	6.00
	Date off flan		1.75	2.00	2.50	3.00

1/2 RUPEE

SILVER, 5.30-5.60 g

Y#	Date	Year	VG	Fine	VF	XF
5	VS1915	1858	6.50	7.00	7.50	8.50
	1930	1873	6.50	7.00	7.50	8.50
	1933	1876	6.50	7.00	7.50	8.50
	1937	1880	6.50	7.00	7.50	8.50
	1940	1883	6.50	7.00	7.50	8.50

Y#	Date	Year	VG	Fine	VF	XF
5	1941	1884	6.50	7.00	7.50	8.50
	1943	1886	6.50	7.00	7.50	8.50
	Date off flan		3.25	3.50	3.75	4.25

Y#	Date	Year	VG	Fine	VF	XF
8	VS1945	1888	6.50	7.50	8.50	10.00
	1946	(1889)	6.50	7.50	8.50	10.00
	1948	(1891)	6.50	7.00	8.00	9.00
	1949	(1892)	6.50	7.00	8.00	9.00
	1953	(1896)	6.50	7.50	8.50	10.00
	1954	(1897)	6.50	7.00	8.00	9.00
	1955	(1898)	6.50	7.00	8.00	9.00
	Date off flan		3.25	3.50	4.00	4.50

RUPEE

SILVER, 10.60-11.20 g

Y#	Date	Year	VG	Fine	VF	XF
6	VS1915	1858	11.50	12.50	14.00	16.50
	1915	1859	11.50	12.50	14.00	16.50
	1916	1859	11.50	13.50	15.00	17.50
	1916	1860	11.50	13.50	15.00	17.50
	1917	1860	11.50	12.50	14.00	16.50
	1918	1861	11.50	12.50	14.00	16.50
	1919	1862	11.50	12.50	14.00	16.50
	1920	1863	11.50	12.50	14.00	16.50
	1921	1864	11.50	12.50	14.00	16.50
	1922	1865	11.50	12.50	14.00	16.50
	1923	1866	11.50	12.50	14.00	16.50
	1924	1867	11.50	12.50	14.00	16.50
	1925	1868	11.50	12.50	14.00	16.50
	1925 (sic)					
		1864	11.50	12.50	14.00	16.50
	1926	1869	11.50	12.50	14.00	16.50
	1927	1870	11.50	12.50	14.00	16.50
	1928	1871	11.50	12.50	14.00	16.50
	1929	1872	11.50	12.50	14.00	16.50
	1930	1873	11.50	12.50	14.00	16.50
	1931	1874	11.50	12.50	14.00	16.50
	1932	1875	11.50	12.50	14.00	16.50
	1933	1876	11.50	12.50	14.00	16.50
	1934	1877	11.50	12.50	14.00	16.50
	1935	1878	11.50	12.50	14.00	16.50
	1936	1879	11.50	12.50	14.00	16.50
	1937	1880	11.50	12.50	14.00	16.50
	1938	1881	11.50	12.50	14.00	16.50
	1940	1883	11.50	12.50	14.00	16.50
	1941	1884	11.50	12.50	14.00	16.50
	1942	1885	11.50	12.50	14.00	16.50
	1943	1886	11.50	12.50	14.00	16.50
	Date off flan		5.50	6.00	7.00	8.50

Y#	Date	Year	VG	Fine	VF	XF
9	VS1943	(1886)	11.50	12.50	14.00	16.50
	1944	(1887)	11.50	12.50	14.00	16.50
	1945	(1888)	11.50	12.50	14.00	16.50
	1946	(1889)	11.50	12.50	14.00	16.50
	1947	(1890)	11.50	12.50	14.00	16.50
	1948	(1891)	11.50	12.50	14.00	16.50
	1949	(1892)	11.50	12.50	14.00	16.50
	1950	(1893)	11.50	12.50	14.00	16.50
	1951	1894	11.50	12.50	14.00	16.50
	1953	(1896)	11.50	12.50	14.00	16.50
	1954	(1897)	11.50	12.50	14.00	16.50
	1955	(1898)	11.50	12.50	14.00	16.50
	1957	(1900)	11.50	12.50	14.00	16.50
	Date off flan		5.50	6.00	7.00	8.50

NAZARANA RUPEE

SILVER, 10.60-11.20 g

Y#	Date	Year	VG	Fine	VF	XF
6a	VS1915	1858	20.00	25.00	32.50	42.50
	1919	1862	20.00	25.00	32.50	42.50
	1925	1868	20.00	25.00	32.50	42.50
	1929	1872	20.00	25.00	32.50	42.50
	1932	1875	20.00	25.00	32.50	42.50

Y#	Date	Year	VG	Fine	VF	XF
6a	1934	1877	20.00	25.00	32.50	42.50
	1935	1878	20.00	25.00	32.50	42.50
	1937	1880	20.00	25.00	32.50	42.50

Y#	Date	Year	VG	Fine	VF	XF
9a	VS1943	(1886)	45.00	60.00	80.00	110.00
	1945	(1888)	45.00	60.00	80.00	110.00
	1946	(1889)	45.00	60.00	80.00	110.00
	1947	(1890)	45.00	60.00	80.00	110.00
	1949	(1892)	45.00	60.00	80.00	110.00
	1951	(1894)	45.00	60.00	80.00	110.00
	1952	(1895)	45.00	60.00	80.00	110.00

Y#	Date	Year	VG	Fine	VF	XF
10	VS1958	(1901)	40.00	60.00	85.00	120.00

In the name of Edward VII

PAISA

COPPER, 4.70-5.10 g

Y#	Date	Year	Good	VG	Fine	VF
A12	VS1963	(1906)	—	Reported, not confirmed		
	1965	(1908)	6.00	9.00	12.50	16.50
	1973	(1916)	6.00	9.00	12.50	16.50
	1974	(1917)	6.00	9.00	12.50	16.50
	1976	(1919)	6.00	9.00	12.50	16.50

1/4 RUPEE

SILVER, 2.65-2.70 g

Y#	Date	Year	VG	Fine	VF	XF
B11	VS1958	(1901)	20.00	25.00	30.00	37.50
	1961	(1904)	20.00	25.00	30.00	37.50
	1962	(1905)	20.00	25.00	30.00	37.50

Y#	Date	Year	VG	Fine	VF	XF
12	VS1963	(1906)	3.50	4.00	4.50	5.50
	1964	(1907)	3.50	4.00	4.50	5.50
	1965	(1908)	3.50	4.00	5.00	6.50
	1966	(1909)	3.50	4.00	4.50	5.50

1/2 RUPEE

SILVER, 16-18mm, 5.30-5.40 g

Y#	Date	Year	VG	Fine	VF	XF
A11	VS1958	(1901)	20.00	25.00	30.00	37.50

Y#	Date	Year	VG	Fine	VF	XF
13	VS1963	(1906)	6.50	7.50	8.50	10.00
	1964	(1907)	6.00	7.00	8.00	9.00
	1965	(1908)	6.00	7.00	8.00	9.00
	1966	(1909)	6.00	7.00	8.00	9.00

RUPEE

SILVER, 10.60-11.70 g

Y#	Date	Year	VG	Fine	VF	XF
11	VS1958	(1901)	11.50	12.50	14.00	16.50
	1959	(1902)	11.50	13.50	15.00	17.50

889 Cambay / INDIAN PRINCELY STATES

Y#	Date	Year	VG	Fine	VF	XF
11	1960	(1903)	11.50	13.50	15.00	17.50
	1961	(1904)	11.50	13.50	15.00	17.50
	1962	(1905)	11.50	13.50	15.00	17.50
	1963	(1906)	12.50	14.50	16.50	20.00

14	VS1963	(1906)	11.50	12.50	14.50	16.50
	1964	(1907)	11.50	12.50	14.50	16.50
	1965	(1908)	11.50	12.50	14.50	16.50
	1966	(1909)	11.50	12.50	14.50	16.50
	1967	(1910)	11.50	13.00	15.00	17.50
	1968	(1911)	11.50	13.00	15.00	17.50
	1969	(1912)	11.50	13.00	15.00	17.50

NAZARANA RUPEE

SILVER, 10.70-11.60 g
Broad square flan

11a	VS1962	(1905)	40.00	55.00	70.00	100.00

Katar type.

14a	VS1966	(1909)	40.00	55.00	70.00	100.00
	1967	(1910)	40.00	55.00	70.00	100.00
	1968	(1911)	40.00	55.00	70.00	100.00
	1969	(1912)	40.00	55.00	70.00	100.00
	1970	(1913)	40.00	55.00	70.00	100.00

Round

14b	VS1967	(1910)	17.50	22.50	30.00	40.00
	1968	(1911)	17.50	22.50	30.00	40.00
	1969	(1912)	17.50	22.50	30.00	40.00

In the name of George V

PAISA

COPPER, rectangular or square, 5.00-5.35 g

Y#	Date	Year	Good	VG	Fine	VF
15	VS1973	(1916)	1.50	2.25	3.00	4.00
	1974	(1917)	1.50	2.25	3.00	4.00
	1976	(1919)	1.50	2.25	3.00	4.00
	1977	(1920)	1.50	2.25	3.00	4.00
	1981	(1924)	1.50	2.25	3.00	4.00
	1982	(1925)	1.50	2.25	3.00	4.00
	1983	(1926)	1.50	2.25	3.00	4.00
	1984	(1927)	1.50	2.25	3.00	4.00
	1986	(1929)	2.00	3.00	4.00	5.00
	1987	(1930)	2.00	3.00	4.00	5.00
	1990	(1933)	3.00	4.00	5.50	7.50
	1992	(1935)	3.00	4.00	5.50	7.50

NOTE: Size and weight vary.

1/4 RUPEE

SILVER, 2.60-2.70 g

Y#	Date	Year	VG	Fine	VF	XF
16	VS1972	(1915)	3.50	4.00	4.50	6.00
	1973	(1916)	3.50	4.00	4.50	6.00
	1974	(1917)	3.50	4.00	4.50	6.00
	1980	(1923)	3.50	4.00	4.50	6.00
	1981	(1924)	3.50	4.00	4.50	6.00
	1982	(1925)	3.50	4.00	4.50	6.00

13mm, similar to 1/2 Rupee, Y#19.

A19	VS1915(sic) 1925		25.00	35.00	40.00	60.00

1/2 RUPEE

SILVER, 5.30-5.40 g

Y#	Date	Year	VG	Fine	VF	XF
17	VS1972	(1915)	6.50	7.00	8.00	10.00
	1973	(1916)	6.50	7.00	8.00	10.00
	1974	(1917)	6.50	7.00	7.50	9.00
	1979	(1922)	6.50	7.00	7.50	9.00
	1980	(1923)	6.50	7.00	7.50	9.00
	1981	(1924)	6.50	7.00	7.50	9.00
	1982	(1925)	6.50	7.00	7.50	9.00
	1983	(1926)	6.50	7.00	7.50	9.00
	1984	(1927)	6.50	7.00	7.50	9.00

19	VS1915(sic) 1925		27.50	35.00	42.50	50.00

RUPEE

SILVER, 10.60-10.70 g

18	VS1972	(1915)	11.50	12.50	13.50	15.00
	1973	(1916)	11.50	12.50	13.50	15.00
	1974	(1917)	11.50	12.50	13.50	15.00
	1979	(1922)	11.50	12.50	13.50	15.00
	1980	(1923)	11.50	12.50	13.50	15.00
	1981	(1924)	11.50	12.50	13.50	15.00
	1982	(1925)	11.50	12.50	13.50	15.00
	1983	(1926)	11.50	12.50	13.50	15.00
	1984	(1927)	11.50	12.50	14.00	16.00
	1987	(1930)	11.50	12.50	14.00	16.00
	1989	(1932)	11.50	12.50	14.00	16.00
	Date off flan		5.50	6.50	7.00	8.00

20	VS1915(sic) 1925		60.00	75.00	100.00	125.00

NAZARANA RUPEE

SILVER, square, 10.50-11.70 g

18a	VS1965	(1908)	32.50	40.00	60.00	80.00
	1971	(1914)	32.50	40.00	60.00	80.00
	1975	(1918)	32.50	40.00	60.00	80.00
	1977	(1920)	32.50	40.00	60.00	80.00
	1979	(1922)	32.50	40.00	60.00	80.00
	1980	(1923)	32.50	40.00	60.00	80.00
	1981	(1924)	32.50	40.00	60.00	80.00
	1983	(1926)	32.50	40.00	60.00	80.00
	1984	(1927)	32.50	40.00	60.00	80.00
	1987	(1930)	32.50	40.00	60.00	80.00
	Date off flan		16.50	20.00	30.00	40.00
20a	VS1915(sic) 1925		75.00	90.00	125.00	150.00

CAMBAY

Khanbayat

Although of very ancient origins as a port, located at the head of the Gulf of Cambay in West India, Cambay did not come into existence as a separate state until about 1730 after the breakdown of Mughal authority in Delhi. The nawabs of Cambay traced their ancestry to Momin Khan II, the last of the Muslim governors of Gujerat. The State came under British control after two decades of Maratha rule.

RULERS

Hussain Yafar Khan
AH1257-1297/1841-1880AD
Ja'far Ali Khan
AH1297-1333/VS1937-1972/1880-1915AD

Mint: Khanbayat

HUSSAIN YAFAR KHAN

AH1257-1297/1841-1880AD

In the name of Shah Alam II

FALUS

COPPER
Obv. c/m: Persian *Shah* on irregular planchets.

Y#	Date	Year	Good	VG	Fine	VF
A1	ND	—	4.00	5.00	6.50	8.00

RUPEE

SILVER, 10.70-11.60 g

Y#	Date	Year	VG	Fine	VF	XF
1	AH1282	—	11.50	13.50	16.50	20.00
	1294	—	11.50	13.50	16.50	20.00

NOTE: Fractional denominations are reported to exist.

JA'FAR ALI KHAN

AH1297-1333/VS1937-1972/1880-1915AD

Anonymous

1/4 PAISA

COPPER
Obv. c/m: Persian *Shah*.

Y#	Date	Year	Good	VG	Fine	VF
2	ND	—	3.00	5.50	7.50	10.00

1/2 PAISA

COPPER, round
Obv. c/m: Persian *Shah*.

3	VS194x	—	3.00	5.50	7.50	9.00
	(19)62	(1905)	3.00	5.50	7.50	9.00

Square

3a	VS194x	—	3.00	5.50	7.50	9.00
	(19)62	(1905)	3.00	5.50	7.50	9.00

14-15mm
Rev: Denomination in words.

5	VS1963	(1906)	3.50	6.50	9.00	12.50
	1964	(1907)	3.50	6.50	9.00	12.50

Rev: Denomination in numerals.

5a	VS1964	(1907)	3.00	5.00	7.50	10.00
	1965	(1908)	3.00	5.00	7.50	10.00
	1966	(1909)	3.00	5.00	7.50	10.00

PAISA

COPPER, round
Obv. c/m: Persian *Shah*.

4	ND	—	1.25	2.00	3.00	4.25

Square

4a	ND	—	1.50	2.25	3.25	4.50

Cambay / INDIAN PRINCELY STATES

Y#	Date	Year	Good	VG	Fine	VF
6	VS1963	(1906)	1.00	1.50	2.00	3.50
	1964	(1907)	1.25	1.75	2.50	4.25
	1965	(1908)	1.00	1.50	2.00	3.50
	1966	(1909)	1.00	1.50	2.00	3.50
	1968	(1911)	1.00	1.50	2.00	3.50
	1970	(1913)	1.65	2.50	4.00	5.00

NOTE: Varieties exist.

In the name of Ja'far Ali Khan

1/8 RUPEE
SILVER, 11mm, 1.34-1.45 g

Y#	Date	Year	VG	Fine	VF	XF
7	AH1313	—	5.00	7.50	11.50	17.50

1/4 RUPEE

SILVER, 14mm, 2.68-2.90 g

8	AH1313	—	6.50	10.00	15.00	25.00

1/2 RUPEE

SILVER, 5.35-5.80 g

9	AH1313	17	12.50	14.00	20.00	27.50

RUPEE

SILVER, 10.70-11.60 g

10	AH1313	17	12.50	20.00	30.00	40.00
	1317	21	12.50	20.00	30.00	40.00
	1319	23	12.50	20.00	30.00	40.00

CANNANORE

Cannanore, on the Malabar Coast in southwest India was ruled by the Cherakal Rajas. Late in the eighteenth century it was overrun by Haider Ali, the Muslim ruler of Mysore. Then, in 1783, Cannanore was captured from Haider Ali's son, Tipu Sultan, by the East India Company. From that time onwards Cannanore was reduced to the status of a British tributary.

RULERS
Ali Rajas, Lord's of the deep.

1/5 RUPEE

SILVER, 2.14-2.32 g

C#	Date	Mintage	VG	Fine	VF	XF
10	AH1220	—	3.00	5.00	7.00	9.00
	1221	—	3.00	5.00	7.00	9.00
	1221	—	3.00	5.00	7.00	9.00
	1231	—	3.00	5.00	7.00	9.00
	1631 error for 1231					
		—	5.00	7.50	10.00	13.50

CHAMBA

The rulers of this mountainous state in north India, the origins of which go back as far as the sixth century, were Rajputs. Although Chamba was sometimes subject to the rulers of Kashmir, and later to the Mughals, even when nominally in subjection the remoteness of the region gave its rulers a considerable degree of autonomy. In 1846 the State came under British protection and in 1948 was merged into Himachal Pradesh.

RULERS
Charhat Singh, 1808-1844AD
Lakar Shah of Basoli, rebel, 1844AD
Sri Singh, 1844-1870AD
Sham Singh, 1870-1904AD

Mint mark:

CHARHAT SINGH
1808-1844AD
PAISA

COPPER

C#	Date	Year	Good	VG	Fine	VF
15	AH—	15	4.00	7.00	10.00	14.00
	—	16	4.00	7.00	10.00	14.00
	—	17	4.00	7.00	10.00	14.00
	ND		3.00	4.50	6.50	8.00

LAKAR SHAH OF BASOLI
Rebel, 1844AD
PAISA

COPPER, 18-22mm
Obv: W/o trident below leg.

20	ND	—	5.00	8.00	11.00	15.00

SRI SINGH
1844-1870AD
PAISA

COPPER
c/m: Trident on 1 Paisa, C#20.

23	ND	—	7.50	15.00	25.00	40.00

Crude, degenerate copy of C#15

25	ND	—	2.75	4.00	5.50	7.50

NOTE: C#25 was also struck during the reign of Shah Singh, 1870-1904AD. It is also found struck over C#15.

CHHOTA UDAIPUR

Formerly one of the non-Aryan-Chota Nagpur states located in Bengal, Chhota Udaipur originated in the late fifteenth century. Its founders were Chauhan Rajputs who, having been expelled from Ajmer, finally re-established themselves in Chhota Udaipur. The rulers were known as Maharawals, and by the nineteenth century became related to the British in India by the usual treaties.

RULERS
Guman Singhji
  SE1744-1773/1822-1851AD
Jitsinghji
  SE1773-1803/VS1908-1938/1851-1881AD
Motisinghji
  VS1938-1952/1881-1905AD

GUMAN SINGHJI
SE1744-1773/1822-1851AD
PAISA

COPPER, 7.40 g

KM#	Date	Year	Good	VG	Fine	VF
10	—	—	4.00	6.00	8.50	11.50

2 PAISA

COPPER, 13.40-14.00 g

KM#	Date	Year	Good	VG	Fine	VF
15.1	SE(1)765	(1843)	3.50	5.50	7.50	10.00
	1767	(1845)	3.50	5.50	7.50	10.00

15.2	SE1797	(1875)	3.50	5.50	7.50	10.00

15.3	ND	—	3.50	5.50	7.50	10.00

JITSINGHJI
SE1773-1803/VS1908-1938/1851-1881AD
PAISA

COPPER, 22mm, 7.40 g

Y#	Date	Year	Good	VG	Fine	VF
1	SE1787	(1865)	2.50	4.50	6.50	8.50

2 PAISA

 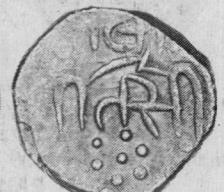

COPPER, 13.40-14.00 g

2	SE1787	—	5.50	7.00	9.00	12.00

3	VS1919	(1862)	7.00	9.00	12.00	16.50
	1924	(1867)	7.00	9.00	12.00	16.50

MOTISINGHJI
VS1938-1952/1881-1905AD
PAISA

COPPER, 7.40 g

4	VS1948	(1891)	6.00	7.50	10.00	13.50

2 PAISA

COPPER, 13.40-14.00 g

5	VS1948	(1891)	5.00	6.50	8.50	11.50

CIS - SUTLEJ STATES

The name Cis-Sutlej States was applied to those states in the tract of land south of the Sutlej and to the north of the Delhi territory. Before 1846 the majority of these chieftains were substantially independent, subject only to the general oversight of an agent of the Governor-General. After the first Sikh war (1845-1846) this independence became somewhat circumscribed and in 1849 the Punjab was annexed and the Cis-Sutlej States were merged into the new province of British India. Perhaps surprisingly, most of these States distinguished themselves on the side of the British during the Great Revolt of 1857.

HANSI
RULER
Raja George Thomas

MINT

Sahibabad

RUPEE

SILVER
Obv: Umbrella. Rev: Sunface.

KM#	Date	Year	VG	Fine	VF	XF
1	AH1214	42	—	—	Rare	—

JIND

State located in the southern Punjab and north Haryana states.

The ruling princes belonged to the same Jat family as the maharajas of Patiala. Like them they traced their ancestry back to Baryam, a revenue collector under Babur (1526). The State was founded by Gajpat Singh after he took part in the Sikh uprising against the Afghan governor of Sirhind in 1763. One of Gajpat Singh's daughters became the mother of Ranjit Singh.

RULERS
Bhag Singh, 1786-1819AD
Sangat Singh, 1822-1834AD
Sarup Singh, 1834-1864AD
Raghbir Singh, 1864-1887AD
Ranbir Singh, VS1943- /1887AD

NOTE: These are believed to have been struck for Gajpat Singh, Sangat Singh and Sarup Singh and are not distinguishable.

Identifying Marks:

On reverse

RAGHBIR SINGH
1864-1887AD

RUPEE
SILVER, 18mm, 10.70-11.60 g
Rev: Similar to 1 Rupee, KM#1 but finer style.

Y#	Date	Year	VG	Fine	VF	XF
1	AH—	4 (frozen)	20.00	30.00	40.00	60.00

MALER KOTLA

State located in the Punjab in northwest India, founded by the Maler Kotla family who were Sherwani Afghans who had travelled to India from Kabul in 1467 as officials of the Delhi emperors.

Coins are imitations of a rupee of Ahmad Shah Durrani, year 4, struck at the Sirhind mint, and except for the last ruler, contain the chief's initial on the reverse. The chiefs were called Ra'is until 1821, Nawabs thereafter.

For similar issues see Patiala.

RULERS
Amir Khan
  AH1237-1261/1821-1845AD
Sube (Mah bub) Khan
  AH1261-1276/1845-1859AD
Sikandar Ali Khan
  AH1276-1288/1859-1871AD
Ibrahim Ali Khan
  AH1288-1326/1871-1908AD
Ahmad Ali Khan
  AH1326-/1908-AD

AMIR KHAN
AH1237-1261/1821-1845AD
Identifying Marks:

On reverse

1/4 RUPEE

SILVER, 2.68-2.90 g

C#	Date	Year	VG	Fine	VF	XF
13	AH—	4 (frozen)	6.50	10.00	15.00	22.50

1/2 RUPEE
SILVER, 16mm, 5.35-5.80 g

14	AH—	4 (frozen)	6.50	10.00	15.00	22.50

RUPEE

SILVER, 17mm, 10.70-11.60 g

15	AH—	4 (frozen)	6.50	9.00	11.50	15.00

SUBE (Mahbub) KHAN
AH1261-1276/1845-1859AD
Identifying Marks:

On reverse

1/2 RUPEE
SILVER, 15mm, 5.35-5.80 g

19	AH—	4 (frozen)	10.00	15.00	20.00	30.00

RUPEE

SILVER, 10.70-11.60 g

20	ND	—	7.50	10.00	12.50	20.00

SIKANDAR ALI KHAN
AH1276-1288/1859-1871AD
Identifying Marks:

On reverse

1/4 RUPEE

SILVER, 2.68-2.90 g

Y#	Date	Year	VG	Fine	VF	XF
1	ND	—	6.00	10.00	15.00	25.00

1/2 RUPEE

SILVER, 5.35-5.80 g

2	ND	—	6.00	10.00	15.00	25.00

RUPEE

SILVER, 10.70-11.60 g

Y#	Date	Year	VG	Fine	VF	XF
3	ND	—	6.50	9.00	11.50	16.50

IBRAHIM ALI KHAN
AH1288-1326/1871-1908AD
Identifying Marks:

On reverse

1/4 RUPEE

SILVER, 2.68-2.90 g

4	ND	—	6.50	10.00	15.00	25.00

1/2 RUPEE
SILVER, 16mm, 5.35-5.80 g

5	ND	—	6.50	10.00	15.00	25.00

RUPEE

SILVER, 10.70-11.60 g

6	ND	—	6.50	9.00	11.50	16.50
	AH1292	—	12.50	15.00	20.00	35.00
	1311	—	12.50	15.00	20.00	35.00

AHMAD ALI KHAN
AH1326-/1908-AD
Identifying Marks:

On reverse

1/2 PAISA

COPPER

Y#	Date	Year	Good	VG	Fine	VF
7	ND	—	2.50	5.00	8.00	15.00

PAISA

COPPER

8	AH3126 (error for 1326)		4.50	7.50	10.00	17.50

RUPEE

SILVER, 10.70-11.60 g

Y#	Date	Year	VG	Fine	VF	XF
9	ND	—	6.50	9.00	11.50	16.50

NAZARANA RUPEE

SILVER, 10.70-11.60 g

Y#	Date	Year	VG	Fine	VF	XF
10	AH1326	—	—	—	Rare	—

NABHA

State located in the Punjab in northwest India and founded in the 18th century.

The ancestry of these rulers was identical to that of Jind. Until 1845 Nabha's history closely paralleled that of Patiala. At this point, however, the raja sided with the Sikhs. It was left to his son to make amends to the British in 1847.

RULERS

Jaswant Singh
  VS1840-1897/1783-1840AD
Bharpur Singh
  VS1903-1920/1846-1863AD
Hira Singh
  VS1927-1968/1870-1911AD

MINT MARKS

Nabha نابها or نابهه

JASWANT SINGH
VS1840-1897/1783-1840AD

Identifying Marks:

On reverse.

RUPEE

SILVER, 10.70-11.60 g
Rev: Cross-like symbol below *Sin*.

C#	Date	Year	VG	Fine	VF	XF
20.1	ND	—	20.00	30.00	40.00	55.00

Rev: Star below *Sin*.

| 20.2 | VS(18)77 | (1820) | 20.00 | 30.00 | 40.00 | 55.00 |

Rev: Branch symbol.

20.3	VS(18)82	(1825)	20.00	30.00	40.00	55.00
	83	(1826)	20.00	30.00	40.00	55.00
	93	(1836)	20.00	30.00	40.00	55.00

NAZARANA RUPEE

SILVER

C#	Date	Year	VG	Fine	VF	XF
25	VS1893	(1836)	—	—	Rare	—

BHARPUR SINGH
VS1903-1920/1846-1863AD

Identifying Marks:

On reverse

In the name of Govind Singh, Sikh Saint

RUPEE

SILVER, 10.70-11.60 g
Rev: Leaf to left of stylized '4'.

Y#	Date	Year	VG	Fine	VF	XF
1	VS1907	(1850)	15.00	25.00	40.00	55.00
	1913	(1856)	15.00	25.00	40.00	55.00
	1917	(1860)	15.00	25.00	40.00	55.00
	1920	(1863)	15.00	25.00	40.00	55.00

MOHUR

GOLD, 10.70-11.60 g

| A2 | VS1907 | (1850) | — | — | — | — |

HIRA SINGH
VS1927-1968/1870-1911AD

Identifying Marks:

On reverse

RUPEE

SILVER, 10.70-11.60 g
Rev: Katar to left of stylized '4'.

2	VS1927	(1870)	15.00	25.00	40.00	55.00
	1928	(1871)	15.00	25.00	40.00	55.00
	1929	(1872)	15.00	25.00	40.00	55.00

PATIALA

State located in the Punjab in northwest India. In the mid-18th century the Raja was given his title and mint right by Ahmad Shah Durrani of Afghanistan, whose coin he copied.

The rulers became Maharajas in 1810AD. The maharaja of Patiala was also recognized as the leader of the Phulkean tribe. Although Patiala's ruling family were Sikhs, they stemmed from the same Jat stock as the rulers of Jind and Nabha. Unlike others, however, Patiala's Sikh rulers had never hesitated to seek British assistance at those times when they felt threatened by their co-religionist neighbors. In 1857 Patiala's forces were immediately made available on the side of the British.

RULERS

Sahib Singh
  AH1196-1229/1781-1813AD
Karm Singh
  AH1229-1261/1813-1845AD
Narindar Singh
  VS1902-1919/1845-1862AD
Mahindar Singh
  VS1919-1933/1862-1876AD
Rajindar Singh
  VS1933-1957/1876-1900AD
Bhupindra Singh
  VS1958-1995/1900-1937AD
Yadvindra Singh
  VS1994-2005/1937-1948AD

MINT

Sirhind سهرند

KARM SINGH
AH1229-1261/1813-1845AD

Identifying Marks:

On reverse

1/4 RUPEE

SILVER, 2.68-2.90 g

C#	Date	Year	VG	Fine	VF	XF
28	AH—	—	10.00	15.00	20.00	30.00

RUPEE

SILVER, 10.70-11.60 g
Rev: W/o symbols around.

| 30.1 | AH— | — | 12.50 | 15.00 | 22.50 | 32.50 |

Rev: *Alif* to left of

| 30.2 | AH— | — | 12.50 | 15.00 | 22.50 | 32.50 |

Rev: Crescent to right of

| 30.3 | AH— | — | 12.50 | 15.00 | 22.50 | 32.50 |

Rev: Three-pointed leaf to right of

| 30.4 | AH— | — | 12.50 | 15.00 | 22.50 | 32.50 |

Rev: Crescent to right, branch to left of

| 30.5 | AH— | — | 12.50 | 15.00 | 22.50 | 32.50 |

Rev: Branch to right of

| 30.6 | AH— | — | 12.50 | 15.00 | 22.50 | 32.50 |

C#	Date	Year	VG	Fine	VF	XF
30.7	AH—		12.50	15.00	22.50	32.50

Rev: Branches both sides of ص

Rev: Scimitar to left of ص

| 31 | AH— | | 13.50 | 20.00 | 30.00 | 45.00 |

NAZARANA RUPEE
SILVER, 24mm, 10.70-11.60 g

| 30a | VS(18)98(1841) | | — | Rare | — | |

MOHUR

GOLD, 10.70-11.60 g

| 35 | AH— | | 175.00 | 225.00 | 265.00 | 300.00 |

NARINDAR SINGH
VS1902-1919/1845-1862AD
Identifying Marks:

On reverse

1/4 RUPEE

SILVER, 2.67-2.90 g

Y#	Date	Year	VG	Fine	VF	XF
A1	ND	—	15.00	27.50	40.00	55.00

RUPEE

SILVER, 10.70-11.60 g

| 1 | VS1902 (1845) | | 15.00 | 27.50 | 40.00 | 55.00 |

w/Sikh leg.

| 3 | ND | | | | | |

MOHUR

GOLD, 17-18mm, 10.70-11.40 g

| 2 | AH— | | 175.00 | 225.00 | 265.00 | 300.00 |

MAHINDAR SINGH
VS1919-1933/1862-1876AD
Identifying Marks:

On reverse

RUPEE

SILVER, 16-17mm, 10.70-11.60 g

| 3 | AH— | | 25.00 | 35.00 | 50.00 | 70.00 |

RAJINDAR SINGH
VS1933-1957/1876-1900AD
Identifying Marks:

On reverse

1/4 RUPEE
SILVER, 13mm, 2.68-2.90 g

Y#	Date	Year	VG	Fine	VF	XF
4	AH—		10.00	15.00	25.00	40.00

1/2 RUPEE
SILVER, 16mm, 5.35-5.80 g

| 5 | AH— | | 10.00 | 15.00 | 25.00 | 40.00 |

RUPEE

SILVER, 10.70-11.60 g

6	VS(19)45	4	15.00	22.50	35.00	50.00
	(19)46	4	15.00	22.50	35.00	50.00
	(19)47	4	15.00	22.50	35.00	50.00
	(19)48	4	17.50	27.50	40.00	60.00

NAZARANA RUPEE

SILVER, 10.70-11.60 g

| 6a | AH— | 4 (frozen) | — | — | Rare | — |

MOHUR

GOLD, 18mm, 10.70-11.40 g

| 9 | ND | — | 160.00 | 200.00 | 275.00 | 375.00 |
| | VS(19)48(1891) | | 160.00 | 200.00 | 275.00 | 375.00 |

BHUPINDRA SINGH
VS1958-1995/1900-1937AD

1/3 MOHUR
(4 Mashas)

GOLD, 3.57-3.80 g
Rev: Katar at left.

KM#	Date	Year	VG	Fine	VF	XF
15	VS(19)50(1893)		85.00	100.00	125.00	175.00

2/3 MOHUR
(8 Mashas)

GOLD, 18mm, 7.14-7.60 g
Rev: Katar at left.

Y#	Date	Year	VG	Fine	VF	XF
16	VS(19)58(1901)		125.00	140.00	165.00	225.00

YADVINDRA SINGH
VS1994-2005/1937-1948AD

1/6 MOHUR
(2 Mashas)

GOLD, 1.78-1.90 g
Rev: Bayoneted rifle at left.

| 19 | (19)94 (1937) | | | | | |

1/3 MOHUR
(4 Mashas)

GOLD, 3.57-3.80 g
Rev: Bayoneted rifle at left.

KM#	Date	Year	VG	Fine	VF	XF
20	VS(19)94(1937)		75.00	100.00	125.00	165.00

2/3 MOHUR
(8 Mashas)

GOLD, 18mm, 7.14-7.60 g
Rev: Bayoneted rifle at left.

Y#	Date	Year	VG	Fine	VF	XF
21	VS(19)94(1937)		150.00	185.00	210.00	250.00

UNCERTAIN ISSUES
Possibly early twentieth century.
Identifying Marks:

On reverse

RUPEE

SILVER, 10.70-11.60 g

KM#	Date	Year	VG	Fine	VF	XF
1	AH—	4 (frozen)	10.00	13.50	20.00	35.00

DATIA

State located in north-central India, governed by Maharajas.

Datia was founded in 1735 by Bhagwan Das, son of Narsingh Dea of the Orchha royal house. In 1804 the State concluded its first treaty with the East India Company and thereafter came under British protection and control.

RULERS
Parachat
  AH1217-1255/1802-1839AD
Vijaya Bahadur
  AH1255-1274/1839-1857AD
Bhawani Singh
  AH1274-1325/1857-1907AD
Govind Singh
  AH1325-1368/1907-1948AD

MINT

Dalipnagar

Gaja Shahi Series
Struck for more than 100 years, with AH date on obverse and frozen regnal year on reverse. These are close copies of Orchha C#24-32 and can only be distinguished by the symbols, which are always different from those of Orchha, except for the Gaja (mace):

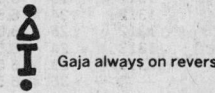

Gaja always on reverse

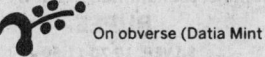

On obverse (Datia Mint Symbol)

On reverse

1/2 PAISA

COPPER, 6.00 g

C#	Date	Year	Good	VG	Fine	VF
22	AH—	4x	2.50	3.50	5.00	7.50
	1320	—	3.00	4.50	6.50	10.00

Datia

PAISA

COPPER, round or squarish, 12.00-13.00 g

C#	Date	Year	Good	VG	Fine	VF
23	AH1246	3x	2.50	3.25	4.00	5.50
	—	39	2.50	3.25	4.00	5.50
	1278	45	2.50	3.25	4.00	5.50
	1320	46	2.50	3.25	4.00	5.50

1/8 RUPEE

SILVER, 1.34-1.45 g

C#	Date	Year	VG	Fine	VF	XF
35	AH—	22	3.00	6.00	10.00	15.00
	—	4x	3.00	6.00	10.00	15.00

1/4 RUPEE

SILVER, 2.68-2.90 g

36	AH1317	23	4.50	6.50	9.00	15.00

1/2 RUPEE

SILVER, 5.35-5.80 g

37	AH1311	19	5.50	8.50	12.50	20.00
	—	23	5.50	8.50	12.50	20.00
	—	29	5.50	8.50	12.50	20.00

RUPEE

SILVER, 10.70-11.60 g

38	AH1215	23	6.50	9.00	11.50	16.50
	1233	24	6.50	9.00	11.50	16.50
	1233	28	6.50	9.00	11.50	16.50
	1249	28	6.50	9.00	11.50	16.50
	1262	29	6.50	9.00	11.50	16.50
	1270	36	6.50	9.00	11.50	16.50
	1271	37	6.50	9.00	11.50	16.50
	1272	38	6.50	9.00	11.50	16.50
	1273	39	6.50	9.00	11.50	16.50
	1277	44	6.50	9.00	11.50	16.50
	1278	45	6.50	9.00	11.50	16.50
	1282	46	6.50	9.00	11.50	16.50
	1311	19	6.50	9.00	11.50	16.50
	1312	24	6.50	9.00	11.50	16.50
	1312	25	6.50	9.00	11.50	16.50
	1313	24	6.50	9.00	11.50	16.50
	1315	23	6.50	9.00	11.50	16.50
	—	35	6.50	9.00	11.50	16.50

In the name of Muhammad Akbar II

RUPEE

SILVER, 10.70-11.60 g

45	AH1270	33	12.50	17.50	25.00	35.00

DEWAS JUNIOR BRANCH

A Maratha state located in west-central India. The raja, the brother of the raja of Dewas Senior Branch had a palace in Dewas City. They descended from two brothers, Tukoji and Jiwaji who were given Dewas City in 1726 by Peshwa Baji Rao as a reward for army services.

Largely due to its geographical location Dewas suffered much at the hands of the armies of Holkar and Sindhia, and from Pindari incursions. In 1818 the State came under British protection.

LOCAL RULERS

Narayan Rao, 1864-1892

NARAYAN RAO
1864-1892AD

1/12 ANNA

COPPER

KM#	Date	Mintage	Fine	VF	XF	Unc
1	1888	.112	15.00	25.00	35.00	50.00
	1888	—	—	—	Proof	125.00

1/4 ANNA

COPPER

3	1888	.484	13.50	22.50	32.50	45.00
	1888	—	—	—	Proof	150.00

SILVER (OMS)

| 3a | 1888 | (restrike) | — | — | Proof | 125.00 |

DEWAS SENIOR BRANCH

A Maratha state located in west-central India. The raja, the brother of the raja of Dewas Junior Branch had a palace in Dewas city. They descended from two brothers, Tukoji and Jiwaji who were given Dewas City in 1726 by Peshwa Baji Rao as a reward for army services.

Largely due to its geographical location Dewas suffered much at the hands of the armies of Holkar and Sindhia, and from Pindari incursions. In 1818 the State came under British protection.

LOCAL RULERS

Krishnaji Rao, 1860-1899AD
Vikrama Simha Rao, 1937-1948AD

ALLOTE MINT
PAISA

COPPER

KM#	Date	Good	VG	Fine	VF
10		2.50	3.50	5.00	7.00

NOTE: Varieties exist.

REGAL ISSUES
Milled Coinage
1/12 ANNA

COPPER

KM#	Date	Mintage	Fine	VF	XF	Unc
11	1888	.112	8.00	12.50	18.50	28.50
	1888	—	—	—	Proof	125.00

SILVER (OMS)

| 11a | 1888 | (restrike) | — | — | Proof | 100.00 |

1/4 ANNA

COPPER

12	1888	.484	8.00	12.50	20.00	30.00
	1888	—	—	—	Proof	150.00

VIKRAMA SIMHA RAO
1937-1948AD

PAISA

COPPER

KM#	Date	Year	Fine	VF	XF	Unc
13	VS2000	1944	45.00	60.00	80.00	100.00
	2001	1944	45.00	60.00	80.00	100.00

DHAR

The territory in central India in which Dhar was located had been controlled by the Paramara clan of Rajputs from the ninth century to the thirteenth, after which it passed into Muslim hands. The modern Princely State of Dhar originated in the first half of the eighteenth century when the Maratha Peshwa, Baji Rao, handed over the region as a fiefdom to Anand Rao Ponwar. Anand Rao Ponwar was of the same stock as the rulers of Dewas and a descendant of the original Paramara Rajputs. Sometimes in conflict with Holkar, sometimes with Sindhia, in 1819 Dhar came under British protection. No silver or gold coinage was ever struck at Dhar. In 1895 the British silver rupee was adopted.

LOCAL RULERS

Jaswant Rao
  AH1250-1274/1834-1857AD
Anand Rao III
  AH1276-1316/1860-1898AD
Anand Rao IV
  AH1363-1368/1943-1948AD

JASWANT RAO
AH1250-1274/1834-1857AD

PAISA

COPPER

KM#	Date	Year	Good	VG	Fine	VF
2	ND	—	2.50	4.00	6.50	9.00

| 1 | AH1266 | — | 2.50 | 4.00 | 6.50 | 9.00 |

ANAND RAO III
AH1276-1316/1860-1898AD

1/2 PAISA

COPPER, 16mm

5	AH1289	—	3.00	5.00	9.00	15.00

PAISA

COPPER

6	AH1289	—	1.25	2.00	3.50	6.50

Milled Coinage
1/12 ANNA

COPPER

KM#	Date	Mintage	Fine	VF	XF	Unc
11	1887	—	4.00	6.50	9.00	13.50
	1887	—	—	—	Proof	125.00

SILVER (OMS)

| 11a | 1887 | (restrike) | — | — | Proof | 100.00 |

GOLD (OMS)

| 11b | 1887 | (restrike) | — | — | Proof | — |

1/2 PICE

COPPER

KM#	Date	Mintage	Fine	VF	XF	Unc
12	1887	—	3.50	5.50	9.00	13.50
	1887	—	—	—	Proof	150.00

SILVER (OMS)

12a	1887	(restrike)	—	—	Proof	125.00

GOLD (OMS)

12b	1887	(restrike)	—	—	Proof	450.00

1/4 ANNA

COPPER

13	1887	—	4.50	8.00	12.50	22.50
	1887	—	—	—	Proof	175.00

SILVER (OMS)

13a	1887	(restrike)	—	—	Proof	150.00

GOLD (OMS)

13b	1887	(restrike)	—	—	Proof	650.00

DHOLPUR

State located in Rajputana, northwest India.

Dholpur had a varied and turbulent history. From the eighth until the twelfth centuries it was ruled by Tonwar Rajputs. Early in the sixteenth century the entire region came under the Mughals. It was included by Akbar in Agra province. With Mughal decline after 1707, Dholpur experienced many masters until, in 1782, it fell into the hands of Sindhia. In 1803 the territory was captured by the British and in 1805 it was returned to the ranas of Gohad, Bamraolia Jats, from whom it had earlier been wrested by Sindhia. The ranas of Gohad opened the mint which operated until 1857.

RULER

Kirat Singh
AH1203-1221 / 1788-1806AD, in Gohad
AH1221-1251 / 1806-1837AD, in Dholpur

DHOLPUR MINT

Mint marks:

On obverse

On reverse Type 1   or Type 2

In the name of Muhammad Akbar II
AH1221-1253 / 1806-1837AD

RUPEE

SILVER, 10.70-11.60 g

C#	Date	Year	VG	Fine	VF	XF
12.1	AH1221	—	20.00	27.50	35.00	50.00
	1225	4	20.00	27.50	35.00	50.00

12.2	AH1226	5	20.00	27.50	35.00	50.00
	1228	—	20.00	27.50	35.00	50.00
	—	17	20.00	27.50	35.00	50.00
	—	19	20.00	27.50	35.00	50.00
	—	21	20.00	27.50	35.00	50.00

GOHAD MINT

Mint marks:

 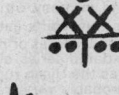
On obverse   or

reverse   or

In the name of Shah Alam II
AH1173-1221 / 1759-1806AD

RUPEE

SILVER, 10.70-11.60 g
Obv: Pistol.

C#	Date	Year	VG	Fine	VF	XF
5	AH1218	46	15.00	25.00	40.00	60.00

RUPEE

Rev: Pistol.

6	AH1245	24	15.00	25.00	40.00	60.00

In the name of Muhammad Akbar II
AH1221-1253 / 1806-1837AD

1/2 RUPEE

SILVER, 5.35-5.80 g

11	AH—	—	14.00	20.00	30.00	40.00

RUPEE

SILVER, 10.70-11.60 g

12a.1	AH1247	26	15.00	25.00	40.00	60.00
	1250	29	15.00	25.00	40.00	60.00
	1251	30	15.00	25.00	40.00	60.00

Rev: Pistol and leaf.

12a.2	AH1252	31	15.00	25.00	40.00	60.00

NOTE: Actually struck in AH1274/1857AD.

NAZARANA RUPEE

SILVER, 10.70-11.60 g
Rev: Pistol and leaf.

12b.2	AH1252	31	50.00	75.00	100.00	150.00

NOTE: Actually struck in AH1274/1857 AD.

MOHUR

GOLD, 10.70-11.60 g
Rev: Pistol and leaf.

15	AH1252	31	—	—	Rare	—

NOTE: Actually struck in AH1274/1857 AD.

DUNGARPUR

A district in northwest India which became part of Rajasthan in 1948.

The maharawals of Dungarpur were descended from the Mewar chieftains of the twelfth century. In 1527 the upper Mahi basin was bifurcated to form the Princely States of Dungarpur and Banswara. Thereafter Dungarpur came successively under Mughal and Maratha control until in 1818 it came under British protection.

RULERS

Bijey Singh
VS1955-1975 / 1898-1918AD
Lakshman Singh
VS1975-2005 / 1918-1948AD

BIJEY SINGH
VS1955-1975 / 1898-1918AD

1/4 PAISA

COPPER, 2.50 g

KM#	Date	Year	Good	VG	Fine	VF
1	VS1917	(1860)	3.50	5.50	8.00	11.50

PAISA

COPPER, 10.35 g

Y#	Date	Year	Good	VG	Fine	VF
A1	VS1911	—	3.00	5.00	7.50	10.00
	1917	(1860)	3.00	5.00	7.50	10.00

LAKSHMAN SINGH
VS1975-2005 / 1918-1948AD

PAISA

COPPER
Rev: 2 bars above *P* of *Paisa*.

Y#	Date	Year	VG	Fine	VF	XF
1.1	VS2001	(1944)	25.00	30.00	37.50	45.00

NOTE: Varieties exist.

Rev: One bar above *P* of *Paisa*.

1.2	VS2001	(1944)	6.50	9.00	12.50	16.50

NOTE: Believed to be a restrike by some authorities.

FARRUKHABAD

Refer to Independent Kingdoms during British rule.

GWALIOR

Sindhia

State located in central India. Capital originally was Ujjain (= Daru-I-fath), but was later transferred to Gwalior in 1810AD.

RULERS

The Gwalior ruling family, the Sindhias, were descendants of the Maratha chief Ranoji Sindhia (d. 1750). His youngest son, Mahadji Sindhia (d. 1794) was anxious to establish his independence from the overlordship of the Peshwas of Poona. Unable to achieve this alone, it was the Peshwa's crushing defeat by Ahmad Shah Durrani at Panipat in 1761 which helped realize his ambitions. Largely in the interests of sustaining this autonomy, but partly as a result of a defeat at East India Company hands in 1781, Mahadji concluded an alliance with the British in 1782. In 1785, he reinstalled the fallen Mughal Emperor, Shah Alam, on the throne at Delhi. Very early in the nineteenth century, Gwalior's relationship with the British began to deteriorate, a situation which culminated in the Anglo-Maratha War of 1803. Gwalior's force under Daulat Rao were defeated. In consequence, and by the terms of the peace treaty which followed, his territory was truncated. In 1818 Gwalior suffered a further loss of land at British hands. In the years that ensued, as the East India Company's possessions became transformed into empire and as the Pax Britannica swept across the subcontinent, the Sindhia family's relationship with their British overlords steadily improved.

Daulat Rao
  AH1209-1243 / 1794-1827AD
Baija Bai, Regent,
  (Widow of Daulat Rao)
  AH1243-1249 / 1827-1833AD
Jankoji Rao
  AH1243-1259 / 1827-1843AD
Jayaji Rao
  AH1259-1304 / 1843-1886AD
Madho Rao
  VS1943-1982 / 1886-1925AD
Jivaji Rao
  VS1982-2005 / 1925-1948AD

Gwalior / INDIAN PRINCELY STATES

Jivaji Rao
VS1982-2005/1925-1948AD

MINTS

Bajranggarh "Jaynagar"	जयनगर
Basoda	بسودہ
Bhilsa "Alamgirpur"	عالم گیرپور
Broach	بروچ
Burhanpur	برہانپور
Dohad	دوہاد
Garhakota "Ravishnagar Sagar"	روش نگر ساگر
Gwalior Fort	گوالیار
Isagarh	عیسی گڑہ
Jhansi "Balwantnagar"	بلونت نگر
Rajod	راجوڑ
Rathgarh "Daulatgarh"	دولت گڑہ
Shadhorah	شاد ہورہ
Sheopur	شیو پور
Sipri "Narwar"	نروار
Ujjain, dar ul Fateh	دارالفتح اجین

NOTE: None of the coins of Gwalior prior to the beginning of machine-struck coinage in 1889AD bears the name of the Sindhia (ruler of Gwalior), but beginning with the reign of Baija Bao, a Nagari letter is used to indicate the ruler under whom it was struck, as follows:

Sri	श्री	Baija Bao
Jo	जे	Jankoji Rao
Ji	जी	Jayaji Rao
Ma	मा	Madho Rao

However, not all the coins bear the initial of the ruler, especially the copper.

The coinage of Gwalior is extremely complicated and not fully understood. Each mint, and there were probably more than twenty in all, maintained its own styles and types, and operated fully independently of every other mint. Hence it is most logical to list the issues of each mint together, rather than attempt to list the coins by reign or denomination. The mints are best identified by the presence of special symbols on the obverse or reverse of the coins, and those symbols are noted whenever possible. Types are listed with designation of reign only when the initial of the ruler appears on the coin; others are assigned a single number for the full duration of their issuance.

Most of the coins of Gwalior are undated, or issued over long periods of time with frozen dates, in order to discourage the nefarious practice of devaluing coins of older dates (for example, one-year old coins might be devalued 1 percent, two-year olds 2 percent, and so forth). Many of the types were struck with frozen dates for several decades, and in many other cases, the dates remained frozen while the ruler's initial changed. The frozen dates may be either AH dates or regnal years, or both.

Regularly dated series often continued over long durations, such as the Ujjain rupees (C#259); the lists of such coins are probably very fragmentary, and many unlisted dates will be discovered. In general, unlisted dates are worth no more than listed dates of the same type.

BAJRANGGARH MINT

For coins issued by Jai Singh, AH1213-1233 refer to Bajranggarh State listings.

AJIT SINGH
AH1235-1274/1819-1857AD

Mintmark: जयनगर

Types of Jai Singh with added mintmarks

 Lotus   Bow and arrow

1/8 RUPEE
SILVER, 16mm, 1.34-1.45 g
Similar to 1 Rupee, KM#16.

KM#	Date	Year	VG	Fine	VF	XF
12 (C9)	ND	—	4.00	6.50	10.00	15.00

1/4 RUPEE

SILVER, 2.68-2.90 g

| 13 (C10) | ND | — | 6.50 | 10.00 | 15.00 | 22.50 |

1/2 RUPEE

SILVER, 5.35-5.80 g

| 14 (C11) | ND | — | 7.50 | 10.00 | 15.00 | 22.50 |

RUPEE
SILVER, 10.70-11.60 g
Rev: Lotus.

| 15 (C12) | AH— | 21 | 10.00 | 15.00 | 21.50 | 30.00 |
| | | 22 | 10.00 | 15.00 | 21.50 | 30.00 |

Obv: Bow and arrow. Rev: Lotus.

16 (C12a)	AH	23	9.00	12.50	17.50	25.00
	—	24	9.00	12.50	17.50	25.00
		25	9.00	12.50	17.50	25.00
		26	9.00	12.50	17.50	25.00
		27	9.00	12.50	17.50	25.00
		28	9.00	12.50	17.50	25.00
		29	9.00	12.50	17.50	25.00
	ND	NRY	9.00	12.50	17.50	25.00

NAZARANA MOHUR
GOLD, octagonal, 10.70-11.40 g

| 17 (C13) | ND | — | 225.00 | 250.00 | 300.00 | 375.00 |

BASODA MINT

Daulat Rao
AH1209-1243/1794-1827AD
In the name of Muhammad Akbar II
AH1221-1253/1806-1837AD

Mint marks:

RUPEE

SILVER, 10.70-11.60 g

KM#	Date	Year	VG	Fine	VF	XF
18 (C20)	AH124x	18	12.50	17.50	23.50	35.00

JANKOJI RAO
AH1243-1259/1833-1843AD
In the name of Muhammad Akbar II
AH1221-1253/1806-1837AD
and Jankoji Rao

With additional marks

RUPEE

SILVER, 10.70-11.60 g

| 19.1 (C20) | AH1252 | 32 | 12.50 | 17.50 | 23.50 | 35.00 |
| | 1254 | 32 | 12.50 | 17.50 | 23.50 | 35.00 |

JAYAJI RAO
AH1259-1304/1843-1886AD
In the name of Muhammad Akbar II
AH1221-1253/1806-1837AD
and Jankoji Rao

RUPEE

SILVER, 10.70-11.60 g

| 19.2 (C20) | AH1274 | 3x | 12.50 | 17.50 | 23.50 | 35.00 |
| | 1274 | 46 | 12.50 | 17.50 | 23.50 | 35.00 |

BHILSA MINT

DAULAT RAO
AH1209-1243/1794-1827AD
In the name of Muhammad Akbar II
AH1221-1253/1806-1837AD

1/8 RUPEE
SILVER

| A20 | — | — | 15.00 | 20.00 | 30.00 | 45.00 |

1/4 RUPEE

SILVER, 2.68-2.90 g

| 20 | AH— | 16 | 3.50 | 4.50 | 5.50 | 7.50 |

1/2 RUPEE

SILVER, 5.35-5.80 g

| 21 | AH— | 15 | 5.00 | 7.50 | 9.00 | 12.50 |

RUPEE

SILVER, 10.70-11.60 g
Obv: Three-leaf symbol. Rev: Regnal year.

| 22 | AH— | 7 | 12.50 | 17.50 | 25.00 | 35.00 |

KM# (C4)	Date	Year	VG	Fine	VF	XF
	—	11	12.50	17.50	25.00	35.00
	—	13	12.50	17.50	25.00	35.00
	—	14	12.50	17.50	25.00	35.00
	—	15	12.50	17.50	25.00	35.00
	—	16	12.50	17.50	25.00	35.00
	—	17	12.50	17.50	25.00	35.00
	—	26	12.50	17.50	25.00	35.00
	—	51	12.50	17.50	25.00	35.00

JAYAJI RAO
AH1259-1304/1843-1886AD

NOTE: The bow & arrow and trident appear on nearly all coins of Bhilsa, Gwalior Fort, and Lashkar Mints, and cannot be used to identify any one of them.

In the name of Shah Alam II
AH1173-1221/1759-1806AD
with additional initial of Jayaji Rao
Frozen date AH(12)25

जी

1/8 RUPEE

SILVER, 1.34-1.45 g
Obv: W/o sword.

23.1 (Y1)	AH(12)25	—	7.50	12.50	20.00	30.00

Obv: W/sword.

| 23.2 (Y1) | AH(12)25 | — | 7.50 | 12.50 | 20.00 | 30.00 |

1/4 RUPEE
SILVER, 12-14mm, 2.68-2.90 g
Obv: W/o sword.

| 24.1 (Y2) | AH(12)25 | — | 3.50 | 4.50 | 5.50 | 7.00 |

Obv: W/sword.

| 24.2 (Y2) | AH(12)25 | — | 3.50 | 4.50 | 5.50 | 7.00 |

1/2 RUPEE

SILVER, 5.35-5.80 g
Obv: W/o sword.

| 25 (Y3.1) | AH(12)25 | — | 5.00 | 7.50 | 9.00 | 12.50 |

Obv: Sword.

| 26 (Y3.2) | AH(12)25 | — | 5.00 | 7.50 | 9.00 | 12.50 |

RUPEE

SILVER, 10.70-11.60 g
Obv: W/o sword. Rev: Bow and arrow.

| 27 (Y4.1) | AH(12)25 | — | 6.00 | 8.50 | 13.50 | 20.00 |

Obv: Sword. Rev: Bow and arrow.

| 28 (Y4.2) | AH(12)25 | — | 5.50 | 7.50 | 10.00 | 16.50 |

With additional initial of Madho Rao II

1/8 RUPEE
SILVER, 9-10mm, 1.34-1.45 g

| 29 (Y5) | AH(12)25 | — | 2.00 | 3.00 | 3.75 | 5.00 |

1/4 RUPEE

SILVER, 2.68-2.90 g

| 30 (Y6) | AH(12)25 | — | 3.50 | 4.50 | 6.00 | 8.00 |

1/2 RUPEE

SILVER, 5.35-5.80 g

KM#	Date	Year	VG	Fine	VF	XF
31 (Y7)	AH(12)25	—	4.50	7.00	9.00	11.50

RUPEE

SILVER, 10.70-11.60 g

| 32 (Y8) | AH(12)25 | — | 11.50 | 13.50 | 16.50 | 20.00 |

BROACH MINT
RUPEE

SILVER, 10.70-11.60 g

34	AH—	27	6.00	8.50	13.50	20.00
	—	32	6.00	8.50	13.50	20.00
	—	35	6.00	8.50	13.50	20.00

BURHANPUR MINT
DAULAT RAO
AH1209-1243/1794-1827AD

In the name of Shah Alam II
AH1173-1221/1759-1806AD

PAISA
COPPER, square, 18.14 g

KM#	Date	Year	Good	VG	Fine	VF
40 (C40)	AH1218	—	2.50	4.00	6.00	8.00

RUPEE
SILVER, 10.70-11.60 g

KM#	Date	Year	VG	Fine	VF	XF
38.2 (C47)	AH1209	—	10.00	14.00	20.00	27.50
	1210	84 (error)				
			10.00	14.00	20.00	27.50
	1211	3x	10.00	14.00	20.00	27.50
	1213	3x	10.00	14.00	20.00	27.50
	1214	—	10.00	14.00	20.00	27.50
	1215	4x	10.00	14.00	20.00	27.50
	1216	4x	10.00	14.00	20.00	27.50
	1217	45	10.00	14.00	20.00	27.50
	1218	—	10.00	14.00	20.00	27.50
	1219	4x	10.00	14.00	20.00	27.50
	1221	4x	10.00	14.00	20.00	27.50
	1222	—	10.00	14.00	20.00	27.50
	1223	4x	10.00	14.00	20.00	27.50
	1224	4x	10.00	14.00	20.00	27.50
	1225	—	10.00	14.00	20.00	27.50
	1227	—	10.00	14.00	20.00	27.50
	1229	—	10.00	14.00	20.00	27.50
	1230	—	10.00	14.00	20.00	27.50
	1232	—	10.00	14.00	20.00	27.50
	1233	—	10.00	14.00	20.00	27.50
	1234	3x	10.00	14.00	20.00	27.50
	1235	39	10.00	14.00	20.00	27.50
	1237	—	10.00	14.00	20.00	27.50
	1238	—	10.00	14.00	20.00	27.50
	1239	—	10.00	14.00	20.00	27.50
	1242	—	10.00	14.00	20.00	27.50
	1243	—	10.00	14.00	20.00	27.50

BAIJA BAI
AH1243-1249/1827-1833AD

RUPEE
SILVER, 10.70-11.60 g

| 38.3 (C47) | AH1247 | — | 10.00 | 14.00 | 20.00 | 30.00 |

JANKOJI RAO
AH1243-1259/1827-1843AD

In the name of Shah Alam II
AH1173-1221/1759-1806AD

RUPEE

SILVER, 10.70-11.60 g

KM#	Date	Year	VG	Fine	VF	XF
38.4 (C47)	AH1255	—	10.00	14.00	20.00	30.00

JAYAJI RAO
AH1243-1249/1827-1833AD

Mint mark:

PAISA

COPPER, 15.23 g

KM#	Date	Year	Good	VG	Fine	VF
41 (C41)	ND	—	2.00	3.00	5.00	7.50

1/4 RUPEE
SILVER, 15mm, 2.68-2.90 g

KM#	Date	Year	VG	Fine	VF	XF
42 (C45)	AH1214	—	8.00	13.50	20.00	30.00

1/2 RUPEE

SILVER, 17mm, 5.35-5.70 g

43 (C46)	AH1214	—	9.00	13.50	21.50	32.50
	1261	—	9.00	13.50	21.50	32.50
	1274	—	9.00	13.50	21.50	32.50

RUPEE

SILVER, 10.70-11.60 g

44 (C47)	AH1259	—	10.00	14.00	20.00	27.50
	AH1260	—	10.00	14.00	20.00	27.50
	1261	—	10.00	14.00	20.00	27.50
	1262	—	10.00	14.00	20.00	27.50
	1266	—	10.00	14.00	20.00	27.50
	1271	—	10.00	14.00	20.00	27.50
	1273	—	10.00	14.00	20.00	27.50
	1274	—	10.00	14.00	20.00	27.50
	1275	—	10.00	14.00	20.00	27.50
	1276	—	10.00	14.00	20.00	27.50
	1277	—	10.00	14.00	20.00	27.50

In the name of Alyjah Bahadur

NOTE: Alyjah Bahadur was the hereditary title of the Sindhia rulers of Gwalior, and was used by all rulers of the dynasty.

Mint marks:

to right of date

Gwalior / INDIAN PRINCELY STATES 898

PAISA

COPPER, 12.44-15.29 g
Rev: Leaf and snake.

KM#	Date	Year	Good	VG	Fine	VF
45	AH1260	—	3.00	4.00	7.00	10.00
(C50)	1273	—	3.00	4.00	7.00	10.00
	1274	—	3.00	4.00	7.00	10.00
	1275	—	3.00	4.00	7.00	10.00

DOHAD MINT

Mint mark:

JAYAJI RAO
AH1259-1304/VS1900-1943/1843-1886AD

1/3 PAISA

COPPER, 1.69-1.88 g

49.1	VS1912	(1855)	2.00	3.00	4.00	5.00
(C68)						

49.2	VS1912	(1855)	2.00	3.00	4.00	5.00

PAISA

COPPER, 16-22mm, 6.00-6.20 g

50	VS1912	(1855)	3.00	4.50	6.50	9.00
(C70)						

GARHAKOTA MINT

Mint marks:

JAYAJI RAO
AH1259-1304/1843-1886AD

1/2 RUPEE
SILVER, 5.35-5.80 g
Similar to 1 Rupee, KM#53.

KM#	Date	Year	VG	Fine	VF	XF
51	AH—	55	7.00	9.00	14.00	20.00

RUPEE

SILVER, 10.70-11.60 g

53	AH—	55	10.00	14.00	20.00	30.00

GWALIOR FORT MINT
DAULAT RAO
AH1209-1243/1794-1827AD

In the name of Shah Alam II
AH1173-1221/1759-1806AD

RUPEE

SILVER, 10.70-11.60 g

KM#	Date	Year	VG	Fine	VF	XF
57.2	AH1216	44	6.50	10.00	13.50	20.00
(C85)	1221	48	6.50	10.00	13.50	20.00

In the name of Muhammad Akbar II
AH1221-1253/1806-1837AD

PAISA

COPPER

KM#	Date	Year	Good	VG	Fine	VF
59	AH1224	3	1.00	1.65	2.50	4.00
	122x	4	1.00	1.65	2.50	4.00
	1232	—	1.00	1.65	2.50	4.00
	1235	14	1.00	1.65	2.50	4.00
	1236	15	1.00	1.65	2.50	4.00
	1241	—	1.00	1.65	2.50	4.00

1/4 RUPEE
SILVER

A60	AH1228	—	15.00	22.50	30.00	40.00

1/2 RUPEE
SILVER, 5.35-5.80 g
Similar to 1 Rupee, KM#61.

KM#	Date	Year	Fine	VF	XF	
60	AH—	—	6.50	13.50		

RUPEE

Mint marks: on obverse

مـ on reverse

SILVER, 10.70-11.60 g

61	AH1222	1	11.50	17.50	25.00	37.50
(C92)						

62	AH1227	6	11.50	13.50	16.50	20.00
(C92)	1228	7	11.50	13.50	16.50	20.00
	1229	8	11.50	13.50	16.50	20.00
	1230	9	11.50	13.50	16.50	20.00
	1231	10	11.50	13.50	16.50	20.00
	1231	11	11.50	13.50	16.50	20.00
	1232	11	11.50	13.50	16.50	20.00
	1234	13	11.50	13.50	16.50	20.00
	1235	14	11.50	13.50	16.50	20.00
	1236	15	11.50	13.50	16.50	20.00
	1239	19	11.50	13.50	16.50	20.00
	1240	19	11.50	13.50	16.50	20.00
	1241	19	11.50	13.50	16.50	20.00

BAIJA BAO
AH1243-1249/1827-1833AD

In the name of Muhammad Shah
With initial *Shri*

NAZARANA 1/3 MOHUR
GOLD, 18mm, 3.57-3.80 g
Nagari *Sri* for Baija Rao

63	AH1130	2 (frozen)				
(C75a)			125.00	165.00	200.00	235.00

NOTE: Struck ca.1827AD.

In the name of Muhammad Akbar
AH1221-1253/1806-1837AD

PAISA

COPPER

KM#	Date	Year	Good	VG	Fine	VF
64	AH1244	24	2.00	3.50	5.50	8.00

With *Sri* for Baija Bao

RUPEE

SILVER, 10.70-11.60 g
Obv. & Rev: Five-flowered symbol.

KM#	Date	Year	VG	Fine	VF	XF
65	AH—	23	11.50	13.50	16.50	20.00
(C95)						

NOTE: The regnal year 23 becomes frozen with this issue on all silver coins of this mint (identified by five-flowered symbol) and of Lashkar Mint.

JANKOJI RAO
AH1243-1259/1827-1843AD

In the name of Muhammad Shah
AH1131-1161/1719-1748AD
With initial *Ja*.

NAZARANA 1/3 MOHUR
GOLD, 3.57-3.80 g
Nagari *Ja* for Jankoji

66	AH1130	2 (frozen)				
(C75b)			125.00	165.00	200.00	235.00

NOTE: Struck ca.1834AD.

In the name of Muhammad Akbar II
AH1221-1253/1806-1837AD
With additional initial of Jankoji Rao
Symbols:

 on obverse

† on rev. (points up or down)

1/8 RUPEE
SILVER, 1.34-1.45 g
Similar to Rupee, KM#72.

67	AH1244	23	2.50	3.50	5.00	8.00

1/4 RUPEE
SILVER, 2.68-2.90 g
Similar to Rupee, KM#72.

68	AH1244	23	2.50	3.50	5.00	8.00

Similar to Rupee, KM#73.

69	AH1244	23	2.50	3.50	5.00	8.00

1/2 RUPEE
SILVER, 5.35-5.70 g

70	AH1244	23	2.50	3.50		8.00

71	AH1244	23	2.50	3.50	5.00	8.00

RUPEE

SILVER, 10.70-11.60 g
Rev: Bow and arrow points down.

72	AH1244	23	6.50	10.00	12.50	21.50
(C100)						

Rev: Bow and arrow points up.

KM#	Date	Year	VG	Fine	VF	XF
73 (C100)	AH1244	23	11.50	13.50	16.50	20.00

JAYAJI RAO
AH1259-1304/1843-1886
In the name of Muhammad Shah
AH1131-1161/1719-1748AD

With initial *Ji*.

NAZARANA 1/3 MOHUR
GOLD, 3.57-3.80 g
Nagari *Ji* for Jayaji

74 (Y14)	AH1130	2 (frozen)				
			125.00	165.00	200.00	235.00

NOTE: Struck ca.1843AD.

MOHUR
GOLD

| A75 (C76) | AH1130 | 2 | 400.00 | 475.00 | 550.00 | 600.00 |

In the name of Muhammad Akbar
AH1221-1253/1806-1837AD
With additional initial of Jayaji Rao
Symbols as on KM#69 and 70, but more stylized.

PAISA

COPPER

KM#	Date	Year	Good	VG	Fine	VF
75 (C87)	AH1269	—	1.00	1.65	2.50	4.00
	127x	42	1.00	1.65	2.50	4.00
	127x	45	1.00	1.65	2.50	4.00
	127x	46	1.00	1.65	2.50	4.00
	127x	47	1.00	1.65	2.50	4.00
	1277	48	1.00	1.65	2.50	4.00
	1278	49	1.00	1.65	2.50	4.00
	1279	—	1.00	1.65	2.50	4.00
	—	54	1.00	1.65	2.50	4.00
	—	56	1.00	1.65	2.50	4.00

Obv: Trisul.

| 76 | AH— | — | 1.00 | 1.65 | 2.50 | 4.00 |

1/16 RUPEE
SILVER, 9mm, 0.67-0.72 g

KM#	Date	Year	VG	Fine	VF	XF
77 (Y9)	AH—	23	3.00	5.00	8.00	11.50

1/8 RUPEE
SILVER, 11mm, 1.34-1.45 g

| 78 (Y10) | AH— | 23 | 2.50 | 3.50 | 5.00 | 8.00 |

1/4 RUPEE
SILVER, 13mm, 2.68-2.90 g

| 79 (Y11) | AH— | 23 | 2.50 | 3.50 | 5.00 | 8.00 |

1/2 RUPEE

SILVER, 15mm, 5.35-5.70 g
Rev: Bow and arrow points down.

| 80 (Y12) | AH— | 23 | 3.50 | 5.50 | 8.00 | 11.50 |

RUPEE

SILVER, 17-19mm, 10.70-11.60 g
Rev: Bow and arrow points up.

KM#	Date	Year	VG	Fine	VF	XF
81 (Y13)	AH—	23	5.00	7.50	9.00	12.50

Rev: Bow and arrow points down.

| 82 (Y13) | AH— | 23 | 5.00 | 7.50 | 9.00 | 12.50 |

NAZARANA RUPEE

SILVER, 10.70-11.60 g

| 83 (Y13a) | AH125x | 23 | 25.00 | 37.50 | 55.00 | 80.00 |

MADHO RAO
AH1304-1313/1886-1925AD
In the name of Muhammad Shah with initial of Madho Rao II

1/3 MOHUR
GOLD, 21mm, 3.57-3.80 g

84 (Y15)	AH1130	2 (frozen)				
			125.00	165.00	200.00	235.00

NOTE: Struck ca.1886AD.

ISAGARH MINT
DAULAT RAO
AH1209-1243/1794-1827AD
In the name of Muhammad Akbar II
AH1221-1253/1806-1837AD

Mint marks: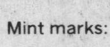

PAISA

COPPER
Obv: Cannon right. Rev: Snake.

| 89 | AH— | 2x | 11.50 | 17.50 | 26.50 | 37.50 |

RUPEE

SILVER, 10.70-11.60 g
Rev: Cannon left.

85	AH122x	8	11.50	17.50	26.50	37.50
	1230	10	11.50	17.50	26.50	37.50
	1230	11	11.50	17.50	26.50	37.50

Obv: Cannon left. Rev: Bhilsa leaf and battle axe.

KM#	Date	Year	VG	Fine	VF	XF
86	AH—	—	11.50	17.50	26.50	37.50

Obv: Cannon right. Rev: Bhilsa leaf, battle axe and snake.

87	AH1229	8	11.50	17.50	26.50	37.50
	1230	10	11.50	17.50	26.50	37.50
	1231	11	11.50	17.50	26.50	37.50
	123x	15	11.50	17.50	26.50	37.50

Obv: Cannon right and snake.
Rev: Bhilsa leaf and battle axe.

| 88 | AH— | — | 11.50 | 17.50 | 26.50 | 37.50 |

JANKOJI RAO
AH1243-1259/1827-1843AD

1/4 RUPEE
SILVER, 2.67-2.90 g
Similar to 1 Rupee, KM#92.

| A90 | AH12xx | 23 | 8.50 | 13.50 | 20.00 | 28.50 |

1/2 RUPEE
Mint marks:  on reverse

SILVER, 5.35-5.80 g
Similar to 1 Rupee, KM#92.

| 90 | AH1243 | 23 | 8.50 | 13.50 | 20.00 | 28.50 |

Similar to 1 Rupee, KM#93.

| 91 | AH1223 (error 1243) | | | | | |
| | | 23 | 8.50 | 13.50 | 20.00 | 28.50 |

RUPEE

SILVER, 10.70-11.60 g

92 (123)	AH1223 (error)					
		23	11.50	16.50	25.00	36.50
	1243	23	11.50	16.50	25.00	36.50

Mint mark:  on obv.

Obv: Lotus bud.

| 93 (127) | ND | — | 11.50 | 13.50 | 16.50 | 20.00 |
| | AH1252 | — | 11.50 | 13.50 | 16.50 | 20.00 |

JAWAD MINT
JANKOJI RAO
AH1243-1259/1827-1843AD

PAISA

COPPER

Gwalior / INDIAN PRINCELY STATES

900

KM#	Date	Year	Good	VG	Fine	VF
103 (130)	ND	—	2.50	4.00	5.50	8.00

Obv: Letter *Ja* and spear.

Obv: Letter *Ja* (retrograde) and spear.

| 104 | ND | — | 2.50 | 4.00 | 5.50 | 8.00 |

Obv: Banner, letter *Ji* and snake. Rev: Trisul.

| 105 | ND | — | 3.50 | 5.00 | 8.00 | 12.50 |

Obv: Letter *Ji*, scimitar and snake. Rev: Trisul.

| 106 (Y1) | ND | — | 2.50 | 4.00 | 5.50 | 7.50 |

Obv: Letters *Ja, Ja, Ja?* and snake. Rev: Trisul.

| 107 | ND | — | 2.50 | 4.00 | 5.50 | 7.50 |

Obv: Snake between letters *S* and *ra*, scimitar. Rev: Trisul.

| 108 | ND | — | 2.50 | 4.00 | 5.50 | 7.50 |

MADHO RAO
AH1304-1313/1886-1925AD

PAISA
With initial of Madho Rao II

COPPER
Obv: Snake between letters *Ji* and *Ma*, scimitar. Rev: Trisul.

| 109 (Y2) | ND | — | 3.00 | 5.00 | 6.50 | 8.50 |

Obv: Letters *Ji* and *Ma*, snake. Rev: Trisul.

| 110 | ND | — | 3.00 | 5.00 | 6.50 | 8.50 |

JHANSI MINT
To Gwalior 1865-1886AD
Regular Jhansi types (q.v.), identifiable as Sindhia issues only by date, and by Persian *Ji* for Jayaji. Similar to coins struck by the Maratha Governors of the Peshwa until 1853AD.

JAYAJI RAO
AH1259-1304/1843-1886AD

PAISA

COPPER, 11.15-15.55 g
Obv: Trisul. Rev: Persian *Ji* over leaf, flywhisk.

KM#	Date	Year	Good	VG	Fine	VF
111	ND	—	3.00	5.00	6.50	8.50

1/8 RUPEE

SILVER, 1.34-1.45 g
Rev: Persian *Ji*.

KM#	Date	Year	VG	Fine	VF	XF
112 (Y16)	ND	—	4.00	7.00	10.00	15.00

RUPEE

SILVER, 10.70-11.60 g
Rev: Persian *Ji*.

113 (Y19)	AH—	48	6.50	10.00	12.50	20.00
	1282	5x	6.50	10.00	12.50	20.00
	1284	5x	6.50	10.00	12.50	20.00

LASHKAR MINT
In the name of Shah Alam II
AH1173-1221/1759-1806AD
NOTE: All the following coins of this mint are in the name of Shah Alam II, with initials and mint marks as shown.
Mint mark:

With regnal years of Shah Alam II

1/8 RUPEE
SILVER, 12mm, 1.34-1.45 g

| 116 (C145) | ND | (1811-21) | 3.00 | 5.00 | 8.50 | 12.50 |

1/4 RUPEE

SILVER, 2.68-2.90 g

| 117 (C146) | ND | (1811-21) | 3.00 | 5.00 | 8.50 | 12.50 |

1/2 RUPEE
SILVER, 16mm, 5.35-5.80 g

| 118 (C147) | ND | (1811-21) | 5.00 | 7.50 | 11.50 | 16.50 |

RUPEE

SILVER, 10.70-11.60 g

| 119 | ND | (1811-21) | | | | |

Mint marks:

With regnal years of Muhammad Akbar II

1/8 RUPEE
SILVER, 1.34-1.45 g

| 120 (C145) | AH— | — | 2.00 | 2.50 | 3.50 | 5.00 |

1/4 RUPEE
SILVER, 2.68-2.90 g
Rev: W/dot in "J" of *Julus*.

| 121.1 (C146) | AH— | — | 3.50 | 4.50 | 6.00 | 8.00 |

Rev: W/o dot in "J" of *Julus*.

KM#	Date	Year	VG	Fine	VF	XF
121.2	AH—	—	3.50	4.50	6.00	8.00

Rev: Lily in *J* of *Julus*.

| 122 (C146) | AH— | 17 | 3.50 | 4.50 | 6.00 | 8.00 |

1/2 RUPEE
SILVER, 5.35-5.80 g
Rev: W/dot in "J" of *Julus*.

| 123.1 (C147) | AH— | — | 6.50 | 7.50 | 9.00 | 12.00 |

Rev: W/o dot in "J" of *Julus*.

| 123.2 | AH— | — | 6.50 | 7.50 | 9.00 | 12.00 |

Rev: Lily blossom in *J* in *Julus*.

| A124 (C147) | AH— | 17 | 6.50 | 7.50 | 9.00 | 12.00 |

RUPEE
SILVER, 10.70-11.60 g
Rev: W/and w/o dot in "J" of *Julus*.

124 (C148)	AH—	16	6.50	9.00	12.50	20.00
	—	17	6.50	9.00	12.50	20.00
	—	18	6.50	9.00	12.50	20.00
	—	19	6.50	9.00	12.50	20.00
	—	21	6.50	9.00	12.50	20.00
	—	22	6.50	9.00	12.50	20.00

Rev: Lily in *J* of *Julus*.

| 125 (C148) | AH— | 17 | 11.50 | 13.50 | 16.50 | 20.00 |

BAIJA BAI
AH1243-1249/1827-1833AD
Struck by Jankoji Rao
AH1243-1259/1827-1843AD

Mint marks:

PAISA

COPPER, 13.35 g
Obv: Trisul. Rev: Flywhisk and spear.

KM#	Date	Year	Good	VG	Fine	VF
131 (C161)	AH—	12	1.25	2.50	3.50	5.50
	—	22	1.25	2.50	3.50	5.50
	—	23	1.25	2.50	3.50	5.50
	—	31	1.25	2.50	3.50	5.50

JAYAJI RAO
AH1259-1304/1843-1886AD

Anonymous Issues
Struck by Jayaji Rao for 30 years, 1869-1899AD.

1/2 PAISA

COPPER, 12mm, 3.00 g

| 142 (Y28) | VS1926 | (1869) | 5.00 | 7.00 | 10.00 | 13.50 |

Gwalior / INDIAN PRINCELY STATES 901

PAISA

COPPER, 6.00 g

KM#	Date	Year	Good	VG	Fine	VF
143 (Y29)	VS1926	(1869)	.35	.75	1.25	2.25

Regular Coinage

In name of Shah Alam II with initials of Jayaji Rao

Copper coins have symbols

 or  on reverse

1/2 PAISA

COPPER

Obv: Trisul. Rev: Flywhisk, *Shri* and spear.

130 (C130)	AH—	23	1.50	3.00	5.00	7.50

PAISA

COPPER, 9.85 g

145 (Y21)	AH—	23	1.00	1.75	3.00	5.00

2 PAISA

COPPER, 17.00-20.00 g

146 (Y22)	AH—	23	2.00	3.75	6.00	10.00

1/16 RUPEE

SILVER, 9mm, 0.67-0.72 g

Rev: Bow and arrow points down, *Ji.*

KM#	Date	Year	VG	Fine	VF	XF
147 (Y23)	AH—	23	2.50	4.00	5.50	7.50

1/8 RUPEE

SILVER, 1.34-1.45 g

Rev: Bow and arrow points down, *Ji.*

148.1 (Y24)	AH—	23	1.75	2.50	3.50	5.00
		25	1.75	2.50	3.50	5.00

Rev: + below *Ji.*

148.2	AH—	—	1.75	2.50	3.50	5.00

1/4 RUPEE

SILVER, 2.68-2.90 g

Rev: Bow and arrow points down, *Ji.*

149 (Y25)	AH—	23	2.00	3.00	4.00	5.50
	—	27	2.00	3.00	4.00	5.50

1/2 RUPEE

SILVER, 5.35-5.80 g

Rev: Bow and arrow points down, *Ji.*

KM#	Date	Year	VG	Fine	VF	XF
150 (Y26)	AH—	23	4.50	6.50	7.50	12.50
	—	26	4.50	6.50	7.50	12.50
	—	27	4.50	6.50	7.50	12.50

Rev: Bow and arrow points up, *Ji.*

151 (Y26)	AH—	2x	4.50	6.50	7.50	12.50

RUPEE

SILVER, 10.70-11.60 g

Rev: Bow and arrow points down, *Ji.*

152 (Y27)	AH—	23	5.00	7.50	10.00	13.50
	—	27	5.00	7.50	10.00	13.50
	—	29	5.00	7.50	10.00	13.50

Rev: Bow and arrow points up, *Ji.*

153 (Y27)	AH—	2x	5.00	7.50	10.00	13.50

NAZARANA RUPEE

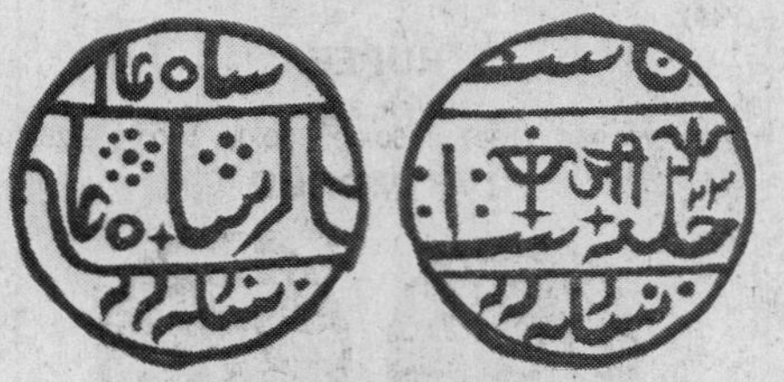

SILVER, 10.70-11.60 g

Rev: Bow and arrow points down, *Ji*, trisul.

154	AH—	23	50.00	65.00	85.00	110.00

MOHUR

GOLD, 10.70-11.40 g

Rev: Bow and arrow points up, *Ji.*

155	AH1130	2	220.00	240.00	265.00	300.00

MADHO RAO

VS1943-1982/1886-1925AD

With initial of Madho Rao II

Symbols as on previous series.

1/16 RUPEE

SILVER, 0.67-0.72 g

Rev: Bow and arrow points down *Ma*, trisul.

A156	AH—	23	1.75	2.25	3.00	4.00

1/8 RUPEE

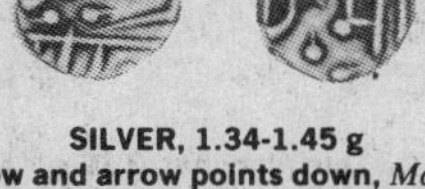

SILVER, 1.34-1.45 g

Rev: Bow and arrow points down, *Ma*, trisul.

156 (Y30)	AH—	23	1.75	2.25	3.00	4.00

1/4 RUPEE

SILVER, 2.68-2.90 g

Rev: Bow and arrow points down, *Ma*, trisul.

KM#	Date	Year	VG	Fine	VF	XF
157 (Y31)	AH—	23	2.00	2.75	4.00	6.50

1/2 RUPEE

SILVER, 5.35-5.80 g

Rev: Bow and arrow points down, *Ma*, trisul.

158 (Y32)	AH—	23	5.00	6.50	8.00	11.50

RUPEE

SILVER, 10.70-11.60 g

Rev: Bow and arrow points down, *Ma*, trisul.

159 (Y33)	AH—	23	5.00	7.50	9.00	11.50

MOHUR

GOLD, 10.70-11.40 g

Rev: Bow and arrow points up, *Ma*, trisul.

160	AH1130	2	220.00	240.00	265.00	300.00

MILLED COINAGE

PIE

COPPER

A161	VS1946	(1889)	—	—	Rare	—

161 (Y41)	VS(19)55(1898)		—	—	Rare	—

1/2 PICE

COPPER, 20mm

162	VS1946	(1889)	15.00	25.00	40.00	65.00

Punched from 1/4 Anna, KM#168.

163 (Y42)	VS1946	(1889)	75.00	125.00	200.00	—

Gwalior / INDIAN PRINCELY STATES   902

KM#	Date	Year	Fine	VF	XF	Unc
164	VS1956	(1899)	.65	1.00	1.50	2.25
(Y45)	1957	(1900)	.65	1.00	1.50	2.25
	1958	(1901)	.65	1.00	1.50	2.25

1/4 ANNA
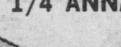

COPPER
Obv: 16 point star, wide nose on sun.

KM#	Date	Year	VG	Fine	VF	XF
165 (Y43)	VS1944	(1887)	15.00	25.00	40.00	65.00

Obv: 18 point star, wide nose on sun.
| 166 (Y43.1) | VS1944 | (1887) | 15.00 | 25.00 | 40.00 | 65.00 |

Obv: 17 point star, wide nose on sun.
| 167 (Y43.2) | VS1945 | (1888) | 15.00 | 25.00 | 40.00 | 65.00 |

Obv: 16 point star, narrow nose on sun.
| 168 (Y43.3) | VS1946 | (1889) | 15.00 | 25.00 | 40.00 | 65.00 |

KM#	Date	Year	Fine	VF	XF	Unc
169	VS1953	(1896)	.50	.75	1.25	1.75
(Y46)	1954	(1897)	.50	.75	1.25	1.75
	1956	(1899)	.50	.75	1.25	1.75
	1957	(1900)	.50	.75	1.25	1.75
	1958	(1901)	.50	.75	1.25	1.75

2.2mm thick planchet, 6.60 g
| 170 (Y48) | VS1970 | (1913) | .50 | 1.00 | 1.50 | 2.00 |

1.6mm thin planchet, 5.10 g
KM#	Date	Year	Fine	VF	XF	Unc
171	VS1970	(1913)	2.50	3.50	5.00	7.00
(Y48a)	1974	(1917)	.35	.75	1.25	1.75

Obv: Continuous legend below portrait.
| 172 (Y48b) | VS1974 | (1917) | 4.00 | 6.00 | 9.00 | 12.00 |

1/2 ANNA

COPPER
| 173 (Y44) | VS1946 | (1889) | 35.00 | 50.00 | 65.00 | 100.00 |

RUPEE
SILVER, 32mm
| 174 | VS1954 | (1897) | 60.00 | 80.00 | 100.00 | 125.00 |

1/3 MOHUR

GOLD, 3.442 g
| 175 (Y47) | VS1959 | (1902) | 165.00 | 250.00 | 400.00 | 500.00 |

JIVAJI RAO
1925-1948AD

1/4 ANNA

COPPER
Thick planchet, 5.10 g
Obv: Ornate robe.
| 176.1 (Y49) | VS1986 | (1929) | .50 | .60 | 1.00 | 2.00 |

Obv: Plainer robe.
| 176.2 | VS1986 | (1929) | .50 | .60 | 1.00 | 2.00 |

Thin planchet, 3.10 g
| 177 | VS1986 | (1929) | 1.50 | 2.50 | 3.50 | 6.00 |
| (Y49a) | 1999 | (1942) | 2.25 | 3.50 | 5.00 | 7.50 |

Rev: W/o inscriptions on side.
Y#	Date	Year	Fine	VF	XF	Unc
178 (Y50)	VS1999	(1942)	.35	.75	1.25	2.25

1/2 ANNA

BRASS
KM#	Date	Year	Fine	VF	XF	Unc
179	VS1999	(1942)	.35	.50	.85	1.50
(Y51)	1999	(1942)	—	—	Proof	50.00

MANDASOR MINT
JAYAJI RAO
AH1259-1304/1843-1886AD

PAISA

COPPER
Obv. leg: Sa Ma Sa.
Rev. leg: A(lijah) Ba(hadur), trisul divides date.
KM#	Date	Year	Good	VG	Fine	VF
180	VS1937	(1880)	1.25	2.75	4.00	6.00
(Y2)	3791	(error-1937)				
		(1880)	1.25	2.75	4.00	6.00
	3711	(error-1937)				
		(1880)	1.25	2.75	4.00	6.00

Rev: Date to left of trisul.
| 181 | VS1937 | (1880) | 1.25 | 2.75 | 4.00 | 6.00 |

Rev. leg: Retrograde.
| 182 | VS1937 | (1880) | 1.25 | 2.75 | 4.00 | 6.00 |

Obv. and rev. leg: Retrograde.
| 183 | VS1937 | (1880) | 1.25 | 2.75 | 4.00 | 6.00 |

NARWAR MINT
To Gwalior from 1805AD
Coins continued to be struck in the types of Narwar state, with dates after AH1221/1806AD. The year AH1230 was retained for several years.

Daulat Rao
AH1209-1243/1794-1827AD

In the name of Shah Alam II
AH1173-1221/1759-1806AD

Mint marks:

Katar 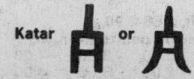 or 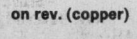 on rev. (copper)

Bhilsa leaf   on rev. (silver)

1/2 PAISA

COPPER, 3.37 g
Rev: Vertical katar.

KM#	Date	Year	Good	VG	Fine	VF
184.2	AH1216	43	1.75	3.00	5.00	8.00
(C10)	1216	44	1.75	3.00	5.00	8.00
	1216	45	1.75	3.00	5.00	8.00
	1217	44	1.75	3.00	5.00	8.00
	1217	45	1.75	3.00	5.00	8.00
	1217	46	1.75	3.00	5.00	8.00
	1219	46	1.75	3.00	5.00	8.00
	1230	7	—	—	—	—
	1230	21	1.75	3.00	5.00	8.00

PAISA

COPPER

185	AH1228	7	2.00	3.50	5.00	7.50
(C198)	1230	12	2.00	3.50	5.00	7.50
	1230	21	2.00	3.50	5.00	7.50

1/16 RUPEE

SILVER, 0.67-0.72 g

KM#	Date	Year	VG	Fine	VF	XF
186	AH1230	—	2.50	—	4.00	6.00

1/8 RUPEE

SILVER, 1.34-1.45 g

187	AH1230	—	2.75	3.50	4.50	7.00

1/4 RUPEE

SILVER, 2.68-2.90 g

188	AH1230	15	7.00	10.00	15.00	22.50
(C199)						

1/2 RUPEE

SILVER, 5.35-5.80 g

189	AH1230	12	7.00	10.00	15.00	22.50
(C200)	1230	21	7.00	10.00	15.00	22.50

RUPEE

SILVER, 10.70-11.60 g

190	AH1228	7	10.00	12.50	17.50	26.50
(C201)	1230	9	10.00	12.50	17.50	26.50
	1230	11	10.00	12.50	17.50	26.50
	1230	12	10.00	12.50	17.50	26.50
	1230	15	10.00	12.50	17.50	26.50
	1230	21	10.00	12.50	17.50	26.50
	—	35	10.00	12.50	17.50	26.50

RAJOD MINT

Symbol: Figure of Hanuman.

1/2 PAISA

COPPER, 7.71 g
Obv: Lingam at right.

KM#	Date	Year	Good	VG	Fine	VF
191 (YA2)	VS1936 (1879)	—	4.00	7.50	12.50	20.00

PAISA

COPPER, 17.10 g

192	VS1930 (1873)	—	6.50	10.00	17.50	30.00

Reduced weight, 11.50-12.30 g
Rev: 9 of date in Sanskrit.

192a (C1)	VS1930 (1873)	—	5.00	8.50	15.00	25.00

Rev: 9 of date in Gujarati.

193	VS1930 (1873)	—	5.00	8.50	15.00	25.00

Obv: Lingam at right.
Rev: 9 of date in sanskrit.

194 (C2)	VS1936 (1879)	—	5.00	8.50	15.00	25.00

Rev: 9 of date in Gujarati.

195	VS1936 (1879)	—	5.00	8.50	15.00	25.00

Obv: Snake at right.

196 (C3)	VS1940 (1883)	—	5.00	8.50	15.00	25.00

RATHGARH MINT

RUPEE

SILVER, 10.70.0011.60 G
Obv: Snake

KM#	Date	Year	VG	Fine	VF	XF
197	AH1221	1	11.50	13.50	16.50	20.00
	12xx	3	11.50	13.50	16.50	20.00
	12xx	4	11.50	13.50	16.50	20.00

KM#	Date	Year	VG	Fine	VF	XF
197	12xx	6	11.50	13.50	16.50	20.00
	12xx	7	11.50	13.50	16.50	20.00
	1232	8	11.50	13.50	16.50	20.00
	12xx	13	11.50	13.50	16.50	20.00
	123x	15	11.50	13.50	16.50	20.00
	12xx	18	11.50	13.50	16.50	20.00
	12xx	22	11.50	13.50	16.50	20.00

SHADORAH MINT

NOTE: Formerly listed as Seondha.
In the name of Muhammad Akbar II
AH1221-1253/1806-1837AD
Mint marks:

on KM#198 and KM#200 obv.

latter has   on rev.

on KM#198 and KM#199 on rev.

KM#199 also has   on rev.

DAULAT RAO

AH1209-1243/1794-1827AD

RUPEE

SILVER, 10.70-11.60 g
Rev: Cannon left, mintname at bottom.

199	AH1228	—	—	—	Rare	—

Obv: Cannon right, mintname at top.

200	ND	—	—	—	Rare	—

SHEOPUR MINT

In the name of Muhammad Akbar II
AH1221-1253/1806-1837AD
Mint mark:

on rev.

DAULAT RAO

AH1209-1243/1794-1827AD

RUPEE

SILVER, 10.70-11.60 g
Rev: Cannon left.

201	AH1228	7	12.50	15.00	18.50	25.00
(C235)	1228	8	12.50	15.00	18.50	25.00
	1228	9	12.50	15.00	18.50	25.00
	1228	10	12.50	15.00	18.50	25.00
	1228	11	12.50	15.00	18.50	25.00
	1228	13	12.50	15.00	18.50	25.00
	1228	15	12.50	15.00	18.50	25.00
	1228	16	12.50	15.00	18.50	25.00
	1228	17	12.50	15.00	18.50	25.00
	1228	18	12.50	15.00	18.50	25.00
	1228	19	12.50	15.00	18.50	25.00
	1228	20	12.50	15.00	18.50	25.00
	1228	22	12.50	15.00	18.50	25.00
	1228	27	12.50	15.00	18.50	25.00
	1228	28	12.50	15.00	18.50	25.00
	1230	—	12.50	15.00	18.50	25.00

BAIJA BAO

AH1243-1249/1827-1833AD

RUPEE

SILVER, 10.70-11.60 g
Rev: Cannon left.

KM#	Date	Year	VG	Fine	VF	XF
202	AH1248	27	11.50	13.50	16.50	20.00
	1248	28	11.50	13.50	16.50	20.00

JAYAJI RAO
AH1259-1304/1843-1886AD

RUPEE

SILVER, 10.70-11.60 g
Rev: Cannon left, *Ji*.

203	AH1270	1	15.00	22.50	27.50	35.00
(Y34.1)	1271	1	15.00	22.50	27.50	35.00
	1274	1	15.00	22.50	27.50	35.00
	1276	1	15.00	22.50	27.50	35.00

Obv: 113. Rev: 113 and *Ji*.

204	AH—	13	15.00	22.50	27.50	35.00
(Y34.2)		15	15.00	22.50	27.50	35.00

SIPRI MINT
Mintname: Narwar

DAULAT RAO
AH1209-1243/1794-1827AD

RUPEE
With regnal years of Muhammad Akbar II
AH1221-1253/1806-1837AD

SILVER, 10.70-11.60 g

208	AH1106	9	12.50	20.00	30.00	45.00

BAIJA BAI
AH1243-1249/1827-1833AD

RUPEE

SILVER, 10.70-11.60 g
Rev: *Shri*.

209	AH1106	17	11.50	13.50	16.50	20.00
(C240)						

JANKOJI RAO
AH1243-1259/1833-1843AD

RUPEE

SILVER, 10.70-11.60 g
Rev: *Ja*.

210	AH—	9	11.50	13.50	16.50	20.00
(C241)						

With regnal years of Muhammad Akbar II

KM#	Date	Year	VG	Fine	VF	XF
211	AH—	35	11.50	13.50	16.50	20.00

UJJAIN MINT
Mint marks:

on most issues

on many copper issues

DAULAT RAO
AH1209-1243/1794-1827

PAISA

COPPER, 12.83-14.00 g

KM#	Date	Year	Good	VG	Fine	VF
219	AH12xx	—	1.50	3.00	5.00	7.50

220	AH—	—	1.50	3.00	5.00	7.50

221	AH—	—	1.50	3.00	5.00	7.50

222	AH1220	—	1.50	3.00	5.00	7.50

1/4 RUPEE
SILVER, 2.67-2.90 g
Obv: AH date below

A223	AH—	62	5.00	7.00	9.00	12.50
		64	5.00	7.00	9.00	12.50

1/2 RUPEE
SILVER, 5.35-5.80 g
Obv: AH date below

B223	AH—	64	5.00	7.00	9.00	12.50

RUPEE

SILVER, 10.70-11.60 g
Obv: AH date below

KM#	Date	Year	VG	Fine	VF	XF
224	AH12xx	44	5.00	7.00	9.00	12.50
	—	45	5.00	7.00	9.00	12.50
	—	46	5.00	7.00	9.00	12.50
	—	48	5.00	7.00	9.00	12.50
	—	51	5.00	7.00	9.00	12.50
	—	52	5.00	7.00	9.00	12.50
	—	55	5.00	7.00	9.00	12.50
	—	57	5.00	7.00	9.00	12.50
	—	58	5.00	7.00	9.00	12.50

KM#	Date	Year	VG	Fine	VF	XF
224	—	59	5.00	7.00	9.00	12.50
	—	60	5.00	7.00	9.00	12.50
	—	62	5.00	7.00	9.00	12.50
	—	63	5.00	7.00	9.00	12.50
123x	—	64	5.00	7.00	9.00	12.50
	—	67	5.00	7.00	9.00	12.50
	—	68	5.00	7.00	9.00	12.50
	—	69	5.00	7.00	9.00	12.50

BAIJA BAI
AH1243-1249/1827-1833AD

1/2 RUPEE
SILVER, 5.35-5.80 g

226	AH—	73	4.50	6.50	9.00	13.50

RUPEE

SILVER, 10.70-11.60 g

227	AH—	71	5.00	7.00	9.00	12.50
		73	5.00	7.00	9.00	12.50

With regnal years of Mohammad Akbar

Rev: *Shri*.

228	AH—	23	—	—	Rare	—
(C267)						

JANKOJI RAO
AH1243-1259/1827-1843AD
With regnal years of Shah Alam

1/4 RUPEE
SILVER, 2.67-2.90 g

A229	AH—	80	3.00	5.00	7.00	10.00

1/2 RUPEE
SILVER, 5.35-5.80 g

229	AH—	77	3.00	5.00	7.00	10.00
		80	3.00	5.00	7.00	10.00

RUPEE

SILVER, 10.70-11.60 g

230	AH—	77	5.00	7.00	9.00	12.50
		78	5.00	7.00	9.00	12.50
		79	5.00	7.00	9.00	12.50
		80	5.00	7.00	9.00	12.50
		84	5.00	7.00	9.00	12.50
		85	5.00	7.00	9.00	12.50

JAYAJI RAO
AH1259-1304/1843-1886AD

PAISA

COPPER, round or square

KM#	Date	Year	Good	VG	Fine	VF
231	AH1262	—	1.50	2.50	3.50	5.00
(Y35)	1263	—	1.50	2.50	3.50	5.00
	1266	—	1.50	2.50	3.50	5.00

Obv: Arrow added.

232	AH1278	—	1.50	2.50	3.50	5.00
	1281	—	1.50	2.50	3.50	5.00
	1292	—	1.50	2.50	3.50	5.00
	1295	—	1.50	2.50	3.50	5.00

Obv: Shri.

KM#	Date	Year	Good	VG	Fine	VF
233	AH1272	—	1.50	2.50	3.50	5.00
	1278	—	1.50	2.50	3.50	5.00
	1287	—	1.50	2.50	3.50	5.00
	1292	—	1.50	2.50	3.50	5.00
	1295	—	1.50	2.50	3.50	5.00

1/8 RUPEE
SILVER, 1.34-1.45 g

KM#	Date	Year	VG	Fine	VF	XF
234	AH—	—	2.00	3.00	4.00	6.00

1/4 RUPEE
SILVER, 2.68-2.90 g

235	AH—	92	3.50	4.50	6.00	9.00

1/2 RUPEE
SILVER, 5.35-5.80 g
Regnal years of Shah Alam

236	AH—	98	3.00	5.00	7.00	10.00

RUPEE

SILVER, 10.70-11.60 g

237	AH—	89	5.00	7.00	9.00	12.50
	—	92	5.00	7.00	9.00	12.50
		93	5.00	7.00	9.00	12.50
		94	5.00	7.00	9.00	12.50
		95	5.00	7.00	9.00	12.50
		98	5.00	7.00	9.00	12.50
		99	5.00	7.00	9.00	12.50
		100	5.00	7.00	9.00	12.50

With regnal years of the British "Raj"

These are a continuation of the thick cruder fabric rupees similar to those issued in the later period with Shah Alam II's regnal years.

1/8 RUPEE
SILVER, 1.34-1.45 g

A238	AH—	26	3.50	4.50	6.00	9.00

1/2 RUPEE
SILVER, 5.35-5.80 g

C238	AH—	28	3.50	4.50	6.00	9.00

RUPEE

SILVER, 10.70-11.60 g

238	AH—	3	5.00	7.00	9.00	12.50
		8	5.00	7.00	9.00	12.50
		9	5.00	7.00	9.00	12.50
		22	5.00	7.00	9.00	12.50
		25	5.00	7.00	9.00	12.50
		26	5.00	7.00	9.00	12.50
		28	5.00	7.00	9.00	12.50

MADHO RAO
AH1304-1344 / 1886-1925AD

With initial of Madho Rao II
Regnal years of the British Raj (Yr. 1 = AD1857)

1/16 RUPEE

SILVER, 0.67-0.72 g

239	AH1312	—	2.50	4.00	6.00	9.00
(Y36)	1313	37	2.50	4.00	6.00	9.00

1/8 RUPEE
SILVER, 1.34-1.45 g

A240	AH—	31	3.50	5.00	7.00	10.00

240	AH1310	34	2.00	3.00	4.00	6.00

KM#	Date	Year	VG	Fine	VF	XF
(Y37)	1311	35	2.00	3.00	4.00	6.00
	1312	36	2.00	3.00	4.00	6.00
	1313	37	2.00	3.00	4.00	6.00

1/4 RUPEE

SILVER, 2.68-2.90 g

241	AH1310	34	3.50	4.50	6.00	9.00
(Y38)	1311	35	3.50	4.50	6.00	9.00
	1312	36	3.50	4.50	6.00	9.00
	1313	37	3.50	4.50	6.00	9.00
	1314	38	3.50	4.50	6.00	9.00

1/2 RUPEE
SILVER, 14-15mm, 5.35-5.80 g

A242	AH—	29	3.50	5.00	7.00	10.00
		31	3.50	5.00	7.00	10.00

242	AH1310	34	3.50	5.00	7.00	10.00
(Y39)	1311	35	3.50	5.00	7.00	10.00
	1312	36	3.50	5.00	7.00	10.00
	1313	37	3.50	5.00	7.00	10.00
	1314	38	3.50	5.00	7.00	10.00

RUPEE

SILVER, 10.70-11.60 g

243	AH—	29	5.00	7.00	9.00	12.50
	—	31	5.00	7.00	9.00	12.50
	—	32	5.00	7.00	9.00	12.50

Obv: AH date below

244	AH130x	33	5.00	7.00	9.00	12.50
	13xx	34	5.00	7.00	9.00	12.50

Obv: AH date in center.

245	AH1310	34	5.00	7.00	9.00	12.50
(Y40)	1310	35	5.00	7.00	9.00	12.50
	1311	34	5.00	7.00	9.00	12.50
	1311	35	5.00	7.00	9.00	12.50
	1311	35	5.00	7.00	9.00	12.50
	1312	34	(error)			
			11.50	13.50	16.50	20.00
	1312	36	5.00	7.00	9.00	12.50
	1313	37	5.00	7.00	9.00	12.50
	1314	38	5.00	7.00	9.00	12.50

UNCERTAIN MINT
PAISA

COPPER

KM#	Date	Year	Good	VG	Fine	VF
246 (Y2)	AH—	23	5.00	8.50	12.50	18.50

247 (Y4)	AH—	ND	5.00	8.00	12.00	16.50

HYDERABAD
Haidarabad

Hyderabad State, the largest Indian State and the last remnant of Mughal suzerainty in South or Central India, traced its foundation to Nizam-ul Mulk, the Mughal viceroy in the Deccan. From about 1724 the first nizam, as the rulers of Hyderabad came to be called, took advantage of Mughal decline in the North to assert an all but ceremonial independence of the emperor. The East India Company defeated Hyderabad's natural enemies, the Muslim rulers of Mysore and the Marathas, with the help of troops furnished under alliances between them and the Nizam. This formed the beginning of a relationship which persisted for a century and a half until India's Independence. Hyderabad was the premier Princely State, with a population (in 1935) of fourteen and a half million. It was not absorbed into the Indian Union until 1948. Hyderabad City is located beside Golkonda, the citadel of the Qutb Shahi sultans until they were overthrown by Aurangzeb in 1687. A beautifully located city on the bank of the Musi river, the mint epithet was appropriately Farkundah Bunyad, "of happy foundation".

Hyderabad exercised authority over a number of feudatories or samasthans. Some of these, such as Gadwal and Shorapur, paid tribute to both the Nizam and the Marathas. These feudatories were generally in the hands of local rajas whose ancestry predated the establishment of Hyderabad State. There were also many mints in the State, both private and government. There was little or no standardization of the purity of silver coinage until the twentieth century. At least one banker, Pestonji Meherji by name, was distinguished by minting his own coins.

RULERS
Nizam Ali Khan
 AH1175-1218 / 1761-1803AD
Sikandar Jah
 AH1218-1244 / 1803-1829AD
Nasir-ad-Daula
 AH1244-1273 / 1829-1857AD
Afzal-ad-Daula
 AH1273-1285 / 1857-1869AD
Mir Mahbub Ali Khan II
 AH1285-1329 / 1869-1911AD
Mir Usman Ali Khan
 AH1329-1367 / 1911-1948AD

MINTS

Amaravati — امراوتی

Aurangabad — اودنگ اباد
Mintname: Khujista Bunyad

Daulatabad — دولت اباد

Farkhanda Bunyad — فرخندہ بنیاد

Mintname: Haidarabad

Haidarabad — حیدراباد

AMARAVATI MINT
RUPEE
SILVER

KM#	Date	Year	Good	VG	Fine	VF
1	AH1240	—	—	—	Rare	
	1241	—	—	—	Rare	

AURANGABAD MINT

Mint marks:

نجستہ بنیاد

Mintname: Khujista Bunyad

RUPEE

SILVER, 10.70-11.60 g

KM#	Date	Year	VG	Fine	VF	XF
5	AH1218	—	12.50	16.50	20.00	30.00

In the name of Muhammad Akbar II
 AH1221-1253 / 1806-1837AD

Obv: W/o Persian letter *S*.

KM#	Date	Year	VG	Fine	VF	XF
45	AH1227	6	12.50	15.00	17.50	21.50
	1230	9	12.50	15.00	17.50	21.50
	—	16	12.50	15.00	17.50	21.50
	1234	17	12.50	15.00	17.50	21.50
	1239	17	12.50	15.00	17.50	21.50
	1240	20	12.50	15.00	17.50	21.50
	1241	2x	12.50	15.00	17.50	21.50
	1242	—	12.50	15.00	17.50	21.50

NASIR AD-DAULA
AH1244-1273/1829-1857AD
In the name of Muhammad Akbar II
AH1221-1253/1806-1837AD

RUPEE
SILVER, 10.70-11.60 g

66a	AH1251	—	12.50	14.50	17.50	21.50

In the name of Bahadur Shah
AH1253-1274/1837-1858AD

Struck by Pestonji Meherji, a Bombay banker in the time of Nasir al-Daula, AD1829-57.

1/8 RUPEE

SILVER, 1.34-1.45 g

C#	Date	Year	VG	Fine	VF	XF
57	AH1256	4	6.00	10.00	15.00	21.50

1/4 RUPEE

SILVER, 2.68-2.90 g

58	AH1256	4	6.00	10.00	15.00	21.50

1/2 RUPEE
SILVER, 17mm, 5.35-5.80 g

59	AH1256	4	7.50	13.50	20.00	30.00

RUPEE

SILVER, 10.70-11.60 g

60	AH1254	2	10.00	13.50	18.50	26.50
	1256	4	10.00	13.50	18.50	26.50
	1264	—	10.00	13.50	18.50	26.50

FARKHANDA BUNYAD MINT
Hyderabad

Mint mark: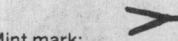

Rev: Persian letter *N*:

SIKANDAR JAH
AH1218-1244/1803-1829AD
In the name of Shah Alam II
AH1173-1221/1759-1806AD

PAISA

COPPER

C#	Date	Year	Good	VG	Fine	VF
40	AH1217	—	1.25	2.00	3.00	4.50
	1218	—	1.25	2.00	3.00	4.50

RUPEE
SILVER, 20-21mm, 10.70-11.60 g

C#	Date	Year	VG	Fine	VF	XF
41	AH1218	—	12.50	17.50	25.00	37.50
	1220	—	12.50	17.50	25.00	37.50

HAIDARABAD MINT

Mint mark:

Persian letter *S*.

SIKANDAR JAH
AH1218-1244/1803-1829AD
In the name of Muhammad Akbar II
AH1221-1253/1806-1837AD

PAISA

 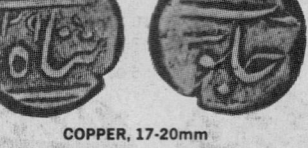

COPPER, 17-20mm

C#	Date	Year	Good	VG	Fine	VF
44	AH1221	—	1.25	2.00	2.75	3.50
(C42)	1229	—	1.25	2.00	2.75	3.50
	1237	—	1.25	2.00	2.75	3.50

1/4 RUPEE

SILVER, 2.68-2.90 g

C#	Date	Year	VG	Fine	VF	XF
46	AH12xx	—	3.50	4.50	6.00	8.00
(C51)	1239	—	5.00	8.00	12.00	18.00

1/2 RUPEE

SILVER, 5.35-5.80 g

47	AH1235	14	5.50	7.50	10.00	16.50
(C52)	1237	—	5.50	7.50	10.00	16.50
	1238	—	5.50	7.50	10.00	16.50
	1242	23	5.50	7.50	10.00	16.50

RUPEE

SILVER, 10.70-11.60 g

48	AH1222	—	7.50	10.00	13.50	18.50
	1225	4	7.50	10.00	13.50	18.50
	1226	4	7.50	10.00	13.50	18.50
	1227	6	7.50	10.00	13.50	18.50
	1227	7	7.50	10.00	13.50	18.50
	1228	7	7.50	10.00	13.50	18.50
	1229	8	7.50	10.00	13.50	18.50
	1230	9	7.50	10.00	13.50	18.50
	1231	10	7.50	10.00	13.50	18.50
	1232	11	7.50	10.00	13.50	18.50
	1234	13	7.50	10.00	13.50	18.50

C#	Date	Year	VG	Fine	VF	XF
48	1235	15	7.50	10.00	13.50	18.50
	1236	15	7.50	10.00	13.50	18.50
	1237	16	7.50	10.00	13.50	18.50
	1238	—	7.50	10.00	13.50	18.50
	1239	21	7.50	10.00	13.50	18.50
	1240	21	7.50	10.00	13.50	18.50
	1240	22	7.50	10.00	13.50	18.50
	1241	22	7.50	10.00	13.50	18.50
	1242	23	7.50	10.00	13.50	18.50
	1243	24	7.50	10.00	13.50	18.50
	1244	25	7.50	10.00	13.50	18.50

NAZARANA RUPEE

SILVER, 10.70-11.60 g

48a	AH1237	16	35.00	55.00	85.00	125.00

1/16 MOHUR
GOLD, 0.67-0.70 g

56	AH123x	—	35.00	50.00	70.00	100.00

1/8 MOHUR
GOLD, 1.34-1.42 g

57	AH123x	—	45.00	65.00	90.00	125.00

1/4 MOHUR
GOLD, 2.68-2.85 g

58	AH1236	15	60.00	90.00	120.00	160.00

NAZARANA 1/4 MOHUR

GOLD, 2.68-2.85 g

A58	AH1236	15	—	—	Rare	—

1/2 MOHUR
GOLD, 5.35-5.70 g

59	AH123x	—	90.00	135.00	185.00	225.00

MOHUR

GOLD, 10.70-11.40 g

60	AH1226	—	185.00	235.00	285.00	325.00
	1227	—	185.00	235.00	285.00	325.00
	1228	—	185.00	235.00	285.00	325.00
	1231	—	185.00	235.00	285.00	325.00
	1234	—	185.00	235.00	285.00	325.00
	1235	—	185.00	235.00	285.00	325.00
	1236	15	185.00	235.00	285.00	325.00
	1237	16	185.00	235.00	285.00	325.00
	1238	—	185.00	235.00	285.00	325.00
	1241	—	185.00	235.00	285.00	325.00
	1242	—	185.00	235.00	285.00	325.00
	1243	—	185.00	235.00	285.00	325.00
	1244	—	185.00	235.00	285.00	325.00

NAZARANA MOHUR

GOLD, 10.70-11.40 g

60a	AH1236	15	—	—	Rare	—

NASIR AD-DAULA
AH1244-1273/1829-1857AD

Mint mark:

Rev: Persian letter *N*:

First Series
In the name of Muhammad Akbar II to AH1252, with his regnal years.

PAISA

COPPER

C#	Date	Year	Good	VG	Fine	VF
61	AH1247	—	2.00	3.00	4.50	7.50
	1250	—	2.00	3.00	4.50	7.50
	Date off flan	—	1.00	2.00	3.50	5.00

1/4 RUPEE

SILVER, 2.68-2.90 g

C#	Date	Year	VG	Fine	VF	XF
64	AH1246	—	3.50	5.00	7.50	12.50
	1247	—	3.50	5.00	7.50	12.50
	1251	—	3.50	5.00	7.50	12.50

1/2 RUPEE
SILVER, 18mm, 5.35-5.80 g

C#	Date	Year	VG	Fine	VF	XF
65	AH1249-51	—	5.00	7.50	11.50	16.50

RUPEE

SILVER, 0.70-11.60 g

C#	Date	Year	VG	Fine	VF	XF
66	AH1245	26	7.50	10.00	15.00	20.00
	1246	—	7.50	10.00	15.00	20.00
	1248	29	7.50	10.00	15.00	20.00
	1249	—	7.50	10.00	15.00	20.00
	1250	31	7.50	10.00	15.00	20.00
	1251	33	7.50	10.00	15.00	20.00
	1252	34	7.50	10.00	15.00	20.00
	1253	35	7.50	10.00	15.00	20.00

1/16 MOHUR
GOLD, 0.67-0.71 g

68	AH—	—	25.00	35.00	45.00	60.00

1/8 MOHUR
GOLD, 1.34-1.42 g

69	AH—	—	35.00	50.00	70.00	100.00

1/4 MOHUR
GOLD, 2.68-2.85 g

70	AH—	—	50.00	85.00	120.00	150.00

1/2 MOHUR
GOLD, 5.35-5.70 g

71	AH—	—	90.00	125.00	165.00	200.00

MOHUR
GOLD, 22-23mm

72	AH1244	—	185.00	235.00	285.00	325.00
	1246	—	185.00	235.00	285.00	325.00
	1248	—	185.00	235.00	285.00	325.00
	1249	—	185.00	235.00	285.00	325.00
	1251	—	185.00	235.00	285.00	325.00

Second Series
In the name of Bahadur Shah
Years 1-22/AH1253-1274

PAISA

COPPER, round or square

C#	Date	Year	Good	VG	Fine	VF
73	AH1257	4	2.00	3.00	4.00	7.00
	1258	—	2.00	3.00	4.00	7.00
	1262	—	2.00	3.00	4.00	7.00
	1272	—	2.00	3.00	4.00	7.00
	1273	—	2.00	3.00	4.00	7.00
	Date off flan	—	1.00	2.00	3.00	4.50

1/16 RUPEE
SILVER, 9-11mm, 0.67-0.72 g

C#	Date	Year	VG	Fine	VF	XF
75	AH1272	—	4.00	7.50	10.00	15.00

1/8 RUPEE
SILVER, 11-13mm, 1.34-1.45 g

76	AH1272	—	4.00	7.50	10.00	15.00

1/4 RUPEE
SILVER, 14-15mm, 2.68-2.90 g

77	AH1257	—	4.00	7.50	10.00	15.00
	1272	17	8.00	15.00	20.00	30.00
	1273	18	4.00	7.50	10.00	15.00

1/2 RUPEE
SILVER, 16-19mm, 5.35-5.80 g

78	AH1257-73	—	6.50	8.00	12.50	20.00

RUPEE

SILVER, 10.70-11.60 g

79	AH1253	1	7.50	10.00	13.50	20.00
	1258	6	7.50	10.00	13.50	20.00
	1261	8	7.50	10.00	13.50	20.00
	1262	9	7.50	10.00	13.50	20.00
	1267	12	7.50	10.00	13.50	20.00
	1268	12	7.50	10.00	13.50	20.00
	1268	13	7.50	10.00	13.50	20.00
	1270	15	7.50	10.00	13.50	20.00
	1270	16	7.50	10.00	13.50	20.00
	1271	16	7.50	10.00	13.50	20.00
	1271	17	7.50	10.00	13.50	20.00
	1272	17	7.50	10.00	13.50	20.00
	1273	18	7.50	10.00	13.50	20.00

1/16 MOHUR
GOLD, 0.67-0.71 g

80	AH—	—	35.00	50.00	70.00	100.00

1/8 MOHUR
GOLD, 1.34-1.42 g

81	AH—	—	40.00	65.00	90.00	125.00

1/4 MOHUR
GOLD, 2.68-2.85 g

82	AH—	—	50.00	85.00	120.00	160.00

1/2 MOHUR
GOLD, 5.35-5.70 g

83	AH—	—	80.00	130.00	185.00	225.00

MOHUR
GOLD, 22mm, 10.70-11.40 gm

84	AH1258	—	175.00	215.00	265.00	300.00
	1260	—	175.00	215.00	265.00	300.00
	1261	—	175.00	215.00	265.00	300.00
	1263	—	175.00	215.00	265.00	300.00
	1264	—	175.00	215.00	265.00	300.00
	1265	—	175.00	215.00	265.00	300.00
	1266	—	175.00	215.00	265.00	300.00
	1267	—	175.00	215.00	265.00	300.00
	1268	—	175.00	215.00	265.00	300.00
	1269	—	175.00	215.00	265.00	300.00
	1270	—	175.00	215.00	265.00	300.00
	1271	—	175.00	215.00	265.00	300.00
	1273	—	175.00	215.00	265.00	300.00

AFZAL AD-DAULA
AH1273-1285/1857-1869AD

First Series
In the name of Bahadur Shah II
Mint marks:

#1

#2 (symbol)

#3 (symbol)

For his last two years, AH1274-75, regnal year 18 w/Persian letter *A* (symbol 3) above *Padishah* on obv.

Copper coins have symbol #1, while silver and gold have #2.

1/2 PAISA

COPPER

C#	Date	Year	Good	VG	Fine	VF
85	AH1275	—	1.50	2.50	3.50	6.00
		19	1.50	2.50	3.50	6.00

PAISA

COPPER

86	AH1275	18	1.50	2.50	3.50	6.00
	1276	19	1.50	2.50	3.50	6.00
	1277	19	1.50	2.50	3.50	6.00
	Date off flan	—	1.25	2.25	3.00	4.50

1/8 RUPEE
SILVER, 13mm, 1.34-1.45 g

C#	Date	Year	VG	Fine	VF	XF
88	AH1275	—	4.00	7.50	10.00	15.00

1/4 RUPEE
SILVER, 14mm, 2.68-2.90 g

89	AH1274	—	4.00	7.50	10.00	15.00

1/2 RUPEE
SILVER, 17mm, 5.35-5.80 g

90	AH1274	—	6.50	10.00	15.00	22.50

RUPEE

SILVER, 10.70-11.60 g

91	AH1273	18	7.50	10.00	13.50	20.00
	1274	18	7.50	10.00	13.50	20.00
	1275	18	7.50	10.00	13.50	20.00

MOHUR
GOLD, 23mm

96	AH1274	—	185.00	225.00	275.00	325.00
	1275	—	185.00	225.00	275.00	325.00

Second Series
In the name of Asaf Jah, Nizam al-Mulk, Founder of the Nizami line (1713-1748AD).
Persian letter *A* for Afzal above *k* of *Mulk* on obv.
All coins bear the numeral '92' on upper obverse.

PAISA
(Dub)
COPPER
Irregular and regular shapes, 16-30mm

Y#	Date	Year	Good	VG	Fine	VF
1	AH1282	—	1.75	2.50	3.50	5.00
	1283	—	1.75	2.50	3.50	5.00
	Date off flan	—	1.00	2.00	3.00	4.00

1/16 RUPEE
(Anna)
SILVER, 9mm, 0.67-0.72 g

Y#	Date	Year	VG	Fine	VF	XF
2	AH1275	—	2.50	4.00	6.50	10.00

1/8 RUPEE

SILVER, 11-13mm, 1.34-1.45 g

3	AH1278	—	2.50	4.00	6.50	10.00
	1279	—	2.50	4.00	6.50	10.00

1/4 RUPEE

908 Hyderabad / INDIAN PRINCELY STATES

SILVER, 2.68-2.90 g

Y#	Date	Year	VG	Fine	VF	XF
4	AH1276	—	2.50	4.50	6.50	10.00
	1278	—	2.50	4.50	6.50	10.00
	1283	10	2.50	4.50	6.50	10.00

1/2 RUPEE

SILVER, 5.35-5.80 g

5	AH1276	—	4.00	5.50	8.00	12.50
	1277	—	4.00	5.50	8.00	12.50

RUPEE

SILVER, 10.70-11.60 g

6	AH1275	2	4.50	5.50	7.50	10.00
	1276	3	4.50	5.50	7.50	10.00
	1276	4	4.50	5.50	7.50	10.00
	1277	4	4.50	5.50	7.50	10.00
	1278	5	4.50	5.50	7.50	10.00
	1279	6	4.50	5.50	7.50	10.00
	1280	7	4.50	5.50	7.50	10.00
	1281	7	4.50	5.50	7.50	10.00
	1281	8	4.50	5.50	7.50	10.00
	1282	9	4.50	5.50	7.50	10.00
	1283	10	4.50	5.50	7.50	10.00
	1284	11	4.50	5.50	7.50	10.00
	1285	12	4.50	5.50	7.50	10.00

1/16 MOHUR

GOLD, 8-9mm, 0.67-0.71 g

7 AH— — Reported, not confirmed

1/8 MOHUR

GOLD, 11mm, 1.34-1.42 g

8	AH1279-81	40.00	55.00	70.00	90.00

1/4 MOHUR

GOLD, 14mm, 2.68-2.85 g

9	AH1281	—	50.00	75.00	110.00	140.00

1/2 MOHUR

GOLD, 16mm, 5.35-5.70 g

10	AH1281	—	90.00	120.00	165.00	200.00

MOHUR

GOLD, 10.70-11.40 g

11	AH1275	—	160.00	185.00	220.00	265.00
	1276	—	160.00	185.00	220.00	265.00
	1277	—	160.00	185.00	220.00	265.00
	1278	—	160.00	185.00	220.00	265.00
	1279	—	160.00	185.00	220.00	265.00
	1280	—	160.00	185.00	220.00	265.00
	1281	—	160.00	185.00	220.00	265.00
	1282	—	160.00	185.00	220.00	265.00
	1283	—	160.00	185.00	220.00	265.00
	1284	—	160.00	185.00	220.00	265.00
	1285	—	160.00	185.00	220.00	265.00

MIR MAHBUB ALI KHAN II

AH1285-1329/1868-1911AD

In the name of Asaf Jah, Nizam al-Mulk, Founder of the Nizami line (1713-1748AD).

Persian letter *M* for Mahbub above *k* of *Mulk* on obv.

1/2 PAISA

COPPER

Y#	Date	Year	Good	VG	Fine	VF
A12	ND	—	—	—	—	—

PAISA (DUB)

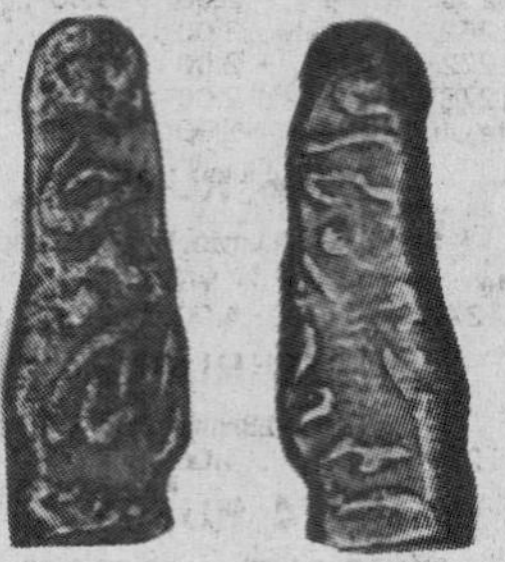

COPPER
Round, rectangular, irregular shape
Many sizes and weights

Y#	Date	Year	Good	VG	Fine	VF
12	AH1290	—	1.50	2.50	3.50	5.00
	1291	—	1.50	2.50	3.50	5.00
	1292	—	1.50	2.50	3.50	5.00
	1296	—	1.50	2.50	3.50	5.00
	1297	—	1.50	2.50	3.50	5.00
	1300	—	1.50	2.50	3.50	5.00
	1301	—	1.50	2.50	3.50	5.00
	1302	18	1.50	2.50	3.50	5.00
	1303	—	1.50	2.50	3.50	5.00
	1308	—	1.50	2.50	3.50	5.00
	1313	—	1.50	2.50	3.50	5.00

1/2 ANNA

COPPER

A13	AH1311	27	—	—	—	—

1/16 RUPEE

.818 SILVER, 0.698 g

Y#	Date	Year	VG	Fine	VF	XF
13	AH1299	15	1.25	1.75	2.50	3.50
	1300	—	1.25	1.75	2.50	3.50
	1304	—	1.25	1.75	2.50	3.50
	1305	—	1.25	1.75	2.50	3.50
	1307	—	1.25	1.75	2.50	3.50
	1313	—	1.25	1.75	2.50	3.50
	1314	30	1.25	1.75	2.50	3.50
	1321	37	1.25	1.75	2.50	3.50

1/8 RUPEE

.818 SILVER, 1.397 g

14	AH1286	—	1.75	2.25	3.00	3.75
	1289	—	1.75	2.25	3.00	3.75
	1290	—	1.75	2.25	3.00	3.75
	1295	—	1.75	2.25	3.00	3.75
	1297	—	1.75	2.25	3.00	3.75
	1298	—	1.75	2.25	3.00	3.75
	1299	—	1.75	2.25	3.00	3.75
	1300	—	1.75	2.25	3.00	3.75
	1301	17	1.75	2.25	3.00	3.75
	1302	17	1.75	2.25	3.00	3.75
	1302	18	1.75	2.25	3.00	3.75
	1304	20	1.75	2.25	3.00	3.75
	1305	—	1.75	2.25	3.00	3.75
	1306	—	1.75	2.25	3.00	3.75
	1307	—	1.75	2.25	3.00	3.75
	1308	24	1.75	2.25	3.00	3.75
	1309	—	1.75	2.25	3.00	3.75
	1316	—	1.75	2.25	3.00	3.75
	1317	33	1.75	2.25	3.00	3.75
	1318	—	1.75	2.25	3.00	3.75
	1321	37	1.75	2.25	3.00	3.75
	Date off flan		1.00	1.50	2.00	2.75

1/4 RUPEE

.818 SILVER, 2.794 g

Y#	Date	Year	VG	Fine	VF	XF
15	AH1286	—	2.00	2.75	4.50	5.50
	1287	—	2.00	2.75	4.50	5.50
	1288	—	2.00	2.75	4.50	5.50
15	1290	—	2.00	2.75	4.50	5.50
	1291	7	2.00	2.75	4.50	5.50
	1294	—	2.00	2.75	4.50	5.50
	1295	—	2.00	2.75	4.50	5.50
	1298	14	2.00	2.75	4.50	5.50
	1299	15	2.00	2.75	4.50	5.50
	1300	16	2.00	2.75	4.50	5.50
	1301	17	2.00	2.75	4.50	5.50
	1302	—	2.00	2.75	4.50	5.50
	1304	—	2.00	2.75	4.50	5.50
	1305	22	2.00	2.75	4.50	5.50
	1306	—	2.00	2.75	4.50	5.50
	1307	23	2.00	2.75	4.50	5.50
	1307	24	2.00	2.75	4.50	5.50
	1308	—	2.00	2.75	4.50	5.50
	1309	—	2.00	2.75	4.50	5.50
	1310	—	2.00	2.75	4.50	5.50
	1313	29	2.00	2.75	4.50	5.50
	1314	—	2.00	2.75	4.50	5.50
	1316	32	2.00	2.75	4.50	5.50
	1316	33	2.00	2.75	4.50	5.50
	1317	33	2.00	2.75	4.50	5.50
	1321	—	2.00	2.75	4.50	5.50

1/2 RUPEE

.818 SILVER, 5.589 g

16	AH1286	7	3.00	4.00	5.50	10.00
	1289	—	3.00	4.00	5.50	10.00
	1291	—	3.00	4.00	5.50	10.00
	1292	—	3.00	4.00	5.50	10.00
	1294	10	3.00	4.00	5.50	10.00
	1295	—	3.00	4.00	5.50	10.00
	1299	15	3.00	4.00	5.50	10.00
	1301	17	3.00	4.00	5.50	10.00
	1302	18	3.00	4.00	5.50	10.00
	1304	—	3.00	4.00	5.50	10.00
	1305	22	3.00	4.00	5.50	10.00
	1306	22	3.00	4.00	5.50	10.00
	1307	23	3.00	4.00	5.50	10.00
	1308	—	3.00	4.00	5.50	10.00
	1310	—	3.00	4.00	5.50	10.00
	1316	32	3.00	4.00	5.50	10.00
	1317	—	3.00	4.00	5.50	10.00

RUPEE

.818 SILVER, 11.178 g

17	AH1286	1	4.50	5.50	6.50	9.00
	1287	—	4.50	5.50	6.50	9.00
	1288	3	4.50	5.50	6.50	9.00
	1289	4	4.50	5.50	6.50	9.00
	1293	—	4.50	5.50	6.50	9.00
	1294	10	4.50	5.50	6.50	9.00
	1295	10	4.50	5.50	6.50	9.00
	1295	11	4.50	5.50	6.50	9.00
	1298	—	4.50	5.50	6.50	9.00
	1299	15	4.50	5.50	6.50	9.00
	1299	16	4.50	5.50	6.50	9.00
	1300	16	4.50	5.50	6.50	9.00
	1301	—	4.50	5.50	6.50	9.00
	1302	18	4.50	5.50	6.50	9.00
	1305	—	4.50	5.50	6.50	9.00
	1306	22	4.50	5.50	6.50	9.00
	1307	23	4.50	5.50	6.50	9.00
	1308	24	4.50	5.50	6.50	9.00
	1308	25	4.50	5.50	6.50	9.00
	1309	25	4.50	5.50	6.50	9.00
	1310	26	4.50	5.50	6.50	9.00
	1315	32	4.50	5.50	6.50	9.00
	1316	32	4.50	5.50	6.50	9.00
	1317	33	4.50	5.50	6.50	9.00
	1317	34	4.50	5.50	6.50	9.00
	1318	34	4.50	5.50	6.50	9.00

1/16 ASHRAFI

.910 GOLD, 0.698 g

18	AH1305	—	20.00	30.00	40.00	60.00
	1314	—	20.00	30.00	40.00	60.00
	1315	—	20.00	30.00	40.00	60.00
	1321	—	20.00	30.00	40.00	60.00

1/8 ASHRAFI

Hyderabad / INDIAN PRINCELY STATES 909

.910 GOLD, 1.397 g

Y#	Date	Year	VG	Fine	VF	XF
19	AH1293	—	25.00	40.00	60.00	75.00
	1302	—	25.00	40.00	60.00	75.00
	1306	—	25.00	40.00	60.00	75.00
	1313	—	25.00	40.00	60.00	75.00
	1318	—	25.00	40.00	60.00	75.00
	1320	—	25.00	40.00	60.00	75.00
	1321	—	25.00	40.00	60.00	75.00

1/4 ASHRAFI

.910 GOLD, 2.794 g

20	AH1301	—	35.00	60.00	80.00	100.00
	1304	—	35.00	60.00	80.00	100.00
	1306	—	35.00	60.00	80.00	100.00
	1314	30	35.00	60.00	80.00	100.00
	1315	—	35.00	60.00	80.00	100.00
	1316	—	35.00	60.00	80.00	100.00
	1318	35	35.00	60.00	80.00	100.00

1/2 ASHRAFI

.910 GOLD, 5.589 g

21	AH1316	—	70.00	85.00	100.00	150.00
	1317	—	70.00	85.00	100.00	150.00

ASHRAFI

.910 GOLD, 11.178 g

22	AH1286	—	150.00	170.00	200.00	250.00
	1287	—	150.00	170.00	200.00	250.00
	1288	—	150.00	170.00	200.00	250.00
	1289	—	150.00	170.00	200.00	250.00
	1290	—	150.00	170.00	200.00	250.00
	1292	—	150.00	170.00	200.00	250.00
	1293	—	150.00	170.00	200.00	250.00
	1294	—	150.00	170.00	200.00	250.00
	1295	—	150.00	170.00	200.00	250.00
	1296	—	150.00	170.00	200.00	250.00
	1297	—	150.00	170.00	200.00	250.00
	1298	14	150.00	170.00	200.00	250.00
	1299	—	150.00	170.00	200.00	250.00
	1300	—	150.00	170.00	200.00	250.00
	1301	—	150.00	170.00	200.00	250.00
	1302	—	150.00	170.00	200.00	250.00
	1303	—	150.00	170.00	200.00	250.00
	1304	—	150.00	170.00	200.00	250.00
	1305	—	150.00	170.00	200.00	250.00
	1306	—	150.00	170.00	200.00	250.00
	1307	—	150.00	170.00	200.00	250.00
	1308	—	150.00	170.00	200.00	250.00
	1309	—	150.00	170.00	200.00	250.00
	1310	—	150.00	170.00	200.00	250.00
	1311	—	150.00	170.00	200.00	250.00
	1312	—	150.00	170.00	200.00	250.00
	1313	—	150.00	170.00	200.00	250.00
	1314	31	150.00	170.00	200.00	250.00
	1315	—	150.00	170.00	200.00	250.00
	1316	—	150.00	170.00	200.00	250.00
	1317	—	150.00	170.00	200.00	250.00
	1318	—	150.00	170.00	200.00	250.00
	1319	—	150.00	170.00	200.00	250.00
	1320	—	150.00	170.00	200.00	250.00
	1321	—	150.00	170.00	200.00	250.00

MILLED COINAGE
PROVISIONAL ISSUES
AH1305-1307

1/4 ANNA

COPPER

KM#	Date	Year	VG	Fine	VF	XF
27	AH1312	27	—	—	—	—
	1312	28	—	—	—	—

1/2 ANNA

COPPER

KM#	Date	Year	VG	Fine	VF	XF
28	AH1311	27	—	—	—	—

ANNA
COPPER

| 32.1 | AH1305 | 21 | 55.00 | 85.00 | 125.00 | 175.00 |

Modified design

| 32.2 | AH1307 | 22 | 55.00 | 85.00 | 125.00 | 175.00 |

2 ANNAS

.818 SILVER, 1.397 g

Y#	Date	Year	VG	Fine	VF	XF
29	AH1318	35	10.00	17.50	27.50	37.50

4 ANNAS

.818 SILVER, 2.794 g

30	AH1318	32	27.50	37.50	50.00	60.00
	1318	34	8.50	16.50	25.00	33.50
	1318	35	8.50	16.50	25.00	33.50

8 ANNAS

.818 SILVER, 5.589 g

31	AH1312	28	10.00	20.00	30.00	40.00
	1318	34	10.00	20.00	30.00	40.00
	1318	35	10.00	20.00	30.00	40.00

COPPER (OMS)

| 31a | AH1312 | 28 | — | — | — | — |

RUPEE

.818 SILVER, 11.178 g

32	AH1312	28	10.00	15.00	20.00	30.00
	1313	29	10.00	15.00	20.00	30.00
	1314	30	10.00	15.00	20.00	30.00
	1318	34	10.00	15.00	20.00	30.00

ASHRAFI

.910 GOLD, 24mm, 11.178 g

Y#	Date	Year	VG	Fine	VF	XF
33	AH1311	27	600.00	800.00	1000.	1250.

REGULAR COINAGE
REGNAL YEAR LOCATION
Copper and Silver Series

Year 20

Gold Series

Year 25

NOTE: The AH date exists with two different regnal years in many cases.

PAI

COPPER

Y#	Date	Year	Fine	VF	XF	Unc
34	AH1326	42	4.00	6.00	9.00	15.00
	1327	42	4.00	6.00	9.00	15.00
	1329	—	—	Reported, not confirmed		

2 PAI

COPPER

35	AH1322	37	1.00	1.25	1.75	2.75
	1322	38	.75	1.00	1.50	2.50
	1322	39	1.00	1.25	1.75	2.75
	1323	38	1.00	1.25	1.75	2.75
	1323	39	.60	.75	1.00	1.50
	1323	40	.75	1.00	1.50	2.50
	1323	41	.75	1.00	1.50	2.50
	1324	39	1.00	1.25	1.75	2.75
	1324	40	.60	.85	1.25	1.75
	1324	41	.75	1.00	1.50	2.50
	1325	40	1.00	1.25	1.75	2.75
	1325	41	.75	1.00	1.50	2.50
	1329	43	.50	.65	1.00	1.75
	1329	44	.50	.65	1.00	1.75
	1329	45	.50	.65	1.00	1.75

1/2 ANNA

COPPER

| 36 | AH1324 | 38 | 2.50 | 4.00 | 6.00 | 10.00 |

Hyderabad / INDIAN PRINCELY STATES 910

Y#	Date	Year	Fine	VF	XF	Unc
36	1324	40	1.50	2.25	3.00	4.00
	1324	41	2.25	3.00	3.50	4.50
	1325	40	2.00	3.25	3.75	5.50
	1325	41	2.00	3.25	3.75	5.50
	1326	41	2.50	3.75	4.50	7.00
	1329	44	1.50	2.50	3.00	4.00

2 ANNAS

.818 SILVER, 1.39 g

37	AH1323	34(SIC)	1.50	2.50	5.00	8.00
	1323	39	.75	1.25	3.00	5.00

4 ANNAS

.818 SILVER, 2.794 g

38	AH1323	39	4.00	4.75	5.50	9.00
	1326	43	8.50	16.50	25.00	32.50
	1328	43	4.00	4.75	6.00	10.00
	1329	44	4.00	4.75	5.50	9.00

8 ANNAS

.818 SILVER, 5.589 g

39	AH1322	38	—	—	Rare	—
	1328	43	6.50	7.50	9.00	15.00
	1329	44	6.50	7.50	9.00	15.00

RUPEE

.818 SILVER, 11.178 g

40	AH1319	35	—	—	—	—
	1321	37	11.50	13.50	16.50	26.50
	1321	38	11.50	13.50	15.00	24.00
	1322	38	11.50	13.50	15.00	24.00
	1322	39	11.50	13.50	15.00	24.00
	1323	39	11.50	13.50	15.00	24.00
	1324	40	11.50	13.50	15.00	24.00
	1325	41	11.50	13.50	15.00	24.00
	1326	41	11.50	13.50	15.00	24.00
	1328	43	11.50	13.50	15.00	24.00
	1329	44	11.50	13.50	15.00	24.00

1/8 ASHRAFI

.910 GOLD, 1.394 g

41	AH1325	41	25.00	35.00	50.00	85.00

1/4 ASHRAFI

.910 GOLD, 2.794 g

42	AH1325	41	40.00	50.00	75.00	125.00
	1329	44	40.00	50.00	75.00	125.00

1/2 ASHRAFI

.910 GOLD, 5.589 g

Y#	Date	Year	Fine	VF	XF	Unc
43	AH1325	41	80.00	100.00	150.00	250.00
	1326	41	80.00	100.00	150.00	250.00
	1329	44	80.00	100.00	150.00	250.00

SILVER (OMS)

43a	AH1324	40	—	—	—	—

ASHRAFI

.910 GOLD, 24mm, 11.178 g

44	AH1325	41	165.00	225.00	300.00	400.00
	1329	—	165.00	225.00	300.00	400.00

SILVER (OMS)

44a	AH1324	40	—	—	—	—

MIR USMAN ALI KHAN
AH1329-1368/1911-1948AD

First Coinage
AH1329-1361

PAI

BRONZE

45	AH1338	—	1.50	2.00	2.50	4.00
	1344	15	.60	.75	1.00	1.50
	1349	20	.60	.75	1.00	1.50
	1352	23	1.00	1.25	1.50	2.50
	1352	24	1.00	1.25	1.50	2.50
	1353	24	.70	.85	1.10	1.75

2 PAI

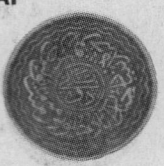

ع

BRONZE
Obv: Short *Ain* in toughra.

46	AH1329	1	10.00	15.00	22.50	35.00
	1330	1	8.00	12.50	20.00	32.50

NOTE: See also 1 Rupee, Y#53 and Y#53a.

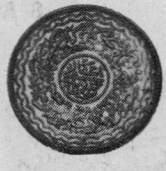

ع

Obv: Full *Ain* in toughra.

46a	AH1330	1	1.50	2.00	2.50	3.50
	1330	2	.35	.50	.65	1.00
	1331	2	.35	.50	.65	1.00
	1331	3	.50	.65	.75	1.00
	1332	3	.35	.50	.65	1.00
	1332	4	.60	.75	1.00	1.50
	1333	3	.60	.75	1.00	1.50
	1333	4	.35	.50	.65	1.00
	1333	5	.75	1.00	1.25	2.00
	1334	3	.60	.75	1.00	1.50
	1335	6	.35	.50	.65	1.00
	1335	7	.35	.50	.65	1.00
	1336	7	.35	.50	.65	1.00
	1336	8	.50	.65	.80	1.25
	1337	7	.75	1.00	1.25	2.00
	1337	8	.60	.75	1.00	1.50
	1338	8	.75	1.00	1.25	2.00
	1338	9	.35	.50	.65	1.00
	1338	11	.50	.75	1.00	1.50
	1339	10	.75	1.00	1.25	2.00
	1339	11	.75	1.00	1.25	2.00
	1342	13	.60	.75	1.00	1.50
	1342	14	.35	.50	.65	1.00
	1343	14	.35	.50	.65	1.00
	1343	15	.40	.60	.75	1.25
	1344	15	.50	.65	.80	1.25
	1345	16	.35	.50	.65	1.00
	1347	18	.75	1.00	1.25	2.00
	1347	19	.75	1.00	1.25	2.00
	1348	19	.35	.50	.65	1.00
	1349	20	.35	.50	.65	1.00

1/2 ANNA

BRONZE

Y#	Date	Year	Fine	VF	XF	Unc
47	AH1332	2	.75	1.00	1.25	2.00
	1332	3	.75	1.00	1.25	2.00
	1334	4	1.25	1.50	2.00	3.25
	1344	15	1.25	1.50	2.00	3.25
	1348	20	1.00	1.35	1.75	2.75

ANNA

COPPER-NICKEL

48	AH1338	—	.50	.75	1.00	1.50
	1339	—	1.00	1.35	1.75	2.75
	1340	—	.60	.85	1.25	1.75
	1341	—	.75	1.00	1.35	2.00
	1344	—	.50	.75	1.00	1.50
	1347	—	.50	.75	1.00	1.50
	1348	—	.60	.85	1.25	1.75
	1349	—	.50	.75	1.00	1.50
	1351	—	.50	.75	1.00	1.50
	1352	—	1.00	1.35	1.75	2.75
	1353	—	.50	.75	1.00	1.50
	1354	—	.50	.75	1.00	1.50

49	AH1356	—	.35	.50	.65	1.00
	1357	—	.50	.65	.85	1.35
	1358	—	.35	.50	.65	1.00
	1359	—	.75	1.00	1.25	2.00
	1360	—	.75	1.00	1.25	2.00
	1361	—	.75	1.00	1.25	2.00

2 ANNAS

.818 SILVER, 1.397 g

50	AH1335	6	1.25	1.75	2.50	4.00
	1337	9	1.00	1.50	2.50	4.00
	1338	10	1.00	1.50	2.50	4.00
	1340	11	1.00	1.50	2.50	4.00
	1341	13	1.00	1.50	2.50	4.00
	1341	14	1.25	2.00	3.00	5.00
	1342	13	1.00	1.50	2.50	4.00
	1343	14	1.00	1.50	2.25	3.50
	1343	15	1.00	1.50	2.25	3.50
	1347	—	1.25	2.00	3.00	5.00
	1348	19	1.00	1.50	2.25	3.50
	1351	22	1.00	1.50	2.50	4.00
	1355	26	1.00	1.50	2.50	4.00

4 ANNAS

.818 SILVER, 2.794 g

51	AH1337	9	1.75	3.00	4.50	7.00
	1340	11	1.75	3.00	4.50	7.00
	1342	13	1.75	3.00	4.50	7.00
	1342	14	1.75	3.00	4.50	7.00
	1348	19	1.75	3.00	4.50	7.00
	1351	22	1.75	3.00	4.50	7.00
	1354	25	1.75	3.00	4.50	7.00
	1358	30	1.75	3.00	4.50	7.00

8 ANNAS

.818 SILVER, 5.589 g

Y#	Date	Year	Fine	VF	XF	Unc
52	AH1337	9	3.50	5.00	8.00	12.00
	1342	13	3.50	5.00	8.00	12.00
	1343	13	3.50	5.00	8.00	12.00
	1354	25	3.50	5.00	8.00	12.00

RUPEE

.818 SILVER, 11.178 g
Obv: Partial initial *Ain* in doorway.

53	AH1330	1	BV	7.50	10.00	25.00

Obv: Full *Ain* in doorway.

53a	AH1330	1	6.00	10.00	12.50	25.00
	1330	2	6.00	10.00	12.50	25.00
	1331	2	BV	7.50	10.00	20.00
	1331	3	BV	7.50	10.00	20.00
	1332	3	BV	7.50	10.00	20.00
	1334	6	BV	7.50	10.00	20.00
	1335	6	BV	7.50	10.00	20.00
	1335	7	BV	7.50	10.00	20.00
	1336	7	BV	7.50	10.00	20.00
	1337	8	BV	7.50	10.00	20.00
	1337	9	11.50	15.00	20.00	25.00
	1338	9	BV	7.50	10.00	20.00
	1339	9	BV	7.50	10.00	20.00
	1340	11	BV	7.50	10.00	20.00
	1341	12	BV	7.50	10.00	20.00
	1342	13	BV	7.50	10.00	20.00
	1343	14	BV	7.50	10.00	20.00

1/8 ASHRAFI
.910 GOLD, 1.394 g

54	AH1329	1	—	—	Rare	—
	1337	8	35.00	50.00	60.00	75.00
	1344	15	35.00	50.00	60.00	75.00
	1354	—	35.00	50.00	60.00	75.00
	1366	37	35.00	50.00	60.00	75.00
	1368	39	35.00	50.00	60.00	75.00

1/4 ASHRAFI

.910 GOLD, 2.794 g

55	AH1337	8	50.00	65.00	85.00	100.00
	1342	13	50.00	65.00	85.00	100.00
	1349	20	50.00	65.00	85.00	100.00
	1357	—	50.00	65.00	85.00	100.00
	1360	31	50.00	65.00	85.00	100.00

1/2 ASHRAFI

.910 GOLD, 21mm, 5.589 g

Y#	Date	Year	Fine	VF	XF	Unc
56	AH1337	8	80.00	100.00	150.00	250.00
	1343	14	80.00	100.00	150.00	250.00
	1345	16	80.00	100.00	150.00	250.00
	1349	20	80.00	100.00	150.00	250.00
	1354	25	80.00	100.00	150.00	250.00
	1357	—	80.00	100.00	150.00	250.00

ASHRAFI
.910 GOLD, 24mm, 11.178 g
Obv: Partial initial *Ain* in doorway.

57	AH1330	1	200.00	250.00	350.00	450.00

Obv: Full *Ain* in doorway.

57a	AH1331	3	150.00	185.00	250.00	350.00
	1333	4	150.00	185.00	250.00	350.00
	1337	8	150.00	185.00	250.00	350.00
	1337	9	150.00	185.00	250.00	350.00
	1338	9	150.00	185.00	250.00	350.00
	1340	11	150.00	185.00	250.00	350.00
	1343	14	150.00	185.00	250.00	350.00
	1344	15	150.00	185.00	250.00	350.00
	1348	19	150.00	185.00	250.00	350.00
	1349	20	150.00	185.00	250.00	350.00
	1354	25	150.00	185.00	250.00	350.00

Second Coinage
AH1361-1368

2 PAI

BRONZE

58	AH1362	33	.25	.35	.50	.75
	1363	34	.25	.35	.50	.75
	1363	35	.20	.25	.50	.75
	1364	35	.20	.25	.50	.75
	1365	36	.20	.25	.50	.75
	1366	37	.20	.25	.50	.75
	1368	39	.20	.25	.50	.75

ANNA

BRONZE

59	AH1361	—	.40	.50	.60	1.00
	1362	—	.40	.50	.60	1.00
	1364	—	.40	.50	.60	1.00
	1365	—	.40	.50	.60	1.00
	1366	—	.40	.50	.60	1.00
	1368	—	.40	.50	.60	1.00

2 ANNAS

SILVER, 1.397 g

60	AH1362	33	.40	.50	.60	1.00

NICKEL

64	AH1366	37	.15	.20	.25	.35	.60
	1368	39	.15	.20	.25	.35	.45	.90

4 ANNAS

SILVER, 2.794 g

Y#	Date	Year	Fine	VF	XF	Unc
61	AH1362	33	.70	.80	1.00	1.65
	1362	34	.75	.90	1.10	1.75
	1364	33	—			
	1364	35	.80	1.00	1.25	2.00
	1364	36	.80	1.00	1.25	2.00
	1365	36	.80	1.00	1.25	2.00

NICKEL

65	AH1366	37	.40	.50	.60	1.00
	1368	39	.40	.50	.60	1.00

8 ANNAS

SILVER, 5.589 g

62	AH1363	34	3.00	5.00	8.50	12.00

NICKEL

66	AH1366	37	.70	.85	1.00	1.65

RUPEE

SILVER, 11.178 g

63	AH1361	31	BV	6.00	7.50	10.00
	1361	32	BV	6.00	7.50	10.00
	1362	34	BV	6.00	7.50	10.00
	1364	35	BV	6.00	7.50	10.00
	1364	36	BV	6.00	7.50	10.00
	1365	36	BV	6.00	7.50	10.00

HYDERABAD FEUDATORIES

AURANGABAD
'TOKA' CASH
COPPER
Rev: Battle-axe in canopy, date below.

C#	Date	Year	Good	VG	Fine	VF
28	FE1241	—	5.00	10.00	16.50	25.00

Date in Nagari numerals.

30	AH1273	—	4.00	8.00	12.50	20.00

NOTE: C#28 and #30 were named after Toka Raj who operated the Aurangabad Mint under a state license from about 1830.

ELICHPUR
ANONYMOUS COINAGE
PAISA

COPPER, 18-20mm, 11.50 g
Obv: Tiger right.

C#	Date	Year	Good	VG	Fine	VF
10	AH1250	—	3.50	4.00	6.00	10.00
	Date off flan	—	2.00	2.75	3.50	5.00

Obv: Tiger left.

10a	AH1250	—	5.00	6.00	8.00	11.50
	1285	—	5.00	6.00	8.00	11.50
	Date off flan	—	2.50	3.00	4.00	5.50

2 PAISA

COPPER
Obv: Tiger left.

15	AH1250	—	5.00	7.50	11.50	20.00

Obv: Tiger right.

15a	AH1250	—	5.00	7.50	12.50	20.00

KALAYANI
Kallian
A town located in north Mysore.

NAWAB
Mohammad Shah Khair al-Din
Mint mark:

كليان

1/8 RUPEE

SILVER, 1.34-1.45 g

KM#	Date	Year	VG	Fine	VF	XF
2	AH1226	—	12.00	15.00	18.50	25.00

RUPEE

SILVER, 10.70-11.60 g
Rev: W/o Persian *Ha* to right of tiger.

5	ND	—	26.50	37.50	50.00	70.00

Rev: Persian *Ha* to right of tiger.

6	AH1226	—	26.50	37.50	50.00	70.00
	ND	—	26.50	37.50	50.00	70.00

NARAYANPETT
Local Rajas
Dilshadabad on coins.

MINT MARKS

ती *Ti* obv. dated AH1186/1186, C#40

क *K* rev. dated AH1186/1186, C#40

गो *Go* obv. dated AH1186/1252, C#37-40

ल *L* rev. dated AH1186/1252, C#37-40

In the name of Shah Alam II
AH1173-1221/1759-1806AD

PAISA

COPPER

C#	Date	Year	Good	VG	Fine	VF
34	AH1202	1252	4.00	6.50	8.00	11.50

1/8 RUPEE

SILVER, 1.34-1.45 g

C#	Date	Year	VG	Fine	VF	XF
37	AH1186	1252	5.00	7.50	10.00	15.00

1/4 RUPEE

SILVER, 13mm, 2.68-2.90 g

38	AH1186	1252	6.00	10.00	15.00	22.50

1/2 RUPEE

SILVER, 16mm, 5.35-5.80 g

39	AH1186	1252	7.00	11.50	16.50	25.00

RUPEE

SILVER, 10.70-11.60 g

40	AH1186	1186	10.00	13.50	15.00	20.00
	1186	1239	12.50	15.00	21.50	30.00
	1186	1245	12.50	15.00	21.50	30.00
	1186	1251	—	—	—	—
	1186	1252	10.00	13.50	15.00	20.00

SHORAPUR
Bahiri Feudatory
1/2 PAISA
COPPER, 14mm
Similar to 1 Paisa, C#63.

C#	Date	Year	Good	VG	Fine	VF
62	ND	—	5.00	6.50	8.00	10.00

COPPER, 13mm
Similar to C#66.

65	AH1262	—	4.00	—	6.50	9.00

PAISA

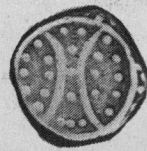

COPPER

63	ND	—	3.00	4.00	5.00	7.00

Rev: Inscribed *Bahiri*.

C#	Date	Year	Good	VG	Fine	VF
64	ND	—	4.00	5.00	6.50	9.00

Rev: *Bahiri*, date.

66	AH1261	—	4.00	5.00	6.50	9.00
	1262	—	4.00	5.00	6.50	9.00

Obv: Different from C#66.

67	AH1262	—	4.00	5.00	6.50	9.00

WANPARTI
Bahiri Rajas
Sagur mintname on coins is Nasirabad. The latter is honorific for the Sagur Mint copied from the rupees of Dharwar.

In the name of Muhammad Akbar II
AH1221-1253/1806-1837AD

1/4 RUPEE
SILVER, 2.67-2.90 g

78	AH1235	14	7.50	11.50	16.50	22.50

RUPEE

SILVER, 10.70-11.60 g
Obv: 'J'. Rev: 'A' in Nagari.

C#	Date	Year	VG	Fine	VF	XF
80	AH1235	14	7.50	11.50	16.50	22.50
	1235	15	7.50	11.50	16.50	22.50

INDORE

The Holkars were one of the three dominant Maratha powers (with the Peshwas and Sindhias), with major land holdings in Central India.

Indore State originated in 1728 with a grant of land north of the Narbada river by the Maratha Peshwa of Poona to Malhar Rao Holkar, a cavalry commander in his service. After Holkar's death (ca.1765) his daughter-in-law, Ahalya Bai, assumed the position of Queen Regent. Together with Tukoji Rao she effectively ruled the State until her death thirty years later. But it was left to Tukoji's son, Jaswant Rao, to challenge the dominance of the Poona Marathas in the Maratha Confederacy, eventually defeating the Peshwa's army in 1802. But at this point the fortunes of the Holkars suffered a serious reverse. Although Jaswant Rao had initially defeated a small British force under Col. William Monson, he was badly beaten by a contingent under Lord Lake. As a result Holkar was forced to cede a considerable portion of his territory and from this time until India's independence in 1947, the residual State of Indore was obliged to accept British protection.

BHS numbers are in reference to A STUDY OF HOLKAR STATE COINAGE, by S.K. Bhatt, R. Holkar and P.K. Sethi.

HOLKAR RULERS
Jaswant Rao
  SE1719-1734/AH1213-1226/
  1798-1811AD
Mulhar Rao II
  AH1226-1248/1811-1833AD
Martand Rao
  AH1249/1834AD
Hari Rao
  AH1250-1260/1834-1843AD
Khande Rao
  AH1260-1261/1843-1844AD
Tukoji Rao II
  VS1891-1943/SE1766-1808/
  AH1261-1304/1844-1886AD
Shivaji Rao
  VS1943-1960/FE1296-1313/
  1886-1903AD
Tukoji Rao III
  VS1960-1983/1903-1926AD
Yashwant Rao
  VS1983-2005/1926-1948AD

REGNAL YEARS
In reference to:
Alamgir II, Year 1/AH1168-1169

Shah Alam II, Year 1/AH1173-1174
Muhammad Akbar II, Year 1/AH1222-1223
Malhar Rao I, as Subehdar, Year 1/
  AH1170-1171

MINTS

Indore اندور or इंदौर

ज़ाफ़राबाद उर्फ़ चांदोर
J'afarabad urf Chandor

Maheshwar (see Malharnagar)

ملهارنگر
Malharnagar

سرونج
Sironj

MUGHAL ISSUES

In the name of Shah Alam II
Until AH1296/1880AD all coinage of Indore was struck in the name of Shah Alam II, with the exception of a few rare special or nazarana issues. The coinage of the individual rulers until 1880AD cannot be told apart except by the date, as no change of type was made for more than a century.

INDORE MINT
JASWANT RAO
SE1719-1734/AH1212-1226
1797-1811AD
NAZARANA RUPEE

SILVER, 10.70-11.60 g

C#	Date	Year	VG	Fine	VF	XF
52	SE1728	(1806)	65.00	80.00	100.00	135.00

In the name of Muhammad Akbar II
AH1221-1253/1806-1837AD
and Jaswant Rao

| 53 | SE1728 | (1806) | — | — | Rare | — |

| 58 | AH1222 | 2 | 20.00 | 35.00 | 55.00 | 85.00 |

Presentation Issues
TUKOJI RAO II
VS1891-1943/SE1766-1808
AH1260-1304/1844-1886AD
COPPER 1/2 MUDRA

COPPER, 4.35-5.10 g

BHS#	Date	Year	Good	VG	Fine	VF
520	SE1780	(1858)	20.00	30.00	40.00	55.00
	1788	VS1923	20.00	30.00	40.00	55.00

COPPER MUDRA

COPPER, 7.80-11.00 g

| 515 | SE1780 | (1858) | — | — | Rare | — |
| | 1788 | VS1923 | — | — | Rare | — |

1/2 ANNA

COPPER, 16.60 g

| 513 | VS1942 | (1885) | — | — | Rare | — |

13.40 g

| 514 | VS1942/SE1807/1885 | | | | | |
| | | | 40.00 | 50.00 | 65.00 | 80.00 |

SILVER MUDRA

SILVER, 11.20 g

BHS#	Date	Year	VG	Fine	VF	XF
388	SE1780	(1858)	40.00	55.00	75.00	100.00

Obv: Blank within wreath.

| 389 | SE1780 | (1858) | 40.00 | 55.00 | 75.00 | 100.00 |

Obv: Two varieties of swirls.

| 391 | SE1780 | (1858) | 50.00 | 80.00 | 120.00 | 150.00 |

| 392 | SE1788 | VS1923 | 40.00 | 55.00 | 75.00 | 100.00 |

BHS#	Date	Year	VG	Fine	VF	XF
393	VS1934	FE1287	60.00	75.00	90.00	110.00

| 393.1 | VS1934 | FE1287 | — | — | Rare | — |

1/2 RUPEE

SILVER, 5.50 g

| 433 | AH1289 | — | 55.00 | 70.00 | 85.00 | 110.00 |
| 394 | ND | — | 55.00 | 70.00 | 85.00 | 110.00 |

RUPEE

SILVER, 11.20 g

| 394 | ND | — | 25.00 | 35.00 | 45.00 | 60.00 |

| 395 | AH1289 | — | 40.00 | 55.00 | 70.00 | 90.00 |

| 399 | AH1295 | — | 40.00 | 55.00 | 70.00 | 90.00 |

MOHUR

GOLD, 10.83 g

C#	Date	Year	VG	Fine	VF	XF
120	VS1941	(1883)	—	—	Rare	—

Milled Coinage
SHIVAJI RAO
VS1943-1960/FE1296-1313/1886-1903AD
Without ruler's name

1/2 PAISA

COPPER
Rev: Denomination in 2 lines: 1/2 Adhela Paisa.

Y#	Date	Year	Good	VG	Fine	VF
9.1	VS1944	(1887)	10.00	15.00	21.50	30.00

Indore / INDIAN PRINCELY STATES 914

Rev: Denomination in 3 lines: *1/2 Dhaleka Paisa.*

Y#	Date	Year	Good	VG	Fine	VF
9.2	VS1944	(1887)	10.00	15.00	21.50	30.00

In the name of Shivaji Rao

Rev: Denomination in 2 lines: *Adha Paisa.*

| 9a | VS1946 | (1889) | 11.50 | 16.50 | 23.50 | 32.50 |

Without ruler's name

1/4 ANNA

COPPER
Obv: Date under bull.

| 10.1 | VS1943 | (1886) | 1.50 | 3.00 | 5.00 | 7.50 |

Rev. leg: Retrograde.

| 10.2 | VS1943 | (1886) | — | — | — | — |

Obv: *Indore* **upside-down below bull.**

10.3	VS1943	(1886)	.35	.75	1.25	2.50
	1944	(1887)	.50	1.00	1.50	3.00
	1945	(1888)	.75	1.25	2.00	4.00

Obv: *Indore* **upright below bull.**

| 10.5 | VS1943 | (1886) | 2.00 | 4.00 | 6.50 | 8.50 |

Obv: Cross w/dot in each quadrant flanking *Indore.*

| 10.4 | VS1943 | (1886) | 1.00 | 2.00 | 3.00 | 6.00 |

In the name of Sivaji Rao

Obv: Name of ruler & *Indore.* **Rev: Date.**

Y#	Date	Year	Good	VG	Fine	VF
10a.1	VS1944	(1887)	.85	1.75	2.50	5.00
	1945	(1888)	.75	1.50	2.00	4.00
	1946	(1889)	.85	1.75	2.50	5.00
	1947	(1890)	.75	1.50	2.00	4.00

Obv: Ruler's name spelled *Sayaji Rao.*

| 10.2a | VS1944 | (1887) | 1.00 | 2.00 | 4.00 | 8.00 |

Obv: Name of ruler and *Bahadur.*
Rev: Date and *Indore.*

10a.3	VS1947	(1890)	.75	1.50	2.25	4.50
	1948	(1891)	.50	1.00	1.50	3.00
	1956	(1899)	.35	.75	1.25	2.50
	1957	(1900)	.65	1.25	1.75	2.50
	1958	(1901)	.65	1.25	1.75	3.50
	1959	(1902)	.65	1.25	1.75	3.50

Obv: Similar to Y#10a.1 but w/o *Indore.*

| 10a.4 | VS1948 | (1891) | 1.00 | 2.00 | 4.00 | 6.00 |

Obv: Similar to Y#10a.3.
Rev: Floral border redesigned.

| 10a.5 | VS1857 | (1900) | .65 | 1.25 | 1.75 | 3.50 |

NOTE: Varieties exist.

Without ruler's name

1/2 ANNA

COPPER
Obv: Date under bull. Rev: *Indore.*

| 11.1 | VS1943 | (1886) | 3.00 | 5.00 | 8.50 | 14.00 |

Obv: *Indore* **upside-down below bull.**

| 11.2 | VS1943 | (1886) | 3.00 | 5.00 | 7.00 | 10.00 |
| | 1944 | (1887) | 3.00 | 5.00 | 7.00 | 10.00 |

Obv. and rev: *Indore.*

Y#	Date	Year	Good	VG	Fine	VF
11.3	VS1943	(1886)	4.00	6.00	8.50	12.50

Obv: *Indore* **upside-down below bull.**

| 11.4 | VS1943 | (1886) | 3.00 | 5.00 | 7.00 | 10.00 |

In the name of Sivaji Rao

Obv: Name of ruler & *Indore.* **Rev: Date.**

11a.1	VS1944	(1887)	3.00	5.00	7.00	10.00
	1945	(1888)	3.00	5.00	7.00	10.00
	1947	(1890)	7.50	13.50	20.00	30.00

Obv: *Bahadur* **upright below bull. Rev:** *State.*

| 11a.2 | VS1943 | (1886) | 3.50 | 5.50 | 8.50 | 11.50 |

Obv: Name of ruler and *Bahadur.*
Rev: Date & *Indore.*

11a.3	VS1945	(1888)	1.00	1.50	2.25	4.50
	1947	(1890)	1.00	1.50	2.00	4.00
	1948	(1891)	1.00	1.50	2.00	3.00
	1956	(1899)	1.00	1.50	2.00	3.00
	1957	(1900)	1.00	1.50	2.00	3.00
	1958	(1901)	1.00	1.50	2.00	4.00
	1959	(1902)	1.00	1.50	2.00	4.00

Rev: Wreath facing clockwise.

| 11a.4 | VS1944 | (1887) | — | — | — | — |

Dump Coinage

First Series
Crossed scimitar and spear below sunface w/Fasli Era and Vikrama Samvat Era dating.

1/4 RUPEE

SILVER, 2.68-2.90 g

Y#	Date	Year	VG	Fine	VF	XF
12	FE1295	VS1945	15.00	20.00	25.00	32.50

1/2 RUPEE

SILVER, 5.35-5.80 g

Y#	Date	Year	VG	Fine	VF	XF
13	FE1295	VS1947	15.00	20.00	25.00	32.50
	1296	VS1947	15.00	20.00	25.00	32.50

RUPEE

SILVER, 10.70-11.60 g
Obv: Large flames.

14.1	FE1294	VS1945	22.50	27.50	35.00	45.00
	1295	VS1945	22.50	27.50	35.00	45.00
	1296	VS1945	22.50	27.50	35.00	45.00

Obv: Small flames.

14.2	FE1295	R.Y.122	20.00	25.00	30.00	38.50
	1296	VS1945	20.00	25.00	30.00	38.50

Obv: W/o flames.

14.3	FE1295	VS1947	20.00	26.50	32.50	40.00
	1296	1947	20.00	26.50	32.50	40.00
	1297	1947	20.00	26.50	32.50	40.00

Second Series
NOTE: There are 2 minor varieties, one w/U-shaped mark on forehead of sunface, the other w/dot on forehead, Vikrama Samvat Era dating.

PAISA
COPPER

A15	VS1948	—	—	Rare	—

1/8 RUPEE

SILVER, 1.34-1.45 g

15	VS1947	(1890)	2.00	2.50	3.25	5.00
	1950	(1893)	2.00	2.50	3.25	5.00
	1951	(1894)	2.00	2.50	3.25	5.00

1/4 RUPEE

SILVER, 2.68-2.90 g

16	VS1947	(1890)	2.50	3.25	4.50	6.50
	1951	(1893)	2.50	3.25	4.50	6.50
	1954	(1897)	2.50	3.25	4.50	6.50
	Date off flan		1.50	2.00	2.75	4.00

1/2 RUPEE

SILVER, 5.35-5.80 g

17	VS1947	(1890)	3.50	4.50	6.00	10.00
	1948	(1891)	3.50	4.50	6.00	10.00
	1949	(1892)	3.50	4.50	6.00	10.00
	1950	(1893)	3.50	4.50	6.00	10.00
	1951	(1894)	3.50	4.50	6.00	10.00
	1952	(1895)	3.50	4.50	6.00	10.00
	1953	(1896)	3.50	4.50	6.00	10.00
	1954	(1897)	3.50	4.50	6.00	10.00
	Date off flan		2.00	2.75	3.50	6.00

RUPEE

SILVER, 10.70-11.60 g

Y#	Date	Year	VG	Fine	VF	XF
18	VS1947	(1890)	BV	6.00	7.50	10.00
	1948	(1891)	BV	6.00	7.50	10.00
	1949	(1892)	BV	6.00	7.50	10.00
	1950	(1893)	BV	6.00	7.50	10.00
	1951	(1894)	BV	6.00	7.50	10.00
	1952	(1895)	BV	6.00	7.50	10.00
	1953	(1896)	BV	6.00	7.50	10.00
	1954	(1897)	BV	6.00	7.50	10.00
	1955	(1898)	BV	6.00	7.50	10.00
	Date off flan		BV	6.00	7.50	10.00

Presentation Issues
NAZARANA RUPEE

SILVER, 11.13-11.21 g

18.1	VS1947	(1890)	35.00	55.00	75.00	100.00

Regular Coinage
Yeshwant Rao
VS1983-2005 / 1926-1948AD

1/4 ANNA

COPPER

Y#	Date	Year	Fine	VF	XF	Unc
20	VS1992	1935	1.00	2.00	3.50	6.00

1/2 ANNA

COPPER

21	VS1992	1935	1.25	2.50	4.00	7.00

MAHESHWAR MINT
Distinctive Marks:

Bilva Leaf   Linga - Yoni.
Silver   Copper and Silver.

1/4 RUPEE

SILVER, 2.68-2.90 g
Rev: Bilva leaf and linga.

BHS#	Date	Year	VG	Fine	VF	XF
80	AH1217	—	8.50	12.50	16.50	21.50

1/2 RUPEE

SILVER, 5.35-5.80 g
Rev: Bilva leaf and linga.

BHS#	Date	Year	VG	Fine	VF	XF
70	AH1216	44	11.00	15.00	20.00	27.50
	1217	—	11.00	15.00	20.00	27.50

RUPEE

SILVER, 10.70-11.60 g
Rev: Bilva leaf and linga.

24	AH1216	44	7.00	9.00	11.50	16.50
	1217	46	7.00	9.00	11.50	16.50

MALHARNAGAR MINT
Mintname: Malharnagar
Distinctive Marks:

Bilva Leaf   Sunface
Copper   Copper and Silver

1/2 PAISA

COPPER, 3.80 g

BHS#	Date	Year	Good	VG	Fine	VF
142	ND	—	5.00	7.50	10.00	13.50

1/4 ANNA

COPPER, 9.60-9.70 g

290	AH1244	—	3.00	4.00	5.50	7.50
	—	88	3.00	4.00	5.50	7.50

COPPER, 12.20-12.40 g
Obv. leg: Hindi leg. *Pau Anna*

518	AH1267	97	5.00	6.50	8.50	11.50

1/2 ANNA

COPPER, 18.70-20.00 g

287	AH1243	1251	3.00	4.00	5.50	7.50
	1244	—	3.00	4.00	5.50	7.50
	—	88	3.00	4.00	5.50	7.50

Indore / INDIAN PRINCELY STATES

COPPER, 12.00-17.30 g
Obv. leg: *Hindi Adha Anna*

BHS#	Date	Year	Good	VG	Fine	VF
484	AH1261	—	2.50	3.25	4.00	6.00
	1266	—	2.50	3.25	4.00	6.00
	1267	97	2.75	3.50	4.50	6.50
	1268	—	2.50	3.25	4.00	6.00
	1269	99	3.00	3.50	4.50	6.50
	1271	—	2.50	3.25	4.00	6.00
	1285	—	1.75	2.50	3.50	5.50
	1286	113	2.25	3.00	4.00	6.00

1286 dated both sides
| | | — | 3.00 | 3.50 | 4.00 | 6.00 |

NAZARANA 1/2 ANNA

COPPER

| 484a | AH12xx | 99 | — | — | — | — |

1/2 ANNA

COPPER

| 494 | — | — | 3.00 | 3.50 | 4.00 | 6.00 |

| 502 | AH1286 | — | 3.00 | 4.00 | 5.00 | 6.50 |

In the name of shah Alam II
AH1173-1221/1759-1806AD

1/8 RUPEE

SILVER, 1.34-1.45 g

BHS#	Date	Year	VG	Fine	VF	XF
251	AH1236	—	3.50	4.00	5.00	7.50
	1237	—	3.50	4.00	5.00	7.50
	1248	—	2.50	3.25	4.00	6.00
	(12)55	—	2.50	3.25	4.00	6.00
	1262	—	2.50	3.25	4.00	6.00
	1268	—	2.50	3.25	4.00	6.00
	1269	—	2.50	3.25	4.00	6.00
	1270	—	2.50	3.25	4.00	6.00
	1278	—	2.50	3.25	4.00	6.00
	1279	—	2.50	3.25	4.00	6.00
	1282	—	2.00	3.25	4.00	6.00
	1289	—	2.50	3.25	4.00	6.00
	1291	—	2.50	3.25	4.00	6.00
	1293	—	2.50	3.25	4.00	6.00
	1294	—	2.50	3.25	4.00	6.00
	1295	—	2.50	3.25	4.00	6.00

1/4 RUPEE

SILVER, 2.68-2.90 g

BHS#	Date	Year	VG	Fine	VF	XF
83	AH1214	—	2.50	3.25	4.50	6.00
	1231	—	2.50	3.25	4.50	6.00
	1232	—	2.50	3.25	4.50	6.00
	1233	—	2.50	3.25	4.50	6.00
	1234	—	2.50	3.25	4.50	6.00
	1235	—	2.50	3.25	4.50	6.00
	1237	—	2.50	3.25	4.50	6.00
	1240	—	2.50	3.25	4.50	6.00
	1241	—	2.50	3.25	4.50	6.00
	1244	—	2.50	3.25	4.50	6.00
	1249	—	2.50	3.25	4.50	6.00
	1250	—	2.50	3.25	4.50	6.00
	1251	—	2.50	3.25	4.50	6.00
	1252	—	2.50	3.25	4.50	6.00
	1253	—	2.50	3.25	4.50	6.00
	1256	—	2.50	3.25	4.50	6.00

BHS#	Date	Year	VG	Fine	VF	XF
83	1261	—	2.50	3.25	4.50	6.00
	1263	—	2.50	3.25	4.50	6.00
	1264	—	2.50	3.25	4.50	6.00
	1265	—	2.50	3.25	4.50	6.00
	1266	—	2.50	3.25	4.50	6.00
	1267	—	2.50	3.25	4.50	6.00
	1268	—	2.50	3.25	4.50	6.00
	1269	—	2.50	3.25	4.50	6.00
	1270	—	2.50	3.25	4.50	6.00
	1272	—	2.50	3.25	4.50	6.00
	1275	—	2.50	3.25	4.50	6.00
	1277	—	2.50	3.25	4.50	6.00
	1278	—	2.50	3.25	4.50	6.00
	1279	—	2.50	3.25	4.50	6.00
	1282	—	2.50	3.25	4.50	6.00
	1285	—	2.50	3.25	4.50	6.00
	1286	—	2.50	3.25	4.50	6.00
	1288	—	2.50	3.25	4.50	6.00
	1289	—	2.50	3.25	4.50	6.00
	1290	—	2.50	3.25	4.50	6.00
	1291	—	2.50	3.25	4.50	6.00
	1292	—	2.50	3.25	4.50	6.00
	1293	—	2.50	3.25	4.50	6.00
	1294	—	2.50	3.25	4.50	6.00
	1295	—	2.50	3.25	4.50	6.00

25mm
Broad, thin planchet

| 451 | AH1280 | 110 | 20.00 | 25.00 | 30.00 | 40.00 |

1/2 RUPEE

SILVER, 5.35-5.80 g

74	AH1227	—	3.25	4.50	6.50	10.00
	1228	—	3.25	4.50	6.50	10.00
	1230	—	3.25	4.50	6.50	10.00
	1233	—	3.25	4.50	6.50	10.00
	1238	—	3.25	4.50	6.50	10.00
	1242	—	3.25	4.50	6.50	10.00
	1246	—	3.25	4.50	6.50	10.00
	1250	—	3.25	4.50	6.50	10.00
	1251	—	3.25	4.50	6.50	10.00
	1255	—	3.25	4.50	6.50	10.00
	1262	—	3.25	4.50	6.50	10.00
	1263	—	3.25	4.50	6.50	10.00
	1264	—	3.25	4.50	6.50	10.00
	1265	—	3.25	4.50	6.50	10.00
	1266	—	3.25	4.50	6.50	10.00
	1267	—	3.25	4.50	6.50	10.00
	1268	—	3.25	4.50	6.50	10.00
	1270	—	3.25	4.50	6.50	10.00
	1272	—	3.25	4.50	6.50	10.00
	1273	—	3.25	4.50	6.50	10.00
	1275	—	3.25	4.50	6.50	10.00
	1276	—	3.25	4.50	6.50	10.00
	1278	—	3.25	4.50	6.50	10.00
	1279	—	3.25	4.50	6.50	10.00
	1280	—	3.25	4.50	6.50	10.00
	1281	—	3.25	4.50	6.50	10.00
	1283	—	3.25	4.50	6.50	10.00
	1285	—	3.25	4.50	6.50	10.00
	1286	—	3.25	4.50	6.50	10.00
	1288	—	3.25	4.50	6.50	10.00
	1289	—	3.25	4.50	6.50	10.00
	1291	—	3.25	4.50	6.50	10.00
	1292	—	3.25	4.50	6.50	10.00
	1293	—	3.25	4.50	6.50	10.00
	1294	—	3.25	4.50	6.50	10.00
	1295	—	3.25	4.50	6.50	10.00
	1296	—	3.25	4.50	6.50	10.00
		121	3.25	4.50	6.50	10.00

NAZARANA 1/2 RUPEE

SILVER, 5.35-5.80 g
Broad, thin planchet

| 418 | AH1236 | 69 | 25.00 | 32.50 | 40.00 | 50.00 |
| | 1280 | 110 | 35.00 | 45.00 | 55.00 | 67.50 |

RUPEE

SILVER, 10.70-11.60 g

33	AH1216	—	3.50	5.50	8.50	13.50
	1217	44	3.50	5.50	8.50	13.50
	1224	—	3.50	5.50	8.50	13.50

BHS#	Date	Year	VG	Fine	VF	XF
33	1225	—	3.50	5.50	8.50	13.50
	1226	60	3.50	5.50	8.50	13.50
	1228	62	3.50	5.50	8.50	13.50
	1230	61	3.50	5.50	8.50	13.50
	1230	62	3.50	5.50	8.50	13.50
	1231	63	3.50	5.50	8.50	13.50
	1232	65	3.50	5.50	8.50	13.50
	1233	66	3.50	5.50	8.50	13.50
	1234	67	3.50	5.50	8.50	13.50
	1235	68	3.50	5.50	8.50	13.50
	1237	70	3.50	5.50	8.50	13.50
	1238	70	3.50	5.50	8.50	13.50
	1242	75	3.50	5.50	8.50	13.50
	1243	76	3.50	5.50	8.50	13.50
	1244	72	3.50	5.50	8.50	13.50
	1246	76	3.50	5.50	8.50	13.50
	1248	77	3.50	5.50	8.50	13.50
	1249	—	3.50	5.50	8.50	13.50
	1251	—	3.50	5.50	8.50	13.50
	1255	—	3.50	5.50	8.50	13.50
	1257	87	3.50	5.50	8.50	13.50
	1258	88	3.50	5.50	8.50	13.50
	1260	9x	3.50	5.50	8.50	13.50
	1262	—	3.50	5.50	8.50	13.50
	1263	—	3.50	5.50	8.50	13.50
	1264	94	3.50	5.50	8.50	13.50
	1265	95	3.50	5.50	8.50	13.50
	1266	9x	3.50	5.50	8.50	13.50
	1266	96	3.50	5.50	8.50	13.50
	1267	97	3.50	5.50	8.50	13.50
	1269	9x	3.50	5.50	8.50	13.50
	1270	—	3.50	5.50	8.50	13.50
	1272	102	3.50	5.50	8.50	13.50
	1273	—	3.50	5.50	8.50	13.50
	1275	—	3.50	5.50	8.50	13.50
	1276	—	3.50	5.50	8.50	13.50
	1277	—	3.50	5.50	8.50	13.50
	1278	—	3.50	5.50	8.50	13.50
	1279	—	3.50	5.50	8.50	13.50
	1280	—	3.50	5.50	8.50	13.50
	1282	111	3.50	5.50	8.50	13.50
	1285	—	3.50	5.50	8.50	13.50
	1286	113	3.50	5.50	8.50	13.50
	1288	—	3.50	5.50	8.50	13.50
	1289	—	3.50	5.50	8.50	13.50
	1292	118	3.50	5.50	8.50	13.50
	1292	120	3.50	5.50	8.50	13.50
	1293	111	3.50	5.50	8.50	13.50
	1293	119	3.50	5.50	8.50	13.50
	1294	120	3.50	5.50	8.50	13.50
	1295	121	3.50	5.50	8.50	13.50
	1295	122	3.50	5.50	8.50	13.50
	1296	122	3.50	5.50	8.50	13.50

Broad, thinner planchet, 28mm

| 10a | AH1280 | 110 | 35.00 | 50.00 | 70.00 | 100.00 |

NAZARANA RUPEE

SILVER, 10.70-11.60 g

| 164 | AH1225 | 59 | — | — | Rare | — |

UNCERTAIN MINTS
1/2 ANNA

Symbol Series

COPPER
Obv: Mace. Rev: Branch w/3 leaves.

KM#	Date	Year	Good	VG	Fine	VF
23	AH1228	—	3.50	4.50	5.50	7.50

Obv: Katar. Rev: Axe.

| 24 | AH1230 | — | 3.50 | 4.50 | 5.50 | 7.50 |

Rev: Jhar and mace.

KM#	Date	Year	Good	VG	Fine	VF
25	AH1230	—	3.50	4.50	5.50	7.50

Obv: Katar. Rev: Broad axe.

26	AH1230	—	3.50	4.50	5.50	7.50

Obv: Broad axe. Rev: Dagger.

27	AH1233	66	3.50	4.50	5.50	7.50
	1241	—	3.50	4.50	5.50	7.50

Obv: Pinwheel. Rev: Geometric design.

28	ND		3.50	4.50	5.50	7.50

Obv: Trisul and double pennant flags.
Rev: Broad axe.

29	AH1220	—	3.50	4.50	5.50	7.50

NOTE: These coins were struck AH1202-1244 with many minor varieties of symbols of which the above are only a sample.

JAIPUR

Tradition has it that the region of Jaipur, located in northwest India, once belonged to an ancient Kachwaha Rajput dynasty which claimed descent from Kush, one of the sons of Rama, King of Ayodhya. But the Princely State of Jaipur originated in the twelfth century. Comparatively small in size, the State remained largely unnoticed until after the sixteenth century when the Jaipur royal house became famous for its military skills and thereafter supplied the Mughals with some of their more distinguished generals. The city of Jaipur was founded about 1728 by Maharaja Jai Singh II who was also well known for his knowledge of mathematics and astronomy. The late eighteenth and early nineteenth centuries were difficult times for Jaipur. They were marked by internal rivalry, exacerbated by Maratha or Pindari incursions. In 1818 this culminated with a treaty whereby Jaipur came under British protection and oversight.

RULERS
Pratap Singh
  AH1192-1218/1778-1803AD
Jagat Singh II
  AH1218-1234/1803-1818AD
Mohan Singh
  AH1234-1235/1818-1819AD
Jai Singh III
  AH1235-1251/1819-1835AD
Ram Singh
  AH1251-1298/1835-1880AD
Madho Singh II, 1880-1922AD
Man Singh II, 1922-1949AD

All coins struck prior to AH1274/1857AD are in the name of the Mughal emperor. The corresponding AH date is listed in ( ) with each regnal year. Some overlapping of AH dates with regnal years will be found. Partial dates and recorded full dates are represented by partial ( ) or without ( ).
Beginning in 1857AD, coins were struck jointly in the names and corresponding AD dates of the British sovereign and the names and regnal years of the Maharajas of Jaipur.
The coins ordinarily bear both AH date before 1857 or the AD date after 1857 as well as the regnal year, but as it is found only at the extreme right of the obverse die, it almost never is visible on the regular coinage but generally legible on the Nazarana coins which were struck utilizing the entire dies.
The listing of regnal years is very incomplete and many more years will turn up. In general, unlisted years are usually worth no more than years listed.

MINTNAMES
Coins were struck at two mints, which bear the following characteristic marks on the reverse:

سواى جى پور
Sawai Jaipur Mint

سواى موهوپور
Sawai Madhopur Mint

(*Sawai* is merely an honorific title accorded each of the two cities.)

Mintmarks:

Jhar   Whisk
Leaf

JAIPUR MINT
Mughal Issues
In the name of Shah Alam II
AH1173-1221/1759-1806AD

PAISA

COPPER
Rev: Large Jhar.

C#	Date	Year	Good	VG	Fine	VF
35	AH—	44	1.00	2.00	3.50	5.50
	—	45	1.00	2.00	3.50	5.50

NAZARANA PAISA
COPPER
Rev: Large Jhar.

35a	AH—	45	8.00	14.00	25.00	40.00

RUPEE

SILVER, 10.70-11.60 g

C#	Date	Year	VG	Fine	VF	XF
36	AH—	44	5.00	7.50	11.50	16.50
	—	45	5.00	7.50	11.50	16.50
	(1218)	46	5.00	7.50	11.50	16.50
	(1219)	47	5.00	7.50	11.50	16.50

In the name of Muhammad Akbar II
AH1221-1253/1806-1837AD

NAZARANA PAISA

COPPER
Rev: Whisk.

C#	Date	Year	Good	VG	Fine	VF
46	AH—	3	9.00	17.50	27.50	45.00
	—	8	9.00	17.50	27.50	45.00
	—	11	9.00	17.50	27.50	45.00

PAISA
COPPER, 18-20mm
Similar to Nazarana Paisa, C#47a.

C#	Date	Year	Good	VG	Fine	VF
47	AH—	12	1.50	2.50	3.50	5.00
	—	13	1.50	2.50	3.50	5.00
	—	17	1.50	2.50	3.50	5.00
	—	22	1.50	2.50	3.50	5.00
	—	26	1.50	2.50	3.50	5.00
	—	27	1.50	2.50	3.50	5.00
	—	29	1.50	2.50	3.50	5.00
	—	35	1.50	2.50	3.50	5.00

NAZARANA PAISA

COPPER
Rev: Jhar.

47a	AH—	4	7.50	12.50	18.50	25.00
	—	9	7.50	12.50	18.50	25.00
	—	11	7.50	12.50	18.50	25.00
	—	15	7.50	12.50	18.50	25.00
	—	16	7.50	12.50	18.50	25.00
	—	22	7.50	12.50	18.50	25.00
	—	28	7.50	12.50	18.50	25.00

1/8 RUPEE
SILVER, 17-18mm, 1.34-1.45 g

C#	Date	Year	VG	Fine	VF	XF
52	AH(1242)	22	6.00	7.50	10.00	17.50

1/4 RUPEE
SILVER, 18-19mm, 2.68-2.90 g

53	AH(1237)	17	6.00	7.50	10.00	17.50
	—	20	6.00	7.50	10.00	17.50
	—	24	7.50	10.00	15.00	25.00
	(1248)	28	6.00	7.50	10.00	17.50

1/2 RUPEE
SILVER, 18-20mm, 5.35-5.80 g

54	AH(1236)	16	6.00	8.50	12.50	20.00
	—	23	6.00	8.50	12.50	20.00
	(1251)	31	6.00	8.50	12.50	20.00

RUPEE

SILVER, 10.70-11.60 g

55	AH1221	1	—	6.00	9.00	15.00
	1222	2	5.00	6.00	9.00	15.00
	122(3)	3	5.00	6.00	9.00	15.00
	1226	4	5.00	6.00	9.00	15.00
	1228	6	5.00	6.00	9.00	15.00
	1229	9	5.00	6.00	9.00	15.00
	1230	10	5.00	6.00	9.00	15.00
	1233	11	5.00	6.00	9.00	15.00
		12	5.00	6.00	9.00	15.00
	1233	13	5.00	6.00	9.00	15.00
	1234	14	5.00	6.00	9.00	15.00
	1235	15	5.00	6.00	9.00	15.00
	1238	18	5.00	6.00	9.00	15.00
	1240	20	5.00	6.00	9.00	15.00
	1246	25	5.00	6.00	9.00	15.00
		26	5.00	6.00	9.00	15.00
	1249	27	5.00	6.00	9.00	15.00
	1250	30	5.00	6.00	9.00	15.00
		31	5.00	6.00	9.00	15.00

Square

55b	AH123x	10	—	—	Rare	

NAZARANA RUPEE

C#	Date	Year	VG	Fine	VF	XF
	1246	25	15.00	25.00	40.00	60.00
	1248	27	15.00	25.00	40.00	60.00
	1249	27	15.00	25.00	40.00	60.00
	1249	29	15.00	25.00	40.00	60.00
	1251	29	15.00	25.00	40.00	60.00
	—	30	15.00	25.00	40.00	60.00

MOHUR

GOLD, 10.70-11.60 g

C#	Date	Year	VG	Fine	VF	XF
62	AH122(1)	1	BV	160.00	225.00	300.00
	(1227)	7	BV	160.00	225.00	300.00
	(1228)	8	BV	160.00	225.00	300.00
	(1229)	9	BV	160.00	225.00	300.00
	(1231)	11	BV	160.00	225.00	300.00
	(1232)	12	BV	160.00	225.00	300.00
	(1236)	16	BV	160.00	225.00	300.00
	(1239)	19	BV	160.00	225.00	300.00
	12(44)	24	BV	160.00	225.00	300.00
	(1249)	29	BV	160.00	225.00	300.00
	(1250)	30	BV	160.00	225.00	300.00

In the name of Bahadur Shah II
AH1253-1274/1837-1858AD

PAISA

COPPER

C#	Date	Year	Good	VG	Fine	VF
85	AH—	13	1.50	3.25	5.00	8.50

NAZARANA PAISA

COPPER

85a	AH—	1	7.50	12.50	20.00	30.00
	—	2	7.50	12.50	20.00	30.00
	—	6	7.50	12.50	20.00	30.00
	—	10	7.50	12.50	20.00	30.00
	—	11	7.50	12.50	20.00	30.00
	—	12	7.50	12.50	20.00	30.00
	—	13	7.50	12.50	20.00	30.00
	—	17	7.50	12.50	20.00	30.00

1/16 RUPEE

SILVER, 0.67-0.72 g

C#	Date	Year	VG	Fine	VF	XF
89	AH(1259)	7	5.00	7.50	12.50	20.00
	(1261)	9	5.00	7.50	12.50	20.00
	(1270)	18	5.00	7.50	12.50	20.00

1/8 RUPEE

SILVER, 15mm, 1.34-1.45 g

90	AH(1270)	18	5.50	7.50	12.50	20.00

1/4 RUPEE

SILVER, 16-18mm, 2.68-2.90 g

91	AH(1259)	7	5.00	7.50	11.50	17.50
	—	19	5.00	7.50	11.50	17.50
	(1272)	20	5.00	7.50	11.50	17.50

1/2 RUPEE

SILVER, 18-19mm, 5.35-5.80 g

92	AH(1257)	5	5.00	7.50	11.50	17.50
	—	11	5.00	7.50	11.50	17.50
	(1270)	18	5.00	7.50	11.50	17.50

RUPEE

SILVER, 10.70-11.60 g

C#	Date	Year	VG	Fine	VF	XF
93	AH1253	1	5.00	6.50	10.00	16.50
	1256	3	5.00	6.50	10.00	16.50
	1257	4	5.00	6.50	10.00	16.50
	1258	5	5.00	6.50	10.00	16.50
	1261	8	5.00	6.50	10.00	16.50
	1262	9	5.00	6.50	10.00	16.50
	1263	10	5.00	6.50	10.00	16.50
	—	11	5.00	6.50	10.00	16.50
	1265	12	5.00	6.50	10.00	16.50
	1268	14	5.00	6.50	10.00	16.50
	—	15	5.00	6.50	10.00	16.50
	1270	17	5.00	6.50	10.00	16.50
	1271	17	5.00	6.50	10.00	16.50
	—	19	5.00	6.50	10.00	16.50
	1273	20	5.00	6.50	10.00	16.50

NAZARANA RUPEE

SILVER, 32-35mm, 10.70-11.60 g

93a	AH(1256)	3	20.00	30.00	40.00	65.00
	1258	4	20.00	30.00	40.00	65.00
	1262	9	20.00	30.00	40.00	65.00
	1264	11	20.00	30.00	40.00	65.00
	1268	8	(error-mule)			
			20.00	30.00	40.00	65.00
	(1266)	13	20.00	30.00	40.00	65.00
	(1271)	19	20.00	30.00	40.00	65.00
	1273	20	20.00	30.00	40.00	65.00

1/4 MOHUR

GOLD, 17mm, 2.68-2.85 g

98	AH(1264)	12	80.00	125.00	150.00	225.00

1/2 MOHUR

GOLD, 18mm, 5.35-5.70 g

99	AH(1264)	12	100.00	150.00	200.00	275.00

MOHUR

GOLD, 10.70-11.40 g

100	AH1253	1	150.00	200.00	250.00	325.00
	(1257)	5	150.00	200.00	250.00	325.00
	12(59)	7	150.00	200.00	250.00	325.00
	1262	9	150.00	200.00	250.00	325.00
	(1262)	10	150.00	200.00	250.00	325.00
	(1264)	12	150.00	200.00	250.00	325.00
	(1265)	13	150.00	200.00	250.00	325.00
	(1266)	14	150.00	200.00	250.00	325.00
	(1267)	15	150.00	200.00	250.00	325.00
	(1271)	19	150.00	200.00	250.00	325.00
	1272	18	150.00	200.00	250.00	325.00
	(1272)	20	150.00	200.00	250.00	325.00

Regal Issues
In the names of Queen Victoria

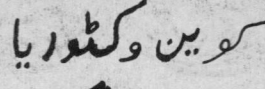

and Ram Singh
Years 22-45 / 1857-1880AD

NEW PAISA

COPPER

Y#	Date	Year	Good	VG	Fine	VF
1	(1871)	36	.60	1.00	1.75	3.00
	(1872)	37	.60	1.00	1.75	3.00
	(1873)	38	.60	1.00	1.75	3.00
	(1874)	39	.60	1.00	1.75	3.00
	(1875)	40	.60	1.00	1.75	3.00
	(1876)	41	.60	1.00	1.75	3.00
	(1877)	42	.60	1.00	1.75	3.00
	(1880)	45	.75	1.25	2.00	3.50

NOTE: Years 36 and 37 are struck on broader flans.

NAZARANA OLD PAISA

COPPER

1a	1858	23	5.00	8.50	15.00	22.50

NAZARANA NEW PAISA

COPPER, 28mm

1b	1862	27	5.00	8.50	15.00	22.50
	1864	29	5.00	8.50	15.00	22.50
	1865	30	5.00	8.50	15.00	22.50
	1872	37	5.00	8.50	15.00	22.50
	1873	38	5.00	8.50	15.00	22.50
	1875	40	5.00	8.50	15.00	22.50
	1876	41	5.00	8.50	15.00	22.50
	1879	44	5.00	8.50	15.00	22.50
	1880	45	5.00	8.50	15.00	22.50

1/8 RUPEE

SILVER, 14mm, 1.34-1.45 g

Y#	Date	Year	VG	Fine	VF	XF
3	(1857)	22	1.50	3.00	5.50	10.00
	(1877)	42	1.50	3.00	5.50	10.00

1/4 RUPEE

SILVER, 2.68-2.90 g

4	(1861)	26	2.00	4.00	6.50	10.00
	(1862)	27	2.00	4.00	6.50	10.00
	(1863)	28	2.00	4.00	6.50	10.00
	(1867)	32	2.00	4.00	6.50	10.00
	(1868)	33	2.00	4.00	6.50	10.00
	(1876)	41	2.00	4.00	6.50	10.00
	(1878)	43	2.00	4.00	6.50	10.00
	(1879)	44	2.00	4.00	6.50	10.00

NAZARANA 1/4 RUPEE

SILVER

4a	(1879)	44	12.50	20.00	32.50	50.00

1/2 RUPEE

SILVER, 18-21mm, 5.35-5.80 g

5	(1857)	22	3.00	5.00	7.50	12.50
	(1862)	27	3.00	5.00	7.50	12.50
	(1868)	33	3.00	5.00	7.50	12.50
	(1869)	35	3.00	5.00	7.50	12.50
	(1871)	36	3.00	5.00	7.50	12.50
	—	42	3.00	5.00	7.50	12.50
	(1879)	44	3.00	5.00	7.50	12.50
	(1880)	45	3.00	5.00	7.50	12.50

NAZARANA 1/2 RUPEE

SILVER

5a	(1865)	30	12.50	20.00	32.50	50.00

RUPEE

SILVER, 10.70-11.60 g

6	(1858)	23	4.00	6.00	8.50	13.50
	(1860)	25	4.00	6.00	8.50	13.50
	(1862)	27	4.00	6.00	8.50	13.50
	(1864)	29	4.00	6.00	8.50	13.50
	(1865)	30	4.00	6.00	8.50	13.50
	1866	31	4.00	6.00	8.50	13.50
	(1867)	32	4.00	6.00	8.50	13.50

Y#	Date	Year	VG	Fine	VF	XF
6	(1868)	33	4.00	6.00	8.50	13.50
	1869	34	4.00	6.00	8.50	13.50
	(1870)	35	4.00	6.00	8.50	13.50
	(1871)	36	4.00	6.00	8.50	13.50
	(1873)	38	4.00	6.00	8.50	13.50
	(1875)	40	4.00	6.00	8.50	13.50
	(1876)	41	4.00	6.00	8.50	13.50
	(1877)	42	4.00	6.00	8.50	13.50
	(1878)	43	4.00	6.00	8.50	13.50
	(1879)	44	4.00	6.00	8.50	13.50
	(1880)	45	4.00	6.00	8.50	13.50

NAZARANA RUPEE

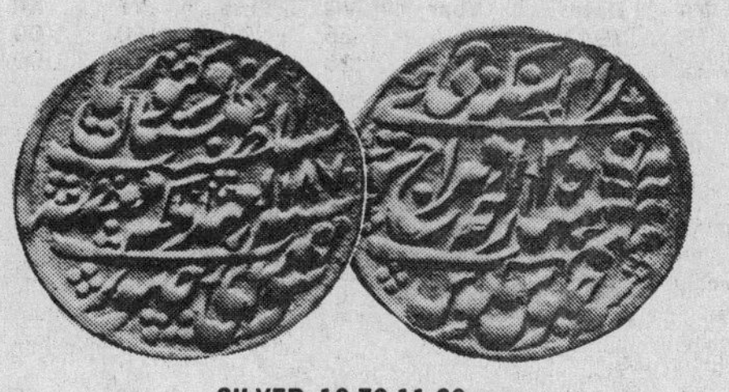

SILVER, 10.70-11.60 g

6a	1858	23	12.50	20.00	32.50	50.00
	1859	24	12.50	20.00	32.50	50.00
	1861	26	12.50	20.00	32.50	50.00
	1864	29	12.50	20.00	32.50	50.00
	1865	30	12.50	20.00	32.50	50.00
	1866	31	12.50	20.00	32.50	50.00
	1867	32	12.50	20.00	32.50	50.00
	1870	35	12.50	20.00	32.50	50.00
	1871	36	12.50	20.00	32.50	50.00
	1875	40	12.50	20.00	32.50	50.00

MOHUR

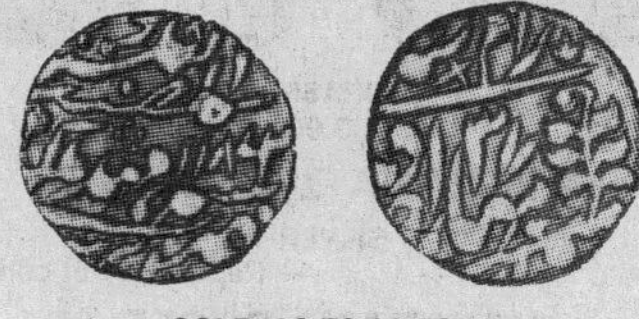

GOLD, 10.70-11.40 g

7	(1856)	21	BV	160.00	225.00	250.00
	18(58)	23	BV	160.00	225.00	250.00
	(1860)	25	BV	160.00	225.00	250.00
	1861	26	BV	160.00	225.00	250.00
	(1864)	29	BV	160.00	225.00	250.00
	(1871)	36	BV	160.00	225.00	250.00
	(1872)	37	BV	160.00	225.00	250.00

In the names of Queen Victoria

کوین وکٹوریا

مادھو سنگھ

and Madho Singh II

Years 1-43/1880-1922AD

NOTE: Queen Victoria's name was retained on Madho Singh II's coinage until 1922AD. No coins were struck with Edward VII's name by Madho Singh II.

1/2 PAISA

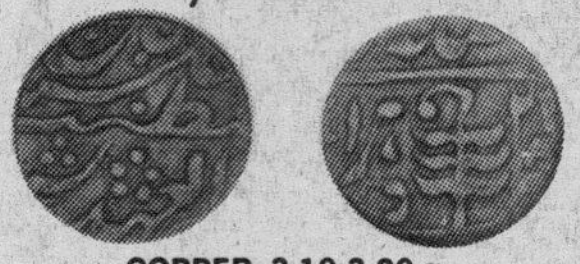

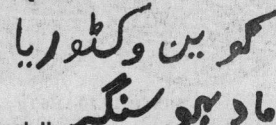

COPPER, 3.10-3.20 g

Y#	Date	Year	Good	VG	Fine	VF
A8	—	22	2.50	5.00	8.50	12.50

PAISA

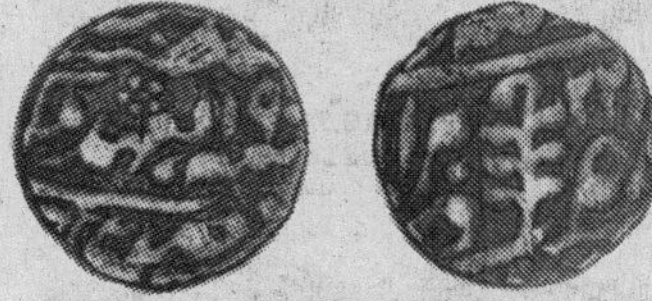

COPPER

Y#	Date	Year	Good	VG	Fine	VF
8	(1882)	3	.30	.50	1.00	2.00
	(1883)	4	.30	.50	1.00	2.00
	(1884)	5	.30	.50	1.00	2.00
	(1887)	8	.30	.50	1.00	2.00
	(1898)	19	.20	.40	.85	1.50
	(1899)	20	.20	.40	.85	1.50
	(1900)	21	.20	.40	.85	1.50
	(1901)	22	.20	.40	.85	1.50
	(1902)	23	.20	.40	.85	1.50
	(1903)	24	.20	.40	.85	1.50
	(1904)	25	.20	.40	.85	1.50
	(1906)	27	.20	.40	.85	1.50
	(1907)	28	.20	.40	.85	1.50
	(1908)	29	.20	.40	.85	1.50
	(1916)	37	.20	.40	.85	1.50
	(1917)	38	.20	.40	.85	1.50

Y#	Date	Year	Good	VG	Fine	VF
8	(1918)	39	.20	.40	.85	1.50
	(1920)	41	.20	.40	.85	1.50

NAZARANA NEW PAISA

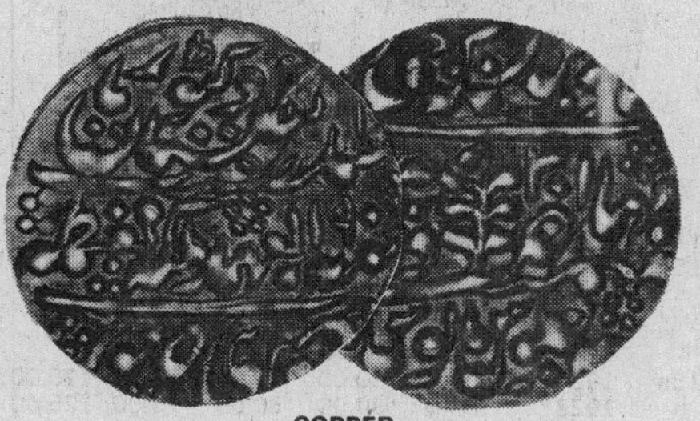

COPPER

Y#	Date	Year	VG	Fine	VF	XF
8a	1880	1	2.50	5.00	8.50	12.50
	1897	17	2.50	5.00	8.50	12.50
	1897	18	2.50	5.00	8.50	12.50
	1899	20	2.50	5.00	8.50	12.50
	1900	21	2.50	5.00	8.50	12.50
	1901	22	2.50	5.00	8.50	12.50
	1902	23	2.50	5.00	8.50	12.50
	1903	24	2.50	5.00	8.50	12.50
	1904	25	2.50	5.00	8.50	12.50
	1905	26	2.50	5.00	8.50	12.50
	1906	27	2.50	5.00	8.50	12.50
	1907	28	2.50	5.00	8.50	12.50
	1908	29	2.50	5.00	8.50	12.50
	1909	30	2.50	5.00	8.50	12.50
	1910	31	2.50	5.00	8.50	12.50
	1911	32	2.50	5.00	8.50	12.50
	1912	33	2.50	5.00	8.50	12.50
	1913	34	2.50	5.00	8.50	12.50
	1914	35	2.50	5.00	8.50	12.50
	1915	36	2.50	5.00	8.50	12.50
	1916	37	2.50	5.00	8.50	12.50

1/16 RUPEE

SILVER, 10mm, 0.67-0.72 g

9	(1881)	2	2.00	4.00	6.50	10.00
	(1889)	10	2.00	4.00	6.50	10.00

1/8 RUPEE

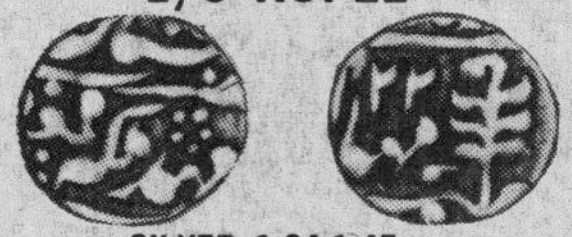

SILVER, 1.34-1.45 g

10	(1883)	4	1.50	3.00	5.50	8.50
	(1885)	6	1.50	3.00	5.50	8.50
	(1890)	11	1.50	3.00	5.50	8.50
	(1891)	12	1.50	3.00	5.50	8.50
	(1897)	18	1.50	3.00	5.50	8.50
	(1898)	19	1.50	3.00	5.50	8.50
	(1900)	21	1.50	3.00	5.50	8.50
	(1901)	22	1.50	3.00	5.50	8.50
	(1902)	23	1.50	3.00	5.50	8.50
	(1905)	26	1.50	3.00	5.50	8.50
	(1906)	27	1.50	3.00	5.50	8.50
	(1907)	28	1.50	3.00	5.50	8.50
	(1908)	29	1.50	3.00	5.50	8.50
	(1920)	41	1.50	3.00	5.50	8.50
	(1921)	42	1.50	3.00	5.50	8.50

1/4 RUPEE

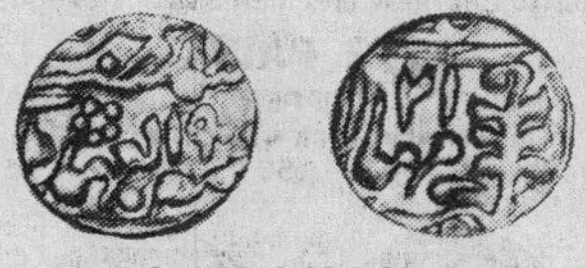

SILVER, 2.68-2.90 g

11	(1880)	1	2.00	4.00	6.50	10.00
	(1881)	2	2.00	4.00	6.50	10.00
	(1883)	4	2.00	4.00	6.50	10.00
	(1886)	7	2.00	4.00	6.50	10.00
	(1887)	8	2.00	4.00	6.50	10.00
	(1889)	10	2.00	4.00	6.50	10.00
	(1890)	11	2.00	4.00	6.50	10.00
	(1891)	12	2.00	4.00	6.50	10.00
	(1893)	14	2.00	4.00	6.50	10.00
	(1894)	15	2.00	4.00	6.50	10.00
	(1895)	16	2.00	4.00	6.50	10.00
	(1896)	17	2.00	4.00	6.50	10.00
	(1897)	18	2.00	4.00	6.50	10.00
	(1898)	19	2.00	4.00	6.50	10.00
	(1899)	20	2.00	4.00	6.50	10.00
	1900	21	2.00	4.00	6.50	10.00
	(1901)	22	2.00	4.00	6.50	10.00
	(1902)	23	2.00	4.00	6.50	10.00
	(1903)	24	2.00	4.00	6.50	10.00
	(1905)	26	2.00	4.00	6.50	10.00
	(1906)	27	2.00	4.00	6.50	10.00
	(1907)	28	2.00	4.00	6.50	10.00
	(1908)	29	2.00	4.00	6.50	10.00
	(1909)	30	2.00	4.00	6.50	10.00
	(1913)	34	2.00	4.00	6.50	10.00
	(1916)	37	2.00	4.00	6.50	10.00
	(1917)	38	2.00	4.00	6.50	10.00
	(1921)	42	2.00	4.00	6.50	10.00

1/2 RUPEE

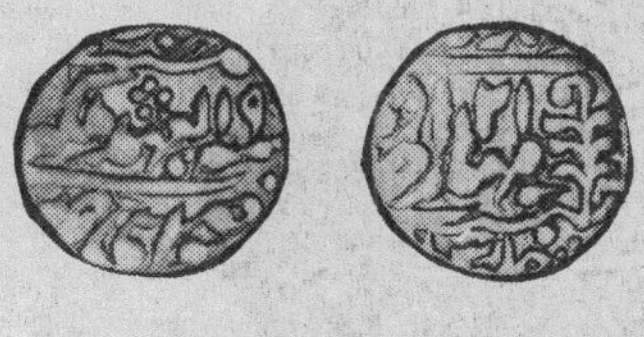

SILVER, 5.35-5.80 g

Y#	Date	Year	VG	Fine	VF	XF
12	(1880)	1	3.00	5.00	7.50	12.50
	(1882)	3	3.00	5.00	7.50	12.50
	(1883)	4	3.00	5.00	7.50	12.50
	(1884)	5	3.00	5.00	7.50	12.50
	(1886)	7	3.00	5.00	7.50	12.50
	(1887)	8	3.00	5.00	7.50	12.50
	(1888)	9	3.00	5.00	7.50	12.50
	(1889)	10	3.00	5.00	7.50	12.50
	(1891)	12	3.00	5.00	7.50	12.50
	(1893)	14	3.00	5.00	7.50	12.50
	(1894)	15	3.00	5.00	7.50	12.50
	(1896)	17	3.00	5.00	7.50	12.50
	(1897)	18	3.00	5.00	7.50	12.50
	(1898)	19	3.00	5.00	7.50	12.50
	(1899)	20	3.00	5.00	7.50	12.50
	190(0)	21	3.00	5.00	7.50	12.50
	(1901)	22	3.00	5.00	7.50	12.50
	(1902)	23	3.00	5.00	7.50	12.50
	(1905)	26	3.00	5.00	7.50	12.50
	(1908)	29	3.00	5.00	7.50	12.50
	(1909)	30	3.00	5.00	7.50	12.50
	(1916)	37	3.00	5.00	7.50	12.50

RUPEE

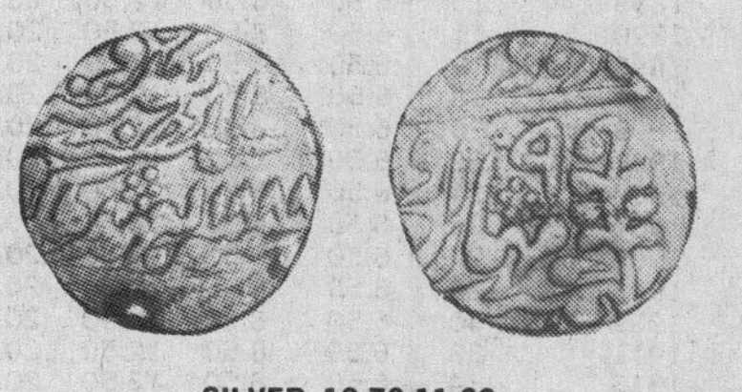

SILVER, 10.70-11.60 g

13	(1880)	1	4.00	6.00	8.50	13.50
	(1881)	2	4.00	6.00	8.50	13.50
	(1882)	3	4.00	6.00	8.50	13.50
	(1883)	4	4.00	6.00	8.50	13.50
	(1884)	5	4.00	6.00	8.50	13.50
	(1885)	6	4.00	6.00	8.50	13.50
	(1886)	7	4.00	6.00	8.50	13.50
	1886	8	4.00	6.00	8.50	13.50
	(1887)	8	4.00	6.00	8.50	13.50
	1888	9	4.00	6.00	8.50	13.50
	(1889)	10	4.00	6.00	8.50	13.50
	(1890)	11	4.00	6.00	8.50	13.50
	(1891)	12	4.00	6.00	8.50	13.50
	(1892)	13	4.00	6.00	8.50	13.50
	(1893)	14	4.00	6.00	8.50	13.50
	(1894)	15	4.00	6.00	8.50	13.50
	(1895)	16	4.00	6.00	8.50	13.50
	(1896)	17	4.00	6.00	8.50	13.50
	(1897)	18	4.00	6.00	8.50	13.50
	(1898)	19	4.00	6.00	8.50	13.50
	(1899)	20	4.00	6.00	8.50	13.50
	(1900)	21	4.00	6.00	8.50	13.50
	(1902)	23	4.00	6.00	8.50	13.50
	(1903)	24	4.00	6.00	8.50	13.50
	(1904)	25	4.00	6.00	8.50	13.50
	(1905)	26	4.00	6.00	8.50	13.50
	(1906)	27	4.00	6.00	8.50	13.50
	(1908)	29	4.00	6.00	8.50	13.50
	(1909)	30	4.00	6.00	8.50	13.50
	(1910)	31	4.00	6.00	8.50	13.50
	(1912)	33	4.00	6.00	8.50	13.50
	(1916)	37	4.00	6.00	8.50	13.50
	191(8)	39	4.00	6.00	8.50	13.50
	(1921)	42	4.00	6.00	8.50	13.50
	1922	43	4.00	6.00	8.50	13.50

NAZARANA RUPEE

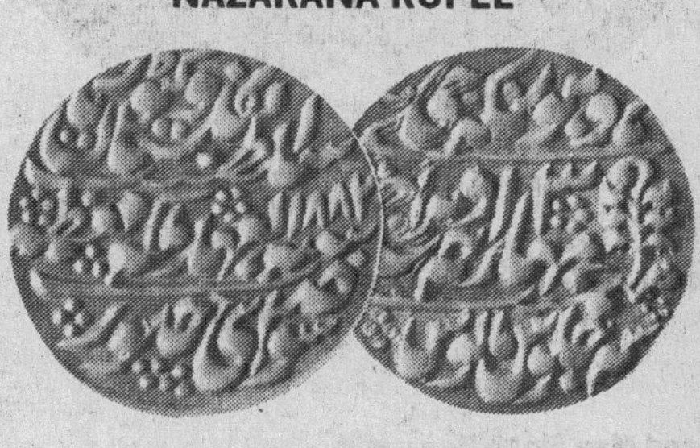

SILVER, 30-31mm, 10.70-11.60 g

13a	1880	1	12.50	20.00	32.50	50.00
	1881	2	12.50	20.00	32.50	50.00
	1882	3	12.50	20.00	32.50	50.00
	1883	4	12.50	20.00	32.50	50.00
	1884	5	12.50	20.00	32.50	50.00

Jaipur / INDIAN PRINCELY STATES

Y#	Date	Year	VG	Fine	VF	XF
13b	1884	5	6.50	8.50	12.50	20.00
	1886	7	6.50	8.50	12.50	20.00
	1887	8	6.50	8.50	12.50	20.00
	1889	10	6.50	8.50	12.50	20.00
	1890	11	6.50	8.50	12.50	20.00
	1891	12	6.50	8.50	12.50	20.00
	1897	18	6.50	8.50	12.50	20.00
	1899	20	6.50	8.50	12.50	20.00
	1901	22	6.50	8.50	12.50	20.00
	1903	24	6.50	8.50	12.50	20.00
	1904	25	6.50	8.50	12.50	20.00
	1906	27	6.50	8.50	12.50	20.00
	1908	29	6.50	8.50	12.50	20.00
	1909	30	6.50	8.50	12.50	20.00
	1911	32	6.50	8.50	12.50	20.00
	1913	34	6.50	8.50	12.50	20.00
	1916	37	6.50	8.50	12.50	20.00

MOHUR

GOLD, 10.70-11.40 g

14	(1881)	2	150.00	200.00	250.00	325.00
	(1884)	5	150.00	200.00	250.00	325.00
	(1895)	16	150.00	200.00	250.00	325.00
	(1896)	17	150.00	200.00	250.00	325.00
	(1899)	20	150.00	200.00	250.00	325.00
	(1916)	37	150.00	200.00	250.00	325.00
	(1919)	40	150.00	200.00	250.00	325.00

NAZARANA MOHUR

GOLD, 29-36mm, 10.70-11.40 g

14a	1880	1	300.00	600.00	1000.	1650.
	1887	8	300.00	600.00	1000.	1650.

In the names of George V

and Man Singh II

Years 1-14/1922-1935AD

RUPEE

SILVER, 10.70 g

Y#	Date	Year	VG	Fine	VF	XF
15	1922	1	20.00	30.00	50.00	80.00

NAZARANA RUPEE

SILVER, 10.70 g

15a	1924	3	30.00	50.00	75.00	125.00
	1928	7	30.00	50.00	75.00	125.00
	1932	11	30.00	50.00	75.00	125.00

MOHUR

GOLD, 10.70-11.40 g

A15	1(924)	3	275.00	325.00	375.00	450.00

In the names of Edward VIII

and Man Singh II

Year 15/1936AD

NAZARANA RUPEE

SILVER, 10.70 g

B15	1936	15	—	—	Rare	—

In the names of George VI

and Man Singh II

Years 15-28/1936-1949AD
NOTE: Refer to George V and Man Singh II legends.

1/2 PAISA

COPPER
Dump struck w/o collar.

16.1	(1942)	21	.50	.75	1.25	2.50

Crude struck in collar.

16.2	(1943)	22	.50	.75	1.25	2.50
	(1944)	23	.50	.75	1.25	2.50

NAZARANA PAISA

COPPER

17	1949	28	4.50	7.50	12.50	20.00

ANNA

BRASS

Y#	Date	Year	VG	Fine	VF	XF
18	1943	—	.25	.40	.60	1.00
	1944	—	.25	.40	.60	1.00

19	1944	—	.10	.20	.40	.65
	1944	—	—	Proof	—	—

2 ANNA

BRASS

20	1942	21	3.00	4.50	6.00	10.00

NAZARANA 1/2 RUPEE

SILVER

B21	—	—	—	—	Reported, not confirmed	

NAZARANA RUPEE

SILVER, 10.70-11.60 g

21	1938	17	12.50	20.00	32.50	50.00
	1941	20	12.50	20.00	32.50	50.00

NAZARANA RUPEE

SILVER, 10.70-11.60 g
Mule. Obv: Y#21a. Rev: Y#13a.

A21	1949	3	—	—	—	—

21a	1939	18	6.50	8.50	12.50	20.00

Y#	Date	Year	VG	Fine	VF	XF
21a	1941	20	6.50	8.50	12.50	20.00
	1943	22	6.50	8.50	12.50	20.00
	1945	24	6.50	8.50	12.50	20.00
	1948	27	6.50	8.50	12.50	20.00
	1949	28	6.50	8.50	12.50	20.00

MOHUR

GOLD, 10.70-11.40 g

22	(1941)	20	175.00	225.00	275.00	350.00
	(1943)	22	175.00	225.00	275.00	350.00
	(1949)	28	175.00	225.00	275.00	350.00

MADHOPUR MINT
In the name of Muhammad Akbar II
AH1221-1253/1806-1837AD

PAISA

COPPER

C#	Date	Year	Good	VG	Fine	VF
71	AH—	13	3.00	5.00	7.50	11.50
	—	14	3.00	5.00	7.50	11.50

RUPEE

SILVER, 10.70-11.60 g

C#	Date	Year	VG	Fine	VF	XF
75	AH1221	1	4.00	6.00	8.50	13.50
	(1222)	2	4.00	6.00	8.50	13.50
	(1224)	4	4.00	6.00	8.50	13.50
	(1225)	5	4.00	6.00	8.50	13.50
	(1226)	6	4.00	6.00	8.50	13.50
	(1227)	7	4.00	6.00	8.50	13.50
	(1228)	8	4.00	6.00	8.50	13.50
	(1229)	9	4.00	6.00	8.50	13.50
	123(0)	10	4.00	6.00	8.50	13.50
	(1231)	11	4.00	6.00	8.50	13.50
	(1232)	12	4.00	6.00	8.50	13.50
	(1233)	13	4.00	6.00	8.50	13.50
	(1234)	14	4.00	6.00	8.50	13.50
	(1235)	15	4.00	6.00	8.50	13.50
	(1236)	16	4.00	6.00	8.50	13.50
	(1237)	17	4.00	6.00	8.50	13.50
	(1238)	18	4.00	6.00	8.50	13.50
	(1239)	20	4.00	6.00	8.50	13.50
	(1241)	21	4.00	6.00	8.50	13.50
	(1242)	22	4.00	6.00	8.50	13.50
	(1243)	23	4.00	6.00	8.50	13.50
	(1244)	24	4.00	6.00	8.50	13.50
	(1246)	26	4.00	6.00	8.50	13.50
	(1249)	29	4.00	6.00	8.50	13.50
	(1250)	30	4.00	6.00	8.50	13.50
	(1251)	31	4.00	6.00	8.50	13.50

In the name of Bahadur Shah II
AH1253-1274/1837-1857AD

RUPEE

SILVER, 10.70-11.60 g

C#	Date	Year	VG	Fine	VF	XF
96	AH(1254)	2	5.00	7.00	10.00	16.50
	125(5)	3	5.00	7.00	10.00	16.50
	(1256)	4	5.00	7.00	10.00	16.50
	(1257)	5	5.00	7.00	10.00	16.50
	(1258)	6	5.00	7.00	10.00	16.50
	(1259)	7	5.00	7.00	10.00	16.50
	(1260)	8	5.00	7.00	10.00	16.50
	(1263)	10	5.00	7.00	10.00	16.50
	(1264)	12	5.00	7.00	10.00	16.50
	(1267)	15	5.00	7.00	10.00	16.50
	(1269)	17	5.00	7.00	10.00	16.50
	(1270)	18	5.00	7.00	10.00	16.50

JAIPUR FEUDATORY STATE
Khetri
A small state in northern Jaipur ruled by the Sadhani chieftains.
Mintname: Muzaffargarh

Mint marks:

In the name of Shah Alam II
AH1173-1221/1759-1806AD

RUPEE

SILVER, 10.70-11.60 g
Obv. leg: *Sahib Qiran.*

KM#	Date	Year	Good	VG	Fine	VF
2	AH12xx	44	13.50	16.50	20.00	27.50
	12xx	45	13.50	16.50	20.00	27.50
	1218	46	13.50	16.50	20.00	27.50
	12xx	47	13.50	16.50	20.00	27.50

In the name of Muhammad Akbar II

3	AH1221	1	20.00	30.00	45.00	65.00
	1222	2	20.00	30.00	45.00	65.00
	1223	3	20.00	30.00	45.00	65.00

JAISALMIR
Although the ruling Rajputs (or rawals) of this desert territory, located in northwest India traced their ancestry back to pre-Asokan times, the State of Jaisalmir was founded by Deoraj, the first rawal, only in the tenth century. Jaisalmir city was established by Rawal Jaisal, after whom both the city and the State were named. Like Jaipur, Jaisalmir reached its zenith in Mughal times. after being forced to acknowledge the supremacy of Delhi in the time of the Emperor Shah Jahan. With Mughal disintegration, Jaisalmir also fell upon hard times and most of its outlying provinces were lost. The state came under British protection in 1818, and on March 30th, 1949 it was merged into Rajasthan.

Anonymous Issues
MINT

Jaisalmir

DODIA PAISA

COPPER, thick

C#	Date	Year	Good	VG	Fine	VF
4	ND		1.00	2.00	3.00	4.50

NOTE: Struck 1660-1863AD.

Mughal Issues
"Akheshahi" Series

In the name of Muhammad Shah
AH1131-1161/1719-1748AD
Struck 1756-1860AD

1/8 RUPEE

SILVER, 11-12mm, 1.34-1.45 g

C#	Date	Year	VG	Fine	VF	XF
7	AH1152	22	2.50	3.50	4.50	6.00

1/4 RUPEE

SILVER, 2.68-2.90 g

8	AH1152	22	2.75	3.75	5.00	6.50

1/2 RUPEE

SILVER, 5.35-5.80 g

C#	Date	Year	VG	Fine	VF	XF
9	AH1153	22	4.00	5.00	7.50	10.00

RUPEE

SILVER, 10.70-11.60 g

10	AH1152	22	10.00	15.00	20.00	30.00
	1153	22	10.00	15.00	20.00	30.00

MOHUR

GOLD, 22mm, 10.70-11.40 g

15	AH1153	22	175.00	250.00	300.00	375.00

Regal Issues
In the Name of Queen Victoria
First Series: Frozen regnal year 22 w/o mint marks.

1/8 RUPEE

SILVER, 1.34-1.45 g

Y#	Date	Year	VG	Fine	VF	XF
1	AH—	22	2.50	3.50	4.50	6.00

1/4 RUPEE

SILVER, 2.68-2.90 g

2	AH—	22	3.00	3.75	5.00	6.50

1/2 RUPEE

SILVER, 5.35-5.80 g

3	AH—	22	4.00	5.00	7.50	10.00

RUPEE

SILVER, 10.70-11.60 g

4	AH—	22	10.00	15.00	20.00	30.00

NAZARANA RUPEE

SILVER, 10.70-11.60 g

4a	AH—	22	60.00	80.00	100.00	125.00

Jaisalmir / INDIAN PRINCELY STATES

Y#	Date	Year	VG	Fine	VF	XF
4b	AH—	22	125.00	150.00	175.00	225.00

Second Series: Frozen regnal year 22 w/ mint marks on rev.

Bird   Umbrella

1/8 RUPEE

SILVER, 1.34-1.45 g

5	AH—	22	2.25	3.00	3.75	5.50

1/4 RUPEE

SILVER, 2.68-2.90 g

6	AH—	22	2.50	3.25	4.00	6.00

1/2 RUPEE

SILVER, 5.35-5.80 g

7	AH—	22	3.50	4.50	6.00	8.00

RUPEE

SILVER, 10.70-11.60 g

8	AH—	22	5.00	7.00	10.00	15.00

NAZARANA RUPEE

SILVER, 10.70-11.60 g

8a	AH—	22	60.00	80.00	100.00	150.00

Y#	Date	Year	VG	Fine	VF	XF
8b	AH—	22	125.00	150.00	185.00	225.00

1/8 MOHUR
GOLD, 12mm, 1.34-1.42 g

9	AH—	22	35.00	65.00	125.00	150.00

1/4 MOHUR
GOLD, 15mm, 2.68-2.85 g

10	AH—	22	50.00	90.00	140.00	165.00

1/2 MOHUR
GOLD, 18mm, 5.35-5.70 g

11	AH—	22	90.00	120.00	160.00	200.00

MOHUR

GOLD, 10.70-11.40 g

12	AH—	22	175.00	225.00	275.00	350.00

JANJIRA ISLAND

Island near Bombay. Dynasty of Nawabs dates from 1489AD.

The origin of the nawabs of Janjira is obscure. They were Sidi or Abyssinian Muslims whose ancestors, serving as admirals to the Muslim rulers of the Deccan, had been granted jagirs (revenue-producing land tenures) under the Adil Shahi sultans of Bijapur. In 1870, Janjira came under direct British rule. Until 1924 the nawabs of Janjira also exercised suzerainty over Jafarabad on the Kathiawar peninsular.

RULERS

Sidi Ibrahim Khan II
   AH1204-06,19-42/1789-92,1804-26AD
Sidi Muhammad Khan
   AH1242-1265/1826-1848AD
Sidi Ibrahim Khan III
   AH1265-1297/1848-1879AD

SIDI IBRAHIM KHAN II
AH1204-1206,1219-1242
1789-1792,1804-1826AD

PAISA

COPPER

C#	Date	Year	Good	VG	Fine	VF
5	ND	—	4.50	7.00	12.50	20.00

SIDI MUHAMMAD KHAN
AH1242-1265/1826-1848AD

PAISA

COPPER

15	ND	—	4.00	6.00	10.00	17.50

SIDI IBRAHIM KHAN III
AH1265-1297/1848-1879AD

PAISA

COPPER
Obv: Date

C#	Date	Year	Good	VG	Fine	VF
20.1	AH1284	—	3.50	5.50	7.50	10.00

Rev: Date

20.2	AH1284	—	3.00	5.00	7.00	9.00

Rev: Date

20.3	AH1288	—	4.25	6.50	10.00	15.00

JAORA

Ghafar Khan (d. 1825), the first Nawab of Jaora, was brother-in-law to Amir Khan, the Pindari leader. Jaora was subordinate to Indore, having been granted control of the territory in central India in return for the maintenance of a body of cavalry and, later, of foot soldiers which were to be made available to Indore when required. The nawabs of Jaora maintained a good relationship with the British which, after 1818, left them in control of the area independently of Indore. In August 1948 Jaora was absorbed into Madhya Pradesh.

RULERS
Muhammad Ismail
   AH1282-1313/1865-1895AD

MINT

Jaora   جاورا

PAISA

COPPER
Obv: Wheel left of flag.

Y#	Date	Year	Good	VG	Fine	VF
A1.1	AH1282	—	7.50	10.00	13.00	18.50

A1.2	AH1284	—	7.50	10.00	13.00	18.50
	1285	—	7.50	10.00	13.00	18.50

Obv: Flag only.

B1	AH1295	—	2.50	4.00	6.00	9.00

Milled Coinage
PAISA

COPPER

Y#	Date	Year	VG	Fine	VF	XF
1	1893/VS1950/AH1310		1.25	2.50	4.50	7.00
	1893/VS1950/AH1311		1.50	3.00	5.50	8.00
	1894/VS1950/AH1310		1.25	2.50	4.00	6.50
	1894/VS1950/AH1311		1.25	2.50	4.00	6.50
	1894/VS1951/AH1311		1.25	2.50	4.00	6.50
	1895/VS1951/AH1311		1.25	2.50	4.50	7.00
	1895/VS1952/AH1311		1.25	2.50	4.00	6.50
	1895/VS1952/AH1312		1.50	3.00	5.50	8.00
	1895/VS1952/AH1313		1.25	2.50	4.00	6.50
	1895/VS1953/AH1313		1.50	3.00	5.50	8.00
	1896/VS1953/AH1313		1.25	2.50	4.00	6.50
	1896/VS1953/AH1331 (error for 1313 w/ second 3 retrograde)		1.75	3.00	5.50	8.00
	1896/VS1953/AH1331 (error for 1313)		2.00	3.50	6.50	10.00

2 PAISA

COPPER

2	1893/VS1950/AH1310		2.00	3.50	6.50	9.00
	1894/VS1950/AH1310		2.00	3.75	7.50	10.00

JHABUA

A state located in northwest India, west of Indore.
Prior to 1818 the Raja of Jhabua was responsible for paying an annual tribute to Indore. The rajas were Rathor Rajputs who had been established in the area since the seventeenth century. They were descended from the rajas of Jodhpur. In 1818 Jhabua came under British protection and control.

RULERS
Gopal Singh
  VS1897-1952/1840-1895AD

MINT
Jhabua

PAISA

COPPER
Obv. leg: Devanagari *Jabuva*.

Rev. leg: Arabic *Jabua*.

KM#	Date	Year	Good	VG	Fine	VF
1	VS(19)29 (1872)		8.50	11.50	15.00	21.50
	(19)35 (1878)		8.50	11.50	15.00	21.50

Obv. leg: Devanagari *Jhabua*. Rev: Date.

| 2 | VS(19)36 (1879) | | 8.50 | 11.50 | 15.00 | 21.50 |

Obv. Devanagari date: Sa(mvat) 21.

| 3 | VS(19)21 (1864) | | 7.00 | 10.00 | 13.50 | 17.50 |
| | (19)22 (1865) | | 7.00 | 10.00 | 13.50 | 17.50 |

Obv: Trident. Rev: Date.

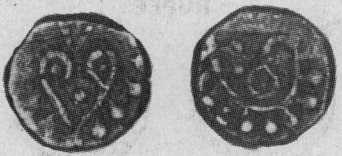

| 4 | VS(19)31 (1874) | | 3.50 | 5.00 | 6.50 | 8.50 |
| | ND | — | 3.50 | 5.00 | 6.50 | 8.50 |

Obv: Four-lobed flower. Rev: Date.

| 5 | VS(19)34 (1877) | | 3.50 | 5.00 | 6.50 | 8.50 |

Obv: Stylized leaf

6	VS(19)22 (1865)		7.50	10.00	12.50	16.50
	(19)23 (1866)		5.00	7.00	10.00	14.00
	(19)24 (1867)		5.00	7.00	10.00	14.00
	(19)28 (1871)		5.00	7.00	10.00	14.00
	(19)32 (1875)		3.00	5.00	7.00	10.00
	(19)33 (1876)		3.00	5.00	7.00	10.00
	(19)35 (1878)		5.00	7.00	10.00	14.00

Rev: Curled branch w/berry.

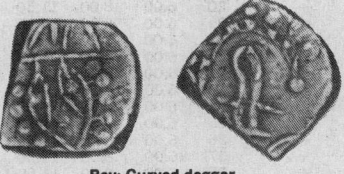

| 7 | ND | | 5.00 | 7.00 | 10.00 | 14.00 |

Rev: Spear point.

| 8 | ND | | 3.00 | 5.00 | 7.00 | 10.00 |

Rev: Curved daggar.

| 9 | ND | | 5.00 | 7.00 | 10.00 | 14.00 |

Rev: Jhar and blossom.

| 10 | ND | | 4.50 | 6.50 | 9.00 | 13.00 |

Rev: Six lobed flower.

KM#	Date	Year	Good	VG	Fine	VF
11	ND		5.00	7.00	10.00	14.00

Rev: Tailed ball.

| 12 | Yr. 30 | | 4.00 | 6.00 | 8.00 | 12.00 |

Obv: Cross. Rev: Tailed ball.

| 13 | ND | | 3.00 | 5.00 | 7.00 | 11.00 |

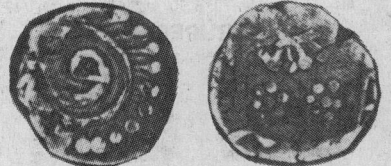

Obv: Square. Rev: Indistinct.

| 14 | ND | | 4.00 | 6.00 | 8.00 | 12.00 |

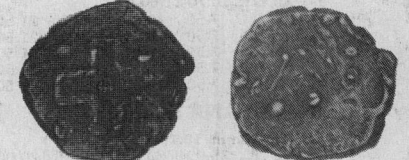

Obv: Arabic *Wa*. Rev: Groups of dots.

| 15 | ND | | 7.00 | 9.00 | 12.00 | 16.00 |

Obv: Cross and dots.

| 16 | ND | — | 7.00 | 9.00 | 12.00 | 16.00 |

NOTE: In addition to the above there are other symbols, and all these occur in different combinations. The crude fabric of these coins and uncommon variety of dies indicate that they were struck by bankers, with or without official sanction. They are commonly found overstruck on earlier types or on coins of other states.

JHALAWAR

State located in Rajputana, northwest India which was originally part of Kotah. Established in memory of services to Kotah of Zalim Singh, long-time administrator of that state. His grandson was given Jhalawar in 1837AD with the title of Raj Rana.
In 1838, at a time of great internal dissention, certain districts were removed from the territory of the Princely State of Kotah to form a principality for Madan Singh, one of the contestants for power. The new state was named Jhalawar. In 1896 the ruling maharaj-rana, Zalim Singh, was deposed by the Government of India for maladministration, and much of the area that had once been ceded to Jhalawar was returned to the sovereignty of the rulers of Kotah. Madan Singh and his successors were Jhala Rajputs from Kathiawar. The residual State of Jhalawar was incorporated into Rajasthan in 1948.

RULERS
Madan Singh
  AH1253-1264/1837-1847AD
Prithvi Singh
  AH1264-1292/1847-1875AD
Zalim Singh
  AH1294-1314/1877-1896AD

MINT MARKS

Both marks on reverse

Jhalawar / INDIAN PRINCELY STATES

Mughal Issues
In the name of Mohammad Akbar
AH1221-1253/1806-1837AD

RUPEE
SILVER, 10.70-11.60 g
W/*Sahib Qiran* leg.

C#	Date	Year	Good	VG	Fine	VF
8	AH—	32				

In the name of Bahadur Shah II
Years 1-22/AH1253-1274/1837-1858AD

PAISA

COPPER

21	AH—	12	2.00	3.00	4.50	6.50
	—	21	2.00	3.00	4.50	6.50

1/8 RUPEE
SILVER, 1.34-1.45 g

C#	Date	Year	VG	Fine	VF	XF
25	AH—	—	4.00	6.00	8.50	12.50

1/4 RUPEE
SILVER, 2.68-2.90 g

26	AH—	—	6.00	—	7.50	11.50

1/2 RUPEE
SILVER, 5.35-5.80 g

27	AH—	—	6.50	8.00	10.00	17.50

RUPEE

SILVER, 10.70-11.60 g

28	AH—	1	7.50	10.00	15.00	21.50
	—	6	7.50	10.00	15.00	21.50
	—	13	7.50	10.00	15.00	21.50
	—	19	7.50	10.00	15.00	21.50
	—	20	7.50	10.00	15.00	21.50

NAZARANA RUPEE
SILVER, 30mm, 10.70-11.60 g

29	AH—	8	35.00	50.00	80.00	120.00
	1263	10	35.00	50.00	80.00	120.00
	—	21	35.00	50.00	80.00	120.00

Regal Issues
In the name of Queen Victoria
Regnal years 1-45 – 1857-1901AD

1/2 PAISA

COPPER, 9.00 g

Y#	Date	Year	Good	VG	Fine	VF
1	AH—	5	2.50	4.50	7.50	12.50

PAISA
COPPER, squarish, 19-21mm, 18.00 g

2	AH—	5	1.25	2.25	4.00	6.50
	—	7	1.25	2.25	4.00	6.50
	—	8	1.25	2.25	4.00	6.50
	—	9	1.25	2.25	4.00	6.50
	—	10	1.25	2.25	4.00	6.50
	—	11	1.25	2.25	4.00	6.50
	—	12	1.25	2.25	4.00	6.50
	—	18	1.25	2.25	4.00	6.50
	—	21	1.25	2.25	4.00	6.50
	—	24	1.25	2.25	4.00	6.50
	—	27	1.25	2.25	4.00	6.50
	—	28	1.25	2.25	4.00	6.50
	—	29	1.25	2.25	4.00	6.50

1/8 RUPEE

SILVER, 13mm, 1.34-1.45 g

Y#	Date	Year	VG	Fine	VF	XF
3	AH—	5	4.00	6.00	10.00	15.00
	—	28	4.00	6.00	10.00	15.00
	—	37	4.00	6.00	10.00	15.00
	—	38	4.00	6.00	10.00	15.00

1/4 RUPEE

SILVER, 2.68-2.90 g

4	AH—	7	4.00	5.50	8.00	10.00
	—	17	4.00	5.50	8.00	10.00
	—	28	4.00	5.50	8.00	10.00
	—	33	4.00	5.50	8.00	10.00
	—	37	4.00	5.50	8.00	10.00
	—	38	4.00	5.50	8.00	10.00

1/2 RUPEE

SILVER, 5.35-5.80 g

5	AH—	1	6.50	8.50	12.50	22.50
	—	11	6.50	8.50	12.50	22.50
	—	22	6.50	8.50	12.50	22.50
	—	35	6.50	8.50	12.50	22.50

NAZARANA 1/2 RUPEE

SILVER, 5.35-5.80 g

5a	AH—	38	—	30.00	45.00	60.00

RUPEE

SILVER, 10.70-11.60 g

6	AH—	1	6.00	8.00	11.50	16.50
	—	2	6.00	8.00	11.50	16.50
	—	3	6.00	8.00	11.50	16.50
	—	5	6.00	8.00	11.50	16.50
	—	7	6.00	8.00	11.50	16.50
	—	9	6.00	8.00	11.50	16.50
	—	11	6.00	8.00	11.50	16.50
	—	12	6.00	8.00	11.50	16.50
	—	13	6.00	8.00	11.50	16.50
	—	14	6.00	8.00	11.50	16.50
	—	17	6.00	8.00	11.50	16.50
	—	18	6.00	8.00	11.50	16.50
	—	19	6.00	8.00	11.50	16.50
	—	20	6.00	8.00	11.50	16.50
	—	21	6.00	8.00	11.50	16.50
	—	22	6.00	8.00	11.50	16.50
	—	24	6.00	8.00	11.50	16.50
	—	27	6.00	8.00	11.50	16.50
	—	29	6.00	8.00	11.50	16.50
	—	34	6.00	8.00	11.50	16.50
	—	35	6.00	8.00	11.50	16.50
	—	36	6.00	8.00	11.50	16.50
	—	37	6.00	8.00	11.50	16.50
	—	38	6.00	8.00	11.50	16.50
	—	41	6.00	8.00	11.50	16.50

NAZARANA RUPEE

SILVER, 10.70-11.60 g

6a	VS1915	2	30.00	50.00	80.00	120.00
	1915	4	30.00	50.00	80.00	120.00
	1915	5	30.00	50.00	80.00	120.00
	1915	7	30.00	50.00	80.00	120.00
	1915	13	30.00	50.00	80.00	120.00
	1915	15	30.00	50.00	80.00	120.00

Y#	Date	Year	VG	Fine	VF	XF
6a	1915	21	30.00	50.00	80.00	120.00
	1915	22	30.00	50.00	80.00	120.00
	1915	25	30.00	50.00	80.00	120.00
	1915	28	30.00	50.00	80.00	120.00
	1915	35	30.00	50.00	80.00	120.00
	1915	38	30.00	50.00	80.00	120.00
	1915	39	30.00	50.00	80.00	120.00

6b	VS1915	3	60.00	80.00	120.00	160.00
	1915	15	60.00	80.00	120.00	160.00
6c	—	30	40.00	60.00	90.00	140.00
	—	31	40.00	60.00	90.00	140.00
	—	33	40.00	60.00	90.00	140.00
	—	36	40.00	60.00	90.00	140.00
	—	37	40.00	60.00	90.00	140.00
	—	40	40.00	60.00	90.00	140.00

JODHPUR

Jodhpur, or Marwar, located in northwest India was the largest Princely State in the Rajputana Agency, its population in 1941 being in excess of two and a half million. The maharajadhirajas of Jodhpur were Rathor Rajputs who claimed an extremely ancient ancestry from Rama, king of Ayodhya. With the collapse of the Rathor rulers of Kanauj in 1194 the family entered Marwar, where they laid the foundation of the new state. The city of Jodhpur was built by Rao Jodha in 1459, and the city and and the state were named after him. In 1561 Akbar invaded Jodhpur, forcing its submission. In 1679 Aurangzeb sacked the city, an experience which stimulated the Rajput royal house to forge a new unity among themselves in order to extricate themselves from Mughal hegemony. Internal dissension once again asserted itself and Rajput unity, which had both benefited from and accelerated Mughal decline, fell apart before the Marathas. In 1818 Jodhpur came under British protection and control and after Indian Union the State was merged into Rajasthan. Jodhpur is best known for its particular style of riding breeches which became very popular in the West in the late nineteenth century.

RULERS

The issues of the first four rulers before 1858AD with the AH and VS dates, as well as the regnal years, are rarely actual dates and years, but were used for many years without change, and were often quite indiscriminately applied. Mismatched regnal years and dates are frequently encountered, as well as blundered dates of all sorts. Dates lying outside the reign of the rulers named on the coin (after 1858AD) were often used. The date or regnal year does not provide an actual dating of the coin.
Coinage of the first four rulers (until 1858AD) is not distinguished by reign, but by type of inscription, mint, and (pseudo-) date.

Bhim Singh
  AH1207-1218/1792-1803AD
Man Singh
  AH1218-1259/1803-1843AD
Takhat Singh
  AH1259-1290/VS1900-1930/
  1843-1873AD
Jaswant Singh
  AH1290-1313/VS1930-1952/
  1873-1895AD
Sardar Singh
  VS1952-1968/1895-1911AD
Sumair Singh
  VS1968-1975/1911-1918AD
Umaid Singh
  VS1975-2004/1918-1947AD
Hanwant Singh, as Titular Ruler
  VS2004-2009/1947-1952AD

MINTNAMES

Jodhpur	جودپور
Dar-ul Mansur	دارالمنصور
Nagor	ناکور
Dar-ul Barkat	دارالبرکات
Pali	پالی
Sujat	سجت or سوجت

MINT MARKS
Before 1858AD

Sujat Mint, always on reverse. (C#30 & C#34)

Sujat, sometimes on obverse. (C#30 & C#34)

(C#34) दा

Pali, sometimes on obverse. (C#30)

Nagor (C#56)

Nagor, Pali, Sujat
Usually on obverse. (C#30 & C#55)

Pali, sometimes on obverse of C#30.

Jodhpur, on obverse of C#59. ध

Issues of 1858-1873AD

After 1858AD, the mint marks vary, and are given for each listing, wherever there is a difference.

All gold coins struck at Jodhpur Mint. All mints except Jodhpur closed by or before 1893 AD. All copper coins were probably struck at the Jodhpur Mint, but if struck elsewhere, they bear no distinguishing marks.

In addition to the mint marks indicating the mint cities, there are also the marks of the Darogas (mint overseers), which are very useful in identifying the mints, especially when the city marks are missing or off the flan. These are given by cat.# and mint: (Only one of the marks appears on any one coin, always on the obverse.)

Jodhpur Y#1.1 रू ह रा

Sujat Y#1.2 ला

Jodhpur Y#3 गं न श्री

Jodhpur Y#19.1 ग रा ष ✽ फ ठ

Sujat Y#1a.2 मा

Pali Y#4.3

Sujat Y#4.3 के

Issues of Jaswant Singh

Jodhpur Y#9.1 & 12 علی

Jodhpur Y#9.1 ड ड रू

Pali Y#9.2 क्र क्र ु मा षा

Sujat Y#9.3 न नं बा बा ग घं

ळ क्र ज 2 ट कि ढ स

Issues of Victoria and Sardar Singh

Jodhpur all व द्रा

Issues of Edward VII and George V and Sardar Singh and Sumair Singh

Jodhpur Y#20-26, 29-31 म

Issues of George V and Sumair Singh

Jodhpur Y#27-28 द

Issues of George V and Umaid Singh

Jodhpur Y#37 & 38 ॐ

Jodhpur Y#38 श्री

Issues of Edward VIII and Umaid Singh

Jodhpur all रं

Issues of George VI and Umaid Singh

Jodhpur Y#40 रं

Jodhpur Y#41 & 42 गो

Issues of George VI and Hanwant Singh

Jodhpur all गो

The Darogas' marks generally consist of a symbol or a single Nagari letter, sometimes inverted, and even lying on its side. Some letters are found on more than one series, so that the mark is not a positive identification, but taken together with the city mark and the style of the coin, will provide a correct attribution.

JODHPUR MINT
Anonymous Issues
With Regnal Years of Shah Alam II
Struck between 1792-1858AD

PAISA

COPPER

C#	Date	Year	Good	VG	Fine	VF
22.2	AH1227	—	2.00	3.00	4.50	7.50
22.2	1267 (error for 1227)					
		—	2.50	4.00	6.00	10.00

NOTE: Some specimens show a wide, floral border.

In the name of Shah Alam II
AH1173-1221/1759-1806AD

RUPEE

SILVER, 10.70-11.60 g

C#	Date	Year	VG	Fine	VF	XF
30	AH1218	45	9.00	11.50	15.00	20.00
	1128(error)	—	9.00	11.50	15.00	20.00
	1228(error)	—	9.00	11.50	15.00	20.00
	128 (error)	—	9.00	11.50	15.00	20.00

NAZARANA RUPEE

SILVER, 20x20mm, square flan, 10.70-11.60 g
Similar to 1 Rupee, C#30, but square.

C#	Date	Year	VG	Fine	VF	XF
30a	AH1218	45	32.50	50.00	70.00	100.00

MOHUR

GOLD, 19mm, 10.70-11.40 g

C#	Date	Year	VG	Fine	VF	XF
40	AH1218	45	200.00	250.00	300.00	360.00

NOTE: Struck ca. 1803-1858AD.

In the name of Muhammad Akbar II
AH1221-1253/1806-1837AD

PAISA

COPPER

C#	Date	Year	Good	VG	Fine	VF
50	AH—	31 on obv., 22 on rev.				
			2.50	3.50	5.50	8.00

1/4 RUPEE

SILVER, 2.67-2.90 g

C#	Date	Year	VG	Fine	VF	XF
53	AH—	22	8.50	11.50	15.00	20.00

RUPEE

SILVER, 10.70-11.60 g

C#	Date	Year	VG	Fine	VF	XF
55	AH—	22	8.50	11.50	15.00	20.00
	—	23	8.50	11.50	15.00	20.00

NOTE: Struck ca. 1816-1859AD.

C#	Date	Year	Good	VG	Fine	VF
56	AH1222	—	11.50	15.00	22.50	30.00
	1227	—	11.50	15.00	22.50	30.00

MOHUR

GOLD, 20mm, 10.70-11.40 g

C#	Date	Year	Good	VG	Fine	VF
59	AH—	22	200.00	240.00	275.00	325.00

Anonymous Issue

PAISA

COPPER, 20mm

C#	Date	Year	Good	VG	Fine	VF
60	AH1267	—	1.75	2.50	3.50	5.00

Jodhpur / INDIAN PRINCELY STATES

In the names of Queen Victoria and Takhat Singh

First Issue
AD1858-1859

RUPEE

SILVER, 10.70-11.60 g
Obv: Jhar, *Jodhpur* in Persian. Rev: Sword.

Y#	Date	Year	VG	Fine	VF	XF
1.1	AH—	22	9.00	12.50	17.50	24.00
		52	9.00	12.50	17.50	24.00

MOHUR
GOLD, 20mm, 10.70-11.40 g

| 2 | AH— | 22 | 200.00 | 250.00 | 300.00 | 350.00 |

Second Issue
RUPEE

SILVER, 21mm, 10.70-11.60 g
Obv: Jhar. Rev: Sword, *Jodhpur* in Persian.

1.3	AH—	22 & 21	8.50	12.50	16.50	20.00
		22 only	8.50	12.50	16.50	20.00
		52 & 16	8.50	12.50	16.50	20.00
		52 only	8.50	12.50	16.50	20.00

NOTE: Struck ca.1860-1869AD.

In the name of Takhat Singh
Queen Victoria mentioned without name, but with title 'Queen, Ruler of India and Europe'. Actual mint names used on this and all subsequent issues.

Third Issue
Nagari legend *Sri Mataji* added on reverse.

RUPEE

SILVER, 21mm, 10.70-11.60 g
Rev. leg: *Nagari Sri Mataji*.

| 3 | AH— | 22 & 61 | 10.00 | 13.50 | 17.50 | 25.00 |
| | | 22 only | 10.00 | 13.50 | 17.50 | 25.00 |

NOTE: Struck ca. 1859-1860AD.

4.1	VS1926	22	10.00	13.50	16.50	23.50
	1927	—	10.00	13.50	16.50	23.50
	1928	—	10.00	13.50	16.50	23.50

In the name of Queen Victoria

PAISA

COPPER, 20-25mm

Y#	Date	Year	Good	VG	Fine	VF
5.1	AH1293	61	1.00	2.00	2.75	3.75
	1305	65	1.25	2.25	3.00	4.00
	Date off flan	—	.50	1.00	1.50	2.25

Y#	Date	Year	Good	VG	Fine	VF
5.2	VS1940	(1883)	1.25	2.25	3.00	4.00
	1940 inverted 1883		2.50	4.00	6.50	9.00
	1941	(1884)	1.00	2.00	2.75	3.75
	1942	(1885)	1.25	2.25	3.00	4.00
	1943	(1886)	1.25	2.25	3.00	4.00
	1944	(1887)	1.25	2.25	3.00	4.00
	1945	(1888)	1.25	2.25	3.00	4.00
	1947	(1890)	1.25	2.25	3.00	4.00
	1948	(1891)	2.00	3.50	5.50	7.00

In the names of Queen Victoria and Jaswant Singh

1/8 RUPEE

SILVER, 1.34-1.45 g

Y#	Date	Year	VG	Fine	VF	XF
6	AH—	22	7.50	12.50	20.00	30.00

1/4 RUPEE

SILVER, 2.68-2.90 g

| 7 | AH— | 22 | 7.50 | 12.50 | 20.00 | 30.00 |

1/2 RUPEE
SILVER, 17mm, 5.35-5.80 g

| 8 | VS1945 | (1888) | 11.50 | 16.50 | 25.00 | 40.00 |

RUPEE

SILVER, 10.70-11.60 g

9.1	AH1293	—	9.00	11.50	15.00	20.00
	Date off flan		9.00	11.50	15.00	20.00
9.2	VS1941	(1884)	9.00	11.50	15.00	20.00
	1942	(1885)	9.00	11.50	15.00	20.00
	2491 error for 1942		9.00	11.50	15.00	20.00
	1943	(1886)	9.00	11.50	15.00	20.00
	8941 error for 1948		9.00	11.50	15.00	20.00
	1950	—	9.00	11.50	15.00	20.00
	Date off flan		7.00	9.00	12.50	17.50

1/4 MOHUR
GOLD, 13mm, 2.68-2.85 g

| 10 | AH1293 | — | 65.00 | 100.00 | 150.00 | 200.00 |

1/2 MOHUR
GOLD, 18mm, 5.35-5.70 g

| 11 | AH1293 | — | 110.00 | 140.00 | 200.00 | 275.00 |

MOHUR
GOLD, 20mm, 10.70-11.40 g

| 12 | AH1293 | — | 210.00 | 260.00 | 300.00 | 375.00 |

In the names of Queen Victoria and Sardar Singh

1/8 RUPEE

SILVER, 1.34-1.45 g

| 13 | VS— | — | 9.00 | 16.50 | 20.00 | 30.00 |

1/4 RUPEE

SILVER, 2.68-2.90 g

| 14 | VS— | — | 8.50 | 11.50 | 17.50 | 25.00 |

1/2 RUPEE

SILVER, 5.35-5.80 g

Y#	Date	Year	VG	Fine	VF	XF
15	VS—	—	12.50	17.50	25.00	35.00

RUPEE

SILVER, 10.70-11.60 g

| 16 | VS1955 | (1898) | 15.00 | 22.50 | 30.00 | 40.00 |
| | 1956 | (1899) | 15.00 | 22.50 | 30.00 | 40.00 |

1/4 MOHUR
GOLD, 15mm, 2.68-2.85 g

| 17 | VS1952 | (1895) | — | — | 125.00 | 150.00 |

1/2 MOHUR
GOLD, 18mm, 5.35-5.70 g

| 18 | VS1952 | (1895) | — | — | 180.00 | 275.00 |

MOHUR
GOLD, 21mm, 10.70-11.40 g

| 19 | VS1952 | 1895 | 200.00 | 240.00 | 300.00 | 350.00 |

In the names of Edward VII and Sardar Singh

1/4 ANNA

COPPER

Y#	Date	Year	Good	VG	Fine	VF
20	1901	—	1.50	2.50	3.75	5.50
	1902	—	1.50	2.50	3.75	5.50
	1903	—	1.50	2.50	3.75	5.50
	1904	—	1.50	2.50	3.75	5.50
	1905	—	1.50	2.50	3.75	5.50
	1906	—	.50	1.00	1.75	2.50
	1609 (error)	—	1.50	2.50	3.75	5.50
	1907	—	1.00	2.00	3.25	4.50
	1908	—	1.00	2.00	3.25	4.50
	1909	—	1.00	2.00	3.25	4.50
	1910	—	1.00	2.00	3.25	4.50
	1290 (error)	—	1.25	2.25	3.00	4.00
	1291 (error)	—	.75	1.50	2.25	3.25
	2091 (error)	—	1.25	2.25	3.00	4.00
	5201 (error)	—	1.25	2.25	3.00	4.00

NOTE: Other blundered dates' exist.

1/2 ANNA

COPPER

| 21 | 1906 | — | 3.50 | 5.00 | 7.00 | 11.50 |
| | 1908 | — | 3.50 | 5.00 | 7.00 | 11.50 |

1/8 RUPEE
SILVER, 1.34-1.45 g

| A22 | — | — | — | — | — | — |

1/4 RUPEE

SILVER, 19mm, 2.68-2.90 g

Y#	Date	Year	VG	Fine	VF	XF
22	VS1965	(1908)	15.00	20.00	30.00	50.00

1/2 RUPEE

SILVER, 5.35-5.80 g

Y#	Date	Year	VG	Fine	VF	XF
A23	ND	—	20.00	25.00	35.00	60.00

1/4 MOHUR
GOLD, 13mm, 2.68-2.85 g

| 23 | 1906 | — | — | — | 150.00 | 200.00 |

1/2 MOHUR
GOLD, 18mm, 5.35-5.70 g

| 24 | 1906 | — | — | — | 215.00 | 275.00 |

MOHUR
GOLD, 20mm, 10.70-11.40 g

| 25 | 1906 | — | 220.00 | 260.00 | 325.00 | 400.00 |

In the names of Edward VII and Sumair Singh

1/2 MOHUR

GOLD, 5.35-5.70 g

| 26 | (1910) | — | 200.00 | 250.00 | 300.00 | 400.00 |

In the names of George V and Sumair Singh

1/4 ANNA

COPPER

Y#	Date	Year	Good	VG	Fine	VF
27	1911	—	6.50	9.00	12.50	17.50
	1914	—	6.50	9.00	12.50	17.50

1/2 ANNA
COPPER, 25mm

| 28 | 1914 | — | 5.00 | 8.50 | 12.50 | 20.00 |
| | 1918 | — | 5.00 | 8.50 | 12.50 | 20.00 |

1/8 RUPEE

SILVER, 1.34-1.45 g

Y#	Date	Year	VG	Fine	VF	XF
29	—	—	10.00	20.00	30.00	40.00

1/4 RUPEE
SILVER, 2.68-2.90 g

| 30 | — | — | 10.00 | 20.00 | 30.00 | 40.00 |

1/2 RUPEE

SILVER, 5.35-5.80 g

| 31 | — | — | 10.00 | 20.00 | 30.00 | 40.00 |

RUPEE
SILVER, 21mm, 10.70-11.60 g

| 32 | — | — | 15.00 | 25.00 | 40.00 | 55.00 |

MOHUR

GOLD, 10.70-11.40 g

Y#	Date	Year	VG	Fine	VF	XF
33	ND	—	220.00	250.00	325.00	400.00

In the names of George V and Umaid Singh

1/4 ANNA
NOTE: Refer to Sirohi State for previously listed 1/4 Anna, Y#34.

1/4 RUPEE
SILVER, 18mm, 2.68-2.90 g

| 35 | — | — | 20.00 | 30.00 | 40.00 | 55.00 |

1/4 MOHUR
GOLD, 16mm, 2.68-2.85 g

| 36 | — | — | 100.00 | 125.00 | 150.00 | 200.00 |

1/2 MOHUR

GOLD, 5.35-5.70 g

| 37 | — | — | 125.00 | 150.00 | 200.00 | 300.00 |

MOHUR

GOLD, 10.70-11.60 g
Obv: *Om*.

| 38.1 | — | — | 225.00 | 275.00 | 375.00 | 450.00 |

Obv: *Shri*.

| 38.2 | — | — | 175.00 | 225.00 | 300.00 | 400.00 |

In the names of Edward VIII and Umaid Singh

1/4 ANNA

COPPER
Obv: W/o Persian '8' to left of Edward.

Y#	Date	Year	Good	VG	Fine	VF
39	1936	—	1.75	2.75	4.00	6.50

Obv: Persian '8' to left of Edward.

| 39.1 | 1936 | — | 1.75 | 2.75 | 4.00 | 6.50 |

NOTE: Blundered legends also exist.

MOHUR
GOLD, 11.01 g

| A40 | 1936 | — | — | — | — | — |

In the names of George VI and Umaid Singh

1/4 ANNA

COPPER, 19mm, thick, 10.00-11.00 g

| 40.1 | AH— | 1937 | 1.25 | 1.75 | 2.50 | 3.50 |
| | — | 1938 | 1.25 | 1.75 | 2.50 | 3.50 |

Y#	Date	Year	Good	VG	Fine	VF
40.2	VS1996	(1939)	2.00	3.00	4.00	6.00

Thin flan, 3.00 g

| 41 | VS2000 | (1943) | 1.75 | 2.75 | 4.00 | 5.50 |
| | Date off flan | | .20 | .30 | .50 | 1.00 |

Obv: Persian '6' below Daroga's mark.

41.1	VS2000	(1943)	1.75	2.75	4.00	5.50
	2001	(1944)	1.75	2.75	4.00	5.50
	2002	(1945)	1.75	2.75	4.00	5.50

NOTE: Varieties exist.

Obv: Persian 2 below Daroga's mark.

| 41.2 | VS— | | — | — | — | — |

Obv: Cock standing left, legend around.
Rev: Date and *Rajya Narvar*.

| 41.3 | VS2000 | | — | — | — | Rare |

MOHUR

GOLD, 10.70-11.40 g

Y#	Date	Year	VG	Fine	VF	XF
42	—	—	220.00	250.00	325.00	425.00

In the names of George VI and Hanwant Singh

1/4 MOHUR
GOLD, 2.68-2.85 g

| 43 | — | — | — | — | — | Rare |

MOHUR

GOLD, 10.70-11.40 g

| 44 | — | — | 250.00 | 300.00 | 400.00 | 525.00 |

COPPER (OMS)

Y#	Date	Year	Good	VG	Fine	VF
44a	—	—	7.50	15.00	30.00	50.00

NAGOR MINT
In the name of Shah Alam II
AH1173-1221 / 1759-1806AD

RUPEE

SILVER, 11.40-11.50 g

Jodhpur / INDIAN PRINCELY STATES 927

Jodhpur / INDIAN PRINCELY STATES

Rev: *Nagore* at top.

C#	Date	Year	VG	Fine	VF	XF
33	AH1218	—	12.50	20.00	28.50	40.00

In the name of Takhat Singh
VS1900-1930/1843-1873AD

RUPEE

SILVER, 11.40-11.50 g

Y#	Date	Year	VG	Fine	VF	XF
4.2	VS1926	(1869)	11.50	15.00	18.50	26.50

PALI MINT

In the names of Queen Victoria and Takhat Singh

RUPEE

SILVER, 10.70-11.60 g
Mark: *Swastika*.

1.5	—	52 & 16	12.50	17.50	22.50	30.00

NAZARANA RUPEE

SILVER
Mark: *Swastika*.

4.5	ND	—	—	—	—	—

In the name of Takhat Singh
VS1900-1930/1843-1873AD

RUPEE

SILVER, 10.70-11.60 g
Rev: *Jhar and sword*.

4.3	VS1926	45	11.50	15.00	20.00	27.50

In the name of Queen Victoria and Jaswant Singh

1/8 RUPEE
SILVER, 1.34-1.45 g

6	AH—	—	6.50	10.00	15.00	25.00

1/4 RUPEE
SILVER, 2.67-2.90 g

7	AH—	—	6.50	10.00	15.00	25.00

1/2 RUPEE
SILVER, 5.35-5.80 g

8	VS1945	(1898)	8.50	13.50	20.00	30.00

RUPEE

SILVER, 19-21mm, 10.70-11.60 g
Rev: *Jhar and sword*.

9.3	VS1930	(1883)	9.00	11.50	15.00	21.50
	1931	(1884)	9.00	11.50	15.00	21.50
	1931	40	9.00	11.50	15.00	21.50
	1932	40	9.00	11.50	15.00	21.50
	1934	40	9.00	11.50	15.00	21.50
	1934	(1887)	9.00	11.50	15.00	21.50
	1935	(1888)	9.00	11.50	15.00	21.50
	1939	(1892)	9.00	11.50	15.00	21.50
	1941	(1894)	9.00	11.50	15.00	21.50

Y#	Date	Year	VG	Fine	VF	XF
9.3	1943	(1896)	9.00	11.50	15.00	21.50
	1944	(1897)	9.00	11.50	15.00	21.50
	1950	(1893)	9.00	11.50	15.00	21.50
	Date off flan		7.50	9.00	13.50	19.00

In the names of Queen Victoria and Sardar Singh

RUPEE
SILVER, 10.70-11.60 g

16.2	—	—	20.00	27.50	35.00	50.00

SUJAT MINT

In the name of Shah Alam II
AH1173-1221/1759-1806AD

RUPEE

SILVER, 10.70-11.60 g

C#	Date	Year	VG	Fine	VF	XF
34	AH1264	23	10.00	13.50	17.50	25.00
	1264	43	10.00	13.50	17.50	25.00

NOTE: Struck ca. 1848-1859.

In the names of Queen Victoria and Takhat Singh

RUPEE
SILVER, 10.70-11.60 g
Rev: *Katar*.

Y#	Date	Year	VG	Fine	VF	XF
1.2	—	16	10.00	14.00	19.00	25.00
	—	22	10.00	14.00	19.00	25.00

Rev: *Katar*.

1.4	—	13	10.00	14.50	20.00	27.50
	—	16	10.00	14.50	20.00	27.50

NOTE: Struck ca. 1869AD.

In the name of Takhat Singh
VS1900-1930/1843-1873AD

RUPEE

SILVER, 10.70-11.60 g

4.4	VS1926	(1869)	11.50	15.00	21.50	28.50
	1928	(1871)	11.50	15.00	21.50	28.50

In the name of Queen Victoria

RUPEE

SILVER, 10.70-11.60 g

9.4	AH1291	(1882)	10.00	12.50	16.50	23.50
	Date off flan		7.50	9.00	13.50	18.50
9.5	VS1929	22	10.00	12.50	16.50	23.50
	1933	(1886)	10.00	12.50	16.50	23.50
	1936	(1889)	10.00	12.50	16.50	23.50
	1938	(1891)	10.00	12.50	16.50	23.50
	Date off flan		7.50	9.00	13.50	18.50

Obv: Devanagari *Sri Maheshji*.

9.6	—	22	11.50	16.50	22.50	32.50

Obv: Devanagari *Sri Ragunathji*.

Y#	Date	Year	VG	Fine	VF	XF
9.7	—	—	12.50	18.50	27.50	37.50

Obv: *Jhar and "X"*.

9.8	VS1932	22	12.50	18.50	27.50	37.50

JODHPUR FEUDATORY STATES

Kuchawan

Kuchawan was a semi-independent feudatory. The thakur of Kuchawan, an Udawat Rajput, was the only feudatory of Jodhpur permitted to strike his own coinage. Refer also to Gwalior-Ajmir Mint and Maratha Confederacy- Ajmir Mint.

In the name of Queen Victoria

1/4 RUPEE
SILVER, 13mm, 2.68-2.90 g

1	1863	—	8.50	12.50	20.00	35.00

1/2 RUPEE
SILVER, 15-16mm, 5.35-5.80 g

2	1863	—	8.50	12.50	20.00	35.00

RUPEE

SILVER, 10.70-11.60 g

3	1863	—	5.00	7.50	11.50	18.50

NAZARANA RUPEE

SILVER, 10.70-11.60 g

3a	1863	—	16.50	22.50	40.00	60.00

JUNAGADH

A state located on the Kathiawar peninsula in west India. Until about 1742 Junagadh was a Rajput state. It was then conquered by the Sultan of Ahmedabad. Under Akbar it became a Mughal dependency. In about 1730, encouraged by Mughal decline, a Mughal officer and military adventurer, Sherkhan Babi, expelled the Mughal governor and asserted his independence. From that time, until Indian Independence, his descendants ruled the territory as the nawabs of Junagadh. The nawabs first entered treaties with the British in 1807.

RULERS

Bahadur Khan,
  AH1226-1256/VS1868-1897/1811-1840AD
Hamid Khan II,
  AH1256-1268/VS1897-1908/1840-1851AD
Mahabat Khan II,
  AH1268-1300/VS1908-1939/1851-1882AD
Bahadur Khan III
  AH1300-1310/VS1939-1949/1882-1892AD
Rasal Khan
  AH1310-1329/VS1949-1968/1892-1911AD
Mahabat Khan III
  AH1329-1368/VS1968-2005/1911-1948AD

Mughal Issues

In the name of Muhammad Akbar II
AH1221-1253/1806-1837AD

With title *Sri Diwana* on obverse, AH and SE dates on reverse.

DOKDO

COPPER

C#	Date	Year	Good	VG	Fine	VF
20	AH1239-48					
	VS1880-89		2.50	5.00	8.00	12.50

1/2 KORI

SILVER, 2.30 g

C#	Date	Year	VG	Fine	VF	XF
27	AH1236	VS1877	2.75	3.50	5.00	7.50
	1245	1885	2.75	3.50	5.00	7.50
	1247	1889	2.75	3.50	5.00	7.50
	1251	1892	2.75	3.50	5.00	7.50
	1267	19xx	2.75	3.50	5.00	7.50
	1268	1908	2.75	3.50	5.00	7.50
	1270	1910	2.75	3.50	5.00	7.50
	1271	1911	2.75	3.50	5.00	7.50
	1272	1912	2.75	3.50	5.00	7.50
	1273	1913	2.75	3.50	5.00	7.50
	1274	1914	2.75	3.50	5.00	7.50
	1275	1915	2.75	3.50	5.00	7.50
	1276	1916	2.75	3.50	5.00	7.50
	1277	1917	2.75	3.50	5.00	7.50
	1278	1918	2.75	3.50	5.00	7.50
	1279	1919	2.75	3.50	5.00	7.50
	1280	1920	2.75	3.50	5.00	7.50

KORI

SILVER, 4.60 g

	Date	Year	VG	Fine	VF	XF
28	AH1235	VS1875	1.75	2.50	4.00	6.50
	1235	1876	1.75	2.50	4.00	6.50
	1236	1877	1.75	2.50	4.00	6.50
	1245	1886	1.75	2.50	4.00	6.50
	1246	1886	1.75	2.50	4.00	6.50
	1247	1887	1.75	2.50	4.00	6.50
	1247	1888	1.75	2.50	4.00	6.50
	1249	1889	1.75	2.50	4.00	6.50
	1249	1890	1.75	2.50	4.00	6.50
	1251	1892	1.75	2.50	4.00	6.50
	1521	1892 (error)				
			1.75	2.50	4.00	6.50
	1252	1892	1.75	2.50	4.00	6.50
35	AH1263	190x	1.75	2.50	4.00	6.50
	1267	1907	1.75	2.50	4.00	6.50
	1268	1908	1.75	2.50	4.00	6.50
43	AH1270	1910	1.75	2.50	4.00	6.50
	1272	1912	1.75	2.50	4.00	6.50
	1273	1913	1.75	2.50	4.00	6.50
	1273	1914	1.75	2.50	4.00	6.50
	1274	1914	1.75	2.50	4.00	6.50
	1275	1915	1.75	2.50	4.00	6.50
	1276	1915	1.75	2.50	4.00	6.50
	1277	1917	1.75	2.50	4.00	6.50
	1278	1918	1.75	2.50	4.00	6.50
	1279	1919	1.75	2.50	4.00	6.50
	1280	1920	1.75	2.50	4.00	6.50

Local Issues
MAHABAT KHAN II
AH1268-1300/VS1908-1939/1851-1882AD

DOKDO

COPPER

Y#	Date	Year	Good	VG	Fine	VF
1	VS1931	(1874)	15.00	25.00	40.00	60.00
	1935	(1878)	13.50	22.50	35.00	50.00

1/2 KORI

SILVER, 2.30 g

Y#	Date	Year	Fine	VF	XF
E1	AH1293	VS1934	4.00	7.50	12.50	20.00
	1299	1938	4.00	7.50	12.50	20.00

KORI

SILVER, 4.60 g

	Date	Year	VG	Fine	VF	XF
2	AH1292	VS1932	1.75	2.50	3.50	6.00
	1293	1933	1.75	2.50	3.50	6.00
	1293	1934	1.75	2.50	3.50	6.00
	1297	1935	1.75	2.50	3.50	6.00
	1297	1936	1.75	2.50	3.50	6.00

Y#	Date	Year	VG	Fine	VF	XF
2	1298	1937	1.75	2.50	3.50	6.00
	1299	1938	1.75	2.50	3.50	6.00

GOLD KORI
GOLD, 15-16mm

	Date	Year	VG	Fine	VF	XF
3	AH1292	VS1932	100.00	130.00	165.00	200.00

BAHADUR KHAN III
AH1300-1310/VS1939-1949/1882-1892AD

1/2 GOLD KORI

GOLD

	Date	Year	VG	Fine	VF	XF
4	AH1309	VS1947	100.00	150.00	225.00	275.00

GOLD KORI

GOLD

	Date	Year	VG	Fine	VF	XF
5	AH1309	VS1947	140.00	225.00	300.00	375.00

RASAL KHAN
AH1310-1329/VS1949-1968/1892-1911AD

DOKDO

COPPER

Y#	Date	Year	Good	VG	Fine	VF
6.1	AH1325	VS1963	4.50	7.00	10.00	13.50

Rev: Date w/o rosettes.

6.2	VS1963	(1906)	1.25	2.00	3.00	4.50
	1964	(1907)	1.25	2.00	3.00	4.50

Rev: Date between rosettes.

6.3	VS1964	(1907)	.50	.85	1.25	1.75
	1965	(1908)	.50	.85	1.25	1.75
	1966	(1909)	.50	.85	1.25	1.75
	1967	(1910)	1.00	1.75	2.50	3.50

6.4	ND	—	1.75	2.75	4.00	5.50

2 DOKDA

COPPER

7	VS1964	(1907)	7.50	12.50	20.00	30.00

KORI
SILVER, 15mm, 4.6 g

Y#	Date	Year	VG	Fine	VF	XF
8	VS1966	(1909)	12.50	25.00	35.00	50.00

MAHABAT KHAN III
AH1329-1368/VS1968-2005/1911-1948AD

DOKDO
COPPER, 19mm

Y#	Date	Year	Good	VG	Fine	VF
9	VS1985	(1928)	10.00	16.50	25.00	40.00
	1990	(1933)	10.00	16.50	25.00	40.00

KALAT
Khelat or Kelat

A state located in Baluchistan, Pakistan.

The Khanate of Kalat had originally been a feudatory of Kabul. Its ruler, the wali, later became a trusted leader in the army of Ahmad Shah Durrani, who in 1761 invaded India and crushed both Mughal and Maratha forces at the battle of Panipat. In 1839 Kalat was taken by the British, and the wali, Mehrab Khan, was killed. The victors then installed his son, Nasir Khan, as ruler and in 1854 a formal treaty was executed. From that time Kalat came under British control, with the Government of India frequently acting as referees in disputes between the wali and his chiefs. In 1893 the wali was deposed for misrule and Kalat's mint was closed.

RULERS

Mehrab Khan
  AH1232-1255/1816-1839AD
Kasir Khan,
  AH1256-1274/1840-1857AD
Khudadad Khan,
  AH1274-1311/1857-1893AD

MINT

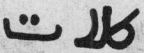

Kalat

MEHRAB KHAN
AH1232-1255/1816-1839AD

FALUS

COPPER

C#	Date	Year	Good	VG	Fine	VF
5	AH1237	—	3.50	6.00	8.50	12.50
	1238	—	—	—	—	—
	1240	—	3.50	6.00	8.50	12.50

KHUDADAD KHAN
AH1274-1311/1857-1893AD
In the name of Mahmud Khan Durrani

FALUS

COPPER
Round, irregular, or rough-cut octagonal

C#	Date	Year	VG	Fine	VF	XF
10	AH1186(error for 1286?)					
		—	2.50	4.00	7.00	11.50
	1290	—	2.50	4.00	7.00	11.50
	1293	—	2.50	4.00	7.00	11.50
	1294	—	2.50	4.00	7.00	11.50
	1295	—	2.00	3.50	6.00	9.00
	1296	—	3.00	4.50	7.00	10.00
	ND	—	1.50	2.00	4.00	6.00

KARAULI

State located in Rajputana, northwest India.

Karauli was established in the eleventh century by Jadon Rajputs, of the same stock as the royal house of Jaisalmir. They are thought to have migrated to Rajasthan from the Mathura region some years earlier. The state passed successively under Mughal and Maratha suzerainty before coming under British authority in 1817.

The maharajas of Karauli first struck coins in the reign of Manak Pal.

RULERS

Manak Pal
  AH1186-1219/1772-1804AD
Harbaksh Pal
  AH1219-1254/1804-1838AD
Pratap Pal
  AH1254-1265/1838-1848AD
Nar Singh Pal
  AH1265-1270/1848-1853AD

Karauli

Madan Pal AH1270-1286/1853-1869AD
Arjun Pal, 1875-1886AD
Bhanwar Pal, 1886-1927

MINT

Karauli کرولی करौली

+ and +
MINT MARKS

 Katar   Jhar on reverse

Mughal Issues

In the name of Muhammad Akbar II
AH1221-1253/1806-1837AD

PAISA
COPPER

C#	Date	Year	VG	Fine	VF	XF
15	AH—	4				

RUPEE

SILVER, 10.70-11.60 g

20	AH—	2	13.50	18.50	27.50	45.00
	1228	7	13.50	18.50	27.50	45.00
	1231	10	13.50	18.50	27.50	45.00
	1239 (retrograde g)					
	—	17	13.50	18.50	27.50	45.00
	—	19	13.50	18.50	27.50	45.00
	1244	—	13.50	18.50	27.50	45.00

In the name of Bahadur Shah II
AH1253-1274/1837-1858AD

RUPEE

SILVER, 10.70-11.60 g

40	AH—	9	13.50	18.50	27.50	45.00
	1265	13	13.50	18.50	27.50	45.00
	1268	15	13.50	18.50	27.50	45.00

Regal Issues

In the name of Queen Victoria
Years of Madan Pal
Years 1-14

PAISA

COPPER

Y#	Date	Year	Good	VG	Fine	VF
1	1852 (error for 1859)	13	2.50	5.00	7.50	11.50

1/4 RUPEE
SILVER, 13mm, 2.68-2.90 g

Y#	Date	Year	VG	Fine	VF	XF
2	1852	7	11.50	15.00	20.00	30.00
	1852	13	11.50	15.00	20.00	30.00
	1859	14	11.50	15.00	20.00	30.00

1/2 RUPEE
SILVER, 18mm, 5.35-5.80 g

3	1852	—	11.50	15.00	20.00	30.00
	1859	—	11.50	15.00	20.00	30.00

RUPEE

SILVER, 10.70-11.60 g

Y#	Date	Year	VG	Fine	VF	XF
4	1859	7	12.50	15.00	22.50	35.00
	1859	9	12.50	15.00	22.50	35.00
	1852	9	12.50	15.00	22.50	35.00
	1852	10	12.50	15.00	22.50	35.00
	1852	11	12.50	15.00	22.50	35.00
	1852	12	12.50	15.00	22.50	35.00
	1852	13	12.50	15.00	22.50	35.00
	1852	14	12.50	15.00	22.50	35.00

In the name of Empress Victoria
Years of Arjun Pal
Years 1-11

1/4 PAISA
COPPER, 13mm, 4.50 g

Y#	Date	Year	Good	VG	Fine	VF
5	—	11	4.50	6.00	10.00	15.00

1/2 PAISA

COPPER, 9.00 g

6	1886	11	1.75	2.75	4.00	7.50

PAISA

COPPER, 18.00 g
Rev: Katar upper right.

7	1881	—	1.75	2.75	4.00	7.50
	1882	11	(error for 1886)			
	1883	—	1.75	2.75	4.00	7.50
	188-	9	1.75	2.75	4.00	7.50
	1885	10	1.75	2.75	4.00	7.50
	1886	11	1.75	2.75	4.00	7.50

RUPEE

SILVER, 10.70-11.60 g

Y#	Date	Year	VG	Fine	VF	XF
8	1882	—	12.50	17.50	25.00	35.00
	1884	—	12.50	17.50	25.00	35.00
	1885	10	12.50	17.50	25.00	35.00
	1886	11	12.50	17.50	25.00	35.00

In the name of Empress Victoria
Years of Bhanwal Pal
Years 1-11

1/2 PAISA

COPPER, 9.00 g

Y#	Date	Year	Good	VG	Fine	VF
9	1886	1	1.75	3.00	5.00	8.00
	1887	2	1.75	3.00	5.00	8.00

PAISA

 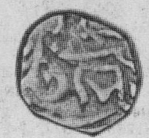

COPPER, 18.00-18.25 g

Y#	Date	Year	Good	VG	Fine	VF
10	1885	—	1.75	2.75	4.50	6.50
	1886	1	1.75	2.75	4.50	6.50
	1887	2	1.75	2.75	4.50	6.50
	1891	6	1.75	2.75	4.50	6.50
	1893	8	1.75	2.75	4.50	6.50

1/4 RUPEE

SILVER, 2.68-2.90 g

Y#	Date	Year	VG	Fine	VF	XF
11	1893	8	8.50	12.50	20.00	30.00
	1896	11	8.50	12.50	20.00	30.00

1/2 RUPEE
SILVER, 18mm, 5.35-5.80 g

12	1893	8	8.50	12.50	20.00	30.00
	1896	10	8.50	12.50	20.00	30.00

RUPEE

SILVER, 10.70-11.60 g

13	1885	1	12.50	16.50	22.50	32.50
	1886	1	12.50	16.50	22.50	32.50
	1886	2	12.50	16.50	22.50	32.50
	1888	2	12.50	16.50	22.50	32.50
	1888	3	12.50	16.50	22.50	32.50
	1889	4	12.50	16.50	22.50	32.50
	1890	4	12.50	16.50	22.50	32.50
	1890	—	12.50	16.50	22.50	32.50
	1891	6	12.50	16.50	22.50	32.50
	1892	8	12.50	16.50	22.50	32.50
	1893	8	12.50	16.50	22.50	32.50
	1894	8	12.50	16.50	22.50	32.50
	1894	9	12.50	16.50	22.50	32.50
	1895	10	12.50	16.50	22.50	32.50
	1896	11	12.50	16.50	22.50	32.50
	1897	11	12.50	16.50	22.50	32.50

Anonymous Issue
1/2 MOHUR

 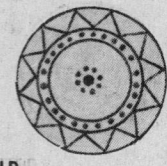

GOLD

KM#	Date	Year	VG	Fine	VF	XF
1	ND	2	—	—	Rare	

KASHMIR

State located in extreme northern India. Part of Afghanistan Durrani Empire 1752-1819AD, under Sikhs of Punjab 1819-1846AD, locally ruled by Dogra Rajas thereafter. For earlier coinage refer to Afghanistan and Sikh Empire.

RULERS
Dogra Rajas

Gulab Singh
VS1903-1913/1846-1856AD
Ranbir Singh
VS1914-1942/1857-1885AD
Pertab Singh
VS1942-1979/1885-1925AD

MINTS

Jammu جموں

Ladakh لداخ

Srinagar سرینگر

JAMMU MINT
Dogra Issues

Anonymous Issues

PAISA

COPPER
Obv: Persian leg. Rev: Gurmukhi leg.

Y#	Date	Year	Good	VG	Fine	VF
1	VS1914	(1857)	.50	1.00	1.75	2.50
	1915	(1858)	.50	1.00	1.75	2.50
	1917	(1860)	.50	1.00	1.75	2.50
	1918	(1861)	.50	1.00	1.75	2.50
	1919	(1862)	.50	1.00	1.75	2.50
	1921	(1864)	.50	1.00	1.75	2.50
	1922	(1865)	.50	1.00	1.75	2.50

Rev: Takari leg.
Machine-punched planchets.

Y#	Date	Year	Good	VG	Fine	VF
2	VS1935	(1876)	3.50	7.50	12.50	20.00
	1936	(1877)	3.50	7.50	12.50	20.00

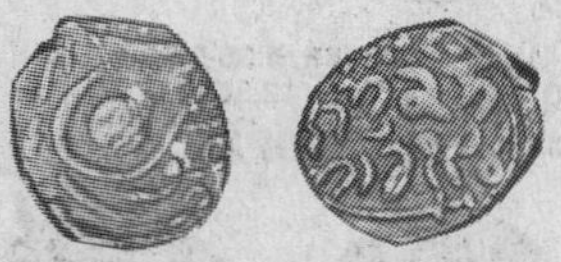

Dump style, uneven planchets.

Y#	Date	Year	Good	VG	Fine	VF
2a	VS1935	(1876)	.50	1.00	1.75	2.50
	1937	(1878)	.50	1.00	1.75	2.50
	1938	(1879)	.50	1.00	1.75	2.50
	1939	(1880)	.50	1.00	1.75	2.50
	1940	(1881)	.50	1.00	1.75	2.50
	1942	(1883)	.50	1.00	1.75	2.50
	1943	(1884)	.50	1.00	1.75	2.50
	1946	(1887)	.50	1.00	1.75	2.50
	1947	(1888)	.50	1.00	1.75	2.50
	1948	(1889)	.50	1.00	1.75	2.50
	1949	(1890)	.50	1.00	1.75	2.50

Anonymous Issue
1/3 MOHUR

GOLD, 3.57-3.80 g

Y#	Date	Year	VG	Fine	VF	XF
3	VS1921	(1864)	225.00	300.00	400.00	600.00

LADAKH MINT

NOTE: For coins struck at the Ladakh Mint refer to Indian Princely State, Ladakh.

SRINAGAR MINT

First Copper Series
Many varieties exist.

PAISA

COPPER
Obv: Fancy leaf.

Y#	Date	Year	Good	VG	Fine	VF
1.1	VS1904	(1847)	2.00	3.50	6.00	10.00

Obv: Trident. Rev: Scimitar through circle.

Y#	Date	Year	Good	VG	Fine	VF
1.2	VS1908	(1851)	2.00	3.50	6.00	10.00

Rev: Fancy leaf.

Y#	Date	Year	Good	VG	Fine	VF
1.3	—	—	2.00	3.50	6.00	10.00

Second Copper Series
Obv: Fancy leaf. Rev: Scimitar through circle.

1/2 ANNA

COPPER

Y#	Date	Year	Good	VG	Fine	VF
8	VS1920	(1863)	4.00	7.50	12.50	20.00

ANNA

COPPER

Y#	Date	Year	Good	VG	Fine	VF
9	VS1920	(1863)	6.00	10.00	15.00	25.00
	1092 (error for 1920)		6.00	10.00	15.00	25.00
	1924	(1867)	6.00	10.00	15.00	25.00

Third Copper Series
Obv: Date in cartouche.

1/2 PAISA

COPPER, 2.50-3.00 g

Y#	Date	Year	Good	VG	Fine	VF
6	VS1922	(1865)	1.75	3.00	4.00	7.50
	1924	(1867)	1.75	3.00	4.00	7.50

PAISA

COPPER, 5.50-6.00 g

Y#	Date	Year	Good	VG	Fine	VF
7	VS1920	(1863)	.75	1.25	1.75	2.50
	1921	(1864)	.75	1.25	1.75	2.50
	1922	(1865)	1.00	1.50	2.00	2.75
	1923	(1866)	1.25	1.75	2.25	3.00
	1926	(1869)	1.25	1.75	2.25	3.00
	1927	(1870)	1.00	1.50	2.00	2.75
	1928	(1871)	1.00	1.50	2.00	2.75
	1930	(1873)	1.00	1.50	2.00	2.75
	1931	(1874)	1.25	1.75	2.25	3.00

Fourth Copper Series
Obv: *JHS*. Rev: Takari leg.

1/4 PAISA

COPPER, 1.50 g

Y#	Date	Year	Good	VG	Fine	VF
17	VS1935	(1878)	2.00	4.50	7.50	12.50
	1941	(1884)	2.00	4.50	7.50	12.50
	Date off flan		1.00	2.25	3.75	6.50

1/2 PAISA

COPPER, 3.00 g

Y#	Date	Year	Good	VG	Fine	VF
18	VS1928	(1871)	2.00	3.00	4.50	6.00
18	1932	(1875)	—	1.00	1.50	3.00
	1933	(1876)	—	1.00	1.50	3.00
	1933 on obv/1934 on rev. (1875/76)		1.75	2.50	3.50	5.00
	1934	(1877)	1.00	1.50	2.00	3.00
	1936	(1879)	1.00	1.50	2.00	3.00
	1937	(1880)	1.00	1.50	2.00	3.00
	1938	(1881)	1.00	1.50	2.00	3.00
	1939	(1882)	1.00	1.50	2.00	3.00
	1940	(1883)	1.00	1.50	2.00	3.00
	1941	(1884)	1.00	1.50	2.00	3.00

PAISA

COPPER, 6.00 g

Y#	Date	Year	Good	VG	Fine	VF
19	VS1938	(1881)	1.75	3.00	5.00	8.00
	1939	(1882)	1.75	3.00	5.00	8.00
	1940	(1883)	1.75	3.00	5.00	8.00

First Silver Series
Rev: Leaf and date, w/o *JHS*.
NOTE: The dot for O in 1903, 1904, 1905 is sometimes omitted.

1/8 RUPEE

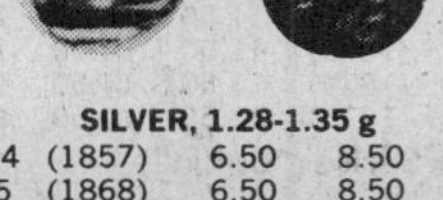

SILVER, 1.28-1.35 g

Y#	Date	Year	VG	Fine	VF	XF
2	VS1903	(1846)	9.00	12.50	16.50	25.00
	1904	(1847)	9.00	12.50	16.50	25.00
	1905	(1848)	9.00	12.50	16.50	25.00

1/4 RUPEE

SILVER, 2.57-2.70 g

Y#	Date	Year	VG	Fine	VF	XF
3	VS1903	(1846)	8.50	10.00	14.00	20.00
	1904	(1847)	8.50	10.00	14.00	20.00

1/2 RUPEE

SILVER, 5.15-5.40 g

Y#	Date	Year	VG	Fine	VF	XF
4	VS1903	(1846)	10.00	15.00	18.50	27.50
	1904	(1847)	10.00	15.00	18.50	27.50
	1905	(1848)	10.00	15.00	18.50	27.50
	1906	(1849)	10.00	15.00	18.50	27.50

RUPEE

SILVER, 10.30-10.80 g

Y#	Date	Year	VG	Fine	VF	XF
5	VS1903	(1846)	11.50	13.00	16.50	25.00
	1904	(1847)	11.50	13.00	16.50	25.00
	1905	(1848)	12.50	14.50	20.00	27.50
	1906	(1849)	12.50	14.50	20.00	27.50

Second Silver Series
Obv. and rev: Persian leg. w/JHS added to rev.

1/16 RUPEE

SILVER, 0.64-0.67 g

Y#	Date	Year	VG	Fine	VF	XF
9	VS—	—	6.50	8.50	11.50	16.50

1/8 RUPEE

SILVER, 1.28-1.35 g

Y#	Date	Year	VG	Fine	VF	XF
10	VS1914	(1857)	6.50	8.50	11.50	16.50
	1925	(1868)	6.50	8.50	11.50	16.50

Kashmir / INDIAN PRINCELY STATES

1/4 RUPEE

SILVER, 2.57-2.70 g

Y#	Date	Year	VG	Fine	VF	XF
11	VS1914	(1857)	7.00	9.00	12.50	17.50
	1922	(1865)	7.00	9.00	12.50	17.50
	1925	(1868)	7.00	9.00	12.50	17.50

1/2 RUPEE

SILVER, 5.15-5.40 g

12	VS1914	(1857)	7.50	9.00	13.50	20.00
	1922	(1865)	7.50	9.00	13.50	20.00

"KHAM" RUPEE

SILVER, 10.30-10.80 g

13	VS1907	(1850)	10.00	11.50	14.00	22.50
	1908	(1851)	10.00	11.50	14.00	22.50
	1909	(1852)	10.00	11.50	14.00	22.50
	1910	(1853)	10.00	11.50	14.00	22.50
	1911	(1854)	10.00	11.50	14.00	22.50
	1912	(1855)	10.00	11.50	14.00	22.50
	1913	(1856)	10.00	11.50	14.00	22.50
	1914	(1857)	10.00	11.50	14.00	22.50
	1915	(1858)	10.00	11.50	14.00	22.50
	1916	(1859)	10.00	11.50	14.00	22.50
	1917	(1860)	10.00	11.50	14.00	22.50
	1918	(1861)	10.00	11.50	14.00	22.50
	1919	(1862)	10.00	11.50	14.00	22.50
	1920	(1863)	10.00	11.50	14.00	22.50
	1921	(1864)	10.00	11.50	14.00	22.50
	1922	(1865)	10.00	11.50	14.00	22.50
	1923	(1866)	10.00	11.50	14.00	22.50
	1924	(1867)	10.00	11.50	14.00	22.50
	1925	(1868)	10.00	11.50	14.00	22.50
	1926	(1869)	10.00	11.50	14.00	22.50
	1927	(1870)	10.00	11.50	14.00	22.50

Third Silver Series
Obv: Persian leg. w/JHS. Rev: Takari leg. Rupee weight reduced to 6.80 g from 10.30-10.80 g.

1/4 RUPEE

SILVER, 15mm, 1.65-1.70 g

14	VS1928	(1871)	15.00	20.00	25.00	40.00

1/2 RUPEE

SILVER, 17mm, 3.30-3.40 g

15	VS1928	(1871)	15.00	20.00	25.00	40.00

RUPEE

SILVER, 6.60-6.80 g
Machine-struck in collar.

16	VS1927	(1870)	40.00	60.00	80.00	120.00

Struck on machine punched planchets.

16a	VS1927	(1870)	10.00	12.50	15.00	25.00
	1928	(1871)	10.00	12.50	15.00	25.00
	1929	(1872)	12.50	15.00	18.50	30.00

Struck on dump planchets.

16b	1929	(1872)	11.50	14.50	17.50	26.50
	1930	(1873)	11.50	14.50	17.50	26.50
	1931	(1874)	11.50	14.50	17.50	26.50
	1932	(1875)	11.50	14.50	17.50	26.50

Fourth Silver Series ("Chilki")
Obv: Persian date in second line. Rev: Davanagari date in second line.

1/2 RUPEE

SILVER, 3.30 g

Y#	Date	Year	VG	Fine	VF	XF
20	VS1946	(1889)	11.50	13.00	16.50	25.00
	1948	(1891)	11.50	13.00	16.50	25.00
	1950	(1893)	11.50	13.00	16.50	25.00
	1951	(1894)	11.50	13.00	16.50	25.00

RUPEE

SILVER, 6.80 g

21	VS1931	(1874)	12.50	17.50	25.00	32.50
	1932	(1875)	12.50	17.50	25.00	32.50
	1933	(1876)	12.50	17.50	25.00	32.50

6.60 g

21a	1934	(1877)	5.00	7.50	10.00	16.50
	1935	(1878)	5.00	7.50	10.00	16.50
	1936	(1879)	5.00	7.50	10.00	16.50
	1937	(1880)	5.00	7.50	10.00	16.50
	1938	(1881)	5.00	7.50	10.00	16.50
	1939	(1882)	5.00	7.50	10.00	16.50
	1940	(1883)	5.00	7.50	10.00	16.50
	1941	(1884)	5.00	7.50	10.00	16.50
	1942	(1885)	5.00	7.50	10.00	16.50
	1943	(1886)	5.00	7.50	10.00	16.50
	1944	(1887)	5.00	7.50	10.00	16.50
	1945	(1888)	5.00	7.50	10.00	16.50
	1946	(1889)	5.00	7.50	10.00	16.50
	1947	(1890)	5.00	7.50	10.00	16.50
	1948	(1891)	5.00	7.50	10.00	16.50
	1949	(1892)	5.00	7.50	10.00	16.50
	1950	(1893)	5.00	7.50	10.00	16.50
	1951	(1894)	5.00	7.50	10.00	16.50
	1952	(1895)	5.00	7.50	10.00	16.50

KISHANGARH

The maharajas of Kishangarh, a small state in northwest India, in the vicinity of Ajmer, belonged to the Rathor Rajputs. The town of Kishangarh, which gave its name to the state, was founded in 1611 and was itself named after Kishen Singh, the first ruler. The maharajas succeeded in reaching terms with Akbar in the late sixteenth century, and again in 1818 with the British. In 1948 the state was merged into Rajasthan.

RULERS
Kalyan Singh
  AH1212-1248 / 1797-1832AD
Mokham Singh
  AH1248-1256 / 1832-1840AD
Prithvi Singh
  AH1256-1297 / 1840-1879AD
Sardul Singh
  AH1297-1318 / 1879-1900AD
Madan Singh
  AH1318-1345 / 1900-1926AD
Yagyanarain
  AH1345-1357 / 1926-1938AD

MINT
Kishangarh

Mintmark:
On reverse

Mughal Issues
In the name of Muhammad Akbar II
AH1221-1253 / 1806-1837AD

PAISA

COPPER, 17.30 g
Crude copy of Jaipur C#47

C#	Date	Year	Good	VG	Fine	VF
25	ND	12	1.00	1.50	2.50	5.00

Regal Issues
In the names of Queen Victoria and Prithvi Singh
1858-1879AD
Frozen regnal year 24 of Shah Alam II.

RUPEE

SILVER, 10.70-11.60 g

Y#	Date	Year	VG	Fine	VF	XF
1	1858	24	10.00	15.00	23.50	35.00
	1859	24	10.00	15.00	23.50	35.00

NOTE: A rare double-thick rupee special strike is known to exist.

In the names of Queen Victoria and probably Sardul Singh
1879-1900AD

1/2 RUPEE

SILVER, 5.35-5.80 g

A2	ND	—	12.50	17.50	25.00	40.00

RUPEE

SILVER, 10.70-11.60 g

2	1880	24	17.50	25.00	35.00	50.00

In the names of Queen Victoria and Madan Singh

1/2 RUPEE

SILVER, 5.35-5.80 g

A3	ND	—	12.50	17.50	25.00	40.00

In the names of Edward VII and probably Madan Singh
1900-1926AD

1/4 RUPEE

SILVER, 2.67-2.90 g

B3	ND	—	12.50	17.50	25.00	40.00

1/2 RUPEE

SILVER, 5.35-5.80 g

3	1902	24	15.00	20.00	27.50	37.50

In the names of George V or VI and Yagyanarain
1926-1938AD

1/4 RUPEE

SILVER, 15mm, 2.68-2.90 g

4	—	24	15.00	20.00	27.50	37.50

1/2 RUPEE

SILVER, 5.35-5.80 g

5	—	24	15.00	20.00	27.50	37.50

RUPEE

SILVER, 10.70-11.60 g

6	—	24	20.00	30.00	40.00	60.00

NAZARANA RUPEE

SILVER, 10.70-11.60 g

Y#	Date	Year	VG	Fine	VF	XF
6a	—	—	75.00	100.00	150.00	200.00

1/2 MOHUR
GOLD, 18mm, 5.35-5.70 g

7	—	24	175.00	225.00	275.00	325.00

MOHUR
GOLD, 19mm, 10.70-11.40 g

8	—	24	225.00	275.00	325.00	400.00

KOLHAPUR

Maratha state in southwest India between Goa and Bombay.
The maharajas of Kolhapur traced their origins and ancestry to Raja Ram, son of Shivaji, the founder of the Maratha kingdom, and to his courageous wife Tarabai who officiated as regent on behalf of her son after Raja Ram's death in 1698. Kolhapur's existence as a separate state dates from about 1730 when a family quarrel left Sambaji, the great-grandson of Sivaji, as the first raja of Kolhapur. In recognition of their special eminence among the Maratha chieftains the rulers of Kolhapur bore the honorific title of "Chhatrapati Maharaja". Between 1811 and 1862 Kolhapur concluded a series of treaties and agreements with the British whereby the state came increasingly under British protection and control.
The mint closed ca. 1850AD.

MINT

Mintname: A'zamnagar Gokak, Pseudo

Mughal Issues
In the name of Muhammad Shah
(struck until ca. 1850AD)

1/4 RUPEE
SILVER, 12mm, 2.68-2.90 g

C#	Date	Year	VG	Fine	VF	XF
14	ND	—	15.00	20.00	27.50	37.50

1/2 RUPEE

SILVER, 15mm, 5.35-5.80 g

15	ND	—	15.00	20.00	27.50	37.50

RUPEE

SILVER, 10.70-11.60 g

16	ND	—	9.00	12.50	15.00	22.50

Fine calligraphy

25	1821	—	11.50	15.00	25.00	40.00

Regal Issues
EAST INDIA COMPANY

Local issue from Shahupur.

1/2 RUPEE
SILVER, 5.35-5.80 g

29	1821	—	18.50	25.00	35.00	55.00

RUPEE

SILVER, 10.70-11.60 g

30	1821	—	18.50	25.00	35.00	55.00

KOTAH

Kotah State, located in northwest India was subdivided out of Bundi early in the seventeenth century when it was given to a younger son of the Bundi raja by the Mughal emperor. The ruler, or maharao, was a Chauhan Rajput. During the years of Maratha ascendancy Kotah fell on hard times, especially from the depredations of Holkar. In 1817 the State came under treaty with the British.

RULERS
Ram Singh,
VS1885-1923/1828-1866AD
Chattar Sal,
VS1923-1946/1866-1889AD
Umed Singh
VS1946-2002/1889-1945AD

MINT

نذركاوٿ

Mintname: Nandgaon

كوڻه عرف نذركاوٿ

Kotah urf Nandgaon

MINTMARKS

1. ⊠   4. ৬
2. ✽
3. ✿   5. ⚛

Mint mark #1 appears beneath #4 on all Kotah coins, and serves to distinguish coins of Kotah from similar issues of Bundi in the pre-Victoria period.
C#28 has mint mark #2 on obv., #1, 3 and 4 on rev. All later issues have #1 on obv., #1, 5 and 4 on rev.

Mughal Issues
In the name of Muhammad Akbar II
AH1221-1253/1806-1837AD

PAISA

COPPER, square

C#	Date	Year	Good	VG	Fine	VF
A29	AH—	25	2.50	3.50	4.50	6.00
		29	2.50	3.50	4.50	6.00

29	AH—	4	1.50	2.50	4.50	7.00
	—	5	1.50	2.50	4.50	7.00
	—	6	1.50	2.50	4.50	7.00
	—	7	1.50	2.50	4.50	7.00
	—	10	1.50	2.50	4.50	7.00
	—	11	1.50	2.50	4.50	7.00
	—	12	1.50	2.50	4.50	7.00
	—	13	1.50	2.50	4.50	7.00
	—	14	1.50	2.50	4.50	7.00
	—	15	1.50	2.50	4.50	7.00
	—	25	1.50	2.50	4.50	7.00
	—	26	1.50	2.50	4.50	7.00

RUPEE

SILVER, 10.70-11.60 g

C#	Date	Year	VG	Fine	VF	XF
30	AH—	1	8.00	10.00	12.50	20.00
	—	12	8.00	10.00	12.50	20.00
	—	16	8.00	10.00	12.50	20.00
	—	20	8.00	10.00	12.50	20.00
	—	23	8.00	10.00	12.50	20.00
	—	28	8.00	10.00	12.50	20.00

NAZARANA RUPEE

SILVER, square, 10.70-11.60 g

C#	Date	Year	VG	Fine	VF	XF
30a	AH—	5	50.00	65.00	85.00	125.00
	—	11	50.00	65.00	85.00	125.00
	—	16	50.00	65.00	85.00	125.00
	—	19	50.00	65.00	85.00	125.00

Round, 27-31mm

30b	AH1239	18	50.00	65.00	85.00	125.00
	—	19	50.00	65.00	85.00	125.00
	—	24	50.00	65.00	85.00	125.00
	—	32	50.00	65.00	85.00	125.00

NOTE: Formerly listed under Bundi State.

In the name of Bahadur Shah II
AH1253-1274/1837-1857AD

1/8 RUPEE
SILVER, 10mm, 1.34-1.45 g

31	AH—	—	8.00	11.00	15.00	25.00

1/4 RUPEE
SILVER, 12mm, 2.68-2.90 g

A31	AH—	—	8.00	11.00	15.00	25.00

1/2 RUPEE
SILVER, 5.35-5.80 g

B31	AH—	—	10.00	12.50	16.50	27.50

RUPEE

SILVER, 10.70-11.60 g

32	AH—	9	8.00	10.00	11.50	17.50
	—	16	8.00	10.00	11.50	17.50
	—	18	8.00	10.00	11.50	17.50
	—	19	8.00	10.00	11.50	17.50
	—	21	8.00	10.00	11.50	17.50

NAZARANA RUPEE

SILVER, 10.70-11.60 g

32a	AH—	4	30.00	45.00	60.00	75.00
	—	5	30.00	45.00	60.00	75.00
	1205	6	30.00	45.00	60.00	75.00
	—	7	30.00	45.00	60.00	75.00
	—	8	30.00	45.00	60.00	75.00
	—	9	30.00	45.00	60.00	75.00
	—	12	30.00	45.00	60.00	75.00
	—	13	30.00	45.00	60.00	75.00
	—	14	30.00	45.00	60.00	75.00
	—	15	30.00	45.00	60.00	75.00

Kotah / INDIAN PRINCELY STATES 934

C#	Date	Year	VG	Fine	VF	XF
32a	—	17	30.00	45.00	60.00	75.00
	—	19	30.00	45.00	60.00	75.00
	—	20	30.00	45.00	60.00	75.00

NOTE: Most specimens show rudimentary traces of AH dates on obverse.

MOHUR
GOLD, 19mm, 10.70-11.40 g

33	AH—	1	225.00	250.00	325.00	400.00
	—	21	225.00	250.00	325.00	400.00

Regal Issues
In the name of Queen Victoria
From 1857AD

1/2 PAISA
COPPER, 12-16mm, 9 g

Y#	Date	Year	Good	VG	Fine	VF
1	AH—	37	1.50	2.50	3.75	6.00
	—	39	1.50	2.50	3.75	6.00
	—	40	1.50	2.50	3.75	6.00

PAISA
COPPER, 15-20mm

2	AH—	27	1.25	2.00	3.25	5.00
	—	28	1.25	2.00	3.25	5.00
	—	29	1.25	2.00	3.25	5.00
	—	31	1.25	2.00	3.25	5.00
	—	32	1.25	2.00	3.25	5.00
	—	37	1.25	2.00	3.25	5.00
	—	38	1.25	2.00	3.25	5.00
	—	39	1.25	2.00	3.25	5.00
	—	40	1.25	2.00	3.25	5.00
	—	41	1.25	2.00	3.25	5.00
	—	51	1.25	2.00	3.25	5.00

1/8 RUPEE
SILVER, 1.34-1.45 g

Y#	Date	Year	VG	Fine	VF	XF
3	AH—	27	2.25	3.75	6.00	10.00
	—	29	2.25	3.75	6.00	10.00
	—	30	2.25	3.75	6.00	10.00
	—	31	2.25	3.75	6.00	10.00
	—	32	2.25	3.75	6.00	10.00
	—	33	2.25	3.75	6.00	10.00
	—	34	2.25	3.75	6.00	10.00
	—	36	2.25	3.75	6.00	10.00
	—	37	2.25	3.75	6.00	10.00
	—	38	2.25	3.75	6.00	10.00

1/4 RUPEE
SILVER, 2.68-2.90 g

4	AH—	1	2.50	3.75	6.00	10.00
	—	2	2.50	3.75	6.00	10.00
	—	8	2.50	3.75	6.00	10.00
	—	22	2.50	3.75	6.00	10.00
	—	27	2.50	3.75	6.00	10.00
	—	29	2.50	3.75	6.00	10.00
	—	30	2.50	3.75	6.00	10.00
	—	31	2.50	3.75	6.00	10.00
	—	32	2.50	3.75	6.00	10.00
	—	33	2.50	3.75	6.00	10.00
	—	35	2.50	3.75	6.00	10.00
	—	37	2.50	3.75	6.00	10.00
	—	38	2.50	3.75	6.00	10.00

1/2 RUPEE
SILVER, 5.35-5.80 g

5	AH—	1	4.00	7.00	10.00	17.50
	—	4	4.00	7.00	10.00	17.50
	—	8	4.00	7.00	10.00	17.50
	—	18	4.00	7.00	10.00	17.50
	—	22	4.00	7.00	10.00	17.50
	—	24	4.00	7.00	10.00	17.50
	—	25	4.00	7.00	10.00	17.50
	—	28	4.00	7.00	10.00	17.50
	—	29	4.00	7.00	10.00	17.50
	—	30	4.00	7.00	10.00	17.50
	—	31	4.00	7.00	10.00	17.50
	—	32	4.00	7.00	10.00	17.50
	—	33	4.00	7.00	10.00	17.50

Y#	Date	Year	VG	Fine	VF	XF
5	—	35	4.00	7.00	10.00	17.50
	—	36	4.00	7.00	10.00	17.50
	—	37	4.00	7.00	10.00	17.50
	—	38	4.00	7.00	10.00	17.50

RUPEE
SILVER, 10.70-11.60 g

6	AH—	1	5.50	7.00	9.00	15.00
	—	2	5.50	7.00	9.00	15.00
	—	4	5.50	7.00	9.00	15.00
	—	6	5.50	7.00	9.00	15.00
	—	8	5.50	7.00	9.00	15.00
	—	9	5.50	7.00	9.00	15.00
	—	15	5.50	7.00	9.00	15.00
	—	16	5.50	7.00	9.00	15.00
	—	17	5.50	7.00	9.00	15.00
	—	18	5.50	7.00	9.00	15.00
	—	19	5.50	7.00	9.00	15.00
	—	20	5.50	7.00	9.00	15.00
	—	21	5.50	7.00	9.00	15.00
	—	22	5.50	7.00	9.00	15.00
	—	26	5.50	7.00	9.00	15.00
	—	28	5.50	7.00	9.00	15.00
	—	31	5.50	7.00	9.00	15.00
	—	32	5.50	7.00	9.00	15.00
	—	34	5.50	7.00	9.00	15.00
	—	35	5.50	7.00	9.00	15.00
	—	38	5.50	7.00	9.00	15.00
	—	40	5.50	7.00	9.00	15.00
	—	41	5.50	7.00	9.00	15.00
	—	44	5.50	7.00	9.00	15.00

Rev: Full year.

7	VS1956 (1899)		16.50	25.00	35.00	50.00

NAZARANA RUPEE
SILVER, 10.70-11.60 g

6a	AH—	1	30.00	40.00	60.00	80.00
	—	2	30.00	40.00	60.00	80.00
	—	3	30.00	40.00	60.00	80.00
	—	4	30.00	40.00	60.00	80.00
	—	6	30.00	40.00	60.00	80.00
	—	7	30.00	40.00	60.00	80.00
	—	8	30.00	40.00	60.00	80.00
	—	9	30.00	40.00	60.00	80.00
	—	14	30.00	40.00	60.00	80.00
	—	15	30.00	40.00	60.00	80.00
	—	17	30.00	40.00	60.00	80.00
	—	18	30.00	40.00	60.00	80.00
	—	21	30.00	40.00	60.00	80.00
	—	22	30.00	40.00	60.00	80.00
	—	23	30.00	40.00	60.00	80.00
	—	24	30.00	40.00	60.00	80.00
	—	25	30.00	40.00	60.00	80.00
	—	26	30.00	40.00	60.00	80.00
	—	27	30.00	40.00	60.00	80.00
	—	28	30.00	40.00	60.00	80.00
	—	29	30.00	40.00	60.00	80.00
	—	30	30.00	40.00	60.00	80.00
	—	31	30.00	40.00	60.00	80.00
	—	32	30.00	40.00	60.00	80.00
	—	39	30.00	40.00	60.00	80.00
	—	43	30.00	40.00	60.00	80.00
	—	44	30.00	40.00	60.00	80.00

Y#	Date	Year	VG	Fine	VF	XF
7a	VS1956 (1899)		40.00	60.00	85.00	125.00

MOHUR
GOLD, 18mm, 10.70-11.40 g

8	AH—	1	220.00	250.00	300.00	375.00
	—	6	220.00	250.00	300.00	375.00
	—	8	220.00	250.00	300.00	375.00
	—	9	220.00	250.00	300.00	375.00
	—	15	220.00	250.00	300.00	375.00
	—	31	220.00	250.00	300.00	375.00
	—	32	220.00	250.00	300.00	375.00
	—	44	220.00	250.00	300.00	375.00

KUTCH

State located in northwest India, consisting of a peninsula north of the Gulf of Kutch.

The rulers of Kutch were Jareja Rajputs who, coming from Tatta in Sind, conquered Kutch in the fourteenth or fifteenth centuries. The capital city of Bhuj is thought to date from the mid-sixteenth century. In 1617, after Akbar's conquest of Gujerat and the fall of the Gujerat sultans, the Kutch ruler, Rao Bharmal I (1586-1632) visited Jahangir and established a relationship which was sufficiently warm as to leave Kutch virtually independent throughout the Mughal period. Early in the nineteenth century internal disorder and the existence of rival claimants to the throne resulted in British intrusion into the state's affairs. Rao Bharmalji II was deposed in favor of Rao Desalji II who proved much more amenable to the Government of India's wishes. He and his successors continued to rule in a manner considered by the British to be most enlightened and, as a result, Maharao Khengarji III was created a Knight Grand Commander of the Indian Empire. In view of its geographical isolation Kutch came under the direct control of the Central Government at India's independence.

First coinage was struck in 1617AD.

RULERS

Rayadhanji II
AH1192-1230/1778-1814AD

राओ श्री रायधनजी
Ra-o Sri Ra-y(a)-dh(a)-n-ji

Bharmalji II
AH1230-1235/1814-1819AD

राओ श्री भारमलजी
Ra-o Sri Bha-r-m(a)-l-ji

Desalji II
AH1235-1277/Vs1876-1917/1819-1860AD

राओ श्री ?सलजी
Ra-o Sri De-s(a)-l-ji

राओ श्री देशलजी
Ra-o Sri De-sa-l-ji

Pragmalji II
VS1917-1932/1860-1875AD

राओ श्री प्रागमलजी
Ra-o Sri Pra-g-m(a)-l-ji

महाराओ श्री प्रागमलजी
M(a)-ha-ra-o Sri Pra-g-m(a)-l-ji

माहाराजाधिराज मिरजा महाराओ श्री
Ma-ha-ra-ja Dhi-ra-j Mi-r-ja M(a)-ha-ra-o Sri

प्रागमलजी बहादुर
Pra-g-m(a)-l-ji B(a)-ha-du-r

Khengarji III
VS1932-1999/1875-1942AD

महाराओ श्री खेंगारजी
M(a)-ha-ra-o Sri Khen-ga-r-ji

माहाराओ खेंगारजी
Ma-ha-ra-o Khen-ga-r-ji

माहाराजाधिराज मिरजा महाराओ श्री
Ma-ha-ra-ja Dhi-ra-j Mi-r-ja M(a)-ha-ra-o Sri

खेंगारजी बहादुर कच्छभुज
Khen-ga-r-ji B(a)-ha-du-r K(a)-chh-bhu-j

मेरजामहाराओश्रीखेंगारजी
Mi-r-jan M(a)-ha-ra-o Sri Khen-ga-r-ji

महाराओश्रीखेंगारजी
M(a)-ha-ra-o Sri Khen-ga-r-ji

महाराजाधिराजामेरजामहाराओ
M(a)-ha-ra-ja Dhi-ra-j Mi-r-jan M(a)-ha-ra-o

श्रीखेंगारजीबहादुर
Sri-Khen-ga-r-ji B(a)-ha-du-r

श्रीखेंगारजीसवाईबहादुर
Sri Khen-ga-r-ji Sa-va-i B(a)-ha-du-r

महाराओश्रीखेंगारजीकच्छभुज
M(a)-ha-ra-o Sri Khen-ga-r-ji K(a)-chchh-bhu-j

Vijayarajji
VS1999-2004/1942-1947AD

विजयराजजी
Vi-j(a)-y(a)-ra-j-ji

महाराओश्रीविजयराजजी
M(a)-ha-ra-o Sri Vi-j(a)-y(a)-ra-j-ji K(a)-chchh 2000

Madanasinhji
VS2004- /1947- AD

मदनसिंहजी
M(a)-d(a)-n(a)-sin-h-ji

MINT

Bhuj (Devavnagri)   or   (Persian)

MONETARY SYSTEM
2 Trambiyo - 1 Dokda
3 Trambiyo - 1 Dhingla
8 Dokda - 1 Kori

NOTE: All coins through Bharmalji II bear a common type, derived from the Gujarati coinage of Muzaffar III (late 16th century AD), and bear a stylized form of the date AH978 (1570AD). The silver issues of Bharmalji II also have the fictitious date AH1165. The rulers name appears in the Devavnagri script on the obverse.

BHARMALJI II
AH1230-1235/1814-1819AD

TRAMBIYO
COPPER, 4.00 g

C#	Date	Good	VG	Fine	VF
31	ND	2.50	4.00	5.50	7.50

DOKDO
COPPER, 16mm, 8.30 g

| 32 | ND | 2.50 | 4.00 | 5.50 | 7.50 |

DHINGLO
COPPER, 17mm, 12.00 g

| 33 | ND | 3.00 | 4.50 | 6.00 | 8.50 |

1/2 KORI
SILVER, 2.10 g

C#	Date	VG	Fine	VF	XF
35	AH1165 (fictitious)	3.00	4.50	6.00	8.50

KORI
SILVER, 4.40 g

| 36 | AH1165 (fictitious) | 2.75 | 3.50 | 4.50 | 6.50 |

DESALJI II
AH1235-1277/VS1876-1917/1819-1860AD

The coins of Desalji II may be divided into four basic series, which may be differentiated as follows:

FIRST SERIES: Similar to coins of Bharmalji, but w/Desalji's name in Devavnagri on rev.

SECOND SERIES: In the name of the Mughal Emperor Akbar II and of Desalji in Devavnagri on obv., mint and both dates in Persian leg. on rev. but actual SE date in Devavnagri numerals. AH date is frozen (12)34, SE dates 1875-1887.

THIRD SERIES: Obv. Persian leg:, rev. in Devavnagri script. AH dates 1250-1266, VS dates 1892-1904. Many subvarieties of type, some w/only AH dates, some w/only SE dates, some w/both. In the name of Muhammad Akbar II.

FOURTH SERIES: Same as third series, but in the name of Bahadur II. VS 1909-1916 on silver and gold issues and AH1267-1274 on copper.

NOTE: Although Muhammad Akbar II was succeeded by Bahadur II on the Mughal throne in AH1253, the change is not acknowledged on Kutch coinage until AH1263 and Bahadur Shah is honored until VS1916/1859AD, the year after he was deposed by the British following the mutiny.

First Series

TRAMBIYO

COPPER, 4.20 g

C#	Date	Good	VG	Fine	VF
38	ND	1.00	1.50	2.50	4.00

DOKDO

COPPER, 8.70 g

| 39 | ND | 1.00 | 1.50 | 2.50 | 4.00 |

DHINGLO
COPPER, 18mm, 12.90 g

| 40 | ND | 1.25 | 2.00 | 3.00 | 4.50 |

Second Series
Obv: Persian leg. w/Devavnagri name below. Rev: Persian leg.

In the name of Muhammad Akbar II
AH1221-1253/1806-1837AD

NOTE: The frozen date AH1234 on this series is the accession date of Desalji II.

TRAMBIYO

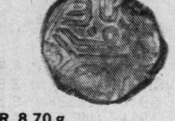

COPPER, 4.00 g

C#	Date	Year	Good	VG	Fine	VF
41	AH1234	VS1880	2.50	3.50	5.00	7.50

DOKDO

COPPER, 7.90 g

| 42 | AH1234 | VS1880 | 2.50 | 3.50 | 5.00 | 7.00 |

DHINGLO

COPPER, 12.30 g

| 43 | AH1234 | VS1880 | 2.75 | 4.00 | 5.50 | 7.50 |

1/2 KORI

SILVER, 2.10-2.20 g

C#	Date	Year	VG	Fine	VF	XF
52	AH1234	VS1877	3.50	5.50	8.50	12.50

KORI

SILVER, 4.40-4.50 g

C#	Date	Year	VG	Fine	VF	XF
53	AH1234	VS1875	3.50	4.00	5.00	7.00
	1234	1876	4.00	4.75	6.00	8.00
	1234	1877	3.50	4.00	5.00	7.00
	1234	1879	4.00	4.75	6.00	8.00
	1234	1880	4.00	4.75	6.00	8.00
	1234	1881	4.00	4.75	6.00	8.00
	1234	1882	3.50	4.00	5.00	7.00
	1234	1884	4.00	4.75	6.00	8.00
	1234	1885	4.00	4.50	5.50	7.50
	1234	1887	4.00	4.50	5.50	7.50

Third Series
Obv: Persian leg. Rev: Devavnagri leg. below Persian mintname on copper; date below Devavnagri leg. on silver.

In the name of Muhammad Akbar II
AH1221-1253/1806-1837AD

TRAMBIYO

COPPER, 4.10 g

C#	Date	Good	VG	Fine	VF
45	AH1255	1.00	1.50	2.50	4.00
	1256	1.00	1.50	2.50	4.00
	1257	1.00	1.50	2.50	4.00
	1258	1.00	1.50	2.50	4.00
	1259	1.00	1.50	2.50	4.00
	1260	1.00	1.50	2.50	4.00
	1261	1.00	1.50	2.50	4.00
	1262	1.00	1.50	2.50	4.00

DOKDO

COPPER, 8.10 g

46	AH1259	1.00	1.50	2.50	4.00
	1261	1.00	1.50	2.50	4.00
	1262	1.00	1.50	2.50	4.00

DHINGLO

COPPER, 12.00-12.50 g

47	AH1255	1.75	3.00	4.00	5.50
	1257	1.25	2.00	3.00	4.50
	1258	1.25	2.00	3.00	4.50
	1259	1.25	2.00	3.00	4.50
	1261	1.25	2.00	3.00	4.50
	1262	1.25	2.00	3.00	4.50
	1266	1.50	2.50	3.50	5.00
	1268	1.50	2.50	3.50	5.00

1/2 KORI

SILVER, 2.10-2.20 g
Rev: Katar below Devavnagri date w/Kutch 9.

C#	Date	Year	VG	Fine	VF	XF
55	VS1891	(1834)	4.00	6.00	8.00	10.00
	1892	(1835)	3.00	5.25	6.50	8.50

Rev: Katar below date.

| 55a | AH1252 | VS1893 | 4.00 | 6.00 | 8.00 | 10.00 |

Rev: Katar to right of Devavnagri date.

| 55b | AH1252 | VS1894 | 4.00 | 6.00 | 8.00 | 10.00 |

Rev: Katar below Kutch date.

| 58 | VS1895 | (1838) | 2.50 | 4.00 | 5.00 | 7.00 |

Obv: AH date at left in middle leg.

| 58a | AH1262 | VS1903 | 3.00 | 5.00 | 6.00 | 8.00 |
| | 1263 | 1904 | 3.00 | 5.00 | 6.00 | 8.00 |

KORI

SILVER, 4.40-4.50 g
Rev: Katar below Devavnagri date w/Kutch *9*.

C#	Date	Year	VG	Fine	VF	XF
56	AH1250	VS1892	4.50	6.00	8.00	11.50
	1251	1892	4.00	5.00	6.50	8.50
	1252	1893	4.00	5.00	6.50	8.50

Rev: Katar to right of Devavnagri date.

56a	AH1252	VS1894	4.00	5.00	6.50	9.00
59	VS1895	—	3.00	5.00	7.00	10.00

Rev: Katar to right of Devavnagri date.

59b	VS1901	—	2.50	4.00	5.50	8.00
	1902	—	2.50	4.00	5.50	8.00

Obv: AH date at left in middle leg.

59a	AH1262	VS1903	4.00	5.00	6.00	7.50

Fourth Series
In name of Bahadur Shah II
AH1253-1274/1837-1858AD

TRAMBIYO

COPPER, 14mm, 4.10 g

C#	Date	Good	VG	Fine	VF
61	AH1263	1.75	2.75	4.00	5.50
	1266	1.75	2.75	4.00	5.50

61a	AH1267	1.00	1.50	2.00	3.50
	1269	1.00	1.50	2.00	3.50
	1274	1.00	1.50	2.00	3.50

DOKDO

COPPER, 17-19mm, 8.10 g

62	AH1263	1.50	2.50	4.00	5.00
	1266	1.50	2.50	4.00	5.00

62a	AH1267	1.50	2.50	4.00	5.00
	1269	1.00	1.50	2.00	2.50
	1274	—	Reported, not confirmed		

DHINGLO

COPPER, 18-21mm, 12.00-12.50 g

63	AH1263	2.50	4.00	5.25	6.50
	1266	2.00	3.50	4.50	5.50

C#	Date	Good	VG	Fine	VF
63a	AH1267	1.25	2.00	2.50	3.00
	1268	1.25	2.00	2.50	3.00
	1269	1.25	2.00	2.50	3.00
	1271	1.75	3.00	3.50	4.00
	1272	1.25	2.00	2.50	3.00
	1274	1.75	3.00	3.50	4.00

1/2 KORI

SILVER, 2.20 g

C#	Date	Year	VG	Fine	VF	XF
65	VS1909	(1852)	2.00	3.50	4.00	6.00
	1910	(1853)	2.00	3.50	4.00	6.00
	1911	(1854)	3.00	5.00	6.00	8.50
	1912	(1855)	2.00	3.50	4.00	6.00
	1913	(1856)	2.00	3.50	4.00	6.00
	1914	(1857)	2.00	3.50	4.00	6.00

KORI

SILVER, 4.40-4.50 g

66	VS1909	(1852)	3.50	4.00	5.50	7.50
	1910	(1853)	3.50	4.00	5.50	7.00
	1911	(1854)	4.00	5.00	6.00	8.50
	1912	(1855)	3.50	4.00	5.50	7.00
	1913	(1856)	3.50	4.00	5.50	7.00
	1914	(1857)	3.50	4.00	5.50	7.00
	1915	(1858)	6.50	8.00	11.00	15.00
	1916	(1859)	8.00	10.00	13.50	17.50

25 KORI

.999 GOLD, 4.67 g

C#	Date	Year	Fine	VF	XF	Unc
67	VS1911	(1854)	110.00	120.00	130.00	150.00
	1912	(1855)	110.00	120.00	130.00	150.00
	1913	(1856)	110.00	120.00	130.00	150.00
	1914	(1857)	110.00	120.00	130.00	150.00
	1915	(1858)	110.00	120.00	130.00	150.00

MILLED COINAGE

Regal Issues

PRAGMALJI II

VS1917-1932/1860-1875AD

Pragmalji II is the first ruler of Kutch to pay homage to Queen Victoria. He experimented with a joint formulation his first year, VS1917/1860AD, see the rare coin type Y#A14. In VS1919/1862AD he settled on a standard type acknowledging "Queen Victoria, Mighty Queen" and himself as "Rao" or "Maharao", see types Y#13, 14 and 17.

TRAMBIYO

COPPER, 4.00 g

Y#	Date	Good	VG	Fine	VF
1	1865	1.25	2.00	3.00	4.50

Rev: 2 characters right of trident.

5	1865	.50	.85	1.50	2.50
	1866	1.50	2.50	3.50	5.00

Rev: Trident above leg.

Y#	Date	Good	VG	Fine	VF
5.1	1865	.75	1.25	1.75	2.50
	1866	.50	.85	1.50	2.50
	1867	1.25	2.00	3.00	4.50
	1767 (error)	.50	.85	1.50	2.50
	1868	.50	.85	1.50	2.50

Obv: Persian leg. w/*Victoria* at bottom.

Y#	Date	Year	Good	VG	Fine	VF
9	1869	VS1925	1.00	1.50	2.50	3.75
	1869	1926	1.50	2.50	3.50	4.50

Obv: Persian leg. w/*Victoria* at top.

9.1	1869	VS1926	.50	1.00	2.00	3.00
	1874	1930	.50	1.00	2.00	3.00

DOKDO

COPPER, 8.00 g

Y#	Date	Good	VG	Fine	VF
6	1865	1.25	2.00	2.50	3.50
	1866	1.00	1.75	2.25	3.00
	1867	.90	1.50	1.75	2.50
	1868	.60	1.00	1.50	2.75
	1869 (retrograde 9)	1.50	2.50	3.75	5.00

Obv: Persian leg. w/*Victoria* at top.

Y#	Date	Year	Good	VG	Fine	VF
10	1869	VS1925	1.25	2.00	3.00	4.50

Obv: Persian leg. w/*Victoria* at bottom.

10.1	1869	VS1925	.60	1.00	1.50	2.50
	1869	1926	1.00	1.50	2.00	3.00
	1869	1927	1.50	2.50	3.50	5.00

Obv: Persian leg. w/*Victoria* right.

10.2	1873	VS1930	1.00	1.50	2.00	3.00
	1874	1930	.60	1.00	1.50	2.50

1-1/2 DOKDA

COPPER, 12.00 g
Obv: Persian leg. w/*Victoria* at top.

11	1869	1926	.75	1.25	1.75	2.25
	1780	1925 (error)				
			1.75	3.00	3.50	4.25
	1780	1926 (error)				
			.90	1.50	2.00	2.50
	1870	1927	.60	1.00	1.50	2.00
	1870	1928	.60	1.00	1.50	2.00
	1780	1928 (error)				
			.75	1.25	1.75	2.25
	1871	1928	.60	1.00	1.50	2.00
	1872	1928	.75	1.25	1.75	2.25

Obv: Persian leg. w/*Victoria* to right.

11.1	1871	VS1928	.90	1.50	2.00	2.50
	1872	1928	.90	1.50	2.00	2.50
	1872	1929	.75	1.25	1.75	2.25
	1873	1929	.60	1.00	1.50	2.25
	1879	1929 (error)				

Obv: Different Persian leg. w/Victoria to right.

Y#	Date	Year	Good	VG	Fine	VF
11.2	1875	1932	.75	1.25	1.75	2.25

Obv: Persian leg. w/Victoria to left.

11.3	1872	VS1928	1.50	2.50	3.75	5.00
	1872	1929	1.50	2.50	3.75	5.00

3 DOKDA

COPPER, 24.00 g
Rev: Sa(m)vat at upper left, date at right.

8	1868	VS1925	2.50	4.00	6.00	7.50

Obv: Similar to Y#8.2. Rev: Sa(m)vat and date at top.

8.1	1868	VS1925	2.50	4.00	6.00	7.50

Rev: Sa(m)vat at top, date at right.

8.2	1868	VS1925	2.50	4.00	6.00	7.50

12	1868	VS1925	2.50	4.00	5.50	6.50
	1869	1925	2.00	3.50	4.50	5.75
	1869	1926	2.00	3.50	4.50	5.75

1/2 KORI

2.3500 g, .610 SILVER, .0460 oz ASW

Y#	Date	Year	VG	Fine	VF	XF
13	1862	VS1919	1.50	2.50	3.50	5.00
	1862	1920	1.25	2.50	3.50	5.00
	1863	1920	1.50	2.50	3.00	5.00
	1763	1920	(error)			
			2.00	3.50	4.50	5.50
	1863	1921	1.25	2.00	2.50	3.50

KORI

4.7000 g, .610 SILVER, .0921 oz ASW
Rev: Rosette after date.

A14	1860	VS1917	—	—	—	—

Y#	Date	Year	VG	Fine	VF	XF
14	1862	VS1918	2.75	3.50	4.00	5.50
	1862	1919	3.00	3.75	5.00	6.50
	1862	1920	2.50	3.00	3.50	5.00
	1863	1920	2.75	3.50	4.00	5.50
	1863	1921	2.50	3.00	3.50	5.00

2-1/2 KORI

6.9350 g, .937 SILVER, .2089 oz ASW

15	1875	VS1931	6.50	7.50	8.50	11.50
	1785	1931	7.50	10.00	12.50	16.00
	1875	1932	6.50	7.50	8.50	11.50

5 KORI

13.8700 g, .937 SILVER, .4178 oz ASW

16	1863	VS1921	20.00	35.00	40.00	55.00

Obv: Leg. rearranged.

16.1	1865	VS1921	13.50	16.50	20.00	27.50
	1865	1922	12.50	15.00	18.50	25.00
	1866	1922	12.00	13.50	15.00	18.50
	1866	1923	12.00	13.50	15.00	18.50
	1870	1927	12.50	14.50	17.50	22.50
	1874	1931	12.00	13.00	14.50	17.50
	1875	1931	12.00	13.00	14.50	17.50
	1875	1932	12.00	13.00	14.50	17.50

25 KORI

4.6750 g, .999 GOLD, .1501 oz AGW

Y#	Date	Year	Fine	VF	XF	Unc
17	1862	VS1919	110.00	120.00	130.00	150.00
	1863	1920	110.00	120.00	130.00	150.00
	1863	1921	110.00	120.00	130.00	150.00

17a	1870	VS1926	110.00	120.00	130.00	150.00
	1870	1927	110.00	120.00	130.00	150.00

50 KORI

9.3500 g, .906 GOLD, .2723 oz AGW

Y#	Date	Year	Fine	VF	XF	Unc
18	1668 (sic - error for 1866)		—	—	—	—
		VS1923				
	1866	1923	165.00	185.00	210.00	250.00
	1873	1930	165.00	185.00	210.00	250.00
	1874	1930	165.00	185.00	210.00	250.00
	1874	1931	165.00	185.00	210.00	250.00

100 KORI

18.7000 g, .906 GOLD, .5446 oz AGW

19	1866	VS1922	375.00	400.00	435.00	500.00
	1866	1923	375.00	400.00	435.00	500.00

KHENGARJI III
VS1932-1999/1875-1942AD

First Series
Obv. leg: *Queen Victoria, Mighty Queen.*

DOKDO

COPPER, 8.00 g

Y#	Date	Year	Good	VG	Fine	VF
22	1878	VS1934	10.00	17.50	20.00	25.00
	1878	1935	13.50	22.50	25.00	30.00
	(1)878	1935	15.00	25.00	27.50	32.50

1-1/2 DOKDA

COPPER, 12.00 g

23	1876	VS1933	.90	1.50	2.00	2.50
	1877	1933	.90	1.50	2.00	2.50
	1877	1934	.90	1.50	2.00	2.50
	1877	1922	(error)			
			.90	1.50	2.00	2.50
	1878	1934	.90	1.50	2.00	2.50
	1878	1935	1.25	2.00	2.50	3.00

Obv: Similar to 1 1/2 Dokda, Y#11.

23.1	1876	VS1933	1.25	2.00	2.50	3.50

KORI

2.3500 g, .610 SILVER, .0460 oz ASW
16mm

Y#	Date	Year	VG	Fine	VF	XF
26	1876	VS1932	60.00	100.00	125.00	150.00
	1876	1933	60.00	100.00	125.00	150.00

5 KORI

13.8700 g, .937 SILVER, .4178 oz ASW

28	1876	VS1933	20.00	30.00	40.00	50.00

Second Series
Obv. leg: *Victoria, Empress of India.*

Kutch / INDIAN PRINCELY STATES 938

TRAMBIYO

COPPER, 4.00 g

Y#	Date	Year	Good	VG	Fine	VF
30	1881	VS1938	.50	.75	1.00	1.50
	1882	1938	.30	.50	.75	1.25
	1883	1939	.30	.50	.75	1.25
	1883	1940	.50	.75	1.00	1.50

Rev: *Kutch* added below date.

| 30.1 | 1883 | VS1940 | .50 | .75 | 1.00 | 1.50 |

DOKDO

COPPER, 8.00 g

31	1882	VS1938	.50	.75	1.00	1.50
	1882	1939	.90	1.50	2.00	2.50
	1883	1939	.50	.75	1.00	1.50

Rev: *Kutch* added below date.

| 31.1 | 1883 | VS1940 | .50 | .75 | 1.00 | 1.50 |
| | 1884 | 1940 | .50 | .75 | 1.00 | 1.50 |

Obv: Leg. similar to Y#31.1 but spaced similar to Y#31.3.

| 31.2 | 1892 | VS1948 | 2.50 | 4.00 | 6.00 | 8.50 |

Obv: Urdu leg. *Victoria* written differently.

| 31.3 | 1899 | VS1956 | .90 | 1.50 | 2.00 | 3.00 |

1-1/2 DOKDA

COPPER, 12.00 g

32	1882	VS1938	.60	1.00	1.25	1.75
	1882	1939	.60	1.00	1.25	1.75
	1883	1939	.60	1.00	1.25	1.75
	1883	1940	.60	1.00	1.25	1.75

Rev: *Kutch* added below date.

32.1	1883	VS1940	.60	1.00	1.25	1.75
	1884	1940	.60	1.00	1.25	1.75
	1884	1941	.60	1.00	1.25	1.75

Finer style

Y#	Date	Year	Good	VG	Fine	VF
32.2	1885	VS1942	.75	1.25	1.50	2.00
	1887	1944	.75	1.25	1.50	2.00
	1888	1944	.75	1.25	1.50	2.00
32.3	1892	1948	.75	1.25	1.50	2.00
	1894	1950	.75	1.25	1.50	2.00

| 32.4 | 1899 | VS1955 | 1.25 | 2.00 | 2.50 | 3.00 |
| | 1899 | 1956 | 1.25 | 2.00 | 2.75 | 3.50 |

3 DOKDA

COPPER, 24.00 g

33	1883	VS1940	1.25	2.00	2.50	3.00
	1885	1942	.90	1.50	2.00	2.50
	1886	1942	1.35	2.25	3.00	4.00
	1887	1944	.90	1.50	2.00	2.50
	1888	1944	1.25	2.00	2.50	3.00

| 33.1 | 1894 | VS1951 | 1.50 | 2.50 | 3.00 | 3.50 |
| | 1899 | 1955 | 1.50 | 2.50 | 3.00 | 3.50 |

1/2 KORI

2.3500 g, .610 SILVER, .0460 oz ASW

Y#	Date	Year	VG	Fine	VF	XF
34	1898	VS1954	1.75	3.00	4.00	5.50
	1899	1955	1.75	3.00	4.00	5.50
	1899	1956	1.75	3.00	4.00	5.50
	1900	1956	1.75	3.00	4.00	5.50
	1900	1957	2.50	4.00	5.00	6.50

KORI

4.7000 g, .610 SILVER, .0921 oz ASW
Rev: Closed crescent.

35	1881	VS1938	3.00	3.50	4.25	5.50
	1882	1938	3.00	3.50	4.25	5.00
	1882	1939	2.75	3.25	4.00	5.00
	1883	1939	2.75	3.25	4.00	5.00
	1883	1940	2.75	3.25	4.00	5.00
	1884	1941	3.00	3.50	4.25	5.50
	1885	1941	2.75	3.00	3.50	5.00

Rev: Open crescent.

Y#	Date	Year	VG	Fine	VF	XF
35.1	1894	VS1950	2.75	3.00	3.50	5.00
	1896	1952	2.75	3.00	3.50	5.00
	1897	1953	2.75	3.00	3.50	4.50
	1897	1954	2.75	3.00	3.50	4.50
	1898	1954	2.75	3.00	3.50	4.50
	1898	1955	2.75	3.00	3.50	4.50
	1899	1955	2.75	3.00	3.50	4.50
	1899	1956	2.75	3.00	3.50	4.50
	1900	1956	2.75	3.00	3.50	4.50
	1900	1957	2.75	3.00	3.50	4.50
	1901	1957	2.75	4.00	5.50	7.00

2-1/2 KORI

6.9350 g, .937 SILVER, .2089 oz ASW
Rev: Closed crescent.

| 36 | 1881 | VS1938 | 6.50 | 7.50 | 9.00 | 12.50 |
| | 1882 | 1938 | 6.50 | 7.50 | 8.50 | 11.50 |

Rev: Open crescent.

36.1	1894	VS1951	6.50	7.50	8.50	12.00
	1895	1951	6.50	7.50	8.50	11.50
	1897	1953	6.50	7.50	8.50	11.50
	1897	1954	6.50	7.50	8.50	11.50
	1898	1954	6.50	7.50	8.50	12.00
	1898	1955	6.50	7.50	8.50	12.00
	1899	1955	6.50	7.50	8.50	12.00

| 36.2 | 1899 | VS1955 | 6.50 | 7.50 | 8.50 | 12.00 |
| | 1899 | 1956 | 6.50 | 7.50 | 8.50 | 11.50 |

5 KORI

13.8700 g, .937 SILVER, .4178 oz ASW
Obv: Leaves of wreath point counter-clockwise.

37	1880	VS1937	12.00	13.00	16.00	20.00
	1881	1937	12.00	13.00	14.50	17.50
	1881	1938	12.00	13.00	14.50	17.50

Obv: Leaves of wreath point clockwise.

| 37.1 | 1881 | VS1937 | 12.00 | 13.00 | 14.50 | 17.50 |
| | 1881 | 1938 | 12.00 | 13.00 | 14.50 | 17.50 |

Rev: Bars to left and right of center leg.

| 37.2 | 1881 | VS1937 | 12.00 | 13.00 | 14.50 | 17.50 |

Obv: Similar to Y#37. Rev: Similar to Y#37.2.

| 37.3 | 1880 | VS1937 | 12.00 | 13.00 | 14.50 | 18.50 |

Obv: Changed wreath. Rev: Closed crescent.

Y#	Date	Year	VG	Fine	VF	XF
37.4	1881	VS1938	12.00	13.00	14.50	17.50
	1882	1938	12.00	13.00	14.50	17.50
	1882	1939	12.00	13.00	14.50	17.50
	1883	1939	12.00	13.00	14.50	17.50
	1883	1940	12.00	13.00	14.50	17.50
	1884	1939	(error)			
	1884	1940	12.00	13.00	14.50	17.50
	1884	1941	12.00	13.00	14.50	17.50
	1885	1941	12.00	13.00	14.50	17.50
	1885	1942	12.00	20.00	30.00	40.00
	1886	1943	12.00	20.00	30.00	40.00

Rev: Open crescent.

Y#	Date	Year	VG	Fine	VF	XF
37.5	1890	VS1947	12.00	17.50	25.00	37.50
	1893	1950	12.00	17.50	22.50	30.00
	1894	1950	12.00	13.00	14.50	17.50
	1894	1951	12.00	13.00	14.50	17.50
	1895	1951	12.00	13.00	14.50	17.50
	1895	1952	12.00	13.00	14.50	17.50
	1896	1952	12.00	13.00	14.50	18.50
	1896	1953	12.00	13.00	14.50	17.50
	1896	1954	(error)			
			12.50	20.00	27.50	35.00
	1897	1951	(error)			
			12.00	13.50	16.50	22.50
	1897	1953	12.00	13.00	14.50	17.50
	1897	1954	12.00	13.00	14.50	17.50
	1898	1951	(error)			
	1898	1953	12.00	13.00	14.50	17.50
	1898	1954	12.00	13.00	14.50	17.50
	1898	1955	12.00	13.00	14.50	17.50
	1899	1955	12.00	13.50	15.00	20.00

Y#	Date	Year	VG	Fine	VF	XF
37.6	1899	VS1955	12.00	13.00	14.50	17.50
	1899	1956	12.00	13.00	14.50	17.50
	1901	1957	18.50	27.50	35.00	45.00

Third Series
In the name of Edward VII

TRAMBIYO

COPPER, 4.00 g

Y#	Date	Year	VG	Fine	VF	XF
38	1908	VS1965	1.50	2.50	3.50	4.50
	1909	1965	.60	1.00	1.50	2.50
	1909	1966	.60	1.00	1.50	2.00
	1910	1966	1.60	2.75	4.25	6.00

DOKDO

COPPER, 8.00 g

Y#	Date	Year	VG	Fine	VF	XF
39	1909	VS1965	.75	1.25	1.50	2.00
	1909	1966	.75	1.25	1.50	2.00

1-1/2 DOKDA
COPPER, 23mm, 12.00 g

Y#	Date	Year	VG	Fine	VF	XF
40	1909	VS1965	60.00	100.00	115.00	150.00

3 DOKDA

COPPER, 24.00 g

| 41 | 1909 | VS1965 | 60.00 | 100.00 | 115.00 | 150.00 |

5 KORI

13.8700 g, .937 SILVER, .4178 oz ASW

Y#	Date	Year	VG	Fine	VF	XF
45	1902	VS1959	80.00	150.00	225.00	375.00
	1903	1960	80.00	150.00	225.00	375.00
	1904	1961	80.00	150.00	225.00	375.00
	1905	1962	80.00	150.00	225.00	375.00
	1906	1963	80.00	150.00	225.00	375.00
	1907	1964	80.00	150.00	225.00	375.00
	1908	1965	65.00	150.00	225.00	375.00
	1909	1966	65.00	150.00	225.00	375.00

Fourth Series
In the name of George V

NOTE: New automatic minting equipment was introduced in 1928 and used to strike the finer style coins from 1928 to 1947 when the mint closed.

TRAMBIYO

COPPER, 4.00 g

Y#	Date	Year	VG	Fine	VF	XF
46	1919	VS1976	.30	.50	.75	1.00
	1920	1976	.30	.50	.75	1.50
	1920	1977	.30	.50	.75	1.50

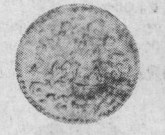 

| 54 | 1928 | VS1984 | .60 | 1.00 | 2.00 | 3.00 |
| | 1928 | 1985 | .30 | .50 | .75 | 1.00 |

DOKDO

COPPER, 8.00 g

Y#	Date	Year	VG	Fine	VF	XF
47	1920	VS1976	.60	1.00	1.25	2.00
	1920	1977	.60	1.00	1.25	2.00

55	1922	VS1982	(error)			
			1.25	1.75	2.50	3.50
	1928	1984	.60	1.00	1.25	1.50
	1929	1985	.60	1.00	1.25	1.50

1-1/2 DOKDA

COPPER, 12.00 g

Y#	Date	Year	VG	Fine	VF	XF
48	1926	VS1982	.90	1.50	2.50	3.00

56	1928	VS1985	.50	.75	1.00	1.50
	1929	1985	.50	.75	1.00	1.50
	1929	1986	.50	.75	1.00	1.50
	1931	1987	.50	.75	1.00	1.50
	1931	1988	.50	.75	1.00	1.50
	1932	1988	1.00	1.50	2.50	4.00
	1932	1989	.50	.75	1.00	1.50

3 DOKDA

COPPER, 24.00 g

| 49 | 1926 | VS1982 | 1.50 | 2.50 | 3.50 | 4.50 |

57	1928	VS1985	.60	1.00	1.50	2.25
	1929	1985	.60	1.00	1.50	2.25
	1929	1986	.60	1.00	1.50	2.25
	1930	1987	.60	1.00	1.50	2.25
	1931	1987	.60	1.00	1.50	2.25
	1934	1990	.60	1.00	1.50	2.25
	1934	1991	.60	1.00	1.50	2.25
	1935	1992	.60	1.00	1.50	2.25

1/2 KORI

2.3500 g, .601 SILVER, .0460 oz ASW

| 58 | 1928 | VS1985 | 1.75 | 2.00 | 2.25 | 3.00 |

KORI

4.7000 g, .601 SILVER, .0921 oz ASW

Y#	Date	Year	Fine	VF	XF	Unc
51	1913	VS1970	2.25	2.00	2.50	3.50
	1923	1979	2.25	2.00	2.50	3.50
	1923	1980	2.25	2.00	2.50	3.50
	1927	1984	2.50	2.50	3.50	4.50
	1927	1985	Reported, not confirmed			

Kutch / INDIAN PRINCELY STATES

Y#	Date	Year	Fine	VF	XF	Unc
59	1928	VS1985	2.25	2.50	3.00	4.00
	1929	1985	2.25	2.50	3.00	4.00
	1931	1987	7.50	12.50	14.50	20.00
	1931	1988	2.25	2.50	3.00	4.00
	1932	1988	2.25	2.50	3.00	4.00
	1932	1989	2.25	2.50	3.00	4.00
	1933	1989	2.25	2.50	3.00	4.00
	1933	1990	2.25	2.50	3.00	4.00
	1934	1990	2.25	2.50	3.00	4.00
	1934	1991	2.25	2.50	3.00	4.00
	1935	1991	2.25	2.50	3.00	4.00
	1935	1992	2.25	2.50	3.00	4.00
	1936	1992	2.50	3.00	4.50	5.50

2-1/2 KORI

6.9350 g, .937 SILVER, .2089 oz ASW

Y#	Date	Year	Fine	VF	XF	Unc
52	1916	VS1973	6.50	7.00	8.00	10.00
	1917	1973	6.50	7.00	8.00	10.00
	1917	1974	6.50	7.00	8.00	10.00
	1918	1974	6.50	7.00	8.00	10.00
	1919	1975	6.50	7.00	8.00	10.00
	1922	1978	6.50	7.00	8.00	10.00
	1922	1979	6.50	7.00	8.00	10.00
	1924	1981	6.50	7.00	8.00	10.00
	1926	1983	6.50	7.00	8.00	10.00

Rev: Smaller leg.

	Date	Year	Fine	VF	XF	Unc
52a	1927	VS1984	6.50	7.50	9.00	12.50
	1928	1985	6.00	7.00	8.00	10.00
	1930	1986	6.00	7.00	8.00	10.00
	1930	1987	6.00	7.00	8.00	10.00
	1932	1988	6.00	7.00	8.00	10.00
	1932	1989	6.00	7.00	8.00	10.00
	1933	1989	6.00	7.00	8.00	10.00
	1933	1990	6.00	7.00	8.00	10.00
	1934	1990	6.00	7.00	8.00	10.00
	1934	1991	6.00	7.00	8.00	10.00
	1935	1991	6.00	7.00	8.00	10.00
	1935	1992	6.00	7.00	8.00	10.00

5 KORI

13.8700 g, .937 SILVER, .4178 oz ASW

Y#	Date	Year	Fine	VF	XF	Unc
53	1913	VS1970	12.00	13.50	15.00	18.50
	1915	1972	12.00	13.50	15.00	18.50
	1916	1973	12.00	13.00	14.50	17.50
	1916	1975	(error)	—	—	—
	1917	1973	12.00	13.00	14.50	17.50
	1917	1974	12.00	13.00	14.50	17.50
	1918	1974	12.00	13.00	14.50	17.50
	1918	1975	12.00	13.00	14.50	17.50
	1919	1975	12.00	13.00	14.50	17.50
	1919	1976	25.00	40.00	50.00	60.00
	1920	1977	12.00	13.50	15.00	18.50
	1921	1977	12.00	13.00	14.50	17.50
	1921	1978	12.00	13.00	14.50	17.50
	1922	1974	(error)	—	—	—
	1922	1978	12.00	13.00	14.50	17.50
	1922	1979	12.00	13.00	14.50	17.50
	1922	1982	(error)	—	—	—
			10.00	13.50	16.50	20.00
	1923	1979	12.00	13.00	14.50	17.50
	1924	1978	(error)	—	—	—
			17.50	30.00	40.00	50.00

Y#	Date	Year	Fine	VF	XF	Unc
53	1924	1980	12.00	13.00	14.50	17.50
	1924	1981	12.00	13.00	14.50	17.50
	1925	1982	12.00	13.00	14.50	17.50
	1926	1978	(error)	—	—	—
	1926	1982	12.00	13.00	14.50	17.50
	1926	1983	12.00	13.00	14.50	17.50
	1927	1984	15.00	27.50	35.00	45.00

NOTE: 5 Kori coins were issued with reeded edges until 1925AD. When the security edge was introduced.

Obv. and rev: Smaller leg.

	Date	Year	Fine	VF	XF	Unc
53a	1928	VS1985	13.50	20.00	30.00	40.00
	1929	1986	12.00	13.00	14.50	18.50
	1930	1986	12.00	13.00	14.50	17.50
	1930	1987	12.00	13.00	14.50	17.50
	1931	1987	12.00	13.00	14.50	17.50
	1931	1988	12.00	13.00	14.50	17.50
	1932	1988	12.00	13.00	14.50	17.50
	1932	1989	12.00	13.00	14.50	17.50
	1933	1989	12.00	13.00	14.50	17.50
	1933	1990	12.00	13.00	14.50	17.50
	1934	1990	12.00	13.00	14.50	17.50
	1934	1991	12.00	13.00	14.50	17.50
	1935	1991	12.00	13.00	14.50	17.50
	1935	1992	12.00	13.00	14.50	17.50
	1936	1992	12.00	13.00	14.50	18.50

Fifth Series
In the name of Edward VIII

3 DOKDA

COPPER, 24.00 g

Y#	Date	Year	VG	Fine	VF	XF
63	1936	VS1993	3.00	5.00	7.50	10.00

KORI

4.7000 g, .601 SILVER, .0921 oz ASW

Y#	Date	Year	Fine	VF	XF	Unc
65	1936	VS1992	2.75	3.00	3.50	4.00
	1936	1993	2.75	3.00	3.25	4.50

2-1/2 KORI

6.9350 g, .937 SILVER, .2089 oz ASW

	Date	Year	Fine	VF	XF	Unc
66	1936	VS1992	10.00	17.50	22.50	28.50
	1936	1993	10.00	17.50	22.50	28.50

5 KORI

13.8700 g, .937 SILVER, .4178 oz ASW

Y#	Date	Year	Fine	VF	XF	Unc
67	1936	VS1992	7.00	8.00	9.00	11.00
	1936	1993	7.00	8.00	9.00	11.00

Sixth Series
In the name of George VI

3 DOKDA

COPPER, 24.00 g

Y#	Date	Year	VG	Fine	VF	XF
71	1937	VS1993	.90	1.50	2.00	3.00

KORI

4.7000 g, .601 SILVER, .0921 oz ASW

Y#	Date	Year	Fine	VF	XF	Unc
73	1937	VS1993	2.75	3.00	3.50	4.00
	1937	1994	2.75	3.00	3.50	4.00
	1938	1995	2.75	3.00	3.50	4.00
	1939	1995	2.75	3.00	3.50	4.00
	1939	1996	2.75	3.00	3.50	4.00
	1940	1996	2.75	3.00	3.50	4.00

2-1/2 KORI

6.9350 g, .937 SILVER, .2089 oz ASW

74	1937	VS1993	6.50	7.00	8.00	10.00

5 KORI

13.8700 g, .937 SILVER, .4178 oz ASW

	Date	Year	Fine	VF	XF	Unc
75	1936	VS1993	12.00	13.00	14.50	18.50
	1937	1993	12.00	13.00	14.50	17.50
	1937	1994	12.00	13.00	14.50	17.50
	1938	1994	12.00	13.00	14.50	17.50
	1938	1995	12.00	13.00	14.50	17.50
	1941	1997	—	—	—	—
	1941	1998	12.00	13.00	14.50	17.50

VIJAYARAJJI
VS1999-2004/1942-1947AD
In the name of George VI

TRAMBIYO

COPPER

Y#	Date	Year	Fine	VF	XF	Unc
76	1943	VS2000	.25	.50	1.00	1.50
	1944	2000	.25	.50	1.00	1.50

DHINGLO
(1/16 Kori = 1-1/2 Dokda)

COPPER

77	1943	VS2000	.20	.35	.60	1.00
	1944	2000	.20	.35	.60	1.00
	1947	2004	.20	.35	.60	1.00
	1948	2004	.50	1.00	2.00	3.50

DHABU
(1/8 Kori = 3 Dokda)

COPPER

78	1943	VS1999	.25	.40	.65	1.00
	1943	2000	.25	.40	.65	1.00
	1944	2000	.25	.40	.65	1.00
	1947	2004	.25	.40	.65	1.00

PAYALO
(1/4 Kori)

COPPER

79	1943	VS1999	.75	1.00	1.50	2.50
	1943	2000	.75	1.00	1.50	2.50
	1944	2000	.75	1.00	1.50	2.50
	1944	2001	.75	1.00	1.50	2.50
	1945	2001	.35	.50	.75	1.25
	1945	2002	.35	.50	.75	1.25
	1946	2002	.35	.50	.75	1.25
	1946	2003	.35	.50	.75	1.25
	1947	2003	.75	1.00	1.50	2.50

ADHIO
(1/2 Kori)

COPPER

80	1943	VS1999	1.50	1.75	2.00	3.50
	1943	2000	1.50	1.75	2.00	3.50
	1944	2001	1.25	1.50	1.75	3.00
	1945	2001	1.50	1.75	2.00	3.50
	1945	2002	1.50	1.75	2.00	3.50
	1946	2002	1.50	1.75	2.00	3.50

KORI
SILVER, 4.66 g

Similar to Y#51.

Y#	Date	Year	Fine	VF	XF	Unc
A81	1942	VS1998	—	—	Rare	

4.7000 g, .601 SILVER, .0921 oz ASW

81	1942	VS1999	2.75	3.00	3.50	4.00
	1943	1999	2.75	3.00	3.50	4.00
	1943	2000	2.75	3.00	3.50	4.00
	1944	2000	2.75	3.00	3.50	4.00
	1944	2001	2.75	3.00	3.50	4.00

5 KORI

13.8700 g, .937 SILVER, .4178 oz ASW

82	1942	VS1998	12.00	13.00	14.50	17.50
	1942	1999	12.00	13.00	14.50	17.50
	1943	1998	Reported, not confirmed			

10 KORI
SILVER, 17.39 g

82A	1943	1999	—	—	—	Rare

MADANASINGHJI
VS2004-2005/1947-1948AD

DHABU
(1/8 Kori)

COPPER

83	VS2004 (1947)	.75	1.25	1.75	3.00

KORI

4.7000 g, .601 SILVER, .0921 oz ASW

84	VS2004 (1947)	4.00	6.50	8.50	11.50

5 KORI

13.8700 g, .937 SILVER, .4178 oz ASW

85	VS2004 (1947)	75.00	125.00	175.00	200.00

LADAKH

Ladakh, a district in northern India, contained the western Himalayas and the valley of the upper Indus river. Area: 45,762 sq. mi. Capital: Leh.

In 1639, the Moghuls marched on Ladakh and defeated them near Karpu. The King Sen-ge-rnam-rgyal promised to pay tribute, if allowed to return home, but never did. In 1665, the Moghul governor of Kashmir demanded the acceptance of Moghul suzerainty under threat of invasion. Knowing the strength of Aurangzeb, King Deb—ldan-rnam-rgyal sent a tribute of gold ashraphis, rupees and other precious objects. It is probable that coins were struck for this occasion in the name of Aurangzeb but no such coins have yet been discovered.

For the next century no further mention is made of coins until in 1781 it is recorded that a Muslim goldsmith from Leh was hired to strike Ladakhi coins called ja'u.

The obverse of the first Ladakhi timashas or ja'u is a close copy of the Farrukhsiyar inscription of the early Garhwali timashas even including the regnal year at the bottom. The reverse has a clearly written Zarb Tibet at the bottom and dots at the top. At the center are crescents and an illegible inscription.

On some of the early Ladakh coins Hejira dates appear which coincide with the period when the Garhwal mint was closed and trade was diverted from Garhwal to Ladakh. No other Ladakh coins of this first issue have been discovered with a literate date. Between 1781 and 1803 it is likely that a considerable number of ja'u were struck. Most specimens were of good silver but later issues were very debased because of the scarcity of silver.

The next type of coin has a different obverse with the Muslim title of the King of Ladakh clearly inscribed as well as the number 14 at the lower left. This issue may have been prompted to demonstrate Ladakhi independence and is the only ja'u to bear a date.

The most remarkable of all Ladakhi coins has a fully legible inscription on the obverse in smaller writing and is enclosed in a circle with no regnal year. The reverse legend refers to the prime minister as well as the title of the king and is the only Ladakhi coin to do so and is very rare.

The appearance of Mahmud Shah on the obverse of the next type coin is thought to acknowledge suzerainty of the ruler of Kashmir. There is a plain circle surrounded by a border of dots. The reverse reverts to the earlier designs but has a finer style with thicker writing.

The next change in type took place after the conquest of Ladakh by Gulab Singh and the Dogra army in 1835. After a crushing defeat of the Dogra army in Tibet, the Ladakhis tried to shake off the Dogra supremacy but the rebellion was crushed. Ladakh was now firmly incorporated within the Empire of Jammu and the monarchy was abolished. Until 1845, Gulab Singh acknowledged Sikh suzerainty but ruled Ladakh as a part of Jammu.

After the defeat of the Sikhs by the British, Gulab Singh offered to pay the war indemnities to the British in exchange for being made independent ruler of Jammu and Kashmir.

Two types of ja'u were struck during the period of the Dogra domination. One combined the tiger knife and Mahmud Shah design and the other the tiger knife and Raja Gulab Singh in Nagari script.

Between 1867 and 1870 an issue of copper coins was made for Ladakh for local use and in 1871 a small issue of ja'u was made. Neither of these coins seemed to have much commercial impact in Ladakh and their issue was suspended after 1871. No special currency was struck in or for Ladakh after this.

JA'U
1815AD

SILVER
Obv: Square around *Siyar* **of Furrukhsiyar.**

KM#	Date	Year	—	Good	VG	Fine	VF
2	ND	—	6.00	10.00	17.50	25.00	

1815-1816AD
In the name of Mahmud Khan

Obv. leg: *Aqibat Mahmud Khan.*

3	ND	—	8.50	15.00	25.00	35.00

Obv. leg: *Aqibat Mahmud Khan* **within circle.**
Rev. leg: *Qalon Seban Tondub, Tibet.*

4	ND	—	50.00	75.00	100.00	150.00

1816-1842AD
In the name of Mahmud Shah

Obv. and rev: Plain border.
Obv. leg: *Mahmud Shah.*

5.1	ND	—	10.00	14.00	18.50	25.00

Ladakh / INDIAN PRINCELY STATES

Obv. and rev: Dotted border.

KM#	Date	Year	Good	VG	Fine	VF
5.2	ND	—	10.00	14.00	18.50	25.00

Obv: Dotted border. Rev: Plain border.

| 5.3 | ND | — | 10.00 | 14.00 | 18.50 | 25.00 |

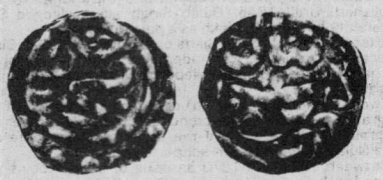

| 5.4 | ND | — | 10.00 | 14.00 | 18.50 | 25.00 |

Obv: Retrograde.

| 5.5 | ND | — | 10.00 | 14.00 | 18.50 | 25.00 |

| 5.6 | ND | — | 10.00 | 14.00 | 18.50 | 25.00 |

1841AD

Obv. leg: *Mahmud Shah* **within circle, dotted border.**
Rev: Katar pointing right, *Zarb Butan* **above and below.**

| 6 | ND | — | 10.00 | 14.00 | 18.50 | 25.00 |

1842-1850AD
In the name of Gulab Singh

Obv. leg: *Raja Gulab Singh* **in Nagari in 3 lines.**

| 7.1 (Y1) | ND | — | 6.00 | 10.00 | 12.50 | 15.00 |

Rev: Dot on blade of Katar.

| 7.2 (Y1) | ND | — | 6.00 | 10.00 | 12.50 | 15.00 |

Rev: Figure 8 on its side on blade of Katar.

KM#	Date	Year	Good	VG	Fine	VF
7.3	ND	—	6.00	10.00	12.50	15.00

Obv. leg: Error, *Raja Galab Bing.*
Rev: Figure 8 on its side on blade of Katar.

| 7.4 | ND | — | 6.00 | 10.00 | 12.50 | 15.00 |

Rev: Legend blundered.

| 7.5 | ND | — | 6.00 | 10.00 | 12.50 | 15.00 |

1871AD

Obv. leg: *1928 Jam-bu'i Par* **in Tibetan script.**
Rev. leg: *Zarb Ladakh, Qilimrao Jamun, Sanah 1928* **in Arabic script.**

| 8 | ND | — | 15.00 | 25.00 | 32.50 | 40.00 |

UNDER DOGRA RULE
After 1834AD

PAISA

COPPER, 19mm

9	VS1924	(1867)	2.50	4.00	5.50	7.50
	1925	(1868)	2.50	4.00	5.50	7.50
	1926	(1869)	2.50	4.00	5.50	7.50
	1927	(1870)	2.50	4.00	5.50	7.50

LUNAVADA

This small state in the Panch Mahal district of western India was ruled by Solanki Rajputs who claimed descent from Sidraj Jaisingh, the ruler of Anhalwara Patan and Gujerat. The rulers, or maharanas, traced their sovereignty to the early decades of the fifteenth century. At different times the State was feudatory to either Baroda or Sindhia.

WAKHAT SINGHJI
VS1924-1986 / 1867-1929AD

1/2 PAISA
NOTE: Struck with paisa dies, either on small planchets, or paisas cut in half.

COPPER, rectangular or round, 3.50-4.00 g
Obv: Open hand.
Rev. leg: Mughal style Persian.

| 2.1 | ND | — | 2.75 | 4.50 | 6.00 | 8.50 |

Obv: Crescent left and star right of hand.

KM#	Date	Year	Good	VG	Fine	VF
2.2	ND	—	—	—	—	—

Obv: Open hand in square, *Lunavada* **around clockwise. Rev: Date & Devanagari leg.**

| 3 | VS1942 | (1885) | 3.00 | 5.00 | 7.50 | 10.00 |

Obv: Lion right *Lunavada* **and date.**
Rev: Devanagari leg. w/ruler's name.

| 4 | VS1949 | (1892) | 2.75 | 4.50 | 6.00 | 8.50 |

PAISA
COPPER, round or rectangular, 6.50-8.30 g
Obv: Two sabres.

| 5 | ND | — | 3.50 | 6.00 | 8.50 | 12.50 |

Obv: Cannon barrel.

| 6 | ND | — | 3.50 | 6.00 | 8.50 | 12.50 |

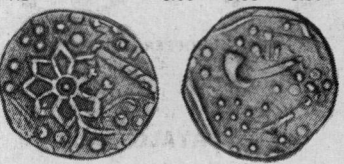

Obv: Lotus blossom. Rev: Persian leg.

| 7 | ND | — | 2.50 | 4.00 | 5.50 | 8.50 |
| | VS1968 | — | 2.50 | 4.00 | 5.50 | 8.50 |

Obv: Open hand, leg. above.

| 8 | ND | — | 2.50 | 4.00 | 5.50 | 8.50 |

Obv: Katar.

| 11 | ND | — | 6.00 | 12.00 | 17.50 | 25.00 |

Obv: Open hand in square.

| 12 | ND | — | 3.50 | 6.00 | 8.50 | 12.50 |

Obv: Open hand in square, on square planchet.

| 9.1 | VS1942 | (1885) | 2.50 | 4.00 | 5.50 | 8.50 |
| | 1249 (error) | | 2.50 | 4.00 | 5.50 | 8.50 |

Similar to KM9.1 but round planchet.

| 9.2 | VS1942 | (1885) | — | — | — | — |

Obv: Lion, *Lunavada* **and date.**

KM#	Date	Year	Good	VG	Fine	VF
10	VS1949	(1892)	2.50	4.00	5.50	8.50

NOTE: Coins of Lunavada are frequently found over struck over earlier types, and over other types of Rampur.

MAKRAI

The rajas of Makrai belong to a very ancient Gond family whose title, Raja Hatiyarai, had been conferred upon them by the emperors of Delhi. This small state of some forty-five villages struggled with varying degrees of success against the Poona Peshwa, Sindhia and the Pindaris before passing under British protection in the nineteenth century.

RULER
Raja Bharat Shah
1886-1920AD

PAISA

COPPER

Y#	Date	Year	Good	VG	Fine	VF
1	ND	—	2.00	3.00	4.50	7.00

MARATHA CONFEDERACY
Refer to Independent Kingdoms during British rule.

MEWAR

State located in Rajputana, northwest India. Capital: Udaipur.

The rulers of Mewar were universally regarded as the highest ranking Rajput house in India. The maharana of Mewar was looked upon as the representative of Rama, the ancient king of Ayodhya - and the family who were Sesodia Rajputs of the Gehlot clan, traced its descent through Rama to Kanak Sen who ruled in the second century. The clan is believed to have migrated to Chitor from Gujarat sometime in the eighth century.

None of the indigenous rulers of India resisted the Muslim invasions into India with greater tenacity than the Rajputs of Mewar. It was their proud boast that they had never permitted a daughter to go into the Mughal harem. Three times the fortress and town of Chitor had fallen to Muslim invaders, to Alauddin Khilji (1303), to Bahadur Shah of Gujarat (1534) and to Akbar (1568). Each time Chitor gradually recovered but the last was the most traumatic experience of all. Rather than to submit to the Mughal onslaught, the women burned themselves on funeral pyres in a fearful rite called jauhar, and the men fell on the swords of the invaders.

After the sacking of Chitor the rana, Udai Singh, retired to the Aravali hills where he founded Udaipur, the capital after 1570. Udai Singh's son, Partab, refused to submit to the Mughal and recovered most of the territory lost in 1568. In the early nineteenth century Mewar suffered much at the hands of Marathas - Holkar, Sindhia and the Pindaris - until, in 1818, the State came under British supervision. In April 1948 Mewar was merged into Rajasthan and the maharana became governor Maharajpramukh of the new province.

RULERS
Bhim Singh,
  AH1192-1244/1777-1828AD
Jawan Singh
  AH1244-1254/1828-1838AD
Sirdar Singh
  AH1254-1258/1838-1842AD
Swarup Singh
  AH1258-1278/1842-1861AD
Shambhu Singh
  AH1278-1291/1861-1874AD
Sajjan Singh
  AH1291-1302/1874-1884AD
Fatteh Singh,
  VS1941-1986/1884-1929AD
Bhupal Singh,
  VS1987-2005/1930-1948AD

MINTS
Chitor   चितोड़
Chitarkot चित्रकूट
Udaipur   उदयपुर

NOTE: All Mewar coinage is struck without ruler's name, and is largely undated. certain types were generally struck over several reigns.

CHITOR MINT
Chitori Series
Struck at Chitor Mint between ca 1760 and the middle of the 19th century.

Mint mark:

Obv: W/o jhar.

1/16 RUPEE
SILVER, 0.67-0.72 g

C#	Date	Year	VG	Fine	VF	XF
22	ND	—	3.00	4.50	7.50	11.50

1/8 RUPEE
SILVER, 1.34-1.45 g

23	ND	—	2.25	3.00	5.00	6.50

1/4 RUPEE

SILVER, 2.68-2.90 g

| 24 | ND | — | 2.50 | 3.00 | 5.00 | 6.50 |

1/2 RUPEE

SILVER, 5.35-5.80 g

| 25 | ND | — | 3.00 | 4.00 | 6.00 | 10.00 |

RUPEE

SILVER, 10.70-11.60 g

| 26 | ND | — | 5.00 | 7.50 | 9.00 | 12.50 |

UDAIPUR MINT
Udaipuri Series
Struck at the Udaipur mint from about 1780 to the middle of the 19th century.

Mint mark: and on obverse.

1/16 RUPEE
SILVER

| 28 | ND | — | — | Reported, not confirmed | | |

1/8 RUPEE
SILVER

| 29 | ND | — | — | Reported, not confirmed | | |

1/4 RUPEE

SILVER, 2.68-2.90 g

| 30 | ND | — | 5.00 | 7.00 | 10.00 | 15.00 |

1/2 RUPEE
SILVER, 5.35-5.80 g

| 31 | ND | — | 5.00 | 7.00 | 10.00 | 15.00 |

RUPEE

SILVER, 10.70-11.60 g

| 32 | ND | — | 6.00 | 9.00 | 11.50 | 16.50 |

Chandori Series
Ordered by Bhim Singh, and struck at the Udaipur Mint until 1842AD. Recalled by Swarup Shah.

Mint mark: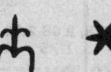
On obverse
On reverse

1/2 RUPEE
SILVER, 5.35-5.80 g

C#	Date	Year	Fine	VF	XF
43	ND	—	8.50	11.50	15.00	25.00

RUPEE

SILVER, 10.70-11.60 g

| 44 | ND | — | 8.50 | 11.50 | 15.00 | 25.00 |

New Chandori Series
Struck at the Udaipur Mint between 1842-1890AD. Many die varieties exist.

Mint mark: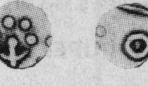

On obverse

1/16 RUPEE
SILVER, 9mm, 0.67-0.72 g

Y#	Date	Year	VG	Fine	VF	XF
1	ND	—	1.50	2.00	3.00	5.00

1/8 RUPEE

SILVER, 1.34-1.45 g

| 2 | ND | — | 1.50 | 2.50 | 3.50 | 6.00 |

1/4 RUPEE

SILVER, 2.68-2.90 g

| 3 | ND | — | 1.50 | 2.50 | 3.50 | 6.00 |

1/2 RUPEE

SILVER, 5.35-5.80 g

| 4 | ND | — | 2.00 | 3.00 | 5.00 | 7.50 |

RUPEE

SILVER, 10.70-11.60 g

| 5 | ND | — | BV | 5.00 | 6.00 | 8.50 |

MOHUR

GOLD, 10.70-11.40 g

| 6 | ND | — | BV | 175.00 | 200.00 | 225.00 |

Swarupshahi Series
Struck at the Udaipur Mint between 1851-1930AD. Many die varieties exist.

Mewar / INDIAN PRINCELY STATES 944

1/16 RUPEE

SILVER, round, 0.67-0.72 g

Y#	Date	Year	VG	Fine	VF	XF
7.1	ND	—	1.50	2.00	2.50	3.55

Irregular shape, 8-10mm.

7.2	ND	—	2.00	2.75	3.50	4.50

1/8 RUPEE

SILVER, 11-12mm, 1.34-1.45 g

8	ND	—	2.00	4.00	6.00	10.00

1/4 RUPEE

SILVER, 2.68-2.90 g

9	ND	—	1.75	2.75	4.00	6.00

1/2 RUPEE

SILVER, 5.35-5.80 g

10	ND	—	BV	3.50	5.00	7.50

RUPEE

SILVER, 10.70-11.60 g

11	ND	—	BV	4.50	5.50	7.50

1/4 MOHUR

GOLD, 2.67-2.90 g

A12	ND	—	—	—	—	—

MOHUR

GOLD, 10.70-11.60 g

12	ND	—	BV	170.00	190.00	225.00

FATTEH SINGH
VS1941-1987 / 1884-1930AD

With names of Chitor and Udaipur.

PIE

COPPER

Y#	Date	Year	Good	VG	Fine	VF
13	VS1975 (1918)	—	7.50	12.50	18.50	27.50

Y#	Date	Year	Good	VG	Fine	VF
14	VS1978 (1921)	—	6.00	10.00	15.00	22.50

Milled Coinage
In the name of 'A Friend of London'.
Dated VS1985 ie. 1928AD, but actually struck at the Alipore Mint in Calcutta between 1931-1932AD, the Y#22 rupee in 1931, the rest in 1932.

1/16 RUPEE

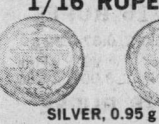

SILVER, 0.95 g

Y#	Date	Mintage	Fine	VF	XF	Unc
18	VS1985 (1928)	3.262	.80	1.25	2.00	4.00

1/8 RUPEE

SILVER, 1.36 g

19	VS1985 (1928)	.800	1.00	2.00	3.00	6.00

1/4 RUPEE

SILVER, 2.72 g

20	VS1985 (1928)	.839	BV	2.50	3.25	6.50

GOLD, 2.68-2.85 g (OMS)

20a	VS1985 (1928)	—	—	—	Proof	250.00

1/2 RUPEE

SILVER, 5.46 g

21	VS1985 (1928)	.648	BV	4.50	6.00	12.50

GOLD, 5.35-5.70 g (OMS)

21a	VS1985 (1928)	—	—	—	Proof	350.00

RUPEE

SILVER, 10.86 g
Obv: Thin legends.

22.1	VS1985 (1928)	14.906	BV	6.00	8.00	16.50

Obv: Thick legends.

22.2	VS1985 (1928)	Inc. Ab.	5.50	8.50	15.00	25.00

GOLD, 10.70-11.40 g (OMS)

Y#	Date	Mintage	Fine	VF	XF	Unc
22a	VS1985 (1928)	—	—	—	Proof	450.00

BHUPAL SINGH
VS1987-2005 / 1930-1948AD

1/4 ANNA

COPPER

Y#	Date	Year	Fine	VF	XF	Unc
15	VS1999 (1942)	—	.50	.85	1.25	2.00

1/2 ANNA

COPPER

16	VS1999 (1942)	—	.50	.85	1.25	2.00

ANNA

COPPER

17	VS2000 (1943)	—	.60	1.00	1.25	2.50

LOCAL ISSUES
Umarda

1/2 PAISA

COPPER

Y#	Date	Year	Good	VG	Fine	VF
23	ND	6	.45	.75	1.00	1.50

NOTE: Varieties exist.

24	ND(1938-41)	—	.75	1.25	1.75	2.50

NOTE: Varieties exist.

FEUDATORY STATES
Bhinda
ZURAWAR SINGH
AH1214-1243 / 1799-1827AD

PAISA

COPPER

C#	Date	Year	Good	VG	Fine	VF
1	ND	—	3.00	5.00	7.50	12.50

Salumba
2 PIES

COPPER

C#	Date	Year	Good	VG	Fine	VF
1	ND(1815-34)	—	3.00	5.00	7.00	11.50
	ND(1835-70)	—	3.00	5.00	7.00	11.50

Shahpur
RULERS
Jagat Singh,
AH1261-1270/1845-1853AD
Lachman Singh,
AH1270-1287/1853-1870AD
Nahat Singh,
AH1287-1351/1870-1932AD

PAISA

COPPER

10	ND(1827-70)	—	2.50	4.00	6.00	10.00

In the name of Alamgir II
AH1167-1173/1754-1759AD

Copy of his Dehli coin with Yr. 12 as a frozen fictitious year. Distinguished by the addition of a small trisul to lower obv.

1/4 RUPEE

SILVER, 14mm, 2.68-2.90 g

C#	Date	Year	VG	Fine	VF	XF
20	AHxxx8	12	10.00	12.50	16.50	25.00

1/2 RUPEE

SILVER, 17mm, 5.35-5.80 g

21	AHxxx8	12	10.00	12.50	16.50	25.00

RUPEE

SILVER, 10.70-11.60 g

22	AHxxx8	12	12.50	16.50	25.00	35.00

MOHUR

GOLD, 18mm, 10.70-11.40 g

29	AHxxx8	12	180.00	225.00	275.00	325.00

MYSORE

Large state in Southern India. Governed until 1761AD by various Hindu dynasties, then by Haider Ali and Tipu Sultan.

In 1831, Krishnaraja being deposed for mal-administration and pensioned off, the administration of Mysore State then came directly under the British. The coinage of Mysore ceased in 1843. After the Great Revolt of 1857, the policy of eliminating Indian princes was discontinued and, as a result, Mysore was returned in 1881 to the control of an adopted son of Krishnaraja Wodeyar. The Wodeyars continued to hold the State until 1947 although they did not issue coins. In November 1956 modern Mysore was inaugurated as a linguistic state within the Indian Union.

NOTE: For earlier issues see Mysore, Independent Kingdoms under British rule.

RULERS
Dewan Purnaiya, regent,
AH1214-1225/1799-1810AD
Krishna Raja Wodeyar,
AH1225-1285/1810-1868AD

MINTS
Mysore
Nagar, or

MONETARY SYSTEM
2 Fanams = 1 Anna
4 Annas = 1 Pavali
4 Pavalis = 1 Rupee

BANGALORE MINT

Type VI
Obv: Lion, date below.

2-1/2 CASH

COPPER

C#	Date	Good	VG	Fine	VF
190.2	1834	3.00	5.00	8.00	12.00
	1839	2.50	4.00	6.50	10.00
	1840	2.50	4.00	6.50	10.00
	1841	2.50	4.00	6.50	10.00
	1842	1.75	3.00	5.00	8.00
	1843	1.75	3.00	5.00	8.00

5 CASH

COPPER

191.2	1834	1.25	2.25	4.00	7.00
	1835	1.25	2.25	4.00	7.00
	1836	1.25	2.25	4.00	7.00
	1837	1.25	2.25	4.00	7.00
	1838	1.25	2.25	4.00	7.00
	1839	1.25	2.25	4.00	7.00
	1840	1.25	2.25	4.00	7.00
	1841	1.25	2.25	4.00	7.00
	1842	1.25	2.25	4.00	7.00
	1843	1.25	2.25	4.00	7.00

10 CASH

COPPER

192.2	1834	3.00	5.00	7.00	11.00
	1835	1.50	2.75	4.00	7.00
	1836	1.50	2.75	4.00	7.00
	1837	1.50	2.75	4.00	7.00
	1838	1.50	2.75	4.00	7.00
	1839	1.50	2.75	4.00	7.00
	1840	1.50	2.75	4.00	7.00
	1841	1.50	2.75	4.00	7.00
	1842	1.50	2.75	4.00	7.00
	1843	1.50	2.75	4.00	7.00

20 CASH

COPPER

193.2	1833	1.50	2.50	4.00	7.00
	1834	1.50	2.50	4.00	7.00
	1835	.75	1.50	2.50	4.00
	1836	.75	1.50	2.50	4.00
	1837	.75	1.50	2.50	4.00
	1838	.75	1.50	2.50	4.00
	1839	.75	1.50	2.50	4.00
	1840	.75	1.50	2.50	4.00
	1841	.75	1.50	2.50	4.00
	1842	.75	1.50	2.50	4.00
	1843	.75	1.50	2.50	4.00

NOTE: All dates have MEILEE on rev.; some 1834 have MILAY, and some 1837 have MILEE.

MYSORE MINT
DEWAN PURNAIYA
Regent for Krishnaraja Wodeyar
AH1214-1225/1799-1810AD
A Sardula (mythical tiger) is illustrated on all of Dewan Purnaiya's coins.

75 CASH

COPPER, 23.59 g

C#	Date	Good	VG	Fine	VF
189	ND(1799-1868)	—	—	—	—

KRISHNA RAJA WODEYAR
1810-1868AD
British control after 1831
(Types I-IV struck 1811-1833)
SRI VARIETIES

Variety I:

Variety II:

Type I, ca. 1811
Obv: Elephant below sun and moon. Rev: Three line Nagari leg.

6-1/4 CASH

COPPER

170	ND	6.00	10.00	15.00	20.00

Type II
Obv: Elephant below Kanarese, *Sri* between sun and moon. Rev: Two lines of Kanarese, denomination in English at the top on the 5 and 10 Cash, at the bottom on the 20 and 40 Cash. The English denomination is often encountered blundered.

5 CASH

COPPER
Obv. leg: *Sri* var. I.

171	ND	1.25	2.25	3.75	6.00
	ND (X CASH in error)	2.50	4.25	7.00	11.00

10 CASH

COPPER
Obv. leg: *Sri* var. I.

174	ND	5.00	7.50	11.50	16.50

20 CASH

COPPER
Obv. leg: *Sri* var. I.

C#	Date	VG	Fine	VF	XF
177	ND	2.50	4.00	6.00	12.50

40 CASH

COPPER
Obv. leg: *Sri* var. I.

180	ND	7.50	15.00	30.00	50.00

Type III
Obv: Elephant below Kanarese, *Sri* between sun and moon. Rev: Three line Kanarese leg., denomination in English at the bottom of the rev. The English denomination is often encountered blundered or retrograde.

Mysore / INDIAN PRINCELY STATES

5 CASH
COPPER
Obv. leg: *Sri* var. I.

C#	Date	Good	VG	Fine	VF
171a.1	ND	3.50	6.00	9.00	14.00

Obv. leg: *Sri* var. II.

| 171a.2 | ND | 3.50 | 6.00 | 9.00 | 14.00 |

10 CASH

COPPER
Obv. leg: *Sri* var. II.

| 174a | ND | 3.00 | 5.50 | 8.50 | 12.50 |
| | ND (X CASH retrograde) | 3.50 | 6.00 | 9.00 | 14.00 |

20 CASH

COPPER
Obv. leg: *Sri* var. II.

| 177a | ND | 1.00 | 1.75 | 2.75 | 4.00 |

Type IV
Obv: Elephant below Kanarese leg. *Sri* between sun and moon/*Chamuni*. Rev: Similar to Type III.

5 CASH

COPPER
Obv. leg: *Sri* var. I.

| 171b | ND | 1.75 | 3.00 | 5.00 | 7.50 |

10 CASH

COPPER

| 174b | ND | 3.00 | 6.00 | 10.00 | 15.00 |

20 CASH

COPPER
Obv. leg: *Sri* var. I.

C#	Date	VG	Fine	VF	XF
177b	ND	3.50	5.00	8.50	17.50

25 CASH

COPPER, 11.20-11.40 g
Obv. leg: *Sri* var. I.

| 179 | ND | — | — | — | — |

Type V
Obv: Sardula (mythical lion) below Kanarese leg. *Sri* between sun and moon/*Chamundi*. Rev. Kanarese leg. *Krishna* in center surrounded by mintname and denomination.

2-1/2 CASH

COPPER

C#	Date	Good	VG	Fine	VF
190.1	1833	4.50	7.50	9.00	13.50

5 CASH

COPPER

| 191.1 | 1833 | 2.50 | 4.00 | 5.50 | 8.00 |
| | 1834 | 2.50 | 4.00 | 5.50 | 8.00 |

10 CASH

COPPER

| 192.1 | 1833 | 3.00 | 5.00 | 6.00 | 9.00 |
| | 1834 | 3.00 | 5.00 | 6.00 | 9.00 |

20 CASH

COPPER

193.1	1833	2.00	3.50	5.00	7.50
	1834	2.00	3.50	5.00	7.50
	1836	2.00	3.50	5.00	7.50
	1838	2.00	3.50	5.00	7.50

NOTE: The 1833 has 2 varieties: W/palm frond before Sardula and w/frond before and above.

1/6 PAVALI

SILVER, 0.45-0.48 g

C#	Date	VG	Fine	VF	XF
199	ND	4.00	6.50	8.00	10.00

1/3 PAVALI

SILVER, 0.89-0.96 g

C#	Date	Year	VG	Fine	VF	XF
200	ND	—	15.00	22.50	35.00	50.00

2/3 PAVALI

SILVER, 1.78-1.92 g

| 201 | ND | — | 12.50 | 18.50 | 25.00 | 37.50 |

1/4 RUPEE (PAVALI)

SILVER, 2.68-2.90 g
Dancing figure (Chamundi)

202	AH1214	—	6.00	12.50	20.00	25.00
	1226	—	6.00	12.50	20.00	25.00
	1229	—	6.00	12.50	20.00	25.00
	1243	—	6.00	12.50	20.00	25.00
	1244	—	6.00	12.50	20.00	25.00
	1245	—	6.00	12.50	20.00	25.00
	1246	—	6.00	12.50	20.00	25.00
	1247	—	6.00	12.50	20.00	25.00
	1248	—	6.00	12.50	20.00	25.00
	3421	—	6.00	12.50	20.00	25.00
	4421	—	6.00	12.50	20.00	25.00

Shah Alam II legends

205	AH1220	44	7.50	11.50	17.50	25.00
	1220	45	7.50	11.50	17.50	25.00
	1221	45	7.50	11.50	17.50	25.00
	—	76	7.50	11.50	17.50	25.00
	—	84	7.50	11.50	17.50	25.00

1/2 RUPEE

SILVER, 5.35-5.80 g

C#	Date	Year	VG	Fine	VF	XF
206	—	35	8.50	13.50	20.00	30.00
	—	39	8.50	13.50	20.00	30.00
	—	76	8.50	13.50	20.00	30.00

RUPEE

SILVER, 10.70-11.60 g

207	AH1214	39	6.00	10.00	14.00	20.00
	1215	39	6.00	10.00	14.00	20.00
	1219	44	6.00	10.00	14.00	20.00
	1221	25	6.00	10.00	14.00	20.00
	1221	45	6.00	10.00	14.00	20.00
	1222	46	6.00	10.00	14.00	20.00
	1221	47	6.00	10.00	14.00	20.00
	1222	64	6.00	10.00	14.00	20.00
	—	48	6.00	10.00	14.00	20.00
	1223	64	6.00	10.00	14.00	20.00
	1224	64	6.00	10.00	14.00	20.00
	1224	74	6.00	10.00	14.00	20.00
	1225	74	6.00	10.00	14.00	20.00
	1225	94	6.00	10.00	14.00	20.00
	1226	94	6.00	10.00	14.00	20.00
	1227	95	6.00	10.00	14.00	20.00
	1228	95	6.00	10.00	14.00	20.00
	1229	96	6.00	10.00	14.00	20.00
	1230	97	6.00	10.00	14.00	20.00
	1231	98	6.00	10.00	14.00	20.00
	1232	99	6.00	10.00	14.00	20.00
	1234	98	6.00	10.00	14.00	20.00
	1235	98	6.00	10.00	14.00	20.00
	1236	98	6.00	10.00	14.00	20.00
	1237	37	6.00	10.00	14.00	20.00
	1238	37	6.00	10.00	14.00	20.00
	1239	3x	6.00	10.00	14.00	20.00
	1240	98	6.00	10.00	14.00	20.00
	1242	37	6.00	10.00	14.00	20.00
	1243	98	6.00	10.00	14.00	20.00
	1247	47	6.00	10.00	14.00	20.00
	1248	48	6.00	10.00	14.00	20.00
	x421	45	6.00	10.00	14.00	20.00
	x421	47	6.00	10.00	14.00	20.00

FANAM

GOLD, 0.33-0.40 g
Narasimha

| 212 | ND | — | 7.50 | 10.00 | 13.50 | 20.00 |

PAGODA

GOLD, 3.40 g
Shiva and Parvati

| 210 | ND | — | BV | 50.00 | 60.00 | 80.00 |

NOTE: Fanams and 1/2 Pagodas of this type are recent fabrications.

1/4 MOHUR

GOLD, 2.68-2.85 g
Mughal type

| 215 | — | 45 | — | Rare | — |

NAGAR MINT
KRISHNA RAJA WODEYAR
1810-1868AD

1/2 RUPEE

SILVER, 5.35-5.80 g

| 206a | — | 74 | 11.50 | 18.50 | 27.50 | 40.00 |
| | — | 84 | 11.50 | 18.50 | 27.50 | 40.00 |

RUPEE

SILVER, 10.70-11.60 g

C#	Date	Year	VG	Fine	VF	XF
207a	—	46	20.00	30.00	50.00	80.00
	AH1225	84	20.00	30.00	50.00	80.00

NAWANAGAR
(Navanagar)

State located on the Kathiawar peninsula, west-central India.

The rulers, or jams, of Kutch were Jareja Rajputs who had entered the Kathiawar peninsular from Kutch and dispossessed the ancient family of Jathwas. Nawanagar was founded about 1535 by Jam Raval, who was possibly the elder brother of the Jam of Kutch. The great fort of Nawanagar was built by Jam Jasaji (d. 1814). The state became tributary to the Gaekwar family and, in the nineteenth century, also to the British. In 1948 the state was merged into Saurashtra.

RULERS

Vibhaji
VS1909-1951/1852-1894AD
Jaswant Singh
VS1951-1964/1894-1907AD

Early Types: Stylized imitations of the coins of Muzaffar III of Gujarat (156-173AD), dated AH978 (= 1570AD), were struck from the end of the 16th century until the early part of the reign of Vibhaji. These show a steady degradation of style over the nearly 300 years of issue, but no types can be dated to specific rulers. The former attribution of these coins to Ranmalji II (1820-1852AD) is incorrect. All are inscribed Sri Jamji, title of all rulers of Nawanagar.

Varieties in this series are the rule, not the exception. These include legend style and small marks in the field such as a crescent, Katar (dagger), etc.

DUMP COINAGE
Crude style; ca. 1570-1850AD

TRAMBIYO

COPPER

C#	Date	Good	VG	Fine	VF
14	AH978 (frozen)	1.25	2.00	3.00	4.50

DOKDO

COPPER

| 15 | AH978 (frozen) | .40 | .75 | 1.00 | 1.50 |

1-1/2 DOKDO

COPPER

| 16 | AH978 (frozen) | 1.25 | 2.00 | 3.00 | 4.00 |

1/2 KORI

SILVER

| 20 | AH978 (frozen) | 1.75 | 3.00 | 4.50 | 6.00 |

KORI

SILVER

C#	Date	Good	VG	Fine	VF
21	AH978 (frozen)	1.50	2.50	3.25	4.00

Finer style from ca. 1850AD.

1/2 DOKDO

COPPER

Y#	Date	Good	VG	Fine	VF
2	AH978 (frozen)	1.00	2.00	3.25	4.50

DOKDO

COPPER, 17-19mm

| 3 | AH978 (frozen) | .65 | 1.15 | 1.75 | 2.50 |

1-1/2 DOKDA

COPPER

| 4 | AH978 (frozen) | 1.00 | 1.75 | 2.50 | 3.50 |

1/2 KORI

SILVER

Y#	Date	VG	Fine	VF	XF
5	AH978 (frozen)	2.50	3.50	5.00	7.00

KORI

SILVER

| 6 | AH978 (frozen) | 1.25 | 1.75 | 2.50 | 4.50 |

VIBHAJI
VS1909-1951/1852-1894AD

1/2 DOKDO

COPPER

Y#	Date	Good	VG	Fine	VF
9	AH978 (frozen)	1.00	1.75	3.00	4.00

Similar to Dokdo, Y#1.

| A1 | VS1919 (1862) | 3.50 | 6.00 | 7.50 | 10.00 |

DOKDO

COPPER

| 10 | AH978 (frozen) | .90 | 1.40 | 2.25 | 3.00 |

Y#	Date	Year	Good	VG	Fine	VF
1	VS1909	(1852)	3.50	6.00	7.50	10.00
	1917	(1860)	3.50	6.00	7.50	10.00
	1919	(1862)	3.50	6.00	7.50	10.00

2 DOKDA

COPPER

| 13 | VS1943 (1886) | 4.00 | 7.00 | 10.00 | 13.50 |

3 DOKDA

COPPER

| 11 | VS1928 (1871) | 3.50 | 5.50 | 7.00 | 10.00 |

| 14 | VS1942 (1885) | 3.00 | 4.50 | 6.50 | 10.00 |

KORI

SILVER
Plain edge

Y#	Date	Year	VG	Fine	VF	XF
12	VS1934	(1877)	3.00	5.00	8.50	15.00
	1935	(1878)	3.00	5.00	8.50	15.00
	1936	(1879)	2.00	3.00	5.00	9.00

2-1/2 KORI

SILVER
Milled edge

15	VS1948 (1891)	6.00	10.00	15.00	23.50
	1949 (1892)	6.00	10.00	15.00	23.50
	1950 (1893)	6.00	10.00	15.00	23.50

5 KORI

Nawanagar / INDIAN PRINCELY STATES

SILVER
Obv. and rev: Large inner circle, milled edge.

Y#	Date	Year	Fine	VF	XF	Unc
16.1	VS1945	(1888)	8.00	12.50	18.50	27.50
	1946	(1889)	8.00	12.50	18.50	27.50
	1947	(1890)	8.00	12.50	18.50	27.50

Obv. and rev. leg: Smaller characters.

16.2	VS1948	(1891)	8.00	12.50	18.50	27.50
	1949	(1892)	8.00	12.50	18.50	27.50
	1950	(1893)	8.00	12.50	18.50	27.50

1/2 GOLDKORI
GOLD, 13mm

Y#	Date	VG	Fine	VF	XF
7	AH978 (frozen)	75.00	100.00	125.00	165.00

GOLDKORI

GOLD

8	AH(9)78 (frozen)	85.00	125.00	185.00	250.00

JASWANT SINGH
VS1951-1964/1894-1907AD

1/2 DOKDO

COPPER

Y#	Date	Year	Good	VG	Fine	VF
17	VS1956	(1899)	10.00	16.50	25.00	40.00

DOKDO

COPPER, 17mm

18	VS1956	(1899)	9.00	15.00	22.50	36.50

1-1/2 DOKDA

COPPER

19	VS1956	(1899)	7.50	12.50	20.00	30.00

2 DOKDA

COPPER

20	VS1956	(1899)	12.50	20.00	33.50	45.00

3 DOKDA

COPPER

Y#	Date	Year	Good	VG	Fine	VF
21	VS1956	(1899)	12.50	22.50	35.00	50.00

ORCHHA

State located in north-central India.

Orchha, the oldest and highest ranking of all the Bundela States, was founded by Rudra Pratap, a Garhwar Rajput, early in the sixteenth century. During the years of Mughal expansion, Orchha came under the supervision of Delhi. A few years later Jujhar Singh (1626-1635) rebelled but was defeated and dispossessed. Shah Jahan installed his brother as ruler in 1641. In the eighteenth century, as the Marathas took control of the region, only Orchha from among the Bundela States was not totally subjugated by the Peshwa. In the nineteenth century Orchha came under British protection.

The Orchha coinage was called Gaja Shahi because of the gaja or mace which was its symbol.

RULERS
Vikramajit Mahendra
  AH1211-1233/1796-1817AD
Dharam Pal
  AH1233-1250/1817-1834AD
Taj Singh
  AH1250-1258/1834-1842AD
Surjain Singh
  AH1258-1265/1842-1848AD
Hamir Singh
  AH1265-1291/1848-1874AD
Pratap Singh
  AH1291-1349/1874-1930AD

MINT MARKS

1 — Reverse. (This is the symbol most characteristic of Orchha's coinage and is copied on the Datia imitations)

2 — Obverse, most common.

3 — Obverse, less common.

4 — Reverse

5 — Reverse

6 — Reverse

7 — Reverse

8 — Reverse

9 — Reverse

10 — Reverse

Marks #4 through #10 are found in addition to Mark #1. The Datia copies can only be distinguished by the mint marks, other than #1, which is common to both series for the list of Datia marks, see listings under that state.

There seems to be no correspondence between AH dates on the obverse and regnal years on the reverse!

In the name of Shah Alam II
AH1173-1221/1759-1806AD

1/2 PAISA
COPPER, 16mm

C#	Date	Year	Good	VG	Fine	VF
24	AH—	—	1.75	3.00	5.00	8.00

PAISA

COPPER

C#	Date	Year	Good	VG	Fine	VF
25	AH1278	45	1.00	2.00	3.25	4.50
	1282	42	1.00	2.00	3.25	4.50

1/4 RUPEE

SILVER, 12mm, 2.68-2.90 g

C#	Date	Year	VG	Fine	VF	XF
30	AH1233	45	2.00	3.50	5.00	7.50
	1233	5x	2.00	3.50	5.00	7.50
	1251	3x	2.00	3.50	5.00	7.50

RUPEE
SILVER, 10.70-11.60 g

32	AH1216	44	5.50	6.50	9.00	14.00
	1216	46	5.50	6.50	9.00	14.00
	1218	46	5.50	6.50	9.00	14.00
	1218	47	5.50	6.50	9.00	14.00
	121x	47	5.50	6.50	9.00	14.00
	1219	48	5.50	6.50	9.00	14.00
	1221	40	5.50	6.50	9.00	14.00
	1232	40	5.50	6.50	9.00	14.00
	1233	40	5.50	6.50	9.00	14.00
	1236	15	5.50	6.50	9.00	14.00
	1245	43	5.50	6.50	9.00	14.00
	1252	32	5.50	6.50	9.00	14.00
	1257	39	5.50	6.50	9.00	14.00

NOTE: Varieties exist with different variations of obverse and reverse symbols.

In the name of Muhammad Akbar II
AH1221-1253/1806-1837AD

PAISA

COPPER

C#	Date	Year	VG	Fine	VF
38	AH—	3x	2.00	4.00	6.00	9.00

RUPEE

SILVER, 20mm, 10.70-11.60 g

C#	Date	Year	Good	Fine	VF	XF
42	AH1219	2	6.50	9.00	13.50	20.00
	1321 (error for 1231)					
		9	8.00	12.50	18.50	25.00
	1232	10	6.50	9.00	13.50	20.00
	1257	48	6.50	9.00	13.50	20.00
	1258	38	6.50	9.00	13.50	20.00
	1270	33	6.50	9.00	13.50	20.00
	1273	39	6.50	9.00	13.50	20.00
	—	41	6.50	9.00	13.50	20.00
	1275	4X	6.50	9.00	13.50	20.00
	1278		6.50	9.00	13.50	20.00

PARTABGARH
Pratapgarh

The rulers of Partabgarh, a state located in northwest India, the maharawals, were Sesodia Rajputs who are believed to have migrated in 1553 from Mewar, where their ancestors once ruled. Arriving in the area they seized control from the local Bhil chieftains but it was not until the early eighteenth century that Partabgarh town was founded by Maharawal Partab Singh. Partabgarh was tributary to Holkar until 1818 when, with the collapse of of the Maratha states, the state came under British protection. The state was then managed through the Rajputana Agency until, in April 1948, it was merged into Rajasthan.

RULERS
Sawant Singh
  AH1189-1241/1775-1825AD
Dulep Singh
  AH1241-1281/1825-1864AD

Udaya Singh
VS1921-1947 / 1864-1890AD
Raganath Singh
VS1947-1986 / 1890-1929AD

MINT MARK

Deogarh, Deogir

DULEP SINGH
AH1241-1281 / 1825-1864AD

In the name of Shah Alam II
Frozen date AH1236/Yr. 45. The meaning of Yr. 45 is not known.

1/8 RUPEE

SILVER, 1.34-1.45 g

C#	Date	Year	VG	Fine	VF	XF
26	AH1236	45	2.50	4.00	6.00	10.00

1/4 RUPEE

SILVER, 2.68-2.90 g

| 27 | AH1236 | 45 | 2.50 | 3.75 | 5.50 | 9.00 |

1/2 RUPEE

SILVER, 5.35-5.80 g

| 28 | AH1236 | 45 | 3.00 | 4.50 | 6.50 | 11.50 |

RUPEE

SILVER, 10.70-11.60 g

| 29 | AH1236 | 45 | 5.50 | 7.50 | 9.00 | 13.50 |

| 29a | AH1236 | 45 | 40.00 | 70.00 | 90.00 | 120.00 |

UDAYA SINGH
VS1921-1947 / 1864-1890AD

PAISA

COPPER

Y#	Date	Year	Good	VG	Fine	VF
1	VS1935	(1878)	1.25	2.25	3.25	5.00

7.60-8.00 g

| 2 | VS1942 | (1885) | 1.00 | 1.75 | 2.50 | 4.00 |
| | 1943 | (1886) | 1.00 | 1.75 | 2.50 | 4.00 |

In the name of the 'Shah of London'
(= Queen Victoria)
Frozen date AH1236/Yr. 45. To be distinguished from the C#27-29 series by the word London directly below the date AH1236.

1/8 RUPEE

SILVER, 1.34-1.45 g

Y#	Date	Year	VG	Fine	VF	XF
3	AH1236	45	2.25	3.50	5.00	8.00

1/4 RUPEE

SILVER, 2.68-2.90 g

| 4 | AH1236 | 45 | 2.00 | 3.50 | 5.00 | 8.50 |

1/2 RUPEE

SILVER, 5.35-5.80 g

| 5 | AH1236 | 45 | 3.25 | 4.25 | 6.00 | 10.00 |

RUPEE

SILVER, 10.70-11.60 g

| 6 | AH1236 | 45 | 5.50 | 7.00 | 9.00 | 14.00 |

| 6a | AH1236 | 45 | 40.00 | 70.00 | 90.00 | 120.00 |

NAZARANA RUPEE

SILVER

| 6b | AH1236 | 45 | — | — | Rare | — |

RAGANATH SINGH
VS1947-1986 / 1890-1929AD

PAISA

COPPER

Y#	Date	Year	Good	VG	Fine	VF
7	VS1953	(1896)	1.50	2.50	3.50	5.00

RADHANPUR

State located on the Kathiawar peninsula. The nawabs of Radhanpur were Pathans of the Babi family who rose to high office in the service of Shah Jahan and Murad Bakhsh in Gujarat. Sometime in the late seventeenth or early eighteenth centuries one of the family was appointed faujdar of Radhanpur and the surrounding area. After Aurangzeb's death, Kamal-ud-din Khan Babi seized the governorship of Ahmadabad, but this was relinquished in 1753 to the forces of the Peshwa of Poona and the Gaekwar of Baroda. Radhanpur, however, remained in Babi control as a Maratha jagir until 1820 when the State came under British protection.

RULERS
Zorawar Khan
AH1241-1291 / 1825-1874AD
Bismilla Khan
AH1291-1313 / 1874-1895AD

MINT

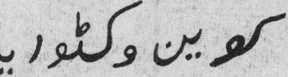

Radhanpur

ZORAWAR KHAN
AH1241-1291 / 1825-1874AD

In the name of Queen Victoria and Zorawar Khan

PAISA

COPPER or BRONZE, uniface

Y#	Date	Good	VG	Fine	VF
2	ND	1.00	1.75	2.50	4.00

2 ANNAS

SILVER, 1.34-1.45 g

Y#	Date	Year	VG	Fine	VF	XF
5	AH1288	1871	20.00	27.50	35.00	50.00

4 ANNAS

SILVER, 2.68-2.90 g

6	AH1287	1869	18.50	25.00	32.50	45.00
	1287	1871	18.50	25.00	32.50	45.00
	1288	1871	18.50	25.00	32.50	45.00
	1288	1872	18.50	25.00	32.50	45.00

8 ANNAS

SILVER, 5.35-5.80 g

7	AH1284	1869	20.00	27.50	35.00	50.00
	1286	1869	20.00	27.50	35.00	50.00
	1287	1869	20.00	27.50	35.00	50.00
	1287	1870	20.00	27.50	35.00	50.00
	1288	1871	20.00	27.50	35.00	50.00
	1289	1871	20.00	27.50	35.00	50.00

50 FALUS

SILVER

| 3 | AH1284 | 1867 | 30.00 | 37.50 | 45.00 | 60.00 |

Radhanpur / INDIAN PRINCELY STATES 950

RUPEE

SILVER, 10.70-11.60 g

Y#	Date	Year	VG	Fine	VF	XF
8	AH1287	1870	18.50	25.00	32.50	45.00
	1287	1871	18.50	25.00	32.50	45.00
	1288	1871	18.50	25.00	32.50	45.00
	1288	1872	18.50	25.00	32.50	45.00
	1289	1872	18.50	25.00	32.50	45.00

100 FALUS

SILVER

4	AH1284	1867	30.00	37.50	45.00	60.00
	1286	1868	30.00	37.50	45.00	60.00
	1286	1869	30.00	37.50	45.00	60.00

MOHUR

GOLD, 27mm, 10.70-11.40 g

9	AH1277	1860	220.00	240.00	265.00	300.00

BISMILLA KHAN
AH1291-1313/1874-1895AD

In the name of Queen Victoria
and Bismillah Khan

PAISA

COPPER or BRONZE

Y#	Date	Good	VG	Fine	VF
1	ND	1.75	2.25	3.00	4.50

2 ANNAS

SILVER, 15mm, 1.34-1.45 g

Y#	Date	Year	VG	Fine	VF	XF
10	AH—	1880	25.00	32.50	40.00	55.00

4 ANNAS

SILVER, 2.68-2.90 g

Obv. leg: Field divided twice, Nawab's name at top. Rev. leg: Field divided once, Queen's name upper left.

11	AH—	1880	20.00	27.50	35.00	50.00

In the name of Empress Victoria
and Bismillah Khan

8 ANNAS

SILVER, 5.35-5.80 g

12.1	AH1291	1875	18.50	25.00	32.50	45.00

In the name of Queen Victoria
and Bismillah Khan

Obv. leg: Field divided twice, Nawab's name at top. Rev. leg: Two field dividers, Queen's name center left, center line three words.

12.2	AH1297	1880	18.50	25.00	32.50	45.00

Rev. leg: W/o field dividers, Queen's name lower left.

Y#	Date	Year	VG	Fine	VF	XF
12.3	AH1297	1881	18.50	25.00	32.50	45.00

Rev. leg: Two field dividers, Queen's name center left, center line three words.

12.4	AH1299	1881	18.50	25.00	32.50	45.00

Obv. leg: Two field dividers, Nawab's name center in one line. Rev. leg: W/o field dividers, Queen's name lower left.

12.5	AH1299	1881	18.50	25.00	32.50	45.00

RUPEE

SILVER, 10.70-11.60 g

Obv. leg: Two field dividers, Nawab's name center in one line. Rev. leg: Field divided once over *Dak*.

13.1	AH1297	1880	25.00	32.50	40.00	55.00
	1298	1880	27.50	35.00	45.00	65.00

Obv. leg: Field divided twice, Nawab's name at top. Rev. leg: Two field dividers, Queen's name center left, center line three words.

13.2	AH1299	1881	25.00	32.50	40.00	55.00

Obv. leg: Two field dividers, Nawab's name center in one line. Rev. leg: Field divided once w/ Queen's titles in different order.

13.3	AH1297	1881	27.50	35.00	45.00	60.00
	1298	1881	25.00	32.50	40.00	55.00

Rev. leg: One field divider, w/o Queen's name, mint name above.

Y#	Date	Year	VG	Fine	VF	XF
13.4	AH1311	1894	25.00	32.50	40.00	55.00

Obv. leg: One field divider, Nawab's name above. Rev. leg: W/o Queen's name, mint name below.

13.5	AH1311	1894	25.00	32.50	40.00	55.00

RAMPUR

This tiny estate of four and a half square miles was held by Chauda Rajputs in the old Gujerat States Agency Area. It was feudatory to Lunavada and the estate was controlled by a thakur or, latterly, by four shareholders.

Anonymous Issues

The following listings may be from Lunavada or from Rampur. They are often found overstruck on coins of Lunavada, and over other states, including Sailana.

1/2 PAISA

COPPER, 3.00-4.00 g
Obv: Open hand in square.
Rev. leg: *Rampar*.

KM#	Date	Year	Good	VG	Fine	VF
1	ND	—	4.00	6.00	10.00	15.00

Obv: Sunbursts. Rev. leg: *Rampar*.

2	ND	—	5.00	7.50	12.00	20.00

PAISA

COPPER, 1.90-4.30 g

3	ND	—	2.50	4.00	6.00	8.50

Obv: Spears. Rev: Spears.

4	ND	—	2.50	4.00	6.00	8.50

Round or square, 8.50 g
Obv: Spears. Rev: *Rampar*.

5	ND	—	2.50	4.00	6.00	8.50

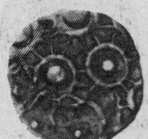

Round or square, 7.50-8.30 g
Obv: Sunbursts. Rev. leg: *Rampar*.

6	ND	—	2.50	4.00	6.00	8.50

PIE

COPPER, 2.30 g

5	ND	—	—	—	—	—

RATLAM

State located northwest of Indore in Madhya Pradesh.
The rajas of Ratlam were Rathor Rajputs, descendants of the younger branch of the Jodhpur ruling family. Ratlam became the premier Rajput state in western Malwa. The founder, Ratan Singh, received the territory as a grant from Shah Jahan in 1631. Before Maratha collapse some fifteen percent of the state's annual revenue went to Sindhia as tribute. Under British protection it was supervised by the Central India Agency and in 1948 Ratlam became a district of Madhya Bharat.

RULERS
Ranjit Singh
VS1921-1950/1864-1893AD

RANJIT SINGH
VS1921-1950/1864-1893AD

PAISA
COPPER, 22mm

Y#	Date	Year	Good	VG	Fine	VF
1	VS1921	(1864)	6.00	9.00	12.50	18.50

2	VS1927	(1870)	3.50	4.50	5.50	7.50
	1928	(1871)	1.50	2.25	3.00	4.50

3	1885	—	2.50	4.00	6.00	9.00

Milled Coinage
PAISA

COPPER
Thick planchet

Y#	Date	Year	VG	Fine	VF	XF
4	VS1945	(1888)	2.50	4.00	5.00	7.00
	1947	(1890)	3.00	5.00	6.50	9.00
	1948	(1891)	.45	.75	1.25	2.00

Thin, crude restrike of Y#4.

| 4a | VS1947 | (1890) | .30 | .50 | .75 | 1.00 |

NOTE: Y#4a was struck c.1942-1945AD.

REWA

State located in eastern north-central India.
The rulers of Rewa were Baghela Rajputs of the Solanki clan who probably migrated from Anhilwara Patan in Gujarat about the eleventh century. Arriving in Bundelkhand they carved out for themselves a substantial kingdom which remained independent until 1597, when they were obliged to become Mughal tributaries under Akbar. With Mughal decline Rewa began to move once more towards independence, this time under the nominal suzerainty of the Peshwa. In 1812 the raja of Rewa, Jai Singh Deo was coerced into a treaty with the British and, failing to observe its conditions, was forced to yield to British control in 1813-1814. In 1948 Rewa was merged into Vindhya Pradesh.

RULERS
Jai Singh Deo
VS1866-1892/1809-1835AD
Vishwanath Singh
VS1892-1900/1835-1843AD
Raghuraj Singh
VS1900-1937/1843-1880AD
Gulab Singh
VS1975-2003/1918-1946AD

JAI SINGH DEO
VS1866-1892/1809-1835AD

PAISA

COPPER, 6.80 g

C#	Date	Year	Good	VG	Fine	VF
20	VS1890	(1823)	2.00	3.00	4.50	7.00

8.80-12.60 g

| 21 | ND | — | 1.75 | 2.75 | 4.00 | 6.00 |

2 PAISA

COPPER

| 22 | ND | — | 2.50 | 4.00 | 7.00 | 11.00 |

VISHVANATH SINGH
VS1892-1900/1835-1843AD

PAISA

COPPER, 7.80 g

| 31 | ND | — | 2.50 | 3.50 | 5.00 | 7.50 |

2 PAISA

COPPER, 16.80 g

| 34 | ND | — | 2.50 | 3.50 | 5.00 | 7.00 |

RAGHURAJ SINGH
VS1900-1937/1843-1880AD

In the name of Agent Bushby Saheb

PAISA

COPPER

| 45 | VS1906 | (1849) | 2.75 | 4.50 | 6.50 | 9.00 |

2 PAISE

COPPER
Obv: Lion left.

| 46.1 | VS1906 | (1849) | 2.75 | 4.50 | 6.50 | 9.00 |

Obv: Lion right.

C#	Date	Year	Good	VG	Fine	VF
46.2	VS1906	(1849)	5.00	7.00	9.00	12.50

GULAB SINGH
VS1975-2003/1918-1946AD

1/2 RUPEE
SILVER, thin flan
Accession Commemorative

Y#	Date	Year	VG	Fine	VF	XF
A1a	VS1975	(1918)	15.00	30.00	42.50	60.00

RUPEE
SILVER, thick flan
Accession Commemorative

| 1b.1 | VS1975 | (1918) | 15.00 | 30.00 | 42.50 | 60.00 |
| (Y1a) | | | | | | |

1/2 MOHUR

GOLD, 5.40 g
Accession Commemorative

| A1 | VS1975 | (1918) | 225.00 | 375.00 | 450.00 | 600.00 |

MOHUR

GOLD, 10.70-11.40 g
Accession Commemorative

| 1 | VS1975 | (1918) | 235.00 | 265.00 | 300.00 | 375.00 |

Reduced weight, 8.80 g

| 1a | VS1977 | (1920) | BV | 30.00 | 50.00 | 75.00 |

ROHILKHAND
Refer to Independent Kingdoms during British rule.

SAILANA

This small state in west-central India, of slightly over one hundred square miles had once been part of Ratlam, but about 1709 it asserted its independence under the leadership of Pratab Singh, the second son of Chhatrasal. The town of Sailana was founded in 1730 by Jai Singh's successor, and from that date the state was named after it. Due to its small size and vulnerability, Sailana was obliged to become tributary to Sindhia to ensure its survival. In 1819 this payment was limited to one-third of the state's revenues. Later, under agreements of 1840 and 1860, the tribute went to the British for the support of British Indian troops in the region. Barmawal was feudatory to Sailana.

LOCAL RULERS
Dule Singh
VS1907-1947/1850-1890AD
Jaswant Singh, 1890-1918AD

ANONYMOUS COINAGE
1/2 PAISA

COPPER, 5.15 g

KM#	Date	Year	Good	VG	Fine	VF
4	ND	—	1.50	2.25	3.25	4.50

PAISA

COPPER
Rev: Pennant points either up or down.

| 5 | ND | — | .50 | .85 | 1.25 | 2.00 |

NOTE: C#5 is known struck over an Egyptian 20 Para Y#3, cut down to an irregular shape. Other combinations could exist.

Sailana / INDIAN PRINCELY STATES 952

2 PAISA

COPPER

KM#	Date	Year	Good	VG	Fine	VF
6	ND	—	—	—	—	—

LOCAL ISSUES
DULE SINGH
VS1907-1947/1850-1890AD

1/2 PAISA

COPPER

10	VS1944	(1887)	3.00	4.50	6.00	8.50

PAISA

COPPER

11	VS1937	(1880)	1.50	2.25	3.00	4.00
	7391 (retrograde)	(1880)	—	—	—	—

Obv: Sprig, Nagari date.

12	VS1940	(1883)	2.25	3.50	4.50	6.00

Rev: Arabic numerals in Samvat date.

13	VS1941	(1884)	2.25	3.50	4.50	6.00

Rev: Trident.

14	VS1944	(1887)	2.25	3.50	4.50	6.00

REGAL ISSUES
JASWANT SINGH
1890-1919AD

1/4 ANNA

COPPER

KM#	Date	Mintage	VG	Fine	VF	XF
15	1908	.224	4.00	7.50	11.50	18.50
	1908	—	—	—	Proof	185.00

KM#	Date	Mintage	VG	Fine	VF	XF
16	1912	.224	2.50	4.50	8.50	12.50
	1912	—	—	—	Proof	175.00

SAILANA FEUDATORY STATE
BARMAWAL
RULER
Raja Handa Singh

PAISA

COPPER

KM#	Date	Year	Good	VG	Fine	VF
1	ND	—	3.50	6.00	9.00	13.50

NOTE: Y#1 was struck prior to 1881AD.

SIKHS
Refer to Sikh Empire, Independent Kingdom during British rule.

SIKKIM
Refer to Independent Kingdom during British rule.

SIND
Refer to Independent Kingdom during British rule.

SIROHI
Formerly Rajputana States Agency; merged in Rajasthan State, except for the tehsils (districts) of Abu Road and Dilawara which were merged with Bombay. Bordered on the north, northeast and west by Jodhpur; on the south by Palanpur, Danta and Idar; and on the east by Mewar.

While the ruling family claims descent from Prithwiraj, the Chauhan King of Delhi, the actual founder of the Sirohi house was one Deoraj, a 13th century figure who was the progenitor of the Deora clan of Rajputs. The present capital, Sirohi, was founded in 1425, about which time the Rana of Chitor is said to have taken refuge at Mount Abu from the army of Kutb-ud-din of Gujarat. The British entered by treaty in 1823, disallowed the claims of Jodhpur to Sirohi lands, ultimately bringing the Minas to submission and the straying thakurs back into line.

RULER
Sheo Singh, VS1873-1919/1816-1862AD

1/4 ANNA

COPPER, 9.75-10.90 g
Rev. leg: *Zarb Raj Sirohi*, scimitar.

Y#	Date	Year	VG	Fine	VF	XF
34	VS1910	(1853)	3.50	5.50	8.50	12.50

NOTE: Previously listed under Jodhpur State.

SIRMUR
Sirmur Nahan

The ruling Rajput family of this Himalayan principality claimed descent from the Jaisalmir royal house and had ruled the region, located in north India, since the end of the eleventh century. From 1803 to 1815, Sirmur came under Gurkha control but on their expulsion by the British during the Nepal War, the original Rajput family was restored to their ancestral dominions as a British feudatory.

NOTE: For earlier issues, see Gurkhas.

RULERS
Fath Prakash, restored
VS1872-1890/1815-1833AD

SITAMAU

PAISA

COPPER

C#	Date	Year	Good	VG	Fine	VF
30	VS1877	(1820)	7.50	12.50	20.00	30.00

SITAMAU
Sitamau, in western Malwa, was founded in 1695 by Raja Kesho Das, a scion of the Rathor rulers of Ratlam. Sitamau was tributary to Sindhia before passing under British protection and control in the nineteenth century.

RULERS
Raja Ram Singh
  VS1859-1924/1802-1867AD
Bahadur Singh
  VS1942-1956/1885-1899AD
Shardul Singh
  VS1956-1957/1899-1900AD

RAJA RAM SINGH
VS1859-1924/1802-1867AD

PAISA

COPPER, 18-20mm

KM#	Date	Year	Good	VG	Fine	VF
1	1844	—	4.50	7.00	10.00	13.50

BAHADUR SINGH
VS1942-1956/1885-1899AD

1/2 PAISA

COPPER

3	ND	—	4.50	7.00	10.00	13.50

PAISA

COPPER

4 (Y4)	VS1948	(1891)	3.00	5.00	7.50	11.50

SHARDUL SINGH
VS1956-1957/1899-1900AD

1/2 PAISA

COPPER, 16-18mm

5 (Y5)	VS1956	(1899)	4.50	7.00	10.00	13.50

NOTE: Varieties exist.

TONK
Tunk

State located partially in Rajputana and in central India. Tonk was founded in 1806 by Amir Khan (d. 1834), the Pathan Pindari leader, who received the territory from Holkar. Amir Khan caused great havoc in Central India by his lightning raids into neighboring states. In 1817 he was forced into submission by the East India Company and remained under British control until India's independence. In March 1948 Tonk was incorporated into Rajasthan.

RULERS
Amir Khan
  AH1213-1250/1798-1834AD
Wazir Muhammad Khan
  AH1250-1281/1834-1864AD
Muhammad Ali Khan
  AH1280-1284/1864-1867AD
Muhammad Ibrahim Ali Khan
  AH1284-1349/1868-1930AD
Muhammad Sa'adat Ali Khan
  AH1349-1368/1930-1949AD

MINT MARKS

Sironj سرونج

Tonk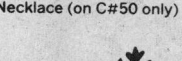

Necklace (on C#50 only)

Flower (on all)

Leaf (several forms)

Beginning with the reign of Muhammad Ibrahim Ali Khan, most coins have both AD and AH dates. Circulation coins with both dates fully legible are worth about 20 per cent more than listed prices. Coins with one date fully legible are worth prices shown. Coins with both dates off are of little value.

There are many minor and major variations of type, varying with location of date, orientation of leaf, arrangement of legend. Although these fall into easily distinguished patterns, they are strictly for the specialist and are omitted here.

SIRONJ MINT
Mughal Issues
In the name of Muhammad Akbar II
AH1221-1253 / 1806-1837AD

PAISA
COPPER, 23mm
Rev: Jhar.

C#	Date	Year	Good	VG	Fine	VF
45	AH1225	—	6.00	10.00	15.00	25.00

Rev: Horse.
| 45a | AH1226 | — | 8.00 | 12.50 | 20.00 | 30.00 |

Rev: Uncertain symbols.
| 45c | AH1247 | — | 4.00 | 6.50 | 10.00 | 17.50 |

Rev: Rosette & katar.
| 45d | AH1250 | — | 4.00 | 6.50 | 10.00 | 17.50 |

20-21mm
Rev: Rosette & pearl loop.
50	AH1252	—	3.50	5.50	8.50	14.00
	1253	—	3.50	5.50	8.50	14.00
	1269	—	3.50	5.50	8.50	14.00

1/4 RUPEE
SILVER, 13mm, 2.68-2.90 g

C#	Date	Year	VG	Fine	VF	XF
58	AH1253	—	7.50	12.50	20.00	30.00

1/2 RUPEE

SILVER, 5.35-5.80 g
| 59 | AH1253 | — | 7.50 | 12.50 | 20.00 | 30.00 |
| | 1267 | — | 7.50 | 12.50 | 20.00 | 30.00 |

RUPEE

SILVER, 10.70-11.60 g
60	AH1219	—	8.50	12.50	17.50	25.00
	1221	—	8.50	12.50	17.50	25.00
	1228	—	8.50	12.50	17.50	25.00
	1233	—	8.50	12.50	17.50	25.00
	1235	—	8.50	12.50	17.50	25.00
	1243	—	8.50	12.50	17.50	25.00
	1245	—	8.50	12.50	17.50	25.00
	1252	—	8.50	12.50	17.50	25.00
	1253	31	8.50	12.50	17.50	25.00
	1264	—	8.50	12.50	17.50	25.00
	1269	—	8.50	12.50	17.50	25.00

Regal Issues
In the names of Queen Victoria and Wazir Muhammad Khan
AH1250-1281 / 1834-1864AD

PAISA
COPPER, 18-20mm
Y#	Date	Year	Good	VG	Fine	VF
1	AH1278	—	4.00	6.25	10.00	16.50

RUPEE

SILVER, 10.70-11.60 g
Y#	Date	Year	VG	Fine	VF	XF
2	AH1276	—	11.50	16.50	23.50	35.00
	1277	—	11.50	16.50	23.50	35.00
	1280	—	11.50	16.50	23.50	35.00

In the names of Queen Victoria and Muhammad Ali Khan
AH1281-1285 / 1864-1867AD

PAISA
COPPER, 23-24mm
Y#	Date	Year	Good	VG	Fine	VF
3	AH1283	—	3.00	5.00	7.50	12.50
	1285	—	3.00	5.00	7.50	12.50
	1286	—	3.00	5.00	7.50	12.50
	1288	—	3.00	5.00	7.50	12.50
	1289	—	3.00	5.00	7.50	12.50

1/8 RUPEE
SILVER, 12mm, 1.34-1.45 g
| 4 | ND (off flan) | — | 7.50 | 12.50 | 20.00 | 30.00 |

1/4 RUPEE
SILVER, 15mm, 2.68-2.90 g
| 5 | AH1289 | — | 7.50 | 12.50 | 20.00 | 30.00 |

1/2 RUPEE
SILVER, 16-17mm, 5.35-5.80 g
Y#	Date	Year	VG	Fine	VF	XF
6	AH1289	—	8.50	12.50	20.00	30.00

RUPEE

SILVER, 10.70-11.60 g
7	AH1282	—	13.50	20.00	27.50	40.00
	1286	—	13.50	20.00	27.50	40.00
	1288	—	13.50	20.00	27.50	40.00
	1289	—	13.50	20.00	27.50	40.00
	1296	—	13.50	20.00	27.50	40.00
	—	1891	13.50	20.00	27.50	40.00

In the names of Victoria Empress and Muhammad Ibrahim Ali Khan
AH1285-1348 / 1867-1930AD

PIE

COPPER, 16mm
Y#	Date	Year	Good	VG	Fine	VF
11	AH1314					

PAISA
COPPER, 23mm
12	AH1298	—	3.50	6.00	10.00	16.50
	1299	—	3.50	6.00	10.00	16.50
	1302	—	3.50	6.00	10.00	16.50
	1308	—	3.50	6.00	10.00	16.50

1/4 RUPEE
SILVER, about 12mm, 2.68-2.90 g
Y#	Date	Year	VG	Fine	VF	XF
13	AH1314	1896	10.00	16.50	22.50	35.00

1/2 RUPEE
SILVER, about 16mm, 5.35-5.80 g
| 14 | AH1310 | 1893 | 10.00 | 16.50 | 22.50 | 35.00 |
| | 1314 | 1896 | 10.00 | 16.50 | 22.50 | 35.00 |

RUPEE

SILVER, 10.70-11.60 g
Y#	Date	Year	VG	Fine	VF	XF
15	AH1299	—	13.50	18.50	26.50	37.50
	1303	—	13.50	18.50	26.50	37.50
	1304	23	13.50	18.50	26.50	37.50
	1306	—	13.50	18.50	26.50	37.50
	1309	1892	13.50	18.50	26.50	37.50
	1310	1893	13.50	18.50	26.50	37.50

In the name of Queen Victoria and Muhammad Ibrahim Ali Khan

TONK MINT
NOTE: All coins with both AH and AD dates clearly readable command about a 50 per cent premium.

PAISA

COPPER
Y#	Date	Year	Good	VG	Fine	VF
8	AH1290	—	3.50	6.00	10.00	17.50

1/8 RUPEE
SILVER, 1.34-1.45 g
Y#	Date	Year	VG	Fine	VF	XF
9	AH-	—	8.50	13.50	20.00	30.00

RUPEE

SILVER, 10.70-11.60 g
10	—	1873	12.50	16.50	21.50	28.50
	AH1290	1873	12.50	16.50	21.50	27.50
	1290	187x	12.50	16.50	21.50	28.50
	1292	187x	12.50	16.50	21.50	28.50
	1293	187x	12.50	16.50	21.50	28.50
	1294	187x	12.50	16.50	21.50	28.50
	1293	1876	12.50	16.50	21.50	28.50
	1294	1877	12.50	16.50	21.50	28.50

NOTE: Var. 1, illustrated above, has no leaf, but a branch on obverse. All others have the leaf, as on the 1 Paisa, Y#8. Six varieties are known.

In the names of Victoria Empress and Muhammad Ibrahim Ali Khan

PAISA

COPPER
Y#	Date	Year	Good	VG	Fine	VF
16	AH1290	187x	1.75	3.25	5.00	8.00
	1292	1876	1.75	3.25	5.00	8.00
	1294	1877	1.75	3.25	5.00	8.00
	1295	187x	1.50	3.00	4.00	6.50
	1298	1880	1.50	3.00	4.00	6.50
	1298	1881	1.50	3.00	4.00	6.50
	1302	1885	1.00	2.50	3.50	5.50
	1303	1885	1.00	2.50	3.50	5.50
	1303	1886	1.00	2.50	3.50	5.50

NOTE: 4 varieties are known.

1/8 RUPEE

SILVER, 1.34-1.45 g
Y#	Date	Year	VG	Fine	VF	XF
17	AH1309	1892	6.00	8.50	12.50	20.00
	1317	1899	6.00	8.50	12.50	20.00

Tonk / INDIAN PRINCELY STATES 954

1/4 RUPEE

SILVER, 14-15mm, 2.68-2.90 g

Y#	Date	Year	VG	Fine	VF	XF
18	AH1305	1888	6.00	8.50	12.50	20.00
	1309	1892	6.00	8.50	12.50	20.00
	1316	189x	6.00	8.50	12.50	20.00
	1317	1899	6.00	8.50	12.50	20.00
	1318	1xxx	6.00	8.50	12.50	20.00

1/2 RUPEE

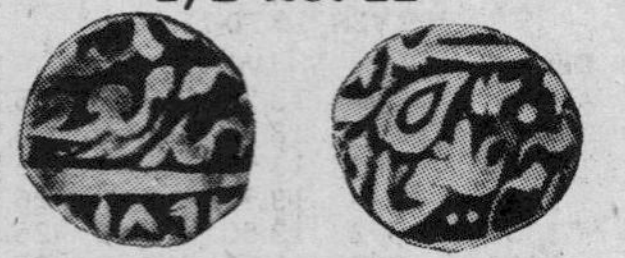

SILVER, 5.35-5.80 g

Y#	Date	Year	VG	Fine	VF	XF
19	AH129x	1882	8.00	10.00	13.50	20.00
	1305	1888	8.00	10.00	13.50	20.00
	1209	1892	8.00	10.00	13.50	20.00
	1309	1892	8.00	10.00	13.50	20.00
	1317	1899	8.00	10.00	13.50	20.00

RUPEE

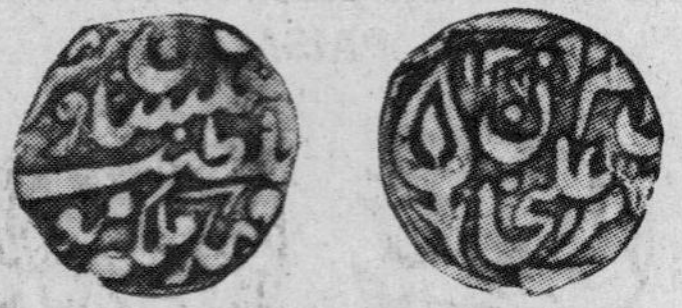

SILVER, 10.70-11.60 g

Y#	Date	Year	VG	Fine	VF	XF
20	AH1293	1876	7.50	10.00	12.50	20.00
	1294	187x	7.50	10.00	12.50	20.00
	1295	187x	7.50	10.00	12.50	20.00
	1295	1878	7.50	10.00	12.50	21.50
	1296	1879	7.50	10.00	12.50	20.00
	1297	1879	7.50	10.00	12.50	20.00
	1297	1880	7.50	10.00	12.50	20.00
	1298	1881	7.50	10.00	12.50	20.00
	1299	1879	7.50	10.00	12.50	20.00
	1301	1884	7.50	10.00	12.50	20.00
	1302	1884	7.50	10.00	12.50	20.00
	1303	188x	—	Reported, not confirmed		
	1304	1887	7.50	10.00	12.50	20.00
	1305	1888	7.50	10.00	12.50	20.00
	1306	18xx	—	Reported, not confirmed		
	1308	1890	7.50	10.00	12.50	20.00
	1308	1891	7.50	10.00	12.50	20.00
	1309	1891	7.50	10.00	12.50	20.00
	1309	1892	7.50	10.00	12.50	20.00
	1310	189x	7.50	10.00	12.50	20.00
	1312	189x	7.50	10.00	12.50	20.00
	1313	1895	7.50	10.00	12.50	20.00
	1315	1897	7.50	10.00	12.50	20.00

NAZARANA 2 RUPEES

SILVER, 32mm, 21.40-23.20 g

Y#	Date	Year	VG	Fine	VF	XF
21	AH1297	1880	125.00	150.00	225.00	300.00
	1298	1881	125.00	150.00	225.00	300.00

MOHUR

GOLD, 19mm, 10.70-11.40 g

Y#	Date	Year	VG	Fine	VF	XF
22	AH1297	1880	200.00	250.00	325.00	400.00
	1298	188x	200.00	250.00	325.00	400.00

NAZARANA 2 MOHURS

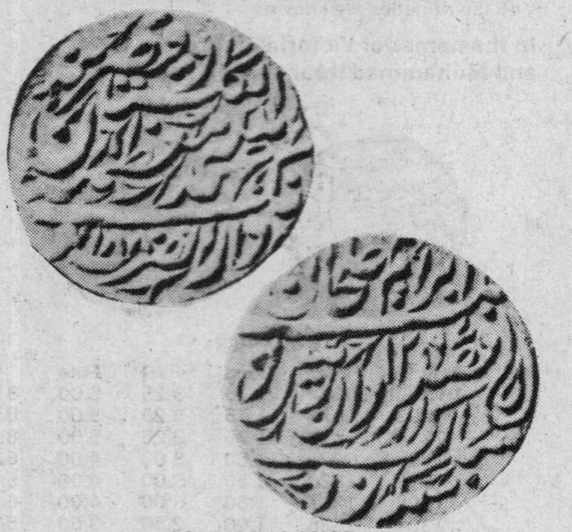

GOLD, 21.40-22.80 g

Y#	Date	Year	VG	Fine	VF	XF
23	AH1297	1880	350.00	600.00	800.00	1000.

In the names of George V and Muhammad Ibrahim Ali Khan

PAISA

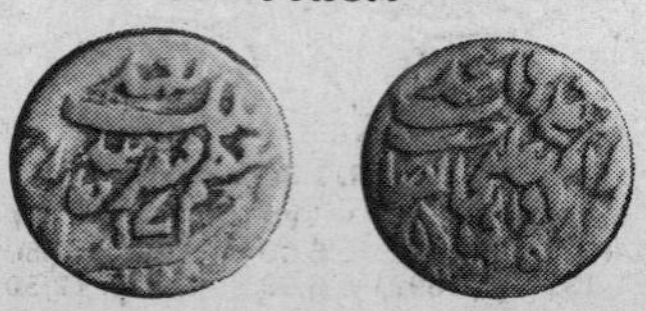

COPPER, 7.30 g

Y#	Date	Year	Good	VG	Fine	VF
24.1	AH1329	1911	1.25	2.00	3.00	4.50
	1329 (sic)	1329	1.25	2.00	3.00	4.50
	1911 (sic)	1911	—	—	—	—
	1329 (sic)	1917	—	—	—	—
	1330	1911	—	—	—	—
	1335	1917	—	—	—	—

Reduced weight, 5.00 g

Y#	Date	Year	Good	VG	Fine	VF
24.2	AH1342	1924	1.25	2.00	3.00	4.50
	1344	1925	1.25	2.00	3.00	4.50
	1344	1926	1.25	2.00	3.00	4.50
	1345	1927	1.25	2.00	3.00	4.50
	134x	1928	1.25	2.00	3.00	4.50

1/4 ANNA

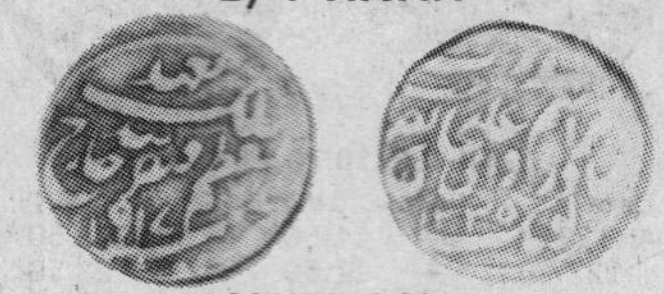

COPPER, 8.30 g

Y#	Date	Year	Good	VG	Fine	VF
A25.1	AH1335	1917	1.25	2.00	3.00	4.50
	1336	1917	1.25	2.00	3.00	4.50

Reduced weight, 5.40 g

Y#	Date	Year	Good	VG	Fine	VF
A25.2	AH1336	1917	—	—	—	—

1/8 RUPEE

SILVER, 11mm, 1.34-1.45 g

Y#	Date	Year	VG	Fine	VF	XF
25	AH1346	1928	4.50	7.50	11.50	18.50

1/4 RUPEE

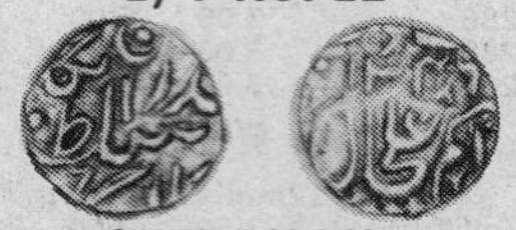

SILVER, 2.68-2.90 g

Y#	Date	Year	VG	Fine	VF	XF
26	AH1346	1928	7.50	10.00	13.50	21.50

1/2 RUPEE

SILVER, 16mm, 5.35-5.80 g

Y#	Date	Year	VG	Fine	VF	XF
27	AH1346	1928	9.00	15.00	22.50	32.50

RUPEE

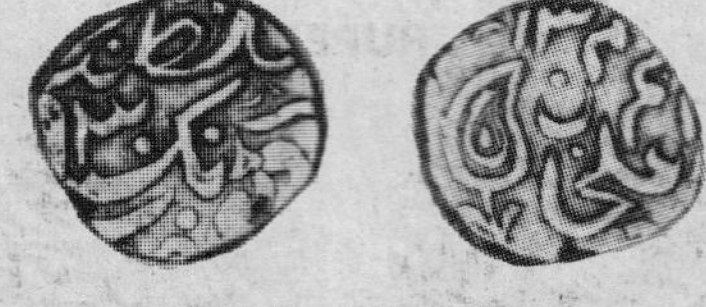

SILVER, 10.70-11.60 g

Y#	Date	Year	VG	Fine	VF	XF
28	AH1329	—	6.50	9.00	12.50	18.50
	1330	1912	6.50	9.00	12.50	18.50
	1341	1923	6.50	9.00	12.50	18.50
	1342	1924	6.50	9.00	12.50	18.50
	1343	1925	6.50	9.00	12.50	18.50
	1344	1925	6.50	9.00	12.50	18.50
	1344	1926	6.50	9.00	12.50	18.50
	1345	1926	6.50	9.00	12.50	18.50
	1346	1926	6.50	9.00	12.50	18.50
	1346	1927	6.50	9.00	12.50	18.50
	1347	1928	6.50	9.00	12.50	18.50
	1348	1928	6.50	9.00	12.50	18.50
	1348	1929	6.50	9.00	12.50	18.50
	134x	1930	6.50	9.00	12.50	18.50

In the names of George V and Muhammad Sa'adat Ali Khan

AH1348-1368/1930-1949AD

1/8 RUPEE

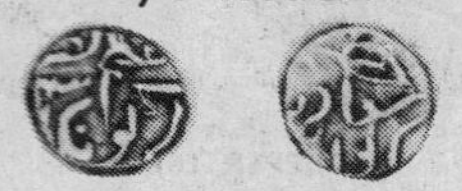

SILVER, 1.34-1.45 g

Y#	Date	Year	VG	Fine	VF	XF
30	AH1351	—	6.00	8.00	10.00	14.00
	1352	—	6.00	8.00	10.00	14.00
	1353	1934	6.00	8.00	10.00	14.00

Milled Coinage

PICE (PAISA)

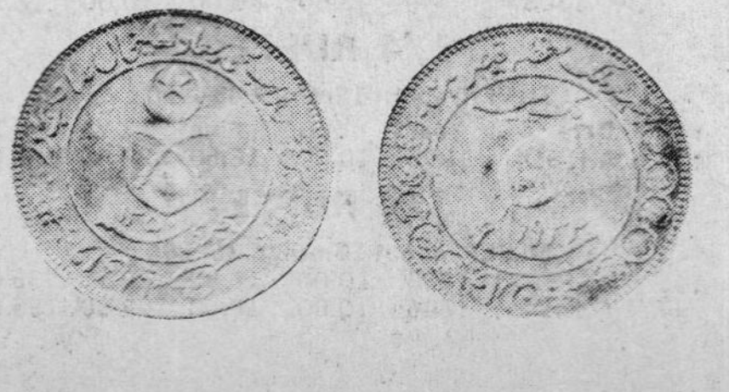

COPPER, 26mm

Y#	Date	Year	Mintage	Fine	VF	XF
29	AH1350	1932	.640	.75	1.25	2.00

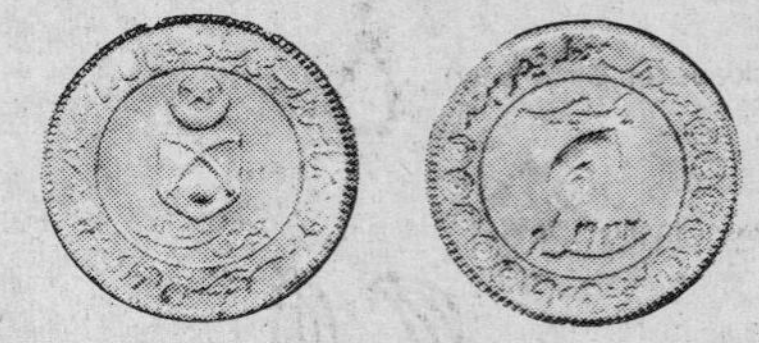

Y#	Date	Year	Mintage	Fine	VF	XF
29a	AH1350	1932	.640	.25	.50	1.00

TRAVANCORE

State located in extreme southwest India. A mint was established in ME965/1789-1790AD.

The region of Travancore had a lengthy history before being annexed by the Vijayanagar kingdom. With Vijayanagar's defeat at the battle of Talikota in 1565, Travancore passed under Muslim control until the late eighteenth century, when it merged as a state in its own right under Raja Martanda Varma. At this time the raja allied himself with British interests as a protection against the Muslim dynasty of Mysore. In 1795 the raja of Travancore officially accepted a subsidiary alliance with the East India Company, and remained within the orbit of British influence from then until India's independence.

RULERS

Bala Rama Varma I
ME973-986/1798-1810AD
Rani Parvathi Bai, regent
ME990-1004/1815-1829AD
Rama Varma III
ME1004-1022/1829-1847AD
Martanda Varma II
ME1022-1035/1847-1860AD
Rama Varma IV
ME1035-1055/1860-1880AD
Rama Varma V
ME1057-1062/1880-1885AD
Rama Varma VI
ME1062-1101/1885-1924AD
Bala Rama Varma II
ME1101-1126/1924-1949AD

MONETARY SYSTEM

16 Cash (Kasu) = 1 Chuckram
4 Chuckram = 1 Fanam
2 Fanams = 1 Anantaraya
7 Fanams = 1 Rupee
52-1/2 Fanam = 1 Pagoda

DATING

ME dates are of the Malabar Era. Add 824 or 825 to the ME date for the AD date. (e.g., ME1112 plus 824-825 = 1936-1937AD).

BALA RAMA VARMA I

ME973-986/1798-1810AD

1/2 CHUCKRAM

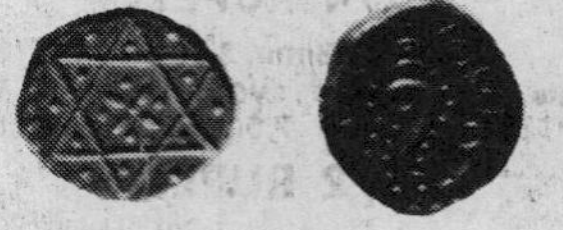

COPPER

KM#	Date	Year	Good	VG	Fine	VF
1	ND	—	2.00	4.00	6.50	11.50

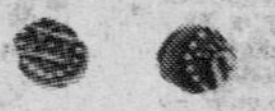

SILVER

C#	Date	Year	VG	Fine	VF	XF
10	ND	(1809-10)	2.50	4.00	5.50	8.00

CHUCKRAM

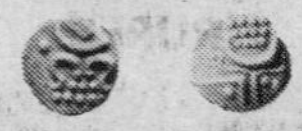

SILVER

C#	Date	Year	VG	Fine	VF	XF
11	ND (1600-1860)		.75	1.25	1.75	2.50

2 CHUCKRAMS

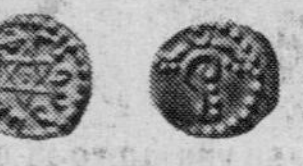

SILVER

C#	Date	Year	VG	Fine	VF	XF
12	ND	(1809-10)	5.00	8.50	11.50	16.50

1/2 ANANTARAYA

(Fanam)

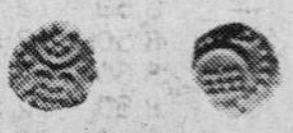

GOLD

C#	Date	Year	VG	Fine	VF	XF
19	ND (1790-1830)		6.00	8.50	12.50	20.00

ANANTARAYA

(2 Fanam)

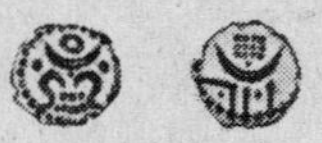

GOLD

C#	Date	Year	VG	Fine	VF	XF
22	ND	(1790-1860)	12.50	17.50	23.50	30.00

NOTE: For similar coins with leaf sprays on the obverse see Yeoman #11.

RANI PARVATHI BAI

Regent, ME990-1004/1815-1829AD

CASH

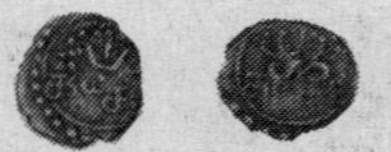

COPPER

C#	Date	Year	Good	VG	Fine	VF
25	ME991-7	(1815-21)	1.50	3.00	5.00	8.50

2 CASH

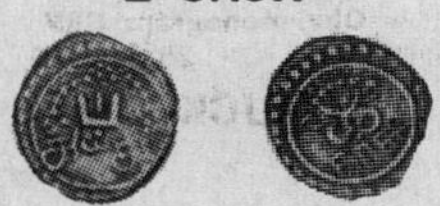

COPPER

26	ME991	(1815)	1.75	3.50	6.00	10.00
	ME997	(1821)	1.75	3.50	6.00	10.00

4 CASH

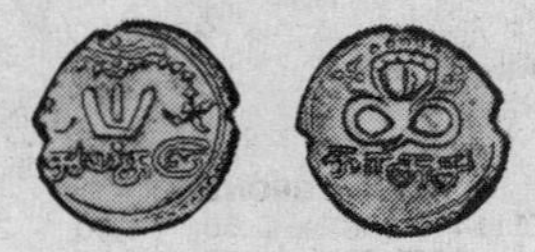

COPPER

27	ME991	(1815)	2.50	4.50	7.50	15.00

8 CASH

COPPER
Similar to 4 Cash, C#27.

28	ME991	(1814)	5.50	10.00	17.50	25.00

RAMA VARMA III

ME1004-1022/1829-1847AD

CASH

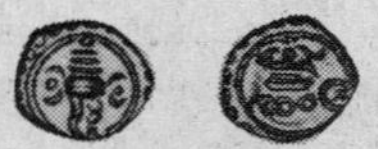

COPPER

36	ME1005	(1830)	1.00	1.75	2.50	5.00

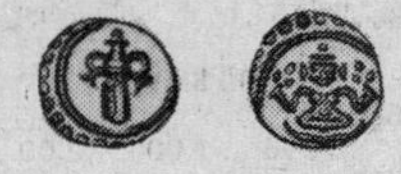

38	ND	(1830-39)	1.00	1.75	2.50	5.50

MARTANDA VARMA II

ME1004-1022/1847-1860AD

CASH

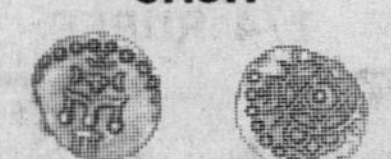

COPPER

Y#	Date	Year	Good	VG	Fine	VF
1	ND	(1848-60)	.50	1.00	1.50	2.25

2 CASH

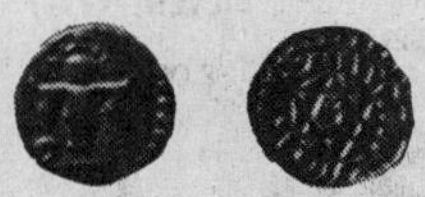

COPPER

2	ND	(1848-49)	1.00	2.00	3.00	4.50

4 CASH

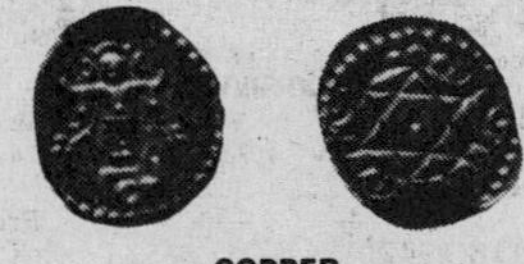

COPPER

3	ND		2.00	4.00	6.00	9.00

8 CASH

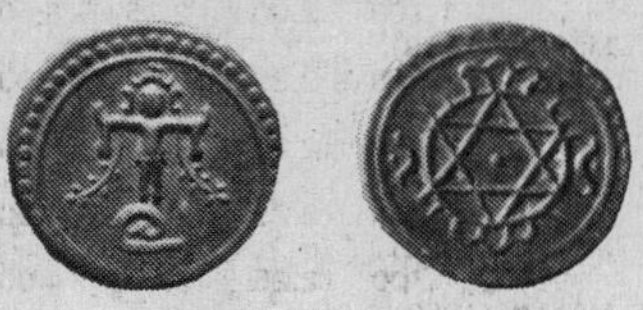

COPPER

Y#	Date	Year	Good	VG	Fine	VF
A4	ND		3.00	6.50	10.00	15.00

RAMA VARMA IV

ME1035-1055/1860-1880AD

CASH

COPPER, 8-10mm

1a	ND	(1860-85)	.25	.50	.75	1.25

CHUCKRAM

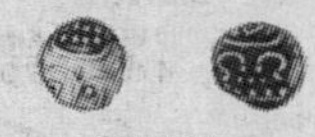

SILVER

8	ND	(1860-1901)	1.25	1.50	1.75	2.25

VELLI FANAM

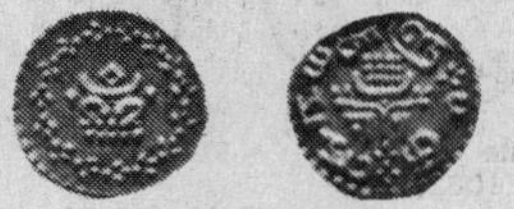

DUMP SILVER

Y#	Date	Year	VG	Fine	VF	XF
9	ND	(1860-61)	2.50	3.25	4.00	7.00

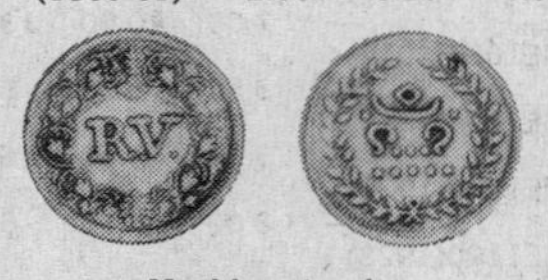

Machine-struck

10	ND	(1864)	2.25	3.00	3.75	6.50

ANATARAYA

(Fanam)

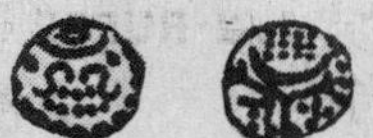

GOLD

11	ND	(1860-90)	9.00	11.50	14.00	17.50

1/2 PAGODA

GOLD

15	1877		35.00	65.00	100.00	140.00

PAGODA

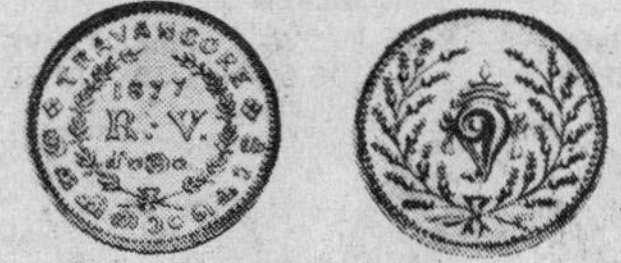

GOLD

16	1877		40.00	80.00	125.00	180.00

2 PAGODA

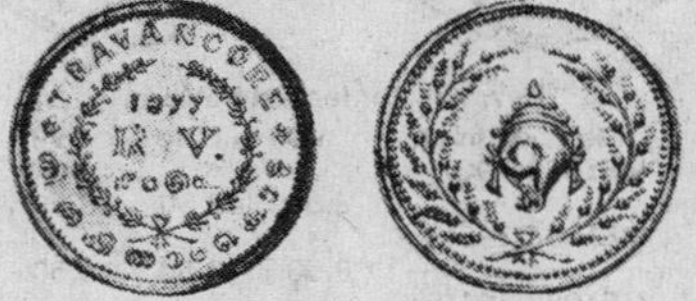

GOLD

17	1877		85.00	150.00	225.00	275.00

RAMA VARMA V

ME1057-1062/1880-1885AD

VIRARAYA FANAM

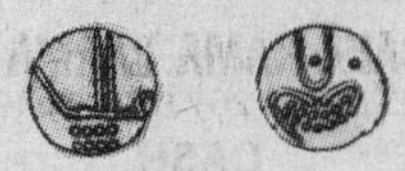

SILVER

18	ND	(1881)	1.75	2.50	3.50	5.00

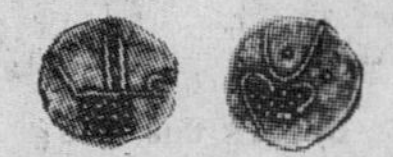

GOLD

19	ND	(1881)	7.00	8.50	11.50	15.00

1/2 SOVEREIGN

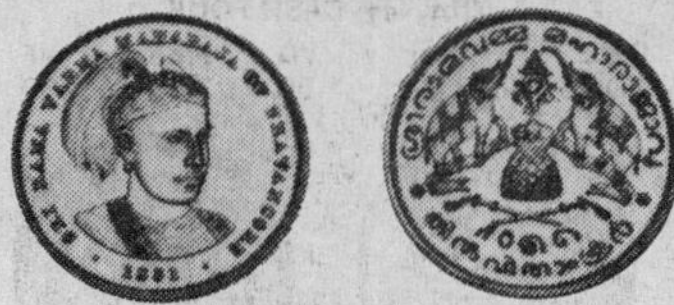

3.9940 g, .917 GOLD, .1177 oz AGW

Y#	Date	Year	Mintage	VF	XF	Unc
20	ME1057	1881	2,000	300.00	400.00	500.00
	WHITE METAL (OMS)					
20a	ME1057	1881	—	—	Proof	125.00

SOVEREIGN

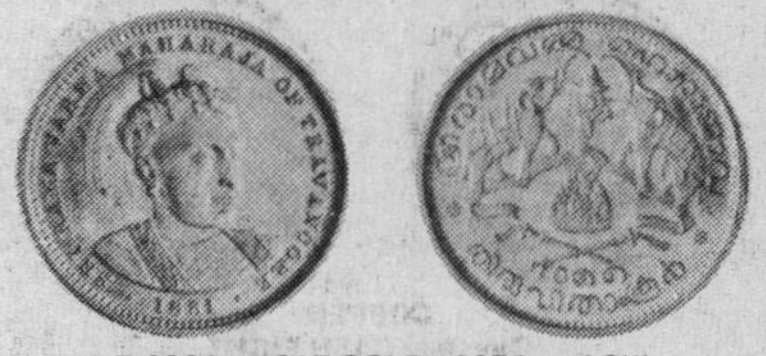

7.9881 g, .917 GOLD, .2354 oz AGW
Obv: Bust of Maharajah. Rev: Arms.

21	ME1057	1881	1,000	375.00	475.00	600.00
	WHITE METAL (OMS)					
21a	ME1057	1881	—	—	Proof	150.00

RAMA VARMA VI

ME1062-1101/1885-1924AD

Dump Coinage

CASH

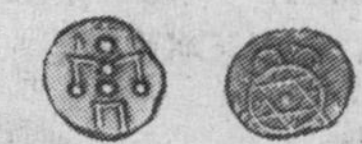

COPPER

Y#	Date	Year	Good	VG	Fine	VF
1b	ND	(1885-95)	.25	.50	.75	1.25

NOTE: Y# 1b is a rather degenerated copy of Y#1.

1/4 CHUCKRAM

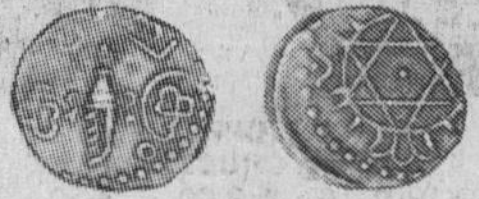

COPPER

22	ND	(1888-89)	1.25	2.00	2.75	5.50

1/2 CHUCKRAM

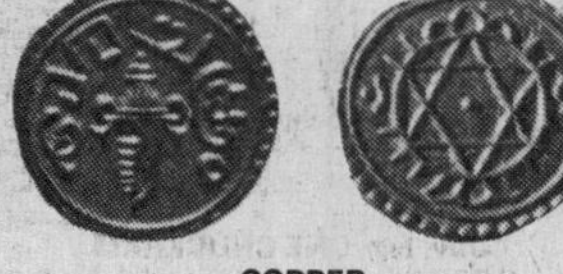

COPPER

23	ND(1888-89)		1.50	2.50	4.00	7.50

KALI FANAM

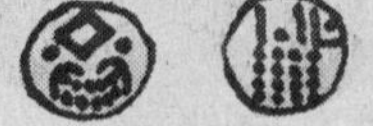

GOLD

Y#	Date	Year	VG	Fine	VF	XF
24	ND	(1890-95)	7.00	8.50	10.00	14.00

Milled Coinage

CASH

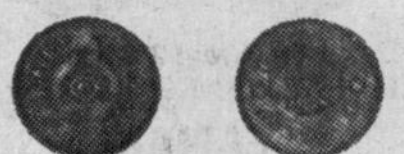

COPPER, 0.65 g
Obv. leg: CASH 1

29	ND	(1901)	5.00	10.00	20.00	30.00
	COPPER, thick, 0.65g					
41.1	ND	—	.25	.50	.75	1.25

NOTE: Refer to Bala Rama Varma II listings for thin variety.

4 CASH

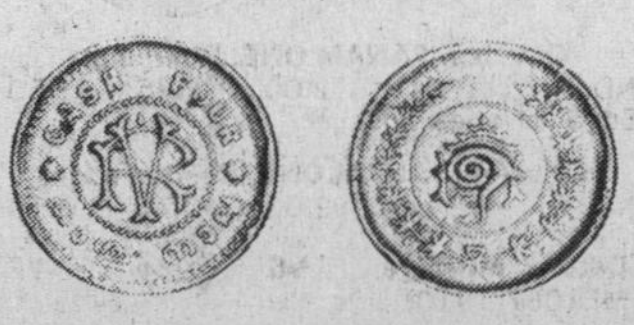

Travancore / INDIAN PRINCELY STATES 956

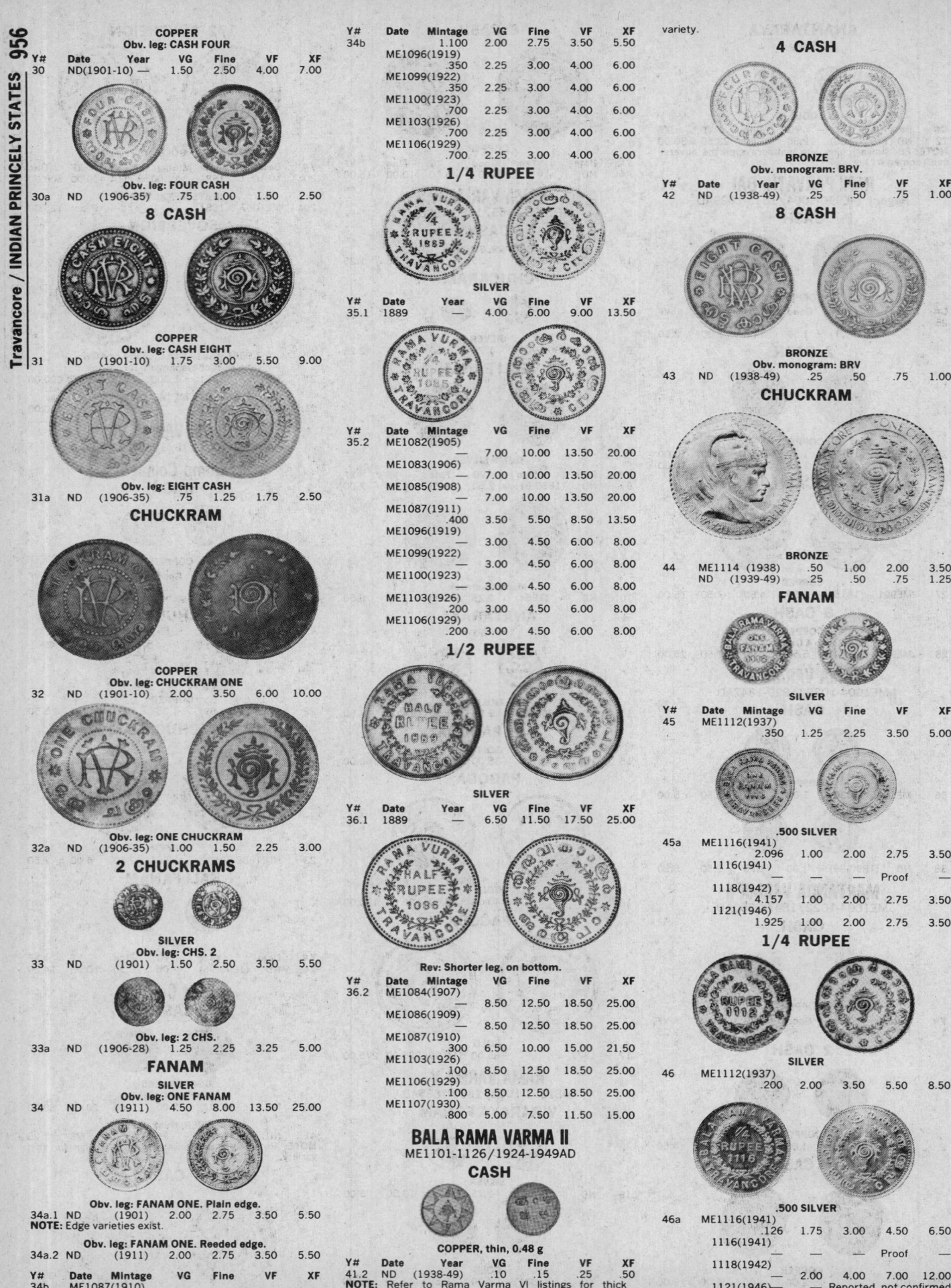

COPPER
Obv. leg: CASH FOUR

Y#	Date	Year	VG	Fine	VF	XF
30	ND(1901-10)	—	1.50	2.50	4.00	7.00

Obv. leg: FOUR CASH

| 30a | ND | (1906-35) | .75 | 1.00 | 1.50 | 2.50 |

8 CASH

COPPER
Obv. leg: CASH EIGHT

| 31 | ND | (1901-10) | 1.75 | 3.00 | 5.50 | 9.00 |

Obv. leg: EIGHT CASH

| 31a | ND | (1906-35) | .75 | 1.25 | 1.75 | 2.50 |

CHUCKRAM

COPPER
Obv. leg: CHUCKRAM ONE

| 32 | ND | (1901-10) | 2.00 | 3.50 | 6.00 | 10.00 |

Obv. leg: ONE CHUCKRAM

| 32a | ND | (1906-35) | 1.00 | 1.50 | 2.25 | 3.00 |

2 CHUCKRAMS

SILVER
Obv. leg: CHS. 2

| 33 | ND | (1901) | 1.50 | 2.50 | 3.50 | 5.50 |

Obv. leg: 2 CHS.

| 33a | ND | (1906-28) | 1.25 | 2.25 | 3.25 | 5.00 |

FANAM

SILVER
Obv. leg: ONE FANAM

| 34 | ND | (1911) | 4.50 | 8.00 | 13.50 | 25.00 |

Obv. leg: FANAM ONE. Plain edge.

| 34a.1 | ND | (1901) | 2.00 | 2.75 | 3.50 | 5.50 |

NOTE: Edge varieties exist.

Obv. leg: FANAM ONE. Reeded edge.

| 34a.2 | ND | (1911) | 2.00 | 2.75 | 3.50 | 5.50 |

Y#	Date	Mintage	VG	Fine	VF	XF
34b	ME1087(1910)	1.100	2.00	2.75	3.50	5.50
	ME1096(1919)	.350	2.25	3.00	4.00	6.00
	ME1099(1922)	.350	2.25	3.00	4.00	6.00
	ME1100(1923)	.700	2.25	3.00	4.00	6.00
	ME1103(1926)	.700	2.25	3.00	4.00	6.00
	ME1106(1929)	.700	2.25	3.00	4.00	6.00

1/4 RUPEE

SILVER

Y#	Date	Year	VG	Fine	VF	XF
35.1	1889	—	4.00	6.00	9.00	13.50

Y#	Date	Mintage	VG	Fine	VF	XF
35.2	ME1082(1905)	—	7.00	10.00	13.50	20.00
	ME1083(1906)	—	7.00	10.00	13.50	20.00
	ME1085(1908)	—	7.00	10.00	13.50	20.00
	ME1087(1911)	.400	3.50	5.50	8.50	13.50
	ME1096(1919)	—	3.00	4.50	6.00	8.00
	ME1099(1922)	—	3.00	4.50	6.00	8.00
	ME1100(1923)	—	3.00	4.50	6.00	8.00
	ME1103(1926)	—	3.00	4.50	6.00	8.00
	ME1106(1929)	.200	3.00	4.50	6.00	8.00
		.200	3.00	4.50	6.00	8.00

1/2 RUPEE

SILVER

Y#	Date	Year	VG	Fine	VF	XF
36.1	1889	—	6.50	11.50	17.50	25.00

Rev: Shorter leg. on bottom.

Y#	Date	Mintage	VG	Fine	VF	XF
36.2	ME1084(1907)	—	8.50	12.50	18.50	25.00
	ME1086(1909)	—	8.50	12.50	18.50	25.00
	ME1087(1910)	.300	6.50	10.00	15.00	21.50
	ME1103(1926)	.100	8.50	12.50	18.50	25.00
	ME1106(1929)	.100	8.50	12.50	18.50	25.00
	ME1107(1930)	.800	5.00	7.50	11.50	15.00

BALA RAMA VARMA II
ME1101-1126/1924-1949AD

CASH

COPPER, thin, 0.48 g

Y#	Date	Year	VG	Fine	VF	XF
41.2	ND	(1938-49)	.10	.15	.25	—

NOTE: Refer to Rama Varma VI listings for thick variety.

4 CASH

BRONZE
Obv. monogram: BRV.

Y#	Date	Year	VG	Fine	VF	XF
42	ND	(1938-49)	.25	.50	.75	1.00

8 CASH

BRONZE
Obv. monogram: BRV

| 43 | ND | (1938-49) | .25 | .50 | .75 | 1.00 |

CHUCKRAM

BRONZE

| 44 | ME1114 (1938) | .50 | 1.00 | 2.00 | 3.50 |
| | ND (1939-49) | .25 | .50 | .75 | 1.25 |

FANAM

SILVER

Y#	Date	Mintage	VG	Fine	VF	XF
45	ME1112(1937)	.350	1.25	2.25	3.50	5.00

.500 SILVER

45a	ME1116(1941)	2.096	1.00	2.00	2.75	3.50
	1116(1941)	—	—	—	Proof	—
	1118(1942)	4.157	1.00	2.00	2.75	3.50
	1121(1946)	1.925	1.00	2.00	2.75	3.50

1/4 RUPEE

SILVER

| 46 | ME1112(1937) | .200 | 2.00 | 3.50 | 5.50 | 8.50 |

.500 SILVER

46a	ME1116(1941)	.126	1.75	3.00	4.50	6.50
	1116(1941)	—	—	—	Proof	—
	1118(1942)	—	2.00	4.00	7.00	12.00
	1121(1946)—	—	Reported, not confirmed			

1/2 RUPEE

SILVER

Y#	Date Mintage	VG	Fine	VF	XF
47	ME1112(1937) .200	5.00	7.50	11.50	16.50

1/2 CHITRA RUPEE

SILVER, reeded edge

| 47a | ME1114(1938/9) | 4.00 | 5.00 | 7.50 | 13.50 |

NOTE: Edge varieties exist.

.500 SILVER, Security edge

47b	ME1116(1941)				
	1.600	3.00	5.00	7.00	12.50
	1118/6(1942) 1.111	—	—	Rare	
	1118(1942) Inc. Ab.	3.00	5.00	7.00	12.50
	1118(1942)			Proof	
	1121(1946) .200	3.00	5.00	7.00	12.50

TULABHARAM MEDALLIC ISSUES (M)

These presentation coins were struck prior to the weighing in ceremony of the Maharajah. The balance of his weight in these gold coins were distributed amongst the learned Brahmins and are referred to as Tulabhara Kasu. The legend reads *Sri Patmanabha*, the National Deity.

1/4 PAGODA

GOLD, uniface, 8.8mm, 0.63 g
Obv: Tamil leg. in 3 lines.

KM#	Date	Year	Fine	VF	XF	Unc
M1 (C42)	ND	(1829,47)	50.00	70.00	100.00	150.00

Uniface, 12.7mm, 0.63 g
Obv: Tamil leg. in 3 lines.

| M5 (Y4) | ND | (1850,55) | 50.00 | 70.00 | 100.00 | 150.00 |

10.9-12.7mm
Obv: Conch shell within wreath.
Rev: Tamil leg. in 3 lines within wreath.

| M9 | ND | (1870-1931) | 45.00 | 65.00 | 90.00 | 135.00 |

1/2 PAGODA

GOLD, uniface, 10.9mm, 1.27 g
Obv: Tamil leg. in 3 lines.

| M2 (C43) | ND | (1829,47) | 60.00 | 80.00 | 110.00 | 165.00 |

Uniface, 14.5mm, 1.27 g
Obv: Tamil leg. in 3 lines.

| M6 (Y5) | ND | (1850,55) | 60.00 | 80.00 | 110.00 | 165.00 |

1.28 g

| M10 | ND | (1870-1931) | 55.00 | 75.00 | 100.00 | 165.00 |

PAGODA

GOLD, uniface, 13mm, 2.54 g
Obv: Tamil leg. in 3 lines.

| M3 (C44) | ND | (1829,47) | 100.00 | 135.00 | 175.00 | 235.00 |

Uniface, 17mm, 2.54 g
Obv: Tamil leg. in 3 lines.

KM#	Date	Year	Fine	VF	XF	Unc
M7 (Y6)	ND	(1850,55)	100.00	135.00	175.00	235.00

2.54 g

| M11 | ND | (1870-1931) | 90.00 | 125.00 | 150.00 | 200.00 |

2 PAGODAS

GOLD, uniface, 15.4mm, 5.06 g
Obv: Tamil leg. in 3 lines.

| M4 (C45) | ND | (1829,47) | 150.00 | 185.00 | 225.00 | 300.00 |

Uniface, 20.3mm, 5.06 g
Obv: Tamil leg. in 3 lines.

| M8 (Y7) | ND | (1850,55) | 150.00 | 185.00 | 225.00 | 300.00 |

20.0-23.9mm, 5.09 g
Obv: Conch shell within wreath.
Rev: Tamil leg. in 3 lines within wreath.

| M12 | ND | (1870-1931) | 125.00 | 170.00 | 200.00 | 265.00 |

TRIPURA
Hill Tipperah

Tripura was a Hindu Kingdom consisting of a strip of the fertile plains east of Bengal, and a large tract of hill territory beyond, which had a reputation for providing wild elephants.

At times when Bengal was weak, Tripura rose to prominence, and extended its rule into the plains, but when Bengal was strong the kingdom consisted purely of the hill area, which was virtually impregnable and not of enough economic worth to encourage the Muslims to conquer it. In this way Tripura was able to maintain its full independence until the 19th century.

The origins of the Kingdom are veiled in legend, but the first coins were struck during the reign of Ratna Manikya (1464-89) and copied the weight and fabric of the contemporary issues of the Sultans of Bengal. He also copied the lion design that had appeared on certain rare tangkas of Nasir-ud-din Mahmud Shah I dated AH849 (1445AD). In other respects the designs were purely Hindu, and the lion was retained on most of the later issues as a national emblem.

Tripura rose to a political zenith during the 16th century, while Muslim rule in Bengal was weak, and several coins were struck to commemorate successful military camps from Chittagong in the south to Sylhet in the north. These conquests were not sustained, and in the early 17th century the Mughal army was able to inflict severe defeats on Tripura, which was forced to pay tribute.

In about 1733AD all the territory in the plains was annexed by the Mughals, and the Raja merely managed his estate there as a zemindar, although he still retained control as independent King of his hill territory.

The situation remained unchanged when the British took over the administration of Bengal in 1765, and it was only in 1871 that the British appointed an agent in the hills, and began to assist the Maharaja in the administration of his hill territory, which became known as the State of Hill Tipperah.

After the middle of the 18th century, coins were not struck for monetary reasons, but merely for ceremonial use at coronations and other ceremonies, and to keep up the treasured right of coinage.

The coins of Tripura are unusual in that the majority have the name of the King together with that of his Queen, and is the only coinage in the world where this was done consistently.

In common with most other Hindu coinages of northeast India, the coins bear fixed dates. Usually the date used was that of the coronation ceremony, but during the 16th century, coins which were struck with a design commemorating a particular event, bore the date of that event, which can be useful as a historical source, where other written evidence is virtually non-existent.

All modern Tripura coins were presentation pieces, more medallic than monetary in nature. They were struck in very limited numbers and although not intended for local circulation, they are often found in worn condition.

RULERS
Rajadhara Manikya
SE1707-1726/1785-1804AD
Rama Ganga Manikya

राम गंगा मानिक्य

SE1728-1731,1735-1748/
1806-1809,1813-1826AD
Queens of Rama Ganga Manikya
Queen Tara
Queen Chandra Tara

চন্দ্র তরা

Durga Manikya

দুর্গা মানিক্য

SE1731-1735/1809-1813AD
Queen of Durga Manikya
Queen Sumitra

সুমিত্র

Kashi Chandra Manikya
SE1748-1752/1826-1830AD
Queens of Kashi Chandra Manikya
Queen Chandraveth
Queen Kirti Lakshmi
Krishna Kishore Manikya

কৃষ্ণ কিশোর মানিক্য

SE1752-1772/1830-1850AD
Queens of Krishna Kishore
Queen Bidumukhi
Queen Ratna Mala

রত্ন মালা

Queen Purnakala
Queen Sudhakshina
Ishana Chandra Manikya
SE1772-1784/1850-1862AD
Queens of Ishana Chandra Manikya
Queen Chandresvari
Queen Muktabani
Queen Rajalakshmi
Vira Chandra Manikya

বীর চন্দ্র মানিক্য

SE1784-1818/TE1272-1306/1862-1896AD
Queens of Vira Chandra Manikya
Queen Bhanumati

ভানুমতী

Queen Rajesvari

রাজেশ্বরী

Queen Manmohini
Radha Kishore Manikya
TE1306-1319/1896-1909AD
Queens of Radha Kishore
Queen Ratnaman Zari
Queen Tulsivati
Virendra Kishore Manikya
TE1319-1333/1909-1923AD
Queen of Virendra Kishore
Queen Prabhavati
Vira Vikrama Kishore Manikya

বীর বিক্রম কিশোর মানিক্য

TE1333-1357/1923-1947AD
Queens of Vira Vikrama Kishore Manikya
Queen Kanchan Prabha

কঞ্চন প্রভা

Queen Kirti Mani

DATING
While the early coinage is dated in the Saka Era (SE) the later issues are dated in the Tripurabda era (TE). To convert, TE date plus 590 = AD date. The dates appear to be accession years.

RAMA GANGA MANIKYA
SE1728-1731/1806-1809AD

RUPEE

SILVER, plain edge, 10.30-10.70 g
Rev. leg: W/Queen Tara

KM#	Date	Year	VG	Fine	VF	XF
259	SE1728	(1806)	40.00	60.00	85.00	110.00

Oblique edge milling

| 260 | SE1728 | (1806) | 80.00 | 100.00 | 125.00 | 150.00 |

MOHUR
GOLD

| 265 | SE1728 | (1806) | 300.00 | 400.00 | 500.00 | 600.00 |

DURGA MANIKYA
SE1731-1735/1809-1813AD

Tripura / INDIAN PRINCELY STATES

RUPEE

SILVER, 10.30-10.70 g
Rev. leg: W/*Srimati Sumitra Maha Devah*

KM#	Date	Year	VG	Fine	VF	XF
275	SE1731	(1809)	40.00	60.00	85.00	110.00

MOHUR
GOLD
| 280 | SE1731 | (1809) | 300.00 | 400.00 | 500.00 | 600.00 |

RAMA GANGA MANIKYA
SE1735-1748/1813-1826AD

RUPEE

SILVER, 10.30-10.70 g
Rev. leg: W/*Sri Srimati Chandra Tara Maha Devi*
| 290 | SE1743 | (1821) | 40.00 | 60.00 | 85.00 | 110.00 |

MOHUR
GOLD
| 295 | SE1743 | (1821) | 300.00 | 400.00 | 500.00 | 600.00 |

KASHI CHANDRA MANIKYA
SE1748-1752/1826-1830AD

RUPEE

SILVER, 10.30-10.70 g
Rev. leg: W/*Queen Chandravethi*
| 305 | SE1748 | (1826) | 80.00 | 100.00 | 125.00 | 150.00 |

Rev. leg: W/*Queen Kirti Lakshmi*
| 306 | SE1748 | (1826) | 80.00 | 100.00 | 125.00 | 150.00 |

KRISHNA KISHORA MANIKYA
SE1752-1772/1830-1850AD

RUPEE

SILVER, 10.30-10.70 g
Rev. leg: W/*Queen Bidumukhi* added.
| 316 | SE1752 | (1830) | 80.00 | 100.00 | 125.00 | 150.00 |

Rev. leg: W/*Queen Purnakala* added.
| 317 | SE1752 | (1830) | 80.00 | 100.00 | 125.00 | 150.00 |

Rev. leg: W/*Sri Srimati Ratna Mala Maha Deva*
KM#	Date	Year	VG	Fine	VF	XF
318	SE1752	(1830)	60.00	75.00	90.00	110.00

MOHUR
GOLD, 11.59 g
Rev. leg: W/*Queen Akhilesvari*
| 323 | SE1752 | (1830) | 300.00 | 400.00 | 500.00 | 600.00 |

Rev. leg: W/*Sri Srimati Ratna Mala Maha Deva*
| 324 | SE1752 | (1830) | 300.00 | 400.00 | 500.00 | 600.00 |

Rev. leg: W/*Queen Sudakshina* added.
| 325 | SE1752 | — | 300.00 | 400.00 | 500.00 | 600.00 |

ISHANA CHANDRA MANIKYA
SE1772-1784/1850-1862AD

RUPEE

SILVER, 10.30-10.70 g
Rev. leg: W/*Queen Chandresvari*
| 335 | SE1771 | (1849) | 60.00 | 75.00 | 90.00 | 110.00 |

Rev. leg: W/*Queen Muktavali*
| 336 | SE1771 | (1849) | 60.00 | 75.00 | 90.00 | 110.00 |

Rev. leg: W/*Queen Raja Lakshmi*
| 337 | SE1771 | (1849) | 60.00 | 75.00 | 90.00 | 110.00 |

MOHUR
GOLD
Rev. leg: W/*Queen Chandresvari*
| 342 | SE1771 | (1849) | 300.00 | 400.00 | 500.00 | 600.00 |

Rev. leg: W/*Queen Muktavali*
| 343 | SE1771 | (1849) | 300.00 | 400.00 | 500.00 | 600.00 |

Rev. leg: W/*Queen Raja Lakshmi*
| 344 | SE1771 | (1849) | 300.00 | 400.00 | 500.00 | 600.00 |

VIRA CHANDRA MANIKYA
SE1784-1818/TE1272-1306/1862-1896AD

RUPEE

SILVER, plain edge, 10.30-10.70 g
Rev. leg: W/*Sri Srimati Bhanumati Maha Devi*
| 354 | SE1791 | (1869) | 60.00 | 75.00 | 85.00 | 110.00 |

Machine struck, milled edge
KM#	Date	Year	VG	Fine	VF	XF
355	TE1279	(1869)	60.00	75.00	85.00	110.00

Rev. leg: W/*Queen Manamohini*
Hand struck.
| 356 | TE1279 | (1869) | 50.00 | 65.00 | 80.00 | 100.00 |

Rev. leg: W/*Sri Srimati Rajesvari Maha Devi*
Hand struck
| 357 | SE1791 | (1869) | 60.00 | 75.00 | 90.00 | 110.00 |

Machine struck
| 358 | TE1279 | (1869) | 50.00 | 65.00 | 80.00 | 100.00 |

MOHUR
GOLD
Similar to 1 Rupee, KM#354.
| 360 | SE1791 | (1869) | 250.00 | 300.00 | 400.00 | 500.00 |

Similar to 1 Rupee, KM#356.
| 363 | TE1279 | (1869) | 250.00 | 300.00 | 400.00 | 500.00 |

Rev. leg: W/*Srimati Sumitra Maha Devah.*
Similar to 1 Rupee, KM#357.
| 364 | SE1791 | (1869) | 300.00 | 400.00 | 500.00 | 600.00 |

RADHA KISHORE MANIKYA
TE1306-1319/1896-1909AD

1/2 RUPEE
SILVER
Rev. leg: W/*Queen Tulsiwati*
| 373 | TE1306 | (1896) | 50.00 | 70.00 | 100.00 | 140.00 |

RUPEE
SILVER, 11.30-11.90 g
Mule. Obv: KM#375. Rev: KM#356.
| 374 | TE1306 | (1896) | 70.00 | 85.00 | 110.00 | 140.00 |

Rev. leg: W/*Queen Ratna Manjari*
| 375 | TE1306 | (1896) | 50.00 | 70.00 | 100.00 | 140.00 |

 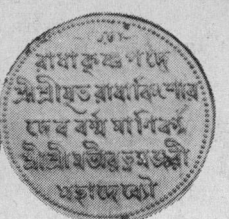

8.80 g
Rev. leg: W/Queen Tulsiwati

KM#	Date	Year	VG	Fine	VF	XF
376	TE1306	(1896)	40.00	60.00	85.00	110.00

MOHUR
GOLD

381	TE1306	(1896)	300.00	400.00	500.00	600.00

VIRENDRA KISHORE MANIKYA
TE1319-1333/1909-1923AD

MOHUR
GOLD
Rev. leg: W/Queen Prabhavati

396	TE1319	(1909)	300.00	400.00	500.00	600.00

VIRA VIKRAMA KISHORE MANIKYA
TE1333-1357/1923-1947AD

RUPEE

SILVER, milled edge, 11.30-11.90 g

406	TE1337	(1930)	25.00	35.00	50.00	70.00

NOTE: Varieties exist.

Security edge

407	TE1337	(1930)	40.00	60.00	90.00	110.00

Rev. leg: W/Queen Kirti Mani

408	TE1341	(1934)	40.00	60.00	85.00	110.00

Rev. leg: W/Sri Srimati Maharani Kanchan Prabha Maha Devi.

409	TE1341	(1934)	20.00	30.00	40.00	52.50

European Influences In India

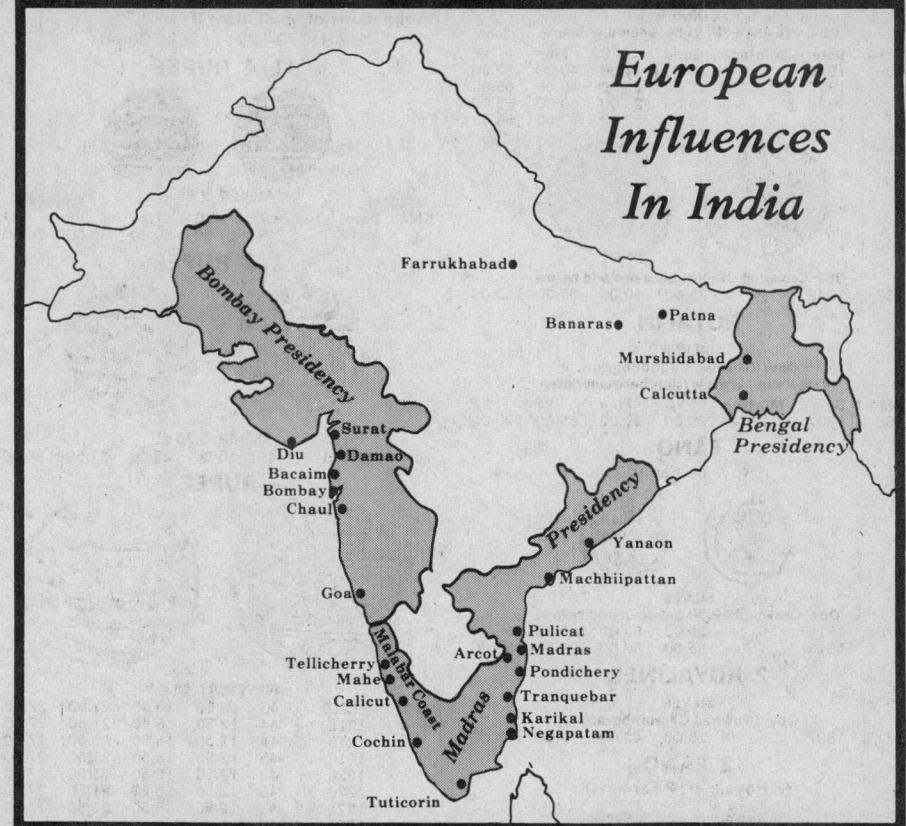

INDIA-DANISH

TRANQUEBAR

Danish India or Tranquebar is a town and former Danish colony on the southeast coast of India. In Danish times, 1620-1845, it was a factory site and seaport operated by the Danish Asiatic Company. Tranquebar and the other Danish settlements in India were sold to the British East India Company in 1845.

RULERS
Danish until 1845

MONETARY SYSTEM
80 Kas (Cash) = Royaliner (Fano or Fanam)
8 Royaliner = 1 Rupee
18 Royaliner = 1 Speciesdaler

DANISH ROYAL COLONY

KAS

COPPER, 0.52 g
Obv: Crowned FVIR monogram.
Rev: Value, date below.

KM#	Date	Mintage	Good	VG	Fine	VF
151	1816	—			Rare	
	1819	—	15.00	25.00	40.00	65.00

IV KAS
COPPER, 2.75 g

155	1807	—	6.50	11.50	21.50	33.50

Obv: Crowned FR, VI below.

158	1815	—	6.50	10.00	17.50	27.50
	1816	—	6.00	9.00	16.50	26.50
	1817	—	7.00	11.00	18.50	28.50
	1820	—	6.00	9.00	16.50	26.50
	1821	—	20.00	32.50	50.00	80.00
	1822	—	6.00	9.00	16.50	26.50
	1823	—	5.50	8.50	15.00	25.00
	1824	—	5.50	8.50	15.00	25.00

Obv: Crown design standardized.

KM#	Date	Mintage	Good	VG	Fine	VF
159.1	1824	—	6.00	9.00	16.00	27.50
	1825	—	7.50	12.50	20.00	35.00
	1830	—	6.50	10.00	18.50	30.00
	1831	—	5.50	8.50	15.00	25.00
	1832	—	5.50	8.50	15.00	25.00
	1833	—	5.50	8.50	15.00	25.00
	1834	—	5.50	8.50	15.00	25.00
	1837	—	3.00	6.00	15.00	25.00
	1838	—	3.00	6.00	15.00	25.00
	1839	—	3.00	6.00	15.00	25.00

Rev: Retrograde S in KAS.

159.2	1817	—	6.00	9.00	15.00	25.00
	1831	—	12.50	20.00	32.50	50.00

160	1824	—	25.00	35.00	60.00	100.00

Obv: Crowned C VIII R monogram.

161	1840	—	3.50	7.00	17.50	27.50
	1841	—	3.50	7.00	17.50	27.50
	1842	—	3.50	7.00	17.50	27.50
	1843	—	3.50	7.00	17.50	27.50
	1844	—	5.00	9.00	22.50	33.50

Obv: Crowned CR monogram.

162	1844	—	3.00	7.00	15.00	25.00
	1845	—	4.00	9.00	20.00	35.00

10 KAS

COPPER
Obv: Crowned FR, VI between and below.

KM#	Date	Mintage	Good	VG	Fine	VF
166	1816	—	15.00	25.00	40.00	65.00
	1822	—	15.00	25.00	40.00	65.00
	1838	—	15.00	25.00	40.00	65.00
	1839	—	13.50	22.50	37.50	60.00

Obv: Crowned CR, VIII between and below.

| 167 | 1842 | — | 25.00 | 40.00 | 65.00 | 100.00 |

ROYALIN
SILVER
Obv: Crowned C7 monogram.
Rev: Value, arms w/lion between date.

KM#	Date	Mintage	VG	Fine	VF	XF
168	1807	—	20.00	35.00	65.00	100.00

FANO
(Royalin, Fanam)

SILVER
Obv: Crowned FR, VI between and below.

| 170 | 1816 | — | 35.00 | 60.00 | 100.00 | 165.00 |
| | 1818 | — | 35.00 | 60.00 | 100.00 | 165.00 |

2 ROYALINER
SILVER
Obv: Crowned C7 monogram.

| 171 | 1807 | — | 25.00 | 40.00 | 75.00 | 125.00 |

2 FANO
(2 Royaliner, 2 Fanams)

SILVER
Obv: Crowned FR, VI between and below.

| 173 | 1816 | — | 50.00 | 80.00 | 125.00 | 200.00 |
| | 1818 | — | 50.00 | 80.00 | 125.00 | 200.00 |

INDIA-FRENCH

It was not until 1664, during the reign of Louis XIV, that the Compagnie des Indes Orientales was formed for the purpose of obtaining holdings on the subcontinent of India. Between 1666 and 1721, French settlements were established at Arcot, Mahe, Surat, Pondichery, Masulipatam, Karikal, Yanam, Murshidabad, Chandernagore, Balasore and Calicut. War with Britain reduced the French holdings to Chandernagore, Pondichery, Karikal, Yanam and Mahe. Chandernagore voted in 1949 to join India and became part of the Republic of India in 1950. Pondichery, Karikal, Yanam and Mahe formed the Pondichery union territory and joined the republic of India in 1954.

RULERS
French until 1945

MINTS
Arcot (Arkat)   اركات

Pondichery   پهلجري

Surat   سورت

MONETARY SYSTEM
Cache Kas or Cash
Doudou = 4 Caches
Biche = 1 Pice
2 Royalins = 1 Fanon Pondichery
5 Heavy Fanons = 1 Rupee Mahe
64 Biches = 1 Rupee
NOTE: The undated coinage was struck ca. 1720 well into the early 19th century.

ARCOT MINT
ARKAT

Mint mark: ☽

Crescent
A crescent moon mint mark is found to left of the regnal year for those struck at the Pondichery Mint. For listings of similar coins with lotus mint mark refer to India—British-Madras Presidency.

In the name of Shah Alam II
AH1173-1221/1759-1806AD

1/4 RUPEE

SILVER, 2.80 g

KM#	Date	Year	VG	Fine	VF	XF
13	AH1221	49	12.50	20.00	35.00	70.00

1/2 RUPEE

SILVER, 5.70 g

| 14 | AH1221 | 49 | 15.00 | 25.00 | 37.50 | 85.00 |

RUPEE

SILVER, 11.40 g

15	AH1218	43	12.50	16.50	21.50	27.50
	1218	44	12.50	16.50	21.50	27.50
	1219	44	12.50	16.50	21.50	27.50
	1219	45	12.50	16.50	21.50	27.50
	1220	43	12.50	16.50	21.50	27.50
	1220	45	12.50	16.50	21.50	27.50
	1221	43	12.50	16.50	21.50	27.50
	1221	49	—	Reported, not confirmed		

PONDICHERY MINT

A city south of Madras on the southeast coast which became the site of the French Mint from 1700 to 1841. Pondichery was settled by the French in 1683. It became their main Indian possession even though it was occupied by the Dutch in 1693-1698 and several times by the British from 1761-1816.

CACHE

BRONZE

KM#	Date	Mintage	Good	VG	Fine	VF
33	ND(1720-1835)	—	3.50	6.50	13.50	25.00

1/2 DOUDOU

COPPER, 2.10 g

| 34 | ND(1720-1835) | — | 2.50 | 5.00 | 8.50 | 15.00 |

DOUDOU

COPPER, 4.20 g

| 35 | ND(1720-1835) | — | 2.00 | 4.00 | 7.00 | 7.50 |

| 52 | 1836 | — | 3.50 | 6.50 | 13.50 | 25.00 |
| | 1837 | — | 3.50 | 6.50 | 13.50 | 25.00 |

1/2 FANON

SILVER, 0.50-0.70 g

KM#	Date	Mintage	VG	Fine	VF	XF
39	ND(1720-1837)	—	10.00	18.50	30.00	50.00
53	1837	—	16.50	28.50	45.00	75.00

FANON

SILVER, 1.500-1.593 g
Obv: Flowered crown.

| 45 | ND | — | 12.50 | 20.00 | 35.00 | 60.00 |

| 54 | 1837 | — | 16.50 | 28.50 | 45.00 | 75.00 |

2 FANON

SILVER, 2.20-2.76 g
Obv: Pearled crown.

| 48 | ND(1720-1837) | — | 16.50 | 28.50 | 45.00 | 75.00 |

Obv: Flowered crown.

| 49 | ND(1720-1837) | — | 16.50 | 28.50 | 45.00 | 75.00 |

| 55 | 1837 | — | 20.00 | 32.50 | 55.00 | 90.00 |

PAGODA

GOLD, 3.40 g
Obv: Flowered crown.

| 51 | ND(1830-48) | — | 225.00 | 300.00 | 350.00 | 400.00 |

SURAT MINT

The French silver coins struck similar to late Mughal issues in two different periods. See also India-British, Bombay Presidency.

1/2 RUPEE

In the name of Shah Alam II (posthumous)

SILVER, 5.70g

KM#	Date	Year	VG	Fine	VF	XF
75	AH122(5)	52	10.00	15.00	25.00	40.00
	Mintname off flan		5.00	7.50	12.50	20.00

NOTE: For listings of coins w/regnal year 46 see India-British, Bombay Presidency.

RUPEE

In the name of Shah Alam II (posthumous)

SILVER, 11.40g

76.1	AH122(4)	51	12.00	20.00	30.00	50.00
	122(5)	52	12.00	20.00	30.00	50.00
	122(6)	53	12.00	20.00	30.00	50.00
	1227	54	12.00	20.00	30.00	50.00
	Mintname off flan		6.00	10.00	15.00	25.00

NOTE: For listings of coins w/regnal year 46 see India-British, Bombay Presidency.

With symbol

KM#	Date	Year	VG	Fine	VF	XF
76.2	AH-	5x	—	—	—	—

INDIA - PORTUGUESE

Vasco da Gama, the Portuguese explorer, first visited India in 1498. Portugal seized control of a number of islands and small enclaves on the west coast of India, and for the next hundred years enjoyed a monopoly on trade. With the arrival of powerful Dutch and English fleets in the first half of the 17th century, Portuguese power in the area declined until virtually all of India that remained under Portuguese control were the west coast enclaves of Goa, Damao and Diu. They were forcibly annexed by India in 1962.

RULERS
Portuguese until 1961

IDENTIFICATION
The undated coppers are best identified by the shape of the coat of arms.

Maria I-Somewhat triangular shield (baroque style)
Joao VI, as Regent: oval shield
Joao VI, as King: square shield superimposed on globe
Maria II: square shield on plain background

DENOMINATION
The denomination of most copper coins appears in numerals on the reverse, though 30 Reis is often given as "1/2 T", and 60 Reis as "T" (T - Tanga). The silver coins have the denomination in words, usually on the obverse until 1850, then on the reverse.

DAMAO
(Daman)

A city located 100 miles north of Bombay. It was captured by the Portuguese in 1559. A mint was opened in Damao in 1611. This mint continued in operation until 1854. While important to early Portuguese trade, Damao dwindled as time passed. It was annexed to India in 1962.

MONETARY SYSTEM
375 Bazacucos = 300 Reis
300 Reis = 1 Pardao
60 Reis = 1 Tanga
2 Pardao (Xerafins) = 1 Rupia

3 REIS
COPPER
Similar to 60 Reis, KM#24.

KM#	Date	Mintage	Good	VG	Fine	VF
21	1834	—	—	—	—	—

15 REIS
COPPER
Similar to 60 Reis, KM#24.

22	1834	—	—	—	—	—

25	1843	—	3.50	7.00	12.50	21.50
26	1854	—	3.00	6.50	11.50	20.00

30 REIS

COPPER

23	1840	—	2.25	4.50	7.50	12.50

Similar to KM#23.

KM#	Date	Mintage	Good	VG	Fine	VF
27	1854	—	3.00	6.00	10.00	17.00

60 REIS

COPPER

24	1840	—	4.00	8.00	13.50	22.50

Similar to KM#24.

28	1854	—	—	—	—	—

DIU

A district in Western India formerly belonging to Portugal. It is 170 miles northwest of Bombay on the Kathiawar peninsula. The Portuguese settled here and built a fort in 1535. A mint was opened in 1685 and was closed in 1859. As with Damao, the importance of Diu diminished with the passage of time. It was annexed to India in 1962.

MONETARY SYSTEM
750 Bazarucos = 600 Reis
40 Atia = 10 Tanga = 1 Rupia

5 BAZARUCOS
LEAD or TIN, 20-23mm
Obv: Crude crowned arms.
Rev: Date in angles of cross.

44	1801	—	6.50	12.50	17.50	25.00

21mm
Similar to 20 Bazarucos, KM#47.

52	1807	—	12.50	25.00	35.00	50.00

20-22mm

56	1827	—	5.00	10.00	15.00	22.50
	1828	—	5.00	10.00	15.00	22.50

10 BAZARUCOS
LEAD or TIN, 27mm

57	1827	—	5.00	10.00	15.00	22.50
	1828	—	5.00	10.00	15.00	22.50

20 BAZARUCOS
TIN, 14.00-16.50 g

47	1801	—	6.00	12.00	20.00	30.00

33-36mm
Similar to KM#47.

53	1807	—	15.00	27.50	40.00	60.00

58	1827	—	5.00	10.00	17.50	26.50
	1828	—	5.00	10.00	17.50	26.50

30 REIS

COPPER

54	1818	—	6.00	11.00	18.00	40.00

60 REIS
COPPER

Similar to 30 Reis, KM#54.

KM#	Date	Mintage	Good	VG	Fine	VF
55	1818	—	7.50	15.00	23.50	50.00

150 REIS
SILVER
Obv: Crowned arms. Rev: Date in angles of cross.

50	1806	—	30.00	50.00	110.00	225.00

60	1859	—	20.00	35.00	70.00	150.00

300 REIS

SILVER

51	1806	—	25.00	40.00	100.00	200.00

61	1859	—	25.00	40.00	100.00	200.00

RUPIA
(600 Reis)
SILVER, 10.63 g
Obv: Crowned arms.
Rev: Date in angles of cross.

49	1804	—	75.00	125.00	250.00	500.00
	1805	—	75.00	125.00	250.00	500.00
	1806	—	75.00	125.00	250.00	500.00

59	1841	—	100.00	150.00	300.00	600.00

GOA

Goa was the capitol of Portuguese India and is located 250 miles south of Bombay on the west coast of India. It was taken by Albuquerque in 1510. A mint was established immediately and operated until closed by the British in 1869. Later coins were struck at Calcutta and Bombay. Goa was annexed by India in 1962.

MONETARY SYSTEM
375 Bazarucos = 300 Reis
240 Reis = 1 Pardao
2 Xerafim = 1 Rupia

NOTE: The silver Xerafim was equal to the silver Pardao, but the gold Xerafim varied according to fluctuations in the gold/silver ratio.

BASTARDO

TIN, 9.30 g
Obv: Arms; dots at sides; star and dots at top in circle.
Rev: Astrolabe in circle.

18	1845	—	4.00	7.00	12.50	25.00

3 REIS
COPPER
Similar to 6 Reis, KM#211.

209	ND	—	5.00	7.50	12.50	25.00

Similar to 4-1/2 Reis, KM#225.

224	ND	—	5.00	7.50	12.50	25.00

Portuguese / INDIA 962

KM#	Date	Mintage	Good	VG	Fine	VF
257	ND	—	5.00	10.00	17.50	35.00
	1842	—	5.00	10.00	17.50	35.00
	1844	—	5.00	10.00	17.50	35.00
	1845	—	5.00	10.00	17.50	35.00
	1846	—	5.00	10.00	17.50	35.00
	1848	—	5.00	10.00	17.50	35.00

4-1/2 REIS
COPPER
Similar to 6 Reis, KM#211.

| 210 | ND | — | 5.00 | 7.50 | 12.50 | 25.00 |

| 225 | ND | — | 5.00 | 7.50 | 12.50 | 25.00 |

258	ND	—	4.00	6.50	11.50	22.50
	1845	—	4.00	7.00	12.50	25.00
	1846	—	4.00	7.00	12.50	25.00
	1847	—	4.00	7.00	12.50	25.00
	1848	—	4.00	7.00	12.50	25.00

6 REIS

COPPER, 3.70-4.30 g

| 211 | ND | — | 6.00 | 10.00 | 15.00 | 30.00 |

| 226 | ND | — | 5.00 | 8.00 | 13.50 | 27.50 |

259	ND	—	4.00	7.00	12.50	25.00
	1845	—	4.00	7.00	12.50	25.00
	1846	—	4.00	7.00	12.50	25.00
	1847	—	4.00	7.00	12.50	25.00
	1848	—	4.00	7.00	12.50	25.00

7-1/2 REIS
COPPER, 4.80 g
Obv: Similar to 6 Reis, KM#211.
Rev. denomination: 7-1/2 REIS

| 212 | ND | — | 6.50 | 12.50 | 17.50 | 35.00 |

Rev. denomination: 7-2/4 REIS

| 213 | ND | — | 12.50 | 25.00 | 35.00 | 70.00 |

Obv: Similar to 6 Reis, KM#226.
Rev. denomination: 7-1/2 REIS

| 227 | ND | — | 6.00 | 11.50 | 17.50 | 35.00 |

COPPER, 4.80 g

260	ND	—	4.00	7.00	12.50	25.00
	1845	—	4.00	7.00	12.50	25.00
	1846	—	4.00	7.00	12.50	25.00
	1847	—	4.50	8.00	13.50	30.00
	1848	—	4.50	8.00	13.50	30.00
	1849	—	4.50	8.00	13.50	30.00

9 REIS
COPPER
Obv: Similar to 6 Reis, KM#226.
Rev. denomination: 9 REIS

| 228 | ND | — | 10.00 | 15.00 | 20.00 | 40.00 |

Rev. denomination: NOVE REIS

KM#	Date	Mintage	Good	VG	Fine	VF
229	ND	—	7.50	12.50	25.00	50.00

10 REIS

COPPER

| 214 | ND | — | 6.00 | 11.00 | 17.50 | 35.00 |

Similar to 6 Reis, KM#226.

| 230 | ND | — | 5.00 | 10.00 | 15.00 | 30.00 |

| 261 | ND | — | 2.00 | 4.00 | 8.50 | 15.00 |
| | 1845 | — | 1.75 | 3.50 | 7.50 | 12.50 |

12 REIS

COPPER

| 215 | ND | — | 7.00 | 12.50 | 20.00 | 40.00 |

Similar to 6 Reis, KM#226.

| 231 | ND | — | 6.00 | 11.50 | 17.50 | 35.00 |

| 262 | ND | — | 7.00 | 12.50 | 20.00 | 40.00 |
| | 1848 | — | 7.00 | 12.50 | 20.00 | 40.00 |

15 REIS

COPPER, 9.30 g

| 216 | ND | — | 6.00 | 11.50 | 17.50 | 35.00 |

| 232 | ND | — | 4.00 | 7.50 | 12.50 | 25.00 |

| 263 | ND | — | 2.00 | 4.00 | 8.50 | 16.50 |

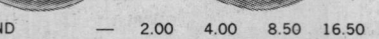

c/m: 15 in circle on earlier coins.

KM#	Date	Mintage	Good	VG	Fine	VF
264	ND(1846)	—	1.75	3.50	7.50	15.00

1/2 TANGA
(30 Reis)

COPPER
Similar to 15 Reis, KM#216.

| 217 | ND | — | 7.50 | 12.50 | 17.50 | 35.00 |

| 233 | ND | — | 7.50 | 12.50 | 17.50 | 35.00 |

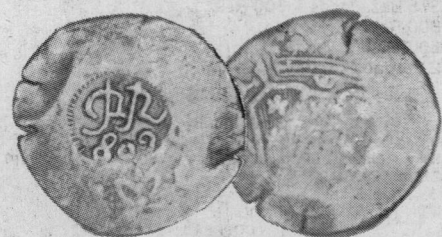

| 249 | ND | — | 5.00 | 8.00 | 12.50 | 25.00 |

c/m: PR 809 in dentilated circle on earlier coins.

| 250 | ND | — | 5.50 | 9.00 | 14.00 | 27.50 |

| 265 | ND | — | 5.00 | 9.00 | 14.00 | 27.50 |

c/m: 30 in circle over earlier coins.

| 274 | ND(1846) | — | 10.00 | 15.00 | 25.00 | 50.00 |

TANGA
(60 Reis)

COPPER
Obv: Head right. Rev: Crowned arms.

| 208 | 1802 | — | 17.50 | 35.00 | 60.00 | 120.00 |
| | 1803 | — | 17.50 | 35.00 | 60.00 | 120.00 |

Obv: Crowned arms. Rev: Value.

| 218 | ND | — | 5.50 | 10.00 | 16.50 | 28.50 |

KM#	Date	Mintage	Good	VG	Fine	VF
234	ND	—	12.50	20.00	30.00	60.00

SILVER, 1.10 g

240	1819	—	35.00	45.00	60.00	85.00
	1823	—	35.00	45.00	60.00	85.00

COPPER

251	ND	—	6.00	10.00	15.00	30.00

c/m: PR 809 in dentilated circle on earlier coins.

253	ND	—	5.00	7.50	12.50	25.00

266	ND	—	8.00	15.00	25.00	50.00

c/m: 60 in circle over earlier coins.

267	ND(1846)	—	7.50	15.00	25.00	50.00

SILVER, 1.03-1.25 g
Pedro V

277	1856	—	25.00	35.00	50.00	90.00
	1858	—	25.00	35.00	50.00	90.00
	1859	—	25.00	35.00	50.00	90.00

1/2 XERAFIM

SILVER, 2.67-2.71 g

KM#	Date	Mintage	Good	VG	Fine	VF
235	1818	—	35.00	45.00	60.00	80.00
	1819	—	35.00	45.00	60.00	80.00

236	1818	—	25.00	35.00	45.00	75.00
	1819/8	—	35.00	45.00	60.00	85.00
	1819	—	25.00	35.00	45.00	75.00
	1820	—	25.00	35.00	45.00	75.00
	1823	—	25.00	35.00	45.00	75.00

255	1831	—	40.00	65.00	100.00	200.00

1/2 PARDAO
(150 Reis)

SILVER, 2.80-2.95 g
Obv: Head right, value: 150 RES.
Rev: Crowned arms.

206	1802	—	10.00	20.00	45.00	85.00
	1803	—	10.00	20.00	45.00	85.00
	1804	—	10.00	20.00	45.00	85.00
	1806	—	10.00	20.00	45.00	85.00

Maria II

271	1845	—	20.00	30.00	40.00	80.00
	1846	—	20.00	30.00	40.00	80.00
	1846/5	—	25.00	35.00	50.00	100.00
	1849	—	20.00	30.00	40.00	80.00

Pedro V
Similar to 60 Reis, KM#277.

280	1857	—	25.00	35.00	50.00	90.00
	1860	—	25.00	35.00	50.00	90.00
	1861	—	25.00	35.00	50.00	90.00

PARDAO
(300 Reis)

SILVER, 5.84-5.95 g
Obv: Head left. Rev: Crowned arms.

204	1801	—	10.00	20.00	40.00	80.00
	1802	—	10.00	20.00	40.00	80.00
	1803	—	10.00	20.00	40.00	80.00
	1804	—	10.00	20.00	40.00	80.00
	1805	—	10.00	20.00	40.00	80.00
	1806	—	10.00	20.00	40.00	80.00

221	1808	—	17.50	27.50	37.50	75.00
	1809	—	17.50	27.50	37.50	75.00
	1810	—	17.50	27.50	37.50	75.00
	1811	—	17.50	27.50	37.50	75.00
	1812/09	—	35.00	60.00	100.00	225.00
	1815/09	—	35.00	60.00	100.00	225.00
	1815	—	17.50	27.50	37.50	75.00
	1816	—	17.50	27.50	37.50	75.00
	1817	—	17.50	27.50	37.50	75.00
	1818	—	17.50	27.50	37.50	75.00

237	1818	—	20.00	30.00	50.00	80.00
	1819	—	20.00	30.00	50.00	80.00
	1820	—	20.00	30.00	50.00	80.00
	1821	—	20.00	30.00	50.00	80.00
	1822	—	20.00	30.00	50.00	80.00
	1823	—	20.00	30.00	50.00	80.00
	1824	—	20.00	30.00	50.00	80.00
	1825	—	20.00	30.00	50.00	80.00

Obv: Diademed head.

KM#	Date	Mintage	Good	VG	Fine	VF
238	ND	—	20.00	30.00	40.00	80.00
247	ND	—	40.00	55.00	70.00	140.00
	1827	—	40.00	55.00	70.00	140.00

256	1831	—	35.00	50.00	65.00	130.00
	1833	—	35.00	50.00	65.00	130.00

268	1839	—	32.50	45.00	60.00	120.00
	1840	—	32.50	45.00	60.00	120.00
	1841	—	32.50	45.00	60.00	120.00

272	1845	—	20.00	30.00	40.00	80.00
	1846	—	20.00	30.00	40.00	80.00
	1847	—	20.00	30.00	40.00	80.00
	1848	—	20.00	30.00	40.00	80.00

Rev: Value and arms.

276	1851	—	30.00	37.50	50.00	100.00

Pedro V

278	1856	—	30.00	40.00	55.00	110.00
	1857	—	30.00	40.00	55.00	110.00
	1860	—	30.00	40.00	55.00	110.00
	1861	—	30.00	40.00	55.00	110.00

Luis I

281	1866	—	30.00	40.00	55.00	110.00
	1868	—	30.00	40.00	55.00	110.00
	1869	—	30.00	40.00	55.00	110.00

XERAFIN

GOLD, 0.40-0.41 g
Obv: Arms on crowned globe.
Rev: Value and date in angles of cross.

KM#	Date	Mintage	VG	Fine	VF	XF
241	1819	—	150.00	300.00	450.00	700.00

RUPIA

SILVER, 11.80 g

KM#	Date	Mintage	Good	VG	Fine	VF
205	1801	—	11.50	18.50	30.00	50.00
	1802	—	11.50	18.50	30.00	50.00
	1803	—	11.50	18.50	30.00	50.00
	1804	—	11.50	18.50	30.00	50.00
	1805	—	11.50	18.50	30.00	50.00
	1806	—	11.50	18.50	30.00	50.00
	1807	—	11.50	18.50	30.00	50.00

Portuguese / INDIA 964

KM#	Date	Mintage	Good	VG	Fine	VF
219	1807 inverted "A" for "V" in "Rupia"					
		—	40.00	55.00	70.00	140.00
	1808	—	40.00	55.00	70.00	140.00
	1809	—	40.00	55.00	70.00	140.00
	1810	—	40.00	55.00	70.00	140.00
	1811	—	40.00	55.00	70.00	140.00
	1812	—	40.00	55.00	70.00	140.00
	1813	—	40.00	60.00	80.00	160.00
	1814	—	40.00	60.00	80.00	160.00
	1815	—	40.00	60.00	80.00	160.00
	1816	—	40.00	55.00	70.00	140.00
	1817	—	40.00	55.00	70.00	140.00
	Mule. Obv: KM#219. Rev: KM#205.					
220	1807	—	40.00	55.00	70.00	140.00

239	1818	—	40.00	55.00	70.00	140.00
	1819	—	40.00	55.00	70.00	140.00
	1820	—	40.00	55.00	70.00	140.00
	1821	—	40.00	55.00	70.00	140.00
	1822	—	40.00	55.00	70.00	140.00
	1823	—	40.00	55.00	70.00	140.00
	1824	—	40.00	55.00	70.00	140.00
	1825	—	40.00	55.00	70.00	140.00
	1826	—	40.00	55.00	70.00	140.00

248	1827	—	80.00	100.00	125.00	250.00
	1828	—	80.00	100.00	125.00	250.00

254	1829	—	70.00	85.00	110.00	225.00
	1830	—	60.00	75.00	90.00	180.00
	1831	—	55.00	65.00	80.00	160.00
	1832	—	55.00	65.00	80.00	160.00
	1833	—	55.00	65.00	80.00	160.00

269	1839	—	22.50	45.00	60.00	75.00
	1840	—	22.50	45.00	60.00	75.00
	1841	—	22.50	45.00	60.00	75.00

273	1845	—	20.00	40.00	55.00	70.00
	1846	—	20.00	40.00	55.00	70.00
	1847	—	20.00	40.00	55.00	70.00
	1848	—	20.00	40.00	55.00	70.00
	1849	—	20.00	40.00	55.00	70.00

KM#	Date	Mintage	Good	VG	Fine	VF
275	1850	—	25.00	50.00	70.00	90.00
	1851	—	25.00	50.00	70.00	90.00

279	1856	—	20.00	40.00	55.00	65.00
	1857	—	20.00	40.00	55.00	65.00
	1858	—	20.00	40.00	55.00	65.00
	1859	—	20.00	40.00	55.00	65.00
	1860	—	20.00	40.00	55.00	65.00
	1861	—	20.00	40.00	55.00	65.00

282	1866	—	25.00	50.00	65.00	80.00
	1867	—	25.00	50.00	65.00	80.00
	1868	—	25.00	50.00	65.00	80.00
	1869	—	25.00	50.00	65.00	80.00

2 XERAFINS
GOLD, 0.81 g

KM#	Date	Mintage	VG	Fine	VF	XF
223	1815	—	175.00	300.00	450.00	650.00
242	1819	—	125.00	200.00	300.00	450.00

4 XERAFINS

GOLD, 1.63 g

202	1803	—	275.00	500.00	725.00	1100.
243	1819	—	250.00	400.00	600.00	900.00

8 XERAFINS
GOLD, 3.25 g

192	1804	—	500.00	850.00	1250.	1850.

Obv: Crowned oval arms.

244	1819	—	300.00	550.00	750.00	1150.

Obv: Similar to 1 Rupia, KM#239.

245	1819	—	450.00	750.00	1100.	1650.

12 XERAFINS

GOLD, 4.87 g

187	1802	—	375.00	650.00	1100.	1500.
	1803	—	250.00	450.00	600.00	900.00
	1804	—	250.00	450.00	600.00	900.00
	1806	—	350.00	600.00	800.00	1200.

222	1808	—	375.00	650.00	1100.	1500.
	1809	—	375.00	650.00	1100.	1500.
	1811	—	375.00	650.00	1100.	1500.
	1812	—	375.00	650.00	1100.	1500.
	1813	—	375.00	650.00	1100.	1500.
	1814	—	375.00	650.00	1100.	1500.
	1815	—	375.00	650.00	1100.	1500.
	1816	—	375.00	650.00	1100.	1500.
246	1819	—	450.00	800.00	1250.	1700.
	1820	—	450.00	800.00	1250.	1700.

KM#	Date	Mintage	VG	Fine	VF	XF
246	1824	—	450.00	800.00	1250.	1700.
	1825	—	450.00	800.00	1250.	1700.
270	1840	—	550.00	1000.	1650.	2250.
	1841	—	550.00	1000.	1650.	2250.

COLONIAL COINAGE
MONETARY SYSTEM
960 Reis = 16 Tanga = 1 Rupia

3 REIS

COPPER

KM#	Date	Mintage	Fine	VF	XF	Unc
1	1871	.052	3.50	7.50	12.50	35.00

5 REIS

COPPER

2	1871	.051	5.00	10.00	15.00	42.50

1/12 TANGA

BRONZE
Roman numeral dating

13	1901	.960	1.50	3.50	7.00	15.00
	1903	.960	1.75	3.75	7.50	18.00

OITAVO (1/8) TANGA

COPPER

7	1881	12.397	1.50	2.50	5.00	12.50
	1884	Inc. Ab.	1.50	2.50	5.50	15.00
	1886	Inc. Ab.	2.00	3.25	6.50	17.50

BRONZE
Roman numeral dating

14	1901	.960	1.00	2.00	5.00	12.50
	1903	.960	2.00	4.00	8.00	17.50

10 REIS

COPPER

3	1871	.051	5.50	11.00	16.50	45.00

QUARTO (1/4) TANGA
(15 Reis)

COPPER

4	1871	.051	7.50	12.50	25.00	65.00

Portuguese / INDIA **965**

KM#	Date	Mintage	Fine	VF	XF	Unc
8	1881	7.242	2.75	5.50	11.50	27.50
	1884	Inc. Ab.	3.25	6.50	12.50	30.00
	1886	Inc. Ab.	2.25	4.50	8.50	22.50
	1888	Inc. Ab.	30.00	50.00	90.00	900.00

BRONZE
Roman numeral dating

15	1901	.800	1.50	3.00	7.00	15.00
	1903	.800	1.75	3.75	8.50	17.50

1/2 TANGA
(30 Reis)

COPPER

5	1871	.050	10.00	15.00	30.00	70.00

BRONZE
Roman numeral dating

16	1901	.800	1.50	3.00	8.50	27.50
	1903	.800	2.00	4.00	10.00	30.00

TANGA
(60 Reis)

COPPER

6	1871	.050	12.50	25.00	40.00	135.00

BRONZE

19	1934	.100	1.00	2.50	5.00	14.00

KM#	Date	Mintage	Fine	VF	XF	Unc
24	1947	1.000	.65	1.25	2.50	6.00

28	1952	9.600	.35	.65	1.25	3.50

OITAVO DE (1/8) RUPIA

1.4600 g, .917 SILVER, .0430 oz ASW

9	1881	.902	3.00	6.00	10.00	32.50

2 TANGAS

COPPER-NICKEL

20	1934	.150	1.25	3.00	6.00	15.00

QUARTO DE (1/4) RUPIA

2.9200 g, .917 SILVER, .0860 oz ASW

10	1881	.471	4.50	8.00	15.00	37.50

COPPER-NICKEL

25	1947	.800	1.00	2.00	3.50	9.00
	1952	4.000	.50	1.00	2.00	5.00

4 TANGAS

COPPER-NICKEL

21	1934	.100	2.00	4.00	8.00	22.50

MEIA (1/2) RUPIA

5.8300 g, .917 SILVER, .1719 oz ASW

11	1881	.357	4.00	8.00	15.00	42.50
	1882	Inc. Ab.	5.00	9.50	18.00	47.50

6.0000 g, .835 SILVER, .1610 oz ASW

KM#	Date	Mintage	Fine	VF	XF	Unc
23	1936	.100	3.50	7.50	10.00	25.00

COPPER-NICKEL

26	1947	.600	1.00	2.00	4.00	8.00
	1952	2.000	.50	1.00	2.50	4.50

UMA (1) RUPIA

11.6600 g, .917 SILVER, .3438 oz ASW

12	1881	1.763	4.00	7.50	16.50	47.50
	1882	Inc. Ab.	3.50	7.00	15.00	45.00

17	1903	.200	4.00	6.50	12.50	40.00
	1904	.100	5.00	8.50	16.00	55.00

18	1912	.100	12.00	25.00	50.00	100.00

12.0000 g, .917 SILVER, .3536 oz ASW

22	1935	.300	5.00	7.00	10.00	22.50

12.0000 g, .500 SILVER, .1929 oz ASW

27	1947	.900	1.50	3.50	7.50	18.00

Portuguese / INDIA 966

6 ESCUDOS

COPPER-NICKEL

KM#	Date	Mintage	Fine	VF	XF	Unc
29	1952	1.000	1.00	2.00	4.00	8.00
	1954	—	25.00	50.00	100.00	200.00

DECIMAL COINAGE
100 Centavos = 1 Escudo

10 CENTAVOS

BRONZE

30	1958	5.000	.20	.40	.85	1.75
	1959	Inc. AB.	.15	.30	.65	1.25
	1961	1.000	.20	.35	.75	1.50

30 CENTAVOS

BRONZE

31	1958	5.000	.20	.35	.75	1.50
	1959	Inc. Ab.	.65	1.25	2.50	5.00

60 CENTAVOS

COPPER-NICKEL

32	1958	5.000	.20	.35	.75	1.50
	1959	Inc. Ab.	.65	1.25	2.50	5.00

ESCUDO

COPPER-NICKEL

33	1958	6.000	.30	.65	1.25	3.00
	1959	Inc. Ab.	.40	.85	1.75	4.00

3 ESCUDOS

COPPER-NICKEL

34	1958	5.000	.40	.85	1.75	4.00
	1959	Inc. Ab.	.65	1.25	2.50	5.50

COPPER-NICKEL

KM#	Date	Mintage	Fine	VF	XF	Unc
35	1959	4.000	1.25	2.50	3.50	8.00

INDIA-BRITISH

The civilization of India, which began about 2500 B.C., flourished under a succession of empires - notably those of Chandragupta, Asoka and the Mughals - until undermined in the 18th and 19th centuries by European Colonial powers.

The Portuguese were the first to arrive, off Calicut in May 1498. It wasn't until 1612, after the Portuguese and Spanish power had begun to wane, that the British East India Company established its initial settlement at Surat. Britain could not have chosen a more propitious time. The northern Mogul Empire, the central girdle of petty states, and the southern Vijayanagar Empire were crumbling and ripe for foreign exploitation. By the end of the century, English traders were firmly established in Bombay, Madras, Calcutta and lesser places elsewhere, and Britain was implementing its announced policy to create such civil and military institutions 'as may be the foundation of secure English domination for all time'. By 1757, following the successful conclusion of a war of colonial rivalry with France during which the military victories of Robert Clive, a young officer with the British East India Company, made him the most powerful man in India, the British were firmly settled in India as not only traders but as conquerors. During the next 60 years, the British East India Company acquired dominion over most of India by bribery and force, and governed it directly or through puppet princelings.

Because of the Sepoy Mutiny of 1857-58, a large scale mutiny among Indian soldiers of the Bengal army, control of the government of India was transferred from the East India Company to the British Crown. At this point in world history, India was the brightest jewel in the imperial diadem of the British lords of the earth, but even then a movement for greater Indian representation in government presaged the Indian Empire's twilight hour less than a century hence - it would pass into history on Aug. 15, 1947.

BENGAL PRESIDENCY
East India Company
(Until 1835 AD)

In 1633 a group of 8 Englishmen obtained a permit to trade in Bengal from the Nawab of Orissa. Shortly thereafter trading factories were established at Balasore and Hariharpur. Although greater trading privileges were granted to the East India Company by the Emperor Shah Jahan in 1634, by 1642 the 2 original factories were abandoned.

In 1651, through an English surgeon named Broughtmon, a permit was acquired to trade at Bengal. Hugli was the first location, followed by Kasimbazar, Balasore and Patna (the last 3 in 1658). Calcutta became of increasing importance in this area and on December 20, 1699 Calcutta was declared a presidency and renamed Fort King William.

During these times there were many conflicts with the Nawab, both diplomatic and military, and the ultimate outcome was the intervention of Clive and the restoration of Calcutta as an important trading center.

During the earlier trading times in Bengal most of the monies used were imported rupees from the Madras factory. These were primarily of the Arcot type. After Clive's victory one of the concessions in the peace treaty was the right to make Mughal type coinage. The Nawab gave specific details as to what form the coinage should take.

In 1765 Emperor Shah Alam gave the East India Company possessions in Bengal, Orissa and Bihar. This made the company responsible only to the Emperor.

In 1777 the "Frozen Year 19" (of Shah Alam) rupees were made at Calcutta and were continued until the advent of the "Arcot" type.

MINTS

Banaras بنارس

Calcutta (Kalkatah) كلكته

Farrukhabad فرخ اباد

Sagar ساكر

BANARAS
(Banares, Varanasi)

NOTE: Coins of similar dates with different legends are listed under Indian Princely States, Awadh.

PICE

COPPER, dump, 9.00-10.00 g
Obv. and rev: Trisul (trident) symbols added.

KM#	Date	Year	Good	VG	Fine	VF
16	(1806-7)	49	2.00	3.00	5.50	8.50

COPPER, dump, 6.40 g
Mint: Banares

KM#	Date	Year	VG	Fine	VF	XF
27	(1815-21)	37	2.00	3.00	6.00	10.00

Reduced weight, 6.15 g

28	(1821-7)	37	1.75	3.75	7.50	12.50

Large flan, 24.5-26.5mm.

29	(1827-9)	37	2.50	4.50	8.50	13.50

Obv. and rev: Crossbar on trisuls, 21-24.5mm.

30	(1827-9)	37	2.50	4.50	8.50	13.50
	(1827-9)	37	—	—	Proof	75.00

1/16 RUPEE
In the name of Shah Alam II

SILVER, dump, 0.67-0.73 g
Mint: Banaras

32	AH1216-1226					
	17/39-49	10.00	25.00	50.00	100.00

1/4 RUPEE
In the name of Shah Alam II

SILVER, dump, 2.68-2.91 g
Mint: Banaras
Struck w/o Darogah's marks

35	AH1229 17/49	8.00	20.00	45.00	75.00

Machine struck, broad flan, w/oblique milling.

36	AH1229 17/49	—	Reported, not confirmed

1/2 RUPEE
In the name of Alamgir II

SILVER, dump, 5.35-5.82 g
Mint: Calcutta
Struck w/o Darogah's marks.

38	AH1229 17/49	18.00	45.00	100.00	150.00

Machine struck, broad flan w/oblique milling.

KM#	Date	Year	Fine	VF	XF	Unc
39	AH1229	17/49	12.50	25.00	75.00	125.00

RUPEE
SILVER, dump, 10.70-11.60 g
Mint: Banaras

KM#	Date	Year	VG	Fine	VF	XF
40	AH1216	17/43	5.00	10.00	25.00	50.00
	1216	17/44	5.00	10.00	25.00	50.00
	1217	17/44	5.00	10.00	25.00	50.00
	1217	17/45	5.00	10.00	25.00	50.00
	1218	17/45	5.00	10.00	25.00	50.00
	1218	17/46	5.00	10.00	25.00	50.00
	1219	17/46	5.00	10.00	25.00	50.00
	1219	17/47	5.00	10.00	25.00	50.00
	1220	17/47	5.00	10.00	25.00	50.00
	1220	17/48	5.00	10.00	25.00	50.00
	1221	17/48	5.00	10.00	25.00	50.00
	1221	17/49	5.00	10.00	25.00	50.00
	1222	17/49	5.00	10.00	25.00	50.00
	1223	17/49	5.00	10.00	25.00	50.00
	1224	17/49	5.00	10.00	25.00	50.00
	1225	17/49	5.00	10.00	25.00	50.00
	1226	17/49	5.00	10.00	25.00	50.00

W/o Darogah's marks.

41	AH1228	17/49	10.00	25.00	50.00	100.00
	1229	17/49	10.00	25.00	50.00	100.00

Machine struck, broad flan w/oblique milling.

KM#	Date	Year	Fine	VF	XF	Unc
42	AH1229	17/49	10.00	20.00	50.00	75.00

NAZARANA RUPEE

SILVER, 11.64 g
Mint: Banaras

KM#	Date	Year	VG	Fine	VF	XF
43	AH1201	17/29	100.00	200.00	350.00	600.00

Large full flan

44	AH1217	17/45	85.00	165.00	275.00	450.00

Small flan

KM#	Date	Year	VG	Fine	VF	XF
45	AH1219	17/45	—	—	500.00	850.00

MOHUR
In the name of Shah Alam II

GOLD, dump, 10.70-11.40 g
Mint: Banaras

31	AH1201	17/29	225.00	500.00	1250.	1750.
	1209	37	225.00	500.00	1250.	1750.
	1213	41	225.00	500.00	1250.	1750.

CALCUTTA
PIE

COPPER

KM#	Date	Year	Fine	VF	XF	Unc
58	(1831)	—	.35	1.00	8.00	20.00
	(1831)				Proof	85.00

PICE
COPPER, 6.54 g.

KM#	Date	Year	VG	Fine	VF	XF
54	(1809)	37	.40	1.00	8.00	45.00

Reduced weight, 6.46 g.

55	(1817)	37	.40	1.00	8.00	45.00

56	(1829)	37	1.25	3.00	6.00	35.00
	(1829)	37	—	—	Proof	200.00

57	(1831)	37	.50	1.50	3.00	25.00
	(1831)	37	—	—	Proof	200.00

1/2 ANNA

COPPER

KM#	Date	Year	Fine	VF	XF	Unc
59	(1831-35)	—	1.00	3.00	15.00	40.00
	(1831-35)				Proof	150.00

FARRUKHABAD
PICE

COPPER

KM#	Date	Year	Good	VG	Fine	VF
64	—	45	—	—	—	—

TRISUL PICE

COPPER, 6.20 g
Mint: Farrukhabad

KM#	Date	Year	VG	Fine	VF	XF
65	(1820)	45	1.50	3.00	10.00	45.00

Mint: Sagar
Obv. & rev: Trident

71	(1826)	45	1.50	3.00	10.00	45.00

Obv: 6-petaled rosette replaces trident

72	(1833)	45	1.50	3.00	10.00	45.00

1/4 RUPEE
.955 SILVER, 2.80 g
Mint: Farrukhabad
Oblique milling (1806-1819)

KM#	Date	Year	Fine	VF	XF	Unc
66	AH—	45	4.00	8.00	20.00	50.00

.909 SILVER, 2.92 g
Vertical milling (1820-1831)

67	AH—	45	4.00	8.00	20.00	50.00

Mints: Calcutta and Banaras

73	AH1204	45	4.00	8.00	20.00	50.00

Mint: Calcutta
Plain edge (1831-1833)

75	AH1204	45	1.50	3.00	15.00	35.00
	1204	45	—	—	Proof	250.00

1/2 RUPEE
.955 SILVER, 5.60 g
Mint: Farrukhabad
Oblique milling (1806-1819)

68	—	45	7.50	15.00	50.00	100.00

.909 SILVER, 5.80 g
Mints: Calcutta and Banaras
Vertical milling (1820-1831)

74	—	45	7.50	8.00	50.00	100.00

Mint: Calcutta
Plain edge (1831-1833)

76	—	45	4.00	8.00	25.00	60.00
	—	45	—	—	Proof	300.00

Bengal Presidency - British / INDIA 968

RUPEE

.955 SILVER, 11.21 g
Mints: Farrukhabad and Calcutta
Oblique milling (1806-1819)

KM#	Date	Year	Fine	VF	XF	Unc
69	—	45	5.00	10.00	30.00	75.00

.909 SILVER, 11.68 g
Mints: Farrukhabad, Calcutta, Banaras, Sagar
Vertical milling (1820-1831)

| 70 | — | 45 | 5.00 | 10.00 | 30.00 | 75.00 |

Mint: Calcutta
Obv. and rev: Large dots; plain edge (1831-1833)

| 77 | — | 45 | 4.00 | 8.00 | 25.00 | 60.00 |
| | — | 45 | — | — | Proof | 400.00 |

Obv. and rev: Small dots; plain edge (1833-1835)

| 78 | — | 45 | 4.00 | 8.00 | 25.00 | 60.00 |
| | — | 45 | — | — | Proof | 400.00 |

MURSHIDABAD
1/4 RUPEE

SILVER, dump, 2.90 g
Mints: Calcutta, Dacca, Murshidabad, Patna
Oblique milling (1793-1818).

| 96 | AH1204 | 19 | 1.00 | 8.00 | 20.00 | 50.00 |
| | 1204 | 19 | — | — | Proof | 300.00 |

Mint: Calcutta
Vertical milling (1819-1829)

| 104 | AH1204 | 19 | 1.00 | 8.00 | 20.00 | 50.00 |

Mint: New Calcutta
Plain edge (1830-1833)

| 115 | AH1204 | 19 | 8.00 | — | 20.00 | 50.00 |

1/2 RUPEE

SILVER, dump, 5.80 g
Mints: Calcutta, Dacca, Murshidabad, Patna
Oblique milling (1793-1818)

KM#	Date	Year	Fine	VF	XF	Unc
97	—	19	3.00	15.00	40.00	80.00
	—	19	—	—	Proof	400.00

Mint: Calcutta
Vertical milling (1819-1829)

| 105 | — | 19 | 2.00 | 12.00 | 30.00 | 75.00 |
| | — | 19 | — | — | Proof | 300.00 |

Mint: New Calcutta
Plain edge (1830-1833)
Rev: Crescent at upper left.

| 116 | — | 19 | 2.00 | 15.00 | 30.00 | 75.00 |
| | — | 19 | — | — | Proof | 300.00 |

RUPEE

SILVER, dump, 11.60 g
Mints: Calcutta, Dacca, Murshidabad, Patna
Machine struck, oblique milling (1792-1818)

| 99 | — | 19 | 15.00 | 35.00 | 75.00 | 125.00 |

Mint: Calcutta
Vertical milling (1819)

| 107 | — | 19 | 2.25 | 8.00 | 20.00 | 50.00 |

Obv: Star added.
Vertical milling (1819-1832)

| 108 | — | 19 | 4.50 | 7.50 | 12.50 | 25.00 |

Rev: Privy mark 'S' at upper left.

| 109 | — | 19 | 30.00 | 60.00 | 150.00 | 300.00 |

Mint: New Calcutta
Plain edge (1830-1833)
Rev: Crescent at upper left.

KM#	Date	Year	Fine	VF	XF	Unc
117	—	19	3.00	15.00	30.00	75.00
	—	19	—	—	Proof	350.00

1/4 MOHUR

.996 GOLD, 3.09 g
Mints: Calcutta, Dacca, Murshidabad, Patna
Oblique milling (1793-1818)

| 100 | AH1204 | 19 | 50.00 | 125.00 | 250.00 | 400.00 |

.917 GOLD, 3.31 g
Mint: Calcutta
Vertical milling (1819-1832)

| 110 | AH1204 | 19 | 50.00 | 125.00 | 250.00 | 400.00 |
| | 1204 | 19 | — | — | Proof | 1250. |

1/2 MOHUR

.996 GOLD, 6.18 g
Mints: Calcutta, Dacca, Murshidabad, Patna
Machine struck, oblique milling (1793-1818)

| 101 | AH1202 | 19 | 100.00 | 200.00 | 350.00 | 500.00 |

.917 GOLD, 6.63 gm.
Mint: Calcutta
Vertical milling (1819-1832)

| 111 | AH1202 | 19 | 100.00 | 200.00 | 350.00 | 500.00 |
| | 1202 | 19 | — | — | Proof | 1500 |

MOHUR

.996 GOLD, 12.36 g
Mints: Calcutta, Dacca, Murshidabad, Patna
Machine struck, oblique milling (1793-1818)

| 103 | AH1202 | 19 | 150.00 | 250.00 | 400.00 | 600.00 |

.917 GOLD, 13.26 g
Mint: Calcutta
Vertical milling (1819-1825)

| 112 | AH1202 | 19 | 175.00 | 300.00 | 450.00 | 600.00 |
| | 1202 | 19 | — | — | Proof | 2000. |

.996 GOLD, 12.36 g
Low relief, oblique left milling (1825)

| 113 | AH1202 | 19 | 150.00 | 200.00 | 350.00 | 500.00 |

Low relief, oblique left milling, crescent added (1830)

KM#	Date	Year	Fine	VF	XF	Unc
114	AH1202	19	150.00	200.00	400.00	600.00
	1202	19	—	—	Proof	1750.

BOMBAY PRESIDENCY

Following a naval victory over the Portuguese on December 24, 1612 negotiations were started that developed into the opening of the first East India Company factory in Surat in 1613. Silver coins for the New World as well as various other foreign coins were used in early trade. Within the decade the Mughal mint at Surat was melting all of these foreign coins and re-minting them as various denominations of Mughal coinage.

Bombay became an English holding as part of the dowry of Catherine of Braganza, Princess of Portugal when she was bethrothed to Charles II of England. Also included in the dowry was Tangier and $500,000. With this acquisition the trading center of the Indian West Coast moved from Surat to Bombay.

Possession of Bombay Island took place on February 8, 1665 and by 1672 the East India Company had a mint in Bombay to serve their trading interests. European designed coins were struck here until 1717. An experimental issue of Mughal style rupees with regnal years pertaining to the reigns of James II and William and Mary. These were not popular and were withdrawn.

From 1717 to 1778 the Mughal style Bombay rupee was the principal coin of the West India trade, although bulk foreign coins were used for striking rupees at Surat.

After the East India Company took over the city of Surat in 1800 they slowed the mint production and finally transferred all activity to Bombay in 1815.

MINTS

Ahmadabad احمد اباد

Bombay (Munbai) منبي

COPPER COINAGE
1/4 PICE

COPPER, dump, 2.65 g

KM#	Date	Year	Good	VG	Fine	VF
219	1816	—	—	15.00	45.00	75.00
	1821	—	—	15.00	45.00	75.00
	1825	—	—	15.00	45.00	75.00

PIE

COPPER
Mint: Bombay
Obv: Center lion on helmet above shield.

KM#	Date	Year	Fine	VF	XF	Unc
230	AH1246	1830	—	—	Proof	300.00
	1246	1831	.75	2.00	25.00	60.00
	1246	1831	—	—	Proof	175.00

Mint: Calcutta
Rev: Tall Persian legend.

| 261 | AH1248 | 1833 | .40 | 1.00 | 12.00 | 45.00 |
| | 1248 | 1833 | — | — | Proof | 100.00 |

Rev: Short Persian legend.

| 262 | AH1248 | 1833 | .40 | 1.00 | 12.00 | 45.00 |

Mule. Obv: KM#261. Rev: KM#230.

| 263 | AH1246 | 1833 | — | — | — | — |

Mule. Obv: KM#230. Rev: KM#261.

| 264 | AH1248 | 1831 | — | — | — | — |

1/2 PICE

COPPER, 9mm, 0.90-1.20 g
Obv: Bale mark. Rev: Date.

KM#	Date	Year	Good	VG	Fine	VF
202	(1)803	—	3.00	10.00	30.00	75.00

COPPER, dump, 5.31 g

KM#	Date	Year	Good	VG	Fine	VF
197	1802	—	3.00	10.00	30.00	75.00
	1803	—	—	Reported, not confirmed		
	1808	—	3.00	10.00	30.00	75.00
	1810	—	3.00	10.00	30.00	75.00
	1813	—	3.00	10.00	30.00	75.00
	1815	—	3.00	10.00	30.00	75.00
	1816	—	3.00	10.00	30.00	75.00
	1818	—	3.00	10.00	30.00	75.00
	1819	—	3.00	10.00	30.00	75.00
	1825	—	3.00	10.00	30.00	75.00
	1826	—	3.00	10.00	30.00	75.00
	1827	—	3.00	10.00	30.00	75.00
	1829	—	3.00	10.00	30.00	75.00

Obv: Center lion on helmet above shield.

KM#	Date	Year	VG	Fine	VF	XF
204	AH1219	1804	.40	1.00	8.00	40.00
	1219	1804	—	—	Proof	50.00

COPPER, machine struck, 3.83 g
Ahmadabad Mint
Similar to 1 Pice, KM#226.

| 255 | AH1234 | 13 | — | — | — | — |

COPPER, dump, 17-18mm, 3.76 g
Mint: Local Southern Concan

KM#	Date	Year	Good	VG	Fine	VF
225	1820	—	3.00	10.00	35.00	100.00
	1821	—	3.00	10.00	35.00	100.00

PICE

COPPER, 2.20-2.85 g

| 203 | 1803 | — | — | — | 30.00 | 75.00 |
| | 1807 | — | 3.00 | 10.00 | 30.00 | 75.00 |

COPPER, dump, 10.62 g

198	1802	—	2.00	5.00	12.00	40.00
	1803	—	2.00	5.00	12.00	40.00
	1804	—	2.00	5.00	12.00	40.00
	1808	—	2.00	5.00	12.00	40.00
	1809	—	2.00	5.00	12.00	40.00
	1810	—	2.00	5.00	12.00	40.00
	1813	—	2.00	5.00	12.00	40.00
	1815	—	2.00	5.00	12.00	40.00
	1816	—	2.00	5.00	12.00	40.00
	1818	—	2.00	5.00	12.00	40.00
	1819	—	2.00	5.00	12.00	40.00
	1825	—	2.00	5.00	12.00	40.00
	1826	—	2.00	5.00	12.00	40.00
	1827	—	2.00	5.00	12.00	40.00
	1828	—	2.00	5.00	12.00	40.00
	1829	—	2.00	5.00	12.00	40.00

KM#	Date	Year	VG	Fine	VF	XF
205	AH1219	1804	.40	1.00	10.00	50.00
	1219	1804	—	—	Proof	65.00

Mint: Ahmadabad
19-20mm, 7.53 g

KM#	Date	Year	Good	VG	Fine	VF
226	AH1233	12	—	—	—	—
	1234	12	—	—	Rare	—
	1236	(14)	—	15.00	45.00	125.00

20mm, 6.7 g

| 227 | 1829 | — | — | 15.00 | 45.00 | 125.00 |

1/4 ANNA

COPPER
Mint: Bombay
Obv. leg: EAST INDIA COMPANY

KM#	Date	Year	Fine	VF	XF	Unc
231.1	AH1246	1830	1.25	3.00	35.00	75.00
	1246	1830	—	—	Proof	250.00
	1246	1832	1.25	3.00	35.00	75.00

Rev: Arabic in different style, medium English letters.

| 231.2 | AH1247 | 1832 | 1.25 | 3.00 | 35.00 | 75.00 |

Mint: Calcutta
Obv: Flat shield, w/o E.I.C. leg.
Rev: Large English letters.

| 232 | AH1249 | 1833 | .75 | — | 30.00 | 75.00 |
| | 1249 | 1833 | — | — | Proof | 200.00 |

Mule. Obv: KM#232. Rev: KM#231.2.
Rev: Small English letters.

| 233 | AH1247 | 1833 | — | — | 150.00 | 350.00 |

Obv: Convex shield w/o E.I.C. leg.
Rev: Small English letters

| 234 | AH1249 | 1833 | .75 | 2.00 | 30.00 | 75.00 |
| | 1249 | 1833 | — | — | Proof | 200.00 |

Mule. Obv: KM#231. Rev: KM#232.

| 235 | AH1249 | 1832 | — | — | 80.00 | 200.00 |

Bombay Presidency - British / INDIA

2 PICE
COPPER, dump, 21.25 g
Rev: Value '2' above *Adil*.

KM#	Date	Year	Good	VG	Fine	VF
199	1802	—	1.50	4.00	7.50	12.50
	1803	—	1.50	4.00	7.50	12.50
	1804	—	1.50	4.00	7.50	12.50

Rev: W/o value '2' above *Adil*.

200	1808	—	1.00	3.00	15.00	45.00
	1809	—	1.00	3.00	15.00	45.00
	1810	—	1.00	3.00	15.00	45.00
	1812	—	Reported, not confirmed			
	1813	—	1.00	3.00	15.00	45.00
	1816	—	1.00	3.00	15.00	45.00
	1818	—	1.00	3.00	15.00	45.00
	1819	—	1.00	3.00	15.00	45.00
	1825	—	1.00	3.00	15.00	45.00
	1826	—	1.00	3.00	15.00	45.00
	1827	—	Reported, not confirmed			
	1828	—	1.00	3.00	15.00	45.00
	1829	—	1.00	3.00	15.00	45.00

KM#	Date	Year	VG	Fine	VF	XF
206	AH1219	1804	.40	1.00	10.00	50.00
	1219	1804	—	—	Proof	120.00

Mule. Obv: KM#206. Rev: Madras 20 Cash, KM#321.
| 207 | — | 1804 | — | — | Proof | 175.00 |

1/2 ANNA

COPPER, 30.5mm, 12.95 g

KM#	Date	Year	Fine	VF	XF	Unc
250	AH1246	1832	—	—	Proof	500.00

Rev: English letters, 2mm.
251	AH1249	1834	2.00	5.00	65.00	125.00
	1249	1834	—	—	Proof	350.00

Rev: English letters, 2.5mm.
| 252 | AH1249 | 1834 | 2.00 | 5.00 | 65.00 | 125.00 |

Rev: English letters, 1mm.
| 253 | AH1249 | 1834 | 2.00 | 5.00 | 65.00 | 125.00 |

SILVER (OMS)
| 253a | AH1249 | 1834 | — | — | Proof | 750.00 |

COPPER, dump, 23-24mm, 15.6 gm.
Mint: Local Southern Concan
Rev: W/Nagari value and date.

KM#	Date	Year	VG	Fine	VF	XF
228	1820	—	5.00	10.00	35.00	100.00
	1821	—	5.00	10.00	35.00	100.00

22.5mm, 13.6 gm.
Rev: Western date.
229	1828	—	7.50	15.00	45.00	125.00
	1829	—	7.50	15.00	45.00	125.00

4 PICE

COPPER, 42.51 gm.
201	1802	—	10.00	20.00	60.00	150.00
	1803	—	10.00	20.00	60.00	150.00
	1804	—	10.00	20.00	60.00	150.00

SILVER COINAGE
PRIVY MARKS

Mint privy marks on dump issues often were intended to be "secret" (= privy marks), indicating changes in standards as well as mint of origin. The following chart is derived from IV Pridmore:

Privy marks involve the 3 diamonds and 4 dots in center line of obverse.

1	∴ ◊	Surat 1800-15
2	∴ ◊	Bombay 1801-02
3	∴ ◊ (1802)	Bombay 1802
4*	∴ ◊ ♛	Bombay 1803-24
4b	∴ ◊	Bombay 1803-24
5*	∴ ◊ ♛	Bombay 1825-31
5b	∴ ◊	Bombay 1825-31
6	∴ ◊	Bombay 1800-24
7	∴ ◊ ♛ } and Bombay 1825
8	∴ ◊ ♛ } on rev. Bombay 1825-31
9	∴ ◊	Unknown

* Crown also may be inverted.

1/16 RUPEE
In the name of Muhammad Akbar II

SILVER, 0.72 g
Mint: Ahmadabad
| 256 | AH1234 | 12 | 4.50 | 6.50 | 9.00 | 12.50 |

See note after Rupee, KM#260.

1/8 RUPEE
In the name of Shah Alam II

SILVER, dump, 1.44 g
Mint: Surat, 1800-1824

KM#	Date	Year	VG	Fine	VF	XF
209	—	46	.65	1.25	3.00	15.00

SILVER, dump, 1.46 g
Privy mark #8.
| 215 | 1825 | 46 | 1.25 | 3.00 | 5.00 | 30.00 |

NOTE: Struck in the period of 1825-1831; the above issue exists with three varieties of privy marks.

In the name of Muhammad Akbar II

11-14mm
Mint: Ahmadabad
| 257 | AH1234 | 12 | 3.00 | 4.50 | 6.50 | 8.50 |
| | 1248 | | 3.00 | 4.50 | 6.50 | 8.50 |

See note after Rupee, KM#260.

1/4 RUPEE
In the name of Shah Alam II

SILVER, dump, 2.88 g
Mint: Surat, 1800-1824
| 210 | — | 46 | .75 | 1.25 | 3.00 | 15.00 |

SILVER, dump, 2.91 g
Privy mark #7
| 216 | 1825 | 46 | 7.50 | 12.50 | 20.00 | 35.00 |

NOTE: Struck in the period of 1825-1831; the above issue exists with four varieties of privy marks.

In the name of Muhammad Akbar II

Machine struck, plain edge.

KM#	Date	Year	Fine	VF	XF	Unc
220	AH1215	46	1.25	3.00	15.00	45.00
	1215	46	—	—	Proof	275.00

Dump
Mint: Ahmadabad

KM#	Date	Year	VG	Fine	VF	XF
258	AH1234	12	2.50	4.00	6.00	10.00

See note after Rupee, KM#260.

1/2 RUPEE
In the name of Shah Alam II

SILVER, dump, 5.76 g
Mint: Surat. Privy mark #6.
| 211 | — | 46 | 1.25 | 2.00 | 12.00 | 25.00 |

NOTE: For listings of coins w/regnal year 52 see India-French.

SILVER, dump, 5.83 g
Mint: Bombay. Privy mark #8.
| 217 | 1825 | 46 | 1.25 | 2.00 | 12.00 | 25.00 |

NOTE: Struck in the period of 1825-1831; the above issue exists with five varieties of privy marks.

Mint: Surat
Machine struck, plain edge.
KM#	Date	Year	Fine	VF	XF	Unc
221	AH1215	46	2.00	5.00	20.00	50.00

KM#	Date	Year	Fine	VF	XF	Unc
221	1215	46	—	—	Proof	350.00

In the name of Muhammad Akbar II

Dump
Mint: Ahmadabad

KM#	Date	Year	VG	Fine	VF	XF
259	AH1239	15	3.50	5.50	8.50	15.00
	1243	—	3.50	5.50	8.50	15.00
	1248	—	3.50	5.50	8.50	15.00

NOTE: See note after Rupee, KM#260.

RUPEE

In the name of Shah Alam II

SILVER, dump, 11.59 g
Mint: Calcutta, 1810-1813
Obv: Inverted crescent privy mark.
Machine struck, plain edge.

KM#	Date	Mintage	VG	Fine	VF	XF
224	—	2.037	20.00	50.00	125.00	175.00

Mint: Surat
Privy mark #1.

KM#	Date	Year	VG	Fine	VF	XF
212	—	46	7.00	10.00	13.50	20.00

NOTE: For listings of coins w/regnal years 51-54 see India- French.

11.66 g
Mint: Bombay
Privy mark #7.

218	1825	46	7.50	12.50	20.00	35.00

Machine struck, vertical milling.
Privy mark #7.

KM#	Date	Year	Fine	VF	XF	Unc
222	AH1215	46	6.00	15.00	75.00	125.00
	1215	46	—	—	Proof	400.00

Mint: Bombay
Plain edge

223	AH1215	46	3.00	5.00	20.00	50.00
	1215	46	—	—	Proof	400.00

In the name of Muhammad Akbar II

Dump
Mint: Ahmadabad

KM#	Date	Year	VG	Fine	VF	XF
260	AH1233	11	6.00	10.00	13.50	20.00
	1233	12	6.00	10.00	13.50	20.00
	1234	12	6.00	10.00	13.50	20.00
	1234	13	6.00	10.00	13.50	20.00
	1235	14	6.00	10.00	13.50	20.00
	1236	13	6.00	10.00	13.50	20.00
	1236	14	6.00	10.00	13.50	20.00
	1239	15	6.00	10.00	13.50	20.00
	1241	16	6.00	10.00	13.50	20.00
	1242	—	6.00	10.00	13.50	20.00
	1243	—	6.00	10.00	13.50	20.00
	1244	—	6.00	10.00	13.50	20.00
	1248	—	6.00	10.00	13.50	20.00
	1249	—	6.00	10.00	13.50	20.00
	1250	—	6.00	10.00	13.50	20.00
	1251	—	6.00	10.00	13.50	20.00

NOTE: Ahmadabad Mint was acquired by the British in 1817AD and finally closed in 1835AD. For other issues, see Mughals, Baroda, and Ahmadabad. Symbols as on Ahmadabad State Issues (q.v.), struck in the name of Muhammad Akbar II.

1/15 MOHUR

In the name of Shah Alam II

GOLD, dump, 7-8mm, 0.77 g
Mint: Surat (1800-1815)

213	—	46	25.00	30.00	60.00	125.00

Mint: Bombay
Privy mark: Crescent.

236	ND(1801-2)	46	25.00	30.00	60.00	125.00

GOLD, dump, 7-8mm, 0.77 g
Mint: Bombay
Privy mark: Star.

237	ND(1803-24)	46	25.00	30.00	60.00	125.00

W/o privy mark

238	ND(1825-31)	46	25.00	30.00	60.00	125.00

PANCHIA
(1/3 Mohur)

GOLD, dump, 3.86 g

239	—	46	75.00	125.00	275.00	500.00

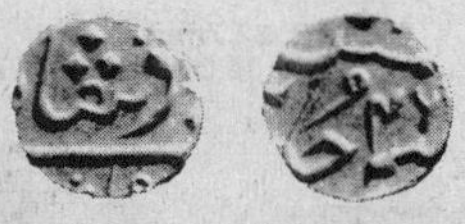

Privy mark: Crescent.

240	ND(1801-2)	46	75.00	125.00	275.00	500.00

241	1802	46	75.00	125.00	275.00	500.00

Privy mark: Normal crown.

243	ND(1803-24)	46	75.00	125.00	275.00	500.00

Privy mark: Inverted crown.

245	—	46	75.00	125.00	275.00	500.00

Privy marks: Normal crown and 6 petal rosette.

247	ND(1825-31)	46	75.00	125.00	275.00	500.00

Privy marks: Inverted crown and 6 petal rosette.

249	—	46	75.00	125.00	275.00	500.00

MOHUR
(15 Rupees)

In the name of Shah Alam II

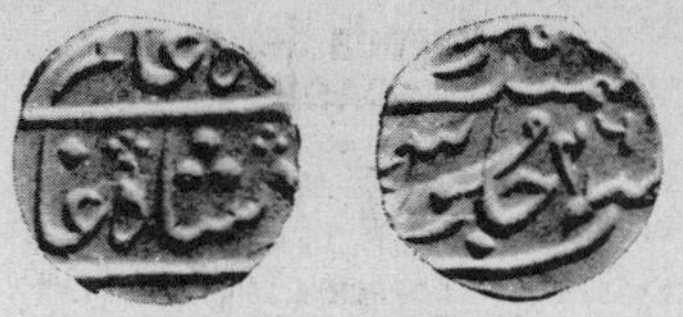

GOLD, dump, 16-19mm, 11.59 g
Mint: Surat (1800-1832)

KM#	Date	Year	VG	Fine	VF	XF
214	—	46	—	125.00	250.00	550.00

Mint: Bombay
Privy mark: Crescent.

242	ND(1803-24)	46	—	125.00	250.00	550.00

Mint: Bombay
Privy mark: Normal crown.

244	ND(1803-24)	46	—	125.00	250.00	550.00

Privy mark: Inverted crown.

246	—	46	—	125.00	250.00	550.00

Privy marks: Normal crown and 6 petal rosette.

248	ND(1825-31)	46	—	125.00	250.00	550.00

MALABAR COAST

Tellicherry
MINT

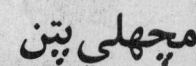

Mintname: Mumbai (Bombay)

1/5 RUPEE

In the name of Alamgir II

SILVER, dump, 2.32 g

277	1805	—	1.00	2.00	5.00	15.00

PAGODA

GOLD, dump, 3.0 g

278	1809	—	75.00	100.00	250.00	400.00

MADRAS PRESIDENCY

English trade was begun on the east coast of India in 1611. The first factory was at Mazulipatam and was maintained intermittently until modern times.

Madras was founded in 1639 and Fort St. George was made the chief factory on the east coast in 1641. A mint was established at Fort St. George where coins of the style of Vijayanagar were struck.

The Madras mint began minting copper coins after the mint had experienced internal rejuvenation. In 1688 silver coins were authorized by the new Board of Directors.

In 1692 the Mughal Emperor Aurangzeb gave permission for Mughal type rupees to be struck at Madras. These circulated locally and were also sent to Bengal. The chief competition for the Madras coins were the Arcot rupees. Some of the bulk coins from Madras were sent to the Nawabs mint to be made into Arcot rupees. In 1742 the East India Company applied for and received permission to make their own Arcot rupees. Coining operations ceased in Madras in 1835.

MINTS

Arcot اركات

مچهلي پتن

Masulipatnam (Machilipatnam)

Pagoda Series
CASH

COPPER, 1.10 g
Obv: Bale mark. Rev: Date.

KM#	Date	Mintage	Good	VG	Fine	VF
314	1803	—	1.75	3.00	12.00	50.00

Machine struck, 11.5mm, 0.64 g

KM#	Date	Mintage	Fine	VF	XF	Unc
315	1803	—	.50	2.00	30.00	100.00
	1803	—			Proof	35.00

SILVER (OMS)

| 315a | 1803 | — | | | Proof | 350.00 |

GILT GOLD (OMS)

| 315b | 1803 | — | | | Proof | 75.00 |

GOLD (OMS)

| 315c | 1803 | — | | | Proof | — |

1/2 DUDU
(5 Cash)

COPPER, 4.43 g

KM#	Date	Mintage	Good	VG	Fine	VF
305	1802	—	—	Reported, not confirmed		
	1804	—	—	Reported, not confirmed		

V (5) CASH

COPPER, 16mm, 1.21 g
Obv: Line of dots above denomination.

KM#	Date	Mintage	VG	Fine	VF	XF
324	ND(1807)	—	4.00	15.00	50.00	175.00

21mm, 3.23 g
Obv: Large lettering.

KM#	Date	Mintage	Fine	VF	XF	Unc
316	1803	—	2.00	4.00	35.00	175.00

Obv: Small lettering.

| 317 | 1803 | — | 2.00 | 4.00 | 35.00 | 175.00 |

Modified design

| 318 | 1803 | — | | | Proof | 70.00 |

SILVER (OMS)

| 318a | 1803 | — | | | Proof | 125.00 |

GILT GOLD (OMS)

| 318b | 1803 | — | | | Proof | — |

GOLD (OMS)

| 318c | 1803 | — | | | Proof | — |

1/4 DUB
(5 Cash)

COPPER, 16.5mm, 2.57 g

| 325 | ND(1807) | — | 25.00 | 75.00 | 150.00 | 250.00 |

DUDU
COPPER, 6.30 g

KM#	Date	Mintage	Good	VG	Fine	VF
306	1801	—	2.00	5.00	15.00	70.00
	1805	—	2.00	5.00	15.00	70.00
	1806	—	—	Reported, not confirmed		

X (10) CASH

COPPER, 23.5mm, 4.83 g

KM#	Date	Mintage	VG	Fine	VF	XF
326	ND(1807)	—	5.00	20.00	100.00	250.00

NOTE: Seven varieties exist; i.e. dividing lines, dots and star, etc. Also exists struck on a XX Cash planchet.

Heavy issue, 25.8mm, 6.47 g

KM#	Date	Mintage	Fine	VF	XF	Unc
319	1803	—	1.75	6.00	45.00	250.00
	1803	—			Proof	90.00
	1808	—	1.75	6.00	45.00	250.00
	1808	—			Proof	90.00

SILVER (OMS)

| 319a | 1808 | — | | | Proof | 600.00 |

GILT GOLD (OMS)

| 319b | 1808 | — | | | Proof | 150.00 |

GOLD (OMS)

| 319c | 1808 | — | | | Proof | — |

COPPER, 25.8mm, 4.66 g

320	1808	—			45.00	250.00
	1808	—	1.50	6.00	45.00	250.00
	1808	—			Proof	90.00

1/2 DUB
(10 Cash)

COPPER, 22.7mm, 5.15 g

| 327 | 1807 | — | 35.00 | 100.00 | 175.00 | 300.00 |

26mm, 4.75 g

KM#	Date	Mintage	Good	VG	Fine	VF
345	1808	—	5.00	10.00	20.00	50.00

XX (20) CASH

COPPER, 26.5mm, 9.65 g

KM#	Date	Mintage	VG	Fine	VF	XF
328	ND(1807)	—	6.50	25.00	125.00	350.00

NOTE: Five varieties exist; i.e. dividing lines, dots and star.

Heavy issue, 30.7mm, 12.95 g

KM#	Date	Mintage	Fine	VF	XF	Unc
321	1803	—	2.50	8.00	60.00	300.00
	1803	—			Proof	120.00
	1808	—	2.50	8.00	60.00	300.00
	1808	—			Proof	120.00

NOTE: For 1804 date see Bombay 2 Pice Mule, KM#207.

SILVER (OMS)

| 321a | 1808 | — | | | Proof | 750.00 |

GILT GOLD (OMS)

| 321b | 1808 | — | | | Proof | 175.00 |

GOLD (OMS)

| 321c | 1808 | — | | | Proof | — |

COPPER, 30.7mm, 9.33 g

| 322 | 1808 | — | 2.00 | 8.00 | 60.00 | 300.00 |
| | 1808 | — | | | Proof | 120.00 |

Mule. Obv: KM#321. Rev: 1/48 Rupee, KM#394.

| 323 | 180x | | | | | |

DUB
(20 Cash)

COPPER, 27.2mm, 7.56 g

KM#	Date	Mintage	VG	Fine	VF	XF
329	1807	—	15.00	75.00	150.00	200.00
	1808	—	15.00	75.00	150.00	200.00

NOTE: An unusual issue referred to as a 'Regulating Dub'. The translation is 'This and three new Dubs are one small Fanam'.

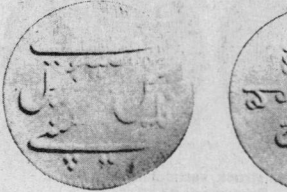 

26.5mm, 10.31 g

KM#	Date	Mintage	Fine	VF	XF	Unc
330	(1807)	—	50.00	125.00	200.00	350.00

26.8mm, 10.00 g

KM#	Date	Mintage	Good	VG	Fine	VF
346	1808	—	7.50	15.00	35.00	75.00

24.3mm, 9.90 g

| 347 | 1808 | — | 7.50 | 15.00 | 35.00 | 75.00 |

XL (40) CASH

COPPER, 36mm, 19.31 g
Obv: Large Persian legend.
Rev: Large legends.

KM#	Date	Mintage	VG	Fine	VF	XF
331	ND(1807)	—	12.50	50.00	200.00	500.00

Obv: Small Persian legend.
Rev: Small legends.
| 332 | ND(1807) | — | 12.50 | 50.00 | 200.00 | 500.00 |

Obv: Dots below "XL CASH".
| 333 | ND(1807) | — | 12.50 | 50.00 | 200.00 | 500.00 |
NOTE: Two other varieties exist.

2 DUBS
(40 Cash)

COPPER, 39.2mm, 20.61 g
| 334 | ND(1807) | — | 50.00 | 150.00 | 250.00 | 600.00 |

36mm, 19.69 gm.

KM#	Date	Mintage	Good	VG	Fine	VF
348	ND(1808)	—	8.00	20.00	75.00	150.00

FANAM

SILVER, 7-8mm, 0.91 g
KM#	Date	Mintage	VG	Fine	VF	XF
307	ND(1764-1807)	3.25	8.00	25.00	60.00

10mm, 0.92 g
| 335 | ND(1807) | .386 | 4.00 | 10.00 | 25.00 | 45.00 |

Obv: W/o center circle.
| 336 | ND(1807) | I.A. | 4.00 | 10.00 | 25.00 | 45.00 |

Obv: W/o branches below star.
| 337 | ND(1807) | I.A. | 4.00 | 10.00 | 25.00 | 45.00 |

11-11.5mm
| 349 | ND(1808) | 1.545 | 1.00 | 2.00 | 5.00 | 12.00 |
NOTE: Two varieties exist of the buckle at the bottom of the obverse.

DOUBLE (2) FANAM

SILVER, 10-11mm, 1.83 g
| 308 | ND(1764-1807) | 4.00 | 10.00 | 35.00 | 75.00 |

12.5mm, 1.85 g
Obv: Center circle. Rev: W/o center circle.
| 338 | ND(1807) | 1.511 | 2.00 | 5.00 | 15.00 | 35.00 |

Obv. and rev: W/o center circle.
| 339 | ND(1807) | I.A. | 2.00 | 5.00 | 15.00 | 35.00 |

Obv. and rev: Center circles.
| 340 | ND(1807) | I.A. | 2.00 | 5.00 | 15.00 | 35.00 |

Obv: W/o center circle. Rev: W/center circle.
| 341 | ND(1807) | I.A. | 2.00 | 5.00 | 15.00 | 35.00 |

| 350 | ND(1808) | 6.044 | 1.50 | 3.00 | 9.00 | 15.00 |
NOTE: Four varieties exist of the buckle at the bottom of the obverse.

5 FANAMS

SILVER, 17.3mm, 4.65 g
| 342 | ND(1807) | .988 | 4.00 | 10.00 | 25.00 | 75.00 |

21-22mm
| 351 | ND(1808) | 3.954 | 2.00 | 5.00 | 15.00 | 35.00 |
NOTE: Eight varieties exist of the buckle at the bottom of the obverse.

1/4 PAGODA

GOLD, 0.837 g
Obv: Single diety.
| A280 | ND(c.1800) | — | — | — | — | — |

SILVER, 27.2mm, 10.58 g
| 343 | ND(1807) | 1.773 | 13.50 | 35.00 | 125.00 | 300.00 |
NOTE: Two varieties exist, one with 9 stars to each side of the Gopuram, the other having 13 stars.

25.5mm
KM#	Date	Mintage	VG	Fine	VF	XF
352	ND(1808)	7.092	4.00	10.00	25.00	75.00
NOTE: Five varieties exist of the buckle at the bottom of the obverse.

1/2 PAGODA

.903 SILVER, 36.5mm, 21.17 g
| 344 | ND(1807) | .501 | 100.00 | 225.00 | 550.00 | 1000. |
NOTE: Four varieties exist; 12, 14, 15 or 18 stars in the field at left and right of the Gopuram. KM#344 can be found overstruck on Spanish or Spanish Colonial 8 reales.

35.5mm
Obv: Large English lettering.
| 353 | ND(1808) | 2.000 | 35.00 | 85.00 | 225.00 | 400.00 |
NOTE: KM#353 can be found overstruck on Spanish or Spanish Colonial 8 reales.

Obv: Small English lettering.
| 354 | ND(1808) | I.A. | 35.00 | 85.00 | 225.00 | 400.00 |
NOTE: KM#354 can be found overstruck on Spanish or Spanish Colonial 8 reales.

Obv: Error "HALF PGODA"
| 355 | ND(1808) | I.A. | 35.00 | 85.00 | 225.00 | 400.00 |
NOTE: KM#355 can be found overstruck on Spanish or Spanish Colonial 8 reales.

PAGODA

GOLD, 10-11mm
Star Pagoda
| 303 | ND(1740-1807) | 50.00 | 125.00 | 200.00 | 300.00 |

 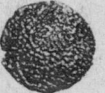

12-14mm, 3.43 g
Obv: Three Swami Pagoda
| 304 | ND(1740-1807) | 50.00 | 125.00 | 200.00 | 300.00 |

17.4mm, 2.97 g

KM#	Date	Mintage	Fine	VF	XF	Unc
356	ND(1808-15)	1.382	75.00	150.00	275.00	450.00

2 PAGODAS

GOLD, 20.5mm, 5.94 g
Obv: 14 stars.

| 357 | ND(1808-15) | 1.064 | 100.00 | 250.00 | 425.00 | 550.00 |

Obv: 18 stars.

| 358 | ND (1808-15) Inc. Ab. | | 100.00 | 250.00 | 425.00 | 550.00 |

TEGNAPATAM
Fort St. David

Rupee Series
1/2 DUB

COPPER, dump, 16mm, 6.60-6.90 g
Obv: Persian *Struck at Machhlipatanbandar*.
Rev: Date, legend.

KM#	Date	Mintage	Good	VG	Fine	VF
385	AH1175-1222	—	5.00	9.00	13.50	20.00

PIE

COPPER

KM#	Date	Year	Mintage	VF	XF	Unc
428	AH1240	1825	4.741	1.00	4.00	15.00
	1240	1825	Inc. Ab.	—	Proof	80.00
	1248	1833	—	10.00	20.00	50.00

DUB

COPPER, dump, 20mm, 13.00-14.00 g
Obv: Persian *Struck at Machhlipatanbandar*.
Rev: Date, legend.

KM#	Date	Mintage	Good	VG	Fine	VF
386	AH1175-1222	—	5.50	11.50	21.50	35.00

Similar to KM#386 but w/ English M on rev.

| 387 | AH1218 | — | 7.50 | 15.00 | 22.50 | 40.00 |

2 PIES

COPPER

KM#	Date	Year	Mintage	VF	XF	Unc
429	AH1240	1825	7.126	2.00	6.00	20.00
	1240	1825	Inc. Ab.	—	Proof	100.00

4 PIES

COPPER
Rev: Right wreath tip points up.

KM#	Date	Year	Mintage	VF	XF	Unc
430	AH1240	1824	7.136	3.00	8.00	25.00
	1240	1824	Inc. Ab.	—	Proof	150.00

Rev: Right wreath tip points down.

| 431 | AH1240 | 1825 | — | 3.00 | 8.00 | 25.00 |
| | 1240 | 1825 | Inc. Ab. | — | Proof | 150.00 |

Rev: Right wreath tip points up.

| 432 | AH1240 | 1825 | — | 3.00 | 8.00 | 25.00 |

Rev: Right wreath tip in straight line.

| 433 | AH1240 | 1825 | Inc. Ab. | 3.00 | 8.00 | 25.00 |

1/16 RUPEE

In the name of Alamgir II

SILVER, 10.5mm
Mint: Madras
(mm: Lotus, 1817-1835)
Oblique milling.

KM#	Date	Year	Fine	VF	XF	Unc
411	AH1172	6	1.00	2.00	10.00	20.00

Mint: Calcutta
(mm: Rose 1823-1825)
Oblique milling

| 423 | AH1172 | 6 | — | 2.00 | 8.00 | 15.00 |

2 ANNAS

SILVER, 16.4mm, 1.48 g

KM#	Date	Mintage	VG	Fine	VF	XF
405	ND(1808)	.065	100.00	250.00	500.00	650.00

Rev: W/o star.

| 406 | ND(1808) | I. A. | 100.00 | 250.00 | 500.00 | 650.00 |

1/8 RUPEE

In the name of Alamgir II

SILVER, 16.5mm, 1.51 g
Mint: Madras
(mm: Lotus 1807)
Oblique milling, 16.5mm, 1.51 g

KM#	Date	Year	Mintage	VF	XF	Unc
399	AH1172	6	.020	45.00	100.00	175.00

(mm: Lotus 1812-1817)
13.5mm, 1.46 g
Oblique milling

| 408 | AH1172 | 6 | .104 | 2.00 | 8.00 | 20.00 |

SILVER, 13.5mm, 1.46 g
Mint: Madras
(mm: Closed form lotus 1817-1835)
Oblique milling

| 412 | AH1172 | 6 | 10.790 | 2.00 | 8.00 | 20.00 |

Mint: Calcutta
(mm: Rose 1823-1825)
Oblique milling

KM#	Date	Year	Mintage	VF	XF	Unc
424	AH1172	6	—	2.00	10.00	20.00

4 ANNAS

SILVER, 17mm, 2.97 g

KM#	Date	Mintage	VG	Fine	VF	XF
407	ND(1808)	.044	125.00	300.00	600.00	750.00

1/4 RUPEE

In the name of Alamgir II

SILVER, 15.5mm, 2.81-2.86 g
Mint: Masulipatnam
(mm: Lotus)

KM#	Date	Year	VG	Fine	VF	XF
388	AH1200	—	10.00	15.00	30.00	100.00
	1210	—	10.00	15.00	30.00	100.00

Mint: Madras
(mm: Lotus 1807)
16.5mm, 3.02 g
Oblique milling

KM#	Date	Year	Mintage	VF	XF	Unc
400	AH1172	6	.018	25.00	100.00	175.00

(mm: Lotus 1812-1817)
17.4mm, 2.91 g
Indented cord milling

| 409 | AH1172 | 6 | .784 | 3.00 | 10.00 | 25.00 |
| | 1176 | 6 | Inc. Ab. | 3.00 | 10.00 | 25.00 |

SILVER, 17.4mm, 2.91 g
Mint: Madras
(mm: Closed form lotus 1817-1835)
Indented cord milling.

| 413 | AH1172 | 6 | 5.227 | 5.00 | 20.00 | 50.00 |

Mint: Calcutta
(mm: Rose 1823-1825)
Vertical milling.

| 425 | AH1172 | 6 | — | 4.00 | 10.00 | 20.00 |

(mm: Rose, crescent added 1830-1835)
Plain edge

| 434 | AH1172 | 6 | — | 2.00 | 10.00 | 20.00 |
| | 1172 | 6 | — | — | Proof | 300.00 |

1/2 RUPEE

In the name of Alamgir II

Madras Presidency / British / INDIA 975

SILVER, 22mm, 6.05 g
Mint: Madras. (mm: Lotus 1807).
Oblique milling

KM#	Date	Year	Mintage	VF	XF	Unc
401	AH1172	6	.108	30.00	75.00	150.00

21.7mm, 5.83 g.
Indented cord milling.

| 402 | AH1172 | 6 | 3.392 | 5.00 | 15.00 | 30.00 |
| | 1176 | 6 | Inc. Ab. | 5.00 | 15.00 | 30.00 |

Mint: Madras
(mm: Closed formed lotus 1817-1835)
Indented cord milling.

| 414 | AH1172 | 6 | 10.674 | 3.00 | 15.00 | 25.00 |

Mint: Calcutta
(mm: Rose 1823-1825)
Vertical milling

| 426 | AH1172 | 6 | — | 5.00 | 35.00 | 65.00 |

(mm: Rose, crescent added 1830-1835)
Plain edge

| 435 | AH1172 | 6 | — | 5.00 | 35.00 | 65.00 |
| | 1172 | 6 | — | — | Proof | 350.00 |

RUPEE

SILVER, 28mm, 12.1 g
Mint: Madras. (mm: Lotus 1807).
Oblique milling

| 403 | AH1172 | 6 | 2.145 | 15.00 | 50.00 | 75.00 |

27.8mm, 11.66 g
(mm: Lotus 1812-1817)
Indented cord milling

| 410 | AH1172 | 6 | 10.939 | 3.00 | 10.00 | 25.00 |
| | 1176 | 6 | Inc. Ab. | 3.00 | 10.00 | 25.00 |

Mint: Madras
(mm: Closed form lotus 1817-1835)
Indented cord milling

KM#	Date	Year	Mintage	VF	XF	Unc
415	AH1172	6	63.116	3.00	15.00	25.00

Mint: Calcutta
(mm: Rose 1823-1825)
Vertical milling

| 427 | AH1172 | 6 | — | 3.00 | 20.00 | 35.00 |

(mm: Rose, crescent added 1830-1835)
Plain edge

| 436 | AH1172 | 6 | — | 3.00 | 20.00 | 35.00 |
| | 1172 | 6 | — | — | Proof | 400.00 |

NOTE: Dump rupees in the name of Alamgir, with a small crescent to left of regnal year and mint name "Arcot", were struck by the French (see India-French) as were Arcot rupees in the names of other Mughal emperors.

2 RUPEES

SILVER, 39.5mm, 24.19 g.
Mint: Madras. (mm: Lotus 1807).

KM#	Date	Year	Mintage	Fine	VF	XF
404.1	AH1172	2	.165	200.00	375.00	700.00

| 404.2 | AH1172 | 6 | Inc. Ab. | 200.00 | 375.00 | 700.00 |

NOTE: Struck over Spanish or Spanish Colonial 8 Reales.

1/4 MOHUR

GOLD, 17.4mm, 2.91 g
Mint: Madras. (mm: Lotus 1817).

KM#	Date	Year	Mintage	VF	XF	Unc
416	AH1172	6	2,000	1000.	1500.	2750.

GOLD, 17mm
Mint: Madras. (mm: Lotus 1817).

KM#	Date	Mintage	Fine	VF	XF	Unc
419	ND(1819)	.092	125.00	250.00	350.00	600.00

5 RUPEES

GOLD, 19.5mm, 3.88 g

| 422 | ND(1820) | 2.180 | 45.00 | 75.00 | 125.00 | 175.00 |

1/2 MOHUR

GOLD, 21.7mm, 5.83 g
Mint: Madras. (mm: Lotus 1817).

KM#	Date	Year	Mintage	VF	XF	Unc
417	AH1172	6	7,500	750.00	1250.	2000.

GOLD, 21.2mm

KM#	Date	Mintage	Fine	VF	XF	Unc
420	ND(1819)	.213	150.00	350.00	550.00	750.00

MOHUR

GOLD, 27.8mm, 11.66 g
Mint: Madras. (mm: Lotus 1817).

KM#	Date	Year	Mintage	VF	XF	Unc
418	AH1172	6	.059	600.00	1000.	1750.

Mint: Madras. (mm: Lotus 1817)

KM#	Date	Mintage	Fine	VF	XF	Unc
421	ND(1819)	1.118	175.00	200.00	425.00	600.00

COLONIAL COINAGE

This section lists the coins of British India from reign of William IV (1835) to the reign of George VI (1947). The issues are divided into two main parts:

Coins struck under the authority of the East India Company (E.I.C.) from 1835 until the trading monopoly of the E.I.C. was abolished in 1853. From August 2, 1858 the property and powers of the Company were transferred to the British Crown. From November 1, 1858 to November 1, 1862 the coins continued to bear the design and inscription of the Company.

Coins struck under the authority of the Crown (Regal issues) from 1862 until 1947.

The first regal issues bear the date 1862 and were struck with the date 1862 unchanged until 1874. From then onward all coins bear the year date. The copper coins dated 1862 have not yet been fully attributed and therefore are not listed by the mint of issue.

In 1877 Queen Victoria was proclaimed Empress of India and the title of the obverse legend was changed accordingly.

For a detailed account of the work of the various mints and the numerous die varieties the general collector and specialist should refer to *The Coins of the British Commonwealth*

of Nations to the end of the reign of King George VI - 1952 - Part 4, India, Vol. 1 and 2 by F. Pridmore, Spink, 1980.

RULERS

British until 1947

MINT MARKS

The coins of British India were struck at the following mints, indicated in the catalogue by either capital letters after the date when the actual letter appears on the coins or small letters in ( ) designating the mint of issue. Plain dates indicate Royal Mint strikes.

B-Bombay, 1835-1947
C or CM-Calcutta, 1835-1947
H - Ralph Heaton & Sons, Birmingham (1857-1858)
I-Bombay, 1918-1919
L-Lahore, 1943-1945
M-Madras, 1869 (closed Sept. 1869)
P-Pretoria, South Africa, 1943-1944
W - J. Watt & Sons, Birmingham (1860)

In 1947 British rule came to an end and India was divided into two self-governing countries, India and Pakistan. In 1971 Bangladash seceded from Pakistan. All are now independent republics and although they are still members of the British Commonwealth of Nations, their coinages do not belong to the British India series.

MONETARY SYSTEM

3 Pies = 1 Pice
4 Pice = 1 Anna
16 Annas = 1 Rupee
15 Rupees = 1 Mohur

The transition from the coins of the Moslem monetary system began with the silver pattern Rupees of William IV, 1834, issued by the East India Company, with the value on the reverse, given in English, Bengali, Persian and Nagari characters. This coinage was struck for several years, as dated, except for the currency Rupee which was struck from 1835 to 1840, all dated 1835.

The portrait coins issued by the East India Company for Victoria show two different head designs on the obverse, which are called Type I and Type II. The coins with Type I head have a continuous obverse legend and were struck from 1840 to 1851. The coins with the Type II head have a divided obverse legend and were struck from 1850 (Calcutta) until 1862. The date on the coins remained unchanged, Rupee, 1/2 Rupee and 1/4 Rupee are dated 1840, the 2 Annas and the Mohur are dated 1841. Both issues were struck at the Calcutta, Bombay and Madras Mints.

Type I coins have on the reverse a dot after the date, those of Type II have no dot, except for some rare 1/4 Rupees and 2 Annas. The latter are mules, struck from reverse dies of the preceding issue.

The following initials appear on the obverse on the truncation:

F - William N. Forbes, Calcutta, 1836-1855
R.S. - Robert Saunders, Calcutta, 1826-1836
S Incuse (Type I)
WW raised or incuse (Type II)
WWS or SWW (Type II)
WWB raised (Type II)

On both issues, the "S" is the initial of Major, later Lt. Col. J. T. Smith, mintmaster at Madras from February 1840 to September 1855.
The 'B' which occurs only on Rupees of Type II, is the initial of Major, later Lt. Col. J.H. Bell (mintmaster at Madras, 1855-1859).
The initials WW which appear on all coins of Type II, are those of William Wyon, Chief Engraver of the Royal Mint, London, who prepared this obverse design in 1849.

Proof and Proof-like restrikes

Original proofs are similar to early English Specimen strikes with wire edges and matte finish busts, arms, etc. Restrikes of most of the coins minted from the period 1835 were regularly supplied until this practice was discontinued on July 1, 1970.

Early proof restrikes are found with slight hairlining from polishing of the old dies. Bust, field, arms etc. are of even smoothness and exhibit a small raised diamond on obverse field behind head.

Modern proof-like (P/L) restrikes are usually heavily hairlined from excessive polishing of the old dies and have a glassy, varnished or proof-like appearance. Many are common while some are quite scarce including some unusual mulings.

East India Company

1/12 ANNA

(1 Pie)

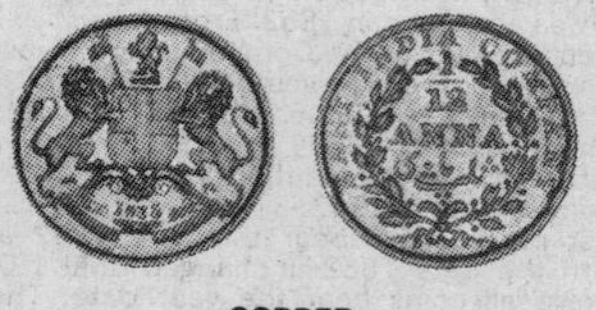

COPPER
Bombay, 18.0mm; Madras, 17.7-17.9mm

KM#	Date	Mintage	Fine	VF	XF	Unc
445	1835(b)	72.313	1.00	2.50	4.00	8.00
	1835(m)	133.788	.75	2.00	3.00	6.00
	1835(c)	—	—	—	Proof	75.00
	1848(c)	14.380	1.25	3.00	5.00	10.00

1/2 PICE

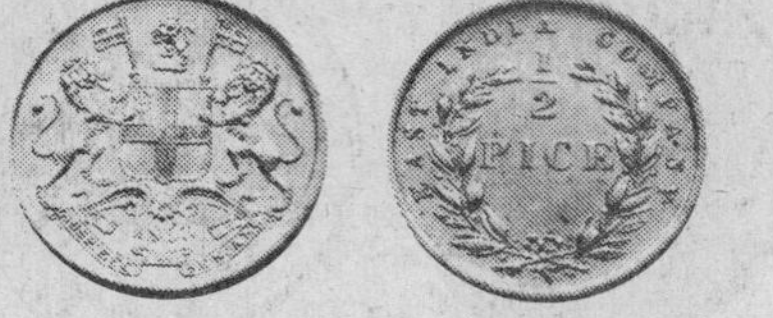

COPPER

KM#	Date	Mintage	Fine	VF	XF	Unc
464	1853(c)	62.408	1.75	3.50	8.00	20.00
	1853(c)	—	—	—	Proof	100.00
	1853(c) (restrike)		—	—	P/L	25.00

1/4 ANNA

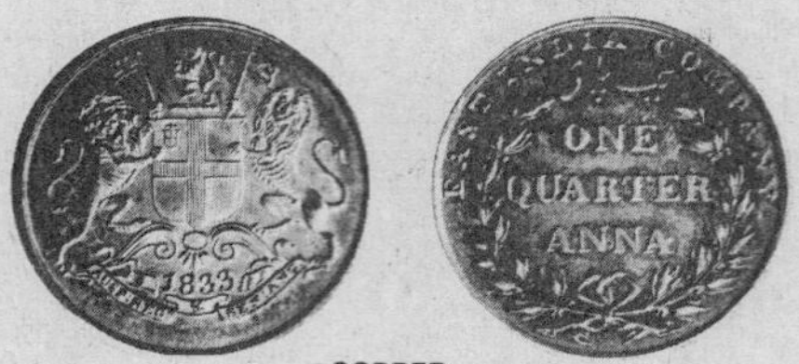

COPPER
Obv: Small shield.
Rev. large leg: ONE QUARTER ANNA.

KM#	Date	Mintage	Fine	VF	XF	Unc
446.1	1833(b)	—	—	—	Proof	175.00
	1835(b)	36.767	1.00	2.00	4.00	10.00
	1835(m)	186.530	1.00	2.00	4.00	10.00

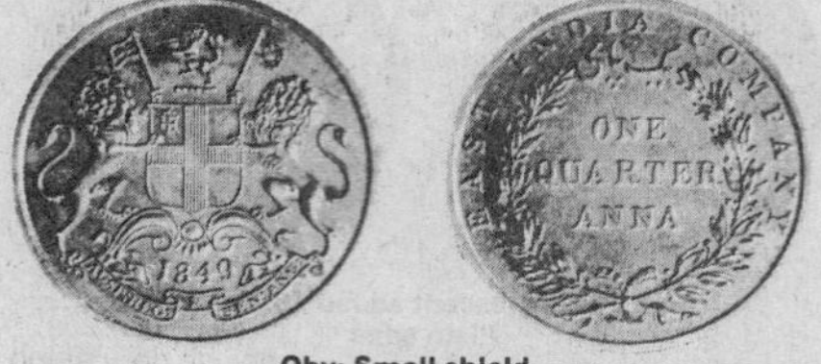

Obv: Small shield.
Rev. small leg: ONE QUARTER ANNA.
Calcutta: 26.2mm; Bombay: 25.2mm; Madras: 25.5mm.

KM#	Date	Mintage	Fine	VF	XF	Unc
446.2	1835(b)	Inc. Ab.	1.00	2.00	4.00	10.00
	1835(c)	755.059	1.00	2.00	4.00	10.00
	1835(c)	—	—	—	Proof	75.00
	1835(m)	Inc. Ab.	1.00	2.00	4.00	10.00
	1849	—	—	—	Proof	250.00

NOTE: 6 varieties for Madras, 2 varieties for Calcutta.

Obv: Large shield.
Rev: Wreath tips are single leaves.

KM#	Date	Mintage	Fine	VF	XF	Unc
463.1	1857(h)	47.040	1.00	2.00	10.00	45.00
	1858(w)	62.720	.85	1.50	2.50	10.00
	1858(w)	—	—	—	Proof	125.00

Rev: Wreath tips are double leaves.

KM#	Date	Mintage	Fine	VF	XF	Unc
463.2	1857(h)	Inc. Ab.	.85	2.00	10.00	45.00
	1857(h)	—	—	—	Proof	125.00
	1858(h)	172.480	1.00	2.00	4.00	10.00
	1858(h)	—	—	—	Proof	125.00

1/2 ANNA

COPPER
Mule. Obv. Bombay KM#251. Rev: KM#447.

KM#	Date	Mintage	Fine	VF	XF	Unc
A447	1834		—	—	275.00	450.00

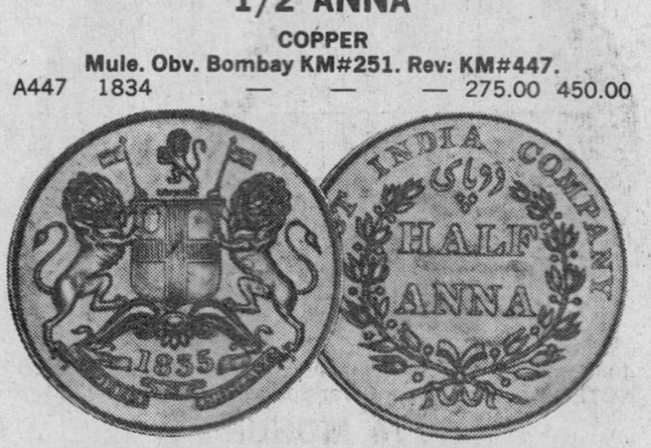

Bombay: 29.7mm; Madras: 30.8mm.

KM#	Date	Mintage	Fine	VF	XF	Unc
447.1	1835(b)	8.658	2.00	4.00	10.00	50.00
	1835(b)	—	—	—	Proof	100.00
	1835(b) (restrike)		—	—	P/L	35.00
	1835(m)	95.203	2.00	4.00	10.00	50.00
	1835(m)	—	—	—	Proof	100.00
	1845C	17.160	2.00	4.00	12.50	65.00

Beaded rim w/milled edge.

KM#	Date	Mintage	Fine	VF	XF	Unc
447.2	1835(c)	—	—	—	Proof	300.00

SILVER (OMS)

KM#	Date	Mintage	Fine	VF	XF	Unc
447.2a	1835(c)	—	—	—	Proof	550.00

2 ANNAS

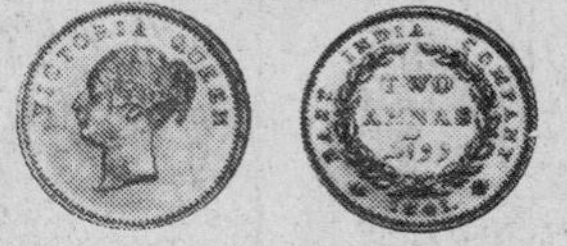

1.4600 g, .917 SILVER, .0430 oz ASW
Type I: Obv. leg. continuous.
Mint: Bombay, 15.8mm

KM#	Date	Mintage	Fine	VF	XF	Unc
459.1	1841(b)	11.431	2.00	4.00	8.50	20.00

Mint: Calcutta, 15.4-15.5mm
Rev: W/crescent on left ribbon bow.

KM#	Date	Mintage	Fine	VF	XF	Unc
459.2	1841(c)	8.385	2.00	4.00	8.50	20.00
	1841(c)	—	—	—	Proof	50.00

Obv: S incuse on truncation, small "v" on right tie of wreath.

KM#	Date	Mintage	Fine	VF	XF	Unc
459.3	1841(m)	10.503	3.50	6.50	12.50	25.00
	1841(b) (restrike)		—	—	P/L	25.00

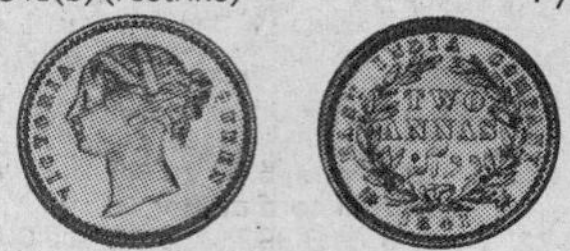

Type II: Obv. leg. divided.
Rev: Type I, dot after date.

KM#	Date	Mintage	Fine	VF	XF	Unc
460.1	1841.(c)	43.002	7.50	12.50	25.00	50.00
	1841.(c) (early restrike)			—	Proof	150.00

Obv: W.W. raised on truncation

KM#	Date	Mintage	Fine	VF	XF	Unc
460.2	1841(c)	Inc. Ab.	1.50	3.00	7.50	15.00
	1841(c)	—	—	—	Proof	150.00

Obv: W.W raised on truncation.

KM#	Date	Mintage	Fine	VF	XF	Unc
460.3	1841(b)	8.427	1.50	3.00	7.50	15.00

Obv: S incuse, W.W. raised.

KM#	Date	Mintage	Fine	VF	XF	Unc
460.4	1841(m)	26.930	2.00	4.00	8.50	17.50
	1841(m)	—	—	—	Proof	150.00

Obv: WW raised.

KM#	Date	Mintage	Fine	VF	XF	Unc
460.5	1849	(early restrike)		—	Proof	250.00
	1849	(restrike)	—	—	P/L	25.00

1/4 RUPEE

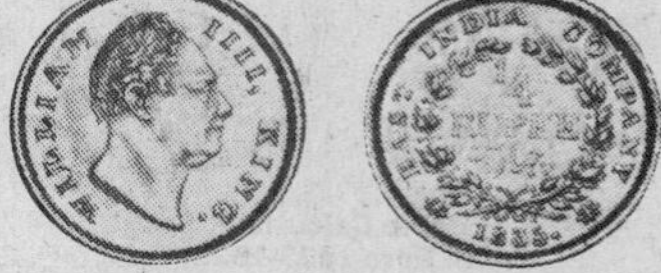

2.9200 g, .917 SILVER, .0860 oz ASW
Obv: F in relief on truncation.

آنا

Rev: "*ana*" in Persian:

KM#	Date	Mintage	Fine	VF	XF	Unc
448.1	1835.(c)	.922	3.50	6.50	12.50	30.00
	1835.(c)	—	—	—	Proof	600.00
	1835.(c) (restrike)		—	—	P/L	25.00

Obv: F incuse on truncation.

KM#	Date	Mintage	Fine	VF	XF	Unc
448.2	1835.(c)	Inc. Ab.	4.50	7.50	15.00	40.00
	1835(c)	Inc. Ab.	3.50	6.50	12.50	35.00

Obv: W/o initial on truncation.

KM#	Date	Mintage	Fine	VF	XF	Unc
448.3	1835(b)	5.760	5.00	10.00	20.00	40.00
	1835(b)	—	—	—	Proof	600.00
	1835(b) (early restrike)			—	Proof	200.00

Obv: RS incuse on truncation.

KM#	Date	Mintage	Fine	VF	XF	Unc
448.4	1835(c)	—	5.00	10.00	20.00	40.00

آنہ

Obv: RS incuse. Rev: "*ana*" in Hindi:

KM#	Date	Mintage	Fine	VF	XF	Unc
448.5	1835(c)	Inc. Ab.	11.50	22.50	45.00	90.00
	1835(c)	—	—	—	Proof	600.00

GOLD (OMS)

KM#	Date	Mintage	Fine	VF	XF	Unc
448a	1835(c)	—	—	—	—	—

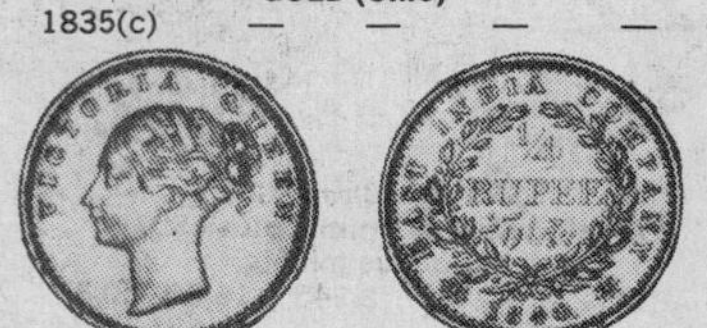

2.9200 g, .917 SILVER, .0860 oz AGW
Type I: Obv. leg. continuous.
Mint: Bombay, 19.7mm
Obv: "Plump" head.

KM#	Date	Mintage	Fine	VF	XF	Unc
453.1	1840(b)	10.617	2.50	5.00	10.00	25.00

Mint: Calcutta, 19.5mm.
Rev: W/crescent on left ribbon bow.
First rev: 20 berries.

KM#	Date	Mintage	Fine	VF	XF	Unc
453.2	1840(c)	12.994	2.50	5.00	10.00	20.00
	1840(c)	—	—	—	Proof	200.00

Obv: S incuse on truncation.
First rev: W/v on right ribbon bow.
First rev: S incuse on truncation.

KM#	Date	Mintage	Fine	VF	XF	Unc
453.3	1840(m)	6.450	3.75	7.50	15.00	30.00

Obv: "Indian" head w/thinner features.

British / INDIA 977

KM#	Date	Mintage	Fine	VF	XF	Unc
		Second rev: 34 berries.				
453.4	1840.(c)	Inc. Ab.	2.50	5.00	10.00	20.00
	1840.(c)		—	—	Proof	200.00

Type II. Obv. leg. divided.
Mule. Rev. KM#453.4.

| 454.1 | 1840.(c) | 32.012 | 10.00 | 20.00 | 40.00 | 80.00 |
| | 1840.(c) | | — | — | Proof | 200.00 |

Obv: W.W. raised on truncation.

| 454.2 | 1840(c) | Inc. Ab. | 2.50 | 5.00 | 10.00 | 20.00 |
| | 1840.(c) | | — | — | Proof | 200.00 |

Obv: W.W. and B raised on truncation.

| 454.3 | 1840.(m) | 13.664 | — | 6.00 | 12.00 | 30.00 |

Obv: W.W. S raised on truncation.

| 454.4 | 1840(m) | Inc. Ab. | 4.00 | 8.00 | 15.00 | 30.00 |

Obv: W.W. on truncation. Plain edge.

| 454.5 | 1849 | (early restrike) | — | — | Proof | 300.00 |
| | 1849 | (restrike) | — | — | P/L | 30.00 |

Milled edge.

| 454.6 | 1849 | (early restrike) | — | — | Proof | 300.00 |
| | 1849 | (restrike) | — | — | P/L | 30.00 |

1/2 RUPEE

5.8300 g, .917 SILVER, .1719 oz ASW
Obv: W/o initial on truncation.

| 449.1 | 1835.(b) | 3.573 | 7.50 | 15.00 | 30.00 | 60.00 |
| | 1835.(b)(restrike) | | — | — | P/L | 18.50 |

Obv: F raised on truncation.

| 449.2 | 1835.(c) | 6.700 | 7.50 | 15.00 | 30.00 | 60.00 |

Obv: F incuse.

| 449.3 | 1835.(c) | | 7.50 | 15.00 | 30.00 | 60.00 |
| | 1835.(c) | (early restrike) | — | — | P/L | 250.00 |

Obv: RS Incuse.

| 449.4 | 1835.(c) | .521 | 10.00 | 20.00 | 40.00 | 80.00 |
| | 1835.(c) | | — | — | Proof | 700.00 |

GOLD (OMS)

| 449a | 1835(c) | | — | — | — | — |

5.8300 g, .917 SILVER, .1719 oz ASW
Type I: Obv. leg. continuous.
Mint: Bombay, 24.5-24.6mm
Obv: "Plump" head.

| 455.1 | 1840.(b) | 9.844 | 5.00 | 10.00 | 20.00 | 45.00 |
| | 1840.(b) | (restrike) | — | — | P/L | 35.00 |

Mint: Calcutta: 24.2-24.4mm
Rev: W/crescent on left ribbon bow.

| 455.2 | 1840.(c) | 8.049 | 5.00 | 10.00 | 20.00 | 45.00 |
| | 1840.(c) | | — | — | Proof | 250.00 |

Obv: S incuse on truncation.

| 455.3 | 1840.(m) | 1.874 | — | — | Rare | — |

Obv: "Indian" head w/thinner features.
Rev: W/mm, crescent, on left ribbon bow.

455.4	1840.(c) Inc. Ab.	5.00	10.00	20.00	45.00
	1840.(c) Inc. Ab.	—	—	Proof	250.00
	1840.(c) (restrike)	—	—	P/L	35.00

Mule. Obv: KM#455.1. Rev: KM#456.1.

| A455 | 1840.(c) | — | 4.50 | 8.50 | 17.50 | 40.00 |

Type II: Obv. leg. divided.
Obv: .W.W incuse.

| 456.1 | 1840(b & c) | | | | | |
| | | 18.551 | 4.00 | 8.00 | 15.00 | 35.00 |

Obv: W.W. incuse and S.

| 456.2 | 1840(m) | 2.507 | 5.00 | 10.00 | 20.00 | 40.00 |

KM#	Date	Mintage	Fine	VF	XF	Unc
		Obv:. W.W incuse. Milled edge.				
456.3	1849	(early restrike)	—	—	Proof	400.00
	1849	(restrike)	—	—	P/L	50.00

Plain edge.

| 456.4 | 1849 | (early restrike) | — | — | Proof | 400.00 |
| | 1849 | (restrike) | — | — | P/L | 50.00 |

Mule. Obv: KM#456.1. Rev: KM#455.4.

| A456 | 1840. | — | 4.50 | 8.50 | 17.50 | 40.00 |

RUPEE

11.6600 g, .917 SILVER, .3438 oz ASW
Obv. leg: Thick lettering. W/o initial on truncation.

450.1	1835.(b)	53.713	8.50	12.50	25.00	50.00
	1835.(b)		—	—	Proof	500.00
	1835.(b) (restrike)	—	—	P/L	40.00

Obv: F raised on truncation.

| 450.2 | 1835.(c) | — | 8.50 | 15.00 | 30.00 | 60.00 |
| | 1835.(c) | | — | — | Proof | 500.00 |

Obv: F incuse on truncation.

450.3	1835.(c)	—	8.50	15.00	30.00	60.00
	1835.(c)		—	—	Proof	850.00
	1835.(c) (early restrike)	—	—	Proof	350.00

Obv: RS incuse on truncation.

| 450.4 | 1835.(c) | 15.759 | 10.00 | 20.00 | 40.00 | 85.00 |
| | 1835.(c) | | — | — | Proof | 850.00 |

| 450.5 | 1840/35.(c) | — | 90.00 | 175.00 | 300.00 | 600.00 |
| 450.6 | 1835.(c) | — | — | — | Rare | — |

Obv. leg: Thin lettering. RS incuse on truncation.

| 450.7 | 1835.(c) | — | 35.00 | 60.00 | 100.00 | 250.00 |

GOLD (OMS)

| 450a | 1835.(c) | — | — | — | — | — |

11.6600 g, .917 SILVER, .3438 oz ASW
Type I: Obv. leg. continuous.

The major reverse varieties occur on the Type I Rupees of all three mints. The first reverse has 19 berries in the wreath, the second reverse has 34 and 35 berries (Calcutta) and 35 berries (Bombay and Madras). There are several minor varieties of the first reverse, but these are not listed. Madras specimens of Type I with the 1st reverse also have a small, raised "V" on the lower part of the right ribbon bow.

Mint: Calcutta, 1st rev. 31.5mm, 2nd rev. 31.1-31.3mm
Obv: "Plump" head.
Rev: 19 berries w/crescent on left ribbon bow.

457.1	1840.(c)					
		179.935	6.00	10.00	17.50	40.00
	1840.(c)		—	—	Proof	325.00

Mint: Bombay, 31.6-31.8mm
Rev: 35 berries.

KM#	Date	Mintage	Fine	VF	XF	Unc
457.2	1840.(b)					
		109.838	7.00	10.00	17.50	40.00

Rev: 19 berries, small diamonds.

| 457.3 | 1840.(b) Inc. Ab. | 7.00 | 10.00 | 17.50 | 40.00 |

Rev: 19 berries, large diamonds.

| 457.4 | 1840.(b) Inc. Ab. | 7.00 | 10.00 | 17.50 | 40.00 |

Mint: Madras, 31.9-32.2mm
Obv: S incuse on truncation. Rev: 19 berries, small diamonds, w/V on right ribbon bow.

| 457.5 | 1840.(m) 21.898 | 9.00 | 18.50 | 37.50 | 75.00 |

Rev: 19 berries, large diamonds.

| 457.6 | 1840.(m) I.A. | 9.00 | 18.50 | 37.50 | 75.00 |

Obv: W/o S.
Rev: 19 berries, w/v on left ribbon bow.

| 457.7 | 1840.(m) I.A. | 9.00 | 18.50 | 37.50 | 75.00 |

Obv: S incuse. Rev: 20 berries, w/o small v.

| 457.8 | 1840.(m) I.A. | 8.00 | 15.00 | 20.00 | 40.00 |

Obv: S incuse. Rev: 35 berries, w/o small v.

| 457.9 | 1840.(m) I.A. | 10.00 | 15.00 | 30.00 | 60.00 |

Obv: "Indian" head w/thinner features.
Rev: 35 berries w/crescent on left ribbon bow.

| 457.10 | 1840.(c) Inc. Ab. | 9.00 | 18.50 | 37.50 | 75.00 |
| | 1840.(c) | — | — | 18.50 | Proof | 350.00 |

Rev: 34 berries.

| 457.11 | 1840.(c) | — | — | — | Proof | 350.00 |

Type II: Obv. leg. divided.
Mint: Calcutta, 30.5mm.
Obv: W.W. raised. Rev: 28 berries, small diamonds.

| 458.1 | 1840(c) 398.554 | 2.50 | 5.00 | 10.00 | 20.00 |

Obv: W.W. raised. Rev: 28 berries, large diamonds.

| 458.2 | 1840.(c) Inc. Ab. | 2.50 | 5.00 | 10.00 | 20.00 |

Mint: Bombay, 30.8mm
Obv: W.W. raised. Rev: 27 berries.

| 458.3 | 1840(b) 312.598 | — | 5.00 | 10.00 | 20.00 |
| | 1840.(b) | — | — | — | Proof | 325.00 |

Obv: W.W.B raised, small B. Rev: 28 berries.

| 458.4 | 1840(m) 55.049 | 2.50 | 5.00 | 10.00 | 20.00 |

Obv: W.W.B raised, large B. Rev: 28 berries.

| 458.5 | 1840(m) Inc. Ab. | 2.50 | 5.00 | 10.00 | 20.00 |

Obv: W.W.B raised, small letters. Rev: 28 berries.

| 458.6 | 1840(m) Inc. Ab. | 2.50 | 5.00 | 10.00 | 20.00 |

Obv: W.W.S raised. Rev: 28 berries.

| 458.7 | 1840(m) | 2.50 | 5.00 | 10.00 | 20.00 |

Obv: W.W. Rev: 25 berries.
Milled edge.

| 458.8 | 1849 | (early restrike) | — | — | Proof | 500.00 |
| | 1849 | (restrike) | — | — | P/L | 50.00 |

Plain edge

| 458.9 | 1849 | (early restrike) | — | — | Proof | 500.00 |
| | 1849 | (restrike) | — | — | P/L | 50.00 |

Mule. Obv: KM#458.1. Rev: 25 berries.

| 458.10 | 1840 | — | — | — | Rare | — |

COPPER (OMS)
Obv: W.W.B

| 458a | 1840(m) | — | — | — | Rare | — |

MOHUR

11.6600 g, .917 GOLD, .3437 oz AGW
Obv: W/o initials.
Milled edge.

| 451.1 | 1835(b) | — | 200.00 | 350.00 | 650.00 | 1000. |
| | 1835(b) (restrike) | — | — | — | P/L | 275.00 |

Obv: RS incuse on truncation.

451.2	1835(c)	.029	275.00	450.00	650.00	1000.
	1835(c)	—	—	—	Proof	—
	1835(c)	—	—	—	P/L	400.00

Obv: F incuse on truncation.

| 451.3 | 1835(c) | .111 | 250.00 | 375.00 | 500.00 | 800.00 |
| | 1835(c) (restrike) | — | — | — | P/L | 500.00 |

Plain edge.
Obv: RS incuse on truncation.

| 451.4 | 1835(c) | — | — | — | Proof | Rare |

978 British / INDIA

Obv: F incuse on truncation.

KM#	Date	Mintage	Fine	VF	XF	Unc
451.5	1835(c)	—	—	—	Proof	Rare

SILVER (OMS)

KM#	Date	Mintage	Fine	VF	XF	Unc
451a	1835(c)	—	—	—	Proof	Rare

COPPER (OMS)

KM#	Date	Mintage	Fine	VF	XF	Unc
451b	1835(c)	—	—	—	Proof	650.00

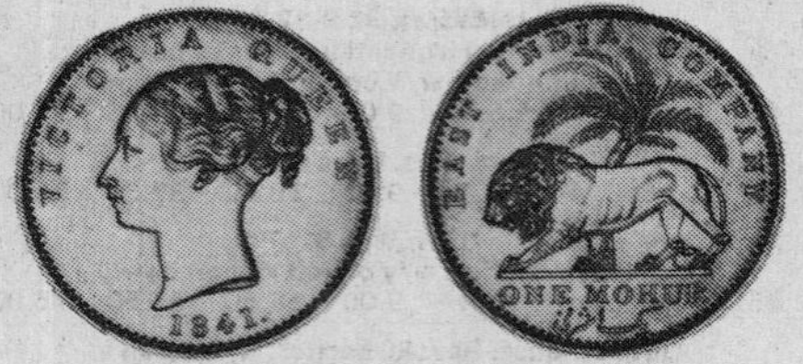

11.6600 g, .917 GOLD, .3437 oz AGW
Type I: Obv. leg. continuous.
Obv: Dot on truncation.

KM#	Date	Mintage	Fine	VF	XF	Unc
461.1	1841.(b)	5,960	—	—	650.00	1000.
461.2	1841.(c)	.601	175.00	225.00	300.00	400.00
	1841.(c)	—	—	—	Proof	1500.

Obv: S incuse on truncation.

KM#	Date	Mintage	Fine	VF	XF	Unc
461.3	1841.(m)	.032	250.00	325.00	450.00	600.00
	1841.(m)	—	—	—	Proof	1500.

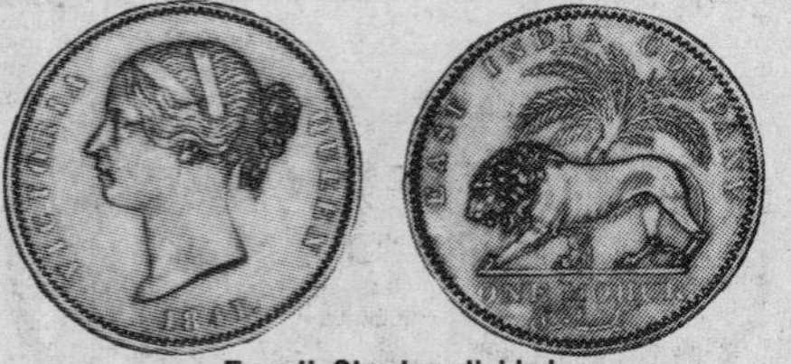

Type II. Obv. leg. divided.

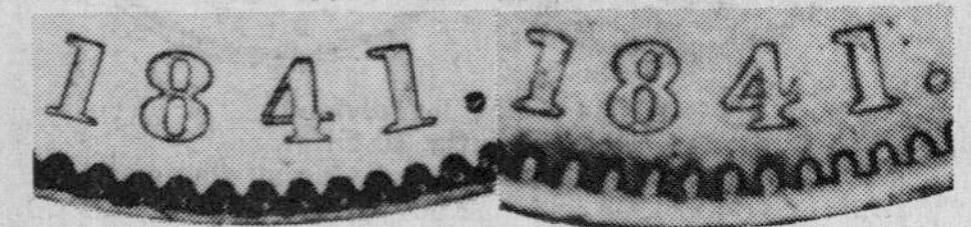

Lg. date normal 4   **lg. date crosslet 4**

Obv: W.W. incuse; lg. leg. and lg. date w/normal 4.

KM#	Date	Mintage	Fine	VF	XF	Unc
462.1	1841.(c)	.442	150.00	200.00	300.00	400.00
	1841.(c) (restrike)		—	—	P/L	450.00

Obv: W.W. incuse; lg. leg. and lg. date w/crosslet 4.

KM#	Date	Mintage	Fine	VF	XF	Unc
462.2	1841.(c)	—	175.00	225.00	300.00	400.00

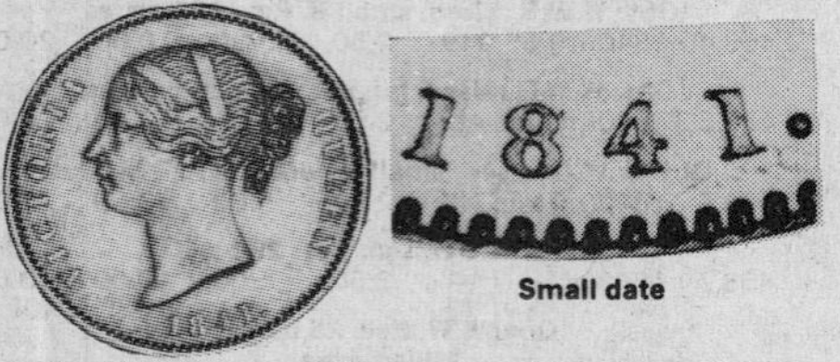

Small date

Obv: W.W. incuse; sm. leg. and sm. date w/normal 4.

KM#	Date	Mintage	Fine	VF	XF	Unc
462.3	1841.	—	200.00	325.00	450.00	600.00

Mule. Obv: KM#462. Rev: KM#451.

KM#	Date	Mintage	Fine	VF	XF	Unc
A462	1841.(c) (restrike)		—	—	P/L	450.00

2 MOHURS

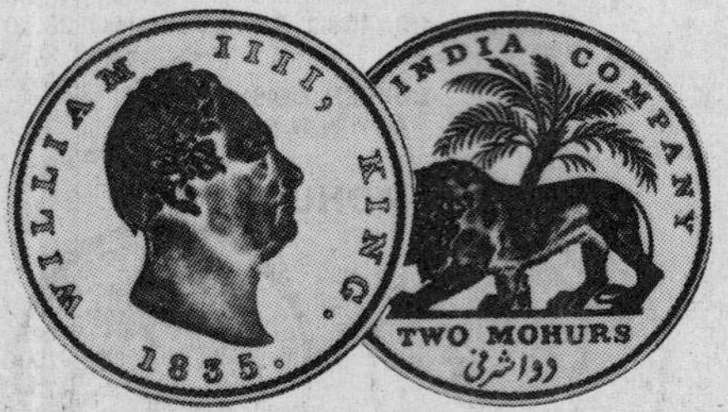

23.3200 g, .917 GOLD, .6873 oz AGW
RS incuse on truncation.
Milled edge.

KM#	Date	Mintage	Fine	VF	XF	Unc
452.1	1835.(c)	1,170	850.00	1250.	1750.	3000.
	1835.(c)	—	—	—	Proof	3500.
	1835.(c) (restrike)		—	—	P/L	1350.

Plain edge.

KM#	Date	Mintage	Fine	VF	XF	Unc
452.2	1835.(c)	—	—	—	Rare	—

SILVER (OMS)

KM#	Date	Mintage	Fine	VF	XF	Unc
452a	1835.(c)	—	—	—	Proof	1500.

COPPER (OMS)

KM#	Date	Mintage	Fine	VF	XF	Unc
452b	1835.(c)	—	—	—	Proof	750.00

REGAL COINAGE

1/12 ANNA

NOTE: The coins dated 1862 were struck at Calcutta, Bombay and Madras but have not yet been attributed to the mint of issue. Calcutta Mint issues 1874-76 are 17.3mm in diameter. From 1877 the coins have a diameter of 17.5mm and the obverse legend at the lower right is distant from the bust. The issues dated 1882 and 1886 have a small incuse "C" on a bead of the circle below the date. Bombay issues 1874-76 have a diameter of 17.9mm. From 1877 the obverse legend at the lower right is close to the bust.

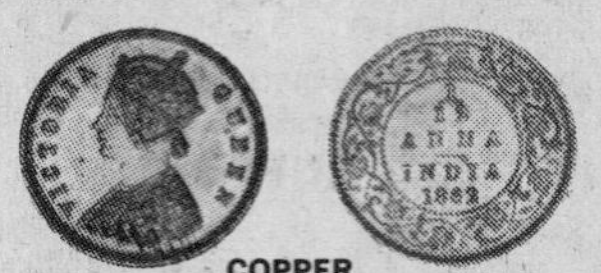

COPPER

KM#	Date	Mintage	Fine	VF	XF	Unc
465	1862(c) 17.4-17.5mm					
		2.502	1.25	2.50	5.00	10.00
	1862(b) 17.9-18.0mm					
		2.999	1.25	2.50	5.00	10.00
	1862(m) 17.6-17.7mm					
		40.487	.75	1.25	2.50	7.50
	1862(c)	—	—	—	Proof	50.00
	1862(c) (restrike)		—	—	P/L	35.00
	1874(c)	4.819	1.25	2.50	5.00	10.00
	1874(b)	2.960	1.25	2.50	5.00	10.00
	1875(c)	4.646	1.25	2.50	5.00	10.00
	1875(c)	—	—	—	Proof	65.00
	1875(b)	3.068	1.25	2.50	5.00	10.00
	1876(c)	20.318	1.00	1.50	2.50	7.50
	1876(b)	Inc. 1875(b)	1.25	2.50	5.00	10.00

GOLD (OMS)

KM#	Date	Mintage	Fine	VF	XF	Unc
465b	1862(c) (restrike)		—	—	P/L	250.00

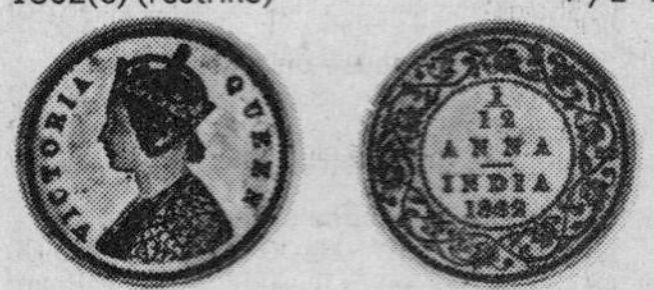

COPPER

KM#	Date	Mintage	Fine	VF	XF	Unc
483	1877(b)	1.551	.50	1.00	2.50	6.00
	1877(b)	—	—	—	Proof	50.00
	1877(c)	5.880	.50	1.00	2.50	6.00
	1877(c)	—	—	—	Proof	50.00
	1877(c) (restrike)		—	—	P/L	25.00
	1878(c)	5.525	.50	1.00	2.50	6.00
	1878(c)	—	—	—	Proof	50.00
	1881(b)	2.954	.50	1.00	2.50	6.00
	1882(c)	4.344	.50	1.00	2.00	5.00
	1883(c)	9.840	.50	1.00	2.00	5.00
	1883(b)	4.794	.35	.75	1.75	4.00
	1883(b)	—	—	—	Proof	50.00
	1884(b)	8.074	.50	1.00	2.50	6.00
	1884(b)	—	—	—	Proof	50.00
	1885(c)	4.783	.50	1.00	2.00	5.00
	1886(c)	18.663	.35	.75	1.75	4.00
	1886(b)	5.783	.50	1.00	2.50	6.00
	1886(b)	—	—	—	Proof	50.00
	1887(c)	8.724	.50	1.00	2.00	5.00
	1887(b)	8.242	.50	1.00	2.50	6.00
	1888(c)	4.662	.50	1.00	2.00	5.00
	1888(b)	2.143	.50	1.00	2.50	6.00
	1889(c)	7.602	.50	1.00	2.00	5.00
	1889(b)	5.660	.50	1.00	2.50	6.00
	1890(b)	—	—	—	Proof	50.00
	1890(c)	21.732	.35	.75	1.75	4.00
	1890 (restrike)		—	—	P/L	20.00
	1891(c)	17.306	.35	.75	1.75	4.00
	1891(c)	—	—	—	Proof	50.00
	1891(c) (restrike)		—	—	P/L	20.00
	1892(c)	13.793	.35	.75	1.75	4.00
	1892(c)	—	—	—	Proof	50.00
	1892(c) (restrike)		—	—	P/L	20.00
	1893(c)	10.034	.35	.75	1.75	4.00
	1893(c)	—	—	—	Proof	50.00
	1893(b) (restrike)		—	—	P/L	20.00
	1894(c)	18.392	.35	.75	1.75	4.00
	1894(c)	—	—	—	Proof	50.00
	1894(c) (restrike)		—	—	P/L	20.00
	1895(c)	15.208	.35	.75	1.75	4.00
	1895(c)	—	—	—	Proof	50.00
	1896(c)	.922	.50	1.25	2.50	6.00
	1896(c)	—	—	—	Proof	50.00
	1896(c) (restrike)		—	—	P/L	20.00
	1897(c)	20.822	.35	.75	1.75	4.00
	1897(c)	—	—	—	Proof	50.00
	1897(c) (restrike)		—	—	P/L	20.00
	1898(c)	13.882	.35	.75	1.75	4.00
	1898(c)	—	—	—	Proof	50.00
	1898(c) (restrike)		—	—	P/L	20.00
	1899(c)	10.056	.35	.75	1.75	4.50
	1899(c)	—	—	—	Proof	50.00
	1899(c) (restrike)		—	—	P/L	20.00
	1901(c)	21.345	.35	.75	1.75	4.00
	1901(c)	—	—	—	Proof	50.00
	1901(c) (restrike)		—	—	P/L	20.00

NOTE: On come Calcutta issues between 1882-1886 a small 'c' can be found on one of the beads of the inner circle on the rev.

ALUMINUM (OMS)

KM#	Date	Mintage	Fine	VF	XF	Unc
483a	1891(b)	—	—	—	Proof	100.00

SILVER (OMS)

KM#	Date	Mintage	Fine	VF	XF	Unc
483b	1892(c) (restrike)		—	—	P/L	75.00
	1893(c) (restrike)		—	—	P/L	75.00
	1894(c) (restrike)		—	—	P/L	75.00
	1895(c) (restrike)		—	—	P/L	75.00
	1896(c) (restrike)		—	—	P/L	75.00
483b	1897(c) (restrike)		—	—	P/L	75.00
	1898(c) (restrike)		—	—	P/L	75.00
	1899(c) (restrike)		—	—	P/L	75.00
	1901(c) (restrike)		—	—	P/L	75.00

GOLD (OMS)

KM#	Date	Mintage	Fine	VF	XF	Unc
483c	1891(c) (restrike)		—	—	P/L	250.00
	1892(c) (restrike)		—	—	P/L	250.00
	1893(c) (restrike)		—	—	P/L	250.00
	1895(c) (restrike)		—	—	P/L	250.00
	1896(c) (restrike)		—	—	P/L	250.00
	1897(c) (restrike)		—	—	P/L	250.00
	1898(c) (restrike)		—	—	P/L	250.00
	1899(c) (restrike)		—	—	P/L	250.00
	1901(c) (restrike)		—	—	P/L	250.00

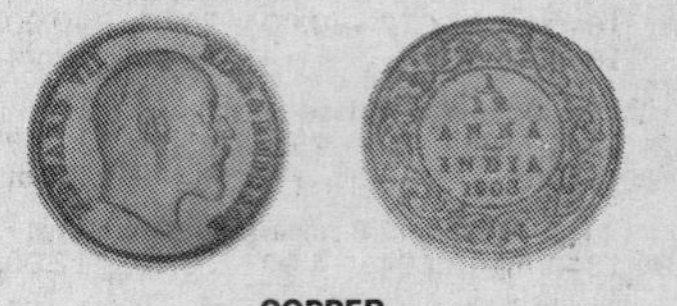

COPPER
Thick planchets

KM#	Date	Mintage	Fine	VF	XF	Unc
497	1903(c)	7.883	.35	1.25	6.00	15.00
	1903(c)	—	—	—	Proof	60.00
	1903(c) (restrike)		—	—	P/L	20.00
	1904(c)	16.506	.25	1.00	4.00	12.00
	1904(c)	—	—	—	Proof	60.00
	1904(c) (restrike)		—	—	P/L	20.00
	1905(c)	13.060	.25	1.00	4.00	12.00
	1905(c) (restrike)		—	—	P/L	20.00
	1906(c)	9.072	.25	1.00	4.00	12.00
	1906(c)	—	—	—	Proof	60.00
	1906(c) (restrike)		—	—	P/L	20.00

SILVER (OMS)

KM#	Date	Mintage	Fine	VF	XF	Unc
497a	1904(c) (restrike)		—	—	P/L	75.00
	1905(c) (restrike)		—	—	P/L	75.00

BRONZE
Thin planchets

KM#	Date	Mintage	Fine	VF	XF	Unc
498	1906(c)	2.184	.35	.75	5.00	15.00
	1906(c)	—	—	—	Proof	50.00
	1907(c)	20.985	.25	.50	3.00	9.00
	1907(c)	—	—	—	Proof	50.00
	1907(c) (restrike)		—	—	P/L	20.00
	1908(c)	22.036	.25	.50	3.00	9.00
	1908(c)	—	—	—	Proof	50.00
	1908(c) (restrike)		—	—	P/L	20.00
	1909(c)	12.316	.25	.50	3.00	9.00
	1909(c) (restrike)		—	—	P/L	20.00
	1910(c)	23.520	.25	.50	3.00	9.00
	1910(c) (restrike)		—	—	P/L	20.00

ALUMINUM (OMS)

KM#	Date	Mintage	Fine	VF	XF	Unc
498a	1909(c)	—	—	—	Proof	75.00

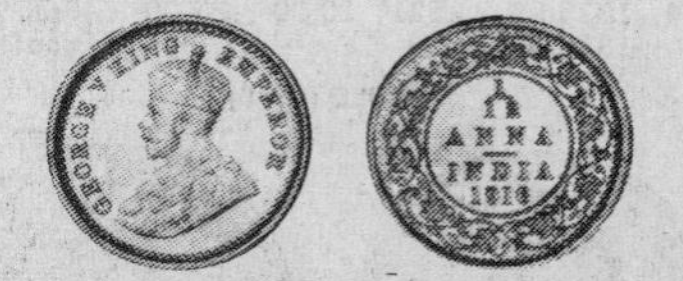

BRONZE

NOTE: Calcutta Mint issues have no mint mark. Bombay Mint issues have a small raised bead or dot below the center of the date.

KM#	Date	Mintage	Fine	VF	XF	Unc
509	1912(c)	—	.50	.75	1.50	4.50
	1912(c)	—	—	—	Proof	50.00
	1912(c) (restrike)		—	—	P/L	20.00
	1913(c)	25.937	.25	.50	1.00	3.00
	1913(c)	—	—	—	Proof	40.00
	1913(c) (restrike)		—	—	P/L	20.00
	1914(c)	29.184	.25	.50	.75	1.50
	1914(c)	—	—	—	Proof	40.00
	1914(c) (restrike)		—	—	P/L	20.00
	1915(c)	20.563	.25	.50	.75	1.50
	1915(c)	—	—	—	Proof	40.00
	1915(c) (restrike)		—	—	P/L	20.00
	1916(c)	12.230	.25	.50	.75	1.50
	1916(c)	—	—	—	Proof	40.00
	1916(c) (restrike)		—	—	P/L	20.00
	1917(c)	26.880	.25	.50	.75	1.50
	1917(c)	—	—	—	Proof	40.00
	1917(c) (restrike)		—	—	P/L	20.00
	1918(c)	29.088	.25	.50	.75	1.50
	1918(c)	—	—	—	Proof	40.00
	1918(c) (restrike)		—	—	P/L	20.00
	1919(c)	20.686	.25	.50	.75	1.50
	1919(c)	—	—	—	Proof	40.00
	1919(c) (restrike)		—	—	P/L	20.00
	1920(c)	42.221	.25	.50	.75	1.50
	1920(c)	—	—	—	Proof	40.00
	1920(c) (restrike)		—	—	P/L	20.00
	1921(c)	19.334	.25	.50	.75	1.50
	1921(c)	—	—	—	Proof	40.00
	1921(c) (restrike)		—	—	P/L	20.00
	1923(c)	6.662	.25	.50	.75	1.50
	1923(c)	—	—	—	Proof	40.00
	1923(b)	4.877	.25	.50	.75	1.50
	1923(b)	—	—	—	Proof	40.00
	1923(b) (restrike)		—	—	P/L	20.00
	1924(c)	2.515	.25	.50	.75	1.50
	1924(c)	—	—	—	Proof	40.00
	1924(b)	11.711	.25	.50	.75	1.50
	1924(b)	—	—	—	Proof	40.00
	1924(b) (restrike)		—	—	P/L	20.00
	1925(c)	6.106	.25	.50	.75	1.50
	1925(c)	—	—	—	Proof	40.00

British / INDIA 979

KM#	Date	Mintage	Fine	VF	XF	Unc
509	1925(b)	5.871	.25	.50	.75	1.50
	1925(b)	—	—	—	Proof	40.00
	1925(b) (restrike)		—	—	P/L	20.00
	1926(c)	4.147	.25	.50	.75	1.50
	1926(c)	—	—	—	Proof	40.00
	1926(b)	18.406	.25	.50	.75	1.50
	1926(b)	—	—	—	Proof	40.00
	1926(b) (restrike)		—	—	P/L	20.00
	1927(c)	2.880	.25	.50	.75	1.50
	1927(c)	—	—	—	Proof	40.00
	1927(b)	4.846	.25	.50	.75	1.50
	1927(b)	—	—	—	Proof	40.00
	1927(b) (restrike)		—	—	P/L	20.00
	1928(c)	11.846	.25	.50	.75	1.50
	1928(c)	—	—	—	Proof	40.00
	1928(b)	8.077	.25	.50	.75	1.50
	1928(b)	—	—	—	Proof	40.00
	1928 (restrike)		—	—	P/L	20.00
	1929(c)	15.130	.25	.50	.75	1.50
	1929(c)	—	—	—	Proof	40.00
	1929(c) (restrike)		—	—	P/L	20.00
	1930(c)	13.498	.25	.50	.75	1.50
	1930(c)	—	—	—	Proof	40.00
	1930(c) (restrike)		—	—	P/L	20.00
	1931(c)	18.278	.25	.50	.75	1.50
	1931(c)	—	—	—	Proof	40.00
	1931(c) (restrike)		—	—	P/L	20.00
	1932(c)	23.213	.25	.50	.75	1.50
	1932(c)	—	—	—	Proof	40.00
	1932(c) (restrike)		—	—	P/L	20.00
	1933(c)	16.896	.25	.50	.75	1.50
	1933(c)	—	—	—	Proof	40.00
	1933(c) (restrike)		—	—	P/L	20.00
	1934(c)	17.146	.25	.50	.75	1.50
	1934(c)	—	—	—	Proof	40.00
	1934(c) (restrike)		—	—	P/L	20.00
	1935(c)	19.142	.25	.50	.75	1.50
	1935(c)	—	—	—	Proof	40.00
	1935(c) (restrike)		—	—	P/L	20.00
	1936(c)	23.213	.25	.50	.75	1.50
	1936(b)	12.887	.25	.50	.75	1.50
	1936(b) (restrike)		—	—	P/L	20.00

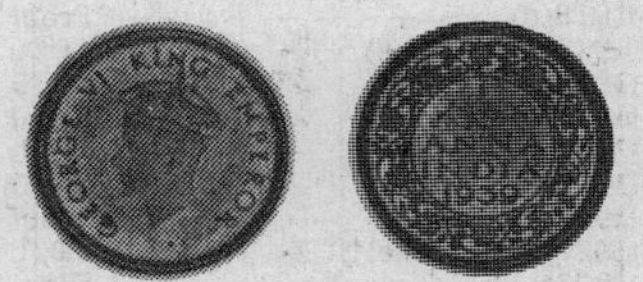

First head

NOTE: Calcutta Mint issues have no mint mark. Bombay Mint issues have a small dot below the date except for those dated 1942 which have a dot on either side of ANNA and the date, and one dot after "INDIA".

KM#	Date	Mintage	Fine	VF	XF	Unc
526	1938(c)	—	—	—	Proof	35.00
	1939(c)	3.571	.25	.50	1.00	2.50
	1939(b)	17.407	.25	.50	1.00	2.50

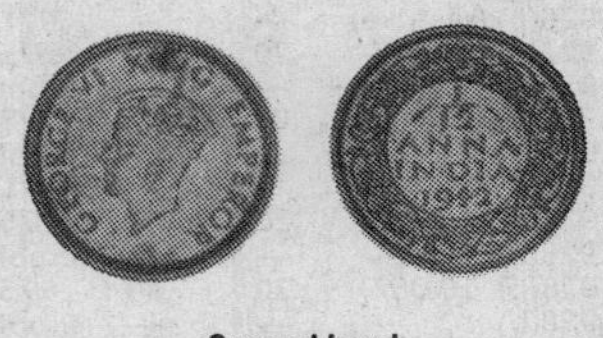

Second head

KM#	Date	Mintage	Fine	VF	XF	Unc
527	1938(c) (restrike)		—	—	P/L	20.00
	1939(c)	5.245	.25	.50	1.00	2.50
	1939(c)	—	—	—	Proof	35.00
	1939(b)	31.306	.25	.50	1.00	2.00
	1939(b)	—	—	—	Proof	35.00
	1939(b) (restrike)		—	—	P/L	20.00
	1941(b)	6.137	.25	.50	.75	1.50
	1942(b)	6.124	1.00	2.25	3.50	7.00
	1942(b)	—	—	—	Proof	35.00
	1942(b) (restrike)		—	—	P/L	20.00

1/2 PICE

NOTE: The 1/2 Pice dated 1862 was struck at all three Indian Government Mints i.e. Calcutta, Bombay and Madras but a correct attribution to the mint of issue has not yet been possible. Two different busts and two reverses have been noted so far.

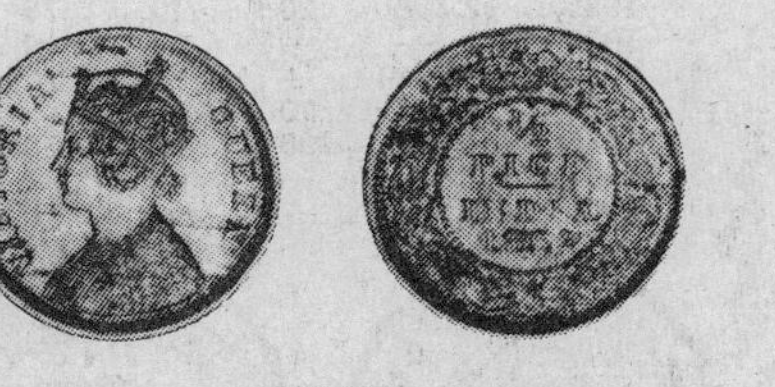

COPPER

KM#	Date	Mintage	Fine	VF	XF	Unc
466	1862(c) (21.25mm)	96.843	1.25	2.50	5.00	15.00
	1862(m) (21.4mm)	6.400	1.50	3.50	6.50	20.00
	1862(c)	—	—	—	Proof	50.00
	1862(c) (restrike)		—	—	P/L	25.00
	1875(c)	—	—	—	Proof	75.00
	1875(c) (restrike)		—	—	P/L	25.00

GOLD (OMS)

KM#	Date	Mintage	Fine	VF	XF	Unc
466b	1862(c)	—	—	—	Proof	250.00

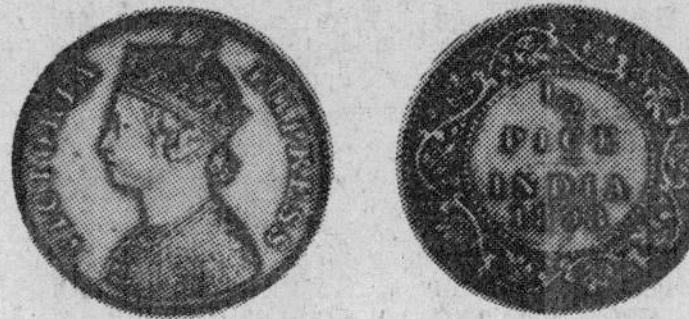

COPPER

KM#	Date	Mintage	Fine	VF	XF	Unc
484	1877(c)	—	—	—	Proof	75.00
	1877(c) (restrike)		—	—	P/L	25.00
	1878(c)	—	—	—	Proof	75.00
	1885(c)	6.206	1.25	2.50	4.00	10.00
	1886(c)	7.733	1.25	2.50	4.00	10.00
	1887(c)	6.464	1.25	2.50	4.00	10.00
	1888(c)	3.190	1.25	2.50	4.00	10.00
	1889(c)	7.587	1.25	2.50	4.00	10.00
	1890(c)	3.504	1.25	2.50	4.00	10.00
	1890(c)	—	—	—	Proof	50.00
	1890(c) (restrike)		—	—	P/L	20.00
	1891(c)	5.139	1.25	2.50	4.00	10.00
	1891(c)	—	—	—	Proof	50.00
	1891(c) (restrike)		—	—	P/L	20.00
	1892(c)	4.774	1.25	2.50	4.00	10.00
	1892(c)	—	—	—	Proof	50.00
	1892(c) (restrike)		—	—	P/L	20.00
	1893(c)	7.005	1.25	2.50	4.00	10.00
	1893(c)	—	—	—	Proof	50.00
	1893(c) (restrike)		—	—	P/L	20.00
	1894(c)	7.777	1.25	2.50	4.00	10.00
	1894(c)	—	—	—	Proof	50.00
	1894(c) (restrike)		—	—	P/L	20.00
	1895(c)	9.874	1.00	1.75	3.50	8.50
	1895(c)	—	—	—	Proof	50.00
	1896(c)	6.113	1.25	2.50	4.00	10.00
	1896(c)	—	—	—	Proof	50.00
	1897(c)	8.484	1.25	2.50	4.00	10.00
	1897(c)	—	—	—	Proof	35.00
	1897(c) (restrike)		—	—	P/L	20.00
	1898(c)	12.940	1.00	1.75	3.50	8.50
	1898(c)	—	—	—	Proof	50.00
	1898(c) (restrike)		—	—	P/L	20.00
	1899(c)	7.936	1.25	2.50	4.00	10.00
	1899(c)	—	—	—	Proof	50.00
	1899(c) (restrike)		—	—	P/L	20.00
	1900(c)	5.219	1.25	2.50	4.00	10.00
	1900(c) (restrike)		—	—	P/L	20.00
	1901(c)	16.057	1.00	1.75	3.50	8.50
	1901(c)	Inc. Ab.	—	—	Proof	50.00
	1901(c) (restrike)		—	—	P/L	20.00

ALUMINUM (OMS)

KM#	Date	Mintage	Fine	VF	XF	Unc
484a	1891(b)	—	—	—	Proof	85.00

SILVER (OMS)

KM#	Date	Mintage	Fine	VF	XF	Unc
484b	1892(c) (restrike)		—	—	P/L	75.00
	1893(c) (restrike)		—	—	P/L	75.00
	1894(c) (restrike)		—	—	P/L	75.00
	1895(c) (restrike)		—	—	P/L	75.00
	1896(c) (restrike)		—	—	P/L	75.00
	1897(c) (restrike)		—	—	P/L	75.00
	1898(c) (restrike)		—	—	P/L	75.00
	1899(c) (restrike)		—	—	P/L	75.00
	1900(c) (restrike)		—	—	P/L	75.00
	1901(c) (restrike)		—	—	P/L	75.00

GOLD (OMS)

KM#	Date	Mintage	Fine	VF	XF	Unc
484c	1891(c) (restrike)		—	—	P/L	300.00
	1892(c) (restrike)		—	—	P/L	300.00
	1893(c) (restrike)		—	—	P/L	300.00
	1895(c) (restrike)		—	—	P/L	300.00
	1896(c) (restrike)		—	—	P/L	300.00
	1897(c) (restrike)		—	—	P/L	300.00
	1898(c) (restrike)		—	—	P/L	300.00
	1899(c) (restrike)		—	—	P/L	300.00
	1901(c) (restrike)		—	—	P/L	300.00

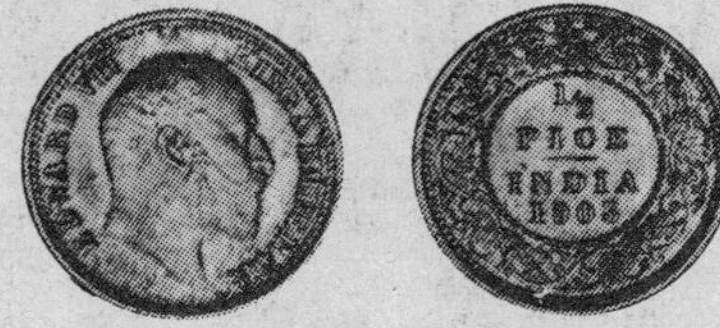

COPPER

KM#	Date	Mintage	Fine	VF	XF	Unc
499	1903(c)	5.376	.75	1.50	5.00	15.00
	1903(c)	—	—	—	Proof	45.00
	1903(c) (restrike)		—	—	P/L	20.00
	1904(c)	8.464	.75	1.50	5.00	15.00
	1904(c)	—	—	—	Proof	45.00
	1904(c) (restrike)		—	—	P/L	20.00
	1905(c)	—	.75	1.50	5.00	15.00
	1905(c) (restrike)		—	—	P/L	20.00
	1906(c)	—	.75	1.50	5.00	15.00
	1906(c)	—	—	—	Proof	45.00
	1906(c) (restrike)		—	—	P/L	20.00

BRONZE
Thinner planchets

KM#	Date	Mintage	Fine	VF	XF	Unc
500	1904(c)	—	—	—	Proof	45.00
	1906(c)	—	.75	1.50	4.50	12.50
	1906(c)	—	—	—	Proof	45.00
	1907(c)	—	.75	1.50	4.50	12.50
	1907(c)	—	—	—	Proof	45.00
	1907(c) (restrike)		—	—	P/L	20.00
	1908(c)	—	.75	1.50	4.50	12.50
	1908(c)	—	—	—	Proof	45.00
	1908(c) (restrike)		—	—	P/L	20.00
	1909(c)	—	.50	1.00	4.00	10.00
500	1909(c) (restrike)		—	—	P/L	20.00
	1910(c)	—	.75	1.50	4.50	12.50

ALUMINUM (OMS)

KM#	Date	Mintage	Fine	VF	XF	Unc
500a	1909(c)	—	—	—	Proof	100.00

NICKEL (OMS)

KM#	Date	Mintage	Fine	VF	XF	Unc
500b	1904(c)	—	—	—	Proof	100.00

SILVER (OMS)

KM#	Date	Mintage	Fine	VF	XF	Unc
500c	1903(c) (restrike)		—	—	P/L	75.00
	1904(c) (restrike)		—	—	P/L	75.00
	1905(c) (restrike)		—	—	P/L	75.00

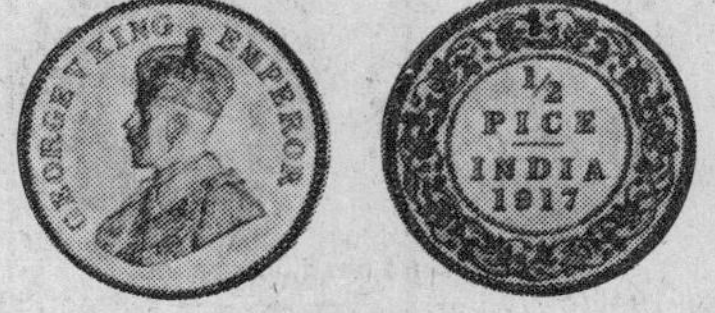

BRONZE

KM#	Date	Mintage	Fine	VF	XF	Unc
510	1912(c)	—	.25	.50	.75	3.00
	1912(c)	—	—	—	Proof	40.00
	1912(c) (restrike)		—	—	P/L	20.00
	1913(c)	12.912	.25	.50	.75	3.00
	1913(c)	—	—	—	Proof	40.00
	1913(c) (restrike)		—	—	P/L	20.00
	1914(c)	10.022	.15	.30	.50	2.50
	1914(c)	—	—	—	Proof	40.00
	1914(c) (restrike)		—	—	P/L	20.00
	1915(c)	8.653	.15	.30	.50	2.50
	1915(c)	—	—	—	Proof	40.00
	1915(c) (restrike)		—	—	P/L	20.00
	1916(c)	5.875	.15	.30	.50	2.50
	1916(c)	—	—	—	Proof	40.00
	1916(c) (restrike)		—	—	P/L	20.00
	1917(c)	13.094	.15	.30	.50	2.50
	1917(c)	—	—	—	Proof	40.00
	1917(c) (restrike)		—	—	P/L	20.00
	1918(c)	4.608	.15	.30	.50	2.50
	1918(c)	—	—	—	Proof	40.00
	1918(c) (restrike)		—	—	P/L	20.00
	1919(c)	13.516	.15	.30	.50	2.50
	1919(c)	—	—	—	Proof	40.00
	1919(c) (restrike)		—	—	P/L	20.00
	1920(c)	7.437	.15	.30	.50	2.50
	1920(c)	—	—	—	Proof	40.00
	1920(c) (restrike)		—	—	P/L	20.00
	1921(c)	6.131	.15	.30	.50	2.50
	1921(c)	—	—	—	Proof	40.00
	1921(c) (restrike)		—	—	P/L	20.00
	1922(c)	4.941	.15	.30	.50	2.50
	1922(c)	—	—	—	Proof	40.00
	1922(c) (restrike)		—	—	P/L	20.00
	1923(c)	6.272	.15	.30	.50	2.50
	1923(c)	—	—	—	Proof	40.00
	1923(c) (restrike)		—	—	P/L	20.00
	1924(c)	10.624	.15	.30	.50	2.50
	1924(c)	—	—	—	Proof	40.00
	1924(c) (restrike)		—	—	P/L	20.00
	1925(c)	3.622	.15	.30	.50	2.50
	1925(c)	—	—	—	Proof	40.00
	1925(c) (restrike)		—	—	P/L	20.00
	1926(c)	6.528	.15	.30	.50	2.50
	1926(c)	—	—	—	Proof	40.00
	1926(c) (restrike)		—	—	P/L	20.00
	1927(c)	6.528	.15	.30	.50	2.50
	1927(c)	—	—	—	Proof	40.00
	1927(c) (restrike)		—	—	P/L	20.00
	1928(c)	7.332	.15	.30	.50	2.50
	1928(c)	—	—	—	Proof	40.00
	1928(c) (restrike)		—	—	P/L	20.00
	1929(c)	7.654	.15	.30	.50	2.50
	1929(c)	—	—	—	Proof	40.00
	1929(c) (restrike)		—	—	P/L	20.00
	1930(c)	7.181	.15	.30	.50	2.50
	1930(c)	—	—	—	Proof	40.00
	1930(c) (restrike)		—	—	P/L	20.00
	1931(c)	8.794	.15	.30	.50	2.50
	1931(c)	—	—	—	Proof	40.00
	1931(c) (restrike)		—	—	P/L	20.00
	1932(c)	5.440	.15	.30	.50	2.50
	1932(c)	—	—	—	Proof	40.00
	1932(c) (restrike)		—	—	P/L	20.00
	1933(c)	9.242	.15	.30	.50	2.50
	1933(c)	—	—	—	Proof	40.00
	1933(c) (restrike)		—	—	P/L	20.00
	1934(c)	8.947	.15	.30	.50	2.50
	1934(c)	—	—	—	Proof	40.00
	1934(c) (restrike)		—	—	P/L	20.00
	1935(c)	15.501	.15	.30	.50	2.00
	1935(c)	—	—	—	Proof	40.00
	1935(c) (restrike)		—	—	P/L	20.00
	1936(c)	26.726	.10	.25	.40	1.25
	1936(c) (restrike)		—	—	P/L	20.00

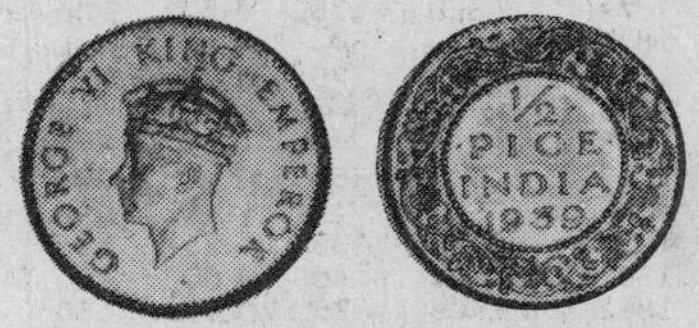

Obv: First head, high relief.

NOTE: Calcutta Mint issues have no mint mark. Bombay Mint issues have a small dot below the date.

KM#	Date	Mintage	Fine	VF	XF	Unc
528	1938(c)	—	—	—	Proof	30.00
	1938(c) (restrike)		—	—	P/L	25.00

KM#	Date	Mintage	Fine	VF	XF	Unc
528	1939(c)	17.357	.15	.40	.65	1.75
	1939(c)	—	—	—	Proof	30.00
	1939(b)	9.343	.15	.40	.65	1.75
	1939(b)	—	—	—	Proof	30.00
	1939(b) (restrike)		—	—	P/L	25.00
	1940(c)	23.770	.15	.40	.65	1.75
	1940(c)	—	—	—	Proof	30.00
	1940(c) (restrike)		—	—	P/L	25.00

NOTE: Calcutta Mint reported 11,161,600 mintage for 1938 but only proof and modern P/L restrikes are known.

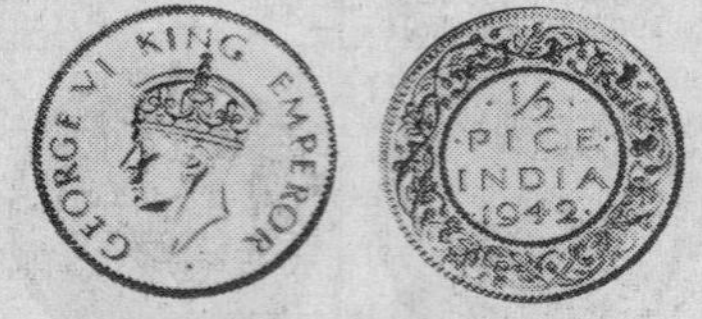

Obv: Second head, low relief.

KM#	Date	Mintage	Fine	VF	XF	Unc
529	1942(b)	—	—	—	Proof	50.00
	1942(b) (restrike)		—	—	P/L	35.00

1/4 ANNA

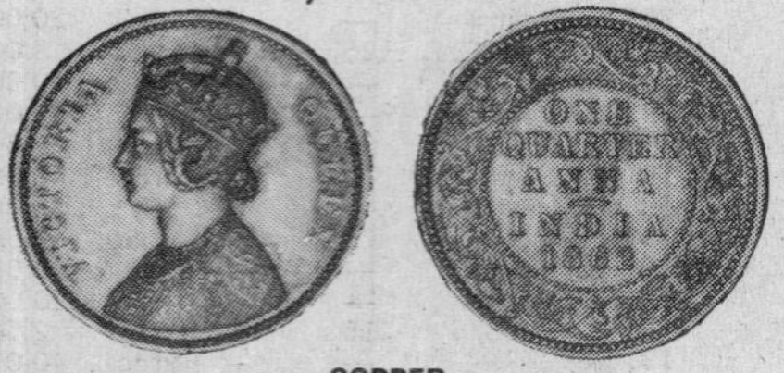

COPPER

NOTE: The one quarter Anna dated 1862 was struck at Calcutta, Bombay and Madras. From 1874 onward the issues from Calcutta and Bombay have a distinctive type of reverse and the coins are identified as follows.

On Calcutta Mint issues the floral design has a leaf below the center of the date. Some specimens dated 1879-1887 have also as a mint mark, a tiny incuse "C" on a bead of the beaded circle, below the center of the date.

On Bombay Mint issues the floral design has a leaf below the first and the last numeral of the date.

KM#	Date	Mintage	Fine	VF	XF	Unc
467	1862(c)	99.504	.75	1.50	3.00	9.00
	1862(c) w/V in bottom of bust	10.654	1.25	2.50	5.00	15.00
	1862(c)	—	—	—	Proof	100.00
	1862(c) (restrike)		—	—	P/L	30.00
	1862(b) w/V in point of shoulder	32.149	1.00	2.00	4.00	12.00
	1862(b) w/dot below date	2.366	2.50	5.00	10.00	25.00
	1862(m) 25.5mm	186.227	.75	1.50	3.00	9.00
	1874(c)	44.678	2.00	4.00	8.00	20.00
	1875(c)	36.237	2.50	5.00	10.00	25.00
	1875(c)	—	—	—	Proof	65.00
	1875(b)	14.494	3.00	6.00	12.00	35.00
	1876(c)	43.581	2.50	5.00	10.00	25.00
	1876	—	—	—	Proof	65.00

GOLD (OMS)

KM#	Date	Mintage	Fine	VF	XF	Unc
467b	1862(c)	—	—	—	Proof	350.00

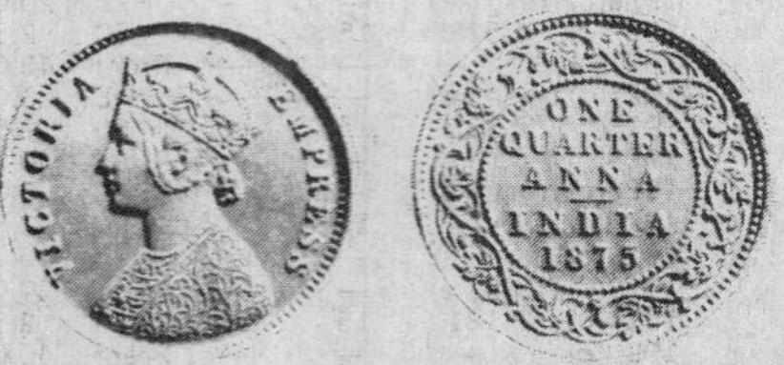

COPPER

Mule. Obv: KM#488. Rev: KM#472.

KM#	Date	Mintage	Fine	VF	XF	Unc
485	1875(c) (restrike)		—	—	P/L	40.00

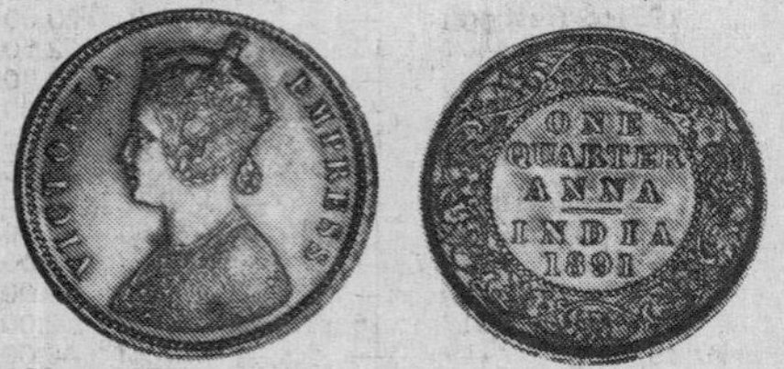

KM#	Date	Mintage	Fine	VF	XF	Unc
486	1877(c)	65.210	.75	1.50	3.00	9.00
	1877(c)	—	—	—	Proof	65.00
	1877(c) (restrike)		—	—	P/L	25.00
	1877(b)	9.320	.75	1.50	3.00	9.00
	1877(b) (restrike)		—	—	P/L	25.00
	1878(c)	40.813	.75	1.50	3.00	9.00
	1878(c)	—	—	—	Proof	65.00
	1878(c) (restrike)		—	—	P/L	25.00
	1879(c)	43.072	.50	1.00	2.00	6.00
	1879(c)	—	—	—	Proof	65.00
	1880(c)	10.278	.35	.75	1.50	4.50
	1882(c)	52.291	.40	1.00	2.00	6.00
	1882(b)	12.409	.75	1.50	2.50	7.50
	1883(c)	57.571	.75	1.50	2.50	7.50
	1883(b)	12.443	.75	1.50	2.50	7.50
	1884(c)	43.196	.50	1.00	2.00	6.00
	1884(c)	—	—	—	Proof	65.00
	1884(b)	16.845	.75	1.50	2.50	7.50
486	1885(c)	36.699	.50	1.00	2.00	6.00
	1886(c)	36.121	.50	1.00	2.00	6.00
	1886(b)	14.390	.75	1.50	2.50	7.50
	1887(c)	59.060	.50	1.00	2.00	6.00
	1887(b)	26.205	.75	1.50	2.50	7.50
	1888(c)	34.531	.75	1.50	2.50	7.50
	1888(b)	8.293	.75	1.50	2.50	7.50
	1889(c)	88.559	.35	.75	1.50	4.50
	1889(b)	19.110	.50	1.00	2.00	6.00
	1890(c)	82.909	.35	.75	1.50	4.50
	1890(c)	—	—	—	Proof	65.00
	1891(c)	86.076	.35	.75	1.50	4.50
	1891(c)	—	—	—	Proof	65.00
	1891(c) (restrike)		—	—	P/L	25.00
	1892(c)	68.131	.35	.75	1.50	4.50
	1892(c)	—	—	—	Proof	65.00
	1892(c) (restrike)		—	—	P/L	25.00
	1893(c)	76.039	.35	.75	1.50	4.50
	1893(c)	—	—	—	Proof	65.00
	1893(c) (restrike)		—	—	P/L	25.00
	1894(c)	45.744	.35	.75	1.50	4.50
	1894(c)	—	—	—	Proof	65.00
	1894(c) (restrike)		—	—	P/L	25.00
	1895(c)	35.744	.35	.75	1.50	4.50
	1895(c)	—	—	—	Proof	65.00
	1896(c)	109.853	.35	.75	1.50	4.50
	1896(c)	—	—	—	Proof	65.00
	1897(c)	82.288	.35	.75	1.50	4.50
	1897(c)	—	—	—	Proof	65.00
	1897(c) (restrike)		—	—	P/L	25.00
	1898(c)	12.118	.35	.75	1.50	4.50
	1898(c)	—	—	—	Proof	65.00
	1898(c) (restrike)		—	—	P/L	25.00
	1899(c)	36.896	.35	.75	1.50	4.50
	1899(c)	Inc. Ab.	—	—	Proof	65.00
	1899(c) (restrike)		—	—	P/L	25.00
	1900(c)	30.534	.35	.75	1.50	4.50
	1900(c)	—	—	—	Proof	65.00
	1900(c) (restrike)		—	—	P/L	25.00
	1901(c)	136.691	.35	.75	1.50	4.50
	1901(c)	—	—	—	Proof	65.00
	1901(c) (restrike)		—	—	P/L	25.00

NOTE: On some Calcutta issues between 1879-1887 a small 'c' can be found on one of the beads of the inner circle on the rev.

ALUMINUM (OMS)

KM#	Date	Mintage	Fine	VF	XF	Unc
486a	1891(b)	—	—	—	Proof	150.00

SILVER (OMS)

KM#	Date	Mintage	Fine	VF	XF	Unc
486b	1891(c) (restrike)		—	—	P/L	75.00
	1892(c) (restrike)		—	—	P/L	75.00
	1893(c) (restrike)		—	—	P/L	75.00
	1894(c) (restrike)		—	—	P/L	75.00
	1895(c) (restrike)		—	—	P/L	75.00
	1896(c) (restrike)		—	—	P/L	75.00
	1897(c) (restrike)		—	—	P/L	75.00
	1898(c) (restrike)		—	—	P/L	75.00
	1899(c) (restrike)		—	—	P/L	75.00
	1900(c) (restrike)		—	—	P/L	75.00
	1901(c) (restrike)		—	—	P/L	75.00

GOLD (OMS)

KM#	Date	Mintage	Fine	VF	XF	Unc
486c	1891(c) (restrike)		—	—	P/L	400.00
	1892(c) (restrike)		—	—	P/L	400.00
	1893(c) (restrike)		—	—	P/L	400.00
	1895(c) (restrike)		—	—	P/L	400.00
	1896(c) (restrike)		—	—	P/L	400.00
	1897(c) (restrike)		—	—	P/L	400.00
	1898(c) (restrike)		—	—	P/L	400.00
	1899(c) (restrike)		—	—	P/L	400.00
	1900(c) (restrike)		—	—	P/L	400.00
	1901(c) (restrike)		—	—	P/L	400.00

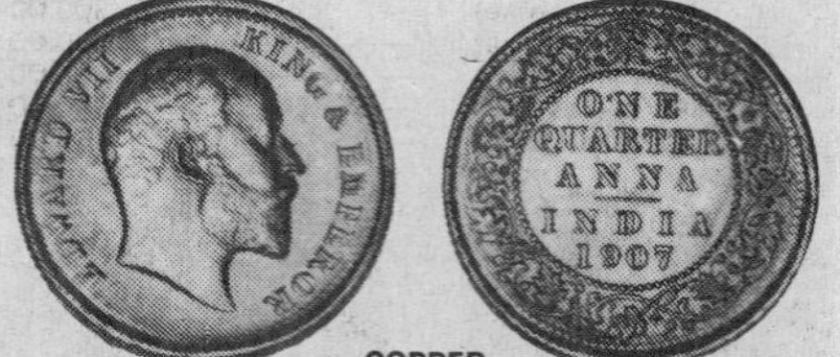

COPPER

KM#	Date	Mintage	Fine	VF	XF	Unc
501	1903(c)	105.974	.35	1.75	7.50	35.00
	1903(c)	—	—	—	Proof	50.00
	1903(c) (restrike)		—	—	P/L	25.00
	1904(c)	104.595	.35	1.75	7.50	35.00
	1904(c)	—	—	—	Proof	50.00
	1904(c) (restrike)		—	—	P/L	25.00
	1905(c)	130.058	.35	1.75	7.50	35.00
	1905(c)	—	—	—	Proof	50.00
	1905(c) (restrike)		—	—	P/L	25.00
	1906(c)	47.229	.35	1.75	7.50	35.00
	1906(c)	—	—	—	Proof	50.00

NICKEL (OMS)

KM#	Date	Mintage	Fine	VF	XF	Unc
501a	1906(c)	—	—	—	Proof	150.00

SILVER (OMS)

KM#	Date	Mintage	Fine	VF	XF	Unc
501b	1903(c) (restrike)		—	—	P/L	100.00
	1904(c) (restrike)		—	—	P/L	100.00
	1905(c) (restrike)		—	—	P/L	100.00

BRONZE

Thinner planchet

KM#	Date	Mintage	Fine	VF	XF	Unc
502	1906(c)	115.786	.35	1.25	6.50	30.00
	1906(c)	—	—	—	Proof	40.00
	1907(c)	234.682	.35	1.25	6.50	30.00
	1907(c)	—	—	—	Proof	40.00
	1907(c) (restrike)		—	—	P/L	20.00
	1908(c)	58.066	.35	1.25	6.50	30.00
	1908(c)	—	—	—	Proof	40.00
502	1908(c) (restrike)		—	—	P/L	20.00
	1909(c)	29.966	.35	1.25	6.50	30.00
	1909(c) (restrike)		—	—	P/L	20.00
	1910(c)	47.265	.35	1.25	6.50	30.00
	1910(c) (restrike)		—	—	P/L	20.00

ALUMINUM (OMS)

KM#	Date	Mintage	Fine	VF	XF	Unc
502a	1908(c)	—	—	—	Proof	150.00

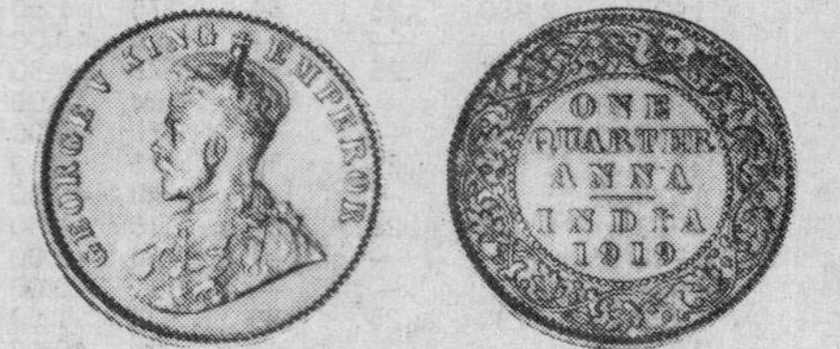

BRONZE

NOTE: Calcutta Mint issues have no mint mark. Bombay Mint issues have a small dot below the date. The pieces dated 1911, like the other coins with that date, show the "Pig" elephant.

KM#	Date	Mintage	Fine	VF	XF	Unc
511	1911(c)	55.918	.75	2.00	5.00	20.00
	1911(c)	—	—	—	Proof	55.00
	1911(c) (restrike)		—	—	P/L	20.00
512	1912(c)	107.456	.20	.40	.75	3.00
	1912(c)	—	—	—	Proof	35.00
	1912(c) (restrike)		—	—	P/L	20.00
	1913(c)	82.061	.25	.50	.85	3.00
	1913(c)	—	—	—	Proof	35.00
	1913(c) (restrike)		—	—	P/L	20.00
	1914(c)	40.576	.20	.40	.75	2.50
	1914(c)	—	—	—	Proof	35.00
	1914(c) (restrike)		—	—	P/L	20.00
	1916(c)	1.632	3.50	7.00	12.00	25.00
	1916(c)	—	—	—	Proof	50.00
	1917(c)	69.370	.20	.40	.75	2.50
	1917(c)	—	—	—	Proof	35.00
	1917(c) (restrike)		—	—	P/L	20.00
	1918(c)	84.045	.20	.40	.75	2.50
	1918(c)	—	—	—	Proof	35.00
	1918(c) (restrike)		—	—	P/L	20.00
	1919(c)	212.467	.20	.40	.75	2.50
	1919(c)	—	—	—	Proof	35.00
	1919(c) (restrike)		—	—	P/L	20.00
	1920(c)	96.019	.20	.40	.75	2.50
	1920(c)	—	—	—	Proof	35.00
	1920(c) (restrike)		—	—	P/L	20.00
	1921(c)	—	—	—	Proof	35.00
	1924(b)	16.322	.20	.40	.75	2.50
	1924(b)	—	—	—	Proof	35.00
	1925(c)	14.253	.20	.40	.75	2.50
	1925(b)	14.588	.20	.40	.75	2.50
	1925(b)	—	—	—	Proof	35.00
	1926(c)	17.389	.20	.40	.75	2.50
	1926(c)	—	—	—	Proof	35.00
	1926(b)	16.073	.20	.40	.75	2.50
	1926(b)	—	—	—	Proof	35.00
	1926(b) (restrike)		—	—	P/L	20.00
	1927(c)	6.925	.20	.40	.75	2.50
	1927(c)	—	—	—	Proof	35.00
	1927(b)	12.440	.20	.40	.75	2.50
	1927(b)	—	—	—	Proof	35.00
	1927(b) (restrike)		—	—	P/L	20.00
	1928(c)	25.779	.20	.40	.75	2.50
	1928(c)	—	—	—	Proof	35.00
	1928(b)	10.057	.20	.40	.75	2.50
	1928(b)	—	—	—	Proof	35.00
	1928(b) (restrike)		—	—	P/L	20.00
	1929(c)	64.000	.20	.40	.75	2.50
	1929(c)	—	—	—	Proof	35.00
	1929(c) (restrike)		—	—	P/L	20.00
	1930(c)	33.485	.20	.40	.75	2.50
	1930(c)	—	—	—	Proof	35.00
	1930(b)	9.646	.20	.40	.75	2.50
	1930(b)	—	—	—	Proof	35.00
	1930(b) (restrike)		—	—	P/L	20.00
	1931(c)	6.560	.20	.40	.75	2.50
	1931(c)	—	—	—	Proof	35.00
	1931(c) (restrike)		—	—	P/L	20.00
	1933(c)	58.800	.20	.40	.75	2.50
	1933(c)	—	—	—	Proof	35.00
	1933(c) (restrike)		—	—	P/L	20.00
	1934(c)	85.862	.20	.40	.75	2.50
	1934(c)	—	—	—	Proof	35.00
	1934(c) (restrike)		—	—	P/L	20.00
	1935(c)	92.768	.20	.40	.75	2.50
	1935(c)	—	—	—	Proof	35.00
	1935(c) (restrike)		—	—	P/L	20.00
	1936(c)	225.344	.20	.40	.75	2.50
	1936(b)	81.812	.20	.40	.75	2.00
	1936(b)	—	—	—	Proof	35.00
	1936(b) (restrike)		—	—	P/L	20.00

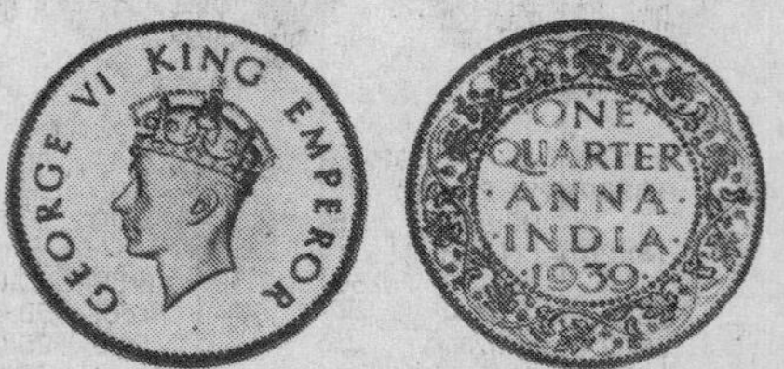

Obv: First head, high relief.

NOTE: Calcutta Mint issues have no mint mark. Bombay Mint issues have a small dot above N of "ONE".

KM#	Date	Mintage	Fine	VF	XF	Unc
530	1938(c)	33.792	.25	.40	.75	1.50

KM#	Date	Mintage	Fine	VF	XF	Unc
530	1938(c)	—	—	—	Proof	35.00
	1938(b)	16.796	.25	.40	.75	1.50
	1938(b) (restrike)		—	—	P/L	30.00
	1939(c)	78.279	.30	.50	1.00	2.00
	1939(c)	—	—	—	Proof	35.00
	1939(b)	60.171	.30	.50	1.00	3.00
	1939(b)	—	—	—	Proof	35.00
	1939(b) (restrike)		—	—	P/L	30.00
	1940(b)	116.721	.35	.75	1.50	3.00

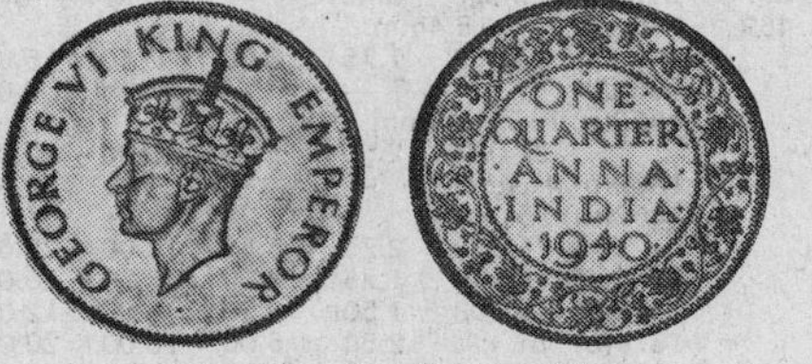

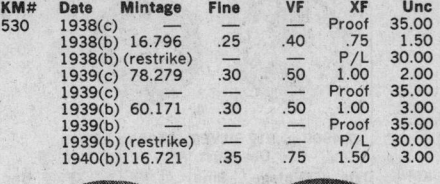

Obv: Second head, low relief.

KM#	Date	Mintage	Fine	VF	XF	Unc
531	1940(c)	140.410	.15	.35	.65	1.00
	1940(c)	—	—	—	Proof	35.00
	1940(b)	Inc. KM530	.15	.35	.65	1.00
	1940(b) (restrike)		—	—	P/L	25.00
	1941(c)	121.107	.15	.35	.65	1.00
	1941(c) (restrike)		—	—	P/L	25.00
	1941(b)	1.446	—	.60	1.50	5.00
	1942(c)	34.298	.15	.35	.65	1.00
	1942(b)	8.768	.15	.35	.65	1.00
	1942(b) (restrike)		—	—	P/L	25.00

PICE

NOTE: There are three types of the crown, which is on the obverse at the top. These are shown below and are designated as (RC) Round Crown, (HC) High Crown, and (FC) Flat Crown. Calcutta Mint issues have no mint mark. The issues from the other mints have the mint mark below the date as following: Lahore, raised "L"; Pretoria, small round dot; Bombay, diamond dot or "large" round dot. On the Bombay issues dated 1944 the mint mark appears to be a large dot over a diamond.

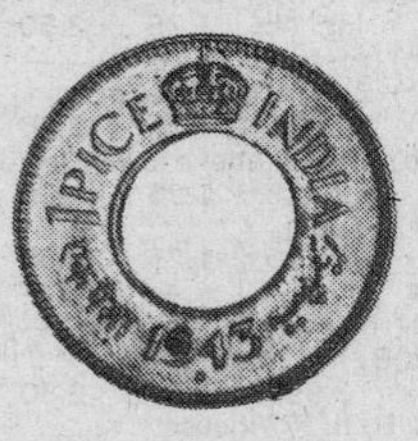

Round Crown (RC)

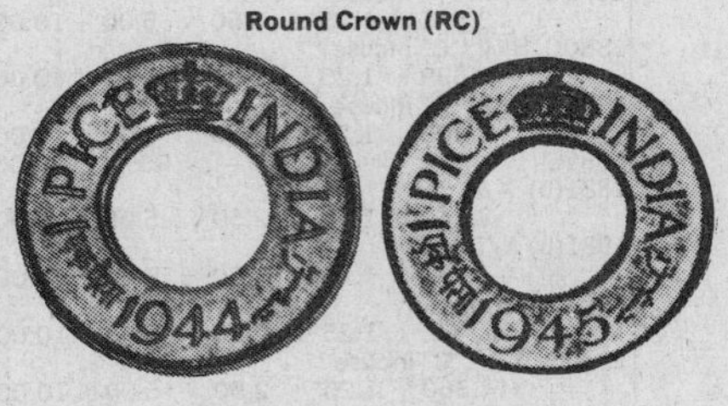

High Crown (HC) **Flat Crown (FC)**

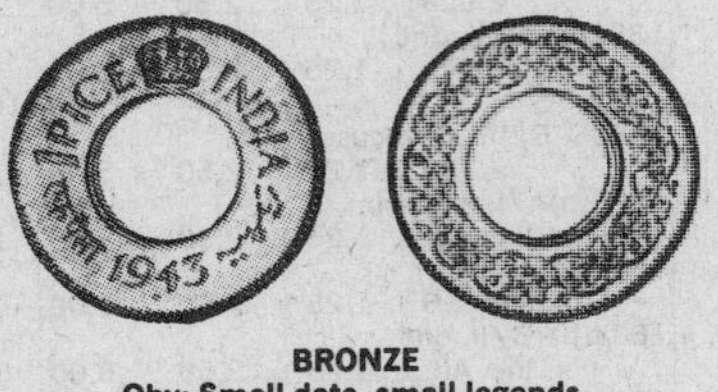

BRONZE
Obv: Small date, small legends.

KM#	Date	Mintage	Fine	VF	XF	Unc
532	1943(b) (RC) diamond	164.659	.25	.40	.85	2.75

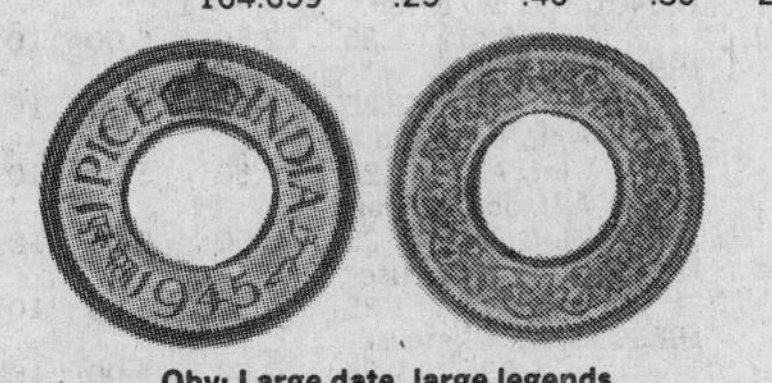

Obv: Large date, large legends.

KM#	Date	Mintage	Fine	VF	XF	Unc
533	1943(b) (HC) large dot	—	.15	.35	.65	1.00
	1943(p) (HC) small dot	98.997	.15	.35	.65	1.00
	1944(c) HC	—	.15	.35	.65	1.00
	1944(c) HC	—	—	—	Proof	25.00
	1944(b) (HC) large dot	195.354	.15	.35	.65	1.00
	1944(b) (HC) diamond	—	.20	.40	.75	1.75
	1944(b) FC large dot	—	.20	.40	.75	1.75
	1944(b) (restrike)	—	—	P/L	20.00	
	1944(p) (HC) small dot	141.003	.20	.40	.75	1.75
	1944L (HC)	29.802	.15	.35	.65	1.00
	1945(c)FC	156.322	.15	.35	.65	1.00
	1945(b) (FC) diamond	237.197	.15	.35	.65	1.00
	1945(b) (FC) large dot	Inc. Ab.	.15	.35	.65	1.00
	1945(b) (restrike)		—	—	P/L	20.00
	1945L (FC)	238.825	.15	.35	.65	1.00
	1947(c)HC	153.702	.15	.35	.65	1.00
	1947(b) (HC) diamond	43.654	.15	.35	.65	1.00
	1947(b)	—	—	—	Proof	25.00
	1947 (restrike)		—	—	P/L	20.00

1/2 ANNA

NOTE: The half Anna dated 1862 was struck at all three Indian Government Mints, i.e. Calcutta, Bombay and Madras but a correct attribution to the mint of issue has not yet been possible. The coins dated 1875-76 were struck at the Calcutta Mint, those dated 1877 were struck at Calcutta and Bombay. Two different busts occur on the 1877 issue.

BUST A - The bottom section of the front dress panel has a small flower in the upper left corner and a large flower at right of center.
BUST C - The bottom section of the front dress panel has a five-dotted flower at right of center.

NOTE: Bust B is the common obverse on 1862 issues and is not described here.

The Bombay issue dated 1877 was identified by the type of the date figure "7" which has a short horizontal stroke and a long downstroke. This type of "7" appears on most Bombay issues but not on any denomination of the Calcutta Mint.

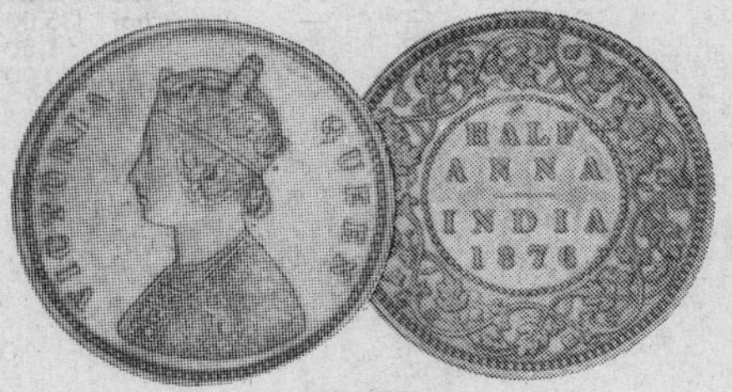

COPPER

KM#	Date	Mintage	Fine	VF	XF	Unc
468	1862(c) 31.3mm	7.235	10.00	20.00	30.00	75.00
	1862(c)	—	—	—	Proof	125.00
	1862(c) (restrike)		—	—	P/L	50.00
	1862(b) 30.5mm	4.802	10.00	20.00	30.00	75.00
	1862(m) 30.7mm	66.515	5.00	10.00	18.50	60.00
	1862(c) 30.9mm w/v in bottom of bust	7.399	10.00	20.00	30.00	75.00
	1862(c)	—	—	—	Proof	125.00
	1862(c) (restrike)		—	—	P/L	35.00
	1875(c), bust A	—	12.50	25.00	50.00	100.00
	1875(c)	—	—	—	Proof	150.00
	1875(c) (restrike)		—	—	P/L	50.00
	1876(c), bust A	3.437	12.50	25.00	50.00	100.00

GOLD (OMS)

KM#	Date	Mintage	Fine	VF	XF	Unc
468b	1862(c)	—	—	—	Proof	650.00

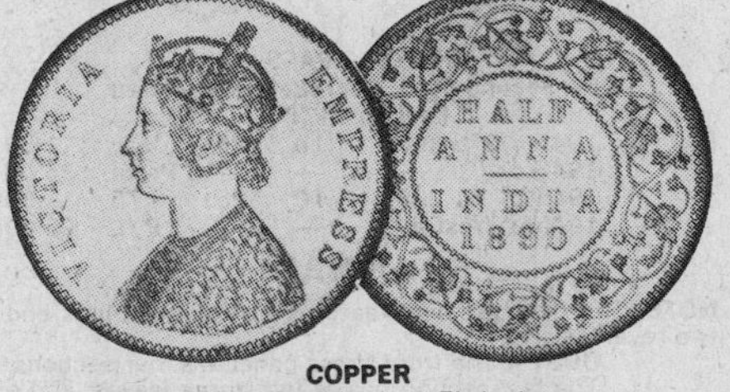

COPPER

KM#	Date	Mintage	Fine	VF	XF	Unc
487	1877(c), bust C, wide short 7's in date	3.584	10.00	20.00	40.00	100.00
	1877(c)	Inc. Ab.	—	—	Proof	100.00
	1877(c) (restrike)		—	—	P/L	40.00
	1877(b), bust A, narrow tall 7's in date	3.454	12.00	20.00	40.00	100.00
	1878(c)	—	—	—	Proof	100.00
	1878(c) (restrike)		—	—	P/L	65.00
	1879(c)	—	—	—	Proof	100.00
	1879(c) (restrike)		—	—	P/L	75.00
	1884(b)	—	—	—	Proof	100.00
	1884(b) (restrike)		—	—	P/L	75.00
	1890(c)	—	—	—	Proof	100.00
	1890(c) (restrike)		—	—	P/L	65.00
	1891(c)	86.077	—	—	Proof	100.00
	1891(c) (restrike)		—	—	P/L	65.00
	1892(c)	—	—	—	Proof	100.00
	1892(c) (restrike)		—	—	P/L	65.00
	1893(c)	76.038	—	—	Proof	100.00
	1893(c) (restrike)		—	—	P/L	65.00
	1894	—	—	Reported, not confirmed		

NOTE: On Calcutta issue 1879 a small incuse 'c' can be found on one of the beads at the inner circle on the rev.

ALUMINUM (OMS)

KM#	Date	Mintage	Fine	VF	XF	Unc
487a	1891(b)	—	—	—	Proof	100.00

SILVER (OMS)

KM#	Date	Mintage	Fine	VF	XF	Unc
487b	1892(c) (restrike)		—	—	P/L	150.00
	1893(c) (restrike)		—	—	P/L	150.00

GOLD (OMS)

KM#	Date	Mintage	Fine	VF	XF	Unc
487c	1891(c) (restrike)		—	—	P/L	500.00
	1892(c) (restrike)		—	—	P/L	500.00
	1893(c) (restrike)		—	—	P/L	500.00

COPPER
Obv: Head of Edward VII. Rev: Similar to KM#487.

KM#	Date	Mintage	Fine	VF	XF	Unc
503	1904(c)	—	—	—	Proof	2000.

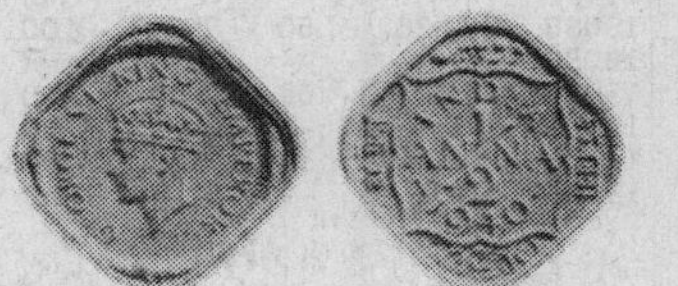

COPPER-NICKEL
Rev. leg: ·INDIA·

KM#	Date	Mintage	Fine	VF	XF	Unc
534	1940(c)	—	—	—	Proof	85.00
(535)	1940(c) (restrike)		—	—	P/L	50.00

GOLD (OMS)

KM#	Date	Mintage	Fine	VF	XF	Unc
534a (535a)	1940(c) (restrike)		—	—	P/L	250.00

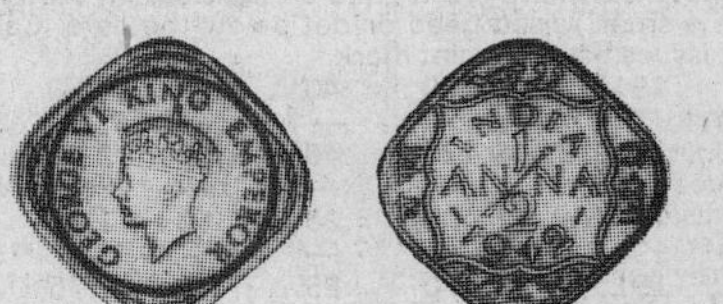

NICKEL-BRASS
Obv: Second head.
Rev. leg: INDIA (w/o dots).

NOTE: Bombay Mint issues dated 1942-1945 are without a dot before and after India and on each side of the date.

KM#	Date	Mintage	Fine	VF	XF	Unc
534b.1	1942(b)	7.945	.15	.35	.65	1.25
(534)	1942(b) (restrike)		—	—	P/L	40.00
	1943(b) (restrike)		—	—	P/L	40.00
	1944(b) (restrike)		—	—	P/L	40.00
	1945(b)	6.264	—	Reported, not confirmed		
	1945(b) (restrike)		—	—	P/L	25.00

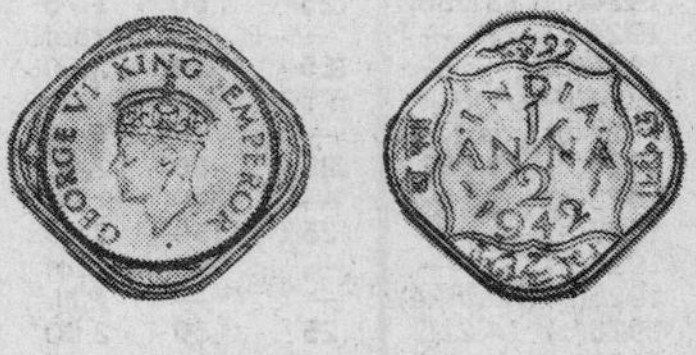

Rev. leg: ·INDIA·

NOTE: Calcutta Mint struck this denomination each year 1942-1945, denoted by a dot before and after the word INDIA on the reverse. Bombay Mint struck only with the dates 1942 and 1945, denoted by INDIA without dots before and after. Calcutta also issued proof coins each year, while Bombay issued none. However, Bombay later produced proof-like restrikes which are difficult to identify because it used old dies from both Bombay and Calcutta indiscriminately; they are all attributed here to Bombay. Source: Pridmore.

KM#	Date	Mintage	Fine	VF	XF	Unc
534b.2	1942(c)	159.000	.10	.15	.35	1.00
(534)	1942(c)	—	—	—	Proof	30.00
	1943(c)	437.760	.10	.15	.35	1.00
	1943(c)	—	—	—	Proof	40.00
	1944(c)	514.800	.10	.15	.35	1.00
	1944(c)	—	—	—	Proof	40.00
	1945(c)	215.732	—	—	Proof	40.00

COPPER-NICKEL

NOTE: Calcutta Mint continued to issue this denomination with the dot before and after INDIA in 1946 and 1947. Bombay also struck in 1946 and 1947, the 1946 issue denoted by a small dot in the center of the dashes before and after the date on the reverse (as well as a dot before and after INDIA, like Calcutta); the characteristics of the 1947 Bombay issue have not been determined but are thought also to resemble the 1946 issue. This denomination is also reported to have been struck in a quantity of 50,829 pieces in 1946 at the new Lahore Mint but no way of distinguishing this issue has been found. The proof issue in 1946 was struck by Bombay, not Calcutta. Source: Pridmore.

KM#	Date	Mintage	Fine	VF	XF	Unc
535.1	1946(b)	48.744	.10	.15	.35	1.00
(535)	1946(b)	—	—	—	Proof	30.00
	1946(b) (restrike)		—	—	P/L	25.00
	1947(b)	24.144	—	Reported, not confirmed		
	1947(b) (restrike)		—	—	P/L	50.00
535.2	1946(c)	75.159	.10	.15	.35	1.00
(535)	1947(c)	126.392	.10	.15	.35	1.00
	1947(c)	—	—	—	Proof	40.00
	1947(c) (restrike)		—	—	P/L	25.00

ANNA

NOTE: Struck only at the Bombay Mint, the pieces have as mint mark a small incuse "B" in the space below the cross pattee of the crown on the obverse.

British / INDIA 982

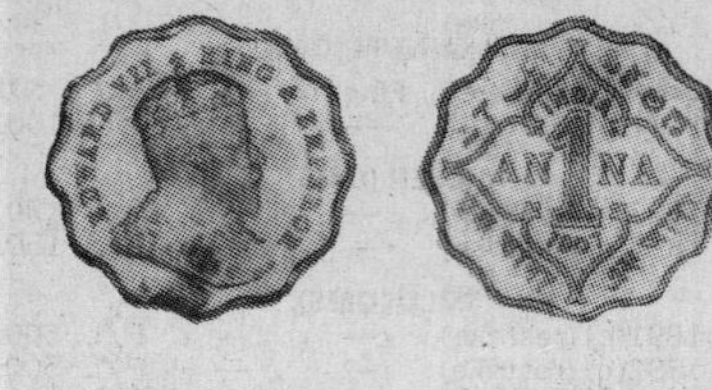

COPPER-NICKEL

KM#	Date	Mintage	Fine	VF	XF	Unc
504	1906B	.200	20.00	50.00	125.00	300.00
	1907B	37.256	.50	1.25	2.00	5.00
	1907B	—	—	—	Proof	60.00
	1908B	22.536	.50	1.25	2.00	5.00
	1908B	—	—	—	Proof	60.00
	1909B	24.800	.50	1.25	2.00	5.00
	1909B	—	—	—	Proof	60.00
	1910B	40.200	.50	1.25	2.00	5.00
	1910B	—	—	—	Proof	60.00

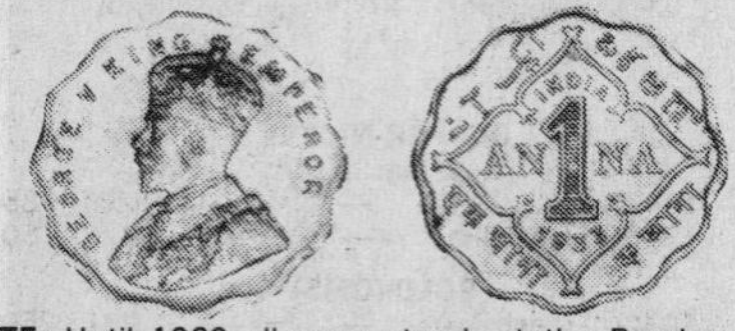

NOTE: Until 1920 all were struck at the Bombay Mint without mint mark. From 1923 on the Bombay Mint issues have a small raised bead or dot below the date. Calcutta Mint issues have no mint mark.

KM#	Date	Mintage	Fine	VF	XF	Unc
513	1912(b)	39.400	.40	1.00	2.50	6.00
	1912	—	—	—	Proof	50.00
	1913(b)	39.776	.40	1.00	2.50	6.00
	1913	—	—	—	Proof	50.00
	1914(b)	48.000	.25	.50	1.75	3.50
	1914	—	—	—	Proof	50.00
	1915(b)	12.470	.25	.50	1.75	3.50
	1915	—	—	—	Proof	50.00
	1916(b)	26.738	.25	.50	1.75	3.50
	1917(b)	50.136	.25	.50	1.75	3.50
	1917	—	—	—	Proof	50.00
	1918(b)	80.360	.25	.50	1.75	3.50
	1918(b)	—	—	—	Proof	50.00
	1919(b)	141.000	.25	.35	1.75	3.00
	1919(b)	—	—	—	Proof	50.00
	1919(c)	—	—	—	Proof	50.00
	1920(b)	11.671	.25	.50	1.50	4.00
	1920(b)	—	—	—	Proof	50.00
	1923(b)	6.438	.25	.50	1.50	4.00
	1923(b)	—	—	—	Proof	50.00
	1924(c)	13.536	.25	.50	1.75	3.00
	1924(c)	—	—	—	Proof	50.00
	1924(b)	—	.25	.50	2.00	5.00
	1924(b)	—	—	—	Proof	50.00
	1924(b) (restrike)	—	—	—	P/L	20.00
	1925(c)	19.832	.25	.50	2.00	5.00
	1925(c)	—	—	—	Proof	50.00
	1925(b)	—	.25	.50	2.00	5.00
	1925(b)	—	—	—	Proof	50.00
	1925(b) (restrike)	—	—	—	P/L	20.00
	1926(c)	14.216	.25	.50	2.00	5.00
	1926(c)	—	—	—	Proof	50.00
	1926(b)	8.988	.25	.50	2.00	5.00
	1926(b)	—	—	—	Proof	50.00
	1926(b) (restrike)	—	—	—	P/L	20.00
	1927(c)	11.080	.25	.50	2.00	5.00
	1927(c)	—	—	—	Proof	50.00
	1927(b)	6.444	.25	.50	2.00	5.00
	1927(b)	—	—	—	Proof	50.00
	1927(b) (restrike)	—	—	—	P/L	20.00
	1928(c)	23.432	.25	.50	2.00	5.00
	1928(c)	—	—	—	Proof	50.00
	1928(b)	11.340	.25	.50	2.00	5.00
	1928(b)	—	—	—	Proof	50.00
	1928(b) (restrike)	—	—	—	P/L	20.00
	1929(c)	43.184	.25	.50	2.00	5.00
	1929(c)	—	—	—	Proof	50.00
	1929(c) (restrike)	—	—	—	P/L	20.00
	1930(c)	27.978	.25	.50	2.00	5.00
	1930(c)	—	—	—	Proof	50.00
	1930(c) (restrike)	—	—	—	P/L	20.00
	1933(c)	8.968	.25	.50	2.00	5.00
	1933(c)	—	—	—	Proof	50.00
	1933(c) (restrike)	—	—	—	P/L	20.00
	1934(c)	37.248	.25	.40	1.50	4.00
	1934(c)	—	—	—	Proof	50.00
	1934(c) (restrike)	—	—	—	P/L	20.00
	1935(c)	18.384	.25	.40	1.50	4.00
	1935(c)	—	—	—	Proof	50.00
	1935(b)	29.221	.25	.40	1.50	4.00
	1935(b)	—	—	—	Proof	50.00
	1935(b) (restrike)	—	—	—	P/L	20.00
	1936(c)	4.008	.25	.40	1.50	4.00
	1936(b)	91.689	.20	.35	1.25	3.00
	1936(b)	—	—	—	Proof	50.00

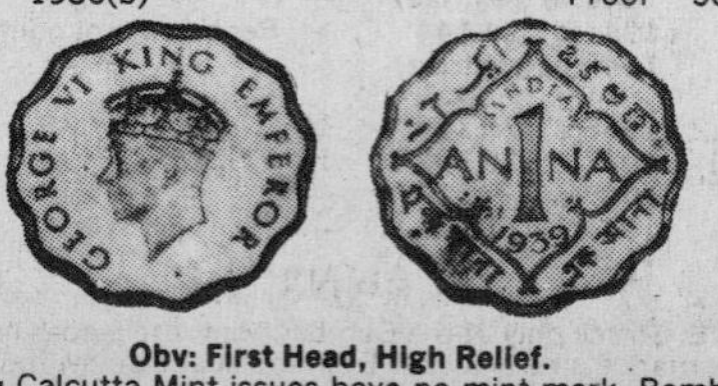

Obv: First Head, High Relief.

NOTE: Calcutta Mint issues have no mint mark. Bombay Mint issues have a small dot below the date.

KM#	Date	Mintage	Fine	VF	XF	Unc
536	1938(c)	7.128	.30	.75	1.50	5.00
	1938(c)	—	—	—	Proof	40.00
	1938(b)	3.126	.30	.75	1.50	3.00
	1938(b) (restrike)	—	—	—	P/L	20.00
	1939(c)	18.192	.15	.40	.75	2.25
	1939(b)	36.157	.15	.40	.75	2.25
	1939(b) (restrike)	—	—	—	P/L	20.00
	1940(c) (restrike)	—	—	—	P/L	20.00
	1940(b)	144.712	.30	.75	1.50	4.00
	1940(b) (restrike)	—	—	—	P/L	20.00

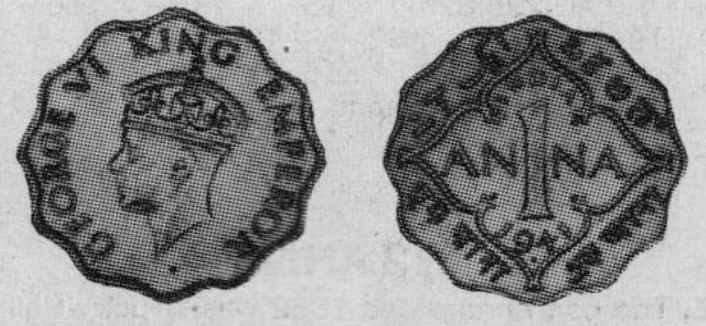

Obv: Second head, low relief, large crown.
Rev: Large "I".

KM#	Date	Mintage	Fine	VF	XF	Unc
537	1940(c)	76.392	.10	.25	.50	1.50
	1940(b)	Inc. Ab.	.10	.25	.50	1.50
	1941(c)	62.480	.10	.15	.25	.75
	1941(b)	40.170	.10	.15	.25	.75
	1941(b) (restrike)	—	—	—	P/L	25.00

NICKEL-BRASS

KM#	Date	Mintage	Fine	VF	XF	Unc
537a	1942(c)	194.056	.10	.25	.50	1.50
	1942(c)	—	—	—	Proof	35.00
	1942(b)	103.240	.10	.25	.50	1.50
	1942(b) (restrike)	—	—	—	P/L	20.00
	1943(c)	352.256	.10	.25	.50	1.50
	1943(c)	—	—	—	Proof	35.00
	1943(b)	134.500	.10	.25	.50	1.50
	1943(b) (restrike)	—	—	—	P/L	20.00
	1944(c)	457.608	.10	.25	.50	1.50
	1944(c)	—	—	—	Proof	35.00
	1944(b)	175.208	.10	.25	.50	1.50
	1944(b) (restrike)	—	—	—	P/L	20.00

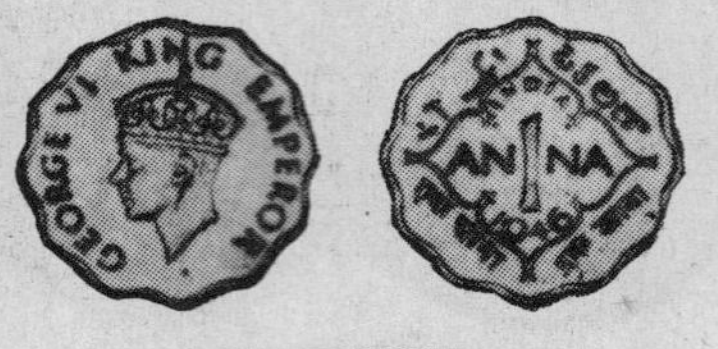

COPPER-NICKEL
Obv: Second head, low relief, small crown.
Rev: Small "I".

KM#	Date	Mintage	Fine	VF	XF	Unc
538	1945(c)	278.360	.10	.25	.50	1.50
	1945(b)	61.228	.10	.25	.50	1.50
	1946(c)	100.820	.10	.15	.35	1.00
	1946(b)	82.052	.10	.15	.35	1.00
	1946(b)	—	—	—	Proof	40.00
	1946(b) (restrike)	—	—	—	P/L	25.00
	1947(c)	148.656	.10	.25	.35	1.00
	1947(c)	—	—	—	Proof	40.00
	1947(b)	50.096	.10	.15	.35	1.00
	1947(b)	—	—	—	Proof	40.00

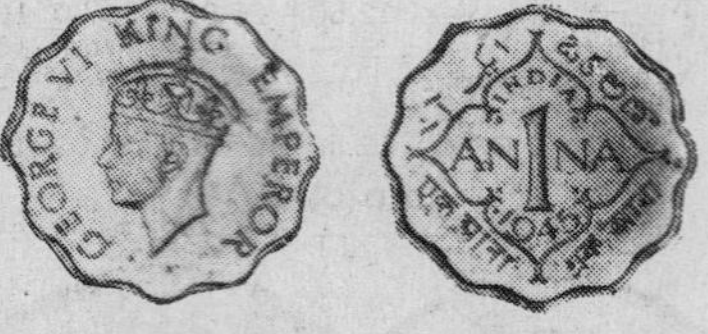

NICKEL-BRASS
Obv: Second head, low relief, large crown.
Rev: Small "I".

KM#	Date	Mintage	Fine	VF	XF	Unc
539	1945(c)	278.360	.10	.25	.75	1.50
	1945(c)	—	—	—	Proof	35.00
	1945(b)	61.228	.10	.25	.75	1.50
	1945(b) (restrike)	—	—	—	P/L	25.00

2 ANNAS

NOTE: The distinguishing features of the two busts and two reverses are:

BUST A-The front dress panel has four sections. The last section has at left, three leaves, and a small indistinct flower in the upper right corner.

BUST B-The front dress panel has 3 1/2 sections. The last, incomplete section shows only three small leaf tops.

REVERSE I-Large top flower; the two large petals above the whorl are long and curved downward.

REVERSE II-Small top flower; the two large petals above the whorl are short and horizontal.

The 2 Annas dated 1862-76 have been re-attributed as a result of latest studies. The 2 Annas, dated 1877 having a bead in the tip of the top flower is now attributed to Calcutta.

Calcutta issues dated 1862-78 have no mint mark. The diameter of the coins is 15.25mm, except for the 1877 issue with the bead in the top flower which is 15.4mm. From 1879 the mint mark is a small incuse "C" in the whorl below the center of the bottom flower. Calcutta coins dated 1874 have not yet been verified.

Bombay issues until 1877 are without mint mark and have a diameter of 15.8mm. From 1877-1883 the mint mark is a small raised bead directly above the bottom flower. From 1884 the coins have a small B raised or incuse, above the whorl of the top flower. Madras issues (1862 only) are 16mm diameter.

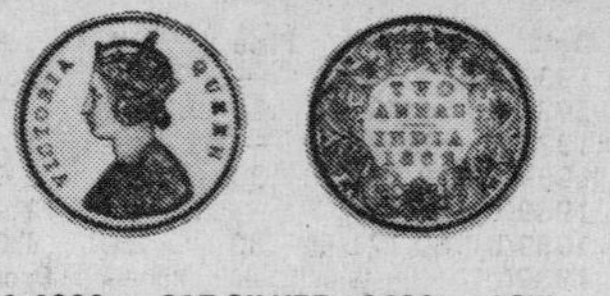

1.4600 g, .917 SILVER, .0430 oz ASW
Obv: Bust "A".

KM#	Date	Mintage	Fine	VF	XF	Unc
469	1862(c) 15.3-15.4mm	29.653	1.75	3.50	7.50	15.00
	1862(c)	—	—	—	Proof	100.00
	1862(b) 15.7-15.9mm	21.037	2.50	5.00	10.00	20.00
	1862(b) (restrike)	—	—	—	P/L	35.00
	1862(m) 16.0mm	4.202	2.75	5.50	11.00	22.00
	1874(c)	5.690	1.75	3.50	7.50	15.00
	1874(b)	9.508	1.50	3.00	6.00	12.00
	1874(b) dot	I.A.	2.50	5.00	10.00	20.00
	1875(c)	6.512	1.50	3.00	6.00	12.00
	1875(c)	—	—	—	Proof	100.00
	1875(b)	1.712	2.50	5.00	10.00	20.00
	1876(c)	10.504	1.00	2.00	4.00	8.00
	1876(b)	3.911	2.00	4.00	8.00	16.00

GOLD (OMS)

KM#	Date	Mintage	Fine	VF	XF	Unc
469a	1862	—	—	—	Proof	350.00

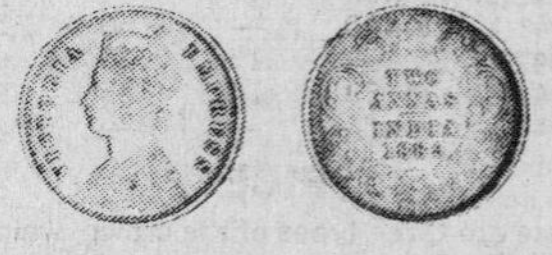

1.4600 g, .917 SILVER, .0430 oz AGW

KM#	Date	Mintage	Fine	VF	XF	Unc
488	1877(c)A/I, w/o mm.	3.575	1.25	2.50	5.00	10.00
	1877(c) A/I, dot below	Inc. Ab.	1.75	3.50	7.00	14.00
	1877(c)	—	—	—	Proof	100.00
	1877(c)B/II, w/o mm.	Inc. Ab	1.75	3.50	7.00	14.00
	1877(c) (restrike)	—	—	—	P/L	30.00
	1877(c) B/II, dot in top flower	Inc. Ab.	1.25	2.50	5.00	10.00
	1877(b) A/I dot above lower flower	2.215	1.25	2.50	5.00	10.00
	1878B A.I, dot	2.215	1.25	2.50	5.00	10.00
	1878B	—	—	—	Proof	100.00
	1878B (restrike)	—	—	—	P/L	30.00
	1878(c)B/II w/o mm.	3.994	1.25	2.50	5.00	10.00
	1879C B/II, "C" incuse	3.541	1.25	2.50	5.00	10.00
	1880C B/II, "C" incuse	2.539	1.25	2.50	5.00	10.00
	1881C B/II, "C" incuse	4.400	1.25	2.50	5.00	10.00
	1881C	—	—	—	Proof	100.00
	1881(b) A/I, dot	2.449	1.25	2.50	5.00	10.00
	1881(b) A/II, dot	—	1.75	3.50	7.00	14.00
	1881(b) B/II, dot	Inc. Ab.	1.25	2.50	5.00	10.00
	1882C B/II, "C" incuse	14.360	1.25	2.50	5.00	10.00
	1882(b) A/I, dot	2.629	1.25	2.50	5.00	10.00
	1882(b) B/II, dot	Inc. Ab.	1.25	2.50	5.00	10.00
	1882	—	—	—	Proof	100.00
	1883C B/II, "C" incuse	2.736	1.25	2.50	5.00	10.00
	1883(b)A/I, w/o mm.	Inc. Ab.	1.25	2.50	5.00	10.00
	1883(b) A/I, dot	4.416	1.25	2.50	5.00	10.00
	1883(b) B/II, dot	Inc. Ab.	1.25	2.50	5.00	10.00
	1884C B/II, "C" incuse	7.200	1.25	2.50	5.00	10.00
	1884(b) A/I, w/o mm.	1.638	1.25	2.50	5.00	10.00
	1884(b) A/I, dot	Inc. Ab.	1.25	2.50	5.00	10.00
	1884B A/I, "B" raised	Inc. Ab.	1.25	2.50	5.00	10.00
	1884B A/I, dot, "B" raised	Inc. Ab.	1.25	2.50	5.00	10.00
	1884B B/II, "B" incuse	Inc. Ab.	1.25	2.50	5.00	10.00
	1885C B/II, "C" incuse	1.335	1.25	2.50	5.00	10.00
	1885B A/I, "B" raised	—	1.75	3.50	7.00	14.00
	1885B B/II, "B" raised	2.262	1.25	2.50	5.00	10.00
	1886C B/II, "C" incuse	10.346	1.25	2.50	5.00	10.00
	1886B B/II, "B" incuse	3.155	1.25	2.50	5.00	10.00
	1887C B/II, "C" incuse	13.927	1.25	2.50	5.00	10.00
	1887B B/II, "B" incuse	3.283	1.25	2.50	5.00	10.00
	1888(c)B/II, w/o mm.	9.307	1.25	2.50	5.00	10.00

983
British / INDIA

KM#	Date	Mintage	Fine	VF	XF	Unc
488	1888B B/II, "B" incuse					
		8.039	1.25	2.50	5.00	10.00
	1888B	—	—	—	Proof	100.00
	1889C B/II, "C" incuse					
		.135	1.75	3.50	7.00	14.00
	1889B B/II, "B" incuse					
		5.895	1.25	2.50	5.00	10.00
	1890C B/II, "C" incuse					
		9.836	1.25	2.50	5.00	10.00
	1890C	—	—	—	Proof	100.00
	1890B B/II, "B" raised					
		7.790	1.25	2.50	5.00	10.00
	1890B B/II, "B" incuse					
		Inc. Ab.	1.25	2.50	5.00	10.00
	1890B	(restrike)	—	—	P/L	30.00
	1891C B/II, "C" incuse					
		8.621	1.25	2.50	5.00	10.00
	1891C	—	—	—	Proof	100.00
	1891B B/II, "B" incuse					
		4.230	1.25	2.50	5.00	10.00
	1891B	(restrike)	—	—	P/L	30.00
	1892C B/II, "C" incuse					
		6.971	1.25	2.50	5.00	10.00
	1892C	—	—	—	Proof	100.00
	1892B B/II, "B" incuse					
		9.347	1.25	2.50	5.00	10.00
	1892B	(restrike)	—	—	P/L	30.00
	1893C B/II, "C" incuse					
		8.003	1.25	2.50	5.00	10.00
	1893C	—	—	—	Proof	100.00
	1893B B/II, "B" incuse					
		10.716	1.25	2.50	5.00	10.00
	1893B	(restrike)	—	—	P/L	30.00
	1894C B/II, "C" incuse					
		2.461	1.25	2.50	5.00	10.00
	1894C	—	—	—	Proof	100.00
	1894B B/II, "B" incuse					
		Inc. Ab.	1.25	2.50	5.00	10.00
	1894B	(restrike)	—	—	P/L	30.00
	1895C B/II, "C" incuse					
		9.668	1.25	2.50	5.00	10.00
	1896C B/II, "C" incuse					
		6.616	1.25	2.50	5.00	10.00
	1896C	—	—	—	Proof	100.00
	1896B B/II, "B" incuse					
		8.235	1.25	2.50	5.00	10.00
	1897C B/II, "C" incuse					
		12.103	1.25	2.50	5.00	10.00
	1897C	—	—	—	Proof	100.00
	1897B B/II, "B" incuse					
		8.041	1.25	2.50	5.00	10.00
	1897B	—	—	—	Proof	100.00
	1897B	(restrike)	—	—	P/L	30.00
	1898C B/II, "C" incuse					
		4.011	1.25	2.50	5.00	10.00
	1898B B/II, "B" incuse					
		3.250	1.25	2.50	5.00	10.00
	1898B	—	—	—	Proof	100.00
	1898B	(restrike)	—	—	P/L	30.00
	1899	—	—	—	Proof	100.00
	1900C B/II, "C" incuse					
		1.705	1.25	2.50	5.00	10.00
	1900	—	—	—	Proof	—
	1900B B/II, "B" raised					
		4.439	1.25	2.50	5.00	10.00
	1900B	—	—	—	Proof	100.00
	1900B	(restrike)	—	—	P/L	30.00
	1901C B/II, "C" incuse					
		8.944	1.25	2.50	5.00	10.00
	1901C	Inc. Ab.	—	—	Proof	35.00
	1901B B/II, "B" incuse					
		1.706	1.25	2.50	5.00	10.00
	1901B	—	—	—	Proof	100.00
	1901B	(restrike)	—	—	P/L	30.00
	1901B B/II, "B" raised					
		Inc. Ab.	1.25	2.50	5.00	10.00

ALUMINUM (OMS)

KM#	Date	Mintage	Fine	VF	XF	Unc
488a	1891(b)	—	—	—	Proof	—

COPPER OR BRONZE (OMS)

KM#	Date	Mintage	Fine	VF	XF	Unc
488b	1884	—	—	—	Proof	75.00
	1891	—	—	—	Proof	75.00
	1892	—	—	—	Proof	75.00

GOLD (OMS)

KM#	Date	Mintage	Fine	VF	XF	Unc
488c	1891	(restrike)	—	—	P/L	250.00
	1892	(restrike)	—	—	P/L	250.00
	1893	(restrike)	—	—	P/L	250.00
	1896	(restrike)	—	—	P/L	250.00
	1897	(restrike)	—	—	P/L	250.00
	1898	(restrike)	—	—	P/L	250.00
	1900	(restrike)	—	—	P/L	250.00

1.4600 g, .917 SILVER, .0430 oz ASW
Mule. Obv: Y#9. Rev: Y#20.

KM#	Date	Mintage	Fine	VF	XF	Unc
489	1877	(restrike)	—	—	P/L	20.00

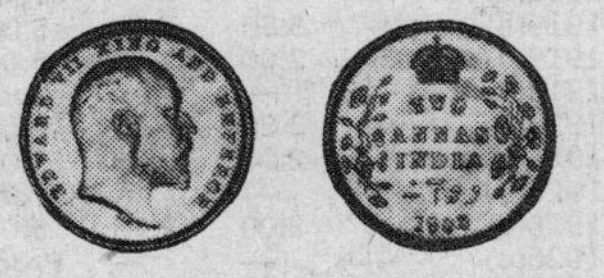

KM#	Date	Mintage	Fine	VF	XF	Unc
505	1903(c)	4.434	1.50	3.00	6.00	12.00
	1903(c)	—	—	—	Proof	65.00
	1903(c)	(restrike)	—	—	P/L	25.00
	1904(c)	14.632	1.50	3.00	6.00	12.00
	1904(c)	—	—	—	Proof	65.00
	1904(c)	(restrike)	—	—	P/L	25.00
	1905(c)	19.303	1.50	3.00	6.00	12.00
	1905(c)	(restrike)	—	—	P/L	25.00
505	1906(c)	1.629	1.50	3.00	6.00	12.00
	1906(c)	(restrike)	—	—	P/L	25.00
	1907(c)	22.145	1.50	3.00	6.00	12.00
	1907(c)	—	—	—	Proof	65.00
	1908(c)	21.600	1.50	3.00	6.00	12.00
	1908(c)	—	—	—	Proof	65.00
	1908(c)	(restrike)	—	—	P/L	25.00
	1909(c)	6.769	1.75	3.50	7.00	14.00
	1909(c)	—	—	—	Proof	65.00
	1909(c)	(restrike)	—	—	P/L	25.00
	1910(c)	1.604	1.25	2.50	5.00	10.00
	1910(c)	—	—	—	Proof	65.00
	1910(c)	(restrike)	—	—	P/L	25.00

GOLD (OMS)

KM#	Date	Mintage	Fine	VF	XF	Unc
505a	1904(c)	(restrike)	—	—	P/L	250.00
	1906(c)	(restrike)	—	—	P/L	250.00
	1910(c)	(restrike)	—	—	P/L	250.00

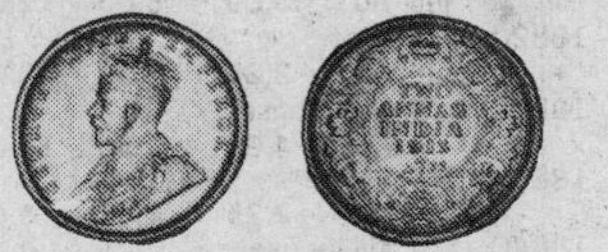

1.4600 g, .917 SILVER, .0430 oz ASW

NOTE: Calcutta Mint issues have no mint mark. Bombay Mint issues have a small raised bead or dot below the lotus flower at the bottom of the reverse. The 2 Annas dated 1911, like the other coins with the same date, has the "Pig" elephant. On these pieces like on the 1/4 Rupee, the King's bust is slightly smaller and has a higher relief than the later issues with the redesigned elephant.

KM#	Date	Mintage	Fine	VF	XF	Unc
514	1911(c)	16.760	1.50	3.00	6.00	12.00
	1911(c)	—	—	—	Proof	75.00
	1911(c)	(restrike)	—	—	P/L	50.00
515	1912(c)	7.724	1.25	2.50	5.00	10.00
	1912(c)	—	—	—	Proof	50.00
	1912(b)	2.462	1.25	2.50	5.00	10.00
	1912(b)	—	—	—	Proof	50.00
	1912(b)	(restrike)	—	—	P/L	25.00
	1913(c)	13.959	1.25	2.50	5.00	10.00
	1913(c)	—	—	—	Proof	50.00
	1913(b)	5.461	1.25	2.50	5.00	10.00
	1913(b)	—	—	—	Proof	50.00
	1913(b)	(restrike)	—	—	P/L	25.00
	1914(c)	8.861	1.25	2.50	5.00	10.00
	1914(c)	—	—	—	Proof	50.00
	1914(b)	3.231	1.25	2.50	5.00	10.00
	1914(b)	(restrike)	—	—	P/L	25.00
	1915(c)	1.620	1.25	2.50	5.00	10.00
	1915(c)	—	—	—	Proof	50.00
	1915(b)	2.711	1.25	2.50	5.00	10.00
	1915(b)	(restrike)	—	—	P/L	25.00
	1916(c)	9.849	1.25	2.00	4.00	8.00
	1916(c)	—	—	—	Proof	50.00
	1916(c)	(restrike)	—	—	P/L	25.00
	1917(c)	35.491	1.25	2.00	4.00	8.00
	1917(c)	—	—	—	Proof	50.00
	1917(c)	(restrike)	—	—	P/L	25.00

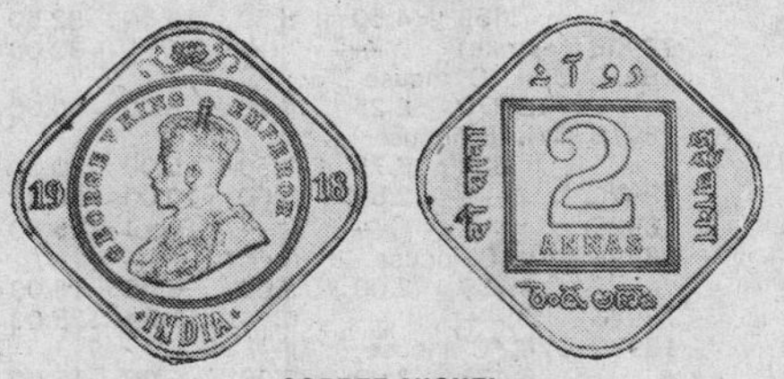

COPPER-NICKEL

NOTE: Calcutta Mint issues have no mint mark. Bombay Mint issues have a small raised dot on the reverse at the bottom near the rim.

KM#	Date	Mintage	Fine	VF	XF	Unc
516	1918(c)	53.412	1.25	1.75	4.00	10.00
	1918(c)	—	—	—	Proof	50.00
	1918(b)	9.191	1.25	1.75	4.00	10.00
	1918(b)	—	—	—	Proof	50.00
	1918(b)	(restrike)	—	—	P/L	20.00
	1919(c)	8.904	1.25	1.75	4.00	10.00
	1919(c)	—	—	—	Proof	50.00
	1919(c)	(restrike)	—	—	P/L	20.00
	1920(b)	—	—	—	Proof	125.00
	1920(c)	13.520	1.25	1.75	4.00	10.00
	1920(c)	—	—	—	Proof	50.00
	1923(c)	7.656	1.25	1.75	4.00	10.00
	1923(c)	—	—	—	Proof	50.00
	1923(b)	6.431	1.25	1.75	4.00	10.00
	1923(b)	—	—	—	Proof	50.00
	1923(b)	(restrike)	—	—	P/L	20.00
	1924(c)	8.384	1.25	1.75	4.00	10.00
	1924(c)	—	—	—	Proof	50.00
	1924(b)	4.818	1.25	1.75	4.00	10.00
	1924(b)	—	—	—	Proof	50.00
	1924(b)	(restrike)	—	—	P/L	20.00
	1925(c)	10.848	1.25	1.75	4.00	10.00
	1925(c)	—	—	—	Proof	50.00
	1925(b)	8.348	1.25	1.75	4.00	10.00
	1925(b)	—	—	—	Proof	50.00
	1925(b)	(restrike)	—	—	P/L	20.00
	1926(c)	8.352	1.25	1.75	4.00	10.00
	1926(c)	—	—	—	Proof	50.00
	1926(b)	2.927	1.25	1.75	4.00	10.00
	1926(b)	—	—	—	Proof	50.00
	1926(b)	(restrike)	—	—	P/L	20.00
	1927(c)	6.424	1.25	1.75	4.00	10.00
	1927(c)	—	—	—	Proof	50.00
	1927(b)	4.835	1.25	1.75	4.00	10.00
	1927(b)	—	—	—	Proof	50.00
516	1927(b)	(restrike)	—	—	P/L	20.00
	1928(c)	7.352	1.25	1.75	4.00	10.00
	1928(c)	—	—	—	Proof	50.00
	1928(b)	4.876	1.25	1.75	4.00	10.00
	1928(b)	—	—	—	Proof	50.00
	1928(b)	(restrike)	—	—	P/L	20.00
	1929(c)	13.408	1.25	1.75	4.00	10.00
	1929(c)	—	—	—	Proof	50.00
	1929(c)	(restrike)	—	—	P/L	20.00
	1930(c)	8.888	1.25	1.75	4.00	10.00
	1930(c)	—	—	—	Proof	50.00
	1930(c)	(restrike)	—	—	P/L	20.00
	1930(b)	—	1.25	1.75	4.00	10.00
	1933(c)	4.300	1.25	1.75	4.00	10.00
	1933(c)	—	—	—	Proof	50.00
	1933(c)	(restrike)	—	—	P/L	20.00
	1934(c)	7.016	1.25	1.75	4.00	10.00
	1934(c)	—	—	—	Proof	50.00
	1934(c)	(restrike)	—	—	P/L	20.00
	1935(c)	12.354	1.25	1.75	4.00	10.00
	1935(b)	21.017	1.00	1.50	3.00	8.00
	1935(b)	—	—	—	Proof	50.00
	1935(b)	(restrike)	—	—	P/L	20.00
	1936(b)	36.295	1.00	1.50	3.00	8.00
	1936(b)	—	—	—	Proof	50.00

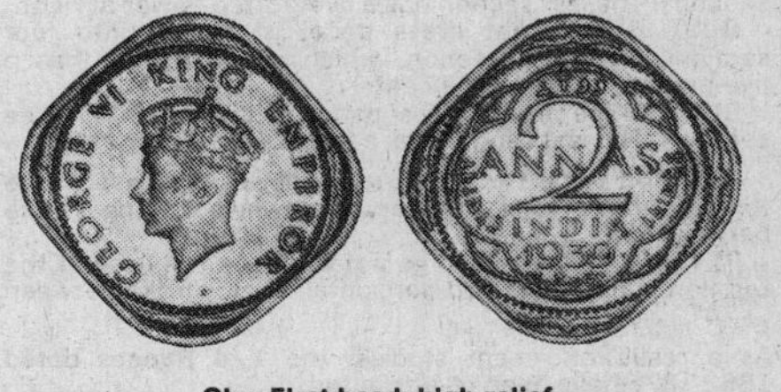

Obv: First head, high relief.

NOTE: Calcutta Mint issues have no mint mark. Bombay Mint issues have a small dot before and after the date.

KM#	Date	Mintage	Fine	VF	XF	Unc
540	1939(c)	4.148	1.25	3.00	6.00	15.00
	1939(b)	3.392	2.00	5.00	10.00	25.00

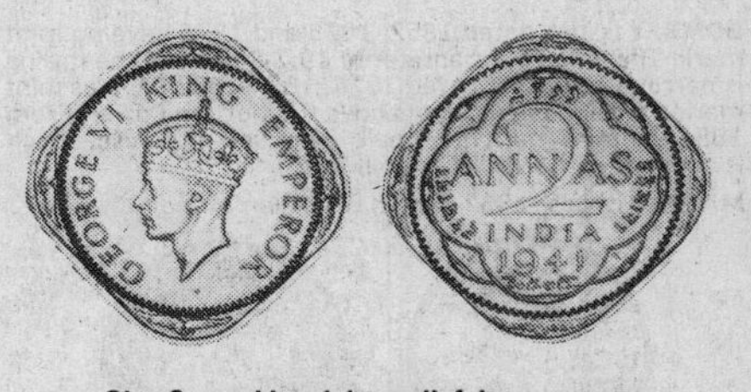

Obv: Second head, low relief, large crown.
Rev: Large "2".

KM#	Date	Mintage	Fine	VF	XF	Unc
541	1939(c)	Inc. Ab.	1.25	2.00	2.50	4.00
	1939(c)	—	—	—	Proof	40.00
	1939(b)	Inc. Ab.	.20	.30	.50	1.00
	1939(b)	—	—	—	Proof	40.00
	1939(b)	(restrike)	—	—	P/L	25.00
	1940(c)	37.636	.20	.30	.50	2.00
	1940(c)	—	—	—	Proof	40.00
	1940(b)	50.599	.20	.30	.50	2.00
	1940(b)	(restrike)	—	—	P/L	25.00
	1941(c)	63.456	.20	.30	.50	1.00
	1941(b)	10.760	.20	.30	.75	2.50
	1941(b)	—	—	—	Proof	40.00
	1941(b)	(restrike)	—	—	P/L	25.00

NICKEL-BRASS

KM#	Date	Mintage	Fine	VF	XF	Unc
541a	1942(b) small 4					
		133.000	.25	.35	.50	2.00
	1942(b) large 4					
		Inc. Ab.	.20	.35	.50	2.00
	1943(b)					
		343.680	.25	.35	.50	2.00
	1944L	6.352	.50	1.25	2.00	5.00
	1944(b)					
		219.700	.25	.35	.50	2.00

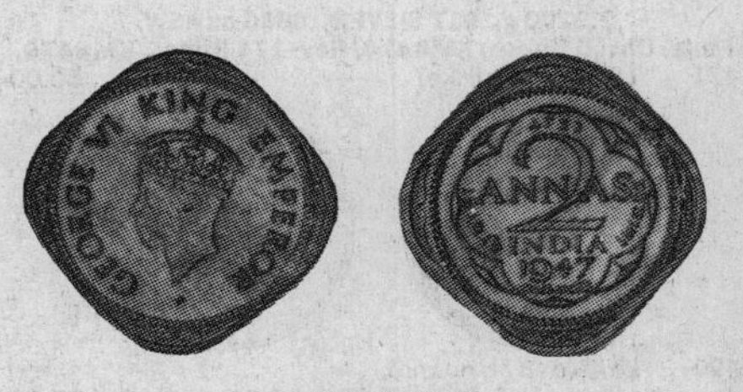

COPPER-NICKEL
Obv: Second head, low relief, small crown.
Rev: Small "2".

KM#	Date	Mintage	Fine	VF	XF	Unc
542	1946(c)	67.276	.20	.30	.50	2.00
	1946(b)	52.500	.20	.30	.50	2.00
	1946(b)	—	—	—	Proof	40.00
	1946(b)	(restrike)	—	—	P/L	25.00
	1946(l)	*25.480	.20	.30	.50	2.00
	1947(c)	57.428	.20	.30	.50	2.00
	1947(b)	38.908	.20	.30	.50	2.00
	1947(b)	—	—	—	Proof	40.00
	1947(b)	(restrike)	—	—	P/L	25.00

NOTE: W/o L mint mark but w/small diamond-shaped marks above "N" at left of "1" on rev.

984 British / INDIA

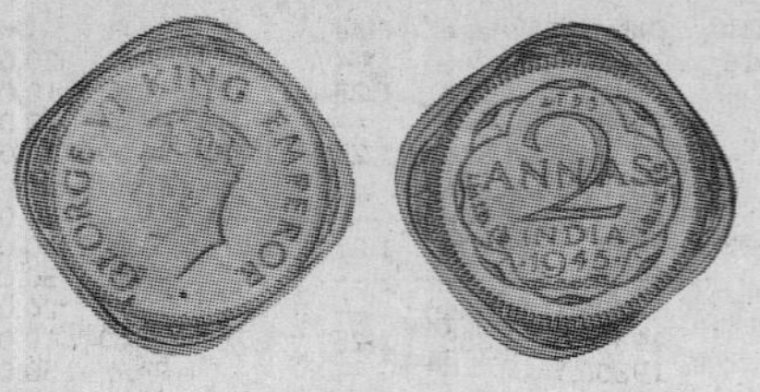

NICKEL-BRASS
Obv: Second head, low relief, large crown.
Rev: Small "2".

KM#	Date	Mintage	Fine	VF	XF	Unc
543	1945(c)	24.260	.25	.75	1.25	2.75
	1945(c)	—	—	—	Proof	40.00
	1945(b)					
		136.688	.25	.35	.50	1.50
	1945(b) (restrike)	—	—	—	P/L	25.00

1/4 RUPEE

NOTE: The distinguishing features of the three busts and two reverses are as following:

BUST A-The front dress panel is divided into four sections. The last section has a five-dotted flower at right.

BUST B-The front dress panel is divided into four sections. The last section, which is incomplete has a five-petalled flower in the center.

BUST C-The front dress panel is divided into three sections. The last section has a five-dotted flower at left.

REVERSE I-The two large petals above the base of the top flower are long and curved downward; long stroke between "1/4".

REVERSE II-The two large petals above the base of the top flower are short and horizontal; short stroke between "1/4".

As a result of recent studies, the 1/4 Rupees dated 1862-1876 have been re-attributed.

CALCUTTA issues dated 1862-1878 have no mint mark. The diameter of the coins is 19-19.2mm and the milling is coarse. From 1879 the mint mark is a small incuse "C" which is in the whorl below the center of the bottom flower.

BOMBAY issues dated 1862, 1875 and 1876 have no mint mark. These have a diameter of 19.7-8mm and the milling is narrow. The coins dated 1874, 1877-1883 have as mint mark a small bead directly above the bottom flower. From 1884 the mint mark is a small "B" raised or incuse, which is above the whorl, in the top flower.

MADRAS issues (1862 only) have a diameter of 20mm.

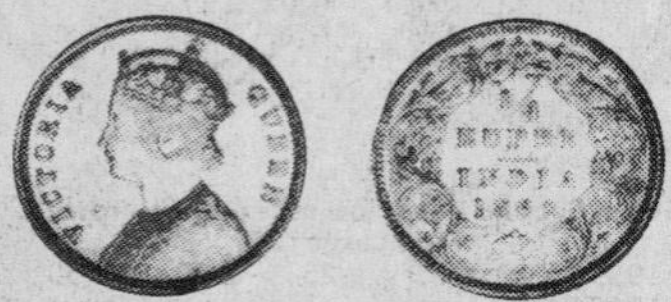

2.9200 g, .917 SILVER, .0860 oz ASW
Obv: Bust A. Rev: I.

KM#	Date	Mintage	Fine	VF	XF	Unc
470	1862(c) 19.3-19.4mm					
		19.412	2.50	5.00	10.00	20.00
	1862(c)	—	—	—	Proof	125.00
	1862(b) 19.7-19.8mm					
		11.390	2.50	5.00	10.00	20.00
	1862(b) (restrike)	—	—	—	P/L	35.00
	1862(m) 19.9-20.0mm					
		5.049	5.00	10.00	20.00	40.00
	1862(m) V1(I)CTORIA (error)					
		Inc. Ab.	5.00	10.00	20.00	40.00
	1874(c)	5.444	3.00	6.00	12.00	24.00
	1874(b)	1.612	3.50	7.50	15.00	30.00
	1875(c)	2.797	3.00	6.00	12.00	24.00
	1875(c)	—	—	—	Proof	125.00
	1875(b)	5.239	3.00	6.00	12.00	24.00
	1876(c)	6.457	3.00	6.00	12.00	24.00
	1876(b)	1.427	3.50	7.50	15.00	30.00

GOLD (OMS)

KM#	Date	Mintage	Fine	VF	XF	Unc
470a	1862(c) (restrike)	—	—	—	P/L	500.00

2.9200 g, .917 SILVER, .0860 oz ASW.
Mule. Obv: 5 Rupee, KM#474. Rev: 1/4 Rupee, KM#470.

KM#	Date	Mintage	Fine	VF	XF	Unc
471	1862(c) (restrike)	—	—	—	P/L	50.00

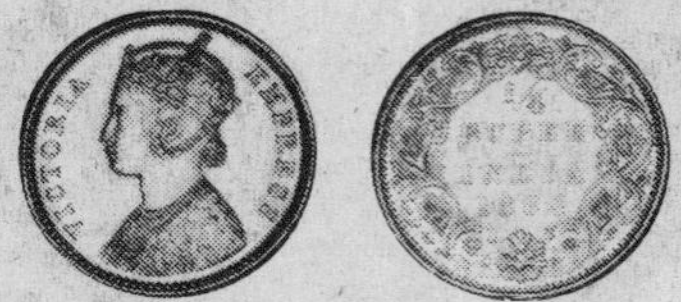

KM#	Date	Mintage	Fine	VF	XF	Unc
490	1877(c) B/I, no mm.					
		3.440	2.50	5.00	10.00	20.00
	1877(c)	—	—	—	Proof	125.00
	1877(b) A/I, dot					
		.884	3.50	7.50	15.00	30.00
	1877(b) B/I, dot					
		Inc. Ab.	3.50	7.50	15.00	30.00
	1877(b)	—	—	—	Proof	125.00
	1877(b) (restrike)	—	—	—	P/L	30.00
	1878C	3.284	2.00	3.50	7.50	15.00
	1878(c) C/II, w/o mm.					
		.044	2.00	3.50	8.00	20.00
	1878(c)	—	—	—	Proof	125.00
	1878(c) (restrike)	—	—	—	P/L	30.00
	1879C C/II, "C" incuse					
		Inc. Ab.	2.00	3.50	8.00	20.00
490	1879(b)	—	—	—	Proof	125.00
	1880C C/II, "C" incuse					
		Inc. Be.	2.00	3.50	8.00	20.00
	1881C C/II, "C" incuse					
		3.244	2.00	3.75	8.00	20.00
	1881C	—	—	—	Proof	125.00
	1881(b) A/II, dot					
		1.444	2.00	3.75	8.00	20.00
	1881(b) B/I, dot					
		Inc. Ab.	4.00	7.50	15.00	30.00
	1882C C/II, "C" incuse					
		.612	2.00	3.50	8.00	20.00
	1882C	—	—	—	Proof	125.00
	1882(b) A/II, dot					
		2.775	2.00	3.75	8.00	20.00
	1882(b) B/I, dot					
		Inc. Ab.	3.00	6.00	12.00	25.00
	1882(b) C/II, dot					
		Inc. Ab.	2.25	4.00	8.00	20.00
	1883C C/II, "C" incuse					
		2.871	4.00	7.50	15.00	30.00
	1883(b) B/I, dot					
		.184	2.25	4.00	8.00	20.00
	1884C C/II "C" incuse					
		3.596	3.75	7.50	15.00	30.00
	1884B B/I, "B" raised					
		1.709	3.75	7.50	15.00	30.00
	1884B C/II, "B" raised					
		Inc. Ab.	3.75	7.50	15.00	30.00
	1884B	—	—	—	Proof	125.00
	1885C C/II, "C" incuse					
		1.024	3.75	7.50	15.00	30.00
	1885B B/I, "B" raised					
		1.118	3.75	7.50	15.00	30.00
	1886C C/II, "C" incuse					
		7.087	2.25	4.00	8.00	20.00
	1886B C/II, "B" raised					
		1.684	3.75	7.50	15.00	30.00
	1887C C/II, "C" incuse					
		6.494	2.25	4.00	8.00	20.00
	1887B C/II, "B" raised					
		4.422	2.50	5.00	10.00	20.00
	1888(c) C/II, no mm.					
		4.945	2.50	5.00	10.00	20.00
	1888B C/II, "B" raised					
		2.278	3.00	6.00	12.00	25.00
	1888B C/II, "B" incuse					
		Inc. Ab.	3.75	7.50	15.00	30.00
	1889C C/II, "C" incuse					
		8.075	2.25	4.00	8.00	20.00
	1889B C/II, "B" incuse					
		4.298	2.50	5.00	10.00	20.00
	1889	—	—	—	Proof	125.00
	1890C C/II, "C" incuse					
		Inc. 1891	2.50	5.00	10.00	20.00
	1890C	—	—	—	Proof	125.00
	1890C C/I, "B" incuse					
		—	4.00	7.50	15.00	30.00
	1890B C/II, "B" incuse					
		.459	4.50	8.50	16.50	32.50
	1890B (restrike)	—	—	—	P/L	30.00
	1891C C/II, "C" incuse					
		13.770	2.25	4.00	8.00	20.00
	1891B C/I, "B" incuse					
		.883	3.75	7.50	15.00	30.00
	1892C	—	2.50	5.00	10.00	20.00
	1892C	—	—	—	Proof	125.00
	1892B C/I, "B" incuse					
		4.059	2.00	3.00	6.00	15.00
	1892B	—	—	—	Proof	125.00
	1893C C/II, "C" incuse					
		6.435	2.00	3.00	6.00	15.00
	1893C	—	—	—	Proof	125.00
	1893B C/I, "B" incuse					
		6.137	2.00	3.00	6.00	15.00
	1893B (restrike)	—	—	—	P/L	30.00
	1894C C/II, "C" incuse					
		2.653	2.00	3.00	6.00	15.00
	1894C	—	—	—	Proof	125.00
	1894B C/I, "B" incuse					
		2.385	2.00	3.00	6.00	15.00
	1894B	—	—	—	Proof	125.00
	1894B (restrike)	—	—	—	P/L	30.00
	1896C C/II, "C" incuse					
		6.811	2.00	3.00	6.00	15.00
	1896C	—	—	—	Proof	125.00
	1897C C/II, "C" incuse					
		5.884	2.00	3.00	6.00	15.00
	1897C	—	—	—	Proof	125.00
	1897B C/I, "B" incuse					
		2.893	2.00	3.00	6.00	15.00
	1897B	—	—	—	Proof	125.00
	1897B (restrike)	—	—	—	P/L	30.00
	1898C C/II, "C" incuse					
		1.330	2.00	3.00	6.00	15.00
	1898C	—	—	—	Proof	125.00
	1898B C/I, "B" incuse					
		2.056	2.00	3.00	6.00	15.00
	1898B	—	—	—	Proof	125.00
	1898B (restrike)	—	—	—	P/L	30.00
	1900C C/II, "C" incuse					
		1.606	2.00	3.00	6.00	15.00
	1900C	—	—	—	Proof	125.00
	1900C (restrike)	—	—	—	P/L	30.00
	1901C C/II, "C" incuse					
		4.476	2.00	3.00	6.00	15.00
	1901C	—	—	—	Proof	125.00
	1901C (restrike)	—	—	—	P/L	30.00

ALUMINUM (OMS)

KM#	Date	Mintage	Fine	VF	XF	Unc
490a	1891B	—	—	—	Proof	100.00

COPPER OR BRONZE (OMS)

KM#	Date	Mintage	Fine	VF	XF	Unc
490b	1884	—	—	—	Proof	100.00
	1891	—	—	—	Proof	100.00
	1892	—	—	—	Proof	100.00

GOLD (OMS)

KM#	Date	Mintage	Fine	VF	XF	Unc
490c	1891	(restrike)	—	—	P/L	350.00
	1892	(restrike)	—	—	P/L	350.00
	1893	(restrike)	—	—	P/L	350.00
	1896	(restrike)	—	—	P/L	350.00
	1897	(restrike)	—	—	P/L	350.00
	1898	(restrike)	—	—	P/L	350.00
	1900	(restrike)	—	—	P/L	350.00

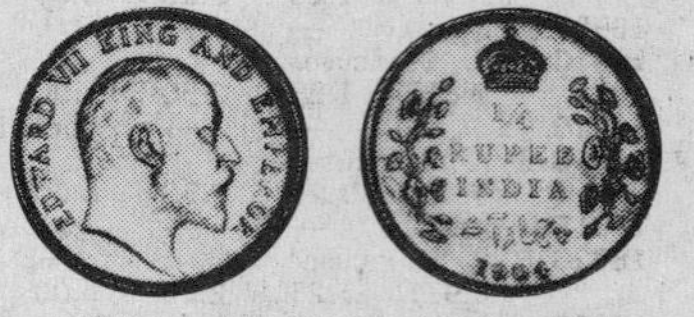

2.9200 g, .917 SILVER, .0860 oz ASW

KM#	Date	Mintage	Fine	VF	XF	Unc
506	1903(c)	2.472	1.50	3.00	8.00	20.00
	1903(c)	—	—	—	Proof	100.00
	1903(c) (restrike)	—	—	—	P/L	30.00
	1904(c)	28.241	1.50	3.00	8.00	20.00
	1904(c)	—	—	—	Proof	100.00
	1904(c) (restrike)	—	—	—	P/L	30.00
	1905(c)	10.026	1.50	3.00	8.00	20.00
	1905(c)	—	—	—	Proof	100.00
	1905(c) (restrike)	—	—	—	P/L	30.00
	1906(c)	16.300	1.50	3.00	8.00	20.00
	1906(c) (restrike)	—	—	—	P/L	30.00
	1907(c)	10.672	1.50	3.00	8.00	20.00
	1907(c)	—	—	—	Proof	100.00
	1907(c) (restrike)	—	—	—	P/L	30.00
	1908(c)	11.464	1.50	3.00	8.00	20.00
	1908(c)	—	—	—	Proof	100.00
	1908(c) (restrike)	—	—	—	P/L	30.00
	1909(c)	—	—	—	Proof	125.00
	1909(c) (restrike)	—	—	—	P/L	30.00
	1910(c)	.802	1.50	3.00	8.00	20.00
	1910(c)	—	—	—	Proof	100.00
	1910(c) (restrike)	—	—	—	P/L	30.00

GOLD (OMS)

KM#	Date	Mintage	Fine	VF	XF	Unc
506a	1910(c) (restrike)	—	—	—	P/L	500.00

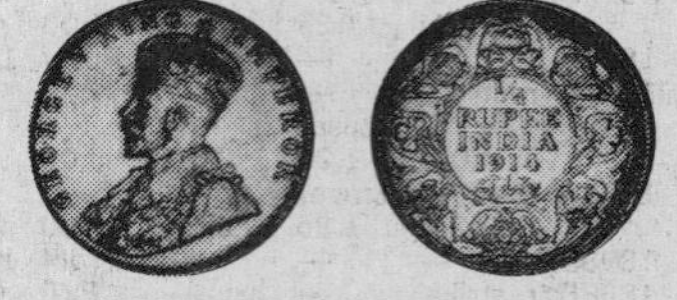

2.9200 g, .917 SILVER, .0860 oz ASW

NOTE: Calcutta Mint issues have no mint mark. Bombay Mint issues have a small raised bead or dot in the space below the lotus flower at the bottom of the reverse. The 1/4 Rupee dated 1911, like the other coins with the same date, has the "Pig" elephant. On these pieces the King's bust is slightly smaller and has a higher relief than later issues with the re-designed elephant.

KM#	Date	Mintage	Fine	VF	XF	Unc
517	1911(c)	8.024	2.00	4.00	8.00	20.00
	1911(c)	—	—	—	Proof	90.00
	1911(c) (restrike)	—	—	—	P/L	60.00
518	1912(c)	2.245	2.00	2.75	5.00	15.00
	1912(c)	—	—	—	Proof	65.00
	1912(b)	1.168	2.00	2.75	5.00	15.00
	1912(b)	—	—	—	Proof	65.00
	1912(b) (restrike)	—	—	—	P/L	25.00
	1913(c)	9.587	2.00	2.75	5.00	15.00
	1913(c)	—	—	—	Proof	65.00
	1913(b)	2.276	2.00	2.75	5.00	15.00
	1913(b)	—	—	—	Proof	65.00
	1913(b) (restrike)	—	—	—	P/L	25.00
	1914(c)	6.014	2.00	2.75	5.00	10.00
	1914(c)	—	—	—	Proof	65.00
	1914(b)	3.967	2.00	2.75	5.00	10.00
	1914(b) (restrike)	—	—	—	P/L	25.00
	1915(c)	.851	2.25	4.00	10.00	35.00
	1915(c)	—	—	—	Proof	65.00
	1915(b)	2.096	2.00	2.75	5.00	15.00
	1915(b) (restrike)	—	—	—	P/L	25.00
	1916(c)	10.716	2.00	2.75	5.00	15.00
	1916(c)	—	—	—	Proof	65.00
	1916(c) (restrike)	—	—	—	P/L	25.00
	1917(c)	21.380	2.00	2.75	5.00	15.00
	1917(c)	—	—	—	Proof	65.00
	1917(c) (restrike)	—	—	—	P/L	25.00
	1918(c)	43.306	2.00	2.75	5.00	15.00
	1918(c)	—	—	—	Proof	65.00
	1919(b)	—	3.50	7.50	15.00	30.00
	1919(c)	35.557	2.00	2.75	5.00	15.00
	1919(c)	—	—	—	Proof	65.00
	1920(b)	—	3.25	6.50	12.50	25.00
	1925(b)	2.003	2.00	2.75	5.00	15.00
	1925(b)	—	—	—	Proof	65.00
	1926(c)	6.117	2.00	2.75	5.00	15.00
	1926(c)	—	—	—	Proof	65.00
	1926(c) (restrike)	—	—	—	P/L	25.00
	1928(b)	4.023	2.00	2.75	5.00	15.00
	1928(b)	—	—	—	Proof	65.00
	1929(c)	4.013	2.00	2.75	5.00	15.00
	1929(c)	—	—	—	Proof	65.00
	1929(c) (restrike)	—	—	—	P/L	25.00
	1930(c)	3.942	2.00	2.75	5.00	15.00
	1930(c)	—	—	—	Proof	65.00
	1930(c) (restrike)	—	—	—	P/L	25.00

KM#	Date	Mintage	Fine	VF	XF	Unc
518	1934(c)	3.947	2.00	2.75	5.00	10.00
	1936(c)	21.771	1.25	2.25	4.00	8.00
	1936(b)	7.142	1.25	2.25	4.00	8.00
	1936(b) (restrike)		—	—	P/L	25.00

NOTE: The silver coinage of George VI is a very complex series with numerous obverse and reverse die varieties. Two different designs of the head appear on the obverse of most denominations struck for George VI. The "First Head" shows the Kings effigy in high relief; the "Second Head" in low relief. In 1941-42 The "Second Head" was slightly reduced in size and this type continued to be used on the silver coins and on some of the smaller denominations.

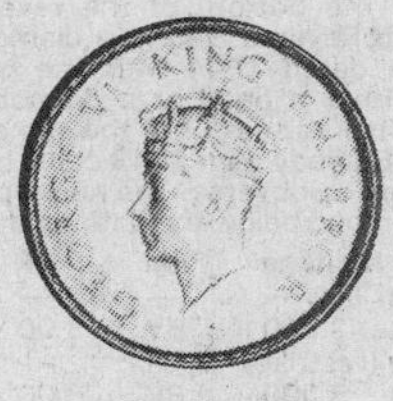

First Head

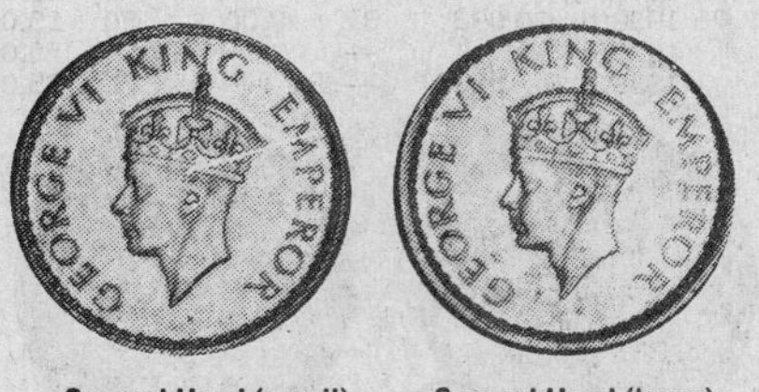

Second Head (small) **Second Head (large)**

From 1942 to 1945 the reverse designs of the silver coins change slightly every year. However, a distinct reverse variety occurs on Rupees and 1/4 Rupees dated 1943-44 and on the half Rupee dated 1944, all struck at Bombay. This variety may be distinguished from the other coins by the design of the center bottom flower as illustrated, and is designated as Reverse B.

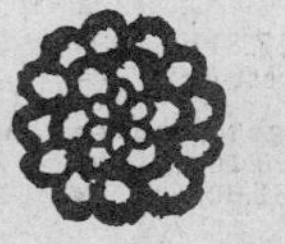

On the normal common varieties dated 1943-44 the three "scalloped circles" are not connected to each other and the bead in the center is not attached to the nearest circle.

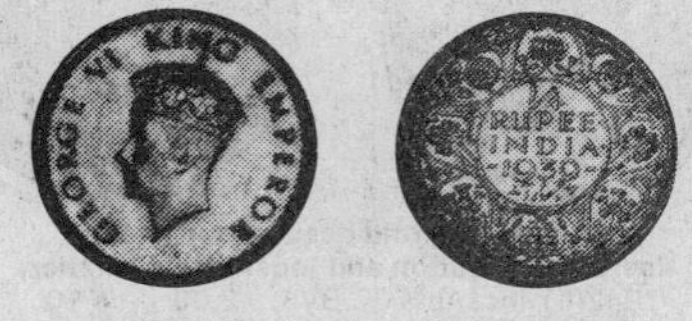

Obv: First head, reeded edge.

NOTE: Calcutta Mint issues have no mint mark. Bombay coins have a small bead below the lotus flower at the bottom on the reverse, except those dated 1943-1944 with reverse B which have a diamond. Lahore Mint issues have a small "L" in the same position. The nickel coins have a diamond below the date on the reverse.

KM#	Date	Mintage	Fine	VF	XF	Unc
544	1938(c)	—	—	—	Proof	65.00
	1938(c) (restrike)		—	—	P/L	25.00
	1939(c)	3.072	2.00	3.50	6.00	12.00
	1939(c)	—	—	—	Proof	65.00
	1939(b)	6.770	2.00	3.50	5.00	10.00
	1939(b) (restrike)		—	—	P/L	25.00

2.9200 g, .500 SILVER, .0469 oz ASW

KM#	Date	Mintage	Fine	VF	XF	Unc
544a	1940(b)	24.635	2.00	3.50	5.00	10.00

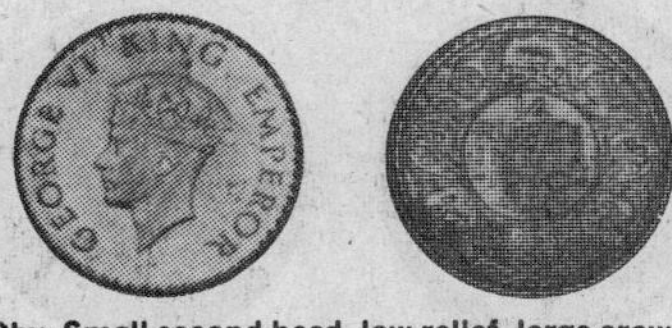

Obv: Small second head, low relief, large crown. Rev: Reeded edge.

KM#	Date	Mintage	Fine	VF	XF	Unc
545	1940(c)	68.675	BV	1.50	2.50	6.00
	1940(c)	—	—	—	Proof	65.00
	1940(b)	28.947	BV	1.50	2.50	6.00

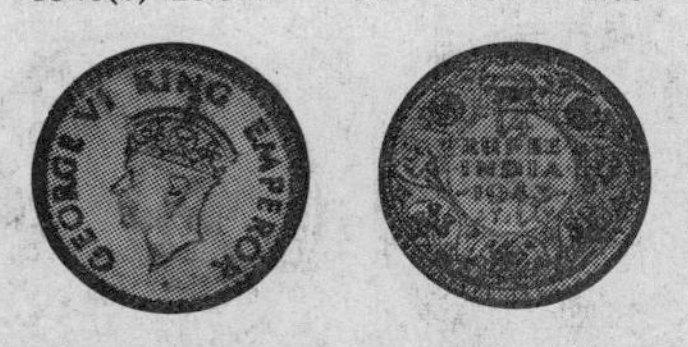

Obv: Small second head, low relief, small crown. Reeded edge.

KM#	Date	Mintage	Fine	VF	XF	Unc
546	1942(c)	88.096	BV	1.50	2.25	4.50
	1943(c)	90.994	BV	1.50	2.25	4.50

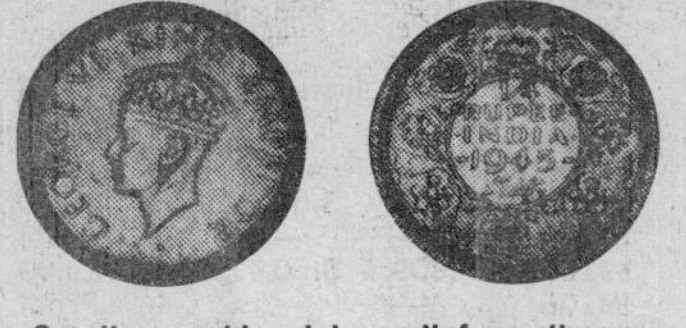

Obv: Small second head, low relief, small crown. Security edge.

KM#	Date	Mintage	Fine	VF	XF	Unc
547	1943B	95.200	BV	1.50	2.25	4.50
	1943B	—	—	—	Proof	60.00
	1943B reverse B					
		Inc. Ab.	BV	1.50	2.25	4.50
	1943L	23.700	BV	1.50	2.25	4.50
	1944B	170.504	BV	1.50	2.25	4.50
	1944B reverse B					
		Inc. Ab.	BV	1.50	2.25	4.50
	1944L	86.400	BV	1.50	2.25	4.50
	1945(b) small 5					
		181.648	BV	1.50	2.25	4.50
	1945(b) large 5					
		Inc. Ab.	BV	.85	1.75	4.00
	1945L small 5					
		29.751	BV	1.50	2.25	4.50
	1945L large 5					
		Inc. Ab.	BV	1.00	2.00	5.00

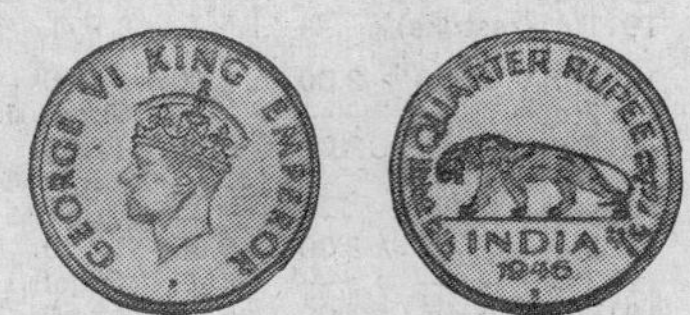

NICKEL

KM#	Date	Mintage	Fine	VF	XF	Unc
548	1946(b)	83.600	.30	.60	1.00	2.75
	1947(b)	109.948	.40	.75	1.50	3.50
	1947(b)	—	—	—	Proof	50.00

4 ANNAS

NOTE: Calcutta Mint issues have no mint mark. Bombay Mint issues have a small raised dot on the reverse at the bottom near the rim.

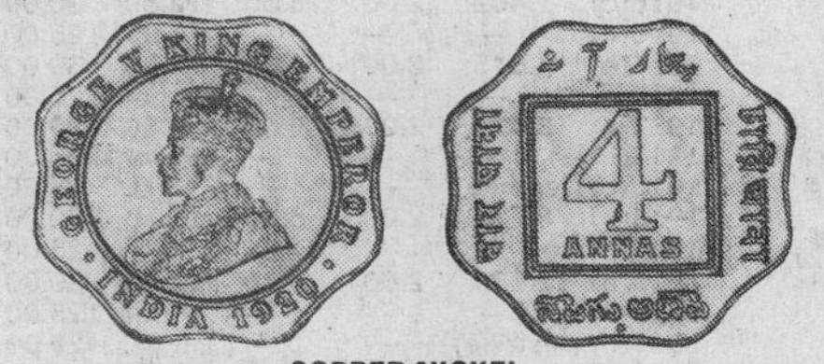

COPPER-NICKEL

KM#	Date	Mintage	Fine	VF	XF	Unc
519	1919(c)	18.632	2.50	5.00	10.00	20.00
	1919(c)	—	—	—	Proof	150.00
	1919(b)	7.672	3.25	6.50	12.50	25.00
	1919 (restrike)		—	—	P/L	25.00
	1920(c)	18.191	2.50	5.00	10.00	20.00
	1920(c)	—	—	—	Proof	150.00
	1920(b)	1.666	2.50	5.00	10.00	20.00
	1920(b)	—	—	—	Proof	150.00
	1920(b) (restrike)		—	—	P/L	25.00
	1921(c)	—	—	—	Proof	150.00
	1921(c) (restrike)		—	—	P/L	75.00
	1921(b)	1.219	3.00	6.50	12.50	25.00
	1921(b)	—	—	—	Proof	150.00
	1921 (restrike)		—	—	P/L	25.00

8 ANNAS

NOTE: Calcutta Mint issues have no mint mark. Bombay Mint issues have a small raised dot on the reverse at the bottom near the rim.

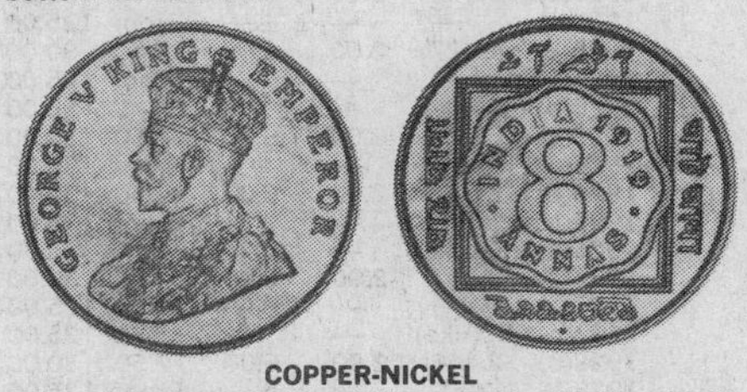

COPPER-NICKEL

KM#	Date	Mintage	Fine	VF	XF	Unc
520	1919(c)	2.980	3.75	7.50	15.00	30.00
	1919(c)	—	—	—	Proof	150.00
	1919(b)	1.400	4.00	8.50	17.50	35.00
	1919(b) (restrike)		—	—	P/L	30.00
	1920(c)	—	—	—	Proof	150.00
	1920(c) (restrike)		—	—	P/L	75.00
	1920(b)	1.000	12.50	25.00	50.00	100.00
	1920(b)	—	—	—	Proof	150.00
	1920(b) (restrike)		—	—	P/L	30.00

1/2 RUPEE

Distinguishing Features

BUST A-The front dress panel has four sections. The last section has a round flower at left and right.

BUST B-The dress panel has 4-1/2 or 4-2/3 sections. The last, incomplete section has a five-petalled flower at left of center.

BUST C-The dress panel is the same as on Bust B but the floral design of the dress differs.

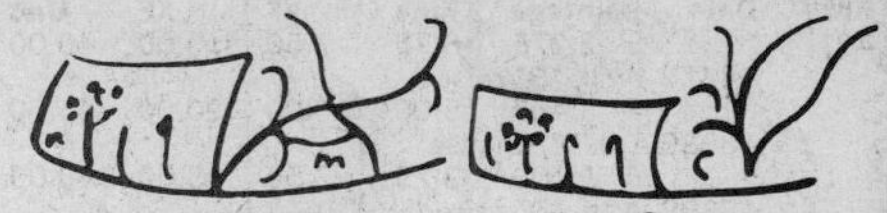

Bust B **Bust C**

REVERSE I-The top flower is open and the two large petals above the whorl are short and horizontal.

REVERSE II-The top flower is closed and the two petals above the whorl are long and curved downward.

CALCUTTA issues have Bust A/Reverse I and Bust C/Reverse II dated 1862-1878 have no mint mark. From 1879 the mint mark is a small incuse "C" located in the whorl, below the center of the bottom flower.

BOMBAY and MADRAS issues dated 1862 have no mint mark. From 1874-1884 the mint mark is a small bead directly above the center of the bottom flower. From 1885 the mint mark is a "B" raised or incuse, in the top flower.

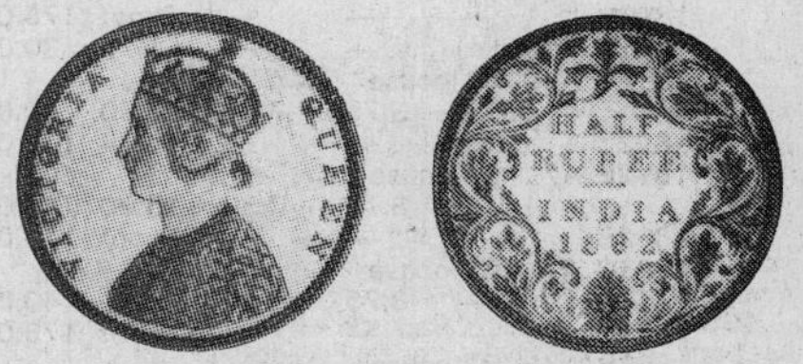

5.8300 g, .917 SILVER, .1719 oz ASW

KM#	Date	Mintage	Fine	VF	XF	Unc
472	1862(c) A/I					
		7.649	5.00	10.00	20.00	50.00
	1862(c)	—	—	—	Proof	175.00
	1862(c) A/II w/V in bottom of bust					
		.736	7.50	15.00	30.00	60.00
	1862(c)	—	—	—	Proof	175.00
	1862(b & m) B/II					
		7.122	5.00	10.00	20.00	40.00
	1862(b) (restrike)		—	—	P/L	35.00
	1862(c) C/II					
		1.623	5.00	10.00	20.00	40.00
	1874(b) B/II, dot					
		1.654	7.50	15.00	30.00	65.00
	1875(c) A/I					
		2.257	5.00	10.00	20.00	50.00
	1875(c)	—	—	—	Proof	175.00
	1875(b) B/II, dot					
		1.023	7.50	15.00	30.00	65.00
	1876(b) B/II, dot					
		.966	7.50	15.00	30.00	65.00

GOLD (OMS)

KM#	Date	Mintage	Fine	VF	XF	Unc
472a	1862(c) (restrike)		—	—	P/L	600.00

5.8300 g, .917 SILVER, .1719 oz ASW

KM#	Date	Mintage	Fine	VF	XF	Unc
491	1877(c) A/1858		5.00	10.00	20.00	45.00
	1877(c)	—	—	—	Proof	175.00
	1877(b) B/II, dot					
		.214	7.50	15.00	30.00	60.00
	1887(b) (restrike)		—	—	P/L	30.00
	1878(c) A/I					
		1.390	5.00	10.00	20.00	45.00
	1878(c)	—	—	—	Proof	175.00
	1878(c) (restrike)		—	—	P/L	30.00
	1879C A/I, "C" incuse					
		1.008	5.00	10.00	20.00	45.00
	1879(b)	—	—	—	Proof	175.00
	1880C A/I, "C" incuse					
		.180	7.50	15.00	30.00	60.00
	1881C A/I, "C" incuse					
		.921	5.00	10.00	20.00	45.00
	1881C	—	—	—	Proof	175.00
	1881(b) B/II, dot					
		1.591	5.00	10.00	20.00	45.00
	1882C A/II, "C" incuse					
		1.161	5.00	10.00	20.00	45.00
	1882C	—	—	—	Proof	175.00
	1882(b) B/II, dot					
		.308	8.00	17.50	35.00	70.00
	1882(b) A/II, dot					
		Inc. Ab.	8.00	17.50	35.00	70.00
	1883C A/I, "C" incuse					
		1.036	5.00	10.00	20.00	45.00
	1884C A/I, "C" incuse					
		—	5.00	10.00	20.00	45.00
	1884(b) A/II, dot					
		1.110	5.00	10.00	20.00	45.00
	1884(b) A/II, no mm.					
		Inc. Ab.	5.00	10.00	20.00	45.00
	1884	—	—	—	Proof	175.00
	1885C A/I, "C" incuse					
		1.408	3.75	7.50	15.00	40.00
	1885B A/II, "B" raised					
		.390	5.00	10.00	20.00	45.00
	1886C A/I, "C" incuse					
		2.645	3.75	7.50	15.00	40.00
	1886B A/II, "B" raised					
		1.116	3.75	7.50	15.00	40.00
	1887C A/I, "C" incuse					

986 British / INDIA

KM#	Date	Mintage	Fine	VF	XF	Unc
491		2.275	3.75	7.50	15.00	40.00
	1887B A/II, "B" raised					
		.407	5.00	10.00	20.00	45.00
	1888C A/I, "C" incuse					
		1.100	3.75	7.50	15.00	40.00
	1888B A/II, "B" raised					
		1.748	5.00	10.00	20.00	45.00
	1888(b) A/II, no mm.					
		Inc. Ab.	5.00	10.00	20.00	45.00
	1889C A/I, "C" incuse					
		2.331	3.75	7.50	15.00	40.00
	1889B A/II, "B" raised					
		1.083	3.75	7.50	15.00	40.00
	1889B A/I, "B" incuse					
		Inc. Ab.	3.75	7.50	15.00	40.00
	1890C	—	—	—	Proof	175.00
	1890C (restrike)		—	—	P/L	30.00
	1891C	—	—	—	Proof	175.00
	1891B A/I, "B" incuse					
		—	—	—	Proof	175.00
	1891B	—	—	—	Proof	175.00
	1891 (restrike)		—	—	P/L	30.00
	1892C A/I, "C" incuse					
		1.761	3.75	7.50	15.00	40.00
	1892C	—	—	—	Proof	175.00
	1892B A/I, "B" incuse					
		1.104	3.75	7.50	15.00	40.00
	1892B	—	—	—	Proof	175.00
	1893C A/I, "C" incuse					
		—	3.75	7.50	15.00	40.00
	1893C	—	—	—	Proof	175.00
	1893B A/I, "B" incuse					
		2.462	3.75	7.50	15.00	40.00
	1893B (restrike)		—	—	P/L	40.00
	1894C A/I, "C" incuse					
		1.277	3.75	7.50	15.00	40.00
	1894C	—	—	—	Proof	175.00
	1894B A/I, "B" incuse					
		—	4.00	10.00	20.00	50.00
	1894B (restrike)		—	—	P/L	40.00
	1896C A/I, "C" incuse					
		2.114	3.75	7.50	15.00	40.00
	1896C	—	—	—	Proof	175.00
	1897C A/I, "C" incuse					
		—	3.75	7.50	15.00	40.00
	1897C	—	—	—	Proof	175.00
	1897B A/I, "B" incuse					
		.560	3.75	7.50	15.00	40.00
	1897B	—	—	—	Proof	175.00
	1897B (restrike)		—	—	P/L	35.00
	1898C A/I, "C" incuse					
		2.057	3.75	7.50	15.00	40.00
	1898C	—	—	—	Proof	175.00
	1898B A/I, "B" incuse					
		.458	5.00	10.00	20.00	45.00
	1898B	—	—	—	Proof	175.00
	1898B (restrike)		—	—	P/L	35.00
	1899C A/I, "C" incuse					
		6.893	3.75	7.50	15.00	40.00
	1899C	—	—	—	Proof	175.00
	1899B A/I, "B" incuse					
		11.174	2.50	5.00	10.00	30.00
	1899B A/I, "B" incuse, inverted B					
		—	5.00	10.00	30.00	60.00
	1899B	Inc. Ab.	—	—	Proof	175.00
	1899B (restrike)		—	—	P/L	35.00
	1900C A/I (restrike)		—	—	P/L	35.00

ALUMINUM (OMS)

KM#	Date	Mintage	Fine	VF	XF	Unc
491a	1891	—	—	—	Proof	—

COPPER OR BRONZE (OMS)

KM#	Date	Mintage	Fine	VF	XF	Unc
491b	1884	—	—	—	Proof	100.00
	1891	—	—	—	Proof	100.00
	1892	—	—	—	Proof	100.00

GOLD (OMS)

KM#	Date	Mintage	Fine	VF	XF	Unc
491c	1891 (restrike)		—	—	P/L	450.00
	1892 (restrike)		—	—	P/L	450.00
	1893 (restrike)		—	—	P/L	450.00
	1896 (restrike)		—	—	P/L	450.00
	1897 (restrike)		—	—	P/L	450.00
	1898 (restrike)		—	—	P/L	450.00
	1899 (restrike)		—	—	P/L	450.00

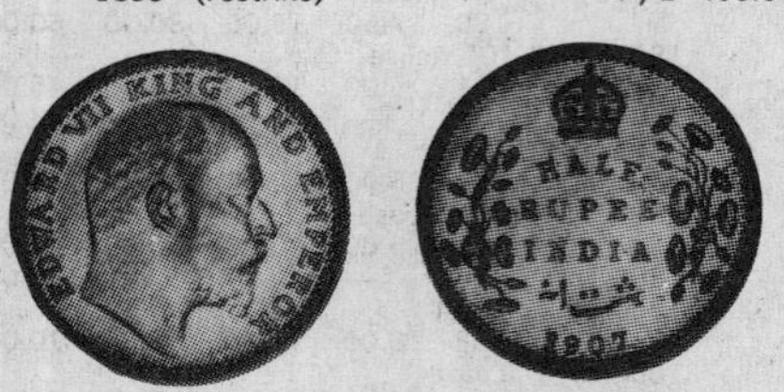

5.8300 g, .917 SILVER, .1719 oz ASW

NOTE: Calcutta Mint issues have no mint mark. Bombay Mint issues have a small incuse "B" in the space below the cross pattee of the crown on the reverse.

KM#	Date	Mintage	Fine	VF	XF	Unc
507	1904(c)	—	—	—	Proof	175.00
	1904(c) (restrike)		—	—	P/L	40.00
	1905(c)	.823	3.50	10.00	25.00	50.00
	1905(c) (restrike)		—	—	P/L	40.00
	1906(c)	3.036	3.50	10.00	25.00	50.00
	1906B	.400	3.75	12.50	30.00	60.00
	1906B (restrike)		—	—	P/L	40.00
	1907(c)	2.786	3.50	10.00	25.00	50.00
	1907(c)	—	—	—	Proof	150.00
	1907B	1.856	3.50	10.00	25.00	50.00
	1907B	—	—	—	Proof	150.00
	1907B (restrike)		—	—	P/L	40.00
	1908(c)	1.577	3.50	10.00	25.00	50.00

KM#	Date	Mintage	Fine	VF	XF	Unc
507	1908(c)	—	—	—	Proof	150.00
	1908(c) (restrike)		—	—	P/L	40.00
	1909(c)	1.569	3.50	10.00	25.00	50.00
	1909(c)	—	—	—	Proof	150.00
	1909(c) (restrike)		—	—	P/L	40.00
	1910(c)	3.413	3.50	10.00	25.00	50.00
	1910(c)	—	—	—	Proof	150.00
	1910B	.809	3.50	10.00	25.00	50.00
	1910B	—	—	—	Proof	150.00
	1910B (restrike)		—	—	P/L	40.00

NOTE: Calcutta Mint issues have no mint marks. Bombay Mint issues have a small raised bead or dot in the space below the lotus flower at the bottom of the reverse. The half Rupee dated 1911 like the Rupee and all other issues of that year has the "Pig" elephant. It was struck only at the Calcutta Mint.

KM#	Date	Mintage	Fine	VF	XF	Unc
521	1911(c)	2.293	2.00	6.00	12.50	30.00
	1911(c)	—	—	—	Proof	175.00
	1911(c) (restrike)		—	—	P/L	75.00
522	1912(c)	3.390	2.00	6.00	12.50	30.00
	1912(c)	—	—	—	Proof	125.00
	1912(b)	1.505	2.00	6.00	12.50	30.00
	1912(b)	—	—	—	Proof	125.00
	1912(b) (restrike)		—	—	P/L	25.00
	1913(c)	Inc. Ab.	2.00	6.00	12.50	30.00
	1913(c)	—	—	—	Proof	125.00
	1913(b)	Inc. Ab.	2.00	6.00	12.50	30.00
	1913(b)	—	—	—	Proof	125.00
	1913(b) (restrike)		—	—	P/L	25.00
	1914(c)	1.639	2.00	6.00	12.50	30.00
	1914(c)	—	—	—	Proof	125.00
	1914(b)	1.919	2.00	6.00	12.50	30.00
	1914(b) (restrike)		—	—	P/L	25.00
	1915(c)	1.600	2.00	6.00	12.50	30.00
	1915(c)	—	—	—	Proof	125.00
	1916(c)	1.402	2.00	6.00	12.50	30.00
	1916(c)	—	—	—	Proof	125.00
	1916(b)	4.615	2.00	6.00	12.50	30.00
	1917(c)	—	—	—	Proof	125.00
	1917(b)	8.422	2.00	6.00	12.50	30.00
	1917(b)	—	—	—	Proof	125.00
	1918(c) (restrike)		—	—	P/L	25.00
	1918(b)	8.768	2.00	6.00	12.50	30.00
	1918(b) (restrike)		—	—	P/L	25.00
	1919(b)	12.180	2.00	6.00	12.50	30.00
	1919(b)	—	—	—	Proof	125.00
	1919(b) (restrike)		—	—	P/L	25.00
	1919(c)	—	4.00	8.00	17.50	40.00
	1921(c)	5.804	2.00	6.00	12.50	30.00
	1921(c)	—	—	—	Proof	125.00
	1921(c) (restrike)		—	—	P/L	25.00
	1922(c)	4.405	2.00	6.00	12.50	30.00
	1922(c)	—	—	—	Proof	125.00
	1922(b)	1.037	2.00	6.00	12.50	30.00
	1922(b)	—	—	—	Proof	125.00
	1922(b) (restrike)		—	—	P/L	25.00
	1923(c)	—	2.00	6.00	12.50	30.00
	1923(c) (restrike)		—	—	P/L	25.00
	1923(b)	1.005	2.00	6.00	12.50	30.00
	1923(b)	—	—	—	Proof	125.00
	1923(b) (restrike)		—	—	P/L	25.00
	1924(c)	3.646	2.00	6.00	12.50	30.00
	1924(c)	—	—	—	Proof	125.00
	1924(b)	2.089	2.00	6.00	12.50	30.00
	1924(b)	—	—	—	Proof	125.00
	1924(b) (restrike)		—	—	P/L	25.00
	1925(c)	3.975	2.00	6.00	12.50	30.00
	1925(c)	—	—	—	Proof	125.00
	1925(b)	1.627	2.00	6.00	12.50	30.00
	1925(b)	—	—	—	Proof	125.00
	1925(b) (restrike)		—	—	P/L	25.00
	1926(c)	6.139	2.00	6.00	12.50	30.00
	1926(c)	—	—	—	Proof	125.00
	1926(b)	2.011	2.00	6.00	12.50	30.00
	1926(b)	—	—	—	Proof	125.00
	1926(b) (restrike)		—	—	P/L	25.00
	1927(c)	2.032	2.00	6.00	12.50	30.00
	1927(c)	—	—	—	Proof	125.00
	1927(c) (restrike)		—	—	P/L	25.00
	1928(b)	2.466	2.00	6.00	12.50	30.00
	1928(b)	—	—	—	Proof	125.00
	1929(c)	4.050	2.00	6.00	12.50	30.00
	1929(c)	—	—	—	Proof	125.00
	1929(c) (restrike)		—	—	P/L	25.00
	1930(c)	2.036	2.00	6.00	12.50	30.00
	1930(c)	—	—	—	Proof	125.00
	1930(c) (restrike)		—	—	P/L	25.00
	1933/2(c)					
		*4.056	2.00	6.00	12.50	30.00
	1933(c)	Inc. Ab.	2.00	6.00	12.50	30.00
	1933(c)	—	—	—	Proof	75.00
	1933(c) (restrike)		—	—	P/L	25.00
	1934(c)	4.056	2.00	6.00	12.50	30.00
	1934(c)	—	—	—	Proof	125.00
	1934(c) (restrike)		—	—	P/L	25.00
	1936(c)	16.919	2.00	6.00	12.50	30.00
	1936(b)	6.693	2.00	6.00	12.50	30.00
	1936(b) (restrike)		—	—	P/L	25.00

***NOTE:** Some 1933C are overdated 1933/32, but no coins dated 1932 were struck.

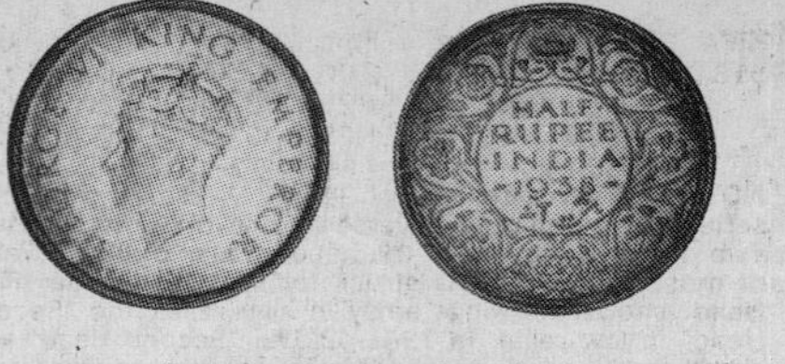

Obv: First head, reeded edge.

NOTE: Calcutta Mint issues have no mint mark. Bombay coins dated 1938-43 and 1945 have a bead below the lotus flower at the bottom of the reverse. Specimens dated 1944 with Reverse B have a diamond in the same position. Those dated 1944 with the normal common reverse have either a bead or a diamond. Lahore Mint issues have a small raised "L" in the same position as the Bombay coins. Bombay Mint 1943 coins have either large or small denticles on obverse. The nickel pieces of the last issue have a diamond below the date on the reverse.

KM#	Date	Mintage	Fine	VF	XF	Unc
549	1938(c)	—	—	—	Proof	100.00
	1938(b)	2.200	BV	3.00	7.50	15.00
	1938(b) (restrike)		—	—	P/L	25.00
	1939(c)	3.300	BV	3.00	7.50	15.00
	1939(c)	—	—	—	Proof	75.00
	1939(b)	10.096	BV	3.00	7.50	15.00
	1939(b)	—	—	—	Proof	75.00
	1939(b) (restrike)		—	—	P/L	25.00

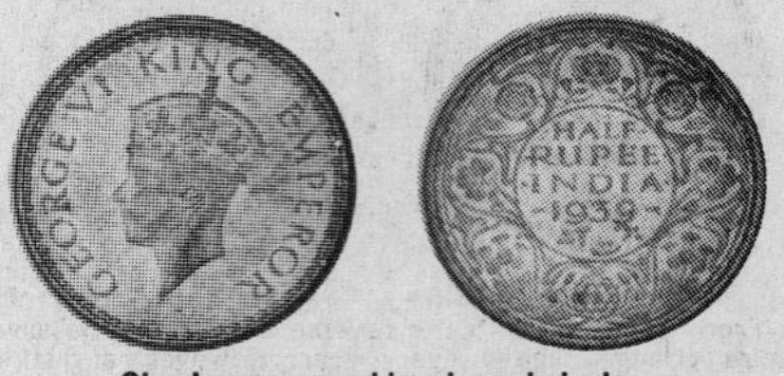

Obv: Large second head, reeded edge.

KM#	Date	Mintage	Fine	VF	XF	Unc
550	1939(c)	Inc. Ab.	BV	3.00	6.50	15.00
	1939(b)	Inc. Ab.	BV	3.00	6.50	13.50

5.8300 g, .500 SILVER, .0937 oz ASW

KM#	Date	Mintage	Fine	VF	XF	Unc
550a	1940(c)	32.898	BV	3.00	6.00	12.00
	1940(c)	—	—	—	Proof	75.00
	1940(b)	17.811	BV	3.00	6.50	13.50
	1940(b) (restrike)		—	—	P/L	25.00

Obv: Large second head, security edge.

KM#	Date	Mintage	Fine	VF	XF	Unc
551	1941(b)	26.100	BV	2.00	5.00	12.50
	1942(b)	61.600	BV	2.00	5.00	12.50

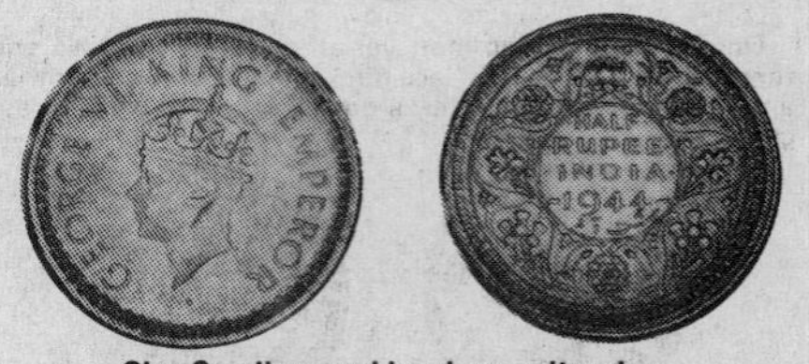

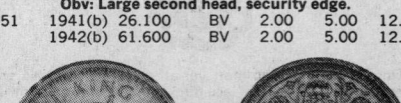

Obv: Small second head, security edge.
Rev: Denomination and inner circle smaller.

KM#	Date	Mintage	Fine	VF	XF	Unc
552	1942(b)	Inc. Ab.	BV	2.00	4.50	9.00
	1943(b)	90.400	BV	2.00	4.50	9.00
	1943(b)	—	—	—	Proof	75.00
	1943B reverse B					
		—	BV	2.00	4.50	9.00
	1943L	9.000	BV	2.00	4.50	9.00
	1943L	—	—	—	Proof	75.00
	1944(b)	46.200	BV	2.00	4.50	9.00
	1944B reverse B					
		Inc. Ab.	BV	2.00	4.50	9.00
	1944L	79.100	BV	2.00	4.50	9.00
	1945(b)	32.722	BV	2.00	4.50	9.00
	1945L small date					
		79.192	BV	2.00	4.50	9.00
	1945L large date					
		Inc. Ab.	2.50	5.00	10.00	20.00

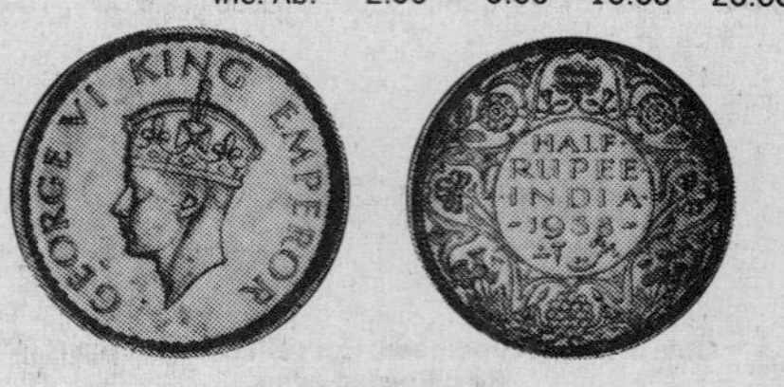

NICKEL (OMS)
Mule. Obv: KM#552. Rev: KM#549.

KM#	Date	Mintage	Fine	VF	XF	Unc
A553	1938(c) (restrike)		—	—	P/L	—

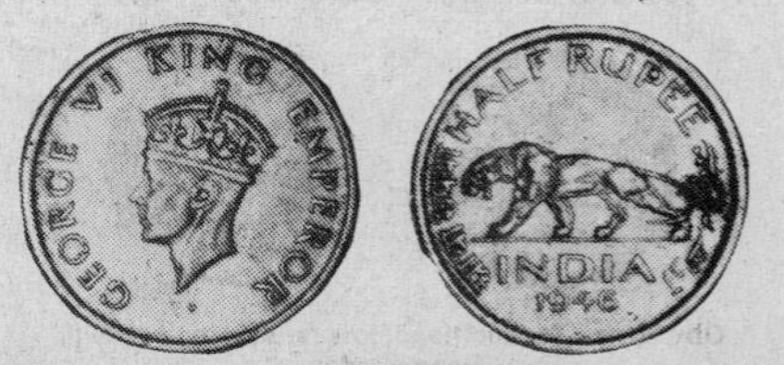

NICKEL

KM#	Date	Mintage	Fine	VF	XF	Unc
553	1946(b)	47.500	.50	1.00	2.25	4.50
	1947(b)	62.724	.50	1.00	2.00	4.00
	1947(b)	—	—	—	Proof	65.00

RUPEE

NOTE: The Rupees dated 1862 were struck with the date unchanged until 1874. However, in 1863 Bombay Mint adopted a method of adding dots or beads to its dies to indicate the exact year of minting.

The beads occur in the following positions:

1. Below the base or whorl of the top flower.
2. Above or around the top of the bottom flower.
3. In both positions together.

The different busts are identified as follows:

BUST A-The front dress panel has 3-3/4 sections with two dividing lines below the lowest string of pearls.
BUST B-The front dress panel has 4-1/4 sections with three dividing lines below the lowest string of pearls.
BUST C-Like Bust A, but shorter at the bottom. The front panel has only 3-1/3 sections.

The reverses are identified by the design of the top center flower as illustrated.

I II III

A variety of Reverse II, designated as IIa, shows the flower buds with a pineapple like pattern above "ONE" and above right of the second "E" of "RUPEE". In the listing of 1862 Rupees, the date column indicates the year in which the coins are believed to have been struck. The variety column lists the Obverse/reverse combination and the bead position. For example, A/I 0/0 means Bust A, Reverse I and no beads. A II 1/2 means Bust A, Reverse II, and one bead at the top and two beads at the bottom.

Mintage for 1862 Rupees

Calcutta	**269,427,222**
Bombay	**408,003,034**
Madras	**29,481,923**

NOTE: The B/II 0/0 coins are attributed to the mint of issues as follows:

CALCUTTA, 30.3mm, round pearls in crown arch.
BOMBAY, 30.5mm, elongated pearls in crown arch. The scroll like floral design of the dress is in flat relief and has a depression around it.
MADRAS, 30.55mm, elongated pearls in crown arch. The floral design is in high relief and shows no depression.

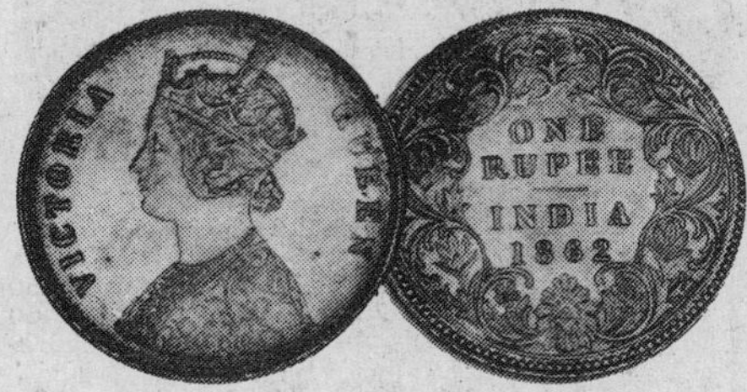

11.6600 g, .917 SILVER, .3438 oz ASW
Common date: 1862

KM#	Date	Year	Fine	VF	XF	Unc
473.1	B/II, 0/0	1862-63(c)	6.50	11.50	15.00	30.00
	B/II, 0/0	1862-63(b)	5.00	7.50	12.50	25.00
	B/II, 0/0	1862-69(m)	5.00	7.50	12.50	25.00
	A/III, 0/0	1863(c)	12.50	20.00	30.00	60.00
	B/III, 0/0	1863(c)	12.50	20.00	30.00	60.00
	A/I, 0/0	1863-74(m)	5.00	7.50	12.50	25.00
	B/II, 1/0	1863(b)	7.50	12.50	16.50	35.00
	A/II, 0/2	1864(b)	12.50	20.00	40.00	80.00
	B/II, 2/0	1864(b)	12.50	20.00	40.00	80.00
	A/II, 2/0	1864(b)	12.50	20.00	32.50	60.00
	B/II, 0/3	1865(b)	5.00	7.50	12.50	30.00
	B/II, 2/3	1865(b)	12.50	20.00	40.00	80.00
	A/I, 0/4	1866(b)	12.50	20.00	40.00	80.00
	B/I, 0/4	1866(b)	12.50	20.00	40.00	80.00
	A/II, 0/4	1866(b)	8.00	15.00	30.00	60.00
	A/II, 2/4	1866(b)	15.00	30.00	50.00	90.00
	B/II, 0/4	1866(b)	8.00	15.00	30.00	60.00
	A/IIa, 0/0	1866-69(c)	7.50	12.50	16.50	35.00

KM#	Date	Year	Fine	VF	XF	Unc
473.1	B/IIa, 0/0	1866-69(b) or (m)	12.50	20.00	32.50	60.00
	A/II, 0/5	1867(b)	5.00	7.50	13.50	30.00
	A/II, 0/0 (30.7mm)	1867-68(b)	12.50	20.00	32.50	60.00
	A/II, 0/6	1868(b)	5.00	7.50	13.50	30.00
	A/II, 0/7	1869(b)	5.00	7.50	13.50	30.00
	B/II, 0/7	1869(b)	12.50	20.00	32.50	60.00
	A/II, 1/7 (top dot in top flower)	1869-70(b)	—	—	Rare	—
	A/II, 1/7 (top dot in normal position)	1872(b)	12.50	20.00	40.00	80.00
	A/II, 0/8	1870(b)	12.50	20.00	40.00	80.00
	A/II, 0/9	1871(b)	12.50	20.00	40.00	80.00
	A/II, 0/10	1872(b)	7.50	12.50	16.50	35.00
	A/II, 1/10 (top dot in top flower)	1872-73(b)	12.50	20.00	40.00	80.00
	A/II, 1/10 (top dot in normal position)	1873(b)	12.50	20.00	40.00	80.00
	A/I, 1/1	1873(b)	7.50	12.50	16.50	35.00
	A/II, 0/1	1873(b)	12.50	20.00	40.00	80.00
	A/II, 1/1	1873(b)	12.50	20.00	40.00	80.00
	A/II, 0/12	1874(b)	12.50	20.00	40.00	80.00
	A/II, 1/2	1874(b)	10.00	17.50	27.50	50.00
	A/I, 1/2	1874(b)	12.50	20.00	40.00	80.00
	C/I, 1/2	1874(b)	12.50	20.00	40.00	80.00
	C/II, 1/2	1874(b)	10.00	17.50	27.50	50.00
		1862(c)	—	—	Proof	200.00
		1862(c) (restrike)	—	—	P/L	35.00

GOLD (OMS)

KM#	Date	Mintage	Fine	VF	XF	Unc
473.1a	1862(c) (restrike)		—	—	P/L	—

From 1874 onward the coins show the year date. The designs are similar to those on the 1862 Rupees but only Bust "A" and the Reverse I and II were used.

CALCUTTA Mint issues dated 1874-78 have no mint mark. From 1879 the mint mark is a small incuse "C" on the whorl below the center of the bottom lotus flower on the reverse. All Calcutta issues have Reverse I.
BOMBAY Mint issues dated 1875-83 have as mint mark a small bead directly above the center of the bottom lotus flower. From 1883 the mint mark is a small "B" raised or incuse above the whorl or base of the top flower. Both mint marks occur on the coins dated 1883. The issues dated 1874-76 have Reverse II only, those dated 1877-85 have both Reverses I and II. Reverse II distinguishes the 1874 coins which have no mint mark from those of Calcutta.

NOTE: There are reverse varieties in most of the following Rupees. Reverse II flowers are found in various sizes. Two bottom rosettes are found rotated, i.e., one petal up or down.

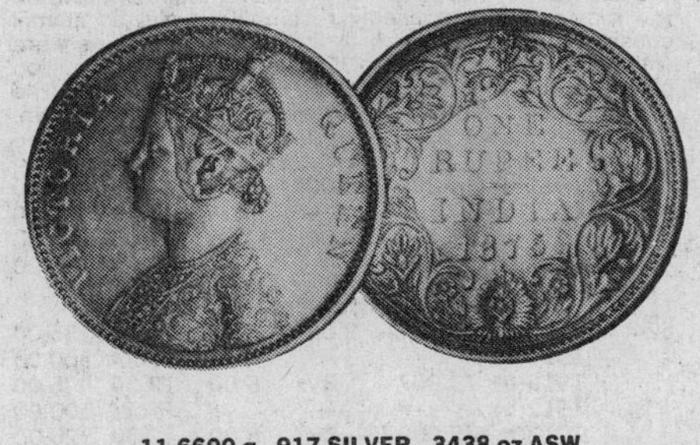

11.6600 g, .917 SILVER, .3438 oz ASW

KM#	Date	Mintage	Fine	VF	XF	Unc
473.2	1874(c) Rev.I	15.014	2.50	8.00	12.00	25.00
	1874(b) Rev.II	25.509	2.50	8.00	12.00	25.00
	1874(b) Rev. II, dot	Inc. Ab.	3.00	10.00	15.00	30.00
	1874(b)		—	—	Proof	175.00
	1874(b) (restrike)		—	—	P/L	35.00
	1875(c) Rev.I	11.632	2.50	8.00	12.00	25.00
	1875(c) Rev.II	—	2.50	8.00	12.00	25.00
	1875(c)		—	—	Proof	175.00
	1875(b) Rev.II, dot	19.360	2.50	8.00	12.00	25.00
	1875(b)		—	—	Proof	175.00
	1875(b) (restrike)		—	—	P/L	35.00
	1875(b) C/II, dot	Inc. Ab.	—	—	—	—
	1876(c) Rev.I	12.001	2.50	8.00	12.00	25.00
	1876(b) Rev.II, dot	28.950	2.50	8.00	12.00	25.00
	1876(b)		—	—	Proof	175.00
	1876(b) (restrike)		—	—	P/L	35.00

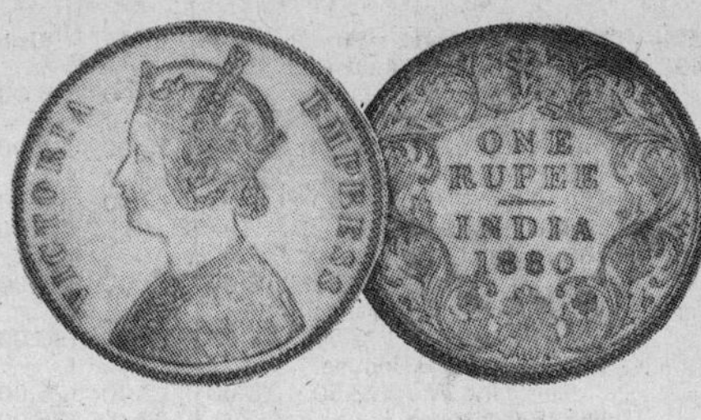

KM#	Date	Mintage	Fine	VF	XF	Unc
492	1877(c) Rev.I	39.252	2.50	8.00	12.00	25.00
	1877(c)	—	—	—	Proof	175.00
	1877(b) Rev.I, dot	95.554	2.50	8.00	12.00	25.00
	1877(b) Rev.II, dot	Inc. Ab.	2.50	8.00	12.00	25.00
	1877(b)		—	—	Proof	175.00
	1877(b) (restrike)		—	—	P/L	35.00
	1878(c) Rev.I	32.658	2.50	8.00	12.00	25.00
	1878(c)	—	—	—	Proof	175.00
	1878(b) Rev.I, dot	63.927	2.50	8.00	12.00	25.00
	1878(b) Rev.II, dot	Inc. Ab.	2.50	8.00	12.00	25.00
	1878(b)		—	—	Proof	175.00
	1878(b) (restrike)		—	—	P/L	35.00
	1879C Rev.I, "C" incuse	15.928	2.50	8.00	12.00	25.00
	1879(b) Rev.I, dot	72.800	6.50	17.50	27.50	50.00
	1879(b) Rev.II, dot	Inc. Ab.	2.50	8.00	12.00	25.00
	1879(b) Rev.II, dot (rosette var.)	Inc. Ab.	2.50	8.00	12.00	25.00
	1879(b)		—	—	Proof	175.00
	1879(b) (restrike)		—	—	P/L	35.00
	1880C Rev.I, "C" incuse	18.400	3.00	10.00	15.00	30.00
	1880(b) Rev.I, dot	53.786	2.50	8.00	12.00	25.00
	1880(b) Rev.II, dot	Inc. Ab.	2.50	8.00	12.00	25.00
	1880(b) (restrike)		—	—	P/L	35.00
	1881C Rev.I, "C" incuse	2.436	3.00	10.00	15.00	35.00
	1881C	—	—	—	Proof	175.00
	1881(b) Rev.I, dot	3.162	6.50	17.50	27.50	50.00
	1881(b) Rev.II, dot	Inc. Ab.	6.50	17.50	27.50	50.00
	1881(b) (restrike)		—	—	P/L	35.00
	1882C Rev.I, "C" incuse	15.090	2.50	8.00	12.00	25.00
	1882C	—	—	—	Proof	175.00
	1882(b) Rev.I, dot	56.397	2.50	8.00	12.00	25.00
	1882(b) (restrike)		—	—	P/L	35.00
	1882 Rev. II, dot	—	—	—	—	—
	1883C Rev.I, "C" incuse	5.123	3.00	10.00	15.00	30.00
	1883(c) Rev.I, no mm.	Inc. Ab.	7.50	20.00	37.50	70.00
	1883(b) Rev.I, dot	18.023	6.50	17.50	27.50	50.00
	1883B Rev.I, "B" raised	Inc. Ab.	6.50	17.50	27.50	50.00
	1883B Rev.I, dot, "B" raised	Inc. Ab.	7.50	20.00	37.50	70.00
	1883B (restrike)		—	—	P/L	35.00
	1884C Rev.I, "C" incuse	11.642	2.50	8.00	12.00	25.00
	1884B Rev.I, "B" raised	35.847	3.00	10.00	17.50	35.00
	1884B Rev. II, "B" raised on whorl below bottom flower	I.A.	6.50	17.50	27.50	50.00
	1884B (restrike)		—	—	P/L	35.00
	1885C Rev.I, "C" incuse	34.152	2.50	8.00	12.00	25.00
	1885C	—	—	—	Proof	175.00
	1885B Rev.I, "B" raised	64.878	2.50	8.00	12.00	25.00
	1885B Rev.II, "B" raised	Inc. Ab.	2.50	8.00	12.00	25.00
	1885B Rev.I, "B" incuse	Inc. Ab	2.50	8.00	12.00	25.00
	1885B Rev. II, "B" incuse	Inc. Ab.	6.50	17.50	27.50	50.00
	1885B (restrike)		—	—	P/L	35.00
	1886C Rev.I, "C" incuse	10.878	2.50	8.00	12.00	25.00
	1886C	—	—	—	Proof	175.00
	1886B Rev.I, "B" incuse	41.146	2.50	8.00	12.00	25.00
	1886B (restrike)		—	—	P/L	35.00
	1887C Rev.I, "C" incuse	40.200	2.50	8.00	12.00	25.00
	1887B Rev.I, "B" raised	48.400	2.50	8.00	12.00	25.00
	1887B Rev.I, "B" incuse	Inc. Ab.	2.50	8.00	12.00	25.00
	1887B Rev.I, "B" incuse, inverted B	Inc. Ab.	3.00	10.00	15.00	30.00
	1887B (restrike)		—	—	P/L	35.00

British / INDIA 988

KM#	Date	Mintage	Fine	VF	XF	Unc
492	1888C Rev.I, "C" incuse					
		7.568	2.50	8.00	12.00	25.00
	1888B Rev.I, "B" raised					
		63.200	2.50	8.00	12.00	25.00
	1888B Rev.I, "B" incuse					
		Inc. Ab.	2.50	8.00	12.00	25.00
	1888B (restrike)		—	—	P/L	35.00
	1889C Rev.I, "C" incuse					
		9.368	2.50	8.00	12.00	25.00
	1889B Rev.I, "B" raised					
		65.300	2.50	8.00	12.00	30.00
	1889B Rev.I, "B" incuse					
		Inc. Ab.	2.50	8.00	12.00	25.00
	1889B (restrike)		—	—	P/L	35.00
	1890C Rev.I, "C" incuse					
		24.742	2.50	8.00	12.00	25.00
	1890C	—	—	—	Proof	175.00
	1890B Rev.I, "B" incuse					
		92.900	2.50	8.00	12.00	25.00
	1890B (restrike)		—	—	P/L	35.00
	1891C Rev.I, "C" incuse					
		14.670	2.50	8.00	12.00	25.00
	1891C	—	—	—	Proof	175.00
	1891B Rev.I, "B" incuse					
		49.500	2.50	8.00	12.00	25.00
	1891B	—	—	—	Proof	175.00
	1892C Rev.I, "C" incuse					
		32.455	2.50	8.00	12.00	25.00
	1892C	—	—	—	Proof	175.00
	1892B Rev.I, "B" raised					
		72.200	2.50	8.00	12.00	25.00
	1892B Rev.I, "B" incuse					
		Inc. Ab.	2.50	8.00	12.00	25.00
	1892B	—	—	—	Proof	175.00
	1892B (restrike)		—	—	P/L	35.00
	1893C Rev.I, "C" incuse					
		9.140	2.50	8.00	12.00	25.00
	1893C	—	—	—	Proof	175.00
	1893B Rev.I, "B" incuse					
		69.590	2.50	8.00	12.00	25.00
	1893B	—	—	—	Proof	175.00
	1893B (restrike)		—	—	P/L	35.00
	1894C	—	—	—	Proof	200.00
	1897C Rev.I, "C" incuse					
		.470	15.00	35.00	70.00	175.00
	1897C	—	—	—	Proof	225.00
	1897B Rev.I, "B" incuse					
		1.055	6.50	17.50	27.50	50.00
	1897B	—	—	—	Proof	175.00
	1897B (restrike)		—	—	P/L	35.00
	1898C Rev.I, "C" incuse					
		1.251	4.00	12.50	22.50	40.00
	1898C	—	—	—	Proof	175.00
	1898B Rev.I, "B" incuse					
		6.268	2.50	8.00	12.00	25.00
	1898B	—	—	—	Proof	175.00
	1898B (restrike)		—	—	P/L	35.00
	1900C Rev.I, "C" incuse					
		5.291	2.50	8.00	12.00	25.00
	1900C	—	—	—	Proof	175.00
	1900B Rev.I, "B" incuse					
		65.237	BV	6.00	12.00	25.00
	1900B	—	—	—	Proof	175.00
	1900B (restrike)		—	—	P/L	35.00
	1901C Rev.I, "C" incuse					
		72.017	BV	6.00	12.00	25.00
	1901C	Inc. Ab.	—	—	Proof	175.00
	1901B Rev.I, "B" incuse					
		103.258	BV	6.00	12.00	25.00
	1901B	—	—	—	Proof	175.00
	1901B (restrike)		—	—	P/L	35.00

ALUMINUM (OMS)

KM#	Date	Mintage	Fine	VF	XF	Unc
492a	1891B	—	—	—	Proof	—

COPPER OR BRONZE (OMS)

KM#	Date	Mintage	Fine	VF	XF	Unc
492b	1884	—	—	—	Proof	100.00
	1885	—	—	—	Proof	100.00
	1887	—	—	—	Proof	100.00
	1891	—	—	—	Proof	100.00
	1892	—	—	—	Proof	100.00

GOLD (OMS)

KM#	Date	Mintage	Fine	VF	XF	Unc
492c	1891 (restrike)		—	—	P/L	500.00
	1892 (restrike)		—	—	P/L	500.00
	1893 (restrike)		—	—	P/L	500.00
	1898 (restrike)		—	—	P/L	500.00
	1900B (restrike)		—	—	P/L	500.00

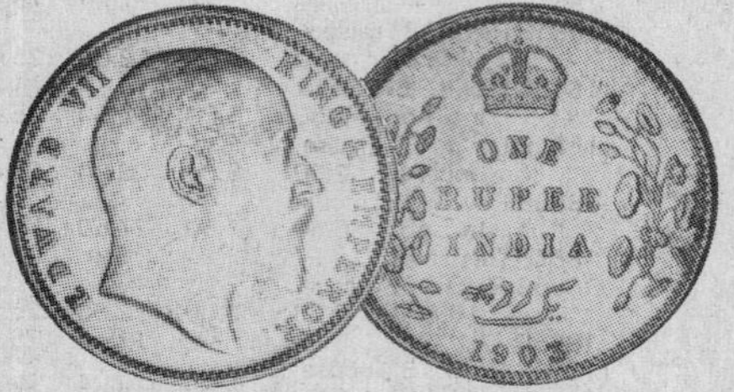

11.6600 g, .917 SILVER, .3438 oz ASW

NOTE: Calcutta Mint issues have no mint mark. Bombay Mint issues have a small incuse "B" in the space below the cross pattee of the crown on the reverse.

KM#	Date	Mintage	Fine	VF	XF	Unc
508	1903(c)	49.403	BV	6.00	12.00	25.00
	1903(c)	—	—	—	Proof	350.00
	1903B (in relief)					
		52.969	BV	6.00	12.00	25.00
	1903B	—	—	—	Proof	350.00
508	1903B (incuse)					
		Inc. Ab.	BV	6.00	12.00	25.00
	1903B (restrike)		—	—	P/L	30.00
	1904(c)	58.339	BV	6.00	12.00	25.00
	1904(c)	—	—	—	Proof	350.00
	1904B	101.949	BV	6.00	12.00	25.00
	1904B	—	—	—	Proof	350.00
	1904B (restrike)		—	—	P/L	30.00
	1905(c)	51.258	BV	6.00	12.00	25.00
	1905(c)	—	—	—	Proof	350.00
	1905B	76.202	BV	6.00	12.00	25.00
	1905B	—	—	—	Proof	350.00
	1905B (restrike)		—	—	P/L	30.00
	1906(c)	104.797	BV	6.00	15.00	30.00
	1906B	158.953	BV	6.00	15.00	30.00
	1906B	—	—	—	Proof	350.00
	1906B (restrike)		—	—	P/L	30.00
	1907(c)	81.338	BV	6.00	15.00	30.00
	1907(c)	—	—	—	Proof	350.00
	1907B	170.912	BV	6.00	15.00	30.00
	1907B	—	—	—	Proof	350.00
	1907B (restrike)		—	—	P/L	30.00
	1908(c)	20.218	BV	6.00	15.00	30.00
	1908(c)	—	—	—	Proof	350.00
	1908B	10.715	5.00	15.00	30.00	60.00
	1908B	—	—	—	Proof	350.00
	1908B (restrike)		—	—	P/L	30.00
	1909(c)	12.759	BV	6.00	15.00	30.00
	1909(c)	—	—	—	Proof	350.00
	1909B	9.539	5.00	15.00	30.00	60.00
	1909B	—	—	—	Proof	350.00
	1909B (restrike)		—	—	P/L	30.00
	1910(c)	12.627	BV	6.00	12.00	25.00
	1910(c)	—	—	—	Proof	350.00
	1910B	10.885	BV	6.00	12.00	25.00
	1910B	—	—	—	Proof	350.00
	1910B (restrike)		—	—	P/L	30.00

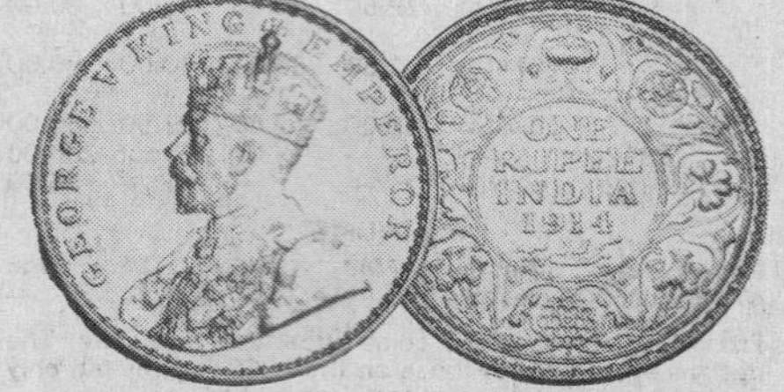

NOTE: Calcutta Mint issues have no mint mark. Bombay Mint issues have a small raised bead or dot in the space below the lotus flower at the bottom of the reverse.

Obverse Dies

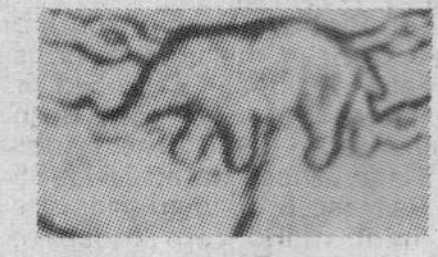

Type I

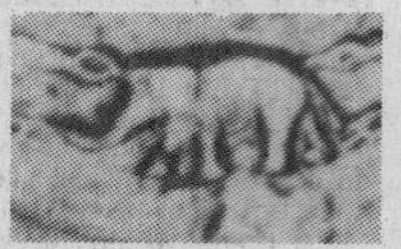

Type II

Type I - Obv. die w/elephant with piglike feet and short tail. Nicknamed "pig rupee".

Type II - Obv. die w/redesigned elephant with outlined ear, heavy feet and long tail.

The Rupees dated 1911 were rejected by the public as the elephant of the Order of the Indian Empire shown on the King's robe supposedly resembled a pig, an animal considered to be unclean by Indians. These coins were withdrawn from circulation. Out of a total of 9.4 million pieces struck at both mint, only 700,000 were issued. The remainder and the withdrawn pieces were melted down. The issues dated 1912 and later have a re-designed elephant.

KM#	Date	Mintage	Fine	VF	XF	Unc
523	1911(c)	4.300	10.00	20.00	40.00	100.00
	1911(c)	—	—	—	Proof	600.00
	1911(b)	5.143	10.00	20.00	40.00	100.00
	1911(b) (restrike)		—	—	P/L	75.00

Redesigned elephant.

KM#	Date	Mintage	Fine	VF	XF	Unc
524	1912(c)	45.122	2.50	7.50	15.00	35.00
	1912(c)	—	—	—	Proof	500.00
	1912(b)	79.067	BV	6.00	12.50	25.00
	1912(b)	—	—	—	Proof	500.00
	1913(c)	75.800	BV	6.00	12.50	25.00
	1913(c)	—	—	—	Proof	500.00
	1913(b)	87.466	BV	6.00	12.50	25.00
	1913(b)	—	—	—	Proof	500.00
	1913(b) (restrike)		—	—	P/L	30.00
	1914(c)	33.100	BV	6.00	12.50	25.00
	1914(c)	—	—	—	Proof	500.00
	1914(b)	15.270	BV	6.00	12.50	25.00
	1914(b)	—	—	—	Proof	500.00
	1914(b) (restrike)		—	—	P/L	30.00
	1915(c)	9.900	5.00	15.00	30.00	60.00
	1915(c)	—	—	—	Proof	500.00
	1915(b)	5.372	7.50	20.00	40.00	80.00
	1915(b)	—	—	—	Proof	500.00
	1915(b) (restrike)		—	—	P/L	30.00
	1916(c)	115.000	BV	6.00	12.50	20.00
	1916(c)	—	—	—	Proof	500.00
	1916(b)	97.900	BV	6.00	12.50	20.00
	1916(b)	—	—	—	Proof	500.00
	1916(b) (restrike)		—	—	P/L	30.00
	1917(c)	114.974	BV	6.00	12.50	20.00
	1917(c)	—	—	—	Proof	500.00
	1917(b)	151.583	BV	6.00	12.50	20.00
	1917(b)	—	—	—	Proof	500.00
	1917(b) (restrike)		—	—	P/L	30.00
	1918(c)	205.420	BV	6.00	12.50	20.00
524	1918(c)	—	—	—	Proof	500.00
	1918(b)	210.550	BV	6.00	12.50	20.00
	1918(b)	—	—	—	Proof	500.00
	1918(b) (restrike)		—	—	P/L	30.00
	1919(c)	211.206	BV	6.00	12.50	20.00
	1919(c)	—	—	—	Proof	500.00
	1919(b)	226.706	BV	6.00	12.50	20.00
	1919(b)	—	—	—	Proof	500.00
	1919(b) (restrike)		—	—	P/L	30.00
	1920(c)	50.500	BV	6.00	12.50	20.00
	1920(c)	—	—	—	Proof	500.00
	1920(b)	55.937	BV	6.00	12.50	20.00
	1920(b)	—	—	—	Proof	500.00
	1921(b)	5.115	25.00	75.00	150.00	250.00
	1921(b)	—	—	—	Proof	500.00
	1922(b)	2.051	25.00	75.00	150.00	250.00
	1922(b)	—	—	—	Proof	500.00
	1935(c)	—	—	—	Proof	500.00
	1935(c) (restrike)		—	—	P/L	125.00
	1936(c)	—	—	—	Proof	500.00

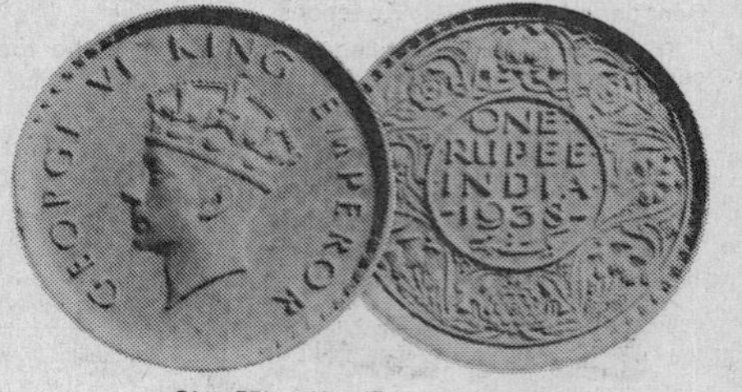

Obv: "First Head", reeded edge.

KM#	Date	Mintage	Fine	VF	XF	Unc
554	1938(c)	—	—	—	Proof	275.00
	1939(c)	—	—	—	Proof	350.00

NOTE: No rupees with the "First Head" were struck for circulation. Those dated 1938-39 were struck in 1940 before the fineness of the silver coins was reduced to .500.

The pieces struck at Calcutta have no mint mark. Bombay issues dated 1938-41 and 1944-45 have a bead below the lotus flower at the bottom of the reverse while those dated 1942-44 have a small diamond mark in the same position. On the specimens dated 1944 with Reverse B the mint mark appears to be a "bead over a diamond". Lahore Mint issues have a small raised "L" in the same position as the Bombay coins. The last issue nickel rupees struck at Bombay have a small diamond below the date on the reverse. The rupees dated 1943 occur with large and small "Second Head" and with large and small date figure "3".

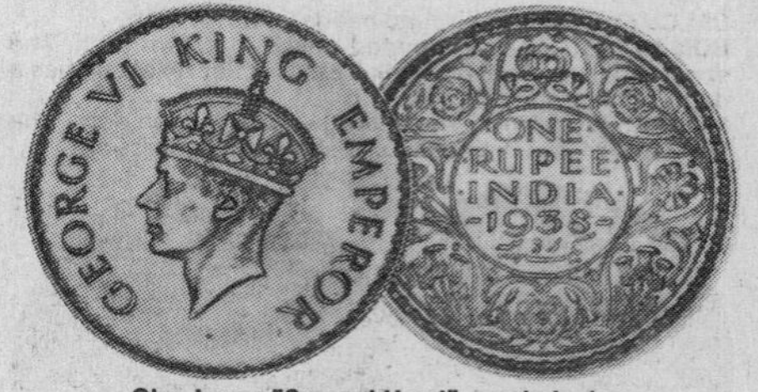

Obv: Large "Second Head", reeded edge.

KM#	Date	Mintage	Fine	VF	XF	Unc
555	1938(b) w/o dot					
		7.352	7.50	11.50	16.50	27.50
	1938(b) dot	I.A.	7.50	11.50	16.50	27.50
	1938(b) (restrike)		—	—	P/L	50.00
	1939(b) dot					
		2.450	150.00	300.00	600.00	1200.

11.6600 g, .500 SILVER, .1874 oz ASW
Security edge

KM#	Date	Mintage	Fine	VF	XF	Unc
556	1939(b)	—	200.00	400.00	800.00	1500.
	1940(b)	153.120	BV	4.00	10.00	20.00
	1941(b)	111.480	BV	4.00	10.00	20.00
	1943(b)	Inc. Be.	BV	4.00	10.00	20.00

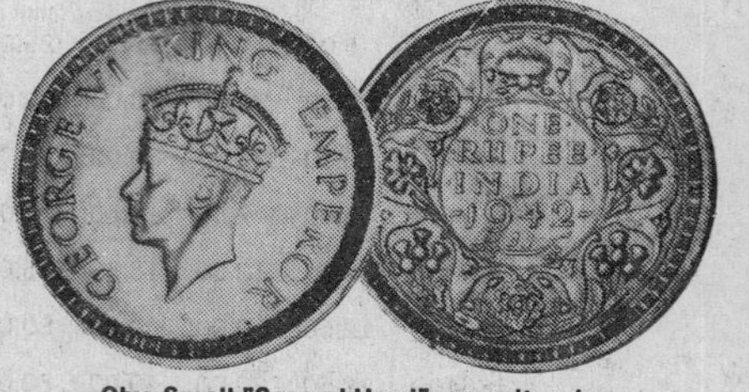

Obv: Small "Second Head", security edge.

KM#	Date	Mintage	Fine	VF	XF	Unc
557	1942(b)	244.500	BV	4.00	10.00	20.00
	1943(b)	65.995	BV	4.00	10.00	20.00
	1943(b) Rev. B					
		Inc. Ab.	BV	4.00	10.00	20.00
	1944(b) Rev. B					
		146.206	BV	4.00	10.00	20.00
	1944(b)	Inc. Ab.	BV	4.00	10.00	20.00
	1944L small L					
		91.400	BV	4.00	10.00	20.00
	1944L large L					
		Inc. Ab.	BV	4.00	10.00	20.00
	1945(b) small date					
		142.666	BV	3.00	6.00	12.50
	1945(b) large date					
		Inc. Ab.	BV	3.00	7.50	15.00
	1945(b)	—	—	—	Proof	—
	1945L	118.126	BV	3.00	6.00	12.50

Reeded edge (error)

KM#	Date	Mintage	Fine	VF	XF	Unc
558	1944(b)	—	—	—	—	—
	1945(b)	—	—	—	—	—

NICKEL (OMS)
Mule. Obv: KM#557. Rev: KM#555.

| A559 | 1938(c) (restrike) | — | — | — | P/L | 125.00 |

NICKEL
Rev: New design, security edge.

559	1947(b)	118.128	1.50	2.50	5.00	10.00
	1947B	—	—	Proof	—	75.00
	1947(l)	41.911	1.50	3.00	6.00	12.00

NOTE: Bombay issue has diamond mark below date, Lahore w/o privy mark.

5 RUPEES

3.8870 g, .917 GOLD, .1146 oz AGW
Obv: Young bust.
Reeded edge

KM#	Date	Year	Fine	VF	XF	Unc
474	1870CM	—	125.00	175.00	300.00	400.00
	1875	—	—	—	Proof	850.00

Plain edge
| 475 | 1870 | — | — | — | Proof | 850.00 |

SILVER (OMS)
| 475a | 1870 | — | — | — | Proof | — |

3.8870 g, .917 GOLD, .1146 oz AGW
Obv: Mature bust.
Reeded edge

476	1870(c)	.013	125.00	175.00	300.00	400.00
	1870(c)	—	—	—	Proof	450.00
	1870(c)	—	—	—	P/L	400.00

Mule. Obv: 1/4 Rupee, Bust A, KM#486. Rev: KM#476.
Obv: Young bust.
| 493.1 | 1879(b) (restrike) | — | — | — | P/L | 400.00 |

Mule. Obv: 1/4 Rupee, Bust B. Rev: KM#476.
| 493.2 | 1879(b) (restrike) | — | — | — | P/L | 400.00 |

Mule. Obv: 1/4 Rupee, Bust C. Rev: KM#476.
| 493.3 | 1879(b) (restrike) | — | — | — | P/L | 400.00 |

Obv: Mature bust.
| 494 | 1879(b) (restrike) | — | — | — | P/L | 275.00 |

10 RUPEES

7.7740 g, .917 GOLD, .2292 oz AGW
Obv: Young bust.

Reeded edge

KM#	Date	Mintage	Fine	VF	XF	Unc
477	1870CM	—	—	—	Proof	500.00
	1870CM (restrike)	—	—	—	P/L	500.00
	1875	—	—	—	Proof	1250.

Plain edge
| 478 | 1870 | — | — | — | Proof | 1250. |

SILVER (OMS)
| 478a | 1870 | — | — | — | Proof | — |

7.7740 g, .917 GOLD, .2292 oz AGW
Obv: Mature bust.
Reeded edge

479	1870(c)	7,932	150.00	275.00	400.00	500.00
	1870(c)	—	—	—	Proof	500.00
	1870(c) (restrike)	—	—	—	P/L	500.00

495	1878(b)	—	—	—	Proof	1250.
	1878(b) (restrike)	—	—	—	P/L	500.00
	1879(b)	—	—	—	Proof	1250.
	1879(b) (restrike)	—	—	—	P/L	500.00

15 RUPEES

7.9881 g, .917 GOLD, .2354 oz AGW

525	1918(b)	2.110	125.00	175.00	250.00	350.00
	1918(b)	12 pcs.	—	—	Proof	1250.
	1918(b) (restrike)	—	—	—	P/L	275.00

NOTE: The above issue was equal in weight and fineness to the British sovereign.

MOHUR

11.6600 g, .917 GOLD, .3437 oz AGW
Obv: Young bust.

480	1862(c)	.153	200.00	275.00	375.00	500.00
	1862(c)	Inc. Ab.	—	—	Proof	850.00
	1862(c) (restrike)	—	—	—	P/L	300.00
	1862(c) w/V on bust Inc. Ab.	200.00	275.00	375.00	500.00
	1862(c) w/V on rev. in design below date Inc. Ab.	200.00	275.00	375.00	500.00
	1862(c) w/V on bust and on rev.	—	200.00	275.00	375.00	500.00
	1862(c) w/V on bust and 2 flowers in bottom panel I.A.	200.00	275.00	375.00	500.00
	1870(c)	—	—	—	Proof	750.00
	1870(c) (restrike)	—	—	—	P/L	400.00
	1875(c) w/V on bust	.011	225.00	300.00	500.00	750.00
	1875(c)	—	—	—	Proof	2500.
	1875(c) (restrike)	—	—	—	P/L	400.00

COPPER OR BRONZE (OMS)
| 480a | 1862(c) | — | — | — | — | 350.00 |

11.6600 g, .917 GOLD, .3437 oz AGW
Obv: Mature bust.

| 481 | 1870(c) | — | — | — | Proof | 2500. |
| | 1870(c) (restrike) | — | — | — | P/L | 400.00 |

Mule. Obv: KM#496. Rev: KM#481.
| 482 | 1870(c) | — | — | — | P/L | 650.00 |

Obv: Young bust.

KM#	Date	Mintage	Fine	VF	XF	Unc
496	1877(c)	.010	175.00	200.00	275.00	450.00
	1878(c) (restrike)	—	—	—	P/L	400.00
	1879C	.019	175.00	200.00	275.00	450.00
	1879(b) modified rev.	—	—	—	Proof	2500.
	1879(b) (restrike)	—	—	—	P/L	400.00
	1881	.023	175.00	200.00	275.00	450.00
	1882C	.012	175.00	200.00	275.00	450.00
	1882(b) w/o C mm (restrike)	—	—	—	P/L	400.00
	1884(c)	8,643	185.00	275.00	375.00	500.00
	1885(c)	.015	175.00	200.00	275.00	450.00
	1888(c)	.015	175.00	200.00	250.00	325.00	450.00
	1889(c)	.015	175.00	200.00	275.00	450.00
	1889(c) (restrike)	—	—	—	P/L	400.00
	1891(c)	.017	175.00	200.00	275.00	450.00

COPPER OR BRONZE (OMS)
| 496a | 1878(b) | — | — | — | — | 350.00 | — |

TRADE COINAGE
SOVEREIGN

7.9881 g, .917 GOLD, .2354 oz AGW

525A	1918I	1.295	125.00	140.00	175.00	225.00
	1918I	—	—	—	Proof	—
	1918I (restrike)	—	—	—	P/L	175.00

NOTE: The Mansfield Commission of 1868 allowed for the admission of British and Australian (see Australian section) sovereigns with shield reverse were struck for export to India) sovereigns as payment for sums due.

The fifth branch of the Royal Mint was established in a section of the Bombay Mint as from December 21, 1917. This was a war-time measure, its purpose being to strike into sovereigns the gold blanks supplied by the Bombay and other Indian mints. The Bombay sovereigns bear the mint mark I and were struck from August 15, 1918 to April 22, 1919. The branch-mint was closed in May, 1919.

BULLION ISSUES
Central Bank of India
Struck at the Bombay Mint.

TOLA

11.7000 g, .996 GOLD, .3747 oz AGW

| 496A | ND(1899-)B | — | — | 165.00 | 185.00 | 225.00 |

5 TOLAS
58.5000 g, .9957 GOLD, 1.8727 oz AGW

| 496B | ND(1899-)B | — | — | 850.00 | 950.00 | 1100. |

10 TOLAS
117.0000 g, .9956 GOLD, 3.7451 oz AGW
Uniface

| 496C | ND(1899-)B | — | — | 1700. | 1900. | 2200. |

MINT SETS (MS)

KM#	Date	Mintage	Identification	Mkt.Val.
MS1	1835c(3)	—	KM448a-450a	—

PROOF SETS (PS)

PS1	1835c(3)	—	KM445-447	500.00
PS2	1875(3)	—	KM474,477,480	4500.
PS3	1904(5)	—	KM497,499,503,Pn70(2)	3000.
PS4	1904(5)	—	KM497,499,501 (bronze) w/'1' c/m on rev.	3000.
PS5	1911c(4)	—	KM514,517,521,523	400.00
PS6	1919c(8)	—	KM513,516,519-520 (2 each)	500.00
PS7	1938c(6)	—	KM527-528,530,536,544,555	350.00
PS8	1947b(7)	—	KM533,535,538,542,548,553,559	300.00

INDIA REPUBLIC

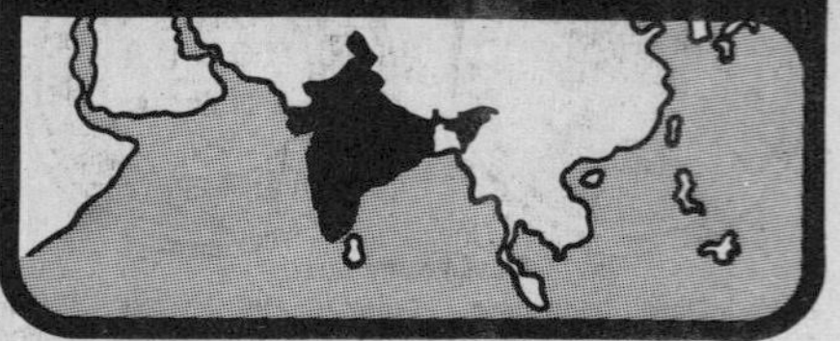

The Republic of India, a subcontinent jutting southward from the mainland of Asia, has an area of 1,269,346 sq. mi. (3,287,590 sq. km.) and a population of *833.4 million, second only to that of the People's Republic of China. Capital: New Delhi. India's economy is based on agriculture and industrial activity. Engineering goods, cotton apparel and fabrics, handicrafts, tea, iron and steel are exported.

The people of India have had a continuous civilization since about 2,500 B.C., when an urban culture based on commerce and trade, and to a lesser extent, agriculture, was developed by the inhabitants of the Indus River Valley. The origins of this civilization are uncertain, but it declined about 1,500 B.C., when the region was conquered by the Aryans. Over the following 2,000 years, the Aryans developed a Brahmanic civilization and introduced the caste system. Several successive empires flourished in India over the following centuries, notably those of the Mauryans, Guptas, and Mughals. In the 8th centuries A.D., the Arabs expanded into western India, bringing with them the Islamic faith. A Muslim dynasty (the Mughal Empire) controlled virtually the entire subcontinent during the period preceding the arrival of the Europeans; an Indo-Islamic style of art and architecture evolved, of which the Taj Mahal is a splendid example.

The Portuguese were the first Europeans to arrive, off Calicut in May 1498. It wasn't until 1612, after Portuguese and Spanish power began to wane, that the British East India Company established its initial settlement at Surat. By the end of the century, English traders were firmly established in Bombay, Madras, and Calcutta, as well as in some parts of the interior, and Britain was implementing a policy to create the civil and military institutions that would insure British dominion over the country. By 1757, following the successful conclusion of a war of colonial rivalry with France, the British were firmly established in India as not only traders, but as conquerors. During the next 60 years, the British East India Company acquired dominion over most of India by intrigue and force, and ruled directly, or through puppet princelings.

The Indian Mutiny (called the first War of Independence by Indian Nationalists) of 1857-58, begun by Indian troops in the service of the British East India Company, revealed the intensity of the growing resentment against British domination. The widespread rebellion against British rule was unsuccessful, but resulted in the transfer of government from the company to the British crown, and was a source of inspiration, to later Indian nationalists. Agitation for representation in the government continued.

Following World War I, in which India sent six million troops to fight at the side of the Allies, Indian nationalism intensified under the banner of the Indian National Congress and the leadership of Mohandas Karamchand Gandhi, who called for non-violent revolt against British authority. The Government of India Act of 1935 proposed a federal status linking the British Indian provinces with the many princely states; in addition, provincial legislatures were to be created. The federal status was never implemented, but the legislatures were created after the election of 1937, with the National Congress winning majorities in most of the provinces.

When Britain declared war on Germany in Sept. 1939, the viceroy declared India also to be at war with a common enemy. The Congress, however, demanded independence as a condition for cooperation; Britain refused. But as the Japanese advanced into Asia, Britain offered to transfer to Indians power over all but military affairs during the war, and set forth a plan for postwar independence. Congress was willing to accept the wartime transfer of power, but both Congress and the Muslim League rejected Britain's plan for independence; Congress because it did not sufficiently safeguard Indian untiy, the Muslims (who wanted a separate Muslim state) because of fears of what would happen to Muslims within a united India.

Early in 1947, Prime Minister Clement Attlee announced that Britain would leave India "by a date not later than June 1948," even though the Hindus and Muslims could not agree among themselves on a plan for self-government. The National Congress, aware that the Muslim League would revolt rather than accept an all-India government, reluctantly agreed to the formation of a separate Muslim state. The Muslim-majority provinces of the North West Frontier. Sindh and West Punjab in the west, and East Bengal in the east were separated from India to form the Muslim state of Pakistan, which became independent on Aug. 14, 1947. India became independent on the following day.

The Republic of India is a member of the Commonwealth of Nations. The president is the Chief of State. The prime minister is the Head of Government.

MINT MARKS

(Most mint marks appear directly below the date.)

B - Bombay, proof issues only
(B) - Bombay, diamond or dot
C - Canadian, Winnipeg
(C) - Calcutta, no mint mark
H - Heaton Mint, Birmingham
(H) - Hyderabad, star
(Hd) - Hyderabad, split diamond
(Hy) - Hyderabad, dot in diamond
(x) - Uncertain, diamond under first date digit
(y) - Uncertain, star under first date digit
(z) - Uncertain, star under last date digit

MONETARY SYSTEM

(Until 1957)

4 Pice = 1 Anna
16 Annas = 1 Rupee

PICE

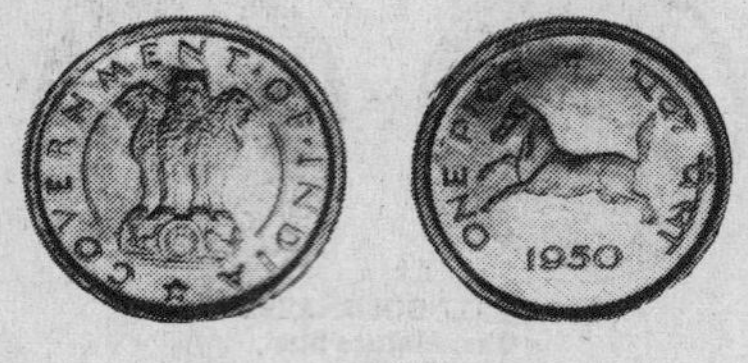

BRONZE
Var. 1: 1.6mm thick, 0.3mm edge rim

KM#	Date	Mintage	VF	XF	Unc
565.1	1950(B)	32.080	.35	.60	1.25

Var. 2: 1.6mm thick, 1.0mm edge rim

KM#	Date	Mintage	VF	XF	Unc
565.2	1950(B)	Inc. Ab.	.20	.30	.60
	1950(B)	—	—	Proof	1.50
	1950(C)	14.000	.20	.30	.60

Var. 3: 1.2mm thick, 0.8mm edge rim

KM#	Date	Mintage	VF	XF	Unc
566	1951(B)	104.626	.10	.15	.35
	1951(C)	127.300	.10	.15	.35
	1952(B)	213.830	.10	.15	.35
	1953(B)	242.358	.10	.15	.35
	1953(C)	111.000	.10	.15	.35
	1953(Hd)	Inc. Ab.	10.00	15.00	20.00
	1954(B)	136.758	.10	.15	.35
	1954(B)	—	—	Proof	1.50
	1954(C)	52.600	.10	.15	.35
	1954(Hd)	Inc. Ab.	5.00	8.00	12.00
	1955(B)	24.423	.15	.25	.50
	1955(Hd)	Inc. Ab.	6.00	10.00	15.00

NOTE: A variety of 1954Hd exists with mint mark split horizontally, instead of vertically.

1/2 ANNA

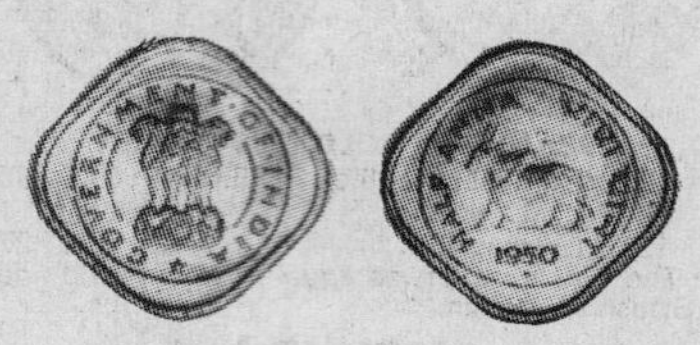

COPPER-NICKEL

KM#	Date	Mintage	VF	XF	Unc
567	1950(B)	26.076	.10	.25	.35
	1950(B)	—	—	Proof	1.50
	1950(C)	3.100	.50	.75	1.50
	1954(B)	14.000	.10	.25	.40
	1954(B)	—	—	Proof	1.50
	1954(C)	20.800	.10	.25	.40
	1955(B)	22.488	.10	.25	.35

NOTE: Varieties of date size exist.

ANNA

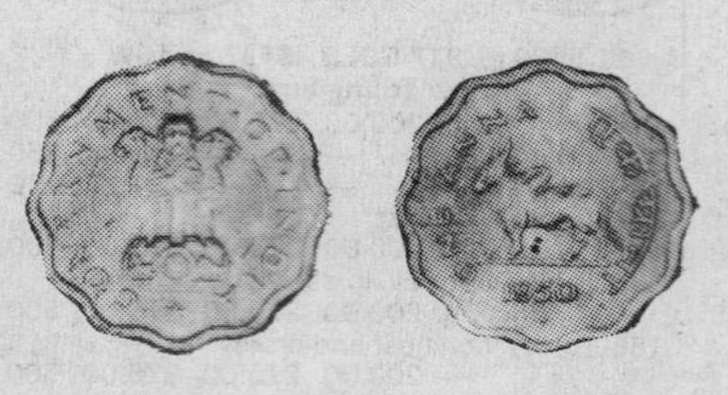

COPPER-NICKEL

KM#	Date	Mintage	VF	XF	Unc
568	1950(B)	9.944	.25	.50	1.00
	1950(B)	—	—	Proof	1.50
	1954(B)	20.388	.10	.25	.50
	1954(B)	—	—	Proof	1.50
	1955(B)	—	4.00	6.00	8.00

2 ANNAS

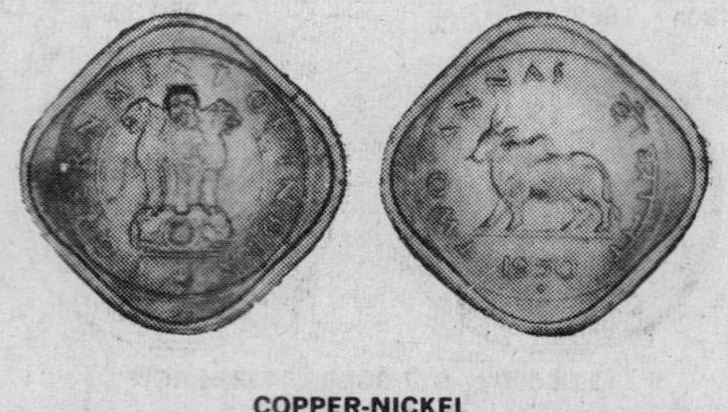

COPPER-NICKEL

KM#	Date	Mintage	VF	XF	Unc
569	1950(B)	7.536	.25	.50	1.50
	1950(B)	—	—	Proof	1.50
	1954(B)	10.548	.25	.50	1.25
	1954(B)	—	—	Proof	1.50
	1955(B)	—	4.00	6.00	8.00

1/4 RUPEE

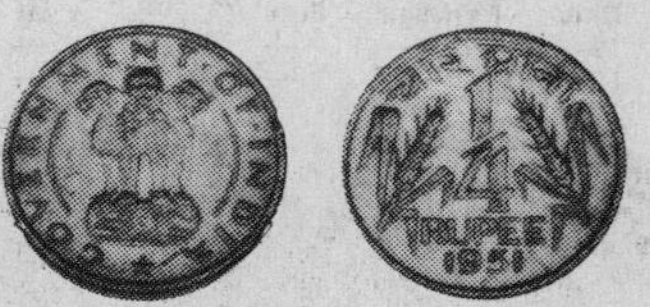

NICKEL
Var. 1: Large lion

KM#	Date	Mintage	VF	XF	Unc
570	1950(B)	7.650	.30	.60	1.50
	1950(B)	—	—	Proof	1.50
	1950(C)	7.800	.30	.60	1.50
	1951(B)	41.439	.25	.50	1.00
	1951(C)	13.500	.25	.50	1.00
	1954(B)	—	—	Proof	1.50
	1954(C)	58.300	.25	.50	1.25
	1955(B)	57.936	.50	1.00	2.50

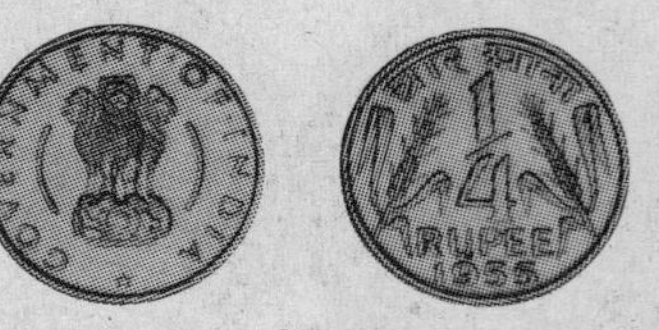

Var. 2: Small lion

KM#	Date	Mintage	VF	XF	Unc
571	1954(C)	Inc. Ab.	.25	.40	.75
	1955(C)	28.900	.25	.40	.75
	1956(C)	22.000	.25	.50	1.00

1/2 RUPEE

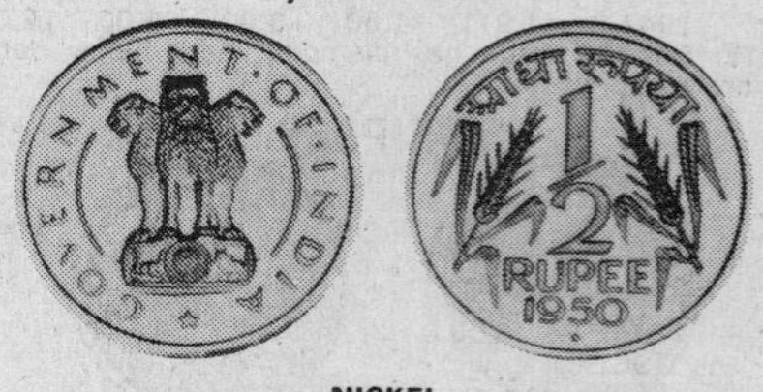

NICKEL
Var. 1: Large lion

KM#	Date	Mintage	VF	XF	Unc
572	1950(B)	12.352	.50	1.00	1.50
	1950(B)	—	—	Proof	2.00
	1950(C)	1.100	.75	1.50	3.00
	1951(B)	9.239	.75	1.50	2.50
	1954(B)	—	—	Proof	2.00
	1954(C)	36.300	.40	1.00	1.50
	1955(B)	18.977	.75	1.50	2.50

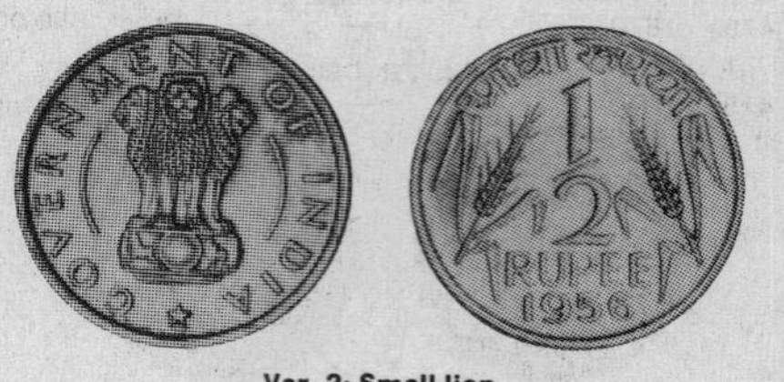

Var. 2: Small lion
Obv: Dots missing between words.

KM#	Date	Mintage	VF	XF	Unc
573	1956(C)	24.900	.25	.40	1.00

RUPEE

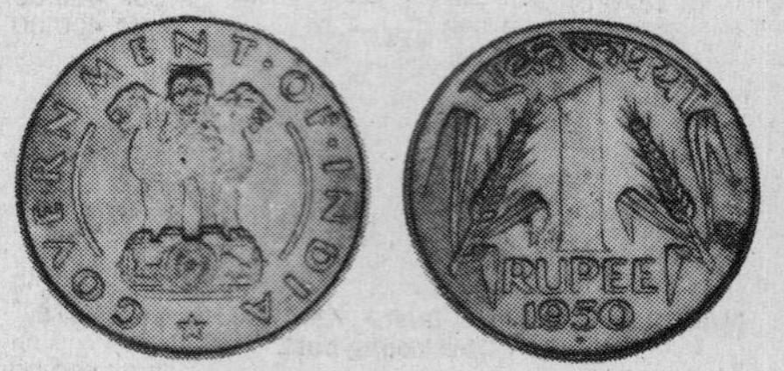

NICKEL

KM#	Date	Mintage	VF	XF	Unc
574	1950(B)	19.412	1.25	2.00	4.00
	1950(B)	—	—	Proof	3.00
	1954(B)	Inc. Ab.	2.00	3.00	5.00
	1954(B)	—	—	Proof	3.00

DECIMAL COINAGE

100 Naye Paise = 1 Rupee (1957-63)
100 Paise = 1 Rupee (1964-)

NOTE: The Paisa was at first called "Naya Paisa" (= New Paisa), so that people would distinguish from the old non-decimal Paisa (or Pice, equal to 1/64 Rupee). After 7 years, the word 'new' was dropped, and the coin was simply called a "Paisa".

NOTE: Many of the Paisa standard types come with two obverse varieties: (three varieties for 25 Paise).

OBV. I: Asoka lion pedestal small. Short, squat 'D' in 'INDIA'.

OBV. II: Asoka lion pedestal larger. Lettering closer to rim. Tall, more elegant "D" in "INDIA". The shape of the "D" in INDIA is the easiest way to distinguish the 2 obverses.

Obv I   Obv II

NOTE: Paisa standard pieces with mint mark B, 1969 to date, were struck only in proof.

NOTE: Indian mintage figures are not divided by mint, and often include dates other than the year in which struck. They should be regarded with reserve.

NAYA PAISA

BRONZE

KM#	Date	Mintage	VF	XF	Unc
575	1957(B)	618.630	—	.10	.25
	1957(C)	Inc. Ab.	—	.10	.25
	1957(Hd)	Inc. Ab.	.10	.20	.35
	1958(B)	468.630	.20	.30	.50
	1958(Hd)	Inc. Ab.	.10	.20	.35
	1959(B)	351.120	.10	.20	.35
	1959(C)	Inc. Ab.	.10	.15	.25
	1959(Hd)	Inc. Ab.	.10	.20	.35
	1960(B)	357.940	—	.10	.20
	1960(C)	—	—	Proof	1.00
	1960(B)	Inc. Ab.	.80	1.50	2.50
	1960(Hd)	Inc. Ab.	3.25	4.00	5.00
	1961(B)	573.170	—	.10	.20
	1961(B)	—	—	Proof	1.00
	1961(C)	Inc. Ab.	.10	.15	.25
	1961(Hy)	Inc. Ab.	.50	.75	1.25
	1962(B)	—	5.00	6.50	8.00

NOTE: 1962(B) has only been found in some of the 1962 uncirculated mint sets.
NOTE: Varieties of the split diamond have been reported.

NICKEL-BRASS

575a	1962(B)	235.103	.10	.15	.25
	1962(B)	—	—	Proof	1.00
	1962(C)	Inc. Ab.	.10	.15	.30
	1962(Hy)	Inc. Ab.	.50	.75	1.25
	1963(B)	343.313	.10	.15	.25
	1963(B)	—	—	Proof	1.00
	1963(C)	Inc. Ab.	.25	.50	1.00
	1963(H)	Inc. Ab.	.10	.25	.40

PAISA

NICKEL-BRASS
Obverse 1

582	1964(B)	539.068	—	.10	.25
	1964(C)	Inc. Ab.	—	.10	.20
	1964(H)	Inc. Ab.	—	.10	.25

BRONZE

582a	1964(H)	Inc. Ab.	.35	.50	1.00

ALUMINUM
Obverse 1

592	1965(B)	223.480	.20	.35	.60
	1965(Hy)	Inc. Ab.	.15	.25	.40
	1966(B)	404.200	.10	.20	.30
	1966(C)	Inc. Ab.	.15	.30	.50
	1966(Hy)	Inc. Ab.	—	.10	.15
	1967(B)	450.433	—	.10	.25
	1967(C)	Inc. Ab.	—	.10	.20
	1967(Hy)	Inc. Ab.	—	.10	.15
	1968(B)	302.720	—	—	.10
	1968(C)	Inc. Ab.	—	.10	.20
	1968(Hy)	Inc. Ab.	—	—	.10
	1969(B)	125.930	.30	.50	.80
	1969B	9,147	—	Proof	
	1969(H)	Inc. Ab.	.30	.50	.80
	1970(B)	15.800	—	.10	.25
	1970B	3,046	—	Proof	.25
	1971B	4,375	—	Proof	.25
	1971(H)	112.100	—	—	.10
	1972(B)	62.090	—	—	.10
	1972B	7,895	—	Proof	.25
	1972(H)	Inc. Ab.	—	—	.10
	1973B	7,562	—	Proof	.10

KM#	Date	Mintage	VF	XF	Unc
592	1974B	—	—	Proof	.10
	1975B	—	—	Proof	.10
	1976B	—	—	Proof	.10
	1977B	—	—	Proof	.10
	1978B	—	—	Proof	.10
	1979B	—	—	Proof	.10
	1980B	—	—	Proof	.10
	1981B	—	—	Proof	.10

NOTE: 1970(B) is found only in the uncirculated sets of that year. It has a mirrorlike surface.

Obverse 2

606	1969(C)	Inc. Ab.	.20	.25	.40
	1970(C)	Inc. Ab.	—	—	.10

2 NAYE PAISE

COPPER-NICKEL

576	1957(B)	406.230	—	.10	.25
	1957(C)	Inc. Ab.	—	.10	.25
	1958(B)	245.660	—	.10	.25
	1958(C)	Inc. Ab.	.10	.15	.30
	1959(B)	171.445	—	.10	.20
	1959(C)	Inc. Ab.	.25	.40	.80
	1960(B)	121.820	—	.10	.25
	1960(B)	—	—	Proof	1.00
	1960(C)	Inc. Ab.	.10	.10	.25
	1961(B)	190.610	—	.10	.20
	1961(B)	—	—	Proof	1.00
	1961(C)	Inc. Ab.	.10	.15	.20
	1962(B)	318.181	—	.10	.20
	1962(B)	—	—	Proof	1.00
	1962(C)	Inc. Ab.	—	.10	.20
	1963(B)	372.380	—	.10	.20
	1963(B)	—	—	Proof	1.00
	1963(C)	Inc. Ab.	—	—	.20

2 PAISE

COPPER-NICKEL
Obverse 1

583	1964(B)	323.504	—	.10	.15
	1964(C)	Inc. Ab.	—	.10	.15

ALUMINUM
Obverse 1. Rev: 10mm '2'.

593	1965(B)	175.770	—	.10	.20
	1965(C)	Inc. Ab.	.10	.20	.35
	1966(B)	386.795	—	.10	.15
	1966(C)	Inc. Ab.	—	.10	.15
	1967(B)	454.593	—	.10	.25

Obverse 1. Rev: 10-1/2mm '2'.

595	1967(C)	Inc. Ab.	—	—	.15

Obverse 2. Rev: 10mm '2'.

596	1967(B)	—	.50	1.00	1.50

Obverse 1. Rev: 11mm '2'.

602	1968(C)	—	.50	1.25	2.50
	1977B	—	—	.10	.15
	1978(B)	—	—	.15	.30

Obverse 2. Rev: 11mm '2'.

603	1968(B)	305.205	—	—	.10
	1968(C)	Inc. Ab.	—	.10	.25
	1969(B)	5.335	1.00	1.50	2.00
	1969B	9,147	—	Proof	.25
	1970(B)	—	.50	1.00	1.50
	1970B	3,046	—	Proof	.25
	1970(C)	79.100	—	—	.10
	1971B	4,375	—	Proof	.25
	1971(C)	207.900	—	—	.10
	1972(B)	7,895	—	Proof	.25
	1972(C)	261.270	—	.10	
	1972(H)	Inc. Ab.	—	—	.10
	1973B	7,562	—	Proof	.15
	1973(C)	—	—	.10	.20
	1973(H)	—	—	—	.10
	1974B	—	—	Proof	.15

KM#	Date	Mintage	VF	XF	Unc
603	1974(C)	—	—	—	.10
	1974(H)	—	—	—	.10
	1975B	—	—	Proof	.15
	1975(C)	184.500	—	—	.10
	1975(H)	Inc. Ab.	—	—	.10
	1976(B)	68.140	—	—	.10
	1976B	—	—	Proof	.15
	1976(H)	—	—	—	.10
	1977(C)	251.955	—	—	.10
	1977B	—	—	Proof	.15
	1977(H)	Inc. Ab.	—	—	.10
	1978(B)	144.010	—	—	.10
	1978B	—	—	Proof	.10
	1978(H)	Inc. Ab.	—	—	.10
	1979B	—	—	Proof	.10
	1980B	—	—	Proof	.10
	1981B	—	—	Proof	.10

NOTE: 1970(B) is found only in the uncirculated sets of that year. It has a mirrorlike surface.

3 PAISE

ALUMINUM
Obverse 1

584	1964(B)	138.890	—	—	.10
	1964(C)	Inc. Ab.	—	.10	.20
	1965(B)	459.825	—	.10	.15
	1965(C)	Inc. Ab.	.10	.20	.35
	1966(B)	390.440	—	—	.10
	1966(C)	Inc. Ab.	—	.10	.15
	1966(Hy)	Inc. Ab.	.20	.35	.50
	1967(B)	167.018	—	.10	.35
	1967(C)	Inc. Ab.	—	—	.10
	1967(H)	Inc. Ab.	.30	.50	.75
	1968(B)	—	.30	.50	1.00

Obverse 2

597	1967(C)	—	.30	.75	1.25
	1967(H)	Inc. Ab.	.30	.75	1.25
	1968(B)	246.390	—	.10	.20
	1968(C)	Inc. Ab.	.30	.45	.70
	1968(H)	Inc. Ab.	—	.10	.20
	1969B	9,147	—	Proof	.25
	1969(C)	7.025	—	.10	.20
	1969(H)	Inc. Ab.	.40	.60	1.00
	1970(B)	—	1.00	1.50	2.50
	1970B	3,046	—	—	.25
	1970(C)	15.300	—	—	.10
	1971B	4,375	—	Proof	.25
	1971(C)	203.100	—	—	.10
	1971(H)	Inc. Ab.	—	—	.10

NOTE: 1970(B) is found only in the uncirculated sets of that year. It has a mirrorlike surface.

Obverse 2

617	1972B	7,895	—	Proof	.25
	1973B	7,562	—	Proof	.20
	1974B	—	—	Proof	.20
	1975B	—	—	Proof	.20
	1976B	—	—	Proof	.20
	1977B	—	—	Proof	.20
	1978B	—	—	Proof	.20
	1979B	—	—	Proof	.20
	1980B	—	—	Proof	.20
	1981B	—	—	Proof	.20

5 NAYE PAISE

COPPER-NICKEL

577	1957(B)	227.210	.10	.20	.40
	1957(C)	Inc. Ab.	.10	.20	.40

Republic / INDIA 992

KM#	Date	Mintage	VF	XF	Unc
577	1958(B)	214.320	.10	.20	.40
	1958(C)	Inc. Ab.	.10	.20	.40
	1959(B)	137.105	.10	.20	.40
	1959(C)	Inc. Ab.	.15	.40	.90
	1960(B)	93.345	.10	.25	.60
	1960(B)	—	—	Proof	1.50
	1960(C)	Inc. Ab.	.10	.30	.75
	1960(Hy)	Inc. Ab.	.50	1.00	2.00
	1961(B)	197.620	.10	.15	.30
	1961(B)	—	—	Proof	1.50
	1961(C)	Inc. Ab.	.25	.50	1.00
	1961(Hy)	Inc. Ab.	1.00	2.00	3.00
	1962(B)	224.277	.10	.15	.35
	1962(B)	—	—	Proof	1.50
	1962(C)	Inc. Ab.	.10	.15	.35
	1962(Hy)	Inc. Ab.	.50	1.00	2.00
	1963(B)	332.600	.10	.15	.30
	1963(B)	—	—	Proof	1.50
	1963(C)	Inc. Ab.	.15	.45	.70
	1963(H)	Inc. Ab.	.75	1.50	2.50

5 PAISE

COPPER-NICKEL
Obverse 1

585	1964(B)	156.000	.40	.60	1.00
	1964(C)	Inc. Ab.	.25	.45	.70
	1964(H)	Inc. Ab.	.75	1.50	2.50
	1965(B)	203.855	.10	.20	.35
	1965(C)	Inc. Ab.	.25	.45	.70
	1965(H)	Inc. Ab.	1.25	2.00	3.00
	1966(B)	101.395	.40	.60	1.00
	1966(C)	Inc. Ab.	.25	.45	.70

ALUMINUM
6mm Short 5   7mm Tall 5
6.5mm Medium 5
Obverse 1
Rev: Short 5.

598.1	1967(B)	608.533	.10	.15	.50

Rev: Medium 5.

598.2	1967(B)	Inc.Ab.	.15	.25	.75
	1967(c)	Inc.Ab.	.15	.25	.75

Rev: Tall 5.

598.3	1967(B)	Inc.Ab.	.25	.50	1.00
	1967(c)	Inc.Ab.	.25	.50	1.00
	1967(H)	Inc.Ab.	—	.10	.20
	1968(B)	—	2.00	3.00	4.00
	1968(C)	—	.75	1.50	3.00
	1968(H)	666.750	.70	1.00	1.50
	1971(H)	499.200	—	.10	.15

Obverse 2

599	1967(H)	—	1.25	1.75	2.75
	1968(B)	Inc. KM598	—	.10	.15
	1968(C)	Inc. KM598	—	.10	.15
	1968(H)	Inc. KM598	.10	.15	.40
	1969(B)	3.740	.75	1.50	2.50
	1969B	9,147	—	Proof	.25
	1970(B)	39.900	.15	.25	.50
	1970B	3,046	—	Proof	.25
	1970(C)	Inc. Ab.	.15	.25	.40
	1970(H)	Inc. Ab.	.20	.40	.60
	1971(B)	Inc. w/1971(H) of KM598			
			—	.10	.15
	1971B	4,375	—	Proof	.25
	1971(C)	Inc. Ab.	—	.10	.15
	1971(H)		—	.10	.15

Obverse 1

618	1972(H)	512.430	—	.10	.15

Rev: Larger 5.

626	1973(B)	—	1.50	2.00	3.00
	1977(B)	—	—	—	.10
	1978(B)	—	—	—	.10

Obverse 2

KM#	Date	Mintage	VF	XF	Unc
619	1972(B)	Inc. KM618	—	.10	.15
	1972B	7,895	—	Proof	.25
	1972(C)	Inc. KM618	—	.10	.15
	1972(H)	—	1.00	2.00	3.00
	1973(B)	—	—	.10	.15
	1973B	7,562	—	Proof	.25
	1973(C)	—	—	.10	.15
	1974(B)	—	—	Proof	.25
	1974(C)	—	—	.10	.15
	1975(B)	—	—	.10	.15
	1976(B)	53.205	—	.10	.20
	1976(H)	—	—	.10	.15
	1979(H)	—	—	.10	.20

Rev: Larger 5.

627	1973(B)	—	—	.10	.15
	1974(B)	—	—	.10	.15
	1974(H)	—	—	.10	.15
	1975(B)	—	—	.10	.15
	1975B	—	—	Proof	.25
	1975(C)	289.080	—	.10	.15
	1975(H)	Inc. Ab.	—	.10	.15
	1976(C)	—	—	.10	.15
	1977(B)	257.900	—	.10	.15
	1977(C)	Inc. Ab.	—	.10	.20
	1977(H)	Inc. Ab.	—	.10	.20
	1978(C)	—	—	.10	.20
	1978(H)	—	—	.10	.20
	1979(B)	—	—	.10	.20
	1980(B)	21.440	—	.10	.20
	1980B	—	—	Proof	.20
	1980(C)	Inc. Ab.	—	.10	.20
	1980(H)	Inc. Ab.	—	.10	.20
	1981B	—	—	Proof	.20
	1981(C)	4.365	—	.10	.20
	1981(H)	Inc. Ab.	—	.10	.20
	1982(B)	3.499	—	Proof	.20
	1982(C)	Inc. Ab.	—	.10	.20
	1982(H)	Inc. Ab.	—	.10	.20
	1983(B)	3.110	—	.10	.20
	1983(C)	Inc. Ab.	—	.10	.20
	1983(H)	Inc. Ab.	—	.10	.20
	1984(B)	28.265	—	.10	.20
	1984(H)	Inc. Ab.	—	.10	.20

NOTE: Due to faulty dies, 1981(H) often resembles the non-existant 1981(B).

F.A.O. Issue, FOOD & WORK FOR ALL

640	1976(B)	34.680	—	.10	.25
	1976B	—	—	Proof	.25
	1976(C)	60.040	—	.10	.25
	1976(H)	60.290	—	.10	.25

F.A.O. Issue, SAVE FOR DEVELOPMENT

644	1977(B)	20.100	—	.10	.20
	1977B	2,224	—	Proof	.25
	1977(C)	40.470	—	.10	.20
	1977(H)	—	—	.10	.20

F.A.O. Issue, FOOD & SHELTER FOR ALL

648	1978(B)	17.440	—	.10	.20
	1978B	—	—	Proof	.25
	1978(C)	30.870	—	.10	.20
	1978(H)	—	—	.10	.20

International Year of the Child

KM#	Date	Mintage	VF	XF	Unc
652	1979(B)	—	—	.10	.15
	1979B	—	—	Proof	.25
	1979(C)	—	—	.10	.15
	1979(H)	—	—	.10	.15

691	1985(B)	—	—	.15	.20
	1985(H)	—	—	.10	.15
	1986(B)	—	—	.15	.15
	1986(C)	—	—	.15	.20
	1986(H)	—	—	.10	.15
	1987(H)	—	—	.15	.15

10 NAYE PAISE

COPPER-NICKEL
Rev: 6.5mm "10".

578.1	1957(B)	139.655	.15	.30	.50
	1957(C)	Inc. Ab.	.15	.30	.50

Rev: 7mm "10".

578.2	1958(B)	123.160	.15	.30	.50
	1958(C)	Inc. Ab.	.25	.50	1.00
	1959(B)	148.570	.15	.30	.50
	1959(C)	Inc. Ab.	.15	.50	.50
	1960(B)	52.335	.15	.30	.50
	1960(B)	—	—	Proof	1.50
	1961(B)	172.545	.15	.30	.50
	1961(B)	—	—	Proof	1.50
	1961(C)	Inc. Ab.	—	.30	.50
	1961(Hy)	Inc. Ab.	1.75	2.50	4.00
	1962(B)	172.777	.15	.30	.50
	1962(B)	—	—	Proof	1.50
	1962(C)	Inc. Ab.	.15	.30	.50
	1962(Hy)	Inc. Ab.	1.00	1.50	2.50
	1963(B)	182.834	.10	.20	.45
	1963(B)	—	—	Proof	1.50
	1963(C)	Inc. Ab.	.10	.20	.45
	1963(H)	Inc. Ab.	.60	1.00	2.00

10 PAISE

COPPER-NICKEL
Obverse 1. Rev: 6.5mm '10'.

586	1964(B) open 4				
		84.112	.10	.20	.45
	1964(B) closed 4				
		Inc. Ab.	1.50	2.00	3.00
	1964(C)	Inc. Ab.	.15	.30	.60
	1964(H)	Inc. Ab.	1.00	1.50	2.50
	1965(B)	253.430	—	.10	.40
	1965(C)	—	—	—	.40
	1965(Hy)	Inc. Ab.	1.00	1.50	2.50
	1965(H)	Inc. Ab.	.75	1.25	2.00
	1966(B)	326.990	—	.10	.40
	1966(C)	Inc. Ab.	—	—	.40
	1966(Hy)	Inc. Ab.	.20	.35	.65
	1967(B)	59.443	.30	.50	.75
	1967(C)	Inc. Ab.	.30	.50	.75
	1967(H)	Inc. Ab.	.40	.75	1.25

NICKEL-BRASS
Obverse 1

604	1968(H)	55.940	2.00	3.00	4.00

Republic / INDIA **993**

Obverse 2. Rev: 6.5mm '10'.

KM#	Date	Mintage	VF	XF	Unc
605	1968(B)	Inc. KM604	.10	.20	.35
	1968(C)	Inc. KM604	.10	.15	.25
	1968(H)	Inc. KM604	.10	.20	.35

Obverse 2. Rev: 7mm '10'.

607	1969(B)	65.405	.10	.15	.25
	1969B	9,147	—	Proof	.25
	1969(C)	Inc. Ab.	.10	.30	.50
	1969(H)	Inc. Ab.	.10	.15	.25
	1970(B)	48.400	.10	.15	.50
	1970B	3,046	—	Proof	.25
	1970(C)	Inc. Ab.	.10	.20	.35
	1971(B)	88.800	.10	.15	.25
	1971B	4,375	—	Proof	.25

ALUMINUM
Obverse 2

615	1971(B)	146.100	—	.10	.15
	1971(C)	Inc. Ab.	—	.10	.15
	1971(H)	Inc. Ab.	.15	.30	.50
	1972(B)	735.090	—	.10	.15
	1972B	7,895	—	Proof	.25
	1972(C)	Inc. Ab.	—	.10	.15
	1973(B)	—	—	.10	.15
	1973B	7,567	—	Proof	.25
	1973(C)	—	—	.10	.15
	1973(H)	—	.10	.15	.30
	1974(B)	—	—	.10	.20
	1974(C)	—	—	.10	.20
	1974(H)	—	.10	.25	.50
	1975(B)	—	.10	.15	.25
	1975	298.830	—	.10	.15
	1976(C)	Inc. Ab.	.25	.50	1.00
	1977(B)	25.288	—	.10	.15
	1977(C)	Inc. Ab.	—	.10	.15
	1978(B)	48.215	—	.10	.15
	1978(C)	Inc. Ab.	—	.10	.15
	1978(H)	Inc. Ab.	—	.10	.15
	1979(B)	—	—	.10	.15
	1979(C)	—	—	.10	.15
	1979(H)	—	—	.10	.15
	1980(B)	—	—	.10	.15
	1980(C)	—	—	.10	.15
	1980(H)	—	—	.10	.15
	1981(B)	—	—	.10	.15
	1981(C)	—	—	.10	.15
	1982(C)	—	—	.10	.15
	1982(H)	—	—	.10	.15

NOTE: Varieties of value size exist.

F. A. O. Issue

631	1974(B)	146.070	—	.10	.15
	1974B	—	—	Proof	.25
	1974(C)	168.500	—	.10	.20
	1974(H)	10.010	.15	.25	.50

F.A.O. Issue, EQUALITY, DEVELOPMENT, PEACE

KM#	Date	Mintage	VF	XF	Unc
635	1975(B)	69.160	—	.10	.15
	1975B	—	—	Proof	.25
	1975(C)	84.820	—	.10	.15

NOTE: Mint mark is below wheat stalk.

F.A.O. Issue, FOOD & WORK FOR ALL

641	1976(B)	36.040	—	.10	.15
	1976B	—	—	Proof	.25
	1976(C)	26.180	—	.10	.15

F.A.O. Issue, SAVE FOR DEVELOPMENT

645	1977(B)	17.040	—	.10	.15
	1977B	2,224	—	Proof	.25
	1977(C)	8.020	—	.10	.15

F.A.O. Issue, FOOD & SHELTER FOR ALL

649	1978(B)	24.470	—	.10	.15
	1978B	—	—	Proof	.25
	1978(C)	26.160	.25	.50	2.00
	1978(H)	Inc. Ab.	—	.10	.15

International Year of the Child

653	1979(B)	—	—	.10	.15
	1979B	—	—	Proof	.25
	1979(C)	—	—	.10	.15
	1979(H)	—	.20	.40	.60

Mule. Obv: KM#649. Rev: KM#653.

| 654 | 1979(B) | — | 5.00 | 7.50 | 10.00 |

Rural Women's Advancement

658	1980(B)	62.639	—	.10	.15
	1980B	—	—	Proof	.25
	1980(C)	Inc. Ab.	—	.10	.15
	1980(H)	Inc. Ab.	—	.10	.15

 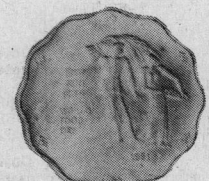

F.A.O. Issue

662	1981(B)	75.905	—	.10	.15
	1981B	—	—	Proof	.25
	1981(C)	Inc. Ab.	—	.10	.15

IX Asian Games

KM#	Date	Mintage	VF	XF	Unc
667	1982(B)	84.128	—	.10	.15
	1982B	—	—	Proof	.25
	1982(C)	Inc. Ab.	—	.10	.15
	1982(H)	Inc. Ab.	—	.10	.15

World Food Day

668	1982(C)	Inc. Ab.	—	.10	.15
	1982(H)	Inc. Ab.	—	.10	.15

677	1983(B)	—	—	.10	.15
	1983(C)	—	—	.10	.15
	1983(H)	—	—	.10	.15
	1984(B)	112.050	—	.10	.15
	1984(C)	Inc. Ab.	—	.10	.15
	1984(H)	Inc. Ab.	—	.10	.15
	1985(B)	—	—	.10	.15
	1985(C)	—	—	.10	.15
	1985(H)	—	—	.10	.15
	1986(B)	—	—	.10	.15
	1986(C)	—	—	.10	.15
	1986(H)	—	—	.10	.15
	1987(C)	—	Reported, not confirmed		
	1987(H)	—	—	.10	.15
	1988(B)	—	—	.10	.15
	1988(C)	—	—	.10	.15

STAINLESS STEEL

| 702 | 1988(c) | — | — | — | .10 |

20 PAISE

NICKEL-BRASS

564	1968(B)	10.585	.15	.25	.50
(605)	1968(C)	Inc. Ab.	.20	.40	.75
	1969(B)	197.940	.10	.15	.35
	1969(C)	—	.10	.15	.35
	1970(B)	Inc. Ab.	.10	.15	.35
	1970(C)	Inc. Ab.	.10	.15	.35
	1970(H)	Inc. Ab.	.10	.15	.35
	1971(B)	124.200	.10	.15	.35

ALUMINUM-BRONZE
Mahatma Gandhi Centennial

608	ND(1969)(B)	45.010	.10	.15	.75
	ND(1969)B	9,147	—	Proof	.25
	ND(1969)(C)	45.070	.10	.15	.75
	ND(1969)(H)	3.000	.25	.50	1.00

NOTE: Struck during 1969 and 1970.

Republic / INDIA 994

F.A.O. Issue, FOOD FOR ALL
Wide rims.

KM#	Date	Mintage	VF	XF	Unc
612	1970(B)	5.160	.25	.50	1.00
	1970B	3,046	—	Proof	.25
	1970(C)	5.010	.25	.50	1.00

Narrow rims.

616	1971(B)	.060	.15	.30	.60
	1971B	4,375	—	Proof	.25

ALUMINUM

669	1982(B)	—	—	.10	.20
	1982(H)	—	—	.10	.20
	1983(C)	28.505	—	.10	.20
	1983(H)	Inc. Ab.	—	.10	.20
	1984(B)	72.163	—	.10	.20
	1984(C)	Inc. Ab.	—	.10	.20
	1984(H)	Inc. Ab.	—	.10	.20
	1985(B)	—	—	.10	.20
	1985(C)	—	—	.10	.20
	1985(H)	—	—	.10	.20
	1986(B)	—	—	.10	.20
	1986(C)	—	—	.10	.20
	1986(H)	—	—	.10	.20
	1987(C)	—	Reported, not confirmed		
	1987(H)	—	—	.10	.20
	1988(B)	—	—	.10	.20
	1988(H)	—	—	.10	.20

FAO - Fisheries

678	1983(B)	Inc. KM669	.10	.20	.50
	1983(C)	Inc. KM669	.10	.20	.50
	1983(H)	Inc. KM669	.10	.20	.50

F.A.O. Issue
Similar to 10 Paise, KM#668.

685	1982(B)	—	.10	.20	.50
	1982(C)	—	.10	.20	.50
	1982(H)	—	.10	.20	.50

25 NAYE PAISE

NICKEL
Rev: Small 25.

579.1	1957(B)	5.640	.40	.75	1.50
	1957(C)	Inc. Ab.	.40	.75	1.50
	1959(B)	43.080	.20	.40	.75
	1959(C)	Inc. Ab.	.15	.30	.50
	1960(B)	115.320	.15	.30	.50
	1960(B)	—	—	Proof	2.00
	1960(C)	Inc. Ab.	.15	.30	.50

Rev: Large 25.

579.2	1961(B)	109.008	.15	.30	.50
	1961(B)	—	.15	Proof	2.00
	1961(C)	Inc. Ab.	.15	.30	.50
	1962(B)	79.242	.15	.30	.50
	1962(B)	—	.15	Proof	2.00
	1962(C)	Inc. Ab.	.15	.30	.50
	1963(B)	101.565	.15	.30	.50
	1963(B)	—	.15	Proof	2.00
	1963(C)	Inc. Ab.	.15	.30	.50

25 PAISE

NICKEL
Obverse 1, Reverse 1

KM#	Date	Mintage	VF	XF	Unc
587	1964(B)	85.321	.10	.25	.50
	1964(C)	Inc. Ab.	.10	.25	.50

Obverse 1, Reverse 2

594	1965(B)	143.662	.10	.20	.40
	1965(C)	Inc. Ab.	.10	.20	.40
	1966(B)	59.040	.10	.20	.40
	1966(C)	Inc. Ab.	.15	.30	.60
	1967(B)	30.027	2.00	3.00	4.00

Obverse 2, Reverse 2

600	1967(C)	Inc. KM594	.15	.30	.60
	1968(C)	Inc. KM594	.20	.40	.80

COPPER-NICKEL
Obverse 1

620	1972(B)	367.640	—	.10	.30
	1972B	7,895	—	Proof	.35
	1972(H)	Inc. Ab.	—	.10	.40
	1973(B)	—	—	.10	.30
	1973B	7,567	—	Proof	.35
	1973(H)	—	—	.10	.30
	1974(B)	—	—	.10	.25
	1974B	—	—	Proof	.35
	1974(H)	—	—	.10	.35
	1975(B)	559.980	—	.10	.25
	1975B	—	—	Proof	.35
	1975(H)	Inc. Ab.	—	.10	.25
	1976(B)	30.016	—	.10	.25
	1976B	Inc. Ab.	—	Proof	.35
	1976(H)	Inc. Ab.	—	.10	.25
	1977(B)	270.520	—	.10	.25
	1977B	Inc. Ab.	—	Proof	.35
	1977(C)	Inc. Ab.	—	.10	.40
	1977(H)	Inc. Ab.	—	.10	.25
	1978(B)	131.632	—	.10	.25
	1978B	Inc. Ab.	—	Proof	.35
	1978(C)	—	—	.10	.25
	1978(H)	—	—	.10	.25
	1979(B)	—	—	.10	.25
	1979(C)	—	—	.10	.25
	1979(H)	—	.20	.35	.75
	1980(B)	6.175	—	.10	.25
	1980(C)	Inc. Ab.	—	.10	.25
	1980(H)	Inc. Ab.	—	.10	.30
	1981(B)	11.048	—	.10	.30
	1981(C)	Inc. Ab.	.50	.75	1.50
	1981(H)	Inc. Ab.	—	.10	.25
	1982(B)	38.288	—	.10	.25
	1983(C)	137.488	—	.10	.20
	1984(B)	98.740	—	.10	.20
	1984(C)	Inc. Ab.	—	.10	.20
	1985(B)	—	—	.10	.20
	1985C	—	—	.10	.20
	1985(H)	—	—	.10	.20
	1986(B)	—	—	.10	.20
	1986(C)	—	—	.10	.20
	1986(H)	—	—	.10	.20
	1987(B)	—	—	.10	.20
	1987(C)	—	—	.10	.20
	1987(H)	—	—	.10	.20
	1988(B)	—	—	.10	.20
	1988(H)	—	—	.10	.20

Obverse 2
9mm between lion nosetips, 15mm across field.

621	1972(C)	—	—	.10	.25
	1977(B)	Inc. KM620	—	.10	.25
	1977B	Inc. KM620	—	Proof	.35
	1978(B)	Inc. KM620	.50	1.00	2.00

Obverse 2
10mm between lion nosetips, 16-16.3mm across field.

622	1972(C)	Inc. KM620	1.00	1.40	2.00
	1973(C)	—	.10	.15	.30
	1974(C)	—	.10	.15	.30
	1975(C)	Inc. KM620	.10	.15	.30
	1976(C)	—	.25	.50	1.00

Rural Women's Advancement

KM#	Date	Mintage	VF	XF	Unc
659	1980(B)	Inc. KM620	.10	.20	.35
	1980B	—	—	Proof	.35
	1980(C)	Inc. KM620	.10	.15	.30
	1980(H)	Inc. KM620	.10	.25	.50

World Food Day

663	1981(B)	Inc. KM620	.10	.25	.35
	1981B	—	—	Proof	.35
	1981(C)	Inc. KM620	.10	.20	.40
	1981(H)	Inc. KM620	.10	.25	.50

IX Asian Games

670	1982(B)	Inc. KM620	.10	.15	.35
	1982B	—	—	Proof	.50
	1982(C)	Inc.KM620	.10	.15	.35
	1982(H)	Inc.KM620	.10	.15	.35

Forestry

692	1985(B)	—	—	.10	.15	.30
	1985(H)	—	—	.10	.15	.30

STAINLESS STEEL

703	1988(C)	—	—	.10	.20

50 NAYE PAISE

NICKEL

580	1960(B)	11.224	.40	.75	1.50
	1960(B)	—	—	Proof	3.00
	1960(C)	Inc. Ab.	.30	.50	1.25
	1961(B)	45.992	.25	.40	.75
	1961(B)	—	—	Proof	3.00
	1961(C)	Inc. Ab.	.25	.40	.75
	1962(B)	64.228	.25	.40	.75
	1962(B)	—	—	Proof	3.00
	1962(C)	Inc. Ab.	.25	.40	.75
	1963(B)	58.168	.25	.40	.75
	1963(B)	—	—	Proof	3.00
	1963(C)	Inc. Ab.	.25	.50	1.00

50 PAISE

NICKEL
Jawaharlal Nehru
Rev. leg: English.

588	ND(1964)(B)	21.900	.30	.65	1.00

Republic / INDIA 995

KM#	Date	Mintage	VF	XF	Unc
588	ND(1964)B	—		Proof	2.50
	ND(1964)(C)	7.160	.50	1.00	2.00

Rev. leg: Hindi.

589	ND(1964)B	36.190	.30	.65	1.00
	ND(1964)(C)	28.350	.50	.75	1.25

NOTE: Nehru commemorative issues were struck until 1967.

Obverse 1, Reverse 1

590	1964(C)	23.361	.35	.60	1.00
	1967(B)	19.267	.25	.45	.75

Obverse 2, Reverse 2

601	1967(C)	—	.40	.75	1.25
	1968(B)	28.076	.20	.30	.60
	1968(C)	Inc. Ab.	.20	.30	.60
	1969(B)	59.388	.20	.30	.60
	1969(C)	Inc. Ab.	.25	.50	1.00
	1970(B)	Inc. Ab.	.20	.30	.50
	1970(C)	Inc. Ab.	.20	.30	.60
	1971(C)	57.900	.20	.30	.50

Obverse 1, Reverse 2

613	1970(B)	Inc. 1969	.20	.30	.75
	1970B	3,046	—	Proof	.60
	1971B	4,375	—	Proof	.60

Mahatma Gandhi Centennial

609	ND(1969)(B)	10.260	—	.30	.60
	ND(1969)B	9,147	—	Proof	.60
	ND(1969)(C)	12.100	.20	.30	.60

NOTE: Struck during 1969 and 1970.

COPPER-NICKEL
25th Anniversary of Independence

623	ND(B)	43.800	.10	.20	.50
	ND B	7,895	—	Proof	.75
	ND(C)	40.080	.10	.20	.50

Obverse 2. Rev: Lettering spaced out.

KM#	Date	Mintage	VF	XF	Unc
624	1972(B)	—	.10	.20	.50
	1972(C)	—	.10	.20	.50
	1973(B)	—	.10	.20	.50
	1973(C)	—	.40	.75	1.25

F.A.O. Issue - Grow More Food

628	1973(B)	28.720	.15	.20	.60
	1973B	.011	—	Proof	.60
	1973(C)	40.100	.15	.25	.60

Obverse 2, Rev. Lettering close.

632	1974(B)	—	.10	.20	.35
	1974B	—	—	Proof	.50
	1974(C)	—	.10	.20	.35
	1975(B)	225.880	.10	.20	.35
	1975B	—	—	Proof	.50
	1975(C)	Inc. Ab.	.10	.20	.35
	1975(H)	—	—	.35	.60
	1976(B)	99.564	.10	.15	.40
	1976B	Inc. Ab.	—	Proof	.50
	1976(C)	Inc. Ab.	.10	.20	.45
	1976(H)	Inc. Ab.	.10	.20	.45
	1977(B)	97.272	—	Proof	.50
	1977B	Inc. Ab.	—	.15	.35
	1977(C)	Inc. Ab.	.10	.20	.45
	1977(H)	Inc. Ab.	.10	.15	.40
	1978B	25.648	—	Proof	.50
	1978(C)	—	.10	.15	.50
	1979B	—	—	Proof	.50
	1980(B)	—	.10	.15	.50
	1980B	—	—	Proof	.50
	1980(C)	—	.10	.15	.50
	1981B	—	—	Proof	.50
	1983(C)	62.634	.10	.15	.50

National Integration

671	1982(B)	9.804	.15	.25	.50
	1982(C)	Inc. Ab.	.35	.55	1.00

Circulation Coinage

680	1984(B)	61.548	.10	.15	.40
	1984(B)	Inc. Ab.	.10	.15	.40
	1984(H)	—	.10	.15	.40
	1984(z)	—	.10	.15	.40
	1985(B)	—	.10	.15	.40
	1985(H)	—	.10	.15	.40
	1985(y)	—	.10	.15	.40
	1986(C)	—	.10	.15	.40
	1987(B)	—	.10	.15	.35
	1987(C)	—	.10	.15	.35
	1987(H)	—	.10	.15	.35
	1988(H)	—	.10	.15	.35

Golden Jubilee of Reserve Bank of India

KM#	Date	Mintage	VF	XF	Unc
681	1985(B)	—	.25	.40	.85
	1985B	—	—	Proof	15.00
	1985(H)	—	.25	.40	.85

Indira Gandhi

686	ND(1985)(B)	—	.15	.30	.70
	ND(1985)B	—	—	Proof	15.00
	ND(1985)(H)	—	.15	.30	.70

F.A.O. Fisheries

696	1986(B)	—	—	—	.75
	1986B	—	—	Proof	15.00

STAINLESS STEEL

704	1988(C)	—	.10	.15	.35

RUPEE

NICKEL, 10.00 g
Obverse 1

581	1962B	—	—	Proof	4.00
	1962(C)	3.689	.50	1.00	2.00
	1970(B)	Inc. Ab.	2.00	3.00	4.00
	1970B	3,046	—	Proof	1.50
	1971B	4,375	—	Proof	1.50
	1972B	7.895	—	Proof	1.50
	1973B	7,567	—	Proof	1.50
	1974B	—	—	Proof	1.50

Jawaharlal Nehru

591	ND(1964)(B)	10.010	.65	1.00	1.75
	ND(1964)B	—	—	Proof	5.00
	ND(1964)(C)	10.020	.65	1.00	1.75

NOTE: Nehru commemorative issues were struck until 1967.

Republic / INDIA 996

Mahatma Gandhi Centennial

KM#	Date	Mintage	VF	XF	Unc
610	ND(1969)(B)	5.180	.25	.40	2.00
	ND(1969)B	9.147	—	Proof	1.00
	ND(1969)(C)	6.690	.50	1.25	2.50

NOTE: Struck during 1969 and 1970.

COPPER-NICKEL, 8.00 g

636	1975(B)	98.850	.20	.35	.75
	1975B	—	—	Proof	1.00
	1975(C)	—	2.00	4.00	7.00
	1976(B)	161.895	.20	.35	.75
	1976B	Inc. Ab.	—	Proof	1.00
	1977(B)	177.105	.20	.35	.75
	1977B	Inc. Ab.	—	Proof	1.00
	1978(B)	127.348	.20	.35	.75
	1978B	Inc. Ab.	—	Proof	1.00
	1978(C)	—	.20	.35	.75
	1979(C)	—	5.00	6.00	7.50

Obverse 2

637	1975(C)	Inc. 636	.25	.50	1.00
	1976(C)	Inc. 636	.25	.50	1.00

Obverse 1
Obv: Letter "I" INDIA has serifs.

655	1979(B)	—	.20	.35	.75
	1979B	—	—	Proof	1.00
	1979(C)	—	1.50	3.00	6.00
	1980(B)	84.768	.20	.35	.75
	1980B	—	—	Proof	1.00
	1980(C)	Inc. Ab.	.25	.40	.85
	1981(B)	82.458	.20	.35	.75
	1981B	—	—	Proof	1.00
	1981(C)	Inc. Ab.	.20	.35	.75
	1982(B)	116.811	.20	.35	.75
	1982(C)	Inc. Ab.	.20	.35	.75
	1983(B)	71.552	.20	.35	.75
	1983(C)	Inc. Ab.	.20	.35	.75
	1984(B)	34.935	.20	.35	.75
	1984(C)	Inc. Ab.	.20	.35	.75

COPPER-NICKEL

679	1983(B)	32.490	.20	.35	.65
	1983(C)	Inc. Ab.	.20	.35	.65
	1984(B)	152.378	.20	.35	.65
	1984(C)	Inc. Ab.	.20	.35	.65
	1984(H)	Inc. Ab.	.20	.35	.65
	1984(x)	—	.20	.35	.65
	1985(C)	—	.20	.35	.65
	1985(y)	—	.20	.35	.65
	1985(z)	—	.20	.35	.65
	1986(B)	—	.20	.35	.65
	1986(C)	—	.20	.35	.65
	1986(H)	—	.20	.35	.65
	1987(B)	—	.20	.35	.65
	1987(C)	—	.20	.35	.65
	1987(H)	—	.20	.35	.65
	1988(B)	—	.20	.35	.65
	1988(H)	—	.20	.35	.65

Youth Year

KM#	Date	Mintage	VF	XF	Unc
693	1985(B)	—	.15	.35	1.25
	1985(C)	—	.15	.35	1.25
	1985(C)	—	—	Proof	5.00

F.A.O. - Small Farmers

699	1978B	—	—	—	1.00
	1978B	—	—	Proof	5.00
	1987(H)	—	—	.20	.35	.50

2 RUPEES

COPPER-NICKEL
IX Asian Games

672	1982(B)	12.720	.20	.40	.75
	1982B	Inc. Ab.	—	Proof	2.00
	1982(C)	Inc. Ab.	.20	.40	.75

National Integration

673	1982(B)	Inc. KM672	.20	.40	.75
	1982(C)	Inc. KM672	.20	.40	.75

Golden Jubilee of Reserve Bank of India

682	1985(B)	—	.20	.50	1.50
	1985B	—	—	Proof	25.00

5 RUPEES

COPPER-NICKEL
Indira Gandhi

687	ND(1985)(B)	—	.50	1.00	3.00
	ND(1985)B	—	—	Proof	25.00
	ND(1985)(H)	—	.80	1.50	4.00

10 RUPEES

15.0000 g, .800 SILVER, .3858 oz ASW
Mahatma Gandhi Centennial

KM#	Date	Mintage	VF	XF	Unc
611	ND(1969)(B)	3.160	—	—	6.00
	ND(1969)B	9.147	—	Proof	7.50
	ND(1969)(C)	.100	—	—	7.50

NOTE: Struck during 1969 and 1970.

F. A. O. Issue

614	1970(B)	.300	—	—	5.50
	1970B	3.046	—	Proof	10.00
	1970(C)	.100	—	—	7.50
	1971(B)	—	—	—	7.50
	1971B	1.594	—	Proof	10.00

22.3000 g, .500 SILVER, .3585 oz ASW
25th Anniversary of Independence

625	1972(B)	1.000	—	—	5.00
	1972B	7.895	—	Proof	6.50
	1972(C)	1.000	—	—	5.00

F. A. O. Issue

629	1973(B)	.064	—	—	6.00
	1973B	.015	—	Proof	7.50

Republic / INDIA 997

COPPER-NICKEL
F.A.O. Issue

KM#	Date	Mintage	VF	XF	Unc
633	1974(B)	.065	—	1.50	2.50
	1974B	.012	—	Proof	3.50

F.A.O. - Women's Year

638	1975(B)	.049	—	1.50	2.50
	1975B	2,531	—	Proof	5.00

F.A.O. Issue

642	1976(B)	.049	—	1.50	2.50
	1976B	3,400	—	Proof	5.00

F.A.O. Issue

646	1977(B)	.020	—	1.50	2.50
	1977B	5,969	—	Proof	5.00

F.A.O. Issue

650	1978(B)	.025	—	1.50	2.50
	1978B	—	—	Proof	5.00

International Year of the Child

KM#	Date	Mintage	VF	XF	Unc
656	1979(B)	—	—	2.00	3.50
	1979B	—	—	Proof	6.00

Rural Women's Advancement

660	1980(B)	—	—	2.00	4.00
	1980B	—	—	Proof	6.00

F.A.O. Issue, World Food Day

664	1981(B)	—	—	2.00	4.00
	1981B	—	—	Proof	6.00

IX Asian Games

KM#	Date	Mintage	VF	XF	Unc
674	1982(B)	—	—	2.00	4.00
	1982B	—	—	Proof	6.00

National Integration

676	1982(B)	—	—	Proof	6.00

Golden Jubilee of Reserve Bank of India

683	1985(B)	—	—	—	18.00
	1985B	—	—	Proof	20.00

Youth Year
Similar to 1 Rupee, KM#693

694	1985(C)	—	—	—	4.00
	1985(C)	—	—	Proof	6.00

20 RUPEES

30.0000 g, .500 SILVER, .4823 oz ASW
F.A.O. Issue

KM#	Date	Mintage	VF	XF	Unc
630	1973(B)	.064	—	—	7.50
	1973B	.012	—	Proof	10.00

COPPER-NICKEL
Indira Gandhi

688	ND(1985)(B)	—	—	—	20.00
	ND(1985)B	—	—	Proof	25.00

F.A.O. Fisheries

697	1986	—	—	—	10.00
	1986	—	—	Proof	15.00

F.A.O. - Small Farmers

700	1987B	—	—	—	10.00
	1987B	—	—	Proof	15.00

50 RUPEES

34.7000 g, .500 SILVER, .5578 oz ASW
F.A.O. Issue

634	1974(B)	.082	—	—	10.00
	1974B	.013	—	Proof	12.50

F.A.O. - Women's Year

KM#	Date	Mintage	VF	XF	Unc
639	1975(B)	.065	—	—	10.00
	1975B	2.691	—	Proof	15.00

F.A.O Issue

643	1976(B)	.042	—	—	10.00
	1976B	3,385	—	Proof	12.50

F.A.O. Issue

647	1977(B)	.026	—	—	10.00
	1977B	2,544	—	Proof	15.00

F.A.O. Issue

651	1978(B)	.025	—	—	10.00
	1978B	—	—	Proof	12.50

International Year of the Child

KM#	Date	Mintage	VF	XF	Unc
657	1979(B)	—	—	—	10.00
	1979B	—	—	Proof	15.00

100 RUPEES

35.0000 g, .500 SILVER, .5627 oz ASW
Rural Women's Advancement

661	1980(B)	.021	—	—	17.50
	1980B	5,811	—	Proof	22.50

F.A.O. ISSUE, World Food Day

665	1981(B)	.022	—	—	17.50
	1981B	2,950	—	Proof	22.50

29.1600 g, .925 SILVER, .8673 oz ASW
International Year of the Child

666	1981(1983)	—	—	Proof	22.50

35.0000 g, .500 SILVER, .5627 oz AGW
IX Asian Games

675	1982(B)	—	—	—	17.50
	1982B	—	—	Proof	22.50

Golden Jubilee of Reserve Bank of India

KM#	Date	Mintage	VF	XF	Unc
684	1985(B)	—	—	—	30.00
	1985B	—	—	Proof	38.00

Indira Gandhi

	Date				
689	ND(1985)(B)	—	—	—	35.00
	ND(1985)B	—	—	Proof	40.00

National Integration

690	1982(B)	—	—	—	16.50
	1982B	—	—	Proof	22.50

Youth Year
Similar to 1 Rupee, KM#693

695	1985(C)	.016	—	—	20.00
	1985(C)	6,267	—	Proof	25.00

F.A.O. Fisheries

KM#	Date	Mintage	VF	XF	Unc
698	1986	—	—	—	25.00
	1986	—	—	Proof	30.00

F.A.O. - Small Farmers

701	1987B	—	—	—	35.00
	1987B	—	—	Proof	50.00

MINT SETS (MS)

KM#	Date	Mintage	Identification	Issue Price	Mkt. Val.
MS1	1950(7)	—	—	3.60	10.00
MS2	1954(7)	—	—	3.60	10.00
MS3	1962(6)	—	KM575a,576-580	1.50	3.00
MS4	1962(7)	—	KM575a,576-581	3.60	3.50
MS5	ND(1964)(B)(2)	—	KM588,591	1.00	3.75
MS6	1967(8)	—	KM581,584-587,590,592-593 (1962 dated Rupee)	1.00	7.00
MS7	1969B(4)	25,281	KM608-611, blue plastic case	2.50	10.00
MS8	1970(B)(8)	—	KM581,584,592-593,599,601, 605,607, brown vinyl case, diamond below date	1.00	10.00
MS9	1970(B)(2)	22,999	KM612,614	2.00	9.00
MS10	1971(B)(2)	9,987	KM614;616	—	8.50
MS11	1972(B)(2)	43,121	KM623,625	2.00	6.50
MS12	1973(B)(2)	48,670	KM629-630	—	13.50
MS13	1974(B)(2)	50,219	KM633-634	10.00	12.50
MS14	1975(B)(2)	40,279	KM638-639	12.00	12.50
MS15	1976(B)(2)	25,105	KM642-643	12.00	12.50
MS16	1977(B)(2)	17,071	KM646-647	12.00	12.50
MS17	1978(B)(2)	15,041	KM650-651	10.00	12.50
MS18	1979(B)(2)	—	KM656-657	—	13.00
MS19	1980(B)(2)	—	KM660-661	—	21.00
MS20	1981(B)(2)	—	KM664-665	—	21.00
MS21	1982(B)(2)	—	KM674-675	—	21.00
MS22	1985(B)(2)	—	KM683-684	48.00	48.00
MS23	ND(1985)(B)(2)	—	KM688-689	43.00	55.00
MS24	ND(1985)(C)(2)	—	KM694-695	—	25.00
MS24	1986(2)	—	KM697-698	45.00	35.00
MS26	1987B(2)	—	KM700-701	45.00	55.00

PROOF SETS (PS)

NOTE: Beginning in 1969, all proof coins have B beneath date, for Bombay Mint. Normal Bombay coins have diamond mint mark.

KM#	Date	Mintage	Identification	Issue Price	Mkt. Val.
PS1	1950B(7)	—*	KM565.1,567-570,572,574	8.40	12.50
PS2	1954B(7)	—*	KM566-570,572,574	8.40	12.50
PS3	1960B(6)	—*	KM575-580	7.00	10.00
PS4	1961B(6)	—*	KM575-580	7.00	10.00
PS5	1962B(7)	—*	KM575a,576-581, (1960 dated 1-50 New Paisa)	8.40	14.00
PS6	1962B(7)	—*	KM575a,576-581	8.40	14.00
PS7	1963B(6)	—*	KM575a,576-580 (1961 dated 1-50 New Paisa	7.00	10.00
PS8	1963B(7)	—*	KM575a,576-581 (1962 Rupee)	8.40	14.00
PS9	ND(1964)B(2)	—*	KM588,591	5.00	7.50
PS10	1969B(9)	9,097	KM592,597,599,603,607, 608-611	15.25	10.00
PS11	1970B(9)	2,900	KM581,584,590,592,596,598, 605,612,614	15.25	14.00
PS12	1971B(9)	4,161	KM581,592,603,615,617, 619-620,623,625	15.25	13.00
PS13	1972B(9)	7,701	KM581,592,596,615,617-618, 620,623,625	15.25	10.00
PS14	1973B(10)	7,563	KM581,592,596,615,617,620, 626,628-630	26.00	20.00
PS15	1973B(9)	3,326	KM581,592,596,615,617,620, 626,628-629	15.25	10.00
PS16	1973B(2)	2,408	KM629-630	17.50	17.50
PS17	1974B(10)	9,138	KM581,592,596,617,620,626, 631-634	29.00	18.00
PS18	1974B(2)	1,712	KM633-634	7.50	16.00
PS19	1975B(10)	2,370	KM592,596,617,620,626,632, 635-636,638-639	35.00	22.50
PS20	1975B(2)	160	KM638-639	22.00	20.00
PS21	1976B(10)	3,209	KM581,592,596,617,620,632, 640-643	35.00	20.00
PS22	1976B(2)	190	KM642-643	22.00	17.50
PS23	1977B(10)	2,222	KM592,596,617,620,632,636, 644-647	35.00	22.50
PS24	1977B(2)	—	KM646-647	—	20.00
PS25	1978B(10)	1,390	KM592,596,617,620,632,636, 648-651	35.00	20.00
PS26	1978B(2)	—	KM650-651	—	17.50
PS27	1979B(9)?	—	KM592,596,617,620,632,636, 652-653,656-657	—	25.00
PS28	1979B(2)	—	KM656-657	—	20.00
PS29	1980B(10)?	—	KM592,596,617,626,632,636, 658-661	—	32.50
PS30	1980B(2)	—	KM660-661	—	29.00
PS31	1981B(10)?	—	KM592,596,617,626,632,636, 662-665	—	32.50
PS32	1981B(2)	—	KM664-665	—	29.00
PS33	1982B(4)	—	KM670,672,674-675	48.00	32.50
PS34	1982B(2)	—	KM674-675	38.00	29.00
PS35	1985B(4)	—	KM681-684	98.00	98.00
PS36	1985B(2)	—	KM683-684	58.00	58.00
PS37	ND(1985)B(4)	—	KM686-689	88.00	105.00
PS38	ND(1985)B(2)	—	KM688-689	48.00	65.00
PS39	1985(C)(3)	—	KM693-695	—	36.00
PS40	1986(3)	—	KM696-698	70.00	60.00
PS41	1986(2)	—	KM697-698	50.00	45.00
PS42	1987(3)	—	KM699-701	65.00	70.00
PS43	1987(2)	—	KM700-701	60.00	65.00

Listings For
INDO-CHINA: refer to French Indo-China

INDONESIA

The Republic of Indonesia, the world's largest archipelago, extends for more than 3,000 miles (4,827 km.) along the equator from the mainland of southeast Asia to Australia. The 13,667 islands comprising the archipelago have a combined area of 788,425 sq. mi. (5,193,250 sq. km.) and a population of 175.6 million, including East Timor. Capital: Djakarta. Petroleum, timber, rubber, and coffee are exported.

Had Columbus succeeded in reaching the fabled Spice Islands, he would have found advanced civilizations a millennium old, and temples still ranked among the finest examples of ancient art. During the opening centuries of the Christian era, the islands were influenced by Hindu priests and traders who spread their culture and religion. Moslem invasions began in the 13th century, fragmenting the island kingdoms into small states which were unable to resist Western colonial infiltration. Portuguese traders established posts in the 16th century, but they were soon outnumbered by the Dutch who arrived in 1596 and gradually asserted control over the islands comprising present-day Indonesia. Dutch dominance, interrupted by British incursions during the Napoleonic Wars, established the Netherlands East Indies as one of the richest colonial possessions in the world.

The Indonesian independence movement, which began between the two world wars, was encouraged by the Japanese during their 3 1/2-year occupation during World War II. Indonesia proclaimed its independence on Aug. 17, 1945, three days after the surrender of Japan, and established it on Dec. 27, 1949, after four years of Dutch effort to reassert control. West Irian, formerly Netherlands New Guinea, came under the administration of Indonesia on May 1, 1963.

On November 28, 1975 the Portuguese Province of Timor, an overseas province occupying the eastern half of the East Indian island of Timor, attained independence as the People's Democratic Republic of East Timor. On December 5, 1975 the government of the People's Democratic Republic was seized by a guerrilla faction sympathetic to the Indonesian territorial claim to East Timor which ousted the constitutional government and replaced it with the Provisional Government of East Timor. On July 17, 1976, the Provisional Government enacted a law which dissolved the free republic and made East Timor the 27th province of Indonesia.

Coinage for the Indonesian Archipelago is varied and extensive. The Dutch struck coins for the islands at various mints in the Netherlands and the islands under the auspices of the VOC (United East India Company), the Batavian Republic and the Kingdom of the Netherlands. The British issued a coinage during the various occupations by the British East Indian Company, 1811-24. Modern coinage issued by the Republic of Indonesia includes separate series for West Irian and for the Riau Archipelago, an area of small islands between Singapore and Sumatra.

NETHERLANDS EAST INDIES

RULERS
Dutch, 1816-1942

MINT MARKS
H - Amsterdam (H)
Hk - Harderwijk (star, rosette, cock, cross, Z)
Hn - Hoorn (star)
E - Einkhuizen (star)
Dt - Dordrecht (rosette)
K - Kampen (eagle)
S - Utrecht
Sa - Surabaya (Sa)

MONETARY SYSTEM
120 Duits = 120 Cents
1 Gulden = 1 Java Rupee
16 Silver Rupees = 1 Gold Mohur

BONKS: Because of the slow delivery of coins from the Netherlands, the government in the East Indies often resorted to the manufacture of "Bonks". These were simply lumps cut from the copper (or tin) rods used for coining. This eliminated the problems inherent in casting round coins and allowed the production of large quantities of legal tender very quickly. The thicker rods were used for the 2 and 8 Stiver Bonks and the thinner rod for the smaller denominations.

DUITS: On many of the Duit and 1/2 Duit coins of the East Indies dated 1802-1826, the value appears as 5-1/32-G (1/2 Duit) and 5-1/16-G (Duit). This is interpreted as; 5 of the pieces equal 1/16 Guilder or 5 equal 1/32 Guilder. However, in 1802 the rate of exchange was set so that 6 Duits should equal 1/16 Guilder which would mean the Duit actually equaled 1/96 Guilder and the 1/2 Duit equaled 1/192 Guilder, but because of the perennial shortage of small coins, the error was ignored and the coins released to circulation.

CENTS: Although some coins in 1833-1841 appear with value as 1 CT (1 Cent) and 2 CT (2 Cent) they are considered Duits and Double Duits and were exchanged at the rate of 1 Duit = 1/96 Guilder, not on a decimal system.

COLONIAL COINAGE
GELDERLAND

MINTMASTER PRIVY MARKS
Date	Privy Mark
1782-1809	Ear of corn, Martin Hendrik Lohse

MONETARY SYSTEM
4 Duits = 1 Stuiver
20 Stuivers = 1 Gulden

DUIT

COPPER
Obv: Crowned arms of Gelderland.

KM#	Date	Mintage	VG	Fine	VF	XF
50	1802	—	2.00	4.00	7.00	14.50
(C24)	1803	—	2.00	4.00	7.00	14.50
	1804	—	3.00	6.00	10.00	17.50
	1805	—	2.00	4.00	7.00	14.50
	1085 (error)	—	—	—	—	—
	1806	—	2.00	4.00	7.00	14.50

NOTE: Varieties exist.

HOLLAND

MINT MARKS
H - Heus, Amsterdam
Rosette - Dordrecht, 1601-1806
Star - Enkhuisen, 1796-1803
Star - Hoorn, 1803-1809

DUIT
COPPER
Obv: Crowned arms of Holland.
Rev: VOC monogram over date.

KM#	Date	Mintage	VG	Fine	VF	XF
70	1802	—	1.50	3.00	5.50	12.00
(C25)	1803	—	1.50	3.00	5.50	12.00
	1804	—	2.00	4.00	7.00	14.50

NOTE: 3 varieties exist.

Batavian Republic
1799-1806
1/2 DUIT
(1/) 5 (of) 1/32 G = 1/160 G

COPPER

KM#	Date	Mintage	VG	Fine	VF	XF
75	1802	.157	.75	1.50	2.50	7.50
(C26)	1803	—	4.00	7.00	10.00	18.00
	1804	—	4.00	7.00	10.00	18.00
	1805	—	.75	1.50	2.50	7.50
	1806	—	.75	1.50	2.50	7.50
(C49)	1807	—	.75	1.50	2.50	7.50
	1808	—	.75	1.50	2.50	7.50
	1809	—	1.00	2.00	3.50	10.00

NOTE: Many varieties of above 3 coins exist.

DUIT
(1/) 5 (of) 1/16 G = 1/80 G

COPPER
Obv: Holland Arms.

KM#	Date	Mintage	VG	Fine	VF	XF
76	1802	.358	1.00	2.00	3.50	10.00
(C27)	1803	—	.75	1.50	2.50	7.50
	1804	—	.75	1.50	2.50	7.50
	1805	—	.75	1.50	2.50	7.50
	1806	—	.75	1.50	2.50	7.50
(C50)	1807	—	.50	1.00	1.50	4.00
	1808	—	.50	1.00	1.50	4.00
	1809/6	—	10.00	20.00	35.00	55.00
	1809/8	—	10.00	20.00	35.00	55.00
	1809	—	5.00	10.00	18.50	30.00

NOTE: Varieties exist.

BRASS (OMS)
| 76a | 1808 | | | | | |

SILVER (OMS)
KM#	Date	Mintage	VG	Fine	VF	XF
76b	1802	—	35.00	60.00	90.00	150.00
(C27a)						

1/16 GULDEN

0.6600 g, .916 SILVER, .0194 oz ASW, 15mm
| 77 | 1802 | — | 10.00 | 17.50 | 30.00 | 60.00 |
| (C38) | | | | | | |

NOTE: 4 varieties exist.

16mm
Obv: W/inner circle.
| 78 | 1802 | — | 10.00 | 17.50 | 30.00 | 60.00 |
| (C38a) | | | | | | |

NOTE: 3 varieties exist.

1/8 GULDEN
1.3250 g, .916 SILVER, .0390 oz ASW, 19mm
| 79 | 1802 | — | 10.00 | 17.50 | 30.00 | 60.00 |
| (C39) | | | | | | |

NOTE: 4 varieties exist.

18mm
Rev: W/o inner circle.
| 80 | 1802 | — | 10.00 | 17.50 | 30.00 | 60.00 |
| (C39a) | | | | | | |

NOTE: 3 varieties exist.

1/4 GULDEN

2.6500 g, .916 SILVER, .0781 oz ASW
| 81 | 1802 | — | 12.00 | 20.00 | 35.00 | 70.00 |
| (C40) | | | | | | |

NOTE: 6 varieties exist.

GOLD (OMS)
| 81a | 1802 | — | — | — | Rare | — |
| (C40a) | | | | | | |

1/2 GULDEN

5.3800 g, .916 SILVER, .1561 oz ASW
Rev: Ship w/INDIAE BATAV, date around.
| 82 | 1802 | — | 15.00 | 30.00 | 47.50 | 85.00 |
| (C40.1) | | | | | | |

NOTE: 2 varieties exist.

GOLD (OMS)
| 82a | 1802 | — | — | — | Rare | — |
| (C40.1a) | | | | | | |

GULDEN

10.6160 g, .916 SILVER, .3127 oz ASW

KM#	Date	Mintage	VG	Fine	VF	XF
83 (C40.2)	1802	—	20.00	40.00	60.00	125.00

NOTE: 5 varieties exist.

GOLD (OMS)

83a (C40.2a)	1802	—	—	—	Rare	—

KINGDOM OF THE NETHERLANDS
1/2 DUIT
(1/) 5 (of) 1/32 G. = 1/160 G.

COPPER
Mint mark: H

85 (C61)	1814	—	—	—	Rare	—
	1815	—	.50	1.00	1.50	4.00
	1816	—	.50	1.00	1.50	4.00

NOTE: Varieties exist.

DUIT
(1/) 5 (of) 1/16 G. = 1/80 G.

COPPER
Mint mark: H

86 (C62)	1814	—	—	—	Rare	—
	1814 w/o H	—	—	—	—	—
	1815	—	2.00	4.50	10.00	16.00
	1816	—	2.00	4.50	10.00	16.00

NOTE: Varieties exist. 1814 dated coins were struck on larger planchets.

OVERYSSEL
MINTMASTER PRIVY MARKS
Heraldic eagle - Nicolaas Wonneman, 1763-1807

Batavian Republic
1799-1806
DUIT

COPPER
Obv: Overyssel arms.

100 (C28)	1803	—	2.00	4.50	10.00	16.00
	1804	—	2.00	4.50	10.00	16.00
	1805	—	2.00	4.50	10.00	16.00
	1806	—	4.50	8.00	13.50	23.50
(C51)	1807	—	4.50	11.00	18.00	30.00

NOTE: Varieties exist.

SILVER (OMS)

100a (C28a)	1804	—	Unique			
	1807 plain edge	—	—	—	—	—
	1807 milled edge	—	—	—	—	—

DECIMAL COINAGE
General Issue
100 Cents = 1 Gulden

MINT MARKS
D - Denver, U.S.A.
P - Philadelphia, U.S.A.
S - San Francisco, U.S.A.
(U) - Caduceus, Utrecht

MINTMASTER PRIVY MARKS

Date	Privy Mark
1818-1840	Torch
1839-1846	Fleur de lis
1846-1874	Sword
1874	Sword in scabbard
1875-1887	Broad axe
1887	Broad axe and star
1888-1909	Halberd
1909	Halberd and star
1909-1933	Sea Horse
1933-1942	Grapes

1/2 CENT

COPPER

KM#	Date	Mintage	Fine	VF	XF	Unc
306 (Y1)	1855(u)	—	—	—	Proof	—
	1856(u)	10.800	1.50	3.00	5.00	8.50
	1857(u)	36.800	1.25	2.50	4.00	7.50
	1858(u)	53.588	1.25	2.50	4.00	7.50
	1859(u)	219.600	1.25	2.50	4.00	7.50
	1860(u)	107.124	1.25	2.50	4.00	7.50
	1902(u)	20.000	.60	1.25	2.50	4.00
	1908(u)	10.600	.75	1.50	3.00	5.00
	1909(u)	4.400	1.25	2.50	4.00	6.00

SILVER (OMS)

306a (Y1a)	1902(u)	—	—	—	Rare	—

GOLD (OMS)

306b (Y1b)	1860(u)	—	—	—	Unique	—
	1902(u)	—	—	—	Rare	—

BRONZE
Mintmaster's mark: Sea horse

314.1 (Y18.1)	1914(u)	50.000	.50	1.00	2.00	3.00
	1916(u)	10.000	.60	1.25	2.50	4.00
	1921(u)	4.000	.80	1.50	3.00	5.00
	1932(u)	10.000	.60	1.25	2.50	4.00
	1933(u)	15.000	.60	1.25	2.50	4.00

Mintmaster's mark: Grapes

314.2 (Y18.2)	1933(u)	5.000	.80	1.50	3.00	5.00
	1934(u)	30.000	.50	1.00	2.00	3.00
	1935(u)	14.000	.60	1.25	2.50	4.00
	1936(u)	12.000	.60	1.25	2.50	4.00
	1937(u)	8.400	.60	1.25	2.50	4.00
	1938(u)	3.600	.80	1.50	3.00	5.00
	1939(u)	2.000	.80	1.50	3.00	5.00
	1945P	400.000	.25	.40	.75	1.25

CENT

COPPER

KM#	Date	Mintage	Fine	VF	XF	Unc
307 (Y2)	1855(u)	.100	27.50	45.00	60.00	85.00
	1855(u)	—	—	—	Proof	—
	1856(u)	67.900	1.50	3.00	5.00	8.00
	1856(u)	—	—	—	Proof	—
	1857(u)	162.000	1.25	2.50	4.00	6.00
	1858(u)	119.431	1.25	2.50	4.00	6.00
	1859(u)	40.800	1.50	3.00	5.00	8.00
	1860(u)	14.455	1.50	3.00	5.00	8.00
	1896(u)	60.400	1.50	3.00	5.00	8.00
	1897(u)	69.600	1.50	3.00	5.00	8.00
	1898(u)	36.600	1.50	3.00	5.00	8.00
	1899(u)	18.400	1.50	3.00	5.00	8.00
	1901(u)	15.000	1.50	3.00	5.00	8.00
	1902(u)	10.000	1.50	3.00	5.00	8.00
	1907(u)	7.500	1.50	3.00	5.00	8.00
	1908(u)	12.500	1.50	3.00	5.00	8.00
	1909(u)	6.000	1.50	2.50	4.00	6.00
	1912(u)	25.000	.75	1.50	3.00	5.00

YELLOW BRONZE (OMS)

307a (Y2a)	1898(u)	—	—	—	Rare	—

SILVER (OMS)

307b (Y2b)	1902(u)	—	—	—	Rare	—

GOLD (OMS)

307c (Y2c)	1860(u)	—	—	—	Unique	—
	1902(u)	—	—	—	Rare	—

BRONZE

KM#	Date	Mintage	Fine	VF	XF	Unc
315 (Y19)	1914(u)	85.000	.50	.75	2.00	5.00
	1916(u)	16.440	.75	1.75	3.00	6.00
	1919(u)	20.000	.75	1.75	3.00	6.00
	1920(u)	120.000	.50	.75	1.75	4.00
	1926(u)	10.000	.75	1.75	3.00	6.00
	1929(u)	50.000	.50	.75	1.75	4.00

317 (Y21)	1936(u)	52.000	.50	.90	1.75	3.50
	1937(u)	120.400	.40	.80	1.50	3.00
	1938(u)	150.000	.40	.80	1.50	3.00
	1939(u)	81.400	.50	.90	1.75	3.50
	1942P	100.000	.25	.60	1.00	2.00
	1945P	335.000	.20	.40	.75	1.25
	1945D	133.800	.25	.60	1.00	2.00
	1945S	102.568	.20	.40	.75	1.50

2-1/2 CENTS

COPPER

308 (Y3)	1856(u)	2.480	5.00	9.00	14.00	20.00
	1856(u)	—	—	—	Proof	—
	1857(u)	36.560	3.00	6.00	10.00	17.50
	1857(u)	—	—	—	Proof	—
	1858(u)	40.990	3.00	6.00	10.00	17.50
	1896(u)	1.120	3.00	6.00	10.00	17.50
	1897(u)	18.105	1.00	1.50	3.00	15.00
	1898(u)	7.600	2.50	5.00	10.00	17.50
	1899(u)	10.400	2.00	4.00	8.00	15.00
	1902(u)	6.000	2.50	5.00	10.00	17.50
	1907(u)	3.000	3.00	6.00	12.50	17.50
	1908(u)	5.940	2.50	5.00	10.00	17.50
	1909(u)	3.060	2.50	5.00	10.00	17.50
	1913(u)	4.000	2.50	5.00	10.00	15.00

SILVER (OMS)

308a (Y3a)	1902(u)	—	—	—	Rare	—

GOLD (OMS)

308b (Y3b)	1858(u)	—	—	—	Unique	—
	1902(u)	—	—	—	Rare	—

BRONZE

316 (Y20)	1914(u)	22.000	.75	3.00	5.00	8.00
	1915(u)	6.000	1.50	4.00	6.00	10.00
	1920(u)	48.000	.75	1.50	3.00	5.00
	1945P	200.000	.50	1.00	1.50	3.50

1/20 GULDEN

.6100 g, .720 SILVER, .0141 oz ASW

303 (Y4)	1854(u)	—	150.00	225.00	350.00	450.00
	1857(u)	—	—	—	Proof	—
	1855(u)	.492	4.00	6.00	12.50	21.50

GOLD (OMS)

303a (Y4a)	1855(u)	—	—	—	Unique	—

5 CENTS

COPPER-NICKEL

KM#	Date	Mintage	Fine	VF	XF	Unc
317	1911(u)	—	—	—	Proof	—
(Y17)	1913(u)	60.000	.75	1.50	3.00	6.00
	1921(u)	40.000	1.00	2.00	4.00	8.00
	1922(u)	20.000	1.00	2.00	4.00	8.00

1/10 GULDEN

 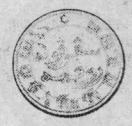

1.2500 g, .720 SILVER, .0289 oz ASW

KM#	Date	Mintage	Fine	VF	XF	Unc
304	1854(u)	3.550	2.25	4.75	10.00	15.00
(Y5)	1854(u)	—	—	—	Proof	—
	1855(u)	6.452	2.00	4.25	8.00	15.00
	1855(u)	—	—	—	Proof	—
	1856(u)	3.000	2.25	4.75	10.00	15.00
	1857(u)	11.000	1.75	3.50	4.50	7.50
	1858(u)	14.000	1.00	2.25	4.00	7.00
	1882(u)	7.500	2.00	4.25	8.00	15.00
	1884(u)	3.550	2.25	4.75	10.00	15.00
	1885(u)	.825	7.50	16.50	25.00	35.00
	1891(u)	5.000	1.50	3.00	4.50	7.50
	1893(u)	5.000	1.25	2.50	4.00	7.00
	1896(u)	3.075	2.25	4.75	10.00	15.00
	1898(u)	2.500	2.25	4.75	10.00	15.00
	1900(u)	6.850	1.75	3.25	4.50	7.50
	1901(u)	5.000	1.75	3.25	4.50	7.50

GOLD (OMS)

| 304a | 1854(u) | — | — | — | Unique | — |
| (Y5a) | 1885(u) | — | — | — | Unique | — |

1.2500 g, .720 SILVER, .0289 oz ASW

309	1903(u)	5.000	2.00	3.00	5.50	8.00
(Y7)	1904(u)	5.000	2.00	3.00	5.50	8.00
	1905(u)	5.000	2.00	3.00	5.50	8.00
	1906(u)	7.500	2.00	3.00	5.50	8.00
	1907(u)	14.000	1.50	2.50	4.50	7.50
	1908(u)	3.000	2.00	4.00	6.50	10.00
	1909(u)	10.000	1.50	2.25	4.75	8.00

GOLD (OMS)

| 309a | 1903(u) | — | — | — | Rare | — |
| (Y7a) | | | | | | |

1.2500 g, .720 SILVER, .0289 oz ASW
Obv. & rev: Wide rims and small leg.

311	1910(u)	15.000	3.00	5.00	8.00	12.00
(Y14)	1911(u)	10.000	5.00	8.00	15.00	25.00
	1912(u)	25.000	1.75	3.50	6.50	10.00
	1913(u)	15.000	2.00	4.00	7.00	11.00
	1914(u)	25.000	1.75	3.50	6.50	10.00
	1915(u)	15.000	2.00	4.00	6.00	11.00
	1918(u)	30.000	1.50	2.00	4.00	6.00
	1919(u)	20.000	1.25	1.75	3.75	5.75
	1920(u)	85.000	1.75	3.75	5.25	8.00
	1928(u)	30.000	.50	1.00	2.50	4.00
	1930(u)	15.000	.75	1.25	2.75	4.50

Obv. & rev: Narrow rims and large leg.

318	1937(u)	20.000	.40	.75	2.00	4.25
(Y14a)	1938(u)	30.000	.40	.75	2.00	4.25
	1939(u)	5.400	1.50	2.00	4.00	6.00
	1940(u)	10.000	1.00	1.50	3.25	5.50
	1941P	41.850	.25	.45	.75	1.75
	1941S	58.150	.25	.45	.75	1.75
	1942S	75.000	.25	.45	.75	1.75
	1945P	100.720	.25	.45	.75	1.75
	1945S	19.280	.25	.45	.75	1.75

1/4 GULDEN

4.0610 g, .568 SILVER, .0742 oz ASW

KM#	Date	Mintage	VG	Fine	VF	XF
301.1	1826(u)	1.238	6.25	10.00	17.50	28.00
(C72.1)	1827(u)	1.003	6.25	11.00	18.50	30.00
	1834/27(u)	.002	11.00	17.00	26.00	40.00
	1834(u)	Inc. Ab.	6.25	11.00	18.50	30.00
	1840(u)	.973	6.50	12.00	20.00	32.50

Coarse milling

| 301.2 | 1826(u) | Inc. Ab. | 15.00 | 30.00 | 45.00 | 65.00 |
| (C72.2) | | | | | | |

GOLD (OMS)

| 301.1a | 1834(u) | — | — | Rare | — |
| (C72a) | | | | | |

3.1800 g, .720 SILVER, .0736 oz ASW

KM#	Date	Mintage	Fine	VF	XF	Unc
305	1854(u)	11.460	2.00	6.00	12.00	20.00
(Y6)	1855(u)	4.541	5.00	9.00	14.00	25.00
	1855(u)	—	—	—	Proof	—
	1857(u)	2.400	6.00	12.00	20.00	30.00
	1858(u)	4.800	5.00	9.00	14.00	25.00
	1858(u)	—	—	—	Proof	—
	1882(u)	2.200	6.00	12.00	20.00	40.00
	1883(u)	.800	12.50	22.50	32.50	55.00
	1885(u)	1.750	11.00	21.00	30.00	45.00
	1890(u)	1.140	10.00	20.00	25.00	35.00
	1891(u)	.860	10.00	20.00	25.00	35.00
	1893(u)	2.000	5.50	10.00	15.00	27.50
	1896(u)	1.230	10.00	20.00	25.00	35.00
	1898(u)	3.000	4.00	9.00	12.50	22.50
	1900(u)	2.800	5.50	10.00	15.00	27.50
	1901(u)	2.000	5.50	10.00	15.00	27.50

GOLD (OMS)

| 305a | 1885(u) | — | — | — | Unique | — |
| (Y6a) | | | | | | |

3.1800 g, .720 SILVER, .0736 oz ASW

310	1903(u)	2.000	5.00	8.50	14.00	25.00
(Y8)	1904(u)	2.000	5.00	8.50	14.00	25.00
	1905(u)	2.000	5.00	8.50	14.00	25.00
	1906(u)	4.000	3.50	7.00	12.50	22.50
	1907(u)	4.400	3.50	7.00	12.50	22.50
	1908(u)	2.000	5.00	8.50	14.00	25.00
	1909(u)	4.000	3.50	7.00	12.50	22.50

GOLD (OMS)

| 310a | 1903(u) | — | — | — | Rare | — |
| (Y8a) | | | | | | |

3.1800 g, .720 SILVER, .0736 oz ASW
Obv. & rev: Wide rims and small leg.

312	1910(u)	6.000	6.00	10.00	17.00	30.00
(Y15)	1911(u)	4.000	8.00	13.50	21.50	40.00
	1912(u)	10.000	5.50	9.00	14.25	27.50
	1913(u)	6.000	7.50	12.00	20.00	35.00
	1914(u)	10.000	5.50	9.00	14.25	27.50
	1915(u)	6.000	6.00	10.00	17.00	30.00
	1917(u)	12.000	2.50	5.00	7.00	12.00
	1919(u)	6.000	8.00	13.50	21.50	40.00
	1920(u)	20.000	2.50	5.00	7.00	12.00
	1921(u)	24.000	2.50	5.00	7.00	12.00
	1929(u)	5.000	4.00	6.00	10.00	20.00
	1930(u)	7.000	2.25	3.50	6.00	10.00

Obv. & rev: Narrow rims and large leg.

KM#	Date	Mintage	Fine	VF	XF	Unc
319	1937(u)	8.000	1.25	2.25	3.50	6.00
(Y15a)	1938(u)	12.000	1.25	2.25	3.50	6.00
	1939(u)	10.400	1.25	2.25	3.50	6.00
	1941P	34.947	.60	.80	1.25	2.25
	1941S	5.053	1.25	2.50	4.00	7.00
	1942S	32.000	.75	1.00	2.00	3.00
	1945S	56.000	.75	1.00	2.00	3.00

1/2 GULDEN

5.3830 g, .893 SILVER
Similar to 1/4 Gulden, KM#301.1.

KM#	Date	Mintage	VG	Fine	VF	XF
302	1826(u)	.517	15.00	22.50	40.00	60.00
(C73)	1827(u)	.037	60.00	125.00	200.00	325.00
	1834(u)	.501	15.00	22.50	40.00	60.00

GOLD (OMS)

| 302a | 1826(u) | — | — | — | Proof | Rare |
| (C73a) | 1834(u) | — | — | — | — | Rare |

GULDEN

10.7700 g, .893 SILVER, .3092 oz ASW

| 300 | 1821(u) | .099 | 80.00 | 175.00 | 300.00 | 425.00 |
| (C74) | | | | | | |

10.0000 g, .945 SILVER, .3038 oz ASW

| 300a | 1839(u) | 2.217 | 10.00 | 18.00 | 32.00 | 62.50 |
| (C74a) | 1840(u) | 1.981 | 10.00 | 18.00 | 32.00 | 62.50 |

WORLD WAR II COINAGE

Netherlands and Netherlands East Indies coins of the 1941-45 period were struck at U.S. Mints (P-Philadelphia, D-Denver, S-San Francisco and bear the mint mark and a palm tree (acorn on Homeland issues) flanking the date. The following issues - Y46a and Y47a are of the usual Netherlands types, being distinguished from similar 1944-45 issues produced in the name of the Homeland by the presence of the palm tree, but were produced for release in the colony. See other related issues under Curacao and Surinam.

HOMELAND COINAGE
GULDEN

10.0000 g, .720 SILVER, .2315 oz ASW

KM#	Date	Mintage	Fine	VF	XF	Unc
330	1943D	20.000	2.25	3.50	6.00	11.50
(Y46a)						

2 1/2 GULDEN

25.0000 g, .720 SILVER, .5787 oz ASW

25.0000 g, .720 SILVER, .5787 oz ASW

KM#	Date	Mintage	Fine	VF	XF	Unc
331 (Y47a)	1943D	2.000	7.50	9.00	13.50	27.50

PROOF SETS (PS)

KM#	Date	Mintage	Identification	Issue Price	Mkt. Val.
PS1	1854/58(12)	—	KM303 (2 pcs. 1854), KM304 (2 pcs. 1855), KM305 (1855 & 1858), KM306 (2 pcs. 1855), KM307 (2 pcs. 1856), KM308 (2 pcs. 1857)		

TRADE COINAGE
DUCAT

.986 GOLD

These gold coins, intended primarily for circulation in the Netherlands East Indies will be found listed as Y#15 in the Netherlands section.

JAPANESE OCCUPATION
10 SEN

TIN ALLOY

Three coins were struck primarily for circulation in the East Indies. The Sen, 5 Sen and 10 Sen are inscribed DAI NIHON (Great Japan) and are found listed under Japan - Occupation Issues as Y#22, Y#24 and Pn48.

LOCAL COINAGE
Batavian Republic
1799-1806

MINTMASTER'S INITIALS
Z - J.A. Zwekkert

1/2 STUIVER

COPPER BONK, 7.72 g
Value and date each in pearled rectangle.

KM#	Date	Mintage	Good	VG	Fine	VF
213 (C30)	1804	—	30.00	50.00	70.00	100.00
	1805	*.545	—	—	—	Rare

NOTE: 3 varieties exist.
*NOTE: Most of these coins were recalled and melted down.

Value and date in lined rectangle.

216 (213)	1818	—	23.50	37.50	60.00	85.00

STUIVER

COPPER BONK, 23.16 g

206 (C31)	1801	—	8.00	14.50	22.50	35.00
	1802	—	5.25	8.25	15.00	22.50
	1803	—	6.50	11.50	17.50	27.50

NOTE: Roman I in date of 1802 issues.

Reduced weight, 19.30 g
Value and date each in pearl rectangle.

210 (C31a)	1803	—	6.00	10.00	22.50	45.00
	1804	—	7.50	12.00	26.00	57.50
	1805	—	6.00	10.00	22.50	45.00
	1806	—	7.50	12.00	26.00	57.50

NOTE: Varieties exist.

2 STUIVER

COPPER BONK, 46.32 g

207 (C32)	1801	—	20.00	35.00	50.00	80.00
	1802	—	6.00	10.00	22.50	45.00
	1803	—	—	—	—	—

NOTE: Roman I in date of 1802 issues.

Reduced weight, 38.60 g

KM#	Date	Mintage	Good	VG	Fine	VF
211 (C32a)	1803	—	7.50	14.00	25.00	50.00
	1804	—	7.75	14.50	26.00	52.50
	1805	—	7.50	14.00	25.00	50.00
	1806	—	8.00	16.50	30.00	60.00

NOTE: Varieties exist.

8 STUIVER

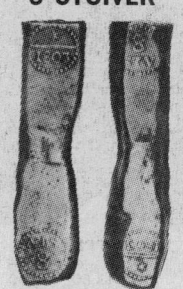

Illustration at 50-percent
COPPER BONK, 154.40 g
Bonk. Value and date in pearl circles.

KM#	Date	Mintage	VG	Fine	VF	XF
212 (C33)	1803	.395	225.00	325.00	450.00	575.00

1/2 RUPEE

6.5750 g, .792 SILVER, .1674 oz ASW

215 (C35)	1805 Z	—	30.00	55.00	100.00	180.00
	1806 Z	—	25.00	45.00	80.00	145.00

NOTE: 12 varieties exist.

RUPEE

13.1500 g, .792 SILVER, .3349 oz ASW

208 (C36)	1801 Z	—	12.00	—	35.50	60.00
	1802 Z	—	18.50	35.00	60.00	110.00
	1803 Z	—	10.00	16.50	30.00	55.00

NOTE: Varieties exist.

214 (C37)	1804	—	15.00	25.00	45.00	80.00
	1805 Z	—	15.00	25.00	45.00	80.00
	1806 Z	—	15.00	25.00	45.00	80.00
(C53)	1808 Z	—	25.00	45.00	80.00	145.00

NOTE: Varieties exist.

1/2 GOLD RUPEE

8.0000 g, .750 GOLD, .1929 oz AGW
Obv: Arabic leg., AD date.

209 (C41)	1801	—	300.00	600.00	900.00	1300.
	1802	—	300.00	600.00	900.00	1300.
	1803	—	—	—	Unique	
	1807 Z	—	600.00	1100.	1600.	2400.

LOCAL COINAGE
Kingdom of Holland
DUIT

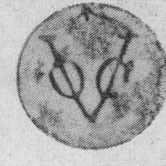

COPPER
Obv: VOC and star above. Rev: JAVA/1806.

KM#	Date	Mintage	VG	Fine	VF	XF
220 (C29)	1806	—	10.00	20.00	34.00	60.00
C42)	1807	—	3.75	7.00	12.00	21.50
	1808	—	3.75	7.00	12.00	21.50
	1809	—	3.00	6.00	13.00	22.50
	1810	—	—	—	Rare	

NOTE: Varieties exist.

Obv: Block LN. Rev: JAVA/date.

223 (C43)	1808	—	3.00	5.00	7.50	13.50
	1809	—	2.00	4.00	7.00	12.50
	1810	—	2.00	4.00	7.00	12.50

NOTE: Varieties exist.

225 (C44)	1810 Z	—	2.00	4.00	7.00	12.50
	1811 Z	—	2.00	4.00	7.00	12.50

NOTE: Several varieties of above 2 coins exist.

Circles of arrowheads around border on both sides.

226 (C44a)	1810 Z	—	8.00	16.50	25.00	40.00

1/2 STUIVER

COPPER
Obv: Ornate LN below value. Rev: JAVA/date.

227 (C45)	1810	—	60.00	160.00	250.00	400.00

NOTE: 3 varieties exist.

228	1810 Z	—	4.50	8.00	14.25	25.50
(C45a)	1811 Z	—	4.50	8.00	14.25	25.50

NOTE: Several varieties exist.

STUIVER

COPPER BONK, 19.30 g

KM#	Date	Mintage	Good	VG	Fine	VF
221 (C47)	1807	—	20.00	35.00	65.00	115.00
	1808	—	—	—	Rare	
	1809	—	7.00	12.50	23.50	42.50
	1810	—	6.50	12.00	21.50	38.50

NOTE: Varieties exist.

11.58 g. Similar to 1 Stuiver, KM#210.

229 (C47a)	1810	—	25.00	40.00	55.00	90.00

NOTE: 2 varieties exist.

Netherlands East Indies / INDONESIA 1004

COPPER
Obv: Ornate LN, value. Rev: JAVA/date.

KM#	Date	Mintage	VG	Fine	VF	XF
230 (C46)	1810	—	80.00	200.00	300.00	450.00

NOTE: 2 varieties exist.

2 STUIVER
COPPER BONK, 38.60 g

KM#	Date	Mintage	Good	VG	Fine	VF
222 (C48)	1807	—	30.00	55.00	85.00	120.00
	1808	—	30.00	55.00	85.00	120.00

Reduced weight, 23.16 g

224.1 (C48.1)	1809	—	12.00	18.00	60.00	150.00
	1810	—	12.00	20.00	30.00	125.00

NOTE: Varieties exist.

15.0-25.0 g
Obv: Retrograde S.

224.2	1809	—	—	—	—	—
	1810	—	5.50	10.00	20.00	35.00

NOTE: Varieties exist. Light weight coins (6.0-10 g) are contemporary forgeries.

Kingdom of the Netherlands
STUIVER

COPPER BONK, 15.44 g
Value and date each in rectangle.

KM#	Date	Mintage	VG	Fine	VF	XF
235 (C68)	1818	—	15.00	35.00	60.00	100.00

NOTE: Varieties exist.

2 STUIVER
COPPER BONK, 30.88 g
Value and date each in rectangle.

236 (C69)	1818	—	10.00	17.50	42.50	80.00
	1819	—	22.50	40.00	72.50	130.00

NOTE: Varieties exist.

BRITISH OCCUPATION
1811-1816
DUIT

COPPER

240 (C54)	1811	—	5.00	10.00	16.50	40.00
	1812	—	3.75	7.50	12.50	35.00

NOTE: At least 5 varieties exist of each date.

BRASS

240a (C54a)	1812	—	7.50	15.00	25.00	45.00

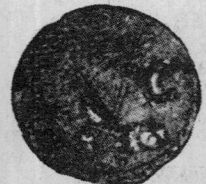 

TIN

244 (C57)	1813	16.747	15.00	35.00	60.00	140.00
	1814	33.656	15.00	30.00	50.00	120.00

1/2 STIVER

COPPER

KM#	Date	Mintage	VG	Fine	VF	XF
241 (C55)	1811	—	5.00	10.00	16.50	40.00
	1812	—	4.00	8.00	13.50	32.50
	1813	—	4.00	8.00	13.50	32.50
	1814	—	5.00	10.00	16.50	40.00
	1815	—	10.00	18.50	30.00	70.00

NOTE: At least 3 varieties exist of each date.

STIVER

COPPER

243 (C56)	1812	—	—	—	Rare	—
	1814	—	13.50	27.50	40.00	70.00
	1815	—	40.00	80.00	120.00	200.00

NOTE: 3 varieties exist of 1814.

1/2 RUPEE

SILVER, 6.57 g
Obv: Javanese leg. and date.
Rev: Arabic leg. and date.

KM#	Date	Year	VG	Fine	VF	XF
246 (C58)	AH1668	AS1740	(1813)error = AH1228)			
	3 or 4 known		—	—	Rare	—
	1229					
	1741	(1814)	175.00	225.00	300.00	375.00

NOTE: The 1/2 Rupee struck in silver is similar to the 1/2 Mohur struck in gold except a five-petaled flower replaces the Christian date on the silver coins.

SUMATRA, Island of

An island, south of the Malay peninsula, was first reached by Europeans for trade in 1599. Competition between European powers for trading rights continued until 1824 at which time it became a Dutch possession. British coins for the island were struck at the Birmingham Mint by Matthew Boulton in 1786 and other issues were struck at Indian mints.

TITLES

فولوفرج

Pulu Percha

MONETARY SYSTEM
100 Kepings = 1 Suku
4 Suku = 1 Dollar (Spanish)

DENOMINATIONS
The following Arabic legends appear for the denomination with an Arabic number above.

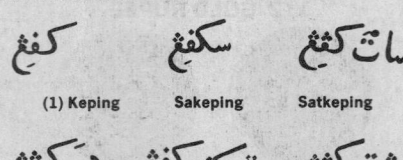

(1) Keping   Sakeping   Satkeping

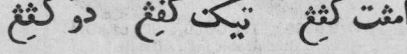

(2) Dua Keping   (3) Tiga Keping   (4) Ampat Keping

EAST INDIA COMPANY
1685 - 1824

KEPING

COPPER
Thick planchet, 3.476 g

KM#	Date	Year	Fine	VF	XF	Unc
262 (C25)	AH1219	1804	2.50	5.00	12.50	20.00
	1219	1804	—	—	Proof	65.00
	1219	1804	—	—	Gilt Proof	85.00

LEAD (OMS)

262a	AH1219	1804	—	—	Proof	250.00

COPPER
Thin planchet, 2.050 g

263 (10)	AH1219	1804	2.50	5.00	12.50	25.00

2 KEPINGS
COPPER
Thick planchet, 6.47 g

264 (13)	AH1219	1804	3.00	6.00	16.50	25.00
		1804	—	—	Proof	75.00
		1804	—	—	Gilt Proof	125.00

LEAD (OMS)

264a	AH1219	1804	—	—	Proof	250.00

COPPER
Thin planchet, 4.40 g

265 (14)	AH1219	1804	2.50	5.00	12.50	20.00

4 KEPINGS

COPPER
Thick planchet, 12.80 g

266 (15)	AH1219	1804	3.75	7.50	20.00	45.00
	1219	1804	—	—	Proof	85.00
	1219	1804	—	—	Gilt Proof	200.00

Thin planchet, 8.50 g

267 (16)	AH1219	1804	3.75	7.50	20.00	45.00

KINGDOM OF THE NETHERLANDS
MINT MARKS
S - Sourabaya Mint

MINTMASTER INITIALS
D - Demmenie
J - L.J. Jeekel
V - K.J. De Vogel
W - C.H. Williams

1/2 DUIT
COPPER
Mint mark: S
Obv: Crowned shield with lion and value as 5 1/32 G
Rev. INDIAE BATAV

KM#	Date	Mintage	VG	Fine	VF	XF
280.1 (C61a)	1816	23.818	.80	2.00	4.00	7.50

W/o mint mark

280.2 (C61b)	1816	—	2.00	5.00	10.00	18.50
	1818	—	.80	2.00	4.00	7.50
	1821	—	.80	2.00	4.00	7.50
	1822	—	2.00	5.00	10.00	17.50

NOTE: Varieties exist.

1/8 STUIVER
(1/2 Duit)

COPPER
Mint mark: S

KM#	Date	Mintage	VG	Fine	VF	XF
286	1822	1.300	1.50	4.00	8.50	15.00
(C64)	1823	33.000	.75	2.00	4.00	7.50
	1824	21.000	.75	2.00	4.00	7.50
	1825	44.000	.75	2.00	4.00	7.50
	1826	69.000	.60	1.50	3.50	6.00

NOTE: Varieties exist. Date 1826 with lion of 1822-1825 with a thick, bushy tail are very rare.

DUIT

COPPER
Mint mark: S

281	1816	64.562	.50	1.25	3.00	5.00
(C62a)						

NOTE: Actually minted 1820-22.

282	1816	—	4.00	10.00	16.50	28.50
(C62b)	1818	—	.50	1.25	2.50	4.00
	1819	—	2.00	5.00	10.00	18.50
	1820	—	.50	1.25	2.50	4.00
	1821	—	.50	1.25	2.50	4.00
	1822	—	.75	2.00	4.00	7.50
	1823	—	1.25	3.00	6.50	11.50
	1824	—	2.00	4.00	8.50	15.00
	1825	—	.75	2.00	4.00	7.50
	1826	—	4.00	10.00	20.00	32.50

NOTE: Varieties exist. 1816 dated coins were actually struck in 1820.

1/4 STUIVER
(Duit)

COPPER
Mint mark: S

287	1822	30.000	.75	2.00	4.00	7.50
(C65)	1823	29.000	.75	2.00	4.00	7.50
	1824	26.000	.75	2.00	4.00	7.50
	1825	125.000	.40	1.00	2.00	3.50
	1826	208.000	.40	1.00	2.00	3.50
	1836	33.453	.75	2.00	4.00	7.50

NOTE: 2 varieties exist and counterfeits w/border of dots.

1/2 STUIVER

COPPER
Obv: G. below shield.

283	1818	—	2.00	4.00	8.50	15.00
(C63)	1819	—	2.00	4.00	8.50	15.00
	1820	—	2.50	5.00	10.00	17.50

NOTE: Varieties exist.

Obv: G. removed.

KM#	Date	Mintage	VG	Fine	VF	XF
284	1820	—	2.00	4.00	8.50	15.00
(C63a)	1821	—	2.00	4.00	8.50	15.00
	1822	—	2.50	5.00	10.00	17.50
	1823	—	2.00	4.00	8.50	15.00
	1824	—	2.00	4.00	8.50	15.00
	1825	—	2.00	4.00	8.50	15.00
	1826	—	4.00	10.00	12.50	22.50

NOTE: Varieties exist.

285	1821S	10.000	.50	2.00	4.00	7.00
(C66)	1822S	7.000	.50	2.00	4.00	7.00
	1823S	19.000	.50	2.00	4.00	7.00
	1824S	5.500	1.00	3.00	6.00	11.50
	1825S	42.000	.50	2.00	4.00	7.00
	1826S	66.000	.50	2.00	4.00	7.00

DECIMAL COINAGE
100 Cents = 1 Gulden

CENT
(Duit)

COPPER

290	1833D	21.778	12.50	30.00	50.00	85.00
(C70)	1833V	Inc. Ab.	1.20	3.00	6.50	11.50
	1834V	66.237	.60	1.50	3.50	6.00
	1835V	48.674	.60	1.50	3.50	6.00
	1836V	94.825	.60	1.50	3.00	6.00
	1837V	182.888	.60	1.50	3.00	6.00
	1837C	Inc. Ab.	—	—	Rare	—
	1837J	Inc. Ab.	—	—	—	5.00
	1838J	235.524	.60	1.50	3.00	5.00
	1839J	314.953	.60	1.50	3.00	5.00
	1839W	Inc. Ab.	.60	1.50	3.00	5.00
	1840W	461.726	.60	1.50	3.00	5.00

NOTE: Varieties exist.

SILVER (OMS)

290a	1833	—	—	—	Rare	—
(C70a)	1834	—	—	—	Rare	—
	1835	—	—	—	Rare	—
	1836	—	—	—	Rare	—
	1837	—	—	—	Rare	—
	1838	—	—	—	Rare	—

2 CENTS
(Double Duit)

COPPER

291	1833D	11.305*	20.00	40.00	80.00	135.00
(C71)	1833V	Inc. Ab.	1.25	3.00	6.00	10.00
	1834V	32.997	.75	2.00	4.00	7.00
	1835V	24.627	.75	2.00	4.00	7.00
	1836V	48.612	.75	2.00	4.00	7.00
	1837J	54.812	1.50	3.00	5.00	9.00
	1837V	Inc. Ab.	.75	2.00	4.00	7.00
	1838J	93.809	.75	2.00	4.00	7.00
	1839J	90.964	.75	2.00	4.00	7.00
	1839W	Inc. Ab.	1.00	3.00	6.00	10.00
	1840W	98.086	2.00	5.00	10.00	17.50
(C75)	1841W	115.321	2.00	5.00	10.00	17.50

NOTE: Varieties exist.

SILVER (OMS)

291a	1836	—	—	—	Unique	—

KM#	Date	Mintage	VG	Fine	VF	XF
(C71a)	1837	—	—	—	Unique	—
	1838	—	—	—	Unique	—

INDONESIA

MONETARY SYSTEM
100 Sen = 1 Rupiah

SEN

ALUMINUM

KM#	Date	Mintage	VF	XF	Unc
7 (Y1)	1952	100.000	.20	.40	.80

5 SEN

ALUMINUM

5 (Y2)	1951	—	.10	.25	.50
	1954	—	.10	.25	.50

10 SEN

ALUMINUM

6 (Y3)	1951	—	.10	.25	.50
	1954	50.000	.10	.20	.40

12 (Y3a)	1957	50.224	.50	.75	1.00

25 SEN

ALUMINUM

8 (Y4)	1952	200.00	.30	.40	.60

11 (Y4a)	1955	25.767	.10	.15	.30
	1957	99.752	.10	.15	.30

50 SEN

COPPER-NICKEL

9 (Y5)	1952	100.000	.10	.15	.30

INDONESIA 1006

KM#	Date	Mintage	VF	XF	Unc
10.1 (Y5a)	1954	1.290	3.00	4.00	6.00
	1955	15.000	.10	.15	.30

Rev: Different head, larger lettering.

10.2	1957	24.977	.10	.15	.30

ALUMINUM

13 (Y7)	1958	100.000	.10	.25	.50

Rev: Modified eagle.

14 (Y7.1)	1959	100.000	.10	.20	.40
	1961	128.528	.10	.20	.40

RUPIAH

ALUMINUM

20 (Y13)	1970	136.010	.10	.15	.20

2 RUPIAH

ALUMINUM

21 (Y14)	1970	139.230	.10	.15	.25

5 RUPIAH

ALUMINUM

22 (Y15)	1970	448.000	.40	.80	1.10

F.A.O. Issue

KM#	Date	Mintage	VF	XF	Unc
37 (Y20)	1974	447.910	—	.10	.15

F.A.O. Issue

43 (Y26)	1979	413.200	.10	.20	.35

10 RUPIAH

COPPER-NICKEL
F.A.O. Issue

33 (Y18)	1971	286.360	—	.10	.15

BRASS-CLAD STEEL
F.A.O. Issue

38 (Y21)	1974	222.910	.10	.15	.20

ALUMINUM
F.A.O. Issue

44 (Y27)	1979	285.670	.10	.20	.35

25 RUPIAH

34 (Y16)	1971	1221.610	.10	.25	.50

COPPER-NICKEL

50 RUPIAH

35 (Y17)	1971	1035.435	.20	.40	.75

COPPER-NICKEL

100 RUPIAH

COPPER-NICKEL

KM#	Date	Mintage	VF	XF	Unc
36 (Y19)	1973	252.868	.25	.50	1.00

F.A.O. Issue

42 (Y25)	1978	907.773	.30	.75	1.50

200 RUPIAH

8.0000 g, .999 SILVER, .2569 oz ASW

23 (1)	1970	5,100	—	Proof	8.50

250 RUPIAH

10.0000 g, .999 SILVER, .3212 oz ASW

24 (2)	1970	5,000	—	Proof	12.50

500 RUPIAH

20.0000 g, .999 SILVER, .6424 oz ASW
Obv: Similar to 10,000 Rupiah, KM#30.

25 (3)	1970	4,800	—	Proof	22.50

750 RUPIAH

30.0000 g, .999 SILVER, .9636 oz ASW
Obv: Similar to 20,000 Rupiah, KM#31.

26 (4)	1970	4,950	—	Proof	40.00

1000 RUPIAH

40.0000 g, .999 SILVER, 1.2848 oz ASW
Obv: Similar to 25,000 Rupiah, KM#32.

Rev: Similar to 750 Rupiah, KM#26.

KM#	Date	Mintage	VF	XF	Unc
27 (5)	1970	4,250	—	Proof	50.00

2000 RUPIAH

4.9300 g, .900 GOLD, .1426 oz AGW

| 28 (7) | 1970 | 2,970 | — | Proof | 100.00 |

25.6500 g, .500 SILVER, .4123 oz ASW
Conservation Series
Rev: Javan Tiger.

| 39 (Y22) | 1974 | .043 | — | — | 15.00 |

28.2800 g, .925 SILVER, .8411 oz ASW

| 39a (Y22a) | 1974 | .018 | — | Proof | 18.00 |

5000 RUPIAH

12.3400 g, .900 GOLD, .3571 oz AGW
Rev: Similar to 2000 Rupiah, KM#28.

| 29 (8) | 1970 | 2,150 | — | Proof | 225.00 |

32.0000 g, .500 SILVER, .5144 oz ASW
Conservation Series
Obv: Similar to 100,000 Rupiah, KM#41.
Rev: Orangutan.

| 40 (Y23) | 1974 | .043 | — | — | 18.00 |

35.0000 g, .925 SILVER, 1.0409 oz ASW

| 40a (Y23a) | 1974 | .017 | — | Proof | 22.00 |

10000 RUPIAH

24.6800 g, .900 GOLD, .7142 oz AGW
Rev: Similar to 500 Rupiah, KM#25.

KM#	Date	Mintage	VF	XF	Unc
30 (9)	1970	1,440	—	Proof	450.00

19.4400 g, .925 SILVER, .5782 oz ASW
Wildlife - Babi Rusa (Wild Pig)
Obv: Similar to 100000 Rupiah, KM#41.

| 45 | 1987 | .025 | — | Proof | 20.00 |

20000 RUPIAH

49.3700 g, .900 GOLD, 1.4391 oz AGW
Rev: Similar to 750 Rupiah, KM#26.

| 31 (10) | 1970 | 1,285 | — | Proof | 950.00 |

25000 RUPIAH

61.7100 g, .900 GOLD, 1.7858 oz AGW
Rev: Similar to 750 Rupiah, KM#26.

| 32 (11) | 1970 | 970 pcs. | — | Proof | 1100. |

100000 RUPIAH

33.4370 g, .900 GOLD, .9676 oz AGW
Conservation Series
Rev: Komodo Lizard.

KM#	Date	Mintage	VF	XF	Unc
41 (Y24)	1974	5,333	—	—	550.00
	1974	1,369	—	Proof	700.00

200000 RUPIAH

10.0000 g, .917 GOLD, .2947 oz AGW
Wildlife - Javan Rhinoceros

| 46 | 1987 | 5,000 | — | Proof | 450.00 |

MINT SETS (MS)

KM#	Date	Mintage	Identification	Issue Price	Mkt. Val.
MS1	1970(3)	—	KM20-22	—	2.00
MS2	1971(3)	—	KM33-35	—	2.00

PROOF SETS (PS)

PS1	1970(10)	970	KM23-32	488.00	2960.
PS2	1970(5)	4,250	KM23-27	45.00	135.00
PS3	1974(2)	30,000	KM39a-40a	50.00	40.00

RIAU ARCHIPELAGO

A group of islands off the tip of the Malay Peninsula. Coins were issued near the end of 1963 (although dated 1962) and recalled as worthless on Sept. 30, 1964. They were legal tender from Oct. 15, 1963 to July 1, 1964.

INSCRIPTION ON EDGE
KEPULAUAN RIAU

SEN

ALUMINUM

KM#	Date	Mintage	VF	XF	Unc
5 (Y8)	1962	—	.50	1.00	1.50

5 SEN

ALUMINUM

| 6 (Y9) | 1962 | — | .30 | .75 | 1.00 |

10 SEN

ALUMINUM

| 7 (Y10) | 1962 | — | .35 | .85 | 1.25 |

Riau Archipelago / INDONESIA 1008

25 SEN

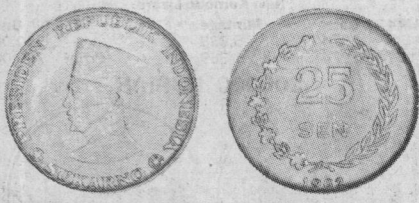

ALUMINUM

KM#	Date	Mintage	VF	XF	Unc
8.1 (Y11.1)	1962	—	.50	1.00	2.00

Rev: Different style "5".

| 8.2 (Y11.2) | 1962 | — | 2.00 | 4.00 | 6.00 |

50 SEN

ALUMINUM
Rev: 17 laurel leaves.

| 9.1 (Y12.1) | 1962 | — | 1.00 | 2.00 | 4.00 |

Rev: 16 laurel leaves.

| 9.2 (Y12.2) | 1962 | — | 4.00 | 7.00 | 12.50 |

IRIAN BARAT
(West Irian, Irian Jaya, Netherlands New Guinea)

A province of Indonesia comprising the western half of the island of New Guinea. A special set of coins dated 1962 were issued in 1964 and were recalled December 31, 1971 and are no longer legal tender.

NO INSCRIPTION ON EDGE

SEN

ALUMINUM
Plain edge

KM#	Date	Mintage	Fine	VF	XF	Unc
5 (Y8a)	1962	—	.25	.75	1.00	1.35

5 SEN

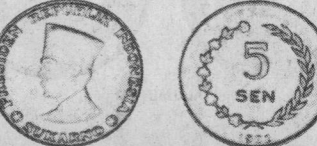

ALUMINUM
Plain edge

KM#	Date	Mintage	Fine	VF	XF	Unc
6 (Y9a)	1962	—	.25	.75	1.00	1.35

10 SEN

ALUMINUM
Plain edge

| 7 (Y10a) | 1962 | — | .30 | .85 | 1.15 | 1.75 |

25 SEN

ALUMINUM
Reeded edge

| 8.1 (Y11a) | 1962 | — | .35 | 1.00 | 1.50 | 2.00 |

Rev: Different style "5".

| 8.2 (Y11a.1) | 1962 | — | 1.00 | 2.75 | 3.75 | 5.25 |

50 SEN

ALUMINUM
Reeded edge

| 9 (Y12a) | 1962 | — | .55 | 1.25 | 1.75 | 2.50 |

TIMOR
(Timur, East Timor)

An island in the Lesser Sunda group, presently part of Indonesia but formerly divided between Portugal and the Netherlands. Portugal discovered and owned the eastern half of the island since 1512 and made coins for this colony. Made part of Indonesia in 1975.

MONETARY SYSTEM
100 Avos = 1 Pataca

COLONIAL COINAGE
10 AVOS

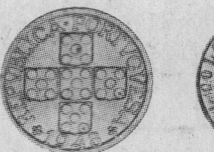

BRONZE

5 (Y1)	1945	.050	15.00	25.00	35.00	65.00
	1948	.500	.60	1.00	2.00	4.00
	1951	6.250	.50	.75	1.50	2.50

---

20 AVOS

NICKEL-BRONZE

KM#	Date	Mintage	Fine	VF	XF	Unc
6 (Y2)	1945	.050	7.50	12.50	25.00	60.00

50 AVOS

3.5000 g, .650 SILVER, .0731 oz ASW

7 (Y3)	1945	.100	20.00	37.50	55.00	85.00
	1948	.200	3.50	7.50	12.50	18.50
	1951	6.250	2.50	5.00	7.50	12.50

MONETARY REFORM
100 Centavos = 1 Escudo

10 CENTAVOS

BRONZE

| 10 (Y4) | 1958 | 1.000 | .50 | 1.00 | 2.50 | 8.00 |

20 CENTAVOS

BRONZE

| 17 (Y12) | 1970 | 1.000 | .10 | .15 | .30 | .60 |

30 CENTAVOS

BRONZE

| 11 (Y5) | 1958 | 2.000 | .50 | 1.00 | 1.50 | 3.00 |

50 CENTAVOS

BRONZE

| 18 (Y13) | 1970 | 1.000 | .10 | .15 | .30 | .75 |

60 CENTAVOS

COPPER-NICKEL

| 12 (Y6) | 1958 | 1.000 | .50 | 1.00 | 1.50 | 3.00 |

ESCUDO

COPPER-NICKEL

KM#	Date	Mintage	Fine	VF	XF	Unc
13 (Y7)	1958	1.200	.50	1.00	2.00	4.00
22 (Y17)	1970	.700	1.00	1.50	3.00	6.00

BRONZE

19 (Y14)	1970	1.200	.15	.35	1.00	2.00

2-1/2 ESCUDOS

COPPER-NICKEL

20 (Y15)	1970	1.000	.25	.50	1.25	2.50

3 ESCUDOS

3.5000 g, .650 SILVER, .0731 oz ASW

14 (Y8)	1958	1.000	2.00	2.50	4.00	7.50

5 ESCUDOS

COPPER-NICKEL

21 (Y16)	1970	1.200	.50	.75	1.50	3.00

6 ESCUDOS

7.0000 g, .650 SILVER, .1463 oz ASW

15 (Y9)	1958	1.000	3.50	5.50	9.00	15.00

10 ESCUDOS

7.0000 g, .650 SILVER, .1463 oz ASW

16 (Y10)	1964	.600	3.50	5.50	9.00	15.00

IRAN

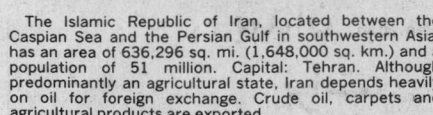

The Islamic Republic of Iran, located between the Caspian Sea and the Persian Gulf in southwestern Asia, has an area of 636,296 sq. mi. (1,648,000 sq. km.) and a population of 51 million. Capital: Tehran. Although predominantly an agricultural state, Iran depends heavily on oil for foreign exchange. Crude oil, carpets and agricultural products are exported.

Iran (historically known as Persia until 1931AD) is one of the world's most ancient and resilient nations. Strategically astride the lower land gate to Asia, it has been conqueror and conquered, sovereign nation and vassal state, ever emerging from its periods of glory or travail with its culture and political individuality intact. Iran (Persia) was a powerful empire under Cyrus the Great (600-529 B.C.), its borders extending from the Indus to the Nile. It has also been conquered by the predatory empires of antique and recent times - Assyrian, Medean, Macedonian, Seljuq, Turk, Mongol - and more recently been coveted by Russia, the Third Reich and Great Britain. Revolts against the absolute power of the Persian shahs resulted in the establishment of a constitutional monarchy in 1906. In 1979, the monarchy was toppled and an Islamic Republic proclaimed.

TITLES

Dar el-Khilafat   دار الخلافة

RULERS

Qajar Dynasty

Fath'ali Shah,
  AH1212-1250/1797-1834AD
Sultan Ali Shah, in Tehran
  AH1250/1834AD (30 days)
Husayn Ali Shah,
  AH1250/1834AD (6 months)
  (in Southern Iran only)
Muhammad Shah,
  AH1250-1264/1834-1848AD
Nasir al-Din Shah,
  AH1264-1313/1848-1896AD
Muzaffar al-Din Shah,
  AH1313-1324/1896-1907AD
Muhammad Ali Shah,
  AH1324-1327/1907-1909AD
Sultan Ahmad Shah,
  AH1327-1344/1909-1925AD

Pahlavi Dynasty

Reza Shah,
  SH1304-1320/1925-1941AD
Mohammad Reza Pahlavi, Shah
  SH1320-1358/1941-1979AD

Islamic Republic, SH1358-/1979-AD

MINTNAMES

Abushahr (Bushire)   ابو شهر

Ardebil   اردبیل

Astarabad   استراباد

Bandar Abbas   بندر عباس

Behbehan   بهبهان

Borujerd   بروجرد

Darband   دربند

Dezful   دزفول

Eravan (Iravan)   ایروان

IRAN 1010

Fouman	
Ganjah (Ganja)	كنجه
Gilan	
Hamadan	بمدان
Herat	برات
Isfahan	اصفهان
Kashan	كاشان
Kerman	كرمان
Kermanshahan (Kermanshah)	كرمانشاهان
Khoy (Khui)	خوى
Lahijan	لاهيجان
Maragheh	مراغه
Mashad	مشهد
Mazandaran	مازندران
Nakhchawan	نخجوان
Naseri	ناصرى
Nihawand	نهاوند
Nukhwi	نخوى
Panahabad	بناه باد
Qazwin	قزوين
Qum	قم
Ra'nash	رعنش
Rasht	رشت
Rekab	ركاب
Reza'iyeh	رظاعيه
Rikab	ركاب
Sarakhs	سرخس
Sari	سارى
Sa'ujbulagh	ساوج بلاق
Shamakha (Caucasia) Shiraz	شيراز
Shushtar	شوشتر
Simnan	سمنان
Sultanabad	سلطاناباد
Tabaristan	طبرستان
Tabriz	تبريز
Tehran	طهران
Tuyserkan	توى سركان
Urumi (Reza'iyeh)	ارومى
Yazd	يزد
Zanjan	زنجان

COIN DATING

Iranian coins were dated according to the Moslem lunar calendar until March 21, 1925 (AD), when dating was switched to a new calendar based on the solar year, indicated by the notation SH. The monarchial calender system was adopted in 1976 = MS2535 and was abandoned in 1978 = MS2537. The previously used solar year calendar was restored at that time.

MONETARY SYSTEM

1798-1825 (AH 1212-1241)
1250 Dinars = 1 Riyal
8 Riyals = 1 Toman

1825-1931 (AH1241-1344, SH1304-09)
50 Dinars = 1 Shahi
20 Shahis = 1 Kran (Qiran)
10 Krans = 1 Toman
NOTE: From AD1830-34 (AH1245-50) the gold Toman was known as a 'Keshwarsetan.'

1932-Date (SH1310-Date)
5 Dinars = 1 Shahi
20 Shahis = 1 Rial (100 Dinars)
10 Rials = 1 Toman
NOTE: The Toman ceased to be an official unit in 1932, but continues to be applied in popular usage. Thus, '135 Rials' is always expressed as '13 Toman, 5 Rials'. The term 'Rial' is often used in conversation, as well as either 'Kran' or 'Ezar' (short for Hazar = 1000) is used.
NOTE: The Law of 18 March 1930 fixed the gold Pahlavi at 20 Rials. No gold coins were struck. The Law of 13 March 1932 divided the Pahlavi into 100 Rials, instead of 20. The Rial's weight was reduced from 0.3661 grams of pure gold to 0.0732. Since 1937 gold has been allowed to float and the Pahlavi is quoted daily in Rials in the marketplaces.

HAMMERED 'DUMP' COINAGE
Copper Coinage

During the nineteenth century, copper coins (falus, flus) were issued at some 40 or more local mints, each of which coined falus for local use only. Copper coins did not circulate generally, but were restricted to the city of their origin and its immediate environs. The local mintmaster, often in collaboration with the local govenor, determined the type, design, and weight of the coinage, and regulated its circulation.

In theory, copper coins were recalled and changed about every year, with a substantial fee payable to the mintmaster for the exchange of old coin for new. To discourage further use the old coin was either demonetized or tariffed at a lower value, usually about half its original.

In order to facilitate the recognition of new and old coin, the type was changed annually, the type being the obverse pictorial design, so that illiterate shopkeepers could tell the difference and not be deceived by obsolete coins. However, after a number of years, the same types would be reinstated for another year. In practice, the system worked more informally, and surviving coins show that at some mints, identical types were struck for several years running and were not recalled annually.

The metrology of the copper Falus is uncertain. While it seems that Falus were intended to follow an assigned weight standard, great tolerance was permitted. The weight standard was frequently changed (or the mint-master issued lighter coins and pocketed the difference), and each mint city maintained its own standard and copper currency policies.

As a result of the frequent recoinage of copper and its frequent demonetization, copper coins were not hoarded or saved, and are consequently quite scarce today. Annual change meant that each mint had a multiplicity of types and varieties, most of which are uncommon today. The following listings are not an attempt at completeness, but give a representative selection of the products of each mint.

IMPORTANT: Most types were used at many different mints. The type can therefore not be used to attribute a coin to the mint of its issue. The ONLY certain way of attributing the coin is to read the mint name on the reverse. Well struck copper falus with clear mintname and date are worth a premium.

LOCAL COPPER FALUS

Abushahr Mint
Obv: Lion.

KM#	Date	Mintage	Good	VG	Fine	VF
2	AH1270	—	4.50	7.50	12.50	20.00

Obv: Two lions facing.

| 56 | AHxxxx | | | | | |

Obv: Bale mark.

| 3 | AH1234 | — | 7.50 | 12.50 | 20.00 | 32.50 |

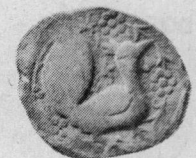

Obv: Peacock.

| 4 | AH1239 | — | 6.00 | 9.00 | 15.00 | 25.00 |

Obv: Two peacocks facing left and right.

| 57 | AH1257 | | | | | |

Obv: Fish.

| 5 | AH1221 | — | 5.50 | 9.00 | 15.00 | 25.00 |
| | 1231 | | | | | |

Ardebil Mint
Obv: Peacock holding worm in beak.

| 6 | AH1232 | — | 6.00 | 10.00 | 17.50 | 30.00 |

Astarabad Mint
Obv: 2 Ibexes.

| 7 | ND | | 6.00 | 10.00 | 17.50 | 30.00 |

Obv: Man horseback.

| A7 | AH1259 | | 6.00 | 10.00 | 17.50 | 30.00 |

Obv: Sun over lion facing right.

| 58 | ND | | 6.00 | 10.00 | 17.50 | 30.00 |

IRAN 1011

Borujerd Mint
Obv: Soldier leaning on his rifle.

KM#	Date	Mintage	Good	VG	Fine	VF
10	AH124x	—	8.00	13.50	21.50	35.00
	1261	—	—	—	—	—

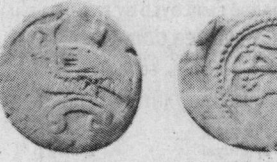

Obv: Small bird.

| 11 | ND | — | 5.50 | 9.00 | 15.00 | 25.00 |

Darband Mint
Obv: Peacock right.

| 59 | AH1228 | — | — | — | — | — |

Ganjah Mint
Obv: Goose.

| 15 | AH1257 | — | 8.00 | 13.50 | 21.50 | 35.00 |

Obv: Horse.

| 60 | AH1220 | — | — | — | — | — |

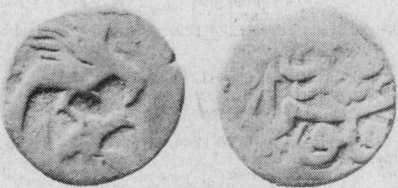

Hamadan Mint
Obv: Eagle carrying off chicken.

| 18 | AH1254 | — | 6.00 | 10.00 | 16.50 | 27.50 |

Iravan Mint
Obv: Camel.

| 19 | AH1223 | — | 8.00 | 13.50 | 21.50 | 35.00 |

Isfahan Mint
Obv: Scales.

| 21 | AH1242 | — | 3.50 | 6.00 | 10.00 | 16.50 |

Kashan Mint
Obv: Lion & sun within wreath.
Denomination: 50 Dinars

| 24 | AH1293 | — | 6.00 | 10.00 | 17.50 | 30.00 |

NOTE: This type was an attempt to reform the copper coinage by Nasir al-Din Shah, and was also struck at Isfahan, Tehran, Tabriz and Shiraz in 1293 and 1294. Kashan is the rarest mint, Tehran and Isfahan the most plentiful.

Kerman Mint
Obv: Lion in wreath.

KM#	Date	Mintage	Good	VG	Fine	VF
27	AH1287	—	4.50	7.50	12.50	20.00

Kermanshahan Mint
Obv: Sunface.

| 28 | AH1245 | — | 4.50 | 7.50 | 12.50 | 20.00 |

Obv: Lion.

| 29 | ND | — | 6.00 | 10.00 | 16.50 | 27.50 |

Obv: Camel and rider.

| 16 | AH1244 | — | 5.50 | 9.00 | 15.00 | 25.00 |

Obv: Horseman riding left. Rev: Lion and sun.

| 62 | AH1231 | — | — | — | — | — |

Khoy Mint
Obv: Gazelle.

| 26 | AH1230 | — | 5.50 | 9.00 | 15.00 | 25.00 |

Maragheh Mint
Obv: Peacock.

| 31 | AH1270 | — | 7.50 | 12.50 | 20.00 | 32.50 |

Mashad Mint
Obv: Elephant and rider.

| 32 | AH1246 | — | 2.50 | 4.50 | 9.00 | 14.50 |

Obv: Sunface.

| 63 | AH1237 | — | — | — | — | — |

Obv: Lion and sun.

| 64 | AH1258 | — | — | — | — | — |
| | 1261 | — | — | — | — | — |

Nihawand Mint
Obv: Lion sitting.

KM#	Date	Mintage	Good	VG	Fine	VF
34	AH1240	—	9.00	15.00	25.00	40.00

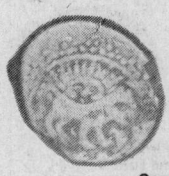 

Qazwin Mint
Obv: Lion and sun.

| 35 | ND | — | 4.50 | 7.50 | 12.50 | 20.00 |

Obv: Lion and sun in wreath.

| A35 | AH129x | — | 4.50 | 7.50 | 12.50 | 20.00 |

Rasht Mint
Obv: Lion and sun.

| 36 | AH1246 | — | 4.50 | 7.50 | 12.50 | 20.00 |

Obv: Lion.

| 37 | AH1233 | — | 4.50 | 8.00 | 13.50 | 22.50 |

Obv: Sunface.

| A37 | AH1247 | — | 4.50 | 7.50 | 12.50 | 20.00 |

Sa'ujbulagh Mint
Obv: 2 Guinea hens.

| 39 | ND | — | 4.50 | 7.50 | 12.50 | 20.00 |

Obv: Lion and sun, stylized.

| 40 | AH1230 | — | 5.50 | 9.00 | 15.00 | 25.00 |

IRAN 1012

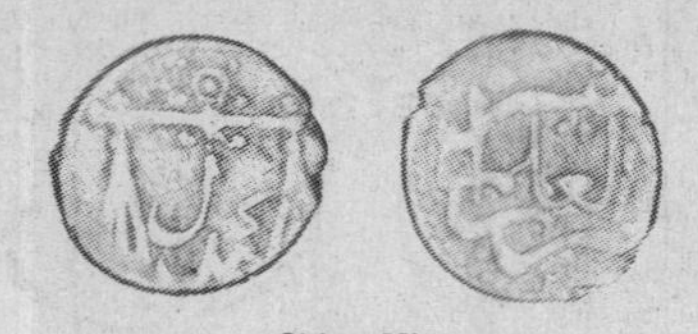

Shiraz Mint
Obv: Scales.

KM#	Date	Mintage	Good	VG	Fine	VF
41	AH126x	—	4.50	7.50	12.50	20.00

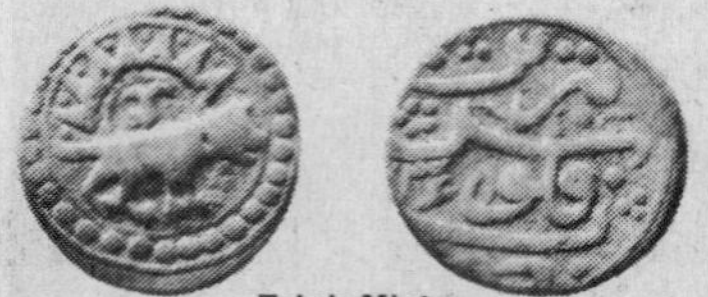

Tabriz Mint
Obv: Lion and sun.

45	AH1235	—	3.50	6.00	10.00	16.50
	1236	—	3.50	6.00	10.00	16.50

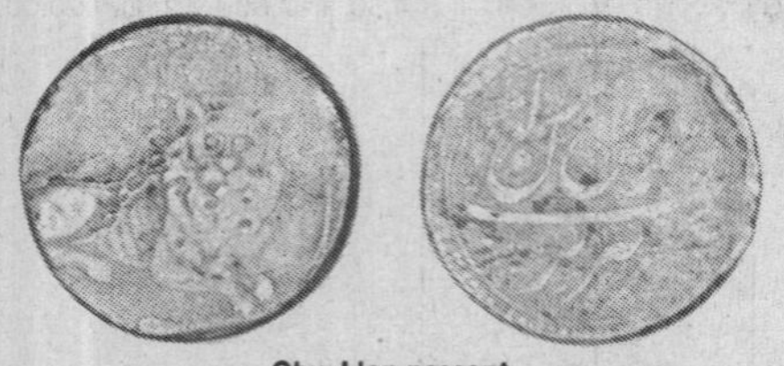

Obv: Lion passant.

47	AH125x	—	3.50	6.00	10.00	16.50

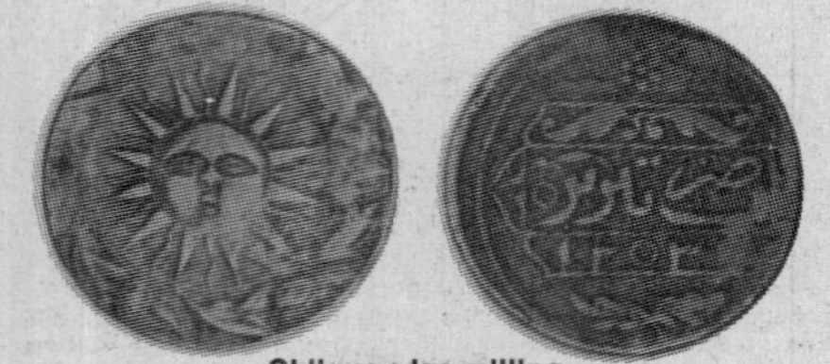

Oblique edge milling
Obv: Radiant sunface within wreath.

A47	AH1229	—	3.50	7.50	12.50	20.00
	1230	—	3.50	7.50	12.50	20.00

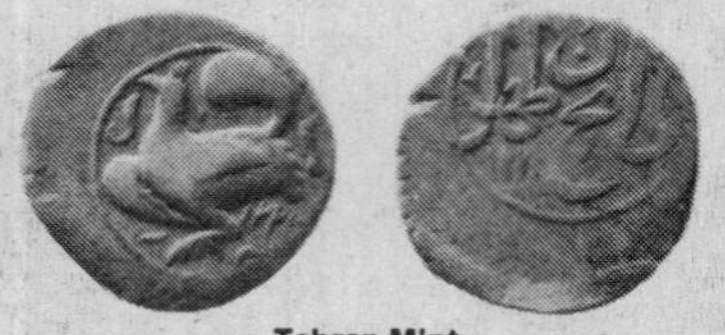

Tehran Mint
Obv: Peacock.

48	AH1222	—	3.50	6.00	10.00	16.50

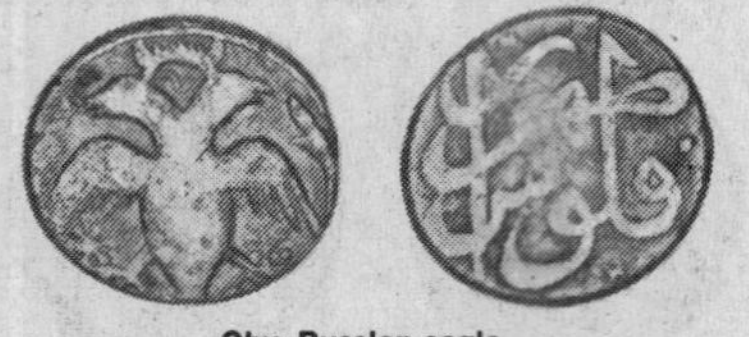

Obv: Russian eagle.

49	ND	—	6.00	10.00	17.50	30.00

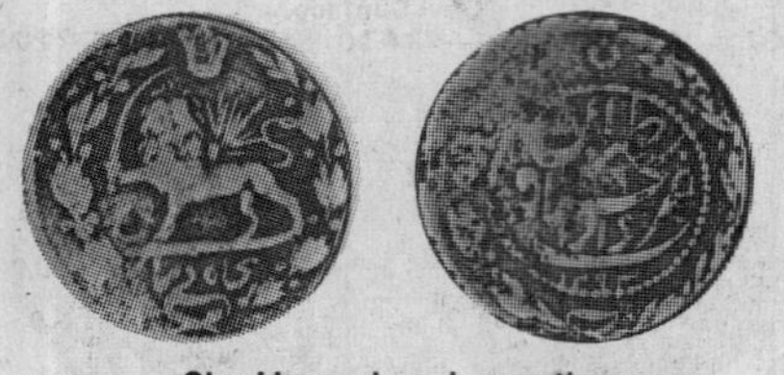

Obv: Lion and sun in wreath.

A49	AH1293	—	4.50	7.50	12.50	20.00

NOTE: Other mints also produced local Falus, for which examples were not available to illustrate. Still other mints operated only or largely at earlier dates. These include Damavand, Damghan, Darabjird, Ja'farafad, Kangan, Ra'nash, Semnan, Tuy, Tus and more.

SILVER AND GOLD COINAGE

The precious metal monetary system of Qajar Persia prior to the reforms of 1878 was the direct descendant of the Mongol system introduced by Ghazan Mahmud in 1297AD, and was the last example of a medieval Islamic coinage. It is not a modern system, and cannot be understood as such. It is not possible to list types, dates, and mints as for other countries, both because of the nature of the coinage, and because very little research has been done on the series. The following comments should help elucidate its nature.

STANDARDS: The weight of the primary silver and gold coins was set by law and was expressed in terms of the Mesqal (about 4.61 g) and the Nokhod (24 Nokhod = 1 Mesqal). The primary silver coin was the Rupee from AH1211-1212, the Riyal from 1212-1241, and the Gheran from 1241-1344. The standard gold coin was the Toman. Currently the price of gold is quoted in Mesqals.

DENOMINATIONS: In addition to the primary denominations, noted in the last paragraph, fractional pieces were coined, valued at one-eighth, one-fourth, and one-half the primary denomination, usually in much smaller quantities. These were ordinarily struck from the same dies as the larger pieces, sometimes on broad, thin flans, sometimes on thick, dumpy flans. On the smaller coins, the denomination can best be determined only by weighing the coin. The denomination is almost never expressed on the coin!

DEVALUATIONS: From time to time, the standard for silver and gold was reduced, and the old coin recalled and replaced with lighter coin, the difference going to the government coffers. The effect was that of a devaluation of the primary silver and gold coins, or inversely regarded, an increase in the price of silver and gold. The durations of each standard varied from about 2 to 20 years. The standards are given for each ruler, as the denomination can only be determined when the standard is known.

LIGHTWEIGHT AND ALLOYED PIECES: Most of the smaller denomination coins were issued at lighter weights than those prescribed by law, with the difference going to the pockets of the mintmasters. Other mints, notably Hamadan, added excessive amounts of alloy to the coins, and some mintmasters lost their heads as a result. Discrepancies in weight of as much as 15 percent and more are observed, with the result that it is often quite impossible to determine the denomination of a coin!

OVERSIZE COINS: Occasionally, multiples of the primary denominations were produced, usually on special occasions for presentation by the Shah to his favorites. These 'coins' did not circulate (except as bullion), and were usually worn as ornaments. They were the 'NCLT's' of their day.

MINTS & EPITHETS: Qajar coinage was struck at 34 mints (plus at least a dozen others striking only copper Falus), which are listed previously, with drawings of the mint names in Persian, as they appear on the coins. However, the Persian script admits of infinite variation and stylistic whimsy, so the forms given are only guides, and not absolute. Only a knowledge of the script will assure correct reading. In addition to the city name, most mint names were given identifying epithets, which occasionally appear in lieu of the mint name, particularly at Iravan and Mashhad.

TYPES: There were no types in the modern sense, but the arrangement of the legends and the ornamental borders were frequently changed. These changes do not coincide with changes in standards, and cannot be used to determine the mint, which must be found by actually reading the reverse inscriptions.

MINTS FOR SILVER AND GOLD

The following mints struck silver and/or gold coins during the period AD1796-1878 (AH1211-1296). All except the Central Mint at Tehran were suppressed by order of Nasir Al-Din Shah in 1295/1878.

The first column lists the mint name and the following three columns provide valuation adjustments for silver coins of each mint for each reign. Special premiums are not applicable to gold coins from the rarer mints. A dash (-) means that no coins are known from the mint for the respective reign.

Relative Scarcity

(For silver coins only)
(plus percent premium)

Mint	Fath'Ali	Muhammad	Nasir Al-din
Ardabil	100	—	—
Astarabad	25	25	None
Borujerd	50	—	—
Ganja	150	—	—
Hamadan	50	None	None
Herat	—	—	100
Iravan	50	—	—
Isfahan	None	None	None
Kashan	None	—	25
Khoy	50	—	50
Kerman	25	50	50
Kirmanshahan	None	None	25
Lahijan	50	—	—
Maragheh	150	—	—
Mashad	None	None	None
Mazandaran	25	—	—
Nihavand	150	—	—
Nukhwi	200	—	—
Qazvin	None	—	25
Qum	75	—	—
Rasht	None	25	25
Rekab	75	—	—
Sarakhs	—	—	200
Shiraz	None	25	25
Shushtar	150	—	See Note
Simnan	100	—	—
Tabaristan	50	25	None
Tabriz	None	None	None
Tehran	None	None	None
Tuyserkan	100	—	—
Urumi	25	—	—
Yazd	None	25	25
Zanjan	75	—	—

NOTE: A coin of Shushtar is reported for Nasir al-Din Shah, but not confirmed.

None = No premium. A dash means coins of that mint for that ruler are unknown.

The following listings are arranged by ruler, first, the various standards are explained. Then, the coins are listed by denomination within each reign. For each denomination, one or more pieces, when available, are illustrated, with the mint and date noted beneath each photo. For each type, a date range is given, but this range indicates the years during which the particular type was current, and does not imply that every year of the interval is known on actual coins. Because dates were carelessly engraved, and old dies were used until they wore out or broke, we occasionally find coins of a particular type dated before or after the indicated interval. Such coins command no premium. No attempt has been made to determine which mints actually exist for which types.

FATH'ALI SHAH

AH1212-1250/1797-1834AD

STANDARDS EMPLOYED BY FATH'ALI SHAH

SILVER COINAGE

I. Rupee Standard, used only for coronation piece (C#188) AH1212. 1 Rupee = 60 Nokhod.

1 Rupee	**11.50 g**

II. First Riyal Standard, AH1212-1232, 1 Riyal = 54 Nokhod.

1/8 Riyal	**1.30 g**
1/4 Riyal	**2.60 g**
1/2 Riyal	**5.20 g**
1 Riyal	**10.40 g**

III. Second Riyal Standard, AH1232-1241, 1 Riyal = 2 Mesqal = 48 Nokhod.

1/8 Riyal	**1.15 g**
1/4 Riyal	**2.30 g**
1/2 Riyal	**4.60 g**
1 Riyal	**9.20 g**

IV. Kran Standard, AH1241-1250, 1 Kran = 1-1/2 Mesqal 36 Nokhod.

1/8 Kran	**0.90 g**
1/4 Kran	**1.70 g**
1/2 Kran	**3.50 g**
1 Kran	**6.90 g**

GOLD COINAGE

I. First Standard, AH1213-?? (after 1214), 1 Toman = 32 Nokhod.

1/2 Toman	**3.10 g**
1 Toman	**6.10 g**

II. Second Standard, AH1220-1224, 1 Toman = 30 Nokhod.

1/4 Toman	**1.50 g**
1/2 Toman	**2.90 g**
1 Toman	**5.80 g**

III. Third Standard, AH1224-1227, 1 Toman = 28 Nokhod.

1/2 Toman	**2.70 g**
1 Toman	**5.40 g**

IV. Fourth Standard, AH1227-1229, 1 Toman = 25 Nokhod.

1/2 Toman	**2.40 g**
1 Toman	**4.80 g**

V. Fifth Standard, AH1230-1244, 1 Toman = 24 Nokhod = 1 Mesqal.

1/4 Toman	**1.15 g**
1/2 Toman	**2.30 g**
1 Toman	**4.60 g**

NOTE: Some mints were using this standard as early as AH1228 if the dates on the coins are correct. However, the similarity of the '2' and '3' in Persian may have led to 1232 being read as 1222, etc.

VI. Sixth Standard, AH1246-1250, 1 Toman = 18 Nokhod.

1/2 Toman	**1.70 g**
1 Toman (Keshvarsetan)	**3.50 g**

NOTE: It is probable that all fractions exist for each standard.

TYPES

Although there are no clearly distinguishable 'types' in the European sense, changes in the obverse legend and calligraphic style enable us to divide the coinage into a sequence of five basic 'types'. Since the same dies, or similar dies, were used for all denominations, gold and silver, the following division applies to all.

TYPE I: With title 'Sultan' and thick, interlaced, coarse calligraphy. Used AH1213-1218.

TYPE II: With title 'Sultan, Son of the Sultan' and thick, coarse calligraphy, but letters separate and flowing (script known as Nasta'liq). Plain background. Used AH1218-22.

TYPE III: As last, but background filled with dots, vines, and tendrils. Used AH1222-1241.

TYPE IV: Style as Type III, but with title 'Sahibqiran' (literally, a title for a person born under an auspicious conjunction of the planets. After the title was assumed by Timor Lang in the 14th century, it lost its astrological meaning and came to denote 'Conqueror'). The coins of this type were named 'Sahibqiran' on account of this title, which was shortened in the popular idiom to 'Ghiran' (Kran). Used AH1241-1245 (but the fifth type never caught on, and most coins dated AH1246-1250 are of the fourth type).

TYPE V: As the third, but with title 'Keshvarsetan' (Conqueror of Nations). Used AH1245-1250.

NOTE: Due to mint carelessness, the use of old dies, and the whims of mintmasters, the above types are found dated before and after their 'official' spans of existence.

NOTE: Type I normally bears dates on obverse and reverse, quite frequently mismatched (no premium for such coins: they are almost as common as those with matched dates!). All other types are normally dated only on the reverse.

NOTE: The obverse is the side bearing the king's name and titles. The reverse is the side with the mint.

All silver coins of the first and second types are on the first Riyal Standard. The third type is divided into two subtypes: III A on the first Riyal Standard (AH1222-1232), III B on the reduced second Riyal Standard (AH1232-41). Types IV and V are on the Kran Standard.

Riyal Standard
1/8 RIYAL

SILVER, 1.30 g

TYPE III A.
C#	Date	Mintage	Good	VG	Fine	VF
191b	AH1222-32	—	4.00	7.50	12.00	25.00

SILVER, 1.15 g

TYPE III B.
| 191c | AH1232-41 | — | 4.00 | 7.50 | 12.00 | 25.00 |

1/4 RIYAL

SILVER, 2.60 g
Tabriz Mint

TYPE III A.
| 192b | AH1222-32 | — | 4.00 | 7.50 | 12.00 | 20.00 |

SILVER, 2.60 g
Tabriz Mint

Borujerd Mint, 2.30 g

TYPE III B.
| 192c | AH1232-41 | — | 3.00 | 5.50 | 9.00 | 15.00 |

1/2 RIYAL

SILVER, 5.20 g
Isfahan Mint

TYPE I
| 193 | AH1213-17 | — | 7.50 | 12.50 | 20.00 | 30.00 |

W/o date.

TYPE II
| 193a | AH1217-22 | — | 5.50 | 9.00 | 12.50 | 18.50 |

Yazd Mint

TYPE III.A
| 193b | AH1222-32 | — | 5.00 | 8.00 | 12.50 | 20.00 |

Kashan Mint, 4.50 g
| 193c.3 | AH123x | — | 6.00 | 10.00 | 15.00 | 25.00 |

SILVER, 5.20 g
Tehran Mint, 4.60 g

TYPE III.B
C#	Date	Mintage	Good	VG	Fine	VF
193c.2	AH1232-41	—	5.00	8.00	11.00	16.50

RIYAL

SILVER, 10.40 g
Tehran Mint

TYPE I
| 194 | AH1212-17 | — | 10.00 | 12.50 | 15.00 | 20.00 |

Khoy Mint

TYPE II
| 194a | AH1217-22 | — | 10.00 | 12.00 | 15.00 | 35.00 |

Isfahan Mint

TYPE III.A
| 194b | AH1222-32 | — | 10.00 | 11.50 | 13.50 | 17.50 |

SILVER, 9.20 g
Isfahan Mint

TYPE III.B
| 194c | AH1232-41 | — | 10.00 | 11.50 | 13.50 | 17.50 |

Kran Standard
1/8 KRAN

SILVER, 0.90 g
Khoy Mint

TYPE IV
| 200 | AH1241-45 | — | 4.00 | 7.00 | 12.00 | 25.00 |

Found both uniface and with two faces.

Isfahan Mint

TYPE V
| 200a | AH1246-50 | — | 7.50 | 15.00 | 25.00 | 40.00 |

NOTE: Use of obsolete dated reverse die.

1/4 KRAN

SILVER, 1.70 g

TYPE IV
| 201 | AH1241-45 | — | 5.00 | 10.00 | 16.50 | 26.50 |

1/2 KRAN

SILVER, 3.50 g
Kashan Mint

TYPE IV
C#	Date	Mintage	Good	VG	Fine	VF
202	AH1241-45	—	5.00	8.00	15.00	25.00

KRAN

SILVER, 6.90 g
Hamadan Mint

Mashad Mint

TYPE IV
| 203 | AH1241-45 | — | 7.00 | 9.00 | 11.50 | 17.50 |

Tabaristan Mint

TYPE V
| 203a | AH1246-50 | — | 8.50 | 15.00 | 25.00 | 50.00 |

GOLD COINAGE

At present, it is not yet possible to determine which types were used with which standard. Until more research is done, and more coins are brought to light, we shall list the gold by standard. The fifth standard comes in two varieties, without 'Sahibaqiran' AH1230-1241 and with 'Sahibqiran' (AH1241-1245), referred to as standards 5A and 5B, respectively.

1/4 TOMAN

GOLD, 1.50 g

SECOND STANDARD
C#	Date	Mintage	VG	Fine	VF	XF
204a	AH1220-24	—	35.00	55.00	85.00	125.00

FOURTH STANDARD, Isfahan
| 204c | AH1228 | — | 35.00 | 55.00 | 85.00 | 125.00 |

GOLD, 1.15 g

FIFTH STANDARD (5A)
| 204d.1 | AH1230-41 | — | 35.00 | 55.00 | 85.00 | 125.00 |

FIFTH STANDARD, 'Sahibqeran' (5B)
| 204d.2 | AH1241-45 | — | 30.00 | 50.00 | 70.00 | 100.00 |

1/2 TOMAN

GOLD, 3.10 g

FIRST STANDARD
| 205 | AH1213-17 | — | 65.00 | 80.00 | 100.00 | 125.00 |

2.90 g

SECOND STANDARD
| 205a | AH1220-24 | — | 65.00 | 80.00 | 100.00 | 125.00 |

2.70 g

THIRD STANDARD
| 205b | AH1224-27 | — | 70.00 | 85.00 | 110.00 | 140.00 |

GOLD, 2.30 g
Tabriz Mint

FIFTH STANDARD, w/o 'Sahibqiran' (5A)
| 205d.1 | AH1230-41 | — | 65.00 | 80.00 | 100.00 | 125.00 |

GOLD, 2.20 g

FIFTH STANDARD, 'Sahibqiran' (5B)
| 205d.2 | AH1241-45 | — | 70.00 | 85.00 | 110.00 | 140.00 |

1.75 g

SIXTH STANDARD, (Keshvarestan)
| 205e | AH1246-50 | — | 75.00 | 100.00 | 135.00 | 175.00 |

TOMAN

GOLD, 6.10 g
Isfahan Mint
FIRST STANDARD

C#	Date	Mintage	VG	Fine	VF	XF
206.1	AH1213-17	—	125.00	145.00	175.00	200.00

Tehran Mint

| 206.2 | AH1216 | — | 125.00 | 145.00 | 175.00 | 200.00 |

Isfahan Mint, 5.80 g
SECOND STANDARD

| 206a | AH1220-24 | — | BV | 90.00 | 100.00 | 150.00 |

5.40 g
THIRD STANDARD

| 206b | AH1224-27 | — | BV | 90.00 | 100.00 | 150.00 |

4.80 g
FOURTH STANDARD

| 206c | AH1227-29 | — | BV | 85.00 | 100.00 | 150.00 |

GOLD, 4.60 g
Iravan Mint
Borujerd
FIFTH STANDARD, w/o 'Sahibqiran' (5A)

| 206d.1 | AH1230-41 | — | BV | 80.00 | 100.00 | 150.00 |

Rasht Mint

| 206d.2 | AH1232 | — | BV | 80.00 | 100.00 | 150.00 |

Tabriz Mint
FIFTH STANDARD, 'Sahibqiran' (5B)

| 206d.3 | AH1241-45 | — | BV | 80.00 | 100.00 | 150.00 |

Tehran Mint, 3.50 g
SIXTH STANDARD (Keshvarsetan)

C#	Date	Mintage	VG	Fine	VF	XF
206e	AH1246-50	—	BV	75.00	100.00	150.00

Zanjan Mint, 4.50 g
SPECIAL ISSUE: King on horseback

| 207 | AH1236 | — | 300.00 | 475.00 | 725.00 | 1200. |

Isfahan Mint, 3.50 g

| 208.1 | AH1245 | — | 325.00 | 475.00 | 750.00 | 1250. |

| 208.2 | AH1245 | — | 325.00 | 475.00 | 750.00 | 1250. |

| 208.3 | AH1249 | — | 325.00 | 475.00 | 750.00 | 1250. |

MINTS OF FATH'ALI SHAH

The following illustrations are of coins, mostly Riyals and Krans, for each of Fath Ali's mints. Usually only one example is shown but considerable variation exists, as die cutters emphasized artistic stylization of legends rather than standardization. In each case, the mint name, date and C# are indicated below the illustration.

Ardebil Mint, AH1245, C#203

Borujerd Mint, AH1244, C#203

Hamadan Mint, AH1250, C#203
NOTE: This AH1250 date is an example of C#203 struck five years after the introduction of C#203a.

Iravan Mint, AH1216, C#194

Isfahan Mint, AH1225, C#194b

Kashan Mint, AH1233, C#194c

Kerman Mint, AH1238, C#193c

Kermanshahan Mint, AH1233, C#194c

Lahijan Mint, AH1219, C#194a

Mashad Mint, AH1222, C#194a
Dated both obverse and reverse

Mazandaran Mint, AH1218, C#194a

Nihawand Mint, AH1242, C#203

Qazwin Mint, AH1227, C#194b

Qum Mint, AH1246, C#203

 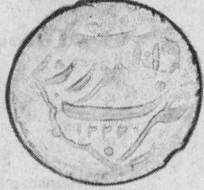
Rasht Mint, AH1222, C#194a

Shushtar Mint, AH1243, C#203

Tabaristan Mint, AH1246, C#203a

Tabriz Mint, AH1221, C#193a

Tehran Mint, AH1217, C#194a

Tuyserkan Mint, AH1241, C#203

Urumi Mint, AH1233, C#194c

Yazd Mint, AH1222, C#194b

Zanjan Mint, AH1244, C#203

For coins of Panahabad struck in the name of Fath'ali Shah, see listings under Russian Caucasia, Khanate of Karabagh.

SULTAN ALI SHAH
AH1250/1834AD
Ruled only 30 days

Silver and gold struck to Fath'ali Shah's Kran and Sixth Gold Standard, respectively. Known only from Mint of Tehran.

KRAN

SILVER, 6.90 g
Tehran Mint

C#	Date	Mintage	VG	Fine	VF	XF
215	AH1250	—	100.00	150.00	250.00	400.00

TOMAN

GOLD, 3.50 g
Tehran Mint

216	AH1250	—	160.00	260.00	425.00	650.00

HUSAIN ALI SHAH
AH1250/1834AD
For six months in southern Iran

Standards as for Sultan Ali mints of Kerman, Shiraz and Yazd struck silver coins. The mint at Shiraz also struck gold coins.

KRAN
SILVER, 6.90 g
219	AH1250	—	100.00	150.00	250.00	400.00

MUHAMMAD SHAH
AH1250-1264/1834-1848AD

SILVER COINAGE
I. FIRST STANDARD AH1250-1251:
    1 Kran – 1-1/2 Mesqal – 36 Nokhod
        1/4 Kran   1.72 g
        1/2 Kran   3.45 g
        1 Kran   6.90 g
II. SECOND STANDARD, AH1252-1255:
    1 Kran – 30 Nokhod
        1/8 Kran   0.72 g
        1/4 Kran   1.50 g
        1/2 Kran   2.90 g
        1 Kran   5.80 g
III. THIRD STANDARD, AH1254-1264:
    1 Kran – 28 Nokhod
        1/8 Kran   0.68 g
        1/4 Kran   1.35 g
        1/2 Kran   2.70 g
        1 Kran   5.40 g
        Krans   10.80 g

GOLD COINAGE
Only one standard
    1 Toman – 18 Nokhod
        1/4 Toman   0.90 g
        1/2 Toman   1.70 g
        1 Toman   3.50 g

NOTE: All coins of Muhammad Shah are essentially of a single type, with the ruler's name on the obverse, the mint & date on the reverse. The exception is the lion & sun type (C#228 below).

1/8 KRAN

SILVER, 0.72 g
Shiraz Mint
SECOND STANDARD
C#	Date	Mintage	Good	VG	Fine	VF
224a	AH1252-55	—	4.50	8.50	15.00	25.00

0.68 g
THIRD STANDARD
| 224b | AH1255-64 | — | 4.00 | 8.00 | 13.50 | 22.50 |

1/4 KRAN
SILVER, 1.70 g
FIRST STANDARD
| 225 | AH1250-51 | — | 5.00 | 10.00 | 17.50 | 27.50 |

1.50 g
SECOND STANDARD
| 225a | AH1252-55 | — | 4.00 | 8.00 | 13.50 | 22.50 |

Kerman Mint, 1.35 g
THIRD STANDARD
| 225b | AH1255-64 | — | 3.00 | 6.00 | 12.00 | 17.50 |

1/2 KRAN

SILVER, 3.50 g
Tehran Mint
FIRST STANDARD
| 226 | AH1250-51 | — | 5.00 | 10.00 | 17.50 | 27.50 |

Tabriz Mint, 2.90 g
SECOND STANDARD
| 226a | AH1252-54 | — | 4.00 | 8.00 | 13.50 | 22.50 |

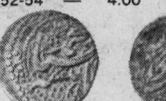 
Tabaristan Mint, 2.70 g
THIRD STANDARD
| 226b | AH1254-64 | — | 3.00 | 6.00 | 11.00 | 16.50 |

KRAN

SILVER, 6.90 g
Tabriz Mint
FIRST STANDARD
| 227 | AH1250-51 | — | 7.50 | 10.00 | 15.00 | 20.00 |

Mashad Mint, 5.80 g
SECOND STANDARD
| 227a | AH1252-55 | — | 7.00 | 8.00 | 9.00 | 14.00 |

Isfahan Mint, 5.40 g
THIRD STANDARD
C#	Date	Mintage	Good	VG	Fine	VF
227b	AH1254-64	—	7.00	8.00	9.00	14.00

Tehran Mint
Machine-milled w/obliquely reeded edge. Possibly a pattern, but found circulated. Tehran Mint only.
| 227r | AH1255 | — | 8.50 | 13.50 | 25.00 | 40.00 |

Lion and sun type
| 228 | AH1258-63 | — | 7.50 | 12.50 | 20.00 | 32.50 |

2 KRANS

SILVER, 10.80 g
Tehran Mint
Lion and sun type
| 229 | AH1263 | — | 30.00 | 50.00 | 100.00 | 165.00 |

1/4 TOMAN
GOLD, 0.90 g
C#	Date	Mintage	VG	Fine	VF	XF
231	AH1250-64	—	45.00	70.00	100.00	135.00

1/2 TOMAN
GOLD, 1.70 g
| 232 | AH1250-64 | — | 80.00 | 110.00 | 140.00 | 185.00 |

TOMAN

GOLD, 3.50 g
Mashad Mint
| 233.1 | AH1250-64 | — | 80.00 | 100.00 | 130.00 | 175.00 |

Rasht Mint
| 233.2 | AH1251 | — | 80.00 | 100.00 | 130.00 | 175.00 |

Tehran Mint
Lion and sun type
| 234 | AH1262-64 | — | 85.00 | 110.00 | 150.00 | 225.00 |

HASAN KHAN SALAR
Rebel, AH1264-1266/1848-1850AD

No coins known. Former C#241 is a coin of Muhammad Shah, dated AH1265 postumously (or error for AH1260).

NASIR AL-DIN SHAH
AH1264-1313/1848-1896AD
Hammered Coinage
AH1264-1296

SILVER COINAGE
FIRST STANDARD, AH1264-1273:
```
1 Kran = 28 Nokhod
1/8 Kran            0.68 g
1/4 Kran            1.35 g
1/2 Kran            2.70 g
1 Kran              5.40 g
```
SECOND STANDARD, AH1273-1296:
```
1 Kran = 26 Nokhod
1/8 Kran            0.63 g
1/4 Kran            1.30 g
1/2 Kran            2.50 g
1 Kran              5.00 g
```
With the introduction of machine-made coinage in AH1296/1879AD, the Kran was reduced to 24 Nokhod (4.60 g).

GOLD COINAGE
Only one standard
```
1 Toman = 18 Nokhod
1/4 Toman           0.86 g
1/2 Toman           1.72 g
1 Toman             3.45 g
2 Tomans            6.90 g
```

25 DINARS
COPPER
C#	Date	Mintage	Good	VG	Fine	VF
249	AH1271-73	—	2.00	3.00	6.00	17.00

This and C#250 bear no mint name. Several variations of type.

50 DINARS
(1 Shahi)

COPPER
| 250 | AH1270-86 | — | 2.00 | 3.00 | 6.00 | 20.00 |

1/8 KRAN

SILVER, uniface, 0.68 g
Rasht Mint
FIRST STANDARD
C#	Date	Mintage	VG	Fine	VF	XF
260	AH1264-73	—	4.00	7.00	12.00	25.00

Uniface, 0.68 g
Tehran Mint
SECOND STANDARD
| 260a | AH1273-94 | — | 3.00 | 6.00 | 10.00 | 17.50 |

1/4 KRAN
SILVER, 1.35 g
Tabriz Mint
FIRST STANDARD
| 261 | AH1264-73 | — | 3.00 | 6.00 | 9.00 | 15.00 |

Tehran Mint

Tehran Mint, 1.30 g
SECOND STANDARD
| 261a | AH1273-94 | — | 2.50 | 5.00 | 8.00 | 15.00 |

1/2 KRAN

SILVER
Isfahan Mint

Khoy Mint

Tabaristan Mint, 2.70 g
FIRST STANDARD
C#	Date	Mintage	VG	Fine	VF	XF
262	AH1264-73	—	4.00	6.00	9.00	22.00

Astarabad Mint

Hamadan Mint, 2.50 g
SECOND STANDARD
| 262a | AH1273-95 | — | 3.00 | 4.50 | 6.50 | 14.00 |

Tehran Mint
Portrait type, 2.50 g
| 265 | AH1273-75 | — | 5.00 | 10.00 | 20.00 | 35.00 |

KRAN

SILVER
Astarabad Mint

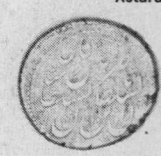

Kerman Mint

Astarabad Mint

Herat Mint, 5.40 g
FIRST STANDARD
| 263 | AH1264-73 | — | 6.50 | 8.00 | 12.50 | 20.00 |

Herat Mint

Astarabad Mint

Hamadan Mint

Tabriz Mint

Tabriz Mint, 5.00 g
SECOND STANDARD

C#	Date	Mintage	VG	Fine	VF	XF
263a	AH1273-96	—	6.50	8.00	12.50	20.00

Mashad Mint
Toughra in wreath, 5.00 g

| 264.1 | AH1286 | — | 10.00 | 20.00 | 35.00 | 50.00 |

Mashad Mint only

Plain toughra, 5.00 g

| 264.2 | AH1287 | — | 10.00 | 20.00 | 35.00 | 50.00 |

Mashad Mint only

Transitional Coinage
KRAN
SILVER
Tehran Mint
Obv: Shah's portrait facing left above wreath between Arabic leg. Rev: Arabic leg. within wreath.

| 266.1 | AH1272 | — | 100.00 | 250.00 | 400.00 | 650.00 |

Kerman Mint
Machine-made planchet, reeded edge, 5.00 g

| 266.2 | AH1282 | — | 9.00 | 15.00 | 27.50 | 40.00 |

Kermanshah Mint, 4.60 g
Broad flan, machine-made planchet, plain edge.

| 266.3 | AH1294 | — | 12.50 | 20.00 | 35.00 | 50.00 |

Yazd Mint
Title Sahibqiran, 5.00 g

C#	Date	Mintage	VG	Fine	VF	XF
267	AH1294	—	12.50	20.00	35.00	55.00

Known only from Yazd, muled w/AH1289-dated reverse.

Tehran Mint, 5.00 g
Machine-struck (?), but crude.

| 268.1 | AH1295 | — | 10.00 | 20.00 | 40.00 | 85.00 |

Rev: Crowned lion and sun, date beneath lion.

| 268.2 | AH1295 | — | 10.00 | 20.00 | 40.00 | 85.00 |

Obv: Date beneath wreath.

| 268.3 | AH1296 | — | 10.00 | 20.00 | 40.00 | 85.00 |

Rev: Crowned mint name.

| 268.4 | AH1296 | — | 20.00 | 35.00 | 50.00 | 95.00 |

All varieties 268.1-4 from Tehran only.

1/4 TOMAN

.900 GOLD, 0.90 g

| 270 | AH1264-93 | — | 50.00 | 80.00 | 110.00 | 140.00 |

1/2 TOMAN

.900 GOLD, 1.70 g
Tehran Mint

| 271 | AH1264-93 | — | 40.00 | 65.00 | 90.00 | 110.00 |

TOMAN
.900 GOLD, 3.50 g
Mashad Mint

| 272.1 | AH1266 | — | 75.00 | 85.00 | 100.00 | 135.00 |

Qazwin Mint

| 272.2 | AH1267 | — | 75.00 | 85.00 | 100.00 | 145.00 |
| | 1269 | — | 75.00 | 85.00 | 100.00 | 145.00 |

Rasht Mint

| 272.3 | AH1269 | — | 75.00 | 80.00 | 90.00 | 120.00 |
| | 1277 | — | 75.00 | 80.00 | 90.00 | 120.00 |

Sarakhs Mint

| 272.4 | AH1264-94 | — | 75.00 | 80.00 | 90.00 | 120.00 |

Shiraz Mint

C#	Date	Mintage	VG	Fine	VF	XF
272.5	AH1269	—	75.00	80.00	90.00	120.00

Tabriz Mint

| 272.6 | AH1272 | — | 75.00 | 80.00 | 90.00 | 120.00 |

Tehran Mint
Obv: Facing portrait.

| 275.1 | AH1271 | — | 175.00 | 275.00 | 485.00 | 925.00 |

Tehran Mint, AH1272
Obv: Portrait left, 3.50 g.

| 275.2 | AH1272-91 | — | 200.00 | 325.00 | 600.00 | 1100 |

Isfahan Mint

| 275.3 | AH1274 | — | 250.00 | 400.00 | 800.00 | 1250. |

2 TOMANS

.900 GOLD, 6.90 g
Kermanshah Mint, AH1271
Obv: Portrait facing.

| 276 | AH1271 | — | 250.00 | 425.00 | 750.00 | 1700. |

Mashad Mint, AH1281
Obv: Toughra, 6.90 g.

| 273 | AH1281 | — | 200.00 | 325.00 | 500.00 | 825.00 |

NOTE: Struck at Mashad mint only.

Milled Coinage
KRAN STANDARD
AH1293-1344, SH1304-1309,
1876-1931AD

12 DINARS
(1/4 Shahi)

COPPER

Y#	Date	Mintage	Good	VG	Fine	VF
1	AH1301	—	20.00	30.00	65.00	85.00
	1303	—	—	Reported, not confirmed		
	ND	—	15.00	25.00	35.00	60.00

25 DINARS
(1/2 Shahi)

COPPER

NOTE: On AH1294 & 1295 coins, initials FP appear on rev.

Y#	Date	Mintage	VG	Fine	VF	XF
2	AH1294	—	10.00	15.00	30.00	50.00
	1294 w/o FP					
		—	25.00	40.00	75.00	
	1295	—	4.00	7.50	20.00	37.50
	1296	—	5.00	10.00	25.00	50.00
	1297	—	7.50	15.00	30.00	60.00
	1298	—	7.50	15.00	30.00	60.00
	1299	—	5.00	10.00	25.00	50.00

IRAN

Y#	Date	Mintage	VG	Fine	VF	XF
2	1300	—	5.00	10.00	25.00	50.00
	1303	—	10.00	20.00	35.00	75.00
	ND	—	2.00	5.00	15.00	35.00

50 DINARS
(1 Shahi)

COPPER

NOTE: On AH1294 & 1295, initials FP appear on rev.

Y#	Date	Mintage	VG	Fine	VF	XF
4	AH1293	—	30.00	45.00	70.00	125.00
	1294	—	4.00	15.00	25.00	75.00
	1295	—	2.00	6.00	15.00	40.00
	1296	—	2.00	6.00	15.00	40.00
	1297	—	2.00	6.00	18.00	50.00
	1298	—	8.00	15.00	35.00	75.00
	1299	—	7.00	12.00	30.00	65.00
	1300	—	2.00	6.00	15.00	40.00
	1301	—	2.00	6.00	15.00	40.00
	1302	—	8.00	15.00	35.00	75.00
	1303	—	2.00	6.00	15.00	40.00
	1304	—	8.00	15.00	35.00	75.00
	1305	—	6.00	10.00	25.00	65.00
	3301 (error) for 1303					
		—	6.00	10.00	25.00	65.00
	1330 (error) for 1303					
		—	10.00	20.00	35.00	75.00
	1792 (error) for 1297					
		—	15.00	25.00	50.00	100.00
	ND	—	4.00	10.00	25.00	50.00

NOTE: AH1293 is probably a mispunched date.

SHAHI

COPPER

Y#	Date	Mintage	Good	VG	Fine	VF
4a	AH1305	—	40.00	60.00	75.00	145.00
	ND	—	30.00	45.00	60.00	100.00

50 DINARS

COPPER-NICKEL

Y#	Date	Mintage	Fine	VF	XF	Unc
23	AH1318	10.000	.75	1.50	4.00	10.00
	1319	12.000	.75	1.50	4.00	10.00
	1321	10.000	.75	1.50	4.00	10.00
	1326	8.000	1.00	2.00	10.00	20.00
	1332	6.000	1.00	4.00	8.00	16.00
	1337	7.000	1.00	3.50	7.00	18.00

95	SH1305	11.000	.80	2.00	6.00	22.00
	1307	2.500	.80	2.00	6.00	22.00

100 DINARS
(2 Shahis)

COPPER

Y#	Date	Mintage	VG	Fine	VF	XF
5	AH1297	—	10.00	20.00	40.00	85.00
	1298	—	15.00	30.00	50.00	100.00
	1299	—	15.00	30.00	50.00	100.00
	1300	—	10.00	20.00	40.00	80.00
	1301	—	10.00	20.00	40.00	80.00
	1302	—	20.00	40.00	60.00	125.00
	1303	—	7.50	15.00	40.00	70.00
	1304	—	20.00	40.00	60.00	125.00
	1305	—	10.00	20.00	35.00	75.00
	1307	—	30.00	50.00	75.00	150.00
	1308	—	30.00	50.00	75.00	150.00
	1313	—	50.00	100.00	200.00	300.00
	1330 (error) for 1303					
		—	10.00	20.00	35.00	75.00
	ND	—	7.50	15.00	30.00	60.00

2 SHAHIS

COPPER

Y#	Date	Mintage	Good	VG	Fine	VF
5a	AH1305	—	30.00	55.00	100.00	175.00
	ND	—	20.00	40.00	70.00	120.00

100 DINARS

COPPER-NICKEL

Y#	Date	Mintage	Fine	VF	XF	Unc
24	AH1318	10.000	1.75	3.00	5.00	10.00
	1319	9.000	1.00	2.50	4.00	8.00
	1321/19					
		5.000	2.50	6.00	10.00	20.00
	1321	Inc. Ab.	1.00	3.00	6.00	15.00
	1326	6.000	1.00	1.50	6.00	15.00
	1332	5.000	1.00	3.00	6.00	15.00
	1337	6.500	1.00	2.50	6.00	8.00

96	SH1305	4.500	1.00	2.00	5.00	25.00
	1307	3.750	1.00	2.00	5.00	25.00

200 DINARS

COPPER

Y#	Date	Mintage	VG	Fine	VF	XF
6	AH1300	—	50.00	125.00	200.00	350.00
	1301	—	20.00	50.00	90.00	140.00

SHAHI SEFID
(White Shahi)

Called the White (i.e., silver) Shahi to distinguish it from the Black or Copper Shahi, the Shahi Sefid was actually worth 3 Shahis. It was used primarily for distribution on New Year's day (Now-Ruz) as good-luck gifts. Since 1926 special privately struck tokens, having no monetary value, have been used instead of coins.

The Shahi Sefid, worth 150 Dinars, was broader, but much thinner, than the 1/4 Kran (Rob'i), worth 250 Dinars.

0.6908 g, .900 SILVER, .0200 oz ASW

Y#	Date	Mintage	VG	Fine	VF	XF
7	AH1296	—	25.00	40.00	75.00	160.00

Date below lion instead of denomination, which is omitted.

Rev: Date below wreath.

7a	AH1297	—	3.00	7.50	15.00	28.00
	1298	—	3.00	6.00	12.50	25.00
	1299	—	4.00	8.00	15.00	35.00
	1300	—	3.00	6.00	12.50	25.00
	1301	—	3.00	6.00	12.50	25.00
	1302	—	7.50	12.50	25.00	50.00
	1303	—	3.00	6.00	12.50	25.00
	1304	—	10.00	15.00	30.00	65.00
	1305	—	3.00	6.00	15.00	30.00
	1307/1	—	7.50	15.00	30.00	60.00
	1307	—	7.50	15.00	30.00	60.00
	1308	—	10.00	15.00	30.00	60.00
	1309/01	—	6.00	15.00	30.00	60.00
	1309	—	6.00	15.00	30.00	60.00
	'13' only	—	10.00	20.00	40.00	90.00
	ND	—	2.00	5.00	10.00	30.00

Rev: Date amidst lion's legs.
(Variations exist)

7b	AH1313	—	20.00	35.00	60.00	100.00
	1--3	—	20.00	35.00	60.00	100.00

Obv. leg: Nasir al-din (Y#7a).
Rev. leg: Sahib al-zaman (Obv. of Y#B44).

8	ND	—	25.00	50.00	80.00	125.00

Obv. leg: Muzaffar al-din Shah.

25	AH1313	—	—	—	Rare	—
	1314	—	10.00	20.00	40.00	75.00
	1315	—	10.00	20.00	40.00	75.00
	1316	—	10.00	20.00	40.00	75.00
	1317	—	15.00	25.00	50.00	100.00
	1318	—	8.00	15.00	30.00	60.00
	1319	—	8.00	15.00	30.00	60.00
	1320	.150	8.00	15.00	30.00	60.00
	8310 (error)	—	8.00	15.00	30.00	60.00
	1039 (error)	—	15.00	25.00	50.00	100.00
	ND	—	4.00	8.00	20.00	40.00

Mule. Obv: Y#25. Rev: Y#7b.

25.1	AH1313	—	20.00	40.00	75.00	165.00

Denomination omitted

25a	AH1319	—	—	—	Rare	—
	ND	—	25.00	50.00	80.00	165.00

NOTE: A number of varieties and mulings of Y#25 and Y#25a with other denominations, esp. 1/4 Krans and 500 Dinar pieces, are reported. These command a premium over others of the same types.

NOTE: Many Shahis of Muzaffar al-din are muled with reverses of Nasir al-din, especially with date 1301 and 1303. Worth $15 in Fine, $25.00 in VF. Many also have the Mouzaffer date of issue engraved amid the legs of old Nasir dies from which the date beneath the wreath wasn't removed. No premium for those showing old Nasir dates.

NOTE: A total of 58,000 pieces were reported struck in AH1322, 1323 and 1324, but none are known with those dates. The specimens were either struck from old dies or were undated types.

Obv. leg: Muzaftar al-din Shah.
Rev. leg: Sahib al-Zaman.

A25	ND	—	25.00	50.00	85.00	165.00

NOTE: Two varieties are known with thick and thin script lettering.

Obv. leg: *Muhammad Ali Shah.*

Y#	Date	Mintage	VG	Fine	VF	XF
44	AH1325	—	15.00	30.00	60.00	100.00
	1326	—	10.00	15.00	25.00	55.00
	1327	—	8.00	10.00	20.00	45.00

Obv. leg: *Sahib al-Zaman.*

B44	AH1326	—	40.00	60.00	125.00	175.00

Obv. Y#44. Rev: Obv. of Y#B44.

A44	ND	—	30.00	50.00	80.00	150.00

Obv. leg: *Ahmad Shah.*
Rev: Date below wreath.

64	AH1328	—	3.00	5.00	10.00	20.00
	1329	—	7.50	12.50	20.00	40.00
	1330	.189	2.00	4.00	10.00	20.00

Rev: Date amidst lion's legs.

A64	AH1332	.010	20.00	30.00	50.00	80.00

Obv. leg: *Ahmad Shah.* Rev. leg: *Sahib-al-Zaman.*

B64	ND	—	40.00	60.00	125.00	185.00

A70	AH1333	.078	2.00	6.00	10.00	20.00
	1334	.006	4.00	12.00	20.00	40.00
	1335	.073	3.00	8.00	15.00	30.00
	1335 dated 1337 on rev. amid legs					
		Inc. Ab.	20.00	40.00	80.00	165.00
	1337	.076	3.00	8.00	15.00	30.00
	1337 also dated on rev.					
		—	20.00	40.00	75.00	150.00
	1339	.010	4.00	12.00	20.00	40.00
	1342	.020	4.00	12.00	20.00	40.00

NOTE: Varieties exist.

Obv: Y#A70. Rev. leg: *Sahib-al-Zaman.*

A70a	AH1335	—	30.00	50.00	80.00	150.00

(Mintage included in Y#A70 of AH1335)

Obv. leg: *Sahib al-Zaman.*

B70	AH1332	Inc. Y#A64				
			5.00	10.00	20.00	40.00
	1333	Inc. Y#A70				
			5.00	10.00	20.00	40.00
	1337	Inc. Y#A70				
			5.00	10.00	20.00	40.00
	1341	.003	10.00	15.00	25.00	50.00
	1342	Inc. Y#A70				
			10.00	15.00	25.00	50.00
	ND	—	5.00	10.00	20.00	40.00

NOTE: Numerous silver Now Ruz tokens, some with dates 1329-1331, are available in Tehran for a fraction of the price of true Shahis.

1/4 KRAN

(Rob'i - 5 Shahis)

ربعی

1.1513 g, .900 SILVER, 15mm, .0333 oz ASW
Rev: Date below wreath.

Y#	Date	Mintage	VG	Fine	VF	XF
9	AH1294	—	30.00	50.00	100.00	175.00
	1296	—	4.00	7.00	15.00	30.00
	1297	—	10.00	20.00	40.00	75.00
	1298	—	10.00	20.00	30.00	50.00
	1299	—	5.00	8.00	20.00	40.00
	1300	—	4.00	7.00	15.00	30.00
	1301	—	3.00	6.00	12.50	30.00
	1303	—	3.00	6.00	12.50	30.00
	1304	—	20.00	40.00	60.00	125.00
	1305	—	8.00	15.00	25.00	50.00
	1306	—	7.00	12.50	20.00	50.00
	1307	—	20.00	40.00	60.00	135.00
	1308	—	20.00	40.00	60.00	135.00
	1309	—	15.00	25.00	50.00	100.00
	1310	—	—	Reported, not confirmed		
	1311	—	20.00	40.00	60.00	135.00
	ND	—	3.00	6.00	15.00	25.00

NOTE: Many examples of Y#9 bear broken or partial dates. These command no premium.

Rev: Date amidst legs.

9d	AH1311	—	20.00	40.00	75.00	160.00
	1312	—	20.00	40.00	75.00	160.00
	1313	—	25.00	50.00	100.00	185.00

Obv. leg: *Muzaffar al-din Shah.*

26	AH1314	—	30.00	50.00	100.00	200.00
	1316	—	6.00	12.50	20.00	35.00
	1318	—	15.00	25.00	50.00	85.00
	1319	—	12.50	20.00	35.00	65.00
	ND	—	3.00	7.50	15.00	25.00

NOTE: 300 specimens reportedly struck in AH1322, but none known to exist.

Obv. leg: *Muhammad Ali Shah.*

45	AH1325	—	20.00	30.00	50.00	100.00
	1326	—	7.50	15.00	27.50	40.00
	1327	—	5.00	10.00	20.00	35.00

Obv. leg: *Ahmad Shah.*

65	AH1327	—	3.00	5.00	10.00	20.00
	1328	—	2.00	4.00	7.50	15.00
	1329	.130	7.50	12.50	20.00	40.00
	1330	.156	2.00	4.00	7.50	15.00
	1331	.030	—	Reported, not confirmed		

Rev: Date amidst legs.

C70.1	AH1332	.252	2.00	5.00	10.00	20.00
(Y-C70)	1333	Inc. Ab.	3.00	6.00	12.00	25.00
	1334	.070	5.00	10.00	20.00	50.00
	1335	.260	2.00	4.00	8.00	15.00
	1336	.160	2.00	4.00	8.00	15.00
	1337	.080	3.00	6.00	12.00	25.00
	1339	.028	4.00	9.00	15.00	30.00
	1341	.022	5.00	12.00	20.00	40.00
	1342	.110	3.00	6.00	12.00	25.00
	1343	.186	2.00	4.00	8.00	15.00

Mule. Obv: Y#C70.1. Rev: Y#45.

C70.2	AH1327	—	30.00	60.00	125.00	175.00
	ND	—	20.00	40.00	60.00	115.00

Obv: Y#C70, date below wreath.

Y#	Date	Mintage	VG	Fine	VF	XF
C70.3	AH1334					
(Y-C70a)	Inc. Y#C70.1		40.00	75.00	150.00	250.00

100	SH1304	.024	7.50	20.00	50.00	95.00

NOTE: 8,000 reported struck in 1305, but that year not yet found and presumed not to exist.

500 DINARS

(10 Shahis - 1/2 Kran)

First Nasir al-din legend — Second Nasir al-din legend with *Sahibqiran* added

Forms of the denomination:

500 DINARS: ۵۰۰ دینار

or

پانصد دینار

10 SHAHIS: ده شاهی

2.3025 g, .900 SILVER, .0666 oz ASW
First leg: *500 Dinars*

10	AH1296	—	—	Reported, not confirmed		
	1297	—	8.00	15.00	30.00	70.00
	1298	—	8.00	15.00	30.00	70.00
	1299	—	—	Reported, not confirmed		
	1301	—	7.00	25.00	55.00	100.00
	1306	—	7.00	15.00	35.00	70.00
	1311	—	25.00	40.00	75.00	140.00
	ND	—	4.00	7.50	15.00	30.00

NOTE: The undated issue is often found in higher grades than dated coins.

First leg: *10 Shahis*
Rev: Date amid legs.

10b	AH1310	—	40.00	75.00	150.00	275.00

Second leg: *10 Shahis*
Obv: Crown added above leg.
Rev: Date amid legs.

10c	AH1310	—	30.00	60.00	125.00	200.00
	1311	—	30.00	60.00	125.00	200.00

First leg: *500 Dinars*
Rev: Date amid legs.

10d	AH1311	—	25.00	50.00	80.00	160.00
	1312	—	20.00	40.00	60.00	110.00
	1313	—	25.00	50.00	80.00	160.00

Second leg: *500 Dinars*
Nasir al-din's Return From Europe

IRAN

Rev: 1306 date.

Y#	Date	Mintage	VG	Fine	VF	XF
A15	AH1307	—	50.00	100.00	175.00	325.00
	1307 w/1306 on rev.					
		—	100.00	200.00	300.00	525.00

Obv. leg: *Muzaffar al-din, 500 Dinars.*
Rev: Date amid legs, arranged variously.

27.1	AH1313	—	25.00	40.00	75.00	150.00
(Y27)	1314	—	10.00	20.00	40.00	100.00
	1315	—	25.00	40.00	75.00	150.00
	1316	—	25.00	40.00	75.00	150.00
	1317	—	—	Reported, not confirmed		
	1318	—	15.00	30.00	50.00	125.00
	1319	—	12.50	20.00	40.00	100.00
	1322	—	10.00	17.50	30.00	50.00
	ND	—	5.00	10.00	20.00	35.00

Mule. Obv: Y#27.1. Rev: Y#10.

| 27.2 | AH1298 | — | 50.00 | 100.00 | 150.00 | 250.00 |

| 30 | AH1323 | .130 | 22.50 | 35.00 | 50.00 | 90.00 |

Obv. leg: *Muhammad Ali Shah.*

46	AH1325	.218	20.00	40.00	75.00	150.00
	1326	.218	15.00	25.00	50.00	100.00
	1336 (error for 1326)					
	Inc. Ab.	20.00	35.00	60.00	125.00	

Obv: Date.

48	AH1326					
	Inc. Y46	20.00	40.00	75.00	150.00	
	1327	—	20.00	40.00	75.00	150.00

Obv: Y#48. Rev: Y#46.
Obv. and rev: Date.

| 48a | AH1325 | — | 75.00 | 125.00 | 175.00 | 320.00 |
| | 1326 | — | 60.00 | 100.00 | 150.00 | 260.00 |

Obv. leg: *Ahmad Shah.*

66	AH1327	—	5.00	10.00	20.00	35.00
	1328	—	5.00	10.00	15.00	30.00
	1329	.044	10.00	15.00	25.00	50.00
	1330	.627	5.00	10.00	20.00	40.00

Obv: Date.

70	AH1331					
	Inc. 1330	2.50	5.00	10.00	20.00	
	1332	.560	1.00	2.00	5.00	10.00
	1333	.292	1.00	2.00	5.00	10.00
	1334	.065	1.50	3.00	6.00	12.00
	1335	.150	4.00	8.00	15.00	30.00
	1336	.240	2.50	4.00	8.00	20.00
	1339	—	10.00	17.50	25.00	40.00
	1343	.160	3.00	6.00	10.00	25.00

NOTE: 10,000 reported struck in AH1337 probably dated AH1336.

Y#	Date	Mintage	VG	Fine	VF	XF
70a	AH1332					
	Inc. Y70	15.00	30.00	50.00	85.00	

Y#	Date	Mintage	Fine	VF	XF	Unc
A101	SH1304	—	130.00	180.00	375.00	675.00

Obv. leg: *Reza Shah.*

| 105 | SH1305 | .010 | 45.00 | 75.00 | 150.00 | 250.00 |

A109	SH1306	.005	40.00	60.00	120.00	160.00
	1307	.046	7.50	15.00	25.00	35.00
	1308	.464	7.50	15.00	25.00	35.00

NOTE: Some of the coins reported in AH1308 were dated 1307.

1000 DINARS
(Kran)

Forms of the denomination:

1000 DINARS:

1 KRAN:

4.6050 g, .900 SILVER, .1332 oz ASW
Obv. leg: *Nasir al-din Shah,* **first leg.,**
1000 Dinars

11	AH1295	—	—	300.00	400.00	
	1296	—	4.00	8.00	20.00	55.00
	1297	—	5.00	10.00	25.00	60.00
	1298/7	—	10.00	20.00	40.00	80.00
	1298	—	10.00	20.00	40.00	80.00
	12—	—	4.00	8.00	25.00	60.00
	129x	—	4.00	8.00	25.00	60.00
	ND	—	4.00	10.00	25.00	60.00

Obv: Second leg, *1000 Dinars*

11a	AH1298	—	5.00	10.00	25.00	60.00
	1299	—	10.00	20.00	50.00	90.00
	1303	—	150.00	250.00	500.00	600.00
	ND	—	5.00	10.00	25.00	45.00

Obv: Second leg, *1 Kran,* **crown above.**

| 11c | AH1310 | — | 100.00 | 150.00 | 250.00 | 425.00 |
| | 1311 | — | 60.00 | 125.00 | 225.00 | 375.00 |

Obv: Second leg, *1 Kran,* **w/o crown.**

| 11b | AH1311 | — | 100.00 | 150.00 | 250.00 | — |

Obv: Second leg., *1000 Dinars,* **w/o crown.**

Y#	Date	Mintage	Fine	VF	XF	Unc
11d	AH1311	—	90.00	135.00	225.00	—
	1312	—	100.00	150.00	250.00	—

Obv. leg: *Muzaffar al-din Shah,*
w/o crown.

| A27 | AH1314 | — | 125.00 | 200.00 | 400.00 | — |

Obv: Crown added above leg.

A27a	AH1317	—	100.00	175.00	250.00	—
	1318	—	100.00	175.00	250.00	—
	1319	—	150.00	225.00	350.00	—
	1322	—	75.00	150.00	225.00	—

Mule. Obv: Y#A27a. Rev: Y#11a.

| B27a | AH1303 | — | — | — | Rare | — |

Mule. Obv: Y#A27a. Rev: Y#11d.

| B27b | AH1312 | — | — | — | Rare | — |

| 31 | AH1323 | .125 | 20.00 | 30.00 | 60.00 | 115.00 |

Obv. leg: *Muhammad Ali Shah.*

| A47 | AH1325 | .289 | 150.00 | 300.00 | 600.00 | — |
| | 1326 | .289 | 150.00 | 300.00 | 600.00 | — |

Obv: Date.

49	AH1326					
	Inc. Y-A47	50.00	100.00	175.00	450.00	
	1327	—	50.00	100.00	175.00	450.00

Obv: Y#49. Rev: Y#47.
Obv. and rev: Date.

| 49a | AH1326 | | | | | |
| | Inc. Y#47 | 125.00 | 200.00 | 350.00 | | |

Transitional Issue
Obv: Y#67. Rev: Y#49a.

| A71 | AH1326 | — | — | Rare | — | |

Obv. leg: *Ahmad Shah.*

67	AH1327	—	15.00	25.00	40.00	70.00
	1328	—	4.00	7.50	20.00	40.00
	1329	3.000	4.00	7.50	20.00	40.00
	1330	—	3.00	7.50	20.00	40.00

24mm

Y#	Date	Mintage	Fine	VF	XF	Unc
67a	AH1330	—	3.00	6.00	15.00	30.00
	1330	—	—	Proof	Rare	

NOTE: Y#67a differs from Y#67 in that it is about 1mm broader and has a much thicker rim and more clearly defined denticles. Struck in Germany, without Iranian authorization, for circulation in western Iran during World War I.) Also, the lion lacks the triangular face & fierce expression of Y#67 and the point of the Talwar (scimitar) does not touch the sunburst as it does on Tehran issues.

23mm

Y#	Date	Mintage	Fine	VF	XF	Unc
71	AH1330 (error) for 1340					
		—	30.00	65.00	125.00	175.00
	1331	1.310	5.00	8.00	25.00	40.00
	1332	1.891	3.00	5.00	12.50	30.00
	1333	2.179	7.50	12.00	25.00	40.00
	1334	1.273	3.00	5.00	12.50	25.00
	1335	2.162	3.00	5.00	12.50	25.00
	1336	1.412	3.50	6.00	15.00	30.00
	1337	3.330	3.00	5.00	12.50	25.00
	1339	.035	12.50	25.00	55.00	90.00
	1340	.028	15.00	30.00	60.00	100.00
	1341	.170	8.00	15.00	35.00	60.00
	1342	.255	3.00	5.00	17.50	30.00
	1343	1.345	3.00	5.00	17.50	30.00
	1344	2.978	4.00	6.00	20.00	35.00

10th Year of Reign

| 73 | AH1337 | .975 | 40.00 | 70.00 | 130.00 | 210.00 |

| 101 | SH1304 | 2.573 | 3.00 | 5.00 | 10.00 | 20.00 |
| | 1305 | 2.265 | 4.00 | 7.00 | 12.50 | 25.00 |

Obv. leg: *Reza Shah.*

106	SH1305	Inc.Y101	3.00	5.00	10.00	20.00
	1306/5	3.130	5.00	8.00	15.00	25.00
	1306	Inc. Ab.	3.00	5.00	10.00	20.00

109	SH1306	Inc.Y106	4.00	8.00	20.00	30.00
	1307	4.300	4.00	6.00	12.50	20.00
	1308	.603	4.00	8.00	15.00	25.00

2000 DINARS
(2 Krans)

Forms of the denomination:

دو قران

2 KRANS:

دو هزار دینار

2000 DINARS:

9.2100 g, .900 SILVER, 27mm, .2665 oz ASW
Obv. leg: *Nasir al-din Shah*, first leg., *2000 Dinars*

Y#	Date	Mintage	Fine	VF	XF	Unc
12	AH1296	—	10.00	20.00	50.00	120.00
	1297	—	8.00	15.00	35.00	95.00
	1298/7	—	15.00	30.00	60.00	110.00
	1298	—	15.00	30.00	60.00	110.00
	ND	—	7.00	15.00	35.00	85.00

Obv: Second leg., *2000 Dinars*

12a	AH1298	—	10.00	20.00	50.00	110.00
	1299	—	12.50	25.00	60.00	120.00
	1299 B on rev.					
		—	—	—	Rare	—
	1300	—	10.00	20.00	50.00	110.00
	1301	—	12.50	25.00	60.00	120.00
	1302	—	20.00	40.00	75.00	140.00
	1303	—	20.00	40.00	75.00	140.00
	1304	—	20.00	40.00	75.00	140.00
	1305	—	10.00	20.00	50.00	110.00
	1306	—	20.00	40.00	75.00	140.00
	1307	—	25.00	50.00	100.00	—
	1308	—	25.00	50.00	100.00	—
	ND	—	10.00	20.00	50.00	110.00

NOTE: All dates after 1301 struck from worn dies and hence incomplete even in high grades.

NOTE: Coins dated AH1300-1305 show a 'b' to the lower left obv., often missing on poorly struck specimens or specimens from filled dies.

Obv: Second leg., *2 Krans.*
Rev: Crown above date below wreath.

12b.1 AH1310 (in blundered form as 13010)
— 100.00 150.00 300.00 —

Obv: W/o crown above *2 Krans.*

12b.2 AH1310 (in blundered form as 13010)
— 100.00 150.00 300.00 —

Obv: Second leg., *2 Krans, w/o crown.*
Rev: Date amid legs.

12c.1 AH1311 — 100.00 150.00 300.00 —

Obv: Crown.

12c.2 AH1310 — 40.00 75.00 125.00 —
| | 1311 | — | 30.00 | 60.00 | 100.00 | — |

Obv: W/o crown above *2000 Dinars.*

12d AH1311 — 40.00 75.00 150.00 —
| | 1312 | — | 40.00 | 75.00 | 150.00 | — |

50th Year of Reign
Special leg: *Dhu'l-Qarneyn.*

C15 AH1313 — 1500. 2500. 5000. —

NOTE: This coin was struck in quantity and was due to be released at Nasir's 50th anniversary as a largesse piece. A number of specimens were passed out to persons close to the royal court before the celebration which accounts for the few known today. Nasir al-din was assassinated just before the fiftieth year of his reign began and the balance of the issue was melted.

Mule. Obv: Y#C15. Rev: Y#12d.

Y#	Date	Mintage	Fine	VF	XF	Unc
12e	AH1312	2 known	—	2500.	—	—

Obv. leg: *Muzaffar al-din Shah,*
w/o crown, leg: *2000 Dinars.*

| 28 | AH1313 | — | 100.00 | 150.00 | 250.00 | — |
| | 1314 | — | 75.00 | 125.00 | 225.00 | — |

Obv: Crown added, leg: *2000 Dinars.*
Rev: Position of date amid legs varies.

28a	AH1314	—	30.00	50.00	125.00	225.00
	1315	—	20.00	35.00	75.00	150.00
	1316	—	15.00	25.00	65.00	130.00
	1317	—	15.00	25.00	65.00	130.00
	1318	—	15.00	25.00	60.00	120.00
	1319	—	15.00	25.00	60.00	120.00
	1320	13.959	12.00	20.00	45.00	110.00

NOTE: Blundered dates exist.

Mule. Obv: Y#28a. Rev: Y#12d.

28c AH1312 — — — Rare —

Obv. leg: *2 Krans.*

28b	AH1320	Inc. Ab.	12.00	20.00	40.00	100.00
	1321 (always '13201')					
		18.108	12.00	20.00	40.00	100.00
	1322	8.640	8.00	15.00	30.00	80.00

32	AH1323					
	Inc. 1322	20.00	35.00	65.00	125.00
	'13'*	—	60.00	100.00	200.00	—

*23 of 1323 filled in or never punched

NOTE: AH1319 is a pattern.

Obv. leg: *Muhammad Ali Shah,*
2 Krans

47	AH1325	3.076	10.00	25.00	50.00	120.00
	1326	3.069	10.00	15.00	30.00	70.00
	1327	—	10.00	15.00	30.00	70.00

Portrait of Shah.

| 50 | AH1326 | | | | | |
| | Inc. Y47 | 750.00 | 1500. | 2000. | — |

BEWARE: Counterfeits exist.

Obv. leg: *Ahmad Shah,*
date below wreath, 2 Krans.

IRAN 1022

Y#	Date	Mintage	Fine	VF	XF	Unc
68	AH1327					
		Inc. 1328	5.00	8.00	15.00	40.00
	1328	30.000	5.00	7.00	12.50	35.00
	1329	29.250	5.00	7.00	12.50	35.00

Obv: Date below wreath, *2000 Dinars,*
Tehran strike. Rev: Fierce, triangular face on lion.

| 68a.1 | AH1330 | 2.901 | 5.00 | 8.00 | 15.00 | 35.00 |

Berlin strike. Rev: Lion's face has friendly expression.

| 68a.2 | AH1330 | — | 4.00 | 7.00 | 10.00 | 27.00 |

Rev: Date amid legs, *2000 Dinars.*

| 68b | AH1330 | Inc.Y68a | 4.00 | 7.00 | 10.00 | 30.00 |
| | 1331 | 13.412 | 5.00 | 10.00 | 17.00 | 40.00 |

72	AH1330 (error) for 1340					
		Inc.Y68a	50.00	100.00	150.00	250.00
	1331	Inc.Y68b	7.00	15.00	25.00	50.00
	1332	12.926	5.00	8.50	16.00	32.00
	1333	Inc. Ab.	5.00	7.50	15.00	30.00
	1334	4.299	5.00	7.50	15.00	30.00
	1335	9.777	5.00	7.50	15.00	30.00
	1336	5.401	5.00	7.50	15.00	30.00
	1337	2.951	5.00	7.50	15.00	30.00
	1339	1.085	6.00	12.50	25.00	50.00
	1340	.254	7.50	15.00	30.00	65.00
	1341	4.460	5.00	7.50	15.00	30.00
	1342	2.245	5.00	8.00	20.00	35.00
	1343	5.205	5.00	8.00	20.00	35.00
	1344/34	12.354	—	—	—	—
	1344	Inc. Ab.	6.00	10.00	25.00	50.00

10th Anniversary of Reign

| 74 | AH1337 | 3.503 | 40.00 | 80.00 | 150.00 | 285.00 |

| 102 | SH1304 | 11.920 | 5.00 | 8.00 | 15.00 | 25.00 |
| | 1305 | 9.785 | 5.00 | 8.00 | 15.00 | 25.00 |

Rev: Date below bow.

Y#	Date	Mintage	Fine	VF	XF	Unc
107	SH1305	Inc.Y102	5.00	10.00	20.00	30.00
	1306	9.380	4.00	6.00	12.50	25.00

Mule. Obv: Y#110. Rev: Y#72.

| A110 | SH1306 | — | — | — | Rare | |

110	SH1306	Inc.Y107	4.00	6.00	12.50	22.00
	1306	—	—	—	Proof	375.00
	1306H	11.714	5.00	7.50	15.00	22.50
	1306L	7.500	3.00	5.00	10.00	20.00
	1307	11.146	3.00	6.00	15.00	25.00
	1308	1.611	5.00	10.00	20.00	30.00

5000 DINARS
(5 Krans)

23.0251 g, .900 SILVER, .6662 oz ASW

| 13 | AH1296 | — | 100.00 | 150.00 | 275.00 | 425.00 |
| | 1297 | — | 90.00 | 135.00 | 250.00 | 400.00 |

Obv: Crown above leg., value: *5 Krans.*

| 13c* | AH1311 | — | 1500. | 2500. | 5000. | — |

Muzaffar al-din Shah

| 29 | AH1320 | .250 | 7.00 | 15.00 | 22.00 | 30.00 |

NOTE: Actual mintage must be considerably greater. Struck in Leningrad.

Royal Birthday

| A40 | AH1322 | — | 450.00 | 830.00 | 1500. | — |

Obv: W/o additional inscriptions flanking head.

| 33 | AH1324 | 3,000 | 650.00 | 1400. | 2250. | — |

(AH1319 is a pattern)

Y#	Date	Mintage	Fine	VF	XF	Unc
A50	AH1327	—	750.00	1350.	2000.	—

69	AH1331	—	60.00	150.00	250.00	500.00
	1332	3.000	8.00	12.00	25.00	85.00
	1333	.667	10.00	15.00	30.00	90.00
	1334	.443	10.00	15.00	30.00	90.00
	1335	1.884	10.00	15.00	30.00	90.00
	1337	.165	12.00	25.00	50.00	110.00
	1339	.090	12.00	25.00	50.00	110.00
	1340	.303	12.00	25.00	50.00	110.00
	1341	.757	10.00	20.00	40.00	95.00
	1342/32	.546	10.00	15.00	30.00	90.00
	1342	Inc. Ab.	10.00	15.00	30.00	90.00
	1343	.935	10.00	15.00	30.00	90.00
	1344/34	2.284	10.00	15.00	30.00	85.00
	1344	Inc. Ab.	15.00	20.00	40.00	95.00

NOTE: Specimens are known dated AH1338 but are believed to be 1337 dated with the 7 inverted. (9000 reported minted in AH1336, but probably dated earlier).

Beware of altered date 1331 specimens.

| 103 | SH1304 | .500 | 15.00 | 25.00 | 40.00 | 80.00 |
| | 1305 | 1.363 | 25.00 | 30.00 | 50.00 | 90.00 |

| 108 | SH1305 | Inc.Y103 | 20.00 | 30.00 | 50.00 | 100.00 |
| | 1306 | 3.186 | 15.00 | 25.00 | 40.00 | 85.00 |

Mule. Obv: Y#111. Rev: Y#69.

| A111 | SH1306 | — | — | — | Rare | — |

| 111 | SH1306 | Inc.Y108 | 6.00 | 10.00 | 17.50 | 30.00 |

IRAN 1023

Y#	Date	Mintage	Fine	VF	XF	Unc
111	1306	—	—	—	Proof	450.00
	1306H	4.711	6.00	10.00	17.50	30.00
	1306L	3.000	6.00	7.50	15.00	30.00
	1307	3.928	6.00	10.00	20.00	35.00
	1308	.584	15.00	30.00	60.00	95.00

(Mintmarks located as on 2000 Dinars Y#110)

GOLD COINAGE

Modern imitations exist of many types, particularly the small 1/5, 1/2 and 1 Toman coins. These are usually underweight (or rarely overweight), and are sold in the bazaars at a small premium over bullion. They are usually crude and probably not intended to deceive collectors, but as a convenient form of bullion. Some are dated outside the reign of the ruler whose name or portrait they bear.

A few deceptive counterfeits are known of the large 10 Toman pieces. Many of the larger pieces are medals, which have been mistaken for coins.

NOTE: Dates in parenthesis are reported, not confirmed.

2000 DINARS
(1/5 Toman)

.6520 g, .900 GOLD, .0188 oz AGW
Obv. leg: First Nasir type. Rev: Lion and sun.

Y#	Date	Mintage	Fine	VF	XF	Unc
A16	AH1295	—	125.00	175.00	350.00	425.00

.5749 g, .900 GOLD, .0166 oz AGW
Obv: Bust of Nasir al-din Shah, AH1292-1305.

Y#	Date	Mintage	Fine	VF	XF	Unc
16	AH1297	—	20.00	40.00	75.00	125.00
	1298	—	22.50	45.00	100.00	150.00
	1299	—	20.00	40.00	75.00	125.00
	1300	—	20.00	40.00	75.00	135.00
	1301	—	20.00	40.00	75.00	135.00

Obv. leg: *Muzaffar-al-din Shah.*
Rev: Lion and sun.

Y#	Date	Mintage	Fine	VF	XF	Unc
A38	AH9301 (error for 1309)		125.00	175.00	275.00	400.00
	AH1305 (error)	—	—	Reported, not confirmed		
A34	ND	—	40.00	75.00	150.00	250.00

Obv: Date and denomination added.

Y#	Date	Mintage	Fine	VF	XF	Unc
A34a	AH1319	—	60.00	125.00	200.00	350.00
	1322	—	60.00	125.00	200.00	350.00
	1323	—	60.00	125.00	200.00	350.00
	1324	—	60.00	125.00	200.00	350.00

Obv: Bust of Muhammad Ali-Shah, AH1326 turned half-left, divided date.
Rev: Leg. in closed wreath.

Y#	Date	Mintage	Fine	VF	XF	Unc
52	AH1326	—	100.00	200.00	300.00	500.00
	1327	—	100.00	200.00	300.00	500.00

Obv. leg: *Ahmad Shah,* **AH1328-1332.**
Rev: Lion and sun.

Y#	Date	Mintage	Fine	VF	XF	Unc
75	AH1328	—	75.00	250.00	400.00	700.00
	1329	—	65.00	125.00	250.00	350.00
	1330	—	—	—	—	—

Obv: Portrait type of Ahmad Shah, AH1332-1343.
Rev: Legend.

Y#	Date	Mintage	Fine	VF	XF	Unc
79	AH1332	—	25.00	40.00	75.00	150.00
	1333	—	20.00	35.00	65.00	125.00
	1335	—	10.00	25.00	35.00	50.00
	1337	—	10.00	25.00	35.00	50.00
	1339	—	15.00	30.00	40.00	75.00
	1340	—	20.00	40.00	60.00	100.00
	1341	—	15.00	30.00	40.00	75.00
	1342	—	15.00	30.00	40.00	75.00
	1343	—	20.00	35.00	48.00	62.50

5000 DINARS
(1/2 Toman)

1.4372 g, .900 GOLD, .0416 oz AGW
Nasir al-din Shah, AH1292-1298
Rev: Lion and sun type.

Y#	Date	Mintage	Fine	VF	XF	Unc
C16	AH1296	—	100.00	200.00	300.00	400.00
	1298	—	—	Reported, not confirmed		
	1309	—	200.00	400.00	750.00	1250.

Obv: First Nasir portrait type, AH1303-1307.

Y#	Date	Mintage	Fine	VF	XF	Unc
17	AH1297	—	60.00	100.00	175.00	275.00
	1299	—	60.00	100.00	175.00	275.00
	1301	—	65.00	150.00	250.00	350.00

Y#	Date	Mintage	Fine	VF	XF	Unc
17	1303	—	65.00	150.00	250.00	350.00
	1305	—	65.00	150.00	250.00	350.00
	13(0)5	—	65.00	150.00	250.00	350.00
	1307	—	125.00	300.00	500.00	750.00
	1213 (error) for 1312	—	100.00	200.00	300.00	450.00
	1313	—	150.00	300.00	500.00	750.00

Obv. leg: *Nasir Dhu'l Garneyn.*

Y#	Date	Mintage	Fine	VF	XF	Unc
—	AH1313	—	—	—	Rare	—

Obv. leg: *Muzaffar al-din Shah,* **AH1313-1314.**
Rev: Lion and sun type.

Y#	Date	Mintage	Fine	VF	XF	Unc
38	AH1314	—	125.00	250.00	350.00	500.00
	1315	—	150.00	300.00	500.00	750.00

Y#	Date	Mintage	Fine	VF	XF	Unc
35	AH1316	—	25.00	50.00	70.00	135.00
	1318	—	25.00	50.00	75.00	150.00
	1319	—	30.00	60.00	100.00	200.00
	1320	—	30.00	60.00	100.00	200.00
	1321	—	30.00	60.00	100.00	200.00
	1322	—	30.00	60.00	100.00	200.00
	1323	—	25.00	50.00	75.00	150.00
	1324	—	25.00	50.00	75.00	150.00

Obv. leg: *Muhammad ali Shah.*
Rev: Lion and sun.

Y#	Date	Mintage	Fine	VF	XF	Unc
56	AH1324	—	125.00	200.00	325.00	450.00
	1325	—	150.00	250.00	400.00	550.00

Obv: Mohammad Ali bust half-left, AH1326 divided date. Rev: Leg. in closed wreath.

Y#	Date	Mintage	Fine	VF	XF	Unc
53	AH1326	—	125.00	250.00	450.00	750.00
	1362 (error)		150.00	350.00	550.00	850.00
	1327	—	125.00	250.00	450.00	750.00

Obv. leg: *Ahmad Shah,* **AH1328-1832.**
Rev: Lion and sun.

Y#	Date	Mintage	Fine	VF	XF	Unc
76	AH1328	—	85.00	150.00	250.00	350.00
	1329	—	75.00	125.00	175.00	250.00
	1330	—	85.00	135.00	190.00	250.00

Obv: Portrait type, AH1332-1343. Rev. leg: Ahmad type.

Y#	Date	Mintage	Fine	VF	XF	Unc
80	AH1331	—	50.00	100.00	150.00	300.00
	1332	—	40.00	60.00	100.00	150.00
	1333	—	25.00	40.00	75.00	125.00
	1334	—	25.00	30.00	50.00	75.00
	1335	—	25.00	30.00	50.00	75.00
	1336	—	25.00	35.00	60.00	100.00
	1337	—	25.00	30.00	50.00	75.00
	1339	—	25.00	35.00	60.00	125.00
	1340	—	25.00	35.00	60.00	125.00
	1341	—	25.00	30.00	50.00	110.00
	1342	—	25.00	30.00	50.00	110.00
	1343	—	25.00	30.00	50.00	110.00

Mule. Obv: Ahmed portrait. Rev. leg: *Sahib al-Zaman.*

Y#	Date	Mintage	Fine	VF	XF	Unc
80a	AH1340	—	100.00	150.00	250.00	400.00

TOMAN

3.4525 g, .900 GOLD, .0988 oz AGW
30th Year of Reign
Obv: Leg. Rev: Lion and sun.

Y#	Date	Mintage	Fine	VF	XF	Unc
—	AH1293	—	200.00	300.00	450.00	600.00

2.8744 g, .900 GOLD, .0832 oz AGW
Obv. leg: First Nasir type.
Rev: Lion and sun.

Y#	Date	Mintage	Fine	VF	XF	Unc
D16	AH1296	—	—	Reported, not confirmed		

Obv: First portrait, w/o leg.
Rev: First Nasir leg.

Y#	Date	Mintage	Fine	VF	XF	Unc
A18	ND	—	100.00	185.00	250.00	350.00
	AH1297	—	110.00	200.00	300.00	450.00

Obv: Portrait.
Rev. leg: First Nasir type.

Y#	Date	Mintage	Fine	VF	XF	Unc
18	AH1297	—	50.00	75.00	150.00	300.00
	1298	—	—	—	Rare	—
	1299	—	50.00	75.00	175.00	350.00
	1301	—	50.00	100.00	200.00	350.00
	1303	—	50.00	125.00	225.00	400.00
	1304	—	70.00	200.00	350.00	600.00
	1305	—	50.00	100.00	200.00	350.00

Y#	Date	Mintage	Fine	VF	XF	Unc
18	1306	—	70.00	200.00	350.00	600.00
	1307	—	60.00	150.00	250.00	450.00
	1309	—	70.00	175.00	300.00	550.00
	1311	—	75.00	200.00	350.00	600.00
	1312	—	75.00	200.00	350.00	600.00
	1313	—	—	Reported, not confirmed		

Shah's return from Europe, AH1307.

Y#	Date	Mintage	Fine	VF	XF	Unc
D15	AH1307	—	400.00	750.00	1250.	1750.

Obv: Second portrait. Rev: First Nasir leg.

Y#	Date	Mintage	Fine	VF	XF	Unc
22	AH1310	—	300.00	550.00	1000.	1500.

Rev: Second Nasir leg.

Y#	Date	Mintage	Fine	VF	XF	Unc
22a	AH1311	—	125.00	225.00	350.00	500.00

Mule. Obv. Y#18. Rev: Y#22.

Y#	Date	Mintage	Fine	VF	XF	Unc
A22	AH1313	—	300.00	500.00	800.00	1250.

Obv. leg: *Muzaffar al-din Shah,* **AH1313-1314.**
Rev: Lion and sun.

Y#	Date	Mintage	Fine	VF	XF	Unc
39	AH1314	—	250.00	450.00	650.00	1000.

Obv: Muzaffar bust 1/2 right, AH1316-1324.

Y#	Date	Mintage	Fine	VF	XF	Unc
36	AH1316	—	45.00	95.00	175.00	300.00
	1318	—	45.00	80.00	150.00	275.00
	1319	—	50.00	100.00	200.00	325.00
	1321	—	50.00	100.00	200.00	325.00

Royal Birthday AH1322
Obv: Mouzaffer bust 3/4 left.

Y#	Date	Mintage	Fine	VF	XF	Unc
40	AH1322	—	—	Reported, not confirmed		

Obv. leg: *Muhammad Ali Shah,* **AH1324.**
Rev: Lion and sun.

Y#	Date	Mintage	Fine	VF	XF	Unc
A56	AH1324	—	350.00	750.00	1000.	1500.

Obv: Mohammad Ali portrait half-left, AH1326.
Rev: Leg. in closed wreath.

Y#	Date	Mintage	Fine	VF	XF	Unc
54	AH1327	—	200.00	350.00	500.00	750.00

Obv. leg: *Ahmad Shah,* **AH1328-1332.**
Rev: Lion and sun.

Y#	Date	Mintage	Fine	VF	XF	Unc
77	AH1329	—	200.00	300.00	500.00	750.00

Obv: Portrait, AH1332-1344
Rev. leg: Ahmad Shah type.

Y#	Date	Mintage	Fine	VF	XF	Unc
81	AH1332	—	—	Reported, not confirmed		
	1333	—	—	—	Rare	—
	1334	—	45.00	60.00	110.00	230.00
	1335	—	45.00	70.00	110.00	230.00
	1337	—	45.00	60.00	110.00	230.00
	1339	—	45.00	70.00	110.00	230.00
	1340	—	45.00	70.00	110.00	230.00
	1341	—	45.00	60.00	110.00	230.00
	1342	—	45.00	60.00	110.00	230.00
	1343	—	45.00	60.00	110.00	230.00

Mule. Obv: Y#81. Rev: Y#41.

Y#	Date	Mintage	Fine	VF	XF	Unc
A41	AH1333	—	300.00	600.00	1000.	1500.

Reza's First New Year Celebration
Obv. leg: Reza type. Rev: Lion and sun.

Y#	Date	Mintage	Fine	VF	XF	Unc
119	SH1305	—	200.00	300.00	400.00	550.00

2 TOMANS

6.5150 g, .900 GOLD, .1885 oz AGW
Discovery of Gold in Kurdistan
Obv: Leg. within wreath, crown above.
Rev: Leg. within wreath.

Y#	Date	Mintage	Fine	VF	XF	Unc
—	AH1295	—	—	—	Rare	—

IRAN 1024

5.7488 g, .900 GOLD, .1663 oz AGW
Obv: First Nasir portrait. Rev. leg: First Nasir type.

Y#	Date	Mintage	Fine	VF	XF	Unc
19	AH1297	—	175.00	300.00	400.00	600.00
	1298	—	250.00	400.00	750.00	1250.
	1299	—	100.00	150.00	250.00	450.00
	1309	—	Reported, not confirmed			

6.5150 g, .900 GOLD, .1885 oz AGW
7th Iman Commemorative
Obv: First Nasir portrait. Rev: Leg. and crown.

—	AH1295	—	—	—	Rare	—

Shah's return from Europe, AH1307
| B15 | AH1307 | — | — | — | Rare | — |

Shah's visit to Tehran Mint, AH1308
| E15 | AH1308 | — | — | — | Rare | — |

Rev: Lion and sun.
| A39 | AH1311 | — | 500.00 | 1000. | 1500. | 2500. |

NOTE: Struck on 1 Toman planchet.

41	AH1322	Royal Birthday				
		—	200.00	400.00	750.00	1350.

10 TOMANS

28.7440 g, .900 GOLD, .8317 oz AGW
Obv: First portrait of Nasir al-din Shah, AH1296-1297.
| 21 | AH1297 | — | 1750. | 2250. | 3500. | 5000. |
| | 1311 | — | 2000. | 3000. | 4000. | 6000. |

Obv: Second portrait of Nasir al-din Shah, AH1311.
| A23 | AH1311 | — | 2000. | 3000. | 5000. | 7500. |
| B34.1 | AH1314 | — | 3000. | 6500. | 9500. | 12,000. |

Rev: W/o denomination, date stamped twice.
| B34.2 | AH1314 | — | 3000. | 6500. | 9500. | 12,000. |

83	AH1331	—	—	—	—	8500.
	1334	—	—	—	Rare	—
	1337/4	—	—	—	Rare	—

5 TOMANS

NOTE: Earlier coins previously mentioned are now published in UNUSUAL WORLD COINS, 2nd edition, Krause Publications, 1988. The following items are all believed to be various commemorative medals.
Y#78 Ahmad Shah, AH1332 - not seen.
Y#82 Ahmad Shah, AH1333 - not seen - Fifth Year of Reign.
Y#86 Ahmad Shah, AH1332 - Obv: Bust w/date AH1337. Rev: Crown in open wreath, dated AH1332. Weight fit for a 5 Toman piece.
Y#87 Ahmad Shah, AH1334 & 1337 - These are medals w/o denomination.
Y#88 Ahmad Shah, AH1337 - Possibly an underweight pattern striking.
Y#89 Ahmad Shah, AH1337 - This is an off-metal strike of the 2000 Dinar coin of Y#74.

MONETARY REFORM
5 Dinars = 1 Shahi
100 Dinars = 1 Rial
100 Rials = 1 Pahlavi

DINAR

BRONZE
Y#	Date	Mintage	Fine	VF	XF	Unc
93	SH1310	10.000	8.00	20.00	35.00	55.00

2 DINARS

BRONZE
| 94 | SH1310 | 5.000 | 5.00 | 12.50 | 30.00 | 65.00 |

5 DINARS

COPPER-NICKEL
| 97 | SH1310 | 3.750 | 8.00 | 15.00 | 25.00 | 75.00 |

COPPER
| 97a | SH1314 | .480 | 50.00 | 75.00 | 100.00 | 140.00 |

ALUMINUM-BRONZE
125	SH1315	5.665	3.00	6.00	13.50	20.00
	1316	Inc. Ab.	1.00	3.00	6.00	10.00
	1317	13.025	.50	1.00	3.00	7.50
	1318	—	.50	1.00	3.00	6.50
	1319	—	.50	1.00	3.00	7.50
	1320	—	.50	1.00	3.00	6.50
	1321	—	.50	1.00	3.00	6.50

10 DINARS

COPPER-NICKEL
| 98 | SH1310 | 3.750 | 8.00 | 20.00 | 45.00 | 100.00 |

COPPER
| 98a | SH1314 | 11.350 | 10.00 | 30.00 | 55.00 | 110.00 |

ALUMINUM-BRONZE
126	SH1315	6.195	2.00	5.00	15.00	25.00
	1316	Inc. Ab.	1.00	3.00	8.00	15.00
	1317	17.120	.50	1.00	3.00	8.00
	1318	—	.50	1.00	2.50	7.50
	1319	—	.75	2.00	4.00	12.00
	1320	—	.50	1.00	3.00	8.00
	1321	—	.50	1.00	3.00	8.00

25 DINARS

COPPER-NICKEL
Y#	Date	Mintage	Fine	VF	XF	Unc
99	SH1310	.750	15.00	25.00	40.00	100.00

COPPER
| 99a | SH1314 | 1.152 | 20.00 | 40.00 | 60.00 | 125.00 |

ALUMINUM-BRONZE
127	SH1326	—	3.00	6.00	15.00	30.00
	1327	—	10.00	15.00	30.00	60.00
	1329	—	4.00	7.00	20.00	40.00

Mule. Obv: 25 Dinars, Y#127. Rev: 1 Rial, Y#129.
| 127a | 1329 | — | 50.00 | 100.00 | 150.00 | 250.00 |

1/4 RIAL

1.2500 g, .828 SILVER, .0332 oz ASW
| 104 | SH1315 | .600 | 1.00 | 2.00 | 3.50 | 6.00 |

(The second '1' is often short, so that the date looks like 1305).

1/2 RIAL

2.5000 g, .828 SILVER, .0665 oz ASW
112	SH1310	2.000	1.50	3.00	7.50	18.00
	1311	—	10.00	20.00	40.00	90.00
	1312	—	1.00	2.00	3.00	11.00
	1313	1.945	1.50	2.00	4.00	12.50
	1314	.100	2.50	7.50	17.50	35.00
	1315	.800	1.50	3.00	7.50	18.00

All 1/2 Rials dated SH1311-1315 are recut dies, usually from SH1310.

10 SHAHIS

COPPER
92	SH1314 small date					
		15.714	4.50	7.00	20.00	50.00
	1314 lg. dt. I.A.	4.50	7.00	20.00	50.00
	1314 plain edge					
		Inc. Ab.	5.00	8.00	25.00	57.50

50 DINARS

ALUMINUM-BRONZE
128	SH1315	15.968	2.00	5.00	12.00	35.00
	1316	34.200	1.00	4.00	9.00	25.00
	1317	17.314	.50	2.00	6.00	20.00
	1318	—	.25	2.00	5.00	15.00
	1319	—	2.00	4.00	10.00	22.50
	1320	—	.25	2.00	5.00	15.00
	1321/0	—	.25	2.00	6.00	18.00
	1322/12	—	.25	1.50	3.00	10.00
	1322/0	—	.25	1.50	3.00	10.00
	1322/1	—	.25	1.50	3.00	10.00
	1331	8.162	2.00	5.00	10.00	25.00
	1332	22.892	.25	1.50	3.00	12.00

COPPER

Y#	Date	Mintage	Fine	VF	XF	Unc
128a	SH1322	—	2.00	4.00	8.00	12.00

ALUMINUM-BRONZE
Reduced thickness

Y#	Date	Mintage	Fine	VF	XF	Unc
137	SH1332	—	10.00	15.00	25.00	40.00
	1333	4.036	.25	1.00	2.50	8.00
	1334	1.370	.25	1.00	3.00	10.00
	1335	.926	.10	.50	2.00	8.00
	1336	-*	.10	.50	2.00	8.00
	1342	.800	.10	.50	2.00	8.00
	1343	1.400	.10	.50	2.00	8.00
	1344	1.600	.10	.25	1.00	6.00
	1345	1.690	.10	.25	1.00	6.00
	1346	153.648**	.10	.25	2.00	4.00
	1347	2.000	.10	.25	2.00	4.00
	1348	1.500	.10	.20	.50	3.00
	1349	.360	1.00	2.00	5.00	12.50
	1350	—	.10	.20	.50	3.00
	1351	—	.10	.20	.50	3.00
	1353	.060	.10	.20	.50	3.00
	1354	.016	.10	.50	2.00	6.00

*Mint reports record 126,500 in SH1337 & 20,000 in SH1338; these were probably dated SH1336.

**Mintage report seems excessive for this and all SH1346 coinage.

BRASS-COATED STEEL

Y#	Date	Mintage	Fine	VF	XF	Unc
137a	MS2535	.027	.25	.50	1.50	5.00
	2536	—	.25	1.00	3.50	5.00
	2537	—	.10	.75	1.25	4.00
	SH1357	—	.10	1.00	1.75	4.00
	1358	—	.10	1.00	2.00	4.00

RIAL

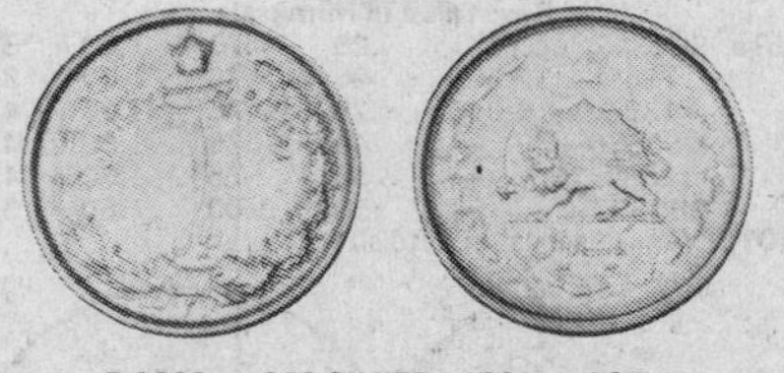

5.0000 g, .828 SILVER, .1331 oz ASW

Y#	Date	Mintage	Fine	VF	XF	Unc
113	SH1310	2.190	BV	2.00	7.00	25.00
	1311	10.256	BV	2.00	5.00	20.00
	1312	25.768	BV	2.00	4.00	15.00
	1313	6.670	BV	2.00	5.00	20.00

All coins dated SH1311-13 cut or punched over SH1310.

1.6000 g, .600 SILVER, .0308 oz ASW

Y#	Date	Mintage	Fine	VF	XF	Unc
129	SH1322	—	.50	1.00	3.00	7.00
	1323	—	BV	1.00	2.00	5.00
	1324/3	—	—	—	—	—
	1324	—	BV	1.00	2.00	6.00
	1325	—	BV	1.50	2.00	6.00
	1326	.567	15.00	25.00	50.00	75.00
	1327	5.795	.75	1.25	2.00	7.50
	1328	1.565	1.00	2.50	4.00	12.50
	1329	.144	22.00	40.00	75.00	120.00
	1330	—	2.00	5.00	10.00	20.00
	1424 (error for 1324)	—	—	—	—	—

COPPER-NICKEL

Y#	Date	Mintage	Fine	VF	XF	Unc
138	SH1331	4.735	.50	2.00	5.00	15.00
	1332	3.320*	4.00	8.00	15.00	30.00
	1333	16.405	.60	1.00	2.00	6.50
	1334	8.980	.60	1.00	2.00	5.00
	1335	8.910	.10	.50	2.00	5.00
	1336	4.450	.50	2.00	8.00	20.00

*Much rarer than mintage would indicate.

Only the last 2 digits of the date appear on Y#138.

2.00 g

Y#	Date	Mintage	Fine	VF	XF	Unc
A140	SH1337	8.005	.50	1.00	2.00	5.00

1.75 g

Y#	Date	Mintage	Fine	VF	XF	Unc
A140a	SH1338	14.940	.10	.20	.40	3.00
	1339	8.400	.25	.50	1.00	4.00
	1340	8.490	.25	.50	1.00	4.00
	1341	8.680	.25	.50	1.00	4.00
	1342	13.332	.10	.20	.40	3.00
	1343	14.746	.10	.15	.25	2.00
A140a	1344	12.050	.10	.20	.50	3.50
	1345	13.786	.10	.15	.20	2.00
	1346	155.321	.10	.15	.20	2.00
	1347	20.664	.10	.15	.25	3.00
	1348	22.960	.10	.15	.20	2.00
	1349	19.918	.10	.15	.20	2.00
	1350	24.248	.10	.20	.65	2.00
	1351/0	21.825	.10	.25	.40	3.00
	1351	Inc. Ab.	.10	.15	.20	2.00
	1352	31.449	.10	.15	.20	2.00
	1353 large date	33.700	.10	.20	.25	3.00
	1353 sm.dt.	I.A.	.10	.15	.20	2.00
	1354	—	.10	.15	.20	2.00
	MS2536	—	.10	.15	.25	3.00

F.A.O. Issue

Y#	Date	Mintage	Fine	VF	XF	Unc
152	SH1350	2.770	.10	.15	.25	1.00
	1351	8.605	.10	.15	.25	1.00
	1353	2.000	.10	.15	.25	1.00
	1354	1.000	.20	.30	.75	2.00

50th Anniversary of Pahlavi Rule

Y#	Date	Mintage	Fine	VF	XF	Unc
154	MS2535	61.945	.50	1.00	1.50	2.50

Obv: *Aryamehr* **added to legend.**

Y#	Date	Mintage	Fine	VF	XF	Unc
154a	MS2536	71.150	.10	.15	.25	2.00
	2537	—	.10	.15	.25	2.00
	2537/6537 (error 2/6)	—	—	—	—	6.00
	SH1357/6	—	.25	.50	.75	5.00
	1357	—	.25	.50	.75	3.00

2 RIALS

10.0000 g, .828 SILVER, .2662 oz ASW

Y#	Date	Mintage	Fine	VF	XF	Unc
114	SH1310	6.145	BV	5.00	10.00	20.00
	1311	8.838	BV	5.00	10.00	20.00
	1312	19.175	BV	5.00	10.00	20.00
	1313	4.015	BV	7.00	15.00	30.00

NOTE: All coins dated SH1311-13 cut or punched over SH1310.

3.2000 g, .600 SILVER, .0617 oz ASW

Y#	Date	Mintage	Fine	VF	XF	Unc
130	SH1322	—	BV	1.00	3.50	7.00
	1323/2	—	10.00	20.00	30.00	50.00
	1323	—	BV	1.00	3.00	6.00
	1324	—	BV	1.00	3.00	6.00
	1325	—	1.25	3.00	5.00	11.00
	1326	.187	15.00	30.00	50.00	90.00
	1327	3.140	BV	2.00	4.00	10.00
	1328	1.198	2.50	5.00	8.00	16.00
	1329	—	20.00	35.00	65.00	120.00
	1330	—	2.50	5.00	9.00	25.00

COPPER-NICKEL

Y#	Date	Mintage	Fine	VF	XF	Unc
139	SH1331	5.335	1.25	3.00	7.00	20.00
139	1332	6.870	1.00	2.00	4.00	8.00
	1333	13.668	.15	.75	2.00	7.00
	1334	7.185	.15	.75	2.00	7.00
	1335	2.400	.15	.75	3.00	12.50
	1336	.325	15.00	25.00	40.00	75.00

Y#	Date	Mintage	Fine	VF	XF	Unc
B140	SH1338	17.610	.10	.25	.75	4.00
	1339	8.575	.10	.25	.50	4.00
	1340	5.668	.10	.25	.50	4.00
	1341	5.820	.10	.25	.75	4.00
	1342	8.570	.10	.25	.50	4.00
	1343	11.250	.10	.25	.50	3.00
	1344	5.155	.10	.25	.50	4.00
	1345	2.267	.15	.30	1.00	5.00
	1346	92.792	—	.10	.20	4.00
	1347	10.300	—	.10	1.00	6.00
	1348	9.319	.20	.45	1.10	4.00
	1349	9.895	.20	.40	1.00	4.00
	1350	9.545	.15	.35	1.00	4.00
	1351	13.305	.15	.35	1.00	3.00
	1352	15.910	—	.10	.20	3.00
	1353	28.477	—	.10	.20	3.00
	1354	41.700	—	.10	.20	3.00
	MS2536	54.725	—	.10	.20	3.00

Obv: *Aryamehr* **added to legend.**

Y#	Date	Mintage	Fine	VF	XF	Unc
B140a	MS2536	Inc. Ab.	.25	.50	1.00	4.00
	2537	—	.25	.50	1.00	4.00
	SH1357	—	.25	.50	1.00	4.00

50th Anniversary of Pahlavi Rule

Y#	Date	Mintage	Fine	VF	XF	Unc
155	MS2535	59.568	—	.10	.30	2.50

5 RIALS

25.0000 g, .828 SILVER, .6655 oz ASW

Y#	Date	Mintage	Fine	VF	XF	Unc
115	SH1310	5.471	BV	10.00	15.00	30.00
	1311	4.527	BV	10.00	15.00	30.00
	1312	5.502	BV	10.00	15.00	30.00
	1313	1.208	BV	12.00	22.00	37.50

NOTE: Most coins dated SH1311-13 are cut or punched over SH1310.

8.0000 g, .600 SILVER, .1543 oz ASW

Y#	Date	Mintage	Fine	VF	XF	Unc
131	SH1322	—	BV	2.00	3.50	12.00
	1323	—	BV	2.50	4.00	7.50
	1324	—	BV	2.00	4.50	10.00
	1325	—	BV	2.00	3.50	12.00
	1326	.061	30.00	50.00	75.00	125.00
	1327	.836	2.00	5.00	7.50	20.00
	1328	.282	2.50	10.00	20.00	40.00
	1329	—	35.00	60.00	90.00	175.00

IRAN 1026

COPPER-NICKEL

Y#	Date	Mintage	Fine	VF	XF	Unc
140	SH1331	3.660	.50	2.00	5.00	20.00
	1332	16.350	.25	1.00	3.00	10.00
	1333	6.582	.25	1.00	3.00	10.00
	1334	.300	10.00	15.00	25.00	50.00
	1336	1.410	.50	2.00	5.00	20.00

7.00 g, 26mm

C140	SH1337	3.660	1.00	2.50	7.50	22.50
	1338	10.467	.50	2.50	8.00	20.00

5.00 g

C140a	SH1338	Inc. Ab.	.25	.40	2.00	6.00
	1339	3.980	.25	.40	2.00	6.00
	1340	3.814	.25	.40	2.00	6.00
	1341	2.332	.25	.40	2.00	6.00
	1342	7.838	.25	.40	1.00	4.00
	1343	9.484	.25	.40	1.00	4.00
	1344	3.468	.25	.40	1.00	4.00
	1345	6.092	.25	.40	1.00	4.00
	1346/36	74.781	.25	.40	1.50	5.00
	1346	Inc. Ab.	.25	.40	1.00	4.00

4.60 g, 24.5mm
Obv. leg: *Aryamehr* added.

C140b	SH1347	7.745	.50	.85	1.50	4.00
	1348	9.193	.50	.75	1.00	4.00
	1349	7.300	.50	.75	1.00	4.00
	1350	10.160	.35	.75	1.00	3.00
	1351	20.582	.25	.75	1.00	3.00
	1352	23.590	.25	.75	1.00	3.00
	1353	28.367	.25	.75	1.00	3.00
	1353 large date	Inc. Ab.	.25	.75	1.00	3.00
	1354	27.294	.25	.75	1.00	3.00
	MS2536	47.906	.20	.50	1.00	3.00
	2537	—	.35	.65	1.00	3.00
	SH1357	—	.50	.75	1.00	3.00

50th Anniversary of Pahlavi Rule

| 156 | MS2535 | 37.144 | .10 | .40 | .75 | 3.00 |

10 RIALS

16.0000 g, .600 SILVER, .3086 oz ASW

132	SH1323/2	—	BV	3.00	6.00	12.00
	1323	—	BV	3.00	5.00	15.00
	1324	—	BV	3.00	5.00	15.00
	1325	—	BV	3.00	6.00	17.50
	1326	—	40.00	75.00	100.00	160.00

NOTE: Counterfeits are known dated SH1322.

COPPER-NICKEL, 12.00 g

Y#	Date	Mintage	Fine	VF	XF	Unc
D140	SH1335	6.225	.50	2.00	5.00	15.00
	1336	4.415	1.00	3.00	7.50	15.00
	1337	.715	3.00	6.00	9.00	20.00
	1338	1.210	.50	2.00	6.00	14.00
	1339	2.775	.50	2.00	4.00	12.00
	1340	3.660	.50	2.00	4.00	12.00
	1341	.744	20.00	35.00	50.00	75.00
	1343	6.874	1.00	3.00	5.00	15.00

Thin flan, 9.00 g

D140a	SH1341	Inc. Y#D140	.35	1.00	2.50	5.00
	1342	3.763	.35	1.00	2.00	4.00
	1343	Inc. Y#D140	.35	.75	1.50	2.50
	1344	1.627	.35	.75	1.50	2.50

Rev: Value in words.

149	SH1345	1.699	.50	.60	2.00	5.00
	1346	38.897	.40	.50	1.00	4.00
	1347	8.220	.40	.65	1.50	8.00
	1348	7.156	.40	.50	1.00	4.00
	1349	7.397	.40	.50	1.00	4.00
	1350	8.972	.40	.50	1.00	4.00
	1351	9.912	.40	.50	1.00	4.00
	1352	28.776	.50	2.00	4.50	7.00

Rev: Value in numerals.

149a	SH1352	Inc. Ab.	.30	.60	1.00	4.00
	1353	22.234	.30	.60	1.00	3.00
	1354	23.482	.30	.60	1.00	4.00
	MS2536	24.324	.30	.60	1.00	3.00
	2537	—	.30	.60	1.00	4.00
	SH1357	—	.30	1.00	1.50	4.00

F.A.O. Issue

| 150 | SH1348 | .150 | .25 | .50 | 1.00 | 3.50 |

50th Anniversary of Pahlavi Rule

| 157 | MS2535 | 29.859 | .25 | .50 | .75 | 3.50 |

20 RIALS

COPPER-NICKEL
Rev: Value in words.

Y#	Date	Mintage	Fine	VF	XF	Unc
151	SH1350	2.349	.25	1.00	3.00	6.00
	1351	11.416	.25	.85	1.00	3.00
	1352	7.172	.25	.85	1.25	5.00

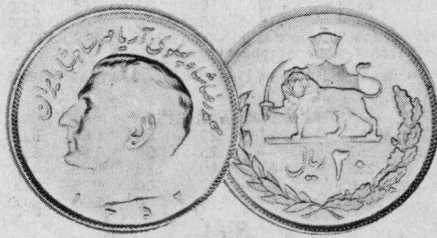

Rev: Value in numerals.

151a	SH1352	Inc.Y151	.25	.75	1.00	3.50
	1353	12.601	.25	.75	1.00	3.75
	1354	16.246	.25	.75	1.00	4.00
	MS2536	—	.40	.75	1.00	4.00
	2537	—	.50	.75	1.00	4.00
	SH1357	—	.50	1.00	1.50	5.00

NOTE: Varieties exist in date size.

7th Asian Games

| 153 | SH1353 | Inc. Ab. | 1.00 | 2.00 | 3.00 | 5.00 |

50th Anniversary of Pahlavi Rule

| 158 | MS2535 | — | .50 | 1.00 | 2.00 | 4.00 |

F.A.O. Issue

| 160 | MS2535 | 10.000 | 1.00 | 2.00 | 3.00 | 5.00 |
| (159) | 2536 | 23.370 | 1.00 | 2.50 | 4.00 | 6.00 |

50th Anniversary of Bank Melli

| 162 | SH1357 | — | 2.00 | 3.00 | 6.00 | 12.00 |
| (160) | | | | | | |

F.A.O. Issue

Y#	Date	Mintage	Fine	VF	XF	Unc
163 (161)	SH1357	5.000	.50	.75	2.00	6.00

25 RIALS

7.5000 g, .999 SILVER, .2409 oz ASW

KM#	Date	Year	Mintage	VF	XF	Unc
2	AH1350	1971	.018	—	Proof	15.00

50 RIALS

15.0000 g, .999 SILVER, .4818 oz ASW

| 3 | AH1350 | 1971 | .018 | — | Proof | 20.00 |

75 RIALS

22.5000 g, .999 SILVER, .7227 oz ASW
Obv: Similar to 50 Rials, KM#3.

| 4 | AH1350 | 1971 | .018 | — | Proof | 25.00 |

100 RIALS

30.0000 g, .999 SILVER, .9636 oz ASW
Obv: Similar to 50 Rials, KM#3.

| 5 | AH1350 | 1971 | .018 | — | Proof | 32.50 |

200 RIALS

60.0000 g, .999 SILVER, 1.9273 oz ASW
Rev: Similar to 2000 Rials, KM#11.

KM#	Date	Year	Mintage	VF	XF	Unc
6	AH1350	1971	.023	—	Proof	60.00

500 RIALS

6.5100 g, .900 GOLD, .1883 oz AGW

| 8 | AH1350 | 1971 | .011 | — | Proof | 150.00 |

750 RIALS

9.7700 g, .900 GOLD, .2827 oz AGW

| 9 | AH1350 | 1971 | .010 | — | Proof | 175.00 |

1000 RIALS

13.0300 g, .900 GOLD, .3770 oz AGW
Polished fields below ruins.

| 10.1 | AH1350 | 1971 | .010 | — | Proof | 225.00 |

Frosted fields below ruins.

| 10.2 | AH1350 | 1971 | Inc. Ab. | — | Proof | 225.00 |

2000 RIALS

26.0600 g, .900 GOLD, .7541 oz AGW

| 11 | AH1350 | 1971 | 9,805 | — | Proof | 500.00 |

1/4 PAHLAVI

2.0340 g, .900 GOLD, 14mm, .0589 oz AGW

Y#	Date	Mintage	Fine	VF	XF	Unc
141	SH1332	.041	BV	35.00	45.00	60.00
	1333	.007	35.00	45.00	100.00	150.00
	1334	—	BV	35.00	60.00	100.00
	1335	.041	BV	35.00	45.00	60.00
	1336	—	—	—	Rare	

Thinner & broader, 16mm

Y#	Date	Mintage	Fine	VF	XF	Unc
141a	SH1336	.007	40.00	60.00	80.00	140.00
	1337	.033	—	BV	35.00	45.00
	1338	.136	—	BV	35.00	45.00
	1339	.156	—	BV	35.00	45.00
	1340	.060	—	BV	35.00	45.00
	1342	.080	—	BV	35.00	45.00
	1343	.040	—	Reported, not confirmed		
	1344	.030	—	35.00	40.00	65.00
	1345	.040	—	BV	35.00	45.00
	1346	.030	—	BV	35.00	45.00
	1347	.060	—	BV	35.00	45.00
	1348	.060	—	BV	35.00	45.00
	1349	.080	—	BV	35.00	45.00
	1350	.080	—	BV	35.00	45.00
	1351	.103	—	BV	35.00	45.00
	1352	.050	—	BV	35.00	45.00
	1353	—	—	BV	35.00	45.00

Obv. leg: *Aryamehr* added.

141b	SH1354	.106	—	BV	30.00	40.00
	1355	.186	—	BV	30.00	40.00
	MS2536	—	—	BV	30.00	40.00
	2537	—	—	BV	30.00	40.00
	SH1358	—	BV	35.00	75.00	115.00

1/2 PAHLAVI

4.0680 g, .900 GOLD, .1177 oz AGW

123	SH1310	696 pcs.	75.00	150.00	275.00	375.00
	1311	286 pcs.	75.00	175.00	300.00	400.00
	1312	892 pcs.	75.00	150.00	250.00	350.00
	1313	531 pcs.	75.00	175.00	300.00	400.00
	1314	—	75.00	175.00	300.00	400.00
	1315	1,042	75.00	175.00	275.00	375.00

133	SH1320	—	75.00	100.00	150.00	300.00
	1322	—	—	BV	60.00	75.00
	1323	.076	—	BV	60.00	75.00
	1324	—	—	Reported, not confirmed		

Obv: High relief head.

135	SH1324	—	BV	60.00	70.00	100.00
	1325	—	BV	60.00	70.00	100.00
	1326	.036	BV	60.00	75.00	125.00
	1327	.036	BV	60.00	75.00	125.00
	1328	—	BV	70.00	85.00	150.00
	1329	75 pcs.	75.00	150.00	250.00	500.00
	1330	.098	—	Reported, not confirmed		

Obv: Low relief head.

142	SH1330	Inc.Y135	BV	55.00	65.00	80.00
	1333	—	BV	75.00	90.00	125.00
	1334	—	—	75.00	90.00	125.00
	1335	—	—	BV	60.00	80.00
	1336	.132	—	BV	60.00	80.00
	1337	.102	—	BV	60.00	70.00
	1338	.140	—	BV	60.00	70.00
	1339	.142	—	BV	60.00	70.00
	1340	.439	—	BV	60.00	70.00
	1342	.040	—	BV	60.00	75.00
	1343	—	—	Reported, not confirmed		
	1344	.030	BV	75.00	90.00	125.00
	1345	.040	—	BV	60.00	72.50
	1346	.040	—	BV	60.00	72.50
	1347	.050	—	BV	60.00	65.00
	1348	.040	—	BV	60.00	70.00
	1349	.080	—	BV	60.00	70.00
	1350	.080	—	BV	60.00	70.00
	1351	.103	—	BV	60.00	70.00
	1352	.067	—	BV	60.00	70.00
	1353	—	—	BV	60.00	70.00

Obv. leg: *Aryamehr* added.

142a	SH1354	.037	—	BV	60.00	70.00
	1355	.153	—	BV	60.00	70.00
	MS2536	—	—	BV	60.00	70.00
	2537	—	—	BV	60.00	70.00
	SH1358	—	—	—	275.00	375.00

PAHLAVI

1.9180 g, .900 GOLD, .0555 oz AGW

Y#	Date	Mintage	Fine	VF	XF	Unc
116	SH1305	5,000	100.00	150.00	250.00	350.00

120	SH1306	.021	50.00	75.00	120.00	170.00
	1307	5,000	60.00	85.00	130.00	200.00
	1308	989 pcs.	80.00	100.00	160.00	275.00

8.1360 g, .900 GOLD, .2354 oz AGW

| 124 | SH1310 | 304 pcs. | 300.00 | 500.00 | 850.00 | 1200. |

134	SH1320	—	—	Rare	—
	1322	—	BV	115.00	130.00
	1323	.311	BV	115.00	130.00
	1324	—	BV	115.00	130.00

Obv: High relief head.

136	SH1324	—	BV	115.00	125.00	170.00
	1325	—	BV	115.00	135.00	190.00
	1326	.151	BV	115.00	150.00	190.00
	1327	.020	BV	130.00	150.00	190.00
	1328	4,000	BV	140.00	195.00	265.00
	1329	4,000	BV	140.00	195.00	265.00
	1330	.048	BV	140.00	195.00	265.00

Obv: Low relief head.

143	SH1330	—	BV	115.00	145.00
	1332	—	—	Rare	—
	1333	—	BV	125.00	150.00	200.00
	1334	—	BV	125.00	150.00	200.00
	1335	—	—	BV	115.00	140.00
	1336	.453	—	BV	115.00	140.00
	1337	.665	—	BV	115.00	120.00
	1338	.776	—	BV	115.00	120.00
	1339	.847	—	BV	115.00	120.00
	1340	.528	—	BV	115.00	120.00
	1342	.020	—	BV	115.00	140.00
	1343	.010	—	Reported, not confirmed
	1344	—	BV	110.00	150.00	190.00
	1345	.020	—	BV	115.00	140.00
	1346	.030	—	BV	115.00	140.00
	1347	.040	—	BV	115.00	120.00
	1348	.070	—	BV	115.00	120.00
	1349	.070	—	BV	115.00	120.00
	1350	.060	—	BV	115.00	120.00
	1351	.100	—	BV	115.00	120.00
	1352	.320	—	BV	115.00	120.00
	1353	—	—	BV	115.00	120.00

Obv. leg: *Aryamehr* **added.**

143a	SH1354	.021	—	BV	115.00	120.00
	1355	.203	—	BV	115.00	120.00
	MS2536	—	—	BV	115.00	120.00
	2537	—	—	BV	115.00	120.00
	SH1358	—	—	—	225.00	325.00

2 PAHLAVI

3.8360 g, .900 GOLD, .1110 oz AGW

Y#	Date	Mintage	Fine	VF	XF	Unc
117	SH1305	1,134	200.00	315.00	475.00	950.00

121	SH1306	2,494	65.00	100.00	175.00	250.00
	1307	7,000	65.00	100.00	175.00	250.00
	1308	789 pcs.	90.00	150.00	225.00	300.00

2-1/2 PAHLAVI

20.3400 g, .900 GOLD, .5885 oz AGW

144	SH1339	1,682	BV	275.00	300.00	350.00
	1340	2,788	BV	275.00	300.00	350.00
	1342	30 pcs.	—	Rare	—
	1347	2,000	—	Reported, not confirmed
	1348	3,000	BV	275.00	300.00	350.00
	1349	3,000	—	Reported, not confirmed
	1350	2,000	BV	275.00	300.00	350.00
	1351	2,500	BV	275.00	300.00	350.00
	1352	3,000	BV	275.00	300.00	350.00
	1353	—	BV	275.00	300.00	350.00

Obv. leg: *Aryamehr* **added.**

144a	SH1354	.018	—	BV	275.00	300.00
	1355	.016	—	BV	275.00	300.00
	MS2536	—	—	BV	275.00	300.00
	2537	—	—	BV	275.00	300.00
	SH1358	—	—	—	Rare	—

5 PAHLAVI

9.5900 g, .900 GOLD, .2775 oz AGW

| 118 | SH1305 | 271 pcs. | 500.00 | 700.00 | 950.00 | 1900. |

122	SH1306	909 pcs.	300.00	500.00	700.00	1400.
	1307	785 pcs.	300.00	500.00	850.00	1600.
	1308	121 pcs.	400.00	600.00	1400.	2200.

40.6799 g, .900 GOLD, 1.1772 oz AGW

| 145 | SH1339 | 2,225 | — | BV | 550.00 | 600.00 |

Y#	Date	Mintage	Fine	VF	XF	Unc
145	1340	2,430	—	BV	550.00	600.00
	1342	20 pcs.	—	—	Rare	—
	1347	500 pcs.	—	Reported, not confirmed
	1348	2,000	—	BV	550.00	600.00
	1349	700 pcs.	—	Reported, not confirmed
	1350	2,000	—	BV	550.00	600.00
	1351	2,500	—	BV	550.00	600.00
	1352	2,100	—	BV	550.00	600.00
	1353	—	—	BV	550.00	600.00

Obv. leg: *Aryamehr* **added.**

145a	SH1354	.010	—	BV	550.00	600.00
	1355	.017	—	BV	550.00	600.00
	MS2536	—	—	BV	550.00	600.00
	2537	—	—	BV	550.00	600.00
	SH1358	—	—	550.00	700.00	1000.

10 PAHLAVI

81.3598 g, .900 GOLD, 2.3544 oz AGW
50th Anniversary of Pahlavi Rule

| 159 | MS2535 | — | — | — | 1200. | 1550. |

Centenary of Reza Shah's Birth

| A159 | MS2536 | — | — | — | 1200. | 1600. |

IRAN

Y#	Date	Mintage	Fine	VF	XF	Unc
161	SH1358	—	—	—	1700.	2250.
	MS2537	—	—	—	1300.	1600.

MINT SETS (MS)

KM#	Date	Mintage	Identification	Issue Price	Mkt. Val.
MS1	SH1342(4)	—	YA140a,B140,C140a,D140a	2.00	15.00
MS2	SH1343(4)	—	YA140a,B140,C140a,D140a	2.00	11.50
MS3	SH1348(5)	—	Y137,A140a,B140,C140b,149	2.00	17.00
MS4	SH1350(5)	—	Y137,A140a,B140,C140b,149	2.00	17.00
MS5	SH1353(6)	—	Y137,A140a,B140, C140b,149a,151a	2.00	19.00
MS6	SH1354(6)	—	Y137,A140a,B140,C140b,149a, 151a,	2.00	22.00
MS7	MS2535(6)	—	Y137a,154-158	2.50	21.50
MS8	MS2536(6)	—	Y137a,B140,C140b,149a,151a, 154a	2.50	20.00

PROOF SETS (PS)

PS1	SH1306	20	Y110,111*	—	1650.

*Two each type.

PS2	1971(9)	9,805	KM2-6, 8-11	261.50	1210.
PS3	1971(5)	18,100	KM2-6	59.50	155.00

ISLAMIC REPUBLIC
50 DINARS

BRASS CLAD STEEL

Y#	Date	Mintage	Fine	VF	XF	Unc
176	SH1358	—	—	5.00	10.00	15.00

RIAL

COPPER-NICKEL
Islamic Republic of Iran

164	SH1358	—	—	.25	.75	2.00
(162)	1359	—	—	.25	.75	1.75
	1360	—	—	.25	.75	1.75
	1361	—	—	.25	.75	1.75
	1364	—	—	.25	.75	1.75
	1365	—	—	.15	.65	1.25

BRONZE CLAD STEEL
Mosque of Omar

Y#	Date	Mintage	Fine	VF	XF	Unc
171	SH1359	—	—	.50	1.75	2.50

2 RIALS

COPPER-NICKEL
Islamic Republic of Iran

165	SH1358	—	—	.50	1.00	3.00
(163)	1359	—	—	.50	1.00	3.00
	1360	—	—	.50	1.00	3.00
	1361	—	—	.40	.75	2.75
	1362	—	—	.35	.50	2.50
	1364	—	—	.35	.50	2.50
	1365	—	—	.25	.50	2.00

5 RIALS

COPPER-NICKEL
Islamic Republic of Iran

166	SH1358	—	—	.75	1.00	3.00
(164)	1359	—	—	.75	1.00	3.00
	1360	—	—	.75	1.00	3.00
	1361	—	—	.75	2.50	3.50

10 RIALS

COPPER-NICKEL
Islamic Republic of Iran

167	SH1358	—	—	1.00	3.00	6.00
(165)	1359	—	—	1.00	3.00	8.00
	1360	—	—	1.00	3.00	6.00
	1361	—	—	1.00	2.00	4.00
	1363	—	—	1.00	2.00	4.00
	1364	—	—	1.00	2.00	4.00
	1365	—	—	.75	1.50	3.00

1st Anniversary of Revolution

169	SH1358	—	—	1.50	3.00	6.00
(167)						

Moslem Unity

175	SH1361	—	—	3.00	4.00	5.50

20 RIALS

COPPER-NICKEL
Islamic Republic of Iran

Y#	Date	Mintage	Fine	VF	XF	Unc
168	SH1358	—	—	2.50	5.00	8.00
(166)	1359	—	—	2.50	5.00	8.00
	1360	—	—	1.25	2.50	5.00
	1361	—	—	1.25	2.50	5.00
	1362	—	—	1.25	2.50	5.00

1400th Anniversary of Mohammed's Flight

170	SH1358	—	—	3.00	4.00	6.00
(168)						

3rd Anniversary of Islamic Revolution

173	SH1360	—	—	3.00	5.00	6.50

174	SH1359	—	—	3.00	5.00	6.50

50 RIALS

ALUMINUM-BRONZE
Oil and Agriculture

172	SH1360	1981	—	8.00	10.00	12.50
	1361	1982	—	8.00	10.00	12.50
	1364	1985	—	5.00	7.50	10.00
	1365	1986	—	5.00	7.50	10.00

TRADE COINAGE
1/4 POUND

2.0339 g, .900 GOLD, .0588 oz AGW
Revolution Commemorative

C163	SH1358	—	—	—	—	175.00

1/2 POUND

4.0680 g, .900 GOLD, .1177 oz AGW
Revolution Commemorative

A163	SH1358	—	—	—	—	100.00

IRAN

POUND

8.1360 g, .900 GOLD, .2354 oz AGW
Revolution Commemorative

Y#	Date	Mintage	Fine	VF	XF	Unc
B163	SH1358	—	—	—	—	150.00
	1363	—	—	—	—	135.00
	1364	—	—	—	—	135.00

2-1/2 POUNDS

20.3400 g, .900 GOLD, .5885 oz AGW
Revolution Commemorative

| D163 | SH1358 | 6 pcs. | — | — | — | 2000. |

IRAQ

The Republic of Iraq, historically known as Mesopotamia, is located in the Near East and is bordered by Kuwait, Iran, Turkey, Syria, Jordan and Saudi Arabia. It has an area of 167,925 sq. mi. (434,924 sq. km.) and a population of 17.6 million. Capital: Baghdad. The economy of Iraq is based on agriculture and petroleum. crude oil accounted for 94 percent of the exports before the war with Iran began in 1980.

Mesopotamia was the site of a number of flourishing civilizations of antiquity - Sumerian, Assyrian, Babylonian, Parthian, Persian - and of the Biblical cities of Ur, Nineveh and Babylon. Desired because of its favored location which embraced the fertile alluvial plains of the Tigris and Euphrates Rivers, Mesopotamia - 'land between the rivers' - was conquered by Cyrus the Great of Persia, Alexander of Macedonia and by Arabs who made the legendary city of Baghdad the capital of the ruling caliphate. Suleiman the Magnificent conquered Mesopotamia for Turkey in 1534, and it formed part of the Ottoman Empire until 1623, and from 1638 to 1917. Great Britain, given a League of Nations mandate over the territory in 1920, recognized Iraq as a kingdom in 1922. Iraq became an independent constitutional monarchy presided over by the Hashemite family, direct descendants of the prophet Mohammed, in 1932. In 1958, the army-led revolution of July 14 overthrew the monarchy and proclaimed a republic.

NOTE: The 'I' mint mark on 1938 and 1943 issues appears on the obverse near the point of the bust. Some of the issues of 1938 have a dot to denote a composition change from nickel to copper-nickel.

RULERS

Turkish, until 1917
British, 1921-1922
Faisal I, 1921-1933
Ghazi I, 1933-1939
Faisal II, 1939-1958

MESOPOTAMIA

MONETARY SYSTEM
40 Para = 1 Piastre (Kurus)

MINTNAME

Baghdad   بغداد

Al Basra   البصرة

Al Hille   الحلة

MAHMUD II
AH1223-1255/1808-1839AD

NOTE: The denominations of the following coins are tentative, and all authorities are not in agreement of the classification. Until a better system is available, that of C. Olcer will be followed. Most types are similar to Turkish coins, but with mintname Baghdad.

2 PARA
COPPER, 16-19mm
Similar to 5 Para, KM#54.

KM#	Date	Year	Good	VG	Fine	VF
80	AH1241	16	—	Reported, not confirmed		

5 PARA

COPPER, 16-23mm

54	AH1238	—	10.00	20.00	25.00	35.00
	1240	—	10.00	20.00	25.00	35.00
	1241	—	10.00	20.00	25.00	35.00
	1244	—	10.00	20.00	25.00	35.00

Obv. and rev: Narrow floral borders.

| 58 | AH1240 | — | 10.00 | 15.00 | 22.50 | 33.50 |

Rev: Year above mintname.

KM#	Date	Year	Good	VG	Fine	VF
63	AH1223	18	—	—	—	—

17-25mm

69	AH1223	23	7.50	15.00	30.00	50.00
	1223	25	7.50	15.00	30.00	50.00

Rev: Year above mintname.

| 70 | AH1223 | 25 | — | — | — | — |

Obv: Star of David. Rev: Similar to KM#70.

| 71 | AH1223 | 25 | — | — | — | — |

Obv: Star of David only, 29mm.

| 72 | AH1248 | — | 8.50 | 17.50 | 35.00 | 60.00 |

Obv: Star and crescent only, 21-25mm.

73	AH1223	25	10.00	15.00	30.00	50.00
	1223	26	10.00	15.00	27.50	45.00

20-22mm

79	AH1223	28	10.00	15.00	25.00	40.00
	1223	29	Reported, not confirmed			

BILLON, 0.80 g, 18mm

| 59 | AH1223 | 17 | 10.00 | 20.00 | 40.00 | 65.00 |

10 PARA

BILLON, 24mm, 2.10 g
Obv: Toughra. Rev: Mint and date within beaded borders.

| 51 | AH1223 | 13 | 25.00 | 60.00 | 125.00 | 200.00 |

26mm, 1.60-1.80 g
Obv: Toughra, mint and date. Rev. leg: 4 lines.

55	AH1223	15	25.00	60.00	125.00	200.00
	1223	17	25.00	60.00	125.00	200.00

Similar to KM#55 w/ornamental borders added.

| 60 | AH1223 | 17 | 18.50 | 37.50 | 75.00 | 125.00 |

22mm, 1.40 g
Similar to KM#51, but floral borders.

| 61 | AH1223 | 17 | 18.50 | 37.50 | 75.00 | 125.00 |

20 PARA

BILLON, 28mm, 3.50-4.20 g

KM#	Date	Year	Good	VG	Fine	VF
52	AH1223	13	30.00	60.00	125.00	200.00

27mm, 3.20 g
Obv: Toughra, mint and date. Rev: 4-line leg.

56	AH1223	15	30.00	60.00	125.00	200.00
	1223	17	30.00	60.00	125.00	200.00

28mm, 3.00 g

62	AH1223	17	60.00	—	150.00	175.00

Reduced weight; 22mm, 1.20-1.60 g

64	AH1223	21	20.00	40.00	80.00	130.00

22mm, 1.80-2.00 g
Similar to KM#52, but extra leg. around central design.

65	AH1223	21	20.00	40.00	80.00	130.00

Similar to KM#56, 26mm, 2.00 g.

68	AH1223	22	20.00	40.00	80.00	130.00

22-24mm
Similar to 5 Para, KM#59.

75	AH1223	26	15.00	25.00	35.00	50.00
	1223	28	15.00	25.00	35.00	50.00
	1223	29	15.00	25.00	35.00	50.00

30 PARA
(Zolota)

BILLON, 31mm, 4.50 g

57	AH1223	15	75.00	100.00	150.00	200.00

PIASTRE
(40 Para)

BILLON, 31mm, 8.00-9.50 g

53	AH1223	13	50.00	100.00	200.00	300.00

Reduced weight; 29mm, 3.20-4.00 g

66	AH1223	21	35.00	65.00	125.00	200.00

Extra leg. added around central device.

67	AH1223	21	35.00	65.00	125.00	200.00

100 PARA

BILLON, 31mm, 3.00-3.20 g

KM#	Date	Year	Good	VG	Fine	VF
76	AH1223	26	35.00	65.00	125.00	200.00

Rev: Arabic legend.

77	AH1223	26	—	—	—	—

5 PIASTRES

BILLON, 36mm, 5.50-6.90 g

78		21 (date error)	—	—	Rare	
	AH1223	26	20.00	30.00	50.00	75.00
	—	27	20.00	30.00	50.00	75.00

HAYRIYE ALTIN

GOLD, 20-21mm, 1.40 g

KM#	Date	Year	VG	Fine	VF	XF
74	AH1223	25	90.00	150.00	250.00	400.00

GOVERNOR SAIT PASA
Coins without name or toughra of Mahmud II

2 PARA

COPPER, 15-18mm

KM#	Date	Year	Good	VG	Fine	VF
82	AH1230	—	15.00	25.00	50.00	80.00

5 PARA

COPPER, 27mm
Obv: Name of Sait Pasa within octagram.

85	AH1231	—	30.00	50.00	100.00	150.00

NOTE: This is the only Ottoman coin ever struck with a governor's name. Sait Pasa was beheaded for this infringement of tradition.

Rev: Similar to KM#85.

KM#	Date	Year	Good	VG	Fine	VF
88	AH1231	—	20.00	30.00	50.00	100.00

NOTE: The Tamgha was originally a sheep and cattle brand, later seal or brand. Each Turkish clan formerly kept its own Tamgha, to use both as a brand and as a seal on documents.

ABDUL MEJID
AH1255-1277 / 1839-1861AD

5 PARA

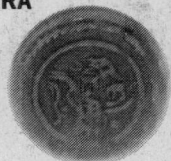

BILLON, 19-21mm

91 (C201)	AH1255	1	150.00	200.00	250.00	350.00

IRAQ

MINT MARKS
I - Bombay

MONETARY SYSTEM
50 Fils = 1 Dirham
200 Fils = 1 Riyal
1000 Fils = 1 Dinar (Pound)

TITLES

العراق
Al-Iraq

المملكة العراقية
Al-Mamlaka al-Iraqiya(t)

الجمهورية العرقية
Al-Jumhuriya(t) Al-Iraqiya(t)

KINGDOM
FILS

BRONZE

KM#	Date	Mintage	Fine	VF	XF	Unc
95	1931	4.000	1.00	3.00	7.50	20.00
	1931	—	—	—	Proof	
	1933	6.000	1.00	3.00	7.50	20.00
	1933	—	—	—	Proof	

102	1936	3.000	1.00	3.00	6.00	20.00
	1936	—	—	—	Proof	
	1938	36.000	.25	.35	.75	1.50
	1938	—	—	—	Proof	
	1938-I	3.000	.50	1.00	4.00	12.00

109	1953	41.000	.25	.40	.60	1.00
	1953	200 pcs.	—	—	Proof	50.00

IRAQ 1032

2 FILS

BRONZE

KM#	Date	Mintage	Fine	VF	XF	Unc
96	1931	2.500	1.25	2.50	7.50	20.00
	1931	—	—	—	Proof	—
	1933	1.000	1.50	3.00	10.00	25.00
	1933	—	—	—	Proof	—

| 110 | 1953 | .500 | .50 | 1.00 | 3.00 | 7.50 |
| | 1953 | 200 pcs. | — | — | Proof | 60.00 |

4 FILS

NICKEL

97	1931	4.500	1.00	2.00	7.50	35.00
	1931	—	—	—	Proof	35.00
	1933	6.500	1.00	2.00	7.50	35.00
	1933	—	—	—	Proof	—

105	1938	1.000	1.25	2.00	4.50	15.00
	1938	—	—	—	Proof	—
	1939	1.000	1.50	2.50	6.50	30.00
	1939	—	—	—	Proof	—

COPPER-NICKEL

105a	1938	2.750	.75	1.00	1.50	4.00
	1938.	—	—	—	Proof	—
	1938-I	2.500	1.00	2.00	7.50	15.00

BRONZE

| 105b | 1938. | 8.000 | .50 | .75 | 1.25 | 2.25 |
| | 1938. | — | — | — | Proof | — |

| 107 | 1943-I | 1.500 | 2.00 | 3.00 | 6.00 | 12.50 |

COPPER-NICKEL

| 111 | 1953 | 20.750 | .60 | .75 | 1.00 | 2.00 |
| | 1953 | 200 pcs. | — | — | Proof | 60.00 |

10 FILS

NICKEL

KM#	Date	Mintage	Fine	VF	XF	Unc
98	1931	2.400	2.00	5.00	15.00	50.00
	1931	—	—	—	Proof	—
	1933	2.200	2.00	5.00	15.00	50.00
	1933	—	—	—	Proof	—

103	1937	.400	3.00	5.00	15.00	50.00
	1937	—	—	—	Proof	—
	1938	.600	2.50	4.00	10.00	35.00
	1938	—	—	—	Proof	—

COPPER-NICKEL

103a	1938.	1.100	1.00	2.00	4.00	10.00
	1938.	—	—	—	Proof	—
	1938-I	1.500	1.50	2.50	6.00	15.00

BRONZE

| 103b | 1938. | 8.250 | .50 | 1.00 | 2.50 | 5.00 |
| | 1938. | — | — | — | Proof | — |

| 108 | 1943-I | 1.500 | 3.00 | 5.00 | 20.00 | 40.00 |

COPPER-NICKEL

| 112 | 1953 | 11.400 | .50 | .75 | 1.00 | 2.00 |
| | 1953 | 200 pcs. | — | — | Proof | 60.00 |

20 FILS

3.6000 g, .500 SILVER, .0579 oz ASW

99	1931	1.500	2.00	6.00	15.00	50.00
	1931	—	—	—	Proof	—
	1933	1.100	2.00	6.00	15.00	50.00
	1933	—	—	—	Proof	—
	1933 (error) 1252
	Inc. Ab.	20.00	60.00	100.00	200.00

| 106 | 1938 | 1.200 | 1.50 | 2.50 | 5.00 | 15.00 |
| | 1938-I | 1.350 | 1.50 | 2.50 | 7.50 | 25.00 |

| 113 | 1953 | .250 | 25.00 | 50.00 | 75.00 | 150.00 |
| | 1953 | 200 pcs. | — | — | Proof | 250.00 |

| 116 | 1955 | 4.000 | 1.50 | 3.00 | 5.00 | 10.00 |
| | 1955 | — | — | — | Proof | 80.00 |

50 FILS

9.0000 g, .500 SILVER, .1447 oz ASW

KM#	Date	Mintage	Fine	VF	XF	Unc
100	1931	8.800	2.00	5.00	15.00	75.00
	1931	—	—	—	Proof	—
	1933	.800	5.00	7.50	25.00	100.00
	1933	—	—	—	Proof	—

104	1937	1.200	2.50	4.00	7.50	25.00
	1937	—	—	—	Proof	—
	1938	5.300	2.00	4.00	5.00	20.00
	1938	—	—	—	Proof	—
	1938-I	7.500	2.00	4.00	5.00	15.00

| 114 | 1953 | .560 | 50.00 | 90.00 | 125.00 | 250.00 |
| | 1953 | 200 pcs. | — | — | Proof | 350.00 |

| 117 | 1955 | 12.000 | 2.50 | 4.00 | 6.00 | 12.50 |
| | 1955 | — | — | — | Proof | 80.00 |

100 FILS

10.0000 g, .900 SILVER, .2893 oz ASW

| 115 | 1953 | 1.200 | 5.00 | 7.50 | 17.50 | 37.50 |
| | 1953 | 200 pcs. | — | — | Proof | 150.00 |

10.0000 g, .500 SILVER, .1607 oz ASW

| 118 | 1955 | 1.000 | — | — | Rare | — |
| | 1955 | — | — | — | Proof | 300.00 |

RIYAL
(200 Fils)

IRAQ

20.0000 g, .500 SILVER, .3215 oz ASW

KM#	Date	Mintage	Fine	VF	XF	Unc
101	1932	.500	7.50	15.00	32.50	250.00
	1932		—	—	Proof	1000.

REPUBLIC
FILS

BRONZE

119	1959	72.000	.15	.25	.40	.75
	1959	400 pcs.	—	—	Proof	30.00

5 FILS

COPPER-NICKEL

120	1959	30.000	.15	.25	.50	1.00
	1959	400 pcs.	—	—	Proof	30.00
125	1967	17.000	.15	.25	.35	.50
	1971	15.000	.15	.25	.35	.50

STAINLESS STEEL

125a	1971	2.000	.20	.30	.50	.75
	1974	15.000	.10	.15	.25	.35
	1975	94.800	.10	.15	.25	.35
	1980	20.160	.10	.15	.25	.35
	1981	29.840	.10	.15	.25	.35

F.A.O. Issue

141	1975	2.000	.10	.15	.25	.50

Babylon - Ruins

159	1982			.10	.15	.25	.50

10 FILS

COPPER-NICKEL

KM#	Date	Mintage	Fine	VF	XF	Unc
121	1959	24.000	.20	.30	.50	1.00
	1959	400 pcs.	—	—	Proof	30.00
126	1967	13.400	.15	.25	.35	.60
	1971	12.000	.15	.25	.35	.60

STAINLESS STEEL

126a	1971	1.550	.15	.25	.50	.75
	1974	12.000	.15	.25	.35	.50
	1975	52.456	.15	.25	.35	.50
	1979	13.800	.15	.25	.35	.50
	1980	11.264	.15	.25	.35	.50
	1981	63.736	.15	.25	.35	.50

F.A.O. Issue

142	1975	1.000	.15	.25	.50	1.00

Babylon - Gate

160	1982					.75

25 FILS

2.5000 g, .500 SILVER, .0401 oz ASW

122	1959	12.000	.50	.75	1.50	3.00
	1959	400 pcs.	—	—	Proof	40.00

COPPER-NICKEL

127	1969	6.000	.15	.25	.35	.50
	1970	6.000	.15	.25	.35	.50
	1972	12.000	.15	.25	.35	.50
	1975	48.000	.15	.25	.35	.50
	1981	60.000	.15	.25	.35	.50

Babylon - Lion

161	1982					1.00

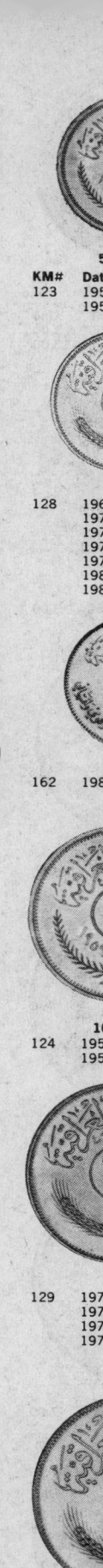

50 FILS

5.0000 g, .500 SILVER, .0803 oz ASW

KM#	Date	Mintage	Fine	VF	XF	Unc
123	1959	24.000	.75	1.25	2.00	4.50
	1959	400 pcs.	—	—	Proof	80.00

COPPER-NICKEL

128	1969	12.000	.20	.30	.50	.75
	1970	12.000	.20	.30	.50	.75
	1972	12.000	.20	.30	.50	.75
	1975	36.000	.20	.30	.50	.75
	1979	1.500	.20	.30	.50	.75
	1980	23.520	.20	.30	.50	.75
	1981	138.995	.20	.30	.50	.75

Babylon - Bull

162	1982		.25	.50	.75	2.00

100 FILS

10.0000 g, .500 SILVER, .1607 oz ASW

124	1959	6.000	2.00	3.25	4.50	8.50
	1959	400 pcs.	—	—	Proof	150.00

COPPER-NICKEL

129	1970	6.000	.35	.50	.75	1.25
	1972	6.000	.35	.50	.75	1.25
	1975	12.000	.35	.50	.75	1.25
	1979	1.000	.35	.75	1.50	3.00

250 FILS

NICKEL
F.A.O. Issue

130	1970	.500	—	1.00	1.50	3.50
	1970	1,000	—	—	Proof	15.00

Edge inscription-FAO-250-repeated three times.

IRAQ

1st Anniversary Peace with Kurds

KM#	Date	Mintage	Fine	VF	XF	Unc
131	1971	.500	—	1.00	1.50	3.00
	1971	1,000	—	—	Proof	15.00

KM#	Date	Mintage	Fine	VF	XF	Unc
147	1980	—	—	1.00	2.00	4.00
	1981	25.568	—	1.00	2.00	4.00

Oil Nationalization

KM#	Date	Mintage	Fine	VF	XF	Unc
139	1973	.260	—	1.75	3.50	5.00
	1973	5,000	—	—	Proof	7.50

Al Baath Party

| 135 | 1972 | .250 | — | 1.00 | 1.50 | 3.00 |

F.A.O. Issue

| 152 | 1981 | 46.432 | — | 1.00 | 2.00 | 4.00 |

| 165 | 1982 | — | — | 1.75 | 2.00 | 2.25 |

Baghdad Conference

| 155 | 1982 | — | — | 1.00 | 1.50 | 3.00 |

25th Anniversary of Central Bank

| 136 | 1972 | .250 | — | 1.00 | 1.50 | 3.00 |

Babylon

| 168 | 1982 | — | — | — | — | 8.50 |

DINAR

Babylon - Sculpture

| 163 | 1982 | — | — | 1.00 | 1.50 | 3.00 |

500 FILS

Oil Nationalization

| 138 | 1973 | .260 | — | 1.00 | 1.50 | 3.00 |
| | 1973 | 5,000 | — | — | Proof | 7.50 |

31.0000 g, .900 SILVER, .8971 oz ASW
50th Anniversary of Iraqi Army

| 133 | 1971 | .020 | — | — | — | 15.00 |
| | 1971 | — | — | — | Proof | 25.00 |

International Year of the Child

| 144 | 1979 | .010 | — | — | Proof | 7.00 |

COPPER-NICKEL
Saddam Hussein

| 146 | 1980 | — | — | 1.00 | 2.00 | 4.00 |

NICKEL
50th Anniversary of Iraqi Army

| 132 | 1971 | .100 | — | 1.75 | 3.50 | 5.00 |
| | 1971 | 5,000 | — | — | Proof | 7.50 |

IRAQ 1035

31.0000 g, .500 SILVER, .4983 oz ASW
25th Anniversary of Central Bank

KM#	Date	Mintage	Fine	VF	XF	Unc
137	1972	.050	—	—	—	15.00
	1972	—	—	—	Proof	25.00

Oil Nationalization

| 140 | 1973 | .060 | — | — | — | 15.00 |
| | 1973 | 5,000 | — | — | Proof | 25.00 |

31.0000 g, .900 SILVER, .8971 oz ASW
1st Anniversary of Tharthat-Euphrates Canal

| 143 | 1977 | 7,000 | — | — | Proof | 25.00 |

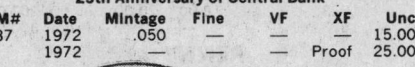

International Year of the Child

KM#	Date	Mintage	Fine	VF	XF	Unc
145	1979	5,000	—	—	Proof	45.00

30.5300 g, .900 SILVER, .8835 oz ASW
15th Century of Hegira

| 148 | 1980 | .025 | — | — | Proof | 40.00 |

NICKEL
Battle of Qadissyiat Saddam

| 149 | 1980 | — | — | — | — | 3.50 | 7.50 |
| | 1980 | — | — | — | — | Proof | 10.00 |

50th Anniversary of Iraq Air Force

| 153 | 1981 | — | — | — | — | 3.50 | 7.50 |

Baghdad Conference

| 156 | 1982 | — | — | — | — | 3.50 | 7.50 |

Tower of Babylon

KM#	Date	Mintage	Fine	VF	XF	Unc
164	1982	—	—	—	3.50	7.50

Circulation Coinage

| 170 | 1981 | — | — | — | — | 3.50 |

5 DINARS

13.5700gm., .917 GOLD, .4001oz AGW
50th Anniversary of Iraqi Army

| 134 | 1971 | .020 | — | — | — | 250.00 |
| | 1971 | — | — | — | Proof | 300.00 |

50 DINARS

13.7000 g, .917 GOLD, .4037 oz AGW
International Year of the Child

| 166 | 1979 | .010 | — | — | Proof | 300.00 |

13.0000 g, .917 GOLD, .3832 oz AGW
15th Century of Hegira

| 150 | 1980 | .013 | — | — | Proof | 250.00 |

16.9650 g, .917 GOLD, .5002 oz AGW
1st Anniversary of Hussein as President
Obv: Portrait 3/4 left above leg. Rev: Arabic leg.

| 169 | 1980 | .010 | — | — | Proof | 300.00 |

13.7000 g, .917 GOLD, .4040 oz AGW
Baghdad Conference

| 157 | 1982 | .010 | — | — | Proof | 250.00 |

100 DINARS

26.0000 g, .917 GOLD, .7665 oz AGW

IRELAND 1036

International Year of the Child

KM#	Date	Mintage	Fine	VF	XF	Unc
167	1979	.010	—	—	Proof	450.00

15th Century of Hegira

151	1980	.014	—	—	Proof	450.00

33.9310 g, .917 GOLD, 1.0000 AGW
Saddam Hussein

154	1981	.010	—	—	Proof	600.00

26.0000 g, .917 GOLD, .7665 oz AGW
Baghdad Conference

158	1982	.010	—	—	Proof	400.00

PROOF SETS (PS)

KM#	Date	Mintage	Identification	Issue Price	Mkt. Val.
PS1	1953(7)	200	KM109-115	—	980.00
PS2	1955(3)	—	KM116-118	—	460.00
PS3	1959(6)	400	KM119-124	—	360.00
PS4	1959(7)	—	KM119-124, plus medallic crown (M1)	—	400.00
PS5	1973(3)	5,000	KM138-140	—	40.00

IRELAND

Ireland, the island located in the Atlantic Ocean west of Great Britain, was settled by a race of tall, red-haired Celts from Gaul about 400 BC. They assimilated the native Erainn and Picts and established a Gaelic civilization. After the arrival of St. Patrick in 432 AD, Ireland evolved into a center of Latin learning which sent missionaries to Europe and possibly North America. In 1154, Pope Adrian IV gave all of Ireland to English King Henry II to administer as a Papal fief. Because of the enactment of pro-Catholic laws and the awarding of vast tracts of Irish land to Protestant absentee land-owners, English control did not become reasonably absolute until 1800 when England and Ireland became the "United Kingdom of Great Britain and Ireland". Religious freedom was restored to the Irish in 1829, but agitation for political autonomy continued until the Irish Free State was established as a Dominion on Dec. 6, 1921 while Northern Ireland remained under the British rule.

RULERS
British to 1921

MONETARY SYSTEM
4 Farthings = 1 Penny
12 Pence = 1 Shilling
5 Shillings = 1 Crown

NOTE: This section has been renumbered to accommodate the numerous earlier listings of the 17th and early 18th century for future publication.

FARTHING

COPPER

KM#	Date	Mintage	Fine	VF	XF	Unc
146 (18)	1806	—	4.00	8.00	45.00	140.00
	1806	—	—	—	Proof	165.00

COPPER GILT

| 146a (18a) | 1805 | — | — | — | Proof | 175.00 |

COPPER BRONZED

| 146b (18b) | 1805 | — | — | — | Proof | 125.00 |

SILVER (OMS)

| 146c (18c) | 1805 | — | — | — | Proof | 1200. |

GOLD (OMS)

| 146d (18d) | 1805 | — | — | — | Proof | Rare |

COPPER
Similar to 1/2 Penny, KM#150.

| 152 (23) | 1823 | — | — | — | Proof | 900.00 |

1/2 PENNY

COPPER

| 147 (19) | 1805 | — | 6.00 | 12.00 | 50.00 | 160.00 |
| | 1805 | — | — | — | Proof | 190.00 |

COPPER, Gilt

| 147a (19a) | 1805 | — | — | — | Proof | 200.00 |

COPPER BRONZED

| 147b (19b) | 1805 | — | — | — | Proof | 125.00 |

SILVER (OMS)

| 147c (19c) | 1805 | — | — | — | Proof | 1250. |

COPPER

KM#	Date	Mintage	Fine	VF	XF	Unc
150 (21)	1822	—	8.00	20.00	85.00	200.00
	1822	—	—	—	Proof	350.00
	1823	—	8.00	20.00	85.00	200.00
	1823	—	—	—	Proof	350.00

PENNY

COPPER

| 148 (20) | 1805 | — | 10.00 | 20.00 | 75.00 | 200.00 |
| | 1805 | — | — | — | Proof | 250.00 |

COPPER, Gilt

| 148a (20a) | 1805 | — | — | — | Proof | 300.00 |

COPPER BRONZED

| 148b (20b) | 1805 | — | — | — | Proof | 150.00 |

SILVER (OMS)

| 148c (20c) | 1805 | — | — | — | Proof | 1400. |

COPPER

151 (22)	1822	—	10.00	25.00	100.00	200.00
	1822	—	—	—	Proof	400.00
	1823	—	10.00	25.00	100.00	200.00
	1823	—	—	—	Proof	400.00

NOTE: For mule obv. KM#151 and rev. Ionian Islands 2 Oboli, KM#33 refer to Greece patterns.

COUNTERMARKED COINAGE
MERCHANT ISSUES
5 SHILLINGS 5 PENCE

.903 SILVER
c/m: PAYABLE AT CASTLE COMER COLLIERY, 5s. 5d.
on Spanish or Spanish Colonial 8 Reales.

KM#	Date	Mintage	Good	VG	Fine	VF
145 (26)	ND(1804)	—	300.00	600.00	900.00	1500.

NOTE: Forgeries of the countermark are frequently encountered.

TOKEN ISSUES (Tn)
Bank of Ireland
5 PENCE

SILVER

KM#	Date	Mintage	Fine	VF	XF	Unc
Tn2	1805	—	7.50	25.00	60.00	150.00
	1806	—	15.00	50.00	125.00	225.00
	1806/5	—	50.00	150.00	500.00	1000.

10 PENCE

SILVER

Tn3	1805	—	15.00	50.00	150.00	400.00
	1806	—	12.50	35.00	85.00	225.00

Tn5	1813	—	7.50	25.00	65.00	200.00
	1813	—	—	—	Proof	—

30 PENCE

SILVER

Tn4	1808	—	17.50	85.00	275.00	500.00

6 SHILLINGS

SILVER

Tn1	1804	—	125.00	250.00	650.00	1200.
	1804	—	—	—	Proof	1750.

NOTE: The silver proofs were struck on specially prepared planchets while circulation strikes were struck over Spanish and Spanish Colonial 8 Reales.

IRELAND/Irish Free State

Ireland, which occupies five-sixths of the island of Ireland located in the Atlantic Ocean west of Great Britain, has an area of 27,136 sq. mi. (70,283 sq. km.) and a population of *3.7 million. Capital: Dublin. Agriculture and dairy farming are the principal industries. Meat, livestock, dairy products and textiles are exported.

A race of tall, red-haired Celts from Gaul arrived in Ireland about 400 B.C., assimilated the native Erainn and Picts, and established a Gaelic civilization. After the arrival of St. Patrick in 432AD, Ireland evolved into a center of Latin learning which sent missionaries to Europe and possibly North America. In 1154, Pope Adrian IV gave all of Ireland to English King Henry II to administer as a Papal fief. Because of the enactment of anti-Catholic laws and the awarding of vast tracts of Irish land to Protestant absentee landowners, English control did not become reasonably absolute until 1800 when England and Ireland became the 'United Kingdom of Great Britain and Ireland'. Religious freedom was restored to the Irish in 1829, but agitation for political autonomy continued until the Irish Free State was established as a dominion on Dec. 6, 1921. Ireland proclaimed itself a republic on April 18, 1949. The government, however, does not use the term "Republic of Ireland", which tacitly acknowledges the partitioning of the island into Ireland and Northern Ireland, but refers to the country simply as "Ireland".

MONETARY SYSTEM

4 Farthings = 1 Penny
12 Pence = 1 Shilling
2 Shillings = 1 Florin
20 Shillings = 1 Pound

NOTE: This section has been renumbered to segregate the coinage of the Irish Free State from the earlier crown coinage of Ireland.

FARTHING

BRONZE

KM#	Date	Mintage	Fine	VF	XF	Unc
1	1928	.300	.25	1.00	3.00	9.00
(Y1)	1928	6,001	—	—	Proof	15.00
	1930	.288	.75	1.50	4.00	17.50
	1931	.192	3.00	6.00	10.00	30.00
	1931	—	—	—	Proof	—
	1932	.192	3.50	7.50	12.50	40.00
	1933	.480	.75	1.50	4.00	17.50
	1935	.192	3.00	6.00	10.00	35.00
	1936	.192	3.00	6.00	10.00	40.00
	1937	.480	.50	1.50	3.00	15.00

9	1939	.768	.50	1.00	1.50	7.00
(Y9)	1939	—	—	—	Proof	700.00
	1940	.192	2.00	4.00	7.50	20.00
	1941	.480	.50	.75	2.50	5.00
	1943	.480	.50	.75	2.00	5.00
	1944	.480	.75	1.25	3.00	10.00
	1946	.480	.50	.75	2.00	4.00
	1946	—	—	—	Proof	—
	1949	.192	.75	3.00	6.00	20.00
	1949	—	—	—	Proof	300.00
	1953	.192	.25	.50	1.25	3.00
	1953	—	—	—	Proof	300.00
	1959	.192	.25	.50	1.25	3.00
	1966	.096	.25	.75	1.50	5.00

1/2 PENNY

BRONZE

KM#	Date	Mintage	Fine	VF	XF	Unc
2	1928	2.880	.50	1.00	4.00	15.00
(Y2)	1928	6,001	—	—	Proof	12.50
	1933	.720	4.50	15.00	75.00	750.00
	1935	.960	1.00	6.00	50.00	250.00
	1937	.960	.75	2.50	10.00	30.00

10	1939	.240	7.50	15.00	50.00	200.00
(Y10)	1939	—	—	—	Proof	1000.
	1940	1.680	.25	4.50	45.00	200.00
	1941	2.400	.20	.50	2.50	25.00
	1942	6.931	.10	.25	1.50	7.50
	1943	2.669	.10	.25	3.00	25.00
	1946	.720	.25	.50	15.00	75.00
	1949	1.344	.10	.25	1.50	15.00
	1949	—	—	—	Proof	—
	1953	2.400	.10	.25	.50	1.50
	1953	—	—	—	Proof	400.00
	1964	2.160	.10	.15	.25	.75
	1965	1.440	.10	.15	.75	1.50
	1966	1.680	.10	.15	.25	.50
	1967	1.200	.10	.15	.25	.50

PENNY

BRONZE

3	1928	9.000	.50	1.00	4.00	20.00
(Y7)	1928	6,001	—	—	Proof	17.50
	1931	2.400	.75	1.50	15.00	80.00
	1931	—	—	—	Proof	1500.
	1933	1.680	1.00	2.50	25.00	150.00
	1935	5.472	.50	1.00	8.00	40.00
	1937	5.400	.50	1.00	15.00	75.00
	1937	—	—	—	Proof	1500.

11	1938	—	—	—	Unique	15,000.
(Y11)	1940	.312	2.50	8.00	75.00	—
	1941	4.680	.20	.50	8.00	50.00
	1942	17.520	.20	.50	1.50	10.00
	1943	3.360	.50	.75	5.00	40.00
	1946	4.800	.20	.50	3.00	20.00
	1948	4.800	.20	.50	3.00	10.00
	1949	4.080	.20	.50	3.00	10.00
	1949	—	—	—	Proof	600.00
	1950	2.400	.20	.50	4.50	15.00
	1950	—	—	—	Proof	600.00
	1952	2.400	.20	.50	1.00	10.00
	1962	1.200	.50	2.00	3.00	15.00
	1962	—	—	—	Proof	125.00
	1963	9.600	.10	.20	.50	1.25
	1963	—	—	—	Proof	125.00
	1964	6.000	.10	.20	.50	.75
	1964	—	—	—	Proof	—
	1965	11.160	.10	.20	.50	.75
	1966	6.000	.10	.20	.30	.50
	1967	2.400	.10	.20	.30	.50
	1968	21.000	.10	.20	.30	.50
	1968	—	—	—	Proof	350.00

NOTE: Varieties exist.

3 PENCE

NICKEL

4	1928	1.500	.50	1.00	3.50	10.00
(Y4)	1928	6,001	—	—	Proof	15.00

IRELAND / Irish Free State

1038

KM#	Date	Mintage	Fine	VF	XF	Unc
(Y4)	1933	.320	1.50	6.00	85.00	400.00
	1934	.800	.50	1.00	10.00	60.00
	1935	.240	2.00	4.00	35.00	200.00

12	1939	.064	6.00	15.00	100.00	500.00
(Y12)	1939	—	—	—	Proof	1500.
	1940	.720	.75	1.50	7.00	45.00

COPPER-NICKEL

12a	1942	4.000	.25	.75	6.00	35.00
(Y12a)	1942	—	—	—	Proof	500.00
	1943	1.360	.50	2.00	15.00	100.00
	1943	—	—	—	Proof	—
	1946	.800	.75	1.50	5.00	35.00
	1946	—	—	—	Proof	200.00
	1948	1.600	.75	1.50	35.00	110.00
	1949	1.200	.25	.50	3.00	30.00
	1949	—	—	—	Proof	200.00
	1950	1.600	.25	.50	3.00	15.00
	1950	—	—	—	Proof	500.00
	1953	1.600	.50	.50	2.00	10.00
	1956	1.200	.25	.50	2.00	7.50
	1961	2.400	.15	.25	.50	4.00
	1962	3.200	.15	.25	.50	6.00
	1963	4.000	.15	.25	.50	1.50
	1964	4.000	.10	.15	.25	.75
	1965	3.600	.10	.15	.25	.75
	1966	4.000	.10	.15	.25	.75
	1967	2.400	.10	.15	.25	.50
	1968	4.000	.10	.15	.25	.50
	1968	—	—	—	Proof	—

6 PENCE

NICKEL

5	1928	3.201	.25	.75	5.00	17.50
(Y5)	1928	6,001	—	—	Proof	20.00
	1934	.600	.50	1.50	15.00	125.00
	1935	.520	1.00	3.00	30.00	300.00

13	1939	.876	.50	1.25	8.00	50.00
(Y13)	1939	—	—	—	Proof	1000.
	1940	1.120	.50	1.25	6.00	45.00

COPPER-NICKEL

13a	1942	1.320	.20	.50	4.50	40.00
(Y13a)	1945	.400	1.00	4.50	50.00	150.00
	1946	.720	1.50	9.00	125.00	500.00
	1947	.800	.75	15.00	50.00	80.00
	1948	.800	.75	1.50	9.00	55.00
	1949	.600	1.00	2.00	8.00	60.00
	1950	.800	.75	5.00	65.00	145.00
	1952	.800	.50	1.00	5.00	27.50
	1952	—	—	—	Proof	175.00
	1953	.800	.50	2.00	5.00	27.50
	1955	.600	.75	2.00	6.00	27.50
	1956	.600	.50	1.50	3.50	15.00
	1958	.600	.50	1.50	5.00	70.00
	1958	—	—	—	Proof	350.00
	1959	2.000	.20	.50	3.00	17.50
	1960	2.020	.20	.50	1.50	12.50
	1961	3.000	.20	.25	1.00	7.50
	1962	4.000	.20	.75	2.50	60.00
	1963	4.000	.15	.25	.50	1.50
	1964	6.000	.10	.15	.25	2.00
	1966	2.000	.10	.15	.20	1.00
	1967	4.000	.10	.15	.20	1.00
	1968	8.000	.10	.15	.20	1.00
	1969	2.000	.10	.15	.25	2.00

SHILLING

5.6552 g, .750 SILVER, .1364 oz ASW

6	1928	2.700	1.50	5.00	10.00	25.00
(Y6)	1928	6,001	—	—	Proof	27.50
	1930	.460	3.00	20.00	125.00	500.00
	1930	—	—	—	Proof	1200.
	1931	.400	3.00	10.00	65.00	140.00

KM#	Date	Mintage	Fine	VF	XF	Unc
(Y6)	1933	.300	4.00	20.00	100.00	325.00
	1935	.400	2.00	7.00	30.00	90.00
	1937	.100	10.00	60.00	400.00	1500

14	1939	1.140	2.50	4.50	10.00	35.00
(Y14)	1939	—	—	—	Proof	750.00
	1940	.580	3.00	5.00	12.50	40.00
	1941	.300	4.00	10.00	20.00	50.00
	1942	.286	3.00	5.00	10.00	30.00

COPPER-NICKEL

14a	1951	2.000	.20	.40	2.50	15.00
(Y14a)	1951	—	—	—	Proof	500.00
	1954	3.000	.20	.40	2.00	10.00
	1954	—	—	—	Proof	—
	1955	1.000	.75	2.00	4.00	12.50
	1955	—	—	—	Proof	—
	1959	2.000	.25	.50	4.00	35.00
	1962	4.000	.20	.40	.75	7.00
	1963	4.000	.20	.40	.75	3.00
	1964	4.000	.15	.30	.50	1.50
	1966	3.000	.15	.30	.50	1.50
	1968	4.000	.15	.30	.50	2.00

FLORIN

11.3104 g, .750 SILVER, .2727 oz ASW

7	1928	2.025	2.50	7.00	15.00	40.00
(Y7)	1928	6,001	—	—	Proof	35.00
	1930	.330	5.00	20.00	150.00	475.00
	1931	.200	7.00	30.00	215.00	575.00
	1933	.300	4.00	20.00	175.00	525.00
	1934	.150	7.50	50.00	300.00	750.00
	1934	—	—	—	Proof	4000.
	1935	.390	4.00	17.50	95.00	200.00
	1937	.150	7.50	30.00	200.00	650.00

15	1939	1.080	2.00	5.00	20.00	40.00
(Y15)	1939	—	—	—	Proof	800.00
	1940	.670	3.00	6.00	15.00	40.00
	1941	.400	3.00	10.00	20.00	40.00
	1942	.109	5.00	10.00	20.00	40.00
	1943	*	1500	2750.	5000.	—

*Approximately 35 known.

COPPER-NICKEL

15a	1951	1.000	.25	.75	6.00	17.50
(Y15a)	1951	—	—	—	Proof	600.00
	1954	1.000	.25	.75	6.00	20.00
	1954	—	—	—	Proof	450.00
	1955	1.000	.25	.75	4.00	15.00
	1955	—	—	—	Proof	450.00
	1959	2.000	.25	.50	2.00	12.00
	1961	2.000	.25	.75	7.00	35.00
	1962	2.400	.25	.50	1.00	12.00
	1963	3.000	.25	.50	.75	7.00
	1964	4.000	.25	.50	.75	3.00
	1965	2.000	.25	.50	.75	3.00
	1966	3.625	.25	.50	.75	3.00
	1968	1.000	.25	.35	.75	3.00

1/2 CROWN

14.1380 g, .750 SILVER, .3409 oz ASW
Rev: Close O and I in COROIN, 8 tufts in horse's tail, w/156 beads in border.

KM#	Date	Mintage	Fine	VF	XF	Unc
8	1928	2.160	2.50	10.00	20.00	50.00
(Y8)	1928	6,001	—	—	Proof	45.00
	1930	.352	3.50	17.50	150.00	475.00
	1931	.160	7.50	25.00	225.00	650.00
	1933	.336	3.50	17.50	175.00	475.00
	1934	.480	3.00	12.00	35.00	140.00
	1937	.040	50.00	150.00	650.00	1500.

Rev: Normal spacing between O and I in COROIN, 7 tufts in horse's tail, w/151 beads in border.

16	1939	.888	2.50	7.00	17.50	55.00
(Y16)	1939	—	—	—	Proof	800.00
	1940	.752	2.50	7.00	15.00	45.00
	1941	.320	3.00	10.00	25.00	75.00
	1942	.286	3.50	10.00	17.50	45.00
	1943	*	100.00	350.00	1000.	2000.

*Approximately 500 known.

COPPER-NICKEL

16a	1951	.800	1.50	3.00	7.50	40.00
(Y16a)	1951	—	—	—	Proof	600.00
	1954	.400	2.00	4.00	10.00	45.00
	1954	—	—	—	Proof	500.00
	1955	1.080	1.00	2.00	5.00	25.00
	1955	—	—	—	Proof	200.00
	1959	1.600	1.00	1.75	3.00	15.00
	1961	1.600	1.00	1.75	3.50	25.00
	1961	—	—	—	Proof	—
	1962	3.200	.50	1.00	2.50	15.00
	1962	—	—	—	Proof	—
	1963	2.400	.50	1.00	1.50	7.50
	1964	3.200	.50	1.00	1.50	4.50
	1966	.700	.75	1.50	3.00	6.00
	1967	2.000	.50	1.00	1.50	3.00

NOTE: 1967 exists struck with a polished reverse die. Estimated value is $10.00 in uncirculated.

KM#8 long base 2   KM#16-16a short base 2
Mule. Obv: KM#8. Rev: KM#16a.

KM#	Date	Mintage	VG	Fine	VF	XF
17 (25)	1961	Inc. Ab.	—	5.00	15.00	225.00

10 SHILLINGS

18.1400 g, .833 SILVER, .4858 oz ASW

KM#	Date	Mintage	Fine	VF	XF	Unc
18	1966	*2.000	—	BV	5.00	7.50
(Y17)	1966	.020	—	—	Proof	15.00

NOTE: *Approximately 1.270 melted down.

DECIMAL COINAGE
5 New Pence = 1 Shilling
10 New Pence = 1 Florin
25 New Pence = 1 Crown
100 Pence = 1 Pound

1/2 PENNY

BRONZE

KM#	Date	Mintage	Fine	VF	XF	Unc
19	1971	100.500	—	—	.10	.20
(Y18)	1971	.050	—	—	Proof	1.00
	1975	10.500	—	—	.10	.15
	1976	5.464	—	—	.10	.15
	1978	33.026	—	—	—	.10
	1980	20.616	—	—	—	.10
	1982	—	—	—	—	.10
	1985	2.784	—	—	—	.10

PENNY

BRONZE

KM#	Date	Mintage	Fine	VF	XF	Unc
20	1971	100.500	—	—	.10	.20
(Y19)	1971	.050	—	—	Proof	1.25
	1974	10.000	—	—	.10	.15
	1975	10.000	—	—	.10	.15
	1976	38.164	—	—	.10	.15
	1978	25.746	—	—	.10	.15
	1979	27.642	—	—	.10	.15
	1980	86.712	—	—	.10	.15
	1982	—	—	—	.10	.15
	1985	19.242	—	—	.10	.15

2 PENCE

BRONZE

KM#	Date	Mintage	Fine	VF	XF	Unc
21	1971	75.500	—	—	.10	1.00
(Y20)	1971	.050	—	—	Proof	1.50
	1975	20.010	—	—	.10	.30
	1976	5.414	—	—	.10	.25
	1978	12.000	—	—	.10	.25
	1979	24.385	—	—	.10	.25
	1980	59.828	—	—	.10	.25
	1982	—	—	—	.10	.25
	1985	14.469	—	—	.10	.25

5 PENCE

COPPER-NICKEL

KM#	Date	Mintage	Fine	VF	XF	Unc
22	1969	5.000	—	.10	.15	1.00
(Y21)	1970	10.000	—	—	.10	.50
	1971	8.000	—	—	—	.45
	1971	.050	—	—	Proof	2.00
	1974	7.000	—	—	.10	.35
	1975	10.000	—	—	.10	.30
	1976	20.616	—	—	.10	.25
	1978	44.966	—	—	.10	.25
	1980	22.190	—	—	.10	.40
	1982	—	—	—	.10	.25
	1985	4.202	—	—	.10	.25

10 PENCE

COPPER-NICKEL

KM#	Date	Mintage	Fine	VF	XF	Unc
23	1969	27.000	—	—	.40	1.00
(Y22)	1971	4.000	—	—	.40	1.00
	1971	.050	—	—	Proof	2.50
	1973	2.500	—	—	.40	1.00
	1974	7.500	—	—	.35	.75
	1975	15.000	—	—	.35	.75
	1976	9.433	—	—	.35	.75
	1978	48.192	—	—	.25	.50
	1980	44.605	—	—	.25	.50
	1982	—	—	—	.25	.50
	1985	4.100	—	—	.25	.50

20 PENCE

NICKEL-BRONZE

KM#	Date				XF	Unc
25 (48)	1986				.50	1.00

50 PENCE

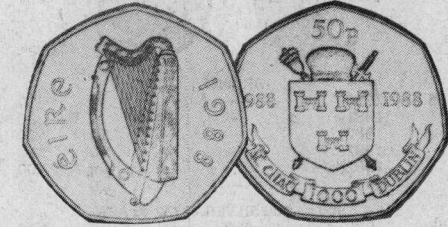

COPPER-NICKEL

KM#	Date	Mintage			XF	Unc
24	1970	9.000	—	—	1.50	5.00
(Y23)	1971	.600	—	—	1.75	6.00
	1971	.050	—	—	Proof	3.50
	1974	1.000	—	—	1.50	6.00
	1975	2.000	—	—	1.50	4.00
	1976	3.000	—	—	1.25	3.00
	1977	4.800	—	—	1.25	3.00
	1978	6.500	—	—	1.25	3.00
	1979	4.000	—	—	1.25	3.00
	1981	6.000	—	—	1.00	2.00
	1982	—	—	—	1.00	2.00
	1983	—	—	—	1.00	1.50

Dublin Millennium

KM#	Date	Mintage			XF	Unc
49	1988	—	—	—	—	3.00
	1988	.050	—	—	Proof	15.00

MINT SETS (MS)

KM#	Date	Mintage	Identification	Issue Price	Mkt. Val.
MS1	1971(6)		KM19-24	1.50	9.00
MS2	Various dates (6)				
		—	KM19-24	—	—
MS3	1982(6)		KM19-24		3.25

PROOF SETS (PS)

PS1	1928(8)	6.001	KM1-8	—	187.50
PS2	1971(6)	50,000	KM19-24	4.40	12.00

Listings For
IRIAN BARAT: refer to Indonesia

ISLE OF MAN

The Isle of Man, a dependency of the British Crown located in the Irish Sea equidistant from Ireland, Scotland and England, has an area of 227 sq. mi. (588 sq. km.) and a population of 68,089. Capital: Douglas. Agriculture, dairy farming, fishing and tourism are the chief industries.

The prevalence of prehistoric artifacts and monuments on the island give evidence that its mild, almost sub-tropical climate was enjoyed by mankind before the dawn of history. Vikings came to the Isle of Man during the 9th century and remained until ejected by Scotland in 1266. The island came under the protection of the British Crown in 1288, and in 1406 was granted, in perpetuity, to the earls of Derby, from whom it was inherited, 1736, by the Duke of Atholl. Rights and title were purchased from the Duke of Atholl in 1765 by the British Crown; the remaining privileges of the Atholl family were transferred to the crown in 1829. The Isle of Man is ruled by its own legislative council and the House of Keys, one of the oldest legislative assemblies in the world. Acts of Parliament passed in London do not affect the island unless it is specifically mentioned.

RULERS
(Commencing 1765)
British

MINT MARKS
PM - Pobjoy Mint

PRIVY MARKS

(b) - Baby Crib - 1982 dates only
(bb) - Big Ben
(f) - FUN logo
(l) - Statue of Liberty
(m) - Queen mother's portrait
(mt) - Mistletoe - Christmas
(p) - Carrier Pigeon - Basel
(pt) - Partridge in a pear tree
(s) - Bridge - SINPEX
(SL) - St. Louis arch
(ss) - Sailing Ship - Sydney
(t) - Stylized triskelion
(v) - Viking ship

PRIVY LETTERS
A - ANA
C - Coinex, London
F - FUN
H - Hong Kong Expo
L - Long Beach
T - Torex, Toronto
X - Ameripex

MONETARY SYSTEM
14 Pence (Manx) = 1 Shilling (Br.)
5 Shillings = 1 Crown
20 Shillings = 1 Pound

FARTHING

COPPER

KM#	Date	Mintage	Fine	VF	XF	Unc
12	1839	.213	3.00	9.00	35.00	70.00
	1839	—	—	—	Proof	200.00
	1841	2 known	—	—	Proof	Rare
	1860	6 known	—	—	Proof	2000.
	1864	3 known	—	—	Proof	Rare

COPPER-GILT (OMS)

| 12a | 1839 | — | — | — | Proof | Rare |
| | 1860 | — | — | — | Proof | Rare |

ISLE OF MAN 1040

1/2 PENNY

COPPER
Obv: Head right. Rev: Triskeles.

KM#	Date	Mintage	Fine	VF	XF	Unc
10	1813	—	10.00	35.00	80.00	175.00
	1813	—	—	—	Proof	300.00

COPPER-GILT (OMS)
| 10a | 1813 | — | — | — | Proof | Rare |

BRONZE (OMS)
| 10b | 1813 | — | — | — | Proof | 300.00 |

13	1839	.214	2.50	7.50	40.00	125.00
	1839	—	—	—	Proof	Rare
	1841	2 known	—	—	Proof	Rare
	1860	7 known	—	—	Proof	2000.

PENNY

COPPER
| 11 | 1813 | — | 7.50 | 35.00 | 100.00 | 225.00 |

BRONZE-GILT (OMS)
| 11a | 1813 | — | — | — | Proof | Rare |

COPPER
14	1839	.081	10.00	25.00	70.00	150.00
	1839	—	—	—	Proof	Rare
	1841	2 known	—	—	Proof	Rare
	1859	7 known	—	—	Proof	3000.

DECIMAL COINAGE
5 New Pence = 1 Shilling
25 New Pence = 1 Crown
100 New Pence = 1 Pound

1/2 NEW PENNY

BRONZE
KM#	Date	Mintage	VF	XF	Unc
19	1971	.495	—	.10	.25
	1971	.010	—	Proof	1.50
	1972	1,000	—	—	20.00
	1973	1,000	—	—	20.00
	1974	1,000	—	—	20.00
	1975	.825	—	.10	.15

2.1000 g, .925 SILVER, .0624 oz ASW
| 19a | 1975 | .020 | — | — | 2.50 |

4.0000 g, .950 PLATINUM, .1221 oz APW
| 19b | 1975 | 600 pcs. | — | Proof | 95.00 |

1/2 PENNY

BRONZE
32	1976	.600	—	.10	.15
	1978	—	—	.10	.15
	1978	—	—	Proof	1.00
	1979(t)	—	—	.10	.15

2.1000 g, .925 SILVER, .0624 oz ASW
32a	1976	.020	—	—	2.00
	1978	.010	—	—	2.00
	1979(t)	.010	—	Proof	2.50

4.0000 g, .950 PLATINUM, .1221 oz APW
32b	1976	600 pcs.	—	Proof	95.00
	1978	600 pcs.	—	Proof	95.00
	1979(t)	500 pcs.	—	Proof	95.00

BRONZE
F.A.O. Issue
| 40 | 1977 PM on rev. | .700 | — | .10 | .20 |
| | 1977 w/o PM on rev. Inc. Ab. | — | — | — | 5.00 |

2.1000 g, .925 SILVER, .0624 oz ASW
| 40a | 1977 | .010 | — | Proof | 2.50 |

BRONZE
58	1980	—	—	.10	.20
	1981	—	—	.10	.20
	1982	—	—	.10	.20
	1982(b)	—	—	.10	.20
	1982(b)	.025	—	Proof	1.00
	1983	—	—	.10	.20

2.1000 g, .500 SILVER, .0337 oz ASW
| 58a | 1980 | .010 | — | Proof | 4.00 |

2.1000 g, .925 SILVER, .0624 oz ASW
| 58b | 1982(b) | .010 | — | Proof | 4.00 |
| | 1983 | 5,000 | — | Proof | 5.00 |

3.5500 g, .917 GOLD, .1046 oz AGW
58c	1980	—	—	Proof	65.00
	1982(b)	500 pcs.	—	Proof	65.00
	1983	—	—	Proof	65.00

4.0000 g, .950 PLATINUM, .1221 oz APW
58d	1980	500 pcs.	—	Proof	95.00
	1982(b)	500 pcs.	—	Proof	95.00
	1983	—	—	Proof	95.00

BRONZE
| 72 | 1981 | — | — | — | .10 |

KM#	Date	Mintage	VF	XF	Unc
111	1984	—	—	—	.10

SILVER
| 111a | 1984 | — | — | Proof | 5.00 |

3.5500 g, .917 GOLD, .1046 oz AGW
| 111b | 1984 | 150 pcs. | — | Proof | 125.00 |

BRONZE
| 142 | 1985 | — | — | — | .10 |
| | 1985 | .050 | — | Proof | 2.00 |

2.1000 g, .925 SILVER, .0625 oz ASW
| 142a | 1985 | .010 | — | — | 3.00 |

3.5500 g, .917 GOLD, .1046 oz AGW
| 142b | 1985 | 300 pcs. | — | Proof | 85.00 |

4.0000 g, .950 PLATINUM, .1221 oz APW
| 142c | 1985 | 200 pcs. | — | Proof | 95.00 |

NEW PENNY

BRONZE
20	1971	.100	—	.10	.35
	1971	.010	—	Proof	2.00
	1972	1,000	—	—	20.00
	1973	1,000	—	—	20.00
	1974	1,000	—	—	20.00
	1975	.855	—	.10	.20

4.2000 g, .925 SILVER, .1249 oz ASW
| 20a | 1975 | .020 | — | — | 5.00 |

8.0000 g, .950 PLATINUM, .2443 oz APW
| 20b | 1975 | 600 pcs. | — | Proof | 200.00 |

PENNY

BRONZE
33	1976	.900	—	.10	.20
	1977	1.000	—	.10	.20
	1978	—	—	.10	.20
	1978	—	—	Proof	1.00
	1979(t)	—	—	.10	.20

4.2000 g, .925 SILVER, .1249 oz ASW
33a	1976	.020	—	—	4.00
	1977	.010	—	Proof	5.00
	1978	.010	—	—	4.00
	1979(t)	.010	—	Proof	5.00

8.0000 g, .950 PLATINUM, .2443 oz APW
33b	1976	600 pcs.	—	Proof	200.00
	1978	600 pcs.	—	Proof	200.00
	1979(t)	500 pcs.	—	Proof	200.00

BRONZE
59	1980	—	—	.10	.20
	1981	—	—	.10	.20
	1982	—	—	.10	.20
	1982(b)	—	—	.10	.20
	1982(b)	.025	—	Proof	1.25
	1983	—	—	.10	.20

4.2000 g, .500 SILVER, .0675 oz ASW
| 59a | 1980 | .010 | — | Proof | 5.00 |

4.2000 g, .925 SILVER, .0675 oz ASW
| 59b | 1982(b) | .010 | — | Proof | 5.00 |
| | 1983 | 5,000 | — | Proof | 5.00 |

7.1000 g, .917 GOLD, .2093 oz AGW
| 59c | 1980 | 300 pcs. | — | Proof | 135.00 |

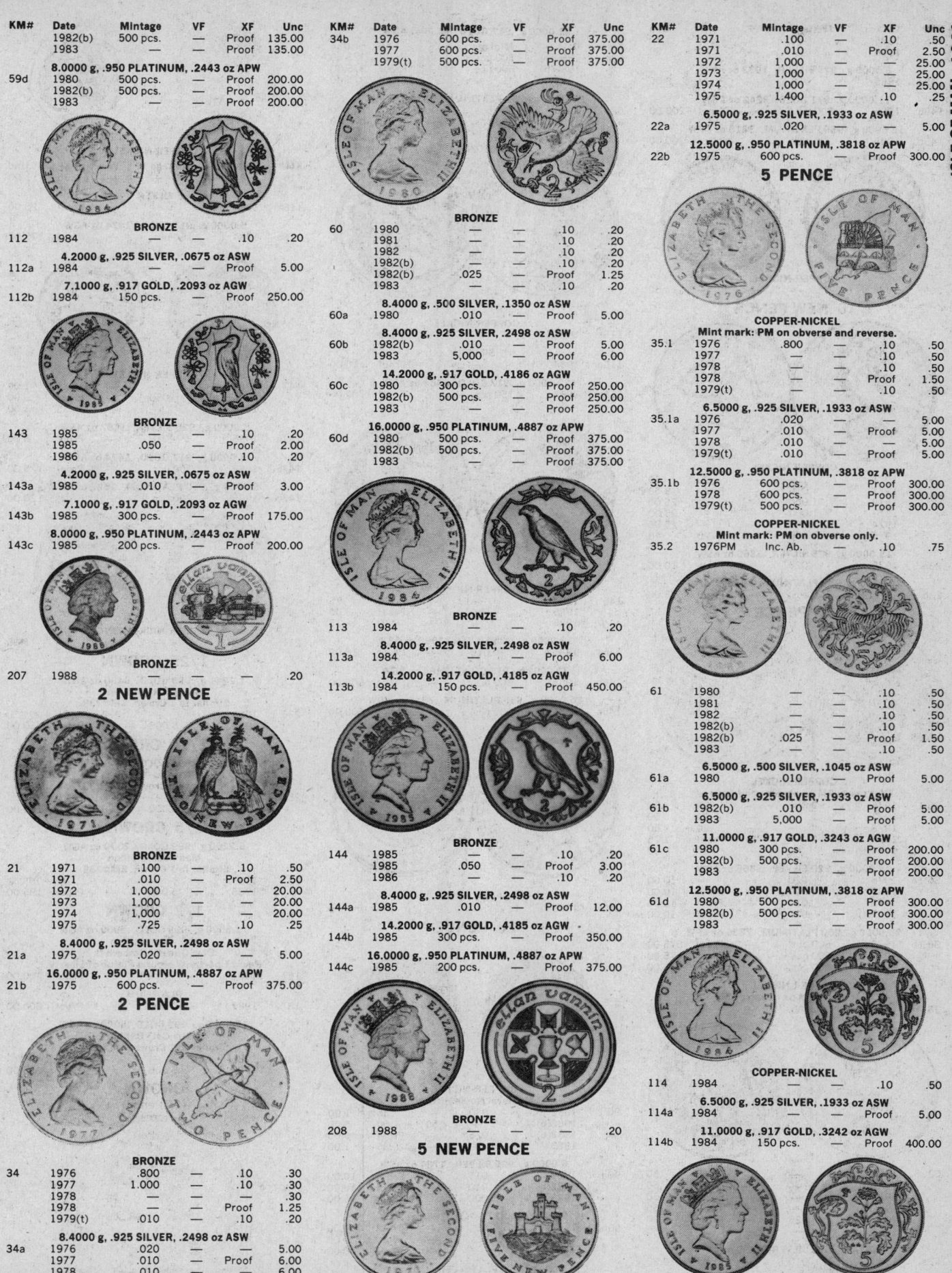

ISLE OF MAN

KM#	Date	Mintage	VF	XF	Unc
145	1985	.050	—	Proof	3.00
	1986	—	—	.10	.50

6.5000 g, .925 SILVER, .1933 oz ASW
| 145a | 1985 | .010 | — | Proof | 8.00 |

11.0000 g, .971 GOLD, .3242 oz AGW
| 145b | 1985 | 300 pcs. | — | Proof | 200.00 |

12.5000 g, .950 PLATINUM, .3818 oz APW
| 145c | 1985 | 200 pcs. | — | Proof | 300.00 |

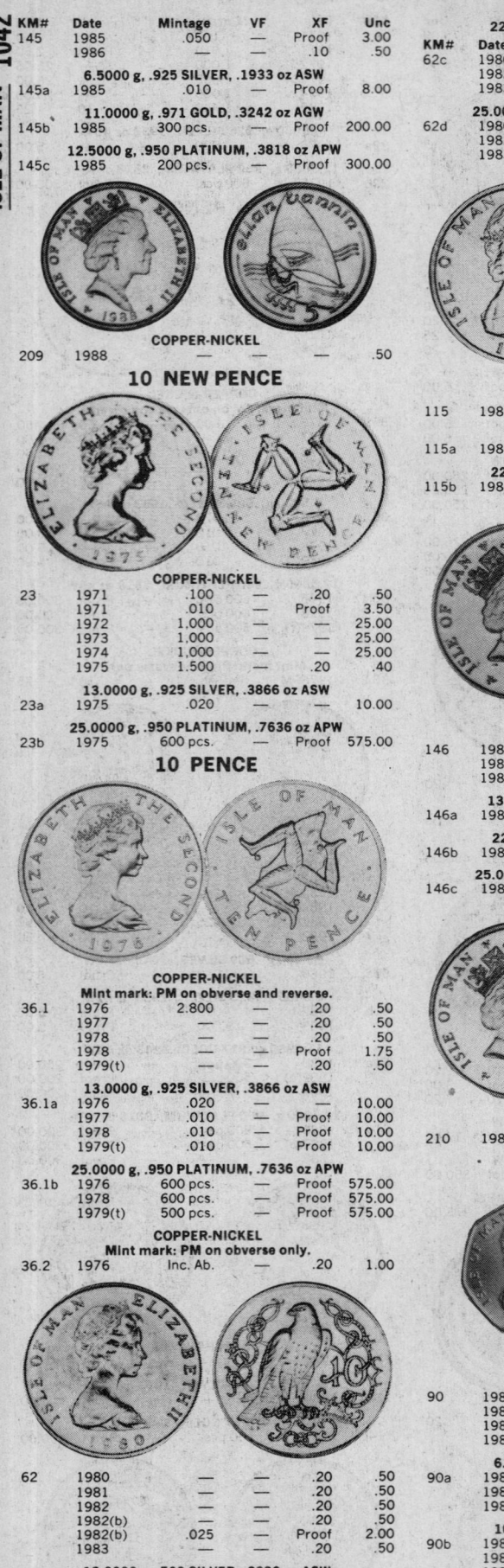

COPPER-NICKEL
| 209 | 1988 | — | — | — | .50 |

10 NEW PENCE

COPPER-NICKEL
23	1971	.100	—	.20	.50
	1971	.010	—	Proof	3.50
	1972	1,000	—	—	25.00
	1973	1,000	—	—	25.00
	1974	1,000	—	—	25.00
	1975	1,500	—	.20	.40

13.0000 g, .925 SILVER, .3866 oz ASW
| 23a | 1975 | .020 | — | — | 10.00 |

25.0000 g, .950 PLATINUM, .7636 oz APW
| 23b | 1975 | 600 pcs. | — | Proof | 575.00 |

10 PENCE

COPPER-NICKEL
Mint mark: PM on obverse and reverse.
36.1	1976	2.800	—	.20	.50
	1977	—	—	.20	.50
	1978	—	—	.20	.50
	1978	—	—	Proof	1.75
	1979(t)	—	—	.20	.50

13.0000 g, .925 SILVER, .3866 oz ASW
36.1a	1976	.020	—	—	10.00
	1977	.010	—	Proof	10.00
	1978	.010	—	Proof	10.00
	1979(t)	.010	—	Proof	10.00

25.0000 g, .950 PLATINUM, .7636 oz APW
36.1b	1976	600 pcs.	—	Proof	575.00
	1978	600 pcs.	—	Proof	575.00
	1979(t)	500 pcs.	—	Proof	575.00

COPPER-NICKEL
Mint mark: PM on obverse only.
| 36.2 | 1976 | Inc. Ab. | — | .20 | 1.00 |

COPPER-NICKEL
62	1980	—	—	.20	.50
	1981	—	—	.20	.50
	1982	—	—	.20	.50
	1982(b)	—	—	.20	.50
	1982(b)	.025	—	Proof	2.00
	1983	—	—	—	.50

13.0000 g, .500 SILVER, .2090 oz ASW
| 62a | 1980 | .010 | — | Proof | 10.00 |

13.0000 g, .925 SILVER, .3866 oz ASW
| 62b | 1982(b) | .010 | — | Proof | 10.00 |
| | 1983 | 5,000 | — | Proof | 12.50 |

22.0000 g, .917 GOLD, .6486 oz AGW
KM#	Date	Mintage	VF	XF	Unc
62c	1980	300 pcs.	—	Proof	375.00
	1982(b)	500 pcs.	—	Proof	375.00
	1983	—	—	Proof	375.00

25.0000 g, .950 PLATINUM, .7636 oz APW
62d	1980	500 pcs.	—	Proof	575.00
	1982(b)	500 pcs.	—	Proof	575.00
	1983	—	—	Proof	575.00

COPPER-NICKEL
| 115 | 1984 | — | — | .20 | .75 |

SILVER
| 115a | 1984 | — | — | Proof | 10.00 |

22.0000 g, .917 GOLD, .6484 oz AGW
| 115b | 1984 | 150 pcs. | — | Proof | 700.00 |

COPPER-NICKEL
146	1985	—	—	.20	.75
	1985	.050	—	Proof	3.00
	1986	—	—	.20	.75

13.0000 g, .925 SILVER, .3866 oz ASW
| 146a | 1985 | .010 | — | Proof | 18.00 |

22.0000 g, .917 GOLD, .6484 oz AGW
| 146b | 1985 | 300 pcs. | — | Proof | 500.00 |

25.0000 g, .950 PLATINUM, .7636 oz APW
| 146c | 1985 | 200 pcs. | — | Proof | 600.00 |

COPPER-NICKEL
| 210 | 1988 | — | — | — | .75 |

20 PENCE

COPPER-NICKEL
Medieval Norse History
90	1982	.030	—	.35	1.00
	1982(b)	—	.50	1.00	5.00
	1982(b)	.025	—	Proof	6.00
	1983	—	—	.35	1.00

6.0000 g, .925 SILVER, .1784 oz ASW
90a	1982	.015	—	Proof	10.00
	1982(b)	.010	—	Proof	10.00
	1983	5,000	—	Proof	15.00

10.0000 g, .917 GOLD, .2948 oz AGW
90b	1982	1,500	—	Proof	200.00
	1982(b)	500 pcs.	—	Proof	200.00
	1983	—	—	Proof	200.00

11.3000 g, .950 PLATINUM, .3452 oz APW
90c	1982	250 pcs.	—	Proof	275.00
	1982(b)	500 pcs.	—	Proof	275.00
	1983	—	—	Proof	275.00

COPPER-NICKEL
KM#	Date	Mintage	VF	XF	Unc
116	1984	—	—	.35	1.00

SILVER
| 116a | 1984 | — | — | Proof | 20.00 |

5.0000 g, .917 GOLD, .1474 oz AGW
| 116b | 1984 | 150 pcs. | — | Proof | 175.00 |

COPPER-NICKEL
147	1985	—	—	.35	1.00
	1985	.050	—	Proof	3.00
	1986	—	—	.35	1.00

5.0000 g, .925 SILVER, .1487 oz ASW
| 147a | 1985 | .010 | — | Proof | 8.00 |

5.0000 g, .917 GOLD, .1474 oz AGW
| 147b | 1985 | 300 pcs. | — | Proof | 125.00 |

5.0000 g, .950 PLATINUM, .1527 oz APW
| 147c | 1985 | 200 pcs. | — | Proof | 120.00 |

COPPER-NICKEL-ZINC
| 211 | 1988 | — | — | — | 1.00 |

1/25 CROWN

1.2441 g, .999 GOLD, .0400 oz AGW
Manx Cat - Bullion
Similar to 1 Crown, KM#239.
| 235 | 1988 | — | — | — | BV + 20% % |
| | 1988 | 5,000 | — | Proof | 50.00 |

1/10 CROWN

3.1100 g, .999 GOLD, .1000 oz AGW
Manx Cat - Bullion
Similar to 1 Crown, KM#239.
| 236 | 1988 | — | — | — | BV + 15% % |
| | 1988 | 5,000 | — | Proof | 100.00 |

1/5 CROWN

6.2200 g, .999 GOLD, .2000 oz AGW
Manx Cat - Bullion
Similar to 1 Crown, KM#239.
| 237 | 1988 | — | — | — | BV + 10% % |
| | 1988 | 5,000 | — | Proof | 185.00 |

1/2 CROWN

15.5500 g, .999 GOLD, .5000 oz AGW
U.S. Constitution
Obv: Queen Elizabeth II.
Rev: 11 portraits around Statue of Liberty.
| 187 | 1987 | .012 | — | — | 400.00 |

PLATINUM
| 187a | 1987 | 250 pcs. | — | Proof | 600.00 |

15.5500 g, .999 GOLD, .5000 oz AGW
Manx Cat - Bullion
Similar to 1 Crown, KM#239.
| 238 | 1988 | — | — | — | BV + 7% |
| | 1988 | 5,000 | — | Proof | 365.00 |

CROWN
(25 Pence)

ISLE OF MAN 1043

COPPER-NICKEL

KM#	Date	Mintage	VF	XF	Unc
18	1970	.150	—	—	5.00

28.2800 g, .925 SILVER, .8411 oz ASW

| 18a | 1970 | .011 | — | Proof | 20.00 |

COPPER-NICKEL
25th Wedding Anniversary

| 25 | 1972 | .078 | — | — | 25.00 |

28.2800 g, .925 SILVER, .8411 oz ASW

| 25a | 1972 | .015 | — | Proof | 15.00 |

COPPER-NICKEL
Winston Churchill Centenary

| 30 | 1974 | .045 | — | — | 2.00 |

28.2800 g, .925 SILVER, .8411 oz ASW

| 30a | 1974 | — | — | — | 12.50 |
| | 1974 | .030 | — | Proof | 15.00 |

COPPER-NICKEL

| 31 | 1975 | .035 | — | — | 2.50 |

28.2800 g, .925 SILVER, .8411 oz ASW

| 31a | 1975 | — | — | — | 12.50 |
| | 1975 | .030 | — | Proof | 17.50 |

COPPER-NICKEL
Bicentenary of American Independence
Obv: Similar to KM#25.

KM#	Date	Mintage	VF	XF	Unc
37	1976	.050	—	—	2.00

28.2800 g, .925 SILVER, .8411 oz ASW

| 37a | 1976 | — | — | — | 12.50 |
| | 1976 | .030 | — | Proof | 15.00 |

COPPER-NICKEL
Centenary of Horse Drawn Tram
Obv: Similar to KM#25.

| 38 | 1976 | .050 | — | — | 2.00 |

28.2800 g, .925 SILVER, .8411 oz ASW

| 38a | 1976 | — | — | — | 12.50 |
| | 1976 | .030 | — | Proof | 15.00 |

COPPER-NICKEL
Silver Jubilee
Obv: Similar to KM#31.

| 41 | 1977 | — | — | — | 3.00 |

28.2800 g, .925 SILVER, .8411 oz ASW

| 41a | 1977 | — | — | — | 12.50 |
| | 1977 | .030 | — | Proof | 15.00 |

COPPER-NICKEL
Queen's Jubilee Appeal
Obv: Similar to KM#25.

| 42 | 1977 | — | — | — | 2.00 |

28.2800 g, .925 SILVER, .8411 oz ASW

| 42a | 1977 | .070 | — | — | 12.50 |
| | 1977 | .030 | — | Proof | 15.00 |

COPPER-NICKEL
25th Anniversary of Coronation
Obv: Similar to KM#31.

KM#	Date	Mintage	VF	XF	Unc
43	1978	—	—	—	2.00
	1978	—	—	Proof	7.50

28.2800 g, .925 SILVER, .8411 oz ASW

| 43a | 1978 | .070 | — | — | 12.50 |
| | 1978 | .030 | — | Proof | 15.00 |

NOTE: For mule of Isle of Man KM#43 obv. with Ascension Island KM#1 rev., refer to Ascension Island listings.

COPPER-NICKEL
300th Anniversary of Manx Coinage
Obv: Similar to KM#25.

| 45 | 1979 | — | — | — | 2.50 |
| | 1979 | — | — | Proof | 7.50 |

28.2800 g, .925 SILVER, .8411 oz ASW

| 45a | 1979 | *.070 | — | — | 12.50 |
| | 1979 | *.030 | — | Proof | 15.00 |

COPPER-NICKEL
Millenium of Tynwald
Obv: Similar to KM#25. Rev: Viking longship.

| 46 | 1979 | *.100 | — | — | 2.50 |

28.2800 g, .925 SILVER, .8411 oz ASW

| 46a | 1979 | *.025 | — | — | 15.00 |
| | 1979 | *.010 | — | Proof | 17.50 |

43.0000 g, .917 GOLD, 1.2678 oz AGW

| 46b | 1979 | *300 pcs. | — | Proof | 700.00 |

52.0000 g, .950 PLATINUM, 1.5884 oz APW

| 46c | 1979 | *100 pcs. | — | Proof | 1200. |

COPPER-NICKEL
Millenium of Tynwald
Obv: Similar to KM#25. Rev: English cog.

| 47 | 1979 | *.100 | — | — | 2.50 |

28.2800 g, .925 SILVER, .8411 oz ASW

| 47a | 1979 | *.025 | — | — | 15.00 |
| | 1979 | *.010 | — | Proof | 17.50 |

43.0000 g, .917 GOLD, 1.2678 oz AGW

| 47b | 1979 | *300 pcs. | — | Proof | 700.00 |

ISLE OF MAN

52.0000 g, .950 PLATINUM, 1.5884 oz APW

KM#	Date	Mintage	VF	XF	Unc
47c	1979	*100 pcs.	—	Proof	1200.

COPPER-NICKEL
Millenium of Tynewald
Obv: Similar to KM#25. Rev: Flemish Carrack.

48	1979	*.100	—	—	2.50

28.2800 g, .925 SILVER, .8411 oz ASW

48a	1979	*.025	—	—	15.00
	1979	*.010	—	Proof	17.50

43.0000 g, .917 GOLD, 1.2678 oz AGW

48b	1979	*300 pcs.	—	Proof	700.00

52.0000 g, .950 PLATINUM, 1.5884 oz APW

48c	1979	*100 pcs.	—	Proof	1200.

COPPER-NICKEL
Millenium of Tynewald
Obv: Similar to KM#25.
Rev: Royalist Soldier and English Man-of-War.

49	1979	*.100	—	—	2.50

28.2800 g, .925 SILVER, .8411 oz ASW

49a	1979	*.025	—	—	15.00
	1979	*.010	—	Proof	17.50

43.0000 g, .917 GOLD, 1.2678 oz AGW

49b	1979	*300 pcs.	—	Proof	700.00

52.0000 g, .950 PLATINUM, 1.5884 oz APW

49c	1979	*100 pcs.	—	Proof	1200.

COPPER-NICKEL
Millenium of Tynewald
Obv: Similar to KM#25.
Rev: Lifeboat and Sir Hillary portrait.

50	1979	*.100	—	—	2.50

28.2800 g, .925 SILVER, .8411 oz ASW

50a	1979	*.025	—	—	15.00
	1979	*.010	—	Proof	17.50

43.0000 g, .917 GOLD, 1.2678 oz AGW

50b	1979	*300 pcs.	—	Proof	700.00

52.0000 g, .950 PLATINUM, 1.5884 oz APW

50c	1979	*100 pcs.	—	Proof	1200.

COPPER-NICKEL
Derby Bicentennial
Obv: Similar to KM#25.

KM#	Date	Mintage	VF	XF	Unc
63	1980	*.100	—	—	3.00

28.2800 g, .925 SILVER, .8411 oz ASW

63a	1980	*.035	—	—	15.00
	1980	*.020	—	Proof	20.00

52.0000 g, .950 PLATINUM, 1.5884 oz APW

63b	1980	*500 pcs.	—	Proof	1000.

COPPER-NICKEL
1980 Winter Olympics - Lake Placid
Obv: Similar to KM#25.

64	1980	*.100	—	—	2.50

28.2800 g, .925 SILVER, .8411 oz ASW

64a	1980	*.050	—	—	12.50
	1980	*.030	—	Proof	20.00

39.8000 g, .917 GOLD, 1.1735 oz AGW

64b	1980	*1,500	—	—	650.00
	1980	*500 pcs.	—	—	675.00

52.0000 g, .950 PLATINUM, 1.5884 oz APW

64c	1980	*100 pcs.	—	Proof	1200.

COPPER-NICKEL
22nd Olympiad Moscow
Obv: Similar to KM#25. Rev: Runner at top.

65	1980	*.030	—	—	3.00

28.2800 g, .925 SILVER, .8411 oz ASW

65a	1980	—	—	—	12.50
	1980	*.010	—	Proof	20.00

39.8000 g, .917 GOLD, 1.1735 oz AGW

65b	1980	*1,500	—	—	650.00

52.0000 g, .950 PLATINUM, 1.5884 oz APW

65c	1980	*100 pcs.	—	Proof	1200.

COPPER-NICKEL
22nd Olympiad Moscow
Obv: Similar to KM#25. Rev: Javelin thrower at top.

66	1980	*.030	—	—	3.00

28.2800 g, .925 SILVER, .8411 oz ASW

KM#	Date	Mintage	VF	XF	Unc
66a	1980	—	—	—	12.50
	1980	*.010	—	Proof	20.00

39.8000 g, .917 GOLD, 1.1735 oz AGW

66b	1980	*1,500	—	—	650.00

52.0000 g, .950 PLATINUM, 1.5884 oz APW

66c	1980	*100 pcs.	—	Proof	1200.

COPPER-NICKEL
22nd Olympiad Moscow
Obv: Similar to KM#25. Rev: Judo match at top.

67	1980	*.030	—	—	3.00

28.2800 g, .925 SILVER, .8411 oz ASW

67a	1980	—	—	—	12.50
	1980	*.010	—	Proof	20.00

39.8000 g, .917 GOLD, 1.1735 oz AGW

67b	1980	*1,500	—	—	650.00

52.0000 g, .950 PLATINUM, 1.5884 oz APW

67c	1980	*100 pcs.	—	Proof	1200.

COPPER-NICKEL, 37mm
80th Birthday of Queen Mother

68		*.100	—	—	2.00

28.2800 g, .500 SILVER, .4546 oz ASW

68a	1980	*.050	—	—	15.00

28.2800 g, .925 SILVER, .8411 oz ASW

68b	1980	*.030	—	—	25.00

5.0000 g, .374 GOLD, .0601 oz AGW

68c	1980	*.050	—	—	75.00

7.9600 g, .917 GOLD, .2347 oz AGW

68d	1980	*1,000	—	—	150.00

COPPER-NICKEL, 37mm
Duke of Edinburgh Award Scheme

73	1981	*.050	—	—	2.50

28.2800 g, .925 SILVER, .8411 oz ASW

73a	1981	*.020	—	—	15.00
	1981	*.015	—	Proof	20.00

52.0000 g, .950 PLATINUM, 1.5884 oz APW

73b	1981	*100 pcs.	—	Proof	1100.

5.1000 g, .374 GOLD, .0613 oz AGW

73c	1981	*.010	—	Proof	75.00

7.9600 g, .917 GOLD, .2347 oz AGW

73d	1981	*1,000	—	Proof	150.00

COPPER-NICKEL, 37mm
Duke of Edinburgh Award Scheme

74	1981	*.050	—	—	2.50

28.2800 g, .925 SILVER, .8411 oz ASW

ISLE OF MAN 1045

KM#	Date	Mintage	VF	XF	Unc
74a	1981	*.020	—	—	15.00
	1981	*.015	—	Proof	20.00

52.0000 g, .950 PLATINUM, 1.5884 oz APW
| 74b | 1981 | *100 pcs. | — | Proof | 1150. |

5.1000 g, .374 GOLD, .0613 oz AGW
| 74c | 1981 | *.010 | — | Proof | 75.00 |

7.9600 g, .917 GOLD, .2347 oz AGW
| 74d | 1981 | *1,000 | — | Proof | 150.00 |

COPPER-NICKEL, 37mm
Duke of Edinburgh Award Scheme
| 75 | 1981 | *.050 | — | — | 2.50 |

28.2800 g, .925 SILVER, .8411 oz ASW
| 75a | 1981 | *.020 | — | — | 15.00 |
| | 1981 | *.015 | — | Proof | 20.00 |

52.0000 g, .950 PLATINUM, 1.5884 oz APW
| 75b | 1981 | *100 pcs. | — | Proof | 1100. |

5.1000 g, .374 GOLD, .0613 oz AGW
| 75c | 1981 | *.010 | — | Proof | 75.00 |

7.9600 g, .917 GOLD, .2347 oz AGW
| 75d | 1981 | *1,000 | — | Proof | 150.00 |

COPPER-NICKEL, 37mm
Duke of Edinburgh Award Scheme
| 76 | 1981 | *.050 | — | — | 2.50 |

28.2800 g, .925 SILVER, .8411 oz ASW
| 76a | 1981 | *.020 | — | — | 15.00 |
| | 1981 | *.015 | — | Proof | 20.00 |

52.0000 g, .950 PLATINUM, 1.5884 oz APW
| 76b | 1981 | *100 pcs. | — | Proof | 1150. |

5.1000 g, .374 GOLD, .0613 oz AGW
| 76c | 1981 | *.010 | — | Proof | 75.00 |

7.9600 g, .917 GOLD, .2347 oz AGW
| 76d | 1981 | *1,000 | — | Proof | 150.00 |

COPPER-NICKEL, 37mm
I.Y.D. - Louis Braille
| 77 | 1981 | *.050 | — | — | 2.50 |

28.2800 g, .925 SILVER, .8411 oz ASW
| 77a | 1981 | *.020 | — | — | 15.00 |
| | 1981 | *.015 | — | Proof | 20.00 |

52.0000 g, .950 PLATINUM, 1.5884 oz APW
| 77b | 1981 | *100 pcs. | — | Proof | 1150. |

5.1000 g, .374 GOLD, .0613 oz AGW
| 77c | 1981 | *.010 | — | Proof | 75.00 |

7.9600 g, .917 GOLD, .2347 oz AGW
KM#	Date	Mintage	VF	XF	Unc
77d	1981	*1,000	—	Proof	150.00

COPPER-NICKEL, 37mm
I.Y.D. - Beethoven
| 78 | 1981 | *.050 | — | — | 2.50 |
| | 1981 | — | — | Proof | — |

28.2800 g, .925 SILVER, .8411 oz ASW
| 78a | 1981 | *.020 | — | — | 15.00 |
| | 1981 | *.015 | — | Proof | 20.00 |

52.0000 g, .950 PLATINUM, 1.5884 oz APW
| 78b | 1981 | *100 pcs. | — | Proof | 1150. |

5.1000 g, .374 GOLD, .0613 oz AGW
| 78c | 1981 | *.010 | — | Proof | 75.00 |

7.9600 g, .917 GOLD, .2347 oz AGW
| 78d | 1981 | *1,000 | — | Proof | 150.00 |

COPPER-NICKEL, 37mm
I.Y.D. - Sir Douglas Bader
| 79 | 1981 | *.050 | — | — | 2.50 |

28.2800 g, .925 SILVER, .8411 oz ASW
| 79a | 1981 | *.020 | — | — | 15.00 |
| | 1981 | *.015 | — | Proof | 20.00 |

52.0000 g, .950 PLATINUM, 1.5884 oz APW
| 79b | 1981 | *100 pcs. | — | Proof | 1150. |

5.1000 g, .374 GOLD, .0613 oz AGW
| 79c | 1981 | *.010 | — | Proof | 75.00 |

7.9600 g, .917 GOLD, .2347 oz AGW
| 79d | 1981 | *1,000 | — | Proof | 150.00 |

COPPER-NICKEL, 37mm
I.Y.D. - Sir Francis Chichester
| 80 | 1981 | *.050 | — | — | 2.50 |
| | 1981 | — | — | Proof | — |

28.2800 g, .925 SILVER, .8411 oz ASW
| 80a | 1981 | *.020 | — | — | 15.00 |
| | 1981 | *.015 | — | Proof | 20.00 |

52.0000 g, .950 PLATINUM, 1.5884 oz APW
| 80b | 1981 | *100 pcs. | — | Proof | 1150. |

5.1000 g, .374 GOLD, .0613 oz AGW
| 80c | 1981 | *.010 | — | Proof | 75.00 |

7.9600 g, .917 GOLD, .2347 oz AGW
| 80d | 1981 | *1,000 | — | Proof | 150.00 |

COPPER-NICKEL, 37mm
Wedding of Prince Charles and Lady Diana
| 81 | 1981 | *.050 | — | — | 2.50 |

28.2800 g, .925 SILVER, .8411 oz ASW
| 81a | 1981 | *.020 | — | — | 20.00 |
| | 1981 | *.015 | — | Proof | 25.00 |

52.0000 g, .950 PLATINUM, 1.5884 oz APW
| 81b | 1981 | *100 pcs. | — | Proof | 1150. |

5.1000 g, .374 GOLD, .0613 oz AGW
| 81c | 1981 | *.010 | — | Proof | 75.00 |

7.9600 g, .917 GOLD, .2347 oz AGW
| 81d | 1981 | *1,000 | — | Proof | 150.00 |

COPPER-NICKEL, 37mm
Wedding of Prince Charles and Lady Diana
KM#	Date	Mintage	VF	XF	Unc
82	1981	*.050	—	—	2.50

28.2800 g, .925 SILVER, .8411 oz ASW
| 82a | 1981 | *.020 | — | — | 15.00 |
| | 1981 | *.015 | — | Proof | 20.00 |

52.0000 g, .950 PLATINUM, 1.5884 oz APW
| 82b | 1981 | — | — | Proof | 1250. |

5.1000 g, .374 GOLD, .0613 oz AGW
| 82c | 1981 | *.010 | — | Proof | 75.00 |

7.9600 g, .917 GOLD, .2347 oz AGW
| 82d | 1981 | *1,000 | — | Proof | 150.00 |

COPPER-NICKEL, 37mm
Soccer-XII World Cup-Spain
| 91 | 1982 | *.050 | — | — | 2.50 |

28.2800 g, .925 SILVER, .8411 oz ASW
| 91a | 1982 | *.020 | — | — | 20.00 |
| | 1982 | *.015 | — | Proof | 25.00 |

52.0000 g, .950 PLATINUM, 1.5884 oz APW
| 91b | 1982 | *100 pcs. | — | Proof | 1100. |

5.1000 g, .374 GOLD, .0613 oz AGW
| 91c | 1982 | *.040 | — | Proof | 75.00 |

7.9600 g, .917 GOLD, .2347 oz AGW
| 91d | 1982 | *4,000 | — | Proof | 150.00 |

COPPER-NICKEL, 37mm
Country Shields-XII World Cup-Spain
| 92 | 1982 | *.050 | — | — | 2.50 |

28.2800 g, .925 SILVER, .8411 oz ASW
| 92a | 1982 | *.020 | — | — | 20.00 |
| | 1982 | *.015 | — | Proof | 25.00 |

52.0000 g, .950 PLATINUM, 1.5884 oz APW
| 92b | 1982 | *100 pcs. | — | Proof | 1350. |

5.1000 g, .374 GOLD, .0613 oz AGW
| 92c | 1982 | *.040 | — | Proof | 75.00 |

7.9600 g, .917 GOLD, .2347 oz AGW
| 92d | 1982 | *4,000 | — | Proof | 150.00 |

COPPER-NICKEL, 37mm
XII World Cup-Spain
| 93 | 1982 | *.050 | — | — | 2.50 |

28.2800 g, .925 SILVER, .8411 oz ASW
| 93a | 1982 | *.020 | — | — | 20.00 |
| | 1982 | *.015 | — | Proof | 25.00 |

52.0000 g, .950 PLATINUM, 1.5884 oz APW
| 93b | 1982 | *100 pcs. | — | Proof | 1100. |

ISLE OF MAN 1046

5.1000 g, .374 GOLD, .0613 oz AGW

KM#	Date	Mintage	VF	XF	Unc
93c	1982	*.040	—	Proof	75.00

7.9600 g, .917 GOLD, .2347 oz AGW
| 93d | 1982 | *4,000 | — | Proof | 150.00 |

COPPER-NICKEL, 37mm
XII World Cup-Spain
| 94 | 1982 | *.050 | — | — | 2.50 |

28.2800 g, .925 SILVER, .8411 oz ASW
| 94a | 1982 | *.020 | — | — | 20.00 |
| | 1982 | *.015 | — | Proof | 25.00 |

52.0000 g, .950 PLATINUM, 1.5884 oz APW
| 94b | 1982 | *100 pcs. | — | Proof | 1100. |

5.1000 g, .374 GOLD, .0613 oz AGW
| 94c | 1982 | *.040 | — | Proof | 75.00 |

7.9600 g, .917 GOLD, .2347 oz AGW
| 94d | 1982 | *4,000 | — | Proof | 150.00 |

COPPER-NICKEL, 37mm
XII World Cup - Spain
Rev: Similar to KM#92 but 1982 above Italian shield.
| 95 | 1982 | — | — | — | 2.50 |

28.2800 g, .925 SILVER, .8411 oz ASW
| 95a | 1982 | — | — | Proof | 25.00 |

52.0000 g, .950 PLATINUM, 1.5884 oz APW
| 95b | 1982 | — | Reported, not confirmed | | |

5.1000 g, .374 GOLD, .0613 oz AGW
| 95c | 1982 | *3,000 | — | Proof | |

7.9600 g, .917 GOLD, .2347 oz AGW
| 95d | 1982 | — | Reported, not confirmed | | |

COPPER-NICKEL, 37mm
Maritime Heritage - Mayflower
| 96 | 1982 | *.050 | — | — | 2.50 |

28.2800 g, .925 SILVER, .8411 oz ASW
| 96a | 1982 | *.015 | — | — | 20.00 |
| | 1982 | *.010 | — | Proof | 25.00 |

52.0000 g, .950 PLATINUM, 1.5884 oz APW
| 96b | 1982 | *50 pcs. | — | Proof | 1250. |

5.1000 g, .374 GOLD, .0613 oz AGW
KM#	Date	Mintage	VF	XF	Unc
96c	1982	*.022	—	Proof	75.00

7.9600 g, .917 GOLD, .2347 oz AGW
| 96d | 1982 | *2,000 | — | Proof | 150.00 |

COPPER-NICKEL, 37mm
Maritime Heritage - H.M.S. Bounty
| 97 | 1982 | *.050 | — | — | 2.50 |

28.2800 g, .925 SILVER, .8411 oz ASW
| 97a | 1982 | *.015 | — | — | 20.00 |
| | 1982 | *.010 | — | Proof | 25.00 |

52.0000 g, .950 PLATINUM, 1.5884 oz APW
| 97b | 1982 | *50 pcs. | — | Proof | 1100. |

5.1000 g, .374 GOLD, .0613 oz AGW
| 97c | 1982 | *.022 | — | Proof | 75.00 |

7.9600 g, .917 GOLD, .2347 oz AGW
| 97d | 1982 | *2,000 | — | Proof | 150.00 |

COPPER-NICKEL, 37mm
Maritime Heritage - H.M.S. Victory
| 98 | 1982 | *.050 | — | — | 2.50 |

28.2800 g, .925 SILVER, .8411 oz ASW
| 98a | 1982 | *.015 | — | — | 20.00 |
| | 1982 | *.010 | — | Proof | 25.00 |

52.0000 g, .950 PLATINUM, 1.5884 oz APW
| 98b | 1982 | *50 pcs. | — | Proof | 1200. |

5.1000 g, .374 GOLD, .0613 oz AGW
| 98c | 1982 | *.022 | — | Proof | 75.00 |

7.9600 g, .917 GOLD, .2347 oz AGW
| 98d | 1982 | *2,000 | — | Proof | 150.00 |

COPPER-NICKEL, 37mm
Maritime Heritage - P.S. Mona's Queen II
| 99 | 1982 | *.050 | — | — | 2.50 |

28.2800 g, .925 SILVER, .8411 oz ASW
| 99a | 1982 | *.015 | — | — | 20.00 |
| | 1982 | *.010 | — | Proof | 25.00 |

52.0000 g, .950 PLATINUM, 1.5884 oz APW
| 99b | 1982 | *50 pcs. | — | Proof | 1100. |

5.1000 g, .374 GOLD, .0613 oz AGW
| 99c | 1982 | *.022 | — | Proof | 75.00 |

7.9600 g, .917 GOLD, .2347 oz AGW
| 99d | 1982 | *2,000 | — | Proof | 150.00 |

COPPER-NICKEL, 37mm
World Cup Soccer - Spain

Rev: Similar to KM#93 w/soccer ball added in upper left field.
KM#	Date	Mintage	VF	XF	Unc
100	1982	—	—	—	2.50

Manned Flight - Balloon
| 103 | 1983 | *.050 | — | — | 2.50 |

28.2800 g, .925 SILVER, .8411 oz ASW
| 103a | 1983 | *.015 | — | — | 20.00 |
| | 1983 | *.011 | — | Proof | 25.00 |

52.0000 g, .950 PLATINUM, 1.5884 oz APW
| 103b | 1983 | *50 pcs. | — | Proof | 1250. |

5.1000 g, .374 GOLD, .0613 oz AGW
| 103c | 1983 | *5,500 | — | Proof | 75.00 |

7.9600 g, .917 GOLD, .2347 oz AGW
| 103d | 1983 | *500 | — | Proof | 150.00 |

COPPER-NICKEL, 37mm
Manned Flight - Biplane
| 104 | 1983 | *.050 | — | — | 2.50 |

28.2800 g, .925 SILVER, .8411 oz ASW
| 104a | 1983 | *.015 | — | — | 20.00 |
| | 1983 | *.011 | — | Proof | 25.00 |

52.0000 g, .950 PLATINUM, 1.5884 oz APW
| 104b | 1983 | *50 pcs. | — | Proof | 1500. |

5.1000 g, .374 GOLD, .0613 oz AGW
| 104c | 1983 | *5,500 | — | Proof | 75.00 |

7.9600 g, .917 GOLD, .2347 oz AGW
| 104d | 1983 | *500 | — | Proof | 150.00 |

COPPER-NICKEL, 37mm
Manned Flight - Jet
| 105 | 1983 | *.050 | — | — | 2.50 |

28.2800 g, .925 SILVER, .8411 oz ASW
| 105a | 1983 | *.015 | — | — | 20.00 |
| | 1983 | *.011 | — | Proof | 25.00 |

52.0000 g, .950 PLATINUM, 1.5884 oz APW
| 105b | 1983 | *50 pcs. | — | Proof | 1500. |

5.1000 g, .374 GOLD, .0613 oz AGW
| 105c | 1983 | *5,500 | — | Proof | 75.00 |

7.9600 g, .917 GOLD, .2347 oz AGW
| 105d | 1983 | *500 | — | Proof | 150.00 |

COPPER-NICKEL, 37mm
Manned Flight - Space Shuttle
| 106 | 1983 | *.050 | — | — | 2.50 |

28.2800 g, .925 SILVER, .8411 oz ASW
| 106a | 1983 | *.015 | — | — | 20.00 |
| | 1983 | *.011 | — | Proof | 25.00 |

52.0000 g, .950 PLATINUM, 1.5884 oz APW
| 106b | 1983 | *50 pcs. | — | Proof | 1500. |

ISLE OF MAN 1047

KM#	Date	Mintage	VF	XF	Unc
		5.1000 g, .374 GOLD, .0613 oz AGW			
106c	1983	*5,500	—	Proof	75.00
		7.9600 g, .917 GOLD, .2347 oz AGW			
106d	1983	*500 pcs.	—	Proof	150.00

COPPER-NICKEL, 37mm
1984 Olympics - Figure Skating

117	1984	—	—	—	2.50
		28.2800 g, .925 SILVER, .8411 oz ASW			
117a	1984	*.020	—	—	15.00
	1984	*.015	—	Proof	25.00

		5.1000 g, .374 GOLD, .0613 oz AGW			
117b	1984	*.010	—	Proof	75.00
		7.9600 g, .917 GOLD, .2347 oz AGW			
117c	1984	*1,000	—	Proof	150.00
		52.0000 g, .950 PLATINUM, 1.5884 oz APW			
117d	1984	—	—	Proof	1500.

COPPER-NICKEL, 37mm
1984 Olympics - Runners

118	1984	—	—	—	2.50
		28.2800 g, .925 SILVER, .8411 oz ASW			
118a	1984	*.020	—	—	15.00
	1984	*.015	—	Proof	25.00

		5.1000 g, .374 GOLD, .0613 oz AGW			
118b	1984	*.010	—	Proof	75.00
		7.9600 g, .917 GOLD, .2347 oz AGW			
118c	1984	*1,000	—	Proof	150.00
		52.0000 g, .950 PLATINUM, 1.5884 oz APW			
118d	1984	—	—	Proof	1500.

COPPER-NICKEL, 37mm
1984 Olympics - Gymnastics

119	1984	—	—	—	2.50
		28.2800 g, .925 SILVER, .8411 oz ASW			
119a	1984	*.020	—	—	15.00
	1984	*.015	—	Proof	25.00

		5.1000 g, .374 GOLD, .0613 oz AGW			
119b	1984	*.010	—	Proof	75.00
		7.9600 g, .917 GOLD, .2347 oz AGW			
119c	1984	*1,000	—	Proof	150.00
		52.0000 g, .950 PLATINUM, 1.5884 oz APW			
119d	1984	—	—	Proof	1500.

COPPER-NICKEL, 37mm
1984 Olympics-Equestrian

120	1984	—	—	—	2.50
		28.2800 g, .925 SILVER, .8411 oz ASW			
120a	1984	*.020	—	—	15.00
	1984	*.015	—	Proof	25.00

		5.1000 g, .374 GOLD, .0613 oz AGW			
120b	1984	*.010	—	Proof	75.00

KM#	Date	Mintage	VF	XF	Unc
		7.9600 g, .917 GOLD, .2347 oz AGW			
120c	1984	*1,000	—	Proof	150.00
		52.0000 g, .950 PLATINUM, 1.5884 oz APW			
120d	1984	—	—	Proof	1500.

COPPER-NICKEL, 37mm
Quincentenary of the College of Arms

121	1984	—	—	—	2.50
		28.2800 g, .925 SILVER, .8411 oz ASW			
121a	1984	—	—	—	20.00
	1984	—	—	Proof	25.00

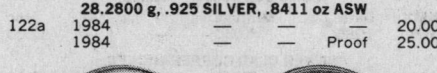

		5.1000 g, .374 GOLD, .0613 oz AGW			
121b	1984	*.010	—	Proof	75.00
		7.9600 g, .917 GOLD, .2347 oz AGW			
121c	1984	*1,000	—	Proof	150.00
		52.0000 g, .950 PLATINUM, 1.5884 oz APW			
121d	1984	—	—	Proof	1100.

COPPER-NICKEL, 37mm
Quincentenary of the College of Arms

122	1984	—	—	—	2.50
		28.2800 g, .925 SILVER, .8411 oz ASW			
122a	1984	—	—	—	20.00
	1984	—	—	Proof	25.00

		5.1000 g, .374 GOLD, .0613 oz AGW			
122b	1984	*.010	—	Proof	75.00
		7.9600 g, .917 GOLD, .2347 oz AGW			
122c	1984	*1,000	—	Proof	150.00
		52.0000 g, .950 PLATINUM, 1.5884 oz APW			
122d	1984	—	—	Proof	1100.

COPPER-NICKEL, 37mm
Quincentenary of the College of Arms

123	1984	—	—	—	2.50
		28.2800 g, .925 SILVER, .8411 oz ASW			
123a	1984	—	—	—	20.00
	1984	—	—	Proof	25.00

		5.1000 g, .374 GOLD, .0613 oz AGW			
123b	1984	*.010	—	Proof	75.00
		7.9600 g, .917 GOLD, .2347 oz AGW			
123c	1984	*1,000	—	Proof	150.00
		52.0000 g, .950 PLATINUM, 1.5884 oz APW			
123d	1984	—	—	Proof	1100.

COPPER-NICKEL, 37mm
Quincentenary of the College of Arms

124	1984	—	—	—	2.50
		28.2800 g, .925 SILVER, .8411 oz ASW			
124a	1984	—	—	—	20.00
	1984	—	—	Proof	25.00

		5.1000 g, .374 GOLD, .0613 oz AGW			
124b	1984	*.010	—	Proof	75.00
		7.9600 g, .917 GOLD, .2347 oz AGW			
124c	1984	*1,000	—	Proof	150.00
		52.0000 g, .950 PLATINUM, 1.5884 oz APW			
124d	1984	—	—	Proof	1100.

COPPER-NICKEL, 37mm
13th Commonwealth Parliamentary Conference

130	1984	—	—	—	2.50
		28.2800 g, .925 SILVER, .8411 oz ASW			

KM#	Date	Mintage	VF	XF	Unc
130a	1984	—	—	—	20.00
	1984	—	—	Proof	25.00

		5.1000 g, .374 GOLD, .0613 oz AGW			
130b	1984	*.010	—	Proof	75.00
		7.9600 g, .917 GOLD, .2347 oz AGW			
130c	1984	*1,000	—	Proof	150.00
		52.0000 g, .950 PLATINUM, 1.5884 oz APW			
130d	1984	—	—	Proof	1100.

COPPER-NICKEL, 37mm
13th Commonwealth Parliamentary Conference

131	1984	—	—	—	2.50
		28.2800 g, .925 SILVER, .8411 oz ASW			
131a	1984	—	—	—	20.00
	1984	—	—	Proof	25.00

		5.1000 g, .374 GOLD, .0613 oz AGW			
131b	1984	*.010	—	Proof	75.00
		7.9600 g, .917 GOLD, .2347 oz AGW			
131c	1984	*1,000	—	Proof	150.00
		52.0000 g, .950 PLATINUM, 1.5884 oz APW			
131d	1984	—	—	Proof	1100.

COPPER-NICKEL, 37mm
13th Commonwealth Parliamentary Conference

132	1984	—	—	—	2.50
		28.2800 g, .925 SILVER, .8411 oz ASW			
132a	1984	—	—	—	20.00
	1984	—	—	Proof	25.00

		5.1000 g, .374 GOLD, .0613 oz AGW			
132b	1984	*.010	—	Proof	75.00
		7.9600 g, .917 GOLD, .2347 oz AGW			
132c	1984	*1,000	—	Proof	150.00
		52.0000 g, .950 PLATINUM, 1.5884 oz APW			
132d	1984	—	—	Proof	1100.

COPPER-NICKEL, 37mm
13th Commonwealth Parliamentary Conference

133	1984	—	—	—	2.50
		28.2800 g, .925 SILVER, .8411 oz ASW			
133a	1984	—	—	—	20.00
	1984	—	—	Proof	25.00

		5.1000 g, .374 GOLD, .0613 oz AGW			
133b	1984	*.010	—	Proof	75.00
		7.9600 g, .917 GOLD, .2347 oz AGW			
133c	1984	*1,000	—	Proof	150.00

ISLE OF MAN

52.0000 g, .950 PLATINUM, 1.5884 oz APW

KM#	Date	Mintage	VF	XF	Unc
133d	1984	—	—	—	Proof 1100.

COPPER-NICKEL
Obv: Portrait of Queen Elizabeth II.
Rev: Queen Mother as a young girl.

216	1985	—	—	—	2.50
	1985	*.050	—	Proof	5.00

SILVER CLAD COPPER-NICKEL

216a	1985	*.020	—	Proof	10.00

28.2800 g, .925 SILVER, .8411 oz ASW

216b	1985	*.015	—	Proof	25.00

5.1000 g, .374 GOLD, .0613 oz AGW

216c	1985	*.010	—	Proof	75.00

7.9600 g, .917 GOLD, .2347 oz AGW

216d	1985	*1,000	—	Proof	150.00

52.0000 g, .950 PLATINUM, 1.5884 oz APW

216e	1985	*100 pcs.	—	Proof	1100.

COPPER-NICKEL
Rev: Portrait of King George VI and Elizabeth

217	1985	—	—	—	2.50
	1985	*.050	—	Proof	5.00

SILVER CLAD COPPER-NICKEL

217a	1985	*.020	—	Proof	10.00

28.2800 g, .925 SILVER, .8411 oz ASW

217b	1985	*.015	—	Proof	25.00

5.1000 g, .374 GOLD, .0613 oz AGW

217c	1985	*.010	—	Proof	75.00

7.9600 g, .917 GOLD, .2347 oz AGW

217d	1985	*1,000	—	Proof	150.00

52.0000 g, .950 PLATINUM, 1.5884 oz APW

217e	1985	*100 pcs.	—	Proof	1100.

COPPER-NICKEL
Rev: Wedding portrait of King George VI and Elizabeth.

218	1985	—	—	—	2.50
	1985	*.050	—	Proof	5.00

SILVER CLAD COPPER-NICKEL

218a	1985	*.020	—	Proof	10.00

28.2800 g, .925 SILVER, .8411 oz ASW

218b	1985	*.015	—	Proof	25.00

5.1000 g, .374 GOLD, .0613 oz AGW

218c	1985	*.010	—	Proof	75.00

7.9600 g, .917 GOLD, .2347 oz AGW

218d	1985	*1,000	—	Proof	150.00

52.0000 g, .950 PLATINUM, 1.5884 oz APW

218e	1985	*100 pcs.	—	Proof	1100.

COPPER-NICKEL
Rev: Queen Mother and child.

219	1985	—	—	—	2.50
	1985	*.050	—	Proof	5.00

SILVER CLAD COPPER-NICKEL

219a	1985	*.020	—	Proof	10.00

28.2800 g, .925 SILVER, .8411 oz ASW

219b	1985	*.015	—	Proof	25.00

5.1000 g, .374 GOLD, .0613 oz AGW

219c	1985	*.010	—	Proof	75.00

7.9600 g, .917 GOLD, .2347 oz AGW

219d	1985	*1,000	—	Proof	150.00

52.0000 g, .950 PLATINUM, 1.5884 oz APW

219e	1985	*100 pcs.	—	Proof	1100.

COPPER-NICKEL
Rev: Queen Mother and two daughters.

220	1985	—	—	—	2.50
	1985	*.050	—	Proof	5.00

SILVER CLAD COPPER-NICKEL

220a	1985	*.020	—	Proof	10.00

28.2800 g, .925 SILVER, .8411 oz ASW

220b	1985	*.015	—	Proof	25.00

5.1000 g, .374 GOLD, .0613 oz AGW

220c	1985	*.010	—	Proof	75.00

7.9600 g, .917 GOLD, .2347 oz AGW

220d	1985	*1,000	—	Proof	150.00

52.0000 g, .950 PLATINUM, 1.5884 oz APW

220e	1985	*100 pcs.	—	Proof	1100.

COPPER-NICKEL
Rev: Queen Mother on 80th Birthday

221	1985	—	—	—	2.50
	1985	*.050	—	Proof	5.00

SILVER CLAD COPPER-NICKEL

221a	1985	*.020	—	Proof	10.00

28.2800 g, .925 SILVER, .8411 oz ASW

221b	1985	*.015	—	Proof	25.00

5.1000 g, .374 GOLD, .0613 oz AGW

221c	1985	*.010	—	Proof	75.00

7.9600 g, .917 GOLD, .2347 oz AGW

221d	1985	*1,000	—	Proof	150.00

52.0000 g, .950 PLATINUM, 1.5884 oz APW

221e	1985	*100 pcs.	—	Proof	1100.

COPPER-NICKEL
World Cup Soccer - Mexico

KM#	Date	Mintage	VF	XF	Unc
160	1986	*.050	—	—	2.00

SILVER CLAD COPPER-NICKEL

160a	1986	*.020	—	Proof	5.00

28.2800 g, .925 SILVER, .8411 oz ASW

160b	1986	*.015	—	Proof	25.00

5.1000 g, .374 GOLD, .0613 oz AGW

160c	1986	*.010	—	Proof	75.00

7.9600 g, .917 GOLD, .2347 oz AGW

160d	1986	*1,000	—	Proof	150.00

52.0000 g, .950 PLATINUM, 1.5884 oz APW

160e	1986	*200 pcs.	—	Proof	1100.

COPPER-NICKEL
World Cup Soccer - Mexico

161	1986	*.050	—	—	2.00

SILVER CLAD COPPER-NICKEL

161a	1986	*.020	—	Proof	5.00

28.2800 g, .925 SILVER, .8411 oz ASW

161b	1986	*.015	—	Proof	25.00

5.1000 g, .374 GOLD, .0613 oz AGW

161c	1986	*.010	—	Proof	75.00

7.9600 g, .917 GOLD, .2347 oz AGW

161d	1986	*1,000	—	Proof	150.00

52.0000 g, .950 PLATINUM, 1.5884 oz APW

161e	1986	*200 pcs.	—	Proof	1100.

COPPER-NICKEL
World Cup Soccer - Mexico

162	1986	*.050	—	—	2.00

SILVER CLAD COPPER-NICKEL

162a	1986	*.020	—	Proof	5.00

28.2800 g, .925 SILVER, .8411 oz ASW

162b	1986	*.015	—	Proof	25.00

5.1000 g, .374 GOLD, .0613 oz AGW

162c	1986	*.010	—	Proof	75.00

7.9600 g, .917 GOLD, .2347 oz AGW

KM#	Date	Mintage	VF	XF	Unc
162d	1986	*1,000	—	Proof	150.00

52.0000 g, .950 PLATINUM, 1.5884 oz APW

162e	1986	*200 pcs.	—	Proof	1100.

COPPER-NICKEL
World Cup Soccer - Mexico

163	1986	*.050	—	—	2.00

SILVER CLAD COPPER-NICKEL

163a	1986	*.020	—	Proof	5.00

28.2800 g, .925 SILVER, .8411 oz ASW

163b	1986	*.015	—	Proof	25.00

5.1000 g, .374 GOLD, .0613 oz AGW

163c	1986	*.010	—	Proof	75.00

7.9600 g, .917 GOLD, .2347 oz AGW

163d	1986	*1,000	—	Proof	150.00

52.0000 g, .950 PLATINUM, 1.5884 oz APW

163e	1986	*200 pcs.	—	Proof	1100.

COPPER-NICKEL
World Cup Soccer - Mexico

164	1986	*.050	—	—	2.00

SILVER CLAD COPPER-NICKEL

164a	1986	*.020	—	Proof	5.00

28.2800 g, .925 SILVER, .8411 oz ASW

164b	1986	*.015	—	Proof	25.00

5.1000 g, .374 GOLD, .0613 oz AGW

164c	1986	*.010	—	Proof	75.00

7.9600 g, .917 GOLD, .2347 oz AGW

164d	1986	*1,000	—	Proof	150.00

52.0000 g, .950 PLATINUM, 1.5884 oz APW

164e	1986	*200 pcs.	—	Proof	1100.

COPPER-NICKEL
World Cup Soccer - Mexico

165	1986	*.050	—	—	2.00

SILVER CLAD COPPER-NICKEL

165a	1986	*.020	—	Proof	5.00

28.2800 g, .925 SILVER, .8411 oz ASW

165b	1986	*.015	—	Proof	25.00

5.1000 g, .374 GOLD, .0613 oz AGW

165c	1986	*.010	—	Proof	75.00

7.9600 g, .917 GOLD, .2347 oz AGW

165d	1986	*1,000	—	Proof	150.00

52.0000 g, .950 PLATINUM, 1.5884 oz APW

165e	1986	*200 pcs.	—	Proof	1100.

ISLE OF MAN 1049

COPPER-NICKEL
Prince Andrew's Wedding - Portraits

KM#	Date	Mintage	VF	XF	Unc
173	1986	—	—	—	4.00
	1986	*.050	—	Proof	6.00

SILVER CLAD COPPER-NICKEL
| 173a | 1986 | *.020 | — | Proof | 10.00 |

28.2800 g, .925 SILVER, .8411 oz ASW
| 173b | 1986 | *.020 | — | — | 25.00 |
| | 1986 | *.015 | — | Proof | 35.00 |

5.1000 g, .374 GOLD, .0613 oz AGW
| 173c | 1986 | *.010 | — | Proof | 75.00 |

7.9600 g, .917 GOLD, .2347 oz AGW
| 173d | 1986 | *1,000 | — | Proof | 150.00 |

52.0000 g, .950 PLATINUM, 1.5884 oz APW
| 173e | 1986 | *100 pcs. | — | Proof | 1200. |

COPPER-NICKEL
Prince Andrew's Wedding - Coats of Arms

| 174 | 1986 | — | — | — | 3.00 |
| | 1986 | *.050 | — | Proof | 5.00 |

SILVER CLAD COPPER-NICKEL
| 174a | 1986 | *.020 | — | Proof | 10.00 |

28.2800 g, .925 SILVER, .8411 oz ASW
| 174b | 1986 | *.020 | — | — | 25.00 |
| | 1986 | *.015 | — | Proof | 35.00 |

5.1000 g, .374 GOLD, .0613 oz AGW
| 174c | 1986 | *.010 | — | Proof | 75.00 |

7.9600 g, .917 GOLD, .2347 oz AGW
| 174d | 1986 | *1,000 | — | Proof | 150.00 |

52.0000 g, .950 PLATINUM, 1.5884 oz APW
| 174e | 1986 | *100 pcs. | — | Proof | 1200. |

COPPER-NICKEL
United States Constitution
Obv: Similar to KM#179.

| 176 | 1987 | — | — | — | 2.00 |

31.1000 g, .999 PALLADIUM, 1.0000 oz APW
U.S. Constitution
| 176a | 1987 | *.028 | — | Proof | 300.00 |

31.1000 g, .995 PLATINUM, 1.0000 oz APW
| 176b | 1987 | *1,000 | — | Proof | 800.00 |

COPPER-NICKEL
America's Cup - Sailboats and Map

KM#	Date	Mintage	VF	XF	Unc
179	1987	—	—	—	2.00

SILVER CLAD COPPER-NICKEL
| 179a | 1987 | *.020 | — | Proof | 12.50 |

28.2800 g, .925 SILVER, .8411 oz ASW
| 179b | 1987 | *.020 | — | — | 26.50 |
| | 1987 | *.015 | — | Proof | 40.00 |

31.1030 g, .999 PALLADIUM, 1.0000 oz APW
| 179c | 1987 | *.025 | — | Proof | 250.00 |

COPPER-NICKEL
America's Cup - Sailboats and Cup
Obv: Similar to KM#179.

| 183 | 1987 | — | — | — | 2.00 |

SILVER CLAD COPPER-NICKEL
| 183a | 1987 | *.020 | — | Proof | 12.50 |

28.2800 g, .925 SILVER, .8411 oz ASW
| 183b | 1987 | *.020 | — | — | 26.50 |
| | 1987 | *.015 | — | Proof | 40.00 |

COPPER-NICKEL
America's Cup - Sailboats - Statue of Liberty
Obv: Similar to KM#179.

| 184 | 1987 | — | — | — | 2.00 |

SILVER CLAD COPPER-NICKEL
| 184a | 1987 | *.020 | — | Proof | 12.50 |

28.2800 g, .925 SILVER, .8411 oz ASW
| 184b | 1987 | *.020 | — | — | 26.50 |
| | 1987 | *.015 | — | Proof | 40.00 |

COPPER-NICKEL
America's Cup - George Steers
Obv: Similar to KM#179.

KM#	Date	Mintage	VF	XF	Unc
185	1987	—	—	—	2.00

SILVER CLAD COPPER-NICKEL
| 185a | 1987 | *.020 | — | Proof | 12.50 |

28.2800 g, .925 SILVER, .8411 oz ASW
| 185b | 1987 | *.020 | — | — | 26.50 |
| | 1987 | *.015 | — | Proof | 40.00 |

COPPER-NICKEL
America's Cup - Sir Thomas Lipton
Obv: Similar to KM#179.

| 186 | 1987 | — | — | — | 2.00 |

SILVER CLAD COPPER-NICKEL
| 186a | 1987 | *.020 | — | Proof | 12.50 |

28.2800 g, .925 SILVER, .8411 oz ASW
| 186b | 1987 | *.020 | — | — | 26.50 |
| | 1987 | *.015 | — | Proof | 40.00 |

Australian Bicentennial - Cockatoo
| 222 | 1988 | — | — | — | 2.50 |

Australian Bicentennial - Koala
| 223 | 1988 | — | — | — | 2.50 |

ISLE OF MAN 1050

Australian Bicentennial - Platypus Duckbill

KM#	Date	Mintage	VF	XF	Unc
224	1988	—	—	—	2.50

225	1988	—	—	—	2.50

Australian Bicentennial - Kangaroo

Australian Bicentennial - Dingo Dog

226	1988	—	—	—	2.50

Australian Bicentennial - Tasmanian Devil

227	1988	—	—	—	2.50

Steam Navigation - Patrick Miller's Number One

KM#	Date	Mintage	VF	XF	Unc
228	1988	—	—	—	2.50

Steam Navigation - Sirius

229	1988	—	—	—	2.50

Steam Navigation - Chaperon

230	1988	—	—	—	2.50

Steam Navigation - Mauretania

231	1988	—	—	—	2.50

Steam Navigation - Queen Mary

232	1988	—	—	—	2.50

Steam Navigation - Queen Elizabeth II

KM#	Date	Mintage	VF	XF	Unc
233	1988	—	—	—	2.50

31.1000 g, .999 SILVER, 1.0000 oz ASW
Manx Cat - Bullion

234	1988	.050	—	Proof	37.50

31.1000 g, .999 GOLD, 1.0000 oz AGW
Similar to KM#234.

239	1988	—	—	—	BV + 4%
	1988	5,000	—	Proof	750.00

COPPER-NICKEL
Obv: Portrait of Queen. Rev: Manx cat.

245	1988	—	—	—	3.50

Mutiny on the Bounty - Captain Bligh and Elizabeth Betham

240	1989	—	—	—	2.50

28.2800 g, .925 SILVER, .8411 oz ASW

240a	1989	—	—	—	25.00

COPPER-NICKEL
Mutiny on the Bounty - H.M.S. Bounty

241	1989	—	—	—	2.50

28.2800 g, .925 SILVER, .8411 oz ASW

241a	1989	—	—	—	25.00

ISLE OF MAN 1051

COPPER-NICKEL
Mutiny on the Bounty - Crew set afloat

KM#	Date	Mintage	VF	XF	Unc
242	1989		—	—	2.50

28.2800 g, .925 SILVER, .8411 oz ASW
| 242a | 1989 | | — | — | 25.00 |

COPPER-NICKEL
Mutiny on the Bounty - Pitcairn Island
| 243 | 1989 | | — | — | 2.50 |

28.2800 g, .925 SILVER, .8411 oz ASW
| 243a | 1989 | | — | — | 25.00 |

50 NEW PENCE

COPPER-NICKEL
24	1971	.100	—	.75	1.50
	1971	.010	—	Proof	7.50
	1972	1,000	—	—	30.00
	1973	1,000	—	—	30.00
	1974	1,000	—	—	30.00
	1975	.227	—	.75	1.50

15.5000 g, .925 SILVER, .4610 oz ASW
| 24a | 1975 | .020 | — | — | 12.50 |

30.4000 g, .950 PLATINUM, .9286 oz APW
| 24b | 1975 | 600 pcs. | — | Proof | 625.00 |

50 PENCE

COPPER-NICKEL
39	1976	.250	—	.75	1.50
	1977	.050	—	.75	1.75
	1978	.025	—	.75	1.75
	1978	—	—	Proof	3.50
	1979(t)	—	—	.75	3.00

15.5000 g, .925 SILVER, .4610 oz ASW
39a	1976	.020	—	—	12.50
	1977	.010	—	Proof	12.50
	1978	.010	—	—	12.50
	1979(t)	.010	—	—	12.50

30.4000 g, .950 PLATINUM, .9286 oz APW
39b	1976	600 pcs.	—	Proof	625.00
	1978	600 pcs.	—	Proof	625.00
	1979(t)	500 pcs.	—	Proof	625.00

COPPER-NICKEL
Manx Millenium of Tynwald
Edge inscription: H.M.Q.E.II ROYAL VISIT I.O.M. JULY 1979

KM#	Date	Mintage	VF	XF	Unc
51	1979 PM	*.050	—	—	3.00

15.5000 g, .925 SILVER, .4610 oz ASW
| 51a | 1979 | .010 | — | — | 10.00 |
| | 1979 | *5,000 | — | Proof | 15.00 |

30.4000 g, .950 PLATINUM, .9286 oz APW
| 51b | 1979 | *500 pcs. | — | Proof | 625.00 |

COPPER-NICKEL
Plain edge
| 53 | 1979 | | — | — | 2.50 |

15.5000 g, .925 SILVER, .4610 oz ASW
| 53a | 1979 | | — | — | 10.00 |
| | 1979 | | — | Proof | 15.00 |

COPPER-NICKEL
Edge inscription: ODINS RAVEN VIKING EXHIBN NEW YORK 1980
| 69 | 1980 | *.020 | — | — | 4.00 |

15.5000 g, .925 SILVER, .4610 oz ASW
| 69a | 1980 | | — | — | 15.00 |
| | 1980 | *5,000 | — | Proof | 20.00 |

26.0000 g, .917 GOLD, .7666 oz AGW
| 69b | 1980 | *250 pcs. | — | Proof | 600.00 |

30.4000 g, .950 PLATINUM, .9286 oz APW
| 69c | 1980 | *50 pcs. | — | Proof | 775.00 |

COPPER-NICKEL
70	1980	*.010	—	.75	2.00
	1981	—	—	.75	2.00
	1982	—	—	.75	2.00
	1982(b)	—	—	.75	2.00
	1982(b)	*.025	—	Proof	2.50
	1983	—	—	.75	2.00

15.5000 g, .500 SILVER, .2491 oz ASW
| 70a | 1980 | *.010 | — | Proof | 10.00 |
| | 1982(b) | *.010 | — | Proof | 15.00 |

15.5000 g, .925 SILVER, .4610 oz ASW
| 70b | 1983 | *5,000 | — | Proof | 17.50 |

26.0000 g, .917 GOLD, .7666 oz AGW
70c	1980	*300 pcs.	—	Proof	600.00
	1982(b)	*500 pcs.	—	Proof	600.00
	1983	—	—	Proof	600.00

30.4000 g, .950 PLATINUM, .9286 oz APW
70d	1980	*500 pcs.	—	Proof	750.00
	1982(b)	*500 pcs.	—	Proof	750.00
	1983	—	—	Proof	750.00

COPPER-NICKEL
Mule. Obv: KM#69. Rev: KM#71.
| 57 | 1980 | | | | |

Christmas 1980
| 71 | 1980 | *.030 | — | — | 2.50 |

15.5000 g, .925 SILVER, .4610 oz ASW
| 71a | 1980 | *5,000 | — | Proof | 15.00 |

26.0000 g, .917 GOLD, .7666 oz AGW
| 71b | 1980 | *250 pcs. | — | Proof | 600.00 |

30.4000 g, .950 PLATINUM, .9286 oz APW
| 71c | 1980 | *50 pcs. | — | Proof | 750.00 |

COPPER-NICKEL
Tourist Trophy Motorcycle Races

KM#	Date	Mintage	VF	XF	Unc
83	1981	*.030	—	—	2.00

15.5000 g, .925 SILVER, .4610 oz ASW
| 83a | 1981 | *5,000 | — | Proof | 15.00 |

26.0000 g, .917 GOLD, .7666 oz AGW
| 83b | 1981 | *250 pcs. | — | Proof | 600.00 |

30.4000 g, .950 PLATINUM, .9286 oz APW
| 83c | 1981 | *50 pcs. | — | Proof | 775.00 |

COPPER-NICKEL
Christmas 1981
| 84 | 1981 | *.030 | — | — | 2.00 |
| | 1981 | — | — | Proof | 4.00 |

15.5000 g, .925 SILVER, .4610 oz ASW
| 84a | 1981 | *5,000 | — | Proof | 15.00 |

26.0000 g, .917 GOLD, .7666 oz AGW
| 84b | 1981 | *250 pcs. | — | Proof | 600.00 |

30.4000 g, .950 PLATINUM, .9286 oz APW
| 84c | 1981 | *50 pcs. | — | Proof | 775.00 |

COPPER-NICKEL
Tourist Trophy Motorcycle Races
| 101 | 1982 | | — | — | 2.00 |
| | 1982 | *.030 | — | Proof | 4.00 |

15.5000 g, .925 SILVER, .4610 oz ASW
| 101a | 1982 | *5,000 | — | Proof | 15.00 |

26.0000 g, .917 GOLD, .7666 oz AGW
| 101b | 1982 | *250 pcs. | — | Proof | 600.00 |

30.4000 g, .950 PLATINUM, .9286 oz APW
| 101c | 1982 | *50 pcs. | — | Proof | 775.00 |

COPPER-NICKEL
Christmas 1982
| 102 | 1982 | *.030 | — | — | 2.00 |
| | 1982 | *250 pcs. | — | Proof | 4.00 |

15.0000 g, .925 SILVER, .4610 oz ASW
| 102a | 1982 | *5,000 | — | Proof | 15.00 |

26.0000 g, .917 GOLD, .7666 oz AGW
| 102b | 1982 | *250 pcs. | — | Proof | 600.00 |

30.4000 g, .950 PLATINUM, .9286 oz APW
| 102c | 1982 | *50 pcs. | — | Proof | 750.00 |

ISLE OF MAN

COPPER-NICKEL
Christmas 1983

KM#	Date	Mintage	VF	XF	Unc
107	1983	*.030	—	—	2.00
	15.5000 g, .925 SILVER, .4610 oz ASW				
107a	1983	*5,000	—	Proof	15.00
	26.000 g, .917 GOLD, .7666 oz AGW				
107b	1983	*250 pcs.	—	Proof	600.00
	30.4000 g, .950 PLATINUM, .9286 oz APW				
107c	1983	*50 pcs.	—	Proof	750.00

COPPER-NICKEL
Tourist Trophy Motorcycle Races

108	1983	*.030	—	—	2.00
	15.5000 g, .925 SILVER, .4610 oz ASW				
108a	1983	*5,000	—	Proof	15.00
	26.0000 g, .917 GOLD, .7666 oz AGW				
108b	1983	*250 pcs.	—	Proof	600.00
	30.4000 g, .950 PLATINUM, .9286 oz APW				
108c	1983	*50 pcs.	—	Proof	775.00

COPPER-NICKEL

125	1984	—	—	—	2.00
	15.5000 g, .925 SILVER, .4610 oz ASW				
125a	1984	—	—	Proof	15.00
	26.0000 g, .917 GOLD, .7666 oz AGW				
125b	1984	*150 pcs.	—	Proof	600.00

COPPER-NICKEL
Tourist Trophy Motorcycle Races

126	1984	*.030	—	—	2.00
	15.5000 g, .925 SILVER, .4610 oz ASW				
126a	1984	*5,000	—	Proof	15.00
	26.0000 g, .917 GOLD, .7666oz AGW				
126b	1984	*250 pcs.	—	Proof	600.00
	30.4000 g, .950 PLATINUM, .9286 oz APW				
126c	1984	*50 pcs.	—	Proof	775.00

COPPER-NICKEL

Christmas 1984

KM#	Date	Mintage	VF	XF	Unc
127	1984	—	—	—	2.00
	15.5000 g, .925 SILVER, .4610 oz ASW				
127a	1984	—	—	Proof	25.00
	26.0000 g, .917 GOLD, .7666 oz AGW				
127b	1984	*250 pcs.	—	Proof	600.00
	30.4000 g, .950 PLATINUM, .9286 oz APW				
127c	1984	—	—	Proof	750.00

COPPER-NICKEL

148	1985	—	—	—	2.00
	1985	*.050	—	Proof	4.00
	1986	—	—	—	2.00
	15.5000 g, .925 SILVER, .4610 oz ASW				
148a	1985	*.010	—	Proof	15.00
	26.0000 g, .917 GOLD, .7666 oz AGW				
148b	1985	*300 pcs.	—	Proof	600.00
	30.4000 g, .950 PLATINUM, .9286 oz APW				
148c	1985	*200 pcs.	—	Proof	750.00

COPPER-NICKEL
Christmas 1985

158	1985	—	—	—	5.00
	15.5000 g, .925 SILVER, .4610 oz ASW				
158a	1985	*5,000	—	Proof	20.00
	26.0000 g, .917 GOLD, .7666 oz AGW				
158b	1985	*250 pcs.	—	Proof	600.00
	30.4000 g, .950 PLATINUM, .9286 oz APW				
158c	1985	—	—	Proof	700.00

COPPER-NICKEL
Christmas 1986

172	1986	—	—	—	5.00
	1986	—	—	Proof	20.00

Christmas 1987

190	1987	—	—	—	2.50
	1987	*.030	—	Proof	5.00
	15.5000 g, .925 SILVER, .4610 oz ASW				
190a	1987	*5,000	—	Proof	20.00
	26.0000 g, .917 GOLD, .7666 oz AGW				
190b	1987	*250 pcs.	—	Proof	450.00
	30.4000 g, .950 PLATINUM, .9286 oz APW				
190c	1987	*50 pcs.	—	Proof	775.00

COPPER-NICKEL

KM#	Date	Mintage	VF	XF	Unc
212	1988	—	—	—	2.50

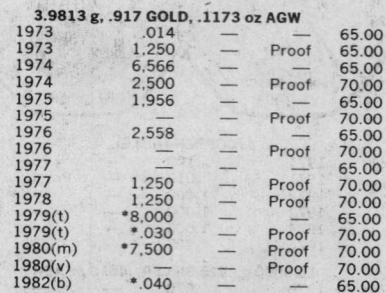

244	1988	—	—	—	2.50
	1988	—	—	Proof	5.00
	15.5000 g, .925 SILVER, .4610 oz ASW				
244a	1988	—	—	—	—
	26.0000 g, .917 GOLD, .7666 oz AGW				
244b	1988	—	—	Proof	400.00
	30.4000 g, .950 PLATINUM, .9286 oz APW				
244c	1988	—	—	Proof	800.00

1/2 SOVEREIGN (1/2 POUND)

3.9940 g, .917 GOLD, .1177 oz AGW
200th Anniversary of Acquisition

15	1965	1,500	—	—	65.00

4.0000 g, .980 GOLD, .1260 oz AGW

15a	1965	1,000	—	Proof	70.00

3.9813 g, .917 GOLD, .1173 oz AGW

26	1973	.014	—	—	65.00
	1973	1,250	—	Proof	65.00
	1974	6,566	—	—	65.00
	1974	2,500	—	Proof	70.00
	1975	1,956	—	—	65.00
	1975	—	—	Proof	70.00
	1976	2,558	—	—	65.00
	1976	—	—	Proof	70.00
	1977	—	—	—	65.00
	1977	1,250	—	Proof	70.00
	1978	1,250	—	Proof	70.00
	1979(t)	*8,000	—	—	65.00
	1979(t)	*.030	—	Proof	70.00
	1980(m)	*7,500	—	—	70.00
	1980(v)	—	—	Proof	70.00
	1982(b)	*.040	—	—	65.00
	1982(b)	*.030	—	Proof	70.00

Wedding of Prince Charles and Lady Diana
Obv: Similar to KM#26.
Rev: Portraits of Royal Couple, joined shields.

85	1981	*.030	—	Proof	70.00

SOVEREIGN (POUND)

7.9881 g, .917 GOLD, .2355 oz AGW
200th Anniversary of Acquisition

16	1965	2,000	—	—	125.00

8.0000 g, .980 GOLD, .2520 oz AGW

16a	1965	1,000	—	Proof	125.00

7.9627 g, .917 GOLD, .2347 oz AGW

27	1973	.040	—	—	125.00
	1973	1,250	—	Proof	135.00
	1974	8,604	—	—	125.00
	1974	2,500	—	Proof	135.00
	1975	956 pcs.	—	—	150.00
	1975	—	—	Proof	135.00
	1976	1,238	—	—	135.00
	1976	—	—	Proof	135.00
	1977	—	—	—	135.00
	1977	1,250	—	Proof	135.00

ISLE OF MAN 1053

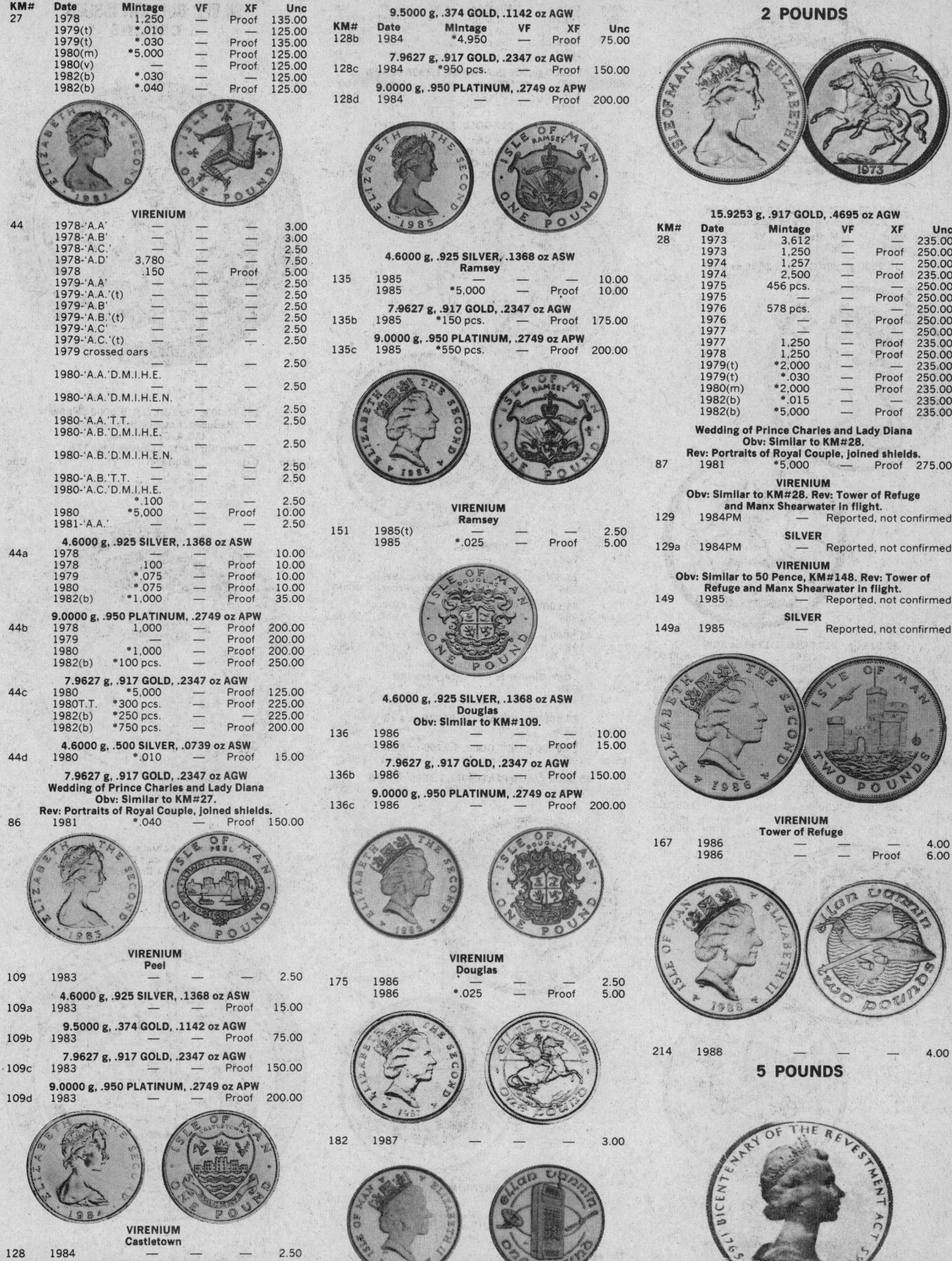

KM#	Date	Mintage	VF	XF	Unc
27	1978	1.250	—	—	135.00
	1979(t)	*.010	—	—	125.00
	1979(t)	*.030	—	Proof	135.00
	1980(m)	*5,000	—	Proof	125.00
	1980(v)	—	—	Proof	125.00
	1982(b)	*.030	—	—	125.00
	1982(b)	*.040	—	Proof	125.00

VIRENIUM

KM#	Date	Mintage	VF	XF	Unc
44	1978-'A.A'	—	—	—	3.00
	1978-'A.B'	—	—	—	3.00
	1978-'A.C.'	—	—	—	2.50
	1978-'A.D'	3,780	—	—	7.50
	1978	.150	—	Proof	5.00
	1979-'A.A'	—	—	—	2.50
	1979-'A.A.'(t)	—	—	—	2.50
	1979-'A.B'	—	—	—	2.50
	1979-'A.B.'(t)	—	—	—	2.50
	1979-'A.C'	—	—	—	2.50
	1979-'A.C.'(t)	—	—	—	2.50
	1979 crossed oars	—	—	—	2.50
	1980-'A.A.'D.M.I.H.E.	—	—	—	2.50
	1980-'A.A.'D.M.I.H.E.N.	—	—	—	2.50
	1980-'A.A.'T.T.	—	—	—	2.50
	1980-'A.B.'D.M.I.H.E.	—	—	—	2.50
	1980-'A.B.'D.M.I.H.E.N.	—	—	—	2.50
	1980-'A.B.'T.T.	—	—	—	2.50
	1980-'A.C.'D.M.I.H.E.	—	—	—	2.50
	1980	*.100	—	—	2.50
	1980	*5,000	—	Proof	10.00
	1981-'A.A.'	—	—	—	2.50

4.6000 g, .925 SILVER, .1368 oz ASW

44a	1978	—	—	—	10.00
	1978	.100	—	Proof	10.00
	1979	*.075	—	Proof	10.00
	1980	*.075	—	Proof	10.00
	1982(b)	*1,000	—	Proof	35.00

9.0000 g, .950 PLATINUM, .2749 oz APW

44b	1978	1,000	—	Proof	200.00
	1979	—	—	Proof	200.00
	1980	*1,000	—	Proof	200.00
	1982(b)	*100 pcs.	—	Proof	250.00

7.9627 g, .917 GOLD, .2347 oz AGW

44c	1980	*5,000	—	Proof	125.00
	1980T.T.	*300 pcs.	—	Proof	225.00
	1982(b)	*250 pcs.	—	—	225.00
	1982(b)	*750 pcs.	—	Proof	200.00

4.6000 g, .500 SILVER, .0739 oz ASW

| 44d | 1980 | *.010 | — | Proof | 15.00 |

7.9627 g, .917 GOLD, .2347 oz AGW
Wedding of Prince Charles and Lady Diana
Obv: Similar to KM#27.
Rev: Portraits of Royal Couple, joined shields.

| 86 | 1981 | *.040 | — | Proof | 150.00 |

VIRENIUM
Peel

| 109 | 1983 | — | — | — | 2.50 |

4.6000 g, .925 SILVER, .1368 oz ASW
| 109a | 1983 | — | — | Proof | 15.00 |

9.5000 g, .374 GOLD, .1142 oz AGW
| 109b | 1983 | — | — | Proof | 75.00 |

7.9627 g, .917 GOLD, .2347 oz AGW
| 109c | 1983 | — | — | Proof | 150.00 |

9.0000 g, .950 PLATINUM, .2749 oz APW
| 109d | 1983 | — | — | Proof | 200.00 |

VIRENIUM
Castletown

| 128 | 1984 | — | — | — | 2.50 |

4.6000 g, .925 SILVER, .1368 oz ASW
| 128a | 1984 | — | — | — | 8.00 |
| | 1984 | — | — | Proof | 8.00 |

9.5000 g, .374 GOLD, .1142 oz AGW
KM#	Date	Mintage	VF	XF	Unc
128b	1984	*4,950	—	Proof	75.00

7.9627 g, .917 GOLD, .2347 oz AGW
| 128c | 1984 | *950 pcs. | — | Proof | 150.00 |

9.0000 g, .950 PLATINUM, .2749 oz APW
| 128d | 1984 | — | — | Proof | 200.00 |

4.6000 g, .925 SILVER, .1368 oz ASW
Ramsey
| 135 | 1985 | — | — | — | 10.00 |
| | 1985 | *5,000 | — | Proof | 10.00 |

7.9627 g, .917 GOLD, .2347 oz AGW
| 135b | 1985 | *150 pcs. | — | Proof | 175.00 |

9.0000 g, .950 PLATINUM, .2749 oz APW
| 135c | 1985 | *550 pcs. | — | Proof | 200.00 |

VIRENIUM
Ramsey
| 151 | 1985(t) | — | — | — | 2.50 |
| | 1985 | *.025 | — | Proof | 5.00 |

4.6000 g, .925 SILVER, .1368 oz ASW
Douglas
Obv: Similar to KM#109.
| 136 | 1986 | — | — | — | 10.00 |
| | 1986 | — | — | Proof | 15.00 |

7.9627 g, .917 GOLD, .2347 oz AGW
| 136b | 1986 | — | — | Proof | 150.00 |

9.0000 g, .950 PLATINUM, .2749 oz APW
| 136c | 1986 | — | — | Proof | 200.00 |

VIRENIUM
Douglas
| 175 | 1986 | — | — | — | 2.50 |
| | 1986 | *.025 | — | Proof | 5.00 |

| 182 | 1987 | — | — | — | 3.00 |

| 213 | 1988 | — | — | — | 3.00 |

2 POUNDS

15.9253 g, .917 GOLD, .4695 oz AGW

KM#	Date	Mintage	VF	XF	Unc
28	1973	3.612	—	—	235.00
	1973	1,250	—	Proof	250.00
	1974	1,257	—	—	250.00
	1974	2,500	—	Proof	235.00
	1975	456 pcs.	—	—	250.00
	1975	—	—	Proof	250.00
	1976	578 pcs.	—	—	250.00
	1976	—	—	Proof	250.00
	1977	—	—	—	250.00
	1977	1,250	—	Proof	235.00
	1978	1,250	—	Proof	250.00
	1979(t)	*2,000	—	—	235.00
	1979(t)	*.030	—	Proof	250.00
	1980(m)	*2,000	—	Proof	235.00
	1982(b)	*.015	—	—	235.00
	1982(b)	*5,000	—	—	235.00

Wedding of Prince Charles and Lady Diana
Obv: Similar to KM#28.
Rev: Portraits of Royal Couple, joined shields.
| 87 | 1981 | *5,000 | — | Proof | 275.00 |

VIRENIUM
Obv: Similar to KM#28. Rev: Tower of Refuge and Manx Shearwater in flight.
| 129 | 1984PM | — | — | Reported, not confirmed |

SILVER
| 129a | 1984PM | — | — | Reported, not confirmed |

VIRENIUM
Obv: Similar to 50 Pence, KM#148. Rev: Tower of Refuge and Manx Shearwater in flight.
| 149 | 1985 | — | — | Reported, not confirmed |

SILVER
| 149a | 1985 | — | — | Reported, not confirmed |

VIRENIUM
Tower of Refuge
| 167 | 1986 | — | — | — | 4.00 |
| | 1986 | — | — | Proof | 6.00 |

| 214 | 1988 | — | — | — | 4.00 |

5 POUNDS

ISLE OF MAN 1054

39.9403 g, .917 GOLD, 1.1776 oz AGW
200th Anniversary of Acquisition

KM#	Date	Mintage	VF	XF	Unc
17	1965	500 pcs.	—	—	625.00

39.9500 g, .980 GOLD, 1.2588 oz AGW

| 17a | 1965 | 1,000 | — | Proof | 650.00 |

39.8134 g, .917 GOLD, 1.1739 oz AGW

29	1973	3,035	—	—	600.00
	1973	1,250	—	Proof	625.00
	1974	481 pcs.	—	—	650.00
	1974	2,500	—	Proof	600.00
	1975	—	—	—	650.00
	1975	306 pcs.	—	Proof	650.00
	1976	370 pcs.	—	—	650.00
	1976	—	—	Proof	650.00
	1977	—	—	—	650.00
	1977	1,250	—	Proof	625.00
	1978	1,250	—	Proof	625.00
	1979(t)	*1,000	—	—	625.00
	1979(t)	*1,000	—	Proof	625.00
	1980(m)	*250 pcs.	—	—	650.00
	1982(b)	*.010	—	—	600.00
	1982(b)	*500 pcs.	—	Proof	625.00

VIRENIUM

| 88 | 1981 | *.030 | — | Proof | 10.00 |
| | 1983 | — | — | — | 20.00 |

23.5000 g, .925 SILVER, .6989 oz ASW

88a	1981	500 pcs.	—	Proof	40.00
	1982(b)	*1,000	—	Proof	35.00
	1983	*5,000	—	Proof	25.00

39.9000 g, .917 GOLD, 1.1764 oz AGW

KM#	Date	Mintage	VF	XF	Unc
88b	1981	*1,000	—	Proof	625.00
	1982(b)	*250 pcs.	—	Proof	650.00
	1982(b)	*750 pcs.	—	Proof	650.00
	1983	—	—	Proof	650.00

45.5000 g, .950 PLATINUM, 1.3898 oz APW

88c	1981	*500 pcs.	—	Proof	1000.00
	1982(b)	*100 pcs.	—	Proof	1100.00
	1983	—	—	Proof	1000.00

39.8134 g, .917 GOLD, 1.1739 oz AGW
Wedding of Prince Charles and Lady Diana
Obv: Similar to KM#29.
Rev: Portraits of Royal Couple, joined shields.

| 89 | 1981 | *1,000 | — | Proof | 650.00 |

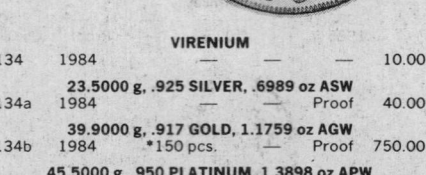

VIRENIUM

| 134 | 1984 | — | — | — | 10.00 |

23.5000 g, .925 SILVER, .6989 oz ASW

| 134a | 1984 | — | — | Proof | 40.00 |

39.9000 g, .917 GOLD, 1.1759 oz AGW

| 134b | 1984 | *150 pcs. | — | Proof | 750.00 |

45.5000 g, .950 PLATINUM, 1.3898 oz APW

| 134c | 1984 | — | — | Proof | 1100.00 |

VIRENIUM
Obv: Similar to 50 Pence, KM#148.

| 150 | 1985 | — | — | — | 10.00 |
| | 1985 | *.025 | — | — | 10.00 |

23.5000 g, .925 SILVER, .6989 oz ASW

| 150a | 1985 | *5,000 | — | Proof | 40.00 |

39.9000 g, .917 GOLD, 1.1759 oz AGW

| 150b | 1985 | *150 pcs. | — | Proof | 750.00 |

45.5000 g, .950 PLATINUM, 1.3898 oz APW

| 150c | 1985 | *100 pcs. | — | Proof | 1200.00 |

VIRENIUM

| 215 | 1988 | — | — | — | 10.00 |

BULLION ISSUES
POBJOY MINT

(M) MATTE - Normal circulation strike.
(U) SPECIAL UNCIRCULATED - Polished or proof-like in appearance, slightly frosted features.
(P) PROOF - The highest quality obtainable having mirror-like fields and frosted features.

SILVER BULLION ISSUES
5 CROWNS

155.5500 g, .999 SILVER, 5.0000 oz ASW
Reduced. Actual size: 65.1mm
U.S.A. Constitution
Obv: Similar to 1 Crown, KM#176.

KM#	Date	Mintage	VF	XF	Unc
177	1987	.012	—	—	175.00

Reduced. Actual size: 65mm
America's Cup
Obv: Similar to 1 Crown, KM#179.

| 180 | 1987 | 7,500 | — | Proof | 140.00 |

Reduced. Actual size: 65mm.
Steam Navigation.
Obv: Similar to 5 Pounds, KM#215.

| 206 | 1988 | — | — | — | 175.00 |

10 CROWNS

311.0350 g, .999 SILVER, 10.0000 oz ASW
Reduced. Actual size: 75mm
America's Cup
Obv: Similar to 1 Crown, KM#179.

KM#	Date	Mintage	VF	XF	Unc
181	1987	5,000	—	Proof	250.00

U.S. Constitution

| 188 | 1987 | 9,000 | — | Proof | 250.00 |

GOLD BULLION ISSUES
1/20 ANGEL

1.6970 g, .917 GOLD, .0500 oz AGW
Christmas

166	1986	—	—	—	40.00
	1986	5,000	—	Proof	50.00
	1987	—	—	—	40.00
	1987	—	—	Proof	50.00

Obv: Similar to 1 Noble, KM#205.

193	1988	—	—	—	35.00
	1988(pt)	—	—	—	45.00

1/10 ANGEL
3.3900 g, .917 GOLD, .1000 oz AGW
Similar to 1 Angel, KM#139.

| 138 | 1984 | 5,000 | — | Proof | 160.00 |

140	1985	8,000	—	—	60.00
	1985	3,000	—	Proof	115.00
	1986	—	—	—	60.00
	1986	—	—	Proof	115.00
	1987	—	—	—	60.00
	1987	—	—	Proof	115.00

159	1985	5,000	—	—	60.00
	1985 A	1,000	—	—	110.00
	1985 C	1,000	—	—	125.00
	1985 H	1,000	—	—	110.00
	1985 L	1,000	—	—	100.00
	1986 A	1,000	—	—	100.00
	1986 T	1,000	—	—	110.00
	1986 X	1,000	—	—	90.00
	1987 A	1,000	—	—	90.00
	1987 F	1,000	—	Proof	115.00
	1987 L	1,000	—	—	90.00
	1987(mt)	3,000	—	Proof	100.00
	1988 A	1,000	—	Proof	85.00

Obv: Similar to 1 Noble, KM#205.

| 194 | 1988 | — | — | — | 60.00 |

1/4 ANGEL

8.4830 g, .917 GOLD, .2500 oz AGW

KM#	Date	Mintage	VF	XF	Unc
152	1985	2,117	—	—	320.00
	1985	51 pcs.	—	Proof	450.00
	1986 L	1,000	—	—	200.00
	1986	—	—	Proof	175.00
	1987	—	—	—	150.00
	1987	—	—	Proof	200.00
	1987(s)	1,000	—	Proof	225.00
	1987(SL)	568 pcs.	—	Proof	180.00
	1987(BB)	1,000	—	Proof	200.00

Obv: Similar to 1 Noble, KM#205.

195	1988	—	—	—	150.00
	1988(f)	1,000	—	Proof	215.00
	1988(p)	1,000	—	Proof	215.00
	1988(ss)	1,000	—	Proof	215.00
	1989(p)	500 pcs.	—	Proof	200.00

1/2 ANGEL
16.9380 g, .917 GOLD, .5000 oz AGW

155	1985	1,776	—	—	270.00
	1985	51 pcs.	—	Proof	520.00
	1986	—	—	—	250.00
	1986	—	—	Proof	450.00
	1987	—	—	—	250.00
	1987	—	—	Proof	400.00

Obv: Similar to 1 Noble, KM#205.

| 196 | 1988 | — | — | — | 250.00 |

ANGEL

33.9300 g, .917 GOLD, 1.0000 oz AGW
Archangel Michael

| 139 | 1984 | 3,000 | — | Proof | 1050. |

141	1985	.028	—	—	450.00
	1985	—	—	P/L	450.00
	1985	3,000	—	Proof	925.00
	1986	—	—	—	450.00
	1986	—	—	Proof	925.00
	1987	—	—	—	450.00
	1987	—	—	Proof	925.00

Hong Kong Coin Show

| 191 | 1987 | 1,000 | — | Proof | 800.00 |

Obv: Similar to 1 Noble, KM#205.

197	1988	—	—	—	450.00
	1988(ss)	1,000	—	Proof	600.00

5 ANGEL
169.6680 g, .917 GOLD, 5.0000 oz AGW

156	1985	104 pcs.	—	—	3500.
	1985	90 pcs.	—	Proof	4000.
	1986	89 pcs.	—	—	3000.
	1986	250 pcs.	—	Proof	4000.
	1987	150 pcs.	—	—	3000.
	1987	27 pcs.	—	Proof	4000.

Obv: Similar to 1 Noble, KM#205.

| 198 | 1988 | 250 pcs. | — | — | 2750. |

10 ANGEL
339.3350 g, .917 GOLD, 10.0000 oz AGW

157	1985	79 pcs.	—	—	5500.
	1985	68 pcs.	—	Proof	8600.
	1986	47 pcs.	—	—	6000.
	1986	250 pcs.	—	Proof	8600.
	1987	150 pcs.	—	—	6000.
	1987	30 pcs.	—	Proof	8600.

Obv: Similar to 1 Noble, KM#205.

KM#	Date	Mintage	VF	XF	Unc
199	1988	250 pcs.	—	Proof	5500.

15 ANGEL
508.9575 g, .917 GOLD, 15.0000 oz AGW

189	1987	150 pcs.	—	—	9000.
	1987	18 pcs.	—	Proof	12,500.

Obv: Similar to 1 Noble, KM#205.

| 200 | 1988 | — | — | Proof | 12,500. |

20 ANGEL

678.6720 g, .917 GOLD, 20.0000 oz AGW
Reduced. Actual size: 75.2mm.

201	1988	250 pcs.	—	—	12,500.
	1988	100 pcs.	—	Proof	16,000.

GILT SILVER (OMS)

| 201a | 1988 | — | — | — | — |

PLATINUM BULLION ISSUES
1/10 NOBLE

3.1100 g, .999 PLATINUM, .1000 oz APW

137	1984	—	—	—	80.00
	1984	5,000	—	Proof	150.00

153	1985	.099	—	—	90.00
	1985	5,000	—	Proof	115.00
	1986	—	—	—	90.00
	1986	5,000	—	Proof	80.00
	1987	—	—	—	90.00
	1987	5,000	—	Proof	125.00

Obv: Similar to 1 Noble, KM#205.

| 202 | 1988 | 5,000 | — | — | 80.00 |

1/4 NOBLE
7.7757 g, .999 PLATINUM, .2500 oz APW

168	1986	2,015	—	Proof	175.00
	1987	—	—	Proof	250.00
	1987(l)	750 pcs.	—	Proof	175.00

Obv: Similar to 1 Noble, KM#205.

203	1988	—	—	—	175.00
	1988(p)	1,000	—	Proof	175.00
	1988(bb)	1,000	—	Proof	175.00
	1989(p)	500 pcs.	—	Proof	200.00

1/2 NOBLE
15.5514 g, .999 PLATINUM, .5000 oz APW

169	1986	15	—	Proof	500.00
	1987	—	—	Proof	350.00

Obv: Similar to 1 Noble, KM#205.

| 204 | 1988 | — | — | — | 400.00 |

ISLE OF MAN

NOBLE

31.1030 g, .999 PLATINUM, .9991 oz APW

KM#	Date	Mintage	VF	XF	Unc
110	1983	1,700	—	—	660.00
	1983	94 pcs.	—	Proof	2150.
	1984	—	—	—	660.00
	1984	2,000	—	Proof	1250.

154	1985	—	—	—	660.00
	1985	3,000	—	Proof	900.00
	1986	—	—	—	650.00
	1986	3,000	—	Proof	775.00
	1987	—	—	—	650.00
	1987	3,000	—	Proof	900.00

205	1988	3,000	—	—	775.00

5 NOBLE

155.5140 g, .999 PLATINUM, 5.0000 oz APW

KM#	Date	Mintage	VF	XF	Unc
170	1986	15 pcs.	—	Proof	4000.
	1987	11 pcs.	—	Proof	3500.
	1988	—	—	Proof	5400.

10 NOBLE

311.0280 g, .999 PLATINUM, 10.0000 oz APW

171	1986	15 pcs.	—	Proof	8000.
	1987	11 pcs.	—	Proof	7500.
	1988	—	—	Proof	10,000.

TOKEN ISSUES (Tn)

1/2 PENNY
COPPER
Obv: Peel Castle. Rev. large leg: DOUGLAS BANK TOKEN.

KM#	Date	Mintage	Fine	VF	XF	Unc
Tn1	1811	—	25.00	75.00	200.00	400.00

Rev. small leg: DOUGLAS BANK TOKEN.

Tn2	1811	—	30.00	100.00	325.00	500.00
	1811	—	—	—	Proof	650.00

Tn3	1811	—	4.00	10.00	40.00	75.00

BRONZE (OMS)

Tn3a	1811	—	—	—	Proof	—

BRASS

Tn3b	1811	—	10.00	25.00	100.00	175.00

Tn21	1831	—	10.00	35.00	100.00	

BRASS (OMS)

Tn21a	1831	—	—	—	Rare	

PENNY

COPPER, normal flan
Rev. leg: DOUGLAS BANK TOKEN.....

Tn6	1811	—	20.00	65.00	200.00	450.00
	1811	—	—	—	Proof	750.00

COPPER, thin flan

Tn7	1811	—	—	—	Proof	Rare

Normal flan.
Obv: Similar to KM#Tn6.
Rev. leg: DOUGLAS TOKEN.....

KM#	Date	Mintage	Fine	VF	XF	Unc
Tn8	1811	—	20.00	60.00	200.00	400.00
	1811	—	—	—	Proof	750.00

Thin flan.

Tn9	1811	—	—	—	Proof	—

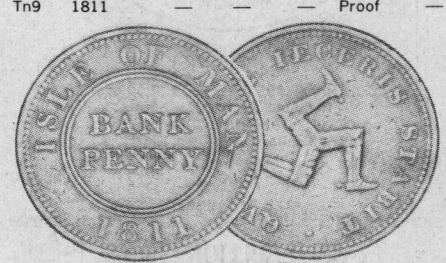

Tn10	1811	—	5.00	15.00	65.00	100.00
	1811	—	—	—	Proof	—

SHILLING
SILVER
Similar to 5 Shillings, KM#Tn14.

Tn12	1811	—	175.00	375.00	750.00	1200.
	1811	—	—	—	Proof	1500.

2 SHILLINGS 6 PENCE
SILVER
Similar to 5 Shillings, KM#Tn14.

Tn13	1811	—	250.00	500.00	1000.	1600.

COPPER

Tn13a	1811	—	—	—	Proof	Rare

5 SHILLINGS

SILVER

Tn14	1811	—	400.00	800.00	1600.	2500.
	1811	—	—	—	Proof	3000.

MINT SETS (MS)

KM#	Date	Mintage	Identification	Issue Price	Mkt. Val.
MS1	1965(3)	1,500	KM15-17	—	800.00
MS2	1971(6)	50,000	KM19-24	3.00	3.00
MS3	1973(4)	2,500	KM26-29	760.00	950.00
MS4	1974(4)	250	KM26-29	—	1100.
MS5	1975(6)	20,000	KM19-24	—	3.00
MS6	1975(6)	20,000	KM19a-24a	56.50	40.00
MS7	1975(4)	200	KM26-29	—	1100.
MS8	1976(6)	20,000	KM32-36,39	—	4.00
MS9	1976(6)	20,000	KM32a-36a,39a	—	37.50
MS10	1976(4)	—	KM26-29	—	1100.
MS11	1977(6)	50,000	KM33-36,39-40	—	4.00
MS12	1977(4)	180	KM26-29	—	1100.
MS13	1978(7)	10,000	KM32a-36a,39a,44a	—	50.00
MS14	1978(6)	—	KM32-36,39	—	4.00
MS15	1979(6)	—	KM32-34,35.1-36.1,39	—	5.00
MS16	1979(4)	—	KM26-29	—	1000.
MS17	1980(7)	—	KM44,58-62,70	—	5.00

KM#	Date	Mintage	Identification	Issue Price	Mkt. Val.
MS18	1981(6)	—	KM58-62,70	—	5.00
MS19	1982(7)	—	—	—	6.00
MS20	1983(9)	—	KM58-62,70,88,90,109	—	20.00

PROOF SETS (PS)

PS1	1965(3)	1,000	KM15a-17a	—	750.00
PS2	1971(6)	10,000	KM19-24	20.00	20.00
PS3	1973(4)	1,250	KM26-29	950.00	1075.
PS4	1974(4)	2,500	KM26-29	900.00	1050.
PS5	1975(6)	600	KM19b-24b	1175.	2175.
PS6	1975(4)	—	KM26-29	—	1100.
PS7	1976(6)	600	KM32b-34b,35.1b,36b,39b	—	2175.
PS8	1976(4)	—	KM26-29	—	1100.
PS9	1977(6)	10,000	KM33a-36a,39a,40a	—	45.00
PS10	1977(4)	1,250	KM26-29	—	1100.
PS11	1978(7)	—	KM32-36,39,44	—	15.00
PS12	1978(7)	600	KM32b-34b,35.1b,36b,39b,44b	—	2375.
PS13	1979(7)	10,000	KM32a-36a,39a,44a	110.00	50.00
PS14	1979(7)	500	KM32b-34b,35.1b,36b,39b,44b	2765.	2375.
PS15	1979(4)	1,000	KM26-29	—	1100.
PS16	1980(7)	—	KM44a,58a-62a,70a	—	50.00
PS17	1980(7)	—	KM44c,58b-62b,70b	—	170.00
PS18	1980(7)	—	KM44b,58c-62c,70c	—	1825.
PS19	1982(9)	1,000	KM44a,58a-62a,88a,90a	—	130.00
PS20	1982(9)	250	KM44c,58b-62b,88b,90b	—	1075.
PS21	1982(9)	100	KM44b,58c-62c,88c,90c	—	2650.
PS22	1982(7)	25,000	KM58-62,70,90	—	15.00
PS23	1982(7)	9,000	KM58a-62a,70a,90a	—	60.00
PS24	1982(7)	250	KM58b-62b,70b,90b	—	245.00
PS25	1982(7)	400	KM58-62,70c,90c	—	1900.
PS26	1983(9)	—	KM58a-62d,90a,109a	—	1575.
PS27	1983(9)	—	KM58b-62b,90b,109b	—	300.00
PS28	1983(9)	—	KM58-62c,90c,109c	—	1450.
PS29	1985(9)	25,000	KM142-148,150-151	36.00	36.00
PS30	1985(9)	5,000	KM135,142a-148a,150a	120.00	120.00
PS31	1985(9)	150	KM135b,142b-148b,150b	3240.	3500.
PS32	1985(9)	100	KM135c,142c-148c,150c	3600.	3850.
PS33	1985(7)	25,000	KM142-148	20.00	20.00
PS34	1985(7)	5,000	KM142a-148a	72.00	72.00
PS35	1985(7)	150	KM142b-148b	2160.	2200.
PS36	1985(7)	100	KM142c-148c	2400.	2450.
PS37	1985(6)	51	KM140-141,152,155-157	—	11,000.
PS38	1986(7)	17	KM140-141,152,155-157,166	—	12,000.
PS39	1986(6)	15	KM153-154,168-171	—	16,000.
PS40	1986(4)	2000	KM153-154,168-169	1950.	2000.
PS41	1986(5)	2500	KM140-141,152,166	—	16.50
PS42	1987(4)	—	KM176a,177,187-188	—	1125.
PS43	1987(4)	30	KM140-141,152,155-157	—	13,000.
PS44	1987(5)	—	KM140-141,152,155,166	—	1800.
PS45	1987(4)	3000	KM140-141,152,155	—	1750.
PS46	1987(6)	11 pcs.	KM153-154,168-169,170-171	—	16,000.
PS47	1987(4)	2500	KM153-154,168-169	—	2000.
PS48	1988(5)	5000	KM235-239	—	1450.

ISRAEL

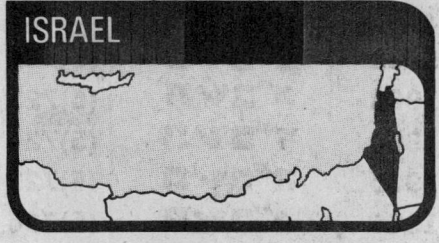

The state of Israel, a Middle Eastern republic at the eastern end of the Mediterranean Sea, bounded by Lebanon on the north, Syria on the northeast, Jordan on the east, and Egypt on the southwest, has an area of 9,000 sq. mi. (23,309 sq. km.) and a population of *4.5 million. Capital: Jerusalem. Finished diamonds, chemicals, citrus, textiles, and minerals are exported.

Palestine, which corresponds to Canaan of the Bible, was settled by the Philistines about the 12th century B.C. and shortly thereafter was invaded by the Jews who established the kingdoms of Israel and Judah. Because of its position as part of the land bridge connecting Asia and Africa, Palestine was invaded and conquered by nearly all of the historic empires of ancient Europe and Asia. In the 16th century it became a part of the Ottoman Empire. After falling to the British in World War I, it, together with Transjordan, was mandated to Great Britain by the League of Nations, 1922.

For more than half a century prior to the termination of the British mandate over Palestine, 1948, Zionist leaders had sought to create a Jewish homeland for Jews dispersed throughout the world. For almost as long, Jews fleeing persecution had immigrated to Palestine. The Nazi persecutions of the 1930s and 1940s increased the Jewish movement to Palestine and generated international support for the creation of a Jewish state, first promulgated by the Balfour Declaration of 1917 which asserted British support for the endeavor. The dream of a Jewish homeland was realized on May 14, 1948 when Palestine was proclaimed the State of Israel.

TITLES

فلسطين

Filastin

MONETARY SYSTEM
1000 Mils = 1 Pound

PALESTINE
MIL

BRONZE

KM#	Date	Mintage	Fine	VF	XF	Unc
1	1927	10.000	.75	1.50	3.00	15.00
	1927	66 pcs.	—	—	Proof	400.00
	1935	.704	1.50	3.00	6.00	25.00
	1937	1.200	2.00	5.00	25.00	100.00
	1939	3.700	1.00	2.00	5.00	25.00
	1939	—	—	—	Proof	300.00
	1940	.396	8.50	15.00	25.00	100.00
	1941	1.920	1.00	2.00	5.00	20.00
	1942	4.480	1.00	2.00	4.00	15.00
	1943	2.800	1.00	2.00	4.00	15.00
	1944	1.400	1.00	2.00	5.00	20.00
	1946	1.632	1.00	3.00	7.00	30.00
	1946	—	—	—	Proof	450.00
	1947	*2.880	—	—	—	10,500.

*NOTE: Only 5 known. The entire issue was to be melted down.

2 MILS

BRONZE

2	1927	5.000	1.00	2.50	8.00	20.00
	1927	66 pcs.	—	—	Proof	350.00
	1941	1.600	1.00	3.00	10.00	30.00
	1941	—	—	—	Proof	250.00
	1942	2.400	1.00	3.00	6.00	20.00
	1945	.960	2.00	10.00	25.00	100.00
	1946	.960	5.00	10.00	25.00	100.00
	1947	*.480				

*NOTE: The entire issue was melted down.

5 MILS

COPPER-NICKEL

KM#	Date	Mintage	Fine	VF	XF	Unc
3	1927	10.000	1.00	2.00	8.00	25.00
	1927	66 pcs.	—	—	Proof	300.00
	1934	.500	10.00	20.00	50.00	200.00
	1935	2.700	1.00	3.00	15.00	40.00
	1939	2.000	1.00	3.00	9.00	30.00
	1939	—	—	—	Proof	300.00
	1941	.400	10.00	20.00	50.00	200.00
	1941	—	—	—	Proof	200.00
	1946	1.000	2.00	4.00	9.00	30.00
	1946	—	—	—	Proof	200.00
	1947	*1.000				

*NOTE: The entire issue was melted down.

BRONZE

3a	1942	2.700	2.00	4.00	15.00	40.00
	1944	1.000	2.00	4.00	15.00	35.00

10 MILS

COPPER-NICKEL

4	1927	5.000	1.00	3.00	15.00	45.00
	1927	66 pcs.	—	—	Proof	275.00
	1933	.500	10.00	30.00	100.00	350.00
	1933	—	—	—	Proof	400.00
	1934	.500	10.00	30.00	100.00	375.00
	1934	—	—	—	Proof	400.00
	1935	1.150	2.00	10.00	50.00	150.00
	1935	—	—	—	Proof	300.00
	1937	.750	4.00	8.00	35.00	150.00
	1937	—	—	—	Proof	300.00
	1939	1.000	2.00	7.00	30.00	100.00
	1939	—	—	—	Proof	275.00
	1940	1.500	2.00	7.00	30.00	100.00
	1940	—	—	—	Proof	250.00
	1941	.400	12.50	25.00	50.00	200.00
	1941	—	—	—	Proof	300.00
	1942	.600	4.00	8.00	30.00	100.00
	1946	1.000	5.00	10.00	20.00	75.00
	1946	—	—	—	Proof	200.00
	1947	*1.000				

*NOTE: The entire issue was melted down.

BRONZE

4a	1942	1.000	2.50	10.00	40.00	150.00
	1943	1.000	4.00	8.00	45.00	200.00

20 MILS

COPPER-NICKEL

5	1927	1.500	7.00	15.00	35.00	100.00
	1927	66 pcs.	—	—	Proof	300.00
	1933	.250	15.00	40.00	100.00	350.00
	1934	.125	55.00	90.00	200.00	600.00
	1934	—	—	—	Proof	
	1935	.575	8.50	50.00	100.00	300.00
	1940	.200	20.00	40.00	90.00	500.00
	1940	—	—	—	*	650.00
	1941	.100	50.00	75.00	175.00	1000.
	1941	—	—	—	Proof	1100.

BRONZE

5a	1942	1.100	8.50	20.00	40.00	150.00
	1944	1.000	20.00	50.00	110.00	500.00

50 MILS

Palestine/ISRAEL

5.8319 g, .720 SILVER, .1350 oz ASW

KM#	Date	Mintage	Fine	VF	XF	Unc
6	1927	8.000	5.00	10.00	15.00	60.00
	1927	66 pcs.			Proof	350.00
	1931	.500	17.50	35.00	85.00	400.00
	1933	1.000	8.50	15.00	30.00	90.00
	1934	.399	15.00	30.00	50.00	125.00
	1935	5.600	5.00	10.00	15.00	45.00
	1939	3.000	3.50	7.50	10.00	25.00
	1939	—	—	—	Proof	175.00
	1940	2.000	6.00	12.50	22.50	60.00
	1940	—	—	—	Proof	150.00
	1942	5.000	3.50	7.50	15.00	40.00

100 MILS

11.6638 g, .720 SILVER, .2700 oz ASW

7	1927	2.000	8.50	15.00	30.00	90.00
	1927	66 pcs.			Proof	600.00
	1931	.250	45.00	100.00	300.00	1250.
	1931	—	—	—	Proof	1250.
	1933	.500	20.00	40.00	100.00	400.00
	1934	.200	90.00	175.00	300.00	750.00
	1935	2.850	8.50	12.50	25.00	75.00
	1939	1.500	8.50	12.50	25.00	65.00
	1939	—	—	—	Proof	300.00
	1940	1.000	8.50	12.50	25.00	65.00
	1942	2.500	8.50	12.50	25.00	75.00

MINT SETS (MS)

KM#	Date	Mintage	Identification	Issue Price	Mkt. Val.
MS1	1927(14)	—	KM1-7, two each	—	1650.

PROOF SETS (PS)

PS1	1927(14)	34	KM1-7, two each, original case	—	6500.
PS2	1927(7)	4	KM1-7, original case	—	4000.

ISRAEL

HEBREW COIN DATING

Modern Israel's coins carry Hebrew dating formed from a combination of the 22 consonant letters of the Hebrew alphabet and read from right to left. The Jewish calendar dates back more than 5700 years, but only five milleniums are assumed in the dating of coins. Thus, the year 5735 (1975AD) appears as 735, with the first two characters from the right indicating the number of years in hundreds; tav (400), plus shin (300). The next is lamedh (30), followed by a separation mark which has the appearance of double quotation marks, then heh (5).

The separation mark - generally similar to a single quotation mark through 5718 (1958 AD), and like a double quotation mark thereafter - serves the purpose of indicating that the letters form a number, not a word, and on some issues can be confused with the character yodh (10), which in a stylized rendering can appear quite similar, although slightly larger and thicker. The separation mark does not appear in either form on a few commemorative issues.

The Jewish New Year falls in September or October by Christian calendar reckoning. Where dual dating is encountered, with but a few exceptions the Hebrew dating on the coins of modern Israel is 3760 years greater than the Christian dating; 5735 is equivalent to 1975AD, with the 5000 assumed until 1981, when full dates appear on the coins. These exceptions are most of the Hanukka coins, (Feast of Lights), the Bank of Israel gold 50 Pound commemorative of 5725 (1964AD) and others. In such special instances the differential from Christian dating is 3761 years, except in the instance of the 5720 Chanuka Pound, which is dated 1960AD, as is the issue of 5721, an arrangement which reflects the fact that the events fall early in the Jewish year and late in the Christian.

The Star of David is not a mint mark. It appears only on some coins sold by the Government Coin and Medal Co. for collectors. It was first used in 1971 on the science coin to signify that it was minted in Jerusalem, but was later used by different mint facilities.

1957	תש"ד	(5)717
1958	תשי"ח	(5)718
1958	תשי"ח	(5)718
1959	תשי"ט	(5)719
1959	תשי"ט	(5)719
1960	תש"ך	(5)720
1960	תשר	(5)720
1961	תשכ"א	(5)721
1962	תשכ"ב	(5)722
1963	תשכ"ג	(5)723
1964	תשכ"ד	(5)724
1965	תשכ"ה	(5)725
1966	תשכ"ו	(5)726
1967	תשכ"ז	(5)727
1968	תשכ"ח	(5)728
1969	תשכ"ט	(5)729
1970	תש"ל	(5)730
1971	תשל"א	(5)731
1972	תשל"ב	(5)732
1973	תשל"ג	(5)733
1974	תשל"ד	(5)734
1975	תשל"ה	(5)735
1976	תשל"ו	(5)736
1977	תשל"ז	(5)737
1978	תשל"ח	(5)738
1979	תשל"ט	(5)739
1980	תש"ם	(5)740
1981	תשמ"א	(5)741
1981	התשמ"א	5741
1982	התשמ"ב	5742
1983	התשמ"ג	5743
1984	התשמ"ד	5744
1985	התשמ"ה	5745
1986	התשמ"ו	5746
1987	התשמ"ד	5757
1988	התשמ"ח	5748
1989	התשמ"ט	5749
1990	התש"ד	5750

MINT MARKS

(o) - Ottawa
None - Jerusalem

(M) MATTE - Normal circulation strike or a dull finish produced by sandblasting special uncirculated (polish finish) or proof quality dies.

(U) SPECIAL UNCIRCULATED - Polished or proof-like in appearance without any frosted features.

(P) PROOF - The highest quality obtainable having mirror-like fields and frosted features.

MONETARY SYSTEM
1000 Mils = 1 Pound

25 MILS

ALUMINUM

KM#	Date	Year	Mintage	VF	XF	Unc
8	5708	(1948)	.043	100.00	250.00	1000.
	5709	(1949)	open link .650	20.00	50.00	150.00
	5709	(1949)	closed link			
				12.50	20.00	35.00

NOTE: Above 3 coins were issued April 6, 1949.

MONETARY REFORM
1000 Prutot = 1 Lira

NOTE: The 1949 Prutot coins, except for the 100 and 500 Prutot values, occur with and without a small pearl under the bar connecting the wreath on the reverse.

PRUTA

ALUMINUM

KM#	Date	Year	Mintage	VF	XF	Unc
9	5709	(1949)	w/pearl 5.185	.50	1.00	2.00
	5709	(1949)	w/o pearl Inc. Ab.	1.00	2.50	10.00

5 PRUTOT

BRONZE

10	5709	(1949)	w/pearl 10.045	.50	1.00	2.00
	5709	(1949)	w/o pearl Inc. Ab.	.50	2.00	8.00

10 PRUTOT

BRONZE

11	5709	(1949)	w/pearl 14.948	2.50	10.00	30.00
	5709	(1949)	w/o pearl Inc. Ab.	.50	1.00	4.00

ALUMINUM

17	5712	(1952)	26.042	.25	.75	2.00

20	5717	(1957)	1.000	.25	.75	2.00

COPPER ELECTROPLATED ALUMINUM

20a	5717	(1957)	1.088	.25	.75	2.00

25 PRUTOT

COPPER-NICKEL

KM#	Date	Year	Mintage	VF	XF	Unc
12	5709	(1949)	w/pearl			
			13.020	.50	.75	2.00
	5709	(1949)	w/o pearl			
			Inc. Ab.	5.00	10.00	30.00

NICKEL-CLAD STEEL

| 12a | 5714 | (1954) | 3.697 | .50 | 1.00 | 2.00 |

50 PRUTOT

COPPER-NICKEL
Reeded edge

13.1	5709	(1949)	w/pearl			
			12.040	5.00	10.00	25.00
	5709	(1949)	w/o pearl			
			Inc. Ab.	.75	1.50	3.00
	5714	(1954)	.250	10.00	17.50	35.00

Plain edge

| 13.2 | 5714 | (1954) | 4.500 | .50 | 1.00 | 2.00 |

NICKEL-CLAD STEEL

| 13.2a | 5714 | (1954) | 17.774 | .50 | 1.00 | 2.00 |

100 PRUTOT

COPPER-NICKEL

14	5709	(1949)	6.062	.75	1.25	2.50
	5715	(1955)	5.868	.75	1.25	2.50

NICKEL-CLAD STEEL
Reduced size, 25.6mm -Bern die-
Rev: Large wreath, close to edge.

| 18 | 5714 | (1954) | .700 | 1.00 | 2.00 | 3.00 |

Utrecht die. Rev: Small wreath, away from edge.

| 19 | 5714 | (1954) | .020 | 300.00 | 450.00 | 1000 |

250 PRUTOT

COPPER-NICKEL

15	5709	(1949)	w/pearl			
			2.020	2.50	7.50	15.00
	5709	(1949)	w/o pearl			
			Inc. Ab.	1.00	2.00	4.00

14.4000 g, .500 SILVER, .2315 oz ASW

| 15a | 5709H | (1949) | .044 | 5.00 | 7.50 | 10.00 |

NOTE: Not placed into circulation.

500 PRUTOT

25.5000 g, .500 SILVER, .4099 oz ASW

KM#	Date	Year	Mintage	VF	XF	Unc
16	5709	(1949)	.034	10.00	15.00	25.00

NOTE: Not placed into circulation.

MONETARY REFORM
Commencing January 1, 1960
100 Agorot = 1 Lira

AGORA

1960 normal date

1960 large date

1961 thick date

1961 wide date

1962 large date

1962 small date

ALUMINUM

24.1	5720	(1960)	"Lamed" w/serif			
			12.768	2.50	5.00	10.00
	5720	(1960)	"Lamed" w/o lower serif			
			Inc. Ab.	10.00	20.00	100.00

KM#	Date	Year	Mintage	VF	XF	Unc
24.1	5720	(1960)	large date			
			300 pcs.	150.00	300.00	750.00
	5721	(1961)	19.262	.50	3.00	7.50
	5721	(1961)	thick date			
			Inc. Ab.	5.00	15.00	100.00
	5721	(1961)	wide date			
			Inc. Ab.	5.00	15.00	100.00
	5722	(1962)	large date			
			14.500	.10		1.00
	5722	(1962)	small date, small serifs			
			Inc. Ab.	2.50	5.00	15.00
	5723	(1963)	14.804	.10	.50	1.00
	5723	(1963)	inverted reverse			
			.010	4.00	8.00	15.00
	5724	(1964)	27.552	—	—	1.00
	5725	(1965)	20.708	—	—	.25
	5726	(1966)	10.165	—	—	.25
	5727	(1967)	6.781	—	—	.25
	5728	(1968)	20.899	—	—	.25
	5729	(1969)	22.120	—	—	.25
	5730	(1970)	17.748	—	—	.25
	5731	(1971)	10.290	.25	—	.25
	5732	(1972)	24.512	—	—	.25
	5733	(1973)	20.496	—	—	.25
	5734	(1974)	42.080	—	—	.25
	5735	(1975)	1.574	—	—	.25
	5736	(1976)	4.512	—	—	.25
	5737	1977	9.680	—	—	.25
	5738	1978	8.864	—	—	.25
	5739	1979	4.048	—	—	.25
	5740	1980	2.600	—	—	1.25

Obv: Star of David in field.

24.2	5731	(1971)	.175	—	—	.25
	5732	(1972)	.100	—	—	.25
	5734	(1974)	.100	—	—	.25
	5735	(1975)	.100	—	—	.25
	5736	(1976)	.070	—	—	.25
	5737	(1977)	.060	—	—	.25
	5738	(1978)	.057	—	.10	.25
	5739	(1979)	.050	—	.10	.25

25th Anniversary of Independence

| 63 | 5733 | (1973) | .100 | In sets only | | .25 |

NICKEL
25th Anniversary of Bank of Israel

| 96 | 5740 | 1980 | .035 | — | — | .25 |
| | 5740 | 1980 | Inc. Ab. | — | Proof | 1.00 |

5 AGOROT

1961 normal   1961 I.C.I.

ALUMINUM-BRONZE

25	5720	(1960)	8.019	2.00	10.00	15.00
	5721	(1961)	sharp, flat date			
			15.090	.25	.50	1.50
	5721	(1961)	I.C.I. issue w/high date w/serifs			
			5.000	15.00	25.00	100.00
	5722	(1962)	large date			
			11.198	.25	.50	1.00
	5722	(1962)	small date			
			Inc. Ab.	4.00	8.00	15.00
	5723	(1963)	1.429	—	—	1.50
	5724	(1964)	.021	15.00	100.00	300.00
	5725	(1965)	.201	—	.10	.25
	5726	(1966)	.291	—	.10	.25
	5727	(1967)	2.195	—	.10	.25
	5728	(1968)	4.020	—	.10	.25
	5729	(1969)	2.200	—	.10	.25
	5730	(1970)	4.004	—	.10	.25
	5731	(1971)	14.010	—	.10	.25
	5732	(1972)	9.005	—	.10	.25
	5733	(1973)	25.720	—	.10	.25
	5734	(1974)	10.470	—	.10	.25
	5735	(1975)	10.232	—	.10	.25

Obv: Star of David in field.

| 25a | 5731 | (1971) | .126 | — | .10 | .25 |
| | 5732 | (1972) | .069 | — | .10 | .25 |

COPPER-NICKEL

25c	5734	(1974)	.093	In sets only		.25
	5735	(1975)	.062	In sets only		.25
	5736	(1976)	—	In sets only		.25
	5737	(1977)	.060	In sets only		.25

ISRAEL 1060

KM#	Date	Year	Mintage	VF	XF	Unc
25c	5738	(1978)	128 pcs.	—	—	.50
	5739	(1979)	.018			.25

ALUMINUM

25b	5736(M)	(1976)	13.156	—	.10	.25
	5737(M)	(1977)	16.800	—	.10	.25
	5737(o)	(1977)	15.000	—	.10	.25
	5738(M)	(1978)	21.480	—	.10	.25
	5738(o)(U)	(1978)	38.760	—	.10	.25
	5739(M)	(1979)	12.836	—	.10	.25

COPPER-NICKEL
25th Anniversary of Independence

64	5733	(1973)	.100	In sets only	.50

NICKEL
25th Anniversary of Bank of Israel

97	5740	1980	.035	—	.10	.25
	5740	1980	Inc. Ab.	—	Proof	1.00

10 AGOROT

ALUMINUM-BRONZE

26	5720	(1960)	14.397	.50	1.00	10.00
	5721	(1961)	12.821	.50	1.00	8.00
	5721	(1961)	"Fatha" in Arabic, leg: "Israel"			
			Inc. Ab.	30.00	80.00	325.00

Large date-thick letters   Small date-thin letters

5722	(1962)	large date, thick letters			
		8.845	.25	.50	1.25
5722	(1962)	small date, thin letters			
		Inc. Ab.	2.50	5.00	15.00
5723	(1963)	3.931	.25	.50	1.25
5724	(1964)	large date			
		3.612	.25	.50	1.25
5724	(1964)	small date			
		Inc. Ab.	5.00	15.00	35.00
5725	(1965)	.201	—	.20	.25
5726	(1966)	7.276	—	.10	.25
5727	(1967)	6.426	—	.10	.25
5728	(1968)	4.825	—	.10	.25
5729	(1969)	6.810	—	.10	.25
5730	(1970)	6.131	—	.10	.25
5731	(1971)	6.810	—	.10	.25
5732	(1972)	19.653	—	.10	.25
5733	(1973)	16.205	—	.10	.25
5734	(1974)	22.040	—	.10	.25
5735	(1975)	25.135	—	.10	.25
5736	(1976)	54.870	—	.10	.25
5737	(1977)	27.886	—	.10	.25

COPPER-NICKEL
Obv: Star of David in field.

26a	5731	(1971)	.175	—	.10	.25
	5732	(1972)	.100	—	.10	.25

COPPER-NICKEL

26c	5734	(1974)	.100	In sets only	.25
	5735	(1975)	.100	In sets only	.25
	5736	(1976)	.070	In sets only	.25
	5737	(1977)	.060	In sets only	.25
	5738	(1978)	.057	In sets only	.25
	5739	(1979)	—	In sets only	.25

ALUMINUM

26b	5737(o)(U)	(1977)	30.100	—	.10	.25
	5738(M)	(1978)	24.050	—	.10	.25
	5738(o)(U)	(1978)	104.336	—	.10	.25
	5739	(1979)	22.201	—	.10	.25
	5740	(1980)	4.752	—	.10	.25

NOTE: Most of the 5740 dated coins were melted down before being issued.

COPPER-NICKEL
25th Anniversary of Independence

65	5733	(1973)	.100	In sets only	.75

NICKEL
25th Anniversary of Bank of Israel

KM#	Date	Year	Mintage	VF	XF	Unc
98	5740	1980	.035	—	.10	.25
	5740	1980	Inc. Ab.	—	Proof	1.00

25 AGOROT

ALUMINUM-BRONZE

27	5720	(1960)	4.391	.25	.50	2.50
	5721	(1961)	5.009	.10	.20	1.00
	5722	(1962)	.882	.15	.30	1.00
	5723	(1963)	.194	.50	1.00	4.00
	5724	(1964)	Five trial pieces only			
	5725	(1965)	.187	.10	.20	.50
	5726	(1966)	.320	—	.10	.40
	5727	(1967)	.325	—	.10	.40
	5728	(1968)	.445	—	.10	.40
	5729	(1969)	.432	—	.10	.40
	5730	(1970)	.417	—	.10	.40
	5731	(1971)	.500	—	.10	.40
	5732	(1972)	1.883	—	.10	.40
	5733	(1973)	3.370	—	.10	.40
	5734	(1974)	2.320	—	.10	.40
	5735	(1975)	3.968	—	.10	.40
	5736	(1976)	3.901	—	.10	.40
	5737	(1977)	1.832	—	.10	.40
	5738	(1978)	12.200	—	.10	.40
	5739	(1979)	10.842	—	.10	.40

Obv: Star of David in field.

27a	5731	(1971)	.126	—	.10	.40
	5732	(1972)	.069	—	.10	.40

COPPER-NICKEL

27b	5734	(1974)	.093	In sets only	.40
	5735	(1975)	.062	In sets only	.40
	5736	(1976)	—	In sets only	.40
	5737	(1977)	.060	In sets only	.40
	5738	(1978)	.057	In sets only	.40
	5739	(1979)	.032	In sets only	.40

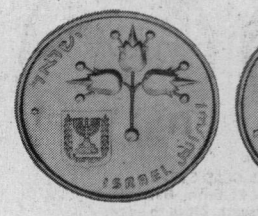

25th Anniversary of Independence

66	5733	(1973)	.100	In sets only	.75

NICKEL
25th Anniversary of Bank of Israel

99	5740	1980	.035	—	.10	.40
	5740	1980	Inc. Ab.	—	Proof	1.00

1/2 LIRA (Pound)

COPPER-NICKEL

36.1	5723	(1963)	large animals			
			5.607	2.00	10.00	15.00
	5723	(1963)	small animals			
			Inc. Ab.	3.00	15.00	30.00
	5724	(1964)	3.762	.10	.75	2.50
	5725	(1965)	1.551	.10	.15	1.00
	5726	(1966)	2.139	.10	.15	.50
	5727	(1967)	1.942	.10	.15	.50
	5728	(1968)	1.183	.10	.15	.50
	5729	(1969)	.450	.10	.20	.60
	5730	(1970)	1.001	.10	.20	.60
	5731	(1971)	.500	.10	.20	.60
	5732	(1972)	.421	.10	.20	.60
	5733	(1973)	3.225	.10	.15	.50
	5734	(1974)	4.275	.10	.15	.50
	5735	(1975)	11.066	.10	.15	.50
	5736	(1976)	4.959	.10	.15	.50
	5737	(1977)	4.983	.10	.15	.50
	5738	(1978)	14.325	.10	.15	.50
	5739	(1979)	21.391	.10	.15	.50

Obv: Star of David in field.

36.2	5731	(1971)	.175	In sets only	.50
	5732	(1972)	.100	In sets only	.50
	5734	(1974)	.100	In sets only	.50
	5735	(1975)	.100	In sets only	.50

KM#	Date	Year	Mintage	VF	XF	Unc
36.2	5736	(1976)	.070	In sets only	.50
	5737	(1977)	.060	In sets only	.50
	5738	(1978)	.057	In sets only	.50
	5739	(1979)	.050	In sets only	.50

25th Anniversary of Independence

67	5733	(1973)	.100	In sets only	.75

NICKEL
25th Anniversary of Bank of Israel

100	5740	1980	.035	.10	.15	.50
	5740	1980	Inc. Ab.	—	Proof	2.00

LIRA (Pound)

COPPER-NICKEL

37	5723	(1963)	large animals			
			4.212	.50	2.00	5.00
	5723	(1963)	small animals			
			Inc. Ab.	1.00	10.00	20.00
	5724	(1964)	Only ten trial pieces struck			
	5725	(1965)	.166	.25	.50	1.00
	5726	(1966)	.290	.25	.50	1.00
	5727	(1967)	.180	.25	.50	1.00

47.1	5727	(1967)	3.830	.10	.25	.75
	5728	(1968)	3.932	.10	.25	.75
	5729	(1969)	12.484	.10	.25	.75
	5730	(1970)	4.794	.10	.25	.75
	5731	(1971)	2.993	.10	.25	.75
	5732	(1972)	2.489	.10	.25	.75
	5733	(1973)	10.265	.10	.25	.75
	5734	(1974)	6.287	.10	.25	.75
	5735	(1975)	13.225	.10	.25	.75
	5736	(1976)	4.268	.10	.25	.75
	5737	(1977)	11.129	.10	.25	.75
	5738	(1978)	61.752	.10	.25	.75
	5739	(1979)	34.815	.10	.25	.75
	5740	(1980)	10.840	.10	.25	.75

NOTE: Most of the 5740 dated coins were melted down before being issued.

Obv: Star of David in field.

47.2	5731	(1971)	.126	In sets only	.75
	5732	(1972)	.069	In sets only	.75
	5734	(1974)	.093	In sets only	.75
	5735	(1975)	.062	In sets only	.75
	5736	(1976)	—	In sets only	.75
	5737	(1977)	Inc. Ab.	In sets only	.75
	5738	(1978)	Inc. Ab.	In sets only	.75
	5739	(1979)	—	In sets only	.75

COMMEMORATIVE COINAGE

NOTE: All proof commemoratives with the exception of the 1 and 5 Lirot issues of 1958 and the gold 100 Lirot Jerusalem 1968 issues are distinguished from the uncirculated editions by the presence of the Hebrew letter "mem".

ISRAEL 1061

1/2 LIRA

COPPER-NICKEL
Feast Of Purim

KM#	Date	Year	Mintage	VF	XF	Unc
31	5721	(1961)	.020	—	—	15.00
	5721	(1961)	4,901	—	Proof	25.00
	5722	(1962)	.020	—	—	10.00
	5722	(1962)	9,894	—	Proof	17.50

LIRA (Pound)

COPPER-NICKEL
Chanuka-Law Is Light

22	5719	1958	.150	—	—	2.50
	5719	1958	5,000	—	Proof	40.00

Deganya

28	5720	1960	.049	—	—	4.00
	5720	1960	4,702	—	Proof	35.00

Henrietta Szold

32	5721	1960	.017	—	—	35.00
	5721	1960	3,000	—	Proof	175.00

Heroism And Sacrifice

34	5722	1961	.019	—	—	12.50
	5722	1961	9,324	—	Proof	20.00

Chanuka - Italian Lamp

38	5723	1962	9,560	—	—	30.00
	5723	1962	5,941	—	Proof	50.00

18th Century
Chanuka-North Africa Lamp

KM#	Date	Year	Mintage	VF	XF	Unc
42	5724	1963	9,928	—	—	30.00
	5724	1963	5,412	—	Proof	50.00

25th Anniversary of Independence

68	5733	(1973)	.100	In sets only	1.00

NICKEL
25th Anniversary of Bank of Israel
Plain edge.

101.1	5740	1980	.035	—	—	3.00

Reeded edge.

101.2	5740	1980	Inc. Ab.	—	Proof	4.00

5 LIROT (POUNDS)

25.0000 g, .900 SILVER, .7234 oz ASW
10th Anniversary-Menora

21	5718	1958	.098	—	—	12.50
	5718	1958	2,000	—	Proof	450.00

11th Anniversary
Ingathering Of The Exiles

23	5719	1959	.027	—	—	22.50
	5719	1959	4,682	—	Proof	40.00

12th Anniversary-Dr. Theodor Herzl

29	5720	1960	.034	—	—	20.00
	5720	1960	4,827	—	Proof	45.00

13th Anniversary-Bar Mitzvah

KM#	Date	Year	Mintage	VF	XF	Unc
33	5721	1961	.019	—	—	50.00
	5721	1961	4,455	—	Proof	70.00

14th Anniversary
Negev Industrialization

35	5722	1962	.010	—	—	40.00
	5722	1962	4,960	—	Proof	60.00

15th Anniversary-Seafaring

39	5723	1963	5,960	—	—	325.00
	5723	1963	4,495	—	Proof	375.00

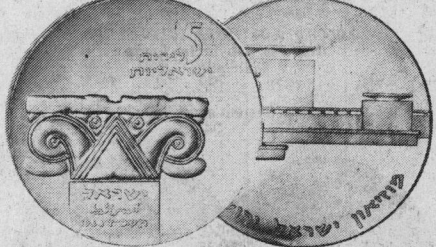

16th Anniversary-Israel Museum

43	5724	1964	.011	—	—	50.00
	5724	1964	4,421	—	Proof	70.00

17th Anniversary-Knesset Building

45	5725	1965	.025	—	—	20.00
	5725	1965	7,537	—	Proof	30.00

18th Anniversary-Israel Lives On

ISRAEL

KM#	Date	Year	Mintage	VF	XF	Unc
46	5726	1966	.032	—	—	12.50
	5726	1966	.010	—	Proof	17.50

19th Anniversary-Port of Eilat

48	5727	1967	.030	—	—	17.50
	5727	1967	7,680	—	Proof	25.00

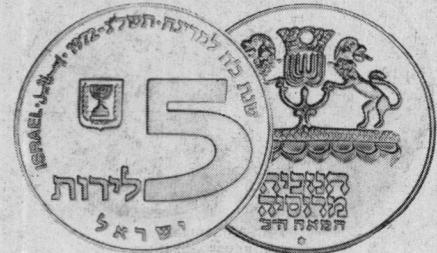

20.0000 g, .750 SILVER, .4823 oz ASW
Chanuka-Russian Lamp
Plain edge.

69.1	5733	1972	.075	—	—	6.00

Reeded edge.

69.2	5733	1972	.022	—	Proof	10.00

20.0000 g, .500 SILVER, .3215 oz ASW
Chanuka-Babylonian Lamp
Plain edge.

75.1	5734	1973	.095	—	—	7.50

Reeded edge.

75.2	5734	1973	.045	—	Proof	9.50

COPPER-NICKEL

90	5738	1978	8.350	.35	.60	1.25
	5739	1979	37.646	.35	.50	1.00

Obv: Star of David in field.

90a	5739	1979	—	.35	.50	1.00

NICKEL
25th Anniversary of Bank of Israel
Reeded edge.

102.1	5740	1980	.035	—	—	2.50

Plain edge.

102.2	5740	1980	Inc. Ab.	—	Proof	5.00

10 LIROT (POUNDS)

26.0000 g, .900 SILVER, .7524 oz ASW
Victory Commemorative

KM#	Date	Year	Mintage	VF	XF	Unc
49	5727	1967	.234	—	—	10.00

26.0000 g, .935 SILVER, .7816 oz ASW

49a	5727	1967	.050	—	Proof	12.50

26.0000 g, .900 SILVER, .7524 oz ASW
20th Anniversary-Jerusalem

51	5728	1968	.050	—	—	12.00
	5728	1968	.020	—	Proof	14.00

21st Anniversary-Shalom

53.1	5729	1969	.040	U.S. Mint
			—	12.50

Rev: K A F under helmet.

53.2	5729	1969	.020	Jerusalem Mint
			—	15.00
	5729	1969	.020	U.S. Mint
			—	Proof 15.00

22nd Anniversary Mikveh Israel School

KM#	Date	Year	Mintage	VF	XF	Unc
55	5730	1970	.048	—	—	10.00
	5730	1970	.022	—	Proof	15.00

Pidyon Haben
Plain edge.

56.1	5730	1970	.049	—	—	10.00

Reeded edge.

56.2	5730	1970	.015	—	Proof	15.00

Plain edge.

57.1	5731	1971	.030	—	—	10.00

Reeded edge.

57.2	5731	1971	.014	—	Proof	15.00

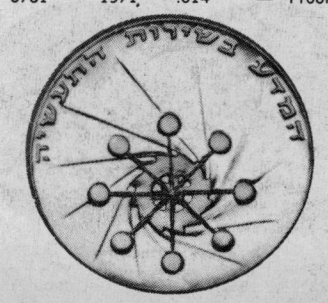

ISRAEL 1063

Star of David
Jerusalem Mint

23rd Anniversary-Science and Industry

KM#	Date	Year	Mintage	VF	XF	Unc
58	5731	1971	.030	—	—	Utrecht Mint 12.00
	5731	1971	star .023	—	—	Jerusalem Mint 12.50
	5731	1971	.018	—	Proof	15.00

Let My People Go
Obv: Legend on rim, closed *Mem*.

59.1	5731	1971	.073	—	—	10.00
	5731	1971	.020	—	Proof	15.00

Obv: Legend away from rim, open *Mem*, (Berne die).

59.2	5731	1971	80 pcs.	—	Proof	775.00

Pidyon Haben
Plain edge.

61.1	5732	1972	star .030	—	—	10.00
	5732	1972	w/o star .015	—	—	15.00

Reeded edge.

61.2	5732	1972	.012	—	Proof	15.00

24th Anniversary-Aviation
Lettered edge.

KM#	Date	Year	Mintage	VF	XF	Unc
62	5732	1972	.050	—	—	12.50
	5732	1972	.015	—	Proof	20.00

Pidyon Haben
Plain edge.

70.1	5733	1973	.101	—	—	10.00

Reeded edge.

70.2	5733	1973	.015	—	Proof	12.50

25th Anniversary of Independence
Lettered edge.

71	5733	1973	.124	—	—	10.00
	5733	1973	.041	—	Proof	12.50

Pidyon Haben
Plain edge.

KM#	Date	Year	Mintage	VF	XF	Unc
76.1	5734	1974	.109	—	—	10.00

Reeded edge.

76.2	5734	1974	.044	—	Proof	12.50

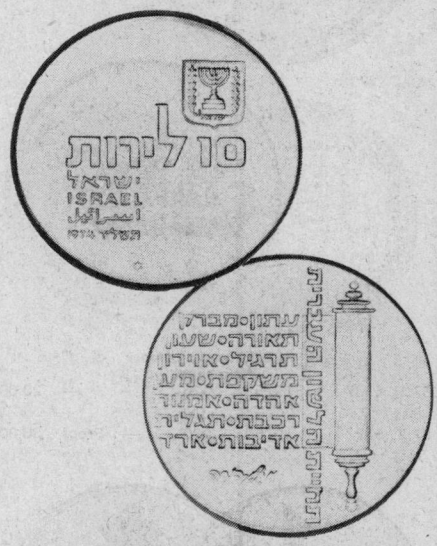

Hebrew Language Revival
Lettered edge.

77	5734	1974	.127	—	—	10.00
	5734	1974	.050	—	Proof	12.00

20.0000 g, .500 SILVER, .3215 oz ASW
Damascus Hannuka Lamp
Plain edge.

78.1	5735	1974	.074	—	—	7.00

Reeded edge.

78.2	5735	1974	.059	—	Proof	10.00

ISRAEL 1064

Holland Hannuka Lamp
Plain edge.

KM#	Date	Year	Mintage	VF	XF	Unc
84.1	5736	1975	.044	—	—	8.00

Reeded edge.

| 84.2 | 5736 | 1975 | .034 | — | Proof | 12.00 |

U.S. Hannuka Lamp
Plain edge.

| 87.1 | 5737 | 1976 | .025 | — | — | 20.00 |

Reeded edge.

| 87.2 | 5737 | 1976 | .020 | — | Proof | 30.00 |

COPPER-NICKEL
Jerusalem Hanukka Lamp
Plain edge.

| 91.1 | 5738 | 1977 | .046 | — | — | 6.00 |

Reeded edge. Open style "mem".

| 91.2 | 5738 | 1977 | .030 | — | Proof | 8.00 |

Closed style "mem"

| 91.3 | 5738 | 1977 | Inc. Ab. | — | Proof | 10.00 |

20 LIROT

7.9880 g, .917 GOLD, .2355 oz AGW
Dr. Theodor Herzl

| 30 | 5720 | 1960 | .010 | — | — | 250.00 |

25 LIROT

26.0000 g, .935 SILVER, .7816 oz ASW
David Ben Gurion
Plain edge.

KM#	Date	Year	Mintage	VF	XF	Unc
79.1	5735	1974	.099	—	—	10.00

Reeded edge.

| 79.2 | 5735 | 1974 | .064 | — | Proof | 14.00 |

26.0000 g, .900 SILVER, .7524 oz ASW
Pidyon Haben
Plain edge.

| 80.1 | 5735 | 1975 | .062 | — | — | 10.00 |

Reeded edge.

| 80.2 | 5735 | 1975 | .049 | — | Proof | 12.50 |

30.0000 g, .800 SILVER, .7717 oz ASW
25th Anniversary of Israel Bond Program

Lettered edge.

KM#	Date	Year	Mintage	VF	XF	Unc
81	5735	1975	.049	—	—	10.00
	5735	1975	.040	—	Proof	12.50

26.0000 g, .900 SILVER, .7524 oz ASW
28th Anniversary of Independence - Strength
Lettered edge.

| 85 | 5736 | 1976 | .038 | — | — | 11.00 |
| | 5736 | 1976 | .027 | — | Proof | 15.00 |

30.0000 g, .800 SILVER, .7717 oz ASW
Pidyon Haben
Plain edge.

| 86.1 | 5736 | 1976 | .037 | — | — | 11.00 |

Reeded edge.

| 86.2 | 5736 | 1976 | .029 | — | Proof | 14.00 |

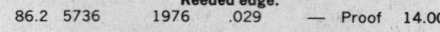

20.0000 g, .500 SILVER, .3215 oz ASW
29th Anniversary of Independence - Brotherhood

ISRAEL 1065

Lettered edge.

KM#	Date	Year	Mintage	VF	XF	Unc
88	5737	1977	.037	—	—	10.00
	5737	1977	.027	—	Proof	12.00

26.0000 g, .900 SILVER, .7524 oz ASW
Pidyon Haben
Plain edge.

| 89.1 | 5737 | 1977 | .032 | — | — | 12.00 |

Reeded edge.

| 89.2 | 5737 | 1977 | .019 | — | Proof | 15.00 |

COPPER-NICKEL
French Hannuka Lamp
Plain edge.

| 94.1 | 5739 | 1978 | .036 | — | — | 5.00 |

Reeded edge.

| 94.2 | 5739 | 1978 | .022 | — | Proof | 8.00 |

50 LIROT

13.3400 g, .917 GOLD, .3933 oz AGW
10th Anniversary of Death of Weizmann

| 40 | 5723 | 1962 | 6,195 | — | Proof | 275.00 |

10th Anniversary of Bank of Israel

| 44 | 5724 | 1964 | 5,975 | — | — | 450.00 |
| | 5724 | 1964*841 pcs. | — | Proof | 3500. |

*The Bank of Israel presented 702 pieces.

7.0000 g, .900 GOLD, .2025 oz AGW
25th Anniversary of Independence

| 72 | 5733 | 1973 | .028 | — | Proof | 140.00 |

20.0000 g, .500 SILVER, .3215 oz ASW
30th Anniversary of Independence - Loyalty
Lettered edge.

KM#	Date	Year	Mintage	VF	XF	Unc
92	5738	1978	.040	—	—	10.00
(92.1)	5738	1978	.022	—	Proof	14.00

31st Anniversary of Independence - Motherhood
Lettered edge.

| 95 | 5739 | 1979 | .024 | — | — | 11.00 |
| | 5739 | 1979 | .016 | — | Proof | 16.00 |

100 LIROT

26.6800 g, .917 GOLD, .7866 oz AGW
10th Anniversary of Death of Weizmann

| 41 | 5723 | 1962 | 6,196 | — | Proof | 400.00 |

Victory Commemorative

| 50 | 5727 | 1967 | 9,004 | — | Proof | 600.00 |

25.0000 g, .800 GOLD, .6430 oz AGW
20th Anniversary - Jerusalem

KM#	Date	Year	Mintage	VF	XF	Unc
52	5728	1968	.012	—	Proof	375.00

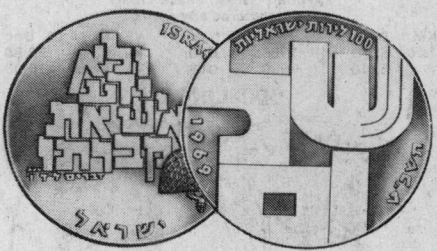

21st Anniversary - Shalom

| 54 | 5729 | 1969 | .013 | — | Proof | 350.00 |

22.0000 g, .900 GOLD, .6366 oz AGW
Let My People Go

| 60 | 5731 | 1971 | 9,956 | — | Proof | 375.00 |

13.5000 g, .900 GOLD, .3906 oz AGW
25th Anniversary of Independence

| 73 | 5733 | 1973 | .028 | — | Proof | 215.00 |

20.0000 g, .500 SILVER, .3215 oz ASW
Hanukka - Egyptian Lamp
Plain edge.

| 103.1 | 5740 | 1979 | .032 | — | — | 15.00 |

Reeded edge.

| 103.2 | 5740 | 1979 | .019 | — | Proof | 22.50 |

200 LIROT

27.0000 g, .900 GOLD, .7813 oz AGW
25th Anniversary of Independence

| 74 | 5733 | 1973 | .018 | — | Proof | 375.00 |

ISRAEL 1066

26.0000 g, .900 SILVER, .7524 oz ASW
Egyptian - Israeli Peace Treaty
Lettered edge.

KM#	Date	Year	Mintage	VF	XF	Unc
104	5740	1980	.020	—	—	22.50
	5740	1980	.013	—	Proof	35.00

500 LIROT

28.0000 g, .900 GOLD, .8102 oz AGW
David Ben Gurion
| 82 | 5735 | 1974 | .048 | — | Proof | 425.00 |

20.0000 g, .900 GOLD, .5787 oz AGW
27th Anniversary of Israel Bond Program
| 83 | 5735 | 1975 | .032 | — | Proof | 300.00 |

1000 LIROT

12.0000 g, .900 GOLD, .3473 oz AGW
30th Anniversary of Independence
| 93 | 5738 | 1978 | .012 | — | Proof | 250.00 |

5000 LIROT

17.2800 g, .900 GOLD, .5000 oz AGW
Israel-Egypt Peace Treaty
| 105 | 5740 | 1980 | 6,382 | — | Proof | 400.00 |

MONETARY REFORM
Commencing February 24, 1980
10 Old Agorot = 1 New Agora
100 New Agorot = 1 Sheqel

NEW AGORA

ALUMINUM

KM#	Date	Year	Mintage	VF	XF	Unc
106	5740	1980	*200.000	—	—	.10
	5741	1981	1.000	—	.10	.20
	5742	1982	1.000	—	.10	.20

*NOTE: 110 million coins were reportedly melted down before being released.

5 NEW AGOROT

ALUMINUM

107	5740	1980	69.532	—	—	.10
	5741	1981	1.000	—	.10	.20
	5742	1982	5.000	—	—	.10

10 NEW AGOROT

ALUMINUM-BRONZE

108	5740	1980	*167.932	—	—	.10
	5741	1981	241.160	—	—	.10
	5742	1982	23.000	—	—	.10
	5743	1983	2.500	—	.10	.15
	5744	1984	.500	—	.10	.20

*NOTE: 70.200 million coins were reportedly melted down before being released.

1/2 SHEQEL

COPPER-NICKEL

109	5740	1980	52.308	—	.25	.50
	5741	1981	53.272	—	.25	.50
	5742	1982	18.808	—	.25	.50
	5743	1983	.250	—	.35	.70
	5744	1984	.250	—	.35	.70

7.2000 g, .850 SILVER, .1967 oz ASW
Holyland Sites - Qumran Caves
| 121 | 5743 | 1982 | .015 | — | — | 15.00 |

Holyland Sites - Herodion
| 126 | 5744 | 1983 | .011 | — | — | 18.00 |

Holyland Sites - Kidron Valley
| 140 | 5745 | 1984 | 7,538 | — | — | 22.00 |

Holyland Sites - Capernaum
| 152 | 5746 | 1985 | 6,010 | — | — | 16.00 |

SHEQEL

14.4000 g, .850 SILVER, .3935 oz ASW
Hanukkah Korfu Lamp
Plain edge.

KM#	Date	Year	Mintage	VF	XF	Unc
110.1	5741	1980	.024	—	—	20.00
	Reeded edge.					
110.2	5741	1980	.015	—	Proof	30.00

COPPER-NICKEL

111	5741	1981	154.540	—	.65	.85
	5742	1982	15.850	—	.65	.85
	5743	1983	26.360	—	.65	.85
	5744	1984	32.205	—	.65	.85
	5745	1985	.500	—	.65	1.00

14.4000 g, .850 SILVER, .3935 oz ASW
Hanukkah Polish Lamp
Plain edge.
116.1	5742	1981	.016	—	—	25.00
	Reeded edge.					
116.2	5742	1981	.011	—	Proof	35.00

Holyland Sites - Qumran Caves
| 122 | 5743 | 1982 | 9,000 | — | Proof | 35.00 |

Hanukkah Yemen Lamp
| 123 | 5743 | 1982 | .014 | — | — | 20.00 |

35th Anniversary of the State of Israel-Valour
| 127 | 5743 | 1983 | .015 | — | — | 25.00 |

ISRAEL 1067

Holyland Sites - Herodion
Rev: Similar to 5 Sheqalim, KM#132.

KM#	Date	Year	Mintage	VF	XF	Unc
128	5744	1983	.010	—	Proof	30.00

Hanukkah Prague Lamp

| 129 | 5744 | 1983 | .013 | — | — | 22.50 |

Ancient Ship Oniyahu

KM#	Date	Year	Mintage	VF	XF	Unc
155	5745	1985	.013	—	P/L	22.50

2 SHEQALIM

Hanukkah Yemen Lamp

KM#	Date	Year	Mintage	VF	XF	Unc
124	5743	1982	8,996	—	Proof	40.00

36th Anniversary of the State of Israel (Kinsmen)

| 135 | 5744 | 1984 | .018 | — | — | 30.00 |

35th Anniversary of the State of Israel-Valour
Rev: Similar to 1 Shequel, KM#127.

| 130 | 5743 | 1983 | .010 | — | Proof | 45.00 |

Holyland Sites - Kidron Valley

| 141 | 5745 | 1984 | 6,798 | — | Proof | 40.00 |

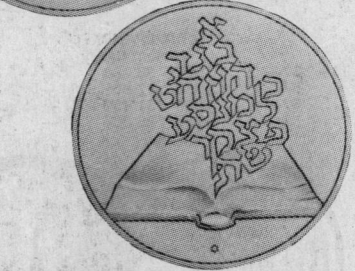

28.8000 g, .825 SILVER, .7639 oz ASW
33rd Anniversary of State of Israel
People of the Book
Lettered edge.

| 112 | 5741 | 1981 | .016 | — | — | 30.00 |
| | 5741 | 1981 | .011 | — | Proof | 45.00 |

Hanukkah Theresianstadt Lamp

| 144 | 5745 | 1984 | .011 | — | — | 25.00 |

Hanukkah Prague Lamp

| 131 | 5744 | 1983 | .011 | — | Proof | 35.00 |

28.8000 g, .850 SILVER, .7871 oz ASW
Baron Edmond de Rothschild
Lettered edge.

| 117 | 5742 | 1982 | .013 | — | — | 30.00 |
| | 5742 | 1982 | 9,506 | — | Proof | 45.00 |

Independence and Science (Scientific Achievement)

| 148 | 5745 | 1985 | 8,520 | — | — | 25.00 |

36th Anniversary of the State of Israel (Kinsmen)

| 136 | 5744 | 1984 | 8,526 | — | Proof | 45.00 |

Holyland Sites - Capernaum

| 153 | 5746 | 1985 | 6,010 | — | Proof | 30.00 |

ISRAEL 1068

Hanukkah Theresienstadt Lamp

KM#	Date	Year	Mintage	VF	XF	Unc
145	5745	1984	.010	—	Proof	55.00

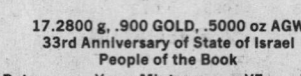

10 SHEQALIM

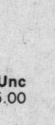

17.2800 g, .900 GOLD, .5000 oz AGW
33rd Anniversary of State of Israel
People of the Book

KM#	Date	Year	Mintage	VF	XF	Unc
113	5741	1981	5,673	—	Proof	425.00

17.2800 g, .900 GOLD, .5000 oz AGW
36th Anniversary of the State of Israel (Kinsmen)

KM#	Date	Year	Mintage	VF	XF	Unc
138	5744	1984	3,798	—	Proof	500.00

Independence and Science (Scientific Achievement)

| 149 | 5745 | 1985 | 8,330 | — | Proof | 45.00 |

5 SHEQALIM

COPPER-ALUMINUM-NICKEL

118	5742	1982	30.000	—	1.00	1.50
	5743	1983	.994	—	1.00	2.00
	5744	1984	17.389	—	1.00	1.50
	5745	1985	.250	—	1.00	2.50

8.6300 g, .900 GOLD, .2497 oz AGW
Holyland Sites - Qumran Caves
Rev: Similar to 1 Sheqel, KM#122.

| 125 | 5743 | 1982 | 4,927 | — | Proof | 300.00 |

Holyland Sites - Herodion

| 132 | 5744 | 1983 | 4,346 | — | Proof | 300.00 |

Holyland Sites - Kidron Valley
Rev: Similar to 1 Sheqel, KM#141.

| 142 | 5745 | 1984 | 2,601 | — | Proof | 650.00 |

Holyland Sites - Capernaum
Similar to 1 Sheqel, KM#153.

| 154 | 5746 | 1985 | 2,633 | — | Proof | 500.00 |

COPPER-NICKEL
Ancient Galley

119	5742	1982	36.084	—	.75	1.25
	5743	1983	17.851	—	.75	1.25
	5744	1984	31.950	—	.75	1.25
	5745	1985	25.864	—	.50	.75

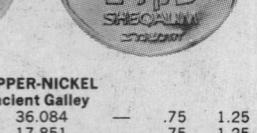

17.2800 g, .900 GOLD, .5000 oz AGW
Baron Edmond de Rothschild

| 120 | 5742 | 1982 | 4,875 | — | Proof | 325.00 |

35th Anniversary of the State of Israel (Valour)

| 133 | 5743 | 1983 | 3,650 | — | Proof | 625.00 |

COPPER-NICKEL
Hanukkah Trade Coin

| 134 | 5744 | 1983 | 2.000 | — | 1.00 | 2.00 |

Herzl

| 137 | 5744 | 1984 | 2.003 | — | 1.00 | 2.00 |

Independence and Science (Scientific Achievement)

| 150 | 5745 | 1985 | 3,240 | — | Proof | 500.00 |

25 SHEQALIM

26.0000 g, .900 SILVER, .7524 oz ASW
Zeev Jabotinsky
Plain edge

| 114.1 | 5740 | 1980 | .014 | — | — | 25.00 |

Reeded edge

| 114.2 | 5740 | 1980 | .012 | — | Proof | 35.00 |

50 SHEQALIM

COPPER-ALUMINUM-NICKEL
Circulation Coins

| 139 | 5744 | 1984 | 13.994 | — | .50 | 1.00 |
| | 5745 | 1985 | 1.000 | — | .75 | 1.50 |

COPPER-NICKEL
David Ben Gurion

| 147 (140) | 5745 | 1985 | 1.000 | — | 1.00 | 2.00 |

100 SHEQALIM

COPPER-NICKEL
Circulation Coins

KM#	Date	Year	Mintage	VF	XF	Unc
143	5744	1984	30.028	—	1.00	2.00
	5745	1985	19.638	—	1.00	2.00

Hanukkah

| 146 | 5745 | (1984) | 2.000 | — | 1.25 | 2.50 |

Zeev Jabotinsky

| 151 | 5745 | 1985 | 2.000 | — | 1.25 | 2.50 |

500 SHEQALIM

17.2800 g, .900 GOLD, .5000 oz AGW
Zeev Jabotinsky

| 115 | 5741 | 1980 | 7.471 | — | Proof | 350.00 |

MONETARY REFORM
September 4, 1985
10 Sheqalim = 1 Agora
1000 Sheqalim = 1 New Sheqel

AGORA

COPPER-ALUMINUM-NICKEL

156	5745	1985	58.144	—	—	.10
	5746	1986	95.272	—	—	.10
	5747	1987	1.080	—	—	.10
	5748	1988		—	—	.10

Hanukkah

KM#	Date	Year	Mintage	VF	XF	Unc
171	5747	1986	1.004	—	.10	.20
	5748	1987		—	.10	.20
	5749	1988		—	.10	.20

40th Anniversary of Israel

| 193 | 5748 | 1988 | .500 | — | — | .10 |

5 AGOROT

COPPER-ALUMINUM-NICKEL

157	5745	1985	34.504	—	.10	.15
	5746	1986	12.384	—	.10	.15
	5747	1987	14.257	—	.10	.15
	5748	1988		—	.10	.15

Hanukkah

172	5747	1986	1.004	—	.10	.30
	5748	1987	.500	—	.10	.30
	5749	1988		—	.10	.30

40th Anniversary of Israel

| 194 | 5748 | 1988 | .500 | — | — | .10 |

10 AGOROT

COPPER-ALUMINUM-NICKEL

158	5745	1985	45.000	—	.10	.20
	5746	1986	92.754	—	.10	.20
	5747	1987	19.351	—	.10	.20
	5748	1988		—	.10	.20

Hanukkah

173	5747	1986	1.004	—	.10	.40
	5748	1987	.800	—	.10	.40
	5749	1988		—	.10	.40

40th Anniversary of Israel

| 195 | 5748 | 1988 | | — | — | .15 |

1/2 NEW SHEQEL

COPPER-ALUMINUM-NICKEL

KM#	Date	Year	Mintage	VF	XF	Unc
159	5745	1985	20.328	—	.35	.50
	5746	1986	4.392	—	.35	.50
	5747	1987	.144	—	.35	2.00
	5748	1988		—	.35	.50

ALUMINUM-BRONZE
Rothschild

| 167 | 5746 | 1986 | 2.000 | — | .35 | .50 |

7.2000 g, .850 SILVER, .1967 oz ASW
Holyland Sites - Akko

| 168 | 5747 | 1986 | 6.224 | — | — | 17.50 |

COPPER-ALUMINUM-NICKEL
Hanukkah

174	5747	1986	1.004	—	.35	.80
	5748	1987	.500	—	.35	.80
	5749	1988		—	.35	.80

7.2000 g, .850 SILVER, .1967 oz ASW
Holyland Sites - Ancient Jericho

| 180 | 5748 | 1987 | 7.590 | — | — | 17.50 |

Holyland Sites - Caesarea

| 188 | 5749 | 1988 | .010 | — | — | 17.50 |

COPPER-ALUMINUM-NICKEL
40th Anniversary of Israel

| 196 | 5748 | 1988 | .500 | — | — | .50 |

NEW SHEQEL

COPPER-NICKEL

160	5745	1985	29.088	—	.65	.85
	5746	1986	20.960	—	.65	.85
	5747	1987	.216	—	.65	3.00
	5748	1988		—	.65	.85

ISRAEL 1070

14.4000 g, .850 SILVER, .3935 oz ASW
Ashkenaz Hanukkah Lamp

KM#	Date	Year	Mintage	VF	XF	Unc
161	5746	1985	9,460	—	—	22.50

COPPER-NICKEL
Hanukkah

163	5746	1985	1.056	—	.65	1.00
	5747	1986	1.004	—	.65	1.00
	5748	1987	.500	—	.65	1.00
	5749	1988	—	—	.65	1.00

14.4000 g, .850 SILVER, .3935 oz ASW
38th Independence Day Tribute to the Arts

164	5746	1986	8,010	—	—	15.00

Holyland Sites - Akko

169	5747	1986	6,117	—	Proof	25.00

Algerian Hanukkah Lamp

175	5747	1986	8,900	—	—	17.50

United Jerusalem

177	5747	1987	8,107	—	—	15.00

Holyland Sites - Jericho

181	5747	1987	8,196	—	Proof	25.00

English Hanukkah Lamp

KM#	Date	Year	Mintage	VF	XF	Unc
183	5748	1987	9,000	—	—	17.50

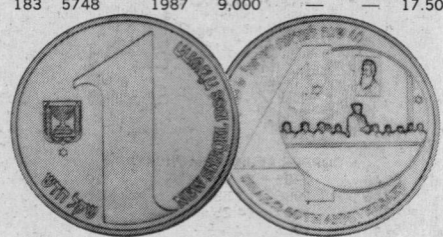

40th Anniversary of Israel

185	5748	1988	*.011	—	—	20.00

Holyland Sites - Caesarea

189	5749	1988	.010	—	Proof	25.00

Hanukkah - Tunisian Lamp

191	5749	1988	*.012	—	—	25.00

COPPER-NICKEL
40th Anniversary of Israel

197	5748	1988	.500	—	—	1.00

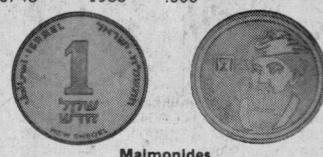

Maimonides

198	5748	1988	—	—	—	1.00

2 NEW SHEQALIM
28.8000 g, .850 SILVER, .7871 oz ASW
Ashkanaz Hanukkah Lamp
Similar to 1 New Sheqel, KM#161.

162	5746	1985	9,225	—	Proof	35.00

38th Anniversary of Independence Day
Tribute to the Arts

165	5746	1986	7,344	—	Proof	35.00

Algerian Hanukkah Lamp

KM#	Date	Year	Mintage	VF	XF	Unc
176	5747	1986	8,850	—	Proof	30.00

United Jerusalem

178	5747	1987	7,788	—	Proof	35.00

English Hanukkah Lamp

184	5748	1987	9,000	—	Proof	30.00

40th Anniversary of Israel

KM#	Date	Year	Mintage	VF	XF	Unc
186	5748	1988	*.010	—	Proof	30.00

Hanukka - Tunisian Lamp

| 192 | 5749 | 1988 | *.011 | — | Proof | 35.00 |

5 NEW SHEQALIM

8.6300 g, .900 GOLD, .2497 oz AGW
Holyland Sites - Akko
Rev: Similar to 1 New Sheqel, KM#169.

| 170 | 5747 | 1986 | 2,800 | — | Proof | 300.00 |

Holyland Sites - Jericho

| 182 | 5748 | 1987 | 4,000 | — | Proof | 300.00 |

Holyland Sites - Caesarea

| 190 | 5749 | 1988 | 5,000 | — | Proof | 225.00 |

10 NEW SHEQALIM

17.2800 g, .900 GOLD, .5000 oz AGW
38th Independence Day Tribute to the Arts

KM#	Date	Year	Mintage	VF	XF	Unc
166	5746	1986	2,485	—	Proof	600.00

United Jerusalem

| 179 | 5747 | 1987 | 3,200 | — | Proof | 450.00 |

40th Anniversary of Israel
Rev: Similar to 2 New Sheqalim, KM#186.

| 187 | 5748 | 1988 | *5,000 | — | Proof | 425.00 |

MINT SETS (MS)

KM#	Date	Mintage	Identification	Issue Price	Mkt. Val.
MS1	1949(10)	—	KM8-12,13.1,14-15,15a,16	—	250.00
MS2	1962(16)	4,000	KM12a,13.2a,17-20,20a,24.1, 25-27	18.50	95.00
MS3	1963(18)	7,000	As above w/KM36.1,37 in presentation holder	22.50	50.00

Trade coin sets as above, and six coin sets of 1964 and 1965 often contained circulated and cleaned coins, thus do not qualify as Mint Sets as usually defined.

| MS4 | 1963(6) | *200 | KM24.1,25-26(1962),27,36.1, 37 (white folder) | 2.50 | 250.00 |

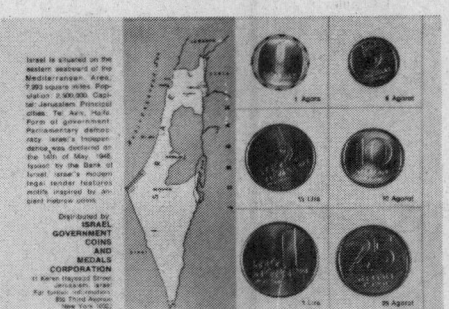

MS5	1963(6)	2,000	KM24.1,25-27,36.1,37 (plain white card)	2.50	125.00
MS6	1963(6)	10,000	KM24.1 w/Inv. Rev., 25-27, 36.1,37 (card w/map)	2.60	20.00
MS7	1963(6)*	10,544	KM24.1,25-27,36.1,37 (card w/map)	2.60	20.00

NOTE: #S7 was issued in 1964.

MS8	1965(6)	153,424	KM24.1,25-27,36.1,37	3.50	2.50
MS9	1966(6)	114,714	As above	3.50	2.50
MS10	1967(6)	128,124	As above (card)	3.50	2.50
MS11	1968(6)	184,552	KM24.1,25-27,36.1,47.1 (card)	3.50	2.50
MS12	1969(6)	158,052	As above(card)	3.50	2.50
MS13	1970(6)	60,045	As above, in red wallet	3.75	2.50
MS13a	1970(6)	64,800	As above (card)	3.75	2.50
MS14	1971(6)	32,543	As above, in blue wallet	3.50	3.00
MS14a	1971(6)	**125,921	As above, in pink plastic case	3.00	3.00
MS15	1972(6)	21,486	As above, in violet wallet	3.00	4.50
MS15a	1972(6)	**68,513	As above, in violet plastic case	3.50	3.00
MS16	1973(6)	98,107	KM63-68, in blue plastic case	3.50	5.00

**W/Star of David

NON STANDARD METALS

MS17	1974(6)	92,868	KM24.1,25a-27a,36.1,47.1 in brown plastic case	3.50	4.00
MS18	1975(6)	61,686	KM24.1,25a-27a,36.2,47.2 in brown plastic case	3.50	4.00
MS19	1976(6)	64,654	KM84-89, in green plastic case	3.50	4.00
MS20	1977(6)	37,208	KM24.1,25a-27a,36.2,47.2	3.50	4.00
MS21	1978(6)	57,200	As above	—	4.00
MS22	1979(7)	31,590	KM24.1,25b-26b,27a,36.2, 47.2,90a	1.80	3.50
MS24	1980(7)	—	KM24.1,26b,47.1,106-109	3.50	7.50
MS26	1982(7)	30,000	KM106-109,111,118-119	—	7.50
MS27	1982(5)	18,735	KM106-109,111,118 pieforts	11.00	25.00
MS28	1983(7)	17,478	KM106-109,111,118-119	11.00	20.00
MS28a	1983(5)	—	KM108-109,111,118-119	—	—
MS29	1984(9)	13,403	KM108-109,111,118-119,134, 137,143	10.00	15.00
MS29a	1984(5)	—	KM108-109,111,118-119 pieforts	—	—
MS30	1985(8)	7,760	KM111,118-119,139-140,143, 146,151	4.50	4.50
MS31	1985(7)	15,224	KM106-109,111,118-119	10.00	15.00
MS32	1985(5)	14,768	KM156-160, pieforts	7.00	20.00
MS33	1986(5)	12,665	KM156-160, pieforts	10.00	20.00
MS34	1986(12)	5746/5747 14,305	KM156-160,163,167,171-174 mixed dates	9.00	9.00
MS35	1986(5)	—	KM163,171-174	—	—
MS36	1987(10)	5747/5748 —	KM156-160,163,171-174 mixed dates	—	—
MS37	1987(5)	30,000	KM163,171-174	—	—
MS38	1987(5)	18,000	KM156-160, pieforts	12.00	20.00
MS39	1988(6)	—	KM156-160, 198 green holder	6.50	7.50
MS40	1988(5)	—	KM156-160, pieforts	—	22.00
MS41	1988(6)	15,000—	KM193-197, blue holder	7.50	8.50
MS42	1988(5)	20,000	KM163,171-174	8.00	10.00

PROOF SETS (PS)

| PS1 | 1980(7) | 31,348 | KM96-102 | 11.00 | 15.00 |
| PS2 | 1981(5) | — | KM106-109,111,pieforts | 10.00 | 25.00 |

SELECT SETS (SS)

| SS1 | 1949(10) | 300 est. | KM8-13.1 w/pearl, 14, 15 w/pearl, 15 w/o pearl, 16 in two piece heavy plastic case (light blue molded bottom and a clear swivel top) | — | 175.00 |

Listings For
Italian Somaliland: refer to Somalia

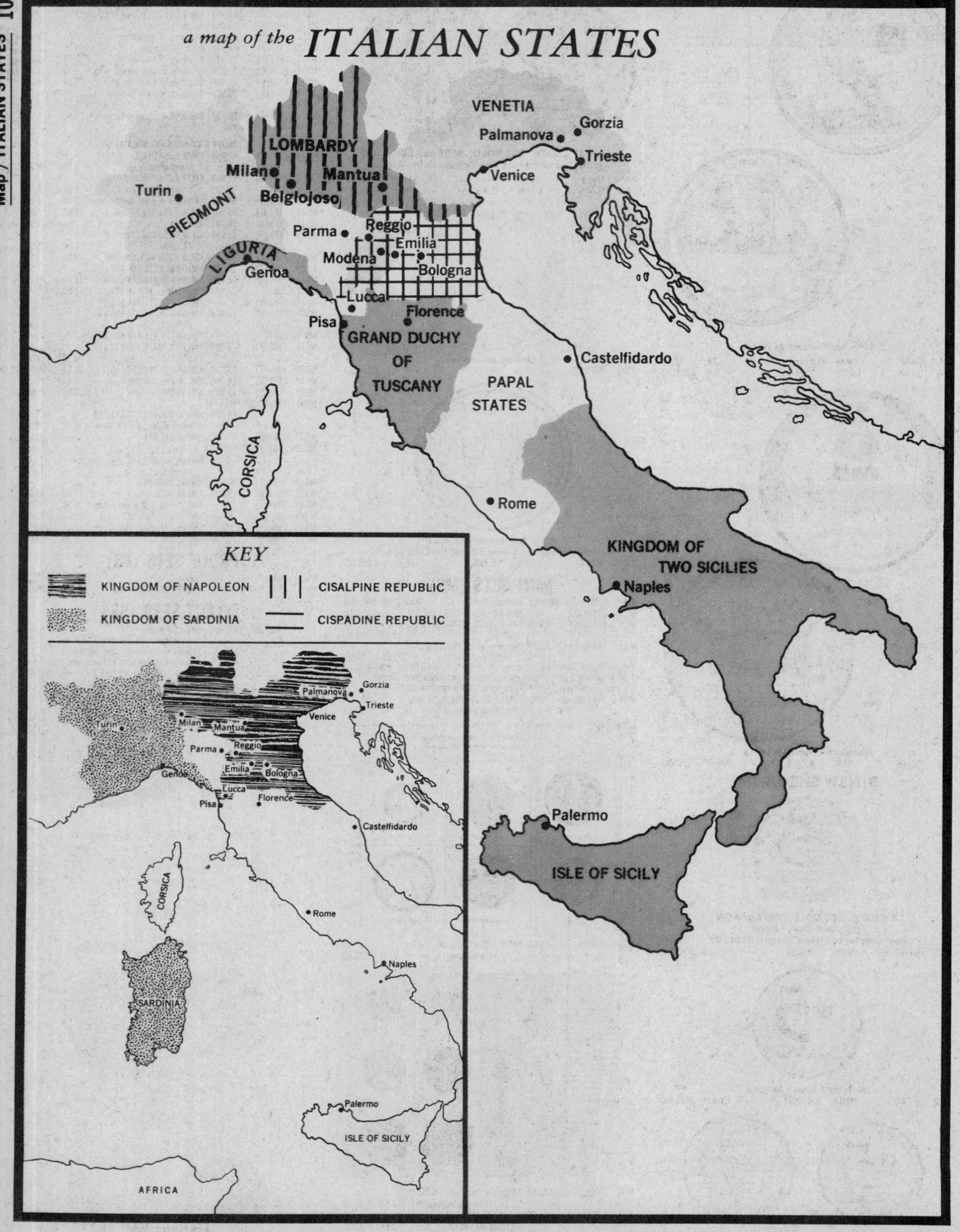

ITALIAN STATES

CISALPINE REPUBLIC
Transpadane Republic

A revolutionary state founded in northern Italy by Napoleon, came into being at Milan, Lombardy, in July 1797. It was subsequently enlarged by the addition of the Cispadine Republic and territory from the Venetian hinterlands and the Swiss Cantons of the Valtellina. It collapsed upon the conquest of Italy by an Austro-Russian army, but was restored by Napoleon in 1800.

MONETARY SYSTEM
20 Soldi = 1 Lira
6 Lire = 1 Scudo

30 SOLDI

7.3300 g, .684 SILVER, .1612 oz ASW

C#	Date	Mintage	VG	Fine	VF	XF
1	(1801) yr. IX	.300	20.00	40.00	65.00	130.00

EMILIA
Emilia-Romagna

A northern division of Italy, came under nominal control of the papacy in 755. In 1796-1814 it was incorporated in the Italian Republic and the Kingdom of Napoleon, returning to the papacy in 1815.

MONETARY SYSTEM
100 Centesimi = 1 Lira

MINT MARKS
B - Bologna
(none) - Birmingham

1 CENTESIMO
COPPER
Obv: Crowned arms in branches.
Rev: Value and date in wreath.

KM#	Date	Mintage	Fine	VF	XF	Unc
1	1826(1860)	—	3.00	5.00	10.00	20.00

3 CENTESIMI
COPPER
Obv: Crowned arms in branches.
Rev: Value and date in wreath.

2	1826(1860)	—	3.00	5.00	10.00	25.00

5 CENTESIMI
COPPER
Obv: Crowned arms in branches.
Rev.: Value and date in wreath.

3	1826(1860)	—	3.00	5.00	10.00	30.00

50 CENTESIMI

2.5000 g, .900 SILVER, .0723 oz ASW
Similar to 1 Lira, C#2.

C#	Date	Mintage	Fine	VF	XF	Unc
1	1859B	—	25.00	50.00	100.00	250.00

LIRA

5.0000 g, .900 SILVER, .1446 oz ASW

2	1859B	—	35.00	75.00	150.00	500.00

2 LIRE

10.0000 g, .900 SILVER, .2892 oz ASW
Similar to 1 Lira, C#2.

3	1859B	—	200.00	350.00	450.00	1100.
	1860B	.013	150.00	250.00	400.00	1100.

5 LIRE

25.0000 g, .900 SILVER, .7320 oz ASW
Rev: Similar to 1 Lira, C#2.

C#	Date	Mintage	Fine	VF	XF	Unc
4	1859	—	150.00	250.00	500.00	2500.
	1860	—	150.00	200.00	400.00	2000.

10 LIRE

3.2200 g, .900 GOLD, .0931 oz AGW

5	1860B	1,145	450.00	950.00	2250.	4000.

20 LIRE

6.4500 g, .900 GOLD, .1866 oz AGW

6	1860B	150 pcs.	—	—	*Rare	

*NOTE: Stack's Hammel sale 9-82 XF realized $24,000. Stack's International sale 3-88 Gem BU realized $16,500.
NOTE: For similar coins of Vittorio Emanuele II, see Sardinia and Tuscany.

GENOA

A seaport in Liguria, was a dominant republic and colonial power in the Middle Ages. In 1798 Napoleon remodeled it into the Ligurian Republic, and in 1805 it was incorporated in the Kingdom of Napoleon. Following a brief restoration of the republic, it was absorbed by the Kingdom of Sardinia, 1815.

MINT MARKS
NOTE: During the occupation by the French forces regular French coins, 1/2, 1, 2, 5, 20 and 40 Francs were struck between 1813 and 1814 with the mint mark C.L.
After Sardinia absorbed Genoa in 1815, regular Sardinian coins were struck until 1860 with a fouled anchor mint mark.

MONETARY SYSTEM
12 Denari = 1 Soldo
20 Soldi = 10 Parpagliola
5 Cavallotti = 1 Lira (Madonnina)

LIGURIAN REPUBLIC
1798-1805

3 DENARI
COPPER
Obv: R.L.A.V. 1802 around D. 3, Rev: Cross.

C#	Date	Year	VG	Fine	VF	XF
25	ND(1802)	V	10.00	20.00	35.00	70.00

4 LIRE

16.6400 g, .889 SILVER, .4756 oz ASW

29	1804	VII	25.00	50.00	100.00	200.00

8 LIRE

33.2700 g, .889 SILVER, .9510 oz ASW

C#	Date	Year	VG	Fine	VF	XF
30.2	1804	VII	60.00	100.00	175.00	300.00

48 LIRE

12.6070 g, .909 GOLD, .3684 oz AGW

C#	Date	Year	Fine	VF	XF	Unc
33	1801	IV	400.00	575.00	1000.	2500.
	1804	VII	400.00	575.00	1000.	2500.

96 LIRE

25.2140 g, .917 GOLD, .7435 oz AGW

34	1801	IV	450.00	750.00	1400.	3500.
	1803	VI	450.00	750.00	1400.	3500.
	1804	VII	450.00	750.00	1400.	3500.
	1805	VIII	450.00	750.00	1400.	3500.

REPUBLIC
1814

QUATTRO (4) DENARI

COPPER

C#	Date	Mintage	VG	Fine	VF	XF
35	1814	—	2.00	4.00	6.50	12.50

2 SOLDI

Kingdom of Napoleon / ITALIAN STATES 1074

BILLON

C#	Date	Mintage	VG	Fine	VF	XF
36	1814	—	2.50	5.50	9.00	20.00

NOTE: Exists with PRAESIDIUM and PRESIDIUM.

4 SOLDI

BILLON

37	1814	—	4.00	8.00	12.00	22.50

10 SOLDI

2.1000 g, .889 SILVER, .0600 oz ASW
Obv: Crowned shield, GENUENSIS.
Rev: John The Baptist standing.

38	1814	—	4.00	10.00	14.00	25.00

Obv. leg: JANUENSIS

38a	1814	—	4.00	10.00	14.00	25.00

GORIZIA

Gorizia, Gorz

A city in Venetia, passed to Maximilian I of Austria in 1500, and became the holding of Charles, son of Austrian emperor Ferdinand I in 1564.

RULERS
Franz II (Austria) 1792-1835

MINT MARKS
A, W - Wien - Vienna
F, H, HA - Hall
G - Graz
G - Nagybanya
H - Gunzburg
K - Kremnitz
O - Oravitza
S - Schmollnitz

MONETARY SYSTEM
20 Soldi = 1 Lira

SOLDO

COPPER
Mint mark: F
Obv: Crowned arms. Rev: Value, date.

8.1	1801	—	—	—	Rare	—

Mint mark: H

8.4	1801	—	3.00	6.00	12.50	30.00
	1802	—	—	—	Rare	—

2 SOLDI

COPPER
Mint mark: F
Obv: Crowned arms. Rev: Value, date.

9.2	1801	—	—	—	Rare	—

Mint mark: H

9.3	1801	—	2.50	5.00	10.00	25.00
	1802	—	2.50	5.00	10.00	25.00

15 SOLDI
(8-1/2 Kreuzer)

BILLON
Mint mark: A

10.1	1802	—	5.00	10.00	20.00	50.00

Mint mark: F

10.2	1802	—	5.00	10.00	20.00	40.00

Mint mark: H

10.3	1802	—	7.50	15.00	35.00	75.00

KINGDOM OF NAPOLEON

Came into being shortly after the first French empire was proclaimed on May 18, 1804; Napoleon's Italian coronation took place at Naples on May 26, 1805.

(French rule)

RULERS
Napoleon I, 1804-1814

MINT MARKS
B - Bologna
M - Milan
V - Venice

MONETARY SYSTEM
100 Centesimi = 20 Soldi
20 Soldi = 1 Lira

CENTESIMO

COPPER
Mint mark: B

C#	Date	Mintage	VG	Fine	VF	XF
1.1	1807	.092	2.00	4.00	7.50	15.00
	1808	2.270	2.00	4.00	7.50	15.00
	1809	4.413	2.00	4.00	7.50	15.00
	1810	3.813	2.00	4.00	7.50	15.00
	1811	1.335	2.00	4.00	7.50	15.00
	1812	4.813	2.00	4.00	7.50	15.00

Mint mark: M

1.2	1807	.097	3.75	7.50	12.50	30.00
	1808	3.372	2.00	4.00	7.50	15.00
	1808 (error) IMPERAPORE					
		.020	6.50	12.50	20.00	42.50
	1809	2.244	2.00	4.00	7.50	15.00
	1810	2.244	2.00	4.00	7.50	15.00
	1811	1.944	2.00	4.00	7.50	15.00
	1812	2.744	2.00	4.00	7.50	15.00
	1813	3.724	2.00	4.00	7.50	15.00

Mint mark: V

1.3	1807	.124	3.75	7.50	12.50	27.50
	1808V/M	.347	3.75	7.50	12.50	27.50
	1808	Inc. Ab.	3.75	7.50	12.50	27.50
	1809	3.017	3.00	6.00	7.50	15.00
	1810	.267	3.75	7.50	12.50	25.00
	1811	7.873	2.00	4.00	7.50	15.00
	1812	1.424	2.00	4.00	7.50	15.00
	1813	4.424	2.00	4.00	7.50	15.00

3 CENTESIMI

COPPER
Mint mark: B

2.1	1807	.063	3.00	8.00	15.00	25.00
	1808	.215	2.00	4.00	7.50	15.00
	1810/9	1.845	4.00	8.00	15.00	30.00
	1810	Inc. Ab.	2.00	4.00	7.50	15.00
	1813/08	.845	2.50	5.00	10.00	20.00
	1813	Inc. Ab.	2.00	4.00	7.50	15.00

Mint mark: M

2.2	1807	.212	2.00	4.00	7.50	15.00
	1808	1.878	2.00	4.00	7.50	15.00
	1809	2.098	2.00	4.00	7.50	15.00
	1810/09	2.798	2.50	5.00	10.00	17.50
	1810	Inc. Ab.	2.00	4.00	7.50	15.00
	1811	2.798	2.00	4.00	7.50	15.00
	1812	3.012	2.00	4.00	7.50	15.00
	1813	2.598	2.00	4.00	7.50	15.00

Mint mark: V

2.3	1807	.117	7.50	12.50	20.00	30.00
	1808	.527	2.00	4.00	8.00	16.00
	1809	.127	2.00	4.00	8.00	16.00
	1810/00	—	2.50	5.00	10.00	20.00
	1810	—	2.00	4.00	8.00	16.00

SOLDO

COPPER
Mint mark: B

3.1	1807	.345	5.00	10.00	20.00	35.00
	1808	.300	2.00	4.00	7.50	15.00
	1809	1.340	2.00	4.00	7.50	15.00

Mint mark: M

3.2	1807	.105	2.50	6.00	12.50	20.00
	1808	1.454	2.00	4.00	7.50	15.00
	1809	1.350	2.00	4.00	7.50	15.00
	1810	1.450	2.00	4.00	7.50	15.00
	1811	2.390	2.00	4.00	7.50	15.00
	1812	2.260	2.00	4.00	7.50	15.00
	1813	2.897	2.00	4.00	7.50	15.00

Mint mark: V

C#	Date	Mintage	VG	Fine	VF	XF
3.3	1807	.265	2.50	5.00	15.00	35.00
	1808	.300	2.50	5.00	10.00	20.00
	1812	1.196	2.50	5.00	15.00	25.00

10 CENTESIMI

2.0000 g, .200 SILVER, .0128 oz ASW
Mint mark: M

4	1808	.012	8.50	17.50	27.50	60.00
	1809	.875	2.00	4.00	7.50	15.00
	1810	.760	2.00	4.00	7.50	15.00
	1811	1.540	2.00	4.00	7.50	15.00
	1812	.740	2.00	4.00	7.50	15.00
	1813	2.670	2.00	4.00	7.50	15.00

5 SOLDI

1.2500 g, .900 SILVER, .0361 oz ASW
Mint mark: M

5.1	1808 stars in relief on edge					
		.130	12.50	25.00	55.00	80.00
	1808 stars incused on edge					
		Inc. Ab.	4.00	6.00	10.00	20.00
	1809	.600	4.00	6.00	10.00	20.00
	1810	1.050	4.00	6.00	10.00	20.00
	1811/0	3.000	4.50	7.00	13.00	25.00
	1811	Inc. Ab.	4.00	6.00	10.00	20.00
	1812	1.700	4.00	6.00	10.00	20.00
	1813	2.800	4.00	6.00	10.00	20.00
	1814	.700	4.00	6.00	10.00	20.00
	1814 (error) IMPERARORE					
		Inc. Ab.	15.00	30.00	45.00	80.00

Mint mark: V

5.2	1812	.110	5.00	10.00	20.00	40.00

Mint mark: B

5.3	1812	.330	4.50	7.00	11.00	22.50
	1812B/M	.390	4.50	7.00	11.00	22.50
	1813	2.800	4.00	6.50	10.00	20.00
	1813B/M	.320	4.50	7.00	11.00	22.50

10 SOLDI

2.5000 g, .900 SILVER, .0722 oz ASW
Mint mark: M

6.1	1808 stars in relief on edge					
		.175	8.50	17.50	35.00	70.00
	1808 stars incused on edge					
		Inc. Ab.	4.50	6.50	10.00	20.00
	1809	.430	4.50	6.50	10.00	20.00
	1810	.550	4.50	6.50	10.00	20.00
	1811	2.050	4.50	6.50	10.00	20.00
	1812	.600	4.50	6.50	10.00	20.00
	1813	.490	4.50	6.50	10.00	20.00
	1814	.450	4.50	6.50	10.00	20.00

Mint mark: V

6.2	1811	.310	10.00	15.00	25.00	50.00
	1812	.160	4.50	7.00	12.50	25.00
	1813	.332	4.50	6.50	10.00	20.00

Mint mark: B

6.3	1812	.018	5.00	10.00	15.00	30.00
	1812B/M	.015	5.00	10.00	15.00	30.00
	1813	.350	4.00	6.00	10.00	20.00

15 SOLDI

3.7500 g, .900 SILVER, .1083 oz ASW
Mint mark: M

7	1808	.038	22.50	40.00	65.00	140.00
	1809	.015	22.50	50.00	100.00	200.00
	1810	9.000	45.00	80.00	200.00	400.00
	1814	370 pcs.	45.00	80.00	150.00	325.00

LIRA

5.0000 g, .900 SILVER, .1444 oz ASW
Mint mark: M

C#	Date	Mintage	VG	Fine	VF	XF
8.1	1808 stars in relief on edge					
		.495	10.00	20.00	30.00	70.00
	1808 stars incused on edge					
		Inc. Ab.	10.00	20.00	30.00	70.00
	1809	.025	5.00	10.00	20.00	40.00
	1810	.495	5.00	10.00	20.00	40.00
	1810 (error) NATOLEON					
		Inc. Ab.	20.00	45.00	70.00	150.00
	1811	1.185	5.00	10.00	20.00	40.00
	1812	.340	5.00	10.00	20.00	40.00
	1813	.230	5.00	10.00	20.00	40.00
	1814	.275	5.00	10.00	20.00	40.00
	1814M/V	I.A.	10.00	25.00	50.00	100.00

Mint mark: B

8.2	1808	.103	6.50	11.50	27.50	55.00
	1810 stars in relief on edge					
		.336	6.50	11.50	27.50	55.00
	1810 stars incused on edge					
		.310	6.50	11.50	27.50	55.00
	1811	.310	6.50	11.50	27.50	55.00
	1812	.310	6.50	11.50	27.50	55.00
	1813	.220	6.50	11.50	27.50	55.00

Mint mark: V

8.3	1811	.045	13.50	22.50	35.00	70.00
	1812	.090	13.50	22.50	35.00	70.00
	1813	.310	12.50	20.00	32.50	65.00

2 LIRE

10.0000 g, .900 SILVER, .2888 oz ASW
Mint mark: M

9.1	1807	.010	20.00	40.00	125.00	250.00
	1808 edge inscription in relief					
		—	125.00	250.00	300.00	450.00
	1808 edge inscription incuse					
		.311	17.50	35.00	70.00	125.00
	1809	.332	15.00	30.00	50.00	90.00
	1810	.370	15.00	30.00	50.00	90.00
	1811	.513	15.00	30.00	50.00	90.00
	1812	.334	15.00	30.00	50.00	90.00
	1813	.223	15.00	30.00	50.00	90.00
	1814	3,100	35.00	60.00	75.00	150.00

Mint mark: B

9.2	1808	2,200	25.00	50.00	200.00	400.00
	1812	.044	10.00	15.00	35.00	60.00
	1813	.348	10.00	15.00	30.00	55.00

Mint mark: V

9.3	1811	.010	15.00	30.00	60.00	125.00
	1812	.239	10.00	20.00	40.00	80.00
	1813	.213	10.00	20.00	40.00	80.00

5 LIRE

25.0000 g, .900 SILVER, .7234 oz ASW
Mint mark: M
DIO PROTEGGE L'ITALIA on edge in relief

10.1	1807	.039	50.00	75.00	150.00	350.00
	1808	3.278	40.00	50.00	60.00	140.00
	1809	2.480	30.00	50.00	80.00	165.00
	1810	.263	35.00	60.00	100.00	200.00

Mint mark: V

10.2	1807	610 pcs.	—	—	Rare	—
	1808	204 pcs.	—	—	Rare	—

Mint mark: B

10.3	1808	.023	30.00	50.00	80.00	165.00
	1809	.221	25.00	40.00	65.00	100.00
	1810	.317	25.00	40.00	65.00	100.00
	1811	—	22.50	35.00	60.00	100.00

Mint mark: M
Edge inscription incuse.

C#	Date	Mintage	VG	Fine	VF	XF
10.4	1809	—	27.50	40.00	80.00	165.00
	1810	—	27.50	40.00	80.00	165.00
	1811	—	27.50	40.00	80.00	165.00
	1812	1.848	27.50	40.00	80.00	165.00
	1813	.772	27.50	40.00	80.00	165.00
	1814	.102	35.00	75.00	150.00	300.00

Mint mark: B

10.5	1810	—	22.50	35.00	50.00	125.00

Mint mark: V

10.6	1811	.367	35.00	65.00	125.00	300.00
	1812	.207	27.50	40.00	80.00	165.00
	1813	.071	30.00	60.00	100.00	225.00

Mint mark: M
Letters in legend smaller, edge inscription incuse.

10.7	1808	—	27.50	40.00	80.00	165.00
	1811	2.820	27.50	40.00	80.00	165.00

Mint mark: V

10.8	1810	.014	27.50	40.00	80.00	165.00

Mint mark: B

10.9	1811	.451	22.50	35.00	50.00	125.00
	1812	.210	22.50	35.00	50.00	125.00
	1813	.110	22.50	35.00	50.00	125.00

20 LIRE

6.4510 g, .900 GOLD, .1866 oz AGW
Mint mark: M

11	1808	.087	100.00	125.00	150.00	400.00
	1809	.053	100.00	125.00	150.00	400.00
	1810	.114	100.00	125.00	150.00	325.00
	1811	.055	100.00	125.00	150.00	325.00
	1812	.045	100.00	125.00	150.00	325.00
	1813	.039	100.00	125.00	150.00	300.00
	1814	.057	100.00	125.00	150.00	300.00

40 LIRE

12.9030 g, .900 GOLD, .3733 oz AGW
Mint mark: M

12	1807	3,430	250.00	300.00	400.00	600.00
	1808 w/o mintmark					
		.352	175.00	200.00	250.00	300.00
	1808 edge inscription in relief					
		Inc. Ab.	175.00	200.00	250.00	300.00
	1808 edge inscription incuse					
		.213	175.00	200.00	250.00	300.00
	1809	.038	175.00	200.00	250.00	300.00
	1810	.158	175.00	200.00	250.00	300.00
	1811	.106	175.00	200.00	250.00	300.00
	1812	.056	175.00	200.00	250.00	300.00
	1813	.041	175.00	200.00	250.00	300.00
	1814	.264	175.00	200.00	250.00	300.00

LOMBARDY - VENETIA

Comprised the northern Italian duchies of Milan and Mantua and the Venetian Republic which were absorbed by the Kingdom of Napoleon in 1805. After Napoleon's fall they were awarded to Austria and incorporated in the Hapsburg monarchy as the Kingdom of Lombardy-Venetia.

RULERS
Franz I (Austria), 1814-1835
Ferdinand, 1835-1848
Franz Joseph, 1848-1866

MINT MARKS
A, W - Vienna
B - Kremnitz
M - Milan
S - Schmollnitz
V - Venice

MONETARY SYSTEM
(Until 1857)
100 Centesimi = 20 Soldi = 1 Lira
6 Lire = 1 Scudo
40 Lire = 1 Sovrano

CENTESIMO

COPPER
Mint mark: A

C#	Date	Mintage	Fine	VF	XF	Unc
1.1	1822	—	—	—	—	250.00

Mint mark: M

1.2	1822	—	3.00	5.00	8.00	30.00
	1834	—	3.00	5.00	8.00	25.00

Mint mark: V

1.3	1822	—	3.00	5.00	8.00	30.00
	1834	—	3.00	5.00	8.00	25.00

12.1	1839	—	3.00	5.00	8.00	25.00
	1843	—	5.00	8.00	12.00	30.00
	1846	—	3.00	5.00	8.00	25.00

Mint mark: V

12.2	1839	—	3.00	5.00	8.00	25.00
	1843	—	3.00	5.00	8.00	25.00
	1846	—	3.00	5.00	8.00	25.00

Mint mark: M

25	1849	—	5.00	8.00	12.00	25.00
	1850	—	5.00	8.00	12.00	25.00
	1852	—	5.00	8.00	12.00	25.00

29.1	1852	—	7.00	10.00	15.00	30.00

Mint mark: V

29.2	1852	—	3.00	5.00	8.00	20.00

5/10 SOLDO

COPPER
Mint mark: A

34.1	1862	12.495	2.00	3.50	6.00	15.00

Mint mark: B

34.2	1862	5.969	3.50	6.00	10.00	20.00

Mint mark: V

34.3	1862	1.915	3.50	6.00	10.00	25.00

3 CENTESIMI

COPPER
Mint mark: A

C#	Date	Mintage	Fine	VF	XF	Unc
2.1	1822	—	—	Reported, not confirmed			
	Mint mark: M						
2.2	1822	—	4.00	6.00	10.00	30.00
	1834	—	6.00	10.00	15.00	35.00
	Mint mark: V						
2.3	1822	—	4.00	6.00	10.00	30.00
	1834	—	4.00	7.00	12.00	35.00

	Mint mark: M						
13.1	1839	—	4.00	7.00	13.00	30.00
	1843	—	5.00	8.00	15.00	35.00
	1846	—	3.00	5.00	10.00	25.00
	Mint mark: V						
13.2	1839	—	3.00	5.00	10.00	25.00
	1843	—	3.00	5.00	10.00	25.00
	1846	—	3.00	5.00	10.00	25.00

	Mint mark: M						
26	1849	—	3.50	6.00	11.00	20.00
	1850	—	3.50	6.00	11.00	20.00
	1852	—	3.50	6.00	11.00	25.00

30.1	1852	—	3.00	6.00	10.00	20.00
	Mint mark: V						
30.2	1852	—	3.00	6.00	10.00	25.00

5 CENTESIMI

COPPER
Mint mark: A

3.1	1822	—	—	Rare	—	
	Mint mark: M						
3.2	1822	—	3.00	5.00	10.00	30.00
	1823	—	—	Reported, not confirmed		
	1834	—	5.00	8.00	15.00	35.00
	Mint mark: V						
3.3	1822	—	3.00	5.00	10.00	30.00
	1834	—	4.00	7.00	12.00	30.00

	Mint mark: M						
14.1	1839	—	6.00	10.00	17.50	35.00

C#	Date	Mintage	Fine	VF	XF	Unc
14.1	1843	—	5.00	8.00	15.00	30.00
	1846	—	5.00	8.00	15.00	30.00
	Mint mark: V						
14.2	1839	—	5.00	8.00	15.00	30.00
	1843	—	5.00	8.00	15.00	30.00
	1846	—	5.00	8.00	15.00	30.00

	Mint mark: M						
27	1849	—	5.00	8.00	15.00	25.00
	1850	—	5.00	8.00	15.00	25.00
31.1	1852	—	5.00	8.00	15.00	25.00
	Mint mark: V						
31.2	1852	—	4.00	7.00	12.00	25.00

SOLDO

COPPER
Mint mark: A

35.1	1862	22.275	1.50	3.00	5.00	10.00
	Mint mark: B						
35.2	1862	8.971	2.00	4.00	6.00	10.00
	Mint mark: V						
35.3	1862	9.395	2.50	4.00	10.00	20.00

10 CENTESIMI

COPPER
Mint mark: M
Similar to 5 Centesimi, C#3.

28	1849	—	30.00	40.00	75.00	150.00

32.1	1852	—	60.00	90.00	150.00	325.00
	Mint mark: V						
32.2	1852	—	5.00	10.00	30.00	50.00

15 CENTESIMI

COPPER
Similar to 10 Centesimi, C#32.1.
Mint mark: M

33.1	1852	—	200.00	250.00	350.00	700.00
	Mint mark: V						
33.2	1852	—	50.00	65.00	100.00	275.00

1/4 LIRA

1.6200 g, .600 SILVER, .0312 oz ASW
Mint mark: A

4.1	1822	—	35.00	50.00	85.00	200.00
	1823	—	150.00	250.00	350.00	800.00
	Mint mark: M						
4.2	1822	—	15.00	20.00	30.00	90.00
	1823/2	—	15.00	20.00	30.00	90.00
	1823	—	15.00	20.00	30.00	90.00
	1824	—	15.00	20.00	30.00	90.00
	Mint mark: V						
4.3	1822	—	15.00	20.00	30.00	90.00
	1823	—	15.00	20.00	30.00	90.00
	1824	—	15.00	20.00	30.00	90.00
	Mint mark: A						

C#	Date	Mintage	Fine	VF	XF	Unc
15.1	1835	—	—	Reported, not confirmed		
	1837	—	—	Reported, not confirmed		
	Mint mark: V						
15.2	1837	—	75.00	100.00	150.00	250.00
	1838	—	75.00	100.00	150.00	300.00
	1839	—	75.00	100.00	150.00	300.00
	1840	—	75.00	100.00	150.00	300.00
	1841	—	75.00	100.00	150.00	300.00
	1842	—	75.00	100.00	150.00	250.00
	1843	—	75.00	100.00	150.00	300.00
	1844	—	75.00	100.00	150.00	300.00
	Obv. leg: FRANZ I. Rev: Arms.						
4a	1843	—	10.00	15.00	30.00	90.00
	Obv. leg: FERDINAND. Rev: Arms.						
—	1837	—	10.00	15.00	30.00	90.00
	1841	—	10.00	15.00	30.00	90.00
	1842	—	10.00	15.00	30.00	90.00

1/2 LIRA

2.1650 g, .900 SILVER, .0626 oz ASW
Mint mark: A

5.1	1822	—	60.00	125.00	250.00	375.00
	1823	—	50.00	100.00	200.00	325.00
	1835	—	—	Reported, not confirmed		
	Mint mark: M						
5.2	1822	—	12.50	20.00	40.00	90.00
	1823	—	12.50	20.00	40.00	90.00
	1824/2	—	12.50	20.00	40.00	90.00
	1824	—	12.50	20.00	40.00	90.00
	Mint mark: V						
5.3	1821	—	—	Reported, not confirmed		
	1822	—	10.00	25.00	40.00	90.00
	1823/2	—	10.00	25.00	40.00	90.00
	1823	—	10.00	25.00	40.00	90.00
	1824	—	—	Reported, not confirmed		
	Mint mark: A						
16.1	1835	—	—	Reported, not confirmed		
	1837	—	—	Reported, not confirmed		
	Mint mark: V						
16.2	1837	—	30.00	50.00	100.00	200.00
	1838	—	30.00	50.00	100.00	200.00
	1839	—	30.00	50.00	100.00	200.00
	1840	—	30.00	50.00	100.00	200.00
	1841	—	30.00	50.00	150.00	225.00
	1842	—	30.00	50.00	150.00	225.00
	1843	—	30.00	50.00	100.00	200.00
	1844	—	30.00	50.00	100.00	200.00
36	1854	—	30.00	50.00	100.00	200.00
	1855	—	30.00	50.00	100.00	200.00

LIRA

4.3300 g, .900 SILVER, .1253 oz ASW
Mint mark: A

6.1	1822	—	75.00	150.00	250.00	550.00
	1823	—	25.00	50.00	100.00	200.00
	1835	—	—	Reported, not confirmed		

	Mint mark: M						
6.2	1822	—	20.00	40.00	75.00	135.00
	1823	—	20.00	40.00	75.00	135.00
	1824/3	—	20.00	40.00	75.00	135.00
	1824	—	20.00	40.00	75.00	135.00
	1825	—	20.00	50.00	85.00	150.00
	Mint mark: V						
6.3	1822	—	20.00	40.00	75.00	100.00
	1823	—	25.00	50.00	85.00	125.00
	Mint mark: A						
17.1	1835	—	—	Reported, not confirmed		
	1837	—	—	Reported, not confirmed		

	Mint mark: V						
17.2	1837	—	50.00	75.00	100.00	200.00
	1838	—	50.00	75.00	100.00	200.00
	1839	—	50.00	75.00	200.00	450.00
	1840	—	50.00	75.00	100.00	225.00
	1841	—	50.00	75.00	100.00	200.00
	1842	—	50.00	75.00	100.00	250.00
	1843	—	50.00	75.00	100.00	250.00
	1844	—	50.00	75.00	100.00	250.00
37.1	1852	—	50.00	75.00	100.00	200.00

C#	Date	Mintage	Fine	VF	XF	Unc
37.2	1853	—	30.00	50.00	100.00	200.00
	1854	—	30.00	50.00	100.00	200.00
	1855	—	50.00	75.00	150.00	300.00
	1856	—	50.00	75.00	150.00	200.00
	1858	—	50.00	75.00	150.00	350.00

1/2 SCUDO

12.3450 g, .900 SILVER, .3527 oz ASW
Mint mark: A

C#	Date	Mintage	Fine	VF	XF	Unc
7.1	1822	—	30.00	50.00	100.00	200.00
	1823	—	30.00	50.00	100.00	200.00
	1824	—	—	—	—	—
	1825	—	—	Reported, not confirmed		
	1835	—	—	Reported, not confirmed		

Mint mark: M

7.2	1822	—	40.00	60.00	100.00	175.00
	1823	—	20.00	30.00	50.00	150.00
	1824	—	20.00	30.00	50.00	150.00
	1825	—	—	—	Rare	—
	1826	—	—	—	Rare	—
	1827	—	—	—	Rare	—

Mint mark: V

7.3	1822	—	20.00	30.00	55.00	150.00
	1823	—	60.00	90.00	150.00	250.00
	1824	—	20.00	30.00	60.00	160.00
	1825	—	20.00	30.00	60.00	160.00
	1826	—	20.00	30.00	60.00	160.00
	1827	—	40.00	60.00	85.00	170.00

Mint mark: A

18.1	1835	—	—	Reported, not confirmed		
	1837	—	—	Reported, not confirmed		

Mint mark: V

18.2	1837	—	75.00	100.00	150.00	300.00
	1838	—	75.00	100.00	150.00	300.00
	1839	—	75.00	100.00	150.00	300.00
	1840	—	75.00	100.00	150.00	300.00
	1841	—	75.00	100.00	150.00	300.00
	1842	—	75.00	100.00	150.00	300.00
	1843	—	75.00	100.00	150.00	300.00
	1844	—	75.00	100.00	150.00	300.00
	1845	—	75.00	100.00	150.00	300.00
	1846	—	75.00	100.00	150.00	300.00

W/o value

| 38 | 1853 | — | 150.00 | 200.00 | 300.00 | 500.00 |

SCUDO

26.0000 g, .900 SILVER, .7524 oz ASW
Mint mark: M

C#	Date	Mintage	Fine	VF	XF	Unc
8.1	1816	—	—	Proof		1500.
	1822	—	25.00	45.00	100.00	250.00
	1823	—	35.00	65.00	125.00	275.00
	1824	—	35.00	65.00	135.00	325.00
	1825	—	30.00	50.00	125.00	325.00
	1826	—	50.00	80.00	180.00	450.00
	1827	—	35.00	65.00	125.00	275.00
	1828	—	125.00	200.00	300.00	600.00
	1829	—	45.00	80.00	150.00	350.00
	1830	—	35.00	70.00	135.00	300.00
	1831	—	30.00	55.00	125.00	275.00

Mint mark: A

8.2	1821	—	—	Proof		—
	1822	—	50.00	80.00	175.00	350.00
	1823	—	50.00	80.00	175.00	350.00
	1824	—	65.00	100.00	200.00	475.00
	1825	—	—	Reported, not confirmed		
	1835	—	—	Reported, not confirmed		

Mint mark: V

8.3	1822	—	35.00	75.00	100.00	225.00
	1823	—	100.00	150.00	200.00	300.00
	1824	—	30.00	65.00	100.00	225.00
	1825	—	30.00	50.00	125.00	325.00
	1826	—	30.00	50.00	110.00	175.00
	1827	—	50.00	80.00	140.00	350.00
	1828	—	90.00	140.00	200.00	600.00
	1829	—	90.00	140.00	200.00	600.00
	1830	—	50.00	75.00	115.00	300.00
	1831	—	40.00	65.00	115.00	275.00
	1832	—	50.00	75.00	115.00	300.00

Mint mark: A

| 19.1 | 1835 | — | — | Reported, not confirmed | | |
| | 1837 | — | — | Reported, not confirmed | | |

Mint mark: M

| 19.2 | 1837 | — | 70.00 | 140.00 | 250.00 | 500.00 |

Mint mark: V

19.3	1837	—	90.00	150.00	210.00	500.00
	1838	—	90.00	150.00	210.00	500.00
	1839	—	90.00	150.00	210.00	500.00
	1840	—	70.00	140.00	175.00	450.00
	1841	—	110.00	180.00	280.00	550.00
	1842	—	90.00	150.00	210.00	500.00
	1843	—	110.00	180.00	280.00	550.00
	1844	—	110.00	180.00	280.00	550.00
	1845	—	90.00	150.00	210.00	500.00
	1846	—	90.00	150.00	210.00	500.00

W/o value

| 39 | 1853 | — | 150.00 | 200.00 | 300.00 | 500.00 |

REVOLUTIONARY PROVISIONAL GOVERNMENT

5 LIRE

25.0000 g, .900 SILVER, .7234 oz ASW
Mint mark: M
Obv: Short stems on branches.

C#	Date	Mintage	Fine	VF	XF	Unc
22.1	1848	—	30.00	40.00	120.00	250.00

Obv: Long stems on branches.

| 22.2 | 1848 | — | 40.00 | 50.00 | 90.00 | 300.00 |

Obv: Short stems on branches. Rev: Star near crown.

| 22.3 | 1848 | — | 30.00 | 40.00 | 120.00 | 250.00 |

20 LIRE

6.4500 g, .900 GOLD, .1866 oz AGW
Mint mark: M

| 23 | 1848 | 4,593 | 300.00 | 400.00 | 950.00 | 2000. |

40 LIRE

12.9000 g, .900 GOLD, .3733 oz AGW
Mint mark: M

| 24 | 1848 | 5,875 | 500.00 | 750.00 | 1100. | 2250. |

TRADE COINAGE
ZECCHINO

3.5000 g, .900 GOLD, .1012 oz AGW
Obv: Doge kneeling before St. Mark, FRANC. I.
Rev: Christ standing.

| 9 | ND(1815) | — | 250.00 | 550.00 | 800.00 | 1500. |

1/2 SOVRANO

5.6700 g, .900 GOLD, .1640 oz AGW
Mint mark: M

10.1	1820	—	250.00	375.00	525.00	1350.
	1822	—	125.00	175.00	250.00	550.00
	1831	—	100.00	150.00	200.00	500.00

Mint mark: A

10.2	1822	—	100.00	160.00	250.00	550.00
	1823	—	100.00	160.00	250.00	600.00
	1831	—	100.00	160.00	250.00	600.00

Mint mark: V

| 10.3 | 1822 | — | 200.00 | 250.00 | 325.00 | 900.00 |
| | 1823 | — | 100.00 | 160.00 | 250.00 | 600.00 |

Mint mark: A

| 10a.1 | 1835 | — | — | Reported, not confirmed | | |

Mint mark: M

| 10a.2 | 1835 | — | 125.00 | 160.00 | 250.00 | 550.00 |

Mint mark: A

| 20.1 | 1837 | — | — | Reported, not confirmed | | |
| | 1839 | — | 175.00 | 300.00 | 500.00 | 1000. |

Mint mark: M

| 20.2 | 1837 | — | 400.00 | 600.00 | 1000. | 1500. |
| | 1838 | — | 175.00 | 300.00 | 400.00 | 600.00 |

Lombardy-Venetia / ITALIAN STATES 1078

C#	Date	Mintage	Fine	VF	XF	Unc
20.2	1839	—	175.00	300.00	400.00	600.00
	1841	—	175.00	300.00	400.00	600.00
	1842	—	200.00	400.00	600.00	800.00
	1843	—	300.00	500.00	750.00	1000.
	1844	—	200.00	300.00	600.00	900.00
	1845	—	200.00	300.00	600.00	900.00
	1846	—	200.00	300.00	600.00	900.00
	1847	—	200.00	300.00	600.00	900.00
	1848	—	175.00	300.00	500.00	800.00

Mint mark: V

20.3	1837	—	175.00	300.00	500.00	700.00
	1838	—	175.00	300.00	500.00	700.00
	1839	—	175.00	300.00	500.00	700.00
	1840	—	175.00	300.00	500.00	700.00
	1841	—	175.00	300.00	500.00	700.00
	1842	—	400.00	600.00	900.00	1250.
	1843	—	175.00	300.00	500.00	700.00
	1844	—	175.00	300.00	500.00	700.00
	1845	—	175.00	300.00	500.00	700.00
	1846	—	400.00	600.00	1000.	1350.
	1847	—	400.00	600.00	1000.	1350.

Mint mark: M

| 20a | 1849 | — | 175.00 | 300.00 | 500.00 | 750.00 |

40.1	1854	—	225.00	325.00	500.00	1100.
	1855	—	225.00	325.00	500.00	1100.
	1856	—	225.00	325.00	500.00	1100.

Mint mark: V

40.2	1854	—	225.00	325.00	500.00	1100.
	1855	—	225.00	325.00	500.00	1100.
	1856	—	225.00	325.00	500.00	1100.

SOVRANO

11.3300 g, .900 GOLD, .3278 oz AGW
Mint mark: M

11.1	1820	—	500.00	800.00	1200.	3000.
	1822	—	200.00	300.00	400.00	1000.
	1823	—	200.00	300.00	400.00	1000.
	1824	—	200.00	300.00	400.00	1000.
	1826	—	350.00	500.00	750.00	1200.
	1827	—	300.00	400.00	650.00	1100.
	1828	—	300.00	400.00	650.00	1100.
	1829	—	200.00	300.00	400.00	1000.
	1830/20	—	—	—	—	—
	1830	—	200.00	300.00	400.00	1000.
	1831/21	—	200.00	350.00	500.00	1100.
	1831	—	200.00	300.00	500.00	900.00

Mint mark: A

11.2	1822	—	200.00	300.00	400.00	850.00
	1823	—	200.00	300.00	400.00	1000.
	1831	—	200.00	300.00	400.00	750.00

Mint mark: V

| 11.3 | 1822 | — | 300.00 | 400.00 | 575.00 | 1000. |

Mint mark: A

| 11a.1 | 1835 | — | — | Reported, not confirmed | | |

Mint mark: M

| 11a.2 | 1835 | — | 400.00 | 550.00 | 800.00 | 2000. |

Mint mark: A

C#	Date	Mintage	Fine	VF	XF	Unc
21.1	1837	—	400.00	550.00	800.00	1600.
	1838	—	—	—	Rare	—
	1839	—	400.00	550.00	800.00	1600.
	1840	—	—	—	Rare	—
	1841	—	500.00	750.00	1000.	1750.
	1842	—	—	Reported, not confirmed		
	1843	—	—	—	Rare	—
	1845	—	—	—	Rare	—
	1847	—	700.00	1000.	1800.	3000.

Mint mark: M

21.2	1837	—	600.00	1000.	1600.	2750.
	1838	—	300.00	400.00	700.00	1250.
	1840	—	300.00	400.00	700.00	1250.
	1841	—	600.00	1000.	1600.	2750.
	1848	—	300.00	400.00	700.00	1250.

Mint mark: V

21.3	1837	—	250.00	350.00	700.00	1250.
	1838	—	250.00	350.00	700.00	1100.
	1839	—	350.00	500.00	800.00	1750.
	1840	—	250.00	350.00	700.00	1250.
	1841	—	250.00	350.00	700.00	1100.
	1842	—	250.00	350.00	700.00	1250.
	1843	—	350.00	500.00	800.00	1600.
	1844	—	350.00	500.00	800.00	1600.
	1845	—	350.00	500.00	800.00	1600.
	1846	—	250.00	350.00	700.00	1250.
	1847	—	250.00	350.00	700.00	1250.

Mint mark: M

41.1	1853	—	500.00	750.00	1200.	2000.
	1855	—	500.00	750.00	1200.	2000.
	1856	—	500.00	750.00	1200.	2000.

Mint mark: V

41.2	1854	—	600.00	1000.	1600.	2500.
	1855	—	500.00	800.00	1400.	2300.
	1856	—	450.00	750.00	1200.	2000.

LUCCA
Luca, Lucensis
Lucca and Piombino

A town in Tuscany and the residence of a marquis, was nominally a fief but managed to maintain a de facto independence until awarded by Napoleon to his sister Elisa in 1805. In 1814 it was occupied by the Neapolitans, and from 1817 to 1847 was a duchy of the queen of Etruria, after which it became a division of Tuscany.

Principality, 1805-1814
Lucca, Duchy, 1817-1847

RULERS
Felix and Elisa (Bonaparte), 1805-1814
Maria Luisa di Borbone
  Duchess, 1817-1824
Carlo Lodovico di Borbone
  Duke, 1824-1847

MONETARY SYSTEM
100 Centesimi = 1 Franco

3 CENTESIMI

COPPER

C#	Date	Mintage	VG	Fine	VF	XF
21	1806	—	6.00	15.00	25.00	60.00

5 CENTESIMI

COPPER

C#	Date	Mintage	VG	Fine	VF	XF
22	1806	—	10.00	20.00	40.00	85.00

FRANCO

5.0000 g, .900 SILVER, .1446 oz ASW

23	1805	—	—	—	Rare	—
	1806	—	12.50	30.00	50.00	110.00
	1807	—	12.50	30.00	50.00	110.00
	1808	—	12.50	30.00	50.00	110.00

5 FRANCHI

24.8400 g, .900 SILVER, .7188 oz ASW

24	1805	—	30.00	50.00	100.00	250.00
	1806	—	30.00	50.00	75.00	200.00
	1807	—	30.00	50.00	75.00	200.00
	1808/7	—	30.00	50.00	75.00	200.00
	1808	—	30.00	50.00	75.00	200.00

MONETARY REFORM
4 Denari = 1 Quattrino
3 Quattrini = 1 Soldo
20 Soldi = 1 Lira

QUATTRINO
COPPER
Obv. leg: DUCATO DI LUCCA. Rev: Value, date.

| 31 | 1826 | — | 3.00 | 6.00 | 12.00 | 25.00 |

MEZZO (1/2) SOLDO
COPPER
Obv. leg: DUCATO DI LUCCA, crown. Rev: Value, date.

32	1826	—	3.00	6.00	12.00	25.00
	1835	—	3.00	6.00	12.00	25.00

2 QUATTRINI

COPPER

| 33 | 1826 | — | 3.00 | 6.00 | 12.00 | 20.00 |

SOLDO
COPPER
Obv. leg: CARLO L. D. B. I. D. S. DUCA DI LUCCA

| 34 | 1826 | — | 3.00 | 6.00 | 12.00 | 25.00 |

C#	Date	Mintage	VG	Fine	VF	XF
34a	1841	—	7.50	15.00	25.00	40.00

5 QUATTRINI
COPPER
Obv: Crowned arms. Rev: Value, date.

| 35 | 1826 | — | 3.00 | 6.00 | 12.00 | 25.00 |

NOTE: Varieties exist.

2 SOLDI
1.4000 g, .200 SILVER, .0090 oz ASW
Obv: Crowned arms. Rev: Value, date.

| 36 | 1835 | — | 7.50 | 12.50 | 20.00 | 35.00 |

3 SOLDI
1.6000 g, .200 SILVER, .0102 oz ASW
Obv: Crowned CL monogram. Rev: Value, date.

| 37 | 1835 | — | 15.00 | 25.00 | 50.00 | 100.00 |

5 SOLDI
3.0000 g, .200 SILVER, .0192 oz ASW
Obv: Crowned shield. Rev: Value, date.

38	1833 flat top 3's	—	6.00	10.00	25.00	50.00
	1833 round top 3's	—	6.00	10.00	25.00	50.00
	1838	—	6.00	10.00	25.00	50.00

10 SOLDI
2.3600 g, .666 SILVER, .0505 oz ASW
Obv: Head right. Rev: Value, date within wreath.

C#	Date	Mintage	Fine	VF	XF	Unc
39	1833	—	10.00	18.00	30.00	75.00
	1838	—	10.00	18.00	30.00	75.00

LIRA

4.7200 g, .666 SILVER, .1010 oz ASW

40	1834	—	10.00	20.00	40.00	100.00
	1837	—	20.00	40.00	100.00	200.00
	1838	—	10.00	20.00	40.00	100.00

2 LIRE

9.4300 g, .666 SILVER, .2019 oz ASW

| 41 | 1837 | — | 35.00 | 60.00 | 150.00 | 250.00 |

NAPLES & SICILY
Two Sicilies

Consists of Sicily and the south of Italy which came into being in 1130. It passed under Spanish control in 1502; Naples was conquered by Austria in 1707. In 1733 Don Carlos of Spain was recognized as king. From then until becoming part of the united Kingdom of Italy, Naples and Sicily, together and separately, were contested for by Spain, Austria, France, and the republican and monarchial factions of Italy.

RULERS
Ferdinando IV
  1799-1805 (2nd reign)
  1815-1816 (restored in Naples)
  1816-1825 (as King of the Two Sicilies)
Joseph Napoleon, 1806-1808
Joachim Murat, 1808-1815
  (Gioacchino Napoleone)

Two Sicilies
Francesco I, 1825-1830
Ferdinand II, 1830-1859
Francesco II, 1859-1869

MONETARY SYSTEM
(Until 1813)
6 Cavalli = 1 Tornese

240 Tornese = 120 Grana = 12 Carlini
 = 6 Tari = 1 Piastra
5 Grana = 1 Cinquina
100 Grana = 1 Ducato (Tallero)

KINGDOM OF NAPLES
3 CAVALLI

COPPER

C#	Date	Mintage	VG	Fine	VF	XF
91	1804	—	2.50	7.50	15.00	30.00

4 CAVALLI
COPPER
Obv: Head right. Rev: Grapes.

| 92 | 1804 LD | — | 2.50 | 7.50 | 15.00 | 30.00 |

TORNESE
(6 Cavalli)
COPPER
Obv: Head right. Rev: Value within wreath.

| 93 | 1804 LD | — | 5.00 | 10.00 | 20.00 | 40.00 |

9 CAVALLI
COPPER
Obv: Head right. Rev: Castle.

94	1801	—	15.00	35.00	60.00	100.00
	1804	—	5.00	10.00	20.00	40.00
	1804 LD	—	5.00	10.00	20.00	40.00

2 GRANA

COPPER

| 101 | 1810 | — | 15.00 | 35.00 | 85.00 | 400.00 |

6 TORNESI

COPPER

96	1801 AP	—	5.00	10.00	20.00	40.00
	1802 AP	—	5.00	10.00	20.00	40.00
	1803 AP	—	5.00	10.00	20.00	40.00
	1803 RC	—	6.00	12.50	25.00	45.00

3 GRANA

COPPER

| 102 | 1810 | — | 15.00 | 30.00 | 60.00 | 250.00 |

Rev: Date below wreath.

C#	Date	Mintage	VG	Fine	VF	XF
102a	1810	—	15.00	30.00	60.00	250.00

60 GRANA

13.7500 g, .833 SILVER, .3682 oz ASW

| 97 | 1805 LD | — | 25.00 | 40.00 | 75.00 | 150.00 |

120 GRANA

27.5000 g, .833 SILVER, .7365 oz ASW

| 98 | 1802 AP | — | 25.00 | 40.00 | 75.00 | 150.00 |

Obv: Head right w/smooth hair.
Rev: Crown above small shield.

| 99.1 | 1805 LD | — | 25.00 | 40.00 | 85.00 | 200.00 |

Plain edge

| 99.2 | 1805 LD | — | 22.50 | 30.00 | 85.00 | 200.00 |

Naples & Sicily / ITALIAN STATES 1080

Obv: Head right w/curly hair.

C#	Date	Mintage	VG	Fine	VF	XF
99.3	1805 LD	—	30.00	65.00	135.00	265.00

NOTE: Varieties exist.

100	1806	—	100.00	175.00	350.00	600.00
	1807/6	—	100.00	175.00	350.00	700.00
	1807	—	80.00	150.00	350.00	500.00
	1808	—	80.00	150.00	325.00	500.00

DODICI (12) CARLINI

27.5300 g, .833 SILVER, .7373 oz ASW

103	1809	—	80.00	150.00	225.00	500.00
	1810	—	80.00	150.00	300.00	650.00

NOTE: Many varieties including mulings exist.

MONETARY REFORM
100 Centesimi = 1 Franco = 1 Lira

3 CENTESIMI
BRONZE
Obv: Head left. Rev: Value.

C#	Date	Mintage	Fine	VF	XF	Unc
105	1813	1.350	500.00	1100.	1500.	3750.

5 CENTESIMI

BRONZE

| 106 | 1813 | 1.280 | 750.00 | 1250. | 1750. | 5250. |

10 CENTESIMI
BRONZE

Obv: Head left. Rev: Value.

C#	Date	Mintage	Fine	VF	XF	Unc
107	1813	.450	750.00	1100.	1500.	2000.

MEZZA (1/2) LIRA

2.5000 g, .900 SILVER, .0723 oz ASW

| 108 | 1813 | .166 | 50.00 | 75.00 | 250.00 | 500.00 |

LIRA

5.0000 g, .900 SILVER, .1446 oz ASW

109	1812	.027	50.00	150.00	300.00	500.00
	1813	.199	30.00	75.00	150.00	250.00

2 LIRE

10.0000 g, .900 SILVER, .2892 oz ASW

110	1812	.028	100.00	200.00	350.00	700.00
	1813	.220	50.00	75.00	175.00	400.00

5 LIRE

25.0000 g, .900 SILVER, .7234 oz ASW

111	1812	2,921	600.00	1200.	2500.	5250.
	1813	.037	100.00	300.00	600.00	1200.

20 LIRE

6.4500 g, .900 GOLD, .1866 oz AGW

| 112 | 1813 | .042 | 200.00 | 400.00 | 550.00 | 800.00 |

40 FRANCHI

12.9000 g, .900 GOLD, .3732 oz AGW

C#	Date	Mintage	Fine	VF	XF	Unc
104	1810	18 pcs.	7500.	10,000.	15,000.	20,000.

40 LIRE

12.9000 g, .900 GOLD, .3732 oz AGW

| 113 | 1813 | .024 | 300.00 | 600.00 | 850.00 | 1200. |

TWO SICILIES

NOTE: Coins bearing legends FERDINANDO IV were for Naples and those with FERDINANDO I were for Two Sicilies.

MONETARY SYSTEM
6 Cavalli = 1 Tornese
240 Tornese = 120 Grana = 12 Carlini = 6 Tari (Naples) = 1 Piastra
5 Grana = 1 Cinquina
100 Grana = 1 Ducato (Tallero)

MEZZO (1/2) TORNESE

COPPER

142	1832	—	3.00	6.00	15.00	30.00
	1833	—	3.00	6.00	15.00	30.00
	1835	—	3.00	6.00	15.00	30.00
	1836	—	3.00	6.00	15.00	30.00
	1838	—	3.00	6.00	15.00	30.00
	1839	—	3.00	6.00	15.00	30.00
	1840	—	6.00	9.00	20.00	35.00
	1844	—	3.00	5.50	10.00	25.00
	1845	—	3.00	5.50	10.00	25.00
	1846	—	3.00	5.50	10.00	25.00
	1847	—	3.00	5.50	10.00	25.00

142a	1848	—	4.00	7.50	12.50	25.00
	1849	—	4.00	7.50	12.50	25.00
	1850	—	4.00	7.50	12.50	25.00
	1851	—	4.00	7.50	12.50	25.00
	1852	—	4.00	7.50	12.50	25.00
	1853	—	4.00	7.50	12.50	25.00
	1854	—	4.00	7.50	12.50	25.00

UNO (1) TORNESE

COPPER

C#	Date	Mintage	VG	Fine	VF	XF
119	1817	—	7.50	15.00	25.00	50.00

| 130 | 1827 | — | 4.00 | 8.00 | 15.00 | 30.00 |

Naples & Sicily / ITALIAN STATES — 1081

Obv: Young head w/o beard, large letters.

C#	Date	Mintage	Fine	VF	XF	Unc
143	1832	—	3.00	6.00	15.00	35.00
	1833	—	3.00	6.00	15.00	35.00
	1835	—	3.50	6.00	15.00	35.00
	1836	—	10.00	17.50	25.00	45.00

Obv: Legend w/small letters.

143a	1838	—	3.00	6.00	15.00	35.00
	1839	—	3.00	6.00	15.00	35.00
	1840	—	3.00	6.00	15.00	35.00
	1843	—	10.00	15.00	20.00	45.00
	1844	—	3.00	6.00	11.00	30.00
	1845	—	3.00	6.00	11.00	30.00
	1846	—	3.00	6.00	11.00	30.00
	1847	—	3.00	6.00	11.00	30.00
	1848	—	10.00	15.00	20.00	45.00

Obv: Older head w/beard.

143b	1845	—	2.50	5.50	10.00	30.00
	1849	—	2.50	5.50	10.00	30.00
	1851	—	2.50	5.50	10.00	30.00
	1852	—	2.50	5.50	10.00	30.00
	1853	—	2.50	5.50	10.00	30.00
	1854	—	2.50	5.50	10.00	30.00
	1855	—	10.00	15.00	20.00	45.00
	1857	—	2.50	5.50	10.00	30.00
	1858	—	2.50	5.50	10.00	30.00
	1859	—	2.50	5.50	10.00	30.00

UNO E MEZZO (1-1/2) TORNESE

COPPER
Obv: Young head w/o beard.

144	1832	—	7.50	15.00	30.00	75.00
	1835	—	7.50	15.00	30.00	75.00
	1836	—	7.50	15.00	30.00	75.00
	1838	—	5.00	12.50	40.00	75.00
	1839	—	7.50	15.00	30.00	75.00
	1840	—	7.50	15.00	30.00	75.00

Obv: Young head w/beard.

144a	1844	—	5.00	12.50	25.00	65.00
	1847	—	5.00	12.50	25.00	65.00
	1848	—	5.00	12.50	25.00	65.00

Obv: Older head w/beard.

144b	1849	—	5.00	12.50	25.00	60.00
	1850	—	5.00	12.50	25.00	60.00
	1851	—	5.00	12.50	25.00	60.00
	1853	—	5.00	12.50	25.00	60.00
	1854	—	5.00	12.50	25.00	60.00

DUE (2) TORNESI

COPPER

C#	Date	Mintage	VG	Fine	VF	XF
131	1825	—	3.00	6.50	12.50	25.00
	1826	—	3.00	6.50	12.50	25.00

Obv: Young head w/o beard.

C#	Date	Mintage	Fine	VF	XF	Unc
145	1832	—	12.00	30.00	75.00	125.00
	1835	—	12.00	30.00	75.00	125.00

Obv: Young head w/beard.

C#	Date	Mintage	Fine	VF	XF	Unc
145a	1838	—	4.00	13.50	20.00	45.00
	1839	—	3.00	8.50	20.00	40.00
	1842	—	3.00	8.50	20.00	40.00
	1843	—	3.00	8.50	20.00	40.00
	1847	—	3.00	8.50	20.00	40.00
	1848	—	3.00	8.50	20.00	40.00
	1849	—	3.00	8.50	20.00	40.00
	1851	—	3.00	8.50	20.00	40.00
	1852	—	3.00	8.50	20.00	40.00
	1853	—	3.00	8.50	20.00	40.00
	1854	—	3.00	8.50	20.00	40.00
	1855	—	3.00	8.50	20.00	40.00
	1856	—	3.00	8.50	20.00	40.00

145b	1857	—	2.50	7.00	20.00	40.00
	1858	—	2.50	7.00	20.00	40.00
	1859	—	2.50	7.00	20.00	40.00

NOTE: Many minor varieties exist such as position of the obverse legend, placement of dots in the legend, large and small dates, etc.

158	1859	—	2.50	7.50	20.00	45.00

TRE (3) TORNESI

COPPER
Obv: Young head w/o beard.

146	1833	—	5.00	15.00	30.00	75.00
	1835	—	5.00	15.00	30.00	75.00
	1837	—	5.00	15.00	30.00	75.00
	1838	—	5.00	15.00	30.00	75.00

Obv: Young head w/beard.

146a	1839	—	5.00	15.00	30.00	75.00
	1842	—	5.00	15.00	30.00	75.00
	1847	—	5.00	15.00	30.00	75.00
	1848	—	5.00	15.00	30.00	60.00
	1849	—	5.00	15.00	30.00	60.00
	1851	—	5.00	15.00	30.00	60.00
	1852	—	5.00	15.00	30.00	60.00
	1854	—	5.00	15.00	30.00	60.00
	1858	—	5.00	15.00	30.00	60.00

QUATTRO (4) TORNESI

COPPER

C#	Date	Mintage	VG	Fine	VF	XF
120	1817	—	15.00	30.00	45.00	90.00

CINQUE (5) TORNESI

COPPER

Obv: FERDINANDVS IV. D. G., etc.

C#	Date	Mintage	VG	Fine	VF	XF
114	1816	—	10.00	25.00	35.00	70.00

Obv: FERD. I.D.G., etc.

121	1816	—	9.00	25.00	45.00	80.00
	1817	—	5.00	10.00	20.00	40.00
	1818	—	5.00	10.00	20.00	40.00

121a	1819	—	7.50	15.00	30.00	55.00

132	1826	—	—	—	Rare	—
	1827	—	—	7.50	15.00	30.00	55.00

NOTE: Many varieties exist of 1827.

Obv: Young head w/o beard.

C#	Date	Mintage	Fine	VF	XF	Unc
147	1831	—	6.00	12.50	25.00	75.00
	1832	—	6.00	12.50	25.00	75.00
	1833	—	6.00	12.50	25.00	75.00
	1838	—	6.00	12.50	25.00	75.00
	1839	—	6.00	12.50	25.00	75.00
	1840	—	6.00	12.50	25.00	75.00
	1841	—	6.00	12.50	25.00	75.00

Obv: Young head w/beard.

147a	1841	—	5.00	10.00	25.00	75.00
	1842	—	5.00	10.00	25.00	75.00
	1843	—	5.00	10.00	25.00	75.00
	1845	—	5.00	10.00	25.00	75.00

Obv: Older head w/beard.

147b	1846	—	5.00	10.00	25.00	75.00
	1847	—	5.00	10.00	25.00	75.00
	1848	—	10.00	20.00	50.00	175.00
	1849	—	5.00	10.00	25.00	75.00
	1851	—	5.00	10.00	25.00	75.00
	1853	—	5.00	10.00	25.00	75.00
	1854	—	5.00	10.00	25.00	75.00
	1857	—	5.00	10.00	25.00	75.00
	1858	—	7.50	15.00	30.00	80.00
	1859	—	5.00	10.00	25.00	75.00

6 TORNESI

BRONZE
Overstruck on 10 Centesimi, 1813, C#107.

107a	ND	—	650.00	900.00	1500.	2500.

OTTO (8) TORNESI

COPPER
Obv: FERDINANDUS IV D. G., etc.
Rev: Similar to C#122

C#	Date	Mintage	VG	Fine	VF	XF
115	1816	—	10.00	20.00	40.00	100.00

Obv: FERD. I. D. G. . . . .

122	1816	—	10.00	20.00	35.00	75.00
	1817	—	10.00	20.00	35.00	75.00
	1818	—	10.00	20.00	35.00	75.00

DIECI (10) TORNESI

COPPER
Rev: Similar to 5 Tornesi, C#121a.

123	1819	—	5.00	10.00	30.00	75.00

Rev: Similar to C#148.

133	1825	—	5.00	10.00	30.00	75.00

Obv: Large head w/o beard.

C#	Date	Mintage	Fine	VF	XF	Unc
148	1831	—	15.00	35.00	75.00	175.00
	1832	—	7.50	17.50	30.00	150.00
	1833	—	7.50	17.50	30.00	150.00
	1834	—	25.00	50.00	100.00	250.00
	1835	—	7.50	17.50	30.00	90.00
	1836	—	16.00	35.00	60.00	160.00
	1837	—	10.00	20.00	40.00	150.00
	1838	—	10.00	20.00	40.00	150.00
	1839	—	10.00	20.00	40.00	100.00

Obv: Medium head w/beard.

148a	1839	—	7.50	17.50	30.00	90.00
	1840	—	12.50	25.00	40.00	95.00
	1841	—	7.50	17.50	30.00	90.00
	1844	—	7.50	17.50	30.00	90.00
	1846	—	7.50	17.50	30.00	90.00
	1847	—	10.00	25.00	50.00	150.00
	1848	—	7.50	17.50	30.00	90.00
	1849	—	7.50	17.50	30.00	90.00
	1851	—	16.00	35.00	60.00	160.00

Obv: Older head w/beard.

148b	1851	—	7.00	15.00	30.00	80.00
	1852	—	7.00	15.00	30.00	80.00
	1853	—	7.00	15.00	30.00	80.00
	1854	—	7.00	15.00	30.00	80.00
	1855	—	7.00	15.00	30.00	80.00
	1856	—	7.00	15.00	30.00	80.00
	1857	—	10.00	20.00	50.00	150.00
	1858	—	7.00	15.00	30.00	80.00
	1859	—	7.00	15.00	30.00	80.00

NOTE: Minor varieties exist, i.e., leg. size, location.

C#	Date	Mintage	Fine	VF	XF	Unc
159	1859	—	12.50	25.00	50.00	125.00

CINQUE (5) GRANA

1.1500 g, .833 SILVER, .0308 oz ASW
Obv: Young head right w/o beard.

149	1836	—	3.50	6.00	15.00	50.00
	1838	—	3.50	6.00	15.00	50.00
	1844	—	3.50	6.00	15.00	50.00
	1845	—	3.50	6.00	15.00	50.00
	1846	—	3.50	6.00	15.00	50.00
	1847	—	3.50	6.00	15.00	50.00

Obv: Young head w/beard.

149a	1848	—	7.50	12.50	20.00	50.00
	1851	—	3.50	6.00	15.00	50.00
	1853	—	3.50	6.00	15.00	50.00

10 GRANA

2.2900 g, .833 SILVER, .0613 oz ASW
Obv: Head right. Rev: Arms.

C#	Date	Mintage	VG	Fine	VF	XF
116	1815	—	7.50	15.00	35.00	65.00
	1816	—	7.50	15.00	35.00	65.00

124	1818	—	5.00	10.00	20.00	50.00

Obv: Head right.

134	1826	—	5.00	10.00	15.00	35.00

Obv: Young head w/o beard, continuous leg.

C#	Date	Mintage	Fine	VF	XF	Unc
150	1832	—	7.50	15.00	30.00	60.00
	1833	—	7.50	12.50	25.00	45.00
	1834	—	7.50	15.00	30.00	60.00
	1835	—	7.50	15.00	30.00	60.00

Obv: Leg. divided over young head w/o beard.

150a	1835	—	6.00	12.50	20.00	50.00
	1836	—	6.00	12.50	20.00	50.00
	1837	—	6.00	12.50	20.00	50.00
	1838	—	6.00	12.50	20.00	50.00
	1839	—	6.00	12.50	20.00	50.00

Obv: Young head w/beard.

150b	1838	—	10.00	18.00	25.00	60.00
	1839	—	6.00	12.50	20.00	50.00
	1840	—	6.00	12.50	20.00	50.00
	1841	—	6.00	12.50	20.00	50.00
	1842	—	6.00	12.50	20.00	50.00
	1843	—	15.00	25.00	40.00	70.00
	1844	—	6.00	12.50	20.00	50.00
	1845	—	6.00	12.50	20.00	50.00
	1846	—	6.00	12.50	20.00	50.00

Obv: Older head w/beard.

C#	Date	Mintage	Fine	VF	XF	Unc
150c	1847	—	5.00	7.50	15.00	40.00
	1848	—	5.00	7.50	15.00	40.00
	1849	—	10.00	20.00	40.00	100.00
	1850	—	6.00	12.50	20.00	50.00
	1851	—	6.00	12.50	20.00	50.00
	1853	—	5.00	7.50	15.00	40.00
	1854	—	5.00	7.50	15.00	40.00
	1855	—	5.00	7.50	15.00	40.00
	1856	—	5.00	7.50	15.00	40.00
	1859	—	5.00	7.50	15.00	40.00

20 GRANA
4.5900 g, .833 SILVER, .1229 oz ASW

C#	Date	Mintage	VG	Fine	VF	XF
135	1826	—	10.00	20.00	40.00	80.00

Obv: Young head w/o beard.

C#	Date	Mintage	Fine	VF	XF	Unc
151	1831	—	10.00	20.00	40.00	150.00
	1832	—	10.00	20.00	40.00	150.00
	1833	—	10.00	20.00	40.00	150.00
	1834	—	10.00	20.00	40.00	150.00
	1835	—	10.00	20.00	40.00	150.00
	1836	—	10.00	20.00	40.00	150.00
	1837	—	10.00	20.00	40.00	150.00
	1838	—	10.00	20.00	40.00	150.00
	1839	—	10.00	20.00	40.00	150.00

Obv: Young head w/beard.

C#	Date	Mintage	Fine	VF	XF	Unc
151a	1839	—	10.00	20.00	40.00	150.00
	1840	—	10.00	20.00	40.00	150.00
	1841	—	10.00	20.00	40.00	150.00
	1842	—	10.00	20.00	35.00	145.00
	1843	—	10.00	20.00	40.00	150.00
	1844	—	10.00	20.00	40.00	150.00
	1845	—	10.00	20.00	40.00	150.00
	1846	—	15.00	30.00	60.00	175.00
	1847	—	10.00	20.00	40.00	150.00
	1848	—	10.00	20.00	40.00	150.00
	1850	—	10.00	20.00	40.00	150.00
	1851	—	10.00	20.00	40.00	150.00
	1852	—	10.00	20.00	40.00	150.00
	1853	—	10.00	20.00	40.00	150.00
	1854	—	10.00	20.00	40.00	150.00
	1855	—	10.00	20.00	40.00	150.00
	1856	—	10.00	20.00	40.00	150.00
	1857	—	10.00	20.00	40.00	150.00
	1858	—	10.00	20.00	40.00	150.00
	1859/8	—	12.50	25.00	50.00	175.00
	1859	—	10.00	20.00	40.00	150.00

160	1859	—	12.50	25.00	50.00	175.00

60 GRANA
13.7500 g, .833 SILVER, .3682 oz ASW
Obv: Head right, FERD IV. D. G., etc.

C#	Date	Mintage	VG	Fine	VF	XF
117	1816	—	15.00	25.00	75.00	175.00

Obv: Crowned head right, FERD I D. G., etc.

| 125 | 1818 | — | 20.00 | 35.00 | 65.00 | 150.00 |

Obv: Head right. Rev: Arms within wreath.

| 136 | 1826 | — | 25.00 | 45.00 | 90.00 | 250.00 |

Obv: Young head w/o beard, leg. continuous.

C#	Date	Mintage	Fine	VF	XF	Unc
152	1831	—	20.00	35.00	75.00	300.00
	1832	—	20.00	35.00	75.00	300.00
	1833	—	20.00	35.00	75.00	300.00
	1834	—	20.00	35.00	75.00	300.00

Obv: Leg. divided.

152a	1835	—	20.00	40.00	80.00	350.00
	1836	—	20.00	35.00	75.00	300.00
	1837	—	50.00	90.00	125.00	600.00
	1838	—	20.00	35.00	75.00	300.00
	1839	—	35.00	60.00	100.00	350.00

Obv: Young head w/beard.

| 152b | 1841 | — | 35.00 | 65.00 | 115.00 | 300.00 |

C#	Date	Mintage	Fine	VF	XF	Unc
152b	1842	—	35.00	65.00	115.00	300.00
	1845	—	35.00	65.00	115.00	300.00

Obv: Older head w/beard.

152c	1846	—	35.00	60.00	100.00	300.00
	1847	—	35.00	60.00	100.00	300.00
	1848	—	35.00	60.00	100.00	300.00
	1850	—	35.00	60.00	100.00	300.00
	1851	—	35.00	60.00	100.00	300.00
	1852	—	35.00	60.00	100.00	300.00
	1854	—	35.00	60.00	100.00	300.00
	1855	—	35.00	60.00	75.00	250.00
	1856	—	35.00	60.00	100.00	300.00
	1857	—	35.00	60.00	100.00	300.00
	1858	—	35.00	60.00	100.00	300.00
	1859	—	35.00	60.00	100.00	300.00

GOLD (OMS)

| 152.5 | 1856 | — | — | — | Proof | 4400. |

120 GRANA

27.5300 g, .833 SILVER, .7373 oz ASW

C#	Date	Mintage	VG	Fine	VF	XF
118	1815	—	45.00	70.00	100.00	185.00
	1816	—	50.00	80.00	125.00	200.00
	1816R	*	55.00	90.00	140.00	250.00

*NOTE: The R(istampato) issues were struck over the coins of Joseph Napoleon and Joachim Murat.

Obv: Large crowned head.

| 126 | 1817 | — | 30.00 | 50.00 | 90.00 | 165.00 |
| | 1818 | — | 20.00 | 30.00 | 50.00 | 145.00 |

Obv: Small crowned head.

C#	Date	Mintage	VG	Fine	VF	XF
126a	1818	—	25.00	35.00	75.00	200.00

27.5300 g, .833 SILVER, .7373 oz ASW

C#	Date	Mintage	Fine	VF	XF	Unc
137	1825	—	35.00	75.00	200.00	600.00
	1825R	—	45.00	90.00	250.00	800.00
	1826	—	35.00	75.00	200.00	600.00
	1826 R	—	45.00	90.00	250.00	800.00
	1828	—	55.00	100.00	275.00	900.00

Rev: Similar to C#153a.

153	1831	—	22.50	30.00	75.00	200.00
	1832	—	22.50	30.00	75.00	200.00
	1833	—	30.00	50.00	90.00	225.00
	1834	—	30.00	50.00	90.00	225.00
	1835	—	22.50	30.00	75.00	200.00

C#	Date	Mintage	Fine	VF	XF	Unc
153a	1835	—	27.50	40.00	90.00	225.00
	1836	—	22.50	30.00	75.00	200.00
	1837	—	30.00	60.00	100.00	300.00
	1838	—	22.50	30.00	75.00	200.00
	1839	—	30.00	60.00	100.00	300.00

Rev: Similar to C#153a.

153b	1840	—	22.50	30.00	70.00	175.00
	1841	—	22.50	30.00	70.00	175.00
	1842	—	22.50	30.00	70.00	175.00
	1843	—	22.50	30.00	70.00	175.00
	1844	—	22.50	30.00	70.00	175.00
	1845	—	22.50	30.00	70.00	175.00
	1846	—	22.50	30.00	70.00	175.00
	1847	—	25.00	50.00	100.00	200.00
	1848	—	25.00	50.00	100.00	200.00
	1849	—	100.00	150.00	500.00	1000.
	1850	—	22.50	30.00	50.00	175.00
	1851	—	22.50	30.00	70.00	175.00

NOTE: Many varieties exist.

Rev: Similar to C#153a.

153c	1851	—	22.50	30.00	60.00	125.00
	1852	—	22.50	30.00	60.00	125.00
	1853	—	22.50	30.00	60.00	125.00
	1854	—	22.50	30.00	60.00	125.00
	1855	—	22.50	30.00	60.00	125.00
	1856	—	22.50	30.00	60.00	125.00
	1857	—	22.50	30.00	60.00	125.00
	1858	—	22.50	30.00	60.00	125.00
	1859	—	22.50	30.00	60.00	125.00

Rev: Similar to C#153a.

| 161 | 1859 | — | 30.00 | 50.00 | 125.00 | 250.00 |

3 DUCATI

3.7900 g, .996 GOLD, .1213 oz AGW

C#	Date	Mintage	VG	Fine	VF	XF
127	1818	—	150.00	225.00	300.00	450.00

Obv: Head right. Rev: Winged Genius.

C#	Date	Mintage	VG	Fine	VF	XF
138	1826	—	300.00	400.00	550.00	1100.

Obv: Young head w/o beard.

C#	Date	Mintage	Fine	VF	XF	Unc
154	1831	—	200.00	250.00	350.00	1000.
	1832	—	200.00	250.00	350.00	1000.
	1835	—	200.00	250.00	350.00	1000.
154a	1837	—	200.00	250.00	350.00	1000.

Obv: Young head w/beard.

| 154b | 1839 | — | 200.00 | 250.00 | 350.00 | 750.00 |
| | 1840 | — | 200.00 | 250.00 | 350.00 | 750.00 |

154c	1842	—	200.00	250.00	350.00	750.00
	1845	—	200.00	250.00	350.00	750.00
	1846	—	200.00	250.00	350.00	750.00
	1848	—	200.00	250.00	350.00	750.00

Obv: Older head w/beard.

154d	1850	—	200.00	250.00	350.00	750.00
	1851	—	200.00	250.00	350.00	750.00
	1852	—	200.00	250.00	350.00	750.00
	1854	—	100.00	175.00	250.00	500.00
	1856	—	200.00	250.00	350.00	750.00

6 DUCATI

7.5700 g, .996 GOLD, .2424 oz AGW

C#	Date	Mintage	VG	Fine	VF	XF
139	1826	—	200.00	400.00	600.00	1400.

Obv: Young head w/o beard. Rev: Winged Genius.

C#	Date	Mintage	Fine	VF	XF	Unc
155	1831	—	150.00	250.00	350.00	800.00
	1833	—	200.00	350.00	500.00	1500.
	1835	—	250.00	450.00	600.00	1750.

Obv: Young head w/beard.

| 155b | 1840 | — | 200.00 | 350.00 | 500.00 | 1250. |

Obv: Older head w/beard.

155c	1842	—	225.00	375.00	525.00	1250.
	1845	—	225.00	375.00	525.00	1250.
	1847	—	225.00	375.00	525.00	1250.
	1848	—	225.00	375.00	650.00	1500.
	1850	—	225.00	375.00	525.00	1250.
	1851	—	225.00	375.00	525.00	1250.
155c	1852	—	225.00	375.00	525.00	1250.
	1854	—	225.00	375.00	525.00	1250.
	1856	—	225.00	375.00	525.00	1250.

15 DUCATI

18.9300 g, .996 GOLD, .6062 oz AGW

C#	Date	Mintage	VG	Fine	VF	XF
128	1818	—	300.00	550.00	750.00	1250.

C#	Date	Mintage	Fine	VF	XF	Unc
140	1825	—	—	—	Rare	—

| 156 | 1831 | — | 500.00 | 800.00 | 1250. | 2750. |

Obv: Young head w/beard. Rev: Winged Genius.

156c	1842	—	550.00	800.00	1550.	3250.
	1844	—	450.00	700.00	850.00	1750.
	1845	—	450.00	700.00	850.00	1750.
	1847	—	450.00	700.00	850.00	1750.

Obv: Older head w/beard.

156d	1848	—	400.00	675.00	1250.	3000.
	1850	—	400.00	675.00	800.00	1750.
	1851	—	400.00	675.00	800.00	1750.
	1852	—	400.00	675.00	800.00	1750.
	1854	—	400.00	675.00	800.00	1750.
	1856	—	400.00	675.00	800.00	1750.

30 DUCATI

37.8700 g, .996 GOLD, 1.2128 oz AGW

C#	Date	Mintage	VG	Fine	VF	XF
129	1818	—	600.00	750.00	1400.	2000.

C#	Date	Mintage	Fine	VF	XF	Unc
157c	1842				Rare	
	1844	—	600.00	900.00	1750.	3250.
	1845	—	600.00	900.00	1750.	3250.
	1847	—	600.00	900.00	1750.	3250.
	1848	—	600.00	900.00	1750.	3250.
	1851	—	600.00	900.00	1750.	3250.
	1854	—	600.00	900.00	1750.	3250.

141	1825	—	600.00	750.00	1500.	3000.
	1826	—	600.00	750.00	1500.	3000.

157e	1850	—	500.00	800.00	1500.	2500.
	1851	—	600.00	900.00	1750.	3250.
	1852	—	600.00	900.00	1750.	3250.

Obv: Small older head w/beard.

157d	1854	—	600.00	900.00	1750.	3250.
	1856	—	600.00	900.00	1750.	3250.

PARMA

A town in Emillia which was a papal possession from 1512 to 1545, was seized by France in 1796, and was attached to the Napoleonic empire in 1808. In 1814 Parma was assigned to Marie Louise, empress of Napoleon I. It was annexed to Sardinia in 1860.

RULERS
Ferdinando di Borbone, 1765-1802
Maria Luigia, Duchess, 1815-1847
Carlo II di Borbone, 1847-1849
Carlo III di Borbone, 1849-1854
Roberto di Borbone, 1854-1858

MONETARY SYSTEM
100 Centesimi = 20 Soldi = 1 Lira

CENTESIMO
COPPER
Similar to 5 Centesimi, C#25.

C#	Date	Mintage	Fine	VF	XF	Unc
157	1831	—	500.00	800.00	1500.	2500.
	1833	—	600.00	900.00	1750.	3250.
	1835	—	600.00	900.00	1750.	3250.

23	1830	2.029	4.00	7.50	12.50	40.00

Obv: Head of Carlo III left. Rev: Oval arms.

33	1854	—	200.00	300.00	375.00	500.00

3 CENTESIMI
COPPER
Similar to 5 Centesimi, C#25.

24	1830	.511	20.00	30.00	50.00	100.00

Obv: Head of Carlo III left. Rev: Oval arms.

34	1854	—	350.00	500.00	600.00	1000.

5 CENTESIMI

COPPER

25	1830	1.506	5.00	10.00	20.00	60.00

Obv: Head of Carlo III left. Rev: Oval arms.

35	1854	—	700.00	1000.	1400.	2000.

157b	1839	—	600.00	900.00	1750.	3250.
	1840	—	600.00	900.00	1750.	3250.

Parma / ITALIAN STATES 1085

5 SOLDI

1.2500 g, .900 SILVER, .0361 oz ASW

C#	Date	Mintage	Fine	VF	XF	Unc
26	1815/3	.682	9.00	15.00	25.00	75.00
	1815	Inc. Ab.	7.50	12.50	20.00	50.00
	1830	—	10.00	15.00	25.00	50.00

10 SOLDI

2.5000 g, .900 SILVER, .0722 oz ASW
Obv: Maria bust left. Rev: ML monogram.

27	1815	.530	12.00	20.00	30.00	85.00
	1830	—	25.00	50.00	100.00	200.00

LIRA

5.0000 g, .900 SILVER, .1444 oz ASW

28	1815	.066	20.00	40.00	80.00	200.00

2 LIRE

10.0000 g, .900 SILVER, .2888 oz ASW

29	1815	.022	50.00	100.00	200.00	500.00

5 LIRE

25.0000 g, .900 SILVER, .7234 oz ASW

30	1815	.093	100.00	150.00	250.00	750.00
	1821	—	—	—	Rare	
	1832	.044	125.00	200.00	400.00	1000.

Parma / ITALIAN STATES 1086

C#	Date	Mintage	Fine	VF	XF	Unc
36	1858	1,000	350.00	500.00	850.00	1500.

20 LIRE

6.4500 g, .900 GOLD, .1866 oz AGW

31	1815	.012	300.00	400.00	575.00	1000.
	1832	1,550	1000.	1500.	2000.	3000.

40 LIRE

12.9000 g, .900 GOLD, .3733 oz AGW

32	1815	.220	200.00	325.00	400.00	700.00
	1821	.037	250.00	400.00	650.00	1500.

PIEDMONT REPUBLIC

Established by Napoleon in 1798 in the Piedmont area of northwest Italy which was the mainland possession of the kingdom of Sardinia, the republic was overthrown by Austro-Russian forces in 1799.

SUBALPINE REPUBLIC
1800-1801

5 FRANCS

25.0000 g, .900 SILVER, .7234 oz ASW

C#	Date	Mintage	VG	Fine	VF	XF
4	L'AN 10(1801)	.033	40.00	60.00	90.00	200.00

20 FRANCS

6.4500 g, .900 GOLD, .1866 oz AGW

5	L'AN 10(1801)	1,492	300.00	500.00	800.00	1250.

SARDINIA

A Roman see in the 11th century occupied by the competitive cities of Pisa and Genoa. In 1297 it was granted to James II of Aragon, and remained under Spanish control until passing to the house of Savoy in 1720. In 1861 it became the nucleus about which the United Kingdom of Italy was formed.

RULERS
Vittorio Emanuele I 1802-1821
Carlo Felice 1821-1831
Carlo Alberto 1831-1849
Vittorio Emanuele II 1849-1878

MINT MARKS
M - Milan
Angel head - Turin

MONETARY SYSTEM
12 Denari = 6 Cagliarese = 1 Soldo
50 Soldi = 10 Reales =
2-1/2 Lire = 1 Scudo Sardo
2 Scudi Sardi = 1 Doppietta
Commencing 1816
100 Centesimi = 1 Lira

TRE (3) CAGLIARESE

COPPER
Obv: Cross on arms. Rev: Value.

C#	Date	Mintage	Fine	VF	XF	Unc
88	ND(1813)	—	40.00	60.00	90.00	150.00

REALE

3.1800 g, .500 SILVER, .0551 oz ASW
Obv: Head right, VIC.EM.D.G.REX.SAR.CYP.ET.IER. around, date.
Rev: Eagle on shield w/head to right, crown above.

89.1	1812	—	60.00	90.00	125.00	250.00

Rev: Eagle's head to left.

89.2	1812	—	60.00	90.00	125.00	250.00

MONETARY REFORM
100 Centesimi = 1 Lira

CENTESIMO

COPPER
Mint mark: Eagle head

118	1842	1.933	40.00	60.00	75.00	140.00

3 CENTESIMI

COPPER
Mint mark: Eagle head
Obv: Arms. Rev: Value and date.

119	1842	2.169	10.00	20.00	40.00	75.00

5 CENTESIMI

COPPER
Mint mark: Eagle head
Obv: Arms. Rev: Value and date.

120	1842	1.845	10.00	25.00	50.00	90.00

SICILY

Has a history of occupation extending back to the ancient Phoenicians. In more recent times it was part of the Kingdom of Naples and Sicily.

RULERS
Ferdinando III, 1759-1825
  (became Ferdinando I in 1816
  as King of Two Sicilies)
Ferdinando II, 1830-1859

MINTMASTER'S INITIALS
Palermo Mint

Letter	Date	Name
JVI	1798-1807	Guiseppe Ugo
VB	1810-1816	Vicenzo Beninati

MONETARY SYSTEM
6 Cavalli = 1 Grano
20 Grani = 2 Carlini = 1 Tari
12 Tari = 1 Piastra
15 Tari = 1 Scudo
2 Scudi = 1 Oncia

MEZZO (1/2) GRANO

COPPER
Obv: Head right. Rev: Value, SICILIANO, date.

C#	Date	Mintage	VG	Fine	VF	XF
52	1836	—	10.00	25.00	60.00	125.00

UN (1) GRANO

COPPER
Obv: Eagle, leg. Rev: Value, date within wreath.

41	1801 JVI	—	6.00	10.00	20.00	35.00
	1802 JVI	—	9.00	15.00	25.00	50.00
	1803 JVI	—	20.00	30.00	50.00	100.00

42	ND(1814) VB	—	20.00	30.00	50.00	100.00
	1814 VB	—	5.00	10.00	20.00	35.00
	1815 VB	—	5.00	10.00	20.00	35.00

NOTE: Varieties exist.

Obv: Head right. Rev: SICILIANO, value, date.

53	1836	—	50.00	100.00	200.00	300.00

DUE (2) GRANI

COPPER
Obv: Eagle, leg. Rev: Value, date within wreath.

43	1801 JVI	—	20.00	30.00	50.00	100.00
	1802 JVI	—	6.00	10.00	20.00	40.00
	1803 JVI	—	6.00	10.00	20.00	40.00
	1804 JVI	—	6.00	10.00	20.00	40.00

44	1814 VB	—	10.00	15.00	25.00	50.00
	1815 VB	—	6.00	10.00	20.00	40.00

NOTE: 1814 exists w/large and small G.2.

Obv: Head right. Rev: SICILIANI, value, date.

54	1836	—	50.00	100.00	200.00	300.00

CINQUE (5) GRANI

COPPER
Obv: Eagle, leg. Rev: Value, date within wreath.

45	1801 JVI	—	30.00	45.00	75.00	150.00
	1802 JVI	—	15.00	22.50	50.00	125.00
	1803 JVI	—	15.00	22.50	50.00	125.00
	1804 JVI	—	15.00	22.50	50.00	125.00

Obv: Large head.

46	ND(1814) VB	—	30.00	45.00	75.00	150.00
	1814 VB	—	12.00	20.00	40.00	90.00
	1815 VB	—	12.00	20.00	40.00	90.00

NOTE: Varieties exist of 1815.

Obv: Small head.

46a	1815 VB	—	12.00	20.00	40.00	90.00
	1816 VB	—	20.00	30.00	50.00	100.00

Obv: Head right. Rev: SICILIANI, crown, value, date.

55	1836	—	100.00	150.00	250.00	400.00

DIECI (10) GRANI

COPPER
Obv: Eagle, leg. Rev: Value, date within wreath.

47	1801 JVI	—	20.00	30.00	50.00	125.00
	1802 JVI	—	20.00	30.00	50.00	125.00
	1803 JVI	—	20.00	30.00	50.00	125.00
	1804 JVI	—	20.00	30.00	50.00	125.00

2 ONCIE

8.8150 g, .906 GOLD, .2567 oz AGW

C#	Date	Mintage	Fine	VF	XF	Unc
51	1814 VB	—	1500.	3000.	5000.	8000.

TUSCANY
Etruria

An Italian territorial division on the west-central peninsula, belonged to the Medici from 1530 to 1737, when it was given to Francis, duke of Lorraine. In 1800 the French established it as part of the Spanish dominions; from 1807 to 1809 it was a French department. After the fall of Napoleon it reverted to its pre-Napoleonic owner, Ferdinand III.

RULERS
Louis I, 1801-1803
Charles Louis, under regency of his mother Maria Louisa, 1803-1807
Annexed To France 1807-1814
Ferdinando III Restored 1814-1824
Leopold II 1824-1848, 1849-1859
Provisional Government 1859
United to Italian Provisional Government 1859-1861

MINT MARKS
Firenze – Florence
Leghorn (Livorno)
Pisa

MONETARY SYSTEM
Until 1826
12 Denari = 3 Quattrini = 1 Soldo
20 Soldi = 1 Lira
10 Lire = 1 Dena
40 Quattrini = 1 Paolo
1-1/2 Paoli = 1 Lira
10 Paoli = 1 Francescone, Scudo, Tallero
3 Zecchini = 1 Ruspone = 40 Lire
1826-1859
100 Quattrini = 1 Fiorino
4 Fiorini = 10 Paoli
1859
100 Centesimi = 1 Lira

QUATTRINO
COPPER
Obv: Square arms. Rev: Value and date.

C#	Date	Mintage	VG	Fine	VF	XF
30	1801	—	3.00	5.00	9.00	25.00

Obv: Crowned arms. Rev: Value.

40	1802	—	12.00	20.00	80.00	125.00
	1803	—	5.00	8.00	35.00	60.00
	1805 (error date)	—	5.50	8.50	36.50	65.00
44	1803	—	5.00	8.00	40.00	80.00
	1804	—	5.00	8.00	40.00	80.00
	1805	—	5.00	8.00	40.00	80.00
	1806	—	5.00	8.00	40.00	80.00
	1807	—	5.00	8.00	40.00	80.00

Obv: Arms, leg: FERD.III.... Rev: Value.

53	1819	—	2.75	4.00	15.00	30.00
	1820	—	2.75	4.00	15.00	30.00
	1821	—	2.75	4.00	15.00	30.00
	1822	—	2.75	4.00	15.00	30.00
	1824	—	2.75	4.00	15.00	30.00

Obv. leg: LEOP. II A.D.'A. GRAND. DI TOSC.

62	1827	—	2.75	4.00	12.00	25.00
	1828	—	2.75	4.00	12.00	25.00
	1829	—	2.75	4.00	12.00	25.00
	1830	—	2.75	4.00	12.00	25.00
	1831	—	2.75	4.00	12.00	25.00
	1832	—	2.75	4.00	12.00	25.00
	1833	—	2.75	4.00	12.00	25.00
	1834	—	2.75	4.00	12.00	25.00
	1835	—	2.75	4.00	12.00	25.00
	1836	—	2.75	4.00	12.00	25.00
	1837	—	2.75	4.00	12.00	25.00
	1838	—	2.75	4.00	12.00	25.00
	1840	—	2.75	4.00	12.00	25.00
	1841	—	5.00	7.50	35.00	60.00
	1843	—	5.00	7.50	35.00	60.00

C#	Date	Mintage	VG	Fine	VF	XF
48	ND(1814) VB	—	30.00	50.00	100.00	200.00
	1814 VB	—	20.00	30.00	50.00	150.00
	1815 VB	—	20.00	30.00	60.00	175.00

NOTE: 1815 exists with G.10. and G.10, and w/lower right tip of bust pointing to E in REX; also tip of bust pointing to X in REX.

Obv: Head right. Rev: SICILIANI, crown, value, date.

56	1835	—	400.00	500.00	750.00	1000.
	1836	—	100.00	150.00	300.00	500.00

12 TARI
27.5330 g, .883 SILVER, .7817 oz ASW
Obv: Bust right, FERDINAN.D.G.SICIL....
Rev: Eagle, date.

49	1801 JVI	—	40.00	75.00	125.00	200.00
	1803 JVI	—	40.00	75.00	125.00	200.00

NOTE: 1801 exists w/REX. and REX

Obv. leg: FERDINAN. III. D.G.SICIL....

49a	1801 JVI	—	40.00	75.00	125.00	200.00
	1802 JVI	—	40.00	75.00	125.00	200.00
	1803 JVI	—	40.00	75.00	125.00	200.00
	1804 JVI	—	40.00	75.00	125.00	200.00

Rev: J.V.I. above eagle within wreath.

50	1805 JVI	—	50.00	100.00	200.00	400.00
	1806 JVI	—	50.00	100.00	200.00	400.00
	1807 JVI	—	50.00	100.00	200.00	400.00

Rev: Eagle between V. and B. within wreath.

50a	1810 VB	—	50.00	100.00	150.00	350.00

NOTE: Seven varieties exist.

Obv. leg: LEOP. II A.D.'A. G-D. DI TOSC.

C#	Date	Mintage	VG	Fine	VF	XF
62a	1842	—	5.00	7.50	35.00	60.00
	1843	—	2.75	4.00	12.00	25.00
	1844	—	2.75	4.00	12.00	25.00
	1845	—	2.75	4.00	12.00	25.00
	1846	—	2.75	4.00	12.00	25.00
	1847	—	2.75	4.00	12.00	25.00
	1848	—	2.75	4.00	12.00	25.00
	1849	—	2.75	4.00	12.00	25.00
	1850	—	2.75	4.00	12.00	25.00
	1851	—	2.75	4.00	12.00	25.00
	1852	—	2.75	4.00	12.00	25.00
	1853	—	2.75	4.00	12.00	25.00
	1854	—	2.75	4.00	12.00	25.00
	1856	—	2.75	4.00	12.00	25.00
	1857	—	2.75	4.00	12.00	25.00

MEZZO (1/2) SOLDO
COPPER

45	ND(1804)	—	3.50	5.00	40.00	65.00

3 QUATTRINI

COPPER

64	1826	—	2.75	4.00	10.00	30.00
	1827	—	2.75	4.00	10.00	30.00
	1828	—	2.75	4.00	10.00	30.00
	1829	—	4.50	9.00	35.00	60.00
	1830	—	2.75	4.00	10.00	30.00
	1832	—	2.75	4.00	10.00	30.00
	1833	—	2.75	4.00	10.00	30.00
	1834	—	2.75	4.00	10.00	30.00
	1835	—	2.75	4.00	10.00	30.00
	1836	—	2.75	4.00	10.00	30.00
	1838	—	2.75	4.00	10.00	30.00
	1839	—	2.75	4.00	10.00	30.00
	1840	—	2.75	4.00	10.00	30.00
	1843	—	2.75	4.00	10.00	30.00
	1845	—	2.75	4.00	10.00	30.00
	1846	—	2.75	4.00	10.00	30.00
	1851	—	2.75	4.00	10.00	30.00
	1853	—	2.75	4.00	10.00	30.00
	1854	—	4.50	9.00	35.00	60.00

SOLDO
COPPER
Obv: Arms, leg: FERD.III..... Rev: Value.

54	1822	—	2.00	4.00	10.00	30.00
	1823	—	2.00	4.00	10.00	30.00

Obv: Arms, leg: LEOP.II..... Rev: Value.

63	1824	—	15.00	30.00	50.00	100.00

5 QUATTRINI

BILLON

65	1826	—	3.50	7.00	30.00	40.00
	1828	—	5.00	10.00	35.00	45.00
	1829	—	3.50	7.00	30.00	40.00
	1830	—	3.50	7.00	30.00	40.00

2 SOLDI
COPPER
Obv: Leg., arms. Rev: Value.

46	1804	—	6.00	12.00	50.00	75.00
	1805	—	6.00	12.00	50.00	75.00

Obv: Arms, leg: FERDINANDUS III..... Rev: Value.

55	1818	—	2.00	4.00	10.00	30.00
	1822	—	2.00	4.00	10.00	30.00

DIECI (10) QUATTRINI
BILLON
Obv: Squarish arms. Rev: Value.

41	1801	—	6.00	10.00	35.00	75.00
	1802	—	6.00	10.00	35.00	75.00

Obv: Arms and date. Rev: Value in field.

41a	1802	—	12.00	20.00	50.00	100.00

Obv: Arms. Rev: Value and date.

41b	1802	—	6.00	10.00	20.00	50.00

Obv: Round arms. Rev: "10 QUATTRINI"

66	1826	—	6.00	10.00	15.00	25.00
	1827	—	6.00	10.00	15.00	25.00
	1853	—	6.00	10.00	15.00	25.00
	1854	—	6.00	10.00	15.00	25.00

Tuscany / ITALIAN STATES 1088

C#	Date	Mintage	VG	Fine	VF	XF
67	1858	—	12.00	20.00	30.00	50.00

1/2 PAOLO

1.3700 g, .920 SILVER, .0405 oz ASW

68	1832	—	7.50	15.00	35.00	65.00
	1839	—	7.50	15.00	25.00	40.00

68a	1853	—	7.50	15.00	35.00	65.00
	1856	—	7.50	15.00	35.00	65.00
	1857	—	7.50	15.00	35.00	65.00
	1859	—	7.50	15.00	35.00	65.00

1/4 DI FIORINO

1.7190 g, .916 SILVER, .0506 oz ASW
Obv: Arms. Rev: Value.

69	1827	—	12.00	20.00	50.00	100.00

10 SOLDI

2.5100 g, .913 SILVER, .0736 oz ASW
Obv: Arms. Rev: Value.

56	1821	—	6.00	10.00	15.00	25.00
	1823	—	6.00	10.00	15.00	25.00

PAOLO

2.7400 g, .920 SILVER, .0810 oz ASW

70	1831	—	7.50	15.00	30.00	50.00
	1832	—	7.50	15.00	30.00	50.00
	1838	—	7.50	15.00	30.00	50.00

70a	1842	—	7.50	15.00	30.00	50.00
	1843	—	7.50	15.00	30.00	50.00
	1845	—	7.50	15.00	30.00	50.00
	1846	—	7.50	15.00	30.00	50.00
	1856	—	7.50	15.00	30.00	50.00
	1857	—	7.50	15.00	30.00	50.00
	1858	—	7.50	15.00	30.00	50.00

LIRA

3.9000 g, .920 SILVER, .1153 oz ASW

47	1803	—	10.00	15.00	30.00	75.00
	1806	—	10.00	15.00	30.00	75.00

4.1030 g, .913 SILVER, .1204 oz ASW
Obv: Head right. Rev: Value.

57	1821	—	12.00	20.00	50.00	100.00
	1822	—	12.00	20.00	50.00	100.00
	1823	—	12.00	20.00	50.00	100.00

1/2 FIORINO

3.4380 g, .916 SILVER, .1012 oz ASW

Obv: Arms. Rev: Value.

C#	Date	Mintage	VG	Fine	VF	XF
71	1827	—	10.00	17.50	35.00	75.00

FIORINO

6.8760 g, .916 SILVER, .2025 oz ASW

72	1826	—	10.00	15.00	25.00	75.00
	1828	—	10.00	15.00	25.00	75.00
	1830	—	10.00	15.00	25.00	75.00
	1840	—	10.00	15.00	25.00	75.00
	1842	—	10.00	15.00	25.00	75.00

72a	1843	—	10.00	15.00	25.00	50.00
	1844	—	10.00	15.00	25.00	50.00
	1847	—	10.00	15.00	25.00	50.00
	1848	—	10.00	15.00	25.00	50.00
	1856	—	10.00	15.00	25.00	50.00
	1857	—	10.00	15.00	25.00	50.00
	1858	—	10.00	15.00	25.00	50.00

5 PAOLI

13.7500 g, .913 SILVER, .4036 oz ASW

58	1819	—	30.00	50.00	200.00	350.00
	1820	—	30.00	50.00	100.00	200.00

Obv: Longer hair.

58a	1823	—	60.00	100.00	250.00	500.00

13.7500 g, .916 SILVER, .4049 oz ASW

73	1827	—	25.00	40.00	100.00	200.00
	1828	—	25.00	40.00	100.00	200.00
	1829 PC	—	25.00	40.00	100.00	200.00

73a	1834	—	125.00	150.00	250.00	600.00

5 LIRE

19.7230 g, .958 SILVER, .6075 oz ASW

C#	Date	Mintage	VG	Fine	VF	XF
48	1803	—	25.00	40.00	125.00	250.00
	1804	—	25.00	40.00	100.00	200.00

FRANCESCONE
(10 Paoli)

27.5000 g, .934 SILVER, .8258 oz ASW
Rev: Modified order chain.

42.1 (C42)	1801	—	200.00	400.00	800.00	1500.
	1802	—	200.00	400.00	800.00	1500.

42.2 (C42.1)	1803	—	65.00	100.00	150.00	300.00

Tuscany / ITALIAN STATES 1089

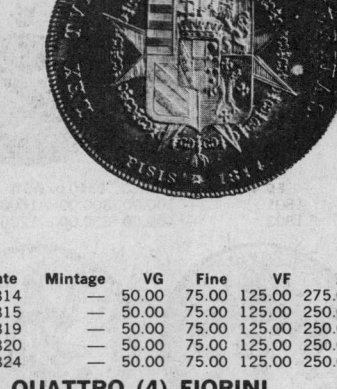

C#	Date	Mintage	VG	Fine	VF	XF
75	1830	—	100.00	300.00	500.00	1450.

Rev: Modified arms.

C#	Date	Mintage	VG	Fine	VF	XF
42.3	1803	—	—	—	—	—

C#	Date	Mintage	VG	Fine	VF	XF
59	1814	—	50.00	75.00	125.00	275.00
	1815	—	50.00	75.00	125.00	250.00
	1819	—	50.00	75.00	125.00	250.00
	1820	—	50.00	75.00	125.00	250.00
	1824	—	50.00	75.00	125.00	250.00

QUATTRO (4) FIORINI

75a	1833	—	35.00	80.00	125.00	200.00
	1834	—	35.00	80.00	125.00	200.00
	1836	—	35.00	80.00	125.00	200.00
	1839	—	50.00	100.00	250.00	635.00
	1840	—	35.00	80.00	125.00	200.00
	1841	—	35.00	80.00	125.00	200.00

27.5000 g, .913 SILVER, .8073 oz ASW
Obv. leg: CAROLVS LVD. . . . .

50.1 (C50)	1803	—	50.00	75.00	125.00	300.00

27.5000 g, .916 SILVER, .8099 oz ASW

74	1826	—	50.00	100.00	200.00	500.00

Obv. leg: CAROLVS LUD. . . . .

50.2 (C50.1)	1806	—	50.00	75.00	125.00	250.00
	1807	—	50.00	75.00	125.00	250.00

75b	1845	—	35.00	70.00	100.00	200.00
	1846	—	35.00	70.00	100.00	200.00
	1856	—	35.00	70.00	100.00	200.00
	1858	—	35.00	70.00	100.00	200.00
	1859	—	35.00	70.00	100.00	200.00

Tuscany / ITALIAN STATES 1090

10 LIRE

39.4470 g, .958 SILVER, 1.2151 oz ASW
Rev. leg: FLORENTIAE - date.

C#	Date	Mintage	VG	Fine	VF	XF
49.1	1803	—	50.00	90.00	150.00	350.00
	1804	—	50.00	90.00	150.00	350.00
	1805	—	50.00	90.00	150.00	350.00
	1806	—	60.00	100.00	175.00	400.00

NOTE: Legend varieties exist.

Rev. leg: FLOR - date.

| 49.2 | 1807 | — | 45.00 | 80.00 | 140.00 | 350.00 |

ZECCHINO
For Levant Trade

3.4900 g, .998 GOLD, .1119 oz AGW
Obv: St. Zenobio kneeling before Christ. Rev: St. John.

| 51 | ND(1805) | — | 800.00 | 1500. | 2500. | 4000. |

| 60 | 1816 | — | 150.00 | 225.00 | 325.00 | 600.00 |
| | 1821 | — | 150.00 | 225.00 | 325.00 | 600.00 |

3.4520 g, .998 GOLD, .1107 oz AGW

C#	Date	Mintage	VG	Fine	VF	XF
76	1824	—	100.00	150.00	200.00	450.00
	1826	—	100.00	150.00	200.00	450.00
	1829	—	100.00	150.00	200.00	450.00
	1832	—	100.00	150.00	200.00	450.00
	1853	—	100.00	150.00	200.00	450.00

RUSPONE
(3 Zecchini)

10.4110 g, .998 GOLD, .3340 oz AGW

| 43 | 1801 | — | 500.00 | 800.00 | 1600. | 3000. |
| | 1803 | — | 400.00 | 650.00 | 1200. | 2000. |

52	1803	—	375.00	600.00	800.00	1250.
	1804	—	375.00	600.00	800.00	1250.
	1805	—	300.00	475.00	725.00	1100.
	1806	—	300.00	475.00	725.00	1100.
	1807	—	300.00	475.00	725.00	1100.

61	1815	—	350.00	550.00	800.00	1250.
	1816	—	350.00	550.00	800.00	1250.
	1818	—	350.00	550.00	800.00	1250.
	1820	—	350.00	550.00	800.00	1250.
	1823	—	350.00	550.00	800.00	1250.

77	1824	—	250.00	400.00	650.00	1000.
	1825	—	250.00	400.00	650.00	1000.
	1829	—	250.00	400.00	650.00	1000.
	1834	—	250.00	400.00	650.00	1000.
	1836	—	250.00	400.00	650.00	1000.

OTTANTA (80) FIORINI

32.6500 g, .999 GOLD, 1.0487 oz AGW

| 78 | 1827 | — | 400.00 | 525.00 | 800.00 | 1500. |
| | 1828 | — | 400.00 | 525.00 | 800.00 | 1500. |

1ST PROVISIONAL GOV'T.
(1859)
FIORINO

6.8800 g, .917 SILVER, .2028 oz ASW

C#	Date	Mintage	VG	Fine	VF	XF
79	1859	—	12.50	25.00	50.00	100.00

RUSPONE

10.4700 g, .998 GOLD, .3359 oz AGW
Obv: Lily. Rev: St. John.

| 80 | 1859 | — | 400.00 | 800.00 | 1500. | 2500. |

2ND PROVISIONAL GOV'T.
(Italian 1859-1861)
CENTESIMO

COPPER

C#	Date	Mintage	Fine	VF	XF	Unc
81	1859	25.000	4.00	8.00	17.50	40.00

2 CENTESIMI

COPPER

| 82 | 1859 | 12.500 | 4.00 | 8.00 | 17.50 | 40.00 |

5 CENTESIMI

COPPER

| 83 | 1859 | 10.000 | 4.00 | 8.00 | 17.50 | 40.00 |

CINQUANTA (50) CENTESIMI

2.5000 g, .900 SILVER, .0723 oz ASW

| 84 | 1860 | 2.430 | 5.00 | 10.00 | 25.00 | 75.00 |
| | 1861 | 1.222 | 100.00 | 200.00 | 400.00 | 1000. |

LIRA

5.0000 g, .900 SILVER, .1446 oz ASW
Rev: W/o dash between FIRENZE and date.

85.1	1859	.061	15.00	30.00	75.00	200.00
	1860/59	—	12.50	22.50	55.00	110.00
	1860	1.655	10.00	20.00	50.00	100.00

Rev: Dash between FIRENZE and date.

| 85.2 | 1860 | INC. Ab. | 7.50 | 15.00 | 30.00 | 80.00 |

2 LIRE

10.0000 g, .900 SILVER, .2892 oz ASW

| 86 | 1860 | .559 | 30.00 | 60.00 | 100.00 | 300.00 |
| | 1861 | .164 | 200.00 | 400.00 | 1000. | 3000. |

VENICE
Venezia

A seaport of Venetia was founded by refugees from the Hun invasions. From that time until the arrival of Napoleon in 1797, it maintained a state of quasi-independence despite the antagonism of jealous Italian states and the Ottoman Turks. Napoleon handed it to Austria. Upon defeat of the Austrians by Prussia in 1860, Venice became a part of the United Kingdom of Italy.

RULERS
Franz II (of Austria) 1798-1806

MINT MARKS
A - Vienna
F - Hall
V - Venice
ZV - Zecca Venezia - Venice
None - Venice

AUSTRIAN OCCUPATION
MEZZA (1/2) LIRA
4.5000 g, .250 SILVER, .0361 oz ASW
Mint mark: V
Rev: Value, date within ornate border.

C#	Date	Mintage	VG	Fine	VF	XF
163.1	1802	—	15.00	25.00	75.00	175.00

Mint mark: A
| 163.2 | 1802 | — | — | Reported, not confirmed | | |

Mint mark: F
| 163.3 | 1802 | — | — | Reported, not confirmed | | |

UNA (1) LIRA

11.3600 g, .250 SILVER, .0913 oz ASW
| 164.1 | 1802 | — | 15.00 | 25.00 | 75.00 | 175.00 |

Mint mark: A
| 164.2 | 1802 | — | — | Reported, not confirmed | | |

Mint mark: F
| 164.3 | 1802 | — | — | Reported, not confirmed | | |

1-1/2 LIRE
8.4900 g, .250 SILVER, .0682 oz ASW
Mint mark: A
Obv: Imperial eagle. Rev: Value, date within ornate border.
| 165.1 | 1802 | — | 10.00 | 15.00 | 35.00 | 75.00 |

Mint mark: F
| 165.2 | 1802 | — | 15.00 | 30.00 | 60.00 | 140.00 |

DUE (2) LIRE
.250 SILVER, 7.95-9.46 g
Mint mark: V
Obv: Large imperial eagle.
Rev: Value, date within wreath.
| 162 | 1801 | — | 25.00 | 40.00 | 80.00 | 200.00 |

NOTE: Three varieties exist.

Obv: Smaller imperial eagle, uncollared strike.
| 162a | 1801 | — | 20.00 | 50.00 | 100.00 | 250.00 |

REVOLUTIONARY ISSUES
(1848-1849)
MONETARY SYSTEM
100 Centesimi = 1 Lire

CENTESIMO

COPPER
Mint mark: ZV
C#	Date	Mintage	Fine	VF	XF	Unc
181	1849	—	3.00	7.00	15.00	30.00

3 CENTESIMI

COPPER
Mint mark: ZV
| 182 | 1849 | — | 3.00 | 6.00 | 10.00 | 25.00 |

5 CENTESIMI

COPPER
Mint mark: ZV
| 183 | 1849 | — | 3.00 | 6.00 | 12.00 | 30.00 |

15 CENTESIMI

1.2600 g, .229 SILVER, .0092 oz ASW
Mint mark: ZV
| 184 | 1848 | — | 10.00 | 15.00 | 25.00 | 50.00 |

25 CENTESIMI
1.2500 g, .900 SILVER, .0361 oz ASW
Mint mark: V
| A184 | 1848 | — | 75.00 | 150.00 | 300.00 | 500.00 |

5 LIRE

25.0000 g, .900 SILVER, .7234 oz ASW
| 185 | 1848 | — | 75.00 | 125.00 | 175.00 | 375.00 |

Mint mark: V
Edge inscription: DIO BENEDITE L'ITALIA.
C#	Date	Mintage	Fine	VF	XF	Unc
186	1848	—	75.00	125.00	175.00	375.00

Edge inscription error: DIO BENEDETE L'ITALIA.
| 186a | 1848 | — | 75.00 | 125.00 | 225.00 | 400.00 |

20 LIRE

6.4500 g, .900 GOLD, .1866 oz AGW
| 187 | 1848 | — | 325.00 | 500.00 | 800.00 | 1600. |

PALMA NOVA
(In Venetia)

Was ceded to France by Austria in 1806 and was returned to Austria in 1814. In 1860 it was incorporated in the United Kingdom of Italy.

SIEGE COINAGE
Issues of French defenders in 1814

50 CENTESIMI

BILLON
C#	Date	Mintage	VG	Fine	VF	XF
2	1814	—	75.00	100.00	150.00	250.00

NOTE: A presentation piece was struck in a collar resulting in a raised rim. They carry a premium.

ITALY

The Italian Republic, a 700-mile-long peninsula extending into the heart of the Mediterranean Sea, has an area of 116,304 sq. mi. (301,225 sq. km.) and a population of 57.4 million. Capital: Rome. The economy centers about agriculture, manufacturing, forestry and fishing. Machinery, textiles, clothing and motor vehicles are exported.

From the fall of Rome until modern times, 'Italy' was little more than a geographical expression. Although nominally included in the Empire of Charlemagne and the Holy Roman Empire, it was in reality divided into a number of independent states and kingdoms presided over by wealthy families, soldiers of fortune or hereditary rulers. The 19th century unification movement fostered by Mazzini, Garibaldi and Cavour attained fruition in 1860-70 with the creation of the Kingdom of Italy and the installation of Victor Emmanuel, king of Sardinia, as king of Italy. Benito Mussolini came to power during the post-World War I period of economic and political unrest, installed a Fascist dictatorship with a figurehead king as titular Head of State, and allied with Germany for the pursuit of World War II. Following the defeat of the Axis powers, the Italian monarchy was dissolved by plebiscite, and the Italian Republic proclaimed.

KINGDOM OF SARDINIA

RULERS
Carlo Emanuele IV 1796-1802
Vittorio Emanuele I 1802-1821
Carlo Felice 1821-1831
Carlo Alberto 1831-1849
Vittorio Emanuele II 1849-1878

MONETARY SYSTEM
Commencing 1816
100 Centesimi = 1 Lira

MINT MARKS
None Before 1802 – Turin (Torino)
Firenze – Florence
B – Bologna
(g) Anchor – Genoa
M – Milan
(t) after 1802 – Eagles head – Turin (Torino)

MINTMASTERS MARKS
P in oval – Andrea O Luca Podesta
L in diamond – Felippo Lavy
P in shield – Giovanni Parodi
B in shield – Tommaso Battilana

2.6 SOLDI
BILLON
Obv: Head right, VICTORIVS EMANVEL around, date.
Rev: Crowned displayed eagle w/arms of Savoy on breast.

C#	Date	Mintage	Fine	VF	XF	Unc
90	1814	—	4.00	8.00	20.00	50.00
	1815	—	4.00	8.00	20.00	50.00

1/2 SCUDO

17.5820 g, .905 SILVER, .5116 oz ASW

C#	Date	Mintage	Fine	VF	XF	Unc
91	1814	—	400.00	600.00	700.00	1500.
	1815	—	600.00	900.00	1250.	2500.

DOPPIA

9.1160 g, .905 GOLD, .2652 oz AGW

94	1814	—	400.00	800.00	1600.	3250.
	1815	—	550.00	1200.	2500.	5000.

MONETARY REFORM
100 Centesimi = 1 Lira

CENTESIMO

COPPER
Mint mark: Anchor

98.1	1826 P	11.485	5.00	10.00	15.00	40.00

Mint mark: Eagle head

98.2	1826 L	—	3.00	5.00	12.00	40.00
	1826 P	4.812	3.00	5.00	12.00	40.00

3 CENTESIMI

COPPER
Mint mark: Anchor

99.1	1826 P	.844	3.00	5.00	12.00	40.00

Mint mark: Eagle head

99.2	1826 L	5.778	3.00	5.00	12.00	40.00

5 CENTESIMI

COPPER
Mint mark: Anchor

100.1	1826 P	10.514	3.00	5.00	12.00	40.00

Mint mark: Eagle head

100.2	1826 L	32.177	3.00	5.00	12.00	40.00
	1826 P	Inc. Ab.	3.00	5.00	12.00	40.00

NOTE: C#98, 99, 100 were struck w/o mint mark at Bologna in 1860. See Emilia 1,2,3.

25 CENTESIMI
1.2500 g, .900 SILVER, .0361 oz ASW
Mint mark: Anchor
Obv: Head right. Rev: Arms.

101.1	1829 P	.450	15.00	25.00	40.00	90.00
	1830 P	.143	15.00	25.00	40.00	90.00

Mint mark: Eagle head

101.2	1829 L	.110	17.50	30.00	50.00	100.00
	1830 L	.234	15.00	25.00	40.00	90.00
	1830 P	Inc. Ab.	20.00	35.00	60.00	150.00

C#	Date	Mintage	Fine	VF	XF	Unc
109.1	1832 P	.120	75.00	150.00	300.00	600.00
	1833 P	—	20.00	35.00	60.00	150.00
	1837 P	.230	75.00	150.00	300.00	600.00

Mint mark: Anchor

109.2	1833 P	7,921	25.00	40.00	60.00	120.00

50 CENTESIMI

2.5000 g, .900 SILVER, .0722 oz ASW
Mint mark: Eagle head

102.1	1823 L	—	—	—	Rare	—
	1824 L	—	—	—	Rare	—
	1825 L	.492	12.50	25.00	50.00	150.00
	1826 L	.640	12.50	25.00	50.00	150.00
	1827 L	.401	12.50	25.00	50.00	150.00
	1828 L	.611	12.50	25.00	50.00	150.00
	1828 P	Inc. Ab.	12.50	25.00	50.00	150.00
	1829 P	.255	35.00	75.00	125.00	200.00
	1830 L	.456	12.50	25.00	50.00	150.00
	1830 P	Inc. Ab.	100.00	150.00	200.00	300.00
	1831 L	.143	12.50	25.00	50.00	150.00
	1831 P	Inc. Ab.	50.00	80.00	150.00	400.00

Mint mark: Anchor

102.2	1826 P	.079	20.00	40.00	75.00	150.00
	1827 P	.143	15.00	30.00	60.00	125.00
	1828 P	.194	35.00	75.00	100.00	175.00
	1829 P	.107	15.00	30.00	60.00	125.00

Mint mark: Eagle head
Obv: Head right. Rev: Arms.

110.1	1832 P	—	—	—	Rare	—
	1833 P	.062	20.00	40.00	75.00	200.00
	1834 P	.061	40.00	80.00	200.00	600.00
	1835 P	—	40.00	80.00	200.00	400.00
	1836 P	.022	40.00	80.00	200.00	600.00
	1837 P	.012	40.00	80.00	200.00	600.00
	1841 P	6,600	40.00	80.00	200.00	600.00
	1842 P	.010	20.00	35.00	75.00	200.00
	1843 P	.014	20.00	35.00	75.00	200.00
	1844 P	9,100	50.00	100.00	300.00	800.00
	1845 P	.016	40.00	75.00	125.00	250.00
	1846 P	.023	50.00	100.00	300.00	800.00
	1847 P	.011	50.00	100.00	200.00	400.00

Mint mark: Anchor

110.2	1833 P	136 pcs.	50.00	100.00	200.00	400.00
	1844 P	.023	50.00	100.00	300.00	800.00

Obv: Head w/beard.

121.1	1850 P	9,268	30.00	60.00	100.00	200.00
	1860 P	15 pcs.	—	—	Rare	—

Mint mark: Eagle head

121.2	1850 B	—	12.50	25.00	50.00	150.00
	1852 B	.055	12.50	25.00	50.00	150.00
	1853 B	.021	12.50	25.00	50.00	150.00
	1855 B	—	30.00	60.00	150.00	300.00
	1856 B	9,754	12.50	25.00	50.00	150.00
	1857 B	.015	12.50	25.00	50.00	150.00
	1858 B	8,114	12.50	25.00	50.00	150.00
	1860 B	6,484	12.50	25.00	50.00	150.00

Mint mark: M

121.3	1860	.982	15.00	30.00	65.00	175.00
	1861	—	50.00	100.00	200.00	500.00

LIRA

5.0000 g, .900 SILVER, .1444 oz ASW
Mint mark: Eagle head

103.1	1823 L	—	—	—	Rare	—
	1824 L	.092	25.00	50.00	100.00	300.00
	1825 L	—	50.00	100.00	200.00	600.00
	1826 L	.547	20.00	40.00	75.00	200.00
	1827 L	.836	20.00	40.00	75.00	200.00
	1828 L	.345	20.00	40.00	75.00	200.00
	1828 P	Inc. Ab.	20.00	40.00	75.00	200.00
	1829 L	.111	20.00	50.00	100.00	400.00
	1830 P	.313	20.00	40.00	75.00	200.00

Mint mark: Anchor

103.2	1824 P	5,670	25.00	50.00	100.00	400.00
	1825 P	—	20.00	40.00	75.00	200.00
	1826 P	.154	20.00	40.00	75.00	200.00
	1827 P	.251	20.00	40.00	75.00	200.00
	1828 P	.388	20.00	40.00	75.00	200.00
	1829 P	.159	20.00	40.00	75.00	200.00
	1830 P	.060	20.00	40.00	75.00	400.00

Obv: Head right. Rev: Arms.

C#	Date	Mintage	Fine	VF	XF	Unc
111.1	1831 P	.019	50.00	100.00	200.00	700.00
	1832 P	.035	35.00	75.00	200.00	600.00
	1833 P	7,620	50.00	100.00	200.00	700.00
	1834 P	.040	—	—	Rare	—
	1835 P	.023	25.00	50.00	100.00	300.00
	1837 P	.018	—	—	Rare	—
	1838 P	—	25.00	50.00	100.00	250.00
	1841 P	.011	—	—	Rare	—
	1844 P	.033	—	—	Rare	—

Mint mark: Eagle head

C#	Date	Mintage	Fine	VF	XF	Unc
111.2	1831 P	5,000	50.00	100.00	200.00	600.00
	1832 P	.030	50.00	100.00	200.00	600.00
	1833 P	85 pcs.	50.00	100.00	200.00	750.00
	1835 P	—	50.00	100.00	200.00	750.00
	1837 P	.028	50.00	100.00	200.00	600.00
	1838 P	.011	50.00	100.00	200.00	600.00
	1839 P	8,558	—	—	Rare	—
	1841 P	.020	—	—	Rare	—
	1842 P	5,184	—	—	Rare	—
	1843 P	.015	20.00	40.00	100.00	300.00
	1844 P	.015	—	—	Rare	—
	1845 P	.010	20.00	40.00	100.00	300.00
	1846 P	.019	—	—	Rare	—
	1847 P	.011	20.00	40.00	100.00	300.00
	1848 P	8,110	175.00	300.00	500.00	1000.
	1849 P	3,037	—	—	Rare	—

Mint mark: Anchor

C#	Date	Mintage	Fine	VF	XF	Unc
122.1	1850 P	—	50.00	75.00	125.00	400.00
	1853 P	7,051	50.00	75.00	150.00	600.00
	1859 P	.012	40.00	75.00	125.00	400.00
	1860 P	—	—	—	Rare	—

Mint mark: Eagle head

C#	Date	Mintage	Fine	VF	XF	Unc
122.2	1850 B	.092	25.00	50.00	150.00	400.00
	1851 B	—	—	—	Rare	—
	1852 B	—	—	—	Rare	—
	1853 B	.022	25.00	50.00	150.00	400.00
	1854 B	—	—	—	Rare	—
	1855 B	.016	25.00	50.00	150.00	400.00
	1856 B	.058	20.00	40.00	100.00	300.00
	1857 B	.031	20.00	40.00	100.00	300.00
	1858 B	—	—	—	Rare	—
	1859 B	5,150	20.00	40.00	100.00	250.00
	1860 B	4,752	40.00	80.00	100.00	300.00

Mint mark: M

C#	Date	Mintage	Fine	VF	XF	Unc
122.3	1859	—	50.00	100.00	200.00	600.00
	1860	.603	50.00	100.00	200.00	600.00

2 LIRE

10.0000 g, .900 SILVER, .2888 oz ASW
Mint mark: Eagle head

C#	Date	Mintage	Fine	VF	XF	Unc
104.1	1823 L	—	—	—	Rare	—
	1825 L	.261	25.00	50.00	100.00	300.00
	1826 L	.235	25.00	50.00	100.00	350.00
	1827 L	.170	25.00	50.00	100.00	350.00
	1828 L	.102	25.00	50.00	200.00	400.00
	1829 L	—	—	—	Rare	—
	1830 L	.049	25.00	50.00	100.00	350.00
	1830 P	Inc. Ab.	25.00	50.00	150.00	400.00

Mint mark: Anchor

C#	Date	Mintage	Fine	VF	XF	Unc
104.2	1825 P	—	25.00	50.00	100.00	400.00
	1826 P	.157	25.00	50.00	100.00	350.00
	1827 P	.366	25.00	50.00	100.00	350.00
	1830 P	.115	25.00	50.00	100.00	350.00
	1831 P	.072	25.00	50.00	100.00	350.00

Obv: Younger head right.

C#	Date	Mintage	Fine	VF	XF	Unc
112.1	1832 P	.035	25.00	50.00	150.00	600.00
	1833 P	187 pcs.	50.00	100.00	200.00	1000.
	1835 P	5,142	50.00	100.00	200.00	1000.
	1836 P	.030	50.00	100.00	200.00	1000.
	1844 P	.030	50.00	100.00	200.00	500.00
	1845 P	.052	50.00	100.00	200.00	750.00
	1847 P	—	50.00	100.00	200.00	750.00

Mint mark: Eagle head

C#	Date	Mintage	Fine	VF	XF	Unc
112.2	1833 P	287 pcs.	250.00	500.00	1000.	2000.
	1834 P	—	250.00	500.00	750.00	1000.
	1835 P	.024	35.00	75.00	150.00	500.00
	1836 P	—	35.00	75.00	150.00	500.00
	1838 P	.020	—	—	Rare	—
	1839 P	.014	—	—	Rare	—
	1841 P	4,259	150.00	250.00	350.00	800.00
	1842 P	.010	35.00	75.00	150.00	500.00

C#	Date	Mintage	Fine	VF	XF	Unc
112.2	1843 P	.012	35.00	75.00	150.00	500.00
	1844 P	.012	35.00	75.00	150.00	500.00
	1845 P	.015	35.00	75.00	150.00	500.00
	1846 P	.015	35.00	75.00	150.00	500.00
	1847 P	.015	—	—	Rare	—
	1848 P	.013	—	—	Rare	—
	1849 P	3,159	—	—	Rare	—

Mint mark: Anchor
Obv: Head w/beard right.

C#	Date	Mintage	Fine	VF	XF	Unc
123.1	1850 P	—	100.00	200.00	400.00	1000.
	1853 P	5,401	—	—	Rare	—
	1854 P	2,748	60.00	125.00	300.00	900.00

Mint mark: Eagle head

C#	Date	Mintage	Fine	VF	XF	Unc
123.2	1850 B	.018	60.00	125.00	300.00	900.00
	1852 B	.023	60.00	125.00	300.00	900.00
	1853 B	4,859	60.00	125.00	300.00	900.00
	1854 B	.018	60.00	125.00	300.00	900.00
	1855 B	9,414	60.00	125.00	300.00	900.00
	1856 B	.011	60.00	125.00	300.00	900.00
	1860 B	8,963	60.00	125.00	300.00	900.00

5 LIRE

25.0000 g, .900 SILVER, .7234 oz ASW
Mint mark: Eagle head
Obv: Similar to C#93.

C#	Date	Mintage	Fine	VF	XF	Unc
92	1816 L	.023	75.00	175.00	325.00	850.00
	1817 L	.044	60.00	125.00	275.00	650.00
	1818 L	.055	60.00	125.00	275.00	650.00
	1819 L	.035	60.00	125.00	275.00	650.00
	1820 L	.101	60.00	125.00	275.00	650.00

C#	Date	Mintage	Fine	VF	XF	Unc
93	1821	—	600.00	1000.	2000.	4000.

C#	Date	Mintage	Fine	VF	XF	Unc
105.1	1821 L	.035	75.00	150.00	200.00	1200.
	1822 L	.037	60.00	110.00	200.00	700.00
	1823 L	.035	60.00	110.00	200.00	500.00
	1824 L	.162	60.00	110.00	200.00	350.00
	1825 L	.395	15.00	30.00	125.00	275.00
	1826 L	.907	30.00	50.00	125.00	275.00
	1827 L	.724	15.00	30.00	125.00	275.00
	1828 L	.253	30.00	50.00	125.00	275.00
	1829 L	.312	30.00	50.00	125.00	275.00
	1830 L	.913	30.00	50.00	125.00	300.00
	1830 P	Inc. Ab.	30.00	50.00	125.00	275.00
	1831 P	.049	60.00	110.00	200.00	500.00

Mint mark: Anchor

C#	Date	Mintage	Fine	VF	XF	Unc
105.2	1824 P	.016	60.00	125.00	250.00	650.00
	1825 P	.017	75.00	150.00	300.00	800.00
	1826 P	.489	30.00	50.00	125.00	275.00
	1827 P	2.137	30.00	50.00	125.00	275.00
	1828 P	1.149	30.00	50.00	125.00	275.00
	1829 P	.597	30.00	50.00	125.00	275.00
	1830 P	1.122	30.00	50.00	125.00	275.00
	1831 P	.451	100.00	175.00	300.00	800.00

Obv: F on truncation. Rev: Arms.

C#	Date	Mintage	Fine	VF	XF	Unc
113.1	1831 P	.451	40.00	60.00	150.00	350.00

Mint mark: Eagle head

C#	Date	Mintage	Fine	VF	XF	Unc
113.2	1831 P	.049	40.00	60.00	150.00	350.00

Mint mark: Anchor
Obv: FERRARIS on truncation.

C#	Date	Mintage	Fine	VF	XF	Unc
113.3	1831 P	—	50.00	90.00	200.00	450.00
	1832 P	.317	25.00	35.00	100.00	300.00
	1833 P	.275	25.00	35.00	100.00	300.00
	1834 P	.154	25.00	35.00	100.00	300.00
	1835 P	.336	25.00	35.00	100.00	300.00
	1836 P	.595	25.00	35.00	100.00	300.00
	1837 P	.359	25.00	35.00	100.00	300.00
	1838 P	.307	25.00	35.00	100.00	300.00
	1839 P	.141	25.00	35.00	100.00	300.00
	1840 P	.193	25.00	35.00	100.00	300.00
	1841 P	.313	25.00	35.00	100.00	300.00
	1842 P	.396	25.00	35.00	100.00	300.00
	1843 P	.787	25.00	35.00	100.00	300.00
	1844 P	1.043	25.00	35.00	100.00	300.00
	1845 P	.302	25.00	35.00	100.00	300.00
	1846 P	.264	25.00	35.00	100.00	300.00
	1847 P	.142	25.00	35.00	100.00	300.00
	1848 P	.778	25.00	35.00	100.00	300.00
	1849 P	.739	25.00	35.00	100.00	300.00

Mint mark: Eagle head

C#	Date	Mintage	Fine	VF	XF	Unc
113.4	1831 P	—	25.00	35.00	100.00	300.00
	1832 P	.095	25.00	35.00	100.00	300.00
	1833 P	.060	25.00	35.00	100.00	300.00
	1834 P	.037	25.00	35.00	100.00	300.00
	1835 P	.069	25.00	35.00	100.00	300.00
	1836 P	.051	25.00	35.00	100.00	300.00
	1837 P	.036	25.00	35.00	100.00	300.00
	1838 P	.042	25.00	35.00	100.00	300.00
	1839 P	.205	25.00	35.00	100.00	300.00
	1840 P	.050	25.00	35.00	100.00	300.00
	1841 P	.015	25.00	35.00	125.00	500.00
	1842 P	.042	25.00	35.00	100.00	300.00
	1843 P	.037	25.00	35.00	100.00	300.00
	1844 P	.171	25.00	35.00	100.00	300.00
	1845 P	.042	25.00	35.00	100.00	300.00
	1846 P	.046	25.00	35.00	100.00	300.00
	1847 P	.037	25.00	35.00	100.00	300.00
	1848 P	.079	25.00	35.00	100.00	300.00
	1849 P	.104	150.00	350.00	600.00	800.00

Sardinia / ITALY 1094

Mint mark: Anchor

C#	Date	Mintage	Fine	VF	XF	Unc
124.1	1850 P	.721	50.00	100.00	200.00	500.00
	1851 P	.316	50.00	100.00	200.00	500.00
	1852 P	.391	50.00	100.00	200.00	500.00
	1853 P	.167	50.00	100.00	200.00	500.00
	1854 P	.284	50.00	100.00	200.00	500.00
	1855 P	.084	50.00	100.00	200.00	500.00
	1856 P	.058	50.00	100.00	200.00	500.00
	1857 P	.035	50.00	100.00	200.00	500.00
	1858 P	.030	50.00	100.00	200.00	500.00
	1859 P	.049	50.00	100.00	200.00	500.00

Mint mark: Eagle head

C#	Date	Mintage	Fine	VF	XF	Unc
124.2	1850 B	.058	50.00	100.00	200.00	500.00
	1851 B	.049	50.00	100.00	200.00	500.00
	1852 B	.097	50.00	100.00	200.00	500.00
	1854 B	.074	50.00	100.00	200.00	500.00
	1855 B	.052	50.00	100.00	200.00	500.00
	1856 B	.037	50.00	100.00	200.00	500.00
	1857 B	.019	50.00	100.00	200.00	500.00
	1858 B	.011	50.00	100.00	200.00	500.00
	1859 B	.012	50.00	100.00	200.00	500.00
	1860 B	5,044	50.00	100.00	200.00	500.00
	1861 B	.012	50.00	100.00	200.00	500.00

10 LIRE

3.2200 g, .900 GOLD, .0931 oz AGW
Mint mark: Eagle head

C#	Date	Mintage	Fine	VF	XF	Unc
114.1	1832 P	—	—	—	Rare	—
	1833 P	5,004	175.00	350.00	500.00	1000.
	1835 P	5,118	250.00	500.00	750.00	1500.
	1838 P	2,826	200.00	400.00	600.00	1200.
	1839 P	2,237	175.00	350.00	500.00	1000.
	1841 P	1,583	175.00	350.00	500.00	1000.
	1842 P	759 pcs.	250.00	500.00	750.00	2000.
	1843 P	950 pcs.	250.00	500.00	750.00	2000.
	1845 P	3,009	250.00	500.00	750.00	2000.
	1846 P	970 pcs.	250.00	500.00	750.00	2000.
	1847 P	405 pcs.	250.00	500.00	750.00	2000.

Mint mark: Anchor

C#	Date	Mintage	Fine	VF	XF	Unc
114.2	1833 P	1,550	200.00	375.00	750.00	1200.
	1835 P	—	—	—	Rare	—
	1841 P	2,809	225.00	425.00	850.00	1250.
	1843 P	4,566	225.00	425.00	850.00	1250.
	1844 P	.011	200.00	350.00	600.00	1000.
	1845 P	1,535	225.00	425.00	850.00	1250.
	1846 P	3,373	225.00	425.00	850.00	1250.
	1847 P	—	—	—	Rare	—
125.1	1850 P	4,141	600.00	1200.	1650.	2200.

Mint mark: Eagle head

C#	Date	Mintage	Fine	VF	XF	Unc
125.2	1850 B	2,326	225.00	400.00	600.00	1000.
	1852 B	—	—	—	Rare	—
	1853 B	—	225.00	400.00	600.00	1000.
	1854 B	1,833	225.00	400.00	600.00	1000.
	1855 B	2,566	225.00	400.00	600.00	1000.
	1856 B	2,526	225.00	400.00	600.00	1000.
	1857 B	7,193	225.00	400.00	600.00	1000.
	1858 B	2,931	225.00	400.00	600.00	1000.
	1859 B	1 known	—	—	7040.	—
	1860 B	6,036	225.00	400.00	600.00	1000.

20 LIRE

6.4500 g, .900 GOLD, .1866 oz AGW
Mint mark: Eagle head

C#	Date	Mintage	Fine	VF	XF	Unc
95	1816	.019	250.00	400.00	500.00	800.00
	1817	.040	150.00	250.00	400.00	650.00
	1818	.035	150.00	250.00	400.00	650.00
	1819	.022	150.00	250.00	400.00	650.00
	1820	.033	150.00	250.00	400.00	650.00

C#	Date	Mintage	Fine	VF	XF	Unc
96	1821	—	1500.	2500.	5000.	8200.

C#	Date	Mintage	Fine	VF	XF	Unc
106.1	1821 L	.018	175.00	225.00	325.00	500.00
	1822 L	7,460	175.00	225.00	325.00	500.00
	1823 L	.022	175.00	225.00	325.00	500.00
	1824 L	2,381	200.00	275.00	375.00	650.00
	1825 L	.028	175.00	225.00	325.00	500.00
	1826 L	.144	175.00	225.00	325.00	500.00
	1827 L	.150	175.00	225.00	325.00	500.00
	1828 L	.095	175.00	225.00	325.00	500.00
	1828 P	—	250.00	350.00	450.00	700.00
	1829 L	.061	250.00	350.00	450.00	700.00
	1829 P	—	250.00	350.00	450.00	700.00
	1830 L	—	250.00	350.00	450.00	700.00
	1830 P	.035	200.00	300.00	400.00	650.00
	1831 P	.042	175.00	225.00	325.00	500.00

Mint mark: Anchor

C#	Date	Mintage	Fine	VF	XF	Unc
106.2	1824 P	2,394	125.00	150.00	200.00	375.00
	1825 P	313 pcs.	375.00	500.00	600.00	1500.
	1827 P	1,766	225.00	300.00	400.00	500.00
	1828 P	—	—	—	Rare	—
	1829 P	—	225.00	300.00	400.00	500.00
	1830 P	3,270	375.00	500.00	600.00	800.00
	1831 P	—	—	—	Rare	—

C#	Date	Mintage	Fine	VF	XF	Unc
115.1	1831 P	—	100.00	125.00	150.00	300.00
	1832 P	.074	100.00	125.00	150.00	300.00
	1833 P	.080	—	—	Rare	—
	1834 P	.133	100.00	125.00	150.00	300.00
	1835 P	.052	100.00	125.00	150.00	300.00
	1836 P	.090	100.00	125.00	150.00	300.00
	1837 P	.056	—	—	Rare	—
	1838 P	.120	100.00	125.00	150.00	300.00
	1839 P	.074	—	—	Rare	—
	1840 P	.176	100.00	125.00	150.00	300.00
	1841 P	.206	125.00	175.00	250.00	400.00
	1842 P	.066	100.00	125.00	150.00	300.00
	1843 P	.045	—	—	Rare	—
	1844 P	.034	—	—	Rare	—
	1845 P	.043	100.00	125.00	150.00	300.00
	1846 P	.043	—	—	Rare	—
	1847 P	.052	100.00	125.00	150.00	300.00
	1848 P	.059	125.00	150.00	175.00	300.00
	1849 P	.111	100.00	125.00	150.00	275.00

Mint mark: Eagle head

C#	Date	Mintage	Fine	VF	XF	Unc
115.2	1831 P	—	100.00	125.00	150.00	300.00
	1832 P	.053	100.00	125.00	150.00	300.00
	1833 P	.016	100.00	125.00	150.00	300.00
	1834 P	.261	100.00	125.00	150.00	300.00
	1836 P	.014	—	—	Rare	—
	1837 P	.015	—	—	Rare	—
	1838 P	.031	100.00	125.00	150.00	300.00
	1839 P	.070	100.00	125.00	150.00	300.00
	1840 P	.028	100.00	125.00	150.00	300.00
	1841 P	.031	—	—	Rare	—
	1842 P	.026	100.00	125.00	150.00	300.00
	1843 P	.024	—	—	Rare	—
	1844 P	.030	100.00	125.00	150.00	300.00
	1845 P	.035	100.00	125.00	150.00	300.00
	1846 P	.030	100.00	125.00	150.00	300.00
	1847 P	.033	100.00	125.00	150.00	300.00
	1848 P	.059	100.00	—	Rare	—
	1849 P	.058	100.00	125.00	150.00	300.00

Unknown Mint

C#	Date	Mintage	Fine	VF	XF	Unc
115.3	1834	—	125.00	150.00	200.00	300.00
	1847	—	125.00	150.00	200.00	300.00

Mint mark: Anchor

C#	Date	Mintage	Fine	VF	XF	Unc
126.1	1850 B	.139	100.00	125.00	175.00	300.00
	1851 B	.296	100.00	125.00	175.00	300.00
	1852 B	.103	100.00	125.00	175.00	300.00
	1853 B	.137	100.00	125.00	175.00	300,00
	1854 B	.142	100.00	125.00	175.00	300.00
	1855 B	.148	100.00	125.00	175.00	300.00
	1856 B	.113	100.00	125.00	175.00	300.00
	1857 B	.059	100.00	125.00	175.00	300.00
	1858 B	.176	100.00	125.00	175.00	300.00
	1859 B	.436	100.00	125.00	175.00	300.00
	1860 B	.163	100.00	125.00	175.00	300.00

Mint mark: Eagle head

C#	Date	Mintage	Fine	VF	XF	Unc
126.2	1850 P	.066	100.00	125.00	175.00	300.00
	1851 P	.163	100.00	125.00	175.00	300.00
	1852 P	.046	100.00	125.00	175.00	300.00
	1853 P	.041	—	—	Rare	—
	1855 P	.041	100.00	125.00	175.00	300.00
	1855 P (error) EMMANVEL H for II					
		—	100.00	125.00	175.00	300.00
	1856 P	.061	375.00	500.00	750.00	1200.
	1857 P	.067	150.00	225.00	300.00	400.00
	1858 P	.103	150.00	250.00	400.00	800.00
	1859 P	.187	100.00	125.00	175.00	300.00
	1860 P	.111	100.00	150.00	200.00	400.00
	1861 P	.156	100.00	150.00	200.00	400.00

Mint mark: M

C#	Date	Mintage	Fine	VF	XF	Unc
126.3	1860	.023	150.00	225.00	325.00	550.00

40 LIRE

12.9000 g, .900 GOLD, .3733 oz AGW
Mint mark: Eagle head

C#	Date	Mintage	Fine	VF	XF	Unc
107.1	1822 L	5,011	300.00	400.00	600.00	1500.
	1823 L	—	—	—	Rare	—
	1825 L	.039	300.00	400.00	500.00	1250.
	1831 L	—	300.00	400.00	500.00	1250.
	1831 P	7,711	300.00	400.00	500.00	1250.

Mint mark: Anchor

C#	Date	Mintage	Fine	VF	XF	Unc
107.2	1825 P	3,994	300.00	400.00	600.00	1750.
	1826 P	2,844	500.00	600.00	900.00	2000.

50 LIRE

16.1200 g, .900 GOLD, .4664 oz AGW
Mint mark: Eagle head

C#	Date	Mintage	Fine	VF	XF	Unc
116.1	1832 P	93 pcs.	—	—	Rare	—
	1833 P	1,773	750.00	1000.	1500.	2500.
	1834 P	657 pcs.	—	—	Rare	—
	1835 P	1,296	—	—	Rare	—
	1836 P	385 pcs.	900.00	1250.	1750.	2750.
	1838 P	992 pcs.	—	—	Rare	—
	1839 P	553 pcs.	—	—	Rare	—
	1840 P	1,402	—	—	Rare	—
	1841 P	2,753	—	—	Rare	—
	1843 P	586 pcs.	—	—	Rare	—

Mint mark: Anchor

C#	Date	Mintage	Fine	VF	XF	Unc
116.2	1833 P	92 pcs.	4000.	5000.	6000.	7500.
	1835 P	—	—	—	Rare	—
	1841 P	562 pcs.	—	—	Rare	—

80 LIRE

25.8000 g, .900 GOLD, .7466 oz AGW
Mint mark: Eagle head

C#	Date	Mintage	Fine	VF	XF	Unc
97	1821	965 pcs.	4500.	8000.	14,000.	23,000.

108.1	1823 L	—	—	—	—	Rare	—
	1824 L	5,919	450.00	550.00	650.00	1000.
	1825 L	.014	400.00	500.00	600.00	900.00
	1826 L	.076	400.00	500.00	600.00	900.00
	1827 L	.038	400.00	500.00	600.00	900.00
	1828 L	.023	400.00	500.00	600.00	900.00
	1828 P	Inc. Ab.	600.00	750.00	1000.	1500.
	1829 P	8,181	400.00	500.00	600.00	900.00
	1830 P	5,972	400.00	500.00	600.00	900.00
	1831 P	740 pcs.	800.00	1000.	1250.	2000.

Mint mark: Anchor

108.2	1824 P	3,904	500.00	700.00	900.00	1500.
	1825 P	8,465	400.00	550.00	725.00	1200.
	1826 P	2,305	700.00	900.00	1100.	1750.
	1827 P	.015	400.00	500.00	600.00	1100.
	1828 P	8,961	400.00	500.00	600.00	1100.
	1829 P	7,436	400.00	500.00	600.00	1100.
	1830 P	.026	400.00	500.00	600.00	1100.
	1831 P	.021	600.00	800.00	1250.	2000.

100 LIRE

32.2500 g, .900 GOLD, .9332 oz AGW
Mint mark: Anchor

117.1	1832 P	—	500.00	600.00	850.00	1800.
	1833 P	2,587	600.00	725.00	1000.	2000.
	1834 P	.012	500.00	600.00	850.00	1800.
	1835 P	8,513	500.00	600.00	850.00	1800.
	1836 P	703 pcs.	700.00	900.00	1100.	2250.
	1837 P	250 pcs.	900.00	1100.	1350.	2750.
	1838 P	4,774	—	—	Rare	—
	1839 P	2,922	—	—	Rare	—
	1840 P	1,003	700.00	900.00	1100.	2250.
	1841 P	8,889	700.00	900.00	1100.	2250.
	1842 P	3,606	700.00	900.00	1100.	2250.
	1843 P	424 pcs.	1500.	2000.	2500.	4000.
	1844 P	2,213	1000.	1500.	2000.	3500.
	1845 P	646 pcs.	1000.	1500.	2000.	3500.

Mint mark: Eagle head

117.2	1832 P	—	475.00	600.00	850.00	1750.
	1833 P	6,769	475.00	600.00	850.00	1750.
	1834 P	.037	475.00	600.00	850.00	1750.
	1835 P	.026	475.00	600.00	850.00	1750.
	1836 P	6,236	475.00	600.00	850.00	1750.
	1837 P	3,885	500.00	700.00	900.00	2000.
	1838 P	3,916	—	—	Rare	—
	1840 P	2,898	500.00	700.00	900.00	2000.
	1841 P	1,207	700.00	1000.	1300.	2750.
	1842 P	864 pcs.	700.00	1000.	1300.	2750.
	1843 P	827 pcs.	800.00	1100.	1500.	3000.
	1844 P	91 pcs.	—	—	Rare	—

KINGDOM OF ITALY

RULERS

Vittorio Emanuele II, 1861-1878
Umberto I, 1878-1900
Vittorio Emanuele III, 1900-1946

MINTMARKS

B - Bologna (1861)
B/I - Birmingham (1893-1894)
FIRENZE - Florence (1861)
H - Birmingham (1866-1867)
KB - Berlin (1894)
M - Milan (1861-1887)
N - Naples (1861-1867)
OM - Strasbourg (1866-1867)
R - Rome (All coins from 1878 have R except where noted).
T - Turin (1861-1867)
No MM - Paris (1862-1866)

MONETARY SYSTEM
100 Centesimi = 1 Lira

CENTESIMO

COPPER
Mint mark: M

KM#	Date	Mintage	Fine	VF	XF	Unc
1.1 (Y6.1)	1861	75.000	.75	1.50	3.00	10.00
	1861 inverted M Inc. Ab.	15.00	30.00	60.00	200.00
	1867	72.759	.75	1.50	3.00	10.00

Mint mark: N

1.2 (Y6.2)	1861	48.280	3.75	8.00	15.00	30.00
	1862/1	37.500	6.00	12.00	20.00	35.00
	1862	Inc. Ab.	1.25	2.00	4.00	15.00

Mint mark: T

| 1.3 (Y6.3) | 1867 | 5.000 | 5.00 | 12.50 | 22.50 | 45.00 |

Mint mark: R

29 (Y22)	1895/8	13.860	1.50	3.00	7.00	22.50
	1895	Inc. Ab.	1.00	2.00	4.00	10.00
	1896	3.730	1.00	2.00	4.00	10.00
	1897	1.845	10.00	17.50	25.00	40.00
	1899	1.287	1.25	2.00	4.00	10.00
	1900	10.000	1.00	2.00	4.00	10.00

35 (Y35)	1902	.026	125.00	200.00	350.00	600.00
	1903	5.655	1.00	2.00	4.00	15.00
	1904/0	14.626	2.00	3.00	7.50	20.00
	1904	Inc. Ab.	1.00	2.00	4.00	10.00
	1905/0	8.531	2.00	3.00	7.50	20.00
	1905	Inc. Ab.	1.00	2.00	4.00	10.00
	1908	3.859	1.00	2.00	4.00	10.00

40 (Y43)	1908	.057	75.00	100.00	200.00	350.00
	1909	3.539	1.00	2.00	4.00	10.00
	1910	3.599	1.00	2.00	4.00	10.00
	1911	.700	5.00	10.00	15.00	25.00
	1912	3.995	1.00	2.00	4.00	10.00
	1913	3.200	1.00	2.00	4.00	10.00
	1914	11.585	1.00	2.00	4.00	10.00
	1915	9.757	1.00	2.00	4.00	10.00
	1916	9.845	1.00	2.00	4.00	10.00
	1917	2.400	1.00	2.00	4.00	10.00
	1918	2.710	5.00	10.00	15.00	25.00

2 CENTESIMI

COPPER
Mint mark: M

2.1 (Y7.1)	1861	37.500	.60	1.50	4.00	15.00
	1867	54.212	.60	1.50	4.00	20.00

Mint mark: N

2.2 (Y7.2)	1861	23.055	.60	1.50	3.50	15.00
	1862	33.195	.60	1.50	3.50	15.00

Mint mark: T

| 2.3 (Y7.3) | 1867 | 5.000 | 2.00 | 4.25 | 8.50 | 17.50 |

ITALY 1095

Mint mark: R

KM#	Date	Mintage	Fine	VF	XF	Unc
30 (Y23)	1895	.305	10.00	17.50	35.00	60.00
	1896	.282	25.00	50.00	100.00	150.00
	1897	4.415	.60	1.50	4.00	12.50
	1898	4.161	.60	1.50	4.00	12.50
	1900	2.735	.60	1.50	4.00	12.50

38 (Y36)	1903	5.000	.60	1.50	4.00	12.50
	1905	1.260	4.00	8.50	18.00	30.00
	1906	3.145	.60	1.50	3.50	7.50
	1907	.230	25.00	50.00	75.00	150.00
	1908	1.518	1.00	2.50	5.00	15.00

41 (Y44)	1908	.298	9.00	15.00	25.00	80.00
	1909	2.419	.60	1.50	3.00	15.00
	1910	.590	2.00	4.00	9.00	30.00
	1911	2.777	.60	1.50	3.00	15.00
	1912	.840	.60	2.00	5.00	16.00
	1914	1.648	.50	1.30	2.00	15.00
	1915	4.860	.50	1.30	2.50	15.00
	1916	1.540	.50	1.30	2.00	15.00
	1917	3.638	.50	1.30	2.00	15.00

5 CENTESIMI

COPPER
Mint mark: B

| 3.1 (Y8.1) | 1861 | 3.809 | 15.00 | 30.00 | 50.00 | 125.00 |

Mint mark: M

3.2 (Y8.2)	1861	210.000	.60	1.50	5.00	35.00
	1867	24.000	.60	1.50	5.00	25.00

Mint mark: N

3.3 (Y8.3)	1861	103.707	.60	1.50	5.00	35.00
	1862	106.293	.60	1.50	5.00	35.00
	1867	46.000	.60	1.50	5.00	35.00

Mint mark: R

31 (Y24)	1895	.508	10.00	17.50	30.00	60.00
	1896	.380	10.00	17.50	30.00	60.00
	1900	2.000	250.00	350.00	500.00	1000.

NOTE: 2,000 of the 1900 dated coins were struck but were remelted and not issued.

42 (Y45)	1908	.824	9.00	15.00	25.00	40.00
	1909	1.734	.75	1.75	3.50	15.00
	1912	.743	1.75	3.00	6.00	30.00
	1913 dot after D					
		1.964	4.00	10.00	15.00	50.00
	1913 w/o dot after D					
		Inc. Ab.	40.00	75.00	150.00	250.00

ITALY 1096

KM#	Date	Mintage	Fine	VF	XF	Unc
(Y45)	1915	1.038	3.50	7.50	12.50	30.00
	1918	4.242	.75	1.75	3.50	15.00

59	1919	13.208	.75	2.00	3.00	10.00
(Y61)	1920	33.372	.30	.75	2.00	5.00
	1921	80.111	.30	.75	2.00	5.00
	1922	42.914	.30	.75	2.00	5.00
	1923	29.614	.30	.75	2.00	5.00
	1924	20.352	.30	.75	2.00	5.00
	1925	40.460	.30	.75	2.00	5.00
	1926	21.158	.30	.75	2.00	5.00
	1927	15.800	.30	.75	2.00	5.00
	1928	16.090	.30	.75	2.00	5.00
	1929	29.000	.30	.75	2.00	5.00
	1930	22.694	.30	.75	2.00	5.00
	1931	20.000	.30	.75	2.00	5.00
	1932	11.456	.30	.75	2.00	5.00
	1933	20.720	.30	.75	2.00	5.00
	1934	16.000	.30	.75	2.00	5.00
	1935	11.000	.30	.75	2.00	5.00
	1936	9.462	.30	.75	2.00	5.00
	1937	.972	4.00	8.00	12.50	25.00

73	1936, yr. XIV					
(Y77)		Inc. Ab.	2.00	4.00	8.00	15.00
	1937, yr. XV					
		7.207	.30	.75	1.00	3.00
	1938, yr. XVI					
		24.000	.20	.65	1.00	3.00
	1939, yr. XVII					
		22.000	.20	.65	1.00	3.00

ALUMINUM-BRONZE

73a	1939, yr. XVII					
(Y77a)		1.000	.30	.75	1.25	3.00
	1940, yr. XVIII					
		9.630	.30	.75	1.00	3.00
	1941, yr. XIX					
		16.340	.30	.75	1.00	3.00
	1942, yr. XX					
		25.200	.30	.75	1.25	3.00
	1943, yr. XXI					
		13.922	2.00	5.00	10.00	20.00

10 CENTESIMI

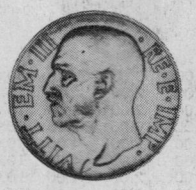

COPPER
Mint mark: M

11.1	1862	40.000	1.50	3.50	7.00	50.00
(Y9.1)	1866	36.000	1.50	3.50	7.00	50.00

Mint mark: None

11.2	1862	—	1.50	3.50	7.00	50.00
(Y9.2)	1863	80.000	1.50	3.50	7.00	50.00
	1866	—	15.00	25.00	35.00	50.00

Mint mark: H

11.3	1866	40.000	1.50	3.50	7.00	50.00
(Y9.3)	1867	50.000	1.50	3.50	7.00	50.00

Mint mark: N

11.4	1866	67.650	1.50	3.50	7.00	50.00
(Y9.4)	1867	31.360	1.50	3.50	7.00	50.00

Mint mark: OM

11.5	1866	20.000	1.50	3.50	7.00	50.00
(Y9.5)	1866.	Inc. Ab.	1.50	3.50	7.00	50.00
	1867	—	1.50	3.50	7.00	50.00
	1867.	—	3.00	5.00	12.50	50.00

Mint mark: T

11.6	1866	16.350	1.50	3.50	7.00	50.00
(Y9.6)	1867	18.640	1.50	3.50	7.00	50.00

Mint mark: B/I

KM#	Date	Mintage	Fine	VF	XF	Unc
27.1	1893	8.547	1.50	3.50	7.00	30.00
(Y25.1)	1894	32.000	1.50	3.50	7.00	30.00

Mint mark: R

27.2	1893	28.000	—	3.50	8.00	50.00
(Y25.2)	1894	5.910	5.00	10.00	25.00	50.00

Similar to 5 Centesimi, KM#42.

43	1908	—	1000.	1800.	2200.	3000.
(Y46)						

50th Anniversary of Kingdom

51	1911	2.000	2.50	5.00	10.00	30.00
(Y57)						

60	1919	.986	20.00	35.00	50.00	100.00
(Y62)	1920	37.995	.50	1.25	4.00	10.00
	1921	66.510	.50	1.25	4.00	10.00
	1922	45.217	.50	1.25	4.00	10.00
	1923	31.529	.50	1.25	4.00	10.00
	1924	35.312	.50	1.25	4.00	10.00
	1925	22.370	.50	1.25	4.00	10.00
	1926	25.190	.50	1.25	4.00	10.00
	1927	22.673	.50	1.25	4.00	10.00
	1928	15.680	.50	2.00	7.50	20.00
	1929	15.593	.50	1.25	4.00	10.00
	1930	17.115	.50	1.25	4.00	10.00
	1931	10.750	.50	1.25	4.00	10.00
	1932	5.678	1.25	2.50	7.50	20.00
	1933	10.250	.50	1.25	4.00	10.00
	1934	18.300	.50	1.25	4.00	10.00
	1935	10.500	.50	1.25	4.00	10.00
	1936	8.770	.50	1.50	4.50	12.50
	1937	5.500	.50	1.50	4.50	12.50

74	1936, yr. XIV					
(Y78)		Inc. Ab.	.75	1.50	3.00	12.50
	1937, yr. XV					
		7.212	.25	.75	1.50	4.00
	1938, yr. XVI					
		18.750	.25	.75	1.50	4.00
	1939, yr. XVII					
		24.750	.25	.75	1.50	4.00

ALUMINUM-BRONZE

74a	1939, yr. XVII					
(Y78a)		.750	.50	1.50	2.00	4.00
	1940, yr. XVIII					
		23.355	.20	.60	1.00	4.00
	1941, yr. XIX					
		27.050	.20	.60	1.00	4.00
	1942, yr. XX					
		18.100	.20	.60	1.00	4.00
	1943, yr. XXI					
		25.400	.25	.60	2.00	5.00

20 CENTESIMI

1.0000 g, .835 SILVER, .0268 oz ASW
Mint mark: T

12	1863NB					
(Y10)		461 pcs.	400.00	750.00	1500.	3000.

Mint mark: M

KM#	Date	Mintage	Fine	VF	XF	Unc
13.1	1863BN	27.845	3.00	5.00	10.00	20.00
(Y15.1)						

Mint mark: T

13.2	1863BN	6.289	4.00	5.50	11.00	25.00
(Y15.2)	1863BN inverted BN					
		Inc. Ab.	7.00	10.00	25.00	75.00
	1867BN	.866	17.50	35.00	65.00	125.00

COPPER-NICKEL
Mint mark: KB

28.1	1894	75.000	.40	1.00	3.00	8.00
(Y26.1)						

Mint mark: R

28.2	1894	13.901	.60	1.50	3.00	12.00
(Y26.2)	1895	11.099	.60	1.50	3.00	12.00

NICKEL

44	1908	14.315	.50	1.00	3.00	10.00
(Y47)	1909	19.280	.50	1.00	3.00	10.00
	1910	21.887	.50	1.00	3.00	10.00
	1911	13.671	.50	1.00	3.00	10.00
	1912	21.040	.50	1.00	3.00	10.00
	1913	20.729	.50	1.00	3.00	10.00
	1914	14.308	.50	1.00	3.00	10.00
	1919	3.475	1.00	3.50	10.00	25.00
	1920	27.284	.50	1.00	3.00	10.00
	1921	50.372	.50	1.00	3.00	10.00
	1922	17.134	.50	1.00	3.00	10.00
	1926	500 pcs.	—	—	—	150.00
	1927	100 pcs.	—	—	—	200.00
	1928	50 pcs.	—	—	—	250.00
	1929	50 pcs.	—	—	—	250.00
	1930	50 pcs.	—	—	—	250.00
	1931	50 pcs.	—	—	—	250.00
	1932	50 pcs.	—	—	—	250.00
	1933	50 pcs.	—	—	—	250.00
	1934	50 pcs.	—	—	—	250.00
	1935	50 pcs.	—	—	—	250.00

COPPER-NICKEL
Plain and reeded edges, overstruck on KM#28.

58	1918	43.097	.50	1.00	3.00	8.00
(Y63)	1919	33.432	.50	1.00	3.00	8.00
	1920	.923	3.00	5.00	10.00	30.00

NICKEL

75	1936, yr. XIV					
(Y79)		.117	10.00	20.00	35.00	75.00
	1937, yr. XV					
		50 pcs.	—	—	—	300.00
	1938, yr. XVII					
		20 pcs.	—	—	—	400.00

STAINLESS STEEL (non-magnetic)
Plain edge, 25mm

75a	1939, yr. XVII					
(Y79a)		.460	.50	1.00	2.50	5.00
	1940, yr. XVIII					
		35.350	.25	.50	1.00	3.00
	1942, yr. XX					
		99.900	.30	.50	1.00	3.00

STAINLESS STEEL (magnetic)
Reeded edge, 21.8mm

| 75b | 1939, yr. XVII | | | | | |

KM# (Y79b)	Date	Mintage	Fine	VF	XF	Unc
		Inc. Ab.	.30	.50	1.00	3.00
	1939, yr. XVIII					
		Inc. Ab.	.35	.50	1.00	3.00
	1940, yr. XVIII					
		Inc. Ab.	.30	.50	1.00	3.00
	1941, yr. XIX					
		107.300	.30	.50	1.00	3.00
	1942, yr. XX					
		Inc. Ab.	.30	.50	1.00	3.00
	1943, yr. XXI					
		57.003	.30	.50	1.00	3.00

25 CENTESIMI

NICKEL
Mint mark: R

| 36 | 1902 | 7.773 | 8.00 | 12.00 | 22.50 | 40.00 |
| (Y37) | 1903 | 5.895 | 7.00 | 10.00 | 20.00 | 35.00 |

50 CENTESIMI

2.5000 g, .900 SILVER, .0723 oz ASW
Mint mark: FIRENZE

| A4 | 1861F | 1.222 | 50.00 | 100.00 | 150.00 | 400.00 |
| (4.1) | | | | | | |

Mint mark: M

| 4.1 | 1861BN | — | — | — | Rare | — |
| (4.2) | | | | | | |

Mint mark: T

4.2	1861B in shield					
(4.3)		.045	—	—	Rare	—
	1862BN	.185	35.00	75.00	150.00	400.00

Mint mark: N

| 4.3 | 1862 | .630 | 20.00 | 45.00 | 100.00 | 250.00 |
| (4.4) | | | | | | |

2.5000 g, .835 SILVER, .0671 oz ASW
Mint mark: M

| 4a.1 | 1863BN | 4.706 | 4.00 | 7.00 | 12.00 | 30.00 |
| (Y11a.1) | | | | | | |

Mint mark: T

| 4a.2 | 1863BN | 2.753 | 7.00 | 15.00 | 35.00 | 75.00 |
| (Y11a.2) | | | | | | |

Mint mark: M

14.1	1863BN	33.760	4.00	7.00	12.00	30.00
(Y16.1)	1866BN	19.199	12.50	20.00	30.00	45.00
	1867BN	10.984	4.00	7.00	12.00	30.00

Mintmark: N

| 14.2 | 1863BN | 16.062 | 5.00 | 10.00 | 15.00 | 30.00 |
| (Y16.2) | 1867BN | 7.838 | 5.00 | 10.00 | 15.00 | 30.00 |

Mint mark: T

| 14.3 | 1863BN | 6.301 | 5.00 | 10.00 | 15.00 | 30.00 |
| (Y16.3) | 1867BN | .396 | 35.00 | 85.00 | 175.00 | 400.00 |

Mint mark: R

| 26 | 1889 | .635 | 25.00 | 40.00 | 75.00 | 200.00 |
| (Y27) | 1892 | .148 | 30.00 | 50.00 | 100.00 | 250.00 |

NICKEL
Plain edge

| 61.1 | 1919 | 3.700 | 2.50 | 5.00 | 20.00 | 50.00 |

KM# (Y64)	Date	Mintage	Fine	VF	XF	Unc
	1920	29.450	.75	1.50	3.00	15.00
	1921	16.849	.75	1.50	3.00	15.00
	1924	.599	40.00	80.00	200.00	400.00
	1925	24.884	1.50	2.50	8.00	20.00
	1926	500 pcs.	—	—	—	185.00
	1927	100 pcs.	—	—	—	300.00
	1928	50 pcs.	—	—	—	350.00

Reeded edge

61.2	1919	Inc. Ab.	2.50	6.25	12.50	100.00
(Y64a)	1920	Inc. Ab.	2.50	6.25	12.50	100.00
	1921	Inc. Ab.	2.50	6.25	12.50	100.00
	1924	Inc. Ab.	25.00	50.00	75.00	250.00
	1925	Inc. Ab.	2.50	5.00	10.00	50.00
	1929	50 pcs.	—	—	—	300.00
	1930	50 pcs.	—	—	—	300.00
	1931	50 pcs.	—	—	—	300.00
	1932	50 pcs.	—	—	—	300.00
	1933	50 pcs.	—	—	—	300.00
	1934	50 pcs.	—	—	—	300.00
	1935	50 pcs.	—	—	—	300.00

76	1936, yr. XIV					
(Y80)		.118	8.00	15.00	30.00	45.00
	1937, yr. XV					
		50 pcs.	—	—	—	300.00
	1938, yr. XVII					
		20 pcs.	—	—	—	400.00

STAINLESS STEEL (non-magnetic)

76a	1939, yr. XVII					
(Y80a)		.370	.25	.75	1.00	3.00
	1939, yr. XVIII					
		Inc. Ab.	.25	.75	1.00	3.00
	1940, yr. XVIII					
		19.005	.20	.35	1.00	3.00

STAINLESS STEEL (magnetic)

76b	1939, yr. XVII					
(Y80b)		Inc. Ab.	.25	.75	1.00	3.00
	1940, yr. XVIII					
		Inc. Ab.	.25	.65	1.00	3.00
	1941, yr. XIX					
		58.100	.25	.55	1.00	3.00
	1942, yr. XX					
		26.450	.25	.60	1.00	3.00
	1943, yr. XXI					
		3.681	10.00	25.00	50.00	75.00

LIRA

5.0000 g, .900 SILVER, .1447 oz ASW
Mint mark: FIRENZE

| A5 | 1861F | .432 | 55.00 | 110.00 | 200.00 | 400.00 |
| (5.1) | | | | | | |

Mint mark: T

5.1	1861B in shield					
(5.2)		.019	—	—	Rare	—
	1862BN	.105	50.00	100.00	200.00	400.00

Mint mark: N

| 5.2 | 1862 | .497 | 30.00 | 65.00 | 150.00 | 300.00 |
| (5.3) | | | | | | |

5.0000 g, .835 SILVER, .1342 oz ASW
Mint mark: M

5a.1	1863BN	24.054	2.00	5.00	10.00	40.00
(Y12a.1)	1867/3BN					
		7.665	6.00	10.00	17.50	60.00
	1867BN	I.A.	4.00	7.50	15.00	50.00

Mint mark: T

| 5a.2 | 1863BN | 2.270 | 4.00 | 7.50 | 15.00 | 50.00 |
| (Y12a.2) | 1867BN | .335 | 25.00 | 50.00 | 150.00 | 300.00 |

Mint mark: M

| 15.1 | 1863BN | 29.837 | 2.00 | 5.00 | 12.50 | 50.00 |
| (Y17.1) | | | | | | |

Mint mark: T

| 15.2 | 1863BN | 3.839 | 60.00 | 125.00 | 200.00 | 375.00 |
| (Y17.2) | | | | | | |

Mint mark: R

KM#	Date	Mintage	Fine	VF	XF	Unc
24.1	1883	5.420	500.00	800.00	1500.	5000.
(Y28.1)	1884	1.995	4.00	10.00	25.00	100.00
	1886	6.095	2.50	6.00	20.00	90.00
	1892	.032	200.00	300.00	500.00	1000.
	1899	1.798	3.00	7.50	20.00	90.00
	1900	.318	25.00	50.00	100.00	500.00

Mint mark: M

| 24.2 | 1887 | 16.305 | 2.50 | 7.50 | 20.00 | 90.00 |
| (Y28.2) | | | | | | |

32	1901	2.590	5.00	12.50	25.00	100.00
(Y38)	1902	4.084	3.50	7.50	20.00	90.00
	1905	.700	30.00	60.00	150.00	400.00
	1906	4.665	3.50	5.00	12.50	50.00
	1907	8.472	2.50	5.00	12.50	50.00

45	1908	2.212	20.00	40.00	80.00	200.00
(Y48)	1909	3.475	3.50	7.50	20.00	100.00
	1910	5.525	2.50	5.00	12.50	60.00
	1912	5.865	2.50	4.00	9.00	35.00
	1913	16.177	2.00	3.50	6.00	25.00

57	1915	5.229	2.75	4.00	12.50	35.00
(Y50)	1916	1.835	5.00	10.00	20.00	60.00
	1917	9.744	2.75	4.00	10.00	25.00

NICKEL

62	1922	82.267	.60	1.00	3.00	15.00
(Y65)	1923	20.175	.60	1.00	3.00	15.00
	1924	29.288	.60	1.00	3.00	15.00
	1926	500 pcs.	—	—	—	175.00
	1927	100 pcs.	—	—	—	225.00
	1928	19.996	1.00	2.00	10.00	30.00
	1929	50 pcs.	—	—	—	300.00
	1930	50 pcs.	—	—	—	300.00
	1931	50 pcs.	—	—	—	300.00
	1932	50 pcs.	—	—	—	300.00
	1933	50 pcs.	—	—	—	300.00
	1934	50 pcs.	—	—	—	300.00
	1935	50 pcs.	—	—	—	300.00

77	1936, yr. XIV					
(Y81)		.119	10.00	15.00	25.00	50.00
	1937, yr. XV					

ITALY 1098

KM#	Date	Mintage	Fine	VF	XF	Unc
(Y81)	1938, yr. XVII	50 pcs.	—	—	—	350.00
		20 pcs.	—	—	—	450.00

STAINLESS STEEL (non-magnetic)

KM#	Date	Mintage	Fine	VF	XF	Unc
77a (Y81a)	1939, yr. XVII	—	.30	.60	1.25	6.00
	1939, yr. XVIII	—	.30	.60	1.25	4.00
	1940, yr. XVIII	25.997	.30	.60	1.25	4.00

STAINLESS STEEL (magnetic)

KM#	Date	Mintage	Fine	VF	XF	Unc
77b (Y81b)	1939, yr. XVII	—	.30	.60	1.25	4.00
	1940, yr. XVIII	Inc. Ab.	.30	.60	1.25	4.00
	1941, yr. XIX	8.550	.30	.60	1.25	4.00
	1942, yr. XX	5.700	.30	.60	1.25	4.00
	1943, yr. XXI	11.500	3.50	6.50	15.00	30.00

2 LIRE

10.0000 g, .900 SILVER, .2893 oz ASW
Mint mark: T

KM#	Date	Mintage	Fine	VF	XF	Unc
6.1 (Y13.1)	1861B in shield	9.871	—	—	Rare	—

Mint mark: N

KM#	Date	Mintage	Fine	VF	XF	Unc
6.2 (Y13.2)	1862	.062	150.00	300.00	600.00	1500.

10.0000 g, .835 SILVER, .2684 oz ASW

KM#	Date	Mintage	Fine	VF	XF	Unc
6a.1 (Y13a.1)	1863BN	10.090	6.50	17.50	40.00	150.00

Mint mark: T

KM#	Date	Mintage	Fine	VF	XF	Unc
6a.2 (Y13a.2)	1863BN	4.910	7.50	20.00	50.00	175.00

Mint mark: N

KM#	Date	Mintage	Fine	VF	XF	Unc
16.1 (Y18.1)	1863BN	—	7.50	20.00	80.00	200.00

Mint mark: T

KM#	Date	Mintage	Fine	VF	XF	Unc
16.2 (Y18.2)	1863BN	—	7.50	25.00	100.00	250.00

Mint mark: R

KM#	Date	Mintage	Fine	VF	XF	Unc
23 (Y29)	1881	4.141	5.00	10.00	40.00	150.00
	1882	2.859	5.00	10.00	40.00	150.00
	1883	3.500	5.00	10.00	40.00	150.00
	1884	4.500	5.00	10.00	40.00	150.00
	1885	.598	25.00	50.00	100.00	300.00
	1886	1.902	5.00	10.00	40.00	150.00
	1887	7.500	5.00	10.00	40.00	150.00
	1897	.848	7.50	12.50	40.00	150.00
	1898	1.320	25.00	50.00	100.00	400.00
	1899	.610	7.50	12.50	35.00	150.00

KM#	Date	Mintage	Fine	VF	XF	Unc
33 (Y39)	1901	.072	200.00	400.00	800.00	1500.
	1902	.549	40.00	80.00	150.00	400.00
	1903	.054	300.00	500.00	1000.	3000.
	1904	.157	125.00	250.00	450.00	700.00
	1905	1.643	10.00	20.00	50.00	200.00
	1906	.970	12.50	25.00	75.00	200.00
	1907	1.245	10.00	20.00	50.00	200.00

KM#	Date	Mintage	Fine	VF	XF	Unc
46 (Y49)	1908	2.283	6.00	15.00	50.00	150.00
	1910	.719	25.00	50.00	125.00	300.00
	1911	.535	30.00	60.00	150.00	400.00
	1912	2.166	6.00	15.00	50.00	150.00

50th Anniversary of Kingdom

KM#	Date	Mintage	Fine	VF	XF	Unc
52 (Y58)	1911	1.000	12.50	25.00	50.00	125.00

KM#	Date	Mintage	Fine	VF	XF	Unc
55 (Y51)	1914	10.390	4.00	6.00	11.00	30.00
	1915	7.948	4.00	6.00	11.00	30.00
	1916	10.923	4.00	6.00	11.00	30.00
	1917	6.123	6.00	12.50	25.00	60.00

NICKEL

KM#	Date	Mintage	Fine	VF	XF	Unc
63 (Y66)	1923	32.260	1.00	2.00	5.00	20.00
	1924	45.051	1.00	2.00	5.00	20.00
	1925	14.628	1.00	2.00	5.00	30.00
	1926	5.101	5.00	10.00	50.00	150.00
	1927	1.632	25.00	50.00	100.00	300.00
	1928	50 pcs.	—	—	—	350.00
	1929	50 pcs.	—	—	—	350.00
	1930	50 pcs.	—	—	—	350.00
	1931	50 pcs.	—	—	—	350.00
	1932	50 pcs.	—	—	—	350.00
	1933	50 pcs.	—	—	—	350.00
	1934	50 pcs.	—	—	—	350.00
	1935	50 pcs.	—	—	—	350.00

KM#	Date	Mintage	Fine	VF	XF	Unc
78 (Y82)	1936, yr. XIV	.120	12.00	16.00	25.00	65.00
	1937, yr. XV	50 pcs.	—	—	—	350.00
	1938, yr. XVII	20 pcs.	—	—	—	450.00

STAINLESS STEEL (non-magnetic)

KM#	Date	Mintage	Fine	VF	XF	Unc
78a (Y82a)	1939, yr. XVII	—	.40	.90	2.00	5.00
	1939, yr. XVIII	—	.40	.90	2.00	5.00
	1940, yr. XVIII	13.483	.40	.90	2.00	5.00

STAINLESS STEEL (magnetic)

KM#	Date	Mintage	Fine	VF	XF	Unc
78b (Y82b)	1940, yr. XVIII	—	.40	.90	2.00	5.00
	1941, yr. XIX	1.865	.40	.90	2.00	5.00
	1942, yr. XX	2.450	20.00	40.00	75.00	175.00
	1943, yr. XXI	.600	15.00	35.00	65.00	125.00

5 LIRE

25.0000 g, .900 SILVER, .7234 oz ASW
Mint mark: FIRENZE
Accession to Throne of Unified Italy

KM#	Date	Mintage	Fine	VF	XF	Unc
7 (Y5)	1861	.021	250.00	500.00	900.00	2000.

Mint mark: T

KM#	Date	Mintage	Fine	VF	XF	Unc
8.1 (Y14.1)	1861B in shield	.160	175.00	375.00	650.00	1200.
	1862BN	.051	50.00	100.00	200.00	550.00
	1865BN	.491	15.00	30.00	70.00	200.00

Mint mark: N

KM#	Date	Mintage	Fine	VF	XF	Unc
8.2 (Y14.2)	1862BN	.142	30.00	65.00	120.00	350.00
	1864BN	.120	20.00	40.00	90.00	225.00
	1865BN	.312	15.00	30.00	70.00	200.00
	1866BN	.460	1000.	1500.	2000.	4000.

Mint mark: M

KM#	Date	Mintage	Fine	VF	XF	Unc
8.3 (Y14.3)	1869BN	3.995	10.00	17.50	40.00	175.00
	1870BN	5.969	10.00	17.50	40.00	150.00
	1871BN	6.697	10.00	17.50	40.00	150.00
	1872BN	7.093	10.00	17.50	40.00	150.00
	1873BN	8.438	10.00	17.50	40.00	150.00
	1874BN	12.000	10.00	17.50	40.00	150.00
	1875BN	8.982	10.00	17.50	40.00	150.00

Mint mark: R

KM#	Date	Mintage	Fine	VF	XF	Unc
8.4 (Y14.4)	1870	—	50.00	100.00	200.00	300.00
	1871	.404	65.00	135.00	250.00	400.00
	1872	.029	300.00	500.00	1000.	2500.
	1873	.017	400.00	700.00	2000.	4000.
	1875	1.018	15.00	30.00	75.00	300.00
	1876	6.390	12.00	20.00	40.00	150.00
	1877	4.410	12.00	20.00	40.00	175.00
	1878	1.700	15.00	25.00	50.00	225.00

ITALY 1099

1.6129 g, .900 GOLD, .0466 oz AGW
Mint mark: T

KM#	Date	Mintage	Fine	VF	XF	Unc
17	1863BN	.197	55.00	100.00	150.00	250.00
(Y-A18)	1865BN	.408	55.00	100.00	150.00	250.00
	1865BN	—	—	—	Proof	450.00

25.0000 g, .900 SILVER, .7234 oz ASW
Mint mark: R

20	1878	.100	200.00	400.00	800.00	2000.
(Y30)	1879	4.000	20.00	40.00	125.00	600.00

34	1901	114 pcs.	—	—	15,000.	20,000.
(Y40)						

50th Anniversary of Kingdom

KM#	Date	Mintage	Fine	VF	XF	Unc
53 (Y59)	1911	.060	175.00	300.00	500.00	800.00

56 (Y52)	1914	.273	500.00	750.00	2250.	3500.

5.0000 g, .835 SILVER, .1342 oz ASW
Edge inscription w/1 asterisk before and after FERT.

67.1	1926	5.405	4.00	7.50	17.50	60.00
(Y67)	1927	92.887	1.50	2.50	4.00	12.50
	1928	9.908	2.50	5.00	12.50	40.00
	1929	33.803	1.50	3.00	4.50	15.00
	1930	19.525	1.50	3.00	4.50	15.00
	1931	50 pcs.	—	—	—	350.00
	1932	50 pcs.	—	—	—	350.00
	1933	50 pcs.	—	—	—	350.00
	1934	50 pcs.	—	—	—	350.00
	1935	50 pcs.	—	—	—	350.00

Edge inscription w/2 asterisks before and after FERT.

67.2	1927	Inc. Ab.	—	—	—	—
	1928	Inc. Ab.				
	1929	Inc. Ab.				

79	1936, yr. XIV	1.016	5.00	9.00	15.00	50.00
(Y89)	1937, yr. XV	.100	10.00	20.00	30.00	75.00
	1938, yr. XVIII	20 pcs.	—	—	—	400.00
	1939, yr. XVIII	20 pcs.	—	—	—	400.00
	1940, yr. XIX	20 pcs.	—	—	—	400.00
	1941, yr. XX	20 pcs.	—	—	—	400.00

10 LIRE

3.2258 g, .900 GOLD, 18mm, .0933 oz AGW
Mint mark: T

9.1	1861B in shield					
(Y-B18.1)		1,916	1500.	3000.	4500.	7500.

18.5mm

KM#	Date	Mintage	Fine	VF	XF	Unc
9.2	1863BN	.543	55.00	70.00	90.00	135.00
(Y-B18.2)	1863BN	—	—	—	Proof	625.00
	1865BN	.444	75.00	125.00	150.00	250.00

19mm

9.3	1863BN	Inc. Ab.	55.00	70.00	90.00	175.00
(Y-B18.3)						

19.5mm

9.4	1863BN	Inc. Ab.	55.00	70.00	90.00	175.00
(Y-B18.4)						

Mint mark: R

47	1910	5.202	—	—	Rare	—
(Y53)	1912	6.796	500.00	1000.	1500.	2500.
	1926	40 pcs.	—	—	—	8800.
	1927	30 pcs.	—	—	—	6850.

10.0000 g, .835 SILVER, .2684 oz ASW
Edge inscription w/1 asterisk before and after FERT.

68.1	1926	1.748	40.00	65.00	125.00	350.00
(Y68)	1927	44.801	4.00	6.00	12.50	40.00
	1928	6.652	10.00	20.00	50.00	150.00
	1929	6.800	10.00	20.00	50.00	150.00
	1930	3.668	25.00	50.00	100.00	200.00
	1931	50 pcs.	—	—	—	450.00
	1932	50 pcs.	—	—	—	450.00
	1933	50 pcs.	—	—	—	450.00
	1934	50 pcs.	—	—	—	450.00

Edge inscription w/2 asterisks before and after FERT.

68.2	1927	Inc. Ab.	—	—	—	—
	1928	Inc. Ab.				
	1929	Inc. Ab.				

80	1936, yr. XIV	.619	10.00	15.00	25.00	50.00
(Y90)	1937, yr. XV	50 pcs.	—	—	—	500.00
	1938, yr. XVII	20 pcs.	—	—	—	800.00
	1939, yr. XVIII	20 pcs.	—	—	—	800.00
	1940, yr. XIX	20 pcs.	—	—	—	800.00
	1941, yr. XX	20 pcs.	—	—	—	800.00

20 LIRE

6.4516 g, .900 GOLD, .1867 oz AGW
Mint mark: T

10.1	1861B in shield					
(Y19.1)		3,267	100.00	120.00	130.00	150.00
	1861T/F	I.A.	BV	100.00	130.00	150.00
	1862BN	1.955	BV	100.00	110.00	135.00
	1863BN	2.981	BV	100.00	110.00	135.00
	1864BN	.609	BV	100.00	110.00	135.00
	1865BN	3.109	BV	100.00	110.00	150.00
	1866BN	.196	BV	100.00	125.00	300.00
	1867BN	.276	BV	100.00	110.00	150.00

ITALY 1100

KM#	Date	Mintage	Fine	VF	XF	Unc
(Y19.1)	1868BN	.340	BV	100.00	110.00	150.00
	1869BN	.185	BV	100.00	110.00	150.00
	1870BN	.055	BV	100.00	125.00	300.00

Mint mark: R

10.2	1870	—	125.00	250.00	500.00	1000.
(Y19.2)	1871	—	BV	125.00	200.00	400.00
	1873	2,174	400.00	800.00	1500.	3000.
	1874	.041	BV	100.00	110.00	155.00
	1875	.051	BV	100.00	110.00	155.00
	1876	.108	BV	100.00	110.00	135.00
	1877	.247	BV	100.00	110.00	135.00
	1878	.316	BV	100.00	110.00	135.00

Mint mark: M

10.3	1872BN	—	100.00	150.00	250.00	500.00
(Y19.3)	1873BN	1.018	BV	100.00	110.00	145.00
	1874BN	.255	BV	100.00	110.00	150.00

Mint mark: R

21	1879	.146	BV	100.00	110.00	135.00
(Y32)	1880	.129	BV	100.00	110.00	135.00
	1881	.843	BV	100.00	110.00	135.00
	1882	6.970	BV	90.00	100.00	115.00
	1883	.182	BV	100.00	110.00	135.00
	1884	9.775	125.00	250.00	500.00	1200.
	1885	.165	BV	100.00	110.00	135.00
	1886	.059	BV	100.00	110.00	135.00
	1888	.111	BV	100.00	110.00	135.00
	1889	—	BV	125.00	200.00	400.00
	1890	.068	BV	100.00	110.00	135.00
	1891	.032	BV	100.00	120.00	160.00
	1893	.041	BV	100.00	110.00	145.00
	1897	.038	BV	100.00	110.00	155.00

RED GOLD

| 21a | 1882 | Inc. Ab. | BV | 110.00 | 125.00 | 175.00 |

6.4516 g, .900 GOLD, .1867 oz AGW

37.1	1902	181 pcs.	—	—	*Rare	
(Y41)	1903	1,800	250.00	500.00	900.00	1450.
	1905	8,715	150.00	250.00	375.00	650.00
	1908	—	—	—	—	100,000.

*NOTE: Stack's International sale 3-88 XF realized $13,200.

Obv: Small anchor bottom indicates gold in coin is from Eritrea.

37.2	1902	115 pcs.	—	5000.	9000.	*14,500.
(Y41a)						

*NOTE: Bowers and Merena Guia sale 3-88 Unc. realized $14,300.

Obv: Uniformed bust.

48	1910	.033	—	—	—	30,000.
(Y54)	1912	.059	150.00	250.00	375.00	700.00
	1926	40 pcs.	—	—	3000.	5500.
	1927	30 pcs.	—	—	—	7250.

1st Anniversary of Fascist Government

64	1923	.020	150.00	250.00	400.00	700.00
(Y72)						

15.0000 g, .800 SILVER, .3858 oz ASW

KM#	Date	Mintage	Fine	VF	XF	Unc
69	1927, yr. V					
(Y69)		100 pcs.	—	—	4000.	5000.
	1927, yr. VI					
		3.518	25.00	50.00	100.00	210.00
	1928, yr. VI					
		2.487	30.00	60.00	120.00	225.00
	1929, yr. VII					
		50 pcs.	—	—	—	1500.
	1930, yr. VIII					
		50 pcs.	—	—	—	1500.
	1931, yr. IX					
		50 pcs.	—	—	—	1500.
	1932, yr. X					
		50 pcs.	—	—	—	1500.
	1933, yr. XI					
		50 pcs.	—	—	—	1500.
	1934, yr. XII					
		50 pcs.	—	—	—	1500.

20.0000 g, .600 SILVER, .3858 oz ASW
10th Anniversary End of World War I

70	1928, yr. VI	—	50.00	100.00	200.00	400.00
(Y75)						

NOTE: Similar 100 Lire pieces struck in gold are modern fantasies. Refer to UNUSUAL WORLD COINS, 2nd edition, Krause Publications, 1988.

15.0000 g, .800 SILVER, .3858 oz ASW

81	1936, yr. XIV					
(Y91)		.010	150.00	300.00	600.00	1000.
	1937, yr. XV					
		50 pcs.	—	—	—	2500.
	1938, yr. XVII					
		20 pcs.	—	—	—	2750.
	1939, yr. XVIII					
		20 pcs.	—	—	—	2750.
	1940, yr. XIX					
		20 pcs.	—	—	—	3000.
	1941, yr. XX					
		20 pcs.	—	—	—	3000.

50 LIRE

16.1290 g, .900 GOLD, .4667 oz AGW
Mint mark: T

18	1864BN					
(Y20)		103 pcs.	—	30,000.	40,000.	—

Mint mark: R

KM#	Date	Mintage	Fine	VF	XF	Unc
25	1884	2,532	650.00	1250.	1750.	3000.
(Y33)	1888	2,125	1000.	2000.	2500.	3500.
	1891	414 pcs.	1250.	2250.	3000.	4500.

49	1910	2,096	—	—	Rare	—
(Y55)	1912	.011	300.00	500.00	750.00	1250.
	1926	40 pcs.	—	—	*Rare	—
	1927	30 pcs.	—	—	—	8750.

*NOTE: Bowers and Merena Guia sale 3-88 Choice Unc. (cleaned) realized $8,250.

50th Anniversary of Kingdom

54	1911	.020	300.00	500.00	750.00	1200.
(Y60)						

4.3995 g, .900 GOLD, .1273 oz AGW

71	1931, yr. IX					
(Y70)		.032	100.00	135.00	175.00	275.00
	1931, yr. X					
		Inc. Ab.	125.00	200.00	300.00	500.00
	1932, yr. X					
		.012	100.00	150.00	225.00	350.00
	1933, yr. XI					
		6,463	150.00	200.00	275.00	450.00

82	1936, yr. XIV					
(Y92)		790 pcs.	—	—	2250.	3250.

100 LIRE

32.2580 g, .900 GOLD, .9334 oz AGW
Mint mark: T

19.1	1864 BN					
(Y21.1)		579 pcs.	—	4000.	7000.	11,000.

Mint mark: R

19.2	1872	661 pcs.	—	3750.	6000.	8000.
(Y21.2)	1878	294 pcs.	—	5000.	9000.	12,500.

ITALY 1101

KM#	Date	Mintage	Fine	VF	XF	Unc
22	1880	145 pcs.	—	10,000.	16,000.*	25,000.
(Y34)	1882	1,229	—	1500.	2500.	3750.
	1883	4,219	—	1250.	2250.	3500.
	1888	1,169	—	1500.	3000.	4500.
	1891	209 pcs.	—	4000.	7000.	10,000.

*NOTE: Bowers and Merena Guia sale 3-88 Choice AU realized $24,200.

39	1903	916 pcs.	—	2500.	4250.	6000.
(Y42)	1905	1,012	—	2500.	4250.	6000.

50	1910	2,013	—	—	—	Rare
(Y56)	1912	4,946	—	1500.	2000.	3000.
	1926	40 pcs.	—	—	—	**Rare
	1927	30 pcs.	—	—	—	*Rare

*NOTE: Stack's International sale 3-88 BU realized $18,700.
**NOTE: Bowers and Merena Guia sale 3-88 Choice Unc. (cleaned) realized $12,650.

1st Anniversary of Fascist Government

65	1923 frosted finish					
(Y73)		.020	550.00	750.00	1100.	1650.
	1923 bright finish	—	—	Rare	—	

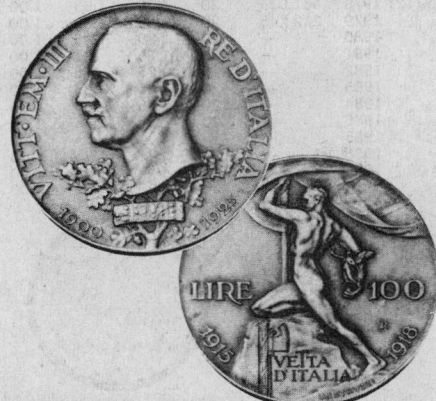

25th Year of Reign-10th Anniv. World War I Entry

66	1925	5,000	700.00	1000.	1500.	3000.
(Y74)	1925	—	—	Matte Proof	3500.	

8.7990 g, .900 GOLD, .2546 oz AGW

KM#	Date	Mintage	Fine	VF	XF	Unc
72	1931, yr. IX					
(Y71)		.034	135.00	200.00	250.00	350.00
	1931, yr. X					
	Inc. Ab.	150.00	250.00	350.00	500.00	
	1932, yr. X					
		9,081	150.00	225.00	325.00	450.00
	1933, yr. XI					
		6,464	150.00	250.00	350.00	475.00

83	1936, yr. XIV					
(Y93)		812 pcs.	—	1500.	2500.	4250.

5.1900 g, .900 GOLD, .1502 oz AGW

84	1937, yr. XVI					
(Y93a)		249 pcs.	—	5000.	9000.*	14,500.
	1940, yr. XVIII					
		2 pcs.	—	—	—	70,000.

*NOTE: Bowers and Merena Guia sale 3-88 Unc realized $14,300.

REPUBLIC
LIRA

ALUMINUM

87	1946	.104	5.00	10.00	20.00	50.00
(Y95)	1947	.012	25.00	40.00	75.00	150.00
	1948	9.000	.40	1.00	2.00	7.50
	1949	13.200	.40	1.00	2.00	7.50
	1950	1.942	1.00	2.00	4.00	10.00

91	1951	3.680	.10	.25	.50	3.00
(Y99)	1952	2.720	.10	.25	.50	5.00
	1953	2.800	.10	.25	.50	3.00
	1954	41.040	.10	.25	.50	2.00
	1955	32.640	.10	.25	.50	2.00
	1956	1.840	.10	.25	.50	5.00
	1957	7.440	.10	.25	.50	2.00
	1958	5.280	.10	.25	.50	2.00
	1959	1.680	.10	.25	.50	2.00
	1968	.100	—	—	—	10.00
	1969	.310	—	—	—	7.50
	1970	1.011	—	—	—	4.00
	1980	1.500	—	—	—	1.00
	1981	.500	—	—	—	1.00
	1982	.085	—	—	—	2.50
	1983	—	—	—	—	6.00
	1984	—	—	—	—	4.00
	1985	—	—	—	—	2.00
	1985	—	—	—	Proof	3.00
	1986	—	—	—	—	2.00
	1986	—	—	—	Proof	3.00

2 LIRE

ALUMINUM

KM#	Date	Mintage	Fine	VF	XF	Unc
88	1946	.123	7.50	12.50	25.00	65.00
(Y96)	1947	.012	25.00	40.00	75.00	175.00
	1948	7.200	.50	1.25	2.50	8.00
	1949	1.350	1.00	2.25	4.00	20.00
	1950	2.640	.60	1.50	2.75	8.00

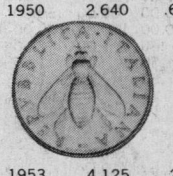

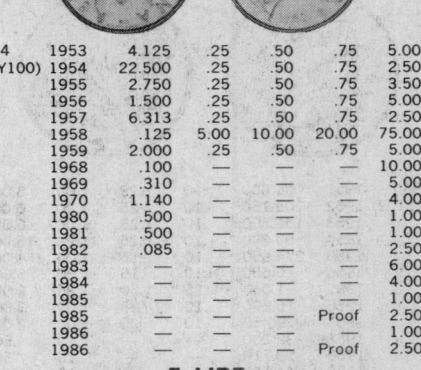

94	1953	4.125	.25	.50	.75	5.00
(Y100)	1954	22.500	.25	.50	.75	2.50
	1955	2.750	.25	.50	.75	3.50
	1956	1.500	.25	.50	.75	5.00
	1957	6.313	.25	.50	.75	2.50
	1958	.125	5.00	10.00	20.00	75.00
	1959	2.000	.25	.50	.75	5.00
	1968	.100	—	—	—	10.00
	1969	.310	—	—	—	5.00
	1970	1.140	—	—	—	4.00
	1980	.500	—	—	—	1.00
	1981	.500	—	—	—	1.00
	1982	.085	—	—	—	2.50
	1983	—	—	—	—	6.00
	1984	—	—	—	—	4.00
	1985	—	—	—	—	1.00
	1985	—	—	—	Proof	2.50
	1986	—	—	—	—	1.00
	1986	—	—	—	Proof	2.50

5 LIRE

ALUMINUM

89	1946	.081	30.00	50.00	80.00	200.00
(Y97)	1947	.017	50.00	75.00	125.00	250.00
	1948	25.125	.30	.75	1.50	7.50
	1949	71.100	.30	.75	1.50	7.50
	1950	114.790	.30	.75	1.50	7.50

92	1951	40.260	.10	.25	.50	3.00
(Y101)	1952	57.400	.10	.25	.50	4.00
	1953	196.200	.10	.25	.50	2.00
	1954	436.400	.10	.25	.50	1.50
	1955	159.000	.10	.25	.50	1.50
	1956	.400	10.00	20.00	30.00	100.00
	1966	1.200	.25	.50	1.00	1.50
	1967	10.600	.10	.25	.50	1.00
	1968	7.500	—	—	.10	.50
	1969	7.910	—	—	.10	.50
	1969 inverted I					
		.969	1.00	2.00	3.00	5.00
	1970	3.200	—	—	.10	.50
	1971	8.600	—	—	.10	.50
	1972	16.400	—	—	.10	.50
	1973	28.800	—	—	.10	.50
	1974	6.600	—	—	.10	.50
	1975	7.000	—	—	.10	.50
	1976	8.800	—	—	.10	.50
	1977	6.700	—	—	.10	.50
	1978	3.600	—	—	.10	.50
	1979	4.200	—	—	.10	.50
	1980	6.000	—	—	.10	.50
	1981	5.000	—	—	.10	.50
	1982	—	—	—	.10	.50
	1983	—	—	—	.10	.50
	1984	—	—	—	.10	.50
	1985	—	—	—	—	1.50
	1985	—	—	—	Proof	1.50
	1986	—	—	—	—	1.50
	1986	—	—	—	Proof	1.50
	1987	—	—	—	.10	.50
	1988	—	—	—	.10	.50

ITALY 1102

10 LIRE

ALUMINUM

KM#	Date	Mintage	Fine	VF	XF	Unc
90	1946	.101	20.00	35.00	50.00	75.00
(Y98)	1947	.012	100.00	150.00	300.00	600.00
	1948	14.400	.40	1.00	2.50	20.00
	1949	49.500	.50	.75	1.50	7.50
	1950	53.311	.50	.75	1.50	7.50

KM#	Date	Mintage	Fine	VF	XF	Unc
93	1951	96.600	.10	.25	1.00	8.00
(Y102)	1952	105.150	.10	.25	1.00	6.00
	1953	151.500	.10	.25	1.00	6.00
	1954	95.250	.10	.25	1.25	15.00
	1955	274.950	.10	.15	1.00	4.00
	1956	76.650	.10	.15	1.00	5.00
	1965	1.050	.25	.50	1.25	6.00
	1966	16.500	.10	.25	1.00	3.00
	1967	29.450	.10	.25	1.00	2.00
	1968	32.200	—	—	.10	.50
	1969	23.710	—	—	.10	.50
	1970	14.100	—	—	.10	.50
	1971	23.550	—	—	.10	.50
	1972	61.300	—	—	.10	.50
	1973	145.800	—	—	.10	.50
	1974	85.000	—	—	.10	.50
	1975	76.800	—	—	.10	.50
	1976	82.000	—	—	.10	.50
	1977	80.750	—	—	.10	.50
	1978	43.800	—	—	.10	.50
	1979	98.000	—	—	.10	.50
	1980	112.000	—	—	.10	.50
	1981	—	—	—	.10	.50
	1982	—	—	—	.10	.50
	1983	—	—	—	.10	.50
	1984	—	—	—	.10	.50
	1985	—	—	—	.10	.50
	1985	—	—	—	Proof	2.50
	1986	—	—	—	.10	.50
	1986	—	—	—	Proof	2.50
	1987	—	—	—	.10	.50
	1988	—	—	—	.10	.50

20 LIRE

ALUMINUM-BRONZE

KM#	Date	Mintage	Fine	VF	XF	Unc
97.1	1957	*60.075	.20	.40	.75	2.50
(Y-A102)	1958	80.550	.20	.40	.75	2.50
	1959	4.005	.50	1.00	2.00	10.00

*NOTE: Two different types of sevens.

Plain edge

KM#	Date	Mintage	Fine	VF	XF	Unc
97.2	1968	.100	—	1.50	2.50	7.50
(Y-A102a)	1969	16.735	.10	.15	.25	.75
	1970	31.500	.10	.15	.25	.50
	1971	12.375	.10	.15	.25	.75
	1972	34.400	.10	.15	.25	.75
	1973	20.000	.10	.15	.25	.75
	1974	17.000	.10	.15	.20	.50
	1975	25.000	.10	.15	.20	.50
	1976	15.000	.10	.15	.20	.50
	1977	10.000	.10	.15	.20	.50
	1978	8.415	.10	.15	.20	.50
	1979	32.000	.10	.15	.20	.50
	1980	33.000	.10	.15	.20	.50
	1981	—	.10	.15	.20	.50
	1982	—	.10	.15	.20	.50
	1983	—	.10	.15	.20	.50
	1984	—	.10	.15	.20	.50
	1985	—	—	—	Proof	3.00
	1986	—	.10	.15	.20	.50
	1986	—	—	—	Proof	3.00
	1987	—	.10	.15	.20	.50
	1988	—	.10	.15	.20	.50

50 LIRE

STAINLESS STEEL

KM#	Date	Mintage	Fine	VF	XF	Unc
95	1954	17.600	.15	.25	.75	5.00
(Y103)	1955	70.500	.15	.25	.75	5.00
	1956	69.400	.15	.25	.75	5.00
	1957	8.925	.15	.25	.75	6.00
	1958	.825	1.00	2.00	5.00	30.00
	1959	8.800	.15	.25	.50	4.00
	1960	2.025	.15	.25	.50	4.00
	1961	11.100	.15	.25	.50	4.00
	1962	17.700	.15	.25	.50	4.00
	1963	31.600	.15	.25	.50	2.00
	1964	37.900	.15	.25	.50	2.00
	1965	25.300	.15	.25	.50	2.00
	1966	27.400	.15	.25	.50	2.00
	1967	28.000	.15	.25	.50	1.00
	1968	17.800	.15	.25	.50	1.00
	1969	23.010	.15	.25	.50	1.00
	1970	21.411	.10	.20	.35	1.00
	1971	33.410	.10	.20	.35	1.00
	1972	39.000	.10	.20	.35	1.00
	1973	48.700	.10	.20	.35	1.00
	1974	64.100	.10	.20	.35	1.00
	1975	87.000	.10	.15	.25	1.00
	1976	180.600	.10	.15	.25	1.00
	1977	293.800	.10	.15	.25	1.00
	1978	416.808	.10	.15	.25	1.00
	1979	256.630	.10	.15	.25	1.00
	1980	—	.10	.15	.25	1.00
	1981	—	.10	.15	.25	1.00
	1982	—	.10	.15	.25	1.00
	1983	—	.10	.15	.25	1.00
	1984	—	.10	.15	.25	1.00
	1985	—	.10	.15	.25	1.00
	1985	—	—	—	Proof	3.00
	1986	—	.10	.15	.25	1.00
	1986	—	—	—	Proof	3.00
	1987	—	.10	.15	.25	1.00
	1988	—	.10	.15	.25	1.00

100 LIRE

STAINLESS STEEL

KM#	Date	Mintage	Fine	VF	XF	Unc
96	1955	8.600	.15	.30	1.00	10.00
(Y104)	1956	99.800	.15	.30	1.00	8.00
	1957	90.600	.15	.30	1.00	8.00
	1958	25.640	.15	.30	1.00	8.00
	1959	19.500	.15	.30	1.00	8.00
	1960	20.700	.15	.30	1.00	8.00
	1961	11.860	.15	.30	1.00	8.00
	1962	21.700	.15	.30	1.00	5.00
	1963	33.100	.15	.30	1.00	4.00
	1964	31.300	.15	.30	1.00	4.00
	1965	37.000	.15	.25	.50	4.00
	1966	52.500	.15	.25	.50	3.00
	1967	23.700	.15	.25	.50	3.00
	1968	34.200	.15	.25	.50	2.00
	1969	27.710	.15	.25	.50	2.00
	1970	25.011	.15	.25	.50	2.00
	1971	25.910	.15	.25	.50	2.00
	1972	31.170	.15	.25	.50	2.00
	1973	30.780	.15	.25	.50	2.00
	1974	83.880	.15	.25	.35	1.00
	1975	106.650	.15	.25	.35	1.00
	1976	160.020	.15	.25	.35	1.00
	1977	253.980	.15	.25	.35	1.00
	1978	343.626	.15	.25	.35	1.00
	1979	187.913	.15	.25	.35	1.00
	1980	—	.15	.25	.35	1.00
	1981	—	.15	.25	.35	1.00
	1982	—	.15	.25	.35	1.00
	1983	—	.15	.25	.35	1.00
	1984	—	.15	.25	.35	1.00
	1985	—	.15	.25	.35	1.00
	1985	—	—	—	Proof	3.50
	1986	—	.15	.25	.35	1.00
	1986	—	—	—	Proof	3.50
	1987	—	.15	.25	.35	1.00
	1988	—	.15	.25	.35	1.00

Guglielmo Marconi

KM#	Date	Mintage	Fine	VF	XF	Unc
102 (Y109)	1974	50.000	.15	.25	.35	1.00

F.A.O. issue

106 (Y113)	1979	78.340	.15	.25	.35	1.00

Centennial of Livorno Naval Acadamy

| 108 (Y117) | 1981 | 40.000 | .15 | .25 | .35 | 1.00 |

8.0000 g, .835 SILVER, .2148 oz ASW
University of Bologna

127	1988	—	—	—	—	5.00
	1988	—	—	—	Proof	10.00

200 LIRE

ALUMINUM-BRONZE

105	1977	15.900	.20	.25	.35	1.00
(Y112)	1978	461.034	.20	.25	.35	1.00
	1979	212.745	.20	.25	.35	1.00
	1980	—	.20	.25	.35	1.00
	1981	—	.20	.25	.35	1.00
	1982	—	.20	.25	.35	1.00
	1983	—	.20	.25	.35	1.00
	1984	—	.20	.25	.35	1.00
	1985	—	.20	.25	.35	1.00
	1985	—	—	—	Proof	4.00
	1986	—	.20	.25	.35	1.00
	1986	—	—	—	Proof	4.00
	1988	—	.20	—	.35	1.00

F.A.O. and International Women's Year

| 107 (Y116) | 1980 | 50.000 | .20 | .25 | .35 | 1.00 |

ITALY 1103

F.A.O. Issue

KM#	Date	Mintage	Fine	VF	XF	Unc
109	1981	50.000	.20	.25	.35	1.00
(Y118)						

5.0000 g, .835 SILVER, .1342 oz ASW
University of Bologna
Obv: Similar to 100 Lire, KM#127.

128	1988	—	—	—	—	7.50
	1988	—	—	—	Proof	15.00

500 LIRE

11.0000 g, .835 SILVER, .2953 oz ASW
Mint mark: R
NOTE: Dates appear on edge of coin in raised lettering.

98	1958	24.240	—	BV	4.50	10.00
(Y105)	1959	19.360	—	BV	4.50	10.00
	1960	24.080	—	BV	4.50	10.00
	1961	6.560	—	BV	10.00	40.00
	1964	4.880	—	BV	4.50	12.50
	1965	3.120	—	BV	4.50	12.50
	1966	13.120	—	BV	4.25	7.00
	1966	—	—	—	Proof	30.00
	1967	1.760	—	BV	4.25	7.00
	1968	.100	—	—	—	100.00
	1969	.310	—	—	—	15.00
	1970	1.140	—	—	—	11.00
	1980	1.500	—	—	—	11.00
	1981	.500	—	—	—	15.00
	1982	.500	—	—	—	15.00
	1983	—	—	—	—	100.00
	1984	—	—	—	—	45.00
	1985	—	—	—	—	30.00
	1986	—	—	—	—	27.50
	1986	—	—	—	Proof	50.00
	1987	—	—	—	—	27.50
	1987	—	—	—	Proof	50.00

*NOTE: Varieties exist in the 1966 issue.

Italian Unification Centennial

99	1961	27.120	—	BV	2.00	4.00
(Y106)	1961	—	—	—	Proof	20.00

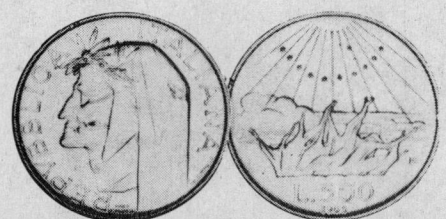

Dante Commemorative

100	1965	5.000	—	BV	2.50	5.00
(Y107)	1965	—	—	—	Proof	12.50

Guglielmo Marconi

KM#	Date	Mintage	Fine	VF	XF	Unc
103	1974	.670	—	—	—	12.00
(Y110)	1974	—	—	—	Proof	15.00

500th Anniversary of Birth of Michelangelo

104	1975	.269	—	—	—	20.00
(Y111)	1975	—	—	—	Proof	30.00

2000th Anniversary of Virgil's Birth

110	1981(1982)	.500	—	—	—	10.00
(Y120)	1981(1982)	—	—	—	Proof	12.50

ACMONITAL RING, BRONZITAL CENTER

111	1982	.218	—	.40	.60	2.00
(Y119)	1983	230.000	—	.40	.60	1.00
	1984	—	—	.40	.60	1.00
	1985	—	—	.40	.60	1.00
	1985	—	—	—	Proof	25.00
	1986	—	—	.40	.60	1.00
	1986	—	—	—	Proof	25.00
	1987	—	—	.40	.60	1.00
	1988	—	—	.40	.60	1.00

11.0000 g, .835 SILVER, .2953 oz ASW
Giuseppe Garibaldi

112	1982(1983)	.500	—	—	—	20.00
(Y121)	1982(1983)	—	—	—	Proof	30.00

Galileo

113	1982(1983)	.500	—	—	—	20.00
(Y122)	1982(1983)	—	—	—	Proof	30.00

Los Angeles Olympics

KM#	Date	Mintage	Fine	VF	XF	Unc
114	1984	.020	—	—	—	22.50
	1984	—	—	—	Proof	32.50

First Italian President of Common Market

115	1985	.132	—	—	—	55.00
	1985	.029	—	—	Proof	60.00

Duino College

116	1985	.050	—	—	—	20.00
	1985	—	—	—	Proof	30.00

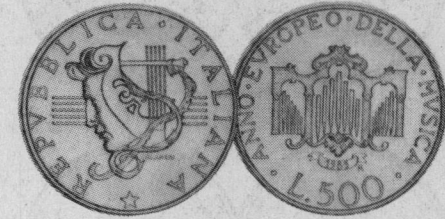

Year of Music

117	1985	—	—	—	—	20.00
	1985	—	—	—	Proof	25.00

Etruscan

118	1985	—	—	—	—	15.00
	1985	—	—	—	Proof	22.50

Alessandro Manzoni

123	1985	—	—	—	—	22.00
	1985	—	—	—	Proof	32.00

ITALY 1104

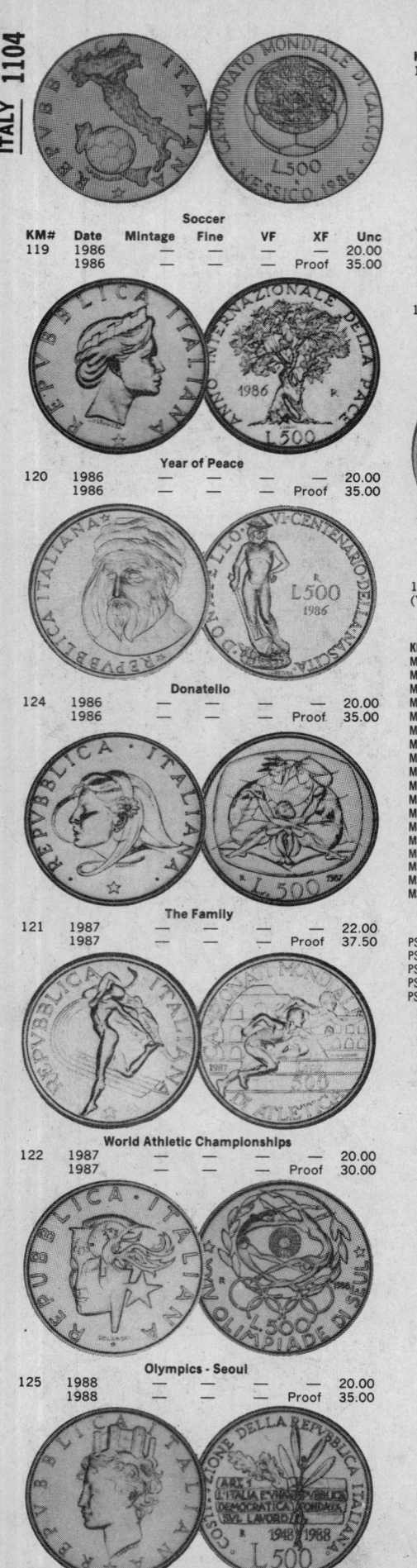

Soccer

KM#	Date	Mintage	Fine	VF	XF	Unc
119	1986	—	—	—	—	20.00
	1986	—	—	—	Proof	35.00

Year of Peace
120	1986	—	—	—	—	20.00
	1986	—	—	—	Proof	35.00

Donatello
124	1986	—	—	—	—	20.00
	1986	—	—	—	Proof	35.00

The Family
121	1987	—	—	—	—	22.00
	1987	—	—	—	Proof	37.50

World Athletic Championships
122	1987	—	—	—	—	20.00
	1987	—	—	—	Proof	30.00

Olympics - Seoul
125	1988	—	—	—	—	20.00
	1988	—	—	—	Proof	35.00

40th Anniversary of Constitution

KM#	Date	Mintage	Fine	VF	XF	Unc
126	1988	—	—	—	—	20.00
	1988	—	—	—	Proof	35.00

University of Bologna
Obv: Similar to 100 Lire, KM#127.

129	1988	—	—	—	—	35.00
	1988	—	—	—	Proof	65.00

1000 LIRE

14.6000 g, .835 SILVER, .3920 oz ASW
Centennial of Rome as Capital

101	1970R	3.011	—	—	—	12.50
(Y108)	1970R	—	—	—	Proof	22.50

MINT SETS (MS)

KM#	Date	Mintage	Identification	Issue Price	Mkt. Val.
MS1	1968(8)	100,000	KM91-96,97.1,98	6.50	110.00
MS2	1969(8)	310,000	KM91-96,97.1,98	6.50	15.00
MS3	1970(9)	1,011,000	KM91-96,97.1,98,101	—	20.00
MS4	1980(10)	—	KM91-96,98,105,107	—	17.50
MS5	1981(11)	—	KM91-96,97.2,98,105,108-109	—	20.00
MS6	1981(8)	—	KM92-93,95-96,97.2,105,108,109	—	6.50
MS7	1982(10)	—	KM91-96,97.2,98,105,111	—	18.00
MS8	1982(7)	—	KM92-93,95-96,97.2,105,111	—	6.50
MS9	1983(10)	—	KM91-96,97.2,98,105,111	—	110.00
MS10	1983(7)	—	KM92-93,95-96,97.2,105,111	—	5.50
MS11	1984(10)	—	KM91-96,97.2,98,105,111	—	50.00
MS12	1984(7)	—	KM92-93,95-96,97.2,105,111	—	5.50
MS13	1985(10)	—	KM91-96,97.2,98,105,111,123	—	15.00
MS14	1985(11)	—	KM91-96,97.2,98,105,111,123	—	45.50
MS14	1985(7)	—	KM92-93,95-96,97.2,105,111	—	5.50
MS16	1986(10)	—	KM91-96,97.2,105,111,124	—	12.50
MS17	1986(11)	—	KM91-96,97.2,98,105,111,124	—	40.00
MS18	1988(3)	—	KM127-129	—	47.50

PROOF SETS (PS)

PS1	1985(10)	—	KM91-96,97.2,105,111,123	—	60.00
PS2	1985(11)	—	KM91-96,97.2,98,105,111,123	—	135.00
PS3	1986(10)	—	KM91-96,97.2,105,111,124	—	60.00
PS4	1986(11)	—	KM91-96,97.2,98,105,111,124	—	135.00
PS5	1988(3)	—	KM127-129	—	90.00

IVORY COAST

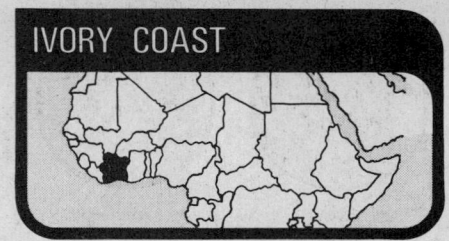

The Republic of the Ivory Coast, a former French Overseas territory located on the south side of the African bulge between Nigeria and Ghana, has an area of 124,504 sq. mi. (322,463 sq. km.) and a population of 11.8 million. Capital: Yamoussoukro. The predominantly agricultural economy is one of Africa's most prosperous. Coffee, tropical woods, cocoa, and bananas are exported.

The Ivory Coast was first visited by French and Portuguese navigators in the 15th century. French traders set up establishments in the 19th century, and gradually extended their influence along the coast and inland. The area was organized as a territory in 1893, and from 1904 to 1958 was a constituent unit of the Federation of French West Africa - as a Colony under the Third Republic and an Overseas Territory under the Fourth. In 1958 Ivory Coast became an autonomous republic within the French Community. Independence was attained on Aug. 7, 1960.

10 FRANCS

25.0000 g, .925 SILVER, .7434 oz ASW

KM#	Date	Mintage	VF	XF	Unc
1	1966	—	—	Proof	25.00

3.2000 g, .900 GOLD, .0926 oz AGW

2	1966	2,000	—	—	100.00

25 FRANCS

8.0000 g, .900 GOLD, .2315 oz AGW

3	1966	2,000	—	Proof	175.00

50 FRANCS

16.0000 g, .900 GOLD, .4630 oz AGW
Similar to 25 Francs, KM#3.

4	1966	—	—	Proof	300.00

100 FRANCS

32.0000 g, .900 GOLD, .9260 oz AGW
Similar to 25 Francs, KM#3.

5	1966	2,000	—	Proof	600.00

PROOF SETS (PS)

KM#	Date	Mintage	Identification	Issue Price	Mkt. Val.
PS1	1966	2,000	KM2-5	—	1200.

JAMAICA

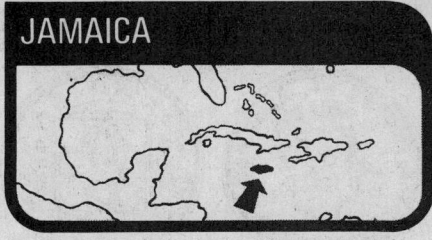

Jamaica, a member of the British Commonwealth situated in the Caribbean Sea 90 miles south of Cuba, has an area of 4,244 sq. mi. (10,991 sq. km.) and a population of *2.4 million. Capital: Kingston. The economy is founded chiefly on mining, tourism and agriculture. Alumina, bauxite, sugar, rum and molasses are exported.

Jamaica was discovered by Columbus on May 3, 1494, and settled by Spain in 1509. The island was captured in 1655 by a British naval force under the command of Admiral William Penn, and ceded to Britain by the Treaty of Madrid, 1670. For more than 150 years, the Jamaican economy of sugar, slaves and piracy was one of the most prosperous in the new world. Dissension between the property-oriented island legislature and the home government prompted parliament to establish a crown colony government for Jamaica in 1866. From 1958 to 1961 Jamaica was a member of the West Indies Federation, withdrawing when Jamaican voters rejected the association. The colony attained independence on Aug. 6, 1962. Jamaica is a member of the Commonwealth of Nations. The Queen of England is Chief of State.

Sterling coinage was introduced in Jamaica in 1825, with the additional silver three halfpence under William IV and Victoria. Certain issues of three pence of William IV and Victoria were intended for colonial use, including Jamaica, as were the last three dates of three pence for George VI.

A decimal standard currency system was adopted on Sept. 8, 1969.

RULERS
British, until 1962

MINT MARKS
H - Heaton
C - Ottawa
FM - Franklin Mint, U.S.A.**
(fm) - Franklin Mint, U.S.A.*
(RM) - Royal Mint

*NOTE: During 1970 the Franklin Mint produced matte and proof coins (1 cent-1 dollar) using dies similar to/or Royal Mint without the FM mintmark.

**NOTE: From 1975 the Franklin Mint has produced coinage in up to 3 different qualities. Qualities of issue are designated in ( ) after each date and are defined as follows:

(M) MATTE - Normal circulation strike or a dull finish produced by sandblasting special uncirculated (polish finish) or proof quality dies.

(U) SPECIAL UNCIRCULATED - Polished or proof-like in appearance without any frosted features.

(P) PROOF - The highest qualitty obtainable having mirror-like fields and frosted features.

MONETARY SYSTEM
4 Farthings = 1 Penny
12 Pence = 1 Shilling
8 Reales = 6 Shillings, 8 Pence
   (Commencing 1969)
100 Cents = 1 Dollar

FARTHING

COPPER-NICKEL

KM#	Date	Mintage	Fine	VF	XF	Unc
15	1880	.192	1.50	2.50	12.00	32.50
	1880	—	—	—	Proof	150.00
	1882H	.384	1.00	1.75	10.00	27.50
	1882H	—	—	—	Proof	125.00
	1884	.096	2.00	4.00	20.00	50.00
	1884	—	—	—	Proof	125.00
	1885	.096	2.00	4.00	20.00	50.00
	1885	—	—	—	Proof	125.00
	1887	.192	1.50	2.50	12.00	32.50
	1887	—	—	—	Proof	125.00
	1888	.192	1.50	2.50	12.00	30.00
	1888	—	—	—	Proof	125.00
	1889	.192	1.50	2.50	12.50	32.50
	1890H	.096	2.00	4.00	20.00	50.00
	1891	.096	2.00	4.00	20.00	80.00
	1893	.096	2.00	4.00	20.00	60.00
	1894	.144	1.75	3.25	15.00	40.00
	1894	—	—	—	Proof	175.00
	1895	.144	1.75	3.25	15.00	40.00
	1897	.144	1.75	3.25	15.00	40.00
	1899	.144	1.75	3.25	15.00	40.00
	1900	.144	1.75	3.25	15.00	40.00

Rev: Horizontal shading in arms.

KM#	Date	Mintage	Fine	VF	XF	Unc
18	1902	.144	1.75	3.25	15.00	40.00
	1903	.144	1.75	3.25	15.00	35.00

Rev: Vertical shading in arms.

21	1904	.192	1.00	2.50	12.00	32.50
	1904	—	—	—	Proof	175.00
	1905	.192	1.00	2.50	12.00	32.50
	1906	.528	1.00	2.00	8.00	25.00
	1907	.192	1.00	2.50	12.00	32.50
	1909	.144	2.00	4.00	15.00	40.00
	1910	.048	2.00	4.00	20.00	45.00

24	1914	.192	1.75	3.25	12.00	32.50
	1916H	.480	.75	1.50	4.00	20.00
	1916H	—	—	—	Proof	250.00
	1918C	.208	1.00	2.00	5.00	25.00
	1918C	—	—	—	Proof	150.00
	1919C	.401	.75	1.50	4.00	20.00
	1926	.240	.75	1.50	4.00	20.00
	1928	.480	.75	1.50	4.00	20.00
	1928	—	—	—	Proof	150.00
	1932	.480	.75	1.50	4.00	20.00
	1932	—	—	—	Proof	—
	1934	.480	.75	1.50	4.00	20.00
	1934	—	—	—	Proof	—

NICKEL-BRASS

27	1937	.480	.50	1.00	1.75	12.00
	1937	—	—	—	Proof	125.00

Obv: Larger head.

30	1938	.480	.20	.40	1.50	8.00
	1938	—	—	—	Proof	—
	1942	.480	.20	.40	1.50	8.00
	1945	.480	.20	.40	1.50	8.00
	1945	—	—	—	Proof	100.00
	1947	.192	.35	.70	2.00	12.00
	1947	—	—	—	Proof	100.00

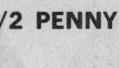

Obv. leg: W/o AND EMPEROR OF INDIA.

33	1950	.288	.10	.25	.80	3.25
	1950	—	—	—	Proof	—
	1952	.288	.10	.25	.80	3.25
	1952	—	—	—	Proof	100.00

1/2 PENNY

COPPER-NICKEL

KM#	Date	Mintage	Fine	VF	XF	Unc
16	1869	.192	1.25	2.50	15.00	40.00
	1869	—	—	—	Proof	250.00
	1870	.240	1.25	2.50	15.00	45.00
	1870	—	—	—	Proof	275.00
	1871	.240	1.25	2.50	15.00	45.00
	1871	—	—	—	Proof	200.00
	1880	.192	1.25	2.50	15.00	45.00
	1880	—	—	—	Proof	250.00
	1882H	.096	2.00	5.00	20.00	70.00
	1882H	—	—	—	Proof	200.00
	1884	.096	2.00	5.00	20.00	50.00
	1884	—	—	—	Proof	200.00
	1885	.096	2.00	5.00	20.00	50.00
	1885	—	—	—	Proof	250.00
	1887	.072	4.00	8.00	40.00	80.00
	1888	.096	1.75	—	20.00	50.00
	1888	—	—	—	Proof	200.00
	1889	.096	2.00	—	25.00	60.00
	1890H	.120	1.75	3.25	20.00	50.00
	1891	.120	1.75	3.25	20.00	70.00
	1893	.144	1.75	3.25	20.00	50.00
	1894	.096	2.00	—	25.00	60.00
	1895	.096	2.00	5.00	25.00	60.00
	1897	.120	1.75	3.25	20.00	50.00
	1899	.120	1.75	3.25	20.00	50.00
	1900	.120	1.75	3.25	20.00	55.00

BRASS (OMS)

16a	1869	—	—	—	Proof	275.00

COPPER-NICKEL
Rev: Horizontal shading in arms.

19	1902	.048	1.25	2.50	15.00	50.00
	1903	.048	1.25	2.50	15.00	50.00

Rev: Vertical shading in arms.

22	1904	.048	1.50	3.00	20.00	70.00
	1905	.048	1.50	3.00	20.00	60.00
	1906	.432	.35	.65	6.50	25.00
	1907	.504	.35	.65	6.50	25.00
	1909	.144	.45	.80	8.00	32.50
	1910	.144	.45	.80	8.00	32.50

25	1914	.096	1.25	2.50	15.00	60.00
	1916H	.192	.35	.65	4.00	20.00
	1918C	.251	.35	.65	4.00	20.00
	1918C	—	—	—	Proof	150.00
	1919C	.312	.35	.65	4.00	20.00
	1920	.480	.35	.65	4.00	20.00
	1926	.240	.35	.65	4.00	30.00
	1928	.120	.35	.65	4.00	20.00
	1928	—	—	—	Proof	150.00

JAMAICA 1106

NICKEL-BRASS

KM#	Date	Mintage	Fine	VF	XF	Unc
28	1937	.960	.50	1.00	2.50	12.00
	1937	—	—	—	Proof	125.00

Obv: Larger head.

31	1938	.960	.25	.50	2.50	12.00
	1938	—	—	—	Proof	125.00
	1940	.960	.25	.50	2.50	12.00
	1940	—	—	—	Proof	125.00
	1942	.960	.25	.50	2.50	12.00
	1945	.960	.25	.50	2.50	12.00
	1945	—	—	—	Proof	125.00
	1947	.960	.25	.50	2.50	12.00
	1947	—	—	—	Proof	125.00

Obv. leg: W/o AND EMPEROR OF INDIA.

34	1950	1.440	.10	.20	.30	3.25
	1950	—	—	—	Proof	125.00
	1952	1.200	.10	.20	.30	3.25
	1952	—	—	—	Proof	125.00

36	1955	1.440	.10	.15	.40	2.00
	1955	—	—	—	Proof	100.00
	1957	.600	.10	.20	.50	2.00
	1957	—	—	—	Proof	—
	1958	.960	.10	.20	.50	2.00
	1958	—	—	—	Proof	100.00
	1959	.960	.10	.20	.50	2.00
	1959	—	—	—	Proof	—
	1961	.480	.20	.40	1.00	4.00
	1961	—	—	—	Proof	—
	1962	.960	.10	.15	.30	2.00
	1962	—	—	—	Proof	100.00
	1963	.960	.10	.15	.30	2.00
	1963	—	—	—	Proof	100.00

Rev: New arms.

38	1964	1.440	.10	.15	.20	.80
	1965	1.200	.10	.15	.20	.80
	1966	1.680	.10	.15	.20	.80

COPPER-NICKEL-ZINC
Jamaican Coinage Centennial

41	1969	.030	.10	.15	.25	.75
	1969	5.000	—	—	Proof	2.50

PENNY

COPPER-NICKEL

KM#	Date	Mintage	Fine	VF	XF	Unc
17	1869	.144	2.00	6.50	25.00	60.00
	1869	—	—	—	Proof	200.00
	1870	.120	2.00	5.00	25.00	65.00
	1870	—	—	—	Proof	300.00
	1871	.120	2.00	5.00	25.00	65.00
	1871	—	—	—	Proof	275.00
	1880	.096	4.00	12.00	50.00	100.00
	1880	—	—	—	Proof	275.00
	1882H	.048	4.00	12.00	50.00	125.00
	1882H	—	—	—	Proof	250.00
	1882	Inc. Ab.	15.00	40.00	120.00	225.00
	1882	—	—	—	Proof	350.00
	1884	.048	4.00	12.00	50.00	100.00
	1884	—	—	—	Proof	250.00
	1885	.048	4.00	12.00	50.00	100.00
	1885	—	—	—	Proof	400.00
	1887	.024	3.00	14.00	60.00	160.00
	1888	.024	4.50	14.00	60.00	180.00
	1888	—	—	—	Proof	250.00
	1889	.024	4.50	14.00	60.00	160.00
	1890	.036	4.00	12.00	50.00	120.00
	1891	.036	4.00	12.00	50.00	120.00
	1893	.024	5.00	14.00	60.00	180.00
	1894	.036	4.00	12.00	50.00	120.00
	1895	.036	4.00	12.00	50.00	120.00
	1897	.024	4.50	14.00	60.00	180.00
	1899	.024	4.50	14.00	60.00	180.00
	1900	.024	4.50	14.00	60.00	160.00

COPPER (OMS)

17a	1869	—	—	—	Proof	275.00
	1870	—	—	—	Proof	325.00

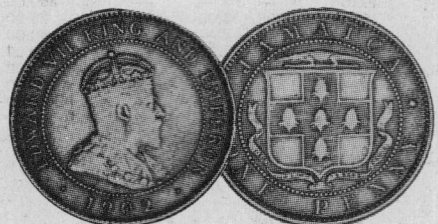

COPPER-NICKEL
Rev: Horizontal shading in arms.

20	1902	.060	2.25	4.75	25.00	60.00
	1903	.060	2.25	4.75	25.00	60.00

Rev: Vertical shading in arms.

23	1904	.024	2.25	6.50	27.50	80.00
	1904	—	—	—	Proof	250.00
	1905	.048	2.00	4.75	22.50	60.00
	1906	.156	1.25	2.50	12.00	40.00
	1907	.108	1.25	2.50	12.00	40.00
	1909	.144	1.25	2.50	12.00	40.00
	1910	.144	1.25	2.50	12.00	40.00

26	1914	.024	8.00	15.00	65.00	175.00
	1916H	.024	6.00	12.00	50.00	150.00
	1918C	.187	2.00	5.00	15.00	60.00
	1918C	—	—	—	Proof	150.00
	1919C	.251	1.25	4.75	12.00	50.00
	1920	.360	.75	2.50	9.50	32.50
	1926	.240	.75	2.50	9.50	30.00

KM#	Date	Mintage	Fine	VF	XF	Unc
26	1928	.360	.75	2.50	9.50	30.00
	1928	—	—	—	Proof	150.00

NICKEL-BRASS

29	1937	1.200	1.00	1.75	3.25	12.00
	1937	—	—	—	Proof	150.00

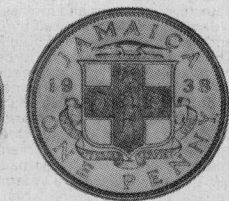

Obv: Larger head.

32	1938	1.200	.35	.65	3.25	12.00
	1938	—	—	—	Proof	160.00
	1940	1.200	.35	.65	3.25	12.00
	1940	—	—	—	Proof	160.00
	1942	1.200	.35	.65	3.25	12.00
	1942	—	—	—	Proof	160.00
	1945	1.200	.35	.65	3.25	12.00
	1945	—	—	—	Proof	160.00
	1947	.480	.35	.65	3.25	12.00
	1947	—	—	—	Proof	160.00

Obv. leg: W/o AND EMPEROR OF INDIA.

35	1950	.600	.20	.35	1.50	8.00
	1950	—	—	—	Proof	120.00
	1952	.725	.20	.35	1.50	8.00
	1952	—	—	—	Proof	120.00

37	1953	1.200	.10	.20	.50	1.00
	1953	—	—	—	Proof	100.00
	1955	.960	.10	.25	1.00	4.00
	1955	—	—	—	Proof	100.00
	1957	.600	.10	.25	1.00	4.00
	1957	—	—	—	Proof	—
	1958	1.080	.10	.20	.30	3.00
	1958	—	—	—	Proof	100.00
	1959	1.368	.10	.20	.30	3.00
	1959	—	—	—	Proof	—
	1960	1.368	.10	.20	.30	3.00
	1960	—	—	—	Proof	—
	1961	1.368	.10	.20	.30	3.00
	1961	—	—	—	Proof	—
	1962	1.920	.10	.20	.30	3.00
	1962	—	—	—	Proof	100.00
	1963	.720	.25	.50	4.00	30.00
	1963	—	—	—	Proof	100.00

39	1964	.480	.10	.15	.25	.75
	1965	1.200	.10	.15	.20	.30
	1966	1.200	.10	.15	.20	.30
	1967	2.760	.10	.15	.20	.30

COPPER-NICKEL-ZINC
Jamaican Coinage Centennial

KM#	Date	Mintage	Fine	VF	XF	Unc
42	1969	.030	.10	.15	.30	.75
	1969	5,000	—	—	Proof	2.50

1-1/2 PENCE

.925 SILVER

From 1834 through 1870 colonial issue 1-1/2 pence were circulated in Ceylon and Jamaica. These are are listed under Great Britain.

5 SHILLINGS

COPPER-NICKEL
VIII Commonwealth Games

KM#	Date	Mintage	VF	XF	Unc
40	1966	.190	—	1.25	1.50	2.50
	1966	.020	—	—	Proof	5.00

DECIMAL COINAGE

NOTE: The Franklin Mint and Royal Mint have both been striking the 1 cent through 1 dollar coinage. The 1970 issues were all struck with dies similar to/or Royal Mint without the FM mint mark. The Royal Mint issues have the name JAMAICA extending beyond the native head dress feathers. Those struck after 1970 by the Franklin Mint have the name JAMAICA within the head dress feathers.

CENT

BRONZE

KM#	Date	Mintage	VF	XF	Unc
45	1969	30.200	—	.10	.25
	1969	.019	—	Proof	.50
	1970(RM) small date				
		10.000	—	.10	.25
	1970FM(M) large date				
		5,000	—	.10	.25
	1970FM(P)	.012	—	Proof	.50
	1971(RM)	5.625	—	.10	.25

KM#	Date	Mintage	VF	XF	Unc
51	1971FM(M)	4,834	—	.10	.25
	1971FM(P)	.014	—	Proof	.50
	1972FM(M)	7,982	—	.10	.25
	1972FM(P)	.017	—	Proof	.50
	1973FM(M)	.029	—	.10	.25
	1973FM(P)	.028	—	Proof	.50
	1974FM(M)	.028	—	.10	.25
	1974FM(P)	.022	—	Proof	.50
	1975FM(M)	.036	—	.10	.25
	1975FM(U)	4,683	—	—	.25
	1975FM(P)	.016	—	Proof	.50

F.A.O. issue

52	1971	.020	—	.10	.25
	1972	5.000	—	.10	.25
	1973	5.500	—	.10	.25
	1974	3.000	—	.10	.25

ALUMINUM
F.A.O. issue

64	1975	15.000	—	.10	.20
	1976	16.000	—	.10	.20
	1977	—	—	.10	.20
	1978	8.400	—	.10	.20
	1980	10.000	—	.10	.20
	1981	8.000	—	.10	.20
	1982	10.000	—	.10	.20
	1983	1.342	—	—	.15
	1984	8.704	—	—	.15
	1985	—	—	Proof	.50
	1986	—	—	—	.15
	1987	—	—	Proof	.50
	1988	—	—	Proof	.50

68	1976FM(M)	.028	—	—	.15
	1976FM(U)	1,802	—	—	.25
	1976FM(P)	.024	—	Proof	.50
	1977FM(M)	.028	—	—	.15
	1977FM(U)	597 pcs.	—	—	1.50
	1977FM(P)	.010	—	Proof	.50
	1978FM(M)	.028	—	—	.15
	1978FM(U)	1,282	—	—	.40
	1978FM(P)	6,058	—	Proof	.60
	1979FM(M)	.028	—	—	.15
	1979FM(U)	2,608	—	—	.40
	1979FM(P)	4,049	—	Proof	.60
	1980FM(M)	.028	—	—	.15
	1980FM(U)	3,668	—	—	.35
	1980FM(P)	2,688	—	Proof	.75
	1981FM(U)	482 pcs.	—	—	1.50
	1981FM(P)	1,577	—	Proof	.75
	1982FM(U)	—	—	—	.35
	1982FM(P)	—	—	Proof	.60
	1984FM(U)	—	—	—	.35
	1984FM(P)	—	—	Proof	.75

Mule. 2 obverses of KM#68.

136	1982 FM	—	—	220.00	250.00

Mule. 2 reverses of KM#68.

137	1982FM	—	—	250.00	300.00

21st Anniversary of Independence

KM#	Date	Mintage	VF	XF	Unc
101	1983FM(U)	—	—	—	.35
	1983FM(P)	—	—	Proof	.75

5 CENTS

COPPER-NICKEL

46	1969	12.008	—	.10	.30
	1969	.030	—	Proof	.60
	1970FM(M)	5,000	—	.10	.30
	1970FM(P)	.012	—	Proof	.60
	1972	6.000	—	.10	.20
	1975	6.010	—	.10	.15
	1977	2.400	—	.10	.15
	1978	2.000	—	.10	.15
	1980	2.272	—	.10	.15
	1981	2.001	—	.10	.15
	1982	2.000	—	.10	.15
	1983	.992	—	.10	.15
	1984	3.508	—	.10	.15
	1985	—	—	.10	.15
	1985	—	—	Proof	.60
	1986	—	—	.10	.15
	1987	—	—	.10	.15
	1987	—	—	Proof	.60
	1988	—	—	Proof	.60

53	1971FM(M)	4,834	—	.10	.30
	1971FM(P)	.014	—	Proof	.60
	1972FM(M)	7,982	—	.10	.30
	1972FM(P)	.017	—	Proof	.60
	1973FM(M)	.017	—	.10	.30
	1973FM(P)	.028	—	Proof	.60
	1974FM(M)	.016	—	.10	.30
	1974FM(P)	.022	—	Proof	.60
	1975FM(M)	6,240	—	.10	.30
	1975FM(U)	4,683	—	—	.30
	1975FM(P)	.016	—	Proof	.60
	1976FM(M)	5,560	—	.10	.30
	1976FM(U)	1,802	—	—	.30
	1976FM(P)	.024	—	Proof	.60
	1977FM(M)	5,560	—	.10	.35
	1977FM(U)	597 pcs.	—	—	1.50
	1977FM(P)	.010	—	Proof	.60
	1978FM(M)	5,560	—	.10	.35
	1978FM(U)	1,282	—	—	.50
	1978FM(P)	6,058	—	Proof	.75
	1979FM(M)	5,560	—	.10	.35
	1979FM(U)	2,608	—	—	.50
	1979FM(P)	4,049	—	Proof	.75
	1980FM(M)	5,560	—	.10	.35
	1980FM(U)	3,668	—	—	.40
	1980FM(P)	2,688	—	Proof	1.00
	1981FM(U)	482 pcs.	—	—	1.50
	1981FM(P)	1,577	—	Proof	1.00
	1982FM(U)	—	—	—	.40
	1982FM(P)	—	—	Proof	1.00
	1984FM(U)	—	—	—	.40
	1984FM(P)	—	—	Proof	1.00

21st Anniversary of Independence

102	1983FM(U)	—	—	—	.40
	1983FM(P)	—	—	Proof	1.00

10 CENTS

COPPER-NICKEL

47	1969	19.508	—	.10	.35
	1969	.030	—	Proof	.75
	1970FM(M)	5,000	—	.10	.35
	1970FM(P)	.012	—	Proof	.75
	1972	6.000	—	.10	.35
	1975	10.010	—	.10	.25
	1977	8.000	—	.10	.25
	1981	8.000	—	.10	.25
	1982	8.000	—	.10	.25

JAMAICA 1107

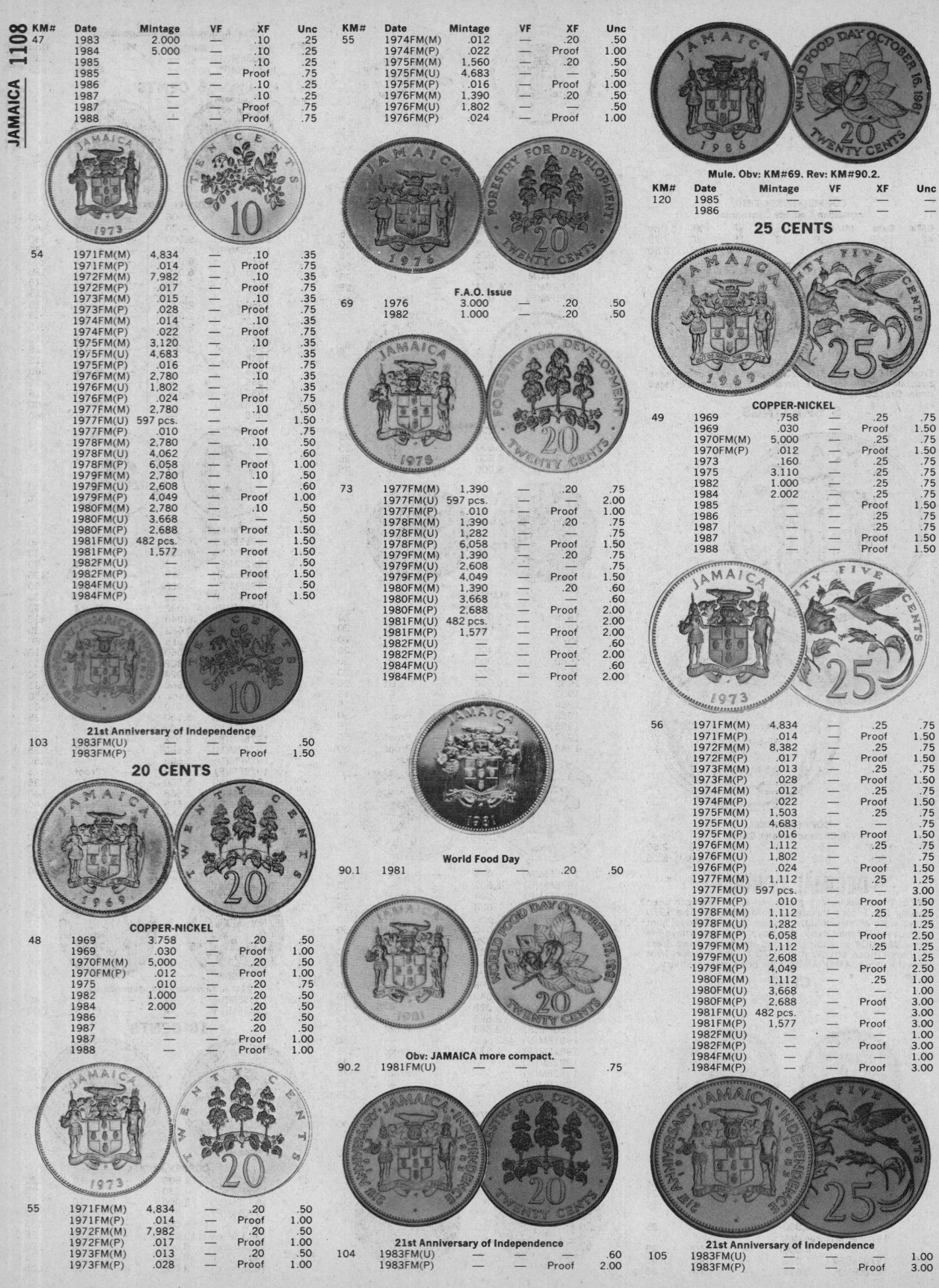

50 CENTS

COPPER-NICKEL
Marcus Garvey

KM#	Date	Mintage	VF	XF	Unc
65	1975	12.010	.15	.50	1.00
	1984	2.000	.15	.50	1.00
	1985	—	.15	.50	1.00
	1985	—	—	Proof	3.00
	1986	—	.15	.50	1.00
	1987	—	.15	.50	1.00
	1988	—	—	Proof	3.00

KM#	Date	Mintage	VF	XF	Unc
70	1976FM(M)	1,112	—	.25	1.50
	1976FM(U)	1,802	—	—	1.50
	1976FM(P)	.024	—	Proof	2.00
	1977FM(M)	556 pcs.	—	.50	3.50
	1977FM(U)	597 pcs.	—	—	3.50
	1977FM(P)	.010	—	Proof	2.00
	1978FM(M)	556 pcs.	—	.50	3.50
	1978FM(U)	1,838	—	—	2.00
	1978FM(P)	6,058	—	Proof	2.50
	1979FM(M)	556 pcs.	—	.50	3.50
	1979FM(U)	1,282	—	—	2.50
	1979FM(P)	4,049	—	Proof	2.00
	1980FM(M)	556 pcs.	—	.50	3.50
	1980FM(U)	3,668	—	—	2.00
	1980FM(P)	2,688	—	Proof	3.00
	1981FM(U)	482 pcs.	—	—	3.50
	1981FM(P)	1,577	—	Proof	2.50
	1982FM(U)	—	—	—	2.00
	1982FM(P)	—	—	Proof	3.00
	1984FM(U)	—	—	—	2.00
	1984FM(P)	—	—	Proof	3.00

21st Anniversary of Independence

106	1983FM(U)	—	—	—	2.00
	1983FM(P)	—	—	Proof	4.00

100th Anniversary of Birth of Marcus Garvey
Obv: Similar to KM#70.
Rev: Similar to 10 Dollars, KM#128.

132	1987	500 pcs.	—	Proof	3.50

DOLLAR

COPPER-NICKEL

50	1969	.047	—	1.00	2.00
	1969	.030	—	Proof	3.00
	1970FM(M)	5,000	—	.30	2.50
	1970FM(P)	.014	—	Proof	3.00

KM#	Date	Mintage	VF	XF	Unc
57	1971FM	5,024	—	.30	2.50
	1971FM(P)	.015	—	Proof	3.00
	1972FM	7,982	—	.30	2.00
	1972FM(P)	.017	—	Proof	3.00
	1973FM	.010	—	.30	2.00
	1973FM(P)	.028	—	Proof	3.00
	1974FM(M)	8,961	—	.30	2.00
	1974FM(P)	.022	—	Proof	3.00
	1975FM(M)	5,312	—	.30	2.50
	1975FM(U)	4,683	—	—	2.50
	1975FM(P)	.016	—	Proof	3.00
	1976FM(M)	284 pcs.	—	.50	17.50
	1976FM(U)	1,802	—	—	4.00
	1976FM(P)	.024	—	Proof	3.00
	1977FM(M)	287 pcs.	—	.50	17.50
	1977FM(U)	597 pcs.	—	—	8.00
	1977FM(P)	.010	—	Proof	3.00
	1978FM(U)	1,566	—	—	4.00
	1978FM(P)	6,058	—	Proof	4.00
	1979FM(M)	284 pcs.	—	.50	17.50
	1979FM(U)	2,608	—	—	4.00
	1979FM(P)	4,049	—	Proof	5.00

Reduced size, 34mm

84	1980FM(M)	284 pcs.	—	.50	15.00
	1980FM(U)	3,668	—	—	3.00
	1980FM(P)	2,688	—	Proof	10.00
	1981FM(U)	482 pcs.	—	—	8.00
	1981FM(P)	1,577	—	Proof	10.00
	1982FM(U)	—	—	—	4.00
	1982FM(P)	—	—	Proof	10.00

84a	1985	—	—	—	3.00
	1987	—	—	Proof	5.00
	1988	—	—	Proof	5.00

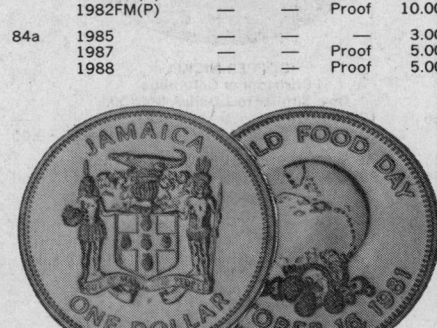

World Food Day

91	1981FM(U)	—	—	—	5.00

Soccer Games

96	1982	—	—	—	2.50

21st Anniversary of Independence

KM#	Date	Mintage	VF	XF	Unc
107	1983FM(U)	3,710	—	—	3.00
	1983FM(P)	609 pcs.	—	Proof	10.00

21st Anniversary of Independence

134	1983FM(P)	—	—	Proof	4.00

100th Anniversary of Birth of Bustamante

113	1984FM(U)	—	—	—	3.00
	1984FM(P)	—	—	Proof	10.00

5 DOLLARS

42.1500 g, .925 SILVER, 1.2536 oz ASW
Norman W. Manley
Obv: Similar to 1 Dollar, KM#50.

58	1971FM	4,072	—	—	12.50
	1971FM(P)	.013	—	Proof	10.00

41.4800 g, .925 SILVER, 1.2336 oz ASW
Obv: Similar to 1 Dollar, KM#50.

59	1972FM	3,232	—	—	15.00
	1972FM(P)	.021	—	Proof	12.00
	1973FM	6,484	—	—	15.00
	1973FM(P)	.036	—	Proof	12.00

COPPER-NICKEL
Similar to KM#59, reduced size, 42mm.

62	1974FM(M)	8,661	—	—	4.00
	1975FM(M)	65 pcs.	—	—	—
	1975FM(U)	4,683	—	—	4.00

JAMACIA 1110

KM#	Date	Mintage	VF	XF	Unc
62	1976FM(M)	56 pcs.	—	—	—
	1976FM(U)	1,802	—	—	6.00
	1977FM(M)	56 pcs.	—	—	—
	1977FM(U)	597 pcs.	—	—	10.00
	1978FM(U)	1,338	—	—	6.00
	1979FM(M)	56 pcs.	—	—	—
	1979FM(U)	2,608	—	—	6.00

37.6000 g, .500 SILVER, .6044 oz ASW

62a	1974FM(P)	.022	—	Proof	10.00
	1975FM(P)	.016	—	Proof	10.00
	1976FM(P)	.023	—	Proof	10.00
	1977FM(P)	.010	—	Proof	10.00
	1978FM(P)	6,058	—	Proof	12.00
	1979FM(P)	4,049	—	Proof	12.00

COPPER-NICKEL
Reduced size, 36mm

85	1980FM(M)	56 pcs.	—	—	—
	1980FM(U)	3,668	—	—	5.00
	1981FM(U)	482 pcs.	—	—	10.00
	1982FM(U)	—	—	—	6.00
	1984FM(U)	—	—	—	6.00

37.6000 g, .500 SILVER, .6044 oz ASW

85a	1980FM(P)	2,688	—	Proof	12.50
	1981FM(P)	1,577	—	Proof	12.50
	1982FM(P)	1,040	—	Proof	12.50
	1984FM(P)	—	—	Proof	12.50
85b	1985	—	—	—	12.50
	1987	—	—	Proof	12.50
	1988	—	—	Proof	12.50

COPPER-NICKEL
21st Anniversary of Independence

108	1983FM(U)	—	—	—	6.00

37.6000 g, .500 SILVER, .6044 oz ASW

108a	1983FM(P)	—	—	Proof	15.00

10 DOLLARS

49.2000 g, .925 SILVER, 1.4632 oz ASW
10th Anniversary of Independence

KM#	Date	Mintage	VF	XF	Unc
60	1972	.042	—	—	14.00
	1972	.033	—	Proof	15.00

COPPER-NICKEL
Sir Henry Morgan
Obv: Similar to 1 Dollar, KM#50.

63	1974FM(M)	.015	—	—	6.00

42.8000 g, .925 SILVER, 1.2728 oz ASW

63a	1974FM(P)	.042	—	Proof	15.00

COPPER-NICKEL
Christopher Columbus
Obv: Similar to 1 Dollar, KM#50.

66	1975FM(M)	30 pcs.	—	—	—
	1975FM(U)	5,758	—	—	9.00

42.8000 g, .925 SILVER, 1.2728 oz ASW

66a	1975FM(P)	.029	—	Proof	16.50

COPPER-NICKEL
Admiral Horatio Nelson
Obv: Similar to 1 Dollar, KM#50.

71	1976FM(M)	27 pcs.	—	—	—
	1976FM(U)	2,302	—	—	10.00

42.8000 g, .925 SILVER, 1.2728 oz ASW

71a	1976FM(P)	.031	—	Proof	18.00

COPPER-NICKEL
Admiral George Rodney

Obv: Similar to 1 Dollar, KM#50.

KM#	Date	Mintage	VF	XF	Unc
74	1977FM(M)	27 pcs.	—	—	—
	1977FM(U)	847 pcs.	—	—	22.50

42.8000 g, .925 SILVER, 1.2728 oz ASW

74a	1977FM(P)	.014	—	Proof	20.00

COPPER-NICKEL
Jamaican Unity
Obv: Similar to 1 Dollar, KM#50.

75	1978FM(U)	1,559	—	—	12.50

42.8000 g, .925 SILVER, 1.2728 oz ASW

75a	1978FM(P)	.012	—	Proof	20.00

COPPER-NICKEL
Homerus Swallowtails
Obv: Similar to 1 Dollar, KM#50.

79	1979FM(M)	27 pcs.	—	—	—
	1979FM(U)	2,608	—	—	20.00

42.8000 g, .925 SILVER, 1.2728 oz ASW

79a	1979FM(P)	8,308	—	Proof	35.00

23.3300 g, .925 SILVER, .6938 oz ASW
International Year of the Child

80	1979	.020	—	Proof	17.50

JAMAICA 1111

COPPER-NICKEL
Trochilus Polytmas Hummingbirds

KM#	Date	Mintage	VF	XF	Unc
86	1980FM(M)	27 pcs.	—	—	—
	1980FM(U)	5,668	—	—	14.00

30.2800 g, .925 SILVER, .9006 oz ASW
| 86a | 1980FM(P) | 5,394 | — | — | 30.00 |

30.2800 g, .500 SILVER, .4868 oz ASW.
10th Anniversary of Caribbean Development Bank
| 87 | 1980FM(P) | 2,327 | — | — | 25.00 |

28.2800 g, .925 SILVER, .8410 oz ASW
Wedding of Prince Charles and Lady Diana
| 92 | 1981 | .040 | — | Proof | 20.00 |

COPPER-NICKEL

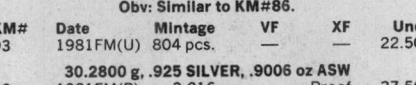

American Crocodile
Obv: Similar to KM#86.
KM#	Date	Mintage	VF	XF	Unc
93	1981FM(U)	804 pcs.	—	—	22.50

30.2800 g, .925 SILVER, .9006 oz ASW
| 93a | 1981FM(P) | 3,216 | — | Proof | 37.50 |

COPPER-NICKEL
Mongoose
| 97 | 1982FM(U) | — | — | — | 20.00 |

30.2800 g, .925 SILVER, .9006 oz ASW
| 97a | 1982FM(P) | 1,852 | — | Proof | 35.00 |

23.2000 g, .925 SILVER, .6899 oz ASW
Soccer Games
| 98 | 1982 | 9,775 | — | Proof | 27.50 |

COPPER-NICKEL
21st Anniversary of Independence
| 109 | 1983FM(U) | 1,350 | — | — | 15.00 |

30.2800 g, .925 SILVER, .9006 oz ASW
| 109a | 1983FM(P) | 1,121 | — | Proof | 35.00 |

23.3300 g, .925 SILVER, .6938 oz ASW

Royal Visit
KM#	Date	Mintage	VF	XF	Unc
111	1983	—	—	Proof	25.00

Summer Olympics
| 125 | 1984 | — | — | Proof | 37.50 |

COPPER-NICKEL
Blue Marlin
Obv: Similar to KM#86.
| 114 | 1984FM(U) | — | — | — | 15.00 |

23.3300 g, .925 SILVER, .6938 oz ASW
| 114a | 1984FM(P) | — | — | Proof | 42.50 |

Decade For Women
| 115 | 1984 | 1,100 | — | Proof | 25.00 |
| | 1985 | 610 pcs. | — | Proof | 30.00 |

28.2800 g, .500 SILVER, .4546 oz ASW
Commonwealth Games
| 121 | 1986 | .050 | — | — | 20.00 |

28.2800 g, .925 SILVER, .8411 oz ASW
| 121a | 1986 | .020 | — | Proof | 25.00 |

JAMAICA

22.4500 g, .925 SILVER, .6677 oz ASW
Year of Youth

KM#	Date	Mintage	VF	XF	Unc
123	1985	1,000	—	Proof	37.50

100th Anniversary of Birth of Marcus Garvey.
| 128 | 1987 | 1,000 | — | Proof | 35.00 |

25th Anniversary of Independence
| 133 | 1987 | *500 pcs. | — | Proof | 40.00 |

COPPER-NICKEL
Year of the Worker
| 138 | 1988 | — | — | — | 5.00 |

22.4500 g, .925 SILVER, .6677 oz ASW
| 138a | 1988 | *1,000 | — | Proof | 45.00 |

20 DOLLARS

15.7484 g, .500 GOLD, .2531 oz AGW
10th Anniversary of Independence
| 61 | 1972 | .030 | — | — | 125.00 |
| | 1972 | .020 | — | Proof | 140.00 |

25 DOLLARS

136.0800 g, .925 SILVER, 4.0473 oz ASW
25th Anniversary of Coronation
KM#	Date	Mintage	VF	XF	Unc
76	1978	.011	—	—	60.00
	1978	.022	—	Proof	65.00

10th Anniversary of Investiture of Prince Charles
| 81 | 1979 | .016 | — | — | 60.00 |
| | 1979 | .025 | — | Proof | 65.00 |

1980 Olympics
KM#	Date	Mintage	VF	XF	Unc
88	1980	—	—	—	95.00
	1980	2,320	—	Proof	95.00

Wedding of Prince Charles and Lady Diana
Obv: Similar to 10 Dollars, KM#92.
| 94 | 1981 | 6,450 | — | Proof | 90.00 |

JAMAICA 1113

Soccer Games
Obv: Similar to 10 Dollars, KM#98.

KM#	Date	Mintage	VF	XF	Unc
99	1982	.030	—	Proof	90.00

112	1983			Proof	80.00

Royal Visit

Summer Olympics
Obv: Similar to 10 Dollars, KM#88.

116	1984	3,300	—	Proof	95.00

23.4400 g, .925 SILVER, .6677 oz ASW
Decade For Women
Mule. Denomination error for 10 Dollars, KM#115.

126	1984				

Humpback Whale
Obv: Similar to KM#112.

KM#	Date	Mintage	VF	XF	Unc
119	1985	2,600	—	Proof	115.00

127	1986				30.00

World Championship Soccer

37.7800 g, .925 SILVER, 1.1236 oz ASW
25 Years of Independence
Obv: Portrait of Queen Elizabeth II right.
Rev: Coat of arms within legend.

130	1987	2,500	—	Proof	45.00

100 DOLLARS

7.8300 g, .900 GOLD, .2265 oz AGW
Christopher Columbus

67	1975FM(M)	100 pcs.	—	—	175.00
	1975FM(U)	.010	—	—	130.00
	1975FM(P)	.021	—	Proof	175.00

Admiral Horatio Nelson

72	1976FM(M)	100 pcs.	—	—	175.00
	1976FM(P)	8,952	—	Proof	175.00

11.3400 g, .900 GOLD, .3281 oz AGW
25th Anniversary of Coronation

KM#	Date	Mintage	VF	XF	Unc
77	1978		—	—	200.00
	1978	5,835	—	Proof	225.00

10th Anniversary of Investiture of Prince Charles

82	1979	2,891	—	Proof	200.00

7.1300 g, .900 GOLD, .2063 oz AGW
21st Anniversary of Independence

110	1983FM(P)	477 pcs.	—	Proof	200.00

100th Anniversary of Birth of Bustamante

117	1984FM(P)	551 pcs.	—	Proof	175.00

Reduced size. Actual size: 63mm
136.0800 g, .925 SILVER, 4.0473 oz ASW
World Soccer

122	1986	.020	—	Proof	110.00

11.3400 g, .900 GOLD, .3281 oz AGW
100th Anniversary of Birth of Marcus Garvey
Obv: Similar to KM#117.
Rev: Similar to 10 Dollars, KM#128.

129	1987	500 pcs.	—	Proof	325.00

136.0800 g, .925 SILVER, 4.0473 oz ASW
Summer Olympics - Relay Race
Reduced. Actual size: 63mm.
Obv: Similar to 10 Dollars, KM#111.

135	1988	.015	—	Proof	150.00

JAMAICA 1114

Mango Hummingbird
Reduced. Actual size: 63mm
Obv: Similar to 250 Dollars KM#124.

KM#	Date	Mintage	VF	XF	Unc
139	1987	—	—	Proof	125.00

250 DOLLARS

43.2200 g, .900 GOLD, 1.2507 oz AGW
25th Anniversary of Coronation

| 78 | 1978 | 3,005 | — | Proof | 600.00 |

10th Anniversary of Investiture of Prince Charles

| 83 | 1979 | 1,650 | — | Proof | 700.00 |

11.3400 g, .900 GOLD, .3281 oz AGW
1980 Olympics

| 89 | 1980 | 902 pcs. | — | Proof | 350.00 |

Wedding of Prince Charles and Lady Diana
Obv: Similar to 10 Dollars, Y#60.

KM#	Date	Mintage	VF	XF	Unc
95	1981	1,491	—	Proof	250.00

Soccer Games

| 100 | 1982 | 694 pcs. | — | Proof | 300.00 |

Decade For Women

| 118 | 1984 | .015 | — | Proof | 250.00 |

11.3200 g, .900 GOLD, .3275 oz AGW
Royal Visit

| 124 | 1983 | 5,000 | — | Proof | 225.00 |

16.0000 g, .900 GOLD, .4630 oz AGW
25 Years of Independence
Obv: Portrait of Queen Elizabeth II right.

| 131 | 1987 | 250 pcs. | — | Proof | 475.00 |

MINT SETS (MS)

KM#	Date	Mintage	Identification	Issue Price	Mkt. Val.
MS1	1969(2)	30,000	KM41-42	.90	2.00
MS2	1969(6)	30,000	KM45-50	—	6.00
MS3	1970(6)	5,000	KM45-50	16.00	6.00
MS4	1971(7)	4,072	KM51,53-58	19.50	20.00
MS5	1971(6)	4,834	KM51,53-57	—	6.00
MS6	1972(7)	2,982	KM51,53-57,59	19.75	20.00
MS7	1972(6)	4,000	KM51,53-57	10.00	6.00
MS8	1973(7)	6,404	KM51,53-57,59	19.75	20.00
MS9	1973(6)	3,000	KM51,53-57	9.95	6.00
MS10	1974(8)	8,361	KM51,53-57,59,63	25.00	15.00
MS11	1975(8)	4,683	KM51,53-57,62,66	27.50	17.50
MS12	1976(7)	1,802	KM53-57,62a,68,70,71	27.50	22.50
MS13	1977(9)	597	KM53-54,56-57,62,68,70,73,74	27.50	47.50
MS14	1978(9)	1,282	KM53-54,56-57,62,68,70,73,75	27.50	27.50
MS15	1979(9)	2,608	KM53-54,56-57,62,68,70,73,79	27.50	32.50
MS16	1980(9)	3,668	KM53-54,56,68,70,73,84-86	30.00	25.00
MS17	1981(9)	482	KM53-54,56,68,70,73,84-85,93	31.00	50.00
MS18	1982(9)	—	KM53-54,56,68,70,73,84-85,97	31.00	35.00
MS19	1983(9)	1,210	KM101-109	37.00	30.00
MS20	1984(9)	—	KM53-54,56,68,70,73,85,113-114	37.00	27.50

PROOF SETS (PS)

| PS1 | 1918C(3) | — | KM24-26 | — | 450.00 |
| PS2 | 1928(3) | 20 | KM24-26 | — | 450.00 |

KM#	Date	Mintage	Identification	Issue Price	Mkt. Val.
PS3	1937(3)	—	KM27-29	—	400.00
PS4	1969(6)	8,530	KM45-50	15.00	5.00
PS5	1969(2)	5,000	KM41-42	2.70	5.00
PS6	1970(6)	11,540	KM45-50	15.00	5.00
PS7	1971(7)	12,739	KM51,53-58	26.50	17.50
PS8	1971(6)	1,048	KM51,53-57	15.00	6.00
PS9	1972(7)	16,967	KM51,53-57,59	27.50	17.50
PS10	1973(7)	28,405	KM51,53-57,59	27.50	17.50
PS11	1974(8)	22,026	KM51,53-57,62a-63a	50.00	27.50
PS12	1975(8)	15,638	KM51,53-57,62a,66a	55.00	30.00
PS13	1976(9)	22,900	KM53-57,62a,68,70,71a	55.00	32.50
PS14	1976(7)	1,503	KM53-57,68,70	22.50	12.50
PS15	1977(9)	10,054	KM53-54,56-57,62a,68,70,73,74a	55.00	35.00
PS16	1978(9)	6,058	KM53-54,56-57,62a,68,70,73,75a	59.00	35.00
PS17	1979(9)	4,049	KM53-54,56-57,62a,68,70,73,79a	59.00	52.50
PS18	1980(9)	2,688	KM53-54,56,68,70,73,84,85a,86a	90.00	50.00
PS19	1981(9)	1,577	KM53-54,56,68,70,73,84,85a,93a	92.00	65.00
PS20	1982(9)	—	KM53-54,56,68,70,73,84,85a,97a	92.00	70.00
PS21	1983(9)	609	KM101-107,108a-109a	—	72.50
PS22	1984(9)	—	KM53-54,56,68,70,73,85a,113,114a	92.00	65.00
PS23	1985(9)	—	KM46-47,49,64-65,84,85b,120,123	—	65.00
PS24	1987(9)	500	KM46-49,64,84a,85b,132,133	90.00	65.00
PS25	1988(9)	500	KM46-49,64-65,84a,85b,138a	115.00	115.00

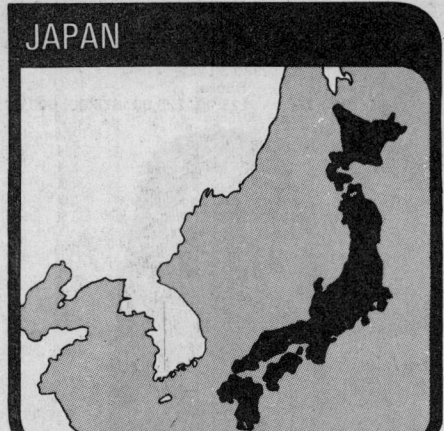

JAPAN

Japan, a constitutional monarchy situated off the east coast of Asia, has an area of 145,809 sq. mi. (377,644 sq. km.) and a population of *123.2 million. Capital: Tokyo. Japan, one of the three major industrial nations of the free world, exports machinery, motor vehicles, textiles and chemicals.

Japan, founded (so legend holds) in 660 B.C. by a direct descendant of the Sun Goddess, was first brought into contact with the west by a storm-blown Portuguese ship in 1542. European traders and missionaries proceeded to enlarge the contact until the Shogunate, sensing a military threat in the foreign presence, expelled all foreigners and restricted relations with the outside world in the 17th century. After Commodore Perry's U.S. flotilla visited in 1854, Japan rapidly industrialized, abolished the Shogunate and established a parliamentary form of government, and by the end of the 19th century achieved the status of a modern economic and military power. A series of wars with China and Russia, and participation with the Allies in World War I, enlarged Japan territorially but brought its interests into conflict with the Far Eastern interests of the United States, Britain and the Netherlands, causing it to align with the Axis Powers for the pursuit of World War II. After its defeat in World War II, Japan renounced military aggression as a political instrument, established democratic self-government, and quickly reasserted its position as an economic world power.

Japanese coinage of concern to this catalog includes those issued for the Ryukyu Islands (also called Liuchu), a chain of islands extending southwest from Japan toward Taiwan (Formosa), before the Japanese government converted the islands into a prefecture under the name Okinawa. Many of the provinces of Japan issued their own definitive coinage under the Shogunate.

RULERS
Shoguns
Iyenari, 1787-1837
Iyeoshi, 1837-1853
Iyesada, 1853-1858
Iyemochi, 1858-1866
Yoshinobu, 1866-1867

Emperors
Komei, 1847-1866
Mutsuhito (Meiji), 1867-1912

Years 1-45 明治 or 治明

Yoshihito (Taisho), 1912-1926

Years 1-15 大正 or 正大

Hirohito (Showa), 1926-1989

Years 1-64 昭和 or 和昭

Akihito (Heisei), 1989-

Years 1- 平成

NOTE: The personal name of the emperor is followed by the name that he chose for his regnal era.

MONETARY SYSTEM
Until 1870

Prior to the Meiji currency reform, there was no fixed exchange rate between the various silver, gold and copper "cash" coins (which previously included Chinese "cash") in circulation. Each coin exchanged on the basis of its own merits and the prevailing market conditions. The size and weight of the copper coins and the weight and fineness of the silver and gold coins varied widely. From time to time the government would declare an official exchange rate, but this was usually ignored. For gold and silver, nominal equivalents were:

16 Shu = 4 Bu = 1 Ryo

Commencing 1870
10 Rin = 1 Sen
100 Sen = 1 Yen

MONETARY UNITS

Momme 匁 Ryo 兩
Bu 分 Shu 朱 Rin 厘
Sen 錢 Yen 円 or 圓 or 圓

MINTMARKS ON MON
A - 文 - Bun - Edo (Tokyo)
B - 佐佐佐 - Sado
C - 十 - Jiuman Tsubo
D - 小 - Koume Mura
E - 一 - Ichi-no-se
F - 川 - Onagi-gawa
G - 元 - Gen-Osaka
H - 長 - Nagasaki
I - 足 - Ashio
J - 仙 - Sendai
K - 千 - Sendai
L - 久 - Kuji (Hitachi Ohta)
M - ト,ド - Mito
N - ノ,イ - Aidzu
O - 一 - Ise
P - 盛 - Morioka
Q - 了 - Hiroshima
R - 山 - Yamanouchi

NOTE: Dates shown in parentheses are the first year of minting. Most pieces were minted for several years afterwards, but the exact years minting took place are not known.

DATING

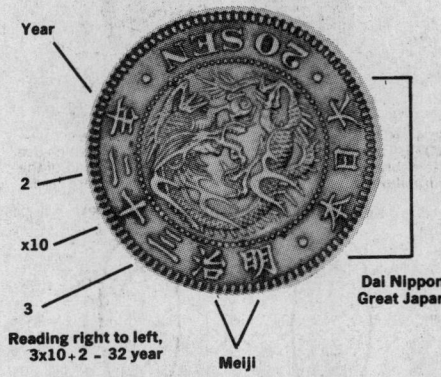

Year
2
x10
3
Reading right to left,
3x10+2 = 32 year
Dai Nippon Great Japan
Meiji

NOTE: In Showa yr. 23 (1948) inscriptions were reversed to read from left to right.

LEGENDS
Reading top-bottom, right-left.

Kan-ei Tsuho

Bunkyu-Eiho

EARLY COINAGE
MON
IRON
Rev: Plain.

C#	Date	Mint	VG	Fine	VF	XF
1.1a	ND(1739-1867)		2.00	5.00	7.50	15.00

Rev: Various mint marks.

1.3a	ND(1862)	B	6.50	12.50	17.50	25.00
1.12	(1739;1838)	K	3.00	5.00	8.00	15.00

NOTE: Most copper 1 Mon pieces predate the coverage of this book. Those with mintmark K are *bosen* - seed or mother coins.

COPPER

| 1.14 | ND(1844) | M | 125.00 | 175.00 | 225.00 | 275.00 |

4 MON

COPPER and BRASS
Rev: 11 waves.

| 4.2 | ND(1769-1860) | — | .30 | .50 | .75 | 1.75 |

| 6 | ND(1863-67) | — | .50 | 1.00 | 1.25 | 2.50 |

IRON

| 6.c | ND(1863-67) | — | 25.00 | 30.00 | 40.00 | |

COPPER and BRASS
Obv: Top character different style. Rev: 11 waves.

| 6.a | ND(1863-67) | — | .50 | .75 | 1.25 | 2.50 |

Obv: As above but character at left abbreviated. Rev: 11 waves.

| 6.b | ND(1863-67) | — | 1.00 | 1.50 | 3.00 | |

IRON
Rev: 11 waves; w/o mint mark.

| 4.2a | ND(1866) | — | 4.00 | 6.00 | 10.00 | 20.00 |

Rev: 11 waves and various mint marks.

4.12	ND(1866)	K	3.00	6.00	12.00	20.00
4.14	(1866)	M	12.00	17.50	25.00	30.00
4.15	(1866)	N	10.00	15.00	22.50	30.00
4.16	(1866)	O	12.00	17.50	25.00	35.00
4.17	(1866)	P	6.00	8.00	12.00	20.00
4.18	(1866)	Q	500.00	600.00	800.00	—
4.19	(1866)	R	500.00	600.00	800.00	—

NOTE: Copper 4 Mon pieces similar to those listed only under iron issues are *bosen* - seed or mother coins.

JAPAN 1116

100 MON
(Tempo Tsuho)

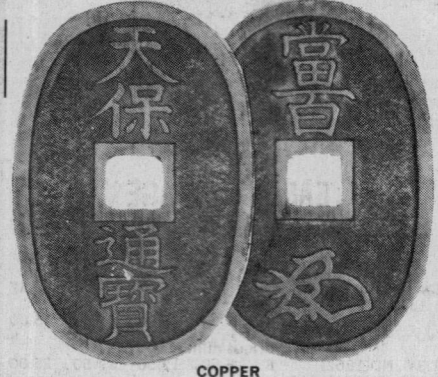

COPPER

C#	Date	Mint	VG	Fine	VF	XF
7	(1835-70)	—	2.50	5.00	7.00	10.00

MAMEITAGIN 'BEAN' SILVER
God of Plenty 'bean' Silver

KEY TO DATING MAMEITA GIN

'BUN'
GENBUN PERIOD
1736-1741
(Used 1736-1818)

'BUN'
BUNSEI PERIOD
1818-1830
(Used 1820-1837)

'HO'
TEMPO PERIOD
1830-1844
(Used 1837-1858)

'SEI'
ANSEI PERIOD
1854-1860
(Used 1859-1865)

One of the above characters is usually found on the obverse of C#8 or both sides of C#8a and C#8b. The same characters are found at both ends of chogin pieces C#9. Era designators were used continuously until the next one was introduced, regardless of intervening eras.

NOTE: Values are for pieces weighing 5-8 grams. Pieces over 10 grams may command up to twice the values shown; pieces under 5 grams somewhat less.

.460 SILVER
Obv: One or more characters, w/or w/o 'God of Plenty'. Rev: Blank.
Genbun

8.1	ND(1736-1818)	—	9.00	15.00	25.00	42.50

.360 SILVER
Obv: One or more characters, w/or w/o "God of Plenty."
Rev: Blank or chopmarked.
Bunsei

8.2	ND(1820-37)	—	9.00	17.50	30.00	50.00

.261 SILVER
Tempo

8.3	ND(1837-58)	—	9.00	15.00	22.50	37.50

.135 SILVER
Ansei

8.4	ND(1859-65)	—	6.00	10.00	18.00	30.00

.460 SILVER
Obv. and rev: 'God of Plenty' design, era designator on belly.
Genbun

C#	Date	Mint	VG	Fine	VF	XF
8a.1	ND(1736-1818)	—	80.00	140.00	215.00	350.00

Obv: "God of Plenty" design.
Rev: Single or multiple era designator.
Genbun

8b.1	ND(1736-1818)	—	—	—	Rare	—

.360 SILVER
Obv. and rev: "God of Plenty" design.
Bunsei

8a.2	ND(1820-37)	—	90.00	150.00	225.00	375.00

Obv: "God of Plenty" design.
Rev: Single or multiple era designator.
Bunsei

8b.2	ND(1820-37)	—	—	—	Rare	—

.261 SILVER
Obv. and rev: "God of Plenty" design.
Tempo

8a.3	ND(1837-58)	—	75.00	125.00	200.00	300.00

Obv: "God of Plenty" design.
Rev: Single or multiple era designator.
Tempo

8b.3	ND(1837-58)	—	—	—	Rare	—

.135 SILVER
Obv. and rev: "God of Plenty" design.
Ansei

8a.4	ND(1859-65)	—	70.00	110.00	175.00	250.00

Obv: "God of Plenty" design.
Rev: Single or multiple era designator.
Ansei

8b.4	ND(1859-65)	—	—	—	Rare	—

NOTE: There are other varieties of Mameita Gin which use the character Ho (treasure) on the reverse instead of the normal era designator (from the obverse). Most are rare.

KEY TO DATING CHO GIN (SILVER)

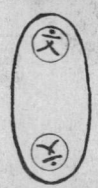 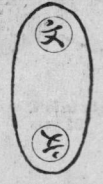

GENBUN, 1736-1741   BUNSEI, 1818-1830

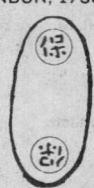 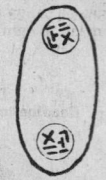

TEMPO, 1830-1844   ANSEI, 1854-1860

CHO GIN
(Long Silver)

.460 SILVER
Obv: Era marks at each end. Miscellaneous marks elsewhere. Rev: Blank except for occasional chopmarks.
Genbun

C#	Date	Mint	VG	Fine	VF	XF
9	ND(1736-1818)	—	130.00	230.00	375.00	600.00

.360 SILVER
Bunsei

9a	ND(1820-37)	—	125.00	225.00	375.00	600.00

.261 SILVER
Tempo

9b	ND(1837-58)	—	100.00	200.00	325.00	450.00

.135 SILVER
Ansei

9c	ND(1859-65)	—	90.00	150.00	250.00	350.00

ISSHU GIN
(One Shu Silver)

.989 SILVER, 2.63 g
Bunsei

C#	Date	Mintage	VG	Fine	VF	XF
11	ND(1829-37)	139.915	37.50	60.00	90.00	125.00

KEY TO DATING LATER ISSHU GIN

 KAEI PERIOD
1848-1854
(Used 1853-1865)

 MEIJI PERIOD
1868-1912
(Used 1868-1869)

.968 SILVER, 1.89 g
Kaie

C#	Date	Mintage	VG	Fine	VF	XF
12	ND(1853-65)	159.245	4.50	6.00	9.00	15.00

.880 SILVER, 1.88 g
Meiji

| 12a | ND(1868-69) | 18.742 | 9.00 | 12.50 | 18.00 | 25.00 |

NOTE: C#12 type Isshu Gin are dated according to how the character illustrated is written on the reverse. Meiji Isshu Gin are also known as Kaheishi Isshu Gin.

NISSHU GIN
(Two Shu Silver)

.978 SILVER, 10.19 g
Meiwa-Ko-Nanryo

| 13 | ND(1772-1824) | 47.464 | 50.00 | 75.00 | 120.00 | 175.00 |

NOTE: Pieces struck on large planchets with edge beads on obverse and reverse command a 50% premium.

.978 SILVER, 7.53 g
Bunsei-Shin-Nanryo

| 13a | ND(1824-30) | 60.624 | 35.00 | 55.00 | 85.00 | 120.00 |

.845 SILVER, 13.62 g
Ansei

| 15 | ND(1859) | .706 | 500.00 | 800.00 | 1200. | 1750. |

KEY TO DATING ICHIBU GIN

 TEMPO PERIOD
1830-1844
(Used 1837-1854)

 ANSEI PERIOD
1854-1860
(Used 1859-1868)

 MEIJI PERIOD
1868-1912
(Used 1868-1869)

NOTE: Ichibu Gin are dated according to how the two characters above are written on the reverse of the piece.

There are other variations as well. Meiji Bu Gin also are known as Kaheishi Bu Gin.

ICHIBU GIN
(One Bu Silver)

.991 SILVER, 8.66 g
Varieties of countermark
Tempo

C#	Date	Mintage	VG	Fine	VF	XF
16	ND(1837-54)	78.917	6.50	10.00	25.00	35.00

.873 SILVER, 8.63 g
Ansei

| 16a | ND(1859-68) | 11.399 | 6.00 | 9.00 | 22.50 | 32.50 |

.807 SILVER, 8.66 g
Meiji

| 16b | ND(1868-69) | 4.267 | 175.00 | 300.00 | 400.00 | 525.00 |

SANBU GIN
(Three Bu Silver)

.903 SILVER
"Ansei Trade Dollar"
c/m: 4 characters on Mexico 8 Reales, KM#377.

KM#	Date	Mintage	VG	Fine	VF	XF
101	ND(1859)	—	2000.	3500.	5000.	7000.

ISSHU KIN
(One Shu Gold)

.123 GOLD/.877 SILVER, 1.39 g
Bunsei

C#	Date	Mintage	VG	Fine	VF	XF
17	ND(1824-32)	46.723	125.00	200.00	300.00	400.00

NISSHU KIN
(Two Shu Gold)

.298 GOLD/.702 SILVER, 1.62 g
Tempo

| 18 | ND(1832-58) | 103.070 | 10.00 | 20.00 | 27.50 | 37.50 |

.229 GOLD/.771 SILVER, 0.75 g
Manen

C#	Date	Mintage	VG	Fine	VF	XF
18a	ND(1860-69)	25.120	15.00	25.00	35.00	50.00

KEY TO DATING ICHIBU AND NIBU KIN

GENBUN PERIOD ICHIBU

 1736-1741
(Used 1736-1818)

BUNSEI PERIOD NIBU

1818-1830
TYPE A DATE MARK
 (Used 1818-1828)

BUNSEI PERIOD ICHIBU and NIBU

1818-1830
TYPE B DATE MARK
 (Used 1819-1829 on Ichibu)
(Used 1828-1832 on Nibu)

TEMPO PERIOD

1830-1844
(Used 1837-1858)

ANSEI PERIOD

1854-1859
(Used 1859)

MANEN PERIOD

1859-1860
(Without era designator)

One of these dating marks will be found in the upper right corner of C#19-21a (except C#20c). C#21b is dated according to its weight. C#21c and C#21d can be distinguished by the character to the left on the reverse.

KEY TO DATING C#21c and C#21d

 MANEN PERIOD
1860-1861
(Used 1860)

 MEIJI PERIOD
1868-1912
(Used 1868-1869)

ICHIBU KIN
(One Bu Gold)

.653 GOLD/.347 SILVER, 3.25 g
Rev: Written as flourish.
Dating mark in upper right corner.
Genbun

| 19 | ND(1736-1818) | — | 32.50 | 60.00 | 100.00 | 150.00 |

.560 GOLD/.440 SILVER, 3.27 g
Bunsei, rev: Type B mark.

| 20 | ND(1819-29) | — | 70.00 | 110.00 | 175.00 | 250.00 |

JAPAN 1118

.568 GOLD/.432 SILVER, 2.80 g
Tempo

C#	Date	Mintage	VG	Fine	VF	XF
20a	ND(1837-58)	—	75.00	125.00	200.00	275.00

.570 GOLD/.430 SILVER, 2.24 g
Ansei

| 20b | ND(1859) | | 1000. | 2000. | 2750. | 3500. |

.574 GOLD/.426 SILVER, 0.82 g
Rev: W/o dating mark.
Manen

| 20c | ND(1860-67) | — | 300.00 | 600.00 | 900.00 | 1200. |

NOTE: Similar pieces without dating mark but weighing about 4 grams were made during the Kyoho era, 1716-34.

NIBU KIN
(Two Bu Gold)

.563 GOLD/.437 SILVER, 6.52 g
Bunsei, rev: Type A mark.

| 21 | ND(1818-28) | | | | | |
| | | 5.972 | 250.00 | 400.00 | 600.00 | 800.00 |

.490 GOLD/.510 SILVER, 6.56 g
Bunsei, rev: Type B mark.

| 21a | ND(1828-32) | | | | | |
| | | 4.066 | 225.00 | 325.00 | 500.00 | 700.00 |

.209 GOLD/.791 SILVER, 5.62 g
Ansei, rev: W/o mark.

| 21b | ND(1856-60) | | | | | |
| | | 7.103 | 45.00 | 90.00 | 125.00 | 175.00 |

A.

B.

.229 GOLD/.771 SILVER, 3.00 g
Manen, obv: Paulownia leaf type A. Rev: W/o mark.

| 21c.1 | ND(1860-) | | | | | |
| | | 100.201 | 225.00 | 350.00 | 500.00 | 650.00 |

Manen, obv: Paulownia leaf type B:

| 21c.2 | ND(1860-) | I.A. | 175.00 | 225.00 | 350.00 | 475.00 |

.223 GOLD/.777 SILVER, 3.00 g
Meiji

| 21d | ND(1868-69) | — | 20.00 | 30.00 | 45.00 | 60.00 |

KOBAN

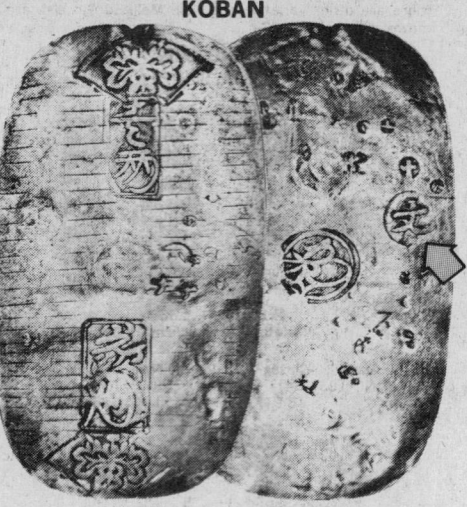

.653 GOLD/.347 SILVER, 13.13 g
Genbun

C#	Date	Mintage	VG	Fine	VF	XF
22	ND(1736-1818)					
		*17.436	1000.	1500.	2000.	2750.

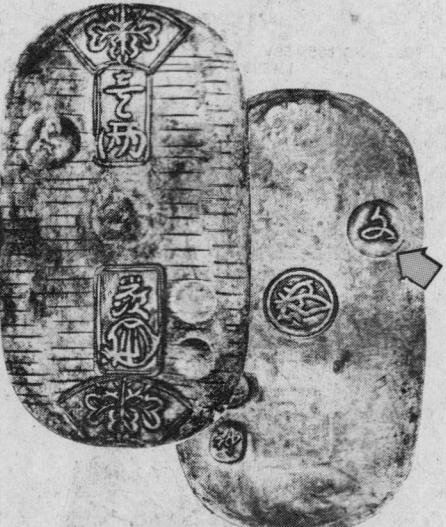

.559 GOLD/.441 SILVER, 13.13 g
Bunsei, rev: Mark B.

| 22a | ND(1819-28) | | | | | |
| | | *11.043 | 1000. | 1500. | 2000. | 2500. |

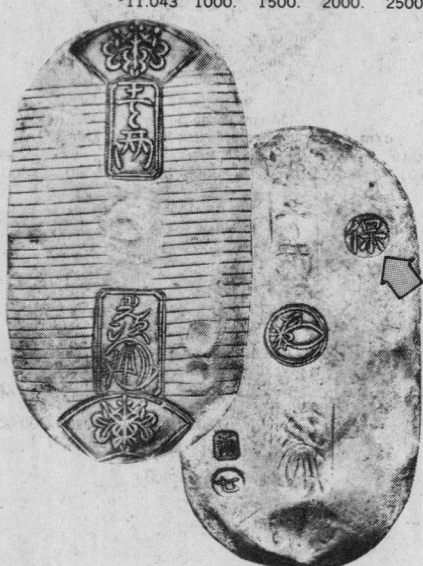

.568 GOLD/.432 SILVER, 11.25 g
Tempo

| 22b | ND(1837-1858) | | | | | |
| | | *8.120 | 650.00 | 950.00 | 1350. | 1750. |

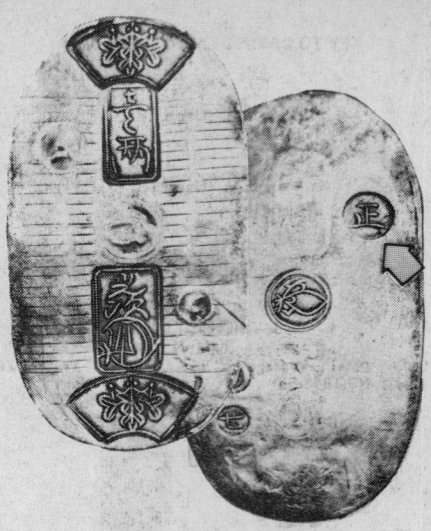

.570 GOLD/.430 SILVER, 8.97 g
Ansei

C#	Date	Mintage	VG	Fine	VF	XF
22c	ND(1859)	.351	3500.	5000.	6500.	7500.

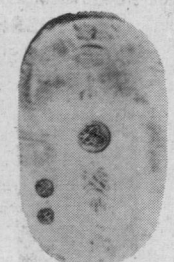

.574 GOLD/.426 SILVER, 3.30 g
Manen, Rev: W/o mark.

| 22d | (1860-67) | .625 | 450.00 | 650.00 | 1000. | 1350. |

*NOTE: Koban mintage figures include Ichibu Kin.

GORYOBAN
(5 Ryo)

.842 GOLD/.158 SILVER, 33.75 g, 51x89mm
Tempo

| 23 | ND(1837-43) | | | | | |
| | | .034 | 3500. | 6000. | 10,000. | 15,000. |

OBAN

NOTE: Oban illustrations are reduced by 50%.

JAPAN 1119

.676 GOLD/.324 SILVER, 165.38 g, 94x153mm
Kyoho

C#	Date	Mintage	VG	Fine	VF	XF
24.1 (C24)	ND(1725-1837)	8,515	—	—	30,000.	45,000.

.674 GOLD/.326 SILVER, 165.38 g, 95x157mm
Tempo

C#	Date	Mintage	VG	Fine	VF	XF
24.2 (C24.3)	ND(1838-60)	1,887	—	—	35,000.	50,000.

Machine made horizontal crenulations.

C#	Date	Mintage	VG	Fine	VF	XF
24a.2 (C24a.1)	ND(1860-62) I.A.	—	—	15,000.	20,000.

DECIMAL COINAGE
10 Rin = 1 Sen
100 Sen = 1 Yen

RIN

COPPER

Y#	Date	Mintage	Fine	VF	XF	Unc
15	Meiji					
	Yr.6(1873)	6.979	4.50	10.00	20.00	60.00
	Yr.7(1874)	I.A.	2.00	6.50	12.50	35.00
	Yr.8(1875)	3.718	4.50	10.00	25.00	72.50
	Yr.9(1876)	.023	300.00	650.00	2000.	3500.
	Yr.10(1877)	I.A.	100.00	250.00	600.00	1000.
	Yr.13(1880)	810 pcs.	750.00	1250.	2500.	4750.
	Yr.15(1882)	3.632	2.00	5.00	8.00	30.00
	Yr.16(1883)	14.128	2.00	5.00	8.00	30.00
	Yr.17(1884)	16.009	2.00	5.00	8.00	30.00
	Yr.25(1892)	—	(none struck for circulation)

NOTE: Two varieties of year 8 exist.

5 RIN

BRONZE

	Taisho					
41	Yr.5(1916)	8.000	.50	2.00	3.50	12.00
	Yr.6(1917)	5.287	.50	2.00	4.00	12.50
	Yr.7(1918)	11.661	.25	1.00	3.00	9.00
	Yr.8(1919)	17.130	.25	1.00	3.00	9.00

1/2 SEN

COPPER
Obv: Square scales on dragon's body.

	Meiji					
16	Yr.6(1873)	16.804	2.50	10.00	50.00	300.00
	Yr.7(1874)	I.A.	2.50	10.00	50.00	350.00
	Yr.8(1875)	17.037	.75	3.50	25.00	250.00
	Yr.9(1876)	24.292	.75	3.50	25.00	250.00
	Yr.10(1877)	29.278	50.00	100.00	300.00	1800

Obv: V scales on dragon's body.

Y#	Date	Mintage	Fine	VF	XF	Unc
16.1	Yr.10(1877)	I.A.	.50	1.50	7.50	60.00
	Yr.12(1879)	29.963	7.50	15.00	25.00	550.00
	Yr.13(1880)	14.090	.50	1.50	7.50	65.00
	Yr.14(1881)	17.929	.50	1.50	7.50	65.00
	Yr.15(1882)	26.458	.50	1.50	7.50	65.00
	Yr.16(1883)	38.202	.50	1.50	7.50	65.00
	Yr.17(1884)	38.480	.50	1.50	7.50	30.00
	Yr.18(1885)	31.166	.50	1.50	7.50	65.00
	Yr.19(1886)	31.831	.50	1.50	7.50	65.00
	Yr.20(1887)	35.651	.50	1.50	7.50	65.00
	Yr.21(1888)	25.744	3.50	7.50	15.00	250.00
	Yr.25(1892)	(none struck for circulation)

SEN

COPPER
Obv: Square scales on dragon's body.

	Meiji					
17	Yr.6(1873)	1.301	7.50	15.00	50.00	300.00
	Yr.7(1874)	25.564	1.00	2.50	10.00	150.00
	Yr.8(1875)	32.832	.75	1.50	7.50	125.00
	Yr.9(1876)	38.048	.75	1.50	7.50	125.00
	Yr.10(1877)	98.041	.75	1.50	7.50	125.00

Obv: V scales on dragon's body.

17.1	Yr.13(1880)	33.947	.50	1.50	5.00	90.00
	Yr.14(1881)	16.123	1.50	3.50	7.50	120.00
	Yr.15(1882)	19.150	.50	1.50	5.00	90.00
	Yr.16(1883)	47.613	.50	1.50	5.00	90.00
	Yr.17(1884)	53.702	.50	1.50	5.00	90.00
	Yr.18(1885)	46.846	.50	1.50	5.00	90.00
	Yr.19(1886)	26.886	.50	1.50	5.00	90.00
	Yr.20(1887)	22.249	.50	1.50	5.00	90.00
	Yr.21(1888)	25.864	.50	1.50	5.00	75.00
	Yr.25(1892)	—	(none struck for circulation)

BRONZE

20	Yr.31(1898)	3.649	2.50	5.00	15.00	150.00
	Yr.32(1899)	9.764	2.00	4.50	12.50	120.00
	Yr.33(1900)	3.086	4.50	12.50	20.00	175.00
	Yr.34(1901)	5.555	2.00	4.50	12.50	120.00
	Yr.35(1902)	4.444	5.00	12.50	20.00	175.00
	Yr.39(1906)	—	(none struck for circulation)
	Yr.42(1909)	(none struck for circulation)

.344 GOLD/.639 SILVER, 112.4 g, 81x137mm
Manen
Hand made horizontal crenulations.

24a.1 (C24a)	ND(1860-62)	.017	—	—	16,000.	22,000.

JAPAN 1120

Y#	Date	Mintage	Fine	VF	XF	Unc
	Taisho					
35	Yr.2(1913)	15.000	2.00	3.00	5.00	45.00
	Yr.3(1914)	10.000	2.00	3.00	5.00	45.00
	Yr.4(1915)	13.000	2.00	3.00	5.00	45.00

42	Yr.5(1916)	19.193	1.50	5.00	20.00	75.00
	Yr.6(1917)	27.183	.50	1.25	7.50	45.00
	Yr.7(1918)	121.794	.25	.50	1.00	12.50
	Yr.8(1919)	209.959	.15	.25	.50	4.50
	Yr.9(1920)	118.829	.15	.25	.50	4.50
	Yr.10(1921)	252.440	.15	.25	.50	4.50
	Yr.11(1922)	253.210	.15	.25	.50	4.50
	Yr.12(1923)	155.500	.15	.25	.50	4.50
	Yr.13(1924)	106.250	.15	.25	.50	4.50

	Showa					
47	Yr.2(1927)	26.500	1.50	3.50	5.50	50.00
	Yr.4(1929)	3.000	7.50	12.50	20.00	60.00
	Yr.5(1930)	5.000	2.50	5.00	15.00	120.00
	Yr.6(1931)	25.001	.50	2.00	5.00	25.00
	Yr.7(1932)	35.066	.50	1.50	3.00	12.50
	Yr.8(1933)	38.936	.25	.50	2.00	5.00
	Yr.9(1934)	100.004	.15	.25	1.50	5.00
	Yr.10(1935)	200.009	.15	.25	.50	4.50
	Yr.11(1936)	109.170	.15	.25	.50	4.50
	Yr.12(1937)	133.196	.15	.25	.50	4.50
	Yr.13(1938)	87.649	.15	.25	.50	4.50

55	Yr.13(1938)	113.605	.25	.50	1.25	2.50

	TYPE A	ALUMINUM		TYPE B		
56	Yr.13(1938)	45.502	—	1.00	3.50	17.50
	Yr.14(1939) Type A	444.602	—	3.00	7.50	22.50
	Yr.14(1939) Type B	Inc. Ab.	—	.25	.50	1.50
	Yr.15(1940)	602.110	—	.25	.50	1.50

0.6500 g

Y#	Date	Mintage	Fine	VF	XF	Unc
59	Yr.16(1941)	1016.620	—	—	.25	.50
	Yr.17(1942)	119.709	—	—	.25	.75
	Yr.18(1943)	1,163.949	—	—	.25	.50

Thinner, 0.5500 g

59a	Yr.18(1943)	627.191	—	—	.50	1.00

 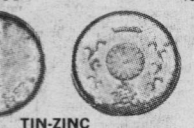

TIN-ZINC

62	Yr.19(1944)	1,641.661	—	—	.25	.50
	Yr.20(1945) I.A.	—	—	.25	.75

REDDISH BROWN BAKED CLAY

KM#	Date	Mintage	Fine	VF	XF	Unc
110	ND(1945)	—	4.00	6.00	12.00	18.00

NOTE: Not issued for circulation.

2 SEN

BRONZE
Obv: Square scales on dragon's body.

Y#	Date	Mintage	Fine	VF	XF	Unc
	Meiji					
18	Yr.6(1873)	3.949	35.00	75.00	150.00	1100.
	Yr.7(1874) I.A.	5.00	25.00	50.00	550.00
	Yr.8(1875)	22.835	1.50	3.50	20.00	300.00
	Yr.9(1876)	25.817	1.50	3.50	20.00	300.00
	Yr.10(1877)	33.897	1.50	3.50	20.00	300.00

Obv: V scales on dragon's body.

18.1	Yr.10(1877)	43.290	1.50	2.50	10.00	150.00
	Yr.13(1880)	33.142	1.50	2.50	10.00	150.00
	Yr.14(1881)	38.475	1.50	2.50	10.00	150.00
	Yr.15(1882)	43.527	1.50	2.50	10.00	150.00
	Yr.16(1883)	19.476	1.50	2.50	10.00	150.00
	Yr.17(1884)	12.090	5.00	15.00	35.00	450.00
	Yr.25(1892)	—	(none struck for circulation)			

5 SEN

1.2500 g, .800 SILVER, .0321 oz ASW

	Meiji					
1	Yr.3(1870) shallow scales	1.501	60.00	125.00	250.00	550.00
	Yr.3(1870) deep scales					

Y#	Date	Mintage	Fine	VF	XF	Unc
1	Inc. Ab.	90.00	200.00	300.00	750.00
	Yr.4(1871) I.A.	100.00	225.00	350.00	850.00

Early variety. Rev: 66 rays, 79 beads.

6.1	Yr.4(1871)	1.665	30.00	85.00	150.00	275.00

Late variety. Rev: 53 rays, 65 beads.

6.2	Yr.4(1871) I.A.	25.00	65.00	100.00	175.00

1.3400 g, .800 SILVER, .0344 oz ASW

22	Yr.6(1873)	5.593	10.00	20.00	45.00	80.00
	Yr.7(1874)	7.806	45.00	80.00	150.00	500.00
	Yr.8(1875)	6.396	10.00	20.00	45.00	80.00
	Yr.9(1876)	5.546	10.00	20.00	50.00	90.00
	Yr.10(1877)	22.024	10.00	20.00	45.00	80.00
	Yr.13(1880)	79 pcs.	1500.	2750.	4500.	8000.
	Yr.25(1892)	—	(none struck for circulation)			

NOTE: Varieties exist.

COPPER-NICKEL

19	Yr.22(1889)	28.841	2.00	4.50	15.00	90.00
	Yr.23(1890)	39.258	2.00	4.50	15.00	90.00
	Yr.24(1891)	15.924	2.50	5.00	17.50	120.00
	Yr.25(1892)	9.510	2.50	5.00	17.50	120.00
	Yr.26(1893)	8.531	2.50	5.00	17.50	120.00
	Yr.27(1894)	14.680	2.50	5.00	17.50	120.00
	Yr.28(1895)	1.030	50.00	100.00	150.00	1500.
	Yr.29(1896)	5.119	3.50	7.50	20.00	250.00
	Yr.30(1897)	7.857	2.50	5.00	17.50	125.00

NOTE: Varieties exist.

21	Yr.30(1897)	4.167	6.50	15.00	35.00	300.00
	Yr.31(1898)	18.197	5.00	10.00	20.00	150.00
	Yr.32(1899)	10.658	5.00	10.00	20.00	150.00
	Yr.33(1900)	2.426	7.50	15.00	25.00	275.00
	Yr.34(1901)	7.124	6.00	12.50	20.00	150.00
	Yr.35(1902)	2.448	10.00	25.00	35.00	300.00
	Yr.36(1903)	.372	150.00	250.00	350.00	1750.
	Yr.37(1904)	1.628	20.00	35.00	50.00	450.00
	Yr.38(1905)	6.000	5.00	10.00	20.00	150.00

	Taisho					
43	Yr.6(1917)	6.781	7.50	15.00	30.00	65.00
	Yr.7(1918)	9.131	5.00	10.00	25.00	50.00
	Yr.8(1919)	44.980	3.00	6.00	12.50	25.00
	Yr.9(1920)	21.906	3.00	6.00	12.50	25.00

19.1mm

44	Yr.9(1920)	100.455	.35	.75	2.00	15.00
	Yr.10(1921)					

JAPAN 1121

Y#	Date	Mintage	Fine	VF	XF	Unc
44	Yr.11(1922)	133.020	.25	.50	1.50	5.00
	Yr.12(1923)	163.908	.25	.50	1.50	5.00
		80.000	.25	.50	1.50	5.00

Showa
| 48 | Yr.7(1932) | 8.000 | .25 | .50 | 1.75 | 10.00 |

NICKEL
53	Yr.8(1933)	16.150	.50	1.50	3.00	5.50
	Yr.9(1934)	33.851	.50	1.00	2.00	4.50
	Yr.10(1935)	13.680	1.00	2.00	3.50	7.50
	Yr.11(1936)	36.321	.50	1.00	2.00	4.50
	Yr.12(1937)	44.402	.50	1.00	2.00	4.50
	Yr.13(1938)	10.000	4 known, balance remelted			

ALUMINUM-BRONZE
57	Yr.13(1938)	40.001	.50	1.00	1.50	4.00
	Yr.14(1939)	97.903	.50	1.00	1.50	4.00
	Yr.15(1940)	34.501	.50	1.00	1.50	4.00

ALUMINUM
Variety 1 - 1.2000 g
| 60 | Yr.15(1940) | 167.638 | — | — | .50 | 2.00 |
| | Yr.16(1941) | 242.361 | — | — | .25 | 1.50 |

Variety 2 - 1.0000 g
| 60a | Yr.16(1941) | 478.023 | 2.50 | 7.50 | 15.00 | 45.00 |
| | Yr.17(1942) I.A. | — | — | — | .25 | 1.00 |

Variety 3 - 0.8000 g
| 60b | Yr.18(1943) | 276.493 | — | — | .25 | 1.00 |

TIN-ZINC
| 63 | Yr.19(1944) | 70.003 | — | .25 | .50 | 1.50 |

| 65 | Yr.20(1945) | 180.008 | — | — | .50 | 2.00 |
| | Yr.21(1946) I.A. | — | — | — | .50 | 2.00 |

REDDISH BROWN BAKED CLAY
KM#	Date	Mintage	Fine	VF	XF	Unc
111	Yr.20(1945)	—	50.00	75.00	100.00	175.00

NOTE: Not issued for circulation.

10 SEN

2.5000 g, .800 SILVER, .0643 oz ASW
Y#	Date	Mintage	Fine	VF	XF	Unc
2	Meiji					
	Yr.3(1870) shallow scales	6.102	12.50	25.00	45.00	125.00
	Yr.3(1870) deep scales	Inc. Ab.	20.00	40.00	65.00	180.00

2.6957 g, .800 SILVER, .0693 oz ASW
| 23 | Yr.6(1873) Type I | 5.109 | 50.00 | 100.00 | 125.00 | 300.00 |
| | Yr.6(1873) Type II | Inc. Ab. | 5.00 | 10.00 | 20.00 | 50.00 |

明　　明

	Type I Character Connected		Type II Character not connected		
Yr.7(1874)	10.221	150.00	250.00	350.00	725.00
Yr.8(1875) Type I	8.977	15.00	30.00	50.00	150.00
Yr.8(1875) Type II	Inc. Ab.	5.00	10.00	20.00	60.00
Yr.9(1876)	11.890	5.00	10.00	20.00	60.00
Yr.10(1877)	20.352	10.00	25.00	45.00	125.00
Yr.13(1880)	77 pcs.	2000.	3750.	5500.	10,000.
Yr.18(1885)	9.763	3.00	7.50	12.00	35.00
Yr.20(1887)	10.421	3.00	7.50	12.00	35.00
Yr.21(1888)	8.177	5.00	10.00	20.00	50.00
Yr.24(1891)	5.000	10.00	20.00	50.00	100.00
Yr.25(1892)	5.000	10.00	20.00	50.00	100.00
Yr.26(1893)	12.000	5.00	10.00	20.00	50.00
Yr.27(1894)	11.000	5.00	10.00	20.00	40.00
Yr.28(1895)	13.719	2.00	5.00	10.00	30.00
Yr.29(1896)	15.080	2.00	5.00	10.00	30.00
Yr.30(1897)	20.357	2.00	5.00	10.00	30.00
Yr.31(1898)	13.643	3.00	7.50	15.00	35.00
Yr.32(1899)	26.216	3.00	7.50	15.00	35.00
Yr.33(1900)	8.183	7.50	15.00	30.00	100.00
Yr.34(1901)	.797	125.00	175.00	225.00	650.00
Yr.35(1902)	1.204	100.00	150.00	200.00	550.00
Yr.37(1904)	11.106	2.50	5.00	7.50	25.00
Yr.38(1905)	34.182	2.50	5.00	7.50	25.00
Yr.39(1906)	4.710	2.50	5.00	7.50	25.00

2.2500 g, .720 SILVER, .0521 oz ASW
29	Yr.40(1907)	12.000	3.00	7.50	17.50	90.00
	Yr.41(1908)	12.273	5.00	8.50	17.50	90.00
	Yr.42(1909)	20.279	1.00	3.50	10.00	45.00
	Yr.43(1910)	20.339	1.00	3.50	10.00	45.00
	Yr.44(1911)	38.729	1.00	3.50	10.00	45.00
	Yr.45(1912)	10.755	1.50	4.50	12.50	80.00

 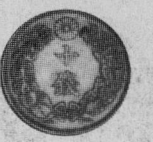

Y#	Date	Mintage	Fine	VF	XF	Unc
36	Taisho					
	Yr.1(1912)	10.344	5.00	8.00	17.50	95.00
	Yr.2(1913)	13.321	1.00	2.50	5.00	15.00
	Yr.3(1914)	10.325	1.00	2.50	5.00	15.00
	Yr.4(1915)	16.836	1.50	3.00	5.00	12.50
	Yr.5(1916)	10.324	1.00	2.50	4.00	12.00
	Yr.6(1917)	35.170	.75	2.00	3.00	10.00

COPPER-NICKEL
45	Yr.9(1920)	4.894	.35	.75	2.50	25.00
	Yr.10(1921)	61.870	.25	.50	1.50	5.00
	Yr.11(1922)	159.770	.25	.50	1.50	5.00
	Yr.12(1923)	190.010	.25	.50	1.50	4.50
	Yr.14(1925)	54.475	.25	.50	1.50	5.00
	Yr.15(1926)	58.675	.25	.50	1.50	5.00

Showa
49	Yr.2(1927)	36.050	.25	.50	1.50	5.00
	Yr.3(1928)	41.450	.25	.50	1.50	5.00
	Yr.4(1929)	10.000	.50	1.00	2.00	20.00
	Yr.6(1931)	1.850	.75	1.50	2.50	7.50
	Yr.7(1932)	23.151	.25	.50	1.50	5.00

NICKEL
54	Yr.8(1933)	14.570	.50	1.00	2.00	5.50
	Yr.9(1934)	37.351	.25	.75	1.50	4.75
	Yr.10(1935)	35.586	.30	1.00	1.75	5.25
	Yr.11(1936)	77.948	.25	.75	1.50	4.75
	Yr.12(1937)	40.001	.30	1.00	1.75	5.25

 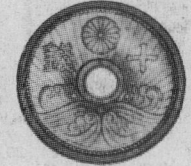

ALUMINUM-BRONZE
58	Yr.13(1938)	47.077	.35	.75	1.50	4.75
	Yr.14(1939)	121.796	.25	.50	1.00	4.50
	Yr.15(1940)	16.135	.50	1.00	2.00	10.00

JAPAN 1122

ALUMINUM, 1.5000 g

Y#	Date	Mintage	Fine	VF	XF	Unc
61	Yr.15(1940)	575.628	—	.20	.35	1.50
	Yr.16(1941)	I.A.	—	.20	.35	1.50

1.2000 g

61a	Yr.16(1941)	944.947	.10	.35	.50	2.00
	Yr.17(1942)	I.A.	.35	.50	1.50
	Yr.18(1943)	I.B.	— Reported, not confirmed

1.0000 g

61b	Yr.17(1942)	—	— Reported, not confirmed
	Yr.18(1943)	756.037	—	.20	.35	1.50

TIN-ZINC

64	Yr.19(1944)	450.022	—	.20	.35	1.50

REDDISH BROWN BAKED CLAY

KM#	Date	Mintage	Fine	VF	XF	Unc
112	Yr.20(1945)	—	50.00	80.00	125.00	175.00

NOTE: Not issued for circulation.

ALUMINUM

Y#	Date	Mintage	Fine	VF	XF	Unc
68	Yr.20(1945)	237.590	—	.20	.35	1.00
	Yr.21(1946)	I.A.	—	.20	.35	1.00

20 SEN

5.0000 g, .800 SILVER, .1286 oz ASW

Meiji

3	Yr.3(1870) shallow scales	4.313	12.50	25.00	50.00	125.00
	Yr.3(1870) deep scales	Inc. Ab.	17.50	35.00	60.00	175.00
	Yr.4(1871)	I.A.	12.50	25.00	40.00	100.00

NOTE: Varieties exist.

5.3800 g, .800 SILVER, .1383 oz ASW

24	Yr.6(1873)	6.214	7.50	15.00	25.00	100.00
	Yr.7(1874)	3.024	20.00	45.00	75.00	210.00
	Yr.8(1875) Type I sm. chrysanthemum rev.
		.612	100.00	150.00	275.00	1000.
	Yr.8(1875) Type II lg. chrysanthemum rev.
		Inc. Ab.	50.00	100.00	150.00	475.00

明 明
Type I   Type II

Y#	Date	Mintage	Fine	VF	XF	Unc
24	Yr.9(1876) Type I char. *Mei* connected
		9.200	20.00	35.00	75.00	250.00
	Yr.9(1876) Type II char. *Mei* not connected
		Inc. Ab.	7.50	15.00	25.00	75.00
	Yr.10(1877)	5.199	20.00	35.00	75.00	250.00
	Yr.13(1880)	96 pcs.	1750.	3250.	5500.	—
	Yr.18(1885)	4.205	6.00	12.00	18.00	45.00
	Yr.20(1887)	4.794	6.00	12.00	18.00	45.00
	Yr.21(1888)	.703	50.00	100.00	250.00	950.00
	Yr.24(1891)	2.500	12.50	20.00	35.00	125.00
	Yr.25(1892)	3.054	7.50	15.00	25.00	100.00
	Yr.26(1893)	3.445	7.50	15.00	25.00	100.00
	Yr.27(1894)	4.500	5.50	12.50	20.00	90.00
	Yr.28(1895)	7.000	3.50	7.50	12.50	35.00
	Yr.29(1896)	2.599	7.50	15.00	25.00	100.00
	Yr.30(1897)	7.516	3.50	7.50	12.50	50.00
	Yr.31(1898)	17.984	3.50	7.50	10.00	30.00
	Yr.32(1899)	15.000	3.50	7.50	10.00	30.00
	Yr.33(1900)	.800	25.00	50.00	75.00	250.00
	Yr.34(1901)	.500	150.00	200.00	300.00	1500.
	Yr.37(1904)	5.250	3.50	7.50	12.50	35.00
	Yr.38(1905)	8.444	3.50	7.50	12.50	35.00

4.0500 g, .800 SILVER, .1042 oz ASW

30	Yr.39(1906)	6.555	3.00	7.00	25.00	175.00
	Yr.40(1907)	20.000	2.25	3.50	7.50	90.00
	Yr.41(1908)	15.000	2.25	3.50	7.50	90.00
	Yr.42(1909)	8.824	2.50	5.00	10.00	95.00
	Yr.43(1910)	21.175	2.25	3.50	7.50	90.00
	Yr.44(1911)	.500	50.00	100.00	150.00	550.00

50 SEN

12.5000 g, .800 SILVER, .3215 oz ASW

Meiji

4	Yr.3(1870)	1.806	32.50	65.00	100.00	300.00
	Yr.4(1871)	I.A.	30.00	60.00	85.00	250.00

NOTE: Varieties exist.

Type II, large dragon

Flame tip overlaps third spine.

Type I, small dragon

Flame tip extends between third & fourth spine.

30.5mm
Type I: 19mm circle of dots around dragon.

Y#	Date	Mintage	Fine	VF	XF	Unc
4a	Yr.4(1871)	2.648	50.00	100.00	150.00	300.00

Type II: 21mm circle of dots around dragon.

| 4a.1 | Yr.4(1871) | I.A. | 400.00 | 600.00 | 800.00 | 1750. |

13.5000 g, .800 SILVER, .3472 oz ASW

25	Yr.6(1873) Type I	3.447	25.00	35.00	65.00	200.00
	Yr.6(1873) Type II	Inc.Ab.	100.00	150.00	200.00	400.00
	Yr.7(1874)	.095	3500.	6000.	8000.	15,000.
	Yr.8(1875)	109 pcs.	4500.	7500.	12,500.	17,500.
	Yr.9(1876)	1,251	2000.	2750.	4000.	9000.
	Yr.10(1877)	.184	850.00	1250.	2000.	4500.
	Yr.13(1880)	179 pcs.	3500.	6500.	8500.	16,500.
	Yr.18(1885)	.409	100.00	150.00	250.00	750.00
	Yr.30(1897)	5.078	7.50	15.00	25.00	175.00
	Yr.31(1898)	22.797	6.50	12.50	20.00	100.00
	Yr.32(1899)	10.254	7.50	15.00	25.00	125.00
	Yr.33(1900)	3.280	12.50	25.00	50.00	200.00
	Yr.34(1901)	1.790	15.00	30.00	60.00	275.00
	Yr.35(1902)	1.023	50.00	100.00	175.00	475.00
	Yr.36(1903)	1.503	25.00	50.00	75.00	300.00
	Yr.37(1904)	5.373	7.50	15.00	25.00	125.00
	Yr.38(1905)	9.566	7.50	15.00	25.00	125.00

NOTE: Two varieties exist for year 6 in the character *Nen* (—year). The type II has a very long lower horizontal stroke.

10.1000 g, .800 SILVER, .2597 oz ASW

31	Yr.39(1906)	12.478	3.00	6.50	20.00	300.00
	Yr.40(1907)	24.062	3.00	6.00	12.50	125.00
	Yr.41(1908)	25.470	3.00	6.00	12.50	125.00
	Yr.42(1909)	21.998	3.00	6.00	12.50	125.00
	Yr.43(1910)	15.323	3.00	6.00	12.50	125.00
	Yr.44(1911)	9.900	3.00	6.00	12.50	125.00
	Yr.45(1912)	3.677	7.50	12.50	32.50	175.00

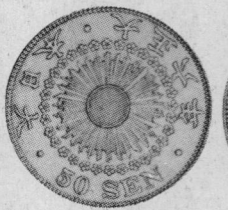 

Taisho

37	Yr.1(1912)	1.928	12.50	25.00	40.00	175.00
	Yr.2(1913)	5.910	3.00	7.50	17.50	65.00
	Yr.3(1914)	1.872	20.00	35.00	50.00	150.00
	Yr.4(1915)	2.011	17.50	32.50	50.00	150.00
	Yr.5(1916)	8.736	3.50	7.50	12.50	42.50
	Yr.6(1917)	9.963	3.50	7.50	12.50	42.50

4.9600 g, .720 SILVER, .1148 oz ASW

Y#	Date	Mintage	Fine	VF	XF	Unc
46	Yr.11(1922)	76.320	BV	1.50	5.00	30.00
	Yr.12(1923)	185.180	BV	1.50	3.00	18.00
	Yr.13(1924)	78.520	BV	1.50	3.00	18.00
	Yr.14(1925)	47.808	BV	1.50	4.00	20.00
	Yr.15(1926)	32.572	BV	1.50	5.00	30.00

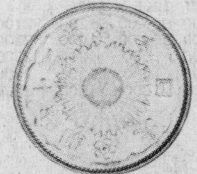 

Showa

Y#	Date	Mintage	Fine	VF	XF	Unc
50	Yr.3(1928)	38.592	BV	1.50	3.00	18.00
	Yr.4(1929)	12.568	BV	1.50	5.00	45.00
	Yr.5(1930)	10.200	BV	2.00	5.50	20.00
	Yr.6(1931)	27.677	BV	1.00	2.50	10.00
	Yr.7(1932)	24.132	BV	1.00	2.50	10.00
	Yr.8(1933)	10.001	BV	2.00	7.00	25.00
	Yr.9(1934)	20.003	BV	1.50	3.00	12.00
	Yr.10(1935)	11.738	BV	1.50	3.00	15.00
	*Yr.11(1936)	44.272	BV	1.50	2.50	7.50
	Yr.12(1937)	48.000	BV	1.50	2.50	7.50
	Yr.13(1938)	3.600	50.00	75.00	125.00	250.00

BRASS

67	Yr.21(1946)	268.187	.25	.50	1.00	2.50
	Yr.22(1947)	I.A.	—	450.00	650.00	1200.

NOTE: Coins dated Showa 22 (1947) were not released to circulation.

*NOTE: Varieties exist.

 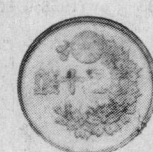

69	Yr.22(1947)	849.234	.10	.20	.40	1.00
	Yr.23(1948)	I.A.	.10	.20	.40	1.00

YEN

1.6700 g, .900 GOLD, 13.5mm, .0482 oz AGW

Meiji

9	Yr.4(1871)	1.841	200.00	350.00	600.00	900.00
	Yr.4(1871)	—	—	—	Proof	6500.

Reduced size, 12mm

9a	Yr.7(1874)	.116	1500.	2500.	3250.	4500.
	Yr.9(1876)	138 pcs.	4500.	7500.	12,000.	16,000.
	Yr.10(1877)	7.246	6500.	12,500.	22,000.	32,000.

Y#	Date	Mintage	Fine	VF	XF	Unc
9a	Yr.13(1880)	112 pcs.	9500.	17,500.	26,000.	36,000.
	Yr.25(1892)	(none struck for circulation)

26.9568 g, .900 SILVER, .7800 oz ASW

Meiji

5	Yr.3(1870) Type 1	3.685	100.00	250.00	350.00	650.00
5.1	Yr.3(1870) Type 2	Inc.Ab.	125.00	300.00	400.00	725.00
5.2	Yr.3(1870) Type 3	Inc. Ab.	450.00	650.00	850.00	2000.

Type I, 38.6mm
Spiral on pearl held by dragon curls in counter clock wise direction from center.

| A25 | Yr.7(1874) | .942 | 350.00 | 650.00 | 1250. | 5000. |

Spiral on pearl curls clockwise from center.

A25.1	Yr.7(1874)	I.A.	300.00	600.00	1200.	2750.
	Yr.8(1875)	.139	2000.	3000.	5000.	11,500.
	Yr.11(1878)	.856	150.00	350.00	750.00	1500.
	Yr.12(1879)	1.913	750.00	1200.	2000.	4250.
	Yr.13(1880)	5.427	50.00	125.00	200.00	550.00
	Yr.14(1881)	2.927	75.00	150.00	225.00	600.00
	Yr.15(1882)	5.089	45.00	75.00	150.00	400.00
	Yr.16(1883)	3.636	45.00	75.00	150.00	450.00
	Yr.17(1884)	3.599	60.00	125.00	200.00	550.00
	Yr.18(1885)	4.296	45.00	75.00	150.00	400.00
	Yr.19(1886)	9.084	45.00	75.00	150.00	550.00
	Yr.20(1887)	8.275	85.00	150.00	325.00	750.00

NOTE: Two varieties of year 7 exist. Year 11 has varieties in the bottom leaf on reverse. Year 19 edge has 198 reeds.

Type II: Reduced size, 38.1mm.

A25.2	Yr.19(1886)	I.A.	500.00	800.00	1200.	2500.
	Yr.20(1887)	I.A.	50.00	100.00	200.00	550.00
	Yr.21(1888)	9.477	25.00	50.00	75.00	200.00
	Yr.22(1889)	9.295	25.00	45.00	65.00	185.00
	Yr.23(1890)	7.292	25.00	45.00	65.00	175.00
	Yr.24(1891)	7.518	15.00	30.00	50.00	150.00
	Yr.25(1892) flame extends between fourth and fifth spine
		11.187	100.00	200.00	400.00	900.00

Y#	Date	Mintage	Fine	VF	XF	Unc
A25.2	Yr.25(1892) flame overlaps third spine of dragon
		I.A.	20.00	35.00	55.00	200.00
	Yr.26(1893)	10.403	20.00	35.00	55.00	200.00
	Yr.27(1894)	22.118	15.00	25.00	45.00	120.00
	Yr.28(1895)	21.098	15.00	25.00	45.00	120.00
	Yr.29(1896)	11.363	15.00	25.00	45.00	120.00
	Yr.30(1897)	2.448	15.00	30.00	50.00	135.00
	Yr.34(1901)	1.256	15.00	30.00	50.00	150.00
	Yr.35(1902)	.668	25.00	50.00	75.00	175.00
	Yr.36(1903)	5.131	15.00	27.50	42.50	110.00
	Yr.37(1904)	6.970	15.00	27.50	42.50	110.00
	Yr.38(1905)	5.031	15.00	27.50	42.50	120.00
	Yr.39(1906)	3.471	35.00	75.00	125.00	350.00
	Yr.41(1908)	.334	50.00	100.00	225.00	950.00
	Yr.45(1912)	5.000	12.50	25.00	42.50	110.00

NOTE: Year 19 is 38.3mm in diameter and the edge has 217 reeds.

Taisho

| 38 | Yr.3(1914) | 11.500 | 12.50 | 22.50 | 35.00 | 90.00 |

'GIN' COUNTERMARKS

c/m: *Gin* right on 1 Yen Meiji Year 3, (1870), Y#5.

c/m: *Gin* left on 1 Yen, Meiji Years 7-30, (1874-1897), Y#A25.

In 1897 Japan demonetized the silver one Yen and Trade Dollar coins, and many were melted to provide bullion from which to produce subsidiary coins. However, some 20 million Trade Dollars and one Yen coins were countermarked with the character *Gin* (meaning silver) and shipped to Taiwan, Korea and Southern Manchuria for use in circulation there. The countermark was applied to indicate that the coin was to be treated simply as bullion and to prevent the coins from returning to Japan where they could be sold to the government for gold.

The actual countermarking was done by the Tokyo and Osaka Mints; the Osaka Mint putting its *Gin* on the left side, the Tokyo Mint putting its *Gin* on the right side. Only 2,100,000 coins were countermarked at the Tokyo Mint as opposed to 18,350,000 countermarked at Osaka, making the Tokyo pieces scarcer than the Osaka pieces.

Formerly *Gin* marked coins were regarded as damaged and sold for about 80 per cent of the price of the same coin without countermark. Now, however, the *Gin* coins are being collected by date and placement of the mark, and some sell for more than a non-countermarked piece.

Mint: Osaka

JAPAN 1124

c/m: *Gin* left on 1 Yen, Y#5.

Y#	Date	Mintage	VG	Fine	VF	XF
28	Yr.3(1870)	—	125.00	250.00	350.00	600.00

Type I, 38.6mm
c/m: *Gin* left on 1 Yen, Y#A25.
Counterclockwise spiral on pearl.

Y#	Date	Mintage	VG	Fine	VF	XF
28a	Yr.7(1874)	—	250.00	400.00	800.00	1200.

Clockwise spiral on pearl.

Y#	Date	Mintage	VG	Fine	VF	XF
28a.1	Yr.7(1874)	—	200.00	350.00	700.00	1000.
	Yr.8(1875)	—	900.00	2000.	3200.	5200.
	Yr.11(1878)	—	100.00	200.00	400.00	720.00
	Yr.12(1879)	—	350.00	750.00	1200.	2000.
	Yr.13(1880)	—	30.00	60.00	120.00	200.00
	Yr.14(1881)	—	35.00	75.00	150.00	225.00
	Yr.15(1882)	—	15.00	35.00	75.00	135.00
	Yr.16(1883)	—	20.00	40.00	80.00	140.00
	Yr.17(1884)	—	35.00	75.00	150.00	225.00
	Yr.18(1885)	—	15.00	35.00	75.00	135.00
	Yr.19(1886)	—	20.00	40.00	80.00	140.00
	Yr.20(1887)	—	40.00	85.00	150.00	325.00

Type II, 38.1mm

Y#	Date	Mintage	VG	Fine	VF	XF
28a.2	Yr.19(1886)	—	300.00	500.00	800.00	1200.
	Yr.20(1887)	—	30.00	50.00	100.00	175.00
	Yr.21(1888)	—	12.00	25.00	45.00	75.00
	Yr.22(1889)	—	10.00	20.00	40.00	65.00
	Yr.23(1890)	—	10.00	20.00	40.00	65.00
	Yr.24(1891)	—	8.00	15.00	35.00	60.00
	Yr.25(1892) early variety		50.00	100.00	200.00	350.00
	Yr.25(1892) late variety		10.00	20.00	40.00	60.00
	Yr.26(1893)	—	10.00	20.00	40.00	60.00
	Yr.27(1894)	—	7.50	15.00	30.00	50.00
	Yr.28(1895)	—	7.50	15.00	30.00	50.00
	Yr.29(1896)	—	7.50	15.00	30.00	50.00
	Yr.30(1897)	—	10.00	20.00	40.00	60.00

Mint: Tokyo
c/m: *Gin* right on 1 Yen, Y#5.

Y#	Date	Mintage	VG	Fine	VF	XF
28.1	YR.3(1870)	—	125.00	250.00	350.00	650.00

Type I, 38.6mm
c/m: *Gin* right on 1 Yen, Y#A25.
Counterclockwise spiral on pearl.

Y#	Date	Mintage	VG	Fine	VF	XF
28a.3	Yr.7(1874)	—	250.00	400.00	800.00	1250.

Clockwise spiral on pearl.

Y#	Date	Mintage	VG	Fine	VF	XF
28a.4	Yr.7(1874)	—	200.00	350.00	750.00	1100.
	Yr.8(1875)	—	1000.	2200.	3250.	5400.
	Yr.11(1878)	—	100.00	200.00	350.00	750.00
	Yr.12(1879)	—	350.00	750.00	1250.	2000.
	Yr.13(1880)	—	30.00	60.00	125.00	200.00
	Yr.14(1881)	—	40.00	80.00	150.00	225.00
	Yr.15(1882)	—	20.00	40.00	75.00	145.00
	Yr.16(1883)	—	25.00	45.00	80.00	150.00
	Yr.17(1884)	—	35.00	75.00	150.00	225.00
	Yr.18(1885)	—	20.00	40.00	75.00	145.00
	Yr.19(1886)	—	25.00	45.00	80.00	150.00
	Yr.20(1887)	—	45.00	90.00	175.00	350.00

Type II, 38.1mm

Y#	Date	Mintage	VG	Fine	VF	XF
28a.5	Yr.19(1886)	—	350.00	550.00	850.00	1250.
	Yr.20(1887)	—	35.00	55.00	115.00	185.00
	Yr.21(1888)	—	15.00	30.00	50.00	85.00
	Yr.22(1889)	—	10.00	20.00	40.00	65.00
	Yr.23(1890)	—	10.00	20.00	40.00	65.00
	Yr.24(1891)	—	8.00	15.00	35.00	60.00
	Yr.25(1892) early variety		50.00	100.00	200.00	400.00
	Yr.25(1892) late variety		10.00	20.00	40.00	60.00
	Yr.26(1893)	—	10.00	20.00	40.00	60.00
	Yr.27(1894)	—	7.50	15.00	30.00	50.00
	Yr.28(1895)	—	7.50	15.00	30.00	50.00
	Yr.29(1896)	—	7.50	15.00	30.00	50.00
	Yr.30(1897)	—	10.00	20.00	40.00	60.00

REGULAR COINAGE
YEN

BRASS

Y#	Year	Date	Mintage	VF	XF	Unc
70	Showa					
	23	(1948)	451.209	.25	.50	2.00
	24	(1949)	Inc. Ab.	.15	.35	1.25
	25	(1950)	Inc. Ab.	.15	.35	1.25

ALUMINUM

Y#		Date	Mintage	VF	XF	Unc
74	30	(1955)	381.700	—	—	.10
	31	(1956)	500.900	—	—	.10

Y#	Year	Date	Mintage	VF	XF	Unc
74	32	(1957)	492.000	—	—	.10
	33	(1958)	374.900	—	—	.10
	34	(1959)	208.600	—	—	.10
	35	(1960)	300.000	—	—	.10
	36	(1961)	432.400	—	—	.10
	37	(1962)	572.000	—	—	.10
	38	(1963)	788.700	—	—	.10
	39	(1964) 1665.100	—	—	.10
	40	(1965) 1743.256	—	—	.10
	41	(1966)	807.344	—	—	.10
	42	(1967)	220.600	—	—	.10
	44	(1969)	184.700	—	—	.10
	45	(1970)	556.400	—	—	.10
	46	(1971)	904.950	—	—	.10
	47	(1972) 1274.950	—	—	.10
	48	(1973) 1470.000	—	—	.10
	49	(1974) 1750.000	—	—	.10
	50	(1975) 1656.150	—	—	.10
	51	(1976)	928.800	—	—	.10
	52	(1977)	895.000	—	—	.10
	53	(1978)	864.000	—	—	.10
	54	(1979) 1015.000	—	—	.10
	55	(1980) 1145.000	—	—	.10
	56	(1981) 1206.000	—	—	.10
	57	(1982) 1017.000	—	—	.10
	58	(1983) 1086.000	—	—	.10
	59	(1984)	981.850	—	—	.10
	60	(1985)	837.150	—	—	.10
	61	(1986)	417.960	—	—	.10
	62	(1987)	955.775	—	—	.10
	62	(1987)	—	—	Proof	1.50
	63	(1988)	—	—	—	.10
	64	(1989)	—	—	—	—

Obv: Large 1 on wide ring in center, date below.
Rev: Small tree.

Y#	Date	Mintage	Fine	VF	XF	Unc
	Heisei					
95	1	(1989)	—	—	—	—

2 YEN

3.3333 g, .900 GOLD, 17.48mm, .0964 oz AGW
Meiji

10	Yr.3(1870)	.883	850.00	1000.	1200.	2000.
	Yr.3(1870)	—	—	Proof	9500.	

Reduced size 16.96mm, same weight

10a	Yr.7(1874)	—	Reported, not confirmed			
	Yr.9(1876) 178 pcs.	—	30,000.	48,000.	64,000.
	Yr.10(1877) 39 pcs.	—	30,000.	48,000.	64,000.
	Yr.13(1880) 87 pcs.	—	30,000.	48,000.	64,000.

5 YEN

8.3333 g, .900 GOLD, 23.8mm, .2411 oz AGW

11	Yr.3(1870)	.273	1250.	1750.	2500.	3500.
	Yr.4(1871)	I.A.	1250.	1650.	2400.	3400.
	Yr.4(1871)	—	—	Proof	10,000.	

Reduced size, 21.8mm, same weight

11a	Yr.5(1872)	1.057	1000.	1250.	1650.	2800.
	Yr.6(1873)	3.148	1000.	1250.	1650.	2800.
	Yr.7(1874)	.728	1500.	1800.	2500.	4000.
	Yr.8(1875)	.181	1750.	2000.	2500.	4000.
	Yr.9(1876)	.146	1850.	2100.	2850.	4000.
	Yr.10(1877)	.136	1900.	2200.	3000.	4750.
	Yr.11(1878)	.101	1900.	2200.	3000.	4750.
	Yr.13(1880)	.078	1900.	2200.	3000.	4750.
	Yr.14(1881)	.149	1900.	2200.	3000.	4750.
	Yr.15(1882)	.113	1900.	2200.	3000.	4750.
	Yr.16(1883)	.108	1900.	2200.	3000.	4750.

Y#	Date	Mintage	Fine	VF	XF	Unc
11a	Yr.17(1884)	.113	1900.	2200.	3000.	4750.
	Yr.18(1885)	.200	1900.	2200.	3000.	4750.
	Yr.19(1886)	.179	1900.	2200.	3000.	4750.
	Yr.20(1887)	.179	1900.	2200.	3000.	4750.
	Yr.21(1888)	.165	1900.	2200.	3000.	4750.
	Yr.22(1889)	.353	1900.	2200.	3000.	4750.
	Yr.23(1890)	.238	1900.	2200.	3000.	4750.
	Yr.24(1891)	.216	1900.	2200.	3000.	4750.
	Yr.25(1892)	.263	1900.	2200.	3000.	4750.
	Yr.26(1893)	.260	1900.	2200.	3000.	4750.
	Yr.27(1894)	.314	1900.	2200.	3000.	4750.
	Yr.28(1895)	.320	1900.	2200.	3000.	4750.
	Yr.29(1896)	.224	1900.	2200.	3000.	4750.
	Yr.30(1897)	.107	1900.	2200.	3000.	4750.

4.1666 g, .900 GOLD, .1205 oz AGW

32	Yr.30(1897)	.111	850.00	950.00	1200.	2100.
	Yr.31(1898)	.055	850.00	950.00	1200.	2100.
	Yr.36(1903)	.021	900.00	1000.	1300.	2300.
	Yr.44(1911)	.059	900.00	1000.	1300.	2200.
	Yr.45(1912)	.059	850.00	1000.	1300.	2200.

Taisho

| 39 | Yr.2(1913) | .040 | 950.00 | 1250. | 1550. | 2550. |
| | Yr.13(1924) | .076 | 850.00 | 1150. | 1450. | 2450. |

Showa

| 51 | Yr.5(1930) | .852 | 10,000. | 20,000. | 40,000. | 52,000. |

BRASS

Y#	Year	Date	Mintage	VF	XF	Unc
71	23	(1948)	74.520	.50	.75	12.50
	24	(1949)	179.692	.15	.40	8.00

Old script

72	24	(1949)	111.896	.15	.25	9.00
	25	(1950)	181.824	.15	.25	6.50
	26	(1951)	197.980	.15	.25	6.50
	27	(1952)	55.000	.30	.60	15.00
	28	(1953)	45.000	.30	.60	6.50
	32	(1957)	10.000	4.00	8.00	15.00
	33	(1958)	50.000	.25	.50	3.50

New script

72a	34	(1959)	33.000	.25	.50	3.00
	35	(1960)	34.800	.20	.40	3.00
	36	(1961)	61.000	.15	.35	2.50
	37	(1962)	126.700	.10	.30	1.50
	38	(1963)	171.800	.10	.30	1.50
	39	(1964)	379.700	.10	.30	1.50
	40	(1965)	384.200	.10	.30	1.50
	41	(1966)	163.100	.10	.30	1.50
	42	(1967)	26.000	.25	.50	1.50
	43	(1968)	114.000	—	.10	.15
	44	(1969)	240.000	—	.10	.15
	45	(1970)	340.000	—	.10	.15
	46	(1971)	362.050	—	.10	.15
	47	(1972)	562.950	—	.10	.15
	48	(1973)	745.000	—	.10	.15
	49	(1974)	950.000	—	.10	.15
	50	(1975)	970.000	—	.10	.15
	51	(1976)	200.000	—	.10	.15
	52	(1977)	340.000	—	.10	.15
	53	(1978)	318.000	—	.10	.15
	54	(1979)	317.000	—	.10	.15
	55	(1980)	385.000	—	.10	.15
	56	(1981)	95.000	—	.10	.15
	57	(1982)	455.000	—	.10	.15

Y#	Year	Date	Mintage	VF	XF	Unc
72a	58	(1983)	410.000	—	.10	.15
	59	(1984)	202.850	—	.10	.15
	60	(1985)	153.150	—	.10	.15
	61	(1986)	113.960	—	.10	.15
	62	(1987)	631.775	—	.10	.15
	62	(1987)	Inc.Ab.	—	Proof	1.75
	63	(1988)	—	—	—	.15
	64	(1989)	—	—	—	.15

Obv: Inscription and date separated by seed leaf.
Rev: Gear around hole, rice stalk above denomination.
Heisei

| 96 | 1 | (1989) | — | — | — | — |

10 YEN

16.6666 g, .900 GOLD, .4823 oz AGW

Y#	Date	Mintage	Fine	VF	XF	Unc
	Meiji					
12	Yr.4(1871)	1.867	3000.	4000.	5400.	8000.
	Yr.4(1871)	—	—	—	Proof	35,000.

Modified design

12a	Yr.9(1876)	1,925	15,000.	25,000.	54,000.	70,000.
	Yr.10(1877)	36 pcs.	20,000.	30,000.	70,000.	85,000.
	Yr.13(1880)	136 pcs.	20,000.	30,000.	70,000.	85,000.
	Yr.25(1892)		(none struck for circulation)			

8.3333 g, .900 GOLD, .2411 oz AGW

33	Yr.30(1897)	2.422	500.00	750.00	1100.	1600.
	Yr.31(1898)	3.176	500.00	750.00	1100.	1600.
	Yr.32(1899)	1.743	500.00	750.00	1100.	1600.
	Yr.33(1900)	1.114	500.00	750.00	1100.	1600.
	Yr.34(1901)	1.654	500.00	800.00	1100.	1600.
	Yr.35(1902)	3.023	500.00	750.00	1100.	1650.
	Yr.36(1903)	2.902	500.00	750.00	1100.	1650.
	Yr.37(1904)	.724	500.00	800.00	1250.	2100
	Yr.40(1907)	.157	500.00	800.00	1250.	2100.
	Yr.41(1908)	1.160	500.00	750.00	1100.	1650.
	Yr.42(1909)	2.165	450.00	850.00	1000.	1600.
	Yr.43(1910)	8,982	5000.	8500.	13,500.	18,000.

BRONZE
Reeded edge

Y#	Year	Date	Mintage	VF	XF	Unc
	Showa					
73	26	(1951)	101.068	.15	.35	45.00
	27	(1952)	486.632	.15	.35	35.00
	28	(1953)	466.300	.15	.35	35.00
	29	(1954)	520.900	.15	.35	45.00
	30	(1955)	123.100	.15	.35	20.00
	32	(1957)	50.000	.25	.65	35.00
	33	(1958)	25.000	.40	1.00	45.00

Plain edge

| 73a | 34 | (1959) | 62.400 | — | .15 | 9.00 |
| | 35 | (1960) | 225.900 | — | .15 | 1.25 |

Y#	Year	Date	Mintage	VF	XF	Unc
73a	36	(1961)	229.900	—	.15	1.25
	37	(1962)	284.200	—	.15	1.25
	38	(1963)	411.300	—	.15	.60
	39	(1964)	479.200	—	.15	.60
	40	(1965)	387.600	—	.15	.60
	41	(1966)	395.900	—	.15	.60
	42	(1967)	158.900	—	.15	.60
	43	(1968)	363.600	—	.15	.30
	44	(1969)	414.800	—	.15	.30
	45	(1970)	382.700	—	.15	.30
	46	(1971)	610.050	—	.15	.30
	47	(1972)	634.950	—	.15	.30
	48	(1973)	1345.000	—	.15	.20
	49	(1974)	1780.000	—	.15	.20
	50	(1975)	1280.260	—	.15	.20
	51	(1976)	1369.740	—	.15	.20
	52	(1977)	1467.000	—	.15	.20
	53	(1978)	1435.000	—	.15	.20
	54	(1979)	1207.000	—	.15	.20
	55	(1980)	1127.000	—	.15	.20
	56	(1981)	1369.000	—	.15	.20
	57	(1982)	890.000	—	.15	.20
	58	(1983)	870.000	—	.15	.20
	59	(1984)	533.850	—	.15	.20
	60	(1985)	335.150	—	.15	.20
	61	(1986)	689.600	—	.15	.20
	62	(1987)	165.775	—	.15	.20
	62	(1987)	Inc. Ab.	—	Proof	1.75
	63	(1988)	—	—	—	.20
	64	(1989)	—	—	—	.20

Obv: Numeral 10 and date in laurel wreath.
Rev: Ancient phoenix temple Hoo-do surrounded by arabesque pattern.
Heisei

| 97 | 1 | (1989) | — | — | — | — |

20 YEN

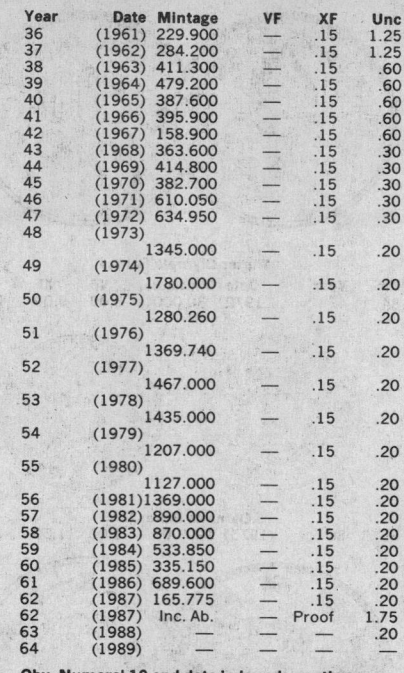

33.3332 g, .900 GOLD, .9646 oz AGW

Y#	Date	Mintage	Fine	VF	XF	Unc
	Meiji					
13	Yr.3(1870)	.046	10,000.	16,500.	30,000.	45,000.
	Yr.3(1870)	—	—	—	Proof	57,500.
	Yr.9(1876)	954 pcs.	12,500.	21,500.	44,500.	65,000.
	Yr.10(1877)	29 pcs.	18,000.	38,000.	78,000	110,000.
	Yr.13(1880)	103 pcs.	16,500.	35,000.	74,000	100,000.
	Yr.25(1892)	—	(none struck for circulation)			

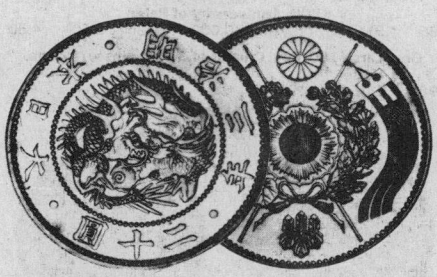

16.6666 g, .900 GOLD, .4823 oz AGW

34	Yr.30(1897)	1.861	600.00	1400.	2100.	3200.
	Yr.36(1903)	—	—	—	Rare	
	Yr.37(1904)	2.759	600.00	1400.	2100.	3200.
	Yr.38(1905)	1.045	600.00	1400.	2100.	3200.
	Yr.39(1906)	1.331	700.00	1500.	2250.	3350.
	Yr.40(1907)	.817	700.00	1500.	2250.	3350.
	Yr.41(1908)	.458	1000.	1500.	2250.	3800.
	Yr.42(1909)	.557	1000.	1500.	2250.	3800.
	Yr.43(1910)	2.163	700.00	1400.	2100.	3200.
	Yr.44(1911)	1.470	600.00	1400.	2100.	3200.
	Yr.45(1912)	1.272	600.00	1400.	2100.	3200.

Y#	Date	Mintage	Fine	VF	XF	Unc
	Taisho					
40	Yr.1(1912)	.177	750.00	1500.	2200.	3500.
	Yr.2(1913)	.869	700.00	1400.	2100.	3100.
	Yr.3(1914)	1.042	700.00	1400.	2100.	3100.
	Yr.4(1915)	1.509	700.00	1400.	2100.	3100.
	Yr.5(1916)	2.376	700.00	1400.	2100.	3100.
	Yr.6(1917)	6.208	600.00	1500.	2000.	2850.
	Yr.7(1918)	3.118	700.00	1400.	2100.	3100.
	Yr.8(1919)	1.531	700.00	1400.	2100.	3100.
	Yr.9(1920)	.370	700.00	1400.	2100.	3250.

Showa

52	Yr.5(1930)	11.055	10,000.	15,000.	30,000.	38,500.
	Yr.6(1931)	7.526	13,000.	17,500.	32,000.	40,000.
	Yr.7(1932)	—	—	—	Rare	

50 YEN

NICKEL

Y#	Year	Date	Mintage	VF	XF	Unc
	Showa					
75	30	(1955)	63.700	.50	1.00	17.50
	31	(1956)	91.300	.50	.75	17.50
	32	(1957)	39.000	.50	1.25	17.50
	33	(1958)	18.000	1.00	2.50	30.00

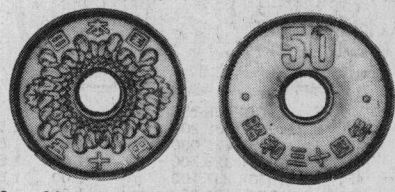

76	34	(1959)	23.900	1.00	2.50	15.00
	35	(1960)	6.000	12.50	22.50	32.50
	36	(1961)	16.000	2.00	4.00	17.50
	37	(1962)	50.300	.50	1.00	5.00
	38	(1963)	55.000	.50	1.00	5.00
	39	(1964)	69.200	.50	1.00	4.00
	40	(1965)	189.300	.50	.75	2.50
	41	(1966)	171.500	.50	1.00	2.50

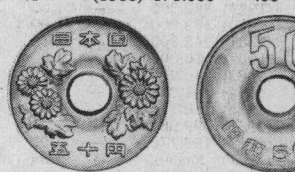

COPPER-NICKEL

81	42	(1967)	238.400	—	.50	.65
	43	(1968)	200.000	—	.50	.65
	44	(1969)	210.900	—	.50	.65
	45	(1970)	269.800	—	.50	.65
	46	(1971)	80.950	—	.50	.65
	47	(1972)	138.980	—	.50	.65
	48	(1973)	200.970	—	.50	.65
	49	(1974)	470.000	—	.50	.65
	50	(1975)	238.120	—	.50	.65
	51	(1976)	241.880	—	.50	.65
	52	(1977)	176.000	—	.50	.65
	53	(1978)	234.000	—	.50	.65
	54	(1979)	110.000	—	.50	.65
	55	(1980)	51.000	—	.50	.65
	56	(1981)	179.000	—	.50	.65
	57	(1982)	30.000	—	.50	.65
	58	(1983)	30.000	—	.50	.65
	59	(1984)	29.850	—	.50	.65

JAPAN 1126

Y#	Year	Date	Mintage	VF	XF	Unc
81	60	(1985)	10.150	—	.50	.65
	61	(1986)	9.960	—	.50	.65
	62	(1987)	.775	—	—	70.00
	62	(1987)	Inc. Ab.	—	Proof	75.00
	63	(1988)	—	—	—	.65

100 YEN

4.8000 g, .600 SILVER .0926 oz ASW

Showa
Y#	Year	Date	Mintage	VF	XF	Unc
77	32	(1957)	30.000	1.00	2.00	9.00
	33	(1958)	70.000	1.00	2.00	6.00

78	34	(1959)	110.000	1.00	2.00	9.00
	35	(1960)	50.000	1.00	2.00	9.00
	36	(1961)	15.000	1.00	2.00	9.00
	38	(1963)	45.000	1.00	2.00	6.00
	39	(1964)	10.000	1.25	3.50	6.00
	40	(1965)	62.500	1.00	2.00	3.75
	41	(1966)	97.500	1.00	2.00	3.75

1964 Olympic Games

79	39	1964	80.000	1.00	2.00	3.50

COPPER-NICKEL

82	42	(1967)	432.200	—	1.00	1.50
	43	(1968)	471.000	—	1.00	1.50
	44	(1969)	323.700	—	1.00	1.50
	45	(1970)	237.100	—	1.00	1.50
	46	(1971)	481.050	—	1.00	1.50
	47	(1972)	468.950	—	1.00	1.50
	48	(1973)	680.000	—	1.00	1.50
	49	(1974)	660.000	—	1.00	1.50
	50	(1975)	437.160	—	1.00	1.50
	51	(1976)	322.840	—	1.00	1.50
	52	(1977)	440.000	—	1.00	1.50
	53	(1978)	292.000	—	1.00	1.50
	54	(1979)	382.000	—	1.00	1.50
	55	(1980)	588.000	—	1.00	1.50
	56	(1981)	348.000	—	1.00	1.50
	57	(1982)	110.000	—	1.00	1.50
	58	(1983)	50.000	—	1.00	1.50
	59	(1984)	41.850	—	1.00	1.50
	60	(1985)	58.150	—	1.00	1.50
	61	(1986)	99.960	—	1.00	1.50
	62	(1987)	193.775	—	1.00	1.50
	62	(1987)	Inc. Ab.	—	Proof	5.00
	63	(1988)	—	—	—	1.50
	64	(1989)	—	—	—	—

NOTE: Varieties exist for Yr.42.

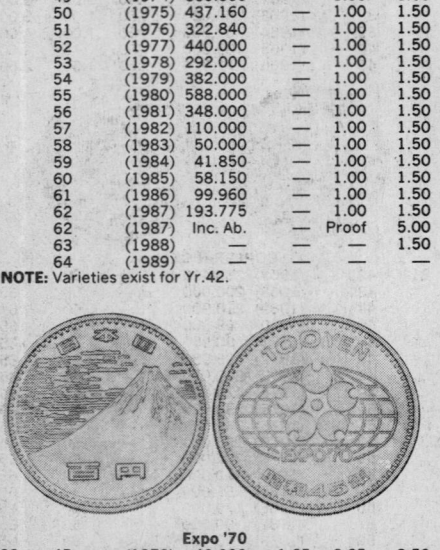

Expo '70

83	45	(1970)	40.000	1.25	2.25	3.50

Winter Olympic Games

Y#	Year	Date	Mintage	VF	XF	Unc
84	47	1972	30.000	3.00	5.00	7.50

Okinawa Expo '75

85	50	(1975)	120.000	1.00	1.50	2.00

50th Anniversary of Reign

86	51	(1976)	70.000	1.25	2.50	4.50

Obv: Large 100. Rev: Cluster of 3 blossoms w/foliage.

	Heisei					
98	1	(1989)	—	—	—	—

500 YEN

COPPER-NICKEL

Showa
87	57	(1982)	300.000	—	4.50	5.50
	58	(1983)	240.000	—	4.50	5.50
	59	(1984)	342.850	—	4.50	5.50
	60	(1985)	97.150	—	4.50	5.50
	61	(1986)	49.960	—	4.25	5.00
	62	(1987)	2.775	5.00	7.00	10.00
	62	(1987)	Inc. Ab.	—	Proof	25.00
	63	(1988)	—	—	—	5.00
	64	(1989)	—	—	—	—

1985 Tsukuba Expo

88	60	(1985)	70.000	—	4.50	6.00

100th Anniversary of Governmental Cabinet System

89	60	(1985)	70.000	—	4.50	6.00

60 Years of Reign of Hirohito

Y#	Year	Date	Mintage	VF	XF	Unc
90	61	(1986)	50.000	—	4.50	6.00
	61	(1986)	Inc. Ab.	—	Proof	—

Opening of Seikan Tunnel

93	63	(1988)	20.000	—	—	8.00

Opening of Seto Bridge

94	63	(1988)	20.000	—	—	8.00

Obv: Large 500, Japanese characters below.
Rev: Spray of flowers.

	Heisei					
99	1	(1989)	—	—	—	—

1000 YEN

20.0000 g, .925 SILVER, .5948 oz ASW
1964 Olympic Games

Showa
80	39	1964	15.000	25.00	35.00	70.00

10000 YEN

20.0000 g, .999 SILVER, .6430 oz ASW
60 Years of Reign of Hirohito

91	61	(1986)	10.000	—	—	100.00
	61	(1986)	Inc. Ab.	—	Proof	120.00

100000 YEN

20.0000 g, .999 GOLD, .6430 oz AGW
60 Years of Reign of Hirohito

Y#	Year	Date	Mintage	VF	XF	Unc
92	61	(1986)	10.000	—	—	900.00
	61	(1986)	Inc. Ab.	—	Proof	1450.
	62	(1987)	—	—	—	900.00
	62	(1987)	—	—	Proof	1450.

OCCUPATION COINAGE

The following issues were struck at the Osaka Mint for use in the Netherlands East Indies. The only inscription found on them is *Dai Nippon:* (Great Japan). The war situation had worsened to the point that shipping the coins became virtually impossible. Consequently, none of these coins were issued in the East Indies and almost the entire issue was lost or were remelted at the mint. Y#'s are for the Netherlands Indies and dates are from the Japanese Shinto dynastic calendar.

SEN

ALUMINUM

Y#	Date	Year	Mintage	VF	XF	Unc
22	2603	1943	233.190	75.00	100.00	150.00
	2604	1944	66.810	65.00	90.00	125.00

10 SEN

TIN ALLOY

24	2603	1943	69.490	25.00	50.00	100.00
	2604	1944	110.510	20.00	40.00	75.00

TRADE COINAGE
TRADE DOLLAR

27.2200 g, .900 SILVER, .7876 oz ASW

Y#	Date	Mintage	Fine	VF	XF	Unc
14	Meiji					
	Yr.8(1875)	.097	300.00	600.00	900.00	1750.
	Yr.9(1876)	1.514	300.00	600.00	900.00	1750.
	Yr.10(1877)	1.125	300.00	600.00	900.00	1800.

'GIN' COUNTERMARKS

Mint: Osaka
c/m: *Gin* left on Trade Dollar, Y#14.

Y#	Date	Mintage	VG	Fine	VF	XF
28b.1	Yr.8(1875)	—	150.00	300.00	500.00	700.00
	Yr.9(1876)	—	150.00	300.00	500.00	700.00
	Yr.10(1877)	—	150.00	300.00	500.00	750.00

Mint: Tokyo
c/m: *Gin* right on Trade Dollar, Y#14.

28b.2	Yr.8(1875)	—	175.00	350.00	550.00	750.00
	Yr.9(1876)	—	175.00	350.00	550.00	750.00
	Yr.10(1877)	—	175.00	350.00	550.00	800.00

MINT SETS (MS)

KM#	Date	Mintage	Identification	Issue Price	Mkt. Val.
MS1	1969(5)	6,162	Y72A,73A,74,81,82	1.25	250.00
MS2	1970(6)	26,000	Y72a,73A,74,81,82,83	2.00	45.00
MS3	1971(5)	14,653	Y72a,73a,74,81,82	1.60	75.00
MS4	1972(6)	30,000	Y72a,73a,74,81,82,84	2.90	42.50
MS5	1975(5)	720,000	Y72a,73a,74,81,82	2.30	6.00
MS6	1976(5)	580,000	Y72a,73a,74,81,82	2.80	6.00
MS7	1977(5)	520,000	Y72a,73a,74,81,82	3.00	7.50
MS8	1978(5)	488,000	Y72a,73a,74,81,82	3.50	7.50
MS9	1979(5)	400,000	Y72a,73a,74,81,82	3.80	9.00
MS10	1980(5)	520,000	Y72a,73a,74,81,82	3.20	8.00
MS11	1981(5)	568,000	Y72a,73a,74,81,82	4.00	7.50
MS12	1982(6)	632,000	Y72a,73a,74,81,82,87	6.80	9.00
MS13	1983(6)	502,000	Y72a,73a,74,81,82,87	6.80	25.00
MS14	1984(6)	520,000	Y72a,73a,74,81,82,87	7.40	25.00
MS15	1985(7)	820,000	Y72a-73a,74,81-82,87-88	8.50	20.00
MS16	1985(7)	746,000	Y72a-73a,74,81-82,87,89	10.50	20.00
MS17	1986(7)	642,000	Y72a-73a,74,81-82,87,90	15.00	20.00
MS18	1986(6)	517,000	Y72a-73a,74,81-82,87	9.20	12.00
MS19	1987(6)	540,000	Y72a-73a,74,81-82,87	12.00	100.00
MS20	1988(6)	—	Y72a-73a,74,81-82,87	12.40	15.00
MS21	1988(2)	—	Y93-94	15.20	65.00

PROOF SETS (PS)

PS1	1987(6)	230,000	Y72a-73a,74,81-82,87	37.40	130.00
PS2	1988(6)	—	Y72a-73a,74,81-82,87	—	75.00

PROVINCIAL COINAGE

AKITA

Capital city of Ugo Province (now Akita Prefecture) in northwest Honshu.

50 MON

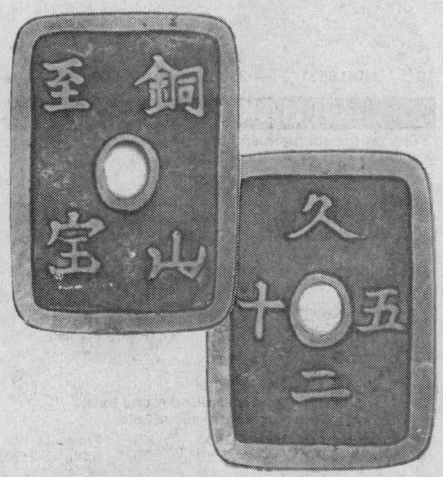

LEAD or COPPER-PLATED LEAD

KM#	Date	Mintage	Good	VG	Fine	VF
2	ND(1862)	—	50.00	80.00	120.00	150.00

100 MON

COPPER

KM#	Date	Mintage	Good	VG	Fine	VF
4	ND(1862)	—	50.00	75.00	100.00	125.00

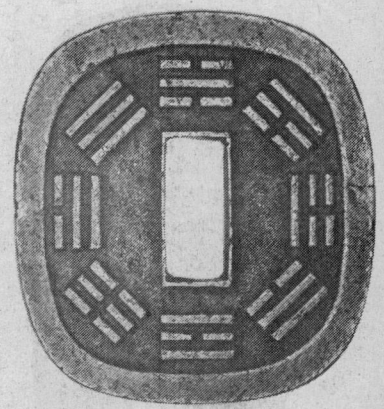

Obv: Short tail phoenix.

6.1	ND(1862)	—	25.00	40.00	55.00	75.00

Akita / JAPAN 1128

Obv: Long tail phoenix.

KM#	Date	Mintage	Good	VG	Fine	VF
6.2	ND(1862)	—	25.00	40.00	55.00	75.00

LEAD or COPPER-PLATED LEAD

| 8 | ND(1862) | — | 50.00 | 80.00 | 120.00 | 150.00 |

BU

SILVER

KM#	Date	Mintage	VG	Fine	VF	XF
9	ND	—	500.00	800.00	1150.	1500.

4 MOMME 6 FUN

SILVER

KM#	Date	Mintage	VG	Fine	VF	XF
10	ND(1863)	—	100.00	150.00	225.00	325.00

9 MOMME 2 FUN

SILVER

| 12 | ND(1863) | — | 250.00 | 400.00 | 550.00 | 700.00 |

HAKODATE

City on the southern end of Hokkaido. One of the ports opened by Perry's Treaty of 1854.

MON

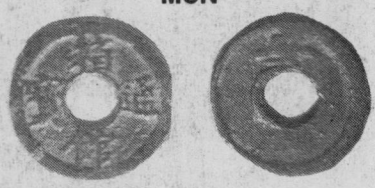

IRON
Obv: 4 characters around round hole.
Rev: 1 character above hole.

KM#	Date	Mintage	Good	VG	Fine	VF
20	ND(1856)	—	2.50	4.00	6.00	12.50

COPPER

| 20a | ND(1856) | — | — | — | 100.00 | 175.00 |

NOTE: KM#20a is the bosen or mother coin used in manufacturing KM#20.

HOSOKURA

A lead mining district in Rikuchu Province (now Iwate Prefecture) in northern Honshu.

100 MON

LEAD

KM#	Date	Mintage	Good	VG	Fine	VF
30	ND(1863)	—	125.00	175.00	250.00	375.00

KAGA

City and province (now Ishikawa Prefecture) on the Asian side of central Honshu.

NAN RYO

SILVER

KM#	Date	Mintage	VG	Fine	VF	XF
35	ND	—	750.00	1200.	1750.	2350.

MIMASAKA

Province in western Honshu, now part of Okayama Prefecture.

BU

SILVER

| 46 | ND | — | 750.00 | 1200. | 1750. | 2400. |

MORIOKA

Chief city of Rikuchu Province (now Iwate Prefecture) in northern Honshu.

Ryukyu Islands / JAPAN 1129

100 MON

COPPER

KM#	Date	Mintage	Good	VG	Fine	VF
50	ND	—	750.00	1250.	2000.	2750.

8 MOMME

SILVER

KM#	Date	Mintage	VG	Fine	VF	XF
52	(1868)	—	600.00	800.00	1200.	1600.

SENDAI
Chief city of Rikuzen Province (now part of Miyagi Prefecture) in northern Honshu.

MON

IRON
Rev: Blank.

KM#	Date	Mintage	Good	VG	Fine	VF
60	ND(1784)	—	6.00	8.00	12.00	17.50

COPPER

| 60a | ND(1784) | — | — | — | 100.00 | 150.00 |

NOTE: KM#60a is the *bosen* or mother coin used in making the sand molds for casting KM#60.

TAJIMA
Province, now part of Hyogo Prefecture, on the Asian side of western Honshu.

NAN RYO

SILVER

KM#	Date	Mintage	VG	Fine	VF	XF
65	ND	—	500.00	800.00	1200.	1600.

TOSA
Province encompassing most of the southern coast of Shikoku, now Kochi Prefecture.

100 MON
COPPER
Similar to 200 Mon, KM#72 but smaller.

KM#	Date	Mintage	Good	VG	Fine	VF
70	ND(1865)	—	—	—	Rare	—

200 MON

COPPER

| 72 | ND(1865) | — | — | — | Rare | — |

NOTE: A total of 8 types are reported for Tosa Province.

YONEZAWA
City in Uzen Province (now in Yamagata Prefecture) in north-central Honshu.

200 MON

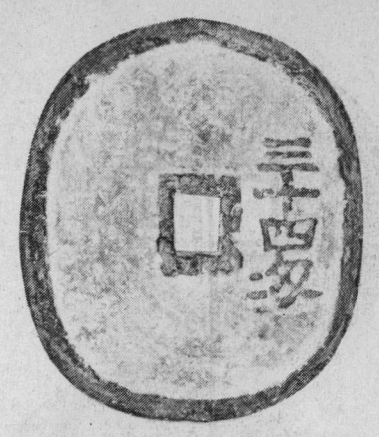

LEAD

KM#	Date	Mintage	Good	VG	Fine	VF
80	ND(1866)	—	80.00	125.00	175.00	250.00

| 82 | ND(1866) | — | 90.00 | 150.00 | 200.00 | 300.00 |

RYUKYU ISLANDS
OKINAWA
(Also called Liu-kiu and Loo-choo)

100 MON

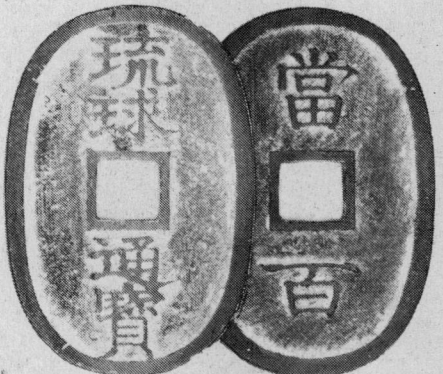

COPPER

C#	Date	Mintage	Good	VG	Fine	VF
100	ND(1862)	—	15.00	25.00	35.00	45.00

1/2 SHU

COPPER

C#	Date	Mintage	Good	VG	Fine	VF
115	ND(1862)	—	30.00	40.00	50.00	70.00

JERSEY

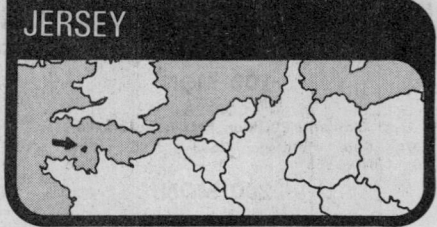

The Bailwick of Jersey, a British Crown dependency located in the English Channel 12 miles (19 km.) west of Normandy, France, has an area of 45 sq. mi. (117 sq. km.) and a population of 72,691. Capital: St. Helier. The economy is based on agriculture and cattle breeding-the importation of cattle is prohibited to protect the purity of the island's world- famous strain of milch cows.

Jersey was occupied by Neanderthal man 100,000 years B.C., and by Iberians of 2000 B.C. who left their chamber tombs in the island's granite cliffs. Roman legions almost certainly visited the island although they left no evidence of settlement. The country folk of Jersey still speak an archaic form of Norman-French, lingering evidence of the Norman annexation of the island in 933 A.D. Jersey was annexed to England in 1206, 140 years after the Norman Conquest. The dependency is administered by its own laws and customs; laws enacted by the British Parliament do not apply to Jersey unless it is specifically mentioned. During World War II, German troops occupied the island from July 1, 1940 until May 9, 1945.

Coins of pre-Roman Gaul and of Rome have been found in abundance on Jersey.

RULERS
British

MINT MARKS
H - Heaton, Birmingham

MONETARY SYSTEM
Until 1877
13 Pence (Jersey) = 1 Shilling
Commencing 1877
12 Pence = 1 Shilling
5 Shillings = 1 Crown
20 Shillings = 1 Pound
100 New Pence = 1 Pound

1/52 SHILLING

COPPER

KM#	Date	Mintage	Fine	VF	XF	Unc
1	1841	.116	10.00	30.00	80.00	150.00
	1841	—	—	—	Proof	500.00
	1861	—	—	—	Proof	1200.

BRONZE

| 1a | 1861 | — | — | — | Proof | Rare |

1/48 SHILLING

BRONZE

6	1877H	*.288	12.00	30.00	60.00	120.00
	1877H	—	—	—	Proof	200.00
	1877	—	—	—	Proof	200.00

*NOTE: Issue withdrawn except for 38,400 pieces.

1/26 SHILLING

COPPER

2	1841	.233	2.50	12.00	40.00	100.00
	1841	—	—	—	Proof	650.00
	1844	.233	3.00	8.00	40.00	100.00
	1851	.160	3.00	12.00	40.00	100.00
	1858	.173	3.00	12.00	40.00	100.00
	1858	—	—	—	Proof	650.00

KM#	Date	Mintage	Fine	VF	XF	Unc
2	1861	.173	3.00	12.00	40.00	100.00
	1861	—	—	—	Proof	650.00

BRONZE

4	1866	.173	1.00	6.00	30.00	50.00
	1866	—	—	—	Proof	275.00
	1870	.160	3.00	12.00	40.00	60.00
	1870	—	—	—	Proof	275.00
	1871	.160	2.00	10.00	35.00	55.00
	1871	—	—	—	Proof	275.00

1/24 SHILLING

BRONZE

7	1877H	.336	1.25	5.00	12.50	30.00
	1877H	—	—	—	Proof	200.00
	1877	—	—	—	Proof	225.00
	1888	.120	1.25	5.00	12.50	30.00
	1894	.120	1.25	5.00	12.50	30.00
	1894	—	—	—	Proof	400.00

| 9 | 1909 | .120 | 1.00 | 3.00 | 12.00 | 25.00 |

11	1911	.072	1.00	3.00	12.00	25.00
	1913	.072	1.00	3.00	12.00	25.00
	1923	.072	1.00	3.00	12.00	25.00

13	1923	.072	.75	4.00	6.00	22.50
	1923	—	—	—	Proof	550.00
	1926	.120	.75	3.00	5.00	20.00
	1926	—	—	—	Proof	550.00

15	1931	.072	.50	1.00	3.50	15.00
	1931	—	—	—	Proof	275.00
	1933	.072	.50	1.00	3.50	15.00
	1933	—	—	—	Proof	275.00
	1935	.072	.50	1.00	3.50	15.00
	1935	—	—	—	Proof	275.00

JERSEY 1131

KM#	Date	Mintage	Fine	VF	XF	Unc
17	1937	.072	.50	1.00	3.50	15.00
	1937	—	—	—	Proof	275.00
	1946	.072	.50	1.00	3.50	15.00
	1946	—	—	—	Proof	275.00
	1947	.072	.50	1.00	3.50	15.00
	1947	—	—	—	Proof	275.00

1/13 SHILLING

BRONZE

KM#	Date	Mintage	Fine	VF	XF	Unc
10	1909	.180	.50	3.00	15.00	45.00

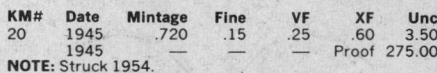

12	1911	.204	.25	1.50	7.00	25.00
	1913	.204	.25	1.50	7.00	25.00
	1923	.204	.25	1.50	7.00	25.00

KM#	Date	Mintage	Fine	VF	XF	Unc
20	1945	.720	.15	.25	.60	3.50
	1945	—	—	—	Proof	275.00

NOTE: Struck 1954.

COPPER

3	1841	.116	1.00	13.50	55.00	120.00
	1841	—	—	—	Proof	800.00
	1844	.027	3.00	20.00	65.00	145.00
	1844	—	—	—	Proof	800.00
	1851	.160	1.50	13.50	50.00	100.00
	1851	—	—	—	Proof	800.00
	1858	.173	1.50	13.50	50.00	100.00
	1858	—	—	—	Proof	600.00
	1861	.173	1.50	13.50	50.00	100.00
	1861	—	—	—	Proof	600.00
	1865	—	—	—	Proof	650.00

14	1923	.301	.25	1.50	7.00	20.00
	1926	.083	.50	2.50	10.00	30.00

21	1957	.720	.10	.15	.25	2.50
	1957	2,100	—	—	Proof	7.50
	1964	1,200	.10	.15	.25	1.00
	1964	.020	—	—	Proof	2.00

300th Anniversary of Accession of King Charles II

23	1960	1.200	.10	.15	.25	1.50
	1960	4,200	—	—	Proof	4.00

BRONZE

5	1866	.173	1.00	6.50	25.00	70.00
	1866	—	—	—	Proof	275.00
	1866 w/o LCW on bust					
		—	—	—	Proof	300.00
	1870	.160	1.00	6.50	25.00	70.00
	1870	—	—	—	Proof	275.00
	1871	.160	1.00	6.50	25.00	70.00
	1871	—	—	—	Proof	400.00

1/12 SHILLING

16	1931	.204	.25	1.00	3.50	12.00
	1931	—	—	—	Proof	275.00
	1933	.204	.25	1.00	3.50	12.00
	1933	—	—	—	Proof	275.00
	1935	.204	.25	1.00	3.50	12.00
	1935	—	—	—	Proof	275.00

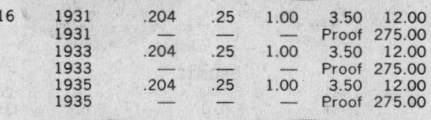

Mule. Obv: KM#20. Rev: KM#23.

24	1960	—	—	—	Proof	100.00

18	1937	.204	.25	.50	3.00	10.00
	1937	—	—	—	Proof	275.00
	1946	.204	.25	.50	3.00	10.00
	1946	—	—	—	Proof	275.00
	1947	.444	.15	.25	1.50	7.50
	1947	—	—	—	Proof	275.00

Norman Conquest

26	1966	1.200	.10	.15	.25	1.00
	1966	.030	—	—	Proof	2.00

1/4 SHILLING
(3 Pence)

BRONZE

8	1877H	.240	.50	3.00	15.00	40.00
	1877H	—	—	—	Proof	250.00
	1877	—	—	—	Proof	300.00
	1881	.075	1.00	7.00	27.50	60.00
	1888	.180	.50	3.00	15.00	40.00
	1894	.180	.50	3.00	15.00	40.00
	1894	—	—	—	Proof	400.00

NICKEL (OMS)

8a	1877-H	—	—	—	Proof	Rare
	1877	—	—	—	Proof	Rare

ALUMINUM (OMS)

8b	1877	—	—	—	Proof	Rare

Liberation Commemorative

19	1945	1.000	.15	.35	.75	5.00
	1945	—	—	—	Proof	275.00

NOTE: Struck between 1949-52.

NICKEL-BRASS

22	1957	2.000	.10	—	.50	3.00
	1957	6,300	—	—	Proof	7.50
	1960	4,200	—	—	Proof	8.50

JERSEY 1132

    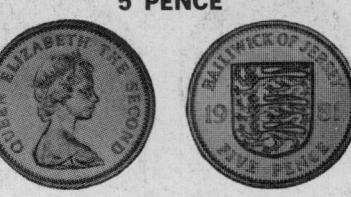

KM#	Date	Mintage	Fine	VF	XF	Unc
25	1964	1.200	.10	.15	.20	.75
	1964	.020	—	—	Proof	2.00

PENNY

BRONZE

KM#	Date	Mintage	VF	XF	Unc
46	1981	—	—	.10	.15
	1981	.010	—	Proof	1.10

5 PENCE

COPPER-NICKEL

KM#	Date	Mintage	VF	XF	Unc
48	1981	—	—	.10	.25
	1981	.101	—	Proof	1.80

54	1983	.050	—	.10	.25
	1984	—	—	.10	.25
	1985	—	—	.10	.25
	1986	—	—	.10	.25
	1987	—	—	.10	.25

4.2000 g, .925 SILVER, .1249 oz ASW
| 54a | 1983 | 5,000 | — | Proof | 5.00 |

56	1983	.150	—	.10	.25
	1984	—	—	.10	.25
	1985	—	—	.10	.25
	1986	—	—	.10	.25
	1987	—	In sets only	—

6.6000 g, .925 SILVER, .1963 oz ASW
| 56a | 1983 | 5,000 | — | Proof | 10.00 |

Norman Conquest

27	1966	1.200	.10	.15	.35	1.25
	1966	.030	—	—	Proof	2.00

5 SHILLINGS

2 NEW PENCE

BRONZE

31	1971	2.250	—	.10	.30
	1975	1.000	—	.10	.40
	1980	—	—	.10	.30
	1980	—	—	Proof	2.25

2 PENCE

10 NEW PENCE

COPPER-NICKEL

33	1968	.400	.20	.35	1.00
	1975	1.022	.20	.30	.90
	1980	—	.20	.30	.75
	1980	—	—	Proof	5.50

10 PENCE

COPPER-NICKEL
Norman Conquest
Obv: Similar to 1/4 Shilling, KM#12.

28	1966	.300	—	1.00	1.25	2.25
	1966	.030	—	—	Proof	5.00

DECIMAL COINAGE
100 New Pence = 1 Pound
Many of the following coins are also struck in silver, gold and platinum for collectors.

1/2 NEW PENNY

BRONZE

KM#	Date	Mintage	VF	XF	Unc
29	1971	3.000	—	.10	.20
	1980	—	—	.10	.20
	1980	—	—	Proof	1.35

1/2 PENNY

BRONZE

45	1981	—	—	—	.10
	1981	.010	—	Proof	.90

NEW PENNY

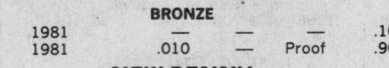

BRONZE

30	1971	4.500	—	.10	.20
	1980	—	—	.10	.20
	1980	—	—	Proof	1.80

BRONZE

47	1981	—	—	.10	.20
	1981	.010	—	Proof	1.35

55	1983	.050	—	.10	.25
	1984	—	—	.10	.25
	1985	—	—	.10	.25
	1986	—	—	.10	.25
	1987	—	—	.10	.25

8.4000 g, .925 SILVER, .2498 oz ASW
| 55a | 1983 | 5,000 | — | Proof | 10.00 |

5 NEW PENCE

COPPER-NICKEL

32	1968	3.600	—	.15	.50
	1980	—	—	.15	.50
	1980	—	—	Proof	2.75

COPPER-NICKEL

49	1981	—	—	.20	.60
	1981	.010	—	Proof	2.25

57	1983	.050	—	.30	.50
	1984	—	—	.30	.50
	1985	—	—	.30	.50
	1986	—	—	.30	.50
	1987	—	—	.30	.50
	1988	—	—	.30	.50

13.2000 g, .925 SILVER, .3926 oz ASW
| 57a | 1983 | 5,000 | — | Proof | 15.00 |

20 PENCE

COPPER-NICKEL
Rev: Date below lighthouse.

KM#	Date	Mintage	VF	XF	Unc
53	1982	.517	—	.40	1.25
	1987	—	—	.40	1.25

5.8300 g, .925 SILVER, .1734 oz ASW

| 53a | 1982 | 1,500 | — | Proof | 15.00 |

COPPER-NICKEL
Obv: Date below bust.

66	1983	.050	—	.50	1.00
	1984	—	—	.50	1.00
	1986	—	—	.50	1.00
	1987	—	—	.50	1.00

5.8300 g, .925 SILVER, .1734 oz ASW

| 66a | 1983 | 5,000 | — | Proof | 15.00 |

25 PENCE

COPPER-NICKEL
Queen's Silver Jubilee

| 44 | 1977 | .262 | .50 | .75 | 2.50 |

28.2800 g, .925 SILVER, .8411 oz ASW

| 44a | 1977 | .025 | — | Proof | 30.00 |

50 NEW PENCE

COPPER-NICKEL

34	1969	.480	—	.90	1.50
	1980	—	—	.90	1.50
	1980	—	—	Proof	9.00

50 PENCE

5.4200 g, .925 SILVER, .1612 oz ASW
25th Wedding Anniversary

35	1972	.024	—	1.25	4.00
	1972	1,500	—	Proof	10.00

COPPER-NICKEL

50	1981	—	—	1.00	1.50
	1981	.010	—	Proof	3.00

KM#	Date	Mintage	VF	XF	Unc
58	1983	.050	—	1.00	1.50
	1984	—	—	1.00	1.50
	1986	—	—	1.00	1.50
	1987	—	—	1.00	1.50
	1988	—	—	1.00	1.50

15.5000 g, .925 SILVER, .4609 oz ASW

| 58a | 1983 | 5,000 | — | Proof | 10.00 |

COPPER-NICKEL
Liberation of 1945

| 63 | 1985 | — | — | 1.00 | 1.50 |

POUND

10.8400 g, .925 SILVER, .3224 oz ASW
25th Wedding Anniversary

36	1972	.024	—	—	7.50
	1972	1,500	—	Proof	25.00

COPPER-NICKEL
Bicentennial Battle of Jersey

51	1981	.200	—	2.00	3.00
	1981	.015	—	Proof	10.00

10.4500 g, .925 SILVER, .3108 oz ASW

| 51a | 1981 | .010 | — | Proof | 25.00 |

17.5500 g, .917 GOLD, .5174 oz AGW

| 51b | 1981 | 5,000 | — | Proof | 300.00 |

NICKEL-BRASS
St. Helier

| 59 | 1983 | .050 | — | 2.00 | 3.00 |

11.6800 g, .925 SILVER, .3474 oz ASW

| 59a | 1983 | .010 | — | Proof | 25.00 |

19.6500 g, .917 GOLD, .5794 oz AGW

| 59b | 1983 | *973 pcs. | — | Proof | 400.00 |

NOTE: 497 pieces were remelted.

NICKEL-BRASS
St. Saviour

| 60 | 1984 | — | — | 2.00 | 3.00 |

11.6800 g, .925 SILVER, .3474 oz ASW

KM#	Date	Mintage	VF	XF	Unc
60a	1984	2,500	—	Proof	35.00

19.6500 g, .917 GOLD, .5794 oz AGW

| 60b | 1984 | 159 pcs. | — | Proof | 500.00 |

NICKEL-BRASS
St. Brelade

| 61 | 1984 | — | — | 2.00 | 3.00 |

11.6800 g, .925 SILVER, .3474 oz ASW

| 61a | 1984 | 2,500 | — | Proof | 35.00 |

19.6500 g, .917 GOLD, .5794 oz AGW

| 61b | 1984 | 133 pcs. | — | Proof | 500.00 |

NICKEL-BRASS
St. Clement

| 62 | 1985 | — | — | 2.00 | 3.00 |

11.6800 g, .925 SILVER, .3474 oz ASW

| 62a | 1985 | 2,500 | — | Proof | 35.00 |

19.6500 g, .917 GOLD, .5794 oz AGW

| 62b | 1985 | 124 pcs. | — | Proof | 450.00 |

NICKEL-BRASS
St. Lawrence

| 65 | 1985 | — | — | 2.00 | 3.00 |

11.6800 g, .925 SILVER, .3474 oz ASW

| 65a | 1985 | 2,500 | — | Proof | 35.00 |

19.6500 g, .917 GOLD, .5794 oz AGW

| 65b | 1985 | 108 pcs. | — | Proof | 450.00 |

NICKEL-BRASS
St. Peter

| 68 | 1986 | — | — | 2.00 | 3.00 |

11.6800 g, .925 SILVER, .3474 oz ASW

| 68a | 1986 | 2,500 | — | Proof | 35.00 |

19.6500 g, .917 GOLD, .5794 oz AGW

| 68b | 1986 | 146 pcs. | — | Proof | 450.00 |

NICKEL-BRASS
Grouville

| 69 | 1986 | — | — | 2.00 | 3.00 |

11.6800 g, .925 SILVER, .3474 oz ASW

| 69a | 1986 | 2,500 | — | Proof | 35.00 |

19.6500 g, .917 GOLD, .5794 oz AGW

| 69b | 1986 | 250 pcs. | — | Proof | 450.00 |

COPPER-ZINC-NICKEL
St. Martin
Obv: Similar to KM#69. Rev: Arms.

| 71 | 1987 | — | — | 2.00 | 3.00 |

11.6800 g, .925 SILVER, .3474 oz ASW

| 71a | 1987 | — | — | Proof | 35.00 |

19.6500 g, .917 GOLD, .5794 oz AGW

| 71b | 1987 | — | — | Proof | 450.00 |

JERSEY 1134

COPPER-ZINC-NICKEL
St. Ouen

KM#	Date	Mintage	VF	XF	Unc
72	1987	—	—	2.00	3.00

11.6800 g, .925 SILVER, .3474 oz ASW
| 72a | 1987 | *2,500 | — | Proof | 35.00 |

19.6500 g, .917 GOLD, .5794 oz AGW
| 72b | 1987 | *250 pcs. | — | Proof | 450.00 |

COPPER-ZINC-NICKEL
Trinity

| 73 | 1988 | — | — | 2.00 | 3.00 |

11.6800 g, .925 SILVER, .3474 oz ASW
| 73a | 1988 | *2,500 | — | Proof | 35.00 |

19.6500 g, .917 GOLD, .5794 oz AGW
| 73b | 1988 | *250 pcs. | — | Proof | 450.00 |

COPPER-ZINC-NICKEL
St. John

| 74 | 1988 | — | — | 2.00 | 3.00 |

11.6800 g, .925 SILVER, .3474 oz ASW
| 74a | 1988 | *2,500 | — | Proof | 35.00 |

19.6500 g, .917 GOLD, .5794 oz AGW
| 74b | 1988 | *250 pcs. | — | Proof | 450.00 |

2 POUNDS

21.9000 g, .925 SILVER, .6513 oz ASW
25th Wedding Anniversary
Obv: Similar to 1 Pound, KM#36.

| 37 | 1972 | .024 | — | — | 15.00 |
| | 1972 | 1,500 | — | Proof | 30.00 |

COPPER-NICKEL
Wedding of Prince Charles and Lady Diana

| 52 | 1981 | .150 | — | — | 5.00 |

28.2800 g, .925 SILVER, .8411 oz ASW
| 52a | 1981 | .035 | — | Proof | 25.00 |

15.9800 g, .917 GOLD, .4712 oz AGW
| 52b | 1981 | 2,000 | — | Proof | 350.00 |

COPPER-NICKEL
Liberation of 1945

KM#	Date	Mintage	VF	XF	Unc
64	1985	.025	—	—	5.00

28.2800 g, .925 SILVER, .8411 oz ASW
| 64a | 1985 | 2,500 | — | Proof | 50.00 |

47.5400 g, .917 GOLD, 1.4011 oz AGW
| 64b | 1985 | 40 pcs. | — | Proof | 2250. |

COPPER-NICKEL
Commonwealth Games
Obv: Similar to KM#70.

| 67.1 | 1986 | 28.2800 g, .500 SILVER, .4546 oz ASW | | | 5.00 |
| 67.1a | 1986 | .050 | — | — | 25.00 |

28.2800 g, .925 SILVER, .8411 oz ASW
| 67.1b | 1986 | .020 | — | Proof | 50.00 |

COPPER-NICKEL
Without edge inscription

| 67.2 | 1986 | | | | 6.25 |

Wildlife Fund - Mauritius Piak Pigeon

| 70 | 1987 | | | | 5.00 |

28.2800 g, .925 SILVER, .8411 oz ASW
| 70a | 1987 | .025 | — | Proof | 50.00 |

2 POUNDS 50 PENCE

27.6000 g, .925 SILVER, .8208 oz ASW

25th Wedding Anniversary
Obv: Similar to 1 Pound, KM#36.

KM#	Date	Mintage	VF	XF	Unc
38	1972	.024	—	—	15.00
	1972	1,500	—	Proof	35.00

5 POUNDS

2.6200 g, .917 GOLD, .0772 oz AGW
25th Wedding Anniversary

| 39 | 1972 | 8,500 | — | — | 40.00 |
| | 1972 | 1,500 | — | Proof | 75.00 |

10 POUNDS

4.6400 g, .917 GOLD, .1368 oz AGW
25th Wedding Anniversary

| 40 | 1972 | 8,500 | — | — | 70.00 |
| | 1972 | 1,500 | — | Proof | 100.00 |

20 POUNDS

9.2600 g, .917 GOLD, .2729 oz AGW
25th Wedding Anniversary

| 41 | 1972 | 8,500 | — | — | 135.00 |
| | 1972 | 1,500 | — | Proof | 175.00 |

25 POUNDS

11.9000 g, .917 GOLD, .3507 oz AGW
25th Wedding Anniversary

| 42 | 1972 | 8,500 | — | — | 175.00 |
| | 1972 | 1,500 | — | Proof | 225.00 |

50 POUNDS

22.6300 g, .917 GOLD, .6670 oz AGW
25th Wedding Anniversary

| 43 | 1972 | 8,500 | — | — | 350.00 |
| | 1972 | 1,500 | — | Proof | 400.00 |

MINT SETS (MS)

KM#	Date	Mintage	Identification	Issue Price	Mkt. Val.
MS1	1972(4)	23,500	KM35-38	24.00	37.50
MS2	1972(9)	—	KM35-43	348.00	800.00
MS3	1983(7)	—	KM53-59		6.00

PROOF SETS (PS)

PS1	1957(4)	1,050	KM21,22 two each	—	30.00
PS2	1960(4)	2,100	KM22,23 two each	—	15.00
PS3	1964(4)	10,000	KM21,25 two each	—	8.00
PS4	1966(4)	15,000	KM26,27 two each	—	8.00
PS5	1966(2)	15,000	KM28 two pcs.	—	8.00
PS6	1972(9)	1,500	KM35-43	648.00	1000.
PS7	1980(6)	10,000	KM29-34	—	20.00
PS8	1981(7)	10,000	KM45-51	31.00	20.00
PS9	1983(7)	5,000	KM53a-59a	—	80.00

JORDAN

The Hashemite Kingdom of Jordan, a constitutional monarchy in southwest Asia, has an area of 37,738 sq. mi. (97,740 sq. km.) and a population of *3 million. Capital: Amman. Agriculture and tourism comprise Jordan's economic base. Chief exports are phosphates, tomatoes and oranges.

Jordan is the Edom and Moab of the time of Moses. It became part of the Roman province of Arabia in 106 A.D., was conquered by the Arabs in 633-36, and was part of the Ottoman Empire from the 16th century until World War I. At that time, the regions presently known as Jordan and Israel were mandated to Great Britain by the League of Nations as Transjordan and Palestine. In 1922 Transjordan was established as the semi-autonomous Emirate of Transjordan, ruled by the Hashemite Prince Abdullah but still nominally a part of the British mandate. The mandate over Transjordan was terminated in 1946, The country becoming the independent Hashemite Kingdom of Transjordan. The kingdom was renamed the Hashemite Kingdom of Jordan in 1950.

NOTE: Several 1964 and 1965 issues were limited to respective quantities of 3,000 and 5,000 examples struck to make up sets for sale to collectors.

TITLES

المملكة الاردنية الهاشمية

El-Mamlakat El-Urduniyat El-Hashemiyat

الاردنية

El-Urduniyat

RULERS
Abdullah Ibn Al Hussein, 1946-1951
Hussein I, 1952—

MONETARY SYSTEM
100 Fils = 1 Dirham
1000 Fils = 10 Dirhams = 1 Dinar

FIL

BRONZE

KM#	Date	Year	Mintage	VF	XF	Unc
1	AH1368	1949	.350	1.00	1.80	3.00
	1368	1949	—	—	Proof	

NOTE: FIL is an error for FILS, the correct Arabic singular.

FILS

BRONZE

2	AH1368	1949	Inc. Ab.	.50	.90	2.00
	1368	1949	25 pcs.	—	Proof	60.00

8	AH1374	1955	.200	.35	.50	1.00
	1374	1955	—	—	Proof	
	1379	1960	.150	.40	.60	1.25
	1379	1960	—	—	Proof	
	1382	1963	.200	.25	.50	1.00
	1382	1963	—	—	Proof	
	1383	1964	3,000	1.50	3.00	5.00
	1385	1965	5,000	1.00	2.00	4.00
	1385	1965	.010	—	Proof	3.00

14	AH1387	1968	.060	.15	.25	.75

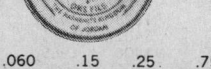

GOLD (OMS)

KM#	Date	Year	Mintage	VF	XF	Unc
14a	AH1387	1968	2 pcs.			

BRONZE

35	AH1398	1978	—	.15	.25	.60
	1398	1978	.020	—	Proof	.75
	1401	1981	.100	.10	.20	.50
	1404	1984	.100	.10	.20	.50
	1406	1985	—	.10	.20	.50
	1406	1985	5,000	—	Proof	.75

5 FILS (1/2 QIRSH)

BRONZE

3	AH1368	1949	3.300	.40	.75	1.50
	1368	1949	25 pcs.	—	Proof	80.00

9	AH1374	1955	3.500	.35	.50	.75
	1374	1955	—	—	Proof	
	1380	1960	.540	.50	.70	1.25
	1380	1960	—	—	Proof	
	1382	1962	.250	.45	.70	1.25
	1382	1962	—	—	Proof	
	1383	1964	3,000	—	4.50	7.50
	1384	1964	2.500	.30	.50	1.00
	1385	1965	5,000	1.25	2.50	4.00
	1385	1965	.010	—	Proof	5.00
	1387	1967	2.000	.10	.20	.40

15	AH1387	1968	.800	.10	.25	.50
	1390	1970	1.400	—	.20	.40
	1392	1972	.400	.10	.25	.65
	1394	1974	2.000	.10	.20	.40
	1395	1975	9.000	.10	.15	.30

GOLD (OMS)

| 15a | AH1387 | 1968 | 2 pcs. | | | |

BRONZE

36	AH1398	1978	60.200	.10	.15	.30
	1398	1978	.020	—	Proof	1.25
	1406	1985	—	.10	.15	.30
	1406	1985	5,000	—	Proof	1.25

10 FILS (QIRSH, PIASTRE)

BRONZE

4	AH1368	1949	2.700	.75	1.25	2.00
	1368	1949	25 pcs.	—	Proof	100.00

KM#	Date	Year	Mintage	VF	XF	Unc
10	AH1374	1955	1.500	.60	1.00	2.00
	1374	1955	—	—	Proof	
	1380	1960	.060	1.25	2.00	3.50
	1380	1960	—	—	Proof	
	1382	1962	2.300	.30	.50	1.00
	1382	1962	—	—	Proof	50.00
	1383	1964	1.253	.30	.50	1.00
	1385	1965	1.003	.20	.40	1.00
	1385	1965	.010	—	Proof	2.00
	1387	1967	1.000	.20	.35	1.00

16	AH1387	1968	.500	.20	.40	.75
	1390	1970	1.000	.20	.35	.60
	1392	1972	.600	.20	.40	.75
	1394	1974	1.000	.20	.40	.65
	1395	1975	5.000	.20	.35	.50

GOLD (OMS)

| 16a | AH1387 | 1968 | 2 pcs. | | | |

BRONZE

37	AH1398	1978	30.000	.10	.15	.40
	1398	1978	.020	—	Proof	1.50
	1404	1984	10.000	.10	.15	.40
	1406	1985	—	.10	.15	.40
	1406	1985	5,000	—	Proof	1.50

20 FILS

COPPER-NICKEL

5	AH1368	1949	1.570	.75	1.25	2.00
	1368	1949	25 pcs.	—	Proof	110.00

13	AH1383	1964	3,000	1.50	3.00	5.00
	1385	1965	5,000	1.50	3.00	5.00
	1385	1965	.010	—	Proof	5.00

25 FILS (1/4 DIRHAM)

COPPER-NICKEL

17	AH1387	1968	.200	.15	.35	.75
	1390	1970	.240	.15	.35	.75
	1394	1974	.800	.15	.35	.75
	1395	1975	2.000	.15	.35	.75
	1397	1977	1.600	.15	.35	.75

GOLD (OMS)

| 17a | AH1387 | 1968 | 2 pcs. | | | |

JORDAN 1136

COPPER-NICKEL

KM#	Date	Year	Mintage	VF	XF	Unc
38	AH1398	1978	—	.20	.30	.75
	1398	1978	.020	—	Proof	2.00
	1401	1981	2.000	.20	.30	.75
	1404	1984	4.000	.20	.30	.75
	1406	1985	—	.20	.30	.75
	1406	1985	5.000	—	Proof	2.00

50 FILS (1/2 DIRHAM)

COPPER-NICKEL

KM#	Date	Year	Mintage	VF	XF	Unc
6	AH1368	1949	2.500	.75	2.00	3.50
	1368	1949	25 Pcs.	—	Proof	125.00

KM#	Date	Year	Mintage	VF	XF	Unc
11	AH1374	1955	2.500	.75	1.50	3.50
	1374	1955	—	—	Proof	—
	1382	1962	.750	.85	1.00	1.50
	1382	1962	—	—	Proof	—
	1383	1964	1.003	.50	.75	1.25
	1385	1965	1.505	.75	1.00	1.50
	1385	1965	.010	—	Proof	3.50

KM#	Date	Year	Mintage	VF	XF	Unc
18	AH1387	1968	.400	.40	.75	1.75
	1390	1970	1.000	.40	.60	1.25
	1393	1973	—	.40	.60	1.25
	1394	1974	1.000	.40	.60	1.25
	1395	1975	2.000	.40	.60	1.25
	1397	1977	6.000	.40	.60	1.25

GOLD (OMS)

| 18a | AH1387 | 1968 | 2 pcs. | — | — | 800.00 |

COPPER-NICKEL

KM#	Date	Year	Mintage	VF	XF	Unc
39	AH1398	1978	6.168	.25	.50	1.25
	1398	1978	.020	—	Proof	2.50
	1401	1981	5.000	.25	.50	1.25
	1404	1984	10.000	.25	.50	1.25
	1406	1985	—	.25	.50	1.25
	1406	1985	5.000	—	Proof	2.50

DIRHAM (100 FILS)

COPPER-NICKEL

KM#	Date	Year	Mintage	VF	XF	Unc
7	AH1368	1949	2.000	2.00	3.00	5.00
	1368	1949	25 pcs.	—	Proof	150.00

KM#	Date	Year	Mintage	VF	XF	Unc
12	AH1374	1955	.500	2.00	2.50	4.00
	1374	1955	—	—	Proof	—
	1382	1962	.600	1.00	1.50	3.00
	1382	1962	—	—	Proof	—
	1383	1964	3.000	1.50	3.00	5.00
	1385	1965	.405	1.00	1.25	2.50
	1385	1965	.010	—	Proof	4.00

KM#	Date	Year	Mintage	VF	XF	Unc
19	AH1387	1968	.175	.75	1.50	2.50
	1395	1975	2.500	.40	1.00	2.00
	1397	1977	2.000	.40	1.00	2.00

GOLD (OMS)

| 19a | AH1387 | 1968 | 2 pcs. | — | — | 1000. |

COPPER-NICKEL

KM#	Date	Year	Mintage	VF	XF	Unc
40	AH1398	1978	3.000	.40	1.00	2.00
	1398	1978	.020	—	Proof	3.00
	1401	1981	4.000	.40	1.00	2.00
	1404	1984	5.000	.40	1.00	1.50
	1406	1985	—	.40	1.00	1.50
	1406	1985	5.000	—	Proof	3.00

1/4 DINAR

COPPER-NICKEL
F.A.O. Issue

KM#	Date	Year	Mintage	VF	XF	Unc
20	AH1389	1969	.060	2.00	2.50	3.50

KM#	Date	Year	Mintage	VF	XF	Unc
28	AH1390	1970	.500	1.00	1.50	3.00
	1394	1974	.400	1.00	1.50	3.00
	1395	1975	.100	1.00	1.50	3.00
	1396	1976	—	1.00	1.50	3.00

19.0400 g, .925 SILVER, .5663 oz ASW
10th Anniversary of Central Bank of Jordan

| 29 | AH1394 | 1974 | 550 pcs. | — | Proof | 60.00 |

.917 GOLD

| 29a | AH1394 | 1974 | 100 pcs. | — | Proof | 550.00 |

COPPER-NICKEL
25th Anniversary of Reign

| 30 | AH1397 | 1977 | .200 | 1.00 | 2.00 | 3.50 |

KM#	Date	Year	Mintage	VF	XF	Unc
41	AH1398	1978	.200	1.00	2.00	3.50
	1398	1978	.020	—	Proof	4.00
	1401	1981	.800	.75	1.50	3.00
	1406	1985	—	.75	1.50	3.00
	1406	1985	5.000	—	Proof	4.00

JORDAN 1137

1/2 DINAR

20.0000 g, .999 SILVER, .6424 oz ASW

KM#	Date	Year	Mintage	VF	XF	Unc
21	AH1389	1969	6,100	—	Proof	25.00

COPPER-NICKEL
1400th Anniversary of Islam

42	AH1400	1980	2.006	1.50	2.50	4.00

3/4 DINAR

30.0000 g, .999 SILVER, .9636 oz ASW
Obv: Similar to 1/2 Dinar, KM#21.

22	AH1389	1969	5,800	—	Proof	45.00

DINAR

40.0000 g, .999 SILVER, 1.2848 oz ASW
Obv: Similar to 1/2 Dinar, KM#21.

KM#	Date	Year	Mintage	VF	XF	Unc
23	AH1389	1969	6,800	—	Proof	65.00

NICKEL-BRONZE
King's 50th Birthday

47	AH1406	1985	—	—	—	7.50
	1406	1985	5,000	—	Proof	10.00

2 DINARS

5.5200 g, .900 GOLD, .1597 oz AGW
Obv: Similar to 1/2 Dinar, KM#21.

24	AH1389	1969	2,425	—	Proof	125.00

2-1/2 DINARS

28.2800 g, .925 SILVER, .8410 oz ASW
Conservation Series
Rev: Rhim Gazelle.

31	AH1397	1977	6,265	—	—	22.50
	AH1397	1977	5,011	—	Proof	30.00

3 DINARS

35.0000 g, .925 SILVER, 1.0409 oz ASW
Conservation Series
Obv: Similar to 2-1/2 Dinars, KM#31.
Rev: Palestine Sunbird.

KM#	Date	Year	Mintage	VF	XF	Unc
32	AH1397	1977	6,263	—	—	27.50
	AH1397	1977	4,897	—	Proof	40.00

23.3300 g, .925 SILVER, .6938 oz ASW
International Year of the Child
Obv: Similar to 1/4 Dinar, KM#41.

43	AH1401	1981	.021	—	Proof	15.00

5 DINARS

13.8200 g, .900 GOLD, .3999 oz AGW
Obv: Similar to 1/2 Dinar, KM#21.

25	AH1389	1969	1,950	—	Proof	300.00

10 DINARS

27.6400 g, .900 GOLD, .7998 oz AGW
Obv: Similar to 1/2 Dinar, KM#21.

26	AH1389	1969	1,870	—	Proof	500.00

30.0000 g, .925 SILVER, .8922 oz ASW
15th Century Hijrah Calendar
Obv: King Hussein. Rev: Mosques.

44	AH1400	1980	.017	—	Proof	27.50

15.0000 g, .925 SILVER, .4610 oz ASW
King's 50th Birthday

48	AH1405	1985	—	—	Proof	27.50

JORDAN 1138

25 DINARS

69.1100 g, .900 GOLD, 1.9999 oz AGW
Obv: Similar to 1/2 Dinar, KM#21.

KM#	Date	Year	Mintage	VF	XF	Unc
27	AH1389	1969	1,000	—	Proof	1200.

15.0000 g, .917 GOLD, .4422 oz AGW
25th Anniversary of Reign

33	AH1397					
	1977FM		4,724	—	Proof	275.00

40 DINARS

14.3100 g, .917 GOLD, .4216 oz AGW
15th Century Hijrah Calendar

| 45 | AH1400 | 1980 | 9,500 | — | Proof | 750.00 |

50 DINARS

15.9800 g, .917 GOLD, .4710 oz AGW
Five Year Plan

| 50 | AH1396 | 1976 | 250 pcs. | — | Proof | 300.00 |

33.4370 g, .900 GOLD, .9676 oz AGW
Conservation Series
Rev: Houbara Bustard.

34	AH1397	1977	829 pcs.	—		600.00
	1397	1977	287 pcs.	—	Proof	850.00

17.0000 g, .917 GOLD, .5013 oz AGW
King's 50th Birthday
Similar to 10 Dinars, KM#48.

| 49 | AH1405 | 1985 | 2,000 | — | Proof | 350.00 |

60 DINARS

17.1700 g, .917 GOLD, .5062 oz AGW
International Year of the Child
Obv: King Hussein. Rev: 2 children gazing at the Palace of Culture in Amman.

KM#	Date	Year	Mintage	VF	XF	Unc
46	AH1401	1981	.020	—	Proof	275.00

SPECIMEN SETS (SS)

KM#	Date	Mintage	Identification	Issue Price	Mkt. Val.
SS1	1964(6)	3,000	KM8-12	—	20.00
SS2	1965(6)	5,000	KM8-12	—	12.50
SS3	1968(6)	50	KM14-19	—	500.00
SS4	1968(6)	2	KM14a-19a	—	—

MINT SETS (MS)

| MS1 | 1985(8) | — | KM35-41,47 | 10.75 | 15.00 |

PROOF SETS (PS)

PS1	1949(6)	25	KM2-7	—	625.00
PS2	1965(6)	10,000	KM8-12	14.40	17.50
PS3	1969(7)	6,000	KM21-27	396.00	2125.
PS4	1969(4)	1,000	KM24-27	—	2125.
PS5	1969(3)	5,800	KM21-23	36.00	135.00
PS6	1977(3)	1,000	KM31a,32a,34	780.00	725.00
PS7	1977(2)	9,000	KM31a,32a	60.00	70.00
PS8	1978(7)	20,000	KM35-41	27.00	15.00
PS9	1980(2)	—	KM44-45	365.00	775.00
PS10	1985(8)	5,000	KM35-41,47	31.00	25.00

Listings For
KAMPUCHEA: refer to Cambodia
KATANGA: refer to Zaire
KEELING-COCOS ISLANDS: refer to Australia

KAMPUCHEA

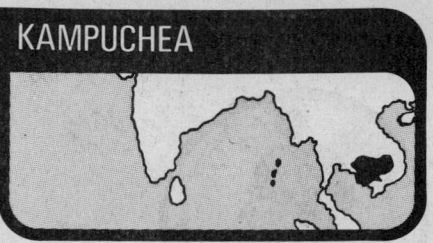

Democratic Kampuchea formerly Cambodia and the Khmer Republic, a land of paddy fields and forest-clad hills located on the Indo-Chinese peninsula, fronting on the Gulf of Thailand, has an area of 69,898 sq. mi. (181,035 sq. km.) and a population of *6.9 million. Capital: Phnom Penh. Agriculture is the basis of the economy, with rice the chief crop. Native industries include cattle breeding, weaving and rice milling. Rubber, cattle, corn, and timber are exported.

The region was the nucleus of the Khmer empire which flourished from the 5th to the 12th century and attained an excellence in art and architecture still evident in the magnificent ruins at Angkor. The Khmer empire once ruled over much of Southeast Asia, but began to decline in the 13th century as the Thai and Vietnamese invaded the region and attached its territories. At the request of the Cambodian king, a French protectorate attached to Cochin-China was established over the country in 1863, saving it from dissolution, and in 1885, Cambodia was included in the French Union of Indo-China. France established a constitutional monarchy for Cambodia within the French Union in 1949. The 1954 Geneva Convention resulted in full independence for the Kingdom of Cambodia. King Sihanouk abdicated to his father and won the office of Prime Minister.

Prince Sihanouk was toppled by a bloodless coup led by Lon Nol in March of 1970. Sihanouk moved to Peking to head a government-in-exile. On Oct. 9, 1970, Cambodia became the Khmer Republic, and Lon Nol its President. The government of Lon Nol was in turn toppled, April 17, 1975, by the Khmer Rouge insurgents who took control of the government and renamed the country Democratic Kampuchea.

The Khmer Rouge completely eliminated the economy and created a state without money, exchange or barter. Everyone worked for the state and was taken care of by the state. The Vietnamese supported People's Republic of Kampuchea was installed in accordance with the constitution of January 5, 1976. The name of the country was changed from Democratic Cambodia to Democratic Kampuchea.

RULERS
Ang Dong (Pra Ong Harizak) 1841-1859
Norodom I, 1859-1905
Sisowath, 1906-1941
Norodom Sihanouk, King, Prince and Prime Minister, 1941-1970
Lon Nol, 1970-1975
Pol Pot, 1975-1978
Heng Samrin, 1978-

MINT MARKS
(a) - Paris, privy marks only

MONETARY SYSTEM
(Until 1860)
2 Att = 1 Pe (Pey)
4 Pe = 1 Fuang (Fuong)
8 Fuang = 1 Tical
4 Salong = 1 Tical
(Commencing 1860)
100 Centimes = 1 Franc

CAMBODIA

KINGDOM

ATT
COPPER, 1.40-2.50 g, uniface
Obv: Similar to 1 Pe, KM#2.

KM#	Date	Year	VG	Fine	VF	XF
1 (C16)	CS1208	(1847)	4.00	6.50	9.00	20.00

PE

COPPER, 4.00-4.60 g, uniface
W/or w/o silver wash

| 2 (C17) | CS1208 | (1847) | 9.00 | 15.00 | 27.50 | 55.00 |

COPPER or BILLON 0.20-0.90 g, uniface

| 3 | ND | | 6.00 | 8.50 | 12.50 | 27.50 |

Uniface
Obv: Cocoa bean.

| 4 | ND | | 6.00 | 9.00 | 15.00 | 30.00 |

KM#	Date	Year	VG	Fine	VF	XF
5	ND		9.00	15.00	27.50	50.00

Uniface

2 PE
(1/2 Fuang)

COPPER or BILLON 1.00-2.00 g, uniface

| 7 | ND | | 3.00 | 4.50 | 7.00 | 12.00 |

Uniface

| 9 | ND | | 5.50 | 8.00 | 12.50 | 27.50 |

Uniface

| 11 (C10) | ND | | 3.00 | 6.00 | 10.00 | 15.00 |

Uniface

| 13 | ND | | 4.00 | 7.00 | 12.00 | 20.00 |

Uniface

| 14 | ND | | 4.00 | 7.00 | 12.00 | 20.00 |

Uniface

| 15 | ND | | 5.50 | 8.00 | 12.50 | 27.50 |

Uniface

| 17 | ND | | 5.50 | 8.00 | 12.50 | 27.50 |

Uniface
Similar to 1 Pe, KM#5.

| 19 | ND | | 10.00 | 15.00 | 27.50 | 55.00 |

Uniface

| 21 | ND | | 10.00 | 15.00 | 27.50 | 55.00 |

Uniface

| 23 | ND | | 10.00 | 15.00 | 27.50 | 55.00 |

Rev: Leg. in Cambodian script. Hand struck.

| 25 | ND | | 5.00 | 8.00 | 15.00 | 25.00 |

Obv: Similar to KM#25 but w/o border around Garuda bird. Machine struck.

KM#	Date	Year	VG	Fine	VF	XF
26 (C14)	ND		2.50	4.00	6.50	12.00

SILVER, 1.85 g, 14.5mm
Uniface
Similar to KM25, but w/o snake in hand.

| 28 | ND | | — | — | — | 300.00 |

BRASS or COPPER, 23mm
Obv: Similar to KM26, but 3 line legend on rev.

| 30 | ND | | 50.00 | 100.00 | 125.00 | 175.00 |

FUANG

COPPER or BILLON, 2.70-3.00 g, uniface

| 27 | ND | | 3.00 | 4.50 | 7.50 | 15.00 |

Uniface
Hippogriff walking to right.
Similar to 2 Pe, KM#21.

| 29 | ND | | 10.00 | 15.00 | 27.50 | 55.00 |

NOTE: KM#'s 1 through 29 above were struck between 1650 and 1850. All are believed to have been struck at Battambang except KM#25 which is thought to have been made at Siem Reap.

1/8 TICAL
(1 Fuang)

BILLON, 1.50-1.75 g, 11-16mm, uniface

| 32.1 | CS1208 | (1847) | 4.00 | 7.00 | 10.00 | 20.00 |

W/o small circle at left.

| 32.2 (C13) | CS1208 | (1847) | — | — | — | — |

SILVER, 14mm
Machine struck

KM#	Date	Year	Fine	VF	XF	Unc
33 (C19)	ND	(1847)	100.00	150.00	250.00	350.00

NOTE: Counterfeits exist in copper, silver and gold.

1/4 TICAL
(1 Salong)

SILVER, 3.20 g, 20mm

| 34 (C20) | CS1208 | (1847) | 150.00 | 250.00 | 400.00 | 550.00 |

3.60 g, 22mm

| 35 | CS1208 | (1847) | 150.00 | 250.00 | 400.00 | 550.00 |

| 39 | CS1209 | (1848) | — | — | — | — |

TICAL

SILVER, 15.00 g, 30mm, thick flan

KM#	Date	Year	Fine	VF	XF	Unc
36 (C22a)	CS1208	(1847)	50.00	100.00	200.00	500.00

35mm, thin flan

| 37 (C22) | CS1208 | (1847) | 50.00 | 100.00 | 275.00 | 750.00 |

4 TICAL

SILVER, 60.50 g
Obv: Similar to 1 Tical, KM#37.

| 38 | CS1209 | (1848) | — | — | — | — |

FRENCH PROTECTORATE
MONETARY SYSTEM
100 Centimes = 1 Franc

REGULAR COINAGE

NOTE: The 1860 dated coins were struck in Belgium in 1875, engraved by C. Wurden whose name appears below the bust.

RESTRIKES
In 1899 after the death of the Queen Mother of Cambodia, all of the 1860 series coins except the 1 Piastre, were restruck with the original dies. These dies were rusty and dirty from long storage and these restrike coins have a grainy appearance to them.

KAMPUCHEA 1140

CINQ (5) CENTIMES

BRONZE

KM#	Date	Mintage	Fine	VF	XF	Unc
42	1860	11.467	5.00	10.00	25.00	60.00
	1860	—	—	—	Proof	90.00

GOLD (OMS)

| 42a | 1860 (restrike) | — | — | — | — | — |

DIX (10) CENTIMES

BRONZE

43.1	1860	10.267	6.00	12.00	30.00	70.00
	1860	—	—	—	Proof	110.00

Local manufacture. Rev: W/error CENTINES

| .43.2 | 1860 | — | — | 15.00 | 40.00 | 75.00 | 150.00 |

GOLD (OMS)

| 43.1a | 1860 | — | — | — | — | — |

25 CENTIMES

1.2500 g, .900 SILVER, .0361 oz ASW

44	1860	—	10.00	30.00	100.00	200.00
	1860	—	—	—	Proof	400.00
	1860 (restrike)	—	5.00	15.00	30.00	75.00

GOLD (OMS)

| 44a | 1860 | — | — | — | — | — |

50 CENTIMES

2.5000 g, .900 SILVER, .0723 oz ASW

45	1860	—	20.00	60.00	110.00	250.00
	1860	—	—	—	Proof	400.00
	1860 (restrike)	—	7.50	20.00	40.00	100.00

GOLD (OMS)

| 45a | 1860 | — | — | — | — | — |

UN (1) FRANC

5.0000 g, .900 SILVER, .1446 oz ASW

46	1860	—	25.00	70.00	125.00	300.00
	1860	—	—	—	Proof	450.00
	1860 (restrike)	—	10.00	35.00	60.00	125.00

GOLD (OMS)

| 46a | 1860 | — | — | — | — | — |

DEUX (2) FRANCS

10.0000 g, .900 SILVER, .2893 oz ASW

KM#	Date	Mintage	Fine	VF	XF	Unc
47	1860	—	35.00	100.00	200.00	400.00
	1860	—	—	—	Proof	600.00
	1860 (restrike)	—	15.00	40.00	75.00	225.00

GOLD (OMS)

| 47a | 1860 | — | — | — | — | — |

QUATRE (4) FRANCS

15.6000 g, .900 SILVER, .4514 oz ASW

48	1860	—	75.00	150.00	250.00	500.00
	1860	—	—	—	Proof	—
	1860 (restrike)	—	40.00	70.00	100.00	225.00

GOLD (OMS)

| 48a | 1860 | — | — | — | — | 2250. |

PIASTRE/PESO

27.0000 g, .900 SILVER, .7812 oz ASW

49	1860	—	400.00	800.00	1600.	3250.
	1860	—	—	—	Proof	—

GOLD (OMS)

| 49a | 1860 | — | — | — | — | — |

SILVERED WHITE METAL (OMS)

| 49b | 1860 | — | — | — | — | 1000. |

COPPER (OMS)
Reeded edge

| 49c.1 | 1860 | — | — | — | — | 650.00 |

Plain edge

| 49c.2 | 1860 | — | — | — | — | 650.00 |

INDEPENDENT KINGDOM
MONETARY SYSTEM

100 Centimes = 1 Riel
100 Sen = 1 Riel (Commencing 1959)

10 CENTIMES

ALUMINUM

KM#	Date	Mintage	Fine	VF	XF	Unc
51	1953(a)	4.000	.25	.50	1.00	2.00

10 SEN

ALUMINUM

| 54 | 1959(a) | 1.000 | .10 | .20 | .40 | .75 |

20 CENTIMES

ALUMINUM

| 52 | 1953(a) | 3.000 | .25 | .65 | 1.50 | 3.00 |

20 SEN

ALUMINUM

| 55 | 1959(a) | 1.004 | .15 | .25 | .60 | 1.00 |

50 CENTIMES

ALUMINUM

| 53 | 1953(a) | 3.170 | .45 | 1.00 | 2.00 | 4.00 |

50 SEN

ALUMINUM

| 56 | 1959(a) | 3.399 | .20 | .35 | .75 | 1.25 |

KHMER REPUBLIC
RIEL

COPPER-NICKEL
F.A.O. Coinage

KM#	Date	Mintage	Fine	VF	XF	Unc
59	1970	5,000	—	—	10.00	20.00

NOTE: According to the Royal Mint of Great Britain, this coin was minted at the Llantrissant Branch Mint in 1972 but dated 1969. According to the FAO, the coin was to have been dated 1971, but was "not minted" due to the fall of the Cambodian government in 1970. However, this coin was released in limited numbers in 1983. The photograph of the coin, supplied by the FAO, is dated 1970.

5000 RIELS

19.0100 g, .925 SILVER, .5654 oz ASW.

KM#	Date	Mintage	VF	XF	Unc
60	1974	500 pcs.	—	—	50.00
	1974	800 pcs.	—	Proof	50.00

Rev: Similar to KM#60.

| 61 | 1974 | 500 pcs. | — | — | 60.00 |
| | 1974 | 800 pcs. | — | Proof | 60.00 |

10,000 RIELS

38.0300 g, .925 SILVER, 1.1310 oz ASW.
President Lon Nol
Rev: Similar to 5,000 Riels, KM#60.

| 62 | 1974 | 500 pcs. | — | — | 85.00 |
| | 1974 | 800 pcs. | — | Proof | 85.00 |

Ancient sculpture
Rev: Similar to 5,000 Riels, KM#60.

KM#	Date	Mintage	VF	XF	Unc
63	1974	500 pcs.	—	—	85.00
	1974	800 pcs.	—	Proof	85.00

50,000 RIELS

6.7100 g, .900 GOLD, .1941 oz AGW

| 64 | 1974 | 3,250 | — | — | 150.00 |
| | 1974 | 2,300 | — | Proof | 200.00 |

Obv: Ancient sculpture

| 65 | 1974 | 450 pcs. | — | — | 175.00 |
| | 1974 | 300 pcs. | — | Proof | 250.00 |

100,000 RIELS

19.1700 g, .900 GOLD, .5547 oz AGW
President Lon Nol
Rev: Similar to 50,000 Riels, KM#65.

| 66 | 1974 | 250 pcs. | — | — | 350.00 |
| | 1974 | 100 pcs. | — | Proof | 600.00 |

NOTE: The above coins were authorized by the Cambodian government shortly before its fall in 1975. The new Communist regime laid claim to the coins and for a time their fate was uncertain. It was not until May 1975, that these coins were offered for sale.

MINT SETS (MS)

KM#	Date	Mintage	Identification	Issue Price	Mkt. Val.
MS1	1974(7)	250	KM60-66	—	950.00
MS2	1974(4)	500	KM60-63	—	280.00

PROOF SETS (PS)

| PS1 | 1974(7) | 100 | KM60-66 | — | 1325. |
| PS2 | 1974(4) | 800 | KM60-63 | — | 280.00 |

PEOPLES REPUBLIC OF KAMPUCHEA
5 SEN

ALUMINUM

KM#	Date	Mintage	VF	XF	Unc
69	1979	—	10.00	15.00	20.00

4 RIELS

COPPER-NICKEL

KM#	Date	Mintage	VF	XF	Unc
71	1988	—	—	—	7.00

20 RIELS

12.0600 g, .999 SILVER, .3855 oz ASW

| 70 | 1988 | 2,000 | — | — | 35.00 |

Soccer

| 72 | 1988 | — | — | — | 30.00 |

Mombasa/KENYA

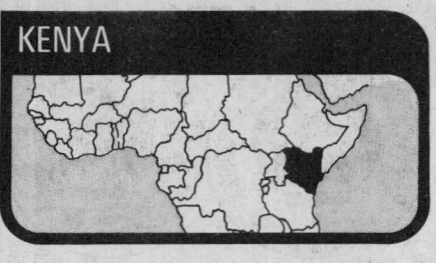

The Republic of Kenya, located on the east coast of Central Africa, has an area of 224,961 sq. mi (582,646 sq. km.) and a population of *23.7 million. Capital: Nairobi. The predominantly agricultural country exports coffee, tea and petroleum products.

The Arabs came to the coast of Kenya in the 8th century and established posts to conduct an ivory and slave trade. The Portuguese, the inveterate wanderers of the Age of Exploration, followed in the 16th century. After a lengthy and bitter struggle with the sultans of Zanzibar who controlled much of the southeastern coast of Africa, the Portuguese were driven away (late 17th century) and for many years Kenya was simply a port of call on the route to India. German and British interests in the 19th century produced agreements defining their respective spheres of influence. The British sphere was administrated by the Imperial East Africa Co. until 1895, when the British government purchased the company's rights in the East Africa Protectorate which, in 1920, was designated as Kenya Colony and protectorate - the latter being a 10-mile wide coastal strip together with Mombasa, Lamu and other small islands nominally retained by the Sultan of Zanzibar. Kenya achieved self-government in June of 1963 as a consequence of the 1952-60 Mau Mau terrorist campaign to secure land reforms and political rights for Africans. Independence was attained on Dec. 12, 1963. Kenya became a republic in 1964. It is a member of the Commonwealth of Nations. The president is Chief of State and Head of Government.

Mombasa was a thriving Arabic commercial center when first visited by Portuguese navigator Vasco da Gama in 1498. During the following two centuries Portugal made repeated efforts to capture the island stronghold but was unable to hold it against the assaults of the Muscat Arabs. In 1823 the ruling Mazuri family placed the city under British protection. Britain repudiated the protectorate and it was then seized by Seyyid Said of Oman, 1837, and annexed to Zanzibar. In 1887 the sultan of Zanzibar relinquished the port of Mombasa to British administration. It was occupied by the Imperial British East Africa Company and for the following two decades was the capital of British East Africa.

MOMBASA

TITLES

Mombasa ممباسه

MINT MARKS
H - Birmingham
C/M - Calcutta

MONETARY SYSTEM
4 Pice = 1 Anna
16 Anna = 1 Rupee

PICE

BRONZE, 24.9mm
Obv. and rev: Small letters.

KM#	Date	Mintage	Fine	VF	XF	Unc
1.1	AH1306/1888C/M	.630	.75	2.50	10.00	25.00
	1306/1888C/M	—	—	—	Proof	125.00

25.4mm
Obv: Small letters. Rev: Medium letters.

| 1.2 | AH1306/1888C/M | Inc. Ab. | .50 | 2.00 | 8.00 | 20.00 |
| | 1306/1888C/M | — | — | — | Proof | 175.00 |

Obv. and rev: Medium letters.
| 1.5 | AH1306/1888C/M | Inc. Ab. | .50 | 2.00 | 8.00 | 20.00 |

Rev: Medium letters.
KM#	Date	Mintage	Fine	VF	XF	Unc
1.3	AH1306/1888H	2.352	.35	1.25	6.00	15.00

Obv. and rev: Large letters w/o serifs, dots between words.
| 1.4 | AH1306/1888H | Inc. Ab. | .25 | 1.00 | 5.00 | 12.50 |
| | 1306/1888H | — | — | — | Proof | 100.00 |

SILVER (OMS)
| 1.4a | AH1306/1888H | — | — | — | Proof | 300.00 |

GOLD (OMS)
| 1.4b | AH1306/1888H | — | — | — | Proof | Rare |

2 ANNAS

1.4600 g, .917 SILVER, .0430 oz ASW
| 2 | 1890H | .016 | 12.00 | 20.00 | 32.50 | 50.00 |
| | 1890H | — | — | — | Proof | 90.00 |

1/4 RUPEE
(4 Annas)

2.9200 g, .917 SILVER, .0860 oz ASW
| 3 | 1890H | .012 | 15.00 | 27.50 | 40.00 | 75.00 |
| | 1890H | — | — | — | Proof | 120.00 |

1/2 RUPEE
(8 Annas)

5.8300 g, .917 SILVER, .1719 oz ASW
| 4 | 1890H | .010 | 20.00 | 40.00 | 70.00 | 120.00 |
| | 1890H | — | — | — | Proof | 140.00 |

RUPEE

11.6600 g, .917 SILVER, .3438 oz ASW
| 5 | 1888H | .094 | 10.00 | 25.00 | 50.00 | 125.00 |
| | 1888H | — | — | — | Proof | 225.00 |

PROOF SETS (PS)

KM#	Date	Mintage	Identification	Issue Price	Mkt. Val.
PS1	1888H(2)	—	KM1.4,5	—	325.00
PS2	1890H(3)	—	KM2-4	—	350.00

KENYA

MONETARY SYSTEM
100 Cents = 1 Shilling

5 CENTS

NICKEL-BRASS
KM#	Date	Mintage	VF	XF	Unc
1	1966	28.000	—	.10	.50
	1966	27 pcs.	—	Proof	65.00
	1967	9.600	—	.10	.50
	1968	12.000	—	.10	.50

10	1969	.800	.50	1.25	3.50
	1969	15 pcs.	—	Proof	100.00
	1970	10.000	—	.10	.30
	1971	29.680	—	.10	.20
	1973	500 pcs.	—	Proof	15.00
	1974	5.599	—	.10	.20
	1975	28.000	—	.10	.20
	1978	23.168	—	.10	.20

| 17 | 1980 | — | — | .10 | .20 |
| | 1984 | — | — | .10 | .25 |

10 CENTS

NICKEL-BRASS
2	1966	26.000	—	.40	1.00
	1966	27 pcs.	—	Proof	65.00
	1967	7.300	—	.30	.75
	1968	12.000	—	.30	.65

11	1969	3.900	—	.10	.25
	1969	15 pcs.	—	Proof	100.00
	1970	7.200	—	.10	.25
	1971	32.400	—	.10	.30
	1973	3.000	—	.10	.25
	1973	500 pcs.	—	Proof	15.00
	1974	3.000	—	.10	.25
	1975	3.000	—	.10	.25
	1977	45.600	—	.10	.25
	1978	22.600	—	.10	.25

KENYA 1143

KM#	Date	Mintage	VF	XF	Unc
18	1980	—	—	.10	1.25
	1984	—	—	.10	1.25
	1986	—	—	.10	1.25

25 CENTS

COPPER-NICKEL

3	1966	4.000	.35	.90	1.75
	1966	27 pcs.	—	Proof	75.00
	1967	4.000	.35	.80	1.50

12	1969	.200	1.00	2.50	6.00
	1969	15 pcs.	—	Proof	110.00
	1973	500 pcs.	—	Proof	15.00

50 CENTS

COPPER-NICKEL

4	1966	4.000	.40	1.00	2.00
	1966	27 pcs.	—	Proof	75.00
	1967	5.120	.40	.85	2.00
	1968	6.000	.25	.60	1.50

13	1969	.400	1.00	2.50	6.00
	1969	15 pcs.	—	Proof	110.00
	1971	9.600	.15	.25	.50
	1973	3.360	.50	1.00	2.00
	1973	500 pcs.	—	Proof	15.00
	1974	12.640	.15	.35	.50
	1975	8.000	.15	.25	.50
	1977	16.000	.15	.25	.50
	1978	20.480	.15	.25	.50

19	1980	—	.15	.25	.40

SHILLING

COPPER-NICKEL

5	1966	20.000	.50	1.00	2.00
	1966	27 pcs.	—	Proof	75.00
	1967	4.000	.50	1.00	2.25
	1968	8.000	.40	.75	1.75

KM#	Date	Mintage	VF	XF	Unc
14	1969	4.000	.30	.70	1.75
	1969	15 pcs.	—	Proof	110.00
	1971	24.000	.20	.30	.85
	1973	2.480	.35	.75	2.50
	1973	500 pcs.	—	Proof	20.00
	1974	13.520	.20	.30	.85
	1975	40.856	.20	.30	.85
	1978	20.000	.20	.30	.60

20	1980	—	.20	.40	1.35

2 SHILLINGS

COPPER-NICKEL

6	1966	3.000	1.50	3.00	5.00
	1966	27 pcs.	—	Proof	95.00
	1968	1.100	1.25	2.50	4.50

15	1969	.100	3.50	7.00	12.50
	1969	15 pcs.	—	Proof	120.00
	1971	1.920	1.25	2.50	5.00
	1973	500 pcs.	—	Proof	25.00

5 SHILLINGS

BRASS
10th Anniversary

16	1973	.100	5.00	7.50	15.00
	1973	1,500	—	Proof	35.00

COPPER-NICKEL

23	1985	—	—	1.50	2.50

100 SHILLINGS

7.6000 g, .917 GOLD, .2240 oz AGW

KM#	Date	Mintage	VF	XF	Unc
7	1966	—	—	—	125.00
	1966	7,500	—	Proof	150.00

200 SHILLINGS

28.2800 g, .925 SILVER, .8410 oz ASW
Obv: President Moi. Rev: Coat of arms.

21	1979	9,500	—	Proof	45.00

250 SHILLINGS

19.0000 g, .917 GOLD, .5602 oz AGW

8	1966	—	—	—	275.00
	1966	1,000	—	Proof	325.00

500 SHILLINGS

38.0000 g, .917 GOLD, 1.1204 oz AGW

9	1966	—	—	—	650.00
	1966	500 pcs.	—	Proof	750.00

3000 SHILLINGS

40.0000 g, .917 GOLD, 1.1787 oz AGW
Obv: President Moi. Rev: Coat of arms.

22	1979	2,000	—	Proof	750.00

MINT SETS (MS)

KM#	Date	Mintage	Identification	Issue Price	Mkt. Val.
MS1	1966(3)	—	KM 7-9	—	1050.

PROOF SETS (PS)

PS1	1966(6)	27	KM 1-6	—	450.00
PS2	1966(3)	500	KM 7-9	152.60	1225.
PS3	1969(6)	15	KM 10-15	—	650.00
PS4	1973(7)	500	KM 10-16	—	140.00

Listings For
KIAO CHAU: refer to China

KIRIBATI

The Republic of Kiribati (formerly the Gilbert Islands), 30 coral atolls and islands spread over more than 1,000,000 sq. mi. (2,590,000 sq. km.) of the southwest Pacific Ocean, has an area of 332 sq. mi. (860 sq. km.) and a population of *65,000. Capital: Bairiki, on Tarawa. In addition to the Gilbert Islands proper, Kiribati includes Ocean Island, the Central and Southern Line Islands, and the Phoenix Islands, though possession of Canton and Enderbury of the Phoenix Islands is disputed with the United States. Most families engage in subsistence fishing. Copra and phosphates are exported, mostly to Australia and New Zealand.

The Gilbert Islands and the group formerly called the Ellice Islands (now Tuvalu) comprised a single British crown colony, the Gilbert and Ellice Islands.

The Islands were first sighted by Spanish mutineers in 1537. Succeeding visits were made by the English navigators John Byron (1764), James Cook (1777), and Thomas Gilbert and John Marshall (1788). An American, Edward Fanning, arrived in 1798. Britain declared a protectorate over the Gilbert and Ellice Islands, and in 1915 began the formation of a colony which was completed with the addition of the Phoenix Islands in 1937. The Central and Southern Line Islands were administratively attached to the Gilbert and Ellice Islands colony in 1972, and remained attached to the Gilberts when Tuvalu was created in 1975. The colony became self-governing in 1971. Kiribati attained independence on July 12, 1979.

RULERS
British until 1979

MONETARY SYSTEM
100 Cents = 1 Dollar

CENT

BRONZE

KM#	Date	Mintage	VF	XF	Unc
1	1979	.090	—	.10	.15
	1979	.010	—	Proof	.75

2 CENTS

BRONZE

2	1979	.025	—	.10	.20
	1979	.010	—	Proof	1.25

5 CENTS

COPPER-NICKEL

3	1979	.020	.10	.15	.50
	1979	.010	—	Proof	2.00

10 CENTS

COPPER-NICKEL

4	1979	.020	.15	.25	1.00
	1979	.010	—	Proof	3.00

20 CENTS

COPPER-NICKEL

KM#	Date	Mintage	VF	XF	Unc
5	1979	.020	.25	.50	1.50
	1979	.010	—	Proof	4.00

50 CENTS

COPPER-NICKEL

6	1979	.020	.50	.75	2.00
	1979	.010	—	Proof	6.00

DOLLAR

COPPER-NICKEL

7	1979	.020	.85	1.25	4.00
	1979	.010	—	Proof	8.00

5 DOLLARS

28.1600 g, .500 SILVER, .4527 oz ASW
Independence
Obv: Similar to 50 Cents, Y#6.

8	1979	1,545	—	—	25.00

28.1600 g, .925 SILVER, .8375 oz ASW

8a	1979	3,326	—	Proof	30.00

COPPER-NICKEL
2nd Anniversary of Independence and Wedding of Prince Charles and Lady Diana

KM#	Date	Mintage	VF	XF	Unc
10	1981	—	—	—	5.00

28.6000 g, .925 SILVER, .8505 oz ASW

10a	1981	.025	—	Proof	25.00

COPPER-NICKEL
Royal Visit

12	1982	—	—	—	4.50

SILVER

12a	1982	—	—	Proof	90.00

10 DOLLARS

28.2800 g, .925 SILVER, .8411 oz ASW
5th Anniversary of Independence

13	1984	2,500	—	Proof	30.00

47.5200 g, .917 GOLD, 1.4012 oz AGW

13a	1984	50 pcs.	—	Proof	2000.

150 DOLLARS

15.9800 g, .917 GOLD, .4711 oz AGW
Independence

9	1979	422 pcs.	—	—	300.00
	1979	386 pcs.	—	Proof	325.00

2nd Anniversary of Independence and Wedding of Prince Charles and Lady Diana

11	1981	750 pcs.	—	—	250.00
	1981	1,500	—	Proof	275.00

PROOF SETS (PS)

KM#	Date	Mintage	Identification	Issue Price	Mkt. Val.
PS1	1979(7)	10,000	KM1-7	34.00	25.00

KOREA

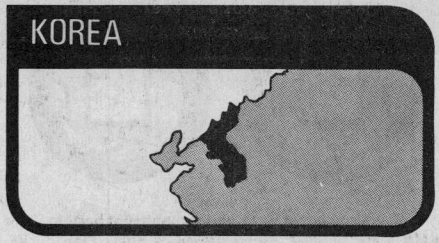

Korea, 'Land of the Morning Calm', occupies a mountainous peninsula in northeast Asia bounded by Manchuria, the Yellow Sea and the Sea of Japan.

According to legend, the first Korean dynasty, that of the House of Tangun, ruled from 2333 B.C. to 1122 B.C. It was followed by the dynasty of Kija, a Chinese scholar, which continued until 193 B.C. and brought a high civilization to Korea. The first recorded period in the history of Korea, the period of the Three Kingdoms, lasted from 57 B.C. to 935 A.D. and achieved the first political unification of the peninsula. The Kingdom of Koryo, from which Korea derived its name, was founded in 935 and continued until 1392, when it was superseded by the Yi Dynasty of King Yi. Sung Kye was to last until the Japanese annexation in 1910.

At the end of the 16th century Korea was invaded and occupied for 7 years by Japan, and from 1627 until the late 19th century it was a semi-independent tributary of China. Japan replaced China as the predominant foreign influence at the end of the Sino-Japanese War (1894-95), only to find her position threatened by Russian influence from 1896 to 1904. The Russian threat was eliminated by the Russo-Japanese War (1904-05) and in 1905 Japan established a direct protectorate over Korea. On Aug. 22, 1910, the last Korean ruler signed the treaty that annexed Korea to Japan as a government general in the Japanese Empire. Japanese suzerainty was maintained until the end of World War II.

From 1633 to 1891 the monetary system of Korea employed cast coins with a square center hole. Fifty-two agencies were authorized to procure these coins from a lesser number of coin foundries. They exist in thousands of varieties. Seed, or mother coins, were used to make the impressions in the molds in which the regular cash coins were cast. Czarist-Russian Korea experimented with Korean coins when Alieexiev of Russia, Korea's Financial Advisor, founded the First Asian Branch of the Russo-Korean Bank on March 1, 1898, and authorized the issuing of a set of new Korean coins with a crowned Russian-style quasi-eagle. British-Japanese opposition and the Russo-Japanese War operated to end the Russian coinage experiment in 1904.

RULERS

Yi Kwang (Sunjo Songhyo), 1801-1835
Yi Whan (Honjong Cholhyo), 1835-1850
Yi Chung (Choljong Yonghyo), 1850-1864
Yi Hyong (Kojong), 1864-1897
    as Emperor Kwang Mu, 1897-1907
Japanese Puppet
Yung Hi (Sunjong), 1907-1910

MONETARY UNITS

 Mun   兩 Yang, Niang

分 Fun   Hwan

錢 Hwan, Chon   圜 Won Won

IDENTIFICATION CHART

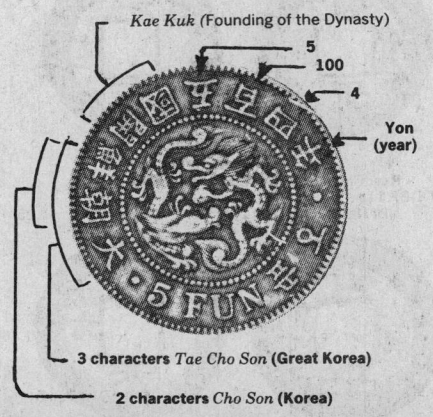

Obverse

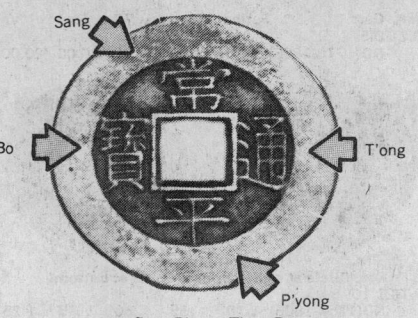

Sang P'yong T'ong Bo
"Always even currency"
Reverse

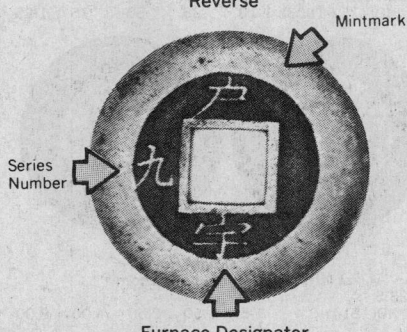

Furnace Designator

NOTE: The series number may be to the left, right or bottom of the center hole. The furnace designator may be either a numeral or a character from the THOUSAND CHARACTER CLASSIC.

SEED COINS

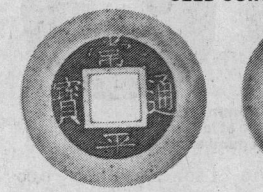

Seed coins are specially prepared examples, perfectly round, with sharp characters, used in the preparation of clay or sand molds.

Kyun	均	Government Tithe Office
Son	宣	Rice & Cloth Department
Chon	典	Central Government Mint
Mu	武	Palace Guard Office
Kum	禁	Court Guard Military Unit
Hun	訓 or 訓	Military Training Command
T'ong	統 or 統	T'ongyong Naval Office Military Office in Seoul
Kyong	経	Government Office of Pukhan Mountain Fortress
Sim	沁	Kanghwa Township Military Office
Kae	開	Kaesong Township Military Office
Song	松	Kaesong Township Military Office
I	利	Iwon Township Military Office
Ch'un	春 or 春	Ch'unch'on Township Military Office
Ch'on	川	Tanch'on Township Military Office
Ch'ang	昌	Ch'angdok Palace Mint Ch'angwon Township Military Office
Ki	圻	Kwangju Township Military Office in Kyonggi Province
Kyong	京	Kyonggi Provincial Office
Kyong Su	京水	Kyonggi Naval Station
P'yong	平	P'yongan Provincial Office
Ham	咸	Hamgyong Provincial Office

TREASURY DEPARTMENT
Ho (Ho Jo)

戶 or 户 or 戶

MUN

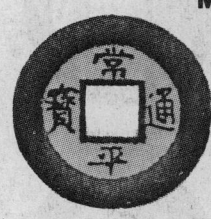 

CAST COPPER or BRONZE, 26mm
Rev: *Ho* at top in different style, series number at bottom.

KM# 9.1-9.10 Date	Series	Good	VG	Fine	VF
ND(1806)	1-10	.25	.40	.60	1.00

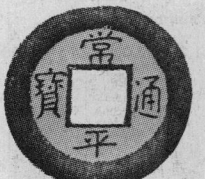 

25mm
Rev: *Sip* (10) at bottom, additional series number at left.

KM# 10.11-10.16					
ND(1806)	11-16	.25	.40	.60	1.00

KOREA 1146

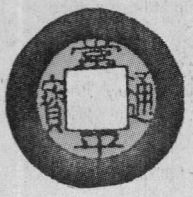 

24mm
Rev: *I (2)* at bottom, series number at right.

KM#	Date	Series	Good	VG	Fine	VF
13.1-13.10	ND(1857)	1-10	2.00	3.50	5.00	10.00

Rev: *I (2)* at bottom, series number at left.
14.1-14.10 ND(1857) 1-10 3.00 4.50 7.50 15.00

25mm
Rev: *Sam (3)* at bottom, series number at right.
15.1-15.10 ND(1832) 1-10 4.00 7.00 10.00 20.00
Rev: Dot in lower right field.
15.14 ND(1832) 4 4.00 7.00 10.00 20.00
Rev: *Sam (3)* at bottom, series number at left.
16.1-16.10 ND(1832) 1-10 4.00 7.00 10.00 20.00

23mm
Rev: *Ho* in different style, *Sam (3)* at bottom, series number at left.
17.1-17.10 ND(1857) 1-10 3.50 6.00 9.00 17.50

 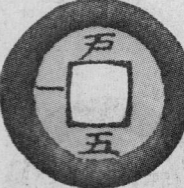

25mm
Rev: *O (5)* at bottom, series number at left.
18.1 ND(1832) 1 1.25 2.25 3.50 5.00

Rev: Dot at right, series number at bottom.
19.1-19.9 ND(1778-1806) 1-9 1.00 2.00 2.75 4.00

Rev: Dot at left, series number at bottom.

KM#	Date	Series	Good	VG	Fine	VF
20.1-20.5	ND(1778-1806)	1-5	4.00	7.00	10.00	20.00

24mm
Rev: Circle at right, series number at bottom.
21.1-21.10 ND(1757-1806) 1-10 .35 .50 .75 1.25
23mm
Rev: Circle at left, series number at bottom.
22.1-22.10 ND(1757-1806) 1-10 .35 .50 .75 1.25

 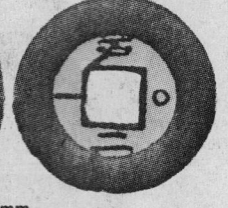

27mm
Rev: Circle at right, *Il (1)* at left, series number at bottom.
23.1-23.5 ND(1814) 1-5 1.50 2.50 4.00 8.00

26mm
Rev: Circle at left, *Il (1)* at right, series number at bottom.
24.1-24.10 ND(1840) 1-10 1.50 2.50 4.00 8.00
Rev: Circle at right, *I (2)* at left, series number at bottom.
25.1-25.10 ND(1814) 1-10 1.25 2.25 3.50 5.00

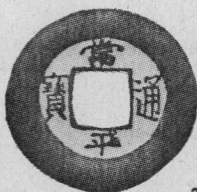 

25mm
Rev: Circle at left, *I (2)* at right, series number at bottom.
26.1-26.10 ND(1814) 1-10 1.25 2.25 3.50 5.00

 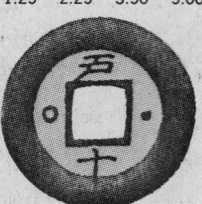

Rev: Dot at right, circle at left, series number at bottom.
27.1-27.10 ND(1778-1806) 1-10 .35 .50 .75 1.25

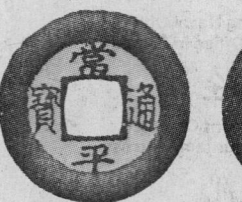 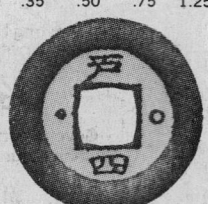

Rev: Circle at right, dot at left, series number at bottom.
28.1-28.4 ND(1778-1806) 1-4 .35 .50 .75 1.25

24mm
Rev: Crescent at right, series number at bottom.

KM#	Date	Series	Good	VG	Fine	VF
29.1-29.10	ND(1757-1806)	1-10	.35	.50	.75	1.25

Rev: Crescent at left, series number at bottom.
30.1-30.10 ND(1757-1806) 1-10 .35 .50 .75 1.25

Rev: Vertical line at right, crescent at left, number 9 at bottom.
31.9 ND(1778-1806) 9 .35 .50 .75 1.25
25mm
Rev: Dot at right, crescent at left, series number at bottom.
32.1-32.10 ND(1778-1806) 1-10 .35 .50 .75 1.25
26mm
Rev: Crescent at right, dot at left, series number at bottom.
33.1-33.10 ND(1778-1806) 1-10 .35 .50 .75 1.25

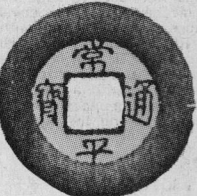 

Rev: Crescent at right, *Il (1)* at left, series number at bottom.
34.1-34.10 ND(1814) 1-10 1.50 2.50 4.00 8.00
Rev: *Il (1)* at right, crescent at left, series number at bottom.
35.1-35.10 ND(1814) 1-10 1.50 2.50 4.00 8.00

25mm
Rev: Crescent at right, *Yuk (6)* at left, series number at bottom.
36.1-36.10 ND(1857) 1-10 4.00 7.00 10.00 20.00

24mm
Small characters.
Rev: *Ch'on* at bottom, series number at right.
37.1-37.11 ND(1832) 1-11 .35 .50 .75 1.25

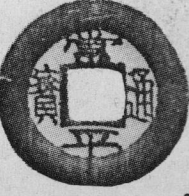 

26mm

KOREA 1147

		Large characters.				
KM#	Date	Series	Good	VG	Fine	VF
38.1-38.11	ND(1852)	1-11	.35	.50	.75	1.25

24mm
Small characters.
Rev: *Ch'on* at bottom, series number at left.

| 39.1-39.10 | ND(1832) | 1-10 | .35 | .50 | .75 | 1.25 |

25mm
Large characters.

| 40.1-40.11 | ND(1857) | 1-11 | .35 | .50 | .75 | 1.25 |

24mm
Rev: *Chi* at bottom, series number at left.

| 41.1-41.10 | ND(1852) | 1-10 | .35 | .50 | .75 | 1.25 |

Rev: *Hyon* at bottom, series number at right.

| 42.1-42.10 | ND(1852) | 1-10 | .35 | .50 | .75 | 1.25 |

26mm
Obv. & rev: Small characters.
Rev: *Hyon* at bottom, series number at left.

| 43.1-43.10 | ND(1852) | 1-10 | .35 | .50 | .75 | 1.25 |

24mm
Obv. and rev: Large characters.
Rev: *Hyon* at bottom, series number at left.

| A43.1-A43.10 | ND(1852) | 1-10 | .35 | .50 | .75 | 1.25 |

Rev: *Hwang* (yellow) at bottom, series number at right.

| 44.1-44.10 | ND(1832) | 1-10 | .35 | .50 | .75 | 1.25 |

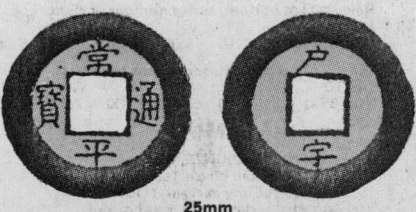

25mm
Rev: *U* at bottom.

| 45 | ND(1814) | — | 1.25 | 2.25 | 3.50 | 5.00 |

Rev: 19mm inner circle, *U* at bottom, series number at right.

KM#	Date	Series	Good	VG	Fine	VF
46.1-46.10	ND(1814)	1-10	.75	1.25	2.00	4.00

23mm
Rev: 16mm inner circle, *U* at bottom, series number at right.

| 47.1-47.10 | ND(1832) | 1-10 | .35 | .50 | .75 | 1.25 |

Rev: *U* at bottom, series number at left.

| 48.1-48.10 | ND(1814) | 1-10 | .35 | .50 | .75 | 1.25 |

25mm
Obv: Smaller *Po*.

| A48.1-A48.10 | | 1-10 | .35 | .50 | .75 | 1.25 |

24mm
Rev: *U* at bottom, *Il* (1) at right, double circle at left.

| 49 | ND(1832) | — | .35 | .50 | .75 | 1.25 |

Rev: *Chu* at bottom, *Chong* at left, series number at right.

| 50.1-50.10 | ND(1832) | 1-10 | .35 | .50 | .75 | 1.25 |

Rev: *Chu* at bottom, series number at left.

| 51.1-51.10 | ND(1852) | 1-10 | .35 | .50 | .75 | 1.25 |

26mm
Rev: *Hong* at bottom, series number at left.

| 52.1-52.10 | ND(1852) | 1-10 | .75 | 1.25 | 2.00 | 4.00 |

22-24mm

KM#	Date	Series	Good	VG	Fine	VF
53.1-53.10	ND(1852)	1-10	.35	.50	.75	1.25

25mm
Rev: *Il* (sun) at bottom, series number at left.

| 54.1-54.10 | ND(1852) | 1-10 | .35 | .50 | .75 | 1.25 |

Rev: *Wol* (moon) at bottom, series number at left.

| 55.1-55.10 | ND(1852) | 1-10 | .35 | .50 | .75 | 1.25 |

Rev: *Chin* at bottom, series number at left.

| 56.1-56.10 | ND(1852) | 1-10 | .35 | .50 | .75 | 1.25 |

24mm
Rev: *Yol* at bottom, series number at left.

| 57.1-57.10 | ND(1852) | 1-10 | .35 | .50 | .75 | 1.25 |

Rev: *Nae* at bottom, series number at left.

| 58.1-58.10 | ND(1852) | 1-10 | .35 | .50 | .75 | 1.25 |

Rev: *Wang* at bottom, series number at left.

| 59.1-59.10 | ND(1852) | 1-10 | .35 | .50 | .75 | 1.25 |

23mm
Rev: *Saeng* at bottom, series number at left.

| 60.1-60.10 | ND(1852) | 1-10 | .35 | .50 | .75 | 1.25 |

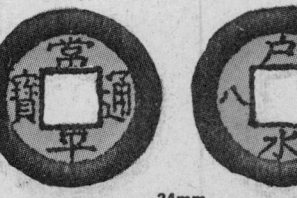

24mm
Rev: *Su* at bottom, series number at left.

KOREA 1148

KM#	Date	Series	Good	VG	Fine	VF
61.1-61.10	ND(1852)	1-10	.35	.50	.75	1.25

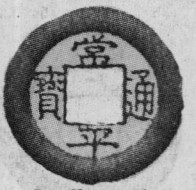

Rev: *Kwang* at bottom, series number at left.

62.1-62.10	ND(1852)	1-10	.35	.50	.75	1.25

Rev: *Kwang* at bottom, dot at right, series number at left.

63.6	ND(1852)	6	.35	.50	.75	1.25

25mm
Rev: *Kwang* at bottom, series number at right.

64.2	ND(1852)	2	.35	.50	.75	1.25

23mm
Rev: *Mun* at bottom, series number at right.

65.1-65.10	ND(1852)	1-10	.35	.50	.75	1.25

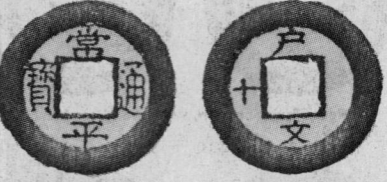

24mm
Rev: *Mun* at bottom, series number at left.

66.1-66.10	ND(1832)	1-10	.35	.50	.75	1.25

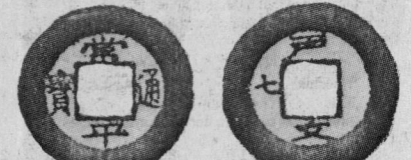

Rev: *Ho* in different style.

67.1-67.10	ND(1832)	1-10	.35	.50	.75	1.25

23mm
Rev: *Mun* at bottom, circle at left, series number at right.

68.1-68.10	ND(1832)	1-10	.35	.50	.75	1.25

25mm
Rev: *Mun* at bottom, circle at right, series number at left.

69.1-69.5	ND(1832)	1-5	.85	1.50	2.00	2.75

24mm
Rev: *Ip* at bottom, series number at right.

70.1-70.10	ND(1814)	1-10	.35	.50	.75	1.25

23mm
Rev: *Ip* at bottom, series number at left.

71.1-71.10	ND(1806-14)	1-10	.35	.50	.75	1.25

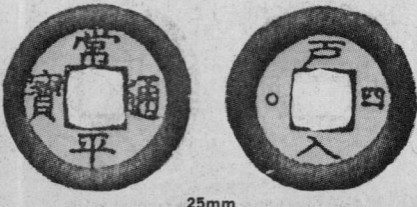

25mm
Rev: *Ip* at bottom, circle at left, series number at right.

KM#	Date	Series	Good	VG	Fine	VF
72.1-72.10	ND(1806-14)	1-10	.35	.50	.75	1.25

Rev: *Ip* at bottom, circle at right, series number at left.

73.1-73.5	ND(1806-14)	1-5	4.00	7.00	10.00	20.00

5 MUN

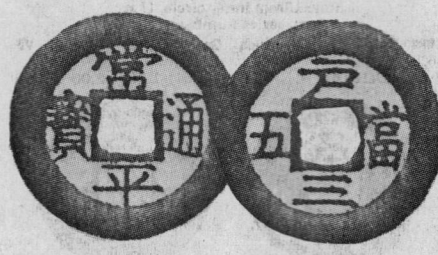

CAST COPPER or BRONZE
30mm
Small characters, inner circle 21-22mm.
Rev: *Tang* at right, *O* (5) at left, series number at bottom.

136.1-136.10	ND(1883)	1-10	1.00	1.75	3.00	4.50

31mm
Medium characters, inner circle 21-22mm.

137.1-137.11	ND(1883)	1-11	1.00	1.75	3.00	4.50

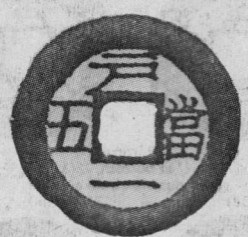

30mm
Large characters, inner circle 21-22mm.

138.1-138.11	ND(1883)	1-11	2.00	3.50	5.00	10.00

31mm
Inner circle 19mm

139.1-139.10	ND(1883)	1-10	2.00	3.50	5.00	10.00

Rev: Small *Ho* at top, crescent under series number at bottom.

140.1-140.10	ND(1883)	1-10	1.00	1.75	3.00	4.50

30mm
Rev: Wide *Ho* at top, crescent under series number at bottom.

KM#	Date	Series	Good	VG	Fine	VF
141.1-141.10	ND(1883)	1-10	1.50	2.50	4.50	8.50

Small characters, inner circle 19mm.
Rev: Crescent under series number at bottom.

142.1-142.10	ND(1883)	1-10	2.00	3.50	5.00	10.00

100 MON

CAST COPPER or BRONZE, 24.00 g, 39-40mm

143	ND(1866)	—	1.25	2.00	3.00	4.50

NOTE: More than 40 varieties exist.

GOVERNMENT TITHE OFFICE
均 Kyun (Kyun Yok Ch'ong)

MUN

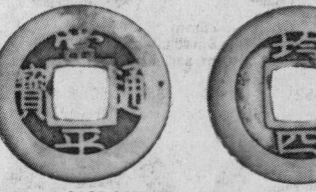

CAST COPPER or BRONZE, 4.00 g
24mm
Rev: *Kyun* at top, series number at bottom.

147.1-147.10	ND(1807)	1-10	.35	.60	1.00	1.50

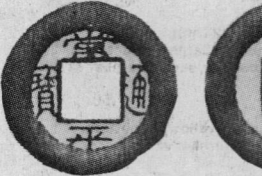

23mm
Rev: *Il* (1) at bottom, series number at right.

148.1-148.10	ND(1857)	1-10	3.00	5.00	7.50	15.00

Rev: *Il* (1) at bottom, series number at left.

149.1-149.10	ND(1857)	1-10	3.00	5.00	7.50	15.00

5 MUN

CAST BRONZE, 31mm
Small characters.
Rev: *Tang* at right, *O* (5) at right, series number at bottom.

150.1-150.11	ND(1883)	1-11	.50	.85	1.50	2.25

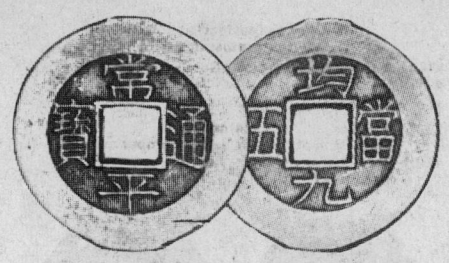

32mm
Medium characters.

KM#	Date	Series	Good	VG	Fine	VF
151.1-151.10	ND(1883)	1-10	.75	1.25	2.25	3.50

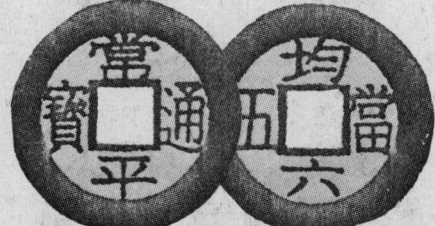

31mm
Large characters.
152.1-152.10
ND(1883)   1-10   1.25   2.00   3.50   5.50

30mm
Different Kyun
153.1-153.11
ND(1883)   1-11   1.25   2.00   3.50   5.50

RICE AND CLOTH DEPARTMENT
宣 Son (Son Hye Ch'ong) 惠
MUN

CAST COPPER or BRONZE, 4.00 g
25mm
Rev: Series number at bottom.
174.1-174.6
ND(1814)   1-6   .50   .85   1.50   2.50

Large characters.
Rev: Hye at top, series number at bottom.
175.1-175.12
ND(1806)   1-12   .50   .85   1.50   2.50

Small characters.
176.1-176.12
ND(1806)   1-12   .50   .85   1.50   2.50

26mm
Rev: I (2) at left, series number at bottom.
177.1-177.7
ND(1836)   1-7   .50   .85   1.50   2.50

CENTRAL GOVERNMENT MINT
典 Chon (Chon Hwan' Guk)
5 MUN

CAST BRONZE, 31mm
Large characters.
Rev: Tang at right, O (5)
at left, series number at bottom.

KM#	Date	Series	Good	VG	Fine	VF
209.1-209.15	ND(1883)	1-15	1.00	1.65	2.50	4.00

32mm
Small characters.
210.1-210.15
ND(1883)   1-15   .75   1.25   2.00   3.00

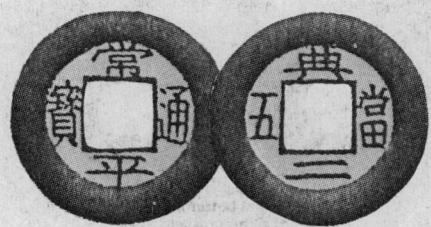

Reduced size, 29mm
211.1-211.10
ND(1883)   1-10   .75   1.25   2.00   3.00

28mm
Rev: Dot below series number at bottom.
212.1-212.3
ND(1883)   1-3   .85   1.35   2.25   3.50

PALACE GUARD OFFICE
武 Mu (Mu Wi Yong)
MUN

CAST BRONZE, 26mm, 4.00 g
Rev: Ch'on at bottom, series number at left.
337.1-337.20
ND(1881)   1-20   1.00   1.75   2.75   4.00

Reduced size, 23-24mm
338.1-338.20
ND(1881)   1-20   .30   .60   1.00   1.50

24mm
Rev: Wan at bottom, series number at left.
339.1 ND(1881)   1   35.00   60.00   100.00   175.00

COURT GUARD
禁 Kum (Kum Wi Yong)
MUN

CAST BRONZE, 4.00 g, 25mm
Large characters.
Rev: Kum at top, series number at bottom.

KM#	Date	Series	Good	VG	Fine	VF
340.1-340.8	ND(1823)	1-8	.30	.60	1.00	1.50

Small characters.
341.1-341.8
ND(1823)   1-8   .30   .60   1.00   1.50

MILITARY TRAINING COMMAND
訓 or 訓 Hun (Hui Ly On Do Gam)
MUN

CAST BRONZE, 4.00 g, 25mm
Rev: Hun at top, series number at bottom.
448.1-448.6
ND(1828)   1-6   .75   1.25   2.00   3.00

24mm
Rev: Ch'on at bottom, series number at left.
449.1-449.10
ND(1857)   1-10   .25   .50   .85   1.25

Rev: Chong at bottom, series number at left.
450.1-450.10
ND(1857)   1-10   .25   .50   .85   1.25

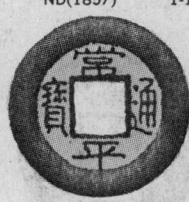 

Rev: Tae at bottom, series number at left.
451.1-451.10
ND(1857)   1-10   .25   .50   .85   1.25

Rev: Kong at bottom, series number at left.
452.1-452.10
ND(1857)   1-10   .25   .50   .85   1.25

25mm
Rev: Mun at bottom, series number at right.
453.1 ND(1857)   1   .25   .50   .85   1.25

KOREA 1150

**24mm
Rev: *Mun* at bottom, series number at left.**

KM#	Date	Series	Good	VG	Fine	VF
454.1-454.10	ND(1857)	1-10	.25	.50	.85	1.25

Rev: *Ch'on* (thousand) at bottom, series number at left.

| 455.1-455.10 | ND(1857) | 1-10 | .25 | .50 | .85 | 1.25 |

**25mm
Rev: *Chung* at bottom, series number at right.**

| 456.1 | ND(1857) | 1 | .35 | .75 | 1.25 | 2.00 |

**24mm
Rev: *Chung* at bottom, series number at left.**

| 457.1-457.10 | ND(1857) | 1-10 | .25 | .50 | .85 | 1.25 |

**25mm
Obv: Small characters.
Rev: *T'o* at bottom, series number at right.**

| 458.1-458.10 | ND(1857) | 1-10 | .25 | .50 | .85 | 1.25 |

Obv: Large characters.

| 459.1-459.10 | ND(1857) | 1-10 | .25 | .50 | .85 | 1.25 |

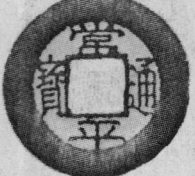 

**Obv: Small characters.
Rev: *T'o* at bottom, series number at left.**

| 460.1-460.10 | ND(1857) | 1-10 | .25 | .50 | .85 | 1.25 |

Obv: Large characters.

| 461.1-461.10 | ND(1857) | 1-10 | .25 | .50 | .85 | 1.25 |

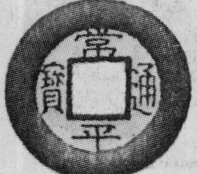 

Rev: *T'o* at bottom, series

number at right, crescent at left.

KM#	Date	Series	Good	VG	Fine	VF
462.1-462.5	ND(1857)	1-5	.25	.50	.85	1.25

**25mm
Obv: Small characters.
Rev: *T'o* at bottom, crescent at right, series number at left.**

463.1	ND(1857)	1	.25	.50	.85	1.25
463.2		2	.25	.50	.85	1.25
463.3		3	.25	.50	.85	1.25
463.4		4	2.00	3.00	4.00	6.50
463.5		5	2.00	3.00	4.00	6.50

**24mm
Obv: Large characters.**

| 464.1-464.5 | ND(1857) | 1-5 | .25 | .50 | .85 | 1.25 |

Rev: *Won* (first) at bottom, series number at right.

| 465.1-465.10 | ND(1857) | 1-10 | .25 | .50 | .85 | 1.25 |

**25mm
Rev: *Won* at bottom, series number at left.**

| 466.1-466.10 | ND(1857) | 1-10 | .25 | .50 | .85 | 1.25 |

Rev: *Won* at bottom, series number at right, crescent at left.

| 467.1-467.5 | ND(1857) | 1-5 | .25 | .50 | .85 | 1.25 |

**26mm
Rev: *Saeng* at bottom, series number at right.**

| 468.1-468.10 | ND(1857) | 1-10 | .25 | .50 | .85 | 1.25 |

**25mm
Rev: *Saeng* at bottom, series number at left.**

| 469.1-469.10 | ND(1857) | 1-10 | .25 | .50 | .85 | 1.25 |

**24mm
Rev: *Saeng* at bottom, crescent at right, series number at left.**

| 470.1-470.5 | ND(1857) | 1-5 | .25 | .50 | .85 | 1.25 |

25mm

Rev: *Chon* (perfect) at bottom, series number at right.

KM#	Date	Series	Good	VG	Fine	VF
471.1-471.10	ND(1857)	1-10	.25	.50	.85	1.25

**24mm
Rev: *Chon* at bottom, series number at left.**

| 472.1-472.10 | ND(1857) | 1-10 | .25 | .50 | .85 | 1.25 |

**25mm
Rev: *Chon* at bottom, crescent at right, series number at left.**

| 473.1-473.5 | ND(1857) | 1-5 | .25 | .50 | .85 | 1.25 |

**24mm
Rev: *Kil* at bottom, series number at right.**

| 474.1-474.10 | ND(1857) | 1-10 | 6.00 | 10.00 | 15.00 | 25.00 |

Rev: *Kil* at bottom, series number at left.

| 475.1-475.10 | ND(1857) | 1-10 | 6.00 | 10.00 | 15.00 | 25.00 |

Rev: *Kil* at bottom, crescent at right, series number at left.

| 476.1-476.5 | ND(1857) | 1-5 | 6.00 | 10.00 | 15.00 | 25.00 |

SEOUL MILITARY OFFICE
統 T'ong (T'ong Wi Yong)
5 MON

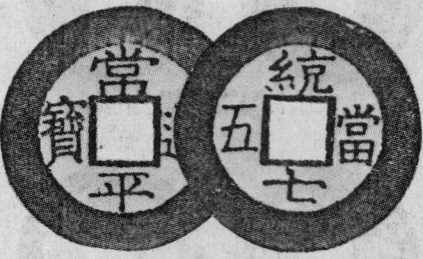

**CAST BRONZE, 32mm
Inside diameter 20-22mm.
Rev: *Tang* at right, *O* (5) at left, series number at bottom.**

| 763.1-763.20 | ND(1883) | 1-20 | .65 | 1.25 | 2.25 | 3.50 |

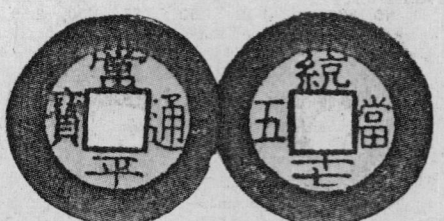

Reduced size, 29mm, inside diameter 18-19mm.

| 764.1-764.20 | ND(1883) | 1-20 | .65 | 1.25 | 2.25 | 3.50 |

KOREA 1151

GOVERNMENT OFFICE
PUKHAN MOUNTAIN FORTRESS
經 Kyong (Kyong Ni Ch'ong)
MUN

CAST BRONZE, 4.00 g, 26mm
Rev: *Kyong* at top, series number at bottom.

KM#	Date	Series	Good	VG	Fine	VF
765.1-765.10	ND(1830)	1-10	.50	.90	1.35	2.00

Rev: *Sip* (10) at bottom and additional series number at left.

| 766.11-766.16 | ND(1830) | 11-16 | .50 | .90 | 1.35 | 2.00 |

KANGWHA TOWNSHIP MILITARY OFFICE
沁 Sim (Kang Hwa Kwal Li Yong)
MUN

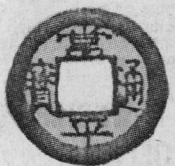 

CAST BRONZE, 4.00 g, 22mm
Rev: *Sim* at top, *Won* (first) at bottom, dot at left.

| 771 | ND(1883) | — | 1.75 | 2.50 | 3.50 | 5.00 |

25mm
Rev: *Won* (first) at bottom, series number at left.

| 772.1-772.10 | ND(1883) | 1-10 | 6.00 | 10.00 | 16.50 | 25.00 |

22mm
Rev: *Won* (first) at bottom, series number at right, circle at left.

| 773 | ND(1883) | 1 | 40.00 | 80.00 | 125.00 | 200.00 |

23mm Wide rim.
Rev: *Won* (first) at bottom, series number at right, crescent at left.

| 774.1-774.10 | ND(1883) | 1-10 | 6.00 | 10.00 | 16.50 | 25.00 |

21mm Narrow rim.
Rev: *Won* (first) at bottom, series number at right, crescent at left.

| A774.1-A774.10 | ND(1883) | 1-10 | 6.00 | 10.00 | 16.50 | 25.00 |

5 MUN

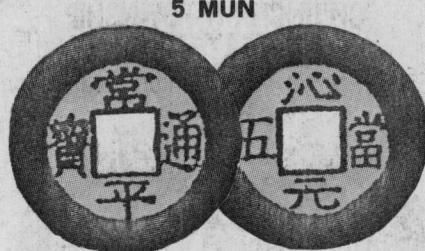

CAST BRONZE, 31mm
Rev: *Sim* at top, *Won* at bottom, *Tang* at right, *O* (5) at left.

KM#	Date	Series	Good	VG	Fine	VF
775	ND(1883)	—	3.50	6.50	10.00	15.00

30mm Large characters.
Rev: Series number at bottom.

| 776.1-776.11 | ND(1883) | 1-11 | 1.25 | 2.00 | 2.75 | 4.00 |

32mm Small characters.

| 777.1-777.10 | ND(1883) | 1-10 | 1.25 | 2.00 | 2.75 | 4.00 |

Rev: Crescent below series number.

| 778.1-778.7 | ND(1883) | 1-7 | 8.00 | 12.00 | 20.00 | 30.00 |

Rev: Crescent at lower left.

| 779.1-779.13 | ND(1883) | 1-13 | 3.00 | 5.00 | 8.00 | 12.00 |

KAESONG TOWNSHIP MILITARY OFFICE
開 Kae (Kae Song Kwal Li Yong)
MUN

CAST BRONZE, 4.00 g, 23.5mm
Large characters.
Rev: Series number at bottom.

| 791.1-791.5 | ND(1836) | 1-5 | .35 | .65 | 1.00 | 1.50 |

24.5mm
Rev: Circle at right, series number at bottom.

| 793.1-793.10 | ND(1816) | 1-10 | .35 | .65 | 1.00 | 1.50 |

24mm
Rev: Circle at left, series number at bottom.

| 794.1-794.10 | ND(1816) | 1-10 | .35 | .65 | 1.00 | 1.50 |

25mm
Rev: Crescent at right, series number at bottom.

KM#	Date	Series	Good	VG	Fine	VF
795.1-795.10	ND(1816)	1-10	.35	.65	1.00	1.50

25.5mm Small characters.
Rev: Crescent at right, series number at bottom.

| A795.1-A795.10 | ND(1836) | 1-10 | 2.50 | 6.00 | 10.00 | 15.00 |

25mm
Rev: Crescent at left, series number at bottom.

| B795.1-B795.10 | ND(1816) | 1-10 | .35 | .65 | 1.00 | 1.50 |

Small characters, wider rims. Small crescent.

| C795.1-C795.10 | ND(1836) | 1-10 | 2.50 | 6.00 | 10.00 | 15.00 |

25mm
Rev: *Ch'on* at bottom, series number at right.

| 796.1-796.10 | ND(1836) | 1-10 | .35 | .65 | 1.00 | 1.50 |

Rev: *Ch'on* at bottom, *Sip* (10) at right, additional series number at left.

| 797.11-797.15 | ND(1836) | 11-15 | .35 | .65 | 1.00 | 1.50 |

Rev: *Ch'on* at bottom, series number at right, crescent at left.

| 798.1-798.3 | ND(1836) | 1-3 | .35 | .65 | 1.00 | 1.50 |

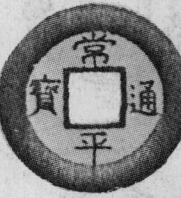 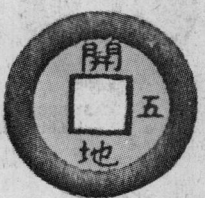

25.5mm
Rev: *Chi* at bottom, series number at right.

| 799.1-799.10 | ND(1836) | 1-10 | 1.00 | 2.00 | 3.00 | 4.50 |

24.5mm
Rev: *Chi* at bottom, *Sip* (10) at right, additional series number at left.

| 800.11-800.19 | ND(1836) | 11-19 | 1.00 | 2.00 | 3.00 | 4.50 |

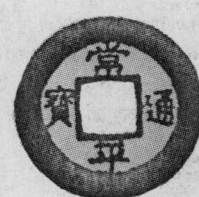 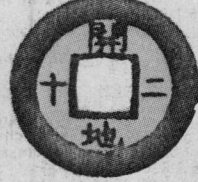 

25mm
Rev: *Chi* at bottom, *I* (2) at right, *Sip* (10) at left.

| 801.20 | ND(1836) | 1 | 1.00 | 2.00 | 3.00 | 4.50 |

KOREA 1152

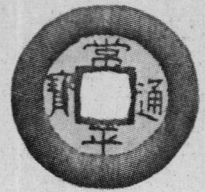 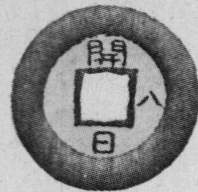

Rev: *Il* (sun) at bottom, series number at right.

KM#	Date	Series	Good	VG	Fine	VF
802.1-802.10	ND(1836)	1-10	1.00	2.00	3.00	4.50

24.5mm
Rev: *Il* (sun) at bottom, series number at left.

| 803.1-803.10 | ND(1836) | 1-10 | 1.00 | 2.00 | 3.00 | 4.50 |

 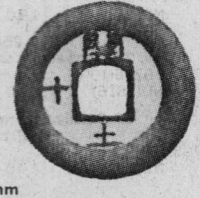

24mm
Rev: *T'o* at bottom, series number at left.

| 804.10 | ND(1836) | 1 | — | — | Rare | — |

松 Song (Song Do Kwal Li Yong)
NOTE: *Song Do* is another name for *Kae Song*.

MUN

CAST BRONZE, 4.00 g, 25mm
Rev: *Song* at top, series number at bottom.

| 805.1-805.10 | ND(1882) | 1-10 | .35 | .65 | 1.00 | 1.75 |

IWON TOWNSHIP MILITARY OFFICE
利 I (I Won Kwal Li Yong)

MUN

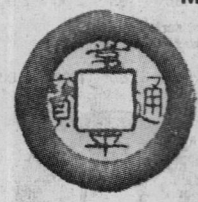 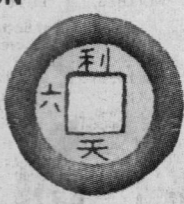

CAST BRONZE, 4.00 g, 24mm
Rev: *Chon* at bottom, series number at left.

| 834.1-834.6 | ND(1882) | 1-6 | 1.75 | 3.00 | 4.50 | 6.50 |

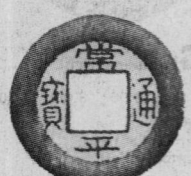 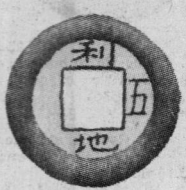

23mm
Large characters.
Rev: *Chi* at bottom, series number at right.

| 835.1-835.5 | ND(1882) | 1-5 | 7.50 | 12.50 | 20.00 | 35.00 |

Small characters.

| A835.1-A835.5 | ND(1882) | 1-5 | 7.50 | 12.50 | 20.00 | 35.00 |

24mm
Large characters.
Rev: *Chi* at bottom, series number at left.

| 836.1-836.5 | ND(1882) | 1-5 | 7.50 | 12.50 | 20.00 | 35.00 |

22mm
Small characters.

| 837.1-837.5 | ND(1882) | 1-5 | 7.50 | 12.50 | 20.00 | 35.00 |

CH'UNCH'ON TOWNSHIP MILITARY OFFICE
春 or 春 Ch'un (Ch'un Ch'on Kwal Li Yong)

5 MUN

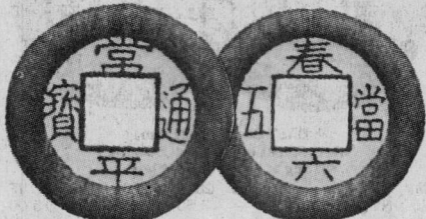

CAST BRONZE, 31mm
Large characters.
Rev: *Ch'un* at top, *Tang* at right,
O (5) at left, series number at bottom.

KM#	Date	Series	Good	VG	Fine	VF
874.1-874.12	ND(1888)	1-12	1.00	1.75	2.75	4.00

30mm
Medium characters.

| 875.1-875.11 | ND(1888) | 1-11 | .50 | 1.00 | 1.50 | 2.50 |

Reduced size, 27mm

| 876.1-876.10 | ND(1888) | 1-10 | 1.00 | 1.75 | 2.75 | 4.00 |

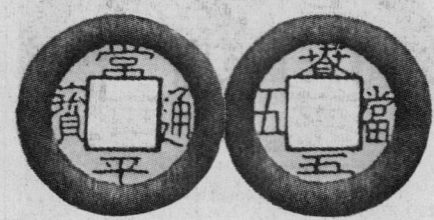

28mm
Rev: *Ch'un* at top in different style.

| 877.1-877.15 | ND(1888) | 1-15 | 1.00 | 1.75 | 2.75 | 4.00 |

29mm
Rev: Crescent at bottom under series number.

| 878.1-878.10 | ND(1888) | 1-10 | 2.00 | 3.00 | 4.00 | 6.00 |

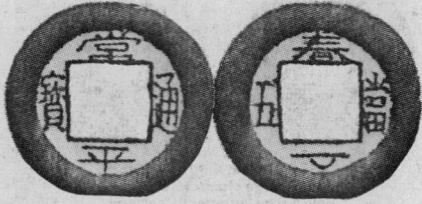

28mm
Rev: Inverted crescent at bottom under series number.

| 879.1-879.10 | ND(1888) | 1-10 | 1.50 | 3.00 | 5.00 | 8.00 |

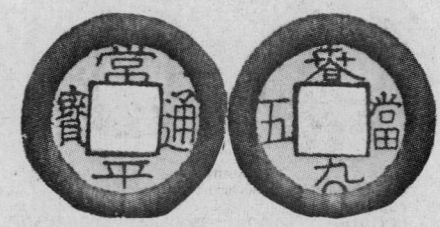

Rev: *Ch'un* at top in different style,
crescent at bottom under series number.

| 880.1-880.20 | ND(1888) | 1-20 | 2.00 | 3.00 | 4.00 | 6.00 |

TANCH'ON TOWNSHIP MILITARY OFFICE
川 Chon (Tan Ch'on Kwal Li Yong)

5 MUN

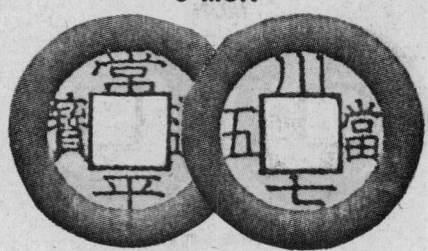

CAST BRONZE, 32mm
Inside diameter 22mm.
Rev: *Ch'on* at top, *Tang* at right,
O (5) at left, series number at bottom.

KM#	Date	Series	Good	VG	Fine	VF
881.1-881.10	ND(1883)	1-10	2.25	4.00	6.00	8.50

28mm
Reduced size, inside diameter 20mm.

| 882.1-882.10 | ND(1883) | 1-10 | 2.75 | 5.00 | 7.50 | 11.00 |

CH'ANG DOK PALACE MINT
昌 Ch'ang (Ch'ang Dok Kung)

MUN

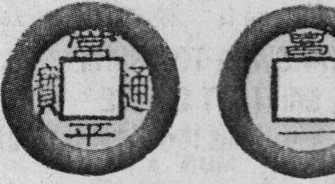

CAST BRONZE, 4.00 g, 23.5mm
Rev: *Ch'ang* at top, series number at bottom.

| 883.1 | ND(1864-95) | 1 | 3.50 | 6.00 | 10.00 | 16.00 |

NOTE: Similar pieces without series number are considered to be spurious.

CH'ANG WON TOWNSHIP MILITARY OFFICE
昌 Ch'ang (Ch'ang Won Kwal Li Yong)

5 MUN

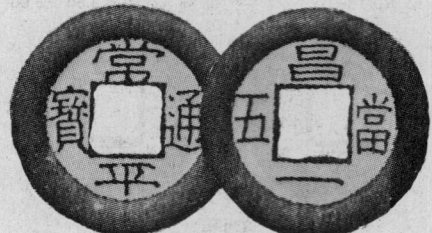

CAST BRONZE, 31mm
Large characters.
Rev: *Ch'ang* at top, *Tang* at right,
O (5) at left, series number at bottom.

| 884.1-884.12 | ND(1887) | 1-12 | 2.00 | 3.50 | 5.50 | 8.50 |

Reduced size, 29mm
Small characters.

| 885.1-885.12 | ND(1887) | 1-12 | 2.00 | 3.50 | 5.50 | 8.50 |

31mm
Large characters.
Rev: Crescent at bottom under series number.

| 886.1-886.9 | ND(1887) | 1-9 | 2.00 | 3.50 | 5.50 | 8.50 |

Reduced size, 29mm
Small characters.
Rev: Crescent at bottom under series number.

| 887.1-887.10 | ND(1887) | 1-10 | 2.00 | 3.50 | 5.50 | 8.50 |

30mm
Rev: Sun or circle at upper right.

| A887.1-A887.10 | ND(1887) | 1-10 | 2.50 | 4.00 | 6.00 | 10.00 |

KWANG JU TOWNSHIP MILITARY OFFICE
Kyonggi Province

圻 **Ki (Kwang Ju Kwal Li Yong)**
MUN

CAST BRONZE, 4.00 g, 25mm
Rev: *Ch'on* at bottom, series number at right.

KM#	Date	Series	Good	VG	Fine	VF
889.1-889.5	ND(1836)	1-5	.75	1.25	2.00	3.00

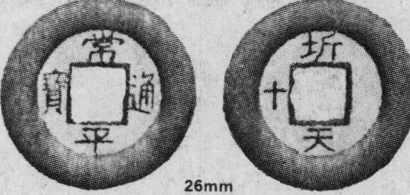

26mm
Large characters.
Rev: *Ch'on* at bottom, series number at left.

| 890.1-890.10 | ND(1836) | 1-10 | .75 | 1.25 | 2.00 | 3.00 |

24mm
Small characters.

| A890.1-A890.10 | ND(1836) | 1-10 | .75 | 1.25 | 2.00 | 3.00 |

27mm
Rev: *Ch'on* at bottom, series number at right, circle at left.

| 891.1-891.5 | ND(1839) | 1-5 | 3.50 | 6.00 | 10.00 | 18.00 |

Rev: Crescent at left, series number at right.

| 892.1-892.10 | ND(1836) | 1-10 | 3.50 | 6.00 | 10.00 | 18.00 |

26.5mm
Rev: Crescent at right, series number at left.

| 893.1-893.10 | ND(1839) | 1-10 | 3.50 | 6.00 | 9.00 | 16.00 |

Rev: *I* (2) at bottom, series number at right.

| 894.1-894.10 | ND(1839) | 1-10 | 5.00 | 8.50 | 13.50 | 20.00 |

Rev: *I* (2) at bottom, series number at left.

| 895.1-895.10 | ND(1839) | 1-10 | 1.50 | 2.50 | 4.50 | 6.50 |

Rev: *I* (2) at bottom, crescent at right, series number at left.

| 896.1-896.10 | ND(1839) | 1-10 | 5.00 | 8.00 | 12.50 | 20.00 |

KYONGGI PROVINCIAL OFFICE
京 **Kyong (Kyong Gi Kam Yong)**
5 MUN

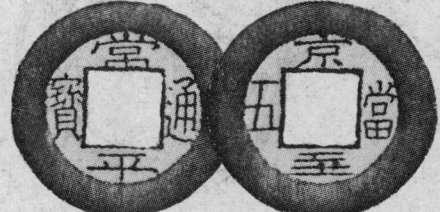

CAST BRONZE, 30mm
Rev: *Kyong* at top, *Tang* at right, *O* (5) at left, series number at bottom.

| 907 | ND(1888) | 1-27 | .65 | 1.25 | 2.00 | 3.00 |

P'YONGAN PROVINCIAL OFFICE
平 **P'yong (P'yong An Kam Yong)**
MUN

CAST BRONZE, 22mm, 4.00 g

KM#	Date	Series	Good	VG	Fine	VF
915.1	ND(1883)	1	.25	.40	.65	1.00
915.2		2	.25	.40	.65	1.00
915.3		3	.25	.40	.65	1.00
915.4		4	.25	.40	.65	1.00
915.5		5	.25	.40	.65	1.00
915.6		6	.25	.40	.65	1.00
915.7		7	.25	.40	.65	1.00
915.8		8	3.50	6.00	9.00	16.00
915.9		9	3.50	6.00	9.00	16.00
915.10		10	3.50	6.00	9.00	16.00
915.11		11	3.50	6.00	9.00	16.00

CAST BRONZE, 26mm, 4.00 g
Rev: Circle at left, series number at bottom.

KM#	Date	Series	Good	VG	Fine	VF
917.1-917.5	ND(1883)	1-5	.25	.40	.60	1.00

23mm
Rev: *Ch'on* at bottom, series number at left.

| 918.1-918.11 | ND(1891) | 1-11 | .25 | .35 | .50 | .75 |

22mm
Rev: *Chi* at bottom, series number at left.

| 919.1 | ND(1891) | 1 | .25 | .40 | .60 | 1.00 |
| 919.4 | | 4 | .25 | .40 | .60 | 1.00 |

21mm
Rev: *Il* (sun) at bottom.

| 920 | ND(1891) | — | .75 | 1.25 | 2.00 | 3.00 |

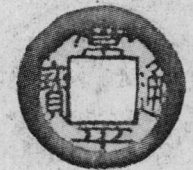 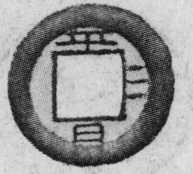

22mm
Rev: *Il* (sun) at bottom, series number at right.

| 921.1-921.10 | ND(1891) | 1-10 | .25 | .40 | .60 | .85 |

Rev: *Il* (sun) at bottom, series number at left.

| 922.1-922.14 | ND(1891) | 1-14 | .25 | .40 | .60 | .85 |

 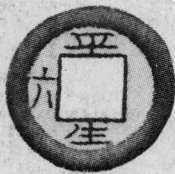

22.5mm
Rev: *Saeng* at bottom, series number at left.

| 923.1-923.13 | ND(1891) | 1-13 | .25 | .40 | .60 | .85 |

22mm
Rev: *Saeng* at bottom, series number at right, circle at left.

| 924.1-924.10 | ND(1891) | 1-10 | .50 | .75 | 1.25 | 2.00 |

5 MUN

CAST BRONZE, 31mm

| A970.1-A970.10 | ND(1883) | 1-10 | 1.00 | 2.00 | 3.00 | 5.00 |

HAMGYONG PROVINCIAL OFFICE
咸 **Ham (Ham Gyong Kam Yong)**
MUN

CAST BRONZE, 4.00 g, 24mm
Rev: *Ham* at top, series number at bottom.

| 974.1-974.4 | ND(1834) | 1-4 | .75 | 1.50 | 2.25 | 3.25 |

TAE DONG
TREASURY DEPARTMENT
CHON

 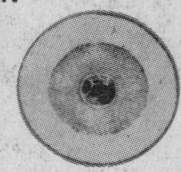

SILVER, 22mm
Rev: *Ho* in green, black or blue cloisonne enameled center circle.

KM#	Date	Mintage	VG	Fine	VF	XF
1081	ND(1882-83)	*	50.00	100.00	150.00	250.00

2 CHON

 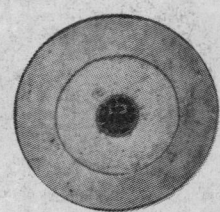

SILVER, 27mm
Rev: *Ho* in green, black or blue cloisonne enameled center circle.

| 1082 | ND(1882-83) | * | 75.00 | 150.00 | 250.00 | 400.00 |

3 CHON

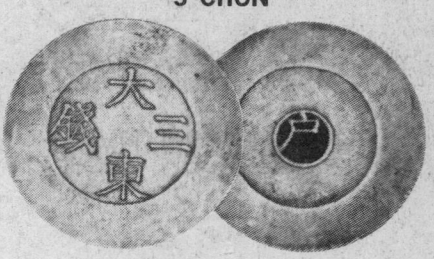

SILVER, 32.5mm
Rev: *Ho* in green, black or blue cloisonne enameled center circle.

| 1083 | ND(1882-83) | * | 250.00 | 400.00 | 550.00 | 800.00 |

*NOTE: Due to the added expense of adding the 'cloisonne' enamel during production the silver one, two & three Chon KM#1081-83 were discontinued in June, 1883. Examples with cloisonne missing are valued at about one half normal valuations. There are many types of trial sets of 1, 2 and 3 Chon in existence.

MILLED COINAGE

During the 1880's and 1890's, Korea experimented with several different types of machine-struck coins including a struck "Cash" coin with round center hole, KM#1100. Some pattern coins of this period exist, some of which may have actually entered circulation.

MONETARY SYSTEM
1888-1891
1000 Mun = 1 Warn

5 MUN

BRASS

KM#	Date	Mintage	Fine	VF	XF	Unc
1100	ND(1891)	—	150.00	300.00	450.00	600.00

COPPER, 3.25 g

KM#	Year	Date	Fine	VF	XF	Unc
1101	497	(1888)	60.00	120.00	200.00	400.00

KOREA 1154

10 MUN

COPPER, 6.50 g

KM#	Year	Date	Fine	VF	XF	Unc
1102	497	(1888)	125.00	250.00	400.00	700.00

WARN

26.9500 g, .900 SILVER, .7798 oz ASW
1103 497 (1888) — — 12,000. 20,000.

MONETARY REFORM
1892-1902
100 Fun = 1 Yang
5 Yang = 1 Whan

FUN

BRASS, 3.50 g
Obv: 3 characters, *Tae Cho-son*
(Great Korea), to left of denomination.

1104	501	(1892)	10.00	35.00	75.00	250.00
	504	(1895)	10.00	35.00	75.00	250.00
	505	(1896)	17.50	65.00	125.00	300.00

Obv: 2 characters, *Cho-son*
(Korea), to left of denomination.

1105	502	(1893)	15.00	50.00	100.00	250.00
	503	(1894)	Reported, not confirmed			
	504	(1895)	8.00	25.00	50.00	150.00
	505	(1896)	Reported, not confirmed			

5 FUN

COPPER, 17.20 g
Obv: Three small characters, *Tae Cho-son*,
leg. above dragon divided into two parts by a dot.

1106	501	(1892)	2.50	6.00	12.50	80.00
	505	(1896)	2.50	6.00	12.50	80.00

Obv: 2 characters, *Cho-son*
(Korea), to left of denomination.

KM#	Year	Date	Fine	VF	XF	Unc
1107	502	(1893)	small characters obv.			
			2.50	6.00	10.00	90.00
	502	(1893)	large characters obv.			
			20.00	40.00	75.00	300.00
	503	(1894)	large characters obv.			
			5.00	9.00	15.00	100.00
	504	(1895)	large characters obv.			
			2.50	6.00	12.00	80.00
	505	(1896)	small characters obv.			
			2.00	5.00	9.00	80.00

Obv: Three large characters, *Tae Cho-son*
(Great Korea) to left of denomination,
w/o dot in leg. above dragon.

1108	504	(1895)	2.00	5.00	10.00	80.00
	505	(1896)	3.00	7.50	16.00	100.00

Obv: Date given as year of Kuang Mu reign.

1116	2	(1898)	small characters obv.			
			2.00	4.00	7.00	80.00
	2	(1898)	medium characters obv.			
			15.00	35.00	70.00	250.00
	2	(1898)	large characters obv.			
			50.00	100.00	200.00	400.00
	3	(1899)	150.00	225.00	500.00	1000.
	6	(1902)	3.50	6.50	12.00	90.00

1/4 YANG

COPPER-NICKEL
Obv: 3 characters, *Tae Cho-son*
(Great Korea), to left of denomination.

1109	501	(1892)	10.00	25.00	50.00	150.00
	504	(1895)	10.00	25.00	50.00	150.00

Obv: 2 characters, *Cho-son*
(Korea), to left of denomination.

1110	502	(1893)	5.00	12.00	25.00	100.00
	503	(1894)	20.00	50.00	150.00	200.00
	504	(1895)	150.00	300.00	500.00	1200.
	505	(1896)	5.00	12.00	25.00	100.00

Obv: Dragon crowded by small tight circle, 11.25mm,
date given as year of Kuang Mu reign.

1117	1	(1897)	100.00	250.00	500.00	1000.
	2	(1898)	.75	1.25	2.00	8.00
	3	(1899)	large characters obv.			
			100.00	250.00	500.00	1000.
	3	(1899)	small characters obv.			
			100.00	250.00	500.00	1000.
	4	(1900)	125.00	300.00	550.00	1100.
	5	(1901)	100.00	250.00	500.00	1000.

NOTE: Many varieties of characters size and style exist for year 2 coins.

Obv: Larger circle around dragon.

1118	2	(1898)	7.50	12.50	25.00	100.00

NOTE: KM#1118 were counterfeits made on machinery supplied by the Japanese. These counterfeits were authorized for circulation by the Korean Government.

YANG

5.2000 g, .800 SILVER, .1338 oz ASW
Obv: 3 characters, *Tae Cho-son*.

KM#	Year	Date	Fine	VF	XF	Unc
1112	501	(1892)	65.00	100.00	150.00	350.00

Obv: 2 characters, *Cho-son*.

1113	502	(1893)	65.00	100.00	150.00	350.00

Obv: Date given as year of Kuang Mu reign.
Rev: Wide spaced *Yang*.

1119	2	(1898)	80.00	150.00	250.00	450.00

Rev: Closely spaced *Yang*.

1120	2	(1898)	75.00	130.00	225.00	400.00

5 YANG

26.9500 g, .900 SILVER, .7798 oz ASW

KM#	Year	Mintage	Fine	VF	XF	Unc
1114	501(1892)	.020	650.00	1000.	1500.	2500.

WHAN

26.9500 g, .900 SILVER, .7798 oz ASW
1115 502(1893) I.A. 2500. 5000. 10,000. 14,000.

MONETARY REFORM
Kuang Mu, Years 5-11 (1901-1907AD)
Yung Hi, Years 1-4 (1907-1910AD)
100 Chon = 1 Won

1/2 CHON

BRONZE, 3.56 g
Obv: Date given as year of Kuang Mu reign.

1124 10(1906)

KOREA 1155

KM#	Year	Mintage	Fine	VF	XF	Unc
1124		24.000	2.00	4.00	9.00	80.00
	11(1907)	*.800	—		Rare	—

2.10 g
Obv: Date given as year of Yung Hi reign.

1136	1(1907)	*I.A.	60.00	150.00	300.00	600.00
	2(1908)	21.000	5.00	12.00	20.00	130.00
	3(1909)	8.200	6.00	13.00	22.50	140.00
	4(1910)	5.070	50.00	125.00	275.00	600.00

*NOTE: Mintage for year 1 is included in the mintage for year 11 of KM#1124.

CHON

BRONZE, 6.80 g
Obv: Date given as year of Kuang Mu reign.

| 1121 | 6(1902) | 3.001 | 1000. | 2000. | 3000. | 5000. |

7.13 g
Obv: Date given as year of Kuang Mu reign.

1125	9(1905)	11.800	8.00	14.00	22.00	100.00
	10(1906)	I.A.	7.50	12.00	18.00	100.00

4.20 g
Obv: Date given as year of Kuang Mu reign.

| 1132 | 11(1907) | 11.200 | 3.50 | 7.00 | 12.00 | 80.00 |

Obv: Date given as year of Yung Hi reign.

1137	1(1907)	I.A.	4.50	10.00	20.00	100.00
	2(1908)	6.800	3.00	6.00	10.00	80.00
	3(1909)	9.200	3.00	6.00	10.00	80.00
	4(1910)	3.500	3.50	8.00	17.00	90.00

5 CHON

COPPER-NICKEL, 4.30 g
Obv: Date given as year of Kuang Mu reign.

| 1122 | 6(1902) | 2.800 | 1000. | 1500. | 2500. | 5000. |

4.50 g
Obv: Date given as year of Kuang Mu reign.

KM#	Year	Mintage	Fine	VF	XF	Unc
1126	9(1905)	20.000	5.00	10.00	20.00	80.00
	11(1907)	160.0000	8.00	12.50	24.00	90.00

Obv: Date given as year of Yung Hi reign.

| 1138 | 3(1909) | — | 900.00 | 1400. | 2400. | — |

10 CHON

2.7000 g, .800 SILVER, .0695 oz ASW, 17.5mm, 1.5mm thick
Obv: Date given as year of Kuang Mu reign.

| 1127 | 10(1906) | 2.000 | 12.00 | 20.00 | 35.00 | 80.00 |

2.25 g, 1.0mm thick
Obv: Date given as year of Kuang Mu reign.

| 1133 | 11(1907) | 2.400 | 13.00 | 22.50 | 40.00 | 100.00 |

2.2500 g, .800 SILVER, .0578 oz ASW
Obv: Date given as year of Yung Hi reign.

1139	2(1908)	6.300	10.00	14.00	22.00	50.00
	3(1909)	—	—		Rare	—
	4(1910)	9.500	7.00	12.00	20.00	45.00

20 CHON

5.3900 g, .800 SILVER, .1386 oz ASW, 22.5mm
Obv: Date given as year of Kuang Mu reign.

1128	9(1905)	1.000	30.00	60.00	120.00	275.00
	10(1906)	2.500	25.00	45.00	70.00	150.00

4.0500 g, .800 SILVER, .1042 oz ASW
Obv: Date given as year of Kuang Mu reign.

| 1134 | 11(1907) | 1.500 | 15.00 | 25.00 | 40.00 | 110.00 |

4.5000 g, .800 SILVER, .1157 oz ASW
Obv: Date given as year of Yung Hi reign.

1140	2(1908)	3.000	15.00	25.00	40.00	100.00
	3(1909)	2.000	15.00	25.00	40.00	100.00
	4(1910)	2.000	15.00	25.00	40.00	100.00

1/2 WON

13.5000 g, .800 SILVER, .3473 oz ASW
Obv: Date given as year of Kuang Mu reign.

| 1123 | 5(1901) | 1.831 | 2000. | 5000. | 7500. | 12,000. |

13.4800 g, .800 SILVER, .3467 oz ASW
Obv: Date given as year of Kuang Mu reign.

KM#	Year	Mintage	Fine	VF	XF	Unc
1129	9(1905)	.600	50.00	100.00	175.00	350.00
	10(1906)	1.200	50.00	100.00	175.00	350.00

10.1300 g, .800 SILVER, .2606 oz ASW
Obv: Date given as year of Kuang Mu reign.

| 1135 | 11(1907) | 1.000 | 60.00 | 100.00 | 175.00 | 375.00 |

Obv: Date given as year of Yung Hi reign.

1141	2(1908)	1.400	65.00	110.00	175.00	375.00
	3(1909)	—	—		Rare	—

5 WON

.900 GOLD
Obv: Date given as year of Yung Hi reign.

1142	2(1908)	.010	—	35,000.	65,000.	100,000.
	3(1909)	—	—		Rare	—

10 WON

.900 GOLD
Obv: Date given as year of Kuang Mu reign.

| 1130 | 10(1906) | 5.012 | — | 20,000. | 30,000. | 42,500. |

Obv: Date given as year of Yung Hi reign.

| 1143 | 3(1909) | — | — | | Rare | — |

20 WON

.900 GOLD
Obv: Date given as year of Kuang Mu reign.

| 1131 | 10(1906) | 2.506 | — | 20,000. | 50,000. | 80,000. |

Obv: Date given as year of Yung Hi reign.

1144	2(1908)	.040	—	20,000.	50,000.	80,000.
	3(1909)	.025	—	20,000.	50,000.	80,000.
	4(1910)	.040	—		Rare	—

KOREA-NORTH

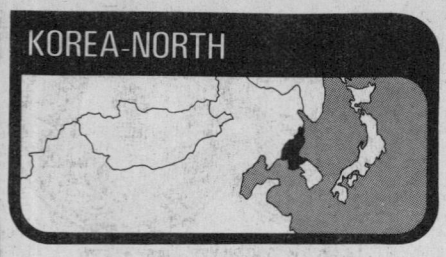

The Democratic People's Republic of Korea, situated in northeastern Asia on the northern half of the Korean peninsula between the People's Republic of China and the Republic of Korea, has an area of 46,540 sq. mi. (120,538 sq. km.) and a population of *22 million. Capital: Pyongyang. The economy is based on heavy industry and agriculture. Metals, minerals and farm produce are exported.

Japan replaced China as the predominant foreign influence in Korea in 1895 and annexed the peninsular country in 1910. Defeat in World War II brought an end to Japanese rule. U.S. troops entered Korea from the south and Soviet forces entered from the north. The Cairo conference (1943) had established that Korea should be 'free and independent'. The Potsdam conference (1945) set the 38th parallel as the line dividing the occupation forces of the United States and Russia. When Russia refused to permit a U.N. commission designated to supervise reunification elections to enter North Korea, an election was held in South Korea which established the Republic of Korea on Aug. 15, 1948. North Korea held an unsupervised election on Aug. 25, 1948, and on the following day proclaimed the establishment of the Democratic People's Republic of Korea.

NOTE: For earlier coinage see Korea.

MONETARY SYSTEM
100 Chon = 1 Won

CHON

ALUMINUM

KM#	Date	Mintage	Fine	VF	XF	Unc
1	1959	—	.50	.75	1.25	1.50
	1970	—	.75	1.00	1.50	1.75

Rev: Stars in field.

| 5 | 1959 | — | — | — | 1.75 | 2.25 |

Rev: Star left of 1.

| 9 | 1959 | — | — | — | 1.75 | 2.25 |

5 CHON

ALUMINUM

| 2 | 1959 | — | 1.00 | 1.50 | 2.00 | 2.50 |
| | 1974 | — | .50 | .75 | 1.00 | 1.75 |

Rev: Stars in field.

| 6 | 1974 | — | — | — | 2.25 | 2.75 |

Rev: Star left of 5.

| 10 | 1974 | — | — | — | 2.25 | 2.75 |

10 CHON

ALUMINUM

KM#	Date	Mintage	Fine	VF	XF	Unc
3	1959	—	.75	1.00	1.50	2.00

Rev: Stars in field.

| 7 | 1959 | — | — | — | 2.50 | 3.00 |

Rev: Star left of 10.

| 11 | 1959 | — | — | — | 2.50 | 3.00 |

50 CHON

ALUMINUM

| 4 | 1978 | — | 1.25 | 1.75 | 2.25 | 3.00 |

Rev: Stars in field.

| 8 | 1978 | — | — | — | 3.50 | 4.50 |

Rev: Star behind rider.

| 12 | 1978 | — | — | — | 3.50 | 4.50 |

NOTE: KM#5-8 were issued to visitors from hard currency countries and KM#9-12 were issued to visitors from Communist countries.

WON

COPPER-NICKEL
Kim Il Sung's Birth Place

| 13 | 1987 | — | — | — | — | 2.00 |

Kim Il Sung's Arch of Triumph

KM#	Date	Mintage	Fine	VF	XF	Unc
14	1987	—	—	—	—	2.00

Kim Il Sung's Tower of Juche

| 15 | 1987 | — | — | — | — | 2.00 |

ALUMINUM

| 18 | 1987 | — | — | — | — | 3.00 |

5 WON

COPPER-NICKEL
World Festival of Youth and Students

| 19 | 1989 | — | — | — | — | 7.00 |

20 WON

14.8000 g, .999 SILVER, .4758 oz ASW
World Festival of Youth and Students

| 20 | 1989 | — | — | — | — | 37.50 |

250 WON

7.7700 g, .999 GOLD, .2500 oz AGW
World Festival of Youth and Students

| 21 | 1989 | — | — | — | — | 300.00 |

500 WON

27.0000 g, .999 SILVER, .8681 oz ASW
Winter Games-Hockey

KM#	Date	Mintage	Fine	VF	XF	Unc
16	1988	.020	—	—	Proof	47.50

30th Anniversary of Gorch Fock

| 17 | 1988 | | | | Proof | 40.00 |

KOREA-SOUTH

The Republic of Korea, situated in northeastern Asia on the southern half of the Korean peninsula between North Korea and the Korean Strait, has an area of 38,025 sq. mi. (98,484 sq. km.) and a population of *45.2 million. Capital Seoul. The economy is based on agriculture and light and medium industry. Some of the world's largest oil tankers are built here. Automobiles, plywood, electronics, and textile products are exported.

Japan replaced China as the predominant foreign influence in Korea in 1895 and annexed the peninsular country in 1910. Defeat in World War II brought an end to Japanese rule. U.S. troops entered Korea from the south and Soviet forces entered from the north. The Cairo conference (1943) had established that Korea should be 'free and independent'. The Potsdam conference (1945) set the 38th parallel as the line dividing the occupation forces of the United States and Russia. When Russia refused to permit a U.N. commission designated to supervise reunification elections to enter North Korea, an election was held in South Korea on May 10, 1948. By its determination, the Republic of Korea was inaugurated on Aug. 15, 1948.

NOTE: For earlier coinage see Korea.

MINT MARKS
(a) - Paris, privy marks only

MONETARY SYSTEM
100 Chon = 1 Hwan

10 HWAN

BRONZE

KM#	Date	Mintage	Fine	VF	XF	Unc
1	4292 (1959)	100.000	.20	.50	1.00	25.00
	4294 (1961)	100.000	.15	.25	.50	2.00

50 HWAN

NICKEL-BRASS

2	4292 (1959)	24.640	.20	.50	1.00	3.00
	4294 (1961)	20.000	.15	.30	.80	2.00

100 HWAN

COPPER-NICKEL

3	4292 (1959)					
(Y3)		49.640	.50	1.00	2.50	6.00

NOTE: Quantities of KM#1-3 dated 4292 in uncirculated condition were countermarked 'SAMPLE' in Korean for distribution to government and banking agencies. KM#3 was withdrawn from circulation June 10, 1962 and melted; KM#1 and KM#2 continued to circulate as 1 Won and 5 Won coins for 9 years respectively until demonitized and withdrawn from circulation March 22, 1975.

MONETARY REFORM
10 Hwan = 1 Won

Prior to the following issue, the Bank of Korea, on its authority, created a number of patterns in 1, 5 and 10 won denominations, for example with the Kyongju Observatory design.

WON

BRASS

KM#	Date	Mintage	VF	XF	Unc
4	1966	7.000	—	.10	4.00
	1967	48.500	—	.10	1.00

ALUMINUM

4a	1968	66.500	—	—	.10
	1969	85.000	—	—	.10
	1970	45.000	—	—	.10
	1974	12.000	—	.10	.15
	1975	10.000	—	.10	.15
	1976	20.000	—	—	.10
	1977	30.000	—	—	.10
	1978	30.000	—	—	.10
	1979	30.000	—	—	.10
	1980	20.000	—	—	.10
	1981	20.000	—	—	.10
	1982	30.000	—	—	.10
	1982	—	—	Proof	

31	1983	40.000	—	—	.10
	1984	20.000	—	—	.10
	1985	10.000	—	—	.10

5 WON

BRONZE

5	1966	4.500	.15	.65	10.00
	1967	18.000	.10	.50	5.00
	1968	20.000	.10	.50	5.00
	1969	25.000	.10	.25	3.00
	1970	50.000	.10	.25	3.00

BRASS

5a	1970	Inc. Ab.	—	.10	2.25
	1971	64.038	—	—	.10
	1972	60.084	—	—	.10
	1977	1.000	—	.10	1.40
	1978	1.000	—	.10	1.30
	1979	1.000	—	.10	1.15
	1980	.100	.25	.50	3.00
	1981	.100	.25	.50	3.00
	1982	.100	.25	.50	3.00
	1982	—	—	Proof	

| 32 | 1983 | 6.000 | — | .10 | .20 |

10 WON

BRONZE

6	1966	10.600	.15	.50	10.00
	1967	22.500	.15	.50	10.00
	1968	35.000	.15	.50	10.00
	1969	46.500	.10	.25	5.00
	1970	157.000	.10	.25	5.00

BRASS

6a	1970	Inc. Ab.	.25	.50	10.00
	1971	220.000	—	.10	.50
	1972	270.000	—	.10	.50
	1973	30.000	—	.10	.80
	1974	15.000	—	.10	.50
	1975	20.000	—	.10	1.00
	1977	1.000	—	.10	1.75
	1978	80.000	—	—	.10
	1979	200.000	—	—	.10
	1980	150.000	—	—	.10
	1981	.100	.25	.50	3.00

South/KOREA 1157

South/KOREA 1158

KM#	Date	Mintage	VF	XF	Unc
6a	1982	20.000	—	.10	.20
	1982	—	—	Proof	—

	1983	25.000	—	.10	.25
33	1985	35.000	—	.10	.25
	1986	195.000	—	.10	.25
	1987	—	—	.10	.35
	1988	—	—	.10	.35

50 WON

2.8000 g, .999 SILVER, .0899 oz ASW

7	1970	4,350	—	Proof	75.00
	1971	—	—	Proof	Rare

COPPER-NICKEL
F.A.O. Issue

20	1972	6.000	.10	.30	3.50
	1973	40.000	.10	.20	1.00
	1974	25.000	.10	.20	1.00
	1977	1.000	.15	.25	2.00
	1978	1.500	.15	.25	1.40
	1979	20.000	—	.10	.25
	1980	10.000	—	.10	.25
	1981	25.000	—	.10	.20
	1982	40.000	—	.10	.20
	1982	—	—	Proof	—

34	1983	50.000	—	.10	.35
	1984	40.000	—	.10	.25
	1985	4.000	—	.10	.35
	1987	—	—	.10	.35
	1988	—	—	.10	.35

100 WON

5.6000 g, .999 SILVER, .1798 oz ASW

8	1970	4,350	—	Proof	100.00

COPPER-NICKEL

9	1970	1.500	.50	.75	4.00
	1971	13.000	.15	.40	2.25
	1972	20.000	.15	.35	1.75
	1973*	80.000	.15	.30	1.00
	1974*	50.000	.15	.30	1.00
	1975	75.000	.15	.25	.60
	1977	30.000	.15	.25	.60
	1978	40.000	.15	.20	.35
	1979	130.000	.15	.20	.35
	1980	60.000	.15	.20	.35
	1981	.100	.25	.50	4.00
	1982	50.000	—	.15	.25
	1982	—	—	Proof	—

*NOTE: Die varieties exist.

30th Anniversary of Liberation

KM#	Date	Mintage	VF	XF	Unc
21	1975	4.998	.25	.50	1.25
	1975	2,000	—	Proof	125.00

1st Anniversary of the 5th Republic

24	1981	4.880	.25	.50	1.00
	1981 unfrosted	.018	—	Proof	30.00
	1981	2,000	—	Proof	175.00

35	1983	8.000	.15	.25	.50
	1984	40.000	.15	.25	.50
	1985	16.000	.15	.25	.50
	1986	131.000	.15	.25	.50

200 WON

11.2000 g, .999 SILVER, .3596 oz ASW

10	1970	4,200	—	Proof	125.00

250 WON

14.0000 g, .999 SILVER, .4497 oz ASW

11	1970	4,100	—	Proof	150.00

500 WON

28.0000 g, .999 SILVER, .8994 oz ASW
Rev: Similar to 200 Won, KM#10.

12	1970	4,700	—	Proof	275.00

COPPER-NICKEL
42nd World Shooting Championships

KM#	Date	Mintage	VF	XF	Unc
22	1978	.980	.75	1.25	4.00
	1978 unfrosted	.018	—	Proof	60.00
	1978	2,000	—	Proof	225.00

27	1982	15.000	—	.85	2.50
	1982	—	—	Proof	—
	1983	64.000	—	.85	2.50
	1984	70.000	—	.85	2.50

1000 WON

56.0000 g, .999 SILVER, 1.7988 oz ASW
Rev: Similar to 200 Won, KM#10.

13	1970	4,050	—	Proof	500.00

3.8700 g, .900 GOLD, .1119 oz AGW
Valcambi Mint

14.1	1970	1,500	—	Proof	750.00

Paris Mint

14.2	1970(a)	100 pcs.	—	Proof	900.00

NICKEL
1st Anniversary of the 5th Republic

25	1981	1.880	1.25	1.50	5.50
	1981 unfrosted	.018	—	Proof	40.00
	1981	2,000	—	Proof	225.00

South/KOREA 1159

COPPER-NICKEL
1988 Olympics - Dancers

KM#	Date	Mintage	VF	XF	Unc
28	1982	1.980	—	1.25	3.50
	1982 unfrosted	.010	—	Proof	25.00
	1982	.010	—	Proof	50.00

1988 Olympics - Drummer

36	1983	.330	—	1.25	4.50
	1983 unfrosted	.056	—	Proof	12.50
	1983	.101	—	Proof	22.50

200 Years of Catholic Church in Korea

39	1984	.572	—	1.25	4.50

Asian Games

41	1986	.930	—	1.25	2.50
	1986	.070	—	Proof	3.25

1988 Olympics - Basketball

46	1986	.560	—	—	7.50
	1986	.140	—	Proof	12.50

1988 Olympics - Tennis

47	1987	.560	—	—	7.50
	1987	.140	—	Proof	12.50

1988 Olympics - Handball

KM#	Date	Mintage	VF	XF	Unc
48	1987	.560	—	—	7.50
	1987	.140	—	Proof	12.50

1988 Olympics - Table Tennis
Obv: Similar to KM#47.

49	1988	.560	—	—	7.50
	1988	.140	—	Proof	12.50

2000 WON

NICKEL
1988 Olympics - Boxing

50	1986	.560	—	—	15.00
	1986	.140	—	Proof	20.00

1988 Olympics - Judo

51	1987	.560	—	—	15.00
	1987	.140	—	Proof	20.00

1988 Olympics - Wrestling

52	1987	.560	—	—	15.00
	1987	.140	—	Proof	20.00

1988 Olympics - Weight Lifting
Obv: Similar to KM#50.

53	1988	.560	—	—	15.00
	1988	.140	—	Proof	20.00

2500 WON

9.6800 g, .900 GOLD, .2801 oz AGW
Valcambi Mint

KM#	Date	Mintage	VF	XF	Unc
15.1	1970	1,750	—	Proof	1000.
		Paris Mint			
15.2	1970(a)	100 pcs.	—	Proof	1200.

5000 WON

19.3600 g, .900 GOLD, .5602 oz AGW
Valcambi Mint

16.1	1970	670 pcs.	—	Proof	2000.
		Paris Mint			
16.2	1970(a)	70 pcs.	—	Proof	2500.

23.0000 g, .900 SILVER, .6655 oz ASW
42nd World Shooting Championships

23	1978	.080	—	—	40.00
	1978 unfrosted	.020	—	Proof	110.00

16.8100 g, .925 SILVER, .5000 oz ASW
1988 Olympics - Tiger Mascot
Obv: Similar to 1000 Won, KM#47.

54	1986	.123	—	—	17.50
	1986	.228	—	Proof	22.50

1988 Olympics - Rope Pulling
Obv: Similar to 1000 Won, KM#47.

55	1986	.123	—	—	17.50
	1986	.228	—	Proof	22.50

South/KOREA 1160

1988 Olympic Stadium
Obv: Similar to KM#67.

KM#	Date	Mintage	VF	XF	Unc
60	1987	.123	—	—	17.50
	1987	.228	—	Proof	22.50

1988 Olympics - Chegi - Kicking
Obv: Similar to KM#67.

61	1987	.123	—	—	17.50
	1987	.228	—	Proof	22.50

1988 Olympics - Tae Kwondo
Obv: Similar to KM#67.

66	1987	.123	—	—	17.50
	1987	.228	—	Proof	22.50

1988 Olympics - Girls on Swing

67	1987	.123	—	—	17.50
	1987	.228	—	Proof	22.50

1988 Olympics - Wrestling
Obv: Similar to KM#67.

70	1988	.123	—	—	17.50
	1988	.228	—	Proof	22.50

1988 Olympics - Boys Spinning Top

Obv: Similar to KM#67.

KM#	Date	Mintage	VF	XF	Unc
71	1988	.123	—	—	17.50
	1988	.228	—	Proof	22.50

10000 WON

38.7200 g, .900 GOLD, 1.1205 oz AGW
Valcambi Mint

17.1	1970	435 pcs.	—	Proof	4000.

Paris Mint

17.2	1970(a)	55 pcs.	—	Proof	5000.

15.0000 g, .900 SILVER, .4340 oz ASW
1988 Olympics - Great South Gate, Seoul

29	1982	.280	—	—	18.00
	1982 unfrosted	.010	—	Proof	45.00
	1982	.010	—	Proof	70.00

1988 Olympics - Pavilion of Kyongbok Palace

37	1983	.137	—	—	18.00
	1983 unfrosted	.056	—	Proof	30.00
	1983	.101	—	Proof	35.00

23.2600 g, .500 SILVER, .3739 oz ASW
200 Years of Catholic Church in Korea

40	1984	.152	—	—	35.00

23.0000 g, .900 SILVER, .6655 oz ASW
Asian Games - Badminton
Obv: Similar to 1000 Won, KM#41.

KM#	Date	Mintage	VF	XF	Unc
42	1986	.130	—	—	30.00
	1986	.070	—	Proof	37.50

Asian Games - Soccer
Obv: Similar to 1000 Won, KM#41.

43	1986	.130	—	—	30.00
	1986	.070	—	Proof	37.50

33.6200 g, .925 SILVER, 1.0000 oz ASW
1988 Olympics - Marathon
Obv: Similar to 1000 Won, KM#47.

56	1986	.123	—	—	35.00
	1986	.228	—	Proof	40.00

1988 Olympics - Diving
Obv: Similar to 1000 Won, KM#47.

57	1987	.123	—	—	35.00
	1987	.228	—	Proof	40.00

South/KOREA 1161

20000 WON

1988 Olympics - Archery

KM#	Date	Mintage	VF	XF	Unc
62	1987	.123	—	—	35.00
	1987	.228	—	Proof	40.00

1988 Olympics - Volleyball
Obv: Similar to KM#62.

63	1987	.123	—	—	35.00
	1987	.228	—	Proof	40.00

1988 Olympics - Gymnastics
Obv: Similar to KM#62.

74	1987	.015	—	—	35.00
	1987	.110	—	Proof	40.00

1988 Olympics - Equestrian Events
Obv: Similar to KM#62.

75	1987	.015	—	—	35.00
	1987	.110	—	Proof	40.00

1988 Olympics - Cycling
Obv: Similar to KM#62.

76	1988	.015	—	—	35.00
	1988	.110	—	Proof	40.00

1988 Olympics - Soccer
Obv: Similar to KM#62.

77	1988	.015	—	—	35.00
	1988	.110	—	Proof	40.00

77.4000 g, .900 GOLD, 2.2398 oz AGW
Valcambi Mint
Rev: Similar to 5000 Won, KM#16.1.

KM#	Date	Mintage	VF	XF	Unc
18.1	1970	382 pcs.	—	Proof	65.00

Paris Mint

| 18.2 | 1970(a) | 52 pcs. | — | Proof | 8000. |

23.0000 g, .900 SILVER, .6655 oz ASW
1st Anniversary of the 5th Republic

26	1981	.080	—	—	45.00
	1981 unfrosted				
		.018	—	Proof	55.00
	1981	2,000	—	Proof	350.00

1988 Olympics - Flame

30	1982	.180	—	—	35.00
	1982 unfrosted				
		.010	—	Proof	65.00
	1982	.010	—	Proof	90.00

1988 Olympics - Wrestlers

KM#	Date	Mintage	VF	XF	Unc
38	1983	.123	—	—	35.00
	1983 unfrosted				
		.056	—	Proof	40.00
	1983	.101	—	Proof	45.00

.900 SILVER
Asian Games - Runner
Obv: Similar to 1000 Won, KM#41.

44	1986	.130	—	—	40.00
	1986	.070	—	Proof	50.00

Asian Games - Pul Guk Temple - Kyong Ju
Obv: Similar to 1000 Won, KM#41.

45	1986	.130	—	—	40.00
	1986	.070	—	Proof	50.00

25000 WON

96.8000 g, .900 GOLD, 2.8012 oz AGW
Valcambi Mint
Reduced. Actual diameter-60mm
Rev: Similar to 5000 Won, KM#16.1.

19.1	1970	325 pcs.	—	Proof	12,000.

South / KOREA 1162

Paris Mint

KM#	Date	Mintage	VF	XF	Unc
19.2	1970(a)	25 pcs.	—	Proof	14,000.

16.8100 g, .925 GOLD, .5000 oz AGW
1988 Olympics - Folk Dancing
Obv: Similar to 1000 Won, KM#47.

58	1986	.043	—	—	300.00
	1986	.118	—	Proof	450.00

1988 Olympics - Fan Dancing
Obv: Similar to 10,000 Won, KM#62.

64	1987	.043	—	—	300.00
	1987	.118	—	Proof	450.00

1988 Olympics - Kite Flying
Obv: Similar to 10,000 Won, KM#62.

68	1987	.043	—	—	300.00
	1987	.118	—	Proof	450.00

1988 Olympics - Korean Seesaw
Obv: Similar to 10,000 Won, KM#62.

72	1988	.043	—	—	300.00
	1988	.118	—	Proof	450.00

50000 WON

33.6200 g, .925 GOLD, 1.0000 oz AGW
1988 Olympics - History - Turtle Ship
Obv: Similar to 1000 Won, KM#47.

59	1986	.030	—	Proof	850.00

1988 Olympics - Grand South Gate
Obv: Similar to 10,000 Won, KM#62.

65	1987	.030	—	Proof	850.00

1988 Olympics - Horse and Rider
Obv: Similar to 10,000 Won, KM#62.

KM#	Date	Mintage	VF	XF	Unc
69	1987	*.030	—	Proof	850.00

1988 Olympics - Pul Guk Temple Pagoda
Obv: Similar to 10,000 Won, KM#62.

73	1988	*.030	—	Proof	850.00

MINT SETS (MS)

KM#	Date	Mintage	Identification	Issue Price	Mkt. Val.
MS1*	Mixed dates (6)	7,500	KM6a(1980) 32,34-35 (1983),27,31 (1984)	—	—
MS2	1986(5)	.130	KM41-45	113.00	145.00

*NOTE: Issued as a presentation set for the World Bank Conference in Seoul, October 1985.

PROOF SETS (PS)

PS1	1970(12)	—	KM7-8,10-13,14.1-19.1	752.00	28,000.
PS2	1970(11)	—	KM7-8,10-13,14.2-18.2	—	27,500.
PS3	1970(6)	—	KM7-8,10-13	53.50	1600.
PS4	1970(6)	300	KM14.1-19.1	698.00	26,250.
PS5	1970(6)	25	KM14.2-19.2	—	32,500.
PS6	1982(6)	2,000*	KM4a-6a,9,20,27. (Presentation Set)		Rare
PS7	1986(5)	.070	KM41-45	170.00	180.00

NOTE: Original, intact sets are worth substantially more than their individual components.

KUWAIT

The State of Kuwait, a constitutional monarchy located on the Arabian Peninsula at the northwestern corner of the Persian Gulf, has an area of 6,880 sq. mi. (17,818 sq. km.) and a population of *2 million. Capital: Kuwait. Petroleum, the basis of the economy, provides 95 per cent of the exports.

The modern history of Kuwait began with the founding of the city of Kuwait, 1740, by tribesmen who wandered northward from the region of the Qatar Peninsula of eastern Arabia. Fearing that the Turks would take over the sheikhdom, Sheikh Mubarak entered into an agreement with Great Britain, 1899, placing Kuwait under the protection of Britain and empowering Britain to conduct its foreign affairs. Britain terminated the protectorate on June 19, 1961, giving Kuwait its independence (by a simple exchange of notes) but agreeing to furnish military aid on request.

The Kuwait dinar, one of the world's strongest currencies, is backed 100 percent by gold and foreign exchange holdings.

TITLES

الكويت

Al-Kuwait

RULERS

Abdullah II, 1866-1892
Abdullah III, 1950-1965
Sabah III, 1965-1977
Jabir, 1977-

MONETARY SYSTEM

1000 Fils = 1 Dinar

BAIZA

COPPER

KM#	Date	Year Mintage	VF	XF	Unc
1	AH1304	(1887)	—	Rare	

MODERN COINAGE
FILS

NICKEL-BRASS

| 2 | 1961 | AH1380 | 2.000 | .50 | 1.00 | 1.75 |
| | 1961 | 1380 | 60 pcs. | — | Proof | 30.00 |

9	1962	AH1382	.500	.10	.15	.25
	1962	1382	60 pcs.	—	Proof	30.00
	1964	1384	.600	.25	.75	2.00
	1966	1385	.500	.25	.75	2.00
	1967	1386	1.875	.25	.75	2.00
	1970	1389	.375	.35	1.00	3.00
	1971	1390	.500	.25	.75	2.00
	1971	1391	.500	.25	.75	2.00
	1972	1392	.500	.25	.75	2.00
	1973	1393	.375	.35	1.00	3.00
	1975	1395	.500	.25	.75	2.00
	1976	1396	2.500	.15	.25	.50
	1977	1397	2.500	.15	.25	.50
	1979	1399	1.500	.15	.25	.50
	1980	1400		.15	.25	.50

5 FILS

NICKEL-BRASS

KM#	Date	Year	Mintage	VF	XF	Unc
3	1961	AH1380	2.400	.60	1.25	2.00
	1961	1380	60 pcs.	—	Proof	35.00

	1962	AH1382	1.800	.10	.20	.35
10	1962	1382	60 pcs.	—	Proof	35.00
	1964	1384	.600	.30	.75	2.00
	1967	1386	1.600	.20	.35	1.00
	1968	1388	.800	.30	.75	2.25
	1969	1389	—	.30	.75	2.25
	1970	1389	.600	.30	.75	2.25
	1971	1390	.600	.30	.75	2.25
	1971	1391	.600	.30	.75	2.25
	1972	1392	.800	.25	.65	1.75
	1973	1393	.800	.25	.65	1.75
	1974	1394	1.200	.10	.15	1.00
	1975	1395	5.020	.10	.15	.50
	1976	1396	.180	.35	1.00	3.00
	1977	1397	4.000	.10	.15	.35
	1979	1399	6.700	.10	.15	.35
	1980	1400	—	.10	.15	.35
	1981	1401	7.000	.10	.15	.35
	1983	1403	—	.10	.15	.35
	1985	1405	—	.10	.15	.35

10 FILS

NICKEL-BRASS

4	1961	AH1380	2.600	.65	1.25	1.75
	1961	1380	60 pcs.	—	Proof	40.00

11	1962	AH1382	1.360	.15	.25	.50
	1962	1382	60 pcs.	—	Proof	40.00
	1964	1384	.800	.35	.85	2.50
	1967	1386	1.360	.30	.75	1.75
	1968	1388	.672	.35	.85	2.50
	1969	1389	.480	.50	1.00	2.75
	1970	1389	.640	.35	.85	2.50
	1971	1390	.480	.50	1.00	2.75
	1971	1391	.800	.35	.85	2.50
	1972	1392	1.120	.15	.40	2.00
	1973	1393	1.440	.15	.40	2.00
	1974	1394	1.280	.15	.40	2.00
	1975	1395	5.280	.15	.25	.75
	1976	1396	2.400	.15	.25	.75
	1977	1397	—	.15	.25	.75
	1979	1399	6.160	.15	.25	.75
	1980	1400	—	.15	.25	.75
	1981	1401	8.320	.15	.25	.75
	1983	1403	—	.15	.25	.75
	1985	1405	—	.15	.25	.75

20 FILS

COPPER-NICKEL

5	1961	AH1380	2.000	.75	1.50	2.50
	1961	1380	60 pcs.	—	Proof	45.00

KM#	Date	Year	Mintage	VF	XF	Unc
12	1962	AH1382	1.200	.25	.35	.75
	1962	1382	60 pcs.	—	Proof	45.00
	1964	1384	.480	.50	1.00	3.00
	1967	1386	1.280	.35	.85	2.00
	1968	1388	.672	.35	.85	2.50
	1969	1389	.800	.35	.85	2.50
	1970	1389	.480	.50	1.00	3.00
	1971	1390	.480	.50	1.00	3.00
	1971	1391	.960	.35	.85	2.00
	1972	1392	1.440	.20	.45	2.00
	1973	1393	1.280	.20	.45	2.00
	1974	1394	1.600	.20	.45	1.50
	1975	1395	2.400	.20	.30	1.25
	1976	1396	3.200	.20	.30	1.25
	1977	1397	3.400	.20	.30	1.25
	1979	1399	5.520	.20	.30	1.25
	1980	1400	—	.20	.30	1.00
	1981	1401	8.960	.20	.30	1.00
	1985	1405	—	.20	.30	1.00

50 FILS

COPPER-NICKEL

6	1961	AH1380	1.720	.85	1.75	2.75
	1961	1380	60 pcs.	—	Proof	60.00

13	1962	AH1382	.900	.50	.75	1.35
	1962	1382	60 pcs.	—	Proof	60.00
	1964	1384	.300	.75	1.50	4.00
	1967	1386	.800	.40	.85	2.50
	1968	1388	.200	1.00	2.00	6.00
	1969	1389	.400	.50	1.00	3.00
	1970	1389	.500	.50	1.00	3.00
	1971	1390	.300	.75	1.50	4.00
	1971	1391	.500	.50	1.00	3.00
	1972	1392	.900	.50	.85	2.50
	1973	1393	.800	.50	.85	2.50
	1974	1394	1.000	.35	.50	2.00
	1975	1395	1.950	.35	.50	2.00
	1976	1396	2.250	.25	.35	2.00
	1977	1397	6.000	.25	.35	1.35
	1979	1399	6.050	.25	.35	1.35
	1980	1400	—	.25	.35	1.35
	1981	1401	3.000	.25	.35	1.35
	1983	1403	—	.25	.35	1.35
	1985	1405	—	.25	.35	1.35

100 FILS

COPPER-NICKEL

7	1961	AH1380	1.260	1.00	2.00	3.00
	1961	1380	60 pcs.	—	Proof	90.00

14	1962	AH1382	.640	.50	.65	1.50
	1962	1382	60 pcs.	—	Proof	90.00
	1964	1384	.160	1.75	3.00	6.00
	1967	1386	.640	1.00	1.50	3.00

KM#	Date	Year	Mintage	VF	XF	Unc
14	1968	1388	.160	1.75	3.00	6.00
	1969	1389	.320	1.00	2.00	4.00
	1971	1391	.240	1.25	2.00	4.00
	1972	1392	.400	1.00	1.50	3.00
	1973	1393	.480	1.00	1.50	3.00
	1974	1394	.480	1.00	1.50	3.00
	1975	1395	3.040	.50	.75	1.75
	1976	1396	—	.50	.75	1.75
	1977	1397	1.600	.50	.75	1.75
	1979	1399	3.040	.50	.75	1.75
	1980	1400	—	.50	.75	1.75
	1981	1401	2.960	.50	.75	1.75
	1983	1403	—	.50	.75	1.75
	1985	1405	—	.50	.75	1.75

2 DINARS

28.2800 g, .500 SILVER, .4546 oz ASW
15th Anniversary of Independence

15	1976	.035	—	35.00

28.2800 g, .925 SILVER, .8411 oz ASW

15a	1976	.072	—	Proof	45.00

5 DINARS

13.5720 g, .917 GOLD, .4001 oz AGW.

8	1961	AH1380	1.000	—	—	400.00

28.2800 g, .925 SILVER, .8411 oz ASW
15th Century of the Hijira

16	1981	AH1401	.030	—	Proof	40.00

20th Anniversary of Independence
Obv: Structures within chain circle.
Rev: Ships, wheel, fishing net and wall below dates.

18	1981	AH1401	.030	—	Proof	40.00

33.6250 g, .925 SILVER, 1.0000 oz ASW
25th Anniversary of Kuwait Currency
Obv: Arabic denomination, buildings, port scene and refinery. Rev: English legend, falcon, dhow, building and map on globe.

20	1986	AH1406	—	—	—	50.00

5th Islamic Summit Conference
Obv: Arabic, English and French inscription, crescent and minaret. Rev: Dhow.

22	1987	AH1407	—	—	—	50.00

KUWAIT 1163

KUWAIT

50 DINARS
16.9660 g, .917 GOLD, .5000 oz AGW
25th Anniversary of Kuwait Independence
Obv: Arabic legend, arched design, falcon, tent, boat and pearl in a shell. Rev: Radiant sun, mosque and assembly building, English and Arabic legends.

KM#	Date	Year	Mintage	VF	XF	Unc
21	1986	AH1406	—	—	—	275.00

5th Islamic Summit Conference
Obv: Arabic, English and French inscription, crescent and minaret. Rev: Dhow.

| 23 | 1987 | AH1407 | — | — | — | 275.00 |

100 DINARS

15.9800 g, .917 GOLD, .4711 oz AGW
15th Century of the Hijira

| 17 | 1981 | AH1401 | .010 | — | Proof | 400.00 |

20th Anniversary of Independence

| 19 | 1981 | AH1401 | — | — | Proof | 450.00 |

MINT SETS (MS)

KM#	Date	Mintage	Identification	Issue Price	Mkt. Val.
MS1	1393-1394(6)	74	KM9-14	1.75	—
MS2	1396-1397(6)	—	KM9-14	3.50	—

PROOF SETS (PS)

| PS1 | 1961(6) | 60 | KM2-7 | — | 300.00 |
| PS2 | 1962(6) | 60 | KM9-14 | — | 300.00 |

LAOS

The Lao People's Democratic Republic, located on the Indo—Chinese Peninsula between the Socialist Republic of Vietnam and the Kingdom of Thailand, has an area of 91,429 sq. mi.(236,800 km.) and a population of *3.9 million. Capital Vientiane. Agriculture employs 95 per cent of the people. Tin, lumber and coffee are exported.

The first United Kingdom of Laos was established in the mid-14th century by King Fa Ngum who ruled an area including present Laos, northeastern Thailand, and the southern part of China's Yunnan province from his capital at Luang Prabang. Thailand and Vietnam obtained control over much of the present Lao territory in the 18th century and remained dominant until France established a protectorate over the area in 1893 and incorporated it into the Union of Indo-China. The Independence of Laos was proclaimed in March of 1945, during the last days of the Japanese occupation of World War II. France reoccupied Laos in 1946, and established it as a constitutional monarchy within the French Union in 1949. In 1953 war erupted between the government and the Pathet Lao, a Communist movement supported by the Vietnamese Communist forces. Peace was declared in 1954 with Laos becoming fully independent in 1955 and the Pathet Lao being permitted to occupy two northern provinces. Civil war broke out again in 1960 with the United States supporting the government of the Kingdom of Laos and the North Vietnamese helping the Communist Pathet Lao, and continued, with intervals of truce and political compromise, until the formation of the Lao People's Democratic Republic on Dec. 2, 1975.

NOTE: For earlier coinage see French Indo-China.

RULERS
Sisavang Vong, 1949-1959
Savang Vatthana, 1959-1975

MONETARY SYSTEM
100 Cents = 1 Piastre
    Commencing 1955
100 Att = 1 Kip

MINT MARKS
(a) - Paris, privy marks only
None - Berlin

NOTE: Private bullion issues previously listed here are now listed under French Indo China.

KINGDOM
10 CENTS

ALUMINUM

KM#	Date	Mintage	VF	XF	Unc
4	1952(a)	2.000	.15	.30	1.00

20 CENTS

ALUMINUM

| 5 | 1952(a) | 3.000 | .20 | .40 | 1.00 |

50 CENTS

ALUMINUM

KM#	Date	Mintage	VF	XF	Unc
6	1952(a)	1.400	.35	.60	1.25

1000 KIP

10.0000 g, .925 SILVER, .2973 oz ASW
King Savang Vatthana Coronation

| 7 | 1971 | — | — | — | 20.00 |
| | 1971 | .020 | — | Proof | 30.00 |

2500 KIP

20.0000 g, .925 SILVER, .5947 oz ASW
King Savang Vatthana Coronation

| 8 | 1971 | — | — | — | 30.00 |
| | 1971 | .020 | — | Proof | 40.00 |

4000 KIP

4.0000 g, .900 GOLD, .1157 oz AGW
King Savang Vatthana Coronation

| 9 | 1971 | .010 | — | Proof | 125.00 |

5000 KIP

40.0000 g, .925 SILVER, 1.1895 oz ASW
King Savang Vatthana Coronation
Obv: Similar to 2500 Kip, KM#8.

| 10 | 1971 | — | — | — | 100.00 |
| | 1971 | .020 | — | Proof | 125.00 |

11.7000 g, .925 SILVER, .3479 oz ASW

KM#	Date	Mintage	VF	XF	Unc
16	1975	400 pcs.	—		50.00
	1975	775 pcs.	—	Proof	65.00

17	1975	400 pcs.	—		50.00
	1975	775 pcs.	—	Proof	65.00

8000 KIP

8.0000 g, .900 GOLD, .2315 oz AGW
King Savang Vatthana Coronation

11	1971	.010	—	Proof	225.00

10000 KIP

80.0000 g, .925 SILVER, 2.3791 oz ASW
King Savang Vatthana Coronation
Obv: Similar to 2500 Kip, KM#8.

12	1971	—	—		150.00
	1971	.020	—	Proof	250.00

23.5000 g, .925 SILVER, .6988 oz ASW

18	1975	300 pcs.	—		100.00
	1975	650 pcs.	—	Proof	115.00

20000 KIP

20.0000 g, .900 GOLD, .5787 oz AGW
King Savang Vatthana Coronation

KM#	Date	Mintage	VF	XF	Unc
13	1971	.010	—	Proof	500.00

40000 KIP

40.0000 g, .900 GOLD, 1.1575 oz AGW
King Savang Vatthana Coronation

14	1971	.010	—	Proof	900.00

50000 KIP

3.6000 g, .900 GOLD, .1041 oz AGW
Obv: Bust of King Savang Vatthana.
Rev. That Luang Temple.

19	1975	100 pcs.	—		150.00
	1975	175 pcs.	—	Proof	200.00

Obv: Similar to 5000 Kip, KM#17.

20	1975	100 pcs.	—		150.00
	1975	175 pcs.	—	Proof	200.00

80000 KIP

80.0000 g, .900 GOLD, 2.3151 oz AGW
King Savang Vatthana Coronation
Obv: Similar to 20000 Kip, KM#13.

15	1971		—	Proof	1850.

100000 KIP

7.3200 g, .900 GOLD, .2118 oz AGW
Obv: Bust of King Savang Vatthana.
Rev: Statue of Buddha.

21	1975	100 pcs.	—		325.00
	1975	100 pcs.	—	Proof	400.00

MINT SETS (MS)

KM#	Date	Mintage	Identification	Issue Price	Mkt. Val.
MS1	1971(4)		KM7,8,10,12	—	300.00
MS1	1975(6)	100	KM16-21	—	825.00
MS2	1975(3)	300	KM16-18	—	200.00

PROOF SETS (PS)

PS1	1971(5)	10,000	KM9,11,13-15	467.00	3600.
PS2	1971(4)	20,000	KM7,8,10,12	163.00	450.00
PS3	1975(6)	100	KM16-21	—	1050.
PS4	1975(3)	650	KM16-18	—	250.00
PS5	1975(3)	100	KM19-21	349.00	800.00

PEOPLE'S DEMOCRATIC REPUBLIC

MINT MARKS
None - Leningrad (50 Kip)

MONETARY SYSTEM
100 Att = 1 Kip

10 ATT

ALUMINUM

KM#	Date	Mintage	VF	XF	Unc
22	1980	—	.25	.50	1.00

20 ATT

ALUMINUM

23	1980	—	.25	.50	1.00

50 ATT

ALUMINUM

24	1980	—	.50	1.00	1.50

50 KIP

38.2000 g, .900 SILVER, 1.1054 oz ASW
10th Anniversary of People's Republic
That Ing Hang

25	1985	2,000	—	Proof	55.00

10th Anniversary of People's Republic - That Luang

26	1985	2,000	—	Proof	55.00

10th Anniversary of People's Republic - Vat Phu

27	1985	2,000	—	Proof	55.00

LAOS

10th Anniversary of People's Republic Valley of Jars

KM#	Date	Mintage	VF	XF	Unc
28	1985	2,000	—	Proof	55.00

PROOF SETS (PS)

KM#	Date	Mintage	Identification	Mkt.Val.
PS1	1985(4)	2,000	KM25-28	220.00

LEBANON

The Republic of Lebanon, situated on the eastern shore of the Mediterranean Sea between Syria and Israel, has an area of 4,015 sq. mi. (10,400 sq. km.) and a population of *2.9 million. Capital: Beirut. The economy is based on agriculture, trade and tourism. Fruit, other foodstuffs and textile's are exported.

Almost at the beginning of recorded history, Lebanon appeared as the well-wooded hinterland of the Phoenicians who exploited its famous forests of cedar. The mountains were a Christian refuge and a Crusader stronghold. Lebanon, the history of which is essentially the same as that of Syria, came under control of the Ottoman Turks early in the 16th century. Following the collapse of the Ottoman Empire after World War I, Lebanon, along with Syria, became a French mandate. The French drew a border around the predominantly Christian Lebanon Sanjak or administrative subdivision in 1926, and proclaimed the area a republic under French control. France announced the independence of Lebanon on Nov. 26, 1941, but factual freedom wasn't attained until Nov. 22, 1943.

TITLES

الجمهورية البنانية

El-Jomhuriyat El-Lubnaniyat

النلنية

El-Lubnaniyat

MINT MARKS
(a) - Paris, privy marks only
(u) - Utrecht, privy marks only

MONETARY SYSTEM
100 Piastres = 1 Livre (Pound)

FRENCH PROTECTORATE

1/2 PIASTRE

COPPER-NICKEL

KM#	Date	Mintage	Fine	VF	XF	Unc
9	1934(a)	.200	2.00	5.00	12.50	40.00
	1936(a)	1.200	1.25	3.00	7.50	25.00

ZINC

| 9a | 1941(a) | 1.000 | .50 | 1.00 | 4.00 | 10.00 |

PIASTRE

COPPER-NICKEL

3	1925(a)	1.500	.50	2.00	7.50	25.00
	1931(a)	.300	1.00	4.00	12.50	45.00
	1933(a)	.500	1.00	4.00	10.00	45.00
	1936(a)	2.200	.50	1.00	6.50	20.00

ZINC

| 3a | 1940(a) | 2.000 | .50 | .75 | 4.00 | 10.00 |

2 PIASTRES

ALUMINUM-BRONZE

KM#	Date	Mintage	Fine	VF	XF	Unc
1	1924(a)	1.800	1.25	3.00	12.50	50.00

| 4 | 1925(a) | 1.000 | 3.00 | 8.00 | 20.00 | 75.00 |

2-1/2 PIASTRES

ALUMINUM-BRONZE

| 10 | 1940(a) | 1.000 | 1.00 | 2.00 | 3.50 | 12.00 |

5 PIASTRES

ALUMINUM-BRONZE

| 2 | 1924(a) | 1.000 | 1.25 | 3.00 | 10.00 | 45.00 |

Rev: Both privy marks to left of '5'.

| 5.1 | 1925(a) | 1.500 | .75 | 1.50 | 8.00 | 30.00 |

Rev: Privy marks to left and right of 5 Piastres.

5.2	1925(a) Inc. Ab.	1.00	2.00	7.50	30.00
	1931(a)	.400	1.50	4.00	12.50	40.00
	1933(a)	.500	1.50	4.00	12.50	40.00
	1936(a)	.900	1.00	2.00	7.50	25.00
	1940(a)	1.000	.75	1.50	5.00	15.00

10 PIASTRES

2.0000 g, .680 SILVER, .0437 oz ASW

| 6 | 1929 | .880 | 3.00 | 10.00 | 30.00 | 90.00 |

25 PIASTRES

5.0000 g, .680 SILVER, .1093 oz ASW

7	1929	.600	3.00	7.00	25.00	85.00
	1933(a)	.200	4.50	15.00	40.00	150.00
	1936(a)	.400	3.50	10.00	27.50	100.00

Listings For
LAHEJ: refer to Yemen Democratic Republic
LATVIA: refer to Baltic Regions

50 PIASTRES

10.0000 g, .680 SILVER, .2186 oz ASW

KM#	Date	Mintage	Fine	VF	XF	Unc
8	1929	.500	5.00	10.00	40.00	150.00
	1933(a)	.100	7.00	20.00	65.00	225.00
	1936(a)	.100	7.00	17.50	50.00	200.00

WORLD WAR II COINAGE
1/2 PIASTRE

BRASS

11	ND	—	1.00	2.50	5.00	10.00

NOTE: Three varieties known. Usually crudely struck, off center, etc. Perfectly struck, centered unc. specimens command a considerable premium. Size of letters also vary.

PIASTRE

BRASS

12	ND	—	1.00	3.00	7.50	15.00

NOTE: Two varieties known. Usually crudely struck, off center, etc. Perfectly struck, centered unc. specimens command a considerable premium.

2-1/2 PIASTRES

ALUMINUM

13	ND	—	1.50	3.00	7.50	15.00

NOTE: Seven varieties known. Usually crudely struck, off center, etc. Perfectly struck, centered unc. specimens command a considerable premium.

REPUBLIC
PIASTRE

ALUMINUM-BRONZE

19	1955(a)	4.000	—	.10	.15	.20

2-1/2 PIASTRES

ALUMINUM-BRONZE

20	1955(a)	5.000	—	.10	.15	.25

5 PIASTRES

ALUMINUM

14	1952(a)	3.600	.50	1.00	1.50	4.00

KM#	Date	Mintage	Fine	VF	XF	Unc
18	1954	4.440	.10	.30	.50	1.00

ALUMINUM-BRONZE

21	1955(a)	3.000	.10	.20	.30	.50
	1961(a)	—	.10	.15	.20	.30

NICKEL-BRASS

25.1	1968	2.000	—	.10	.15	.20
	1969	4.000	—	.10	.15	.20
	1970	—	—	—	.10	.15
	1972(a)	12.000	—	—	.10	.15

25.2	1975(a)	—	—	—	.10	.15
	1980	—	—	—	.10	.15

10 PIASTRES

ALUMINUM

15	1952(a)	3.600	.50	1.00	5.00	17.50

ALUMINUM-BRONZE

22	1955	2.175	.20	.40	.60	1.00

23	1955(a)	6.000	.10	.25	.50	.75

COPPER-NICKEL

24	1961	7.000	—	.10	.20	.40
	1961	—	—	—	Proof	

NICKEL-BRASS

KM#	Date	Mintage	Fine	VF	XF	Unc
26	1968(a)	2.000	—	.10	.15	.25
	1969(a)	5.000	—	—	.10	.20
	1970(a)	8.000	—	—	.10	.20
	1972(a)	12.000	—	—	.10	.20
	1975(a)	—	—	—	.10	.20

25 PIASTRES

ALUMINUM-BRONZE

16	1952(u)	7.200	.10	.40	.60	1.00
	1961(u)	5.000	.10	.40	.60	.75

NOTE: The 1961 issue was actually struck by the Berne Mint and has a larger date.

NICKEL-BRASS

27	1968	1.500	.10	.15	.25	.50
	1969	2.500	.10	.15	.20	.40
	1970	—	.10	.15	.20	.40
	1972	8.000	.10	.15	.20	.30
	1975	—	.10	.15	.20	.30
	1980	—	.10	.15	.20	.30

50 PIASTRES

4.9710 g, .600 SILVER, .0959 oz ASW

17	1952(u)	7.200	BV	1.00	1.50	3.50

NICKEL

28	1968	2.000	.20	.40	.60	1.00
	1969	3.488	.10	.25	.40	.75
	1970	2.000	.10	.25	.40	.50
	1971	2.000	.10	.25	.40	.50
	1975	—	.10	.25	.40	.50
	1978	22.400	.10	.25	.40	.50
	1980	—	.10	.25	.40	.50

LIVRE

NICKEL
F.A.O. Issue

29	1968	.300	.25	.50	1.00	2.00

30	1975	—	.20	.40	.60	1.00
	1975	—	—	—	Proof	
	1977	8.000	.20	.40	.60	1.00

LEBANON 1168

KM#	Date	Mintage	Fine	VF	XF	Unc
30	1980	12.000	.20	.40	.60	1.00
	1981	—	.20	.40	.60	1.00

COPPER-NICKEL
1980 Winter Olympics

| 32 | 1980 | .040 | — | — | Proof | 4.00 |

5 LIVRES

NICKEL
F.A.O. Issue

| 31 | 1978 | 1.000 | — | — | — | 3.50 |

10 LIVRES

19.0000 g, .500 SILVER, .3054 oz ASW
1980 Winter Olympics

| 33 | 1980 | .020 | — | — | Proof | 20.00 |

COPPER-NICKEL
F.A.O. Issue

| 35 | 1981 | .015 | — | — | — | 5.00 |

400 LIVRES

8.0000 g, .900 GOLD, .2315 oz AGW
1980 Winter Olympics

KM#	Date	Mintage	Fine	VF	XF	Unc
34	1980	1,000	—	—	Proof	275.00

LESOTHO

The Kingdom of Lesotho, a constitutional monarchy located within the east-central part of the Republic of South Africa, has an area of 11,720 sq. mi. (30,355 sq. km.) and a population of *1.7 million. Capital: Maseru. The economy is based on subsistence agriculture and livestock raising. Wool, mohair, and cattle are exported.

Lesotho (formerly Basutoland) was sparsely populated until the end of the 16th century. Between the 16th and 19th centuries an influx of refugees from tribal wars led to the development of a distinct Basotho group. During the reign of tribal chief Moshesh I (1823-70), a series of wars with the Orange Free State resulted in the loss of large areas of territory to South Africa. Moshesh appealed to the British for help, and Basutoland was constituted a native state under British protection. In 1871 it was annexed to Cape Colony, but was restored to direct control by the Crown in 1884. From 1884 to 1959 legislative and executive authority was vested in a British High Commissioner. The constitution of 1959 recognized the expressed wish of the people for independence, which was attained on Oct. 4, 1966.

Lesotho is a member of the Commonwealth of Nations. The King of Lesotho is Chief of State.

RULERS
Moshoeshoe II, 1966-

MONETARY SYSTEM
100 Licente/Lisente = 1 Maloti/Loti

SENTE

NICKEL-BRASS

KM#	Date	Mintage	VF	XF	Unc
16	1979	4.500	—	.10	.25
	1979	.010	—	Proof	.50
	1980	—	—	.10	.25
	1980	.010	—	Proof	.50
	1981	2,500	—	Proof	.50
	1983	—	—	.10	.25

2 LISENTE

NICKEL-BRASS

17	1979	3.000	—	.10	.50
	1979	.010	—	Proof	1.00
	1980	—	—	.10	.50
	1980	.010	—	Proof	1.00
	1981	2,500	—	Proof	2.00

5 LICENTE/LISENTE

2.8900 g, .900 SILVER, .0836 oz ASW

| 1 | 1966 | 5,000 | — | Proof | 6.00 |

NICKEL-BRASS

18	1979	2.700	—	.10	.50
	1979	.010	—	Proof	1.25
	1980	—	—	.10	.50
	1980	.010	—	Proof	1.25
	1981	2,500	—	Proof	2.50

10 LICENTE/LISENTE

5.6800 g, .900 SILVER, .1643 oz ASW

KM#	Date	Mintage	VF	XF	Unc
2	1966	5,000	—	Proof	6.00

COPPER-NICKEL
19	1979	2.000	.10	.15	1.00
	1979	.010	—	Proof	1.75
	1980	—	.10	.15	1.00
	1980	.010	—	Proof	1.75
	1981	2,500	—	Proof	3.00

20 LICENTE

11.2800 g, .900 SILVER, .3263 oz ASW
3	1966	5,000	—	Proof	12.00

25 LISENTE

COPPER-NICKEL
20	1979	1.200	.10	.20	1.50
	1979	.010	—	Proof	2.00
	1980	—	.10	.20	1.50
	1980	.010	—	Proof	2.00
	1981	2,500	—	Proof	3.50

50 LICENTE/LISENTE

28.1000 g, .900 SILVER, .8131 oz ASW
Rev: Small 900/1000 at right of date.
4.1	1966	—	—	—	15.00
	1966	—	—	Proof	17.50

Rev: Large 900/1000 at right of date.
4.2	1966	—	—	—	15.00
	1966	5,000	—	Proof	17.50

Rev: Mint mark and fineness below date.
KM#	Date	Mintage	VF	XF	Unc
4.3	1966	—	—	—	15.00
	1966	—	—	Proof	17.50

COPPER-NICKEL
21	1979	.480	.35	.50	1.50
	1979	.010	—	Proof	2.50
	1980	—	.35	.50	1.50
	1980	.010	—	Proof	2.50
	1981	2,500	—	Proof	4.00
	1983	—	.35	.50	1.50

MALOTI/LOTI

3.9940 g, .917 GOLD, .1177 oz AGW
5	1966	3,500	—	Proof	75.00

F.A.O. Issue
8	1969	3,000	—	Proof	75.00

COPPER-NICKEL
22	1979	1.275	.60	.80	1.50
	1979	.010	—	Proof	4.00
	1980	—	.60	.80	2.00
	1980	.010	—	Proof	4.00
	1981	2,500	—	Proof	6.00

11.3100 g, .925 SILVER, .3363 oz ASW
Silver Jubilee of King Moshoeshoe II
46	1985	2,500	—	Proof	25.00

18.9800 g, .917 GOLD, .5626 oz AGW
46a	1985	500 pcs.	—	Proof	400.00

2 MALOTI

7.9880 g, .917 GOLD, .2355 oz. AGW
6	1966	3,500	—	Proof	150.00

F.A.O. Issue
KM#	Date	Mintage	VF	XF	Unc
9	1969	3,000	—	Proof	150.00

4 MALOTI

15.9760 g, .917 GOLD, .4710 oz AGW
7	1966	3,500	—	Proof	300.00

F.A.O. Issue
10	1969	3,000	—	Proof	300.00

10 MALOTI

39.9400 g, .917 GOLD, 1.1776 oz AGW
F.A.O. Issue
11	1969	3,000	—	Proof	750.00

25.0800 g, .925 SILVER, .7459 oz ASW

LESOTHO 1170

10th Anniversary of Independence

KM#	Date	Mintage	VF	XF	Unc
13	1976	2,300	—	—	30.00
	1976	2,100	—	Proof	35.00

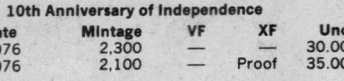

28.2800 g, .925 SILVER, .8411 oz ASW

23	1979	.010	—	—	20.00
	1979	5,000	—	Proof	25.00

12.0000 g, .500 SILVER, .1929 oz ASW

23a	1979	.010	—	—	10.00
	1979	5,000	—	Proof	15.00

28.2800 g, .925 SILVER, .8411 oz ASW
International Year of the Child
Similar to 15 Maloti, KM#25.

24	1979(1981)	—	—	—	20.00
	1979(1981)	.037	—	Proof	25.00

23.3300 g, .925 SILVER, .6938 oz ASW
Soccer Games

32	1982	3,582	—	Proof	35.00

Soccer Games

34	1982	3,000	—	Proof	35.00

31.1000 g, .500 SILVER, .5000 oz ASW
George Washington
Obv: Similar to KM#34.
Rev: Washington facing left.

40	1982	7,355	—	Proof	35.00

George Washington
Obv: Similar to KM#34.
Rev: Washington kneeling on one knee.

41	1982	4,200	—	Proof	35.00

George Washington
Obv: Similar to KM#34.

42	1982	.015	—	Proof	25.00

COPPER-NICKEL
International Games - Field Hockey

KM#	Date	Mintage	VF	XF	Unc
47	1984	—	—	Proof	25.00

23.3300 g, .925 SILVER, .6939 oz ASW
Decade For Women

49	1985	1,000	—	Proof	35.00

28.2800 g, .925 SILVER, .8411 oz ASW
Papal Visit

50	1988	*.015	—	Proof	45.00

15 MALOTI

33.4000 g, .925 SILVER, .9933 oz ASW
International Year of the Child
Obv: Similar to 25 Maloti, KM#35.

25	1979	.018	—	—	17.50
	1979	7,500	—	Proof	25.00

.500 SILVER
15th Anniversary of Commonwealth Membership

37	1983	2,500	—	Proof	30.00

20 MALOTI

79.8810 g, .917 GOLD, 2.3553 oz AGW
F.A.O. Issue
Obv: Similar to 10 Maloti, KM#11.

KM#	Date	Mintage	VF	XF	Unc
12	1969	3,000	—	Proof	1450.

25 MALOTI

16.8200 g, .925 SILVER, .5003 oz ASW
Duke of Edinburgh Youth Awards

35	1981	5,000	—	Proof	35.00

28.2800 g, .925 SILVER, .8411 oz ASW
International Games

43	1982	650 pcs.	—	Proof	60.00

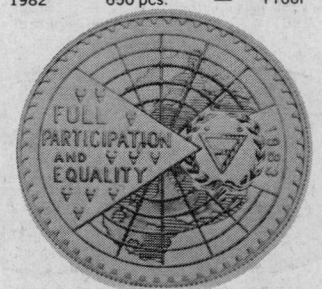

International Year of Disabled Persons

44	1983	—	—	—	20.00
	1983	—	—	Proof	25.00

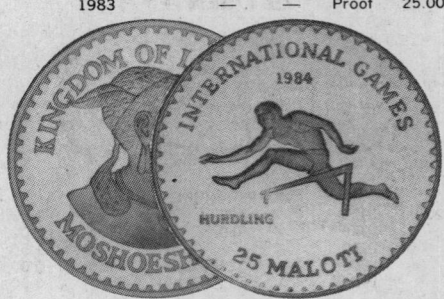

28.3500 g, SILVER
International Games - Hurdling

48	1984	—	—	Proof	25.00

30 MALOTI

.925 SILVER
Wedding of Prince Charles and Lady Diana

30	1981	.010	—	Proof	25.00

50 MALOTI

4.5000 g, .900 GOLD, .1302 oz AGW
10th Anniversary of Independence

14	1976	700 pcs.	—	—	125.00
	1976	1,910	—	Proof	125.00

33.6200 g, .925 SILVER, .9999 oz ASW
110th Anniversary of Death of King Moshoeshoe I

KM#	Date	Mintage	VF	XF	Unc
27	1980	2,500	—	—	30.00
	1980	1,400	—	Proof	45.00

15.7500 g, .995 PLATINUM, .5039 oz APW
KM#	Date	Mintage	VF	XF	Unc
31a	1981	200 pcs.	—	Proof	500.00

15th Anniversary of Commonwealth Membership
KM#	Date	Mintage	VF	XF	Unc
39	1981	500 pcs.	—	Proof	700.00

.995 PLATINUM
| 39a | 1981 | 200 pcs. | — | Proof | 825.00 |

MINT SETS (MS)
KM#	Date	Mintage	Identification	Issue Price	Mkt. Val.
MS1	1976(3)	450	KM13-15	—	330.00

PROOF SETS (PS)
PS1	1966(7)	1,500	KM1-7	301.00	575.00
PS2	1966(5)	7	KM Pn5-9	—	—
PS3	1966(4)	2	KM Pn1-4	—	—
PS4	1966(4)	3,500	KM1-4	28.00	42.50
PS5	1966(3)	2,000	KM5-7	301.00	525.00
PS6	1969(5)	3,000	KM8-12	450.00	2725.
PS7	1976(3)	1,410	KM13-15	285.00	335.00
PS8	1976(2)	—	KM14-15	270.00	300.00
PS9	1979(7)	10,000	KM16-22	34.00	15.00
PS10	1980(8)	10,000	KM16-22,23a	51.00	25.00
PS11	1981(8)	2,500	KM16-22,30	55.00	45.00

15th Anniversary of Commonwealth Membership
| 38 | 1981 | 5,000 | — | Proof | 40.00 |

100 MALOTI

9.0000 g, .900 GOLD, .2604 oz AGW
10th Anniversary of Independence
| 15 | 1976 | 450 pcs. | — | — | 175.00 |
| | 1976 | 1,410 | — | Proof | 175.00 |

200 MALOTI
15.9800 g, .900 GOLD, .4624 oz AGW
International Year of Disabled Persons
Obv: Similar to 250 Maloti, KM#33.
Rev: IYDP logo supported by hands.
| 45 | 1983 | 500 pcs. | — | — | 400.00 |
| | 1983 | 500 pcs. | — | Proof | 450.00 |

250 MALOTI
33.9300 g, .917 GOLD, 1.0000 oz AGW
International Year of the Child
Similar to 15 Maloti, KM#25.
| 26 | 1979 | 2,500 | — | — | 550.00 |
| | 1979 | 2,000 | — | Proof | 650.00 |

7.1300 g, .900 GOLD, .2063 oz AGW
Soccer Games
| 33 | 1982 | 551 pcs. | — | Proof | 225.00 |

16.9600 g, .917 GOLD, .5001 oz AGW
Duke of Edinburgh Youth Award
| 36 | 1981 | 1,500 | — | Proof | 300.00 |

15.7500 g, .995 PLATINUM, .5039 oz APW
| 36a | 1981 | 200 pcs. | — | Proof | 500.00 |

15.9800 g, .917 GOLD, .4708 oz AGW
Papal Visit
| 51 | 1988 | *750 pcs. | — | Proof | 500.00 |

500 MALOTI

31.1000 g, .917 GOLD, .9170 oz AGW
110th Anniversary of Death of King Moshoeshoe I
Obv: Similar to 50 Maloti, KM#27.
| 28 | 1980 | 1,500 | — | — | 500.00 |
| | 1980 | 3,000 | — | Proof | 550.00 |

33.9300 g, .917 GOLD, 1.000 oz AGW
110th Anniversary of Death of King Moshoeshoe I
Obv: Similar to 50 Maloti, KM#27.
| 29 | 1980 | 1,500 | — | — | 550.00 |
| | 1980 | 3,000 | — | Proof | 600.00 |

15.9000 g, .917 GOLD, .4688 oz AGW
Wedding of Prince Charles and Lady Diana
| 31 | 1981 | 1,000 | — | — | 250.00 |
| | 1981 | 1,500 | — | Proof | 325.00 |

LIBERIA 1172

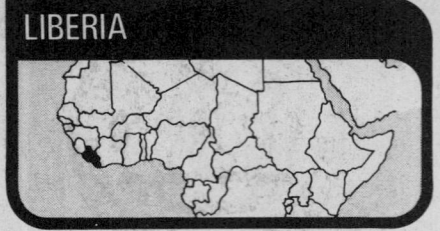

The Republic of Liberia, located on the southern side of the west African bulge between Sierra Leone and Ivory Coast, has an area of 43,000 sq. mi. (111,369 sq. km) and a population of *2.5 million. Capital: Monrovia. The major industries are agriculture, mining and lumbering. Iron ore, diamonds, rubber, coffee and coca are exported.

The Liberian coast was explored and charted by Portuguese navigator Pedro de Cintra in 1461. For the following three centuries Portuguese traders visited the area regularly to trade for gold, slaves and pepper. The modern country of Liberia, Africa's first republic, was settled in 1822 by the American Colonization Society as a homeland for American freed slaves, with the U.S. government furnishing funds and assisting in negotiations for procurement of land from the native chiefs. The various settlements united in 1839 to form the Commonwealth of Liberia, and in 1847 established the country as a republic with a constitution modeled after that of the United States.

U.S. money was declared legal tender in Liberia in 1943, replacing British West African currency.

Most of the Liberian pattern series, particularly of the 1888-90 period are acknowledged to have been 'unofficial' privately sponsored issues, but they are without exception avidly collected by most collectors of Liberian coins. The 'K' number designations on these pieces refer to a listing of Liberian patterns compiled and published by Ernst Kraus.

MINT MARKS
B - Bern, Switzerland
H - Heaton, Birmingham
(d) - Denver, U.S.
(l) - London
(s) - San Francisco, U.S.
FM - Franklin Mint, U.S.A.*

*NOTE: During 1975-77 the Franklin Mint produced coinage in up to 3 different qualities. Qualities of issue are designated in ( ) after each date and are defined as follows:

(M) MATTE - Normal circulation strike or a dull finish produced by sandblasting special uncirculated (polish finish) or proof quality dies.

(U) SPECIAL UNCIRCULATED - Polished or prooflike in appearance without any frosted features.

(P) PROOF - The highest quality obtainable having mirror-like fields and frosted features.

MONETARY SYSTEM
100 Cents = 1 Dollar

1/2 CENT

BRASS

KM#	Date	Mintage	Fine	VF	XF	Unc
10	1937	1.000	.10	.25	.35	.50

COPPER-NICKEL

| 10a | 1941 | .025 | .15 | .35 | .50 | .75 |

CENT

COPPER
Rev: 2 stars.

1	1847	—	5.00	12.50	20.00	50.00
	1847	—	—	—	Proof	65.00

Rev: 4 stars.

KM#	Date	Mintage	Fine	VF	XF	Unc
3	1862	—	5.00	12.50	22.50	60.00
	1862	—	—	—	Proof	70.00

BRONZE

5	1896H	.358	2.00	5.00	12.50	27.50
	1896H	—	—	—	Proof	135.00
	1906H	.180	3.50	7.50	17.50	45.00
	1906H	—	—	—	Proof	135.00

BRASS

| 11 | 1937 | 1.000 | .20 | .50 | 1.50 | 6.00 |

COPPER-NICKEL

| 11a | 1941 | .250 | .50 | 2.50 | 7.50 | 40.00 |

BRONZE

13	1960	.500	—	—	.10	.25
	1961	7.000	—	—	.10	.30
	1968(L)	3.000	—	—	.10	.15
	1968(S)	.014	—	—	Proof	.50
	1969	5.056	—	—	Proof	.50
	1970	3.464	—	—	Proof	1.00
	1971	3.032	—	—	Proof	1.00
	1972(D)	10.000	—	—	.10	.25
	1972(S)	4.866	—	—	Proof	.50
	1973	.011	—	—	Proof	.50
	1974	9.362	—	—	Proof	.50
	1975	5.000	—	—	.10	.15
	1975	4.056	—	—	Proof	.50
	1976	2.131	—	—	Proof	.50
	1977	2.500	—	—	.10	.35
	1977	920 pcs.	—	—	Proof	.50
	1978FM	7.311	—	—	Proof	.50
	1983FM	2.500	—	—	.10	.35
	1984	2.500	—	—	.10	.35

Edge inscription: O.A.U. July 1979.

| 13a | 1979FM | 1.857 | — | — | Proof | 1.00 |

2 CENTS

COPPER
Rev: 2 stars.

KM#	Date	Mintage	Fine	VF	XF	Unc
2	1847	—	5.00	10.00	20.00	50.00
	1847	—	—	—	Proof	75.00

Rev: 4 stars.

| 4 | 1862 | — | 5.00 | 10.00 | 25.00 | 75.00 |
| | 1862 | — | — | — | Proof | 175.00 |

BRONZE

6	1896H	.323	2.00	4.00	10.00	30.00
	1896H	—	—	—	Proof	160.00
	1906H	.108	4.00	8.00	20.00	60.00
	1906H	—	—	—	Proof	160.00

BRASS

| 12 | 1937 | 1.000 | .10 | .25 | .75 | 5.00 |

COPPER-NICKEL

| 12a | 1941 | .810 | .10 | .25 | .50 | 2.00 |
| | 1978FM | 7.311 | — | — | Proof | 1.50 |

Edge inscription: O.A.U. July 1979.

| 12b | 1979FM | 1.857 | — | — | Proof | 2.00 |

5 CENTS

COPPER-NICKEL

14	1960	1.000	—	.10	.15	.50
	1961	3.200	—	.10	.15	.40
	1968	.015	—	—	Proof	.75
	1969	5.056	—	—	Proof	.75
	1970	3.464	—	—	Proof	1.25
	1971	3.032	—	—	Proof	1.25
	1972(D)	3.000	—	.10	.15	.25
	1972(S)	4.866	—	—	Proof	.75
	1973	.011	—	—	Proof	.75
	1974	9.362	—	—	Proof	.75
	1975	3.000	—	.10	.15	.25
	1975	4.056	—	—	Proof	.75
	1976	2.131	—	—	Proof	.75
	1977	—	—	.10	.15	.50
	1977	920 pcs.	—	—	Proof	.75
	1978FM	7.311	—	—	Proof	.75
	1983FM	1.000	—	.10	.15	.25
	1984	1.000	—	.10	.15	.25

Edge inscription: O.A.U. July 1979.

| 14a | 1979FM | 1.857 | — | — | Proof | 2.00 |

10 CENTS

2.0700 g, .925 SILVER, .0616 oz ASW

7	1896H	.020	4.00	—	22.50	100.00
	1896H	—	—	—	Proof	175.00
	1906H	.035	4.00	10.00	22.50	100.00
	1906H	—	—	—	Proof	175.00

LIBERIA

2.0700 g, .900 SILVER, .0599 oz ASW

KM#	Date	Mintage	Fine	VF	XF	Unc
15	1960	1.000	BV	.75	1.25	3.00
	1961	1.200	BV	.75	1.25	3.00

COPPER-NICKEL

15a	1966	2.000	—	.15	.25	.50
	1968	.014	—	—	Proof	1.25
	1969	5,056	—	—	Proof	1.25
	1970(D)	2.500	—	.15	.25	.50
	1970(S)	3,464	—	—	Proof	1.50
	1971	3,032	—	—	Proof	1.50
	1972	4,866	—	—	Proof	1.25
	1973	.011	—	—	Proof	1.00
	1974	9,362	—	—	Proof	1.00
	1975	4,500	—	.15	.20	.35
	1975	4,056	—	—	Proof	1.00
	1976	2,131	—	—	Proof	1.00
	1977	—	—	.15	.25	.75
	1977	920 pcs.	—	—	Proof	1.00
	1978FM	7,311	—	—	Proof	1.00
	1983FM	.500	—	.15	.25	.75
	1984	.500	—	.15	.25	.75

Edge inscription: O.A.U. July 1979.

15b	1979FM	1,857	—	—	Proof	2.00

25 CENTS

5.1800 g, .925 SILVER, .1541 oz ASW

8	1896H	.015	4.00	10.00	30.00	110.00
	1896H	—	—	—	Proof	250.00
	1906H	.034	6.00	12.50	35.00	120.00
	1906H	—	—	—	Proof	250.00

5.1800 g, .900 SILVER, .1499 oz ASW

16	1960	.900	BV	1.50	2.00	4.50
	1961	1.200	BV	1.50	2.00	4.50

COPPER-NICKEL

16a	1966	.800	—	.25	.65	1.25
	1968(D)	1.600	—	.25	.50	1.00
	1968(S)	.014	—	—	Proof	1.50
	1969	5,056	—	—	Proof	1.50
	1970	3,464	—	—	Proof	1.75
	1971	3,032	—	—	Proof	1.75
	1972	4,866	—	—	Proof	1.50
	1973	2.000	—	.25	.40	.75
	1973	.011	—	—	Proof	1.25
	1974	9,362	—	—	Proof	1.25
	1975	1.600	—	.25	.40	.75
	1975	4,056	—	—	Proof	1.25
	1976	.800	—	.25	.65	1.25
	1976	100 pcs.	—	—	Proof	25.00

F.A.O. Issue

30	1976	.800	—	.25	.75	1.50
	1976	2,131	—	—	Proof	3.50
	1977	920 pcs.	—	—	Proof	3.50
	1978FM	7,311	—	—	Proof	2.25

Edge inscription: O.A.U. July 1979.

30a	1979FM	1,857	—	—	Proof	3.50

50 CENTS

10.9600 g, .925 SILVER, .3260 oz ASW

KM#	Date	Mintage	Fine	VF	XF	Unc
9	1896H	5,000	7.50	15.00	45.00	250.00
	1896H	—	—	—	Proof	400.00
	1906H	.024	7.50	15.00	45.00	250.00
	1906H	—	—	—	Proof	400.00

10.9600 g, .900 SILVER, .3171 oz ASW

17	1960	1.100	BV	3.00	4.00	8.00
	1961	.800	BV	3.00	4.00	8.00

COPPER-NICKEL

17a	1966	.200	—	.75	1.00	1.50
	1968(L)	1.000	—	.60	.80	1.50
	1968(S)	.014	—	—	Proof	1.50
	1969	5,056	—	—	Proof	1.50
	1970	3,464	—	—	Proof	2.50
	1971	3,032	—	—	Proof	2.50
	1972	4,866	—	—	Proof	1.50
	1973	1.000	—	.60	.75	1.00
	1973	.011	—	—	Proof	1.50
	1974	9,362	—	—	Proof	1.50
	1975	.800	—	.60	.75	1.00
	1975	4,056	—	—	Proof	1.50
	1976	1.000	—	.60	.75	1.00
	1976	100 pcs.	—	—	Proof	35.00

31	1976	—	—	.60	1.00	2.00
	1976	2,131	—	—	Proof	5.00
	1977	920 pcs.	—	—	Proof	5.00
	1978FM	7,311	—	—	Proof	3.50

Edge inscription: O.A.U. July 1979.

31a	1979FM	1,857	—	—	Proof	5.00

DOLLAR

20.7400 g, .900 SILVER, .6001 oz ASW

18	1961	.200	BV	5.00	6.50	13.00
	1962	1.000	BV	5.00	6.50	12.00

COPPER-NICKEL

18a	1966	1.000	—	1.00	1.50	2.25
	1968(L)	1.000	—	1.00	1.50	2.25
	1968(S)	.014	—	—	Proof	2.00
	1969	5,056	—	—	Proof	2.00
	1970(D)	2.000	—	1.00	1.50	3.00
	1970(S)	3,464	—	—	Proof	8.00
	1971	3,032	—	—	Proof	4.50
	1972	4,866	—	—	Proof	4.50
	1973	.011	—	—	Proof	3.00
	1974	9,362	—	—	Proof	3.00
	1975	.400	—	1.25	1.75	3.00
	1975	4,056	—	—	Proof	3.00
	1976	2.000	—	1.50	2.00	3.50
	1976	100 pcs.	—	—	Proof	50.00

KM#	Date	Mintage	Fine	VF	XF	Unc
32	1976	—	—	1.25	1.75	3.50
	1976	2,131	—	—	Proof	9.00
	1977	920 pcs.	—	—	Proof	11.50
	1978FM	7,311	—	—	Proof	12.50

Edge inscription: O.A.U. July 1979.

32a	1979FM	1,857	—	—	Proof	15.00

2 DOLLARS

COPPER-NICKEL
FAO World Fisheries Conference

47	1983	.100	—	—	—	6.00

28.2800 g, .925 SILVER, .8411 oz ASW

47a	1983	.020	—	—	Proof	25.00

47.5400 g, GOLD

47b	1983	600 pcs.	—	—	Proof	1500

2-1/2 DOLLARS

4.1796 g, .900 GOLD, .1209 oz AGW
Obv: The capitol. Rev: Arms.

24	1972	—	—	—	—	100.00

5 DOLLARS

8.3592 g, .900 GOLD, .2419 oz AGW
Obv: Ship. Rev: Arms.

25	1972	—	—	—	—	175.00

LIBERIA 1174

34.1000 g, .900 SILVER, .9868 oz ASW

KM#	Date	Mintage	Fine	VF	XF	Unc
29	1973	500 pcs.	—	—	—	30.00
	1973	.028	—	—	Proof	12.50
	1974	.020	—	—	Proof	12.50
	1975	9,017	—	—	Proof	17.50
	1976	3,683	—	—	Proof	17.50
	1977	1,640	—	—	Proof	20.00
	1978FM	7,311	—	—	Proof	17.50

Edge Inscription: O.A.U. July 1979.

| 29a | 1979FM | 1,857 | — | — | Proof | 25.00 |

COPPER-NICKEL

| 44 | 1982 | 4.000 | — | 5.00 | 6.50 | 8.00 |
| | 1985 | — | — | 5.00 | 6.50 | 8.00 |

10 DOLLARS

16.7185 g, .900 GOLD, .4838 oz AGW

| 26 | 1972 | — | — | — | — | 400.00 |

23.3300 g, .925 SILVER, .6939 oz ASW
Decade For Women
Rev: Coat of arms, denomination.

| 53 | 1985 | — | — | — | — | 25.00 |

31.1000 g, .999 SILVER, 1.0000 oz ASW
John F. Kennedy

KM#	Date	Mintage	Fine	VF	XF	Unc
54	1988	*.0255	—	—	Proof	35.00

President Samuel K&nyon Doe
Similar to 250 Dollars, KM#56.

| 55 | 1988 | *.025 | — | — | Proof | 35.00 |

12 DOLLARS

6.0000 g, .900 GOLD, .1736 oz AGW
President Tubman 70th Birthday

| 20 | 1965 | 400 pcs. | — | — | Proof | 150.00 |

20 DOLLARS

18.6500 g, .900 GOLD, .5397 oz AGW

| 19 | 1964B | .010 | — | — | — | 250.00 |

.999 GOLD

| 19a | 1964B-L | 100 pcs. | — | — | Proof | 400.00 |

NOTE: Of the total issue, 10,200 were struck of .900 fine gold and bear the "B" mint mark of the Bern Mint below the date, while 100 were struck (restrikes suspected) as proofs of .999 fine gold and are designated by the presence of a small "L" above date.

33.4370 g, .900 GOLD, .9675 oz AGW
President Tolbert Inauguration

| 27 | 1972 | — | — | — | — | 520.00 |

28.2800 g, .925 SILVER, .8411 oz ASW
Year of the Scout
Obv: Coat of arms.

| 45 | 1983 | .010 | — | — | — | 20.00 |
| | 1983 | .010 | — | — | Proof | 30.00 |

International Year of Disabled Persons

KM#	Date	Mintage	Fine	VF	XF	Unc
48	1983	—	—	—	—	20.00
	1983	—	—	—	Proof	30.00

25 DOLLARS

23.3120 g, .900 GOLD, .6746 oz AGW
President Tubman 70th Birthday

| 21 | 1965B | 3,000 | — | — | — | 350.00 |
| | 1965B | — | — | — | Proof | 375.00 |

.999 GOLD

| 21a | 1965B-L | 100 pcs. | — | — | — | 450.00 |

President Tubman 75th Birthday

| 23 | 1970 | — | — | — | Proof | 375.00 |

23.3700 g, .910 GOLD, .6838 oz AGW
Sesquicentennial of Founding of Liberia

| 28 | 1972 | 3,000 | — | — | Proof | 375.00 |

31.3700 g, SILVER
International Games - Basketball

| 51 | 1984 | — | — | — | Proof | 40.00 |

30 DOLLARS

15.0000 g, .900 GOLD, .4340 oz AGW
President Tubman 70th Birthday

KM#	Date	Mintage	Fine	VF	XF	Unc
22	1965	400 pcs.	—	—	—	Proof 300.00

100 DOLLARS

6.0000 g, .900 GOLD, .1736 oz AGW
Obv: President Tolbert. Rev: People stretching upward.

| 33 | 1976 | 175 pcs. | — | — | — | Proof 175.00 |

10.9300 g, .900 GOLD, .3163 oz AGW
130th Anniversary of the Republic

| 36 | 1977FM(U) | 787 pcs. | — | — | — | 200.00 |
| | 1977FM(P) | 4,250 | — | — | — | Proof 175.00 |

Organization of African Unity Summit Conference

| 37 | 1979FM | 1,656 | — | — | — | Proof 200.00 |

11.2000 g, .900 GOLD, .3241 oz AGW
Organization of African Unity

| 38 | 1979FM(P) | — | — | — | — | Proof 325.00 |

10.9300 g, .900 GOLD, .3163 oz AGW
5th Anniversary of Government

| 50 | 1985FM(P) | 409 pcs. | — | — | — | Proof 275.00 |

200 DOLLARS

12.0000 g, .900 GOLD, .3472 oz AGW
Obv: President Tolbert. Rev: President Tolbert blowing a horn.

| 34 | 1976 | 100 pcs. | — | — | — | Proof 300.00 |

15.9800 g, .917 GOLD, .4712 oz AGW
Year of the Scout
Obv: Coat of arms. Rev: Scout saluting.

| 46 | 1983 | — | — | — | — | 400.00 |
| | 1983 | — | — | — | — | Proof 500.00 |

15.9800 g, .900 GOLD, .4624 oz AGW
International Year of Disabled Persons
Similar to 20 Dollars, KM#48.
Obv: Disabled people.

| 49 | 1983 | 500 pcs. | — | — | — | 350.00 |
| | 1983 | 500 pcs. | — | — | — | Proof 450.00 |

250 DOLLARS

15.5000 g, .999 GOLD, .5000 oz AGW
John F. Kennedy Memorial

KM#	Date	Mintage	Fine	VF	XF	Unc
52	1988	5,000	—	—	—	Proof 885.00

15.5000 g, .999 GOLD, .5000 oz AGW
President Samuel Kanyon Doe

| 56 | 1988 | *5,000 | — | — | — | Proof 500.00 |

400 DOLLARS

24.0000 g, .900 GOLD, .6945 oz AGW
Obv: President Tolbert. Rev: Map of Liberia.

| 35 | 1976 | 25 pcs. | — | — | — | Proof 1000. |

PROOF SETS (PS)

KM#	Date	Mintage	Identification	Issue Price	Mkt. Val.
PS1	1896H(5)	—	KM5-9	—	1125.
PS2	1906H(5)	—	KM5-9	—	1125.
PS3	1968(6)	14,396	KM13,14,15a-18a	15.25	7.50
PS4	1969(6)	5,056	KM13,14,15a-18a	15.25	7.50
PS5	1970(6)	3,464	KM13,14,15a-18a	15.25	16.00
PS6	1971(6)	3,032	KM13,14,15a-18a	15.25	12.50
PS7	1972(6)	4,866	KM13,14,15a-18a	15.50	10.00
PS8	1972(4)	—	KM24-27	—	1200.
PS9	1973(7)	10,542	KM13,14,15a-18a,29	27.00	20.00
PS10	1974(7)	9,362	KM13,14,15a-18a,29	27.00	20.00
PS11	1975(7)	4,056	KM13,14,15a-18a,29	31.50	25.00
PS12	1976(7)	2,131	KM13,14,15a,29-32	45.00	37.50
PS13	1977(7)	920	KM13,14,15a,29-32	45.00	42.50
PS14	1978(8)	7,311	KM12a,13,14,15a,29-30,31-32	47.00	40.00
PS15	1979(8)	1,857	KM12b,13a,14a,15b,29a-30a,31a-32a		
			marked O.A.U. JULY,1979	45.00	53.00

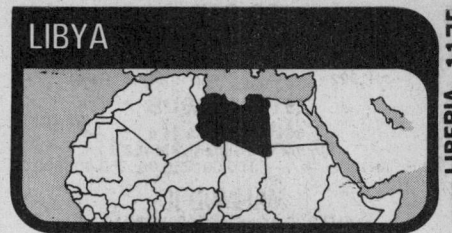

LIBYA

The Socialist People's Libyan Arab Jamahiriya, located on the north-central coast of Africa between Tunisia and Egypt, has an area of 679,362 sq. mi. (1,759,540 sq. km.) and a population of *4.3 million. Capital: Tripoli. Crude oil, which accounts for 90 per cent of the export earnings, is the mainstay of the economy.

Libya has been subjected to foreign rule throughout most of its history, various parts of it having been ruled by the Phoenicians, Carthaginians, Vandals, Byzantines, Greeks, Romans, Egyptians, and in the following centuries the Arabs' language, culture and religion were adopted by the indigenous population. Libya was conquered by the Ottoman Turks in 1553, and remained under Turkish domination, becoming a Turkish vilayet in 1835, until it was conquered by Italy and made into a colony in 1911. The name 'Libya', the ancient Greek name for North Africa exclusive of Egypt, was given to the colony by Italy in 1934. Libya came under Allied administration after the fall of Tripoli on Jan. 23, 1943, divided into zones of British and French control. On Dec. 24, 1951, in accordance with a United Nations resolution, Libya proclaimed its independence as a constitutional monarchy, thereby becoming the first country to achieve independence through the United Nations. The monarchy was overthrown by a coup d'etat on Sept. 1, 1969, and Libya was established as a republic.

TITLES

المملكة الليبية

Al-Mamlaka(t) Al-Libiya

الجمهورية الليبية

Al-Jomhuriya(t) Al-Libiya

TRIPOLI

Tripoli (formerly Ottoman Empire Area of antique Tripolitania, 700-146 B.C.), the capital city and chief port of the Libyan Arab Jamahiriya, is situated on the North African coast on a promontory stretching out into the Mediterranean Sea. It was probably founded by Phoenicians from Sicily, but was under Roman control from 146 B.C. until 450 A.D. Invasion by Vandals and conquest by the Byzantines preceded the Arab invasions of the 11th century which, by destroying the commercial centers of Sabratha and Leptis, greatly enhanced the importance of Tripoli, an importance maintained through periods of Norman and Spanish control. Tripoli fell to the Turks, who made it the capital of the vilayet of Tripoli in 1551 and remained in their hands until 1911, when it was occupied by the Italians who made it the capital of the Italian province of Tripolitania. British forces entered the city on Jan. 23, 1943, and administered it until establishment of the independent Kingdom of Libya on Dec. 24, 1951.

RULERS

Ottoman, until 1911

LOCAL PASHAS

Yusuf Pasha Qaramanli,
AH1210-1248 / 1796-1833AD (resigned)
Ali Pasha Qaramanli II,
AH1248-1250 / 1833-1835AD

MINTNAME

طرابلس غرب

Tarabalus Gharb - Tripoli West

The appellation *west* serving to distinguish it from Tripoli in Lebanon, which had been an Ottoman Mint in the 16th century. On some of the copper coins, *Gharb* is omitted; several types come both with and without *Gharb*. The mint closed between the 28th and 29th year of the reign of Mahmud II.

MONETARY SYSTEM

The monetary system of Tripoli was confused and is poorly understood. Theoretically, 40 Para were equal to one Piastre, but due to the debasement of the silver coinage, later issues are virtually pure copper, though the percentage of alloy varies radically even within a given year. The 10 Para and 20 Para pieces were a little heavier than the copper Paras, with which they could easily be confounded, except that the copper Paras were generally thicker, and bear simpler inscriptions. It is not known how many of the coppers were tariffed to the debased Piastre and its fractions. Some authorities consider the copper pieces to be Beshliks (5 Para coins).

The gold coinage came in two denominations, the Zeri Mahbub (2.4-2.5 g) and the Sultani Altin (3.3-3.4 g). The ratio of the billon Piastres to the gold coins fluctuated from day to day.

OTTOMAN COINAGE

MUSTAFA IV

AH1222-1223 / 1807-1808AD

Tripoli / LIBYA 1176

30 PARA
SILVER, 35mm, 12.50 g

KM#	Date	Year	VG	Fine	VF	XF
70	AH1222			Rare	—	

ZERI MAHBUB
GOLD, 21mm, 2.45 g
Similar to 1 Sultani, KM#62.

| 73 | AH1222 | — | 150.00 | 250.00 | 350.00 | 500.00 |

MAHMUD II
AH1223-1255/1808-1839AD

COPPER COINAGE

Under this rubric are included all pieces intended as paras. Many of the billon coins are so debased as to be nearly pure copper, but they can be distinguished from those coins intended as paras as they are much thinner, and bear different devices and inscriptions. Some pieces are also struck in brass.

In addition to pieces bearing no regnal year, the issuance of coppers seems to be restricted to two series, the first bearing years 12 & 13, the other years 20-27. The first group is related to an anomalous billon issue in the same years (Type D below), the second issue seems to be connected to the reduced weight series of years 21-25. The undated pieces were most probably struck during one of these two periods.

All of the following pieces appear to be of one denomination, probably a para, but vary in size from about 17-23mm.

PARA

COPPER

KM#	Date	Year	Good	VG	Fine	VF
75	AH1223	—	2.75	4.50	7.50	20.00
		13	4.50	9.00	18.50	35.00
		20	3.00	6.00	12.00	30.00

Obv. leg: *Sultan/Mahmud Khan/Azza Nashruhu.*

| 77 | AH1223 | — | 3.75 | 7.50 | 15.00 | 22.50 |
| | | 20 | 4.00 | 8.00 | 16.50 | 25.00 |

Obv. leg: *Sultan/1223.* **Rev. leg:** *Mahmud/24.*

| 79 | AH1223 | 24 | 4.00 | 8.00 | 16.50 | 30.00 |

Obv: Toughra. **Rev:** Similar to KM#75, w/*Gharb.*

81	AH1222(error)					
		—	7.50	12.50	20.00	45.00
	1223	—	2.50	5.00	10.00	30.00

Rev: W/o *Gharb.*

| 83 | AH1223 | — | 2.50 | 5.00 | 10.00 | 20.00 |

Obv: Toughra and rev. leg. within lozenges.

| 85 | AH1223 | 2 | 3.75 | 7.50 | 15.00 | 25.00 |

COPPER or BRASS

| 87 | AH1223 | 18 | 5.00 | 10.00 | 20.00 | 35.00 |

COPPER
Obv. leg: *Sultan Mahmud 1223* around arabesque.

KM#	Date	Year	Good	VG	Fine	VF
89	AH1223	25	3.00	6.00	10.00	20.00
		26	3.75	7.50	15.00	25.00
		62	(error) for year 26			
			3.75	7.50	15.00	35.00

NOTE: Several variations are found in the arrangement of the obverse legend. Year 29 is reported, but is likely a misreading of year 26. Center ornament on obverse small.

Obv. leg: *Duriba.* **Rev. leg:** *Fi Trablus.*

| 91 | ND | — | 3.00 | 6.00 | 12.00 | 20.00 |

Obv. and rev. leg. within lozenge.

| 93 | AH1223 | — | 5.00 | 10.00 | 20.00 | 30.00 |

COPPER or BRASS
Obv. and rev. leg. arranged differently.

| 95 | AH1223 | 23 | 3.00 | 6.00 | 12.00 | 45.00 |

COPPER
Obv. and rev. leg. within 10-pointed stars.

| 97 | AH1223 | 23 | 3.75 | 7.50 | 15.00 | 25.00 |

Obv. leg: *Duriba/Fi/1223.* **Rev:** *Tarabalus.*

99	AH1223	12	4.00	8.50	16.50	25.00
		13	4.00	8.50	16.50	25.00
		20	4.00	8.50	16.50	25.00

Obv. leg: *Duriba/Fi/1223.* **Rev:** *Tarabalus 21.*

| 101 | AH1223 | 12 | 4.00 | 8.50 | 16.50 | 30.00 |
| | | 21 | 4.00 | 8.50 | 16.50 | 25.00 |

3.79g, 20mm
Rev: *Tarabalus 22* in star of David.

| 102 | AH1123 | — | 10.00 | 15.00 | 20.00 | 35.00 |

Obv: Similar to rev. of KM#75.
Rev: 5 dots within wreath.

| 103 | AH1223 | 20 | 3.75 | 7.50 | 15.00 | 22.50 |

Rev: Arabesque.

| 105 | AH1223 | 21 | 4.00 | 8.00 | 16.00 | 24.00 |

Obv: W/o *Gharb.*
Rev: Rosette within knotted border.

KM#	Date	Year	Good	VG	Fine	VF
107	AH1223	22	3.75	7.50	15.00	22.50

Rev: 5 stars.

| 109 | AH1223 | 25 | 4.50 | 9.00 | 16.50 | 25.00 |

Obv. leg: *Duriba/Fi/Tarabalus/1223.* **Rev:** *Gharb.*

| 111 | AH1223 | 21 | 4.50 | 6.00 | 12.00 | 20.00 |

Obv. and rev. leg. enclosed within wavy hexagrams.

| 113 | AH1223 | 22 | 4.00 | 8.00 | 16.00 | 25.00 |

Obv. leg: *Duriba/Fi/Tarabalus/1223.*
Rev: Hexagram.

| 115 | AH1223 | 27 | 3.75 | 7.50 | 15.00 | 22.50 |

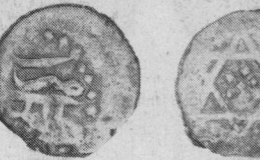

Rev: Hexagram w/dots.

| 117 | AH1223 | — | 2.00 | 3.50 | 10.00 | 20.00 |

Obv: Similar to KM#111. **Rev:** Hexagram w/*23.*

| 119 | AH1223 | 23 | 4.50 | 9.00 | 18.00 | 24.00 |

BILLON COINAGE

The billon coinage of Mahmud II is extremely varied, with a plethora of types deriving largely from contemporary Turkish, Egyptian, and Tunisian prototypes. There is considerable controversy over the denominations of these coins, although they seem to be based on a Piastre (40 Paras, Kuruns) of about 16 grams from yrs. 1-13, of about 12 grams from yrs. 13-21, and of 10 grams from yrs. 21-25. A new style coinage was introduced in yr. 28, but it was apparently never issued in sizable quantities and confined to the one year.

There is considerable weight variation within each denomination, in some cases up to 20 percent higher or lower than the theoretical norm. There is not yet discernible correlation between type, denomination, year, and standard. Recent evidence indicates that the net silver content was frequently and repeatedly reduced, probably in rather small increments. Thus the existence of several types for a single denomination and regnal year may indicate a multiplicity of issues with a single year, but as the full series is still not known, the complete sequence for each denomination cannot yet be reconstructed. Debasements were frequent: In the 4-year period covering years 21-24, ten changes in the coinage are recorded, but not all changes need have referred to all denominations.

Except for a few isolated miscellaneous types, all of the billon coinage can be classed into five basic types:

TYPE A: Obv: Toughra, sometimes with adjacent symbol.
Rev: Year/mintname/*1223.*

TYPE B: Obv: Toughra/mintname/*1223.*
Rev: 4-line leg. giving Sultan's titles: *Sultan al-Bahrayn Wa Khaqan al-Bahrayn al Sultan Ibn al Sultan.*

TYPE C: Obv: Sultan's name/benediction/mintname/*1223.* (4-line leg.)
Rev: Same as rev. of Type B.

TYPE D: Obv: Sultan's name (sometimes with *1223*).
Rev: Year/mintname/*1223* (1223 omitted when on obv.)

TYPE E: Obv: 4-line leg: *Sultan al Barrayn wa Khaqan al Bahrayn al Sultan Mahmud Khan Azza Nasruhu* & year.
Rev: Mintname/*1223* (this type copied from

Tunis piastre & fractions).

In addition to the variations in type, there is considerable variation in the borders. No attempt has been made in these listings to distinguish the various types of borders, though it is quite possible that such distinctions may have been monetarily important.

STANDARD COINAGE

The following listings are arranged by standard, and then by denomination within each standard. The sizes of the coins can vary considerably within each issue. The weight can vary by up to 20 percent higher or lower than the amounts shown.

All of the coins were struck in low-grade billon, tending toward pure copper on some of the later issues. Most of the coins originally were lightly silver-washed, and specimens with the silver wash intact are now quite scarce.

FIRST STANDARD
Based on a Piastre (40 Para) of about 16.00 g.

5 PARA

BILLON, 22-23mm, Type B

KM#	Date	Year	Good	VG	Fine	VF
126	AH1223	2	20.00	35.00	60.00	100.00
		7	20.00	35.00	60.00	100.00
		8	25.00	40.00	75.00	125.00
		9	20.00	35.00	60.00	100.00
		10	20.00	35.00	60.00	100.00
		11	20.00	35.00	60.00	100.00

SILVER, 1.35 g, 18mm
Obv: Ornament right of toughra.
Rev: Ornament in circle for regnal year.

| 127 | AH1223 | — | — | — | Rare | — |

10 PARA

BILLON, 22-24mm, Type A
| 128 | AH1223 | — | 12.50 | 25.00 | 75.00 | 125.00 |

3.35 g
| 130 | AH1223 | 7 | 12.50 | 25.00 | 75.00 | 125.00 |

31mm
| 132 | | 10 | 12.50 | 25.00 | 75.00 | 125.00 |

29-31mm
| 134 | AH1223 | — | 7.50 | 15.00 | 60.00 | 100.00 |

20 PARA

BILLON, 31mm, 6.65 g, Type A
| 136 | AH1223 | 7 | 12.50 | 25.00 | 75.00 | 125.00 |

KM#	Date	Year	Good	VG	Fine	VF
138	AH1223	9	—	—	Rare	—

40 PARA
BILLON, 37mm, 15.68 g, Type A
| 140 | AH1223 | ND | 17.50 | 40.00 | 100.00 | 200.00 |

100 PARA
BILLON, 25.00 g, 44mm
Ornament w/dot on either side.
| 142 | AH1223 | ND | 100.00 | 175.00 | 275.00 | 400.00 |

Obv: Ornament right of toughra.
| 143 | AH1223 | 4 | — | — | Rare | — |

Obv: Flower right of toughra.
| 144 | AH1223 | 5 | — | — | Rare | — |

SECOND STANDARD
Years 12-13
Based on a Piastre of about 14.00 g.

10 PARA
BILLON, 19mm, Type D
| 145 | AH1223 | 12 | 15.00 | 25.00 | 75.00 | 125.00 |

15 PARA
BILLON, 23mm, Type D
| 147 | AH1223 | 12 | 12.50 | 25.00 | 60.00 | 100.00 |
| | | 13 | 12.50 | 25.00 | 60.00 | 100.00 |

20 PARA
BILLON, 28mm, Type B
| 149 | AH1223 | 13 | 25.00 | 50.00 | 100.00 | 150.00 |

THIRD STANDARD
Years 14-21
Based on a Piastre of about 12.00 g.

10 PARA
BILLON, 26mm, Type A
| 154 | AH1223 | 19 | 15.00 | 30.00 | 60.00 | 100.00 |

Type B, 26-27mm
156	AH1223	16	15.00	25.00	50.00	100.00
		17	15.00	25.00	50.00	100.00
		18	17.50	30.00	60.00	125.00

Type C, 25mm
| 158 | AH1223 | 14 | 20.00 | 40.00 | 75.00 | 125.00 |

NOTE: The authenticity of KM#158 is questionable, but if counterfeit, it is contemporary.

22mm
Obv. and rev: Devices in center within marginal leg.
| 160 | AH1223 | 20 | 20.00 | 40.00 | 75.00 | 125.00 |

15 PARA
BILLON, 29mm, Type E
| 162 | AH1223 | 17 | 20.00 | 40.00 | 75.00 | 125.00 |

20 PARA
BILLON, 23mm, Type A
| 164 | AH1223 | 20 | 15.00 | 30.00 | 50.00 | 100.00 |

Type A, 31mm
| 166 | AH1223 | 21 | 20.00 | 40.00 | 65.00 | 125.00 |

Type B
| 168 | AH1223 | 15 | 27.50 | 50.00 | 100.00 | 150.00 |

Type C, 29mm
| 170 | AH1222 | — | 20.00 | 40.00 | 80.00 | 120.00 |
| | 1223 | 20 | 10.00 | 20.00 | 40.00 | 60.00 |

Type D, 28mm
| 172 | AH1223 | 20 | 10.00 | 20.00 | 40.00 | 60.00 |

30 PARA
BILLON, 34mm, Type A
| 174 | AH1223 | 3 | 100.00 | 150.00 | 250.00 | 400.00 |

29mm, Type A
KM#	Date	Year	Good	VG	Fine	VF
176	AH1223	20	15.00	30.00	60.00	100.00

Type E, 33-34mm
| 178 | AH1223 | 17 | 15.00 | 30.00 | 60.00 | 125.00 |
| | | 18 | 15.00 | 30.00 | 60.00 | 125.00 |

40 PARA
BILLON, 35mm, Type A, lozenge borders
| 180 | AH1223 | 21 | 30.00 | 50.00 | 90.00 | 150.00 |

32mm, Type A, plain borders
| 182 | AH1223 | 20 | 30.00 | 50.00 | 90.00 | 150.00 |

36-39mm, Type A, circular ornate borders
| 184 | AH1223 | 19 | 30.00 | 50.00 | 90.00 | 150.00 |
| | | 21 | 30.00 | 50.00 | 90.00 | 150.00 |

35-37mm, Type B
186	AH1223	14	30.00	50.00	90.00	150.00
		18	30.00	50.00	90.00	150.00
		20	30.00	50.00	90.00	150.00

36mm, Type C
| 188 | AH1223 | 19 | 30.00 | 50.00 | 90.00 | 150.00 |

34mm, Type D
| 190 | AH1223 | 20 | 30.00 | 50.00 | 90.00 | 150.00 |

33mm, Type E
| 192 | AH1243 | — | 30.00 | 50.00 | 90.00 | 150.00 |

NOTE: KM#192 is dated to the actual year, as on similar coins of Tunis.

50 PARA
BILLON, 37mm, Type A
| 194 | AH1243 | — | 75.00 | 125.00 | 200.00 | 300.00 |

NOTE: Refer to KM#182. The denomination of the above coin is very uncertain.

60 PARA

Tripoli / LIBYA

BILLON, 18.27 g, Type A

KM#	Date	Year	Good	VG	Fine	VF
196	AH1223	20	20.00	35.00	60.00	100.00
	1243	—	100.00	150.00	250.00	400.00

FOURTH STANDARD
Years 21-25
Based on a Piastre of approximately 10.00 g.

10 PARA
BILLON, 24mm, Type B

201	AH1223	22	12.50	22.50	35.00	75.00
		23	35.00	50.00	70.00	100.00
		24	12.50	22.50	35.00	75.00
		25	12.50	22.50	35.00	75.00

20 PARA
BILLON, 29-30mm, Type A

203	AH1223	23	18.50	35.00	50.00	70.00

Type B

205	AH1223	22	16.50	30.00	45.00	65.00
		24	16.50	30.00	45.00	65.00
		25	16.50	30.00	45.00	65.00

30 PARA
BILLON, 32mm, Type D

207	AH1223	22	35.00	60.00	100.00	150.00

34mm

209	AH1223	23	30.00	50.00	85.00	125.00

35mm
Similar to Type A, but w/large crescents at both sides similar to Turkey 10 Para, C#197 but w/o wreaths.

211	AH1223	24	30.00	60.00	100.00	125.00

40 PARA
BILLON, Type A

213	AH1223	13	25.00	45.00	100.00	150.00
		14	—	Reported, not confirmed		
		21	25.00	45.00	75.00	100.00
		22	25.00	40.00	60.00	85.00
		24	25.00	40.00	60.00	85.00

Type B

KM#	Date	Year	Good	VG	Fine	VF
215	AH1223	21	65.00	100.00	150.00	225.00
		22	30.00	50.00	75.00	120.00
		25	20.00	35.00	60.00	100.00

FIFTH STANDARD
Year 28 only
Uncertain metrology

5 PARA
BILLON, 1.855 g

216	AH1223	28	—	—	Rare	—

10 PARA

BILLON, 3.680 g
Obv: Toughra w/*Nuhas* (= copper) to right, year 28 to left.
Rev. leg: *Duriba/Fi/Tarabalus Gharb/1223*.

217	AH1223	28	10.00	20.00	40.00	75.00

NOTE: Varieties exist.

20 PARA
BILLON, 7.054 g

218	AH1223	28	—	—	Rare	—

40 PARA
BILLON, 14.813 g

219	AH1223	28	—	—	Rare	—

1-1/2 PIASTRES
(60 Para)
BILLON, 7.73 g, 30mm
Similar to 3 Piastres, KM#220.

KM#	Date	Year	VG	Fine	VF	XF
221	AH1223	28	—	—	Rare	—

3 PIASTRES
(120 Para)
BILLON, 14.50 g, 38mm.
Type A, but obv. and rev. leg. within wreaths.
W/*Fidda* (= Silver) to right of toughra, regnal year at left.

KM#	Date	Year	Good	VG	Fine	VF
220	AH1223	28	—	—	Rare	—

ZERI MAHBUB

GOLD, 21-24mm, 2.30-2.50 g, Type B

KM#	Date	Year	VG	Fine	VF	XF
222	AH1223	12	75.00	110.00	250.00	350.00
		13	75.00	110.00	250.00	350.00

Type E
Obv. leg: 4 lines. Rev: Mintname over date.

224	AH1223	18	75.00	110.00	250.00	350.00

226	AH1223	20	75.00	110.00	250.00	350.00

SULTANI

GOLD, 24-26mm, 3.20-3.40 g, Type C (variant)

KM#	Date	Year	VG	Fine	VF	XF
228	AH1223	6	100.00	150.00	250.00	350.00

Similar, but broader and thinner.

230	AH1223	19	110.00	135.00	200.00	300.00

Rev: W/o lines dividing leg.

232	AH1223	—	110.00	165.00	240.00	350.00

LIBYA

RULERS
Idris I, 1951-1969

MONETARY SYSTEM
10 Milliemes = 1 Piastre
100 Piastres = 1 Pound

MILLIEME

BRONZE

KM#	Date	Year	Mintage	VF	XF	Unc
1	—	1952	7.750	.10	.15	.50
	—	1952	32 pcs.	—	Proof	75.00

NICKEL-BRASS

6	AH1385	1965	11.000	.10	.15	.25

2 MILLIEMES

BRONZE

2	—	1952	6.650	.10	.25	.75
	—	1952	32 pcs.	—	Proof	75.00

5 MILLIEMES

BRONZE

LIBYA 1179

KM#	Date	Year	Mintage	VF	XF	Unc
3	—	1952	7.680	.10	.35	1.00
	—	1952	32 pcs.	—	Proof	75.00

NICKEL-BRASS
| 7 | AH1385 | 1965 | 8.500 | .10 | .15 | .30 |

PIASTRE

COPPER-NICKEL
| 4 | — | 1952 | 10.200 | .35 | .60 | 1.50 |
| | — | 1952 | 32 pcs. | — | Proof | 100.00 |

10 MILLIEMES

COPPER-NICKEL
| 8 | AH1385 | 1965 | 17.000 | .10 | .20 | .40 |

2 PIASTRES

COPPER-NICKEL
| 5 | — | 1952 | 6.075 | .35 | .75 | 2.00 |
| | — | 1952 | 32 pcs. | — | Proof | 125.00 |

20 MILLIEMES

COPPER-NICKEL
| 9 | AH1385 | 1965 | 8.750 | .15 | .35 | 2.00 |

50 MILLIEMES

COPPER-NICKEL
| 10 | AH1385 | 1965 | 8.000 | .25 | .50 | 3.00 |

100 MILLIEMES

COPPER-NICKEL
| 11 | AH1385 | 1965 | 8.000 | .50 | 1.00 | 3.50 |

REPUBLIC
MONETARY SYSTEM
1000 Dirhams = 1 Dinar

DIRHAM

BRASS-CLAD STEEL
KM#	Date	Year	Mintage	VF	XF	Unc
12	AH1395	1975	20.000	.10	.25	1.00

| 18 | AH1399 | 1979 | 1.000 | .20 | .50 | 1.50 |

5 DIRHAMS

BRASS-CLAD STEEL
| 13 | AH1395 | 1975 | 23.000 | .10 | .35 | 1.50 |

| 19 | AH1399 | 1979 | 2.000 | .25 | .65 | 2.00 |

10 DIRHAMS

COPPER-NICKEL-CLAD STEEL
| 14 | AH1395 | 1975 | 52.750 | .10 | .45 | 1.50 |

| 20 | AH1399 | 1979 | 4.000 | .15 | .65 | 2.50 |

20 DIRHAMS

COPPER-NICKEL-CLAD STEEL
| 15 | AH1395 | 1975 | 25.500 | .25 | .75 | 3.50 |

| 21 | AH1399 | 1979 | 6.000 | .35 | 1.00 | 4.00 |

50 DIRHAMS

COPPER-NICKEL
KM#	Date	Year	Mintage	VF	XF	Unc
16	AH1395	1975	25.640	.40	1.25	4.50

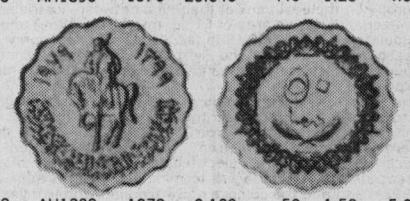

| 22 | AH1399 | 1979 | 9.120 | .50 | 1.50 | 5.00 |

100 DIRHAMS

COPPER-NICKEL
| 17 | AH1395 | 1975 | 15.433 | .75 | 2.00 | 5.00 |

| 23 | AH1399 | 1979 | 15.000 | .75 | 2.50 | 6.00 |

5 DINARS

28.2800 g, .925 SILVER, .8410 oz ASW
International Year of Disabled Persons
| 24 | — | 1981 | .020 | — | — | 25.00 |
| | — | 1981 | .021 | — | Proof | 30.00 |

70 DINARS
15.9800 g, .917 GOLD, .4712 oz AGW
International Year of Disabled Persons
Similar to 5 Dinars, KM#24.
| 25 | — | 1981 | 4,000 | — | — | 400.00 |
| | — | 1981 | 4,000 | — | Proof | 500.00 |

PROOF SETS (PS)

KM#	Date	Mintage	Identification	Issue Price	Mkt. Val.
PS1	1952(5)	32	KM1-5	—	450.00

LIECHTENSTEIN

The Principality of Liechtenstein, located in central Europe on the east bank of the Rhine between Austria and Switzerland, has an area of 61 sq. mi. (157 sq. km.) and a population of *30,000. Capital: Vaduz. The economy is based on agriculture and light manufacturing. Canned goods, textiles, ceramics and precision instruments are exported.

The lordships of Schellenburg and Vaduz were merged into the principality of Liechtenstein. It was a member of the Rhine Confederation from 1806 to 1815, and of the German Confederation from 1815 to 1866 when it became independent. Liechtenstein's long and close association with Austria was terminated by World War I. In 1921 it adopted the coinage of Switzerland, and two years later entered into a customs union with the Swiss, who also operate its postal and telegraph systems and represent it in international affairs. The tiny principality abolished its army in 1868 and has avoided involvement in all European wars since that time.

RULERS
Prince John II, 1858-1929
Prince Franz I, 1929-1938
Prince Franz Josef II, 1938-

MINT MARKS
A - Vienna
B - Bern
M - Munich (restrikes)

MONETARY SYSTEM
(1857-1868)
1-1/2 Florins = 1 Vereinsthaler

EIN (1) THALER
(Vereins)

18.5200 g, .900 SILVER, .5358 oz ASW

Y#	Date	Mintage	Fine	VF	XF	Unc
1	1862A	1,920	1400.	2200.	3000.	3500.
	1862A-M	—	(restrike)	—	25.00	

29.5000 g, .900 GOLD, .8536 oz AGW

| 1a | 1862A-M | .050 | (restrike) | Proof 600.00 |

33.34g, PLATINUM

| 1b | 1862A-M | — | (restrike) | — | 1250. |

MONETARY REFORM
100 Heller = 1 Krone

KRONE

5.0000 g, .835 SILVER, .1342 oz ASW

2	1900A	.050	12.00	20.00	25.00	55.00
	1904A	.075	10.00	18.00	22.50	50.00
	1910A	.045	12.00	20.00	25.00	55.00
	1915A	.075	12.00	20.00	25.00	55.00

2 KRONEN

10.0000 g, .835 SILVER, .2684 oz ASW

Y#	Date	Mintage	Fine	VF	XF	Unc
3	1912A	.050	15.00	20.00	35.00	65.00
	1915A	.038	15.00	20.00	35.00	65.00

5 KRONEN

24.0000 g, .900 SILVER, .6944 oz ASW

4	1900A	5,000	350.00	500.00	625.00	700.00
	1904A	.015	75.00	95.00	150.00	250.00
	1910A	.010	75.00	110.00	175.00	275.00
	1915A	.010	75.00	100.00	175.00	275.00

10 KRONEN

3.3875 g, .900 GOLD, .0980 oz AGW

| 5 | 1900A | 1,500 | — | 2250. | 3500. | 5000. |

20 KRONEN

6.7750 g, .900 GOLD, .1960 oz AGW

| 6 | 1898A | 1,500 | — | 2250. | 3000. | 4350. |

MONETARY REFORM
100 Rappen = 1 Frank

1/2 FRANK

2.5000 g, .835 SILVER, .0751 oz ASW

| 7 | 1924B | *.030 | 65.00 | 125.00 | 150.00 | 200.00 |

*NOTE: 15,745 pieces were remelted.

FRANK

5.0000 g, .835 SILVER, .1342 oz ASW

| 8 | 1924B | *.060 | 45.00 | 70.00 | 90.00 | 150.00 |

*NOTE: 45,355 pieces were remelted.

2 FRANKEN

10.0000 g, .835 SILVER, .2684 oz ASW

Y#	Date	Mintage	Fine	VF	XF	Unc
9	1924B	*.050	50.00	95.00	140.00	175.00

*NOTE: 41,707 pieces were remelted.

5 FRANKEN

25.0000 g, .900 SILVER, .7234 oz ASW

| 10 | 1924B | *.015 | 200.00 | 400.00 | 650.00 | 1000. |

*NOTE: 11,260 pieces were remelted.

10 FRANKEN

3.2258 g, .900 GOLD, .0933 oz AGW

| 11 | 1930B | 2,500 | — | 700.00 | 1000. | 1250. |

| 13 | 1946B | .010 | — | 100.00 | 150.00 | 250.00 |

30.0000 g, .900 SILVER, .8682 oz ASW
50th Anniversary of Reign
Obv: Similar to 50 Franken, Y#21.

| 20 | 1988 | .035 | — | — | — | 20.00 |

20 FRANKEN

6.4516 g, .900 GOLD, .1867 oz AGW

Y#	Date	Mintage	Fine	VF	XF	Unc
12	1930B	2,500	—	700.00	1000.	2500.

| 14 | 1946B | .010 | — | 125.00 | 175.00 | 300.00 |

25 FRANKEN

5.6450 g, .900 GOLD, .1633 oz AGW
Franz Josef II and Princess Gina

| 15 | 1956B | .015 | — | — | 150.00 | 225.00 |

100th Anniversary of National Bank

| 18 | 1961 | .020 | — | — | — | 250.00 |

50 FRANKEN

11.2900 g, .900 GOLD, .3267 oz AGW
Franz Josef II and Princess Gina

| 16 | 1956 | .015 | — | — | 225.00 | 300.00 |

100th Anniversary of National Bank

| 19 | 1961 | .020 | — | — | — | 300.00 |

10.0000 g, .900 GOLD, .2894 oz AGW
50th Anniversary of Reign

| 21 | 1988 | .035 | — | — | — | 200.00 |

100 FRANKEN

32.2580 g, .900 GOLD, .9335 oz AGW
Franz Josef II and Princess Gina

Y#	Date	Mintage	Fine	VF	XF	Unc
17	1952	4,000	—	—	2250.	3000.

LUXEMBOURG

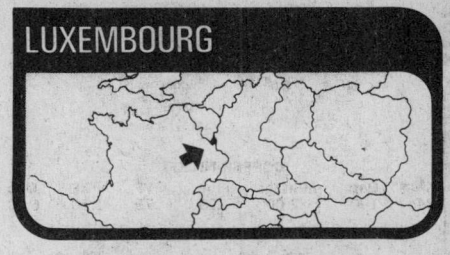

The Grand Duchy of Luxembourg is located in western Europe between Belgium, Germany and France, has an area of 998 sq. mi.(2,586 sq. km.) and a population of *369,000. Capital: Luxembourg. The economy is based on steel - Luxembourg's per capita production of 16 tons is the highest in the world.

Founded about 963, Luxembourg was a prominent country of the Holy Roman Empire; one of its sovereigns became Holy Roman Emperor as Henry VII, 1308. After being made a duchy by Emperor Charles IV, 1354, Luxembourg passed under the domination of Burgundy, Spain, Austria and France, 1443-1815, regaining autonomy under the Treaty of Vienna, 1815, as a grand duchy in union with the Netherlands, though ostensibly a member of the German Confederation. When Belgium seceded from the Kingdom of the Netherlands, 1830, Luxembourg was forced to cede its greater western section to Belgium. The tiny duchy left the German Confederation in 1867 when the Treaty of London recognized it as an independent state and guaranteed its perpetual neutrality. Luxembourg was occupied by Germany and liberated by American troops in both World Wars, and is the resting place of 5,000 American soldiers, including Gen. George S. Patton.

RULERS
William III (Netherlands), 1849-1890
Adolphe, 1890-1905
William IV, 1905-1912
Marie Adelaide, 1912-1919
Charlotte, 1919-1964
Jean, 1964-

MINT MARKS
A - Paris
(b) - Brussels, privy marks only
(u) - Utrecht, privy marks only

PRIVY MARKS
Angels head, two headed eagle - Brussels
Anchor, hand - Paris, (1846-60)
Anchor, bee - Paris, (1860-79)
Sword, Caduceus - Utrecht (1846-74 although struck at Brussels until 1909)

MONETARY SYSTEM
100 Centimes = 1 Franc

2-1/2 CENTIMES

BRONZE

KM#	Date	Mintage	Fine	VF	XF	Unc
21	1854(u)	.640	1.00	3.00	7.50	25.00
	1870(u) dot above BARTH on rev.					
		.210	2.00	8.00	15.00	30.00
	1870(u) w/o dot above BARTH on rev.					
	Inc. Ab.	2.50	10.00	18.50	42.50
	1901(u)	.800	1.00	2.00	3.50	12.50
	1908(u)	.400	1.00	2.50	4.00	14.00

5 CENTIMES

BRONZE

22.1	1854(u)	.680	1.50	4.00	12.50	30.00
	1870(u)	.304	2.00	4.50	12.50	30.00

Mint mark: A

22.2	1855	.600	1.50	4.00	12.50	30.00
	1860	.200	7.50	15.00	25.00	60.00

LUXEMBOURG

COPPER-NICKEL

KM#	Date	Mintage	Fine	VF	XF	Unc
24	1901	2,000	.25	.75	1.50	6.00
26	1908	1,500	.35	1.00	1.75	7.50

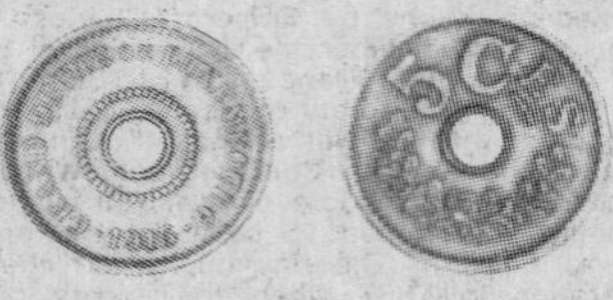

ZINC

KM#	Date	Mintage	Fine	VF	XF	Unc
27	1915	1,200	1.00	2.50	5.50	15.00

IRON

30	1918	1,200	1.00	2.50	5.00	15.00
	1921	.600	1.75	3.50	7.50	22.50
	1922	.400	12.00	20.00	40.00	80.00

COPPER-NICKEL

33	1924	3,000	.15	.35	.75	4.00

BRONZE

40	1930	5,000	.10	.25	.60	2.00

10 CENTIMES

BRONZE
Mint mark: Sword

23.1	1854(u)	.500	2.50	5.00	10.00	35.00
	1870(u) dot above BARTH on rev.					
		1.313	1.25	3.00	12.50	30.00
	1870(u) w/o dot above BARTH on rev.					
	Inc. Ab.	1.25	3.00	12.50	30.00	

Mint mark: A

23.2	1855	1,200	1.25	3.00	12.50	30.00
	1860	.900	1.50	3.50	12.50	30.00
	1865	1,000	1.25	3.00	12.50	30.00

COPPER-NICKEL

25	1901	4,000	.25	.75	1.50	7.50

ZINC

KM#	Date	Mintage	Fine	VF	XF	Unc
28	1915	1,400	1.25	3.00	5.00	15.00

31	1918	1,603	1.50	3.50	7.50	20.00
	1921	.626	2.00	4.50	9.00	22.50
	1923	.350	12.00	20.00	40.00	85.00

COPPER-NICKEL

34	1924	3,500	.20	.50	1.00	4.00

BRONZE

41	1930	5,000	.10	.25	.75	2.25

25 CENTIMES

ZINC

29	1916	.800	1.50	3.50	7.50	15.00

IRON

32	1919	.804	2.75	5.50	11.00	30.00
	1920	.800	2.25	4.00	8.50	25.00
	1922	.600	2.25	4.00	8.50	25.00

COPPER-NICKEL

37	1927	2,500	.35	.65	1.25	3.50

BRONZE

42	1930	1,000	.25	.75	1.50	5.00

COPPER-NICKEL

42a	1938	2,000	1.00	2.00	4.00	7.00

BRONZE

KM#	Date	Mintage	Fine	VF	XF	Unc
45	1946	4,000	—	.15	.25	.75
	1947	4,000	—	.15	.25	.75

ALUMINUM

45a	1954	7,000	—	—	—	.10
	1957	3,020	—	—	—	.10
	1960	3,020	—	—	—	.10
	1963	4,000	—	—	—	.10
	1965	2,000	—	—	—	.10
	1967	3,000	—	—	—	.10
	1968	.600	.10	.25	.50	1.00
	1970	4,000	—	—	—	.10
	1972	4,000	—	—	—	.10

2.9600 g, .925 SILVER, .0880 oz ASW

45b	1980	3,000	—	—	Proof	12.00

50 CENTIMES

NICKEL

43	1930	2,000	.25	.50	1.00	5.00

FRANC

NICKEL

35	1924	1,000	.25	.75	1.25	8.00
	1928	2,000	.20	.50	1.00	7.00
	1935	1,000	.25	.75	1.25	6.00

COPPER-NICKEL

44	1939	5,000	.25	.75	1.50	5.00

46.1	1946	4,000	.15	.35	.50	1.00
	1947	2,000	.20	.40	.75	1.00

46.2	1952	5,000	.10	.25	.50	1.00

46.3	1953	2,000	—	.10	.15	.40
	1955	1,000	—	.10	.15	.40
	1957	2,000	—	.10	.15	.40
	1960	2,000	—	.10	.15	.40
	1962	2,000	—	.10	.15	.40
	1964	2,000	—	.10	.15	.40

4.4500 g, .925 SILVER, .1323 oz ASW

46.3a	1980	3,000	—	—	Proof	20.00

COPPER-NICKEL

KM#	Date	Mintage	Fine	VF	XF	Unc
55	1965	3.000	—	—	.10	.15
	1966	1.000	—	—	.10	.15
	1968	3.000	—	—	.10	.15
	1970	3.000	—	—	.10	.15
	1972	3.000	—	—	.10	.15
	1973	3.000	—	—	.10	.15
	1976	3.000	—	—	.10	.15
	1977	1.000	—	—	.10	.15
	1978	3.000	—	—	.10	.15
	1979	2.775	—	—	.10	.15
	1980	4.000	—	—	.10	.15
	1981	5.000	—	—	.10	.15
	1982	3.000	—	—	.10	.15
	1983	3.000	—	—	.10	.15
	1984	3.000	—	—	.10	.15

4.4700 g, .925 SILVER, .1329 oz ASW

| 55a | 1980 | 3.000 | — | — | Proof | 20.00 |

COPPER-NICKEL

59	1986	3.000	—	—	.10	.20
	1987	3.000	—	—	.10	.20

NICKEL-STEEL

| 63 | 1988 | — | — | — | — | .25 |

2 FRANCS

NICKEL

| 36 | 1924 | 1.000 | 1.00 | 2.25 | 4.00 | 15.00 |

5 FRANCS

8.0000 g, .750 SILVER, .1929 oz ASW

| 38 | 1929 | 2.000 | BV | 2.50 | 5.00 | 15.00 |

COPPER-NICKEL

| 50 | 1949 | 2.000 | .30 | .60 | 1.00 | 2.50 |

| 51 | 1962 | 2.000 | .10 | .25 | .40 | .75 |

6.7400 g, .925 SILVER, .2004 oz ASW

| 51a | 1980 | 3.000 | — | — | Proof | 27.50 |

COPPER-NICKEL

KM#	Date	Mintage	Fine	VF	XF	Unc
56	1971	1.000	—	—	.15	.50
	1976	1.000	—	—	.15	.50
	1979	1.000	—	—	.15	.50
	1981	1.000	—	—	.15	.50

6.7800 g, .925 SILVER, .2016 oz ASW

| 56a | 1980 | 3.000 | — | — | Proof | 27.50 |

BRASS

60.1	1986	9.000	—	—	.15	.35
	1987	7.000	—	—	.15	.35
	1988	2.000	—	—	.15	.35

Rev: Larger crown w/cross touching rim.

| 60.2 | 1988 | Inc. Ab. | — | — | .15 | .35 |

10 FRANCS

13.3900 g, .750 SILVER, .3228 oz ASW

| 39 | 1929 | 1.000 | BV | 4.50 | 9.00 | 25.00 |

NICKEL

57	1971	3.000	—	—	.30	.60
	1972	3.000	—	—	.30	.60
	1974	3.000	—	—	.30	.60
	1976	3.000	—	—	.30	.60
	1977	3.000	—	—	.30	.60
	1978	3.000	—	—	.30	.60
	1979	1.000	—	—	.30	.60
	1980	3.000	—	—	.30	.60

8.7900 g, .925 SILVER, .2614 oz ASW

| 57a | 1980 | 3.000 | — | — | Proof | 30.00 |

20 FRANCS

8.5000 g, .835 SILVER, .2282 oz ASW
600th Anniversary John the Blind

| 47 | 1946 | .100 | — | — | 7.50 | 15.00 |

BRONZE

| 58 | 1980 | 3.000 | — | — | .60 | 1.00 |

KM#	Date	Mintage	Fine	VF	XF	Unc
58	1981	3.000	—	—	.60	1.00
	1982	3.000	—	—	.60	1.00
	1983	2.000	—	—	.60	1.00

10.2100 g, .925 SILVER, .3036 oz ASW

| 58a | 1980 | 3.000 | — | — | Proof | 35.00 |

50 FRANCS

12.5000 g, .835 SILVER, .3356 oz ASW
600th Anniversary John the Blind

| 48 | 1946 | .100 | — | — | 12.50 | 18.00 |

NICKEL

62	1987	3.000	—	—	1.50	2.50
	1988	1.200	—	—	1.50	2.50
	1989	—	—	—	1.50	2.50

100 FRANCS

25.0000 g, .835 SILVER, .6711 oz ASW
600th Anniversary John the Blind

49	1946	.098	—	—	22.50	40.00
	1946 w/o designer's name					
	(restrike)	2,000	—	—	—	120.00

18.0000 g, .835 SILVER .4832 oz ASW

| 52 | 1963 | .050 | — | — | 10.00 | 15.00 |

| 54 | 1964 | .054 | — | — | 7.50 | 12.50 |

LUXEMBOURG 1184

250 FRANCS

25.0000 g, .900 SILVER, .7234 oz ASW
Millennium Commemorative

KM#	Date	Mintage	Fine	VF	XF	Unc
53.1	1963	.011	—	—	60.00	75.00

"Dark toned" by the mint

KM#	Date	Mintage	Fine	VF	XF	Unc
53.2	1963	8,500	—	—	65.00	85.00

PROOF SETS (PS)

KM#	Date	Mintage	Identification	Issue Price	Mkt. Val.
PS1	1980(7)	3,000	KM45b,46.3a,51a,55a-58a	—	175.00

MACAO

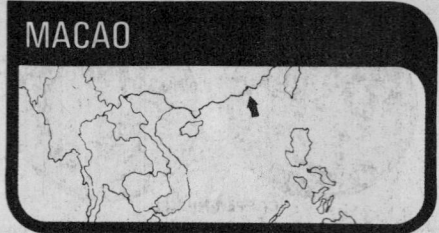

The Province of Macao, a Portuguese overseas province located in the South China Sea 40 miles southwest of Hong Kong, consists of the peninsula of Macao and the islands of Taipa and Coloane. It has an area of 6.2 sq. mi. (16 sq. km.) and a population of *433,000. Capital: Macao. Macao's economy is based on light industry, commerce, tourism, fishing, and gold trading -- Macao is one of the few entirely free markets for gold in the world. Cement, textiles, fireworks, vegetable oils, and metal products are exported.

Established by the Portuguese in 1557, Macao is the oldest European settlement in the Far East. The Chinese, while agreeing to Portuguese settlement, did not recognize Portuguese sovereign rights and the Portuguese remained largely under control of the Chinese until 1849, when the Portuguese abolished the Chinese custom house and declared the independence of the port. The Manchu government formally recognized the Portuguese right to 'perpetual occupation' of Macao in 1887.

In 1987, Portugal and China agreed that Macao will become a Chinese Territory from 1999 on.

RULERS
Portuguese

MONETARY SYSTEM
100 Avos = 1 Pataca

5 AVOS

BRONZE

KM#	Date	Mintage	VF	XF	Unc
1	1952	1.032	.50	1.00	3.00

NICKEL-BRASS

| 1a | 1967 | 5.000 | — | .10 | .25 |

10 AVOS

BRONZE

| 2 | 1952 | 6.825 | .25 | .50 | 1.25 |

NICKEL-BRASS

2a	1967	5.525	.15	.20	.30
	1968	6.975	.15	.20	.30
	1975	20.000	—	.10	.25
	1976	Inc. Ab.	—	.10	.25

BRONZE

| 20 | 1982 | 24.580 | — | .10 | .15 |
| | 1983 | — | — | .10 | .15 |

3.2000 g, .925 SILVER, .0952 oz ASW

20a	1982	2,000	—	Proof	7.50
	1983	2,500	—	Proof	5.00
	1984	2,500	—	Proof	5.00
	1985	2,500	—	Proof	5.00

4.0000 g, .917 GOLD, .1179 oz AGW

| 20b | 1982 | 150 pcs. | — | Proof | 100.00 |

4.5000 g, .950 PLATINUM, .1374 oz APW

| 20c | 1982 | 375 pcs. | — | Proof | 125.00 |

20 AVOS

BRONZE

KM#	Date	Mintage	VF	XF	Unc
21	1982	9.960	—	.10	.20
	1983	—	—	.10	.20

4.6000 g, .925 SILVER, .1368 oz ASW

21a	1982	2,000	—	Proof	10.00
	1983	2,500	—	Proof	7.50
	1984	2,500	—	Proof	7.50
	1985	2,500	—	Proof	7.50

5.5000 g, .917 GOLD, .1621 oz AGW

| 21b | 1982 | 150 pcs. | — | Proof | 150.00 |

6.2000 g, .950 PLATINUM, .1893 oz APW

| 21c | 1982 | 375 pcs. | — | Proof | 175.00 |

50 AVOS

COPPER-NICKEL

| 3 | 1952 | 2.560 | .35 | .75 | 2.50 |

| 7 | 1972 | 1.600 | .15 | .35 | .75 |
| | 1973 | 4.840 | .25 | .35 | .75 |

| 9 | 1978 | 3.000 | .10 | .30 | .65 |

BRONZE

| 22 | 1982 | 16.952 | — | .10 | .25 |
| | 1983 | — | — | .10 | .25 |

5.7000 g, .925 SILVER, .1695 oz ASW

22a	1982	2,000	—	Proof	12.50
	1983	2,500	—	Proof	10.00
	1984	2,500	—	Proof	10.00
	1985	2,500	—	Proof	10.00

7.4000 g, .917 GOLD, .2181 oz AGW

| 22b | 1982 | 150 pcs. | — | Proof | 175.00 |

8.4000 g, .950 PLATINUM, .2565 oz APW

| 22c | 1982 | 375 pcs. | — | Proof | 200.00 |

PATACA

3.0000 g, .720 SILVER, .0694 oz ASW

| 4 | 1952 | .522 | 1.50 | 2.50 | 5.00 |

NICKEL

| 6 | 1968 | 5.000 | .35 | .50 | 1.25 |
| | 1975 | 6.000 | .20 | .30 | 1.00 |

COPPER-NICKEL

| 6a | 1980 | — | — | .20 | .30 | 1.00 |

KM#	Date	Mintage	VF	XF	Unc
23	1982	6.427	.20	.35	.75
	1983	—	.20	.35	.75

9.0000 g, .925 SILVER, .2677 oz ASW

23a	1982	2,000	—	Proof	15.00
	1983	2,500	—	Proof	12.50
	1984	2,500	—	Proof	12.50
	1985	2,500	—	Proof	12.50

11.6000 g, .917 GOLD, .3420 oz AGW

23b	1982	150 pcs.	—	Proof	250.00

13.2000 g, .950 PLATINUM, .4032 oz APW

23c	1982	375 pcs.	—	Proof	325.00

5 PATACAS

15.0000 g, .720 SILVER, .3472 oz ASW

5	1952	.500	4.50	5.50	9.00

10.0000 g, .650 SILVER, .2089 oz ASW

5a	1971	.500	3.00	4.00	6.50

COPPER-NICKEL

24	1982	1.102	.75	1.00	2.00
	1983	—	.75	1.00	2.00

10.7000 g, .925 SILVER, .3182 oz ASW

24a	1982	2,000	—	Proof	30.00
	1983	2,500	—	Proof	25.00
	1984	2,500	—	Proof	25.00
	1985	2,500	—	Proof	25.00

16.3000 g, .917 GOLD, .4808 oz AGW

24b	1982	150 pcs.	—	Proof	350.00

18.4000 g, .950 PLATINUM, .5620 oz APW

24c	1982	375 pcs.	—	Proof	425.00

20 PATACAS

18.0000 g, .650 SILVER, .3762 oz ASW
Opening of Macao-Taipa Bridge

KM#	Date	Mintage	VF	XF	Unc
8	1974	1.000	—	7.50	12.50

100 PATACAS

28.2800 g, .925 SILVER, .8411 oz ASW
25th Anniversary of Grand Prix

10	1978	610 pcs.	—	—	Proof 100.00

COPPER-NICKEL

10a	1978	—	—	—	325.00

28.2800 g, .925 SILVER, .8411 oz ASW
Rev: Racing car w/o advertising.

11	1978	5,500	—	Proof	45.00

Year of the Goat

14	1979	5,500	—	Proof	45.00

Year of the Monkey

16	1980	—	—	—	35.00
	1980	—	—	Proof	45.00

Year of the Cockerel

KM#	Date	Mintage	VF	XF	Unc
18	1981	1,450	—	—	35.00
	1981	1,450	—	Proof	45.00

Year of the Dog

25	1982	500 pcs.	—	—	35.00
	1982	500 pcs.	—	Proof	45.00

Year of the Pig

27	1983	2,500	—	—	35.00
	1983	2,500	—	Proof	45.00

Year of the Rat

29	1984	2,000	—	—	35.00
	1984	5,000	—	Proof	45.00

MACAO 1186

Year of the Ox

KM#	Date	Mintage	VF	XF	Unc
31	1985	.010	—	—	35.00
	1985	5,000	—	Proof	45.00

Visit of Portugal's President Eanes

33	1985	3,000	—	—	30.00
	1985	2,000	—	Proof	40.00

Year of the Tiger

34	1986	2,000	—	—	35.00
	1986	3,000	—	Proof	45.00

Year of the Rabbit

36	1987	—	—	—	50.00
	1987	5,000	—	Proof	60.00

Year of the Dragon
Similar to 1000 Patacas, KM#39.

38	1988	—	—	—	50.00
	1988	5,000	—	Proof	60.00

35th Anniversary of Grand Prix
Rev: Similar to 500 Patacas, KM#42.

KM#	Date	Mintage	VF	XF	Unc
40	1988	5,000	—	Proof	45.00

Year of the Snake
Similar to 1000 Patacas, KM#45.

44	1989	2,000	—	—	40.00
	1989	3,000	—	Proof	50.00

500 PATACAS

7.9600 g, .917 GOLD, .2347 oz AGW
25th Anniversary of Grand Prix

12	1978	550 pcs.	—	Proof	350.00

Rev: Racing car w/o advertising.

13	1978	5,500	—	Proof	200.00

Year of the Goat

15	1979	5,500	—	Proof	225.00

155.5150 g, .999 SILVER, 5.0000 oz ASW
35th Anniversary of Grand Prix
Similar to KM#42.

41	1988	2,000	—	Proof	150.00

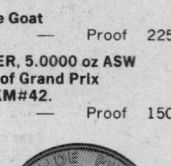

7.9881 g, .917 GOLD, .2354 oz AGW
35th Anniversary of Grand Prix

42	1988	4,500	—	Proof	225.00

1000 PATACAS

15.9760 g, .917 GOLD, .4711 oz AGW
Year of the Monkey

17	1980	5,500		Proof	400.00

Year of the Cockerel

KM#	Date	Mintage	VF	XF	Unc
19	1981	2,500	—	—	350.00
	1981	Inc. Ab.	—	Proof	400.00

Year of the Dog

26	1982	256 pcs.	—	—	350.00
	1982	255 pcs.	—	Proof	450.00

Year of the Pig

28	1983	400 pcs.	—	—	350.00
	1983	500 pcs.	—	Proof	450.00

Year of the Rat

30	1984	2,000	—	—	350.00
	1984	3,000	—	Proof	400.00

Year of the Ox

32	1985	.010	—	—	350.00
	1985	5,000	—	Proof	400.00

Year of the Tiger

35	1986	2,000	—	—	350.00
	1986	3,000	—	Proof	450.00

Year of the Rabbit

37	1987	—	—	—	350.00
	1987	5,000	—	Proof	400.00

Year of the Dragon

KM#	Date	Mintage	VF	XF	Unc
39	1988	5,000	—	Proof	400.00

Year of the Snake

| 45 | 1989 | 2,000 | — | — | 350.00 |
| | 1989 | 3,000 | — | Proof | 500.00 |

10,000 PATACAS
155.5150 g, .999 GOLD, 5.0000 oz AGW
25th Anniversary of Grand Prix
Similar to 500 Patacas, KM#42.

| 43 | 1988 | 500 pcs. | — | Proof | 2500. |

PROOF SETS (PS)

KM#	Date	Mintage	Identification	Issue Price	Mkt. Val.
PS1	1982(5)	2,000	KM20a-24a	—	75.00
PS1b	1982(5)	150	KM20b-24b	—	1025.
PS1c	1982(5)	375	KM20c-24c	—	1250.
PS2	1983(5)	2,500	KM20a-24a	55.00	60.00
PS3	1984(5)	2,500	KM20a-24a	55.00	60.00
PS4	1985(5)	2,500	KM20a-24a	55.00	60.00

MADAGASCAR

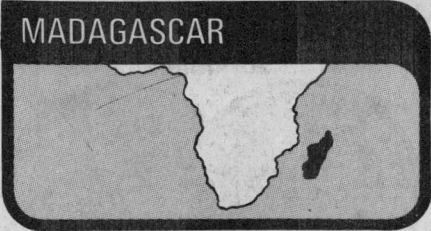

The Democratic Republic of Madagascar, an independent member of the French Community located in the Indian Ocean 250 miles (402 km.) off the southeast coast of Africa, has an area of 226,658 sq. mi. (587,041 sq. km.) and a population of *11.1 million. Capital: Antananarivo. The economy is primarily agricultural; large bauxite deposits are presently being developed. Coffee, vanilla, graphite, and rice are exported.

Diago Diaz, a Portuguese navigator, sighted the island of Madagascar on Aug. 10, 1500, when his ship became separated from an India-bound fleet. Attempts at settlement by the British during the reign of Charles I and by the French during the 17th and 18th centuries were of no avail, and the island became a refuge and supply base for Indian Ocean pirates. Despite considerable influence on the island, the British accepted the imposition of a French protectorate in 1886 in return for French recognition of Britain's sphere of influence in Zanzibar. Madagascar was made a French colony in 1896 after absolute control had been established by military force. Britain occupied the island after the fall of France, 1942, to prevent its seizure by the Japanese, returning it to the Free French in 1943. On Oct. 14, 1958, following a decade of intermittent but bitter warfare, Madagascar, as the Malagasy Republic, became an autonomous state within the French Community. On June 27, 1960, it became a sovereign, independent nation, though remaining nominally within the French Community. The Malagasy Republic was renamed the Democratic Republic of Madagascar in 1975.

MONETARY SYSTEM
100 Centimes = 1 Franc

MINT MARKS
(a) - Paris, privy marks only
Pretoria

50 CENTIMES

BRONZE
Pretoria Mint

KM#	Date	Mintage	VF	XF	Unc
1	1943	2.000	1.50	7.50	22.00

FRANC

BRONZE
Pretoria Mint

| 2 | 1943 | 5.000 | 5.00 | 12.00 | 48.00 |

ALUMINUM

| 3 | 1948(a) | 7.400 | .30 | .50 | 2.00 |
| | 1958(a) | 2.600 | .30 | .50 | 2.25 |

2 FRANCS

ALUMINUM

KM#	Date	Mintage	VF	XF	Unc
4	1948(a)	10.000	.35	.65	1.75

5 FRANCS

ALUMINUM

| 5 | 1953(a) | 30.012 | .55 | .75 | 1.75 |

10 FRANCS

ALUMINUM-BRONZE

| 6 | 1953(a) | 25.000 | .60 | .80 | 2.00 |

20 FRANCS

ALUMINUM-BRONZE

| 7 | 1953(a) | 15.000 | 1.50 | 2.50 | 4.00 |

MALAGASY REPUBLIC

MINT MARKS
(a) - Paris, privy marks only

MONETARY SYSTEM
100 Centimes = 1 Franc

FRANC

STAINLESS STEEL

8	1965(a)	1.170	.10	.25	.50
	1966(a)	—	.10	.25	.50
	1970(a)	—	.10	.25	.50
	1974(a)	1.250	.10	.25	.50
	1975(a)	7.355	.10	.25	.50
	1976(a)	—	.10	.25	.50
	1977(a)	—	.10	.25	.50
	1979(a)	—	.10	.25	.50
	1980(a)	—	.10	.25	.50
	1982(a)	—	.10	.25	.50
	1983(a)	—	.10	.25	.50
	1986(a)	—	.10	.25	.50

2 FRANCS

STAINLESS STEEL

9	1965(a)	.760	.15	.40	.75
	1970(a)	—	.10	.30	.60
	1974(a)	1.250	.10	.30	.60
	1975(a)	8.250	.10	.30	.60
	1976(a)	—	.10	.30	.60
	1977(a)	—	.10	.30	.60
	1981(a)	—	.10	.30	.60
	1982(a)	—	.10	.30	.60
	1983(a)	—	.10	.30	.60
	1984(a)	—	.10	.30	.60
	1986(a)	—	.10	.30	.60

Democratic Republic / MADAGASCAR 1188

5 FRANCS

STAINLESS STEEL

KM#	Date	Mintage	VF	XF	Unc
10	1966(a)	—	.10	.50	.85
	1967(a)	—	.10	.50	.85
	1968(a)	7.500	.10	.50	.85
	1970(a)	—	.10	.50	.85
	1972(a)	19.100	.10	.50	.85
	1976(a)	—	.10	.50	.85
	1977(a)	—	.10	.50	.85

10 FRANCS

ALUMINUM-BRONZE
F.A.O. Issue

11	1970(a)	25.000	.15	.60	1.00
	1971(a)	Inc. Ab.	.15	.60	1.00
	1972(a)	Inc. Ab.	.15	.60	1.00
	1973(a)	Inc. Ab.	.15	.60	1.00
	1974(a)	—	.15	.60	1.00
	1975(a)	—	.15	.60	1.00
	1976(a)	9.500	.15	.60	1.00
	1977(a)	—	.15	.60	1.00
	1978(a)	—	.15	.60	1.00

20 FRANCS

ALUMINUM-BRONZE
F.A.O. Issue

12	1970(a)	15.000	.20	.60	1.35
	1971(a)	Inc. Ab.	.20	.60	1.35
	1972(a)	Inc. Ab.	.20	.60	1.35
	1973(a)	Inc. Ab.	.20	.60	1.35
	1974(a)	—	.20	.60	1.35
	1975(a)	—	.20	.60	1.35
	1976(a)	2.700	.20	.60	1.35
	1977(a)	—	.20	.60	1.35
	1978(a)	—	.20	.60	1.35

FLEUR DE COIN SETS (SS)

KM#	Date	Mintage	Identification	Issue Price	Mkt. Val.
SS1	1970(5)	1,500	KM8-12	2.75	10.00

DEMOCRATIC REPUBLIC
MONETARY SYSTEM
5 Francs = 1 Ariary

10 ARIARY

NICKEL
F.A.O. Issue

KM#	Date	Mintage	VF	XF	Unc
13	1978	8.001	.50	1.50	3.50

9.0000 g, .925 SILVER, .2676 oz ASW

| 13a | 1978 | 3,800 | — | Proof | 20.00 |

10.0000 g, .917 GOLD, .2947 oz AGW

World Wildlife Fund - Ibis

KM#	Date	Mintage	VF	XF	Unc
16	1988	*5,000	—	Proof	200.00

20 ARIARY

NICKEL
F.A.O. Issue

| 14 | 1978 | 8.001 | 1.00 | 2.00 | 5.00 |

12.0000 g, .925 SILVER, .3569 oz ASW

| 14a | 1978 | 3,800 | — | Proof | 25.00 |

19.4400 g, .925 SILVER, .5782 oz ASW
World Wildlife Fund - Lemur

| 15 | 1988 | *.025 | — | Proof | 45.00 |

PROOF SETS (PS)

KM#	Date	Mintage	Identification	Issue Price	Mkt. Val.
PS1	1978	3,800	KM13a,14a	38.00	45.00

MADEIRA

The Madeira Islands, which belong to Portugal, are located 360 miles (492 km.) off the northwest coast of Africa. They have an area of 307 sq. mi. (795 sq. km.) and a population of *267,000. The group consists of two inhabited islands named Madeira and Porto Santo and two groups of uninhabited rocks named Desertas and Selvagens. Capital: Funchal. The two staple products are wine and sugar. Bananas and pineapples are also produced for export.

Although the evidence is insufficient, it is thought that the Phoenicians visited Madeira at an early period. It is also probable that the entire archipelago was explored in early times by Genoese adventurers; an Italian map dated 1351 shows the Madeira Islands quite clearly. The Portuguese navigator Goncalvez Zarco first sighted Porto Santo in 1418, having been driven there by a storm while he was exploring the coast of West Africa. Madeira itself was discovered in 1420. The islands were uninhabited when visited by Zarco, but their colonization was immediately begun by Prince Henry the Navigator, aided by the knights of the Order of Christ. British troops occupied the islands in 1801, and again in 1807-14.

RULERS
Portuguese

V (5) REIS

COPPER

KM#	Date	Mintage	VG	Fine	VF	XF
1	1850	—	35.00	75.00	150.00	300.00

X (10) REIS

COPPER

2	1842	—	7.50	15.00	30.00	60.00
	1850	—	—	—	Rare	—
	1852	—	7.50	15.00	30.00	60.00

SILVER (OMS)

| 2a | 1842 | — | — | — | Rare | — |

GOLD (OMS)

| 2b | 1842 | — | — | — | Rare | — |

XX (20) REIS

COPPER

| 3 | 1842 | — | 10.00 | 20.00 | 40.00 | 80.00 |
| | 1852 | — | — | — | Rare | — |

MODERN COINAGE
25 ESCUDOS

COPPER-NICKEL
Autonomy of Madeira - Zarco

KM#	Date	Mintage	Fine	VF	XF	Unc
4	1981	.750	—	—	—	3.50

11.0000 g, .925 SILVER, .3272 oz ASW

| 4a | 1981 | .020 | — | — | Proof | 12.00 |

100 ESCUDOS

COPPER-NICKEL
Autonomy of Madeira - Zarco

| 5 | 1981 | .250 | — | — | — | 7.50 |

16.5000 g, .925 SILVER, .4908 oz ASW

| 5a | 1981 | .020 | — | — | Proof | 18.00 |

PROOF SETS (PS)

KM#	Date	Mintage	Identification	Issue Price	Mkt. Val.
PS1	1981 (2)	20,000	KM4a-5a	42.00	30.00

MALAWI

The Republic of Malawi (formerly Nyasaland), located in southeastern Africa to the west of Lake Malawi (Nyasa), has an area of 45,747 sq. mi. (118,484 sq. km.) and a population of *8 million. Capital: Lilongwe. The economy is predominantly agricultural. Tobacco, tea, peanuts and cotton are exported.

Although the Portuguese, heirs to the restless spirit of Prince Henry, were the first Europeans to reach the Malawi area, the first meaningful contact was made by missionary-explorer Dr. David Livingstone who arrived at Lake Malawi on Sept. 16, 1859, and remained to make extensive explorations in the 1860's. Subsequent clashes between settlements of Scottish missionaries and Arab slave traders, and the procurement of development rights by Cecil Rhodes, 1884, stimulated British interest and brought about the establishment of the Nyasaland protectorate in 1891. In 1953 Nyasaland reluctantly joined the Federation of Rhodesia and Nyasaland and, after prolonged protest, was granted self-government within the federation. Nyasaland became the independent nation of Malawi on July 6, 1964, and became a republic two years later. Malawi is a member of the Commonwealth of Nations. The president is the Chief of State and Head of Government.

NOTE: For earlier coinage see Rhodesia and Nyasaland.

MONETARY SYSTEM
12 Pence = 1 Shilling
2 Shillings = 1 Florin
5 Shillings = 1 Crown
20 Shillings = 1 Pound

PENNY

BRONZE

KM#	Date	Mintage	VF	XF	Unc
6	1967	6.000	.65	1.25	2.50
	1968	3.600	5.00	8.00	15.00

6 PENCE

COPPER-NICKEL-ZINC

1	1964	14.800	.50	1.00	2.00
	1964	.010	—	Proof	1.25
	1967	6.000	1.00	2.50	5.00

SHILLING

COPPER-NICKEL-ZINC

2	1964	11.900	.75	1.50	2.50
	1964	.010	—	Proof	1.25
	1968	3.000	1.50	3.00	4.50

FLORIN

COPPER-NICKEL-ZINC

KM#	Date	Mintage	VF	XF	Unc
3	1964	6.500	1.00	2.25	4.00
	1964	.010	—	Proof	2.00

1/2 CROWN

COPPER-NICKEL-ZINC

4	1964	6.400	1.75	3.50	6.00
	1964	.010	—	Proof	3.00

CROWN

NICKEL-BRASS
Republic Day

5	1966	.020	—	Proof	6.50

DECIMAL COINAGE
100 Tambala = 1 Kwacha

TAMBALA

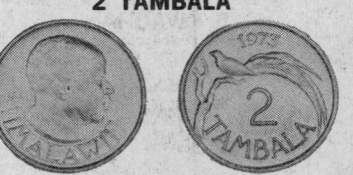

BRONZE

7	1971	15.000	—	.10	.20
	1971	4.000	—	Proof	.50
	1973	5.000	—	.10	.20
	1974	12.500	—	.10	.15
	1975	—	—	.10	.15
	1976	10.000	—	.10	.15
	1977	10.000	—	.10	.15
	1979	15.000	—	.10	.15
	1982	15.000	—	.10	.15

COPPER PLATED STEEL

7a	1984	.201	—	.10	.15
	1985	—	—	.10	.15
	1985	.010	—	Proof	3.00

2 TAMBALA

BRONZE

8	1971	10.000	—	.10	.25
	1971	4.000	—	Proof	.50
	1973	5.000	—	.10	.25
	1974	5.000	—	.10	.25
	1975	—	—	.10	.25
	1976	5.000	—	.10	.25
	1977	5.000	—	.10	.25
	1979	7.637	—	.10	.25
	1982	15.000	—	.10	.25

MALAWI 1190

5 TAMBALA
COPPER PLATED STEEL

KM#	Date	Mintage	VF	XF	Unc
8a	1984	.150	—	.10	.25
	1985	—	—	.10	.25
	1985	.010	—	Proof	4.00

10 TAMBALA
COPPER-NICKEL

9	1971	7.000	.10	.30	.60
	1971	4,000	—	Proof	1.50
	1985	.010	—	Proof	5.00

20 TAMBALA
COPPER-NICKEL

10	1971	4,000	.50	1.00	2.00
	1971	4,000	—	Proof	2.00
	1985	.010	—	Proof	6.00

KWACHA
COPPER-NICKEL

11	1971	3.000	1.00	1.75	3.00
	1971	4,000	—	Proof	3.00
	1985	.010	—	Proof	7.00

5 KWACHA
COPPER-NICKEL
Obv: Similar to 20 Tambala, KM#11.

12	1971	.020	2.00	3.75	6.00
	1971	4,000	—	Proof	6.00

28.2800 g, .925 SILVER, .8410 oz ASW
Conservation Series
Rev: Crawshay's Zebra.

KM#	Date	Mintage	VF	XF	Unc
15	1978	4,048	—	—	25.00
	1978	3,622	—	Proof	55.00

10 KWACHA

35.0000 g, .925 SILVER, 1.0409 oz ASW
10th Anniversary of Independence

13	1974	7,556	—	—	15.00
	1974	4,937	—	Proof	25.00

10th Anniversary of the Reserve Bank
Obv: Similar to KM#13.

14	1975	6,870	—	—	12.50
	1975	Inc. Ab.	—	Proof	20.00

.900 GOLD

| 14a | 1975 | — | — | — | 1000. |

35.0000 g, .925 SILVER, 1.0409 oz ASW
Conservation Series
Obv: Similar to 250 Kwacha, KM#17.
Rev: Sabie Antelope.

16	1978	4,009	—	—	30.00
	1978	3,416	—	Proof	65.00

28.2800 g, .925 SILVER, .8410 oz ASW
20th Anniversary of Reserve Bank

KM#	Date	Mintage	VF	XF	Unc
18	1985	4,000	—	Proof	30.00

47.5400 g, .917 GOLD, 1.4011 oz AGW

| 18a | 1985 | 50 pcs. | — | Proof | 1500. |

250 KWACHA

33.4370 g, .900 GOLD, .9676 oz AGW
Conservation Series
Rev: Nyala.

17	1978	566 pcs.	—	—	650.00
	1978	208 pcs.	—	Proof	850.00

MINT SETS (MS)

KM#	Date	Mintage	Identification	Issue Price	Mkt. Val.
MS1	1971(6)	10,000	KM7-12	3.30	12.00
MS2	1978(2)	—	KM15,16	—	55.00

PROOF SETS (PS)

PS1	1964(4)	10,000	KM1-4	10.00	7.50
PS2	1971(6)	4,000	KM7-12	8.70	13.50
PS3	1978(2)	—	KM15a,16a	—	120.00
PS4	1985(5)	10,000	KM7a-8a,9-11	30.00	25.00

Listings for
MALAYA: refer to Malaysia
MALAYA & BRITISH BORNEO: refer to Malaysia

MALAYSIA

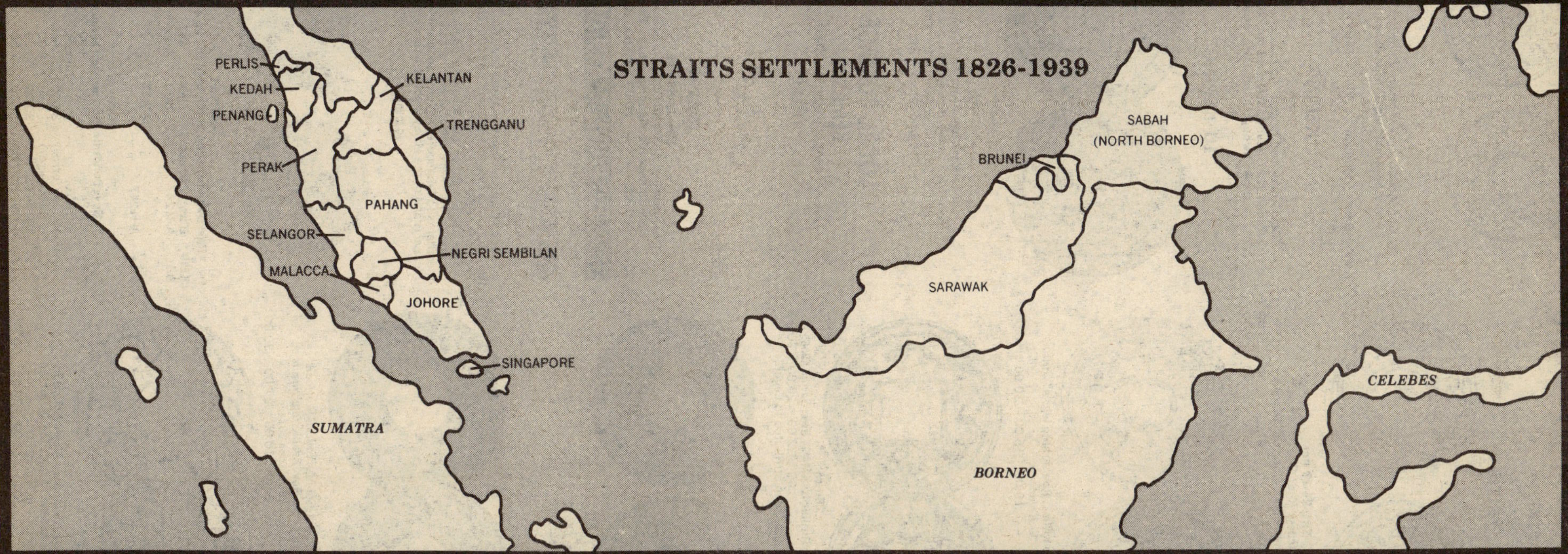

STRAITS SETTLEMENTS 1826-1939

SABAH (NORTH BORNEO)
BRUNEI
SARAWAK
BORNEO
CELEBES
PERLIS
KEDAH
PENANG
PERAK
SELANGOR
MALACCA
KELANTAN
TRENGGANU
PAHANG
NEGRI SEMBILAN
JOHORE
SINGAPORE
SUMATRA

MALAYA  1939-1952

MALAYA & BR. BORNEO 1952-1963

MALAYSIA 1963—

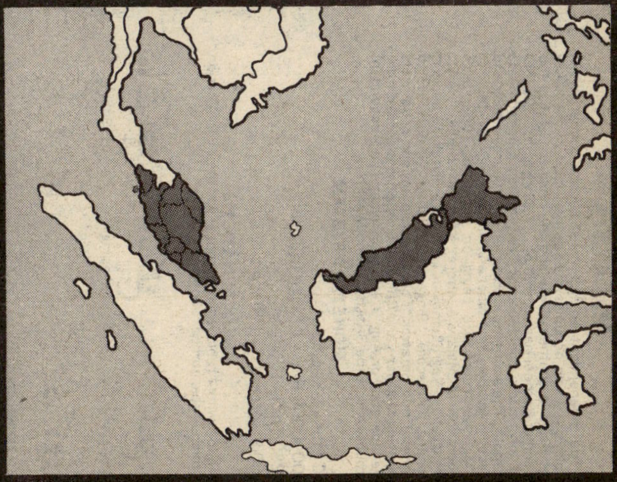

MALAYSIA

The independent limited constitutional monarchy of Malaysia, which occupies the southern part of the Malay Peninsula in southeast Asia and the northern part of the island of Borneo, has an area of 127,317 sq. mi. (329,749 sq. km.) and a population of *16.9 million. Capital: Kuala Lumpur. The economy is based on agriculture, mining and forestry. Rubber, tin, timber and palm oil are exported.

Malaysia came into being on Sept. 16, 1963, as a federation of Malaya (Johore, Kelantan, Kedah, Perlis, Trengganu, Negri-Sembilan, Pahang, Perak, Selangor, Penang, Malacca), Singapore, Sabah (British North Borneo) and Sarawak. Following two serious racial riots involving Malayans and Chinese, Singapore withdrew from the federation on Aug. 9, 1965, to become an independent republic within the British Commonwealth.

MONETARY SYSTEM

10 Pitis = 1 Keping
900-4,000 Pitis = 1 Ringgit (Dollar)
1280 Trah = 1 Ringgit
100 Pice(cents) = 1 Ringgit

DENOMINATIONS

The following Arabic legends appear for the denomination with an Arabic number above.

(1) Keping   Sakeping   Satkeping

(2) Dua Keping

NOTE: Many local merchant tokens, inscribed mainly in Chinese, exist for most of the Malay states. These have not been listed.

KEDAH

A state in northwestern Malaysia. Islam introduced in 15th century. Subject to Thailand from 1821-1909. Coins issued under Governor Tengku Anum.

TITLES

Kedah

SULTANS

Ahmad Taju'd-din Halim Shah, 1798-1843
Zainal Rashid al-Muazzam Shah, 1843-1854
Ahmad Taju'd-din Mukarram Shah, 1854-1879
Abdul-Hamim, 1882-1909

From 1821-1843, Kedah was actually under the control of the Siamese, and was ruled by Governor Tengku Anum.

TRA

TIN, 23mm
Obv. Arabic leg: *Tahun Alif 1224.* Rev: Arabic leg: *Balad Kedah Daru'l/Aman.* Irregular center hole.

KM#	Date	Mintage	Good	VG	Fine	VF
3	AH1224	—	20.00	35.00	50.00	75.00

24mm
Obv: Five-petaled lotus blossom. Rev: Arabic leg: *Belanja Balad al-Perlis Kedah-Sanat 1262.* Irregular center hole.

| 4 | AH1262 | — | 20.00 | 35.00 | 50.00 | 75.00 |

18mm
Obv: Crude 12-pointed star. Rev: Arabic leg: *Belanja Balad Kedah Daru'l-Aman.* Irregular center hole.

| 5 | ND | — | 20.00 | 30.00 | 45.00 | 65.00 |

KELANTAN

A state in northern Malaysia. Colonized by Japanese in 1300's. Subject to Thailand from 1780 to 1909.

TITLES

Kelantan

Khalifat Al-Mu'minin

SULTANS

Muhammed I, 1800-1835
Muhammed II, 1835-1886
Ahmad, 1886-1889
Muhammed III, 1889-1891
Mansur, 1891-1899
Interregnum, 1899-1902
Muhammed IV, 1902-1919

PITIS

TIN, 24-29mm
Obv. Arabic leg: *Khalifat al-Mu'minin.* Rev: Same. Many minor variations.

KM#	Date	Mintage	VG	Fine	VF	XF
1	ND	—	5.00	8.00	15.00	25.00

Obv: Similar to KM#1. Rev. Arabic leg: *Al-Julus Kelantan.*

| 2 | ND | — | 10.00 | 15.00 | 30.00 | 50.00 |

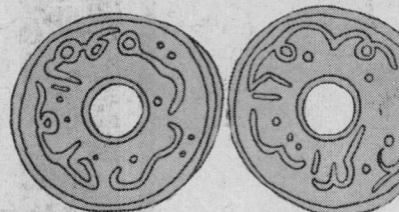

28mm
Obv. Arabic leg: Similar to KM#1. Rev: *Sanat 1256.*

| 4 | AH1256 | — | 8.00 | 12.00 | 20.00 | 30.00 |

NOTE: This type has also been attributed to Legeh.

Obv. Arabic leg: *Duriba Fi Jamadal Akhir 1300.* Rev. Arabic leg: *Dama Sama Mulka Daulat Kelantan.*

| 5 | AH1300 | — | 8.00 | 12.00 | 20.00 | 30.00 |

Obv. Arabic leg: *Adim Mulkahu Belanjaan Kera Jaan Kelantan.* Rev. Arabic leg: *Sunia Fi Jumadal Ula Sanat 1314.*

| 10 | AH1314 | — | 5.00 | 10.00 | 17.00 | 30.00 |

Obv. Arabic leg: *Belanjaan Negri Kelantan Adama Mulkahu.* Rev. Arabic leg: *Sunia Fi Jumadal Ula Sanat 1321.*

| 12 | AH1321 | — | 8.00 | 12.00 | 20.00 | 30.00 |

Obv. Arabic leg: *Belanjaan Kerajaan Kelan Tan.* Rev. Arabic leg: *Duriba Fi Dhul Hijja Sanat 1321.*

KM#	Date	Mintage	VG	Fine	VF	XF
15	AH1321	—	1.50	2.50	3.50	7.00

KEPING

TIN
Obv. Arabic leg: *Negri Kelantan Satu Keping Sanat 1323.* Rev: Uninscribed but obv. leg. shows through in negative form.

| 18 | AH1323 | — | 15.00 | 25.00 | 35.00 | 50.00 |

10 KEPING

TIN
Obv. Arabic leg: *Belanjaan Kerajaan Kelantin Sepuloh Keping.* Rev. Arabic leg: *Sunia Fi Dhul Hijja Sanat 1321.* Border of diamonds around leg.

| 20 | AH1321 | — | 5.00 | 10.00 | 20.00 | 30.00 |

LOCAL COINAGE

KEMASIN
Town in Kelantan State

TITLES

Kemasin

JOKOH

TIN, 29-30mm
Obv. Jawi leg: *Ini Pakai Di Kemasin Sanat 1300.* Rev: Chinese inscription & 5 c/m. Two vars.

| 30 | AH1300 | — | 20.00 | 40.00 | 60.00 | 100.00 |

PATANI, PATTANI

Refer to Thailand Local Issues.

MALACCA

A state of Malaysia on the west coast. It was settled from Sumatra in the 1300's. Occupied by the Portuguese in 1511. Captured by the Dutch in 1641. Held by the British from 1795 to 1802 and 1811 to 1818. Ceded to Britain in 1824.

The attribution of the following coins to Malacca is uncertain. All were struck in England, on behalf of merchants in Singapore. All have an Arabic legend *Tanah Melayu* (Land of the Malays) above a rooster.

KEPING

COPPER
Rev: Denomination at top written like a fraction.

KM#	Date	Mintage	Fine	VF	XF	Unc
8.1	AH1247	—	1.00	3.00	7.00	25.00
8.1a	AH1247	**BRASS**				

COPPER
Rev: Denomination written simply 1.

8.2	AH1247	—	1.00	3.00	7.00	25.00
	AH1251	Reported, not confirmed				
	AH1147(error)		30.00	50.00	70.00	100.00
	AH1219(error)		2.50	6.00	15.00	30.00
	AH1241(error)		30.00	50.00	70.00	100.00
	AH1411(error)		4.00	7.50	15.00	40.00

2 KEPING

COPPER

KM#	Date	Mintage	Fine	VF	XF	Unc
14	AH1247	—	12.50	20.00	30.00	60.00

PAHANG

A state on the east coast of Malaysia. Subject to the Suyyaya kingdom in Sumatra in the 1200's. Shuttled from native kingdom to native kingdom after 1450. Became one of the Federated Malay States in 1895.

The following coins were minted by prominent Chinese in Pahang by permission of Sultan Ahmed. They were intended for general circulation within Pahang. Many other pieces issued by merchants and gambling houses exist, but will not be listed here.

TITLES

Pahang

GOVERNORS
Bendahara Sewa Raja Tun Ali, 1806-1857
Bendahara Sewa Raja Tun Mutahir, 1857-1863

SULTANS
Ahmed Al Muazzam, 1884-1914 ruled as Governor Bendahara Sewa Raja Ahmad from 1863 to 1884

Pahang Company
1/2 CENT

TIN
Obv: Four Chinese characters *Ch'ien Sheng T'ung Pao*. Rev: value and Arabic leg: *Pahang Company* and *1/2C*.

KM#	Date	Mintage	Good	VG	Fine	VF
6	ND	—	15.00	20.00	40.00	60.00

Minted between 1884 and 1896.

CENT

TIN
Rev: 1 C
9 ND — 15.00 20.00 40.00 60.00
Minted between 1884 and 1896.

PENANG
Pulu Penang-Prince of Wales Island

Obv: Value and Chinese *Ch'ien Sheng T'ung Pao*.
Rev: Date and Arabic leg.

KM#	Date	Mintage	Good	VG	Fine	VF
11	AH1301	—	10.00	15.00	30.00	50.00

An island off the west coast of Malaysia. Ceded to the British in 1791 by the sultan of Kedah and was the first British settlement in Malaya. Also known as Pulu Penang and Prince of Wales Island - which title it retained until 1867.

The currency system depended on the Spanish dollar divided into 100 pice (or cents) until 1826 when 48 pice were deemed the equivalent of one Bengal rupee until 1830. The coins are considered in three groups:

(a) The Company bale mark series, consisting of copper 1/10th, 1/2 and 1 pice of 1786/1787, and silver tenth, quarter and half dollars, dated 1788;
(b) Company coat of arms issues in copper between 1810 and 1828 in denominations of 1/2, 1 and double pice pieces; and
(c) Tin issues of local mintage pice pieces of 1800-1809, which are extremely rare.

TITLES

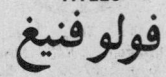

Pulu Penang

MONETARY SYSTEM
100 Cents (Pice) = 1 Dollar

1/2 CENT
(1/2 Pice)

COPPER
Royal Mint

KM#	Date	Mintage	Fine	VF	XF	Unc
11	1810	1.720	20.00	30.00	60.00	125.00
	1810	—	—	—	Proof	400.00

Madras Mint
| 12 | 1825 | .145 | 60.00 | 90.00 | 150.00 | 300.00 |
| | 1828 | .414 | 50.00 | 80.00 | 140.00 | 280.00 |

NOTE: Wreath varies from 21 to 26 lily cups.

CENT
(Pice)

Tin, uniface, 40.35 g
Initial GL (Governor Leith) in ring.
c/m: Chinese character *Yuan*.

KM#	Date	Mintage	VG	Fine	VF	XF
8	ND(c.1800-03)	—	350.00	650.00	950.00	1250

TIN, uniface, 30.50 g
Initials GF (Governor Farquhar) in ring,
c/m: Chinese character *Ch'i*.

KM#	Date	Mintage	VG	Fine	VF	XF
9	ND(c.1805)	—	600.00	1000.	1700.	2700.

TIN, uniface, 30.00-32.00 g
Initials A & C (Anderson & Clubley)
c/m: Chinese character *Mei*.

| 10 | 1809 | — | 800.00 | 1400. | 2300. | 3600. |

NOTE: Varieties exist.

COPPER
Royal Mint
Rev: Leaves on wreath go clockwise.

KM#	Date	Mintage	Fine	VF	XF	Unc
13	1810 small date, small shield	1.827	17.50	35.00	70.00	100.00
	1810	—	—	—	Proof	200.00

Madras Mint
| 14 | 1825 | .137 | 40.00 | 80.00 | 140.00 | 240.00 |
| | 1828 | .236 | 35.00 | 75.00 | 130.00 | 225.00 |

NOTE: Wreath varies from 21 to 27 lily cups.

2 CENTS
(2 Pice)

COPPER
Madras Mint

| 15 | 1825 | .130 | 40.00 | 80.00 | 140.00 | 240.00 |
| | 1828 | .720 | — | 50.00 | 120.00 | 180.00 |

NOTE: Wreath varies from 24 to 28 lily cups.

PERAK

A state on the west coast of Malaysia. Important tin deposits are in this state. Part of Malay kingdoms from early times. Perak was an independent state from 1824-1874. The only coin is one made in Birmingham, England and distributed by a Singapore importer.

TITLES

Negri Peraq

SULTANS

Ahmadin, ?-1806
Abdul-Malik Mansur, 1806-1825
Abdullah Muazzam, 1825-1830
Shahabud-Din Riayat, 1831-1851
Abdullah Muhammad, 1851-1857
Jafar Muazzam, 1857-1865
Ali Al-Mukammal Inayat, 1865-1871
Ismail Muabidin, 1871-1874
Abdullah Muhammad, 1874-1877
Yusuf Sharifud-Din Mufzal, 1877-1887
Sir Idris Murshid Al-Azzam, 1887-1916
Abdul-Jalil, 1916-1918
Iskander, 1918-?

KEPING

COPPER
Obv. Arabic leg: *Negri Perak* (State of Perak).
Rev. Arabic leg: *Satu Kepang 1251* (one Keping AH 1251).

KM#	Date	Mintage	Fine	VF	XF	Unc
4	AH1251	—	2.50	5.00	15.00	35.00
	1251	—	—	—	Proof	120.00

TIN (OMS)
| 4a | AH1251 | | | | | |

SILVERED BRONZE (OMS)
| 4b | AH1251 | — | — | — | Proof | — |

PERLIS

See State of Kedah

SELANGOR

A state on the west coast of Malaysia. Played a part in the trading programs of both the Dutch and the British. Signed a treaty with Britain in 1818 and Britain took control of the state in 1874.

TITLES

Negeri Selangor

SULTANS

Ibrahim, 1777-1826
Muhammad, 1826-1857
Abdul-Samad, 1857-1898
Sulaiman, 1898-1938

PITIS

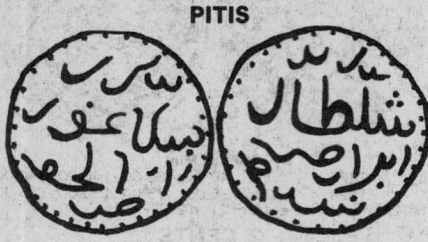

TIN
Obv. leg: Arabic *Negari Selangor Darul Ihsan*.
Rev. leg: Arabic *Baginda Sultan Ibrahim Shah*.

| 1 | ND | | | | | |

KEPING

COPPER
Obv. Arabic leg: *Negri Selangor*.
Rev. Arabic leg: *Satu Keping 1251*.

| 3 | AH1251 | — | 2.50 | 5.00 | 15.00 | 35.00 |

TRENGGANU

A state in eastern Malaysia on the shore of the south China Sea. Area of dispute between Malacca and Thailand with the latter emerging with possession. Trengganu became a British dependency in 1909.

TITLES

Khalifat Al-Mu'minin

Trengganu

SULTANS

Zainal Abidin II, 1793-1808
Ahmad I, 1808-1827
Abdul Rahman, 1827-1831
Daud, 1831
Mansur II, 1831-1836
Muhammed, 1836-1839
Baginda Omar, 1839-1876
Ahmad II, 1876-1881
Zainal Abidin III, 1881-1918
Muhammed, 1918-1920
Sulaiman, 1920-1942

PITIS

TIN

KM#	Date	Mintage	VG	Fine	VF	XF
9	AH1222	—	17.50	27.50	40.00	60.00

Legend points outward instead of inward.
| 10 | AH1222 | — | 20.00 | 35.00 | 50.00 | 75.00 |

Obv: *Khalifat al-Muminin 1251 Malik al-Adil*.
| 11 | AH1251 | — | 30.00 | 50.00 | 75.00 | 100.00 |

| 13 | AH1265 | — | 25.00 | 40.00 | 65.00 | 90.00 |

Obv: *Belanja Trengganu Sanat 1299*.
| 14 | AH1299 | — | 25.00 | 40.00 | 65.00 | 90.00 |

KEPING

COPPER

Obv. Arabic leg: *Negri Trengganu* (State of Trengganu). Rev. Arabic leg: *Satu Keping 1251*.

KM#	Date	Mintage	VG	Fine	VF	XF
12	AH1251	—	5.00	8.00	20.00	40.00
	AH1251	—	—	—	Proof	125.00

10 KEPING

TIN
| 15 | AH1310 | — | 10.00 | 20.00 | 30.00 | 55.00 |

1/4 CENT

TIN
Similar to 1/2 Cent, KM#16.
| 17 | AH1325 | — | — | — | Rare | — |

1/2 CENT

TIN
| 16 | AH1322 (recast) | — | — | — | — | 15.00 |

| 18 | AH1325 (recast) | — | — | — | — | 15.00 |

NOTE: Originals are rare.

CENT

TIN
| 19 | AH1325 | — | 4.50 | 8.25 | 15.00 | 25.00 |

| 20 | AH1325 | — | 4.50 | 8.25 | 15.00 | 25.00 |

Although dated AH1325 (1907) this coin was actually struck in 1920 under Sultan Sulaiman. Authorized mintage was one million pieces. Beware of thin lead counterfeits.

STRAITS SETTLEMENTS

Straits Settlements, a former British crown colony situated on the Malay Peninsula of Asia, was formed in 1826 by combining the territories of Singapore, Penang and Malacca. The colony was administered by the East India Company until its abolition in 1853. Straits Settlements was a part of British India from 1858 to 1867 at which time it became a Crown Colony. This name was changed to Malaya in 1939.

RULERS

British

MINT MARKS

H - Heaton, Birmingham
W - Soho Mint
B - Bombay

MONETARY SYSTEM
100 Cents = 1 Dollar

EAST INDIA COMPANY
1826-1858
1/4 CENT

COPPER
Rev. leg: EAST INDIA COMPANY

KM#	Date	Mintage	Fine	VF	XF	Unc
1	1845	34.327	4.00	12.00	20.00	50.00
	1845 WW on base of bust		—	—	Proof	300.00

1/2 CENT

COPPER

2	1845	18.737	4.50	12.50	30.00	65.00
	1845		—	—	Proof	300.00
	1845 WW on truncation					
	Inc. Ab.	4.50	12.50	30.00	62.50
	1845 WW on truncation		—	—	Proof	300.00

CENT

COPPER

3	1845	18.526	3.00	10.00	22.50	50.00
	1845 WW on truncation		—	—	Proof	350.00

BRITISH INDIA GOVERNMENT
1858-1867
1/4 CENT

COPPER
Rev. leg: INDIA STRAITS

4	1862	3.368	50.00	125.00	225.00	475.00
	1862		—	—	Proof	800.00

1/2 CENT

COPPER

5	1862	4.590	25.00	45.00	120.00	250.00
	1862		—	—	Proof	600.00

CENT

COPPER

KM#	Date	Mintage	Fine	VF	XF	Unc
6	1862	9.321	7.50	18.00	40.00	120.00
	1862		—	—	Proof	350.00

COLONIAL ISSUES
1867-1939
1/4 CENT

COPPER
Rev. leg: STRAITS SETTLEMENTS, plain edge.

7	1872	—	—	—	Proof	350.00
	1872H	9.240	6.50	12.50	35.00	100.00
	1872H	—	—	—	Proof	250.00
	1873	—	120.00	160.00	300.00	700.00
	1873	—	—	—	Proof	750.00
	1875	—	—	—	Proof	625.00
	1875W	—	—	—	Proof	625.00
	1883	.200	300.00	600.00	1000.	1800.

BRONZE

7a	1884	8.000	2.50	10.00	30.00	60.00
	1884	—	—	—	Proof	250.00

Reeded edge

14	1889	2.000	2.50	7.50	30.00	60.00
	1889	—	—	—	Proof	250.00
	1890	—	—	—	Proof	625.00
	1891	—	—	—	Proof	400.00
	1898	1.600	2.00	5.00	22.00	55.00
	1898	—	—	—	Proof	250.00
	1899	2.400	2.00	4.00	20.00	50.00
	1901	2.000	2.00	4.00	20.00	50.00

SILVER (OMS)

14a	1891	—	—	—	Proof	1500.
	1898	—	—	—	Proof	1500.

GOLD (OMS)

14b	1891	—	—	—	Proof	3200.

COPPER

17	1904 plain edge					
		—	—	—	Proof	500.00
	1904 milled edge					
		—	—	—	Proof	500.00
	1905	2.008	1.25	6.00	15.00	40.00
	1905	—	—	—	Proof	250.00
	1908	1.200	1.25	6.00	17.50	45.00

27	1916	4.000	1.00	2.00	4.00	10.00
	1916	—	—	—	Proof	220.00

1/2 CENT

COPPER
Plain edge

8	1872	—	—	—	Proof	350.00
	1872H	5.610	18.00	30.00	60.00	120.00
	1872H	—	—	—	Proof	350.00
	1873	—	35.00	65.00	140.00	400.00
	1874	—	—	—	Proof	400.00
	1875	—	—	—	Proof	400.00
	1875W	—	—	—	Proof	400.00
	1883	2.740	50.00	75.00	250.00	500.00

BRONZE

8a	1884	4.000	6.00	12.00	40.00	90.00
	1884	—	—	—	Proof	400.00

Reeded edge

15	1889	2.000	10.00	22.00	50.00	110.00
	1890	—	—	—	Proof	400.00
	1891	—	—	—	Proof	400.00

SILVER (OMS)

15a	1891	—	—	—	Proof	1750.

GOLD (OMS)

15b	1891	—	—	—	Proof	3600.

COPPER

KM#	Date	Mintage	Fine	VF	XF	Unc
18	1904	—	—	—	Proof	350.00
	1908	2.000	2.50	5.00	15.00	45.00

28	1916	3.000	1.00	2.50	7.50	15.00
	1916	—	—	—	Proof	300.00

BRONZE

37	1932	5.000	.75	1.00	2.50	8.00
	1932	—	—	—	Proof	240.00

CENT

COPPER
Plain edge

9	1872	—	—	—	Proof	350.00
	1872H	5.770	3.00	12.50	35.00	90.00
	1872H	—	—	—	Proof	350.00
	1873	—	7.00	18.00	45.00	95.00
	1874	10.000	4.00	12.50	35.00	65.00
	1874H	10.000	4.00	12.50	35.00	65.00
	1874H	—	—	—	Proof	250.00
	1875	6.000	7.00	18.00	40.00	70.00
	1875	—	—	—	Proof	250.00
	1875W	—	5.00	14.00	25.00	75.00
	1875 W on truncation					
		—	—	—	Proof	250.00
	1876	—	6.50	15.00	32.50	65.00
	1877	—	6.50	15.00	32.50	65.00
	1878	—	60.00	175.00	400.00	800.00
	1883	8.640	6.50	15.00	40.00	90.00

BRONZE

9a	1884	6.000	1.00	5.00	15.00	45.00
	1884	—	—	—	Proof	220.00
	1885	7.412	10.00	25.00	60.00	150.00
	1886	1.512	20.00	40.00	100.00	200.00

Reeded edge

16	1887	8.988	1.25	4.50	15.00	50.00
	1888	10.000	1.25	4.50	15.00	50.00
	1889	6.010	1.25	4.50	15.00	50.00
	1890	11.006	1.25	4.50	15.00	50.00
	1890	—	—	—	Proof	220.00
	1891	6.004	1.00	4.50	15.00	50.00
	1894	9.034	1.00	4.50	15.00	50.00
	1895	4.446	1.00	4.50	15.00	50.00
	1897	18.040	1.00	4.50	15.00	50.00
	1898	2.086	4.00	10.00	25.00	70.00
	1898	—	—	—	Proof	220.00
	1900	2.914	1.00	4.00	15.00	50.00
	1901	15.230	1.00	4.00	12.50	37.50

SILVER (OMS)

16a	1890	—	—	—	Proof	1500.
	1891	—	—	—	Proof	1500.
	1898	—	—	—	Proof	1200.

GOLD (OMS)

16b	1891	—	—	—	Proof	3600.

Straits Settlements / MALAYSIA 1196

COPPER

KM#	Date	Mintage	Fine	VF	XF	Unc
19	1903	7.053	1.50	4.50	13.50	37.50
	1903	—	—	—	Proof	200.00
	1904	6.467	1.50	4.50	13.50	37.50
	1904	—	—	—	Proof	250.00
	1906	7.504	3.00	6.00	20.00	60.00
	1907	5.015	1.00	3.00	10.00	40.00
	1908	Inc. Ab.	1.00	2.50	5.00	22.50
	1908	—	—	—	Proof	200.00

KM#	Date	Mintage	Fine	VF	XF	Unc
32	1919	20.165	.50	.75	5.00	17.50
	1919	—	—	—	Proof	175.00
	1920	55.000	.50	.75	3.00	12.50
	1920	—	—	—	Proof	150.00
	1926/0	5.000	2.00	5.00	10.00	25.00
	1926	Inc. Ab.	.50	.75	7.50	22.50

5 CENTS

1.3600 g, .800 SILVER, .0349 oz ASW

KM#	Date	Mintage	Fine	VF	XF	Unc
10	1871	.062	320.00	700.00	1150.	1850.
	1871	—	—	—	Proof	2800.
	1873	.060	540.00	1200.	1600.	2300.
	1874H	.060	75.00	125.00	225.00	375.00
	1876H	.040	500.00	1000.	1500.	2000.
	1877	.060	400.00	660.00	1100.	1800.
	1878	.260	15.00	35.00	90.00	200.00
	1878	—	—	—	Proof	350.00
	1879H	.100	120.00	200.00	400.00	600.00
	1880H	.090	140.00	300.00	550.00	800.00
	1881	.180	20.00	40.00	120.00	200.00
	1881	—	—	—	Proof	350.00
	1882H	.380	12.50	25.00	55.00	160.00
	1882H	—	—	—	Proof	350.00
	1883	.080	100.00	200.00	350.00	720.00
	1884	.440	5.00	12.00	35.00	90.00
	1884	—	—	—	Proof	350.00
	1885	.200	15.00	35.00	100.00	240.00
	1885	—	—	—	Proof	350.00
	1886	.340	7.50	12.50	28.00	80.00
	1887	.440	6.00	10.00	22.00	70.00
	1888	.590	5.00	10.00	20.00	65.00
	1889	1.000	2.00	4.00	15.00	35.00
	1889	—	—	—	Proof	350.00
	1890H	.440	6.00	17.50	48.00	80.00
	1890H	—	—	—	Proof	350.00
	1891	.800	2.50	5.00	15.00	40.00
	1893	.440	3.50	6.00	20.00	50.00
	1894	.340	3.50	6.00	20.00	45.00
	1895	1.480	2.50	5.00	10.00	40.00
	1896	.960	2.50	5.00	10.00	40.00
	1897	.320	5.00	8.00	20.00	60.00
	1897H	.440	5.00	8.00	22.00	70.00
	1898	1.200	1.50	2.50	12.50	40.00
	1899	.078	3.00	6.00	20.00	50.00
	1900	2.720	1.50	2.50	12.50	40.00
	1900H	.400	5.00	10.00	22.00	60.00
	1901	3.000	1.50	2.50	12.50	40.00

KM#	Date	Mintage	Fine	VF	XF	Unc
20	1902	1.920	5.00	12.00	50.00	90.00
	1902	—	—	—	Proof	350.00
	1903	2.270	5.00	12.00	50.00	90.00
	1903	—	—	—	Proof	350.00

1.3600 g, .600 SILVER, .0262 oz ASW

KM#	Date	Mintage	Fine	VF	XF	Unc
20a	1910B	13.012	1.25	2.25	5.50	12.00
	1910B	—	—	—	Proof	350.00

1.3600 g, .400 SILVER, .0174 oz ASW

KM#	Date	Mintage	Fine	VF	XF	Unc
31	1918	3.100	.50	1.25	5.00	12.00
	1919	6.900	.50	1.25	5.00	12.00
	1920	4.000	120.00	250.00	600.00	1200.

COPPER-NICKEL

KM#	Date	Mintage	Fine	VF	XF	Unc
34	1920	20.000	1.00	10.00	50.00	100.00
	1920	—	—	—	Proof	525.00

1.3600 g, .600 SILVER, .0262 oz ASW
Similar to KM#31, smaller bust, broader rim.

KM#	Date	Mintage	Fine	VF	XF	Unc
36	1926	10.000	.50	.75	5.00	12.00
	1926	—	—	—	Proof	240.00
	1935	3.000	.50	.75	5.00	9.00
	1935	—	—	—	Proof	240.00

10 CENTS

2.7100 g, .800 SILVER, .0697 oz ASW

KM#	Date	Mintage	Fine	VF	XF	Unc
11	1871	.248	15.00	25.00	72.50	150.00
	1871	—	—	—	Proof	250.00
	1872H	.230	15.00	25.00	70.00	130.00
	1872H	—	—	—	Proof	200.00
	1873	.210	25.00	45.00	110.00	180.00
	1874H	.180	13.50	20.00	45.00	90.00
	1876H	.120	20.00	65.00	130.00	250.00
	1877	.160	15.00	35.00	55.00	120.00
	1878	.470	5.00	10.00	25.00	60.00
	1878	—	—	—	Proof	250.00
	1879H	.250	13.50	20.00	45.00	90.00
	1879H	—	—	—	Proof	250.00
	1880H	.235	16.50	28.00	60.00	130.00
	1881	.460	5.00	8.00	25.00	60.00
	1881	—	—	—	Proof	250.00
	1882H	.430	5.00	8.00	25.00	60.00
	1882H	—	—	—	Proof	250.00
	1883	.160	25.00	50.00	100.00	200.00
	1883H	.610	100.00	180.00	350.00	725.00
	1883H	—	—	—	Proof	1000.
	1884 crosslet 4	1.240	3.00	5.00	12.00	50.00
	1884 plain 4	Inc. Ab.	3.00	5.00	12.00	50.00
	1884	—	—	—	Proof	250.00
	1885	.400	10.00	15.00	25.00	90.00
	1885	—	—	—	Proof	250.00
	1886	.790	3.00	5.00	12.00	45.00
	1886	—	—	—	Proof	250.00
	1887	.640	3.00	5.00	12.00	45.00
	1888	1.075	3.00	5.00	12.00	45.00
	1888	—	—	—	Proof	250.00
	1889	1.500	2.00	3.00	7.50	40.00
	1889	—	—	—	Proof	250.00
	1890H	.730	3.50	6.00	15.00	50.00
	1890H	—	—	—	Proof	250.00
	1891	1.380	2.00	3.00	7.50	30.00
	1891	—	—	—	Proof	250.00
	1893	.980	2.00	3.00	7.50	30.00
	1893	—	—	—	Proof	250.00
	1894	1.640	2.00	3.00	7.50	30.00
	1895	2.324	2.00	3.00	7.50	25.00
	1896	2.256	2.00	3.00	7.50	25.00
	1897	.700	2.50	5.00	10.00	35.00
	1897H	.390	4.00	8.00	20.00	50.00
	1898	1.960	2.00	3.50	8.00	30.00
	1899	.286	2.00	3.50	8.00	30.00
	1900	2.960	2.00	3.50	8.00	30.00
	1900H	1.000	2.50	5.00	15.00	50.00
	1900H	—	—	—	Proof	250.00
	1901	2.700	2.00	3.00	7.00	25.00

COPPER (OMS)

KM#	Date	Mintage	Fine	VF	XF	Unc
11a	1872H	—	—	—	Proof	250.00
	1873	—	—	—	—	300.00

2.7100 g, .800 SILVER, .0697 oz ASW

KM#	Date	Mintage	Fine	VF	XF	Unc
21	1902	6.118	2.50	10.00	25.00	60.00
	1902	—	—	—	Proof	250.00
	1903	1.401	3.00	12.00	32.50	80.00
	1903	—	—	—	Proof	250.00

2.7100 g, .600 SILVER, .0522 oz ASW

KM#	Date	Mintage	Fine	VF	XF	Unc
21a	1909B	11.088	5.00	17.50	35.00	85.00
	1910B	1.657	1.00	2.00	3.00	10.00
	1910B	—	—	—	Proof	250.00

KM#	Date	Mintage	Fine	VF	XF	Unc
29	1916	.600	3.00	7.00	20.00	35.00
	1917	5.600	1.00	2.00	7.00	22.00

2.7100 g, .400 SILVER, .0348 oz ASW

KM#	Date	Mintage	Fine	VF	XF	Unc
29a	1918	7.500	1.00	2.50	8.00	22.00
	1919	11.500	1.00	2.50	8.00	22.00
	1920	4.000	5.00	15.00	27.50	100.00

2.7100 g, .600 SILVER, .0522 oz ASW

KM#	Date	Mintage	Fine	VF	XF	Unc
29b	1926	20.000	1.00	1.50	5.00	15.00
	1926	—	—	—	Proof	225.00
	1927	23.000	.50	.75	1.00	3.25
	1927	—	—	—	Proof	225.00

20 CENTS

5.4300 g, .800 SILVER, .1396 oz ASW

KM#	Date	Mintage	Fine	VF	XF	Unc
12	1871	.016	400.00	800.00	1200.	1900.
	1871	—	—	—	Proof	2800.
	1872H	.040	120.00	250.00	450.00	700.00
	1873	.030	375.00	700.00	1100.	1750.
	1874H	.045	75.00	110.00	200.00	350.00
	1876H	.030	100.00	220.00	400.00	750.00
	1877	.055	65.00	110.00	200.00	400.00
	1878	.150	15.00	20.00	60.00	150.00
	1878	—	—	—	Proof	400.00
	1879H	.050	60.00	120.00	220.00	400.00
	1879H	—	—	—	Proof	450.00
	1880H	.085	30.00	55.00	110.00	250.00
	1880H	—	—	—	Proof	400.00
	1881/71	.100	25.00	40.00	100.00	250.00
	1881	Inc. Ab.	20.00	35.00	90.00	200.00
	1882H	.245	12.00	20.00	50.00	120.00
	1882H	—	—	—	Proof	400.00
	1883	.200	15.00	22.00	55.00	130.00
	1884	.220	5.00	10.00	27.50	65.00
	1884	—	—	—	Proof	400.00
	1885	.100	20.00	35.00	90.00	200.00
	1886	.245	5.00	7.50	20.00	50.00
	1886	—	—	—	Proof	400.00
	1887	.220	5.00	7.50	15.00	40.00
	1888	.295	5.00	7.50	15.00	40.00
	1888	—	—	—	Proof	400.00
	1889	.420	3.00	5.00	15.00	40.00
	1890H	.270	7.50	15.00	35.00	70.00
	1890H	—	—	—	Proof	300.00
	1891	.510	3.25	5.00	13.50	35.00
	1893	.310	3.25	5.00	13.50	35.00
	1894	.495	3.25	5.00	13.50	35.00
	1895	.580	3.25	5.00	13.50	35.00
	1896	.600	3.25	5.00	13.50	35.00
	1897	.150	8.00	15.00	30.00	80.00
	1897H	.185	8.00	15.00	30.00	80.00
	1898	.580	3.00	4.50	12.50	35.00
	1899	.204	3.00	4.50	12.50	35.00
	1900	.620	3.00	4.50	12.50	35.00
	1900H	.300	6.00	9.00	25.00	70.00
	1900H	—	—	—	Proof	400.00
	1901	.600	3.00	4.50	12.50	35.00

COPPER (OMS)
Plain edge

KM#	Date	Mintage	Fine	VF	XF	Unc
12a	1873	—	—	—	Proof	1000.

5.4300 g, .800 SILVER, .1396 oz ASW

KM#	Date	Mintage	Fine	VF	XF	Unc
22	1902	1.105	6.00	15.00	50.00	120.00
	1902	—	—	—	Proof	300.00
	1903	1.150	6.00	15.00	50.00	120.00
	1903	—	—	—	Proof	300.00

5.4300 g, .600 SILVER, .1047 oz ASW

KM#	Date	Mintage	Fine	VF	XF	Unc
22a	1910B	3.276	2.00	3.50	10.00	25.00
	1910B	—	—	—	Proof	300.00

RULERS
James Brooke, Rajah, 1841-1868
Charles J. Brooke, Rajah, 1868-1917
Charles V. Brooke, Rajah, 1917-1946

MINT MARKS
H - Heaton, Birmingham

MONETARY SYSTEM
100 Cents = 1 Dollar

1/4 CENT

KM#	Date	Mintage	Fine	VF	XF	Unc
30	1916B	.545	4.00	10.00	30.00	70.00
	1916B		—	—	Proof	250.00
	1917B	.652	2.50	4.50	25.00	55.00

5.4300 g, .400 SILVER, .0698 oz ASW

30a	1919B	2.500	2.50	4.50	12.00	35.00
	1919B	—	—	—	Proof	250.00

5.4300 g, .600 SILVER, .1047 oz ASW

30b	1926	2.500	1.50	3.00	12.00	35.00
	1926	—	—	—	Proof	250.00
	1927	3.000	1.50	2.50	6.00	12.00
	1927	—	—	—	Proof	250.00
	1935 round top 3					
		1.000	1.50	2.50	3.50	7.00
	1935 flat top 3					
		Inc. Ab.	1.50	2.50	3.50	7.00

50 CENTS

13.5769 g, .800 SILVER, .3492 oz ASW

13	1886	.060	50.00	120.00	270.00	850.00
	1886	—	—	—	Proof	2200.
	1887	.094	40.00	75.00	180.00	400.00
	1887	—	—	—	Proof	2200.
	1888	.096	40.00	75.00	180.00	400.00
	1889	.032	800.00	1350.	1600.	3200.
	1890H	.042	100.00	200.00	325.00	850.00
	1891	.112	35.00	50.00	125.00	300.00
	1891	—	—	—	Proof	2200.
	1893	.024	400.00	750.00	1250.	2100.
	1893	—	—	—	Proof	2750.
	1894	.052	50.00	150.00	250.00	500.00
	1895	.056	50.00	150.00	250.00	500.00
	1896	.120	25.00	50.00	120.00	280.00
	1897	.036	100.00	200.00	320.00	800.00
	1897H	.044	85.00	150.00	250.00	600.00
	1898	.160	25.00	50.00	120.00	280.00
	1899	.136	25.00	50.00	120.00	280.00
	1900	.088	35.00	70.00	150.00	320.00
	1900H	.040	100.00	175.00	350.00	775.00
	1901	.120	25.00	50.00	120.00	280.00

23	1902	.148	50.00	80.00	175.00	280.00
	1902	—	—	—	Proof	850.00
	1903	.193	50.00	80.00	175.00	280.00
	1903	—	—	—	Proof	850.00
	1904	—	—	—	Proof	1000.
	1905B raised					
		.498	35.00	65.00	135.00	260.00
	1905B raised	—	—	—	Proof	1000.
	1905B incuse	—	—	—	Proof	1000.

10.1000 g, .900 SILVER, .2922 oz ASW

24	1907	.464	5.50	10.00	22.00	60.00
	1907H	2.667	5.50	10.00	22.00	60.00
	1907H	—	—	—	Proof	200.00
	1908	2.869	7.00	12.50	27.50	80.00
	1908H					
		Inc. 1907H	7.00	10.00	22.00	60.00

8.4200 g, .500 SILVER, .1353 oz ASW
Obv: Cross under bust.

KM#	Date	Mintage	Fine	VF	XF	Unc
35.1	1920	3.900	1.50	2.50	4.00	8.00
	1920	—	—	—	Proof	250.00
	1921	2.579	2.00	3.00	5.00	10.00
	1921	—	—	—	Proof	250.00

Obv: Dot under bust.

35.2	1920	Inc. Ab.	120.00	185.00	275.00	500.00

DOLLAR

26.9500 g, .900 SILVER, .7799 oz ASW

25	1903	—	—	—	Proof	1000.
	1903B incuse					
		15.010	18.00	25.00	50.00	100.00
	1903B raised					
		Inc. Ab.	70.00	120.00	250.00	600.00
	1903B raised	—	—	—	Proof	1100.
	1904B	20.365	15.00	20.00	40.00	90.00
	1904B	—	—	—	Proof	1000.

20.2100 g, .900 SILVER, .5848 oz ASW
Reduced size, 34.5mm.

26	1907	6.842	7.50	10.00	20.00	65.00
	1907H	4.000	7.50	10.00	20.00	65.00
	1907H	—	—	—	Proof	550.00
	1908	4.152	7.50	10.00	20.00	65.00
	1908	—	—	—	Proof	550.00
	1909	1.014	10.00	15.00	25.00	85.00
	1909	—	—	—	Proof	550.00

16.8500 g, .500 SILVER, .2709 oz ASW

33	1919	6.000	15.00	30.00	70.00	120.00
	1919(restrike)	—	—	—	Proof	80.00
	1920	8.164	10.00	20.00	30.00	70.00
	1920(restrike)	—	—	—	Proof	80.00
	1925	—	450.00	850.00	1250.	—
	1925	—	—	—	Proof	3500.
	1925(restrike)	—	—	—	Proof	600.00
	1926	—	450.00	850.00	1250.	—
	1926	—	—	—	Proof	3500.
	1926(restrike)	—	—	—	Proof	600.00

NOTE: For later coinage see Brunei and Singapore.

SARAWAK

Sarawak is a former British colony located on the northwest coast of Borneo. Japanese occupation during World War II so thoroughly devastated the country that rajah Sir Charles Vyner Brooke ceded it to Great Britain on July 1, 1946. In September, 1963 the colony joined the Federation of Malaysia.

COPPER

KM#	Date	Mintage	Fine	VF	XF	Unc
1	1863	—	40.00	80.00	150.00	300.00
	1863	—	—	—	Proof	550.00

BRONZED COPPER

1a	1863	—	—	—	Proof	500.00

COPPER

4	1870	.100	8.00	20.00	50.00	120.00
	1870	—	—	—	Proof	350.00
	1896H	.283	6.00	15.00	35.00	100.00
	1896H	—	—	—	Proof	350.00

1/2 CENT

COPPER

2	1863	—	12.50	35.00	85.00	200.00
	1863	—	—	—	Proof	550.00

BRONZED COPPER

2a	1863	—	—	—	Proof	720.00

COPPER

5	1870	.250	6.00	18.00	40.00	95.00
	1879	.640	6.00	18.00	40.00	95.00
	1879	—	—	—	Proof	350.00
	1896H	.327	4.00	12.00	30.00	85.00
	1896H	—	—	—	Proof	350.00

20	1933H	2.000	1.00	2.00	3.50	9.00
	1933H	—	—	—	Proof	240.00

CENT

COPPER

3	1863	—	7.00	18.00	40.00	120.00
	1863	—	—	—	Proof	400.00

BRONZED COPPER

3a	1863	—	—	—	Proof	600.00

Sarawak / MALAYSIA 1198

COPPER

KM#	Date	Mintage	Fine	VF	XF	Unc
6	1870	—	2.50	6.00	15.00	40.00
	1870	—	—	—	Proof	200.00
	1870	—	—	—	Gilt Proof	200.00
	1879	.750	3.50	8.00	20.00	65.00
	1879	—	—	—	Proof	200.00
	1880	1.070	3.00	7.00	18.00	60.00
	1882	1.070	2.50	6.00	16.50	50.00
	1882	—	—	—	Proof	200.00
	1884	1.070	2.50	6.00	16.50	50.00
	1884	—	—	—	Proof	200.00
	1885	2.140	2.50	6.00	16.50	50.00
	1885	—	—	—	Proof	200.00
	1886	3.210	2.50	6.00	16.50	40.00
	1887	1.605	2.50	6.00	16.50	40.00
	1887	—	—	—	Proof	200.00
	1888	2.140	2.50	6.00	16.50	40.00
	1888	—	—	—	Proof	200.00
	1889	.535	2.50	6.00	16.50	40.00
	1889/8H	2.675	3.00	7.00	17.50	45.00
	1889H	Inc. Ab.	2.50	6.00	16.50	40.00
	1889H	—	—	—	Proof	200.00
	1890H	3.210	2.50	6.00	16.50	40.00
	1891	.535	5.00	10.00	25.00	55.00
	1891H	1.070	2.50	6.00	16.50	40.00

NOTE: Varieties exist.

7	1892H	2.178	2.50	6.00	15.00	40.00
	1892H	—	—	—	Proof	200.00
	1893H	1.634	2.50	6.00	15.00	40.00
	1894H	1.633	2.50	6.00	15.00	40.00
	1896H	2.178	2.50	6.00	15.00	40.00
	1896H	—	—	—	Proof	200.00
	1897H	1.089	2.50	6.00	15.00	40.00

COPPER-NICKEL

12	1920H	5.000	3.00	7.50	18.00	60.00

BRONZE

18	1927H	5.000	1.25	2.25	4.50	8.00
	1927H	—	—	—	Proof	210.00
	1929H	2.000	1.25	2.25	4.50	10.00
	1930H	3.000	1.25	2.25	4.50	10.00
	1930H	—	—	—	Proof	210.00
	1937H	3.000	1.25	2.25	4.50	8.00
	1941H*	3.000	250.00	350.00	525.00	900.00
	1942	—	—	Reported, not confirmed

*NOTE: Estimate 50 pcs. exist.

5 CENTS

1.3500 g, .800 SILVER, .0347 oz ASW

8	1900H	.200	20.00	40.00	65.00	120.00
	1900H	—	—	—	Proof	375.00
	1908H	.040	30.00	50.00	90.00	140.00
	1908H	—	—	—	Proof	375.00
	1911H	.040	30.00	50.00	90.00	140.00
	1913H	.100	25.00	50.00	80.00	120.00
	1913H	—	—	—	Proof	375.00

KM#	Date	Mintage	Fine	VF	XF	Unc
8	1915H	.100	25.00	50.00	90.00	130.00
	1915H	—	—	—	Proof	350.00

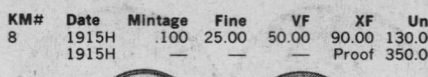

1.3500 g, .400 SILVER, .0174 oz ASW

13	1920H	.100	40.00	60.00	100.00	180.00
	1920H	—	—	—	Proof	400.00

COPPER-NICKEL

14	1920H	.400	2.00	4.00	8.00	20.00
	1927H	.600	2.00	4.00	8.00	20.00
	1927H	—	—	—	Proof	275.00

10 CENTS

2.7100 g, .800 SILVER, .0697 oz ASW

9	1900H	.150	15.00	20.00	45.00	90.00
	1900H	—	—	—	Proof	350.00
	1906H	.050	18.00	27.50	55.00	100.00
	1906H	—	—	—	Proof	350.00
	1910H	.050	18.00	27.50	55.00	100.00
	1910H	—	—	—	Proof	350.00
	1911/10H	.100	20.00	30.00	60.00	120.00
	1911H	Inc. Ab.	15.00	20.00	45.00	90.00
	1913H	.100	15.00	20.00	45.00	90.00
	1913H	—	—	—	Proof	350.00
	1915H	.100	35.00	50.00	90.00	200.00
	1915H	—	—	—	Proof	350.00

15	1920H	.150	16.00	25.00	55.00	90.00
	1920H	—	—	—	Proof	350.00

COPPER-NICKEL

16	1920H	.800	2.00	4.00	8.00	17.50
	1927H	1.000	2.00	3.00	6.00	17.50
	1927H	—	—	—	Proof	300.00
	1934H	2.000	2.00	3.00	6.00	17.50
	1934H	—	—	—	Proof	300.00

20 CENTS

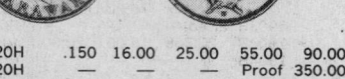

5.4300 g, .800 SILVER, .1396 oz ASW

10	1900H	.075	20.00	40.00	75.00	160.00
	1900H	—	—	—	Proof	400.00
	1906H	.025	22.50	55.00	100.00	210.00
	1906H	—	—	—	Proof	400.00
	1910H	.025	22.50	55.00	100.00	210.00
	1910H	—	—	—	Proof	400.00
	1911H	.015	22.50	55.00	110.00	225.00
	1913H	.025	22.50	55.00	100.00	210.00
	1913H	—	—	—	Proof	400.00
	1915H	.025	125.00	175.00	300.00	500.00
	1915H	—	—	—	Proof	700.00

5.4300 g, .400 SILVER, .0699 oz ASW

KM#	Date	Mintage	Fine	VF	XF	Unc
17	1920H	.025	65.00	120.00	220.00	400.00
	1920H	—	—	—	Proof	600.00
	1927H	.250	5.00	10.00	20.00	45.00
	1927H	—	—	—	Proof	400.00

50 CENTS

13.5700 g, .800 SILVER, .3490 oz ASW

11	1900H	.040	70.00	130.00	220.00	350.00
	1900H	—	—	—	Proof	1250.
	1906H	.010	165.00	270.00	400.00	780.00
	1906H	—	—	—	Proof	1250.

13.5700 g, .500 SILVER, .2181 oz ASW

19	1927H	.200	10.00	17.50	35.00	90.00
	1927H	—	—	—	Proof	400.00

BRITISH NORTH BORNEO

British North Borneo (now known as Sabah), a former British protectorate and crown colony, occupies the northern tip of the island of Borneo. The island of Labuan, which lies 6 miles off the northwest coast of the island of Borneo, was attached to Singapore settlement in 1907. It became an independent settlement of the Straits Colony in 1912 and was incorporated with British North Borneo in 1946.

RULERS

British

MINT MARKS

H - Heaton, Birmingham

MONETARY SYSTEM

100 Cents = 1 Straits Dollar

1/2 CENT

BRONZE

1	1885H	.500	4.00	12.50	27.50	70.00
	1885H	—	—	—	Proof	150.00
	1886H	1.000	3.50	7.00	22.50	60.00
	1886H	—	—	—	Proof	150.00
	1887H	.500	3.50	7.00	22.50	60.00
	1891H	2.000	3.50	7.00	20.00	50.00
	1891H	—	—	—	Proof	150.00
	1907H	1.000	12.50	25.00	60.00	120.00

CENT

BRONZE

KM#	Date	Mintage	Fine	VF	XF	Unc
2	1882H	2.000	2.00	4.00	15.00	45.00
	1882H	—	—	—	Proof	120.00
	1884H	2.000	2.00	4.00	15.00	45.00
	1884H	—	—	—	Proof	120.00
	1885H	1.750	2.00	5.00	17.00	50.00
	1886H	5.000	2.00	4.00	15.00	45.00
	1886H	—	—	—	Proof	120.00
	1887H	6.000	2.00	4.00	15.00	45.00
	1887H	—	—	—	Proof	120.00
	1888H	6.000	2.00	4.00	15.00	45.00
	1888H	—	—	—	Proof	120.00
	1889H	9.000	2.00	4.00	15.00	45.00
	1890H	8.003	2.00	4.00	15.00	45.00
	1890H	—	—	—	Proof	120.00
	1891H	3.000	2.00	4.00	15.00	45.00
	1891H	—	—	—	Proof	120.00
	1894H	1.000	12.50	25.00	45.00	90.00
	1896H	1.000	12.50	25.00	45.00	90.00
	1907H	1.000	18.00	45.00	70.00	120.00
	1907H	—	—	—	Proof	400.00

COPPER-NICKEL

KM#	Date	Mintage	Fine	VF	XF	Unc
3	1904H	2.000	1.75	3.25	7.50	22.50
	1921H	1.000	1.75	3.25	7.50	22.50
	1935H	1.000	1.00	2.00	5.00	20.00
	1938H	1.000	1.00	2.00	5.00	20.00
	1941H	1.000	1.00	2.00	5.00	20.00

2-1/2 CENTS

COPPER-NICKEL

KM#	Date	Mintage	Fine	VF	XF	Unc
4	1903H	2.000	2.50	5.00	17.50	50.00
	1903H	—	—	—	Proof	300.00
	1920H	.280	5.00	15.00	30.00	65.00

5 CENTS

COPPER-NICKEL

KM#	Date	Mintage	Fine	VF	XF	Unc
5	1903H	1.000	1.25	3.50	12.00	30.00
	1920H	.100	3.00	7.50	25.00	45.00
	1921H	.500	1.25	3.50	12.00	30.00
	1927H	.150	1.50	4.00	12.00	30.00
	1928H	.150	1.50	4.00	12.00	30.00
	1938H	.500	1.25	2.50	6.00	12.50
	1940H	.500	1.25	2.50	6.00	12.50
	1941H	1.000	1.25	2.50	6.00	12.50

25 CENTS

2.8300 g, .500 SILVER, .0454 oz ASW

KM#	Date	Mintage	Fine	VF	XF	Unc
6	1929H	.400	8.00	15.00	22.00	45.00
	1929H	—	—	—	Proof	150.00

MALAYA

Malaya, a former member of the British Commonwealth located in the southern part of the Malay peninsula, consisted of 11 states: the unfederated Malay states of Johore, Kelantan, Kedah, Perlis and Trengganu; the federated Malay states of Negri-Sembilan, Pahang, Perak and Selangor; former members of the Straits Settlements Penang and Malacca. Malaya was occupied by the Japanese during the years 1942-1945. The only local opposition to the Japanese had come mainly from the Chinese Communists who then continued their guerilla operations after the Japanese had surrendered. They were finally defeated in 1956. Malaya was granted full independence on Aug. 31, 1957.

British

RULERS

MINT MARKS

I - Calcutta Mint(1941)
I - Bombay Mint(1945)
No Mint mark - Royal Mint

MONETARY SYSTEM

100 Cents = 1 Dollar

1/2 CENT

BRONZE

KM#	Date	Mintage	Fine	VF	XF	Unc
1	1940	6.000	.50	1.00	1.50	4.00
	1940	—	—	—	Proof	150.00

CENT

BRONZE

2	1939	20.000	.25	.40	.60	1.50
	1939	—	—	—	Proof	150.00
	1940	23.600	.25	.40	.60	1.50
	1940	—	—	—	Proof	—
	1941-I	33.620	.15	.35	.50	1.00

Reduced size.

6	1943	50.000	.10	.20	.35	.80
	1943	—	—	—	Proof	180.00
	1945	40.033	.10	.20	.35	.80
	1945	—	—	—	Proof	180.00

5 CENTS

1.3600 g, .750 SILVER, .0327 oz ASW

3	1939	2.000	.50	1.00	1.50	2.50
	1939	—	—	—	Proof	240.00
	1941	4.000	.40	.50	1.20	2.00
	1941	—	—	—	Proof	240.00
	1941-I	Inc. Ab.	.40	.50	1.50	2.00

1.3600 g, .500 SILVER, .0218 oz ASW

3a	1943	10.000	.30	.40	.65	1.50
	1943	—	—	—	Proof	240.00
	1945	8.800	.30	.40	.65	1.50
	1945	—	—	—	Proof	240.00
	1945-I	4.600	.30	.50	.75	2.50

COPPER-NICKEL

7	1948	30.000	.10	.25	.75	2.00
	1948	—	—	—	Proof	200.00
	1950	40.000	.10	.25	.75	2.00
	1950	—	—	—	Proof	200.00

10 CENTS

2.7100 g, .750 SILVER, .0653 oz ASW

KM#	Date	Mintage	Fine	VF	XF	Unc
4	1939	10.000	.75	1.00	1.25	2.50
	1939	—	—	—	Proof	275.00
	1941	17.000	.75	1.00	1.25	2.50
	1941	—	—	—	Proof	275.00
	1941-I	—	—	—	Proof	Rare

2.7100 g, .500 SILVER, .0435 oz ASW

4a	1943	5.000	.75	1.00	1.50	2.50
	1943	—	—	—	Proof	275.00
	1945	3.152	1.00	1.50	2.50	4.00
	1945-I	—	—	—	Proof	Rare

COPPER-NICKEL

8	1948	23.885	.15	.30	.75	2.25
	1948	—	—	—	Proof	275.00
	1949	26.115	.25	.50	1.20	3.00
	1949	—	—	—	Proof	275.00
	1950	65.000	.15	.30	.75	2.25
	1950	—	—	—	Proof	275.00

20 CENTS

5.4300 g, .750 SILVER, .1309 oz ASW

5	1939	8.000	1.50	2.00	2.50	5.00
	1939	—	—	—	Proof	275.00

5.4300 g, .500 SILVER, .0872 oz ASW

5a	1943	5.000	1.25	2.00	2.50	5.00
	1943	—	—	—	Proof	250.00
	1945	10.000	2.00	3.50	7.50	10.00
	1945-I	—	—	—	Proof	Rare

COPPER-NICKEL

9	1948	40.000	.30	.50	1.50	5.00
	1948	—	—	—	Proof	275.00
	1950	20.000	.30	.50	1.50	5.00
	1950	—	—	—	Proof	275.00

MALAYA & BRITISH BORNEO

Malaya & British Borneo, a Currency Commission named the Board of Commissioners of Currency, Malaya and British Borneo, was initiated on Jan. 1, 1952, for the purpose of providing a common currency for use in Johore, Kelantan, Kedah, Perlis, Trengganu, Negri Sembilan, Pahang, Perak, Selangor, Penang, Malacca, Singapore, North Borneo, Sarawak and Brunei.

British

RULERS

MINT MARKS

KN - King's Norton, Birmingham
H - Heaton, Birmingham
No Mint mark - Royal Mint

MONETARY SYSTEM

100 Cents = 1 Dollar

CENT

Malaya & British Borneo / MALAYSIA

BRONZE

KM#	Date	Mintage	VF	XF	Unc
5	1956	6.250	.10	.25	.50
	1956	—	—	Proof	125.00
	1957	12.500	.10	.25	.50
	1957	—	—	Proof	—
	1958	5.000	.10	.25	.50
	1958	—	—	Proof	125.00
	1961	10.000	.10	.20	.50
	1961	—	—	Proof	125.00

6	1962	45.000	—	.10	.35
	1962	*25 pcs.	—	Proof	125.00

5 CENTS

COPPER-NICKEL

KM#	Date	Mintage	VF	XF	Unc
1	1953	20.000	.25	.50	1.50
	1953	—	—	Proof	200.00
	1957	10.000	.50	.75	2.00
	1957	—	—	Proof	—
	1957H	10.000	.50	.75	2.00
	1957KN	Inc. Ab.	1.25	1.75	3.00
	1958	10.000	.25	.50	1.50
	1958	—	—	Proof	200.00
	1958H	10.000	.50	.75	2.00
	1961	95.000	.15	.50	1.50
	1961	—	—	Proof	—
	1961H	5.000	2.00	4.00	9.00
	1961KN	Inc. Ab.	1.00	2.50	5.00

10 CENTS

COPPER-NICKEL

KM#	Date	Mintage	VF	XF	Unc
2	1953	20.000	.40	1.00	2.50
	1953	—	—	Proof	200.00
	1956	10.000	.40	1.00	2.50
	1956	—	—	Proof	200.00
	1957H	10.000	.40	1.00	3.00
	1957H	—	—	Proof	200.00
	1957KN	10.000	.40	1.00	2.50
	1958	10.000	.40	.80	2.00
	1958	—	—	Proof	200.00
	1960	10.000	.40	.80	2.00
	1960	—	—	Proof	200.00
	1961	60.780	.20	.40	1.20
	1961	—	—	Proof	200.00
	1961H	69.220	.20	.40	1.20
	1961KN	Inc. Ab.	.50	.80	2.75

20 CENTS

COPPER-NICKEL

KM#	Date	Mintage	VF	XF	Unc
3	1954	10.000	.75	1.25	2.50
	1954	—	—	Proof	220.00
	1956	5.000	.75	1.25	2.00
	1956	—	—	Proof	220.00
	1957H	2.500	1.00	1.50	3.00
	1957KN	2.500	1.00	1.50	4.00
	1961	32.000	.50	.75	2.00
	1961	—	—	Proof	200.00
	1961H	23.000	.75	1.25	2.00

50 CENTS

COPPER-NICKEL, security edge

KM#	Date	Mintage	VF	XF	Unc
4.1	1954	8.000	1.00	2.00	4.50
	1954	—	—	Proof	280.00
	1955H	4.000	1.25	2.25	5.00
	1956	3.440	1.50	2.25	5.00
	1956	—	—	Proof	280.00
	1957H	2.000	1.50	2.50	6.00
	1957KN	2.000	2.00	2.75	6.00
	1958H	4.000	1.00	1.50	5.00
	1961	17.000	1.00	1.50	4.00
	1961	—	—	Proof	280.00
	1961H	4.000	1.50	2.50	5.00

Error, w/o security edge.

4.2	1954	Inc. Ab.	65.00	100.00	220.00
	1958H	Inc. Ab.	65.00	100.00	220.00
	1961	Inc. Ab.	65.00	100.00	220.00

MALAYSIA

MINT MARKS
FM - Franklin Mint, U.S.A.*

*NOTE: From 1975 the Franklin Mint has produced coinage in up to 3 different qualities. Qualities of issue are designated in ( ) after each date and are defined as follows:

(M) MATTE - Normal circulation strike or a dull finish produced by sandblasting special uncirculated (polish finish) or proof quality dies.

(U) SPECIAL UNCIRCULATED - Polished or proof-like in appearance without any frosted features.

(P) PROOF - The highest quality obtainable having mirror-like fields and frosted features.

MONETARY SYSTEM
100 Sen = 1 Ringgit Dollar

SEN

BRONZE

KM#	Date	Mintage	VF	XF	Unc
1	1967	45.000	—	.10	.15
	1967	500 pcs.	—	Proof	5.00
	1968	10.500	—	.10	.15
	1970	2.535	.15	.35	1.00
	1971	30.012	—	.10	.15
	1973	39.264	—	.10	.15
	1981FM(P)	—	—	Proof	—

COPPER-CLAD STEEL

1a	1973	Inc. Ab.	.15	.45	.65
	1976	24.694	—	.10	.15
	1977	24.437	—	.10	.15
	1978	30.861	—	.10	.15
	1979	15.714	—	.10	.15
	1980	16.151	—	.10	.15
	1981	24.633	—	.10	.15
	1982	37.295	—	.10	.15
	1983	12.140	—	.10	.15
	1984	26.260	—	.10	.15
	1985	52.402	—	.10	.15
	1986	48.920	—	.10	.15
	1987	35.284	—	.10	.15

BRONZE

1c	1976	100 pcs.	20.00	60.00	100.00

COPPER-NICKEL

1b	1980FM(P)	6,628	—	Proof	1.00
	1981FM(P)	—	—	Proof	1.00

5 SEN

COPPER-NICKEL

KM#	Date	Mintage	VF	XF	Unc
2	1967	75.464	—	.10	.20
	1967	500 pcs.	—	Proof	10.00
	1968	74.536	—	.10	.20
	1971	16.668	—	.30	.50
	1973	102.942	—	.10	.15
	1976	65.659	—	.10	.15
	1977	10.609	—	.30	.50
	1978	50.012	—	.10	.15
	1979	38.824	—	.10	.15
	1980	33.898	—	.10	.15
	1980FM(P)	6,628	—	Proof	2.00
	1981	51.490	—	.10	.15
	1981FM(P)	—	—	Proof	—
	1982	118.594	—	.10	.15
	1985	15.553	—	.10	.15
	1987	16.723	—	.10	.15

10 SEN

COPPER-NICKEL

KM#	Date	Mintage	VF	XF	Unc
3	1967	106.708	.10	.15	.25
	1967	500 pcs.	—	Proof	12.50
	1968	20.000	.10	.15	.25
	1971	.042	35.00	45.00	65.00
	1973	214.865	.10	.15	.25
	1976	148.809	.10	.15	.25
	1977	52.724	.10	.15	.25
	1978	21.154	.10	.15	.25
	1979	50.663	.10	.15	.25
	1980	51.802	.10	.15	.25
	1980FM(P)	6,628	—	Proof	3.00
	1981	236.639	.10	.15	.25
	1981FM(P)	—	—	Proof	—
	1982	145.639	—	.10	.20
	1983	30.840	—	.10	.20

20 SEN

COPPER-NICKEL

KM#	Date	Mintage	VF	XF	Unc
4	1967	19.560	.10	.30	.40
	1967	500 pcs.	—	Proof	17.50
	1968	35.440	.10	.30	.40
	1969	15.000	.15	.35	.50
	1970	1.054	.50	.75	1.00
	1971	9.968	.10	.25	.35
	1973	116.075	.10	.20	.30
	1976	61.534	.10	.20	.30
	1977	52.002	.10	.20	.30
	1978	6.847	.10	.20	.30
	1979	17.346	.10	.20	.30
	1980	32.842	.10	.20	.30
	1980FM(P)	6,628	—	Proof	4.00
	1981	144.128	.10	.20	.30
	1981FM(P)	—	—	Proof	—
	1982	97.905	—	.10	.20
	1983	—	—	.10	.20
	1987	26.225	—	—	—

50 SEN

COPPER-NICKEL

KM#	Date	Mintage	VF	XF	Unc
5.1	1967	15.000	.25	.50	1.00
(5)	1967	500 pcs.	—	Proof	20.00
	1968	12.000	.25	.50	1.00
	1969	2.000	.50	.75	1.50

Error, w/o security edge.

5.2	1967	Inc. Ab.	65.00	115.00	180.00
(6)	1968	Inc. Ab.	65.00	115.00	180.00
	1969	Inc. Ab.	200.00	280.00	400.00

Lettered edge

5.3	1971	8.414	.30	.60	.85
(8)	1973	48.250	.25	.50	.75
	1976	—	.25	.40	.60
	1977	17.721	.25	.40	.60
	1978	11.033	.25	.40	.60
	1979	5.361	.25	.40	.60
	1980	15.916	.25	.40	.60
	1980FM(P)	6,628	—	Proof	5.00
	1981	22.969	—	.25	.50
	1982	20.585	—	.25	.50
	1983	11.560	—	.25	.50
	1984	10.140	—	.25	.50
	1985	7.115	—	.25	.50
	1986	8.193	—	.25	.50
	1987	7.696	—	.25	.50

Plain edge

5.4	1981FM(P)	—	—	Proof	—

RINGGIT

MALAYSIA 1201

COPPER-NICKEL
10th Anniversary Bank Negara

KM#	Date	Mintage	VF	XF	Unc
7	1969	1.000	1.00	1.50	3.00
	17.000 g, .925 SILVER, .5055 oz ASW				
7a	1969	1,000	—	Proof	400.00

9.1	1971	2.379	—	.50	1.00
	1971	500 pcs.	—	Proof	800.00
	1980	.472	.60	.85	1.50
	1980FM(P)	6,628	—	Proof	10.00
	1981	.765	.60	.85	1.50
	1982	.202	.60	.85	1.50
	1984	.356	.60	.85	1.50
	1985	.302	.60	.85	1.50
	1986	1.500	.60	.85	1.50
	1987	.177	.60	.85	1.50

Plain edge

9.2	1981FM(P)	—	Proof	—

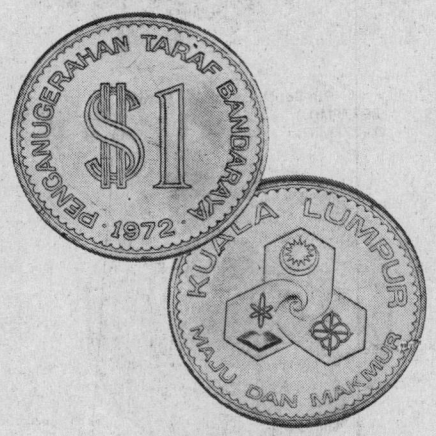

Kuala Lumpur Anniversary

12	1972	.500	.60	.85	2.50
	1972	500 pcs.	—	Proof	350.00

25th Anniversary Employee Provident Fund

KM#	Date	Mintage	VF	XF	Unc
13	1976	.500	.60	.85	2.50
	1976FM(P)	7,810	—	Proof	18.00

Malaysian 3rd Five Year Plan

16	1976	1.000	.60	.75	2.00
	1976FM(P)	.017	—	Proof	12.00

9th South-East Asian Games

22	1977	1.000	.60	.75	2.00
	1977FM(P)	.011	—	Proof	15.00

20th Anniversary of Independence

25	1977	.500	.60	.75	2.00
	1977FM(P)	3,102	—	Proof	35.00

100th Anniversary of Natural Rubber Production

26	1977	.500	.60	.75	2.00

20th Anniversary of Bank Negara

KM#	Date	Mintage	VF	XF	Unc
27	1979	.300	.60	.75	2.00
	17.0000 g, .925 SILVER, .5055 oz ASW				
27a	1979	8,000	—	Proof	25.00
	1980FM(P)	6,628	—	Proof	30.00

COPPER-NICKEL
15th Century of Hegira

28	1981	.050		.60	1.50

Tun Hussein Onn

29	1981	1.000		.60	1.50
	1981	.010	—	Proof	15.00

25th Anniversary of Independence

32	1982	1.500		.60	1.50
	1982	.015	—	Proof	12.00

5th Malaysian 5 Year Plan

36	1986	1.000		—	1.50
	1986	8,000	—	Proof	10.00

MALAYSIA 1202

PATA Conference

KM#	Date	Mintage	VF	XF	Unc
39	1986	.500	—	—	1.50

16.8500 g, .500 SILVER, .2709 oz ASW

| 39a | 1986 | .011 | — | Proof | 10.00 |

COPPER-ZINC-TIN
30 Years of Independence

| 43 | 1987 | 1.000 | — | — | 1.75 |
| | 1987 | 2.000 | — | Proof | 10.00 |

5 RINGGIT

COPPER-NICKEL

| 10 | 1971 | 2.000 | 2.25 | 2.75 | 4.00 |
| | 1971 | 500 pcs. | — | Proof | 850.00 |

29.0300 g, .500 SILVER, .4662 oz ASW
PATA Conference

| 40 | 1986 | .011 | — | Proof | 22.50 |

10 RINGGIT

10.8200 g, .925 SILVER, .3218 oz ASW
Malaysian 3rd Five Year Plan

KM#	Date	Mintage	VF	XF	Unc
17	1976FM(U)	.200	—	—	7.50
	1976FM(P)	.010	—	Proof	15.00
	1980FM(P)	6.628	—	Proof	20.00

10.8200 g, .500 SILVER, .1740 oz ASW
30 Years of Independence

| 44 | 1987 | .050 | — | — | 6.00 |
| | 1987 | .010 | .010 | Proof | 12.00 |

15 RINGGIT

28.2800 g, .925 SILVER, .8411 oz ASW
Conservation Series
Rev: Malaysian Gaur.

| 19 | 1976 | .040 | — | — | 22.50 |
| | 1976 | 8,113 | — | Proof | 60.00 |

20 RINGGIT

16.2300 g, .500 SILVER, .2609 oz ASW
Tun Hussein Onn
Obv: Similar to 1 Ringgit, KM#29.

| 30 | 1981FM(U) | .100 | — | — | 12.50 |
| | 1981FM(P) | 5,000 | — | Proof | 25.00 |

25 RINGGIT

35.0000 g, .925 SILVER, 1.0409 oz ASW
25th Anniversary Employee Provident Fund

| 14 | 1976FM(U) | .100 | — | — | 15.00 |
| | 1976FM(P) | 7,796 | — | Proof | 45.00 |

Conservation Series
Obv: Similar to 500 Ringgit, KM#21.
Rev: Rhinoceros Hornbill.

KM#	Date	Mintage	VF	XF	Unc
20	1976	.040	—	—	40.00
	1976	8,008	—	Proof	125.00

9th South-East Asian Games

| 23 | 1977FM(U) | .100 | — | — | 20.00 |
| | 1977FM(P) | 5,877 | — | Proof | 65.00 |

25th Anniversary of Independence
Rev: Similar to 1 Ringgit, KM#32.

| 33 | 1982 | .154 | — | — | 15.00 |
| | 1982 | 7,000 | — | Proof | 30.00 |

MALAYSIA 1203

35.0000 g, .500 SILVER, .5627 oz ASW
25th Anniversary of the National Bank

KM#	Date	Mintage	VF	XF	Unc
35	1984	.098	—	—	15.00
	1984	.010	—	Proof	35.00

5th Malaysian 5 Year Plan

| 37 | 1986 | .080 | — | — | 15.00 |
| | 1986 | 5,000 | — | Proof | 30.00 |

23.3300 g, .925 SILVER, .6939 oz ASW
Women's Decade

| 41 | 1986 | 2,000 | — | Proof | 47.50 |

100 RINGGIT

18.6600 g, .917 GOLD, .5502 oz AGW
Prime Minister Abdul Rahman Putra Al-haj

KM#	Date	Mintage	VF	XF	Unc
11	1971	.100	—	—	320.00
	1971	500 pcs.	—	Proof	1200.

200 RINGGIT

7.3000 g, .900 GOLD, .2112 oz AGW
Malaysian 3rd Five Year Plan

| 18 | 1976FM(U) | .051 | — | — | 100.00 |
| | 1976FM(P) | 3,102 | — | Proof | 200.00 |

7.2200 g, .900 GOLD, .2089 oz AGW
9th South-East Asian Games

| 24 | 1977FM(U) | .012 | — | — | 125.00 |
| | 1977FM(P) | 975 pcs. | — | Proof | 265.00 |

250 RINGGIT

10.1100 g, .900 GOLD, .2925 oz AGW
25th Anniversary Employee Provident Fund

| 15 | 1976FM(U) | .030 | — | — | 175.00 |
| | 1976FM(P) | 7,706 | — | Proof | 250.00 |

8.1000 g, .900 GOLD, .2344 oz AGW
Women's Decade

| 42 | 1985 | 1,500 | — | Proof | 225.00 |

7.4300 g, .900 GOLD, .2150 oz AGW
30 Years of Independence

| 45 | 1987 | 5,000 | — | — | 125.00 |
| | 1987 | 2,000 | — | Proof | 150.00 |

500 RINGGIT

33.4370 g, .900 GOLD, .9676 oz AGW
Conservation Series

Rev: Malayan Tapir.

KM#	Date	Mintage	VF	XF	Unc
21	1976	2,894	—	—	650.00
	1976	508 pcs.	—	Proof	900.00

10.2600 g, .900 GOLD, .2969 oz AGW
Tun Hussein Onn

| 31 | 1981FM(U) | .020 | — | — | 275.00 |
| | 1981FM(P) | 1,000 | — | Proof | 375.00 |

26.0000 g, .900 GOLD, .7524 oz AGW
25th Anniversary of Independence
Similar to 1 Ringgit, KM#32.

| 34 | 1982 | .020 | — | — | 250.00 |
| | 1982 | 1,000 | — | Proof | 350.00 |

10.2600 g, .900 GOLD, .2969 oz AGW
5th Malaysian 5 Year Plan

| 38 | 1986 | .010 | — | — | 250.00 |
| | 1986 | 1,000 | — | Proof | 350.00 |

MINT SETS (MS)

KM#	Date	Mintage	Identification	Issue Price	Mkt. Val.
MS1	1967(5)	10,000	KM1-5.1	—	10.00
MS2	1973(5)	2,000	KM1-5.3	—	2.00
MS3	1976(2)	—	KM19-20	35.00	62.50

PROOF SETS (PS)

PS1	1967(5)	500	KM1-5.1	—	200.00
PS2	1976(3)	508	KM19-21	808.00	1600.
PS3	1976(2)	7,500	KM19-20	—	375.00
PS4	1976(3)	2,641	KM16-18	—	250.00
PS5	1976(3)	1,000	KM13-15	—	375.00
PS6	1977(3)	975	KM22-24	164.00	500.00
PS7	1980(9)	5,000	KM1b,2-5.3,9.1,17,23,27a	132.00	150.00
PS8	1981(6)		KM1-5,29	—	—
PS9	1981(3)	3,000	KM29-31	—	420.00
PS10	1982(3)	4,000	KM32-34	—	400.00
PS11	1986(3)	2,000	KM36-38	—	390.00
PS12	1986(2)	11,000	KM39a,40	—	32.50

MALDIVE ISLANDS

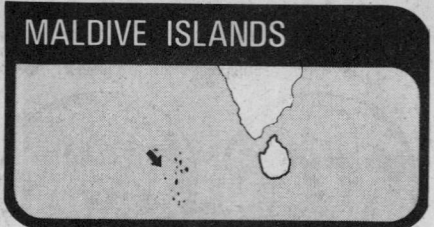

The Republic of Maldives, an archipelago of 2,000 coral islets in the northern Indian Ocean 417 miles (671 km.) west of Ceylon, has an area of 115 sq. mi. (298 sq. km.) and a population of *202,000. Capital: Male. Fishing employs 95 percent of the male work force. Dried fish, copra and coir yarn are exported.

The Maldive Islands were visited by Arab traders and converted to Islam in 1153. After being harassed in the 16th and 17th centuries by Mopla pirates of the Malabar coast and Portuguese raiders, the Maldivians voluntarily placed themselves under the suzerainty of Ceylon. In 1887 the islands became an internally self-governing British protectorate and a nominal dependency of Ceylon. Traditionally a sultanate, the Maldives became a republic in 1953 but restored the sultanate in 1954. The Sultanate of the Maldive Islands attained complete internal and external autonomy on July 26, 1965, and on Nov. 11, 1968, became again a republic.

The coins of the Maldives, issued by request of the Sultan and without direct British sponsorship, are not definitively coins of the British Commonwealth.

RULERS

Muhammad Mu'in al-Din,
 AH1213-1250/1798-1835AD
Muhammad Imad al-Din IV,
 AH1250-1300/1835-1882AD
Ibrahim Nur al-Din,
 AH1300-1318/1882-1900AD
Muhammad Imad al-Din V,
 AH1318-1322/1900-1904AD
Muhammad Shams al-Din III,
 AH1322-1353/1904-1935AD
Hasan Nur al-Din II,
 AH1353-1364/1935-1945AD
Abdul-Majid Didi,
 AH1364-1371/1945-1953AD
First Republic,
 AH1371-1372/1953-1954AD
Muhammad Farid Didi,
 AH1372-1388/1954-1968AD
Second Republic, AH1388 to
 date/1968AD to date

MONETARY SYSTEM
100 Lari = 1 Rupee (Rufiya)

NOTE: The metrology of the early coinage is problematical. There seem to have been three denominations: a double Larin of 8-10 g, a Larin of 4.8 g, and a half Larin that varied from 1.1 to 2.3 g, known as the Bodu Larin, Larin and Kuda Larin, respectively. In some years, probably when copper was cheap (AH1276 & 1294), the Kuda (1/2) Larin is found with weights as high as 3.7 g.

MUHAMMAD MU'IN AL-DIN ISKANDAR
AH1213-1250/1798-1835AD

KUDA (1/2) LARIN

BRONZE, 1.40-2.30 g

KM#	Date	Good	VG	Fine	VF
32	AH1216	3.00	5.00	7.50	10.00
	1219	3.00	5.00	7.50	10.00
	1221	3.00	5.00	7.50	10.00
	1230	5.00	7.50	12.00	18.00
	1238	3.50	6.00	9.00	12.50
	1239	4.00	6.50	10.00	15.00
	1248	3.00	5.00	7.50	10.00

NOTE: Some specimens are struck on lightweight planchets, some being square in shape. The date on the reverse occurs in various places.

MUHAMMAD IMAD AL-DIN IV ISKANDAR
AH1250-1300/1835-1882AD

1/4 LARIN

BRONZE, 1.10 g

KM#	Date	Good	VG	Fine	VF
34	AH1251	5.00	7.50	12.00	17.50
	1292	5.00	7.50	12.00	17.50
	1298	4.00	6.50	10.00	15.00

NOTE: These lightweight coins are believed to have been intended as 1/4 larins since the dies with which they were struck are smaller than those for the kuda (1/2) larin, below. The issue dated AH1251 is square or round.

KUDA (1/2) LARIN

BRONZE, 1.50-3.50 g

KM#	Date	Good	VG	Fine	VF
35.1	AH1252	4.00	6.50	10.00	15.00
	1257	2.50	3.50	6.00	9.00
	1276	2.50	3.50	6.00	9.00
	1286	2.50	3.00	5.00	8.00
	1287	4.00	6.50	10.00	15.00
	1292	2.50	3.50	6.00	9.00
	1294	3.00	5.00	7.50	10.00
	1298	.50	1.25	2.50	4.50

NOTE: The date on the reverse occurs in various places.

Rev: Date in top line.

35.2	AH1286	4.00	6.50	10.00	15.00

Obv: Leg. within quadrifoil.
Rev: Leg. within border of small circles.

35.3	AH1286	—	—	Rare	—

BODU (2) LARI

BRONZE, 8.20-9.00 g

36.1	AH1294	5.00	8.50	12.50	17.50

36.2	AH1298	7.50	12.50	20.00	30.00

IBRAHIM NUR AL-DIN ISKANDAR
AH1300-1318/1882-1900AD

1/4 LARIN/LARIN

BRONZE, 1.10 g

KM#	Date	Fine	VF	XF	Unc
37	AH1300	2.00	3.00	4.50	6.00

NOTE: Toward the end of this reign the standard was reportedly revised by a factor of four, making this denomination officially one larin. The date occurs in different places on the reverse.

MUHAMMAD IMAD AL-DIN V ISKANDAR
AH1318-1322/1900-1904AD

LARIN

COPPER/BRASS, 1.00 g

38	AH1318	1.00	1.50	2.00	4.00
	1319	3.00	4.50	6.00	8.00

2 LARIAT

COPPER/BRASS, 1.80 g

KM#	Date	Fine	VF	XF	Unc
39	AH1311 (error for 1319)	3.00	5.00	9.00	15.00
	1319	1.50	3.50	5.00	7.50

4 LARIAT

COPPER/BRASS, 3.70 g

40.1	AH1320	1.50	2.50	4.50	8.00

Rev: Arabic Sanat below date.

40.2	AH1320	4.00	8.00	12.00	16.00

NOTE: A pattern or presentation piece is reported to exist in silver or with silver plating.

MUHAMMAD SHAMS AL-DIN III ISKANDAR
AH1322-1353/1904-1935AD

LARIN

BRONZE, 0.90 g

41	AH1331	.75	1.00	1.25	2.50

Struck at Birmingham, England, Mint.

4 LARIAT

BRONZE, 3.30 g

42	AH1331	1.00	1.50	2.50	5.00

Struck at Birmingham, England, Mint.

REPUBLIC
MONETARY SYSTEM
100 Laari = 1 Rupee

LAARI

BRONZE

KM#	Date	Year	Mintage	VF	XF	Unc
43	AH1379	1960	.300	.15	.25	.50
	1379	1960	1,270	—	Proof	2.25

ALUMINUM

49	AH1389	1970	.500	.10	.15	.30
	1399	1979	—	.10	.15	.30
	1399	1979	.100	—	Proof	1.00

68	AH1404	1984	—	—	.10	.15
	1404	1984	—	—	Proof	2.00

2 LAARI

MALDIVES 1205

BRONZE

KM#	Date	Year	Mintage	VF	XF	Unc
44	AH1379	1960	.600	.20	.35	.60
	1379	1960	1,270	—	Proof	2.75

ALUMINUM

50	AH1389	1970	.500	.15	.25	.40
	1399	1979	—	.15	.25	.40
	1399	1979	.100	—	Proof	1.00

5 LAARI

NICKEL-BRASS

45	AH1379	1960	.300	.25	.40	.75
	1379	1960	1,270	—	Proof	3.50

BRONZE

45b	AH1379	1960	—	—	—	—

NICKEL-BRASS

51	AH1389	1970	.300	.20	.30	.40

ALUMINUM

45a	AH1399	1979	—	—	.10	.15
	1399	1979	—	—	Proof	2.00

69	AH1404	1984	—	—	.10	.15
	1404	1984	—	—	Proof	2.00

10 LAARI

NICKEL-BRASS

46	AH1379	1960	.600	.50	.75	1.50
	1379	1960	1,270	—	Proof	4.50

ALUMINUM

46a	AH1399	1979	—	—	.10	.20
	1399	1979	—	—	Proof	2.00

70	AH1404	1984	—	—	.10	.20
	1404	1984	—	—	Proof	2.50

25 LAARI

NICKEL-BRASS

47	AH1379	1960	.300	.60	1.00	1.50
	1379	1960	1,270	—	Proof	5.00
	1399	1979	—	—	.10	.25
	1399	1979	.100	—	Proof	3.00

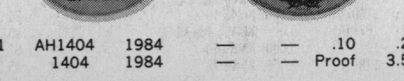

71	AH1404	1984	—	—	.10	.25
	1404	1984	—	—	Proof	3.50

50 LAARI

NICKEL-BRASS

KM#	Date	Year	Mintage	VF	XF	Unc
48	AH1379	1960	.300	1.00	1.75	2.50
	1379	1960	1,270	—	Proof	7.00
	1399	1979	—	.10	.20	.40
	1399	1979	.100	—	Proof	6.00

72	AH1404	1984	—	.10	.20	.40
	1404	1984	—	—	Proof	5.00

RUFIYAA

COPPER-NICKEL

73	AH1402	1982	—	—	.20	.40
	1404	1984	—	.15	.25	.50
	1404	1984	—	—	Proof	10.00

5 RUFIYAA

COPPER-NICKEL
F.A.O. Issue

55	AH1397	1977	.015	—	2.00	3.50

F.A.O. Issue

57	AH1398	1978	7,000	—	3.00	5.00

SILVER

57a	AH1398	1978	1,887	—	Proof	30.00

GOLD

57b	AH1398	1978	—	—	Proof	750.00

10 RUFIYAA

COPPER-NICKEL
F.A.O. Issue

KM#	Date	Year	Mintage	VF	XF	Unc
59	AH1399	1979	—	—	3.50	9.00

25.0000 g, .925 SILVER, .7435 oz ASW

59a	AH1399	1979	3,000	—	Proof	27.50

COPPER-NICKEL
F.A.O. Issue

62	AH1400	1980	—	—	3.00	8.00

20 RUFIYAA

28.2800 g, .500 SILVER, .4546 oz ASW
F.A.O. Issue

56	AH1397	1977	.015	—	—	12.50

28.2800 g, .925 SILVER, .8410 oz ASW
International Year of the Child

61	AH1399	1979	.012	—	Proof	25.00

MALDIVES 1206

COPPER-NICKEL
World Fisheries Conference

KM#	Date	Year	Mintage	VF	XF	Unc
65	AH1404	1984	.100	—	—	5.00

28.2800 g, .925 SILVER, .8410 oz ASW

| 65a | AH1404 | 1984 | .020 | — | Proof | 30.00 |

19.4400 g, .925 SILVER, .5782 oz ASW
Decade for Women

| 74 | AH1405 | 1984 | 500 pcs. | — | Proof | 40.00 |

25 RUFIYAA

28.0500 g, .500 SILVER, .4509 oz ASW
F.A.O. Issue

| 58 | AH1398 | 1978 | 7,140 | — | — | 30.00 |
| | 1398 | 1978 | 2,000 | — | — | 40.00 |

GOLD

| 58a | AH1398 | 1978 | — | — | — | 1000. |

COPPER-NICKEL
International Games - Football

KM#	Date	Year	Mintage	VF	XF	Unc
77	AH1405	1984	—	—	Proof	20.00

International Games - Swimming

| 79 | AH1405 | 1984 | — | — | Proof | 20.00 |

100 RUFIYAA

28.2800 g, .800 SILVER, .7274 oz ASW
F.A.O. Issue

| 60 | AH1399 | 1979 | 6,000 | — | — | 30.00 |

28.2800 g, .925 SILVER, .8411 oz ASW

| 60a | AH1399 | 1979 | 8,000 | — | Proof | 35.00 |

28.2800 g, .800 SILVER, .7274 oz ASW
F.A.O. Issue

| 63 | AH1400 | 1980 | 6,501 | — | — | 30.00 |

28.2800 g, .925 SILVER, .8411 oz ASW

| 63a | AH1400 | 1980 | 3,003 | — | Proof | 45.00 |

World Food Day
Obv: Similar to KM#60.

| 64 | AH1401 | 1981 | .010 | — | — | 30.00 |
| | 1401 | 1981 | 5,000 | — | Proof | 40.00 |

15.9800 g, .917 GOLD, .4712 oz AGW
Obv: Similar to KM#60.
Rev: Disabled people under umbrella.

KM#	Date	Year	Mintage	VF	XF	Unc
67	AH1403	1983	500 pcs.	—	—	400.00
	1403	1983	500 pcs.	—	Proof	450.00

28.2800 g, .925 SILVER, .8411 oz ASW
International Year of Disabled Persons
Rev: Ancient Yin and Yang symbols.

| 66 | AH1404 | 1984 | — | — | — | 25.00 |
| | 1404 | 1984 | — | — | Proof | 35.00 |

15.9800 g, .917 GOLD, .4712 oz AGW
Commonwealth Finance Ministers Meeting

| 75 | AH1404 | 1984 | 100 pcs. | — | Proof | 500.00 |

28.2800 g, .925 SILVER, .8411 oz ASW
Opening of Grand Mosque and Islamic Centre

| 78 | AH1404 | 1984 | 500 pcs. | — | Proof | 70.00 |

28.2800 g, .925 SILVER, .8410 oz ASW
Commonwealth Finance Ministers Meeting

| 76 | AH1405 | 1985 | 300 pcs. | — | Proof | 75.00 |

MINT SETS (MS)

KM#	Date	Mintage	Identification	Issue Price	Mkt. Val.
MS1	1984(6)	—	KM68-73	8.75	7.50

PROOF SETS (PS)

PS1	1960(6)	1,270	KM43-48	—	25.00
PS2	1979(6)	—	KM45a,46a,47-50	30.00	15.00
PS3	1979(2)	3,000	KM59,60	—	62.50
PS4	1984(6)	2,500	KM68-73	30.00	25.00

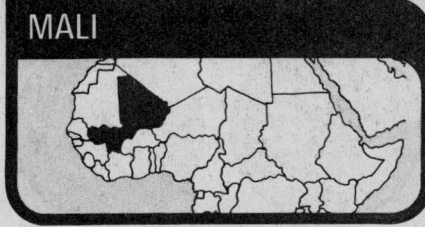

MALI

The Republic of Mali, a landlocked country in the interior of West Africa southwest of Algeria, has an area of 478,767 sq. mi. (1,240,000 sq. km.) and a population of *8.5 million. Capital: Bamako. Livestock, fish, cotton and peanuts are exported.

Malians are descendants of the ancient Malinke Kingdom of Mali that controlled the middle Niger from the 11th to the 17th centuries. The French penetrated the Sudan (now Mali) about 1880, and established their rule in 1898 after subduing fierce native resistance. In 1904 the area became the colony of Upper Senegal-Niger (changed to French Sudan in 1920), and became part of the French Union in 1946. In 1958 French Sudan became the Sudanese Republic with complete internal autonomy. Senegal joined with the Sudanese Republic in 1959 to form the Mali Federation which, in 1960, became a fully independent member of the French Community. Upon Senegal's subsequent withdrawal from the Federation, the Sudanese, on Sept. 22, 1960, proclaimed their nation the fully independent Republic of Mali and severed all ties with France.

MINT MARKS
(a) - Paris, privy marks only

5 FRANCS

ALUMINUM

KM#	Date	Mintage	VF	XF	Unc
2	1961	—	.35	.70	1.00

10 FRANCS

25.0000 g, .900 SILVER, .7234 oz ASW
Independence Day
1   1960   .010   —   Proof   32.50

ALUMINUM
3   1961   —   .35   .70   1.00

3.2000 g, .900 GOLD, .0926 oz AGW
Similar to 25 Francs, KM#6.
5   1967   —   —   Proof   75.00

10 FRANCS

ALUMINUM

KM#	Date	Mintage	VF	XF	Unc
11	1976(a)	5.000	.15	.25	.60

25 FRANCS

ALUMINUM
4   1961   —   .50   1.25   2.00

8.0000 g, .900 GOLD, .2315 oz AGW
6   1967   —   —   Proof   150.00

ALUMINUM
12   1976(a)   5.000   .35   .75   1.25

50 FRANCS

16.0000 g, .900 GOLD, .4630 oz AGW
7   1967   —   —   Proof   300.00

NICKEL-BRASS
F.A.O. Issue
9   1975(a)   10.000   .50   .75   1.25
    1977(a)   —   .50   .75   1.50

100 FRANCS

32.0000 g, .900 GOLD, .9260 oz AGW
8   1967   —   —   Proof   600.00

NICKEL-BRASS
F.A.O. Issue

KM#	Date	Mintage	VF	XF	Unc
10	1975(a)	23.000	.75	1.50	2.50

PROOF SETS (PS)

KM#	Date	Mintage	Identification	Issue Price	Mkt. Val.
PS1	1967(4)	—	KM5-8	—	1125.

MALTA

The Republic of Malta, an independent parliamentary democracy within the British Commonwealth, is situated in the Mediterranean Sea between Sicily and North Africa. With the islands of Gozo and Comino, Malta has an area of 122 sq. mi. (316 sq. km.) and a population of *358,000. Capital: Valletta. Malta has no proven mineral resources, an agriculture insufficient to its needs, and a small, but expanding, manufacturing facility. Clothing, textile yarns and fabrics, and knitted wear are exported.

For more than 3,500 years Malta was ruled, in succession, by Phoenicians, Carthaginians, Romans, Arabs, Normans, the Knights of Malta, France and Britain. Napoleon seized Malta by treachery in 1798. The French were ousted by a Maltese insurrection assisted by Britain, and in 1814 Malta, of its own free will, became a part of the British Empire. Malta obtained full independence in Sept., 1964; electing to remain within the Commonwealth with the British monarch as the nominal head of state.

Malta became a republic on Dec. 13, 1974, but remained a member of the Commonwealth of Nations. The president is Chief of State. The prime minister is the Head of Government.

RULERS
British, until 1964

BRITISH COINAGE
MONETARY SYSTEM
4 Farthings = 1 Penny

1/3 FARTHING

COPPER

NOTE: From 1827 through 1913 homeland type 1/3 Farthing along with other coinage of Great Britain circulated in Malta. The 1/3 Farthing corresponded to the copper Grano or 1/12 penny. These are found listed under Great Britain.

DECIMAL COINAGE
10 Mils = 1 Cent
100 Cents = 1 Pound

MINT MARKS
FM - Franklin Mint, U.S.A.*

*NOTE: From 1975 the Franklin Mint has produced coinage in up to 3 different qualities. Qualities of issue are designated in ( ) after each date and are defined as follows:

(M) MATTE - Normal circulation strike or a dull finish produced by sandblasting special uncirculated (polish finish) or proof quality dies.

(U) SPECIAL UNCIRCULATED - Polished or prooflike in appearance without any frosted features.

(P) PROOF - The highest quality obtainable having mirror-like fields and frosted features.

2 MILS

ALUMINUM

KM#	Date	Mintage	VF	XF	Unc
5	1972	.030	.10	.15	.35
	1972	.013	—	Proof	.50
	1976FM(M)	5,000	—	—	2.00
	1976FM(P)	.026	—	Proof	.50
	1977FM(U)	5,252	—	—	1.00
	1977FM(P)	6,884	—	Proof	1.00
	1978FM(U)	5,252	—	—	1.00
	1978FM(P)	3,244	—	Proof	1.00
	1979FM(U)	537 pcs.	—	—	3.00
	1979FM(P)	6,577	—	Proof	1.00
	1980FM(U)	385 pcs.	—	—	3.00
	1980FM(P)	3,451	—	Proof	1.00
	1981FM(U)	444 pcs.	—	—	3.00
	1981FM(P)	1,453	—	Proof	1.00

10th Anniversary of Decimalization

KM#	Date	Mintage	VF	XF	Unc
54	1982FM(U)	850 pcs.	—	—	3.00
	1982FM(P)	1,793	—	Proof	1.00

3 MILS

ALUMINUM

6	1972	—	.10	.15	.35
	1972	8,000	—	Proof	.75
	1976FM(M)	5,000	—	—	2.50
	1976FM(P)	.026	—	Proof	.75
	1977FM(U)	5,252	—	—	1.50
	1977FM(P)	6,884	—	Proof	1.25
	1978FM(U)	5,252	—	—	2.50
	1978FM(P)	3,244	—	Proof	1.25
	1979FM(U)	537 pcs.	—	—	5.00
	1979FM(P)	6,577	—	Proof	1.25
	1980FM(U)	385 pcs.	—	—	5.00
	1980FM(P)	3,451	—	Proof	1.25
	1981FM(U)	449 pcs.	—	—	5.00
	1981FM(P)	1,453	—	Proof	1.25

10th Anniversary of Decimalization

55	1982FM(U)	850 pcs.	—	—	4.00
	1982FM(P)	1,793	—	Proof	1.25

5 MILS

ALUMINUM

7	1972	4.320	.10	.15	.35
	1972	.013	—	Proof	1.00
	1976FM(M)	5,000	—	—	3.00
	1976FM(P)	.026	—	Proof	1.00
	1977FM(U)	5,252	—	—	2.00
	1977FM(P)	6,884	—	Proof	1.50
	1978FM(U)	5,252	—	—	2.00
	1978FM(P)	3,244	—	Proof	1.50
	1979FM(U)	537 pcs.	—	—	7.00
	1979FM(P)	6,577	—	Proof	1.50
	1980FM(U)	385 pcs.	—	—	7.00
	1980FM(P)	3,451	—	Proof	1.50
	1981FM(U)	449 pcs.	—	—	7.00
	1981FM(P)	1,453	—	Proof	1.50

10th Anniversary of Decimalization

56	1982FM(U)	850 pcs.	—	—	5.00
	1982FM(P)	1,793	—	Proof	1.50

CENT

BRONZE

KM#	Date	Mintage	VF	XF	Unc
8	1972	5.650	.10	.15	.25
	1972	.013	—	Proof	1.25
	1975	1.500	.10	.20	.30
	1976FM(M)	5,000	—	—	3.50
	1976FM(P)	.026	—	Proof	1.25
	1977	2.793	.10	.15	.25
	1977FM(U)	5,252	—	—	2.50
	1977FM(P)	6,884	—	Proof	1.75
	1978FM(U)	5,252	—	—	2.50
	1978FM(P)	3,244	—	Proof	1.75
	1979FM(U)	537 pcs.	—	—	9.00
	1979FM(P)	6,577	—	Proof	1.75
	1980FM(U)	385 pcs.	—	—	9.00
	1980FM(P)	3,451	—	Proof	1.75
	1981FM(U)	449 pcs.	—	—	9.00
	1981FM(P)	1,453	—	Proof	1.75
	1982	—	.10	.15	.25

10th Anniversary of Decimalization

57	1982FM(U)	850 pcs.	—	—	7.50
	1982FM(P)	1,793	—	Proof	1.75

COPPER-ZINC
Obv: Similar to 1 Pound, KM#82. Rev: Weasel.

78	1986	—	—	—	.10
	1986	.010	—	Proof	2.00

2 CENTS

COPPER-NICKEL

9	1972	5.640	.10	.15	.30
	1972	.013	—	Proof	1.50
	1976	1.000	.15	.20	.40
	1976FM(M)	2,500	—	—	4.50
	1976FM(P)	.026	—	Proof	1.50
	1977	6.105	.10	.15	.30
	1977FM(U)	2,752	—	—	4.50
	1977FM(P)	6,884	—	Proof	2.50
	1978FM(U)	2,752	—	—	4.50
	1978FM(P)	3,244	—	Proof	2.50
	1979FM(U)	537 pcs.	—	—	12.00
	1979FM(P)	6,577	—	Proof	2.50
	1980FM(U)	385 pcs.	—	—	12.00
	1980FM(P)	3,451	—	Proof	2.50
	1981FM(U)	449 pcs.	—	—	12.00
	1981FM(P)	1,453	—	Proof	2.50
	1982	—	.10	.15	.30

10th Anniversary of Decimalization

58	1982FM(U)	850 pcs.	—	—	10.00
	1982FM(P)	1,793	—	Proof	2.50

Obv: Similar to 1 Pound, KM#82. Rev: Olive branch.

79	1986	—	—	—	.15
	1986	.010	—	Proof	3.00

5 CENTS

COPPER-NICKEL

KM#	Date	Mintage	VF	XF	Unc
10	1972	4.180	.20	.30	.50
	1972	.013	—	Proof	1.75
	1976	1.009	.20	.30	.60
	1976FM(M)	2,500	—	—	5.00
	1976FM(P)	.026	—	Proof	2.00
	1977	—	.20	.30	.50
	1977FM(U)	2,752	—	—	5.00
	1977FM(P)	6,884	—	Proof	3.00
	1978FM(U)	2,752	—	—	5.00
	1978FM(P)	3,244	—	Proof	3.00
	1979FM(U)	537 pcs.	—	—	15.00
	1979FM(P)	6,577	—	Proof	3.00
	1980FM(U)	385 pcs.	—	—	15.00
	1980FM(P)	3,451	—	Proof	3.00
	1981FM(U)	449 pcs.	—	—	15.00
	1981FM(P)	1,453	—	Proof	3.00

10th Anniversary of Decimalization

59	1982FM(U)	850 pcs.	—	—	12.50
	1982FM(P)	1,793	—	Proof	3.00

77	1986	—	—	—	.25
	1986	.010	—	Proof	3.50

10 CENTS

COPPER-NICKEL

11	1972	10.680	.40	.60	1.00
	1972	.013	—	Proof	2.25
	1976FM(M)	1,000	—	—	6.00
	1976FM(P)	.026	—	Proof	2.50
	1977FM(U)	1,252	—	—	6.00
	1977FM(P)	6,884	—	Proof	3.50
	1978FM(U)	1,252	—	—	6.00
	1978FM(P)	3,244	—	Proof	3.50
	1979FM(U)	537 pcs.	—	—	17.50
	1979FM(P)	6,577	—	Proof	3.50
	1980FM(U)	385 pcs.	—	—	15.00
	1980FM(P)	3,451	—	Proof	3.50
	1981FM(U)	449 pcs.	—	—	15.00
	1981FM(P)	1,453	—	Proof	3.50

10th Anniversary of Decimalization

60	1982FM(U)	850 pcs.	—	—	13.00
	1982FM(P)	1,793	—	Proof	3.50

KM#	Date	Mintage	VF	XF	Unc
76	1986	—	—	.40	.60
	1986	.010	—	Proof	4.00

25 CENTS

BRASS
1st Anniversary of Republic of Malta

29	1975	4.750	1.00	1.50	2.50
	1975	—	Matte Proof		150.00

BRONZE

29a	1975	6,000	—	Proof	12.50

COPPER-NICKEL

29b	1976FM(M)	300 pcs.	—	—	40.00
	1976FM(P)	.026	—	Proof	3.00
	1977FM(U)	552 pcs.	—	—	20.00
	1977FM(P)	6,884	—	Proof	4.50
	1978FM(U)	552 pcs.	—	—	20.00
	1978FM(P)	3,244	—	Proof	4.50
	1979FM(U)	537 pcs.	—	—	20.00
	1979FM(P)	6,577	—	Proof	4.50
	1980FM(U)	385 pcs.	—	—	20.00
	1980FM(P)	3,451	—	Proof	4.50
	1981FM(U)	449 pcs.	—	—	20.00
	1981FM(P)	1,453	—	Proof	4.50

10th Anniversary of Decimalization

61	1982FM(U)	850 pcs.	—	—	15.00
	1982FM(P)	1,793	—	Proof	4.50

Obv: Similar to 1 Pound, KM#82. Rev: Ghirlanda flower.

80	1986	—	—	—	1.00
	1986	.010	—	Proof	5.00

50 CENTS

COPPER-NICKEL

12	1972	5.500	1.75	2.00	2.50
	1972	.013	—	Proof	3.50
	1976FM(M)	150 pcs.	—	—	90.00
	1976FM(P)	.026	—	Proof	5.00
	1977FM(U)	402 pcs.	—	—	25.00
	1977FM(P)	6,884	—	Proof	6.00
	1978FM(U)	402 pcs.	—	—	25.00
	1978FM(P)	3,244	—	Proof	6.00
	1979FM(U)	537 pcs.	—	—	25.00
	1979FM(P)	6,577	—	Proof	6.00
	1980FM(U)	385 pcs.	—	—	25.00
	1980FM(P)	3,451	—	Proof	6.00
	1981FM(U)	449 pcs.	—	—	25.00
	1981FM(P)	1,453	—	Proof	6.00

10th Anniversary of Decimalization

KM#	Date	Mintage	VF	XF	Unc
62	1982FM(U)	850 pcs.	—	—	20.00
	1982FM(P)	1,793	—	Proof	6.00

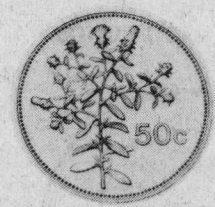

Obv: Similar to 1 Pound, KM#82. Rev: Tulliera plant.

81	1986	—	—	—	1.75
	1986	.010	—	Proof	7.00

POUND

10.0000 g, .987 SILVER, .3173 oz ASW
Manwel Dimech

13	1972	.055	—	5.00	10.00

Sir Temi Zammit

19	1973	.030	—	5.00	10.00

5.6600 g, .925 SILVER, .1683 oz ASW
Kelb tal-Fenek, an ancient Maltese dog.

45	1977	.066	—	3.50	7.00
	1977	2,500	—	Proof	20.00

Departure of Foreign Forces

51	1979FM(U)	.050	—	3.50	7.00
	1979FM(P)	7,871	—	Proof	10.00

COPPER-NICKEL
World Fisheries Conference
Obv: Similar to KM#51.
Rev: Similar to 5 Pounds KM#64.

63	ND(1984)	.120	—	3.50	5.50

MALTA 1210

NICKEL
Rev: Merill bird.

KM#	Date	Mintage	VF	XF	Unc
82	1986	—	—	—	3.50
	1986	.010	—	Proof	8.00

2 POUNDS

20.0000 g, .987 SILVER, .6347 oz ASW
Fort St. Angelo

| 14 | 1972 | .053 | — | 8.00 | 14.00 |

Tal-Imdina Gate
Obv: Similar to KM#14.

| 20 | 1973 | .030 | — | 8.00 | 14.00 |

10.0000 g, .987 SILVER, .3173 oz ASW
Giovanni Francesco Abela

| 24 | 1974 | .025 | — | 6.50 | 8.00 |

Obv: Similar to KM#24. Rev: Similar to KM#31.

| 30 | 1975 | 2.000 | — | 8.00 | 14.00 |

Alfonso Maria Galea

KM#	Date	Mintage	VF	XF	Unc
31	1975	.018	—	6.50	8.00

Guze Ellul Mercer

| 40 | 1976 | .011 | — | 7.00 | 10.00 |

11.3100 g, .925 SILVER, .3363 oz ASW
Sir Luigi Preziosi

| 46 | 1977 | .015 | — | — | 10.00 |
| | 1977 | 3.692 | — | Proof | 17.50 |

F.A.O. Issue

| 52 | 1981 | 1,500 | — | — | 17.50 |
| | 1981 | .012 | — | Proof | 10.00 |

4 POUNDS

20.0000 g, .987 SILVER, .6347 oz ASW
Cottonera Gate

| 25 | 1974 | .024 | — | 13.00 | 15.00 |

Obv: Same as KM#25. Rev: Similar to KM#33.

| 32 | 1975 | 2,000 | — | 15.00 | 27.50 |

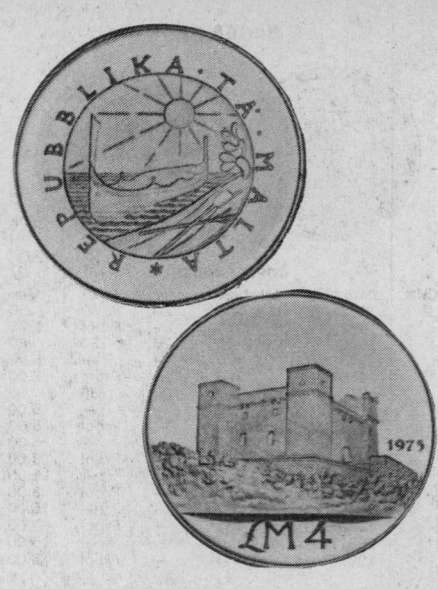

St. Agatha's Tower at Qammieh

KM#	Date	Mintage	VF	XF	Unc
33	1975	.018	—	13.00	15.00

Fort Manoel Gate

| 41 | 1976 | .010 | — | 13.00 | 15.00 |

5 POUNDS

3.0000 g, .916 GOLD, .0883 oz AGW
Rev: Hand holding torch, map of Malta.

| 15 | 1972 | .018 | — | — | 60.00 |

28.2800 g, .925 SILVER, .8411 oz ASW
Windmill of Xarolla

| 47 | 1977 | .015 | — | — | 25.00 |
| | 1977 | 3.938 | — | Proof | 40.00 |

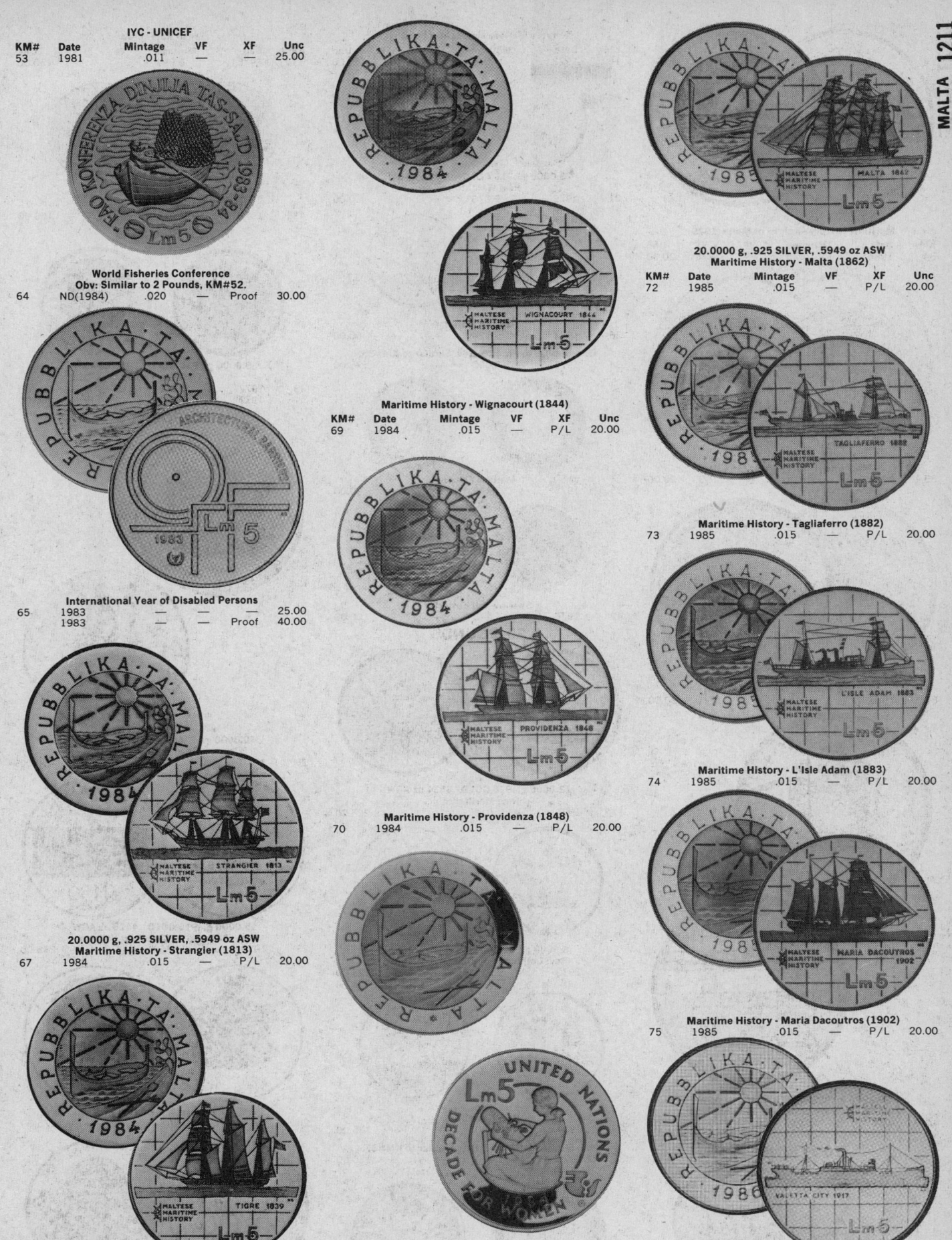

MALTA 1211

IYC - UNICEF

KM#	Date	Mintage	VF	XF	Unc
53	1981	.011	—	—	25.00

World Fisheries Conference
Obv: Similar to 2 Pounds, KM#52.

64	ND(1984)	.020	—	Proof	30.00

International Year of Disabled Persons

65	1983	—	—	—	25.00
	1983	—	—	Proof	40.00

20.0000 g, .925 SILVER, .5949 oz ASW
Maritime History - Strangier (1813)

67	1984	.015	—	P/L	20.00

Maritime History - Tigre (1839)

68	1984	.015	—	P/L	20.00

Maritime History - Wignacourt (1844)

KM#	Date	Mintage	VF	XF	Unc
69	1984	.015	—	P/L	20.00

Maritime History - Providenza (1848)

70	1984	.015	—	P/L	20.00

28.2800 g, .925 SILVER, .8411 oz ASW
Decade for Women

71	1984	.017	—	Proof	25.00

20.0000 g, .925 SILVER, .5949 oz ASW
Maritime History - Malta (1862)

KM#	Date	Mintage	VF	XF	Unc
72	1985	.015	—	P/L	20.00

Maritime History - Tagliaferro (1882)

73	1985	.015	—	P/L	20.00

Maritime History - L'Isle Adam (1883)

74	1985	.015	—	P/L	20.00

Maritime History - Maria Dacoutros (1902)

75	1985	.015	—	P/L	20.00

Maritime History - Valetta City (1917)

83	1986	.015	—	P/L	20.00

MALTA 1212

Maritime History - Knight of Malta (1929)
KM#	Date	Mintage	VF	XF	Unc
84	1986	.015	—	P/L	20.00

Maritime History - Saver (1943)
| 85 | 1986 | .015 | — | P/L | 20.00 |

Maritime History - Dwe Jra II (1969)
| 86 | 1986 | .015 | — | P/L | 20.00 |

28.2800 g, .925 SILVER, .8411 oz ASW
20th Anniversary of Central Bank of Malta
| 87 | 1988 | *5,000 | — | — | 25.00 |
| | 1988 | *2,000 | — | Proof | 45.00 |

10 POUNDS

6.0000 g, .916 GOLD, .1767 oz AGW

Kenur, a Maltese stone charcoal stove.
KM#	Date	Mintage	VF	XF	Unc
16	1972	.016	—	—	100.00

3.0000 g, .916 GOLD, .0883 oz AGW
Rev: Watchtower.
| 21 | 1973 | 9,078 | — | — | 60.00 |

Zerafa Flower
| 26 | 1974 | 9,124 | — | — | 60.00 |

Obv: Similar to KM#26. Rev: Similar to KM#35.
| 34 | 1975 | 2,000 | — | — | 75.00 |

Maltese Falcon
| 35 | 1975 | 6,448 | — | — | 90.00 |

Swallow-tail butterfly
| 42 | 1976 | 4,448 | — | — | 100.00 |

20 POUNDS

12.0000 g, .916 GOLD, .3534 oz AGW
Rev: Merill bird.
| 17 | 1972 | .016 | — | — | 225.00 |

6.0000 g, .916 GOLD, .1767 oz AGW
Rev: Dolphins Fountain at Floriana.
| 22 | 1973 | 9,075 | — | — | 125.00 |

Rev: Gozo boat.
| 27 | 1974 | 8,700 | — | — | 125.00 |

Obv: Similar to KM#27. Rev: Similar to KM#37.
| 36 | 1975 | 2,000 | — | — | 150.00 |

Fresh water crab.
KM#	Date	Mintage	VF	XF	Unc
37	1975	5,698	—	—	150.00

Storm Petrel bird.
| 43 | 1976 | 4,098 | — | — | 150.00 |

25 POUNDS

8.0000 g, .916 GOLD, .2356 oz AGW
First Gozo coin.
| 48 | 1977 | 4,000 | — | — | 125.00 |
| | 1977 | 3,249 | — | Proof | 150.00 |

50 POUNDS

30.0000 g, .916 GOLD, .8836 oz AGW
Rev: Neptune.
| 18 | 1972 | .016 | — | — | 450.00 |

15.0000 g, .916 GOLD, .4418 oz AGW
Rev: Auberge de Castille at Valletta.
| 23 | 1973 | 9,075 | — | — | 275.00 |

Rev: First Maltese coin.
| 28 | 1974 | 8,667 | — | — | 275.00 |

| 38 | 1975 | 2,000 | — | — | 300.00 |

Ornamental stone balcony.

KM#	Date	Mintage	VF	XF	Unc
39	1975	5,500	—	—	275.00

Obv: Similar to KM#28.
Ornamental door knocker.

| 44 | 1976 | 3,748 | — | — | 275.00 |

Mnara

| 49 | 1977 | 4,000 | — | — | 275.00 |
| | 1977 | 846 pcs. | — | Proof | 325.00 |

100 POUNDS

32.0000 g, .916 GOLD, .9425 oz AGW
Sculpture of Les Gavroches.

| 50 | 1977 | 4,000 | — | — | 500.00 |
| | 1977 | 846 pcs. | — | Proof | 650.00 |

15.9800 g, .917 GOLD, .4709 oz AGW
International Year of Disabled Persons

| 66 | 1983 | 700 pcs. | — | — | 400.00 |
| | 1983 | 600 pcs. | — | Proof | 500.00 |

MINT SETS (MS)

KM#	Date	Mintage	Identification	Issue Price	Mkt. Val.
MS1	1972(8)	8,000	KM5-12	—	5.00
MS2	1972(4)	8,000	KM15-18	210.00	800.00
MS3	1972(2)	—	KM13,14	8.50	27.50
MS4	1973(3)	9,078	KM21-23	—	400.00
MS5	1973(2)	—	KM19,20	—	27.50
MS6	1974(3)	—	KM26-28	256.00	400.00
MS7	1974(2)	—	KM24,25	19.60	22.50
MS8	1975(5)	2,000	KM30,32,34,36,38	276.00	550.00
MS9	1975(3)	—	KM34,36,38	256.00	475.00
MS10	1975(2)	—	KM30,32	20.00	45.00
MS11	1975(3)	—	KM35,37,39	—	425.00
MS12	1976(3)	—	KM42-44	—	425.00
MS13	1976(2)	—	KM40-41	—	25.00
MS14	1977(9)	252	KM5-12,29b	—	65.00
MS15	1977(3)	4,000	KM48-50	610.00	900.00
MS16	1977(3)	15,000	KM45-47	34.50	36.50
MS17	1978(9)	252	KM5-12,29b	—	65.00
MS18	1979(9)	537	KM5-12,29b	—	110.00
MS19	1980(9)	385	KM5-12,29b	11.00	110.00
MS20	1981(9)	449	KM5-12,29b	13.25	110.00
MS21	1982(9)	850	KM54-62	13.25	20.00
MS22	1984(4)	—	KM67-70	—	70.00
MS23	1985(4)	15,000	KM72-75	—	75.00

PROOF SETS (PS)

PS1	1972(8)	8,000	KM5-12 (plastic case)	—	12.50
PS2	1976(9)	26,248	KM5-12,29b	27.50	15.00
PS3	1977(9)	6,884	KM5-12,29b	31.50	25.00
PS4	1977(3)	750	KM48-50	909.00	1125.
PS5	1977(3)	2,500	KM45-47	72.00	80.00
PS6	1978(9)	3,244	KM5-12,29b	—	20.00
PS7	1979(10)	6,577	KM5-12,29b,51	41.50	30.00
PS8	1980(9)	3,451	KM5-12,29b	30.00	20.00
PS9	1981(9)	1,453	KM5-12,29b	25.30	25.00
PS10	1982(9)	1,793	KM54-62	32.00	25.00
PS11	1986(7)	10,000	KM76-82	29.75	32.50

ORDER OF MALTA

The Order of Malta, modern successor to the Sovereign Military Hospitaller Order of St. John of Jerusalem (the crusading Knights Hospitallers), derives its sovereignty from grants of extraterritoriality by Italy (1928) and the Vatican City (1953), and from its supranational character as a religious military Order owing suzerainty to the Holy See. Its territory is confined to Palazzo Malta on Via Condotti, Villa Malta and the crest of the Aventine Hill, all in the city of Rome. The Order maintains diplomatic relations with about 35 governments, including Italy, Spain, Austria, State of Malta, Portugal, Brazil, Guatemala, Panama, Peru, Iran, Lebanon, Philippines, Liberia, Ethiopia, etc.

The Knights Hospitallers were founded in 1099 just before the crusaders' capture of Jerusalem. Father Gerard (died 1120) was the founder and first rector of the Jerusalem hospital. The headquarters of the Order was successively at Jerusalem 1099-1187; Acre 1187-1291; Cyprus 1291-1310; Rhodes 1310-1522; Malta 1530-1798; Trieste 1798-1799; St. Petersburg 1799-1803; Catania 1803-1825; Ferrara 1826-1834; Rome 1834-Present.

The symbolic coins issued by the Order since 1961 are intended to continue the last independent coinage of the Order on Malta in 1798. In traditional tari and scudi denominations, they are issued only in proof condition. They have a theoretical fixed exchange value with the Italian lira, but are not used in commerce.

The modern medallic issues are perhaps the world's last major symbolic coinage, just as their issuer is the world's last sovereign order of knighthood. Proceeds from the sale of this coinage maintain the Order's hospitals, clinics and leprosariums around the world.

RULERS
Ernesto Paterno-Castello di Carcaci,
 Lieutenant Grand Master, 1955-1962
FR. Angelo de Mojana di Cologna,
 Grand Master, 1962-1988
FRA. Giancarlo Pallavicini
 Temporary Grand Master, 1988
FR. Andreas Bertie
 Grand Master, 1988-

MINT MARKS
Rome (no mark) 1961
Paris (no mark) 1962
Arezzo (no mark) 1963
Order of Malta Mint in Rome - SMOM
 in angles of a cross - 1964-

MONETARY SYSTEM
(Until ca. 1800)
20 Grani = 1 Tari
12 Tari = 1 Scudo

NOTICE
Catalog Numbering Revised

MEDALLIC ISSUES (M)
10 GRANI

BRONZE

KM#	Date	Mintage	Fine	VF	XF	Unc
M17 (M1)	1967	.010	—	—	Proof	5.00

| M29 (MA1) | 1969 | 3,000 | — | — | Proof | 5.50 |

Order of MALTA 1214

KM#	Date	Mintage	Fine	VF	XF	Unc
M35 (MB1)	1970	3,000	—	—	Proof	4.50

KM#	Date	Mintage	Fine	VF	XF	Unc
M40 (M2)	1971	3,000	—	—	Proof	4.50

Obv. leg: F. ANGELVS DE MOJANA....

Battle of Lepanto
FR. Petrus de Monte

| M46 (M3) | 1971 | 5,000 | — | — | Proof | 5.00 |

FR. Angelvs de Mojana

| M48 (M4) | 1972 | 3,000 | — | — | Proof | 4.50 |
| | 1973 | 3,000 | — | — | Proof | 4.50 |

M56 (M5)	1974	3,000	—	—	Proof	5.00
	1975	3,000	—	—	Proof	5.00
(MA5)	1976	3,000	—	—	Proof	5.00
	1977	3,000	—	—	Proof	5.00

| M70 (M55) | 1978 | 3,000 | — | — | Proof | 6.00 |

KM#	Date	Mintage	Fine	VF	XF	Unc
M74 (MA55)	1979	3,000	—	—	Proof	4.50

| M80 (M64) | 1980 | 3,000 | — | — | Proof | 7.50 |

International Year of Disabled Persons

| M85 (M70) | 1981 | 3,000 | — | — | Proof | 8.50 |

20th Anniversary of Grand Master

| M90 (M76) | 1982 | 2,000 | — | — | Proof | 7.50 |

Obv: Similar to KM#M90.
Rev: Similar to KM#M108.

| M96 (M82) | 1983 | 2,000 | — | — | Proof | 7.50 |

Piranesi

| M102 (M88) | 1984 | 2,000 | — | — | Proof | 7.50 |

| M108 (M94) | 1985 | 2,000 | — | — | Proof | 7.50 |

Grotto of Apparitions at Lourdes

| M113 (M100) | 1986 | 2,000 | — | — | Proof | 7.50 |

25th Anniversary of Grand Master

| M118 | 1987 | 2,000 | — | — | Proof | 6.50 |

Obv: Shoulder length portrait of FRA. A. Mojana left.
Rev: Ship, similar to KM#M74.

| M124 | 1988 | 2,000 | — | — | Proof | 6.50 |

FRA. Giancarlo Pallavicini (Interregnum)
Obv: Maltese cross w/leg: SVB.HOC....
Rev: St. John the Baptist.

KM#	Date	Mintage	Fine	VF	XF	Unc
M130	1988	—	—	—	Proof	6.50

FR. Andreas Bertie

| M136 | 1988 | — | — | — | Proof | 6.50 |
| M142 | 1989 | — | — | — | Proof | 6.50 |

2 TARI

BRONZE, 1mm thick
F.A.O. Issue

| M23 (M6.1) | 1968 | .020 | — | — | Proof | 5.00 |

2mm thick

| M23a (M6.2) | 1968 | Inc. Ab. | — | — | Proof | 5.00 |

9 TARI

9.0000 g, .900 SILVER, .2604 oz ASW
Obv. leg: F. ANGELVS DE MOJANA....

| M18 (M7) | 1967 | .010 | — | — | Proof | 10.00 |

| M30 (M8) | 1969 | 3,000 | — | — | Proof | 10.00 |

Rev: Head of St. John the Baptist.

| M36 (M9) | 1970 | 3,000 | — | — | Proof | 10.00 |

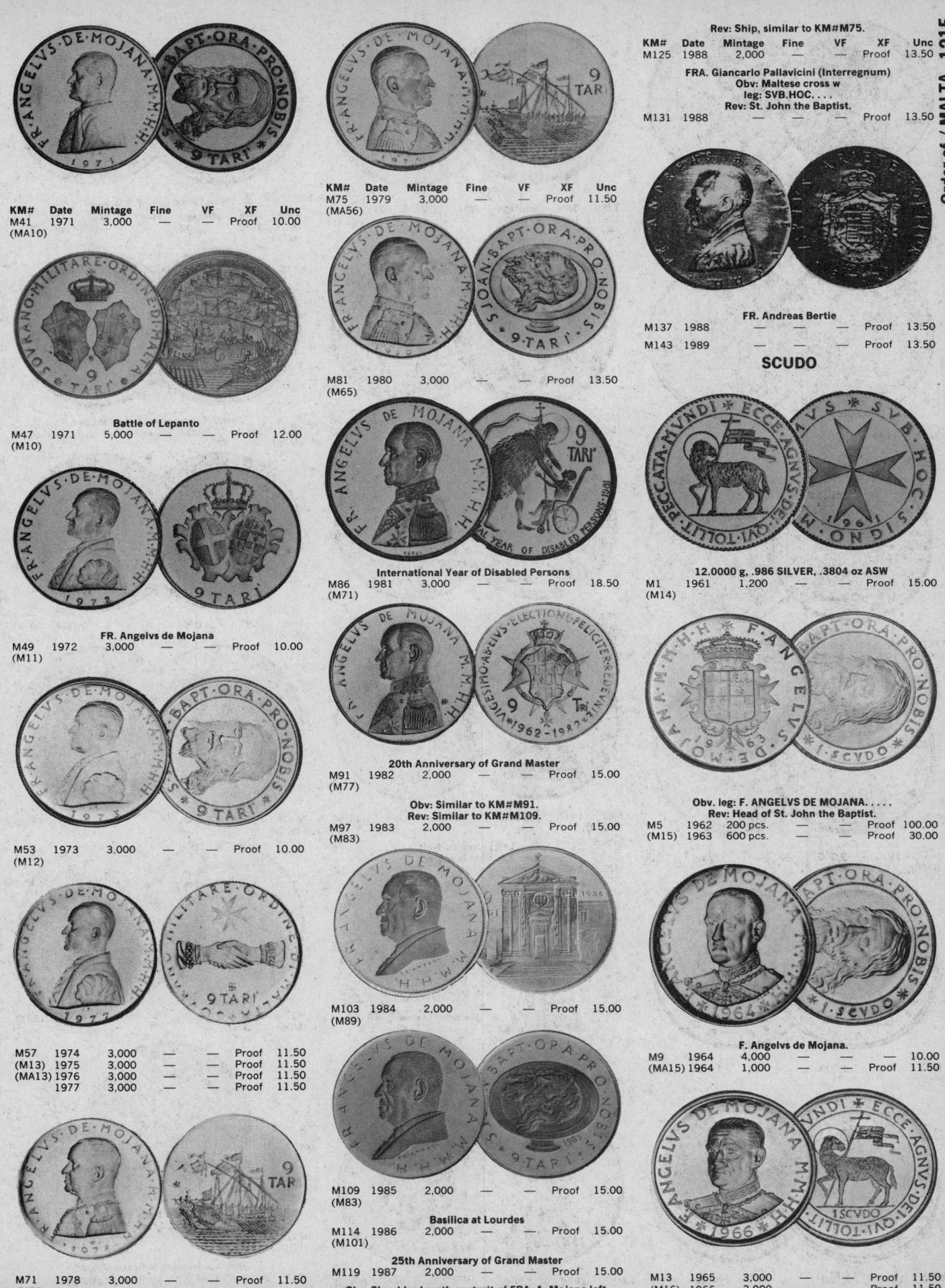

Order of / MALTA 1216

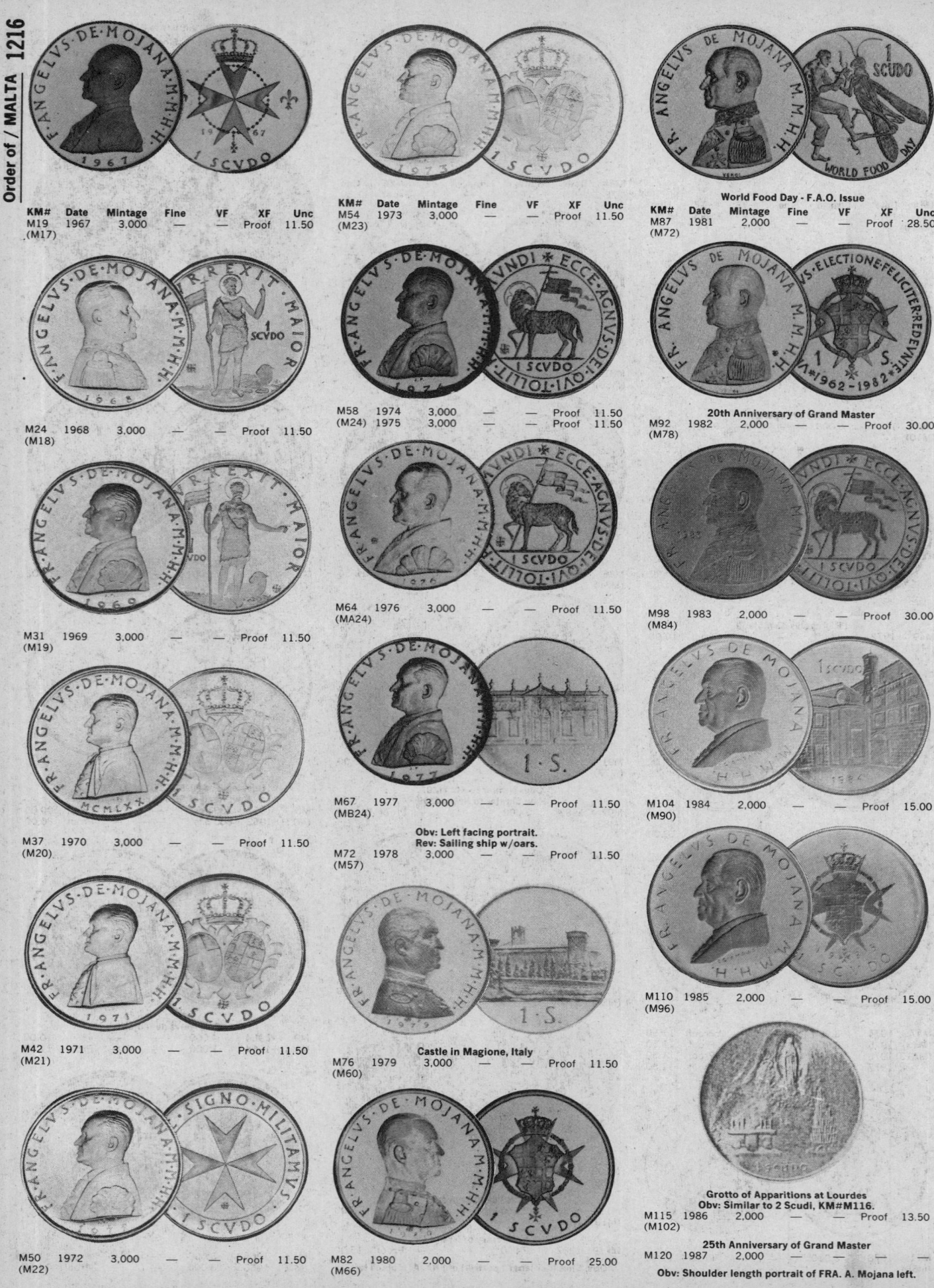

KM#	Date	Mintage	Fine	VF	XF	Unc
M19 (M17)	1967	3,000	—	—	Proof	11.50

KM#	Date	Mintage	Fine	VF	XF	Unc
M54 (M23)	1973	3,000	—	—	Proof	11.50

World Food Day - F.A.O. Issue

KM#	Date	Mintage	Fine	VF	XF	Unc
M87 (M72)	1981	2,000	—	—	Proof	28.50

| M24 (M18) | 1968 | 3,000 | — | — | Proof | 11.50 |

| M58 (M24) | 1974 | 3,000 | — | — | Proof | 11.50 |
| | 1975 | 3,000 | — | — | Proof | 11.50 |

20th Anniversary of Grand Master

| M92 (M78) | 1982 | 2,000 | — | — | Proof | 30.00 |

| M31 (M19) | 1969 | 3,000 | — | — | Proof | 11.50 |

| M64 (MA24) | 1976 | 3,000 | — | — | Proof | 11.50 |

| M98 (M84) | 1983 | 2,000 | — | — | Proof | 30.00 |

| M37 (M20) | 1970 | 3,000 | — | — | Proof | 11.50 |

| M67 (MB24) | 1977 | 3,000 | — | — | Proof | 11.50 |

Obv: Left facing portrait.
Rev: Sailing ship w/oars.

| M72 (M57) | 1978 | 3,000 | — | — | Proof | 11.50 |

| M104 (M90) | 1984 | 2,000 | — | — | Proof | 15.00 |

| M42 (M21) | 1971 | 3,000 | — | — | Proof | 11.50 |

Castle in Magione, Italy

| M76 (M60) | 1979 | 3,000 | — | — | Proof | 11.50 |

| M110 (M96) | 1985 | 2,000 | — | — | Proof | 15.00 |

Grotto of Apparitions at Lourdes
Obv: Similar to 2 Scudi, KM#M116.

| M115 (M102) | 1986 | 2,000 | — | — | Proof | 13.50 |

25th Anniversary of Grand Master

| M120 | 1987 | 2,000 | — | — | — | — |

Obv: Shoulder length portrait of FRA. A. Mojana left.

| M50 (M22) | 1972 | 3,000 | — | — | Proof | 11.50 |

| M82 (M66) | 1980 | 2,000 | — | — | Proof | 25.00 |

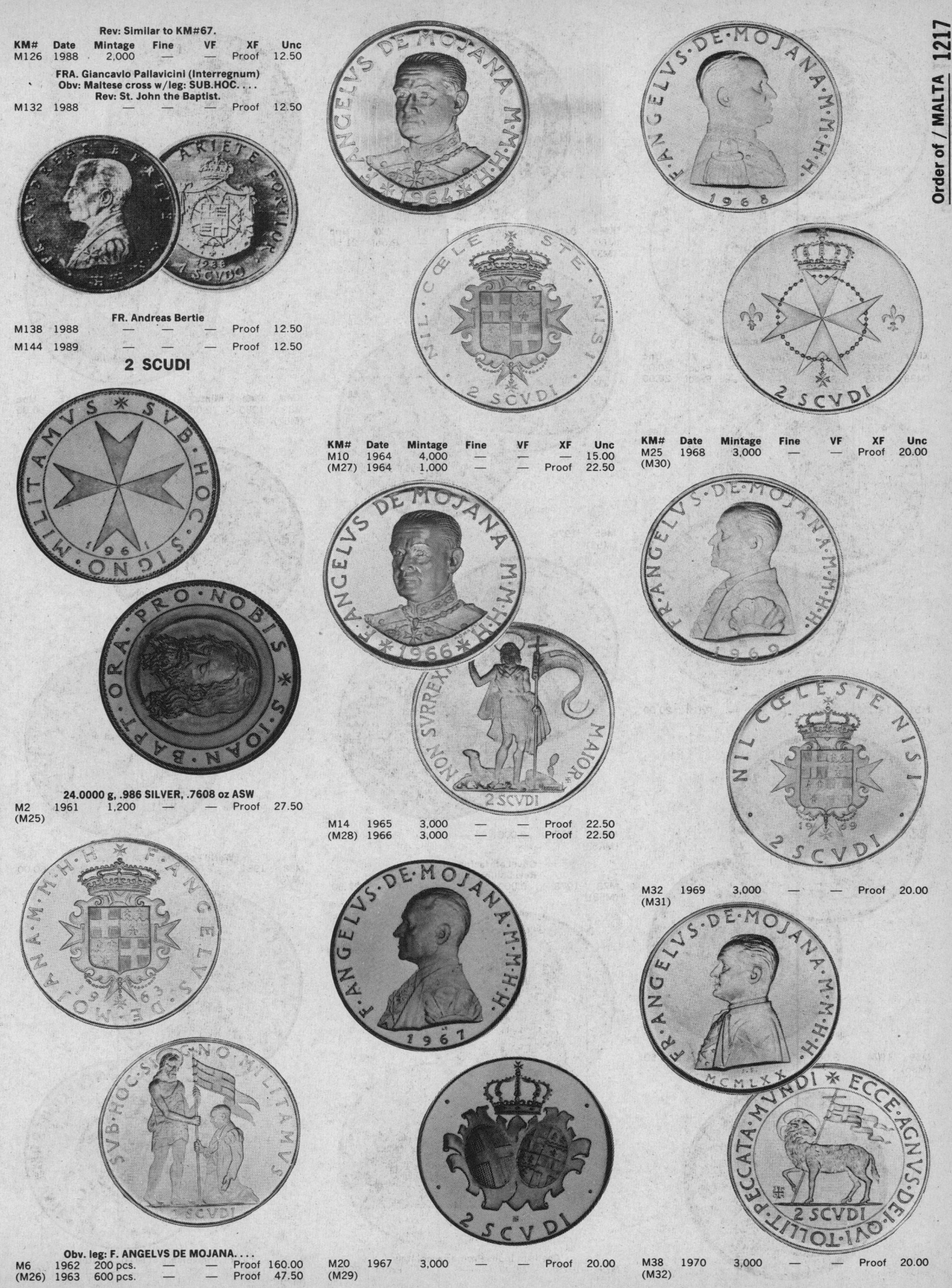

Rev: Similar to KM#67.

KM#	Date	Mintage	Fine	VF	XF	Unc
M126	1988	2,000	—	—	Proof	12.50

FRA. Giancavlo Pallavicini (Interregnum)
Obv: Maltese cross w/leg: SUB.HOC. . . .
Rev: St. John the Baptist.

| M132 | 1988 | — | — | — | Proof | 12.50 |

FR. Andreas Bertie

| M138 | 1988 | — | — | — | Proof | 12.50 |
| M144 | 1989 | — | — | — | Proof | 12.50 |

2 SCUDI

24.0000 g, .986 SILVER, .7608 oz ASW

| M2 (M25) | 1961 | 1,200 | — | — | Proof | 27.50 |

Obv. leg: F. ANGELVS DE MOJANA . . . .

| M6 | 1962 | 200 pcs. | — | — | Proof | 160.00 |
| (M26) | 1963 | 600 pcs. | — | — | Proof | 47.50 |

KM#	Date	Mintage	Fine	VF	XF	Unc
M10	1964	4,000	—	—	—	15.00
(M27)	1964	1,000	—	—	Proof	22.50

| M14 | 1965 | 3,000 | — | — | Proof | 22.50 |
| (M28) | 1966 | 3,000 | — | — | Proof | 22.50 |

| M20 (M29) | 1967 | 3,000 | — | — | Proof | 20.00 |

KM#	Date	Mintage	Fine	VF	XF	Unc
M25 (M30)	1968	3,000	—	—	Proof	20.00

| M32 (M31) | 1969 | 3,000 | — | — | Proof | 20.00 |

| M38 (M32) | 1970 | 3,000 | — | — | Proof | 20.00 |

Order of / MALTA

KM#	Date	Mintage	Fine	VF	XF	Unc
M43	1971	3,000	—	—	Proof	20.00
(M33)	1973	3,000	—	—	Proof	20.00

KM#	Date	Mintage	Fine	VF	XF	Unc
M60 (M37)	1975	3,000	—	—	Proof	21.50

KM#	Date	Mintage	Fine	VF	XF	Unc
M83 (M67)	1980	2,000	—	—	Proof	50.00

M51 (M34)	1972	3,000	—	—	Proof	20.00

M65 (M53)	1976	3,000	—	—	Proof	21.50

M68 (MA53)	1977	3,000	—	—	Proof	18.50

Obv: Left facing portrait.
Rev: Sailing ship w/oars.

M73 (M58)	1978	3,000	—	—	Proof	27.50

World Food Day - F.A.O. Issue

M88 (M73)	1981	2,000	—	—	Proof	50.00

M59 (M36)	1974	3,000	—	—	Proof	23.50

Castle in Ipplis Premariacco, Italy

M77 (M61)	1979	3,000	—	—	Proof	22.50

20th Anniversary of Grand Master

M93 (M79)	1982	2,000	—	—	Proof	50.00

Order of / MALTA 1219

KM#	Date	Mintage	Fine	VF	XF	Unc
M99 (M85)	1983	2,000	—	—	Proof	30.00

M105 1984 2,000 — — Proof 30.00
(M91)

M111 1985 2,000 — — Proof 30.00
(M97)

Grotto of Apparitions at Lourdes

KM#	Date	Mintage	Fine	VF	XF	Unc
M116 (M103)	1986	2,000	—	—	Proof	27.50

25th Anniversary of Grand Master
M121 1987 2,000 — — Proof 25.00
Obv: Shoulder length portrait of FRA. A. Mojana.
Rev: Similar to KM#M59.
M127 1988 2,000 — — Proof 25.00
FRA. Giancarlo Pallavicini (Interregnum)
Obv: Maltese Cross w/leg: SVB.HOC....
Rev: St. John the Baptist.
M133 1988 — — — Proof 25.00

FR. Andreas Bertie.
M139 1988 — — — Proof 25.00
M145 1989 — — — Proof 25.00

3 SCUDI

12.0000 g, .800 SILVER, .3086 oz ASW
F.A.O. Issue
M38 1968 .020 — — Proof 11.50

5 SCUDI

4.0000 g, .916 GOLD, .1179 oz AGW

KM#	Date	Mintage	Fine	VF	XF	Unc
M3 (M39)	1961	1,200	—	—	Proof	100.00

4.0000 g, .920 GOLD, .1183 oz AGW
Obv. leg: F. ANGELVS MOJANA.
M7 1962 200 pcs. — — Proof 325.00
(M40) 1963 600 pcs. — — Proof 120.00

4.0000 g, .900 GOLD, .1157 oz AGW
F. Angelvs Mojana
M11 1964 1,000 — — Proof 100.00
(M41)

M15 1965 1,000 — — Proof 100.00
(MA42) 1966 600 pcs. — — Proof 110.00

M21 1967 1,000 — — Proof 100.00
(M42)

M27 1968 1,000 — — Proof 100.00
(MA43)

M33.1 1969 1,000 — — Proof 100.00
(M43)

M33.2 1970 1,000 — — Proof 100.00

M44 1971 1,000 — — Proof 100.00
    1972 1,000 — — Proof 100.00
    1973 1,000 — — Proof 100.00
    1974 1,000 — — Proof 100.00
    1975 1,000 — — Proof 100.00

Order of / MALTA 1220

KM#	Date	Mintage	Fine	VF	XF	Unc
M66 (M54)	1976	1,000	—	—	Proof	100.00
	1977	1,000	—	—	Proof	100.00
	1978	1,000	—	—	Proof	100.00
M78 (M62)	1979	1,000	—	—	Proof	100.00
	1980	600 pcs.	—	—	Proof	135.00
	1981	1,000	—	—	Proof	140.00

20th Anniversary of Grand Master

KM#	Date	Mintage	Fine	VF	XF	Unc
M94 (M80)	1982	600 pcs.	—	—	Proof	150.00
M100 (M86)	1983	600 pcs.	—	—	Proof	125.00
M106 (M92)	1984	600 pcs.	—	—	Proof	125.00
	1985	600 pcs.	—	—	Proof	110.00
	1986	600 pcs.	—	—	Proof	110.00

25th Anniversary of Grand Master

KM#	Date	Mintage	Fine	VF	XF	Unc
M122	1987	600 pcs.	—	—	Proof	110.00

**Obv: Shoulder length portrait of FRA. Mojana left.
Rev: Similar to KM#M106.**

| M128 | 1988 | 600 pcs. | — | — | Proof | 110.00 |

**FRA. Giancarlo Pallavicini (Interregnum)
Obv: Maltese cross w/leg: SVB.HOC. . . .
Rev: St. John the Baptist.**

| M134 | 1988 | — | — | — | Proof | 110.00 |

FR. Andreas Bertie

| M140 | 1988 | — | — | — | Proof | 110.00 |
| M146 | 1989 | — | — | — | Proof | 110.00 |

10 SCUDI

8.0000 g, .916 GOLD, .2358 oz AGW

KM#	Date	Mintage	Fine	VF	XF	Unc
M4 (M45)	1961	1,200	—	—	Proof	170.00

**8.0000 g, .920 GOLD, .2366 oz AGW
Obv. leg: F. ANGELVS DE MOJANA. . . . .**

KM#	Date	Mintage	Fine	VF	XF	Unc
M8 (M46)	1962	200 pcs.	—	—	Proof	500.00
	1963	600 pcs.	—	—	Proof	200.00

8.0000 g, .900 GOLD, .2314 oz AGW

M12 (M47)	1964	1,000	—	—	Proof	170.00
M16 (MA48)	1965	1,000	—	—	Proof	170.00
	1966	600 pcs.	—	—	Proof	200.00
M22 (M48)	1967	1,000	—	—	Proof	170.00
M28 (MA49)	1968	1,000	—	—	Proof	170.00
M34 (M49)	1969	1,000	—	—	Proof	170.00
	1970	1,000	—	—	Proof	170.00

**Obv: Bust of Angelvs de Mojana left.
Rev: Lamb of God w/banner.**

M45 (M50)	1971	1,000	—	—	Proof	170.00
M52 (M51)	1972	1,000	—	—	Proof	170.00
	1974	1,000	—	—	Proof	170.00
M55 (MA52)	1973	1,000	—	—	Proof	170.00

**Obv: Similar to KM#M52. Rev: Coat of arms
superimposed on center of Maltese Cross.**

| M61 (M52) | 1975 | 1,000 | — | — | Proof | 170.00 |
| | 1976 | 1,000 | — | — | Proof | 170.00 |

**Obv: Bust of Angelvs de Mojana.
Rev: St. John baptizing Jesus.**

KM#	Date	Mintage	Fine	VF	XF	Unc
M69 (M59)	1977	1,000	—	—	Proof	170.00
	1978	1,000	—	—	Proof	170.00

Castle in Chignolo, Italy

| M79 (M63) | 1979 | 1,000 | — | — | Proof | 170.00 |
| M84 (M69) | 1980 | 600 pcs. | — | — | Proof | 275.00 |

World Food Day - F.A.O. Issue

| M89 (M75) | 1981 | 1,000 | — | — | Proof | 275.00 |

20th Anniversary of Grand Master

| M95 (M81) | 1982 | 600 pcs. | — | — | Proof | 285.00 |
| M101 (M87) | 1983 | — | — | — | Proof | 225.00 |

Altar of Chiesa di Santa Maria all Aventino

| M107 (M93) | 1984 | 600 pcs. | — | — | Proof | 225.00 |
| M112 (M99) | 1985 | 600 pcs. | — | — | Proof | 225.00 |

**Grotto of Apparitions at Lourdes
Obv: Similar to KM#M112. Rev: Maltese Cross.**

| M117 (M105) | 1986 | 600 pcs. | — | — | Proof | 225.00 |

25th Anniversary of Grand Master

| M123 | 1987 | 600 pcs. | — | — | Proof | 225.00 |

Obv: Shoulder length portrait of FRA. A. Mojana left.
Rev: Similar to KM#M112.

KM#	Date	Mintage	Fine	VF	XF	Unc
M129	1988	600 pcs.	—	—	—	Proof 225.00

FRA. Giancarlo Pallavicini (Interregnum)
Obv: Maltese cross w/leg: SVB.HOC....
Rev: St. John the Baptist.

| M135 | 1988 | — | — | — | — | Proof 225.00 |

FR. Andreas Bertie

| M141 | 1988 | — | — | — | — | Proof 225.00 |
| M147 | 1989 | — | — | — | — | Proof 225.00 |

SOVRANO

8.0500 g, .900 GOLD, .2329 oz AGW
FR. Angelvs de Mojana

| M39 (M106) | 1970 | .015 | — | — | — | Proof 150.00 |

MINT SETS (MS)

KM#	Date	Mintage	Identification	Issue Price	Mkt. Val.
MS1	1964(2)	4,000	MA9,M10	—	35.00

PROOF SETS (PS)

KM#	Date	Mintage	Identification	Issue Price	Mkt. Val.
PS1	1961(4)	1,200	KM-M1-M4	—	320.00
PS3	1962(4)	200	KM-M5-M8	—	1100.
PS4	1963(4)	600	KM-M5-M8	—	400.00
PS5	1963(2)	1,000	KM-M5,M6	—	800.00
PS6	1964(4)	1,000	KM-M9-M12	—	310.00
PS7	1965(4)	1,000	KM-M13-M16	—	400.00
PS8	1965(2)	4,000	KM-M13,M14	—	35.00
PS9	1966(4)	600	KM-M13-M16	—	350.00
PS10	1966(2)	4,000	KM-M13,M14	—	35.00
PS11	1967(4)	1,000	KM-M19-M22	62.50	300.00
PS12	1967(2)	2,000	KM-M19,M20	14.00	32.50
PS13	1967(2)	10,000	KM-M17,M18	3.50	15.00
PS14	1968(4)	1,000	KM-M24,M25,M27,M28	62.50	300.00
PS15	1968(2)	2,000	KM-M24,M25	14.00	32.50
PS16	1968(2)	20,000	KM-M23,M26	3.00	17.50
PS17	1969(4)	1,000	KM-M31,M34	75.00	300.00
PS18	1969(2)	2,000	KM-M31,M32	17.00	32.50
PS19	1969(2)	10,000	KM-M29,M30	3.00	15.00
PS20	1970(4)	1,000	KM-M33,M34,M37,M38	75.00	300.00
PS21	1970(2)	2,000	KM-M37,M38	17.00	32.50
PS22	1970(2)	3,000	KM-M35,M36	3.00	15.00
PS23	1971(6)	1,000	KM-M40-M45	78.00	320.00
PS24	1971(2)	2,000	KM-M42,M43	17.00	32.50
PS25	1971(2)	2,000	KM-M40,M41	3.00	15.00
PS26	1971(2)	5,000	KM-M46,M47	5.00	17.50
PS27	1972(4)	1,000	KM-M44,M50-M52	82.00	300.00
PS28	1972(2)	2,000	KM-M50,M51	18.00	32.50
PS29	1972(2)	3,000	KM-M49,M50	5.00	22.50
PS30	1973(6)	1,000	KM-M43,M44,M48,M53-M55	110.00	225.00
				110.00	225.00
PS31	1973(2)	2,000	KM-M43,M54	12.00	32.50
PS32	1973(2)	3,000	KM-M48,M53	6.00	15.00
PS33	1974(6)	1,000	KM-M44,M52,M56-M59	170.00	320.00
PS34	1974(2)	3,000	KM-M58,M59	33.00	35.00
PS35	1974(2)	2,000	KM-M56,M57	8.00	17.50
PS36	1975(4)	1,000	KM-M44,M58,M60,M61	170.00	310.00
PS37	1975(2)	2,000	KM-M58,M60	30.00	32.50
PS38	1975(2)	3,000	KM-M56,M57	8.00	17.50
PS39	1976(4)	1,000	KM-M61,M64-M66	180.00	310.00
PS40	1976(2)	2,000	KM-M64,M65	35.00	33.50
PS41	1976(2)	3,000	KM-M56,M57	10.00	17.50
PS42	1977(4)	1,000	KM-M66-M69	—	310.00
PS43	1977(2)	2,000	KM-M67,M68	—	30.00
PS44	1977(2)	3,000	KM-M56,M57	—	17.50
PS45	1978(4)	1,000	KM-M66,M69,M72,M73	—	310.00
PS46	1978(2)	2,000	KM-M72,M73	—	30.00
PS47	1978(2)	3,000	KM-M70,M71	—	17.50
PS48	1979(4)	1,000	KM-M76-M79	—	310.00
PS49	1979(2)	2,000	KM-M76,M77	—	35.00
PS50	1979(2)	3,000	KM-M74,M75	—	15.00
PS51	1980(4)	600	KM-M78,M82-M84	—	385.00
PS52	1980(2)	1,400	KM-M82,M83	—	40.00
PS53	1980(2)	3,000	KM-M80,M81	—	21.50
PS54	1981(4)	1,000	KM-M78,M87-M89	—	400.00
PS55	1981(2)	1,000	KM-M87,M88	—	80.00
PS56	1981(2)	3,000	KM-M85,M86	—	27.50
PS57	1982(2)	600	KM-M92-M95	—	525.00
PS58	1982(2)	1,400	KM-M92,M93	—	80.00
PS59	1982(2)	2,000	KM-M90,M91	—	22.50
PS60	1983(4)	600	KM-M98-M101	—	385.00
PS61	1983(2)	1,400	KM-M98,M99	—	60.00
PS62	1983(2)	2,000	KM-M96,M97	—	22.50
PS63	1984(4)	600	KM-M104-M107	—	375.00
PS64	1984(2)	1,400	KM-M104-M105	—	30.00
PS65	1984(2)	2,000	KM-M102,M103	—	22.50
PS66	1985(4)	600	KM-M106,M110-M112	—	325.00
PS67	1985(2)	2,000	KM-M110,M111	—	45.00
PS68	1985(2)	2,000	KM-M108,M109	—	22.50
PS69	1986(6)	600	KM-M106,M115-M117	200.00	325.00
PS70	1986(2)	2,000	KM-M115,M116	40.00	40.00
PS71	1986(2)	2,000	KM-M113,M114	18.00	22.50
PS72	1987(2)	600	KM-M122,M123	—	325.00
PS73	1987(2)	2,000	KM-M120,M121	—	37.50
PS74	1987(2)	2,000	KM-M118,M119	—	22.50
PS75	1988(2)	600	KM-M128,M129	—	310.00
PS76	1988(2)	2,000	KM-M126,M127	—	37.50
PS77	1988(2)	2,000	KM-M124,M125	—	20.00
PS78	1988(2)	—	KM-M134,M135	—	325.00
PS79	1988(2)	—	KM-M132,M133	—	37.50
PS80	1988(2)	—	KM-M130,M131	—	20.00
PS81	1988(2)	—	KM-M140,M141	—	325.00
PS82	1988(2)	—	KM-M138,M139	—	37.50
PS83	1988(2)	—	KM-M136,M137	—	20.00
PS84	1989(2)	—	KM-M146,M147	—	325.00
PS85	1989(2)	—	KM-M144,M145	—	37.50
PS86	1989(2)	—	KM-M142,M143	—	20.00

Listings For
MANCHUKUO: refer to China-Japanese Puppet States

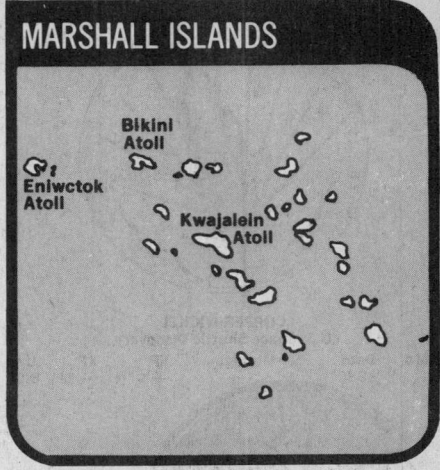

MARSHALL ISLANDS

The Republic of the Marshall Islands, an archipelago which is one of the four island groups that make up what is commonly known as Micronesia, consists of 33 coral atolls comprised of over 1,150 islands or islets. It is located east of the Caroline Islands and west north-west of the Gilbert Islands half way between Hawaii and Australia. The Ratak chain to the east and the Ralik chain to the west comprise a total land area of 70 sq. mi. with a population of 20,206 of which about 10 percent includes Americans who work at Kwajalein Missile Range. Majuro Atoll is the government and commercial center of the Republic.

Very little is known of the history of the islands before the 16th century. It is believed that many countries vessels visited the islands while searching for new trade routes to the East. In 1788, John Marshall, a British sea captain for whom the islands were named, explored them. The Marshalls have undergone successive domination by the Spanish, Germans, Japanese and Americans. It was the site of some of the fiercest fighting of the entire Pacific theater during World War II. At the conclusion of the war, the United States, under the direction of the United Nations administered the affairs of the Marshall Islands.

A constitutional government was formed on May 1, 1979 with Amata Kabua being elected as the head of the government. On October 1, 1986, the United States notified the United Nations that the Marshall Islands were to be recognized as a separate nation.

The monetary system is based on the U.S. dollar.

1/2 DOLLAR

15.5510 g, .999 SILVER, .5000 oz ASW
Independence and Bullion - Pandanus Fruit

KM#	Date	Mintage	VF	XF	Unc
1	1986	.010	—	Proof	16.50

DOLLAR

31.1030 g, .999 SILVER, 1.0000 oz ASW
Independence and Bullion - Triton Shell
Obv: Similar to 1/2 Dollar, KM#1.

| 2 | 1986 | .010 | — | Proof | 32.50 |

5 DOLLARS

MARSHALL ISLANDS

COPPER-NICKEL
U.S. Space Shuttle Discovery

KM#	Date	Mintage	VF	XF	Unc
6	1988	—	—	—	6.00

First Men on the Moon

| 13 | 1989 | — | — | — | 6.00 |

20 DOLLARS

3.1100 g, .999 GOLD, .1000 oz AGW
Independence and Bullion - Sun
Obv: Similar to 5 Dollars, KM#6.

| 3 | 1986 | *5,000 | — | Proof | 90.00 |

50 DOLLARS

7.7750 g, .999 GOLD, .2500 oz AGW
Independence and Bullion - Coconut
Obv: Similar to 5 Dollars, KM#6.

| 4 | 1986 | *5,000 | — | Proof | 210.00 |

31.1000 g, .999 SILVER, 1.0000 oz ASW
U.S. Space Shuttle Discovery
Similar to 5 Dollars, KM#6.

| 12 | 1988 | *.050 | — | Proof | 55.00 |

John Glenn in Space Orbit
Obv: Similar to 5 Dollars, KM#6.

| 7 | 1989 | *.025 | — | Proof | 55.00 |

Neil Armstrong on the Moon
Obv: Similar to 5 Dollars, KM#6.

KM#	Date	Mintage	VF	XF	Unc
8	1989	*.025	—	Proof	55.00

Amierican Space Station - Skylab
Obv: Similar to 5 Dollars, KM#6.

| 9 | 1989 | *.025 | — | Proof | 55.00 |

Apollo - Sojus Joint Mission
Obv: Similar to 5 Dollars, KM#6.

| 10 | 1989 | *.025 | — | Proof | 55.00 |

First Space Shuttle Flight
Obv: Similar to 5 Dollars, KM#6.

| 11 | 1989 | *.025 | — | Proof | 55.00 |

200 DOLLARS

31.1030 g, .999 GOLD, 1.0000 oz AGW
Independence and Bullion - Stick Chart
Obv: Similar to 5 Dollars, KM#6.

| 5 | 1986 | *5,000 | — | Proof | 825.00 |

PROOF SETS (PS)

KM#	Date	Mintage	Identification	Mkt.Val.
PS1	1986(3)	—	KM3-5	1125.
PS2	1986(2)	—	KM1-2	50.00

MARTINIQUE

The French Overseas Department of Martinique, located in the Lesser Antilles of the West Indies between Dominica and Saint Lucia, has an area of 425 sq. mi. (1,101 sq. km.) and a population of *329,000. Capital: Fort-de-France. Agriculture and tourism are the major sources of income. Bananas, sugar, and rum are exported.

Christopher Columbus discovered Martinique, probably on June 15, 1502. France took possession on June 25, 1635, and has maintained possession since that time except for three short periods of British occupation during the Napoleonic Wars. A French department since 1946, Martinique voted a reaffirmation of that status in 1958, remaining within the new French Community. Martinique was the birthplace of Napoleon's Empress Josephine, and the site of the eruption of Mt. Pelee in 1902 that claimed 40,000 lives.

The official currency of Martinique is the French franc. The 1897-1922 coinage of the Colony of Martinique is now obsolete.

RULERS
British, 1793-1801
French, 1802-1809

MONETARY SYSTEM
15 Sols = 1 Escalin
20 Sols = 1 Livre
66 Livres = 4 Escudos = 6400 Reis

French Occupation
1802-1809

MONETARY SYSTEM
6400 Reis = 22 Livres

20 LIVRES

GOLD
c/m: 20 over eagle on lightweight Brazil 6400 Reis.

KM#	Date	Mintage	VG	Fine	VF	XF
32	ND(1805)	—	1100.	1350.	1650.	2500.

22 LIVRES

GOLD
c/m: 22 over eagle on Brazil 6400 Reis, C#75.

| 35 | (1789-1805) | — | 800.00 | 1200. | 1400. | 2250. |

c/m: 22 over eagle on Portugal 4 Escudos, C#16.
| 36 | | | | | | |

NOTE: There are many merchant c/m from Martinique during this period, but the above are probably the only official issues. There are also many counterfeits or fantasies attributed to the West Indies.

MONETARY REFORM
100 Centimes = 1 Franc

50 CENTIMES

COPPER-NICKEL

KM#	Date	Mintage	VG	Fine	VF	XF
40	1897	.600	5.00	10.00	25.00	50.00
	1922	.500	5.00	10.00	20.00	40.00

FRANC

COPPER-NICKEL

41	1897	.300	7.50	15.00	35.00	70.00
	1922	.350	7.50	15.00	30.00	60.00

MAURITANIA

The Islamic Republic of Mauritania, located in northwest Africa bounded by Spanish Sahara, Mali, Algeria, Senegal and the Atlantic Ocean, has an area of 397,955 sq. mi. (1,030,700 sq. km.) and a population of *1.8 million. Capital: Nouakchott. The economy centers about herding, agriculture, fishing and mining. Iron ore, copper concentrates and fish products are exported.

The indigenous Negroid inhabitants were driven out of Mauritania by Berber invaders of the Islamic faith in the 11th century. The Berbers in turn were conquered by Arab invaders, the Beni Hassan, in the 16th century. Arab traders carried on a gainful trade in gum arabic, gold and slaves with Portuguese, Dutch, English and French traders until late in the 19th century when France took control of the area and made it a part of French West Africa, in 1920. Mauritania became a part of the French Union in 1946 and was made an autonomous republic within the new French Community in 1958, when the Islamic Republic of Mauritania was proclaimed. The republic became independent on November 28, 1960, and withdrew from the French Community in 1966.

On June 28, 1973, in a move designed to emphasize its non-alignment with France, Mauritania converted its currency from the old French-supported C.F.A. franc unit to a new unit called the Ouguiya.

MONETARY SYSTEM
5 Khoum = 1 Ouguiya
100 Ouguiya = 500 CFA Francs

1/5 OUGUIYA
(Khoum)

ALUMINUM

KM#	Date	Year	Mintage	VF	XF	Unc
1	AH1393	1973	1,000	6.00	8.00	12.00
	1394	1974	—	6.00	8.00	12.00

OUGUIYA

COPPER-NICKEL-ALUMINUM
Rev: Arabic leg. in one line.

2	AH1393	1973	—	6.50	12.50	20.00

Rev: Arabic leg. in two lines.

6	AH1394	1974	—	6.50	11.50	20.00
	1401	1981	—	5.50	11.00	15.00
	1403	1983	—	4.00	6.50	12.00
	1406	1986	—	2.50	5.00	8.00

5 OUGUIYA

COPPER-NICKEL-ALUMINUM

3	AH1393	1973	—	7.50	11.00	15.00
	1394	1974	—	7.50	11.50	20.00
	1401	1981	—	5.00	7.50	13.50
	1404	1984	—	5.00	7.50	13.50
	1407	1987	—	3.00	6.00	10.00

10 OUGUIYA

COPPER-NICKEL

KM#	Date	Year	Mintage	VF	XF	Unc
4	AH1393	1973	—	7.50	11.00	20.00
	1394	1974	—	7.50	11.50	25.00
	1401	1981	—	5.00	7.50	15.00
	1403	1983	—	5.00	7.50	15.00
	1407	1987	—	3.00	6.00	10.00

20 OUGUIYA

COPPER-NICKEL

5	AH1393	1973	—	7.50	11.00	20.00
	1394	1974	—	7.50	11.50	25.00
	1403	1983	—	6.00	8.50	15.00

500 OUGUIYA

26.0800 g, .920 GOLD, .7714 oz AGW
15th Anniversary of Independence

7	1975(a)	1,800	—	—	—	550.00

COPPER-NICKEL
International Athletics - Runners

8	1984	—	—	Proof	25.00

International Athletics - Fencing

9	1984	—	—	Proof	25.00

MINT SETS (MS)

KM#	Date	Mintage	Identification	Issue Price	Mkt. Val.
MS1	1973(10)	—	KM1-5, two each	20.00	175.00

MAURITIUS

The island of Mauritius, a member nation of the British Commonwealth located in the Indian Ocean 500 miles (805 km.) east of Madagascar, has an area of 790 sq. mi. (2,045 sq. km.) and a population of *1 million. Capital: Port Louis. Sugar provides 90 percent of the export revenue.

Cartographic evidence indicates that Arabs and Malays arrived at Mauritius during the Middle Ages. Domingo Fernandez, a Portuguese navigator, visited the island in the early 16th century, but Portugal made no attempt at settlement. The Dutch took possession, and named the island, in 1598. Their colony failed to prosper and was abandoned in 1710. France claimed Mauritius in 1715 and developed a strong and prosperous colony that endured until the island was captured by the British, 1810, during the Napoleonic Wars. British possession was confirmed by the Treaty of Paris, 1814. Mauritius became independent on March 12, 1968. It is a member of the Commonwealth of Nations. The Queen of England is Chief of State.

The first coins struck under British auspices for Mauritius were undated (1822) and bore French legends.

RULERS

British

MINT MARKS

H - Heaton, Birmingham
SA - Pretoria Mint

MONETARY SYSTEM

20 Sols (Sous) = 1 Livre
100 Cents = 1 Rupee

25 SOUS

.500 SILVER

KM#	Date	Mintage	VG	Fine	VF	XF
1	ND(1822)	—	15.00	25.00	40.00	100.00
	ND(1822)	—	—	—	Proof	400.00

50 SOUS

.500 SILVER

KM#	Date	Mintage	VG	Fine	VF	XF
2	ND(1822)	—	20.00	30.00	55.00	125.00
	ND(1822)	—	—	—	Proof	500.00

ANCHOR COINAGE

(1/16, 1/8, 1/4 & 1/2 Dollar)

NOTE: Coins dated 1820 were struck for Mauritius and colonies of the British West Indies. These circulated in Mauritius until 1826 when they were shipped to the British West Indies where they will be found listed.

REGULAR COINAGE

100 Cents = 1 Rupee

CENT

BRONZE

KM#	Date	Mintage	Fine	VF	XF	Unc
7	1877	—	—	—	Proof	175.00
	1877H	.700	2.00	4.00	25.00	80.00
	1877H	—	—	—	Proof	175.00
	1878	.250	2.00	10.00	50.00	120.00
	1878	—	—	—	Proof	175.00
	1882H	.300	1.50	5.00	30.00	75.00
7	1883	.500	1.25	2.50	20.00	60.00
	1883	—	—	—	Proof	175.00
	1884	.500	1.25	2.50	20.00	60.00
	1884	—	—	—	Proof	175.00
	1888	.500	1.25	2.50	20.00	60.00
	1890H	.500	1.25	2.50	20.00	60.00
	1896	.500	1.25	2.50	20.00	60.00
	1897	1.000	1.00	2.00	12.00	40.00
	1897	—	—	—	Proof	175.00

KM#	Date	Mintage	Fine	VF	XF	Unc
12	1911	1.000	.75	1.50	12.00	40.00
	1912	.500	1.25	2.50	20.00	60.00
	1917	.500	.75	1.50	12.00	35.00
	1920	.500	1.50	3.00	25.00	60.00
	1921	.500	3.00	5.00	35.00	70.00
	1922	1.800	.50	1.00	8.00	25.00
	1923	.200	3.00	5.00	30.00	55.00
	1924	.200	3.00	5.00	30.00	55.00

KM#	Date	Mintage	Fine	VF	XF	Unc
21	1943SA	.520	.50	1.25	4.00	10.00
	1944SA	.500	.50	1.25	4.00	10.00
	1945SA	.500	.50	1.25	4.00	10.00
	1946SA	.500	.50	1.25	4.00	10.00
	1947SA	.500	.50	1.25	4.00	10.00

KM#	Date	Mintage	Fine	VF	XF	Unc
25	1949	.500	.75	1.25	2.50	7.50
	1949	—	—	—	Proof	100.00
	1952	.500	.75	1.25	2.50	7.50
	1952	—	—	—	Proof	100.00

KM#	Date	Mintage	Fine	VF	XF	Unc
31	1953	.500	.10	.25	.50	2.00
	1953	—	—	—	Proof	75.00
	1955	.501	.10	.25	.50	3.00
	1955	—	—	—	Proof	75.00
	1956	.500	.10	.20	.50	3.00
	1956	—	—	—	Proof	75.00
	1957	.501	.10	.20	.50	4.00
	1959	.501	.10	.20	.50	4.00
	1959	—	—	—	Proof	75.00
	1960	.500	.10	.20	.50	4.00
	1960	—	—	—	Proof	75.00
	1961	.500	.10	.20	.50	4.00
	1961	—	—	—	Proof	75.00
	1962	.500	.10	.20	.50	2.00
	1962	—	—	—	Proof	75.00
	1963	.500	.10	.20	.50	2.00
	1963	—	—	—	Proof	50.00
	1964	1.500	—	.10	.20	.50
	1964	—	—	—	Proof	50.00
	1965	1.500	—	.10	.20	.50
	1969	.500	—	.10	.15	.30
	1970	1.500	—	—	.10	.20
	1971	1.000	—	—	.10	.20
	1971	750 pcs.	—	—	Proof	25.00
	1975	.400	—	—	.10	.20
	1978	9.268	—	—	Proof	1.00

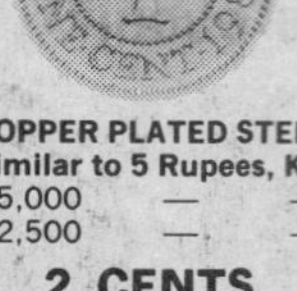

COPPER PLATED STEEL
Obv: Similar to 5 Rupees, KM#56.

KM#	Date	Mintage	Fine	VF	XF	Unc
51	1987	*5,000	—	—	—	.15
	1987	*2,500	—	—	Proof	1.00

2 CENTS

BRONZE

KM#	Date	Mintage	Fine	VF	XF	Unc
8	1877	—	—	—	Proof	200.00
	1877H	.350	1.00	6.50	27.50	100.00
	1877H	—	—	—	Proof	200.00
	1878	.130	2.50	12.00	60.00	140.00
	1878	—	—	—	Proof	200.00
	1882H	.150	2.00	8.00	30.00	125.00
	1883	.250	1.00	6.50	27.50	100.00
	1884	.250	1.00	6.50	27.50	100.00
	1884	—	—	—	Proof	200.00
	1888	.250	.75	4.00	20.00	50.00
	1888	—	—	—	Proof	250.00
	1890H	.250	1.00	5.00	25.00	75.00
	1896	.188	1.00	6.50	27.50	100.00
	1897	1.000	.75	4.00	20.00	50.00
	1897	—	—	—	Proof	200.00

KM#	Date	Mintage	Fine	VF	XF	Unc
13	1911	.500	2.00	4.00	15.00	45.00
	1911	—	—	—	Proof	300.00
	1912	.250	3.00	5.00	30.00	70.00
	1917	.250	1.25	2.50	12.00	40.00
	1920	.250	1.50	3.00	20.00	50.00
	1921	.250	1.50	3.00	20.00	50.00
	1922	.900	.50	1.00	8.00	30.00
	1923	.400	1.25	2.50	20.00	50.00
	1924	.400	1.25	2.50	20.00	50.00

KM#	Date	Mintage	Fine	VF	XF	Unc
22	1943SA	.290	.75	2.00	4.00	10.00
	1944SA	.500	.75	2.00	4.00	10.00
	1945SA	.250	.75	2.00	4.00	10.00
	1946SA	.400	.75	2.00	4.00	10.00
	1947SA	.250	.75	2.00	4.00	10.00

KM#	Date	Mintage	Fine	VF	XF	Unc
26	1949	.250	.75	1.25	2.50	7.50
	1949	—	—	—	Proof	150.00
	1952	.250	.75	1.25	2.50	7.50
	1952	—	—	—	Proof	150.00

KM#	Date	Mintage	Fine	VF	XF	Unc
32	1953	.250	.10	.25	.50	3.00
	1953	—	—	—	Proof	100.00
	1954	—	—	—	Proof	300.00
	1955	.501	.10	.25	.50	3.00
	1955	—	—	—	Proof	100.00
	1956	.250	.10	.25	.50	4.00
	1956	—	—	—	Proof	100.00
	1957	.501	.10	.25	.50	4.00
	1959	.503	.10	.25	.50	4.00
	1959	—	—	—	Proof	100.00
	1960	.250	.10	.25	.50	4.00
	1960	—	—	—	Proof	100.00
	1961	.500	.10	.25	.50	4.00
	1961	—	—	—	Proof	100.00
	1962	.500	.10	.25	.50	2.00
	1962	—	—	—	Proof	100.00
	1963	.500	.10	.25	.50	2.00
	1963	—	—	—	Proof	100.00
	1964	1.00	—	.10	.25	.50
	1964	—	—	—	Proof	100.00
	1965	.750	.10	.20	.40	.60
	1966	.500	.10	.20	.40	.50
	1967	.250	.10	.20	.40	.50
	1969	.500	.10	.20	.40	.50
	1971	1.000	—	.10	.20	.50
	1971	750 pcs.	—	—	Proof	25.00
	1975	5.200	—	—	.10	.35
	1978	9.268	—	—	Proof	1.50

5 CENTS

BRONZE

KM#	Date	Mintage	Fine	VF	XF	Unc
9	1877	—	—	—	Proof	350.00
	1877H	3.00	3.00	12.00	65.00	200.00
	1877H	—	—	—	Proof	250.00
	1878	.050	6.00	20.00	90.00	300.00
	1878	—	—	—	Proof	200.00
	1882H	.060	5.00	15.00	80.00	150.00
	1883	.100	3.00	12.00	65.00	150.00
	1884	.100	3.00	12.00	65.00	200.00
	1884	—	—	—	Proof	250.00
	1888	.100	1.00	7.50	40.00	90.00
	1890H	.100	2.00	12.00	70.00	180.00
	1897	.600	1.00	7.50	50.00	120.00
	1897	—	—	—	Proof	250.00

KM#	Date	Mintage	Fine	VF	XF	Unc
14	1917	.600	2.00	4.50	27.50	80.00
	1920	.200	2.00	4.50	32.50	100.00
	1921	.100	3.00	6.50	35.00	120.00
	1922	.360	2.00	4.50	32.50	100.00
	1923	.400	3.00	6.50	35.00	120.00
	1924	.400	2.00	4.50	32.50	100.00

KM#	Date	Mintage	Fine	VF	XF	Unc
20	1942SA	.940	1.25	2.50	6.50	15.00
	1944SA	1.000	1.00	1.75	4.00	10.00
	1945SA	.500	1.00	1.75	4.00	12.00

KM#	Date	Mintage	Fine	VF	XF	Unc
34	1956	.201	.25	.50	.75	5.00
	1956	—	—	—	Proof	125.00
	1957	.203	.25	.50	2.00	8.00
	1957	—	—	—	Proof	125.00
	1959	.801	.25	.50	1.00	4.00
	1959	—	—	—	Proof	125.00
	1960	.400	.25	.50	1.00	4.00
	1960	—	—	—	Proof	125.00
	1963	.200	.25	.50	1.00	2.00
	1963	—	—	—	Proof	125.00
	1964	.600	.25	.50	1.00	2.00
	1964	—	—	—	Proof	125.00
	1965	.200	.25	.50	.75	2.00
	1966	.200	.25	.50	.75	1.50
	1967	.200	.25	.50	.75	2.00
	1969	.500	.10	.15	.25	.50
	1970	.800	.10	.15	.25	.50
	1971	.500	.10	.15	.25	.50
	1971	750 pcs.	—	—	Proof	25.00
	1975	3.700	.10	.15	.25	.50
	1978	8.000	—	.10	.20	.50
	1978	9,268	—	—	Proof	2.00

COPPER PLATED STEEL

Obv: Similar to 5 Rupees, KM#56.

KM#	Date	Mintage	Fine	VF	XF	Unc
52	1987	*5,000	—	—	—	.30
	1987	*2,500	—	—	Proof	2.00

10 CENTS

1.4100 g, .800 SILVER, .0362 oz ASW

KM#	Date	Mintage	Fine	VF	XF	Unc
10	1877	—	—	—	Proof	300.00
	1877H	.250	1.25	6.50	27.50	100.00
	1877H	—	—	—	Proof	275.00
	1878	.050	3.00	12.00	40.00	160.00
	1878	—	—	—	Proof	250.00
	1882H	.030	15.00	35.00	150.00	250.00
	1883	.100	3.00	12.00	45.00	200.00
	1883	—	—	—	Proof	250.00
	1886	.750	1.25	6.50	27.50	100.00
	1886	—	—	—	Proof	250.00
	1889H	.500	1.50	7.50	30.00	125.00
	1889	—	—	—	Proof	250.00
	1897	.500	1.50	7.50	25.00	60.00
	1897	—	—	—	Proof	250.00

COPPER-NICKEL

KM#	Date	Mintage	Fine	VF	XF	Unc
24	1947	.500	.75	1.50	8.00	35.00
	1947	—	—	—	Proof	200.00

KM#	Date	Mintage	Fine	VF	XF	Unc
30	1952	.250	.50	.75	1.50	6.50
	1952	—	—	—	Proof	175.00

KM#	Date	Mintage	Fine	VF	XF	Unc
33	1954	.252	.20	.35	.75	3.00
	1954	—	—	—	Proof	250.00
	1957	.250	.20	.35	.75	3.00
	1959	.253	.20	.35	.75	3.00
	1959	—	—	—	Proof	175.00
	1960	.050	.20	.35	.75	2.50
	1960	—	—	—	Proof	175.00
	1963	.200	.15	.30	.60	2.00
	1963	—	—	—	Proof	175.00
	1964	.200	.15	.30	.60	1.00
	1965	.200	.15	.30	.60	1.00
	1966	.200	.10	.25	.50	.75
	1969	.200	.10	.25	.50	.75
	1970	.500	.10	.25	.50	.75
	1971	.300	.10	.25	.50	.75
	1971	750 pcs.	—	—	Proof	25.00
	1975	6.675	.10	.25	.50	.75
	1978	13.000	.10	.25	.50	.75
	1978	9,268	—	—	Proof	2.50

20 CENTS

2.8300 g, .800 SILVER, .0727 oz ASW

KM#	Date	Mintage	Fine	VF	XF	Unc
11	1877	—	—	—	Proof	500.00
	1877H	.375	5.00	20.00	75.00	200.00
	1877H	—	—	—	Proof	300.00
	1878	.050	8.00	27.50	140.00	350.00
	1878	—	—	—	Proof	300.00
	1882H	.015	15.00	40.00	200.00	400.00
	1883	.100	6.00	22.50	100.00	275.00
	1883	—	—	—	Proof	300.00
	1886	.750	4.00	16.00	45.00	125.00
	1886	—	—	—	Proof	300.00
	1889H	.250	5.00	20.00	60.00	180.00
	1899	.500	4.00	16.00	55.00	150.00
	1899	—	—	—	Proof	300.00

NICKEL PLATED STEEL

Obv: Similar to 5 Rupees, KM#56.

KM#	Date	Mintage	Fine	VF	XF	Unc
53	1987	*5,000	—	—	—	.50
	1987	*2,500	—	—	Proof	3.00

1/4 RUPEE

2.8300 g, .916 SILVER, .0833 oz ASW

KM#	Date	Mintage	Fine	VF	XF	Unc
15	1934	.400	2.00	9.00	20.00	60.00
	1934	—	—	—	Proof	250.00
	1935	.400	2.00	9.00	20.00	60.00
	1935	—	—	—	Proof	250.00
	1936	.400	2.00	9.00	18.00	50.00
	1936	—	—	—	Proof	250.00

KM#	Date	Mintage	Fine	VF	XF	Unc
18	1938	2.000	3.00	10.00	30.00	80.00
	1938	—	—	—	Proof	200.00

2.8300 g, .500 SILVER, .0454 oz ASW

KM#	Date	Mintage	Fine	VF	XF	Unc
18a	1946	2.000	4.00	15.00	35.00	100.00
	1946	—	—	—	Proof	200.00

COPPER-NICKEL

KM#	Date	Mintage	Fine	VF	XF	Unc
27	1950	2.000	.50	1.00	2.00	9.50
	1950	—	—	—	Proof	200.00
	1951	1.000	.50	1.00	2.00	9.50
	1951	—	—	—	Proof	200.00

KM#	Date	Mintage	Fine	VF	XF	Unc
36	1960	1.000	.35	.75	1.00	2.50
	1960	—	—	—	Proof	250.00
	1964	.400	.25	.50	.75	1.75
	1964	—	—	—	Proof	200.00
	1965	.400	.25	.50	.75	1.50
	1970	.400	.20	.35	.60	1.25
	1971	.540	.25	.50	.75	1.50
	1971	750 pcs.	—	—	Proof	25.00
	1975	8.940	.15	.30	.60	1.00
	1978	*8.800	.15	.30	.60	1.00
	1978	9,268	—	—	Proof	3.50

***NOTE:** Variety exists with lower hole in 8 filled.

1/2 RUPEE

5.6600 g, .916 SILVER, .1667 oz ASW

KM#	Date	Mintage	Fine	VF	XF	Unc
16	1934	1.000	2.50	5.00	15.00	50.00
	1934	—	—	—	Proof	350.00

5.6600 g, .500 SILVER, .0909 oz ASW

KM#	Date	Mintage	Fine	VF	XF	Unc
23	1946	1.000	10.00	25.00	125.00	200.00
	1946	—	—	—	Proof	300.00

MAURITIUS 1226

COPPER-NICKEL

KM#	Date	Mintage	Fine	VF	XF	Unc
28	1950	1.000	.50	1.00	1.75	9.50
	1950	—	—	—	Proof	200.00
	1951	.570	.75	1.25	2.00	9.50
	1951	—	—	—	Proof	200.00

37.1	1965	.200	.50	1.00	2.00	6.00
	1971	.400	.25	.50	1.25	2.50
	1971	750 pcs.	—	—	Proof	30.00
	1975	4.160	.25	.50	.75	1.50
	1978	.400	.35	.60	.85	1.50
	1978	9.268	—	—	Proof	4.00

Error. W/o security edge.
| 37.2 | 1971 | Inc. Ab. | — | — | — | — |

NICKEL PLATED STEEL
Obv: Similar to 5 Rupees, KM#56.
54	1987	*5,000	—	—	—	2.00
	1987	*2,500	—	—	Proof	5.00

RUPEE

11.3100 g, .916 SILVER, .3331 oz ASW
17	1934	1.500	5.00	7.50	20.00	50.00
	1934	—	—	—	Proof	350.00

19	1938	.200	6.00	10.00	30.00	90.00
	1938	—	—	—	Proof	350.00

COPPER-NICKEL
29.1	1950	1.500	.75	1.50	3.00	16.00
	1950	—	—	—	Proof	200.00
	1951	1.000	.50	1.25	2.00	12.00
	1951	—	—	—	Proof	200.00

Error. W/o security edge.
| 29.2 | 1951 | Inc. Ab. | — | — | — | — |

KM#	Date	Mintage	Fine	VF	XF	Unc
35.1	1956	1.000	.25	.75	1.50	6.50
	1956	—	—	—	Proof	250.00
	1964	.200	.50	1.00	3.00	5.00
	1971	.600	.25	.60	1.00	2.00
	1971	750 pcs.	—	—	Proof	50.00
	1975	4.525	.25	.60	1.00	2.00
	1978	2.000	.25	.60	1.00	2.00
	1978	9.268	—	—	—	5.00

Error. W/o security edge.
| 35.2 | 1971 | Inc. Ab. | .25 | .75 | 1.25 | 2.50 |

Obv: Similar to 5 Rupees, KM#56.
55	1987	*5,000	—	—	—	3.00
	1987	*2,500	—	—	Proof	10.00

5 RUPEES

COPPER-NICKEL
56	1987	*5,000	—	—	—	11.00
	1987	*2,500	—	—	Proof	16.00

10 RUPEES

COPPER-NICKEL
Independence Commemorative
38	1971	.050	—	1.00	2.00	4.00

20.0000 g, .925 SILVER, .5948 oz ASW
| 38a | 1971 | 750 pcs. | — | — | Proof | 250.00 |

COPPER-NICKEL
Wedding of Prince Charles and Lady Diana
KM#	Date	Mintage	Fine	VF	XF	Unc
46	1981	—	—	1.00	1.50	2.50

28.2800 g, .925 SILVER, .8411 oz ASW
| 46a | 1981 | 2,090 | — | — | Proof | 30.00 |

World Food Day
Obv: Similar to KM#46.
48	1981	.010	—	—	—	15.00
	1981	5,000	—	—	Proof	20.00

25 RUPEES

25.4000 g, .500 SILVER, .4083 oz ASW
Conservation Series
Rev: Blue swallowtail.
KM#	Date	Mintage	VF	XF	Unc
40	1975	—	—	—	22.50

28.2800 g, .925 SILVER, .8411 oz ASW
| 40a | 1975(error) | 12 pcs. | — | — | — |
| | 1975 | 9,869 | — | Proof | 27.50 |

28.4000 g, .500 SILVER, .4565 oz ASW
Queen's Silver Jubilee
| 43 | 1977 | — | — | — | 10.00 |

MAURITIUS & REUNION

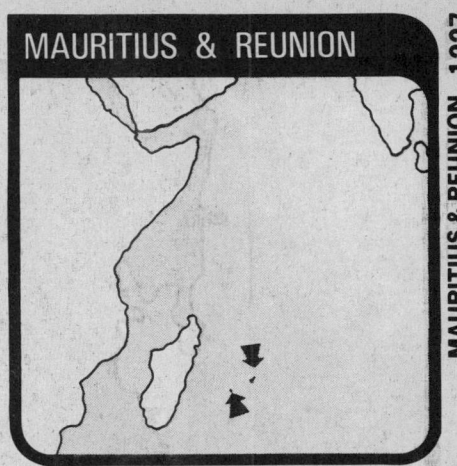

Mauritius and Reunion (Isles de France et de Bourbon), located in the Indian Ocean about 500 miles east of Madagascar, were at one time administered by France as a single colony. Ownership of Mauritius passed to Great Britain in 1810-14. Isle de Bourbon, renamed Reunion in 1793, remained a French possession and is now an overseas department.

RULERS
French until 1810

MONETARY SYSTEM
20 Sols (Sous) = 1 Livre

ISLE DE FRANCE ET BONAPARTE

Reunion became the official name in 1792 but after the French Revolution and the beginning of the Napoleonic era the name was changed to Isle de Bonaparte (1801-1814).

DIX (10) LIVRES

SILVER

KM#	Date	Mintage	VG	Fine	VF	XF
1	1810	—	200.00	300.00	425.00	650.00

NOTE: This coin was weakly struck on the obverse and reverse centers. Well struck examples command a premium.

28.2800 g, .925 SILVER, .8411 oz ASW

KM#	Date	Mintage	VF	XF	Unc
43a	1977	.047	—	Proof	15.00

10th Anniversary of Independence
Obv: Similar to 1000 Rupees, Y#39.

44	1978	.020	—	—	15.00
	1978	5,100	—	Proof	25.00

International Year of Disabled Persons

49	1982	.011	—	—	17.50
	1982	.010	—	Proof	20.00

50 RUPEES

32.1500 g, .500 SILVER, .5168 oz ASW
Conservation Series
Rev: Mauritius Kestrel.

41	1975	—	—	—	25.00

35.0000 g, .925 SILVER, 1.0409 oz ASW

41a	1975	12 pcs.	—	—	—
	1975	9,513	—	Proof	35.00

200 RUPEES

15.5600 g, .917 GOLD, .4587 oz AGW
Independence Commemorative

KM#	Date	Mintage	VF	XF	Unc
39	1971	2,500	—	—	300.00
	1971	750 pcs.	—	Proof	400.00

1000 RUPEES

33.4370 g, .900 GOLD, .9676 oz AGW
Conservation Series
Rev: Mauritius Flycatcher.

42	1975	1,966	—	—	600.00
	1975	716 pcs.	—	Proof	850.00

15.9800 g, .917 GOLD, .4711 oz AGW
10th Anniversary of Independence

45	1978	1,000	—	—	300.00
	1978	1,016	—	Proof	350.00

Wedding of Prince Charles and Lady Diana

47	1981	28 pcs.	—	—	500.00
	1981	22 pcs.	—	Proof	750.00

International Year of Disabled Persons
Obv: Queen Elizabeth II. Rev: IYDP logo, map.

50	1982	45 pcs.	—	—	750.00
	1982	48 pcs.	—	Proof	1000.

MINT SETS (MS)

KM#	Date	Mintage	Identification	Issue Price	Mkt. Val.
MS1	1987(6)	*5,000	KM51-56	16.95	37.50

PROOF SETS (PS)

PS1	1971(9)	750	KM31-37,38a,39	200.00	850.00
PS2	1972(2)	30,000	KM40a-41a	50.00	62.50
PS3	1978(7)	9,268	KM31-37	22.00	20.00
PS4	1987(6)	*2,500	KM51-56	36.95	17.50

MINTS OF MEXICO

Locations of the various mints where coins were produced in Mexico.

Casas De Moneda De Mexico
Colocaciones de las varias casas de moneda donde las monedas producida en mexico.

MEXICO

The United Mexican States, located immediately south of the United States has an area of 764,000 sq. mi. (1,978,750 sq. km.) and a population of *88.1 million. Capital: Mexico City. The economy is based on agriculture, manufacturing and mining. Oil, cotton, silver, coffee, and shrimp are exported.

Mexico was the site of highly advanced Indian civilizations. 1,500 years before conquistador Hernando Cortes conquered the wealthy Aztec empire of Montezuma, 1519-21, and founded a Spanish colony which lasted for nearly 300 years. During the Spanish period, Mexico, then called New Spain, stretched from Guatemala to the present states of Wyoming and California, its present northern boundary having been established by the secession of Texas (1836) and the 1846-48 war with the United States.

Independence from Spain was declared by Father Miguel Hidalgo on Sept. 16, 1810, (Mexican Independence Day) and was achieved by General Agustin de Iturbide in 1821. Iturbide became emperor in 1822 but was deposed when a republic was established a year later. For more than half a century following the birth of the republic, the political scene of Mexico was characterized by turmoil which saw two emperors (including the unfortunate Maximilian), several dictators and an average of one new government every nine months passing swiftly from obscurity to oblivion. The land, social, economic and labor reforms promulgated by the Reform Constitution of 1917 established the basis for sustained economic development and participative democracy that have made Mexico one of the most politically stable countries of modern Latin America.

COLONIAL MILLED COINAGE

RULERS

Charles IV, 1788-1808
Ferdinand VII, 1808-1821

MINT MARKS

Mo, MX - Mexico City Mint

ASSAYER'S INITIALS

Letter	Date	Name
F	1777-1803	Francisco Arance Cobos
M	1784-1801	Mariano Rodriguez
T	1801-1810	Tomas Butron Miranda
H	1803-1814	Henrique Buenaventura Azorin
J	1809-1833	Joaquin Davila Madrid
J	1812-1833	Jose Garcia Ansaldo

MONETARY SYSTEM

16 Pilones = 1 Real
8 Tlaco = 1 Real
16 Reales = 1 Escudo

1/8 (PILON)

(1/16 Real)

COPPER
Obv: Crowned F VII monogram.
Rev: Castles and lions in wreath.

KM#	Date	VG	Fine	VF	XF
59	1814	8.00	15.00	30.00	100.00
	1815	8.00	15.00	30.00	100.00

1/4 (TLACO)

(1/8 Real)

COPPER
Obv. leg: FERDIN. VII. . around crowned F.VII.

KM#	Date	VG	Fine	VF	XF
63	1814	10.00	20.00	40.00	125.00
	1815	10.00	20.00	40.00	125.00
	1816	10.00	20.00	40.00	125.00

2/4 (2 TLACO)

(1/4 Real)

COPPER
Obv. leg: FERDIN. VII. . around crowned F.VII.

KM#	Date	VG	Fine	VF	XF
64	1814	6.00	12.00	25.00	100.00
	1815/4	8.00	15.00	35.00	125.00
	1815	6.00	12.00	25.00	100.00
	1816	6.00	12.00	25.00	100.00
	1821	15.00	30.00	50.00	175.00

1/4 REAL

.8450 g, .903 SILVER, .0245 oz ASW
Obv: Castle. Rev: Lion.

KM#	Date	VG	Fine	VF	XF
62	1801	10.00	15.00	27.50	60.00
	1802	12.50	20.00	27.50	60.00
	1803	12.50	20.00	27.50	60.00
	1804	10.00	20.00	27.50	70.00
	1805/4	12.50	22.50	40.00	65.00
	1805	10.00	20.00	35.00	60.00
	1806	10.00	20.00	35.00	70.00
	1807/797	15.00	30.00	40.00	75.00
	1807	12.50	25.00	35.00	70.00
	1808	12.50	25.00	35.00	70.00
	1809/8	12.50	25.00	35.00	70.00
	1809	12.50	25.00	35.00	70.00
	1810	12.50	25.00	35.00	60.00
	1811	12.50	25.00	35.00	60.00
	1812	12.50	25.00	35.00	60.00
	1813	10.00	20.00	27.50	60.00
	1815	10.00	20.00	35.00	60.00
	1816	10.00	20.00	30.00	50.00

1/2 REAL

1.6900 g, .903 SILVER, .0490 oz ASW
Obv: Armored bust of Charles IIII.
Rev: Pillars and arms.

KM#	Date	VG	Fine	VF	XF
72	1801 FM	6.50	10.00	20.00	75.00
	1801 FT	4.00	6.00	10.00	45.00
	1802 FT	4.00	6.00	10.00	45.00
	1803 FT	5.00	9.00	15.00	45.00
	1804 TH	4.00	6.00	10.00	45.00
	1805 TH	4.00	6.00	10.00	45.00
	1806 TH	4.00	6.00	10.00	45.00
	1807/6 TH	4.50	6.50	11.50	50.00
	1807 TH	4.00	6.00	10.00	45.00
	1808/7 TH	4.50	6.50	11.50	50.00
	1808 TH	4.00	6.00	10.00	45.00

Obv: Armored bust of Ferdinand VII.

KM#	Date	VG	Fine	VF	XF
73	1808 TH	3.00	5.00	10.00	30.00
	1809 TH	3.00	5.00	10.00	30.00
	1810 TH	5.00	8.00	12.00	35.00
	1810 HJ	3.00	5.00	10.00	30.00
	1811 HJ	3.00	5.00	10.00	30.00
	1812 HJ	3.00	5.00	10.00	30.00
	1813 TH	3.50	6.00	10.00	30.00
	1813 JJ	10.00	20.00	40.00	100.00
	1813 HJ	7.50	15.00	30.00	90.00
	1814 JJ	5.00	8.00	12.00	35.00

Obv: Draped bust of Ferdinand VII.

KM#	Date	VG	Fine	VF	XF
74	1814 JJ	3.00	5.00	12.00	45.00
	1815 JJ	3.00	5.00	10.00	40.00
	1816 JJ	3.00	5.00	10.00	40.00
	1817/6 JJ	—	—	—	—
	1817 JJ	3.00	5.00	12.00	45.00
	1818/7 JJ	3.00	5.00	15.00	50.00
	1818 JJ	3.00	5.00	15.00	50.00
	1819 JJ	3.00	5.00	10.00	40.00
	1820 JJ	3.00	5.00	15.00	50.00
	1821 JJ	3.00	5.00	10.00	40.00

REAL

3.3800 g, .903 SILVER, .0981 oz ASW
Obv: Armored bust of Charles IIII.

KM#	Date	VG	Fine	VF	XF
81	1801 FM	8.00	15.00	25.00	80.00
	1801 FT	3.00	8.50	16.50	60.00
	1802 FM	3.00	8.50	16.50	60.00
	1802 FT	3.00	7.50	12.50	60.00
	1803 FT	3.00	8.50	16.50	60.00
	1804 TH	3.00	7.50	12.50	60.00
	1805 TH	3.00	8.50	16.50	60.00
	1806 TH	3.00	7.50	12.50	60.00
	1807/6 TH	3.50	8.50	13.50	65.00
	1807 TH	3.00	7.50	12.50	60.00
	1808/7 TH	3.50	8.50	13.50	65.00
	1808 TH	3.00	7.50	12.50	60.00

Obv: Imaginary bust of Ferdinand VII.

KM#	Date	VG	Fine	VF	XF
82	1809 TH	4.00	7.50	15.00	100.00
	1810/09 TH	4.00	7.50	15.00	100.00
	1810 TH	4.00	7.50	15.00	100.00
	1810 HJ	6.00	10.00	20.00	125.00
	1811 HJ	4.00	7.50	15.00	100.00
	1811 TH	25.00	35.00	60.00	250.00
	1812 HJ	4.00	7.50	15.00	80.00
	1812 JJ	6.00	10.00	20.00	125.00
	1813 HJ	5.50	8.50	17.50	125.00
	1813 JJ	50.00	100.00	150.00	250.00
	1814 HJ	50.00	100.00	200.00	300.00
	1814 JJ	50.00	100.00	200.00	300.00

Obv: Draped bust of Ferdinand VII.

KM#	Date	VG	Fine	VF	XF
83	1814 JJ	25.00	50.00	100.00	350.00
	1815 JJ	5.50	8.50	17.50	125.00
	1815 HJ	15.00	30.00	60.00	150.00
	1816 JJ	4.00	7.50	12.50	75.00
	1817 JJ	4.00	7.50	12.50	75.00
	1818 JJ	30.00	60.00	125.00	500.00
	1819 JJ	5.50	8.50	17.50	75.00
	1820 JJ	5.00	8.50	17.50	75.00
	1821/0 JJ	7.50	12.50	27.50	110.00
	1821 JJ	5.00	8.50	12.50	50.00

2 REALES

6.7700 g, .903 SILVER, .1965 oz ASW
Obv: Armored bust of Carolus IIII.

KM#	Date	VG	Fine	VF	XF
91	1801 FT	5.00	10.00	15.00	100.00
	1801 FM	20.00	40.00	75.00	250.00
	1802 FT	5.00	10.00	15.00	100.00
	1803 FT	5.00	10.00	15.00	100.00
	1804 TH	5.00	10.00	15.00	100.00
	1805 TH	5.00	10.00	15.00	100.00
	1806/5 TH	5.50	11.50	16.50	110.00
	1806 TH	5.00	10.00	15.00	100.00
	1807/5 TH	5.50	11.50	16.50	110.00
	1807/6 TH	15.00	30.00	60.00	200.00
	1807 TH	5.00	10.00	15.00	100.00
	1808/7 TH	5.50	11.50	16.50	110.00
	1808 TH	5.00	10.00	15.00	100.00

Obv: Imaginary bust of Ferdinand VII.

KM#	Date	VG	Fine	VF	XF
92	1809 TH	6.50	12.50	30.00	150.00
	1810 TH	6.50	12.50	30.00	150.00
	1810 HJ	6.50	12.50	30.00	150.00
	1811 HJ	6.50	12.50	30.00	150.00
	1811 HJ/TH	40.00	80.00	150.00	300.00
	1811 TH	100.00	200.00	300.00	750.00

Obv: Draped bust of Ferdinand VII.

KM#	Date	VG	Fine	VF	XF
93	1812 HJ	15.00	30.00	100.00	300.00
	1812 TH	60.00	125.00	250.00	500.00
	1812 JJ	10.00	20.00	60.00	200.00
	1813 HJ	15.00	30.00	100.00	400.00
	1813 JJ	20.00	60.00	125.00	350.00
	1813 TH	15.00	30.00	100.00	400.00
	1814/13 JJ	15.00	30.00	100.00	400.00
	1814 JJ	15.00	30.00	100.00	400.00
	1815 JJ	5.00	10.00	30.00	100.00
	1816 JJ	5.00	10.00	30.00	100.00
	1817 JJ	5.00	10.00	30.00	100.00
	1818 JJ	5.00	10.00	30.00	100.00
	1819 JJ	5.00	10.00	30.00	100.00
	1820 JJ	—	—	Rare	—
	1821/0 JJ	5.00	10.00	30.00	110.00
	1821 JJ	5.00	10.00	30.00	100.00

4 REALES
13.5400 g, .903 SILVER, .3931 oz ASW
Obv: Armored bust of Charles IIII.
Rev: Pillars, arms.

KM#	Date	VG	Fine	VF	XF
100	1801 FM	25.00	40.00	80.00	350.00
	1801 FT	60.00	100.00	150.00	500.00
	1802 FT	200.00	300.00	500.00	1000.
	1803 FT	60.00	125.00	200.00	550.00
	1803 FM	350.00	450.00	650.00	1250.
	1804 TH	25.00	50.00	150.00	450.00
	1805 TH	25.00	40.00	80.00	350.00
	1806 TH	25.00	40.00	80.00	350.00
	1807 TH	25.00	40.00	80.00	350.00
	1808/7 TH	25.00	50.00	150.00	450.00
	1808 TH	25.00	50.00	150.00	450.00

Obv: Imaginary bust Ferdinand VII.

101	1809 HJ	75.00	125.00	175.00	450.00
	1810 TH	75.00	125.00	175.00	450.00
	1810 HJ	75.00	125.00	175.00	450.00
	1811 HJ	75.00	125.00	175.00	450.00
	1812 HJ	500.00	750.00	1000.	2000.

Obv: Draped bust of Ferdinand VII.

102	1816 JJ	150.00	200.00	350.00	600.00
	1817 JJ	250.00	400.00	500.00	1000.
	1818/7 JJ	250.00	400.00	500.00	1000.
	1818 JJ	250.00	400.00	500.00	1000.
	1819 JJ	175.00	250.00	350.00	700.00
	1820 JJ	175.00	250.00	350.00	700.00
	1821 JJ	75.00	125.00	200.00	425.00

8 REALES

27.0700 g, .903 SILVER, .7859 oz ASW
Obv: Armored bust of Charles IIII.

109	1801/791 FM	35.00	60.00	100.00	225.00
	1801/0 FM	35.00	60.00	100.00	225.00
	1801/0 FT/FM	20.00	40.00	50.00	100.00
	1801 FM	20.00	40.00	100.00	225.00
	1801 FT/M	20.00	40.00	50.00	100.00
	1801 FT	20.00	40.00	50.00	100.00
	1802/1 FT	20.00	40.00	50.00	100.00
	1802 FT	20.00	40.00	50.00	100.00

KM#	Date	VG	Fine	VF	XF
109	1802 FT/FM	20.00	40.00	50.00	100.00
	1803 FT	20.00	40.00	50.00	100.00
	1803 FT/FM	20.00	40.00	50.00	100.00
	1803 TH	50.00	100.00	150.00	300.00
	1804/3 TH	20.00	40.00	50.00	100.00
	1804 TH	20.00	40.00	50.00	100.00
	1805/4 TH	20.00	40.00	50.00	100.00
	1805 TH	20.00	40.00	50.00	100.00
	1806 TH	20.00	40.00	50.00	100.00
	1807 TH	20.00	40.00	50.00	100.00
	1870 TH(error 1807)				
		150.00	250.00	350.00	700.00
	1808/7 TH	20.00	40.00	50.00	100.00
	1808 TH	20.00	40.00	50.00	100.00

Obv: Armored bust of Ferdinand VII.

110	1808 TH	25.00	40.00	65.00	125.00
	1809/8 TH	25.00	40.00	65.00	125.00
	1809 HJ	25.00	40.00	65.00	125.00
	1809 HJ/TH	20.00	40.00	50.00	100.00
	1809 TH/JH	20.00	40.00	50.00	100.00
	1809 TH	20.00	40.00	50.00	100.00
	1810/09 HJ	25.00	40.00	65.00	125.00
	1810 HJ	25.00	40.00	65.00	125.00
	1810 HJ/TH	25.00	40.00	65.00	125.00
	1810 TH	75.00	125.00	200.00	400.00
	1811/0 HJ	20.00	40.00	50.00	80.00
	1811 HJ	20.00	40.00	50.00	80.00

Obv: Draped bust of Ferdinand VII.

111	1811 HJ	50.00	75.00	125.00	250.00
	1812 HJ	50.00	75.00	125.00	250.00
	1812 JJ/HJ	20.00	40.00	50.00	75.00
	1812 JJ	20.00	40.00	50.00	75.00
	1813 HJ	50.00	75.00	125.00	250.00
	1813 JJ	20.00	40.00	50.00	75.00
	1814/3 HJ	500.00	800.00	1500.	3000.
	1814/3 JJ/HJ				
		20.00	40.00	50.00	75.00
	1814/3 JJ	20.00	40.00	50.00	75.00
	1814 JJ	20.00	40.00	50.00	75.00
	1814 HJ	500.00	800.00	1500.	3000.
	1815/4 JJ	20.00	40.00	50.00	75.00
	1815 JJ	20.00	40.00	50.00	75.00
	1816/5 JJ	20.00	40.00	50.00	75.00
	1816 JJ	20.00	40.00	50.00	75.00
	1817 JJ	20.00	40.00	50.00	75.00
	1818 JJ	20.00	40.00	50.00	75.00
	1819 JJ	20.00	40.00	50.00	75.00
	1820 JJ	20.00	40.00	50.00	75.00
	1821 JJ	20.00	40.00	50.00	75.00

1/2 ESCUDO

1.6900 g, .875 GOLD, .0475 oz AGW
Obv. leg: FERD.VII.D.G.HISP.ET IND.

KM#	Date	VG	Fine	VF	XF
112	1814 JJ	250.00	350.00	450.00	600.00
	1815/4 JJ	150.00	200.00	250.00	350.00
	1815 JJ	150.00	200.00	250.00	350.00
	1816 JJ	100.00	150.00	200.00	300.00
	1817 JJ	150.00	200.00	250.00	350.00
	1818 JJ	150.00	200.00	250.00	350.00
	1819 JJ	150.00	200.00	250.00	350.00
	1820 JJ	200.00	300.00	450.00	600.00

ESCUDO

3.3800 g, .875 GOLD, .0950 oz AGW
Obv: Armored bust of Charles IV.

120	1801 FT	125.00	200.00	250.00	350.00
	1801 FM	125.00	200.00	250.00	350.00
	1802 FT	125.00	200.00	250.00	350.00
	1803 FT	125.00	200.00	250.00	350.00
	1804/3 TH	125.00	200.00	250.00	350.00
	1804 TH	125.00	200.00	250.00	350.00
	1805 TH	125.00	200.00	250.00	350.00
	1806 TH	125.00	200.00	250.00	350.00
	1807 TH	125.00	200.00	250.00	350.00
	1808 TH	125.00	200.00	250.00	350.00

Obv: Imaginary bust of Ferdinand VII.

121	1809 HJ	125.00	200.00	250.00	400.00
	1810 HJ	125.00	200.00	250.00	400.00
	1811 HJ	125.00	200.00	250.00	400.00
	1812 HJ	150.00	250.00	350.00	550.00

Obv: Undraped bust of Ferdinand VII.

122	1814 HJ	100.00	150.00	225.00	400.00
	1815 JJ	100.00	150.00	225.00	400.00
	1815 HJ	100.00	150.00	225.00	400.00
	1816 JJ	125.00	175.00	275.00	500.00
	1817 JJ	100.00	150.00	225.00	400.00
	1818 JJ	100.00	150.00	225.00	400.00
	1819 JJ	100.00	150.00	225.00	400.00
	1820 JJ	100.00	150.00	225.00	400.00

2 ESCUDOS

6.7700 g, .875 GOLD, .1904 oz AGW
Obv: Armored bust of Charles IV.

132	1801 FM	125.00	250.00	350.00	600.00
	1802 FT	125.00	250.00	350.00	600.00
	1803 FT	125.00	250.00	350.00	600.00
	1804 TH	125.00	250.00	350.00	600.00
	1805 TH	125.00	250.00	350.00	600.00
	1806 TH	125.00	250.00	350.00	600.00
	1807 TH	125.00	250.00	350.00	600.00
	1808 TH	125.00	250.00	350.00	600.00

Obv: Imaginary bust of Ferdinand VII.

133	1808 TH	400.00	600.00	800.00	1400.
	1809 HJ	350.00	500.00	750.00	1200.
	1810 HJ	350.00	500.00	750.00	1200.
	1811 HJ	300.00	400.00	600.00	1000.

War of Independence / MEXICO 1231

Obv: Undraped bust of Ferdinand VII.

KM#	Date	VG	Fine	VF	XF
134	1814 HJ	250.00	400.00	650.00	1200.
	1814 JJ	250.00	400.00	650.00	1200.
	1815 JJ	250.00	400.00	650.00	1200.
	1816 JJ	250.00	400.00	650.00	1200.
	1817 JJ	250.00	400.00	650.00	1200.
	1818 JJ	250.00	400.00	650.00	1200.
	1819 JJ	250.00	400.00	650.00	1200.
	1820 JJ	250.00	400.00	650.00	1200.

4 ESCUDOS
13.5400 g, .875 GOLD, .3809 oz AGW
Obv: Armored bust of Charles IIII.

144	1801 FM	300.00	500.00	750.00	1400.
	1801 FT	300.00	500.00	750.00	1400.
	1802 FT	300.00	500.00	750.00	1400.
	1803 FT	300.00	500.00	750.00	1400.
	1804/3 TH	300.00	500.00	750.00	1400.
	1804 TH	300.00	500.00	750.00	1400.
	1805 TH	300.00	500.00	750.00	1400.
	1806/5 TH	300.00	500.00	750.00	1400.
	1806 TH	300.00	500.00	750.00	1400.
	1807 TH	300.00	500.00	750.00	1400.
	1808/0 TH	300.00	500.00	750.00	1400.
	1808 TH	300.00	500.00	750.00	1400.

Obv: Imaginary bust of Ferdinand VII.

145	1810 HJ	450.00	600.00	950.00	1600.
	1811 HJ	350.00	500.00	850.00	1400.
	1812 HJ	350.00	500.00	850.00	1400.

Obv: Undraped bust of Ferdin. VII.

146	1814 HJ	400.00	650.00	900.00	1600.
	1815 HJ	400.00	650.00	900.00	1600.
	1815 JJ	400.00	650.00	900.00	1600.
	1816 JJ	400.00	650.00	900.00	1600.
	1817 JJ	400.00	650.00	900.00	1600.
	1818 JJ	400.00	650.00	900.00	1600.
	1819 JJ	400.00	650.00	900.00	1600.
	1820 JJ	400.00	650.00	900.00	1600.

8 ESCUDOS
27.0700 g, .875 GOLD, .7616 oz AGW
Obv: Armored bust of Charles IIII.
Rev. leg: IN UTROQ. FELIX., arms, order chain.

159	1801/0 FT	400.00	500.00	700.00	1000.
	1801 FM	375.00	475.00	650.00	800.00
	1801 FT	375.00	475.00	650.00	800.00
	1802 FT	375.00	475.00	650.00	800.00
	1803 FT	375.00	475.00	650.00	800.00
	1804/3 TH	400.00	500.00	700.00	1000.
	1804 TH	375.00	475.00	650.00	800.00
	1805 TH	375.00	475.00	650.00	800.00
	1806 TH	375.00	475.00	650.00	800.00
	1807/6 TH	400.00	500.00	700.00	1000.
	1807 TH	450.00	550.00	750.00	1000.
	1808 TH	450.00	600.00	800.00	1100.

Obv: Imaginary bust of Ferdinand VII.

KM#	Date	VG	Fine	VF	XF
160	1808 TH	400.00	500.00	750.00	1000.
	1809 HJ	400.00	500.00	750.00	1000.
	1810 HJ	375.00	475.00	650.00	850.00
	1811/0 HJ	400.00	500.00	750.00	1000.
	1811 HJ	400.00	500.00	750.00	1000.
	1811 JJ	375.00	475.00	650.00	850.00
	1812 JJ	375.00	475.00	650.00	850.00

Obv: Undraped bust of Ferdinand VII.

161	1814 JJ	375.00	475.00	650.00	850.00
	1815/4 JJ	400.00	500.00	700.00	1000.
	1815/4 HJ	400.00	500.00	700.00	1000.
	1815 JJ	375.00	475.00	650.00	850.00
	1815 HJ	375.00	475.00	650.00	850.00
	1816/5 JJ	400.00	500.00	700.00	1000.
	1816 JJ	375.00	475.00	650.00	850.00
	1817 JJ	375.00	475.00	650.00	850.00
	1818/7 JJ	375.00	475.00	650.00	850.00
	1818 JJ	375.00	475.00	650.00	850.00
	1819 JJ	375.00	475.00	650.00	850.00
	1820 JJ	375.00	475.00	650.00	850.00
	1821 JJ	400.00	500.00	700.00	1000.

WAR OF INDEPENDENCE
ROYALIST ISSUES
(1810-1821)
Provisional Mints
RULER
Ferdinand VII, 1808-1821
MINT MARKS
CA - Chihuahua
D - Durango
GA - Guadalajara
GO - Guanajuato
ZS - Zacatecas
MONETARY SYSTEM
16 Reales = 1 Escudo

CHIHUAHUA
The Chihuahua Mint was established by a decree of October 8, 1810 as a temporary mint. Their first coins were cast 8 reales using Mexico City coins as patterns and obliterating/changing the mint mark and moneyer initials. Two c/m were placed on the obverse-on the left, a T designating its having been received by the Royal Treasurer and on the right crowned pillars of Hercules with pomegranate beneath: the symbol of the comptroller.

In 1814 standard dies were available and from 1814 to 1822 standard 8 reales were struck. Only the one denomination was made at this mint.

MINT MARK: CA

8 REALES

CAST SILVER
Obv: Imaginary bust of Ferdinand VII; leg: FERDIN.VII. DEI. GRATIA. c/m: 'T' at left and pomegranate pillars at right.

KM#	Date	Good	VG	Fine	VF
123	1810 RP	—	—	Rare	—
	1811 RP	45.00	60.00	100.00	150.00
	1812 RP	30.00	40.00	60.00	90.00
	1813/2 RP	32.50	45.00	70.00	100.00
	1813 RP	30.00	40.00	60.00	90.00

27.0700 g, .903 SILVER, .7860 oz ASW
Obv: Draped bust of Ferdinand VII.
Rev: Similar to KM#123.

KM#	Date	VG	Fine	VF	XF
111.1	1813 RP	Reported, not confirmed			
	1814 RP	Reported, not confirmed			
	1815 RP	200.00	275.00	350.00	500.00
	1816 RP	80.00	125.00	150.00	275.00
	1817 RP	100.00	150.00	185.00	275.00
	1818 RP	100.00	150.00	185.00	275.00
	1819 RP	125.00	175.00	250.00	350.00
	1820 RP	200.00	275.00	350.00	500.00
	1821 RP	200.00	275.00	350.00	500.00
	1822 RP	400.00	600.00	800.00	1100.

NOTE: KM#111.1 is normally found counterstamped over earlier cast 8 Reales, KM#123.

DURANGO
The Durango mint was authorized as a temporary mint at the same time as the Chihuahua Mint, October 8, 1810. The mint opened sometime in 1811 and made coins of 6 denominations - 5 silver and 1 copper - during the period 1811 to 1822.

MINT MARK: D

1/8 REAL

COPPER
Obv: Crown over double F7 monogram.
Rev: EN DURANGO, value, date.

60	1812	—	35.00	75.00	125.00	225.00
	1813	—	—	—	Rare	—
	1814	—	—	—	Rare	—

Rev: Spray added above date.

KM#	Date	VG	Fine	VF	XF
61	1814	15.00	25.00	50.00	85.00
	1815	15.00	25.00	50.00	85.00
	1816	15.00	25.00	50.00	85.00
	1817	15.00	25.00	50.00	80.00
	1818	15.00	25.00	50.00	80.00
	1818 OCTAVO DD REAL (error)				
		45.00	75.00	—	—

1/2 REAL

1.6900 g, .903 SILVER, .0491 oz ASW
Obv: Draped bust of Ferdinand VII.

74.1	1813 RM	250.00	350.00	600.00	1500.
	1814 MZ	250.00	350.00	600.00	1500.
	1816 MZ	250.00	350.00	600.00	1500.

REAL

3.3800 g, .903 SILVER, .0981 oz ASW
Obv: Draped bust of Ferdinand VII.

83.1	1813 MZ	250.00	350.00	500.00	1250.
	1814 MZ	250.00	350.00	500.00	1250.
	1815 MZ	250.00	300.00	500.00	1250.

2 REALES

6.7700 g, .903 SILVER, .1966 oz ASW
Obv: Armored bust of Ferdinand VII.

92.2	1811 RM	200.00	300.00	400.00	1500.
	1812 RM	—	—	Rare	—

Obv: Draped bust of Ferdinand VII.

93.1	1812 MZ	200.00	300.00	400.00	1500.
	1812 RM	—	—	Rare	—
	1813 MZ	300.00	500.00	800.00	2500.
	1813 RM	300.00	500.00	800.00	2500.
	1814 MZ	300.00	500.00	800.00	2500.
	1815 MZ	300.00	500.00	800.00	2500.
	1816 MZ	300.00	500.00	800.00	2500.
	1817 MZ	300.00	500.00	800.00	2500.

4 REALES

13.5400 g, .903 SILVER, .3931 oz ASW
Obv: Draped bust of Ferdinand VII.

102.1	1814 MZ	500.00	1000.	1500.	4000.
	1816 MZ	400.00	800.00	1200.	3000.
	1817 MZ	400.00	800.00	1200.	3000.

8 REALES

27.0700 g, .903 SILVER, .7860 oz ASW
Obv: Armored bust of Ferdinand VII.

110.1	1811 RM	500.00	800.00	1200.	4000.
	1812 RM	300.00	500.00	800.00	3000.
	1813 MZ	300.00	500.00	800.00	3000.
	1814 MZ	300.00	500.00	800.00	3000.

Obv: Draped bust of Ferdinand VII.

KM#	Date	VG	Fine	VF	XF
111.2	1812 MZ	300.00	400.00	600.00	1500.
	1812 RM	125.00	175.00	275.00	800.00
	1813 RM	150.00	200.00	325.00	850.00
	1813 MZ	125.00	175.00	275.00	750.00
	1814 MZ	150.00	225.00	275.00	750.00
	1815 MZ	75.00	125.00	225.00	600.00
	1816 MZ	50.00	75.00	125.00	325.00
	1817 MZ	30.00	50.00	90.00	250.00
	1818 MZ	50.00	75.00	125.00	350.00
	1818 RM	50.00	75.00	125.00	325.00
	1818 CG/RM	100.00	125.00	150.00	350.00
	1818 CG	50.00	75.00	125.00	325.00
	1819 CG/RM	50.00	100.00	150.00	300.00
	1819 CG	30.00	60.00	100.00	250.00
	1820 CG	30.00	60.00	100.00	250.00
	1821 CG	30.00	40.00	50.00	150.00
	1822 CG	30.00	50.00	75.00	160.00

NOTE: Occasionally these are found struck over Guadalajara 8 reales and are very rare in general, specimens dated prior to 1816 are rather weakly struck.

GUADALAJARA

The Guadalajara Mint made its first coins in 1812 and the mint operated until April 30, 1815. It was to reopen in 1818 and continue operations until 1822. It was the only Royalist mint to strike gold coins, both 4 and 8 escudos. In addition to these it struck the standard 5 denominations in silver.

MINT MARK: GA

1/2 REAL

1.6900 g, .903 SILVER, .0491 oz ASW
Obv: Draped bust of Ferdinand VII.

74.2	1812 MR	—	—	Rare	—
	1814 MR	40.00	100.00	200.00	300.00
	1815 MR	200.00	350.00	500.00	1000.

REAL

3.3800 g, .903 SILVER, .0981 oz ASW
Obv: Draped bust of Ferdinand VII.

83.2	1814 MR	125.00	175.00	275.00	600.00
	1815 MR	—	—	Rare	—

2 REALES

6.7700 g, .903 SILVER, .1966 oz ASW
Obv: Draped bust of Ferdinand VII.

93.2	1812 MR	300.00	500.00	800.00	2500.
	1814 MR	75.00	125.00	200.00	600.00
	1815/4 MR	425.00	725.00	1100.	3600.
	1815 MR	400.00	700.00	1000.	3500.
	1821 FS	200.00	250.00	350.00	900.00

4 REALES

13.5400 g, .903 SILVER, .3931 oz ASW
Obv: Draped bust of Ferdinand VII.

102.2	1814 MR	40.00	65.00	150.00	250.00
	1815 MR	80.00	150.00	300.00	500.00

Obv: Large bust.

KM#	Date	VG	Fine	VF	XF
102.3	1814 MR	50.00	100.00	200.00	400.00

Obv: Large bust w/berries in wreath of crown.

102.4	1814 MR	—	—	Rare	—

8 REALES

27.0700 g, .903 SILVER, .7860 oz ASW
Obv: Draped bust of Ferdinand VII.

111.3	1812 MR	1000.	1500.	3000.	4500.
	1813/2 MR	60.00	100.00	150.00	400.00
	1813 MR	60.00	100.00	150.00	400.00
	1814 MR	20.00	30.00	50.00	175.00
	1815 MR	150.00	200.00	250.00	750.00
	1818 FS	30.00	50.00	65.00	200.00
	1821/18 FS	30.00	50.00	75.00	200.00
	1821 FS	25.00	35.00	50.00	150.00
	1822/1 FS	30.00	50.00	75.00	200.00
	1822 FS	30.00	50.00	75.00	200.00

4 ESCUDOS

13.5400 g, .875 GOLD, .3809 oz ASW
Obv: Uniformed bust of Ferdinand VII.

147	1812 MR	—	—	Rare	—

8 ESCUDOS

27.0700 g, .875 GOLD, .7616 oz AGW
Obv: Large uniformed bust of Ferdinand VII.

162	1812 MR	3500.	5000.	8000.	13,000.
	1813 MR	2750.	4000.	7000.	12,000.

Obv: Small uniformed bust of Ferdinand VII.

KM#	Date	VG	Fine	VF	XF
163	1813 MR	2750.	4000.	7000.	12,000.

Obv: Undraped bust of Ferdinand VII.

| 161.1 | 1821 FS | 1250. | 1500. | 3000. | 5000. |

Obv: Draped bust of Ferdinand VII.

| 164 | 1821 FS | 1500. | 2500. | 4000. | 7000. |

GUANAJUATO

Guanajuato Mint was authorized December 24, 1812 and started production shortly thereafter. For unknown reasons it closed on May 15, 1813. The mint was reopened in April of 1821 by the insurgent forces. They continued to make coins of the Spanish design to pay their army. After independence coins were made into the year 1822. Only the 2 and 8 reales coins were made.

MINT MARK: Go

2 REALES

6.7700 g, .903 SILVER, .1966 oz ASW
Obv: Draped bust of Ferdinand VII.

93.3	1821 JM	30.00	60.00	90.00	175.00
	1822 JM	25.00	45.00	65.00	125.00

8 REALES

27.0700 g, .903 SILVER, .7860 oz ASW
Obv: Draped bust of Ferdinand VII.

111.4	1812 JJ	750.00	1250.	1750.	2500.
	1813 JJ	125.00	175.00	275.00	600.00
	1821 JM	25.00	50.00	75.00	200.00
	1822/0 JM	40.00	100.00	150.00	300.00
	1822 JM	20.00	30.00	50.00	175.00

NUEVA VISCAYA
(Later became Durango State)

This 8 reales, intended for the province of Nueva Viscaya was minted in the newly opened Durango Mint during the months of February and March of 1811 before the regular coinage of Durango was started.

8 REALES

.903 SILVER
**Obv. leg: MON.PROV. DE NUEV.VIZCAYA,
arms of Durango. Rev: Royal arms.**

KM#	Date	Good	VG	Fine	VF
181	1811 RM	1250.	2000.	2750.	4500.

NOTE: Several varieties exist.

OAXACA

The city of Oaxaca was in the midst of a coin shortage when it became apparent the city would be taken by insurgent forces. The Royalist forces under Lt. Gen. Saravia had some coins made. They were cast in a blacksmith shop and were made in 3 denominations - 1/2, 1 and 8 reales. They were made only briefly in 1812 before the city fell to the opposing forces.

1/2 REAL

.903 SILVER
**Obv: Cross separating castle, lion, F,7O.
Rev. leg: OAXACA around shield.**

| 166 | 1812 | 1000. | 1500. | 2500. | 3500. |

REAL

.903 SILVER

| 167 | 1812 | 300.00 | 600.00 | 1000. | 2000. |

8 REALES

.903 SILVER

168	1812 c/m:A	1200.	1800.	3000.	4500.
	1812 c/m:B	1200.	1800.	3000.	4500.
	1812 c/m:C	1200.	1800.	3000.	4500.
	1812 c/m:D	1200.	1800.	3000.	4500.
	1812 c/m:K	1200.	1800.	3000.	4500.
	1812 c/m:L	1200.	1800.	3000.	4500.
	1812 c/m:Mo	1200.	1800.	3000.	4500.
	1812 c/m:N	1200.	1800.	3000.	4500.
	1812 c/m:O	1200.	1800.	3000.	4500.
	1812 c/m:R	1200.	1800.	3000.	4500.
	1812 c/m:V	1200.	1800.	3000.	4500.
	1812 c/m:Z	1200.	1800.	3000.	4500.

NOTE: The above issue usually has a second c/m: O between crowned pillars.

REAL DEL CATORCE
(City in San Luis Potosi)

Real del Catorce is an important mining center in the state of San Luis Potosi. In 1811 an 8 reales coin was issued under very tedious conditions while the city was still in Royalist hands. Few survive.

8 REALES

.903 SILVER
**Obv. leg: EL R.D. CATORC. POR FERNA. VII.
Rev. leg: MONEDA. PROVISIONAL.VALE.8R.**

KM#	Date	VG	Fine	VF	XF
169	1811	2000.	4000.	7500.	15,000.

SAN FERNANDO DE BEXAR

Struck by Jose Antonio de la Garza, the 'jolas' are the only known coins issued under Spanish rule in the continental United States of America.

1/8 REAL

COPPER

KM#	Date	Mintage	Good	VG	Fine	VF
170	1818	8,000	500.00	750.00	1200.	1600.

| 171 | 1818 | Inc. Ab. | 500.00 | 750.00 | 1200. | 1600. |

SAN LUIS POTOSI

Sierra De Pinos
Villa

1/4 REAL

COPPER

KM#	Date	Good	VG	Fine	VF
A172	1814	85.00	125.00	185.00	250.00

SILVER

| A172a | 1814 | — | — | Rare | — |

SOMBRERETE
(Under Royalist Vargas)

The Sombrerete Mint opened on October 8, 1810 in an area that boasted some of the richest mines in Mexico. The mint operated until July 16, 1811 when it closed only to reopen in 1812 and finally to close for good at the end of 1812. The man in charge of the mines, Fernando Vargas, was also in charge of the coinage. All of the coins bear his name.

1/2 REAL

.903 SILVER
Obv. leg: FERDIN.VII.SOMBRERETE..., around crowned globes. Rev. leg: VARGAS over lys in oval, sprays.

KM#	Date	Good	VG	Fine	VF
172	1811	35.00	60.00	100.00	175.00
	1812	50.00	90.00	150.00	225.00

REAL

.903 SILVER
Obv. leg: FERDIN.VII.SOMBRERETE..., around crowned globes. Rev. leg: VARGAS over lys in oval, sprays.

173	1811	40.00	60.00	100.00	160.00
	1812	30.00	50.00	80.00	125.00

2 REALES

.903 SILVER
Obv: R.CAXA.DE.SOMBRERETE, royal arms.
Rev. c/m: VARGAS, 1811, S between crowned pillars.

174	1811 SE	65.00	120.00	400.00	650.00

4 REALES

.903 SILVER
Obv. leg: R.CAXA.DE.SOMBRERETE, royal arms.
Rev. leg: VARGAS/1811 or 1812.

175	1811	100.00	200.00	400.00	750.00
	1812	50.00	150.00	250.00	400.00

8 REALES

.903 SILVER
Obv. leg: R.CAXA. DE SOMBRERETE.
Rev. c/m: VARGAS, date, S between crowned pillars.

176	1810	1000.	1500.	2500.	3500.
	1811	200.00	300.00	400.00	500.00

Obv. leg: R.CAXA DE SOMBRETE, crowned arms.
Rev. leg: VARGAS/date/3

KM#	Date	Good	VG	Fine	VF
177	1811	100.00	150.00	200.00	300.00
	1812	100.00	150.00	200.00	300.00

VALLADOLID MICHOACAN
(Now Morelia)

Valladolid, capitol of Michoacan province, was a strategically important center for military thrusts into the adjoining provinces. The Royalists made every effort to retain the position. In 1813, with the advance of the insurgent forces, it became apparent that to maintain the position would be very difficult. During 1813 it was necessary to make coins in the city due to lack of traffic with other areas. These were made only briefly before the city fell and were also used by the insurgents with appropriate countermarks.

8 REALES

.903 SILVER
Obv: Royal arms in wreath, value at sides.
Rev: PROVISIONAL/DE VALLADOLID/1813.

178	1813	1000.	2000.	3000.	5000.

Obv: Bust, leg: FERDIN. VII.
Rev: Arms, pillars.

179	1813	1500.	2500.	3500.	5500.

ZACATECAS

The city of Zacatecas, in a rich mining area, has a long history of providing silver for the world. From the mid-1500's silver poured from its mines. On November 14, 1810 a mint began production for the Royalist cause. Zacatecas was the most prolific of the mints during the War of Independence. The 4 silver denominations were made here. The first type was a local type with the mountains of silver shown on the coins. These were made only in 1810 and 1811. Some of the 1811 were made by the insurgents after the town fell on April 15, 1811. The town was retaken by the Royalists on May 21, 1811. From then until 1822 the standard bust type of Ferdinand VII was made.

MINT MARKS: Z, ZS, Zs

1/2 REAL

.903 SILVER
Similar to KM#181 but w/local arms.
Flowers 1 and 4, castles 2 and 3.

180	1810	75.00	125.00	200.00	400.00
	1811	30.00	50.00	75.00	150.00

Obv: Royal arms.
Rev. leg: MONEDA PROVISIONAL DE ZACATECAS., mountain.

181	1811	30.00	50.00	75.00	100.00

Obv: Provincial bust FERDIN. VII.
Rev. leg: MONEDA PROVISIONAL DE ZACATECAS.

182	1811	30.00	40.00	60.00	80.00
	1812	25.00	35.00	50.00	70.00

1.6900 g, .903 SILVER, .0491 oz ASW
Obv: Armored bust of Ferdinand VII.

73.1	1813 FP	30.00	60.00	100.00	175.00
	1813 AG	20.00	40.00	60.00	100.00
	1814 AG	15.00	30.00	60.00	100.00
	1815 AG	12.50	25.00	40.00	60.00
	1816 AG	10.00	15.00	25.00	50.00

KM#	Date	Good	VG	Fine	VF
73.1	1817 AG	10.00	15.00	25.00	50.00
	1818 AG	10.00	15.00	25.00	50.00
	1819 AG	10.00	15.00	25.00	50.00

Obv: Draped bust Ferdinand VII.

KM#	Date	Good	VG	Fine	VF
74.3	1819 AG	8.00	12.00	25.00	50.00
	1820 AG	8.00	12.00	25.00	50.00
	1820 RG	5.00	10.00	20.00	45.00
	1821 AG	50.00	100.00	150.00	250.00
	1821 RG	5.00	10.00	20.00	45.00

REAL

.903 SILVER
Similar to KM#184 but w/local arms.
Flowers 1 and 4, castles 2 and 3.

KM#	Date	Good	VG	Fine	VF
183	1810	100.00	150.00	300.00	500.00
	1811	20.00	40.00	75.00	125.00

Obv: Royal arms.
Rev. leg: MONEDA PROVISIONAL DE ZACATECAS., mountain.

184	1811	15.00	30.00	50.00	100.00
	1811	15.00	30.00	50.00	100.00

Obv: Provincial bust, leg: FERDIN. VII.
Rev. leg: MONEDA PROVISIONAL DE ZACATECAS, arms, pillars.

185	1811	45.00	75.00	100.00	175.00
	1812	45.00	75.00	100.00	175.00

3.3800 g, .903 SILVER, .0981 oz ASW
Obv: Imaginary bust of Ferdinand VII.

82.1	1813 FP	50.00	100.00	150.00	250.00
	1814 FP	20.00	35.00	50.00	75.00
	1814 AG	20.00	35.00	50.00	75.00
	1815 AG	20.00	35.00	50.00	75.00
	1816 AG	10.00	20.00	30.00	60.00
	1817 AG	6.50	12.50	20.00	40.00
	1818 AG	6.50	12.50	20.00	40.00
	1819 AG	5.00	9.00	15.00	30.00
	1820 AG	4.00	7.50	12.50	25.00

Obv: Draped bust of Ferdinand VII.

KM#	Date	VG	Fine	VF	XF
83.3	1820 AG	5.00	10.00	17.50	40.00
	1820 RG	5.00	10.00	17.50	40.00
	1821 AG	15.00	30.00	45.00	75.00
	1821 AZ	10.00	20.00	30.00	60.00
	1821 RG	6.00	12.00	17.50	45.00
	1822 AZ	6.00	12.00	17.50	45.00
	1822 RG	15.00	30.00	45.00	75.00

2 REALES

.903 SILVER
Obv: Local arms.
Flowers 1 and 4, castles 2 and 3.

KM#	Date	Good	VG	Fine	VF
186	1810	—	—	Rare	—
	1811	25.00	40.00	60.00	100.00

War of Independence / MEXICO 1235

Obv: Royal arms.
Rev. leg: MONEDA PROVISIONAL DE ZACATECAS.,
mountain over L.V.O.

KM#	Date	Good	VG	Fine	VF
187	1811	15.00	30.00	50.00	75.00

Obv: Provincial bust, leg: FERDIN. VII.
Rev. leg: MONEDA PROVISIONAL DE
ZACATECAS, crowned arms, pillars.

188	1811	40.00	75.00	150.00	225.00
	1812	30.00	60.00	125.00	200.00

6.7700 g, .903 SILVER, .1966 oz ASW
Obv: Large armored bust of Ferdinand VII.

92.1	1813 FP	37.50	50.00	75.00	125.00
	1814 FP	37.50	50.00	75.00	125.00
	1814 AG	37.50	50.00	75.00	125.00
	1815 AG	6.50	12.50	25.00	50.00
	1816 AG	6.50	12.50	25.00	50.00
	1817 AG	6.50	12.50	25.00	50.00
	1818 AG	6.50	12.50	25.00	50.00

Obv: Small armored bust of Ferdinand VII.

A92	1819 AG	25.00	50.00	100.00	200.00

Obv: Draped bust of Ferdinand VII.

KM#	Date	VG	Fine	VF	XF
93.4	1818 AG	6.50	12.50	20.00	40.00
	1819 AG	10.00	20.00	40.00	75.00
	1820 AG	10.00	20.00	40.00	75.00
	1820 RG	10.00	20.00	40.00	75.00
	1821 AG	10.00	20.00	40.00	75.00
	1821 AZ/RG	10.00	20.00	40.00	75.00
	1821 AZ	10.00	20.00	40.00	75.00
	1821 RG	10.00	20.00	40.00	75.00
	1822 AG	10.00	20.00	40.00	75.00
	1822 AZ	15.00	30.00	60.00	120.00
	1822 RG	10.00	20.00	40.00	75.00

8 REALES

.903 SILVER
Rev: Similar to KM#190.

KM#	Date	Good	VG	Fine	VF
189	1810	300.00	450.00	600.00	800.00
	1811	100.00	150.00	225.00	300.00

Obv. leg: FERDIN.VII.DEI. ., royal arms.
Rev. leg: MONEDA PROVISIONAL DE
ZACATECAS, mountain over L.V.O.

190	1811	75.00	125.00	150.00	225.00

Obv: Imaginary bust of Ferdinand VII.
Rev. leg: MONEDA PROVISIONAL DE ZACATECAS,
crowned arms, pillars.

191	1811	35.00	50.00	100.00	150.00
	1812	35.00	50.00	100.00	150.00

Obv: Draped bust of Ferdinand VII.
Rev. leg: MONEDA PROVISIONAL DE ZACATECAS
crowned arms, pillars.

192	1812	50.00	75.00	125.00	200.00

27.0700 g, .903 SILVER, .7860 oz ASW
Obv: Draped bust of Ferdinand VII.

KM#	Date	VG	Fine	VF	XF
111.5	1813 AG	125.00	200.00	250.00	350.00
	1813 FP	75.00	125.00	175.00	275.00
	1814 AG	100.00	150.00	200.00	300.00
	1814 AG Dover horizontal D in IND				
		125.00	175.00	225.00	325.00
	1814 AG/FP	100.00	150.00	200.00	300.00
	1814 FP	150.00	250.00	350.00	450.00
	1815 AG	50.00	100.00	150.00	250.00
	1816 AG	35.00	50.00	65.00	125.00
	1817 AG	35.00	50.00	65.00	125.00
	1818 AG	30.00	40.00	50.00	100.00
	1819 AG	30.00	40.00	50.00	100.00
	1820 AG	30.00	40.00	50.00	100.00
	1820 RG	30.00	40.00	50.00	100.00
	1821 RG	15.00	25.00	35.00	65.00
	1821/81 RG	75.00	150.00	200.00	300.00
	1821 AZ	50.00	100.00	150.00	200.00
	1822 RG	40.00	60.00	100.00	175.00

COUNTERMARKED COINAGE
Crown and Flag
(Refer to Multiple Countermarks)

LCM - La Comandancia Militar
NOTE: This countermark exists in 15 various sizes.

2 REALES

.903 SILVER
c/m: LCM on Mexico KM#92.

KM#	Date	Good	VG	Fine	VF
193.1	1809 TH	100.00	150.00	200.00	275.00

c/m: LCM on Zacatecas KM#187.

193.2	1811	100.00	150.00	200.00	275.00

8 REALES
CAST SILVER
c/m: LCM on Chihuahua KM#123.

194.1	1811 RP	100.00	200.00	300.00	450.00
	1812 RP	100.00	200.00	300.00	450.00

War of Independence / MEXICO 1236

.903 SILVER
c/m: LCM on Chihuahua KM#111.1 struck over KM#123.

KM#	Date	Good	VG	Fine	VF
194.2	1815 RP	200.00	275.00	400.00	550.00
	1817 RP	125.00	175.00	225.00	300.00
	1820 RP	125.00	175.00	225.00	300.00
	1821 RP	125.00	175.00	225.00	300.00

c/m: LCM on Durango KM#111.2.
| 194.3 | 1812 RM | 70.00 | 125.00 | 190.00 | 250.00 |
| | 1821 CG | 70.00 | 125.00 | 190.00 | 250.00 |

c/m: LCM on Guadalajara KM#111.3.
| 194.4 | 1813 MR | 150.00 | 225.00 | 300.00 | 475.00 |
| | 1820 FS | — | — | Rare | — |

c/m: LCM on Guanajuato KM#111.4.
| 194.5 | 1813 JM | 225.00 | 350.00 | 475.00 | 650.00 |

c/m: LCM on Nueva Vizcaya KM#165.
| 194.6 | 1811 RM | — | — | RARE | — |

c/m: LCM on Mexico KM#111.
194.7	1811 HJ	125.00	225.00	350.00	600.00
	1812 JJ	110.00	135.00	190.00	325.00
	1817 JJ	50.00	65.00	85.00	125.00
	1818 JJ	50.00	65.00	85.00	125.00
	1820 JJ				

c/m: LCM on Sombrerete KM#176.
| 194.8 | 1811 | — | — | Rare | — |
| | 1812 | — | — | Rare | — |

c/m: LCM on Zacatecas KM#190.
| 194.9 | 1811 | 225.00 | 350.00 | 450.00 | — |

c/m: LCM on Zacatecas KM#111.5.
194.10	1813 FP				
	1814 AG				
	1822 RG				

LCV - Las Cajas de Veracruz
(The Royal Treasury of the City of Veracruz)

L.C.V.

7 REALES
SILVER
c/m: LCV and 7 on underweight 8 Reales.
| 195 | — | — | — | Rare | — |

7-1/4 REALES
SILVER
c/m: LCV and 7-1/4 on underweight 8 Reales.
| 196 | — | — | — | Rare | — |

7-1/2 REALES
SILVER
c/m: LCV and 7-1/2 on underweight 8 Reales.
KM#	Date	Good	VG	Fine	VF
197	—	—	—	Rare	—

7-3/4 REALES

SILVER
c/m: LCV and 7-3/4 on underweight 8 Reales.
| 198 | — | 300.00 | 375.00 | 450.00 | 600.00 |

8 REALES
CAST SILVER
c/m: LCV on Chihuahua KM#123.
| A198 | 1811 RP | 150.00 | 250.00 | 400.00 | 500.00 |

SILVER
c/m: LCV on Zacatecas KM#191.
| 199 | 1811 | 175.00 | 225.00 | 275.00 | 350.00 |
| | 1812 | 175.00 | 225.00 | 275.00 | 350.00 |

MS (Monogram) - Manuel Salcedo

8 REALES

SILVER
c/m: MS monogram on Mexico KM#110.
KM#	Date	Good	VG	Fine	VF
200	1809 TH	150.00	250.00	400.00	500.00
	1810 HJ	150.00	250.00	400.00	500.00
	1811 HJ	150.00	250.00	400.00	500.00

MVA - Monclova

8 REALES
SILVER
c/m: MVA/1811 on Chihuahua KM#111.1; struck over cast Mexico KM#110.
201	1809	—	—	Rare	—
	1816 RP	—	—	Rare	—
	1821 RP	—	—	Rare	—

c/m: MVA/1812 on Chihuahua KM#111.1; struck over cast Mexico KM#109.
| 202.1 | — | 125.00 | 175.00 | 250.00 | 350.00 |

c/m: MVA/1812 on cast Mexico KM#109.
| 202.2 | 1798 FM | 100.00 | 150.00 | 250.00 | 350.00 |
| | 1802 FT | 100.00 | 150.00 | 250.00 | 350.00 |

c/m: MVA/1812 on cast Mexico KM#110.
202.3	1809 HJ	100.00	150.00	250.00	350.00
	1809 TH	100.00	150.00	250.00	350.00
	1810 HJ	100.00	150.00	250.00	350.00

c/m: MVA/1812 on Zacatecas KM#189.
| 202.5 | 1813 | 300.00 | 350.00 | 450.00 | 550.00 |

War of Independence / MEXICO 1237

2 REALES

		CAST SILVER			
KM#	Date	Good	VG	Fine	VF
206	1811	150.00	250.00	350.00	500.00
	1812	150.00	250.00	350.00	500.00
		STRUCK SILVER			
207	1811	—	Rare	—	—
	1812	300.00	600.00	1000.	1500.

		COPPER			
KM#	Date	Good	VG	Fine	VF
212	1812	100.00	150.00	200.00	250.00
	1813	25.00	50.00	75.00	100.00
	1814	35.00	75.00	110.00	150.00

.903 SILVER
213 1813 125.00 250.00 300.00 400.00
NOTE: These dies were believed to be intended for the striking of 2 Escudos.

4 REALES

c/m: MVA/1812 on Chihuahua KM#111.1.

KM#	Date	Good	VG	Fine	VF
202.6	1816	—	—	—	—

PDV - Provisional de Valladolid
VTIL - (Util = useful)
(Refer to Multiple countermarks)

INSURGENT COINAGE
Supreme National Congress
Of America
1/2 REAL
COPPER
Obv. leg: FERDIN. VII DEI GRATIA, eagle on bridge.
Rev. leg: S.P.CONG.NAT.IND.
GUV.T., value, bow, quiver, etc.
203 1811 30.00 45.00 60.00 100.00

REAL
SILVER
Similar to 1/2 Real, KM#203.
204 1811 50.00 75.00 125.00 200.00

2 REALES

SILVER
205 1812 250.00 350.00 500.00 700.00

8 REALES

COPPER
Obv. leg: FERDIN.VII. . . ., eagle on bridge.
Rev. leg: PROVICIONAL POR LA SUPREMA JUNTA DE AMERICA, bow, sword and quiver.
208 1811 100.00 150.00 225.00 450.00
     1812 100.00 150.00 225.00 450.00

National Congress
1/2 REAL

COPPER
Obv. leg: VICE FERD. VII DEI GRATIA ET, eagle on bridge.
Rev. leg: S. P. CONG. NAT. IND.
GUV. T., value, bow, quiver, etc.
209 1811 50.00 100.00 150.00 200.00
     1812 30.00   60.00 100.00 150.00
     1813 30.00   60.00 100.00 150.00
     1814 50.00 100.00 150.00 200.00

.903 SILVER
210 1812 30.00 60.00 100.00 150.00
     1813 50.00 100.00 175.00 275.00
NOTE: 1812 exists with the date reading inwards and outwards.

REAL

.903 SILVER
211 1812 25.00 45.00 65.00 100.00
     1813 25.00 45.00 65.00 100.00
NOTE: 1812 exists with the date reading inward and outward.

.903 SILVER
214 1813 500.00 1000. 2000. 3000.

8 REALES
.903 SILVER
Similar to 4 Reales, KM#214.
215 1812 500.00 1000. 2000. 3500.
     1813 500.00 1000. 2000. 3500.

American Congress
REAL

.903 SILVER
Obv: Eagle on cactus,
leg: CONGRESO AMERICANO.
Rev: F.7 on spread mantle,
leg: DEPOSIT D.L.AUCTORI J.
216 ND (1813) 35.00 65.00 100.00 150.00

Obv: Eagle on cactus, leg: CONGR.AMER.
Rev: F.7 on spread mantle,
leg: DEPOS.D.L.AUT.D.
217 ND(1813) 35.00 65.00 100.00 150.00

NUEVA GALICIA
(Later became Jalisco State)

Nueva Galicia was a province in early colonial times that was similar to modern Zacatecas, etc. The name was adopted again during the War of Independence. The only issue was an 1812 2 reales of rather enigmatic origin.

War of Independence / MEXICO 1238

2 REALES

.903 SILVER
Obv. leg: PROVYCIONAL....., N.G. in center, date.

KM#	Date	Good	VG	Fine	VF
218	1813	1000.	3000.	6000.	10,000.

OAXACA

Oaxaca was the hub of insurgent activity in the south. The issues of Oaxaca represent various episodic strikings of coins, usually under dire circumstances, by various individuals. The copper coins were made because of urgency and were to be redeemed at its face value in gold or silver. The silver coins were made after the copper coins when silver was available to the insurgent forces. Coinage started in July, 1811 and ran until October 1814.

SUD
(Under General Morelos)

1/2 REAL

COPPER
Obv: Bow, SUD.
Rev: Morelos monogram Mo, date.

KM#	Date	Good	VG	Fine	VF
219	1811	7.50	12.50	20.00	30.00
	1812	7.50	12.50	20.00	30.00
	1813	6.00	10.00	17.50	25.00
	1814	10.00	17.50	25.00	35.00

NOTE: Uniface strikes exist of #219.

STRUCK SILVER

220.1	1811	—	—	—	—
	1812	—	—	—	—
	1813	—	—	—	—

CAST SILVER

220.2	1811	—	—	—	—
	1812	—	—	—	—
	1813	25.00	50.00	100.00	150.00

NOTE: Most silver specimens available on today's market are considered spurious.

SILVER
Obv. leg: PROVICIONAL DE OAXACA, bow, arrow.
Rev. leg: AMERICA MORELOS, lion.

221	1812	35.00	60.00	100.00	150.00
	1813	35.00	60.00	100.00	150.00

COPPER

221a	1812	27.50	42.50	70.00	100.00
	1813	20.00	35.00	60.00	85.00

Obv: Similar to KM#220.
Rev: Similar to KM#221 but w/1/2 at left of lion.

A222	1813	27.50	42.50	70.00	100.00

REAL

COPPER

222	1811	5.00	10.00	20.00	40.00
	1812	4.00	8.00	15.00	30.00
	1813	4.00	8.00	15.00	30.00

STRUCK SILVER

222a	1812	—	—	—	—
	1813	—	—	—	—

CAST SILVER

KM#	Date	Good	VG	Fine	VF
223	1812	—	—	—	—
	1813	40.00	75.00	125.00	175.00

NOTE: Most silver specimens available on today's market are considered spurious.

COPPER
Obv: Bow, arrow/SUD.
Rev. leg: AMERICA MORELOS, lion.

224	1813	27.50	42.50	75.00	110.00

SILVER

225	1813	—	—	Rare	—

2 REALES

COPPER

226.1	1811	12.50	25.00	50.00	100.00
	1812	2.50	3.75	5.00	10.00
	1813	2.50	3.75	5.00	10.00

Obv: Three large stars added.

226.2	1814	10.00	20.00	40.00	60.00

Obv. leg: SUD-OXA, bow, arrow.
Rev: Morelos monogram, value, date.

227	1813	60.00	100.00	200.00	300.00
	1814	60.00	100.00	200.00	300.00

Obv. leg: SUD. OAXACA

228	1814	60.00	100.00	200.00	325.00

CAST SILVER

229	1812	60.00	100.00	150.00	225.00
	1812 filled D in SUD				
		60.00	100.00	150.00	225.00

NOTE: Most silver specimens available on today's market are considered spurious.

4 REALES

CAST SILVER

230	1811	—	—	—	—
	1812	—	—	—	—

NOTE: Most silver specimens available on today's market are considered spurious.

Obv. leg: SUD-OXA, bow, arrow.
Rev: Morelos monogram.

KM#	Date	Good	VG	Fine	VF
231	1813	125.00	250.00	400.00	800.00

COPPER
Obv. leg: SUD-OXA, bow, arrow.
Rev: Morelos monogram.

232	1814	100.00	150.00	200.00	400.00

8 REALES

COPPER
Plain fields

233.1	1812	15.00	30.00	60.00	90.00

233.2	1812	6.00	8.00	12.00	15.00
	1813	6.00	8.00	12.00	15.00
	1814	10.00	12.00	15.00	20.00

Similar to KM#233.4 but lines below bow slant left.

233.3	1813	10.00	17.50	30.00	50.00

Obv: Lines below bow slant right.

233.4	1813	10.00	17.50	30.00	50.00

Ornate flowery fields

234	1811	75.00	125.00	150.00	225.00
	1812	4.00	5.00	7.50	15.00
	1813	4.00	5.00	7.50	15.00
	1814	10.00	15.00	25.00	50.00

War of Independence / MEXICO 1239

CAST SILVER

KM#	Date	Good	VG	Fine	VF
235	1811				
	1812	100.00	200.00	300.00	400.00
	1813	75.00	150.00	250.00	350.00
	1814				

NOTE: Most silver specimens available on today's market are considered spurious.

.903 SILVER, struck
Obv: PROV. D. OAXACA, M monogram.
Rev: Lion shield w/or w/o bow above.

| 236 | 1812 | — | — | Rare | — |

Obv: W/o leg.

| 237 | 1813 | — | — | Rare | — |

Obv: Bow/M/SUD.
Rev: PROV. DE. . . . . ., arms.

| 238 | 1813 | — | — | Rare | — |

CAST SILVER
Similar to 4 Reales, KM#231.

| 239 | 1814 | — | — | Rare | — |

COPPER

| 240 | 1814 | 30.00 | 60.00 | 125.00 | 200.00 |

OAXACA spelled out

| 241 | 1814 | — | — | Rare | — |

Huautla
8 REALES

COPPER
Obv. leg: MONEDA PROVI.CIONAL PS.ES. around bow, arrow/SUD.
Rev. leg: FABRICADO EN HUAUTLA

KM#	Date	Good	VG	Fine	VF
242	1812	500.00	800.00	1200.	1750.

Tierra Caliente
(Hot Country)
Under General Morelos
1/2 REAL

COPPER
Obv: Bow, T.C., SUD.
Rev: Morelos monogram, value, date.

| 243 | 1813 | 40.00 | 70.00 | 125.00 | 200.00 |

REAL
COPPER
Similar to 1/2 Real, KM#243.

| 244 | 1813 | 15.00 | 50.00 | 50.00 | 80.00 |

2 REALES
COPPER
Similar to 1/2 Real, KM#243.

| 245 | 1813 | 10.00 | 25.00 | 35.00 | 50.00 |

| 246 | 1814 | 25.00 | 50.00 | 100.00 | 175.00 |

CAST SILVER

| 247 | 1814 | — | — | Rare | — |

8 REALES

COPPER

| 248 | 1813 | 10.00 | 20.00 | 40.00 | 75.00 |

CAST SILVER

| 249 | 1813 | — | — | — | — |

NOTE: Most specimens available on todays market are considered spurious.

PUEBLA

The coins of Puebla emanated from Zacatlan, the headquarters of the hit-and-run insurgent leader Osorno. The mint opened in April of 1812 and operated until the end of 1813. The coins were 2 reales in silver and 1 and 1/2 reales in copper.

Zacatlan
(Struck by General Osorno)
1/2 REAL

COPPER
Obv: Osorno monogram, ZACATLAN, date.
Rev: Crossed arrows, wreath, value.

KM#	Date	Good	VG	Fine	VF
250	1813	—	—	Rare	—

REAL

| 251 | 1813 | 100.00 | 150.00 | 250.00 | 450.00 |

2 REALES
COPPER

| 252 | 1813 | 125.00 | 200.00 | 325.00 | 550.00 |

VERACRUZ

Veracruz was the province that housed the town of Zongolica. In this town 2 priests and a lawyer decided to raise an army to fight for independence. Because of their isolation from other insurgent forces they decided to make coins for their area. Records show that they planned to or did mint coins of 1/2, 1, 2, 4, and 8 reales denominations. Extant specimens are known for only the three higher values.

Zongolica
2 REALES

.903 SILVER
Obv. leg: VIVA FERNANDO VII Y AMERICA, bow and arrow.
Rev. leg: ZONGOLICA, value, crossed palm branch, sword, date.

| 253 | 1812 | 100.00 | 200.00 | 300.00 | 600.00 |

4 REALES
.903 SILVER
Similar to 2 Reales, KM#253.

| 254 | 1812 | 600.00 | 800.00 | 1200. | 2000. |

8 REALES

War of Independence / MEXICO

.903 SILVER

KM#	Date	Good	VG	Fine	VF
255	1812	1200.	1600.	3000.	6000.

COUNTERMARKED COINAGE
Congress Of Chilpanzingo

Type A: Hand holding bow and arrow between quiver w/arrows, sword and bow.

Type B: Crowned eagle on bridge.

1/2 REAL
SILVER
c/m: Type A on cast Mexico City KM#72.

256.1	1812	45.00	70.00	90.00	120.00

c/m: Type A on Zacatecas KM#181.

256.2	1811	55.00	75.00	100.00	125.00

REAL
SILVER
c/m: Type A on cast Mexico City KM#81.

A257	1803	20.00	30.00	50.00	80.00

2 REALES

SILVER
c/m: Type B on 1/4 cut of 8 Reales.

257.1	—	—	—	Unique	—

c/m: Type B on Zacatecas KM#186.

257.2	1811	—	—	Unique	—

8 REALES

SILVER
c/m: Type A on cast Mexico City KM#109.

KM#	Date	Good	VG	Fine	VF
258.1	1805 TH	45.00	65.00	85.00	125.00

c/m: Type A on cast Mexico City KM#110.

258.2	1810 HJ	50.00	75.00	100.00	150.00

c/m: Type A on cast Mexico City KM#111.

258.3	1811 HJ	45.00	65.00	85.00	125.00
	1812 HJ	100.00	125.00	175.00	275.00

c/m: Type B on Chihuahua KM#111.1.

259.1	1816 RP	200.00	250.00	300.00	350.00

c/m: Type B on cast Mexico City KM#111.

259.2	1811 HJ	130.00	140.00	150.00	175.00

c/m: Type B on Valladolid KM#178.

259.3	1813	1000.	2000.	3000.	5000.

c/m: Type B on Zacatecas KM#190.

259.4	1810	400.00	500.00	600.00	750.00

Ensaie
8 REALES
SILVER
c/m: Eagle over ENSAIE on Mexico City KM#110.

260.1	1811 HJ	150.00	200.00	275.00	350.00

c/m: Eagle over ENSAIE crude sling below on Zacatecas KM#189.

260.2	1811	200.00	400.00	600.00	800.00

c/m: Eagle over ENSAIE, crude sling below on Zacatecas KM#190.

260.3	1810				
	1811	100.00	150.00	200.00	300.00

c/m: Eagle over ENSAIE, crude sling below on Zacatecas KM#191.

KM#	Date	Good	VG	Fine	VF
260.4	1810	500.00	700.00	900.00	1200.
	1811	275.00	325.00	400.00	500.00
	1812	225.00	275.00	300.00	400.00

Jose Maria Liceaga

J.M.L. with banner on cross, crossed olive branches.
(J.M.L./V., D.s, S.M.,S.Y.S.L., Ve, A.P.,
s.r.a., Sea, P.G.,S.,S.M.,E.)

1/2 REAL
SILVER
c/m: JML/SM on cast Mexico City 1/2 Real.

A260	—	100.00	150.00	200.00	275.00

2 REALES

SILVER
c/m: J.M.L./Ve on 1/4 cut of 8 Reales.

261.1	ND	175.00	225.00	300.00	—

c/m: J.M.L./V. on Zacatecas KM#186-187.

261.2	1811	200.00	225.00	250.00	300.00

c/m: J.M.L./DS on Zacatecas KM#186-187.

261.3	1811	200.00	235.00	275.00	325.00

c/m: J.M.L./S.M. on Zacatecas KM#186-187.

261.4	1811	200.00	235.00	275.00	325.00

c/m: J.M.L./S.Y. on Zacatecas KM#186-187.

261.5	1811	200.00	235.00	275.00	325.00

8 REALES

SILVER
c/m: J.M.L./D.S. on Zacatecas KM#189-190.

262.1	1811	250.00	325.00	425.00	550.00

c/m: J.M.L./E on Zacatecas KM#189-190.

KM#	Date	Good	VG	Fine	VF
262.2	1811	225.00	300.00	400.00	550.00

c/m: J.M.L./P.G. on Durango KM#111.2.
| 262.3 | 1813 RM | | 300.00 | 275.00 | 375.00 | 525.00 |

c/m: J.M.L./S.F. on Zacatecas KM#189-190.
| 262.4 | 1811 | 200.00 | 275.00 | 375.00 | 525.00 |

c/m: J.M.L./S.M. on Zacatecas KM#189-190.
| 262.5 | 1811 | 200.00 | 275.00 | 375.00 | 525.00 |

c/m: J.M.L./V.E. on Zacatecas KM#189-190.
| 262.6 | 1811 | 200.00 | 275.00 | 375.00 | 525.00 |

Don Jose Maria De Linares

8 REALES

SILVER
c/m: LINA/RES* on Mexico City KM#110.
KM#	Date	Good	VG	Fine	VF
263.1	1808 TH	300.00	350.00	425.00	525.00

c/m: LINA RES * on Zacatecas KM#189-190.
| 263.2 | 1811 | 350.00 | 425.00 | 500.00 | 600.00 |

c/m: LINA RES* on Zacatecas, KM#191-192.
| 263.3 | 1812 | 300.00 | 350.00 | 425.00 | 525.00 |

L.V.S. - Labor Vincit Semper

NOTE: Some authorities believe L.V.S. is for 'La Villa de Sombrerete'.

8 REALES

CAST SILVER
c/m: L.V.S. on Chihuahua KM#123.
| 264.1 | 1811 RP | 275.00 | 350.00 | 450.00 | 550.00 |
| | 1812 RP | 200.00 | 250.00 | 300.00 | 375.00 |

c/m: L.V.S. on Chihuahua KM#111.1 overstruck on KM#123.
264.2	1816 RP	250.00	300.00	325.00	375.00
	1817 RP	250.00	300.00	325.00	375.00
	1818 RP	250.00	300.00	325.00	375.00
	1819 RP	400.00	450.00	500.00	600.00
	1820 RP	450.00	500.00	550.00	650.00

c/m: L.V.S. on Guadalajara KM#111.3.
| 264.3 | 1817 | 185.00 | 220.00 | 250.00 | 310.00 |

c/m: L.V.S. on Nueva Vizcaya KM#165.
| 264.4 | 1811 RM | 1150. | 3150. | 5250. | 8250. |

c/m: L.V.S. on Sombrerete KM#177.
| 264.5 | 1811 | 300.00 | 350.00 | 450.00 | 550.00 |
| | 1812 | 300.00 | 350.00 | 450.00 | 550.00 |

c/m: L.V.S. on Zacatecas KM#189-190.
| 264.6 | 1811 | 350.00 | 400.00 | 450.00 | 550.00 |

c/m: L.V.S. on Zacatecas KM#192.
KM#	Date	Good	VG	Fine	VF
264.7	1813	350.00	400.00	450.00	550.00

Morelos
Morelos monogram

Type A: Stars above and below monogram in circle.

Type B: Dots above and below monogram in oval.

Type C: Monogram in rectangle.

NOTE: Many specimens of Type C available in today's market are considered spurious.

8 REALES

SILVER
c/m: Type A on cast Mexico City KM#109.
265.1	1797 FM	45.00	50.00	55.00	75.00
	1798 FM	45.00	50.00	55.00	75.00
	1800 FM	45.00	50.00	55.00	75.00
	1807 TH	45.00	50.00	55.00	75.00

c/m: Type A on Mexico City KM#110.
| 265.2 | 1809 TH | 55.00 | 65.00 | 75.00 | 100.00 |
| | 1811 HJ | 55.00 | 65.00 | 75.00 | 100.00 |

c/m: Type A on Mexico City KM#111.
| 265.3 | 1812 JJ | 50.00 | 55.00 | 60.00 | 70.00 |

COPPER
c/m: Type A on Oaxaca Sud KM#233.
265.4	1811	12.50	17.50	25.00	35.00
	1812	12.50	17.50	25.00	35.00
	1813	12.50	17.50	25.00	35.00
	1814	12.50	17.50	25.00	35.00

War of Independence / MEXICO 1242

CAST SILVER
c/m: Type A on Supreme National Congress KM#206.

KM#	Date	Good	VG	Fine	VF
265.5	1811	200.00	250.00	300.00	450.00

SILVER
c/m: Type A on Zacatecas KM#189-190.

| 265.6 | 1811 | 200.00 | 250.00 | 350.00 | 450.00 |

c/m: Type A on Zacatecas KM#191.

| 265.7 | 1811 | 200.00 | 250.00 | 350.00 | 450.00 |

c/m: Type B on Guatemala 8 Reales, C#67.

| 266.1 | 1810 M | — | — | — | Rare |

c/m: Type B on Mexico City KM#110.

| 266.2 | 1809 TH | 45.00 | 55.00 | 65.00 | 90.00 |

c/m: Type C on Zacatecas KM#189-190.

| 267 | 1811 | 300.00 | 350.00 | 400.00 | 500.00 |

Norte
Issued by the Supreme National Congress and the Army of the North.

c/m: Eagle on cactus; star to left; NORTE below.

1/2 REAL
SILVER
c/m: On Zacatecas KM#180.

| 268 | 1811 | 250.00 | 300.00 | 375.00 | 450.00 |

2 REALES

SILVER
c/m: On Zacatecas KM#187.

| 269 | 1811 | 225.00 | 275.00 | 325.00 | 400.00 |

c/m: On Zacatecas KM#188.

| A269 | 1812 | — | — | — | — |

4 REALES
SILVER
c/m: On Sombrerete KM#175.

| B269 | 1812 | 100.00 | 150.00 | 200.00 | 275.00 |

8 REALES
SILVER
c/m: On Chihuahua KM#111.1.

| 270.1 | 1813 RP | 250.00 | 350.00 | 450.00 | 550.00 |

c/m: On Guanajuato KM#111.4.

KM#	Date	Good	VG	Fine	VF
270.2	1813 JM	400.00	550.00	700.00	800.00

c/m: On Zacatecas KM#189-190.

| 270.3 | 1811 | 300.00 | 400.00 | 500.00 | 650.00 |

c/m: On Zacatecas KM#191.

| 270.4 | 1811 | 200.00 | 300.00 | 400.00 | 550.00 |
| | 1812 | 200.00 | 300.00 | 400.00 | 550.00 |

Osorno

c/m: Osorno monogram.
(Jose Francisco Osorno)

1/2 REAL

SILVER
c/m: On Mexico City KM#72.

271.1	1798 FM	65.00	100.00	150.00	200.00
	1802 FT	65.00	100.00	150.00	200.00
	1806	65.00	100.00	150.00	200.00

c/m: On Mexico City KM#73.

| 271.2 | 1809 | 65.00 | 100.00 | 150.00 | 200.00 |

REAL

SILVER
c/m: On Mexico City KM#81.

KM#	Date	Good	VG	Fine	VF
272.1	1803 FT	65.00	100.00	150.00	200.00
	1803 FT	65.00	100.00	150.00	200.00

c/m: On Potosi Real.

| 272.2 | ND | 65.00 | 100.00 | 150.00 | 200.00 |

2 REALES
SILVER
c/m: On cast Mexico City KM#92.

| A272.1 | 1809 TH | 75.00 | 125.00 | 175.00 | 250.00 |

c/m: On Zacatlan KM#252.

| A272.2 | 1813 | 150.00 | 200.00 | 300.00 | 400.00 |

4 REALES

SILVER
c/m: On Mexico City KM#97.

| 273 | 1782 FF | — | — | — | — |

8 REALES
SILVER
c/m: On Lima 8 Reales, C#101.

| 274.1 | 1811 JP | 200.00 | 225.00 | 250.00 | 300.00 |

c/m: On Mexico City KM#110.

274.2	1809 TH	125.00	150.00	225.00	300.00
	1810 HJ	125.00	150.00	225.00	300.00
	1811 HJ	125.00	150.00	225.00	300.00

S.J.N.G. - Suprema Junta National Gubernativa
(Refer to Multiple countermarks)

VILLA/GRAN

(Julian Villagran)

2 REALES

SILVER
c/m: On cast Mexico City KM#91.

KM#	Date	Good	VG	Fine	VF
298	1799 FM	150.00	200.00	250.00	350.00
	1802 FT	150.00	200.00	250.00	350.00

8 REALES

SILVER
c/m: VILLA/GRAN on cast Mexico City KM#109.

275	1796 FM	200.00	250.00	300.00	350.00
	1806 TH	200.00	250.00	300.00	350.00

UNCLASSIFIED COUNTERMARKS

General Vicente Guerrero

The countermark of an eagle facing left within a pearled oval has been attributed by some authors as that of General Vicente Guerrero, a leader of the insurgents in the south, 1816-1821.

1/2 REAL

SILVER
c/m: Eagle on Mexico City 1/2 Real.

276	—	40.00	60.00	80.00	175.00

REAL

SILVER
c/m: Eagle on Mexico City KM#78.

277	1772 FM	35.00	50.00	75.00	150.00

2 REALES

SILVER
c/m: Eagle on Mexico City KM#88.

278.1	1784 FM	50.00	75.00	125.00	250.00

c/m: Eagle on Mexico City KM#91.

278.2	1807 PJ	35.00	65.00	85.00	200.00

8 REALES

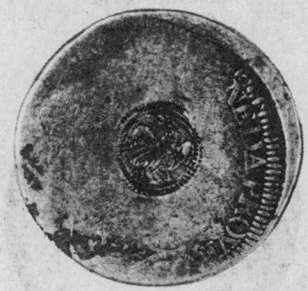

SILVER
c/m: Eagle on Zacatecas KM#191.

KM#	Date	Good	VG	Fine	VF
279	1811	100.00	150.00	200.00	350.00

ZMY
8 REALES

SILVER
c/m: ZMY on Zacatecas KM#191.

286	1812	100.00	150.00	210.00	275.00

MULTIPLE COUNTERMARKS

Many combinations of Royalist and Insurgent countermarks are found usually on the cast copies produced by the Chihuahua and Mexico City Mints and also the crude provisional mint issues of this period. Struck Mexico Mint coins were used for molds to cast necessity coinage and were countermarked to show issuing authority. Some were marked again by opposing forces or by friendly forces to allow circulation in their area of occupation. Some countermarks are only obtainable with companion markings.

Chilpanzingo Crown and Flag
8 REALES

SILVER
c/m: Chilpanzingo Type B and crown and flag on Zacatecas KM#189-190.

280	1811

Chilpanzingo/LVA
8 REALES

SILVER
c/m: Chilpanzingo Type A and LVA on Mexico City KM#109.

KM#	Date	Good	VG	Fine	VF
297	1805 TH	—	—	—	—

Chilpanzingo/LVS
8 REALES

SILVER
c/m: Chilpanzingo Type A and script LVS on cast Mexico City KM#110.

281	1809 HJ	50.00	75.00	150.00	250.00

Chilpanzingo/Morelos
8 REALES

SILVER
c/m: Chilpanzingo Type A and Morelos monogram Type A on cast Mexico City KM#109.

284	1806 TH	35.00	45.00	55.00	150.00
	1807 TH				

c/m: Chilpanzingo Type A and Morelos monogram Type A on struck Mexico City KM#110.

285.1	1809 TH	35.00	50.00	100.00	250.00

c/m: Chilpanzingo Type A and Morelos monogram Type A on cast Mexico City KM#110.

285.2	1810 HJ	35.00	45.00	55.00	150.00
	1811 HJ				

c/m: Chilpanzingo Type A and Morelos monogram Type A on cast Mexico City KM#111.

285.3	1811 HJ	—	—	—	—

War of Independence / MEXICO 1244

Chilpanzingo/Morelos/LVS
8 REALES

SILVER
c/m: Chilpanzingo Type A, Morelos Type A and LVS monogram on cast Mexico City KM#110.

KM#	Date	Good	VG	Fine	VF
286	1809 HJ	35.00	50.00	75.00	200.00

Chilpanzingo/P.D.V.
8 REALES

SILVER
c/m: Chilpanzingo Type B and P.D.V. (Provisional De Valladolid) on Valladolid KM#178.

287	1813	—	—	—	—

Chilpanzingo/S.J.N.G.
8 REALES

SILVER
c/m: Chilpanzingo Type B and S.J.N.G. (Suprema Junta Nacional Gubernativa) on Zacatecas KM#189-190.

288	1811	—	—	—	—

C.M.S./S.C.M.
2 REALES

SILVER
c/m: C.M.S. (Comandancia Militar Suriana) and eagle w/S.C.M. (Soberano Congreso Mexicano) on Mexico City 2 Reales.

289	—	—	—	—	—

ENSAIE/VTIL
8 REALES

SILVER
c/m: ENSAIE and VTIL on Zacatecas KM#189-190.

KM#	Date	Good	VG	Fine	VF
290	1811	—	—	—	—

J.M.L./VTIL
2 REALES

SILVER
c/m: J.M.L./D.S. and VTIL on Zacatecas, KM#186.

A286	1811	75.00	125.00	175.00	250.00

c/m: J.M.L./V.E. and VTIL on Zacatecas KM#186.

B286	1810	75.00	125.00	175.00	250.00
	1811	75.00	125.00	175.00	250.00

8 REALES

SILVER
c/m: J.M.L./D.S. and VTIL on Mexico City KM#110.

291	1810 HJ	—	—	—	—

L.C.M./Morelos
8 REALES

SILVER
c/m: LCM and Morelos monogram Type A on cast Mexico City KM#109.

282	1792 FM	—	—	—	—

Morelos/Morelos
8 REALES

SILVER
c/m: Morelos Type A and C on cast Mexico City KM#109.

KM#	Date	Good	VG	Fine	VF
283	1806 TH	—	—	—	—

LCM/MVA-1812
8 REALES

SILVER
c/m: LCM and MVA/1812 on Chihuahua KM#123.

292	1810 RP	—	—	—	—

c/m: LCM and MVA 1812 on Chihuahua KM#110.

A293	1810 HJ	—	—	—	—

c/m: LCM and MVA/1812 on Chihuahua KM#111.1.

293	1818	200.00	300.00	450.00	700.00

L.V.A./Morelos
8 REALES

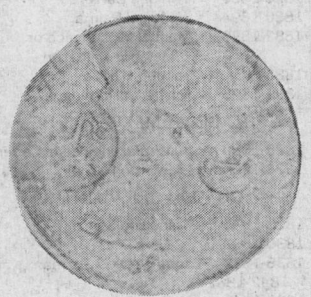

SILVER
c/m: Script LVA and Morelos monogram Type A
on cast Mexico City KM#110.

KM#	Date	Good	VG	Fine	VF
294	- HJ				

M.d.S./S.C.M.
2 REALES

SILVER
c/m: M.d.S. (Militar del Sur) and eagle w/S.C.M.
(Soberano Congreso Mexicano) on Mexico City 2 Reales.

295	—				

OSORNO/VILLAGRAN
8 REALES

SILVER
c/m: Osorno monogram and VILLA/GRAN on cast
Mexico City KM#110.

296	1809 TH				

S.J.N.G./VTIL
8 REALES

SILVER
c/m: S.J.N.G. and VTIL on Zacatecas KM#191.

297	ND	35.00	50.00	75.00	200.00

EMPIRE OF ITURBIDE
RULERS
Augustin I Iturbide, 1822-1823
MINT MARKS
Mo - Mexico City Mint
ASSAYER'S INITIALS
JA - Jose Garcia Ansaldo, 1812-1833
JM - Joaquin Davila Madrid,
  1809-1833

1/8 REAL

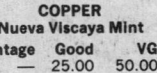

COPPER
Nueva Viscaya Mint

KM#	Date	Mintage	Good	VG	Fine	VF
299	1821	—	25.00	50.00	85.00	150.00
	1822	—	7.50	12.50	25.00	45.00
	1823	—	7.50	12.50	25.00	45.00

1/4 REAL

COPPER
Nueva Viscaya Mint

300	1822	—	175.00	275.00	425.00	500.00

1/2 REAL

.903 SILVER
Mint mark: Mo

KM#	Date	Mintage	Fine	VF	XF	Unc
301	1822 JM	—	17.50	40.00	75.00	325.00
	1823 JM	—	12.50	20.00	55.00	275.00

REAL

.903 SILVER
Mint mark: Mo

302	1822 JM	—	75.00	125.00	250.00	700.00

2 REALES

.903 SILVER
Mint mark: Mo

303	1822 JM	—	30.00	60.00	250.00	800.00
	1823 JM	—	20.00	50.00	200.00	800.00

8 REALES

.903 SILVER
Mint mark: Mo

KM#	Date	Mintage	Fine	VF	XF	Unc
304	1822 JM	—	70.00	150.00	275.00	900.00

Obv: Bust similar to 8 Escudos, KM#313.
Rev: Similar to KM#304.

305	1822 JM	—	75.00	150.00	350.00	950.00

Type I. Obv: Leg. divided. Rev: 8 R.J.M. at upper
left of eagle.

306	1822 JM	—	75.00	150.00	300.00	1250.

Type II. Obv: Similar to KM#306.
Rev: Similar to KM#310.

307	1822 JM	—	150.00	350.00	600.00	2250.

Type III. Obv: Continuous leg. w/long smooth
truncation. Rev: Similar to KM#306.

308	1822 JM	—	200.00	525.00	1000.	1500.

Type IV. Obv: Similar to KM#308.
Rev: Similar to KM#310.

309	1822 JM	—	50.00	120.00	250.00	900.00

Empire of Iturbide / MEXICO 1246

Type V. Obv. continuous leg. w/short irregular truncation. Rev: 8 R.J.M. below eagle.

KM#	Date	Mintage	Fine	VF	XF	Unc
310	1822 JM	—	55.00	135.00	250.00	800.00
	1823 JM	—	55.00	135.00	250.00	800.00

Type VI. Obv. Bust w/long truncation. Rev: Similar to KM#310.

| 311 | 1823 JM | — | — | — | Rare | — |

4 SCUDOS

.875 GOLD
Mint mark: Mo

| 312 | 1823 JM | — | 1000. | 1750. | 2500. | 4500. |

8 SCUDOS

.875 GOLD
Mint mark: Mo
Obv. leg: AUGUSTINUS.

| 313.1 | 1822 JM | — | 1000. | 1750. | 2500. | 4500. |

Obv. leg: AUGSTINUS.

| 313.2 | 1822 JM | — | 1250. | 2000. | 3000. | 5500. |

KM#	Date	Mintage	Fine	VF	XF	Unc
314	1823 JM	—	1000.	1750.	2500.	4500.

REPUBLIC

MINT MARKS

- A, AS - Alamos
- CE - Real de Catorce
- C, CH, CL - Chihuahua
- C, Cn, Gn(error) - Culiacan
- D, Do - Durango
- EoMo - Estado de Mexico
- Ga - Guadalajara
- GC - Guadalupe y Calvo
- G, Go - Guanajuato
- H, Ho - Hermosillo
- M, Mo - Mexico City
- O, OA - Oaxaca
- SLP, PI, P, I/P - San Luis Potosi
- Z, Zs - Zacatecas

ASSAYER'S INITIALS

ALAMOS MINT

Initials	Years	Mintmaster
PG	1862-1868	Pascual Gaxiola
DL, L	1866-1879	Domingo Larraguibel
AM	1872-1874	Antonio Moreno
ML, L	1878-1895	Manuel Larraguibel

REAL DE CATORCE MINT

| ML | 1863 | Mariano Leon |

CHIHUAHUA MINT

MR	1831-1834	Mariano Cristobal Ramirez
AM	1833-1839	Jose Antonio Mucharraz
MJ	1832	Jose Mariano Jimenez
RG	1839-1856	Rodrigo Garcia
JC	1856-1865	Joaquin Campa
BA	1858	Bruno Arriada
FP	1866	Francisco Potts
JG	1866-1868	Jose Maria Gomez del Campo
MM, M	1868-1895	Manuel Merino
AV	1873-1880	Antonio Valero
EA	1877	Eduardo Avila
JM	1877	Jacobo Mucharraz
GR	1877	Guadalupe Rocha
MG	1880-1882	Manuel Gameros

CULIACAN MINT

CE	1846-1870	Clemente Espinosa de los Monteros
C	1870	???
PV	1860-1861	Pablo Viruega
MP, P	1871-1876	Manuel Onofre Parodi
GP	1876	Celso Gaxiola & Manuel Onofre Parodi
CG, G	1876-1878	Celso Gaxiola
JD, D	1878-1882	Juan Dominguez
AM, M	1882-1899	Antonio Moreno
F	1870	Fernando Ferrari
JQ, Q	1899-1903	Jesus S. Quiroz
FV, V	1903	Francisco Valdez
MH, H	1904	Merced Hernandez
RP, P	1904-1905	Ramon Ponce de Leon

DURANGO MINT

RL	1825-1832	???
RM	1830-1848	Ramon Mascarenas
OMC	1840	Octavio Martinez de Castro
CM	1848-1876	Clemente Moron
JMR	1849-1852	Jose Maria Ramirez
CP, P	1853-1864, 1867-1873	Carlos Leon de la Pena

Initials	Years	Mintmaster
LT	1864-1865	???
JMP, P	1877	Carlos Miguel de la Palma
PE, E	1878	Pedro Espejo
TB, B	1878-1880	Trinidad Barrera
JP	1880-1894	J. Miguel Palma
MC, C	1882-1890	Manuel M. Canseco or Melchor Calderon
JB	1885	Jacobo Blanco
ND, D	1892-1895	Norberto Dominguez

ESTADO DE MEXICO MINT

| L | 1828-1830 | Luis Valazquez de la Cadena |
| F | 1828-1830 | Francisco Parodi |

GUADALAJARA MINT

FS	1818-1835	Francisco Suarez
JM	1830-1832	???
JG	1836-1839, 1842-1867	Juan de Dios Guzman
MC	1839-1846	Manuel Cueras
JM	1867-1869	Jesus P. Manzano
IC, C	1869-1877	Ignacio Canizo y Soto
MC	1874-1875	Manuel Contreras
JA, A	1877-1881	Julio Arancivia
FS, S	1880-1882	Fernando Sayago
TB, B	1883-1884	Trinidad Barrera
AH, H	1884-1885	Antonio Hernandez y Prado
JS, S	1885-1895	Jose S. Schiafino

GUADALUPE Y CALVO MINT

| MP | 1844-1852 | Manuel-Onofre Parodi |

GUANAJUATO MINT

JJ	1825-1826	Jose Mariano Jimenez
MJ, MR, JM, PG, PJ, PF	???	
PM	1841-1848, 1853-1861	Patrick Murphy
YF	1862-1868	Yldefonso Flores
YE	1862-1863	Ynocencio Espinoza
FR	1870-1878	Faustino Ramirez
SB, RR	???	
RS	1891-1900	Rosendo Sandoval

HERMOSILLO MINT

PP	1835-1836	Pedro Peimbert
FM	1871-1876	Florencio Monteverde
MP	1866	Manuel Onofre Parodi
PR	1866-1875	Pablo Rubio
R	1874-1875	Pablo Rubio
GR	1877	Guadalupe Rocha
AF, F	1876-1877	Alejandro Fourcade
JA, A	1877-1883	Jesus Acosta
FM, M	1883-1886	Fernando Mendez
FG, G	1886-1895	Fausto Gaxiola

MEXICO CITY MINT

Because of the great number of assayers for this mint (Mexico City is a much larger mint than any of the others) there is much confusion as to which initial stands for which assayer at any one time. Therefore we feel that it would be of no value to list the assayers.

OAXACA MINT

AE	1859-1891	Agustin Endner
E	1889-1890	Agustin Endner
FR	1861-1864	Francisco de la Rosa
EN	1890	Eduardo Navarro Luna
N	1890	Eduardo Navarro Luna

POTOSI MINT

JS	1827-1842	Juan Sanabria
AM	1838, 1843-1849	Jose Antonio Mucharraz
PS	1842-1843, 1848-1849, 1857-1861, 1867-1870	Pomposo Sanabria
S	1869-1870	Pomposo Sanabria
MC	1849-1859	Mariano Catano
RO	1859-1865	Romualdo Obregon
MH, H	1870-1885	Manuel Herrera Rozo
O	1870-1873	Juan R. Ochoa
CA, G	1867-1870	Carlos Aguirre Gomez
BE, E	1879-1881	Blas Escontria
LC, C	1885-1886	Uis Cievas
MR, R	1886-1893	Mariano Reyes

ZACATECAS MINT

A	1825-1829	Adalco
Z	1825-1826	Mariano Zaldivar
V	1824-1831	Jose Mariano Vela
O	1829-1867	Manuel Ochoa
M	1831-1867	Manuel Miner
VL	1860-1866	Vicente Larranaga
JS	1867-1868, 1876-1886	J.S. de Santa Ana
YH	1868-1874	Ygnacio Hierro
JA	1874-1876	Juan H. Acuna
FZ	1886-1905	Francisco de P. Zarate
FM	1904-1905	Francisco Mateos

State and Federal Issues
1/16 REAL
(Medio Octavo)

COPPER
Jalisco Mint
Obv. leg: DEPARTAMENTO DE JALISCO

KM#	Date	Mintage	Good	VG	Fine	VF
316	1860	—	3.00	5.00	10.00	50.00

Obv. leg: ESTADO LIBRE DE JALISCO

| 317 | 1861 | — | 3.00 | 5.00 | 10.00 | 50.00 |

Mexico City Mint
Obv. leg: REPUBLICA MEXICANA

KM#	Date	Mintage	VG	Fine	VF	XF
315	1831	—	10.00	15.00	35.00	100.00
	1832/1	—	12.00	17.50	35.00	125.00
	1832	—	10.00	15.00	35.00	100.00
	1833	—	10.00	15.00	35.00	100.00

BRASS

| 315a | 1832 | — | 15.00 | 22.50 | 60.00 | 150.00 |
| | 1833 | — | 12.00 | 17.50 | 50.00 | 100.00 |

1/8 REAL
(Octavo Real)

COPPER
Chihuahua Mint
Obv. leg: ESTADO SOBERANO DE CHIHUAHUA

KM#	Date	Mintage	Good	VG	Fine	VF
318	1833	—	—	—	Rare	—
	1834	—	—	—	Rare	—
	1835/3	—	—	—	Rare	—

Obv. leg: ESTADO DE CHIHUAHUA

| 319 | 1855 | — | 3.50 | 5.00 | 18.00 | 60.00 |

Durango Mint
Rev. leg: LIBERTAD

| 320 | 1824 | — | 5.00 | 10.00 | 35.00 | 100.00 |
| | 1828 | — | 150.00 | 250.00 | 400.00 | 900.00 |

NOTE: These pieces were frequently struck over 1/8 Real, dated 1821-23 of Nueva Vizcaya. All known examples are collectable contemporary counterfeits.

Rev. leg: OCTo.DE.R.DE DO., date.

| 321 | 1828 | — | 6.00 | 15.00 | 35.00 | 100.00 |

Obv. leg: ESTADO DE DURANGO

| 322 | 1833 | — | — | — | Rare | — |

Obv. leg: REPUBLICA MEXICANA

| 323 | 1842/33 | — | 15.00 | 20.00 | 40.00 | 125.00 |
| | 1842 | — | 10.00 | 15.00 | 30.00 | 100.00 |

Obv. leg: REPUBLICA MEXICANA
Rev. leg: DEPARTAMENTO DE DURANGO

| 324 | 1845 | — | 25.00 | 50.00 | 100.00 | 250.00 |

KM#	Date	Mintage	Good	VG	Fine	VF
324	1846	—	—	—	Rare	—
	1847	—	3.00	5.00	8.00	35.00

Obv. leg: REPUBLICA MEXICANA
Rev. leg: ESTADO DE DURANGO

325	1851	—	3.00	5.00	8.00	30.00
	1852/1	—	3.00	5.00	8.00	30.00
	1852	—	3.00	5.00	8.00	30.00

Guanajuato Mint
Obv. leg: ESTADO LIBRE DE GUANAJUATO

326	1829	—	3.00	5.00	10.00	30.00
	1829 error w/GUANJUATO					
		—	5.00	10.00	30.00
	1830	—	8.00	12.00	20.00	75.00

BRASS

| 327 | 1856 | — | 8.00 | 12.00 | 20.00 | 75.00 |

25mm

| 328 | 1856 | — | 4.00 | 6.00 | 10.00 | 30.00 |
| | 1857 | — | 4.00 | 6.00 | 10.00 | 30.00 |

COPPER

| 328a | 1857 | — | 10.00 | 20.00 | 35.00 | 60.00 |

Jalisco Mint
Obv. leg: ESTADO LIBRE DE JALISCO

329	1828	—	3.00	5.00	8.00	25.00
	1831	—	100.00	200.00	300.00	400.00
	1832/28	—	3.00	5.00	8.00	25.00
	1832	—	3.00	5.00	8.00	25.00
	1833	—	3.00	5.00	8.00	25.00
	1834	—	50.00	100.00	175.00	300.00

330	1856	—	4.00	7.00	10.00	25.00
	1857	—	4.00	7.00	10.00	25.00
	1858	—	4.00	7.00	10.00	25.00
	1861	—	100.00	200.00	300.00	400.00
	1862/1	—	4.00	7.00	10.00	25.00
	1862	—	4.00	7.00	10.00	25.00

Obv. leg: DEPARTAMENTO DE JALISCO

KM#	Date	Mintage	Good	VG	Fine	VF
331	1858	—	3.00	5.00	8.00	20.00
	1859	—	3.00	5.00	8.00	20.00
	1860/59	—	3.00	5.00	8.00	20.00
	1860	—	3.00	5.00	8.00	20.00
	1862	—	6.00	10.00	20.00	60.00

Mexico City Mint
27mm
Obv. leg: REPUBLICA MEXICANA

| 332 | 1829 | — | — | — | Rare | — |

21mm
Obv. leg: REPUBLICA MEXICANA

333	1829	—	10.00	15.00	30.00	60.00
	1830	—	2.00	3.00	5.00	15.00
	1831	—	2.00	4.00	6.00	20.00
	1832	—	2.00	4.00	6.00	20.00
	1833/2	—	2.00	4.00	6.00	20.00
	1833	—	2.00	3.00	5.00	15.00
	1834	—	2.00	3.00	5.00	15.00
	1835/4	—	2.25	4.00	6.00	20.00
	1835	—	2.00	3.00	5.00	15.00

Obv. leg: LIBERTAD

334	1841	—	7.00	15.00	30.00	75.00
	1842	—	3.00	5.00	10.00	30.00
	1850	—	15.00	20.00	30.00	80.00
	1861	—	8.00	12.00	25.00	70.00

Occidente Mint
Obv. leg: ESTADO DE OCCIDENTE

| 335 | 1828 reverse S | — | 15.00 | 30.00 | 45.00 | 100.00 |
| | 1829 | — | 15.00 | 30.00 | 45.00 | 100.00 |

Potosi Mint
Obv. leg: ESTADO LIBRE DE SAN LUIS POTOSI

336	1829	—	6.00	9.00	15.00	50.00
	1830	—	8.00	12.00	20.00	60.00
	1831	—	5.00	8.00	12.00	40.00
	1859	—	5.00	8.00	12.00	40.00

Sonora Mint
Obv. leg: ESTO LIBE Y SOBO DE SONORA, 28mm.

| 337 | 1859 | — | — | — | Rare | — |

Zacatecas Mint

Republic / MEXICO 1248

Obv. leg: ESTo LIBe FEDo DE ZACATECAS

KM#	Date	Mintage	Good	VG	Fine	VF
338	1825	—	3.00	5.00	10.00	25.00
	1827	—	3.00	5.00	10.00	25.00
	1827 inverted A for V in OCTAVO					
		—	12.00	20.00	40.00	100.00
	1829	—			Rare	—
	1830	—	3.00	5.00	8.00	20.00
	1831	—	4.00	6.00	10.00	25.00
	1832	—	3.00	5.00	8.00	20.00
	1833	—	3.00	5.00	8.00	20.00
	1835	—	4.00	6.00	10.00	25.00
	1846	—	4.00	6.00	10.00	25.00
	1851	—	125.00	175.00	250.00	350.00
	1852	—	4.00	6.00	10.00	25.00
	1858	—	3.00	5.00	8.00	20.00
	1859	—	3.00	5.00	8.00	20.00
	1862	—	3.00	5.00	8.00	20.00
	1863 reversed 6 in date					
		—	3.00	5.00	8.00	20.00

Obv. leg: DEPARTAMENTO DE ZACATECAS

339	1836	—	4.00	8.00	15.00	40.00
	1845	—	6.00	10.00	20.00	50.00
	1846	—	4.00	8.00	15.00	40.00

1/4 REAL
(Un Quarto / Una Quartilla)
(Copper/Brass Series)

COPPER
Chihuahua Mint
Obv. leg: ESTADO SOBERANO DE CHIHUAHUA

KM#	Date	Mintage	Good	VG	Fine	VF
340	1833	—	8.00	12.00	35.00	75.00
	1834	—	5.00	8.00	12.00	50.00
	1835	—	5.00	8.00	12.00	50.00

Obv. leg: ESTADO LIBRE DE CHIHUAHUA

341	1846	—	4.00	6.00	12.00	50.00

NOTE: Varieties with or without fraction bar.

Obv. leg: ESTADO DE CHIHUAHUA

342	1855	—	3.00	5.00	10.00	50.00
	1856	—	3.00	5.00	10.00	50.00

Obv. leg: DEPARTAMENTO DE CHIHUAHUA

343	1855	—	3.00	5.00	10.00	50.00
	1855 DE/reversed D and E					
		—	3.00	5.00	10.00	50.00

Obv. leg: E. CHIHA LIBERTAD

KM#	Date	Mintage	Good	VG	Fine	VF
344	1860	—	2.00	4.00	8.00	25.00
	1861	—	2.00	4.00	8.00	25.00
	1865/1	—	2.50	5.50	10.00	30.00
	1865	—	10.00	20.00	35.00	95.00
	1866	—	2.00	4.00	8.00	25.00

Durango Mint
Obv. leg: REPUBLICA MEXICANA

345	1845	—			Rare	—

Obv. leg: REPUBLICA MEXICANA
Rev: DURANGO, date, value.

346	1858	—			Rare	—

Obv. leg: ESTADO DE DURANGO
Rev. leg: CONSTITUCION

347	1858	—	3.00	6.00	12.00	50.00

NOTE: Variety exists in brass.

Obv. leg: DEPARTAMENTO DE DURANGO
Rev. leg: LIBERTAD EN EL ORDEN.

348	1860	—	2.00	5.00	15.00	45.00
	1866	—	2.00	5.00	15.00	45.00

Obv. leg: ESTADO DE DURANGO
Rev. leg: INDEPENDENCIA Y LIBERTAD

349	1866	—	3.00	5.00	12.00	45.00

Rev. leg: SUFRAGIO LIBRE

KM#	Date	Mintage	Good	VG	Fine	VF
350	1872	—	2.00	4.00	10.00	20.00

NOTE: Variety exists in brass.

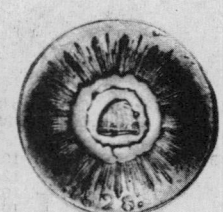

Guanajuato Mint
Obv. leg: ESTADO LIBRE DE GUANAJUATO

351	1828	—	4.00	7.00	10.00	45.00
	1828 error w/GUANJUATO					
		—	4.00	7.00	10.00	45.00
	1829	—	4.00	7.00	10.00	45.00

Obv. leg: EST. LIB. DE GUANAXUATO
Rev. leg: OMNIA VINCIT LABOR

352	1856	—	12.00	25.00	50.00	100.00
	1857	—	6.00	9.00	15.00	45.00

BRASS

352a	1856	—	4.00	7.00	10.00	30.00
	1857	—	4.00	7.00	10.00	30.00

COPPER
Jalisco Mint
Obv. leg: ESTADO LIBRE DE JALISCO

353	1828	—	4.00	6.00	12.00	35.00
	1829/8	—	3.00	5.00	8.00	35.00
	1829	—	3.00	5.00	8.00	35.00
	1830/20	—	3.00	5.00	8.00	30.00
	1830/29	—	3.00	5.00	8.00	30.00
	1830	—	3.00	5.00	8.00	30.00
	1831	—	—	—	Rare	—
	1832/20	—	3.00	5.00	8.00	30.00
	1832/28	—	3.00	5.00	8.00	30.00
	1832	—	3.00	5.00	8.00	30.00
	1833/2	—	3.00	5.00	8.00	30.00
	1834	—	3.00	5.00	8.00	30.00
	1835/3	—	3.00	5.00	8.00	30.00
	1835	—	3.00	5.00	8.00	30.00
	1836	—	—	—	Rare	—

Obv. leg: DEPARTAMENTO DE JALISCO

354	1836	—			Rare	—

Republic / MEXICO 1249

Obv. leg: ESTADO LIBRE DE JALISCO

KM#	Date	Mintage	Good	VG	Fine	VF
355	1858	—	3.00	5.00	8.00	20.00
	1861	—	3.00	5.00	10.00	25.00
	1862	—	3.00	5.00	8.00	20.00

Obv. leg: DEPARTAMENTO DE JALISCO

356	1858	—	3.00	5.00	8.00	20.00
	1859/8	—	3.00	5.00	8.00	20.00
	1859	—	3.00	5.00	8.00	20.00
	1860	—	3.00	5.00	8.00	20.00

Mexico City Mint
Obv. leg: REPUBLICA MEXICANA.

KM#	Date	Mintage	VG	Fine	VF	XF
357	1829	—	8.00	20.00	60.00	150.00

Reduced size.

358	1829	—	12.00	25.00	50.00	150.00
	1830	—	2.00	3.00	4.00	10.00
	1831	—	2.00	3.00	4.00	10.00
	1832	—	5.50	10.00	20.00	35.00
	1833	—	2.00	3.00	4.00	10.00
	1834/3	—	2.00	3.00	4.00	10.00
	1834	—	2.00	3.00	4.00	10.00
	1835	—	2.00	3.00	4.00	10.00
	1836	—	2.00	3.00	4.00	10.00
	1837	—	5.00	10.00	20.00	40.00

BRASS
c/m: JM

358a.1	1831	—	8.00	15.00	35.00	75.00

W/o countermark

358a.2	1831	—	—	—	—	—

COPPER
Potosi Mint
Obv. leg: ESTADO LIBRE DE SAN LUIS POTOSI
Rev. leg: MEXICO LIBRE

KM#	Date	Mintage	Good	VG	Fine	VF
359	1828	—	3.00	4.00	6.00	15.00
	1829	—	3.00	4.00	6.00	15.00
	1830	—	3.00	4.00	6.00	15.00
	1832	—	3.00	4.00	6.00	15.00
	1859 large LIBRE					
		—	3.00	4.00	6.00	15.00
	1859 small LIBRE					
		—	3.00	4.00	6.00	15.00
	1860	—	3.00	4.00	6.00	15.00

Rev. leg: REPUBLICA MEXICANA

KM#	Date	Mintage	Good	VG	Fine	VF
360	1862	1,367	3.00	4.00	6.00	10.00
	1862 LIBR					
		Inc. Ab.	3.00	4.00	6.00	10.00

Milled edge
Obv. leg: ESTADO LIBRE Y SOBERANO DE S.L. POTOSI
Rev. leg: LIBERTAD Y REFORMA

361	1867	3,177	3.00	4.00	7.00	20.00
	1867 AFG I.A.	3.00	4.00	7.00	20.00

Plain edge

362	1867 Inc. Ab.	3.00	4.00	7.00	20.00
	1867 AFG I.A.	3.00	4.00	7.00	20.00

Sinaloa Mint
Obv. leg: ESTADO LIBRE Y SOBERANO DE SINALOA

363	1847	—	3.00	5.00	8.00	20.00
	1848	—	3.00	5.00	8.00	20.00
	1859	—	2.00	3.00	4.00	9.00
	1861	—	2.00	3.00	4.00	9.00
	1862	—	2.00	3.00	4.00	9.00
	1863	—	2.50	3.50	5.00	10.00
	1864/3	—	2.50	3.50	5.00	10.00
	1864	—	2.00	3.00	4.00	9.00
	1865	—	2.00	3.00	4.00	9.00
	1866/5	7,401	2.50	3.50	5.00	10.00
	1866 Inc. Ab.	2.00	3.00	4.00	9.00

BRASS

363a	1847	—	5.00	10.00	20.00	50.00

COPPER
Sonora Mint
Obv. leg: EST.D.SONORA UNA CUART

364	1831	—	—	—	Rare	—
	1832	—	3.00	5.00	9.00	50.00
	1833/2	—	2.50	4.00	7.00	40.00
	1833	—	2.50	4.00	7.00	40.00
	1834	—	2.50	4.00	7.00	40.00
	1835/3	—	2.50	4.00	7.00	40.00
	1835	—	2.50	4.00	7.00	40.00
	1836	—	2.50	4.00	7.00	40.00

Obv. leg: ESTO.LIBE.Y SOBO.DE SONORA

365	1859	—	3.00	5.00	8.00	20.00
	1861/59	—	4.00	6.50	11.00	25.00
	1861	—	3.00	5.00	8.00	20.00
	1862	—	3.00	5.00	8.00	20.00
	1863/2	—	7.00	15.00	30.00	50.00

Zacatecas Mint
Obv. leg: ESTO LIBE FEDO DE ZACATECAS

KM#	Date	Mintage	Good	VG	Fine	VF
366	1824	—	—	—	Rare	—
	1825	—	3.00	5.00	8.00	20.00
	1826	—	100.00	150.00	200.00	300.00
	1827/17	—	3.00	5.00	8.00	20.00
	1829	—	3.00	5.00	8.00	20.00
	1830	—	3.00	5.00	8.00	20.00
	1831	—	50.00	100.00	125.00	250.00
	1832	—	3.00	5.00	8.00	20.00
	1833	—	3.00	5.00	8.00	20.00
	1834	—	—	—	Rare	—
	1835	—	3.00	5.00	8.00	20.00
	1846	—	3.00	5.00	8.00	20.00
	1847	—	3.00	5.00	8.00	20.00
	1852	—	3.00	5.00	8.00	20.00
	1853	—	3.00	5.00	8.00	20.00
	1855	—	5.00	10.00	20.00	65.00
	1858	—	3.00	5.00	8.00	20.00
	1859	—	3.00	5.00	8.00	20.00
	1860	—	100.00	150.00	200.00	300.00
	1862/57	—	3.50			
	1862/59	—	10.00	20.00	40.00	80.00
	1862	—	3.00	5.00	8.00	20.00
	1863/2	—	3.00	5.00	8.00	20.00
	1863	—	3.00	5.00	8.00	20.00
	1864/58	—	5.00	10.00	25.00	60.00

Obv. leg: DEPARTAMENTO DE ZACATECAS

367	1836	—	5.00	8.00	12.00	25.00
	1845	—	—	—	Rare	—
	1846	—	3.00	5.00	8.00	20.00

SILVER SERIES

0.8450 g, .903 SILVER, .0245 oz ASW
Mint mark: CA

KM#	Date	Mintage	VG	Fine	VF	XF
368	1843 RG	—	75.00	125.00	300.00	500.00

Mint mark: C

368.1	1855 LR	—	50.00	100.00	200.00	400.00

Mint mark: Do

368.2	1842 LR	—	12.00	20.00	40.00	125.00
	1843 LR	—	20.00	25.00	60.00	150.00

Mint mark: Ga

368.3	1842 JG	—	2.50	5.50	8.00	20.00
	1843 JG	—	6.00	9.00	12.50	30.00
	1843 MC	—	4.00	6.50	9.00	25.00
	1844 MC	—	4.00	6.50	9.00	25.00
	1844 LR	—	2.50	5.00	7.50	15.00
	1845 LR	—	2.50	4.50	7.50	15.00
	1846 LR	—	5.00	8.00	10.00	25.00
	1847 LR	—	4.00	6.50	9.00	25.00
	1848 LR	—	—	—	Rare	—
	1850 LR	—	—	—	Rare	—
	1851 LR	—	6.00	10.00	20.00	50.00
	1852 LR	—	50.00	100.00	135.00	200.00
	1854/3 LR	—	50.00	100.00	135.00	200.00
	1854 LR	—	5.00	10.00	12.50	30.00
	1855 LR	—	5.00	8.00	10.00	30.00
	1857 LR	—	6.50	10.00	15.00	27.50
	1862 LR	—	5.50	10.00	15.00	30.00

Mint mark: GC

368.4	1844 LR	—	50.00	75.00	125.00	200.00

Mint mark: Go

368.5	1842 PM	—	4.00	6.00	10.00	20.00
	1842 LR	—	2.00	4.00	8.00	15.00
	1843/2 LR	—	4.00	6.00	10.00	20.00
	1843 LR	—	2.00	4.00	8.00	15.00
	1844 LR	—	2.00	4.00	8.00	15.00
	1845 LR	—	8.00	15.00	30.00	60.00
	1846 LR	—	4.00	6.00	10.00	20.00
	1847 LR	—	2.00	4.00	8.00	15.00
	1848/7 LR	—	2.00	4.00	8.00	15.00
	1848 LR	—	2.00	4.00	8.00	15.00
	1849/7 LR	—	8.00	15.00	30.00	60.00
	1849 LR	—	2.00	4.00	8.00	15.00
	1850 LR	—	2.00	4.00	8.00	15.00

KM#	Date	Mintage	VG	Fine	VF	XF
368.5	1851 LR	—	2.00	4.00	8.00	15.00
	1852 LR	—	2.00	4.00	8.00	15.00
	1853 LR	—	2.00	4.00	8.00	15.00
	1855 LR	—	4.00	8.00	15.00	30.00
	1856 LR	—	5.00	10.00	20.00	35.00
	1862/1 LR	—	3.00	5.00	10.00	20.00
	1862 LR	—	2.00	4.00	8.00	15.00
	1863 LR	—	2.00	4.00	8.00	15.00

Mint mark: Mo

KM#	Date	Mintage	VG	Fine	VF	XF
368.6	1842 LR	—	2.00	4.00	8.00	15.00
	1843 LR	—	2.00	4.00	8.00	15.00
	1844/3 LR	—	8.00	12.00	20.00	40.00
	1844 LR	—	4.00	6.00	10.00	20.00
	1845 LR	—	4.00	6.00	10.00	20.00
	1846 LR	—	2.00	4.00	8.00	15.00
	1850 LR	—	5.00	10.00	20.00	35.00
	1858 LR	—	4.00	8.00	15.00	30.00
	1859 LR	—	4.00	6.00	10.00	20.00
	1860 LR	—	4.00	6.00	10.00	20.00
	1861 LR	—	4.00	6.00	10.00	20.00
	1862 LR	—	4.00	6.00	10.00	20.00
	1863 LR	—	4.00	6.00	10.00	20.00

Mint mark: S.L.Pi

KM#	Date	Mintage	VG	Fine	VF	XF
368.7	1842	—	2.00	4.00	8.00	15.00
	1843/2	—	2.00	4.00	8.00	15.00
	1843	—	2.00	4.00	8.00	15.00
	1844	—	2.00	4.00	8.00	15.00
	1845/3	—	4.00	6.00	10.00	25.00
	1845/4	—	4.00	6.00	10.00	25.00
	1845	—	2.00	4.00	8.00	15.00
	1847/5	—	4.00	6.00	10.00	20.00
	1847	—	2.00	4.00	8.00	15.00
	1851	—	4.00	8.00	15.00	30.00
	1854	—	125.00	200.00	275.00	400.00
	1856	—	4.00	8.00	15.00	30.00
	1857	—	5.00	10.00	20.00	35.00
	1862/57	—	10.00	20.00	40.00	85.00

Mint mark: Zs

KM#	Date	Mintage	VG	Fine	VF	XF
368.8	1842/1 LR	—	4.00	8.00	15.00	30.00
	1842 LR	—	4.00	6.00	10.00	20.00

1/2 REAL

1.6900 g, .903 SILVER, .0490 oz ASW
Mint mark: Mo
Obv: Hooked neck eagle

KM#	Date	Mintage	Fine	VF	XF	Unc
369	1824 JM	—	40.00	60.00	125.00	500.00

Obv: Facing eagle
Mint mark: Ca

KM#	Date	Mintage	Fine	VF	XF	Unc
370.1	1844 RG	—	75.00	125.00	175.00	275.00
	1845 RG	—	75.00	125.00	150.00	250.00

Mint mark: C, Co

KM#	Date	Mintage	Fine	VF	XF	Unc
370.2	1846 CE	—	30.00	50.00	75.00	150.00
	1848/7 CE	—	15.00	25.00	45.00	90.00
	1849/8 CE	—	15.00	25.00	45.00	90.00
	1852 CE	—	12.50	20.00	40.00	80.00
	1853/1 CE	—	12.50	20.00	40.00	80.00
	1854 CE	—	20.00	35.00	50.00	100.00
	1856 CE	—	12.50	20.00	40.00	80.00
	1857/6 CE	—	20.00	35.00	50.00	100.00
	1857 CE	—	15.00	25.00	45.00	90.00
	1858 CE (error 1 for 1/2)	—	12.50	20.00	40.00	80.00
	1860/59 PV	—	20.00	35.00	50.00	100.00
	1860 PV	—	12.50	20.00	40.00	80.00
	1861 PV	—	12.50	20.00	40.00	80.00
	1863 CE (error 1 for 1/2)	—	15.00	25.00	45.00	90.00
	1867 CE	—	12.50	20.00	40.00	80.00
	1869 CE (error 1 for 1/2)	—	12.50	20.00	40.00	80.00

Mint mark: D, Do

KM#	Date	Mintage	Fine	VF	XF	Unc
370.3	1832 RM	—	125.00	225.00	350.00	600.00
	1833/2 RM/L	—	75.00	100.00	150.00	225.00
	1833/1 RM/L	—	12.50	20.00	40.00	80.00
	1833 RM	—	25.00	40.00	75.00	150.00
	1834/1 RM	—	25.00	40.00	75.00	150.00
	1834 RM	—	12.50	20.00	40.00	80.00
	1837/1 RM	—	12.50	20.00	40.00	80.00
	1837/4 RM	—	12.50	20.00	40.00	80.00
	1837/6 RM	—	12.50	20.00	40.00	80.00
	1841/33 RM	—	15.00	25.00	50.00	100.00
	1842/32 RM	—	12.50	20.00	40.00	80.00
	1842 RM	—	12.50	20.00	40.00	80.00
	1842 RM 8R (error)	—	12.50	20.00	40.00	80.00
	1842 RM 1/2/8R	—	12.50	20.00	40.00	80.00
	1843/33 RM	—	15.00	25.00	50.00	100.00
	1845/31 RM	—	12.50	20.00	40.00	80.00
	1845/34 RM	—	12.50	20.00	40.00	80.00
	1845/35 RM	—	12.50	20.00	40.00	80.00
	1845 RM	—	15.00	25.00	50.00	100.00
	1846 RM	—	30.00	50.00	80.00	150.00
	1848/5 RM	—	35.00	55.00	110.00	200.00
	1848/6 RM	—	25.00	40.00	75.00	150.00
	1849 JMR	—	25.00	40.00	75.00	150.00

KM#	Date	Mintage	Fine	VF	XF	Unc
370.3	1850 JMR	—	25.00	40.00	75.00	150.00
	1851 JMR	—	20.00	35.00	50.00	100.00
	1852/1 JMR	—	65.00	125.00	225.00	500.00
	1852 JMR	—	30.00	50.00	80.00	150.00
	1853 CP	—	12.50	20.00	40.00	80.00
	1854 CP	—	25.00	40.00	75.00	150.00
	1855 CP	—	25.00	40.00	60.00	125.00
	1856/5 CP	—	20.00	35.00	50.00	100.00
	1857 CP	—	20.00	35.00	50.00	100.00
	1858/7 CP	—	20.00	35.00	50.00	100.00
	1859 CP	—	20.00	35.00	50.00	100.00
	1860/59 CP	—	40.00	60.00	125.00	225.00
	1861 CP	—	125.00	200.00	300.00	500.00
	1862 CP	—	25.00	40.00	60.00	125.00
	1864 LT	—	50.00	100.00	200.00	350.00
	1869 CP	—	40.00	75.00	125.00	225.00

Mint mark: EoMo

KM#	Date	Mintage	Fine	VF	XF	Unc
370.4	1829 LF	—	175.00	300.00	450.00	1250.

Mint mark: Ga

KM#	Date	Mintage	Fine	VF	XF	Unc
370.5	1825 FS	—	25.00	40.00	75.00	150.00
	1826 FS	—	10.00	15.00	35.00	70.00
	1828/7 FS	—	12.50	20.00	40.00	80.00
	1829 FS	—	7.50	15.00	30.00	60.00
	1830/29 FS	—	40.00	60.00	100.00	200.00
	1831 LP	—	—	—	Rare	—
	1832 FS	—	10.00	20.00	35.00	70.00
	1834/3 FS	—	65.00	100.00	175.00	250.00
	1834 FS	—	10.00	20.00	35.00	70.00
	1835/4/3 FS/LP	—	15.00	25.00	40.00	80.00
	1837/6 JG	—	50.00	100.00	150.00	250.00
	1838/7 JG	—	15.00	25.00	40.00	80.00
	1839/8 JG/FS	—	35.00	75.00	150.00	250.00
	1839 MC	—	10.00	20.00	35.00	70.00
	1840 MC	—	15.00	25.00	40.00	80.00
	1841 MC	—	20.00	35.00	50.00	100.00
	1842/1 JG	—	15.00	25.00	40.00	80.00
	1842 JG	—	10.00	20.00	35.00	70.00
	1843/2 JG	—	15.00	30.00	50.00	100.00
	1843 JG	—	10.00	20.00	35.00	70.00
	1843 MC/JG	—	10.00	20.00	35.00	70.00
	1843 MC	—	10.00	20.00	35.00	70.00
	1844 MC	—	10.00	20.00	35.00	70.00
	1845 MC	—	10.00	20.00	35.00	70.00
	1845 JG	—	10.00	20.00	35.00	70.00
	1846 MC	—	10.00	20.00	35.00	70.00
	1846 JG	—	10.00	20.00	35.00	70.00
	1847 JG	—	10.00	20.00	35.00	70.00
	1848/7 JG	—	10.00	20.00	35.00	70.00
	1849 JG	—	10.00	20.00	35.00	70.00
	1850 JG	—	10.00	20.00	35.00	70.00
	1851/0 JG	—	10.00	20.00	35.00	70.00
	1852 JG	—	10.00	20.00	35.00	70.00
	1853 JG	—	10.00	20.00	35.00	70.00
	1854 JG	—	10.00	20.00	35.00	70.00
	1855/4 JG	—	10.00	20.00	35.00	70.00
	1855 JG	—	10.00	20.00	35.00	70.00
	1856 JG	—	10.00	20.00	35.00	70.00
	1857 JG	—	10.00	20.00	35.00	70.00
	1858/7 JG	—	10.00	20.00	35.00	70.00
	1858 JG	—	10.00	20.00	35.00	70.00
	1859/7 JG	—	10.00	20.00	35.00	70.00
	1860/59 JG	—	10.00	20.00	35.00	70.00
	1861 JG	—	5.00	12.50	25.00	50.00
	1862/1 JG	—	15.00	25.00	40.00	80.00

Mint mark: GC

KM#	Date	Mintage	Fine	VF	XF	Unc
370.6	1844 MP	—	50.00	100.00	150.00	350.00
	1845 MP	—	25.00	50.00	100.00	200.00
	1846 MP	—	25.00	50.00	100.00	200.00
	1847 MP	—	25.00	50.00	100.00	300.00
	1848 MP	—	20.00	40.00	75.00	150.00
	1849 MP	—	25.00	50.00	100.00	200.00
	1850 MP	—	30.00	60.00	125.00	250.00
	1851 MP	—	25.00	50.00	100.00	200.00

Mint mark: Go

KM#	Date	Mintage	Fine	VF	XF	Unc
370.7	1826 MJ	—	125.00	250.00	400.00	1000.
	1827/6 MJ	—	7.50	15.00	30.00	75.00
	1828/7 MJ	—	7.50	15.00	30.00	75.00
	1828 MJ denomination 2/1	—	—	—	—	—
	1828 MR	—	50.00	100.00	150.00	250.00
	1829/8 MJ	—	5.00	10.00	25.00	50.00
	1829 MJ	—	5.00	10.00	25.00	50.00
	1829 MJ reversed N in MEXICANA	—	5.00	10.00	25.00	50.00
	1830 MJ	—	5.00	10.00	25.00	50.00
	1831/29 MJ	—	15.00	30.00	60.00	150.00
	1831 MJ	—	10.00	20.00	40.00	80.00
	1832/1 MJ	—	7.50	15.00	30.00	75.00
	1832 MJ	—	7.50	15.00	30.00	75.00
	1833 MJ round top 3	—	10.00	20.00	40.00	80.00
	1833 MJ flat top 3	—	10.00	20.00	40.00	80.00
	1834 PJ	—	5.00	10.00	25.00	50.00
	1835 PJ	—	5.00	10.00	25.00	50.00
	1836/5 PJ	—	7.50	15.00	30.00	75.00
	1836 PJ	—	5.00	10.00	25.00	50.00
	1837 PJ	—	5.00	10.00	25.00	50.00
	1838/7 PJ	—	5.00	10.00	25.00	50.00
	1839 PJ	—	5.00	10.00	25.00	50.00
	1839 PJ (error: REPUBLIGA)	—	5.00	10.00	25.00	50.00
	1840/39 PJ	—	7.50	10.00	25.00	75.00
	1840 PJ straight J	—	5.00	10.00	25.00	50.00
	1840 PJ curved J					

KM#	Date	Mintage	Fine	VF	XF	Unc
370.7		—	5.00	10.00	25.00	50.00
	1841/31 PJ	—	5.00	10.00	25.00	50.00
	1841 PJ	—	5.00	10.00	25.00	50.00
	1842/1 PJ	—	5.00	10.00	25.00	50.00
	1842/1 PM	—	5.00	10.00	25.00	50.00
	1842 PM/J	—	5.00	10.00	25.00	50.00
	1842 PJ	—	5.00	10.00	25.00	50.00
	1842 PM	—	5.00	10.00	25.00	50.00
	1843/33 PM 1/2 over 8	—	5.00	10.00	25.00	50.00
	1843 PM convex wings	—	5.00	10.00	25.00	50.00
	1843 PM concave wings	—	5.00	10.00	25.00	50.00
	1844/3 PM	—	5.00	10.00	25.00	50.00
	1844 PM	—	10.00	20.00	40.00	90.00
	1845/4 PM	—	5.00	10.00	25.00	50.00
	1845 PM	—	5.00	10.00	25.00	50.00
	1846/4 PM	—	5.00	10.00	25.00	50.00
	1846/5 PM	—	5.00	10.00	25.00	50.00
	1846 PM	—	5.00	10.00	25.00	50.00
	1847/6 PM	—	7.50	15.00	30.00	60.00
	1847 PM	—	7.50	15.00	30.00	60.00
	1848/35 PM	—	5.00	10.00	25.00	50.00
	1848 PM	—	5.00	10.00	25.00	50.00
	1848 PF/M	—	5.00	10.00	25.00	50.00
	1849/39 PF	—	5.00	10.00	25.00	50.00
	1849 PF	—	5.00	10.00	25.00	50.00
	1849 PF (error: MEXCANA)	—	5.00	10.00	25.00	50.00
	1850 PF	—	5.00	10.00	25.00	50.00
	1851 PF	—	5.00	10.00	25.00	50.00
	1852/1 PF	—	5.00	10.00	25.00	50.00
	1852 PF	—	2.50	7.50	17.50	40.00
	1853 PF/R	—	5.00	10.00	25.00	50.00
	1853 PF	—	5.00	10.00	25.00	50.00
	1854 PF	—	5.00	10.00	25.00	50.00
	1855 PF	—	5.00	10.00	25.00	50.00
	1856/4 PF	—	5.00	10.00	25.00	50.00
	1856/5 PF	—	5.00	10.00	25.00	50.00
	1856 PF	—	5.00	10.00	25.00	50.00
	1857/6 PF	—	5.00	10.00	25.00	50.00
	1857 PF	—	5.00	10.00	25.00	50.00
	1858/7 PF	—	7.50	15.00	30.00	60.00
	1858 PF	—	5.00	10.00	25.00	50.00
	1859 PF	—	5.00	10.00	25.00	50.00
	1860 PF small 1/2	—	5.00	10.00	25.00	50.00
	1860 PF large 1/2	—	5.00	10.00	25.00	50.00
	1860/59 PF	—	5.00	10.00	25.00	50.00
	1861 PF small 1/2	—	5.00	10.00	25.00	50.00
	1861 PF large 1/2	—	5.00	10.00	25.00	50.00
	1862/1 YE	—	5.00	10.00	25.00	50.00
	1862 YE	—	2.50	7.50	17.50	40.00
	1862 YF	—	5.00	10.00	25.00	50.00
	1867 YF	—	2.50	7.50	17.50	40.00
	1868 YF	—	2.50	7.50	17.50	40.00

NOTE: Varieties exist.

Mint mark: Ho

KM#	Date	Mintage	Fine	VF	XF	Unc
370.8	1839 PP	—	—	—	Unique	—
	1862 FM	—	65.00	125.00	200.00	400.00
	1867 PR/FM 6/inverted 6, & 7/1	—	100.00	175.00	250.00	450.00

Mint mark: Mo

KM#	Date	Mintage	Fine	VF	XF	Unc
370.9	1825 JM	—	10.00	20.00	40.00	80.00
	1826/5 JM	—	10.00	20.00	40.00	80.00
	1826 JM	—	5.00	10.00	20.00	60.00
	1827/6 JM	—	5.00	10.00	20.00	60.00
	1827 JM	—	5.00	10.00	20.00	60.00
	1828/7 JM	—	7.50	15.00	25.00	75.00
	1828 JM	—	10.00	20.00	40.00	80.00
	1829 JM	—	7.50	15.00	25.00	75.00
	1830 JM	—	5.00	10.00	20.00	60.00
	1831 JM	—	5.00	10.00	20.00	60.00
	1832 JM	—	7.50	12.50	27.50	60.00
	1833 MJ	—	7.50	12.50	27.50	60.00
	1834 ML	—	5.00	10.00	20.00	60.00
	1835 ML	—	5.00	10.00	20.00	60.00
	1836/5 ML/MF	—	7.50	15.00	25.00	65.00
	1836 ML	—	7.50	15.00	25.00	65.00
	1838 ML	—	5.00	10.00	20.00	60.00
	1839/8 ML	—	5.00	10.00	20.00	65.00
	1839 ML	—	5.00	10.00	20.00	50.00
	1840 ML	—	5.00	10.00	20.00	50.00
	1841 ML	—	5.00	10.00	20.00	50.00
	1842 ML	—	5.00	10.00	20.00	50.00
	1842 MM	—	5.00	10.00	20.00	50.00
	1843 MM	—	10.00	20.00	40.00	80.00
	1844 MF	—	5.00	10.00	20.00	50.00
	1845/4 MF	—	5.00	10.00	25.00	60.00
	1845 MF	—	5.00	10.00	20.00	50.00
	1846 MF	—	5.00	10.00	20.00	50.00
	1847 RC	—	10.00	20.00	40.00	80.00
	1848/7 GC/RC	—	5.00	10.00	20.00	50.00
	1849 GC	—	5.00	10.00	20.00	50.00
	1850 GC	—	5.00	10.00	20.00	50.00
	1851 GC	—	5.00	10.00	20.00	50.00
	1852 GC	—	5.00	10.00	20.00	50.00
	1853 GC	—	5.00	10.00	20.00	50.00
	1854 GC	—	5.00	10.00	20.00	50.00
	1855 GC	—	5.00	10.00	20.00	50.00
	1855 GF/GC	—	7.50	12.50	25.00	65.00
	1856/5 GF	—	7.50	12.50	25.00	65.00
	1857 GF	—	5.00	10.00	20.00	50.00
	1858 FH	—	3.00	5.00	12.50	40.00

KM#	Date	Mintage	Fine	VF	XF	Unc
370.9	1859 FH	—	3.00	6.00	15.00	50.00
	1860 FH/GC	—	5.00	10.00	20.00	50.00
	1860/59 FH	—	7.50	12.50	25.00	65.00
	1860 FH	—	3.00	6.00	15.00	50.00
	1860 TH	—	5.00	10.00	20.00	50.00
	1861 CH	—	3.00	6.00	15.00	45.00
	1862/52 CH	—	5.00	10.00	20.00	50.00
	1862 CH	—	3.00	6.00	15.00	45.00
	1863/55 TH/GC	—	5.00	10.00	20.00	50.00
	1863 CH/GC	—	5.00	10.00	20.00	50.00
	1863 CH	—	3.00	6.00	15.00	45.00

Mint mark: Pi

KM#	Date	Mintage	Fine	VF	XF	Unc
370.10	1831 JS	—	7.50	12.50	25.00	65.00
	1841/36 JS	—	20.00	40.00	75.00	125.00
	1842/1 PS	—	20.00	40.00	75.00	125.00
	1842 PS/JS	—	50.00	75.00	125.00	250.00
	1842 JS	—	20.00	40.00	75.00	125.00
	1843/2 PS	—	17.50	25.00	40.00	80.00
	1843 PS	—	15.00	25.00	35.00	70.00
	1843 AM	—	10.00	15.00	25.00	60.00
	1844 AM	—	10.00	15.00	30.00	65.00
	1845 AM	—	250.00	375.00	500.00	1500.
	1846/5 AM	—	40.00	75.00	125.00	200.00
	1847/6 AM	—	15.00	25.00	40.00	80.00
	1848 AM	—	15.00	25.00	40.00	80.00
	1849 MC/AM	—	15.00	25.00	40.00	80.00
	1849 MC	—	12.50	20.00	35.00	70.00
	1850 MC	—	10.00	15.00	25.00	60.00
	1851 MC	—	10.00	15.00	25.00	60.00
	1852 MC	—	10.00	20.00	30.00	65.00
	1853 MC	—	7.50	12.50	20.00	60.00
	1854 MC	—	7.50	12.50	20.00	60.00
	1855 MC	—	15.00	20.00	35.00	70.00
	1856 MC	—	15.00	25.00	50.00	100.00
	1857 MC	—	7.50	12.50	20.00	60.00
	1857 PS	—	10.00	15.00	30.00	65.00
	1858 MC	—	12.50	20.00	35.00	70.00
	1858 PS	—	12.50	20.00	35.00	70.00
	1859 MC	—	—	—	Rare	—
	1860/59 PS	—	12.50	20.00	35.00	70.00
	1861 RO	—	10.00	15.00	30.00	60.00
	1862/1 RO	—	15.00	25.00	50.00	125.00
	1862 RO	—	15.00	25.00	50.00	125.00
	1863/2 RO	—	15.00	25.00	45.00	100.00

Mint mark: Z, Zs

KM#	Date	Mintage	Fine	VF	XF	Unc
370.11	1826 AZ	—	5.00	10.00	20.00	60.00
	1826 AO	—	5.00	10.00	20.00	60.00
	1827 AO	—	5.00	10.00	20.00	60.00
	1828/7 AO	—	5.00	10.00	20.00	60.00
	1829 AO	—	5.00	10.00	20.00	60.00
	1830 OV	—	5.00	10.00	20.00	60.00
	1831 OV	—	25.00	50.00	75.00	150.00
	1831 OM	—	5.00	10.00	20.00	60.00
	1832 OM	—	5.00	10.00	20.00	60.00
	1833 OM	—	5.00	10.00	20.00	60.00
	1834 OM	—	5.00	10.00	20.00	60.00
	1835/4 OM	—	5.00	10.00	20.00	60.00
	1835 OM	—	5.00	10.00	20.00	60.00
	1836 OM	—	5.00	10.00	20.00	60.00
	1837 OM	—	10.00	20.00	40.00	80.00
	1838 OM	—	5.00	10.00	20.00	60.00
	1839 OM	—	7.50	15.00	30.00	65.00
	1840 OM	—	10.00	25.00	45.00	90.00
	1841 OM	—	10.00	25.00	45.00	90.00
	1842/1 OM	—	5.00	10.00	20.00	60.00
	1842 OM	—	5.00	10.00	20.00	60.00
	1843 OM	—	40.00	75.00	115.00	250.00
	1844 OM	—	5.00	10.00	20.00	60.00
	1845 OM	—	5.00	10.00	20.00	60.00
	1846 OM	—	7.50	15.00	30.00	65.00
	1847 OM	—	5.00	10.00	20.00	50.00
	1848 OM	—	5.00	10.00	20.00	50.00
	1849 OM	—	5.00	10.00	20.00	50.00
	1850 OM	—	5.00	10.00	20.00	50.00
	1851 OM	—	5.00	10.00	20.00	50.00
	1852 OM	—	5.00	10.00	20.00	50.00
	1853 OM	—	5.00	10.00	20.00	50.00
	1854/3 OM	—	5.00	10.00	20.00	50.00
	1854 OM	—	5.00	10.00	20.00	50.00
	1855/3 OM	—	7.50	15.00	30.00	65.00
	1855 OM	—	5.00	10.00	20.00	50.00
	1856 OM	—	5.00	10.00	20.00	50.00
	1857 MO	—	5.00	10.00	20.00	50.00
	1858 MO	—	5.00	10.00	20.00	50.00
	1859 MO	—	6.00	8.50	17.50	35.00
	1859 VL	—	6.00	8.50	17.50	40.00
	1860/59 VL inverted A for V		5.00	10.00	20.00	50.00
	1860 MO	—	5.00	10.00	20.00	50.00
	1860 VL	—	5.00	10.00	20.00	50.00
	1861/0 VL inverted A for V	—	7.50	15.00	30.00	65.00
	1861 VL inverted A for V	—	5.00	10.00	20.00	50.00
	1862 VL inverted A for V	—	5.00	10.00	20.00	50.00
	1863/1 VL inverted A for V	—	7.50	15.00	30.00	65.00
	1863 VL inverted A for V	—	5.00	10.00	20.00	50.00
	1869 YH	—	5.00	10.00	20.00	50.00

REAL

3.3800 g, .903 SILVER, .0981 oz ASW
Mint mark: Do

KM#	Date	Mintage	Fine	VF	XF	Unc
371	1824 RL	—	2750.	3250.	4000.	5500.

Mint mark: Ca

KM#	Date	Mintage	Fine	VF	XF	Unc
372	1844 RG	—	500.00	1000.	1500.	2500.
	1845 RG	—	500.00	1000.	1500.	2500.
	1855 RG	—	100.00	150.00	225.00	400.00

Mint mark: C

KM#	Date	Mintage	Fine	VF	XF	Unc
372.1	1846 CE	—	12.50	25.00	40.00	110.00
	1848 CE	—	12.50	25.00	40.00	110.00
	1850 CE	—	12.50	25.00	40.00	110.00
	1851/0 CE	—	12.50	25.00	40.00	110.00
	1852/1 CE	—	7.50	15.00	30.00	100.00
	1853/2 CE	—	7.50	15.00	30.00	100.00
	1854 CE	—	7.50	15.00	30.00	100.00
	1856 CE	—	40.00	65.00	100.00	225.00
	1857/4 CE	—	10.00	20.00	35.00	100.00
	1857/6 CE	—	10.00	20.00	35.00	100.00
	1858 CE	—	5.00	7.50	15.00	100.00
	1859 CE	—	—	—	—	—
	1860 PV	—	5.00	7.50	15.00	100.00
	1861 PV	—	5.00	7.50	15.00	100.00
	1869 CE	—	5.00	7.50	15.00	100.00

Mint mark: Do

KM#	Date	Mintage	Fine	VF	XF	Unc
372.2	1832/1 RM	—	5.00	10.00	20.00	90.00
	1832 RM/RL	—	10.00	15.00	30.00	100.00
	1832 RM	—	5.00	10.00	20.00	100.00
	1834/24 RM/RL	—	15.00	25.00	50.00	150.00
	1834/3 RM/RL	—	15.00	25.00	50.00	150.00
	1834 RM	—	10.00	20.00	40.00	110.00
	1836/4 RM	—	5.00	7.50	15.00	100.00
	1836 RM	—	5.00	7.50	15.00	100.00
	1837 RM	—	12.50	20.00	40.00	110.00
	1841 RM	—	7.50	15.00	30.00	100.00
	1842/32 RM	—	10.00	20.00	40.00	110.00
	1842 RM	—	7.50	15.00	30.00	100.00
	1843 RM	—	5.00	7.50	15.00	100.00
	1844/34 RM	—	15.00	25.00	45.00	125.00
	1845 RM	—	5.00	7.50	15.00	100.00
	1846 RM	—	7.50	15.00	30.00	100.00
	1847 RM	—	10.00	15.00	35.00	100.00
	1848/31 RM	—	10.00	15.00	35.00	100.00
	1848/33 RM	—	10.00	15.00	35.00	100.00
	1848/5 RM	—	10.00	15.00	35.00	100.00
	1848 RM	—	7.50	12.50	20.00	100.00
	1849/8 CM	—	10.00	15.00	30.00	100.00
	1850 JMR	—	15.00	25.00	45.00	125.00
	1851 JMR	—	15.00	25.00	45.00	120.00
	1852 JMR	—	15.00	25.00	45.00	120.00
	1853 CP	—	12.50	20.00	35.00	100.00
	1854/1 CP	—	10.00	15.00	25.00	100.00
	1854 CP	—	7.50	12.50	20.00	100.00
	1855 CP	—	10.00	15.00	25.00	100.00
	1856 CP	—	12.50	20.00	35.00	100.00
	1857 CP	—	12.50	20.00	35.00	100.00
	1858 CP	—	12.50	20.00	35.00	100.00
	1859 CP	—	7.50	12.50	20.00	100.00
	1860/59 CP	—	10.00	15.00	25.00	100.00
	1861 CP	—	15.00	25.00	40.00	110.00
	1862/1 CP	—	225.00	300.00	450.00	1250.
	1864 LT	—	15.00	25.00	40.00	110.00

Mint mark: EoMo

KM#	Date	Mintage	Fine	VF	XF	Unc
372.3	1828 LF	—	200.00	300.00	450.00	1500.

Mint mark: Ga

KM#	Date	Mintage	Fine	VF	XF	Unc
372.4	1826 FS	—	15.00	30.00	50.00	125.00
	1828/7 FS	—	15.00	30.00	50.00	125.00
	1829/8/7 FS	—	—	—	—	—
	1829 FS	—	15.00	30.00	50.00	125.00
	1830 FS	—	250.00	350.00	500.00	—
	1831 LP	—	15.00	30.00	50.00	125.00
	1831 LP/FS	—	300.00	450.00	600.00	—
	1832 FS	—	250.00	350.00	500.00	—
	1833/2 G FS	—	100.00	150.00	275.00	550.00
	1833 FS	—	75.00	125.00	225.00	500.00
	1834/3 FS	—	75.00	125.00	225.00	500.00
	1835 FS	—	—	—	—	—
	1837/6 JG/FS	—	12.50	20.00	35.00	100.00
	1838/7 JG/FS	—	12.50	20.00	35.00	100.00
	1839 JG	—	250.00	350.00	500.00	—
	1840 JG	—	12.50	20.00	35.00	100.00
	1840 MC	—	7.50	12.50	25.00	70.00
	1841 MC	—	50.00	75.00	125.00	250.00
	1842/0 JG/MC	—	10.00	15.00	30.00	100.00
	1842 JG	—	7.50	12.50	20.00	100.00
	1843 JG	—	150.00	200.00	300.00	750.00
	1843 MC	—	5.00	7.50	15.00	100.00
	1844 MC	—	7.50	12.50	20.00	100.00
	1845 MC	—	10.00	15.00	25.00	100.00
	1845 JG	—	5.00	7.50	20.00	100.00
	1846 JG	—	12.50	20.00	35.00	100.00
	1847/6 JG	—	10.00	15.00	25.00	100.00
	1847 JG	—	10.00	15.00	25.00	100.00
	1848 JG	—	400.00	550.00	700.00	—
	1849 JG	—	7.50	12.50	20.00	100.00
	1850 JG	—	175.00	275.00	400.00	—
	1851 JG	—	10.00	15.00	25.00	100.00
	1852 JG	—	10.00	15.00	25.00	100.00
	1853/2 JG	—	10.00	15.00	25.00	100.00
	1854 JG	—	10.00	15.00	25.00	100.00
	1855 JG	—	15.00	25.00	40.00	100.00
	1856 JG	—	7.50	12.50	20.00	100.00
	1857/6 JG	—	12.50	20.00	35.00	100.00
	1858/7 JG	—	15.00	25.00	40.00	110.00
	1859/8 JG	—	25.00	50.00	75.00	150.00
	1860/59 JG	—	30.00	60.00	90.00	225.00
	1861/0 JG	—	20.00	30.00	50.00	125.00
	1861 JG	—	25.00	50.00	100.00	250.00
	1862 JG	—	7.50	12.50	20.00	100.00

Mint mark: GC

KM#	Date	Mintage	Fine	VF	XF	Unc
372.5	1844 MP	—	40.00	60.00	100.00	250.00
	1845 MP	—	40.00	60.00	100.00	250.00
	1846 MP	—	40.00	60.00	100.00	250.00
	1847 MP	—	40.00	60.00	100.00	250.00
	1848 MP	—	40.00	60.00	100.00	250.00
	1849/7 MP	—	40.00	60.00	100.00	250.00
	1849/8 MP	—	40.00	60.00	100.00	250.00
	1849 MP	—	40.00	60.00	100.00	250.00
	1850 MP	—	40.00	60.00	100.00	250.00
	1851 MP	—	40.00	60.00	100.00	250.00

Mint mark: Go

KM#	Date	Mintage	Fine	VF	XF	Unc
372.6	1826/5 JJ	—	5.00	7.50	15.00	85.00
	1826 MJ	—	4.00	6.00	15.00	85.00
	1827 MJ	—	4.00	6.00	15.00	65.00
	1827 JM	—	10.00	15.00	25.00	75.00
	1828/7 MR	—	4.00	6.00	15.00	85.00
	1828 MJ, straight J, small 8	—	4.00	6.00	15.00	85.00
	1828Go MJ, full J, large 8	—	4.00	6.00	15.00	85.00
	1828G MJ, full J, large 8	—	4.00	6.00	15.00	85.00
	1828 MR	—	4.00	6.00	15.00	85.00
	1829/8 MG small eagle	—	4.00	6.00	15.00	85.00
	1829 MJ small eagle	—	4.00	6.00	15.00	85.00
	1829 MJ large eagle	—	4.00	6.00	15.00	85.00
	1830 MJ small initials	—	4.00	6.00	15.00	85.00
	1830 MJ medium initials	—	4.00	6.00	15.00	85.00
	1830 MJ large initials	—	4.00	6.00	15.00	85.00
	1830 MJ reversed N in MEXICANA	—	4.00	6.00	15.00	85.00
	1831/0 MJ reversed N in MEXICANA	—	4.00	6.00	15.00	85.00
	1831 MJ	—	4.00	6.00	15.00	85.00
	1832/1 MJ	—	15.00	30.00	50.00	125.00
	1832 MJ	—	15.00	30.00	50.00	125.00
	1833 MJ top of 3 round	—	4.00	6.00	15.00	85.00
	1833 MJ top of 3 flat	—	4.00	6.00	15.00	85.00
	1834 PJ	—	4.00	6.00	15.00	85.00
	1835 PJ	—	7.50	12.50	20.00	85.00
	1836 PJ	—	4.00	6.00	15.00	85.00
	1837 PJ	—	15.00	30.00	50.00	125.00
	1838/7 PJ	—	10.00	20.00	35.00	85.00
	1839 PJ	—	4.00	6.00	15.00	85.00
	1840/39 PJ	—	4.00	6.00	15.00	85.00
	1840 PJ	—	4.00	6.00	15.00	85.00
	1841/31 PJ	—	10.00	20.00	35.00	85.00
	1841 PJ	—	4.00	6.00	15.00	85.00
	1842 PJ	—	4.00	6.00	15.00	85.00
	1842 PM	—	4.00	6.00	15.00	85.00
	1843 PM convex wings	—	4.00	6.00	15.00	85.00
	1843 PM concave wings	—	4.00	6.00	15.00	85.00
	1844 PM	—	4.00	6.00	15.00	85.00
	1845/4 PM	—	4.00	6.00	15.00	85.00
	1845 PM	—	4.00	6.00	15.00	85.00
	1846/5 PM	—	7.50	12.50	20.00	85.00
	1846 PM	—	4.00	6.00	15.00	85.00
	1847/6 PM	—	4.00	6.00	15.00	85.00
	1847 PM	—	4.00	6.00	15.00	85.00
	1848 PM	—	4.00	6.00	15.00	85.00
	1849 PF	—	10.00	20.00	35.00	85.00
	1850 PF	—	4.00	6.00	15.00	85.00
	1851 PF	—	10.00	20.00	35.00	100.00
	1853/2 PF	—	7.50	12.50	20.00	75.00
	1853 PF	—	4.00	6.00	15.00	75.00
	1854/3 PF	—	4.00	6.00	15.00	75.00
	1854 PF large eagle	—	4.00	6.00	15.00	75.00
	1854 PF small eagle	—	4.00	6.00	15.00	75.00
	1855/3 PF	—	4.00	6.00	15.00	75.00
	1855/4 PF	—	4.00	6.00	15.00	75.00

Republic / MEXICO 1252

KM#	Date	Mintage	Fine	VF	XF	Unc
372.6	1855 PF	—	4.00	6.00	15.00	75.00
	1856/5 PF	—	4.00	6.00	15.00	75.00
	1856 PF	—	4.00	6.00	15.00	75.00
	1857/6 PF	—	4.00	6.00	15.00	75.00
	1857 PF	—	4.00	6.00	15.00	75.00
	1858 PF	—	4.00	6.00	15.00	75.00
	1859 PF	—	4.00	6.00	15.00	75.00
	1860/50 PF	—	4.00	6.00	15.00	75.00
	1860 PF	—	4.00	6.00	15.00	75.00
	1861 PF	—	4.00	6.00	15.00	75.00
	1862 YE	—	4.00	6.00	15.00	75.00
	1862/1 YF	—	7.50	12.50	20.00	75.00
	1862 YF	—	4.00	6.00	15.00	75.00
	1867 YF	—	4.00	6.00	15.00	75.00
	1868/7 YF	—	4.00	6.00	15.00	75.00

Mint mark: Ho

KM#	Date	Mintage	Fine	VF	XF	Unc
372.7	1867 small 7/1 PR	—	50.00	65.00	100.00	250.00
	1867 large 7/small 7 PR	—	50.00	65.00	100.00	250.00
	1868 PR	—	50.00	65.00	100.00	250.00

Mint mark: Mo

KM#	Date	Mintage	Fine	VF	XF	Unc
372.8	1825 JM	—	10.00	20.00	40.00	110.00
	1826 JM	—	7.50	15.00	30.00	100.00
	1827/6 JM	—	7.50	15.00	30.00	75.00
	1827 JM	—	5.00	10.00	20.00	70.00
	1828 JM	—	7.50	15.00	30.00	100.00
	1830/29 JM	—	5.00	10.00	20.00	100.00
	1830 JM	—	5.00	12.50	25.00	100.00
	1831 JM	—	100.00	200.00	300.00	750.00
	1832 JM	—	5.00	10.00	20.00	100.00
	1833/2 MJ	—	5.00	10.00	20.00	100.00
	1850 GC	—	5.00	10.00	20.00	100.00
	1852 GC	—	275.00	425.00	575.00	—
	1854 GC	—	10.00	20.00	40.00	100.00
	1855 GF	—	5.00	10.00	20.00	80.00
	1856 GF	—	5.00	10.00	20.00	80.00
	1857 GF	—	5.00	10.00	20.00	80.00
	1858 FH	—	5.00	10.00	20.00	80.00
	1859 FH	—	5.00	10.00	20.00	80.00
	1861 CH	—	5.00	10.00	20.00	80.00
	1862 CH	—	5.00	10.00	20.00	80.00
	1863/2 CH	—	7.50	12.50	25.00	80.00

Mint mark: Pi

KM#	Date	Mintage	Fine	VF	XF	Unc
372.9	1831 JS	—	5.00	10.00	20.00	125.00
	1837 JS	—	750.00	850.00	1000.	—
	1838/7 JS	—	250.00	300.00	375.00	—
	1838 JS	—	20.00	35.00	60.00	125.00
	1840/39 JS	—	7.50	15.00	30.00	125.00
	1840 JS	—	7.50	15.00	30.00	125.00
	1841 JS	—	7.50	15.00	30.00	125.00
	1842 JS	—	15.00	30.00	55.00	150.00
	1842 PS	—	5.00	10.00	20.00	125.00
	1843 PS	—	12.50	20.00	35.00	125.00
	1843 AM	—	40.00	60.00	80.00	150.00
	1844 AM	—	40.00	60.00	80.00	150.00
	1845 AM	—	7.50	15.00	30.00	125.00
	1846/5 AM	—	7.50	15.00	30.00	125.00
	1847/6 AM	—	7.50	15.00	30.00	125.00
	1847 AM	—	7.50	15.00	30.00	125.00
	1848/7 AM	—	7.50	15.00	30.00	125.00
	1849 PS	—	7.50	15.00	30.00	125.00
	1849/8 SP	—	60.00	100.00	150.00	—
	1849 SP	—	15.00	25.00	40.00	125.00
	1850 MC	—	5.00	10.00	20.00	125.00
	1851/0 MC	—	7.50	15.00	30.00	125.00
	1851 MC	—	7.50	15.00	30.00	125.00
	1852/1/0 MC	—	10.00	20.00	35.00	125.00
	1852 MC	—	7.50	15.00	30.00	125.00
	1853/1 MC	—	12.50	20.00	35.00	125.00
	1853 MC	—	10.00	20.00	35.00	125.00
	1854/3 MC	—	20.00	40.00	60.00	150.00
	1855/4 MC	—	20.00	40.00	60.00	150.00
	1855 MC	—	15.00	25.00	45.00	125.00
	1856 MC	—	15.00	25.00	45.00	125.00
	1857 PS	—	20.00	35.00	55.00	135.00
	1857 MC	—	20.00	40.00	60.00	150.00
	1858 MC	—	12.50	20.00	35.00	125.00
	1859 PS	—	10.00	15.00	30.00	125.00
	1860/59 PS	—	10.00	15.00	30.00	125.00
	1861 PS	—	7.50	12.50	20.00	125.00
	1861 RO	—	12.50	20.00	35.00	125.00
	1862/1 RO	—	12.50	20.00	35.00	90.00
	1862 RO	—	7.50	12.50	20.00	125.00

Mint mark: Zs

KM#	Date	Mintage	Fine	VF	XF	Unc
372.10	1826 AZ	—	5.00	12.50	35.00	120.00
	1826 AO	—	5.00	12.50	35.00	120.00
	1827 AO	—	5.00	12.50	35.00	120.00
	1828/7 AO	—	5.00	12.50	35.00	120.00
	1828 AO	—	5.00	12.50	35.00	120.00
	1828 AO inverted V for A	—	5.00	12.50	35.00	120.00
	1829 AO	—	5.00	12.50	35.00	120.00
	1830 ZsOV	—	5.00	12.50	35.00	120.00
	1830 ZOV	—	5.00	12.50	35.00	120.00
	1831 OV	—	5.00	12.50	35.00	120.00
	1831 OM	—	5.00	12.50	30.00	120.00
	1832 OM	—	5.00	12.50	30.00	120.00
	1833/2 OM	—	5.00	12.50	30.00	120.00
	1833 OM	—	5.00	12.50	30.00	120.00
	1834/3 OM	—	5.00	12.50	30.00	120.00
	1834 OM	—	5.00	12.50	30.00	120.00
	1835/4 OM	—	20.00	35.00	60.00	150.00
	1835 OM	—	4.00	8.00	20.00	65.00
	1836/5 OM	—	4.00	8.00	20.00	85.00
	1836 OM	—	4.00	8.00	20.00	85.00
	1837 OM	—	4.00	8.00	20.00	85.00
372.10	1838 OM	—	4.00	8.00	20.00	85.00
	1839 OM	—	4.00	8.00	20.00	85.00
	1840 OM	—	4.00	8.00	20.00	85.00
	1841 OM	—	20.00	40.00	60.00	150.00
	1842/1 OM	—	4.00	8.00	20.00	85.00
	1842 OM	—	4.00	8.00	20.00	85.00
	1843 OM	—	4.00	8.00	20.00	85.00
	1844 OM	—	4.00	8.00	20.00	85.00
	1845/4 OM	—	5.00	12.50	30.00	100.00
	1845 OM	—	4.00	8.00	20.00	85.00
	1846 OM old font and obv.	—	4.00	8.00	20.00	85.00
	1846 OM new font and obv.	—	4.00	8.00	20.00	85.00
	1847 OM	—	4.00	8.00	20.00	85.00
	1848 OM	—	4.00	8.00	20.00	85.00
	1849 OM	—	10.00	25.00	50.00	125.00
	1850 OM	—	4.00	6.00	15.00	85.00
	1851 OM	—	4.00	6.00	15.00	85.00
	1852 OM	—	4.00	6.00	15.00	85.00
	1853 OM	—	4.00	6.00	15.00	85.00
	1854/2 OM	—	4.00	6.00	15.00	85.00
	1854/3 OM	—	4.00	6.00	15.00	85.00
	1854 OM	—	4.00	6.00	15.00	85.00
	1855/4 OM	—	4.00	6.00	15.00	85.00
	1855 OM	—	4.00	6.00	15.00	85.00
	1855 MO	—	4.00	6.00	15.00	85.00
	1856 MO	—	4.00	6.00	15.00	85.00
	1856 MO/OM	—	4.00	6.00	15.00	85.00
	1857 MO	—	4.00	6.00	15.00	85.00
	1858 MO	—	4.00	6.00	15.00	85.00
	1859 MO	—	4.00	6.00	15.00	75.00
	1860 VL	—	4.00	6.00	15.00	75.00
	1861 VL	—	4.00	6.00	15.00	75.00
	1862 VL	—	5.00	12.50	30.00	100.00
	1868 JS	—	25.00	45.00	90.00	175.00
	1869 YH	—	4.00	8.00	20.00	75.00

2 REALES

6.7600 g, .903 SILVER, .1962 oz ASW
Mint mark: D, Do
Obv: Hooked-neck eagle.

KM#	Date	Mintage	Fine	VF	XF	Unc
373	1824 Do RL	—	50.00	125.00	300.00	750.00
	1824 D RL	—	100.00	200.00	500.00	1500.

Mint mark: Mo

KM#	Date	Mintage	Fine	VF	XF	Unc
373.1 (373.2)	1824 JM	—	20.00	50.00	100.00	300.00

REPUBLICA MEXICANA
2R. G. 1861. C. H. 10 D. 20

Mint mark: A
Obv: Facing eagle, reeded edge.

KM#	Date	Mintage	Fine	VF	XF	Unc
374	1872 AM	.015	40.00	60.00	100.00	350.00

Mint mark: Ce

KM#	Date	Mintage	Fine	VF	XF	Unc
374.1	1863 ML	—	125.00	200.00	325.00	675.00

Mint mark: Ca

KM#	Date	Mintage	Fine	VF	XF	Unc
374.2	1832 MR	—	30.00	60.00	100.00	200.00
	1833 MR	—	30.00	60.00	125.00	500.00
	1834 MR	—	35.00	75.00	125.00	500.00
	1834 AM	—	35.00	75.00	125.00	500.00
	1835 AM	—	35.00	75.00	125.00	500.00
	1836 AM	—	20.00	40.00	80.00	200.00
	1844 RG	—	—	—	Unique	—
	1845 RG	—	20.00	40.00	80.00	200.00
	1855 RG	—	20.00	40.00	80.00	200.00

Mint mark: C

KM#	Date	Mintage	Fine	VF	XF	Unc
374.3	1846/1146 CE	—	25.00	50.00	100.00	225.00
	1847 CE	—	12.50	20.00	40.00	200.00
	1848 CE	—	12.50	20.00	40.00	200.00
	1850 CE	—	25.00	50.00	75.00	200.00
	1851 CE	—	12.50	20.00	40.00	200.00
	1852/1 CE	—	12.50	20.00	40.00	200.00
	1853/2 CE	—	15.00	20.00	40.00	200.00
	1854 CE	—	15.00	30.00	50.00	200.00
	1856 CE	—	20.00	35.00	70.00	200.00
	1857 CE	—	12.50	20.00	40.00	200.00
	1860 PV	—	12.50	20.00	40.00	200.00
	1861 PV	—	12.50	20.00	40.00	200.00
	1869 CE	—	12.50	20.00	40.00	200.00

Mint mark: Do

KM#	Date	Mintage	Fine	VF	XF	Unc
374.4	1826 RL	—	20.00	40.00	60.00	200.00
	1832 RM style of pre-1832	—	20.00	40.00	60.00	200.00
	1832 RM style of post-1832	—	20.00	40.00	60.00	200.00
	1834/2 RM	—	20.00	40.00	60.00	200.00
374.4	1834/3 RM	—	20.00	40.00	60.00	200.00
	1835/4 RM/RL	—	200.00	300.00	500.00	—
	1841/31 RM	—	50.00	75.00	125.00	250.00
	1841 RM	—	50.00	75.00	125.00	250.00
	1842/32 RM	—	12.50	20.00	40.00	200.00
	1843 RM/RL	—	12.50	20.00	40.00	200.00
	1844 RM	—	35.00	50.00	80.00	200.00
	1845/34 RM/RL	—	12.50	20.00	40.00	200.00
	1846/36 RM	—	100.00	150.00	200.00	350.00
	1848/36 RM	—	12.50	20.00	40.00	200.00
	1848/37 RM	—	12.50	20.00	40.00	200.00
	1848/7 RM	—	12.50	20.00	40.00	200.00
	1848 RM	—	12.50	20.00	40.00	200.00
	1849 CM/RM	—	12.50	20.00	40.00	200.00
	1849 CM	—	12.50	20.00	40.00	200.00
	1851 JMR/RL	—	12.50	20.00	40.00	200.00
	1852 JMR	—	12.50	20.00	40.00	200.00
	1854 CP/CR	—	30.00	50.00	80.00	200.00
	1855 CP	—	250.00	350.00	500.00	—
	1856 CP	—	100.00	150.00	250.00	500.00
	1858 CP	—	12.50	20.00	40.00	200.00
	1859/8 CP	—	12.50	20.00	40.00	200.00
	1861 CP	—	12.50	20.00	40.00	200.00

Mint mark: EoMo

KM#	Date	Mintage	Fine	VF	XF	Unc
374.5	1828 LF	—	325.00	525.00	900.00	2500.

Mint mark: Ga

KM#	Date	Mintage	Fine	VF	XF	Unc
374.6	1825 FS	—	20.00	40.00	80.00	200.00
	1826 FS	—	20.00	40.00	80.00	200.00
	1828/7 FS	—	100.00	150.00	225.00	400.00
	1829 FS	—	—	—	Rare	—
	1832/0 FS	—	100.00	150.00	225.00	350.00
	1832 FS	—	12.50	20.00	40.00	200.00
	1833/2 FS/LP	—	12.50	20.00	40.00	200.00
	1834/27 FS	—	—	—	Rare	—
	1834 FS	—	12.50	20.00	40.00	200.00
	1835 FS	—	2100.	—	—	—
	1837 JG	—	12.50	20.00	40.00	200.00
	1838 JG	—	12.50	20.00	40.00	200.00
	1840/30 MC	—	12.50	20.00	40.00	200.00
	1841 MC	—	12.50	20.00	40.00	200.00
	1842/32 JG/MC	—	35.00	50.00	100.00	200.00
	1842 JG	—	20.00	40.00	80.00	200.00
	1843 JG	—	12.50	20.00	40.00	200.00
	1843 MC/JG	—	12.50	20.00	40.00	200.00
	1844 MC	—	12.50	20.00	40.00	200.00
	1845/3 MC/JG	—	12.50	20.00	40.00	200.00
	1845/4 MC/JG	—	12.50	20.00	40.00	200.00
	1845 JG	—	12.50	20.00	40.00	200.00
	1846 JG	—	12.50	20.00	40.00	200.00
	1847/6 JG	—	25.00	40.00	80.00	200.00
	1848/7 JG	—	12.50	20.00	40.00	200.00
	1849 JG	—	12.50	20.00	40.00	200.00
	1850/40 JG	—	12.50	20.00	40.00	200.00
	1851 JG	—	250.00	350.00	500.00	—
	1852 JG	—	12.50	20.00	40.00	200.00
	1853/1 JG	—	12.50	20.00	40.00	200.00
	1854 JG	—	250.00	350.00	500.00	—
	1855 JG	—	35.00	50.00	80.00	200.00
	1856 JG	—	12.50	20.00	40.00	200.00
	1857 JG	—	250.00	350.00	500.00	—
	1859/8 JG	—	12.50	20.00	40.00	200.00
	1859 JG	—	12.50	20.00	40.00	200.00
	1862/1 JG	—	12.50	20.00	40.00	200.00

Mint mark: GC

KM#	Date	Mintage	Fine	VF	XF	Unc
374.7	1844 MP	—	40.00	60.00	125.00	275.00
	1845 MP	—	40.00	60.00	125.00	275.00
	1846 MP	—	50.00	100.00	150.00	300.00
	1847 MP	—	35.00	50.00	100.00	250.00
	1848 MP	—	50.00	100.00	150.00	300.00
	1849 MP	—	50.00	100.00	150.00	300.00
	1850 MP	—	50.00	100.00	150.00	300.00
	1851/0 MP	—	50.00	100.00	150.00	300.00
	1851 MP	—	50.00	100.00	150.00	300.00

Mint mark: Go

KM#	Date	Mintage	Fine	VF	XF	Unc
374.8	1825 JJ	—	7.50	15.00	30.00	150.00
	1826/5 JJ	—	7.50	15.00	30.00	150.00
	1826 JJ	—	7.50	10.00	25.00	150.00
	1826 MJ	—	7.50	10.00	25.00	150.00
	1827/6 MJ	—	7.50	10.00	25.00	150.00
	1827 MJ	—	7.50	10.00	25.00	150.00
	1828/7 MR	—	7.50	15.00	30.00	150.00
	1828 MJ	—	7.50	10.00	20.00	150.00
	1828 JM	—	7.50	10.00	20.00	150.00
	1829 MJ	—	7.50	10.00	20.00	150.00
	1831 MJ	—	7.50	10.00	20.00	150.00
	1832 MJ	—	7.50	10.00	20.00	150.00
	1833 MJ	—	7.50	10.00	20.00	150.00
	1834 PJ	—	7.50	10.00	20.00	150.00
	1835/4 PJ	—	7.50	15.00	30.00	150.00
	1835 PJ	—	7.50	10.00	20.00	150.00
	1836 PJ	—	7.50	10.00	20.00	150.00
	1837/6 PJ	—	7.50	10.00	20.00	150.00
	1837 PJ	—	7.50	10.00	20.00	150.00
	1838/7 PJ	—	7.50	10.00	20.00	150.00
	1838 PJ	—	7.50	10.00	20.00	150.00
	1839/8 PJ	—	7.50	15.00	30.00	150.00
	1839 PJ	—	7.50	10.00	20.00	150.00
	1840 PJ	—	7.50	10.00	20.00	150.00
	1841 PJ	—	7.50	10.00	20.00	150.00
	1842 PJ	—	7.50	10.00	20.00	150.00
	1842 PM/PJ	—	7.50	10.00	20.00	150.00

KM#	Date	Mintage	Fine	VF	XF	Unc
374.8	1842 PM	—	7.50	10.00	20.00	150.00
	1843/2 PM concave wings, thin rays, sm. letters	—	7.50	10.00	20.00	150.00
	1843 PM convex wings, thick rays, lg. letters	—	7.50	10.00	20.00	150.00
	1844 PM	—	7.50	10.00	20.00	150.00
	1845/4 PM	—	7.50	10.00	20.00	150.00
	1845 PM	—	7.50	10.00	20.00	150.00
	1846/5 PM	—	10.00	15.00	35.00	150.00
	1846 PM	—	7.50	10.00	20.00	150.00
	1847 PM	—	7.50	10.00	20.00	150.00
	1848/7 PM	—	7.50	15.00	30.00	150.00
	1848 PM	—	7.50	15.00	30.00	150.00
	1848 PF	—	100.00	150.00	250.00	500.00
	1849/8 PF/PM	—	7.50	10.00	20.00	150.00
	1849 PF	—	7.50	10.00	20.00	150.00
	1850/40 PF	—	7.50	10.00	20.00	150.00
	1850 PF	—	7.50	10.00	20.00	150.00
	1851 PF	—	7.50	10.00	20.00	150.00
	1852/1 PF	—	7.50	10.00	20.00	150.00
	1852 PF	—	7.50	10.00	20.00	150.00
	1853 PF	—	7.50	10.00	20.00	150.00
	1854/3 PF	—	7.50	10.00	20.00	150.00
	1854 PF old font and obv.	—	7.50	10.00	20.00	150.00
	1854 PF new font and obv.	—	7.50	10.00	20.00	150.00
	1855 PF	—	7.50	10.00	20.00	150.00
	1855 PF star in G of mint mark	—	7.50	10.00	20.00	150.00
	1856/5 PF	—	10.00	15.00	35.00	150.00
	1856 PF	—	10.00	15.00	25.00	150.00
	1857/6 PF	—	7.50	10.00	20.00	150.00
	1857 PF	—	7.50	10.00	20.00	150.00
	1858/7 PF	—	7.50	10.00	20.00	150.00
	1858 PF	—	7.50	10.00	20.00	150.00
	1859/7 PF	—	7.50	10.00	20.00	150.00
	1859 PF	—	7.50	10.00	20.00	150.00
	1860/50 PF	—	7.50	10.00	20.00	150.00
	1860/59 PF	—	7.50	10.00	20.00	150.00
	1860 PF	—	7.50	10.00	20.00	150.00
	1861/51 PF	—	7.50	10.00	20.00	150.00
	1861/57 PF	—	7.50	10.00	20.00	150.00
	1861/0 PF	—	7.50	10.00	20.00	150.00
	1861 PF	—	7.50	10.00	20.00	150.00
	1862/1 YE	—	7.50	10.00	20.00	125.00
	1862 YE	—	7.50	10.00	20.00	125.00
	1862/57 YE	—	7.50	10.00	20.00	125.00
	1862 YE/PF	—	7.50	10.00	20.00	125.00
	1862 YF	—	7.50	10.00	20.00	125.00
	1863/52 YF	—	7.50	10.00	20.00	125.00
	1863 YF	—	7.50	10.00	20.00	125.00
	1867/57 YF	—	7.50	10.00	20.00	125.00
	1868/57 YF	—	10.00	15.00	25.00	125.00

NOTE: Varieties exist.

Mint mark: Ho

KM#	Date	Mintage	Fine	VF	XF	Unc
374.9	1861 FM	—	200.00	300.00	400.00	650.00
	1862/52 Ho FM/C. CE	—	250.00	350.00	500.00	—
	1867/1 PR/FM	—	75.00	150.00	250.00	500.00

Mint mark: Mo

KM#	Date	Mintage	Fine	VF	XF	Unc
374.10	1825 JM	—	10.00	15.00	30.00	175.00
	1826 JM	—	10.00	15.00	30.00	175.00
	1827 JM	—	10.00	15.00	30.00	175.00
	1828 JM	—	10.00	15.00	30.00	175.00
	1829/8 JM	—	10.00	15.00	30.00	175.00
	1829 JM	—	10.00	15.00	30.00	175.00
	1830 JM	—	40.00	60.00	125.00	250.00
	1831 JM	—	10.00	15.00	30.00	175.00
	1832 JM	—	100.00	200.00	400.00	—
	1833/2 MJ/JM	—	10.00	15.00	30.00	175.00
	1834 ML	—	50.00	100.00	200.00	400.00
	1836 ML	—	10.00	15.00	30.00	175.00
	1836 MF	—	10.00	15.00	30.00	175.00
	1837 ML	—	10.00	15.00	30.00	175.00
	1840 ML	—	150.00	225.00	350.00	—
	1841 ML	—	10.00	15.00	30.00	175.00
	1842 ML	—	—	—	Rare	—
	1847 RC	—	10.00	15.00	30.00	175.00
	1848 GC	—	10.00	15.00	30.00	175.00
	1849 GC	—	10.00	15.00	30.00	175.00
	1850 GC	—	10.00	15.00	30.00	175.00
	1851 GC	—	40.00	60.00	125.00	250.00
	1852 GC	—	10.00	15.00	30.00	175.00
	1853 GC	—	10.00	15.00	30.00	175.00
	1854/44 GC	—	10.00	15.00	30.00	175.00
	1855 GC	—	10.00	15.00	30.00	175.00
	1855 GF/GC	—	10.00	15.00	30.00	175.00
	1855 GF	—	10.00	15.00	30.00	175.00
	1856/5 GF/GC	—	10.00	15.00	30.00	175.00
	1857 GF	—	10.00	15.00	30.00	175.00
	1858 FH	—	7.50	12.50	25.00	150.00
	1858 FH/GF	—	7.50	12.50	25.00	150.00
	1859 FH	—	7.50	12.50	25.00	150.00
	1860 FH	—	7.50	12.50	25.00	150.00
	1860 TH	—	7.50	12.50	25.00	150.00
	1861 TH	—	7.50	12.50	25.00	150.00
	1861 CH	—	7.50	12.50	25.00	150.00
	1862 CH	—	7.50	12.50	25.00	150.00
	1863 CH	—	7.50	12.50	25.00	150.00
	1863 TH	—	7.50	12.50	25.00	150.00
	1867 CH	—	7.50	12.50	25.00	150.00
	1868 CH	—	10.00	15.00	30.00	150.00
	1868 PH	—	7.50	12.50	25.00	150.00

NOTE: Varieties exist.

Mint mark: Pi

KM#	Date	Mintage	Fine	VF	XF	Unc
374.11	1829 JS	—	10.00	15.00	30.00	200.00
	1830/20 JS	—	20.00	30.00	60.00	200.00
	1837 JS	—	10.00	15.00	30.00	200.00
	1841 JS	—	10.00	15.00	30.00	200.00
	1842/1 JS	—	10.00	15.00	30.00	200.00
	1842 JS	—	10.00	15.00	30.00	200.00
	1842 PS	—	20.00	35.00	60.00	200.00
	1843 PS	—	12.50	20.00	40.00	200.00
	1843 AM	—	10.00	15.00	30.00	200.00
	1844 AM	—	10.00	15.00	30.00	200.00
	1845 AM	—	10.00	15.00	30.00	200.00
	1846 AM	—	10.00	15.00	30.00	200.00
	1849 MC	—	10.00	15.00	30.00	200.00
	1850 MC	—	10.00	15.00	30.00	200.00
	1856 MC	—	40.00	60.00	125.00	250.00
	1857 MC	—	—	—	—	—
	1858 MC	—	12.50	20.00	40.00	200.00
	1859 MC	—	50.00	70.00	100.00	200.00
	1861 PS	—	10.00	15.00	30.00	200.00
	1862 RO	—	12.50	20.00	40.00	200.00
	1863 RO	—	100.00	250.00	350.00	500.00
	1868 PS	—	10.00	15.00	30.00	200.00
	1869/8 PS	—	10.00	15.00	30.00	200.00
	1869 PS	—	10.00	15.00	30.00	200.00

Mint mark: Zs

KM#	Date	Mintage	Fine	VF	XF	Unc
374.12	1825 AZ	—	10.00	15.00	30.00	150.00
	1826 AV (A is inverted V)	—	7.50	10.00	25.00	150.00
	1826 AZ (A is inverted V)	—	7.50	10.00	25.00	150.00
	1826 AO	—	10.00	15.00	30.00	150.00
	1827 AO (A is inverted V)	—	6.00	8.00	12.00	150.00
	1828/7 AO	—	15.00	30.00	60.00	175.00
	1828 AO	—	7.50	10.00	25.00	100.00
	1828 AO (A is inverted V)	—	7.50	10.00	25.00	150.00
	1829 AO	—	7.50	10.00	25.00	150.00
	1829 OV	—	7.50	10.00	25.00	150.00
	1830 OV	—	7.50	10.00	25.00	150.00
	1831 OV	—	7.50	10.00	25.00	150.00
	1831 OM/OV	—	7.50	10.00	25.00	150.00
	1831 OM	—	7.50	10.00	25.00	150.00
	1832/1 OM	—	15.00	30.00	60.00	150.00
	1832 OM	—	7.50	10.00	25.00	150.00
	1833/27 OM	—	7.50	10.00	25.00	150.00
	1833/2 OM	—	7.50	10.00	25.00	150.00
	1833 OM	—	7.50	10.00	25.00	150.00
	1834 OM	—	40.00	60.00	125.00	200.00
	1835 OM	—	7.50	10.00	25.00	150.00
	1836 OM	—	7.50	10.00	25.00	150.00
	1837 OM	—	7.50	10.00	25.00	150.00
	1838 OM	—	15.00	30.00	60.00	150.00
	1839 OM	—	7.50	10.00	20.00	150.00
	1840 OM	—	7.50	10.00	20.00	150.00
	1841/0 OM	—	7.50	10.00	20.00	150.00
	1841 OM	—	7.50	10.00	20.00	150.00
	1842 OM	—	7.50	10.00	20.00	150.00
	1843 OM	—	7.50	10.00	20.00	150.00
	1844 OM	—	7.50	10.00	20.00	150.00
	1845 OM small letter S and leaves	—	7.50	10.00	20.00	150.00
	1845 OM large letter S and leaves	—	7.50	10.00	20.00	150.00
	1846 OM	—	7.50	10.00	20.00	150.00
	1847 OM	—	7.50	10.00	20.00	150.00
	1848 OM	—	7.50	10.00	20.00	150.00
	1849 OM	—	7.50	10.00	20.00	150.00
	1850 OM	—	7.50	10.00	20.00	150.00
	1851 OM	—	7.50	10.00	20.00	150.00
	1852 OM	—	7.50	10.00	20.00	150.00
	1853 OM	—	7.50	10.00	20.00	150.00
	1854/3 OM	—	7.50	10.00	20.00	150.00
	1854 OM	—	7.50	10.00	20.00	150.00
	1855/4 OM	—	7.50	10.00	20.00	150.00
	1855 OM	—	7.50	10.00	20.00	150.00
	1855 MO	—	7.50	10.00	20.00	150.00
	1856/5 MO	—	7.50	10.00	20.00	150.00
	1856 MO	—	7.50	10.00	20.00	150.00
	1857 MO	—	7.50	10.00	20.00	150.00
	1858 MO	—	7.50	10.00	20.00	150.00
	1859 MO	—	7.50	10.00	20.00	150.00
	1860/59 MO	—	7.50	10.00	20.00	150.00
	1860 MO	—	7.50	10.00	20.00	100.00
	1860 VL	—	7.50	10.00	20.00	150.00
	1861 VL	—	7.50	10.00	20.00	150.00
	1862 VL	—	7.50	10.00	20.00	100.00
	1863 MO	—	12.50	20.00	40.00	150.00
	1863 VL	—	7.50	10.00	20.00	150.00
	1864 MO	—	7.50	10.00	20.00	150.00
	1864 VL	—	7.50	10.00	20.00	150.00
	1865 MO	—	7.50	10.00	20.00	150.00
	1867 JS	—	7.50	10.00	20.00	150.00
	1868 JS	—	10.00	15.00	35.00	150.00
	1868 YH	—	7.50	10.00	20.00	150.00
	1869 YH	—	7.50	10.00	20.00	150.00
	1870 YH	—	7.50	10.00	20.00	150.00

NOTE: Varieties exist.

4 REALES

13.5400 g, .903 SILVER, .3925 oz ASW
Mint mark: Ce
Obv: Facing eagle.

KM#	Date	Mintage	Fine	VF	XF	Unc
375	1863 ML large C	—	200.00	500.00	850.00	3200.
	1863 ML small C	—	350.00	650.00	1000.	3500.

Mint mark: C

KM#	Date	Mintage	Fine	VF	XF	Unc
375.1	1846 CE	—	400.00	550.00	900.00	—
	1850 CE	—	75.00	125.00	250.00	600.00
	1852 CE	—	200.00	300.00	500.00	1000.
	1857 CE	—	—	—	Rare	—
	1858 CE	—	100.00	200.00	350.00	800.00
	1860 PV	—	25.00	50.00	125.00	500.00

Mint mark: Ga

KM#	Date	Mintage	Fine	VF	XF	Unc
375.2	1842/1 JG	—	35.00	50.00	80.00	400.00
	1842 JG	—	35.00	50.00	80.00	400.00
	1843 MC	—	20.00	40.00	80.00	400.00
	1844/3 MC	—	30.00	60.00	125.00	400.00
	1844 MC	—	20.00	40.00	80.00	400.00
	1845 MC	—	20.00	40.00	80.00	400.00
	1845 JG	—	20.00	40.00	80.00	400.00
	1846 JG	—	20.00	40.00	80.00	400.00
	1847 JG	—	40.00	80.00	150.00	400.00
	1848/7 JG	—	40.00	80.00	150.00	400.00
	1849 JG	—	40.00	80.00	150.00	400.00
	1850 JG	—	65.00	125.00	250.00	550.00
	1852 JG	—	—	—	Rare	—
	1854 JG	—	—	—	Rare	—
	1855 JG	—	100.00	200.00	400.00	1000.
	1856 JG	—	—	—	Rare	—
	1857/6 JG	—	65.00	125.00	250.00	550.00
	1858 JG	—	125.00	250.00	450.00	1000.
	1859/8 JG	—	125.00	250.00	450.00	1000.
	1860 JG	—	—	—	Rare	—
	1863/2 JG	—	150.00	300.00	1250.	5000.
	1863 JG	—	150.00	300.00	1250.	5000.

Mint mark: GC

KM#	Date	Mintage	Fine	VF	XF	Unc
375.3	1844 MP	—	400.00	600.00	1000.	2000.
	1845 MP	—	3000.	4000.	5000.	8000.
	1846 MP	—	400.00	600.00	1000.	2000.
	1847 MP	—	400.00	600.00	1000.	2000.
	1849 MP	—	400.00	600.00	1000.	2000.
	1850 MP	—	400.00	600.00	1000.	2000.

Mint mark: Go

KM#	Date	Mintage	Fine	VF	XF	Unc
375.4	1835 PJ	—	12.50	25.00	60.00	350.00
	1836/5 PJ	—	15.00	30.00	75.00	350.00
	1836 PJ	—	15.00	30.00	75.00	350.00
	1837 PJ	—	12.50	25.00	60.00	350.00
	1838/7 PJ	—	15.00	30.00	75.00	350.00
	1838 PJ	—	12.50	30.00	75.00	350.00
	1839 PJ	—	12.50	25.00	60.00	350.00
	1840/30 PJ	—	20.00	50.00	100.00	350.00
	1841/31 PJ	—	150.00	250.00	450.00	1000.
	1842 PJ	—	—	—	Rare	—
	1842 PM	—	15.00	30.00	75.00	350.00
	1843/2 PM eagle w/convex wings, thick rays	—	12.50	25.00	60.00	350.00
	1843 PM eagle w/concave wings, thin rays	—	12.50	25.00	60.00	350.00
	1844/3 PM	—	15.00	30.00	75.00	350.00
	1844 PM	—	20.00	50.00	100.00	350.00
	1845/4 PM	—	20.00	50.00	100.00	350.00
	1845 PM	—	20.00	50.00	100.00	350.00
	1846/5 PM	—	15.00	30.00	75.00	350.00
	1846 PM	—	15.00	30.00	75.00	350.00
	1847/6 PM	—	15.00	30.00	75.00	350.00
	1847 PM	—	15.00	30.00	75.00	350.00
	1848/7 PM	—	20.00	50.00	100.00	350.00
	1848 PM	—	20.00	50.00	100.00	350.00
	1849 PF	—	20.00	50.00	100.00	350.00
	1850 PF	—	12.50	25.00	60.00	350.00
	1851 PF	—	12.50	25.00	60.00	350.00
	1852 PF	—	15.00	30.00	75.00	350.00
	1853 PF	—	15.00	30.00	75.00	350.00
	1854 PF large eagle	—	15.00	30.00	75.00	350.00
	1854 PF small eagle	—	15.00	30.00	75.00	350.00
	1855/4 PF	—	15.00	30.00	75.00	350.00
	1855 PF	—	12.50	25.00	60.00	350.00
	1856 PF	—	12.50	25.00	60.00	350.00
	1857 PF	—	20.00	50.00	100.00	350.00
	1858 PF	—	20.00	50.00	100.00	350.00
	1859 PF	—	20.00	50.00	100.00	350.00
	1860/59 PF	—	15.00	30.00	75.00	350.00
	1860 PF	—	15.00	30.00	75.00	350.00
	1861/51 PF	—	15.00	30.00	75.00	350.00
	1861 PF	—	20.00	50.00	100.00	350.00
	1862/1 YE	—	15.00	30.00	75.00	350.00
	1862/1 YF	—	15.00	30.00	75.00	350.00
	1862 YE/PF	—	15.00	30.00	75.00	350.00

1254 Republic / MEXICO

KM#	Date	Mintage	Fine	VF	XF	Unc
375.4	1862 YE	—	15.00	30.00	75.00	350.00
	1862 YF	—	15.00	30.00	75.00	350.00
	1863/53 YF	—	15.00	30.00	75.00	350.00
	1863 YF/PF	—	15.00	30.00	75.00	350.00
	1863 YF	—	15.00	30.00	75.00	350.00
	1867/57 YF/PF	—	15.00	30.00	75.00	350.00
	1868/58 YF/PF	—	15.00	30.00	75.00	350.00
	1870 FR	—	15.00	30.00	75.00	350.00

NOTE: Varieties exist. Some 1862 dates appear to be 1869 because of weak dies.

Mint mark: Ho

KM#	Date	Mintage	Fine	VF	XF	Unc
375.5	1861 FM	—	200.00	350.00	500.00	1500.
	1867/1 PR/FM	—	150.00	275.00	400.00	1500.

Mint mark: Mo

KM#	Date	Mintage	Fine	VF	XF	Unc
375.6	1827/6 JM	—	100.00	200.00	350.00	800.00
	1850 GC	—	—	—	Rare	—
	1852 GC	—	—	—	Rare	—
	1854 GC	—	—	—	Rare	—
	1855 GF/GC	—	50.00	100.00	200.00	500.00
	1855 GF	—	100.00	200.00	350.00	800.00
	1856 GF/GC	—	20.00	50.00	100.00	350.00
	1856 GF	—	—	—	Rare	—
	1859 FH	—	20.00	50.00	100.00	350.00
	1861 CH	—	15.00	30.00	75.00	300.00
	1862 CH	—	20.00	50.00	100.00	350.00
	1863/2 CH	—	20.00	50.00	100.00	350.00
	1863 CH	—	75.00	150.00	300.00	650.00
	1867 CH	—	20.00	50.00	100.00	350.00
	1868 CH/PH	—	30.00	75.00	150.00	400.00
	1868 CH	—	20.00	50.00	100.00	350.00
	1868 PH	—	30.00	75.00	150.00	400.00

Mint mark: O

KM#	Date	Mintage	Fine	VF	XF	Unc
375.7	1861 FR ornamental edge	—	225.00	450.00	700.00	—
	1861 FR herringbone edge	—	275.00	550.00	800.00	—
	1861 FR obliquely reeded edge	—	200.00	400.00	650.00	—

Mint mark: Pi

KM#	Date	Mintage	Fine	VF	XF	Unc
375.8	1837 JS	—	—	—	Rare	—
	1838 JS	—	150.00	250.00	400.00	800.00
	1842 PS	—	50.00	100.00	200.00	450.00
	1843/2 PS	—	50.00	100.00	200.00	450.00
	1843/2 PS 3 cut from 8 punch	—	50.00	100.00	200.00	450.00
	1843 AM	—	30.00	75.00	150.00	450.00
	1843 PS	—	50.00	100.00	200.00	450.00
	1844 AM	—	30.00	75.00	150.00	450.00
	1845/4 AM	—	20.00	50.00	100.00	450.00
	1845 AM	—	20.00	50.00	100.00	450.00
	1846 AM	—	20.00	50.00	100.00	450.00
	1847 AM	—	75.00	150.00	250.00	550.00
	1848 AM	—	—	—	Rare	—
	1849 MC/AM	—	20.00	50.00	100.00	450.00
	1849 MC	—	20.00	50.00	100.00	450.00
	1849 PS	—	20.00	50.00	100.00	450.00
	1850 MC	—	20.00	50.00	100.00	450.00
	1851 MC	—	20.00	50.00	100.00	450.00
	1852 MC	—	20.00	50.00	100.00	450.00
	1853 MC	—	20.00	50.00	100.00	450.00
	1854 MC	—	100.00	200.00	400.00	900.00
	1855 MC	—	200.00	350.00	500.00	1250.
	1856 MC	—	300.00	450.00	700.00	—
	1857 MC	—	—	—	Rare	—
	1857 PS	—	—	—	Rare	—
	1858 MC	—	100.00	200.00	400.00	850.00
	1859 MC	—	—	—	Rare	—
	1860 PS	—	300.00	450.00	700.00	—
	1861 PS	—	30.00	75.00	150.00	450.00
	1861 RO/PS	—	30.00	75.00	150.00	450.00
	1861 RO	—	50.00	100.00	200.00	450.00
	1862 RO	—	30.00	75.00	150.00	450.00
	1863 RO	—	30.00	75.00	150.00	450.00
	1864 RO	—	—	—	Rare	—
	1868 PS	—	30.00	75.00	150.00	450.00
	1869/8 PS	—	30.00	75.00	150.00	450.00
	1869 PS	—	30.00	75.00	150.00	450.00

Mint mark: Zs

KM#	Date	Mintage	Fine	VF	XF	Unc
375.9	1831 OM	—	15.00	30.00	75.00	350.00
	1832/1 OM	—	20.00	50.00	100.00	350.00
	1832 OM	—	20.00	50.00	100.00	350.00
	1833/2 OM	—	20.00	50.00	100.00	350.00
	1833/27 OM	—	15.00	30.00	75.00	350.00
	1833 OM	—	15.00	30.00	75.00	350.00
	1834/3 OM	—	20.00	50.00	100.00	350.00
	1834 OM	—	15.00	30.00	75.00	350.00
	1835 OM	—	15.00	30.00	75.00	350.00
	1836 OM	—	15.00	30.00	75.00	350.00
	1837/5 OM	—	20.00	50.00	100.00	350.00
	1837/6 OM	—	20.00	50.00	100.00	350.00
	1837 OM	—	20.00	50.00	100.00	350.00
	1838/7 OM	—	15.00	30.00	75.00	350.00
	1839 OM	—	250.00	375.00	500.00	—
	1840 OM	—	—	—	Rare	—
	1841 OM	—	15.00	30.00	75.00	350.00
	1842 OM small letters	—	75.00	150.00	300.00	700.00
	1842 OM large letters	—	15.00	30.00	75.00	350.00
	1843 OM	—	15.00	30.00	75.00	350.00
	1844 OM	—	20.00	50.00	100.00	350.00
	1845 OM	—	20.00	50.00	100.00	350.00
	1846/5 OM	—	25.00	60.00	125.00	350.00
	1846 OM	—	20.00	50.00	100.00	350.00
	1847 OM	—	15.00	30.00	75.00	350.00

KM#	Date	Mintage	Fine	VF	XF	Unc
375.9	1848/6 OM	—	50.00	75.00	125.00	350.00
	1848 OM	—	20.00	50.00	100.00	350.00
	1849 OM	—	20.00	50.00	100.00	350.00
	1850 OM	—	20.00	50.00	100.00	350.00
	1851 OM	—	15.00	30.00	75.00	350.00
	1852 OM	—	15.00	30.00	75.00	350.00
	1853 OM	—	20.00	50.00	100.00	350.00
	1854/3 OM	—	30.00	75.00	150.00	350.00
	1855/4 OM	—	20.00	50.00	100.00	350.00
	1855 OM	—	15.00	30.00	75.00	350.00
	1856 OM	—	15.00	30.00	75.00	350.00
	1856 MO	—	20.00	50.00	100.00	350.00
	1857/5 MO	—	20.00	50.00	100.00	350.00
	1857 O/M	—	20.00	50.00	100.00	350.00
	1857 MO	—	15.00	30.00	75.00	350.00
	1858 MO	—	20.00	50.00	100.00	350.00
	1859 MO	—	15.00	30.00	75.00	350.00
	1860/59 MO	—	20.00	50.00	100.00	350.00
	1860 MO	—	15.00	30.00	75.00	350.00
	1860 VL	—	20.00	50.00	100.00	350.00
	1861/0 VL	—	20.00	50.00	100.00	350.00
	1861 VL	—	15.00	30.00	75.00	350.00
	1862/1 VL	—	20.00	50.00	100.00	350.00
	1862 VL	—	20.00	50.00	100.00	350.00
	1863 VL	—	20.00	50.00	100.00	350.00
	1863 MO	—	20.00	50.00	100.00	350.00
	1864 VL	—	15.00	30.00	75.00	350.00
	1868 JS	—	20.00	50.00	100.00	350.00
	1868 YH	—	15.00	30.00	75.00	350.00
	1869 YH	—	15.00	30.00	75.00	350.00
	1870 YH	—	15.00	30.00	75.00	350.00

8 REALES

27.0700 g, .903 SILVER, .7859 oz ASW

Mint mark: Do

Obv: Hooked-neck eagle.

KM#	Date	Mintage	Fine	VF	XF	Unc
376	1824 RL	—	200.00	350.00	1250.	2250.

NOTE: Varieties exist.

Mint mark: Go

KM#	Date	Mintage	Fine	VF	XF	Unc
376.1	1824 JM	—	200.00	325.00	1000.	3000.
	1825/4 JJ	—	550.00	800.00	1500.	5000.
	1825 JJ	—	500.00	750.00	1400.	4500.

Mint mark: Mo

KM#	Date	Mintage	Fine	VF	XF	Unc
376.2	1823 JM	—	150.00	300.00	650.00	2000.
	1824 JM	—	125.00	250.00	450.00	1500.
	1824 JM (error) REPULICA	—	—	—	Rare	—

NOTE: These are rarely found with detail on the eagles breast and bring a premium if even slight feather detail is present there.

Mint mark: A, As

KM#	Date	Mintage	Fine	VF	XF	Unc
377	1864 PG	—	650.00	900.00	1200.	—
	1865/4 PG	—	—	—	Rare	—
	1865 PG	—	500.00	750.00	1000.	—
	1866/5 PG	—	—	—	Rare	—
	1866 PG	—	—	—	Rare	—
	1866 DL	—	—	—	Rare	—
	1867 DL	—	—	—	Rare	—
	1867 PG	—	—	—	—	—
	1868 DL	—	50.00	100.00	150.00	300.00
	1869/8 DL	—	50.00	100.00	150.00	—
	1869 DL	—	60.00	85.00	150.00	300.00
	1870 DL	—	30.00	60.00	150.00	300.00
	1871 DL	—	20.00	35.00	75.00	200.00
	1872 AM/DL	—	25.00	50.00	100.00	300.00
	1872 AM	—	25.00	50.00	100.00	250.00
	1873 AM	.509	15.00	30.00	60.00	175.00
	1874 DL	—	15.00	30.00	60.00	175.00
	1875A DL 7/7	—	40.00	80.00	150.00	300.00
	1875A DL	—	15.00	25.00	50.00	150.00
	1875AsDL	—	30.00	60.00	125.00	250.00
	1876 DL	—	15.00	25.00	50.00	150.00
	1877 DL	.515	15.00	25.00	50.00	150.00
	1878 DL	.513	15.00	25.00	50.00	150.00
	1879 DL	—	20.00	35.00	75.00	175.00
	1879 ML	—	30.00	60.00	125.00	300.00
	1880 ML	—	12.00	15.00	25.00	125.00
	1881 ML	.966	12.00	15.00	25.00	125.00
	1882 ML	.480	12.00	15.00	25.00	125.00
	1883 ML	.464	12.00	15.00	25.00	125.00
	1884 ML	—	12.00	15.00	25.00	125.00
	1885 ML	.280	12.00	15.00	25.00	125.00
	1886 ML	.857	12.00	15.00	20.00	100.00
	1887 ML	.650	12.00	15.00	20.00	100.00
	1888 ML	.508	12.00	15.00	20.00	100.00
	1889 ML	.427	12.00	15.00	20.00	100.00
	1890 ML	.450	12.00	15.00	20.00	100.00
	1891 ML	.533	12.00	15.00	20.00	100.00
	1892 ML	.465	12.00	15.00	20.00	100.00
	1893 ML	.734	10.00	12.00	18.00	75.00
	1894 ML	.725	10.00	12.00	18.00	75.00
	1895 ML	.477	10.00	12.00	18.00	75.00

NOTE: Varieties exist.

Mint mark: Ce

KM#	Date	Mintage	Fine	VF	XF	Unc
377.1	1863 ML	—	375.00	625.00	1000.	2250.
	1863 CeML/PiMC	—	375.00	650.00	1100.	2750.

Mint mark: Ca

KM#	Date	Mintage	Fine	VF	XF	Unc
377.2	1831 MR	—	1000.	1750.	2250.	3250.
	1832 MR	—	125.00	200.00	300.00	600.00
	1833 MR	—	500.00	750.00	1250.	—
	1834 MR	—	—	—	Rare	—
	1834 AM	—	—	—	Rare	—
	1835 AM	—	150.00	250.00	400.00	800.00
	1836 AM	—	100.00	150.00	225.00	450.00
	1837 AM	—	—	—	Rare	—
	1838 AM	—	100.00	200.00	300.00	600.00
	1839 RG	—	—	—	Rare	—

Republic / MEXICO 1255

KM#	Date	Mintage	Fine	VF	XF	Unc
377.2	1840 RG 1 dot after date	—	400.00	600.00	800.00	1500.
	1840 RG 3 dots after date	—	400.00	600.00	800.00	1500.
	1841 RG	—	50.00	100.00	150.00	300.00
	1842 RG	—	25.00	40.00	65.00	125.00
	1843 RG	—	40.00	80.00	125.00	250.00
	1844/1 RG	—	35.00	70.00	100.00	200.00
	1844 RG	—	25.00	40.00	65.00	125.00
	1845 RG	—	25.00	40.00	65.00	125.00
	1846 RG	—	50.00	100.00	150.00	300.00
	1847 RG	—	40.00	80.00	125.00	250.00
	1848 RG	—	30.00	60.00	100.00	200.00
	1849 RG	—	50.00	100.00	150.00	300.00
	1850/40 RG	—	40.00	80.00	125.00	250.00
	1850 RG	—	30.00	60.00	100.00	200.00
	1851/41 RG	—	100.00	200.00	300.00	500.00
	1851 RG	—	150.00	250.00	400.00	750.00
	1852/42 RG	—	150.00	250.00	400.00	750.00
	1852 RG	—	150.00	250.00	400.00	750.00
	1853/43 RG	—	150.00	250.00	400.00	750.00
	1853 RG	—	150.00	250.00	400.00	750.00
	1854/44 RG	—	100.00	200.00	300.00	500.00
	1854 RG	—	50.00	100.00	150.00	300.00
	1855/45 RG	—	100.00	200.00	350.00	650.00
	1855 RG	—	75.00	125.00	200.00	400.00
	1856/45 RG	—	200.00	400.00	600.00	1000.
	1856/5 JC	—	600.00	1000.	1250.	1750.
	1857 JC/RG	—	40.00	80.00	125.00	250.00
	1857 JC	—	50.00	100.00	150.00	250.00
	1858 JC	—	20.00	30.00	50.00	100.00
	1858 BA	—	—	—	Rare	—
	1859 JC	—	40.00	80.00	125.00	250.00
	1860 JC	—	20.00	40.00	90.00	175.00
	1861 JC	—	15.00	25.00	50.00	100.00
	1862 JC	—	20.00	35.00	75.00	150.00
	1863 JC	—	20.00	35.00	75.00	150.00
	1864 JC	—	20.00	35.00	75.00	150.00
	1865 JC	—	100.00	200.00	350.00	600.00
	1865 FP	—	—	—	Rare	—
	1866 JC	—	—	—	Rare	—
	1866 FP	—	—	—	Rare	—
	1866 JG	—	—	—	Rare	—
	1867 JG	—	100.00	200.00	350.00	600.00
	1868 JG	—	75.00	150.00	200.00	350.00
	1868 MM	—	50.00	100.00	150.00	300.00
	1869 MM	—	20.00	35.00	65.00	125.00
	1870 MM	—	20.00	35.00	65.00	125.00
	1871/0 MM	—	15.00	25.00	50.00	100.00
	1871 MM	—	15.00	25.00	50.00	100.00
	1871 MM first M/inverted M	—	20.00	35.00	65.00	125.00
	1873 MM	—	20.00	35.00	65.00	125.00
	1873 MM/T	—	15.00	25.00	50.00	100.00
	1874 MM	—	12.00	15.00	30.00	100.00
	1875 MM	—	12.00	15.00	30.00	100.00
	1876 MM	—	12.00	15.00	30.00	100.00
	1877 EA	.472	12.00	15.00	30.00	100.00
	1877 GR	I.A.	25.00	45.00	65.00	150.00
	1877 JM	I.A.	12.00	15.00	30.00	100.00
	1877 AV	I.A.	100.00	200.00	350.00	750.00
	1878 AV	.439	12.00	15.00	25.00	75.00
	1879 AV	—	12.00	15.00	25.00	75.00
	1880 AV	—	250.00	400.00	600.00	1200.
	1880 PM	—	500.00	750.00	1000.	1500.
	1880 MG normal initials	—	12.00	15.00	25.00	100.00
	1880 MG tall initials	—	12.00	15.00	25.00	100.00
	1880 MM	—	12.00	15.00	25.00	100.00
	1881 MG	1.085	10.00	12.00	20.00	60.00
	1882 MG	.779	10.00	12.00	20.00	60.00
	1882 MM	I.A.	10.00	12.00	20.00	60.00
	1882 MM M sideways	Inc. Ab.	20.00	40.00	90.00	150.00
	1883/2 MM	.818	—	—	—	—
	1883 MM	I.A.	10.00	12.00	20.00	60.00
	1884/3 MM	—	12.00	15.00	30.00	75.00
	1884 MM	—	10.00	12.00	20.00	60.00
	1885/4 MM	1.345	15.00	25.00	50.00	100.00
	1885/6 MM	I.A.	15.00	25.00	50.00	100.00
	1885 MM	I.A.	10.00	12.00	20.00	60.00
	1886 MM	2.483	10.00	12.00	20.00	60.00
	1887 MM	2.625	10.00	12.00	20.00	60.00
	1888/7 MM	2.434	15.00	25.00	50.00	100.00
	1888 MM	I.A.	10.00	12.00	20.00	60.00
	1889 MM	2.681	10.00	12.00	20.00	60.00
	1890 MM	2.137	10.00	12.00	20.00	60.00
	1891/0 MM	2.268	15.00	25.00	50.00	100.00
	1891 MM	I.A.	10.00	12.00	20.00	80.00
	1892 MM	2.527	10.00	12.00	20.00	60.00
	1893 MM	2.632	10.00	12.00	20.00	60.00
	1894 MM	2.642	10.00	12.00	20.00	60.00
	1895 MM	1.112	10.00	12.00	20.00	60.00

NOTE: Varieties exist.

Mint mark: C, Cn

KM#	Date	Mintage	Fine	VF	XF	Unc
377.3	1846 CE	—	150.00	300.00	800.00	1500.
	1847 CE	—	600.00	1000.	1500.	—
	1848 CE	—	150.00	300.00	600.00	1000.
	1849 CE	—	75.00	125.00	200.00	400.00
	1850 CE	—	75.00	125.00	200.00	400.00
	1851 CE	—	150.00	300.00	500.00	1000.
	1852/1 CE	—	100.00	150.00	250.00	500.00
	1852 CE	—	100.00	200.00	350.00	650.00
	1853/0 CE	—	200.00	350.00	700.00	1300.
377.3	1853/2/0	—	200.00	400.00	750.00	1400.
	1853 CE thick rays	—	100.00	175.00	300.00	600.00
	1853 CE (error:) MEXIGANA	—	300.00	450.00	650.00	—
	1854 CE	—	150.00	300.00	600.00	1000.
	1854 CE large eagle & hat	—	150.00	300.00	600.00	1000.
	1855/6 CE	—	40.00	60.00	100.00	200.00
	1855 CE	—	25.00	40.00	60.00	125.00
	1856 CE	—	50.00	100.00	175.00	350.00
	1857 CE	—	20.00	30.00	45.00	100.00
	1858 CE	—	30.00	40.00	60.00	125.00
	1859 CE	—	20.00	30.00	45.00	100.00
	1860/9 PV/CV	—	50.00	70.00	100.00	200.00
	1860/9 PV/E	—	50.00	70.00	100.00	200.00
	1860 CE	—	25.00	40.00	55.00	100.00
	1860 PV	—	40.00	60.00	80.00	150.00
	1861/0 CE	—	40.00	60.00	100.00	250.00
	1861 PV/CE	—	75.00	125.00	200.00	350.00
	1861 CE	—	20.00	35.00	50.00	150.00
	1862 CE	—	20.00	35.00	50.00	150.00
	1863/2 CE	—	30.00	50.00	75.00	200.00
	1863 CE	—	20.00	30.00	50.00	150.00
	1864 CE	—	30.00	60.00	100.00	300.00
	1865 CE	—	125.00	200.00	325.00	650.00
	1866 CE	—	—	—	Rare	—
	1867 CE	—	125.00	200.00	375.00	750.00
	1868/7 CE	—	30.00	40.00	75.00	150.00
	1868/8	—	50.00	100.00	150.00	300.00
	1868 CE	—	30.00	40.00	75.00	150.00
	1869 CE	—	30.00	40.00	75.00	175.00
	1870 CE	—	35.00	50.00	90.00	200.00
	1873 MP	—	50.00	100.00	150.00	300.00
	1874C MP	—	20.00	30.00	45.00	100.00
	1874CN MP	—	125.00	200.00	300.00	600.00
	1875 MP	—	12.00	15.00	20.00	75.00
	1876 GP	—	12.00	15.00	30.00	90.00
	1876 CG	—	12.00	15.00	20.00	75.00
	1877 CG	.339	12.00	15.00	20.00	75.00
	1877 GnCG (error)	—	65.00	125.00	200.00	400.00
	1877 JA	Inc. Ab.	35.00	75.00	125.00	250.00
	1878/7 CG	.483	35.00	75.00	125.00	250.00
	1878 CG	Inc. Ab.	15.00	25.00	35.00	125.00
	1878 JD	Inc. Ab.	15.00	20.00	30.00	125.00
	1878 JD D/retrograde D	Inc. Ab.	20.00	30.00	40.00	150.00
	1879 JD	—	12.00	15.00	30.00	90.00
	1880/70 JD	—	15.00	20.00	30.00	90.00
	1880 JD	—	12.00	15.00	20.00	75.00
	1881/0 JD	1.032	15.00	20.00	30.00	90.00
	1881C JD	Inc. Ab.	12.00	15.00	20.00	75.00
	1881CnJD	I.A.	40.00	60.00	90.00	150.00
	1882 JD	.397	12.00	15.00	20.00	75.00
	1882 AM	I.A.	12.00	15.00	20.00	75.00
	1883 AM	.333	12.00	15.00	20.00	125.00
	1884 AM	—	12.00	15.00	20.00	75.00
	1885/6 AM	.227	20.00	30.00	45.00	100.00
	1885C AM	I.A.	75.00	125.00	250.00	500.00
	1885CnAM	I.A.	12.00	15.00	20.00	75.00
	1885GnAM (error)	Inc. Ab.	60.00	100.00	150.00	300.00
	1886 AM	.571	12.00	15.00	20.00	75.00
	1887 AM	.732	12.00	15.00	20.00	75.00
	1888 AM	.768	12.00	15.00	20.00	75.00
	1889 AM	1.075	12.00	15.00	20.00	75.00
	1890 AM	.874	10.00	12.00	18.00	60.00
	1891 AM	.777	10.00	12.00	18.00	60.00
	1892 AM	.681	10.00	12.00	18.00	60.00
	1893 AM	1.144	10.00	12.00	18.00	60.00
	1894 AM	2.118	10.00	12.00	18.00	60.00
	1895 AM	1.834	10.00	12.00	18.00	60.00
	1896 AM	2.134	10.00	12.00	18.00	60.00
	1897 AM	1.580	10.00	12.00	18.00	60.00

NOTE: Varieties exist.

Mint mark: Do

KM#	Date	Mintage	Fine	VF	XF	Unc
377.4	1825 RL	—	30.00	55.00	85.00	175.00
	1826 RL	—	40.00	100.00	250.00	500.00
	1827/6 RL	—	35.00	60.00	80.00	175.00
	1827 RL	—	30.00	50.00	75.00	150.00
	1828/7 RL	—	35.00	60.00	80.00	175.00
	1828 RL	—	25.00	50.00	75.00	150.00
	1829 RL	—	25.00	50.00	75.00	150.00
	1830 RM	—	25.00	50.00	75.00	150.00
	1831 RM	—	20.00	30.00	50.00	125.00
	1832 RM Mexican dies	—	25.00	50.00	100.00	200.00
	1832 RM/RL European dies	—	25.00	35.00	75.00	150.00
377.4	1833/2 RM/RL	—	20.00	35.00	75.00	150.00
	1833 RM	—	15.00	30.00	50.00	125.00
	1834/3/2 RM/RL	—	20.00	35.00	75.00	150.00
	1834 RM	—	15.00	25.00	45.00	100.00
	1835/4 RM/RL	—	25.00	40.00	80.00	150.00
	1835 RM	—	20.00	35.00	55.00	125.00
	1836/1 RM	—	20.00	30.00	50.00	125.00
	1836/4 RM	—	20.00	30.00	50.00	125.00
	1836/5/4 RM/RL	—	75.00	150.00	250.00	500.00
	1836 RM	—	20.00	30.00	50.00	125.00
	1836 RM M on snake	—	20.00	30.00	50.00	125.00
	1837/1 RM	—	20.00	30.00	50.00	125.00
	1837 RM	—	20.00	30.00	50.00	125.00
	1838/1 RM	—	20.00	30.00	50.00	125.00
	1838/7 RM	—	20.00	30.00	50.00	125.00
	1838 RM	—	20.00	30.00	50.00	125.00
	1839/1 RM/RL	—	20.00	30.00	50.00	125.00
	1839/1 RM	—	20.00	30.00	50.00	125.00
	1839 RM	—	20.00	30.00	50.00	125.00
	1840/38/31 RM	—	20.00	30.00	50.00	125.00
	1840/39 RM	—	20.00	30.00	50.00	125.00
	1840 RM	—	20.00	30.00	50.00	125.00
	1841/31 RM	—	25.00	50.00	75.00	175.00
	1842/31 RM B below cactus	—	125.00	250.00	400.00	750.00
	1842/31 RM	—	40.00	80.00	125.00	250.00
	1842/32 RM	—	40.00	80.00	125.00	250.00
	1842 RM eagle of 1832-41	—	20.00	30.00	50.00	125.00
	1842 RM pre 1832 eagle resumed	—	20.00	30.00	50.00	125.00
	1842 RM	—	40.00	80.00	125.00	250.00
	1843/33 RM	—	50.00	90.00	150.00	250.00
	1844/34 RM	—	100.00	200.00	300.00	500.00
	1844/35 RM	—	100.00	200.00	300.00	500.00
	1845/31 RM	—	35.00	75.00	125.00	250.00
	1845/34 RM	—	35.00	75.00	125.00	250.00
	1845/35 RM	—	35.00	75.00	125.00	250.00
	1845 RM	—	20.00	30.00	50.00	125.00
	1846/31 RM	—	20.00	30.00	50.00	125.00
	1846/36 RM	—	20.00	30.00	50.00	125.00
	1846 RM	—	20.00	30.00	50.00	125.00
	1847 RM	—	25.00	50.00	75.00	150.00
	1848/7 RM	—	125.00	250.00	400.00	750.00
	1848/7 CM/RM	—	100.00	200.00	350.00	700.00
	1848 CM/RM	—	100.00	200.00	350.00	700.00
	1848 RM	—	100.00	200.00	300.00	600.00
	1848 CM	—	50.00	100.00	200.00	400.00
	1849/39 CM	—	100.00	200.00	350.00	700.00
	1849 CM	—	100.00	200.00	350.00	700.00
	1849 JMR/CM oval O	—	200.00	325.00	450.00	800.00
	1849 DoJMR oval O	—	200.00	400.00	600.00	1000.
	1849 DoJMR round O	—	200.00	400.00	600.00	1000.
	1850 JMR	—	100.00	150.00	250.00	500.00
	1851/0 JMR	—	100.00	150.00	250.00	500.00
	1851 JMR	—	100.00	150.00	250.00	500.00
	1852 CP/JMR	—	—	—	Rare	—
	1852 CP	—	—	—	Rare	—
	1852 JMR	—	175.00	250.00	375.00	550.00
	1853 CP/JMR	—	175.00	275.00	400.00	700.00
	1853 CP	—	200.00	400.00	600.00	1200.
	1854 CP	—	25.00	35.00	65.00	300.00
	1855 CP eagle type of 1854	—	50.00	100.00	175.00	350.00
	1855 CP eagle type of 1856	—	50.00	100.00	175.00	350.00
	1856 CP	—	50.00	100.00	175.00	350.00
	1857 CP	—	35.00	75.00	175.00	350.00
	1858/7 CP	—	25.00	35.00	70.00	150.00
	1858 CP	—	20.00	30.00	60.00	150.00
	1859 CP	—	20.00	30.00	60.00	150.00
	1860/59 CP	—	30.00	50.00	100.00	200.00
	1860 CP	—	20.00	30.00	60.00	150.00
	1861/0 CP	—	30.00	50.00	100.00	200.00
	1861 CP	—	20.00	30.00	50.00	125.00
	1862/1 CP	—	25.00	35.00	60.00	125.00
	1862 CP	—	20.00	30.00	55.00	100.00
	1863/2 CP	—	25.00	50.00	75.00	175.00
	1863/53 CP	—	30.00	60.00	90.00	200.00
	1863 CP	—	25.00	50.00	75.00	175.00
	1864 CP	—	100.00	150.00	225.00	400.00
	1864 LT	—	25.00	40.00	80.00	175.00
	1865 LT	—	—	—	Rare	—
	1866 CM	—	—	—	Rare	—
	1867/6 CP	—	200.00	400.00	600.00	1200.
	1867 CP	—	20.00	30.00	50.00	125.00
	1867 CP/CM	—	20.00	30.00	50.00	125.00
	1867 CP/LT	—	20.00	30.00	50.00	125.00
	1867 CM	—	25.00	35.00	55.00	125.00
	1868 CP	—	25.00	40.00	80.00	175.00
	1869 CP	—	20.00	30.00	50.00	125.00
	1870/69 CP	—	20.00	30.00	50.00	125.00
	1870/9 CP	—	20.00	30.00	50.00	125.00
	1870 CP	—	20.00	30.00	50.00	125.00
	1873 CP	—	125.00	225.00	325.00	600.00
	1873 CM	—	30.00	50.00	100.00	200.00
	1874/3 CM	—	12.00	15.00	20.00	100.00
	1874 CM	—	10.00	15.00	20.00	60.00

1256 Republic / MEXICO

KM#	Date	Mintage	Fine	VF	XF	Unc
377.4	1874 JH	—	—	—	Rare	—
	1875 CM	—	10.00	15.00	20.00	75.00
	1875 JH	—	100.00	175.00	275.00	500.00
	1876 CM	—	10.00	15.00	20.00	75.00
	1877 CM	.431	—	—	Rare	—
	1877 CP	Inc. Ab.	10.00	15.00	20.00	75.00
	1877 JMP	I.A.	—	—	Rare	—
	1878 PE	.409	15.00	25.00	40.00	90.00
	1878 TB	Inc. Ab.	10.00	15.00	20.00	75.00
	1879 TB	—	10.00	15.00	20.00	75.00
	1880/70 TB	—	150.00	250.00	375.00	650.00
	1880/70 TB/JP	—	150.00	250.00	375.00	650.00
	1880/70 JP	—	15.00	25.00	40.00	90.00
	1880 TB	—	150.00	250.00	375.00	650.00
	1880 JP	—	10.00	15.00	20.00	75.00
	1881 JP	.928	10.00	15.00	20.00	75.00
	1882 JP	.414	10.00	15.00	20.00	75.00
	1882 MC/JP	Inc. Ab.	30.00	60.00	100.00	200.00
	1882 MC	I.A.	25.00	50.00	75.00	150.00
	1883/73 MC	.452	15.00	25.00	40.00	90.00
	1883 MC	I.A.	10.00	15.00	20.00	75.00
	1884/3 MC	—	20.00	30.00	60.00	110.00
	1884 MC	—	10.00	15.00	20.00	75.00
	1885 MC	.547	10.00	12.00	18.00	65.00
	1885 JB	Inc. Ab.	25.00	35.00	50.00	125.00
	1886/3 MC	.955	15.00	25.00	40.00	90.00
	1886 MC	I.A.	10.00	12.00	18.00	65.00
	1887 MC	1.004	10.00	12.00	18.00	65.00
	1888 MC	.996	10.00	12.00	18.00	65.00
	1889 MC	.874	10.00	12.00	18.00	65.00
	1890 MC	1.119	10.00	12.00	18.00	65.00
	1890 JP	Inc. Ab.	10.00	12.00	18.00	65.00
	1891 JP	1.487	10.00	12.00	18.00	65.00
	1892 JP	1.597	10.00	12.00	18.00	65.00
	1892 ND	Inc. Ab.	25.00	50.00	100.00	200.00
	1893 ND	1.617	10.00	12.00	18.00	65.00
	1894 ND	1.537	10.00	12.00	18.00	65.00
	1895/3 ND	.761	15.00	25.00	40.00	90.00
	1895 ND	I.A.	10.00	12.00	18.00	65.00

NOTE: Varieties exist.

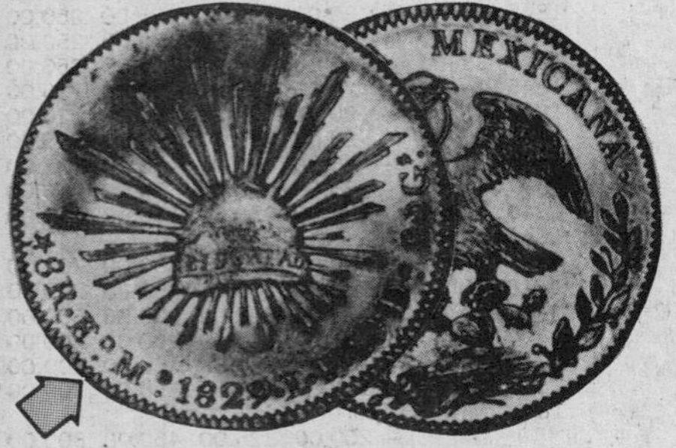

Mint mark: EoMo

KM#	Date	Mintage	Fine	VF	XF	Unc
377.5	1828 LF/LP	—	500.00	1000.	2500.	—
	1828 LF	—	500.00	1000.	2500.	—
	1829 LF	—	400.00	800.00	1500.	—
	1830/20 LF	—	—	—	Rare	—
	1830 LF	—	1000.	2000.	3000.	—

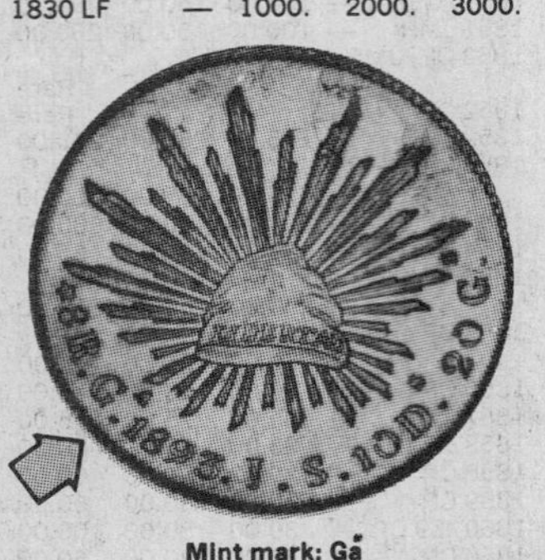

Mint mark: Gá

KM#	Date	Mintage	Fine	VF	XF	Unc
377.6	1825 FS	—	150.00	275.00	425.00	850.00
	1826/5 FS	—	125.00	250.00	400.00	800.00
	1827/87 FS	—	125.00	250.00	400.00	800.00
	1827 FS	—	225.00	350.00	500.00	1000.
	1828 FS	—	200.00	375.00	550.00	1100.
	1829/8 FS	—	200.00	375.00	550.00	1100.
	1829 FS	—	175.00	325.00	475.00	950.00
	1830/29 FS	—	175.00	300.00	450.00	900.00
	1830 FS	—	100.00	175.00	300.00	600.00
	1830 LP/FS	—	—	—	Rare	—
	1831 LP	—	200.00	400.00	600.00	1200.
	1831 FS/LP	—	300.00	500.00	750.00	1500.
	1831 FS	—	—	—	—	—
	1832/1 FS	—	50.00	100.00	175.00	300.00
	1832/1 FS/LP	—	60.00	125.00	200.00	350.00
	1832 FS	—	25.00	50.00	100.00	200.00
	1833/2/1 FS/LP	—	45.00	75.00	125.00	250.00
	1833/2 FS	—	25.00	50.00	100.00	200.00
	1834/2 FS	—	60.00	125.00	200.00	350.00
	1834/3 FS	—	60.00	125.00	200.00	350.00
	1834/0 FS	—	60.00	125.00	200.00	350.00
	1834 FS	—	50.00	100.00	150.00	300.00
	1835 FS	—	25.00	50.00	100.00	200.00

KM#	Date	Mintage	Fine	VF	XF	Unc
377.6	1836/1 JG/FS	—	40.00	80.00	125.00	250.00
	1836 FS	—	—	—	Rare	—
	1836 JG/FS	—	25.00	50.00	100.00	200.00
	1836 JG	—	25.00	50.00	100.00	200.00
	1837/6 JG/FS	—	50.00	100.00	175.00	300.00
	1837 JG	—	40.00	80.00	125.00	250.00
	1838/7 JG	—	100.00	175.00	300.00	550.00
	1838 JG	—	100.00	150.00	275.00	500.00
	1839 MC	—	100.00	200.00	300.00	550.00
	1839 MC/JG	—	100.00	200.00	300.00	550.00
	1839 JG	—	60.00	125.00	200.00	350.00
	1840/30 MC	—	50.00	75.00	150.00	275.00
	1840 MC	—	30.00	60.00	125.00	250.00
	1841 MC	—	30.00	60.00	125.00	250.00
	1842/1 JG/MG	—	100.00	150.00	250.00	450.00
	1842/1 JG/MC	—	100.00	150.00	250.00	450.00
	1842 JG	—	25.00	50.00	100.00	200.00
	1842 JG/MG	—	25.00	50.00	100.00	200.00
	1843/2 MC/JG	—	25.00	50.00	100.00	200.00
	1843 MC/JG	—	25.00	50.00	100.00	200.00
	1843 JG	—	400.00	600.00	800.00	1500.
	1843 MC	—	50.00	100.00	150.00	300.00
	1844 MC	—	50.00	100.00	150.00	300.00
	1845 MC	—	75.00	150.00	250.00	450.00
	1845 JG	—	600.00	1000.	1500.	—
	1846 JG	—	40.00	80.00	150.00	300.00
	1847 JG	—	100.00	150.00	225.00	400.00
	1848/7 JG	—	55.00	85.00	125.00	250.00
	1848 JG	—	50.00	75.00	100.00	200.00
	1849 JG	—	90.00	125.00	175.00	300.00
	1850 JG	—	50.00	100.00	150.00	300.00
	1851 JG	—	125.00	200.00	350.00	650.00
	1852 JG	—	100.00	150.00	250.00	450.00
	1853/2 JG	—	125.00	175.00	250.00	475.00
	1853 JG	—	90.00	125.00	175.00	300.00
	1854/3 JG	—	65.00	90.00	125.00	250.00
	1854 JG	—	50.00	75.00	125.00	250.00
	1855/4 JG	—	50.00	100.00	150.00	275.00
	1855 JG	—	25.00	50.00	100.00	200.00
	1856/4 JG	—	60.00	125.00	175.00	300.00
	1856 JG	—	50.00	100.00	150.00	275.00
	1857 JG	—	50.00	100.00	225.00	400.00
	1858 JG	—	100.00	150.00	300.00	500.00
	1859/7 JG	—	25.00	50.00	100.00	175.00
	1859/8 JG	—	25.00	50.00	100.00	175.00
	1859 JG	—	20.00	40.00	80.00	125.00
	1860 JG w/o dot	—	400.00	800.00	1200.	2000.
	1860 JG dot in loop of eagles tail (base alloy)	—	—	—	Rare	—
	1861 JG	—	—	—	Rare	—
	1862 JG	—	—	—	Rare	—
	1863/52 JG	—	—	—	—	—
	1863/59 JG	—	45.00	50.00	85.00	135.00
	1863/2 JG	—	30.00	50.00	90.00	175.00
	1863/4 JG	—	40.00	60.00	125.00	200.00
	1863 JG	—	25.00	45.00	75.00	150.00
	1863 FV	—	—	—	Rare	—
	1867 JM	—	—	—	Rare	—
	1868/7 JM	—	50.00	75.00	125.00	200.00
	1868 JM	—	50.00	75.00	125.00	200.00
	1869 JM	—	50.00	75.00	125.00	200.00
	1869 IC	—	75.00	125.00	200.00	375.00
	1870/60 IC	—	60.00	90.00	150.00	275.00
	1870 IC	—	60.00	90.00	150.00	275.00
	1873 IC	—	15.00	25.00	50.00	125.00
	1874 IC	—	10.00	15.00	20.00	85.00
	1874 MC	—	25.00	50.00	100.00	200.00
	1875 IC	—	15.00	30.00	60.00	125.00
	1875 MC	—	10.00	15.00	20.00	85.00
	1876 IC	.559	15.00	30.00	50.00	100.00
	1876 MC	Inc. Ab.	125.00	175.00	250.00	375.00
	1877 IC	.928	10.00	15.00	20.00	85.00
	1877 JA	Inc. Ab.	10.00	15.00	20.00	85.00
	1878 JA	.764	10.00	15.00	20.00	85.00
	1879 JA	—	10.00	15.00	20.00	85.00
	1880/70 FS	—	15.00	25.00	50.00	125.00
	1880 JA	—	10.00	15.00	20.00	85.00
	1880 FS	—	10.00	15.00	20.00	85.00
	1881 FS	1.300	10.00	15.00	20.00	85.00
	1882/1 FS	.537	15.00	25.00	50.00	125.00
	1882 FS	I.A.	10.00	15.00	20.00	85.00
	1882 TB/FS	I.A.	75.00	150.00	250.00	450.00
	1882 TB	I.A.	50.00	100.00	175.00	300.00
	1883 TB	.561	50.00	100.00	150.00	275.00
	1884 TB	—	10.00	12.00	18.00	85.00
	1884 AH	—	10.00	12.00	18.00	85.00
	1885 AH	.443	10.00	12.00	18.00	85.00
	1885 JS	Inc. Ab.	30.00	60.00	100.00	200.00
	1886 JS	1.039	10.00	12.00	18.00	85.00
	1887 JS	.878	10.00	12.00	18.00	85.00
	1888 JS	1.159	10.00	12.00	18.00	85.00
	1889 JS	1.583	10.00	12.00	18.00	85.00
	1890 JS	1.658	10.00	12.00	18.00	85.00
	1891 JS	1.507	10.00	12.00	18.00	85.00
	1892/1 JS	1.627	15.00	25.00	50.00	125.00
	1892 JS	I.A.	10.00	12.00	18.00	75.00
	1893 JS	1.952	10.00	12.00	18.00	75.00
	1894 JS	2.046	10.00	12.00	18.00	75.00
	1895 JS	1.146	10.00	12.00	18.00	60.00

NOTE: Varieties exist. The 1830 LP/FS is currently only known with a Philippine countermark.

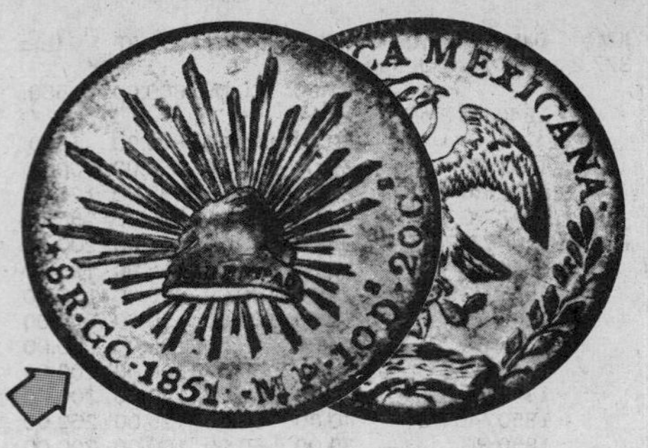

Mint mark: GC

KM#	Date	Mintage	Fine	VF	XF	Unc
377.7	1844 MP	—	350.00	500.00	1000.	2000.
	1844 MP (error) reversed S in Ds, Gs	—	400.00	600.00	1200.	2250.
	1845 MP eagle's tail square	—	125.00	225.00	300.00	600.00
	1845 MP eagle's tail round	—	225.00	450.00	650.00	1200.
	1846 MP eagle's tail square	—	100.00	150.00	350.00	750.00
	1846 MP eagle's tail round	—	100.00	150.00	350.00	750.00
	1847 MP	—	150.00	250.00	400.00	800.00
	1848 MP	—	175.00	300.00	500.00	900.00
	1849 MP	—	175.00	300.00	525.00	1000.
	1850 MP	—	175.00	300.00	575.00	1100.
	1851 MP	—	400.00	600.00	900.00	1600.
	1852 MP	—	500.00	800.00	1250.	2250.

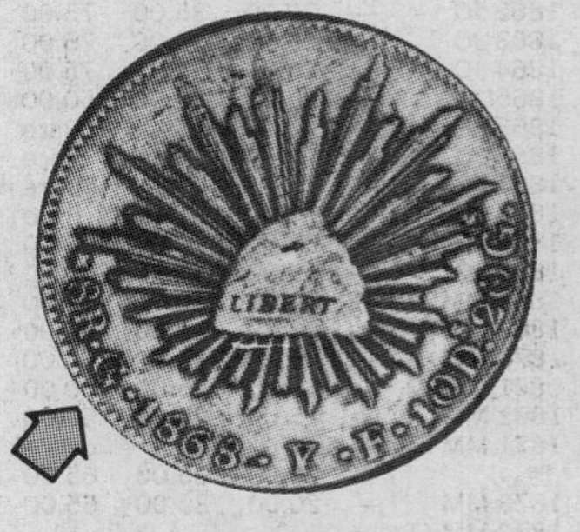

Mint mark: Go

KM#	Date	Mintage	Fine	VF	XF	Unc
377.8	1825 JJ	—	40.00	70.00	150.00	300.00
	1826 JJ straight J's	—	40.00	80.00	175.00	350.00
	1826 JJ full J's	—	30.00	60.00	125.00	250.00
	1826 MJ	—	—	—	Rare	—
	1827 MJ	—	40.00	75.00	125.00	250.00
	1827 MJ/JJ	—	40.00	75.00	125.00	250.00
	1827 MR	—	100.00	200.00	350.00	600.00
	1828 MJ	—	30.00	60.00	125.00	250.00
	1828/7 MR	—	200.00	400.00	600.00	1200.
	1828 MR	—	200.00	400.00	600.00	1200.
	1829 MJ	—	20.00	35.00	55.00	150.00
	1830 MJ oblong beading and narrow J	—	20.00	30.00	55.00	150.00
	1830 MJ regular beading and wide J	—	20.00	30.00	55.00	150.00
	1831 MJ colon after date	—	12.00	20.00	30.00	100.00
	1831 MJ 2 stars after date	—	12.00	20.00	30.00	100.00
	1832 MJ	—	12.00	20.00	30.00	100.00
	1832 MJ 1 of date over inverted 1	—	20.00	35.00	65.00	125.00
	1833 MJ	—	12.00	20.00	30.00	100.00
	1833 JM	—	1000.	1500.	2000.	2500.
	1834 PJ	—	12.00	20.00	30.00	100.00
	1835 PJ	—	12.00	20.00	30.00	100.00
	1836 PJ	—	12.00	20.00	30.00	100.00
	1837 PJ	—	12.00	20.00	30.00	100.00
	1838 PJ	—	12.00	20.00	30.00	100.00
	1839 PJ/JJ	—	12.00	20.00	30.00	100.00
	1839 PJ	—	12.00	20.00	30.00	100.00
	1840/30 PJ	—	20.00	30.00	50.00	150.00
	1840 PJ	—	12.00	20.00	30.00	125.00
	1841/31 PJ	—	12.00	20.00	30.00	100.00
	1841 PJ	—	12.00	20.00	30.00	100.00
	1842/31 PM/PJ	—	25.00	35.00	60.00	150.00
	1842 PJ	—	20.00	30.00	50.00	125.00
	1842 PM/PJ	—	12.00	20.00	30.00	100.00
	1842 PM	—	12.00	20.00	30.00	100.00
	1843 PM dot after date	—	12.00	20.00	30.00	100.00
	1843 PM triangle of dots after date	—	12.00	20.00	30.00	100.00
	1844 PM	—	12.00	20.00	30.00	100.00
	1845 PM	—	12.00	20.00	30.00	100.00
	1846/5 PM eagle type of 1845	—	20.00	30.00	50.00	150.00
	1846 PM early type of 1847	—	15.00	25.00	35.00	125.00
	1847 PM	—	12.00	20.00	30.00	75.00
	1848/7 PM	—	20.00	35.00	65.00	150.00
	1848 PM	—	20.00	35.00	65.00	150.00
	1848 PF	—	12.00	20.00	30.00	75.00

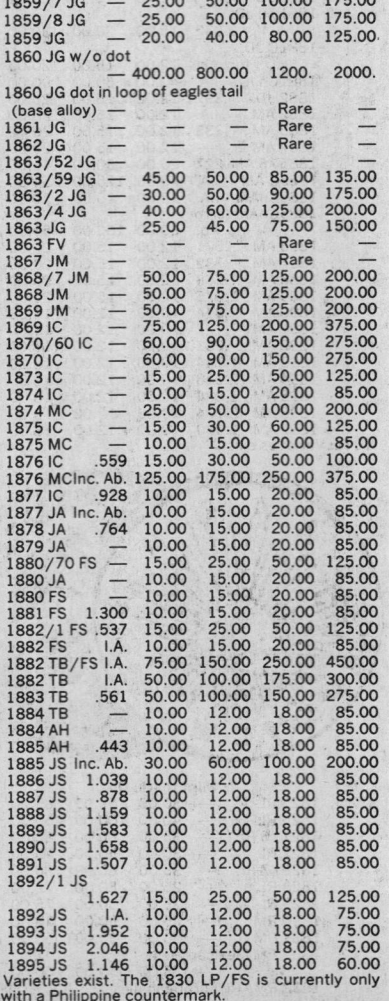

KM#	Date	Mintage	Fine	VF	XF	Unc
377.8	1849 PF	—	12.00	20.00	30.00	75.00
	1850 PF	—	12.00	20.00	30.00	75.00
	1851/0 PF	—	20.00	30.00	50.00	100.00
	1851 PF	—	12.00	20.00	30.00	75.00
	1852/1 PF	—	20.00	30.00	50.00	100.00
	1852 PF	—	12.00	20.00	30.00	75.00
	1853/2 PF	—	20.00	30.00	50.00	100.00
	1853 PF	—	12.00	20.00	30.00	75.00
	1854 PF	—	12.00	20.00	30.00	75.00
	1855 PF large letters	—	12.00	20.00	30.00	75.00
	1855 PF small letters	—	12.00	20.00	30.00	75.00
	1856/5 PF	—	20.00	30.00	50.00	100.00
	1856 PF	—	12.00	20.00	30.00	75.00
	1857/5 PF	—	20.00	30.00	50.00	100.00
	1857/6 PF	—	20.00	30.00	50.00	100.00
	1857 PF	—	12.00	20.00	30.00	75.00
	1858 PF	—	12.00	20.00	30.00	75.00
	1859/7 PF	—	20.00	30.00	50.00	100.00
	1859/8 PF	—	20.00	30.00	50.00	100.00
	1859 PF	—	12.00	20.00	30.00	75.00
	1860/50 PF	—	20.00	30.00	50.00	100.00
	1860/59 PF	—	12.00	18.00	25.00	85.00
	1860 PF	—	12.00	15.00	20.00	75.00
	1861/51 PF	—	15.00	20.00	30.00	100.00
	1861/0 PF	—	12.00	15.00	20.00	75.00
	1861 PF	—	12.00	15.00	20.00	75.00
	1861 YE	—	12.00	15.00	20.00	75.00
	1862 YE/PF	—	12.00	15.00	20.00	75.00
	1862 YE	—	12.00	15.00	20.00	75.00
	1862 YF	—	12.00	15.00	20.00	75.00
	1862 YF/PF	—	12.00	15.00	20.00	75.00
	1863/53 YF	—	12.00	18.00	25.00	75.00
	1863/54 YF	—	15.00	20.00	30.00	100.00
	1863 YE	—	—	—	Rare	—
	1863 YF	—	12.00	15.00	20.00	75.00
	1867/57 YF	—	15.00	20.00	30.00	100.00
	1867 YF	—	12.00	15.00	20.00	75.00
	1868/58 YF	—	15.00	20.00	30.00	100.00
	1868 YF	—	12.00	15.00	20.00	75.00
	1870/60 FR	—	20.00	30.00	50.00	150.00
	1870 YF	—	—	—	Rare	—
	1870 FR/YF	—	12.00	18.00	25.00	85.00
	1870 FR	—	12.00	15.00	20.00	75.00
	1873 FR	—	12.00	15.00	20.00	75.00
	1874/3 FR	—	15.00	20.00	30.00	85.00
	1874 FR	—	15.00	25.00	35.00	100.00
	1875/6 FR	—	15.00	20.00	30.00	85.00
	1875 FR	—	12.00	15.00	20.00	75.00
	1876/5 FR	—	15.00	20.00	30.00	85.00
	1876 FR	—	12.00	15.00	20.00	60.00
	1877 FR	2.477	12.00	15.00	20.00	60.00
	1878/7 FR	2.273	15.00	20.00	30.00	75.00
	1878/7 SM	—	15.00	20.00	30.00	75.00
	1878 FR	I.A.	12.00	15.00	20.00	65.00
	1878 SM,S/F	—	15.00	20.00	25.00	70.00
	1878 SM	—	12.00	15.00	20.00	65.00
	1879/7 SM	—	15.00	20.00	30.00	75.00
	1879/8 SM	—	15.00	20.00	30.00	75.00
	1879/8 SM/FR	—	15.00	20.00	30.00	75.00
	1879 SM	—	12.00	15.00	20.00	65.00
	1879 SM/FR	—	15.00	20.00	30.00	75.00
	1880/70 SB	—	15.00	20.00	30.00	75.00
	1880 SB/SM	—	12.00	15.00	20.00	65.00
	1881/71 SB —	3.974	15.00	20.00	30.00	75.00
	1881/0 SB	I.A.	15.00	20.00	30.00	75.00
	1881 SB	I.A.	12.00	15.00	20.00	65.00
	1882 SB	2.015	12.00	15.00	20.00	75.00
	1883 SB	2.100	35.00	75.00	125.00	250.00
	1883 BR	I.A.	12.00	15.00	20.00	65.00
	1883 BR/SR	—	12.00	15.00	20.00	65.00
	1883 BR/SB	Inc. Ab.	12.00	15.00	20.00	65.00
	1884/73 BR	—	20.00	30.00	40.00	100.00
	1884/74 BR	—	20.00	30.00	40.00	100.00
	1884/3 BR	—	20.00	30.00	40.00	100.00
	1884 BR	—	12.00	15.00	20.00	65.00
	1884/74 RR	—	50.00	100.00	175.00	350.00
	1884 RR	—	12.00	15.00	20.00	65.00
	1885/75 RR	2.363	15.00	20.00	30.00	75.00
	1885 RR	I.A.	12.00	15.00	20.00	65.00
	1886/75 RR	4.127	15.00	20.00	25.00	70.00
	1886/76 RR	Inc. Ab.	12.00	15.00	20.00	65.00
	1886/5 RR/BR	Inc. Ab.	12.00	15.00	20.00	65.00
	1886 RR	I.A.	12.00	15.00	20.00	65.00
	1887 RR	4.205	10.00	15.00	20.00	65.00
	1888 RR	3.985	10.00	15.00	20.00	65.00
	1889 RR	3.646	10.00	15.00	20.00	65.00
	1890 RR	3.615	10.00	15.00	20.00	65.00
	1891 RS	3.197	10.00	15.00	20.00	65.00
	1891 RR	—	—Contemporary counterfeit			
	1892 RS	3.672	10.00	15.00	20.00	65.00
	1893 RS	3.854	10.00	15.00	20.00	65.00
	1894 RS	4.127	10.00	15.00	20.00	65.00
	1895/1 RS	3.768	15.00	20.00	25.00	75.00
	1895/3 RS	I.A.	15.00	20.00	25.00	75.00
	1895 RS	I.A.	10.00	15.00	20.00	65.00
	1896 RS/AS 1891 ML	5.229	15.00	20.00	25.00	75.00
	1896/1 RS	I.A.	12.00	15.00	20.00	65.00
	1896 RS	Inc. Ab.	10.00	12.00	18.00	60.00
	1897 RS	4.344	10.00	12.00	18.00	60.00

NOTE: Varieties exist.

Mint mark: Ho

KM#	Date	Mintage	Fine	VF	XF	Unc
377.9	1835 PP	—	—	—	—	—
	1836 PP	—	—	Unique	—	—
	1839 PR	—	—	Unique	—	—
	1861 FM	—	—	—	Rare	—
	1862 FM	—	—	—	Rare	—
	1862 FM reeded edge	—	—	—	Rare	—
	1863 FM	—	150.00	300.00	800.00	—
	1864 FM	—	—	—	Rare	—
	1864 PR	—	—	—	Rare	—
	1865 FM	—	250.00	500.00	950.00	—
	1866 FM	—	—	—	Rare	—
	1866 MP	—	—	—	Rare	—
	1867 PR	—	100.00	175.00	275.00	500.00
	1868 PR	—	20.00	35.00	65.00	175.00
	1869 PR	—	40.00	60.00	125.00	250.00
	1870 PR	—	50.00	80.00	150.00	300.00
	1871/0 PR	—	50.00	75.00	125.00	250.00
	1871 PR	—	30.00	50.00	90.00	200.00
	1872/1 PR	—	35.00	60.00	90.00	200.00
	1872 PR	—	30.00	50.00	75.00	175.00
	1873 PR	.351	30.00	50.00	85.00	150.00
	1874 PR	—	15.00	20.00	40.00	125.00
	1875 PR	—	15.00	20.00	40.00	125.00
	1876 AF	—	15.00	20.00	40.00	125.00
	1877 AF	.410	20.00	30.00	50.00	150.00
	1877 GR	I.A.	100.00	150.00	225.00	400.00
	1877 JA	I.A.	25.00	50.00	85.00	175.00
	1878 JA	.451	15.00	20.00	40.00	100.00
	1879 JA	—	15.00	20.00	40.00	100.00
	1880 JA	—	15.00	20.00	40.00	100.00
	1881 JA	.586	15.00	20.00	40.00	100.00
	1882 HoJA O above H	.240	25.00	40.00	65.00	125.00
	1882 HoJA O after H	Inc. Ab.	25.00	40.00	65.00	125.00
	1883/2 JA	.204	225.00	375.00	550.00	1000.
	1883/2 FM/JA	Inc. Ab.	25.00	40.00	75.00	150.00
	1883 FM	Inc. Ab.	20.00	30.00	60.00	125.00
	1883 JA	Inc. Ab.	200.00	350.00	500.00	1000.
	1884/3 FM	—	20.00	25.00	50.00	125.00
	1884 FM	—	15.00	20.00	40.00	100.00
	1885 FM	.132	15.00	20.00	40.00	100.00
	1886 FM	.225	20.00	30.00	45.00	125.00
	1886 FG	Inc. Ab.	20.00	30.00	45.00	125.00
	1887 FG	.150	20.00	35.00	65.00	150.00
	1888 FG	.364	12.00	18.00	25.00	100.00
	1889 FG	.490	12.00	18.00	25.00	100.00
	1890 FG	.565	12.00	18.00	25.00	100.00
	1891 FG	.738	12.00	18.00	25.00	100.00
	1892 FG	.643	12.00	18.00	25.00	100.00
	1893 FG	.518	12.00	18.00	25.00	100.00
	1894 FG	.504	12.00	18.00	25.00	100.00
	1895 FG	.320	12.00	18.00	25.00	100.00

NOTE: Varieties exist.

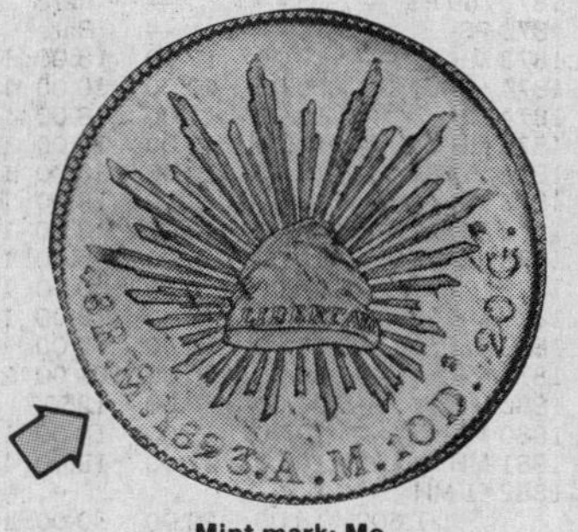

Mint mark: Mo

KM#	Date	Mintage	Fine	VF	XF	Unc
377.10	1824 JM round tail	—	75.00	125.00	250.00	500.00
	1824 JM square tail	—	75.00	125.00	250.00	500.00
	1825 JM	—	25.00	35.00	50.00	150.00
	1826/5 JM	—	25.00	40.00	75.00	150.00
	1826 JM	—	20.00	30.00	50.00	125.00
	1827 JM medal alignment	—	25.00	35.00	50.00	125.00
	1827 JM coin alignment	—	25.00	35.00	50.00	125.00
	1828 JM	—	30.00	60.00	100.00	200.00
	1829 JM	—	20.00	30.00	50.00	125.00
	1830/20 JM	—	35.00	55.00	100.00	200.00
	1830 JM	—	30.00	50.00	90.00	175.00
	1831 JM	—	30.00	50.00	100.00	200.00
	1832/1 JM	—	25.00	40.00	60.00	125.00

KM#	Date	Mintage	Fine	VF	XF	Unc
377.10	1832 JM	—	20.00	30.00	40.00	100.00
	1833 MJ	—	25.00	40.00	80.00	175.00
	1833 ML	—	500.00	750.00	950.00	2000.
	1834/3 ML	—	25.00	35.00	50.00	125.00
	1834 ML	—	20.00	30.00	40.00	100.00
	1835 ML	—	20.00	30.00	40.00	125.00
	1836 ML	—	50.00	100.00	150.00	300.00
	1836 ML/MF	—	50.00	100.00	150.00	300.00
	1836 MF	—	30.00	50.00	80.00	175.00
	1836 MF/ML	—	35.00	60.00	90.00	200.00
	1837/6 ML	—	30.00	50.00	75.00	150.00
	1837/6 MM	—	30.00	50.00	75.00	150.00
	1837/6 MM/ML	—	30.00	50.00	75.00	150.00
	1837/6 MM/MF	—	30.00	50.00	75.00	150.00
	1837 ML	—	30.00	50.00	75.00	150.00
	1837 MM	—	75.00	125.00	175.00	325.00
	1838 MM	—	30.00	50.00	75.00	150.00
	1838 ML	—	20.00	35.00	60.00	125.00
	1838 ML/MM	—	20.00	35.00	60.00	125.00
	1839 ML	—	15.00	25.00	35.00	100.00
	1840 ML	—	15.00	25.00	35.00	100.00
	1841 ML	—	15.00	25.00	35.00	75.00
	1842 ML	—	15.00	25.00	35.00	75.00
	1842 MM	—	15.00	25.00	35.00	75.00
	1843 MM	—	15.00	25.00	35.00	75.00
	1844 MF/MM	—	—	—	—	—
	1844 MF	—	15.00	25.00	35.00	75.00
	1845/4 MF	—	15.00	25.00	35.00	75.00
	1845 MF	—	15.00	25.00	35.00	75.00
	1846/5 MF	—	15.00	25.00	35.00	100.00
	1846 MF	—	15.00	25.00	35.00	100.00
	1847/6 MF	—	—	—	Rare	—
	1847 MF	—	—	—	Rare	—
	1847 RC	—	20.00	30.00	40.00	100.00
	1847 RC/MF	—	15.00	25.00	35.00	75.00
	1848 GC	—	15.00	25.00	35.00	75.00
	1849/8 GC	—	20.00	35.00	50.00	100.00
	1849 GC	—	15.00	25.00	35.00	75.00
	1850/40 GC	—	25.00	50.00	100.00	200.00
	1850/49 GC	—	25.00	50.00	100.00	200.00
	1850 GC	—	20.00	40.00	75.00	150.00
	1851 GC	—	20.00	40.00	60.00	125.00
	1852 GC	—	15.00	30.00	45.00	100.00
	1853 GC	—	15.00	25.00	40.00	100.00
	1854 GC	—	15.00	25.00	40.00	100.00
	1855 GC	—	20.00	35.00	65.00	125.00
	1855 GF	—	12.00	15.00	20.00	75.00
	1855 GF/GC	—	12.00	15.00	20.00	75.00
	1856/4 GF	—	15.00	25.00	40.00	100.00
	1856/5 GF	—	15.00	25.00	40.00	100.00
	1856 GF	—	12.00	15.00	20.00	75.00
	1857 GF	—	10.00	15.00	20.00	75.00
	1858/7 FH/GF	—	10.00	15.00	20.00	75.00
	1858 FH	—	10.00	15.00	20.00	75.00
	1859 FH	—	10.00	15.00	20.00	75.00
	1860/59 FH	—	15.00	20.00	25.00	75.00
	1860 FH	—	10.00	15.00	20.00	65.00
	1860 TH	—	12.00	18.00	30.00	100.00
	1861 TH	—	10.00	15.00	20.00	75.00
	1861 CH	—	10.00	15.00	20.00	75.00
	1862 CH	—	10.00	15.00	20.00	75.00
	1863 CH	—	10.00	15.00	20.00	75.00
	1863 CH/TH	—	10.00	15.00	20.00	75.00
	1863 TH	—	10.00	15.00	20.00	75.00
	1867 CH	—	10.00	15.00	20.00	65.00
	1868 CH	—	10.00	15.00	20.00	65.00
	1868 CH/PH	—	10.00	15.00	20.00	65.00
	1868 PH	—	10.00	15.00	20.00	65.00
	1869 CH	—	10.00	15.00	20.00	65.00
	1873 MH	—	10.00	15.00	20.00	65.00
	1873 MH/HH	—	12.00	18.00	25.00	75.00
	1874 CP	—	—	—	—	—
	1874/69 MH	—	15.00	25.00	45.00	100.00
	1874 MH	—	12.00	18.00	25.00	75.00
	1874 BH/MH	—	12.00	15.00	20.00	65.00
	1874 BH	—	10.00	15.00	20.00	65.00
	1875 BH	—	10.00	15.00	20.00	65.00
	1875 MB	—	100.00	150.00	225.00	350.00
	1876/4 BH	—	12.00	18.00	25.00	75.00
	1876/5 BH	—	12.00	18.00	25.00	75.00
	1876 BH	—	10.00	15.00	20.00	65.00
	1877 MH	.898	10.00	15.00	20.00	65.00
	1877 MH/BH	Inc. Ab.	12.00	18.00	25.00	75.00
	1878 MH	2.154	10.00	15.00	20.00	65.00
	1879/8 MH	—	10.00	15.00	20.00	75.00
	1879 MH	—	10.00	15.00	20.00	65.00
	1880/79 MH	—	15.00	20.00	30.00	75.00
	1880 MH	—	10.00	15.00	20.00	75.00
	1881 MH	5.712	10.00	15.00	20.00	65.00
	1882/1 MH	2.746	12.00	15.00	20.00	75.00
	1882 MH	I.A.	10.00	15.00	20.00	65.00
	1883/2 MH	2.726	12.00	18.00	25.00	85.00
	1883 MH	I.A.	10.00	15.00	20.00	65.00
	1884/3 MH	—	15.00	20.00	30.00	75.00
	1884 MH	—	10.00	15.00	20.00	65.00
	1885 MH	3.649	10.00	15.00	20.00	65.00
	1886 MH	7.558	10.00	12.00	18.00	60.00
	1887 MH	7.681	10.00	12.00	18.00	60.00
	1888 MH	7.179	10.00	12.00	18.00	60.00
	1889 MH	7.332	10.00	15.00	20.00	65.00
	1890 MH	7.412	10.00	12.00	18.00	60.00
	1890 AM	I.A.	10.00	12.00	18.00	60.00
	1891 AM	8.076	10.00	12.00	18.00	60.00
	1892 AM	9.392	10.00	12.00	18.00	60.00
	1893 AM	10.773	10.00	12.00	18.00	55.00

1258 Republic / MEXICO

KM#	Date	Mintage	Fine	VF	XF	Unc
377.10	1894 AM	12.394	10.00	12.00	18.00	45.00
	1895 AM	10.474	10.00	12.00	18.00	45.00
	1895 AB	I.A.	10.00	12.00	18.00	60.00
	1896 AB	9.327	10.00	12.00	18.00	60.00
	1896 AM	I.A.	10.00	12.00	18.00	60.00
	1897 AM	8.621	10.00	12.00	18.00	60.00

NOTE: Varieties exist. 1874 CP is a die struck counterfeit.

Mint mark: O, Oa

KM#	Date	Mintage	Fine	VF	XF	Unc
377.11	1858O AE	—	—	—	Rare	—
	1858OaAE	—	—	—	Rare	—
	1859 AE A in O of mm	—	250.00	550.00	1000.	—
	1860 AE A in O of mm	—	200.00	400.00	600.00	—
	1861 O FR	—	125.00	250.00	500.00	1000.
	1861OaFR	—	200.00	400.00	600.00	—
	1862O FR	—	50.00	100.00	200.00	375.00
	1862OaFR	—	75.00	150.00	250.00	450.00
	1863O FR	—	30.00	60.00	100.00	250.00
	1863O AE	—	30.00	60.00	100.00	250.00
	1863OaAE A in O of mm	—	100.00	150.00	250.00	450.00
	1863OaAE A above O in mm	—	—	—	Rare	—
	1864 FR	—	25.00	50.00	75.00	200.00
	1867 AE	—	40.00	80.00	150.00	400.00
	1868 AE	—	25.00	50.00	100.00	250.00
	1869 AE	—	30.00	60.00	100.00	250.00
	1873 AE	—	200.00	300.00	600.00	1250.
	1874 AE	.142	15.00	30.00	50.00	200.00
	1875/4 AE	.131	25.00	50.00	75.00	200.00
	1875 AE	I.A.	15.00	30.00	40.00	125.00
	1876 AE	.140	20.00	35.00	55.00	200.00
	1877 AE	.139	20.00	30.00	50.00	200.00
	1878 AE	.125	15.00	25.00	50.00	200.00
	1879 AE	.153	15.00	30.00	45.00	150.00
	1880 AE	.143	15.00	30.00	45.00	150.00
	1881 AE	.134	20.00	35.00	60.00	150.00
	1882 AE	.100	20.00	35.00	60.00	150.00
	1883 AE	.122	15.00	30.00	45.00	150.00
	1884 AE	.142	15.00	30.00	50.00	150.00
	1885 AE	.158	15.00	25.00	40.00	125.00
	1886 AE	.120	15.00	30.00	45.00	150.00
	1887/6 AE	.115	25.00	50.00	80.00	200.00
	1887 AE	I.A.	15.00	25.00	40.00	125.00
	1888 AE	.145	15.00	25.00	40.00	125.00
	1889 AE	.150	20.00	30.00	60.00	175.00
	1890 AE	.181	20.00	30.00	60.00	175.00
	1891 EN	.160	15.00	25.00	40.00	125.00
	1892 EN	.120	15.00	25.00	40.00	125.00
	1893 EN	.066	45.00	75.00	115.00	225.00

NOTE: Varieties exist.

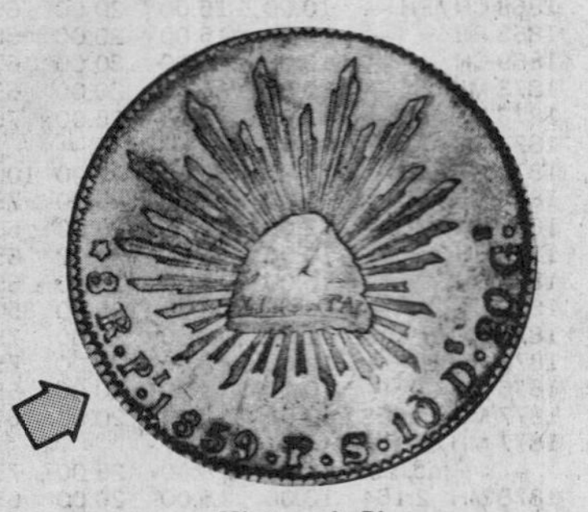

Mint mark: Pi

KM#	Date	Mintage	Fine	VF	XF	Unc
377.12	1827 JS	—	—	—	Rare	—
	1828/7 JS	—	250.00	400.00	600.00	1200.
	1828 JS	—	200.00	350.00	500.00	1000.
	1829 JS	—	35.00	65.00	125.00	250.00
	1830 JS	—	30.00	50.00	100.00	200.00
	1831/0 JS	—	30.00	60.00	125.00	250.00
	1831 JS	—	25.00	35.00	65.00	200.00
	1832/22 JS	—	25.00	35.00	55.00	150.00
	1832 JS	—	25.00	35.00	55.00	150.00
	1833/2 JS	—	30.00	40.00	50.00	150.00
	1833 JS	—	20.00	30.00	40.00	125.00
	1834/3 JS	—	25.00	35.00	50.00	125.00
	1834 JS	—	15.00	25.00	40.00	125.00
	1835 JS denomination 8R	—	15.00	25.00	40.00	125.00
	1835 JS denomination 8Rs	—	15.00	25.00	40.00	125.00
	1836 JS	—	20.00	30.00	45.00	125.00
	1837 JS	—	30.00	50.00	80.00	175.00
	1838 JS	—	20.00	30.00	45.00	125.00
	1839 JS	—	20.00	40.00	60.00	125.00
	1840 JS	—	20.00	30.00	50.00	125.00

KM#	Date	Mintage	Fine	VF	XF	Unc
377.12	1841PiJS	—	25.00	40.00	80.00	175.00
	1841iPJS (error)	—	50.00	100.00	200.00	400.00
	1842/1 JS	—	40.00	60.00	90.00	175.00
	1842/1 PS/JS	—	35.00	55.00	85.00	175.00
	1842 JS eagle type of 1843	—	30.00	50.00	75.00	150.00
	1842 PS	—	30.00	50.00	75.00	150.00
	1842 PS/JS eagle type of 1841	—	30.00	50.00	75.00	150.00
	1843/2 PS round top 3	—	50.00	75.00	150.00	250.00
	1843 PS flat top 3	—	30.00	60.00	125.00	225.00
	1843 AM round top 3	—	20.00	30.00	50.00	125.00
	1843 AM flat top 3	—	20.00	30.00	50.00	125.00
	1844 AM	—	20.00	30.00	50.00	125.00
	1845/4 AM	—	25.00	50.00	100.00	225.00
	1845 AM	—	25.00	50.00	100.00	225.00
	1846/5 AM	—	25.00	35.00	50.00	125.00
	1846 AM	—	15.00	25.00	40.00	125.00
	1847 AM	—	30.00	50.00	80.00	150.00
	1848/7 AM	—	30.00	60.00	90.00	175.00
	1848 AM	—	30.00	50.00	80.00	150.00
	1849/8 PS/AM	—	—	—	Rare	—
	1849 PS/AM	—	—	—	Rare	—
	1849 MC/PS	—	60.00	125.00	250.00	500.00
	1849 AM	—	—	—	Rare	—
	1849 MC	—	60.00	125.00	250.00	500.00
	1850 MC	—	40.00	80.00	150.00	300.00
	1851 MC	—	125.00	200.00	300.00	600.00
	1852 MC	—	75.00	125.00	200.00	400.00
	1853 MC	—	125.00	175.00	300.00	600.00
	1854 MC	—	100.00	150.00	250.00	500.00
	1855 MC	—	100.00	150.00	250.00	500.00
	1856 MC	—	65.00	100.00	200.00	400.00
	1857 MC	—	—	—	Rare	—
	1857 PS/MC	—	150.00	225.00	375.00	700.00
	1857 PS	—	125.00	200.00	350.00	650.00
	1858 MC/PS	—	250.00	400.00	650.00	1200.
	1858 MC	—	250.00	400.00	650.00	1200.
	1858 PS	—	—	—	Rare	—
	1859/8 MC/PS	—	—	—	Rare	—
	1859 MC/PS	—	—	—	Rare	—
	1859 PS/PC	—	—	—	Rare	—
	1859 PS	—	—	—	Rare	—
	1860 MC	—	600.00	1000.	1500.	2000.
	1860 PS	—	400.00	600.00	900.00	1750.
	1861 PS	—	30.00	60.00	90.00	175.00
	1861 RS	—	20.00	30.00	50.00	125.00
	1861 RO	—	25.00	35.00	55.00	125.00
	1862/1 RO	—	20.00	25.00	50.00	125.00
	1862 RO	—	15.00	20.00	40.00	100.00
	1862 RO oval O in RO	—	15.00	20.00	40.00	100.00
	1862 RO round O in RO, 6 is inverted 9	—	20.00	30.00	50.00	125.00
	1863/2 RO	—	25.00	35.00	65.00	150.00
	1863 RO	—	15.00	20.00	40.00	125.00
	1863 6/inverted 6	—	25.00	35.00	55.00	125.00
	1863 FC	—	—	—	Rare	—
	1864 RO	—	—	—	Rare	—
	1867 CA	—	—	—	Rare	—
	1867 LR	—	—	—	Rare	—
	1867 PS	—	30.00	60.00	125.00	275.00
	1868/7 PS	—	30.00	60.00	125.00	250.00
	1868 PS	—	20.00	30.00	50.00	125.00
	1869/8 PS	—	20.00	25.00	45.00	125.00
	1869 PS	—	15.00	20.00	40.00	100.00
	1870/69 PS	—	—	—	Rare	—
	1870 PS	—	—	—	Rare	—
	1873 MH	—	10.00	12.00	18.00	100.00
	1874/3 MH	—	15.00	20.00	30.00	125.00
	1874 MH	—	10.00	12.00	18.00	100.00
	1875 MH	—	10.00	12.00	18.00	100.00
	1876/5 MH	—	15.00	20.00	30.00	125.00
	1876 MH	—	10.00	12.00	18.00	100.00
	1877 MH	1.018	10.00	12.00	18.00	100.00
	1878 MH	1.046	12.00	15.00	25.00	100.00
	1879/8 MH	—	15.00	20.00	30.00	125.00
	1879 MH	—	10.00	12.00	18.00	100.00
	1879 BE	—	25.00	50.00	75.00	150.00
	1879 MR	—	30.00	50.00	100.00	200.00
	1880 MR	—	500.00	750.00	1250.	—
	1880 MH	—	10.00	12.00	18.00	100.00
	1881 MH	2.100	10.00	12.00	18.00	100.00
	1882/1 MH	1.602	15.00	20.00	30.00	125.00
	1882 MH	I.A.	10.00	12.00	18.00	100.00
	1883 MH	1.545	10.00	12.00	18.00	100.00
	1884/3 MH	—	15.00	20.00	30.00	125.00
	1884 MH/MM	—	12.00	15.00	20.00	85.00
	1884 MH	—	10.00	12.00	18.00	75.00
	1885/4 MH	1.736	15.00	20.00	30.00	125.00
	1885/8 MH	I.A.	15.00	20.00	30.00	125.00
	1885 MH	I.A.	10.00	12.00	18.00	75.00
	1885 LC	I.A.	12.00	18.00	25.00	100.00
	1886 LC	3.347	10.00	12.00	18.00	75.00
	1886 MR	I.A.	10.00	12.00	18.00	75.00
	1887 MR	2.922	10.00	12.00	18.00	75.00
	1888 MR	2.438	10.00	12.00	18.00	75.00
	1889 MR	2.103	10.00	12.00	18.00	75.00
	1890 MR	1.562	10.00	12.00	18.00	65.00

KM#	Date	Mintage	Fine	VF	XF	Unc
377.12	1891 MR	1.184	10.00	12.00	18.00	65.00
	1892 MR	1.336	10.00	12.00	18.00	65.00
	1893 MR	.530	10.00	12.00	18.00	75.00

NOTE: Varieties exist.

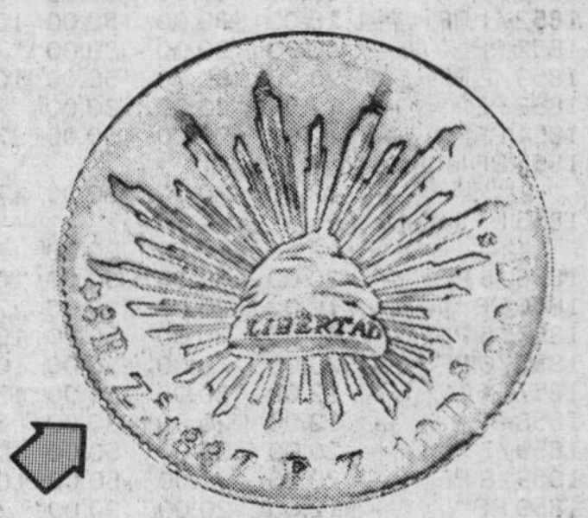

Mint mark: Zs

KM#	Date	Mintage	Fine	VF	XF	Unc
377.13	1825 AZ	—	25.00	35.00	60.00	150.00
	1826/5 AZ	—	25.00	45.00	75.00	175.00
	1826 AZ	—	20.00	35.00	60.00	150.00
	1826 AV	—	225.00	450.00	700.00	1500.
	1826 AO	—	350.00	650.00	1000.	2000.
	1827 AO/AZ	—	35.00	50.00	125.00	250.00
	1827 AO	—	25.00	45.00	85.00	175.00
	1828 AO	—	15.00	20.00	40.00	125.00
	1829 AO	—	15.00	20.00	40.00	125.00
	1829 OV	—	50.00	90.00	150.00	300.00
	1830 OV	—	15.00	20.00	40.00	125.00
	1831 OV	—	25.00	50.00	90.00	175.00
	1831 OM	—	15.00	25.00	50.00	125.00
	1832/1 OM	—	20.00	25.00	40.00	125.00
	1832 OM	—	15.00	20.00	35.00	100.00
	1833/2 OM	—	20.00	30.00	40.00	125.00
	1833 OM/MM	—	15.00	25.00	35.00	100.00
	1833 OM	—	15.00	20.00	30.00	100.00
	1834 OM	—	15.00	20.00	30.00	100.00
	1835 OM	—	15.00	20.00	35.00	100.00
	1836/4 OM	—	20.00	30.00	45.00	125.00
	1836/5 OM	—	20.00	30.00	45.00	125.00
	1836 OM	—	15.00	20.00	30.00	100.00
	1837 OM	—	15.00	20.00	30.00	100.00
	1838/7 OM	—	20.00	30.00	40.00	125.00
	1838 OM	—	15.00	20.00	30.00	100.00
	1839 OM	—	15.00	20.00	30.00	100.00
	1840 OM	—	15.00	20.00	30.00	100.00
	1841 OM	—	15.00	20.00	30.00	100.00
	1842 OM	—	15.00	20.00	30.00	100.00
	1843 OM	—	15.00	20.00	30.00	100.00
	1844 OM	—	15.00	20.00	30.00	100.00
	1845 OM	—	15.00	20.00	30.00	100.00
	1846 OM	—	15.00	20.00	30.00	100.00
	1847 OM	—	15.00	20.00	30.00	100.00
	1848/7 OM	—	20.00	30.00	40.00	125.00
	1848 OM	—	15.00	20.00	30.00	100.00
	1849 OM	—	15.00	20.00	30.00	100.00
	1850 OM	—	15.00	20.00	30.00	100.00
	1851 OM	—	15.00	20.00	30.00	100.00
	1852 OM	—	15.00	20.00	30.00	100.00
	1853 OM	—	30.00	45.00	65.00	200.00
	1854/3 OM	—	20.00	30.00	50.00	150.00
	1854 OM	—	15.00	25.00	40.00	125.00
	1855 OM	—	20.00	30.00	60.00	125.00
	1855 MO	—	30.00	60.00	90.00	175.00
	1856/5 MO	—	20.00	30.00	40.00	125.00
	1856 MO	—	15.00	20.00	30.00	100.00
	1857/5 MO	—	20.00	30.00	40.00	125.00
	1857 MO	—	15.00	20.00	30.00	100.00
	1858/7 MO	—	15.00	20.00	30.00	100.00
	1858 MO	—	15.00	20.00	30.00	100.00
	1859/8 MO	—	15.00	20.00	30.00	100.00
	1859 MO	—	15.00	20.00	30.00	100.00
	1859 VL/MO	—	25.00	50.00	75.00	150.00
	1859 VL	—	20.00	40.00	60.00	125.00
	1860/50 MO	—	10.00	12.00	18.00	75.00
	1860/59 MO	—	10.00	12.00	18.00	75.00
	1860 MO	—	10.00	12.00	18.00	75.00
	1860 VL/MO	—	10.00	12.00	18.00	75.00
	1860 VL	—	10.00	12.00	18.00	75.00
	1861/0 VL/MO	—	10.00	12.00	18.00	75.00
	1861/0 VL	—	10.00	12.00	18.00	75.00
	1861 VL	—	10.00	12.00	18.00	75.00
	1862/1 VL	—	15.00	20.00	30.00	100.00
	1862 VL	—	10.00	12.00	18.00	75.00
	1863 VL	—	10.00	12.00	18.00	75.00
	1863 MO	—	10.00	12.00	18.00	75.00
	1864/3 VL	—	15.00	20.00	30.00	100.00
	1864 VL	—	10.00	12.00	18.00	75.00
	1864 MO	—	15.00	20.00	30.00	100.00
	1865/4 MO	—	200.00	450.00	700.00	1500.
	1865 MO	—	175.00	400.00	600.00	1250.
	1866 VL	—	Contemporary counterfeit			
	1867 JS	—	—	—	Rare	—
	1868 JS	—	10.00	12.00	18.00	75.00
	1868 YH	—	10.00	12.00	18.00	75.00
	1869 YH	—	10.00	12.00	18.00	75.00
	1870 YH	—	—	—	Rare	—
	1873 YH	—	10.00	12.00	18.00	75.00
	1874 YH	—	10.00	12.00	18.00	75.00
	1874 JA/YA	—	10.00	12.00	18.00	75.00
	1874 JA	—	10.00	12.00	18.00	75.00
	1875 JA	—	10.00	12.00	18.00	75.00
	1876 JA	—	10.00	12.00	18.00	75.00
	1876 JS	—	10.00	12.00	18.00	75.00

KM#	Date	Mintage	Fine	VF	XF	Unc
377.13	1877 JS	2.700	10.00	12.00	18.00	75.00
	1878 JS	2.310	10.00	12.00	18.00	75.00
	1879/8 JS	—	15.00	20.00	30.00	100.00
	1879 JS	—	10.00	12.00	18.00	75.00
	1880 JS	—	10.00	12.00	18.00	75.00
	1881 JS	5.592	10.00	12.00	18.00	75.00
	1882/1 JS	2.485	15.00	20.00	30.00	100.00
	1882 JS straight J	Inc. Ab.	10.00	12.00	18.00	60.00
	1882 JS full J	Inc. Ab.	10.00	12.00	18.00	60.00
	1883/2 JS	2.563	15.00	20.00	30.00	100.00
	1883 JS	I.A.	10.00	12.00	18.00	75.00
	1884 JS	—	10.00	12.00	18.00	75.00
	1885 JS	2.252	10.00	12.00	18.00	60.00
	1886/5 JS	5.303	15.00	20.00	30.00	100.00
	1886/8 JS	I.A.	15.00	20.00	30.00	100.00
	1886 JS	I.A.	10.00	12.00	18.00	60.00
	1886 FZ	I.A.	10.00	12.00	18.00	60.00
	1887ZsFZ	4.733	10.00	12.00	18.00	60.00
	1887Z FZ	I.A.	20.00	30.00	50.00	100.00
	1888/7 FZ	5.132	12.00	15.00	25.00	75.00
	1888 FZ	I.A.	10.00	12.00	18.00	60.00
	1889 FZ	4.344	10.00	12.00	18.00	60.00
	1890 FZ	3.887	10.00	12.00	18.00	60.00
	1891 FZ	4.114	10.00	12.00	18.00	60.00
	1892/1 FZ	4.238	12.00	15.00	25.00	75.00
	1892 FZ	I.A.	10.00	12.00	18.00	60.00
	1893 FZ	3.872	10.00	12.00	18.00	60.00
	1894 FZ	3.081	10.00	12.00	18.00	60.00
	1895 FZ	4.718	10.00	12.00	18.00	60.00
	1896 FZ	4.226	10.00	12.00	18.00	50.00
	1897 FZ	4.877	10.00	12.00	18.00	50.00

NOTE: Varieties exist.

1/2 ESCUDO

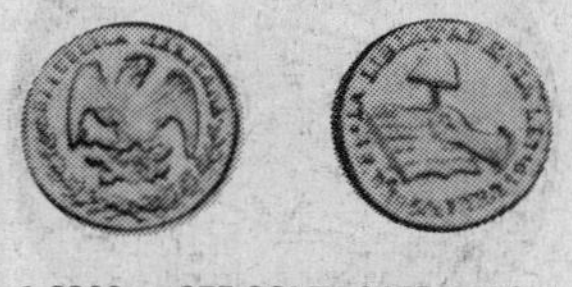

1.6900 g, .875 GOLD, .0475 oz AGW
Mint mark: C
Obv: Facing eagle.

KM#	Date	Mintage	VG	Fine	VF	XF
378	1848 CE	—	35.00	50.00	75.00	150.00
	1853 CE	—	35.00	50.00	75.00	150.00
	1854 CE	—	35.00	50.00	75.00	150.00
	1856 CE	—	50.00	100.00	150.00	250.00
	1857 CE	—	35.00	50.00	75.00	150.00
	1859 CE	—	35.00	50.00	75.00	150.00
	1860 CE	—	35.00	50.00	75.00	150.00
	1862 CE	—	35.00	50.00	75.00	125.00
	1863 CE	—	35.00	50.00	75.00	125.00
	1866 CE	—	35.00	50.00	75.00	125.00
	1867 CE	—	35.00	50.00	75.00	125.00
	1870 CE	—	—	—	—	—

Mint mark: Do

KM#	Date	Mintage	VG	Fine	VF	XF
378.1	1833 RM/RL	—	35.00	50.00	75.00	150.00
	1834/3 RM	—	35.00	50.00	75.00	150.00
	1835/3 RM	—	35.00	50.00	75.00	150.00
	1836/4 RM	—	35.00	50.00	75.00	150.00
	1837 RM	—	35.00	50.00	75.00	150.00
	1838 RM	—	40.00	60.00	100.00	175.00
	1843 RM	—	40.00	60.00	100.00	175.00
	1844/33 RM	—	40.00	60.00	100.00	175.00
	1844/33 RM/RL	—	40.00	60.00	100.00	175.00
	1846 RM	—	40.00	60.00	100.00	175.00
	1848 RM	—	40.00	60.00	100.00	175.00
	1850/33 JMR	—	40.00	60.00	100.00	175.00
	1851 JMR	--	40.00	60.00	100.00	200.00
	1852 JMR	—	40.00	60.00	100.00	175.00
	1853/33 CP	—	75.00	150.00	300.00	500.00
	1853 CP	—	35.00	50.00	75.00	150.00
	1854 CP	—	35.00	50.00	75.00	150.00
	1855 CP	—	35.00	50.00	75.00	150.00
	1859 CP	—	35.00	50.00	75.00	150.00
	1861 CP	—	35.00	50.00	75.00	150.00
	1864 LT	—	75.00	125.00	250.00	400.00

Mint mark: Ga

KM#	Date	Mintage	VG	Fine	VF	XF
378.2	1825 FS	—	40.00	60.00	100.00	175.00
	1829 FS	—	40.00	60.00	100.00	175.00
	1831 FS	—	40.00	60.00	100.00	175.00
	1834 FS	—	40.00	60.00	100.00	175.00
	1835 FS	—	40.00	60.00	100.00	175.00
	1837 JG	—	40.00	60.00	100.00	175.00
	1838 JG	—	40.00	60.00	100.00	175.00
	1839 JG	—	40.00	60.00	100.00	175.00
	1842 JG	—	40.00	60.00	100.00	175.00
	1847 JG	—	40.00	60.00	100.00	175.00
	1850 JG	—	35.00	50.00	75.00	150.00
	1852 JG	—	35.00	50.00	75.00	150.00
	1859 JG	—	40.00	60.00	100.00	175.00
	1861 JG	—	35.00	50.00	75.00	150.00

Mint mark: GC

KM#	Date	Mintage	VG	Fine	VF	XF
378.3	1843/2 MP	—	—	—	—	—
	1846 MP	—	50.00	75.00	100.00	175.00
	1847 MP	—	50.00	75.00	100.00	175.00
	1848/7 MP	—	50.00	75.00	100.00	200.00
	1851 MP	—	50.00	75.00	100.00	175.00

Mint mark: Go

KM#	Date	Mintage	VG	Fine	VF	XF
378.4	1845 PM	—	30.00	40.00	65.00	125.00
	1849 PF	—	30.00	40.00	65.00	125.00
	1851/41 PF	—	30.00	40.00	65.00	125.00
	1851 PF	—	30.00	40.00	65.00	125.00
	1852 PF	—	30.00	40.00	65.00	125.00
	1853 PF	—	30.00	40.00	65.00	125.00
	1855 PF	—	30.00	50.00	80.00	150.00
	1857 PF	—	30.00	40.00	65.00	125.00
	1858/7 PF	—	30.00	40.00	65.00	125.00
	1859 PF	—	30.00	40.00	65.00	125.00
	1860 PF	—	30.00	40.00	65.00	125.00
	1861 PF	—	30.00	40.00	65.00	125.00
	1862/1 YE	—	30.00	40.00	65.00	125.00
	1863 YF	—	30.00	40.00	65.00	125.00

Mint mark: Mo

KM#	Date	Mintage	VG	Fine	VF	XF
378.5	1825/1 JM	—	50.00	75.00	125.00	200.00
	1825/4 JM	—	50.00	75.00	125.00	200.00
	1825 JM	—	30.00	40.00	80.00	150.00
	1827/6 JM	—	30.00	40.00	80.00	150.00
	1827 JM	—	30.00	40.00	80.00	150.00
	1829 JM	—	30.00	40.00	80.00	150.00
	1831/0 JM	—	30.00	40.00	80.00	150.00
	1831 JM	—	30.00	40.00	60.00	125.00
	1832 JM	—	30.00	40.00	60.00	125.00
	1833 MJ olive & oak branches reversed	—	30.00	50.00	90.00	175.00
	1834 ML	—	30.00	40.00	60.00	125.00
	1835 ML	—	30.00	40.00	80.00	150.00
	1838 ML	—	30.00	50.00	90.00	175.00
	1839 ML	—	30.00	50.00	90.00	175.00
	1840 ML	—	30.00	40.00	60.00	125.00
	1841 ML	—	30.00	40.00	60.00	125.00
	1842 ML	—	30.00	40.00	80.00	150.00
	1842 MM	—	30.00	40.00	80.00	150.00
	1843 MM	—	30.00	40.00	60.00	125.00
	1844 MF	—	30.00	40.00	60.00	125.00
	1845 MF	—	30.00	40.00	60.00	125.00
	1846/5 MF	—	30.00	40.00	60.00	125.00
	1846 MF	—	30.00	40.00	60.00	125.00
	1848 GC	—	30.00	40.00	60.00	125.00
	1850 GC	—	30.00	40.00	60.00	125.00
	1851 GC	—	30.00	40.00	60.00	125.00
	1852 GC	—	30.00	40.00	60.00	125.00
	1853 GC	—	30.00	40.00	60.00	125.00
	1854 GC	—	30.00	40.00	60.00	125.00
	1855 GF	—	30.00	40.00	60.00	125.00
	1856/4 GF	—	30.00	40.00	60.00	125.00
	1857 GF	—	30.00	40.00	60.00	125.00
	1858 FH	—	30.00	40.00	60.00	125.00
	1859 FH	—	30.00	40.00	60.00	125.00
	1860/59 FH	—	30.00	40.00	60.00	125.00
	1861 CH/FH	—	30.00	40.00	80.00	150.00
	1862 CH	—	30.00	40.00	60.00	125.00
	1863/57 CH/GF	—	30.00	40.00	60.00	125.00
	1868/58 PH	—	30.00	40.00	80.00	150.00
	1869/59 CH	—	30.00	40.00	80.00	150.00

Mint mark: Zs

KM#	Date	Mintage	VG	Fine	VF	XF
378.6	1860 VL	—	35.00	50.00	75.00	150.00
	1862/1 VL	—	35.00	50.00	75.00	150.00
	1862 VL	—	30.00	40.00	65.00	125.00

ESCUDO

3.3800 g, .875 GOLD, .0950 oz AGW
Mint mark: C
Obv: Facing eagle.

KM#	Date	Mintage	VG	Fine	VF	XF
379	1846 CE	—	75.00	100.00	200.00	350.00
	1847 CE	—	50.00	75.00	125.00	175.00
	1848 CE	—	50.00	75.00	125.00	175.00
	1849/8 CE	—	60.00	100.00	150.00	225.00
	1850 CE	—	50.00	75.00	125.00	175.00
	1851/0 CE	—	60.00	100.00	150.00	225.00
	1853/1 CE	—	60.00	100.00	150.00	225.00
	1854 CE	—	50.00	75.00	125.00	175.00
	1856/5/4 CE	—	60.00	100.00	150.00	225.00
	1856 CE	—	50.00	75.00	125.00	175.00
	1857/1 CE	—	60.00	100.00	150.00	225.00
	1857 CE	—	50.00	75.00	125.00	175.00
	1861 PV	—	50.00	75.00	125.00	175.00
	1862 CE	—	50.00	75.00	125.00	175.00
	1863 CE	—	50.00	75.00	125.00	175.00
	1866 CE	—	50.00	75.00	125.00	175.00
	1870 CE	—	50.00	75.00	125.00	175.00

Mint mark: Do

KM#	Date	Mintage	VG	Fine	VF	XF
379.1	1833/2 RM/RL	—	75.00	125.00	200.00	300.00
	1834 RM	—	60.00	100.00	150.00	200.00
	1835 RM	—	—	—	—	—
	1836 RM/RL	—	60.00	100.00	150.00	200.00
	1838 RM	—	60.00	100.00	150.00	200.00
	1846/38 RM	—	75.00	125.00	200.00	300.00
	1850 JMR	—	75.00	125.00	175.00	225.00
	1851/31 JMR	—	75.00	125.00	200.00	300.00
	1851 JMR	—	75.00	125.00	175.00	225.00
	1853 CP	—	75.00	125.00	175.00	225.00
	1854/34 CP	—	75.00	125.00	175.00	225.00
	1854/44 CP/RP	—	75.00	125.00	175.00	225.00
	1855 CP	—	75.00	125.00	175.00	225.00
	1859 CP	—	75.00	125.00	175.00	225.00
	1861 CP	—	75.00	125.00	175.00	225.00
	1864 LT/CP	—	75.00	125.00	175.00	225.00

Mint mark: Ga

KM#	Date	Mintage	VG	Fine	VF	XF
379.2	1825 FS	—	60.00	90.00	125.00	200.00
	1826 FS	—	60.00	90.00	125.00	200.00
	1829 FS	—	—	—	—	—
	1831 FS	—	60.00	90.00	125.00	200.00
	1834 FS	—	60.00	90.00	125.00	200.00
	1835 JG	—	60.00	90.00	125.00	200.00
	1842 JG/MC	—	60.00	90.00	125.00	200.00
	1843 MC	—	60.00	90.00	125.00	200.00
	1847 JG	—	60.00	90.00	125.00	200.00
	1848/7 JG	—	60.00	90.00	125.00	200.00
	1849 JG	—	60.00	90.00	125.00	200.00
	1850/40 JG	—	60.00	125.00	225.00	325.00
	1850 JG	—	60.00	90.00	125.00	200.00
	1852/1 JG	—	60.00	90.00	125.00	200.00
	1856 JG	—	60.00	90.00	125.00	200.00
	1857 JG	—	60.00	90.00	125.00	200.00
	1859/7 JG	—	60.00	90.00	125.00	200.00
	1860/59 JG	—	60.00	90.00	125.00	200.00
	1860 JG	—	60.00	90.00	125.00	200.00

Mint mark: GC

KM#	Date	Mintage	VG	Fine	VF	XF
379.3	1844 MP	—	75.00	100.00	175.00	250.00
	1845 MP	—	75.00	100.00	175.00	250.00
	1846 MP	—	75.00	100.00	175.00	250.00
	1847 MP	—	75.00	100.00	175.00	250.00
	1848 MP	—	75.00	100.00	175.00	250.00
	1849 MP	—	75.00	100.00	175.00	250.00
	1850 MP	—	75.00	100.00	175.00	250.00
	1851 MP	—	75.00	100.00	175.00	250.00

Mint mark: Go

KM#	Date	Mintage	VG	Fine	VF	XF
379.4	1845 PM	—	60.00	75.00	125.00	200.00
	1849 PF	—	60.00	75.00	125.00	200.00
	1851 PF	—	60.00	75.00	125.00	200.00
	1853 PF	—	60.00	75.00	125.00	200.00
	1860 PF	—	75.00	125.00	200.00	300.00
	1862 YE	—	60.00	75.00	125.00	200.00

Mint mark: Mo

KM#	Date	Mintage	VG	Fine	VF	XF
379.5	1825 JM	—	50.00	70.00	100.00	150.00
	1827/6 JM	—	50.00	70.00	100.00	150.00
	1827 JM	—	50.00	70.00	100.00	150.00
	1830/29 JM	—	50.00	70.00	100.00	150.00
	1831 JM	—	50.00	70.00	100.00	150.00
	1832 JM	—	50.00	70.00	125.00	175.00
	1833 MJ	—	50.00	70.00	100.00	150.00
	1834 ML	—	50.00	70.00	125.00	175.00
	1841 ML	—	50.00	70.00	125.00	175.00
	1843 MM	—	50.00	70.00	100.00	150.00
	1845 MF	—	50.00	70.00	100.00	150.00
	1846/5 MF	—	50.00	70.00	100.00	150.00
	1848 GC	—	50.00	70.00	125.00	175.00
	1850 GC	—	50.00	70.00	125.00	175.00
	1856/4 GF	—	50.00	70.00	100.00	150.00
	1856/5 GF	—	50.00	70.00	100.00	150.00
	1856 GF	—	50.00	70.00	100.00	150.00
	1858 FH	—	50.00	70.00	125.00	175.00
	1859 FH	—	50.00	70.00	100.00	150.00
	1860 TH	—	50.00	70.00	125.00	175.00
	1861 CH	—	50.00	70.00	100.00	150.00
	1862 CH	—	50.00	70.00	125.00	175.00
	1863 TH	—	50.00	70.00	100.00	150.00
	1869 CH	—	50.00	70.00	100.00	150.00

Mint mark: Zs

KM#	Date	Mintage	VG	Fine	VF	XF
379.6	1853 OM	—	100.00	125.00	200.00	300.00
	1860/59 VL V is inverted A	—	75.00	100.00	200.00	350.00
	1860 VL	—	75.00	100.00	150.00	200.00
	1862 VL	—	75.00	100.00	150.00	200.00

2 ESCUDOS

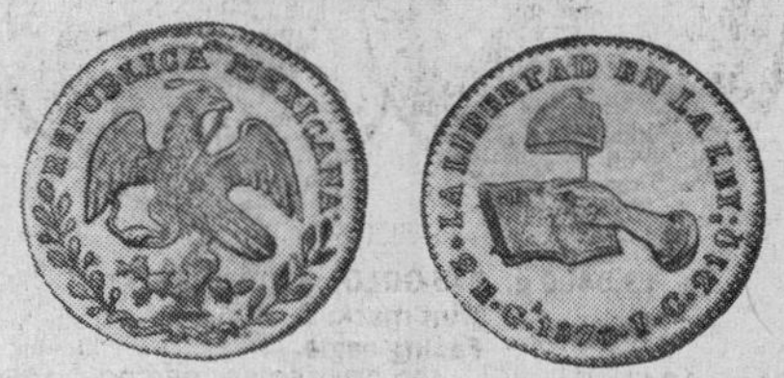

6.7700 g, .875 GOLD, .1904 oz AGW
Mint mark: C
Obv: Facing eagle.

KM#	Date	Mintage	VG	Fine	VF	XF
380	1846 CE	—	100.00	150.00	225.00	325.00
	1847 CE	—	100.00	150.00	225.00	325.00
	1848 CE	—	100.00	150.00	225.00	325.00
	1852 CE	—	100.00	150.00	225.00	325.00
	1854 CE	—	100.00	175.00	250.00	375.00
	1856/1 CE	—	100.00	175.00	250.00	375.00
	1857 CE	—	100.00	150.00	225.00	325.00

Mint mark: Do

KM#	Date	Mintage	VG	Fine	VF	XF
380.1	1833 RM	—	300.00	450.00	700.00	1200.
	1837/4 RM	—	—	—	—	—
	1837 RM	—	—	—	—	—
	1844 RM	—	275.00	400.00	600.00	1000.

Mint mark: EoMo

KM#	Date	Mintage	VG	Fine	VF	XF
380.2	1828 LF	—	700.00	1000.	1750.	2500.

Mint mark: Ga

KM#	Date	Mintage	VG	Fine	VF	XF
380.3	1835 FS	—	100.00	150.00	225.00	325.00
	1836/5 JG	—	100.00	150.00	225.00	300.00
	1839/5 JG	—	—	—	—	—
	1839 JG	—	100.00	150.00	200.00	275.00

1260 Republic / MEXICO

KM#	Date	Mintage	VG	Fine	VF	XF
380.3	1840 MC	—	100.00	150.00	200.00	275.00
	1841 MC	—	100.00	150.00	250.00	400.00
	1847/6 JG	—	100.00	150.00	225.00	300.00
	1848/7 JG	—	100.00	150.00	225.00	300.00
	1850 JG	—	100.00	150.00	200.00	250.00
	1851 JG	—	100.00	150.00	200.00	275.00
	1852 JG	—	100.00	150.00	225.00	325.00
	1853 JG	—	100.00	150.00	200.00	275.00
	1854/2 JG	—	—	—	—	—
	1858 JG	—	100.00	150.00	200.00	275.00
	1859/8 JG	—	100.00	150.00	225.00	300.00
	1859 JG	—	100.00	150.00	200.00	275.00
	1860/50 JG	—	100.00	150.00	225.00	300.00
	1860 JG	—	100.00	150.00	225.00	300.00
	1861/59 JG	—	100.00	150.00	200.00	275.00
	1861/0 JG	—	100.00	150.00	200.00	275.00
	1863/1 JG	—	100.00	150.00	200.00	275.00
	1870 IC	—	100.00	150.00	200.00	275.00
	Mint mark: GC					
380.4	1844 MP	—	150.00	200.00	275.00	400.00
	1845 MP	—	750.00	1250.	2000.	3000.
	1846 MP	—	750.00	1250.	2000.	3000.
	1847 MP	—	125.00	175.00	350.00	500.00
	1848 MP	—	150.00	200.00	350.00	450.00
	1849 MP	—	150.00	200.00	300.00	400.00
	1850 MP	—	150.00	200.00	300.00	400.00
	Mint mark: Go					
380.5	1845 PM	—	100.00	150.00	250.00	400.00
	1849 PF	—	100.00	150.00	250.00	400.00
	1853 PF	—	100.00	150.00	250.00	400.00
	1856 PF	—	100.00	150.00	250.00	400.00
	1859 PF	—	100.00	150.00	250.00	400.00
	1860/59 PF	—	100.00	150.00	250.00	400.00
	1860 PF	—	100.00	150.00	250.00	400.00
	1862 YE	—	100.00	150.00	250.00	400.00
	Mint mark: Ho					
380.6	1861 FM	—	500.00	1000.	1500.	2000.
	Mint mark: Mo					
380.7	1825 JM	—	100.00	150.00	200.00	275.00
	1827/6 JM	—	100.00	150.00	200.00	275.00
	1827 JM	—	100.00	150.00	200.00	275.00
	1830/29 JM	—	100.00	150.00	200.00	275.00
	1831 JM	—	100.00	150.00	200.00	275.00
	1833 ML	—	100.00	150.00	200.00	275.00
	1841 ML	—	100.00	150.00	200.00	275.00
	1844 MF	—	100.00	150.00	200.00	275.00
	1845 MF	—	100.00	150.00	200.00	275.00
	1846 MF	—	125.00	200.00	400.00	600.00
	1848 GC	—	100.00	150.00	200.00	275.00
	1850 GC	—	100.00	150.00	200.00	275.00
	1856/5 GF	—	100.00	150.00	200.00	275.00
	1856 GF	—	100.00	150.00	200.00	275.00
	1858 FH	—	100.00	150.00	200.00	275.00
	1859 FH	—	100.00	150.00	200.00	275.00
	1861 TH	—	100.00	150.00	200.00	275.00
	1861 CH	—	100.00	150.00	200.00	300.00
	1862 CH	—	100.00	150.00	200.00	300.00
	1863 TH	—	100.00	150.00	200.00	300.00
	1868 PH	—	100.00	150.00	200.00	300.00
	1869 CH	—	100.00	150.00	200.00	300.00
	Mint mark: Zs					
380.8	1860 VL	—	150.00	300.00	600.00	1200.
	1862 VL	—	250.00	500.00	800.00	1200.
	1864 MO	—	150.00	300.00	600.00	1200.

4 ESCUDOS

REPUBLICA MEXICANA
LA LIBERTAD EN LA LEY.

13.5400 g, .875 GOLD, .3809 oz AGW

KM#	Date	Mintage	VG	Fine	VF	XF
	Mint mark: C					
	Facing eagle					
381	1847 CE	—	400.00	650.00	850.00	1250.
	1848 CE	—	600.00	900.00	1250.	1750.
	Mint mark: Do					
381.1	1832 RM/LR	—	—	—	Rare	—
	1832 RM	—	600.00	900.00	1250.	1750.
	1833 RM	—	—	—	Rare	—
	1852 JMR	—	—	—	Rare	—
	Mint mark: Ga					
381.2	1844 MC	—	500.00	750.00	1000.	1500.
	1844 JG	—	400.00	650.00	850.00	1250.
	Mint mark: GC					
381.3	1844 MP	—	400.00	650.00	850.00	1250.
	1845 MP	—	350.00	500.00	700.00	1000.
	1846 MP	—	400.00	650.00	850.00	1250.
	1848 MP	—	400.00	650.00	850.00	1250.
	1850 MP	—	500.00	750.00	1000.	1500.
	Mint mark: Go					
381.4	1829/8 MJ	—	250.00	400.00	550.00	750.00
	1829 JM	—	250.00	400.00	550.00	750.00
	1829 MJ	—	250.00	400.00	550.00	750.00
	1831 MJ	—	250.00	400.00	550.00	750.00
	1832 MJ	—	250.00	400.00	550.00	750.00

KM#	Date	Mintage	VG	Fine	VF	XF
381.4	1833 MJ	—	250.00	400.00	600.00	850.00
	1834 PJ	—	300.00	500.00	700.00	1000.
	1835 PJ	—	300.00	500.00	700.00	1000.
	1836 PJ	—	250.00	400.00	600.00	850.00
	1837 PJ	—	250.00	400.00	600.00	850.00
	1838 PJ	—	250.00	400.00	600.00	850.00
	1839 PJ	—	300.00	500.00	700.00	1000.
	1840 PJ	—	250.00	400.00	600.00	850.00
	1841 PJ	—	300.00	500.00	700.00	1000.
	1845 PM	—	250.00	400.00	600.00	850.00
	1847/5 YE	—	300.00	500.00	700.00	1000.
	1847 PM	—	300.00	500.00	700.00	1000.
	1849 PF	—	300.00	500.00	700.00	1000.
	1851 PF	—	300.00	500.00	700.00	1000.
	1852 PF	—	250.00	400.00	600.00	850.00
	1855 PF	—	250.00	400.00	600.00	850.00
	1857/5 PF	—	250.00	400.00	600.00	850.00
	1858/7 PF	—	250.00	400.00	600.00	850.00
	1858 PF	—	250.00	400.00	600.00	850.00
	1859/7 PF	—	300.00	500.00	700.00	1000.
	1860 PF	—	300.00	500.00	800.00	1200.
	1862 YE	—	250.00	400.00	600.00	850.00
	1863 YF	—	250.00	400.00	600.00	850.00
	Mint mark: Ho					
381.5	1861 FM	—	1000.	1500.	2500.	3500.
	Mint mark: Mo					
381.6	1825 JM	—	250.00	400.00	600.00	900.00
	1827 JM	—	250.00	400.00	550.00	850.00
	1829 JM	—	250.00	450.00	700.00	1000.
	1831 JM	—	250.00	450.00	700.00	1000.
	1832 JM	—	300.00	500.00	800.00	1200.
	1844 MF	—	250.00	450.00	700.00	1000.
	1850 GC	—	250.00	450.00	700.00	1000.
	1856 GF	—	250.00	400.00	550.00	850.00
	1857/6 GF	—	250.00	400.00	550.00	850.00
	1857 GF	—	250.00	400.00	550.00	850.00
	1858 FH	—	250.00	450.00	700.00	1000.
	1859/8 FH	—	250.00	450.00	700.00	1000.
	1861 CH	—	400.00	800.00	1200.	1600.
	1863 CH	—	250.00	450.00	700.00	1000.
	1868 PH	—	250.00	400.00	550.00	850.00
	1869 CH	—	250.00	400.00	500.00	800.00
	Mint mark: O, Oa					
381.7	1861 FR	—	1500.	2500.	4000.	6500.
	Mint mark: Zs					
381.8	1862 VL	—	750.00	1250.	2250.	3500.

8 ESCUDOS

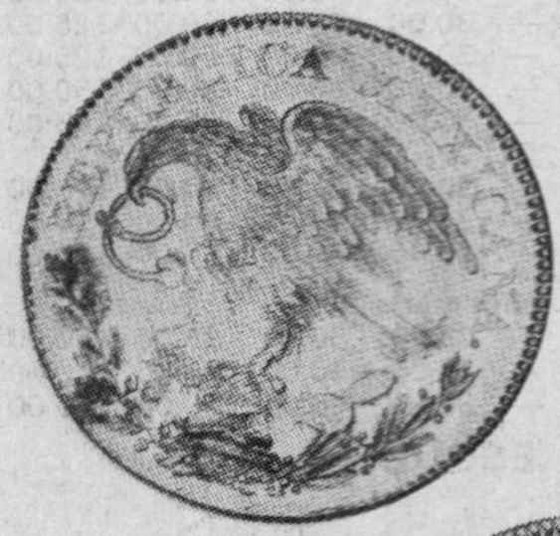
REPUBLICA MEXICANA

LA LIBERTAD EN LA LEY.

27.0700 g, .875 GOLD, .7616 oz AGW
Mint mark: Mo
Obv: Hooked-neck eagle.

KM#	Date	Mintage	Fine	VF	XF	Unc
382	1823 JM	—	3500.	6500.	10,000.	—

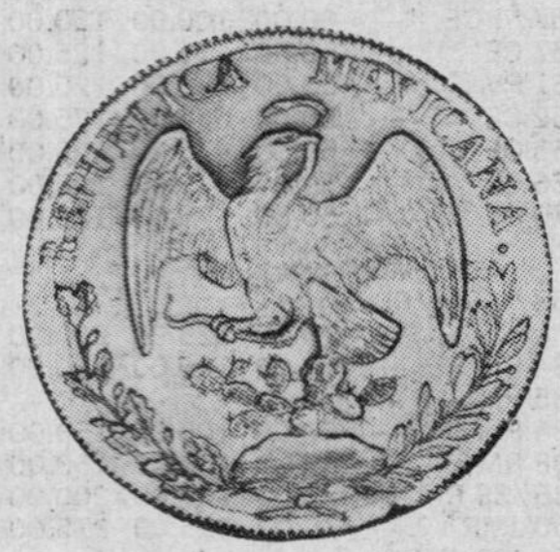
REPUBLICA MEXICANA

Mint mark: A
Obv: Facing eagle.

KM#	Date	Mintage	Fine	VF	XF	Unc
383	1864 PG	—	650.00	1250.	2250.	—
	1866 DL	—	—	—	7500.	—
	1868/7 DL	—	1500.	2250.	3250.	—
	1869 DL	—	650.00	1250.	2250.	—
383	1870 DL	—	1500.	2250.	3250.	—
	1872 AM	—	—	—	Rare	—
	Mint mark: Ca					
383.1	1841 RG	—	400.00	750.00	1250.	1750.
	1842 RG	—	375.00	500.00	1000.	1500.
	1843 RG	—	375.00	500.00	1000.	1500.
	1844 RG	—	350.00	500.00	1000.	1500.
	1845 RG	—	350.00	500.00	1000.	1500.
	1846 RG	—	500.00	1250.	1500.	2000.
	1848 RG	—	350.00	500.00	1000.	1500.
	1849 RG	—	350.00	500.00	1000.	1500.
	1850/40 RG	—	350.00	500.00	1000.	1500.
	1851/41 RG	—	350.00	500.00	1000.	1500.
	1852/42 RG	—	350.00	500.00	1000.	1500.
	1853/43 RG	—	350.00	500.00	1000.	1500.
	1854/44 RG	—	350.00	500.00	1000.	1500.
	1855/43 RG	—	400.00	650.00	1250.	1750.
	1856 RG	—	350.00	500.00	750.00	1250.
	1857 JC/RG	—	350.00	500.00	750.00	1250.
	1858 JC	—	350.00	500.00	750.00	1250.
	1858 BA/RG	—	350.00	500.00	750.00	1250.
	1859 JC/RC	—	350.00	500.00	750.00	1250.
	1860 JC/RC	—	350.00	500.00	1000.	1500.
	1861 JC	—	375.00	500.00	750.00	1250.
	1862 JC	—	375.00	500.00	750.00	1250.
	1863 JC	—	500.00	1000.	1750.	2250.
	1864 JC	—	400.00	750.00	1250.	1750.
	1865 JC	—	750.00	1500.	2500.	3500.
	1866 JC	—	375.00	500.00	1000.	1500.
	1866 FP	—	600.00	1250.	2000.	2500.
	1866 JG	—	375.00	500.00	1000.	1500.
	1867 JG	—	375.00	500.00	750.00	1250.
	1868 JG	—	375.00	500.00	750.00	1250.
	1869 MM	—	375.00	500.00	750.00	1250.
	1870 MM	—	375.00	500.00	750.00	1250.
	1871/61 MM	—	375.00	500.00	1000.	1500.

LA LIBERTAD EN LA LEY.

KM#	Date	Mintage	Fine	VF	XF	Unc
	Mint mark: C					
383.2	1846 CE	—	375.00	500.00	1000.	1750.
	1847 CE	—	375.00	500.00	800.00	1250.
	1848 CE	—	375.00	500.00	1000.	1750.
	1849 CE	—	375.00	450.00	700.00	1250.
	1850 CE	—	375.00	450.00	700.00	1250.
	1851 CE	—	375.00	500.00	800.00	1250.
	1852 CE	—	375.00	500.00	800.00	1250.
	1853/1 CE	—	375.00	450.00	700.00	1250.
	1854 CE	—	375.00	450.00	700.00	1250.
	1855/4 CE	—	375.00	500.00	1000.	1750.
	1855 CE	—	375.00	500.00	800.00	1250.
	1856 CE	—	375.00	450.00	700.00	1250.
	1857 CE	—	375.00	450.00	700.00	1250.
	1858 CE	—	375.00	450.00	700.00	1250.
	1859 CE	—	375.00	450.00	700.00	1250.
	1860 CE	—	375.00	500.00	800.00	1250.
	1860 PV	—	375.00	450.00	700.00	1250.
	1861 PV	—	375.00	500.00	800.00	1250.
	1861 CE	—	375.00	500.00	800.00	1250.
	1862 CE	—	375.00	500.00	800.00	1250.
	1863 CE	—	375.00	500.00	800.00	1250.
	1864 CE	—	375.00	450.00	700.00	1250.
	1865 CE	—	375.00	500.00	800.00	1250.
	1866/5 CE	—	375.00	450.00	700.00	1250.
	1866 CE	—	375.00	450.00	700.00	1250.
	1867 CE	—	375.00	450.00	700.00	1250.
	1868 CE	—	375.00	500.00	800.00	1250.
	1869 CE	—	375.00	500.00	800.00	1250.
	1870 CE	—	375.00	500.00	800.00	1250.

KM#	Date	Mintage	Fine	VF	XF	Unc
	Mint mark: Do					
383.3	1832 RM	—	850.00	1750.	2000.	3000.
	1833 RM/RL	—	375.00	500.00	800.00	1250.
	1834 RM	—	375.00	500.00	800.00	1250.
	1835 RM	—	375.00	500.00	800.00	1250.
	1836 RM/RL	—	375.00	500.00	800.00	1250.
	1836 RM M on snake					
		—	375.00	500.00	800.00	1250.
	1837 RM	—	375.00	500.00	800.00	1250.
	1838/6 RM	—	375.00	500.00	800.00	1250.

KM#	Date	Mintage	Fine	VF	XF	Unc
383.3	1838 RM	—	375.00	500.00	800.00	1250.
	1839 RM	—	375.00	450.00	700.00	1250.
	1840/30 RM/RL	—	400.00	600.00	1000.	1750.
	1841/31 RM	—	375.00	500.00	800.00	1250.
	1841/34 RM	—	375.00	500.00	800.00	1250.
	1841 RM/RL	—	375.00	500.00	800.00	1250.
	1842/32 RM	—	375.00	500.00	800.00	1250.
	1843/1 RM	—	375.00	500.00	800.00	1250.
	1843 RM	—	375.00	500.00	800.00	1250.
	1844/34 RM/RL	—	500.00	1000.	1500.	2500.
	1844 RM	—	450.00	800.00	1250.	2000.
	1845/36 RM	—	400.00	600.00	1000.	1750.
	1845 RM	—	400.00	600.00	1000.	1750.
	1846 RM	—	375.00	500.00	800.00	1250.
	1847 RM	—	375.00	500.00	800.00	1250.
	1848/37 RM	—	—	—	—	—
	1848 CM	—	375.00	500.00	800.00	1250.
	1849/39 CM	—	375.00	500.00	800.00	1250.
	1849 JMR	—	400.00	750.00	1250.	2000.
	1850 JMR	—	400.00	750.00	1250.	2000.
	1851 JMR	—	400.00	750.00	1250.	2000.
	1852/1 JMR	—	450.00	800.00	1250.	2000.
	1852 CP	—	450.00	800.00	1250.	2000.
	1853 CP	—	450.00	800.00	1250.	2000.
	1854 CP	—	400.00	600.00	1000.	1750.
	1855/4 CP	—	375.00	500.00	800.00	1250.
	1856 CP	—	400.00	600.00	1000.	1750.
	1857 CP French style eagle, 1832-57	—	375.00	500.00	800.00	1250.
	1857 CP Mexican style eagle	—	375.00	500.00	800.00	1250.
	1858 CP	—	375.00	500.00	800.00	1250.
	1859 CP	—	375.00	500.00	800.00	1250.
	1861/0 CP	—	400.00	600.00	1000.	1750.
	1862/52 CP	—	375.00	500.00	800.00	1250.
	1862 CP	—	375.00	500.00	800.00	1250.
	1863 CP	—	375.00	500.00	800.00	1250.
	1864 LT	—	375.00	500.00	800.00	1250.
	1865 LT	—	—	—	—	—
	1866/4 CM	—	1250.	2000.	2500.	—
	1866 CM	—	400.00	600.00	1000.	1750.
	1867/56 CP	—	400.00	600.00	1000.	1750.
	1868/4 CP/LT	—	—	—	—	—
	1869 CP	—	500.00	1250.	1750.	2750.
	1870 CP	—	400.00	600.00	1000.	1750.

Mint mark: EoMo

KM#	Date	Mintage	Fine	VF	XF	Unc
383.4	1828 LF	—	2500.	5000.	7500.	—
	1829 LF	—	2500.	5000.	7500.	—

Mint mark: Ga

KM#	Date	Mintage	Fine	VF	XF	Unc
383.5	1825 FS	—	500.00	1000.	1250.	1750.
	1826 FS	—	500.00	1000.	1250.	1750.
	1830 FS	—	500.00	1000.	1250.	1750.
	1836 FS	—	750.00	1500.	2000.	3000.
	1837 JG	—	1000.	2500.	3500.	—
	1840 MC	—	750.00	1500.	2000.	3000.
	1842 JG	—	—	—	—	—
	1843 MC	—	—	—	—	—
	1845 MC	—	400.00	750.00	1000.	1500.
	1849 JG	—	500.00	1000.	1250.	1750.
	1850 JG	—	400.00	750.00	1000.	1500.
	1851 JG	—	400.00	750.00	1000.	1500.
	1852/1 JG	—	500.00	1000.	1250.	1750.
	1855 JG	—	1000.	2500.	3500.	—
	1856 JG	—	400.00	750.00	1000.	1500.
	1857 JG	—	400.00	750.00	1000.	1500.
	1861/0 JG	—	500.00	1000.	1250.	1750.
	1863/1 JG	—	500.00	1000.	1250.	1750.
	1866 JG	—	400.00	750.00	1000.	1500.

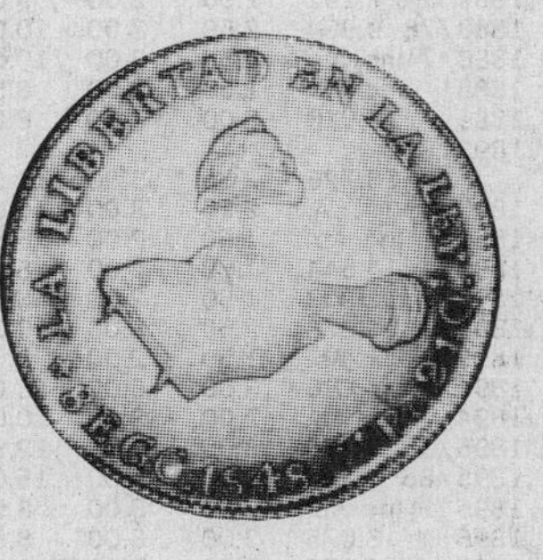

Mint mark: GC

KM#	Date	Mintage	Fine	VF	XF	Unc
383.6	1844 MP	—	550.00	750.00	1250.	2000.
	1845 MP eagle's tail square	—	550.00	750.00	1250.	2000.
	1845 MP eagle's tail round	—	550.00	750.00	1250.	2000.
	1846 MP eagle's tail square	—	450.00	650.00	1000.	1750.
	1846 MP eagle's tail round	—	450.00	650.00	1000.	1750.
	1847 MP	—	450.00	650.00	1000.	1750.
	1848 MP	—	550.00	750.00	1250.	2000.
	1849 MP	—	550.00	750.00	1250.	2000.
	1850 MP	—	450.00	650.00	1000.	1750.
	1851 MP	—	450.00	650.00	1000.	1750.
	1852 MP	—	550.00	750.00	1250.	2000.

Mint mark: Go

KM#	Date	Mintage	Fine	VF	XF	Unc
383.7	1828 MJ	—	700.00	1750.	2250.	3000.
	1829 MJ	—	600.00	1500.	2000.	2750.
	1830 MJ	—	375.00	500.00	750.00	1000.
	1831 MJ	—	600.00	1500.	2000.	2750.
	1832 MJ	—	500.00	1250.	1750.	2500.
	1833 MJ	—	375.00	500.00	750.00	1000.
	1834 PJ	—	375.00	500.00	750.00	1000.
	1835 PJ	—	375.00	500.00	750.00	1000.
	1836 PJ	—	400.00	650.00	900.00	1250.
	1837 PJ	—	400.00	650.00	900.00	1250.
	1838/7 PJ	—	375.00	500.00	750.00	1000.
	1839/8 PJ	—	375.00	500.00	750.00	1000.
	1840 PJ	—	375.00	500.00	750.00	1000.
	1841 PJ	—	375.00	500.00	750.00	1000.
	1842 PJ	—	375.00	475.00	650.00	1000.
	1842 PM	—	375.00	500.00	750.00	1000.
	1843 PM	—	375.00	500.00	750.00	1000.
	1844/3 PM	—	400.00	650.00	900.00	1250.
	1844 PM	—	375.00	500.00	750.00	1000.
	1845 PM	—	375.00	500.00	750.00	1000.
	1846 PM	—	375.00	500.00	750.00	1000.
	1847 PM	—	400.00	650.00	900.00	1250.
	1848/7 PM	—	375.00	500.00	750.00	1000.
	1848 PM	—	375.00	500.00	750.00	1000.
	1848 PF	—	375.00	500.00	750.00	1000.
	1849 PF	—	375.00	425.00	650.00	900.00
	1850 PF	—	375.00	425.00	650.00	900.00
	1851 PF	—	375.00	500.00	750.00	1000.
	1852 PF	—	375.00	500.00	750.00	1000.
	1853 PF	—	375.00	425.00	650.00	900.00
	1854 PF	—	375.00	500.00	750.00	1000.
	1855/4 PF	—	400.00	650.00	900.00	1250.
	1855 PF	—	375.00	500.00	750.00	1000.
	1856 PF	—	375.00	500.00	750.00	1000.
	1857 PF	—	375.00	500.00	750.00	1000.
	1858 PF	—	375.00	500.00	750.00	1000.
	1859 PF	—	375.00	400.00	550.00	750.00
	1860/50 PF	—	375.00	425.00	650.00	900.00
	1860/59 PF	—	400.00	650.00	900.00	1250.
	1860 PF	—	375.00	500.00	750.00	1100.
	1861/0 PF	—	375.00	400.00	500.00	750.00
	1861 PF	—	375.00	400.00	500.00	750.00
	1862/1 YE	—	375.00	500.00	750.00	1000.
	1862 YE	—	375.00	500.00	750.00	1000.
	1863 YF	—	375.00	500.00	750.00	1000.
	1863 PF	—	375.00	500.00	750.00	1000.
	1867 6/5 YF/YP	—	375.00	500.00	750.00	1000.
	1867 YF	—	375.00	500.00	750.00	1000.
	1868 YF	—	375.00	500.00	750.00	1000.
	1870 FR	—	375.00	425.00	650.00	900.00

Mint mark: Ho

KM#	Date	Mintage	Fine	VF	XF	Unc
383.8	1863 FM	—	400.00	650.00	1000.	2000.
	1864 FM	—	600.00	1250.	1750.	2750.
	1864 PR/FM	—	400.00	650.00	1000.	2000.
	1865 FM/PR	—	500.00	800.00	1250.	2500.
	1867 PR	—	400.00	650.00	1000.	2000.
	1868 PR	—	500.00	800.00	1250.	2500.
	1868 PR/FM	—	500.00	800.00	1250.	2500.
	1869 PR/FM	—	400.00	650.00	1000.	2000.
	1869 PR	—	400.00	650.00	1000.	2000.
	1870 PR	—	400.00	650.00	1000.	2000.
	1871 PR	—	500.00	800.00	1250.	2500.
	1872/1 PR	—	600.00	1250.	1750.	2750.
	1873 PR	—	400.00	650.00	1000.	2000.

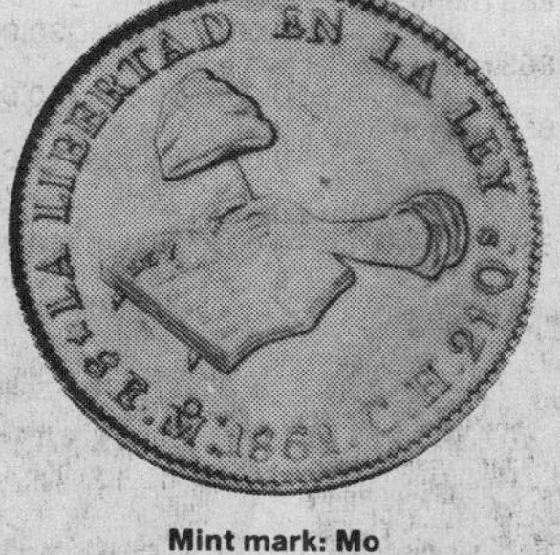

Mint mark: Mo

KM#	Date	Mintage	Fine	VF	XF	Unc
383.9	1824 JM	—	500.00	1000.	1250.	2000.
	1825/3 JM	—	400.00	750.00	1000.	1500.
	1825 JM	—	375.00	450.00	600.00	1000.
	1826/5 JM	—	700.00	1750.	2250.	3000.
	1827 JM	—	375.00	600.00	725.00	1000.
	1828 JM	—	375.00	600.00	725.00	1000.
	1829 JM	—	375.00	600.00	725.00	1000.
	1830 JM	—	375.00	600.00	725.00	1000.
	1831 JM	—	375.00	600.00	725.00	1000.

KM#	Date	Mintage	Fine	VF	XF	Unc
383.9	1832/1 JM	—	375.00	600.00	725.00	1000.
	1832 JM	—	375.00	600.00	725.00	1000.
	1833 MJ	—	400.00	750.00	1000.	1500.
	1833 ML	—	375.00	450.00	600.00	900.00
	1834 ML	—	375.00	450.00	600.00	900.00
	1835/4 ML	—	500.00	1000.	1250.	2000.
	1836 ML	—	375.00	450.00	600.00	900.00
	1837/6 ML	—	375.00	450.00	600.00	900.00
	1838 ML	—	375.00	450.00	600.00	900.00
	1839 ML	—	375.00	450.00	600.00	900.00
	1840 ML	—	375.00	450.00	600.00	900.00
	1841 ML	—	375.00	450.00	600.00	900.00
	1842/1 ML	—	—	—	—	—
	1842 ML	—	375.00	450.00	600.00	900.00
	1842 MM	—	—	—	—	—
	1843 MM	—	375.00	450.00	600.00	900.00
	1844 MF	—	375.00	450.00	600.00	900.00
	1845 MF	—	375.00	450.00	600.00	900.00
	1846 MF	—	500.00	1000.	1250.	2000.
	1847 RC	—	375.00	500.00	800.00	1250.
	1848 GC	—	375.00	450.00	600.00	900.00
	1849 GC	—	375.00	450.00	600.00	900.00
	1850 GC	—	375.00	450.00	600.00	900.00
	1851 GC	—	375.00	450.00	600.00	900.00
	1852 GC	—	375.00	450.00	600.00	900.00
	1853 GC	—	375.00	450.00	600.00	900.00
	1854/44 GC	—	375.00	450.00	600.00	900.00
	1854/3 GC	—	375.00	450.00	600.00	900.00
	1855 GF	—	375.00	450.00	600.00	900.00
	1856/5 GF	—	375.00	450.00	600.00	900.00
	1856 GF	—	375.00	450.00	600.00	900.00
	1857 GF	—	375.00	450.00	600.00	900.00
	1858 FH	—	375.00	450.00	600.00	900.00
	1859 FH	—	400.00	750.00	1000.	1500.
	1860 FH	—	375.00	450.00	600.00	900.00
	1860 TH	—	375.00	450.00	600.00	900.00
	1861/51 CH	—	375.00	450.00	600.00	900.00
	1862 CH	—	375.00	450.00	600.00	900.00
	1863/53 CH	—	375.00	450.00	600.00	900.00
	1863/53 TH	—	375.00	450.00	600.00	900.00
	1867 CH	—	375.00	450.00	600.00	900.00
	1868 CH	—	375.00	450.00	600.00	900.00
	1868 PH	—	375.00	450.00	600.00	900.00
	1869 CH	—	375.00	450.00	600.00	900.00

Mint mark: O

KM#	Date	Mintage	Fine	VF	XF	Unc
383.10	1858 AE	—	2000.	3000.	4000.	6000.
	1859 AE	—	1000.	2500.	3750.	5500.
	1860 AE	—	1000.	2500.	3750.	5500.
	1861 FR	—	450.00	900.00	1500.	2750.
	1862 FR	—	450.00	900.00	1500.	2750.
	1863 FR	—	450.00	900.00	1500.	2750.
	1864 FR	—	450.00	900.00	1500.	2750.
	1867 AE	—	450.00	900.00	1500.	2750.
	1868 AE	—	450.00	900.00	1500.	2750.
	1869 AE	—	450.00	900.00	1500.	2750.

Mint mark: Zs

KM#	Date	Mintage	Fine	VF	XF	Unc
383.11	1858 MO	—	400.00	750.00	1000.	2000.
	1859 MO	—	375.00	450.00	650.00	900.00
	1860/9 MO	—	400.00	750.00	1000.	2000.
	1860 MO	—	375.00	500.00	700.00	1000.
	1861/0 VL	—	375.00	500.00	700.00	1000.
	1861 VL	—	375.00	500.00	700.00	1000.
	1862 VL	—	375.00	500.00	700.00	1100.
	1863 VL	—	375.00	500.00	700.00	1000.
	1863 MO	—	375.00	500.00	700.00	1000.
	1864 MO	—	750.00	1000.	1500.	3000.
	1865 MO	—	375.00	500.00	700.00	1000.
	1865 MP	—	Contemporary counterfeit			
	1868 JS	—	400.00	600.00	800.00	1250.
	1868 YH	—	400.00	600.00	800.00	1250.
	1869 YH	—	400.00	600.00	800.00	1250.
	1870 YH	—	400.00	600.00	800.00	1250.
	1871 YH	—	400.00	600.00	800.00	1250.

EMPIRE OF MAXIMILIAN

RULER

Maximilian, Emperor, 1864-1867

MINT MARKS

Refer To Republic Coinage

MONETARY SYSTEM

100 Centavos = 1 Peso (8 Reales)

Empire of Maximilian / MEXICO 1262

CENTAVO

COPPER
Mint mark: M

KM#	Date	Mintage	Fine	VF	XF	Unc
384	1864	—	40.00	75.00	200.00	1000.

5 CENTAVOS

1.3537 g, .903 SILVER, .0393 oz ASW
Mint mark: G

385	1864	.090	17.50	30.00	75.00	300.00
	1865	—	22.50	35.00	75.00	275.00
	1866	—	90.00	160.00	325.00	2000.

Mint mark: M

385.1	1864	—	12.50	20.00	50.00	225.00
	1866/4	—	25.00	50.00	90.00	425.00
	1866	—	22.50	45.00	85.00	400.00

Mint mark: P

| 385.2 | 1864 | — | 150.00 | 300.00 | 1100. | 2250. |

Mint mark: Z

| 385.3 | 1865 | — | 20.00 | 40.00 | 125.00 | 375.00 |

10 CENTAVOS

2.7073 g, .903 SILVER, .0786 oz ASW
Mint mark: G

386	1864	.045	17.50	40.00	80.00	250.00
	1865	—	25.00	50.00	100.00	300.00

Mint mark: M

386.1	1864	—	12.50	25.00	50.00	225.00
	1866/4	—	20.00	30.00	70.00	300.00
	1866/5	—	20.00	35.00	75.00	300.00
	1866	—	20.00	30.00	75.00	300.00

Mint mark: P

| 386.2 | 1864 | — | 60.00 | 125.00 | 225.00 | 600.00 |

Mint mark: Z

| 386.3 | 1865 | — | 25.00 | 50.00 | 150.00 | 500.00 |

50 CENTAVOS

13.5365 g, .903 SILVER, .3929 oz ASW
Mint mark: Mo

| 387 | 1866 | .031 | 30.00 | 60.00 | 125.00 | 600.00 |

PESO

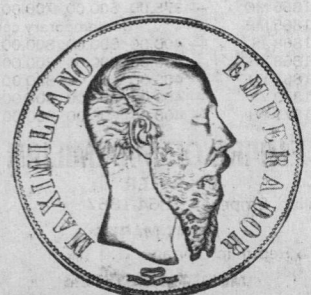

27.0700 g, .903 SILVER, .7857 oz ASW
Mint mark: Go

KM#	Date	Mintage	Fine	VF	XF	Unc
388	1866	—	350.00	500.00	750.00	2250.

Mint mark: Mo

388.1	1866	2.148	25.00	45.00	100.00	300.00
	1867	1.238	35.00	65.00	150.00	400.00

Mint mark: Pi

| 388.2 | 1866 | — | 40.00 | 75.00 | 150.00 | 650.00 |

20 PESOS

33.8400 g, .875 GOLD, .9520 oz AGW
Mint mark: Mo

| 389 | 1866 | 8,274 | 500.00 | 900.00 | 1500. | 2500. |

REPUBLIC
DECIMAL COINAGE

100 Centavos = 1 Peso

UN (1) CENTAVO

COPPER
Mint mark: Mo
Obv: Seated Liberty.

390	1863 round top 3, reeded edge					
		—	10.00	15.00	30.00	150.00
	1863 round top 3, plain edge					
		—	10.00	15.00	30.00	150.00
	1863 flat top 3					
		—	8.00	12.50	25.00	150.00

Mint mark: SLP

| 390.1 | 1863 | 1.025 | 10.00 | 25.00 | 50.00 | 300.00 |

Mint mark: As
Obv: Standing eagle.

391	1876	.050	75.00	100.00	175.00	650.00
	1880	—	25.00	50.00	100.00	400.00
	1881	—	30.00	60.00	125.00	250.00

Mint mark: Cn

KM#	Date	Mintage	Fine	VF	XF	Unc
391.1	1874	.266	12.50	17.50	35.00	150.00
	1875/4	.153	15.00	20.00	45.00	150.00
	1875	Inc. Ab.	10.00	15.00	25.00	150.00
	1876	.154	5.00	8.00	15.00	125.00
	1877/6	.993	7.50	11.50	17.50	175.00
	1877	Inc. Ab.	6.00	9.00	15.00	150.00
	1880	.142	7.50	10.00	12.50	150.00
	1881	.167	7.50	10.00	25.00	175.00
	1897 large N in mm.					
		.300	2.50	5.00	12.00	50.00
	1897 small N in mm.					
		Inc. Ab.	2.50	5.00	9.00	45.00

Mint mark: Do

391.2	1879	.110	10.00	17.50	35.00	150.00
	1880	.069	40.00	90.00	175.00	500.00
	1891	—	8.00	11.00	30.00	150.00
	1891 Do/Mo	—	8.00	11.00	30.00	150.00

Mint mark: Ga

391.3	1872	.263	15.00	30.00	60.00	200.00
	1873	.333	6.00	9.00	25.00	150.00
	1874	.076	15.00	25.00	50.00	175.00
	1875	—	10.00	15.00	30.00	150.00
	1876	.303	3.00	6.00	17.50	150.00
	1877	.108	4.00	6.00	20.00	150.00
	1878	.543	4.00	6.00	15.00	150.00
	1881/71	.975	7.00	9.00	20.00	175.00
	1881	Inc. Ab.	7.00	9.00	20.00	175.00
	1889 Ga/Mo	—	3.50	5.00	25.00	125.00
	1890	—	4.00	7.50	20.00	100.00

Mint mark: Go

391.4	1874	—	20.00	40.00	80.00	250.00
	1875	.190	11.50	20.00	60.00	200.00
	1876	—	125.00	200.00	350.00	750.00
	1877	—	—	—	Rare	—
	1878	.576	8.00	11.00	30.00	175.00
	1880	.890	6.00	10.00	25.00	175.00

Mint mark: Ho

391.5	1875	3,500	—	—	Rare	—
	1876	8,508	50.00	100.00	225.00	500.00
	1880 short H, round O					
		.102	6.75	10.00	35.00	150.00
	1880 tall H, oval O					
		Inc. Ab.	6.75	10.00	35.00	150.00
	1881	.459	5.00	10.00	25.00	150.00

Mint mark: Mo

391.6	1869	1.874	7.50	25.00	60.00	200.00
	1870/69	1.200	10.00	25.00	60.00	225.00
	1870	Inc. Ab.	8.00	20.00	50.00	200.00
	1871	.918	8.00	15.00	40.00	200.00
	1872/1	1.625	6.50	10.00	30.00	200.00
	1872	Inc. Ab.	6.00	9.00	25.00	200.00
	1873	1.605	4.00	7.50	20.00	200.00
	1874/3	1.700	5.00	7.00	15.00	100.00
	1874.	Inc. Ab.	3.00	5.50	15.00	100.00
	1874.	Inc. Ab.	5.00	10.00	25.00	200.00
	1875	1.495	6.00	8.00	30.00	100.00
	1876	1.600	3.00	5.50	12.50	100.00
	1877	1.270	3.00	5.50	13.50	100.00
	1878/5	1.900	7.50	11.00	22.50	125.00
	1878/6	Inc. Ab.	7.50	11.00	22.50	125.00
	1878/7	Inc. Ab.	7.50	11.00	20.00	125.00
	1878	Inc. Ab.	6.00	9.00	13.50	100.00
	1879/8	1.505	4.50	6.50	13.50	100.00
	1879	Inc. Ab.	3.00	5.50	11.50	75.00
	1880/70	1.130	5.50	7.50	15.00	100.00
	1880/72	I.A.	20.00	50.00	100.00	250.00
	1880/79	I.A.	15.00	35.00	75.00	175.00
	1880	Inc. Ab.	4.25	6.00	12.50	75.00
	1881	1.060	4.50	7.00	15.00	75.00
	1886	12.687	1.50	2.00	8.50	40.00
	1887	7.292	1.50	2.00	5.00	35.00
	1888/78	9.984	2.50	3.00	10.00	30.00
	1888/7	Inc. Ab.	2.50	3.00	10.00	30.00
	1888	Inc. Ab.	1.50	2.00	8.50	30.00
	1889	19.970	2.00	3.00	8.00	30.00
	1890/89					
		18.726	2.50	3.00	10.00	40.00
	1890/990	I.A.	2.50	3.00	10.00	40.00
	1890	Inc. Ab.	1.50	2.00	8.50	30.00
	1891	14.544	1.50	2.00	8.50	30.00
	1892	12.908	1.50	2.00	8.50	30.00
	1893/2	5.078	2.50	3.00	10.00	35.00
	1893	Inc. Ab.	1.50	2.00	8.50	30.00
	1894/3	1.896	3.00	6.00	15.00	50.00
	1894	Inc. Ab.	2.00	3.00	10.00	35.00
	1895/3	3.453	3.00	4.50	12.50	35.00
	1895/85	I.A.	3.00	6.00	15.00	50.00
	1895	Inc. Ab.	2.00	3.00	8.50	25.00
	1896	3.075	2.00	3.00	8.50	25.00
	1897	4.150	1.50	2.00	8.50	25.00

NOTE: Varieties exist.

Mint mark: Oa

391.7	1872	.016	300.00	500.00	1200.	—
	1873	.011	—	—	Rare	—
	1874	4,835	—	—	Rare	—
	1875	2,860	—	—	Rare	—

Mint mark: Pi

391.8	1871	—	—	—	Rare	—
	1877	.249	—	—	Rare	—
	1878	.751	12.50	25.00	50.00	200.00
	1891 Pi/Mo	—	10.00	17.50	35.00	150.00
	1891	—	8.00	15.00	30.00	150.00

Mint mark: Zs

| 391.9 | 1872 | .055 | 22.50 | 30.00 | 100.00 | 300.00 |

KM#	Date	Mintage	Fine	VF	XF	Unc
391.9	1873	1.460	4.00	8.00	25.00	150.00
	1874/3	.685	5.50	11.00	30.00	250.00
	1874	Inc. Ab.	4.00	8.00	25.00	200.00
	1875/4	.200	8.50	17.00	45.00	250.00
	1875	Inc. Ab.	7.00	14.00	35.00	200.00
	1876	—	5.00	10.00	25.00	200.00
	1877	—	50.00	125.00	300.00	750.00
	1878		4.50	9.00	25.00	200.00
	1880	.100	5.00	10.00	30.00	200.00
	1881	1.200	4.25	8.00	25.00	150.00

COPPER-NICKEL
Mint: Mexico City

392	1882	99.955	7.50	12.50	17.50	35.00
	1883	Inc. Ab.	.50	.75	1.00	1.50

Obv: Restyled eagle.

393	1898	1.529	4.00	6.00	15.00	40.00

NOTE: Varieties exist.

Mint mark: C
Reduced size

394	1901	.220	15.00	22.50	35.00	75.00
	1902	.320	15.00	22.50	55.00	100.00
	1903	.536	7.50	12.50	20.00	45.00
	1904/3	.148	35.00	50.00	75.00	125.00
	1905	.110	100.00	150.00	300.00	550.00

NOTE: Varieties exist.

Mint mark: M, Mo

394.1	1899	.051	150.00	175.00	300.00	800.00
	1900	4.010	2.50	4.00	7.50	25.00
	1901	1.494	3.00	8.00	17.50	50.00
	1902/899					
		2.090	30.00	60.00	100.00	175.00
	1902	Inc. Ab.	2.25	4.00	10.00	35.00
	1903	8.400	1.50	2.25	4.00	20.00
	1904	10.250	1.50	2.00	4.00	20.00
	1905	3.643	2.25	4.00	10.00	40.00

NOTE: Varieties exist.

2 CENTAVOS

COPPER-NICKEL
Mint: Mexico City

395	1882	50.023	2.00	3.00	7.50	15.00
	1883/2	Inc. Ab.	2.00	3.00	7.50	15.00
	1883	Inc. Ab.	.50	.75	1.00	2.50

5 CENTAVOS

1.3530 g, .903 SILVER, .0392 oz ASW
Mint mark: Ca
Obv: Facing eagle. Rev: Denomination in wreath.

396	1868	—	40.00	65.00	125.00	400.00
	1869	*.030	25.00	40.00	100.00	350.00
	1870	.035	30.00	50.00	100.00	350.00

Mint mark: SLP

| 396.1 | 1863 | — | 75.00 | 125.00 | 350.00 | 1200. |

Mint mark: Mo
Rev: Cap and rays.

397	1867/3	—	25.00	50.00	125.00	275.00
	1867	—	20.00	40.00	100.00	250.00
	1868/7	—	25.00	50.00	150.00	325.00
	1868	—	20.00	40.00	100.00	250.00

NOTE: Varieties exist.

Mint mark: P

397.1	1868/7	.034	25.00	50.00	125.00	300.00
	1868	Inc. Ab.	20.00	45.00	100.00	250.00
	1869	.014	200.00	300.00	600.00	—

Mint mark: As
Obv: Standing eagle.

398	1874 DL	—	7.50	15.00	30.00	100.00
	1875 DL	—	7.50	15.00	30.00	100.00
	1876 L	—	20.00	40.00	60.00	150.00
	1878 L mule, gold peso obverse					
		—	250.00	350.00	650.00	—
	1879 L mule, gold peso obverse					
		—	30.00	60.00	100.00	250.00
	1880 L mule, gold peso obverse					
		.012	50.00	75.00	125.00	300.00
	1886 L	.043	10.00	20.00	40.00	150.00
	1886 L mule, gold peso obverse					
		Inc. Ab.	—	75.00	125.00	200.00
	1887 L	.020	25.00	50.00	75.00	150.00
	1888 L	.032	10.00	20.00	40.00	100.00
	1889 L	.016	25.00	50.00	100.00	200.00
	1890 L	.030	25.00	50.00	75.00	150.00
	1891 L	8,000	50.00	75.00	125.00	350.00
	1892 L	.013	20.00	40.00	60.00	125.00
	1893 L	.024	10.00	20.00	40.00	80.00
	1895 L	.020	10.00	20.00	40.00	80.00

Mint mark: CH, Ca

398.1	1871 M	.014	20.00	40.00	100.00	250.00
	1873 M crude date					
		—	100.00	150.00	250.00	500.00
	1874 M crude date					
		—	25.00	50.00	75.00	150.00
	1886 M	.025	10.00	15.00	30.00	100.00
	1887 M	.037	7.50	15.00	30.00	100.00
	1887 Ca/MoM					
		Inc. Ab.	10.00	20.00	40.00	125.00
	1888 M	.145	1.50	3.00	6.00	25.00
	1889 M	.044	5.00	10.00	20.00	50.00
	1890 M	.102	1.50	3.00	6.00	25.00
	1891 M	.164	1.50	3.00	6.00	25.00
	1892 M	.085	1.50	3.00	6.00	25.00
	1892 M 9/inverted 9					
		Inc. Ab.	2.00	4.00	7.50	30.00
	1893 M	.133	1.50	3.00	6.00	25.00
	1894 M	.108	1.50	3.00	6.00	25.00
	1895 M	.074	2.00	4.00	7.50	30.00

Mint mark: Cn

398.2	1871 P	—	125.00	200.00	350.00	—
	1873 P	4,992	50.00	100.00	200.00	400.00
	1874 P	—	25.00	50.00	100.00	200.00
	1875 P	—	—	—	Rare	—
	1876 P	—	25.00	50.00	100.00	200.00
	1886 M	.010	25.00	50.00	100.00	200.00
	1887 M	.010	25.00	50.00	100.00	200.00
	1888 M	.119	1.50	3.00	6.00	30.00
	1889 M	.066	4.00	7.50	15.00	50.00
	1890 M	.180	1.50	3.00	6.00	25.00
	1890 D (error)					
		Inc. Ab.	125.00	175.00	250.00	—
	1891 M	.087	2.00	4.00	7.50	25.00
	1894 M	.024	4.00	7.50	15.00	40.00
	1896 M	.016	7.50	12.50	25.00	75.00
	1897 M	.223	1.50	2.50	5.00	20.00

Mint mark: Do

398.3	1874 M	—	100.00	150.00	225.00	500.00
	1877 P	4,795	75.00	125.00	225.00	450.00
	1878/7 E/P					
		4,300	200.00	300.00	450.00	—
	1879 B	—	125.00	200.00	350.00	—
	1880 B	—	—	—	Rare	—
	1881 P	3,020	300.00	500.00	800.00	—
	1887 C	.042	5.00	8.00	17.50	60.00
	1888/9 C	.091	6.00	10.00	30.00	70.00
	1888 C	Inc. Ab.	4.00	7.50	15.00	55.00
	1889 C	.049	3.50	6.00	12.50	50.00
	1890 C	.136	4.00	7.50	15.00	55.00
	1890 P	Inc. Ab.	5.00	8.00	17.50	60.00
	1891/0 P	.048	3.50	6.00	12.50	50.00
	1891 P	Inc. Ab.	3.00	5.00	10.00	45.00
	1894 D	.038	3.50	5.00	12.50	50.00

Mint mark: Ga

398.4	1877 A	—	15.00	30.00	60.00	150.00
	1881 S	.156	4.00	7.50	15.00	60.00
	1886 S	.087	2.00	4.00	7.50	25.00
	1888 S lg.G	.262	2.00	4.00	10.00	30.00
	1888 S sm.g	I.A.	2.00	4.00	10.00	30.00
	1889 S	.178	1.50	3.00	7.50	30.00
	1890 S	.068	4.00	7.50	12.50	35.00
	1891 S	.050	4.00	6.50	10.00	35.00
	1892 S	.078	2.00	4.00	7.50	25.00
	1893 S	.044	4.00	7.50	15.00	45.00

Mint mark: Go

398.5	1869 S	.080	15.00	30.00	75.00	175.00
	1871 S	.100	5.00	10.00	25.00	75.00
	1872 S	.030	15.00	30.00	60.00	125.00
	1873 S	.040	30.00	60.00	125.00	250.00
	1874 S	—	7.00	12.00	25.00	75.00
	1875 S	—	8.00	15.00	30.00	75.00
	1876 S	—	8.00	15.00	30.00	75.00
	1877 S	—	7.00	12.00	20.00	75.00
	1878/7 S	.020	8.00	15.00	25.00	75.00
	1879 S	—	8.00	15.00	25.00	75.00
	1880 S	.055	15.00	30.00	60.00	200.00
	1881/0 S	.160	5.00	8.00	17.50	60.00
	1881 S	Inc. Ab.	4.00	6.00	12.00	45.00
	1886 R	.230	1.50	3.00	6.00	30.00
	1887 R	.230	1.50	2.50	5.00	30.00
	1888 R	.320	1.50	2.50	6.00	30.00
	1889 R	.060	4.00	6.00	12.00	45.00
	1890 R	.250	1.50	2.50	5.00	20.00
	1891/0 R	.168	1.80	3.00	6.00	30.00
	1891 R	Inc. Ab.	1.50	2.50	5.00	20.00
	1892 R	.138	1.50	3.00	6.00	20.00
	1893 R	.200	1.25	2.50	5.00	20.00
	1894 R	.200	1.25	2.50	5.00	20.00
	1896 R	.525	1.25	2.00	4.00	15.00
	1897 R	.596	1.50	2.00	4.00	15.00

Mint mark: Ho

398.6	1874/69 R	—	125.00	225.00	350.00	—
	1874 R	—	100.00	200.00	325.00	—
	1878/7 A	.022	—	—	Rare	—
	1878 A	Inc. Ab.	20.00	40.00	80.00	175.00
	1878 A mule, gold peso obverse					
		Inc. Ab.	40.00	80.00	150.00	300.00
	1880 A	.043	7.50	15.00	30.00	75.00
	1886 G	.044	5.00	10.00	20.00	75.00
	1887 G	.020	5.00	10.00	20.00	75.00
	1888 G	.012	7.50	15.00	30.00	85.00
	1889 G	.067	3.00	6.00	12.50	40.00
	1890 G	.050	3.00	6.00	12.50	40.00
	1891 G	.046	3.00	6.00	12.50	40.00
	1893 G	.084	2.50	5.00	10.00	30.00
	1894 G	.068	2.00	4.00	10.00	30.00

Mint mark: Mo

398.7	1869/8 C	.040	8.00	15.00	40.00	120.00
	1870 C	.140	4.00	7.00	20.00	60.00
	1871 C	.103	9.00	20.00	40.00	100.00
	1871 M	Inc. Ab.	7.50	12.50	25.00	60.00
	1872 M	.266	5.00	8.00	20.00	55.00
	1873 M	.020	40.00	60.00	100.00	225.00
	1874/69 M	—	7.50	15.00	30.00	75.00
	1874 M	—	4.00	7.00	17.50	50.00
	1874/3 B	—	5.00	8.00	22.50	55.00
	1874 B	—	5.00	8.00	22.50	55.00
	1875 B	—	4.00	7.00	15.00	50.00
	1875 B/M	—	6.00	9.00	17.50	60.00
	1876/5 B	—	4.00	7.00	15.00	50.00
	1876 B	—	4.00	7.00	12.50	50.00
	1877/6 M	.080	4.00	7.00	15.00	60.00
	1877 M	Inc. Ab.	4.00	7.00	15.00	55.00
	1878/7 M	.100	4.00	7.00	15.00	55.00
	1878 M	Inc. Ab.	2.50	5.00	12.50	45.00
	1879/8 M	—	8.00	12.50	22.50	55.00
	1879 M	—	4.50	7.00	15.00	50.00
	1879 M 9/inverted 9					
		—	10.00	15.00	25.00	75.00
	1880/76 M/B					
		—	5.00	7.50	15.00	50.00
	1880/76 M	—	5.00	7.50	15.00	50.00
	1880 M	—	4.00	6.00	12.00	40.00
	1881/0 M	.180	4.00	6.00	10.00	35.00
	1881 M	Inc. Ab.	3.00	4.50	9.00	35.00
	1886/0 M	.398	2.00	2.75	7.50	25.00
	1886/1 M	I.A.	2.00	2.75	7.50	25.00
	1886 M	Inc. Ab.	1.75	2.25	6.00	20.00
	1887 m	.720	1.75	2.00	6.00	20.00
	1887 M/m	I.A.	1.75	2.00	6.00	20.00
	1888/7 M	1.360	2.25	2.50	6.00	20.00
	1888 M	Inc. Ab.	1.75	2.00	6.00	20.00
	1889/8 M	1.242	2.25	2.50	6.00	20.00
	1889 M	Inc. Ab.	1.75	2.00	6.00	20.00
	1890/00 M					
		1.694	1.75	2.75	6.00	20.00
	1890 M	Inc. Ab.	1.50	2.00	5.00	20.00
	1891 M	1.030	1.75	2.00	5.00	20.00
	1892 M	1.400	1.75	2.00	5.00	20.00
	1892 M 9/inverted 9					
		Inc. Ab.	2.00	2.75	7.50	20.00
	1893 M	.220	1.75	2.00	5.00	15.00
	1894 M	.320	1.75	2.00	5.00	15.00
	1895 M	.078	3.00	5.00	8.00	25.00
	1896 B	.080	1.75	2.00	5.00	20.00
	1897 M	.160	1.75	2.00	5.00	15.00

NOTE: Varieties exist.

Mint mark: Oa

398.8	1890 E	.048	—	—	Rare	—
	1890 N	Inc. Ab.	65.00	125.00	200.00	350.00

Mint mark: Pi

398.9	1869 S	—	300.00	400.00	500.00	—
	1870 G/MoC					
		.020	—	—	Rare	—
	1870 O	Inc. Ab.	200.00	300.00	400.00	—
	1871 O	5,400	—	—	Rare	—
	1872 O	—	75.00	100.00	175.00	400.00
	1873	5,000	—	—	Rare	—
	1874 H	—	30.00	50.00	100.00	225.
	1875 H	—	7.50	12.50	30.00	
	1876 H	—	10.00	20.00	45.	
	1877 H	—	—	7.50	12.50	
	1878/7 H					
	1878 H	—	60.00	9		
	1880 H	6,200				
	1881 H	4,500				
	1886 R	.033	12.50	25.0		
	1887/0 R	.169	4.00	7.50		

1264 Decimal-Republic / MEXICO

KM#	Date	Mintage	Fine	VF	XF	Unc
398.9	1887 R	Inc. Ab.	3.00	5.00	10.00	35.00
	1888 R	.210	2.00	4.00	9.00	30.00
	1889/7 R	.197	2.50	5.00	10.00	35.00
	1889 R	Inc. Ab.	2.00	4.00	9.00	30.00
	1890 R	.221	2.00	3.00	6.00	25.00
	1891/89 R/B					
		.176	2.00	4.00	8.00	25.00
	1891 R	Inc. Ab.	2.00	3.00	6.00	20.00
	1892/89 R	.182	2.00	4.00	8.00	25.00
	1892/0 R	I.A.	2.00	4.00	8.00	25.00
	1892 R	Inc. Ab.	2.00	3.00	6.00	20.00
	1893 R	.041	5.00	10.00	20.00	60.00

NOTE: Varieties exist.

Mint mark: Zs

KM#	Date	Mintage	Fine	VF	XF	Unc
398.10	1870 H	.040	12.50	25.00	50.00	125.00
	1871 H	.040	12.50	25.00	50.00	125.00
	1872 H	.040	12.50	25.00	50.00	125.00
	1873/2 H	.020	35.00	65.00	125.00	275.00
	1873 H	Inc. Ab.	25.00	50.00	100.00	250.00
	1874 H	—	7.50	12.50	25.00	75.00
	1874 A	—	40.00	75.00	150.00	300.00
	1875 A	—	7.50	12.50	25.00	75.00
	1876 A	—	50.00	75.00	100.00	200.00
	1876 S	—	12.50	25.00	50.00	125.00
	1877 S	—	3.00	6.00	12.00	40.00
	1878 S	.060	3.00	6.00	12.00	40.00
	1879/8 S	—	3.00	6.00	15.00	50.00
	1879 S	—	3.00	6.00	12.00	40.00
	1880/79 S	.130	6.00	10.00	20.00	60.00
	1880 S	Inc. Ab.	5.00	8.00	16.00	45.00
	1881 S	.210	2.50	5.00	10.00	35.00
	1886/4 S	.360	6.00	10.00	20.00	60.00
	1886 S	Inc. Ab.	2.00	3.00	6.00	20.00
	1886 Z	Inc. Ab.	5.00	10.00	25.00	65.00
	1887 Z	.400	2.00	3.00	6.00	25.00
	1888/7 Z	.500	2.00	3.00	6.00	25.00
	1888 Z	Inc. Ab.	2.00	3.00	6.00	25.00
	1889 Z	.520	2.00	3.00	6.00	25.00
	1889 Z 9/inverted 9					
		Inc. Ab.	2.00	3.00	6.00	25.00
	1889 ZsZ/MoM					
		Inc. Ab.	2.00	3.00	6.00	25.00
	1890 Z	.580	1.75	2.50	5.00	20.00
	1890 ZsZ/MoM					
		Inc. Ab.	2.00	3.00	6.00	25.00
	1891 Z	.420	1.75	2.50	5.00	20.00
	1892 Z	.346	1.75	2.50	5.00	20.00
	1893 Z	.258	1.75	2.50	5.00	20.00
	1894 Z	.228	1.75	2.50	5.00	20.00
	1894 ZoZ (error)					
		Inc. Ab.	2.00	4.00	8.00	30.00
	1895 Z	.260	1.75	2.50	5.00	20.00
	1896 Z	.200	1.75	2.50	5.00	20.00
	1896 6/inverted 6					
		Inc. Ab.	2.00	3.00	6.00	25.00
	1897/6 Z	.200	2.00	3.00	6.00	25.00
	1897 Z	Inc. Ab.	1.75	2.50	5.00	20.00

COPPER-NICKEL
Mint: Mexico City

KM#	Date	Mintage	Fine	VF	XF	Unc
399	1882	Inc. Ab.	.50	1.00	2.50	7.50
	1883	Inc. Ab.	25.00	75.00	100.00	300.00

.903 SILVER
Mint mark: Cn
Obv: Restyled eagle.

KM#	Date	Mintage	Fine	VF	XF	Unc
400	1898 M	.044	1.75	4.00	8.00	20.00
	1899 M	.111	5.50	8.50	20.00	50.00
	1899 Q	Inc. Ab.	1.75	2.25	4.50	12.50
	1900/800 Q					
		.239	3.50	5.00	12.50	30.00
	1900 Q round Q, single tail					
		Inc. Ab.	1.75	2.50	6.00	15.00
	1900 Q narrow C, oval Q					
		Inc. Ab.	1.75	2.50	6.00	15.00
	1900 Q wide C, oval Q					
		Inc. Ab.	1.75	2.50	6.00	15.00
	1901 Q	.148	1.75	2.25	4.50	12.50
	1902 Q narrow C, heavy serifs					
		.262	1.75	2.50	6.00	15.00
	1902 Q wide C, light serifs					
		Inc. Ab.	1.75	2.50	6.00	15.00
	1903/1 Q	.331	2.00	2.50	6.00	15.00
	1903 Q	Inc. Ab.	1.75	2.25	4.50	12.50
	1903/898 V					
		Inc. Ab.	3.50	4.50	9.00	22.50
	1903 V	Inc. Ab.	1.75	2.25	4.50	12.50
	1904 H	.352	1.75	2.25	5.00	15.00

NOTE: Varieties exist.

Mint mark: Go

KM#	Date	Mintage	Fine	VF	XF	Unc
400.1	1898 R mule, gold peso obverse					
		.180	7.50	15.00	30.00	75.00
	1899 R	.260	1.75	2.25	4.50	12.50
	1900 R	.200	1.75	2.25	4.50	12.50

NOTE: Varieties exist.

Mint mark: Mo

KM#	Date	Mintage	Fine	VF	XF	Unc
00.2	1898 M	.080	2.00	4.00	7.00	25.00
	1899 M	.168	1.75	2.25	4.50	12.50
	1900/800 M					
		.300	4.50	6.50	10.00	30.00
	1900 M	Inc. Ab.	1.75	2.25	4.50	12.50

KM#	Date	Mintage	Fine	VF	XF	Unc
400.2	1901 M	.100	1.75	2.25	4.50	12.50
	1902 M	.144	1.25	2.00	3.75	10.00
	1903 M	.500	1.25	2.00	3.75	10.00
	1904/804 M					
		1.090	1.75	2.50	6.00	15.00
	1904/94 M	I.A.	1.75	2.50	6.00	15.00
	1904 M	Inc. Ab.	1.25	2.00	6.00	12.50
	1905 M	.344	1.75	3.75	7.50	17.50

Mint mark: Zs

KM#	Date	Mintage	Fine	VF	XF	Unc
400.3	1898 Z	.100	1.75	2.25	4.50	12.50
	1899 Z	.050	2.00	3.00	7.00	20.00
	1900 Z	.055	1.75	2.50	5.00	15.00
	1901 Z	.040	1.75	2.50	5.00	15.00
	1902/1 Z	.034	2.00	4.50	9.00	22.50
	1902 Z	Inc. Ab.	1.75	3.75	7.50	17.50
	1903 Z	.217	1.25	2.00	5.00	12.50
	1904 Z	.191	1.75	2.50	5.00	12.50
	1904 M	Inc. Ab.	1.75	2.50	6.00	15.00
	1905 M	.046	2.00	4.50	9.00	22.50

10 CENTAVOS

2.7070 g, .903 SILVER, .0785 oz ASW
Mint mark: Ca
Obv: Eagle. Rev: Value within wreath.

KM#	Date	Mintage	Fine	VF	XF	Unc
401	1868/7	—	30.00	60.00	150.00	500.00
	1868	—	30.00	60.00	150.00	500.00
	1869	.015	25.00	50.00	125.00	500.00
	1870	.017	22.50	45.00	100.00	500.00

Mint mark: SLP

KM#	Date	Mintage	Fine	VF	XF	Unc
401.2	1863	—	100.00	200.00	300.00	800.00

Mint mark: Mo

KM#	Date	Mintage	Fine	VF	XF	Unc
402	1867/3	—	50.00	100.00	150.00	400.00
	1867	—	20.00	40.00	60.00	225.00
	1868/7	—	20.00	40.00	80.00	250.00
	1868	—	20.00	45.00	75.00	225.00

Mint mark: P

KM#	Date	Mintage	Fine	VF	XF	Unc
402.1	1868/7	.038	45.00	90.00	175.00	600.00
	1868	Inc. Ab.	20.00	40.00	100.00	500.00
	1869/7	4,900	55.00	125.00	250.00	700.00

Mint mark: As

KM#	Date	Mintage	Fine	VF	XF	Unc
403	1874 DL	—	20.00	40.00	80.00	175.00
	1875 L	—	5.00	10.00	25.00	75.00
	1876 L	—	7.50	12.50	35.00	100.00
	1878/7 L	—	7.50	12.50	35.00	110.00
	1878 L	—	5.00	10.00	30.00	100.00
	1879 L	—	7.50	12.50	35.00	100.00
	1880 L	.013	7.50	12.50	35.00	100.00
	1882 L	.022	7.50	12.50	35.00	100.00
	1883 L	8,520	25.00	50.00	100.00	225.00
	1884 L	—	5.00	10.00	30.00	100.00
	1885 L	.015	5.00	10.00	25.00	100.00
	1886 L	.045	5.00	10.00	25.00	100.00
	1887 L	.015	5.00	10.00	25.00	100.00
	1888 L	.038	5.00	10.00	25.00	100.00
	1889 L	.020	5.00	10.00	25.00	100.00
	1890 L	.040	5.00	10.00	25.00	100.00
	1891 L	.038	5.00	10.00	25.00	100.00
	1892 L	.057	3.00	6.00	20.00	100.00
	1893 L	.070	7.50	12.50	35.00	100.00

NOTE: Varieties exist.

Mint mark: CH,Ca

KM#	Date	Mintage	Fine	VF	XF	Unc
403.1	1871 M	8,150	15.00	30.00	60.00	150.00
	1873 M crude date					
		—	35.00	75.00	125.00	175.00
	1874 M	—	10.00	17.50	35.00	100.00
	1880/70 G					
		7,620	20.00	40.00	80.00	175.00
	1880 G/g	I.A.	15.00	25.00	50.00	125.00
	1881	340 pcs.	—	—	Rare	—
	1883 M	9,000	10.00	20.00	40.00	125.00
	1884 M	—	10.00	20.00	40.00	125.00
	1886 M	.045	7.50	12.50	30.00	100.00
	1887/3 M/G					
		.096	5.00	10.00	20.00	75.00
	1887 M	Inc. Ab.	2.00	4.00	8.00	75.00
	1888 M	.299	1.50	2.50	5.00	75.00
	1888 Ca/Mo					
		Inc. Ab.	1.50	2.50	5.00	75.00
	1889/8 M	.115	2.00	4.00	8.00	75.00
	1889 M small 89 (5 Centavo font)					
		Inc. Ab.	2.00	4.00	8.00	75.00
	1890/80 M	.140	2.00	4.00	8.00	75.00
	1890/89 M	I.A.	2.00	4.00	8.00	75.00

KM#	Date	Mintage	Fine	VF	XF	Unc
403.1	1890 M	Inc. Ab.	1.50	3.00	7.00	75.00
	1891 M	.163	1.50	3.00	7.00	75.00
	1892 M	.169	1.50	3.00	7.00	75.00
	1892 M 9/inverted 9					
		Inc. Ab.	2.00	4.00	8.00	75.00
	1893 M	.246	1.50	3.00	7.00	75.00
	1894 M	.163	1.50	3.00	7.00	75.00
	1895 M	.127	1.50	3.00	7.00	75.00

NOTE: Varieties exist.

Mint mark: Cn

KM#	Date	Mintage	Fine	VF	XF	Unc
403.2	1871 P	—	—	—	Rare	—
	1873 P	8,732	20.00	50.00	100.00	225.00
	1881 D	9,440	75.00	175.00	325.00	500.00
	1882 D	.012	75.00	125.00	200.00	400.00
	1885 M mule gold 2-1/2 Peso obv.					
		.018	25.00	50.00	100.00	200.00
	1886 M mule, gold 2-1/2 Peso obv.					
		.013	50.00	100.00	150.00	300.00
	1887 M	.011	20.00	40.00	75.00	175.00
	1888 M	.056	5.00	10.00	25.00	125.00
	1889 M	.042	5.00	10.00	20.00	75.00
	1890 M	.132	2.00	4.00	7.50	75.00
	1891 M	.084	5.00	10.00	20.00	75.00
	1892/1 M	.037	4.00	8.00	15.00	75.00
	1892 M	Inc. Ab.	2.50	5.00	10.00	75.00
	1894 M	.043	2.50	5.00	10.00	75.00
	1895 M	.023	2.50	5.00	10.00	60.00
	1896 M	.121	1.50	2.50	5.00	50.00

Mint mark: Do

KM#	Date	Mintage	Fine	VF	XF	Unc
403.3	1878 E	2,500	100.00	175.00	300.00	600.00
	1879 B	—	—	—	Rare	—
	1880/70 B	—	—	—	Rare	—
	1880/79 B	—	—	—	Rare	—
	1884 C	—	30.00	60.00	100.00	225.00
	1886 C	.013	75.00	150.00	300.00	500.00
	1887 C	.081	4.00	8.00	15.00	100.00
	1888 C	.031	6.00	12.00	30.00	100.00
	1889 C	.055	4.00	8.00	15.00	100.00
	1890 C	.050	4.00	8.00	15.00	100.00
	1891 P	.139	2.00	4.00	8.00	80.00
	1892 P	.212	2.00	4.00	8.00	80.00
	1892 D	Inc. Ab.	2.00	4.00	8.00	80.00
	1893 D	.258	2.00	4.00	8.00	80.00
	1893 D/C	I.A.	2.50	5.00	10.00	80.00
	1894 D	.184	1.50	3.00	6.00	80.00
	1894 D/C	I.A.	2.00	4.00	8.00	80.00
	1895 D	.142	1.50	3.00	6.00	80.00

Mint mark: Ga

KM#	Date	Mintage	Fine	VF	XF	Unc
403.4	1871 C	4,734	75.00	125.00	200.00	500.00
	1873/1 C	.025	10.00	15.00	35.00	150.00
	1873 C	Inc.Ab.	10.00	15.00	35.00	150.00
	1874 C	—	10.00	15.00	35.00	150.00
	1877 A	—	10.00	15.00	30.00	150.00
	1881 A	.115	5.00	10.00	25.00	150.00
	1881 S	Inc. Ab.	5.00	10.00	25.00	150.00
	1883 B	.090	4.00	8.00	15.00	90.00
	1884 B	—	5.00	10.00	20.00	90.00
	1884 B/S	—	6.00	12.50	25.00	90.00
	1884 H	—	3.00	5.00	10.00	90.00
	1885 H	.093	3.00	5.00	10.00	90.00
	1886 S	.151	2.50	4.00	9.00	90.00
	1887 S	.162	1.50	3.00	6.00	90.00
	1888 S	.225	1.50	3.00	6.00	90.00
	1888 GaS/HoG					
		Inc. Ab.	1.50	3.00	6.00	90.00
	1889 S	.310	1.50	3.00	6.00	40.00
	1890 S	.303	1.50	3.00	6.00	40.00
	1891 S	.199	5.00	10.00	20.00	45.00
	1892 S	.329	1.50	3.00	6.00	40.00
	1893 S	.225	1.50	3.00	6.00	40.00
	1894 S	.243	3.00	6.00	12.00	40.00
	1895 S	.080	1.50	3.00	6.00	40.00

NOTE: Varieties exist.

Mint mark: Go

KM#	Date	Mintage	Fine	VF	XF	Unc
403.5	1869 S	7,000	20.00	40.00	80.00	200.00
	1871/0 S	.060	15.00	25.00	50.00	125.00
	1872 S	.060	15.00	25.00	50.00	125.00
	1873 S	.050	15.00	25.00	50.00	125.00
	1874 S	—	15.00	25.00	50.00	125.00
	1875 S	—	250.00	350.00	500.00	800.00
	1876 S	—	10.00	20.00	40.00	100.00
	1877 S	—	80.00	120.00	200.00	400.00
	1878/7 S	.010	10.00	20.00	45.00	110.00
	1878 S	Inc. Ab.	7.50	12.00	20.00	75.00
	1879 S	—	7.50	12.00	20.00	75.00
	1880 S	—	100.00	200.00	300.00	450.00
	1881/71 S	.100	3.00	5.00	10.00	75.00
	1881/0 S	I.A.	3.50	5.00	10.00	75.00
	1881 S	Inc. Ab.	3.00	5.00	10.00	75.00
	1882/1 S	.040	3.00	6.00	12.00	75.00
	1883 B	—	3.00	5.00	10.00	75.00
	1884 B	—	1.50	3.00	6.00	75.00
	1884 S	—	6.00	12.50	25.00	90.00
	1885 R	.100	1.50	3.00	6.00	75.00
	1886 R	.095	3.00	5.00	10.00	75.00
	1887 R	.330	2.50	5.00	10.00	75.00
	1888 R	.270	1.50	3.00	6.00	75.00
	1889 R	.205	2.00	4.00	8.00	75.00
	1889 GoR/HoG					
		Inc. Ab.	3.00	5.00	10.00	75.00
	1890 R	.270	1.50	3.00	6.00	35.00
	1890 GoR/Cn M					
		Inc. Ab.	1.50	3.00	6.00	35.00
	1891 R	.523	1.50	3.00	6.00	35.00
	1891 GoR/HoG					
		Inc. Ab.	1.50	3.00	6.00	35.00
	1891 GoR/G					
		Inc. Ab.	1.50	3.00	6.00	35.00

KM#	Date	Mintage	Fine	VF	XF	Unc
403.5	1892 R	.440	1.50	3.00	6.00	35.00
	1893/1 R	.389	3.00	5.00	10.00	35.00
	1893 R	Inc. Ab.	1.50	3.00	6.00	35.00
	1894 R	.400	1.50	2.50	5.00	35.00
	1895 R	.355	1.50	2.50	5.00	35.00
	1896 R	.190	1.50	2.50	5.00	35.00
	1897 R	.205	1.50	2.50	5.00	35.00

NOTE: Varieties exist.

Mint mark: Ho

KM#	Date	Mintage	Fine	VF	XF	Unc
403.6	1874 R	—	30.00	60.00	100.00	200.00
	1876 F	3,140	200.00	300.00	450.00	750.00
	1878 A	—	5.00	10.00	15.00	85.00
	1879 A	—	25.00	50.00	90.00	175.00
	1880 A	—	3.00	6.00	12.50	85.00
	1881 A	.028	4.00	7.00	15.00	85.00
	1882/1 A	.025	5.00	10.00	20.00	85.00
	1882/1 a	I.A.	6.00	12.50	25.00	85.00
	1882 A	Inc. Ab.	4.00	7.00	15.00	85.00
	1883	7,000	65.00	100.00	200.00	400.00
	1884 A	—	35.00	75.00	150.00	300.00
	1884 M	—	7.50	15.00	30.00	85.00
	1885 M	.021	12.50	25.00	50.00	100.00
	1886 M	.010	—	—	Rare	—
	1886 G	Inc. Ab.	7.50	12.50	25.00	85.00
	1887 G	—	25.00	50.00	75.00	150.00
	1888 G	.025	6.00	12.50	25.00	85.00
	1889 G	.042	3.00	6.00	10.00	85.00
	1890 G	.048	3.00	6.00	10.00	85.00
	1891/80 G	.136	3.00	6.00	10.00	85.00
	1891/0 G	I.A.	3.00	6.00	10.00	85.00
	1891 G	Inc. Ab.	3.00	6.00	10.00	85.00
	1892 G	.067	3.00	6.00	10.00	85.00
	1893 G	.067	3.00	6.00	10.00	85.00

Mint mark: Mo

KM#	Date	Mintage	Fine	VF	XF	Unc
403.7	1869/8 C	.030	10.00	20.00	40.00	100.00
	1869 C	Inc. Ab.	8.00	17.50	35.00	90.00
	1870 C	.110	3.00	7.50	15.00	50.00
	1871 C	.084	50.00	75.00	125.00	250.00
	1871 M	Inc. Ab.	12.00	17.50	45.00	125.00
	1872/69 M	.198	10.00	20.00	35.00	100.00
	1872 M	Inc. Ab.	3.00	7.50	15.00	65.00
	1873 M	.040	10.00	15.00	30.00	75.00
	1874 M	—	5.00	10.00	20.00	65.00
	1874/64 B	—	5.00	10.00	20.00	65.00
	1874 B/M	—	20.00	40.00	60.00	125.00
	1874 B	—	5.00	10.00	15.00	65.00
	1875 B	—	20.00	40.00	60.00	125.00
	1876/5 B	—	3.00	5.00	9.00	65.00
	1876/5 B/M	—	3.00	5.00	9.00	65.00
	1877/6 M	—	3.00	5.00	9.00	65.00
	1877/6 M/B	—	3.00	5.00	9.00	65.00
	1877 M	—	3.00	5.00	9.00	65.00
	1878/7 M	.100	3.00	5.00	9.00	65.00
	1878 M	Inc. Ab.	3.00	5.00	9.00	65.00
	1879/69 M	—	3.00	5.00	9.00	65.00
	1879 M/C	—	3.00	5.00	9.00	65.00
	1880/79 M	—	3.00	5.00	9.00	65.00
	1881/0 M	.510	3.00	5.00	9.00	35.00
	1881 M	Inc. Ab.	3.00	5.00	9.00	35.00
	1882/1 M	.550	3.00	5.00	9.00	35.00
	1882 M	Inc. Ab.	3.00	5.00	9.00	35.00
	1883/2 M	.250	3.00	5.00	9.00	35.00
	1884 M	—	3.00	5.00	9.00	35.00
	1885 M	.470	3.00	5.00	9.00	35.00
	1886 M	.603	3.00	5.00	9.00	35.00
	1887 M	.580	3.00	5.00	9.00	35.00
	1888/7 MoM					
		.710	3.00	5.00	9.00	35.00
	1888 MoM	I.A.	3.00	5.00	9.00	35.00
	1888 MOM	I.A.	3.00	5.00	9.00	35.00
	1889/8 M	.622	3.00	5.00	9.00	35.00
	1889 M	Inc. Ab.	3.00	5.00	9.00	35.00
	1890/89 M	.815	3.00	5.00	9.00	35.00
	1890 M	Inc. Ab.	3.00	5.00	9.00	35.00
	1891 M	.859	1.50	2.50	7.00	25.00
	1892 M	1.030	1.50	2.50	7.00	25.00
	1893 M	.310	1.50	2.50	7.00	25.00
	1893 M/C	I.A.	1.50	2.50	7.00	25.00
	1894 M	.350	5.00	10.00	20.00	60.00
	1895 M	.320	1.50	2.50	7.00	25.00
	1896 B/G	.340	1.50	2.50	7.00	25.00
	1896 M	Inc. Ab.	35.00	70.00	100.00	150.00
	1897 M	.170	1.50	2.50	5.00	20.00

NOTE: Varieties exist.

Mint mark: Oa

KM#	Date	Mintage	Fine	VF	XF	Unc
403.8	1889 E	.021	200.00	400.00	600.00	—
	1890 E	.031	100.00	150.00	250.00	500.00
	1890 N	Inc. Ab.	—	—	Rare	—

Mint mark: Pi

KM#	Date	Mintage	Fine	VF	XF	Unc
403.9	1869/8 S	4,000	—	—	Rare	—
	1870/69 O	.018	—	—	Rare	—
	1870 G	Inc. Ab.	125.00	200.00	325.00	600.00
	1871 O	.021	50.00	100.00	150.00	300.00
	1872 O	.016	150.00	225.00	350.00	650.00
	1873 O	4,750	—	—	Rare	—
	1874 H	—	25.00	50.00	100.00	200.00
	1875 H	—	75.00	125.00	200.00	400.00
	1876 H	—	75.00	125.00	200.00	400.00
	1877 H	—	75.00	125.00	200.00	400.00
	1878 H	—	250.00	500.00	750.00	—
	1879 H	—	—	—	—	—
	1880 H	—	150.00	250.00	350.00	—
	1881 H	7,600	250.00	350.00	500.00	—
	1882 H	4,000	—	—	Rare	—
	1883 H	—	125.00	200.00	300.00	500.00
	1884 H	—	25.00	50.00	100.00	200.00
	1885 H	.051	25.00	50.00	100.00	200.00
	1885 C	Inc. Ab.	—	—	Rare	—
403.9	1886 C	.052	15.00	30.00	60.00	150.00
	1886 R	Inc. Ab.	5.00	10.00	20.00	65.00
	1887 R	.118	2.50	5.00	10.00	50.00
	1888 R	.136	2.50	5.00	10.00	50.00
	1889/7 R	.131	7.50	12.50	20.00	60.00
	1890 R	.204	1.50	3.00	7.50	40.00
	1891/89 R	.163	2.50	5.00	10.00	40.00
	1891 R	Inc. Ab.	1.50	3.50	6.00	30.00
	1892/0 R	.200	2.00	4.00	8.00	40.00
	1892 R	Inc. Ab.	1.50	2.50	5.00	40.00
	1893 R	.048	7.50	10.00	17.50	60.00

NOTE: Varieties exist.

Mint mark: Zs

KM#	Date	Mintage	Fine	VF	XF	Unc
403.10	1870 H	.020	100.00	150.00	200.00	400.00
	1871/0 H	.010	—	—	—	—
	1871 H	Inc. Ab.	—	—	—	—
	1872 H	.010	150.00	200.00	275.00	500.00
	1873 H	.010	—	—	Rare	—
	1874/3 H	—	250.00	350.00	500.00	—
	1874 H	—	250.00	350.00	500.00	—
	1874 A	—	50.00	75.00	150.00	300.00
	1875 A	—	5.00	10.00	25.00	100.00
	1876 A	—	5.00	10.00	25.00	100.00
	1876 S	—	100.00	200.00	300.00	500.00
	1877 S small S					
		—	7.50	12.50	25.00	100.00
	1877 S regular S					
		—	7.50	12.50	25.00	100.00
	1878/7 S	.030	5.00	10.00	20.00	80.00
	1878 S	Inc. Ab.	5.00	10.00	20.00	80.00
	1879 S	—	5.00	10.00	20.00	80.00
	1880 S	—	5.00	10.00	20.00	80.00
	1881/0 S	.120	3.00	6.00	12.50	50.00
	1881 S	Inc. Ab.	3.00	6.00	12.50	50.00
	1882/1 S	.064	12.50	25.00	50.00	125.00
	1882 S	Inc. Ab.	12.50	25.00	50.00	125.00
	1883/73 S	.102	2.00	4.00	8.00	50.00
	1883 S	Inc. Ab.	2.00	4.00	8.00	50.00
	1884/3 S	—	2.00	4.00	8.00	50.00
	1884 S	—	2.00	4.00	8.00	50.00
	1885 S	.297	1.50	2.50	5.00	50.00
	1885 S small S in mint mark					
		Inc. Ab.	2.50	4.00	8.00	50.00
	1885 Z w/o assayer's initial (error)					
		Inc. Ab.	3.50	7.50	15.00	65.00
	1886 S	.274	1.50	2.50	5.00	30.00
	1886 Z	I.A.	12.50	25.00	50.00	125.00
	1887 ZsZ	.233	1.50	2.50	5.00	30.00
	1887 Z Z (error)					
		Inc. Ab.	3.50	7.50	15.00	50.00
	1888 ZsZ	.270	1.50	2.50	5.00	30.00
	1888 Z Z (error)					
		Inc. Ab.	3.50	7.50	15.00	40.00
	1889/7 Z/S					
		.240	4.00	8.00	12.50	40.00
	1889 Z/S	I.A.	1.50	4.00	8.00	30.00
	1889 Z	Inc. Ab.	1.50	2.50	5.00	30.00
	1890 ZsZ	.410	1.50	2.50	5.00	30.00
	1890 Z Z (error)					
		Inc. Ab.	3.75	7.50	15.00	40.00
	1891 Z	1.105	1.50	2.50	5.00	30.00
	1891 ZsZ double s					
		Inc. Ab.	2.00	4.00	7.00	30.00
	1892 Z	1.102	1.50	2.50	5.00	30.00
	1893 Z	1.011	1.50	2.50	5.00	25.00
	1894 Z	.892	1.50	2.50	5.00	30.00
	1895 Z	.920	1.50	2.50	5.00	30.00
	1896/5 ZsZ	.700	1.50	2.50	5.00	30.00
	1896 ZsZ	I.A.	1.50	2.50	5.00	30.00
	1896 Z Z (error)					
		Inc. Ab.	3.75	7.50	15.00	40.00
	1897/6 ZsZ	.900	2.00	5.00	10.00	30.00
	1897/6 Z Z (error)					
		Inc. Ab.	3.75	7.50	15.00	40.00
	1897 Z	Inc. Ab.	1.50	2.50	5.00	30.00

NOTE: Varieties exist.

Mint mark: Cn

Obv: Restyled eagle.

KM#	Date	Mintage	Fine	VF	XF	Unc
404	1898 M	9,870	50.00	100.00	150.00	300.00
	1899 Q round Q, single tail					
		.080	5.00	7.50	15.00	40.00
	1899 Q oval Q, double tail					
		Inc. Ab.	5.00	7.50	15.00	40.00
	1900 Q	.160	1.50	2.50	5.00	20.00
	1901 Q	.235	1.50	2.50	5.00	20.00
	1902 Q	.186	1.50	2.50	5.00	20.00
	1903 Q	.256	1.50	2.50	6.00	20.00
	1903 V	Inc. Ab.	1.50	2.50	5.00	15.00
	1904 H	.307	1.50	2.50	5.00	15.00

NOTE: Varieties exist.

Mint mark: Go

KM#	Date	Mintage	Fine	VF	XF	Unc
404.1	1898 R	.435	1.50	2.50	5.00	20.00
	1899 R	.270	1.50	2.50	5.00	25.00
	1900 R	.130	7.50	12.50	25.00	60.00

Mint mark: Mo

KM#	Date	Mintage	Fine	VF	XF	Unc
404.2	1898 M	.130	1.50	2.50	5.00	17.50
	1899 M	.190	1.50	2.50	5.00	17.50
	1900 M	.311	1.50	2.50	5.00	17.50
	1901 M	.080	2.50	3.50	7.00	20.00
	1902 M	.181	1.50	2.50	5.00	17.50
	1903 M	.581	1.50	2.50	5.00	17.50
404.2	1904 M	1.266	1.25	2.00	4.50	15.00
	1904 MM (error)					
		Inc. Ab.	2.50	5.00	10.00	25.00
	1905 M	.266	2.00	3.75	7.50	20.00

Mint mark: Zs

KM#	Date	Mintage	Fine	VF	XF	Unc
404.3	1898 Z	.240	1.50	2.50	7.50	20.00
	1899 Z	.105	1.50	3.00	10.00	22.00
	1900 Z	.219	7.50	10.00	20.00	45.00
	1901 Z	.070	2.50	5.00	10.00	25.00
	1902 Z	.120	2.50	5.00	10.00	25.00
	1903 Z	.228	1.50	3.00	10.00	20.00
	1904 Z	.368	1.50	3.00	10.00	20.00
	1904 M	Inc. Ab.	1.50	3.00	10.00	25.00
	1905 M	.066	7.50	15.00	30.00	60.00

20 CENTAVOS

5.4150 g, .903 SILVER, .1572 oz ASW

Mint mark: Cn

Obv: Restyled eagle.

KM#	Date	Mintage	Fine	VF	XF	Unc
405	1898 M	.114	5.00	10.00	30.00	100.00
	1899 M	.044	12.00	20.00	45.00	225.00
	1899 Q	Inc. Ab.	20.00	35.00	100.00	250.00
	1900 Q	.068	6.50	10.00	30.00	100.00
	1901 Q	.185	4.00	7.50	25.00	75.00
	1902/802 Q					
		.098	6.00	10.00	30.00	100.00
	1902 Q	Inc. Ab.	4.00	8.00	30.00	100.00
	1903 Q	.093	4.00	7.50	25.00	80.00
	1904/3 H	.258	—	—	—	—
	1904 H	Inc. Ab.	5.00	10.00	30.00	100.00

Mint mark: Go

KM#	Date	Mintage	Fine	VF	XF	Unc
405.1	1898 R	.135	4.00	8.00	20.00	90.00
	1899 R	.215	4.00	8.00	20.00	90.00
	1900/800 R					
		.038	10.00	20.00	50.00	125.00

Mint mark: Mo

KM#	Date	Mintage	Fine	VF	XF	Unc
405.2	1898 M	.150	4.00	8.00	20.00	60.00
	1899 M	.425	4.00	8.00	20.00	60.00
	1900/800 M					
		.295	4.00	8.00	20.00	60.00
	1901 M	.110	4.00	8.00	20.00	60.00
	1902 M	.120	4.00	8.00	20.00	60.00
	1903 M	.213	4.00	8.00	20.00	60.00
	1904 M	.276	4.00	8.00	20.00	60.00
	1905 M	.117	6.50	20.00	40.00	125.00

NOTE: Varieties exist.

Mint mark: Zs

KM#	Date	Mintage	Fine	VF	XF	Unc
405.3	1898 Z	.195	5.00	10.00	20.00	80.00
	1899 Z	.210	5.00	10.00	20.00	80.00
	1900/800 Z					
		.097	5.00	10.00	20.00	100.00
	1901/0 Z	.130	25.00	50.00	100.00	250.00
	1901 Z	Inc. Ab.	5.00	10.00	20.00	100.00
	1902 Z	.105	5.00	10.00	20.00	100.00
	1903 Z	.143	5.00	10.00	20.00	80.00
	1904 Z	.246	5.00	10.00	20.00	80.00
	1904 M	Inc. Ab.	5.00	10.00	20.00	80.00
	1905 M	.059	10.00	20.00	50.00	150.00

25 CENTAVOS

6.7680 g, .903 SILVER, .1965 oz ASW

Mint mark: A,As

KM#	Date	Mintage	Fine	VF	XF	Unc
406	1874 L	—	20.00	40.00	80.00	200.00
	1875 L	—	15.00	30.00	60.00	200.00
	1876 L	—	30.00	50.00	90.00	200.00
	1877 L	.011	25.00	50.00	125.00	250.00
	1877.	Inc. Ab.	10.00	25.00	50.00	200.00
	1878 L	.025	10.00	25.00	50.00	200.00
	1879 L	—	10.00	25.00	50.00	200.00
	1880 L	—	10.00	25.00	50.00	200.00
	1880.L	—	10.00	25.00	50.00	200.00
	1881 L	8,800	—	—	Rare	—
	1882 L	7,777	15.00	35.00	75.00	200.00
	1883 L	.028	10.00	25.00	50.00	200.00
	1884 L	—	10.00	25.00	50.00	200.00
	1885 L	—	20.00	40.00	80.00	200.00
	1886 L	.046	10.00	25.00	60.00	200.00
	1887 L	.012	10.00	25.00	50.00	200.00
	1888 L	.020	10.00	25.00	50.00	200.00
	1889 L	.014	10.00	25.00	50.00	200.00
	1890 L	.023	10.00	25.00	50.00	200.00

Mint mark: CA,CH,Ca

KM#	Date	Mintage	Fine	VF	XF	Unc
406.1	1871 M	.018	25.00	50.00	100.00	200.00
	1872 M very crude date					
		.024	50.00	100.00	150.00	300.00
	1883 M	.012	10.00	25.00	50.00	175.00

KM#	Date	Mintage	Fine	VF	XF	Unc
406.1	1885/3 M	.035	10.00	25.00	50.00	175.00
	1885 M	Inc.Ab.	10.00	25.00	50.00	175.00
	1886 M	.022	10.00	25.00	50.00	175.00
	1887/6 M	.026	10.00	15.00	30.00	175.00
	1887 M	Inc. Ab.	10.00	15.00	30.00	175.00
	1888 M	.014	10.00	25.00	50.00	175.00
	1889 M	.050	10.00	15.00	30.00	175.00

Mint mark: Cn

KM#	Date	Mintage	Fine	VF	XF	Unc
406.2	1871 P	—	250.00	500.00	750.00	—
	1872 P	2,780	300.00	550.00	800.00	—
	1873 P	.020	100.00	150.00	250.00	500.00
	1874 P	—	20.00	50.00	125.00	250.00
	1875 P	—	250.00	500.00	750.00	—
	1876 P	—	—	—	Rare	—
	1878/7 D/S	—	100.00	150.00	250.00	500.00
	1878 D	—	100.00	150.00	250.00	500.00
	1879 D	—	15.00	35.00	70.00	175.00
	1880 D	—	250.00	500.00	750.00	—
	1881/0 D	.018	15.00	30.00	60.00	175.00
	1882 D	—	250.00	500.00	750.00	—
	1882 M	—	—	—	Rare	—
	1883 M	.015	50.00	100.00	150.00	300.00
	1884 M	—	20.00	40.00	80.00	175.00
	1885/4 M	.019	20.00	40.00	80.00	175.00
	1886 M	.022	12.50	20.00	50.00	175.00
	1887 M	.032	12.50	20.00	50.00	175.00
	1888 M	.086	7.50	15.00	30.00	175.00
	1889 M	.050	10.00	25.00	50.00	175.00
	1890 M	.091	7.50	17.50	40.00	175.00
	1892/0 M	.016	20.00	40.00	80.00	200.00
	1892 M	Inc. Ab.	20.00	40.00	80.00	200.00

Mint mark: Do

KM#	Date	Mintage	Fine	VF	XF	Unc
406.3	1873 P	892 pcs.	—	—	Rare	—
	1877 P	—	25.00	50.00	100.00	200.00
	1878/7 E	—	250.00	500.00	750.00	—
	1878 B	—	—	—	Rare	—
	1879 B	—	50.00	75.00	125.00	250.00
	1880 B	—	—	—	Rare	—
	1882 C	.017	25.00	50.00	100.00	225.00
	1884/3 C	—	25.00	50.00	100.00	200.00
	1885 C	.015	20.00	40.00	80.00	200.00
	1886 C	.033	15.00	30.00	60.00	200.00
	1887 C	.027	10.00	20.00	50.00	200.00
	1888 C	.025	10.00	20.00	50.00	200.00
	1889 C	.029	10.00	20.00	50.00	200.00
	1890 C	.068	7.50	15.00	40.00	200.00

Mint mark: Ga

KM#	Date	Mintage	Fine	VF	XF	Unc
406.4	1880 A	.038	25.00	50.00	100.00	200.00
	1881/0 S	.039	25.00	50.00	100.00	200.00
	1881 S	Inc. Ab.	25.00	50.00	100.00	200.00
	1882 S	.018	25.00	50.00	100.00	200.00
	1883/2 B/S	—	50.00	100.00	150.00	300.00
	1884 B	—	20.00	40.00	80.00	150.00
	1889 S	.030	20.00	40.00	80.00	150.00

Mint mark: Go

KM#	Date	Mintage	Fine	VF	XF	Unc
406.5	1870 S	.128	10.00	20.00	50.00	125.00
	1871 S	.172	10.00	20.00	50.00	125.00
	1872/1 S	.178	10.00	20.00	50.00	125.00
	1872 S	Inc. Ab.	10.00	20.00	50.00	125.00
	1873 S	.120	10.00	20.00	50.00	125.00
	1874 S	—	15.00	30.00	60.00	150.00
	1875/4 S	—	15.00	30.00	60.00	150.00
	1875 S	—	10.00	20.00	50.00	125.00
	1876 S	—	20.00	40.00	80.00	175.00
	1877 S	.124	10.00	20.00	50.00	125.00
	1878 S	.146	10.00	20.00	50.00	125.00
	1879 S	—	10.00	20.00	50.00	125.00
	1880 S	—	20.00	40.00	80.00	175.00
	1881 S	.408	7.50	17.50	45.00	125.00
	1882 S	.204	7.50	17.50	45.00	125.00
	1883 B	.168	7.50	17.50	45.00	125.00
	1884/69 B	—	7.50	17.50	45.00	125.00
	1884/3 B	—	7.50	17.50	45.00	125.00
	1884 B	—	7.50	17.50	45.00	125.00
	1885/65 R	.300	7.50	17.50	45.00	125.00
	1885/69 R	I.A.	7.50	17.50	45.00	125.00
	1885 R	Inc. Ab.	7.50	17.50	45.00	125.00
	1886/66 R	.322	7.50	17.50	45.00	125.00
	1886/69 R/S	Inc. Ab.	7.50	17.50	45.00	125.00
	1886/5/69R	Inc. Ab.	7.50	15.00	45.00	125.00
	1886 R	Inc. Ab.	7.50	15.00	45.00	125.00
	1887 R	.254	7.50	15.00	45.00	125.00
	1887 Go/Cn R/D	Inc. Ab.	7.50	15.00	45.00	125.00
	1888 R	.312	7.50	15.00	45.00	125.00
	1889/8 R	.304	7.50	15.00	45.00	125.00
	1889/8 Go/Cn R/D	Inc. Ab.	7.50	15.00	45.00	125.00
	1889 R	Inc. Ab.	7.50	15.00	45.00	125.00
	1890 R	.236	7.50	15.00	45.00	125.00

NOTE: Varieties exist.

Mint mark: Ho

KM#	Date	Mintage	Fine	VF	XF	Unc
406.6	1874 R	.023	10.00	20.00	40.00	125.00
	1874/64 R	I.A.	10.00	20.00	40.00	125.00
	1875 R	—	—	—	Rare	—
	1876/4 F/R	.034	10.00	20.00	50.00	150.00
	1876 F/R	I.A.	10.00	25.00	60.00	150.00
	1876 F	Inc. Ab.	10.00	25.00	55.00	135.00
	1877 F	—	10.00	20.00	50.00	125.00
	1878 A	.023	10.00	20.00	50.00	125.00
	1879 A	—	10.00	20.00	50.00	125.00
	1880 A	—	15.00	30.00	60.00	125.00
	1881 A	.019	15.00	30.00	60.00	125.00
	1882 A	8,120	20.00	40.00	80.00	150.00
	1883 M	2,000	100.00	200.00	300.00	600.00
406.6	1884 M	—	12.50	25.00	50.00	150.00
	1885 M	—	10.00	20.00	50.00	125.00
	1886 G	6,400	30.00	60.00	125.00	250.00
	1887 G	.012	10.00	20.00	40.00	125.00
	1888 G	.020	10.00	20.00	40.00	125.00
	1889 G	.028	10.00	20.00	40.00	125.00
	1890/80 G	.018	25.00	50.00	100.00	125.00
	1890 G	Inc. Ab.	25.00	50.00	100.00	125.00

NOTE: Varieties exist.

Mint mark: Mo

KM#	Date	Mintage	Fine	VF	XF	Unc
406.7	1869 C	.076	10.00	25.00	50.00	125.00
	1870/9 C	.136	6.00	12.00	30.00	125.00
	1870 C	Inc. Ab.	6.00	12.00	30.00	125.00
	1871 M	.138	6.00	12.00	30.00	125.00
	1872 M	.220	6.00	12.00	30.00	125.00
	1873/1 M	.048	10.00	25.00	50.00	125.00
	1873 M	Inc. Ab.	10.00	25.00	50.00	125.00
	1874/69 B/M	—	10.00	25.00	50.00	125.00
	1874/3 M	—	10.00	25.00	50.00	125.00
	1874/3 B	—	10.00	25.00	50.00	125.00
	1874 M	—	6.00	12.00	30.00	125.00
	1874 B/M	—	10.00	25.00	50.00	125.00
	1875 B	—	6.00	12.00	30.00	125.00
	1876/5 B	—	7.50	15.00	40.00	125.00
	1876 B	—	6.00	12.00	30.00	125.00
	1877 M	.056	10.00	25.00	50.00	125.00
	1878/1 M	.120	10.00	25.00	50.00	125.00
	1878/7 M	I.A.	10.00	25.00	50.00	125.00
	1878 M	Inc. Ab.	6.00	12.00	30.00	125.00
	1879 M	—	10.00	20.00	40.00	125.00
	1880 M	—	7.50	15.00	35.00	125.00
	1881/0 M	.300	10.00	25.00	50.00	125.00
	1881 M	Inc. Ab.	10.00	25.00	50.00	125.00
	1882 M	.212	7.50	15.00	35.00	125.00
	1883 M	.108	7.50	15.00	35.00	125.00
	1884 M	—	10.00	20.00	40.00	125.00
	1885 M	.216	10.00	20.00	40.00	125.00
	1886/5 M	.436	7.50	15.00	35.00	125.00
	1886 M	Inc. Ab.	7.50	15.00	35.00	125.00
	1887 M	.376	7.50	15.00	35.00	125.00
	1888 M	.192	7.50	15.00	35.00	125.00
	1889 M	.132	7.50	15.00	35.00	125.00
	1890 M	.060	10.00	20.00	40.00	125.00

NOTE: Varieties exist.

Mint mark: Pi

KM#	Date	Mintage	Fine	VF	XF	Unc
406.8	1869 S	—	25.00	75.00	150.00	300.00
	1870 G	.050	10.00	30.00	75.00	150.00
	1870 O	Inc. Ab.	15.00	35.00	85.00	175.00
	1871 O	.030	10.00	30.00	75.00	150.00
	1872 O	.046	10.00	30.00	75.00	150.00
	1873 O	.013	15.00	40.00	90.00	175.00
	1874 H	—	15.00	40.00	90.00	200.00
	1875 H	—	10.00	20.00	60.00	150.00
	1876/5 H	—	15.00	30.00	80.00	175.00
	1876 H	—	10.00	25.00	65.00	150.00
	1877 H	.019	10.00	25.00	65.00	150.00
	1878 H	—	15.00	30.00	60.00	150.00
	1879/8 H	—	10.00	25.00	60.00	150.00
	1879 H	—	10.00	25.00	60.00	150.00
	1879 E	—	100.00	200.00	300.00	600.00
	1880 H	—	20.00	40.00	100.00	200.00
	1881 H	.050	20.00	40.00	80.00	175.00
	1881 E	Inc. Ab.	—	—	Rare	—
	1882 H	.020	10.00	20.00	60.00	150.00
	1883 H	.017	10.00	25.00	65.00	150.00
	1884 H	—	10.00	25.00	65.00	150.00
	1885 H	.043	10.00	20.00	60.00	150.00
	1886 C	.078	10.00	25.00	65.00	150.00
	1886 R	Inc. Ab.	7.50	20.00	50.00	150.00
	1886 R 6/inverted 6	Inc. Ab.	7.50	20.00	50.00	150.00
	1887 Pi/ZsR	.092	7.50	20.00	50.00	150.00
	1887 Pi/ZsB	Inc. Ab.	100.00	150.00	300.00	500.00
	1888 R	.106	7.50	20.00	50.00	150.00
	1888 Pi/ZsR	Inc. Ab.	10.00	20.00	50.00	150.00
	1888 R/B	I.A.	10.00	20.00	50.00	150.00
	1889 R	.115	7.50	15.00	40.00	150.00
	1889 Pi/ZsR	Inc. Ab.	10.00	20.00	50.00	150.00
	1889 R/B	I.A.	10.00	20.00	50.00	150.00
	1890 R	.064	10.00	20.00	50.00	150.00
	1890 Pi/ZsR/B	Inc. Ab.	7.50	15.00	40.00	150.00
	1890 R/B	I.A.	10.00	20.00	50.00	150.00

NOTE: Varieties exist.

Mint mark: Zs

KM#	Date	Mintage	Fine	VF	XF	Unc
406.9	1870 H	.152	6.00	15.00	50.00	125.00
	1871 H	.250	6.00	15.00	50.00	125.00
	1872 H	.260	6.00	15.00	50.00	125.00
	1873 H	.132	6.00	15.00	50.00	125.00
	1874 H	—	10.00	20.00	60.00	125.00
	1874 A	—	10.00	20.00	60.00	125.00
	1875 A	—	7.00	20.00	60.00	125.00
	1876 A	—	6.00	15.00	50.00	125.00
	1876 S	—	6.00	15.00	50.00	125.00
	1877 S	.350	6.00	15.00	50.00	125.00
	1878 S	.252	6.00	15.00	50.00	125.00
	1879 S	—	6.00	15.00	50.00	125.00
	1880 S	—	6.00	15.00	50.00	125.00
	1881/0 S	.570	6.00	15.00	50.00	125.00
	1881 S	Inc. Ab.	6.00	15.00	50.00	125.00
	1882/1 S	.300	10.00	17.50	55.00	125.00
	1882 S	Inc. Ab.	6.00	15.00	50.00	125.00
	1883/2 S	.193	10.00	17.50	55.00	125.00
	1883 S	Inc. Ab.	6.00	15.00	50.00	125.00
406.9	1884/3 S	—	10.00	17.50	55.00	125.00
	1884 S	—	6.00	15.00	50.00	125.00
	1885 S	.309	6.00	15.00	50.00	125.00
	1886/5 S	.613	6.00	15.00	50.00	125.00
	1886 S	Inc. Ab.	6.00	15.00	50.00	125.00
	1886 Z	Inc. Ab.	6.00	15.00	55.00	125.00
	1887 Z	.389	6.00	15.00	50.00	125.00
	1888 Z	.408	6.00	15.00	50.00	125.00
	1889 Z	.400	6.00	15.00	50.00	125.00
	1890 Z	.269	6.00	15.00	50.00	125.00

NOTE: Varieties exist.

50 CENTAVOS

13.5360 g, .903 SILVER, .3930 oz ASW

Mint mark: A,As

Rev: Balance scale.

KM#	Date	Mintage	Fine	VF	XF	Unc
407	1875 L	—	12.00	25.00	60.00	400.00
	1876/5 L	—	25.00	40.00	100.00	450.00
	1876 L	—	12.00	25.00	60.00	400.00
	1877 L	.026	15.00	30.00	75.00	450.00
	1878 L	—	12.00	25.00	60.00	400.00
	1879 L	—	25.00	50.00	100.00	450.00
	1880 L	.057	12.00	25.00	60.00	400.00
	1881 L	.018	15.00	30.00	75.00	450.00
	1884 L	6,286	75.00	125.00	250.00	650.00
	1885 As/HoL	.021	15.00	35.00	80.00	450.00
	1888 L	—	Contemporary counterfeits			

Mint mark: Ca, CHa

KM#	Date	Mintage	Fine	VF	XF	Unc
407.1	1883 M	.012	30.00	60.00	125.00	500.00
	1884 M	—	25.00	50.00	125.00	500.00
	1885 M	.013	15.00	35.00	90.00	400.00
	1886 M	.018	20.00	40.00	100.00	450.00
	1887 M	.026	25.00	65.00	150.00	500.00

Mint mark: Cn

KM#	Date	Mintage	Fine	VF	XF	Unc
407.2	1871 P	—	400.00	550.00	750.00	1500.
	1873 P	—	400.00	550.00	750.00	1500.
	1874 P	—	200.00	300.00	500.00	1000.
	1875/4 P	—	20.00	40.00	75.00	450.00
	1875 P	—	12.00	25.00	50.00	450.00
	1876 P	—	15.00	30.00	60.00	450.00
	1877/6 G	—	15.00	30.00	60.00	450.00
	1877 G	—	12.00	25.00	50.00	450.00
	1878 G	.018	20.00	40.00	75.00	450.00
	1878 D Cn/Mo	Inc. Ab.	30.00	60.00	100.00	450.00
	1878 D	Inc. Ab.	15.00	35.00	75.00	450.00
	1879 D	—	12.00	25.00	50.00	450.00
	1879 D/G	—	12.00	25.00	50.00	450.00
	1880 D	—	15.00	30.00	60.00	450.00
	1881/0 D	.188	15.00	30.00	60.00	450.00
	1881 D	Inc. Ab.	15.00	30.00	60.00	450.00
	1881 G	Inc. Ab.	125.00	175.00	275.00	550.00
	1882 D	—	175.00	225.00	325.00	1000.
	1882 G	—	100.00	250.00	300.00	1000.
	1883 D	.019	25.00	50.00	100.00	500.00
	1885/3 M/G	9,254	30.00	60.00	100.00	500.00
	1886 M/G	7,030	50.00	100.00	150.00	800.00
	1886 M	Inc. Ab.	40.00	80.00	150.00	800.00
	1887 M	.076	20.00	40.00	100.00	450.00
	1888 M	—	Contemporary counterfeits			
	1892 M	8,200	40.00	80.00	150.00	800.00

Mint mark: Do

KM#	Date	Mintage	Fine	VF	XF	Unc
407.3	1871 P	591 pcs.	—	—	Rare	—
	1873 P	4,010	150.00	250.00	500.00	1250.
	1873 M/P	I.A.	150.00	250.00	500.00	1250.
	1874 M	—	20.00	40.00	175.00	750.00
	1875 M	—	20.00	40.00	80.00	350.00
	1875 H	—	150.00	250.00	450.00	1000.
	1876/5 M	—	35.00	70.00	150.00	500.00
	1876 M	—	35.00	70.00	150.00	500.00
	1877 P	2,000	30.00	45.00	150.00	1250.
	1878 B	—	—	—	Rare	—
	1879 B	—	—	—	Rare	—
	1880 P	—	30.00	60.00	125.00	500.00
	1881 P	.010	40.00	80.00	150.00	550.00
	1882 C	8,957	30.00	75.00	200.00	800.00
	1884/2 C	—	20.00	50.00	125.00	600.00
	1884 C	—	—	—	—	—
	1885 B	—	15.00	40.00	100.00	500.00
	1886 C	.016	15.00	40.00	100.00	500.00
	1887 Do/MoC	.028	15.00	40.00	100.00	500.00

Mint mark: Go

KM#	Date	Mintage	Fine	VF	XF	Unc
407.4	1869 S	—	15.00	35.00	75.00	550.00
	1870 S	.166	12.00	25.00	50.00	450.00
	1871 S	.148	12.00	25.00	50.00	450.00
	1872/1 S	.144	15.00	30.00	60.00	500.00
	1872 S	Inc. Ab.	12.00	25.00	50.00	450.00
	1873 S	.050	12.00	25.00	50.00	450.00
	1874 S	—	12.00	25.00	50.00	450.00
	1875 S	—	15.00	35.00	75.00	450.00
	1876 S	—	12.00	25.00	50.00	450.00
	1877 S	.076	12.00	25.00	60.00	450.00
	1878 S	.037	15.00	30.00	75.00	550.00

KM#	Date	Mintage	Fine	VF	XF	Unc
407.4	1879 S	—	12.00	25.00	50.00	450.00
	1880 S	—	12.00	25.00	50.00	450.00
	1881/79 S	.032	15.00	30.00	60.00	500.00
	1881 S	Inc. Ab.	12.00	25.00	50.00	450.00
	1882 S	.018	12.00	25.00	50.00	450.00
	1883/2 B/S	—	15.00	30.00	60.00	500.00
	1883 B	—	12.00	25.00	50.00	450.00
	1883 S	—	—	—	Rare	—
	1884 B/S	—	15.00	30.00	75.00	500.00
	1885 R	.053	12.00	25.00	50.00	450.00
	1886/5 R/B	.059	15.00	30.00	60.00	500.00
	1886/5 R/S	Inc. Ab.	20.00	40.00	75.00	500.00
	1886 R	Inc. Ab.	20.00	40.00	75.00	450.00
	1887 R	.018	20.00	40.00	75.00	550.00
	1888 R	—	Contemporary counterfeits			

NOTE: Varieties exist.

Mint mark: Ho

KM#	Date	Mintage	Fine	VF	XF	Unc
407.5	1874 R	—	20.00	40.00	100.00	600.00
	1875/4 R	—	20.00	50.00	125.00	600.00
	1875 R	—	20.00	50.00	125.00	600.00
	1876/5 F/R	—	15.00	35.00	100.00	550.00
	1876 F	—	15.00	35.00	100.00	550.00
	1877 F	—	50.00	75.00	150.00	650.00
	1880/70 A	—	15.00	35.00	100.00	550.00
	1880 A	—	15.00	35.00	100.00	550.00
	1881 A	.013	15.00	35.00	100.00	550.00
	1882 A	—	75.00	150.00	250.00	750.00
	1888 G	—	Contemporary counterfeits			
	1894 G	.059	15.00	30.00	100.00	450.00
	1895 G	8,000	250.00	350.00	500.00	1250.

NOTE: Varieties exist.

Mint mark: Mo

KM#	Date	Mintage	Fine	VF	XF	Unc
407.6	1869 C	.046	15.00	35.00	95.00	600.00
	1870 C	.052	15.00	30.00	90.00	550.00
	1871 C	.014	40.00	75.00	150.00	650.00
	1871 M/C	I.A.	35.00	75.00	150.00	600.00
	1872/1 M	.060	35.00	75.00	150.00	550.00
	1872 M	Inc. Ab.	35.00	75.00	150.00	550.00
	1873 M	6,000	35.00	75.00	150.00	600.00
	1874/3 M	—	200.00	400.00	600.00	1250.
	1874/2 B	—	15.00	30.00	75.00	500.00
	1874/3 B/M	—	15.00	30.00	75.00	500.00
	1874 B	—	15.00	30.00	75.00	500.00
	1875 B	—	15.00	30.00	75.00	550.00
	1876/5 B	—	15.00	30.00	75.00	500.00
	1876 B	—	12.00	25.00	75.00	500.00
	1877/2 M	—	20.00	40.00	100.00	550.00
	1877 M	—	15.00	30.00	90.00	500.00
	1878/7 M	8,000	25.00	50.00	125.00	600.00
	1878 M	Inc. Ab.	15.00	35.00	100.00	550.00
	1879 M	—	25.00	50.00	125.00	550.00
	1880 M	—	100.00	150.00	250.00	750.00
	1881 M	.016	25.00	50.00	125.00	600.00
	1882/1 M	2,000	30.00	60.00	150.00	750.00
	1883 M	4,000	150.00	225.00	350.00	1000.
	1884 M	—	150.00	225.00	350.00	1000.
	1885 M	.012	30.00	60.00	150.00	600.00
	1886/5 M	.066	15.00	35.00	90.00	450.00
	1886 M	Inc. Ab.	12.00	25.00	75.00	400.00
	1887/6 M	.088	15.00	35.00	90.00	450.00
	1887 M	Inc. Ab.	15.00	35.00	75.00	450.00
	1888 M	—	Contemporary counterfeits			

Mint mark: Pi

KM#	Date	Mintage	Fine	VF	XF	Unc
407.7	1870/780 G	.050	25.00	45.00	110.00	500.00
	1870 G	Inc. Ab.	20.00	40.00	100.00	450.00
	1870 O	Inc. Ab.	20.00	40.00	100.00	450.00
	1871 O/G	.064	15.00	30.00	80.00	400.00
	1872 O	.052	15.00	30.00	80.00	400.00
	1872 O/G	I.A.	15.00	30.00	80.00	400.00
	1873 O	.032	20.00	40.00	100.00	450.00
	1873 H	Inc. Ab.	25.00	50.00	125.00	550.00
	1874 H/O	—	15.00	30.00	80.00	400.00
	1875 H	—	15.00	30.00	80.00	400.00
	1876 H	—	30.00	60.00	150.00	700.00
	1877 H	.034	20.00	40.00	100.00	450.00
	1878 H	9,700	20.00	40.00	100.00	450.00
	1879/7 H	—	15.00	35.00	90.00	450.00
	1879 H	—	15.00	35.00	90.00	400.00
	1880 H	—	20.00	40.00	100.00	450.00
	1881 H	.028	20.00	40.00	100.00	450.00
	1882 H	.022	15.00	30.00	80.00	400.00
	1883 H 8/8	.029	50.00	100.00	200.00	750.00
	1883 H	Inc. Ab.	15.00	30.00	80.00	400.00
	1884 H	—	50.00	100.00	175.00	600.00
	1885/0 H	.045	20.00	40.00	100.00	450.00
	1885/4 H	I.A.	20.00	40.00	100.00	450.00
	1885 H	Inc. Ab.	25.00	50.00	125.00	450.00
	1885 C	Inc. Ab.	15.00	30.00	80.00	400.00
	1886/1 R	.092	50.00	100.00	175.00	600.00
	1886 C	Inc. Ab.	15.00	30.00	80.00	400.00
	1886 R	Inc. Ab.	15.00	30.00	80.00	400.00
	1887 R	.032	15.00	30.00	90.00	450.00
	1888 R	—	Contemporary counterfeits			

Mint mark: Zs

KM#	Date	Mintage	Fine	VF	XF	Unc
407.8	1870 H	.086	12.00	25.00	60.00	450.00
	1871 H	.146	12.00	25.00	50.00	400.00
	1872 H	.132	12.00	25.00	50.00	400.00
	1873 H	.056	12.00	25.00	50.00	400.00
	1874 H	—	12.00	25.00	50.00	400.00
	1874 A	—	—	—	Rare	—
	1875 A	—	12.00	25.00	50.00	400.00
	1876/5 A	—	15.00	30.00	60.00	450.00
407.8	1876 A	—	12.00	25.00	50.00	400.00
	1876 S	—	100.00	200.00	350.00	750.00
	1877 S	.100	12.00	25.00	50.00	400.00
	1878/7 S	.254	15.00	30.00	60.00	450.00
	1878 S	Inc. Ab.	15.00	30.00	60.00	400.00
	1879 S	—	12.00	25.00	50.00	400.00
	1880 S	—	12.00	25.00	50.00	400.00
	1881 S	.201	12.00	25.00	50.00	400.00
	1882/1 S	2,000	50.00	100.00	250.00	650.00
	1882 S	Inc. Ab.	50.00	100.00	250.00	650.00
	1883 Zs/Za S	.031	30.00	60.00	100.00	450.00
	1883 S	Inc. Ab.	25.00	50.00	100.00	450.00
	1884/3 S	—	15.00	30.00	60.00	450.00
	1884 S	—	12.00	25.00	50.00	400.00
	1885/4 S	2,000	25.00	50.00	125.00	450.00
	1885 S	Inc. Ab.	25.00	50.00	125.00	450.00
	1886 Z	2,000	150.00	275.00	400.00	1000.
	1887 Z	.063	30.00	60.00	125.00	450.00

NOTE: Varieties exist.

PESO

27.0730 g, .903 SILVER, .7860 oz ASW
Mint mark: CH
Rev: Balance scale.

KM#	Date	Mintage	Fine	VF	XF	Unc
408	1872 P/M	.747	—	—	Rare	—
	1872 P	Inc. Ab.	—	—	Rare	—
	1872/1 M	I.A.	25.00	40.00	75.00	400.00
	1872 M	Inc. Ab.	17.50	25.00	50.00	250.00
	1873 M	.320	20.00	30.00	60.00	250.00
	1873 M/P	I.A.	25.00	40.00	75.00	350.00

Mint mark: Cn

KM#	Date	Mintage	Fine	VF	XF	Unc
408.1	1870 E	—	40.00	80.00	150.00	500.00
	1871/11 P	.478	25.00	45.00	90.00	350.00
	1871 P	Inc. Ab.	20.00	40.00	80.00	300.00
	1872 P	.209	20.00	40.00	80.00	300.00
	1873 P	.527	20.00	40.00	80.00	300.00

Mint mark: Do

KM#	Date	Mintage	Fine	VF	XF	Unc
408.2	1870 P	—	50.00	100.00	175.00	450.00
	1871 P	.427	25.00	50.00	75.00	300.00
	1872 P	.296	20.00	40.00	75.00	350.00
	1872 PT	Inc. Ab.	100.00	175.00	300.00	675.00
	1873 P	.203	25.00	45.00	85.00	350.00

Mint mark: Ga

KM#	Date	Mintage	Fine	VF	XF	Unc
408.3	1870 C	—	650.00	850.00	—	—
	1871 C	.829	35.00	75.00	150.00	600.00
	1872 C	.485	40.00	90.00	175.00	650.00
	1873/2 C	.277	40.00	90.00	175.00	700.00
	1873 C	Inc. Ab.	35.00	75.00	150.00	600.00

Mint mark: Go

KM#	Date	Mintage	Fine	VF	XF	Unc
408.4	1871/0 S	3.946	75.00	125.00	225.00	400.00
	1871/3 S	I.A.	20.00	35.00	70.00	250.00
	1871 S	Inc. Ab.	12.00	20.00	40.00	200.00
	1872 S	4.067	12.00	20.00	40.00	250.00
	1873/2 S	1.560	15.00	25.00	50.00	250.00
	1873 S	Inc. Ab.	12.00	20.00	45.00	200.00
	1873/Go/Mo/S/M	Inc. Ab.	12.00	20.00	45.00	250.00

Mint mark: Mo

KM#	Date	Mintage	Fine	VF	XF	Unc
408.5	1869 C	—	35.00	65.00	135.00	450.00
	1870/69 C	5.115	15.00	25.00	50.00	275.00
	1870 C	Inc. Ab.	12.00	20.00	40.00	250.00
	1870 M/C	I.A.	18.00	30.00	50.00	275.00
	1870 M	Inc. Ab.	18.00	30.00	50.00	275.00
	1871/0 M	6.974	15.00	25.00	50.00	275.00
	1871 M	Inc. Ab.	12.00	20.00	40.00	250.00
	1872/1 M/C	4.801	15.00	25.00	50.00	275.00
	1872 M	Inc. Ab.	12.00	20.00	40.00	250.00
	1873 M	1.765	12.00	20.00	40.00	250.00

NOTE: The 1869 C with large LEY on the scroll is a pattern.

Mint mark: Oa

KM#	Date	Mintage	Fine	VF	XF	Unc
408.6	1869 E	—	275.00	400.00	600.00	2000.
	1870 OAE small A	Inc. Ab.	15.00	30.00	75.00	400.00
	1870 OA E large A	Inc. Ab.	100.00	150.00	300.00	900.00
	1871/69 E	.140	30.00	50.00	125.00	550.00
	1871 OaE small A	Inc. Ab.	15.00	30.00	60.00	300.00
	1871 OA E large A	Inc. Ab.	15.00	30.00	75.00	400.00
	1872 OaE small A	.180	15.00	30.00	75.00	400.00
	1872 OA E large A	Inc. Ab.	50.00	100.00	200.00	450.00
	1873 E	.105	15.00	30.00	75.00	350.00

Mint mark: Pi

KM#	Date	Mintage	Fine	VF	XF	Unc
408.7	1870 S	1.967	200.00	350.00	500.00	1000.
	1870 S/A	I.A.	200.00	350.00	500.00	1000.
	1870 G	Inc. Ab.	25.00	50.00	125.00	450.00
	1870 H	Inc. Ab.	Contemporary counterfeit			
	1870 O/G	I.A.	25.00	35.00	125.00	450.00
	1870 O	Inc. Ab.	20.00	30.00	100.00	350.00
	1871/69 O	2.103	20.00	40.00	100.00	350.00
	1871 O/G	I.A.	15.00	30.00	60.00	300.00
	1872 O	1.873	15.00	30.00	60.00	300.00
	1873 O	.893	15.00	30.00	60.00	300.00
	1873 H	Inc. Ab.	15.00	30.00	60.00	300.00

NOTE: Varieties exist.

Mint mark: Zs

KM#	Date	Mintage	Fine	VF	XF	Unc
408.8	1870 H	4.519	12.00	30.00	40.00	200.00
	1871 H	4.459	12.00	20.00	40.00	200.00
	1872 H	4.039	12.00	20.00	40.00	200.00
	1873 H	1.782	12.00	20.00	40.00	200.00

NOTE: Varieties exist.

Mint mark: Cn
Liberty cap

KM#	Date	Mintage	Fine	VF	XF	Unc
409	1898 AM	1.720	10.00	15.00	30.00	75.00
	1898 Cn/MoAM	Inc. Ab.	15.00	30.00	90.00	150.00
	1899 AM	1.722	25.00	50.00	90.00	175.00
	1899 JQ	Inc. Ab.	10.00	15.00	50.00	125.00
	1900 JQ	1.804	10.00	15.00	30.00	80.00
	1901 JQ	1.473	10.00	15.00	30.00	80.00
	1902 JQ	1.194	10.00	15.00	45.00	125.00
	1903 JQ	1.514	10.00	15.00	30.00	80.00
	1903 FV	Inc. Ab.	25.00	50.00	100.00	225.00
	1904 MH	1.554	10.00	15.00	30.00	80.00
	1904 RP	I.A.	50.00	100.00	150.00	300.00
	1905 RP	.598	25.00	50.00	100.00	225.00

Mint mark: Go

KM#	Date	Mintage	Fine	VF	XF	Unc
409.1	1898 RS	4.256	10.00	15.00	35.00	85.00
	1898 Go/MoRS	Inc. Ab.	20.00	30.00	60.00	125.00
	1899 RS	3.207	10.00	15.00	30.00	75.00
	1900 RS	1.489	25.00	50.00	100.00	250.00

NOTE: Varieties exist.

Mint mark: Mo

KM#	Date	Mintage	Fine	VF	XF	Unc
409.2	1898 AM original strike - rev. w/139 Beads	10.156	7.50	10.00	17.50	60.00
	1898 AM restrike (1949) - rev. w/134 Beads	10.250	7.50	10.00	15.00	40.00
	1899 AM	7.930	10.00	12.50	20.00	70.00
	1900 AM	8.226	10.00	12.50	20.00	70.00
	1901 AM	14.505	7.50	10.00	20.00	70.00
	1902/1 AM	16.224	150.00	300.00	500.00	950.00
	1902 AM	I.A.	7.50	10.00	20.00	70.00
	1903 AM	22.396	7.50	10.00	20.00	70.00
	1903 MA (error)	Inc. Ab.	2000.	3000.	4000.	8000.
	1904 AM	14.935	7.50	10.00	20.00	70.00
	1905 AM	3.557	15.00	25.00	55.00	125.00
	1908 AM	7.575	10.00	12.50	20.00	60.00
	1908 GV	I.A.	10.00	12.50	17.50	45.00
	1909 GV	2.924	10.00	12.50	17.50	45.00

NOTE: Varieties exist.

Mint mark: Zs

KM#	Date	Mintage	Fine	VF	XF	Unc
409.3	1898 FZ	5.714	10.00	12.50	20.00	60.00
	1899 FZ	5.618	10.00	12.50	20.00	65.00
	1900 FZ	5.357	10.00	12.50	20.00	65.00
	1901 AZ	5.706	4000.	6500.	10,000.	—
	1901 FZ	Inc. Ab.	10.00	12.50	20.00	70.00
	1902 FZ	7.134	10.00	12.50	20.00	65.00
	1903/2 FZ	3.080	12.50	15.00	50.00	125.00
	1903 FZ	Inc. Ab.	10.00	12.50	20.00	65.00
	1904 FZ	2.423	10.00	15.00	25.00	70.00

Decimal-Republic / MEXICO 1268

KM#	Date	Mintage	Fine	VF	XF	Unc
409.3	1904 FM	Inc. Ab.	10.00	15.00	25.00	85.00
	1905 FM	.995	20.00	40.00	60.00	150.00

NOTE: Varieties exist.

1.6920 g, .875 GOLD, .0476 oz AGW

Mint mark: As

KM#	Date	Mintage	Fine	VF	XF	Unc
410	1888 L	—	—	—	Rare	—
	1888 AsL/MoM	—	—	—	Rare	—

Mint mark: Ca

KM#	Date	Mintage	Fine	VF	XF	Unc
410.1	1888 Ca/MoM	104 pcs.	—	—	Rare	—

Mint mark: Cn

KM#	Date	Mintage	Fine	VF	XF	Unc
410.2	1873 P	1,221	75.00	100.00	150.00	250.00
	1875 P	—	85.00	125.00	150.00	250.00
	1878 G	248 pcs.	100.00	175.00	225.00	450.00
	1879 D	—	100.00	150.00	175.00	275.00
	1881/0 D	338 pcs.	100.00	150.00	175.00	275.00
	1882 D	340 pcs.	100.00	150.00	175.00	275.00
	1883 D	—	100.00	150.00	175.00	275.00
	1884 M	—	100.00	150.00	175.00	275.00
	1886/4 M	277 pcs.	100.00	150.00	225.00	450.00
	1888/7 M	2,586	100.00	175.00	225.00	450.00
	1888 M	Inc. Ab.	65.00	100.00	150.00	250.00
	1889 M	—	—	—	Rare	—
	1891/89 M	969 pcs.	75.00	100.00	150.00	250.00
	1892 M	780 pcs.	75.00	100.00	150.00	250.00
	1893 M	498 pcs.	85.00	125.00	150.00	250.00
	1894 M	493 pcs.	80.00	125.00	150.00	250.00
	1895 M	1,143	65.00	100.00	150.00	250.00
	1896/5 M	1,028	65.00	100.00	150.00	250.00
	1897 M	785 pcs.	65.00	100.00	150.00	250.00
	1898 M	3,521	65.00	100.00	150.00	225.00
	1898 Cn/MoM	Inc. Ab.	65.00	100.00	150.00	250.00
	1899 Q	2,000	65.00	100.00	150.00	225.00
	1901/0 Q	2,350	65.00	100.00	150.00	225.00
	1902 Q	2,480	65.00	100.00	150.00	225.00
	1902 Cn/MoQ/C	Inc. Ab.	65.00	100.00	150.00	225.00
	1904 H	3,614	65.00	100.00	150.00	225.00
	1904 Cn/Mo/H	Inc. Ab.	65.00	100.00	150.00	250.00
	1905 P	1,000	—	Reported, not confirmed		

Mint mark: Go

KM#	Date	Mintage	Fine	VF	XF	Unc
410.3	1870 S	—	100.00	125.00	150.00	250.00
	1871 S	500 pcs.	100.00	175.00	225.00	450.00
	1888 R	210 pcs.	125.00	200.00	250.00	500.00
	1890 R	1,916	75.00	100.00	150.00	250.00
	1892 R	533 pcs.	100.00	150.00	175.00	325.00
	1894 R	180 pcs.	150.00	200.00	250.00	500.00
	1895 R	676 pcs.	100.00	150.00	175.00	300.00
	1896/5 R	4,671	65.00	100.00	150.00	250.00
	1897/6 R	4,280	65.00	100.00	150.00	250.00
	1897 R	Inc. Ab.	65.00	100.00	150.00	250.00
	1898 R regular obv.	5,193	65.00	100.00	150.00	250.00
	1898 R mule, 5 Centavos obv., normal rev.	Inc. Ab.	75.00	100.00	150.00	250.00
	1899 R	2,748	65.00	100.00	150.00	250.00
	1900/800 R	864 pcs.	75.00	125.00	150.00	275.00

Mint mark: Ho

KM#	Date	Mintage	Fine	VF	XF	Unc
410.4	1874 R	—	—	Reported, not confirmed		
	1875 R	310 pcs.	—	—	Rare	—
	1876 F	—	—	—	Rare	—
	1888 G/MoM	—	—	—	Rare	—

Mint mark: Mo

KM#	Date	Mintage	Fine	VF	XF	Unc
410.5	1870 C	2,540	50.00	80.00	125.00	200.00
	1871 M/C	1,000	50.00	100.00	150.00	225.00
	1872 M/C	3,000	50.00	80.00	125.00	200.00
	1873/1 M	2,900	50.00	80.00	125.00	200.00
	1873 M	Inc. Ab.	50.00	80.00	125.00	200.00
	1874 M	—	50.00	80.00	125.00	200.00
	1875 B/M	—	50.00	80.00	125.00	200.00
	1876/5 B/M	—	50.00	80.00	125.00	200.00
	1877 M	—	50.00	80.00	125.00	200.00
	1878 M	2,000	50.00	80.00	125.00	200.00
	1879 M	—	50.00	80.00	125.00	200.00
	1880/70 M	—	50.00	80.00	125.00	200.00
	1881/71 M	1,000	50.00	80.00	125.00	200.00
	1882/72 M	—	50.00	80.00	125.00	200.00
		—	50.00	80.00	125.00	225.00
	1883/72 M	1,000	50.00	80.00	125.00	200.00
	1884 M	—	50.00	80.00	125.00	200.00
	1885/71 M	—	50.00	80.00	125.00	200.00
	1885 M	—	50.00	80.00	125.00	200.00
	1886 M	1,700	50.00	80.00	125.00	200.00
	1887 M	2,200	50.00	80.00	125.00	200.00
	1888 M	1,000	50.00	80.00	125.00	200.00
	1889 M	500 pcs.	100.00	150.00	200.00	275.00
	1890 M	570 pcs.	100.00	150.00	200.00	275.00
	1891 M	746 pcs.	100.00	150.00	200.00	275.00
410.5	1892/0 M	2,895	50.00	80.00	125.00	200.00
	1893 M	5,917	50.00	80.00	125.00	200.00
	1894 M	6,244	50.00	80.00	125.00	200.00
	1895 M	8,994	50.00	80.00	125.00	200.00
	1895 B	Inc. Ab.	50.00	80.00	125.00	200.00
	1896 B	7,166	50.00	80.00	125.00	200.00
	1896 M	Inc. Ab.	50.00	80.00	125.00	200.00
	1897 M	5,131	50.00	80.00	125.00	200.00
	1898/7 M	5,368	50.00	80.00	125.00	200.00
	1899 M	9,515	50.00	80.00	125.00	200.00
	1900/800 M	9,301	50.00	80.00	125.00	200.00
	1900/880 M	Inc. Ab.	50.00	80.00	125.00	200.00
	1900/890 M	Inc. Ab.	50.00	80.00	125.00	200.00
	1900 M	Inc. Ab.	50.00	80.00	125.00	200.00
	1901/801 M	8,293	50.00	80.00	125.00	200.00
	1901 M	Inc. Ab.	50.00	80.00	120.00	180.00
	1902 M large date	.011	50.00	80.00	120.00	180.00
	1902 M small date	Inc. Ab.	50.00	80.00	125.00	200.00
	1903 M	.010	50.00	80.00	120.00	180.00
	1904 M	9,845	50.00	80.00	120.00	180.00
	1905 M	3,429	50.00	80.00	125.00	200.00

Mint mark: Zs

KM#	Date	Mintage	Fine	VF	XF	Unc
410.6	1872 H	2,024	125.00	150.00	175.00	250.00
	1875/3 A	—	125.00	150.00	200.00	300.00
	1878 S	—	125.00	150.00	175.00	250.00
	1888 Z	280 pcs.	175.00	225.00	300.00	650.00
	1889 Z	492 pcs.	150.00	175.00	225.00	425.00
	1890 Z	738 pcs.	150.00	175.00	225.00	425.00

2-1/2 PESOS

4.2300 g, .875 GOLD, .1190 oz AGW

Mint mark: As

KM#	Date	Mintage	Fine	VF	XF	Unc
411	1888 As/MoL	—	—	—	Rare	—

Mint mark: Cn

KM#	Date	Mintage	Fine	VF	XF	Unc
411.1	1893 M	141 pcs.	1500.	2000.	2500.	3500.

Mint mark: Do

KM#	Date	Mintage	Fine	VF	XF	Unc
411.2	1888 C	—	—	—	Rare	—

Mint mark: Go

KM#	Date	Mintage	Fine	VF	XF	Unc
411.3	1871 S	600 pcs.	1250.	2000.	2500.	3250.
	1888 Go/MoR	110 pcs.	1750.	2250.	2750.	3500.

Mint mark: Ho

KM#	Date	Mintage	Fine	VF	XF	Unc
411.4	1874 R	—	—	—	Rare	—
	1888 G	—	—	—	Rare	—

Mint mark: Mo

KM#	Date	Mintage	Fine	VF	XF	Unc
411.5	1870 C	820 pcs.	150.00	250.00	350.00	650.00
	1872 M/C	800 pcs.	150.00	250.00	350.00	650.00
	1873/2 M	—	200.00	350.00	750.00	1250.
	1874 M	—	200.00	350.00	750.00	1250.
	1874 B/M	—	200.00	350.00	750.00	1250.
	1875 B	—	200.00	350.00	750.00	1250.
	1876 B	—	250.00	500.00	1000.	1500.
	1877 M	—	200.00	350.00	750.00	1250.
	1878 M	400 pcs.	200.00	350.00	750.00	1250.
	1879 M	—	200.00	350.00	750.00	1250.
	1880/79 M	—	200.00	350.00	750.00	1250.
	1881 M	400 pcs.	200.00	350.00	750.00	1250.
	1882 M	—	200.00	350.00	750.00	1250.
	1883/73 M	400 pcs.	200.00	350.00	750.00	1250.
	1884 M	—	250.00	500.00	1000.	1500.
	1885 M	—	200.00	350.00	750.00	1250.
	1886 M	400 pcs.	200.00	350.00	750.00	1250.
	1887 M	400 pcs.	200.00	350.00	750.00	1250.
	1888 M	540 pcs.	200.00	350.00	750.00	1250.
	1889 M	240 pcs.	150.00	300.00	525.00	850.00
	1890 M	420 pcs.	200.00	350.00	750.00	1250.
	1891 M	188 pcs.	200.00	350.00	750.00	1250.
	1892 M	240 pcs.	200.00	350.00	750.00	1250.

Mint mark: Zs

KM#	Date	Mintage	Fine	VF	XF	Unc
411.6	1872 H	1,300	200.00	350.00	500.00	1000.
	1873 H	—	175.00	325.00	450.00	700.00
	1875/3 A	—	200.00	350.00	750.00	1250.
	1877 S	—	200.00	350.00	750.00	1250.
	1878 S	300 pcs.	200.00	350.00	750.00	1250.
	1888 Zs/MoS	80 pcs.	300.00	500.00	1000.	1750.
	1889 Zs/MoZ	184 pcs.	250.00	450.00	950.00	1500.
	1890 Z	326 pcs.	200.00	350.00	750.00	1250.

CINCO (5) PESOS

8.4600 g, .875 GOLD, .2380 oz AGW

Mint mark: As

KM#	Date	Mintage	Fine	VF	XF	Unc
412	1875 L	—	—	—	—	—
	1878 L	383 pcs.	900.00	1700.	3000.	4500.

Mint mark: Ca

KM#	Date	Mintage	Fine	VF	XF	Unc
412.1	1888 M	120 pcs.	—	—	Rare	—

Mint mark: Cn

KM#	Date	Mintage	Fine	VF	XF	Unc
412.2	1873 P	—	300.00	600.00	1000.	1500.
	1874 P	—	—	—	—	—
	1875 P	—	300.00	500.00	700.00	1250.
	1876 P	—	300.00	500.00	700.00	1250.
	1877 G	—	300.00	500.00	700.00	1250.
	1882	174 pcs.	—	—	Rare	—
	1888 M	—	500.00	1000.	1350.	2000.
	1890 M	435 pcs.	250.00	500.00	750.00	1250.
	1891 M	1,390	250.00	400.00	500.00	1000.
	1894 M	484 pcs.	250.00	500.00	750.00	1600.
	1895 M	142 pcs.	500.00	750.00	1500.	2500.
	1900 Q	1,536	200.00	300.00	400.00	950.00
	1903 Q	1,000	200.00	300.00	400.00	800.00

Mintmark: Do

KM#	Date	Mintage	Fine	VF	XF	Unc
412.3	1873/2 P	—	700.00	1250.	1800.	3000.
	1877 P	—	700.00	1250.	1800.	3000.
	1878 E	—	700.00	1250.	1800.	3000.
	1879/7 B	—	700.00	1250.	1800.	3000.
	1879 B	—	700.00	1250.	1800.	3000.

Mint mark: Go

KM#	Date	Mintage	Fine	VF	XF	Unc
412.4	1871 S	1,600	400.00	800.00	1250.	2500.
	1887 R	140 pcs.	600.00	1200.	1500.	2750.
	1888 R	65 pcs.	—	—	Rare	—
	1893 R	16 pcs.	—	—	Rare	—

Mint mark: Ho

KM#	Date	Mintage	Fine	VF	XF	Unc
412.5	1874 R	—	1750.	2500.	3000.	4500.
	1877 R	990 pcs.	750.00	1250.	2000.	3000.
	1877 A	Inc. Ab.	650.00	1100.	1750.	2750.
	1888G	—	—	—	Rare	—

Mint mark: Mo

KM#	Date	Mintage	Fine	VF	XF	Unc
412.6	1870 C	550 pcs.	200.00	400.00	550.00	900.00
	1871/69 M	1,600	175.00	350.00	475.00	750.00
	1871/9 M	I.A.	175.00	350.00	475.00	750.00
	1871 M	Inc. Ab.	175.00	350.00	475.00	750.00
	1872 M	1,600	175.00	350.00	475.00	750.00
	1873/2 M	—	200.00	400.00	550.00	850.00
	1874 M	—	200.00	400.00	550.00	850.00
	1875/3 B/M	—	200.00	400.00	550.00	950.00
	1875 B	—	200.00	400.00	550.00	950.00
	1876/5 B/M	—	200.00	400.00	550.00	1000.
	1877 M	—	250.00	450.00	750.00	1250.
	1878/7 M	400 pcs.	200.00	400.00	550.00	1250.
	1878 M	Inc. Ab.	200.00	400.00	550.00	1250.
	1879/8 M	—	200.00	400.00	550.00	1250.
	1880 M	—	200.00	400.00	550.00	1250.
	1881 M	—	200.00	400.00	550.00	1250.
	1882 M	200 pcs.	250.00	450.00	750.00	1250.
	1883 M	200 pcs.	250.00	450.00	750.00	1250.
	1884 M	—	250.00	450.00	750.00	1250.
	1886 M	200 pcs.	250.00	450.00	750.00	1250.
	1887 M	200 pcs.	250.00	450.00	750.00	1250.
	1888 M	250 pcs.	200.00	400.00	550.00	1250.
	1889 M	190 pcs.	250.00	450.00	750.00	1250.
	1890 M	149 pcs.	250.00	450.00	750.00	1250.
	1891 M	156 pcs.	250.00	450.00	750.00	1250.
	1892 M	214 pcs.	250.00	450.00	750.00	1250.
	1893 M	1,058	200.00	400.00	500.00	800.00
	1897 M	370 pcs.	200.00	400.00	550.00	1000.
	1898 M	376 pcs.	200.00	400.00	550.00	1000.
	1900 M	1,014	175.00	350.00	450.00	750.00
	1901 M	1,071	175.00	350.00	450.00	750.00
	1902 M	1,478	175.00	350.00	450.00	750.00
	1903 M	1,162	175.00	350.00	450.00	750.00
	1904 M	1,415	175.00	350.00	450.00	750.00
	1905 M	563 pcs.	200.00	400.00	550.00	1500.

Mint mark: Zs

KM#	Date	Mintage	Fine	VF	XF	Unc
412.7	1874 A	—	200.00	400.00	500.00	750.00
	1875 A	—	200.00	400.00	500.00	1000.
	1877 S/A	—	200.00	400.00	600.00	1000.
	1878/7 S/A	—	200.00	400.00	600.00	1000.
	1883 S	—	175.00	375.00	500.00	750.00
	1888 Z	70 pcs.	1000.	1500.	2000.	3000.
	1889 Z	373 pcs.	200.00	300.00	500.00	850.00
	1892 Z	1,229	200.00	300.00	450.00	750.00

DIEZ (10) PESOS

16.9200 g, .875 GOLD, .4760 oz AGW

Mint mark: As

Rev: Balance scale.

KM#	Date	Mintage	Fine	VF	XF	Unc
413	1874 DL	—	—	—	Rare	—
	1875 L	642 pcs.	600.00	1250.	2500.	3500.
	1878 L	977 pcs.	500.00	1000.	2000.	3000.
	1879 L	1,078	500.00	1000.	2000.	3000.
	1880 L	2,629	500.00	1000.	2000.	3000.
	1881 L	2,574	500.00	1000.	2000.	3000.
	1882 L	3,403	500.00	1000.	2000.	3000.

KM#	Date	Mintage	Fine	VF	XF	Unc
413	1883 L	3,597	500.00	1000.	2000.	3000.
	1884 L	—	—	—	Rare	—
	1885 L	4,562	500.00	1000.	2000.	3000.
	1886 L	4,643	500.00	1000.	2000.	3000.
	1887 L	3,667	500.00	1000.	2000.	3000.
	1888 L	4,521	500.00	1000.	2000.	3000.
	1889 L	5,615	500.00	1000.	2000.	3000.
	1890 L	4,920	500.00	1000.	2000.	3000.
	1891 L	568 pcs.	500.00	1000.	2000.	3000.
	1892 L	—	—	—	—	—
	1893 L	817 pcs.	500.00	1000.	2000.	3000.
	1894/3 L	1,658	—	—	—	—
	1894 L	Inc. Ab.	500.00	1000.	2000.	3000.
	1895 L	1,237	500.00	1000.	2000.	3000.
	Mint mark: Ca					
413.1	1888 M	175 pcs.	—	—	7500.	—
	Mint mark: Cn					
413.2	1881 D	—	400.00	600.00	1000.	1750.
	1882 D	874 pcs.	400.00	600.00	1000.	1750.
	1882 E	Inc. Ab.	400.00	600.00	1000.	1750.
	1883 D	221 pcs.	—	—	—	—
	1883 M	Inc. Ab.	400.00	600.00	1000.	1750.
	1884 D	—	400.00	600.00	1000.	1750.
	1884 M	—	400.00	600.00	1000.	1750.
	1885 M	1,235	400.00	600.00	1000.	1750.
	1886 M	981 pcs.	400.00	600.00	1000.	1750.
	1887 M	2,289	400.00	600.00	1000.	1750.
	1888 M	767 pcs.	400.00	600.00	1000.	1750.
	1889 M	859 pcs.	400.00	600.00	1000.	1750.
	1890 M	1,427	400.00	600.00	1000.	1750.
	1891 M	670 pcs.	400.00	600.00	1000.	1750.
	1892 M	379 pcs.	400.00	600.00	1000.	1750.
	1893 M	1,806	400.00	600.00	1000.	1750.
	1895 M	179 pcs.	500.00	1000.	1500.	2500.
	1903 Q	774 pcs.	400.00	600.00	1000.	1750.
	Mint mark: Do					
413.3	1872 P	1,755	350.00	550.00	850.00	1250.
	1873/2 P	1,091	350.00	550.00	900.00	1500.
	1873/2 M/P	Inc. Ab.	350.00	550.00	900.00	1500.
	1874 M	—	350.00	550.00	900.00	1500.
	1875 M	—	350.00	550.00	900.00	1500.
	1876 M	—	450.00	750.00	1250.	2000.
	1877 P	—	350.00	550.00	900.00	1500.
	1878 E	582 pcs.	350.00	550.00	900.00	1500.
	1879/8 B	—	350.00	550.00	900.00	1500.
	1879 B	—	350.00	550.00	900.00	1500.
	1880 P	2,030	350.00	550.00	900.00	1500.
	1881/79 P	2,617	350.00	550.00	900.00	1500.
	1882 P	1,528	—	—	Rare	—
	1882 C	Inc. Ab.	350.00	550.00	900.00	1500.
	1883 C	793 pcs.	450.00	750.00	1250.	2000.
	1884 C	108 pcs.	450.00	750.00	1250.	2000.
	Mint mark: Ga					
413.4	1870 C	490 pcs.	500.00	800.00	1000.	1500.
	1871 C	1,910	400.00	800.00	1500.	2250.
	1872 C	780 pcs.	500.00	1000.	2000.	2500.
	1873 C	422 pcs.	500.00	1000.	2000.	3000.
	1874/3 C	477 pcs.	500.00	1000.	2000.	3000.
	1875 C	710 pcs.	500.00	1000.	2000.	3000.
	1878 A	183 pcs.	600.00	1200.	2500.	3500.
	1879 A	200 pcs.	600.00	1200.	2500.	3500.
	1880 S	404 pcs.	500.00	1000.	2000.	3000.
	1881 S	239 pcs.	600.00	1200.	2500.	3500.
	1891 S	196 pcs.	600.00	1200.	2500.	3500.
	Mint mark: Go					
413.5	1872 S	1,400	800.00	1500.	2000.	3000.
	1887 R	80 pcs.	1250.	2000.	2500.	3500.
	1888 R	68 pcs.	1500.	2500.	3000.	4000.
	Mint mark: Ho					
413.6	1874 R	—	—	—	Rare	—
	1876 F	357 pcs.	—	—	Rare	—
	1878 A	814 pcs.	1750.	3000.	3500.	5000.
	1879 A	—	1000.	2000.	2500.	3500.
	1880 A	—	1000.	2000.	2500.	3500.
	1881 A	—	—	—	Rare	—
	Mint mark: Mo					
413.7	1870 C	480 pcs.	500.00	900.00	1200.	2000.
	1872/1 M/C	2,100	350.00	550.00	900.00	1400.
	1873 M	—	400.00	600.00	950.00	1500.
	1874/3 M	—	400.00	600.00	950.00	1500.
	1875 B/M	—	400.00	600.00	950.00	1500.
	1876 B	—	—	—	Rare	—
	1878 M	300 pcs.	400.00	600.00	950.00	1500.
	1879 M	—	—	—	—	—
	1881 M	100 pcs.	500.00	1000.	1600.	2500.
	1882 M	—	400.00	600.00	950.00	1500.
	1883 M	100 pcs.	600.00	1000.	1600.	2500.
	1884 M	—	600.00	1000.	1600.	2500.
	1885 M	—	400.00	600.00	950.00	1500.
	1886 M	100 pcs.	600.00	1000.	1600.	2500.
	1887 M	100 pcs.	600.00	1000.	1625.	2750.
	1888 M	144 pcs.	450.00	750.00	1200.	2000.
	1889 M	88 pcs.	600.00	1000.	1600.	2500.
	1890 M	137 pcs.	600.00	1000.	1600.	2500.
	1891 M	133 pcs.	600.00	1000.	1600.	2500.
	1892 M	45 pcs.	600.00	1000.	1600.	2500.
	1893 M	1,361	350.00	550.00	900.00	1400.
	1897 M	239 pcs.	400.00	600.00	950.00	1500.
	1898/7 M	244 pcs.	425.00	625.00	1000.	1750.
	1900 M	733 pcs.	400.00	600.00	950.00	1500.
	1901 M	562 pcs.	350.00	500.00	800.00	1400.
413.7	1902 M	719 pcs.	350.00	500.00	800.00	1400.
	1903 M	713 pcs.	350.00	500.00	800.00	1400.
	1904 M	694 pcs.	350.00	500.00	800.00	1400.
	1905 M	401 pcs.	400.00	600.00	950.00	1500.
	Mint mark: Oa					
413.8	1870 E	4,614	400.00	600.00	900.00	1350.
	1871 E	2,705	400.00	600.00	900.00	1350.
	1872 E	5,897	400.00	600.00	900.00	1350.
	1873 E	3,537	400.00	600.00	950.00	1500.
	1874 E	2,205	400.00	600.00	1200.	1800.
	1875 E	312 pcs.	450.00	750.00	1400.	2250.
	1876 E	766 pcs.	450.00	750.00	1400.	2250.
	1877 E	463 pcs.	450.00	750.00	1400.	2250.
	1878 E	229 pcs.	450.00	750.00	1400.	2250.
	1879 E	210 pcs.	450.00	750.00	1400.	2250.
	1880 E	238 pcs.	450.00	750.00	1400.	2250.
	1881 E	961 pcs.	400.00	600.00	1200.	2000.
	1882 E	170 pcs.	600.00	1000.	1500.	2500.
	1883 E	111 pcs.	600.00	1000.	1500.	2500.
	1884 E	325 pcs.	450.00	750.00	1400.	2250.
	1885 E	370 pcs.	450.00	750.00	1400.	2250.
	1886 E	400 pcs.	450.00	750.00	1400.	2250.
	1887 E	—	700.00	1250.	2250.	3750.
	1888 E	—	—	—	—	—
	Mint mark: Zs					
413.9	1871 H	2,000	350.00	550.00	850.00	1200.
	1872 H	3,092	350.00	550.00	750.00	1000.
	1873 H	936 pcs.	400.00	600.00	950.00	1500.
	1874 H	—	400.00	600.00	950.00	1500.
	1875/3 A	—	400.00	600.00	1000.	1750.
	1876/5 S	—	400.00	600.00	1000.	1750.
	1877 S/H	506 pcs.	400.00	600.00	1000.	1750.
	1878 S	711 pcs.	400.00	600.00	1000.	1750.
	1879/8 S	—	450.00	750.00	1400.	2250.
	1879 S	—	450.00	750.00	1400.	2250.
	1880 S	2,089	350.00	550.00	950.00	1500.
	1881 S	736 pcs.	400.00	600.00	1000.	1750.
	1882 S	1,599	350.00	550.00	950.00	1500.
	1883/2 S	256 pcs.	450.00	700.00	1200.	2000.
	1884/3 S	—	350.00	550.00	1000.	1750.
	1884 S	—	350.00	550.00	1000.	1750.
	1885 S	1,588	350.00	550.00	950.00	1500.
	1886 S	5,364	350.00	550.00	950.00	1500.
	1887 S	2,330	—	—	—	—
	1887 Z	Inc. Ab.	350.00	550.00	950.00	1500.
	1888 Z	4,810	350.00	550.00	950.00	1500.
	1889 Z	6,154	350.00	550.00	950.00	1500.
	1890 Z	1,321	350.00	550.00	950.00	1500.
	1891 Z	1,930	350.00	550.00	950.00	1500.
	1892 Z	1,882	350.00	550.00	950.00	1500.
	1893 Z	2,899	350.00	550.00	950.00	1500.
	1894 Z	2,501	350.00	550.00	950.00	1500.
	1895 Z	1,217	350.00	550.00	950.00	1500.

VEINTE (20) PESOS

33.8400 g, .875 GOLD, .9520 oz AGW
Mint mark: As
Rev: Balance scale.

KM#	Date	Mintage	Fine	VF	XF	Unc
414	1876 L	276 pcs.	—	—	Rare	—
	1877 L	166 pcs.	—	—	Rare	—
	1878 L	—	—	—	—	—
	1888 L	—	—	—	Rare	—
	Mint mark: CH,Ca					
414.1	1872 M	995 pcs.	500.00	650.00	950.00	2500.
	1873 M	950 pcs.	500.00	650.00	950.00	2500.
	1874 M	1,116	500.00	650.00	950.00	2500.
	1875 M	750 pcs.	500.00	650.00	950.00	2500.
	1876 M	600 pcs.	500.00	800.00	1250.	2750.
	1877	55 pcs.	—	—	Rare	—
	1882 M	1,758	500.00	650.00	950.00	2500.
	1883 M	161 pcs.	600.00	1000.	1500.	3000.
	1884 M	496 pcs.	500.00	650.00	950.00	2500.
	1885 M	122 pcs.	600.00	1000.	1500.	3000.
	1887 M	550 pcs.	500.00	650.00	950.00	2500.
	1888 M	351 pcs.	500.00	650.00	950.00	2500.
	1889 M	464 pcs.	500.00	650.00	950.00	2500.
	1890 M	1,209	500.00	650.00	950.00	2500.
	1891 M	2,004	500.00	600.00	900.00	2250.
	1893 M	418 pcs.	500.00	650.00	950.00	2500.
	1895 M	133 pcs.	600.00	1000.	1500.	3000.
	Mint mark: Cn					
414.2	1870 E	3,749	500.00	650.00	950.00	2000.
	1871 P	3,046	500.00	650.00	950.00	2000.
	1872 P	972 pcs.	500.00	650.00	950.00	2000.
	1873 P	1,317	500.00	650.00	950.00	2000.
	1874 P	—	500.00	650.00	950.00	2000.
	1875 P	—	600.00	1200.	1800.	2500.
	1876 P	—	500.00	650.00	950.00	2000.
	1876 G	—	500.00	650.00	950.00	2000.
	1877 G	167 pcs.	600.00	1000.	1500.	2500.
	1878	842 pcs.	—	—	Rare	—
	1881/0 D	2,039	—	—	—	—
414.2	1881 D	Inc. Ab.	500.00	650.00	950.00	2000.
	1882/1 D	736 pcs.	500.00	650.00	950.00	2000.
	1883 M	1,836	500.00	650.00	950.00	2000.
	1884 M	—	500.00	650.00	950.00	2000.
	1885 M	544 pcs.	500.00	650.00	950.00	2000.
	1886 M	882 pcs.	500.00	650.00	950.00	2000.
	1887 M	837 pcs.	500.00	650.00	950.00	2000.
	1888 M	473 pcs.	500.00	650.00	950.00	2000.
	1889 M	1,376	500.00	650.00	950.00	2000.
	1890 M	—	500.00	650.00	950.00	2000.
	1891 M	237 pcs.	500.00	900.00	1200.	2250.
	1892 M	526 pcs.	500.00	650.00	950.00	2000.
	1893 M	2,062	500.00	650.00	950.00	2000.
	1894 M	4,516	500.00	650.00	950.00	2000.
	1895 M	3,193	500.00	650.00	950.00	2000.
	1896 M	4,072	500.00	650.00	950.00	2000.
	1897/6 M	959 pcs.	500.00	650.00	950.00	2000.
	1897 M	Inc. Ab.	500.00	650.00	950.00	2000.
	1898 M	1,660	500.00	650.00	950.00	2000.
	1899 M	1,243	500.00	650.00	950.00	2000.
	1899 Q	Inc. Ab.	500.00	900.00	1200.	2250.
	1900 Q	1,558	500.00	650.00	950.00	2000.
	1901/0 Q	1,496	—	—	—	—
	1901 Q	Inc. Ab.	500.00	650.00	950.00	2000.
	1902 Q	1,059	500.00	650.00	950.00	2000.
	1903 Q	1,121	500.00	650.00	950.00	2000.
	1904 H	4,646	500.00	650.00	950.00	2000.
	1905 P	1,738	500.00	900.00	1200.	2250.
	Mint mark: Do					
414.3	1870 P	416 pcs.	1000.	1500.	2000.	2500.
	1871/0 P	1,073	1000.	1750.	2250.	2750.
	1871 P	Inc. Ab.	1000.	1500.	2000.	2500.
	1872/1 PT	—	1500.	3000.	4500.	6500.
	1876 M	—	1000.	1500.	2000.	2500.
	1877 P	94 pcs.	1500.	2250.	2750.	3250.
	1878	258 pcs.	—	—	Rare	—
	Mint mark: Go					
414.4	1870 S	3,250	500.00	650.00	900.00	1250.
	1871 S	.020	500.00	650.00	900.00	1250.
	1872 S	.018	500.00	650.00	900.00	1250.
	1873 S	7,000	500.00	650.00	900.00	1250.
	1874 S	—	500.00	650.00	900.00	1250.
	1875 S	—	500.00	650.00	900.00	1250.
	1876 S	—	500.00	650.00	900.00	1250.
	1876 M	—	—	—	—	—
	1877 M/S	.015	—	—	Rare	—
	1877 R	Inc. Ab.	500.00	650.00	900.00	1250.
	1877 S	Inc. Ab.	—	—	Rare	—
	1878/7 M/S	.013	650.00	1250.	2000.	2500.
	1878 M	Inc. Ab.	650.00	1250.	2000.	2500.
	1878 S	Inc. Ab.	500.00	650.00	900.00	1250.
	1879 S	8,202	500.00	800.00	1200.	2250.
	1880 S	7,375	500.00	650.00	900.00	1250.
	1881 S	4,909	500.00	650.00	900.00	1250.
	1882 S	4,020	500.00	650.00	900.00	1250.
	1883/2 B	3,705	550.00	750.00	1150.	1800.
	1883 B	Inc. Ab.	500.00	650.00	900.00	1250.
	1884 B	1,798	500.00	650.00	900.00	1250.
	1885 R	2,660	500.00	650.00	900.00	1250.
	1886 R	1,090	500.00	800.00	1200.	2000.
	1887 R	1,009	500.00	800.00	1200.	2000.
	1888 R	1,011	500.00	800.00	1200.	2000.
	1889 R	956 pcs.	500.00	800.00	1200.	2000.
	1890 R	879 pcs.	500.00	800.00	1200.	2000.
	1891 R	818 pcs.	500.00	800.00	1200.	2000.
	1892 R	730 pcs.	500.00	800.00	1200.	2000.
	1893 R	3,343	500.00	650.00	950.00	1600.
	1894/3 R	6,734	500.00	650.00	900.00	1250.
	1894 R	Inc. Ab.	500.00	650.00	900.00	1250.
	1895/3 R	7,118	500.00	650.00	900.00	1250.
	1895 R	Inc. Ab.	500.00	650.00	900.00	1250.
	1896 R	9,219	500.00	650.00	900.00	1250.
	1897/6 R	6,781	500.00	650.00	900.00	1250.
	1897 R	Inc. Ab.	500.00	650.00	900.00	1250.
	1898 R	7,710	500.00	650.00	900.00	1250.
	1899 R	8,527	500.00	650.00	900.00	1250.
	1900 R	4,512	500.00	650.00	900.00	1250.
	Mint mark: Ho					
414.5	1874 R	—	—	—	Rare	—
	1875 R	—	—	—	Rare	—
	1876 F	—	—	—	Rare	—
	1888 G	—	—	—	Rare	—
	Mint mark: Mo					
414.6	1870 C	.014	500.00	600.00	800.00	1000.
	1871 M	.021	500.00	600.00	800.00	1000.
	1872/1 M	.011	500.00	600.00	800.00	1600.
	1872 M	Inc. Ab.	500.00	600.00	800.00	1000.
	1873 M	5,600	500.00	600.00	800.00	1000.
	1874/2 M	—	500.00	600.00	800.00	1350.
	1874/2 B	—	500.00	750.00	1000.	1600.
	1875 B	—	500.00	650.00	900.00	1250.
	1876 B	—	500.00	650.00	900.00	1500.
	1876 M	—	—	—	—	—
	1877 M	2,000	500.00	650.00	900.00	1250.
	1878 M	7,000	500.00	650.00	900.00	1500.
	1879 M	—	500.00	650.00	900.00	1750.
	1880 M	—	500.00	650.00	900.00	1750.
	1881/0 M	.011	500.00	600.00	800.00	1350.
	1881 M	Inc. Ab.	500.00	600.00	800.00	1350.
	1882/1 M	5,800	500.00	600.00	800.00	1350.
	1882 M	Inc. Ab.	500.00	600.00	800.00	1350.
	1883/1 M	4,000	500.00	600.00	800.00	1350.
	1883 M	Inc. Ab.	500.00	600.00	800.00	1250.
	1884/3 M	—	500.00	650.00	900.00	1400.
	1884 M	—	500.00	650.00	900.00	1400.

1270 Decimal-Republic / MEXICO

KM#	Date	Mintage	Fine	VF	XF	Unc
414.6	1885 M	6,000	500.00	650.00	900.00	1750.
	1886 M	.010	500.00	600.00	800.00	1500.
	1887 M	.012	500.00	600.00	800.00	1500.
	1888 M	7,300	500.00	650.00	900.00	1500.
	1889 M	6,477	500.00	650.00	900.00	1500.
	1890 M	7,852	500.00	650.00	900.00	1500.
	1891/0 M	8,725	500.00	650.00	900.00	1500.
	1891 M	Inc. Ab.	500.00	650.00	900.00	1500.
	1892 M	.011	500.00	650.00	900.00	1300.
	1893 M	.015	500.00	600.00	900.00	1300.
	1894 M	.014	500.00	600.00	900.00	1300.
	1895 M	.013	500.00	650.00	900.00	1300.
	1896 B	.014	500.00	650.00	900.00	1300.
	1897/6 M	.012	500.00	650.00	900.00	1300.
	1897 M	Inc. Ab.	500.00	650.00	900.00	1300.
	1898 M	.020	500.00	650.00	900.00	1300.
	1899 M	.023	500.00	650.00	900.00	1300.
	1900 M	.021	500.00	650.00	900.00	1300.
	1901 M	.029	500.00	650.00	900.00	1300.
	1902 M	.038	500.00	650.00	900.00	1300.
	1903/2 M	.031	500.00	650.00	900.00	1300.
	1903 M	Inc. Ab.	500.00	650.00	900.00	1300.
	1904 M	.052	500.00	650.00	900.00	1300.
	1905 M	9,757	500.00	650.00	900.00	1300.

Mint mark: Oa

414.7	1870 E	1,131	750.00	1500.	2500.	4000.
	1871 E	1,591	750.00	1500.	2500.	4000.
	1872 E	255 pcs.	1000.	1750.	3000.	5000.
	1888 E	170 pcs.	2000.	3000.	5000.	—

Mint mark: Zs

414.8	1871 H	1,000	3500.	6500.	7000.	8500.
	1875 A	—	4000.	6000.	7500.	9000.
	1878 S	441 pcs.	4000.	6000.	7500.	9000.
	1888 Z	50 pcs.	—	—	Rare	—
	1889 Z	640 pcs.	3500.	5500.	7000.	8500.

UNITED STATES

MINT MARK

o
M - Mexico City

CENTAVO

BRONZE, 20mm

415	1905	6.040	3.50	6.50	13.50	87.50
	1906	*67.505	.40	.75	1.50	12.00
	1910	8.700	2.00	3.00	10.00	80.00
	1911	16.450	.75	1.25	2.50	18.50
	1912	12.650	.90	1.50	3.50	30.00
	1913	12.850	.85	1.10	3.00	30.00
	1914	17.350	.75	1.00	2.50	12.00
	1915	2.277	10.00	20.00	70.00	300.00
	1916	.500	50.00	80.00	330.00	1150.
	1920	1.433	20.00	35.00	75.00	350.00
	1921	3.470	6.00	15.00	45.00	150.00
	1922	1.880	7.50	15.00	50.00	300.00
	1923	4.800	.75	1.00	2.00	13.50
	1924/3	2.000	45.00	70.00	200.00	450.00
	1924	Inc. Ab.	4.50	7.50	22.50	160.00
	1925	1.550	5.00	10.00	22.50	210.00
	1926	5.000	1.00	2.00	4.50	25.00
	1927/6	6.000	20.00	30.00	60.00	125.00
	1927	Inc. Ab.	.65	1.75	3.50	20.00
	1928	5.000	.50	1.00	3.00	18.00
	1929	4.500	.75	1.00	2.00	18.00
	1930	7.000	.55	1.00	2.00	19.00
	1933	10.000	.25	.35	.75	15.00
	1934	7.500	.30	.75	2.00	30.00
	1935	12.400	.15	.25	.40	10.00
	1936	20.100	.15	.20	.30	9.00
	1937	20.000	.15	.25	.35	3.75
	1938	10.000	.10	.15	.30	2.25
	1939	30.000	.10	.15	.30	1.25
	1940	10.000	.20	.30	.60	6.50
	1941	15.800	.15	.25	.35	2.25
	1942	30.400	.15	.20	.30	1.25
	1943	4.310	.25	.50	.75	8.00
	1944	5.645	.15	.25	.50	7.50
	1945	26.375	.10	.15	.25	1.00
	1946	42.135	—	.10	.15	.45
	1947	13.445	—	.10	.15	1.00
	1948	20.040	—	.10	.15	1.00
	1949	6.235	.10	.20	.30	1.25

***NOTE:** 50,000,000 pcs. were struck at the Birmingham Mint.
NOTE: Varieties exist.

Zapata Issue
Reduced size, 16mm

416	1915	.179	10.00	20.00	40.00	75.00

BRASS, 16mm

KM#	Date	Mintage	Fine	VF	XF	Unc
417	1950	12.815	.10	.15	.30	1.75
	1951	25.740	.10	.15	.25	.95
	1952	24.610	—	.10	.15	.40
	1953	21.160	—	.10	.15	.40
	1954	25.675	—	.10	.15	.65
	1955	9.820	.10	.15	.35	.85
	1956	11.285	—	.10	.15	.60
	1957	9.805	—	.10	.15	1.10
	1958	12.155	—	.10	.15	.60
	1959	11.875	—	.10	.15	.65
	1960	10.360	—	—	.10	.25
	1961	6.385	—	—	.10	.45
	1962	4.850	—	—	.10	.40
	1963	7.775	—	—	.10	.25
	1964	4.280	—	—	.10	.15
	1965	2.255	—	.10	.20	.25
	1966	1.760	—	.10	.15	.35
	1967	1.290	—	.10	.15	.40
	1968	1.000	—	.10	.15	.75
	1969	1.000	—	.10	.15	.70

Reduced size, 13mm.

418	1970	1.000	.10	.20	.35	1.25
	1972	1.000	.10	.25	.40	1.50
	1973	1.000	1.00	1.50	3.50	7.00

2 CENTAVOS

BRONZE, 25mm

419	1905	.050	125.00	200.00	350.00	750.00
	1906/inverted 6	9.998	10.00	20.00	40.00	175.00
	1906	*Inc. Ab.	6.50	12.00	20.00	75.00
	1920	1.325	7.50	15.00	35.00	225.00
	1921	4.275	2.75	4.50	11.00	95.00
	1922	—	250.00	500.00	1500.	4000.
	1924	.750	10.00	20.00	50.00	400.00
	1925	3.650	1.50	3.25	6.00	32.00
	1926	4.750	1.25	2.75	5.50	30.00
	1927	7.250	.75	1.25	2.25	22.50
	1928	3.250	1.00	1.75	4.00	25.00
	1929	.250	30.00	55.00	375.00	800.00
	1935	1.250	5.00	10.00	35.00	125.00
	1939	5.000	.45	.85	1.50	18.50
	1941	3.550	.40	.50	1.50	18.50

***NOTE:** 5,000,000 pcs. were struck at the Birmingham Mint.

Zapata Issue
Reduced size, 20mm

420	1915	.487	5.00	7.50	10.00	50.00

5 CENTAVOS

NICKEL

421	1905	1.420	5.00	10.00	25.00	145.00
	1906/5	10.615	10.00	17.50	45.00	—
	1906	*Inc. Ab.	.75	1.25	3.25	40.00
	1907	4.000	1.00	3.50	12.00	165.00
	1909	2.052	3.50	9.00	55.00	315.00
	1910	6.181	.90	1.25	4.00	65.00
	1911	4.487	.75	1.50	5.00	80.00
	1912 small mint mark	.420	60.00	80.00	175.00	650.00
	1912 large mint mark	Inc. Ab.	50.00	75.00	165.00	475.00
	1913	2.035	1.75	4.50	10.00	100.00
	1914	2.000	1.00	2.00	4.00	50.00

NOTE: 5,000,000 pcs. appear to have been struck at the Birmingham Mint in 1914 and all of 1909-1911. The Mexican Mint report does not mention receiving the 1914 dated coins.
NOTE: Varieties exist.

BRONZE

KM#	Date	Mintage	Fine	VF	XF	Unc
422	1914	2.500	7.50	20.00	45.00	235.00
	1915	11.424	1.50	5.00	16.00	145.00
	1916	2.860	15.00	35.00	175.00	675.00
	1917	.800	75.00	175.00	375.00	800.00
	1918	1.332	37.50	90.00	225.00	600.00
	1919	.400	135.00	185.00	300.00	900.00
	1920	5.920	3.50	8.00	45.00	225.00
	1921	2.080	11.00	25.00	65.00	250.00
	1924	.780	40.00	90.00	250.00	600.00
	1925	4.040	5.00	12.00	40.00	125.00
	1926	3.160	6.00	12.00	45.00	150.00
	1927	3.600	4.00	8.00	30.00	150.00
	1928 large date	1.740	9.00	16.00	65.00	175.00
	1928 small date	Inc. Ab.	20.00	40.00	90.00	300.00
	1929	2.400	6.00	10.00	35.00	145.00
	1930 large oval 0 in date	2.600	5.00	9.00	35.00	175.00
	1930 small square 0 in date	Inc. Ab.	45.00	95.00	200.00	550.00
	1931	—	500.00	700.00	1150.	3000.
	1933	8.000	1.25	2.00	3.00	25.00
	1934	10.000	1.25	1.75	2.25	22.50
	1935	21.980	.75	1.25	3.00	17.50

NOTE: Varieties exist.

COPPER-NICKEL

423	1936	46.700	.25	.50	1.00	6.50
	1937	49.060	.25	.40	1.00	5.50
	1938	3.340	3.25	4.50	6.25	42.00
	1940	22.800	.60	.90	1.50	7.00
	1942	7.100	1.00	1.50	2.75	24.00

BRONZE
'Josefa' Ortiz de Dominguez

424	1942	.900	6.25	22.50	65.00	300.00
	1943	54.660	.30	.50	.75	3.75
	1944	53.463	.10	.15	.20	.75
	1945	44.262	.15	.25	.30	.85
	1946	49.054	.35	.50	.90	2.00
	1951	50.758	.50	.75	1.00	3.25
	1952	17.674	1.00	1.50	2.50	9.00
	1953	31.568	.30	.50	1.00	2.75
	1954	58.680	.30	.50	1.00	2.75
	1955	31.114	1.00	1.25	2.00	11.00

COPPER-NICKEL
'White Josefa'

425	1950	5.700	.50	.75	1.50	6.00

BRASS

426	1954 dot	—	5.00	9.00	20.00	200.00
	1954 w/o dot	—	5.00	8.00	16.00	175.00
	1955	12.136	.60	.90	1.75	10.00
	1956	60.216	.10	.15	.20	.80
	1957	55.288	.10	.15	.20	.90
	1958	104.624	.10	.15	.20	.40
	1959	106.000	.10	.15	.20	.90
	1960	99.144	—	.10	.15	.25
	1961	61.136	—	.10	.15	.40

United States / MEXICO 1271

KM#	Date	Mintage	Fine	VF	XF	Unc
426	1962	47.232	—	.10	.15	.30
	1963	156.680	—	—	.10	.15
	1964	71.168	—	—	.10	.15
	1965	155.720	—	—	.10	.15
	1966	124.944	—	—	.10	.30
	1967	118.816	—	—	.10	.25
	1968	189.588	—	—	.10	.25
	1969	210.492	—	—	.10	.25

COPPER-NICKEL (OMS)

| 426a | 1962 | — | — | 300.00 | — | — |

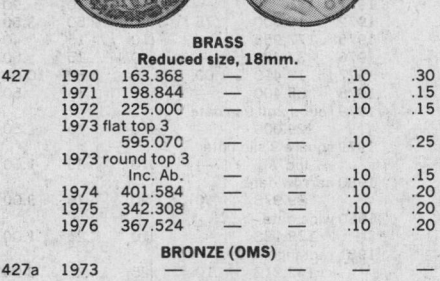

BRASS
Reduced size, 18mm.

427	1970	163.368	—	—	.10	.30
	1971	198.844	—	—	.10	.15
	1972	225.000	—	—	.10	.15
	1973 flat top 3					
		595.070	—	—	.10	.25
	1973 round top 3					
		Inc. Ab.	—	—	.10	.15
	1974	401.584	—	—	.10	.20
	1975	342.308	—	—	.10	.20
	1976	367.524	—	—	.10	.20

BRONZE (OMS)

| 427a | 1973 | — | — | — | — | — |

10 CENTAVOS

2.5000 g, .800 SILVER, .0643 oz ASW

428	1905	3.920	4.00	6.00	7.50	35.00
	1906	8.410	2.00	4.00	6.00	17.50
	1907/6	5.950	20.00	50.00	100.00	200.00
	1907	Inc. Ab.	3.00	6.00	8.25	20.00
	1909	2.620	5.00	9.00	12.00	55.00
	1910/00	3.450	5.00	10.00	17.50	80.00
	1910	Inc. Ab.	5.50	7.50	10.00	22.50
	1911	2.550	—	7.50	10.00	37.50
	1912	1.350	8.00	10.00	12.50	115.00
	1913/2	1.990	4.00	7.00	10.00	32.50
	1913	Inc. Ab.	4.00	7.00	10.00	32.50
	1914	3.110	2.00	4.50	6.75	14.00

NOTE: Varieties exist.

1.8125 g, .800 SILVER, .0466 oz ASW
Reduced size, 15mm.

| 429 | 1919 | 8.360 | 6.00 | 9.50 | 17.50 | 75.00 |

NOTE: Varieties exist.

BRONZE

430	1919	1.232	20.00	40.00	80.00	375.00
	1920	6.612	8.50	15.00	45.00	350.00
	1921	2.255	15.00	35.00	75.00	750.00
	1935	5.970	8.00	17.00	30.00	95.00

1.6600 g, .720 SILVER, .0384 oz ASW

431	1925/15	5.350	7.50	15.00	30.00	100.00
	1925/19	I.A.	15.00	30.00	85.00	160.00
	1925/3	Inc. Ab.	10.00	20.00	35.00	90.00
	1925	Inc. Ab.	1.25	2.50	4.00	30.00
	1926/16	2.650	15.00	30.00	60.00	150.00
	1926	Inc. Ab.	1.50	3.00	7.25	50.00
	1927	2.810	1.25	2.25	3.50	20.00
	1928	5.270	1.00	1.50	2.50	11.00
	1930	2.000	1.50	3.00	6.00	22.50
	1933	5.000	1.50	2.00	3.00	7.50
	1934	8.000	1.00	1.25	2.00	9.50
	1935	3.500	2.50	3.50	5.00	12.50

NOTE: Varieties exist.

COPPER-NICKEL

KM#	Date	Mintage	Fine	VF	XF	Unc
432	1936	33.030	.20	.40	.90	7.00
	1937	3.000	1.25	5.00	15.00	215.00
	1938	3.650	.75	1.50	3.00	40.00
	1939	6.920	.50	1.00	2.00	20.00
	1940	12.300	.20	.50	1.25	5.00
	1942	14.380	.40	.75	1.75	7.00
	1945	9.558	.20	.35	.60	3.50
	1946	46.230	.15	.25	.50	2.50

BRONZE
Benito Juarez

433	1955	1.818	.60	1.00	3.50	22.50
	1956	5.255	.20	.50	2.25	20.00
	1957	11.925	.15	.20	.50	5.00
	1959	26.140	.10	.15	.20	.50
	1966	5.873	—	.10	.15	.45
	1967	32.318	—	.10	.15	.40

COPPER-NICKEL
Variety I
Rev: 5 full rows of kernels, sharp stem.

434.1	1974	6.000	—	—	.10	.40
	1975	5.550	—	.10	.15	.45
	1976	7.680	—	.10	.20	.40
	1977	144.650	.25	.50	2.00	3.50
	1978	271.870	—	—	2.00	3.50
	1979 wide date					
		375.660	—	—	.10	.45
	1979 narrow date					
		Inc. Ab.	—	.10	.50	2.00
	1980	21.290	.50	.75	2.00	4.00

Variety II
Rev: 5 full, plus 1 partial row at left, blunt stem.

434.2	1977	Inc. Ab.	—	—	.10	.25
	1978	Inc. Ab.	—	—	.10	.25

20 CENTAVOS

5.0000 g, .800 SILVER, .1286 oz ASW

435	1905	2.565	6.50	10.00	17.50	150.00
	1906	6.860	—	7.00	12.00	55.00
	1907 straight 7					
		9.435	7.00	10.00	15.00	50.00
	1907 curved 7					
		Inc. Ab.	5.00	8.00	12.00	50.00
	1908	.350	25.00	70.00	150.00	1500.
	1910	1.135	6.00	11.00	17.50	75.00
	1911	1.150	7.00	13.00	21.00	125.00
	1912	.625	17.50	35.00	75.00	325.00
	1913	1.000	7.00	14.00	21.00	85.00
	1914	1.500	5.00	10.00	15.00	60.00

NOTE: Varieties exist.

3.6250 g, .800 SILVER, .0932 oz ASW
Reduced size, 19mm.

| 436 | 1919 | 4.155 | 12.50 | 30.00 | 50.00 | 200.00 |

BRONZE

KM#	Date	Mintage	Fine	VF	XF	Unc
437	1920	4.835	12.50	35.00	80.00	400.00
	1935	20.000	2.50	5.00	8.00	65.00

NOTE: Varieties exist.

3.3300 g, .720 SILVER, .0770 oz ASW

438	1920	3.710	2.50	5.00	12.00	135.00
	1921	6.160	2.50	5.00	12.00	80.00
	1925	1.450	5.50	9.00	21.00	135.00
	1926/5	1.465	7.50	12.50	35.00	300.00
	1926	Inc. Ab.	2.50	5.00	10.00	100.00
	1927	1.405	2.00	4.00	7.50	90.00
	1928	3.630	1.50	2.50	3.50	15.00
	1930	1.000	2.00	3.50	7.00	25.00
	1933	2.500	1.50	2.50	3.25	12.00
	1934	2.500	1.50	2.50	3.25	12.00
	1935	2.460	1.50	2.50	3.25	10.00
	1937	10.000	1.00	1.50	2.50	4.50
	1939	8.800	1.00	1.50	2.25	4.00
	1940	3.000	1.00	1.50	2.25	4.00
	1941	5.740	1.00	1.50	2.00	3.50
	1942	12.460	1.00	1.50	2.00	3.50
	1943	3.955	1.00	1.50	2.00	3.50

NOTE: Varieties exist.

BRONZE

439	1943	46.350	.30	.60	3.00	18.00
	1944	83.650	.25	.50	.75	9.00
	1945	26.801	.20	.40	1.75	10.00
	1946	25.695	.25	.45	1.25	6.00
	1951	11.385	1.50	3.00	6.50	70.00
	1952	6.560	1.25	2.00	4.50	20.00
	1953	26.948	.20	.30	.50	6.50
	1954	40.108	.20	.30	.50	9.00
	1955	16.950	1.50	3.00	6.50	55.00

440	1955 Inc. KM439	.40	.75	1.75	10.00
	1956	22.431	.15	.25	.35	3.50
	1957	13.455	.20	.50	1.00	9.00
	1959	6.017	2.00	4.50	9.00	50.00
	1960	39.756	.10	.15	.20	.75
	1963	14.869	.10	.20	.30	.90
	1964	28.654	—	.10	.15	.50
	1965	74.162	—	.10	.15	.65
	1966	43.745	.10	.15	.20	.70
	1967	46.487	.10	.15	.20	.60
	1968	15.477	.10	.25	.90	
	1969	63.647	.10	.15	.20	.85
	1970	76.287	.10	.15	.20	.60
	1971	49.892	.10	.25	.35	1.50

| 441 | 1971 Inc. KM440 | .10 | .15 | .25 | .75 |

1272

KM#	Date	Mintage	Fine	VF	XF	Unc
441	1973	78.398	—	.10	.15	.50
	1974	34.200	.10	.20	.40	1.00

COPPER-NICKEL
Madero

442	1974	112.000	—	—	.10	.25
	1975	611.000	—	.10	.15	.25
	1976	394.000	—	.10	.15	.25
	1977	394.350	—	.10	.15	.30
	1978	527.950	—	.10	.15	.25
	1979	524.615	—	—	.10	.25
	1980	326.500	—	—	.10	.40
	1981 open 8					
		106.205	—	.10	.25	1.00
	1981 closed 8					
		248.500	—	.10	.25	1.00
	1982/1286.855	—	—	Rare		
	1982	Inc. Ab.	—	.10	.25	1.00
	1983	100.930	—	.10	.25	1.75
	1983	998 pcs.	—	—	Proof	45.00

BRONZE
Olmec Culture

491	1983	260.000	—	.10	.25	.90
	1983	50 pcs.	—	—	Proof	185.00
	1984	180.320	—	.10	.25	1.50

25 CENTAVOS

3.3300 g, .300 SILVER, .0321 oz ASW

443	1950	77.060	—	BV	.50	2.00
	1951	41.172	—	BV	.50	1.75
	1952	29.264	—	BV	.60	2.00
	1953	38.144	—	BV	.50	1.65

COPPER-NICKEL
Francisco Madero

444	1964	20.686	—	—	.10	.25
	1966	.180	.25	.50	1.00	2.75

50 CENTAVOS

12.5000 g, .800 SILVER, .3215 oz ASW

445	1905	2.446	7.50	15.00	22.50	150.00
	1906	16.966	4.00	6.00	10.00	25.00
	1907 straight 7					
		33.761	3.50	5.75	8.50	25.00
	1907 curved 7					
		Inc. Ab.	3.00	5.00	7.50	23.00
	1908	.488	40.00	75.00	135.00	575.00
	1912	3.736	4.50	7.50	12.50	45.00
	1913/0710.510	15.00	25.00	50.00	175.00
	1913/2	7.50	12.50	25.00	50.00
	1913	Inc. Ab.	3.00	6.50	10.00	25.00
	1914	7.710	3.00	6.50	10.00	25.00
	1916	.480	30.00	60.00	75.00	225.00
	1917	37.112	3.00	5.00	7.00	17.50
	1918	1.320	30.00	60.00	100.00	250.00

NOTE: Varieties exist.

Reduced size, 27mm.

KM#	Date	Mintage	Fine	VF	XF	Unc
446	1918/7	2.760	—	—	625.00	1250.
	1918	Inc. Ab.	12.50	20.00	55.00	325.00
	1919	29.670	5.00	10.00	20.00	100.00

8.3300 g, .720 SILVER, .1928 oz ASW

447	1919	10.200	4.00	8.50	17.50	85.00
	1920	27.166	3.00	6.00	10.00	70.00
	1921	21.864	3.00	6.00	10.00	75.00
	1925	3.280	6.00	10.00	25.00	110.00
	1937	20.000	2.00	4.00	6.00	7.50
	1938	.100	15.00	55.00	80.00	300.00
	1939	10.440	2.00	4.00	6.50	9.00
	1942	.800	2.00	4.00	5.00	8.00
	1943	41.512	—	BV	3.50	5.50
	1944	55.806	—	BV	3.50	5.50
	1945	56.766	—	BV	3.50	5.00

NOTE: Varieties exist.

7.9730 g, .420 SILVER, .1076 oz ASW

448	1935	70.800	BV	1.50	3.00	5.00

6.6600 g, .300 SILVER, .0642 oz ASW
Cuauhtemoc

449	1950	13.570	BV	1.00	2.00	3.75
	1951	3.650	BV	1.00	2.00	4.00

BRONZE

450	1955	3.502	.50	1.00	2.50	22.00
	1956	34.643	.25	.75	1.25	2.75
	1957	9.675	.20	.40	.60	4.00
	1959	4.540	.10	.20	.50	1.25

COPPER-NICKEL

451	1964	43.806	—	—	.10	.25
	1965	14.326	—	—	.10	.30
	1966	1.726	.10	.20	.40	1.10
	1967	55.144	—	—	.10	.50
	1968	80.438	—	—	.10	.50
	1969	87.640	—	.10	.20	.75

Obv: Stylized eagle.

KM#	Date	Mintage	Fine	VF	XF	Unc
452	1970	76.236	—	—	.10	1.00
	1971	125.288	—	—	.10	.90
	1972	16.000	.75	1.00	2.50	3.50
	1975	177.958	—	.10	.15	.40
	1976	37.480	—	—	.10	.50
	1977	12.410	1.00	3.50	5.50	10.00
	1978	85.400	—	—	.10	.50
	1979 round 2nd 9 in date					
		229.000	—	—	.10	.50
	1979 square 9's in date					
		Inc. Ab.	—	.10	.35	1.60
	1980 narrow date					
		89.978	.10	.20	.75	3.00
	1980 wide date					
		178.188	—	—	.10	1.00
	1981 rectangular 9					
		142.212	.10	.25	.85	3.00
	1981 round 9					
		Inc. Ab.	—	.10	.50	1.00
	1982	45.474	—	.10	.25	1.25
	1983	90.318	—	.10	.50	2.00
	1983	998 pcs.	—	—	Proof	45.00

STAINLESS STEEL
Palenque

492	1983	66.148	—	—	.10	.75
	1983	50 pcs.	—	—	Proof	185.00
	1984	33.392	—	—	.10	.50
	1985		—	—	.10	.50

UN (1) PESO

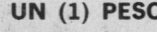

27.0700 g, .903 SILVER, .7859 oz ASW
'Caballito'

453	1910	3.814	22.50	35.00	50.00	185.00
	1911 long lower left ray on rev.					
		1.227	30.00	40.00	70.00	275.00
	1911 short lower left ray on rev.					
		Inc. Ab.	60.00	125.00	175.00	550.00
	1912	.322	40.00	80.00	100.00	325.00
	1913/2	2.880	25.00	40.00	60.00	275.00
	1913	Inc. Ab.	22.50	35.00	70.00	195.00
	1914	.120	400.00	530.00	800.00	2250.00

18.1300 g, .800 SILVER, .4663 oz ASW

KM#	Date	Mintage	Fine	VF	XF	Unc
454	1918	3.050	20.00	35.00	100.00	2500.
	1919	6.151	12.50	22.50	50.00	1500.

16.6600 g, .720 SILVER, .3856 oz ASW

455	1920/10	8.830	20.00	30.00	50.00	250.00
	1920	Inc. Ab.	4.00	6.00	15.00	150.00
	1921	5.480	4.00	6.00	15.00	150.00
	1922	33.620	BV	4.00	5.50	24.00
	1923	35.280	BV	4.00	5.50	24.00
	1924	33.060	BV	4.00	5.50	24.00
	1925	9.160	BV	5.00	11.00	40.00
	1926	28.840	BV	4.00	5.50	22.00
	1927	5.060	BV	4.00	9.00	40.00
	1932	50.770	BV	3.50	4.50	6.00
	1933/2	43.920	10.00	15.00	25.00	80.00
	1933	Inc. Ab.	BV	3.50	4.50	6.00
	1934	22.070	BV	3.50	4.50	10.00
	1935	8.050	BV	3.50	5.50	12.00
	1938	30.000	BV	3.50	4.00	7.50
	1940	20.000	BV	3.50	4.00	6.50
	1943	47.662	BV	3.50	4.00	5.50
	1944	39.522	BV	3.50	4.00	5.50
	1945	37.300	BV	3.50	4.00	5.50

NOTE: Varieties exist.

14.0000 g, .500 SILVER, .2250 oz ASW
Morelos

456	1947	61.460	BV	1.50	3.00	5.00
	1948	22.915	BV	2.00	4.00	5.00
	1949	*4.000	—	—	1400.	2400.
	1949	—	—	—	Proof	4000.

*NOTE: Not released for circulation.

13.3300 g, .300 SILVER, .1285 oz ASW
Morelos

457	1950	3.287	BV	1.75	2.25	6.00

16.0000 g, .100 SILVER, .0514 oz ASW
Juarez-Constitution

KM#	Date	Mintage	Fine	VF	XF	Unc
458	1957	.500	1.25	3.00	4.50	14.00

Morelos

459	1957	28.273	—	BV	.60	2.50
	1958	41.899	—	BV	.80	2.00
	1959	27.369	—	BV	1.50	5.00
	1960	26.259	—	BV	.80	3.50
	1961	52.601	—	BV	.80	2.50
	1962	61.094	—	BV	.60	2.25
	1963	26.394	—	BV	.60	1.50
	1964	15.615	—	BV	.60	1.50
	1965	5.004	—	BV	.60	2.00
	1966	30.998	—	BV	.60	2.00
	1967	9.308	—	BV	.60	3.00

NOTE: Varieties exist.

COPPER-NICKEL

460	1970 narrow date					
		102.715	.10	.15	.35	.65
	1970 wide date					
		Inc. Ab.	.15	.30	.50	1.25
	1971	426.222	.10	.15	.20	.50
	1972	120.000	.10	.15	.20	.40
	1974	63.700	.10	.20	.25	.70

1975 tall narrow date
205.979 .10 .15 .20 .60

	1975 short wide date					
		Inc. Ab.	.10	.15	.20	.75
	1976	94.489	.10	.15	.20	.50
	1977 thick date					
		94.364	.10	.15	.20	1.00
	1977 thin date					
		Inc. Ab.	.25	1.00	2.25	12.50
	1978 closed 8					
		208.300	.10	.15	.35	1.00
	1978 open 8					
		55.140	.20	.60	.80	1.50
	1979 thin date					
		117.884	.10	.15	.20	.70
	1979 thick date					
		Inc. Ab.	.15	.40	.50	1.00
	1980 closed 8					
		318.800	—	.15	.25	.80
	1980 open 8					
		23.865	.25	.50	1.00	6.00
	1981 closed 8					
		413.349	.10	.20	.25	.75
	1981 open 8					
		58.616	.25	.50	1.00	5.00
	1982	235.000	.20	.50	1.00	2.25
	1983	100.000	.10	.20	.30	1.50
	1983	1,048	—	—	Proof	50.00
	1984 thin date					
		47.358	.10	.20	.35	1.75

KM#	Date	Mintage	Fine	VF	XF	Unc
460	1984 thick date		.50	1.00	2.00	5.00
		Inc. Ab.				

STAINLESS STEEL
Morelos

496	1984	722.802	—	—	.10	1.00
	1985	985.000	—	—	.10	.60
	1986	740.000	—	—	.10	.65
	1987	—	—	—	.10	.60

DOS (2) PESOS

1.6666 g, .900 GOLD, .0482 oz AGW

461	1919	1.670	—	BV	27.50	32.50
	1920	4.282	—	BV	27.50	40.00
	1944	.010	27.50	35.00	50.00	65.00
	1945	*.140	—	—	BV + 20%	
	1946	.168	30.00	50.00	55.00	100.00
	1947	.025	27.50	40.00	50.00	65.00
	1948	.045		no specimens known		

*NOTE: During 1951-1972 a total of 4,590,493 pieces were restruck, most likely dated 1945.

26.6667 g, .900 SILVER, .7717 oz ASW
Independence Commemorative

462	1921	1.278	25.00	35.00	60.00	450.00

DOS Y MEDIO (2-1/2) PESOS

2.0833 g, .900 GOLD, .0602 oz AGW

463	1918	1.704	—	BV	32.50	45.00
	1919	.984	—	BV	32.50	55.00
	1920/10	.607	—	BV	65.00	100.00
	1920	Inc. Ab.	—	BV	32.50	55.00
	1944	.020	32.50	40.00	50.00	75.00
	1945	*.180	—	—	BV + 18%	
	1946	.163	32.50	40.00	50.00	60.00
	1947	.024	200.00	250.00	300.00	550.00
	1948	.063	32.50	40.00	50.00	65.00

*NOTE: During 1951-1972 a total of 5,025,087 pieces were restruck, most likely dated 1945.

CINCO (5) PESOS

4.1666 g, .900 GOLD, .1205 oz AGW

KM#	Date	Mintage	Fine	VF	XF	Unc
464	1905	.018	100.00	150.00	225.00	700.00
	1906	4.638	—	BV	60.00	80.00
	1907	1.088	—	BV	60.00	80.00
	1910	.100	BV	60.00	70.00	90.00
	1918/7	.609	60.00	65.00	75.00	90.00
	1918	Inc. Ab.	—	BV	60.00	80.00
	1919	.506	—	BV	60.00	80.00
	1920	2.385	—	BV	60.00	75.00
	1955	*.048	—	—	BV + 11%

*NOTE: During 1955-1972 a total of 1,767,645 pieces were restruck, most likely dated 1955.

30.0000 g, .900 SILVER, .8681 oz ASW
Cuauhtemoc

465	1947	5.110	—	BV	7.50	11.50
	1948	26.740	—	BV	7.00	10.50

27.7800 g, .720 SILVER, .6431 oz ASW
Southeast Railroad

466	1950	.200	20.00	30.00	40.00	60.00

Miguel Hidalgo y Costilla

467	1951	4.958	—	BV	6.00	9.00
	1952	9.595	—	BV	6.00	8.00
	1953	20.376	—	BV	5.50	8.00
	1954	.030	—	50.00	80.00	100.00

Bicentennial of Hidalgo Birth

KM#	Date	Mintage	Fine	VF	XF	Unc
468	1953	1.000	—	BV	7.50	10.00

18.0500 g, .720 SILVER, .4178 oz ASW
Reduced size, 36mm.

469	1955	4.271	BV	4.00	5.00	6.50
	1956	4.596	BV	4.00	5.00	6.50
	1957	3.464	BV	4.00	5.00	6.50

Juarez-Constitution

470	1957	.200	4.00	5.50	8.50	13.00

Centennial of Carranza Birth

471	1959	1.000	—	BV	5.00	9.50

Small date / Large date
COPPER-NICKEL
Guerrero

472	1971	28.457	.10	—	.50	.75	2.50
	1972	75.000	.10	—	.50	.75	2.00
	1973	19.405	1.00	—	1.50	3.00	6.00
	1974	34.500	.10	—	.20	.50	1.75
	1976 small date						
		26.121	.25	—	1.00	2.25	4.50
	1976 large date						
		121.550	—	—	.10	.50	1.50
	1977	102.000	—	—	.10	.75	1.50
	1978	25.700	.25	—	.50	1.50	6.00

KM#	Date	Mintage	Fine	VF	XF	Unc
485	1980	266.900	—	.10	.20	1.75
	1981	30.500	—	.10	.25	2.25
	1982	20.000	—	.10	.25	3.50
	1982	1,048	—	—	Proof	50.00
	1984	16.300	.50	1.00	2.00	4.00
	1985	76.900	.60	1.25	2.25	4.50

BRASS
Circulation Coinage

502	1985	30.000	—	—	.10	.50
	1988		—	—	.10	.35

DIEZ (10) PESOS

8.3333 g, .900 GOLD, .2411 oz AGW

473	1905	.039	120.00	135.00	150.00	225.00
	1906	2.949	—	BV	120.00	135.00
	1907	1.589	—	BV	120.00	135.00
	1908	.890	—	BV	120.00	135.00
	1910	.451	—	BV	120.00	135.00
	1916	.026	120.00	135.00	175.00	325.00
	1917	1.967	—	BV	120.00	135.00
	1919	.266	—	BV	120.00	135.00
	1920	.012	175.00	300.00	500.00	750.00
	1959	*.050	—	—	BV + 7%	

*NOTE: During 1961-1972 a total of 954,983 pieces were restruck, most likely dated 1959.

28.8800 g, .900 SILVER, .8357 oz ASW
Hidalgo

474	1955	.585	—	—	BV	7.50	13.50
	1956	3.535	—	—	BV	6.50	12.00

1275 United States / MEXICO

Juarez-Constitution

KM#	Date	Mintage	Fine	VF	XF	Unc
475	1957	.100	10.00	15.00	30.00	50.00

Hidalgo-Madero

476	1960	1.000	—	BV	7.00	10.00

COPPER-NICKEL
Hidalgo
Thin flan, 1.6mm.

477.1	1974	3.900	.25	.50	1.75	3.75
	1974	—	—	—	Proof	600.00
	1975	1.000	.35	1.00	3.50	6.75
	1976	74.500	.10	.25	.75	1.75
	1977	79.620	.10	.30	1.00	2.25

Thick flan, 2.3mm.

477.2	1978	124.850	.10	.35	1.00	2.50
	1979	57.200	.10	.35	1.00	2.50
	1980	55.200	—	.10	.50	2.25
	1981	222.768	—	.10	.50	2.25
	1982	151.770	—	.10	.60	3.00
	1982	1,048	—	—	Proof	55.00
	1985	58.000	—	—	.75	4.75

STAINLESS STEEL
Miguel Hidalgo y Costilla

512	1985	257.000	—	—	.15	.65
	1986	392.000	—	—	.15	.65
	1987	—	—	—	.10	.50
	1988	—	—	—	.10	.35
	1989	—	—	—	.10	.35

VEINTE (20) PESOS

16.6666 g, .900 GOLD, .4823 oz AGW

KM#	Date	Mintage	Fine	VF	XF	Unc
478	1917	.852	—	BV	230.00	265.00
	1918	2.831	—	BV	230.00	275.00
	1919	1.094	—	BV	230.00	265.00
	1920/10	.462	—	BV	230.00	275.00
	1920	Inc. Ab.	—	BV	230.00	275.00
	1921/11	.922	—	BV	230.00	285.00
	1921	Inc. Ab.	—	BV	230.00	265.00
	1959	*.013				BV + 4%

*NOTE: During 1960-1971 a total of 1,158,414 pieces were restruck, most likely dated 1959.

COPPER-NICKEL

486	1980	84.900	—	.10	.50	2.50
	1981	250.573	—	.10	.50	2.75
	1982	236.892	—	.10	.75	3.50
	1982	1,048	—	—	Proof	60.00
	1984	55.000	—	—	.75	3.00

BRASS
Guadalupe Victoria, First President

508	1985 wide date					
		25.000	—	.10	.20	1.25
	1985 narrow date					
		Inc. Ab.	—	.10	.25	2.00
	1986	10.000	—	—	.10	.45
	1988	—	—	—	.10	.45

VEINTICINCO (25) PESOS

22.5000 g, .720 SILVER, .5209 oz ASW
Type I, rings aligned.

479.1	1968	27.182	—	—	BV	4.00	6.50

Type II, center ring low.

KM#	Date	Mintage	Fine	VF	XF	Unc
479.2	1968	Inc. Ab.	—	BV	5.00	9.50

Normal tongue   **Long curved tongue**
Type III, center rings low.
Snake with long curved tongue.

479.3	1968	Inc. Ab.	—	BV	6.00	10.50

Benito Juarez

480	1972	2.000	—	BV	4.75	8.00

7.7760 g, .720 SILVER, .1800 oz ASW, 24mm
1986 World Cup Soccer Games

497	1985	.354	—	—	—	8.00
	1986	—	—	—	—	8.00

8.4060 g, .925 SILVER, .2500 oz ASW
Rev: W/o fineness statement.

497a	1985	—	—	—	Proof	16.00
	1986	—	—	—	Proof	16.00

7.7760 g, .720 SILVER, .1800 oz ASW
1986 World Cup Soccer Games

503	1985	.190	—	—	—	8.00

8.4060 g, .925 SILVER, .2500 oz ASW
Rev: W/o fineness statement.

503a	1985	.277	—	—	Proof	16.00

7.7760 g, .720 SILVER, .1800 oz ASW
1986 World Cup Soccer Games

514	1985	.234	—	—	—	8.00

8.4060 g, .925 SILVER, .2500 oz ASW
Rev: W/o fineness statement.

514a	1985	Inc. Ab.	—	—	Proof	16.00

United States / MEXICO 1276

7.7760 g, .720 SILVER, .1800 oz ASW
1986 World Cup Soccer Games

KM#	Date	Mintage	Fine	VF	XF	Unc
519	1986	—	—	—	—	8.00

8.4060 g, .925 SILVER, .2500 oz ASW
Rev: W/o fineness statement.

| 519a | 1986 | — | — | — | Proof | 16.00 |

50 PESOS

41.6666 g, .900 GOLD, 1.2057 oz AGW

481	1921	.180	—	—	BV	775.00
	1922	.463	—	—	BV	650.00
	1923	.432	—	—	BV	650.00
	1924	.439	—	—	BV	650.00
	1925	.716	—	—	BV	650.00
	1926	.600	—	—	BV	650.00
	1927	.606	—	—	BV	650.00
	1928	.538	—	—	BV	650.00
	1929	.458	—	—	BV	650.00
	1930	.372	—	—	BV	650.00
	1931	.137	—	—	BV	700.00
	1944	.593	—	—	BV	650.00
	1945	1.012	—	—	BV	650.00
	1946	1.588	—	—	BV	650.00
	1947	.309	—	—	BV + 3%	
	1947	—	—	—	Specimen	6500.

NOTE: During 1949-1972 a total of 3,975,654 pieces were restruck, most likely dated 1947.

COPPER-NICKEL

490	1982	222.890	—	—	.75	3.25
	1983	45.000	—	1.00	2.00	4.50
	1983	1.048	—	—	Proof	65.00
	1984	73.537	—	.75	1.25	3.50

Benito Juarez

495	1984	94.216	—	.25	1.00	2.00
	1985	296.000	—	.25	.75	2.00
	1986	50.000	—	—	—	2.50
	1987	—	—	—	—	1.25

STAINLESS STEEL

| 495a | 1988 | — | — | — | .10 | .60 |

15.5520 g, .720 SILVER, .3601 oz ASW
1986 World Cup Soccer Games

KM#	Date	Mintage	Fine	VF	XF	Unc
498	1985	.347	—	—	—	11.00
	1986	—	—	—	—	11.00

16.8130 g, .925 SILVER, .5000 oz ASW
Rev: W/o fineness statement.

| 498a | 1985 | .010 | — | — | Proof | 24.00 |
| | 1986 | — | — | — | Proof | 24.00 |

15.5520 g, .720 SILVER, .3601 oz ASW
1986 World Cup Soccer Games

| 504 | 1985 | .347 | — | — | — | 11.00 |

16.8130 g, .925 SILVER, .5000 oz ASW
Rev: W/o fineness statement.

| 504a | 1985 | — | — | — | Proof | 24.00 |

15.5520 g, .720 SILVER, .3601 oz ASW
1986 World Cup Soccer Games

| 515 | 1985 | .234 | — | — | — | 11.00 |

16.8130 g, .925 SILVER, .5000 oz ASW
Rev: W/o fineness statement.

| 515a | 1985 | Inc. Ab. | — | — | Proof | 24.00 |

15.5520 g, .720 SILVER, .3601 oz ASW
1986 World Cup Soccer Games

| 523 | 1986 | .190 | — | — | — | 11.00 |

16.8130 g, .925 SILVER, .5000 oz ASW
Rev: W/o fineness statement.

| 523a | 1986 | Inc. Ab. | — | — | Proof | 24.00 |

15.5500 g, .999 SILVER, .5000 oz ASW
50th Anniversary of Nationalization of Oil Industry

| 532 | 1988 | — | — | — | — | 7.50 |

CIEN (100) PESOS

Low 7's   High 7's

27.7700 g, .720 SILVER, .6429 oz ASW

KM#	Date	Mintage	Fine	VF	XF	Unc
483	1977 low 7's, sloping shoulder					
		5.225	—	BV	6.50	9.50
	1977 high 7's, sloping shoulder					
		Inc. Ab.	—	BV	7.50	12.00

484	1977 date in line, redesigned higher right shoulder					
		Inc. KM483	—	BV	6.00	7.50
	1978	9.879	—	BV	5.00	8.25
	1979	.784	—	BV	6.00	9.00
	1979	—	—	—	Proof	500.00

ALUMINUM-BRONZE
Venustiana Carranza

493	1984	227.809	—	.20	.50	2.50
	1985	377.423	—	.15	.40	2.00
	1986	43.000	—	.75	1.25	4.00
	1987	—	—	—	.20	1.50
	1988	—	—	—	.20	1.00

31.1030 g, .720 SILVER, .7201 oz ASW
1986 World Cup Soccer Games

| 499 | 1985 | .302 | — | — | — | 16.50 |

United States / MEXICO 1277

33.6250 g, .925 SILVER, 1.0000 oz ASW
Rev: W/o fineness statement.

KM#	Date	Mintage	Fine	VF	XF	Unc
499a	1985	9,006	—	—	Proof	35.00

31.1030 g, .720 SILVER, .7201 oz ASW
1986 World Cup Soccer Games

| 505 | 1985 | .302 | — | — | — | 16.50 |

33.6250 g, .925 SILVER, 1.0000 oz ASW
Rev: W/o fineness statement.

| 505a | 1985 | 9,006 | — | — | Proof | 35.00 |

31.1030 g, .720 SILVER, .7201 oz ASW
1986 World Cup Soccer Games
Obv: Similar to KM#499.

| 521 | 1986 | .208 | — | — | — | 16.50 |

33.6250 g, .925 SILVER, 1.0000 oz ASW
Rev: W/o fineness statement.

| 521a | 1986 | Inc. Ab. | — | — | Proof | 35.00 |

31.1030 g, .720 SILVER, .7201 oz ASW
1986 World Cup Soccer Games
Obv: Similar to KM#499.

| 524 | 1986 | .190 | — | — | — | 16.50 |

33.6250 g, .925 SILVER, 1.0000 oz ASW
Rev: W/o fineness statement.

| 524a | 1986 | Inc. Ab. | — | — | Proof | 35.00 |

31.1030 g, .720 SILVER, .7201 oz ASW
World Wildlife Fund

KM#	Date	Mintage	Fine	VF	XF	Unc
537	1987	*.030	—	—	—	25.00

31.1030 g, .999 SILVER, 1.0000 oz ASW
50th Anniversary of Nationalization of Oil Industry

| 533 | 1988 | — | — | — | — | 12.50 |

200 PESOS

COPPER-NICKEL
175th Anniversary of Independence

| 509 | 1985 | 75.000 | — | — | .25 | 3.00 |

75th Anniversary of 1910 Revolution

| 510 | 1985 | 98.590 | — | — | .25 | 2.00 |

1986 World Cup Soccer Games

| 525 | 1986 | 50.000 | — | — | .25 | 2.00 |

62.2060 g, .999 SILVER, 2.0000 oz ASW
1986 World Cup Soccer Games

KM#	Date	Mintage	Fine	VF	XF	Unc
526	1986	—	—	—	Proof	50.00

250 PESOS

8.6400 g, .900 GOLD, .2500 oz AGW
1986 World Cup Soccer Games
Obv: Eagle facing left w/snake in beak.

| 500.1 | 1985 | .100 | — | — | — | 170.00 |
| | 1986 | — | — | — | — | 170.00 |

Rev: W/o fineness statement.

| 500.2 | 1985 | 4,506 | — | — | Proof | 225.00 |
| | 1986 | — | — | — | Proof | 225.00 |

1986 World Cup Soccer Games

| 506.1 | 1985 | .088 | — | — | — | 175.00 |

Rev: W/o fineness statement.

| 506.2 | 1985 | — | — | — | Proof | 225.00 |

500 PESOS

17.2800 g, .900 GOLD, .5000 oz AGW
1986 World Cup Soccer Games
Obv: Eagle facing left w/snake in beak.

| 501.1 | 1985 | .102 | — | — | — | 350.00 |
| | 1986 | — | — | — | — | 350.00 |

Rev: W/o fineness statement.

| 501.2 | 1985 | 5,506 | — | — | Proof | 450.00 |
| | 1986 | — | — | — | Proof | 450.00 |

1278 United States / MEXICO

1986 World Cup Soccer Games

KM#	Date	Mintage	Fine	VF	XF	Unc
507.1	1985	—	—	—	—	350.00

Rev: W/o fineness statement.

| 507.2 | 1985 | — | — | — | Proof | 450.00 |

33.4500 g, .925 SILVER, 1.0000 oz ASW
75th Anniversary of 1910 Revolution

| 511 | 1985 | .040 | — | — | Proof | 40.00 |

COPPER-NICKEL
Madero

529	1986	20.000	—	—	.50	1.75
	1987	—	—	—	.50	1.75
	1988	—	—	—	.35	1.50

17.2800 g, .900 GOLD, .5000 oz AGW
50th Anniversary of Nationalization of Oil Industry
Similar to 5000 Pesos, KM#531.

| 534 | 1988 | — | — | — | — | 225.00 |

1000 PESOS

17.2800 g, .900 GOLD, .5000 oz AGW
175th Anniversary of Independence

| 513 | 1985 | — | — | — | — | Proof 475.00 |

31.1030 g, .999 GOLD, 1.0000 oz AGW
1986 World Cup Soccer Games
Similar to 200 Pesos, KM#526.

| 527 | 1986 | — | — | — | — | 675.00 |

34.5590 g, .900 GOLD, 1.0000 oz AGW
50th Anniversary of Nationalization of Oil Industry
Similar to 5000 Pesos, KM#531.

| 535 | 1988 | — | — | — | — | Proof 550.00 |

ALUMINUM-BRONZE
Juana de Asbaje

| 536 | 1988 | — | — | — | .75 | 1.75 |
| | 1989 | — | — | — | .75 | 1.75 |

2000 PESOS

62.2000 g, .999 GOLD, 2.0000 oz AGW
1986 World Cup Soccer Games
Similar to 200 Pesos, KM#526.

| 528 | 1986 | — | — | — | — | 1250. |

5000 PESOS

COPPER-NICKEL
50th Anniversary of Nationalization of Oil Industry

KM#	Date	Mintage	Fine	VF	XF	Unc
531	1988	—	—	—	2.75	4.50

SILVER BULLION ISSUES
ONZA TROY de PLATA
(Troy Ounce of Silver)

33.6250 g, .925 SILVER, 1.0000 oz ASW
One Troy ounce of pure silver

| M49a | 1949 | 1.000 | 10.00 | 12.50 | 17.50 | 30.00 |

Type 1. Obv: Wide spacing between DE MONEDA

| M49b.1 | 1978 | .280 | — | BV | 8.00 | 18.50 |

Type 2. Obv: Close spacing between DE MONEDA

| M49b.2 | 1978 | Inc. Ab. | — | — | BV | 11.00 |

Type 3. Rev: Left scale pan points to U in UNA.

| M49b.3 | 1979 | 4.508 | — | — | BV | 12.50 |

Type 4. Rev: Left scale pan points between U and N of UNA.

| M49b.4 | 1979 | Inc. Ab. | — | — | BV | 11.50 |

Type 5.

| M49b.5 | 1980 | 6.104 | — | — | BV | 11.50 |
| | 1980/70 | I.A. | — | — | BV | 15.00 |

LIBERTAD
(Onza Troy de Plata)

31.1000 g, .999 SILVER, 1.0000 oz ASW
Libertad

KM#	Date	Mintage	Fine	VF	XF	Unc
494	1982	1.050	—	—	BV	10.00
	1983	1.268	—	—	BV	10.00
	1983	998 pcs.	—	—	Proof	325.00
	1984	1.014	—	—	BV	10.00
	1985	2.017	—	—	BV	10.00
	1986	—	—	—	BV	10.00
	1986	.030	—	—	Proof	32.50
	1987	—	—	—	BV	10.00
	1987	.012	—	—	Proof	40.00
	1988	—	—	—	BV	10.00
	1989	—	—	—	BV	10.00

GOLD BULLION ISSUES
1/20 ONZA ORO PURO
(1/20 Ounce of Pure Gold)

1.7500 g, .900 GOLD, .0500 oz AGW
Obv: Winged Victory. Rev: Calendar stone.

| 530 | 1987 | — | — | — | — | BV + 30% |
| | 1988 | — | — | — | — | BV + 30% |

1/4 ONZA ORO PURO
(1/4 Ounce of Pure Gold)

8.6396 g, .900 GOLD, .2500 oz AGW

| 487 | 1981 | .313 | — | — | — | BV + 11% |

1/2 ONZA ORO PURO
(1/2 Ounce of Pure Gold)

17.2792 g, .900 GOLD, .5000 oz AGW

| 488 | 1981 | .193 | — | — | — | BV + 8% |

ONZA ORO PURO
(1 Ounce of Pure Gold)

34.5585 g, .900 GOLD, 1.0000 oz AGW

489	1981	.596	—	—	—	BV + 3%
	1985	—	—	—	—	BV + 3%
	1988	—	—	—	—	BV + 3%

(50 PESOS)

41.6666 g, .900 GOLD, 1.2057 oz AGW

KM#	Date	Mintage	Fine	VF	XF	Unc
482	1943	.089	—	—	BV	575.00

MINT SETS (MS)

KM#	Date	Mintage	Identification	Issue Price	Mkt. Val.
MS1	1977(16)	500	—	—	600.00
MS2	1978(9)	500	KM434.1,434.2,442,452, 460 open 8, 460 closed 8, 472,477,484, Type 1 flat pack	—	200.00
MS3	1978(9)	—	KM434.1,434.2,442,452, 460 open 8, 460 closed 8, 472,477,484, Type 2 for 3 ring binder	—	200.00
MS4	1979(8)	—	KM434.1,434.2,442,452 square 9, 452 round 9, 460, 477,484, Type 1 flat pack	11.00	17.50
MS5	1979(8)	—	KM434.1,434.2,442,452 square 9, 452 round 9, 460,477,484, Type 2 for 3 ring binder	11.00	12.00
MS6	1980	—	—	4.20	12.00
MS7	1981(9)	—	KM442 open 8, 442 closed 8, 452 rectangular 9, 452 round 9, 460 open 8, 460 closed 8, 477, 485, 486	—	7.50
MS8	1982(7)	—	KM442,452,460,477,485,486,490	—	7.50
MS9	1983(9)	—	—	—	7.50
MS10	1983(9)	—	KM446(2),460(2),490(1),491(2), 492(2) for 3 ring binder	—	11.00
MS11	1984(8)	—	KM485-486,490-491,493,495(2), 496	—	10.00
MS12	1985(12)	—	KM477.2,485,493(2),495(2), 496,502,508,509,510,512	—	22.50
MS13	1986(7)	—	KM493,495,496,508,512,525,529	—	18.50

NOTE: The 1978 and 1979 sets were issued in 2 varieties of plastic holders, one of which has holes for insertion in an official 3 ring binder which was sold for $3.30.

PROOF SETS (PS)

PS1	1982/1983(8)	998	KM442,452,460,485,477.2 486,490,494	495.00	695.00
PS2	1982/1983(7)	*25	KM460,477.2,485,486,490, 491,492 (in white box with Mo in gold)	—	650.00
PS3	1982/1983(7)	*17	KM460,477.2,485,486,490,491, 492 (in white box)	—	650.00
PS4	1982/1983(7)	*8	KM460,477.2,485,486,490,491, 492 (in blue pouch)	—	650.00
PS5	1985/1986(12)	—	KM497a-499a,503a-505a,514a-515a, 519a,521a,523a-524a	—	300.00
PS6	1985(4)	—	KM500.2-501.2,506.2,507.2	—	1600.
PS7	1985(2)	—	500,1000 Peso Independence	—	525.00

*NOTE: KM#PS2, PS3 and PS4 are commonly referred to as pattern proof sets.

LOCAL COINAGE

This representation of local coinage is not to be considered as complete. Correspondence is welcomed by our editorial staff on any new varieties.

Ahualulco
OCTAVO - 1/8 REAL

COPPER, uniface
AHUALULCO and 1813 around 1/8 in circle.

KM#	Date	Good	VG	Fine	VF
L1	1813	17.50	25.00	35.00	50.00

Script AHO, 1/8 below.
| L2 | ND | 12.50 | 17.50 | 25.00 | 35.00 |

Ameca
OCTAVO - 1/8 REAL
COPPER, uniface
Church flanked by trees.
| L6 | 1824 | 12.50 | 17.50 | 25.00 | 35.00 |

TLACO DE AMECA around QTG monogram in circle.
KM#	Date	Good	VG	Fine	VF
L7	ND	12.50	17.50	25.00	35.00

AME/CA 1811 in circle.
| L8 | 1811 | 17.50 | 25.00 | 35.00 | 50.00 |

Octagonal planchet.
| L9 | 1811 | 17.50 | 25.00 | 35.00 | 50.00 |

F 1/8 Z within wavy circle.
| L10 | ND | 17.50 | 25.00 | 35.00 | 50.00 |

T.Z. AMECA 1833 around value.
| L11 | 1833 | 12.50 | 17.50 | 25.00 | 35.00 |

V.F AMECA 1858 below value.
| L12 | 1858 | 12.50 | 17.50 | 25.00 | 35.00 |

Amescua
OCTAVO - 1/8 REAL

COPPER, uniface
Mexican Eagle
| L15 | 1828 | 12.50 | 17.50 | 25.00 | 35.00 |

Date below eagle.
| L16 | 1838 | 13.50 | 20.00 | 28.50 | 40.00 |

Atencinco
OCTAVO - 1/8 REAL
COPPER, uniface
ATENCINCO in outer border, 8 leaved rosette over branch in center.
| L19 | ND | 12.50 | 17.50 | 25.00 | 35.00 |

Atotonilco
OCTAVO - 1/8 REAL
COPPER, uniface
ATOTONILCO ANO DE 1808 in outer border, L.S.S./JUSU/ESES in circle.
| L22 | 1808 | 27.50 | 37.50 | 52.50 | 75.00 |

Obv. leg: ATOTONILCO ANO DE in outer border, 1821 in center. Rev. leg: E T P D Z around outer border.
| L23 | 1821 | 17.50 | 25.00 | 35.00 | 50.00 |

Obv. leg: VILL ATOTONILCO in outer border, 1826 in center. Rev. leg: 1/8 in center, stars in outer border.
| L24 | 1826 | 17.50 | 25.00 | 35.00 | 50.00 |

Campeche
CENTAVO

BRASS
KM#	Date	Good	VG	Fine	VF
L27	1861	12.50	17.50	25.00	35.00

Catorce
1/4 REAL

COPPER
Obv. leg: FONDOS PUBLICO around border, 1/4 below flower and raised rectangle.
Rev. leg: DE CATORCE 1822 around border, eagle on cactus.
| L30 | 1822 | 13.50 | 20.00 | 28.50 | 40.00 |

Celaya
OCTAVO - 1/8 REAL
COPPER
Obv. leg: EN/CELAYA/DE/1803.
Rev. leg: LUIS/VASQUE/S, branches below, flower above.
| L33 | 1803 | 27.50 | 37.50 | 52.50 | 75.00 |

COPPER, uniface
VINDERI/QUE/CELALLA/1808
| L34 | 1808 | 27.50 | 37.50 | 52.50 | 75.00 |

VISCARA/CELAYA/1814 w/ornament above.
| L35 | 1814 | 17.50 | 25.00 | 35.00 | 50.00 |

Chilchota
OCTAVO - 1/8 REAL

COPPER
Obv: Head to right, leg: CHILCHOTA UN OCTAVO, date below. Rev: Wreath in center, leg: RESPONSAVIDAD DE MURGVIA.
| L38 | 1858 | 17.50 | 25.00 | 35.00 | 50.00 |

Colima
OCTAVO - 1/8 REAL
COPPER
Obv. leg: VILLA DE COLIMA around border as continuous leg. Rev: Blank.
| L41 | 1813 | 17.50 | 25.00 | 35.00 | 50.00 |

Obv. leg: VILLA DE COLIMA and date in 3 lines. Rev: Blank.
| L42 | 1814 | 17.50 | 25.00 | 35.00 | 50.00 |

Obv. leg: QUART COLIMA 1816 in 3 lines in wreath. Rev: Colima monogram in wreath.
| L43 | 1816 | 17.50 | 25.00 | 35.00 | 50.00 |

Local Coinage / MEXICO 1280

KM#	Date	Good	VG	Fine	VF
L44	1819	21.50	30.00	42.50	60.00

Obv. leg: QUARTo DE COLIMA around border; date in center circle. Rev: Colima monogram in wreath.

| L45 | 1824 | 21.50 | 30.00 | 42.50 | 60.00 |

Obv. leg: OCTO DE COLIMA around border, date in center circle. Rev. leg: OCTAVO within wreath, pellet in center.

| L46 | 1824 | 21.50 | 30.00 | 42.50 | 60.00 |

Obv. leg: OCTO DE COLA in 3 lines.
Rev. leg: ANO DE 1824 in 3 lines.

| L47 | 1824 | 21.50 | 30.00 | 42.50 | 60.00 |
| | 1828 | 21.50 | 30.00 | 42.50 | 60.00 |

Obv. leg: OCTO DE COLIMA in 3 lines.
Rev. leg: ANO DE 1830 in 3 lines.

| L48 | 1830 | 21.50 | 30.00 | 42.50 | 60.00 |

Cotija
OCTAVO - 1/8 REAL

COPPER
Obv: Seated Liberty w/staff and liberty cap,
leg: DE.D.JOSE NUNES. Rev: Value and date in wreath,
leg: COMMERCIO. D. COTIJA.

| L51 | ND | 13.50 | 20.00 | 28.50 | 40.00 |

Lagos
1/4 REAL

BRONZE
Obv: Two globes w/crown above, wreath and 1/4 below.
Rev: Coat of arms of Lagos.

| L59 | ND | | 100.00 | 150.00 | 200.00 | 250.00 |

SILVER
| L59a | ND | | 150.00 | 200.00 | 300.00 | 500.00 |

Merida
1/2 GRANO

LEAD
Obv. leg: PART/DE LA SO/CIED in center. MERIDADE YUCATAN around border, 1859 below.
Rev. leg: 1/2/GRANO/DE PESO/FUERTE.

KM#	Date	Good	VG	Fine	VF
L60	1859	12.50	17.50	25.00	35.00

Pazcuaro
OCTAVO - 1/8 REAL

COPPER
Obv: Town at base of mountains, lake in foreground, value 1/8 above. Rev: Woman walking right, carrying bag, fish net and fish.

| L63 | ND | 12.50 | 17.50 | 25.00 | 35.00 |

NOTE: Also in brass and cast in bronze.

Obv: 1/8 PAZCUARO. Rev: Crude portrait?.

| L64 | ND | 12.50 | 17.50 | 25.00 | 35.00 |

Progreso
OCTAVO - 1/8 REAL

COPPER
Obv: Radiant star above open book.
Rev: Value 1/8 in double wreath.

| L66 | 1858 | 17.50 | 25.00 | 35.00 | 50.00 |

CENTAVO
LEAD
Obv. leg: MUNICIPALIDAD DE PROGRESO UN CENT, 1873 in center. Rev: Flank in oval band.

| L67 | 1873 | 12.50 | 17.50 | 27.50 | 40.00 |

Quitupan
OCTAVO - 1/8 REAL

COPPER
Obv: Bow and 2 arrows in center,
leg: QUITUPAN. .1854. Rev: 1/8 in center,
leg: IGNACIO BUENROSTO, monogram c/m.

| L69 | 1854 | 17.50 | 25.00 | 35.00 | 50.00 |

Tacambaro
OCTAVO - 1/8 REAL

COPPER
Obv: Winged caduceus in sprays.
Rev: Value 1/8 in sprays.

KM#	Date	Good	VG	Fine	VF
L72	ND	13.50	20.00	28.50	40.00

Taretan
OCTAVO - 1/8 REAL

COPPER
Obv: Head of man right. Rev: Tree.

| L75 | 1858 | 21.50 | 30.00 | 42.50 | 60.00 |

Tlazasalca
OCTAVO - 1/8 REAL

COPPER
Obv: 2 mountains, date below.
Rev: Value 1/8 in wreath.

| L78 | 1853 | 17.50 | 25.00 | 35.00 | 50.00 |

XALOSTOTITLAN
OCTAVO - 1/8 REAL

COPPER
Obv: Crown in center, leg: AYVNTAMIENTO ILVSTRE.
Rev: 4 in center, leg: DE XALOSTOTITLAN. 1820.

| L54 | 1820 | 27.50 | 37.50 | 52.50 | 75.00 |

Zamora
OCTAVO - 1/8 REAL

COPPER
L80	1842	17.50	25.00	35.00	50.00
	1848	17.50	25.00	35.00	50.00
	1854	17.50	25.00	35.00	50.00
	1858	17.50	25.00	35.00	50.00

COPPER or BRONZE
Obv: Eagle on cactus above sprays.
Rev: Liberty cap, bow and arrows above sprays.
W/or w/o various c/m.

| L81 | 1852 | 17.50 | 25.00 | 35.00 | 50.00 |
| | 1853 | 17.50 | 25.00 | 35.00 | 50.00 |

KM#	Date	Good	VG	Fine	VF
L81	1856	17.50	25.00	35.00	50.00
	1857	17.50	25.00	35.00	50.00
	1858	17.50	25.00	35.00	50.00

NOTE: These pieces are also found with various countermarks. "Za" in a dentilated circle is the most common. "1/8" in a circular c/m is also encountered.

Zapotlan
OCTAVO - 1/8 REAL

COPPER, uniface
ZAPO/TLAN/1813

L84	1813		18.50	30.00	42.50	60.00

ZAPOTLAM/A.DE 1814

L85	1814		21.50	32.50	50.00	75.00

REVOLUTION 1910-1917

The Mexican independence movement, which is of interest and concern to collectors because of the warfare-induced activity of local and state mints, began with the Sept. 16, 1810 march on the capital led by Father Miguel Hidalgo, a well-intentioned man of imagination and courage who proved to be an inept organizer and leader. Hidalgo was captured and executed within 10 months. His revolution, led by such as Morelos, Guerrero and Iturbide, continued and culminated in Mexican independence in 1821. Turbulent years followed. From 1821 to 1877 there were two emperors, several dictators and enough presidents to provide a change of government on the average of once every nine months. Porfirio Diaz, who had the longest tenure of any dictator in Latin American history, seized power in 1877 and did not relinquish it until 1911.

The final phase of Mexico's lengthy revolutionary period began in 1910 and lasted through the adoption of a liberal constitution and the election of a new congress in 1917. The 1910-1917 revolution was agrarian in character and intended to destroy the regime of Diaz and to make Mexico economically and diplomatically independent. The republic experienced a state of upheaval that saw most of the leading figures of the revolution (Villa, Carranza, Obregon, Zapata, Calles) fighting each other at one time or another. Carranza eventually emerged as the most powerful figure of the early revolution. As de facto president in 1916, he convened a constitutional convention which produced a constitution in which the aims of the revolution were formulized. Obregon, perhaps the ablest general and wiliest politician of the lot, became Mexico's elected president in 1920, bringing the most disasterous but significant decade in Mexico's history to an end.

AGUASCALIENTES

Aguascalientes is a state in central Mexico. Its coin issues, struck by authority of Pancho Villa, represent his deepest penetration into the Mexican heartland. Lack of silver made it necessary to make all denominations in copper.

CENTAVO

COPPER

KM#	Date	VG	Fine	VF	XF
601	1915 lg. date	25.00	40.00	60.00	90.00
	1915 sm. date reeded edge				
		20.00	30.00	50.00	75.00
	1915 sm. date plain edge				
		30.00	50.00	75.00	115.00

SILVER (OMS)

601a	1915 lg. date	—	—	275.00	450.00
	1915 sm. date	—	—	275.00	450.00

2 CENTAVOS

COPPER

602	1915 round front 2				
		40.00	100.00	200.00	350.00
	1915 square front 2, reeded edge				
		35.00	60.00	85.00	200.00
	1915 square front 2, plain edge				
		40.00	70.00	100.00	225.00

SILVER (OMS)

602a	1915	—	—	600.00	1000.

5 CENTAVOS

COPPER

603	1915	10.00	15.00	25.00	35.00

604	1915 reeded edge				
		10.00	15.00	25.00	35.00
	1915 plain edge				
		100.00	150.00	225.00	325.00

KM#	Date	VG	Fine	VF	XF
604a	1915			1000.	1500.

20 CENTAVOS

COPPER
Rev: With flat bottomed 2.

605	1915	4.50	6.00	9.00	22.00

SILVER (OMS)

605a	1915	—	—	1200.	2000.

COPPER
Rev: With wavy bottomed 2.

606	1915	4.50	6.00	9.00	20.00

NOTE: Varieties exist with both plain and milled edges and many variations in the shading of the numerals.

CHIHUAHUA

Chihuahua is a northern state of Mexico bordering the U.S. It was the arena that introduced Pancho Villa to the world. Villa, an outlaw, was given a title when asked by Madero to participate in maintaining order during Madero's presidency. After Madero's death in February 1913 Villa became a persuasive leader. Chihuahua was where he made his first coins - the Parral series. The "Army of the North" pesos also came from this state. This coin helped Villa recruit soldiers because of his ability to pay in silver while others were paying in worthless paper.

HIDALGO DEL PARRAL
"FUERZAS CONSTITUCIONALISTAS"

2 CENTAVOS

COPPER

607	1913	2.50	4.00	8.00	15.00

BRASS

607a	1913	—	—	Rare	—

50 CENTAVOS

SILVER
Reeded edge

608	1913	9.00	15.00	20.00	35.00

Plain edge

609	1913	40.00	60.00	80.00	160.00

Chihuahua / MEXICO 1282

PESO

SILVER
Rev: 1 through PESO and ball BOLITA.

KM#	Date	VG	Fine	VF	XF
610	1913	1200.	1750.	2250.	3600.

Rev: 1 above PESO.
Obv: Similar to KM#610.

| 611 | 1913 | 35.00 | 50.00 | 75.00 | 150.00 |

CONSTITUTIONALIST ARMY
"EJERCITO CONSTITUCIONALISTA"

5 CENTAVOS

COPPER
Rev: Ornaments at each side of 1914.

| 612 | 1914 | 20.00 | 30.00 | 50.00 | 80.00 |

| 613 | 1914 | 1.00 | 2.50 | 3.50 | 4.50 |
| | 1915 | 1.00 | 2.50 | 3.50 | 4.50 |

NOTE: Numerous varieties exist.

BRASS

| 613a | 1914 | — | — | — | — |
| | 1915 | — | — | — | — |

NOTE: Numerous varieties exist.

COPPER

KM#	Date	VG	Fine	VF	XF
614	1915	150.00	250.00	325.00	400.00

10 CENTAVOS

COPPER

| 615 | 1915 | 1.25 | 2.50 | 3.50 | 5.00 |

BRASS

| 615a | 1915 | — | — | — | — |

NOTE: Many varieties exist.

ARMY OF THE NORTH
"EJERCITO DEL NORTE"

SILVER

| 619 | 1915 | 15.00 | 25.00 | 35.00 | 50.00 |

DURANGO

A state in north central Mexico. Another area of operation for Pancho Villa. The "Muera Huerta" peso originates in this state. The coins were made in Cuencame under the orders of Generals Cemceros and Contreras.

CUENCAME
"MUERA HUERTA"
(Death to Huerta)

PESO

SILVER
Rev: 1914 below UN PESO with 3 stars at each side.

KM#	Date	VG	Fine	VF	XF
620	1914	1250.	1000.	1500.	2750.

Obv. and rev: Continuous border.

| 621 | 1914 | 60.00 | 100.00 | 125.00 | 250.00 |

COPPER

| 621a | 1914 | 175.00 | 250.00 | 350.00 | 450.00 |

SILVER
Obv: Dot and dash border.

| 622 | 1914 | 50.00 | 75.00 | 100.00 | 200.00 |

20 PESOS

NOTE: The so called 20 Pesos gold Muera Huerta pieces are modern fantasies. Refer to *Unusual World Coins*, 2nd edition, 1989, Krause Publications, Inc.

ESTADO DE DURANGO
CENTAVO

KM#	Date	VG	Fine	VF	XF
		COPPER			
625	1914	2.00	3.00	5.00	7.50
		BRASS			
625a	1914	9.00	15.00	20.00	30.00
		LEAD			
625b	1914	20.00	40.00	65.00	90.00

		COPPER			
626	1914	15.00	30.00	45.00	60.00
		BRASS			
626a	1914	12.50	20.00	30.00	45.00
		LEAD			
626b	1914	20.00	35.00	50.00	75.00

		COPPER			
627	1914	6.00	10.00	15.00	25.00
		LEAD			
627a	1914	20.00	35.00	50.00	65.00

		ALUMINUM			
628	1914	.65	1.00	2.00	3.00

5 CENTAVOS

COPPER
Obv. leg: ESTADO DE DURANGO.
629	1914	1.25	2.00	4.00	7.50

Obv. leg: E. DE DURANGO. Rev: Thin 5.
630	1914	20.00	30.00	40.00	60.00

Rev: Thick 5.
631	1914	1.25	2.00	4.00	7.50
		BRASS			
631a	1914	50.00	75.00	100.00	130.00
		LEAD			
631b	1914	45.00	70.00	90.00	120.00

KM#	Date	VG	Fine	VF	XF
		COPPER			
632	1914	3.00	5.00	9.00	15.00
		LEAD			
632a	1914	30.00	45.00	60.00	80.00

Obv: 3 stars below 1914. Rev: 5 CVS.
633	1914	—	400.00	800.00	—

		BRASS			
634	1914	.50	1.00	1.50	2.00

NOTE: There are numerous varieties of these general types of the Durango 1 and 5 Centavo pieces.

GUERRERO

Guerrero is a state on the southwestern coast of Mexico. It was one of the areas of operation of Zapata and his forces in the south of Mexico. Seven different mints were operated by the Zapata forces in this state. The date ranges were from 1914 to 1917 and denominations from 2 centavos to 2 pesos. Some were cast but most were struck and the rarest coin of the group is the Suriana 1915 2 pesos.

3 CENTAVOS

		COPPER			
635	1915	500.00	1000.	1500.	2000.

5 CENTAVOS

		COPPER			
636	1915GRO	600.00	1000.	1300.	1750.

10 CENTAVOS

		COPPER			
637	1915GRO	4.50	7.50	10.00	12.50

20 CENTAVOS
Previously listed #638 dated 1915GRO existing in copper and in silver has been determined to be spurious.

25 CENTAVOS

KM#	Date	VG	Fine	VF	XF
		SILVER			
639	1915	300.00	400.00	525.00	650.00

50 CENTAVOS

		SILVER			
640	1915	900.00	1500.	2100.	3000.

UN (1) PESO

0.30 g, 1.000 FINE GOLD/SILVER
Obv: Star before UN PESO.
641	1914	15.00	25.00	35.00	65.00

NOTE: Many die varieties exist.

Obv: Star before and after UN PESO.
642	1914	50.00	75.00	100.00	150.00
	1915	600.00	1000.	1500.	2000.

DOS (2) PESOS

Guerrero / MEXICO 1284

KM#	Date	VG	Fine	VF	XF
	0.595 g, 1.000 FINE GOLD/SILVER				
643	1914GRO	12.50	22.50	35.00	75.00

NOTE: Many varieties exist.

644	1915GRO	65.00	85.00	160.00	250.00
	COPPER				
644a	1915GRO	400.00	600.00	800.00	1000.

ATLIXTAC
10 CENTAVOS

	COPPER				
645	1915	3.00	4.00	6.50	9.00

Obv: Stars in leg.
646	1915	3.00	4.00	6.50	9.00

CACAHUATEPEC
5 CENTAVOS

	COPPER				
648	1917	25.00	45.00	90.00	150.00

20 CENTAVOS

	SILVER				
649	1917	75.00	125.00	200.00	250.00

50 CENTAVOS

KM#	Date	VG	Fine	VF	XF
	SILVER				
650	1917	50.00	75.00	100.00	150.00

UN (1) PESO

	SILVER				
651	1917 L.V.Go	1500.	2500.	3750.	4500.

CACALOTEPEC
20 CENTAVOS

	SILVER				
652	1917	1000.	1500.	2000.	2500.

CAMPO MORADO
C.M., C.M.GRO, CoMoGro, CAMPO Mo
5 CENTAVOS

	COPPER				
653	1915C.M.	9.00	15.00	22.50	35.00

10 CENTAVOS

	COPPER				
654	1915C.M.GRO	6.00	10.00	17.50	27.50

20 CENTAVOS

KM#	Date	VG	Fine	VF	XF
	COPPER				
655	1915C.M.GRO	15.00	25.00	35.00	50.00

50 CENTAVOS

	COPPER				
	Obv: UN PESO effaced below eagle.				
656	1915C.M.GRO	12.00	20.00	27.50	32.50

	Regular obverse				
657	1915C.M.GRO	6.00	10.00	13.50	20.00
	BASE SILVER				
657a	1915C.M.GRO	165.00	275.00	400.00	575.00

UN (1) PESO

.300 g, 1.000 FINE GOLD/SILVER
Obv: Date below eagle.
658	1914Co Mo Gro	450.00	650.00	850.00	1100.

Rev: Date below Liberty cap.
659	1914 CAMPO Mo	15.00	30.00	45.00	60.00

DOS (2) PESOS

.595 g, 1.000 FINE GOLD/SILVER

KM#	Date	VG	Fine	VF	XF
660	1915 Co. Mo.	15.00	25.00	35.00	55.00

Rev: Star before and after Co. Mo.
| 661 | 1915 Co.Mo. | 1200. | 2000. | 3000. | 4500. |

| 662 | 1915 C.M.GRO | 20.00 | 30.00 | 50.00 | 65.00 |

CHILPANCINGO
10 CENTAVOS

SILVER (cast)
KM#	Date	VG	Fine	VF	XF
663	1914	—	—	Rare	

20 CENTAVOS

SILVER (cast)
| 664 | 1914 | — | — | Rare | |

SURIANA
DOS (2) PESOS

0.595 g, 1.000 FINE GOLD/SILVER*
| 665 | 1915 | — | — | 23,000.* | |

*Munoz Part 1 sale by Superior Galleries June, 1978 (The Bothamely Specimen).

TAXCO
2 CENTAVOS

COPPER
| 666 | 1915 | 75.00 | 150.00 | 300.00 | 500.00 |

Obv. leg: EDO.DE.GRO above eagle.
| 667 | 1915 O/T | 25.00 | 40.00 | 60.00 | 90.00 |

5 CENTAVOS

COPPER
KM#	Date	VG	Fine	VF	XF
668	1915	9.00	15.00	20.00	25.00

10 CENTAVOS

COPPER
| 669 | 1915 | 9.00 | 15.00 | 20.00 | 30.00 |

50 CENTAVOS
COPPER
Obv. leg: Large letters.
| 670 | 1915 | 15.00 | 25.00 | 50.00 | 65.00 |

SILVER
| 671 | 1915 | 20.00 | 30.00 | 40.00 | 70.00 |

UN (1) PESO

.300 g, 1.000 FINE GOLD/SILVER
Obv: Star before UN PESO and star before G.
| 672 | 1915 | 12.00 | 20.00 | 25.00 | 35.00 |

Obv: Star before UN PESO, w/o star before G.
| 673 | 1915 | 250.00 | 300.00 | 400.00 | 500.00 |

Obv: W/o star before UN PESO.
| 674 | 1915 | 75.00 | 150.00 | 275.00 | 400.00 |

JALISCO

Jalisco is a state on the west coast of Mexico. The few coins made for this state show that the "Army of the North" did not restrict their operations to the northern border states. The coins were made in Guadalajara under the watchful eye of General Dieguez, commander of this segment of Villa's forces.

GUADALAJARA
CENTAVO

COPPER

KM#	Date	VG	Fine	VF	XF
675	1915	9.50	15.00	20.00	25.00

2 CENTAVOS

COPPER

| 676 | 1915 | 9.50 | 15.00 | 17.50 | 22.50 |

5 CENTAVOS

COPPER

| 677 | 1915 | 6.50 | 12.00 | 15.00 | 20.00 |

10 CENTAVOS

COPPER

| 678 | 1915 | — | — | 1600. | — |

PESO

COPPER

| A678 | 1915 | — | — | 8000. | — |

MEXICO, ESTADO DE

Estado de Mexico is a state in central Mexico that surrounds the Federal District on 3 sides. The issues by the Zapata forces in this state have two distinctions - the Amecameca pieces are the crudest and the Toluca cardboard piece is the most unusual. General Tenorio authorized the crude incuse Amecameca pieces.

AMECAMECA
5 CENTAVOS

BRASS, hand stamped

| 679 | ND | — | — | Unique | — |

| 680 | ND | 75.00 | 100.00 | 150.00 | 200.00 |

10 CENTAVOS

BRASS, hand stamped

KM#	Date	VG	Fine	VF	XF
681	ND	60.00	90.00	125.00	160.00

20 CENTAVOS

BRASS, hand stamped

| 682 | ND | 15.00 | 22.50 | 35.00 | 60.00 |

COPPER, hand stamped
Obv: Eagle over A.D.J.

| 683 | ND | 7.50 | 12.50 | 20.00 | 35.00 |

BRASS

| 683a | ND | — | — | 125.00 | 175.00 |

25 CENTAVOS

BRASS, hand stamped

| 684 | ND | — | — | Unique | — |

COPPER, hand stamped
Obv: Eagle over sprays.

| 685 | ND | 15.00 | 25.00 | 40.00 | 80.00 |

BRASS, hand stamped

| 685a | ND | — | — | 50.00 | 100.00 |

50 CENTAVOS

COPPER, hand stamped
Obv: Eagle over sprays.

| 686 | ND | 5.00 | 8.00 | 12.00 | 20.00 |

BRASS, hand stamped

| 686a | ND | 75.00 | 100.00 | 150.00 | 200.00 |

COPPER
Contemporary counterfeit, hand engraved.

KM#	Date	VG	Fine	VF	XF
687	ND	12.00	20.00	32.50	50.00

NOTE: KM#687 - ¢ clears top of 5 while KM#686a has the stem of ¢ above the 5.

MEXICO, DISTRITO FEDERAL

See also general listings for 1 Centavo, KM#416 and 2 Centavos, KM#417 dated 1915 struck by Revolutionary forces under E. Zapata.

TENANCINGO, TOWN
2 CENTAVOS

COPPER

| 688 | 1915 | — | — | 350.00 | — |

5 CENTAVOS

COPPER

| 689 | 1915 | 5.00 | 10.00 | 15.00 | 25.00 |

10 CENTAVOS

COPPER

| 690 | 1916 | 10.00 | 15.00 | 20.00 | 30.00 |

20 CENTAVOS

COPPER

| 691 | 1915 | 25.00 | 40.00 | 55.00 | 75.00 |

TOLUCA, CITY
5 CENTAVOS

GREY CARDBOARD

| 692 | 1915 | 15.00 | 25.00 | 35.00 | 45.00 |

20 CENTAVOS

COPPER
20 within C in circular countermark on regular 1 Centavo.

KM#	Date	VG	Fine	VF	XF
693	ND	20.00	30.00	45.00	60.00

40 CENTAVOS

COPPER
40 within C in circular countermark on regular 2 Centavos.

694	ND	25.00	40.00	55.00	70.00

MORELOS

Morelos is a state in south central Mexico, adjoining the federal district on the south. It was the headquarters of Emiliano Zapata. His personal quarters were at Tlatizapan in Morelos. The Morelos coins from 2 centavos to 1 peso were all copper except one type of 1 peso in silver. The 2 operating Zapatista mints in Morelos were Atlihuayan and Tlaltizapan.

2 CENTAVOS

COPPER
E.L.DE MORELOS

695	1915	1200.	1500.	2000.	2500.

5 CENTAVOS

COPPER
E. DE MOR. 1915.

696	1915	200.00	350.00	500.00	700.00

10 CENTAVOS

COPPER

697	1915	12.00	20.00	27.50	35.00

Date effaced from die

698	ND	12.00	20.00	32.50	50.00

699	1915	1000.	1500.	2000.	2500.

KM#	Date	VG	Fine	VF	XF
700	1916	10.00	15.00	20.00	

20 CENTAVOS

COPPER

701	1915	9.00	15.00	21.50	30.00

50 CENTAVOS

COPPER
Obv: MOR beneath eagle. Rev: 50C monogram.

702	1915	300.00	500.00	900.00	1300.

Obv: Sprays beneath eagle.

703	1915	12.50	17.50	27.50	32.50

NOTE: The above exists with a silver and also a brass wash.

Obv: MORELOS below eagle.

704	1916	12.50	17.50	27.50	32.50

UN (1) PESO

SILVER

708	1916	450.00	750.00	1000.	1500.

COPPER

708a	1916	450.00	750.00	1000.	1500.

OAXACA

Oaxaca is one of the southern states in Mexico. The coins issued in this state represent the most prolific series of the Revolution. Most of the coins bear the portrait of Benito Juarez and were issued by a provisional government in the state. The exceptions are the rectangular 1 and 3 centavos pieces that begin the series.

UN (1) CENTAVO

 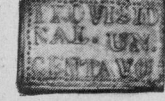

COPPER

709	1915	60.00	90.00	125.00	150.00

KM#	Date	VG	Fine	VF	XF
710	1915	12.00	17.50	25.00	35.00

TRES (3) CENTAVOS

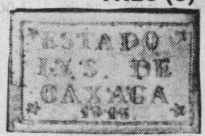 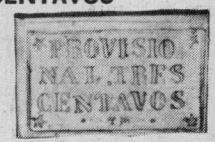

COPPER

711	1915	60.00	100.00	125.00	150.00

 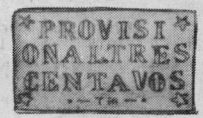

712	1915	600.00	1000.	1500.	2000.

713	1915	3.00		9.00	15.00

714	1915	6.00	9.00	14.00	20.00

5 CENTAVOS

COPPER
JAN.15 1915, incuse lettering

715	1915	—	—	Rare	—

Obv: Facing bust of Juarez.

716	1915	—	—	1800.	

Obv: 2nd bust, low relief w/long pointed truncation.

717	1915	1.50	3.00	4.50	7.00

Obv: 5th bust, heavy w/short unfinished lapels.

718	1915	1.50	2.50	4.00	6.00

Obv: 6th bust, curved bottom.

719	1915	1.50	2.50	4.00	6.00

Oaxaca/Revolution/MEXICO 1288

Obv: 7th bust, short truncation w/closed lapels.

KM#	Date	VG	Fine	VF	XF
720	1915	1.50	3.00	4.50	7.00

Obv: 8th bust, short curved truncation.

| 721 | 1915 | 1.50 | 2.50 | 4.00 | 6.00 |

10 CENTAVOS

COPPER
Obv: 2nd bust, low relief w/long-pointed truncation.

| 722 | 1915 | 1.50 | 2.50 | 4.00 | 6.00 |

Obv. and rev. leg: Retrograde.

| 723 | 1915 | — | — | Rare | — |

Obv: 4th bust, bold, unfinished truncation using 1 Peso obv. die of KM#740.

| 724 | 1915 | 3.00 | 5.00 | 7.00 | 9.00 |

Obv: 5th bust, heavy w/short unfinished lapels centered high.

| 725 | 1915 | 1.50 | 2.50 | 4.00 | 6.00 |

Obv: 6th bust, curved bottom.

| 726 | 1915 | 1.50 | 2.50 | 4.00 | 6.00 |

Obv: 7th bust, short truncation w/closed lapels.

| 727 | 1915 | 1.50 | 2.50 | 4.00 | 6.00 |

20 CENTAVOS

SILVER
Obv: 2nd bust, low relief w/long-pointed truncation.

| 728 | 1915 | 500.00 | 750.00 | 1200. | 1500. |

COPPER
Obv: 4th bust, bold unfinished truncation using 1 Peso obv. die

KM#	Date	VG	Fine	VF	XF
729	1915	1.50	3.00	4.50	7.00

Obv: 5th bust, heavy, w/short unfinished lapels using 20 Pesos obv. die.

| 730 | 1915 | 5.00 | 7.00 | 10.00 | 15.00 |

Obv: 6th bust, curved bottom.

| 731 | 1915 | 1.50 | 2.50 | 4.00 | 6.00 |

Obv: 6th bust.

| 732 | 1915 | 1.50 | 2.50 | 4.00 | 6.00 |

Obv: 7th bust, short truncation w/closed lapels.

| 733 | 1915 | 1.50 | 3.00 | 4.50 | 7.00 |

50 CENTAVOS

SILVER
Obv: 5th bust, heavy w/short unfinished lapels, centered high.

| 734 | 1915 | 10.00 | 20.00 | 45.00 | 100.00 |

Obv: 6th bust, curved bottom.

| 735 | 1915 | 6.00 | 9.00 | 14.00 | 22.50 |

Obv: 7th bust, short truncation w/closed lapels.

| 736 | 1915 | 5.00 | 7.50 | 12.50 | 17.50 |

Obv: 8th bust, short truncation w/pronounced curve.

| 737 | 1915 | 6.00 | 9.00 | 14.00 | 22.50 |

BILLON
Obv: 9th bust, high nearly straight truncation.

KM#	Date	VG	Fine	VF	XF
739	1915	—	—	—	2000.

COPPER

| 739a | 1915 | — | — | — | — |

UN (1) PESO

SILVER
Obv: 4th bust, w/heavy unfinished truncation.

| 740 | 1915 | 3.00 | 5.00 | 8.50 | 14.00 |

Obv: 5th bust, heavy, w/short unfinished lapels, centered high.

| 741 | 1915 | 6.00 | 9.00 | 14.00 | 22.50 |

Obv: 6th bust, curved bottom line.

| 742 | 1915 | 6.00 | 9.00 | 14.00 | 22.50 |

Obv: 7th bust, short truncation w/closed lapels.

| 743 | 1915 | 4.00 | 6.00 | 10.00 | 16.00 |

DOS (2) PESOS

SILVER
Obv: 4th bust, using 1 Peso obv. die.

| 744 | 1915 | 12.00 | 20.00 | 25.00 | 35.00 |

.902 SILVER/.010 GOLD, 22mm
Obv: 5th bust. Rev: Curved bottomed 2 over PESOS.

| 745 | 1915 | 12.00 | 20.00 | 27.50 | 37.50 |

COPPER

| 745a | 1915 | 50.00 | 75.00 | 110.00 | 160.00 |

SILVER

Obv: 6th bust. Rev: 2 PESOS.

KM#	Date	VG	Fine	VF	XF
746	1915	10.00	15.00	27.50	45.00

Obv: 6th bust. Rev: DOS PESOS.
| 747 | 1915 | 10.00 | 15.00 | 25.00 | 40.00 |

.902 SILVER
Obv: 7th bust, short truncation w/closed lapels, 22mm.
| 748 | 1915 | 12.00 | 20.00 | 40.00 | 60.00 |

SILVER
Obv: 10th, small nude bust.
| 749 | 1915 | — | — | Unique | 2300. |

5 PESOS

.175 GOLD
Obv: 3rd bust, heavy, w/short unfinished lapels.
| 750 | 1915 | 150.00 | 200.00 | 275.00 | 375.00 |

.902 SILVER
Obv: 7th bust, short truncation w/closed lapels.
| 751 | 1915 | 30.00 | 50.00 | 75.00 | 125.00 |

COPPER
| 751a | 1915 | 25.00 | 45.00 | 65.00 | 100.00 |

10 PESOS

.150 GOLD
Obv: 4th bust.
| A752 | 1915 | — | — | Rare | — |

.175 GOLD
Obv: 5th bust.
| 752 | 1915 | 225.00 | 300.00 | 450.00 | 550.00 |

20 PESOS

.150 GOLD
Obv: 4th bust.
| A753 | 1915 | — | — | Unique | — |

.175 GOLD
Obv: 5th bust, heavy, w/short unfinished lapels, centered high.
KM#	Date	VG	Fine	VF	XF
753	1915	400.00	600.00	800.00	1000.

Obv: 7th bust, short truncation w/closed lapels.
| 754 | 1915 | 200.00 | 300.00 | 450.00 | 600.00 |

60 PESOS

.854 GOLD
| 755 | 1916 originals (Yellow Gold) | 5000. | 7000. | 9000. | 12,000. |
| | 1916 restrikes (Red Gold) | 1000. | 1400. | 1800. | 2250. |

PUEBLA

A state of central Mexico. Puebla was a state that occassionally saw Zapata forces active within its boundaries. Also active, and an issuer of coins, was the Madero brigade who issued coins with their name 2 years after Madero's death. The state issue of 2, 5, 10 and 20 centavos saw limited circulation and recent hoards have been found of some values.

CHICONCUAUTLA
MADERO BRIGADE
10 CENTAVOS

COPPER
| 756 | 1915 | 7.50 | 12.50 | 17.50 | 25.00 |

20 CENTAVOS

COPPER
Rev: TRANSITORIO between rosettes.
KM#	Date	VG	Fine	VF	XF
757	1915	2.50	4.00	6.00	9.00

Rev: TRANSITORIO w/o rosettes.
| 758 | 1915 | 7.00 | 12.00 | 17.00 | 25.00 |

TETELA DEL ORO Y OCAMPO
2 CENTAVOS

COPPER, 17mm
| 759 | 1915 | 2.00 | 3.00 | 5.00 | 7.50 |

Rev. leg. ends: E.DE PU.
| 760 | 1915 | 15.00 | 25.00 | 35.00 | 55.00 |

Rev. leg. ends: E.DE PUE.
| 761 | 1915 | 9.00 | 15.00 | 22.50 | 35.00 |

5 CENTAVOS

COPPER
| 762 | 1915 | 50.00 | 100.00 | 150.00 | 250.00 |

20 CENTAVOS

COPPER
| 764 | 1915 | 50.00 | 100.00 | 150.00 | 225.00 |

SINALOA

A state along the west coast of Mexico. The cast pieces of this state have been attributed to two people - Generals Rafael Buelna and Juan Carrasco. The cap and rays 8 reales is usually attributed to General Buelna and the rest

Sinaloa/MEXICO 1289

of the series to Carrasco. Because of their crude nature it is questionable whether separate series or mints can be determined.

BUELNA/CARRASCO ISSUES

NOTE: These are all crude sand cast coins using regular coins to prepare the mold. Prices below give a range for how much of the original coin from which the mold was prepared is visible.

20 CENTAVOS

SILVER (cast)
Sand molded using regular 20 Centavos.

KM#	Date	Good	VG	Fine	VF
765	ND(1898-1905)	200.00	300.00	—	—

50 CENTAVOS

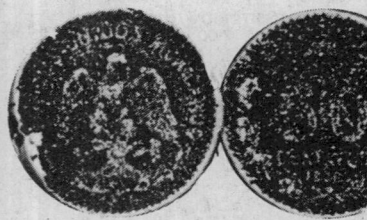

SILVER (cast)
Sand molded using regular 50 Centavos, KM#445.

| 766 | ND(1905-18) | 200.00 | 300.00 | — | — |

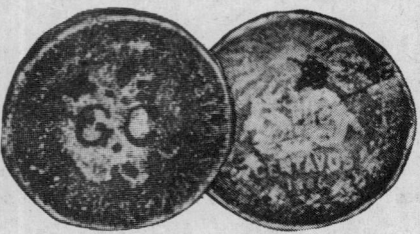

Obv: W/additional c/m: G.C.
| 767 | ND(1905-18) | 200.00 | 350.00 | 500.00 | 600.00 |

PESO

SILVER (cast)
Sand molded using regular 8 Reales, KM#377.
| 768 | ND(1824-97) | 17.50 | 35.00 | 45.00 | 65.00 |

Sand molded using regular Peso, KM#409.
KM#	Date	Good	VG	Fine	VF
769	ND(1898-1909)	17.50	35.00	45.00	65.00

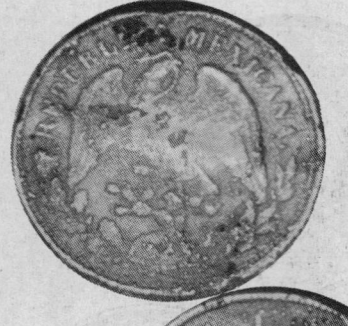

Rev: W/additional c/m: G.C.
| 770 | ND(1898-1909) | 30.00 | 60.00 | 140.00 | 200.00 |

Listings For
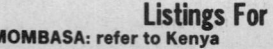
MOMBASA: refer to Kenya

MONACO

The Principality of Monaco, located on the Mediterranean coast nine miles from Nice, has an area of 0.58 sq. mi. (1.49 sq. km.) and a population of *29,000. Capital: Monaco-Ville. The economy is based on tourism and the manufacture of cosmetics, gourmet foods and highly specialized electronics. Monaco also derives its revenue from a tobacco monopoly and the sale of postage stamps for philatelic purpose. Gambling in Monte Carlo accounts for only a small fraction of the country's revenue.

Monaco derives its name from 'Monoikos', the Greek surname for Hercules, the mythological strong man who, according to legend, formed the Monacan headland during one of his twelve labors. Monaco has been ruled by the Grimaldi dynasty since 1297 - Prince Rainier III, the present and 31st monarch of Monaco, is still of that line - except for a period during the French Revolution until Napoleon's downfall when the Principality was annexed to France. Since 1865, Monaco has maintained a customs union with France which guarantees its privileged position as long as the royal line remains intact. Under the new constitution proclaimed on December 17, 1962, the Prince shares his power with an 18-member unicameral National Council.

RULERS

Honore IV, 1795-1819
Honore V, 1819-1841
Florestan I, 1841-1856
Charles III, 1856-1889
Albert I, 1889-1922
Louis II, 1922-1949
Rainier III, 1949-

MINT MARKS

M - Monaco
A - Paris

PRIVY MARKS

(a) - Paris (privy marks only)
C and clasped hands - Francois Cabinas, mint director, 1837-1838
(p) - Thunderbolt - Poissy

MONETARY SYSTEM

10 Centimes = 1 Decime
10 Decimes = 1 Franc

CINQ (5) CENTIMES

BRASS, struck
Mint mark: M
Obv: Large head, BORREL F. below.

KM#	Date	Mintage	VG	Fine	VF	XF
95.1 (C1.1)	1837 C	—	5.00	9.00	20.00	70.00

COPPER, struck
| 95.1a (C1.1a) | 1837 C | — | 3.50 | 7.00 | 15.00 | 55.00 |

BRASS, struck
Obv: Small head, BORREL F. below.
| 95.2 (C1.2) | 1837 C | — | 5.00 | 9.00 | 17.50 | 65.00 |

COPPER, struck
| 95.2a (C1.2a) | 1837 C | — | 3.50 | 7.00 | 15.00 | 55.00 |
| | 1838 C | — | 10.00 | 15.00 | 25.00 | 75.00 |

MONACO 1291

UN (1) DECIME

COPPER, struck
Mint mark: M
Obv: BORREL F. below head. Rev: Knot of wreath tied.

KM#	Date	Mintage	VG	Fine	VF	XF
97.1 (C2.1)	1838 C	—	10.00	20.00	60.00	125.00

BRASS, struck

| 97.1a (C2.1a) | 1838 C | — | 7.50 | 12.00 | 45.00 | 90.00 |

COPPER, struck
Obv: Smaller head, BORREL F. below.
Rev: Knot of wreath untied.

| 97.2 (C2.2) | 1838 C | — | 20.00 | 35.00 | 75.00 | 150.00 |

BRASS, struck

| 97.2a (C2.2a) | 1838 C | — | — | Reported, not confirmed | | |

50 CENTIMES

ALUMINUM-BRONZE

KM#	Date	Mintage	VF	XF	Unc
110 (Y2)	1924(p)	.150	12.00	20.00	45.00

| 113 (Y5) | 1926(p) | .100 | 15.00 | 25.00 | 50.00 |

FRANC

ALUMINUM-BRONZE

| 111 (Y3) | 1924(p) | .150 | 10.00 | 18.00 | 40.00 |

| 114 (Y6) | 1926(p) | .100 | 13.50 | 25.00 | 55.00 |

ALUMINUM

KM#	Date	Mintage	VF	XF	Unc
120 (Y8a)	ND(1943a)	2.500	1.00	2.00	7.50

ALUMINUM-BRONZE

| 120a (Y8) | ND(1945a) | 1.509 | 1.00 | 1.50 | 5.00 |

2 FRANCS

ALUMINUM-BRONZE

| 112 (Y4) | 1924(p) | .075 | 20.00 | 35.00 | 80.00 |

| 115 (Y7) | 1926(p) | .075 | 20.00 | 35.00 | 80.00 |

ALUMINUM

| 121 (Y9a) | ND(1943a) | 1.250 | 1.50 | 5.00 | 12.00 |

ALUMINUM-BRONZE

| 121a (Y9) | ND(1945a) | 1.080 | 1.00 | 2.00 | 8.00 |

5 FRANCS

25.0000 g, .900 SILVER, .7234 oz ASW
Mint mark: M

KM#	Date	Mintage	Fine	VF	XF	Unc
96 (C3)	1837	—	300.00	600.00	1000.	3000.

ALUMINUM

KM#	Date	Mintage	VF	XF	Unc
122 (Y10)	1945(a)	1.000	2.50	5.00	10.00

10 FRANCS

COPPER-NICKEL

| 123 (Y11) | 1946(a) | 1.000 | 3.00 | 6.00 | 12.00 |

ALUMINUM-BRONZE

| 130 (Y13) | 1950(a) | .500 | 1.00 | 1.50 | 3.50 |
| | 1951(a) | .500 | 1.00 | 1.50 | 3.50 |

VINGT (20) FRANCS

6.4516 g, .900 GOLD, .1867 oz AGW

| 98 (Y-A1) | 1878A | .025 | 200.00 | 300.00 | 600.00 |
| | 1879A | .050 | 175.00 | 250.00 | 500.00 |

COPPER-NICKEL

| 124 (Y12) | 1947(a) | 1.000 | 3.00 | 6.50 | 15.00 |

ALUMINUM-BRONZE

| 131 (Y14) | 1950(a) | .500 | 1.00 | 1.50 | 4.00 |
| | 1951(a) | .500 | 1.00 | 1.50 | 4.00 |

CINQUANTE (50) FRANCS

ALUMINUM-BRONZE

| 132 (Y15) | 1950(a) | .500 | 2.50 | 5.00 | 10.00 |

MONACO 1292

CENT (100) FRANCS

32.2580 g, .900 GOLD, .9335 oz AGW

KM#	Date	Mintage	VF	XF	Unc
99 (Y-B1)	1882A	5,000	600.00	1000.	2000.
	1884A	.015	500.00	650.00	850.00
	1886A	.015	500.00	650.00	850.00

105 (Y1)	1891A	.020	500.00	600.00	750.00
	1895A	.020	500.00	600.00	750.00
	1896A	.020	500.00	600.00	750.00
	1901A	.015	500.00	600.00	750.00
	1904A	.010	500.00	600.00	750.00

COPPER-NICKEL

133 (Y16)	1950(a)	.500	3.00	6.00	15.00

134 (Y17)	1956(a)	.500	2.00	4.00	10.00

MONETARY REFORM
100 Old Francs = 1 New Franc

CENTIME

STAINLESS STEEL

155 (Y34)	1976(a)	.025	.10	.25	3.50
	1977(a)	.025	.10	.25	3.50
	1978(a)	.075	.10	.25	3.50
	1979(a)	.075	.10	.25	3.50
	1982(a)	.010	.10	.25	3.50

5 CENTIMES

COPPER-ALUMINUM-NICKEL

KM#	Date	Mintage	VF	XF	Unc
156 (Y35)	1976(a)	.025	.15	.30	4.00
	1977(a)	.025	.15	.30	4.00
	1978(a)	.075	.15	.30	4.00
	1979(a)	.075	.15	.30	4.00
	1982(a)	.010	.15	.30	4.00

10 CENTIMES

ALUMINUM-BRONZE

142 (Y20)	1962(a)	.750	.10	.20	1.00
	1974(a)	.179	.10	.20	2.00
	1975(a)	.172	.10	.20	2.00
	1976(a)	.178	.10	.20	2.00
	1977(a)	.172	.10	.20	2.00
	1978(a)	.112	.10	.20	2.00
	1979(a)	.112	.10	.20	2.00
	1982(a)	.100	.10	.20	2.00

20 CENTIMES

ALUMINUM-BRONZE

143 (Y21)	1962(a)	.750	.15	.25	1.25
	1974(a)	.104	.15	.25	3.00
	1975(a)	.097	.15	.25	3.00
	1976(a)	.103	.15	.25	3.00
	1977(a)	.097	.15	.25	3.00
	1978(a)	.081	.15	.25	3.00
	1979(a)	.081	.15	.25	3.00
	1982(a)	.100	.15	.25	3.00

50 CENTIMES

ALUMINUM-BRONZE

144 (Y22)	1962(a)	.375	1.00	2.00	4.50

1/2 FRANC

NICKEL

145 (Y-A18)	1965(a)	.375	.50	1.00	2.00
	1968(a)	.250	.50	1.00	2.00
	1974(a)	.069	.50	1.00	3.00
	1975(a)	.070	.50	1.00	3.00
	1976(a)	.068	.50	1.00	3.00
	1977(a)	.062	.50	1.00	3.00
	1978(a)	.414	.50	1.00	3.00
	1979(a)	.414	.50	1.00	3.00
	1982(a)	.457	.50	1.00	3.00

FRANC

NICKEL

KM#	Date	Mintage	VF	XF	Unc
140 (Y18)	1960(a)	.500	.65	1.25	3.25
	1966(a)	.175	.75	1.50	3.50
	1968(a)	.250	.75	1.50	3.50
	1974(a)	.194	.75	1.50	3.50
	1975(a)	.195	.75	1.50	3.50
	1976(a)	.193	.75	1.50	3.50
	1977(a)	.188	.75	1.50	3.50
	1978(a)	.783	.75	1.50	3.50
	1979(a)	.783	.75	1.50	3.50
	1982(a)	.525	.75	1.50	3.50
	1986(a)	—	.75	1.50	3.50

2 FRANCS

NICKEL

157 (Y36)	1979(a)	.162	.75	1.50	3.50
	1981(a)	.275	.75	1.50	3.50
	1982(a)	.446	.75	1.50	3.50

5 FRANCS

12.0000 g, .835 SILVER, .3221 oz ASW

141 (Y19)	1960(a)	.125	—	7.50	11.00
	1966(a)	.125	—	7.50	11.00

NICKEL-CLAD COPPER-NICKEL

150 (Y26)	1971(a)	.250	1.00	2.00	4.50
	1974(a)	.152	1.00	2.00	4.50
	1975(a)	8,000	2.00	5.00	10.00
	1976(a)	8,000	2.00	5.00	10.00
	1977(a)	.042	2.00	5.00	10.00
	1978(a)	.022	2.00	5.00	10.00
	1979(a)	.022	2.00	5.00	10.00
	1982(a)	.152	2.00	5.00	10.00

10 FRANCS

25.0000 g, .900 SILVER, .7234 oz ASW

146 (Y25)	1966(a)	.038	—	—	25.00

COPPER-NICKEL-ALUMINUM
25th Anniversary of Reign

KM#	Date	Mintage	VF	XF	Unc
151 (Y27)	1974(a)	.025	2.00	3.00	7.50

154 (Y33)	1975(a)	.025	2.00	3.00	7.50
	1976(a)	.016	2.50	3.50	8.50
	1977(a)	.050	—	2.50	4.00
	1978(a)	.228	2.00	2.50	4.00
	1979(a)	.228	2.00	2.50	4.00
	1981(a)	.235	2.00	2.50	4.00
	1982(a)	.230	2.00	2.50	4.00

Princess Grace

160 (Y37)	1982(a)	.030	—	—	10.00

50 FRANCS

30.0000 g, .900 SILVER, .8681 oz ASW
25th Anniversary of Reign
Commemorative edge inscription.

152.1 (Y28)	1974(a)	.025	—	—	45.00
		Plain edge			
152.2	1975(a)	7,500	—	—	60.00
(Y28a)	1976(a)	6,000	—	—	65.00

100 FRANCS

15.0000 g, .900 SILVER, .4340 oz ASW
Heir Apparent Prince Albert

KM#	Date	Mintage	VF	XF	Unc
161 (Y38)	1982(a)	.030	—	Proof	45.00

SPECIMEN SETS (SS)
Fleur de Coin

KM#	Date	Mintage	Identification	Issue Price	Mkt. Val.
SS1	1974(7)	*7,000	KM140,142-143,145,150-151, 152.1	45.00	100.00
SS2	1975(7)	7,500	KM140,142-143,145,150,152.2, 154	—	90.00
SS3	1976(9)	6,000	KM140,142-143,145,150,152.2, 154-156	—	110.00
SS6	1982(11)	10,000	KM140,142-143,145,150,154-157, 160-161	—	80.00

*NOTE: 3,000 of the above sets were not released.

MONGOLIA

The Mongolian People's Republic, a landlocked country in central Asia between the Soviet Union and the People's Republic of China, has an area of 604,250 sq. mi. (1,565,000 sq. km.) and a population of *2.1 million. Capital: Ulan Bator. Animal herds and flocks are the chief economic asset. Wool, cattle, butter, meat and hides are exported.

Mongolia (often referred to as Outer Mongolia), one of the world's oldest countries, attained its greatest power in the 13th century when Genghis Khan and his successors conquered all of China and extended their influence westward as far as Hungary and Poland. The empire dissolved in later centuries and in 1691 was brought under suzerainty of the Manchus, who had conquered China in 1644. After the Chinese republican movement led by Sun Yat-sen overthrew the Manchus and set up the Chinese Republic in 1911, Mongolia, with the support of Russia, proclaimed its independence from China and, on March 13, 1921, established the Mongolian People's Republic.

MONETARY SYSTEM
100 Mongo = 1 Tukhrik

MONGO

COPPER

KM#	Year	Date	Fine	VF	XF	Unc
1	15	(1925)	5.00	7.00	10.00	17.50

ALUMINUM-BRONZE

9	27	(1937)	2.50	3.50	6.00	12.00

15	35	(1945)	2.00	3.00	5.00	10.00

ALUMINUM

KM#	Date	Mintage	Fine	VF	XF	Unc
21	1959	—	.25	.75	1.25	2.00

 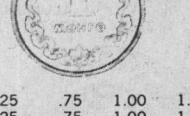

27	1970	—	.25	.75	1.00	1.50
	1977	—	.25	.75	1.00	1.50
	1980	—	.25	.75	1.00	1.50
	1981	—	.25	.75	1.00	1.50

2 MONGO

COPPER

KM#	Year	Date	Fine	VF	XF	Unc
2	15	(1925)	5.00	8.00	10.00	18.00

MONGOLIA 1293

MONGOLIA 1294

ALUMINUM-BRONZE

KM#	Year	Date	Fine	VF	XF	Unc
10	27	(1937)	2.50	3.50	5.00	10.00

| 16 | 35 | (1945) | 1.00 | 2.00 | 3.50 | 6.00 |

ALUMINUM

KM#	Date	Mintage	Fine	VF	XF	Unc
22	1959	—	.25	1.00	2.00	3.00

28	1970	—	.25	1.00	2.00	3.00
	1977	—	.25	1.00	2.00	3.00
	1980	—	.25	1.00	2.00	3.00

5 MONGO

COPPER

KM#	Year	Date	Fine	VF	XF	Unc
3	15	(1925)	6.00	12.50	17.50	30.00

ALUMINUM-BRONZE

| 11 | 27 | (1937) | 2.75 | 3.50 | 5.00 | 10.00 |

| 17 | 35 | (1945) | 2.25 | 3.50 | 4.50 | 7.50 |

ALUMINUM

KM#	Date	Mintage	Fine	VF	XF	Unc
23	1959	—	.25	1.00	2.00	3.00

29	1970	—	.25	1.00	2.00	3.00
	1977	—	.25	1.00	2.00	3.00
	1980	—	.25	1.00	2.00	3.00
	1981	—	.25	1.00	2.00	3.00

10 MONGO

1.7996 g, .500 SILVER, .0289 oz ASW

4	Yr.15(1925)					
		1.500	3.00	5.00	8.00	15.00

COPPER-NICKEL

KM#	Year	Date	Fine	VF	XF	Unc
12	27	(1937)	2.00	3.50	6.00	12.00

| 18 | 35 | (1945) | 2.00 | 3.50 | 5.00 | 9.00 |

ALUMINUM

KM#	Date	Mintage	Fine	VF	XF	Unc
24	1959	—	.75	1.50	3.00	5.00

COPPER-NICKEL

30	1970	—	.75	1.50	2.50	4.00
	1977	—	.75	1.50	2.50	4.00
	1980	—	.75	1.50	2.50	4.00
	1981	—	.75	1.50	2.50	4.00

15 MONGO

2.6994 g, .500 SILVER, .0433 oz ASW

5	Yr.15(1925)					
		.417	3.50	6.00	10.00	17.50

COPPER-NICKEL

KM#	Year	Date	Fine	VF	XF	Unc
13	27	(1937)	2.00	3.00	5.00	10.00

KM#	Year	Date	Fine	VF	XF	Unc
19	35	(1945)	2.25	2.75	4.00	7.00

ALUMINUM

KM#	Date	Mintage	Fine	VF	XF	Unc
25	1959	—	.25	1.00	2.00	3.50

COPPER-NICKEL

31	1970	—	.25	1.00	2.00	3.00
	1977	—	.25	1.00	2.00	3.00
	1980	—	.25	1.00	2.00	3.00

20 MONGO

3.5992 g, .500 SILVER, .0578 oz ASW

6	Yr.15(1925)					
		1.625	5.00	8.00	12.00	20.00

COPPER-NICKEL

KM#	Year	Date	Fine	VF	XF	Unc
14	27	(1937)	3.00	5.00	8.00	16.00

| 20 | 35 | (1945) | 2.00 | 3.50 | 5.00 | 9.00 |

ALUMINUM

KM#	Date	Mintage	Fine	VF	XF	Unc
26	1959	—	.75	1.50	2.50	3.50

COPPER-NICKEL

32	1970	—	.50	1.00	2.00	3.00
	1977	—	.50	1.00	2.00	3.00
	1980	—	.50	1.00	2.00	3.00

MONGOLIA

50 MONGO

9.9979 g, .900 SILVER, .2893 oz ASW

KM#	Date	Mintage	Fine	VF	XF	Unc
7	Yr.15(1925)	.920	8.50	12.50	20.00	35.00

COPPER-NICKEL

33	1970	—	.50	1.50	2.50	5.00
	1977	—	.50	1.50	2.50	5.00
	1980	—	.50	1.50	2.50	5.00
	1981	—	.50	1.50	2.50	5.00

TUKHRIK

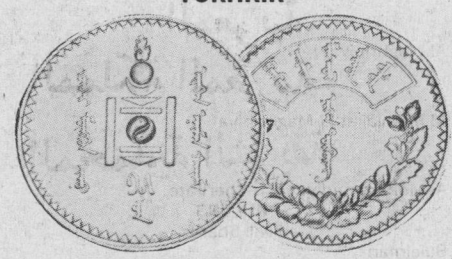

19.9957 g, .900 SILVER, .5786 oz ASW

8	Yr.15(1925)	.400	15.00	18.00	25.00	42.50

ALUMINUM-BRONZE
50th Anniversary of Republic
Date on edge.

34	1971	—	5.00	7.00	9.00	12.00

COPPER-NICKEL

34a	1971	—	5.00	7.00	9.00	12.00

18.4000 g, SILVER

34b	1971	—	—	Proof	50.00

30.3000 g, GOLD

34c	1971	5-10 pcs.	—	Proof	1500.

ALUMINUM-BRONZE
60th Anniversary of Independence
Obv: Arms. Rev: Warrior on horse.

41	1981	—	—	4.50	8.00

Soviet - Mongolian Space Flight

42	1981	—	—	3.50	6.00

60th Anniversary of the Revolution

KM#	Date	Mintage	Fine	VF	XF	Unc
43	1984	—	—	—	3.50	6.00

60th Anniversary of the State Bank

44	1984	—	—	3.50	6.00

Year of Peace

48	1986	—	—	3.50	6.00

65th Anniversary of Independence

49	1986	—	—	3.50	6.00

10 TUKHRIK

COPPER-NICKEL
State Bank

KM#	Date	Mintage	VF	XF	Unc
35	1974	—	—	—	7.50

International Games - Archery

KM#	Date	Mintage	VF	XF	Unc
46	1984	—	—	Proof	25.00

International Games - Equestrian

51	1984	—	—	Proof	25.00

25 TUKHRIK

28.2800 g, .925 SILVER, .8411 oz ASW
Conservation Series
Rev: Wild Mountain Sheep.

36	1976	5,348	—	—	22.50
	1976	6,096	—	Proof	30.00

19.4400 g, .925 SILVER, .5781 oz ASW
International Year of the Child

39	1980	.014	—	Proof	30.00

Decade For Women

47	1984	1,249	—	Proof	35.00

28.2800 g, .925 SILVER, .8411 oz ASW
World Wildlife Fund - Panther
Obv: Similar to KM#36.

50	1987	.025	—	Proof	40.00

MONGOLIA

50 TUKHRIK

35.0000 g, .925 SILVER, 1.0409 oz ASW
Conservation Series
Obv: Similar to 25 Tukhrik, KM#36.
Rev: Bactrian Camel.

KM#	Date	Mintage	VF	XF	Unc
37	1976	5,328	—	—	27.50
	1976	5,900	—	Proof	37.50

250 TUKHRIK

7.1300 g, .900 GOLD, .2062 oz AGW
Decade for Women

45	1984	500 pcs.	—	Proof	250.00

750 TUKHRIK

33.4370 g, .900 GOLD, .9676 oz AGW
Conservation Series
Rev: Przewalski's horse.

38	1976	929 pcs.	—	—	600.00
	1976	374 pcs.	—	Proof	900.00

18.7900 g, .900 GOLD, .5437 oz AGW
International Year of the Child

40	1980	.032	—	Proof	300.00

Listings For
MONTENEGRO: refer to Yugoslavia

MONTSERRAT

Montserrat, a British crown colony located in the Lesser Antilles of the West Indies 27 miles (43 km.) southwest of Antigua, has an area of 38 sq. mi. (98 sq. km.) and a population of 11,600. Capital: Plymouth. The island - actually a range of volcanic peaks rising from the Caribbean - exports cotton, limes and vegetables.
Columbus discovered Montserrat in 1493 and named it after Monserrado, a mountain in Spain. It was colonized by the English in 1632 and, except for brief periods of French occupancy in 1667 and 1782-83, has remained a British possession from that time. Until becoming a separate colony in 1956, Montserrat was a presidency of the Leeward Islands.

RULERS
British

MONETARY SYSTEM
1798-1840
12 Bits = 1 Dollar

4 DOLLARS

COPPER-NICKEL
F.A.O. Issue

KM#	Date	Mintage	Fine	VF	XF	Unc
16	1970	.013	—	—	6.00	8.00
	1970	2,000	—	—	Proof	20.00

MOROCCO

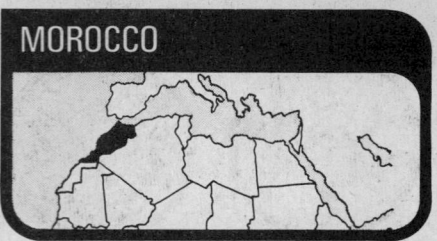

The Kingdom of Morocco, situated on the northwest corner of Africa, has an area of 275,117 sq. mi. (712,550 sq. km.) and a population of *25.4 million. Capital: Rabat. The economy is essentially agricultural. Phosphates, fresh and preserved vegetables, canned fish, and raw materials are exported.
Morocco's strategic position at the gateway to western Europe has been the principal determinant of its violent, frequently unfortunate history. Time and again the fertile plain between the rugged Atlas Mountains and the sea has echoed the battle's trumpet as Phoenicians, Romans, Vandals, Visigoths, Byzantine Greeks and Islamic Arabs successively conquered and occupied the land. Modern Morocco is a remnant of an early empire formed by the Arabs at the close of the 7th century which encompassed all of northwest Africa and most of the Iberian Peninsula. During the 17th and 18th centuries, while under the control of native dynasties, it was the headquarters of the famous Sale pirates. Morocco's strategic position involved it in the competition of 19th century European powers for political influence in Africa, and resulted in the division of Morocco into French and Spanish spheres of interest which were established as protectorates in 1912. Morocco became independent on March 2, 1956, after France agreed to end its protectorate. Spain signed similar agreements on April 7 of the same year.

TITLES

المغربية
Al-Maghribiyat

المملكة المغربية
Al-Mamlakat El-Maghribiyat

المحمدية الشريفة
Al-Mohammediyat Esh-Sherifate

RULERS
Filali Sharifs

Suleiman
  AH1207-1238/1793-1822AD
'Abd Al-Rahman
  AH1238-1276/1822-1859AD
Mohammed IV
  AH1276-1290/1859-1873AD
Al-Hasan
  AH1290-1312/1873-1895AD
'Abd Al-Aziz
  AH1312-1325/1895-1907AD
Al-Hafiz
  AH1325-1330/1907-1912AD
   French Protectorate
  AH1330/1912AD
Yusuf
  AH1330-1345/1912-1927AD
Mohammed V
  AH1345-1375/1927-1955AD
   Kingdom
Mohammed V
  AH1376-1381/1956-1962AD
Al-Hasan II
  AH1381- /1962AD

EARLY COINAGE

Prior to the introduction of modern machine-struck coinage in Morocco in AH1299 (= 1882AD), a variety of primitive cast bronze coins and crudely hammered silver and gold were in circulation, together with considerable quantities of foreign coins.
The cast bronze were produced in several denominations, multiples of the basic unit, the Falus. The size of the coins is variable, and the distinction of the various denominations is not always clear, particularly on the issues of Sulaiman. The early types are varied, but beginning about AH1218, the reverse bears the seal of Solomon, and the obverse contains the date and/or mint. The date is inscribed in European numerals, the mint, when present, is written out in Arabic script. Many of the issues are quite barbarous, with illegible dates and mints, and occasionally light in weight. These barbarous issues may have been contemporary counterfeits, and are of little numismatic value. The bronze pieces were cast in trees, and occasionally, entire or partial 'trees' are found on the market.
The silver and gold coins usually have the mint name on one side and the date on the other. The silver unit was the dirham of about 2.7 grams (but only about 2.0 grams from circa AH 1266-78), and the gold unit was the benduqi of about 3.25 grams. There were no fixed rates of exchange between coins of different metals.
Prices are for specimens with clearly legible dates and mint names (if any). Illegible, barbarous, and defectively produced pieces are worth much less.

MINTS
(a) - Paris privy marks only

Lr - Al-'Araish (Larache)	العرايش
Lr - Al-'Araisah (Larache)	العرايشة
Bi - Angland (Birmingham)	بانكلند
Ln - Bi-Angland (London)	بانكلند
Pa - Bi-Bariz (Paris)	بباريز
Be - Berlin	برلين
EM - Essaouir Mogador	الصويرة - الصوير
Fs - Fes (Fas, Fez)	فاس
FH - Fes Hazrat	فاس حضرة
KH - El Kitaoua Hazrat	حضرة الكتوة
MH - Marakesh Hazrat	مراكش
Mr - Marrakesh (Marakesh)	مراكش
Mk - Meknes (Miknas)	مكناس
Miknasah	مكناسة

(Py) - Poissy Inscribed "Paris" but with thunderbolt privy mark.

Rb - Rabat	رباط
RF - Rabat al-Fath	رباط الفتح
Si - Sijilmasah	سجلماسه
Sus	سوس
Sr - Al-Suwair	الصوير
Sh - Al-Suwairah	الصويرة
Tg - Tanjah (Tangier)	طنجة
Te - Tetuan	تطوان

(NM) = No mint name on coin.

NOTE: Some of the above forms of the mint names are shown as they appear on the coins, not in regular Arabic script.

The following coins are listed by Craig's numbers, and are therefore divided by reign. However, all of the coins are anonymous, and the distinction by reign is purely artificial. There is much variation within each type, and several of the subtypes overlap more than one reign. The coinage of Sulaiman II and Abd al-Rahman II are listed only by type (dates through AH1276 inclusive); those of Muhammad XVII (beginning AH1277 inclusive) and those of Mulai Hasan III are broken down by mint and date. However, the date listings for these two rulers are believed to be very incomplete.

Suleiman
AH1207-1238/1793-1822AD
FALUS

BRONZE

C#	Date	Good	VG	Fine	VF
95	AH1209-38	1.50	2.50	6.00	15.00

NOTE: Many varieties exist.

2 FALUS

BRONZE

96	AH1209-38	2.00	3.00	6.00	15.00

3 FALUS

BRONZE

97	AH1212-17	6.00	10.00	15.00	25.00

DIRHAM

SILVER, 17-20mm, 2.70 g

108	AH1211-37	4.00	7.00	11.00	20.00

BENDUQI

GOLD, 3.40 g
Fez Mint

KM#	Date	Mintage	VG	Fine	VF	XF
115	AH1216	—	50.00	70.00	100.00	150.00

'Abd al Rahman
AH1238-1276/1822-1859AD
1/2 FALUS
(Zelagh)

BRONZE, 13-14mm
Rev: Flower design.

C#	Date	Good	VG	Fine	VF
120	ND	2.00	3.50	6.00	10.00

Rev: Date.

121	AH1245	5.00	10.00	20.00	40.00
	1270				

FALUS

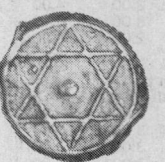 

BRONZE
Obv: Mint name above date.

C#	Date	Good	VG	Fine	VF
122	AH1240-76	1.00	2.00	3.50	8.00

NOTE: Many varieties exist.

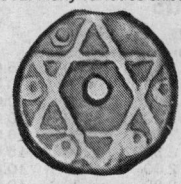 

126	AH1240-76	1.00	2.00	3.50	6.00

NOTE: Many varieties exist.

3 FALUS

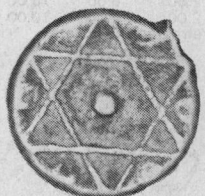 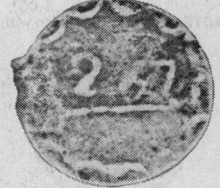

BRONZE

128	AH1264-69	2.50	4.50	7.50	12.50

1/2 DIRHAM

SILVER, 15-18mm, 1.30-1.40 g

135	AH1241-64	3.50	6.00	10.00	17.50

DIRHAM

SILVER, 17-20mm, 2.70 g

140	AH1240-52	4.00	7.00	11.00	20.00

Reduced standard, 2.00 g.

140a	AH1266-76	3.25	6.00	10.00	20.00

1/2 BENDUQI

GOLD, 1.60-1.70 g
Fez Mint

KM#	Date	Mintage	VG	Fine	VF	XF
145	AH12xx	—	50.00	70.00	100.00	150.00

BENDUQI

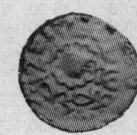 

GOLD, 3.20-3.40 g
Fez Mint

150	AH1251	—	55.00	70.00	100.00	150.00
	1269	—	55.00	70.00	100.00	150.00
	1270	—	55.00	70.00	100.00	150.00
	1271	—	55.00	70.00	100.00	150.00

Mohammed IV
AH1276-1290/1859-1873AD
FALUS

BRONZE
Early types.

C#	Date	Good	VG	Fine	VF
160	AH1277(NM)	1.00	2.00	4.00	10.00
	1277Fs	1.00	2.00	4.00	10.00
	1278(NM)	1.00	2.00	4.00	10.00
	1278Te	2.00	3.00	6.00	15.00
	1278Fs	1.00	2.00	4.00	10.00
	1279Te	2.00	3.00	6.00	15.00

MOROCCO 1298

C#	Date	Good	VG	Fine	VF
160	1280	1.00	2.00	4.00	10.00
	1281Te	2.00	3.00	6.00	15.00
	1281(Nl♦)	1.00	2.00	4.00	10.00

NOTE: Many varieties exist.

Reform type
Similar to 2 Falus, C#163a.

160a	AH1283Fs	2.00	3.00	10.00	20.00
	1283Mr	2.00	3.00	10.00	20.00
	1284Fs	2.00	3.00	10.00	20.00
	1285Fs	2.00	3.00	10.00	20.00
	1286Fs	2.00	3.00	10.00	20.00
	1287Fs	2.00	3.00	10.00	20.00
	1288Fs	2.00	3.00	10.00	20.00
	1289Fs	2.00	3.00	10.00	20.00

2 FALUS
BRONZE
Early types.

163	AH1277Te	1.25	2.50	6.00	15.00
	1277Fs	1.00	2.00	4.00	10.00
	1277Mr	1.00	2.00	4.00	10.00
	1277(NM)	1.00	2.00	4.00	10.00
	1278Fs	1.00	2.00	4.00	10.00
	1278Te	1.25	2.50	6.00	15.00
	1278(NM)	1.00	2.00	4.00	10.00
	1279Fs	1.00	2.00	4.00	10.00
	1279(NM)	1.00	2.00	4.00	10.00
	1280(NM)	1.00	2.00	4.00	10.00
	1281Fs	1.00	2.00	4.00	10.00
	1281Te	1.25	2.50	6.00	15.00
	1281(NM)	1.00	2.00	4.00	10.00

NOTE: 1281 Fz found also with retrograde '2' in date.

Reform type

163a	AH1283Fs	2.50	4.50	6.50	11.00
	1283Mr	2.00	3.00	5.00	10.00
	1284Fs	2.00	3.00	5.00	10.00
	1285Fs	2.00	3.00	5.00	10.00
	1285Mr	2.00	3.00	5.00	10.00
	1286Fs	2.00	3.00	5.00	10.00
	1287Fs	2.00	3.00	5.00	10.00
	1288Fs	2.00	3.00	5.00	10.00
	1288Mr	2.00	3.00	5.00	10.00
	1289Fs	2.00	3.00	5.00	10.00
	1290Fs	2.00	3.00	5.00	10.00

3 FALUS

BRONZE
Reform types.

166	AH1278Mr	2.00	3.00	5.00	8.00
	1280Fs	2.00	3.00	5.00	8.00
	1283Fs	1.75	3.25	5.00	8.00
	1283Mr	2.00	3.50	5.50	9.00
	1284Fs	1.50	3.00	4.50	7.50
	1284Mr	1.25	2.25	3.50	6.00
	1285Fs	1.50	2.75	4.00	6.50
	1285Mr	1.50	2.75	4.00	6.50
	1286/5Mr	1.75	3.25	5.00	8.00
	1286Fs	2.25	4.00	7.00	12.00
	1286Mr	1.00	1.75	2.75	4.50
	1287Fs	2.00	3.50	5.50	9.00
	1287Mr	2.00	3.50	5.50	9.00
	1288/7Fs	2.25	4.00	6.00	10.00
	1288Fs	.75	1.50	2.50	4.00
	1288Mr	1.00	1.75	3.00	5.00
	1289/79Mr	1.20	2.00	3.50	6.00
	1289/8Mr	1.20	2.00	3.50	6.00
	1289Fs	1.00	1.75	3.00	5.00
	1289Mr	1.50	2.75	4.00	6.50
	1290Fs	1.00	1.75	3.00	5.00

NOTE: Some AH1280 Fs are a poorly engraved 1284 Fs.

1/4 DIRHAM
(Mazuna)
SILVER, 0.65 g, 13mm
Muhammad XVII

170	AH1284Fs	4.00	6.50	10.00	16.50
	1284Mr	4.00	6.50	10.00	16.50
	1286Fs	4.00	6.50	10.00	16.50
	1288Fs	3.50	6.00	10.00	15.00

1/2 DIRHAM
SILVER, 15-18mm, 1.30-1.40 g

175	AH1283Fs	3.00	5.50	8.50	15.00
	1284Fs	3.00	5.50	8.50	15.00
	1284Mr	4.00	7.00	11.00	20.00
	1284Rb	4.25	8.00	12.50	20.00

C#	Date	Good	VG	Fine	VF
175	1286Fs	3.00	5.50	8.50	15.00
	1288Fs	3.00	5.50	8.50	15.00

DIRHAM
SILVER, 17-20mm, 2.70 g
Light standard, 2.00 g.

176	AH1277Fs	4.50	8.00	12.50	20.00
	1278Fs	4.50	8.00	12.50	20.00

Heavy standard restored, 2.70 g.

176a	AH1283Fs	4.00	7.00	12.00	20.00
	1284Fs	3.25	6.00	11.00	18.00
	1284Mr	3.75	7.00	12.00	20.00
	1284Rb	3.75	7.00	12.00	20.00
	1285Fs	4.00	7.00	12.00	20.00
	1286Fs	3.25	6.00	11.00	18.00
	1288Rb	4.00	7.00	12.00	20.00

Al-Hasan
AH1290-1312/1873-1895AD

2 FALUS
BRONZE
182	AH1295 uncertain mint	—	—	—	—

NOTE: All known specimens appear to be counterfeits.

3 FALUS
BRONZE

183	AH1291Mr	—	—	—	—
	1291Fs	5.00	8.00	12.50	20.00
	1295Mr	3.50	6.50	10.00	16.50
	1295Fs	3.50	6.50	10.00	16.50

	AH1311Fs	—	—	Rare	

1/2 DIRHAM
SILVER, 15-18mm, 1.30-1.40 g
186	AH1299Fs	15.00	20.00	30.00	50.00

DIRHAM
SILVER
187	AH1291Fs	10.00	15.00	30.00	50.00

MONETARY REFORM
MONETARY SYSTEM
Until 1921

50 Mazunas = 1 Dirham
10 Dirhams = 1 Rial

NOTES
Various copper and silver coins dated AH1297-1309 are believed to be patterns. Copper coins similar to Y#14-17, but without denomination on reverse, are patterns. On the silver coins the denominations are written in words and each series has its own characteristic names:
Y#4-8 (1299-1314) Denomination in Shar'i Dirhams.
Y#9-13 (1313-1319) Denomination in 'Preferred' Dirhams.
Y#18-22 (1320-1323) Denomination in fractions of a Rial, but on the 3 larger sizes, the equivalent is given in "Urti parts", 1 Rial 20 – Urti parts.
Y#23-25 (1329) Denomination in Dirhams and in fraction of a Rial.
Y#30-33 (1331-1336) Denomination in Yusuti or "Treasury" Dirhams.
On most of the larger denominations, the denomination is given in the form of a rhymed couplet.

1/2 MAZUNA

BRONZE

Y#	Date	Mintage	Fine	VF	XF	Unc
C1	AH1306Fs	—	—	—	Rare	
	1310Fs	—	175.00	275.00	475.00	750.00

NOTE: Some authorities consider Y#C1 to be a Mazuna.

MAZUNA

BRONZE

Y#	Date	Mintage	Fine	VF	XF	Unc
B1	AH1310Fs	—	125.00	200.00	350.00	600.00

NOTE: Some authorities regard Y#B1 as a 2 Mazuna.

2-1/2 MAZUNAS

BRONZE

1	AH1310Fs	—	125.00	200.00	350.00	600.00

NOTE: Some authorities consider Y#1 to be a 3 Mazuna.

5 MAZUNAS

2	AH1306Fs	—	—	—	Rare	
	1310Fs	—	125.00	200.00	350.00	600.00

10 MAZUNAS

BRONZE

3	AH1306Fs	—	40.00	60.00	125.00	360.00
	1310Fs					

1/2 DIRHAM
(1/20 Rial)

1.4558 g, .835 SILVER, .0391 oz ASW

4	AH1299Pa	2.200	1.25	2.00	6.00	17.50
	1309Pa	1.700	2.25	5.00	12.00	27.50
	1310Pa	1.700	2.00	4.00	9.00	20.00
	1311Pa	1.700	2.00	4.00	9.00	20.00
	1312Pa	1.700	2.00	4.00	9.00	20.00
	1313Pa	1.700	2.00	4.00	9.00	20.00
	1314Pa	1.700	5.00	12.50	22.50	45.00

DIRHAM
(1/10 Rial)

2.9116 g, .835 SILVER, .0782 oz ASW

5	AH1299Pa	6.800	2.00	4.00	8.00	20.00
	1309Pa	1.700	2.75	8.00	20.00	35.00
	1310Pa	1.800	2.75	7.00	17.50	30.00
	1311Pa	.800	2.75	7.00	17.50	30.00
	1312Pa	.800	2.75	7.00	17.50	30.00
	1313Pa	.800	3.00	8.00	22.50	30.00
	1314Pa	Inc. Y10	10.00	20.00	35.00	75.00

2-1/2 DIRHAMS
(1/4 Rial)

MOROCCO 1299

7.2790 g, .835 SILVER, .1954 oz ASW

Y#	Date	Mintage	Fine	VF	XF	Unc
6	AH1299Pa	2.100	3.00	10.00	20.00	30.00
	1299Pa	—	—	—	Proof	225.00
	1309Pa	.700	4.00	12.00	30.00	55.00
	1310Pa	.400	4.00	12.00	30.00	55.00
	1311Pa	.800	4.00	12.00	30.00	55.00
	1312Pa	.300	4.00	12.00	30.00	55.00
	1313Pa	.300	4.00	12.00	30.00	55.00
	1314Pa	—	20.00	45.00	75.00	140.00

5 DIRHAMS
(1/2 Rial)

14.5580 g, .835 SILVER, .3908 oz ASW

Y#	Date	Mintage	Fine	VF	XF	Unc
7	AH1299Pa	1.400	8.00	15.00	30.00	60.00
	1299Pa	—	—	—	Proof	400.00
	1309Pa	.280	12.00	22.50	40.00	125.00
	1310Pa	.170	8.00	20.00	35.00	90.00
	1311Pa	.170	8.00	20.00	35.00	90.00
	1312Pa	.170	8.00	20.00	35.00	90.00
	1313Pa	.170	15.00	30.00	55.00	150.00
	1314Pa					
	Inc. Y12	100.00	175.00	300.00	750.00	

10 DIRHAMS
(Rial)

29.1160 g, .900 SILVER, .8425 oz ASW

| 8 | AH1299Pa | .870 | 15.00 | 30.00 | 50.00 | 140.00 |

'Abd Al-Aziz
AH1312-1325/1895-1907AD

MAZUNA

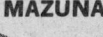 

BRONZE

14	AH1320Be	5 pcs.	—	—	Proof	700.00
	1320Bi	3.000	2.00	5.00	9.00	20.00
	1320Fz	—	20.00	35.00	50.00	120.00
	1321Bi	.900	2.50	6.00	12.00	35.00

NOTE: 5 million examples of 1320 Pa were struck and melted, but at least one specimen is known to exist.

2 MAZUNAS

BRONZE

Y#	Date	Mintage	Fine	VF	XF	Unc
15.1	AH1320Be	5 pcs.	—	—	Proof	700.00
	1320Bi	1.500	2.00	5.00	10.00	25.00
	1320Bi	—	—	—	Proof	250.00
	1321Bi	.450	2.00	5.00	10.00	25.00
	1321Pa	6.500	2.00	5.00	10.00	25.00

NOTE: Varieties exist.

Rev: Rim design reversed.

15.2	AH1320Fs	—	10.00	25.00	35.00	50.00
	1322Fs	—	10.00	25.00	35.00	75.00
	1323Fs	—	15.00	35.00	50.00	100.00

5 MAZUNAS

BRONZE

16	AH1320Be	*5 pcs.	—	—	Proof	700.00
	1320Bi	2.400	1.00	3.00	8.00	25.00
	1320Bi	—	—	—	Proof	300.00
	1320Fs	—	15.00	35.00	50.00	100.00
	1321Bh	.720	1.00	3.00	8.00	30.00
	1321Fs	—	Reported, not confirmed			
	1321Pa	7.950	5.00	10.00	20.00	35.00
	1322Fs	—	25.00	60.00	100.00	150.00

*NOTE: An additional 799,764 pieces are reported struck, but very few are known.
NOTE: Varieties exist.

10 MAZUNAS

BRONZE

17	AH1320Be	2.400	1.25	2.50	6.00	25.00
	1320Bi	1.200	1.50	4.00	6.50	25.00
	1320Fs	—	12.00	20.00	55.00	125.00
	1320Pa	—	1.50	3.50	6.00	25.00
	1321Be	2.600	1.25	3.00	6.00	25.00
	1321Bi	.360	1.00	2.00	3.25	25.00
	1321Fs	—	8.00	20.00	45.00	100.00
	1323Fs lg.10	—	35.00	60.00	75.00	150.00
	1323Fs sm.10					
		—	35.00	60.00	75.00	150.00

1/2 DIRHAM

1.4558 g, .835 SILVER, .0391 oz ASW

9	AH1313Be	.560	15.00	17.50	22.50	40.00
	1314Pa	2.200	7.50	12.50	17.50	35.00
	1315Pa	1.190	2.50	4.00	7.50	20.00
	1316Pa	2.280	2.50	7.00	12.50	25.00
	1317Pa	1.700	2.00	4.00	7.50	25.00
	1318Pa	1.715	4.00	8.00	12.00	25.00
	1319Pa	—	2.50	5.00	10.00	25.00

1.2500 g, .835 SILVER, .0336 oz ASW

18	AH1320Ln	3.920	1.25	4.00	10.00	27.50
	1320Pa	2.400	1.50	4.00	10.00	27.50
	1321Ln	2.105	Inc. 1320Ln			
			3.00	5.00	10.00	25.00

DIRHAM

2.9116 g, .835 SILVER, .0782 oz AGW
Rev: Arrow heads point outwards.

Y#	Date	Mintage	Fine	VF	XF	Unc
10.1	AH1313Be	.430	6.00	12.50	20.00	40.00

Rev: Arrow heads point inwards.

10.2	AH1314Pa	1.400	3.00	7.00	15.00	30.00
	1315Pa	.860	3.00	7.00	15.00	30.00
	1316Pa	.860	3.00	7.00	15.00	30.00
	1317Pa	.860	3.00	7.00	15.00	30.00
	1318Pa	.858	3.00	7.00	15.00	30.00

2.5000 g, .835 SILVER, .0671 oz ASW

19	AH1320Ln	2.940	3.00	8.00	15.00	40.00
	1321Ln	.770	3.00	8.00	15.00	40.00

2-1/2 DIRHAMS

7.2790 g, .835 SILVER, .1954 oz ASW

11	AH1313Be	.220	7.50	15.00	25.00	75.00
	1314Pa	1.036	5.00	8.00	20.00	20.00
	1315Be	.640	5.00	10.00	15.00	50.00
	1315Pa	.340	5.00	10.00	15.00	50.00
	1316Pa	.400	5.00	15.00	50.00	75.00
	1317Pa	.340	5.00	15.00	50.00	75.00
	1318Be	.146	10.00	40.00	75.00	125.00
	1318Pa	.340	10.00	35.00	60.00	100.00

6.2500 g, .835 SILVER, .1678 oz ASW

20	AH1320Be	.380	4.00	12.50	20.00	45.00
	1320Ln	3.056	4.00	10.00	12.50	35.00
	1320Pa	.640	4.00	11.00	17.50	40.00
	1321Be	4.450	4.00	8.00	12.50	30.00
	1321Ln	1.889	4.00	8.00	12.50	30.00
	1321Ln	—	—	—	Proof	350.00
	1321Pa	—	40.00	60.00	125.00	250.00

5 DIRHAMS

14.5580 g, .835 SILVER, .3908 oz ASW

12	AH1313Be	.110	15.00	30.00	60.00	125.00
	1314Pa	.517	10.00	20.00	50.00	85.00
	1315Be	.360	10.00	16.00	35.00	75.00
	1315Pa	.160	10.00	16.00	35.00	80.00
	1316Pa	.225	10.00	20.00	35.00	100.00
	1317Pa	.170	10.00	20.00	35.00	100.00
	1318Be	.073	20.00	50.00	85.00	150.00
	1318Pa	.177	12.50	30.00	50.00	125.00

MOROCCO 1300

12.5000 g, .835 SILVER, .3356 oz ASW

Y#	Date	Mintage	Fine	VF	XF	Unc
21	AH1320Be	2.510	7.00	15.00	30.00	75.00
	1320Ln	.900	7.00	15.00	30.00	75.00
	1321Be	—	—	—	Rare	—
	1321Ln	1.041	7.00	15.00	30.00	75.00
	1321Ln	—	—	—	Proof	450.00
	1321Pa	1.800	7.00	17.50	35.00	85.00
	1322Pa	.540	7.00	20.00	40.00	100.00
	1323Pa	1.090	7.00	20.00	40.00	100.00

10 DIRHAMS

29.1160 g, .900 SILVER, .8425 oz ASW

13	AH1313Be	.050	75.00	150.00	225.00	320.00
	1313Be	—	—	—	Proof	750.00

25.0000 g, .900 SILVER, .7234 oz ASW

22	AH1320Ln	.330	17.50	25.00	40.00	150.00
	1320Ln	—	—	—	Proof	Rare
	1321Pa	.300	20.00	27.50	40.00	150.00

Al-Hafiz
AH1325-1330/1907-1912AD

2-1/2 DIRHAMS

6.2500 g, .835 SILVER, .1678 oz ASW

Y#	Date	Mintage	Fine	VF	XF	Unc
23	AH1329Pa	3.130	4.00	8.50	18.00	40.00

5 DIRHAMS

12.5000 g, .835 SILVER, .3356 oz ASW

24	AH1329Pa	4.660	7.00	10.00	30.00	100.00

10 DIRHAMS

25.0000 g, .900 SILVER, .7234 oz ASW

25	AH1329Pa	7.040	10.00	20.00	40.00	100.00

Yusuf
AH1330-1345 / 1912-1927AD

MAZUNA

BRONZE

26	AH1330Pa	1.850	2.00	5.00	17.00	32.50

2 MAZUNAS

BRONZE

27	AH1330Pa	2.790	2.00	4.00	12.00	32.50

NOTE: Coins reportedly dated 1331 Pa probably bore date 1330.

5 MAZUNAS

BRONZE

Y#	Date	Mintage	Fine	VF	XF	Unc
28.1	AH1330Pa	3.180	2.00	5.00	11.00	25.00

Rev: Privy marks.

28.2	1340Pa	2.000	1.00	2.00	5.00	25.00
	1340Py	2.010	2.00	5.00	8.00	27.50

10 MAZUNAS

BRONZE

29.1	AH1330Pa	1.500	.75	3.00	12.00	30.00

Rev: Privy marks.

29.2	1340Pa	1.000	.75	1.50	7.50	25.00
	1340Py	1.000	1.25	3.00	12.50	35.00

DIRHAM

2.5000 g, .835 SILVER, .0671 oz ASW

30	AH1331Pa	.500	30.00	45.00	75.00	200.00

2-1/2 DIRHAMS

6.2500 g, .835 SILVER, .1678 oz ASW

31	AH1331Pa	2.500	30.00	45.00	85.00	275.00

5 DIRHAMS

.835 SILVER

32	AH1331Pa	1.500	7.00	16.00	25.00	60.00
	1336Pa	11.500	6.00	11.00	20.00	50.00

10 DIRHAMS

25.0000 g, .900 SILVER, .7234 oz ASW

Y#	Date	Mintage	Fine	VF	XF	Unc
33	AH1331Pa	7.000	9.00	20.00	35.00	90.00
	1336Pa	2.600	9.00	17.50	25.00	65.00

FRENCH PROTECTORATE
MONETARY SYSTEM
100 Centimes = 1 Franc
100 Francs = 1 Dirham

NOTE: Y46-51 were struck for more than 20 years without change of date, until a new currency was introduced in 1974. Final mintage statistics are not yet available.

25 CENTIMES

COPPER-NICKEL
Obv. and rev: W/o privy marks.

34.1	ND (1921)Pa	13.000	1.00	2.50	5.00	40.00

Rev: Thunderbolt above CENTIMES.

34.2	ND (1924)Py	6.020	1.00	2.50	6.00	40.00

Rev: Thunderbolt and torch at left and right of CENTIMES.

34.3	ND(1924)Py	Inc. Ab.	1.00	2.50	6.00	40.00

50 CENTIMES

NICKEL
Obv. and rev: W/o privy marks.

35.1	ND(1921)Pa	11.000	.50	1.00	3.50	45.00

Rev: Thunderbolt at bottom.

35.2	ND(1924)Py	3.000	1.00	2.00	6.00	45.00

FRANC
NICKEL
Obv. and rev: W/o privy marks.

36.1	ND(1921)Pa	13.510	.50	1.00	3.50	45.00

Rev: Thunderbolt below 1.

Y#	Date	Mintage	Fine	VF	XF	Unc
36.2	ND(1924)Py	3.000	1.25	2.50	7.50	55.00

Mohammed
AH1345-1375 / 1927-1955AD

50 CENTIMES

ALUMINUM-BRONZE

Y#	Date	Year	Mintage	VF	XF	Unc
40	AH1364(a)	1945	—	.20	1.50	2.50

FRANC

ALUMINUM-BRONZE

41	AH1364(a) 1945	12.000	.25	1.00	2.50

ALUMINUM

46	AH1370(a) 1951	—	.10	.25	1.00

2 FRANCS

ALUMINUM-BRONZE

42	AH1364(a) 1945	12.000	.50	2.50	6.00

ALUMINUM

47	AH1370(a) 1951	—	.10	.50	2.00

5 FRANCS

5.0000 g, .680 SILVER, .1093 oz ASW

37	AH1347(a)	4.000	2.50	5.00	30.00
	1352(a)	5.000	1.50	3.00	15.00

ALUMINUM-BRONZE

Y#	Date	Mintage	Fine	VF	XF	Unc
43	AH1365(a)	20.000	.15	.35	.60	1.50

ALUMINUM

Y#	Date	Mintage	Fine	VF	XF	Unc
48	AH1370(a)	—	.10	.15	.30	1.00

10 FRANCS

10.0000 g, .680 SILVER, .2186 oz ASW

38	AH1347(a)	1.600	4.00	10.00	22.00	80.00
	1352(a)	2.900	2.25	3.00	8.00	27.50

COPPER-NICKEL

44	AH1366(a)	20.000	.35	.75	1.00	1.50

ALUMINUM-BRONZE

49	AH1371(a)	—	.10	.35	.75	2.00

20 FRANCS

20.0000 g, .680 SILVER, .4372 oz ASW

39	AH1347(a)	—	5.00	12.00	32.50	80.00
	1352(a)	2.000	3.00	8.00	25.00	50.00

COPPER-NICKEL

45	AH1366(a)	6.000	.25	.50	1.00	2.00
	1366	—	—	—	—	Proof 50.00

MOROCCO 1302

ALUMINUM-BRONZE

Y#	Date	Mintage	Fine	VF	XF	Unc
50	AH1371(a)			.10	.25	.75	1.50

50 FRANCS

ALUMINUM-BRONZE

| 51 | AH1371(a) | | .25 | .50 | .65 | 1.00 |

100 FRANCS

4.0000 g, .720 SILVER, .0926 oz ASW

Y#	Date	Year	Mintage	VF	XF	Unc
A54	AH1370(a)	1951	10.000	—	—	175.00

NOTE: Most were remelted.

| 52 | AH1372(a) | 1953 | 5.000 | 2.50 | 3.50 | 5.00 |

200 FRANCS

8.0000 g, .720 SILVER, .1851 oz ASW

| 53 | AH1372(a) | 1953 | 9.200 | 2.00 | 4.00 | 8.00 |

KINGDOM
1956-
Mohammed V
AH1376-1381 / 1956-1962AD

500 FRANCS

22.5000 g, .900 SILVER, .6511 oz ASW

| 54 | AH1376(a) | 1956 | 2.000 | 8.50 | 12.50 | 17.50 |

MONETARY REFORM
100 Francs = 1 Dirham

DIRHAM
(100 Francs)

6.0000 g, .600 SILVER, .1157 oz ASW

Y#	Date	Year	Mintage	VF	XF	Unc
55	AH1380(a)	1960	30.600	1.00	2.50	6.00

Al-Hasan II
AH1381- /1962- AD

DIRHAM
(100 Francs)

NICKEL

56	AH1384(a)	1965	35.000	.40	.75	1.00
	1388(a)	1968	—	.40	.75	1.00
	1389(a)	1969	—	.40	.75	1.00

5 DIRHAM
(500 Francs)

11.7500 g, .720 SILVER, .2720 oz ASW

| 57 | AH1384(a) | 1965 | 1.800 | 5.00 | 7.00 | 12.50 |
| | 1384(a) | 1965 | 200 pcs. | — | Proof | 60.00 |

MONETARY REFORM
1974-
100 Santimat = 1 Dirham

SANTIM

ALUMINUM

58	AH1394	1974	14.200	—	.75	1.50
	1394	1974	.020	—	Proof	1.00
	1395	1975	1.700	—	.10	1.00
	1395	1975	.014	—	Proof	2.50

.917 GOLD

| 58a | AH1394 | 1974 | 30 pcs. | — | Proof | 400.00 |

5 SANTIMAT

BRASS
F.A.O. Issue

59	AH1394	1974	71.800	—	.20	.40
	1394	1974	.020	—	Proof	1.00
	1395	1975	11.000	—	.10	.25
	1398	1978	12.600	—	.10	.25

.917 GOLD

| 59a | AH1394 | 1974 | 30 pcs. | — | Proof | 400.00 |

BRASS
F.A.O. Issue
Obv: Arms. Rev: Wheat ears, value and date.

| 83 | AH1407 | 1987 | | | | .25 |

10 SANTIMAT

BRASS
F.A.O. Issue

Y#	Date	Year	Mintage	VF	XF	Unc
60	AH1394	1974	93.800	—	.20	.40
	1394	1974	.020	—	Proof	1.50
	1395	1975	10.900	—	.10	.20
	1398	1978	1.000	—	.10	.30

.917 GOLD

| 60a | AH1394 | 1974 | 30 pcs. | — | Proof | 500.00 |

BRASS
F.A.O. Issue
Obv: Arms. Rev: Ear of corn, value and date.

| 84 | AH1407 | 1987 | | | | .25 |

20 SANTIMAT

BRASS

61	AH1394	1974	25.000	.30	.40	.50
	1394	1974	—	—	Proof	2.00
	1395	1975	10.700	.10	.15	.35
	1397	1977	22.800	.10	.15	.35
	1398	1978	2.200	.10	.15	.35

.917 GOLD

| 61a | AH1394 | 1974 | 30 pcs. | — | Proof | 600.00 |

BRASS
F.A.O. Issue
Obv: Arms. Rev: Ornamental design, value and date.

| 85 | AH1407 | 1987 | | | | .35 |

50 SANTIMAT

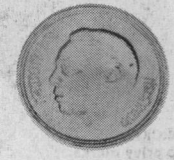 

COPPER-NICKEL

62	AH1394	1974	48.900	.20	.40	.60
	1394	1974	.020	—	Proof	2.50
	1398	1978	1.100	.25	.50	.75

.917 GOLD

| 62a | AH1394 | 1974 | 30 pcs. | — | Proof | 600.00 |

DIRHAM

COPPER-NICKEL

63	AH1394	1974	21.900	.30	.50	.75
	1394	1974	.020	—	Proof	4.00
	1398	1978	18.100	.15	.35	.75

.917 GOLD

| 63a | AH1394 | 1974 | 30 pcs. | — | Proof | 700.00 |

5 DIRHAMS

COPPER-NICKEL
F.A.O. Issue: World Food Conference

| 64 | AH1395 | 1975 | .500 | — | 1.00 | 3.50 |
| | 1395 | 1975 | 500 pcs. | — | Proof | 7.00 |

12.0000 g, .925 SILVER, .3569 oz ASW

| 64a | AH1395 | 1975 | 200 pcs. | — | — | Proof |

23.6500 g, .900 GOLD, .6844 oz AGW

| 64b | AH1395 | 1975 | 20 pcs. | — | Proof | 950.00 |

MOROCCO 1303

COPPER-NICKEL

Y#	Date	Year	Mintage	VF	XF	Unc
72 (A63)	AH1400	1980	10.000	1.00	4.00	6.00

STAINLESS STEEL RING, ALUMINUM-BRONZE CENTER
| 82 | AH1407 | 1987 | — | — | — | 1.00 |

50 DIRHAMS

35.0000 g, .925 SILVER, 1.0409 oz ASW
20th Anniversary Independence
| 65 | AH1395 | 1975 | 6,000 | — | — | 30.00 |
| | 1395 | 1975 | 4,400 | — | Proof | 50.00 |

60.1400 g, .900 GOLD, 1.7404 oz AGW
| 65a | AH1395 | 1975 | 40 pcs. | — | Proof | 2250. |

35.0000 g, .925 SILVER, 1.0409 oz ASW
International Women's Year
Obv: Similar to Y#65.
| 67 | AH1395 | 1975 | 6,000 | — | — | 27.50 |
| | 1395 | 1975 | 4,400 | — | Proof | 60.00 |

60.1400 g, .900 GOLD, 1.7404 oz AGW
| 67a | AH1395 | 1975 | 20 pcs. | — | Proof | 2500. |

35.0000 g, .925 SILVER, 1.0409 oz ASW
Anniversary Green March
Obv: Similar to Y#65.
Y#	Date	Year	Mintage	VF	XF	Unc
68	AH1396	1976	.011	—	—	20.00
	1396	1976	4,400	—	Proof	55.00
	1397	1977	3,500	—	—	30.00
	1397	1977	200 pcs.	—	Proof	50.00
	1398	1978	5,000	—	—	25.00
	1398	1978	300 pcs.	—	Proof	45.00
	1399	1979	3,000	—	—	30.00
	1399	1979	300 pcs.	—	Proof	45.00
	1400	1980	1,000	—	—	35.00
	1400	1980	200 pcs.	—	Proof	50.00

60.1400 g, .900 GOLD, 1.7404 oz AGW
68a	AH1396	1976	20 pcs.	—	Proof	2250.
	1397	1977	20 pcs.	—	Proof	2250.
	1398	1978	70 pcs.	—	Proof	2000.
	1399	1979	70 pcs.	—	Proof	2000.
	1400	1980	30 pcs.	—	Proof	2100.

35.0000 g, .925 SILVER, 1.0409 oz ASW
International Year of the Child
Obv: Similar to Y#65.
| 70 | AH1399 | 1979 | 5,000 | — | — | 25.00 |
| | 1399 | 1979 | 500 pcs. | — | Proof | 50.00 |

60.1400 g, .900 GOLD, 1.7404 oz AGW
| 70a | AH1399 | 1979 | 70 pcs. | — | Proof | 2000. |

35.0000 g, .925 SILVER, 1.0409 oz ASW
50th Birthday King Hassan
| 76 | AH1399 | 1979 | 5,000 | — | — | 30.00 |
| | 1399 | 1979 | 500 pcs. | — | Proof | 50.00 |

60.1400 g, .900 GOLD, 1.7404 oz AGW
| 76a | AH1399 | 1979 | 70 pcs. | — | Proof | 2000. |

100 DIRHAMS

25.0000 g, .925 SILVER, .7436 oz ASW
9th Mediterranean Games
Obv: Similar to 50 Dirhams, Y#65.
Y#	Date	Year	Mintage	VF	XF	Unc
75	AH1403	1983	5,000	—	—	25.00
	1403	1983	500 pcs.	—	Proof	50.00

15.0000 g, .925 SILVER, .4461 oz ASW
Olympic Games
| 77 | AH1405 | 1985 | 2,300 | — | — | 25.00 |
| | 1405 | 1985 | 300 pcs. | — | Proof | 65.00 |

| 78 | AH1406 | 1985 | 1,200 | — | — | 25.00 |
| | 1406 | 1985 | 200 pcs. | — | Proof | 75.00 |

Anniversary Green March
| 79 | AH1406 | 1986 | — | — | — | 25.00 |

Visit of the Pope
| 80 | AH1406 | 1986 | 2,000 | — | Proof | 45.00 |

150 DIRHAMS

35.0000 g, .925 SILVER, 1.0409 oz ASW
15th Hijrah Calendar Century
Obv: Similar to Y#73.
| 74 | AH1401 | 1980 | 3,000 | — | — | 30.00 |
| | 1401 | 1980 | 300 pcs. | — | Proof | 50.00 |

60.1400 g, .900 GOLD, 1.7404 oz AGW
| 74a | AH1401 | 1980 | 30 pcs. | — | Proof | 2250. |

MOZAMBIQUE 1304

35.0000 g, .925 SILVER, 1.0409 oz ASW
20th Anniversary King Hassan's Coronation

Y#	Date	Year	Mintage	VF	XF	Unc
73	AH1401	1981	3,000	—	—	35.00
	1401	1981	300 pcs.	—	Proof	55.00

60.1400 g, .900 GOLD, 1.7404 oz AGW

| 73a | AH1401 | 1981 | 30 pcs. | — | Proof | 2250. |

200 DIRHAMS

15.0000 g, .925 SILVER, .4461 oz ASW
Moroccan - American Friendship Treaty

| 81 | AH1408 | 1987 | *5,000 | — | Proof | 55.00 |

250 DIRHAMS

6.4500 g, .900 GOLD, .1867 oz AGW
Birthday of King Hassan

66	AH1395	1975	5,000	—	—	100.00
	1395	1975	1,270	—	Proof	125.00
	1396	1976	3,200	—	—	100.00
	1396	1976	450 pcs.	—	Proof	175.00
	1397	1977	3,000	—	—	100.00
	1397	1977	800 pcs.	—	Proof	150.00
	1398	1978	2,000	—	—	100.00
	1398	1978	150 pcs.	—	Proof	200.00
	1399	1979	508 pcs.	—	—	150.00
	1399	1979	398 pcs.	—	Proof	175.00

500 DIRHAMS

12.9000 g, .900 GOLD, .3733 oz AGW
Birthday of King Hassan

71	AH1399	1979	3,000	—	—	200.00
	1399	1979	300 pcs.	—	Proof	300.00
	1400	1980	100 pcs.	—	—	450.00
	1400	1980	100 pcs.	—	Proof	500.00
	1401	1981	100 pcs.	—	—	450.00
	1401	1981	100 pcs.	—	Proof	500.00
	1402	1982	100 pcs.	—	—	450.00
	1402	1982	100 pcs.	—	Proof	500.00

Y#	Date	Year	Mintage	VF	XF	Unc
71	1403	1983	2,500	—	—	250.00
	1403	1983	Inc. Ab.	—	Proof	250.00
	1404	1984	100 pcs.	—	—	450.00
	1404	1984	100 pcs.	—	Proof	500.00
	1405	1985	275 pcs.	—	—	275.00
	1405	1985	125 pcs.	—	Proof	500.00

MINT SETS (MS)
Fleur de Coin

KM#	Date	Mintage	Identification	Issue Price	Mkt. Val.
MS1	1951-65(8)	—	Y46-51,56,57	—	17.50

PROOF SETS (PS)

| PS1 | 1974-75(7) | .020 | Y58-64 | 20.00 | 20.00 |
| PS2 | 1974(6) | 30 | Y58a-63a | — | 3200. |

MOZAMBIQUE

The People's Republic of Mozambique, a former overseas province of Portugal stretching for 1,430 miles (2,301 km.) along the southeast coast of Africa, has an area of 302,330 sq. mi. (783,030 sq. km.) and a population of 15.3 million, 99 percent of whom are native Africans of the Bantu tribes. Capital: Maputo. Agriculture is the chief industry. Cashew nuts, cotton, sugar, copra and tea are exported.

Vasco de Gama explored all the coast of Mozambique in 1498 and found Arab trading posts already established along the coast. Portuguese settlement dates from the establishment of the trading post of Mozambique in 1505. Within five years Portugal absorbed all the former Arab sultanates along the east African coast. The area was organized as a colony in 1907 and became an overseas province in 1952. In Sept. of 1974, after more than a decade of guerrilla warfare with the forces of the Mozambique Liberation Front, Portugal agreed to the independence of Mozambique, effective June 25, 1975.

Maria Theresa talers and other foreign coins stamped with PM or with crowned PM served as an emergency coinage from about 1888 to 1895.

RULERS
Portuguese, until 1975

MINT MARKS
R - Rio

MONETARY SYSTEM
2880 Reis = 6 Cruzados = 1 Onca

REAL

COPPER

KM#	Date	Mintage	VG	Fine	VF	XF
24 (29)	1853	.100	1.75	4.00	8.00	13.50

II (2) REIS

COPPER

| 25 (30) | 1853 | .100 | 3.50 | 7.50 | 12.50 | 20.00 |

NOTE: The V Reis, X Reis and XX Reis pieces dated 1853 were issued for circulation in Mozambique. These are also attributed to Portugal and will be found under their appropriate listings.

20 REIS
COPPER

| 18 | 1820 Rio | — | 4.50 | 7.50 | 15.00 | 25.00 |

NOTE: For coins with c/m '10' refer to Brazil listings. Some 20 Reis coins previously listed here are now listed in St. Thomas and Prince Islands.

| 21 | 1840 | .040 | 4.00 | 6.00 | 15.00 | 30.00 |

40 REIS
COPPER

| 19 | 1820 Rio | — | 2.75 | 5.00 | 10.00 | 15.00 |

NOTE: For coins with c/m '20' refer to Brazil listings. Some 40 Reis coins previously listed here are now listed in St. Thomas and Prince Islands.

| 22 | 1840 | .020 | 4.00 | 6.00 | 15.00 | 30.00 |

80 REIS

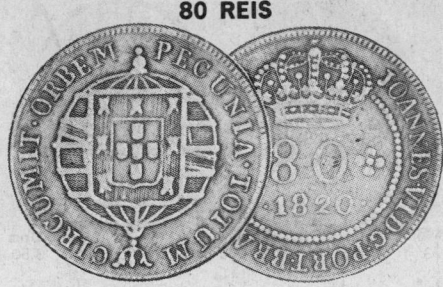

COPPER

KM#	Date	Mintage	VG	Fine	VF	XF
20	1820 Rio	—	6.00	10.00	15.00	22.50

NOTE: Other 80 Reis coins previously listed here are now listed in St. Thomas and Prince Islands.

| 23 | 1840 | .010 | | 15.00 | 25.00 | 35.00 |

ONCA

SILVER
Obv: Small date, lettering.

| 26.1 | 1843 | — | 50.00 | 150.00 | 300.00 | — |

Obv: Large date, lettering.

| 26.2 | 1845 | — | 70.00 | 165.00 | 350.00 | — |
| | 1847 | — | 50.00 | 150.00 | 300.00 | — |

1-1/4 MATICAES

7.20 g, GOLD, Rectangular, 11x17mm

| 31 (34) | ND(1835) | — | 550.00 | 1300. | 3000. | — |

c/m: Rosette on KM#31.

| 32 (36) | ND(1851) | — | 300.00 | 700.00 | 1500. | |

2-1/2 MATICAES

14.50 g, GOLD

| 33 (35) | ND(1835) | — | 700.00 | 1000. | 2000. | |

c/m: Rosette on KM#33.

KM#	Date	Mintage	VG	Fine	VF	XF
34 (37)	ND(1851)	—	300.00	500.00	800.00	—

COUNTERMARKED COINAGE
Decree of January 5, 1889

This decree ordained that all foreign silver coinage circulating in Mozambique was to be countermarked with a crowned PM within a circle. These coins were eventually to be replaced or exchanged by current Portuguese coinage upon their entry into the public treasury. The following list is a basic guide. Caution should be exercised as counterfeits exist. Grades noted are for the basic coin as the countermark is normally found in better condition than the coin bearing it.

6 PENCE
.925 SILVER
c/m: Crowned PM on Great Britain 6 Pence, KM#751.

KM#	Date	Mintage	Good	VG	Fine	VF
35	ND(1870)	—	25.00	40.00	65.00	100.00

SHILLING
.925 SILVER
c/m: Crowned PM on Great Britain 1 Shilling, KM#734.

| 36 | ND(1860) | — | 25.00 | 40.00 | 65.00 | 100.00 |

1/2 RUPEE
.917 SILVER
c/m: Crowned PM on India 1/2 Rupee, KM#455.

| A37 | ND(1840) | — | 12.50 | 20.00 | 32.50 | 50.00 |

c/m: Crowned PM on India 1/2 Rupee, KM#456.

| 37 | ND(1840) | — | 12.50 | 20.00 | 32.50 | 50.00 |

c/m: Crowned PM on India 1/2 Rupee, KM#472.

| A38 | ND(1862-76) | — | 10.00 | 15.00 | 25.00 | 40.00 |

c/m: Crowned PM on India 1/2 Rupee, KM#491.

| 38 (51) | ND(1877-88) | — | 10.00 | 15.00 | 25.00 | 40.00 |

RUPEE

.917 SILVER
c/m: Crowned PM on India Rupee, KM#450.

| 39 | ND(1835) | — | 35.00 | 60.00 | 100.00 | 150.00 |

c/m: Crowned PM on India Rupee, KM#457.

| A40 | ND(1840) | — | 20.00 | 30.00 | 50.00 | 80.00 |

c/m: Crowned PM on India Rupee, KM#458.

| 40 | ND(1840) | — | 20.00 | 30.00 | 50.00 | 80.00 |

c/m: Crowned PM on India Rupee, KM#473.

| A41 (54) | ND(1862-76) | — | 10.00 | 15.00 | 25.00 | 40.00 |

c/m: Crowned PM on India Rupee, KM#492.

| 41 | ND(1877-88) | — | 10.00 | 15.00 | 25.00 | 40.00 |

c/m: Crowned PM on India-Portuguese Rupia, KM#12.

| 42 | ND(1881-82) | — | 30.00 | 50.00 | 80.00 | |

c/m: Crowned PM on Mombasa Rupee, KM#5.

| 43 | ND(1888) | — | 25.00 | 37.50 | 62.50 | 100.00 |

8 REALES
SILVER
c/m: Crowned PM on Mexico 8 Reales, KM#377.

| 44 | ND(1825-88) | — | 40.00 | 75.00 | 125.00 | 200.00 |

THALER

SILVER
c/m: Crowned PM on Austria Maria Theresa Thaler, KM#T1.

KM#	Date	Mintage	Good	VG	Fine	VF
45 (57)	ND(1780)	—	25.00	40.00	65.00	100.00

c/m: Crowned PM on Austria Thaler, KM#473.

| A46 | ND(1811-15) | — | 30.00 | 50.00 | 80.00 | 140.00 |

c/m: Crowned PM on Austria Thaler, KM#493.

| 46 | ND(1817-24) | — | 30.00 | 50.00 | 80.00 | 140.00 |

c/m: Crowned PM on Austria Thaler, KM#494.

| 47 | ND(1824-30) | — | 30.00 | 50.00 | 80.00 | 140.00 |

Decree of January 19, 1889
1889-1895

During the reign of D. Carlos I, a substitution of an indented PM (Provincia de Mocambique) which replaced the crowned PM of D. Luis I, was countermarked on all foreign silver coinage circulating in Mozambique. These coins were to be replaced or exchanged by Portuguese coinage on their entry into the public treasury.

1/4 RUPEE

 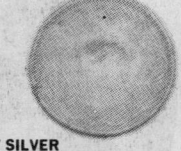

.917 SILVER
c/m: PM on India 1/4 Rupee, KM#470.

| A48 | ND(1862-76) | — | 15.00 | 22.50 | 37.50 | 60.00 |

c/m: PM on India 1/4 Rupee, KM#490.

| 48 | ND(1877-88) | — | 15.00 | 22.50 | 37.50 | 60.00 |

1/2 RUPEE
.917 SILVER
c/m: PM on India 1/2 Rupee, KM#455.

| A49 | ND(1840) | — | 12.50 | 20.00 | 32.50 | 50.00 |

c/m: PM on India 1/2 Rupee, KM#456.

| 49 | ND(1840) | — | 12.50 | 20.00 | 32.50 | 50.00 |

c/m: PM on India 1/2 Rupee, KM#472.

| 50 | ND(1862-76) | — | 10.00 | 15.00 | 25.00 | 40.00 |

c/m: PM on German East Africa 1/2 Rupie, KM#4.

| 51 | ND(1891) | — | 40.00 | 75.00 | 125.00 | 200.00 |

RUPEE
.917 SILVER
c/m: PM on India Rupee, KM#450.

| 52 | ND(1835) | — | 35.00 | 60.00 | 100.00 | 150.00 |

c/m: PM on India Rupee, KM#457.

| A53 | ND(1840) | — | 20.00 | 30.00 | 50.00 | 80.00 |

MOZAMBIQUE 1306

c/m: PM on India Rupee, KM#458.

KM#	Date	Mintage	Good	VG	Fine	VF
53	ND(1840)	—	20.00	30.00	50.00	80.00

c/m: PM on India Rupee, KM#473.

| A54 (53) | ND(1862-76) | — | 20.00 | 30.00 | 50.00 | 80.00 |

c/m: PM on India Rupee, KM#492.

| 54 | ND(1877-88) | — | 20.00 | 30.00 | 50.00 | 80.00 |

c/m: PM on India-Portuguese Rupia, KM#12.

| 55 | ND(1881) | — | 20.00 | 30.00 | 50.00 | 80.00 |

c/m: PM on Mombasa Rupee, KM#5.

| 56 | ND(1888) | — | 25.00 | 37.50 | 62.50 | 100.00 |

c/m: PM on German East Africa Rupie, KM#2.

| 57 | ND(1890-94) | — | 40.00 | 75.00 | 125.00 | 200.00 |

THALER

SILVER
c/m: PM on Austria Maria Theresa Thaler, KM#T1.

| 58 (56) | ND(1780) | — | 25.00 | 40.00 | 65.00 | 100.00 |

c/m: PM on Austria Thaler, KM#473.

| 59 | ND(1817-24) | — | 30.00 | 50.00 | 80.00 | 140.00 |

c/m: PM on Austria Thaler, KM#494.

| 60 | ND(1824-30) | — | 30.00 | 50.00 | 80.00 | 140.00 |

DECIMAL COINAGE
100 Centavos = 1 Escudo

10 CENTAVOS

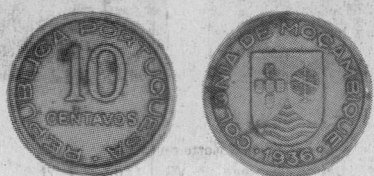

BRONZE

KM#	Date	Mintage	VF	XF	Unc
63	1936	2.000	1.25	3.00	10.00

| 72 | 1942 | 2.000 | 1.00 | 2.00 | 5.50 |

| 83 | 1960 | 3.750 | .10 | .15 | .40 |
| | 1961 | 10.300 | | .10 | .40 |

20 CENTAVOS

BRONZE

| 64 | 1936 | 2.500 | 2.00 | 3.50 | 12.50 |

| 71 | 1941 | 2.000 | 2.00 | 5.00 | 18.00 |

| 75 | 1949 | 8.000 | .50 | 1.25 | 2.25 |
| | 1950 | 12.500 | .50 | .75 | 1.50 |

| 85 | 1961 | 12.500 | .10 | .15 | 1.00 |

Reduced size, 16mm

| 88 | 1973 | 1.798 | 50.00 | 75.00 | 100.00 |
| | 1974 | 13.044 | 50.00 | 75.00 | 100.00 |

50 CENTAVOS

COPPER-NICKEL

| 65 | 1936 | 2.500 | 1.50 | 3.75 | 14.50 |

BRONZE

KM#	Date	Mintage	VF	XF	Unc
73	1945	2.500	.50	1.50	3.50

NICKEL-BRONZE

| 76 | 1950 | 20.000 | .35 | .75 | 1.75 |
| | 1951 | 16.000 | .35 | .75 | 1.75 |

BRONZE

| 81 | 1953 | 5.010 | .15 | .35 | 1.25 |
| | 1957 | 24.990 | .10 | .15 | .50 |

| 89 | 1973 | 6.841 | .10 | .20 | .50 |
| | 1974 | 23.810 | .10 | .20 | .50 |

ESCUDO

COPPER-NICKEL

| 66 | 1936 | 2.000 | 1.50 | 4.00 | 30.00 |

BRONZE

| 74 | 1945 | 2.000 | 1.25 | 2.50 | 6.00 |

NICKEL-BRONZE

| 77 | 1950 | 10.000 | .75 | 1.25 | 3.50 |
| | 1951 | 10.000 | .75 | 1.25 | 3.50 |

BRONZE

KM#	Date	Mintage	VF	XF	Unc
82	1953	2.013	.50	.75	2.00
	1957	2.987	.35	.50	1.50
	1962	.600	.50	.75	2.50
	1963	3.258	.10	.35	1.50
	1965	5.000	.10	.35	1.50
	1968	4.500	.10	.35	1.50
	1969	1.642	.15	.50	1.75
	1973	.501	.50	.75	3.00
	1974	25.281	.10	.30	1.00

2-1/2 ESCUDOS

3.5000 g, .650 SILVER, .0731 oz ASW

61	1935	1.200	2.50	5.00	20.00

68	1938	1.000	1.75	2.50	6.50
	1942	1.200	1.75	2.50	6.00
	1950	4.000	1.25	1.75	4.50
	1951	4.000	1.25	1.75	4.50

COPPER-NICKEL

78	1952	4.000	.25	.50	1.50
	1953	4.000	.25	.50	1.50
	1954	4.000	.25	.50	1.00
	1955	4.000	.25	.50	1.00
	1965	8.000	.25	.50	1.00
	1973	1.767	.50	.75	2.00

5 ESCUDOS

7.0000 g, .650 SILVER, .1463 oz ASW

62	1935	1.000	3.50	12.50	30.00

69	1938	.800	5.50	16.50	35.00
	1949	8.000	2.50	5.00	12.50

4.0000 g, .650 SILVER, .0835 oz ASW

84	1960	8.000	.75	1.25	3.00

COPPER-NICKEL

KM#	Date	Mintage	VF	XF	Unc
86	1971	8.000	.50	1.00	2.25
	1973	3.352	.50	1.75	3.50

10 ESCUDOS

12.5000 g, .835 SILVER, .3356 oz ASW

67	1936	.497	8.00	12.00	35.00

70	1938	.530	8.00	12.00	32.50

5.0000 g, .720 SILVER, .1157 oz ASW

79	1952	1.503	1.50	3.00	7.00
	1954	1.335	1.50	3.00	7.00
	1955	1.162	1.50	3.00	7.00
	1960	2.000	1.50	2.50	5.25

5.0000 g, .680 SILVER, .1093 oz ASW

79a	1966	.500	2.00	5.00	11.50

COPPER-NICKEL

79b	1968	5.000	.50	1.50	3.00
	1970	4.000	.50	1.25	2.50
	1974	3.366	.50	1.50	4.00

20 ESCUDOS

10.0000 g, .720 SILVER, .2315 oz ASW

80	1952	1.004	3.00	5.00	8.00
	1955	.996	3.25	5.50	8.50
	1960	2.000	2.50	4.50	7.00

10.0000 g, .680 SILVER, .2186 oz ASW

80a	1966	.250	3.50	6.50	10.00

NICKEL

KM#	Date	Mintage	VF	XF	Unc
87	1971	2.000	.75	1.75	3.50
	1972	1.158	.75	1.75	3.50

MONETARY REFORM
100 Centimos = 1 Metica

CENTIMO

ALUMINUM

90	1975	15.050	—	150.00	225.00
	1975	—	—	P/L	500.00

2 CENTIMOS

COPPER-ZINC
Obv: Similar to 50 Centimos, KM#95.

91	1975	8.242	—	100.00	150.00
	1975	—	—	P/L	280.00

5 CENTIMOS

COPPER-ZINC

92	1975	14.898	—	100.00	150.00
	1975	—	—	P/L	250.00

10 CENTIMOS

COPPER-ZINC
Obv: Similar to 50 Centimos, KM#95.

93	1975	18.000	—	100.00	150.00
	1975	—	—	P/L	280.00

20 CENTIMOS

COPPER-NICKEL
Obv: Similar to 50 Centimos, KM#95.

94	1975	8.050	—	165.00	275.00
	1975	—	—	P/L	500.00

50 CENTIMOS

COPPER-NICKEL

95	1975	3.050	—	175.00	300.00
	1975	—	—	P/L	325.00

MOZAMBIQUE 1308

METICA

COPPER-NICKEL

KM#	Date	Mintage	VF	XF	Unc
96	1975	2.550	—	90.00	125.00
	1975	—	—	P/L	165.00

2-1/2 METICAS

COPPER-NICKEL

97	1975	1.500	—	175.00	250.00
	1975	—	—	P/L	275.00

MONETARY REFORM
100 Centavos = 1 Metical

50 CENTAVOS

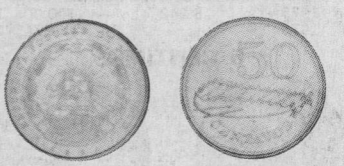

ALUMINUM

98	1980	5.160	.30	.60	1.00
	1982	—	.30	.60	1.00

METICAL

BRASS

99	1980	.032	.50	1.00	1.50
	1982	—	.50	1.00	1.50

2-1/2 METICAIS

COPPER-NICKEL

100	1980	1.088	.50	1.25	2.50

5 METICAIS

ALUMINUM

101	1980	7.736	.75	1.50	3.00
	1982	—	.75	1.50	3.00

10 METICAIS

COPPER-NICKEL

KM#	Date	Mintage	VF	XF	Unc
102	1980	.152	1.00	2.00	4.00

20 METICAIS

COPPER-NICKEL

103	1980	.078	1.50	2.50	5.00

50 METICAIS

COPPER-NICKEL
World Fisheries Conference

106	1983	.130	5.00	7.00	10.00

22.0000 g, .925 SILVER, .6543 oz ASW

106a	1983	.021	—	Proof	30.00

22.0000 g, .900 GOLD, .6366 oz AGW

106b	1983	135 pcs.	—	Proof	1200.

250 METICAIS

28.2800 g, .925 SILVER, .8411 oz ASW
10th Anniversary of Independence

107	1985	2,000	—	Proof	40.00

500 METICAIS

19.4000 g, .800 SILVER, .4990 oz ASW
5th Anniversary of Independence

KM#	Date	Mintage	VF	XF	Unc
104	1980	5,000	—	Proof	35.00

1000 METICAIS

COPPER-NICKEL
Pope's Visit

109	1988	*.080	—	—	7.50

28.2800 g, .925 SILVER, .8411 oz ASW

109a	1988	*3,500	—	Proof	40.00

2000 METICAIS

17.5000 g, .917 GOLD, .5158 oz AGW
10th Anniversary of Independence

108	1985	100 pcs.	—	Proof	750.00

5000 METICAIS

17.2790 g, .900 GOLD, .5000 oz AGW
5th Anniversary of Independence
Obv: State emblem above denomination.
Rev: Figure at left, corn plants in background, tractor above.

105	1980	2,000	—	Proof	300.00
	1980	2,000	—	Proof	400.00

SPECIMEN SETS (SS)

KM#	Date	Mintage	Identification	Issue Price	Mkt. Val.
SS1	1975 (8)	—	KM90-97	—	2400.

Listings For

MUKALLA: refer to Yemen Democratic Republic
MUSCAT & OMAN: refer to Oman
NEJD: refer to Saudi Arabia

NEPAL

The Kingdom of Nepal, the world's only surviving Hindu kingdom, is a landlocked country occupying the southern slopes of the Himalayas. It has an area of 56,136 sq. mi. (145,391 sq. km.) and a population of *18.8 million. Capital: Kathmandu. Nepal has deposits of coal, copper, iron and cobalt, but they are largely unexploited. Agriculture is the principal economic activity. Rice, timber and jute are exported, with tourism the other major foreign exchange earner.

Apart from a brief Muslim invasion in the 14th century, Nepal was able to avoid the mainstream of Northern Indian politics, because of its impregnable position in the mountains. It is therefore a unique survivor of the medieval Hindu and Buddhist culture of Northern India, which was largely destroyed by the successive waves of Muslim invasions.

Prior to the late 18th century, Nepal, as we know it today, was divided among a number of small states. Unless otherwise stated, the term "Nepal" applies to the small fertile valley, about 4,500 ft. above sea level, in which the three main cities of Kathmandu, Patan and Bhatgaon are situated.

During the reign of King Yaksha Malla (1428-1482AD), the Nepalese kingdom, with capital at Bhatgaon, was extended northwards into Tibet, and also controlled a considerable area to the south of the hills. After Yaksha Malla's death, the Kingdom was divided among his four sons, so four kingdoms were established with capitals at Bhatgaon, Patan, Kathmandu and Banepa, all situated within the small valley, less than 20 miles square. Banepa was quickly absorbed within the territory of Bhatgaon, but the other 3 kingdoms remained until 1769. The internecine strife between the 3 kings effectively stopped Nepal from becoming a major military force during this period, although with its fertile land and strategic position, it was by far the wealthiest and most powerful of the Himalayan states.

Apart from agriculture, Nepal owed its prosperity to its position on one of the easiest trade routes between the great monasteries of central Tibet, and India. Nepal made full use of this, and a trading community was set up in Lhasa during the 16th century, and Nepalese coins became the accepted currency medium in Tibet.

The seeds of discord between Nepal and Tibet were sown during the first half of the 18th century, when the Nepalese debased the coinage, and the fate of the Malla kings of Nepal was sealed when Prithvi Narayan Shah, King of the small state of Gorkha, to the west of Kathmandu, was able to gain control of the trans-shimalayan trade routes during the years after 1750.

Prithvi Narayan spent several years consolidating his position in hill areas before he finally succeeded in conquering the Kathmandu Valley in 1768, where he established the Shah dynasty, and moved his capital to Kathmandu.

After Prithvi Narayan's death a period of political instability ensued which lasted until the 1840's when the Rana family reduced the monarch to a figurehead and established the post of hereditary Prime Minister. A popular revolution in 1950 toppled the Rana family and reconstituted power in the throne. In 1959 King Mahendra declared Nepal a constitutional monarchy, and in 1962 a new constitution set up a system of panchayat (village council) democracy.

DATING

Nepal Samvat Era (NS)

All coins of the Malla kings of Nepal are dated in the Nepal Samvat era (NS). Year 1 NS began in 881, so to arrive at the AD date add 880 to the NS date. This era was exclusive to Nepal, except for one gold coin of Prana Narayan of Cooch Behar.

Saka Era (SE)

Up until 1888AD all coins of the Gorkha Dynasty were dated in the Saka era (SE). To convert from Saka to AD take Saka date + 78 - AD date. Coins dated with this era have SE before the date in the following listing.

Vikrama Samvat Era (VS)

From 1888AD most copper coins were dated in the Vikram Samvat (VS) era. To convert take VS date - 57 - AD date. Coins with this era have VS before the year in the listing. With the exception of a few gold coins struck in 1890 & 1892, silver and gold coins only changed to the VS era in 1911AD, but now this era is used for all coins struck in Nepal.

RULERS

SHAH DYNASTY

Girvan Yuddha Vikrama

गीर्वाण युद्ध विक्रम सा

SE1720-1738/1799-1816AD

Queens of Girvan Yuddha Vikrama: Siddhi Lakshmi

सिद्धि लद्मी

Goraksha Rajya Lakshmi

गोरच्छ राज्य लद्मी

Rajendra Vikrama

राजेन्द्र विक्रम

SE1738-1769/1816-1847AD

Queens of Rajendra Vikrama: Samrajya Lakshmi

साम्राज्य लद्मी

Rajya Lakshmi

राज्य लद्मी

Surendra Vikrama

सुरेन्द्र विक्रम सा

SE1769-1803/1847-1881AD

Queens of Surendra Vikrama: Trailokyaraja Lakshmi

त्रैलोक्य राज्य लद्मी

Sura Raja Lakshmi

सुर राज लद्मी

Deva Raja Lakshmi

देवराज लद्मी

Punyakumari Raja Lakshmi

पुरायकुमारी राज लद्मी

Prithvi Vira Vikrama

पृथ्वी वीर विक्रम

SE1803-1833/1881-1911AD
VS1938-1968/

Queens of Prithvi Vira Vikrama: Lakshmi Divyeswari

लद्मी दिव्येश्वरी

Tribhuvana Vira Vikrama

त्रिभुवनवीर विक्रम

VS1968-2007, 2007-2011/
1911-1950, 1951-1955AD

Jnanendra Vira Vikrama

ज्ञानेन्द वीर विक्रम

VS2007/1950-1951AD

Mahendra Vira Vikrama

महेन्द्रवीर विक्रम

VS2012-2028/1955-1972AD

Queens of Mahendra Vira Vikrama: Ratna Rajya Lakshmi

रन्न राज लद्मी

Birendra Bir Bikram

वीरेन्द्र वीर विक्रम

VS2028/1972-AD

Queen of Birendra Aishvarya Rajya Lakshmi

ऐश्वर्य राज्य लद्मी देवी

VS2028-/1972-AD

MONETARY SYSTEM

COPPER

Initially the copper paisa was not fixed in value relative to the silver coins, and generally fluctuated in value from 1/32 mohar in 1865AD to around 1/50 mohar after c1880AD, and was fixed at that value in 1903AD.

4 Dam - 1 Paisa
2 Paisa - 1 Dyak, Adhani

COPPER and SILVER
Decimal Series

100 Paisa - 1 Rupee

Although the value of the copper paisa was fixed at 100 paisa to the rupee in 1903, it was not until 1932 that silver coins were struck in the decimal system.

GOLD COINAGE

Nepalese gold coinage until recently did not carry any denominations and was traded for silver, etc. at the local bullion exchange rate. The three basic weight standards used in the following listing are distinguished for convenience, although all were known as Asarphi (gold coin) locally as follows:

GOLD MOHAR

5.60 g Multiples and Fractions

TOLA

12.48 g Multiples and Fractions

GOLD RUPEE or ASARPHI

11.66 g Multiples and Fractions
(Reduced to 10.00 g in 1966)

NOTE: In some instances the gold and silver issues were struck from the same dies.

NUMERALS

Nepal has used more variations of numerals on their coins than any other nation. The commonest are illustrated in the numeral chart in the introduction. The chart below illustrates some variations encompassing the last four centuries.

1	2	3	4	5	6	7	8	9	0
१	२	३	४	५	६	७	८	९	०
१	२		५	६	७		८		
१		३	५	५		७	८		
			४	६		७	८	९	
				६			८	९	
			१				८	९	
			९					९	

NUMERICS

Half	आधा
One	एक
Two	दइ
Four	चार
Five	पाच
Ten	दस
Twenty	विस
Twenty-five	पचीसा
Fifty	पचासा
Hundred	शय

DENOMINATIONS

Paisa	पैसा
Dam	दाम
Mohar	मोरु
Rupee	रुपैयाँ
Ashrapi	असार्फो
Asarphi	अश्रफो

DIE VARIETIES

Although some dies were used both for silver and gold coinage the gold Mohar is easily recognized being less ornate. The following illustrations are of a silver Mohar, KM#602 and a gold Mohar KM#615 issued by Surendra Vikrama Saha Deva in the period SE1769-1803/1847-1881AD. Note the similar reverse legend. The obverse usually will start with the character for the word Shri either in single or multiples, the latter as Shri Shri Shri or Shri 3.

NEPAL 1310

OBVERSE

SILVER SE1791   GOLD SE1793

LEGEND

श्री श्री श्री सुरेन्द्र बिक्रम साहदेव

Shri Shri Shri Surendra Vikrama Saha Deva (date).

REVERSE

SILVER   GOLD

LEGEND (in center)

श्री ३ भवानी

Shri 3 Bhavani (around outer circle)

श्री श्री श्री गोरषनाथ

Shri Shri Shri Gorakhanatha

SHAH DYNASTY

1/4 MOHAR
GIRVAN YUDDHA VIKRAMA
SE1720-1738 / 1799-1816AD

Copper Coinage
DAM

COPPER, 1.00 g

KM#	Date	Year	VG	Fine	VF	XF
517	VS1861	(1804)	.75	1.25	2.25	3.50

2 DAM
COPPER, 2.00 g

| A517 | VS1861 | (1804) | 1.50 | 2.00 | 4.00 | 8.00 |

2 PAISA (Dyak)
COPPER, 4.00 g

| B517 | ND | — | 3.00 | 5.00 | 10.00 | 15.00 |

Silver Coinage
DAM

Actual Size   2 x Actual Size
SILVER, uniface, 0.04 g

| 518 | ND (1799-1816) | 4.00 | 8.00 | 11.50 | 16.00 |

1/32 MOHAR

SILVER, uniface, 0.18 g

| 519 | ND (1799-1816) | 8.00 | 13.50 | 18.50 | 25.00 |

1/16 MOHAR

SILVER, 0.35 g

KM#	Date	Year	VG	Fine	VF	XF
520	ND (1799-1816)		7.50	11.50	16.50	22.50

NOTE: Varieties exist.

1/8 MOHAR

SILVER, 0.70 g
Obv: Shri above sword.

| 521 | ND (1799-1816) | 6.00 | 10.00 | 13.50 | 18.50 |

Obv: Umbrella above sword.

| 522 | ND (1799-1816) | 6.00 | 10.00 | 13.50 | 18.50 |

Obv: Wreath above sword.

| 523 | ND (1799-1816) | 6.00 | 10.00 | 13.50 | 18.50 |

In the name of Queen Siddhi Lakshmi

1/4 MOHAR

SILVER, 1.40 g

524	SE1730	(1808)	10.00	13.50	18.50	25.00
	1733	(1811)	10.00	13.50	18.50	25.00
	1735	(1813)	10.00	13.50	18.50	25.00

In the name of Queen Goraksha Rajya Lakshmi

| 525 | SE1738 | (1816) | 65.00 | 75.00 | 85.00 | 100.00 |

1/2 MOHAR

SILVER, 2.77 g

526	1728	(1806)	7.50	12.50	20.00	30.00
	1729	(1807)	7.50	12.50	20.00	30.00
	1730	(1808)	5.00	8.50	15.00	22.50
	1733	(1811)	7.50	12.50	20.00	30.00

3/4 MOHAR

SILVER, 4.20 g

| 527 | SE1727 | (1805) | 50.00 | 80.00 | 100.00 | 125.00 |

MOHAR

SILVER, 5.60 g
Obv: 3 Shri's above square.

KM#	Date	Year	VG	Fine	VF	XF
529	SE1723	(1801)	4.50	6.50	9.00	11.50
	1724	(1802)	4.50	6.50	9.00	11.50
	1725	(1803)	4.50	6.50	9.00	11.50
	1728	(1806)	4.50	6.50	9.00	11.50
	1729	(1807)	4.50	6.50	9.00	11.50
	1730	(1808)	4.50	6.50	9.00	11.50
	1731	(1809)	4.50	6.50	9.00	11.50
	1732	(1810)	4.50	6.50	9.00	11.50
	1733	(1811)	4.50	6.50	9.00	11.50
	1734	(1812)	4.50	6.50	9.00	11.50
	1735	(1813)	4.50	6.50	9.00	11.50
	1736	(1814)	4.50	6.50	9.00	11.50
	1737	(1815)	4.50	6.50	9.00	11.50
	1738	(1816)	4.50	6.50	9.00	11.50

Mule. Obv: KM#547. Rev: KM#529.

| 530 | SE1728 | (1806) | 50.00 | 80.00 | 100.00 | 125.00 |
| | 1729 | (1807) | 50.00 | 80.00 | 100.00 | 125.00 |

1-1/2 MOHARS

SILVER, 8.40 g

| 531 | SE1725 | (1803) | 15.00 | 25.00 | 35.00 | 50.00 |
| | 1726 | (1804) | 15.00 | 25.00 | 35.00 | 50.00 |

| 532 | SE1727 | (1805) | 30.00 | 50.00 | 75.00 | 100.00 |

3 MOHARS

SILVER, 16.80 g
Obv: Flourishes outside central legend.

| A533 | SE1725 | (1803) | — | 150.00 | 200.00 | 250.00 |

Obv: W/o flourishes outside central legend.

| 533 | SE1725 | (1803) | — | 150.00 | 200.00 | 250.00 |

Similar to 1-1/2 Mohars, KM#532.

| 534 | SE1726 | (1804) | — | 200.00 | 300.00 | 400.00 |

Gold Coinage
DAM

GOLD, uniface, 0.044 g

| 535 | ND (1799-1816) | 10.00 | 14.00 | 20.00 | 27.50 |

NEPAL 1311

1/32 MOHAR

GOLD, uniface, 0.175 g

KM#	Date	Year	VG	Fine	VF	XF
536	ND	(1799-1816)	14.00	20.00	25.00	32.50

1/16 MOHAR

GOLD, 0.35 g

KM#	Date	Year	VG	Fine	VF	XF
537	ND	(1799-1816)	14.00	20.00	25.00	32.50

NOTE: Three varieties exist.

1/8 MOHAR

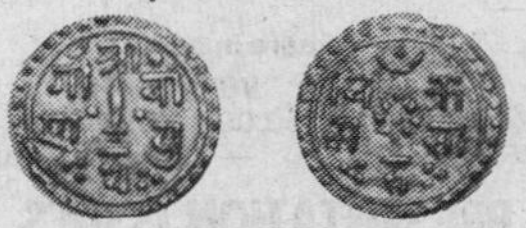

GOLD, 0.70 g
Obv: *Shri* **above sword.**

KM#	Date	Year	VG	Fine	VF	XF
538	ND	(1799-1816)	22.50	27.50	35.00	45.00

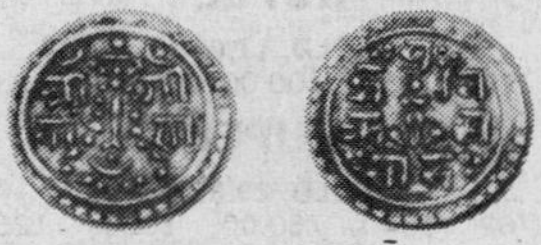

Obv: Umbrella above sword.

KM#	Date	Year	VG	Fine	VF	XF
539	ND	(1799-1816)	22.50	27.50	35.00	45.00

In the name of Queen Siddhi Lakshmi

1/4 MOHAR

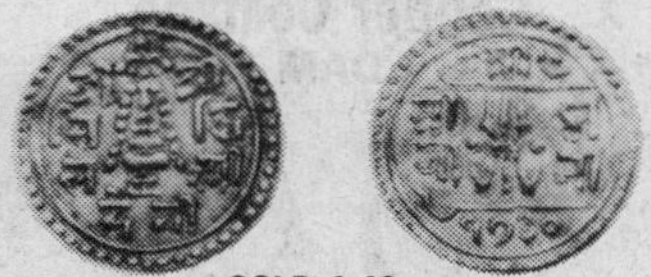

GOLD, 1.40 g

KM#	Date	Year	VG	Fine	VF	XF
540.1	SE1730	(1808)	40.00	50.00	65.00	85.00

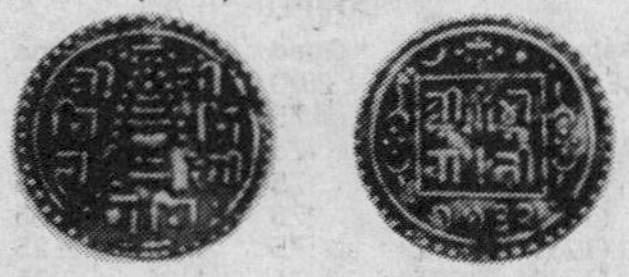

KM#	Date	Year	VG	Fine	VF	XF
540.3	SE1732	(1810)	40.00	50.00	65.00	85.00
	1733	(1811)	40.00	50.00	65.00	85.00

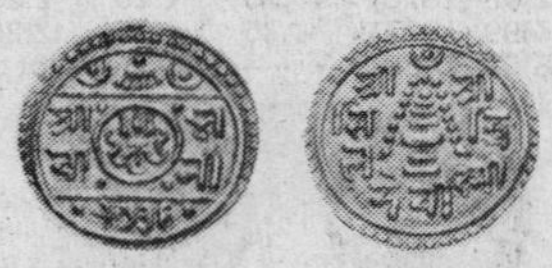

KM#	Date	Year	VG	Fine	VF	XF
540.4	SE1736	(1814)	40.00	50.00	65.00	85.00

In the name of Queen Goraksha Rajyalakshmi

KM#	Date	Year	VG	Fine	VF	XF
540.2	SE1738	(1816)	120.00	150.00	170.00	200.00

1/2 MOHAR

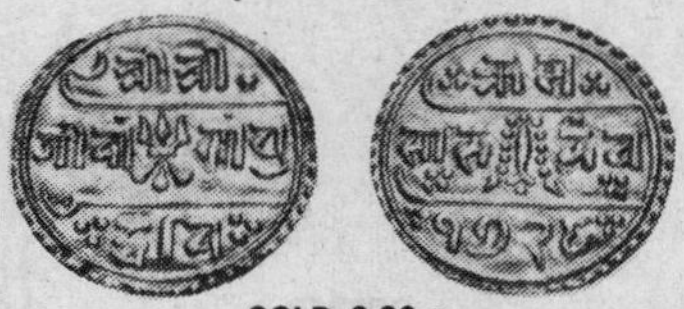

GOLD, 2.80 g

KM#	Date	Year	VG	Fine	VF	XF
541	SE1728	(1806)	70.00	80.00	100.00	125.00
	1729	(1807)	70.00	80.00	100.00	125.00
	1730	(1808)	70.00	80.00	100.00	125.00

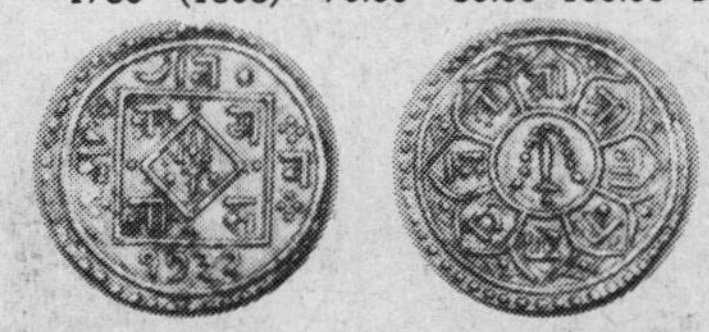

KM#	Date	Year	VG	Fine	VF	XF
542	SE1732	(1810)	70.00	80.00	100.00	125.00
	1733	(1811)	70.00	80.00	100.00	125.00
543	SE1736	(1814)	70.00	80.00	100.00	125.00

MOHAR

GOLD, 5.60 g
Similar to KM#529.

KM#	Date	Year	VG	Fine	VF	XF
544	SE1723	(1801)	115.00	125.00	140.00	165.00
	1724	(1802)	115.00	125.00	140.00	165.00
	1728	(1806)	115.00	125.00	140.00	165.00

Obv: Square in center.

KM#	Date	Year	VG	Fine	VF	XF
546	SE1733	(1811)	115.00	125.00	140.00	165.00

1-1/2 MOHARS

GOLD, 8.40 g
Similar to KM#531.

KM#	Date	Year	VG	Fine	VF	XF
547	SE1726	(1804)	185.00	225.00	275.00	350.00
	1728	(1806)	185.00	225.00	275.00	350.00
	1729	(1807)	185.00	225.00	275.00	350.00

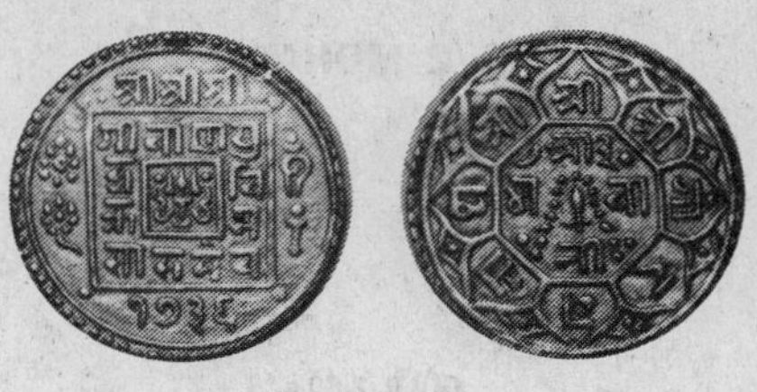

Rev: Hexagon.

KM#	Date	Year	VG	Fine	VF	XF
548	SE1736	(1814)	185.00	225.00	275.00	350.00

2 MOHARS

GOLD, 11.20 g
Obv: Square in center.

KM#	Date	Year	VG	Fine	VF	XF
550	SE1733	(1811)	250.00	275.00	325.00	375.00

PRESENTATION ISSUES

In the name of Queen Goraksha Rajya Lakshmi

RUPEE

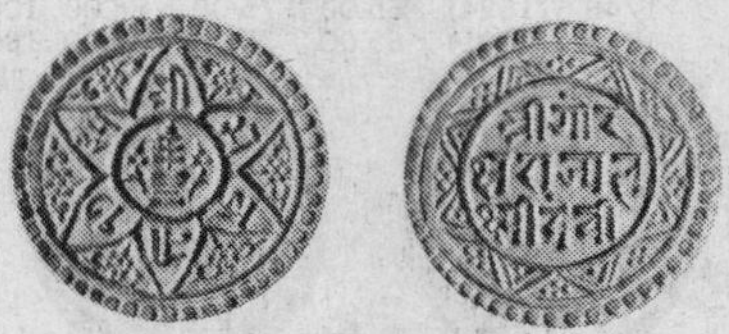

GOLD, 11.66 g

KM#	Date	Year	VG	Fine	VF	XF
551	SE1735	(1813)	400.00	500.00	550.00	600.00

RAJENDRA VIKRAMA

SE1738-1769/1816-1847AD

Silver Coinage

DAM

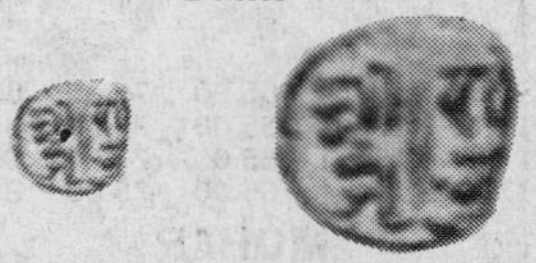

Actual Size — 2 x Actual Size

SILVER, uniface, 0.04 g

KM#	Date	Year	VG	Fine	VF	XF
553	ND	(1816-47)	4.00	6.00	8.00	12.50

1/32 MOHAR

SILVER, uniface, 0.18 g

KM#	Date	Year	VG	Fine	VF	XF
554	ND	(1816-47)	5.50	9.00	12.50	17.50

1/16 MOHAR

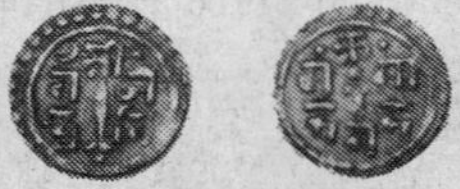

SILVER, 0.35 g

KM#	Date	Year	VG	Fine	VF	XF
555	ND	(1816-47)	5.00	8.50	12.00	17.00

1/8 MOHAR

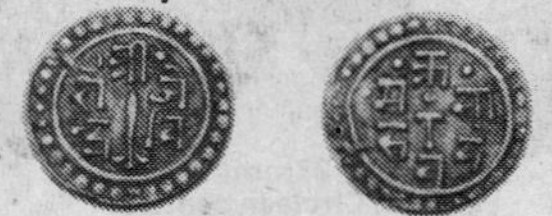

SILVER, 0.70 g

KM#	Date	Year	VG	Fine	VF	XF
556	ND	(1816-47)	3.00	5.00	8.50	15.00

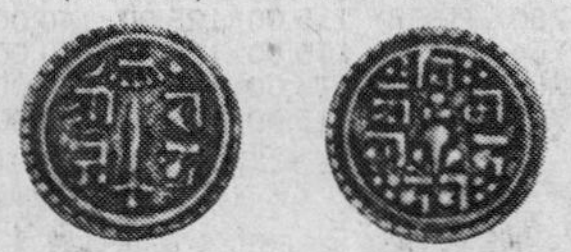

Obv: Umbrella above sword.

KM#	Date	Year	VG	Fine	VF	XF
557	ND	(1816-47)	3.00	5.00	8.50	15.00

In the name of Queen Samrajya Lakshmi

1/4 MOHAR

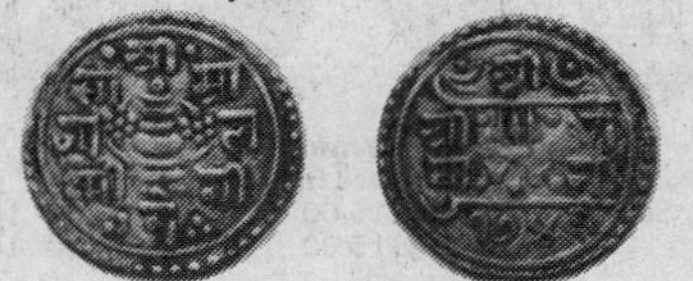

SILVER, 1.40 g

KM#	Date	Year	VG	Fine	VF	XF
558	SE1745	(1823)	8.50	12.50	18.50	25.00
	1746	(1824)	5.00	8.50	12.50	18.50
	1753	(1831)	5.00	8.50	12.50	18.50
	1755	(1833)	5.00	8.50	12.50	18.50

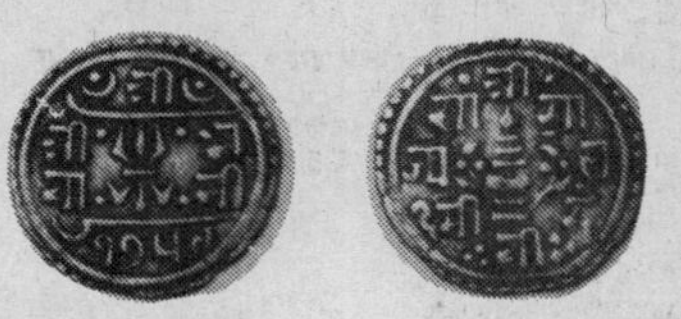

KM#	Date	Year	VG	Fine	VF	XF
559	SE1746	(1824)	5.00	8.50	12.50	18.50
	1759	(1837)	5.00	8.50	12.50	18.50

Obv: Wreath above vase.

KM#	Date	Year	VG	Fine	VF	XF
560	SE1746	(1824)	5.00	8.50	12.50	18.50
	1753	(1831)	5.00	8.50	12.50	18.50
	1759	(1837)	5.00	8.50	12.50	18.50

In the name of Queen Rajya Lakshmi

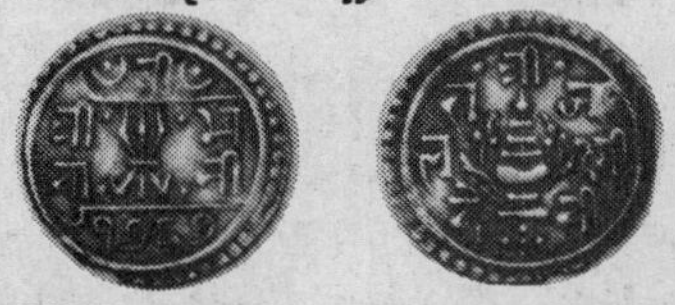

KM#	Date	Year	VG	Fine	VF	XF
561.1	SE1764	(1842)	8.50	12.50	18.50	25.00
	1766	(1844)	8.50	12.50	18.50	25.00
	1767	(1845)	8.50	12.50	18.50	25.00

Struck w/gold dies. Rev: Circle.

KM#	Date	Year	VG	Fine	VF	XF
561.2	SE1764	(1842)	30.00	40.00	55.00	75.00

1/2 MOHAR

SILVER, 2.80 g
Mule. Obv: KM#563. Rev: KM#526.

KM#	Date	Year	VG	Fine	VF	XF
562	SE1730	(1808)	15.00	25.00	40.00	60.00

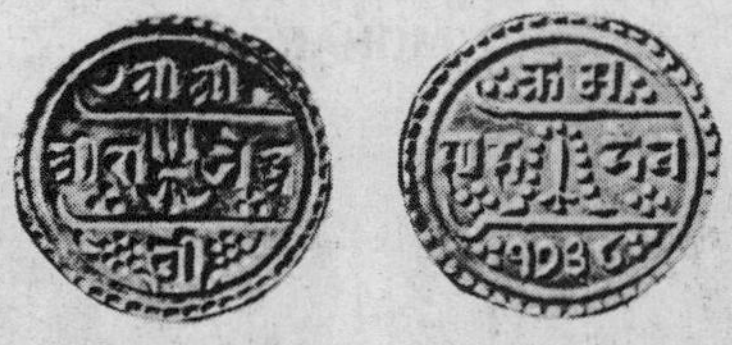

KM#	Date	Year	VG	Fine	VF	XF
563	SE1738	(1816)	3.50	6.50	10.00	15.00
	1744	(1822)	7.50	12.50	20.00	30.00
	1746	(1824)	4.50	6.50	12.50	17.50

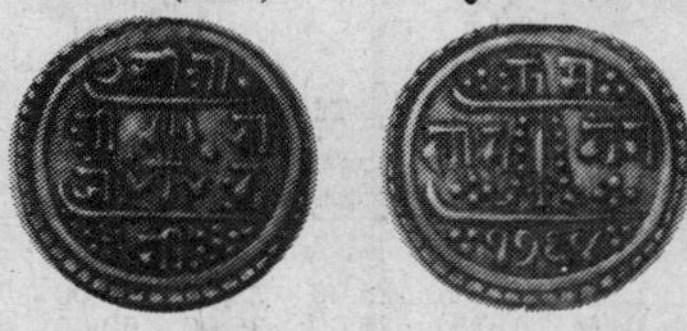

KM#	Date	Year	VG	Fine	VF	XF
564	SE1746	(1824)	3.50	6.50	10.00	15.00
	1753	(1831)	3.50	6.50	10.00	15.00
	1755	(1833)	3.50	6.50	10.00	15.00
	1757	(1835)	3.50	6.50	10.00	15.00
	1759	(1837)	3.50	6.50	10.00	15.00
	1762	(1840)	3.50	7.50	12.50	16.50
	1764	(1842)	3.50	7.50	12.00	16.50
	1765	(1843)	3.50	7.50	12.00	16.50
	1766	(1844)	3.50	7.50	12.00	16.50

MOHAR

SILVER, 5.60 g

KM#	Date	Year	VG	Fine	VF	XF
565	SE1738	(1816)	4.50	6.50	9.00	11.50
	1739	(1817)	4.50	6.50	9.00	11.50
	1740	(1818)	4.50	6.50	9.00	11.50
	1741	(1819)	4.50	6.50	9.00	11.50
	1742	(1820)	4.50	6.50	9.00	11.50
	1743	(1821)	4.50	6.50	9.00	11.50
	1744	(1822)	4.50	6.50	9.00	11.50
	1745	(1823)	4.50	6.50	9.00	11.50
	1746	(1824)	4.50	6.50	9.00	11.50
	1747	(1825)	4.50	6.50	9.00	11.50
	1748	(1826)	4.50	6.50	9.00	11.50
	1749	(1827)	4.50	6.50	9.00	11.50
	1750	(1828)	4.50	6.50	9.00	11.50
	1751	(1829)	4.50	6.50	9.00	11.50
	1752	(1830)	4.50	6.50	9.00	11.50
	1753	(1831)	4.50	6.50	9.00	11.50
	1754	(1832)	4.50	6.50	9.00	11.50
	1755	(1833)	4.50	6.50	9.00	11.50
	1756	(1834)	4.50	6.50	9.00	11.50
	1757	(1835)	4.50	6.50	9.00	11.50
	1758	(1836)	4.50	6.50	9.00	11.50
	1759	(1837)	4.50	6.50	9.00	11.50
	1760	(1838)	4.50	6.50	9.00	11.50
	1761	(1839)	7.00	10.00	13.50	17.50
	1762	(1840)	7.00	10.00	13.50	17.50
	1764	(1842)	4.50	6.50	9.00	11.50
	1765	(1843)	7.00	10.00	13.50	17.50

NEPAL 1312

KM#	Date	Year	VG	Fine	VF	XF
565	1766	(1844)	4.50	6.50	9.00	11.50
	1767	(1845)	4.50	6.50	9.00	11.50
	1768	(1846)	4.50	7.50	12.50	16.50
	1769	(1847)	7.00	10.00	13.50	17.50

Obv: Sri 3 at top.
| 566 | SE1740 | (1818) | 7.00 | 10.00 | 13.50 | 17.50 |

Obv: Ornamentation reversed.
| 567 | SE1762 | (1840) | 7.00 | 10.00 | 13.50 | 17.50 |

2 MOHARS

SILVER, 11.20 g
568	SE1738	(1816)	25.00	35.00	50.00	75.00
	1740	(1818)	25.00	35.00	50.00	75.00
	1742	(1820)	25.00	35.00	50.00	75.00
	1743	(1821)	25.00	35.00	50.00	75.00
	1744	(1822)	25.00	35.00	50.00	75.00
	1753	(1831)	25.00	35.00	50.00	75.00
	1757	(1835)	25.00	35.00	50.00	75.00
	1764	(1842)	25.00	35.00	50.00	75.00

Gold Coinage
DAM
GOLD, uniface, 0.04 g
| 569 | ND | (1816-47) | 10.00 | 14.00 | 20.00 | 27.50 |

1/32 MOHAR
GOLD, uniface, 0.18 g
| 570 | ND | (1816-47) | 14.00 | 20.00 | 25.00 | 32.50 |

1/16 MOHAR
GOLD, 0.35 g
| 571 | ND | (1816-47) | 14.00 | 20.00 | 25.00 | 32.50 |

1/8 MOHAR
GOLD, 0.70 g
| 572 | ND | (1816-47) | 22.50 | 27.50 | 35.00 | 45.00 |

In the name of Queen Samrajya Lakshmi
1/4 MOHAR

GOLD, 1.40 g
573	SE1746	(1824)	40.00	50.00	65.00	85.00
	1757	(1835)	40.00	50.00	65.00	85.00
	1758	(1836)	40.00	50.00	65.00	85.00
	1759	(1837)	40.00	50.00	65.00	85.00

NOTE: Varieties exist.
In the name of Queen Rajya Lakshmi

| 574 | SE1764 | (1842) | 40.00 | 50.00 | 65.00 | 85.00 |

1/2 MOHAR

GOLD, 2.80 g
KM#	Date	Year	VG	Fine	VF	XF
575	SE1741	(1819)	70.00	80.00	100.00	125.00

576	SE1744	(1822)	65.00	75.00	85.00	100.00
	1746	(1824)	65.00	75.00	85.00	100.00
	1753	(1831)	65.00	75.00	85.00	100.00

| 577 | SE1757 | (1835) | 65.00 | 75.00 | 85.00 | 100.00 |

578	SE1757	(1835)	65.00	75.00	85.00	100.00
	1758	(1836)	65.00	75.00	85.00	100.00
	1764	(1842)	65.00	75.00	85.00	100.00
	1766	(1844)	65.00	75.00	85.00	100.00

MOHAR

GOLD, 5.60 g
Obv: Square in center.
| 579 | SE1738 | (1816) | 115.00 | 125.00 | 140.00 | 165.00 |

27mm
Obv: Circle in center.
580	SE1741	(1819)	115.00	125.00	140.00	165.00
	1758	(1836)	115.00	125.00	140.00	165.00
	1760	(1838)	115.00	125.00	140.00	165.00
	1764	(1842)	115.00	125.00	140.00	165.00
	1766	(1844)	115.00	125.00	140.00	165.00
	1768	(1846)	115.00	125.00	140.00	165.00

27mm
Obv: Square in center.
| 581 | SE1746 | (1824) | 115.00 | 125.00 | 140.00 | 165.00 |
| | 1757 | (1835) | 115.00 | 125.00 | 140.00 | 165.00 |

2 MOHARS
GOLD, 11.20 g
582	SE1738	(1816)	250.00	275.00	325.00	375.00
	1741	(1819)	250.00	275.00	325.00	375.00
	1768	(1846)	250.00	275.00	325.00	375.00

Obv: Square in center.
KM#	Date	Year	VG	Fine	VF	XF
583	SE1746	(1824)	250.00	275.00	325.00	375.00
	1757	(1835)	—	Reported, not confirmed		

PRESENTATION ISSUES
In the name of Queen Samrajya Lakshmi
RUPEE
GOLD, 11.66 g
| 584 | SE1759 | (1837) | 400.00 | 500.00 | 550.00 | 600.00 |

2 RUPEES
GOLD, 23.32 g
| 585 | SE1762 | (1840) | 750.00 | 1000. | 1250. | 1500. |

SURENDRA VIKRAMA
SE1769-1803 / 1847-1881AD

Copper Coinage
DAM

COPPER
KM#	Date	Year	Good	VG	Fine	VF
586	SE(17)88	(1866)	2.00	3.50	5.00	7.50
	(17)90	(1868)	.75	1.25	2.25	3.50
	(17)91	(1869)	.75	1.25	2.25	3.50
	(17)92	(1870)	.75	1.25	2.25	3.50
	(17)93	(1871)	.75	1.25	2.25	3.50
	(17)94	(1872)	.75	1.25	2.25	3.50
	(17)96	(1874)	.75	1.25	2.25	3.50
	(17)97	(1875)	.75	1.25	2.25	3.50
	(17)98	(1876)	.75	1.25	2.25	3.50
	(17)99	(1877)	.75	1.25	2.25	3.50
	(18)02	(1880)	—	Reported, not confirmed		

Machine struck
| 586.1 | SE(17)90 | (1868) | 30.00 | 45.00 | 85.00 | 175.00 |

1/2 PAISA

COPPER
| 587 | SE1802 | (1880) | 20.00 | 30.00 | 35.00 | 50.00 |

PAISA

COPPER
Rev. leg: 12 characters.
| 588 | SE1787 | (1865) | 1.75 | 3.00 | 5.00 | 8.00 |

Obv. and rev: Border of dots.
| 589 | SE1787 | (1865) | 3.00 | 5.00 | 7.50 | 10.00 |

Rev. leg: 9 characters.

KM#	Date	Year	Good	VG	Fine	VF
590	SE1787	(1865)	1.50	2.00	3.50	5.00
	1788	(1866)	1.50	2.00	3.50	5.00
	1789	(1867)	1.50	2.00	3.50	5.00
	1790	(1868)	1.50	2.00	3.50	5.00
	1791	(1869)	1.50	2.00	3.50	5.00
	1792	(1870)	1.50	2.00	3.50	5.00
	1793	(1871)	1.50	2.00	3.50	5.00
	1794	(1872)	1.50	2.00	3.50	5.00
	1796	(1874)	1.50	2.00	3.50	5.00
	1797	(1875)	1.50	2.00	3.50	5.00
	1798	(1876)	1.50	2.00	3.50	5.00
	1799	(1877)	1.50	2.00	3.50	5.00
	1802	(1880)	15.00	20.00	25.00	35.00

2 PAISA
(Dak)

COPPER
Rev. leg: 12 characters.

| 591 | SE1787 | (1865) | 30.00 | 40.00 | 50.00 | 75.00 |

Rev. leg: 9 characters.

592	SE1788	(1866)	2.00	3.50	5.00	10.00
	1790	(1868)	1.50	2.50	3.50	6.00
	1791	(1869)	1.50	2.50	3.50	6.00
	1796	(1874)	1.75	3.00	4.00	8.00
	1798	(1876)	1.75	3.00	4.00	8.00
	1802	(1880)	30.00	40.00	50.00	75.00

NOTE: Varieties exist.

Silver Coinage
DAM

SILVER, uniface, 0.04 g

KM#	Date	Year	VG	Fine	VF	XF
593	ND	(1847-81)	5.00	7.50	10.00	15.00

1/32 MOHAR

SILVER, uniface, 0.18 g

| 594 | ND | (1847-81) | 6.00 | 10.00 | 13.50 | 18.50 |

1/16 MOHAR

SILVER, 0.35 g

| 595 | ND | (1847-81) | 6.00 | 10.00 | 13.50 | 18.50 |

1/8 MOHAR

SILVER, 0.70 g

| 596 | ND | (1847-81) | 5.00 | 8.50 | 12.50 | 17.50 |

In the name of Queen Trailokyaraja Lakshmi

1/4 MOHAR

SILVER, 1.40 g

KM#	Date	Year	VG	Fine	VF	XF
597	SE1769	(1847)	15.00	20.00	30.00	40.00
	1770	(1848)	15.00	20.00	30.00	40.00
	1772	(1850)	15.00	20.00	30.00	40.00

In the name of Queen Sura Raja Lakshmi

598.1	SE1769	(1847)	15.00	25.00	35.00	45.00
	1770	(1848)	15.00	25.00	35.00	45.00
	1772	(1850)	15.00	25.00	35.00	45.00
	1775	(1853)	15.00	25.00	35.00	45.00
	1776	(1854)	15.00	25.00	35.00	45.00
	1782	(1860)	15.00	25.00	35.00	45.00
	1787	(1865)	15.00	25.00	35.00	45.00
	1788	(1866)	15.00	25.00	35.00	45.00

Struck with gold dies

| 598.2 | SE1777 | (1855) | 40.00 | 50.00 | 75.00 | 100.00 |

In the name of Queen Deva Raja Lakshmi

599	SE1769	(1847)	9.00	13.50	20.00	30.00
	1770	(1848)	9.00	13.50	20.00	30.00
	1773	(1851)	9.00	13.50	20.00	30.00
	1775	(1853)	9.00	13.50	20.00	30.00
	1776	(1854)	9.00	13.50	20.00	30.00

In the name of Queen Punyakumari Raja Lakshmi

| 600 | SE1802 | (1880) | 40.00 | 50.00 | 75.00 | 100.00 |

1/2 MOHAR

SILVER, 2.80 g

601	SE1769	(1847)	5.00	8.50	13.50	20.00
	1770	(1848)	5.00	8.50	13.50	20.00
	1771	(1849)	5.00	8.50	13.50	20.00
	1772	(1850)	5.00	8.50	13.50	20.00
	1773	(1851)	15.00	20.00	25.00	30.00
	1775	(1853)	15.00	20.00	25.00	30.00
	1776	(1854)	15.00	20.00	25.00	30.00
	1787	(1865)	15.00	20.00	25.00	30.00
	1802	(1880)	15.00	20.00	25.00	30.00

MOHAR

SILVER, 5.60 g

602	SE1769	(1847)	4.50	6.50	9.00	11.50
	1770	(1848)	4.50	6.50	9.00	11.50
	1771	(1849)	4.50	6.50	9.00	11.50
	1772	(1850)	4.50	6.50	9.00	11.50
	1773	(1851)	4.50	6.50	9.00	11.50

KM#	Date	Year	VG	Fine	VF	XF
602	1774	(1852)	7.00	10.00	13.50	17.50
	1775	(1853)	4.50	6.50	9.00	11.50
	1776	(1854)	4.50	6.50	9.00	11.50
	1777	(1855)	4.50	6.50	9.00	11.50
	1778	(1856)	4.50	6.50	9.00	11.50
	1779	(1857)	4.50	6.50	9.00	11.50
	1780	(1858)	4.50	6.50	9.00	11.50
	1781	(1859)	4.50	6.50	9.00	11.50
	1782	(1860)	4.50	7.50	12.50	16.50
	1785	(1863)	7.00	10.00	13.50	17.50
	1786	(1864)	4.50	6.50	9.00	11.50
	1787	(1865)	4.50	6.50	9.00	11.50
	1788	(1866)	4.50	6.50	9.00	11.50
	1789	(1867)	4.50	6.50	9.00	11.50
	1790	(1868)	4.50	6.50	9.00	11.50
	1791	(1869)	4.50	6.50	9.00	11.50
	1792	(1870)	4.50	6.50	9.00	11.50
	1793	(1871)	4.50	6.50	9.00	11.50
	1794	(1872)	4.50	6.50	9.00	11.50
	1796	(1874)	4.50	6.50	9.00	11.50
	1797	(1875)	4.50	6.50	9.00	11.50
	1800	(1878)	4.50	6.50	9.00	11.50
	1801	(1879)	4.50	6.50	9.00	11.50
	1802	(1880)	4.50	6.50	9.00	11.50
	1803	(1881)	4.50	6.50	9.00	11.50

Machine struck, plain edge

602.1	SE1786	(1864)	12.50	15.00	20.00	27.50
	1787	(1865)	7.50	10.00	15.00	22.50
	1788	(1866)	12.50	15.00	20.00	27.50
	1789	(1867)	12.50	15.00	20.00	27.50

Struck using gold dies.

| 602.2 | SE1801 | (1879) | 12.50 | 15.00 | 20.00 | 27.50 |

2 MOHARS

SILVER, 11.20 g

603	SE1769	(1847)	22.50	30.00	40.00	55.00
	1770	(1848)	22.50	30.00	40.00	55.00
	1771	(1849)	22.50	30.00	40.00	55.00
	1772	(1850)	22.50	30.00	40.00	55.00
	1777	(1855)	22.50	30.00	40.00	55.00
	1782	(1860)	22.50	30.00	40.00	55.00
	1796	(1874)	22.50	30.00	40.00	55.00
	1797	(1875)	22.50	30.00	40.00	55.00
	1801	(1879)	17.50	20.00	25.00	40.00
	1802	(1880)	22.50	30.00	40.00	55.00

Machine struck, milled edge

| 603.1 | SE1786 | (1864) | — | — | Rare |

26mm
Struck w/regular gold dies

| 603.2 | SE1801 | (1879) | 10.00 | 18.50 | 25.00 | 40.00 |
| | 1802 | (1880) | 22.50 | 30.00 | 40.00 | 55.00 |

28mm

| 603.3 | SE1801 | (1879) | 11.50 | 20.00 | 28.50 | 50.00 |

Gold Coinage
DAM

Actual Size   2 x Actual Size
GOLD, uniface, 0.04 g

NEPAL

KM#	Date	Year	VG	Fine	VF	XF
604	ND	(1847-81)	10.00	14.00	20.00	27.50

Legend in 2 lines.

Actual Size   2 X Actual Size

Legend in 3 lines.
| A604 | ND | (1847-81) | — | — | — | — |

1/32 MOHAR
GOLD, uniface, 0.18 g
| 605 | ND | (1847-81) | 14.00 | 20.00 | 25.00 | 32.50 |

1/16 MOHAR
GOLD, 0.35 g
| 606 | ND | (1847-81) | 14.00 | 20.00 | 25.00 | 32.50 |

1/8 MOHAR
GOLD, 0.70 g
| 607 | ND | (1847-81) | 22.50 | 27.50 | 35.00 | 45.00 |

In the name of Queen Trailokya Raja Lakshmi

1/4 MOHAR

GOLD, 1.40 g
| A608 | SE1769 | (1847) | 40.00 | 50.00 | 65.00 | 85.00 |
| | 1770 | (1848) | 40.00 | 50.00 | 65.00 | 85.00 |

In the name of Queen Sura Raja Lakshmi

608	SE1769	(1847)	40.00	50.00	65.00	85.00
(C178)	1787	(1865)	40.00	50.00	65.00	85.00
	1790	(1868)	40.00	50.00	65.00	85.00

In the name of Queen Deva Raja Lakshmi

| 609 | SE1770 | (1848) | 40.00 | 50.00 | 65.00 | 85.00 |

In the name of Queen Punyakumari Raja Lakshmi

| 610 | SE1802 | (1880) | 55.00 | 75.00 | 100.00 | 135.00 |

1/2 MOHAR
GOLD, 2.80 g
611	SE1769	(1847)	65.00	75.00	85.00	100.00
	1770	(1848)	65.00	75.00	85.00	100.00
	1802	(1880)	65.00	75.00	85.00	100.00

Rev: W/o horizontal lines.
| 612 | SE1790 | (1868) | 65.00 | 75.00 | 85.00 | 100.00 |

In the name of Queen Deva Raja Lakshmi

MOHAR
GOLD, 5.60 g
613	SE1769	(1847)	115.00	125.00	145.00	175.00
	1791	(1869)	115.00	125.00	145.00	175.00
	1794	(1872)	115.00	125.00	145.00	175.00
	1802	(1880)	115.00	125.00	145.00	175.00

1/2 TOLA

GOLD, 6.24 g

KM#	Date	Year	VG	Fine	VF	XF
614	SE1773	(1851)	125.00	135.00	160.00	200.00
	1786	(1864)	125.00	135.00	160.00	200.00
	1787	(1865)	125.00	135.00	160.00	200.00

TOLA

GOLD, 12.48 g
615	SE1769	(1847)	265.00	285.00	310.00	350.00
	1773	(1851)	265.00	285.00	310.00	350.00
	1774	(1852)	265.00	285.00	310.00	350.00
	1778	(1856)	265.00	285.00	310.00	350.00
	1780	(1858)	265.00	285.00	310.00	350.00
	1786	(1864)	265.00	285.00	310.00	350.00
	1787	(1865)	265.00	285.00	310.00	350.00
	1791	(1869)	265.00	285.00	310.00	350.00
	1793	(1871)	265.00	285.00	310.00	350.00
	1794	(1872)	265.00	285.00	310.00	350.00
	1802	(1880)	265.00	285.00	310.00	350.00

2 RUPEES
GOLD
Similar to 1 Tola, KM#615.
| 616 | SE1794 | (1872) | 450.00 | 525.00 | 650.00 | 800.00 |

PRESENTATION ISSUES
In the name of Queen Trailokyaraja Lakshmi

RUPEE
GOLD, 11.66 g
| 617 | SE1769 | (1847) | 400.00 | 500.00 | 550.00 | 600.00 |

| 617.1 | SE1771 | (1849) | 285.00 | 350.00 | 425.00 | 500.00 |

2 RUPEES
SILVER
| 618 | SE1769 | (1847) | | Reported, not confirmed | | |

GOLD, 23.32 g
| 619 | SE1769 | (1847) | 750.00 | 1000. | 1250. | 1500. |
| | 1771 | (1849) | 750.00 | 1000. | 1250. | 1500. |

PRITHVI VIRA VIKRAMA
SE1803-1833/VS1938-1968
1881-1911AD

Copper Coinage
DAM

COPPER
KM#	Date	Year	Fine	VF	XF	Unc
620	SE(18)18	(1896)	7.50	12.00	15.00	20.00
	(18)19	(1897)	7.50	12.00	15.00	20.00

| 620.1 | VS(19)64 | (1907) | 7.50 | 12.00 | 15.00 | 20.00 |

1/2 PAISA
KM#	Date	Year	Fine	VF	XF	Unc
621	VS(19)68	(1911)	4.50	7.50	10.00	17.50

COPPER
| 622 | VS(19)64 | (1907) | 4.50 | 7.50 | 10.00 | 17.50 |
| | (19)68 | (1911) | 4.50 | 7.50 | 10.00 | 17.50 |

PAISA

COPPER
Obv: Trident. Rev. leg: 4 lines.
KM#	Date	Year	Good	VG	Fine	VF
623	SE1810	(1888)	30.00	50.00	75.00	100.00

Obv: Crossed khukris, circular leg. border of flowers.
| 624 | VS1945 | (1888) | 30.00 | 50.00 | 75.00 | 100.00 |

Obv: 2 footprints above khukris.
| 625 | VS1945 | (1888) | 3.00 | 5.00 | 8.50 | 13.50 |
| | 1948 | (1891) | 9.00 | 15.00 | 22.50 | 35.00 |

Obv. and rev: Border of XXX's.
| 626 | VS1948 | (1891) | 1.00 | 1.50 | 3.00 | 5.00 |
| | 1949 | (1892) | 2.00 | 3.00 | 5.00 | 8.00 |

Obv. and rev: Border of crescents.
627	VS1949	(1892)	1.00	1.50	3.00	5.00
	1950	(1893)	1.00	1.50	3.00	5.00
	1951	(1894)	1.25	1.75	3.50	6.00

Obv. and rev: Leg. within wreaths.
628	VS1949	(1892)	1.00	1.50	3.00	5.00
	1950	(1893)	1.00	1.50	3.00	5.00
	1951	(1894)	1.00	1.50	3.00	5.00
	1952	(1895)	1.00	1.50	3.00	5.00

KM#	Date	Year	Good	VG	Fine	VF
628	1953	(1896)	1.00	1.50	3.00	5.00
	1954	(1897)	1.00	1.50	3.00	5.00
	1955	(1898)	1.00	1.50	3.00	5.00
	1956	(1899)	1.00	1.50	3.00	5.00
	1957	(1900)	1.00	1.50	3.00	5.00
	1959	(1902)	1.00	1.50	3.00	5.00
	1960	(1903)	1.00	1.50	3.00	5.00
	1961	(1904)	1.00	1.50	3.00	5.00
	1962	(1905)	1.00	1.50	3.00	5.00
	1963	(1906)	1.00	1.50	3.00	5.00
	1964	(1907)	1.00	1.50	3.00	5.00

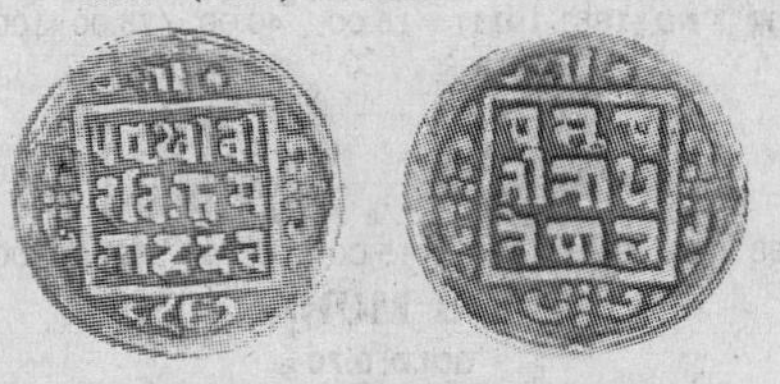

Obv. and rev: Leg. within squares.

KM#	Date	Year	Good	VG	Fine	VF
629	VS1959	(1902)	1.00	1.50	2.50	4.00
	1962	(1905)	1.00	1.50	2.50	4.00
	1963	(1906)	1.00	1.50	2.50	4.00
	1964	(1907)	1.00	1.50	2.50	4.00
	1965	(1908)	1.00	1.50	2.50	4.00
	1966	(1909)	1.00	1.50	2.50	4.00
	1967	(1910)	1.00	1.50	2.50	4.00
	1968	(1911)	1.00	1.50	2.50	4.00

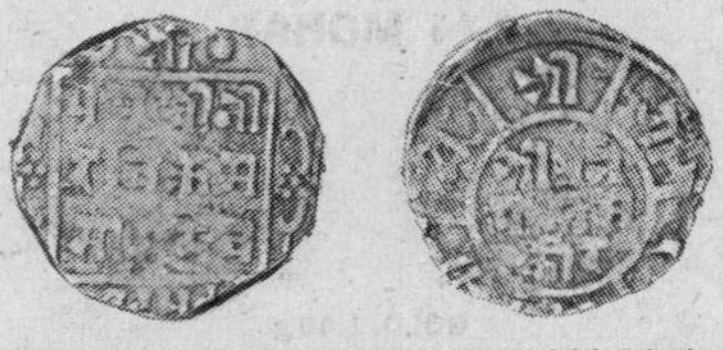

Obv: Leg. within square. Rev: Leg. within circle.

KM#	Date	Year	Good	VG	Fine	VF
630	VS1959	(1902)	7.50	12.50	20.00	33.50

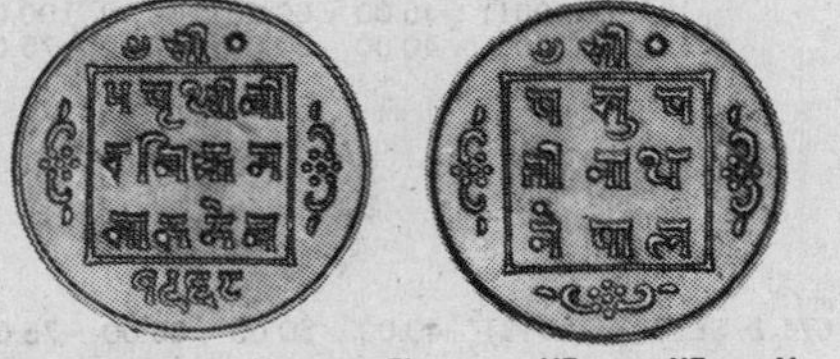

KM#	Date	Year	Fine	VF	XF	Unc
631	VS1964	(1907)	5.50	9.00	15.00	22.50
	1968	(1911)	8.50	13.50	20.00	30.00

2 PAISA
(Dak)

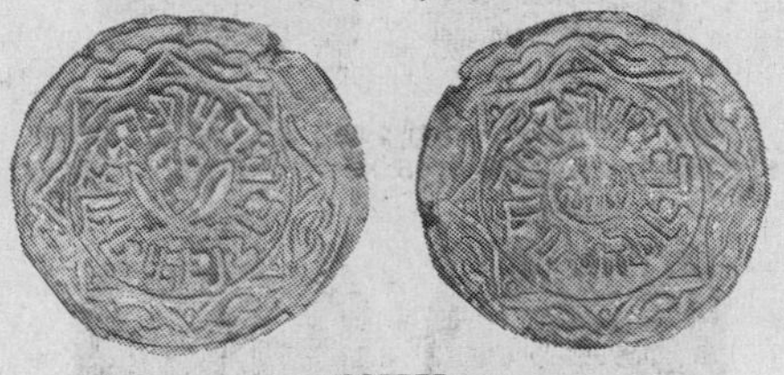

COPPER
Obv. and rev: Circular legends.

KM#	Date	Year	Good	VG	Fine	VF
632	VS1948	(1891)	2.00	3.00	5.00	8.00
	1949	(1892)	2.50	3.50	5.00	8.00
	1950	(1893)	2.50	3.50	5.00	8.00

Obv: Leg. within square. Rev: Leg. within circle.

KM#	Date	Year	Good	VG	Fine	VF
633	VS1959	(1902)	12.50	17.50	25.00	50.00

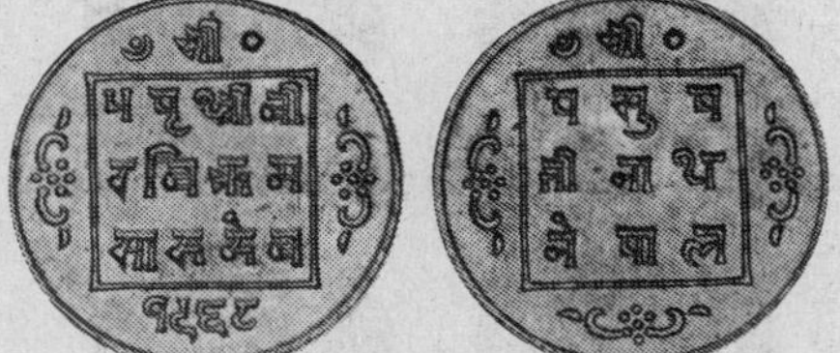

KM#	Date	Year	Fine	VF	XF	Unc
634	VS1964	(1907)	8.50	13.50	20.00	30.00
	1968	(1911)	9.00	15.00	22.50	35.00

Silver Coinage

DAM

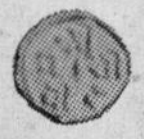

SILVER, uniface, 0.04 g
5 characters around sword

KM#	Date	Fine	VF	XF	Unc
635	ND (1881-1911)	8.00	10.00	15.00	25.00

4 characters around sword

KM#	Date	Year	Fine	VF	XF	Unc
636	ND (1881-1911)		15.00	25.00	30.00	40.00

1/32 MOHAR

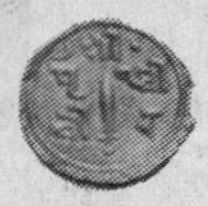

SILVER, uniface, 0.18 g
Sun and moon

KM#	Date	Year	VG	Fine	VF	XF
637	ND (1881-1911)		5.00	8.50	12.50	16.50

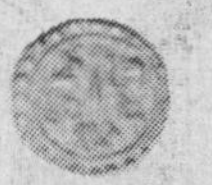

W/o sun and moon

KM#	Date	Year	VG	Fine	VF	XF
638	ND (1881-1911)		5.00	8.50	12.50	16.50

1/16 MOHAR

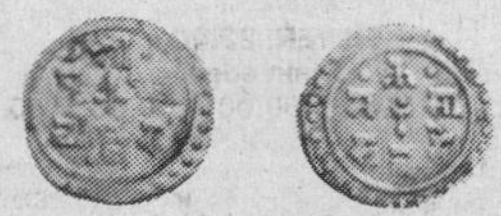

SILVER, 0.35 g

KM#	Date	Year	Fine	VF	XF	Unc
639	ND (1881-1911)		6.00	10.00	13.50	20.00

NOTE: Varieties exist.

1/8 MOHAR

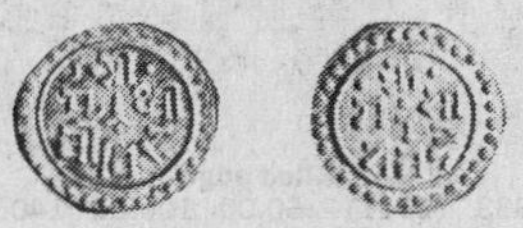

SILVER, 0.70 g

KM#	Date	Year	Fine	VF	XF	Unc
640	ND (1881-1911)		7.50	12.50	18.50	27.50

NOTE: Varieties exist.

1/4 MOHAR

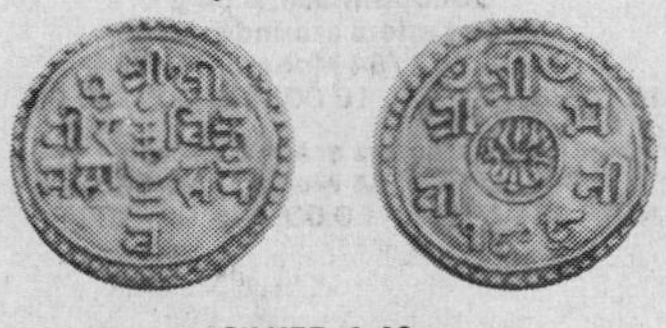

SILVER, 1.40 g
Rev: Two moons.

KM#	Date	Year	VG	Fine	VF	XF
641	SE1804	(1882)	15.00	17.50	25.00	35.00
	1806	(1884)	20.00	25.00	35.00	45.00
	1808	(1886)	15.00	17.50	25.00	35.00
	1811	(1889)	20.00	25.00	35.00	45.00

Rev: Moon and spiral sun.

KM#	Date	Year	VG	Fine	VF	XF
642	SE1816	(1894)	1.75	3.00	5.00	7.00
	1817	(1895)	1.75	3.00	5.00	7.00

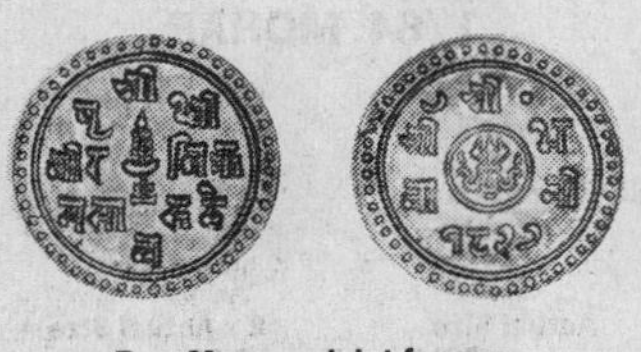

Rev: Moon and dot for sun.

KM#	Date	Year	VG	Fine	VF	XF
643	SE1827	(1905)	1.75	3.00	5.00	7.00

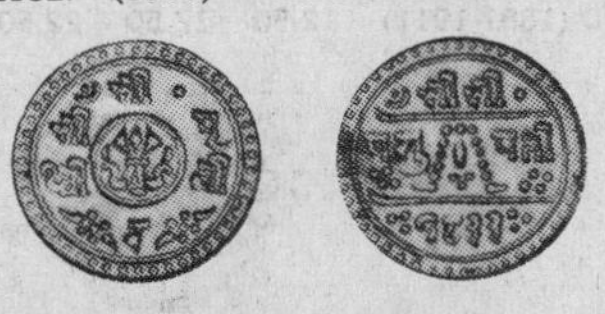

Machine struck

KM#	Date	Year	VG	Fine	VF	XF
644	SE1833	(1911)	1.75	3.00	5.00	7.00
	1833	(1911)	—	—	Proof	25.00

1/2 MOHAR

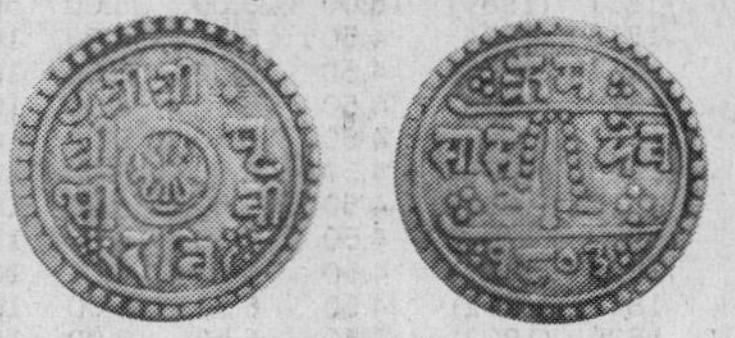

SILVER, 2.77 g

KM#	Date	Year	VG	Fine	VF	XF
645	SE1803	(1881)	15.00	20.00	25.00	30.00
	1804	(1882)	15.00	20.00	25.00	30.00

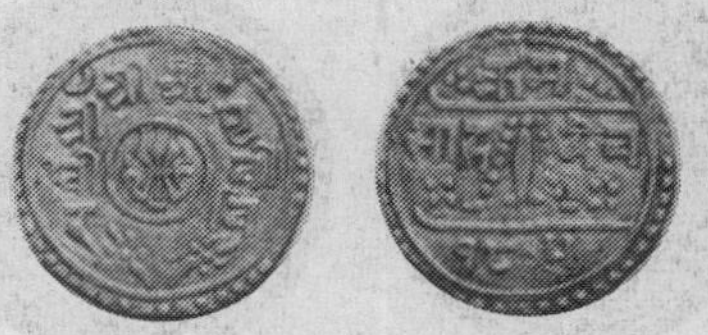

Obv: Leg. modified.

KM#	Date	Year	VG	Fine	VF	XF
646	SE1805	(1883)	15.00	20.00	25.00	30.00

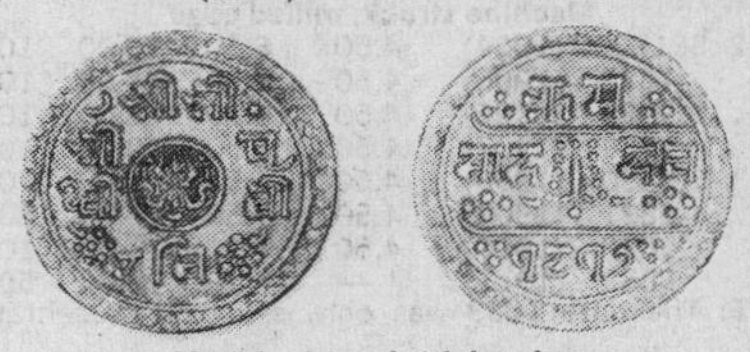

Machine struck, plain edge.

KM#	Date	Year	Fine	VF	XF	Unc
647	SE1816	(1894)	3.00	5.00	7.00	10.00
	1817	(1895)	3.00	5.00	7.00	10.00
	1824	(1902)	20.00	25.00	30.00	35.00

NOTE: Varieties exist.

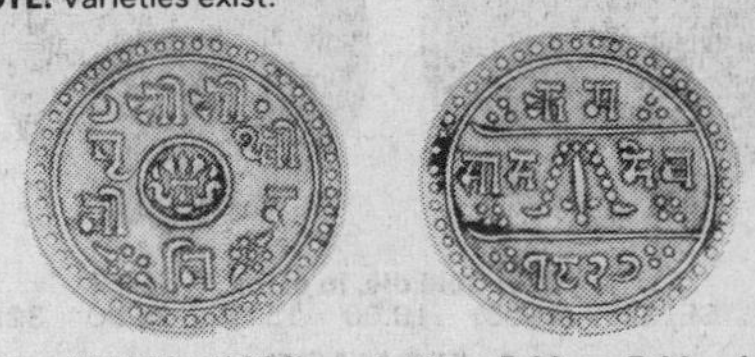

KM#	Date	Year	Fine	VF	XF	Unc
648	SE1826	(1904)	3.00	5.00	7.00	10.00
	1827	(1905)	3.00	5.00	7.00	10.00
	1829	(1907)	3.50	5.50	8.50	11.50

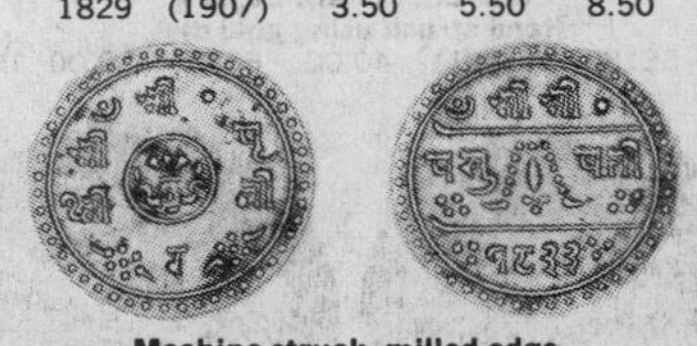

Machine struck, milled edge.

KM#	Date	Year	Fine	VF	XF	Unc
649	SE1832	(1910)	20.00	25.00	30.00	35.00
	1833	(1911)	2.25	3.50	5.00	7.00
	1833	(1911)	—	—	Proof	35.00

MOHAR

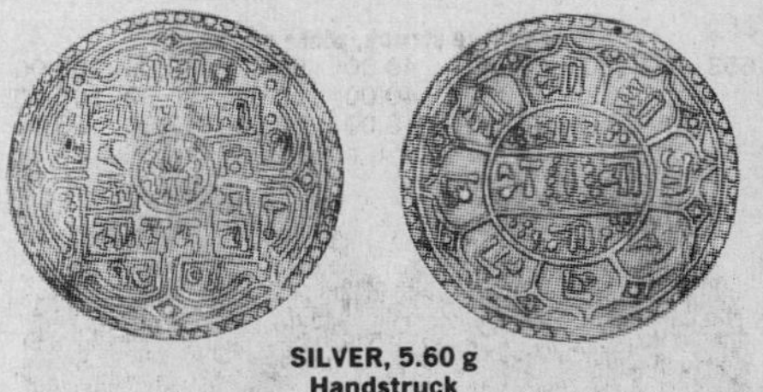

SILVER, 5.60 g
Handstruck

KM#	Date	Year	VG	Fine	VF	XF
650	SE1803	(1881)	4.50	6.50	9.00	11.50
	1804	(1882)	4.50	6.50	9.00	11.50

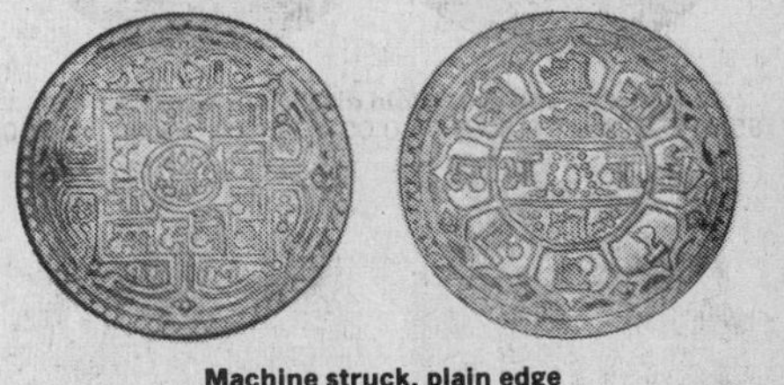

Machine struck, plain edge

KM#	Date	Year	Fine	VF	XF	Unc
651.1	SE1803	(1881)	15.00	25.00	35.00	50.00
	1804	(1882)	4.50	6.50	8.00	10.00
	1805	(1883)	4.50	6.50	8.00	10.00
	1806	(1884)	4.50	6.50	8.00	10.00
	1807	(1885)	4.50	6.50	8.00	10.00
	1808	(1886)	4.50	6.50	8.00	10.00
	1809	(1887)	4.50	6.50	8.00	10.00
	1810	(1888)	4.50	6.50	8.00	10.00

NEPAL 1316

KM#	Date	Year	Fine	VF	XF	Unc
651.1	1811	(1889)	15.00	25.00	35.00	50.00
	1816	(1894)	4.50	6.50	8.00	10.00
	1817	(1895)	4.50	6.50	8.00	10.00
	1818	(1896)	4.50	6.50	8.00	10.00
	1819	(1897)	4.50	6.50	8.00	10.00
	1820	(1898)	4.50	6.50	8.00	10.00
	1821	(1899)	4.50	6.50	8.00	10.00
	1822	(1900)	4.50	6.50	8.00	10.00
	1823	(1901)	4.50	6.50	8.00	10.00
	1824	(1902)	4.50	6.50	8.00	10.00
	1825	(1903)	4.50	6.50	8.00	10.00
	1826	(1904)	4.50	6.50	8.00	10.00
	1827	(1905)	4.50	6.50	8.00	10.00

Machine struck, milled edge

651.2	SE1826	(1904)	4.50	6.50	8.00	10.00
	1827	(1905)	4.50	6.50	8.00	10.00
	1828	(1906)	4.50	6.50	8.00	10.00
	1829	(1907)	4.50	6.50	8.00	10.00
	1830	(1908)	4.50	6.50	8.00	10.00
	1831	(1909)	4.50	6.50	8.00	10.00
	1832	(1910)	4.50	6.50	8.00	10.00
	1833	(1911)	—	25.00	35.00	50.00

NOTE: The date 1833 was only issued in presentation sets.

Rev: Gold die, in error.

| 652 | SE1825 | (1903) | 10.00 | 15.00 | 25.00 | 32.50 |

2 MOHARS
SILVER, 27mm, 11.20 g
Hand struck using gold dies.

| A653 | SE1803 | (1881) | 40.00 | 60.00 | 80.00 | 100.00 |

Machine struck, plain edge.

653	SE1804	(1882)	40.00	60.00	80.00	100.00
	1811	(1889)	40.00	60.00	80.00	100.00
	1817	(1895)	8.00	12.50	17.50	25.00

Machine struck using gold dies, plain edge, 29mm.

| 654 | SE1821 | (1899) | 10.00 | 15.00 | 25.00 | 45.00 |

Machine struck, milled edge, 27mm

655	SE1829	(1907)	15.00	27.50	40.00	60.00
	1831	(1909)	6.00	9.00	12.50	20.00

Machine struck, 29mm

KM#	Date	Year	Fine	VF	XF	Unc
656	SE1832	(1910)	7.00	9.00	11.50	18.50
	1833	(1911)	—	8.00	10.00	16.50

4 MOHARS

SILVER, 22.40 g
Plain edge

| 657 | SE1817 | (1895) | 60.00 | 100.00 | 140.00 | 200.00 |

Milled edge

| 658 | SE1833 | (1911) | 60.00 | 100.00 | 140.00 | 200.00 |

Gold Coinage
DAM
GOLD, uniface, 0.04 g
5 characters around sword.
Similar to 1/64 Mohar, KM#664.

| 659 | ND | (1881-1911) | 10.00 | 14.00 | 20.00 | 27.50 |

4 characters around sword.
Similar to 1/64 Mohar, KM#663.

| 660 | ND | (1881-1911) | 10.00 | 14.00 | 20.00 | 27.50 |

Actual Size   2 x Actual Size
Circle around characters.

| 661 | ND | (1881-1911) | 10.00 | 14.00 | 20.00 | 27.50 |

Actual Size   2 x Actual Size
2 characters under sword.

| 662 | ND | (1881-1911) | 10.00 | 14.00 | 20.00 | 27.50 |

1/64 MOHAR

Actual Size   2 x Actual Size
GOLD, uniface, 0.09 g
Obv: 4 characters around sword.

| 663 | ND | (1881-1911) | 12.50 | 17.50 | 22.50 | 30.00 |

Actual Size   2 x Actual Size
Obv: 5 characters around sword.

| 664 | ND | (1881-1911) | 12.50 | 17.50 | 22.50 | 30.00 |

1/32 MOHAR
GOLD, uniface, 0.18 g
5 characters around sword.

KM#	Date	Year	Fine	VF	XF	Unc
665	ND	(1881-1911)	20.00	40.00	75.00	100.00

4 characters around sword.

| 666 | ND | (1881-1911) | 15.00 | 30.00 | 75.00 | 100.00 |

1/16 MOHAR
GOLD, 0.35 g

| 667 | ND | (1881-1911) | 15.00 | 40.00 | 75.00 | 100.00 |

| 668 | SE(18)33 | (1911) | 15.00 | 30.00 | 75.00 | 100.00 |

1/8 MOHAR
GOLD, 0.70 g

| 669 | ND | (1881-1911) | 22.50 | 40.00 | 75.00 | 100.00 |

NOTE: Varieties exist.

| 670 | SE(18)33 | (1911) | 22.50 | 40.00 | 75.00 | 100.00 |

1/4 MOHAR

GOLD, 1.40 g

671.1	SE1808	(1886)	45.00	60.00	80.00	100.00
	1811	(1889)	45.00	60.00	80.00	100.00
	1817	(1895)	40.00	50.00	60.00	75.00
	1823	(1901)	45.00	60.00	80.00	100.00
	1829	(1907)	40.00	50.00	60.00	75.00

| 671.2 | SE1833 | (1911) | 40.00 | 50.00 | 60.00 | 75.00 |

1/2 MOHAR

GOLD, 2.80 g

| 672.1 | SE1805 | (1883) | 65.00 | 75.00 | 85.00 | 100.00 |

| 672.2 | SE1817 | (1895) | 65.00 | 75.00 | 85.00 | 100.00 |

| 672.3 | SE1823 | (1901) | 70.00 | 80.00 | 100.00 | 125.00 |

| 672.4 | SE1829 | (1907) | 65.00 | 75.00 | 85.00 | 100.00 |

| 672.5 | SE1833 | (1911) | 65.00 | 75.00 | 85.00 | 100.00 |

MOHAR

GOLD, 5.60 g

KM#	Date	Year	Fine	VF	XF	Unc
673.1	SE1804	(1882)	115.00	125.00	145.00	175.00
	1805	(1883)	115.00	125.00	145.00	175.00
	1809	(1887)	115.00	125.00	145.00	175.00
	1817	(1895)	115.00	125.00	145.00	175.00
	1820	(1898)	115.00	125.00	140.00	165.00
	1823	(1901)	115.00	125.00	140.00	165.00
	1825	(1903)	115.00	125.00	140.00	165.00
	1826	(1904)	115.00	125.00	140.00	165.00
	1827	(1905)	115.00	125.00	140.00	165.00

Milled edge

KM#	Date	Year	Fine	VF	XF	Unc
673.2	SE1828	(1906)	115.00	125.00	140.00	165.00
	1829	(1907)	115.00	125.00	140.00	165.00
	1831	(1909)	115.00	125.00	140.00	165.00
	1833	(1911)	115.00	125.00	140.00	165.00
673.3	VS1949	(1892)	115.00	125.00	145.00	175.00

TOLA

GOLD, 12.48 g
Oblique edge milling.

KM#	Date	Year	Fine	VF	XF	Unc
674.1	SE1803	(1881)	250.00	275.00	300.00	335.00
	1805	(1883)	250.00	275.00	300.00	335.00
	1811	(1889)	250.00	275.00	300.00	335.00

Vertical edge milling.

KM#	Date	Year	Fine	VF	XF	Unc
674.2	SE1803	(1881)	250.00	275.00	300.00	335.00
	1804	(1882)	250.00	275.00	300.00	335.00

Plain edge.

KM#	Date	Year	Fine	VF	XF	Unc
674.3	SE1807	(1885)	250.00	275.00	300.00	325.00
	1817	(1895)	250.00	275.00	300.00	325.00
	1820	(1898)	250.00	275.00	300.00	325.00
	1823	(1901)	250.00	275.00	300.00	325.00
	1824	(1902)	250.00	275.00	300.00	325.00
	1825	(1903)	250.00	275.00	300.00	325.00
	1826	(1904)	250.00	275.00	300.00	325.00

Vertical edge milling.

KM#	Date	Year	Fine	VF	XF	Unc
675.1	SE1828	(1906)	250.00	275.00	300.00	325.00
	1829	(1907)	250.00	275.00	300.00	325.00
	1831	(1909)	250.00	275.00	300.00	325.00
	1832	(1910)	250.00	275.00	300.00	325.00
	1833	(1911)	250.00	275.00	300.00	325.00

Plain edge.

KM#	Date	Year	Fine	VF	XF	Unc
675.2	VS1947	(1890)	250.00	275.00	300.00	325.00

Oblique edge milling.

KM#	Date	Year	Fine	VF	XF	Unc
675.3	VS1949	(1892)	250.00	275.00	300.00	325.00

DUITOLA ASARPHI

GOLD, 23.32 g

KM#	Date	Year	Fine	VF	XF	Unc
676	SE1811	(1889)	600.00	700.00	800.00	1000.

Rev: Die of 4 Mohars, KM#657.

KM#	Date	Year	Fine	VF	XF	Unc
677	SE1817	(1895)	600.00	700.00	800.00	1000.

Plain edge.

KM#	Date	Year	Fine	VF	XF	Unc
678	SE1817	(1895)	600.00	700.00	800.00	1000.
	1825	(1902)	600.00	700.00	800.00	1000.

Milled edge, 27mm.

KM#	Date	Year	Fine	VF	XF	Unc
679	SE1829	(1907)	600.00	650.00	750.00	800.00

Milled edge, 29mm.

KM#	Date	Year	Fine	VF	XF	Unc
680	SE1833	(1911)	600.00	650.00	750.00	800.00

QUEEN LAKSHMI DIVYESWARI
(Regent for Tribhuvana Vira Vikrama)

Silver Coinage
1/2 MOHAR

SILVER, 2.77 g

KM#	Date	Year	Fine	VF	XF	Unc
681	VS1971	(1914)	4.00	6.00	9.00	11.50

MOHAR

SILVER, 5.60 g

KM#	Date	Year	Fine	VF	XF	Unc
682	VS1971	(1914)	4.50	6.50	9.00	11.50

Gold Coinage
MOHAR

GOLD, 5.60 g

KM#	Date	Year	Fine	VF	XF	Unc
683	VS1971	(1914)	100.00	125.00	145.00	175.00

TRIBHUVANA VIRA VIKRAMA
VS1968-2007 / 1911-1950AD

Copper Coinage
1/2 PAISA

COPPER

KM#	Date	Year	Fine	VF	XF	Unc
684	VS1978	(1921)	—	—	50.00	75.00
	1985	(1928)	—	—	50.00	75.00

NOTE: Struck only for presentation sets.

PAISA

COPPER
Machine struck

KM#	Date	Year	Good	VG	Fine	VF
685.1	VS1968	(1911)	10.00	20.00	50.00	75.00

Hand struck

KM#	Date	Year	Good	VG	Fine	VF
685.2	VS1969	(1912)	1.00	1.50	2.25	3.50
	1970	(1913)	1.00	1.50	2.25	3.50
	1971	(1914)	1.00	1.50	2.25	3.50
	1972	(1915)	1.00	1.50	2.25	3.50
685.2	1973	(1916)	1.00	1.50	2.25	3.50
	1974	(1917)	1.00	1.50	2.25	3.50
	1975	(1918)	1.00	1.50	2.25	3.50
	1976	(1919)	1.00	1.50	2.25	3.50
	1977	(1920)	1.00	1.50	2.25	3.50

KM#	Date	Year	Fine	VF	XF	Unc
686	VS1975	(1918)	—	—	37.50	50.00

NOTE: The above issue is believed to be a pattern.

Crude, hand struck

KM#	Date	Year	Good	VG	Fine	VF
687.1	VS1978	(1921)	2.00	3.00	4.50	7.50
	1979	(1922)	2.00	3.00	4.50	7.50
	1980	(1923)	4.00	5.00	7.50	12.50
	1981	(1924)	4.00	5.00	7.50	12.50
	1982	(1925)	4.00	5.00	7.50	12.50
	1983	(1926)	4.00	5.00	7.50	12.50

Machine struck, 3.75 g

KM#	Date	Year	Fine	VF	XF	Unc
687.2	VS1975	(1918)	1.25	1.75	3.00	6.00
	1976	(1919)	1.25	1.75	3.00	6.00
	1977	(1920)	1.25	1.75	3.00	6.00
	1977 inverted date					
		(1920)	3.00	4.50	7.50	15.00

Reduced weight, 2.80 g

KM#	Date	Year	Fine	VF	XF	Unc
688	VS1978	(1921)	1.25	1.75	3.00	6.00
	1979	(1922)	1.25	1.75	3.00	6.00
	1980	(1923)	1.50	3.00	5.00	10.00
	1981	(1924)	1.50	3.00	5.00	10.00
	1982	(1925)	1.25	1.75	3.00	6.00
	1984	(1927)	1.25	1.75	3.00	6.00
	1985	(1928)	1.25	1.75	3.00	6.00
	1986	(1929)	1.25	1.75	3.00	6.00
	1987	(1930)	1.25	1.75	3.00	6.00

2 PAISA

COPPER
Crude struck

KM#	Date	Year	Good	VG	Fine	VF
689.1	VS1978	(1921)	1.00	2.00	3.50	6.00
	1979	(1922)	1.00	2.00	3.50	6.00
	1980	(1923)	1.00	2.00	3.50	6.00
	1981	(1924)	1.00	2.00	3.50	6.00
	1982	(1925)	1.00	2.00	3.50	6.00
	1983	(1926)	1.00	2.00	3.50	6.00
	1984	(1927)	1.00	2.00	3.50	6.00
	1985	(1928)	1.00	2.00	3.50	6.00
	1986	(1929)	1.50	2.50	4.00	7.00
	1987	(1930)	1.50	2.50	4.00	7.00
	1988	(1931)	2.00	3.00	5.00	8.50

NOTE: Varieties of the Khukris exist.

NEPAL 1318

Machine struck, 7.50 g

KM#	Date	Year	VG	Fine	VF	XF
689.2	VS1976	(1919)	1.00	2.00	3.00	5.00
	1977	(1920)	1.00	2.00	3.00	5.00
	1977 inverted date					
		(1920)	3.50	5.00	8.50	13.50

Reduced weight, 5.00 g

689.3	VS1978	(1921)	1.00	2.00	3.00	4.50
	1979	(1922)	1.00	2.00	3.00	4.50
	1980	(1923)	1.00	2.00	3.00	4.50
	1981	(1924)	1.00	2.00	3.00	4.50
	1982	(1925)	1.00	2.00	3.00	4.50
	1983	(1926)	1.00	2.00	3.00	4.50
	1984	(1927)	1.00	2.00	3.00	4.50
	1991	(1934)	1.50	2.50	4.00	6.00

5 PAISA

**COPPER
Crude struck**

KM#	Date	Year	Fine	VF	XF	Unc
690.1	VS1978	(1921)	1.75	3.00	5.00	7.50
	1979	(1922)	1.75	3.00	5.00	7.50
	1980	(1923)	1.75	3.00	5.00	7.50
	1981	(1924)	1.75	3.00	5.00	7.50
	1982	(1925)	1.75	3.00	5.00	7.50
	1983	(1926)	1.75	3.00	5.00	7.50
	1984	(1927)	1.75	3.00	5.00	7.50
	1985	(1928)	1.75	3.00	5.00	7.50
	1986	(1929)	1.75	3.00	5.00	7.50
	1987	(1930)	1.75	3.00	5.00	7.50
	1988	(1931)	6.00	10.00	14.00	20.00

NOTE: Varieties of the Khukris exist.

Machine struck, 18.00 g

690.2	VS1975	(1918)	50.00	75.00	100.00	125.00
	1976	(1919)	6.00	10.00	14.00	20.00
	1977	(1920)	1.25	2.25	3.50	6.00
	1977 inverted date					
		(1920)	3.00	5.00	8.50	12.50

Reduced weight, 14.00 g

690.3	VS1978	(1921)	1.25	2.25	3.50	5.00
	1979	(1922)	1.25	2.25	3.50	5.00
	1980	(1923)	1.25	2.25	3.50	5.00
	1981	(1924)	1.25	2.25	3.50	5.00
	1982	(1925)	1.25	2.25	3.50	5.00
	1983	(1926)	1.25	2.25	3.50	5.00
	1984	(1927)	1.25	2.25	3.50	5.00
	1991	(1934)	15.00	20.00	25.00	30.00

NOTE: Varieties exist with both open and closed handles on Khukris.

Silver Coinage
DAM

SILVER, uniface, 0.04 g

691	ND	(1911-1950)	15.00	25.00	30.00	50.00

1/4 MOHAR

SILVER, 1.40 g

KM#	Date	Year	VG	Fine	VF	XF
692	VS1969	(1912)	1.75	3.00	5.00	7.00
	1970	(1913)	1.75	3.00	5.00	7.00

1/2 MOHAR

SILVER, 2.80 g

KM#	Date	Year	Fine	VF	XF	Unc
693	VS1968	(1911)	2.25	3.50	5.00	7.00
	1970	(1913)	2.25	3.50	5.00	7.00

MOHAR

SILVER, 5.60 g

694	VS1968	(1911)	4.50	6.50	8.00	10.00
	1969	(1912)	4.50	6.50	8.00	10.00
	1971	(1914)	4.50	6.50	8.00	10.00

2 MOHARS

SILVER, 11.20 g

695	VS1968	(1911)	BV	7.50	10.00	16.50
	1969	(1912)	BV	7.50	10.00	16.50
	1970	(1913)	BV	7.50	10.00	16.50
	1971	(1914)	BV	7.50	10.00	16.50
	1972	(1915)	BV	7.50	10.00	16.50
	1973	(1916)	BV	7.50	10.00	16.50
	1974	(1917)	BV	7.50	10.00	16.50
	1975	(1918)	BV	7.50	10.00	16.50
	1976	(1919)	BV	7.50	10.00	16.50
	1977	(1920)	BV	7.50	10.00	16.50
	1978	(1921)	BV	7.50	10.00	16.50
	1979	(1922)	BV	7.50	10.00	16.50
	1980	(1923)	BV	7.50	10.00	16.50
	1982	(1925)	BV	7.50	10.00	16.50
	1983	(1926)	BV	7.50	10.00	16.50
	1984	(1927)	BV	7.50	10.00	16.50
	1985	(1928)	BV	7.50	10.00	16.50
	1986	(1929)	BV	7.50	10.00	16.50
	1987	(1930)	BV	7.50	10.00	16.50
	1988	(1931)	BV	7.50	10.00	16.50
	1989	(1932)	BV	7.50	10.00	16.50

4 MOHARS

SILVER, 22.40 g

696	VS1971	(1914)	40.00	75.00	125.00	175.00

Gold Coinage
DAM

GOLD, uniface, 0.04 g

697	ND	(1911-50)	25.00	40.00	75.00	100.00

1/32 MOHAR

GOLD, uniface, 0.18 g

698	ND	(1911-50)	35.00	60.00	90.00	125.00

1/16 MOHAR

GOLD, 0.35 g

699	VS(19)77	(1920)	50.00	90.00	120.00	150.00

1/8 MOHAR

GOLD, 0.70 g

KM#	Date	Year	Fine	VF	XF	Unc
700	VS(19)76	(1919)	75.00	120.00	150.00	200.00

1/2 MOHAR

GOLD, 2.80 g

701	VS1969	(1912)	—	Reported, not confirmed		
717	VS1995	(1938)	—	Reported, not confirmed		

MOHAR

GOLD, 5.60 g

702	VS1969	(1912)	100.00	125.00	140.00	165.00
	1975	(1918)	100.00	125.00	140.00	165.00
	1978	(1921)	100.00	125.00	140.00	165.00
	1979	(1922)	100.00	125.00	140.00	165.00
	1981	(1924)	100.00	125.00	140.00	165.00
	1983	(1926)	100.00	125.00	140.00	165.00
	1985	(1928)	100.00	125.00	140.00	165.00
	1986	(1929)	100.00	125.00	140.00	165.00
	1987	(1930)	100.00	125.00	140.00	165.00
	1989	(1932)	100.00	125.00	140.00	165.00
	1990	(1933)	100.00	125.00	140.00	165.00
	1991	(1934)	100.00	125.00	140.00	165.00
	1998	(1941)	100.00	125.00	140.00	165.00
	1999	(1942)	100.00	125.00	140.00	165.00
	2000	(1943)	100.00	125.00	140.00	165.00
	2003	(1946)	100.00	125.00	140.00	165.00
	2005	(1948)	100.00	125.00	140.00	165.00

KM#	Date	Mintage	Fine	VF	XF	Unc
722	VS1993(1936)	.376	—	Reported, not confirmed		
	1994(1937)	.283	—	Reported, not confirmed		

TOLA

GOLD, 12.48 g

KM#	Date	Year	Fine	VF	XF	Unc
703	VS1969	(1912)	225.00	275.00	300.00	325.00
	1974	(1917)	225.00	275.00	300.00	325.00
	1975	(1918)	225.00	275.00	300.00	325.00
	1976	(1919)	225.00	275.00	300.00	325.00
	1977	(1920)	225.00	275.00	300.00	325.00
	1978	(1921)	225.00	275.00	300.00	325.00
	1979	(1922)	225.00	275.00	300.00	325.00
	1980	(1923)	225.00	275.00	300.00	325.00
	1981	(1924)	225.00	275.00	300.00	325.00
	1982	(1925)	225.00	275.00	300.00	325.00
	1983	(1926)	225.00	275.00	300.00	325.00
	1984	(1927)	225.00	275.00	300.00	325.00
	1985	(1928)	225.00	275.00	300.00	325.00
	1986	(1929)	225.00	275.00	300.00	325.00
	1987	(1930)	225.00	275.00	300.00	325.00
	1988	(1931)	225.00	275.00	300.00	325.00
	1989	(1932)	225.00	275.00	300.00	325.00
	1990	(1933)	225.00	275.00	300.00	325.00
	1991	(1934)	225.00	275.00	300.00	325.00
	1998	(1941)	225.00	275.00	300.00	325.00
	1999	(1942)	225.00	275.00	300.00	325.00
	2000	(1943)	225.00	275.00	300.00	325.00
	2003	(1946)	225.00	275.00	300.00	325.00
	2005	(1948)	225.00	275.00	300.00	325.00

Obv: Trident in center.

727	VS1992	(1935)	235.00	250.00	285.00	325.00

DUITOLA ASARPHI
GOLD

Similar to 1 Tola, KM#703.

KM#	Date	Year	Fine	VF	XF	Unc
728	VS2005	(1948)	450.00	500.00	550.00	650.00

DECIMAL COINAGE
100 Paisa = 1 Rupee

1/4 PAISA

COPPER

KM#	Date		Fine	VF	XF	Unc
704	VS2000	(1943)	15.00	25.00	30.00	40.00
	2004	(1947)	15.00	25.00	30.00	40.00

1/2 PAISA

COPPER

KM#	Date	Year	Mintage	VF	XF	Unc
705	VS2004	(1947)	—	25.00	30.00	40.00

PAISA

COPPER

KM#	Date	Mintage	Fine	VF	XF	Unc
706	VS1990(1933)		.75	1.50	3.00	5.00
	1991(1934)		.75	1.50	3.00	5.00
	1992(1935)		.75	1.50	3.00	5.00
	1993(1936)		.75	1.50	3.00	5.00
	1994(1937)	.456	.75	1.50	3.00	5.00
	1995(1938)		.75	1.50	3.00	5.00
	1996(1939)		.75	1.50	3.00	5.00
	1997(1940)		.75	1.50	3.00	5.00

KM#	Date	Year	Fine	VF	XF	Unc
707	VS2005	(1948)	.75	1.25	1.75	2.50

BRASS

707a	VS2001	(1944)	.30	.50	.75	1.00
	2003	(1946)	.30	.50	.75	1.00
	2004	(1947)	3.00	5.00	7.00	10.00
	2005	(1948)	.30	.50	.75	1.00
	2006	(1949)	.60	1.00	1.25	1.75

2 PAISA

COPPER

KM#	Date	Year	VG	Fine	VF	XF
708	VS1992	(1935)	3.00	5.00	8.50	13.50

KM#	Date	Mintage	Fine	VF	XF	Unc
709	VS1992(1935)		2.00	4.00	6.50	10.00

KM#	Date	Mintage	Fine	VF	XF	Unc
709	VS1993(1936)	.473	1.00	2.00	3.00	5.00
	1994(1937)	1.133	1.00	2.00	3.00	5.00
	1995(1938)	—	1.00	2.00	3.00	5.00
	1996(1939)		1.00	2.00	3.00	5.00
	1997(1940)		2.00	4.00	6.50	10.00

KM#	Date	Year	Fine	VF	XF	Unc
709.1	VS1992	(1935)	.60	1.00	1.75	3.00
	1994	(1937)	.50	.75	1.50	2.50
	1995	(1938)	2.00	3.50	5.00	7.50
	1996	(1939)	.30	.50	1.00	1.50
	1997	(1940)	.50	.75	1.50	2.50
	1998	(1941)	.50	.75	1.50	2.50
	1999	(1942)	.50	.75	1.50	2.50

710	VS1999	(1942)	.30	.50	1.00	2.00
	2000	(1943)	.30	.50	1.00	2.00
	2003	(1945)	.30	.50	1.00	2.00
	2005	(1948)	3.00	5.00	7.00	10.00

BRASS

710a	VS1999	(1942)	.30	.50	1.00	2.00
	2000	(1943)	.30	.50	1.00	2.00
	2001	(1944)	.30	.50	1.00	2.00
	2005	(1948)	1.75	3.00	5.00	7.50
	2008	(1951)	.30	.50	1.00	2.00
	2009	(1952)	.30	.50	1.00	2.00
	2010	(1953)	.30	.50	1.00	2.00

5 PAISA

COPPER

KM#	Date	Mintage	Fine	VF	XF	Unc
711	VS1992(1935)		1.50	3.00	4.50	6.50
	1993(1936)	.878	1.50	3.00	4.50	6.50
	1994(1937)	.403	1.50	3.00	4.50	6.50
	1995(1938)		1.00	2.00	3.00	5.00
	1996(1939)		1.50	3.00	4.50	6.50
	1997(1940)		1.50	3.00	4.50	6.50
	1998(1941)		—	Reported, not confirmed		

COPPER-NICKEL-ZINC

KM#	Date	Year	Fine	VF	XF	Unc
712	VS2000	(1943)	.65	1.00	1.50	2.50
	2009	(1952)	1.75	3.00	5.00	8.50
	2010	(1953)	1.25	2.00	3.00	5.00

NOTE: The original issues were struck in German silver (copper-nickel-zinc) while restrikes were struck in copper-nickel.

1/16 RUPEE

SILVER

KM#	Date	Year	Fine	VF	XF	Unc
713	VS(19)96	(1939)	12.50	20.00	32.50	50.00

20 PAISA

21.2161 g, .333 SILVER, .0237 oz ASW

714	VS1989	(1932)	2.25	4.00	5.00	6.50
	1991	(1934)	1.75	3.50	4.50	6.00
	1992	(1935)	1.75	3.50	4.50	6.00
	1993	(1936)	1.75	3.50	4.50	6.00
	1994	(1937)	3.75	6.50	10.00	15.00
	1995	(1938)	1.75	3.50	4.50	6.00
	1996	(1939)	1.75	3.50	4.50	6.00
	1997	(1940)	1.75	3.50	4.50	6.00
	1998	(1941)	1.75	3.50	4.50	6.00
	1999	(1942)	1.75	3.50	4.50	6.00
	2000	(1943)	1.75	3.50	4.50	6.00
	2001	(1944)	1.75	3.50	4.50	6.00
	2003	(1945)	1.75	3.50	4.50	6.00
	2004	(1947)	1.75	3.50	4.50	6.00
715	VS1989	(1932)	2.25	4.00	6.00	8.50

*****NOTE:** The date SE1989 is given in different style characters. Refer to 50 Paisa KM#719 and 1 Rupee, KM#724 for style.

716	VS2006	(1949)	.75	1.00	1.25	1.75
	2007	(1950)	—	Reported, not confirmed		
	2009	(1952)	.75	1.00	1.50	2.50
	2010	(1953)	.75	1.00	1.50	2.50

50 PAISA

5.5403 g, .800 SILVER, .1425 oz ASW

718	VS1989	(1932)	5.50	6.50	8.00	10.00
	1991	(1934)	2.50	4.50	7.00	10.00
	1992	(1935)	2.50	4.50	7.00	10.00
	1993	(1936)	2.50	4.50	7.00	10.00
	1994	(1937)	2.50	4.50	7.00	10.00
	1995	(1938)	2.50	4.50	7.00	10.00
	1996	(1939)	2.50	4.50	7.00	10.00
	1997	(1940)	2.50	4.50	7.00	10.00
	1998	(1941)	2.50	4.50	7.00	10.00
	1999	(1942)	2.50	4.50	7.00	10.00
	2000	(1943)	2.50	4.50	7.00	10.00
	2001	(1944)	2.50	4.50	7.00	10.00
	2003	(1946)	2.50	4.50	7.00	10.00
	2004	(1947)	2.50	4.50	7.00	10.00
	2005	(1948)	2.50	4.50	7.00	10.00

719	VS1989	(1932)	2.50	4.50	7.00	9.00

NOTE: The date is given in different characters.

5.5403 g, .333 SILVER, .0593 oz ASW
Obv: 4 dots around trident.

720	VS2005	(1948)	45.00	65.00	90.00	125.00

NEPAL 1320

Obv: W/o dots around trident.

KM#	Date	Year	Fine	VF	XF	Unc
721	VS2006	(1949)	1.50	2.00	2.75	4.50
	2007	(1950)	1.50	2.00	2.75	4.50
	2009	(1952)	1.50	2.00	2.75	4.50
	2010	(1953)	1.50	2.00	2.75	4.50

RUPEE

11.0806 g, .800 SILVER, .2850 oz ASW

KM#	Date	Mintage	Fine	VF	XF	Unc
723	VS1989(1932)	—	2.50	5.00	8.00	20.00
	1991(1934)	—	2.50	5.00	8.00	16.50
	1992(1935)	—	2.50	5.00	8.00	16.50
	1993(1936)	1.717	2.50	5.00	8.00	16.50
	1994(1937)	2.097	2.50	5.00	8.00	16.50
	1995(1938)	—	2.50	5.00	8.00	16.50
	1996(1939)	—	2.50	5.00	8.00	16.50
	1997(1940)	—	2.50	5.00	8.00	16.50
	1998(1941)	—	2.50	5.00	8.00	16.50
	1999(1942)	—	2.50	5.00	8.00	16.50
	2000(1943)	—	2.50	5.00	8.00	16.50
	2001(1944)	—	2.50	5.00	8.00	16.50
	2003(1946)	—	2.50	5.00	8.00	16.50
	2005(1948)	—	2.50	5.00	8.00	16.50

KM#	Date	Year	Fine	VF	XF	Unc
724	VS1989	(1932)	7.50	10.00	12.50	15.00

NOTE: The date is given in different characters.

11.0806 g, .333 SILVER, .1186 oz ASW
Obv: 4 dots around trident.

| 725 | VS2005 | (1948) | 5.00 | 7.50 | 10.00 | 13.50 |

Obv: W/o dots around trident.

KM#	Date	Year	Fine	VF	XF	Unc
726	VS2006	(1949)	2.50	3.50	5.00	7.50
	2007	(1950)	2.50	3.50	5.00	7.50
	2008	(1951)	2.50	3.50	5.00	7.50
	2009	(1951)	2.50	3.50	5.00	7.50
	2010	(1952)	2.50	3.50	5.00	7.50

JNANENDRA VIRA VIKRAMA
VS2007/1950-1951AD

50 PAISA

5.5403 g, .333 SILVER, .0593 oz ASW

KM#	Date	Year	Mintage	VF	XF	Unc
729	VS2007	(1950)	26 pcs.	175.00	275.00	350.00

RUPEE

11.0806 g, .333 SILVER, .1186 oz ASW

KM#	Date	Year	Fine	VF	XF	Unc
730	VS2007	(1950)	4.50	6.50	9.00	12.50

MOHAR
GOLD

| 731 | VS2007 | (1950) | — | — | Rare | — |

TOLA
GOLD

| 732 | VS2007 | (1950) | — | — | Rare | — |

TRIVHUVANA VIRA VIKRAMA
VS2007-2011/1951-1955AD

50 PAISA

COPPER-NICKEL

| 740 | VS2010 | (1953) | .50 | 1.00 | 2.00 | 3.00 |
| | 2011 | (1954) | .35 | .75 | 1.50 | 2.00 |

RUPEE

COPPER-NICKEL
Equal denticles at rim.

| 742 | VS2010 | (1953) | .75 | 1.25 | 2.00 | 3.50 |
| | 2011 | (1954) | .75 | 1.25 | 2.00 | 3.50 |

Unequal denticles at rim.
| 743 | VS2011 | (1954) | .75 | 1.25 | 2.00 | 3.50 |

ANONYMOUS COINAGE
PAISA

BRASS, 18mm

KM#	Date	Year	Fine	VF	XF	Unc
733	VS2010	(1953)	8.00	15.00	20.00	25.00
	2011	(1954)	17.50	25.00	35.00	40.00
	2011	(1954)	(restrike)	1.00	1.50	2.00

17.5mm
| 734 | VS2012 | (1955) | 1.25 | 2.00 | 2.50 | 3.50 |

2 PAISA

BRASS

735	VS2010	(1953)	12.50	20.00	37.50	60.00
	2011	(1954)	30.00	40.00	50.00	75.00
	2011	(1954)	(restrike)		1.50	2.50

749	VS2012	(1955)	.30	.50	.75	1.50
	2013	(1956)	.30	.50	.75	1.50
	2014	(1957)	.30	.50	.75	1.50

4 PAISA

BRASS
| 754 | VS2012 | (1955) | 1.00 | 1.75 | 3.00 | 5.00 |

5 PAISA

BRONZE, 3.89 g

736	VS2010	(1953)	2.75	4.50	7.00	10.00
	2011	(1954)	.65	1.00	2.75	5.00
(755)	2012	(1955)	.30	.50	.75	1.00
	2013	(1956)	.30	.50	.75	1.00
	2014	(1957)	.30	.50	.75	1.00

COPPER-NICKEL, 4.04 g (OMS?)
| 736a (755a) | VS2014 | (1957) | — | — | — | — |

10 PAISA

BRONZE

737	VS2010	(1953)	2.75	4.50	7.00	10.00
	2011	(1954)	.15	.25	.50	1.00
(760)	2012	(1955)	.15	.25	.50	1.00

20 PAISA

COPPER-NICKEL

KM#	Date	Year	Fine	VF	XF	Unc
738	VS2010	(1953)	12.50	20.00	30.00	40.00
	2010	(1953)		(restrike)	2.50	3.00
	2011	(1954)	32.50	40.00	50.00	60.00

25 PAISA

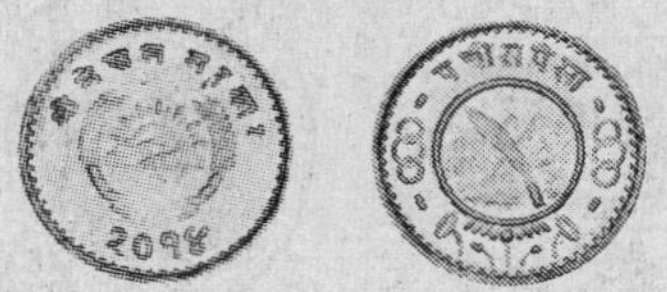

COPPER-NICKEL

KM#	Date	Year	Fine	VF	XF	Unc
739	VS2010	(1953)	2.00	3.50	4.50	6.00
	2011	(1954)	2.00	3.50	4.50	6.00
(769)	2012	(1955)	1.25	2.00	2.50	3.50
	2014	(1957)	1.25	2.00	2.50	3.50

1/2 ASARPHI

GOLD, 5.80 g
Portrait type.

KM#	Date	Year	Mintage	VF	XF	Unc
741	VS2010	(1953)	—	120.00	140.00	160.00

NOTE: KM#741 is believed to be a restrike.

ASARPHI

GOLD, 11.66 g

KM#	Date	Year	Mintage	VF	XF	Unc
744	VS2010	(1953)	—	175.00	200.00	250.00

MAHENDRA VIRA VIKRAMA

VS2012-2028/1955-1972AD

PAISA

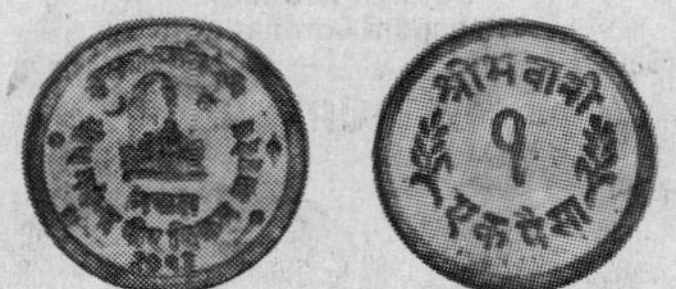

BRASS
Mahendra Coronation

KM#	Date	Year	Fine	VF	XF	Unc
745	VS2013	(1956)	.30	.50	.75	1.00

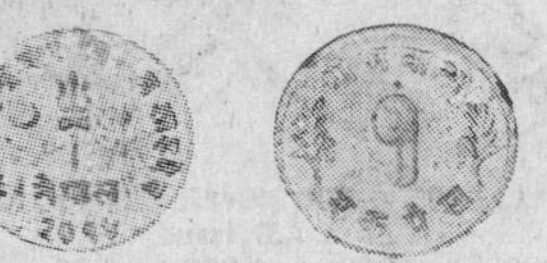

Rev: Numerals w/shading.

KM#	Date	Year	Fine	VF	XF	Unc
746	VS2014	(1957)	.10	.15	.25	.40
	2015	(1958)	.10	.15	.25	.40
	2018	(1961)	.10	.15	.25	.40
	2019	(1962)	.10	.15	.25	.40
	2020	(1963)	.10	.15	.25	.40

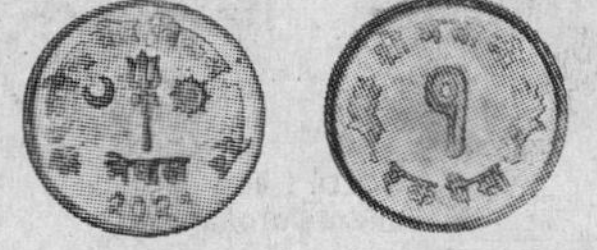

Rev: Numerals w/o shading.

KM#	Date	Year	Fine	VF	XF	Unc
747	VS2021	(1964)	.10	.15	.20	.30
	2022	(1965)	.10	.15	.25	.40

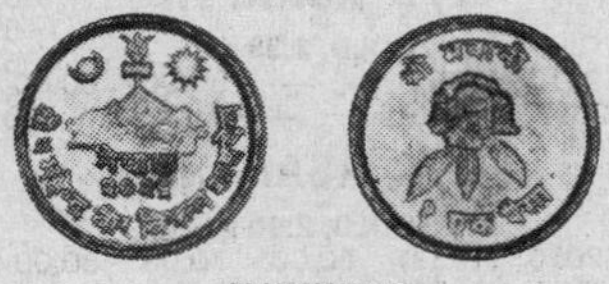

ALUMINUM

KM#	Date	Year	Mintage	VF	XF	Unc
748	VS2023	(1966)	—	.10	.15	.25
	2025	(1968)	—	.10	.15	.25
	2026	(1969)	—	.10	.15	.25
	2027	(1970)	2,187	—	Proof	1.25
	2028	(1971)	—	.10	.15	.25
	2028	(1971)	2,380	—	Proof	1.25

2 PAISA

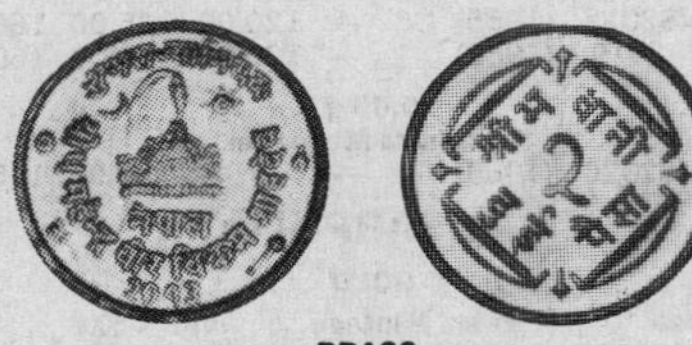

BRASS
Mahendra Coronation
Narrow rim

KM#	Date	Year	Fine	VF	XF	Unc
750.1	VS2013	(1956)	.30	.50	.75	1.00

Wide rim

KM#	Date	Year	Fine	VF	XF	Unc
750.2	VS2013	(1956)	.30	.50	.75	1.00

Rev: Numerals w/shading.

KM#	Date	Year	Fine	VF	XF	Unc
751	VS2014	(1957)	.10	.15	.25	.40
	2015	(1958)	.10	.15	.25	.40
	2016	(1959)	.10	.15	.25	.40
	2018	(1961)	.10	.15	.25	.40
	2019	(1962)	.10	.15	.25	.40
	2020	(1963)	.10	.15	.25	.40

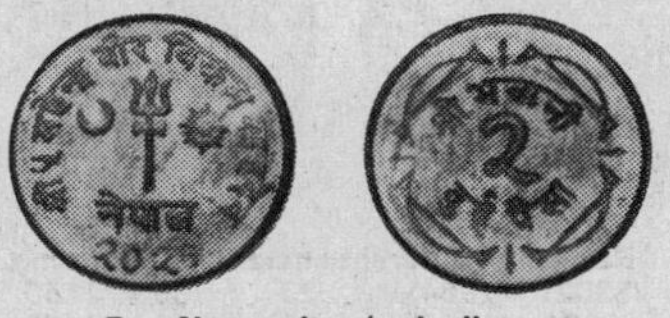

Rev: Numerals w/o shading.

KM#	Date	Year	Fine	VF	XF	Unc
752	VS2021	(1964)	.10	.15	.20	.35
	2022	(1965)	.10	.15	.25	.50
	2023	(1966)	.10	.15	.25	.50

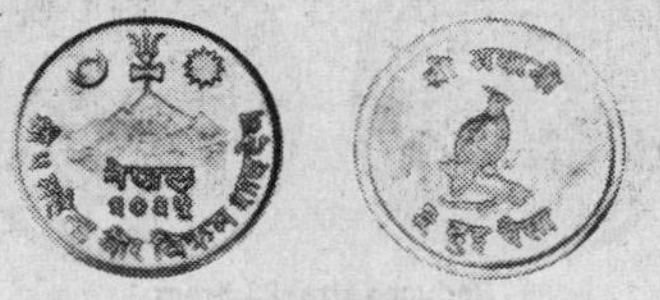

ALUMINUM

KM#	Date	Year	Mintage	VF	XF	Unc
753	VS2023	(1966)	—	.10	.15	.25
	2024	(1967)	—	.10	.15	.25
	2025	(1968)	—	.10	.15	.25
	2026	(1969)	—	.10	.15	.25
	2027	(1970)	—	.10	.15	.25
	2027	(1970)	2,187	—	Proof	1.50
	2028	(1971)	—	.10	.15	.25
	2028	(1971)	2,380	—	Proof	1.50

5 PAISA

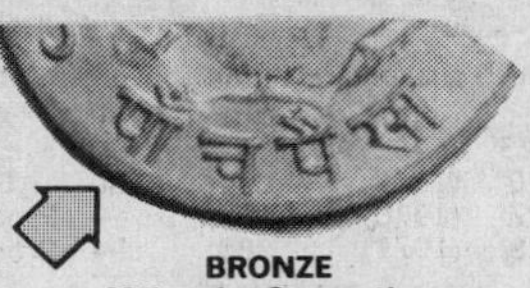

BRONZE
Mahendra Coronation
Wide rim w/accent mark.

KM#	Date	Year	Fine	VF	XF	Unc
756.1	VS2013	(1956)	10.00	20.00	30.00	40.00

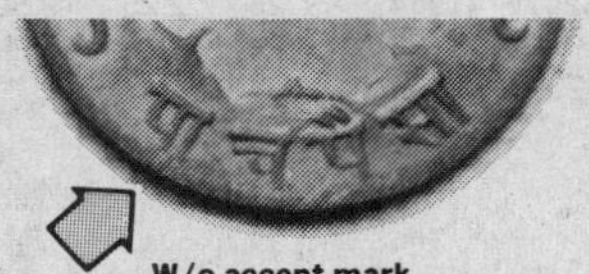

W/o accent mark.

KM#	Date	Year	Fine	VF	XF	Unc
756.3	VS2013	(1956)	1.00	2.00	3.00	5.00

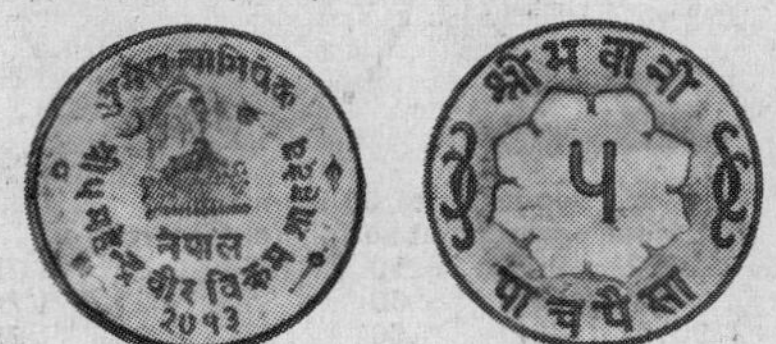

Narrow rim

KM#	Date	Year	Fine	VF	XF	Unc
756.2	VS2013	(1956)	(restrike) .35	.60	1.00	1.50

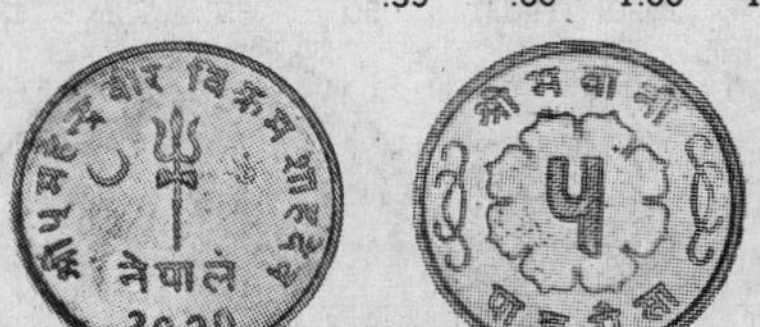

Rev: Numerals w/shading.

KM#	Date	Year	Fine	VF	XF	Unc
757	VS2014	(1957)	.10	.20	.30	.75
	2015	(1958)	.10	.20	.30	.75
	2016	(1959)	.10	.30	.50	1.00
	2017	(1960)	.10	.20	.30	.75
	2018	(1961)	.10	.20	.30	.75
	2019	(1962)	.10	.20	.30	.75
	2020	(1963)	.10	.20	.30	.75

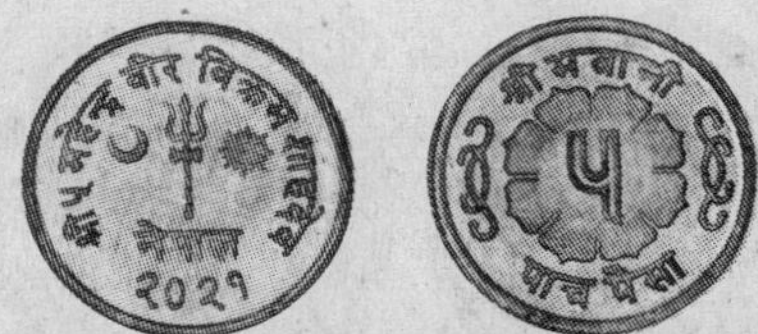

ALUMINUM BRONZE
Rev: Numerals w/o shading.

KM#	Date	Year	Fine	VF	XF	Unc
758	VS2021	(1964)	.50	1.00	1.50	2.50

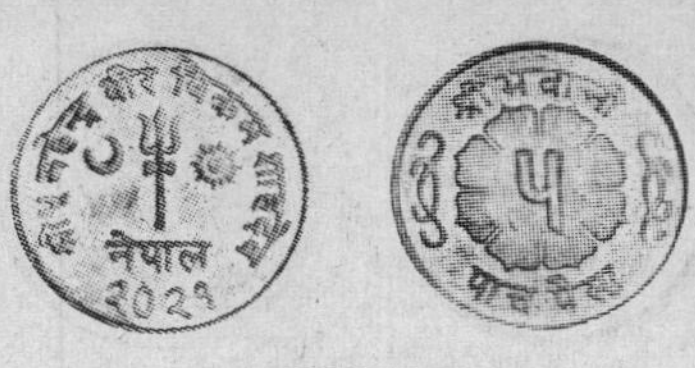

BRONZE

KM#	Date	Year	Fine	VF	XF	Unc
758a	VS2021	(1964)	.10	.15	.25	.50
	2022	(1965)	.10	.15	.30	.60
	2023	(1966)	.10	.15	.30	.60

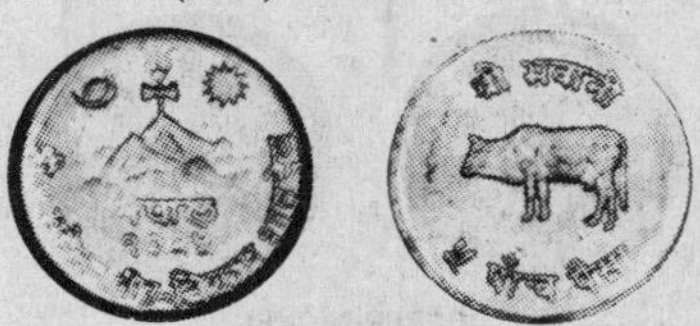

ALUMINUM

KM#	Date	Year	Mintage	VF	XF	Unc
759	VS2023	(1966)	—	.15	.25	.50
	2024	(1967)	—	.10	.20	.35
	2025	(1968)	—	.10	.20	.35
	2026	(1969)	—	.10	.20	.25
	2027	(1970)	—	.10	.20	.35
	2027	(1970)	2,187	—	Proof	1.75
	2028	(1971)	—	.10	.20	.35
	2028	(1971)	2,038	—	Proof	1.75

10 PAISA

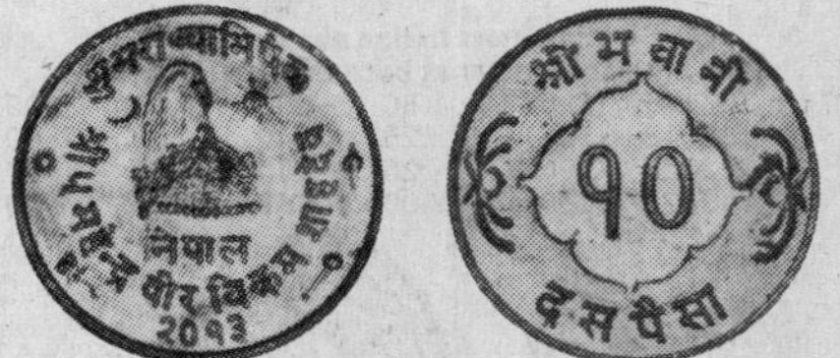

BRONZE
Mahendra Coronation

KM#	Date	Year	Fine	VF	XF	Unc
761	VS2013	(1956)	.25	.50	.75	1.50

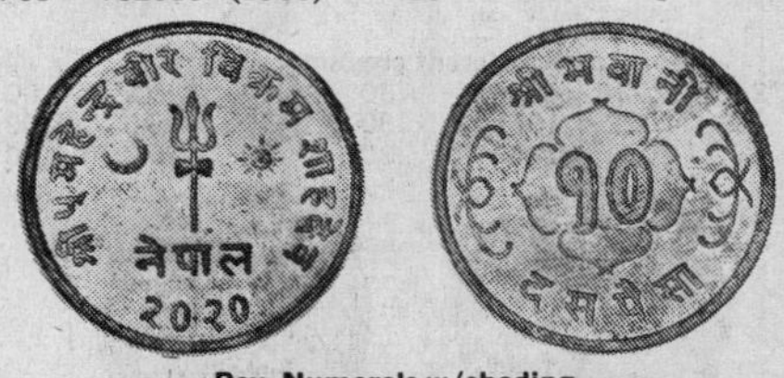

Rev: Numerals w/shading.

KM#	Date	Year	Fine	VF	XF	Unc
762	VS2014	(1957)	2.75	4.50	7.00	10.00
	2015	(1958)	.15	.25	.50	.75
	2016	(1959)	3.00	5.00	7.00	10.00
	2018	(1961)	.15	.25	.50	.75
	2019	(1962)	.15	.25	.50	.75
	2020	(1963)	.15	.25	.50	.75

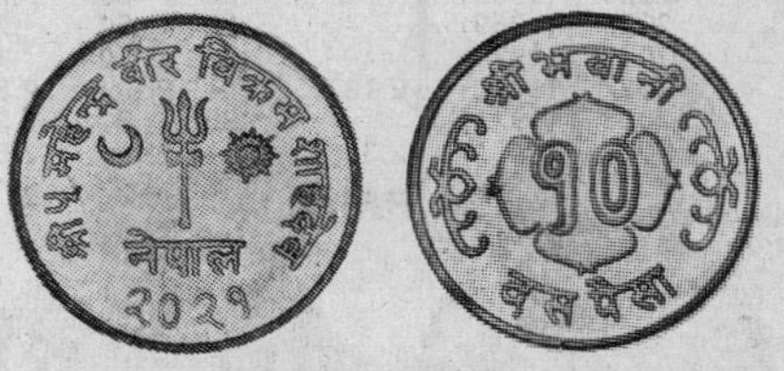

ALUMINUM-BRONZE
Rev: Numerals w/o shading.

KM#	Date	Year	Fine	VF	XF	Unc
763	VS2021	(1964)	.75	1.25	2.00	3.00

BRONZE, 25mm
Modified design

KM#	Date	Year	Fine	VF	XF	Unc
764	VS2021	(1964)	.10	.15	.25	.50
	2022	(1965)	.10	.15	.25	.50
	2023	(1966)	.10	.15	.25	.50

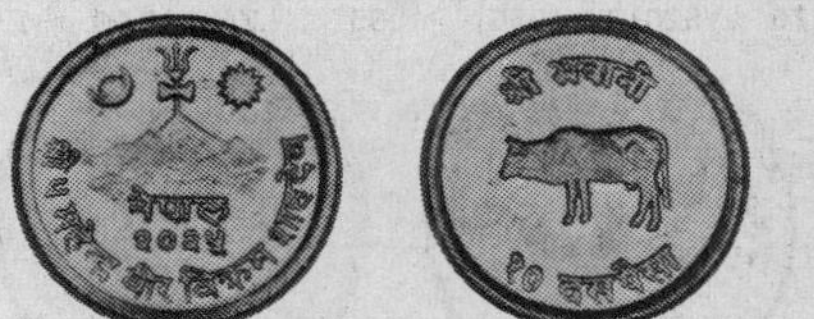

BRASS

KM#	Date	Year	Mintage	VF	XF	Unc
765	VS2023	(1966)	—	.15	.25	.50
	2024	(1967)	—	.15	.25	.50
	2025	(1968)	—	.10	.20	.35
	2026	(1969)	—	.10	.20	.35
	2027	(1970)	—	.10	.20	.35
	2027	(1970)	2,187	—	Proof	2.00
	2028	(1971)	—	.10	.20	.35
	2028	(1971)	2,380	—	Proof	2.00

NEPAL 1322

F.A.O. Issue

KM#	Date	Year	Mintage	VF	XF	Unc
766	VS2028	(1971)	1.500	.10	.15	.20

25 PAISA

COPPER-NICKEL
Mahendra Coronation

KM#	Date	Year	Fine	VF	XF	Unc
770	VS2013	(1956)	.30	.50	.70	1.00

Obv: 4 characters in line above trident.
Rev: Small character at bottom (outer circle).

771	VS2015	(1958)	1.50	2.50	4.00	6.00
	2018	(1961)	.25	.40	.60	.80
	2020	(1963)	.25	.40	.60	.80
	2022	(1965)	2.00	3.50	6.00	9.00

Rev: Large different character at bottom.

772	VS2021	(1964)	.30	.50	.70	1.00
	2022	(1965)	.30	.50	.70	1.00
	2023	(1966)	.30	.50	.70	1.00

Obv: 5 characters in line above trident.

KM#	Date	Year	Mintage	VF	XF	Unc
773	VS2024	(1967)	—	.35	.50	.75
	2025	(1968)	—	.35	.50	.75
	2026	(1969)	—	.35	.50	.75
	2027	(1970)	—	.35	.50	.75
	2027	(1970)	2,187	—	Proof	2.50
	2028	(1971)	—	.35	.50	.75
	2028	(1971)	2,380	—	Proof	2.50

50 PAISA

COPPER-NICKEL
Mahendra Coronation

KM#	Date	Year	Fine	VF	XF	Unc
776	VS2013	(1956)	.35	.75	1.00	1.50

Rev: Small character at bottom (outer circle).

777	VS2011	(1954)	.50	1.00	1.50	3.00
	2012	(1955)	.25	.50	.75	1.00
	2013	(1956)	.25	.50	1.00	2.00
	2014	(1957)	.25	.50	1.00	2.00
	2015	(1958)	.25	.50	1.00	2.00
	2016	(1959)	.25	.50	1.00	2.00

KM#	Date	Year	Fine	VF	XF	Unc
777	2017	(1960)	.25	.30	.75	1.25
	2018	(1961)	.25	.50	1.00	2.00
	2020	(1963)	.25	.30	.75	1.50

Rev: Large different character at bottom.

778	VS2021	(1964)	.25	.35	.50	.75
	2022	(1965)	.25	.50	.75	1.50
	2023	(1966)	.25	.50	.75	1.00

Reduced size, 23.5mm
Obv: 4 characters in line above trident.

779	VS2023	(1966)	.25	.50	.75	1.50

Obv: 5 characters in line above trident.

KM#	Date	Year	Mintage	VF	XF	Unc
780	VS2025	(1968)	—	.30	.50	1.00
	2026	(1969)	—	.30	.50	.85
	2027	(1970)	2,187	—	Proof	3.00
	2028	(1971)	2,380	—	Proof	3.00

RUPEE

COPPER-NICKEL, 29.6mm

KM#	Date	Year	Fine	VF	XF	Unc
784	VS2011	(1954)	1.25	2.25	3.50	5.00
	2012	(1955)	1.00	1.75	2.50	4.00

Reduced size, 28.8mm.
Rev: Small character at bottom (outer circle).

785	VS2012	(1955)	.50	.85	1.25	1.75
	2013	(1956)	.50	.85	1.25	1.75
	2014	(1957)	.50	.85	1.25	1.75
	2015	(1958)	.50	.85	1.25	1.75
	2016	(1959)	.50	.85	1.25	1.75
	2018	(1961)	.50	.85	1.25	1.75
	2020	(1963)	.50	.85	1.25	1.75

Rev: Large character at bottom.

786	VS2021	(1964)	.50	.75	1.00	1.50
	2022	(1965)	.50	1.00	1.50	2.50
	2023	(1966)	4.50	7.50	10.00	15.00

Reduced size, 27mm.
Obv: 4 characters in line above trident.

KM#	Date	Year	Fine	VF	XF	Unc
787	VS2023	(1966)	.75	1.00	1.35	2.00

Obv: 5 characters in line above trident.

KM#	Date	Year	Mintage	VF	XF	Unc
788	VS2025	(1968)	—	1.00	1.50	2.00
	2026	(1969)	—	1.00	1.40	2.00
	2027	(1970)	2,187	—	Proof	4.50
	2028	(1971)	2,380	—	Proof	4.50

COPPER-NICKEL
Mahendra Coronation

790	VS2013	(1956)	—	1.25	1.75	2.50

10 RUPEES

15.6000 g, .600 SILVER, .3009 oz ASW
F.A.O. Issue

794	VS2025	(1968)	1.000	3.00	4.00	8.00

1/6 ASARPHI

GOLD, 1.90 g
Mahendra Coronation

KM#	Date	Year	Fine	VF	XF	Unc
767	VS2013	(1956)	—	50.00	60.00	100.00

1/5 ASARPHI

GOLD, 2.33 g

768	VS2010	(1953)	—	50.00	60.00	100.00
	2012	(1955)	—	Reported, not confirmed

1/4 ASARPHI

GOLD, 2.90 g

774	VS2010	(1953)	60.00	70.00	80.00	100.00
	2012	(1955)	—	Reported, not confirmed

NOTE: Coins dated VS2010 are believed to be restrikes.

Reduced weight, 2.50 g.

775	VS2026	(1969)	—	—	75.00	100.00

1/2 ASARPHI

GOLD, 5.80 g
Mahendra Coronation

781	VS2013	(1956)	—	120.00	135.00	160.00
782	VS2012	(1955)	—	120.00	135.00	160.00
	2019	(1962)	—	120.00	135.00	160.00

5.00 g
Virendra Marriage

783	VS2026	(1969)	—	—	150.00	175.00

ASARPHI

GOLD

KM#	Date	Year	Mintage	VF	XF	Unc
789	VS2012	(1955)	—	225.00	250.00	300.00
	2019	(1962)	—	225.00	250.00	300.00

Mahendra Coronation

791	VS2013	(1956)	—	225.00	250.00	300.00

10.00 g

792	VS2026	(1969)	—	225.00	250.00	300.00

2 ASARPHI
GOLD

KM#	Date	Year	Fine	VF	XF	Unc
793	VS2012	(1955)	—	500.00	550.00	625.00

In the name of Queen Ratna Rajya Lakshmi

50 PAISA

COPPER-NICKEL
| 795 | VS2012 | (1955) | 3,000 | 100.00 | 125.00 | 150.00 |

RUPEE
COPPER-NICKEL

KM#	Date	Year	Mintage	VF	XF	Unc
797	VS2012	(1955)	2,000	100.00	150.00	175.00

1/2 ASARPHI
GOLD
| 796 | VS2012 | (1955) | — Reported, not confirmed |

ASARPHI
GOLD, 11.66 g
| 798 | VS2012 | (1955) | — Reported, not confirmed |

VIRENDRA VIR VIKRAMA
VS2028-/1972-AD

PAISA

ALUMINUM
799	VS2028	(1972)	.010	.20	.30	.40
	2029	(1972)	3.036	.10	.15	.25
	2029	(1972)	3.943	—	Proof	.60
	2030	(1973)	1.279	.10	.15	.25
	2030	(1973)	8.891	—	Proof	.40
	2031	(1974)	.430	.10	.15	.25
	2031	(1974)	.011	—	Proof	.40
	2032	(1975)	.324	.10	.15	.25
	2033	(1976)	.217	—	.10	.25
	2034	(1977)	1.040	.10	.15	.25
	2035	(1978)	.394	.10	.15	.25
	2036	(1979)	—	.10	.15	.25

Virendra Coronation
| 800 | VS2031 | (1974) | .075 | .10 | .15 | .25 |

COPPER-NICKEL
| 800a | VS2031 | (1974) | 1,000 | — | Proof | 2.50 |

ALUMINUM
| 1012 | VS2039 | (1982) | — | — | .10 | .20 |
| | 2040 | (1983) | .042 | — | .10 | .20 |

2 PAISA

ALUMINUM
801	VS2028	(1972)	8,319	.20	.30	.50
	2029	(1972)	5.206	.10	.15	.25
	2029	(1972)	3.943	—	Proof	.70
	2030	(1973)	2.563	.10	.15	.25
	2030	(1973)	8.891	—	Proof	.50
	2031	(1974)	.011	—	Proof	.50
	2033	(1976)	.072	.10	.15	.30
	2035	(1978)	.026	.10	.15	.30

5 PAISA

ALUMINUM
KM#	Date	Year	Mintage	VF	XF	Unc
802	VS2028	(1972)	3.700	.10	.20	.35
	2029	(1972)	23.578	.10	.20	.35
	2029	(1972)	3.943	—	Proof	.85
	2030	(1973)	12.320	.10	.20	.35
	2030	(1973)	8.891	—	Proof	.60
	2031	(1974)	15.730	.10	.20	.35
	2031	(1974)	.011	—	Proof	.60
	2032	(1975)	19.747	.10	.20	.35
	2033	(1976)	29.619	.10	.20	.30
	2034	(1977)	27.222	.10	.20	.30
	2035	(1978)	27.613	.10	.20	.30
	2036	(1979)	—	.10	.20	.30
	2037	(1980)	13.235	.10	.20	.30
	2038	(1981)	15.137	.10	.20	.30

F.A.O. Issue
| 803 | VS2031 | (1974) | 4.584 | — | .10 | .15 |

Virendra Coronation
| 804 | VS2031 | (1974) | 2.869 | .10 | .25 | .50 |
COPPER-NICKEL
| 804a | VS2031 | (1974) | 1,000 | — | Proof | 3.00 |

Rural Women's Advancement
| 805 | SE2036 | (1979) | — | .10 | .25 | .50 |

ALUMINUM
1013	VS2039	(1982)	8.971	—	.10	.25
	2040	(1983)	6.430	—	.10	.25
	2041	(1984)	9.634	—	.10	.25
	2042	(1985)	—	—	.10	.25
	2043	(1986)	—	—	.10	.25

10 PAISA

BRASS
| 806 | VS2028 | (1972) | 5.035 | .25 | .40 | .70 |

807	VS2029	(1972)	3.297	.15	.25	.40
	2029	(1972)	3.943	—	Proof	1.00
	2030	(1973)	5.670	.15	.25	.40
	2030	(1973)	8.891	—	Proof	.70
	2031	(1974)	.011	—	Proof	.70

ALUMINUM

Virendra Coronation
KM#	Date	Year	Mintage	VF	XF	Unc
808	VS2031	(1974)	.192	.10	.20	.35
COPPER-NICKEL
| 808a | VS2031 | (1974) | 1,000 | — | Proof | 3.50 |

BRASS
International Women's Year
| 809 | VS2032 | (1975) | 2.500 | .10 | .15 | .25 |

Agricultural Development
| 810 | VS2033 | (1976) | 10.000 | .10 | .15 | .25 |

ALUMINUM
International Year of the Child
| 811 | VS2036 | (1979) | — | .10 | .15 | .25 |

Education for Village Women
| 812 | VS2036 | (1979) | — | .10 | .15 | .50 |

1014	VS2041	(1984)	7.834	—	.10	.30
	2042	(1985)	—	—	.10	.30
	2043	(1986)	—	—	.10	.30
	2044	(1987)	—	—	.10	.30

20 PAISA

BRASS
| 813 | VS2035 | (1978) | .234 | .35 | .75 | 1.00 |

International Year of the Child
| 814 | VS2036 | (1979) | .030 | .35 | .75 | 1.00 |

25 PAISA

COPPER-NICKEL
815	VS2028	(1972)	5.691	.40	.60	.80
	2029	(1972)	3.943	—	Proof	1.25
	2030	(1973)	8.676	.30	.40	.50
	2030	(1973)	8.891	—	Proof	.80

NEPAL 1323

NEPAL 1324

KM#	Date	Year	Mintage	VF	XF	Unc
815	2031	(1974)	1.172	.35	.50	.75
	2031	(1974)	.011	—	Proof	.80
	2032	(1975)	4.584	.30	.40	.50
	2033	(1976)	1.837	.30	.40	.50
	2034	(1977)	3.808	.30	.40	.50
	2035	(1978)	5.964	.30	.40	.50
	2036	(1979)	—	.30	.40	.50
	2037	(1980)	2.047	.30	.40	.50
	2038	(1981)	1.580	.30	.40	.50
	2039	(1982)	7.185	.30	.40	.50

Virendra Coronation

816	VS2031	(1974)	.431	.35	.50	.75
	2031	(1974)	1,000	—	Proof	4.00

BRASS
World Food Day

817	VS2038	(1981)	2.000	—	.10	.30

International Year of Disabled Persons

818	VS2038	(1981)	—	.10	.25	.50

ALUMINUM

1015	VS2039	(1982)	—	.10	.25	.50
	2040	(1983)	7.603	.10	.25	.50
	2041	(1984)	15.534	.10	.25	.50
	2042	(1985)	—	.10	.25	.50
	2043	(1986)	—	.10	.25	.50
	2044	(1987)	—	.10	.25	.50
	2045	(1988)	—	.10	.25	.50

50 PAISA

COPPER-NICKEL

821	VS2028	(1972)	5.343	.35	.50	1.00
	2029	(1972)	.347	.35	.50	.90
	2029	(1972)	3.943	—	Proof	1.50
	2030	(1973)	.998	.35	.50	.90
	2030	(1973)	8.891	—	Proof	1.00
	2031	(1974)	.016	.35	.50	1.00
	2031	(1974)	.011	—	Proof	1.00
	2032	(1975)	.227	.35	.50	.90
	2033	(1976)	3.446	.35	.50	.75
	2034	(1977)	6.016	.35	.50	.75
	2035	(1978)	2.355	.35	.50	.75
	2036	(1979)	—	.35	.50	.75
	2037	(1980)	4.861	.35	.50	.75
	2038	(1981)	.929	.35	.50	.75
	2039	(1982)	2.954	.35	.50	.75

Virendra Coronation

822	VS2031	(1974)	.136	.50	.75	1.25
	2031	(1974)	1,000	—	Proof	5.00

World Food Day

KM#	Date	Year	Mintage	VF	XF	Unc
823	VS2038	(1981)	2.000	.10	.30	.60

International Year of Disabled Persons

824	VS2038	(1981)	—	.50	.75	1.25

Family Planning

1016	VS2041	(1984)	—	.10	.25	.50

19mm

1018	VS2039	(1982)	Inc. Ab.	.10	.25	.50
	2040	(1983)	.072	.10	.25	.50
	2041	(1984)	5.917	.10	.25	.50

STAINLESS STEEL, 23.5mm

1018a	VS2044	(1987)	—	.10	.25	.50
	2045	(1988)	—	.10	.25	.50

RUPEE

COPPER-NICKEL

828	VS2028	(1972)	5.030	.50	1.00	2.00
	2029	(1972)	.022	.50	1.00	1.50
	2029	(1972)	3.943	—	Proof	2.50
	2030	(1973)	5.667	.50	1.00	2.00
	2030	(1973)	8.891	—	Proof	2.00
	2031	(1974)	.011	—	Proof	1.50
	2033	(1976)	.058	.50	1.00	1.50
	2034	(1977)	30.000	.25	.50	1.00
	2035	(1978)	—	.25	.50	1.00
	2036	(1979)	—	.25	.50	1.00
	2036	(1980)	30.000	.25	.50	1.00

Virendra Coronation

829	VS2031	(1974)	—	.75	1.25	1.75
	2031	(1974)	1,000	—	Proof	6.00

F.A.O. Issue and International Women's Year

KM#	Date	Year	Mintage	VF	XF	Unc
831	VS2032	(1975)	1.500	.75	1.00	1.50

Family Planning

1019	VS2041	(1984)	9.224	—	—	.75

2 RUPEES

COPPER-NICKEL
World Food Day

832	VS2038	(1981)	1.000	.50	.75	1.25

Family Planning

1020	VS2041	(1984)	.011	—	—	1.00

F.A.O. Issue

1025	VS2039	(1982)	.366	—	—	1.00

5 RUPEES

COPPER-NICKEL
F.A.O. and Rural Women

833	VS2037	(1980)	.050	.75	1.25	2.50

National Bank Silver Jubilee

834	VS2038	(1981)	.062	.75	1.25	2.75

Circulation Coinage

1009	VS2040	(1983)	.478	.30	.50	1.00

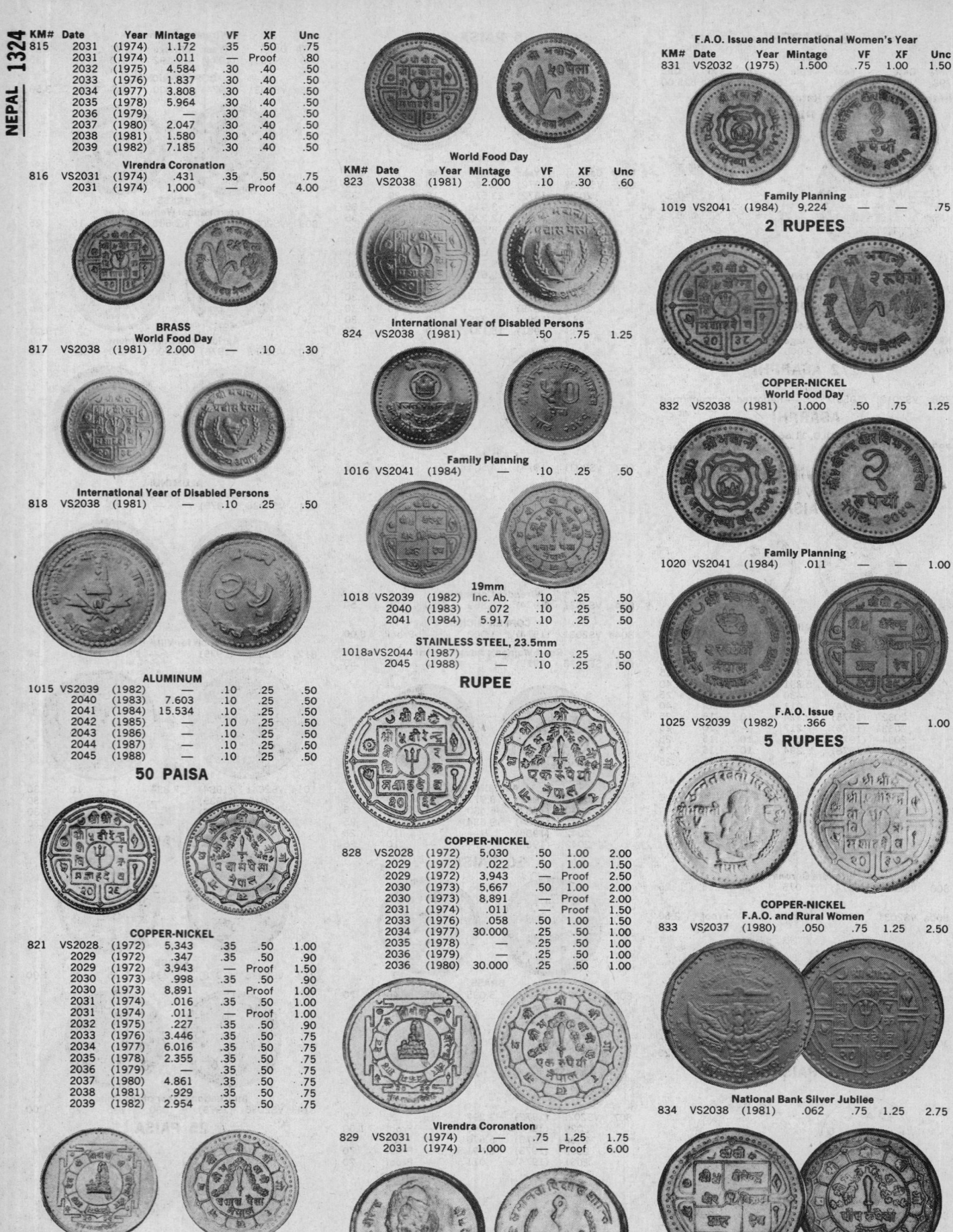

NEPAL 1325

Family Planning

KM#	Date	Year	Mintage	VF	XF	Unc
1017	VS2041	(1984)	.458	.50	1.00	2.00

Year of Youth

| 1023 | VS2042 | (1985) | — | — | — | 3.00 |

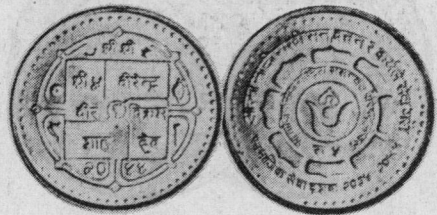

F.A.O. Issue

| 1028 | VS2043 | (1986) | — | — | — | 2.50 |

10th Year of National Social Security Administration

| 1030 | VS2044 | (1987) | — | — | — | 2.50 |

10 RUPEES

7.8500 g, .600 SILVER, .1514 oz ASW
F.A.O. Issue

| 835 | VS2031 | (1974) | .039 | — | 4.00 | 6.00 |

COPPER-NICKEL
30th Anniversary of Ascent of Mt. Everest
Obv: Similar to 5 Rupees, KM#833.

| 1004 | VS2040 | 1983 | 2,000 | — | — | 12.50 |

20 RUPEES

14.8500 g, .500 SILVER, .2387 oz ASW
International Women's Year

KM#	Date	Year	Mintage	VF	XF	Unc
836	VS2032	(1975)	.050	—	3.50	7.00

International Year of the Child

| 837 | VS2036 | (1979) | — | — | 2.50 | 5.00 |

15.0000 g, .925 SILVER, .4461 oz ASW

| 837a | VS2036 | (1979) | 1,000 | — | Proof | 27.50 |

25 RUPEES

25.6000 g, .500 SILVER, .4115 oz ASW
Virendra Coronation

| 838 | VS2031 | (1974) | .075 | — | 4.00 | 8.00 |

28.2800 g, .925 SILVER, .8411 oz ASW

| 838a | VS2031 | (1974) | 1,000 | — | Proof | 37.50 |

NOTE: Struck in 1979.

25.6000 g, .500 SILVER, .4115 oz ASW
Conservation Series
Rev: Monal Pheasant.

KM#	Date	Year	Mintage	VF	XF	Unc
839	VS2031	(1974-75)	.011	—	—	15.00

28.2800 g, .925 SILVER, .8411 oz ASW

| 839a | VS2031 | (1974-75) | .011 | — | Proof | 20.00 |

50 RUPEES

31.8000 g, .500 SILVER, .5112 oz ASW
Conservation Series
Obv: Similar to 25 Rupees, KM#839.
Rev: Red Panda.

| 841 | VS2031 | (1974-75) | .011 | — | — | 20.00 |

35.0000 g, .925 SILVER, 1.0409 oz ASW

| 841a | VS2031 | (1974-75) | .010 | — | Proof | 30.00 |

25.0000 g, .500 SILVER, .4018 oz ASW
Education for Village Women

| 842 | VS2036 | (1979) | .015 | — | — | 12.50 |

25.0000 g, .925 SILVER, .7436 oz ASW

| 842a | VS2036 | (1979) | 1,000 | — | Proof | 32.50 |

NEPAL 1326

14.9000 g, .500 SILVER, .2395 oz ASW
International Year of Disabled Persons

KM#	Date	Year	Mintage	VF	XF	Unc
843	VS2038	(1981)	.016	—	—	10.00

15.0000 g, .400 SILVER, .1929 oz ASW
International Year of the Child
Similar to 100 Rupees, KM#851.

| A851 | VS2038 | (1981) | 8,765 | — | — | 15.00 |

100 RUPEES

25.4900 g, .500 SILVER, .4050 oz ASW
World Food Day

| 850 | VS2038 | (1981) | .021 | — | — | 10.00 |
| | 2038 | (1981) | .010 | — | Proof | 15.00 |

19.4400 g, .500 SILVER, .3125 oz ASW
International Year of the Child

| 851 | VS2038 | (1981) | 9,270 | — | Proof | 25.00 |

31.1000 g, .925 SILVER, .9250 oz ASW
30th Anniversary of Ascent of Mt. Everest
Obv: Similar to 5 Rupees, KM#833.

KM#	Date	Year	Mintage	VF	XF	Unc
1005	VS2040	(1983)	1,500	—	Proof	60.00

15.0000 g, .500 SILVER, .2411 oz ASW
Year of Youth

| 1024 | VS2042 | (1985) | — | — | — | 10.00 |
| | 2042 | (1985) | — | — | Proof | 13.50 |

200 RUPEES

15.0000 g, .600 SILVER, .2894 oz ASW
10th Year of National Social Security Administration
Similar to 5 Rupees, KM#1030.

| 1031 | VS2044 | (1987) | .010 | — | — | 25.00 |

250 RUPEES

28.2800 g, .925 SILVER, .8411 oz ASW
10th Anniversary of Reign

| 1007 | VS2038 | (1982) | .010 | — | Proof | 30.00 |

Year of the Scout

KM#	Date	Year	Mintage	VF	XF	Unc
1010	VS2039	(1982)	.010	—	—	27.50
	2039	(1982)	Inc. Ab.	—	Proof	35.00

19.4400 g, .925 SILVER, .5749 oz ASW
Wildlife Preservation - Deer

| 1026 | VS2043 | (1986) | .020 | — | Proof | 30.00 |

300 RUPEES

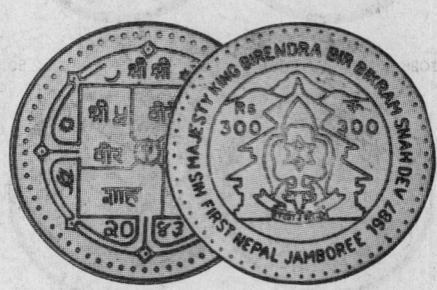

25.2900 g, .500 SILVER, .4066 oz ASW
First Scout Jamboree in Nepal

| 1029 | VS2043 | 1987 | — | — | — | 27.50 |

350 RUPEES

23.3000 g, .500 SILVER, .3746 oz ASW
Crown Prince, Sacred Thread Ceremony

| 1032 | VS2044 | (1987) | — | — | — | 45.00 |

500 RUPEES

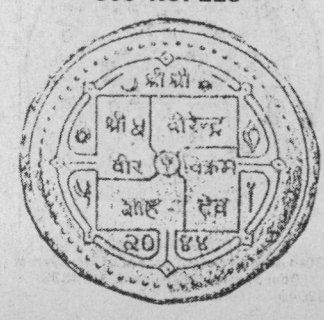

35.0000 g, .500 SILVER, .5627 oz ASW
National Bank

KM#	Date	Year	Mintage	VF	XF	Unc
1035	VS2044	(1987)	—	—	—	50.00

600 RUPEES

31.1030 g, .999 SILVER, 1.0000 oz ASW
60th Birthday - Queen Mother
1041 VS2045 (1988) — Proof 55.00

1000 RUPEES

33.4370 g, .900 GOLD, .9676 oz AGW
Conservation Series
Rev: Great Indian Rhinoceros.

844	VS2031					
		(1974-75)	2,166	—	—	550.00
	2031					
		(1974-75)	668 pcs.	—	Proof	750.00

10.0000 g, .500 WHITE GOLD, .1608 oz AGW
5th Anniversary of Coronation
845 VS2036 (1979) 55 pcs. — Proof 300.00

F.A.O. World Food Day

KM#	Date	Year	Mintage	VF	XF	Unc
1000	VS2037	(1980)	500 pcs.	—	Proof	175.00

155.5150 g, .999 SILVER, 5.0000 oz ASW
Snow Leopard
Reduced: Actual size: 65mm

KM#	Date	Mintage	VF	XF	Unc
1036	1988	*5,000	—	Proof	175.00

1/10 ASARFI

3.1100 g, .999 GOLD, .1000 oz AGW
Snow Leopard
Similar to 1 Asarfi, KM#1040.

1037	1988	*.010	—	—	50.00
	1988	2,000	—	Proof	100.00

1/4 ASARPHI

GOLD
Virendra Coronation

KM#	Date	Year	Mintage	VF	XF	Unc
816a	VS2031	(1974)	—	—	—	100.00

2.91 g

819	VS2028	(1971)	4 pcs.	—	—	—
	2030	(1973)	—	—	—	90.00
	2031	(1974)	—	—	—	90.00
	2036	(1979)	—	—	—	90.00
	2037	(1980)	—	—	—	90.00

7.7700 g, .999 GOLD, .2500 oz AGW
Snow Leopard
Similar to 1 Asarfi, KM#1040.

KM#	Date	Mintage	VF	XF	Unc
1038	1988	*8,000	—	—	125.00
	1988	*2,000	—	Proof	200.00

1/2 ASARPHI

GOLD
Virendra Coronation

KM#	Date	Year	Mintage	VF	XF	Unc
822a	VS2031	(1974)	—	—	—	150.00

KM#	Date	Year	Mintage	VF	XF	Unc
825	VS2028	(1971)	4 pcs.	—	—	—
	2030	(1973)	—	—	—	150.00
	2031	(1974)	—	—	—	150.00
	2036	(1979)	—	—	—	150.00
	2037	(1980)	—	—	—	150.00

5.00 g
Similar to KM#1018.
1021 VS2039 (1982) — — — 150.00

5.0000 g, .960 GOLD, .1543 oz AGW
Crown Prince, Sacred Thread Ceremony
1033 VS2044 (1987) — — — 110.00

15.5500 g, .999 GOLD, .5000 oz AGW
Snow Leopard
Similar to 1 Asarfi, KM#1040.

KM#	Date	Mintage	VF	XF	Unc
1039	1988	*8,000	—	—	250.00
	1988	*2,000	—	Proof	400.00

ASARPHI

GOLD
Similar to 1 Rupee, KM#828.

KM#	Date	Year	Mintage	VF	XF	Unc
827	VS2028	(1971)	*4 pcs.	—	—	—
	2030	(1973)	50 pcs.	—	—	325.00
	2031	(1974)	—	—	—	325.00
	2033	(1976)	—	—	—	325.00
	2036	(1979)	—	—	—	325.00
	2037	(1980)	—	—	—	325.00

Virendra Coronation
829a VS2031 (1974) 195 pcs. — Proof 300.00

11.6600 g, .900 GOLD, .3374 oz AGW
International Year of the Child
852 VS2038 (1981) 4,055 — Proof 225.00

10.0000 g, .500 GOLD, .1608 oz AGW
30th Anniversary of Ascent of Mt. Everest
Obv: Similar to 5 Rupees, KM#833.
1006 VS2040 (1983) 350 pcs. — Proof 250.00

15.9800 g, .900 GOLD, .4624 oz AGW
10th Anniversary of Reign

1008	VS2038	(1982)	27 pcs.	—	—	450.00
	2038	(1982)	5,092	—	Proof	300.00

NEPAL 1328

15.9800 g, .917 GOLD, .4712 oz AGW
Year of the Scout

KM#	Date	Year	Mintage	VF	XF	Unc
1011	VS2039	(1984)	2,000	—	—	400.00
	VS2039	(1984)	2,000	—	Proof	500.00

GOLD, 10.00 g
Similar to 50 Paisa, KM#1018.

| 1022 | VS2039 | (1982) | — | — | — | 250.00 |

11.6600 g, .900 GOLD, .3374 oz AGW
Wildlife Protection - Ganges River Dolphins

| 1027 | VS2041 | (1986) | 5,000 | — | Proof | 450.00 |

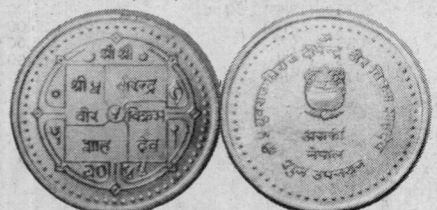

10.0000 g, .960 GOLD, .3086 oz AGW
Crown Prince, Sacred Thread Ceremony

| 1034 | VS2044 | (1987) | — | — | — | 220.00 |

31.1000 g, .999 GOLD, 1.0000 oz AGW
Snow Leopard

KM#	Date	Mintage	VF	XF	Unc
1040	1988	*.010	—	—	500.00
	1988	2,000	—	Proof	800.00

In the name of Queen Aishvarya Rajya Lakshmi

1/2 RUPEE
COPPER-NICKEL

KM#	Date	Year	Mintage	VF	XF	Unc
846	VS2031	(1974)	—	—	Rare	—

RUPEE
COPPER-NICKEL

| 848 | VS2031 | (1974) | — | — | Rare | — |

1/2 ASARPHI
GOLD

| 847 | VS2031 | (1974) | — | — | Rare | — |

ASARPHI
GOLD

| 849 | VS2031 | (1981) | — | — | Rare | — |

NOTE: The above coins were struck and sent to the Royal Palace. Few, if any, have emerged.

MINT SETS (MS)

KM#	Date	Mintage	Identification	Issue Price	Mkt. Val.
MS1	1932(3)	—	—	—	—
MS2	1949(3)	—	KM716,718,723 restrikes	—	8.00
MS3	1953(8)	—	KM733,735-740,742	—	160.00
MS4	1955(3)	—	KM712(2000),733,749(2012)	.85	5.00
MS5	1956(7)	—	KM745,750,756.2,761,770,776,790	—	50.00
MS6	1956(7)	—	KM745,750,756.3,761,770,776,790 restrikes	—	13.50
MS7	1957(4)	—	KM740(2011),742,738(2010),769(2014)	2.05	12.00
MS8	1957(6)	—	KM709.1(1996),755(2014)760(2011) 2 pcs. each	.85	7.00
MS9	1964(7)	—	KM747,752,758,763,772,778,785	—	10.00
MS10	1964(7)	—	KM747,752,758a,764,772,778,785	—	5.00
MS11	1965(7)	—	KM747,752(2022),758,763,772,778,786(2021)	2.75	10.00
MS12	1972(7)	—	KM799,801,802,806,815,821,828	—	5.00
MS13	1974(7)	—	KM800,804,808,816,822,829,838	—	12.50
MS14	1974(2)	—	KM839,841	32.50	35.00
MS15	1975(5)	—	KM808,816,822,829,838	—	13.00
MS16	1975(3)	—	KM809,831,836	—	9.00

PROOF SETS (PS)

PS1	1911	—	Copper, Silver	—	—
PS2	1911	—	Gold	—	—
PS3	1970(7)	2,187	KM748,753,759,765,773,780,788	10.00	16.50
PS4	1971(7)	2,380	KM748,753,759,765,773,780,788	10.00	16.50
PS5	1972(7)	3,943	KM799,801,802,807,815,821,828	10.00	8.50
PS6	1973(7)	8,891	KM799,801,802,807,815,821,828	10.00	6.00
PS7	1974(7)	10,543	KM799,801,802,807,815,821,828	10.00	5.50
PS8	1974(2)	30,000	KM839a,841a	50.00	50.00
PS9	(1979)(7)*	1,000	KM800a,804a,808a,816,822,829,838a (dated 1974)	62.00	62.00

*****NOTE:** Coins dated 2031 (1974) but this set was issued in 1979 ostensibly to celebrate the 5th Anniversary of the Coronation.

NETHERLANDS

The Kingdom of the Netherlands, a country of western Europe fronting on the North Sea and bordered by Belgium and Germany, has an area of 15,770 sq. mi. (40,844 sq. km.) and a population of 14.5 million. Capital: Amsterdam, but the seat of government is at The Hague. The economy is based on dairy farming and a variety of industrial activities. Chemicals, yarns and fabrics, and meat products are exported.

After being a part of Charlemagne's empire in the 8th and 9th centuries, the Netherlands came under control of Burgundy and the Austrian Hapsburgs, and finally was subjected to Spanish dominion in the 16th century. Led by William of Orange, the Dutch revolted against Spain in 1568. The seven northern provinces formed the Union of Utrecht and declared their independence in 1581, becoming the Republic of the United Netherlands. In the following century, the 'Golden Age' of Dutch history, the Netherlands became a great sea and colonial power, a patron of the arts and a refuge for the persecuted. In 1814, all the provinces of Holland and Belgium were merged into the Kingdom of the United Netherlands under William I. The Belgians withdrew in 1830 to form their own kingdom, the last substantial change in the configuration of European Netherlands.

WORLD WAR II COINAGE

Coinage of the Netherlands Homeland Types - Y#36, Y#34, Y#43, Y#44 and Y#46 - were minted by U.S. mints in the name of the government in exile and its remaining Curacao and Surinam Colonies during the years 1941-45. The Curacao and Surinam strikings, distinguished by the presence of a palm tree in combination with a mint mark (P-Philadelphia; D-Denver; S-San Francisco) flanking the date, are incorporated under those titles in this volume. Pieces of this period struck in the name of the homeland bear an acorn and mint mark and are incorporated in the following tabulation.

NOTE: Excepting the World War II issues struck at U.S. mints, all of the modern coins were struck at the Utrecht Mint and bear the caduceus mint mark of that facility. They also bear the mintmaster's marks.

RULERS

BATAVIAN REPUBLIC
French domination, 1795-1806

KINGDOM OF HOLLAND
French Protectorate
Louis Napoleon, 1806-1810

FRENCH ANNEXATION
Napoleon I, 1810-1814

KINGDOM OF THE NETHERLANDS
William I, 1815-1840
William II, 1840-1849
William III, 1849-1890
Wilhelmina I, 1890-1948
Juliana, 1948-1980
Beatrix, 1980-

MINT MARKS
B - Brussels (Belgium), 1821-1830
D - Denver, 1943-1945
P - Philadelphia, 1941-1945
S - San Francisco, 1944-1945

MINT PRIVY MARKS
Harderwijk (Gelderland)

Date	Privy Mark
1782-1806	Ear of corn

Dordrecht (Holland)

| 1600-1806 | Rosette |
| 1795-1806 | None |

Enkhuizen (West Friesland)

| 1796-1803 | Star |

Hoorn (West Friesland)

| 1803-1809 | Star |

Utrecht (Utrecht)

| 1738-1805 | Shield |

Utrecht

| 1806-present | Caduceus |

MINTMASTERS PRIVY MARKS
Brussels Mint

Date	Privy Mark
1821-1830	Palm branch

U. S. Mints

Date	Privy Mark
1941-1945	Palm tree

Utrecht Mint

Date	Privy Mark
1806-1810	Bee
1810-1813	Mast
1815-1816	Cloverleaf
1817	Child in swaddling clothes
1818-1840	Torch
1839-1846	Fleur de lis
1846-1874	Sword
1874	Sword in scabbard
1875-1887	Broadaxe
1887	Broadaxe and star
1888-1909	Halberd
1909	Halberd and star
1909-1933	Seahorse
1933-1942	Grapes
1943-1945	No privy mark
1945-1969	Fish
1969-1979	Cock
1980	Cock and star (temporal)
1980-1988	Anvil with hammer
1989-	Bow and arrow

NOTE: A star adjoining the privy mark indicates that the piece was struck at the beginning of the term of office of a successor. (The star was used only if the successor had not chosen his own mark yet.)

MONETARY SYSTEM
8 Duits = 1 Stuiver (Stiver)
6 Stuivers = 1 Schelling
20 Stuivers = 1 Gulden (Guilder or Florin)
50 Stuivers = 1 Rijksdaalder (Silver Ducat)
60 Stuivers = 1 Ducaton (Silver Rider)
14 Gulden = 1 Golden Rider
Commencing 1815
100 Cents = 1 Gulden
2-1/2 Gulden = 1 Rijksdaalder

BATAVIAN REPUBLIC

Prior to 1806, the Netherlands was a confederation of seven provinces, each producing coins similar in design but differing in the coat of arms or inscription. Generally the coins of each province contained an abbreviation of the name of the province somewhere in the inscription. Under the Batavian Republic, the following abbreviations were used.

MINT MARKS
G, GEL - Gelderland
HOL, HOLL - Holland
TRANSI - Overijsel
TRA, TRAI, TRAIECTUM - Utrecht
WESTF, WESTRI - Westfriesland
ZEL, ZEELANDIA - Zeeland

3 GULDEN
.915 SILVER
Mint mark: HOL, HOLL

KM#	Date	Mintage	Fine	VF	XF	Unc
9.2 (C-C36)	1801	—	100.00	160.00	200.00	300.00

RIJKSDAALDER
.868 SILVER
Mint mark: G, GEL

KM#	Date	Mintage	Fine	VF	XF	Unc
10.1 (C-A37)	1801	—	350.00	450.00	600.00	750.00
	1802	—	350.00	450.00	600.00	750.00

Mint mark: HOL, HOLL

KM#	Date	Mintage	Fine	VF	XF	Unc
10.2 (C-C37)	1801/0	—	200.00	300.00	400.00	550.00
	1801	—	175.00	250.00	350.00	450.00
	1802	—	175.00	250.00	350.00	450.00
	1806	—	950.00	1400.	1800.	2200.

Mint mark: TRAIECTUM, TRA, TRAI

KM#	Date	Mintage	Fine	VF	XF	Unc
10.4 (C-F37)	1801	—	65.00	100.00	125.00	175.00
	1801 small 8-0	—	65.00	100.00	125.00	175.00
	1802	—	65.00	100.00	125.00	175.00
	1803 long sword	—	65.00	100.00	125.00	175.00
	1803 short sword					
	1804	—	65.00	100.00	125.00	175.00
	1805/797	—	65.00	100.00	125.00	175.00
	1805	—	65.00	100.00	125.00	175.00

TRADE COINAGE
DUCAT
3.5000 g, .986 GOLD, .1109 oz AGW
Mint mark: GELDERLAND (G, GEL)

KM#	Date	Mintage	Fine	VF	XF	Unc
11.1 (C-A40)	1801	—	150.00	250.00	300.00	400.00
	1802	—	150.00	250.00	300.00	400.00
	1803	—	650.00	1300.	1750.	2250.

Mint mark: HOL, HOLL

KM#	Date	Mintage	Fine	VF	XF	Unc
11.2 (C-C40)	1801 w/o star	—	90.00	155.00	180.00	220.00
	1801 star	—	220.00	475.00	600.00	750.00
	1802 w/o star	—	90.00	165.00	200.00	250.00
	1802 star	—	220.00	425.00	500.00	600.00
	1803 w/o star	—	100.00	220.00	275.00	400.00
	1804 w/o star	—	100.00	220.00	275.00	400.00
	1805 w/o star	—	220.00	475.00	600.00	750.00

NOTE: Coins with the star were struck at the Enkhuizen Mint with a total mintage of 630,455. Coins without the star were struck at the Dordrecht Mint with a total mintage of 2,861,825.

Mint mark: TRAIECTUM, TRA, TRAI

KM#	Date	Mintage	Fine	VF	XF	Unc
11.3	1801	.960	70.00	130.00	175.00	220.00
	1802	1.705	70.00	130.00	175.00	220.00
	1803	2.089	70.00	130.00	175.00	220.00
	1804/3	.870	80.00	170.00	200.00	250.00
	1804	Inc. Ab.	80.00	170.00	200.00	250.00
	1805	1.300	70.00	130.00	175.00	220.00

2 DUCAT
7.0000 g, .986 GOLD, .2219 oz AGW
Mint mark: HOL, HOLL

KM#	Date	Mintage	Fine	VF	XF	Unc
12.1 (C-C41)	1802	—	700.00	1300.	1700.	2250.

Mint mark: TRAIECTUM, TRA, TRAI
Similar to 1 Ducat, KM#11.3.

KM#	Date	Mintage	Fine	VF	XF	Unc
12.2	1801	.215	350.00	700.00	900.00	1000.
	1802	.115	500.00	1000.	1400.	1800.
	1803	.365	350.00	700.00	900.00	1000.
	1804	.250	350.00	700.00	900.00	1000.
	1805	.301	350.00	700.00	900.00	1000.

KINGDOM OF HOLLAND
10 STUIVERS

SILVER

KM#	Date	Mintage	Fine	VF	XF	Unc
30 (C51)	1808	—	—	—	Rare	
	1809	—	425.00	700.00	1000.	1250.

FLORIN

SILVER

KM#	Date	Mintage	Fine	VF	XF	Unc
29 (C51a)	1807	—	450.00	1000.	1400.	1700.

GULDEN

SILVER

KM#	Date	Mintage	Fine	VF	XF	Unc
31 (C52)	1808	—	400.00	700.00	1000.	1225.
	1809	—	400.00	700.00	1000.	1225.
	1810	—	400.00	700.00	1000.	1225.

RIJKSDAALDER

.868 SILVER
Obv. leg: .....TRAI.

KM#	Date	Mintage	Fine	VF	XF	Unc
25 (C55)	1806	.580	125.00	220.00	300.00	350.00
	1807	.151	150.00	250.00	325.00	400.00
	1808	.343	125.00	220.00	300.00	350.00
	1816					

SILVER

KM#	Date	Mintage	Fine	VF	XF	Unc
36 (C56)	1809	—	900.00	1600.	2100.	3000.

KM#	Date	Mintage	Fine	VF	XF	Unc
37 (C57)	1809	—	1200.	1900.	3000.	3500.

Kingdom of Holland / NETHERLANDS 1330

50 STUIVERS

SILVER

KM#	Date	Mintage	Fine	VF	XF	Unc
28	1807	300 pcs.	900.00	1650.	2250.	2800.
(C54)	1808	2.466	100.00	175.00	250.00	325.00

2-1/2 GULDEN

SILVER

32	1808	—	1000.	2000.	2500.	3000.
(C53)						

10 GULDEN

6.8250 g, .917 GOLD, .2012 oz AGW

33	1808	—	2100.	3500.	5000.	7500.
(C62)	1810	—	2100.	3500.	5000.	7500.

20 GULDEN

13.6500 g, .917 GOLD, .4024 oz AGW

34	1808	—	3200.	5300.	8000.	10,000.
(C63)	1810	—	3200.	5300.	8000.	10,000.

TRADE COINAGE
DUCAT

3.5000 g, .986 GOLD, .1109 oz AGW
Mint mark: HOL, HOLL

26.1	1806	526 pcs.	425.00	650.00	800.00	1200.
(C58)						

Mint mark: TRAIECTUM, TRA, TRAI

Utrecht Mint

KM#	Date	Mintage	Fine	VF	XF	Unc
26.2	1806 sm.dt.	.794	110.00	190.00	260.00	350.00
(C58a)	1807 small date, straight 7	.622	110.00	190.00	260.00	350.00
	1808/7	.037	175.00	300.00	350.00	450.00
	1808	Inc. Ab.	140.00	250.00	325.00	375.00

Leningrad Mint

26.3	1806 lg.dt.	1.300	110.00	190.00	260.00	350.00
(26.2)	1807 large date, curved 7	1.940	110.00	190.00	260.00	350.00

35	1808	.283	200.00	375.00	525.00	700.00
(C60)	1809	Inc. Ab.	200.00	375.00	525.00	700.00

38	1809	2.371	200.00	375.00	525.00	700.00
(C61)	1810	Inc. Ab.	200.00	375.00	525.00	700.00

2 DUCATS

7.0000 g, .986 GOLD, .2218 oz AGW
Utrecht Mint

27	1806	.199	500.00	775.00	900.00	1100.
(C59)	1807	.156	500.00	775.00	900.00	1100.
	1808	—	500.00	775.00	900.00	1100.

FRENCH ANNEXATION

From 1810 to 1814, the Netherlands were a part of France. During this period, homeland type coins were not minted. Regular French coins were struck at the Utrecht Mint at this time, and are identified by the fish and mast privy marks. These coins are listed under France.

KINGDOM OF THE NETHERLANDS

1/2 CENT
COPPER

51	1818	—	450.00	1150.	1750.	2500.
(C71)	1819	.144	150.00	450.00	600.00	850.00
	1821	3.500	35.00	75.00	100.00	150.00
	1821B	.271	85.00	150.00	250.00	450.00
	1822	9.888	17.50	35.00	65.00	85.00
	1822B	3.969	35.00	75.00	100.00	150.00
	1823	10.000	15.00	35.00	65.00	85.00
	1823B	13.228	15.00	35.00	65.00	85.00
	1824	2.402	35.00	75.00	100.00	155.00
	1824B	3.430	35.00	75.00	100.00	155.00
	1826	—	140.00	220.00	325.00	500.00
	1826B	2.076	35.00	90.00	110.00	160.00
	1827	4.574	15.00	35.00	65.00	85.00
	1827B	3.337	15.00	35.00	65.00	85.00
	1828	1.358	15.00	75.00	100.00	150.00
	1828B	4.034	15.00	35.00	65.00	85.00
	1829	3.347	15.00	35.00	65.00	85.00
	1831	3.850	15.00	35.00	65.00	85.00
	1832	10.328	15.00	35.00	65.00	85.00
	1833	.150	150.00	300.00	500.00	650.00
	1837	2.602	15.00	30.00	60.00	85.00

SILVER (OMS)

51a	1818	—	—	—	Rare	—
(C71b)						

GOLD (OMS)

51b	1819	—	—	—	Rare	—
(C71a)	1822	—	—	—	Rare	—
	1824	—	—	—	Rare	—

COPPER

68	1841	2.600	20.00	45.00	90.00	120.00
(C86)	1843	3.120	20.00	45.00	90.00	120.00
	1846	.600	25.00	60.00	110.00	160.00
	1847	2.000	25.00	50.00	90.00	130.00

90	1850	2.000	10.00	25.00	45.00	65.00

KM#	Date	Mintage	Fine	VF	XF	Unc
(Y1)	1851	2.051	10.00	25.00	45.00	65.00
	1852	2.028	40.00	80.00	115.00	140.00
	1853	2.000	10.00	25.00	45.00	65.00
	1854	3.000	10.00	25.00	35.00	60.00
	1855	.999	80.00	200.00	300.00	400.00
	1857	4.155	10.00	25.00	30.00	55.00
	1859	4.052	10.00	25.00	30.00	55.00
	1861	1.446	20.00	40.00	70.00	90.00
	1862	2.026	8.00	20.00	30.00	55.00
	1863	2.428	8.00	20.00	30.00	55.00
	1864	2.016	8.00	20.00	30.00	55.00
	1865	2.006	8.00	20.00	30.00	55.00
	1867	2.008	8.00	20.00	30.00	55.00
	1869	2.014	8.00	20.00	30.00	55.00
	1870	2.004	8.00	20.00	30.00	55.00
	1872	2.026	8.00	20.00	30.00	55.00
	1873	2.026	8.00	20.00	30.00	55.00
	1875	2.026	8.00	20.00	30.00	55.00
	1876	2.020	8.00	20.00	30.00	55.00
	1877	1.400	15.00	35.00	50.00	75.00

SILVER (OMS)

90a	1872	—	—	—	Rare	—
(Y1a)						

GOLD (OMS)

90b	1872	—	—	—	Rare	—
(Y1b)						

BRONZE
Obv: 17 small shields in field, leg: KONINKRIJK.

109	1878	4.000	5.00	10.00	20.00	35.00
(Y3)	1883	.800	50.00	100.00	160.00	200.00
	1884	17.200	2.50	5.00	10.00	17.50
	1885	7.800	3.00	7.50	12.50	20.00
	1886	2.200	25.00	60.00	110.00	140.00
	1891	5.000	5.00	10.00	20.00	35.00
	1894	5.000	5.00	10.00	20.00	35.00
	1898	2.000	20.00	50.00	100.00	140.00
	1900	3.000	14.00	25.00	50.00	70.00
	1901	6.000	3.00	7.00	12.50	25.00

GOLD (OMS)

109a	1884	—	—	—	Rare	—
(Y3a)						

BRONZE
Obv: 15 large shields in field around larger lion, smaller date and leg. Rev: CENT in larger letters.

133	1903	10.000	2.00	4.50	6.00	15.00
(Y3c)	1906	10.000	2.00	4.50	6.00	15.00

GOLD (OMS)

133a	1903	—	—	—	Rare	—
(Y3d)						

BRONZE

138	1909	5.000	2.00	4.00	7.00	11.00
(Y35)	1911	5.000	2.00	4.00	7.00	11.00
	1912	5.000	2.00	4.00	7.00	11.00
	1914	5.000	2.00	4.00	7.00	11.00
	1915	2.500	8.00	17.50	30.00	40.00
	1916	4.000	3.00	6.00	11.00	15.00
	1917	5.000	2.00	4.00	7.00	11.00
	1921	1.500	9.00	22.50	35.00	50.00
	1922	2.500	7.00	15.00	25.00	35.00
	1928	4.000	2.00	4.00	7.00	11.00
	1930	6.000	2.00	4.00	7.00	11.00
	1934	5.000	1.50	3.50	6.00	7.50
	1936	5.000	1.50	3.50	6.00	7.50
	1937	1.600	2.00	5.00	8.00	12.00
	1938	8.400	1.25	3.00	5.00	7.50
	1940	6.000	1.25	3.00	5.00	7.50

SILVER (OMS)

138a	1911	—	—	—	Rare	—
(Y35a)						

CENT

COPPER

47	1817	—	300.00	1750.	2300.	3000.
(C72)	1818	—	300.00	1750.	2300.	3000.
	1819	.165	220.00	600.00	1250.	1850.
	1821	10.325	15.00	30.00	60.00	85.00
	1821B	.113	220.00	600.00	1150.	1750.
	1822	18.462	15.00	30.00	60.00	85.00
	1822B	6.718	17.50	45.00	90.00	120.00
	1823	22.300	15.00	30.00	60.00	85.00
	1823B	11.272	17.50	45.00	90.00	120.00
	1824	5.450	40.00	90.00	140.00	200.00
	1824B	.144	175.00	450.00	850.00	1400.
	1826	4.600	17.50	45.00	90.00	120.00
	1826B	7.824	17.50	45.00	90.00	120.00
	1827	27.450	15.00	30.00	60.00	85.00

KM#	Date	Mintage	Fine	VF	XF	Unc
(C72)	1827B	20.966	15.00	30.00	60.00	85.00
	1828	8.261	15.00	30.00	60.00	85.00
	1828B	7.608	17.50	45.00	90.00	120.00
	1830	1.750	40.00	90.00	115.00	140.00
	1831	4.161	17.50	45.00	90.00	120.00
	1837	5.203	12.50	30.00	55.00	85.00

SILVER (OMS)

| 47a (C72a) | 1823 | — | — | — | Rare | — |

GOLD (OMS)

47b (C72b)	1823	—	—	—	Rare	—
	1826	—	—	—	Rare	—
	1827	—	—	—	Rare	—

BRONZE

100 (Y2)	1860	2.032	10.00	25.00	45.00	75.00
	1861	2.050	10.00	25.00	45.00	75.00
	1862	2.026	10.00	25.00	45.00	75.00
	1863	10.246	4.00	9.00	16.00	25.00
	1864	2.026	10.00	25.00	45.00	75.00
	1870	4.010	7.00	15.00	30.00	45.00
	1873	3.026	9.00	17.50	35.00	55.00
	1875	3.015	9.00	17.50	35.00	55.00
	1876	13.047	4.00	9.00	16.00	25.00
	1877	11.026	4.00	9.00	16.00	25.00

SILVER (OMS)

| 100a (Y2a) | 1875 | — | — | — | Rare | — |
| | 1876 | — | — | — | Rare | — |

GOLD (OMS)

100b (Y2b)	1875	—	—	—	Rare	—
	1876	—	—	—	Rare	—
	1877	—	—	—	Rare	—

BRONZE
Obv: 15 small shields in field, leg: KONINGRIJK

107 (Y4)	1877	6.100	6.00	13.00	30.00	45.00
	1878	53.900	1.50	4.00	9.00	15.00
	1880	20.000	2.50	6.00	16.50	30.00
	1881	10.000	2.50	6.00	16.50	30.00
	1882	5.000	5.00	10.00	25.00	35.00
	1883	15.000	2.50	6.00	16.50	30.00
	1884	10.000	2.50	6.00	16.50	30.00
	1892	5.000	6.00	15.00	30.00	55.00
	1896	3.000	10.00	30.00	60.00	80.00
	1897	2.500	10.00	30.00	60.00	80.00
	1898	5.000	6.00	15.00	25.00	50.00
	1899	5.100	6.00	15.00	25.00	50.00
	1900 large date	12.400	4.00	10.00	20.00	40.00
	1900 small date	Inc. Ab.	4.00	10.00	20.00	40.00

GOLD (OMS)

| 107a (Y4d) | 1884 | — | — | — | Rare | — |

BRONZE
Obv: 15 large shields in field, leg: KONINKRIJK

| 130 (Y4a) | 1901 | 10.000 | 3.00 | 7.00 | 20.00 | 35.00 |

Obv: 10 large shields in field, leg: KONINGRIJK.

| 131 (Y4b) | 1901 | 10.000 | 3.00 | 7.00 | 20.00 | 35.00 |

Obv: 15 medium shields in field, leg: KONINGRIJK.

132 (Y4c)	1902	10.000	2.00	5.00	10.00	25.00
	1904	15.000	2.00	5.00	10.00	25.00
	1905	10.000	2.00	5.00	10.00	25.00
	1906	9.000	2.00	5.00	10.00	25.00
	1907	6.000	15.00	35.00	65.00	90.00

GOLD (OMS)

| 132a (Y4e) | 1902 | — | — | — | Rare | — |

BRONZE

152 (Y36)	1913	5.000	6.00	15.00	30.00	45.00
	1914	9.000	2.00	5.00	10.00	20.00
	1915	10.800	2.00	5.00	10.00	20.00
	1916	21.700	1.00	3.00	6.00	12.00
	1917	20.000	1.00	3.00	6.00	12.00
	1918	10.000	1.00	3.00	10.00	15.00
	1919	6.000	3.00	6.00	15.00	20.00
	1920	11.400	1.00	3.00	6.00	12.00
	1921	12.600	1.00	3.00	6.00	12.00

KM#	Date	Mintage	Fine	VF	XF	Unc
(Y36)	1922	20.000	1.00	3.00	6.00	12.00
	1924	1.400	25.00	50.00	100.00	120.00
	1925	18.600	1.00	3.00	6.00	12.00
	1926	10.000	1.00	3.00	6.00	12.00
	1927	10.000	1.00	3.00	6.00	12.00
	1928	10.000	1.00	3.00	6.00	12.00
	1929	20.000	1.00	3.00	6.00	12.00
	1930	10.000	1.00	3.00	6.00	12.00
	1931	3.400	8.00	20.00	35.00	50.00
	1937	10.000	1.00	3.00	5.00	7.50
	1938	16.600	1.00	2.50	3.50	7.00
	1939	22.000	1.00	2.50	3.50	7.00
	1940	24.600	1.00	2.50	3.50	7.00
	1941	66.600	.50	1.00	2.00	3.00

NOTE: For similar coins dated 1942P see Netherlands Antilles (Curacao); 1943P, 1957-1960 see Surinam.

ZINC

170 (Y48)	1941	31.800	2.50	6.00	15.00	22.00
	1942	241.000	.25	.75	2.00	4.50
	1943	71.000	1.00	3.00	5.00	10.00
	1944	29.600	2.50	6.00	15.00	22.00

BRONZE

KM#	Date	Mintage	Fine	VF	XF	BU
175 (Y53)	1948	130.400	.25	.50	1.50	10.00
	1948				Proof	40.00

180 (Y57)	1950	91.000	.10	.25	.50	3.25
	1950	—	—	—	Proof	20.00
	1951	45.800	.10	.25	.50	3.25
	1951	—	—	—	Proof	15.00
	1952	68.000	.10	.25	.50	3.25
	1952	—	—	—	Proof	25.00
	1953	54.000	.10	.25	.50	3.25
	1953	—	—	—	Proof	25.00
	1954	54.000	.10	.25	.50	3.25
	1954	—	—	—	Proof	15.00
	1955	52.000	.10	.25	.50	3.25
	1955	—	—	—	Proof	15.00
	1956	34.800	.10	.25	.50	3.25
	1956	—	—	—	Proof	15.00
	1957	48.000	.10	.25	.50	3.25
	1957	—	—	—	Proof	15.00
	1958	34.000	.10	.25	.50	3.25
	1958	—	—	—	Proof	15.00
	1959	36.000	.10	.25	.50	3.25
	1959	—	—	—	Proof	15.00
	1960	40.000	.10	.25	.50	3.25
	1960	—	—	—	Proof	15.00
	1961	52.000	—	.10	.25	2.75
	1961	—	—	—	Proof	15.00
	1962	57.000	—	.10	.25	2.75
	1962	—	—	—	Proof	15.00
	1963	70.000	—	.10	.25	2.75
	1963	—	—	—	Proof	20.00
	1964	73.000	—	.10	.25	2.75
	1964	—	—	—	Proof	20.00
	1965	91.000	—	.10	.25	1.75
	1965	—	—	—	Proof	20.00
	1966 large date	104.000	—	.10	.25	1.75
	1966 large date	—	—	—	Proof	20.00
	1966 small date	Inc. Ab.	—	.10	.25	1.75
	1966 small date	—	—	—	Proof	20.00
	1967	140.000	—	.10	.25	1.75
	1967	—	—	—	Proof	25.00
	1968	28.000	—	.10	.25	1.75
	1968	—	—	—	Proof	20.00
	1969 fish privy mark	50.000	—	.10	.25	1.75
	1969 fish privy mark	—	—	—	Proof	20.00
	1969 cock privy mark	50.000	—	.10	.15	1.50
	1969 cock privy mark	—	—	—	Proof	20.00
	1970	100.000	—	.10	.15	1.50
	1970	—	—	—	Proof	20.00
	1971	70.000	—	.10	.15	1.50
	1972	40.000	—	—	.10	1.00
	1973	34.000	—	—	.10	1.00
	1974	46.000	—	—	.10	1.00
	1975	25.000	—	—	.10	.50
	1976	15.000	—	—	.10	.25
	1977	15.000	—	—	.10	.25
	1978	15.000	—	—	.10	.25
	1979	15.000	—	—	.10	.25

KM#	Date	Mintage	Fine	VF	XF	BU
(Y57)	1980 cock & star privy mark	15.300	—	—	—	.10	.25

2-1/2 CENTS

BRONZE
Obv: 17 small shields in field, leg: KONINGRIJK.

KM#	Date	Mintage	Fine	VF	XF	Unc
108 (Y5)	1877	4.000	2.50	7.50	17.50	35.00
	1880	4.000	2.50	7.50	17.50	35.00
	1881	4.000	2.50	7.50	17.50	35.00
	1883	.400	20.00	50.00	75.00	100.00
	1884	3.600	3.50	9.00	20.00	45.00
	1886	2.000	7.50	20.00	35.00	50.00
	1890	2.000	7.50	20.00	35.00	50.00
	1894	1.000	20.00	55.00	100.00	130.00
	1898	1.600	15.00	35.00	65.00	85.00

GOLD (OMS)

| 108a (Y5a) | 1884 | — | — | — | Rare | — |

BRONZE
Obv: 15 large shields in field.

134 (Y5c)	1903	4.000	2.50	5.00	15.00	30.00
	1904	4.000	2.50	5.00	15.00	30.00
	1905	4.000	2.50	5.00	15.00	30.00
	1906	8.000	2.50	5.00	15.00	30.00

GOLD (OMS)

| 134a (Y5d) | 1903 | — | — | — | Rare | — |

BRONZE

150 (Y37)	1912	2.000	7.50	20.00	35.00	45.00
	1913	4.000	3.50	7.50	15.00	25.00
	1914	2.000	7.50	20.00	35.00	45.00
	1915	3.000	6.50	14.00	25.00	35.00
	1916	8.000	3.00	5.00	12.50	20.00
	1918	4.000	3.50	7.50	15.00	25.00
	1919	2.000	7.50	15.00	30.00	40.00
	1929	8.000	2.00	4.00	8.00	12.50
	1941	19.800	1.00	2.00	3.00	5.00

ZINC

| 171 (Y49) | 1941 | 27.600 | 2.50 | 7.50 | 10.00 | 25.00 |
| | 1942 | .200* | 575.00 | 1250. | 1800. | 2400. |

***NOTE:** Almost entire issue melted, about 30 pcs. known.

5 CENTS

.8200 g, .569 SILVER, .0150 oz ASW

52 (C73)	1818	2.500	450.00	750.00	900.00	1100.
	1819	3.000	300.00	600.00	750.00	900.00
	1822	.047	220.00	440.00	650.00	800.00
	1825B	.900	35.00	60.00	120.00	150.00
	1826B	1.021	35.00	60.00	120.00	150.00
	1827	.534	25.00	50.00	75.00	100.00
	1827B	.284	40.00	80.00	130.00	175.00
	1828B	.397	35.00	70.00	120.00	150.00

GOLD (OMS)

| 52a (C73a) | 1818 | — | — | — | Rare | — |
| | 1822 | — | — | — | Proof | 3000. |

.6850 g, .640 SILVER, .0141 oz ASW

| 74 (C87) | 1848 | 100 pcs. | 600.00 | 1300. | 2000. | 2600. |

GOLD (OMS)

| 74a (C87a) | 1848 | — | — | — | Rare | — |

.6850 g, .640 SILVER, .0141 oz ASW

KM#	Date	Mintage	Fine	VF	XF	Unc
91 (Y6)	1850	3.037	3.00	7.00	15.00	25.00
	1853	.011	200.00	450.00	600.00	900.00
	1855	.515	5.00	12.00	20.00	35.00
	1859	.400	5.00	12.00	20.00	35.00
	1862. dot after date	.400	5.00	12.00	20.00	35.00
	1862 w/o dot after date	Inc. Ab.	5.00	12.00	20.00	35.00
	1863	.640	5.00	12.00	20.00	35.00
	1868	.200	30.00	55.00	125.00	175.00
	1869	.500	5.00	12.00	20.00	35.00
	1876	.200	7.00	20.00	35.00	50.00
	1879	.200	7.00	20.00	35.00	50.00
	1887	.100	25.00	45.00	75.00	90.00

NOTE: Varieties exist for 1850 dated coins.

.718 SILVER
c/m: 718

KM#	Date	Mintage	Fine	VF	XF	Unc
91a (Y6b)	1853	—	—	—	Rare	—

GOLD (OMS)

KM#	Date	Mintage	Fine	VF	XF	Unc
91b (Y6a)	1879	—	—	—	Rare	—

COPPER-NICKEL

KM#	Date	Mintage	Fine	VF	XF	Unc
137 (Y33)	1907	6.000	4.00	12.00	22.50	35.00
	1908	5.430	5.00	15.00	27.50	45.00
	1909	2.570	30.00	70.00	110.00	135.00

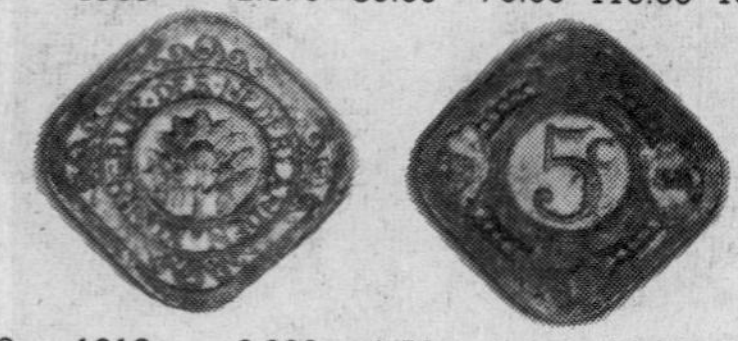

KM#	Date	Mintage	Fine	VF	XF	Unc
153 (Y34)	1913	6.000	1.50	2.50	10.00	25.00
	1914	7.400	1.50	2.50	10.00	25.00
	1923	10.000	1.50	2.50	10.00	25.00
	1929	8.000	1.50	2.50	12.50	25.00
	1932	2.000	10.00	25.00	40.00	60.00
	1933	1.400	40.00	70.00	110.00	135.00
	1934	2.600	7.50	17.50	27.50	45.00
	1936	2.600	7.50	17.50	27.50	45.00
	1938	4.200	3.00	7.00	15.00	25.00
	1939	4.600	3.00	7.00	15.00	25.00
	1940	7.200	2.50	5.00	12.50	25.00

NOTE: For a similar coin dated 1943, see Netherlands Antilles (Curacao).

ZINC

KM#	Date	Mintage	Fine	VF	XF	Unc
172 (Y50)	1941	32.200	2.00	4.00	10.00	20.00
	1942	11.800	4.00	8.00	15.00	30.00
	1943	7.000	10.00	22.50	40.00	70.00

BRONZE

KM#	Date	Mintage	Fine	VF	XF	BU
176 (Y54)	1948	23.600	.50	.75	2.00	15.00
	1948	—	—	—	Proof	40.00

KM#	Date	Mintage	Fine	VF	XF	BU
181 (Y58)	1950	20.000	.10	.25	.50	3.25
	1950	—	—	—	Proof	20.00
	1951	16.200	.10	.25	.50	3.25
	1951	—	—	—	Proof	15.00
	1952	14.400	.10	.25	.50	3.25
	1952	—	—	—	Proof	25.00
(Y58)	1953	12.000	.10	.25	.50	3.25
	1953	—	—	—	Proof	25.00
	1954	14.000	.10	.25	.50	3.25
	1954	—	—	—	Proof	15.00
	1955	11.400	.10	.25	.50	3.25
	1955	—	—	—	Proof	15.00
	1956	7.400	.15	.35	.75	5.00
	1956	—	—	—	Proof	15.00
	1957	16.000	.10	.25	.50	3.25
	1957	—	—	—	Proof	15.00
	1958	9.000	.10	.25	.50	5.00
	1958	—	—	—	Proof	15.00
	1960	11.000	.10	.25	.50	3.25
	1960	—	—	—	Proof	15.00
	1961	12.000	.10	.25	.50	2.00
	1961	—	—	—	Proof	15.00
	1962	15.000	.10	.25	.50	2.00
	1962	—	—	—	Proof	15.00
	1963	18.000	.10	.25	.50	2.00
	1963	—	—	—	Proof	20.00
	1964	21.000	.10	.25	.50	2.00
	1964	—	—	—	Proof	20.00
	1965	28.000	.10	.25	.50	2.00
	1965	—	—	—	Proof	20.00
	1966	22.000	.10	.25	.50	2.00
	1966	—	—	—	Proof	20.00
	1967 leaves far from rim	32.000	—	.10	.25	2.00
	1967 leaves far from rim	—	—	—	Proof	25.00
	1967 leaves touching rim	Inc. Ab.	.15	.50	1.00	3.00
	1967 leaves touching rim	—	—	—	Proof	25.00
	1969 fish privy mark	5.000	.15	.50	1.00	3.50
	1969 fish privy mark	—	—	—	Proof	20.00
	1969 cock privy mark	11.000	—	.10	.25	2.00
	1969 cock privy mark	—	—	—	Proof	20.00
	1970	22.000	—	.10	.25	1.00
	1970	—	—	—	Proof	20.00
	1970 date close to rim	Inc. Ab.	—	.10	.25	1.00
	1970 date close to rim	—	—	—	Proof	20.00
	1971	25.000	—	.10	.25	1.00
	1972	25.000	—	.10	.25	1.00
	1973	22.000	—	.10	.25	1.00
	1974	20.000	—	—	.10	.50
	1975	46.000	—	—	.10	.50
	1976	50.000	—	—	.10	.50
	1977	50.000	—	—	.10	.50
	1978	60.000	—	—	.10	.50
	1979	80.000	—	—	.10	.50
	1980 cock & star privy mark	252.500	—	—	.10	.30

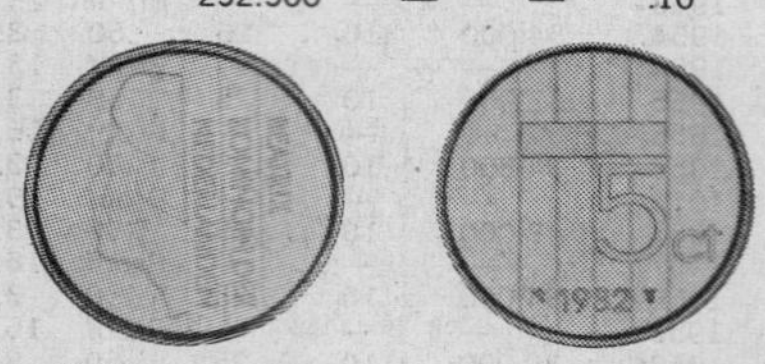

KM#	Date	Mintage	Fine	VF	XF	BU
202 (Y69)	1982	47.100	—	—	.10	.20
	1982	.010	—	—	Proof	10.00
	1983	60.200	—	—	.10	.20
	1983	.015	—	—	Proof	7.50
	1984	70.700	—	—	.10	.20
	1984	.020	—	—	Proof	4.00
	1985	36.100	—	—	.10	.20
	1985	.017	—	—	Proof	4.00
	1986	14.900	—	—	.10	.20
	1986	.020	—	—	Proof	4.00
	1987	33.200	—	—	—	.10
	1987	.018	—	—	Proof	4.00
	1988	*43.000	—	—	—	.10
	1988	.020—	—	—	Proof	4.00
	1989	—	—	—	—	.10

10 CENTS

1.6900 g, .569 SILVER, .0309 oz ASW

KM#	Date	Mintage	Fine	VF	XF	Unc
53 (C74)	1818	60 pcs.	750.00	1400.	1800.	2200.
	1819	.025	275.00	600.00	900.00	1200.
	1822	.113	200.00	400.00	700.00	800.00
	1823B	.178	110.00	220.00	325.00	450.00
	1825	.972	30.00	45.00	90.00	110.00
	1825B	1.727	30.00	50.00	100.00	130.00
	1826	2.138	25.00	40.00	85.00	110.00
	1826B	1.430	25.00	40.00	85.00	110.00
	1827	5.895	17.50	32.50	70.00	110.00
	1827B	1.711	25.00	40.00	85.00	110.00
	1828	2.036	25.00	40.00	85.00	110.00
	1828B	1.168	25.00	40.00	85.00	110.00

GOLD (OMS)

KM#	Date	Mintage	Fine	VF	XF	Unc
53a (C74a)	1822	—	—	—	Rare	3500.

1.4000 g, .640 SILVER, .0288 oz ASW

KM#	Date	Mintage	Fine	VF	XF	Unc
75 (C88)	1848	6.859	20.00	55.00	120.00	160.00
	1849. dot after date	4.051	15.00	45.00	90.00	110.00
	1849 w/o dot after date	Inc. Ab.	30.00	80.00	160.00	200.00

KM#	Date	Mintage	Fine	VF	XF	Unc
80 (Y7)	1849	6.204	20.00	55.00	90.00	150.00
	1850	7.270	20.00	55.00	90.00	150.00
	1853	1.104	45.00	90.00	130.00	200.00
	1855	.745	50.00	100.00	150.00	220.00
	1855 low 5	Inc. Ab.	50.00	100.00	150.00	220.00
	1856	1.000	20.00	55.00	90.00	150.00
	1859	1.000	20.00	55.00	90.00	150.00
	1862	.800	45.00	100.00	160.00	220.00
	1863	1.240	20.00	55.00	80.00	125.00
	1868	.200	100.00	300.00	500.00	600.00
	1869	1.000	20.00	55.00	80.00	125.00
	1871	1.000	20.00	55.00	80.00	125.00
	1873	1.000	20.00	55.00	80.00	125.00
	1874 sword privy mark	.800	90.00	250.00	400.00	500.00
	1874 sword in scabbard privy mark	2.000	40.00	100.00	150.00	200.00
	1876	1.000	12.50	35.00	70.00	100.00
	1877	1.000	12.50	35.00	70.00	100.00
	1878	1.000	12.50	35.00	70.00	100.00
	1879	1.000	12.50	35.00	70.00	100.00
	1880	1.000	12.50	35.00	70.00	100.00
	1881	2.000	12.50	35.00	70.00	100.00
	1882	2.000	12.50	35.00	70.00	100.00
	1884	1.000	12.50	35.00	70.00	100.00
	1885	2.000	12.50	35.00	70.00	100.00
	1887	1.600	12.50	35.00	70.00	100.00
	1889	2.800	10.00	30.00	60.00	80.00
	1890	2.600	10.00	30.00	60.00	80.00

.718 SILVER (OMS)
c/m: 718

KM#	Date	Mintage	Fine	VF	XF	Unc
80a (Y7b)	1853	—	—	—	Rare	—

GOLD (OMS)

KM#	Date	Mintage	Fine	VF	XF	Unc
80b (Y7a)	1884	—	—	—	Rare	—
	1885	—	—	—	Rare	—

1.4000 g, .640 SILVER, .0288 oz ASW

KM#	Date	Mintage	Fine	VF	XF	Unc
116 (Y20)	1892 thin head	2.000	12.00	35.00	70.00	90.00
	1893	2.000	12.00	35.00	70.00	90.00
	1894	1.500	12.00	35.00	70.00	90.00
	1895	1.000	17.50	55.00	90.00	135.00
	1896	2.000	12.00	35.00	70.00	90.00
	1897	7.850	6.00	20.00	40.00	60.00

Obv: Small head, divided legend.

KM#	Date	Mintage	Fine	VF	XF	Unc
119 (Y23)	1898	2.000	22.50	60.00	120.00	180.00
	1901	2.000	20.00	55.00	100.00	160.00

Obv: Large head.

KM#	Date	Mintage	Fine	VF	XF	Unc
135 (Y23a)	1903	6.000	8.00	25.00	45.00	70.00

GOLD (OMS)

KM#	Date	Mintage	Fine	VF	XF	Unc
135a (Y23c)	1903	—	—	—	Rare	—

1.4000 g, .640 SILVER, .0288 oz ASW
Obv: Small head, continuous legend.

KM#	Date	Mintage	Fine	VF	XF	Unc
136	1904	3.000	10.00	32.50	65.00	80.00
(Y23b)	1905	2.000	15.00	40.00	80.00	110.00
	1906	4.000	9.00	25.00	45.00	65.00

145	1910	2.250	25.00	60.00	100.00	135.00
(Y39)	1911	4.000	9.00	25.00	55.00	70.00
	1912	4.000	9.00	25.00	55.00	70.00
	1913	5.000	9.00	25.00	55.00	70.00
	1914	9.000	3.00	10.00	20.00	35.00
	1915	5.000	3.00	10.00	20.00	35.00
	1916	5.000	3.00	10.00	20.00	35.00
	1917	10.000	2.00	7.50	15.00	30.00
	1918	20.000	1.50	5.00	12.50	25.00
	1919	10.000	2.00	7.50	15.00	30.00
	1921	5.000	3.00	10.00	20.00	35.00
	1925	5.000	3.00	10.00	20.00	35.00

GOLD (OMS)

145a (Y39a)	1910	—	—	—	Rare	—

1.4000 g, .640 SILVER, .0288 oz ASW

163	1926	2.700	7.00	18.00	30.00	50.00
(Y43)	1927	2.300	7.00	18.00	30.00	50.00
	1928	10.000	.75	3.00	7.50	15.00
	1930	5.000	1.50	4.50	10.00	17.50
	1934	2.000	9.00	20.00	35.00	60.00
	1935	8.000	1.00	3.00	7.50	15.00
	1936	15.000	.50	1.00	2.00	5.00
	1937	18.600	.50	1.00	2.00	5.00
	1938	21.400	.50	1.00	2.00	5.00
	1939	20.000	.50	1.00	2.00	5.00
	1941	43.000	.50	.75	1.50	4.00
	1943P acorn privy mark					
		Inc. Be.	4.00	12.00	20.00	30.00
	1944P	120.000	.50	.75	1.00	2.50
	1944D	25.400	1150.	2250.	3000.	4500.
	1944S	64.040	6.00	12.00	20.00	32.50
	1945P	90.560	175.00	350.00	500.00	600.00

NOTE: For similar coins dated 1941P-1943P with palm tree privy mark, see Netherlands Antilles (Curacao) and Surinam.

ZINC

173	1941	29.800	1.00	2.00	7.50	12.50
(Y51)	1942	95.600	.25	.50	2.50	10.00
	1943	29.000	1.00	2.00	7.50	12.50

NICKEL

KM#	Date	Mintage	Fine	VF	XF	BU
177	1948	69.200	.25	.50	1.00	7.00
(Y55)	1948	—	—	—	Proof	60.00

182	1950	56.600	.10	.25	.50	3.50
(Y59)	1950	—	—	—	Proof	30.00
	1951	54.200	.10	.25	.50	3.50
	1951	—	—	—	Proof	25.00
	1954	8.200	.10	.35	.75	4.50
	1954	—	—	—	Proof	15.00
	1955	18.200	.10	.25	.50	3.50
	1955	—	—	—	Proof	15.00
	1956	12.000	.10	.25	.50	3.50
	1956	—	—	—	Proof	15.00
	1957	18.600	.10	.25	.50	3.50

KM#	Date	Mintage	Fine	VF	XF	BU
(Y59)	1957	—	—	—	Proof	15.00
	1958	34.000	.10	.25	.50	3.50
	1958	—	—	—	Proof	15.00
	1959	44.000	.10	.25	.50	3.50
	1959	—	—	—	Proof	15.00
	1960	12.000	.10	.25	.50	3.50
	1960	—	—	—	Proof	25.00
	1961	25.000	—	.10	.25	3.50
	1961	—	—	—	Proof	25.00
	1962	30.000	—	.10	.25	3.50
	1962	—	—	—	Proof	25.00
	1963	35.000	—	.10	.25	3.50
	1963	—	—	—	Proof	30.00
	1964	41.000	—	.10	.25	3.50
	1964	—	—	—	Proof	30.00
	1965	59.000	—	.10	.25	3.50
	1965	—	—	—	Proof	30.00
	1966	44.000	—	—	.10	2.00
	1966	—	—	—	Proof	30.00
	1967	39.000	—	—	.10	2.00
	1967	—	—	—	Proof	30.00
	1968	42.000	—	—	.10	2.00
	1968	—	—	—	Proof	30.00
	1969 fish privy mark					
		28.000	—	—	.10	2.00
	1969 fish privy mark					
		—	—	—	Proof	30.00
	1969 cock privy mark					
		24.000	—	—	.10	2.00
	1969 cock privy mark					
		—	—	—	Proof	30.00
	1970	50.000	—	—	.10	2.00
	1970	—	—	—	Proof	30.00
	1971	55.000	—	—	.10	2.00
	1972	60.000	—	—	.10	2.00
	1973	90.000	—	—	.10	2.00
	1974	75.000	—	—	.10	1.00
	1975	110.000	—	—	.10	1.00
	1976	85.000	—	—	.10	1.00
	1977	100.000	—	—	.10	1.00
	1978	110.000	—	—	.10	1.00
	1979	120.000	—	—	.10	1.00
	1980 cock & star privy mark					
		195.300	—	—	.10	.50

203	1982	10.300	—	—	.10	.25
(Y70)	1982	.010	—	—	Proof	10.00
	1983	38.200	—	—	—	.25
	1983	.015	—	—	Proof	8.00
	1984	42.000	—	—	.10	.25
	1984	.020	—	—	Proof	4.00
	1985	29.000	—	—	.10	.25
	1985	.017	—	—	Proof	4.00
	1986	23.100	—	—	.10	.25
	1986	.020	—	—	Proof	4.00
	1987	4.600	—	—	.10	.25
	1987	.018	—	—	Proof	4.00
	1988	*22.000	—	—	.10	.25
	1988	.020	—	—	Proof	4.00
	1989	—	—	—	—	.25

25 CENTS

4.2300 g, .569 SILVER, .0773 oz ASW

KM#	Date	Mintage	Fine	VF	XF	Unc
48	1817	—	525.00	1500.	2000.	2500.
(C75)	1818	—	525.00	1500.	2000.	2500.
	1819	.013	300.00	600.00	900.00	1250.
	1822	.116	220.00	400.00	550.00	700.00
	1823B	1.334	35.00	70.00	100.00	130.00
	1824B	6.033	25.00	45.00	70.00	100.00
	1825	10.311	25.00	45.00	70.00	100.00
	1825B	2.608	35.00	70.00	100.00	130.00
	1826	12.282	25.00	45.00	70.00	100.00
	1826B	7.299	25.00	45.00	70.00	100.00
	1827B	1.822	35.00	70.00	100.00	130.00
	1828B	.334	150.00	300.00	550.00	725.00
	1829	.106	150.00	300.00	550.00	725.00
	1829B	1.256	45.00	90.00	145.00	185.00
	1830	1.534	45.00	90.00	145.00	185.00
	1830B	.902	50.00	90.00	145.00	185.00

3.5750 g, .640 SILVER, .0736 oz ASW

76	1848. dot after date					
(C89)		10.730	20.00	50.00	100.00	150.00
	1848 w/o dot after date					

KM#	Date	Mintage	Fine	VF	XF	Unc
(C89)		Inc. Ab.	25.00	90.00	150.00	175.00
	1849/89	8.059	150.00	330.00	500.00	625.00
	1849	Inc. Ab.	15.00	40.00	85.00	115.00

81	1849	Inc.KM76	140.00	300.00	400.00	525.00
(Y8)	1850	2.207	110.00	270.00	300.00	500.00
	1853	7,974	250.00	500.00	800.00	1000.
	1887	.100	140.00	300.00	400.00	525.00
	1889	.200	125.00	270.00	350.00	550.00
	1890. dot after date					
		.600	80.00	175.00	275.00	450.00
	1890 w/o dot after date					
		Inc. Ab.	110.00	250.00	400.00	475.00

GOLD (OMS)

81a (Y8a)	1849	—	—	—	Rare	—

.718 SILVER (OMS)
c/m: 718

81b (Y8b)	1853	—	—	—	Rare	—

3.5750 g, .640 SILVER, .0736 oz ASW

115	1891	2 pcs.	—	—	—	—
(Y21)	1892	.800	17.50	50.00	90.00	130.00
	1893	.800	17.50	50.00	90.00	130.00
	1894	1.000	15.00	50.00	90.00	130.00
	1895	1.200	15.00	50.00	90.00	130.00
	1895 slanted mint mark					
		Inc. Ab.	75.00	150.00	350.00	450.00
	1896	.600	35.00	110.00	180.00	250.00
	1897	3.100	10.00	40.00	70.00	100.00

Obv: Bust w/small truncation.

120.1	1898	.400	140.00	375.00	550.00	725.00
(Y24)	1901	1.600	12.50	45.00	90.00	120.00

Obv: Bust w/wider truncation.

120.2	1901	Inc. Ab.	50.00	150.00	275.00	350.00
(Y24.1)	1902	1.200	15.00	45.00	80.00	110.00
	1903	1.200	15.00	45.00	80.00	110.00
	1904	1.600	15.00	45.00	80.00	110.00
	1905	1.200	15.00	45.00	80.00	110.00
	1906	2.000	12.00	40.00	65.00	90.00

GOLD (OMS)

120.2a (Y24a)	1903	—	—	—	Rare	—

3.5750 g, .640 SILVER, .0736 oz ASW

146	1910	.880	30.00	90.00	160.00	225.00
(Y40)	1911	1.600	15.00	45.00	75.00	120.00
	1912	1.600	15.00	45.00	75.00	120.00
	1913	1.200	20.00	60.00	100.00	150.00
	1914	5.600	5.00	25.00	50.00	80.00
	1915	2.000	6.00	25.00	50.00	100.00
	1916	2.000	6.00	25.00	50.00	100.00
	1917	4.000	5.00	22.50	45.00	85.00
	1918	6.000	4.00	17.50	35.00	60.00
	1919	4.000	5.00	22.50	45.00	85.00
	1925	2.000	5.00	25.00	50.00	85.00

164	1926	2.000	12.50	35.00	50.00	100.00
(Y44)	1928	8.000	1.50	3.00	7.50	20.00
	1939	4.000	1.50	4.00	6.00	10.00
	1940	9.000	1.00	2.00	4.00	7.50
	1941	40.000	.75	1.00	2.00	4.00
	1943P acorn privy mark					
		Inc. Be.	1.50	4.00	7.50	15.00
	1944P acorn privy mark					

Kingdom of the Netherlands / NETHERLANDS 1334

KM# (Y44)	Date	Mintage	Fine	VF	XF	Unc
			.75	1.00	2.00	4.00
	1945P acorn privy mark	40.000				
		92.000	80.00	180.00	350.00	450.00

NOTE: For similar coins dated 1941P and 1943P with palm tree privy mark, see Netherlands Antilles (Curacao).

ZINC

KM#	Date	Mintage	Fine	VF	XF	Unc
174 (Y52)	1941	34.600	.50	1.50	5.00	20.00
	1942	27.800	.50	1.50	5.00	20.00
	1943	13.600	5.00	17.50	30.00	50.00

NICKEL

KM#	Date	Mintage	Fine	VF	XF	BU
178 (Y56)	1948	27.400	.25	.50	1.50	10.00
	1948	—	—	—	Proof	60.00

183 (Y60)	1950	43.000	.15	.25	.50	5.00
	1950	—	—	—	Proof	30.00
	1951	33.200	.15	.25	.50	5.00
	1951	—	—	—	Proof	25.00
	1954	6.400	.50	1.50	2.50	8.00
	1954	—	—	—	Proof	25.00
	1955	10.000	.15	.25	.50	5.00
	1955	—	—	—	Proof	25.00
	1956	8.000	.15	.25	.50	4.00
	1956	—	—	—	Proof	25.00
	1957	8.000	.15	.25	.50	4.00
	1957	—	—	—	Proof	25.00
	1958	15.000	.15	.25	.50	4.00
	1958	—	—	—	Proof	25.00
	1960	9.000	.15	.25	.50	4.00
	1960	—	—	—	Proof	30.00
	1961	6.000	.40	1.25	2.00	7.50
	1961	—	—	—	Proof	30.00
	1962	12.000	.15	.25	.50	3.50
	1962	—	—	—	Proof	30.00
	1963	18.000	.15	.25	.50	3.50
	1963	—	—	—	Proof	30.00
	1964	25.000	.15	.25	.50	3.50
	1964	—	—	—	Proof	30.00
	1965	18.000	.15	.25	.50	3.50
	1965	—	—	—	Proof	30.00
	1966	25.000	—	.15	.25	1.50
	1966	—	—	—	Proof	30.00
	1967	18.000	—	.15	.25	1.50
	1967	—	—	—	Proof	35.00
	1968	26.000	—	.15	.25	1.50
	1968	—	—	—	Proof	35.00
	1969 fish privy mark	14.000	—	.15	.25	1.50
	1969 fish privy mark	—	—	—	Proof	35.00
	1969 cock privy mark	21.000	—	.15	.25	1.50
	1969 cock privy mark	—	—	—	Proof	35.00
	1970	39.000	—	.15	.25	1.50
	1970	—	—	—	Proof	35.00
	1971	40.000	—	.15	.25	1.50
	1972	50.000	—	.15	.25	1.50
	1973	45.000	—	.15	.25	1.50
	1974	10.000	—	.15	.25	1.50
	1975	25.000	—	.15	.25	1.00
	1976	64.000	—	.15	.25	1.00
	1977	55.000	—	.15	.25	1.00
	1978	35.000	—	.15	.25	1.00
	1979	45.000	—	.15	.25	1.00
	1980 cock & star privy mark	159.300	—	—	.15	.75

ALUMINUM

| 183a (Y60a) | 1980 | 15 pcs. | — | — | — | 400.00 |

NICKEL

KM# (Y71)	Date	Mintage	Fine	VF	XF	BU
204	1982	18.300	—	—	.15	.25
	1982	.010	—	—	Proof	15.00
	1983	18.200	—	—	.15	.25
	1983	.015	—	—	Proof	12.00
	1984	19.000	—	—	.15	.25
	1984	.020	—	—	Proof	6.00
	1985	29.000	—	—	.15	.25
	1985	.017	—	—	Proof	6.00
	1986	20.300	—	—	.15	.25
	1986	.020	—	—	Proof	6.00
	1987	36.000	—	—	.15	.25
	1987	.018	—	—	Proof	6.00
	1988	*33.000	—	—	.15	.25
	1988	.020	—	—	Proof	6.00
	1989	—	—	—	—	.25

1/2 GULDEN
(50 Cents)

5.3800 g, .893 SILVER, .1544 oz ASW

KM# (C76)	Date	Mintage	Fine	VF	XF	Unc
54	1818	.051	130.00	250.00	650.00	800.00
	1819	.043	130.00	250.00	650.00	800.00
	1822 engraver's name below bust	.119	130.00	250.00	450.00	600.00
	1822 w/o engraver's name	Inc. Ab.	250.00	475.00	700.00	900.00
	1829B	.180	130.00	250.00	450.00	600.00
	1830B	.100	130.00	250.00	450.00	600.00

5.0000 g, .945 SILVER, .1519 oz ASW
Reeded edge.

73.1 (C90)	1846	—	600.00	1500.	2500.	3500.
	1846	—	—	—	Proof	—
	1847	1.111	35.00	100.00	200.00	300.00
	1848	4.050	15.00	60.00	150.00	250.00

Lettered edge.

| 73.2 (C90.1) | 1846 | — | — | — | Proof | — |

92 (Y9)	1850	—	750.00	1750.	2250.	3000.
	1853/43	1.711	300.00	850.00	1750.	2500.
	1857	3.606	15.00	40.00	75.00	135.00
	1858	7.604	12.50	35.00	60.00	115.00
	1859	3.001	15.00	40.00	75.00	140.00
	1860	6.603	12.50	35.00	60.00	125.00
	1861	6.001	12.50	35.00	60.00	125.00
	1862	4.002	12.50	35.00	60.00	125.00
	1863	5.152	12.50	35.00	60.00	125.00
	1864	4.001	12.50	35.00	60.00	125.00
	1866	1.402	25.00	70.00	125.00	200.00
	1868 open 8	4.004	12.50	35.00	60.00	125.00
	1868 closed 8	Inc. Ab.	12.50	35.00	60.00	120.00

GOLD (OMS)

| 92a (Y9a) | 1868/58 | — | — | — | Rare | — |

5.0000 g, .945 SILVER, .1519 oz ASW

| 121.1 (Y25) | 1898 | 2.000 | 25.00 | 60.00 | 150.00 | 200.00 |
| | 1898 | — | — | — | Proof | 600.00 |

GOLD (OMS)

| 121.1a (Y25b) | 1898 | — | — | — | Rare | — |

5.0000 g, .945 SILVER, .1519 oz ASW
Rev: W/o 50 C. under shield.

KM#	Date	Mintage	Fine	VF	XF	Unc
121.2 (Y25a)	1904	1.000	35.00	75.00	125.00	225.00
	1905	4.000	10.00	25.00	50.00	100.00
	1906	1.000	35.00	85.00	130.00	225.00
	1907	3.300	10.00	25.00	50.00	100.00
	1908	4.000	10.00	25.00	50.00	100.00
	1909	3.000	10.00	25.00	50.00	100.00

GOLD (OMS)

| 121.2a (Y25c) | 1905 | — | — | — | Rare | — |

5.0000 g, .945 SILVER, .1519 oz ASW

147 (Y41)	1910	4.000	10.00	30.00	70.00	125.00
	1912	4.000	10.00	30.00	70.00	125.00
	1913	8.000	8.00	17.50	40.00	90.00
	1919	8.000	8.00	17.50	40.00	90.00

5.0000 g, .720 SILVER, .1157 oz ASW

160 (Y45)	1921	5.000	1.50	3.00	6.00	22.50
	1921	—	—	—	Proof	200.00
	1922	11.240	1.25	2.50	5.00	15.00
	1928	5.000	1.50	3.00	6.00	22.50
	1929	9.500	1.25	2.50	5.00	12.50
	1930	18.500	1.25	2.50	4.00	10.00

GULDEN
(100 Cents)

10.7600 g, .893 SILVER, .3089 oz ASW

KM# (C77)	Date	Mintage	Fine	VF	XF	Unc
55	1818	.043	400.00	750.00	1500.	2000.
	1819	.252	160.00	400.00	600.00	800.00
	1820	.543	85.00	175.00	275.00	450.00
	1821	1.239	85.00	175.00	275.00	450.00
	1822	.080	300.00	700.00	1500.	2000.
	1823	.732	85.00	175.00	275.00	450.00
	1823B	.025	650.00	1500.	2000.	2500.
	1824	1.096	85.00	175.00	275.00	400.00
	1824 dash between crown & shield	Inc. Ab.	85.00	160.00	225.00	325.00
	1828	.062	300.00	600.00	1250.	1700.
	1829B	.383	200.00	400.00	750.00	1000.
	1831/21	.120	200.00	400.00	750.00	1000.
	1831	Inc. Ab.	200.00	400.00	750.00	1000.
	1832/21	1.362	80.00	160.00	275.00	450.00
	1832/23	I.A.	80.00	160.00	275.00	450.00
	1832/24	I.A.	80.00	160.00	275.00	450.00
	1832/24 dash between crown & shield		80.00	160.00	275.00	450.00
	1832/28	I.A.	80.00	160.00	275.00	450.00
	1832	Inc. Ab.	80.00	160.00	275.00	450.00
	1837	.383	80.00	160.00	275.00	450.00

GOLD (OMS)

| 55a (C77a) | 1820 | — | — | — | Rare | — |
| | 1821 | — | — | — | Rare | — |

Kingdom of the Netherlands / NETHERLANDS 1335

10.0000 g, .945 SILVER, .3038 oz ASW

KM#	Date	Mintage	Fine	VF	XF	Unc
65	1840	.099	60.00	130.00	250.00	425.00
(C80)	1840	—	—	—	Proof	1500.

KM#	Date	Mintage	Fine	VF	XF	Unc
66	1840	2 pcs.	—	—	Rare	—
(C91)	1842	.661	80.00	225.00	375.00	550.00
	1842 shorter bust					
		Inc. Ab.	175.00	375.00	600.00	950.00
	1843	1.720	60.00	135.00	200.00	300.00
	1844	1.575	60.00	135.00	200.00	300.00
	1845	3.803	20.00	50.00	90.00	115.00
	1845 dash between crown & shield					
		.221	60.00	115.00	200.00	300.00
	1846 fleur de lis privy mark					
		.901	30.00	80.00	130.00	175.00
	1846 sword privy mark					
		3.772	20.00	45.00	90.00	115.00
	1847	8.280	15.00	35.00	65.00	100.00
	1848	13.615	15.00	35.00	65.00	100.00
	1849	.650	55.00	140.00	200.00	300.00

KM#	Date	Mintage	Fine	VF	XF	Unc
93	1850	10 pcs.	—	—	Rare	—
(Y10)	1850 reeded edge					
		—	—	—	Rare	—
	1851	2.125	22.50	60.00	120.00	175.00
	1853/0	.652	275.00	350.00	500.00	700.00
	1853/1	Inc. Ab.	275.00	350.00	500.00	700.00
	1853	Inc. Ab.	250.00	325.00	500.00	750.00
	1854	4.511	17.50	35.00	55.00	100.00
	1855	5.133	17.50	35.00	55.00	100.00
	1856	4.955	17.50	35.00	55.00	100.00
	1857	2.125	22.50	40.00	80.00	120.00
	1858	4.199	17.50	35.00	70.00	110.00
	1859	2.717	17.50	35.00	70.00	120.00
	1860	4.036	17.50	30.00	65.00	110.00
	1861	5.079	15.00	30.00	65.00	110.00
	1863	7.986	15.00	30.00	65.00	110.00
	1864	3.600	15.00	30.00	65.00	110.00
	1865	6.402	15.00	30.00	65.00	110.00
	1866	1.002	27.50	65.00	100.00	175.00
	1867	*4 pcs.	—	—	Proof	10,000.

GOLD (OMS)

| 93a | 1867 | — | — | — | Rare | — |
| (Y10a) | | | | | | |

10.0000 g, .945 SILVER, .3038 oz ASW

117	1892	3.500	10.00	30.00	80.00	150.00
(Y22)	1896	.100	100.00	260.00	500.00	850.00
	1897	2.500	15.00	35.00	100.00	175.00

KM#	Date	Mintage	Fine	VF	XF	Unc
122.1	1898	2.000	40.00	90.00	175.00	325.00
(Y26)	1901	2.000	35.00	65.00	130.00	200.00

GOLD (OMS)

| 122.1a | 1898 | 2 pcs. | — | — | Rare | — |
| (Y26b) | | | | | | |

10.0000 g, .945 SILVER, .3038 oz ASW
Rev: W/o 100 C. under shield.

122.2	1904	2.000	17.50	35.00	70.00	135.00
(Y26a)	1905	1.000	35.00	65.00	110.00	190.00
	1906	.500	200.00	350.00	450.00	600.00
	1907	5.100	12.00	30.00	65.00	110.00
	1908	4.700	12.00	30.00	65.00	110.00
	1909	2.000	20.00	45.00	80.00	140.00

148	1910	1.000	45.00	90.00	175.00	300.00
(Y42)	1911	2.000	70.00	150.00	300.00	450.00
	1912	3.000	12.50	25.00	55.00	100.00
	1913	8.000	10.00	25.00	55.00	100.00
	1914	15.785	10.00	20.00	50.00	100.00
	1915	14.215	10.00	20.00	50.00	100.00
	1916	5.000	25.00	50.00	80.00	150.00
	1917	2.300	30.00	50.00	80.00	150.00

10.0000 g, .720 SILVER, .2315 oz ASW

161	1922	9.550	4.00	9.00	18.00	30.00
(Y46)	1922	—	—	—	Proof	350.00
	1923	8.050	4.00	9.00	18.00	30.00
	1924	8.000	4.00	12.50	25.00	45.00
	1928	6.150	4.00	7.50	15.00	25.00
	1929	32.350	BV	5.00	7.50	15.00
	1930	13.500	BV	5.00	7.50	17.50
	1931	38.100	BV	5.00	7.50	15.00
	1938	5.000	6.00	12.50	20.00	30.00
	1939	14.200	BV	5.00	7.50	15.00
	1940	21.300	BV	5.00	7.50	15.00
	1944P acorn privy mark					
		105.125	20.00	30.00	50.00	65.00
	1944P acorn privy mark, leg. further under truncation					
		I.A.	70.00	150.00	225.00	275.00
	1945P acorn privy mark					
		25.375	350.00	700.00	1000.	1350.

NOTE: For similar coins dated 1943D with palm tree privy mark, see Netherlands East Indies.

6.5000 g, .720 SILVER, .1504 oz ASW

KM#	Date	Mintage	Fine	VF	XF	BU
184	1954	6.600	—	BV	4.00	10.00
(Y61)	1954	—	—	—	Proof	65.00
	1955	37.500	—	BV	2.50	8.00
	1955	—	—	—	Proof	65.00
	1956	38.900	—	BV	2.50	8.00
	1956	—	—	—	Proof	65.00
	1957	27.000	—	BV	2.50	8.00
	1957	—	—	—	Proof	65.00
	1958	30.000	—	BV	2.50	8.00
	1958	—	—	—	Proof	65.00
	1963	5.000	—	BV	4.00	12.50
	1963	—	—	—	Proof	75.00
	1964	9.000	—	BV	2.50	5.00
	1964	—	—	—	Proof	75.00
	1965	21.000	—	BV	2.00	4.00
	1965	—	—	—	Proof	75.00
	1966	5.000	—	BV	3.00	6.00
	1966	—	—	—	Proof	75.00
	1967	7.000	—	BV	4.00	11.00
	1967	—	—	—	Proof	100.00

NICKEL

184a	1967	31.000	—	—	.75	2.50
(Y61a)	1967	—	—	—	Proof	55.00
	1968	61.000	—	—	.75	2.50
	1969 fish	27.500	—	—	.75	2.50
	1969 fish	—	—	—	Proof	50.00
	1969 cock					
		15.500	—	—	.75	2.50
	1969 cock	—	—	—	Proof	50.00
	1970	18.000	—	—	.75	2.50
	1970	—	—	—	Proof	50.00
	1971	50.000	—	—	.65	1.75
	1972	60.000	—	—	.65	1.75
	1973	27.000	—	—	.65	1.75
	1975	9.000	—	—	.65	1.75
	1976	32.000	—	—	.65	1.75
	1977	38.000	—	—	.65	1.75
	1978	30.000	—	—	.65	1.50
	1979	25.000	—	—	.65	1.50
	1980 cock & star privy mark					
		118.300	—	—	.65	1.25

Investiture of New Queen

| 200 | 1980 | 30.500 | — | — | .65 | 1.25 |
| (Y67) | | | | | | |

SILVER

| 200a | 1980 | 157 pcs. | — | — | Rare | — |
| (Y67a) | | | | | | |

GOLD (OMS)

| 200b | 1980 | 7 pcs. | — | — | Rare | — |
| (Y67b) | | | | | | |

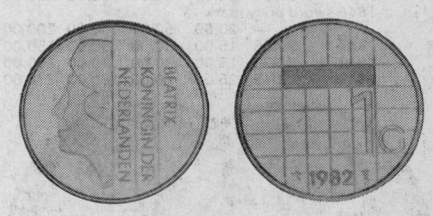

NICKEL

205	1982	31.300	—	—	—	1.00
(Y72)	1982	.010	—	—	Proof	20.00
	1983	5.200	—	—	—	1.00
	1983	.015	—	—	Proof	15.00
	1984	4.000	—	—	—	1.00
	1984	.020	—	—	Proof	7.50
	1985	3.000	—	—	—	1.00
	1985	.017	—	—	Proof	7.50
	1986	12.100	—	—	—	1.00
	1986	.018	—	—	Proof	7.50
	1987	20.000	—	—	—	1.00
	1987	.020	—	—	Proof	7.50
	1988	*22.000	—	—	—	1.00
	1988	.020	—	—	Proof	7.50
	1989	—	—	—	—	1.00

RIJKSDAALDER

.868 SILVER

KM#	Date	Mintage	Fine	VF	XF	Unc
46	1815	12 pcs.	—	—	Proof	8000.
(C78)	1816	.174	550.00	900.00	1200.	1450.

GOLD (OMS)

| 46a | 1814 | — | — | — | Rare | — |
| (C78a) | 1816 | — | — | — | Rare | — |

2-1/2 GULDEN

25.0000 g, .945 SILVER, .7596 oz ASW

KM#	Date	Mintage	Fine	VF	XF	Unc
67 (C81)	1840	.044	125.00	250.00	500.00	750.00
	1840	—	—	—	Proof	Rare

GOLD (OMS)

| 67a (C81a) | 1840 | 2 pcs. | — | — | — | Rare |

25.0000 g, .945 SILVER, .7596 oz ASW
Rev: Similar to KM#67.

69 (C92)	1841	.054	200.00	500.00	1100.	1500.
	1842	1.010	50.00	100.00	225.00	350.00
	1843	.643	60.00	125.00	250.00	400.00
	1844	.279	100.00	200.00	400.00	600.00
	1845	3.270	25.00	50.00	100.00	200.00
	1845 dash between crown & shield					
		.504	40.00	75.00	150.00	300.00
	1845 dot on band of privy mark					
		.154	50.00	75.00	150.00	250.00
	1846 Fleur de lis privy mark					
		3.630	20.00	50.00	150.00	200.00
	1846 sword privy mark					
		—	20.00	50.00	150.00	200.00
	1847	9.465	15.00	30.00	90.00	150.00
	1848	8.333	15.00	30.00	90.00	150.00
	1849	2.049	25.00	70.00	160.00	275.00

Rev: Similar to KM#67.

82 (Y11)	1849	.439	60.00	175.00	300.00	400.00
	1850	5.008	18.00	35.00	90.00	150.00
	1851	3.647	18.00	35.00	90.00	150.00
	1852	4.547	18.00	35.00	90.00	150.00
	1853/2	.234	100.00	300.00	425.00	550.00
	1853	Inc. Ab.	75.00	200.00	325.00	425.00
	1854/2	4.335	60.00	100.00	275.00	400.00
	1854	Inc. Ab.	18.00	35.00	90.00	150.00
	1855	2.082	18.00	35.00	90.00	150.00
	1856	.909	45.00	110.00	200.00	275.00
	1857	3.353	18.00	35.00	90.00	150.00
	1858	8.357	18.00	35.00	90.00	140.00
	1859	4.307	18.00	35.00	100.00	160.00
	1860	.847	50.00	100.00	200.00	300.00
	1861	.876	40.00	100.00	200.00	300.00
	1862	3.304	20.00	35.00	100.00	160.00
	1863	.051	300.00	600.00	1200.	1800.

KM#	Date	Mintage	Fine	VF	XF	Unc
(Y11)	1864	2.034	18.00	30.00	60.00	110.00
	1865	2.288	18.00	30.00	60.00	110.00
	1866	3.563	18.00	30.00	60.00	110.00
	1867	4.949	15.00	25.00	60.00	95.00
	1868	4.040	15.00	25.00	60.00	95.00
	1869	5.046	15.00	25.00	60.00	95.00
	1870	6.640	12.00	22.50	45.00	75.00
	1871	6.875	12.00	22.50	45.00	75.00
	1872	13.416	12.00	22.50	45.00	75.00
	1873	5.515	12.00	22.50	45.00	75.00
	1874 sword privy mark					
		3.040	12.00	22.50	45.00	75.00
	1874 sword in scabbard privy mark					
		9.756	12.00	22.50	45.00	75.00

GOLD (OMS)

| 82a (Y11a) | 1874 sword in scabbard privy mark | | | | | |
| | | — | — | — | — | Rare |

25.0000 g, .945 SILVER, .7596 oz ASW

| 123 | 1898 | .100 | 175.00 | 275.00 | 550.00 | 800.00 |
| (Y27) | 1898 | — | — | — | Proof | 2000. |

GOLD (OMS)

| 123a (Y27a) | 1898 | — | — | — | — | Rare |

25.0000 g, .720 SILVER, .5787 oz ASW

165	1929	4.400	7.00	12.00	20.00	45.00
(Y47)	1930	11.600	5.00	9.00	14.00	20.00
	1931	4.400	5.00	9.00	14.00	20.00
	1932	6.320	5.00	10.00	16.00	25.00
	1932 deep hair lines					
		Inc. Ab.	100.00	175.00	225.00	300.00
	1933	3.560	9.00	15.00	25.00	45.00
	1937	4.000	7.00	10.00	17.50	30.00
	1938	2.000	9.00	15.00	25.00	45.00
	1938 deep hair lines					
		Inc. Ab.	90.00	150.00	200.00	275.00
	1939	3.760	7.00	11.00	17.50	30.00
	1940	4.640	30.00	50.00	90.00	130.00

NOTE: For similar coins dated 1943D with palm tree privy mark, see Netherlands East Indies.

15.0000 g, .720 SILVER, .3472 oz ASW

KM#	Date	Mintage	Fine	VF	XF	BU
185	1959	7.200	—	BV	5.00	12.50
(Y62)	1959	—	—	—	Proof	115.00
	1960	12.800	—	BV	5.00	12.50
	1960	—	—	—	Proof	115.00
	1961	10.000	—	BV	5.00	12.50
	1961	—	—	—	Proof	115.00
	1962	5.000	—	BV	6.25	15.00
	1962	—	—	—	Proof	115.00
	1963	4.000	BV	6.25	12.50	25.00
	1963	—	—	—	Proof	125.00

KM#	Date	Mintage	Fine	VF	XF	BU
(Y62)	1964	2.800	BV	7.50	12.50	25.00
	1964	—	—	—	Proof	125.00
	1966	5.000	—	BV	6.25	15.00
	1966	—	—	—	Proof	125.00

NICKEL

191	1969 fish privy mark					
(Y62a)		1.200	1.50	3.50	5.00	7.50
	1969 fish privy mark					
		—	—	—	Proof	70.00
	1969 cock privy mark					
		15.600	—	—	1.50	3.00
	1969 cock privy mark					
		—	—	—	Proof	70.00
	1970	22.000	—	—	1.50	3.00
	1970	—	—	—	Proof	70.00
	1971	8.000	—	—	1.50	3.00
	1972	20.000	—	—	1.50	3.00
	1978	5.000	—	1.50	2.00	5.00
	1980 cock & star privy mark					
		37.300	—	—	1.50	2.00

400th Anniversary of the Union of Utrecht

| 197 (Y66) | 1979 | 25.000 | — | — | 1.50 | 2.00 |

Investiture of New Queen

| 201 (Y68) | 1980 | 30.500 | — | — | — | 2.00 |

SILVER

| 201a (Y68a) | 1980 | 157 pcs. | — | — | — | Rare |

GOLD (OMS)

| 201b (Y68b) | 1980 | 7 pcs. | — | — | — | Rare |

NICKEL

206	1982	14.300	—	—	—	2.00
(Y73)	1982	.010	—	—	Proof	35.00
	1983	3.800	—	—	—	2.00
	1983	.015	—	—	Proof	27.50
	1984	5.000	—	—	—	2.00
	1984	.020	—	—	Proof	16.00
	1985	7.000	—	—	—	2.00
	1985	.017	—	—	Proof	16.00
	1986	5.800	—	—	—	2.00
	1986	.020	—	—	Proof	16.00
	1987	2.320	—	—	—	2.00
	1987	.018	—	—	Proof	16.00
	1988	*7.000	—	—	—	2.00
	1988	.020	—	—	Proof	16.00
	1989	—	—	—	—	2.00

3 GULDEN

39.2900 g, .893 SILVER, .9270 oz ASW

KM#	Date	Mintage	Fine	VF	XF	Unc
49	1817	12 pcs.	—	—	Rare	—
(C79)	1818	.116	300.00	450.00	800.00	1000.
	1819/8	.151	750.00	1000.	1400.	1800.
	1819	Inc. Ab.	270.00	450.00	800.00	1000.
	1820	.713	270.00	450.00	800.00	1000.
	1821	.277	270.00	450.00	800.00	1000.
	1821 w/o engraver's name					
		Inc. Ab.	500.00	750.00	1000.	1250.
	1822	.296	500.00	750.00	1000.	1500.
	1822 w/o engraver's name					
		Inc. Ab.	500.00	750.00	1000.	1500.
	1823	.255	500.00	750.00	850.00	1000.
	1823B	.014	1500.	3000.	6000.	7500.
	1824	.644	300.00	450.00	800.00	1000.
	1824 dash between crown & shield					
		Inc. Ab.	300.00	450.00	800.00	1000.
	1830/20	.246	300.00	450.00	800.00	1000.
	1830/24	I.A.	300.00	450.00	800.00	1000.
	1830/24 dash between crown & shield					
		Inc. Ab.	325.00	500.00	900.00	1200.
	1830	Inc. Ab.	300.00	450.00	800.00	1000.
	1831/24	.117	300.00	450.00	800.00	1000.
	1831/24 dash between crown & shield					
		Inc. Ab.	300.00	450.00	800.00	1000.
	1831	Inc. Ab.	300.00	450.00	800.00	1000.
	1832/21	.371	300.00	450.00	800.00	1000.
	1832/22	I.A.	300.00	450.00	800.00	1000.
	1832/23	I.A.	300.00	450.00	800.00	1000.
	1832/24	I.A.	300.00	450.00	800.00	1000.
	1832/24 dash between crown & shield					
		Inc. Ab.	300.00	450.00	800.00	1000.
	1832	Inc. Ab.	300.00	450.00	800.00	1000.

GOLD (OMS)

49a	1823	—	—	—	Rare	—
(C79a)						

5 GULDEN

3.3645 g, .900 GOLD, .0973 oz AGW

60	1826B	.843	175.00	275.00	375.00	600.00
(C82)	1827	.518	175.00	275.00	375.00	750.00
	1827B	1.629	175.00	275.00	375.00	600.00

72	1843	1,595	300.00	900.00	1500.	1800.
(C93)						

Obv: Bust right. Rev: Crowned arms within branches.

77	1848	50 pcs.	600.00	1500.	2000.	2500.
(1)						

94	1850	—	600.00	1200.	1500.	2200.
(Y12)	1851	.010	250.00	700.00	1000.	1500.

KM#	Date	Mintage	Fine	VF	XF	Unc
151	1912	1.000	50.00	75.00	125.00	175.00
(Y31)	1912	120 pcs.	—	—	Matte Proof	500.00

BRONZE CLAD NICKEL

210	1988	75.000	—	—	—	2.50
	1988	.020	—	—	Proof	5.00

10 GULDEN

6.7290 g, .900 GOLD, .1947 oz AGW

56	1818	—	1000.	1400.	1750.	3500.
(C83)	1819	.107	600.00	850.00	1200.	2000.
	1820	.033	600.00	850.00	1200.	2000.
	1822	.048	600.00	850.00	1200.	2000.
	1823	.266	150.00	275.00	350.00	800.00
	1824	.336	150.00	275.00	350.00	800.00
	1824B	3.735	150.00	275.00	350.00	800.00
	1825	.228	150.00	275.00	350.00	800.00
	1825B	3.821	150.00	275.00	350.00	800.00
	1826	—	1000.	1400.	1750.	3500.
	1826B	.079	600.00	850.00	1200.	2000.
	1827	.134	450.00	575.00	700.00	1200.
	1827B	—	600.00	850.00	1200.	2000.
	1828	.015	900.00	1250.	1600.	2700.
	1828B	.562	150.00	275.00	350.00	800.00
	1829	9,484	600.00	850.00	1200.	2000.
	1829B	.084	600.00	850.00	1200.	2000.
	1830/28	.568	1000.	1200.	1500.	3000.
	1830	Inc.Ab.	150.00	275.00	350.00	800.00
	1831/0	.099	600.00	850.00	1200.	2000.
	1831	Inc. Ab.	150.00	275.00	350.00	800.00
	1832/1	1.372	600.00	850.00	1200.	2000.
	1832	Inc. Ab.	150.00	275.00	350.00	800.00
	1833	.721	150.00	275.00	350.00	800.00
	1837	.458	150.00	275.00	350.00	800.00
	1839	.326	150.00	275.00	350.00	800.00
	1840	2.760	150.00	275.00	350.00	600.00

71	1842	860 pcs.	1100.	1800.	2500.	3500.
(C94)						

78	1848	*50 pcs.	1000.	1500.	2000.	3250.
(2)	1848	—	—	—	Proof	5000

95	1850	—	800.00	1750.	2250.	3000.
(Y13)	1850	—	—	—	Proof	3500.
	1851	.010	450.00	900.00	1250.	1750.

KM#	Date	Mintage	Fine	VF	XF	Unc
105	1875	4.110	—	BV	100.00	115.00
(Y-B16)						

106	1876	1.581	—	BV	100.00	120.00
(Y-A16)	1877	1.108	—	BV	100.00	120.00
	1879/7	.581	125.00	175.00	250.00	350.00
	1879	Inc. Ab.	—	BV	100.00	120.00
	1880	.050	BV	110.00	145.00	175.00
	1885	.067	BV	110.00	145.00	175.00
	1886	.054	100.00	125.00	165.00	200.00
	1887	.041	100.00	125.00	165.00	200.00
	1888	.036	125.00	250.00	350.00	450.00
	1889	.205	—	BV	100.00	120.00

118	1892	61 pcs.	1400.	2500.	4000.	5000.
(Y28)	1892	—	—	—	Proof	7000.
	1895/1	149 pcs.	1400.	2500.	3500.	4500.
	1895	Inc. Ab.	900.00	2000.	3000.	4000.
	1897	.454	—	BV	100.00	150.00

124	1898	.099	125.00	175.00	250.00	375.00
(Y29)						

149	1911	.775	—	BV	100.00	120.00
(Y30)	1911	8 pcs.	—	—	Proof	1750
	1912	3.000	—	BV	100.00	120.00
	1913	1.133	—	BV	100.00	120.00
	1917	4.000	—	BV	100.00	120.00

162	1925	2.000	—	BV	100.00	120.00
(Y32)	1925	12 pcs.	—	—	Proof	1500.
	1926	2.500	—	BV	100.00	120.00
	1926	—	—	—	Proof	1300.
	1927	1.000	—	BV	100.00	120.00
	1932	4.324	—	BV	100.00	120.00
	1933	2.462	—	BV	100.00	120.00

1338 Kingdom of the Netherlands / NETHERLANDS

25.0000 g, .720 SILVER, .5787 oz ASW
25th Anniversary of Liberation

KM#	Date	Mintage	Fine	VF	XF	Unc
195	1970	6.000	—	—	7.00	9.00
(Y64)	1970	.020	—	—	P/L	27.50
	1970	40 pcs.	—	—	Proof	300.00

196	1973	4.500	—	—	7.00	9.00
(Y65)	1973	.106	—	—	Proof	22.50

25th Anniversary of Reign

20 GULDEN

13.4580 g, .900 GOLD, .3894 oz AGW
Obv: Bust right. Rev: Crowned arms within branches.

79	1848	*50 pcs.	1250.	3000.	3500.	4000.
(3)						

96	1851	2,500	600.00	1350.	1750.	2000.
(Y14)	1853	136 pcs.	1000.	2250.	3000.	3750.

50 GULDEN

25.0000 g, .925 SILVER, .7435 oz ASW
Dutch-American Friendship

KM#	Date	Mintage	Fine	VF	XF	Unc
207	1982	.190	—	—	—	40.00
(Y74)	1982	.050	—	—	Proof	55.00

GOLD (OMS)

207a	1982	2 pcs.	—	—	—	2000.
(Y74a)						

25.0000 g, .925 SILVER, .7435 oz ASW
William of Orange

208	1984	1.125	—	—	P/L	32.50
(Y75)	1984	.060	—	—	Proof	42.50

Golden Wedding of Queen Mother and Prince Bernhard

209	1987	1.580	—	—	—	35.00
	1987	.053	—	—	Proof	45.00

300th Anniversary of William and Mary

KM#	Date	Mintage	Fine	VF	XF	Unc
212	1988	1.080	—	—	—	35.00
	1988	.050	—	—	Proof	50.00

TRADE COINAGE
DUCAT

3.5000 g, .983 GOLD, .1106 oz AGW
Utrecht Mint

45	1814	2.930	100.00	200.00	250.00	350.00
(C84)	1815	.673	120.00	225.00	275.00	375.00
	1815 cloverleaf					
		.614	120.00	225.00	275.00	375.00
	1816	.221	130.00	250.00	325.00	450.00

50.1	1817	.495	220.00	400.00	550.00	650.00
(C85)	1818	1.552	80.00	130.00	175.00	250.00
	1819	.111	100.00	200.00	275.00	350.00
	1820	.010	200.00	350.00	425.00	600.00
	1821	.015	200.00	350.00	425.00	600.00
	1822	.012	200.00	350.00	425.00	600.00
	1824B	8,000	350.00	600.00	900.00	1200.
	1825	.119	100.00	200.00	275.00	350.00
	1825B	.056	200.00	350.00	500.00	600.00
	1827	.138	130.00	250.00	325.00	450.00
	1827B	.027	220.00	400.00	500.00	600.00
	1828/7	.622	120.00	225.00	275.00	375.00
	1828	Inc. Ab.	120.00	225.00	275.00	375.00
	1828B	.534	100.00	200.00	275.00	350.00
	1829/8B	.247	200.00	350.00	500.00	600.00
	1829B	Inc. Ab.	200.00	350.00	500.00	600.00
	1829	1.153	80.00	130.00	175.00	200.00
	1830B	.011	300.00	425.00	550.00	750.00
	1831	.411	80.00	130.00	175.00	200.00
	1833	.247	100.00	200.00	275.00	350.00
	1836/5	.236	150.00	325.00	600.00	750.00
	1836	Inc. Ab.	110.00	225.00	325.00	450.00
	1839	.151	80.00	170.00	250.00	300.00
	1840 Fleur de lis privy mark					
		.103	110.00	225.00	300.00	425.00

Leningrad Mint

50.2	1818	1.350	80.00	130.00	175.00	250.00
	1827	.350	130.00	250.00	325.00	450.00
	1828	1.300	120.00	225.00	275.00	375.00
	1829	.150	80.00	130.00	175.00	200.00
	1830	2.000	80.00	130.00	175.00	200.00
	1831	1.000	80.00	130.00	175.00	200.00
	1832	1.000	100.00	200.00	275.00	350.00
	1833	.350	100.00	200.00	275.00	350.00
	1834	.150	200.00	350.00	450.00	600.00
	1835	.650	110.00	225.00	325.00	425.00
	1836	.300	110.00	225.00	325.00	450.00
	1837	1.400	80.00	170.00	250.00	350.00
	1838	1.200	80.00	170.00	250.00	350.00
	1839	1.350	80.00	170.00	250.00	350.00
	1840 torch privy mark					
		—	80.00	175.00	250.00	350.00

70.1	1841 torch privy mark					
(C95)		4.000	80.00	100.00	150.00	225.00

Utrecht Mint

70.2	1841 Fleur de lis privy mark					
		.096	100.00	150.00	200.00	350.00

83.1	1849	.014	70.00	140.00	200.00	300.00
(Y15)	1872	.030	150.00	400.00	700.00	1000.
	1873	.040	150.00	400.00	700.00	1000.
	1874	.044	150.00	400.00	700.00	1000.
	1876	.044	150.00	400.00	700.00	1000.
	1877	.015	150.00	400.00	700.00	1000.
	1878	.087	150.00	400.00	700.00	1000.
	1879	.020	150.00	400.00	700.00	1000.
	1880	.025	150.00	400.00	700.00	1000.
	1885	.081	125.00	350.00	600.00	800.00

KM#	Date	Mintage	Fine	VF	XF	Unc
	1894	.030	110.00	225.00	300.00	450.00
	1895/55	.058	110.00	225.00	300.00	450.00
	1895/59	I.A.	110.00	225.00	300.00	450.00
	1895	Inc. Ab.	90.00	175.00	270.00	350.00
	1899	.061	90.00	175.00	270.00	350.00
	1901	.029	110.00	220.00	275.00	500.00
	1903	.091	90.00	180.00	270.00	450.00
	1905	.088	90.00	180.00	270.00	450.00
	1906	.029	110.00	220.00	275.00	450.00
	1908	.091	90.00	180.00	270.00	350.00
	1909	halberd w/star privy mark				
		.106	80.00	150.00	250.00	350.00
	1909	sea horse privy mark				
		.030	130.00	250.00	300.00	450.00
	1910	.421	80.00	150.00	225.00	350.00
	1910	—	—	—	Proof	700.00
	1912	.148	80.00	150.00	225.00	350.00
	1913	.205	80.00	150.00	225.00	350.00
	1914	.247	80.00	150.00	225.00	350.00
	1916	.117	80.00	150.00	225.00	350.00
	1916	—	—	—	Proof	450.00
	1917	.217	BV	65.00	80.00	120.00
	1920	.293	BV	65.00	80.00	120.00
	1921	.409	BV	60.00	70.00	100.00
	1922	.050	80.00	150.00	225.00	400.00
	1923	.107	BV	75.00	150.00	250.00
	1924	.084	BV	75.00	150.00	250.00
	1925	.573	BV	60.00	70.00	100.00
	1925	Inc. Ab.	—	—	Proof	250.00
	1926	.191	BV	60.00	80.00	120.00
	1927	.654	—	BV	55.00	75.00
	1928	.572	—	BV	55.00	75.00
	1932	.088	100.00	200.00	350.00	450.00
	1937	.117	BV	—	90.00	110.00	150.00

Leningrad Mint

| 83.2 | 1849 | 4.750 | 70.00 | 140.00 | 200.00 | 300.00 |

Similar to KM#190.2 but knight w/right leg bent.

190.1 (Y63)	1960	3,605	—	—	P/L	475.00
	1972	.029	—	—	P/L	75.00
	1974	.087	—	—	P/L	70.00
	1974 medal struck					
		2,000	—	—	P/L	200.00
	1975	.205	—	—	P/L	65.00
	1976	*.038	—	—	P/L	180.00
	1978	.029	—	—	P/L	100.00
	1985	.104	—	—	P/L	85.00

*NOTE: Of the original 37,844 pieces struck, 32,000 were melted.

Obv: Knight w/left leg bent, larger letters in legend.

| 190.2 | 1986 | .095 | — | — | P/L | 85.00 |
| | 1989 | — | — | — | Proof | 85.00 |

2 DUCATS
6.9880 g, .983 GOLD, .2209 oz AGW

| 97 | 1854 | — | — | — | 8000. | 10,000. |
| (Y16) | 1867 | — | — | — | — | 18,000. |

| 211 | 1988 | .024 | — | — | P/L | 200.00 |
| | 1989 | — | — | — | Proof | 150.00 |

SELECT SETS (SS)
Fleur de Coin

KM#	Date	Mintage	Identification	Issue Price	Mkt. Val.
SS1	1971(6)	1,000	KM180-183,184a,191	—	30.00
SS1a	1972(1)	2,000	KM191	—	6.00
SS2	1972(5)	2,000	KM180-183,184a	—	35.00
SS3	1973(5)	10,000	KM180-183,184a	—	27.50
SS4	1974(3)	10,000	KM180-182	—	12.50
SS5	1975(6)	12,000	*KM180-183,184a	—	30.00
SS6	1976(5)	15,000	KM180-183,184a	—	45.00
SS7	1977(5)	17,000	KM180-183,184a	—	40.00
SS8	1978(6)	21,500	KM180-183,184a,191	6.50	25.00
SS9	1979(6)	50,000	KM180-183,184a,197	6.50	12.50
SS10	1980(6)	249,732	KM180-183,184a,191	—	10.00
SS11	1980(2)	504,000	KM200-201	—	10.00
SS12	1980(2)	157 pcs.	KM200-201, Silver	—	750.00
SS13	1980(2)	7 pcs.	KM200b-201b	—	—
SS14	1982(5)	242,701	KM202-206	12.00	7.50
SS15	1983(5)	156,165	KM202-206	—	10.00
SS16	1984(5)	131,748	KM202-206	12.00	10.00
SS17	1985(5)	113,079	KM202-206	—	12.50
SS18	1986(5)	112,190	KM202-206	—	8.50
SS19	1987(5)	120,323	KM202-206	—	15.00
SS20	1988(6)	133,100	KM202-206,210	16.00	17.50

*NOTE: Set also includes 1974 25 cents.

PROOF SETS (PS)

KM#	Date	Mintage	Identification	Issue Price	Mkt. Val.
PS1	1948(4)	50	KM175-178 w/Proof	—	500.00
PS2	1948(4)	—	KM175-178	—	150.00
PS3	1949(4)	—	KM180-183 head left	—	Rare
PS4	1950(4)	—	KM180-183 w/Proof	—	400.00
PS5	1950(4)	—	KM180-183	—	100.00
PS6	1951(4)	—	KM180-183	—	80.00
PS7	1952(2)	—	KM180-181	—	50.00
PS8	1953(2)	—	KM180-181	—	50.00
PS9	1954(5)	—	KM180-184	—	135.00
PS10	1955(5)	—	KM180-184	—	135.00
PS11	1956(5)	—	KM180-184	—	135.00
PS12	1957(5)	—	KM180-184	—	135.00
PS13	1958(5)	—	KM180-184	—	135.00
PS14	1959(3)	—	KM180,182,185	—	145.00
PS15	1960(5)	—	KM180-183,185	—	200.00
PS16	1961(5)	—	KM180-183,185	—	200.00
PS17	1962(5)	40	KM180-183,185	—	200.00
PS18	1963(6)	40	KM180-185	—	300.00
PS19	1964(6)	40	KM180-185	—	300.00
PS20	1965(5)	—	KM180-184	—	150.00
PS21	1966(5)	—	KM180-185	—	200.00
PS22	1967(5)	—	KM180-183,184a	—	125.00
PS23	1968(3)	—	KM180,182-183	—	100.00
PS24	1969(6) Cock	—	KM180-183,184a,191	—	200.00
PS25	1969(6) Fish	—	KM180-183,184a,191	—	225.00
PS26	1970(6)	—	KM180-183,184a,191	—	200.00

NOTE: From 1970 until 1982 no proof sets were struck for collectors. Approximately 60 sets per year had been struck and presented to various officials, etc.

PS27	1982(5)	10,000	KM202-206	35.00	145.00
PS28	1983(5)	15,000	KM202-206	35.00	70.00
PS29	1984(5)	20,406	KM202-206	35.00	60.00
PS30	1985(5)	17,100	KM202-206	35.00	60.00
PS31	1986(5)	19,500	KM202-206	35.00	50.00
PS32	1987(5)	18,100	KM202-206	35.00	50.00
PS33	1988(6)	19,550	KM202-206,210	53.50	55.00

NETHERLANDS ANTILLES

The Netherlands Antilles, comprise two groups of islands in the West Indies: Aruba, Bonaire and Curacao and their dependencies near the Venezuelan coast and St. Eustatius, Saba, and the southern part of St. Martin (St. Maarten) southeast of Puerto Rico. The island group has an area of 371 sq. mi. (961 sq. km.) and a population of *176,000. Capital: Willemstad. Chief industries are the refining of crude oil and tourism. Petroleum products and phosphates are exported.

On Dec. 15, 1954, the Netherlands Antilles were given complete domestic autonomy and granted equality within the Kingdom with Surinam and the Netherlands.

SAINT EUSTATIUS

St. Eustatius (Sint Eustatius, Statia), a Netherlands West Indian island located in the Leeward Islands of the Lesser Antilles nine miles northwest of St. Kitts, has an area of 12 sq. mi. (21 sq. km.) and a population of about 2,000. It is part of the Netherlands Antilles. The island's capital is Oranjestad. The chief industries are farming, fishing, and tourism.

Between 1630 and 1640 the Dutch seized Curacao, Saba, St. Martin and St. Eustatius, all valuable as piloting and smuggling depots. The territorial acquisitions were confirmed to the Dutch by the Treaty of Munster in 1648. Under the guidance of merchants from Flushing, St. Eustatius became a prosperous entrepot of neutral trade. On Feb. 3, 1781, British Admiral George Rodney, acting under orders, captured the island and confiscated much valuable booty. Before passing permanently into Dutch hands, St. Eustatius was attacked or captured several times by the French and English, and was in English hands during the Napoleonic Wars from 1810 to 1814.

RULERS
Dutch

MONETARY SYSTEM
6 Stuivers = 1 Reaal

COUNTERMARKED COINAGE

SE incuse countermark on French Guiana 2 Sous coins were official.

These were followed by raised SE countermarks on a variety of worn billon & silver coins generally thought to be forgeries.

From 1809 all coins had to be revalidated with a P countermark. Both raised and incuse SE varieties as well as unmarked coins were revalidated.

STUIVER

COPPER
c/m: Raised SE.

KM#	Date	Mintage	Good	VG	Fine	VF
1.2	ND(1797-1809)	—	40.00	65.00	90.00	125.00

BILLON

| 1.2a | ND(1797-1809) | — | 40.00 | 65.00 | 90.00 | 125.00 |

SILVER

| 1.2b | ND(1797-1809) | — | 100.00 | 150.00 | 200.00 | 250.00 |

BRITISH OCCUPATION
STUIVER

VARIOUS METALS
c/m: P revalidation on older SE.

| 4 | ND(1809-12) | — | 25.00 | 45.00 | 65.00 | 85.00 |

2 REALES
SILVER
c/m: P in circle of dots.

| 7.1 | ND(1810-12) | — | — | — | Rare | — |

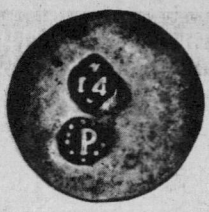

c/m: P in circle of dots on St. Bartholomew
14 Stuivers, KM#11.

KM#	Date	Mintage	Good	VG	Fine	VF
7.2	ND(1810-12)	—	—	—	Rare	

SAINT MARTIN

St. Martin (Sint Maarten), the only island in the Antilles owned by two European powers (France and the Netherlands), is located in the Leeward Islands of the Lesser Antilles five miles south of the British island of Anguilla. The French northern section of the island (St. Martin) is a dependency of the French Department of Guadeloupe. It has an area of 20 sq. mi. (51 sq. km.) and a population of about 4,500. Capital: Le Marigot. The Dutch southern section of the island (Sint Maarten) has an area of 17 sq. mi. (34 sq. km.) and a population of about 8,000. Capital: Philipsburg. The chief industries are farming, fishing, and tourism. Salt, horses, and mules are exported.

Although nominally a Spanish possession at the time, St. Martin was occupied by French freebooters in 1638, but when Spain relinquished claim to the island in 1648 it was peaceably divided between France and Holland in recognition of the merchant communities already established on the island by nationals of both powers. St. Martin has remained under dual French-Dutch ownership to the present time, except for a period during the Napoleonic Wars when the British seized and occupied it.

MONETARY SYSTEM
6 Stuivers = 1 Reaal
20 Stuivers = 1 Gulden
12 (later 15) Reaals = 1 Peso

COUNTERMARKED COINAGE
2 STUIVERS

BILLON
c/m: StM in beaded circle plus Incuse M
on French Guiana 2 Sous.

| 3 | ND(1820) | — | 80.00 | 120.00 | 150.00 | 180.00 |

c/m: Incuse Fleur-de-Lys on French Guiana 2 Sous.

| 4 | ND(1805) | — | 100.00 | 150.00 | 200.00 | 250.00 |

SILVER
c/m: Raised Fleur-de-Lis

| 5 | ND(1805) | — | 30.00 | 50.00 | 75.00 | 100.00 |

18 STUIVERS

SILVER
c/m: ST. MARTIN and arrows on 1/5 cut of Spanish or
Spanish Colonial 8 Reales.

| 12 | ND(1809) | — | 125.00 | 200.00 | 350.00 | 500.00 |

CURACAO

The island of Curacao, the largest of the Netherlands Antilles, which is an autonomous part of the Kingdom of the Netherlands located in the Caribbean Sea 40 miles off the coast of Venezuela, has an area of 173 sq. mi. (472 sq. km.) and a population of 150,000. Capital: Willemstad. The chief industries are the refining of crude oil imported from Venezuela and Colombia and tourism. Petroleum products, salt, phosphates and cattle are exported.

Curacao was discovered by Spanish navigator Alonso de Ojeda in 1499 and was settled by Spain in 1527. The Dutch West India Company took the island from Spain in 1634 and administered it until 1787, when it was surrendered to the crown. The Dutch held it thereafter except for two periods during the Napoleonic Wars, 1800-1803 and 1807-16, when it was occupied by the British. During World War II, Curacao refined 60 percent of the oil used by the Allies; the refineries were protected by U.S. troops after Germany invaded the Netherlands in 1940.

During the second occupation of the Napoleonic period, the British created an emergency coinage for Curacao by cutting the Spanish dollar into five equal segments and countermarking each piece with a rosette indent.

BATAVIAN REPUBLIC
MONETARY SYSTEM
1799-1803

1 Cent (U.S.) = 2-1/2 Stuivers
6 Stuivers = 1 Reaal
12 Realen = 1 Peso
20 Stuivers = 1 Gulden
20 Gulden = 8 Pesos = 1 Johannes
(1/2 Dobra)

9 STUIVERS

SILVER
c/m: 9 in oval indent on Spanish Colonial 1 Real.

KM#	Date	Mintage	Good	VG	Fine	VF
4	ND 1801	—	40.00	60.00	75.00	85.00

NOTE: The above coins along with similar coins bearing the numbers 3, 5, 14-18 are of questionable origin. Thus, they are not listed in Craig. Pridmore states these as unattributable.

3 REAAL

SILVER
c/m: Five-petalled rosace in circle on 1/4 cut of
Spanish or Spanish Colonial 8 Reales

KM#	Date	Mintage	VG	Fine	VF	XF
7	ND(c.1810)	.030	55.00	135.00	250.00	300.00

BRITISH OCCUPATION
1807-1816

MONETARY SYSTEM
1807-1825

15 Reales = 1 Peso
6 Stuivers = 1 Reaal
27 Gulden = 6 Pesos = 1 Johannes

3 REAAL

SILVER
Reconstructed 5 segments
c/m: Five-petalled rosace in circle on 1/5 cut of Spanish
or Spanish Colonial 8 reales

| 13 | ND(1815) | .040 | 50.00 | 75.00 | 250.00 | 300.00 |

3-1/2 REAAL

SILVER
c/m: Additional 21 in oval indent on KM#13.

| 16 | ND(1814) | — | 180.00 | 450.00 | 725.00 | 900.00 |

22 GULDEN

GOLD
c/m: 22 in square on Brazilian 1/2 Dobra.

| 19 | ND | — | — | — | Rare | |

NETHERLANDS RESTORED
1816

STUIVER

.300 SILVER

KM#	Date	Mintage	Fine	VF	XF	Unc
24	1822	.529	80.00	125.00	200.00	400.00

NOTE: Struck also in 1840-41, circulating at that time as a 2 Cent piece.

1/4 REAAL

SILVER

KM#	Date	Mintage	Fine	VF	XF	Unc
25	1821	Unique?	—	—	—	—

REAAL

SILVER
Rev: 4 acorns.

| 26.1 | 1821 | .121 | 130.00 | 275.00 | 360.00 | 675.00 |

Rev: 7 acorns.
| 26.2 | 1821 | Inc. Ab. | 130.00 | 275.00 | 360.00 | 675.00 |

Rev: 8 acorns.
| 26.3 | 1821 | Inc. Ab. | 130.00 | 275.00 | 360.00 | 675.00 |

Rev: 9 acorns.
| 26.4 | 1821 | Inc. Ab. | 130.00 | 275.00 | 360.00 | 675.00 |

Rev: 12 acorns.
| 26.5 | 1821 | Inc. Ab. | 130.00 | 275.00 | 360.00 | 675.00 |

1/4 GUILDER

SILVER
Reconstructed 4 segments
c/m: C in oval indent on 1/4 cut of Netherlands
1 Gulden.

KM#	Date	Mintage	VG	Fine	VF	XF
27	ND(1838)	.024	80.00	250.00	400.00	500.00

3 REAAL

SILVER
Reconstructed 5 segments
c/m: 3 in circle on 1/5 cut of Spanish or Colonial
8 Reales.

| 28 | ND(1818) | .078 | 70.00 | 140.00 | 210.00 | 300.00 |

c/m: 3 in dentilated circle on 1/5 cut of Spanish or
Colonial 8 Reales.

| 29 | ND(1819-25) | — | 35.00 | 75.00 | 125.00 | 250.00 |

5 REAAL

SILVER
c/m: 5 in circle on 1/3 cut of Spanish or Colonial

8 Reales.

KM#	Date	Mintage	VG	Fine	VF	XF
30	ND(1818)	3,000	725.00	2150.	3500.	4500.

MODERN COINAGE
MONETARY SYSTEM
100 Cents = 1 Gulden
CENT

BRONZE

KM#	Date	Mintage	Fine	VF	XF	Unc
39	1942P	2.500	3.50	7.50	15.00	37.50

NOTE: This coin was also circulated in Surinam. For similar coins dated 1943P & 1957-1960, see Surinam.

41	1944D	3.000	.75	1.25	4.00	8.00
	1947	1.500	.75	1.50	5.00	10.00
	1947	80 pcs.	—	—	Proof	25.00

2-1/2 CENTS

BRONZE

42	1944D	1.000	.75	1.25	4.00	8.00
	1947	.500	.75	1.25	4.00	8.00
	1947	80 pcs.	—	—	Proof	25.00
	1948	1.000	.50	.75	1.50	3.00
	1948	75 pcs.	—	—	Proof	25.00

5 CENTS

COPPER-NICKEL

40	1943	8.595	1.75	3.00	6.00	12.00

NOTE: The above piece does not bear either a palm tree privy mark or a mint mark, but it was struck expressly for use in Curacao and Surinam. This homeland type of Y#34 was last issued in the Netherlands in 1940.

47	1948	1.000	.75	2.00	4.00	6.00
	1948	75 pcs.	—	—	Proof	100.00

1/10 GULDEN

1.4000 g, .640 SILVER, .0288 oz ASW

36	1901	.300	15.00	45.00	75.00	100.00
	1901	40 pcs.	—	—	Proof	200.00

43	1944D	1.500	1.00	2.50	4.00	8.50
	1947	1.000	.75	2.00	3.00	7.00
	1947	80 pcs.	—	—	Proof	100.00

KM#	Date	Mintage	Fine	VF	XF	Unc
48	1948	1.000	1.75	3.00	6.00	12.00
	1948	75 pcs.	—	—	Proof	100.00

10 CENTS

1.4000 g, .640 SILVER, .0288 oz ASW

37	1941P	.800	10.00	15.00	30.00	42.50
	1943P	4.500	6.50	9.50	20.00	30.00

NOTE: Both these coins were also circulated in Surinam. For coins dated 1942P, see Surinam.

1/4 GULDEN

3.5800 g, .640 SILVER, .0736 oz ASW

35	1900	.480	10.00	30.00	50.00	100.00
	1900	40 pcs.	—	—	Proof	200.00

44	1944D	1.500	.75	2.00	4.00	6.00
	1947	1.000	.75	2.50	5.00	7.50
	1947	80 pcs.	—	—	Proof	100.00

25 CENTS

3.5800 g, .640 SILVER, .0736 oz ASW

38	1941P	1.100	3.50	5.50	9.00	13.00
	1943/1P	2.500	4.25	6.50	10.00	20.00
	1943P	Inc.Ab.	3.00	5.00	8.00	10.00

NOTE: Both these coins were also circulated in Surinam. For similar coins dated 1943, 1944 & 1945-P with acorn mintmark see Netherlands.

GULDEN

10.0000 g, .720 SILVER, .2315 oz ASW

45	1944D	.500	4.50	7.50	12.50	26.50

2-1/2 GULDEN

25.0000 g, .720 SILVER, .5787 oz ASW

KM#	Date	Mintage	Fine	VF	XF	Unc
46	1944D	.200	4.25	6.00	8.50	15.00

PROOF SETS (PS)

KM#	Date	Mintage	Identification	Issue Price	Mkt. Val.
PS1	1901(2)	40	KM36(1901), KM35(1900)	—	400.00
PS2	1947(4)	80	KM41-44	—	250.00
PS3	1948(3)	75	KM42,47-48	—	225.00

NETHERLANDS ANTILLES

RULERS
Juliana, 1948-1980
Beatrix, 1980-

MINT MARKS
Utrecht - privy marks only
FM - Franklin Mint, U.S.A.*

*NOTE: From 1975 the Franklin Mint has produced coinage in up to 3 different qualities. Qualities of issue are designated in ( ) after each date and are defined as follows:

(M) MATTE - Normal circulation strike or a dull finish produced by sandblasting special uncirculated (polish finish) or proof quality dies.

(U) SPECIAL UNCIRCULATED - Polished or proof-like in appearance without any frosted features.

(P) PROOF - The highest quality obtainable having mirror-like fields and frosted features.

MONETARY SYSTEM
100 Cents = 1 Gulden

CENT

BRONZE

KM#	Date	Mintage	Fine	VF	XF	Unc
1	1952 fish	1.000	.75	2.75	3.50	6.00
	1952	100 pcs.	—	—	Proof	75.00
	1954	1.000	.50	2.25	3.25	5.75
	1954	200 pcs.	—	—	Proof	20.00
	1957	1.000	.50	2.25	3.25	5.75
	1957	250 pcs.	—	—	Proof	20.00
	1959	1.000	.25	.75	1.75	3.25
	1959	250 pcs.	—	—	Proof	20.00
	1960	300 pcs.	—	—	Proof	20.00
	1961	1.000	.25	.50	1.75	3.25
	1963	1.000	.25	.50	1.75	3.25
	1963	—	—	—	Proof	20.00
	1964	—	—	—	Proof	25.00
	1965	1.200	.25	.50	1.75	3.25
	1965	—	—	—	Proof	20.00
	1967	.850	.50	2.00	3.00	6.00
	1967	—	—	—	Proof	20.00
	1968 fish	.900	.75	2.00	3.00	4.00
	1968 star & fish	.700	1.50	3.00	6.75	12.50
	1970 cock	.200	.75	2.00	2.75	6.00
	1970	—	—	—	Proof	20.00

8	1970 cock	1.200	.10	.25	.50	1.00
	1970	—	—	—	Proof	17.50
	1971	3.000	.10	.25	.50	1.00
	1971	—	—	—	Proof	17.50
	1972	1.000	.10	.25	.50	1.00
	1973	3.000	.10	.20	.35	.75
	1973	—	—	—	Proof	17.50
	1974	3.000	.10	.20	.35	.75
	1974	—	—	—	Proof	17.50
	1975	2.000	.10	.20	.50	1.00
	1975	—	—	—	Proof	17.50
	1976	3.000	—	.10	.25	.50
	1977	4.000	—	.10	.25	.50
	1978	2.000	—	.10	.25	.50

ALUMINUM

8a	1979 cock	7.500	—	.10	.20	.35
	1979	—	—	—	Proof	7.50
	1980 cock & star	2.500	—	.10	.20	.35
	1981 anvil	2.400	—	.10	.20	.35
	1982	2.400	—	.10	.20	.35
	1983	2.900	—	.10	.20	.35
	1984	3.600	—	.10	.20	.35
	1985	—	—	.10	.20	.35

NETHERLANDS ANTILLES 1342

2-1/2 CENTS

BRONZE

KM#	Date	Mintage	Fine	VF	XF	Unc
5	1956 fish	.400	.50	1.00	4.00	8.00
	1956	500 pcs.	—	—	Proof	20.00
	1959	1.000	.25	.75	2.75	6.00
	1959	250 pcs.	—	—	Proof	25.00
	1965 fish	.500	.25	.75	3.50	7.50
	1965	—	—	—	Proof	25.00
	1965 star & fish	.150	.75	1.50	5.00	10.00

KM#	Date	Mintage	Fine	VF	XF	Unc
9	1970 cock	.500	.20	.30	.75	1.50
	1970	—	—	—	Proof	20.00
	1971	3.000	.20	.30	.50	.75
	1971	—	—	—	Proof	20.00
	1973	1.000	—	.25	.50	.75
	1973	—	—	—	Proof	20.00
	1974	1.000	.20	.25	.50	.75
	1974	—	—	—	Proof	20.00
	1975	1.000	.20	.25	.50	.75
	1976	1.000	.20	.25	.50	.75
	1977	1.000	.20	.25	.50	.75
	1978	1.500	.20	.25	.50	.75

ALUMINUM

KM#	Date	Mintage	Fine	VF	XF	Unc
9a	1979 cock	2.000	—	.10	.25	.50
	1979	—	—	—	Proof	10.00
	1980 cock & star	2.000	—	.10	.25	.50
	1981 anvil	1.000	—	.10	.25	.50
	1982	1.000	—	.10	.25	.50
	1983	1.000	—	.10	.25	.50
	1984	1.000	—	.10	.25	.50
	1985	—	—	.10	.25	.50

5 CENTS

COPPER-NICKEL

KM#	Date	Mintage	Fine	VF	XF	Unc
6	1957	.500	.75	1.00	2.75	5.50
	1957	250 pcs.	—	—	Proof	25.00
	1962	.250	1.25	5.50	10.00	15.00
	1962	200 pcs.	—	—	Proof	25.00
	1963	.400	.75	1.00	2.75	5.50
	1963	—	—	—	Proof	25.00
	1965	.500	.75	1.00	2.75	5.50
	1965	—	—	—	Proof	25.00
	1967	.600	.75	2.00	4.50	6.75
	1967	—	—	—	Proof	25.00
	1970	.450	.75	1.00	2.75	5.50
	1970	—	—	—	Proof	25.00

KM#	Date	Mintage	Fine	VF	XF	Unc
13	1971 cock	2.000	.10	.20	.35	.75
	1971	—	—	—	Proof	22.50
	1974	.500	.50	1.50	3.00	5.00
	1974	—	—	—	Proof	22.50
	1975	2.000	.10	.20	.35	.75
	1975	—	—	—	Proof	22.50
	1976	1.500	.10	.20	.35	.75
	1977	1.000	.10	.25	.50	1.00
	1978	1.500	.10	.20	.35	.75
	1979	1.500	—	.10	.35	.75
	1979	—	—	—	Proof	12.50
	1980 cock & star	1.500	—	.10	.35	.75
	1981 anvil	1.000	—	.10	.35	.75
	1982	1.000	—	.10	.35	.75
	1983	1.000	—	.10	.35	.75
	1984	1.500	—	.10	.35	.75
	1985	—	—	.10	.35	.75

1/10 GULDEN

1.4000 g, .640 SILVER, .0288 oz ASW

KM#	Date	Mintage	Fine	VF	XF	Unc
3	1954 fish	.200	2.50	5.00	10.00	17.50
	1954	200 pcs.	—	—	Proof	30.00
	1956	.250	.50	2.50	5.00	10.00
	1956	500 pcs.	—	—	Proof	30.00
	1957	.250	.50	2.50	5.00	10.00
	1957	250 pcs.	—	—	Proof	35.00
	1959	.250	.50	2.50	5.00	10.00
	1959	250 pcs.	—	—	Proof	30.00
	1960	.400	.50	1.25	3.50	7.50
	1960	300 pcs.	—	—	Proof	25.00
	1962	.400	.50	1.25	3.50	7.50
	1962	200 pcs.	—	—	Proof	30.00
	1963	.900	.50	1.00	1.50	3.00
	1963	—	—	—	Proof	30.00
	1966 fish	1.000	.50	1.00	1.50	3.00
	1966 star & fish	.200	1.00	2.50	4.00	7.00
	1970 cock	.300	1.00	2.50	4.00	7.00
	1970	—	—	—	Proof	30.00

10 CENTS

NICKEL

KM#	Date	Mintage	Fine	VF	XF	Unc
10	1970 cock	1.000	.10	.20	.50	1.00
	1970	—	—	—	Proof	25.00
	1971	3.000	.10	.20	.35	.75
	1971	—	—	—	Proof	25.00
	1974	1.000	.10	.20	.50	1.00
	1974	—	—	—	Proof	25.00
	1975	1.500	.10	.20	.35	.75
	1975	—	—	—	Proof	25.00
	1976	2.000	.10	.20	.35	.75
	1977	1.000	.10	.20	.35	.75
	1978	1.500	.10	.20	.35	.75
	1979 cock	1.500	.10	.20	.35	.75
	1979	—	—	—	Proof	12.50
	1980 cock & star	1.500	—	.20	.35	.75
	1981 anvil	1.000	—	.20	.35	.75
	1982	1.000	—	.20	.35	.75
	1983	1.000	—	.20	.35	.75
	1984	1.000	—	.20	.35	.75
	1985	—	—	.20	.35	.75

1/4 GULDEN

3.5800 g, .640 SILVER, .0736 oz ASW

KM#	Date	Mintage	Fine	VF	XF	Unc
4	1954 fish	.200	2.00	5.00	7.00	15.00
	1954	200 pcs.	—	—	Proof	40.00
	1956	.200	1.00	3.00	7.00	15.00
	1956	500 pcs.	—	—	Proof	40.00
	1957	.200	1.00	3.00	7.00	15.00
	1957	250 pcs.	—	—	Proof	45.00
	1960	.240	.50	1.50	5.00	10.00
	1960	300 pcs.	—	—	Proof	30.00
	1962	.240	.50	1.50	5.00	10.00
	1962	200 pcs.	—	—	Proof	35.00
	1963	.300	.50	1.50	5.00	10.00
	1963	—	—	—	Proof	35.00
	1965	.500	.50	1.50	5.00	10.00
	1965	—	—	—	Proof	35.00
	1967 fish	.310	.50	1.50	5.00	10.00
	1967	—	—	—	Proof	35.00
	1967 star & fish	.200	.50	1.50	5.00	12.50
	1970 cock	.150	1.25	3.25	8.50	18.50
	1970	—	—	—	Proof	35.00

25 CENTS

NICKEL

KM#	Date	Mintage	Fine	VF	XF	Unc
11	1970 cock	.750	.25	.50	1.50	2.25
	1970	—	—	—	Proof	30.00
	1971	3.000	.25	.50	.75	1.00
	1971	—	—	—	Proof	30.00
	1975	1.000	.25	.50	.75	1.00
	1975	—	—	—	Proof	30.00
	1976	1.000	.25	.50	.75	1.00
	1977	1.000	.25	.50	.75	1.00
	1978	1.000	.25	.50	.75	1.00
	1979	1.000	.25	.50	.75	1.00
	1979	—	—	—	Proof	17.50
	1980 cock & star	1.000	—	.50	.75	1.00

KM#	Date	Mintage	Fine	VF	XF	Unc
11	1981 anvil	1.000	—	.50	.75	1.00
	1982	1.000	—	.50	.75	1.00
	1983	1.000	—	.50	.75	1.00
	1984	1.000	—	.50	.75	1.00
	1985	—	—	.50	.75	1.00

GULDEN

10.0000 g, .720 SILVER, .2315 oz ASW

2	1952 fish	1.000	1.75	5.50	12.00	20.00
	1952	100 pcs.	—	—	Proof	150.00
	1963	.100	3.00	6.50	10.00	17.50
	1963	—	—	—	Proof	100.00
	1964 fish	.300	2.00	3.00	5.00	9.00
	1964 star & fish	.200	2.00	4.00	7.00	12.00
	1964	—	—	—	Proof	100.00
	1970 cock	.050	2.50	6.00	8.50	25.00
	1970	—	—	—	Proof	100.00

NICKEL

12	1970 cock	.500	.75	1.50	2.50	4.00
	1970	—	—	—	Proof	50.00
	1971	3.000	—	.75	1.50	2.50
	1971	—	—	—	Proof	50.00
	1978	.500	—	.75	1.50	2.50
	1979	.500	—	.75	1.50	2.50
	1979	—	—	—	Proof	25.00
	1980 cock & star	.500	—	.75	1.50	2.50

24	1980 anvil	.200	—	.75	1.00	2.00
	1981	.200	—	.75	1.00	2.00
	1982	.500	—	.75	1.00	2.00
	1983	.500	—	.75	1.00	2.00
	1984	.500	—	.75	1.00	2.00
	1985	—	—	.75	1.00	2.00

2-1/2 GULDEN

25.0000 g, .720 SILVER, .5787 oz ASW

7	1964 fish	.200	7.00	10.00	12.50	15.00
	1964 fish	—	—	—	Proof	200.00

NETHERLANDS ANTILLES 1343

KM#	Date	Mintage	Fine	VF	XF	Unc
19	1978 cock	.100	1.50	2.00	3.50	6.50
	1979 cock	.200	1.50	2.00	3.00	5.00
	1979 cock	—	—	—	Proof	35.00
	1980 cock & star	.200	1.50	2.00	2.50	4.00

25	1980 anvil	.100	—	1.50	3.50	5.00
	1981	.100	—	1.50	3.50	5.00
	1982	.100	—	1.50	1.75	4.00
	1983	—	—	1.50	1.75	4.00
	1984	.013	—	1.50	1.75	4.00
	1985	—	—	1.50	1.75	4.00

5 GULDEN

3.3600 g, .900 GOLD, .0972 oz AGW
Obv: Bust of Queen Beatrix left.

26	1980(1982)	.016	—	—	Proof	65.00

10 GULDEN

25.0000 g, .720 SILVER, .5787 oz ASW
150th Anniversary of Bank

20	1978 cock	.035	—	—	—	12.50
	1978	.015	—	—	Proof	27.50

6.7200 g, .900 GOLD, .1945 oz AGW
Obv: Bust of Queen Beatrix left.

27	1980(1982)	6,000	—	—	Proof	150.00

25 GULDEN

41.7000 g, .925 SILVER, 1.2401 oz ASW
25th Anniversary of Reign

KM#	Date	Mintage	Fine	VF	XF	Unc
14	1973	.040	—	—	—	20.00
	1973	.020	—	—	Proof	25.00

U.S. Bicentennial

15	1976FM(M)	200 pcs.	—	—	—	175.00
	1976FM(U)	9,425	—	—	—	45.00
	1976FM(P)	.013	—	—	Proof	60.00

Peter Stuyvesant
Obv: Similar to KM#15.

17	1977FM(U)	2,000	—	—	Proof	200.00

27.2200 g, .925 SILVER, .8095 oz ASW
International Year of the Child

KM#	Date	Mintage	Fine	VF	XF	Unc
22	1979	1,000	—	—	—	125.00
	1979	4,000	—	—	P/L	60.00
	1979	.017	—	—	Proof	25.00

50 GULDEN

3.3600 g, .900 GOLD, .0972 oz AGW
75th Anniversary of the Royal Covenant

23	1979	.011	—	—	—	65.00
	1979	.064	—	—	Proof	80.00

24.0000 g, .500 SILVER, .3859 oz ASW

28	1980	.015	—	—	—	32.50
	1980	.024	—	—	Proof	35.00

25.0000 g, .925 SILVER, .7435 oz ASW
Dutch-American Friendship

30	1982	.010	—	—	Proof	40.00

NETHERLANDS ANTILLES 1344

Mikve Israel Emanuel Synagogue

KM#	Date	Mintage	Fine	VF	XF	Unc
31	1982	.010	—	—	— Proof	60.00

100 GULDEN

6.7200 g, .900 GOLD, .1944 oz AGW
150th Anniversary of Bank

| 21 | 1978 | .027 | — | — | — | 125.00 |
| | 1978 | .024 | — | — | Proof | 150.00 |

200 GULDEN

7.9500 g, .900 GOLD, .2300 oz AGW
U.S. Bicentennial

16	1976FM(M)	100 pcs.	—	—	—	300.00
	1976FM(U)	5,726	—	—	—	175.00
	1976FM(P)	.015	—	—	Proof	200.00

Peter Stuyvesant

18	1977FM(M)	2,000	—	—	—	225.00
	1977FM(U)	654 pcs.	—	—	—	300.00
	1977FM(P)	6,878	—	—	Proof	200.00

300 GULDEN

5.0400 g, .900 GOLD, .1458 oz AGW
Abdication of Queen Juliana

| 29.1 | 1980(U) | .012 | — | — | — | 175.00 |
| | 1980(U) | .037 | — | — | Proof | 200.00 |

Rev: W/o mint mark.

| 29.2 | 1980 | — | — | — | Proof | 225.00 |

MINT SETS (MS)

KM#	Date	Mintage	Identification	Issue Price	Mkt. Val.
MS1	1971(7)	—	KM8-13 + Curacao KM46	—	22.00
MS2	1979(7)	11,500	KM8a,9a,10-13,19	—	11.00
MS3	1980(7)	18,500	KM8a,9a,10-13,19	—	10.00
MS4	1980(2)	23,000	KM24-25	—	6.50
MS5	1981(7)	23,500	KM8a,9a,10-12,24,25	—	10.25
MS6	1982(7)	10,000	KM8a,9a,10-12,24,25	—	9.50
MS7	1983(6)	25,000	KM8a,9a,10-12,24 + medallion	14.00	5.25
MS8	1984(7)	—	KM8a,9a,10-12,24,25	14.50	9.50
MS9	1985(7)	—	KM8a,9a,10-12,24,25	—	9.50

PROOF SETS (PS)

PS1	1952(2)	100	KM1,2	—	225.00
PS2	1954(3)	200	KM1,3-4	—	90.00
PS3	1956(3)	500	KM3-5	—	60.00
PS4	1957(4)	250	KM1,3-4,6	—	100.00
PS5	1959(3)	250	KM1,3,5	—	70.00
PS6	1960(3)	300	KM1,3-4,6	—	65.00
PS7	1962(3)	200	KM3-4,6	—	70.00
PS8	1963(5)	—	KM1-4,6	—	90.00
PS9	1964(3)	—	KM1,2,7	—	325.00
PS10	1965(4)	—	KM1,4-6	—	105.00
PS11	1967(3)	—	KM1,4,6	—	80.00
PS12	1970(10)	—	KM1-4,6,8-12	—	350.00
PS13	1971(6)	—	KM8-13	—	165.00
PS14	1973(3)	—	KM8,9,14	—	87.50
PS15	1974(4)	—	KM8-10,13	—	85.00
PS16	1975(4)	—	KM8,10-11,13	—	240.00
PS17	1976(2)	.013	KM15,16	187.50	325.00
PS18	1979(7)	—	KM8a,9a,10-13,19	—	120.00

Listings For
NETHERLANDS EAST INDIES: refer to Indonesia
NEW BRUNSWICK: refer to Canada

NEW CALEDONIA

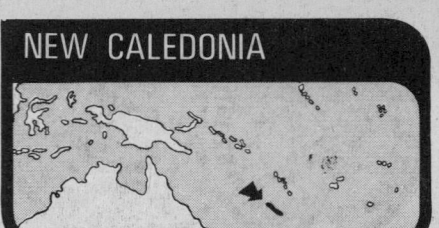

The French Overseas Territory of New Caledonia, a group of about 25 islands in the South Pacific, is situated about 750 miles (1,207 km.) east of Australia. The territory, which includes the dependencies of Ile des Pins, Loyalty Islands, Ile Huon, Isles Belep, Isles Chesterfield, and Ile Walpole, has a total land area of 7,358 sq. mi. (19,058 sq. km.) and a population of *152,000. Capital: Noumea. The islands are rich in minerals; New Caledonia has the world's largest known deposit of nickel. Nickel, nickel castings, coffee and copra are exported.

The first European to sight New Caledonia was the British navigator Capt. James Cook in 1774. The French took possession in 1853, and established a penal colony on the island in 1854. The European population of the colony remained disproportionately convict until 1894. New Caledonia became an overseas territory within the French Community in 1946, and in 1958 and 1972 chose to remain affiliated with France.

MINT MARKS
(a) - Paris, privy marks only

MONETARY SYSTEM
100 Centimes = 1 Franc

50 CENTIMES

ALUMINUM

KM#	Date	Mintage	VF	XF	Unc
1	1949(a)	1.000	.50	1.00	3.50

FRANC

ALUMINUM

| 2 | 1949(a) | 4.000 | .20 | .50 | 2.00 |

| 8 | 1971(a) | 1.000 | .25 | .75 | 2.00 |

Obv. leg: I.E.O.M. added.

10	1972(a)	.600	.25	.75	2.50
	1973(a)	1.000	.15	.25	.75
	1977(a)	1.500	.15	.25	.75
	1979(a)	—	.10	.20	.50
	1981(a)	1.000	.10	.20	.50
	1982(a)	1.000	.10	.20	.50

2 FRANCS

ALUMINUM

KM#	Date	Mintage	VF	XF	Unc
3	1949(a)	3.000	.50	1.50	4.50
9	1971(a)	1.000	.25	1.00	2.00

Obv. leg: I.E.O.M. added.

14	1973(a)	.400	.20	.75	2.50
	1977(a)	1.500	.20	.50	1.00
	1979(a)	—	.20	.40	.50
	1982(a)	1.000	.20	.35	.50

5 FRANCS

ALUMINUM

4	1952(a)	4.000	.50	1.00	3.50

10 FRANCS

NICKEL

5	1967(a)	.400	1.00	2.00	4.50
	1970(a)	1.000	.50	.75	2.50

Obv. leg: I.E.O.M. added.

11	1972(a)	.600	.50	.75	2.00
	1973(a)	.400	.50	.75	2.00
	1977(a)	1.000	.50	.75	1.00
	1979(a)	—	.35	.50	1.00
	1983(a)	—	.35	.50	1.00

20 FRANCS

NICKEL

6	1967(a)	.300	1.25	2.50	6.00
	1970(a)	1.200	.60	1.00	2.00

Obv. leg: I.E.O.M. added.

12	1972(a)	.700	.75	1.00	2.00
	1977(a)	.350	.75	1.00	3.00
	1979(a)	—	.50	.85	1.50
	1983(a)	—	.50	.85	1.50

50 FRANCS

NICKEL

KM#	Date	Mintage	VF	XF	Unc
7	1967(a)	.700	1.50	3.00	7.00

Obv. leg: I.E.O.M. added.

13	1972(a)	.300	1.50	2.00	5.00
	1979(a)	—	1.50	2.00	5.00
	1983(a)	—	1.50	2.00	5.00

100 FRANCS

NICKEL-BRONZE

15	1976(a)	2.000	1.50	2.50	6.00
	1979(a)	—	1.50	2.50	6.00

FLEUR DE COIN SETS (SS)

KM#	Date	Mintage	Identification	Issue Price	Mkt. Val.
SS1	1967(a)(3)	2,200	KM5-7	10.00	17.50

NOTE: This set issued with New Hebrides and French Polynesia 1967 set.

Listings For

NEWFOUNDLAND: refer to Canada
NEW GUINEA: refer to Papua New Guinea
NEW HEBRIDES: refer to Vanuatu

NEW ZEALAND

New Zealand, a parliamentary state located in the Southwestern Pacific 1,250 miles (2,011 km.) east of Australia, has an area of 103,883 sq. mi. (269,056 sq.km.) and a population of *3.4 million. Capital: Wellington. Wool, meat, dairy products and some manufactured items are exported.

The first European to sight New Zealand was the Dutch navigator Abel Tasman in 1642. The islands were explored by British navigator Capt. James Cook who surveyed it in 1769 and annexed the land to Great Britain. The British government disavowed the annexation and for the next 70 years the only white settlers to arrive were adventurers attracted by the prospects of lumbering, sealing and whaling. Great Britain annexed the land in 1840 by treaty with the native chiefs and made it a dependency of New South Wales. The colony was granted self-government in 1852, a ministerial form of government in 1856, and full dominion status on Sept. 26, 1907. Full internal and external autonomy, which New Zealand had in effect possessed for many years, was formally extended in 1947. New Zealand is a member of the Commonwealth of Nations. The Queen of England is Chief of State.

Prior to 1933 English coins were the official legal tender but Australian coins were accepted in small transactions. Currency fluctuations caused a distinctive New Zealand coinage to be introduced in 1933. The 1935 Waitangi crown and proof set were originally intended to mark the introduction but delays caused their date to be changed to 1935. The 1940 halfcrown marked the centennial of British rule, the 1949 and 1953 crowns commemorated Royal visits and the 1953 proof set marked the coronation of Queen Elizabeth.

Decimal Currency was introduced in 1967 with special sets commemorating the last issued of pound sterling and the first of the decimal issues. Since then dollars and sets of coins have been issued nearly every year.

RULERS
British

MONETARY SYSTEM
12 Pence = 1 Shilling
2 Shillings = 1 Florin
2 Shillings & 6 Pence = Half Crown
5 Shillings = 1 Crown
20 Shillings = 1 Pound
2 Dollars = 1 Pound

1/2 PENNY

BRONZE

KM#	Date	Mintage	Fine	VF	XF	Unc
12	1940	3.432	.35	1.00	3.00	20.00
	1940	—	—	—	Proof	200.00
	1941	.960	.25	1.00	4.00	25.00
	1941	—	—	—	Proof	250.00
	1942	1.960	.35	1.50	12.50	65.00
	1944	2.035	.25	.75	3.00	20.00
	1945	1.516	.25	.75	3.00	18.50
	1945	—	—	—	Proof	200.00
	1946	3.120	.25	.50	2.00	12.50
	1946	—	—	—	Proof	200.00
	1947	2.726	.25	.50	2.00	12.50
	1947	—	—	—	Proof	175.00

20	1949	1.766	.10	.50	2.00	12.50
	1949	—	—	—	Proof	175.00
	1950	1.426	.10	.50	2.50	16.50
	1950	—	—	—	Proof	200.00
	1951	2.342	.10	.50	1.50	10.00
	1951	—	—	—	Proof	175.00
	1952	2.400	.10	.35	1.00	5.00
	1952	—	—	—	Proof	175.00

NEW ZEALAND 1346

Obv: W/o shoulder strap.

KM#	Date	Mintage	Fine	VF	XF	Unc
23.1	1953	.720	.10	.50	2.50	8.50
	1953	7,000	—	—	Proof	10.00
	1954	.240	1.00	2.50	8.00	45.00
	1954	—	—	—	Proof	150.00
	1955	.240	.75	2.50	8.00	45.00
	1955	—	—	—	Proof	150.00

Obv: W/shoulder strap.

KM#	Date	Mintage	Fine	VF	XF	Unc
23.2	1956	1.200	.10	.50	1.50	15.00
	1956	—	—	—	Proof	150.00
	1957	1.440	.10	.50	1.25	7.50
	1957	—	—	—	Proof	150.00
	1958	1.920	.10	.40	1.25	7.50
	1958	—	—	—	Proof	150.00
	1959	1.920	.10	.20	1.00	6.50
	1959	—	—	—	Proof	150.00
	1960	2.400	.10	.15	.50	3.50
	1960	—	—	—	Proof	150.00
	1961	2.880	.10	.15	.50	3.50
	1961	—	—	—	Proof	150.00
	1962	2.880	.10	.15	.40	3.00
	1962	—	—	—	Proof	150.00
	1963	1.680	.10	.15	.30	2.00
	1963	—	—	—	Proof	150.00
	1964	2.885	.10	.15	.20	.75
	1964	—	—	—	Proof	150.00
	1965	5.177	.10	.15	.20	.75
	1965	.025	—	—	Proof	2.00

PENNY

BRONZE

KM#	Date	Mintage	Fine	VF	XF	Unc
13	1940	5.424	.35	2.00	4.00	35.00
	1940	—	—	—	Proof	250.00
	1941	1.200	.25	1.50	14.00	75.00
	1942	3.120	.35	2.00	15.00	80.00
	1942	—	—	—	Proof	300.00
	1943	8.400	.25	1.00	6.50	25.00
	1943	—	—	—	Proof	250.00
	1944	3.696	.25	1.00	5.25	20.00
	1944	—	—	—	Proof	250.00
	1945	4.764	.25	.75	5.25	20.00
	1945	—	—	—	Proof	250.00
	1946	6.720	.25	.75	5.00	20.00
	1946	—	—	—	Proof	250.00
	1947	5.880	.25	.75	5.00	20.00
	1947	—	—	—	Proof	250.00

BRONZE, burnished

KM#	Date	Mintage	Fine	VF	XF	Unc
13a	1945	—	—	—	40.00	120.00

NOTE: Struck in error by Royal Mint on Great Britain blanks.

BRONZE

KM#	Date	Mintage	Fine	VF	XF	Unc
21	1949	2.016	.20	.75	5.00	27.50
	1949	—	—	—	Proof	250.00
	1950	5.784	.15	.50	3.00	20.00
	1950	—	—	—	Proof	200.00
	1951	6.888	.15	.50	3.00	20.00
	1951	—	—	—	Proof	200.00
	1952	10.800	.15	.50	2.00	15.00
	1952	—	—	—	Proof	175.00

Obv: W/o shoulder strap.

KM#	Date	Mintage	Fine	VF	XF	Unc
24.1	1953	2.400	.10	.25	2.50	12.00
	1953	7,000	—	—	Proof	15.00
	1954	1.080	.25	1.00	12.00	50.00
	1954	—	—	—	Proof	200.00
	1955	3.720	.10	.25	3.00	18.50
	1955	—	—	—	Proof	175.00
	1956	Inc. Be.	20.00	30.00	150.00	450.00

Obv: W/shoulder strap.

KM#	Date	Mintage	Fine	VF	XF	Unc
24.2	1956	3.600	.10	.20	2.00	15.00
	1956	—	—	—	Proof	175.00
	1957	2.400	.10	.20	1.50	10.00
	1957	—	—	—	Proof	175.00
	1958	10.800	.10	.20	1.00	8.00
	1958	—	—	—	Proof	175.00
	1959	8.400	.10	.20	1.00	8.00
	1959	—	—	—	Proof	175.00
	1960	7.200	.10	.20	1.00	5.00
	1960	—	—	—	Proof	150.00
	1961	7.200	.10	.20	.50	3.00
	1961	—	—	—	Proof	150.00
	1962	6.000	—	.10	.45	2.00
	1962	—	—	—	Proof	150.00
	1963	2.400	—	.10	.20	1.00
	1963	—	—	—	Proof	150.00
	1964	18.000	—	.10	.15	.50
	1964	—	—	—	Proof	150.00
	1965	.175	—	.10	.50	2.50
	1965	.025	—	—	Proof	2.50

3 PENCE

1.4100 g, .500 SILVER, .0226 oz ASW

KM#	Date	Mintage	Fine	VF	XF	Unc
1	1933	6.000	.50	2.00	10.00	30.00
	1933	*20 pcs.	—	—	Proof	500.00
	1934	6.000	.50	2.00	10.00	30.00
	1934	*20 pcs.	—	—	Proof	500.00
	1935	.040	35.00	100.00	250.00	600.00
	1935	364 pcs.	—	—	Proof	600.00
	1936	2.760	.50	1.00	7.50	30.00
	1936	—	—	—	Proof	500.00

KM#	Date	Mintage	Fine	VF	XF	Unc
7	1937	2.880	.50	2.00	4.00	25.00
	1937	—	—	—	Proof	450.00
	1939	3.000	.50	2.00	4.00	25.00
	1939	—	—	—	Proof	450.00
	1940	2.000	.50	2.50	12.00	35.00
	1940	—	—	—	Proof	450.00
	1941	1.760	.65	3.00	16.00	65.00
	1941	—	—	—	Proof	400.00
	1942	3.120	.50	1.00	10.00	27.50
	1942 w/1 dot	Inc. Ab.	1.50	15.00	125.00	350.00
	1943	4.400	.50	1.00	3.00	17.50
	1944	2.840	.50	1.50	4.00	20.00
	1944	—	—	—	Proof	400.00
	1945	2.520	.50	1.25	3.00	17.50
	1945	—	—	—	Proof	400.00
	1946	6.080	.50	1.00	3.00	15.00
	1946	—	—	—	Proof	400.00

COPPER-NICKEL

KM#	Date	Mintage	Fine	VF	XF	Unc
7a	1947	6.400	.15	.35	7.50	30.00
	1947	*20 pcs.	—	—	Proof	350.00

KM#	Date	Mintage	Fine	VF	XF	Unc
15	1948	4.000	.15	.35	8.50	35.00
	1948	—	—	—	Proof	200.00
	1950	.800	.25	3.00	30.00	75.00
	1950	—	—	—	Proof	250.00
	1951	3.600	.15	.35	4.00	17.50
	1951	—	—	—	Proof	200.00
	1952	8.000	.15	.35	3.00	16.50
	1952	—	—	—	Proof	200.00

Obv: W/o shoulder strap.

KM#	Date	Mintage	Fine	VF	XF	Unc
25.1	1953	4.000	.15	.35	2.00	10.00
	1953	7,000	—	—	Proof	12.00
	1954	4.000	.15	.35	2.00	15.00
	1954	—	—	—	Proof	200.00
	1955	4.000	.15	.35	2.00	15.00
	1955	—	—	—	Proof	200.00
	1956	Inc. Be.	1.25	2.50	9.00	100.00
	1956	—	—	—	Proof	300.00

Obv: W/shoulder strap.

KM#	Date	Mintage	Fine	VF	XF	Unc
25.2	1956	4.800	.10	.20	1.50	7.00
	1956	—	—	—	Proof	200.00
	1957	8.000	.10	.20	.75	5.00
	1957	—	—	—	Proof	200.00
	1958	4.800	.10	.20	.75	5.00
	1958	—	—	—	Proof	200.00
	1959	4.000	.10	.20	.75	5.00
	1959	—	—	—	Proof	200.00
	1960	4.000	.10	.20	.50	3.50
	1960	—	—	—	Proof	200.00
	1961	4.800	.10	.15	.30	2.00
	1961	—	—	—	Proof	200.00
	1962	6.000	.10	.15	.30	2.00
	1962	—	—	—	Proof	200.00
	1963	4.000	.10	.15	.25	1.00
	1963	—	—	—	Proof	200.00
	1964	6.400	.10	.15	.25	1.00
	1964	—	—	—	Proof	200.00
	1965	4.175	—	.10	.15	1.00
	1965	.027	—	—	Proof	1.50

6 PENCE

2.8300 g, .500 SILVER, .0454 oz ASW

KM#	Date	Mintage	Fine	VF	XF	Unc
2	1933	3.000	1.00	3.00	17.50	60.00
	1933	*20 pcs.	—	—	Proof	500.00
	1934	3.600	1.00	3.00	18.50	60.00
	1934	*20 pcs.	—	—	Proof	500.00
	1935	.560	2.50	15.00	80.00	250.00
	1935	364 pcs.	—	—	Proof	300.00
	1936	1.480	1.75	4.50	22.50	60.00
	1936	—	—	—	Proof	—

KM#	Date	Mintage	Fine	VF	XF	Unc
8	1937	1.280	1.00	4.00	18.00	55.00
	1937	—	—	—	Proof	400.00
	1939	.700	1.00	4.00	18.00	55.00
	1939	—	—	—	Proof	400.00
	1940	.800	1.00	5.00	25.00	70.00
	1940	—	—	—	Proof	400.00
	1941	.440	2.50	25.00	125.00	450.00
	1941	—	—	—	Proof	600.00
	1942	.360	2.50	12.50	80.00	300.00
	1943	1.800	.75	2.50	10.00	37.50
	1944	1.160	.75	2.50	10.00	40.00
	1944	—	—	—	Proof	350.00
	1945	.940	.75	2.50	10.00	40.00
	1945	—	—	—	Proof	350.00
	1946	2.120	.75	2.50	8.00	35.00
	1946	—	—	—	Proof	350.00

COPPER-NICKEL

KM#	Date	Mintage	Fine	VF	XF	Unc
8a	1947	3.200	.30	1.00	15.00	75.00
	1947	*20 pcs.	—	—	Proof	350.00

KM#	Date	Mintage	Fine	VF	XF	Unc
16	1948	2.000	.30	.75	15.00	55.00
	1948	—	—	—	Proof	300.00
	1950	.800	.75	2.50	45.00	250.00
	1950	—	—	—	Proof	300.00
	1951	1.800	.30	.75	1.00	6.50
	1951	—	—	—	Proof	300.00
	1952	3.200	.30	.75	7.00	40.00
	1952	—	—	—	Proof	250.00

NEW ZEALAND 1347

KM#	Date	Mintage	Fine	VF	XF	Unc
18	1949	—	—	—	Proof	450.00
	1950	3.500	.75	2.00	7.00	35.00
	1950	—	—	—	Proof	450.00
	1951	1.000	.75	2.00	5.00	32.50
	1951	—	—	—	Proof	450.00

Obv: W/o shoulder strap.

KM#	Date	Mintage	Fine	VF	XF	Unc
26.1	1953	1.200	.15	.50	2.00	14.50
	1953	7.000	—	—	Proof	16.50
	1954	1.200	.15	.50	4.50	20.00
	1954	—	—	—	Proof	200.00
	1955	1.600	.15	.50	4.50	20.00
	1957	Inc. Be.	2.00	3.75	60.00	225.00
	1957	—	—	—	Proof	500.00

Obv: W/shoulder strap.

KM#	Date	Mintage	Fine	VF	XF	Unc
26.2	1955	—	—	—	Proof	2800.
	1956	2.000	.20	.50	2.50	15.00
	1956	—	—	—	Proof	200.00
	1957	2.400	.20	.50	2.00	12.50
	1957	—	—	—	Proof	200.00
	1958	3.000	.15	.50	1.50	10.00
	1958	—	—	—	Proof	200.00
	1959	2.000	.15	.50	1.50	10.00
	1959	—	—	—	Proof	200.00
	1960	1.600	.15	.25	.75	5.00
	1960	—	—	—	Proof	200.00
	1961	.800	.15	.20	.65	4.50
	1961	—	—	—	Proof	200.00
	1962	1.200	.10	.15	.50	3.50
	1962	—	—	—	Proof	200.00
	1963	.800	.10	.15	.25	3.00
	1963	—	—	—	Proof	200.00
	1964	7.800	—	.10	.15	2.00
	1964	—	—	—	Proof	200.00
	1965	8.575	—	—	.10	1.50
	1965	.025	—	—	Proof	1.25

SHILLING

5.6500 g, .500 SILVER, .0908 oz ASW

KM#	Date	Mintage	Fine	VF	XF	Unc
3	1933	3.000	3.50	8.50	30.00	150.00
	1933	*20 pcs.	—	—	Proof	650.00
	1934	3.600	3.50	8.50	27.50	125.00
	1934	*20 pcs.	—	—	Proof	650.00
	1935	.560	4.00	10.00	60.00	225.00
	1935	364 pcs.	—	—	Proof	300.00

9	1937	.890	2.50	8.50	20.00	100.00
	1937	—	—	—	Proof	600.00
	1940	.500	2.50	8.50	25.00	150.00
	1940	—	—	—	Proof	600.00
	1941	.360	2.50	10.00	60.00	300.00
	1941	—	—	—	Proof	600.00
	1942	.240	2.50	8.00	50.00	250.00
	1943	.900	1.25	5.50	20.00	90.00
	1944	.480	1.25	5.50	20.00	100.00
	1944	—	—	—	Proof	600.00
	1945	1.030	1.50	3.00	15.00	55.00
	1945	—	—	—	Proof	600.00
	1946	1.060	1.50	3.00	15.00	55.00
	1946	—	—	—	Proof	600.00

COPPER-NICKEL

9a	1947	2.800	.60	2.00	35.00	150.00
	1947	—	—	—	Proof	400.00

17	1948	1.000	.60	2.00	32.50	150.00
	1948	—	—	—	Proof	400.00
	1950	.600	.60	2.00	30.00	150.00
	1950	—	—	—	Proof	400.00
	1951	1.200	.60	2.00	25.00	100.00
	1951	—	—	—	Proof	400.00
	1952	.600	.60	2.00	20.00	90.00
	1952	—	—	—	Proof	400.00

Obv: W/o shoulder strap.

KM#	Date	Mintage	Fine	VF	XF	Unc
27.1	1953	.200	.75	1.25	5.00	15.00
	1953	7.000	—	—	Proof	18.00
	1955	.200	.75	2.50	18.00	150.00
	1955	—	—	—	Proof	400.00

Obv: W/shoulder strap.

27.2	1956	.800	.60	1.00	4.00	20.00
	1956	—	—	—	Proof	400.00
	1957	.800	.60	1.00	4.00	20.00
	1957	—	—	—	Proof	400.00
	1958	1.000	.30	.60	2.00	12.00
	1958	—	—	—	Proof	400.00
	1959	.600	.30	.60	2.00	10.00
	1959	—	—	—	Proof	400.00
	1960	.600	.30	.60	2.00	10.00
	1960	—	—	—	Proof	400.00
	1961	.400	.15	.30	1.00	6.50
	1961	—	—	—	Proof	400.00
	1962	1.000	.15	.30	.75	5.00
	1962	—	—	—	Proof	400.00
	1963	.600	.15	.30	.75	4.00
	1963	—	—	—	Proof	400.00
	1964	3.400	.10	.15	.30	1.00
	1964	—	—	—	Proof	400.00
	1965	4.475	.10	.15	.30	.75
	1965	.025	—	—	Proof	1.75

FLORIN

11.3100 g, .500 SILVER, .1818 oz ASW

4	1933	2.100	2.00	—	40.00	225.00
	1933	*20 pcs.	—	—	Proof	700.00
	1934	2.850	2.00	10.00	40.00	225.00
	1934	*20 pcs.	—	—	Proof	700.00
	1935	.755	3.00	15.00	100.00	275.00
	1935	364 pcs.	—	—	Proof	350.00
	1936	.150	8.00	45.00	400.00	1400.
	1936	—	—	—	—	1500.

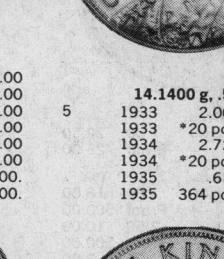

10.1	1937	1.190	2.00	6.00	30.00	150.00
(10)	1937	—	—	—	Proof	700.00
	1940	.500	4.00	25.00	200.00	750.00
	1940	—	—	—	Proof	900.00
	1941	.820	2.00	6.00	25.00	100.00
	1941	—	—	—	Proof	700.00
	1942	.150	2.00	10.00	70.00	225.00
	1943	1.400	2.00	5.00	20.00	90.00
	1944	.140	3.00	15.00	100.00	400.00
	1944	—	—	—	Proof	900.00
	1945	.515	2.00	4.00	25.00	95.00
	1945	—	—	—	Proof	700.00
	1946	1.200	2.00	4.00	25.00	95.00
	1946	—	—	—	Proof	700.00

Rev: Flat back on kiwi.

10.2	1946	Inc. Ab.	3.00	25.00	200.00	550.00

COPPER-NICKEL

10.1a	1947	2.500	.75	3.25	50.00	225.00
(10a)	1947	—	—	—	Proof	500.00

18	1948	1.750	.75	2.75	35.00	165.00
	1948	—	—	—	Proof	450.00
	1949	3.500	.75	2.75	30.00	150.00

Obv: W/o shoulder strap.

28.1	1953	.250	.50	1.50	5.00	18.50
	1953	7.000	—	—	Proof	20.00

Obv: W/shoulder strap.

28.2	1961	1.500	.30	.60	1.25	8.75
	1961	—	—	—	Proof	400.00
	1962	1.500	.15	.60	1.25	8.75
	1962	—	—	—	Proof	400.00
	1963	.100	.30	.60	1.25	6.00
	1963	—	—	—	Proof	400.00
	1964	7.000	.15	.30	.60	3.00
	1964	—	—	—	Proof	400.00
	1965	9.425	.15	.20	.30	1.00
	1965	.025	—	—	Proof	2.00

1/2 CROWN

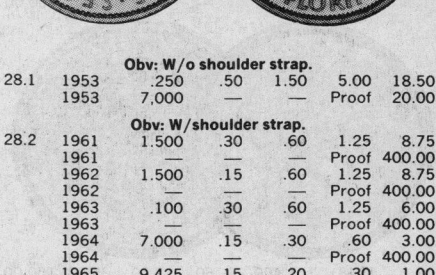

14.1400 g, .500 SILVER, .2273 oz ASW

5	1933	2.000	3.00	12.00	70.00	600.00
	1933	*20 pcs.	—	—	Proof	750.00
	1934	2.720	3.00	12.00	40.00	225.00
	1934	*20 pcs.	—	—	Proof	750.00
	1935	.612	3.00	22.50	100.00	550.00
	1935	364 pcs.	—	—	Proof	650.00

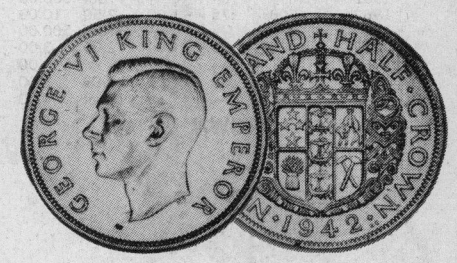

11	1937	.672	3.00	9.00	45.00	160.00
	1937	—	—	—	Proof	750.00
	1941	.776	3.00	10.00	40.00	150.00
	1941	—	—	—	Proof	750.00
	1942	.240	3.00	9.00	50.00	225.00
	1943	1.120	3.00	9.50	35.00	100.00
	1944	.180	7.00	22.50	100.00	550.00
	1944	—	—	—	Proof	750.00
	1945	.420	3.00	6.00	35.00	150.00
	1945	—	—	—	Proof	750.00
	1946	.960	3.00	6.00	25.00	100.00
	1946	—	—	—	Proof	750.00

New Zealand Centennial

14	1940	.101	5.00	12.50	18.00	35.00
	1940	—	—	—	Proof	5500.

NEW ZEALAND 1348

COPPER-NICKEL

KM#	Date	Mintage	Fine	VF	XF	Unc
11a	1947	1.600	.60	2.50	45.00	225.00
	1947	*20 pcs.	—	—	Proof	600.00

19	1948	1.400	.60	2.50	35.00	150.00
	1948	—	—	—	Proof	550.00
	1949	2.800	.60	2.50	35.00	150.00
	1949	—	—	—	Proof	550.00
	1950	3.600	.60	1.50	7.50	35.00
	1950	—	—	—	Proof	550.00
	1951	1.200	.60	1.00	6.50	32.50
	1951	—	—	—	Proof	550.00

Obv: W/o shoulder strap.

29.1	1953	.120	1.00	2.00	7.00	22.50
	1953	7,000	—	—	Proof	25.00

Obv: W/shoulder strap.

29.2	1961	.080	.75	1.00	3.00	18.00
	1961	—	—	—	Proof	500.00
	1962	.600	.75	1.00	2.50	10.00
	1962	—	—	—	Proof	500.00
	1963	.400	.50	1.00	2.00	3.00
	1963	—	—	—	Proof	500.00
	1965	.175	.50	1.00	2.00	3.00
	1965	.025	—	—	Proof	4.00

CROWN

28.2800 g, .500 SILVER, .4546 oz ASW
Waitangi

6	1935	764 pcs.	1250.	1500.	2000.	2500.
	1935	364 pcs.	—	—	Proof	2750.

Proposed Royal Visit

KM#	Date	Mintage	Fine	VF	XF	Unc
22	1949	.200	5.00	6.00	8.00	20.00
	1949	*2 pcs.	—	—	Proof	5500.

COPPER-NICKEL
Queen Elizabeth II Coronation

30	1953	.250	1.50	3.50	5.00	10.00
	1953	7,000	—	—	Proof	32.50

DECIMAL COINAGE

MINTS
(c) Royal Mint, Canberra
(l) Royal Mint, Llantrisant
(o) Royal Mint, Ottawa

MONETARY SYSTEM
100 Cents = 1 Dollar

CENT

BRONZE

KM#	Date	Mintage	VF	XF	Unc
31	1967	120.250	—	.10	.25
	1967	.050	—	Proof	1.50
	1968	.035	—	.10	1.25
	1968	.040	—	Proof	2.00
	1969	.050	—	.10	1.25
	1969	.050	—	Proof	2.00
	1970	10.090	—	.10	.50
	1970	.020	—	Proof	1.25
	1971(c) serifs on date numerals				
		10.000	—	.10	3.75
	1971(l) w/o serifs				
		.015	—	.10	3.50
	1971(l)	5,000	—	Proof	15.00

KM#	Date	Mintage	VF	XF	Unc
31	1972	10.055	—	.10	2.00
	1972	8,045	—	Proof	6.00
	1973	15.055	—	.10	1.75
	1973	8,000	—	Proof	6.00
	1974	35.035	—	.10	1.00
	1974	8,000	—	Proof	5.00
	1975	60.015	—	.10	.60
	1975	.010	—	Proof	5.00
	1976	20.016	—	.10	.60
	1976	.011	—	Proof	5.00
	1977	.020	—	.10	5.00
	1977	.012	—	Proof	5.50
	1978(o)	15.023	—	.10	1.00
	1978(o)	.015	—	Proof	4.00
	1979(o)	35.025	—	.10	.35
	1979(o)	.016	—	Proof	4.00
	1980(l) round 0 in date				
		.027	—	.10	1.25
	1980(l)	.017	—	Proof	4.00
	1980(o) oval 0 in date				
		40.000	—	.10	.50
	1981(o) serif on 1				
		10.000	—	.10	.30
	1981(l) flat 1	.025	—	.10	1.00
	1981(l) flat 1	.018	—	Proof	4.00
	1982(o) shaped 2				
		10.000	—	.10	.15
	1982(l) straight 2				
		.025	—	.10	1.00
	1982(l) straight 2				
		.018	—	Proof	3.00
	1983(o) blunt 3				
		40.000	—	.10	.25
	1983(l) stylized 3				
		.025	—	.10	.85
	1983(l) stylized 3				
		.018	—	Proof	3.00
	1984(o)	30.000	—	.10	.15
	1984(l)	.025	—	—	.25
	1984(l)	.015	—	Proof	1.75
	1985(o)	40.000	—	—	.10
	1985(c)	.020	—	—	.25
	1985(l)	.012	—	—	1.25

Obv: Similar to 1 Dollar, KM#57.

58	1986(o)	25.000	—	—	.10
	1986(l)	.018	—	—	.25
	1986(l)	.010	—	Proof	1.25
	1987(o)	27.500	—	—	.10
	1987(l)	.018	—	—	.25
	1987(l)	.010	—	Proof	1.25
	1988(l)	.015	—	—	.25
	1988(l)	9,000	—	Proof	1.25

2 CENTS

BRONZE

32	1967	75.250	—	.10	.25
	1967	.050	—	Proof	1.00
	1968	.035	—	.10	1.25
	1968	.040	—	Proof	1.50
	1969	20.560	—	.10	1.00
	1969	.050	—	Proof	1.50
	1970	.030	—	.10	2.00
	1970	.020	—	Proof	1.50
	1971(c) serifs on date numerals				
		15.050	—	.10	4.00
	1971(l) w/o serifs				
		.015	—	.10	3.00
	1971(l)	5,000	—	Proof	17.00
	1972	17.525	—	.10	2.00
	1972	8,045	—	Proof	6.50
	1973	38.565	—	.10	2.50
	1973	8,000	—	Proof	6.25
	1974	50.015	—	.10	1.10
	1974	8,000	—	Proof	4.00
	1975	20.015	—	.10	1.00
	1975	.010	—	Proof	4.00
	1976	15.016	—	.10	1.00
	1976	.011	—	Proof	4.00
	1977	20.000	—	.10	.85
	1977	.012	—	Proof	4.00
	1978	.023	—	.10	3.00
	1978	.015	—	Proof	4.00
	1979	.025	—	.10	3.50
	1979	.016	—	Proof	4.00
	1980(l) round 0 in date				
		.027	—	.10	1.25
	1980(l)	.017	—	Proof	3.50
	1980(o) oval 0 in date				
		10.000	—	.10	1.00
	1981(o) serif on 1				
		25.000	—	.10	.35
	1981(l) flat 1	.025	—	.10	1.00
	1981(l) flat 1	.018	—	Proof	3.50
	1982(o) shaped 2				
		50.000	—	.10	.25
	1982(l) straight 2				
		.025	—	.10	1.00
	1982(l) straight 2				
		.018	—	Proof	3.50
	1983(o) blunt 3				

NEW ZEALAND 1349

KM#	Date	Mintage	VF	XF	Unc
32		15.000	—	.10	.25
	1983(I) stylized 3				
		.025	—	.10	1.00
	1983(I) stylized 3				
		.018	—	Proof	3.50
	1984(o)	10.000	—	.10	.25
	1984(I)	.025	—	.10	1.25
	1984(I)	.015	—	Proof	2.00
	1985(o)	22.500	—	.10	.15
	1985(c)	.020	—	—	.50
	1985(c)	.012	—	Proof	1.50

Mule. Obv: Bahamas 5 Cent, KM#3. Rev: KM#32.

| 33 | ND(1967) | *.050 | 10.00 | 15.00 | 35.00 |

Obv: Similar to 1 Dollar, KM#57.

59	1986(o)	.018	—	.10	1.25
	1986(I)	.018	—	—	.50
	1986(I)	.010	—	Proof	1.50
	1987(o)	36.250	—	—	.50
	1987(I)	.018	—	—	.25
	1987(I)	.010	—	Proof	1.50
	1988(I)	.015	—	—	.50
	1988(I)	9,000	—	Proof	1.50

5 CENTS

COPPER-NICKEL

34	1967	26.250	—	.10	.50
	1967 w/o sea line				
	Inc. Ab.	.50	1.75	25.00	
	1967	.050	—	Proof	1.25
	1968	.035	—	.10	1.25
	1968	.040	—	Proof	2.00
	1969	10.310	—	.10	.65
	1969	.050	—	Proof	1.60
	1970	11.182	—	.10	.70
	1970	.020	—	Proof	2.00
	1971(c) serifs on date numerals				
		11.520	—	.10	4.50
	1971(I) w/o serifs				
		.015	—	.10	3.50
	1971(I)	5,000	—	Proof	20.00
	1972	20.015	—	.10	2.25
	1972	8.045	—	Proof	7.00
	1973	4.039	—	.10	1.25
	1973	8.000	—	Proof	6.50
	1974	18.015	—	.10	1.50
	1974	8.000	—	Proof	5.00
	1975	32.015	—	.10	1.25
	1975	.010	—	Proof	5.50
	1976	.016	—	.10	9.00
	1976	.011	—	Proof	5.00
	1977	.020	—	.10	6.00
	1977	.012	—	Proof	5.00
	1978	20.023	—	.10	1.00
	1978	.015	—	Proof	5.00
	1979	.025	—	.10	3.75
	1979	.016	—	Proof	5.00
	1980(I) round 0 in date				
		.027	—	.10	1.25
	1980(I)	.017	—	Proof	5.00
	1980(o) oval 0 in date				
		12.000	—	.10	1.00
	1981(o) serif on 1				
		20.000	—	.10	.50
	1981(I) flat 1	.025	—	.10	1.15
	1981(I) flat 1	.018	—	Proof	4.00
	1982(o) shaped 2				
		50.000	—	.10	.35
	1982(I) straight 2				
		.025	—	.10	1.15
	1982(I) straight 2				
		.018	—	Proof	4.00
	1983(I)	.025	—	.10	1.50
	1983(I)	.018	—	Proof	4.00
	1984(I)	.025	—	.10	1.80
	1984(I)	.015	—	Proof	4.00
	1985(o)	14.000	—	.10	.30
	1985(c)	.020	—	—	.75
	1985(c)	.012	—	Proof	4.00

Mule. Obv: KM#34. Rev: Canada 10 Cent, KM#77.

| 64 | 1981(o) serif on 1 | | | | |
| | | — | — | — | — |

Obv: Similar to 1 Dollar, KM#57.

60	1986(o)	18.000	—	.10	.30
	1986(I)	.018	—	—	.75
	1986(I)	.010	—	Proof	4.00
	1987(o)	60.000	—	.10	.30
	1987(I)	.018	—	—	.75
	1987(I)	.010	—	Proof	4.00
	1988(o)	16.000	—	.10	.30

KM#	Date	Mintage	VF	XF	Unc
60	1988(I)	.015	—	—	.75
	1988(I)	9,000	—	Proof	4.00

10 CENTS

COPPER-NICKEL

35	1967	17.250	—	.10	.40
	1967	.050	—	Proof	1.50
	1968	.035	—	.10	1.50
	1968	.040	—	Proof	2.50
	1969	3.050	—	.10	.75
	1969	.050	—	Proof	2.00

41	1970	2.076	—	.10	.75
	1970	.020	—	Proof	2.00
	1971(c) serifs on date numerals				
		2.800	1.00	3.50	10.00
	1971(I) w/o serifs				
		.015	—	.10	3.50
	1971(I)	5,000	—	Proof	30.00
	1972	2.039	—	.10	2.50
	1972	8.000	—	Proof	10.00
	1973	3.525	—	.10	1.75
	1973	8.000	—	Proof	7.50
	1974	4.619	—	.10	1.75
	1974	8.000	—	Proof	7.50
	1975	7.015	—	.10	1.50
	1975	.010	—	Proof	6.00
	1976	5.016	—	.10	1.25
	1976	.011	—	Proof	6.00
	1977	5.000	—	.10	1.00
	1977	.012	—	Proof	6.00
	1978	16.023	—	.10	1.15
	1978	.015	—	Proof	5.00
	1979	6.000	—	.10	.80
	1979	.016	—	Proof	5.00
	1980(I) round 0 in date				
		.027	—	.10	1.50
	1980(I)	.017	—	Proof	5.00
	1980(o) oval 0 in date				
		28.000	—	.10	1.00
	1981(o)	5.000	—	.10	.60
	1981(I)	.025	—	.10	1.25
	1981(I)	.018	—	Proof	5.00
	1982(o)	18.000	—	.10	.50
	1982(I)	.025	—	.10	1.25
	1982(I)	.018	—	Proof	5.00
	1983(I)	.025	—	.10	1.75
	1983(I)	.018	—	Proof	4.50
	1984(I)	.025	—	.10	1.75
	1984(I)	.015	—	Proof	4.50
	1985(o)	8.000	—	—	.50
	1985(c)	.020	—	—	1.75
	1985(c)	.012	—	Proof	4.50

Obv: Similar to 1 Dollar, KM#57.

61	1986(I)	.018	—	.10	1.00
	1986(I)	.010	—	Proof	4.50
	1987(o)	21.000	—	—	.50
	1987(I)	.018	—	.10	1.00
	1987(I)	.010	—	Proof	4.50
	1988(o)	24.000	—	.10	.50
	1988(I)	.015	—	.10	1.00
	1988(I)	9,000	—	Proof	4.50

20 CENTS

COPPER-NICKEL

36	1967	13.250	—	.15	.75
	1967	.050	—	Proof	1.75
	1968	.035	—	.15	1.75
	1968	.040	—	Proof	3.00
	1969	2.500	—	.15	1.00
	1969	.050	—	Proof	2.50
	1970	.030	—	.15	2.50
	1970	.020	—	Proof	3.00
	1971(c) serifs on date numerals				

KM#	Date	Mintage	VF	XF	Unc
36		1.600	1.00	4.50	20.00
	1971(I) w/o serifs				
		.015	—	.15	4.00
	1971(I)	5,000	—	Proof	50.00
	1972	1.531	—	.15	2.75
	1972	8.000	—	Proof	15.00
	1973	3.043	—	.15	2.00
	1973	8.000	—	Proof	8.00
	1974	4.527	—	.15	2.00
	1974	8.000	—	Proof	9.00
	1975	5.015	—	.15	2.00
	1975	.012	—	Proof	7.50
	1976	7.516	—	.15	1.50
	1976	.011	—	Proof	7.00
	1977	7.500	—	.15	1.50
	1977	.012	—	Proof	7.50
	1978	2.523	—	.15	1.50
	1978	.015	—	Proof	6.00
	1979	8.000	—	.15	1.00
	1979	.016	—	Proof	6.00
	1980(I) round 0 in date				
		.027	—	.15	1.75
	1980(I)	.017	—	Proof	6.00
	1980(o) oval 0 in date				
		9.000	—	.15	1.25
	1981(o) serif on 1				
		7.500	—	.15	.75
	1981(I) flat 1	.025	—	.15	1.50
	1981(I) flat 1	.018	—	Proof	5.00
	1982(o) shaped 2				
		17.500	—	.15	.50
	1982(I) straight 2				
		.025	—	.15	1.50
	1982(I) straight 2				
		.018	—	Proof	5.00
	1983(o) blunt 3				
		2.500	—	.15	1.00
	1983(I) stylized 3				
		.025	—	.15	2.00
	1983(I) stylized 3				
		.018	—	Proof	5.00
	1984(o)	1.500	—	.15	.75
	1984(I)	.025	—	.15	2.00
	1984(I)	.018	—	Proof	5.00
	1985(o)	6.000	—	.15	.50
	1985(c)	.020	—	.15	2.00
	1985(c)	.012	—	Proof	5.00

Obv: Similar to 1 Dollar, KM#57.

62	1986(o)	12.500	—	.15	.50
	1986(I)	.018	—	.25	1.25
	1986(I)	.010	—	Proof	5.00
	1987(o)	14.000	—	.15	.50
	1987(I)	.018	—	.25	1.25
	1987(I)	.010	—	Proof	5.00
	1988(o)	12.500	—	.15	.50
	1988(I)	.015	—	.25	1.25
	1988(I)	9,000	—	Proof	5.00

50 CENTS

COPPER-NICKEL

37	1967	10.250	—	.35	.75
	1967 dot above 1				
	Inc. Ab.	.75	1.75	28.00	
	1967	.050	—	Proof	2.50
	1968	.035	—	.35	2.00
	1968	.040	—	Proof	3.50
	1970	.030	—	.35	2.75
	1970	.050	—	Proof	3.50
	1971(c) serifs on date numerals				
		1.123	1.00	5.00	30.00
	1971(I) w/o serifs				
		.015	—	.35	4.50
	1971(I)	5,000	—	Proof	50.00
	1972	1.423	—	.35	3.25
	1972	8.045	—	Proof	20.00
	1973	2.523	—	.35	2.50
	1973	8.000	—	Proof	12.50
	1974	1.215	—	.35	2.50
	1974	8.000	—	Proof	12.50
	1975	3.815	—	.35	2.50
	1975	.010	—	Proof	9.00
	1976	2.016	—	.35	2.00
	1976	.011	—	Proof	9.00
	1977	2.000	—	.35	2.00
	1977	.012	—	Proof	9.00
	1978	2.023	—	.35	1.75
	1978	.015	—	Proof	7.00
	1979	2.400	—	.35	1.45
	1979	.016	—	Proof	7.00
	1980(I) round 0 in date				
		.027	—	.35	2.00
	1980(I)	.017	—	Proof	7.00
	1980(o) oval in date				
		8.000	—	.35	1.50
	1981(o) serif on 1				

NEW ZEALAND 1350

KM#	Date	Mintage	VF	XF	Unc
37		4.000	—	.35	1.00
	1981(l) flat 1	.025	—	.35	2.00
	1981(l) flat 1	.018	—	Proof	7.00
	1982(o) shaped 2	6.000	—	.35	.60
	1982(l) straight 2	.025	—	.35	2.00
	1982(l) straight 2	.018	—	Proof	7.00
	1983(l)	.025	—	.35	2.00
	1983(l)	.018	—	Proof	7.00
	1984(o)	2.000	—	.35	1.00
	1984(l)	.025	—	.35	2.00
	1984(l)	.015	—	Proof	6.00
	1985(o)	2.000	—	.35	.75
	1985(c)	.020	—	.35	1.50
	1985(c)	.012	—	Proof	6.00

200th Anniversary Captain Cook's Voyage
Similar to KM#37.
Edge inscribed COOK BI-CENTENARY 1769-1969

| 39 | 1969 | .050 | — | .75 | 2.50 |
| | 1969 | .050 | — | Proof | 4.00 |

Obv: Similar to 1 Dollar, KM#57.

63	1986(o)	5.200	—	.35	.75
	1986(l)	.018	—	.50	1.50
	1986(l)	.010	—	Proof	6.00
	1987(o)	3.600	—	.35	.75
	1987(l)	.018	—	.50	1.50
	1987(l)	.010	—	Proof	6.00
	1988(o)	8.800	—	.35	.75
	1988(l)	.015	—	.50	1.50
	1988(l)	9.000	—	Proof	6.00

DOLLAR

COPPER-NICKEL
Decimalization Commemorative, lettered edge

| 38.1 | 1967 | .450 | — | .75 | 1.50 |
| | 1967 | .050 | — | Proof | 3.00 |

Regular Issue, reeded edge

38.2	1971	.045	—	3.00	10.00
	1971	5.000	—	Proof	75.00
	1972	.042	—	2.00	7.50
	1972	8.045	—	Proof	28.00
	1972 RAM case	3.000	—	Proof	125.00
	1973	.037	—	2.00	7.00
	1973	.016	—	Proof	13.50
	1975	.035	—	2.50	6.00
	1975	.020	—	Proof	10.00
	1976	.036	—	2.50	8.50
	1976	.022	—	Proof	10.00

200th Anniversary Captain Cook's Voyage

| 40 | 1969 | .450 | — | 1.00 | 1.75 |
| | 1969 | .050 | — | Proof | 3.50 |

Royal Visit

KM#	Date	Mintage	VF	XF	Unc
42	1970	.315	—	1.00	1.75
	1970	.020	—	Proof	4.00

Cook Islands

| 43 | 1970 | .025 | — | 10.00 | 25.00 |
| | 1970 | 5.030 | — | Proof | 90.00 |

Commonwealth Games

| 44 | 1974 | .502 | — | 1.00 | 2.00 |

27.2160 g, .925 SILVER, .8095 oz ASW

| 44a | 1974 | .018 | — | Proof | 35.00 |

COPPER-NICKEL
New Zealand Day

| 45 | 1974 | .050 | — | 4.00 | 17.50 |
| | 1974 | 5,000 | — | Proof | 175.00 |

Waitangi Day

KM#	Date	Mintage	VF	XF	Unc
46	1977	.090	—	2.75	6.00

27.2160 g, .925 SILVER, .8095 oz ASW

| 46a | 1977 | .027 | — | Proof | 22.50 |

COPPER-NICKEL
25th Anniversary of Coronation

| 47 | 1978 | .123 | — | 1.25 | 3.00 |

27.2160 g, .925 SILVER, .8095 oz ASW

| 47a | 1978 | .033 | — | Proof | 17.50 |

COPPER-NICKEL

| 48 | 1979 | .110 | — | 1.25 | 2.50 |

27.2160 g, .925 SILVER, .8095 oz ASW

| 48a | 1979 | .035 | — | Proof | 15.00 |

COPPER-NICKEL
Fan Tail

| 49 | 1980 | .112 | — | 1.25 | 3.25 |

27.2160 g, .925 SILVER, .8095 oz ASW

| 49a | 1980 | .037 | — | Proof | 15.00 |

NEW ZEALAND 1351

COPPER-NICKEL
Royal Visit

KM#	Date	Mintage	VF	XF	Unc
50	1981	.100	—	1.25	3.25

27.2160 g, .925 SILVER, .8095 oz ASW
| 50a | 1981 | .038 | — | Proof | 15.00 |

COPPER-NICKEL
Takahe

| 51 | 1982 | .065 | — | 1.50 | 4.00 |

27.2160 g, .925 SILVER, .8095 oz ASW
| 51a | 1982 | .035 | — | Proof | 18.00 |

COPPER-NICKEL
Royal Visit

| 52 | 1983 | .040 | — | 3.00 | 6.00 |

27.6800 g, .925 SILVER, .8233 oz ASW
| 52a | 1983 | .017 | — | Proof | 35.00 |

COPPER-NICKEL
New Zealand Coinage

KM#	Date	Mintage	VF	XF	Unc
53	1983	.065	—	1.25	3.25

28.2800 g, .925 SILVER, .8411 oz ASW
| 53a | 1983 | .035 | — | Proof | 20.00 |

COPPER-NICKEL
Chatham Island Black Robin

| 54 | 1984 | .065 | — | 1.25 | 4.00 |

28.2800 g, .925 SILVER, .8411 oz ASW
| 54a | 1984 | .030 | — | Proof | 18.00 |

COPPER-NICKEL
Black Stilt
Obv: Similar to KM#38.1.

| 55 | 1985 | .060 | — | 1.25 | 3.25 |

27.2200 g, .925 SILVER, .8095 oz ASW
| 55a | 1985 | .025 | — | Proof | 18.00 |

COPPER-NICKEL
Royal Visit

| 56 | 1986 | .040 | — | 1.25 | 4.00 |

28.2800 g, .925 SILVER, .8411 oz ASW
| 56a | 1986 | .013 | — | Proof | 45.00 |

COPPER-NICKEL
Kakapo

KM#	Date	Mintage	VF	XF	Unc
57	1986	.053	—	1.25	3.25

28.2800 g, .925 SILVER, .8411 oz ASW
| 57a | 1986 | .021 | — | Proof | 18.00 |

COPPER-NICKEL
National Parks Centennial

| 65 | 1987 | .053 | — | — | 3.00 |

28.2800 g, .925 SILVER, .8411 oz ASW
| 65a | 1987 | .021 | — | Proof | 15.00 |

COPPER-NICKEL
Yellow-eyed Penguin

| 66 | 1988 | *.045 | — | — | 3.00 |

28.2800 g, .925 SILVER, .8411 oz ASW
| 66a | 1988 | *.019 | — | Proof | 15.00 |

SELECT SETS (SS)

KM#	Date	Mintage	Identification	Issue Price	Mkt. Val.
SS1	1965(7)	75,000	KM23.2-29.2	2.50	13.50

MINT SETS (MS)

MS1	1965(7)	100,000	KM23.2-29.2	2.00	12.50
MS2	1967(7)	250,000	KM31-32,34-37,38.1	4.50	4.50
MS4	1968(6)	35,000	KM31-32,34-37	2.15	9.00
MS5	1969(7)	50,000	KM31-32,34-36,39-40	3.25	9.00
MS7	1970(7)	30,000	KM31-32,34-36,37,41-42	3.50	11.00
MS10	1971(7)	15,000	KM31-32,34,36-37,38.2,41	3.50	25.00
MS12	1972(7)	15,000	KM31-32,34,36-37,38.2,41	3.50	22.50
MS14	1973(7)	15,000	KM31-32,34,36-37,38.2,41	3.50	20.00
MS17	1974(7)	15,000	KM31-32,34,36-37,41,44	4.35	15.00
MS20	1975(7)	15,000	KM31-32,34,36-37,38.2,41	4.50	12.00
MS22	1976(7)	16,000	KM31-32,34,36-37,38.2,41	5.00	15.00
MS23	1977(7)	20,000	KM31-32,34,36-37,41,46	5.00	18.00
MS24	1978(7)	23,000	KM31-32,34,36-37,41,47	5.00	7.50
MS25	1979(7)	25,000	KM31-32,34,36-37,41,48	5.50	7.50
MS26	1980(7)	27,000	KM31-32,34,36-37,41,49	5.75	7.50
MS27	1981(7)	25,000	KM31-32,34,36-37,41,50	5.75	7.50
MS28	1982(7)	25,000	KM31-32,34,36-37,41,51	6.00	7.50
MS29	1983(7)	25,000	KM31-32,34,36-37,41,53	4.25	7.50
MS30	1984(7)	25,000	KM31-32,34,36-37,41,54	4.00	7.50
MS31	1985(7)	20,000	KM31-32,34,36-37,41,55	4.00	7.50
MS32	1986(7)	18,000	KM57-63	4.00	6.00
MS33	1987(7)	18,000	KM58-65	7.50	7.50
MS34	1988(7)	15,000	KM58-63,66	7.50	7.50

PROOF SETS (PS)

| PS1 | 1933(5) | *20 pcs. | KM1-5 | — | 3000. |
| PS2 | 1934(5) | *20 pcs. | KM1-5 | — | 3000. |

NEW ZEALAND 1352

KM#	Date	Mintage	Identification	Issue Price	Mkt. Val.
PS3	1935(6)	364 pcs.	KM1-6	—	4500.
PS4	1937(5)	*20 pcs.	KM7-11	—	3000.
PS5	1947(5)	*20 pcs.	KM7a-11a	—	2500.
PS6	1953(8)	7,000	KM23-30	—	100.00
PS7	1954(4)	—	KM23-26	—	1000.
PS8	1964(6)	—	KM23-28	—	1500.
PS9	1965(7)	25,000	KM23.2-29.2 flat pack	—	12.00
PS9a	1965(7)	400	KM23.2-29.2 red plush case	—	140.00
PS10	1967(7)	50,000	KM31-32,34-38 flat pack	10.00	10.00
PS10a	1967(7)	400	KM31-32,34-38 blue plush case	—	140.00
PS11	1968(6)	40,000	KM31-32,34-37	7.00	11.00
PS12	1969(7)	50,000	KM31-32,34-36,39-40	7.00	10.00
PS13	1970(7)	20,000	KM31-32,34,36-37,41-42	7.00	10.00
PS14	1971(7)	5,000	KM31-32,34,36-37,38.2,41	15.00	225.00
PS15	1972(7)	8,045	KM31-32,34,36-37,38.2,41	16.00	80.00
PS16	1973(7)	8,000	KM31-32,34,36-37,38.2,41	16.00	45.00
PS17	1974(7)	8,000	KM31-32,34,36-37,41,44a	14.00	65.00
PS18	1975(7)	10,000	KM31-32,34,36-37,38.2,41	14.00	30.00
PS19	1976(7)	11,000	KM31-32,34,36-37,38.2,41	15.00	30.00
PS20	1977(7)	12,000	KM31-32,34,36-37,41,46a	19.50	45.00
PS21	1978(7)	15,000	KM31-32,34,36-37,41,47a	20.00	35.00
PS22	1979(7)	16,000	KM31-32,34,36-37,41,48a	22.00	32.00
PS23	1980(7)	17,000	KM31-32,34,36-37,41,49a	—	35.00
PS24	1981(7)	18,000	KM31-32,34,36-37,41,50a	37.00	32.00
PS25	1982(7)	18,000	KM31-32,34,36-37,41,51a	33.00	32.00
PS26	1983(7)	18,000	KM31-32,34,36-37,41,53a	28.00	35.00
PS27	1984(7)	15,000	KM31-32,34,36-37,41,54a	25.00	32.00
PS28	1985(7)	11,500	KM31-32,34,36-37,41,55a	27.00	32.00
PS29	1986(7)	10,000	KM57a,58-63	25.00	35.00
PS30	1987(7)	10,000	KM58-63,65a	38.00	38.00
PS31	1988(7)	9,000	KM58-63,66a	38.00	38.00

NICARAGUA

The Republic of Nicaragua, situated in Central America between Honduras and Costa Rica, has an area of 50,193 sq. mi. (130,000 sq. km.) and a population of *3.7 million. Capital: Managua. Agriculture, mining (gold and silver) and hardwood logging are the principal industries. Cotton, meat, coffee and sugar are exported.

Columbus sighted the coast of Nicaragua in 1502 during the course of his last voyage of discovery. It was first visited in 1522 by conquistadores from Panama, under command of Gonzalez Davola. After the first settlements were established in 1524 at Granada and Leon. Nicaragua was incorporated, for administrative purpose, in the Captaincy General of Guatemala, which included every Central American state but Panama. The Captaincy General declared its independence from Spain on Sept. 15, 1821. The next year Nicaragua united with the Mexican Empire of Agustin de Iturbide, then in 1823 with the Central American Republic. When the federation was dissolved, Nicaragua declared itself an independent republic in 1838.

MINT MARKS
H - Heaton, Birmingham
Mo - Mexico City
 - Sherritt

MONETARY SYSTEM
100 Centavos = 1 Peso

CENTAVO

COPPER-NICKEL

KM#	Date	Mintage	Fine	VF	XF	Unc
1	1878	.500	2.00	5.00	15.00	50.00
	1878	—	—	—	Proof	400.00

5 CENTAVOS

1.2500 g, .800 SILVER, .0322 oz ASW

2	1880H	.256	2.50	5.00	20.00	125.00
	1880H	—	—	—	Proof	250.00

5	1887H	1.000	1.00	3.00	10.00	45.00

COPPER-NICKEL

8	1898	2.000	.50	1.50	7.00	25.00

9	1899	2.000	.75	2.00	8.00	35.00

10 CENTAVOS

2.5000 g, .800 SILVER, .0643 oz ASW

KM#	Date	Mintage	Fine	VF	XF	Unc
3	1880H	.552	2.50	7.50	20.00	75.00
	1880H	—	—	—	Proof	275.00

6	1887H	1.500	1.00	2.50	10.00	60.00

20 CENTAVOS

5.0000 g, .800 SILVER, .1286 oz ASW

4	1880H	.288	3.00	7.50	35.00	125.00
	1880H	—	—	—	Proof	350.00

7	1887H	1.000	2.00	5.00	20.00	40.00

MONETARY REFORM
100 Centavos = 1 Cordoba
12-1/2 Pesos = 1 Cordoba

1/2 CENTAVO

BRONZE

10	1912H	.900	1.00	2.50	10.00	30.00
	1912H	—	—	—	Proof	275.00
	1915H	.320	1.50	4.00	15.00	50.00
	1916H	.720	1.50	4.00	10.00	40.00
	1917	.720	1.50	4.00	10.00	35.00
	1922	.400	1.00	3.00	8.00	35.00
	1924	.400	1.00	3.00	8.00	30.00
	1934	.500	1.00	2.00	5.00	25.00
	1936	.600	.50	.75	3.00	15.00
	1937	1.000	.40	.60	3.00	15.00

SILVER (OMS)

| 10a | 1912H | 2 pcs. | — | — | — | — |

GOLD (OMS)

| 10b | 1912H | 1 pc. | — | — | — | — |

CENTAVO

BRONZE

11	1912H	.450	1.00	3.00	10.00	35.00
	1912H	—	—	—	Proof	275.00
	1914H	.300	6.00	15.00	30.00	60.00
	1915H	.500	2.00	5.00	12.50	40.00
	1916H	.450	2.00	5.00	12.50	35.00
	1917	.450	2.00	5.00	12.50	35.00
	1919	.750	1.00	4.00	10.00	35.00
	1920	.700	1.00	4.00	10.00	35.00
	1922	.500	1.00	4.00	10.00	35.00
	1924	.300	1.00	5.00	12.50	40.00
	1927	.250	1.50	7.50	12.50	40.00
	1928	.500	1.00	4.00	9.50	25.00
	1929	.500	1.00	4.00	9.50	25.00
	1930	.250	1.50	7.50	15.00	50.00
	1934	.500	.50	2.00	4.00	13.00
	1935	.500	.50	2.00	4.00	12.00
	1936	.500	.50	2.00	4.00	12.00
	1937	1.000	.10	.50	2.00	12.00
	1938	2.000	.10	.50	3.00	10.00
	1940	2.000	.10	.50	3.00	10.00

SILVER (OMS)

| 11a | 1912H | 2 pcs. | — | — | — | 2000. |

GOLD (OMS)

| 11b | 1912H | 1 pc. | — | — | — | — |

KM#	Date	Mintage	Fine	VF	XF	Unc
20	1943	1.000	.50	1.50	4.50	18.00

5 CENTAVOS

COPPER-NICKEL

12	1912H	.460	1.00	3.00	10.00	40.00
	1912H	—	—	—	Proof	400.00
	1914H	.300	1.00	4.00	15.00	50.00
	1915H	.160	2.00	5.00	20.00	75.00
	1919	.100	1.00	4.00	17.50	65.00
	1920	.150	1.00	3.00	12.50	50.00
	1927	.100	1.00	3.00	15.00	40.00
	1928	.100	1.00	3.00	15.00	40.00
	1929	.100	1.00	3.00	12.50	35.00
	1930	.100	1.00	3.00	12.50	35.00
	1934	.200	.75	2.00	10.00	25.00
	1935	.200	.75	2.00	6.50	20.00
	1936	.300	.50	1.00	5.00	15.00
	1937	.300	.50	1.00	5.00	15.00
	1938	.800	.50	1.00	5.00	12.50
	1940	.800	.50	1.00	5.00	12.50

SILVER (OMS)

| 12a | 1912H | 2 pcs. | — | — | — | — |

GOLD (OMS)

| 12b | 1912H | 1 pc. | — | — | — | — |

BRASS
Plain edge

| 21.1 | 1943 | 2.000 | .50 | 2.50 | 7.00 | 25.00 |

Reeded edge.

| 21.2 | 1943 | — | — | — | Reported, not confirmed |

COPPER-NICKEL
B.N.N. on edge

24.1	1946	4.000	.10	.25	2.50	7.50
	1946	—	—	—	Proof	300.00
	1952	4.000	.10	.15	2.00	9.00
	1952	—	—	—	Proof	100.00
	1954	4.000	.10	.15	.25	2.50
	1954	—	—	—	Proof	100.00
	1956	5.000	.10	.15	.25	1.50
	1956	—	—	—	Proof	100.00

B.C.N. on edge

24.2	1962	3.000	—	.10	.15	.75
	1962	—	—	—	Proof	150.00
	1964	4.000	—	.10	.15	.75
	1965	10.000	—	.10	.15	.75

Reeded edge

| 24.3 | 1972 | .020 | — | — | Proof | 2.50 |

NICKEL CLAD STEEL

| 24.3a | 1972 | 10.000 | — | — | .10 | .25 |

ALUMINUM
F.A.O. Issue

| 27 | 1974 | 2.000 | — | — | .40 | 1.00 |

KM#	Date	Mintage	Fine	VF	XF	Unc
28	1974	16.200	—	—	.10	.25

| 49 | 1981 | — | — | — | .50 | 2.00 |

| 55 | 1987 | — | — | — | .20 | .50 |

10 CENTAVOS

2.5000 g, .800 SILVER, .0643 oz ASW

13	1912H	.230	1.50	3.50	15.00	50.00
	1912H	—	—	—	Proof	450.00
	1914H	.220	2.50	7.50	25.00	80.00
	1927	.500	1.00	2.00	7.50	40.00
	1928	1.000	.50	1.50	6.00	30.00
	1930	.150	1.50	3.00	12.50	50.00
	1935	.250	1.00	2.00	5.00	25.00
	1936	.250	1.00	2.00	5.00	25.00

GOLD (OMS)

| 13b | 1912H | 1 pc. | — | — | — | — |

COPPER-NICKEL
B.N.N. on edge

17.1	1939	2.500	.50	1.00	4.00	20.00
	1939	—	—	—	Proof	300.00
	1946	2.000	.25	.50	2.00	8.50
	1946	—	—	—	Proof	75.00
	1950	2.000	.25	.50	3.00	15.00
	1950	—	—	—	Proof	75.00
	1952	1.500	.25	.50	3.00	15.00
	1952	—	—	—	Proof	75.00
	1954	3.000	.10	.25	1.50	3.00
	1954	—	—	—	Proof	75.00
	1956	5.000	.10	.20	1.00	2.00
	1956	—	—	—	Proof	75.00

B.C.N. on edge

17.2	1962	4.000	—	.10	.15	1.25
	1962	—	—	—	Proof	225.00
	1964	4.000	—	.10	.15	1.50
	1965	12.000	—	.10	.15	.75

Reeded edge

| 17.3 | 1972 | .020 | — | — | Proof | 2.50 |

NICKEL CLAD STEEL

| 17.3a | 1972 | 10.000 | — | .10 | .15 | .30 |

BRASS
Reeded edge

| 22 | 1943 | 2.000 | .50 | 1.00 | 5.00 | 35.00 |

ALUMINUM
F.A.O. Issue

KM#	Date	Mintage	Fine	VF	XF	Unc
29	1974	2.000	—	—	.10	.25

| 30 | 1974 | 20.000 | — | — | .10 | .50 |

COPPER-NICKEL

31	1975	2.000	—	—	.25	.75
	1978	—	—	—	.40	1.25

ALUMINUM

| 50 | 1981 | — | — | — | .15 | .50 |

| 56 | 1987 | — | — | — | .15 | .50 |

25 CENTAVOS

6.2500 g, .800 SILVER, .1607 oz ASW

14	1912H	.320	2.00	5.00	30.00	65.00
	1912H	—	—	—	Proof	450.00
	1914H	.100	4.00	6.00	35.00	90.00
	1928	.200	2.00	5.00	20.00	30.00
	1929	.020	5.00	10.00	35.00	75.00
	1930	.020	5.00	10.00	30.00	75.00
	1936	.100	2.00	3.00	15.00	40.00

GOLD (OMS)

| 14b | 1912H | 1 pc. | — | — | — | — |

COPPER-NICKEL
B.N.N. on edge

18.1	1939	1.000	.50	1.50	6.50	20.00
	1939	—	—	—	Proof	325.00
	1946	1.000	.25	.50	1.50	5.00
	1946	—	—	—	Proof	100.00
	1950	*1.000	.25	.50	1.50	5.00
	1950	—	—	—	Proof	—
	1952	1.000	.25	.50	1.50	5.00
	1952	—	—	—	Proof	100.00
	1954	2.000	.10	.20	.50	4.00
	1954	—	—	—	Proof	100.00
	1956	3.000	.10	.20	.50	2.50
	1956	—	—	—	Proof	100.00

B.C.N. on edge

18.2	1964	3.000	.10	.20	.40	2.00
	1965	4.400	.10	.20	.30	.75

Reeded edge

18.3	1972	4.000	—	.10	.15	.35
	1972	.020	—	—	Proof	2.50
	1974	6.000	—	.10	.15	.35

BRASS
Reeded edge

| 23 | 1943 | 1.000 | .50 | 1.50 | 7.50 | 35.00 |

NICARAGUA 1353

NICARAGUA 1354

NICKEL CLAD STEEL
Sherritt Mint

KM#	Date	Mintage	Fine	VF	XF	Unc
51	1981	—	—	—	.25	.75
	1985	—	—	—	.25	.50

ALUMINUM

| 57 | 1987 | — | — | — | .25 | .50 |

50 CENTAVOS

12.5000 g, .800 SILVER, .3215 oz ASW

15	1912H	.260	5.00	12.50	30.00	100.00
	1912H	—	—	—	Proof	600.00
	1929	.020	7.00	15.00	50.00	200.00

GOLD (OMS)

| 15b | 1912H | 1 pc. | — | — | — | — |

COPPER-NICKEL
B.N.N. on edge

19.1	1939	1.000	.50	2.00	7.50	30.00
	1939	—	—	—	Proof	425.00
	1946	.500	.50	1.00	4.00	15.00
	1946	—	—	—	Proof	120.00
	1950	.500	.50	1.50	7.50	30.00
	1950	—	—	—	Proof	120.00
	1952	1.000	.25	1.00	5.00	20.00
	1952	—	—	—	Proof	120.00
	1954	2.000	.15	.50	2.00	5.00
	1954	—	—	—	Proof	120.00
	1956	2.000	.15	.25	1.00	4.00
	1956	—	—	—	Proof	120.00

B.C.N. on edge

| 19.2 | 1965 | .600 | .50 | 1.25 | 3.50 | 8.00 |
| | 1965 | — | — | — | Proof | 35.00 |

Reeded edge

| 19.3 | 1972 | .020 | — | — | Proof | 2.50 |
| | 1974 | 2.000 | .10 | .25 | .50 | 2.00 |

| 42 | 1980 Mo | 5.000 | .10 | .25 | .50 | 1.75 |

NICKEL CLAD STEEL

42a	1982	—	—	—	.40	1.25
	1983	—	—	—	.40	1.00
	1985	—	—	—	.40	1.00

ALUMINUM-BRONZE

KM#	Date	Mintage	Fine	VF	XF	Unc
58	1987	—	—	—	.40	1.00

UN (1) CORDOBA

25.0000 g, .900 SILVER, .7234 oz ASW

| 16 | 1912H | .035 | 20.00 | 45.00 | 200.00 | 1350. |
| | 1912H | — | — | — | Proof | 1500. |

GOLD (OMS)

| 16b | 1912H | 1 pc. | — | — | Proof | — |

COPPER-NICKEL
Reeded edge

| 26 | 1972 | 20.000 | .10 | .20 | .50 | 2.00 |
| | 1972 | — | — | — | Proof | 5.00 |

| 43 | 1980 Mo | 10.000 | .10 | .20 | .50 | 2.50 |
| | 1983 | — | .10 | .20 | .50 | 2.50 |

NICKEL CLAD STEEL

| 43a | 1984 | — | — | .10 | .50 | 2.00 |
| | 1985 | — | — | .10 | .50 | 2.00 |

ALUMINUM-BRONZE

| 59 | 1987 | — | — | — | .50 | 2.00 |

5 CORDOBAS

COPPER-NICKEL

| 44 | 1980 Mo | 10.000 | .15 | .25 | 1.00 | 2.50 |

NICKEL CLAD STEEL

KM#	Date	Mintage	Fine	VF	XF	Unc
44a	1984	—	—	.25	1.00	2.50

ALUMINUM-BRONZE

| 60 | 1987 | — | — | — | 1.00 | 2.50 |

20 CORDOBAS

5.0300 g, .925 SILVER, .1496 oz ASW
Earthquake Relief Issue

KM#	Date	Mintage	VF	XF	Unc
32	1975	2,500	—	—	7.50
	1975	2,000	—	Proof	10.00

50 CORDOBAS

35.6000 g, .900 GOLD, 1.0300 oz AGW
Ruben Dario

| 25 | 1967 | *.017 | — | Proof | BV + 4% |

*NOTE: Originally 500 pcs. were issued in green boxes with certificates. An additional 16,000 pieces were struck later on. Boxed originals command a premium.

12.5700 g, .925 SILVER, .3738 oz ASW
U.S. Bicentennial

| 33 | 1975 | 2,000 | — | — | 10.00 |
| | 1975 | 2,000 | — | Proof | 15.00 |

Earthquake Relief Issue

| 34 | 1975 | 2,500 | — | — | 9.00 |
| | 1975 | 2,000 | — | Proof | 12.50 |

16.6000 g, .825 SILVER, .4403 oz ASW
Olympics - Skier

KM#	Date	Mintage	VF	XF	Unc
61	1988	.010	—	Proof	10.00

Olympics - Sailboat

| 62 | 1988 | .010 | — | Proof | 10.00 |

100 CORDOBAS

25.1400 g, .925 SILVER, .6668 oz ASW
U.S. Bicentennial

| 35 | 1975 | 2,000 | — | — | 25.00 |
| | 1975 | 2,000 | — | Proof | 35.00 |

Earthquake Relief Issue

| 36 | 1975 | 2,700 | — | — | 20.00 |
| | 1975 | 2,000 | — | Proof | 30.00 |

200 CORDOBAS

2.1000 g, .900 GOLD, .0608 oz AGW
Pieta

KM#	Date	Mintage	VF	XF	Unc
37	1975	1,200	—	—	60.00
	1975	1,650	—	Proof	75.00

500 CORDOBAS

5.4000 g, .900 GOLD, .1563 oz AGW
Colonial Church

| 38 | 1975 | 320 pcs. | — | — | 125.00 |
| | 1975 | 100 pcs. | — | Proof | 175.00 |

Earthquake Relief Issue

| 39 | 1975 | 1,000 | — | — | 100.00 |
| | 1975 | 1,650 | — | Proof | 150.00 |

14.0000 g, .925 SILVER, .4164 oz ASW
A.C. Sandino

| 45 | 1980 Mo | .021 | — | — | 20.00 |

20.0000 g, .900 GOLD, .5788 oz AGW

| 45a | 1980 | 6,000 | — | Proof | 350.00 |

14.0000 g, .925 SILVER, .4164 oz ASW
Dobas Carlos Fonseca

| 46 | 1980 Mo | .021 | — | — | 20.00 |

20.0000 g, .900 GOLD, .5788 oz AGW

| 46a | 1980 | 6,000 | — | Proof | 350.00 |

14.0000 g, .925 SILVER, .4164 oz ASW
Rigoberto Lopez Perez

| 47 | 1980 Mo | .021 | — | — | 20.00 |

20.0000 g, .900 GOLD, .5788 oz AGW

| 47a | 1980 | 6,000 | — | Proof | 350.00 |

1000 CORDOBAS

9.5000 g, .900 GOLD, .2749 oz AGW
U.S. Bicentennial

| 40 | 1975 | 3,380 | — | — | 200.00 |
| | 1975 | 2,270 | — | Proof | 225.00 |

20.0000 g, .900 GOLD, .5788 oz AGW
1979 Revolution

KM#	Date	Mintage	VF	XF	Unc
48	1980 Mo	6,000	—	Proof	350.00

20.0000 g, .917 GOLD, .5896 oz AGW
Rev: Portrait of General Augusto Cesar Sandino.

| 52 | 1984 | 1,000 | — | Proof | 350.00 |

Rev: Birthplace of Augusto Cesar Sandino.

| 53 | 1984 | 1,000 | — | Proof | 350.00 |

Rev: Generals Sandino, Estrada and Umanzor.

| 54 | 1984 | 1,000 | — | Proof | 350.00 |

2000 CORDOBAS

19.2000 g, .900 GOLD, .5556 oz AGW
U.S. Bicentennial

| 41 | 1975 | 320 pcs. | — | — | 450.00 |
| | 1975 | 100 pcs. | — | Proof | 750.00 |

MINT SETS (MS)

KM#	Date	Mintage	Identification	Issue Price	Mkt. Val.
MS1	1975(5)	—	KM37-41	—	925.00
MS2	1975(5)	2,250	KM32-36	—	72.50

PROOF SETS (PS)

PS1	1912(7)	10	KM10-16	—	3250.
PS2	1912(7)	2	KM10a-16a	—	—
PS3	1912(7)	1	KM10b-16b	—	—
PS4	1972(5)	20,000	KM17.3-19.3,24,3,26	8.00	15.00
PS5	1975(7)	—	KM32,33,35,37,38,40,41	—	1165.
PS6	1975(5)	2,000	KM32-36	—	110.00
PS7	1975(3)	—	KM32,33,35	115.00	60.00
PS8	1975(3)	—	KM34,36,39	—	170.00

NIGER 1356

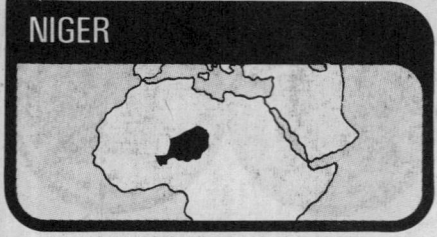

The Republic of Niger, located in West Africa's Sahara region 1,000 miles (1,609 km.) from the Mediterranean shore, has an area of 489,191 sq. mi. (1,267,000 sq. km.) and a population of *7.4 million. Capital: Niamey. The economy is based on subsistence agriculture and livestock raising. Peanuts, peanut oil, and livestock are exported.

Although four-fifths of Niger is arid desert, it was, some 6,000 years ago inhabited and an important economic crossroads. Its modern history began in the 19th century with the beginning of contacts with British and German explorers searching for the mouth of the Niger River. Niger was incorporated into French West Africa in 1896, but it was 1922 before all native resistance was quelled and Niger became a French colony. In 1958 the voters approved the new French Constitution and elected to become an autonomous republic within the French Community. On Aug. 3, 1960, Niger withdrew from the Community and proclaimed its independence.

10 FRANCS

3.2000 g, .900 GOLD, .0926 oz AGW

KM#	Date	Mintage	VF	XF	Unc
1	1960	1,000	—	Proof	75.00

| 7 | 1968 | 1,000 | — | Proof | 125.00 |

24.5400 g, .900 SILVER, .7100 oz ASW
Sharp details, raised rim.
| 8.1 | 1968 | 1,000 | — | Proof | 50.00 |

20.2000 g, .900 SILVER, .5845 oz ASW
Dull details, machined down rim.
| 8.2 | 1968 | (restrike) | — | — | — |

25 FRANCS

8.0000 g, .900 GOLD, .2315 oz AGW
| 2 | 1960 | 1,000 | — | Proof | 160.00 |

| 9 | 1968 | 1,000 | — | Proof | 300.00 |

50 FRANCS

16.0000 g, .900 GOLD, .4630 oz AGW
KM#	Date	Mintage	VF	XF	Unc
3	1960	1,000	—	Proof	265.00

| 10 | 1968 | 1,000 | — | Proof | 450.00 |

100 FRANCS

32.0000 g, .900 GOLD, .9260 oz AGW
| 4 | 1960 | 1,000 | — | Proof | 700.00 |

| 11 | 1968 | 1,000 | — | Proof | 750.00 |

500 FRANCS

10.0000 g, .900 SILVER, .2893 oz ASW
| 5 | 1960 | — | — | Proof | 25.00 |

1000 FRANCS

20.0000 g, .900 SILVER, .5787 oz ASW
KM#	Date	Mintage	VF	XF	Unc
6	1960	—	—	Proof	45.00

PROOF SETS (PS)

KM#	Date	Mintage	Identification	Issue Price	Mkt. Val.
PS1	1960(4)	1,000	KM1-4	—	1200.
PS2	1968(4)	—	KM7,9-11	—	1625.

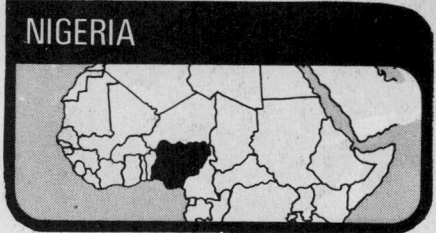
NIGERIA

The Federal Republic of Nigeria, situated on the Atlantic coast of Africa between Benin and Cameroon, has an area of 356,669 sq. mi. (923,768 sq. km.) and a population of *115.2 million. Capital: Lagos. The economy is based on petroleum and agriculture. Crude oil, cocoa, tobacco and tin are exported.

Following the Napoleonic Wars, the British expanded their trade with the interior of Nigeria. British claims to a sphere of influence in that area were recognized by the Berlin Conference of 1885, and in the following year the Royal Niger Company was chartered. Direct British control of the territory was initiated in 1900, and in 1914 the amalgamation of Northern and Southern Nigeria into the Colony and Protectorate of Nigeria was effected. In 1960, following a number of territorial and constitutional changes, Nigeria was granted independence within the British Commonwealth as a federation of the Northern, Western and Eastern regions. Nigeria altered its political relationship with Great Britain on Oct. 1, 1963, by proclaiming itself a republic. It did, however, elect to remain a member of the Commonwealth of Nations. The Supreme Commander of Armed Forces is the Head of the Federal Military Government.

On May 30, 1967, the Eastern Region of the republic - an area occupied principally by the proud and resourceful Ibo tribe - seceded from Nigeria and proclaimed itself the independent Republic of Biafra with Odumegwu Ojukwu as Chief of State. Civil war erupted and raged for 31 months. Casualties, including civilian, were about two million, the majority succumbing to malnutrition and disease. Biafra surrendered to the federal government on January 15, 1970.

For earlier coinage refer to British West Africa.

RULERS
Elizabeth II, 1952-1963

MONETARY SYSTEM
12 Pence = 1 Shilling
20 Shillings = 1 Pound

1/2 PENNY

BRONZE

KM#	Date	Mintage	VF	XF	Unc
1	1959	52.800	.10	.15	.35
	1959	6,031	—	Proof	2.00

PENNY

BRONZE

2	1959	93.368	.10	.15	.25
	1959	6,031	—	Proof	2.50

3 PENCE

NICKEL-BRASS

3	1959	52.000	.15	.25	.60
	1959	6,031	—	Proof	3.50

6 PENCE

COPPER-NICKEL

KM#	Date	Mintage	VF	XF	Unc
4	1959	35.000	.20	.40	.80
	1959	6,031	—	Proof	5.00

SHILLING

COPPER-NICKEL

5	1959	18.000	.50	1.00	2.00
	1959	6,031	—	Proof	6.50
	1961	48.584	.50	1.00	2.00
	1961	—	—	Proof	—
	1962	39.416	.50	1.00	2.00

2 SHILLINGS

COPPER-NICKEL
Reeded edge

6.1	1959	15.000	.50	1.00	2.50
	1959	6,031	—	Proof	9.00

Security edge

6.2	1959	Inc. Ab.	.50	1.00	2.50

REPUBLIC
100 Kobo = 1 Naira
(10 Shillings)

1/2 KOBO

BRONZE

7	1973	166.618	.10	.15	.40
	1973	.010	—	Proof	1.00

KOBO

BRONZE

8	1973	586.944	.10	.15	.60
	1973	.010	—	Proof	1.50
	1974	14.500	.10	.20	.75

5 KOBO

COPPER-NICKEL

9	1973	96.920	.10	.20	.80
	1973	.010	—	Proof	2.50
	1974	—	.10	.20	.80
	1976	9.800	.10	.20	.80
	1987	—	.10	.20	.80

10 KOBO

COPPER-NICKEL

KM#	Date	Mintage	VF	XF	Unc
10	1973	340.870	.15	.25	1.25
	1973	.010	—	Proof	4.00
	1974	—	.15	.25	1.25
	1976	7.000	.15	.25	1.25

25 KOBO

COPPER-NICKEL

11	1973	4.616	.35	.75	2.00
	1973	.010	—	Proof	6.00
	1975	—	.35	.75	2.00

PROOF SETS (PS)

KM#	Date	Mintage	Identification	Issue Price	Mkt. Val.
PS1	1959(6)	1,031	KM1-6, red case, originals	—	35.00
PS2	1959(6)	5,000	KM1-6, blue case, restrikes	—	15.00
PS3	1973(5)	10,200	KM7-11	14.70	15.00

BIAFRA

MONETARY SYSTEM
12 Pence = 1 Shilling

3 PENCE

ALUMINUM

KM#	Date	Mintage	VF	XF	Unc
1	1969	—	22.50	37.50	55.00

SHILLING

ALUMINUM

2	1969	—	10.00	15.00	22.50

Obv. value: ONE SHILLING

3	1969	—	—	Rare	—

2-1/2 SHILLINGS

ALUMINUM

4	1969	—	20.00	30.00	45.00

Biafra / NIGERIA 1358

CROWN

SILVER
Independence and Liberty

KM#	Date	Mintage	VF	XF	Unc
5	1969	—	—	Rare	—

POUND

		SILVER			
6	1969	—	—	65.00	90.00

3.9940 g, .917 GOLD, .1177 oz AGW
2nd Anniversary of Independence
Obv: Similar to 25 Pounds, KM#11.

7	1969	3,000	—	Proof	70.00

2 POUNDS

7.9881 g, .917 GOLD, .2354 oz AGW
2nd Anniversary of Independence
Obv: Similar to 25 Pounds, KM#11.

8	1969	3,000	—	Proof	140.00

5 POUNDS

15.9761 g, .917 GOLD, .4710 oz AGW
2nd Anniversary of Independence
Obv: Similar to 25 Pounds, KM#11.

KM#	Date	Mintage	VF	XF	Unc
9	1969	3,000	—	Proof	275.00

10 POUNDS

39.9403 g, .917 GOLD, 1.1776 oz AGW
2nd Anniversary of Independence
Obv: Similar to 25 Pounds, KM#11.

10	1969	3,000	—	Proof	700.00

25 POUNDS

79.8805 g, .917 GOLD, 2.3553 oz AGW
2nd Anniversary of Independence

11	1969	3,000	—	Proof	1375.

PROOF SETS (PS)

KM#	Date	Mintage	Identification	Issue Price	Mkt. Val.
PS1	1969(5)	3,000	KM7-11	464.00	2560.

Listings For
NIGERIA - BRITISH WEST AFRICA: refer to British West Africa

NIUE

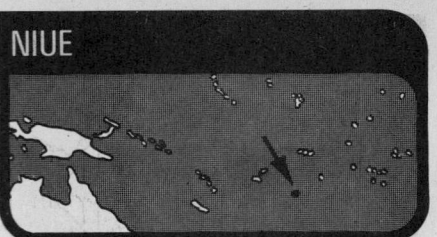

Niue, or Savage Island, a dependent state of New Zealand is located in the Pacific Ocean east of Tonga and south-east of Samoa. The size is 100 sq. mi. with a population of *3,148. Chief village and port is Alofi. Bananas and copra are exported.

Discovered by Captain Cook in 1774, it was originally part of the Cook Islands administration but has been separate since 1922.

5 DOLLARS

COPPER-NICKEL
Olympic Tennis - Boris Becker

KM#	Date	Mintage	VF	XF	Unc
1	1987	.080	—	—	4.00

Olympic Tennis - Steffi Graf

5	1987	.050	—	—	4.00

Tennis - Steffi Graf

11	1988	—	—	—	5.50

Soccer - Franz Beckenbauer

12	1988	—	—	—	4.50

Tennis - Navratilova, Graf and Evert

KM#	Date	Mintage	VF	XF	Unc
15	1988	—	—	—	5.50

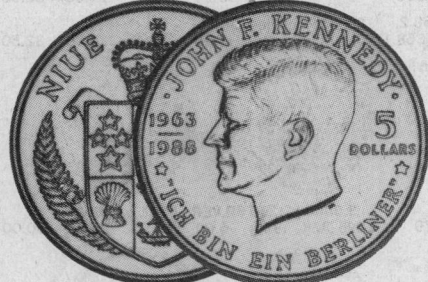

John F. Kennedy

| 17 | 1988 | .080 | — | — | 5.50 |

50 DOLLARS

27.1000 g, .625 SILVER, .5446 oz ASW
Olympic Tennis - Boris Becker

| 2 | 1987 | .020 | — | Proof | 42.50 |

Olympic Tennis - Steffi Graf
Similar to 5 Dollars, KM#5.

| 6 | 1987 | .020 | — | Proof | 42.50 |

Tennis - Steffi Graf
Similar to 5 Dollars, KM#11.

| 13 | 1988 | *.020 | — | Proof | 42.50 |

Soccer - Franz Beckenbauer
Similar to 5 Dollars, KM#12.

| 14 | 1988 | *.020 | — | Proof | 42.50 |

Tennis - Navratilova, Graf and Evert
Similar to 5 Dollars, KM#15.

| 16 | 1988 | *.020 | — | Proof | 42.50 |

28.2800 g, .925 SILVER, .8411 oz ASW
John F. Kennedy
Similar to 5 Dollars, KM#17.

| 18 | 1988 | .020 | — | Proof | 42.50 |

100 DOLLARS

155.5175 g, .999 SILVER, 5.0000 oz ASW
Illustration reduced. Actual size: 65mm

Olympic Tennis - Boris Becker

KM#	Date	Mintage	VF	XF	Unc
3	1987	*5,000	—	Proof	125.00

Illustration reduced. Actual size: 65mm
Olympic Tennis - Steffi Graf

| 7 | 1987 | *5,000 | — | Proof | 125.00 |

155.5170 g, .999 SILVER, 5.0000 oz ASW
John F. Kennedy
Similar to 5 Dollars, KM#17.

| 19 | 1988 | 3,000 | — | Proof | 125.00 |

Soccer - Franz Beckenbauer
Similar to 5 Dollars, KM#12.

| 21 | 1988 | — | — | Proof | 125.00 |

200 DOLLARS

311.0350 g, .999 SILVER, 10.0000 oz ASW
Olympic Tennis - Boris Becker
Similar to 50 Dollars, KM#2.

| 4 | 1987 | *3,000 | — | Proof | 165.00 |

Olympic Tennis - Steffi Graf
Similar to 50 Dollars, KM#2.

| 8 | 1987 | *3,000 | — | Proof | 165.00 |

250 DOLLARS

8.4830 g, .917 GOLD, .2500 oz AGW
Olympic Tennis - Boris Becker

| 9 | 1987 | *5,000 | — | Proof | 200.00 |

Olympic Tennis - Steffi Graf

| 10 | 1987 | *5,000 | — | Proof | 200.00 |

10.0000 g, .917 GOLD, .2948 oz AGW
John F. Kennedy

| 20 | 1988 | 5,000 | — | Proof | 200.00 |

Listings For
NORTH KOREA: refer to Korea
NORTH VIETNAM: refer to Vietnam

NORWAY

The Kingdom of Norway, a constitutional monarchy located in northwestern Europe, has an area of 150,000 sq. mi. (388,500 sq. km.), including the island territories of Spitzbergen (Svalbard) and Jan Mayen, and a population of *4.2 million. Capital: Oslo. The diversified economic base of Norway includes shipping, fishing, forestry, agriculture, and manufacturing. Nonferrous metals, paper and paperboard, paper pulp, iron, steel and oil are exported.

A united Norwegian kingdom was established in the 9th century, the era of the indomitable Norse Vikings who ranged far and wide, visiting the coasts of northwestern Europe, the Mediterranean, Greenland and North America. In the 13th century the Norse kingdom was united briefly with Sweden, then passed through inheritance in 1380 to the rule of Denmark which was maintained until 1814. In 1814 Norway fell again under the rule of Sweden. The union lasted until 1905 when the Norwegian Parliament arranged a peaceful separation and invited a Danish prince (King Haakon VII) to ascend the throne of an independent Kingdom of Norway.

RULERS
Christian VII, 1766-1808
Frederik VI, 1808-1814
Carl XIII, 1814-1818
Carl XIV, 1818-1844
Oscar I, 1844-1859
Carl XV, 1859-1872
Oscar II, 1872-1905
Haakon VII, 1905-1957
Olav V, 1957-

MINTMASTERS

Letter	Date	Name
AB,B	1961-1980	Arne Bakken
AB*	1980	Ole R. Kolberg
B	1861	Brynjulf Bergslien
CHL	1836-1844	Caspar Herman Langberg
I,IT	1880-1926	Ivar Trondsen, engraver
IGM	1797-1806	Johan Georg Madelung
IGP	1807-1824	Johan Georg Prahm
JMK	1825-1836	Johan Michael Kruse
K	1981-	Ole R. Kolberg
M	1815-1830	Gregorius Middelthun
OH	1959—	Oivind Hansen, engraver

MONETARY SYSTEM
Until 1873
120 Skilling = 1 Speciedaler
(Rigsdaler Specie)

1/2 SKILLING

COPPER

C#	Date	Mintage	VG	Fine	VF	XF
71.1	1839	.613	2.00	4.00	10.00	25.00
(C71)	1840	2.558	1.50	3.00	6.00	20.00
	1841	1.683	1.50	3.00	6.00	20.00

Rev: Star under hammers.

| 71.2 | 1841 | Inc. Ab. | 1.00 | 2.50 | 5.00 | 14.00 |
| (C71.1) | | | | | | |

Y#	Date	Mintage	Fine	VF	XF	Unc
1	1863	.480	5.00	12.50	35.00	75.00

| 2 | 1867 | 3.600 | 1.00 | 2.00 | 7.00 | 20.00 |

SKILLING
COPPER, 25mm

NORWAY 1360

Obv: Crowned FR monogram.
Rev: 5-petalled rosettes, by 1 and below date.

C#	Date	Mintage	VG	Fine	VF	XF
51.1 (C51)	1809	.346	7.50	12.50	20.00	50.00

Rev: 8-petalled rosettes, by 1 and below date.

| 51.2 (C51.1) | 1809 | Inc. Ab. | 7.50 | 12.50 | 20.00 | 50.00 |

Rev: Ovals by 1 and below date.

| 51.3 (C51.2) | 1809 | Inc. Ab. | 7.50 | 12.50 | 20.00 | 50.00 |

| 52 | 1812 | 5.453 | 1.00 | 2.50 | 5.00 | 10.00 |

*1812 w/o crossed hammers under date

| | | Inc. Ab. | 15.00 | 30.00 | 60.00 | 100.00 |

*Beware of removed mint mark or altered coin.

| 61 | 1816 | 1.659 | 4.00 | 9.00 | 25.00 | 70.00 |

72	1819	3.817	4.00	10.00	20.00	50.00
	1820	Inc. Ab.	3.00	7.00	15.00	50.00
	1824	6,000	30.00	50.00	100.00	250.00
	1825	—	250.00	500.00	750.00	1500.
	1827	.034	30.00	50.00	100.00	225.00
	1828	.038	500.00	850.00	—	—
	1831/28	1.440	35.00	60.00	140.00	260.00
	1831	Inc. Ab.	35.00	60.00	135.00	255.00
	1832	Inc. Ab.	22.50	40.00	80.00	170.00
	1833	.126	22.50	40.00	80.00	170.00
	1834	—	1000.	—	—	—

Y#	Date	Mintage	Fine	VF	XF	Unc
3	1870	1.200	2.00	5.00	15.00	50.00

2 SKILLING

1.5000 g, .250 SILVER, .0120 oz ASW

C#	Date	Mintage	VG	Fine	VF	XF
18	1801 IGM	1.109	2.00	5.00	9.00	18.00
	1802 IGM	2.854	2.00	5.00	9.00	18.00
	1803 IGM	2.419	2.00	5.00	9.00	18.00
	1804 IGM	3.634	3.00	8.00	16.00	30.00
	1805 IGM	2.412	2.50	6.00	10.00	25.00
	1807 IGP	3.507	2.00	5.00	9.00	18.00

COPPER
Rev: 8-petalled rosettes by 2 and below date.

| 53.1 (C53) | 1810 | 3.449 | 2.00 | 4.00 | 8.00 | 20.00 |

Rev: Cross.

| 53.2 (C53.1) | 1810 | Inc. Ab. | 2.00 | 4.00 | 6.00 | 20.00 |
| | 1811 | 1.191 | 2.50 | 6.00 | 12.00 | 25.00 |

C#	Date	Mintage	VG	Fine	VF	XF
73	1822	.963	7.00	15.00	40.00	90.00
	1824	.549	7.00	15.00	40.00	90.00
	1825	.510	12.00	30.00	65.00	150.00
	1827	.288	12.00	27.50	65.00	150.00
	1828	.453	10.00	20.00	50.00	125.00
	1831	Inc. Ab.	7.00	15.00	35.00	100.00
	1832	Inc. Ab.	7.00	15.00	35.00	100.00
	1833	.060	8.00	20.00	40.00	100.00
	1834	.880	35.00	80.00	125.00	275.00

1.5000 g, .250 SILVER, .0120 oz ASW, 17mm

| 78 | 1825 | .240 | 7.00 | 15.00 | 30.00 | 60.00 |

| 93 | 1842 | 1.500 | 2.00 | 4.00 | 10.00 | 20.00 |
| | 1843 | Inc. Ab. | 3.00 | 7.50 | 15.00 | 25.00 |

Rev: Rosettes.

Y#	Date	Mintage	Fine	VF	XF	Unc
4.1 (Y4.1)	1870	.900	3.00	5.00	10.00	25.00
	1871	.900	3.00	5.00	10.00	25.00

Rev: Stars.

| 4.2 (Y4.2) | 1871 | 1.140 | 3.00 | 5.00 | 10.00 | 25.00 |

3 SKILLING

2.2500 g, .250 SILVER, .0181 oz ASW
Rev: Rosettes.

| 5.1 (Y5.1) | 1868 | .499 | 5.00 | 8.00 | 16.00 | 35.00 |
| | 1869 | .103 | 10.00 | 16.00 | 32.50 | 60.00 |

Rev: Stars.

| 5.2 (Y5.2) | 1869 | .600 | 5.00 | 8.00 | 16.00 | 35.00 |

Rev: Rosettes.

| 11.1 (Y11) | 1872 | .504 | 5.00 | 8.00 | 16.00 | 35.00 |

Rev: Stars.

| 11.2 (Y11) | 1872 | .576 | 5.00 | 8.00 | 16.00 | 35.00 |
| | 1873 | .600 | 5.00 | 8.00 | 16.00 | 35.00 |

4 SKILLING

COPPER

Rev: Rosettes by 4 and below date.

C#	Date	Mintage	VG	Fine	VF	XF
54.1 (C54)	1809	.251	12.50	30.00	70.00	150.00

Rev: Stars by 4 and below date.

54.2 (C54.1)	1809	Inc. Ab.	17.50	40.00	85.00	190.00
	1810					
	2 pcs. known		—	—	Rare	

2.0500 g, .250 SILVER, .0165 oz ASW

| 58.1 (C58) | 1809 IGP rev. leg: SKILLI: | 2.228 | 3.00 | 6.00 | 14.00 | 32.50 |
| 58.2 (C58.1) | 1809 IGP rev. leg: SKILLE – | Inc. Ab. | 3.00 | 6.00 | 14.00 | 32.50 |

3.0000 g, .250 SILVER, .0241 oz ASW

| 79 | 1825 JMK | .333 | 6.00 | 12.50 | 25.00 | 50.00 |

| 94 | 1842 | .750 | 3.00 | 7.00 | 20.00 | 50.00 |

Y#	Date	Mintage	Fine	VF	XF	Unc
6	1871	.559	7.00	12.50	25.00	50.00

6 SKILLING
COPPER
Obv: Crowned shield. Rev: Value.

C#	Date	Mintage	VG	Fine	VF	XF
55	1813	.109	3.00	6.00	15.00	32.50

8 SKILLING

 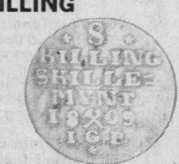

2.7300 g, .375 SILVER, .0329 oz ASW

C#	Date	Mintage	VG	Fine	VF	XF
59	1809 IGP	1.349	5.00	10.00	20.00	45.00

3.3700 g, .500 SILVER, .0542 oz ASW

| 67 | 1817 IGP | .241 | 8.00 | 20.00 | 45.00 | 120.00 |

| 80 | 1819 IGP | .101 | 15.00 | 30.00 | 70.00 | 150.00 |

1.9300 g, .875 SILVER, .0543 oz ASW

| 87 | 1825 | .016 | 15.00 | 30.00 | 60.00 | 110.00 |
| | 1827/5 | .014 | 15.00 | 30.00 | 60.00 | 110.00 |

1/15 SPECIE DALER

3.3700 g, .500 SILVER, .0542 oz ASW
Obv: Value, crowned oval arms. Rev: Value, date.

C#	Date	Mintage	VG	Fine	VF	XF
26	1801 IGM	.382	5.00	12.50	17.50	50.00
	1802 IGM	.149	5.00	12.50	17.50	50.00

12 SKILLING

COPPER
Obv: Crowned shield. Rev: Value.

C#	Date	Mintage	VG	Fine	VF	XF
56	1813	.739	3.00	6.00	12.50	30.00

2.8900 g, .875 SILVER, .0813 oz ASW
Plain border

C#	Date	Mintage	VG	Fine	VF	XF
101.1	1845	.631	6.00	10.00	22.50	50.00
(C101)	1846	.250	6.50	10.00	25.00	55.00
	1847	.256	6.50	10.00	25.00	55.00
	1848	.316	6.50	10.00	25.00	55.00

Beaded border

C#	Date	Mintage	VG	Fine	VF	XF
101.2	1850 leg: V KONGE					
(C101.1)		.287	6.50	10.00	25.00	55.00
	1850 leg: V.KONGE					
	Inc. Ab.		7.00	13.00	25.00	60.00
	1852	.313	5.00	10.00	22.50	50.00
	1853	.360	5.00	10.00	22.50	50.00
	1854	.301	5.00	10.00	22.50	50.00
	1855	.450	5.00	10.00	22.50	50.00
	1856/5	.812	4.50	9.00	20.00	40.00
	1856 Inc. Ab.		4.00	7.00	18.00	35.00

Obv: Small head.

Y#	Date	Mintage	Fine	VF	XF	Unc
7	1861	2,500	400.00	700.00	1350.	2200.
	1862	2,500	400.00	700.00	1350.	2200.

Obv: Large head.

| 7a | 1865 | .152 | 50.00 | 90.00 | 200.00 | 375.00 |

| 12 | 1873 | .490 | 30.00 | 45.00 | 75.00 | 200.00 |

24 SKILLING

7.3100 g, .687 SILVER, .1615 oz ASW

C#	Date	Mintage	VG	Fine	VF	XF
81	1819 IGP	.050	20.00	40.00	80.00	150.00

5.7300 g, .875 SILVER, .1612 oz ASW

| 81a | 1823 IGP | .125 | 37.50 | 75.00 | 125.00 | 250.00 |
| | 1824 JMK | 7,800 | 40.00 | 80.00 | 175.00 | 325.00 |

C#	Date	Mintage	VG	Fine	VF	XF
88	1825	4,600	45.00	90.00	200.00	325.00
	1827/5	.027	30.00	65.00	135.00	250.00
	1827 Inc. Ab.		30.00	65.00	135.00	250.00
	1830	5,800	55.00	110.00	225.00	400.00
	1831/0	2,400	—	—	Rare	
	1833	—	110.00	225.00	450.00	800.00
	1834	—	110.00	225.00	450.00	800.00
	1835	2,500	90.00	175.00	375.00	650.00
	1836	2,500	90.00	175.00	400.00	700.00

5.7800 g, .875 SILVER, .1626 oz ASW
Plain border

102.1	1845	.359	8.00	17.50	40.00	75.00
(C102)	1846	.383	9.00	20.00	45.00	85.00
	1847	.217	9.00	20.00	45.00	85.00
	1848	.150	11.00	25.00	50.00	95.00

Beaded border

102.2	1850	.102	11.00	25.00	50.00	100.00
(C102.1)	1852	.254	9.00	20.00	45.00	85.00
	1853	.327	9.00	20.00	45.00	85.00
	1854	.212	11.00	25.00	50.00	100.00
	1855	.204	8.00	17.50	40.00	80.00

Obv: Small head.

Y#	Date	Mintage	Fine	VF	XF	Unc
8	1861	13 pcs.	—	—	Rare	
	1862	1,200	450.00	850.00	1600.	2500.

Obv: Large head.

| 8a | 1865 | .079 | 75.00 | 125.00 | 275.00 | 500.00 |

1/5 SPECIE DALER

7.3100 g, .687 SILVER, .1615 oz ASW

C#	Date	Mintage	VG	Fine	VF	XF
32	1801 IGM	.163	15.00	30.00	60.00	110.00
	1803 IGM	.092	15.00	30.00	60.00	110.00

1/3 SPECIE DALER

9.6300 g, .875 SILVER, .2709 oz ASW
Similar to KM#34.2.

34.1	1801 IGM	.108	25.00	55.00	110.00	225.00
(C34)	1802 IGM	.065	35.00	70.00	140.00	300.00
	1803 IGM	.024	50.00	100.00	200.00	400.00

Obv: Bust right w/o bow, P.G. below portrait.

| 34.2 | 1803 IGM | I.A. | 125.00 | 250.00 | 500.00 | 1000. |
| (C34.1) | | | | | | |

1/2 SPECIE DALER

14.4500 g, .875 SILVER, .4065 oz ASW

C#	Date	Mintage	VG	Fine	VF	XF
83	1819	.010	60.00	120.00	250.00	475.00
	1821	.069	40.00	70.00	120.00	230.00
	1823/1	6,100	90.00	180.00	325.00	650.00
	1824/1	.033	40.00	80.00	150.00	275.00
	1824 Inc. Ab.		40.00	80.00	150.00	275.00

89	1827 SKI:	.070	40.00	75.00	135.00	290.00
	1827. SKI. I.A.		40.00	75.00	135.00	290.00
	1829	5,100	150.00	275.00	425.00	800.00
	1830	8,000	90.00	180.00	300.00	550.00
	1831	9,000	90.00	180.00	300.00	550.00
	1832	4,700	90.00	180.00	300.00	550.00
	1833	1,500	90.00	180.00	300.00	550.00
	1834/29	.018	50.00	90.00	175.00	325.00
	1834 Inc. Ab.		50.00	90.00	175.00	325.00
	1835	9,000	50.00	90.00	175.00	325.00
	1835 star under mint mark					
	Inc. Ab.		—	—	Rare	
	1836	4,000	60.00	120.00	225.00	350.00

| 95 | 1844 | .231 | 35.00 | 65.00 | 120.00 | 230.00 |

103	1846	.146	35.00	65.00	120.00	230.00
	1847	.047	35.00	65.00	120.00	230.00
	1848	.015	40.00	70.00	140.00	275.00
	1849	.142	30.00	65.00	120.00	230.00
	1850 Inc. Ab.		30.00	65.00	120.00	230.00
	1855	.010	100.00	200.00	325.00	575.00

Y#	Date	Mintage	Fine	VF	XF	Unc
9	1861	500 pcs.	—	—	Rare	
	1861 B under bust					
	13 pcs.	—	—	Rare	
	1862	.064	135.00	225.00	385.00	750.00
9a	1865	700 pcs.	—	—	Rare	
13	1873	4,200	4000.	5000.	6000.	8250.

NORWAY 1361

NORWAY 1362

SPECIE DALER

28.8900 g, .875 SILVER, .8127 oz ASW

C#	Date	Mintage	VG	Fine	VF	XF
84	1819 IGP	.024	125.00	300.00	500.00	700.00
	1821 IGP	.101	60.00	120.00	235.00	450.00
	1823 IGP	.016	200.00	350.00	650.00	1150.
	1824/1 JMK	.121	60.00	125.00	250.00	475.00
	1824 JMK	I.A.	60.00	125.00	250.00	475.00

90	1826	.025	70.00	140.00	275.00	475.00
	1826 initial M Inc. Ab.	750.00	1500.	3000.	—
	1827/6	.132	60.00	120.00	230.00	425.00
	1827	Inc. Ab.	60.00	120.00	230.00	425.00
	1829/7	.016	75.00	150.00	300.00	525.00
	1829	Inc. Ab.	75.00	150.00	300.00	525.00
	1830	.026	60.00	120.00	240.00	450.00
	1831	.031	80.00	165.00	350.00	600.00
	1832	.024	80.00	165.00	350.00	600.00
	1833	2.732	500.00	1000.	2000.	3000.
	1834	.103	60.00	120.00	230.00	425.00
	1835	.040	60.00	120.00	230.00	425.00
	1835 star under mint mark Inc. Ab.	200.00	425.00	750.00	1200.
	1836	.052	65.00	150.00	275.00	500.00

C#	Date	Mintage	VG	Fine	VF	XF
96	1844	.302	60.00	120.00	230.00	435.00

104	1846	.067	50.00	100.00	200.00	350.00
	1847	.140	50.00	100.00	200.00	350.00
	1848	.081	50.00	100.00	200.00	350.00
	1849	.114	50.00	100.00	200.00	350.00
	1850	.124	50.00	100.00	200.00	350.00
	1855	.148	50.00	100.00	200.00	350.00
	1856	.114	55.00	110.00	220.00	350.00
	1857	.160	55.00	110.00	220.00	350.00

Rev: Similar to C#96.

Y#	Date	Mintage	Fine	VF	XF	Unc
10	1861	.044	225.00	350.00	650.00	1250.
	1861 B under bust 13 pcs.	—	—	Rare	—
	1862	.062	225.00	350.00	575.00	1250.

Rev: Similar to C#96.

10a	1864	.130	150.00	250.00	400.00	825.00
	1865	.086	150.00	250.00	400.00	825.00
	1867	.030	250.00	500.00	1000.	2000.
	1868	.114	160.00	300.00	550.00	1200.
	1869	.057	150.00	250.00	475.00	1000.

DECIMAL COINAGE
100 Ore = 1 Krone (30 Skilling)

ORE

BRONZE

19	1876	8.000	4.00	8.00	15.00	45.00
	1877	2.166	15.00	25.00	45.00	85.00
	1878	1.834	22.50	37.50	60.00	125.00
	1884	3.378	6.00	8.00	15.00	45.00
	1885	.622	60.00	110.00	150.00	250.00
	1889	3.000	5.00	8.00	17.50	35.00
	1891	3.000	5.00	8.00	17.50	35.00
	1893	3.000	5.00	8.00	17.50	35.00
	1897	3.000	5.00	8.00	17.50	35.00

Y#	Date	Mintage	Fine	VF	XF	Unc
19	1899	4.500	2.00	4.00	10.00	25.00
	1902	4.500	2.00	4.00	10.00	25.00

30	1906	3.000	2.00	4.00	9.00	17.50
	1907	2.550	2.00	5.00	10.00	22.50

35	1908	1.450	8.00	15.00	25.00	75.00
	1910	2.480	1.00	2.50	7.00	25.00
	1911	3.270	1.00	2.50	7.00	30.00
	1912	2.850	3.00	7.00	15.00	65.00
	1913	2.840	1.00	2.50	6.00	20.00
	1914	5.020	1.00	2.50	5.00	20.00
	1915	1.540	8.00	15.00	25.00	90.00
	1921	3.805	17.50	35.00	50.00	125.00
	1922	Inc. Ab.	.50	2.00	12.00	35.00
	1923	.770	6.00	12.00	25.00	65.00
	1925	3.000	.50	1.50	10.00	35.00
	1926	2.200	.50	1.50	10.00	35.00
	1927	.800	4.00	7.00	17.50	60.00
	1928	3.000	.25	.75	4.00	18.00
	1929	4.990	.25	.75	4.00	15.00
	1930	2.010	.50	1.00	5.00	20.00
	1931	2.000	.50	1.00	5.00	20.00
	1932	2.500	.50	1.00	5.00	20.00
	1933	2.000	.50	1.00	5.00	15.00
	1934	2.000	.50	1.00	5.00	15.00
	1935	5.495	.25	.75	2.00	10.00
	1936	6.855	.25	.75	2.00	10.00
	1937	6.020	.20	.50	1.25	6.00
	1938	4.920	.20	.50	1.25	6.00
	1939	2.500	.20	.50	1.25	8.00
	1940	5.010	.20	.50	1.25	6.00
	1941	12.260	.10	.25	1.25	6.00
	1946	2.200	.10	.25	.75	5.00
	1947	4.870	.10	.25	.75	4.00
	1948	9.405	.10	.25	.75	3.50
	1949	2.785	.10	.25	.75	5.00
	1950	5.730	.10	.25	.75	3.50
	1951	16.670	.10	.25	.75	3.50
	1952	Inc. Ab.	.10	.25	.75	2.50

IRON

35a	1918	6.000	5.00	8.00	15.00	30.00
	1919	12.930	1.50	3.50	9.00	18.00
	1920	4.445	6.00	10.00	20.00	40.00
	1921	2.270	30.00	35.00	55.00	95.00

World War II German Occupation

53	1941	13.410	.15	.50	1.50	5.00
	1942	37.710	.15	.50	1.50	4.00
	1943	33.030	.15	.50	1.50	4.00
	1944	8.820	.25	.75	2.00	6.00
	1945	1.740	4.00	8.00	12.50	25.00

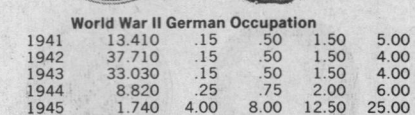

BRONZE

59	1952	Inc. Y#35	—	.10	.80	3.00
	1953	7.440	—	.10	.80	3.00
	1954	7.650	—	.10	.80	3.00
	1955	8.635	—	.10	.80	3.00
	1956	11.705	—	.10	.80	3.00
	1957	15.750	—	.10	.60	2.00

66	1958	2.820	.25	.50	2.00	6.00
	1959	9.120	.10	.20	.75	4.00
	1960	7.890	—	.10	.25	2.00
	1961	5.671	—	.10	.25	2.00
	1962	12.180	—	.10	.20	1.00
	1963	8.010	—	.10	.25	2.00
	1964	11.020	—	—	.10	.60
	1965	8.081	—	—	.10	1.25
	1966	12.431	—	—	.10	.80
	1967	13.026	—	—	.10	.60
	1968	.126	.50	1.00	2.00	6.00
	1969	6.291	—	—	.10	.40
	1970	6.608	—	—	.10	.40
	1971	18.966	—	—	.10	.30
	1972	21.103	—	—	.10	.30

2 ORE

Y#	Date	Mintage	Fine	VF	XF	Unc
	BRONZE					
20	1876	1.774	4.00	7.00	18.00	45.00
	1877	1.976	3.00	6.00	15.00	40.00
	1884	1.000	5.00	9.00	20.00	50.00
	1889	1.000	3.00	6.00	12.50	35.00
	1891	1.000	2.00	5.00	9.00	32.50
	1893	1.000	2.00	5.00	9.00	32.50
	1897	1.000	2.00	5.00	9.00	32.50
	1899	1.000	2.00	5.00	9.00	32.50
	1902	1.005	1.50	4.00	8.00	30.00

Y#	Date	Mintage	Fine	VF	XF	Unc
31	1906	.500	5.00	7.00	16.00	65.00
	1907	.980	3.00	4.00	10.00	35.00

Y#	Date	Mintage	Fine	VF	XF	Unc
36	1909	.520	6.00	10.00	30.00	90.00
	1910	.500	6.00	10.00	30.00	150.00
	1911	.195	6.00	10.00	30.00	110.00
	1912	.805	6.00	10.00	30.00	120.00
	1913	2.010	.75	2.00	6.00	35.00
	1914	2.990	.75	2.00	6.00	35.00
	1915	Inc. Ab.	4.00	8.00	20.00	100.00
	1921	2.028	.50	1.00	10.00	45.00
	1922	2.288	.50	1.00	10.00	45.00
	1923	.745	1.00	2.00	10.00	70.00
	1928	2.250	.50	1.00	5.00	25.00
	1929	.750	1.00	2.00	12.00	35.00
	1931	1.570	.50	1.00	5.00	25.00
	1932	.630	3.50	6.00	15.00	55.00
	1933	.750	.50	1.50	6.00	35.00
	1934	.500	.50	1.50	6.00	35.00
	1935	2.223	.25	1.00	4.00	15.00
	1936	4.533	.25	1.00	4.00	15.00
	1937	3.790	.20	.50	2.25	10.00
	1938	3.765	.20	.50	2.25	10.00
	1939	4.420	.20	.50	2.25	10.00
	1940	2.655	.20	.50	2.25	10.00
	1946	1.575	.20	.50	3.00	10.00
	1947	4.679	.10	.25	1.00	5.00
	1948	1.003	1.00	3.00	4.00	13.00
	1949	1.455	.10	.25	1.00	6.00
	1950	5.790	.10	.25	1.00	5.00
	1951	10.540	.10	.25	1.00	5.00
	1952	Inc. Ab.	.10	.25	1.00	5.00
		IRON				
36a	1917	.720	75.00	115.00	175.00	350.00
	1918	1.280	35.00	50.00	80.00	150.00
	1919	3.365	10.00	15.00	35.00	70.00
	1920	2.635	10.00	15.00	45.00	85.00

World War II German Occupation

Y#	Date	Mintage	Fine	VF	XF	Unc
54	1943	6.575	.50	.75	1.50	7.00
	1944	9.805	.50	.75	1.50	7.00
	1945	2.520	1.50	3.00	5.00	15.00

BRONZE

Y#	Date	Mintage	Fine	VF	XF	Unc
60	1952	Inc. Ab.	—	.10	.80	6.00
	1953	6.705	—	.10	.80	4.00
	1954	2.805	—	.10	.80	4.00
	1955	3.600	—	.10	.80	4.00
	1956	6.780	—	.10	.80	4.00
	1957	6.090	—	.10	.80	4.00

Rev: Small lettering.

Y#	Date	Mintage	Fine	VF	XF	Unc
67	1958	2.700	.20	.50	1.50	6.00

Rev: Large lettering.

Y#	Date	Mintage	Fine	VF	XF	Unc
67a	1959	4.125	.10	.20	1.00	5.00
	1960	3.735	—	.10	.75	3.00
	1961	4.477	—	.10	.30	1.50
	1962	6.205	—	.10	.30	1.50
	1963	4.840	—	.10	.30	1.50
	1964	7.250	—	.10	.15	1.00
	1965	6.241	—	.10	.25	2.00
	1966	10.485	—	—	.10	1.50
	1967	11.993	—	—	.10	1.00
	1968	3,467		In mint sets only		800.00
	1969	.316	.50	1.00	1.50	4.00
	1970	6.794	—	—	.10	.50
	1971	15.462	—	—	.10	.40
	1972	15.898	—	—	.10	.30

5 ORE

BRONZE

Y#	Date	Mintage	Fine	VF	XF	Unc
21	1875	.354	22.00	35.00	90.00	300.00
	1876	1.647	3.50	8.00	30.00	100.00
	1878	.500	6.00	20.00	45.00	200.00
	1896	1.000	2.50	6.00	30.00	90.00
	1899	.700	2.50	6.00	30.00	100.00
	1902	.705	2.50	6.00	30.00	100.00

Y#	Date	Mintage	Fine	VF	XF	Unc
32	1907	.200	3.50	9.00	35.00	125.00

Y#	Date	Mintage	Fine	VF	XF	Unc
37	1908	.600	20.00	35.00	60.00	175.00
	1911	.480	2.00	7.50	30.00	100.00
	1912	.520	4.00	10.00	40.00	200.00
	1913	1.000	1.25	2.50	17.50	80.00
	1914	1.000	1.25	2.50	17.50	80.00
	1915	Inc. Ab.	8.00	17.50	45.00	200.00
	1916	.300	6.00	12.50	25.00	150.00
	1921	.683	1.50	6.00	35.00	150.00
	1922	2.296	1.25	5.00	25.00	70.00
	1923	.456	2.50	7.50	40.00	150.00
	1928	.848	.60	3.00	15.00	60.00
	1929	.452	3.00	9.00	30.00	100.00
	1930	1.292	.60	2.50	17.50	60.00
	1931	.808	.60	2.50	17.50	60.00
	1932	.500	3.00	10.00	30.00	90.00
	1933	.300	3.00	10.00	35.00	120.00
	1935	.496	1.50	5.00	15.00	60.00
	1936	.760	1.00	2.50	12.50	35.00
	1937	1.552	.50	1.50	10.00	30.00
	1938	1.332	.50	1.50	10.00	30.00
	1939	1.370	.50	1.50	8.00	25.00
	1940	2.554	.30	1.00	6.00	22.50
	1941	3.576	.30	1.00	5.00	17.50
	1951	8.128	.25	.50	2.00	10.00
	1952	Inc. Ab.	1.50	3.50	8.00	30.00

IRON

Y#	Date	Mintage	Fine	VF	XF	Unc
37a	1917	1.700	25.00	40.00	60.00	100.00
	1918/7	.432	125.00	185.00	325.00	550.00
	1918	Inc. Ab.	115.00	175.00	300.00	500.00
	1919	3.464	15.00	35.00	55.00	100.00
	1920	1.629	30.00	60.00	90.00	200.00

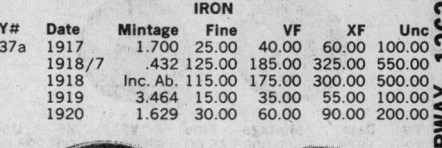

World War II German Occupation

Y#	Date	Mintage	Fine	VF	XF	Unc
55	1941	6.608	.50	1.50	4.50	25.00
	1942	10.312	.50	1.50	4.00	11.00
	1943	6.184	.75	2.00	6.00	17.50
	1944	4.256	1.25	5.00	10.00	25.00
	1945	.408	75.00	150.00	225.00	350.00

BRONZE

Y#	Date	Mintage	Fine	VF	XF	Unc
61	1952	Inc. Y#37	.10	1.00	2.00	12.50
	1953	6.216	.10	1.00	2.00	10.00
	1954	4.536	.10	1.00	2.00	10.00
	1955	6.570	.10	1.00	2.00	10.00
	1956	2.959	.10	1.00	2.00	12.50
	1957	5.624	.10	1.00	2.00	8.00

Y#	Date	Mintage	Fine	VF	XF	Unc
68	1958	2.205	1.00	2.00	5.00	20.00
	1959	3.208	.10	.50	2.00	10.00
	1960	5.519	.10	.20	1.00	8.00
	1961	4.554	.10	.20	1.00	7.00
	1962	7.764	.10	.15	.75	5.00
	1963	3.204	.10	.15	.75	5.00
	1964	6.108	—	.10	.50	2.00
	1965	6.841	—	.10	.50	2.00
	1966	8.415	—	.10	.50	2.00
	1967	9.071	—	.10	.50	2.00
	1968	4.286	—	.10	.80	3.00
	1969	4.328	—	.10	.30	1.25
	1970	7.351	—	.10	.30	1.00
	1971	13.450	—	.10	.30	1.25
	1972	19.002	—	—	.10	.50
	1973	9.584	—	—	.10	.50

Y#	Date	Mintage	Fine	VF	XF	Unc
76	1973	52.886	—	—	.10	.30
	1974	37.150	—	—	.10	.30
	1975	32.479	—	—	.10	.30
	1976	24.233	—	—	.10	.20
	1977	29.646	—	—	.10	.20
	1978	13.838	—	—	.10	.20
	1979	25.255	—	—	.10	.20
	1980	12.315	—	—	.10	.20
	1980 w/o star					
		27.515	—	—	.10	.20
	1981	24.529	—	—	.10	.20
	1982	16.849	—	—	.10	.20

10 ORE

(3 Skilling)

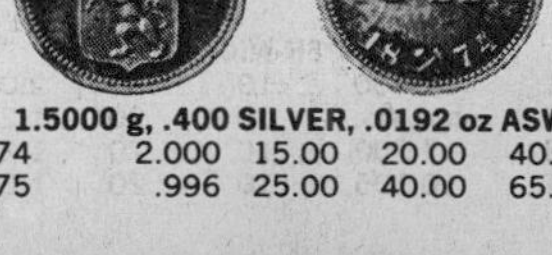

1.5000 g, .400 SILVER, .0192 oz ASW

Y#	Date	Mintage	Fine	VF	XF	Unc
14	1874	2.000	15.00	20.00	40.00	100.00
	1875	.996	25.00	40.00	65.00	150.00

NORWAY 1364

Y#	Date	Mintage	Fine	VF	XF	Unc
22	1875	1.008	45.00	65.00	125.00	225.00
	1876	1.992	10.00	20.00	40.00	85.00
	1877	.588	50.00	90.00	140.00	225.00
	1878	.612	30.00	50.00	80.00	175.00
	1880	.600	25.00	40.00	60.00	120.00
	1882	.760	17.50	30.00	45.00	85.00
	1883	1.250	12.50	20.00	40.00	65.00
	1888	.500	18.00	35.00	55.00	100.00
	1889	.750	12.50	17.50	32.50	65.00
	1890	1.000	10.00	15.00	32.50	55.00
	1892	2.000	8.00	12.50	27.50	50.00
	1894	1.500	8.00	12.50	27.50	50.00
	1897	1.500	5.00	7.50	22.50	45.00
	1898	2.000	5.00	7.50	22.50	45.00
	1899	2.500	5.00	7.50	22.50	45.00
	1901	2.021	5.00	7.50	22.50	45.00
	1903	1.501	5.00	7.50	22.50	45.00

38	1909	2.000	4.00	7.50	17.50	40.00
	1911	1.650	5.00	8.50	17.50	40.00
	1912	2.350	4.00	7.50	17.50	40.00
	1913	2.000	4.00	6.00	17.50	35.00
	1914	1.180	7.00	11.00	20.00	40.00
	1915	2.820	1.50	3.00	6.00	15.00
	1916	1.500	6.00	9.00	15.00	37.50
	1917	5.950	1.00	2.00	4.00	7.50
	1918	1.650	1.50	2.50	7.50	15.00
	1919	7.800	1.00	2.00	4.00	7.50

COPPER-NICKEL

46	1920	2.535	12.50	17.50	22.50	35.00
	1921	6.465	5.00	10.00	12.50	25.00
	1922	3.965	5.00	10.00	12.50	25.00
	1923	7.135	10.00	15.00	20.00	35.00

49	1924	12.079	.30	.75	7.50	35.00
	1925	7.051	.30	.75	7.50	35.00
	1926	11.764	.30	.75	7.50	35.00
	1927	.527	5.00	12.50	80.00	200.00
	1937	5.000	.30	.75	4.00	15.00
	1938	3.413	.30	.75	4.00	15.00
	1939	1.538	1.00	2.50	8.00	35.00
	1940	4.800	.30	.75	1.50	9.00
	1941	10.150	.30	.75	1.50	7.50
	1945	1.719	.10	.25	1.50	15.00
	1946	3.723	.10	.25	1.50	6.00
	1947	7.257	.10	.25	1.50	5.00
	1948	3.105	.10	.25	2.00	4.00
	1949	11.546	.10	.25	1.50	5.00
	1951	5.150	.10	.25	1.50	5.00

NICKEL-BRASS
World War II Government in exile.

49a	1942	*6.000	—	—	100.00	150.00

NOTE: All melted down except for 9,667.

ZINC
World War II Nazi Occupation

56	1941	15.310	.75	2.00	5.00	15.00
	1942	50.388	.35	1.00	3.00	6.00
	1943	13.378	.75	2.00	4.50	12.00
	1944	3.549	7.50	12.50	65.00	65.00
	1945	5.646	4.00	8.00	15.00	30.00

COPPER-NICKEL

62	1951	17.400	.10	.30	2.00	10.00
	1952	Inc. Ab.	.10	.20	1.25	5.00
	1953	7.700	.10	.20	1.25	5.00
	1954	10.105	.10	.20	1.25	7.00

Y#	Date	Mintage	Fine	VF	XF	Unc
62	1955	9.830	.10	.20	1.25	12.00
	1956	10.066	.10	.20	1.25	5.00
	1957	22.900	.10	.20	1.25	5.00

Rev: Small lettering.

69	1958	1.425	.50	1.50	2.50	8.00

Rev: Large lettering.

69a	1959	2.500	—	.75	2.50	7.50
	1960	12.490	—	.10	.50	3.00
	1961	10.386	—	.10	.50	3.00
	1962	16.210	—	.10	.50	2.50
	1963	17.560	—	.10	.50	2.50
	1964	9.781	—	.10	.25	1.00
	1965	10.561	—	.10	.50	2.50
	1966	16.610	—	.10	.50	2.00
	1967	18.243	—	.10	.30	2.00
	1968	24.698	—	.10	.30	2.00
	1969	27.157	—	.10	.20	1.50
	1970	.639	.50	1.00	2.00	4.00
	1971	8.904	—	.10	.15	1.00
	1972	24.834	—	—	.10	.50
	1973	22.301	—	—	.10	.50

77	1974	30.995	—	—	.10	.40
	1975	21.845	—	—	.10	.40
	1976	42.403	—	—	.10	.30
	1977	43.304	—	—	.10	.30
	1978	37.395	—	—	.10	.30
	1979	25.808	—	—	.10	.30
	1980	28.620	—	—	.10	.30
	1980 w/o star					
		14.050	—	—	.10	.30
	1981	43.083	—	—	.10	.30
	1982	40.974	—	—	.10	.30
	1983	45.637	—	—	.10	.30
	1984	100.066	—	—	.10	.25
	1985	103.108	—	—	.10	.25
	1986	146.392	—	—	.10	.25
	1987	166.040	—	—	.10	.25
	1988	—	—	—	.10	.25

25 ORE

2.4000 g, .600 SILVER, .0463 oz ASW

23	1876	3.200	8.00	15.00	40.00	100.00

24	1896	.400	15.00	30.00	65.00	165.00
	1898	.400	15.00	30.00	65.00	165.00
	1899	.600	10.00	16.00	40.00	90.00
	1900	.400	15.00	30.00	65.00	165.00
	1901	.607	10.00	16.00	40.00	90.00
	1902	.612	10.00	16.00	40.00	90.00
	1904	.600	10.00	16.00	40.00	90.00

39	1909	.600	10.00	20.00	40.00	90.00
	1911	.400	20.00	30.00	55.00	120.00
	1912	.200	50.00	75.00	130.00	200.00
	1913	.400	15.00	25.00	50.00	120.00
	1914	.400	15.00	25.00	55.00	130.00
	1915	1.032	6.00	10.00	20.00	45.00
	1916	.368	20.00	30.00	55.00	130.00
	1917	.400	17.50	30.00	50.00	120.00
	1918/6	.800	10.00	17.50	32.50	70.00
	1918	Inc. Ab.	7.00	10.00	20.00	40.00
	1919	1.600	5.00	8.00	15.00	30.00

COPPER-NICKEL

47	1921	4.800	8.00	12.50	20.00	30.00
	1922	4.200	8.00	12.50	20.00	30.00
	1923	5.200	15.00	20.00	27.50	50.00

Y#	Date	Mintage	Fine	VF	XF	Unc
47a	1921	Inc. Y47	3.00	5.00	25.00	200.00
	1922	Inc. Y47	3.00	4.00	18.00	140.00
	1923	Inc. Y47	1.50	3.00	15.00	100.00

50	1924	4.000	.50	2.00	6.00	45.00
	1927	6.200	.50	1.50	6.00	45.00
	1929	.800	1.50	5.00	17.50	90.00
	1939	1.220	.25	.75	3.00	20.00
	1940	1.160	.25	.75	3.00	20.00
	1946	1.850	.20	.50	1.50	7.50
	1947	2.592	.20	.50	1.50	5.00
	1949	2.602	.20	.50	1.50	5.00
	1950	2.800	.20	.50	1.50	5.00

NICKEL-BRASS
World War II Government in exile.

50a	1942	*2.400	—	—	100.00	150.00

*NOTE: All melted down except for 10,300 pieces.

ZINC
World War II German Occupation

57	1943	14.105	1.00	1.50	3.50	12.50
	1944	3.031	4.00	7.50	17.50	35.00
	1945	3.010	6.00	10.00	20.00	40.00

COPPER-NICKEL

63	1952	4.060	.10	.25	1.00	5.00
	1953	3.320	.10	.25	1.00	7.50
	1954	3.140	.10	.25	1.00	5.00
	1955	2.000	.10	.25	1.00	15.00
	1956	3.980	.10	.25	1.00	5.00
	1957	7.660	.10	.25	1.00	5.00

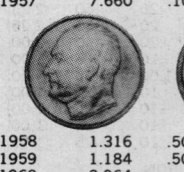 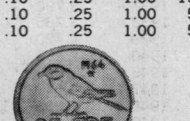

70	1958	1.316	.50	1.00	2.50	10.00
	1959	1.184	.50	1.00	2.50	10.00
	1960	3.964	—	.10	1.00	5.50
	1961	4.656	—	.10	.90	4.50
	1962	6.304	—	.10	.90	4.50
	1963	3.640	—	.10	.90	4.50
	1964	4.953	—	.10	.40	1.50
	1965	2.798	—	.10	.60	2.50
	1966	6.075	—	.10	.60	2.00
	1967	6.641	—	.10	.60	2.00
	1968	4.963	—	.10	.40	1.75
	1969	12.427	—	.10	.15	1.00
	1970	1.545	—	.10	.60	4.00
	1971	5.247	—	—	.10	.75
	1972	7.929	—	—	.10	.75
	1973	8.516	—	—	.10	.60

78	1974	8.048	—	—	.10	.40
	1975	15.595	—	—	.10	.40
	1976	24.721	—	—	.10	.30
	1977	20.150	—	—	.10	.30
	1978	11.259	—	—	.10	.30
	1979	16.666	—	—	.10	.30
	1980	6.289	—	—	.10	.30
	1980 w/o star					
		8.176	—	—	.10	.30
	1981	17.971	—	—	.10	.30
	1982	16.863	—	—	.10	.30

50 ORE
(15 Skilling)

5.0000 g, .600 SILVER, .0964 oz ASW

Y#	Date	Mintage	Fine	VF	XF	Unc
15	1874	.160	60.00	90.00	190.00	425.00
	1875	.640	70.00	100.00	200.00	450.00

Rev: W/o 15 SK.

25	1877	.800	12.50	35.00	125.00	300.00
	1880	.120	75.00	125.00	250.00	500.00
	1885	.100	75.00	125.00	250.00	500.00
	1887	.200	30.00	55.00	100.00	225.00
	1888	.100	50.00	80.00	175.00	350.00
	1889	.200	17.50	35.00	75.00	160.00
	1891	.400	10.00	25.00	50.00	120.00
	1893	.600	7.50	20.00	45.00	120.00
	1895	.200	12.50	25.00	55.00	130.00
	1896	.500	12.50	25.00	60.00	140.00
	1897	.200	22.50	40.00	75.00	180.00
	1898	.300	12.50	25.00	60.00	140.00
	1899	.200	12.50	25.00	60.00	140.00
	1900	.300	7.50	20.00	50.00	130.00
	1901	.404	7.50	20.00	50.00	130.00
	1902	.301	7.50	20.00	50.00	130.00
	1904	.101	60.00	90.00	150.00	250.00

40	1909	.200	20.00	35.00	65.00	125.00
	1911	.200	30.00	40.00	75.00	150.00
	1912	.200	40.00	60.00	100.00	200.00
	1913	.200	30.00	40.00	75.00	160.00
	1914	.800	5.00	9.00	17.50	50.00
	1915	.300	17.50	25.00	50.00	100.00
	1916	.700	6.00	9.00	17.50	50.00
	1918	3.090	2.00	4.00	8.00	20.00
	1919	1.219	2.50	4.50	10.00	25.00

COPPER-NICKEL

48	1920	1.236	25.00	35.00	45.00	85.00
	1921	7.345	8.00	12.50	20.00	35.00
	1922	3.000	8.00	12.50	20.00	35.00
	1923	4.540	45.00	65.00	85.00	125.00

48a	1920	Inc. Y48	30.00	50.00	100.00	500.00
	1921	Inc. Y48	3.00	8.00	50.00	350.00
	1922	Inc. Y48	2.50	6.00	35.00	250.00
	1923	Inc. Y48	2.50	6.00	30.00	150.00

51	1926	2.000	.35	1.50	12.50	50.00
	1927	2.502	.35	1.50	10.00	45.00
	1928/7	1.458	.75	2.50	17.50	60.00
	1928	Inc. Ab.	.35	1.50	12.50	50.00
	1929	.600	1.50	5.00	30.00	200.00

Y#	Date	Mintage	Fine	VF	XF	Unc
51	1939	.900	.25	.60	4.00	20.00
	1940	2.193	.20	.50	3.00	15.00
	1941	2.373	.20	.50	3.00	12.50
	1945	1.354	.25	.50	2.00	20.00
	1946	1.533	.25	.50	3.00	12.00
	1947	2.465	.25	.50	3.00	10.00
	1948	5.911	.25	.40	1.50	10.00
	1949	1.030	.25	1.00	4.00	15.00

NICKEL-BRASS
World War II Government in Exile

51a	1942	*1.600	—	—	110.00	160.00

***NOTE:** All melted down except for 9,238.

ZINC
World War II Nazi Occupation

58	1941	7.761	1.25	3.00	7.50	25.00
	1942	7.606	1.00	2.50	6.00	15.00
	1943	3.349	15.00	20.00	50.00	125.00
	1944	1.542	10.00	15.00	30.00	70.00
	1945	.226	150.00	250.00	375.00	600.00

COPPER-NICKEL

64	1953	2.370	.20	.60	1.50	10.00
	1954	.230	3.50	9.00	50.00	200.00
	1955	1.930	.10	.40	2.00	30.00
	1956	1.630	.10	.40	2.00	20.00
	1957	1.800	.10	.40	2.00	12.00

71	1958	1.560	.25	.75	2.50	12.50
	1959	.340	1.00	2.00	10.00	45.00
	1960	1.584	—	.10	1.50	6.50
	1961	2.425	—	.10	.75	5.00
	1962	3.064	—	.10	.75	5.00
	1963	2.168	—	.10	.75	5.00
	1964	2.692	—	.10	.50	3.50
	1965	1.248	—	.10	1.00	12.00
	1966	4.262	—	.10	.25	2.00
	1967	4.001	—	.10	.25	2.00
	1968	5.431	—	.10	.25	2.00
	1969	7.591	—	.10	.25	1.25
	1970	.481	.25	.75	2.00	6.00
	1971	2.489	—	.10	.15	1.00
	1972	4.453	—	.10	.15	.75
	1973	3.317	—	.10	.15	.75

79	1974	8.494	—	.10	.15	.50
	1975	10.123	—	.10	.15	.50
	1976	15.177	—	.10	.15	.40
	1977	19.412	—	.10	.15	.30
	1978	15.305	—	.10	.15	.30
	1979	10.152	—	.10	.15	.30
	1980	7.082	—	.10	.15	.30
	1980 w/o star	7.066	—	.10	.15	.30
	1981	3.402	—	.10	.15	.30
	1982	11.157	—	.10	.15	.30
	1983	15.762	—	.10	.15	.30
	1984	8.615	—	.10	.15	.30
	1985	4.444	—	.10	.15	.30
	1986	4.178	—	.10	.15	.30
	1987	5.167	—	.10	.15	.30
	1988	—	—	.10	.15	.30

KRONE

(30 Skilling)

7.5000 g, .800 SILVER, .1929 oz ASW

Y#	Date	Mintage	Fine	VF	XF	Unc
16	1875	.600	100.00	170.00	275.00	525.00

Rev: W/o 30 SK.

26	1877	1.000	12.50	50.00	150.00	350.00
	1878	.060	300.00	650.00	1200.	2500.
	1879	.140	50.00	125.00	350.00	700.00
	1881	.080	70.00	125.00	400.00	800.00
	1882	.120	50.00	100.00	350.00	700.00
	1885	.100	40.00	75.00	250.00	500.00
	1887	.100	40.00	75.00	225.00	475.00
	1888	.075	65.00	125.00	375.00	750.00
	1889	.200	25.00	45.00	100.00	235.00
	1890	.200	25.00	45.00	100.00	235.00
	1892	.150	30.00	50.00	110.00	265.00
	1893	.100	30.00	50.00	110.00	265.00
	1894	.100	30.00	50.00	125.00	275.00
	1895/4	.100	32.50	60.00	135.00	300.00
	1895	Inc. Ab.	32.50	60.00	135.00	300.00
	1897	.250	35.00	40.00	80.00	190.00
	1898	.150	37.50	50.00	110.00	235.00
	1900	.250	20.00	40.00	80.00	165.00
	1901	.152	20.00	40.00	80.00	180.00
	1904	.100	50.00	90.00	175.00	325.00

41	1908 crossed hammers on shield	.180	35.00	50.00	85.00	165.00
	1908 crossed hammers w/o shield	.170	20.00	40.00	70.00	145.00
	1910	.100	55.00	100.00	175.00	350.00
	1912	.200	35.00	60.00	100.00	225.00
	1913	.230	25.00	40.00	85.00	165.00
	1914	.602	10.00	20.00	40.00	80.00
	1915	.498	12.50	22.50	45.00	90.00
	1916	.400	15.00	25.00	50.00	120.00
	1917	.600	10.00	17.50	25.00	70.00

COPPER-NICKEL

52	1925	8.686	.30	3.00	15.00	70.00
	1926	1.939	.50	4.00	20.00	100.00
	1927	1.000	1.00	4.50	20.00	175.00
	1936	.700	1.25	5.00	35.00	175.00
	1937	1.000	1.00	4.00	25.00	110.00
	1938	.926	.60	2.50	15.00	100.00
	1939	2.253	.60	1.50	7.50	50.00
	1940	3.890	.30	1.00	5.00	35.00
	1946	5.499	.25	.50	2.50	15.00
	1947	.802	1.00	2.00	10.00	50.00
	1949	7.846	.20	.50	2.50	11.00
	1950	9.942	.20	.50	2.50	10.00
	1951	4.761	.20	.50	2.50	11.00

NORWAY 1366

Y#	Date	Mintage	Fine	VF	XF	Unc
65	1951	3.819	.20	.50	2.00	12.00
	1953	1.465	.20	.50	2.00	20.00
	1954	3.045	.20	.50	2.00	20.00
	1955	1.970	.20	.50	2.00	25.00
	1956	4.300	.20	.50	2.00	18.00
	1957	7.630	.20	.50	2.00	15.00

Y#	Date	Mintage	Fine	VF	XF	Unc
72	1958	.540	3.00	7.00	30.00	110.00
	1959	4.450	—	.20	2.00	20.00
	1960	1.790	—	.20	2.00	15.00
	1961	3.934	—	.20	.75	9.00
	1962	6.015	—	.20	.75	9.00
	1963	4.677	—	.20	.75	9.00
	1964	3.469	—	.20	.50	4.50
	1965	3.222	—	.20	.75	15.00
	1966	3.084	—	.20	.40	4.50
	1967	6.680	—	.20	.40	4.50
	1968	6.149	—	.20	.50	6.00
	1969	5.186	—	.20	.35	2.50
	1970	8.637	—	.20	.40	9.00
	1971	10.258	—	.20	.35	1.75
	1972	13.179	—	.20	.35	1.25
	1973	9.140	—	.20	.35	1.25

Y#	Date	Mintage	Fine	VF	XF	Unc
80	1974	16.537	—	.20	.35	.80
	1975	26.044	—	.20	.35	.80
	1976	35.927	—	.20	.35	.50
	1977	26.264	—	.20	.35	.50
	1978	23.360	—	.20	.35	.50
	1979	15.897	—	.20	.35	.50
	1980	5.918	—	.20	.35	2.00
	1981	16.308	—	.20	.35	.50
	1982	29.187	—	.20	.35	.50
	1983	34.293	—	.20	.35	.50
	1984	3.677	—	.20	.35	1.00
	1985	10.985	—	.20	.35	.50
	1986	5.612	—	.20	.35	.50
	1987	11.015	—	.20	.35	.50
	1988	—	—	.20	.35	.50

2 KRONER

15.0000 g, .800 SILVER, .3858 oz ASW

Y#	Date	Mintage	Fine	VF	XF	Unc
27	1878	.300	25.00	75.00	220.00	525.00
	1885	.025	225.00	375.00	900.00	1800.
	1887*	.025	225.00	375.00	900.00	1800.
	1888	.025	250.00	400.00	1000.	2200.
	1890	.100	35.00	55.00	135.00	300.00
	1892	.050	60.00	100.00	245.00	600.00
	1893	.075	40.00	80.00	175.00	500.00
	1894	.075	40.00	80.00	175.00	500.00
	1897	.050	60.00	100.00	200.00	700.00
	1898	.050	60.00	100.00	200.00	550.00
	1900	.125	30.00	50.00	120.00	250.00
	1902	.153	35.00	55.00	135.00	300.00
	1904	.076	45.00	75.00	150.00	300.00

NOTE: Restrikes are made by the Royal Mint, Norway in gold, silver and bronze.

Norway Independence
Obv: Large shield.

| 33 | 1906 | .100 | 10.00 | 15.00 | 30.00 | 50.00 |

Obv: Smaller shield.

Y#	Date	Mintage	Fine	VF	XF	Unc
33a	1907	.055	20.00	30.00	50.00	85.00

Border Watch

| 34 | 1907 | .028 | 60.00 | 125.00 | 225.00 | 400.00 |

42	1908	.200	20.00	30.00	60.00	125.00
	1910	.150	35.00	50.00	100.00	200.00
	1912	.150	30.00	45.00	90.00	175.00
	1913	.270	15.00	25.00	50.00	100.00
	1914	.255	17.50	30.00	60.00	110.00
	1915	.225	17.50	30.00	60.00	110.00
	1916	.250	35.00	50.00	90.00	150.00
	1917	.378	10.00	17.50	30.00	70.00

Constitution Centennial

| 45 | 1914 | .226 | 6.00 | 10.00 | 17.50 | 37.50 |

5 KRONER

COPPER-NICKEL

73	1963	7.074	—	1.00	3.00	12.00
	1964	7.346	—	1.00	2.00	7.00
	1965	2.233	—	1.00	2.50	40.00
	1966	2.502	—	1.00	2.50	20.00
	1967	.583	1.00	1.75	5.00	17.50
	1968	1.813	—	1.00	2.00	9.00
	1969	2.404	—	1.00	2.00	7.00
	1970	.202	1.50	2.50	5.00	12.50
	1971	.178	1.50	2.50	6.00	15.00
	1972	2.281	—	—	1.00	2.50
	1973	2.778	—	—	1.00	2.50

Y#	Date	Mintage	Fine	VF	XF	Unc
81	1974	1.983	—	—	1.00	2.25
	1975	2.946	—	—	1.00	1.75
	1976	9.056	—	—	1.00	1.50
	1977	4.630	—	—	1.00	1.25
	1978	5.853	—	—	1.00	1.25
	1979	6.818	—	—	1.00	1.25
	1980	1.578	—	—	1.00	2.00
	1981	1.105	—	—	1.00	1.50
	1982	3.920	—	—	1.00	1.25
	1983	2.932	—	—	1.00	1.25
	1984	1.233	—	—	1.00	1.50
	1985	1.441	—	—	1.00	1.25
	1987	.900	—	—	1.00	2.00
	1988	—	—	—	1.00	1.25

100th Anniversary of Krone System

| 82 | 1975 | 1.192 | — | 1.00 | 1.50 | 2.50 |

150th Anniversary Emmigration to America

| 83 | 1975 | 1.223 | — | 1.00 | 1.50 | 2.50 |

350th Anniversary of Norwegian Army

| 84 | 1978 | 2.990 | — | 1.00 | 1.50 | 2.00 |

300th Anniversary of the Mint

| 89 | 1986 | 2.345 | — | 1.00 | 1.50 | 2.00 |
| | 1986 | 5,000 | — | — | P/L | 40.00 |

10 KRONER
(2-1/2 Speciedaler)

4.4803 g, .900 GOLD, .1296 oz AGW

| 17 | 1874 | .024 | 350.00 | 600.00 | 900.00 | 1300. |

Y#	Date	Mintage	Fine	VF	XF	Unc
28	1877	.020	350.00	600.00	900.00	1300.
	1902	.025	275.00	475.00	650.00	900.00

| 43 | 1910 | .053 | 175.00 | 275.00 | 400.00 | 550.00 |

20.0000 g, .900 SILVER, .5787 oz ASW
Constitution Sesquicentennial

| 74 | 1964 | 1.408 | — | — | 6.00 | 7.00 |

NOTE: Edge lettering varieties exist.

COPPER-ZINC-NICKEL

88	1983	20.193	—	—	1.75	3.50
	1984	26.169	—	—	1.75	2.50
	1985	22.458	—	—	1.75	2.50
	1986	29.060	—	—	1.75	2.50
	1987	8.809	—	—	1.75	2.50
	1988		—	—	1.75	2.50

20 KRONER
(5 Speciedaler)

8.9606 g, .900 GOLD, .2593 oz AGW

| 18 | 1874 | .198 | 250.00 | 425.00 | 650.00 | 850.00 |
| | 1875 | .105 | 250.00 | 425.00 | 650.00 | 850.00 |

29	1876	.109	225.00	350.00	550.00	700.00
	1877	.038	250.00	425.00	650.00	850.00
	1878	.139	225.00	350.00	550.00	700.00
	1879	.046	225.00	350.00	550.00	700.00
	1883	.036	2750.	5500.	8500.	12,000.
	1886	.101	225.00	350.00	550.00	700.00
	1902	.050	225.00	350.00	550.00	700.00

Y#	Date	Mintage	Fine	VF	XF	Unc
44	1910	.250	200.00	275.00	400.00	600.00

25 KRONER

29.0000 g, .875 SILVER, .8159 oz ASW
25th Anniversary of Liberation

| 75 | 1970 | 1.204 | — | — | — | 9.00 |

50 KRONER

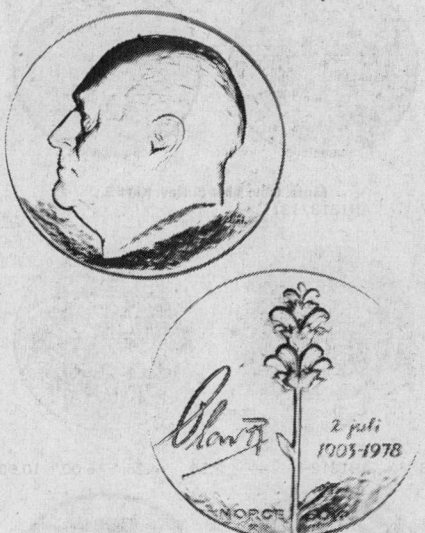

27.0000 g, .925 SILVER, .8030 oz ASW
75th Birthday of King Olav V

| 85 | 1978 | .800 | — | — | — | 12.50 |

100 KRONER

24.7300 g, .925 SILVER, .7355 oz ASW
25th Anniversary of King Olaf's Reign

| 87 | 1982 | .800 | — | — | — | 20.00 |

200 KRONER

26.8000 g, .625 SILVER, .5385 oz ASW
35th Anniversary of Liberation

Y#	Date	Mintage	Fine	VF	XF	Unc
86	1980	.298	—	—	—	37.50

MINT SETS (MS)

KM#	Date	Mintage	Identification	Issue Price	Mkt. Val.
MS1	1960(7)	200	Y66,67a,68,69a,70-72	—	—
MS2	1961(7)	475	Y66,67a,68,69a,70-72	—	—
MS3	1962(7)	570	Y66,67a,68,69a,70-72	—	—
MS4	1963(8)	370	Y66,67a,68,69a,70-73	—	—
MS6	1964(8)	1,260	Y66,67a,68,69a,70-73	—	—
MS7	1965(8)	1,800	Y66,67a,68,69a,70-73,plastic	—	150.00
MS8	1966(8)	1,400	Y66,67a,68,69a,70-73,plastic	—	100.00
MS9	1967(8)	2,490	Y66,67a,68,69a,70-73,soft plastic	—	100.00
MS11	1968(8)	1,167	Y66,67a,68,69a,70-73,soft plastic	—	850.00
MS12	1968(8)	2,300	Y66,67a,68,69a,70-73,sandhill	—	875.00
MS13	1969(8)	3,140	Y66,67a,68,69a,70-73,soft plastic	—	20.00
MS14	1969(8)	7,450	Y66,67a,68,69a,70-73,sandhill	—	40.00
MS15	1970(8)	2,005	Y66,67a,68,69a,70-73,soft plastic	—	50.00
MS16	1970(8)	7,311	Y66,67a,68,69a,70-73,sandhill	—	70.00
MS17	1971(8)	2,010	Y66,67a,68,69a,70-73,soft plastic	—	50.00
MS18	1971(8)	4,055	Y66,67a,68,69a,70-73,sandhill	—	75.00
MS19	1972(8)	6,549	Y66,67a,68,69a,70-73,soft plastic	—	15.00
MS20	1972(8)	6,435	Y66,67a,68,69a,70-73,sandhill	—	35.00
MS21	1973(7)	7,085	Y68,69a,70-73,76,soft plastic	—	12.00
MS22	1973(7)	13,090	Y68,69a,70-73,76,sandhill	—	25.00
MS23	1974(6)	10,275	Y76-81,soft plastic	—	8.00
MS24	1974(6)	29,695	Y76-81,sandhill	—	12.00
MS25	1975(6)	30,207	Y76-83,sandhill	5.00	27.50
MS26	1975(7)	5,287	Y76-82,soft plastic	5.00	20.00
MS27	1976(6)	5,000	Y76-81,soft plastic	3.00	7.00
MS28	1976(6)	25,000	Y76-81,sandhill	3.00	10.00
MS29	1977(6)	5,000	Y76-81,soft plastic	3.40	12.00
MS30	1977(6)	25,000	Y76-81,sandhill	3.40	25.00
MS31	1978(6)	5,000	Y76-81,soft plastic	3.40	14.00
MS32	1978(6)	30,000	Y76-81,sandhill	3.40	25.00
MS33	1979(6)	8,000	Y76-81,soft plastic	3.40	6.00
MS34	1979(6)	50,000	Y76-81,sandhill	3.40	9.00
MS35	1980(6)	10,000	Y76-81,soft plastic	3.40	7.00
MS36	1980(6)	70,000	Y76-81,sandhill	3.40	9.00
MS37	1981(6)	100,000	Y76-81,hard plastic	4.25	8.00
MS38	1982(6)	102,650	Y76-81	4.50	8.00
MS39	1983(4)	102,300	Y77,79-81	5.00	8.00
MS40	1984(5)	101,000	Y77,79-81,88	5.00	8.00
MS41	1985(5)	110,000	Y77,79-81,88	5.00	8.00
MS42	1986(5)	100,000	Y77,79-80,88-89	7.00	10.00
MS43	1987(5)	85,000	Y77,79-81,88	7.00	10.00
MS44	1988(5)	90,000	Y77,79-81,88	7.00	8.00

Listings For
NOVA SCOTIA: refer to Canada

OMAN

The Sultanate of Oman (formerly Muscat and Oman), an independent monarchy located in the southeastern part of the Arabian Peninsula, has an area of 82,030 sq. mi. (212,457 sq. km.) and a population of *1.4 million. Capital: Muscat. The economy is based on agriculture, herding and petroleum. Petroleum products, dates, fish and hides are exported.

The first European contact with Muscat and Oman was made by the Portuguese who captured Muscat, the capital and chief port, in 1508. They occupied the city, utilizing it as a naval base and factory and holding it against land and sea attacks by Arabs and Persians until finally ejected by local Arabs in 1650. It was next occupied by the Persians who maintained control until 1741, when it was taken by Ahmed ibn Sa'id of the present ruling family. Muscat and Oman was the most powerful state in Arabia during the first half of the 19th century, until weakened by the persistent attack of interior nomadic tribes. British influence, initiated by the signing of a treaty of friendship with the Sultanate in 1798, remains a dominant fact of the civil and military phases of the government, although Britain recognizes the Sultanate as a sovereign state and there is no colonial relationship between them.

Sultan Said bin Taimur was overthrown by his son, Qabus bin Said, on July 23, 1970. The new sultan changed the nation's name to Sultanate of Oman.

TITLES

Muscat   مسقط

Oman   عمان

MUSCAT & OMAN

RULERS

Feisal Bin Turkee,
  AH1285-1332/1888-1913AD
Sa'id Bin Taimur,
  AH1351-1390/1932-1970AD
Qabus Bin Sa'id, AH1390-/1970-AD

MONETARY SYSTEM
Until 1970

4 Baisa = 1 Anna
64 Baisa = 1 Rupee
200 Baisa = 1 Riyal
    Commencing 1970
1000 Baisa = 1 Riyal

COLONIAL COINAGE
1/12 ANNA

COPPER

KM#	Date	Mintage	VG	Fine	VF	XF
1	AH1311	—	25.00	35.00	60.00	125.00

1/4 ANNA

COPPER

KM#	Date	Mintage	Good	VG	Fine	VF
2	AH1311	—	6.00	10.00	18.00	40.00

Birmingham Mint

KM#	Date	Mintage	Good	VG	Fine	VF
3	AH1315	19.110	.20	.50	1.00	2.00

NOTE: Large and small inscriptions.

LOCAL COINAGE
1/4 ANNA

COPPER

4	AH1312	—	2.00	3.25	5.00	8.50

5	AH1312	—	2.50	4.25	6.00	10.00

6	AH1312	—	—	—	—	—
	1313	—	2.50	4.25	6.00	10.00

Mule. Obv: KM#6. Rev: KM#5.

7	AH1313/1311					

8	AH1312	—	2.50	4.25	6.00	10.00

9	AH1313	—	2.50	4.25	6.00	10.00

10	AH1314	—	3.00	5.00	7.00	12.50

KM#	Date	Mintage	Good	VG	Fine	VF
11	AH1314	—	3.00	5.00	7.00	12.50

12	AH1315	—	2.00	3.25	5.00	8.50

13	AH5131 (error) date retrograde					
			4.00	6.50	10.00	17.50

14	AH1316	—	2.50	4.00	6.00	10.00
15	AH1316	—	12.50	20.00	30.00	50.00
16	AH1318					

Mule. Obv: KM#6. Rev: KM#14.

17	AH1315					

NOTE: There are numerous varieties of each year of the native issues, varying in both obverse and reverse legends, in the presence or absence of wreath borders, etc.

COUNTERMARKED COINAGE
1/4 ANNA

COPPER
c/m: *ST* in Arabic on 1/4 Anna, Y#3.

19	ND(AH1311-18)		15.00	25.00	40.00	60.00

MONETARY REFORM
2 BAISA

COPPER-NICKEL

KM#	Date	Mintage	Fine	VF	XF	Unc
25	AH1365		.50	.75	1.00	2.00
	1365				Proof	4.00

NOTE: Coins of AH1365 have the monetary unit spelled Baiza; on all other coins it is spelled Baisa.

NOTE: Most of the proof issues of the AH1359 and 1365 dated coins of Muscat & Oman now on the market are probably later restrikes produced by the Bombay Mint.

BRONZE

KM#	Date	Mintage	Fine	VF	XF	Unc
36	AH1390	4.000	.10	.15	.25	.40
	1390	—	—	—	Proof	1.50

3 BAISA

BRONZE

30	AH1378	8.000	.50	.75	1.25	2.00
	1378	—	—	—	Proof	—

32	AH1380	10.000	.35	.50	.60	.75
	1380	—	—	—	Proof	—
	1381 Inc. Ab.		.25	.35	.60	1.00

5 BAISA

COPPER-NICKEL

26	AH1365	—	1.00	1.25	1.50	2.00
	1365	—	—	—	Proof	5.00

33	AH1380	5.000	.40	.60	1.00	1.50
	1381 Inc. Ab.		.40	.60	1.00	1.50
	1381	—	—	—	Proof	—

BRONZE

37	AH1390	3.400	—	.10	.15	.25
	1390	—	—	—	Proof	2.00

10 BAISA

COPPER-NICKEL

22	AH1359	—	2.50	3.25	4.00	5.00
	1359	—	—	—	Proof	7.50

Struck for use in Dhofar province.

BRONZE

38	AH1390	4.500	.10	.15	.20	.35
	1390	—	—	—	Proof	2.00

20 BAISA

COPPER-NICKEL

KM#	Date	Mintage	Fine	VF	XF	Unc
23	AH1359	—	3.00	5.00	7.50	10.50
	1359	—	—	—	Proof	13.50

Struck for use in Dhofar province.

27	AH1365	—	1.00	2.00	2.75	4.00
	1365	—	—	—	Proof	6.50

Mule. Obv: KM#23. Rev: KM#27.

28	AH1359/1365 (restrike)		—	—	—	17.50

25 BAISA

COPPER-NICKEL

39	AH1390	—	.10	.15	.30	.50
	1390	—	—	—	Proof	2.50

.916 GOLD

39a	AH1390 350 pcs.		—	—	Proof	150.00

NOTE: An issue of 250 circulation strikes and 50 proof strikes of Y#39a, 40a, and 41a in gold, and bearing the date AH1392, were reported to have been struck by the Royal Mint in 1973, but no specimens of this issue bearing the date AH1392 have yet been reported.

50 BAISA

COPPER-NICKEL

24	AH1359	.20	6.50	8.50	12.50	
	1359	—	—	—	Proof	16.50

NOTE: Struck for use in Dhofar province.

40	AH1390	1.600	.15	.30	.50	.75
	1390	—	—	—	Proof	4.00

.916 GOLD

40a	AH1390 350 pcs.		—	—	Proof	200.00

See note after KM#39a.

100 BAISA

COPPER-NICKEL

41	AH1390	1.000	.30	.45	.60	1.00
	1390	—	—	—	Proof	5.00

.916 GOLD

41a	AH1390 350 pcs.		—	—	Proof	350.00

See note after KM#39a.

1/2 DHOFARI RIYAL

SILVER

KM#	Date	Mintage	Fine	VF	XF	Unc
29	AH1367	—	12.50	15.00	20.00	27.50
	1367	—	—	—	Proof	40.00

1/2 SAIDI RIYAL

.500 SILVER

34	AH1380	.396	3.00	3.50	4.75	7.50
	1380	—	—	—	Proof	75.00
	1381	.454	3.00	3.50	4.75	6.50
	1381	—	—	—	Proof	—

25.6000 g, .916 GOLD, 33mm, .7540 oz AGW

34a	AH1381 100 pcs.		—	—	Proof	550.00
	1382 100 pcs.		—	—	Proof	550.00
	1390 350 pcs.		—	—	Proof	500.00

NOTE: An additional 224 proof pieces are reported to have been struck in gold bearing the date AH1391, but none have yet been observed.

SAIDI RIYAL

28.0700 g, .833 SILVER, .7518 oz ASW

31	AH1378	1.000	—	12.00	15.00	20.00
	1378 100 pcs.		—	—	Proof	650.00

28.0700 g, .500 SILVER, .4512 oz ASW

31a	AH1378	.400	—	10.00	12.50	15.00

OMAN 1370

46.6500 g, .916 GOLD, 33.7mm, 1.3740 oz AGW

KM#	Date	Mintage	Fine	VF	XF	Unc
31b	AH1378	100 pcs.	—	—	Proof	1000.
	1390	350 pcs.	—	—	Proof	800.00

NOTE: An additional 224 proof pieces are reported struck in gold with date AH1391, but none have been seen to date.

15 SAIDI RIYALS

7.9900 g, .916 GOLD, .2353 oz AGW

35	AH1381	2,100	—	—	—	135.00
	1381		—	—	Proof	250.00

NOTE: An additional 460 pieces reported struck in 1971 and 1972, bearing the date AH1391.

MINT SETS (MS)

KM#	Date	Mintage	Identification	Issue Price	Mkt. Val.
MS1	AH1390(6)	5,500	KM36-41	—	3.50

PROOF SETS (PS)

PS1	AH1359,65,67 (6)		KM22-26,29	—	75.00
PS2	AH1359,65,67 (6)		KM22,24-27,29	—	70.00
PS3	AH1390(6)	2,102	KM36-41	11.00	16.50
PS4	AH1390(3)	350	KM39a-41a	—	700.00

NOTE: Sets of 5 coins comprising KM22,24,25,26 and 27 or 28 have been marketed in recent years. They are Bombay mint restrikes.

SULTANATE OF OMAN

5 BAIZA

BRONZE

KM#	Date	Year	Mintage	VF	XF	Unc
50	AH1395	(1975)	3.000	.10	.15	.30
	1400	(1980)	5.000	.10	.15	.30

10 BAIZA

BRONZE F.A.O. Issue

51	AH1395	(1975)	3.000	.10	.15	.30

52	AH1395	(1975)	2.555	.10	.15	.30
	1400	(1980)	5.250	.10	.15	.30

25 BAIZA

5.9600 g, .917 GOLD, 18mm, .1757 oz AGW

45	AH1394	—	250 pcs.	—	—	175.00

NOTE: Struck for presentation purposes.

COPPER-NICKEL

KM#	Date	Year	Mintage	VF	XF	Unc
53	AH1395	(1975)	3.500	.15	.25	.50
	1400	(1980)	3.330	.15	.25	.50

.917 GOLD Similar to 10 Baiza, Y#9.

54	AH1395	(1975)	250 pcs.	—	—	200.00
	1397	(1977)	1,000	—	—	150.00

50 BAIZA

12.8900 g, .917 GOLD, 24mm, .3801 oz AGW

46	AH1394	—	250 pcs.	—	—	350.00

NOTE: Struck for presentation purposes.

COPPER-NICKEL

55	AH1395	(1975)	2.000	.20	.40	1.00
	1400	(1980)	4.510	.20	.40	1.00

.917 GOLD Similar to 10 Baiza, Y#9.

56	AH1395	(1975)	250 pcs.	—	—	350.00

75 BAIZA

12.0000 g, .917 GOLD, .3537 oz AGW Tenth National Day of Oman

69	AH1404	(1984)	500 pcs.	—	Proof	300.00

100 BAIZA

22.7400 g, .917 GOLD, 28.5mm, .6705 oz AGW

47	AH1394	(1974)	250 pcs.	—	—	600.00
	1395	(1975)	250 pcs.	—	—	600.00

NOTE: Struck for presentation purposes.

COPPER-NICKEL

68	AH1404	(1984)	4.000	.35	.50	1.50

1/4 OMANI RIAL

12.8900 g, .917 GOLD, .3799 oz AGW Fort Al Hazam Obv: Similar to 1/2 Omani Rial, KM#58. Rev: Fort.

57	AH1397	(1977)	1,000	—	Proof	300.00

ALUMINUM-BRONZE

66	AH1400	1980	2.000	.75	1.00	2.00

1/2 OMANI RIAL

25.6000 g, .917 GOLD, .7548 oz AGW

48	AH1394	(1974)	250 pcs.	—	—	650.00
	1397	(1977)	1,000	—	—	600.00

NOTE: Struck for presentation purposes.

19.6700 g, .917 GOLD, .5797 oz AGW Fort Marbat

KM#	Date	Year	Mintage	VF	XF	Unc
58	AH1397	(1977)	1,000	—	Proof	500.00

COPPER-NICKEL F.A.O. Issue

64	AH1398	1978	.015	2.75	3.50	5.00

ALUMINUM-BRONZE

67	AH1400	1980	—	2.75	3.50	5.00

10.0000 g, .917 GOLD, .2947 oz AGW Youth Year

70	AH1404	(1984)	400 pcs.	—	Proof	300.00

OMANI RIAL

46.6500 g, .917 GOLD, 1.3755 oz AGW

44	AH1391	(1971)	224 pcs.	—	Proof	900.00
	1392	(1972)		—	Proof	900.00
	1394	(1974)	250 pcs.	—	Proof	900.00

NOTE: Struck for presentation purposes.

25.6000 g, .917 GOLD, .7545 oz AGW Fort Buraimi Obv: Similar to 1/2 Omani Rial, Y#22. Rev: Fort.

59	AH1397	(1977)	1,000	—	Proof	600.00

		15.0000 g, .500 SILVER, .2412 oz ASW F.A.O. Issue				
KM#	Date	Year	Mintage	VF	XF	Unc
65	AH1398	1978	.015	—	7.50	10.00

		20.0000 g, .917 GOLD, .5894 oz AGW Youth Year				
71	AH1404	(1984)	300 pcs.	—	Proof	500.00

2-1/2 OMANI RIALS

		25.3100 g, .925 SILVER, .7528 oz ASW Conservation Series Rev: Caracal.				
60	AH1397	(1977)	4,407	—	—	30.00

		28.2800 g, .925 SILVER, .8411 oz ASW				
60a	AH1397	(1977)	4,539	—	Proof	40.00

World Wildlife Fund - Eagles
Obv: Similar to 25 Omani Rials, KM#74.

73	AH1407	1987	.025	—	Proof	25.00

5 OMANI RIALS

		31.6500 g, .925 SILVER, .9414 oz ASW Conservation Series Rev: Arabian Whit Oryx.				
61	AH1397	(1977)	4,401	—	—	35.00

		35.0000 g, .925 SILVER, 1.0409 oz ASW				
61a	AH1397	(1977)	4,359	—	Proof	45.00

45.6500 g, .917 GOLD, 1.3454 oz AGW

Sultan Qabus bin Said

KM#	Date	Year	Mintage	VF	XF	Unc
62	AH1397	(1977)	1,000	—	Proof	1200.

15 OMANI RIALS

7.9900 g, .917 GOLD, .2355 oz AGW, 22mm

49	AH1394	(1974)	300 pcs.	—	—	200.00

NOTE: Struck for presentation purposes.

25 OMANI RIALS

10.0000 g, .917 GOLD, .2947 oz AGW
World Wildlife Fund - Masked Booby

74	AH1407	1987	5,000	—	Proof	200.00

75 OMANI RIALS

33.4370 g, .900 GOLD, .9676 oz AGW
Conservation Series
Rev: Arabian Tahr.

63	AH1397	(1977)	825 pcs.	—	—	600.00
	1397	(1977)	325 pcs.	—	Proof	900.00

World Wildlife

72	AH1404	(1984)	200 pcs.	—	Proof	1000.

PROOF SETS (PS)

KM#	Date	Mintage	Identification	Issue Price	Mkt. Val.
PS1	1977(3)	—	KM60a,61a,63	780.00	985.00
PS2	1977(2)	—	KM60a,61a	60.00	85.00

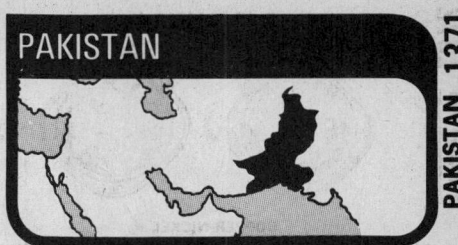

PAKISTAN

The Islamic Republic of Pakistan, located on the Indian sub-continent between India and Afghanistan, has an area of 310,404 sq. mi. (803,943 sq. km.) and a population of *110.4 million. Capital: Islamabad. Pakistan is mainly an agricultural land. Yarn, cotton, rice, and leather are exported.

Afghan and Turkish intrusions into northern India between the 11th and 18th centuries resulted in large numbers of Indians being converted to Islam. The idea of a separate Moslem state independent of the Islamic Republic of Hindu India developed in the 1930's and was agreed to by Britain in 1946. The Islamic majority areas of India, consisting of the separate geographic entities known as East and West Pakistan, achieved self-government as Pakistan, with dominion status in the British Commonwealth, when the British withdrew from India on Aug. 14, 1947, and became a republic in 1956. When a basic constitutional crisis initiated by the election of Dec. 1, 1970 - the first direct general election in Pakistani history - could not be resolved by the leaders of East and West Pakistan, the East Pakistanis seceded from the Islamic Republic of Pakistan (March 26, 1971) and formed the independent People's Republic of Bangladesh. After many years of vacillation between civilian and military regimes, the people of Pakistan held a free national election in November, 1988 and installed a democratic government under a parliamentary system.

TITLE

باکستان

Pakistan

MONETARY SYSTEM

3 Pies = 1 Pice
4 Pice = 1 Anna
16 Annas = 1 Rupee

PIE

BRONZE

KM#	Date	Mintage	Fine	VF	XF	Unc
11	1951	2.950	.10	.20	.30	.50
	1951	—	—	—	Proof	1.25
	1953	.110	.10	.40	.60	1.00
	1953	—	—	—	Proof	1.00
	1955	.211	.10	.40	.60	1.00
	1956	3.390	.10	.15	.25	.35
	1957	—	.10	.15	.25	.35

PICE

BRONZE

1	1948	101.070	.10	.15	.20	.40
	1948	—	—	—	Proof	1.50
	1949	25.740	.10	.15	.20	.35
	1951	14.050	.10	.15	.20	.40
	1952	41.680	.10	.15	.20	.35

NICKEL-BRASS

12	1953	47.540	.10	.15	.20	.35
	1953	—	—	—	Proof	1.25
	1955	31.280	.10	.15	.20	.35
	1956	9.710	.15	.20	.25	.50
	1957	57.790	.10	.15	.20	.35
	1958	52.470	.10	.15	.20	.35
	1959	41.620	.10	.15	.20	.35

PAKISTAN

1/2 ANNA

COPPER-NICKEL

KM#	Date	Mintage	Fine	VF	XF	Unc
2	1948	73.920	.10	.15	.20	.25
	1948	—	—	—	Proof	1.50
	1949 dot after date	—				
		16.940	.20	.25	.35	.50
	1951	75.360	.10	.15	.20	.25

NICKEL-BRASS

13	1953	8.350	.10	.20	.25	.35
	1953	—	—	—	Proof	1.25
	1955	17.310	.10	.15	.20	.30
	1958	38.250	.10	.15	.20	.25

ANNA

COPPER-NICKEL

3	1948	73.460	.10	.20	.30	.50
	1948	—	—	—	Proof	1.50
	1949	11.140	.10	.20	.25	.50
	1949 dot after date	—				
		Inc. Y#3a	.15	.25	.30	.50
	1951	40.800	.10	.20	.25	.40
	1952	15.430	.10	.20	.25	.35

 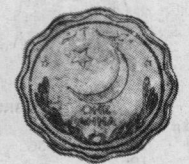

8	1950	94.830	3.00	4.50	6.50	10.00
	1950	—	—	—	Proof	15.00

14	1953	9.350	.10	.15	.20	.30
	1953	—	—	—	Proof	1.50
	1954	35.360	.10	.15	.20	.25
	1955	6.230	.10	.15	.20	.30
	1956	4.580	.10	.15	.20	.35
	1957	12.500	.10	.15	.20	.25
	1958	44.320	.10	.15	.20	.25

2 ANNAS

COPPER-NICKEL

4	1948	55.930	.15	.25	.35	.60
	1948	—	—	—	Proof	1.50
	1949	19.720	.15	.25	.35	.60
	1949 dot after date	—				
		Inc. Y#4a	.20	.30	.40	.75
	1951	33.130	.15	.25	.35	.60

KM#	Date	Mintage	Fine	VF	XF	Unc
9	1950	21.190	3.50	5.00	7.50	12.50
	1950	—	—	—	Proof	20.00

15	1953	7.910	.10	.15	.20	.50
	1953	—	—	—	Proof	1.50
	1954	5.740	.10	.15	.20	.50
	1955	6.230	.10	.15	.20	.50
	1956	1.370	.10	.20	.35	.75
	1957	2.570	.10	.15	.30	.60
	1958	6.200	.10	.15	.20	.50
	1959	8.010	.10	.15	.20	.50

1/4 RUPEE

NICKEL

5	1948	52.680	.20	.30	.40	.65
	1948	—	—	—	Proof	2.25
	1949	46.000	.20	.30	.35	.40
	1951	19.120	.20	.30	.35	.40

10	1950	19.400	5.00	7.50	12.00	20.00
	1950	—	—	—	Proof	25.00

1/2 RUPEE

NICKEL

6	1948	33.260	.40	.60	.75	1.00
	1948	—	—	—	Proof	2.00
	1949	20.300	.40	.60	.75	1.00
	1951	11.430	.40	.65	.90	1.25

RUPEE

NICKEL

7	1948	46.200	.75	1.25	2.00	3.50
	1948	—	—	—	Proof	4.00
	1949	37.100	.75	1.25	2.00	3.50

DECIMAL COINAGE
100 Paisa (Pice) = 1 Rupee

PICE

BRONZE

KM#	Date	Mintage	Fine	VF	XF	Unc
16	1961	74.910	—	.10	.20	.25	.35

PAISA

BRONZE

17	1961	134.650	—	.10	.15	.20
	1961	—	—	—	Proof	1.50
	1962	149.380	—	.10	.15	.20
	1963	127.810	—	.10	.15	.20

24	1964	39.890	.10	.25	.50	1.00
	1964	—	—	—	Proof	1.50
	1965	69.660	.10	.25	.50	1.00
24a	1965	32.950	—	.10	.15	.20
	1966	179.370	—	.10	.15	.20

ALUMINUM

29	1967	170.070	—	—	.10	.15
	1968	—	—	—	.10	.15
	1969	—	—	—	.10	.15
	1970	204.606	—	—	.10	.15
	1971	191.880	—	—	.10	.15
	1972	108.510	—	—	.10	.15
	1973	Inc. Ab.	—	—	.10	.15

F.A.O. Issue

33	1974	14.230	—	—	—	.10
	1975	43.000	—	—	—	.10
	1976	49.180	—	—	—	.10
	1977	62.750	—	—	—	.10
	1978	20.380	—	—	—	.10
	1979	5.630	—	—	—	.10

2 PAISA

BRONZE

25	1964	67.660	.10	—	.15	.20	.25
	1964	—	—	.15	Proof	1.50
	1965	27.880	.10	.15	.20	.25
	1966	50.590	.10	.15	.20	.25

ALUMINUM

28	1966	11.940	.10	.15	.20	.25
	1967	73.970	—	.10	.15	.20
	1968		—	—	.10	.15	.20

25a	1968	—	—	—	.10	.15

PAKISTAN

KM#	Date	Mintage	Fine	VF	XF	Unc
25a	1969	—	—	—	.10	.15
	1970	24.401	—	—	.10	.15
	1971	10.140	—	—	.10	.20
	1972	4.040	—	.10	.15	.25
	1974	3.600	—	.10	.15	.25

F.A.O. Issue

34	1974	3.600	—	—	.10	.15
	1975	4.020	—	—	.10	.15
	1976	5.750	—	—	.10	.15

5 PICE
NICKEL-BRASS

18	1961	40.050	—	.10	.15	.25
	1961	—	—	Proof		1.50

5 PAISA
NICKEL-BRASS

19	1961	40.790	—	—	.10	.20
	1961	—	—	Proof		1.50
	1962	48.200	—	—	.10	.20
	1963	45.020	—	—	.10	.20

26	1964	82.730	—	—	.10	.20
	1965	72.570	—	—	.10	.20
	1966	32.900	—	—	.10	.20
	1967	24.470	—	—	.10	.20
	1968	—	—	.10	.15	.35
	1969	5.690	—	.10	.15	.35
	1970	24.655	—	—	.10	.30
	1971	23.860	—	—	.10	.30
	1972	40.345	—	—	.10	.30
	1973	Inc. Ab.	—	—	.10	.30
	1974	7.695	—	—	.15	.30

ALUMINUM
F.A.O. Issue

35	1974	23.395	—	—	.10	.25
	1975	50.030	—	—	.10	.25
	1976	58.255	—	—	.10	.25
	1977	32.840	—	—	.10	.15
	1978	61.940	—	—	.10	.15
	1979	65.485	—	—	.10	.15
	1980	55.940	—	—	.10	.15
	1981	18.290	—	—	.10	.15

52	1981	16.730	—	—	—	.10
	1982	51.210	—	—	—	.10
	1983	42.915	—	—	—	.10
	1984	45.105	—	—	—	.10
	1985	—	—	—	—	.10
	1987	—	—	—	—	.10

10 PICE
COPPER-NICKEL

KM#	Date	Mintage	Fine	VF	XF	Unc
20	1961	22.230	.10	.15	.25	.35

10 PAISA
COPPER-NICKEL

21	1961	31.090	—	.10	.15	.35
	1961	—	—	Proof		2.00
	1962	29.440	—	.10	.15	.35
	1963	19.760	—	.10	.15	.35

27	1964	52.580	—	—	.10	.25
	1965	51.540	—	—	.10	.25
	1966	—	—	—	.10	.25
	1967	16.430	—	—	.10	.25
	1968	—	—	—	.10	.25

Reduced size

31	1969	—	—	—	.10	.25
	1970	30.250	—	—	.10	.25
	1971	26.270	—	—	.10	.25
	1972	24.845	—	—	.10	.25
	1973	Inc. Ab.	—	—	.10	.25
	1974	4.780	—	—	.10	.25

ALUMINUM
F.A.O. Issue

36	1974	18.640	—	—	—	.10
	1975	28.875	—	—	.10	.25
	1976	43.755	—	—	.10	.25
	1977	29.045	—	—	.10	.20
	1978	55.185	—	—	.10	.20
	1979	56.100	—	—	.10	.20
	1980	40.985	—	—	.10	.20
	1981	15.500	—	—	.10	.20

53	1981	7.995	—	—	.10	.15
	1982	39.770	—	—	.10	.15
	1983	44.705	—	—	.10	.15
	1984	35.255	—	—	.10	.15

25 PAISA
NICKEL

KM#	Date	Mintage	Fine	VF	XF	Unc
22	1963	16.900	.10	.15	.20	.25
	1964	7.990	.10	.15	.25	.35
	1965	9.290	.10	.15	.25	.35
	1966	6.650	.10	.15	.25	.35
	1967	3.740	.10	.15	.25	.35

COPPER-NICKEL

30	1967	(?)5.500	.10	.15	.20	.30
	1968	(?)5.500	.10	.15	.20	.30
	1969	—	.10	.15	.20	.30
	1970	30.392	—	.10	.15	.25
	1971	12.664	—	.10	.15	.25
	1972	10.824	—	.10	.15	.25
	1973	—	—	.10	.15	.25
	1974	9.756	—	.10	.15	.25

37	1975	14.264	—	.10	.15	.25
	1976	20.440	—	.10	.15	.25
	1977	22.092	—	.10	.15	.25
	1978	33.544	—	.10	.15	.25
	1979	29.648	—	.10	.15	.25
	1980	49.556	—	.10	.15	.25
	1981	33.952	—	.10	.15	.25

58	1981	5.648	—	.10	.15	.25
	1982	28.940	—	.10	.15	.25
	1983	40.844	—	.10	.15	.25
	1984	50.988	—	.10	.15	.25
	1986	—	—	.10	.15	.25
	1987	—	—	.10	.15	.25

50 PAISA
NICKEL

23	1963	8.110	.10	.20	.30	.50
	1964	4.580	.15	.25	.40	.60
	1965	8.980	.10	.20	.30	.50
	1966	2.860	.15	.25	.50	1.00
	1967	Reported, not confirmed
	1968	—	.10	.20	.30	.50
	1969	—	.10	.20	.30	.50

COPPER-NICKEL

32	1969	—	.10	.20	.30	.70
	1970	—	.10	.15	.25	.50
	1971	4.670	.10	.15	.25	.50
	1972	4.900	.10	.15	.25	.50
	1974	1.128	.15	.20	.30	.70

PAKISTAN 1373

PAKISTAN 1374

KM#	Date	Mintage	Fine	VF	XF	Unc
38	1975	9.180	.10	.15	.25	.50
	1976	—	.10	.15	.25	.50
	1977	5.548	.10	.15	.25	.50
	1978	18.252	.10	.15	.25	.50
	1979	14.596	.10	.15	.25	.50
	1980	22.332	.10	.15	.25	.50
	1981	13.552	.10	.15	.25	.50

Mohammad Ali Jinnah

39	1976	5.600	.10	.15	.25	.60

Hegira Anniversary

KM#	Date Year	Mintage	VF	XF	Unc
51	AH1401 (1980)	—	.10	.25	.75

KM#	Date	Mintage	Fine	VF	XF	Unc
54	1981	4.612	—	.10	.15	.50
	1982	15.844	—	.10	.15	.50
	1983	9.608	—	.10	.15	.50
	1984	17.520	—	.10	.15	.50
	1987	—	—	.10	.15	.50

RUPEE

COPPER-NICKEL
Islamic Summit Minar

45	1977	5.074	.25	.50	1.00	1.50

Allama Mohammad Iqbal

46	1977	5.000	.25	.50	1.00	1.50

Hegira Anniversary

KM#	Date Year	Mintage	VF	XF	Unc
55	AH1401 (1981)	.045	—	—	3.00

World Food Day

KM#	Date	Mintage	Fine	VF	XF	Unc
56	1981	.045	—	—	—	2.50

26.5mm

57.1	1979	—	—	.10	.25	1.00
	1980	14.522	—	.10	.25	1.00
	1981	12.038	—	.10	.25	1.00

25mm

57.2	1981	4.084	—	.10	.25	1.00
	1982	27.878	—	.10	.25	1.00
	1983	18.746	—	.10	.25	1.00
	1984	14.562	—	.10	.25	1.00
	1987	—	—	.10	.25	1.00

100 RUPEES

28.2800 g, .925 SILVER, .8411 oz ASW
Conservation Series
Rev: Western Tragopan Pheasant.

40	1976	5,120	—	—	—	30.00
	1976	5,837	—	—	Proof	35.00

20.4400 g, .925 SILVER, .6079 oz ASW

Mohammad Ali Jinnah

KM#	Date	Mintage	Fine	VF	XF	Unc
41	1976	1,300	—	—	—	30.00
	1976	2,800	—	—	Proof	30.00

Islamic Summit Minar

47	1977	1,500	—	—	—	25.00
	1977	2,500	—	—	Proof	25.00

Allama Mohammad Iqbal

48	1977	3,000	—	—	—	30.00
	1977	300 pcs.	—	—	Proof	50.00

150 RUPEES

35.0000 g, .925 SILVER, 1.0409 oz ASW
Conservation Series
Obv: Similar to 3000 Rupees, KM#44.
Rev: Gavial Crocodile.

42	1976	5,119	—	—	—	35.00
	1976	5,637	—	—	Proof	40.00

500 RUPEES

4.5000 g, .917 GOLD, .1325 oz AGW

Mohammad Ali Jinnah

KM#	Date	Mintage	Fine	VF	XF	Unc
43	1976	500 pcs.	—	—	—	90.00
	1976	500 pcs.	—	—	Proof	125.00

3.6400 g, .917 GOLD, .1073 oz AGW
Allama Mohammad Iqbal

49	1977	500 pcs.	—	—	—	90.00
	1977	200 pcs.	—	—	Proof	150.00

1000 RUPEES

9.0000 g, .917 GOLD, .2650 oz AGW
Islamic Summit Minar

50	1977	400 pcs.	—	—	—	175.00
	1977	400 pcs.	—	—	Proof	300.00

3000 RUPEES

33.4370 g, .900 GOLD, .9676 oz AGW
Conservation Series
Rev: Astor Markhor.

44	1976	902 pcs.	—	—	—	600.00
	1976	273 pcs.	—	—	Proof	900.00

MIXED DATE MINT SETS (MS)

KM#	Date	Mintage	Identification	Issue Price	Mkt. Val.
MS1	1948/51/53(8)	—	KM5-7,11-15	4.00	5.00
MS2	1948/61(6)	—	KM5-7,17,19,21	2.00	4.00
MS3	1948/64(7)	—	KM7,22-27	2.00	4.00
MS4	1948/74(7)	—	KM7,30,32-36	2.00	4.00
MS5	1948/75(7)	—	KM7,33-38	—	4.50
MS6	1951/53(5)	—	KM11-15	—	4.00

NOTE: Restrikes have been issued for most of these sets.

MINT SETS (MS)

MS7	1976(2)	—	KM41,43	63.00	125.00
MS8	1976(2)	—	KM40,42	—	65.00
MS9	1977(2)	—	KM47,50	—	200.00

PROOF SETS (PS)

PS1	1948(7)	5,000	KM1-7	4.00	14.50
PS2	1950(3)	—	KM8-10	—	60.00
PS3	1953(5)	—	KM11-15	2.00	6.50
PS4	1961(3)	—	KM17,19,21	1.00	5.00
PS5	1976(2)	—	KM41,43	90.50	130.00
PS6	1976(2)	—	KM40a,42a	—	75.00
PS7	1977(2)	—	KM47,50	—	325.00

Listings For
PALESTINE: refer to Israel

PANAMA

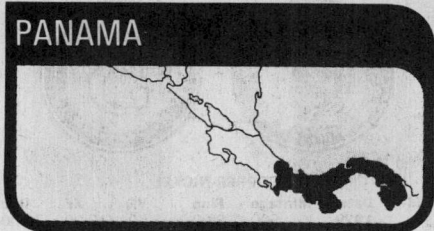

The Republic of Panama, a Central American country situated between Costa Rica and Colombia, has an area of 29,762 sq. mi. (77,083 sq. km.) and a population of *2.4 million. Capital: Panama City. The Panama Canal is the country's biggest asset; servicing world related transit trade and international commerce. Bananas, refined petroleum, sugar and shrimp are exported.

Panama was visited by Christopher Columbus in 1502 during his fourth voyage to America, and explored by Vasco Nunez de Balboa in 1513. Panama City, founded in 1519, was a primary transshipment center for treasure and supplies to and from Spain's American colonies. Panama declared its independence in 1821 and joined the Confederation of Greater Colombia. In 1903, after Colombia rejected a treaty enabling the United States to build a canal across the Isthmus, Panama with the support of the United States proclaimed its independence from Colombia and became a sovereign republic.

The 1904 2-1/2 centesimos known as the 'Panama Pill' or 'Panama Pearl' is one of the world's smaller silver coins and a favorite with collectors.

MINT MARKS
FM - Franklin Mint, U.S.A.*
CHI in circle - Valcambi Mint, Balerna, Switzerland
*NOTE: From 1975 the Franklin Mint has produced coinage in up to 3 different qualities. Qualities of issue are designated in ( ) after each date and are defined as follows:

(M) MATTE - Normal circulation strike or a dull finish produced by sandblasting special uncirculated (polish finish) or proof quality dies.

(U) SPECIAL UNCIRCULATED - Polished or proof-like in appearance without any frosted features.

(P) PROOF - The highest quality obtainable having mirror-like fields and frosted features.

MONETARY SYSTEM
100 Centesimos = 1 Balboa

1/2 CENTESIMO

COPPER-NICKEL

KM#	Date	Mintage	Fine	VF	XF	Unc
6	1907	1.000	1.00	1.50	2.00	5.00
	1907/1907	—	1.00	1.50	2.00	7.50
	1907	—	—	—	Proof	

CENTESIMO

BRONZE

14	1935	.200	1.00	3.00	7.00	50.00
	1937	.200	1.00	2.50	6.00	45.00

50th Anniversary of the Republic

17	1953	1.500	.10	.15	.35	3.00

KM#	Date	Mintage	VF	XF	Unc
22	1961	2.500	—	.10	1.00
	1962	2.000	—	.10	.75
	1962	*50 pcs.	—	Proof	200.00
	1966	3.000	.10	.15	.50
	1966	.013	—	—	1.00
	1967	7.600	.10	.15	.50
	1967	.020	—	Proof	1.00
	1968	25.000	.10	.15	.50

KM#	Date	Mintage	VF	XF	Unc
22	1968	.023	—	Proof	1.00
	1969	.014	—	Proof	1.00
	1970	9.528	—	Proof	1.00
	1971	.011	—	Proof	1.00
	1972	.013	—	Proof	1.00
	1973	.017	—	Proof	1.00
	1974	*10.000	.10	.15	.25
	1974	*.018	—	Proof	1.00
	1975	10.000	.10	.15	.25
	1977	10.000	.10	.15	.25
	1978	10.000	.10	.15	.25
	1979	10.000	.10	.15	.25
	1980	20.500	.10	.15	.25
	1982	20.000	.10	.15	.25
	1983FM(P)	—	—	Proof	1.50
	1983	5.000	.10	.15	.25
	1984FM(P)	—	—	Proof	1.50
	1985FM(P)	**	—	Proof	1.50
	1986	20.000	.10	.15	.25
	1987	20.000	—	—	.10

ZINC

22a	1983	45.000	.10	.15	.25

*1974 circulation coins struck at West Point and by the Royal Canadian Mint, proof coins at San Francisco.
**NOTE: Unauthorized striking.

33.1	1975(RCM)	.500	.10	.20	.50
	1975FM(M)	.125	.10	.25	1.00
	1975FM(U)	1,410	—	—	2.00
	1975FM(P)	.041	—	Proof	.50
	1976(RCM)	.050	.10	.20	.50
	1976FM(M)	.063	.10	.20	1.00
	1976FM(P)	.012	—	Proof	.50
	1977FM(U)	.063	—	.20	.50
	1977FM(P)	9,548	—	Proof	.50
	1979FM(U)	.020	.10	.20	.50
	1979FM(P)	5,949	—	Proof	.50
	1980FM(U)	.040	.10	.20	1.00
	1981FM(P)	1,973	—	Proof	1.00
	1982FM(U)	5,000	.50	1.00	2.00
	1982FM(P)	1,480	—	Proof	1.00

Edge lettering: 1830 BOLIVAR 1980

33.2	1980FM(P)	2,629	—	Proof	1.00

75th Anniversary of Independence

45	1978FM(U)	.050	.10	.20	1.00
	1978FM(P)	.011	—	Proof	1.25

1-1/4 CENTESIMOS

BRONZE

KM#	Date	Mintage	Fine	VF	XF	Unc
15	1940	1.600	.50	1.00	3.50	12.00

2-1/2 CENTESIMOS

1.2500 g, .900 SILVER, .0362 oz ASW

1	1904	.400	6.00	8.00	12.50	22.50
	1904	12 pcs.	—	—	Proof	800.00

NOTE: The above piece is popularly referred to as the Panama Pill or Panama Pearl.

COPPER-NICKEL
Rev. leg: DOS Y MEDIOS

7.1	1907	.800	1.00	3.50	12.50	65.00
	1907	5 pcs.	—	—	Proof	

PANAMA 1376

Rev. leg: DOS Y MEDIO

KM#	Date	Mintage	Fine	VF	XF	Unc
7.2	1916	.800	1.50	3.50	20.00	100.00
	1918*	—	—	—	Rare	—

*NOTE: Unauthorized issue, 1 million pieces melted June, 1918.

KM#	Date	Mintage	Fine	VF	XF	Unc
8	1929	1.000	2.00	5.00	20.00	100.00
	1929	—	—	—	Proof	—

KM#	Date	Mintage	Fine	VF	XF	Unc
16	1940	1.200	.50	1.00	3.50	12.50

COPPER-NICKEL CLAD COPPER
F.A.O. Issue

KM#	Date	Mintage	VF	XF	Unc
32	1973	2.000	—	.10	.20
	1975	1.000	—	.10	.50

KM#	Date	Mintage	VF	XF	Unc
34.1	1975(RCM)	.040	.35	.60	1.00
	1975FM(M)	.050	.35	.60	1.00
	1975FM(U)	1,410	1.00	1.75	2.50
	1975FM(P)	.041	—	Proof	1.00
	1976(RCM)	.020	.35	.60	1.00
	1976FM(M)	.025	.35	.60	1.00
	1976FM(P)	.024	—	Proof	1.00
	1977FM(U)	.025	.35	.60	1.00
	1977FM(P)	9,548	—	Proof	1.00
	1979FM(U)	.012	.35	.60	1.00
	1979FM(P)	5,949	—	Proof	1.00
	1980FM(U)	.040	.35	.60	1.00
	1981FM(P)	1,973	—	Proof	2.00
	1982FM(U)	2,000	.60	1.00	1.50
	1982FM(P)	1,480	—	Proof	2.00

Edge lettering: 1830 BOLIVAR 1980

KM#	Date	Mintage	VF	XF	Unc
34.2	1980FM(P)	2,629	—	Proof	1.00

75th Anniversary of Independence

KM#	Date	Mintage	VF	XF	Unc
46	1978FM(U)	.040	.25	.50	1.00
	1978FM(P)	.011	—	Proof	1.00

KM#	Date	Mintage	VF	XF	Unc
85	1983FM(P)	—	—	Proof	2.50
	1984FM(P)	—	—	Proof	2.50
	1985FM(P)	*	—	Proof	2.50

*NOTE: Unauthorized striking.

5 CENTESIMOS

2.5000 g, .900 SILVER, .0723 oz ASW

KM#	Date	Mintage	Fine	VF	XF	Unc
2	1904	1.500	2.50	6.50	15.00	60.00
	1904	12 pcs.	—	—	Proof	1000.
	1916	.100	45.00	65.00	135.00	275.00

COPPER-NICKEL

KM#	Date	Mintage	Fine	VF	XF	Unc
9	1929	.500	2.00	3.50	10.00	75.00
	1932	.332	2.00	3.50	12.50	75.00

KM#	Date	Mintage	VF	XF	Unc
23.1	1961	1.000	.50	1.25	2.50

KM#	Date	Mintage	VF	XF	Unc
23.2	1962	2.600	.10	.20	1.00
	1962	*25 pcs.	—	Proof	350.00
	1966	4.900	.10	.20	.50
	1966	.013	—	Proof	1.00
	1967	2.600	.10	.20	.50
	1967	.020	—	Proof	1.00
	1968	6.000	.10	.20	.50
	1968	.023	—	Proof	1.00
	1969	.014	—	Proof	1.00
	1970	5.000	.10	.20	.50
	1970	9,528	—	Proof	1.00
	1971	.011	—	Proof	1.00
	1972	.013	—	Proof	1.00
	1973	5.000	.10	.20	.50
	1973	.017	—	Proof	1.00
	1974	.019	—	Proof	1.00
	1975	5.000	.10	.15	.40
	1982	8.000	.10	.15	.40
	1983	7.500	.10	.15	.40

NOTE: The 1962 & 1966 Royal Mint strikes are normally sharper in detail. The stars on the reverse above the eagle are flat while previous dates are raised.

KM#	Date	Mintage	VF	XF	Unc
35.1	1975(RCM)	.080	.25	.50	1.00
	1975FM(M)	.015	.25	.50	1.00
	1975FM(U)	1,410	—	—	2.50
	1975FM(P)	.041	—	Proof	1.00
	1976(RCM)	.020	.25	.50	1.00
	1976FM(M)	.013	.25	.50	1.00
	1976FM(P)	.012	—	Proof	1.00
	1977FM(U)	.013	.25	.50	1.00
	1977FM(P)	9,548	—	Proof	1.00
	1979FM(U)	.012	.25	.50	1.00
	1979FM(P)	5,949	—	Proof	1.00
	1980FM(U)	.043	.25	.50	1.00
	1981FM(P)	1,973	—	Proof	1.50
	1982FM(U)	3,000	.75	1.25	2.00
	1982FM(P)	1,480	—	Proof	1.50

Edge lettering: 1830 BOLIVAR 1980

KM#	Date	Mintage	VF	XF	Unc
35.2	1980FM(P)	2,629	—	Proof	1.50

COPPER-NICKEL CLAD COPPER
75th Anniversary of Independence

KM#	Date	Mintage	VF	XF	Unc
47	1978FM(U)	.030	—	—	1.00
	1978FM(P)	.011	—	Proof	1.00

KM#	Date	Mintage	VF	XF	Unc
86	1983FM(P)	—	—	Proof	2.50
	1984FM(P)	—	—	Proof	2.50
	1985FM(P)	*	—	Proof	3.50

*NOTE: Unauthorized striking.

10 CENTESIMOS

5.0000 g, .900 SILVER, .1447 oz ASW

KM#	Date	Mintage	Fine	VF	XF	Unc
3	1904	1.100	2.50	5.00	12.50	75.00
	1904	12 pcs.	—	—	Proof	1200.

1/10 BALBOA

2.5000 g, .900 SILVER, .0723 oz ASW

KM#	Date	Mintage	Fine	VF	XF	Unc
10	1930	.500	1.75	3.00	9.50	35.00
	1930	20 pcs.	—		Matte Proof	1500.
	1931	.200	2.50	5.00	15.00	100.00
	1932	.150	3.00	6.00	15.00	120.00
	1933	.100	4.00	8.50	22.50	150.00
	1934	.075	7.50	15.00	40.00	250.00
	1947	1.000	.75	1.50	3.00	10.00
	1962	5.000	—	BV	1.00	1.50
	1962	*25 pcs.	—	—	Proof	500.00

NOTE: Coins dated 1962 vary somewhat in detail from those of 1930-1947.

COPPER-NICKEL CLAD COPPER

KM#	Date	Mintage	VF	XF	Unc
10a	1966TI	6.955	.25	.35	1.00
	1966TII	1.000	.50	2.00	8.00
	1966	.013	—	Proof	1.00
	1967	.020	—	Proof	1.00
	1968	5.000	.20	.30	1.00
	1968	.023	—	Proof	1.00
	1969	.014	—	Proof	1.00
	1970	7.500	.15	.25	.50
	1970	9,528	—	Proof	1.00
	1971	.011	—	Proof	1.00
	1972	.013	—	Proof	1.00
	1973	10.000	.15	.20	.50
	1973	.017		Proof	1.00
	1974	.018	—	Proof	1.00
	1975	.500	.25	.50	1.00
	1980	5.000	.15	.25	.50
	1982	7.740	.10	.20	.35
	1983	7.750	.10	.20	.35
	1986	1.000	.10	.20	.35

NOTE: The 1966 exists in two varieties, Type I is similar to the 1962 strike on a thick flan (London) with diamonds on both sides of DE and Type II is similar to the 1947 strikes on a thin flan (U.S.) with elongated diamonds on both sides of DE.

2.5000 g, .900 SILVER, .0723 oz ASW
50th Anniversary of the Republic

KM#	Date	Mintage	Fine	VF	XF	Unc
18	1953	3.300	BV	.75	1.50	2.50

KM#	Date	Mintage	Fine	VF	XF	Unc
24	1961	2.500	BV	.75	1.50	2.00

COPPER-NICKEL CLAD COPPER

KM#	Date	Mintage	VF	XF	Unc
87	1983FM(P)	—	—	Proof	3.00
	1984FM(P)	—	—	Proof	3.00
	1985FM(P)	*	—	Proof	5.00

*NOTE: Unauthorized striking.

10 CENTESIMOS

COPPER-NICKEL CLAD COPPER

KM#	Date	Mintage	VF	XF	Unc
36.1	1975(RCM)	.050	.20	.50	1.00
	1975FM(M)	.013	.20	.50	1.00
	1975FM(U)	1,410	—	—	2.50
	1975FM(P)	.041	—	Proof	1.00
	1976(RCM)	.020	.20	1.00	1.50
	1976FM(M)	6,250	.50	1.25	2.00
	1976FM(P)	.012	—	Proof	1.00
	1977FM(U)	6,250	.50	1.25	2.00
	1977FM(P)	9,548	—	Proof	1.00
	1979FM(U)	.010	.20	.50	1.00
	1979FM(P)	5,949	—	Proof	1.00
	1980FM(U)	.040	.20	.50	1.00
	1981FM(P)	1,973	—	Proof	1.50
	1982FM(U)	2,500	.75	1.50	2.50
	1982FM(P)	1,480	—	Proof	1.50

Edge lettering: 1830 BOLIVAR 1980

| 36.2 | 1980FM(P) | 2,629 | — | Proof | 2.50 |

75th Anniversary of Independence

| 48 | 1978FM(U) | .020 | .20 | .50 | 1.00 |
| | 1978FM(P) | .011 | — | Proof | 1.25 |

25 CENTESIMOS

12.5000 g, .900 SILVER, .3617 oz ASW

KM#	Date	Mintage	Fine	VF	XF	Unc
4	1904	1.600	5.00	10.00	25.00	125.00
	1904	12 pcs.	—	—	Proof	1500.

1/4 BALBOA

6.2500 g, .900 SILVER, .1809 oz ASW

11	1930	.400	2.75	5.00	15.00	65.00
	1930	20 pcs.	—	Matte Proof		2000.
	1931	.048	20.00	50.00	150.00	1500.
	1932	.126	2.50	10.00	35.00	300.00
	1933	.120	2.50	10.00	30.00	200.00
	1934	.090	2.50	10.00	30.00	175.00
	1947	.700	1.50	3.00	6.00	20.00
	1962	4.000	BV	1.50	2.00	3.00
	1962	25 pcs.	—	—	Proof	500.00

NOTE: Coins dated 1962 vary somewhat in detail of the helmet from those of 1930-1947.

COPPER-NICKEL CLAD COPPER

KM#	Date	Mintage	VF	XF	Unc
11a	1966	7.400	.35	.50	1.00
	1966	.013	—	Proof	2.00
	1967	.020	—	Proof	1.50
	1968	1.200	.35	.60	1.25
	1968	.023	—	Proof	1.50

KM#	Date	Mintage	VF	XF	Unc
11a	1969	.014	—	Proof	1.50
	1970	2.000	.35	.50	1.00
	1970	9,528	—	Proof	2.00
	1971	.011	—	Proof	1.50
	1972	.013	—	Proof	1.50
	1973	.800	.40	1.00	1.50
	1973	.017	—	Proof	1.50
	1974	.018	—	Proof	1.50
	1975	1.500	.35	.50	.75
	1979	2.000	.25	.35	.50
	1980	2.000	.25	.35	.50
	1982	3.000	.25	.35	.50
	1983	6.000	.25	.35	.50
	1986 (RCM)	3.000	—	—	.35

6.2500 g, .900 SILVER, .1809 oz ASW
50th Anniversary of the Republic

KM#	Date	Mintage	Fine	VF	XF	Unc
19	1953	1.200	BV	2.00	4.50	15.00

| 25 | 1961 | 2.000 | BV | 1.50 | 2.00 | 4.00 |

COPPER-NICKEL CLAD COPPER

KM#	Date	Mintage	VF	XF	Unc
88	1983FM(P)	—	—	Proof	4.00
	1984FM(P)	—	—	Proof	4.00
	1985FM(P)	*	—	Proof	7.50

*NOTE: Unauthorized striking.

25 CENTESIMOS

COPPER-NICKEL CLAD COPPER

KM#	Date	Mintage	VF	XF	Unc
37.1	1975(RCM)	.040	.25	.50	1.00
	1975FM(M)	5,000	1.00	1.75	3.00
	1975FM(U)	1,410	—	—	4.00
	1975FM(P)	.041	—	Proof	1.00
	1976(RCM)	.012	.35	.50	1.00
	1976FM(M)	2,500	.75	1.50	2.50
	1976FM(P)	.012	—	Proof	1.00
	1977FM(U)	2,500	.75	1.50	2.50
	1977FM(P)	9,548	—	Proof	1.00
	1979FM(U)	4,000	.50	1.00	1.50
	1979FM(P)	5,949	—	Proof	1.50
	1980FM(U)	4,000	.50	1.00	1.50
	1981FM(P)	1,973	—	Proof	2.00
	1982FM(U)	2,000	.75	1.50	2.00
	1982FM(P)	1,480	—	Proof	2.00

Edge lettering: 1830 BOLIVAR 1980

| 37.2 | 1980FM(P) | 2,629 | — | Proof | 2.00 |

75th Anniversary of Independence

| 49 | 1978FM(U) | 8,000 | .35 | .50 | 1.00 |
| | 1978FM(P) | .011 | — | Proof | 1.50 |

50 CENTESIMOS

25.0000 g, .900 SILVER, .7235 oz ASW

KM#	Date	Mintage	Fine	VF	XF	Unc
5	1904	1.800*	15.00	27.50	65.00	275.00
	1904	12 pcs.	—	—	Proof	3000
	1905	1.000*	20.00	35.00	90.00	350.00

*NOTE: 1,000,000 melted in 1931 to issue 1 Balboa coin at San Francisco Mint.

1/2 BALBOA

12.5000 g, .900 SILVER, .3617 oz ASW

12	1930	.300	5.00	7.50	20.00	95.00
	1930	20 pcs.	—	Matte Proof		2500.
	1932	.063	7.50	20.00	125.00	950.00
	1933	.120	6.00	10.00	45.00	300.00
	1934	.090	6.00	10.00	50.00	350.00
	1947	.450	BV	5.00	10.00	35.00
	1962	.700	BV	3.00	4.50	6.50
	1962	25 pcs.	—	—	Proof	750.00

NOTE: Coins dated 1962 vary somewhat in detail from those of 1930-1947.

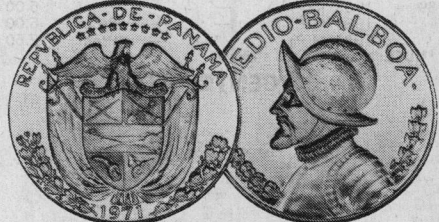

12.5000 g, .400 CLAD SILVER, .1608 oz ASW
Obv: Normal helmet.

KM#	Date	Mintage	VF	XF	Unc
12a.1	1966	1.000	1.50	2.00	4.00
	1966	.013	—	Proof	4.50
	1967	.300	1.50	2.00	4.50
	1967	.020	—	Proof	3.00
	1968	1.000	1.50	2.00	3.50
	1968	.023	—	Proof	3.00
	1969	.014	—	Proof	3.00
	1970	.610	1.50	2.00	3.00
	1970	9,528	—	Proof	4.00
	1971	.011	—	Proof	3.00
	1972	.013	—	Proof	3.00

PANAMA 1378

Error: Type II helmet rim incomplete

KM#	Date	Mintage	Fine	VF	XF	Unc
12a.2	1966	Inc. Ab.	3.50	5.00	7.50	17.50

COPPER-NICKEL CLAD COPPER

KM#	Date	Mintage	VF	XF	Unc
12b	1973	1.000	1.00	1.25	1.50
	1973	.017	—	Proof	2.00
	1974	.018	—	Proof	2.00
	1975	1.200	.75	1.25	1.50
	1979	1.000	—	.75	1.00
	1980	.400	—	.75	1.00
	1982	.400	—	.75	1.00
	1983	1.850	—	.75	1.00
	1986	.200	—	.75	1.00

12.5000 g, .900 SILVER, .3617 oz ASW
50th Anniversary of the Republic

KM#	Date	Mintage	Fine	VF	XF	Unc
20	1953	.600	—	BV	3.00	5.00

| 26 | 1961 | .350 | — | BV | 4.00 | 7.00 |

COPPER-NICKEL CLAD COPPER

KM#	Date	Mintage	VF	XF	Unc
89	1983FM(P)	—	—	Proof	6.00
	1984FM(P)	—	—	Proof	6.00
	1985FM(P)	*	—	Proof	12.50

*NOTE: Unauthorized striking.

50 CENTESIMOS

COPPER-NICKEL CLAD COPPER

KM#	Date	Mintage	VF	XF	Unc
38.1	1975(RCM)	.020	1.00	1.50	2.00
	1975FM(M)	2,000	1.50	3.00	5.00
	1975FM(U)	1,410	—	—	6.50
	1975FM(P)	.041	—	Proof	2.00
	1976(RCM)	.012	1.00	1.50	2.00
	1976FM(M)	1,250	1.00	2.00	3.00
	1976FM(P)	.012	—	Proof	2.00
	1977FM(U)	1,250	1.00	2.00	3.00
	1977FM(P)	9,548	—	Proof	2.00
	1979FM(U)	2,000	1.00	2.00	3.00
	1979FM(P)	5,949	—	Proof	2.00
	1980FM(U)	2,000	1.00	2.00	3.00
	1981FM(P)	1,973	—	Proof	3.00
	1982FM(U)	1,000	1.00	2.00	3.00
	1982FM(P)	1,480	—	Proof	3.00

Edge lettering: 1830 BOLIVAR 1980

38.2	1980FM(P)	2,629	—	Proof	3.00
	1980FM(P) (error) w/o edge lettering				
		Inc. Ab.	—	Proof	65.00

75th Anniversary of Independence

KM#	Date	Mintage	VF	XF	Unc
50	1978FM(U)	8,000	1.00	2.00	4.00
	1978FM(P)	.011	—	Proof	5.00

BALBOA

26.7300 g, .900 SILVER, .7735 oz ASW

KM#	Date	Mintage	Fine	VF	XF	Unc
13	1931	.200	6.50	9.00	17.50	75.00
	1931	20 pcs.	—	Matte Proof	3000.
	1934	.225	6.50	8.00	15.00	75.00
	1947	.500	BV	6.00	9.00	15.00

50th Anniversary of the Republic
Obv: Similar to KM#13.

| 21 | 1953 | .050 | 6.50 | 9.00 | 12.50 | 25.00 |

KM#	Date	Mintage	VF	XF	Unc
27	1966	.300	—	—	10.00
	1966	.013	—	Proof	15.00
	1967	.020	—	Proof	12.00
	1968	.023	—	Proof	12.00
	1969	.014	—	Proof	12.00
	1970	.013	—	Proof	15.00
	1971	.018	—	Proof	12.00
	1972	.023	—	Proof	12.00
	1973	.030	—	Proof	12.00
	1974	.030	—	Proof	12.00

NOTE: More than 200,000 of 1966 dates were melted down in 1971 for silver for the 20 Balboas.

COPPER-NICKEL CLAD COPPER

KM#	Date	Mintage	VF	XF	Unc
39.1	1975FM(M)	4,035	—	—	15.00
	1975FM(U)	1,410	—	—	25.00
	1976FM(M)	625 pcs.	—	—	35.00
	1977FM(M)	625 pcs.	—	—	35.00
	1979FM(U)	1,000	—	—	25.00
	1980FM(U)	1,000	—	—	25.00
	1982FM(U)	500 pcs.	—	—	30.00

26.7300 g, .925 SILVER, .7950 oz ASW

39.1a	1975FM(P)	.045	—	Proof	12.00
	1976FM(P)	.014	—	Proof	12.00
	1977FM(P)	.011	—	Proof	12.00
	1979FM(P)	7,160	—	Proof	12.00

20.7400 g, .500 SILVER, .3334 oz ASW

| 39.1b | 1981FM(P) | 2,633 | — | Proof | 20.00 |
| | 1982FM(P) | 1,480 | — | Proof | 20.00 |

COPPER-NICKEL CLAD COPPER
Obv: Erroroneous silver content (LEY .925) below arms.

| 39.2 | 1975 | .010 | — | — | 8.00 |
| | 1976 | .012 | — | — | 8.00 |

20.7400 g, .500 SILVER, .3334 oz ASW
Edge lettering: 1830 BOLIVAR 1980

| 39.3 | 1980FM(P) | 2,629 | — | Proof | 20.00 |

COPPER-NICKEL CLAD COPPER
Obv: Erroneous silver content (LEY. 500) below arms.

| 39.4 | 1982FM(U) | 9 pcs. | — | — | 850.00 |

75th Anniversary of Independence

| 51 | 1978FM(U) | 4,000 | — | — | 10.00 |

.925 SILVER

| 51a | 1978FM(P) | .013 | — | Proof | 20.00 |

COPPER-NICKEL
General Omar Torrijos

76	1982	.200	—	—	2.50
	1982	*250 pcs.	—	Proof	100.00
	1983	.200	—	—	2.50
	1984	.200	—	—	2.50

*NOTE: 50 pieces with frosted obverse only and 200 pieces with frosted obverse and reverse.

PANAMA 1379

KM#	Date	Mintage	VF	XF	Unc
90	1983FM(M)	—	—	—	5.00

20.7400 g, .500 SILVER, .3334 oz ASW

90a	1983FM(P)	1,602	—	Proof	22.50
	1984FM(P)	1,098	—	Proof	22.50
	1985FM(P)	*	—	Proof	40.00

*NOTE: Unauthorized striking.

5 BALBOAS

35.7400 g, .925 SILVER, 1.0617 oz ASW
11th Central American and Caribbean Games

28	1970FM(M)	.666	—	—	8.50
	1970FM(P)	.059	—	Proof	12.00

35.0000 g, .900 SILVER, 1.0128 oz ASW
F.A.O. Issue
Obv: Similar to Y#28.

30	1972	.070	—	—	10.00
	1972	.010	—	Proof	30.00

COPPER-NICKEL CLAD COPPER
Obv: Similar to KM#28.

40.1	1975FM(M)	5,125	—	—	10.00
	1975FM(U)	1,410	—	—	20.00
	1976FM(M)	125 pcs.	—	—	75.00
	1977FM(M)	125 pcs.	—	—	75.00
	1979FM(U)	1,000	—	—	15.00
	1980FM(U)	1,000	—	—	15.00
	1982FM(U)	1,200	—	—	15.00

35.1200 g, .925 SILVER, 1.0446 oz ASW

40.1a	1975FM(P)	.041	—	Proof	15.00
	1976FM(P)	.012	—	Proof	15.00
	1977FM(P)	9,548	—	Proof	15.00
	1979FM(P)	5,949	—	Proof	15.00

23.3300 g, .500 SILVER, .3751 oz ASW

KM#	Date	Mintage	VF	XF	Unc
40.1b	1981FM(P)	1,973	—	Proof	30.00
	1982FM(P)	1,480	—	Proof	30.00

COPPER-NICKEL CLAD COPPER
Obv: Erroneous silver content (LEY .925) below arms.

40.2	1975	4,000	—	—	8.50
	1976	5,000	—	—	8.50

23.3300 g, .500 SILVER, .3751 oz ASW
Edge lettering: 1830 BOLIVAR 1980

40.3	1980FM(P)	2,629	—	Proof	20.00

Obv: Erroneous silver content (LEY.925) below arms.

40.4	1982FM(P)	—	—	Proof	75.00

COPPER-NICKEL CLAD COPPER
Obv: Erroneous silver content (LEY .500) below arms.

40.5	1982FM(U)	200 pcs.	—	—	45.00

75th Anniversary of Independence

52	1978FM(U)	2,000	—	—	15.00

35.1200 g, .925 SILVER, 1.0446 oz ASW

52a	1978FM(P)	.011	—	Proof	20.00

Panama Canal Treaty Implementation

58	1979FM(P)	6,854	—	Proof	20.00

24.1100 g, .500 SILVER, .3875 oz ASW
Champions of Boxing

63	1980	1,261	—	Proof	30.00

24.1600 g, .925 SILVER, .7186 oz ASW
Champions of Soccer

KM#	Date	Mintage	VF	XF	Unc
77	1982	9,446	—	Proof	20.00

23.3300 g, .500 SILVER, .3751 oz ASW

91	1983FM(P)	1,776	—	Proof	27.50
	1984FM(P)	909 pcs.	—	Proof	27.50

Discovery of the Pacific Ocean

104	1985FM(P)	*	—	Proof	25.00

*NOTE: Unauthorized striking.

10 BALBOAS

42.4800 g, .925 SILVER, 1.2635 oz ASW
Panama Canal Treaty Ratification

53	1978FM(P)	.012	—	—	25.00

NICKEL

53a	1978	.300	—	—	15.00

PANAMA 1380

42.4800 g, .925 SILVER, 1.2635 oz ASW
Panama Canal Treaty Implementation

KM#	Date	Mintage	VF	XF	Unc
59	1979FM(P)	7,229	—	Proof	25.00

26.4800 g, .500 SILVER, .4257 oz ASW
Balseria Game

64	1980	1,267	—	Proof	30.00

26.2600 g, .925 SILVER, .7811 oz ASW
Champions of Soccer

78	1982	9,076	—	Proof	25.00

International Year of the Child

79	1982	8,460	—	Proof	35.00

20 BALBOAS

129.5900 g, .925 SILVER, 3.8544 oz ASW
150th Anniversary of Central American Independence
Obv: Similar to 5 Balboas, KM#28.

KM#	Date	Mintage	VF	XF	Unc
29	1971FM(M)	.069	—	—	35.00
	1971FM(U)		—	—	60.00
	1971FM(P)	.040	—	Proof	40.00

Actual size of this and following Panama listings - KM#29, 31 and 44 - is 61mm.

Regular Issue, Simon Bolivar
Obv: Similar to 5 Balboas, KM#28.

31	1972FM(M)	.037	—	—	35.00
	1972FM(P)	.048	—	Proof	40.00
	1973FM(M)	.094	—	—	35.00
	1973FM(P)	.074	—	Proof	40.00
	1974FM(M)	.099	—	—	35.00
	1974FM(P)	.161	—	Proof	40.00
	1975FM(M)	2,500	—	—	55.00
	1975FM(P)	.062	—	Proof	40.00
	1976FM(M)	2,500	—	—	55.00
	1976FM(P)	.022	—	Proof	45.00

Obv: Similar to 5 Balboas, KM#28.

44	1977FM(U)	2,879	—	—	70.00
	1977FM(P)	.024	—	Proof	55.00
	1979FM(U)	2,500	—	—	70.00
	1979FM(P)	.013	—	Proof	65.00

75th Anniversary of Independence
Rev: Similar to KM#44.

KM#	Date	Mintage	VF	XF	Unc
54	1978FM(U)	2,500	—	—	70.00
	1978FM(P)	.023	—	Proof	60.00

119.8800 g, .500 SILVER, 1.9273 oz ASW
150th Anniversary of Simon Bolivar
Obv: Similar to 5 Balboas, KM#28.

65	1980FM(U)	1,000	—	—	120.00
	1980FM(P)	3,714	—	Proof	85.00

118.5700 g, .500 SILVER, 1.9060 oz ASW
Simon Bolivar, El Libertador

71	1981FM(U)	500 pcs.	—	—	135.00
	1981FM(P)	3,528	—	Proof	85.00

2.1400 g, .500 GOLD, .0344 oz AGW
Figure of Eight Butterfly

72	1981FM(U)	205 pcs.	—	—	125.00
	1981FM(P)	4,445	—	Proof	55.00

PANAMA 1381

Christmas 1983

KM#	Date	Mintage	VF	XF	Unc
94	1983FM(U)	—	—	—	150.00
	1983FM(P)	—	—	Proof	115.00

119.8800 g, .500 SILVER, 1.9273 oz ASW
Balboa, Discoveror of the Pacific

KM#	Date	Mintage	VF	XF	Unc
80	1982FM(P)	2,352	—	Proof	120.00

119.8800 g, .500 SILVER, 1.9273 oz ASW
Balboa and Indian Guide

KM#	Date	Mintage	VF	XF	Unc
98	1984FM(P)	1,402	—	Proof	150.00

Peace of Christmas

	1984FM(P)	—	—	Proof	175.00

75 BALBOAS

2.1400 g, .500 GOLD, .0344 oz AGW
Hummingbird

81	1982FM(U)	140 pcs.	—	—	125.00
	1982FM(P)	3,445	—	Proof	60.00

Banded Butterfly Fish

92	1983FM(U)	—	—	—	125.00
	1983FM(P)	—	—	Proof	70.00

2.1400 g, .500 GOLD, .0344 oz AGW
Harpy Eagle

102	1985FM(P)	817 pcs.	—	Proof	90.00

10.6000 g, .500 GOLD, .1704 oz AGW
75th Anniversary of Independence

55	1978FM(U)	410 pcs.	—	—	140.00
	1978FM(P)	9,161	—	Proof	100.00

100 BALBOAS

8.1600 g, .900 GOLD, .2361 oz AGW
500th Anniversary of Balboa

41	1975FM(U)	.044	—	—	125.00
	1975FM(P)	.075	—	Proof	125.00
	1976FM(M)	50 pcs.	—	—	350.00
	1976FM(U)	3,013	—	—	125.00
	1976FM(P)	.011	—	Proof	125.00
	1977FM(M)	50 pcs.	—	—	350.00
	1977FM(U)	324 pcs.	—	—	150.00
	1977FM(P)	5,092	—	Proof	135.00

119.8800 g, .500 SILVER, 1.9273 oz ASW
Discovery of the Pacific Ocean

105	1985FM(P)	1,746	—	Proof	150.00

50 BALBOAS

5.3700 g, .500 GOLD, .0861 oz AGW
Christmas 1981

73	1981FM(U)	154 pcs.	—	—	150.00
	1981FM(P)	1,940	—	Proof	80.00

Dove - Orchid

56	1978FM(M)	50 pcs.	—	—	350.00
	1978FM(U)	300 pcs.	—	—	200.00
	1978FM(P)	6,086	—	Proof	175.00

118.5700 g, .500 SILVER, 1.9060 oz ASW
200th Anniversary of Birth of Bolivar
Obv: Similar to 5 Balboas, KM#77.

93	1983FM(U)	500 pcs.	—	—	90.00
	1983FM(P)	3,186	—	Proof	65.00

2.1400 g, .500 GOLD, .0344 oz AGW
Puma

97	1984FM(U)	100 pcs.	—	—	175.00
	1984FM(P)	357 pcs.	—	Proof	100.00

Christmas 1982

82	1982FM(U)	60 pcs.	—	—	175.00
	1982FM(P)	1,361	—	Proof	90.00

Golden Turtle

60	1979FM(M)	50 pcs.	—	—	350.00
	1979FM(U)	240 pcs.	—	—	225.00
	1979FM(P)	4,829	—	Proof	175.00

PANAMA 1382

Golden Condor

KM#	Date	Mintage	VF	XF	Unc
66	1980FM(U)	209 pcs.	—	—	275.00
	1980FM(P)	2,411	—	Proof	175.00

7.1300 g, .500 GOLD, .1146 oz AGW
Panama Canal Centennial

67	1980FM(U)	77 pcs.	—	—	250.00
	1980FM(P)	2,468	—	Proof	125.00

Cocle Indian Ceremonial Mask

74	1981FM(U)	174 pcs.	—	—	250.00
	1981FM(P)	1,841	—	Proof	150.00

Pre-Columbian Indian Design

83	1982FM(U)	26 pcs.	—	—	275.00
	1982FM(P)	578 pcs.	—	Proof	175.00

Cocle Indian Birds

95	1983FM(U)	—	—	—	250.00
	1983FM(P)	—	—	Proof	150.00

Indian Art

100	1984FM(U)	—	—	—	275.00
	1984FM(P)	—	—	Proof	160.00

150 BALBOAS

9.3000 g, .999 PLATINUM, .2987 oz APW
150th Anniversary Pan-American Congress

KM#	Date	Mintage	VF	XF	Unc
43	1976FM(M)	30 pcs.	—	—	850.00
	1976FM(U)	510 pcs.	—	—	250.00
	1976FM(P)	.013	—	Proof	250.00

7.6700 g, .500 GOLD, .1233 oz AGW
Simon Bolivar Sesquicentenarium

68	1980FM(U)	169 pcs.	—	—	275.00
	1980FM(P)	1,837	—	Proof	175.00

200 BALBOAS

9.5000 g, .980 PLATINUM, .2994 oz APW
Panama Canal Treaties

61	1979FM(P)	2,178	—	Proof	245.00

9.3300 g, .980 PLATINUM, .2940 oz APW
Champions of Boxing

69	1980	219 pcs.	—	Proof	400.00

500 BALBOAS

41.7000 g, .900 GOLD, 1.2067 oz AGW
500th Anniversary of Balboa
Obv: Similar to 200 Balboas, KM#69.

42	1975FM(M)	10 pcs.	—	—	1500.
	1975FM(U)	1,496	—	—	575.00
	1975FM(P)	9,824	—	Proof	600.00
	1976FM(M)	10 pcs.	—	—	1500.
	1976FM(U)	160 pcs.	—	—	650.00
	1976FM(P)	2,669	—	Proof	600.00
	1977FM(M)	10 pcs.	—	—	1500.
	1977FM(U)	59 pcs.	—	—	750.00
	1977FM(P)	1,980	—	Proof	600.00

30th Anniversary of Organization of American States
Obv: Similar to KM#42.

57	1978FM(M)	10 pcs.	—	—	1500.
	1978FM(U)	106 pcs.	—	—	675.00
	1978FM(P)	2,009	—	Proof	650.00

Golden Jaguar
Obv: Similar to KM#42.

KM#	Date	Mintage	VF	XF	Unc
62	1979FM(U)	130 pcs.	—	—	900.00
	1979FM(P)	1,657	—	Proof	800.00

37.1800 g, .500 GOLD, .5977 oz AGW
White Herons
Obv: Similar to KM#42.

70	1980FM(U)	54 pcs.	—	—	900.00
	1980FM(P)	612 pcs.	—	Proof	950.00

Sailfish
Obv: Similar to KM#42.

75	1981FM(U)	41 pcs.	—	—	900.00
	1981FM(P)	487 pcs.	—	Proof	1000.

General Omar Torrijos
Obv: Similar to KM#42.

84	1982FM(U)	97 pcs.	—	—	900.00
	1982FM(P)	398 pcs.	—	Proof	800.00

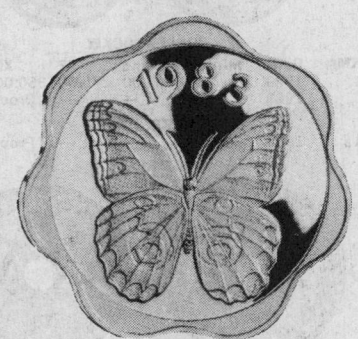

KM#	Date	Mintage	VF	XF	Unc
96	1983FM(U)	100 pcs.	—	—	1000.
	1983FM(P)	300 pcs.	—	Proof	1450.

Owl Butterfly

37.1200 g, .500 GOLD, .5968 oz AGW
Golden Eagle

101	1984FM(U)	10 pcs.	—	—	2000.
	1984FM(P)	156 pcs.	—	Proof	1600.

37.1800 g, .500 GOLD, .5977 oz AGW
National Eagle

KM#	Date	Mintage	VF	XF	Unc
103	1985FM(P)	184 pcs.	—	Proof	1750.

MINT SETS (MS)

KM#	Date	Mintage	Identification	Issue Price	Mkt. Val.
MS1	1975(8)	1,410	KM33.1-40.1	25.00	65.00

PROOF SETS (PS)

PS1	1904(5)	12	KM1-5	—	7500.
PS2	1930(3)	20	KM10-12	—	6000.
PS3	1962(5)	25	KM10-12,22,23.2	—	2300.
PS4	1966(6)	12,701	KM10a-11a,12a.1,22,23.2,27	15.25	25.00
PS5	1967(6)	19,983	KM10a-11a,12a.1,22,23.2,27	15.25	20.00
PS6	1968(6)	23,210	KM10a-11a,12a.1,22,23.2,27	15.25	20.00
PS7	1969(6)	14,000	KM10a-11a,12a.1,22,23.2,27	15.25	20.00
PS8	1970(6)	9,528	KM10a-11a,12a.1,22,23.2,27	15.25	25.00
PS9	1971(6)	10,696	KM10a-11a,12a.1,22,23.2,27	15.25	20.00
PS10	1972(6)	13,322	KM10a-11a,12a.1,22,23.2,27	15.50	20.00
PS11	1973(6)	16,946	KM10a-11a,12b,22,23.2,27	17.50	19.00
PS12	1974(6)	17,521	KM10a-11a,12b,22,23.2,27	17.50	19.00
PS13	1975(9)	37,041	KM31.1,33.1-38.1,39.1a-40.1a	130.00	80.00
PS14	1975(8)	4,057	KM34.1-38.1,39.1a-40.1a	50.00	25.00
PS15	1976(9)	10,610	KM31.1,33.1-38.1,39.1a-40.1a	102.00	80.00
PS16	1976(8)	1,792	KM33.1-38.1,39.1a-40.1a	50.00	30.00
PS17	1976(2)	11,479	KM31,34.1	51.00	40.00
PS18	1977(9)	8,093	KM33.1-38.1,39.1a-40.1a,44	100.00	90.00
PS19	1977(8)	1,455	KM33.1-38.1,39.1a-40.1a	50.00	30.00
PS20	1978(9)	9,667	KM45-50,51a,52a,54	110.00	110.00
PS21	1978(5)	1,122	KM45-50,51a,52a,54	—	40.00
PS22	1979(9)	4,974	KM33.1-38.1,39.1a-40.1a,44	132.00	90.00
PS23	1979(8)	975	KM33.1-38.1,39.1a-40.1a	60.00	30.00
PS24	1979(2)	1,775	KM58-59	125.00	45.00
PS25	1980(9)	1,686	KM33.2-38.2,39.3-40.3,65	287.00	150.00
PS26	1980(8)	943	KM33.2-38.2,39.3-40.3	87.00	40.00
PS27	1981(9)	1,279	KM33.1-38.1,39.1b-40.1b,71	212.00	160.00
PS28	1981(8)	694	KM33.1-38.1,39.1b-40.1b	87.00	35.00
PS29	1982(9)	746	KM33.1-38.1,39.1b-40.1b,80	212.00	200.00
PS30	1982(9)	Error set	KM33-38,39.1b,40.4,80	212.00	250.00
PS31	1982(8)	734	KM33-38,39.1b-40.1b	87.00	35.00
PS32	1982(8)	Error set	KM33-38,39.1b,40.4	—	140.00
PS33	1983(8)	—	KM22,85-89,90a,91,93	87.00	155.00
PS34	1983(8)	—	KM22,85-89,90a,91	—	70.00
PS35	1984(9)	—	KM22,85-89,90a,91,98	—	200.00
PS36	1984(8)	—	KM22,85-89,90a,91	72.00	70.00
PS37	1985(8)	*	KM22,85-89,90a,104	72.00	100.00

*****NOTE:** Unauthorized striking.

PALO SECO

Palo Seco Leper Colony was established in Balboa, Canal Zone in 1907. It is known today as Palo Seco Hospital. The original issue of tokens totaled $1,800.00 of which $1,492.75 was destroyed on November 28, 1955. The issue was backed by United States Currency and was replaced by United States silver coinage.

Leprosarium Token Coinage (Tn)
CENT

COPPER

KM#	Date	Mintage	VG	Fine	VF
Tn1	ND(1919)	—	20.00	35.00	50.00

5 CENTS

BRASS

Tn2	ND(1919)	—	25.00	40.00	60.00

10 CENTS

ALUMINUM

KM#	Date	Mintage	VG	Fine	VF
Tn3	ND(1919)	—	50.00	75.00	100.00

25 CENTS

ALUMINUM

Tn4	ND(1919)	—	60.00	100.00	125.00

50 CENTS

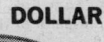

ALUMINUM

Tn5	ND(1919)	—	75.00	125.00	175.00

DOLLAR

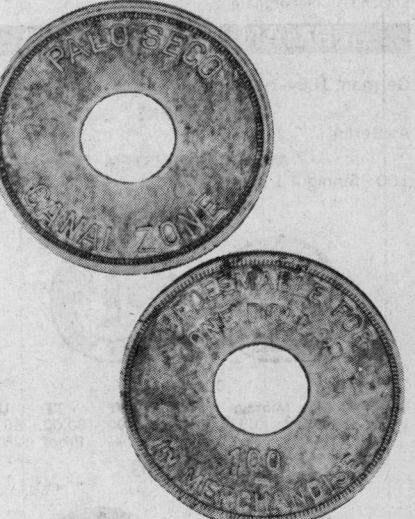

ALUMINUM

Tn6	ND(1919)	—	125.00	200.00	250.00

PAPUA NEW GUINEA

Papua New Guinea, an independent member of the British Commonwealth, occupies the eastern half of the island of New Guinea. It lies north of Australia near the equator and borders on West Irian. The country, which includes nearby Bismark archipelago, Buka and Bougainville, has an area of 178,260 sq. mi. (461,691 sq. km.) and a population of *3.6 million who are divided into more than 1,000 seperate tribes speaking more than 700 mutually unintelligible languages. Capital: Port Moresby. The economy is agricultural, and exports copra, rubber, cocoa, coffee, tea, gold and copper.

In 1884 Germany annexed the area known as German New Guinea (also Neu Guinea or Kaiser Wilhelmsland) comprising the northern section of eastern New Guinea, and granted its administration and development to the Neu-Guinea Compagnie. Administration reverted to Germany in 1889 following the failure of the company to exercise adequate administration. While a German protectorate, German New Guinea had an area of 92,159 sq. mi. (238,692 sq. km.) and a population of about 250,000. Capital: Hebertshohe, later named Rabaul. Copra was the chief crop. Australian troops occupied German New Guinea in Aug. 1914, shortly after Great Britain declared war on Germany. It was mandated to Australia by the League of Nations in 1920, known as the Territory of New Guinea. The territory was invaded and occupied by Japan in 1942. Following the Japanese surrender, it came under U.N. trusteeship, Dec. 13, 1946, with Australia as the administering power.

The Papua and New Guinea act, 1949, provided for the government of Papua and New Guinea as one administrative unit. On Dec. 1, 1973, Papua New Guinea became selfgoverning with Australia retaining responsibility for defense and foreign affairs. Full independence was achieved on Sept. 16, 1975. Papua New Guinea is a member of the Commonwealth of Nations. The Queen of England is Chief of State.

GERMAN NEW GUINEA

RULERS
German, 1884-1918

MINT MARKS
A - Berlin

MONETARY SYSTEM
100 Pfennig = 1 Mark

PFENNIG

COPPER

KM#	Date	Mintage	Fine	VF	XF	Unc
1	1894A	.033	20.00	30.00	50.00	80.00
	1894A	—	—	—	Proof	125.00

2 PFENNIG

COPPER

2	1894A	.017	25.00	45.00	70.00	90.00
	1894A	—	—	—	Proof	150.00

10 PFENNIG

COPPER

3	1894A	.024	20.00	45.00	85.00	150.00
	1894A	—	—	—	Proof	250.00

1/2 MARK

2.7780 g, .900 SILVER, .0804 oz ASW

KM#	Date	Mintage	Fine	VF	XF	Unc
4	1894A	.016	50.00	80.00	125.00	225.00
	1894A	—	—	—	Proof	325.00

MARK

5.5560 g, .900 SILVER, .1608 oz ASW

5	1894A	.033	50.00	80.00	130.00	250.00
	1894A	—	—	—	Proof	350.00

2 MARK

11.1110 g, .900 SILVER, .3215 oz ASW

6	1894A	.013	100.00	175.00	325.00	500.00
	1894A	—	—	—	Proof	650.00

5 MARK

27.7780 g, .900 SILVER, .8039 oz ASW

7	1894A	.019	—	700.00	900.00	1500.
	1894A	—	—	—	Proof	2400.

10 MARK

3.9820 g, .900 GOLD, .1152 oz AGW

8	1895A	2,000	—	4500.	8250.	11,500.
	1895A	—	—	—	Proof	14,000.

20 MARK

7.9650 g, .900 GOLD, .2305 oz AGW

9	1895A	1,500	—	4500.	10,000.	14,000.
	1895A	—	—	—	Proof	17,500.

PROOF SETS (PS)

KM#	Date	Mintage	Identification	Issue Price	Mkt. Val.
PS1	1894 (7)	—	KM1-7	—	4250.

NEW GUINEA

New Guinea, the world's largest island after Greenland, was discovered by Spanish navigator Jorge de Menezes, who landed on the northwest shore in 1527. European interests, attracted by exaggerated estimates of the resources of the area, resulted in the island being claimed in whole or part by Spain, the Netherlands, Great Britain and Germany.

RULERS
British 1910-1952

MONETARY SYSTEM
12 Pence = 1 Shilling
20 Shillings = 1 Pound

1/2 PENNY

COPPER-NICKEL

KM#	Date	Mintage	Fine	VF	XF	Unc
1	1929	.025	200.00	275.00	350.00	500.00
	1929	—	—	—	Proof	750.00

NICKEL (OMS)

1a	1929	20 pcs.	—	—	Proof	750.00

PENNY

COPPER-NICKEL

2	1929	.063	200.00	275.00	350.00	500.00
	1929	—	—	—	Proof	750.00

NICKEL (OMS)

2a	1929	20 pcs.	—	—	Proof	750.00

BRONZE

6	1936	.360	1.00	1.50	3.00	6.25
	1936	—	—	—	Proof	300.00

7	1938	.360	2.50	4.50	6.00	10.00
	1944	.240	1.50	2.75	5.00	9.00

3 PENCE

COPPER-NICKEL

3	1935	1.200	3.00	6.00	10.00	35.00
	1935	—	—	—	Proof	250.00

10	1944	.500	2.00	4.00	8.50	27.50

6 PENCE

COPPER-NICKEL

4	1935	2.000	3.50	7.50	10.00	40.00
	1935	—	—	—	Proof	250.00

KM#	Date	Mintage	Fine	VF	XF	Unc
9	1943	.130	6.00	9.00	12.50	45.00

SHILLING

5.3800 g, .925 SILVER, .1600 oz ASW

5	1935	2.100	1.50	3.00	4.00	8.00
	1936	1.360	1.50	3.00	4.00	8.00

8	1938	3.400	1.50	3.00	4.00	8.00
	1945	2.000	1.50	3.00	4.00	8.00

PROOF SETS (PS)

KM#	Date	Mintage	Identification	Issue Price	Mkt. Val.
PS1	1929(2)	—	KM1,2	—	1500.
PS2	1929(2)	20	KM1a,2a	—	1500.

PAPUA NEW GUINEA

MINT MARKS

FM - Franklin Mint, U.S.A.*

*NOTE: From 1975 the Franklin Mint has produced coinage in up to 3 different qualities. Qualities of issue are designated in ( ) after each date and are defined as follows:

(M) MATTE - Normal circulation strike or a dull finish produced by sandblasting special uncirculated (polish finish) or proof quality dies.

(U) SPECIAL UNCIRCULATED - Polished or proof-like in appearance without any frosted features.

(P) PROOF - The highest quality obtainable having mirror-like fields and frosted features.

MONETARY SYSTEM

100 Toea = 1 Kina

TOEA

BRONZE

KM#	Date	Mintage	VF	XF	Unc
1	1975	14.400	—	.10	.15
	1975FM(M)	.083	—	—	.15
	1975FM(U)	4,134	—	—	1.00
	1975FM(P)	.067	—	Proof	1.00
	1976	25.175	—	—	.10
	1976FM(M)	.084	—	—	.10
	1976FM(U)	976 pcs.	—	—	1.00
	1976FM(P)	.016	—	Proof	1.00
	1977FM(M)	.084	—	—	.10
	1977FM(U)	603 pcs.	—	—	1.50
	1977FM(P)	7,721	—	Proof	1.50
	1978		—	—	.10
	1978FM(M)	.083	—	—	.10
	1978FM(U)	777 pcs.	—	—	1.00
	1978FM(P)	5,540	—	Proof	1.50
	1979FM(M)	.084	—	—	.10
	1979FM(U)	1,366	—	—	1.00
	1979FM(P)	2,728	—	Proof	1.50
	1980FM(U)	1,160	—	—	1.00
	1980FM(P)	2,125	—	Proof	1.50
	1981FM(M)		—	—	1.00
	1981FM(M)		—	—	.10
	1981FM(P)	.010	—	Proof	2.00
	1982		—	—	1.00
	1982FM(P)		—	Proof	2.00
	1983FM(M)		—	—	.10
	1983FM(P)		—	Proof	2.00
	1984		—	—	.10
	1984FM(P)		—	Proof	2.00

2 TOEA

BRONZE

KM#	Date	Mintage	VF	XF	Unc
2	1975	11.400	—	.10	.20
	1975FM(M)	.042	—	—	.25
	1975FM(U)	4,134	—	—	1.25
	1975FM(P)	.067	—	Proof	1.25
	1976	15.175	—	.10	.15
	1976FM(M)	.042	—	—	.15
	1976FM(U)	976 pcs.	—	—	1.25
	1976FM(P)	.016	—	Proof	1.25
	1977FM(M)	.042	—	—	.15
	1977FM(U)	603 pcs.	—	—	1.75
	1977FM(P)	7,721	—	Proof	2.00
	1978FM(M)	.042	—	—	.15
	1978FM(U)	777 pcs.	—	—	1.25
	1978FM(P)	5,540	—	Proof	2.00
	1979FM(M)	.042	—	—	.15
	1979FM(U)	1,366	—	—	1.25
	1979FM(P)	2,728	—	Proof	2.00
	1980FM(U)	1,160	—	—	1.25
	1980FM(P)	2,125	—	Proof	2.00
	1981FM(P)	.010	—	Proof	3.00
	1982FM(M)	—	—	—	1.25
	1982FM(P)	—	—	Proof	3.00
	1983		—	—	.15
	1983FM(M)		—	—	.15
	1983FM(P)		—	Proof	3.00
	1984FM(P)		—	Proof	3.00

5 TOEA

COPPER-NICKEL

KM#	Date	Mintage	VF	XF	Unc
3	1975	11.000	.10	.20	.40
	1975FM(M)	.017	—	—	.50
	1975FM(U)	4,134	—	—	1.50
	1975FM(P)	.067	—	Proof	1.50
	1976	24.000	.10	.20	.40
	1976FM(M)	.017	—	—	.50
	1976FM(U)	976 pcs.	—	—	1.50
	1976FM(P)	.016	—	Proof	1.50
	1977FM(M)	.017	—	—	.55
	1977FM(U)	603 pcs.	—	—	2.00
	1977FM(P)	7,721	—	Proof	2.50
	1978	2.000	—	—	3.00
	1978FM(M)	.017	—	—	.55
	1978FM(U)	777 pcs.	—	—	1.50
	1978FM(P)	5,540	—	Proof	2.50
	1979		—	—	.40
	1979FM(M)	.017	—	—	.55
	1979FM(U)	1,366	—	—	1.50
	1979FM(P)	2,728	—	Proof	2.50
	1980FM(U)	1,160	—	—	1.50
	1980FM(P)	2,125	—	Proof	2.50
	1981FM(P)	.010	—	Proof	4.00
	1982		—	—	.40
	1982FM(M)		—	—	1.50
	1982FM(P)		—	Proof	4.00
	1983FM(M)		—	—	.55
	1983FM(P)		—	Proof	4.00
	1984FM(P)		—	Proof	4.00

10 TOEA

COPPER-NICKEL

KM#	Date	Mintage	VF	XF	Unc
4	1975	8.600	.15	.30	.60
	1975FM(M)	8,300	—	—	1.00
	1975FM(U)	4,134	—	—	1.75
	1975FM(P)	.067	—	Proof	2.00
	1976		.15	.30	.60
	1976FM(M)	8,300	—	—	1.00
	1976FM(U)	976 pcs.	—	—	1.75
	1976FM(P)	.016	—	Proof	2.00
	1977FM(M)	8,300	—	—	1.00
	1977FM(U)	603 pcs.	—	—	2.25
	1977FM(P)	7,721	—	Proof	3.00
	1978FM(M)	8,300	—	—	1.00
	1978FM(U)	777 pcs.	—	—	1.75
	1978FM(P)	5,540	—	Proof	3.00
	1979FM(M)	8,300	—	—	1.00
	1979FM(U)	1,366	—	—	1.75
	1979FM(P)	2,728	—	Proof	3.00

KM#	Date	Mintage	VF	XF	Unc
4	1980FM(U)	1,160	—	—	1.75
	1980FM(P)	2,125	—	Proof	3.00
	1981FM(P)	.010	—	Proof	5.00
	1982FM(M)	—	—	—	1.75
	1982FM(P)	—	—	Proof	5.00
	1983FM(M)	—	—	—	1.00
	1983FM(P)	—	—	Proof	5.00
	1984FM(P)	—	—	Proof	5.00

20 TOEA

COPPER-NICKEL

KM#	Date	Mintage	VF	XF	Unc
5	1975	15.500	.25	.50	1.00
	1975FM(M)	4,150	—	—	2.25
	1975FM(U)	4,134	—	—	2.25
	1975FM(P)	.067	—	Proof	3.00
	1976FM(M)	4,150	—	—	2.25
	1976FM(U)	976 pcs.	—	—	2.25
	1976FM(P)	.016	—	Proof	3.00
	1977FM(M)	4,150	—	—	2.25
	1977FM(U)	603 pcs.	—	—	2.75
	1977FM(P)	7,721	—	Proof	4.00
	1978	2.500	.35	.75	1.25
	1978FM(M)	4,150	—	—	2.25
	1978FM(U)	777 pcs.	—	—	2.25
	1978FM(P)	5,540	—	Proof	4.00
	1979FM(M)	4,150	—	—	2.25
	1979FM(U)	1,366	—	—	2.25
	1979FM(P)	2,728	—	Proof	4.00
	1980FM(U)	1,160	—	—	2.25
	1980FM(P)	2,125	—	Proof	4.00
	1981		.25	.50	1.00
	1981FM(P)	.010	—	Proof	6.00
	1982FM(M)	—	—	—	2.25
	1982FM(P)	—	—	Proof	6.00
	1983FM(M)	—	—	—	2.25
	1983FM(P)	—	—	Proof	6.00
	1984		.25	.50	1.00
	1984FM(P)	—	—	Proof	6.00

50 TOEA

COPPER-NICKEL
South Pacific Festival of Arts

KM#	Date	Mintage	VF	XF	Unc
15	1980FM(U)	1,160	—	—	15.00
	1980FM(P)	2,125	—	Proof	10.00

KINA

COPPER-NICKEL

KM#	Date	Mintage	VF	XF	Unc
6	1975	2.000	1.25	1.75	2.50
	1975FM(M)	829 pcs.	—	—	10.00
	1975FM(U)	4,134	—	—	3.00
	1975FM(P)	.067	—	Proof	3.00
	1976FM(M)	829 pcs.	—	—	10.00
	1976FM(U)	976 pcs.	—	—	3.00
	1976FM(P)	.016	—	Proof	4.00
	1977FM(M)	829 pcs.	—	—	10.00
	1977FM(U)	603 pcs.	—	—	15.00
	1977FM(P)	7,721	—	Proof	5.00
	1978FM(M)	829 pcs.	—	—	10.00
	1978FM(U)	777 pcs.	—	—	3.00
	1978FM(P)	5,540	—	Proof	5.00
	1979FM(M)	829 pcs.	—	—	10.00
	1979FM(U)	1,366	—	—	3.00
	1979FM(P)	2,728	—	Proof	6.50
	1980FM(U)	1,160	—	—	3.00
	1980FM(P)	2,125	—	Proof	6.50
	1981FM(P)	.010	—	Proof	3.00
	1982FM(M)	—	—	—	3.00
	1982FM(P)	—	—	Proof	8.00

PAPUA NEW GUINEA 1386

KM#	Date	Mintage	VF	XF	Unc
6	1983FM(M)	—	—	—	3.00
	1983FM(P)	—	—	Proof	8.00
	1984FM(P)	—	—	Proof	8.00

5 KINA

COPPER-NICKEL

7	1975FM(M)	166 pcs.	—	—	40.00
	1975FM(U)	4,134	—	—	7.50
	1976FM(M)	166 pcs.	—	—	40.00
	1976FM(U)	976 pcs.	—	—	12.50
	1977FM(M)	166 pcs.	—	—	40.00
	1977FM(U)	603 pcs.	—	—	25.00
	1978FM(M)	166 pcs.	—	—	40.00
	1978FM(U)	777 pcs.	—	—	12.50
	1979FM(M)	166 pcs.	—	—	40.00
	1979FM(U)	1,366	—	—	10.00
	1980FM(U)	1,160	—	—	10.00

27.6000 g, .500 SILVER, .4436 oz ASW

7a	1975FM(P)	.067	—	Proof	6.50
	1976FM(P)	.016	—	Proof	7.50
	1977FM(P)	7,721	—	Proof	10.00
	1978FM(P)	5,540	—	Proof	10.00
	1979FM(P)	2,728	—	Proof	12.50
	1980FM(P)	2,125	—	Proof	12.50

28.2800 g, .500 SILVER, .4656 oz ASW
International Year of the Child

| 18 | 1981 | 8,775 | — | — | 20.00 |

COPPER-NICKEL
Defense of the Kokoda Trail
Obv: Similar to 20 Toea, KM#5.

| 20 | 1982FM(M) | — | — | — | 10.00 |

28.2800 g, .925 SILVER, .8411 oz ASW

| 20a | 1982FM(P) | 1,795 | — | Proof | 40.00 |

COPPER-NICKEL
10th Anniversary of Bank of Papua New Guinea

Obv: Similar to 20 Toea, KM#5.

KM#	Date	Mintage	VF	XF	Unc
23	1983FM(U)	360 pcs.	—	—	10.00

28.2800 g, .925 SILVER, .8411 oz ASW

| 23a | 1983FM(P) | 673 pcs. | — | Proof | 40.00 |

New Parliament Building

| 25a | 1984FM(P) | — | — | Proof | 40.00 |

Decade for Women

| 28 | 1984FM(P) | 1,050 | — | Proof | 25.00 |

10 KINA

COPPER-NICKEL

8	1975FM(M)	82 pcs.	—	—	75.00
	1975FM(U)	4,134	—	—	12.50
	1976FM(M)	82 pcs.	—	—	75.00
	1976FM(U)	976 pcs.	—	—	15.00
	1978FM(M)	168 pcs.	—	—	60.00
	1978FM(U)	777 pcs.	—	—	17.50
	1979FM(M)	82 pcs.	—	—	75.00
	1979FM(U)	1,366	—	—	15.00
	1980FM(U)	776 pcs.	—	—	15.00
	1983FM(M)	360 pcs.	—	—	17.50

41.6000 g, .925 SILVER, 1.2371 oz ASW

8a	1975FM(P)	.079	—	Proof	15.00
	1976FM(P)	.021	—	Proof	17.50
	1978FM(P)	7,352	—	Proof	22.50
	1979FM(P)	4,147	—	Proof	25.00
	1980FM(P)	2,752	—	Proof	27.50
	1982FM(P)	1,025	—	Proof	30.00
	1983FM(P)	1,025	—	Proof	30.00

COPPER-NICKEL
Silver Jubilee

KM#	Date	Mintage	VF	XF	Unc
11	1977FM(M)	82 pcs.	—	—	80.00
	1977FM(U)	603 pcs.	—	—	30.00

40.5000 g, .925 SILVER, 1.2046 oz ASW

| 11a | 1977FM(P) | .014 | — | Proof | 20.00 |

COPPER-NICKEL
Royal Visit
Obv: Similar to 5 Kina, KM#7.

| 21 | 1982FM(M) | — | — | — | 20.00 |

40.5000 g, .925 SILVER, 1.2046 oz ASW

| 21a | 1982FM(P) | 1,185 | — | Proof | 60.00 |

35.6000 g, .925 SILVER, 1.0587 oz ASW
Papal Visit
Obv: Similar to 5 Kina, KM#7.

| 26a | 1984FM(P) | — | — | Proof | 55.00 |

100 KINA

9.5700 g, .900 GOLD, .2769 oz AGW

9	1975FM(M)	100 pcs.	—	—	250.00
	1975FM(U)	8,081	—	—	150.00
	1975FM(P)	.018	—	Proof	175.00

1st Anniversary of Independence

KM#	Date	Mintage	VF	XF	Unc
10	1976FM(M)	100 pcs.	—	—	250.00
	1976FM(U)	250 pcs.	—	—	150.00
	1976FM(P)	8,020	—	Proof	175.00

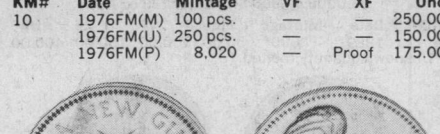

12	1977FM(M)	100 pcs.	—	—	250.00
	1977FM(U)	362 pcs.	—	—	150.00
	1977FM(P)	3,460	—	Proof	175.00

13	1978FM(U)	400 pcs.	—	—	250.00
	1978FM(P)	4,751	—	Proof	475.00

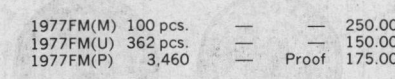

14	1979FM(M)	102 pcs.	—	—	250.00
	1979FM(U)	286 pcs.	—	—	150.00
	1979FM(P)	3,492	—	Proof	175.00

7.8300 g, .500 GOLD, .1258 oz AGW
South Pacific Festival of Arts

| 16 | 1980 | 7,500 | — | Proof | 150.00 |

9.5700 g, .900 GOLD, .2769 oz AGW
5th Anniversary of Independence

17	1980FM(M)	30 pcs.	—	—	300.00
	1980FM(P)	1,118	—	Proof	200.00

Prime Minister, Sir Julius Chan

| 19 | 1981FM(P) | 685 pcs. | — | Proof | 225.00 |

Royal Visit

KM#	Date	Mintage	VF	XF	Unc
22	1982FM(P)	484 pcs.	—	Proof	300.00

10th Anniversary of Bank of Papua New Guinea

| 24 | 1983FM(P) | 378 pcs. | — | Proof | 350.00 |

100th Anniversary of Founding of British and German Protectorates

| 27 | 1984FM(P) | 274 pcs. | — | Proof | 400.00 |

MINT SETS (MS)

KM#	Date	Mintage	Identification	Issue Price	Mkt. Val.
MS1	1975FM(8)	4,134	KM1-8	30.00	27.50
MS2	1976FM(8)	976	KM1-8	30.00	37.50
MS3	1977FM(8)	603	KM1-7,11	30.00	60.00
MS4	1978FM(8)	777	—	30.00	40.00
MS5	1979FM(8)	1,366	KM1-8	31.00	35.00
MS6	1980FM(9)	—	KM1-8,15	35.00	35.00
MS7	1982FM(8)	—	KM1-6,20,21	36.00	35.00
MS8	1983FM(8)	360	KM1-6,8,23	36.00	35.00

PROOF SETS (PS)

PS1	1975FM(8)	42,340	KM1-6,7a,8a	60.00	35.00
PS2	1976FM(8)	16,323	KM1-6,7a,8a	60.00	35.00
PS3	1977FM(8)	7,721	KM1-6,7a,11a	60.00	55.00
PS4	1978FM(8)	5,540	KM1-6,7a,8a	70.00	45.00
PS5	1979FM(8)	2,728	KM1-6,7a,8a	72.00	50.00
PS6	1980FM(9)	—	KM1-6,7a,8a,15	130.00	65.00
PS7	1981FM(6)	10,000	KM1-6	29.00	12.50
PS8	1982FM(8)	—	KM1-6,20a,21a	92.00	100.00
PS9	1983FM(8)	—	KM1-6,8a,23a	132.00	120.00
PS10	1984FM(8)	—	KM1-6,25a-26a	133.00	120.00

PARAGUAY

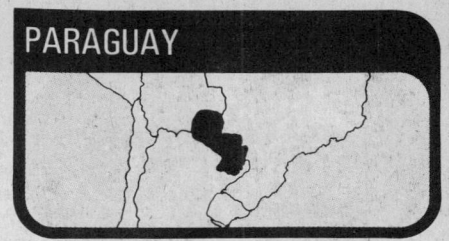

The Republic of Paraguay, a landlocked country in the heart of South America surrounded by Argentina, Bolivia and Brazil, has an area of 157,048 sq. mi. (406,752 sq. km.) and a population of *4.5 million, 95 percent of whom are of mixed Spanish and Indian descent. Capital: Asuncion. The country is predominantly agrarian, with no important mineral deposits or oil reserves. Meat, timber, oilseeds, tobacco and cotton account for 70 percent of Paraguay's export revenue.

Paraguay was first visited by Alejo Garcia, a shipwrecked Spaniard, in 1524. The interior was explored by Sebastian Cabot in 1527 and 1528, when he sailed up the Parana and Paraguay rivers. Asuncion, which would become the center of a province embracing much of southern South America, was established by the Spanish explorer Juan de Salazar on Aug. 15, 1537. For a century and a half the history of Paraguay was largely the history of the agricultural colonies established by the Jesuits in the south and east to Christianize the Indians. In 1811, following the outbreak of the South American wars of independence, Paraguayan patriots overthrew the local Spanish authorities and proclaimed their country's independence.

MINT MARKS
HF - LeLocle

CONTRACTORS
(Chas. J.) SHAW - for Ralph Heaton, Birmingham Mint

MONETARY SYSTEM
100 Centesimos = 1 Peso

1/12 REAL

COPPER

KM#	Date	Mintage	Fine	VF	XF	Unc
1.1*	1845 Birmingham					
		3.168	5.00	15.00	50.00	100.00

Crude issue struck at Asuncion Mint.

| 1.2* | 1845 | — | 5.00 | 25.00 | 75.00 | 150.00 |

*NOTE: Struck with medal die alignment - coin strike varieties exist. After 1847 then were revalued at 1/24th Real.

4 PESOS FUERTES

10.3000 g, .900 GOLD, .2980 oz AGW

| A2 | 1867 | — | — | — | Rare |

DECIMAL COINAGE
100 Centavos (Centesimos) = 1 Peso

CENTESIMO

COPPER
Rev: SHAW to right of date.

| 2 | 1870 | — | 2.00 | 5.00 | 20.00 | 40.00 |

PARAGUAY 1388

2 CENTESIMOS

COPPER
Rev: SHAW to right of date.

KM#	Date	Mintage	Fine	VF	XF	Unc
3	1870	—	2.50	7.50	25.00	50.00

4 CENTESIMOS

COPPER
Rev: SHAW to right of date.

4.1	1870	—	3.00	10.00	30.00	75.00

Crude issue struck at Asuncion.
Obv: W/o ribbon bow on sprays.
Rev: W/o Shaw to right of date.

KM#	Date	Mintage	VG	Fine	VF	XF
4.2	1870	—	50.00	100.00	200.00	500.00

Rev: SAEZ to right of date.

| 4.3 | 1870 | — | 50.00 | 75.00 | 150.00 | 300.00 |

5 CENTAVOS

COPPER-NICKEL

KM#	Date	Mintage	Fine	VF	XF	Unc
6	1900	.400	1.00	2.00	10.00	20.00
	1903	.600	1.00	2.00	7.50	15.00

| 9 | 1908 | .400 | 1.50 | 5.00 | 30.00 | 75.00 |

10 CENTAVOS

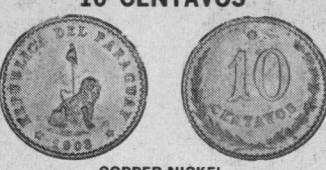

COPPER-NICKEL

KM#	Date	Mintage	Fine	VF	XF	Unc
7	1900	.800	1.00	2.50	10.00	20.00
	1903	1.200	1.00	2.00	7.50	17.50

| 10 | 1908 | .800 | 2.50 | 5.00 | 25.00 | 70.00 |

20 CENTAVOS

COPPER-NICKEL

8	1900	.500	1.00	3.00	10.00	20.00
	1903	.750	1.00	2.00	7.50	17.50

| 11 | 1908 | 1.000 | 2.50 | 5.00 | 25.00 | 70.00 |

50 CENTAVOS

COPPER-NICKEL

| 12 | 1925 | 4.000 | .50 | 1.50 | 5.00 | 10.00 |

ALUMINUM

| 15 | 1938 | .400 | .50 | 1.00 | 3.50 | 7.50 |

PESO

25.0000 g, .900 SILVER, .7233 oz ASW

KM#	Date	Mintage	Fine	VF	XF	Unc
5	1889	.600*	50.00	100.00	150.00	400.00

*Unknown quantity melted.

COPPER-NICKEL

| 13 | 1925 | 3.500 | .50 | 1.00 | 5.00 | 8.00 |

ALUMINUM

| 16 | 1938 | — | .50 | 1.50 | 3.00 | 6.50 |

2 PESOS

COPPER-NICKEL

| 14 | 1925 | 2.500 | .50 | 1.00 | 6.00 | 9.00 |

ALUMINUM

| 17 | 1938 | — | .50 | 1.50 | 3.00 | 6.50 |

5 PESOS

COPPER-NICKEL

| 18 | 1939 | 4.000 | 1.00 | 2.50 | 7.50 | 15.00 |

10 PESOS

COPPER-NICKEL

| 19 | 1939 | 4.000 | 1.00 | 2.00 | 7.00 | 14.00 |

MONETARY REFORM
100 Centimos = 1 Guarani

CENTIMO

ALUMINUM-BRONZE

20	1944	3.500	.10	.50	1.00	2.00
	1948HF	2.000	.10	.50	1.00	2.00
	1950HF	1.096	.10	.25	1.00	2.00

5 CENTIMOS

ALUMINUM-BRONZE

KM#	Date	Mintage	Fine	VF	XF	Unc
21	1944	2.195	.10	.50	1.00	2.50
	1947HF	13.111	.10	.20	.50	1.00

10 CENTIMOS

ALUMINUM-BRONZE

22	1944	.975	.25	.75	2.50	5.00
	1947HF	6.656	.10	.25	.50	1.00

25	1953	5.000	.10	.15	.25	.50

NOTE: Medal rotation dies.

15 CENTIMOS

ALUMINUM-BRONZE

26	1953	5.000	.10	.15	.25	.50

NOTE: Medal rotation dies.

25 CENTIMOS

ALUMINUM-BRONZE

23	1944	.700	.25	1.00	3.00	10.00
	1948HF	.600	.25	.75	2.50	7.00
	1951HF	1.000	.25	.75	1.25	3.00

27	1953	2.000	.10	.15	.25	.75

NOTE: Medal rotation dies.

50 CENTIMOS

ALUMINUM-BRONZE

24	1944	2.485	.25	1.00	2.00	5.00
	1951	2.893	.25	.75	1.50	2.50

 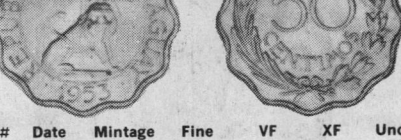

KM#	Date	Mintage	Fine	VF	XF	Unc
28	1953	2.000	.10	.15	.25	.75

NOTE: Medal rotation dies.

GUARANI

STAINLESS STEEL

151	1975	10.000	—	—	.10	.30
(31)	1975	1.000	—	—	Proof	—
	1976	12.000	—	—	.10	.50
	1976	1.000	—	—	Proof	—

F.A.O. Issue

165	1978	15.000	—	—	.10	.30
(35)	1980	3.450	—	—	.10	.30
	1980	1.000	—	—	Proof	—
	1984	15.000	—	—	.10	.25
	1986	15.000	—	—	.10	.25
	1988	15.000	—	—	.10	.25

5 GUARANIES

STAINLESS STEEL

152	1975	7.500	—	—	.10	.30
(32)	1975	1.000	—	—	Proof	—

F.A.O. Issue

166	1978	10.000	—	—	.10	.30
(36)	1980	2.875	—	—	.10	.30
	1980	1.000	—	—	Proof	—
	1984	15.000	—	—	.10	.25
	1986	15.000	—	—	.10	.25

10 GUARANIES

STAINLESS STEEL

153	1975	10.000	—	.10	.15	.30
(33)	1975	1.000	—	—	Proof	—
	1976	10.000	—	.10	.15	.50
	1976	1.000	—	—	Proof	—

F.A.O. Issue

167	1978	15.000	—	.10	.15	.30
(37)	1980	3.770	—	.10	.15	.35
	1980	1.000	—	—	Proof	—
	1984	20.000	—	.10	.15	.30
	1986	35.000	—	.10	.15	.30
	1988	40.000	—	.10	.15	.30

50 GUARANIES

STAINLESS STEEL

KM#	Date	Mintage	Fine	VF	XF	Unc
154	1975	9.500	.20	.40	.60	1.00
(34)	1975	1.000	—	—	Proof	—

General Estigarribia
Rev: Dam.

169	1980	5.692	.20	.40	.60	1.00
(38)	1980	1.000	—	—	Proof	—
	1986	15.000	.20	.40	.60	1.00
	1988	25.000	.20	.40	.60	1.00

150 GUARANIES

25.0000 g, .999 SILVER, .8030 oz ASW
General A. Stroessner
Obv: Arms.

KM#	Date	Mintage	VF	XF	Unc
31	1972	*.010	—	Proof	65.00
(M1)					

Munich Olympics

32	1972	*.010	—	Proof	125.00
(M2)					

Munich Olympics
Obv: Arms. Rev: Broad jumper.

33	1972	*.010	—	Proof	125.00
(M3)					

Munich Olympics
Obv: Arms. Rev: Relay runner.

34	1972	*.010	—	Proof	125.00
(M4)					

PARAGUAY 1390

Munich Olympics
Obv: Arms.

KM#	Date	Mintage	VF	XF	Unc
35 (M5)	1972	*.010	—	Proof	125.00

Munich Olympics
Obv: Arms. Rev: Pole vaulter.

| 36 (M6) | 1972 | *.010 | — | Proof | 125.00 |

Munich Olympics
Obv: Arms.

| 37 (M7) | 1972 | *.010 | — | Proof | 125.00 |

Mariscal Jose F. Estigarriba
Obv: Arms.

| 59 (M29) | 1973 | *.010 | — | Proof | 65.00 |

Mariscal Francisco Solano Lopez
Obv: Arms.

| 60 (M30) | 1973 | *.010 | — | Proof | 65.00 |

General Jose E. Diaz
Obv: Arms.

KM#	Date	Mintage	VF	XF	Unc
61 (M31)	1973	*.010	—	Proof	65.00

General Bernardino Caballero
Obv: Arms.

| 62 (M32) | 1973 | *.010 | — | Proof | 65.00 |

Teotihucana Culture
Obv: Arms.

| 63 (M33) | 1973 | *.010 | — | Proof | 65.00 |

Huasteca Culture
Obv: Arms.

| 64 (M34) | 1973 | *.010 | — | Proof | 65.00 |

Mixteca Culture
Obv: Arms.

| 65 (M35) | 1973 | *.010 | — | Proof | 65.00 |

Veracruz Ceramica
Obv: Arms.

KM#	Date	Mintage	VF	XF	Unc
66 (M36)	1973	*.010	—	Proof	65.00

Veracruz Culture
Obv: Arms.

| 67 (M37) | 1973 | *.010 | — | Proof | 65.00 |

Albrecht Durer
Obv: Arms.

| 68 (M38) | 1973 | *.010 | — | Proof | 65.00 |

Johann Wolfgang Goethe
Obv: Arms.

| 69 (M39) | 1973 | *.010 | — | Proof | 65.00 |

Abraham Lincoln
Obv: Arms.

| 107 (M77) | 1974 | *.010 | — | Proof | 75.00 |

Ludwig van Beethoven
Obv: Arms.

| 108 (M78) | 1974 | *.010 | — | Proof | 65.00 |

PARAGUAY 1391

KM#	Date	Mintage	VF	XF	Unc
109 (M79)	1974	*.010	—	Proof	75.00

Otto von Bismarck — Obv: Arms.

KM#	Date	Mintage	VF	XF	Unc
114 (M84)	1974	*.010	—	Proof	85.00

John F. Kennedy — Obv: Arms.

KM#	Date	Mintage	VF	XF	Unc
155 (M89)	1975	*.010	—	Proof	65.00

Parliament of Paraguay — Obv: Arms.

| 110 (M80) | 1974 | *.010 | — | Proof | 100.00 |

Albert Einstein — Obv: Arms.

| 115 (M85) | 1974 | *.010 | — | Proof | 75.00 |

Konrad Adenauer — Obv: Arms.

| 156 (M122) | 1975 | *.010 | — | Proof | 85.00 |

Apollo 11 — Obv: Arms.

| 111 (M81) | 1974 | *.010 | — | Proof | 65.00 |

Giuseppe Garibaldi — Obv: Arms.

| 116 (M86) | 1974 | *.010 | — | Proof | 65.00 |

Winston Churchill — Obv: Arms.

| 157 (M123) | 1975 | *.010 | — | Proof | 75.00 |

Apollo 15 — Obv: Arms.

| 112 (M82) | 1974 | *.010 | — | Proof | 65.00 |

Alessandro Manzoni — Obv: Arms.

| 117 (M87) | 1974 | *.010 | — | Proof | 75.00 |

Pope John XXIII — Obv: Arms.

| 158 (M124) | 1975 | *.010 | — | Proof | 65.00 |

Friendship Bridge — Obv: Arms.

| 113 (M83) | 1974 | *.010 | — | Proof | 65.00 |

William Tell — Obv: Arms.

| 118 (M88) | 1974 | *.010 | — | Proof | 65.00 |

Pope Paul VI — Obv: Arms.

| 159 (M125) | 1975 | *.010 | — | Proof | 65.00 |

Holy Trinity Church — Obv: Arms.

PARAGUAY 1392

Ruins of Humaita
Obv: Arms.

KM#	Date	Mintage	VF	XF	Unc
160 (M126)	1975	*.010	—	Proof	65.00

300 GUARANIES

26.6000 g, .720 SILVER, .6157 oz ASW
Stroessner

KM#	Date	Mintage	Fine	VF	XF	Unc
29	1968	.250	—	—	6.00	12.50

1500 GUARANIES

10.7000 g, .900 GOLD, .3096 oz AGW
General A. Stroessner
Obv: Arms.

KM#	Date	Mintage	VF	XF	Unc
38 (M8)	1972	*1,500	—	Proof	450.00

Munich Olympics
Obv: Arms. Rev: Runner.

| 39 (M9) | 1972 | *1,500 | — | Proof | 450.00 |

Munich Olympics
Obv: Arms. Rev: Broad jumper.

| 40 (M10) | 1972 | *1,500 | — | Proof | 450.00 |

Munich Olympics
Obv: Arms. Rev: Relay runner.

| 41 (M11) | 1972 | *1,500 | — | Proof | 450.00 |

Munich Olympics
Obv: Arms. Rev: Hurdler.

| 42 (M12) | 1972 | *1,500 | — | Proof | 450.00 |

Munich Olympics
Obv: Arms. Rev: Pole vaulter.

| 43 (M13) | 1972 | *1,500 | — | Proof | 450.00 |

Munich Olympics
Obv: Arms. Rev: Boxer.

| 44 (M14) | 1972 | *1,500 | — | Proof | 450.00 |

Estigarribia
Obv: Arms.

| 70 (M40) | 1973 | *1,500 | — | Proof | 450.00 |

Mariscal Francisco Solano Lopez
Obv: Arms.

| 71 (M41) | 1973 | *1,500 | — | Proof | 450.00 |

General Jose E. Diaz
Obv: Arms.

KM#	Date	Mintage	VF	XF	Unc
72 (M42)	1973	*1,500	—	Proof	450.00

General Bernardino Caballero
Obv: Arms.

| 73 (M43) | 1973 | *1,500 | — | Proof | 450.00 |

Teotihucana Culture
Obv: Arms. Rev: Sculpture.

| 74 (M44) | 1973 | *1,500 | — | Proof | 450.00 |

Huasteca Culture
Obv: Arms. Rev: Sculpture.

| 75 (M45) | 1973 | *1,500 | — | Proof | 450.00 |

Mixteca Culture
Obv: Arms. Rev: Pitcher in shape of animal.

| 76 (M46) | 1973 | *1,500 | — | Proof | 450.00 |

Veracruz Ceramica
Obv: Arms. Rev: Vase.

| 77 (M47) | 1973 | *1,500 | — | Proof | 450.00 |

Veracruz Culture
Obv: Arms. Rev: Sculpted head.

| 78 (M48) | 1973 | *1,500 | — | Proof | 450.00 |

Albrecht Durer
Obv: Arms.

| 79 (M49) | 1973 | *1,500 | — | Proof | 450.00 |

Johann Wolfgang Goethe
Obv: Arms.

| 80 (M50) | 1973 | *1,500 | — | Proof | 450.00 |

Abraham Lincoln
Obv: Arms.

| 119 (M90) | 1974 | *1,500 | — | Proof | 450.00 |

Ludwig van Beethoven
Obv: Arms.

| 120 (M91) | 1974 | *1,500 | — | Proof | 450.00 |

Otto von Bismarck
Obv: Arms.

| 121 (M92) | 1974 | *1,500 | — | Proof | 450.00 |

Albert Einstein
Obv: Arms.

| 122 (M93) | 1974 | *1,500 | — | Proof | 450.00 |

Giuseppe Garibaldi
Obv: Arms.

| 123 (M94) | 1974 | *1,500 | — | Proof | 450.00 |

Alessandro Manzoni
Obv: Arms.

| 124 (M95) | 1974 | *1,500 | — | Proof | 450.00 |

William Tell
Obv: Arms.

| 125 (M96) | 1974 | *1,500 | — | Proof | 450.00 |

John F. Kennedy
Obv: Arms.

| 126 (M97) | 1974 | *1,500 | — | Proof | 450.00 |

Konrad Adenauer
Obv: Arms.

| 127 (M98) | 1974 | *1,500 | — | Proof | 450.00 |

Winston Churchill
Obv: Arms.

| 128 (M99) | 1974 | *1,500 | — | Proof | 450.00 |

Pope John XXIII
Obv: Arms.

| 129 (M100) | 1974 | *1,500 | — | Proof | 450.00 |

Pope Paul VI
Obv: Arms.

| 130 (M101) | 1974 | *1,500 | — | Proof | 450.00 |

3000 GUARANIES

21.3000 g, .900 GOLD, .6164 oz AGW
General A. Stroessner

KM#	Date	Mintage	VF	XF	Unc
45 (M15)	1972	*1,500	—	Proof	750.00

Munich Olympics
Obv: Arms. Rev: Runner.

| 46 (M16) | 1972 | *1,500 | — | Proof | 750.00 |

Munich Olympics
Obv: Arms. Rev: Broad jumper.

| 47 (M17) | 1972 | *1,500 | — | Proof | 750.00 |

Munich Olympics
Obv: Arms. Rev: Relay runner.

| 48 (M18) | 1972 | *1,500 | — | Proof | 750.00 |

Munich Olympics
Obv: Arms. Rev: Hurdler.

| 49 (M19) | 1972 | *1,500 | — | Proof | 750.00 |

Munich Olympics
Obv: Arms. Rev: Pole vaulter.

| 50 (M20) | 1972 | *1,500 | — | Proof | 750.00 |

Munich Olympics
Obv: Arms. Rev: Boxer.

| 51 (M21) | 1972 | *1,500 | — | Proof | 750.00 |

Estigarribia

| 81 (M51) | 1973 | *1,500 | — | Proof | 750.00 |

Mariscal Francisco Solano Lopez

| 82 (M52) | 1973 | *1,500 | — | Proof | 750.00 |

General Jose E. Diaz

| 83 (M53) | 1973 | *1,500 | — | Proof | 750.00 |

PARAGUAY

General Bernardino Caballero

KM#	Date	Mintage	VF	XF	Unc
84 (M54)	1973	*1,500	—	Proof	750.00

Teotihucana Culture
Obv: Arms. Rev: Sculpture.
| 85 (M55) | 1973 | *1,500 | — | Proof | 750.00 |

Huasteca Culture
Obv: Arms. Rev: Sculpture.
| 86 (M56) | 1973 | *1,500 | — | Proof | 750.00 |

Mixteca Culture
Obv: Arms. Rev: Pitcher in shape of animal.
| 87 (M57) | 1973 | *1,500 | — | Proof | 750.00 |

Veracruz Ceramica
Obv: Arms. Rev: Vase.
| 88 (M58) | 1973 | *1,500 | — | Proof | 750.00 |

Veracruz Culture
Obv: Arms. Rev: Sculpted head.
| 89 (M59) | 1973 | *1,500 | — | Proof | 750.00 |

Albrecht Durer
| 90 (M60) | 1973 | *1,500 | — | Proof | 750.00 |

Johann Wolfgang Goethe
| 91 (M61) | 1973 | *1,500 | — | Proof | 750.00 |

Abraham Lincoln
| 131 (M102) | 1974 | *1,500 | — | Proof | 750.00 |

Ludwig van Beethoven
Obv: Arms.
| 132 (M103) | 1974 | *1,500 | — | Proof | 750.00 |

Otto von Bismarck

KM#	Date	Mintage	VF	XF	Unc
133 (M104)	1974	*1,500	—	Proof	750.00

Albert Einstein
Obv: Arms.
| 134 (M105) | 1974 | *1,500 | — | Proof | 750.00 |

Giuseppe Garibaldi
| 135 (M106) | 1974 | *1,500 | — | Proof | 750.00 |

Alessandro Manzoni
| 136 (M107) | 1974 | *1,500 | — | Proof | 750.00 |

William Tell
| 137 (M108) | 1974 | *1,500 | — | Proof | 750.00 |

John F. Kennedy
| 138 (M109) | 1974 | *1,500 | — | Proof | 750.00 |

Konrad Adenauer

KM#	Date	Mintage	VF	XF	Unc
139 (M110)	1974	*1,500	—	Proof	750.00

Winston Churchill
| 140 (M111) | 1974 | *1,500 | — | Proof | 750.00 |

Pope John XXIII
| 141 (M112) | 1974 | *1,500 | — | Proof | 750.00 |

Pope Paul VI
| 142 (M113) | 1974 | *1,500 | — | Proof | 750.00 |

Iglesia De Santisima Trinidad
| 161 (M127) | 1975 | — | — | Proof | 700.00 |

Parliament of Paraguay
| 162 (M128) | 1975 | — | — | Proof | 700.00 |

Friendship Bridge
| 163 (M129) | 1975 | — | — | Proof | 700.00 |

PARAGUAY 1394

Humaita Ruins

KM#	Date	Mintage	VF	XF	Unc
164 (M130)	1975	—		Proof	700.00

4500 GUARANIES
31.9000 g, .900 GOLD, .9231 oz AGW
General A. Stroessner
Obv: Arms.

52 (M22)	1972	*1,500	—	Proof	1150.

Munich Olympics
Obv: Arms.

53 (M23)	1972	*1,500	—	Proof	1150.

Munich Olympics
Obv: Arms. Rev: Broad jumper.

54 (M24)	1972	*1,500	—	Proof	1150.

Munich Olympics
Obv: Arms. Rev: Relay runner.

55 (M25)	1972	*1,500	—	Proof	1150.

Munich Olympics
Obv: Arms. Rev: Hurdler.

56 (M26)	1972	*1,500	—	Proof	1150.

Munich Olympics
Obv: Arms. Rev: Pole vaulter.

57 (M27)	1972	*1,500	—	Proof	1150.

Munich Olympics
Obv: Arms. Rev: Boxer.

58 (M28)	1972	*1,500	—	Proof	1150.

Mariscal Jose F. Estigarribia
Obv: Arms.

92 (M62)	1973	*1,500	—	Proof	1150.

Mariscal Francisco Solano Lopez
Obv: Arms.

93 (M63)	1973	*1,500	—	Proof	1150.

General Jose E. Diaz
Obv: Arms.

94 (M64)	1973	*1,500	—	Proof	1150.

General Bernardino Caballero
Obv: Arms.

95 (M65)	1973	*1,500	—	Proof	1150.

Teotihucana Culture
Obv: Arms. Rev: Sculpture.

96 (M66)	1973	*1,500	—	Proof	1150.

Huasteca Culture
Obv: Arms. Rev: Sculpture.

97 (M67)	1973	*1,500	—	Proof	1150.

Mixteca Culture
Obv: Arms. Rev: Pitcher in shape of animal.

98 (M68)	1973	*1,500	—	Proof	1150.

Veracruz Ceramica
Obv: Arms. Rev: Vase.

99 (M69)	1973	*1,500	—	Proof	1150.

Veracruz Culture
Obv: Arms. Rev: Sculpted head.

100 (M70)	1973	*1,500	—	Proof	1150.

Albrecht Durer
Obv: Arms.

KM#	Date	Mintage	VF	XF	Unc
101 (M71)	1973	*1,500		Proof	1150.

Johann Wolfgang Goethe
Obv: Arms.

102 (M72)	1973	*1,500		Proof	1150.

Ludwig van Beethoven
Obv: Arms.

103 (M73)	1973	*1,500		Proof	1150.

Otto von Bismarck
Obv: Arms.

104 (M74)	1973	*1,500		Proof	1150.

Giuseppe Garibaldi
Obv: Arms.

105 (M75)	1973	*1,500		Proof	1150.

Alessandro Manzoni

106 (M76)	1973	*1,500	—	Proof	1150.

Abraham Lincoln
Obv: Arms.

143 (M114)	1974	*1,500	—	Proof	1150.

Albert Einstein
Obv: Arms.

144 (M115)	1974	*1,500	—	Proof	1150.

William Tell
Obv: Arms.

145 (M116)	1974	*1,500	—	Proof	1150.

John F. Kennedy
Obv: Arms.

146 (M117)	1974	*1,500	—	Proof	1150.

Konrad Adenauer
Obv: Arms.

147 (M118)	1974	*1,500	—	Proof	1150.

Winston Churchill
Obv: Arms.

148 (M119)	1974	*1,500	—	Proof	1150.

Pope John XXIII
Obv: Arms.

149 (M120)	1974	*1,500	—	Proof	1150.

Pope Paul VI
Obv: Arms.

150 (M121)	1974	*1,500	—	Proof	1150.

NOTE: Most Paraguayan gold coins have been melted. All may be considered very scarce.

10,000 GUARANIES
46.0100 g, .900 GOLD, 1.3315 oz AGW
Stroessner
Similar to 300 Guaranies KM#29.

KM#	Date	Mintage	Fine	VF	XF	Unc
30 (39)	1968	*50 pcs.			Proof	4500.

*NOTE: KM#30 struck for presentation.

28.7000 g, .999 SILVER, .9219 oz ASW
Caballero and Stroessner

KM#	Date	Mintage	Fine	VF	XF	Unc
171	1987	1,000			Proof	45.00

Stroessner

173	1988	1,000		—	Proof	45.00

70,000 GUARANIES

46.0000 g, .900 GOLD, 1.3310 oz AGW
Stroessner

168	1978	300 pcs.			Proof	1000.

100,000 GUARANIES

46.0000 g, .900 GOLD, 1.3310 oz AGW
Stroessner

KM#	Date	Mintage	Fine	VF	XF	Unc
170 (40)	1983	300 pcs.	—	—	Proof	1000.

250,000 GUARANIES

46.0000 g, .917 GOLD, 1.3561 oz AGW
Caballero - Stroessner

KM#	Date	Mintage	Fine	VF	XF	Unc
172 (41)	1987	500 pcs.	—	—	Proof	1100.

300,000 GUARANIES

46.0000 g, .917 GOLD, 1.3561 oz AGW
Stroessner

KM#	Date	Mintage	Fine	VF	XF	Unc
174	1988	500 pcs.	—	—	Proof	1100.

PROOF SETS (PS)

KM#	Date	Mintage	Identification	Issue Price	Mkt. Val.
PS5	1975(4)	1,000	KM61-64	—	25.00
PS6	1976(2)	1,000	KM61,63	—	13.50
PS7	1980(4)	1,000	KM65-68	—	25.00

Listings For

PERSIA: refer to Iran

PERU

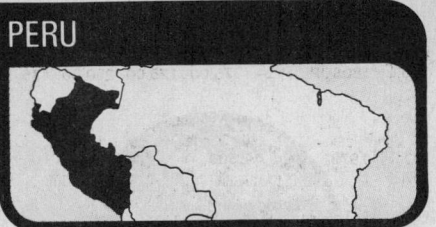

The Republic of Peru, located on the Pacific coast of South America, has an area of 496,225 sq. mi. (1,285,216 sq. km.) and a population of *21.8 million. Capital: Lima. The diversified economy includes mining, fishing and agriculture. Fish meal, copper, sugar, zinc and iron ore are exported.

Once part of the great Inca Empire that reached from northern Ecuador to central Chile, Peru was conquered in 1531-33 by Francisco Pizarro. Desirable as the richest of the Spanish viceroyalties, it was torn by warfare between avaricious Spaniards until the arrival in 1569 of Francisco de Toledo, who initiated 2-1/2 centuries of efficient colonial rule which made Lima the most aristocratic colonial capital and the stronghold of Spain's American possessions. Jose de San Martin of Argentina proclaimed Peru's independence on July 28, 1821; Simon Bolivar of Venezuela secured it in December, 1824 when he defeated the last Spanish army in South America. After several futile attempts to re-establish its South American empire, Spain recognized Peru's independence in 1879.

Andres de Santa Cruz, whose mother was a high-ranking Inca, was the best of Bolivia's early presidents, and temporarily united Peru and Bolivia 1836-39, thus realizing his dream of a Peruvian/Bolivian confederation. This prompted the separate coinages of North and South Peru. Peruvian resistance and Chilean intervention finally broke up the confederation, sending Santa Cruz into exile. A succession of military strongman presidents ruled Peru until Marshall Castilla revitalized Peruvian politics in the mid-19th century and repulsed Spain's attempt to reclaim its one-time colony. Subsequent loss of southern territory to Chile in the War of the Pacific, 1879-81, and gradually increasing rejection of foreign economic domination, combined with recent serious inflation, affected the country numismatically.

RULERS
Spanish, until 1822

MINT MARKS
AREQUIPA, AREQ = Arequipa
AYACUCHO = Ayacucho
(B) = Brussels
CUZCO (monogram), Cuzco, Co. = Cuzco
L, LIMAE (monogram), Lima (monogram), LIMA = Lima
(L) = London
PASCO (monogram), Pasco, Paz, Po = Pasco
P,(P) = Philadelphia
S = San Francisco
(W) = Waterbury, CT, USA

NOTE: The LIMAE monogram appears in three forms. The early LM monogram form looks like a dotted L with M. The later LIMAE monogram has all the letters of LIMAE more readily distinguishable. The third form appears as an M monogram during early Republican issues.

MINT ASSAYER'S INITIALS
The letter(s) following the dates of Peruvian coins are the assayer's initials appearing on the coins. They generally appear at the 11 o'clock position on the Colonial coinage and at the 5 o'clock position along the rim on the obverse or reverse on the Republican coinage.

MONETARY SYSTEM
16 Reales = 2 Pesos = 1 Escudo

DATING
Peruvian 5, 10 and 20 centavos, issued from 1918-1944, bear the dates written in Spanish. The following table translates those written dates into numerals:

1918 - UN MIL NOVECIENTOS DIECIOCHO
1919 - UN MIL NOVECIENTOS DIECINUEVE
1920 - UN MIL NOVECIENTOS VEINTE
1921 - UN MIL NOVECIENTOS VEINTIUNO
1923 - UN MIL NOVECIENTOS VEINTITRES
1926 - UN MIL NOVECIENTOS VEINTISEIS
1934 - UN MIL NOVECIENTOS TREINTICUATRO
1935 - UN MIL NOVECIENTOS TREINTICINCO
1937 - UN MIL NOVECIENTOS TREINTISIETE
1939 - UN MIL NOVECIENTOS TREINTINUEVE
1940 - UN MIL NOVECIENTOS CUARENTA
1941 - UN MIL NOVECIENTOS CUARENTIUNO
U. S. Mints
1942 - MIL NOVECIENTOS CUARENTA Y DOS
Lima Mint
1942 - UN MIL NOVECIENTOS CUARENTIDOS
U. S. Mints
1943 - MIL NOVECIENTOS CUARENTA Y TRES
1944 - MIL NOVECIENTOS CUARENTA Y CUATRO
Lima Mint
1944 - MIL NOVECIENTOS CUARENTICUATRO

MILLED COINAGE
1/4 REAL
.8500 g, .903 SILVER, .0247 oz ASW
Mint mark: L
Obv: Castle. Rev: Lion.

KM#	Date	Mintage	VG	Fine	VF	XF
102	1801	—	7.50	12.50	20.00	40.00
	1802	—	10.00	15.00	30.00	60.00
	1803	—	10.00	15.00	30.00	60.00
	1804	—	10.00	15.00	30.00	60.00
	1805	—	10.00	15.00	30.00	60.00
	1806	—	7.50	12.50	20.00	40.00
	1807	—	7.50	12.50	20.00	40.00
	1808	—	7.50	12.50	20.00	40.00

KM#	Date	Mintage	VG	Fine	VF	XF
108	1809	—	25.00	45.00	65.00	80.00
	1810	—	6.00	10.00	20.00	35.00
	1811	—	8.00	13.50	30.00	45.00
	1812	—	8.00	13.50	30.00	45.00
	1813	—	6.00	10.00	20.00	35.00
	1814	—	6.00	10.00	20.00	35.00
	1815	—	9.00	15.00	30.00	45.00
	1816	—	6.00	10.00	22.50	35.00
	1817	—	6.00	10.00	22.50	35.00
	1818	—	6.00	10.00	22.50	35.00
	1819	—	6.00	10.00	22.50	35.00
	1820	—	6.00	10.00	22.50	35.00
	1821	—	6.00	10.00	22.50	35.00
	1823	—	30.00	45.00	70.00	100.00
	1825	—	45.00	75.00	100.00	150.00

NOTE: Most 1809 dates found are actually dated 1802, where the base of the 2 is weakly struck.

1/2 REAL
1.6500 g, .903 SILVER, .0479 oz ASW
Mint mark: LIMAE (monogram)
Obv. leg: CAROLUS IIII, bust. Rev: Arms, pillars.

KM#	Date	Mintage	VG	Fine	VF	XF
93	1801 IJ	—	3.00	6.00	10.00	22.50
	1802 IJ	—	3.00	6.00	10.00	22.50
	1803 IJ	—	4.50	9.00	15.00	30.00
	1803 JP	—	3.00	6.00	9.00	20.00
	1804 JP	—	3.00	6.00	9.00	20.00
	1805 JP	—	3.00	6.00	10.00	22.50
	1805 IJ	—	10.00	18.50	35.00	50.00
	1806 JP	—	3.00	6.00	10.00	22.50
	1807 JP	—	3.00	6.00	9.00	20.00
	1808 JP	—	3.00	6.00	10.00	20.00

Obv. leg: FERDND. VII..., Lima bust.
Rev: Arms, pillars.

KM#	Date	Mintage	VG	Fine	VF	XF
103.1	1808 JP	—	40.00	65.00	100.00	150.00

Obv. leg: FERDIN. VII.

103.2	1809 JP	—	13.50	22.50	37.50	75.00
	1810 JP	—	7.50	12.50	22.50	55.00
	1811 JP	—	7.50	12.50	22.50	55.00

Obv: Standard bust.

113	1811 JP	—	6.00	10.00	20.00	45.00
	1812 JP	—	2.75	5.00	10.00	20.00
	1813 JP	—	2.75	5.00	10.00	20.00
	1814 JP	—	3.50	7.00	13.50	30.00
	1815 JP	—	2.75	5.00	10.00	20.00
	1816 JP	—	2.75	5.00	10.00	20.00
	1817 JP	—	2.75	5.00	10.00	20.00
	1818 JP	—	2.75	5.00	10.00	20.00
	1819 JP	—	2.75	5.00	10.00	20.00
	1820 JP	—	2.75	5.00	10.00	20.00
	1821 JP	—	2.75	5.00	10.00	20.00

REAL
3.2500 g, .903 SILVER, .0944 oz ASW
Obv. leg: CAROLUS IIII..., bust of Charles IV.
Rev: Similar to KM#109.

KM#	Date	Mintage	VG	Fine	VF	XF
94	1801 IJ	—	6.00	10.00	20.00	40.00
	1802 IJ	—	15.00	25.00	40.00	65.00
	1803 IJ	—	12.00	20.00	40.00	100.00
	1803 JP	—	9.00	15.00	35.00	100.00
	1804 IJ	—	12.00	20.00	50.00	100.00
	1804 JP	—	12.00	20.00	50.00	100.00
	1805 JP	—	9.00	15.00	35.00	100.00
	1806 JP	—	6.00	10.00	20.00	50.00
	1807 JP	—	6.00	10.00	20.00	50.00
	1808 JP	—	25.00	40.00	100.00	140.00

Obv. leg: FERDIN VII..., Lima bust.

109	1808 JP	—	—	—	Rare	
	1809 JP	—	—	Reported, not confirmed		
	1810 JP	—	12.00	20.00	30.00	65.00
	1811 JP	—	12.00	20.00	30.00	65.00

Obv. leg: FERDIN. VII..., standard bust.

| 114.1 | 1811 JP | — | 25.00 | 40.00 | 70.00 | 125.00 |
| | 1812 JP | — | 5.00 | 9.00 | 15.00 | 30.00 |

PERU 1396

KM#	Date	Mintage	VG	Fine	VF	XF
114.1	1813 JP	—	5.00	9.00	15.00	35.00
	1814 JP	—	3.50	7.00	12.50	30.00
	1815 JP	—	7.00	12.00	16.00	35.00
	1816 JP	—	4.00	7.00	12.50	30.00
	1817 JP	—	4.00	7.00	12.50	30.00
	1818 JP	—	4.00	7.00	12.50	30.00
	1819 JP	—	4.00	7.00	12.50	30.00
	1820 JP	—	4.00	7.00	12.50	30.00
	1821 JP	—	4.00	7.00	12.50	30.00
	1823 JP	—	15.00	25.00	60.00	110.00

Mint mark: CUZCO (monogram)

114.2	1824/3 T	—	37.50	65.00	150.00	275.00
	1824 T	—	50.00	100.00	175.00	350.00

2 REALES
6.5000 g, .903 SILVER, .1887 oz ASW
Obv. leg: CAROLUS IIII, bust of Charles IV.
Rev: Similar to KM#104.2.

95	1801 IJ	—	6.00	10.00	15.00	30.00
	1802 IJ	—	6.00	10.00	15.00	25.00
	1803 IJ	—	15.00	25.00	45.00	75.00
	1803 JP	—	6.00	10.00	15.00	30.00
	1804 IJ	—	9.00	15.00	25.00	50.00
	1804 JP	—	6.00	10.00	15.00	25.00
	1805 JP	—	5.00	9.00	12.50	22.50
	1806 JP	—	6.00	10.00	15.00	25.00
	1807 JP	—	6.00	10.00	15.00	30.00
	1808 JP	—	6.00	10.00	15.00	30.00

Obv. leg: FERDND. VII..., Lima bust.
Rev: Arms, pillars.

104.1	1808 JP	—	35.00	60.00	150.00	250.00
	1809 JP	—	—	—	Rare	—

Obv. leg: FERDIN. VII..., Lima bust.

104.2	1808 JP	—	9.00	15.00	25.00	40.00
	1809 JP	—	9.00	15.00	25.00	40.00
	1810 JP	—	6.00	10.00	15.00	30.00
	1811 JP	—	15.00	25.00	45.00	75.00

Obv. leg: FERDIN. VII..., standard bust.

115.1	1811 JP	—	12.00	20.00	35.00	85.00
	1812 JP	—	4.75	8.50	12.50	17.50
	1813 JP	—	4.75	8.50	12.50	17.50
	1814 JP	—	6.00	10.00	14.00	25.00
	1815 JP	—	6.00	10.00	15.00	25.00
	1816 JP	—	4.75	8.50	12.50	17.50
	1817 JP	—	4.75	8.50	12.50	17.50
	1818 JP	—	4.75	8.50	12.50	17.50
	1819 JP	—	4.75	8.50	12.50	17.50
	1820 JP	—	4.75	8.50	12.50	17.50
	1821 JP	—	4.75	8.50	12.50	17.50
	1823 JP	—	6.00	10.00	15.00	25.00

Mint mark: CUZCO (monogram)

115.2	1824 T	—	125.00	200.00	300.00	500.00

Mint mark: LIMAE (monogram)

115.3	1826 IR	—	75.00	125.00	250.00	375.00

NOTE: KM#115.3 was struck in Callao by Royalists prior to final capitulation on January 22, 1826.

4 REALES

13.0000 g, .903 SILVER, .3774 oz ASW
Obv. leg: CAROLUS IIII...

96	1801 IJ	—	25.00	45.00	90.00	150.00
	1802 IJ	—	30.00	50.00	100.00	175.00
	1803 IJ	—	75.00	125.00	200.00	350.00
	1803 JP	—	45.00	75.00	125.00	250.00
	1804 JP	—	25.00	45.00	100.00	175.00
	1805 JP	—	25.00	40.00	100.00	175.00
	1806 JP	—	25.00	40.00	100.00	175.00
	1807 JP	—	25.00	45.00	100.00	175.00
	1808 JP	—	45.00	75.00	125.00	250.00

Obv. leg: FERDND. VII..., Lima bust.
Rev: Arms, pillars.

KM#	Date	Mintage	VG	Fine	VF	XF
105.1	1808 JP	—	75.00	125.00	250.00	475.00

Obv. leg: FERDIN. VII..., Lima bust.

105.2	1810 JP	—	65.00	125.00	250.00	500.00
	1811 JP	—	65.00	125.00	250.00	500.00

Obv. leg: FERDIN. VII..., standard bust.

116	1811 JP	—	—	—	Rare	—
	1812 JP	—	25.00	40.00	100.00	150.00
	1813 JP	—	75.00	125.00	200.00	350.00
	1814 JP	—	75.00	125.00	200.00	350.00
	1815 JP	—	60.00	100.00	175.00	250.00
	1816 JP	—	20.00	30.00	100.00	150.00
	1817 JP	—	20.00	30.00	100.00	150.00
	1818 JP	—	20.00	30.00	100.00	150.00
	1819 JP	—	20.00	30.00	100.00	150.00
	1820 JP	—	20.00	30.00	75.00	100.00
	1821 JP	—	20.00	30.00	75.00	150.00

8 REALES

25.0000 g, .903 SILVER, .7259 oz ASW
Obv. leg: CAROLUS IIII..., bust of Charles IV.
Rev: Similar to KM#117.2.

97	1801 IJ	—	25.00	32.50	45.00	75.00
	1802 IJ	—	25.00	32.50	45.00	75.00
	1803 IJ	—	35.00	60.00	100.00	125.00
	1803 JP	—	25.00	32.50	45.00	75.00
	1804 JP	—	25.00	32.50	45.00	75.00
	1805 JP	—	25.00	32.50	45.00	75.00
	1806 JP	—	25.00	32.50	45.00	75.00
	1807 JP	—	25.00	32.50	45.00	75.00
	1808 JP	—	25.00	32.50	45.00	75.00

Obv. leg: FERDND. VII..., imaginary bust.
Rev: Arms, pillars.

106.1	1808 JP	—	150.00	250.00	425.00	700.00
	1809 JP	—	100.00	200.00	280.00	450.00

Obv. leg: FERDIN. VII..., imaginary bust.

KM#	Date	Mintage	VG	Fine	VF	XF
106.2	1809 JP	—	25.00	50.00	75.00	225.00
	1810 JP	—	25.00	50.00	75.00	225.00
	1811 JP	—	25.00	45.00	60.00	150.00

Obv. leg: FERDIN. VII..., standard bust.
Rev: Similar to KM#117.2.

117.1	1811 JP	—	50.00	90.00	140.00	225.00
	1812 JP	—	25.00	32.50	45.00	75.00
	1813 JP	—	25.00	32.50	45.00	75.00
	1814 JP	—	25.00	32.50	45.00	75.00
	1815 JP	—	25.00	32.50	45.00	75.00
	1816 JP	—	25.00	32.50	45.00	75.00
	1817 JP	—	25.00	32.50	45.00	75.00
	1818 JP	—	25.00	32.50	45.00	75.00
	1819 JP	—	25.00	32.50	45.00	75.00
	1820 JP	—	25.00	32.50	45.00	75.00
	1821 JP	—	25.00	32.50	45.00	75.00
	1822 JP	—	275.00	450.00	650.00	950.00
	1823 JP	—	100.00	175.00	250.00	400.00
	1824 JP	—	225.00	350.00	500.00	750.00
	1824 JM	—	100.00	150.00	300.00	500.00

Mint mark: CUZCO (monogram)
Obv: Similar to KM#117.1.

117.2	1824 T	—	60.00	100.00	175.00	350.00
	1824 G	—	90.00	150.00	250.00	550.00
	1824 G/T	—	—	—	Rare	—

1/2 ESCUDO

1.6875 g, .875 GOLD, .0475 oz AGW
Mint mark: LIMAE (monogram)

125	1814 JP	—	225.00	450.00	800.00	1400.
	1815 JP	—	225.00	450.00	800.00	1400.
	1816 JP	—	225.00	450.00	800.00	1400.
	1817 JP	—	225.00	450.00	800.00	1400.
	1818 JP	—	225.00	450.00	800.00	1400.
	1819 JP	—	225.00	450.00	800.00	1400.
	1820 JP	—	225.00	450.00	800.00	1400.
	1821 JP	—	225.00	450.00	800.00	1400.

ESCUDO
3.3750 g, .875 GOLD, .0949 oz AGW
Obv. leg: CAROL. IIII..., bust of Charles IV.
Rev: Similar to KM#126.

89	1801 IJ	—	100.00	150.00	250.00	350.00
	1802 IJ	—	100.00	150.00	250.00	350.00
	1803 IJ	—	100.00	150.00	250.00	350.00
	1803 JP	—	100.00	150.00	250.00	350.00
	1804 JP	—	100.00	150.00	250.00	350.00
	1805 JP	—	100.00	150.00	250.00	350.00

KM#	Date	Mintage	VG	Fine	VF	XF
89	1806 JP	—	100.00	150.00	250.00	350.00
	1807 JP	—	100.00	150.00	250.00	350.00
	1808 JP	—	100.00	150.00	250.00	350.00

Obv. leg: FERDIN. VII..., uniformed Lima bust.

110	1809 JP	—				
	1810 JP	—	200.00	400.00	650.00	900.00
	1811 JP	—	200.00	400.00	650.00	900.00
	1812 JP	—	200.00	400.00	650.00	900.00

Obv. leg: FERDIN. VII..., standard bust.

119	1812 JP	—	125.00	250.00	400.00	600.00
	1813 JP	—	125.00	250.00	400.00	600.00
	1814 JP	—	125.00	250.00	400.00	600.00

Obv. leg: FERDIN. VII..., laureate undraped bust.

126	1814 JP	—	150.00	225.00	350.00	450.00
	1815 JP	—	100.00	150.00	250.00	350.00
	1816 JP	—	100.00	150.00	250.00	350.00
	1817 JP	—	100.00	150.00	250.00	350.00
	1818 JP	—	100.00	150.00	250.00	350.00
	1819 JP	—	150.00	225.00	350.00	450.00
	1820 JP	—	100.00	150.00	250.00	350.00
	1821 JP	—	125.00	200.00	300.00	400.00

2 ESCUDOS
6.7500 g, .875 GOLD, .1899 oz AGW
Obv. leg: CAROL IIII, bust of Charles IV.

100	1804 JP	—	125.00	225.00	400.00	550.00
	1805 JP	—	175.00	275.00	500.00	650.00
	1806 JP	—	175.00	275.00	500.00	650.00
	1808 PJ	—	225.00	325.00	600.00	750.00

Obv. leg: FERDIN. VII..., uniformed Lima bust.
Rev: Crowned arms, order chain.

111	1809 JP	—	300.00	550.00	1000.	1500.
	1810 JP	—	300.00	550.00	1000.	1500.
	1811 JP	—	300.00	550.00	1000.	1500.

Obv. leg: FERDIN. VII..., standard bust.

| 120 | 1812 JP | — | 225.00 | 450.00 | 700.00 | 1100. |
| | 1813 JP | — | 225.00 | 450.00 | 700.00 | 1100. |

Obv. leg: FERDIN. VII..., laureate undraped bust

127	1814 JP	—	200.00	350.00	550.00	900.00
	1815 JP	—	200.00	350.00	550.00	900.00
	1816 JP	—	200.00	350.00	550.00	900.00
	1817 JP	—	200.00	350.00	550.00	900.00
	1818 JP	—	200.00	350.00	550.00	900.00
	1819 JP	—	200.00	350.00	550.00	900.00
	1820 JP	—	200.00	350.00	550.00	900.00
	1821 JP	—	200.00	350.00	550.00	900.00

4 ESCUDOS
13.5000 g, .875 GOLD, .3798 oz AGW
Obv. leg: CAROL. IV..., bust of Charles IV.

98	1801 IJ	—	500.00	750.00	1300.	2000.
	1804 JP	—	500.00	750.00	1300.	2000.
	1805 JP	—	500.00	750.00	1300.	2000.
	1806 JP	—	500.00	750.00	1300.	2000.
	1807 JP	—	500.00	750.00	1300.	2000.

13.5000 g, .875 GOLD, .3798 oz AGW
Obv. leg: FERDIN. VII...

| 112 | 1809 JP | — | 1250. | 1750. | 2500. | 4000. |
| | 1810 JP | — | 1000. | 1500. | 2250. | 3500. |

Obv: Laureate, draped bust of Ferdinand VII.

| 121 | 1812 JP | — | 1250. | 1750. | 2250. | 3500. |

Obv: Smaller bust of Ferdinand VII.

| 122 | 1812 JP | — | 800.00 | 1250. | 1750. | 2500. |
| | 1813 JP | — | 800.00 | 1250. | 1750. | 2500. |

Obv: Laureate, undraped bust of Ferdinand VII.

128	1814 JP	—	600.00	1000.	1500.	2250.
	1815 JP	—	500.00	750.00	1250.	2000.
	1816 JP	—	600.00	1000.	1500.	2250.
	1817 JP	—	1200.	1750.	2250.	3500.
	1818 JP	—	600.00	1000.	1500.	2250.
	1819 JP	—	800.00	1200.	1750.	2500.
	1820 JP	—	800.00	1200.	1750.	2500.
	1821 JP	—	800.00	1200.	1750.	2500.

8 ESCUDOS
27.0000 g, .875 GOLD, .7596 oz AGW
Obv. leg: CAROL. IIII, bust of Charles IV.
Rev: Crowned arms.

KM#	Date	Mintage	VG	Fine	VF	XF
101	1801 IJ	—	400.00	500.00	800.00	1100.
	1802 IJ	—	400.00	500.00	800.00	1100.
	1803 IJ	—	400.00	500.00	800.00	1100.
	1803 JP	—	400.00	500.00	900.00	1300.
	1804 IJ	—	600.00	900.00	1800.	3000.
	1804 JP	—	400.00	500.00	900.00	1300.
	1805 JP	—	400.00	500.00	800.00	1100.
	1806 JP	—	400.00	500.00	800.00	1100.
	1807 JP	—	400.00	500.00	800.00	1100.
	1808 JP	—	400.00	500.00	800.00	1100.

27.0000 g, .875 GOLD, .7596 oz AGW
Obv: Local, uniformed bust of Ferdinand VII.
Rev: Crowned arms, order chain.

107	1808 JP	—	900.00	1800.	3000.	4500.
	1809 JP	—	600.00	1000.	1750.	2500.
	1810 JP	—	600.00	1000.	1750.	2500.
	1811 JP	—	600.00	1000.	1750.	2500.
	1812 JP	—	800.00	1250.	2500.	3500.

Obv: Larger bust of Ferdinand VII.

| 118 | 1811 JP | — | 900.00 | 1750. | 3000. | 5000. |
| | 1812 JP | — | 600.00 | 1000. | 1750. | 2500. |

Obv: Laureate draped bust of Ferdinand VII.
Rev: Arms, order chain.

123	1812 JP	—	500.00	750.00	1200.	2000.
	1814 JP	—	1250.	2500.	4000.	7000.
	1815 JP	—	2000.	4000.	7000.	10,000.

Obv: Smaller bust of Ferdinand VII.

| 124 | 1812 JP | — | 750.00 | 1250. | 2000. | 2500. |
| | 1813 JP | — | 750.00 | 1250. | 2000. | 2500. |

129.1	1814 JP	—	400.00	500.00	800.00	1100.
	1815 JP	—	400.00	500.00	800.00	1100.
	1816 JP	—	400.00	500.00	900.00	1300.
	1817 JP	—	400.00	500.00	800.00	1100.
	1818 JP	—	400.00	500.00	800.00	1100.
	1819 JP	—	400.00	500.00	800.00	1100.
	1820 JP	—	400.00	500.00	800.00	1100.
	1821 JP	—	400.00	500.00	900.00	1300.

Mint mark: Co
Obv: Similar to 8 Reales, KM#117.1.

KM#	Date	Mintage	VG	Fine	VF	XF
129.2	1824 G	—	800.00	1250.	2500.	4000.

COUNTERMARKED COINAGE
(Royalist)
8 REALES

SILVER
c/m: Crown above 1824 on KM#136.

KM#	Date	Year	VG	Fine	VF	XF
130	1824	1822 JP	65.00	115.00	200	275.00
(132)	1824	1823 JP	50.00	100.00	175.00	250.00

PROVISIONAL COINAGE
1/4 REAL

COPPER

KM#	Date	Mintage	VG	Fine	VF	XF
135	1822	—	4.50	10.00	17.50	35.00

OCTAVO DE (1/8) PESO
(1 Real)

COPPER

| 137 | 1823 | — | 3.00 | 6.00 | 12.00 | 25.00 |
| | 1823 V | — | 15.00 | 35.00 | 50.00 | 80.00 |

QUARTO DE (1/4) PESO
(2 Reales)

COPPER
Obv. denomination: QUARTO DE PESO

| 138 | 1823 | — | 2.00 | 5.00 | 7.50 | 25.00 |
| | 1823 V | — | 5.00 | 10.00 | 20.00 | 50.00 |

8 REALES

PERU 1398

25.0000 g, .903 SILVER, .7259 oz ASW
Mint mark: LIMAE (monogram)
Peru Libre Type

KM#	Date	Mintage	VG	Fine	VF	XF
136	1822 JP	—	30.00	50.00	100.00	225.00
	1823 JP	—	30.00	50.00	100.00	200.00

REPUBLIC
1/4 REAL

.8400 g, .903 SILVER, .0243 oz ASW
Lima Mint

KM#	Date	Mintage	VG	Fine	VF	XF
143.1	1826	—	3.50	6.50	14.00	27.50
	1827	—	2.50	4.75	10.00	17.50
	1828	—	3.50	6.50	14.00	27.50
	1829/8	—	4.75	8.50	17.50	37.50
	1830/28	—	3.00	6.00	14.00	27.50
	1831/0	—	2.50	4.75	10.00	17.50
	1831	—	3.50	6.00	13.00	25.00
	1832	—	5.25	11.00	22.50	45.00
	1833	—	3.00	5.75	12.00	25.00
	1834/3	—	5.00	7.50	15.00	30.00
	1834	—	3.50	6.00	13.00	27.50
	1835	—	6.50	13.50	26.00	55.00
	1836/5	—	10.00	15.00	30.00	50.00
	1836	—	5.00	10.00	22.50	45.00
	1837	—	5.00	10.00	22.50	45.00
	1839/8	—	5.00	10.00	22.50	45.00
	1839	—	4.25	8.50	17.00	35.00
	1840	—	4.25	8.50	17.00	35.00
	1841/0	—	3.50	6.00	13.00	25.00
	1841	—	—	—	—	—
	1842	—	2.50	4.75	10.00	17.50
	1843/33	—	—	—	—	—
	1843	—	2.50	4.75	10.00	17.50
	1845	—	3.00	5.75	12.00	22.50
	1846	—	2.50	4.75	10.00	17.50
	1846/3	—	2.50	5.00	12.00	20.00
	1847	—	3.50	7.00	16.00	30.00
	1848	—	4.25	8.50	20.00	40.00
	1849/8	—	4.25	8.50	20.00	40.00
	1849	—	3.50	7.00	16.00	30.00
	1850	—	2.50	5.00	12.00	20.00
	1851/21	—	2.00	4.00	10.00	18.00
	1851/31	—	2.00	4.00	10.00	18.00
	1853/1	—	2.50	5.00	12.00	20.00
	1855/35	—	1.50	2.75	5.00	12.00
	1855/3	—	1.50	2.75	5.00	12.00
	1855	—	1.25	2.50	4.50	10.00
	1856	—	1.50	2.75	5.00	12.00

Arequipa Mint

| 143.2 | 1839 | — | 100.00 | 175.00 | 350.00 | 550.00 |

1/2 REAL

1.6900 g, .903 SILVER, .0490 oz ASW
Mint mark: LIMAE (monogram)
Obv. leg: REPUB.PERUANA.

144.1	1826 JM	—	3.50	7.50	15.00	25.00
	1827 JM	—	5.50	12.50	25.00	40.00
	1828 JM	—	3.50	7.50	15.00	25.00
	1829/8 JM	—	7.00	15.00	35.00	60.00
	1830 JM	—	7.00	15.00	35.00	60.00
	1831 MM	—	4.00	7.50	17.50	30.00
	1832 MM	—	4.00	7.50	17.50	30.00
	1833/2	—	4.00	7.50	17.50	30.00
	1833 MM	—	2.50	6.00	12.50	20.00
	1834 MM	—	2.50	6.00	12.50	20.00
	1835/3 MM	—	4.50	9.00	18.50	32.00
	1835 MM	—	4.50	9.00	18.50	32.00
	1835 MT/M	—	7.00	15.00	35.00	60.00
	1836 MT	—	3.50	7.50	17.50	30.00
	1839 MB	—	3.00	6.50	15.00	25.00
	1840 MB	—	3.00	6.50	15.00	25.00

Mint mark: CUZCO (monogram)

144.2	1827 GM	—	12.50	25.00	50.00	95.00
	1828 G	—	12.50	25.00	50.00	95.00
	1829/8 G	—	10.00	20.00	40.00	80.00
	1829 G	—	12.50	25.00	50.00	95.00
	1830/28	—	10.00	20.00	40.00	80.00
	1830 G	—	6.00	12.00	20.00	50.00
	1831 G	—	4.00	8.00	15.00	45.00
	1835 B	—	4.00	8.00	15.00	45.00

Mint mark: CUZCO

| 144.3 | 1833 B | — | 3.00 | 5.50 | 10.00 | 30.00 |
| | 1834 B | — | 3.50 | 6.50 | 12.00 | 35.00 |

1.6500 g, .667 SILVER, .0354 oz ASW
Mint mark: AREQ
Obv. leg: REPUB. PERUANA

| 144.4 | 1836 M | — | 5.00 | 12.00 | 25.00 | 50.00 |

1.6500 g, .903 SILVER, .0479 oz ASW
Mint mark: LIMAE (monogram)

| 144.5 | 1840 MMB | — | 10.00 | 20.00 | 35.00 | 65.00 |
| | 1841/0 MMB | — | 15.00 | 30.00 | 50.00 | 85.00 |

Obv. leg: REP. PERUANA 10D. 20G

144.7	1840 MB	—	5.50	12.00	25.00	55.00
	1841 MB	—	5.50	12.00	25.00	45.00
	1842 MB	—	5.50	12.00	25.00	45.00
	1843 MB	—	4.00	8.00	16.00	32.00
	1845 MB	—	3.00	6.00	12.00	25.00
	1846 MB	—	3.00	7.00	14.00	28.00
	1847 MB	—	—	—	—	—
	1849 MB	—	6.00	12.00	25.00	55.00
	1850 MB	—	3.00	6.00	12.00	25.00
	1851 MB	—	4.00	7.50	15.00	30.00
	1852 MB	—	—	—	—	—
	1853/1 MB	—	15.00	20.00	30.00	75.00
	1853/2 MB	—	—	—	—	—
	1854 MB	—	3.00	7.00	14.00	28.00
	1855 MB	—	3.00	5.50	10.00	17.50
	1856 MB	—	3.00	5.50	10.00	17.50

NOTE: Varieties exist.

REAL

3.3800 g, .903 SILVER, .0981 oz ASW
Mint mark: LIMAE (monogram)
Obv. leg: REPUB. PERUANA

145.1	1826 JM	—	5.00	10.00	20.00	40.00
	1827 JM	—	4.50	9.00	16.00	30.00
	1828 JM	—	4.50	9.00	16.00	30.00
	1829 JM	—	—	Reported, not confirmed		
	1830 JM	—	8.50	17.50	35.00	60.00
	1831 JM	—	10.00	20.00	42.50	80.00
	1831 MM	—	—	—	—	—
	1832 MM	—	7.50	15.00	27.50	50.00
	1833/2 MM	—	10.00	20.00	40.00	75.00
	1834 MM	—	5.50	10.00	18.00	35.00
	1835/3	—	10.00	20.00	40.00	75.00
	1836 MT	—	10.00	20.00	40.00	75.00
	1839 MB	—	7.50	15.00	27.50	50.00
	1840 MB	—	6.00	10.00	16.00	30.00

Mint mark: CUZco (monogram)
Obv. leg: REPUB. PERUANA

145.2	1827 GM	—	20.00	40.00	65.00	100.00
	1828 G	—	20.00	40.00	65.00	100.00
	1829/8 G	—	25.00	45.00	80.00	125.00
	1829 G	—	25.00	45.00	80.00	125.00
	1830 G	—	25.00	45.00	80.00	125.00
	1831/21 G	—	25.00	45.00	80.00	125.00
	1831 G	—	25.00	45.00	80.00	125.00

Mint mark: CUZCO

| 145.3 | 1834 B | — | 60.00 | 120.00 | 170.00 | 275.00 |

Obv. leg: REP. PERUANA 10D 20G
Mint mark: LIMAE: (monogram)

145.4	1841 MB	—	—	—	—	—
	1842 MB	—	10.00	20.00	40.00	75.00
	1843 MB	—	10.00	20.00	40.00	75.00
	1846 MB	—	10.00	20.00	40.00	75.00
	1847/6 MB	—	12.00	25.00	47.50	90.00
	1849 MB	—	5.50	10.00	18.00	35.00
	1850 MB	—	3.50	7.00	12.50	20.00
	1851 MB	—	4.00	8.00	14.00	25.00
	1855 MB	—	4.50	9.00	16.00	30.00
	1856/5 MB	—	3.50	7.00	12.50	20.00

2 REALES

6.7700 g, .903 SILVER, .1965 oz ASW
Mint mark: LIMAE (monogram)
Obv. leg: REPUB. PERUANA

KM#	Date	Mintage	VG	Fine	VF	XF
141.1	1825 JM	—	12.00	25.00	40.00	80.00
	1826 JM	—	4.00	7.00	14.00	30.00
	1827 JM	—	5.00	10.00	18.00	40.00
	1828 JM	—	3.00	6.50	11.00	22.50
	1829 JM	—	16.00	35.00	65.00	125.00
	1830/29 JM	—	9.00	17.50	35.00	75.00
	1830 JM	—	9.00	17.50	35.00	75.00
	1831 MM	—	9.00	17.50	35.00	75.00
	1832/1 MM	—	9.00	17.50	35.00	75.00
	1832 MM	—	5.00	10.00	18.00	40.00
	1833 MM	—	—	—	—	—
	1834 MM	—	8.00	15.00	25.00	50.00
	1835 MM	—	150.00	300.00	—	—
	1836 MT	—	150.00	350.00	—	—
	1839 MB	—	8.00	15.00	25.00	50.00
	1840 MB	—	4.00	8.00	15.00	35.00

Mint mark: CUZco (monogram)
Obv. leg: REPUB. PERUANA

141.2	1827 GM	—	20.00	40.00	60.00	100.00
	1828 G	—	25.00	50.00	75.00	125.00
	1829 G	—	25.00	50.00	75.00	125.00
	1830 G	—	30.00	60.00	85.00	150.00
	1831 G	—	20.00	40.00	60.00	100.00

6.7700 g, .667 SILVER, .1452 oz ASW

| 141.2a | 1835 B | — | 6.00 | 10.00 | 15.00 | 37.50 |

Mint mark: LIMAE (monogram)
Obv. leg: REP. PERUANA 10D 20G

141.3	1840 MB	—	12.00	25.00	40.00	80.00
	1841/0 MB	—	10.00	22.00	35.00	65.00
	1841 MB	—	4.50	10.00	20.00	45.00
	1842 MB	—	4.50	10.00	20.00	45.00
	1843 MB	—	8.00	15.00	25.00	60.00
	1845 MB	—	10.00	20.00	40.00	80.00
	1846 MB	—	—	—	—	—
	1848/6 MB	—	5.00	12.00	22.00	50.00
	1848 MB	—	5.00	12.00	22.00	50.00
	1849 MB	—	4.00	8.00	15.00	30.00
	1850 MB	—	4.00	8.00	15.00	30.00
	1851 MB	—	4.50	10.00	20.00	45.00
	1854 MB	—	8.00	15.00	25.00	60.00
	1855 MB	—	10.00	20.00	40.00	80.00
	1856 MB	—	8.00	15.00	25.00	60.00

NOTE: Varieties exist.

Pasco Mint
Obv. leg: REPUB. PERUANA

| 141.4 | 1843 M | — | 400.00 | 750.00 | — | — |

4 REALES

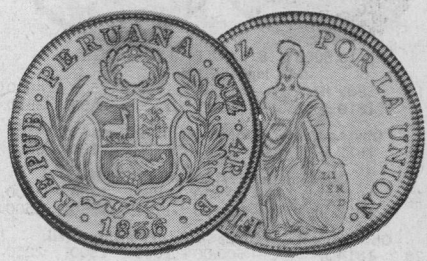

13.0000 g, .667 SILVER, .2788 oz ASW
Mint mark: CUZco (monogram)

| 151.1 | 1835 B | — | 3.00 | 7.00 | 16.50 | 50.00 |
| | 1836 B | — | 2.00 | 3.75 | 9.00 | 42.50 |

NOTE: Many die varieties.

PERU 1399

	Mint mark: AREQ Obv. leg: REPUB PERUANA				
KM#	Date Mintage	VG	Fine	VF	XF
151.2	1836 M —	25.00	45.00	100.00	200.00
	1839 MV —	25.00	45.00	100.00	200.00
	1840 MV —	25.00	45.00	100.00	200.00

	Obv. leg: REP. PERUANA.				
KM#	Date Mintage	VG	Fine	VF	XF
151.10	1856 Z in O —	75.00	175.00	300.00	—
	1857 Z in O —	8.50	17.50	32.50	75.00
	1857 AF —	75.00	175.00	300.00	—
	1857 —	50.00	125.00	200.00	—

8 REALES

13.5400 g, .903 SILVER, .3931 oz ASW
Mint mark: LIMAE (monogram)
Obv. leg: REPUB. PERUANA

151.3	1842 MB	—	15.00	27.50	50.00	125.00
	1843/2 MB	—	10.00	17.50	35.00	85.00
	1843 MB	—	10.00	17.50	35.00	85.00
	1845 MB	—	15.00	25.00	50.00	125.00
	1846 MB	—	20.00	35.00	70.00	150.00
	1848 MB	—	7.00	15.00	30.00	50.00
	1849 MB	—	15.00	25.00	50.00	125.00
	1850 MB	—	9.00	20.00	35.00	75.00
	1851 MB	—	8.00	17.50	32.50	70.00
	1854 MB	—	4.00	8.00	15.00	40.00
	1855/4 MB	—	4.00	8.00	15.00	40.00
	1855 MB	—	10.00	15.00	30.00	65.00
	1856 MB	—	40.00	75.00	125.00	250.00

Mint mark: PAZO (monogram)
Obv. leg: REPUB. PERUANA, 10Ds20Gs.

| 151.4 | 1843 M | — | 20.00 | 45.00 | 120.00 | 250.00 |

Mint mark: PASCO
Obv. leg: REPUB. PERUANA 10Ds20Gs.

| 151.5 | 1844 M | — | 8.50 | 17.50 | 47.50 | 115.00 |

Obv. leg: REPUBLICA PERUANA, w/o fineness.

| 151.6 | 1844 M | — | 10.00 | 22.50 | 65.00 | 165.00 |
| | 1845 M
4 known | — | — | — | — | — |

Mint mark: PASCO (monogram)
Obv. leg: REP. PERUANA 10Ds20Gs.

| 151.7 | 1844 M | — | — | Reported, not confirmed |
| | 1855 N.S. | — | — | Rare |

Mint mark: PASCO
Obv. leg: REPUB. PERUANA. 10Ds20Gs.

| 151.8 | 1855 | — | 20.00 | 45.00 | 100.00 | 250.00 |

Obv. leg: REP. PERUANA 10D 20G

| 151.9 | 1855 M | — | 8.50 | 17.50 | 35.00 | 85.00 |

NOTE: All known coins of this variety have small engraver's initial B in wreath above arms.

27.0700 g, .903 SILVER, .7859 oz ASW
Mint mark: LIMAE (monogram)
Obv. leg: REPUB. PERUANA
Rev: Small figure of Liberty.

142.1	1825 JM	—	12.00	20.00	35.00	100.00
	1826 JM	—	10.00	15.00	30.00	75.00
	1827 JM	—	10.00	15.00	30.00	75.00
	1828 JM	—	40.00	65.00	125.00	250.00

Mint mark: CUZco (monogram)
Rev: Similar to KM#142.1.

142.2	1826 GM	—	35.00	55.00	100.00	225.00
	1826 G	—	15.00	27.50	55.00	100.00
	1827 GM	—	15.00	27.50	55.00	100.00
	1827 G	—	35.00	55.00	100.00	225.00
	1828/7 G	—	15.00	30.00	60.00	120.00
	1828 G	—	15.00	27.50	55.00	100.00
	1829 G	—	35.00	55.00	100.00	225.00
	1829 G REPMB	—	—	—	Rare	—

Mint mark: LIMAE (monogram)
Rev: Large figure of Liberty.

KM#	Date Mintage	VG	Fine	VF	XF
142.3	1828 JM —	8.00	14.00	25.00	65.00
	1829 JM —	10.00	16.00	30.00	75.00
	1830 JM —	10.00	16.00	30.00	75.00
	1831 JM —	35.00	60.00	115.00	250.00
	1831 MM —	10.00	16.00	30.00	75.00
	1832 MM —	8.00	14.00	25.00	60.00
	1833 MM —	8.00	14.00	25.00	60.00
	1833 MM Por al Union				
	—	—	—	Rare	—
	1834 MM —	8.00	14.00	25.00	60.00
	1835 MM —	10.00	16.00	30.00	75.00
	1835 MT —	10.00	16.00	30.00	75.00
	1836 MT —	8.00	14.00	25.00	60.00
	1836 TM —	30.00	50.00	100.00	250.00
	1838 MB —	20.00	30.00	55.00	125.00
	1839 MB —	12.00	20.00	40.00	90.00
	1840 MB —	8.00	14.00	25.00	60.00

Mint mark: CUZCO
Rev: Similar to KM#142.2.

142.4	1830 G —	10.00	18.00	32.50	70.00
	1831 G —	10.00	18.00	32.50	70.00
	1832 B —	12.00	20.00	35.00	80.00
	1833 B —	15.00	25.00	45.00	100.00
	1833 BoAr —	12.00	22.00	40.00	90.00
	1834 BoAr —	12.00	22.00	40.00	90.00

Mint mark: CUZco (monogram)

| 142.5 | 1835 B — | 30.00 | 50.00 | 100.00 | 200.00 |

Mint mark: AREQ
Rev: Similar to KM#142.3.

| 142.7 | 1839 MV — | 800.00 | 1500. | 3250. | 6500. |
| | 1840 MV — | 600.00 | 1200. | 3000. | 6000. |

PERU 1400

Mint mark: LIMAE (monogram)
Obv. leg: REP. PERUANA 10DS 20GS
Rev: Similar to KM#142.3.

KM#	Date	Mintage	VG	Fine	VF	XF
142.8	1840 MB	—	30.00	55.00	100.00	200.00
	1841/0 MB	—	25.00	50.00	85.00	100.00
	1841 MB	—	12.00	22.00	32.00	75.00

Mint mark: CUZco (monogram)
Obv. leg: 10Ds20Gs.

| 142.9 | 1840 A | — | 15.00 | 30.00 | 60.00 | 125.00 |

Mint mark: LIMAE (monogram)
Obv. leg: REPUB. PERUANA 10Ds 20Gs.

142.10	1841 MB	—	—	—	Rare	—
	1842 MB	—	8.00	20.00	60.00	175.00
	1843 MB	—	8.00	17.50	50.00	140.00
	1844 MB	—	20.00	35.00	85.00	250.00
	1845 MB	—	8.00	17.50	50.00	140.00
	1846 MB	—	10.00	25.00	75.00	200.00
	1847/6 MB	—	25.00	50.00	100.00	325.00
	1847 MB	—	25.00	50.00	100.00	325.00
	1848/7 MB	—	10.00	25.00	75.00	200.00
	1848 MB	—	10.00	25.00	75.00	200.00
	1849/8/7 MB					
		—	50.00	125.00	300.00	600.00
	1849 MB	—	50.00	125.00	300.00	600.00
	1850/49 MB					
		—	50.00	100.00	200.00	300.00
	1850 MB ornamented edge					
		—	10.00	25.00	75.00	200.00
	1850 MB roped edge					
		—	30.00	60.00	150.00	450.00
	1851 MB	—	15.00	35.00	95.00	250.00
	1852 MB	—	20.00	45.00	120.00	300.00
	1855 MB reeded edge					
		—	8.00	17.50	40.00	75.00

Mint mark: AREQ
Obv. leg: REPUB. PERUANA . . . . . 10Ds20Gs.

| 142.11 | 1841 M | — | 2000. | 3500. | 6000. | 10,000. |

Pasco Mint
Obv. leg: REPUB. PERUANA

| 142.6 | 1836 MO | — | — | — | Rare | — |

Mint mark: LIMAE (monogram)
Obv. leg: Small REPUBLICA PERUANA, small date.
Rev: Small letters in legend.

KM#	Date	Mintage	VG	Fine	VF	XF
142.12	1853 MB	—	20.00	40.00	100.00	250.00

Pasco Mint
Obv. leg: REPUB PERUANA. 10Ds20Gs.

142.13	1857 Z in O	—	—	—	10,000.	20,000.
	1857 Z in O POR LA UNION					
		—	—	—	10,000.	

1/2 ESCUDO

1.6875 g, .875 GOLD, .0475 oz AGW
Mint mark: LIMAE (monogram)

146.1	1826 JM	—	45.00	90.00	150.00	200.00
	1827 JM	—	60.00	125.00	225.00	300.00
	1828 JM	—	35.00	70.00	115.00	150.00
	1829 JM	—	30.00	50.00	80.00	100.00
	1833 MM	—	35.00	70.00	115.00	150.00
	1836 TM	—	35.00	70.00	115.00	150.00
	1839 MB	—	60.00	125.00	225.00	300.00
	1840 MB	—	30.00	50.00	80.00	100.00
	1841 MB	—	35.00	70.00	115.00	150.00
	1842 MB	—	60.00	125.00	225.00	300.00
	1850 MB	—	35.00	70.00	115.00	150.00
	1856 MB	—	45.00	90.00	150.00	200.00

NOTE: For coins of this type dated 1838 M, see North Peru.

Mint mark: CUZCO

| 146.2 | 1826 GM | — | 35.00 | 60.00 | 95.00 | 125.00 |

ESCUDO
3.3750 g, .875 GOLD, .0949 oz AGW
Mint mark: LIMAE (monogram)
Obv. leg: REPUBLICA PERUANA

KM#	Date	Mintage	VG	Fine	VF	XF
147.1	1826 JM	—	70.00	120.00	200.00	300.00
	1827 JM	—	95.00	165.00	265.00	350.00
	1828/7 JM	—	70.00	120.00	200.00	300.00
	1828 JM	—	70.00	120.00	200.00	300.00
	1829 JM	—	55.00	85.00	135.00	200.00
	1833 MM	—	—	Reported, not confirmed		

Mint mark: CUZCO

| 147.2 | 1826 GM | — | 100.00 | 160.00 | 240.00 | 400.00 |
| | 1830 G | — | 100.00 | 160.00 | 240.00 | 400.00 |

Mint mark: CUZco (monogram)

147.3	1840 A	—	55.00	85.00	135.00	200.00
	1845 A	—	55.00	70.00	95.00	150.00
	1846 A	—	55.00	85.00	135.00	200.00

Mint mark: LIMAE (monogram)
Obv. leg: REPUB. PERUANA

| 147.4 | 1855 MB | — | 70.00 | 120.00 | 200.00 | 300.00 |

---

2 ESCUDOS

6.7500 g, .875 GOLD, .1899 oz AGW
Mint mark: LIMAE (monogram)
Obv. leg: REPUBLICA PERUANA

KM#	Date	Mintage	VG	Fine	VF	XF
149.1	1828 JM	—	150.00	200.00	275.00	500.00
	1829 JM	—	100.00	130.00	150.00	250.00

Obv. leg: REPUB. PERUANA

149.2	1850 MB	—	125.00	175.00	250.00	400.00
	1851 MB	—	110.00	150.00	200.00	300.00
	1853 MB	—	95.00	115.00	140.00	200.00
	1854 MB	—	125.00	175.00	250.00	400.00
	1855 MB	—	125.00	175.00	250.00	400.00

4 ESCUDOS
13.5000 g, .875 GOLD, .3798 oz AGW
Mint mark: LIMA

| 150.1 | 1828 JM | — | — | — | — | Rare |

Mint mark: LIMAE (monogram)

150.2	1850 MB	—	225.00	350.00	500.00	750.00
	1853 MB	—	300.00	475.00	650.00	1000.
	1854 MB	—	200.00	300.00	450.00	650.00

Obv. leg: REPUB. PERUANA

| 150.3 | 1855 MB | — | 185.00 | 210.00 | 300.00 | 450.00 |

8 ESCUDOS

27.0000 g, .875 GOLD, .7596 oz AGW
Mint mark: LIMAE (monogram)
Obv. leg: REPUBLICA PERUANA

148.1	1826 JM	—	350.00	375.00	500.00	800.00
	1827 JM	—	350.00	400.00	550.00	1000.
	1828 JM	—	350.00	500.00	800.00	1500.
	1829/8 JM	—	350.00	400.00	550.00	1000.
	1829 JM	—	350.00	400.00	550.00	1000.
	1833 MM	—	350.00	375.00	500.00	800.00
	1840 MB	—	350.00	500.00	800.00	1500.

Mint mark: CUZCO

KM#	Date	Mintage	VG	Fine	VF	XF
148.2	1826 GM	—	350.00	550.00	750.00	1400.
	1827 G	—	350.00	550.00	750.00	1400.
	1828/7 G	—	350.00	450.00	600.00	1100.
	1828 G	—	350.00	450.00	600.00	1100.
	1829 G	—	350.00	550.00	750.00	1400.
	1830 G	—	350.00	450.00	600.00	1100.
	1831 G	—	350.00	375.00	550.00	900.00
	1832 VOARSH					
		—	350.00	400.00	600.00	1000.
	1833 BoAr	—	350.00	375.00	550.00	900.00
	1834 BoAr	—	350.00	400.00	600.00	1000.

Mint mark: CUZco (monogram)

148.3	1835 B	—	350.00	450.00	650.00	1200.
	1836 B	—	350.00	500.00	800.00	1500.
	1839 A	—	350.00	500.00	800.00	1500.
	1840 A	—	350.00	400.00	600.00	1000.
	1843 A	—	350.00	450.00	650.00	1200.
	1844 A	—	350.00	500.00	800.00	1500.
	1845 A	—	350.00	375.00	550.00	900.00

Mint mark: LIMA (monogram)
Small legends

148.4	1853 MB	—	400.00	600.00	900.00	1500.
	1854 MB	—	350.00	375.00	450.00	750.00
	1855 MB	—	350.00	375.00	500.00	850.00

Obv. leg: REPUB. PERUANA

148.5	1855 MB	—	350.00	375.00	450.00	750.00

NORTH PERU
Nor-Peruano

STATE COINAGE
1/2 REAL

1.6900 g, .903 SILVER, .0490 oz ASW
Lima Mint

KM#	Date	Mintage	VG	Fine	VF	XF
154.1	1836 TM	—	12.50	30.00	70.00	225.00
	1837 TM	—	7.50	22.50	45.00	100.00
	1837 M	—	11.00	27.50	55.00	130.00
	1838 M	—	11.00	27.50	55.00	130.00
	1838 MB	—	11.00	27.50	55.00	130.00

REAL

3.3800 g, .903 SILVER, .0981 oz ASW

158	1838 MB	—	65.00	150.00	250.00	400.00

2 REALES
6.7700 g, .903 SILVER, .1965 oz ASW

157	1837 JM	—	—	—	—	—
	1838 MB	—	—	—	—	—

8 REALES

27.0700 g, .903 SILVER, .7859 oz ASW

155	1836 TM	—	10.00	17.50	35.00	100.00
	1837 TM	—	7.50	12.50	22.00	65.00
	1837 M	—	10.00	17.50	32.00	100.00
	1838 M	—	10.00	17.50	32.00	100.00
	1838 MB	—	7.50	12.50	22.00	55.00
	1839 M	—	10.00	17.50	32.00	100.00

1/2 ESCUDO
1.6875 g, .875 GOLD, .0475 oz AGW

159	1838 M	—	75.00	150.00	250.00	350.00

NOTE: This coin is identical to the Republic type, KM#146.1 and can only be identified by the date.

ESCUDO

3.3750 g, .875 GOLD, .0949 oz AGW

160	1838 M	—	500.00	1000.	1500.	2000.

2 ESCUDOS

6.7500 g, .875 GOLD, .1899 oz AGW

161	1838 M	—	1500.	2000.	2500.	3000.

4 ESCUDOS

13.5000 g, .875 GOLD, .3798 oz AGW

162	1838 M	—	2000.	3000.	5000.	10,000.

8 ESCUDOS

27.0000 g, .875 GOLD, .7596 oz AGW

KM#	Date	Mintage	VG	Fine	VF	XF
156	1836 TM	—	—	—	Rare	—
	1838 M	—	1500.	2500.	3500.	5000.

REPUBLIC COINAGE
1/2 REAL

1.6900 g, .903 SILVER, .0490 oz ASW

163	1839 MB	—	42.50	100.00	175.00	300.00

8 REALES

27.0700 g, .903 SILVER, .7859 oz ASW

164	1839 MB	—	250.00	450.00	800.00	1500.

SOUTH PERU
Sud Peruano

STATE COINAGE
1/2 REAL

1.6900 g, .667 SILVER, .0490 oz ASW
Cuzco Mint

166	1837 B	—	8.75	17.50	32.50	75.00

8 ESCUDOS

27.0000 g, .875 GOLD, .7596 oz AGW

167	1837 BA	—	400.00	600.00	900.00	1550.

REPUBLIC COINAGE
1/2 REAL

1.6500 g, .667 SILVER, .0354 oz ASW

South / PERU 1402

Mint mark: AREQ(uipa)

KM#	Date	Mintage	VG	Fine	VF	XF
168	1837	—	10.00	17.50	35.00	80.00

2 REALES

6.5000 g, .667 SILVER, .1391 oz ASW
Cuzco Mint

| 169.1 | 1837 BA | — | 5.00 | 10.00 | 22.50 | 50.00 |

Arequipa Mint

| 169.2 | 1838 | — | 7.00 | 15.00 | 35.00 | 80.00 |

4 REALES

13.5400 g, .667 SILVER, .2899 oz ASW
Mint mark: AREQ (uipa).

| 172 | 1838 MV | — | 8.00 | 15.00 | 35.00 | 80.00 |

8 REALES

27.0700 g, .903 SILVER, .7859 oz ASW
Mint mark: CUZCO
Rev. leg: FEDERACION

170.1	1837 BA incuse edge lettering
		—	20.00	45.00	80.00	175.00
	1837 BA raised edge lettering
	5 known	—	—	Rare	—

Rev. leg: Small letters, CONFEDERACION.

| 170.2 | 1837 BA | — | 25.00 | 55.00 | 90.00 | 200.00 |

Rev. leg: Large letters, CONFEDERACION.

KM#	Date	Mintage	VG	Fine	VF	XF
170.4	1837 MS	—	45.00	70.00	140.00	275.00
	1838 BA	—	20.00	45.00	75.00	125.00
	1838 MS	—	20.00	45.00	75.00	125.00
	1839 MS	—	50.00	85.00	200.00	350.00

Mint mark: AREQ(uipa)

| 170.3 | 1838 MV | — | 500.00 | 1000. | 2000. | 4000. |
| | 1839 MV | — | — | Rare | — | |

1/2 ESCUDO

1.6875 g, .875 GOLD, .0475 oz AGW
Mint mark: CUZCO (monogram)

| 173 | 1838 MS | — | 100.00 | 150.00 | 250.00 | 450.00 |

ESCUDO

3.3750 g, .875 GOLD, .0949 oz AGW

| 174 | 1838 MS | — | 125.00 | 200.00 | 350.00 | 600.00 |

8 ESCUDOS

27.0000 g, .875 GOLD, .7596 oz AGW

| 171 | 1837 BA | — | 400.00 | 600.00 | 900.00 | 1750. |
| | 1838 MS | — | 400.00 | 550.00 | 800.00 | 1600. |

TRANSITIONAL COINAGE
Issued during the changeover to the decimal system.

MEDIO (1/2) REAL

1.2500 g, .900 SILVER, .0361 oz ASW

KM#	Date	Mintage	Fine	VF	XF	Unc
177	1858 MB	—	5.00	10.00	20.00	50.00

180	1859 YB	—	4.50	10.00	20.00	50.00
	1860/59 YB	—	4.50	10.00	20.00	50.00
	1860 YB	—	3.00	6.00	15.00	35.00
	1861 YB	—	4.50	10.00	20.00	50.00

NOTE: Die varieties exist.

REAL

2.5000 g, .900 SILVER, .0723 oz ASW

181	1859 YB	—	5.00	12.00	25.00	55.00
	1860 YB	—	3.50	7.00	12.50	25.00
	1861 YB	—	6.50	14.00	30.00	65.00

NOTE: Die varieties exist.

25 CENTAVOS

6.2500 g, .900 SILVER, .1808 oz ASW

| 182 | 1859/8 YB | — | 22.50 | 60.00 | 120.00 | 300.00 |
| | 1859 YB | — | 50.00 | 100.00 | 175.00 | 450.00 |

NOTE: Die varieties exist.

50 CENTIMOS

12.1000 g, .900 SILVER, .3501 oz ASW

| 178 | 1858 MB | — | 12.50 | 27.50 | 50.00 | 135.00 |
| | 1858 MB | — | — | — | Proof | — |

50 CENTAVOS

12.1000 g, .900 SILVER, .3501 oz ASW
Rev: Liberty w/short hair.

179.1	1858 MB	—	18.00	35.00	70.00	275.00
	1858 YB	—	10.00	20.00	47.50	135.00
	1859 YB	—	17.50	42.50	100.00	215.00

Rev: Liberty w/long hair.

179.2	1858 YB	—	9.00	22.00	45.00	150.00
	1859/8 YB	—	9.00	22.00	45.00	150.00
	1859 YB	—	8.50	20.00	42.50	130.00

NOTE: Die varieties exist.

4 ESCUDOS

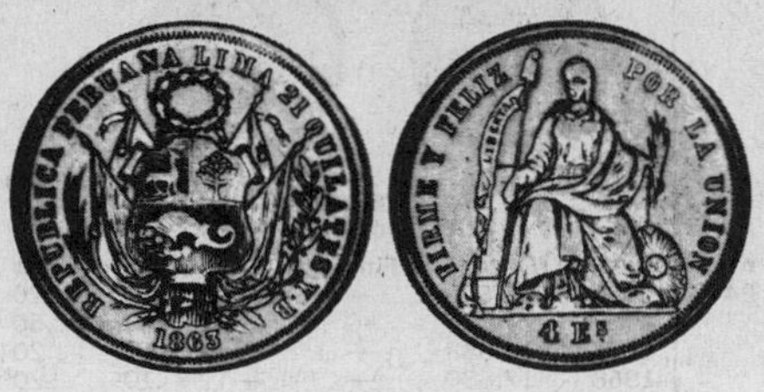

13.5000 g, .875 GOLD, .3798 oz AGW

KM#	Date	Mintage	Fine	VF	XF	Unc
184	1863 YB	—	—	—	Rare	—

8 ESCUDOS

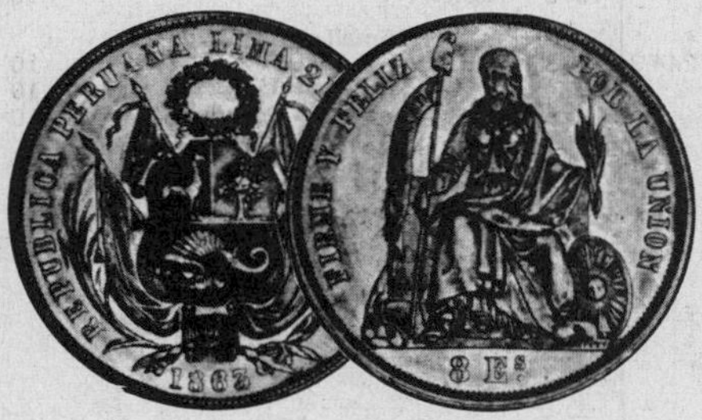

27.0000 g, .875 GOLD, .7596 oz AGW

KM#	Date	Mintage	Fine	VF	XF	Unc
183	1862 YB	—	400.00	500.00	700.00	1250.
	1862/2 YB	—	350.00	450.00	550.00	900.00
	1863 YB	—	350.00	450.00	550.00	900.00

DECIMAL COINAGE

100 Centavos (10 Dineros) = 1 Sol
10 Soles = 1 Libra

CENTAVO

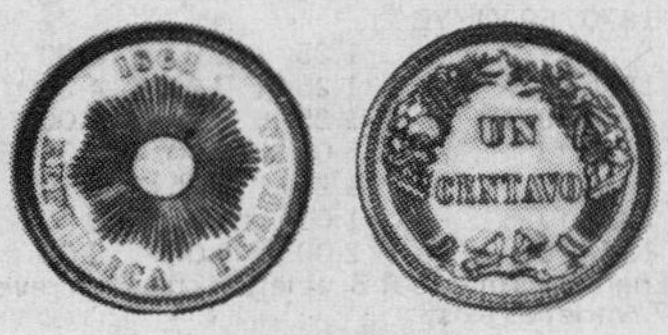

COPPER-NICKEL

KM#	Date	Mintage	Fine	VF	XF	Unc
187.1	1863	1.000	1.00	2.50	6.00	22.50
	1864	Inc. Ab.	1.25	3.50	7.50	25.00

BRONZE

KM#	Date	Mintage	Fine	VF	XF	Unc
187.1a	1875	—	1.50	3.50	6.00	20.00
	1876	—	1.00	3.00	5.00	15.00
	1877	—	2.00	5.00	10.00	30.00
	1878	—	10.00	15.00	25.00	65.00

NOTE: Date varieties exist.

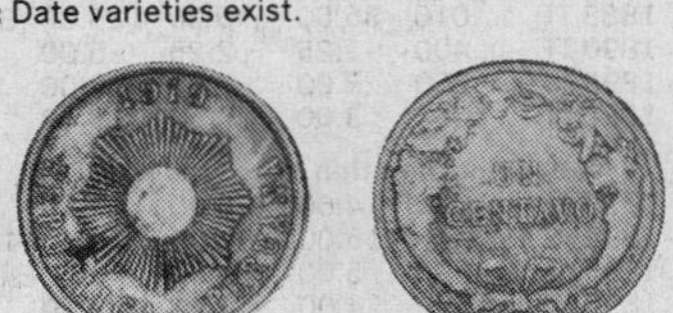

Sharper diework

KM#	Date	Mintage	Fine	VF	XF	Unc
187.2	1919 (P)	4.000	.50	1.00	2.50	8.50

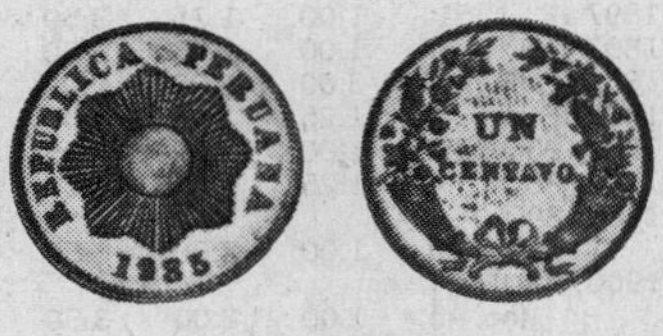

Thick planchet
Small date and legend.

KM#	Date	Mintage	Fine	VF	XF	Unc
208.1	1901	.600	1.00	2.50	4.00	14.00
	1904	1.000	4.50	8.00	14.00	45.00

Large date and legend.

KM#	Date	Mintage	Fine	VF	XF	Unc
208.2	1933	.275	1.50	3.00	5.50	16.00
	1934	1.185	.75	1.50	2.50	7.50
	1935	1.105	.75	1.50	2.50	7.50
	1936	.565	1.50	3.00	5.50	16.00
	1937/6	.735	1.00	2.00	4.00	12.00
	1937	Inc. Ab.	.75	1.50	2.50	7.50
	1938	.340	.75	1.50	2.50	7.50
	1939	1.225	1.50	3.00	5.50	15.00
	1940	1.250	1.50	3.00	5.50	15.00
	1941	2.593	.40	.75	1.50	6.00

Thin Planchet

KM#	Date	Mintage	Fine	VF	XF	Unc
208a	1941	Inc.KM208	.40	.75	1.50	6.00
	1942	2.865	.50	1.00	1.75	7.50
	1943	—	—	Reported, not confirmed		
	1944	—	4.00	9.00	16.00	40.00

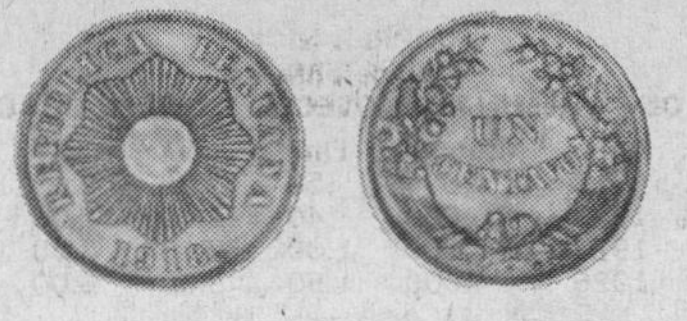

KM#	Date	Mintage	Fine	VF	XF	Unc
211	1909	.252	7.50	15.00	20.00	50.00
	1909/999 R	I.A.	7.50	15.00	20.00	50.00
	1909 R	Inc. Ab.	7.50	15.00	20.00	50.00
	1915	.250	3.00	6.00	10.00	25.00
	1916	.360	1.00	2.00	4.50	14.00
	1916 R	Inc. Ab.	1.00	2.00	4.50	14.00
	1917	.830	1.00	2.00	4.00	14.00
	1917 R	Inc. Ab.	1.00	2.00	4.00	14.00
	1918	1.060	1.00	2.00	4.00	12.00
	1918 R	Inc. Ab.	1.00	2.00	4.00	12.00
	1920 R	.360	1.00	2.50	4.50	15.00
	1933 R	Inc. KM208	1.00	2.50	4.50	15.00
	1934	Inc.KM208	4.50	8.00	14.00	45.00
	1935 R	Inc. KM208	4.00	7.00	12.00	40.00
	1936 R	Inc. KM208	1.50	3.50	6.00	15.00
	1937	—	—	—	—	—
	1937 R	Inc. KM208	1.50	3.50	6.00	15.00
	1939 R	Inc. KM208	4.50	8.00	14.00	45.00

NOTE: Engraver's initial R appeared below ribbon on most or all new dies, but often became weak or filled. Most coins show at least a faint trace of R. Date varieties also exist.

KM#	Date	Mintage	Fine	VF	XF	Unc
211a	1941	Inc.KM208	1.00	2.00	3.50	12.50
	1942	Inc. KM208a	.50	1.00	1.75	7.50
	1943	—	2.50	5.00	12.50	30.00
	1944	2.490	.15	.40	.75	2.50
	1945	2.157	.15	.40	.75	2.50
	1946	3.198	.15	.40	.75	2.00
	1947	2.976	.15	.40	.75	2.50
	1948	3.195	.15	.40	.75	2.00
	1949	1.104	.25	.65	1.25	3.50

NOTE: Many varieties exist.

ZINC (OMS)

KM#	Date	Mintage	Fine	VF	XF	Unc
211b	1949	—	—	—	30.00	50.00

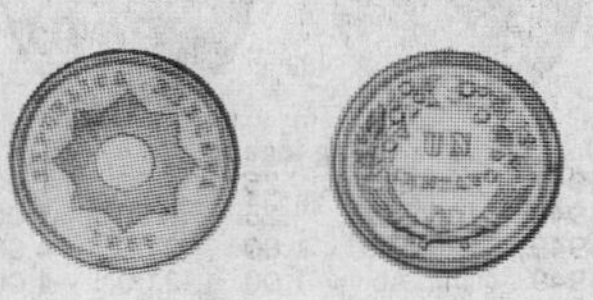

ZINC

KM#	Date	Mintage	Fine	VF	XF	Unc
227	1950	3.196	.35	.75	1.25	4.00
	1951	3.289	.25	.40	.65	2.00
	1952	3.050	.25	.40	.65	2.00
	1953	3.260	.35	.60	1.00	3.00
	1954	3.215	.75	1.50	2.50	8.00
	1955	3.400	.25	.40	.65	2.00
	1956	2.500	.25	.40	.65	2.00
	1957	4.400	.40	.85	1.50	5.00
	1958	2.600	.35	.60	1.00	3.00
	1959	3.200	.25	.40	.65	2.00
	1960/50	3.060	.35	.60	1.00	3.00
	1961/51	2.600	.35	.60	1.00	3.00
	1962/52	2.600	.25	.40	.65	2.00
	1963/53	2.400	.25	.40	.65	2.00
	1963	Inc. Ab.	.25	.40	.65	2.00
	1965	.360	.65	1.25	2.50	8.00

NOTE: Varieties exist. Copper plated examples of type dated 1951 are known.

2 CENTAVOS

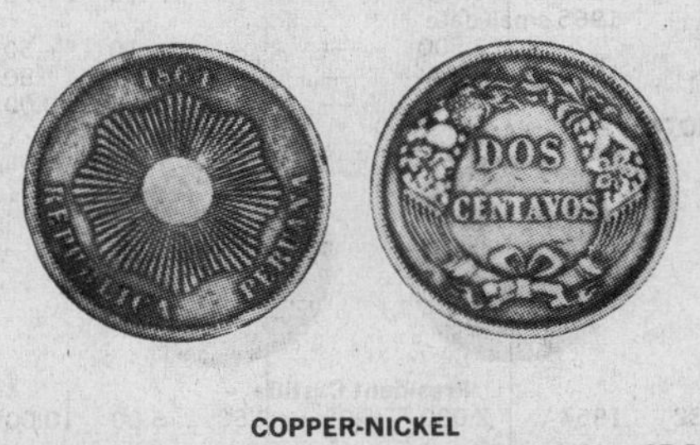

COPPER-NICKEL

KM#	Date	Mintage	Fine	VF	XF	Unc
188.1	1863	1.000	1.50	4.00	12.50	27.50
	1864	Inc. Ab.	1.50	4.00	12.50	27.50

COPPER or BRONZE

KM#	Date	Mintage	Fine	VF	XF	Unc
188.1a	1876	—	1.00	3.00	6.00	17.50
	1877	—	1.00	4.00	8.50	25.00
	1878	—	1.00	3.00	7.00	20.00
	1879	—	1.00	3.00	7.00	20.00
	1879 B	—	—	—	—	—

Modified dies.

KM#	Date	Mintage	Fine	VF	XF	Unc
188.2	1895 (W)	—	.75	1.75	4.00	9.50

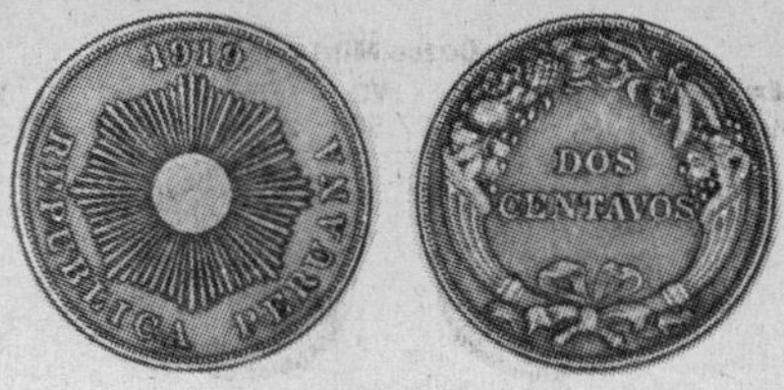

Sharper diework

KM#	Date	Mintage	Fine	VF	XF	Unc
188.3	1919 (P)	3.000	.35	.75	2.00	6.50

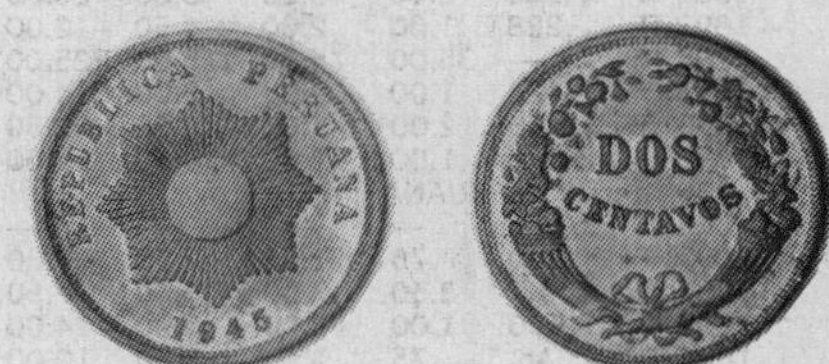

Thick planchet

KM#	Date	Mintage	Fine	VF	XF	Unc
212.1	1917 C	.073	4.00	6.50	10.00	25.00
	1918/17	.580	3.50	6.00	9.00	22.50
	1918/17 C	I.A.	3.50	6.00	9.00	22.50
	1918	Inc. Ab.	3.50	6.00	12.00	30.00
	1918 C	Inc. Ab.	3.50	6.00	12.00	30.00
	1920	.328	1.00	1.75	3.00	10.00
	1920 C	Inc. Ab.	1.00	1.75	3.00	10.00
	1933	.285	1.00	1.75	3.00	10.00
	1933 C	Inc. Ab.	1.00	1.75	3.00	10.00
	1934	.973	.75	1.50	2.50	9.00
	1934 C	Inc. Ab.	.75	1.50	2.50	9.00
	1935	.950	.75	1.50	2.50	9.00
	1935 C	Inc. Ab.	.75	1.50	2.50	9.00
	1936	.763	.75	1.50	2.50	9.00
	1936/5 C	I.A.	1.50	2.50	4.50	15.00
	1936 C	Inc. Ab.	.75	1.25	2.25	7.50
	1937	.963	.75	1.50	2.50	9.00
	1937 C	Inc. Ab.	.75	1.50	2.50	9.00
	1938 C	.428	1.00	1.75	3.00	10.00
	1939/8 C	—	—	Reported, not confirmed		
	1939 C	.783	.75	1.50	2.50	9.00
	1940 C	.565	1.00	1.75	3.00	10.00
	1941/0	I.A.	—	—	—	—
	1941/0 C	I.A.	—	—	—	—
	1941/22	—	—	—	—	—
	1941 C	Inc. Ab.	2.00	5.00	10.00	15.00

NOTE: Engraver's initial C appeared below ribbon on most or all new dies, but often became weak or filled. Most coins show at least a faint trace of C. Other varieties also exist.

Thin planchet

KM#	Date	Mintage	Fine	VF	XF	Unc
212.2	1941/32	.870	—	—	—	—
	1941/33 C	I.A.	1.00	2.00	3.50	10.00
	1941/33	I.A.	—	—	—	—
	1941/38	I.A.	—	—	—	—
	1941/38 C	I.A.	1.00	2.00	3.50	10.00
	1941/39 C	I.A.	1.00	2.00	3.50	10.00
	1941/0	I.A.	1.00	2.00	3.50	10.00
	1941	Inc. Ab.	.35	.75	1.25	4.00
	1942/22	4.418	—	—	—	—
	1942/32	4.418	—	—	—	—
	1942	Inc. Ab.	.25	.50	1.00	3.00
	1943/2	1.829	.50	1.00	2.00	7.00
	1943	Inc. Ab.	.50	1.00	2.00	7.00
	1944	2.068	.75	1.50	3.00	9.00
	1945	2.288	.75	1.50	3.00	9.00
	1946	2.121	.25	.50	.75	2.50
	1947	1.280	.25	.50	.75	2.50
	1948	1.518	.25	.50	.75	3.00
	1949/8	.938	.25	.60	3.50	5.00
	1949	Inc. Ab.	—	—	—	—

NOTE: Varieties exist.

ZINC, 19mm (OMS)

KM#	Date	Mintage	Fine	VF	XF	Unc
212.2a	1949	—	—	—	30.00	50.00

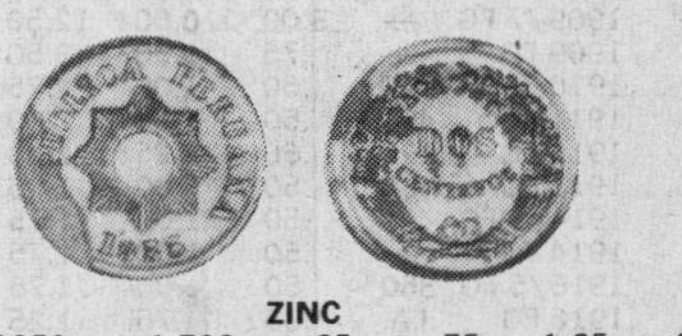

ZINC

KM#	Date	Mintage	Fine	VF	XF	Unc
228	1950	1.702	.35	.75	1.25	4.00
	1951	3.289	.35	.75	1.25	4.00
	1952	1.155	.35	.75	1.25	4.00
	1953	1.150	.40	.85	1.50	5.00
	1954	—	2.50	5.00	9.00	30.00
	1955	1.185	.35	.75	1.25	4.00
	1956	.400	.50	1.00	2.00	6.00
	1957	.520	1.50	3.00	6.00	20.00
	1958	.200	1.25	2.50	4.50	15.00

NOTE: Copper plated examples of type dated 1951 exist.

1/2 DINERO

1.2500 g, .900 SILVER, .0362 oz ASW
Lima Mint
Obv: Small wreath. Rev: Denomination in curved line.

KM#	Date	Mintage	Fine	VF	XF	Unc
189	1863 YB	—	1.00	2.00	5.00	15.00
	1864 YB	—	1.50	3.00	7.50	25.00

NOTE: Engraver's initials RB appear left of shield on reverse.

PERU 1404

Cuzco Mint

KM#	Date	Mintage	VG	Fine	VF	XF
189a	1885 JM	—	27.50	45.00	90.00	175.00

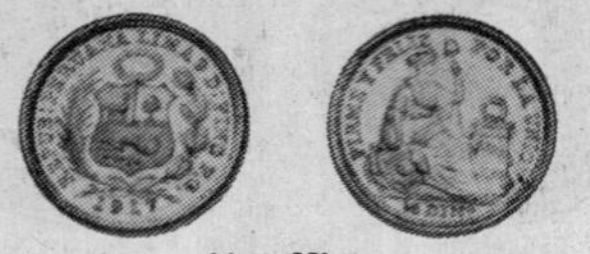

Lima Mint

Obv: Large wreath. Rev: Denomination in straight line.

KM#	Date	Mintage	Fine	VF	XF	Unc
206	1890 TF	.870	1.50	3.00	6.00	15.00
	1891 TF	.160	2.00	3.50	8.00	20.00
	1892 TF	.228	1.00	2.00	4.50	12.00
	1893 TF	—	35.00	75.00	125.00	225.00
	1895 TF	.422	1.00	2.00	5.00	14.00
	1896 TF	.456	2.00	4.00	9.00	22.50
	1896 F	Inc. Ab.	1.00	2.00	4.50	12.00
	1896 F (error) PBRUANA	Inc. Ab.	—	—	—	—
	1897 JF	.320	.75	1.25	2.50	7.00
	1897 VN	Inc. Ab.	3.50	7.00	16.00	37.50
	1898/7 VN	.600	1.00	2.00	5.00	14.00
	1898 VN	Inc. Ab.	.75	1.50	3.50	10.00
	1898 JF	Inc. Ab.	.60	1.25	2.50	7.00
	1899/8 JF	.500	1.00	1.75	4.00	11.00
	1899 JF	Inc. Ab.	.60	1.25	2.50	7.00
	1900/890 JF	.400	.60	1.25	2.50	7.00
	1901/801	.500	—	—	—	—
	1901/891 JF	Inc. Ab.	.60	1.25	2.00	6.00
	1901 JF	Inc. Ab.	.75	1.50	3.50	9.00
	1902/802 JF	.616	.60	1.25	2.00	6.00
	1902/892 JF	Inc. Ab.	.60	1.25	2.00	6.00
	1902/92	I.A.	—	—	—	—
	1902 JF	Inc. Ab.	.75	1.50	3.50	9.00
	1903/803 JF	1.798	.50	1.00	1.75	4.50
	1903/893 JF	Inc. Ab.	.50	1.00	1.75	4.50
	1903/897 JF	Inc. Ab.	1.00	1.75	4.00	11.00
	1903 JF	Inc. Ab.	.75	1.50	3.00	7.50
	1904/804 JF	.723	.60	1.25	2.00	6.00
	1904/804 JF (error FFLIZ)	Inc. Ab.	2.00	4.50	8.00	12.50
	1904/893 JF	Inc. Ab.	.60	1.25	2.00	6.00
	1904/894 JF	Inc. Ab.	.60	1.25	2.00	6.00
	1904/894 JF (error FFLIZ)	Inc. Ab.	2.00	4.50	8.00	12.50
	1904 JF	Inc. Ab.	.75	1.50	3.00	7.50
	1904 JF (error FFLIZ)	Inc. Ab.	2.00	4.50	8.00	12.50
	1905/805 JF	1.400	.75	1.50	3.50	9.00
	1905/893 JF	Inc. Ab.	1.00	2.00	4.50	12.00
	1905/894	Inc. Ab.	1.00	2.00	4.50	12.00
	1905/895 JF	Inc. Ab.	.50	1.25	2.00	6.00
	1905/3 JF	I.A.	1.00	2.00	4.50	12.00
	1905 JF	Inc. Ab.	.75	1.50	3.00	7.50
	1906/806 JF	.900	.75	1.50	3.50	9.00
	1906/886 JF	Inc. Ab.	.75	1.50	3.50	9.00
	1906/895 JF	Inc. Ab.	.75	1.50	3.50	9.00
	1906/896 JF	Inc. Ab.	.50	1.25	2.00	6.00
	1906 JF	Inc. Ab.	.75	1.50	3.00	9.00
	1907 FG	.600	.60	1.25	2.00	6.00
	1908/7 FG	.200	1.50	3.00	6.00	15.00
	1908 FG	Inc. Ab.	.75	1.50	3.50	9.00
	1909/7 FG	—	3.00	6.00	12.50	27.50
	1909 FG	—	.75	1.50	3.50	9.00
	1910 FG	.640	.50	1.00	1.75	4.50
	1911 FG	.460	.50	1.25	2.00	6.00
	1912 FG	.120	.60	1.25	2.50	7.00
	1913 FG	.480	.50	1.00	1.75	4.50
	1914/3 FG	—	.50	1.00	1.75	4.50
	1914 FG	—	.50	1.00	1.75	4.50
	1916/5 FG	.860	.50	1.00	1.75	4.50
	1916 FG	I.A.	.35	.75	1.25	3.00
	1916/5 FG (error) FERUANA	Inc. Ab.	—	—	—	—
	1916 FG(error FERUANA)	Inc. Ab.	1.00	2.00	4.50	12.00
	1917 FG	.140	.50	1.00	1.75	4.50

NOTE: Most coins 1900-06 show faint to strong traces of 9/8 or 90/89 in date. Non-overdates without such traces are scarce. Most coins of 1907-17 have engraver's initial R at left of shield tip on reverse. Many varieties exist.

5 CENTAVOS

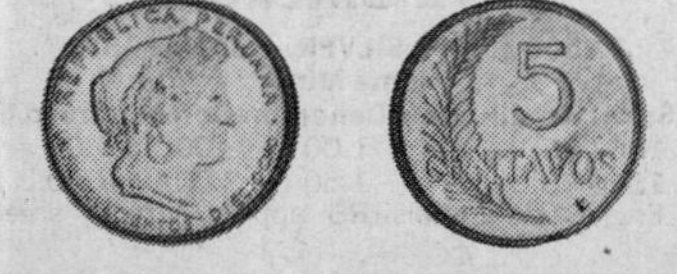

COPPER-NICKEL

Philadelphia Mint

Obv. date: UN MIL NOVECIENTOS DIECIOCHO.

KM#	Date	Mintage	Fine	VF	XF	Unc
213.1	1918	4.000	.50	1.25	2.50	10.00
	1919	10.000	.40	1.00	2.00	7.00
	1923	2.000	1.00	2.00	3.50	12.50
	1926	4.000	1.50	3.00	6.00	20.00

London Mint

213.2	1934	4.000	.75	2.00	3.00	8.50
	1934	—	—	—	Proof	—
	1935	4.000	.50	1.25	2.00	6.00
	1935	—	—	—	Proof	—
	1937	2.000	.75	2.00	3.00	8.50
	1937	—	—	—	Proof	—
	1939	2.000	.50	1.25	2.00	6.00
	1939	—	—	—	Proof	—
	1940	2.000	.50	1.25	2.00	6.00
	1940	—	—	—	Proof	—
	1941	2.000	.50	1.25	2.00	6.00
	1941	—	—	—	Proof	—

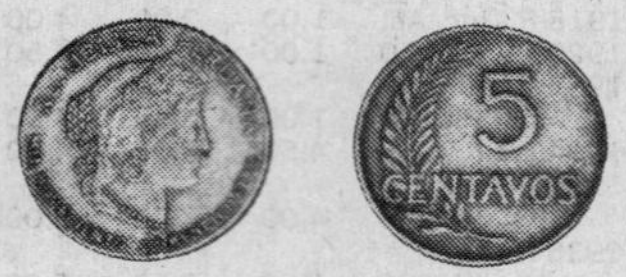

BRASS

Philadelphia Mint

Obv. date: MIL NOVECIENTOS CUARENTA Y DOS.

213.2a.1	1942	4.000	1.00	3.00	5.00	12.00
	1943	4.000	1.00	3.00	5.00	12.00
	1944	4.000	1.00	2.75	4.50	10.00

Mint mark: S

213.2a.2	1942	4.000	1.00	3.00	5.00	12.00
	1943	4.000	2.50	4.50	8.00	20.00

Lima Mint

Obv. date: MIL NOVECIENTOS CUARENTICUATRO.

213.2a.3	1944	1.106	1.50	3.50	6.00	15.00

Thick planchet, short legend.

223.1	1945	2.768	.35	.75	1.50	4.00
	1946/5	4.270	1.00	2.50	5.00	14.00
	1946	Inc. Ab.	.25	.50	1.00	3.50

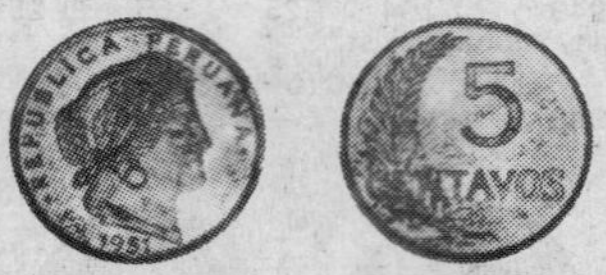

Long legend.

223.3	1947	7.683	.25	.50	1.00	3.00
	1948	6.711	.25	.50	1.00	3.00
	1949/8	5.550	1.00	2.00	4.00	10.00
	1949	Inc. Ab.	1.00	2.00	4.00	10.00
	1950	7.933	.25	.50	1.00	3.00
	1951	8.064	.25	.50	1.00	3.00

Thin planchet

223.2	1951	Inc. Ab.	.10	.25	.50	2.50
	1952	7.840	.10	.25	.50	2.50
	1953	6.976	.10	.25	.50	2.50
	1953 AFP	—	—	—	—	—
	1954	6.244	.10	.20	.40	1.00
	1955	8.064	.10	.20	.40	2.00
	1956	16.200	—	.10	.35	1.50
	1957 small date	16.000	—	.10	.25	.75
	1957 sm.dt.	I.A.	—	.10	.25	.75
	1958	4.600	—	.10	.25	1.00
	1959	8.300	—	.10	.25	1.00
	1960/50	9.900	—	—	Rare	—
	1960	Inc. Ab.	—	.10	.25	.75
	1961	10.200	—	.10	.20	.75
	1962	11.064	—	.10	.20	.75
	1963	12.012	—	.10	.20	.75
	1964/3	12.304	—	.10	.35	1.50
	1964	Inc. Ab.	—	—	.10	.75
	1965 small date	12.500	—	—	.10	.50
	1965 lg. dt.	I.A.	—	—	.10	.50
	1965	—	—	—	Proof	20.00

NOTE: Varieties exist.

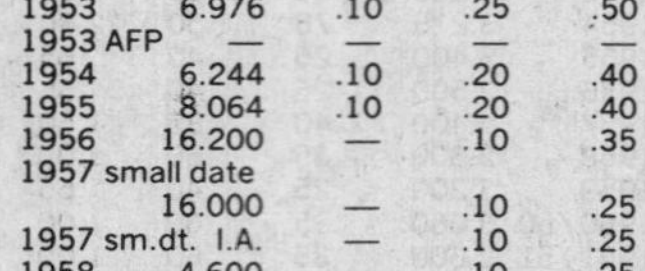

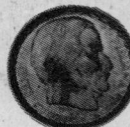

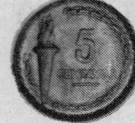

President Castilla

232	1954	2.080	1.25	2.50	5.00	10.00

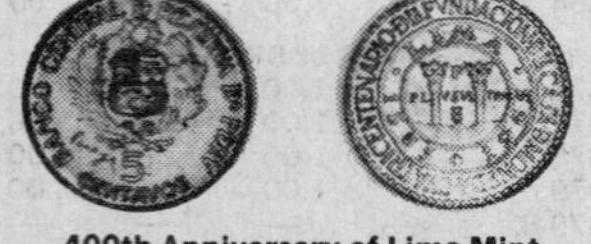

400th Anniversary of Lima Mint

290	1965	.712	—	—	.10	.25
(236)	1965	—	—	—	Proof	100.00

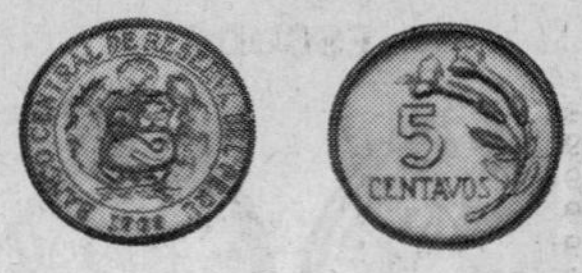

Obv: Large arms.

Reeded edge

KM#	Date	Mintage	Fine	VF	XF	Unc
244.1	1966	14.620	—	—	.10	.20
	1966	1,000	—	—	Proof	2.50
	1967	14.088	—	—	.10	.20
	1968	17.880	—	—	.10	.20

Plain edge

244.2	1969	17.880	—	—	—	.10
	1970	—	—	—	—	.10
	1971	24.320	—	—	—	.10
	1972	24.342	—	—	—	.10
	1973	25.074	—	—	—	.10

Obv: Small arms.

244.3	1973	Inc. Ab.	—	—	—	.10
	1974	—	—	—	—	.10
	1975	—	—	—	—	.10

DINERO

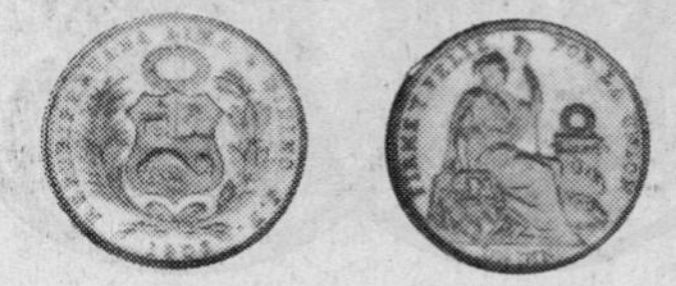

2.5000 g, .900 SILVER, .0723 oz ASW

Lima Mint

Obv: Small wreath. Rev: Denomination in curved line.

190	1863 YB	—	1.25	2.25	4.50	17.50
	1864/3 YB	—	1.25	2.25	4.00	15.00
	1864 YB	—	1.50	2.50	5.00	22.00
	1865 YB	—	2.00	5.00	10.00	45.00
	1866/5 YB	—	1.25	2.25	4.00	15.00
	1866 YB	—	1.00	1.75	3.50	12.50
	1870/60 YJ	—	3.00	6.00	15.00	45.00
	1870/60 YJ/YB	—	—	—	—	—
	1870/69 YJ/YB	—	1.25	2.25	4.00	15.00
	1870 YJ	—	1.25	2.25	4.50	17.50
	1870 YJ/B	—	1.25	2.25	4.00	15.00
	1872 YJ	—	35.00	75.00	125.00	300.00
	1874 YJ	—	1.25	2.25	4.50	17.50
	1875 YJ	—	1.00	1.75	3.50	12.50
	1877 YJ	—	2.00	4.00	8.00	30.00

NOTE: Engraver's initials R.B. at left of shield on reverse of 1863-77. Varieties exist.

Cuzco Mint

KM#	Date	Mintage	VG	Fine	VF	XF
190a	1886	—	22.50	37.50	75.00	150.00

Lima Mint

Obv: Large wreath.

Rev: Denomination in straight line.

KM#	Date	Mintage	Fine	VF	XF	Unc
204.1	1888 TF	.010	35.00	75.00	125.00	300.00
	1890 TF	.400	1.25	2.25	5.00	20.00
	1891 TF	.060	3.00	7.50	15.00	38.00
	1892 TF	.069	3.00	7.50	15.00	38.00

Rev: Denomination in curved line.

204.2	1893 TF	.023	4.00	8.00	17.50	60.00
	1894/3 TF	—	15.00	30.00	60.00	180.00
	1895/3 TF	.090	5.00	15.00	25.00	45.00
	1895 TF	Inc. Ab.	4.00	8.00	17.50	70.00
	1896/5 TF	.534	2.50	6.00	12.50	25.00
	1896 TF	Inc. Ab.	3.00	6.00	12.00	30.00
	1896/5 F	I.A.	1.00	1.75	3.50	10.00
	1896 F	Inc. Ab.	3.00	6.00	12.00	28.00
	1897 JF	.511	1.00	1.75	3.50	10.00
	1897 VN	Inc. Ab.	1.00	1.75	3.50	10.00
	1898/7 JF	.200	3.00	6.00	12.00	28.00
	1898 JF	Inc. Ab.	1.25	2.25	4.00	12.50
	1900/90 JF	.550	1.00	2.00	3.25	10.00
	1900/98 JF	I.A.	1.25	2.25	4.00	12.50
	1900/890 JF	Inc. Ab.	1.00	2.00	3.50	10.00
	1900/89 JF	Inc. Ab.	1.00	2.00	3.50	10.00
	1900 JF	Inc. Ab.	1.00	2.00	3.50	10.00
	1902/1 JF	.375	1.00	2.00	3.50	10.00
	1902/892 JF	Inc. Ab.	1.00	2.00	3.50	10.00
	1902/897 JF	Inc. Ab.	—	—	—	—
	1902 JF	Inc. Ab.	1.00	2.00	3.50	10.00
	1903/892 JF	.887	.75	2.00	3.50	8.00
	1903/92 JF	I.A.	.75	2.00	3.50	8.00
	1903 JF	Inc. Ab.	.75	1.75	2.50	6.00
	1904 JF	.380	1.00	2.00	4.00	12.50
	1905/3 JF	.700	1.00	2.50	4.00	10.00
	1905 JF	Inc. Ab.	.75	2.00	3.50	8.00
	1906 JF	.826	.75	2.00	3.50	8.00
	1907 JF	.500	—	—	Rare	—
	1907 FG/JF	Inc. Ab.	1.25	2.50	4.50	10.00
	1907 FG	Inc. Ab.	1.00	1.75	3.00	8.00
	1908 FG/JF	.200	1.00	2.25	4.00	10.00

KM#	Date	Mintage	Fine	VF	XF	Unc
204.2	1908 FG Inc. Ab.		1.00	1.75	3.00	8.00
	1909 FG	—	2.00	4.00	8.00	15.00
	1909 FG/FO	—	2.00	4.00	8.00	15.00
	1910 FG	.210	.60	1.25	2.50	8.00
	1910 FG/JF I.A.		1.00	2.25	4.00	12.50
	1910 FG/JG I.A.		1.00	2.25	4.00	12.50
	1911 FG	.200	.75	1.50	3.00	8.00
	1911 FG/JF I.A.		—	—	—	—
	1911 FG/JG I.A.		—	—	—	—
	1912 FG	.400	.60	1.25	2.50	8.00
	1912/02 FG/JF					
	Inc. Ab.		—	—	—	—
	1912 FG/JF I.A.		—	—	—	—
	1913/2 FG	.360	—	—	—	—
	1913 FG Inc. Ab.		.60	1.25	2.50	8.00
	1913 FG/G I.A.		.60	1.25	2.50	8.00
	1913 FG/JB I.A.		.60	1.25	2.50	8.00
	1916 FG large date					
		.430	1.25	2.50	4.50	10.00
	1916 FG small date					
	Inc. Ab.		.60	1.25	2.00	6.00

NOTE: Varieties exist.

10 CENTAVOS

COPPER-NICKEL
Philadelphia Mint
Obv. date: UN MIL NOVECIENTOS DIECIOCHO.

KM#	Date	Mintage	Fine	VF	XF	Unc
214.1	1918	3.000	.40	1.00	2.00	7.00
	1919	2.500	.40	1.00	2.00	7.00
	1920	3.080	.35	.75	1.50	6.00
	1921	6.920	.35	.75	1.50	6.00
	1926	3.000	2.50	5.00	8.50	22.50

London Mint

214.2	1935	1.000	.75	1.50	3.00	12.00
	1935	—	—	—	Proof	—
	1937	1.000	.40	1.00	2.00	7.00
	1937	—	—	—	Proof	—
	1939	2.000	.35	.75	1.25	5.00
	1939	—	—	—	Proof	—
	1940	2.000	.35	.75	1.25	5.00
	1940	—	—	—	Proof	—
	1941	2.000	.35	.75	1.25	5.00
	1941	—	—	—	Proof	—

BRASS
Philadelphia Mint
Date is spelled out w/a "Y".

214a.1	1942	2.000	1.50	3.00	6.00	16.00
	1943	2.000	1.50	3.00	6.00	16.00
	1944	2.000	1.50	3.50	7.00	20.00

Mint mark: S

214a.2	1942	2.000	6.00	12.00	20.00	45.00
	1943	2.000	1.50	3.00	6.00	16.00

Lima Mint
Date is spelled out with an I.

214a.3	1942	—	5.00	9.00	15.00	35.00
	1944	—	3.50	7.00	12.00	30.00

Thick planchet
Obv: Short legend.

224.1	1945	2.810	.25	.50	1.50	4.00
	1946/5	4.863	.50	1.00	2.50	8.00
	1946	Inc. Ab.	.35	.75	2.00	7.00

Thin Planchet, 1.3mm
Obv: Long legend.

224.2	1951	Inc. Ab.	.10	.20	.40	2.00
	1952	6.694	.10	.20	.40	3.00
	1952 AFP	—	—	—	—	—
	1953	5.668	.10	.20	.40	2.00
	1953 AFP	—	—	—	—	—
	1954	7.786	—	.10	.35	1.50

KM#	Date	Mintage	Fine	VF	XF	Unc
224.2	1954 AFP	—	—	—	—	—
	1955	6.690	—	.10	.35	1.50
	1955 AFP	—	—	—	—	—
	1956/5	8.410	.10	.35	.75	3.50
	1956	Inc. Ab.	—	.10	.25	.75
	1957	8.420	—	.10	.25	.75
	1957 AFP	—	—	—	—	—
	1958	10.380	—	.10	.25	1.00
	1958 AFP	—	—	—	—	—
	1959	8.300	—	.10	.25	.75
	1960	12.600	—	.10	.25	.50
	1961	12.700	—	.10	.15	.60
	1962	14.598	—	.10	.15	.50
	1963	16.100	—	.10	.15	.50
	1964	16.504	—	.10	.15	.60
	1965	17.808	—	.10	.15	.50
	1965	—	—	—	Proof	25.00

NOTE: Date varieties exist.

Thick planchet.
Obv: Long legend.

226	1947	6.806	.25	.50	1.00	3.00
	1948	5.771	.25	.50	1.25	4.00
	1949/8	4.730	.50	1.00	1.50	7.50
	1949	Inc. Ab.	.25	.50	1.25	4.00
	1950	5.298	.25	.50	1.00	3.00
	1951	7.324	6.00	10.00	15.00	35.00
	1951/0 AFP	—	—	—	—	—
	1951 AFP	—	—	—	—	—

NOTE: Varieties exist.

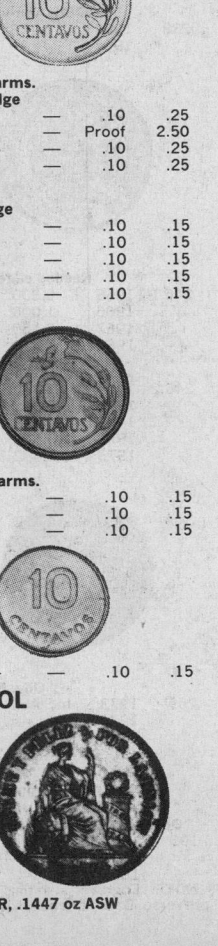

President Castilla

233	1954	1.818	1.50	3.00	6.00	12.50

400th Anniversary of Lima Mint

237	1965	.572	—	—	.10	.35
	1965	—	—	—	Proof	150.00

Obv: Large arms.
Reeded edge

245.1	1966	14.930	—	—	.10	.25
	1966	1.000	—	—	Proof	2.50
	1967	19.330	—	—	.10	.25
	1968	24.390	—	—	.10	.25

NOTE: Date varieties exist.

Plain edge

245.2	1969	24.390	—	—	.10	.15
	1970	29.110	—	—	.10	.15
	1971	30.590	—	—	.10	.15
	1972	34.442	—	—	.10	.15
	1973	33.864	—	—	.10	.15

NOTE: Date varieties exist.

Obv: Small arms.

245.3	1973	Inc. Ab.	—	—	.10	.15
	1974	—	—	—	.10	.15
	1975	10.430	—	—	.10	.15

263	1975	—	—	—	.10	.15

1/5 SOL

5.0000 g, .900 SILVER, .1447 oz ASW

Lima Mint
Obv: Small wreath. Rev: Denomination in curved line.

KM#	Date	Mintage	Fine	VF	XF	Unc
191	1863 YB	—	1.75	4.00	8.00	40.00
	1864/3 YB	—	2.00	5.00	10.00	50.00
	1864/3 YB-DD					
		—	—	25.00	55.00	200.00
	1864 YB	—	1.50	3.50	7.00	30.00
	1864 YB-DD	—	—	25.00	55.00	200.00
	1865/4 YB	—	2.00	5.00	10.00	50.00
	1865 YB	—	1.50	3.50	7.00	40.00
	1866/5 YB	—	2.00	4.50	8.50	35.00
	1866 YB	—	1.50	3.00	6.00	25.00
	1867 YB	—	1.50	3.50	7.00	30.00
	1869 YB	—	8.00	14.00	24.00	75.00
	1874 YJ	—	1.75	4.00	7.50	35.00
	1874 YJ/YB	—	—	—	—	—
	1875 YB	—	—	—	—	—
	1875/65 YJ	—	2.50	5.00	10.00	50.00
	1875 YJ	—	1.75	4.00	7.50	35.00

NOTE: Engraver's initials RB appear left of shield on reverse. Varieties exist.

Arequipa Mint

191a	1885 A.C.	—	175.00	300.00		

Lima Mint
Obv: Large wreath. Rev: Denomination in straight line.

205	1888 TF	.550	1.75	3.50	6.00	17.50
	1889 TF	—	—	—	Rare	—
	1890/88 TF	.085	4.50	9.00	18.00	45.00
	1890 TF Inc. Ab.		3.50	7.00	15.00	40.00
	1891 TF	.064	5.00	10.00	20.00	60.00
	1892 TF	.128	1.75	3.50	7.00	20.00
	1893 TF-JR	.049	5.00	10.00	20.00	60.00
	1895 TF-JR I.A.		7.00	15.00	30.00	75.00
	1896 TF-JR	.586	1.50	3.00	5.50	14.00
	1896 F-JR I.A.		1.75	3.50	7.00	20.00
	1897 JF	.745	1.50	3.00	5.50	14.00
	1897 JF-JR					
	Inc. Ab.		1.50	3.00	5.50	14.00
	1897 VN Inc. Ab.		1.75	3.50	6.00	15.00
	1898 JF	.350	1.50	3.00	5.50	14.00
	1899/88 JF					
		.700	1.50	3.00	5.50	12.50
	1899 JF Inc. Ab.		1.50	3.00	5.50	12.00
	1900/800 JF					
		.750	1.75	3.50	6.00	15.00
	1900/800 JF-JR					
	Inc. Ab.		1.75	3.50	6.00	15.00
	1900/890 JF					
	Inc. Ab.		1.75	3.50	6.00	15.00
	1900 JF Inc. Ab.		1.50	3.00	5.50	12.00
	1901 JF	.638	1.50	3.00	5.50	12.00
	1903/1 JF	.702	1.75	3.50	6.00	15.00
	1903/13 JF I.A.		1.75	3.50	6.00	15.00
	1903 JF Inc. Ab.		1.50	3.00	5.50	12.00
	1906 JF	.660	1.50	3.00	5.50	12.00
	1907 JF	1.370	1.25	2.00	4.00	6.00
	1907 FG Inc. Ab.		1.50	3.00	5.50	12.00
	1908/7 FG	.560	1.75	3.50	6.00	15.00
	1908 FG Inc. Ab.		1.50	3.00	5.50	12.00
	1909 FG	.042	2.00	4.00	9.00	27.50
	1910 FG	.165	3.00	7.00	12.00	25.00
	1911 FG	.250	1.50	3.00	5.50	9.00
	1911 FG-R I.A.		1.50	3.00	5.50	9.00
	1912 FG	.300	1.25	2.00	4.50	9.00
	1912 FG-R I.A.		1.50	3.00	5.50	9.00
	1913 FG	.223	1.75	3.50	6.00	15.00
	1913 FG-R I.A.		1.75	3.50	6.00	15.00
	1914 FG	.010	5.00	10.00	20.00	40.00
	1915 FG	—	20.00	30.00	50.00	85.00
	1916 FG	.425	2.00	5.00	10.00	20.00
	1916 FG-R I.A.		1.50	3.00	5.50	9.00
	1917 FG-R	.020	8.00	15.00	30.00	60.00

NOTE: Some coins 1893-1900 have engraver's initials JR left of shield tip on reverse and some 1911-17 have R in same location. Die varieties exist.

20 CENTAVOS

COPPER-NICKEL

PERU 1406

Obv. date: UN MIL NOVECIENTOS DIECIOCHO.

KM#	Date	Mintage	Fine	VF	XF	Unc
215.1	1918	2.500	.40	1.00	2.50	8.00
	1919	1.250	.50	1.25	3.00	10.00
	1920	1.464	.50	1.25	3.00	10.00
	1921	8.536	.35	.85	2.00	7.00
	1926	2.500	.75	2.50	6.00	20.00

London Mint

215.2	1940	1.000	.25	.75	1.75	5.50
	1940	—	—	—	Proof	125.00
	1941	1.000	.35	1.00	2.50	7.50
	1941	—	—	—	Proof	125.00

BRASS
Philadelphia Mint
Obv. date: MIL NOVECIENTOS CUARENTA Y TRES.

215a.1	1942	.500	3.00	6.00	12.50	50.00
	1943	.500	3.00	6.00	12.50	50.00
	1944	.500	4.00	7.50	15.00	55.00

Mint mark: S

215a.2	1942	.500	12.00	25.00	90.00	
	1943	.500	3.00	6.00	12.50	60.00

Lima Mint
Thick planchet
Obv: Large head, divided leg.

221.1	1942	.300	1.00	2.50	5.00	12.50
	1943	1.900	.75	1.50	2.50	7.50
	1944	2.963	.60	1.25	2.00	6.00

Obv: Large head w/AFP on truncation, continuous leg.

221.2	1945	—	—	—	—	—
	1946	3.410	.25	.50	.85	3.00
	1947	4.307	.25	.50	.85	3.00
	1948	3.578	.25	.50	.85	3.00
	1949/8	2.709	.75	1.50	2.50	6.50
	1949	Inc. Ab.	.50	1.00	1.75	4.50
	1950	2.427	1.00	1.75	3.00	8.00
	1951	2.941	3.00	7.50	12.50	30.00

NOTE: Date varieties exist.

COPPER (OMS)

221.2a	1947	300 pcs.	—	—	—	75.00

BRASS
Thin planchet, 1.3mm, AFP

221.2b	1951	Inc. Ab.	.20	.40	.75	2.00
	1952	4.410	.20	.40	.75	2.50
	1952 w/o AFP	Inc. Ab.	—	—	—	—
	1953	2.615	—	—	.75	2.00
	1954	1.816	1.50	2.50	4.00	9.00
	1955 lg.dt.	4.050	.10	.15	.30	1.50
	1955 sm.dt.	I.A.	.15	.25	.50	2.00
	1956	3.760	.10	.15	.30	1.50
	1957	3.680	.10	.15	.30	1.00
	1958	3.100	.10	.15	.30	1.00
	1959	5.450	—	.10	.20	.75
	1960	6.750	—	.10	.20	.75
	1960 w/o AFP	—	—	—	—	—
	1961	6.800	—	.10	.20	.75
	1961 w/o AFP	—	—	—	—	—
	1962	7.357	—	.10	.20	.75
	1963/2	8.843	.15	.25	.50	2.00
	1963	Inc. Ab.	—	.10	.20	1.00
	1964	9.550	—	.10	.20	.75
	1965	—	—	.10	.20	.75
	1965	—	—	—	Proof	30.00

NOTE: Date varieties exist.

Obv: Small head, continuous leg.

KM#	Date	Mintage	Fine	VF	XF	Unc
225	1945	3.043	.25	.50	.75	1.50
	1946/5	Inc. Ab.	.25	.65	1.00	2.00
	1946	Inc. Ab.	.25	.50	.75	1.50

President Castilla

234	1954	.799	2.00	4.00	8.00	12.50

264	1975	—	—	—	.10	.20

25 CENTAVOS

BRASS
400th Anniversary of Lima Mint

238	1965	1.113	—	.10	.15	.35
	1965	—	—	—	Proof	200.00

Reeded edge. Obv: Large arms.

246.1	1966	9.300	—	.10	.15	.25
	1966	1.000	—	—	Proof	2.50
	1967	8.150	—	.10	.15	.25
	1968	7.440	—	.10	.15	.25

Plain edge.

246.2	1969	7.440	—	.10	.15	.25
	1970	6.341	—	.10	.15	.25
	1971	3.196	—	.10	.15	.25
	1972	5.523	—	.10	.15	.25
	1973	7.492	.10	.15	.20	.50

Obv: Small arms.

259	1973	Inc. Ab.	—	.10	.15	.25
	1974	—	—	.10	.15	.25
	1975	—	—	.10	.15	.25

1/2 SOL

12.5000 g, .900 SILVER, .3617 oz ASW
Lima Mint
Obv: Small wreath. Rev: Denomination in curved line.

195	1864 YB	—	4.00	8.50	15.00	60.00
	1864 YB-D	—	100.00	200.00	300.00	500.00
	1865 YB	—	4.00	8.50	15.00	55.00

NOTE: Engraver's initials RB appear left of shield on reverse. Date varieties exist.

Obv: Large wreath. Rev: Denomination in straight line.

KM#	Date	Mintage	Fine	VF	XF	Unc
203	1907 FG-JR	1.000	BV	4.00	6.50	14.00
	1908/7 FG-JR	.030	8.00	15.00	35.00	100.00
	1908 FG-JR I.A.	12.00	25.00	45.00	125.00	
	1914 FG-JR	.173	BV	4.50	9.00	20.00
	1915 FG-JR	.570	BV	3.50	5.50	12.00
	1916 FG	.384	BV	3.50	5.50	12.00
	1916 FG-JR	—	BV	3.50	5.50	12.00
	1917 FG-JR	.178	BV	4.00	7.50	20.00

NOTE: Most coins 1907-17 have engraver's initials JR left of shield tip on reverse. Date varieties exist.

12.5000 g, .500 SILVER, .2009 oz ASW

216	1922 LIBERTAD incuse, J.R. on rev.					
		.465	2.50	4.50	8.00	30.00
	1922 LIBERTAD in relief					
		Inc. Ab.	2.50	4.50	8.00	30.00
	1923 LIBER/TAD GM round top 3					
		2.520	BV	2.50	6.00	20.00
	1923 flat top 3					
		Inc. Ab.	BV	2.50	5.50	17.50
	1924 GM	.238	3.00	6.00	12.00	40.00
	1926 GM	.694	BV	3.50	7.00	25.00
	1927 GM	2.640	BV	2.50	5.50	15.00
	1928/7 GM	3.028	—	—	—	—
	1928 GM	Inc.Ab.	BV	2.50	5.50	15.00
	1929 GM	3.068	BV	2.50	5.50	15.00
	1935 AP	2.653	BV	2.50	5.00	14.00
	1935	—	—	—	—	—

NOTE: Engraver's initials appear on stems of obverse wreath. Date varieties exist.

BRASS
London Mint
Obv: 3 palm leaves point to llama on shield.

220.1	1935	10.000	.50	1.25	2.25	7.00
	1941	4.000	—	1.25	2.25	7.00

Philadelphia Mint

220.2	1942	4.000	1.50	3.00	5.00	15.00
	1943	—	3.00	6.50	12.50	35.00
	1944	4.000	1.50	3.00	5.00	15.00

Mint mark: S

220.3	1942	1.668	1.50	3.00	5.00	15.00
	1943	6.332	1.50	3.00	5.00	15.00

NOTE: The coins struck in Philadelphia and San Francisco have a serif on the "4" of the date; the Lima and London coins do not.

Lima Mint
Obv: 1 palm leaf points to llama on shield.

220.4	1941	2.000	3.00	6.50	12.50	35.00
	1942	Inc. Ab.	1.50	3.00	5.00	15.00
	1942 AP					
	1943	2.000	.50	1.00	2.00	8.00
	1944	—	.40	.85	1.75	7.00
	1945	4.000	.75	1.50	3.00	10.00

NOTE: Dates 1941-44 have thick flat-top 4 w/o serifs. 1945 has narrow 4 like KM#220.5.

Obv: 3 palm leaves point to llama on shield.

220.5	1942 long-top 2					
		Inc. Ab.	1.50	3.00	5.00	15.00
	1944	Inc. Ab.	.75	1.50	3.00	10.00
	1944 AP Inc. Ab.	.50	1.00	2.00	7.00
	1945	Inc. Ab.	.75	1.50	3.00	10.00
	1945 AP Inc. Ab.	.75	1.50	3.00	10.00
	1946/5 AP					
		3.744	2.00	3.50	6.50	17.50
	1946 AP Inc. Ab.	.40	.75	1.25	4.00

KM#	Date	Mintage	Fine	VF	XF	Unc
220.5	1947 AP	6.066	.40	.75	1.25	5.00
	1947	Inc. Ab.	.40	.75	1.25	5.00
	1948	3.324	.40	.75	1.25	4.00
	1949/8	.420	1.00	2.00	4.00	12.00
	1949	Inc. Ab.	.75	1.50	3.00	10.00
	1950	.091	1.00	2.25	4.50	15.00
	1951/8	.930	.50	1.00	2.00	7.00
	1951	Inc. Ab.	.50	1.00	2.00	7.00
	1952	.935	.75	1.50	3.00	10.00
	1953	.817	.50	1.00	2.00	7.00
	1954	.637	.75	1.50	3.00	10.00
	1955	1.383	.15	.35	.75	4.00
	1956	2.309	.10	.25	.40	1.50
	1957	2.700	.10	.25	.50	2.00
	1958	2.691	.10	.20	.40	1.50
	1959	3.609	.10	.25	.40	1.50
	1960	5.600	.10	.20	.35	.75
	1961	4.400	.10	.20	.35	.75
	1962	3.540	.10	.20	.35	1.00
	1963	4.345	.10	.20	.35	.75
	1964	5.315	.10	.20	.35	1.50
	1965	7.090	.10	.20	.35	1.75
	1965				Proof	50.00

NOTE: 1942, 1944 AP and all 1945-49 have narrow 4 w/o serif on crossbar. 1944 w/o AP has flat-top 4 like KM#220.4. Engraver's initials AP appear on wreath stems of some 1944-45, all 1946 and some 1947 coins. Varieties exist.

400th Anniversary Of Lima Mint

239	1965	10.971	—	.10	.15	.35
	1965	—	—		Proof	400.00

Obv: Large arms. Rev: Llama in high relief.

247.1	1966	13.720	—	.10	.20	.40
	1966	1,000	—		Proof	4.00
	1967	15.500	—	.10	.20	.35
	1968	13.890	—	.10	.20	.40
	1969	13.890	—	.10	.20	.40
	1970	11.901	—	.10	.20	.40
	1971	7.524	—	.15	.20	.40

Rev: Llama in low relief.

247.2	1972	19.441	—	.10	.20	.40
	1973	14.951	—	.10	.20	.40

Obv: Small arms.

260	1973	Inc. Ab.	—	.10	.20	.40
	1974/1	—	—	.10	.20	.40
	1974	14.518	—	.10	.20	.40
	1975	—	—	.10	.20	.40

265	1975	62.682	—	.10	.20	.30
	1976	369.828	—	.10	.20	.30
	1977	18.943	—	.10	.20	.30

9.3500 g, .900 GOLD, .2706 oz AGW
150th Anniversary Battle of Ayacucho

268	1976	.010	—	—	110.00	175.00

SOL

25.0000 g, .900 SILVER, .7234 oz ASW
Lima Mint
Type I
Obv: Small wreath above shield has ribbon ties.
Rev: Shield below liberty's hand is tilted.
Santiago issues have LIMA on the coin.

KM#	Date	Mintage	Fine	VF	XF	Unc
196.1	1864/54 YB	—	6.00	8.50	12.00	55.00
	1864/54 Y.B	—	6.00	8.50	12.00	55.00
	1864/54 Y.B Roman I in date					
		—	6.00	8.50	12.00	55.00
	1864/54 Y.B Y.B upside down					
		—	6.00	8.50	12.00	55.00
	1864/54 Y.B R-B on stems/ribbon by date					
		—	9.00	16.00	30.00	90.00
	1865/55 YB	—	6.00	9.00	14.00	65.00
	1865/55 Y.B	—	6.00	9.00	14.00	65.00
	1865/55 Y.B/B.B					
		—	6.00	9.00	14.00	65.00
	1866/56 YB	—	6.00	8.00	11.00	40.00
	1866/56 Y.B	—	6.00	9.00	12.00	65.00
	1866/56 Y.B	—	6.00	8.00	11.00	40.00
	1867/57 Y.B	—	6.00	8.00	11.00	40.00
	1868/58 Y.B	—	6.00	8.00	11.00	40.00
	1868/58 Y.B BP on rev., left side					
		—	6.00	9.00	14.00	65.00

NOTE: Many minor die varieties, all coins are overdates.

Obv: DERTEANO on bottom row of coins falling from cornucopia.

196.2	1864/54 Y.B Arabic date					
		—	60.00	150.00	400.00	1500.
	1864/54 Y.B Roman I in date					
		—	100.00	175.00	500.00	2000.
	1864 Y.B Arabic date					
		—	—	—	—	Rare

NOTE: There are numerous minor die varieties such as D's in the denticles around the border on the obv.

Type II

196.3	1868 YB Roman I					
		—	6.00	9.00	14.00	65.00
	1868 YB Arabic 1/Roman I					
	1868 YB Arabic 1					
		—	10.00	20.00	35.00	100.00
	1868 YB Arabic 1 BP on rev., left side					
		—	6.00	8.00	11.00	40.00
	1868 YB Arabic 1 Llama has 5 legs					
		—	6.00	9.00	14.00	70.00
	1869 YB Arabic 1					
		—	6.00	7.50	10.00	30.00
	1869 YB Arabic 1 BP on rev., left side					
		—	6.00	7.50	11.00	40.00
	1869 YB Roman I					
		—	6.00	8.00	11.00	40.00
	1870 YJ	—	6.00	7.50	11.00	40.00
	1870 YJ dot below 7 in date					
		—	6.00	7.50	11.00	40.00
	1871 YJ	—	6.00	7.50	10.00	30.00
	1871 YJ dot above 1 in date					
		—	6.00	7.50	10.00	30.00
	1871 YJ dot below 1 in date					
		—	6.00	7.50	10.00	30.00
	1872 YJ	—	6.00	7.50	10.00	30.00
	1873 YJ	—	10.00	17.50	32.50	120.00
	1874 YJ	—	6.00	7.50	10.00	30.00
	1875 YJ	—	6.00	7.50	10.00	35.00

NOTE: Many minor die varieties exist.

Santiago Mint

196.4	1873 LD Arabic 1					
		.445	7.00	14.00	22.00	60.00
	1873 LD/backwards D, Arabic 1					
		—	10.00	17.00	30.00	90.00
	1873 LD Roman I					
		—	8.00	15.00	25.00	70.00

NOTE: Many minor die varieties exist.

Type III
Letters R.B. on stems flanking date.

196.5	1879 YJ	—	6.00	8.50	12.00	55.00
	1880/70 YJ	—	17.50	37.50	75.00	300.00
	1880/8 YJ	—	12.00	25.00	50.00	200.00
	1880 YJ	—	12.00	25.00	50.00	200.00

Letters R.B. on ribbon of wreath, 3 berries in bunch.

KM#	Date	Mintage	Fine	VF	XF	Unc
196.6	1880 YJ	—	20.00	45.00	85.00	350.00

2 berries in bunch.

196.7	1880 YJ	—	20.00	45.00	85.00	350.00

W/o extra letters, 2 berries in bunch.

196.8	1880 YJ	—	12.00	25.00	50.00	200.00

NOTE: Many minor die varieties exist.

Type IV

196.9	1881 BF	—	6.00	12.00	20.00	60.00

Rev: Letters R.L. on base of column.

196.10	1881 BF	—	6.00	12.00	20.00	60.00

NOTE: Many minor die varieties exist.

Type V
B.F. on rev., left side.

196.11	1881 BF	—	6.00	9.00	14.00	65.00

R.B. on rev., left side.

196.12	1881 BF	—	6.00	9.00	14.00	65.00
	1882 BF	—	6.00	8.50	12.00	55.00

F.D. on rev., left side.

196.13	1882 BF	—	6.00	8.50	12.00	55.00

FD on rev. at base of column.

196.14	1882 BF	—	6.00	9.00	14.00	65.00
	1882 FN	—	6.00	10.00	16.00	70.00

NOTE: Many minor die varieties exist.

Type VI
F.D. on rev., left side.

196.15	1882 FN	—	6.00	9.00	14.00	65.00

FD on rev. at base of column.

196.16	1882 FN	—	6.00	9.00	14.00	65.00

FD on rev., RB at base of column.

196.17	1882 FN	—	6.00	9.00	14.00	65.00

NOTE: Many minor die varieties exist.

Type VII
B.F. on rev., left side.

196.18	1883 FN	—	6.00	8.50	12.00	55.00

F.D. on rev., left side.

196.19	1883 FN	—	6.00	8.50	12.00	55.00
	1884 BD	—	6.00	7.50	10.00	35.00
	1884 RD	—	6.00	7.50	10.00	35.00

NOTE: Many minor die varieties exist.

Type VIII
F.D. on rev., left side.

196.20	1884 BD	—	6.00	7.50	10.00	35.00
	1884 BD/BF	—	6.00	8.00	11.00	40.00
	1884 RD	—	6.00	7.50	10.00	35.00

Type IX
W/o extra initials.

196.21	1884 RD	—	7.00	9.00	12.00	50.00

Type X

196.22	1885 RD	—	6.00	7.50	15.00	30.00
	1885 RD/BD	—	6.00	7.50	15.00	30.00
	1885 RD/BF	—	6.00	7.50	15.00	30.00
	1885 TD	—	6.00	7.50	15.00	30.00
	1885 TD/BD	—	6.00	7.50	15.00	30.00
	1885 TD/BF	—	6.00	7.50	15.00	30.00
	1885 TD/TF	—	6.00	7.50	15.00	30.00
	1886/5 TF	—	17.50	37.50	75.00	300.00
	1886/5 TF/BR					
		—	17.50	37.50	100.00	350.00
	1886 TF	—	6.00	8.50	12.00	55.00
	1887/6 TF	—	6.00	7.50	10.00	30.00
	1887/6 TF/BF					
		—	6.00	7.50	10.00	30.00
	1887 TF	—	6.00	7.00	9.50	27.50
	1887 TF/BF	—	6.00	7.00	9.50	27.50

NOTE: Many minor die varieties exist.

Rev: R on base of column.

196.23	1885 RD	—	6.00	8.50	12.00	50.00

PERU 1408

Type XI
Rev: Shield below Liberty's hand is tilted. UN SOL is in a straight line.

KM#	Date	Mintage	Fine	VF	XF	Unc
196.24	1888 TF	3.147	6.00	7.00	10.00	30.00
	1888 TF/BF I.A.		6.00	7.00	10.00	30.00
	1889 TF	2.842	6.00	7.00	10.00	27.50
	1889 TF/BF I.A.		6.00	7.00	10.00	27.50
	1890/80 TF/BF	2.304	6.00	9.00	14.00	55.00
	1890 TF/BF Inc. Ab.		6.00	7.00	10.00	27.50
	1890 TF Inc. Ab.		6.00	7.00	10.00	27.50
	1891/81 TF	2.981	6.00	8.00	11.00	32.50
	1891 TF/BF Inc. Ab.		6.00	7.00	10.00	27.50
	1891 TF Inc. Ab.		6.00	7.00	10.00	27.50
	1892 TF	2.270	6.00	7.00	10.00	27.50
	1892 TF/BF Inc. Ab.		6.00	7.00	10.00	27.50

NOTE: Date varieties exist.

Rev. leg: Inverted V for A in LA.

| 196.25 | 1889 TF/BF | | 6.00 | 8.00 | 11.00 | 32.50 |

NOTE: Many minor die varieties exist, especially for the 1888 issues.

Type XII
Legends have smaller lettering, 37mm.

196.26	1893 TF (error date)		35.00	50.00	95.00	200.00
	1893 TF	—	6.00	7.00	10.00	27.50
	1894 TF	4.358	6.00	7.00	10.00	27.50
	1895 TF	4.111	6.00	7.00	10.00	27.50
	1896 TF	2.511	6.00	8.00	11.00	40.00
	1896 F Inc. Ab.		6.00	7.00	10.00	27.50
	1897 JF	.234	7.00	12.00	20.00	90.00
	1914 FG	.620	6.00	7.00	8.00	22.50
	1915/4 FG	1.736	—	—	—	—
	1915 FG Inc. Ab.		6.00	7.00	8.00	20.00

NOTE: Varieties exist.

Rev: LIBERTAD incuse, 36.5mm.

| 196.27 | 1916 FG | 1.927 | 6.00 | 7.00 | 8.00 | 20.00 |

Type XIII
Rev: LIBERTAD in relief.

| 196.28 | 1916 FG Inc. Ab. | | 6.00 | 7.00 | 8.00 | 20.00 |

25.0000 g, .500 SILVER, .4019 oz ASW
Obv: Fineness omitted. Rev: LIBERTAD in relief.

KM#	Date	Mintage	Fine	VF	XF	Unc
217.1	1922				Rare	
	1923	3,600	15.00	32.50	75.00	300.00

Rev: LIBERTAD incuse.

| 217.2 | 1923 | 1,400 | 30.00 | 75.00 | 200.00 | 600.00 |

Philadelphia Mint
Small letters

218.1	1923	*2.369	BV	4.00	8.00	15.00
	1924/3	*3.113	5.00	10.00	20.00	40.00
	1924	Inc. Ab.	BV	4.00	8.00	15.00
	1925	*1.291	BV	4.00	8.00	17.50
	1926	*2.157	BV	4.00	8.00	15.00

*NOTE: The Philadelphia and Lima strikings may be distinguished by the fact that the letters in the legends are smaller on those pieces produced at Philadelphia. All bear the name of the Lima Mint.

Lima Mint
Large letters
Obv: Engraver's initials on stems flanking date.

218.2	1924	.096	5.00	10.00	20.00	65.00
	1925	1.005	BV	4.00	8.00	15.00
	1930	.076	BV	4.00	8.00	15.00
	1931	.024	BV	4.00	9.00	18.00
	1933	5.000	6.00	12.00	20.00	40.00
	1934	2.855	BV	3.00	6.00	12.00
	1935	.695	BV	4.00	8.00	17.50

BRASS

222	1943	10.000	.35	1.25	3.00	8.00
	1944	Inc. Ab.	.35	1.25	3.00	7.00
	1945	—	.50	1.50	3.50	9.00
	1946	1.752	.50	1.50	3.00	8.00
	1947	3.302	.35	1.00	2.00	6.00
	1948	1.992	.35	1.00	2.00	6.00
	1949/8	.751	2.00	4.00	7.00	20.00
	1949	Inc. Ab.	3.00	5.00	8.00	22.00
	1950	1.249	7.00	10.00	15.00	25.00
	1951/0	2.094	.25	.50	1.50	6.00
	1951	Inc. Ab.	.25	.50	1.50	6.00
	1952	2.037	.25	.50	1.50	6.00
	1953	1.243	3.00	6.00	10.00	25.00
	1954	1.220	.35	.75	1.75	6.00
	1955	1.323	.35	.75	1.75	6.00
	1956	3.450	.15	.35	.75	3.00

KM#	Date	Mintage	Fine	VF	XF	Unc
222	1957	3.086	.15	.35	1.00	5.00
	1958	3.390	.15	.35	.75	3.00
	1959	4.975	.15	.35	1.00	5.00
	1960	5.800	.15	.35	.75	1.50
	1961	5.200	.15	.35	.75	2.00
	1962	5.102	.15	.35	.75	1.50
	1963	5.499	.15	.35	.75	2.00
	1964	5.888	.15	.35	.75	2.00
	1965	5.504	.15	.35	.75	2.00
	1965	—	—	—	Proof	75.00

NOTE: Date varieties exist.

400th Anniversary Of Lima Mint

| 240 | 1965 | 3.103 | — | — | .10 | .30 | .75 |
| | 1965 | — | — | — | — | Proof | 650.00 |

248	1966	16.410	—	—	.10	.25	.50
	1966	1.000	—	—	—	Proof	5.00
	1967	13.920	—	—	.10	.25	.50
	1968	12.260	—	—	.10	.25	.50
	1969	12.260	—	—	.10	.25	.50
	1970	12.336	—	—	.10	.25	.50
	1971	11.927	—	—	.10	.25	.50
	1972	3.945	—	—	.10	.25	.50
	1973	12.856	—	—	.10	.25	.50
	1974	14.966	—	—	.10	.25	.50
	1975	—	—	—	.10	.25	.50

21mm

| 266.1 | 1975 | 354.485 | — | — | .10 | .25 |
| | 1976 | 114.660 | — | — | .10 | .25 |

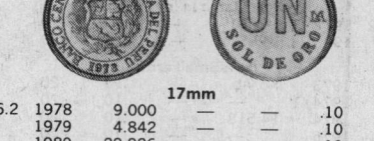

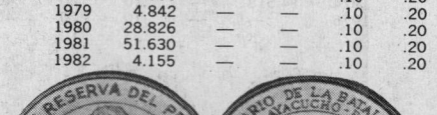

17mm

266.2	1978	9.000	—	—	.10	.20
	1979	4.842	—	—	.10	.20
	1980	28.826	—	—	.10	.20
	1981	51.630	—	—	.10	.20
	1982	4.155	—	—	.10	.20

23.4000 g, .900 GOLD, .6772 oz AGW
150th Anniversary Battle of Ayacucho

| 269 | 1976 | .010 | — | — | — | 450.00 |

5 SOLES

8.0645 g, .900 GOLD, .2334 oz AGW

| 192 | 1863 Y.B. | — | 125.00 | 175.00 | 275.00 | 375.00 |

2.3404 g, .900 GOLD, .0677 oz AGW
Lima Mint

KM#	Date	Mintage	Fine	VF	XF	Unc
235	1956	4,510	—	—	—	50.00
	1957	2,146	—	—	—	50.00
	1958	3,325	— Reported, not confirmed			
	1959	1,536	—	—	—	50.00
	1960	8,133	—	—	—	50.00
	1961	1,154	—	—	—	50.00
	1962	1,550	—	—	—	50.00
	1963	3,945	—	—	—	50.00
	1964	2,063	—	—	—	50.00
	1965	.014	—	—	—	50.00
	1966	4,738	—	—	—	50.00
	1967	3,651	—	—	—	50.00
	1968	129 pcs.	— Reported, not confirmed			
	1969	127 pcs.	—	—	—	175.00

COPPER-NICKEL

252	1969	10.000	.20	.40	.60	1.50

150th Anniversary of Independence

254	1971	3.480	.20	.40	.80	2.00

Regular Issue

257	1972	2.068	—	.10	.35	1.00
	1973	.475	—	.10	.35	1.00
	1974		—	.10	.35	1.50
	1975		—	.10	.35	1.50

267	1975	—	—	.10	.35	1.00
	1976	17.016	—	.10	.35	1.00
	1977	94.272	—	.10	.35	1.00

BRASS

271	1978	38.016	—	.10	.20	.50
	1979	64.524	—	.10	.20	.50
	1980	76.964	—	.10	.20	.50
	1981	31.632	—	.10	.20	.50
	1982	23.262	—	.10	.20	.50
	1983	650 pcs.	—	—	—	—

10 SOLES

16.1290 g, .900 GOLD, .4667 oz AGW

KM#	Date	Mintage	Fine	VF	XF	Unc
193	1863YB	—	225.00	250.00	300.00	500.00

4.6807 g, .900 GOLD, .1354 oz AGW
Lima Mint

236	1956	5,410	—	—	BV	75.00
	1957	1,300	—	—	BV	75.00
	1958	3,325	— Reported, not confirmed			
	1959	1,103	—	—	BV	75.00
	1960	7,178	—	—	BV	75.00
	1961	1,634	—	—	BV	75.00
	1962	1,676	—	—	BV	75.00
	1963	3,372	—	—	BV	75.00
	1964	1,554	—	—	BV	75.00
	1965	.014	—	—	BV	75.00
	1966	2,601	—	—	BV	75.00
	1967	3,002	—	—	BV	75.00
	1968	100 pcs.	—	—	BV	100.00	200.00
	1969	100 pcs.	—	—	BV	100.00	200.00

COPPER-NICKEL

253	1969	15.000	—	.25	.50	.75	1.75

150th Anniversary of Independence

255	1971	2.460	—	.25	.50	1.00	2.50

258	1972	2.235	—	.10	.40	1.25
	1973	1.765	—	.10	.40	1.25
	1974		—	.10	.40	1.25
	1975		—	.10	.40	1.25

BRASS
Obv: Large arms, small letters.

272.1	1978	46.970	—	.10	.40	.75

Obv: Small arm, large letters.

272.2	1979	82.220	—	.10	.40	.75
	1980	99.595	—	.10	.40	.75

KM#	Date	Mintage	Fine	VF	XF	Unc
272.2	1981	25.660	—	.10	.40	.75
	1982	61.035	—	.10	.40	.75
	1983	15.820	—	.10	.40	.75

Admiral Grau

287	1984	30.000	—	—	.10	.25

20 SOLES

32.2581 g, .900 GOLD, .9334 oz AGW

194	1863 YB	—	450.00	475.00	500.00	650.00

9.3614 g, .900 GOLD, .2709 oz AGW
Lima Mint

229	1950	1,800	—	—	BV	150.00
	1951	9,264	—	—	BV	150.00
	1952	424 pcs.	—	—	BV	200.00
	1953	1,435	—	—	BV	150.00
	1954	1,732	—	—	BV	150.00
	1955	1,971	—	—	BV	150.00
	1956	1,201	—	—	BV	150.00
	1957	.011	—	—	BV	150.00
	1958	.011	—	—	BV	150.00
	1959	.012	—	—	BV	150.00
	1960	7,753	—	—	BV	150.00
	1961	1,825	—	—	BV	150.00
	1962	2,282	—	—	BV	150.00
	1963	3,892	—	—	BV	150.00
	1964	1,302	—	—	BV	150.00
	1965	.012	—	—	BV	150.00
	1966	4,001	—	—	BV	150.00
	1967	5,003	—	—	BV	150.00
	1968	640 pcs.	—	—	BV	200.00
	1969	640 pcs.	—	—	BV	200.00

8.0000 g, .900 SILVER, .2315 oz ASW
400th Anniversary of Lima Mint

241	1965	.150	—	—	—	5.00

7.9700 g, .900 SILVER, .2306 oz ASW
1866 Peru-Spain Naval Battle

249	1966	4,001	—	—	—	20.00

PERU 1410

50 SOLES

33.4363 g, .900 GOLD, .9675 oz AGW

KM#	Date	Mintage	Fine	VF	XF	Unc
219	1930	5,584	475.00	625.00	950.00	1600.
	1931	5,538	475.00	625.00	950.00	1500.
	1967	.010	—	—	—	600.00
	1968	300 pcs.	—	—	—	1000.
	1969	403 pcs.	—	—	—	1000.

23.4056 g, .900 GOLD, .6772 oz AGW
Lima Mint

230	1950	1,927	—	—	BV	400.00
	1951	5,292	—	—	BV	400.00
	1952	1,201	—	—	BV	400.00
	1953	1,464	—	—	BV	400.00
	1954	1,839	—	—	BV	400.00
	1955	1,898	—	—	BV	400.00
	1956	.011	—	—	BV	400.00
	1957	.011	—	—	BV	400.00
	1958	.011	—	—	BV	400.00
	1959	5,734	—	—	BV	400.00
	1960	2,139	—	—	BV	400.00
	1961	1,110	—	—	BV	400.00
	1962	3,319	—	—	BV	400.00
	1963	3,089	—	—	BV	400.00
	1964/3	2,425	—	—	BV	400.00
	1964	Inc. Ab.	—	—	BV	400.00
	1965	.023	—	—	BV	400.00
	1966	3,409	—	—	BV	400.00
	1967	5,805	—	—	BV	400.00
	1968	443 pcs.	—	—	BV	500.00
	1969	443 pcs.	—	—	BV	500.00
	1970	553 pcs.	—	—	BV	500.00

400th Anniversary of Lima Mint

242	1965	.017	—	—	BV	400.00

Peru-Spain Naval Battle

250	1966	6,409	—	—	BV	550.00

21.4500 g, .800 SILVER, .5517 oz ASW
150th Anniversary of Independence

256	1971	.100	—	—	—	8.00

ALUMINUM-BRONZE

KM#	Date	Mintage	Fine	VF	XF	Unc
273	1979	1.323	—	.10	.20	.35
	1980	42.573	—	.10	.20	.35
	1981	19.923	—	.10	.20	.35
	1982 LIMA	18.471	—	.10	.20	.35
	1982		—	.10	.20	.35
	1983	8.175	—	.10	.20	.35

BRASS
Admiral Grau

297	1984	—	—	—	—	.10
	1985	—	—	—	—	.10

100 SOLES

46.8071 g, .900 GOLD, 1.3544 oz AGW
Lima Mint

231	1950	1,176	—	—	BV	750.00
	1951	8,241	—	—	BV	700.00
	1952	126 pcs.	—	—	2000.	3000.
	1953	498 pcs.	—	—	BV	800.00
	1954	1,808	—	—	BV	700.00
	1955	901 pcs.	—	—	BV	700.00
	1956	1,159	—	—	BV	700.00
	1957	550 pcs.	—	—	BV	800.00
	1958	101 pcs.	—	—	5000.	7000.
	1959	4,710	—	—	BV	700.00
	1960	2,207	—	—	BV	700.00
	1961	6,982	—	—	BV	700.00
	1962	9,678	—	—	BV	700.00
	1963	7,342	—	—	BV	700.00
	1964	.011	—	—	BV	700.00
	1965	.023	—	—	BV	700.00
	1966	3,409	—	—	BV	700.00
	1967	6,431	—	—	BV	700.00
	1968	540 pcs.	—	—	BV	800.00
	1969	540 pcs.	—	—	BV	800.00
	1970	425 pcs.	—	—	BV	800.00

400th Anniversary of Lima Mint

243	1965	.027	—	—	BV	700.00

1866 Peru-Spain Naval Battle

251	1966	6,253	—	—	BV	825.00

22.4500 g, .800 SILVER, .5774 oz AGW
Centennial Peru-Japan Trade Relations

KM#	Date	Mintage	Fine	VF	XF	Unc
261	1973	.375	—	—	—	9.50

COPPER-NICKEL

283	1980	100.000	—	.10	.35	.70
	1982		—	.10	.35	.70

BRASS
Admiral Grau

288	1984	20.000	—	.10	.20	.50

200 SOLES

22.0000 g, .800 SILVER, .5659 oz ASW
Aviation Heroes

262	1974	.025	—	—	—	15.00
	1975	.090	—	—	—	12.00
	1976	.025	—	—	—	15.00
	1977	3,000	—	—	—	20.00
	1978	3,000	—	—	—	20.00

400 SOLES

28.1000 g, .900 SILVER, .8131 oz ASW
150th Anniversary Battle of Ayacucho
Obv: Similar to 200 Soles, Y#77.

270	1976	—	—	—	—	12.50

500 SOLES

BRASS
Admiral Grau

KM#	Date	Mintage	Fine	VF	XF	Unc
289	1984	16.962	—	.10	.20	.75
	1985	—	—	.10	.20	.75

1000 SOLES
15.5500 g, .500 SILVER, .2500 oz ASW
Battle of Iquique
Similar to 5000 Soles, KM#276.

274	1979	.200	—	Reported, not confirmed

National Congress

275	1979	.200	—	—	—	5.00

5000 SOLES

33.6300 g, .925 SILVER, 1.0000 oz ASW
Battle of Iquique

276	1979	.100	—	—	—	18.50

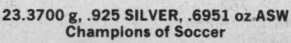

23.3700 g, .925 SILVER, .6951 oz ASW
Champions of Soccer

284	1982	8,250	—	—	Proof	40.00

Champions of Soccer

KM#	Date	Mintage	Fine	VF	XF	Unc
285	1982	8,300	—	—	Proof	40.00

10000 SOLES

16.8000 g, .925 SILVER, .4997 oz ASW
Battle of La Brena and General Caceres

286	1982	.100	—	—	—	5.50

50000 SOLES

16.9700 gm., .917 GOLD, .5004 oz AGW
Alfonso Urgarte

277	1979	.010	—	—	—	300.00

Elias Aguirre

278	1979	.010	—	—	—	300.00

F. Garcia Calderon

279	1979	.010	—	—	—	300.00

100000 SOLES

33.9000 g, .917 GOLD, .9995 oz AGW
Francisco Bolognese

280	1979	.010	—	—	—	550.00

Andres A. Caceres
Obv: Similar to KM#280.

KM#	Date	Mintage	Fine	VF	XF	Unc
281	1979	.010	—	—	—	550.00

Miguel Grau

282	1979	.010	—	—	—	550.00

PROVISIONAL COINAGE
5 CENTAVOS

COPPER-NICKEL

197	1879	12.000	1.00	1.75	3.50	6.00
	1880	2.000	1.50	3.00	6.00	10.00

10 CENTAVOS

COPPER-NICKEL

198	1879	3.005	1.00	2.00	6.00	10.00
	1880	4.000	1.00	1.50	2.50	5.00

20 CENTAVOS

COPPER-NICKEL

199	1879	.498	4.00	8.00	20.00	75.00

1/2 REAL

1.2500 g, .900 SILVER, .0362 oz ASW
Ayacucho Mint

202	1882 LM	—	200.00	400.00	750.00	1500.

NOTE: Most specimens have been holed (and sometimes repaired) and are worth much less than market valuations shown.

PERU

PESETA

5.0000 g, .900 SILVER, .1447 oz ASW

KM#	Date	Mintage	Fine	VF	XF	Unc
200	1880 B.F.	—	2.00	4.00	8.00	20.00

5 PESETAS

25.0000 g, .900 SILVER, .7234 oz ASW
Lima Mint
Obv: B under wreath.

201.1	1880 BF	—	17.50	22.50	37.50	150.00

Obv: W/dot after B under wreath.

201.2	1880 BF	—	10.00	16.00	32.00	125.00

Ayacucho Mint
Rev: Similar to KM#201.1.

201.3	1881 B	—	80.00	200.00	375.00	900.00
	1882 LM	—	45.00	90.00	150.00	400.00

MONETARY REFORM
100 Centimos = 1 Inti

CENTIMO

BRASS

KM#	Date	Mintage	Fine	VF	XF	Unc
291	1985	—	—	—	—	.10

5 CENTIMOS

BRASS

292	1985	—	—	—	—	.10

10 CENTIMOS

BRASS

293	1985	—	—	—	—	.10
	1986	—	—	—	—	.10
	1987	—	—	—	—	.10

20 CENTIMOS

BRASS

KM#	Date	Mintage	Fine	VF	XF	Unc
294	1985	—	—	—	—	.15
	1986	—	—	—	—	.15

50 CENTIMOS

BRASS

295	1985	—	—	—	—	.20
	1986	—	—	—	—	.20

INTI

COPPER-NICKEL

296	1985	—	—	—	—	.50
	1986	—	—	—	—	.50
	1987	—	—	—	—	.50

100 INTIS

11.1100 g, .925 SILVER, .3271 oz ASW
150th Anniversary of Birth of Marshal Caceres

298	1986	.010	—	—	—	5.50

200 INTIS

22.0400 g, .925 SILVER, .6543 oz ASW
150th Anniversary of Birth of Marshal Caceres

299	1986	—	—	—	—	9.50

TRADE COINAGE

1/5 LIBRA (POUND)

1.5976 g, .917 GOLD, .0471 oz AGW
Lima Mint

KM#	Date	Mintage	Fine	VF	XF	Unc
210	1905 ROZF	.045	—	BV	27.50	35.00
	1905 GOZF	I.A.	—	BV	27.50	35.00
	1906 GOZF	.106	—	BV	27.50	35.00
	1907 GOZF	.031	—	BV	27.50	35.00
	1907 GOZG	—	—	BV	27.50	35.00
	1908	—	—	Reported, not confirmed		
	1909	—	—	Reported, not confirmed		
	1910 GOZG	—	—	BV	27.50	35.00
	1911 GOZF	.062	—	BV	27.50	35.00
	1911 GOZG	—	—	BV	27.50	35.00
	1912 GOZG	—	—	BV	27.50	35.00
	1912 POZG	—	—	BV	27.50	35.00
	1913 POZG	.060	—	BV	27.50	35.00
	1914 POZG	.025	—	BV	27.50	35.00

KM#	Date	Mintage	Fine	VF	XF	Unc
210	1914 PBLG	I.A.	—	BV	27.50	35.00
	1915	.010	—	BV	27.50	35.00
	1916	.013	—	Reported, not confirmed		
	1917	3,896	—	BV	27.50	35.00
	1918	.016	—	BV	27.50	35.00
	1919	.010	—	BV	27.50	35.00
	1920	.072	—	BV	27.50	35.00
	1921	—	—	Reported, not confirmed		
	1922	8,110	—	BV	27.50	35.00
	1923	.027	—	BV	27.50	35.00
	1924	—	—	BV	27.50	35.00
	1925	.020	—	BV	27.50	35.00
	1926	.011	—	BV	27.50	35.00
	1927	.014	—	BV	27.50	35.00
	1928	9,322	—	BV	27.50	35.00
	1929	8,971	—	BV	27.50	35.00
	1930	9,991	—	BV	27.50	35.00
	1931	8,722	—	Reported, not confirmed		
	1932	8,430	—	Reported, not confirmed		
	1946	.010	—	Reported, not confirmed		
	1947	.010	—	Reported, not confirmed		
	1948	.015	—	Reported, not confirmed		
	1949	.011	—	Reported, not confirmed		
	1951 BBR	4,637	—	Reported, not confirmed		
	1952 BBR	6,337	—	Reported, not confirmed		
	1953 BBR	9,821	—	—	—	40.00
	1954	9,473	—	Reported, not confirmed		
	1955 ZBR	.010	—	—	—	40.00
	1956 ZBR	8,116	—	Reported, not confirmed		
	1957 ZBR	6,345	—	Reported, not confirmed		
	1958 ZBR	5,098	—	—	—	32.50
	1959 ZBR	6,308	—	—	—	32.50
	1960 ZBR	6,083	—	—	—	32.50
	1961 ZBR	.012	—	—	—	32.50
	1962 ZBR	5,431	—	—	—	32.50
	1963 ZBR	.011	—	—	—	32.50
	1964 ZBR	.025	—	—	—	32.50
	1965 ZBR	.019	—	—	—	32.50
	1966 ZBR	.060	—	—	—	32.50
	1967 BBR	9,914	—	—	—	32.50
	1968 BBR	4,781	—	—	—	32.50
	1968 BBB	I.A.	—	—	—	32.50
	1969 BBB	.015	—	—	—	32.50

1/2 LIBRA (POUND)

3.9940 g, .917 GOLD, .1177 oz AGW

209	1902 ROZF	7,800	—	BV	60.00	70.00
	1903 ROZF	7,245	—	BV	60.00	70.00
	1904 ROZF	8,360	—	BV	60.00	70.00
	1905 ROZF	8,010	—	BV	60.00	70.00
	1905 GOZF	I.A.	—	BV	60.00	70.00
	1906 GOZF	9,176	—	BV	60.00	70.00
	1907 GOZF	.010	—	BV	60.00	70.00
	1907 GOZG	I.A.	—	BV	60.00	70.00
	1908 GOZG	8,180	—	BV	60.00	70.00
	1909 GOZG	6,799	—	Reported, not confirmed		
	1910 GOZG	4,221	—	Reported, not confirmed		
	1911 GOZG	.014	—	Reported, not confirmed		
	1912 GOZG	.016	—	Reported, not confirmed		
	1912 POZG	—	—	Reported, not confirmed		
	1913 POZG	.020	—	BV	60.00	70.00
	1914 PBLG	—	—	Reported, not confirmed		
	1915	—	—	Reported, not confirmed		
	1916	1,900	—	Reported, not confirmed		
	1917	8,133	—	Reported, not confirmed		
	1918	8,800	—	Reported, not confirmed		
	1919	8,765	—	Reported, not confirmed		
	1925	—	—	Reported, not confirmed		
	1926	—	—	Reported, not confirmed		
	1927	—	—	Reported, not confirmed		
	1928	—	—	Reported, not confirmed		
	1930	1,889	—	Reported, not confirmed		
	1940	—	—	Reported, not confirmed		
	1941	—	—	Reported, not confirmed		
	1946	7,750	—	Reported, not confirmed		
	1947	3,146	—	Reported, not confirmed		
	1948	.012	—	Reported, not confirmed		
	1949	.020	—	Reported, not confirmed		
	1950	5,890	—	Reported, not confirmed		
	1951	.018	—	Reported, not confirmed		
	1952 BBR	8,345	—	Reported, not confirmed		
	1953 BBR	9,210	—	—	—	65.00
	1954 BBR	9,220	—	Reported, not confirmed		
	1955 ZBR	.014	—	—	—	65.00
	1956 ZBR	7,385	—	Reported, not confirmed		
	1957 ZBR	8,472	—	Reported, not confirmed		
	1958 ZBR	.011	—	Reported, not confirmed		
	1959 ZBR	5,236	—	Reported, not confirmed		
	1960 ZBR	.016	—	Reported, not confirmed		
	1961 ZBR	752 pcs.	—	—	BV	100.00
	1962 ZBR	4,286	—	VF	BV	65.00
	1963 ZBR	908 pcs.	—	—	BV	100.00

KM#	Date	Mintage	Fine	VF	XF	Unc
209	1964 ZBR	.010	—	—	BV	65.00
	1965 ZBR	5,490	—	—	BV	65.00
	1966 ZBR	.044	—	—	BV	65.00
	1967 ZBR	—	—	—	BV	65.00
	1968 BBB	.014	—	—	BV	65.00
	1968 PBB	I.A.	—	—	BV	65.00
	1969 BBB	4,400	—	—	BV	65.00

LIBRA (POUND)

7.9881 g, .917 GOLD, .2354 oz AGW

KM#	Date	Mintage	Fine	VF	XF	Unc
207	1898 ROZF	—	—	—	BV	120.00	140.00
	1899 ROZF	—	—	—	BV	120.00	140.00
	1900 ROZF	.064	—	—	BV	120.00	140.00
	1901 ROZF	.081	—	—	BV	120.00	140.00
	1902 ROZF	.089	—	—	BV	120.00	140.00
	1903 ROZF	.100	—	—	BV	120.00	140.00
	1904 ROZF	.033	—	—	BV	120.00	140.00
	1905 ROZF	.141	—	—	BV	120.00	140.00
	1905 GOZF	—	—	—	BV	120.00	140.00
	1906 GOZF	.201	—	—	BV	120.00	140.00
	1907 GOZF	.123	—	—	BV	120.00	140.00
	1907 GOZG	I.A.	—	—	BV	120.00	140.00
	1908 GOZG	.036	—	—	BV	120.00	140.00
	1909 GOZG	.052	—	—	BV	120.00	140.00
	1910 GOZG	.047	—	—	BV	120.00	140.00
	1911 GOZG	.042	—	—	BV	120.00	140.00
	1912 GOZG	.054	—	—	BV	120.00	140.00
	1912 POZG	I.A.	—	—	BV	120.00	140.00
	1913 POZG	—	—	—	BV	120.00	140.00
	1914 POZG	—	—	—	BV	120.00	140.00
	1914 PBLG	.119	—	—	BV	120.00	140.00
	1915 PVG	.091	—	—	BV	120.00	140.00
	1915	Inc. Ab.	—	—	BV	120.00	140.00
	1916	.582	—	—	BV	120.00	140.00
	1917	1,928	—	—	BV	120.00	140.00
	1918	.600	—	—	BV	120.00	140.00
	1919	Inc. Ab.	—	—	BV	120.00	140.00
	1920	.152	—	—	BV	120.00	140.00
	1921	Inc. Ab.	—	—	BV	120.00	140.00
	1922	.013	—	—	BV	120.00	140.00
	1923	.015	—	—	BV	120.00	140.00
	1924	8,113	—	—	BV	120.00	140.00
	1925	9,068	—	—	BV	120.00	140.00
	1926	4,596	—	—	BV	120.00	140.00
	1927	8,360	—	—	BV	120.00	140.00
	1928	2,184	—	—	BV	120.00	140.00
	1929	3,119	—	—	BV	120.00	140.00
	1930	1,050	—	—	BV	120.00	140.00
	1931	—	—	Reported, not confirmed
	1932	—	—	Reported, not confirmed
	1940	—	—	Reported, not confirmed
	1951	—	—	Reported, not confirmed
	1959 ZBR	605 pcs.	—	—	BV	175.00
	1961 ZBR	402 pcs.	—	—	BV	175.00
	1962 ZBR	6,203	—	—	BV	140.00
	1963 ZBR	302 pcs.	—	—	BV	175.00
	1964 ZBR	.013	—	—	BV	140.00
	1965 ZBR	9,917	—	—	BV	140.00
	1966 ZBR	.039	—	—	BV	140.00
	1967 BBR	2,002	—	—	BV	140.00
	1968 BBB	7,307	—	—	BV	140.00
	1969 BBB	7,307	—	—	BV	140.00

PROOF SETS (PS)

KM#	Date	Mintage	Identification	Issue Price	Mkt. Val.
PS2	1965(5)	*10	KM237-240,290	—	1500.
PS3	1965(5)	—	KM220.5,221.2b,222,223.2-224.2	—	200.00
PS4	1966(5)	*1,000	KM244.1-247.1,248	—	16.50

*Estimated mintage.

PHILIPPINES

The Republic of the Philippines, an archipelago in the western Pacific 500 miles (805 km.) from the southeast coast of Asia, has an area of 115,830 sq. mi. (300,000 sq. km.) and a population of *62 million. Capital: Manila. The economy of the 7,000—island group is based on agriculture, forestry and fishing. Timber, coconut products, sugar and hemp are exported.

Migration to the Philippines began about 30,000 years ago when land bridges connected the islands with Borneo and Sumatra. Ferdinand Magellan claimed the islands for Spain in 1521. The first permanent settlement was established by Miguel de Legazpi at Cebu in April of 1565; Manila was established in 1572. A British expedition captured Manila and occupied the Spanish colony in Oct. of 1762, but it was returned to Spain by the treaty of Paris, 1763. Spain held the Philippines amid a growing movement of Filipino nationalism until 1898 when they were ceded to the United States at the end of the Spanish-American War. The Philippines became a self-governing commonwealth of the United States in 1935, and attained independence as the Republic of the Philippines on July 4, 1946.

RULERS
Spanish until 1898

MINT MARKS
(b) Brussels, privy marks only
BSP - Bangko Sentral Pilipinas
D - Denver, 1944-1945
(Lt) - Llantrisant
M, MA - Manila
S - San Francisco, 1903-1947
SGV - Madrid
(Sh) - Sherritt
(US) - United States
FM - Franklin Mint, U.S.A.*
(VDM) - Vereinigte Deutsche Metall Werks; Altona, W. Germany

*NOTE: From 1975 the Franklin Mint has produced coinage in up to 3 different qualities. Qualities of issue are designated in ( ) after each date and are defined as follows:

(M) MATTE - Normal circulation strike or a dull finish produced by sandblasting special uncirculated (polish finish) or proof quality dies.

(U) SPECIAL UNCIRCULATED - Polished or proof-like in appearance without any frosted features.

(P) PROOF - The highest quality obtainable having mirror-like fields and frosted features.

MONETARY SYSTEM
8 Octavos = 4 Quartos = 1 Real
8 Reales = 1 Peso

OCTAVO

COPPER
Mint mark: M

KM#	Date	Mintage	Good	VG	Fine	VF
5	1805F	—	15.00	30.00	50.00	80.00
	1806F	—	15.00	30.00	50.00	80.00

KM#	Date	Mintage	Fine	VF	XF	Unc
8	1820F	—	10.00	20.00	40.00	100.00
	1829F	—	60.00	80.00	150.00	500.00
	1830F	—	12.00	25.00	50.00	250.00

QUARTO

COPPER
Mint mark: M.
Similar to KM#7.

KM#	Date	Mintage	Good	VG	Fine	VF
6	1805F	—	8.00	12.50	25.00	40.00
	1806F	—	8.00	12.50	25.00	40.00
	1807F	—	8.00	12.50	25.00	40.00

KM#	Date	Mintage	VG	Fine	VF	XF
7	1817F	—	40.00	60.00	125.00	200.00
	1819 (retrograde) P181
		—	100.00	160.00	325.00	500.00
	1820F	—	10.00	20.00	40.00	60.00
	1821F	—	10.00	20.00	40.00	60.00
	1822F	—	—	—	Rare	—
	1822 (error) 2281 w/backwards 2's
		—	30.00	50.00	80.00	150.00
	1823F	—	15.00	25.00	45.00	100.00
	1824F	—	—	—	Rare	—
	1826F	—	10.00	20.00	40.00	60.00
	1827F	—	—	—	Rare	—
	1828F	—	10.00	20.00	45.00	80.00
	1829F	—	10.00	20.00	40.00	65.00
	1830F	—	10.00	20.00	40.00	65.00
	1831F	—	40.00	60.00	80.00	150.00
	1833F	—	40.00	60.00	80.00	150.00

KM#	Date	Mintage	Good	VG	Fine	VF
9	1822F	—	25.00	40.00	60.00	150.00
	1823F	—	15.00	25.00	45.00	90.00
	1824F	—	30.00	50.00	80.00	200.00

Mint mark: MA

10	1834F	—	12.00	20.00	40.00	60.00

13	1835F	—	30.00	50.00	80.00	150.00

2 QUARTOS

COPPER
Mint mark: MA

11	1834F	—	60.00	120.00	200.00	325.00

14	1835F	—	50.00	80.00	150.00	225.00

4 QUARTOS

COPPER
Mint mark: MA

KM#	Date	Mintage	Good	VG	Fine	VF
12	1834F	—	100.00	150.00	225.00	450.00

| 15 | 1835F | — | 80.00 | 120.00 | 180.00 | 300.00 |

COUNTERSTAMPED COINAGE
(8 REALES)
MANILA/1828

Type I
Obv. c/s: MANILA/1828 within serrated circle.
Rev. leg: HABILITADO POR EL REY N.S.D. FERN. VII.
around crowned Spanish royal arms.

This counterstamp was inaugurated on October 13, 1828 by the Captain-General of the Philippines. The outer serrated border was intended to obliterate the legends on the foreign dollars being overstruck. This failed to work satisfactorily and this method was soon discontinued.

SILVER
c/s: Type I on Bolivia 8 Soles, KM#97.

KM#	Date	Year	Good	VG	Fine	VF
16	1828	(1827 JM)	125.00	200.00	300.00	500.00

c/s: Type I on Bolivia 8 Reales, KM#84.
| 17 | 1828 | (1808-25) | 125.00 | 200.00 | 225.00 | 300.00 |

c/s: Type I on Mexico 8 Reales, KM#376.
| 18 | 1828 | (1823-5) | 125.00 | 200.00 | 250.00 | 400.00 |

c/s: Type I on Mexico 8 Reales, KM#309.
| 19 | 1828 | (1822 JM) | — | — | Rare | — |

c/s: Type I on Mexico 8 Reales, KM#310.
| 20 | 1828 | | | | | |
| | (1822-23 JM) | 225.00 | 400.00 | 600.00 | 800.00 |

c/s: Type I on Mexico 8 Reales, KM#376.
| 38 | 1828 | (1823-24) | 100.00 | 175.00 | 300.00 | 300.00 |

c/s: Type I on Mexico 8 Reales, KM#377.
| 21 | 1828 | (1824-8) | 100.00 | 175.00 | 200.00 | 300.00 |

c/s: Type I on Peru (Lima) 8 Reales, KM#117.1.
| 22 | 1828 | (1810-24) | 100.00 | 160.00 | 200.00 | 300.00 |

c/s: Type I on Peru (Lima) 8 Reales, KM#136.
| 23 | 1828 | (1822-3) | 100.00 | 160.00 | 200.00 | 300.00 |

c/s: Type I on Peru (Lima) 8 Reales, KM#142.1.
| 24 | 1828 | (1825-8) | 80.00 | 150.00 | 200.00 | 350.00 |

c/s: Type I on Peru (Lima) 8 Reales, KM#142.3.
| 25 | 1828 | (1828) | 65.00 | 125.00 | 175.00 | 300.00 |

c/s: Type I on Peru (Cuzco) 8 Reales, KM#142.2.
| 26 | 1828 | (1826-28) | 80.00 | 150.00 | 200.00 | 300.00 |

NOTE: Other coin types may exist with this particular counterstamp.

MANILA/1828

Type II
Obv. c/s: MANILA/1828. Rev: Crowned Spanish royal arms without legends and serrated circles.

SILVER
c/s: Type II on Bolivia 8 Reales, KM#84.
| 27 | 1828 | (1808-25) | 90.00 | 160.00 | 200.00 | 300.00 |

c/s: Type II on Mexico 8 Reales, KM#376.
| 28 | 1828 | (1823-25) | 100.00 | 175.00 | 200.00 | 300.00 |

c/s: Type II on Mexico 8 Reales, KM#377.
| 29 | 1828 | (1824-28) | 90.00 | 160.00 | 200.00 | 300.00 |

c/s: Type II on Peru 8 Reales, KM#117.1.
| 30 | 1828 | (1810-24) | 70.00 | 130.00 | 200.00 | 300.00 |

c/s: Type II on Peru 8 Reales, KM#136.
| 31 | 1828 | (1822-23) | 70.00 | 130.00 | 200.00 | 300.00 |

c/s: Type II on Peru 8 Reales, KM#142.1.
| 32 | 1828 | (1825-28) | 80.00 | 150.00 | 200.00 | 325.00 |

c/s: Type II on Peru 8 Reales, KM#142.3.
| 33 | 1828 | (1828) | 60.00 | 90.00 | 130.00 | 200.00 |

NOTE: Other coin types may exist with this particular counterstamp.

(8 ESCUDOS)
MANILA/1829

Type III
c/s: MANILA/1829. Rev: Crowned Spanish royal arms.

GOLD
c/s: Type III on Mexico, 8 Escudos, KM#383.
| 34 | 1829 | (1825JM) | | | | |

NOTE: The above is in the collection of Fabrica Nacional de Moneda y Timbre de Madrid (Spain).

(8 REALES)
MANILA/1830

Type IV
c/s: MANILA/1830 within serrated circle.
Rev. leg. HABILITADO POR EL REY N.S.D.FERN.VII.
around crowned Spanish royal arms.

SILVER
Type IV on Bolivia 8 Sueldos, KM#97.
| 35 | 1830 | (1827-30) | 1500. | 1800. | 2200. | 2500. |

c/s: Type IV on Mexico 8 Reales, KM#376.
| 36 | 1830 | (1823-25) | 1500. | 1800. | 2200. | 2500. |

c/s: Type IV on Mexico 8 Reales, KM#377.
| 37 | 1830 | (1824-30) | 1500. | 1800. | 2200. | 2500. |

NOTE: Other coin types may exist with this particular counterstamp.

COUNTERMARKED COINAGE
(8 REALES)
FERDINAND VII

SILVER
Oval Type V   Round Type V
Actual size 9-10mm

These countermarks were introduced by decree of October 27, 1832 due to the problems encountered with the larger countermarks of 1828-1830. Pierced or holed coins were declared non valid but later were countermarked directly over the hole with Type V or Type VI countermarks and circulated freely. The latter types exist countermarked on both sides directly over the hole and are very scarce. These countermarks were retired in 1834 after the death of Ferdinand VII and replaced with a new die of Isabel II, Type VI. Coins with either Type V countermark dated after 1834 can be considered counterfeit.

(REAL)
SILVER
c/m: F.7.o on Mexico 1 Real.
KM#	Date	Year	Good	VG	Fine	VF
40	ND				Rare	—

(2 REALES)
SILVER
c/m: F.7.o on Mexico 2 Reales, KM#372.
| 41 | ND | (1825-34) | 75.00 | 100.00 | 200.00 | 300.00 |

c/m: F.7.o on Peru 2 Reales, KM#141.
| 42 | ND | (1825-34) | 75.00 | 100.00 | 200.00 | 300.00 |

(4 REALES)
SILVER
c/m: F.7.o on Mexico 4 Reales.
| 43 | ND | — | 200.00 | 300.00 | 400.00 | 700.00 |

(8 REALES)
SILVER
c/m: F.7.o on Argentina 8 Reales, KM#5.
| 44 | ND | (1813-5) | 50.00 | 80.00 | 150.00 | 250.00 |

c/m: F.7.o on Argentina 8 Soles, KM#15.
| 45 | ND | (1815) | 50.00 | 80.00 | 150.00 | 250.00 |

c/m: F.7.o on Argentina 8 Reales, KM#20.
| 46 | ND | (1826-34) | 60.00 | 100.00 | 175.00 | 275.00 |

c/m: F.7.o on Bolivia 8 Reales, KM#55.
| 47 | ND | (1773-89) | 75.00 | 110.00 | 200.00 | 300.00 |

c/m: F.7.o on Bolivia 8 Reales, KM#64.
| 48 | ND | (1789-91) | 60.00 | 100.00 | 190.00 | 275.00 |

c/m: F.7.o on Bolivia 8 Reales, KM#73.
| 49 | ND | (1791-1808) | 60.00 | 100.00 | 160.00 | 250.00 |

c/m: F.7.o on Bolivia 8 Reales, KM#84.
| 50 | ND | (1808-25) | 60.00 | 100.00 | 160.00 | 250.00 |

c/m: F.7.o on Bolivia 8 Sueldos, KM#97.
| 51 | ND | (1827-34) | 25.00 | 40.00 | 60.00 | 80.00 |

c/m: F.7.o on Brazil 960 Reis, KM#307.
| 52 | ND | (1809-18) | 75.00 | 120.00 | 300.00 | 500.00 |

c/m: F.7.o on Brazil 960 Reis, KM#326.
| 53 | ND | (1818-22) | 100.00 | 170.00 | 400.00 | 600.00 |

c/m: F.7.o on Brazil 960 Reis, KM#368.
| 54 | ND | (1823-7) | 75.00 | 120.00 | 300.00 | 500.00 |

c/m: F.7.o on Chile 1 Peso, KM#82.
| 55 | ND | (1817-34) | 50.00 | 75.00 | 100.00 | 150.00 |

c/m: F.7.o on France 5 Francs, C#189.
| 56 | 1826D | — | 350.00 | 500.00 | 800.00 | 1200. |

c/m: F.7.o on Central American Rep. 8 Reales, KM#4.

KM#	Date	Year	Good	VG	Fine	VF
57	ND	(1824-34)	75.00	120.00	180.00	250.00

c/m. in oval: F.7.o on Kingdom of Italy 5 Lire, C#10.1.

| 58 | 1809 | — | — | — | Rare |

c/m: F.7.o on Mexico 8 Reales, KM#105.

| 59 | ND | (1760-71) | 100.00 | 150.00 | 240.00 | 400.00 |

c/m: F.7.o on Mexico 8 Reales, KM#106.

| 60 | ND | (1772-89) | 80.00 | 100.00 | 175.00 | 225.00 |

c/m: F.7.o on Mexico 8 Reales, KM#107.

| 61 | ND(1789-90FM) | 60.00 | 100.00 | 175.00 | 225.00 |

c/m: F.7.o on Mexico 8 Reales, KM#108.

| 62 | ND | (1790FM) | 60.00 | 100.00 | 175.00 | 225.00 |

c/m: F.7.o on Mexico 8 Reales, KM#109.

| 63 | ND (1791-1808) | 50.00 | 90.00 | 150.00 | 215.00 |

c/m: F.7.o on Mexico 8 Reales, KM#110.

| 64 | ND | (1808-11) | 60.00 | 100.00 | 175.00 | 220.00 |

c/m: F.7.o on Mexico 8 Reales, KM#111.

KM#	Date	Year	Good	VG	Fine	VF
65	ND	(1811-21)	60.00	110.00	150.00	220.00

c/m: F.7.o on Mexico 8 Reales, KM#304.

| 66 | ND | (1822JM) | 50.00 | 100.00 | 150.00 | 250.00 |

c/m: F.7.o on Mexico 8 Reales, KM#305.

| 67 | ND | (1822JM) | 50.00 | 100.00 | 150.00 | 250.00 |

c/m: F.7.o on Mexico 8 Reales, KM#306.

| 68 | ND | (1822JM) | 50.00 | 100.00 | 150.00 | 250.00 |

c/m: F.7.o on Mexico 8 Reales, KM#307.

| 69 | ND | (1822JM) | 50.00 | 100.00 | 150.00 | 250.00 |

c/m: F.7.o on Mexico 8 Reales, KM#308.

| 70 | ND | (1822JM) | 50.00 | 100.00 | 150.00 | 250.00 |

c/m: F.7.o on Mexico 8 Reales, KM#309.

| 71 | ND | (1822JM) | — | — | — | Rare |

c/m: F.7.o on Mexico 8 Reales, KM#310.

| 72 | ND | (1822-3JM) | 50.00 | 100.00 | 150.00 | 250.00 |

c/m: F.7.o on Mexico 8 Reales, KM#376.

| 73 | ND | (1823-5) | 45.00 | 80.00 | 125.00 | 200.00 |

c/m: F.7.o on Mexico 8 Reales, KM#377.

| 74 | ND | (1824-34) | 30.00 | 50.00 | 60.00 | 80.00 |

c/m: F.7.o on Peru 8 Reales, KM#78.

| 75 | ND | (1772-89) | 60.00 | 100.00 | 150.00 | 250.00 |

c/m: F.7.o on Peru 8 Reales, KM#87.

| 76 | ND | (1789-91) | 60.00 | 100.00 | 150.00 | 250.00 |

c/m: F.7.o on Peru 8 Reales, KM#97.

| 77 | ND (1791-1808) | 60.00 | 80.00 | 125.00 | 200.00 |

c/m: F.7.o on Peru 8 Reales, KM#106.

| 78 | ND | (1808-11) | 60.00 | 85.00 | 130.00 | 200.00 |

c/m: F.7.o on Peru 8 Reales, KM#117.1.

| 79 | ND | (1810-24) | 60.00 | 80.00 | 125.00 | 175.00 |

c/m: F.7.o on Peru 8 Reales, KM#136.

| 80 | ND | (1822-3) | 35.00 | 60.00 | 90.00 | 125.00 |

c/m: F.7.o on Peru 8 Reales, KM#130.

| 81 | ND | (1824) | 60.00 | 90.00 | 150.00 | 200.00 |

c/m. in oval: F.7.o on Peru 8 Reales, KM#142.1.

| 82 | ND | (1825-8) | — | — | Rare | — |

c/m: F.7.o on Peru 8 Reales, KM#142.3.

KM#	Date	Year	Good	VG	Fine	VF
83	ND	(1828-34)	30.00	45.00	60.00	75.00

8 ESCUDOS
GOLD

c/m: F.7.o on Chile 8 Escudos, KM#84.

| 85 | ND | 1822FD | 3000. | 3500. | 4000. | 5000. |

c/m: F.7.o on Colombia 8 Escudos, KM#82.2.

| A86 | ND | 1825 | — | — | Rare | *— |

*NOTE: Superior Ebsen sale 6-87 VF realized $13,750.

c/m: F.7.o on Mexico 8 Escudos, KM#383.4.

| 86 | ND | 1829LF | — | — | — | Unique |

NOTE: Other coin types may exist with this particular countermark.

ISABEL II

SILVER
Type VI

This countermark was introduced after the death of Ferdinand VII on December 20, 1834. It exists with several varieties of crowns. Countermarking of foreign coins was halted in Manila by the edict of March 31, 1837 after Spain had recognized the independence of Mexico, Peru, Colombia, Bolivia, Chile and other former colonies in Central and South America. Coins with the Type VI countermarked after 1837 can be considered counterfeit.

(REAL)
SILVER

c/m: Y.II on Mexico Real.

| 87 | ND | — | — | — | Rare | — |

(2 REALES)

SILVER

c/m: Y.II on Mexico Zacatecas 2 Reales, KM#374.12.

| 88 | ND | (1825-37) | 60.00 | 100.00 | 150.00 | 250.00 |

c/m: Y.II on Peru 2 Reales, KM#141.

KM#	Date	Year	Good	VG	Fine	VF
90	ND	(1825-37)	60.00	100.00	150.00	200.00

(GULDEN)

.920 SILVER
c/m: Y.II on Netherlands-Holland 1 Gulden, Cr#C13.

| 89 | ND | (1793) | 120.00 | 150.00 | 200.00 | 300.00 |

(4 REALES)

SILVER
c/m: Y.II on Bolivia 4 Reales, KM#54.

| 91 | ND | (1788) | 250.00 | 400.00 | 600.00 | 900.00 |

c/m: Y.II on Mexico Zacatecas 4 Reales, KM#375.9.

| 92 | ND | (1832) | 200.00 | 300.00 | 450.00 | 750.00 |

(8 REALES)

SILVER
c/m: Y.II on Argentina 8 Reales, KM#5.

| 93 | ND | (1813-5) | 60.00 | 100.00 | 150.00 | 200.00 |

c/m: Y.II on Argentina 8 Soles, KM#15.

| 94 | ND | (1815) | 60.00 | 100.00 | 150.00 | 350.00 |

c/m: Y.II on Argentina 8 Reales, KM#20.

| 95 | ND | (1826-37) | 60.00 | 100.00 | 150.00 | 250.00 |

c/m: Y.II on Bolivia 8 Reales, KM#55.

| 96 | ND | (1773-89) | 65.00 | 110.00 | 160.00 | 250.00 |

c/m: Y.II on Bolivia 8 Reales, KM#64.

| 97 | ND | (1789-91) | 65.00 | 110.00 | 160.00 | 250.00 |

c/m: Y.II on Bolivia 8 Reales, KM#73.

| 98 | ND | (1791-1808) | 65.00 | 100.00 | 150.00 | 200.00 |

c/m: Y.II on Bolivia 8 Reales, KM#84.

| 99 | ND | (1808-25) | 60.00 | 90.00 | 140.00 | 190.00 |

c/m: Y.II on Bolivia 8 Sueldos, KM#97.

| 100 | ND | (1827-37) | 25.00 | 35.00 | 45.00 | 80.00 |

c/m: Y.II on Brazil 960 Reis, KM#307.

| 101 | ND | (1809-18) | 90.00 | 150.00 | 200.00 | 300.00 |

c/m: Y.II on Brazil 960 Reis, KM#326.

| 102 | ND | (1818-22) | 90.00 | 150.00 | 200.00 | 300.00 |

c/m: Y.II on Brazil 960 Reis, KM#368.

| 103 | ND | (1823-30) | 90.00 | 150.00 | 200.00 | 300.00 |

c/m: Y.II on Brazil 960 Reis, KM#385.

| 104 | ND | (1832-4) | — | — | Rare | — |

c/m: Y.II on Brazil 1200 Reis, KM#454.

| 105 | ND | (1834-7) | 100.00 | 150.00 | 200.00 | 300.00 |

c/m: Y.II on Central American Rep. 8 Reales, KM#4.

KM#	Date	Year	Good	VG	Fine	VF
106	ND	(1824-37)	60.00	100.00	150.00	200.00

c/m: Y.II on Central American Rep. 8 Reales, KM#22.

| 107 | ND | (1831) | 150.00 | 300.00 | 400.00 | 600.00 |

c/m: Y.II on Chile 1 Peso, KM#82.

| 108 | ND | (1817-34) | 50.00 | 75.00 | 100.00 | 125.00 |

c/m: Y.II on Colombia 8 Reales, KM#89.

| 109 | ND | (1834-6) | 40.00 | 60.00 | 80.00 | 120.00 |

c/m: Y.II on Mexico 8 Reales, KM#104.

| 110 | ND | (1747-60) | — | — | Rare | — |

c/m: Y.II on Mexico 8 Reales, KM#105.

| 111 | ND | (1760-71) | — | — | Rare | — |

c/m: Y.II on Mexico 8 Reales, KM#106.

| 112 | ND | (1772-89) | 60.00 | 120.00 | 160.00 | 250.00 |

c/m: Y.II on Mexico 8 Reales, KM#107.

| 113 | ND | (1789-90FM) | 60.00 | 120.00 | 150.00 | 200.00 |

c/m: Y.II on Mexico 8 Reales, KM#108.

| 114 | ND | (1790FM) | 60.00 | 120.00 | 170.00 | 250.00 |

c/m: Y.II on Mexico 8 Reales, KM#109.

| 115 | ND | (1791-1808) | 50.00 | 100.00 | 150.00 | 200.00 |

c/m: Y.II on Mexico 8 Reales, KM#110.

| 116 | ND | (1808-11) | 50.00 | 100.00 | 150.00 | 200.00 |

c/m: Y.II on Mexico 8 Reales, KM#111.2.

| 117 | ND | (1811-21) | 50.00 | 100.00 | 150.00 | 200.00 |

c/m: Y.II on Mexico 8 Reales, KM#111.5.

| 118 | ND | (1813-22) | 50.00 | 100.00 | 150.00 | 200.00 |

c/m: Y.II on Mexico 8 Reales, KM#111.

| 119 | ND | (1811-21) | 50.00 | 100.00 | 150.00 | 200.00 |

c/m: Y.II on Mexico 8 Reales, KM#189.

| 120 | ND | (1811) | 100.00 | 150.00 | 200.00 | 300.00 |

c/m: Y.II on Mexico 8 Reales, KM#304.

KM#	Date	Year	Good	VG	Fine	VF
121	ND	(1822JM)	50.00	85.00	135.00	175.00

c/m: Y.II on Mexico 8 Reales, KM#305.

| 122 | ND | (1822JM) | 50.00 | 100.00 | 140.00 | 200.00 |

c/m: Y.II on Mexico 8 Reales, KM#306.

| 123 | ND | (1822JM) | 50.00 | 100.00 | 140.00 | 200.00 |

c/m: Y.II on Mexico 8 Reales, KM#307.

| 124 | ND | (1822JM) | 50.00 | 100.00 | 140.00 | 180.00 |

c/m: Y.II on Mexico 8 Reales, KM#308.

| 125 | ND | (1822JM) | 50.00 | 100.00 | 140.00 | 180.00 |

c/m: Y.II on Mexico 8 Reales, KM#309.

| 126 | ND | (1822JM) | — | — | Rare | — |

c/m: Y.II on Mexico 8 Reales, KM#310.

| 127 | ND | (1822-3JM) | 40.00 | 80.00 | 125.00 | 180.00 |

c/m: Y.II on Mexico 8 Reales, KM#376.

| 128 | ND | (1823-4) | 50.00 | 100.00 | 140.00 | 200.00 |

c/m: Y.II on Mexico 8 Reales, KM#377.

| 129 | ND | (1824-37) | 30.00 | 45.00 | 60.00 | 90.00 |

c/m: Y.II on Peru 8 Reales, KM#78.

| 131 | ND | (1772-89) | 50.00 | 100.00 | 150.00 | 200.00 |

c/m: Y.II on Peru 8 Reales, KM#87.

| 132 | ND | (1789-91) | 60.00 | 110.00 | 175.00 | 250.00 |

c/m: Y.II on Peru 8 Reales, KM#97.

| 133 | ND | (1791-1808) | 50.00 | 100.00 | 150.00 | 200.00 |

c/m: Y.II on Peru 8 Reales, KM#106.

| 134 | ND | (1808-11) | 50.00 | 100.00 | 150.00 | 200.00 |

c/m: Y.II on Peru 8 Reales, KM#117.1.

| 135 | ND | (1810-24) | 45.00 | 65.00 | 85.00 | 125.00 |

c/m: Y.II on Peru 8 Reales, KM#136.

| 136 | ND | (1822-3) | 35.00 | 50.00 | 75.00 | 100.00 |

c/m: Y.II on Peru 8 Reales, KM#132.

| 137 | ND | (1824) | 50.00 | 60.00 | 80.00 | 110.00 |

c/m: Y.II on Peru 8 Reales, KM#142.1.

| 138.1 | ND | (1825-8) | 25.00 | 35.00 | 45.00 | 60.00 |

c/m: Y.II on Peru 8 Reales, KM#142.3.

| 138.2 (139) | ND | (1828-37) | 25.00 | 35.00 | 45.00 | 60.00 |

c/m: Y.II on Peru 8 Reales, KM#142.4.

| 138.4 (84) | ND | (1830-34) | 30.00 | 45.00 | 60.00 | 75.00 |

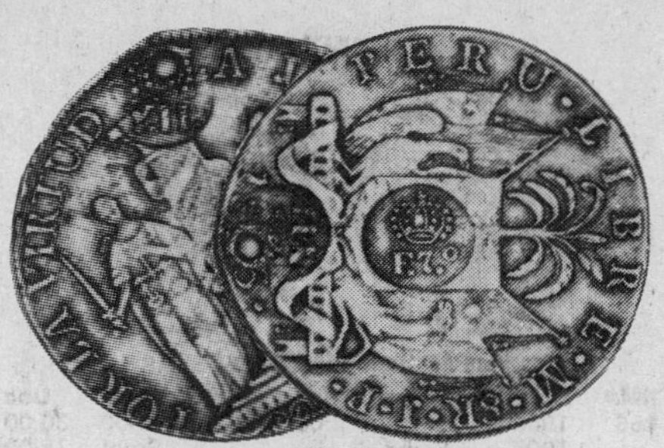

c/m: Y.II. on Philippines, KM#80.

KM#	Date	Year	Good	VG	Fine	VF
139	ND	(1822-3)	90.00	135.00	225.00	300.00

ESCUDO

GOLD

c/m: Y.II. on Colombia 1 Escudo, KM#81.2.

KM#	Date	Year	Good	VG	Fine	VF
140	ND	1827FM	—	—	Unique	—

8 ESCUDO

GOLD

c/m: Y.II. on Colombia 8 Escudos, KM#82.

KM#	Date	Year	Good	VG	Fine	VF
141	ND	1826JF	3000.	3500.	4000.	5000.

NOTE: The above countermarks have been reported on other coins, (i.e. U.S. 1/2 Dollar, Dollar, and Spanish 20 Reales). Coins bearing both Type V or Type VI countermarks with other countermarks are considered rare. Certain holed or pierced coins are sometimes found with an additional set of countermarks usually struck on both sides over the hole to approve it for normal circulation. These are very scarce and rarely offered at two to three times the value of single countermarked pieces.

DECIMAL COINAGE

1861-1897

100 Centavos = 1 Peso

CENTAVO

COPPER, 25mm.

Obv: Boy head of Alfonso XIII of Spain .

Rev: Crowned arms between branches.

KM#	Date	Mintage	Fine	VF	XF	Unc
152	1894	—	1600.	2000.	2500.	3000.

2 CENTAVOS

COPPER, 30mm.

Obv: Boy head of Alfonso XIII of Spain.

Rev: Crowned arms between branches.

KM#	Date	Mintage	Fine	VF	XF	Unc
153	1894	—	2000.	2400.	2750.	3500.

10 CENTIMOS

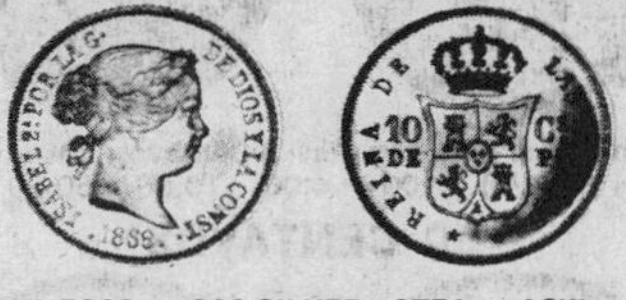

2.5960 g, .900 SILVER, .0751 oz ASW

KM#	Date	Mintage	Fine	VF	XF	Unc
145	1864	4,586	75.00	150.00	400.00	1600.
	1865	.082	20.00	50.00	125.00	1000.
	1866	.039	30.00	60.00	150.00	1200.
	1867/6	.124	20.00	50.00	125.00	1000.
	1867	Inc. Ab.	20.00	40.00	100.00	950.00
	1868	*.139	6.00	12.00	25.00	125.00

NOTE: An additional 450,000 pieces were struck between 1870-74, all dated 1868.

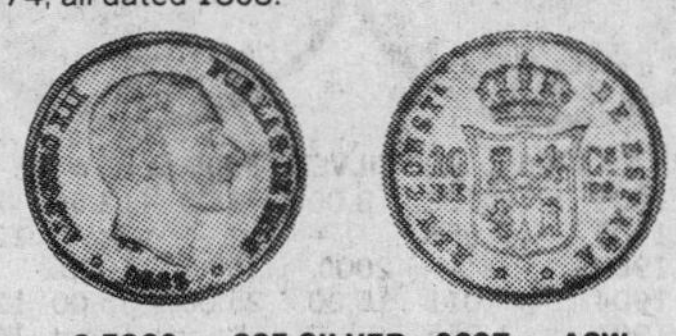

2.5960 g, .835 SILVER, .0697 oz ASW

KM#	Date	Mintage	Fine	VF	XF	Unc
148	1880	.015	150.00	250.00	600.00	2500.
	1881/0	.624	15.00	30.00	85.00	400.00
	1881	Inc. Ab.	10.00	25.00	80.00	350.00
	1882/1	.525	10.00	30.00	85.00	400.00
	1882	Inc. Ab.	10.00	25.00	85.00	400.00
	1883/1	.983	12.00	25.00	90.00	350.00
	1883/2	Inc. Ab.	11.00	22.00	80.00	350.00
	1883	Inc. Ab.	10.00	20.00	80.00	300.00
	1884	.010	150.00	200.00	500.00	2000.
	1885	*5.625	3.00	6.00	12.00	50.00

***NOTE:** An additional 5,432,614 pieces were struck between 1886-1898, all dated 1885.

20 CENTIMOS

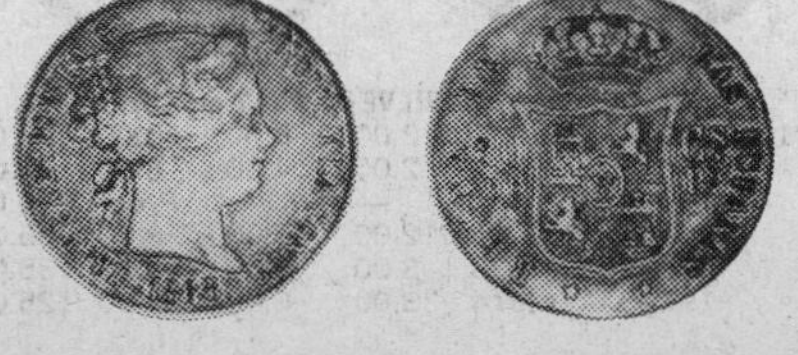

5.1920 g, .900 SILVER, .1502 oz ASW

KM#	Date	Mintage	Fine	VF	XF	Unc
146	1864	.067	40.00	60.00	120.00	1600.
	1865	.239	10.00	25.00	65.00	1000.
	1866/5	.134	15.00	35.00	90.00	1200.
	1866	Inc. Ab.	20.00	40.00	100.00	1250.
	1867	.138	15.00	30.00	80.00	1200.
	1868	*.418	5.00	8.00	15.00	150.00

***NOTE:** An additional 708,400 pieces were struck between 1869-1874, all dated 1868.

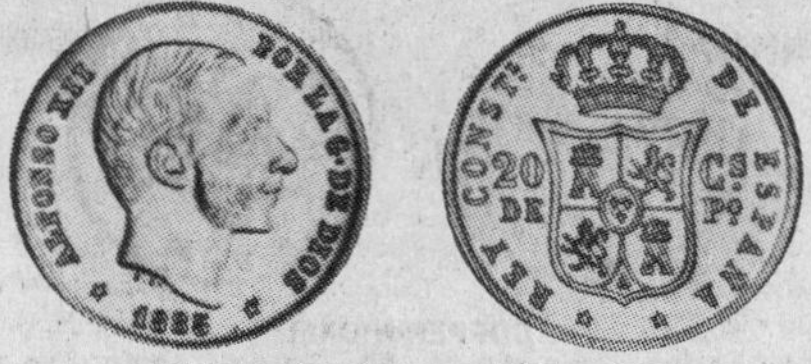

5.1920 g, .835 SILVER, .1394 oz ASW

KM#	Date	Mintage	Fine	VF	XF	Unc
149	1880	.070	30.00	60.00	120.00	1250.
	1881/0	1.029	10.00	20.00	40.00	300.00
	1881	Inc. Ab.	10.00	18.00	50.00	300.00
	1882/1	.968	12.00	20.00	50.00	500.00
	1882	Inc. Ab.	12.00	24.00	55.00	500.00
	1883/2	1.972	12.00	18.00	30.00	350.00
	1883/horizontal 8	Inc. Ab.	12.00	18.00	30.00	300.00
	1883	Inc. Ab.	10.00	16.00	30.00	300.00
	1884	.859	20.00	35.00	75.00	500.00
	1885	*1.344	5.00	10.00	15.00	70.00

***NOTE:** An additional 4,092,205 pieces were struck between 1886-1898, all dated 1885.

50 CENTIMOS

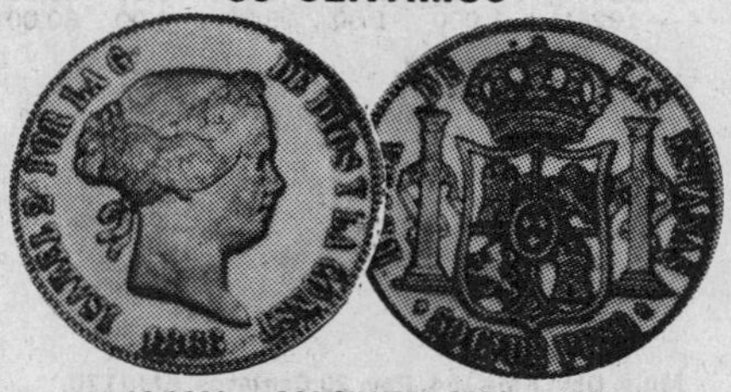

12.9800 g, .900 SILVER, .3756 oz ASW

KM#	Date	Mintage	Fine	VF	XF	Unc
147	1865	.081	30.00	60.00	150.00	1500.
	1866	7,442	300.00	450.00	700.00	5000.
	1867	6,870	250.00	400.00	600.00	4000.
	1868/58	*.423	10.00	18.00	50.00	200.00
	1868/7	Inc. Ab.	10.00	18.00	50.00	200.00
	1868	Inc. Ab.	7.50	15.00	45.00	200.00

***NOTE:** An additional 200,800 pieces were struck between 1869-1874, all dated 1868.

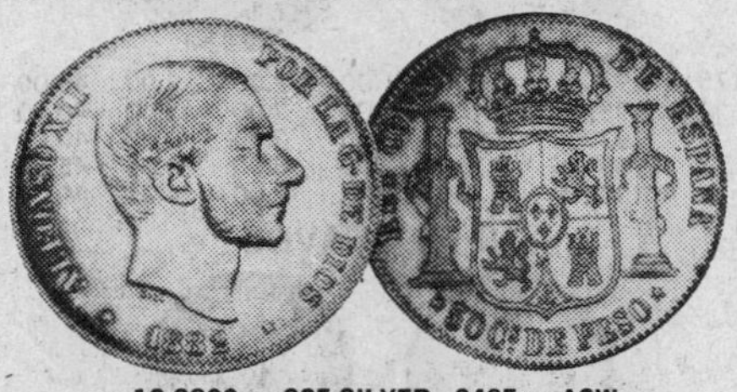

12.9800 g, .835 SILVER, .3485 oz ASW

KM#	Date	Mintage	Fine	VF	XF	Unc
150	1880	.127	100.00	125.00	275.00	2200.
	1881	2.480	10.00	20.00	40.00	500.00
	1882/0	1.890	12.50	22.50	40.00	650.00
	1882/1	Inc. Ab.	12.50	22.50	40.00	650.00
	1882	Inc. Ab.	10.00	20.00	40.00	650.00
	1883	2.221	10.00	20.00	40.00	500.00
	1884	.023	80.00	125.00	250.00	2000.
	1885/3	*22.700	5.00	10.00	20.00	75.00
	1885	I.A.	3.50	7.50	15.00	65.00

***NOTE:** An additional 22,649,115 pieces were struck between 1886-1898, all dated 1885.

PESO

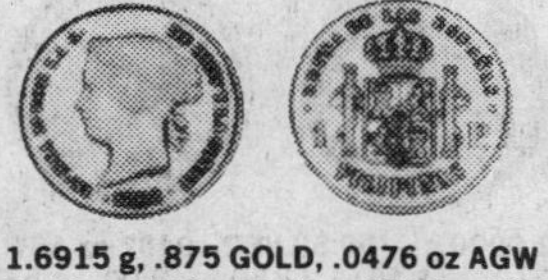

1.6915 g, .875 GOLD, .0476 oz AGW

KM#	Date	Mintage	Fine	VF	XF	Unc
142	1861/0	.237	45.00	65.00	90.00	225.00
	1861	Inc. Ab.	45.00	65.00	90.00	225.00
	1862/1	.143	45.00	65.00	90.00	225.00
	1862	Inc. Ab.	45.00	65.00	90.00	225.00
	1863/2	.236	45.00	65.00	90.00	225.00
	1863	Inc. Ab.	45.00	65.00	90.00	225.00
	1864/0	.274	45.00	65.00	90.00	225.00
	1864	Inc. Ab.	50.00	75.00	100.00	250.00
	1865/0	.189	55.00	90.00	125.00	250.00
	1865	Inc. Ab.	45.00	65.00	90.00	225.00
	1866/5	.077	160.00	200.00	300.00	1250.
	1866	Inc. Ab.	160.00	200.00	300.00	1250.
	1867	.012	450.00	800.00	1250.	3000.
	1868/6	*.028	45.00	70.00	100.00	200.00
	1868/7	Inc. Ab.	45.00	70.00	100.00	200.00
	1868	Inc. Ab.	40.00	50.00	70.00	125.00

***NOTE:** An additional 372,724 pieces were struck between 1869-1874, all dated 1868.

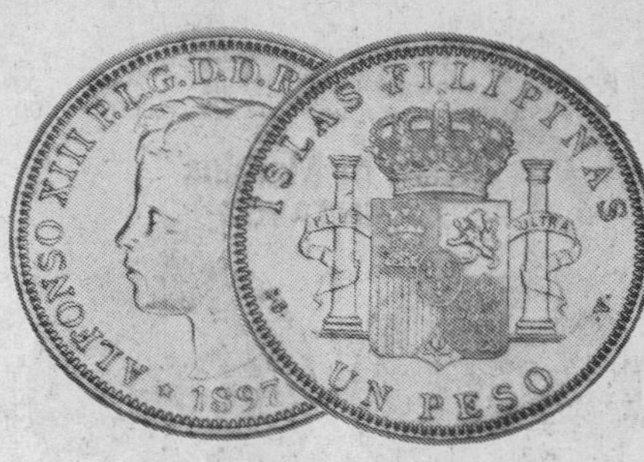

25.0000 g, .900 SILVER, .7234 oz ASW

KM#	Date	Mintage	Fine	VF	XF	Unc
154	1897 SGV	6.000	25.00	35.00	75.00	300.00

2 PESOS

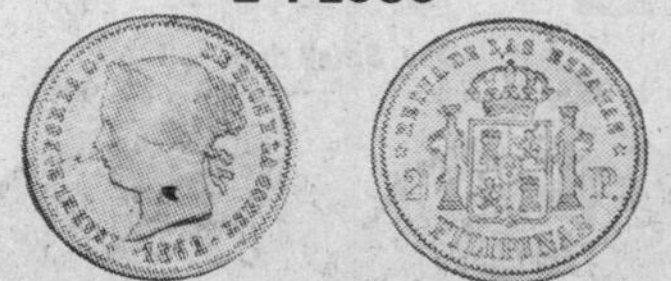

3.3830 g, .875 GOLD, .0952 oz AGW

KM#	Date	Mintage	Fine	VF	XF	Unc
143	1861/0	.265	60.00	90.00	110.00	325.00
	1861	Inc. Ab.	60.00	90.00	110.00	325.00
	1862/1	.237	60.00	90.00	110.00	325.00
	1862	Inc. Ab.	60.00	90.00	110.00	325.00
	1863/2	.176	60.00	90.00	110.00	325.00
	1863	Inc. Ab.	60.00	90.00	110.00	325.00
	1864/0	.181	60.00	90.00	110.00	325.00
	1864/3	Inc. Ab.	60.00	90.00	110.00	325.00
	1864	Inc. Ab.	70.00	100.00	140.00	350.00
	1865	.034	150.00	225.00	350.00	750.00
	1866/5	.016	600.00	800.00	1250.	2500.
	1866	Inc. Ab.	600.00	800.00	1250.	2500.
	1868/6	*.048	55.00	70.00	90.00	200.00
	1868	Inc. Ab.	60.00	75.00	100.00	225.00

NOTE: An additional 304,691 pieces were struck between 1869-1873, all dated 1868.

4 PESOS

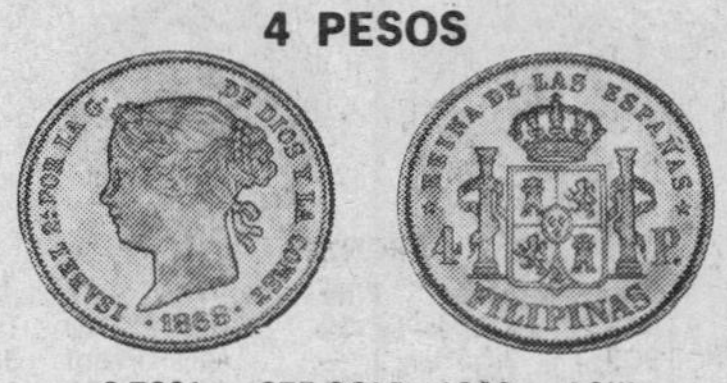

6.7661 g, .875 GOLD, .1903 oz AGW

KM#	Date	Mintage	Fine	VF	XF	Unc
144	1861	.183	120.00	150.00	190.00	375.00
	1862/1	.507	120.00	150.00	170.00	300.00
	1862	Inc. Ab.	120.00	150.00	170.00	300.00
	1863	.475	120.00	150.00	170.00	300.00
	1864	.461	120.00	150.00	175.00	350.00
	1865	.241	120.00	200.00	275.00	600.00
	1866/65	.044	500.00	750.00	1500.	3000.
	1866	Inc. Ab.	500.00	750.00	1500.	3000.
	1867	1,530	—	—	Rare	—
	1868	.036	100.00	120.00	170.00	325.00

NOTE: 1,521,505 were struck between 1869-1873, all dated 1868.

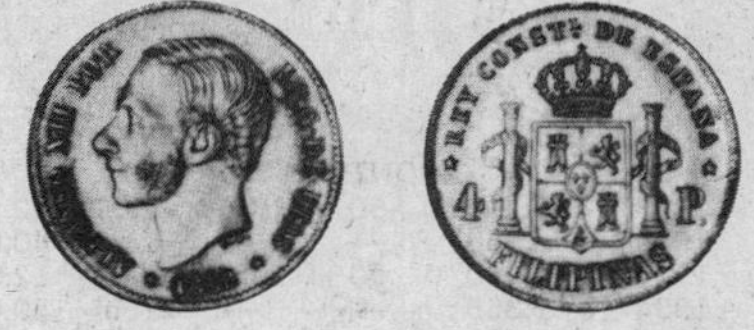

KM#	Date	Mintage	Fine	VF	XF	Unc
151	1880	—	—	Rare	—	—
	1881	—	2500.	3500.	6000.	8000.
	1882	—	500.00	750.00	1000.	1800.
	1883	—	—	Reported, not confirmed		
	1884	—	—	Reported, not confirmed		
	1885	—	2500.	3500.	6000.	8000.

REVOLUTIONARY COINAGE

Island of Panay

CENTAVO

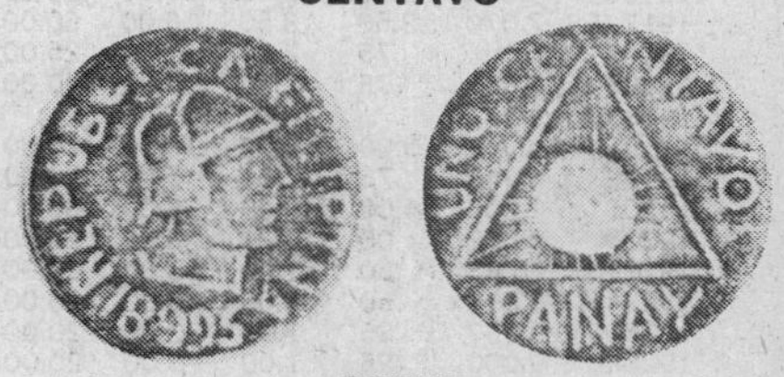

COPPER

Obv: Helmeted head right, leg.

Rev: Sun in triangle, leg.

KM#	Date	Mintage	VG	Fine	VF	XF
156	1899	—	—	—	2000.	2400.

PHILIPPINES 1418

c/m: M behind head.

#	Date	Mintage	VG	Fine	VF	XF
	1899	—	—	—	2000.	2400.

Town of Malolos
2 CENTAVOS

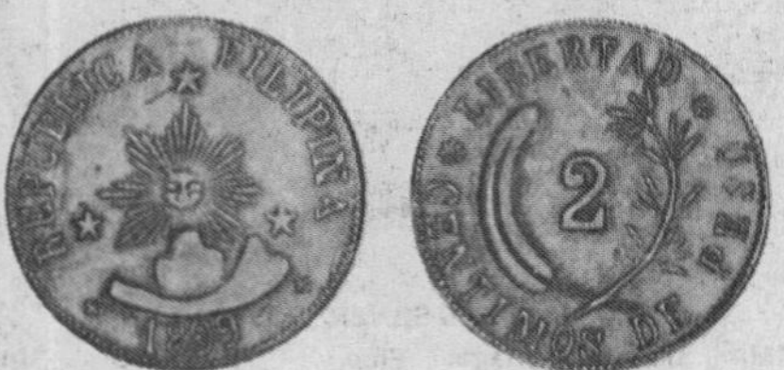

COPPER

KM#	Date	Mintage	VG	Fine	VF	XF
		Obv: Large date.				
158.1	1899	—	—	—	2000.	2400.
		Obv: Small date.				
158.2	1899	—	—	—	2000.	2400.

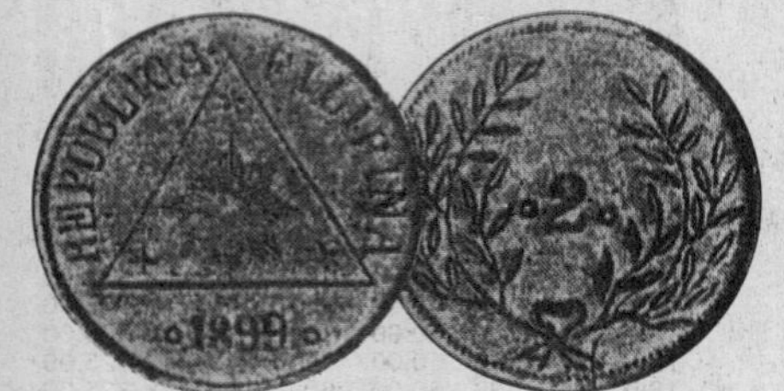

KM#	Date	Mintage	VG	Fine	VF	XF
159	1899	—	—	—	2000.	2400.

UNITED STATES ADMINISTRATION

1903-1935

100 Centavos = 1 Peso

1/2 CENTAVO

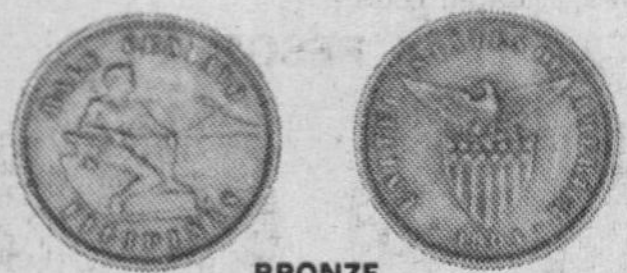

BRONZE

KM#	Date	Mintage	Fine	VF	XF	Unc
162	1903	12.084	.50	1.00	2.00	10.00
	1903	2,558	—	—	Proof	35.00
	1904	5.654	.50	1.00	2.50	15.00
	1904	1,355	—	—	Proof	45.00
	1905	471 pcs.	—	—	Proof	100.00
	1906	500 pcs.	—	—	Proof	75.00
	1908	500 pcs.	—	—	Proof	75.00

CENTAVO

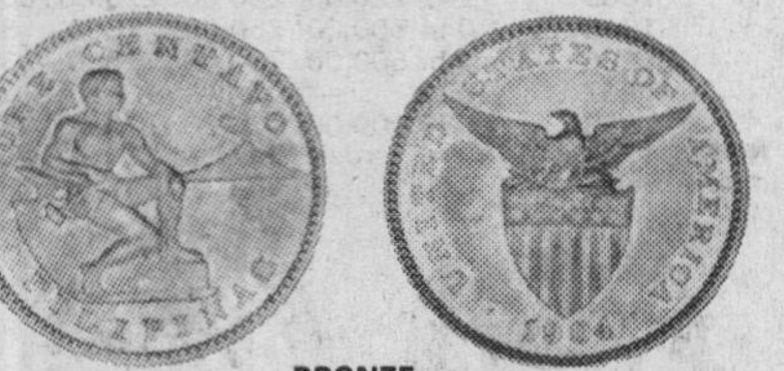

BRONZE

KM#	Date	Mintage	Fine	VF	XF	Unc
163	1903	10.790	.50	1.00	2.00	12.50
	1903	2,558	—	—	Proof	40.00
	1904	17.040	.50	1.00	2.00	12.50
	1904	1,355	—	—	Proof	50.00
	1905	10.000	.50	1.00	2.00	20.00
	1905	471 pcs.	—	—	Proof	90.00
	1906	500 pcs.	—	—	Proof	50.00
	1908	500 pcs.	—	—	Proof	50.00
	1908S	2.187	1.00	2.00	6.00	30.00
	1909S	1.738	2.00	6.00	10.00	65.00
	1910S	2.700	1.00	2.00	6.00	30.00
	1911S	4.803	.50	2.00	6.00	25.00
	1912S	3.000	1.00	2.00	6.00	30.00
	1913S	5.000	.75	2.00	6.00	25.00
	1914S	5.000	.50	2.00	5.00	25.00
	1915S	2.500	10.00	15.00	35.00	175.00
	1916S	4.330	4.00	8.00	16.00	90.00
	1917/6S	7.070	2.50	3.50	6.00	60.00
	1917S	Inc. Ab.	.75	2.00	4.00	25.00
	1918S	11.660	.75	2.00	3.00	20.00
	1918S large S					
		Inc. Ab.	5.00	10.00	18.00	120.00
	1919S	4.540	.75	2.00	5.00	20.00
	1920S	2.500	4.00	8.00	16.00	80.00
	1920M	3.552	1.00	2.00	3.00	20.00
	1921M	7.283	.50	1.00	3.00	20.00
	1922M	3.519	.50	1.00	3.00	20.00
	1925M	9.332	.25	1.00	3.00	20.00
	1926M	9.000	.25	1.00	3.00	20.00
	1927M	9.270	.25	1.00	3.00	20.00
	1928M	9.150	.25	1.00	3.00	20.00
	1929M	5.657	.75	1.50	3.00	20.00
	1930M	5.577	.75	1.50	3.00	20.00
	1931M	5.659	.75	1.50	3.00	20.00

KM#	Date	Mintage	Fine	VF	XF	Unc
163	1932M	4.000	.75	2.00	3.00	25.00
	1933M	8.393	.50	.75	3.00	20.00
	1934M	3.179	1.00	2.00	3.00	25.00
	1936M	17.455	.50	1.00	3.00	12.00
		SILVER (OMS)				
163a	1922M	—	—	—	Proof	—

5 CENTAVOS

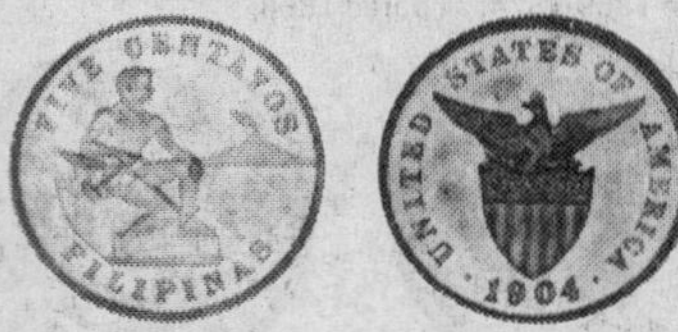

COPPER-NICKEL

KM#	Date	Mintage	Fine	VF	XF	Unc
164	1903	8.910	.50	1.00	2.50	12.50
	1903	2,558	—	—	Proof	60.00
	1904	1.075	.60	1.50	3.50	20.00
	1904	1,355	—	—	Proof	60.00
	1905	471 pcs.	—	—	Proof	135.00
	1906	500 pcs.	—	—	Proof	85.00
	1908	500 pcs.	—	—	Proof	85.00
	1916S	.300	8.00	15.00	35.00	250.00
	1917S	2.300	1.00	2.00	4.00	50.00
	1918S	2.780	1.00	2.00	4.00	50.00
	1919S	1.220	1.00	3.00	6.00	60.00
	1920M	1.421	2.00	4.00	8.00	80.00
	1921M	2.132	2.00	4.00	8.00	75.00
	1925M	1.000	2.00	4.00	8.00	75.00
	1926M	1.200	2.00	4.50	8.00	60.00
	1927M	1.000	1.00	3.00	6.00	35.00
	1928M	1.000	1.00	3.00	8.00	60.00

Mule. Obv: KM#164. Rev: 20 Centavos, KM#170.

KM#	Date	Mintage	Fine	VF	XF	Unc
173	1918S	—	100.00	200.00	400.00	1600.

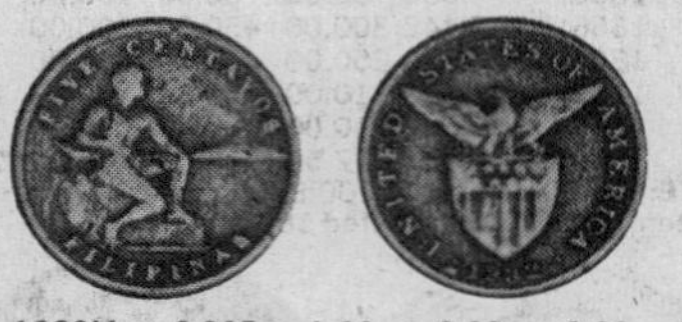

KM#	Date	Mintage	Fine	VF	XF	Unc
175	1930M	2.905	1.00	2.00	3.00	40.00
	1931M	3.477	1.00	2.00	3.00	40.00
	1932M	3.956	1.00	2.00	3.00	40.00
	1934M	2.154	1.00	3.00	5.00	45.00
	1935M	2.754	1.00	2.00	4.00	40.00

10 CENTAVOS

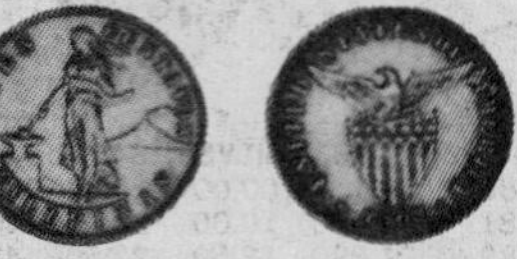

2.6924 g, .900 SILVER, .0779 oz ASW

KM#	Date	Mintage	Fine	VF	XF	Unc
165	1903	5.103	1.50	2.00	3.00	25.00
	1903	2,558	—	—	Proof	75.00
	1903S	1.200	6.00	10.00	17.50	100.00
	1904	.011	7.50	12.50	17.50	70.00
	1904	1,355	—	—	Proof	90.00
	1904S	5.040	1.50	2.00	3.00	40.00
	1905	471 pcs.	—	—	Proof	135.00
	1906	500 pcs.	—	—	Proof	115.00

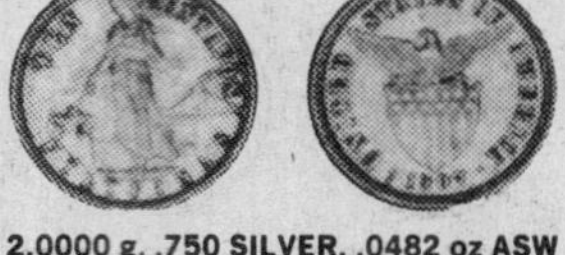

2.0000 g, .750 SILVER, .0482 oz ASW

KM#	Date	Mintage	Fine	VF	XF	Unc
169	1907	1.501	1.50	3.00	5.00	45.00
	1907S	4.930	1.00	2.50	3.50	40.00
	1908	500 pcs.	—	—	Proof	125.00
	1908S	3.364	1.00	1.75	3.50	40.00
	1909S	.312	8.00	20.00	40.00	220.00
	1910S	5-10 pcs.	Unknown in any collection			
	1911S	1.101	1.50	3.50	8.00	45.00
	1912S	1.010	1.50	4.00	8.00	50.00
	1913S	1.361	1.50	4.50	8.50	50.00
	1914S	1.180	2.50	5.00	12.50	150.00
	1915S	.450	7.00	15.00	30.00	200.00
	1917S	5.991	.75	1.75	2.50	20.00
	1918S	8.420	.75	1.75	2.50	20.00
	1919S	1.630	1.00	1.75	3.50	30.00
	1920M	.520	4.00	5.00	10.00	45.00
	1921M	3.863	.75	1.50	2.50	22.50
	1929M	1.000	.75	1.50	2.50	25.00
	1935M	1.280	.75	1.25	2.50	22.50

20 CENTAVOS

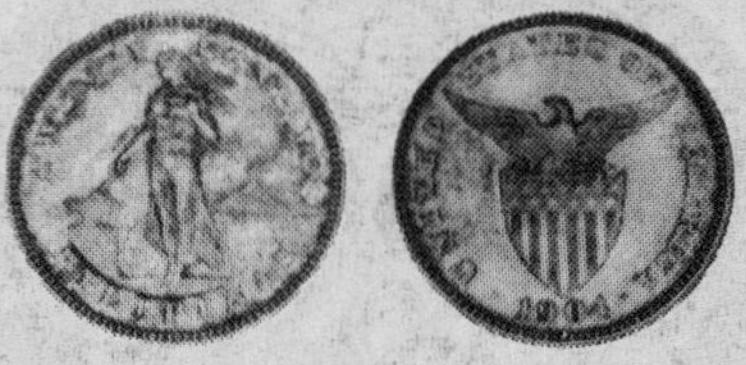

5.3849 g, .900 SILVER, .1558 oz ASW

KM#	Date	Mintage	Fine	VF	XF	Unc
166	1903	5.353	2.00	3.00	4.00	30.00
	1903	2,558	—	—	Proof	75.00
	1903S	.150	7.50	15.00	35.00	120.00
	1904	.011	10.00	15.00	20.00	80.00
	1904	1,355	—	—	Proof	90.00
	1904S	2.060	2.00	3.00	4.00	35.00
	1905	471 pcs.	—	—	Proof	200.00
	1905S	.420	6.00	8.00	17.50	80.00
	1906	500 pcs.	—	—	Proof	150.00

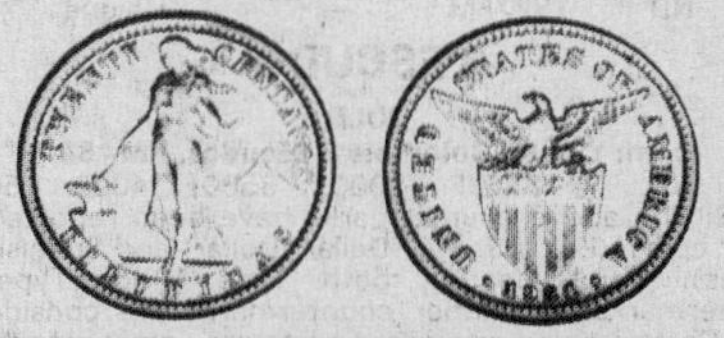

4.0000 g, .750 SILVER, .0965 oz ASW

KM#	Date	Mintage	Fine	VF	XF	Unc
170	1907	1.251	2.00	4.00	6.00	50.00
	1907S	3.165	2.00	3.00	5.00	35.00
	1908	500 pcs.	—	—	Proof	150.00
	1908S	1.535	2.00	3.00	5.00	35.00
	1909S	.450	3.00	8.00	20.00	185.00
	1910S	.500	3.00	8.00	20.00	200.00
	1911S	.505	3.00	8.00	20.00	150.00
	1912S	.750	2.00	5.00	8.00	75.00
	1913S/S	.949	5.00	9.00	12.00	85.00
	1913S	Inc. Ab.	2.00	5.00	8.00	75.00
	1914S	.795	1.50	3.00	8.00	75.00
	1915S	.655	1.50	3.00	15.00	100.00
	1916S	1.435	.80	2.00	8.00	90.00
	1917S	3.151	.80	2.00	4.00	20.00
	1918S	5.560	.80	2.00	4.00	20.00
	1919S	.850	.80	2.00	6.00	40.00
	1920	1.046	1.00	3.00	8.00	80.00
	1921	1.843	.80	2.00	3.00	22.50
	1929M	1.970	.80	2.00	3.00	22.50

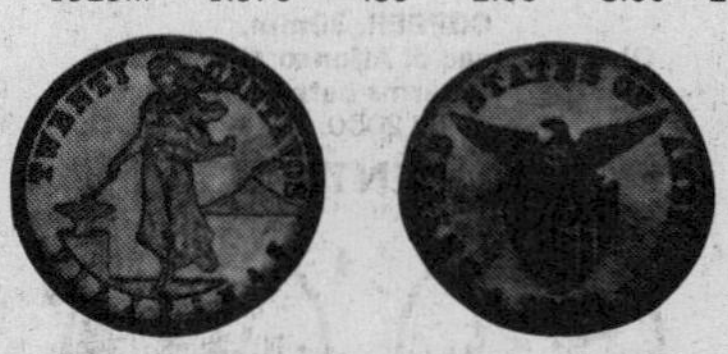

Mule. Obv: KM#170. Rev: 5 Centavos, KM#164.

KM#	Date	Mintage	Fine	VF	XF	Unc
174	1928/7M	.100	4.00	10.00	50.00	300.00

50 CENTAVOS

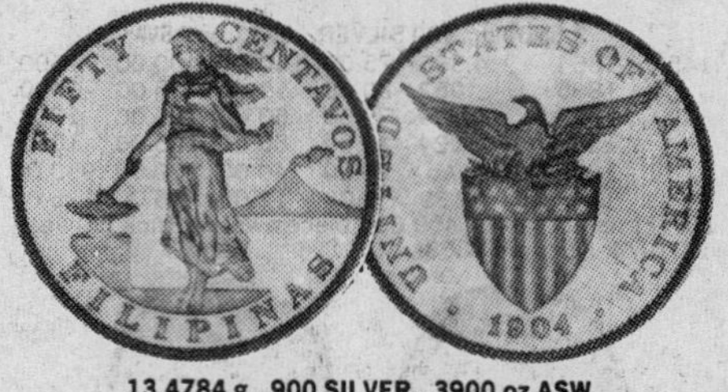

13.4784 g, .900 SILVER, .3900 oz ASW

KM#	Date	Mintage	Fine	VF	XF	Unc
167	1903	3.102	3.00	6.00	12.50	75.00
	1903	2,558	—	—	Proof	125.00
	1903S	—	2000.	3500.	5000.	—
	1904	.011	15.00	25.00	35.00	125.00
	1904	1,355	—	—	Proof	165.00
	1904S	2.160	3.00	6.50	12.50	125.00
	1905	471 pcs.	—	—	Proof	325.00
	1905S	.852	3.00	8.00	20.00	150.00
	1906	500 pcs.	—	—	Proof	275.00

10.0000 g, .750 SILVER, .2411 oz ASW

KM#	Date	Mintage	Fine	VF	XF	Unc
171	1907	1.201	2.00	5.00	10.00	75.00
	1907S	2.112	2.00	4.00	8.00	65.00
	1908	500 pcs.	—	—	Proof	275.00
	1908S	1.601	2.00	4.00	8.00	65.00
	1909S	.528	3.00	6.00	10.00	135.00
	1917S	.674	3.00	6.00	10.00	125.00

KM#	Date	Mintage	Fine	VF	XF	Unc
171	1918S	2.202	2.00	4.00	6.00	45.00
	1919S	1.200	2.00	4.50	6.50	50.00
	1920M	.420	3.00	5.00	7.00	55.00
	1921	2.317	2.00	4.00	6.00	25.00

PESO

26.9568 g, .900 SILVER, .7800 oz ASW

168	1903	2.791	6.00	12.00	25.00	150.00
	1903	2.558	—	—	Proof	250.00
	1903S	11.361	6.00	10.00	20.00	120.00
	1904	.011	35.00	60.00	100.00	225.00
	1904	1.355	—	—	Proof	260.00
	1904S	6.600	6.00	12.00	25.00	125.00
	1905	471 pcs.	—	—	Proof	600.00
	1905S	6.056	10.00	12.00	20.00	135.00
	1906	500 pcs.	—	—	Proof	475.00
	1906S	.201	350.00	625.00	1000.	4000.

20.0000 g, .800 SILVER, .5144 oz ASW

172	1907	2 pcs. known	—	—	Proof	`Rare
	1907S	10.276	BV	5.00	10.00	80.00
	1908	500 pcs.	—	—	Proof	350.00
	1908S	20.955	BV	5.00	10.00	75.00
	1909S	7.578	BV	5.00	10.00	80.00
	1910S	3.154	BV	6.00	12.50	130.00
	1911S	.463	10.00	16.00	60.00	450.00
	1912S	.680	10.00	16.00	60.00	500.00

COMMONWEALTH
CENTAVO

BRONZE
Commonwealth

179	1937M	15.790	.25	1.00	1.75	12.00
	1938M	10.000	.25	.75	1.50	10.00
	1939M	6.500	.25	1.00	2.00	15.00
	1940M	4.000	.25	.75	1.25	8.00
	1941M	5.000	.50	1.00	2.00	15.00
	1944S	58.000	.10	.15	.20	.50

5 CENTAVOS

COPPER-NICKEL
Commonwealth

180	1937M	2.494	.75	1.50	3.00	17.50
	1938M	4.000	.50	1.25	2.00	10.00
	1941M	2.750	.75	1.50	2.50	15.00

COPPER-NICKEL-ZINC

180a	1944	21.198	.10	.15	.50	2.00
	1944S	14.040	.10	.15	.25	.75
	1945S	72.796	.10	.15	.20	.50

10 CENTAVOS

2.0000 g, .750 SILVER, .0482 oz ASW
Commonwealth

KM#	Date	Mintage	Fine	VF	XF	Unc
181	1937M	3.500	.50	1.00	2.50	15.00
	1938M	3.750	.50	.75	1.75	10.00
	1941M	2.500	.50	1.00	2.00	12.00
	1944D	31.592	—	BV	.75	1.50
	1945D	137.208	—	BV	.50	1.00

20 CENTAVOS

4.0000 g, .750 SILVER, .0965 oz ASW
Commonwealth

182	1937M	2.665	BV	1.00	2.25	12.00
	1938M	3.000	BV	1.00	2.00	8.00
	1941M	1.500	BV	1.00	2.00	8.00
	1944D	28.596	—	BV	1.00	2.50
	1944D/S	—	—	—	—	—
	1945D	82.804	—	BV	.75	1.50

50 CENTAVOS

10.0000 g, .750 SILVER, .2411 oz ASW
Establishment of the Commonwealth

176	1936	.020	15.00	25.00	35.00	65.00

183	1944S	19.187	—	BV	2.50	4.50
	1945S	18.120	—	BV	2.50	4.50

PESO

20.0000 g, .900 SILVER, .5787 oz ASW
Establishment of the Commonwealth
Presidents Roosevelt And Quezon

177	1936	.010	40.00	50.00	65.00	125.00

Establishment of the Commonwealth
Governor General Murphy And President Quezon
Rev: Similar to KM#177.

178	1936	.010	40.00	50.00	65.00	125.00

REPUBLIC
CENTAVO

BRONZE
Republic

KM#	Date	Mintage	Fine	VF	XF	Unc
186	1958	20.000	—	—	.10	.25
	1960	40.000	—	—	.10	.15
	1962	30.000	—	—	.10	.15
	1963	130.000	—	—	.10	.15

5 CENTAVOS

BRASS
Republic

187	1958	10.000	—	—	.10	.20
	1959	10.000	—	—	.10	.20
	1960	40.000	—	—	.10	.15
	1962	40.000	—	—	.10	.20
	1963	50.000	—	—	.10	.15
	1964	100.000	—	—	—	.10
	1966	10.000	—	—	.10	.20

10 CENTAVOS

NICKEL-BRASS
Republic

188	1958	10.000	—	.10	.15	.25
	1960	70.000	—	.10	.15	.20
	1962	50.000	—	.10	.15	.20
	1963	50.000	—	.10	.15	.20
	1964	100.000	—	—	.10	.20
	1966	110.000	—	—	.10	.20

25 CENTAVOS

NICKEL-BRASS
Republic
Obv: 8 smoke rings from volcano.

189.1	1958	10.000	.10	.20	.25	.50
	1960	10.000	.10	.20	.30	.50
	1962	40.000	—	.10	.25	.50
	1964	49.800	—	.10	.20	.35
	1966	10.000	—	.10	.20	.40

Obv: 6 smoke rings from volcano.

189.2	1966	40.000	—	.10	.20	.40

50 CENTAVOS

10.0000 g, .750 SILVER, .2411 oz ASW
General Douglas Mac Arthur

184	1947S	.200	—	BV	3.50	5.00

PHILIPPINES 1420

NICKEL-BRASS
Republic

KM#	Date	Mintage	Fine	VF	XF	Unc
190	1958	5.000	.20	.30	.45	1.00
	1964	25.000	.10	.20	.30	.60

1/2 PESO

12.5000 g, .900 SILVER, .3617 oz ASW
Dr. Jose Rizal

191	1961	.100	—	—	3.00	5.00

PESO

20.0000 g, .900 SILVER, .5787 oz ASW
General Douglas Mac Arthur

185	1947S	.100	—	BV	8.00	15.00

26.6000 g, .900 SILVER, .7697 oz ASW
Dr. Jose Rizal

192	1961	.100	—	—	7.00	10.00

Andres Bonifacio

193	1963	.100	—	—	7.00	10.00

Apolinario Mabini

KM#	Date	Mintage	Fine	VF	XF	Unc
194	1964	.100	—	—	7.00	10.00

25th Anniversary of Bataan Day

195	1967	.100	—	—	7.00	10.00

NOTE: KM#195 is a proof-like issue.

MONETARY REFORM
100 Sentimos = 1 Piso

SENTIMO

ALUMINUM

KM#	Date	Mintage	VF	XF	Unc
196	1967	10.000	—	—	.10
	1968	27.940	—	—	.10
	1969	12.060	—	—	.10
	1970	130.000	—	—	.10
	1974	165.000	—	—	.10
	1974	.010	—	Proof	5.00

205	1975	9.241	—	—	.10
	1975FM(M)	.108	—	—	.10
	1975FM(U)	5.875	—	—	2.00
	1975FM(P)	.037	—	Proof	1.50
	1975 Lt	—	—	—	.10
	1975(US)	105.000	—	—	.10
	1976FM(M)	.010	—	—	.10
	1976FM(U)	1.826	—	1.00	2.50
	1976FM(P)	9.901	—	Proof	2.00
	1976	10.000	—	—	.10
	1976(US)	108.000	—	—	.10
	1977	4.808	—	—	.10
	1977FM(M)	.010	—	—	1.00
	1977FM(U)	354 pcs.	—	—	4.00
	1977FM(P)	4.822	—	Proof	2.00
	1978	24.813	—	—	.10
	1978FM(M)	.010	—	—	1.00
	1978FM(P)	4.792	—	Proof	2.00

Rev: Redesigned seal

224	1979BSP	—	—	—	.10
	1979FM(M)	.010	—	—	1.00
	1979FM(P)	3,645	—	Proof	2.00
	1980BSP	—	—	—	.10
	1980FM(M)	.010	—	—	1.00
	1980FM(P)	3,133	—	Proof	2.00
	1981BSP	—	—	—	.10
	1981FM(M)	—	—	—	1.00
	1981FM(P)	1,795	—	Proof	2.00
	1982FM(P)	—	—	Proof	2.00

Obv: Lapu-Lapu. Rev: Sea shell.

KM#	Date	Mintage	VF	XF	Unc
238	1983	62.090	—	—	.10
	1983	—	—	Proof	2.00
	1984	.320	—	—	.10
	1985	.016	—	—	.10
	1986	—	—	—	.10
	1987	—	—	—	.10

5 SENTIMOS

BRASS

197	1967	40.000	—	—	.10
	1968	50.000	—	—	.10
	1970	5.000	—	.10	.20
	1972	71.744	—	—	.10
	1974	90.025	—	—	.10
	1974	.010	—	Proof	5.00

206	1975	9.995	—	—	.10
	1975FM(M)	.104	—	—	.10
	1975FM(U)	5,875	—	—	2.50
	1975FM(P)	.037	—	Proof	2.00
	1975(US)	90.035	—	—	.10
	1975 US	.010	—	Proof	2.50
	1975 Lt	—	—	—	.10
	1976FM(M)	.010	—	—	1.50
	1976FM(U)	1,826	—	—	5.00
	1976FM(P)	9,901	—	Proof	2.50
	1976	10.000	—	—	.10
	1976(US)	100.026	—	—	.10
	1977	19.367	—	—	.10
	1977FM(M)	.010	—	—	1.50
	1977FM(U)	354 pcs.	—	—	4.00
	1977FM(P)	4,822	—	Proof	2.50
	1978	61.838	—	—	.10
	1978FM(M)	.010	—	—	1.50
	1978FM(P)	4,792	—	Proof	2.50
	1982BSP	—	—	—	.10

Rev: Redesigned seal

225	1979BSP	12.805	—	—	.10
	1979FM(M)	.010	—	—	1.00
	1979FM(P)	3,645	—	Proof	2.50
	1980BSP	—	—	—	.10
	1980FM(M)	.010	—	—	1.00
	1980FM(P)	3,133	—	Proof	2.50
	1981BSP	—	—	—	.10
	1981FM(M)	—	—	—	1.00
	1981FM(P)	1,795	—	Proof	3.00
	1982FM(P)	—	—	Proof	3.00

ALUMINUM
Melchora Aquino

239	1983	100.016	—	—	.10
	1983	—	—	Proof	2.00
	1984	141.744	—	—	.10
	1985	50.416	—	—	.10
	1986	—	—	—	.10
	1987	—	—	—	.10

10 SENTIMOS

COPPER-NICKEL

198	1967	50.000	—	—	.10
	1968	60.000	—	—	.10

KM#	Date	Mintage	VF	XF	Unc
198	1969	40.000	—	—	.10
	1970	50.000	—	—	.10
	1971	80.000	—	—	.10
	1972	121.390	—	—	.10
	1974	60.208	—	—	.10
	1974	.010	—	Proof	7.50

207	1975	10.000	—	—	.10
	1975FM(M)	.104	—	—	.10
	1975FM(U)	5,875	—	—	2.50
	1975FM(P)	.037	—	Proof	2.00
	1975(VDM)	—	—	—	.10
	1975(US)	60.000	—	—	.10
	1976FM(M)	.010	—	—	.15
	1976FM(U)	1,826	—	—	6.00
	1976FM(P)	9,901	—	Proof	3.00
	1976	10.000	—	—	.10
	1976(US)	50.010	—	—	.10
	1977	29.314	—	—	.10
	1977FM(M)	.010	—	—	1.50
	1977FM(U)	354 pcs.	—	—	6.50
	1977FM(P)	4,822	—	Proof	3.00
	1978	60.042	—	—	.10
	1978FM(M)	.010	—	—	2.00
	1978FM(P)	4,792	—	Proof	3.00

Rev: Redesigned seal

226	1979BSP	6.446	—	—	.10
	1979FM(M)	.010	—	—	1.00
	1979FM(P)	3,645	—	Proof	3.00
	1980BSP	—	—	—	.10
	1980FM(M)	.010	—	—	1.00
	1980FM(P)	3,133	—	Proof	3.25
	1981BSP	—	—	—	.10
	1981FM(M)	—	—	—	1.00
	1981FM(P)	1,795	—	Proof	3.50
	1982BSP	—	—	—	.10
	1982FM(P)	—	—	Proof	3.50

ALUMINUM
World Conference on Fisheries - F.A.O.
Rev: Fish's name in error: PANDAKA PYGMEA

240.1	1983	95.640	—	—	.10
	1983	—	—	Proof	3.00
	1987	—	—	—	.10

Rev: Fish's name: PANDAKA PYGMAEA

240.2	1984	235.900	—	—	.10
	1985	90.169	—	—	.10
	1986	—	—	—	.10
	1987	—	—	—	.10

25 SENTIMOS

COPPER-NICKEL
Republic

199	1967	40.000	—	.10	.20
	1968	10.000	—	.10	.20
	1969	10.000	—	.10	.20
	1970	40.000	—	.10	.20
	1971	60.000	—	.10	.20
	1972	59.572	—	.10	.20
	1974	10.000	—	.10	.20
	1974	.010	—	Proof	15.00

208	1975	10.000	—	.10	.20
	1975FM(M)	.104	—	—	.40
	1975FM(U)	5,875	—	—	3.50
	1975FM(P)	.037	—	Proof	3.00

KM#	Date	Mintage	VF	XF	Unc
208	1975(US)	10.000	—	.10	.20
	1975(VDM)	—	—	.10	.20
	1976FM(M)	.010	—	.10	.20
	1976FM(U)	1,826	—	—	8.00
	1976FM(P)	9,901	—	Proof	3.50
	1976	10.000	—	.10	.20
	1976(US)	10.010	—	.10	.20
	1977	24.654	—	.10	.20
	1977FM(M)	.010	—	—	1.50
	1977FM(U)	354 pcs.	—	—	8.00
	1977FM(P)	4,822	—	Proof	4.50
	1978	40.466	—	.10	.20
	1978FM(M)	.010	—	—	2.50
	1978FM(P)	4,792	—	Proof	4.00

Rev: Redesigned seal

227	1979BSP	20.725	—	.10	.20
	1979FM(M)	.010	—	—	1.50
	1979FM(P)	3,645	—	Proof	4.50
	1980BSP	—	—	.10	.20
	1980FM(M)	.010	—	—	1.50
	1980FM(P)	3,133	—	Proof	4.50
	1981BSP	—	—	.10	.20
	1981FM(M)	—	—	—	1.50
	1981FM(P)	1,795	—	Proof	5.00
	1982BSP	—	—	.10	.20
	1982FM(P)	—	—	Proof	5.00

BRASS
Juan Luna

241	1983	92.944	—	.10	.20
	1983	—	—	Proof	3.00
	1984	254.324	—	.10	.20
	1985	84.922	—	.10	.20
	1986	—	—	.10	.20
	1987	—	—	.10	.20

50 SENTIMOS

COPPER-NICKEL-ZINC

200	1967	20.000	—	.20	.50
	1971	10.000	.10	.20	.60
	1972 serif on 2	20.517	.10	.20	.50
	1972 plain 2	—	.10	.20	.50
	1974	5.004	.10	.20	.60
	1974	.010	—	Proof	25.00
	1975	5.714	.10	.20	.60

COPPER-NICKEL
Marcelo H. Del Pilar
Eagle's name - PITHECOPHAGA

242.1	1983	27.644	—	.10	.25
	1983	—	—	Proof	5.00
	1984	121.408	—	.10	.25
	1985	107.048	—	.10	.25
	1986	—	—	.10	.25
	1987	—	—	.10	.25

Error. Eagle's name - PITHECOBHAGA

| 242.2 | 1983 | Inc. Ab. | — | — | — |

PISO

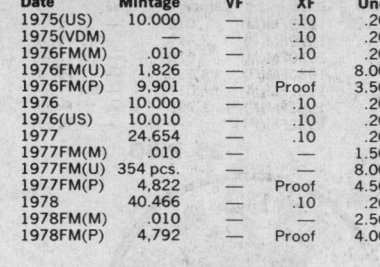

26.4500 g, .900 SILVER, .7653 oz ASW
Centennial Birth of Aguinaldo

KM#	Date	Mintage	VF	XF	Unc
201	1969	.100	—	7.00	9.00

NOTE: These coins are 'proof-like' issues.

NICKEL
Pope Paul VI Visit

202	1970	.070	—	1.00	2.00

26.4500 g, .900 SILVER, .7653 oz ASW

202a	1970	.030	—	7.00	12.50

19.3000 g, .917 GOLD, .5691 oz AGW

202b	1970	1,000	—	—	500.00

COPPER-NICKEL
Regular Issue

203	1972	121.821	.15	.25	.75
	1974	45.631	.15	.25	.75
	1974	.010	—	Proof	37.50

209.1	1975	10.000	.15	.25	.75
	1975FM(M)	.104	—	—	1.00
	1975FM(U)	5,877	—	—	3.50
	1975FM(P)	.037	—	Proof	3.00
	1975(VDM)	—	.15	.25	.75
	1975(US)	44.080	.15	.25	.75
	1976FM(M)	.010	—	—	1.00
	1976FM(U)	1,826	—	—	10.00
	1976FM(P)	9,901	—	Proof	5.00
	1976(VDM)	—	.15	.25	.75
	1976(US)	30.010	.15	.25	.75
	1977	14.771	.15	.25	.75
	1977FM(M)	.012	—	—	4.00

PHILIPPINES 1422

KM#	Date	Mintage	VF	XF	Unc
209.1	1977FM(U)	354 pcs.	—	—	10.00
	1977FM(P)	4,822	—	Proof	5.50
	1978	19.408	.15	.25	.75
	1978FM(M)	.010	—	—	4.00
	1978FM(P)	4,792	—	Proof	5.50

Rev. leg: ISANG BANSA ISANG DIWA below shield.

209.2	1979BSP	.321	.15	.25	1.00
	1979FM(M)	.010	—	—	2.50
	1979FM(P)	3,645	—	Proof	6.00
	1980BSP	—	.15	.25	.75
	1980FM(M)	.010	—	—	2.50
	1980FM(P)	3,133	—	Proof	12.50
	1981BSP	—	.15	.25	.75
	1981FM	—	—	—	3.00
	1981FM(P)	1,795	—	Proof	6.00
	1982FM(P)	—	—	Proof	6.00
	1982BSP lg.dt.	—	.15	.25	.75
	1982BSP sm.dt.	—	.15	.25	.75

Jose Rizal

243	1983	55.869	.10	.20	.50
	1983	—	—	Proof	7.00
	1984	4.997	.10	.20	.50
	1985	182.596	.10	.20	.50
	1986	—	.10	.20	.50
	1987	—	.10	.20	.50

2 PISO

COPPER-NICKEL
Andres Bonifacio

244	1983	15.640	.15	.30	1.00
	1983	—	—	Proof	10.00
	1984	121.111	.15	.30	1.00
	1985	115.215	.15	.30	1.00
	1986	—	.15	.30	1.00
	1987	—	.15	.30	1.00

5 PISO

NICKEL

210.1	1975FM(M)	3,850	—	—	15.00
	1975FM(U)	7,875	—	—	10.00
	1975FM(P)	.039	—	Proof	7.50
	1975(Sh)	20.000	.50	.75	1.50
	1976FM(M)	.010	—	—	5.00
	1976FM(U)	1,826	—	—	17.50
	1976FM(P)	9,901	—	Proof	7.50
	1977FM(M)	.010	—	—	5.00
	1977FM(U)	354 pcs.	—	—	15.00
	1977FM(P)	4,822	—	Proof	7.50
	1978FM(M)	.010	—	—	5.00
	1978FM(P)	4,792	—	Proof	7.50
	1982	—	.50	.75	1.50

Obv. leg: ISANG BANSA ISANG DIWA below shield.

KM#	Date	Mintage	VF	XF	Unc
210.2	1979FM(M)	.010	—	—	3.00
	1979FM(P)	3,645	—	Proof	8.00
	1980FM(M)	.010	—	—	3.00
	1980FM(P)	3,133	—	Proof	8.00
	1981FM(M)	.011	—	—	3.00
	1981FM(P)	1,795	—	Proof	10.00
	1982FM(P)	—	—	Proof	10.00

25 PISO

26.4000 g, .900 SILVER, .7639 oz ASW
25th Anniversary of Bank

204	1974	.090	—	—	10.00
	1974	.010	—	Proof	17.50

25.0000 g, .500 SILVER, .4018 oz ASW
Emilio Aguinaldo
Obv: Similar to KM#204.

211	1975FM(M)	.010	—	—	10.00
	1975FM(U)	5,875	—	—	15.00
	1975FM(P)	.037	—	Proof	15.00

F.A.O. Issue
Obv: Similar to KM#204.

214	1976FM(M)	.022	—	—	12.00
	1976FM(U)	1,826	—	—	40.00
	1976FM(P)	9,901	—	Proof	20.00

Banawie Rice Terraces
Obv: Similar to KM#204.

217	1977FM(M)	.010	—	—	15.00
	1977FM(U)	354 pcs.	—	—	50.00
	1977FM(P)	4,822	—	Proof	30.00

100th Anniversary of Birth of Quezon
Obv: Similar to KM#204.

KM#	Date	Mintage	VF	XF	Unc
221	1978FM(M)	.010	—	—	15.00
	1978FM(P)	9,930	—	Proof	17.50

UN Conference on Trade and Development

228	1979FM(M)	.010	—	—	15.00
	1979FM(P)	7,093	—	Proof	20.00

Gen. Douglas MacArthur

230	1980FM(M)	9,800	—	—	17.50
	1980FM(P)	6,318	—	Proof	40.00

World Food Day

232	1981FM(M)	.010	—	—	15.00
	1981FM(P)	3,033	—	Proof	22.50

Presidents Marcos and Reagan

235	1982	8,000	—	—	60.00
	1982	250 pcs.	—	Proof	525.00

PHILIPPINES 1423

18.4100 g, .925 SILVER, .5475 oz ASW
Aquino Visit

KM#	Date	Mintage	VF	XF	Unc
246	1986	—	—	Proof	35.00

50 PISO

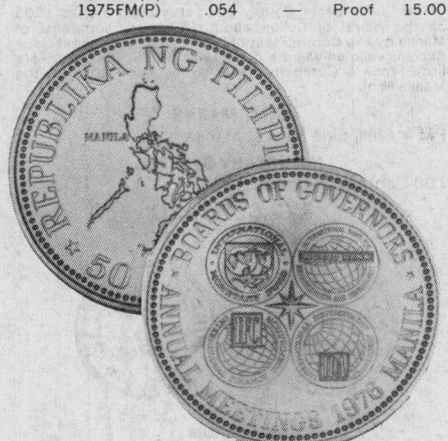

27.4000 g, .925 SILVER, .8148 oz ASW

212	1975FM(M)	.010	—	—	15.00
	1975FM(U)	7,875	—	—	17.50
	1975FM(P)	.054	—	Proof	15.00

I.M.F. Meeting

215	1976	5,477	—	Proof	17.50
	1976FM(M)	.010	—	—	15.00
	1976FM(U)	1,826	—	—	60.00
	1976FM(P)	.015	—	Proof	15.00

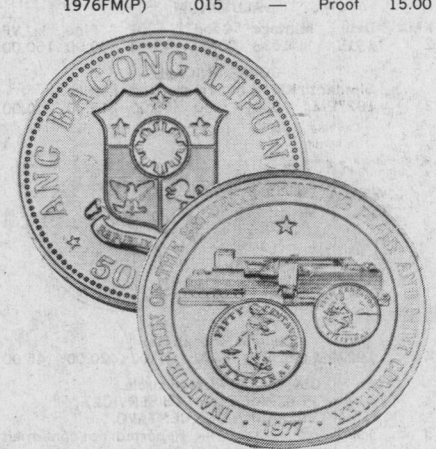

Inauguration of New Mint Facilities

218	1977FM(M)	.010	—	—	17.50
	1977FM(U)	354 pcs.	—	—	80.00
	1977FM(P)	6,704	—	Proof	25.00

100th Anniversary of Birth of Quezon

KM#	Date	Mintage	VF	XF	Unc
222	1978FM(M)	.010	—	—	15.00
	1978FM(P)	9,969	—	Proof	30.00

International Year of the Child

229	1979FM(M)	.010	—	—	15.00
	1979FM(P)	.027	—	Proof	15.00

Pope John Paul II Visit

233	1981FM(M)	.010	—	—	30.00
	1981FM(P)	3,353	—	Proof	60.00

40th Anniversary of Bataan-Corregidor

236	1982FM(M)	—	—	—	12.50
	1982FM(P)	4,626	—	Proof	40.00

100 PISO

25.0000 g, .500 SILVER, .4019 oz ASW
Philippine National University

KM#	Date	Mintage	VF	XF	Unc
245	1983	.015	—	—	15.00
	1983	2,000	—	Proof	35.00

200 PISO

25.0000 g, .925 SILVER, .7436 oz ASW
World Wildlife Fund - Mindoro Buffalo

248	1987	.025	—	Proof	20.00

500 PISO

28.0000 g, .925 SILVER, .8328 oz ASW

PHILIPPINES 1424

People Power Revolution

KM#	Date	Mintage	VF	XF	Unc
249	1988	*7,500		Proof	45.00

1000 PISO

9.9500 g, .900 GOLD, .2879 oz AGW
3rd Anniversary of the New Society

213	1975	.023	—	—	135.00
	1975	.013	—	Proof	150.00

1500 PISO

20.5500 g, .900 GOLD, .5947 oz AGW
I.M.F. Meeting

216	1976	5,500	—	—	300.00
	1976	6,500	—	Proof	350.00

219	1977	4,000	—	—	300.00
	1977	6,000	—	Proof	325.00

Security Printing & Mint

223	1978	3,000	—	—	300.00
	1978	3,000	—	Proof	350.00

9.9500 g, .900 GOLD, .2879 oz AGW
Pope John Paul II Visit

234	1981	1,000	—	Proof	375.00

9.7800 g, .900 GOLD, .2830 oz AGW
40th Anniversary of Bataan-Corregidor

237	1982FM(U)	—	—	—	250.00
	1982FM(P)	445 pcs.	—	Proof	400.00

2500 PISO

14.5700 g, .500 GOLD, .2342 oz AGW
Gen. Douglas MacArthur

KM#	Date	Mintage	VF	XF	Unc
231	1980FM(P)	3,073	—	Proof	450.00

15.0000 g, .500 GOLD, .2414 oz AGW
Aquino Visit

247	1986	250 pcs.	—	Proof	400.00

5000 PISO

68.7400 g, .900 GOLD, 1.9893 oz AGW
5th Anniversary of the New Society

220	1977FM(U)	100 pcs.	—	—	1100.
	1977FM(P)	3,832	—	Proof	1100.

MINT SETS (MS)

KM#	Date	Mintage	Identification	Issue Price	Mkt. Val.
MS1	1936(3)	—	KM176-178	—	325.00
MS2	1947(2)	—	KM184-185	—	20.00
MS3	1958(5)	—	KM186-190	—	2.50
MS4	1970(2)	—	KM202,202a	—	15.00
MS5	1975(8)	5,877*	KM205-208,209.1,210-212	33.50	35.00
MS6	1975(8)	3,850	KM205-208,209.1,210-212	—	55.00
MS7	1976(8)	1,826*	KM205-210,214-215	—	150.00
MS8	1976(8)	10,000	KM205-210,214-215	—	35.00
MS9	1977(8)	354*	KM205-210,217-218	—	175.00
MS10	1977(8)	10,000	KM205-210,217-218	—	35.00
MS11	1978(8)	10,000	KM205-210,221-222	—	35.00
MS12	1979(8)	10,000	KM209.2-210.2,224-229	—	35.00
MS13	1980(7)	9,800	KM209.2-210.2,224-227,230	—	25.00
MS14	1981(8)	10,000	KM209.2-210.2,224-227,232-233	—	50.00

*NOTE: Enclosed in Franklin Mint folder.

PROOF SETS (PS)

PS1	1903(7)	2,558	KM162-168	—	600.00
PS1i	1903(7)	Inc. Ab.	KM162-168 (impaired)	—	350.00
PS2	1904(7)	1,355	KM162-168	—	800.00
PS2i	1904(7)	Inc. Ab.	KM162-168 (impaired)	—	450.00
PS3	1905(7)	471	KM162-168	—	1250.
PS3i	1905(7)	Inc. Ab.	KM162-168 (impaired)	—	550.00
PS4	1906(7)	500	KM162-168	—	1100.
PS4i	1906(7)	Inc. Ab.	KM162-168 (impaired)	—	500.00
PS5	1908(7)	500	KM162-164,169-172	—	1000.
PS5i	1908(7)	Inc. Ab.	KM162-164,169-172 (impaired)	—	500.00
PS6	1958(5)	—	KM186-190	—	—
PS7	1974(6)	*10,000	KM196-200,203	—	95.00
PS8	1975(8)	36,516	KM205-208,209.1-210.1,211-212	67.00	50.00
PS9	1975(6)	—	KM205-208,209.1-210.1	—	—
PS10	1976(8)	9,901	KM205-208,209.1-210.1,214-215	67.00	60.00
PS11	1977(8)	4,822	KM205-208,209.1-210.1,217-218	70.00	80.00
PS12	1978(8)	4,792	KM205-208,209.1-210.1,220-221	70.00	75.00
PS13	1978(2)	3,911	KM221-222	46.00	50.00
PS14	1979(8)	3,645	KM209.2-210.2,224-229	68.00	60.00
PS15	1979(2)	2,448	KM228-229	47.50	35.00
PS16	1980(7)	3,133	KM209.2-210.2,224-227,230	65.00	50.00
PS17	1981(7)	1,795	KM209.2-210.2,224-227,232-233	—	115.00
PS18	1982(7)	—	KM209.2-210.2,224-227,236	52.00	70.00
PS19	1983(8)	—	KM238-239,240.1,241,242.1,243-245	50.00	70.00

LEPROSARIUM COINAGE
Culion Leper Colony

The Culion Leper Colony was established around 1903 on the island of Culion about 150 miles southeast of Manila by the Commission of Public Health. The first issue of coins valid only in the colony was produced by a private firm, Frank & Company. Later issues were struck at the Manila Mint.

MINT MARKS
PM - Philippine Mint at Manila

MONETARY SYSTEM
100 Centavos = 1 Peso

1/2 CENTAVO

ALUMINUM

KM#	Date	Mintage	Fine	VF	XF	Unc
1	1913	.017	.50	1.00	2.00	5.00

NOTE: Some authorities doubt that this coin circulated.

CENTAVO

ALUMINUM

KM#	Date	Mintage	Good	VG	Fine	VF
2	1913	.033	25.00	45.00	80.00	150.00

COPPER-NICKEL
Similar to KM#4 but 1st die; better strike.

3	1927PM	.030	5.00	10.00	15.00	40.00

2nd die, poor strike.

4	1927PM	Inc. Ab.	6.00	12.00	20.00	45.00

Obv: Bust of Rizal in circle.
Rev: PHILIPPINE HEALTH SERVICE/ LEPER COIN ONE CENTAVO.

5	1930	—	—	Reported, not confirmed		

5 CENTAVOS

ALUMINUM
Similar to 1/2 Centavo, KM#1.

6	1913	6,600	30.00	60.00	150.00	250.00

COPPER-NICKEL

KM#	Date	Mintage	Good	VG	Fine	VF
7	1927	.016	2.50	5.00	8.00	15.00

10 CENTAVOS
ALUMINUM
Similar to 1/2 Centavo, KM#1.

8	1913	6.600	4.00	6.50	10.00	35.00

Similar to 1 Peso, KM#14.

9	1920	.020	2.50	5.00	7.50	20.00

COPPER-NICKEL

KM#	Date	Mintage	VG	Fine	VF	XF
10	1930	.017	1.00	2.00	3.50	10.00

NOTE: One pattern exists in copper, but it has not been authenticated.

20 CENTAVOS
ALUMINUM
Similar to 1/2 Centavo, KM#1.

KM#	Date	Mintage	Good	VG	Fine	VF
11	1913	.010	5.00	10.00	18.00	50.00

Similar to 1 Peso, KM#14.

12	1920	.010	2.50	5.00	10.00	20.00

COPPER-NICKEL
Obv: CULION LEPER COLONY
20/CENTAVOS/PHILIPPINE ISLANDS.
Rev: A caduceus and PHILIPPINE HEALTH SERVICE.

KM#	Date	Mintage	VG	Fine	VF	XF
13	1922PM	.010	5.00	10.00	17.50	30.00

PESO

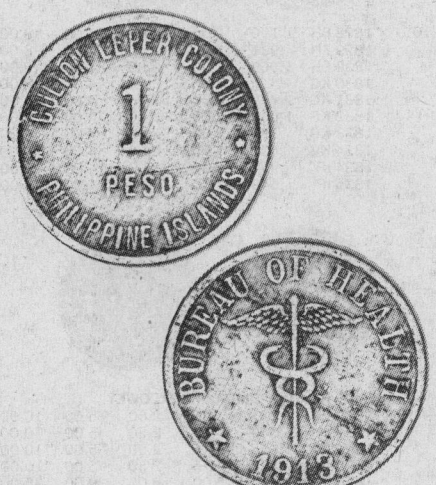

ALUMINUM

14	1913	8,600	1.50	3.50	7.50	25.00

NOTE: This coin exists with thick and thin planchets.

15	1920	4,000	3.00	8.00	15.00	35.00

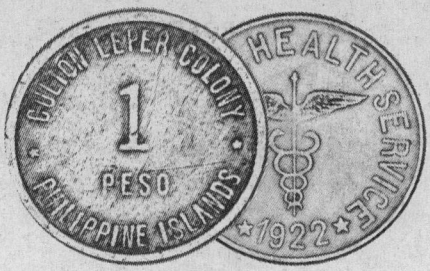

COPPER-NICKEL

KM#	Date	Mintage	VG	Fine	VF	XF
16	1922PM	8,280	3.00	7.00	12.00	20.00

Similar to KM#16, but caduceus has curved wings.

17	1922PM Inc. Ab.	.020	20.00	35.00	50.00	100.00

18	1925	.020	1.00	2.50	5.00	10.00

PITCAIRN ISLANDS

A small volcanic island, along with the uninhabited islands of Oeno, Henderson, and Ducie, constitute the British Colony of Pitcairn Islands. The main island has an area of about 2 sq. mi. and a population of 61. It is located 1350 miles southeast of Tahiti. The islanders subsist on fishing, garden produce and crops. The sale of postage stamps and carved curios to passing ships brings cash income.

Discovered in 1767 by a British naval officer, Pitcairn was not occupied until 1790 when Fletcher Christian and nine mutineers from the British ship, HMS Bounty, along with some Tahitian men and women went ashore, and survived in obscurity until discovered by American Whalers in 1880.

Adamstown is the chief settlement, located on the north coast, one of the few places that island-made longboats can land. The primary religion is Seventh-day Adventist and a public school provides basic education. In 1898 the settlement was placed under the jurisdication of the Commissioner for the Western Pacific. Since 1952, the colony has been administered by the governor of Fiji through locally elected officers and an island council.

New Zealand currency has been used since July 10, 1967.

DOLLAR
COPPER-NICKEL
Drafting of Pitcairn Islands Constitution
Similar to 250 Dollars, KM#2.

KM#	Date	Mintage	VF	XF	Unc
3	1988	—	—	—	6.00

28.2800 g, .925 SILVER, .8411 oz ASW

3a	1988	—	—	Proof	48.00

COPPER-NICKEL
Mutiny on the Bounty
Obv: Similar to 250 Dollars, KM#2.

4	1989	*.050	—	—	6.00

28.2800 g, .925 SILVER, .8411 oz ASW

4a	1989	*.020	—	Proof	48.00

50 DOLLARS
155.6000 g, .999 SILVER, 5.0000 oz ASW
Drafting of Pitcairn Islands Constitution
Similar to 250 Dollars, KM#2.

1	1988	*.010	—	Proof	150.00

Mutiny on the Bounty
Obv: Similar to 250 Dollars, KM#2.
Rev: Similar to 1 Dollar, KM#4.

5	1989	*.010	—	Proof	150.00

250 DOLLARS

15.9800 g, .917 GOLD, .4708 oz AGW
Drafting of Pitcairn Islands Constitution

2	1988	*2,500	—	Proof	575.00

Mutiny on the Bounty
Obv: Similar to KM#2.
Rev: Similar to 1 Dollar, KM#4.

6	1989	*2,500	—	Proof	575.00

POLAND

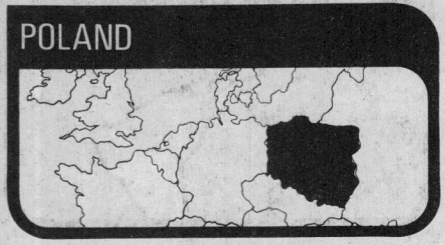

The Polish People's Republic, located in central Europe, has an area of 120,725 sq. mi. (312,677 sq. km.) and a population of *38.4 million. Capital: Warsaw. The economy is essentially agricultural, but industrial activity provides the products for foreign trade. Machinery, coal, coke, iron, steel and transport equipment are exported.

Poland, which began as a Slavic duchy in the 10th century and reached its peak of power between the 14th and 16th centuries, has had a turbulent history of invasion, occupation or partition by Mongols, Turkey, Hungary, Sweden, Austria, Prussia and Russia.

The first partition took place in 1772. Prussia took Polish Pomerania. Russia took part of the eastern provinces. Austria took Galicia, in which lay the fortress city of Cracow (Krakow). The second partition occurred in 1793 when Russia took another slice of the eastern provinces and Prussia took what remained of western Poland. The third partition, 1795, literally removed Poland from the map. Russia took what was left of the eastern provinces. Prussia seized most of central Poland, including Warsaw. Austria took what was left of the south. Napoleon restored to Poland much of the territory lost to Prussia and Austria, but after his defeat another partition returned the Duchy of Warsaw to Prussia, made Cracow into a tiny republic, and declared what remained to be the Kingdom of Poland under the czar and in permanent union with Russia.

Poland re-emerged as an independent state recognized by the Treaty of Versailles on June 28, 1919, and maintained its independence until 1939 when it was invaded by, and partitioned between, Germany and Russia. Poland's present boundaries were determined by the U.S.-British-Russian agreement of Aug. 16, 1945. The Polish Communist-Socialist faction won a decisive victory at the polls in 1947 and established a 'People's Republic' of the Soviet type in 1952.

RULERS

Friedrich August I, King of Saxony,
  As Grand Duke, 1807-1814
Alexander I, Czar of Russia,
  As King, 1815-1825
Nicholas (Mikolay) I, Czar of Russia,
  As King, 1825-1855

MINT MARKS

MV, MW, MW-monogram - Warsaw Mint
FF - Stuttgart Germany 1916-1917
(w) Arrow-Warsaw 1925-39
Other letters appearing with date denote the Mint Master at the time the coin was struck.

MINTMASTER'S INITIALS
WARSAW MINT

Letter	Date	Name
IB	1811-27	Jakub Benik
IP	1834-35	Jerzy (George) Pusch
JS	1810-11	John Stockmann
KG	1829-34	Carl Gronau

MONETARY SYSTEM
Until 1815

1 Solidus = 1 Schilling
3 Solidi = 2 Poltura = 1 Grosz
3 Poltura = 1-1/2 Grosze = 1 Polturak
6 Groszy = 1 Szostak
18 Groszy = 1 Tympf
30 Groszy = 4 Silbergroschen
  = 1 Zloty
1 Talara = 1 Zloty
6 Zlotych = 1 Reichsthaler
8 Zlotych = 1 Speciesthaler
5 Speciesthaler = 1 August D'or
3 Ducats = 1 Stanislaus D'or

GRAND DUCHY OF WARSAW
GROSZ

COPPER

C#	Date	Mintage	VG	Fine	VF	XF
81	1810 IS	.743	1.75	3.00	6.00	12.50
	1811 IS	4.358	1.75	2.50	5.00	10.00
	1811 IB	Inc. Ab.	1.75	2.50	5.00	10.00
	1812 IB	6.346	1.75	2.50	5.00	10.00
	1814 IB	3.072	1.75	2.50	5.00	10.00

3 GROSZE

COPPER

C#	Date	Mintage	VG	Fine	VF	XF
82	1810 IS	1.008	2.00	4.50	9.00	18.00
	1811 IS	5.479	2.00	3.00	7.50	15.00
	1811 IB	Inc. Ab.	2.00	3.00	7.50	15.00
	1812 IB	6.816	2.00	3.00	7.50	15.00
	1813 IB	1.139	2.00	3.00	7.50	15.00
	1814 IB	3.427	2.00	3.00	7.50	15.00

5 GROSZY

2.2000 g, .210 SILVER, .0148 oz ASW

83	1811 IS	11.595	4.00	7.00	15.00	25.00
	1811 IB	Inc. Ab.	4.00	7.00	15.00	25.00
	1812 IB	3.405	4.00	7.00	15.00	25.00

10 GROSZY

2.9900 g, .245 SILVER, .0235 oz ASW

84	1810 IS	—	6.00	15.00	30.00	60.00
	1812 IB	.951	5.00	10.00	16.50	35.00
	1813 IB	3.549	5.00	10.00	15.00	30.00

1/6 TALARA

4.9800 g, .535 SILVER, .0856 oz ASW

85	1811 IS	.113	9.00	15.00	45.00	90.00
	1812 IB	.223	9.00	15.00	45.00	90.00
	1813 IB	.106	15.00	25.00	50.00	100.00
	1814 IB	1.491	9.00	15.00	45.00	90.00

1/3 TALARA

8.6600 g, .625 SILVER, .1740 oz ASW

86	1810 IS	.123	10.00	15.00	45.00	90.00
	1811 IS	.993	10.00	15.00	30.00	60.00
	1812 IB	2.804	10.00	15.00	30.00	60.00
	1813 IB	1.916	10.00	15.00	30.00	60.00
	1814 IB	4.611	10.00	15.00	30.00	60.00

TALAR

22.9200 g, .720 SILVER, .5305 oz ASW

87	1811 IB	4.488	60.00	100.00	250.00	500.00
	1812 IB	.036	60.00	100.00	200.00	400.00
	1814 IB	.014	60.00	100.00	200.00	400.00

TRADE COINAGE
DUCAT

3.5000 g, .986 GOLD, .1109 oz AGW

C#	Date	Mintage	VG	Fine	VF	XF
88	1812 IB	8,456	250.00	400.00	700.00	1100.
	1813 IB	3,000	450.00	800.00	1400.	2000.

CONGRESS KINGDOM OF POLAND
MONETARY SYSTEM

30 Groszy = 15 Russian Kopeks = 1 Zloty
10 Zlotych = 1-1/2 Rubles

GROSZ

COPPER

93	1816 IB	1.873	1.00	2.00	4.00	8.00
	1817 IB	3.092	1.00	2.00	4.00	8.00
	1818 IB	4.035	1.00	2.00	4.00	8.00
	1818	Inc. Ab.	1.00	7.50	12.50	20.00
	1819 IB	Inc. Bl.	1.00	2.50	5.00	8.00
	1820 IB	.372	1.00	2.50	5.00	8.00
	1821 IB	.571	1.00	2.50	5.00	8.00
	1822 IB					
		Inc. C#94	6.00	10.00	17.50	35.00

NOTE: Varieties of eagles exist.

105	1828 FH	1.190	1.00	2.00	4.00	8.00
	1829 FH	.931	1.00	2.00	4.00	8.00
	1830 FH	1.569	1.00	2.00	4.00	8.00
	1830 KG	I.A.	1.00	2.00	4.00	8.00
	1831 KG	1.777	1.00	2.00	4.00	8.00
	1832 KG	1.559	1.00	2.00	4.00	8.00
	1833 KG	.375	1.00	2.00	4.00	8.00
	1834 KG	.427	1.00	2.00	4.00	8.00
	1834 IP	I.A.	1.00	2.00	4.00	8.00
	1835 IP	.542	1.00	2.00	4.00	8.00
	(Mining)					

Rev. leg: Z MIEDZI KRALOWEY.

94	1822 IB	2.721	1.75	2.50	5.00	10.00
	1823 IB	5.046	1.75	2.50	5.00	10.00
	1824 IB	5.413	1.75	2.50	5.00	10.00
	1825 IB	2.108	1.75	2.50	5.00	10.00
	1826 IB	—	5.00	10.00	20.00	35.00

106	1835 MW	.542	2.00	4.00	8.00	15.00
	1836 MW	.839	2.00	4.00	8.00	15.00
	1837 MW	1.016	1.00	2.00	4.00	8.00
	1837 WM	I.A.	—	—	Rare	—
	1838 MW	.488	1.00	2.00	4.00	8.00
	1839 MW	.670	1.00	2.00	4.00	8.00
	1840 MW					
		.243	1.00	2.00	4.00	8.00

Rev: W/wreath, pearl rim.

| 106a | 1840 | Inc. Ab. | 7.50 | 12.50 | 17.50 | 30.00 |

Rev: JEDEN or IEDEN above value.

107	1840 MW					
		Inc. C106	—	—	Rare	—
	1841 MW	.372	—	—	Rare	—

3 GROSZE

COPPER
Plain edge, struck w/o collar

C#	Date	Mintage	VG	Fine	VF	XF
95.1	1817 IB	.843	2.00	4.00	8.00	16.00
(C95)	1818 IB	.157	4.00	8.00	17.50	25.00

NOTE: Varieties of eagles exist.

Reeded edge, struck in collar

C#	Date	Mintage	VG	Fine	VF	XF
95.2	1818 IB	—	—	—	Rare	—
(C95.1)	1819 IB	.187	2.00	4.00	8.00	16.00
	1820 IB	.089	2.00	5.00	10.00	20.00

(Mining)

Rev. leg: Z MIEDZI KRAIOWEY.

C#	Date	Mintage	VG	Fine	VF	XF
108	1826 IB	.570	7.00	10.00	15.00	25.00
	1827 IB	Inc. Ab.	7.00	10.00	15.00	25.00

Rev. leg: 3/GROSZE/POLSKI.

C#	Date	Mintage	VG	Fine	VF	XF
109	1827 FH	.495	2.50	5.00	10.00	20.00
	1828 FH	1.159	2.00	4.00	8.00	16.00
	1829 FH	1.057	2.00	4.00	8.00	16.00
	1829	—	7.00	10.00	15.00	25.00
	1830 FH	.891	2.00	4.00	8.00	16.00
	1830 KG	I.A.	12.50	20.00	35.00	75.00
	1831 FH	1.112	—	—	Rare	—
	1831 KG	1.343	2.00	4.00	8.00	16.00
	1832 FH	.030	—	—	Rare	—
	1832 KG	7.117	2.00	4.00	8.00	16.00
	1833 KG	.515	2.00	4.00	8.00	16.00
	1834 KG	.346	2.50	5.00	10.00	20.00
	1834 IP	I.A.	2.50	5.00	10.00	20.00
	1835 IP	.185	4.00	8.00	16.00	30.00

Rev: Wreath surrounds value.

C#	Date	Mintage	VG	Fine	VF	XF
110.1	1835 MW	I.A.	2.00	4.00	8.00	16.00
(C110)	1836 MW	.244	2.00	4.00	8.00	16.00
	1837 MW	.398	2.00	4.00	8.00	16.00
	1838 MW	.288	2.00	4.00	8.00	16.00
	1839 MW	.333	2.00	4.00	8.00	16.00

Obv: Eagle's heads larger, shield smaller.

C#	Date	Mintage	VG	Fine	VF	XF
110.2	1840 MW	.118	2.00	4.00	8.00	16.00
(C110.1)	1840 WW	I.A.	7.00	10.00	15.00	25.00
	1841 MW	.242	4.00	7.50	15.00	25.00

5 GROSZY

1.4500 g, .192 SILVER, .0090 oz ASW
Obv: Eagle's wings smaller. Rev. value: 5 GROSZY.
Smooth edge

C#	Date	Mintage	VG	Fine	VF	XF
96.1 (C96)	1816 IB	2.700	6.00	8.50	12.00	22.50

Reeded edge

C#	Date	Mintage	VG	Fine	VF	XF
96.2 (C96.1)	1817 IB	—	—	—	Rare	—

Obv: Redesigned shield.

C#	Date	Mintage	VG	Fine	VF	XF
96.3	1818 IB	3.056	2.50	5.00	12.00	22.50
(C96.2)	1819 IB	5.532	2.50	5.00	12.00	22.50
	1820 IB	3.481	2.50	5.00	12.00	22.50
	1821 IB	1.651	2.50	5.00	12.00	22.50
	1822 IB	1.282	2.50	5.00	12.00	22.50
	1823 IB	2.098	2.50	5.00	12.00	22.50
	1824 IB	.235	5.00	10.00	25.00	50.00
	1825 IB	.350	2.50	5.00	12.00	22.50
111	1826 IB	2.079	2.50	5.00	12.00	22.50
	1827 IB	1.904	2.50	5.00	12.00	22.50
	1827 FH	I.A.	2.50	5.00	15.00	25.00
	1828 FH	.403	2.50	5.00	15.00	25.00
	1829 FH	.714	2.50	5.00	15.00	25.00

C#	Date	Mintage	VG	Fine	VF	XF
111	1829 KG	—	—	—	Rare	—
	1830 FH	.571	2.50	5.00	15.00	25.00
	1831 KG	.359	3.00	8.00	17.50	30.00
	1832 KG	.154	10.00	20.00	40.00	80.00

C#	Date	Mintage	VG	Fine	VF	XF
111a	1836 MW	.159	2.50	5.00	15.00	25.00
	1838 MW	.173	2.50	5.00	15.00	25.00
	1839 MW	.380	2.50	5.00	15.00	25.00
	1840 MW	.127	2.50	5.00	17.50	20.00

Obv: Similar to 25 Zlotych, C#118.

C#	Date	Mintage	VG	Fine	VF	XF
112	1841	—	—	—	Proof	Rare

10 GROSZY

2.9000 g, .192 SILVER, .0180 oz ASW
Obv: Eagle.

C#	Date	Mintage	VG	Fine	VF	XF
97	1816 IB	.750	5.00	10.00	15.00	25.00
	1820 IB	.793	8.00	12.00	17.50	35.00
	1821 IB	.707	5.00	10.00	15.00	25.00
	1822 IB	1.238	5.00	10.00	15.00	25.00
	1823 IB	.262	10.00	15.00	20.00	40.00
	1825 IB	.750	7.50	10.00	15.00	30.00
113	1826 IB	.750	4.00	7.50	12.50	25.00
	1827 IB	.737	4.00	7.50	12.50	25.00
	1827 FH	I.A.	8.00	12.50	20.00	40.00
	1828 FH	.529	4.00	7.50	12.50	25.00
	1830 FH	.145	6.00	10.00	15.00	30.00
	1830 KG	I.A.	4.00	7.50	12.50	25.00
	1831 KG	16.604	6.00	10.00	15.00	30.00
	1832 KG	—	—	—	Rare	—
	1833 KG	—	—	—	Rare	—

C#	Date	Mintage	VG	Fine	VF	XF
113a	1835 MW	.869	4.00	7.50	12.50	25.00
	1836 MW	1.736	4.00	7.50	12.50	25.00
	1837 MW	.767	4.00	7.50	12.50	25.00
	1838 MW	1.735	4.00	7.50	12.50	25.00
	1839 MW	.060	4.00	7.50	12.50	25.00
	1840 MW	63.349	3.00	6.00	10.00	15.00
	1840 WW	I.A.	6.00	12.00	15.00	30.00

ZLOTY

4.5500 g, .593 SILVER, .0872 oz ASW
Obv: Large head. Rev: Eagle, lettered edge.

C#	Date	Mintage	VG	Fine	VF	XF
98	1818 IB	2.523	6.00	10.00	20.00	40.00
	1818 IB struck in collar		—	—	Rare	—
	1819 IB	1.208	6.00	10.00	20.00	40.00
	1819 IB struck in collar		—	—	Rare	—

Obv: Smaller head.

C#	Date	Mintage	VG	Fine	VF	XF
98a	1818 IB	Inc. Ab.	—	—	Rare	—
	1822 IB	.287	6.00	10.00	20.00	40.00
	1823 IB	.052	6.00	10.00	20.00	40.00
	1824 IB	.119	6.00	10.00	20.00	40.00
	1825 IB	.084	6.00	10.00	20.00	40.00

Obv: Large head.

C#	Date	Mintage	VG	Fine	VF	XF
114.1	1827 IB	.106	6.00	10.00	20.00	35.00
(C114)	1828 FH	.092	6.00	10.00	20.00	35.00
	1829 FH	.124	6.00	10.00	20.00	35.00
	1830 FH	.614	6.00	10.00	20.00	35.00
	1831 KG	—	6.00	10.00	20.00	35.00
	1832 KG	1.112	6.00	10.00	20.00	35.00

Obv: Small head.

C#	Date	Mintage	VG	Fine	VF	XF
114.2)	1832 KG	I.A.	6.00	10.00	20.00	35.00
(C114.1)	1833 KG	.041	6.50	11.00	25.00	40.00
	1834 IP	.201	6.00	10.00	20.00	35.00

ZLOTY-15 KOPEKS

3.0700 g, .868 SILVER, .0857 oz ASW

C#	Date	Mintage	VG	Fine	VF	XF
129	1832 НГ	.049	6.50	10.00	15.00	30.00
	1833 НГ	.655	6.50	10.00	15.00	30.00
	1834 НГ	.030	7.50	12.50	20.00	40.00
	1834 MW	.042	15.00	30.00	60.00	100.00
	1835 НГ	.150	6.50	10.00	15.00	30.00
	1835 MW	2.192	5.00	7.50	10.00	25.00
	1836 НГ	1.450	6.50	10.00	15.00	30.00
	1836 MW	3.331	5.00	7.50	10.00	25.00
	1837 НГ	.080	6.50	10.00	15.00	30.00
	1837 MW	3.028	5.00	7.50	10.00	25.00
	1838 НГ	1.410	10.00	20.00	40.00	80.00
	1838 MW	3.617	5.00	7.50	10.00	25.00
	1839 НГ	1.510	6.50	10.00	15.00	30.00
	1839 MW	3.586	5.00	7.50	10.00	25.00
	1840 НГ	1.060	6.50	10.00	15.00	30.00
	1840 MW	.487	6.50	10.00	15.00	30.00
	1841 НГ	1.060	—	—	Proof	Rare
	1841 MW	1.320	10.00	17.50	30.00	60.00

NOTE: Varieties exist.

40 GROSZY-20 KOPEKS

4.1000 g, .868 SILVER, .1144 oz ASW

C#	Date	Mintage	VG	Fine	VF	XF
130	1842 MW	.051	10.00	15.00	20.00	35.00
	1843 MW	.037	10.00	15.00	20.00	35.00
	1844 MW	—	10.00	15.00	20.00	35.00
	1845 MW	.062	10.00	15.00	20.00	35.00
	1846 MW	—	—	—	Rare	—
	1848 MW	.027	10.00	15.00	20.00	35.00
	1850 MW	.038	10.00	15.00	20.00	35.00

50 GROSZY-25 KOPEKS

5.1800 g, .868 SILVER, .1445 oz ASW

C#	Date	Mintage	VG	Fine	VF	XF
131	1842 MW	—	10.00	15.00	25.00	50.00
	1843 MW	—	10.00	15.00	25.00	40.00
	1844 MW	—	10.00	20.00	45.00	90.00
	1845 MW	—	10.00	15.00	25.00	40.00
	1846 MW	—	10.00	15.00	25.00	40.00
	1847 MW	—	10.00	15.00	25.00	40.00
	1848 MW	.168	10.00	15.00	25.00	40.00
	1850 MW	1.489	10.00	15.00	25.00	40.00

2 ZLOTE

9.0900 g, .593 SILVER, .1733 oz ASW
Lettered edge.

C#	Date	Mintage	VG	Fine	VF	XF
99	1816 IB	1.393	10.00	15.00	25.00	50.00
	1817 IB	1.084	10.00	15.00	25.00	50.00
	1818 IB	1.321	10.00	15.00	25.00	50.00
	1819 IB	1.241	10.00	15.00	25.00	50.00
	1820 IB	1.970	10.00	20.00	40.00	80.00

Obv: Medium head. Reeded edge, struck in collar.

C#	Date	Mintage	VG	Fine	VF	XF
99a	1819 IB	—			Rare	
	1820 IB	Inc. Ab.	10.00	15.00	25.00	60.00
	1821 IB	.997	10.00	15.00	25.00	50.00
	1822 IB	.093	10.00	15.00	25.00	60.00
	1823 IB	.446	10.00	15.00	25.00	50.00
	1824 IB	.348	10.00	15.00	25.00	50.00
	1825 IB	.229	10.00	15.00	25.00	50.00

Obv: Laureated head

C#	Date	Mintage	VG	Fine	VF	XF
115	1826 IB	.065	10.00	15.00	30.00	60.00
	1828 FH	.119	10.00	15.00	25.00	50.00
	1830 FH	.306	10.00	15.00	25.00	50.00

2 ZLOTE-30 KOPEKS

6.2100 g, .868 SILVER, .1733 oz ASW

C#	Date	Mintage	VG	Fine	VF	XF
132	1834 MW	.024	12.00	20.00	35.00	65.00
	1835 MW	2.229	7.50	10.00	20.00	40.00
	1836 MW	2.589	7.50	10.00	20.00	40.00
	1837 MW	1.544	10.00	15.00	25.00	50.00
	1838 MW	1.978	10.00	15.00	25.00	50.00
	1839 MW	2.037	10.00	15.00	25.00	50.00
	1840 MW	.306	10.00	15.00	25.00	50.00
	1841 MW	1.261	10.00	15.00	25.00	50.00

5 ZLOTYCH

15.5900 g, .868 SILVER, .4351 oz ASW

C#	Date	Mintage	VG	Fine	VF	XF
100	1816 IB	.971	30.00	60.00	120.00	250.00
	1817 IB	2.585	30.00	50.00	120.00	225.00
	1818 IB	.201	30.00	60.00	130.00	275.00

NOTE: Large and small crown varieties exist.

C#	Date	Mintage	VG	Fine	VF	XF
116	1829 FH	1.234	15.00	25.00	45.00	80.00
	1830 FH	.287	22.50	32.50	55.00	100.00
	1830 KG	I.A.	22.50	32.50	55.00	100.00
	1831 KG	.023	22.50	32.50	55.00	100.00
	1832 KG	.639	15.00	25.00	45.00	80.00
	1833 KG	.445	15.00	25.00	45.00	80.00
	1834 KG	.414	22.50	32.50	60.00	120.00
	1834 IP	—	22.50	32.50	55.00	100.00

NOTE: Large and small bust varieties exist.

Obv. leg. w/retrograde 'S'

116a	1833 KG	Inc. Ab.	22.50	32.50	55.00	100.00

5 ZLOTYCH-3/4 RUBLE

15.5400 g, .868 SILVER, .4337 oz ASW

C#	Date	Mintage	VG	Fine	VF	XF
133	1833 НГ	.258	12.00	20.00	30.00	60.00
	1834 НГ	.206	12.00	20.00	30.00	60.00
	1834 MW	.086	12.00	20.00	30.00	60.00
	1835 НГ	.107	12.00	20.00	30.00	60.00
	1835 MW	.540	10.00	15.00	20.00	50.00
	1836 НГ	.078	12.00	20.00	30.00	60.00
	1836 MW	1.196	10.00	15.00	20.00	50.00
	1837 НГ	.262	12.00	20.00	30.00	60.00
	1837 MW	1.000	10.00	15.00	20.00	50.00
	1838 НГ	.012	50.00	85.00	135.00	225.00
	1838 MW	1.996	10.00	15.00	20.00	50.00
	1839 НГ	—	—	—	Rare	—
	1839 MW	2.689		15.00		50.00
	1840 НГ	2.001	—	—	Rare	—
	1840 MW	2.482	10.00	15.00	20.00	50.00
	1841 НГ	—	—	—	Rare	—
	1841 MW	1.274	10.00	15.00	20.00	50.00

10 ZLOTYCH

31.1000 g, .868 SILVER, .8679 oz ASW

C#	Date	Mintage	VG	Fine	VF	XF
101.1	1820 IB	534 pcs.	—	—	Rare	—
(C101)	1821 IB	1,195	150.00	250.00	400.00	550.00
	1822 IB	233 pcs.	—	—	Rare	—

101.2	1823 IB	1,124	150.00	250.00	400.00	550.00
(C101.1)	1824 IB	513 pcs.	—	—	Rare	—
	1825 IB	—	—	—	Rare	—

Obv: Laureated head.

117	1827 IB	123 pcs.	—	—	Rare	—
	1827 FH	I.A.	—	—	Rare	—

10 ZLOTYCH-1-1/2 RUBLES

31.1000 g, .868 SILVER, .8679 oz ASW

C#	Date	Mintage	VG	Fine	VF	XF
134	1833 НГ	.127	20.00	30.00	60.00	100.00
	1834 НГ	.064	20.00	40.00	80.00	150.00
	1835 НГ	.262	20.00	35.00	60.00	100.00
	1835 MW	3,081	40.00	80.00	120.00	200.00
	1836 НГ	.134	20.00	35.00	60.00	100.00
	1836 MW	.220	20.00	35.00	60.00	100.00
	1837 НГ	.036	40.00	80.00	120.00	200.00
	1837 MW	.194	20.00	35.00	60.00	100.00
	1838 НГ	13 pcs.	—	—	Rare	—
	1838 MW	.010	100.00	200.00	325.00	475.00
	1839 НГ	7,006	125.00	275.00	450.00	750.00
	1839 MW	2,295	40.00	80.00	175.00	350.00
	1840 НГ	2,001	—	—	Rare	—
	1840 MW	2,747	40.00	80.00	175.00	350.00
	1841 НГ	—	—	—	Rare	—
	1841 MW	.037	40.00	80.00	120.00	200.00

20 ZLOTYCH-3 RUBLES

3.8900 g, .917 GOLD, .1147 oz AGW

C#	Date	Mintage	Fine	VF	XF	Unc
136.1	1834 MW	243 pcs.	250.00	500.00	1000.	2000.
(C136)	1835 MW	350	250.00	500.00	1000.	2000.
	1836 MW	307 pcs.	250.00	500.00	1000.	2000.
	1837 MW	423 pcs.	250.00	500.00	1000.	2000.
	1838 MW	66 pcs.	500.00	900.00	1500.	3000.
	1839 MW	57 pcs.	500.00	900.00	1500.	3000.
	1840 MW	—	800.00	1500.	2000.	3500.

Mintmark: St. Petersburg СПБ

136.2	1834 ПД	.077	150.00	225.00	300.00	425.00
(C136.1)	1835 ПД	.052	150.00	225.00	300.00	425.00
	1836 ПД	.010	175.00	275.00	350.00	450.00
	1837 ПД	.030	150.00	225.00	300.00	425.00
	1838 ПД	.017	175.00	275.00	350.00	450.00
	1839 ПД	.011	175.00	300.00	375.00	475.00

136.3	1840 ПД	5.473	225.00	375.00	450.00	525.00
(C136.2)	1841 ПД	—	—	—	Proof	*Unique

*NOTE: Superior Pipito sale 12-87 Proof realized $12,100.

25 ZLOTYCH

4.8900 g, .916 GOLD, .1443 oz AGW

102	1817 IB	.096	175.00	350.00	475.00	700.00
	1818 IB	.055	150.00	250.00	375.00	550.00
	1819 IB	.086	150.00	250.00	375.00	550.00

POLAND 1429

Struck in collar

C#	Date	Mintage	Fine	VF	XF	Unc
102a	1818 IB	Inc. Ab.	—	—	Rare	—
	1822 IB	1,124	300.00	550.00	1000.	1500.
	1823 IB	479 pcs.	500.00	900.00	1500.	2000.
	1824 IB	612 pcs.	400.00	600.00	1200.	1800.
	1825 IB	1,155	400.00	600.00	1200.	1800.

118	1828 FH	241 pcs.	500.00	900.00	1500.	2000.
	1829 FH	684 pcs.	600.00	1000	1600.	2200.
	1832 KG	304 pcs.	500.00	900.00	1500.	2000.
	1833 KG	304 pcs.	500.00	900.00	1500.	2000.

50 ZLOTYCH

9.7800 g, .916 GOLD, .2880 oz AGW

103	1817 IB	.017	250.00	400.00	600.00	1000.
	1818 IB	.050	250.00	500.00	700.00	1150.
	1819 IB	.020	250.00	500.00	750.00	1250.

Obv: Small head.

103a	1819 IB	Inc. Ab.	250.00	400.00	600.00	1000.
	1820 IB	7,098	250.00	400.00	650.00	1000.
	1821 IB	2,638	250.00	500.00	750.00	1250.
	1822 IB	1,610	250.00	500.00	750.00	1250.
	1823 IB	251 pcs.	450.00	800.00	1500.	2500.

119	1827 FH	299 pcs.	700.00	1200.	1700.	2800.
	1829 FH	238 pcs.	500.00	1100.	1500.	2500.

REVOLUTIONARY COINAGE
1830-1831
3 GROSZE

COPPER

C#	Date	Mintage	VG	Fine	VF	XF
120	1831 KG	1.112	3.50	7.50	15.00	30.00

10 GROSZY

2.9000 g, .192 SILVER, .0180 oz ASW

C#	Date	Mintage	VG	Fine	VF	XF
121	1831 KG	6.038	10.00	15.00	25.00	50.00

NOTE: Varieties in eagle exist.

2 ZLOTE

9.0090 g, .593 SILVER, .1733 oz ASW

123	1831 KG	.171	15.00	25.00	45.00	70.00

5 ZLOTYCH

15.5900 g, .868 SILVER, .4351 oz ASW

124	1831	.023	25.00	50.00	100.00	150.00

TRADE COINAGE
DUCAT

3.5000 g, .986 GOLD, .1109 oz AGW

C#	Date	Mintage	Fine	VF	XF	Unc
125	1831	.156	175.00	275.00	375.00	650.00

WWI OCCUPATION COINAGE

Germany released a 1, 2 and 3 Kopek coinage series in 1916 which circulated during their occupation of Poland. They will be found listed as Germany Y#A18, B18 and C18.

GERMAN-AUSTRIAN REGENCY
100 Fenigow = 1 Marka
FENIG

IRON

Y#	Date	Mintage	Fine	VF	XF	Unc
4	1918 FF	51.484	1.00	2.50	5.00	10.00

5 FENIGOW

IRON

5	1917 FF	18.700	.50	1.00	1.50	4.00
	1917 FF	—	—	—	Proof	100.00
	1918 FF	22.690	.50	1.00	1.50	4.00

Obv: German Y#21. Rev: Muling of Y#6.

5.1	1917 FF	—	50.00	100.00	150.00	200.00

10 FENIGOW

IRON

Y#	Date	Mintage	Fine	VF	XF	Unc
6	1917 FF obv. leg. touches edge					
		33.000	7.50	15.00	20.00	25.00
	1917 FF	—	—	—	Proof	100.00
	1917 FF obv. leg. away from edge					
			.50	1.00	2.00	6.50
	1918 FF obv. leg. touches edge					
		14.990	.50	1.00	2.00	6.50
	1918 FF obv. leg. away from edge					
			.50	1.00	2.00	6.50

ZINC

6a	1917 FF	—	25.00	45.00	85.00	150.00

Mule. Obv: German 10 Pfennig, Y#22. Rev: Poland 10 Fenigow, Y#6.

6.1	1917 FF	—	50.00	100.00	150.00	200.00

20 FENIGOW

IRON

7	1917 FF	1.900	2.00	4.00	6.00	10.00
	1918 FF	19.260	1.00	2.00	3.00	5.00

ZINC

7a	1917FF	—	35.00	60.00	100.00	200.00

REPUBLIC COINAGE
100 Groszy = 1 Zloty
GROSZ

BRASS

8	1923	—	18.00	25.00	45.00	100.00

BRONZE

8a	1923(a)	30.000	.25	.50	.75	5.00
	1925(w)	38.164	.25	.50	.75	5.00
	1927(w)	17.000	.25	.50	.75	5.00
	1928(w)	13.600	.25	.50	.75	5.00
	1930(w)	22.500	.25	.50	.75	5.00
	1931(w)	9.000	.50	1.00	7.00	15.00
	1932(w)	10.000	.50	1.00	5.00	10.00
	1933(w)	7.000	.50	1.00	5.00	10.00
	1934(w)	5.900	1.25	3.50	6.00	20.00
	1935(w)	7.300	.75	1.50	3.50	8.00
	1936(w)	12.600	.25	.50	2.00	5.00
	1937(w)	17.370	.25	.50	.75	2.50
	1938(w)	20.530	.25	.50	.75	2.50
	1939(w)	12.000	.25	.50	.75	2.50

2 GROSZE

BRASS

9	1923	20.500	.30	.75	2.50	6.00

BRONZE

9a	1923	Inc. Ab.	2.50	5.00	10.00	30.00
	1925(w)	39.000	.20	.40	.75	5.00

POLAND 1430

Y#	Date	Mintage	Fine	VF	XF	Unc
9a	1927(w)	15.300	.20	.40	.75	5.00
	1928(w)	13.400	.20	.40	.75	5.00
	1930(w)	20.000	.20	.40	.75	5.00
	1931(w)	9.500	1.75	2.50	4.50	10.00
	1932(w)	6.500	2.00	5.00	10.00	20.00
	1933(w)	7.000	2.00	5.00	10.00	20.00
	1934(w)	9.350	1.75	3.00	7.50	15.00
	1935(w)	5.800	.20	.40	.75	5.00
	1936(w)	5.800	.20	.40	.60	2.50
	1937(w)	17.360	.20	.40	.60	2.50
	1938(w)	20.530	.20	.40	.60	2.50
	1939(w)	12.000	.20	.40	.60	2.50

5 GROSZY

BRASS

| 10 | 1923 | 32.000 | .50 | 1.00 | 2.00 | 5.00 |

BRONZE

10a	1923	350 pcs.	10.00	20.00	30.00	50.00
	1925(w)	45.500	.20	.40	.50	5.00
	1928(w)	8.900	.20	.40	.50	7.50
	1930(w)	14.200	.20	.40	.60	7.50
	1931(w)	1.500	.50	.75	2.00	10.00
	1934(w)	.420	5.00	7.50	15.00	30.00
	1935(w)	4.660	.20	.40	.60	5.00
	1936(w)	4.660	.20	.40	.60	2.25
	1937(w)	9.050	.20	.40	.60	2.25
	1938(w)	17.300	.20	.40	.60	2.25
	1939(w)	10.000	.20	.40	.60	2.25

10 GROSZY

NICKEL

| 11 | 1923 | 100.000 | .20 | .45 | .80 | 1.25 |

20 GROSZY

NICKEL

| 12 | 1923 | 150.000 | .35 | .75 | 1.25 | 2.00 |

50 GROSZY

NICKEL

| 13 | 1923 | 101.000 | .40 | .80 | 1.25 | 3.00 |

ZLOTY

5.0000 g, .750 SILVER, .1206 oz ASW

15	1924 (Paris) torches at sides of date					
		16.000	1.50	5.00	15.00	40.00
	1925 (London) dot after date					
		24.000	1.50	4.00	10.00	32.50
	1924 (Birmingham)					
		—	—	—	Proof	600.00

NICKEL

Y#	Date	Mintage	Fine	VF	XF	Unc
14	1929	32.000	.50	1.00	1.75	5.00

2 ZLOTE

10.0000 g, .750 SILVER, .2411 oz ASW

16	1924 (Paris) torches at sides of date					
		8.200	5.00	10.00	17.50	60.00
	1924H (Birmingham)					
		1.200	17.50	35.00	100.00	250.00
	1924 (Birmingham)					
		—	—	—	Proof	600.00
	1924 (Philadelphia) w/o torches					
		.800	10.00	20.00	40.00	100.00
	1925 (London) dot after date					
		11.000	5.00	10.00	20.00	50.00
	1925 (Philadelphia)					
		5.200	7.50	17.50	30.00	65.00

4.4000 g, .750 SILVER, .1061 oz ASW

20	1932	15.700	1.50	2.00	4.00	14.00
	1933	9.250	1.50	2.00	4.00	14.00
	1934	.250	3.00	5.00	8.00	20.00

| 27 | 1934 | 10.425 | 2.00 | 5.00 | 10.00 | 30.00 |
| | 1936 | .075 | 20.00 | 35.00 | 65.00 | 150.00 |

| 30 | 1936 | 3.918 | 3.00 | 5.00 | 8.00 | 20.00 |

5 ZLOTYCH

25.0000 g, .900 SILVER, .7234 oz ASW
Rev: 81 pearls in circle w/monogram by date.

Y#	Date	Mintage	Fine	VF	XF	Unc
17.1 (Y17)	1925	1,000	125.00	250.00	400.00	700.00

Rev: W/o monogram by date.

| 17.2 (Y17.1) | 1925 | 1,000 | 125.00 | 250.00 | 400.00 | 700.00 |

BRONZE (OMS)

| 17.2a (Y17.1a) | 1925 | 100 pcs. | — | — | 200.00 | 300.00 |

25.0000 g, .900 SILVER, .7234 oz ASW
Rev: 100 pearls in circle.

| 17.3 (Y17.2) | 1925 | 1,000 | 125.00 | 250.00 | 400.00 | 700.00 |

BRASS (OMS)

| 17.3a (Y17.2a) | 1925 | 60 pcs. | — | — | 225.00 | 350.00 |

GOLD (OMS)

| 17.3b (Y17.2b) | 1925 | 1 pc. | — | — | — | — |

18.0000 g, .750 SILVER, .4340 oz ASW

18	1928 Warsaw conjoined arrow and 'K' mint mark					
		13.200	12.50	22.50	45.00	140.00
	1928 error 'SUPRMA' edge inscription					
	Inc. Ab.	40.00	75.00	100.00	225.00
	1928 (London) w/o mint mark					
		4.300	12.50	22.50	45.00	140.00
	1930	5.900	20.00	40.00	75.00	200.00
	1931	2.200	40.00	90.00	175.00	350.00
	1932	3.100	90.00	175.00	250.00	—

1830 Revolution

| 19.1 (Y19) | 1930 | 1.000 | 15.00 | 30.00 | 60.00 | 160.00 |

High relief.

| 19.2 (Y19.1) | 1930 | 200 pcs. | 70.00 | 100.00 | 175.00 | 350.00 |

11.0000 g, .750 SILVER, .2652 oz ASW

21	1932 (Warsaw)					
		1.000	10.00	20.00	40.00	80.00
	1932 (London) w/o mint mark					
		3.000	4.00	5.00	7.50	25.00
	1933	11.000	3.50	4.50	7.50	22.50
	1933	—	—	—	Proof	—
	1934	.250	5.00	7.50	10.00	35.00

Rifle Corps Aug. 6, 1914

Y#	Date	Mintage	Fine	VF	XF	Unc
25	1934	.300	4.00	6.00	12.50	30.00

28	1934	6.510	3.00	5.00	9.00	20.00
	1935	1.800	4.00	5.00	9.00	20.00
	1936	1.000	4.00	5.00	9.00	20.00
	1938	.289	5.00	7.50	15.00	30.00

31	1936	1.000	6.00	8.00	14.00	25.00

10 ZLOTYCH

3.2258 g, .900 GOLD, .0933 oz AGW
Boleslaus I

Y#	Date	Mintage	VF	XF	Unc
32	1925	.050	55.00	75.00	100.00

22.0000 g, .750 SILVER, .5305 oz ASW

Y#	Date	Mintage	Fine	VF	XF	Unc
22	1932 (Warsaw)	3.100	6.00	9.00	14.00	35.00
	1932 (London) w/o mintmark					
		6.000	6.00	9.00	14.00	35.00
	1932	—	—	—	Proof	—
	1933	2.800	6.00	9.00	14.00	35.00
	1933	—	—	—	Proof	—

Jan III Sobieski's Victory Over the Turks
Obv: Similar to Y#22.

23	1933	.300	10.00	20.00	40.00	85.00
	1933	100 pcs.	—	—	Proof	—

1863 Insurrection
Obv: Similar to Y#23.

Y#	Date	Mintage	Fine	VF	XF	Unc
24	1933	.300	10.00	20.00	50.00	100.00
	1933	100 pcs.	—	—	Proof	—

Rifle Corps Aug. 6, 1914

26	1934	.300	7.50	12.50	35.00	70.00

29	1934	.200	10.00	20.00	40.00	85.00
	1935	1.670	7.50	10.00	17.50	45.00
	1936	2.130	7.50	10.00	17.50	45.00
	1937	.908	7.50	15.00	25.00	55.00
	1938	.234	10.00	20.00	35.00	80.00
	1939	—	10.00	15.00	30.00	65.00

20 ZLOTYCH

6.4516 g, .900 GOLD, .1867 oz AGW
Boleslaus I

Y#	Date	Mintage	VF	XF	Unc
33	1925	.027	100.00	110.00	150.00

GERMAN OCCUPATION
GROSZ

ZINC
German Occupation Issue W W II

Y#	Date	Mintage	Fine	VF	XF	Unc
34	1939	33.909	.50	1.25	2.50	5.00

5 GROSZY

ZINC
German Occupation Issue W W II

35	1939	15.324	1.75	3.50	4.00	6.50

10 GROSZY

ZINC
German Occupation Issue W W II

Y#	Date	Mintage	Fine	VF	XF	Unc
36	1923	42.175	.10	.20	.30	1.50

Above piece actually struck in 1941-44.

20 GROSZY

ZINC
German Occupation Issue W W II

37	1923	40.025	.15	.25	.50	1.50

Above piece actually struck in 1941-44.

50 GROSZY

NICKEL PLATED IRON
German Occupation Issue W W II

38	1938 w/arrow					
		32.000	1.00	2.00	4.00	7.50

IRON

38a	1938 w/o arrow				
		—	1.25	2.50	5.00	8.50

POST WAR COINAGE
GROSZ

ALUMINUM

39	1949	400.116	—	—	.50	1.00

2 GROSZE

ALUMINUM

40	1949	300.106	—	—	.75	1.50

5 GROSZY

BRONZE

41	1949	300.000	.10	.25	.50	1.00

ALUMINUM

41a	1949	200.000	.10	.25	1.00	2.00

10 GROSZY

COPPER-NICKEL

42	1949	200.000	.20	.40	.60	1.00

ALUMINUM

42a	1949	31.047	.10	.25	1.00	2.00

POLAND 1432

20 GROSZY

COPPER-NICKEL

Y#	Date	Mintage	Fine	VF	XF	Unc
43	1949	133.383	.30	.60	.75	1.00

ALUMINUM

| 43a | 1949 | 197.472 | .10 | .25 | 1.00 | 2.00 |

50 GROSZY

COPPER-NICKEL

| 44 | 1949 | 109.000 | .50 | .75 | 1.00 | 1.50 |

ALUMINUM

| 44a | 1949 | 59.393 | .10 | .25 | 1.50 | 3.00 |

ZLOTY

COPPER-NICKEL

| 45 | 1949 | 87.053 | 1.00 | 1.50 | 2.25 | 3.00 |

ALUMINUM

| 45a | 1949 | 43.000 | .10 | .25 | 2.50 | 5.00 |

PEOPLE'S REPUBLIC
5 GROSZY

ALUMINUM

Y#	Date	Mintage	VF	XF	Unc
A46	1958	53.521	—	.10	.20
	1959	28.564	—	.10	.15
	1960	12.246	—	.50	1.00
	1961	29.502	—	.10	.20
	1962	90.257	—	.10	.15
	1963	20.878	—	.10	.15
	1965MW	5.050	—	1.00	2.00
	1967MW	10.056	—	.50	1.00
	1968MW	10.196	—	.50	1.00
	1970MW	20.095	—	.10	.20
	1971MW	20.000	—	.10	.20
	1972MW	10.000	—	.10	.20

10 GROSZY

ALUMINUM

AA47	1961	73.400	—	.50	1.00
	1962	25.362	—	2.00	4.00
	1963	40.434	—	.50	1.50
	1965MW	50.521	—	1.00	2.00
	1966MW	70.749	—	.50	1.50
	1967MW	62.059	—	.50	1.50
	1968MW	62.204	—	.50	1.50
	1969MW	71.566	—	.50	1.00
	1970MW	38.844	—	.10	.50
	1971MW	50.000	—	.10	.50
	1972MW	60.000	—	.10	.50
	1973MW	80.000	—	.10	.25
	1974MW	50.000	—	.10	.20
	1975MW	50.000	—	.10	.15
	1976MW	100.000	—	—	.10
	1977MW	100.000	—	—	.10
	1978MW	71.204	—	—	.10
	1979MW	73.191	—	—	.10
	1980MW	60.623	—	—	.10
	1981MW	70.000	—	—	.10
	1983MW	9.600	—	—	.10
	1985MW	9.957	—	—	.10

20 GROSZY

ALUMINUM

Y#	Date	Mintage	VF	XF	Unc
A47	1957	3.940	—	2.00	10.00
	1961	53.108	—	.75	2.00
	1962	19.140	—	1.00	3.00
	1963	41.217	—	.50	2.00
	1965MW	32.022	—	.50	2.00
	1966MW	23.860	—	.50	2.00
	1967MW	29.099	—	.50	2.00
	1968MW	29.191	—	.50	2.00
	1969MW	40.227	—	.50	1.50
	1970MW	20.028	—	.10	1.00
	1971MW	20.000	—	.10	1.00
	1972MW	60.000	—	.10	1.00
	1973	50.000	—	.10	.50
	1973MW	65.000	—	.10	.50
	1975MW	50.000	—	.10	.50
	1976MW large date	100.000	—	.10	.50
	1976MW small date	Inc. Ab.	—	.10	.50
	1977MW	80.730	—	.10	.20
	1978MW	50.730	—	.10	.20
	1979MW	45.252	—	.10	.20
	1980MW	30.020	—	.10	.20
	1981MW	60.082	—	.10	.20
	1983MW	10.041	—	.10	.20
	1985	16.227	—	.10	.20

50 GROSZY

ALUMINUM

48	1957	91.316	.10	1.00	2.50
	1965MW	22.090	.10	.50	1.00
	1967MW	2.065	.15	1.50	4.00
	1968MW	2.027	.15	1.50	4.00
	1970MW	3.273	.15	.30	1.50
	1971MW	7.000	.10	.25	1.00
	1972MW	10.000	.10	.25	.50
	1973MW	39.000	.10	.20	.50
	1974MW	33.000	.10	.20	.50
	1975MW	25.000	.10	.20	.50
	1976	25.000	.10	.20	.40
	1977MW	50.000	.10	.20	.40
	1978	18.600	.10	.20	.40
	1978MW	50.020	.10	.20	.40
	1982MW	16.067	.10	.20	.40
	1983MW	39.667	.10	.20	.40
	1984MW	44.217	.10	.20	.40
	1985MW	49.052	.10	.20	.40
	1986	45.796	.10	.20	.40

ZLOTY

ALUMINUM

49	1957	58.631	.10	1.50	3.00
	1965MW	15.015	.10	1.00	2.00
	1966MW	18.185	.15	1.00	2.00
	1967MW	1.002	.25	1.50	3.00
	1968MW	1.176	.25	1.50	3.00
	1969MW	3.024	.20	1.00	2.00
	1970MW	6.016	.15	.50	1.50
	1971MW	6.000	.15	.50	1.50
	1972MW	7.000	.15	.50	1.00
	1973MW	15.000	.10	.50	1.00
	1974MW	42.000	.10	.15	.50
	1975	25.000	.10	.15	.50
	1975MW	33.000	.10	.15	.50
	1976	22.000	.10	.50	1.00
	1977MW	65.000	.10	.50	1.00
	1978	16.400	.10	.50	1.50
	1978MW	80.000	.10	.50	1.00
	1980MW	100.002	.10	.15	.50
	1981MW	4.082	.10	.15	1.00
	1982MW	59.643	.10	.15	.30
	1983MW	49.636	.10	.15	.25
	1984MW	61.036	.10	.15	.25
	1985MW	167.939	.10	.15	.25
	1986MW	130.697	.10	.15	.25
	1987MW	—	.10	.15	.25
	1988MW	—	.10	.15	.25

2 ZLOTE

ALUMINUM

Y#	Date	Mintage	VF	XF	Unc
46	1958	82.640	.20	1.50	3.00
	1959	7.170	.30	2.00	4.00
	1960	36.131	.20	.40	1.00
	1970MW	2.014	.30	1.00	2.00
	1971MW	3.000	.20	1.00	2.00
	1972MW	3.000	.20	1.00	2.00
	1973MW	10.000	.15	.50	1.50
	1974MW	46.000	.15	.30	1.00

BRASS

80	1975	25.000	.15	.25	.50
	1976	60.000	.15	.25	.50
	1977	50.000	.15	.25	.50
	1978	2.600	.15	.25	.50
	1978MW	2.382	.15	.25	.50
	1979MW	85.752	.10	.20	.40
	1980MW	66.610	.10	.20	.40
	1981MW	40.306	.10	.20	.40
	1982MW	45.318	.10	.20	.40
	1983MW	35.244	.10	.20	.40
	1984MW	59.999	.10	.20	.40
	1985MW	100.300	.10	.20	.40
	1986MW	60.718	.10	.20	.40
	1987MW	—	.10	.20	.40
	1988MW	—	.10	.20	.40

5 ZLOTYCH

ALUMINUM

47	1958	1.328	7.50	12.50	20.00
	1959	56.811	.25	1.50	3.00
	1960	16.301	.25	1.50	3.00
	1971MW	1.000	.35	2.00	4.00
	1973MW	5.000	.25	1.00	2.00
	1974MW	46.000	.20	.50	1.00

BRASS

81	1975	25.000	.20	.35	.65
	1976	60.000	.20	.35	.65
	1977	50.000	.20	.35	.65
	1979MW	5.098	.20	.35	.65
	1980MW	10.100	.20	.35	.65
	1981MW	4.008	.20	.35	.65
	1982MW	25.379	.20	.35	.65
	1983MW	30.531	.20	.35	.65
	1984MW	85.598	.20	.35	.65
	1985MW	20.501	.20	.35	.65
	1986MW	57.108	.20	.35	.65
	1987MW	—	.20	.35	.65
	1988MW	—	.20	.35	.65

10 ZLOTYCH

COPPER-NICKEL, 31mm
Tadeusz Kosciuszko

Y#	Date	Mintage	VF	XF	Unc
50	1959	13.107	.50	1.75	2.50
	1960	27.551	.50	1.00	2.00
	1966MW	4.157	.50	5.00	10.00

Reduced size, 28mm.

50a	1969MW	5.428	.50	1.50	3.00
	1970MW	13.783	.50	1.00	1.75
	1971MW	12.000	.50	1.00	1.75
	1972MW	10.000	.50	1.00	1.75
	1973MW	3.900	.50	2.00	4.00

Mikolaj Kopernik

51	1959	12.559	.75	1.25	2.50
	1965MW	3.000	1.00	4.00	8.00

Reduced size

51a	1967MW	2.128	.75	2.00	4.00
	1968MW	9.389	.75	1.25	2.00
	1969MW	8.612	.75	1.25	2.00

600th Anniversary of Jagiello University
Legends raised

52	1964	2.612	.50	1.25	2.50

Legends incuse

52a	1964	2.610	.50	1.25	2.50

700th Anniversary of Warsaw

54	1965MW	3.492	.50	1.25	2.50

700th Anniversary of Warsaw

Y#	Date	Mintage	VF	XF	Unc
55	1965MW	2.000	.50	1.25	2.50

200th Anniversary of Warsaw Mint

56	1966MW	.102	2.00	7.50	15.00

20th Anniversary of Death of General Swierczewski

58	1967MW	2.000	.50	1.00	2.00

Marie Curie Centennial of Birth

59	1967MW	2.000	.50	1.00	2.00

25th Anniversary Peoples Army

60	1968MW	2.000	.50	1.00	2.00

25th Anniversary Peoples Republic

61	1969MW	2.000	.50	1.00	2.00

25th Anniversary Provincial Annexations

62	1970MW	2.000	.50	1.00	2.00

POLAND 1433

F. A. O. issue

Y#	Date	Mintage	VF	XF	Unc
63	1971MW	2.000	.50	1.00	2.00

Battle of Upper Silesia 50th Anniversary

64	1971MW	2.000	.50	1.00	2.00

50th Anniversary Gdynia Seaport

65	1972MW	2.000	.50	1.00	2.00

Boleslaw Prus

73	1975MW	35.000	.25	.65	1.00
	1976MW	20.000	.25	.65	1.00
	1977MW	25.000	.25	.65	1.00
	1978MW	4.007	.25	.65	1.50
	1981MW	2.655	.25	1.00	2.00
	1982MW	16.341	.25	.65	1.00
	1983MW	14.248	.25	.65	1.00
	1984MW	19.064	.25	.65	1.00

Adam Mickiewicz

74	1975MW	35.000	.25	.65	1.00
	1976MW	20.000	.25	.65	1.00

Circulation Coinage

152	1984MW	15.756	.10	.20	.40
	1985MW	5.282	.10	.20	.40
	1986MW	31.043	.10	.20	.40
	1987MW	—	.10	.20	.40
	1988MW	—	.10	.20	.40

POLAND 1434

20 ZLOTYCH

COPPER-NICKEL

Y#	Date	Mintage	VF	XF	Unc
67	1973	25.000	.25	1.00	2.00
	1974	12.000	.25	.75	1.50
	1976	20.000	.25	.75	1.50

Marceli Nowotko

69	1974MW	10.000	.25	1.00	2.00
	1975	10.000	.25	1.00	2.00
	1976	20.000	.25	.75	1.50
	1976MW	30.000	.25	.75	1.50
	1977MW	16.000	.25	1.00	2.00
	1983MW	.152	.25	5.00	12.50

25th Anniversary Comcon

70	1974MW	2.000	.75	1.25	2.00

International Woman's Year

75	1975MW	2.000	.75	1.25	2.00

Maria Konopnicka

95	1978MW	2.010	.75	1.50	2.50

First Polish Cosmonaut

97	1978MW	2.009	.75	1.50	2.50

Year of the Child

Y#	Date	Mintage	VF	XF	Unc
99	1979MW	2.007	.75	1.50	2.50

1980 Olympics

108	1980MW	2.000	1.00	1.75	3.00

50th Anniversary of Ship "Dar Pomorza"

112 (107)	1980MW	2.007	1.00	1.75	3.00

Circulation Coinage

153	1984MW	12.703	.25	.50	.75
	1985MW	15.514	.25	.50	.75
	1986MW	37.959	.25	.50	.75
	1987MW	—	.25	.50	.75
	1988MW	—	.25	.50	.75

50 ZLOTYCH

12.6400 g, .750 SILVER, .3048 OZ ASW
Fryderyk Chopin

66	1972	.050	1.50	3.00	6.00
	1972	20 pcs.	—	Proof	—
	1974	.010	1.75	3.50	7.50

COPPER-NICKEL
Prince Mieszko I

100	1979MW	2.640	—	1.50	3.00

Boleslaw I Chrobry

Y#	Date	Mintage	VF	XF	Unc
114 (109)	1980MW	2.564	—	1.50	3.00

Kazimierz I Odnowiciel

117 (115)	1980MW	2.504	—	1.50	3.00

General Broni Wladyslaw Sikorski

122	1981MW	2.505	—	1.50	4.00

Boleslaw II Smialy

124	1981MW	2.538	—	1.50	3.00

World Food Day

127	1981MW	2.524	—	1.50	3.00

Wladyslaw I Herman

128	1981MW	2.500	—	—	3.00

POLAND 1435

Boleslaw III
Y#	Date	Mintage	VF	XF	Unc
133	1982MW	2.616	—	—	4.00

150th Anniversary of Great Theater
142	1983MW	.615	1.00	4.00	8.00

Jan III Sobieski
145	1983MW	2.576	—	—	4.00

Ignacy Lukasiewicz
146	1983MW	.612	1.00	4.00	8.00

100 ZLOTYCH

20.0000 g, .900 SILVER, .5787 oz ASW
Polish Millenium
57	1966MW	.198	—	—	15.00

16.5000 g, .625 SILVER, .3316 oz ASW
Mikolaj Kopernik
68	1973MW	.051	—	—	Proof 7.50
	1974MW	.050	—	—	Proof 7.50

Maria Sklodowska Curie
Y#	Date	Mintage	VF	XF	Unc
71	1974MW	.050	—	Proof	7.50

Royal Castle in Warsaw
76	1975MW	.050	—	Proof	7.50

Ignacy Jan Paderewski
77	1975MW	.060	—	Proof	7.50

Helena Modrzejewska
78	1975MW	.060	—	Proof	7.50

Tadeusz Kosciuszko
82	1976MW	.100	—	Proof	7.50

Kazimierz Pulaski
84	1976MW	.100	—	Proof	7.50

Enviroment Protection
Y#	Date	Mintage	VF	XF	Unc
87	1977MW	.030	—	Proof	10.00

Henryk Sienkiewicz
88	1977MW	.020	—	Proof	7.50

Wladyslaw Reymont
89	1977MW	.020	—	Proof	7.50

Wawel Castle in Krakow
91	1977MW	.030	—	Proof	12.50

Adam Mickiewicz
92	1978MW	.030	—	Proof	10.00

Environment Protection - Moose
93	1978MW	.030	—	Proof	12.50

POLAND 1436

Janusz Korczak

Y#	Date	Mintage	VF	XF	Unc
94	1978MW	.030	—	Proof	10.00

Jan Kochanowski

Y#	Date	Mintage	VF	XF	Unc
120 (111)	1980MW	.010	—	Proof	12.50

16.5000 g, .625 SILVER, .3316 oz ASW
Environment Protection - Stork

Y#	Date	Mintage	VF	XF	Unc
141	1982MW	6,000	—	Proof	17.50

Environment Protection - Beaver

| 96 | 1978MW | .027 | — | Proof | 12.50 |

1980 Olympics
Rev: Olympic rings and runner.

| 109 | 1980MW | .010 | — | Proof | 17.50 |

Wildlife Protection - Bear

| 147 | 1983MW | 8,000 | — | Proof | 25.00 |

Henryk Wieniawski

| 98 | 1979MW | .030 | — | Proof | 10.00 |

Environment Protection - Cappercaillie

| 121 (112) | 1980MW | .018 | — | Proof | 15.00 |

COPPER-NICKEL
Wincenty Witos

| 148 | 1984MW | 1.530 | — | — | 4.00 |

Ludwik Zamenhof

| 103 (102) | 1979MW | .030 | — | Proof | 10.00 |

General Broni Wladyslaw Sikowski

| 123 | 1981MW | .012 | — | Proof | 15.00 |

40th Anniversary of People's Republic

| 151 | 1984MW | 2.595 | — | — | 3.00 |

Environment Protection - Lynx

| 104 (103) | 1979MW | .020 | — | Proof | 12.50 |

Environment Protection - Horse

| 126 | 1981MW | .012 | — | Proof | 15.00 |

Przemyslaw II

| 155 | 1985MW | 2.924 | — | — | 4.00 |

Environment Protection - Chamois

| 105 (104) | 1979MW | .020 | — | Proof | 12.50 |

14.1700 g, .750 SILVER, .3417 oz ASW
Visit of Pope John Paul II

136	1982	8,700	—	—	20.00
	1982	3,750	—	Proof	40.00
	1986	80 pcs.	—	—	—
	1986	128 pcs.	—	Proof	—

Polish Women's Memorial Hospital Center

| 157 | 1985MW | 1.927 | — | — | 4.00 |

POLAND 1437

Y#	Date	Mintage	VF	XF	Unc
160	1986MW	2,540	—	—	4.00

Władysław I Łokietek

| 167 | 1987MW | — | — | — | 4.00 |

King Kazimierz III

200 ZLOTYCH

14.4700 g, .625 SILVER, .2907 oz ASW
30th Anniversary Polish People's Republic

| 72 | 1974MW | 13,600 | — | — | 4.00 |
| | 1974MW | 6,000. | — | Proof | 10.00 |

14.4700 g, .750 SILVER, .3490 oz ASW
30th Anniversary Victory Over Fascism

| 79 | 1975 | 1,700 | — | — | 5.00 |
| | 1975MW | 2,600 | — | Proof | 17.50 |

14.4700 g, .625 SILVER, .2907 oz ASW
XXI Olympics

| 86 | 1976MW | 2,072 | — | — | 5.00 |
| | 1976MW | .011 | — | Proof | 15.00 |

Mieszko I

| 101 | 1979MW | 2,500 | — | Proof | 17.50 |

17.6000 g, .750 SILVER, .4244 oz ASW
Winter Olympics
Rev: Torch mint mark.

Y#	Date	Mintage	VF	XF	Unc
110 (113)	1980MW	.028	—	Proof	15.00

Rev: W/o mint mark.

| 110a (112a) | 1980MW | .032 | — | proof | 15.00 |

Bolesław I

| 115 (110) | 1980MW | .012 | — | Proof | 17.50 |

Kazimierz I

| 118 (116) | 1980MW | .012 | — | Proof | 12.50 |

Bolesław II Smiały

| 125 | 1981MW | .012 | — | Proof | 15.00 |

Władysław I Herman

| 129 | 1981MW | .012 | — | Proof | 15.00 |

Soccer Games in Spain

Y#	Date	Mintage	VF	XF	Unc
130	1982MW	.021	—	Proof	15.00

Bolesław III Krzywousty

| 132 | 1982MW | .012 | — | Proof | 15.00 |

28.1300 g, .750 SILVER, .6784 oz ASW
Visit of Pope John Paul II
Obv: Similar to Y#132.

137	1982	3,000	—	—	30.00
	1982	3,650	—	Proof	40.00
	1986	32 pcs.	—	—	—
	1986	75 pcs.	—	Proof	—

17.6000 g, .750 SILVER, .4244 oz ASW
Jan III Sobieski

| 143 | 1983MW | .011 | — | Proof | 15.00 |

Winter Olympics

| 149 | 1984MW | .015 | — | Proof | 17.50 |

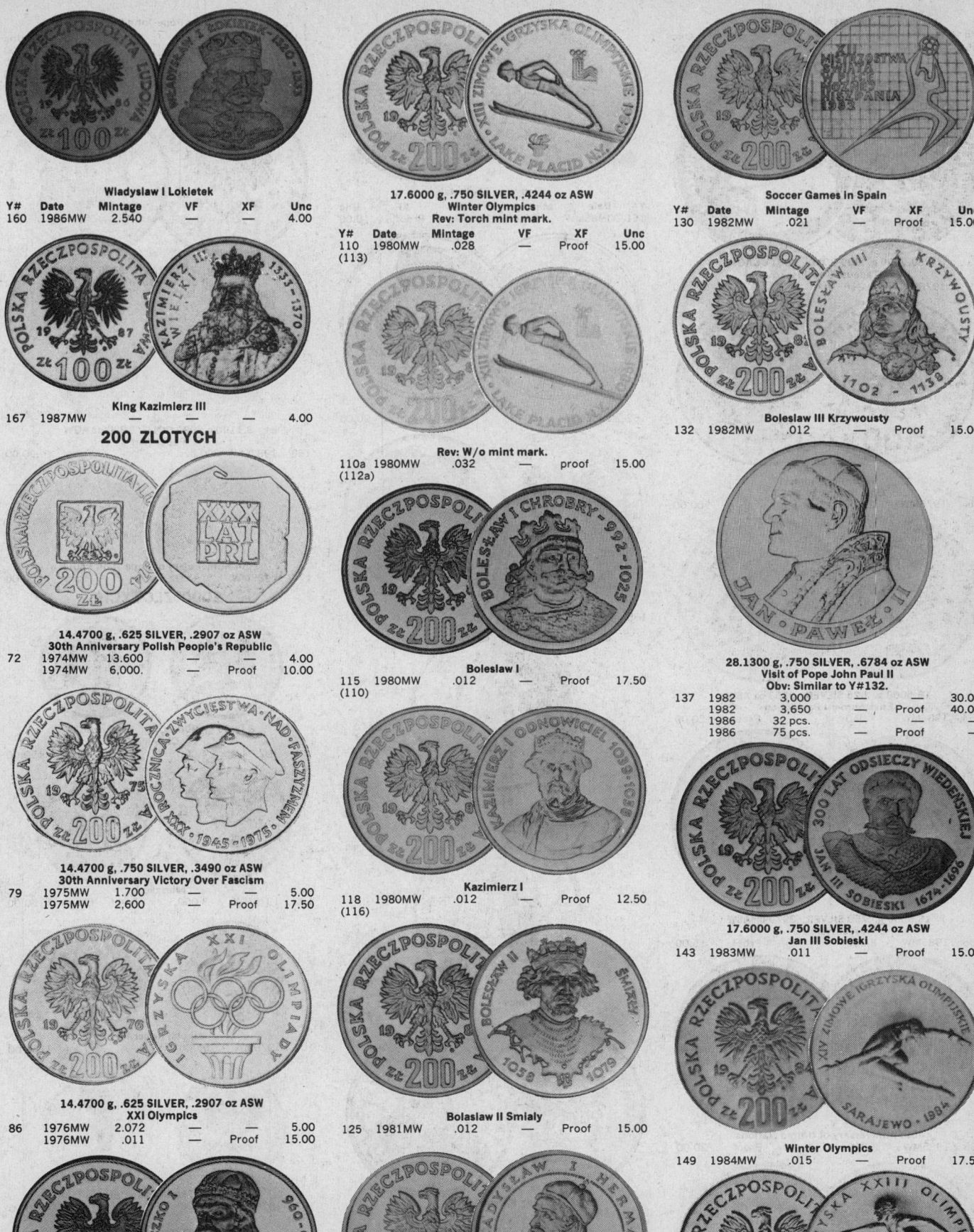

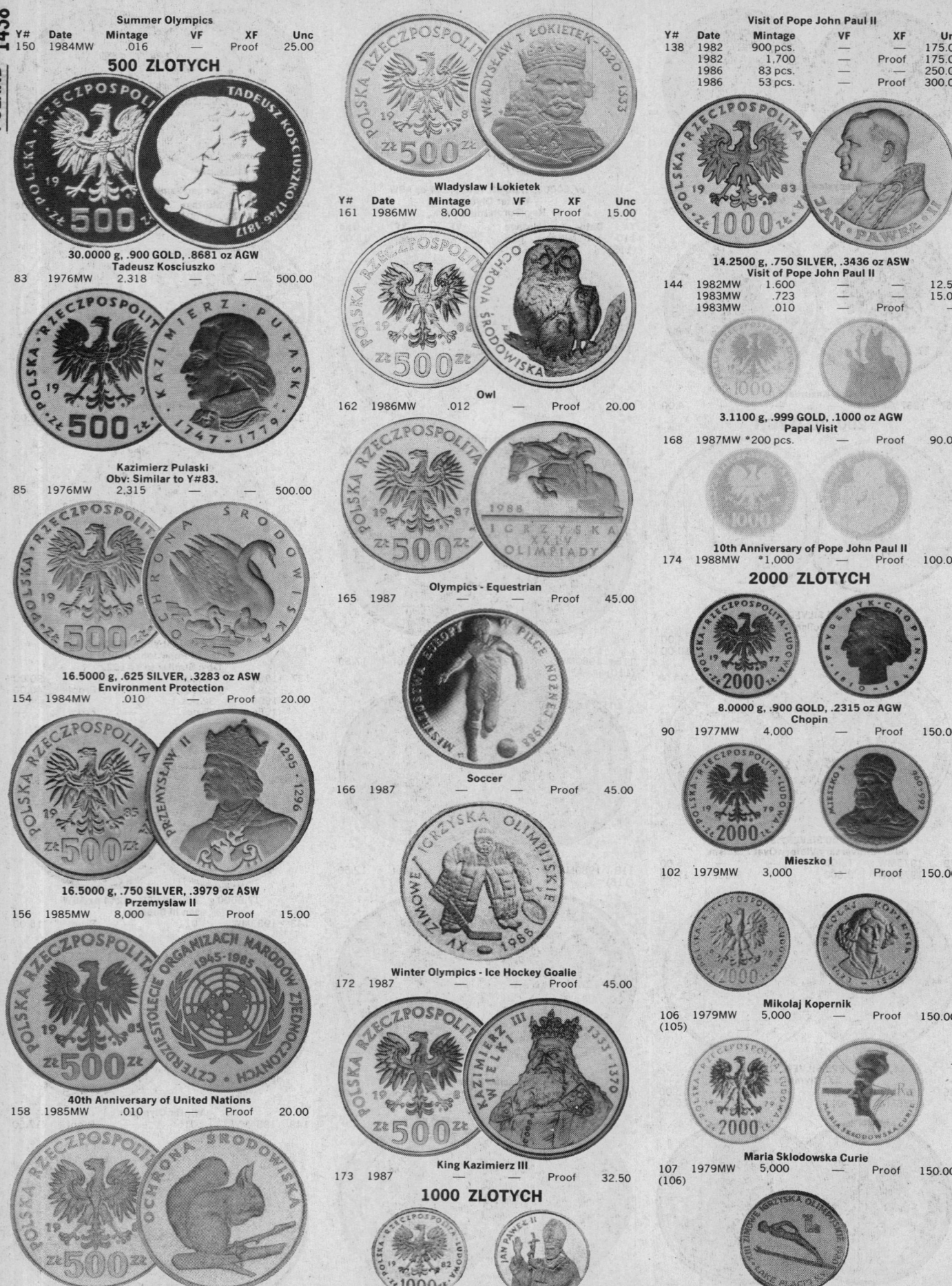

Obv: Similar to Y#107.

Y#	Date	Mintage	VF	XF	Unc
111 (114)	1980MW	5,250	—	Proof	140.00

Boleslaw I
| 116 | 1980 | 2,500 | | Proof | 160.00 |

Kazimierz I
| 119 | 1980MW | 2,500 | | Proof | 160.00 |

Boleslaw II
| 126 | 1981MW | 3,000 | | Proof | 160.00 |

Wladyslaw I Herman
Similar to 200 Zlotych, Y#129.
| 131 | 1981MW | 3,113 | | Proof | 160.00 |

6.8000 g, .900 GOLD, .1968 oz AGW
Visit of Pope John Paul II
139	1982	500 pcs.	—	—	250.00
	1982	1,250	—	Proof	250.00
	1986	54 pcs.	—	—	350.00
	1986	79 pcs.	—	Proof	400.00

7.7700 g, .999 GOLD, .2500 oz AGW
Papal Visit
| 169 | 1987MW | *200 pcs. | — | Proof | 215.00 |

10th Anniversary of Pope John Paul II
| 175 | 1988 | *1,000 | — | Proof | 300.00 |

5000 ZLOTYCH

15.5500 g, .999 GOLD, .5000 oz AGW
Papal Visit
| 170 | 1987MW | *200 pcs. | — | Proof | 430.00 |

10th Anniversary of Pope John Paul II
| 176 | 1988MW | *1,000 | — | Proof | 500.00 |

10000 ZLOTYCH

34.5000 g, .900 GOLD, .9984 oz AGW
Visit of Pope John Paul II

Y#	Date	Mintage	VF	XF	Unc
140	1982	200 pcs.	—	—	800.00
	1982	700 pcs.	—	Proof	1000.
	1986	6 pcs.	—	—	2000.
	1986	13 pcs.	—	Proof	2500.

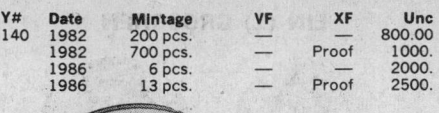

19.0600 g, .750 SILVER, .4582 oz ASW
Papal Visit
| 164 | 1987MW | — | — | — | 35.00 |

31.1030 g, .999 GOLD, 1.0000 oz AGW
Papal Visit
| 171 | 1987MW | *200 pcs. | — | Proof | 860.00 |

10th Anniversary of Pope John Paul II
| 177 | 1988MW | — | — | — | 475.00 |
| | 1988MW | *1,000 | — | Proof | 700.00 |

31.1000 g, .999 SILVER, 1.0000 oz ASW
| 177a | 1988MW | — | — | — | 45.00 |
| | 1988MW | — | — | Proof | 50.00 |

Pope John Paul - Christmas
| 179 | 1988MW | — | — | Proof | 45.00 |

50000 ZLOTYCH

19.3000 g, .750 SILVER, .4654 oz ASW
70 Years of Polish Independence
Y#	Date	Mintage	VF	XF	Unc
180	1988				

200,000 ZLOTYCH

373.2420 g, .999 GOLD, 12.0000 oz AGW
Papal Visit
Illustration reduced. Actual size: 70mm
| 163 | 1987 | 100 pcs. | — | — | 8800. |

POLAND 1439

POLAND

10th Anniversary of Pope John Paul II
Illustration reduced. Actual size: 70mm

Y#	Date	Mintage	VF	XF	Unc
178	1988MW	300 pcs.	—	Proof	8950.

SPECIMEN SETS (SS)

KM#	Date	Mintage	Identification	Mkt.Val.
SS1	1831 (5)	—	C120,121,123-125, includes 1 Zloty banknote	1500.

DANZIG

A seaport on the nothern coast of Poland giving access to the Baltic Sea. An important port from early times. Has at different times belonged to the Teutonic Knights, Pomerania, Russia, and Prussia. Danzig was a free city from 1919 to 1939 during which most of its modern coinage was made.

RULERS
Friedrich Wilhelm III (of Prussia), 1797-1840
Marshal Lefebvre (as Duke), 1807-1814

MINT MARKS
A - Berlin

MINTMASTER'S INITIALS
Letter	Date	Name
M	—	Jan Ludwig Meyer

MONETARY SYSTEM
3 Schilling = 1 Groschen

SCHILLING

COPPER

KM#	Date	Mintage	VG	Fine	VF	XF
135 (C15)	1801A	—	6.00	12.00	25.00	40.00

| 136 (C16) | 1808M | — | 6.00 | 12.00 | 25.00 | 40.00 |
| | 1812M | — | 6.00 | 12.00 | 25.00 | 40.00 |

EIN (1) GROSCHEN

COPPER

KM#	Date	Mintage	VG	Fine	VF	XF
137 (C17)	1809M	—	7.50	15.00	25.00	50.00
	1812M	—	7.50	15.00	25.00	50.00

FREE STATE
MONETARY SYSTEM
Until 1923
100 Pfennig = 1 Mark
Commencing 1923
100 Pfennig, Pfennige = 1 Gulden

PFENNIG

BRONZE

KM#	Date	Mintage	Fine	VF	XF	Unc
140 (Y3)	1923	4.000	1.00	3.00	5.00	10.00
	1923	—	—	—	Proof	50.00
	1926	1.500	1.50	4.00	8.00	16.00
	1929	1.000	2.50	6.50	11.00	18.50
	1930	2.000	1.25	3.50	6.50	11.00
	1937	3.000	1.25	3.50	6.50	11.00

2 PFENNIG

BRONZE

141 (Y4)	1923	1.000	1.75	4.50	7.25	14.00
	1923	—	—	—	Proof	65.00
	1926	1.750	1.75	4.50	7.25	14.00
	1937	.500	2.75	6.50	11.00	18.50

5 PFENNIG

COPPER-NICKEL

142 (Y5)	1923	3.000	1.25	3.50	6.00	11.00
	1923	—	—	—	Proof	100.00
	1928	1.000	3.75	8.25	14.00	27.50
	1928	—	—	—	Proof	175.00

ALUMINUM-BRONZE

| 151 (Y13) | 1932 | 4.000 | 1.25 | 2.75 | 6.00 | 16.00 |

10 PFENNIG

COPPER-NICKEL

| 143 (Y6) | 1923 | 5.000 | 3.00 | 3.50 | 8.00 | 17.50 |
| | 1923 | — | — | — | Proof | 115.00 |

ALUMINUM-BRONZE

KM#	Date	Mintage	Fine	VF	XF	Unc
152 (Y14)	1932	4.000	2.75	3.25	7.50	17.00

1/2 GULDEN

2.5000 g, .750 SILVER, .0603 oz ASW

144 (Y7)	1923	1.000	6.00	16.00	30.00	50.00
	1923	—	—	—	Proof	150.00
	1927	.400	14.00	27.50	55.00	100.00
	1927	—	—	—	Proof	250.00

NICKEL

| 153 (Y15) | 1932 | 1.400 | 8.00 | 25.00 | 37.50 | 60.00 |

GULDEN

5.0000 g, .750 SILVER, .1206 oz ASW

| 145 (Y8) | 1923 | 2.500 | 11.00 | 22.50 | 40.00 | 65.00 |
| | 1923 | — | — | — | Proof | 225.00 |

NICKEL

| 154 (Y16) | 1932 | 2.500 | 8.00 | 27.50 | 35.00 | 55.00 |

2 GULDEN

10.0000 g, .750 SILVER, .2411 oz ASW

| 146 (Y9) | 1923 | 1.250 | 25.00 | 60.00 | 100.00 | 175.00 |
| | 1923 | — | — | — | Proof | 250.00 |

10.0000 g, .500 SILVER, .1608 oz ASW

| 155 (Y17) | 1932 | 1.250 | — | 200.00 | 250.00 | 300.00 |

5 GULDEN

25.0000 g, .750 SILVER, .6028 oz ASW

KM#	Date	Mintage	Fine	VF	XF	Unc
147	1923	.700	75.00	150.00	210.00	325.00
(Y10)	1923	—	—	—	Proof	500.00
	1927	.160	150.00	250.00	375.00	600.00
	1927	—	—	—	Proof	1000.

14.8200 g, .500 SILVER, .2382 oz ASW

156	1932	.430	150.00	250.00	400.00	950.00
(Y18)						

157	1932	.430	150.00	350.00	850.00	1500.
(Y19)						

NICKEL

158	1935	.800	100.00	175.00	250.00	450.00
(Y20)						

10 GULDEN

NICKEL

159	1935	.380	300.00	500.00	750.00	1350.
(Y21)						

25 GULDEN

7.9881 g, .917 GOLD, .2354 oz AGW

148	1923	200 pcs.	—	1500.	1800.	2500.
(Y11)	1923	800 pcs.	—	—	Proof	3250.

NOTE: This issue was presented to members of the Senate.

KM#	Date	Mintage	Fine	VF	XF	Unc
150	1930	*4,000	—	—	7000.	10,000.
(Y12)						

NOTE: Not released for circulation; a few were given in presentation cases on September 1, 1939.

PROOF SETS (PS)

KM#	Date	Mintage	Identification	Issue Price	Mkt. Val.
PS1	1923(8)	—	KM140-147	—	1300.

EAST PRUSSIA

An area on the southeastern coast of the Baltic Sea. Part of the area is in present day Poland and part in the U.S.S.R. A possession of Prussia from 1525 until 1945. Coinage for the area made by the Prussian kings except for brief occupation by Russia from 1756-1762 when Russia produced special coin types for the area.

RULERS
Friedrich Wilhelm III (of Prussia) 1797-1840

MINT MARKS
A - Berlin
E - Konigsberg
G - Glatz, Silesia

For gold listings refer to Konigsberg Mint under Brandenburg and Prussia (German States).

PRUSSIAN COINAGE
SCHILLING
COPPER

C#	Date	Mintage	VG	Fine	VF	XF
53	1804A	—	1.50	3.25	6.00	11.00
	1805A	—	1.50	3.25	6.00	10.00
	1806A	—	1.50	3.25	6.00	11.00

54	1810A	—	1.50	3.25	6.00	11.00

1/2 GROSCHEN
COPPER

56	1811A	—	3.25	6.50	12.50	25.00

GROSCHEN

COPPER

58	1810	—	2.00	4.00	8.00	14.00
	1811A	—	2.00	4.00	8.00	14.00

3 GROSCHEN

BILLON

60	1800A	—	6.00	10.00	15.00	25.00
	1801A	—	6.00	10.00	15.00	25.00
	1802A	—	6.00	10.00	15.00	25.00
	1803A	—	6.00	10.00	15.00	25.00
	1805A	—	6.00	10.00	15.00	25.00
	1806A	—	6.00	10.00	15.00	25.00
	1807A	—	6.00	10.00	15.00	25.00
60a	1807G	—	6.00	10.00	15.00	25.00
	1808G	—	6.00	10.00	15.00	25.00

KRAKOW

A city in southern Poland, the third largest in the country. Formed an independent republic in 1815 that lasted until 1846 at which time the city reverted to Austria. Coins made for the republic in 1835.

MONETARY SYSTEM
30 Groszy = 1 Zloty

5 GROSZY

BILLON

C#	Date	Mintage	VG	Fine	VF	XF
11	1835	—	10.00	20.00	30.00	50.00

10 GROSZY

SILVER

12	1835	—	10.00	20.00	30.00	50.00

ZLOTY

SILVER

13	1835	—	15.00	22.50	35.00	55.00

POSEN

One of the oldest cities in Poland, was an active member of the Hanseatic League. Was a province of Prussia from 1793-1918. Became part of the Grand Duchy of Warsaw. Returned to Prussia after the Congress of Vienna (1815). A special coin issue was made as a provincial issue for the Grand Duchy of Posen by Prussia immediately after repossession.

RULERS
Friedrich Wilhelm III (of Prussia) 1797-1840

MINT MARKS
A - Berlin
B - Breslau

GROSCHEN

COPPER

KM#	Date	Mintage	VG	Fine	VF	XF
30	1816A	—	5.00	10.00	15.00	25.00
(C1)	1816B	—	5.00	10.00	15.00	25.00
	1817A	—	5.00	10.00	15.00	25.00

3 GROSCHEN

COPPER

31	1816A	—	—	—	Rare	—
(C2)	1816B	—	5.00	15.00	20.00	30.00
	1817A	—	5.00	15.00	20.00	40.00

ZAMOSC

A commune in eastern Poland.

MONETARY SYSTEM
30 Groszy = 1 Zloty

6 GROSZY

BRONZE

C#	Date	Mintage	VG	Fine	VF	XF
1	1813	1,330	300.00	500.00	750.00	1000.

NOTE: Varieties exist.

10 GROSZY
BILLON
Obv. leg: BOZE DOPOMOZ..... around arms.
Rev. leg: W.OBLEZENJU. ZAMOSCIA/value/date.

6	1831					

NOTE: A crude contemporary fantasy.

2 ZLOTY

SILVER

	Date	Mintage	VG	Fine	VF	XF
2	1813	7,930	200.00	300.00	400.00	500.00

Obv: Legend in 4 lines.

| 2a | 1813 | Inc. Ab. | 225.00 | 400.00 | 500.00 | 600.00 |

NOTE: Varieties exist.

PORTUGAL

The Portuguese Republic, located in the western part of the Iberian Peninsula in southwestern Europe, has an area of 35,553 sq. mi. (92,082 sq. km.) and a population of *10.2 million. Capital: Lisbon. Portugal's economy is based on agriculture and a small but expanding industrial sector. Textiles, machinery, chemicals, wine and cork are exported.

After centuries of domination by Romans, Visigoths and Moors, Portugal emerged in the 12th century as an independent kingdom financially and philosophically prepared for the great period of exploration that would follow. Attuned to the inspiration of Prince Henry the Navigator (1394-1460), Portugal's daring explorers of the 15th and 16th centuries roamed the world's oceans from Brazil to Japan in an unprecendented burst of energy and endeavor that culminated in 1494 with Portugal laying claim to half the transoceanic world. Unfortunately for the fortunes of the tiny kingdom, the Portuguese proved to be inept colonizers. Less than a century after Portugal laid claim to half the world, English, French and Dutch trading companies had seized the lion's share of the world's colonies and commerce, and Portugal's place as an imperial power was lost forever. The monarchy was overthrown in 1910 and a republic established.

On April 25, 1974, the government of Portugal was seized by a military junta which reached agreements providing for independence for the Portuguese overseas provinces of Portuguese Guinea (Guinea-Bissau), Mozambique, Cape Verde Islands, Angola, and St. Thomas and Prince Islands (Sao Tome and Principe).

On January 1, 1986, Portugal became the eleventh member of the European Economic Community.

RULERS
Joao, As Prince Regent, 1799-1816
Joao, As King (Joao VI), 1816-1826
Pedro IV, 1826-1828
Miguel, 1828-1834
Maria II, 1834-1853
Pedro V, 1853-1861
Luiz I, 1861-1889
Carlos I, 1889-1908
Manuel II, 1908-1910
Republic, 1910 to date

MINT MARKS
A - Paris (1891-1892, Copper only)
L - Lisbon
P - Porto
No Mint mark - Lisbon

MONETARY SYSTEM
1826-1836
7500 Reis = 1 Peca
Beginning in 1836 all coins were expressed in terms of Reis and arranged in a decimal sequence. (until 1910).
Commencing 1836
20 Reis = 1 Vintem
100 Reis = 1 Tostao
480 Reis = 24 Vintens = 1 Cruzado
1600 Reis = 1 Escudo
6400 Reis = 4 Escudos = 1 Peca
Commencing 1910
100 Centavos = 1 Escudo

NOTE: The primary denomination was the Peca, weighing 14.34 g, tariffed at 6400 Reis until 1825, and at 7500 Reis after 1826. The weight was not changed.

III (3) REIS
COPPER
Obv: JOANNES...., around shield. Rev: Leg. around wreath, date and denomination within.

KM#	Date	Mintage	VG	Fine	VF	XF
334 (C48)	1804	.123	4.25	8.50	17.50	40.00

Obv: Crowned arms. Rev: Value and date in branches.

| 354 (C65) | 1818 | — | 15.00 | 35.00 | 70.00 | 135.00 |

V (5) REIS
COPPER
Obv. leg: JOANNES..., arms. Rev. leg. ends: PRINCEPS.

| 325 (C49) | 1800 | — | 15.00 | 30.00 | 60.00 | 125.00 |
| | 1801 | — | 20.00 | 40.00 | 85.00 | 175.00 |

Rev. leg. ends: REGENS.

| 335 (C49b) | 1804 | — | — | Reported, not confirmed | | |

KM#	Date	Mintage	VG	Fine	VF	XF
346 (C49c)	1812	.399	1.00	2.00	4.00	8.00
	1813	.539	2.00	3.00	6.00	12.50
	1814	.448	2.25	4.50	9.00	20.00

Mule. Obv: KM#305. Rev: KM#346.

| 347 (C49d) | 1812 | — | 5.25 | 11.25 | 22.50 | 45.00 |

Obv: Arms, JOANNES VI.
Rev: PORTUGALIAE... REX, value in wreath.

355 (C66)	1818	—	50.00	110.00	225.00	450.00
	1819	.011	4.00	8.00	17.50	35.00
	1820		3.50	7.00	15.00	30.00
	1823	.032	4.00	8.00	17.50	35.00
	1824	.098	1.50	3.00	6.00	12.50

Obv. leg: MICHAEL I DEI GRATIA, crowned arms.
Rev: Leg. around wreath, value within, date below.

| 389 (C88) | 1829 | .037 | 1.25 | 2.50 | 5.00 | 12.50 |

NOTE: For similar coins dated 1830 but w/titles of Maria II see Azores.

Titles of Maria II
Obv: Square shield.

| 398 (C99a) | 1833 | — | 65.00 | 125.00 | 250.00 | 400.00 |

(Struck at Porto.)

| 408 (C99b) | 1836 | 5,593 | 15.00 | 25.00 | 40.00 | 80.00 |

X (10) REIS
COPPER
Obv. leg: JOANNES..., arms.
Rev. leg. ends: PRINCEPS.

| 327 (C50) | 1800 | — | 15.00 | 30.00 | 60.00 | 125.00 |
| | 1801 | — | — | | Rare | — |

Rev. leg. ends: REGENS.

| 333 (C50a) | 1803 | — | 20.00 | 37.50 | 75.00 | 150.00 |

| 348 (C50b) | 1812 | .332 | 1.25 | 2.50 | 5.00 | 11.25 |
| | 1813 | .276 | 1.25 | 2.50 | 5.00 | 11.25 |

Obv. leg: JOANNES VI..., arms.
Rev. leg: PORTUGALIAE... REX, value in wreath.

356 (C67)	1818	—	20.00	40.00	80.00	150.00
	1819	.806	1.50	3.00	6.00	12.50
	1820	6,773	10.00	22.50	45.00	90.00
	1822	.021	10.00	20.00	40.00	80.00
	1823	.044	2.00	4.25	9.00	20.00
	1824	.064	2.00	3.50	7.00	15.00
	1825		—	—	Reported, not confirmed	

PORTUGAL 1443

KM#	Date	Mintage	VG	Fine	VF	XF
390	1829	.056	2.00	3.50	6.00	15.00
(C89)	1831	.345	1.00	4.25	10.00	7.50
	1833	.070	5.50	11.50	22.50	45.00

NOTE: For similar coins dated 1830 but with titles of Maria II see Azores.

Similar to 5 Reis, KM#408.

399	1833	—	50.00	100.00	175.00	300.00
(C100a)						

(Struck at Porto.)

Obv: Large crowned shield.

406	1835	.287	2.50	6.00	12.00	25.00
(C100b)	1836	.227	1.50	3.50	7.50	15.00
	1837	.360	—	10.00	17.50	35.00

Obv: Small crowned shield.

409	1837	Inc. Ab.	2.00	4.25	8.50	17.50
(C100c)	1838	.645	1.50	3.00	6.50	12.50
	1839	.469	1.50	3.00	6.50	12.50

20 REIS
(Vintem)

COPPER, 34mm
Obv. leg: JOANNES..., arms.
Rev. leg: PORTUGALIAE..., date, value within wreath.

328	1800	—	17.50	30.00	60.00	125.00
(C51)	1801	—	Reported, not confirmed			

Large planchet, 37mm.

329	1800	—	15.00	27.50	50.00	100.00
(C51a)						

SILVER
Obv: Globe. Rev: Cross w/rosettes in angles.

330	ND(1799-1816)	2.25	4.25	8.50	17.50
(C53)						

BRONZE
Titles of Maria II

400	1833	—	10.00	20.00	35.00	75.00
(C102)						

(Struck at Porto.)

40 REIS
(Pataco)

BRONZE
Plain edge

345.1	1811	.163	6.25	12.50	20.00	45.00

KM#	Date	Mintage	VG	Fine	VF	XF
(C52)	1812	1.384	3.25	6.25	12.50	30.00
	1813	1.762	2.50	5.00	10.00	25.00
	1814	.542	2.50	5.00	10.00	25.00
	1815	.118	10.00	20.00	35.00	75.00
	1817	—	Reported, not confirmed			

Milled edge

345.2	1814	Inc. Ab.	8.50	17.50	35.00	90.00
365	1819	.422	3.00	6.00	12.50	35.00
(C68)						

370	1820	1.579	2.00	3.50	6.25	25.00
(C68a)	1821	1.575	2.00	3.50	6.25	25.00
	1822	2.370	2.00	3.50	6.25	25.00
	1823	2.621	2.00	3.50	6.25	25.00
	1824	3.051	2.00	3.50	6.25	25.00
	1825	1.124	2.50	4.00	7.50	30.00

Similar to KM#345.1.

371	1821	—	25.00	60.00	115.00	225.00
(C68b)	1823	—	20.00	50.00	90.00	175.00

Rev: Similar to KM#345.1.

373	1826	1.253	3.25	6.25	12.50	40.00
(C81)	1827	1.447	2.50	5.00	10.00	30.00
	1828	1.378	2.50	5.00	10.00	30.00

Obv: Large high crown.

380	1828	1.378	4.00	8.00	15.00	40.00
(C90.1)	1829	1.678	3.00	5.00	10.00	35.00

Obv: Small lower crown.

391	1829	Inc. KM380	2.25	4.25	7.50	20.00
(C90.2)	1830	1.783	2.25	4.25	7.50	20.00
	1831	1.391	2.25	4.25	7.50	20.00
	1832	1.780	2.25	4.25	7.50	20.00
	1833	1.631	2.25	4.25	7.50	20.00
	1834	—	Reported, not confirmed			

Titles of Maria II
Similar to 20 Reis, C#102, shield flared outward at upper corners, value in wreath.

401	1833	—	6.25	12.50	20.00	45.00
(C103)						

(Struck at Porto.)

Shield w/right-angle upper corners.

402	1833	—	2.00	3.75	7.50	22.50
(C103a)	1834	—	2.00	3.75	7.50	22.50
	1847	—	3.50	7.50	17.50	45.00

The 1833-34 coins were struck at Lisbon, the 1847 at Porto. Varieties of the 1833 and 1834 coins have a vertical axis instead of horizontal. Values are 1833 $27.50 in XF, 1834 $35.00 in XF.

200 REIS

SILVER
Obv. leg: JOANNES .... P. REGENS., arms.

KM#	Date	Mintage	VG	Fine	VF	XF
340	1806	—	60.00	100.00	170.00	325.00
(C58)	1807	—	—	—	Rare	—
	1808	—	20.00	35.00	60.00	125.00
	1809	.022	35.00	60.00	100.00	200.00
	1816	—	50.00	90.00	150.00	300.00

357	1818	.021	30.00	60.00	120.00	225.00
(C73)	1819	.024	30.00	65.00	135.00	250.00
	1820	2.818	30.00	60.00	125.00	225.00
	1821	2,293	80.00	175.00	350.00	650.00
	1822	6,483	40.00	85.00	175.00	325.00

Obv. leg: MICHAEL I..., crowned arms.

392	1829	3,584	17.50	30.00	50.00	100.00
(C95)	1830	6,594	22.50	40.00	65.00	125.00

400 REIS

SILVER
Obv. leg. ends: ET. ALG.
Rev: Similar to KM#331.

318	1801	.196	50.00	90.00	150.00	300.00
(C59)	1802	—	—	—	Rare	—

Obv. leg. ends: P.REGENS

331	1802	—	25.00	40.00	65.00	125.00
(C59a)	1805	—	15.00	25.00	40.00	80.00
	1807	—	9.00	15.00	25.00	50.00
	1808	—	9.00	15.00	25.00	50.00
	1809	—	9.00	15.00	25.00	50.00
	1810	—	9.00	15.00	25.00	50.00
	1811	—	9.00	17.50	30.00	60.00
	1812	—	9.00	15.00	25.00	50.00
	1813	—	9.00	15.00	25.00	50.00
	1814	—	9.00	15.00	25.00	50.00
	1815	—	9.00	15.00	25.00	50.00
	1816	—	9.00	15.00	25.00	50.00
	1816 VINECS (error for VINCES)					
		—	50.00	100.00	175.00	350.00

358	1818	2.337	9.00	15.00	25.00	50.00
(C74)	1819	1.432	9.00	15.00	25.00	50.00
	1820	1.845	9.00	15.00	25.00	50.00
	1821	1.937	9.00	15.00	25.00	50.00
	1822	.568	10.00	20.00	40.00	80.00
	1823	.667	15.00	30.00	60.00	125.00
	1825	.028	32.50	55.00	90.00	175.00

Obv. leg: PETRUS IV .... REX., arms.

PORTUGAL 1444

KM#	Date	Mintage	VG	Fine	VF	XF
377 (C85)	1826	.257	32.50	55.00	90.00	175.00
	1827	—	None known to have survived			

.906 SILVER
Similar to KM#331.

KM#	Date	Mintage	VG	Fine	VF	XF
386 (C96)	1828	.135	50.00	90.00	150.00	300.00
	1829	.022	250.00	500.00	1000.	2000.
	1830	.029	40.00	65.00	115.00	225.00
	1831	.065	35.00	60.00	100.00	200.00
	1832	.108	35.00	60.00	100.00	200.00
	1833	.798	35.00	60.00	100.00	200.00
	1834	.705	—	—	Rare	

Obv. leg: *MARIA II . . . . REGINA*, arms.

| 403.1 (C106) | 1833 | — | 500.00 | 1000. | 1750. | 3000. |

(Struck in Porto.)

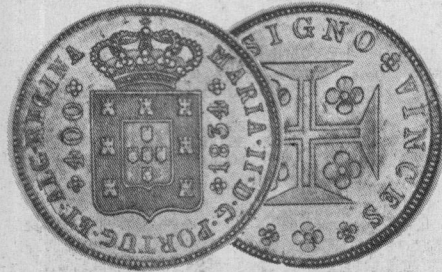

403.2 (C106a)	1833	.798	10.00	17.50	30.00	75.00
	1834	1,864	9.00	15.00	25.00	50.00
	1835	3,433	9.00	15.00	25.00	45.00
	1836	.829	9.00	15.00	25.00	55.00
	1837	.194	100.00	200.00	350.00	650.00

Obv. leg: Stars removed (Lisbon issues).

(Pinto)
(480 Reis)

1.0720 g, .917 GOLD, .0316 oz AGW
Obv. leg: JOANNES P.R. in crowned wreath.

| 341 (C60) | 1807 | 8,857 | 65.00 | 125.00 | 225.00 | 350.00 |

Obv. leg: JOAN VI in crowned wreath.

359 (C75)	1818	4,401	85.00	150.00	200.00	325.00
	1819	1,387	100.00	175.00	250.00	400.00
	1820	200 pcs.	200.00	350.00	550.00	825.00
	1821	266 pcs.	200.00	300.00	450.00	675.00

1000 REIS
(Quartinho)
(1200 Reis)

2.6800 g, .917 GOLD, .0790 oz AGW

360 (C77)	1818	3,144	125.00	250.00	375.00	600.00
	1819	1,247	150.00	300.00	475.00	700.00
	1820	270 pcs.	250.00	425.00	600.00	1000.
	1821	275 pcs.	250.00	425.00	600.00	1000.

1/2 ESCUDO
(800 Reis)

1.7920 g, .917 GOLD, .0528 oz AGW
Obv. leg: JOANNES D.G. PORT. ET ALG. P. REGENS.

337 (C61)	1805	3,278	75.00	150.00	275.00	450.00
	1806	—	100.00	200.00	375.00	600.00
	1807	5,253	75.00	150.00	275.00	450.00

Obv. leg: JOANNES VI D.G. PORT...

361 (C76)	1818	270 pcs.	200.00	350.00	500.00	1000.
	1819	5,536	100.00	250.00	400.00	600.00
	1820	82 pcs.	—	—	Rare	
	1821	286 pcs.	200.00	350.00	500.00	1000.

ESCUDO
(1600 Reis)

3.5850 g, .917 GOLD, .1057 oz AGW
Obv. leg: JOANNES D.G. PORT ET ALG. P. REGENS.

KM#	Date	Mintage	VG	Fine	VF	XF
338 (C62)	1805	—	—	—	Rare	
	1807	800 pcs.	200.00	450.00	750.00	1200.

Obv. leg: JOANNES VI D.G. PORT . . . . REX, bust.

362 (C78)	1818	1,804	200.00	350.00	550.00	850.00
	1819	1,523	200.00	350.00	550.00	850.00
	1821	270 pcs.	300.00	500.00	700.00	1000.

1/2 PECA
(3200 Reis)
Revalued to 3750 Reis in 1826.

7.1500 g, .917 GOLD, .2107 oz AGW
Obv. leg: JOANNES D.G. PORT ET ALG. P. REGENS, bust.

| 339 (C63) | 1805 | 74 pcs. | — | — | Rare | |

| 342 (C63a) | 1807 | 483 pcs. | 250.00 | 400.00 | 600.00 | 1000. |

363 (C79)	1818	100 pcs.	300.00	500.00	750.00	1200.
	1819	1,700	200.00	350.00	500.00	1000.
	1820	242 pcs.	—	—	Rare	—
	1821	196 pcs.	—	—	Rare	—
	1822	.014	150.00	250.00	375.00	600.00
	1823	—	—	—	Rare	

| 379 (C86) | 1827 | 1,713 | 300.00 | 500.00 | 750.00 | 1200. |

| 387 (C97) | 1828 | 242 pcs. | 450.00 | 750.00 | 1250. | 2000. |

KM#	Date	Mintage	VG	Fine	VF	XF
396 (C97a)	1830	525 pcs.	500.00	800.00	1250.	2500.
	1831	225 pcs.	500.00	900.00	1500.	3000.

PECA
(6400 Reis)
Revalued to 7500 Reis in 1826.

14.3420 g, .917 GOLD, .4228 oz AGW

| 332 (C64) | 1802 | .030 | 500.00 | 1000. | 1500. | 2250. |

336 (C64a)	1804	476 pcs.	500.00	1000.	2000.	4000.
	1805	.027	225.00	375.00	550.00	900.00
	1806	.041	225.00	350.00	500.00	750.00
	1807	.036	250.00	425.00	750.00	1100.
	1808	.027	250.00	425.00	750.00	1100.
	1809	.013	250.00	425.00	750.00	1100.
	1812	.025	250.00	425.00	750.00	1100.
	1813	5,590	275.00	500.00	900.00	1400.
	1814	21 pcs.	—	—	Rare	
	1815	305 pcs.	500.00	1000.	2000.	4000.
	1816	—	—	—	Rare	
	1817	620 pcs.	—	Reported, not confirmed		

NOTE: Similar pieces with "R" after date were struck in Rio de Janeiro and are found listed under Brazil.

Similar to KM#372.

364 (C80)	1818	291 pcs.	400.00	800.00	1250.	2000.
	1819	1,727	250.00	500.00	750.00	1400.
	1820	1,687	225.00	450.00	650.00	1200.
	1821	391 pcs.	400.00	800.00	1250.	2000.

372 (C80a)	1822	.030	225.00	300.00	425.00	600.00
	1823	.027	225.00	300.00	425.00	600.00
	1824	1,553	300.00	400.00	500.00	800.00

NOTE: Similar pieces with "R" after date were struck in Rio de Janeiro and are listed under Brazil.

| 378 (C87) | 1826 | 10,883 | 350.00 | 650.00 | 1100. | 1800. |
| | 1828 | 1,255 | 500.00 | 1000. | 1500. | 2500. |

NOTE: Similar pieces dated 1826 with square shield on reverse are patterns.

KM#	Date	Mintage	VG	Fine	VF	XF
388 (C98)	1828	Inc. KM378	500.00	1000.	1500.	2750.

Modified design

397 (C98a)	1830	2,274	300.00	600.00	900.00	1500.
	1831	1,618	400.00	800.00	1250.	2000.

Obv: Bare head of queen.

404 (C112)	1833	1,265	600.00	1250.	2500.	5000.

405 (C112a)	1833	—	500.00	1000.	1500.	2750.
	1834	.032	250.00	450.00	700.00	1000.

Obv. leg. continuous.

407 (C112b)	1835	2,989	350.00	600.00	850.00	1400.

COUNTERMARKED COINAGE
40 REIS

COPPER

c/m: GCP in a circle on 40 Reis, KM#402.

C#	Date	Mintage	Good	VG	Fine	VF
415.1 (C103b)	1833	—	5.00	15.00	25.00	35.00
	1847	—	2.00	4.00	7.00	10.00

c/m: Dot added below GCP on 40 Reis, KM#402.

415.2 (C103c)	1847	—	3.00	6.00	10.00	20.00

870 REIS

In 1834, the Portuguese government ordered that the countermarking of all Spanish and Spanish American 8 Reales in circulation with the crowned arms of Portugal, to indicate a revaluation to 870 Reis.

SILVER

c/m: On Bolivia (Potosi) 8 Reales, KM#55.

KM#	Date	Mintage	Good	VG	Fine	VF
440.1 (C113.1)	ND(1773-89)	—	50.00	100.00	150.00	200.00

c/m: On Bolivia (Potosi) 8 Reales, KM#74.
| 440.2 (C113.2) | ND(1789-91) | — | 60.00 | 125.00 | 175.00 | 250.00 |

c/m: On Bolivia (Potosi) 8 Reales, KM#73.
| 440.3 (C113.3) | ND(1791-1808) | — | 40.00 | 75.00 | 110.00 | 150.00 |

c/m: On Bolivia (Potosi) 8 Reales, KM#84.
| 404.4 (C113.4) | ND(1808-25) | — | 35.00 | 70.00 | 100.00 | 135.00 |

c/m: On Brazil 960 Reis, KM#326.
| 440.5 (C113.5) | ND(1818-22) | — | 65.00 | 125.00 | 200.00 | 250.00 |

c/m: On Chile 8 Reales, KM#51.
| 440.6 (C113.6) | ND(1791-1808) | — | 125.00 | 225.00 | 350.00 | 500.00 |

c/m: On Guatemala 8 Reales, KM#69.
| 440.7 (C113.7) | ND(1808-22) | — | 125.00 | 200.00 | 250.00 | 400.00 |

c/m: On Mexico 8 Reales, KM#103.
| 440.8 (C113.8) | ND(1732-47) | — | 100.00 | 175.00 | 225.00 | 300.00 |

c/m: On Mexico 8 Reales, KM#104.
| 440.9 (C113.9) | ND(1747-60) | — | 80.00 | 135.00 | 200.00 | 300.00 |

c/m: On Mexico 8 Reales, KM#105.
| 440.10 (C113.10) | ND(1760-72) | — | 100.00 | 150.00 | 200.00 | 350.00 |

c/m: On Mexico 8 Reales, KM#106.
| 440.11 (C113.11) | ND(1772-89) | — | 25.00 | 50.00 | 75.00 | 100.00 |

c/m: On Mexico 8 Reales, KM#107.
| 440.12 (C113.12) | ND(1789-90) | — | 35.00 | 65.00 | 85.00 | 125.00 |

c/m: On Mexico 8 Reales, KM#109.
| 440.13 (C113.13) | ND(1791-1808) | — | 25.00 | 50.00 | 75.00 | 100.00 |

c/m: On Mexico 8 Reales, KM#110.
| 440.14 (C113.14) | ND(1808-11) | — | 25.00 | 50.00 | 75.00 | 100.00 |

c/m: On Mexico 8 Reales, KM#111.
| 440.15 (C113.15) | ND(1811-21) | — | 25.00 | 50.00 | 75.00 | 100.00 |

c/m: On Mexico (Durango) 8 Reales KM#111.2.
| 440.16 (C113.16) | ND(1812-22) | — | 125.00 | 225.00 | 350.00 | 500.00 |

c/m: On Mexico (Guadalajara) 8 Reales, KM#111.3.
| 440.17 (C113.17) | ND(1812-22) | — | 60.00 | 125.00 | 150.00 | 250.00 |

c/m: On Mexico (Guanajuato) 8 Reales, KM#111.4.
| 440.18 (C113.18) | ND(1812-22) | — | 60.00 | 125.00 | 150.00 | 250.00 |

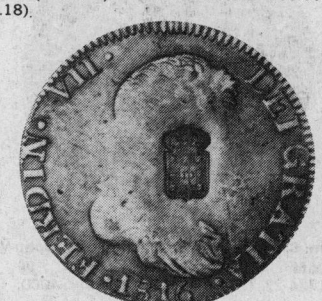

c/m: On Mexico (Zacatecas) 8 Reales, KM#111.5.
| 440.19 (C113.19) | ND(1813-22) | — | 35.00 | 75.00 | 100.00 | 150.00 |

c/m: On Peru (Lima) 8 Reales, KM#87.
| 440.20 (C113.20) | ND(1789-91) | — | 40.00 | 75.00 | 100.00 | 150.00 |

c/m: On Peru (Lima) 8 Reales, KM#97.
| 440.21 (C113.21) | ND(1791-1808) | — | 35.00 | 65.00 | 95.00 | 125.00 |

c/m: On Peru (Lima) 8 Reales, KM#106.
| 440.22 (C113.22) | ND(1808-11) | — | 35.00 | 65.00 | 95.00 | 125.00 |

c/m: On Peru (Lima) 8 Reales, KM#117.
| 440.33 (C113.33) | ND(1810-24) | — | 30.00 | 60.00 | 90.00 | 125.00 |

c/m: On Spain (Cadiz), C#136.
| 440.34 (C113.34) | ND(1810-15) | — | 60.00 | 100.00 | 150.00 | 250.00 |

c/m: On Spain (Madrid) 8 Reales, C#71.
| 440.35 (C113.35) | ND(1789-1808) | — | 65.00 | 125.00 | 175.00 | 275.00 |

c/m: On Spain (Madrid) 20 Reales, C#92.
| 440.36 (C113.36) | ND(1808-13) | — | 65.00 | 125.00 | 175.00 | 275.00 |

c/m: On Spain (Madrid) 8 Reales, C#136.
| 440.37 (C113.37) | ND(1812-33) | — | 35.00 | 65.00 | 95.00 | 125.00 |

c/m: On Spain (Seville) 8 Reales, C#40.
| 440.38 (C113.38) | ND(1772-88) | — | 125.00 | 250.00 | 350.00 | 500.00 |

PORTUGAL 1446

c/m: On Spain (Seville) 8 Reales, C#71.

KM#	Date	Mintage	Good	VG	Fine	VF
440.39 (C113.39)	ND(1788-1808)	—	85.00	150.00	225.00	300.00

c/m: On Spain (Seville) 8 Reales, C#136.

| 440.40 (C113.40) | ND(1809-30) | — | 45.00 | 75.00 | 110.00 | 150.00 |

c/m: On Spain (Valencia) 8 Reales, C#136a.

| 440.41 (C113.41) | ND(1809-11) | — | 125.00 | 175.00 | 250.00 | 500.00 |

(30,000 REIS)

In 1847, the same countermark was applied to the Dobrao of John V, indicating a revaluation from 20,000 to 30,000 Reis.

GOLD
c/m: Crowned arms on 20,000 Reis of John V.

KM#	Date	VG	Fine	VF	XF
467 (C115)	1724-27 (1847)	1500.	2500.	4000.	5500.

DECIMAL COINAGE

New denominations, all expressed in terms of Reis, were introduced by Maria II in 1836, to bring Portugal's currency into decimal form. Some of the coins retained old names, as follows:

1000 Reis Silver - Coroa
100 Reis Silver - Tostao

NOTE: The diameter of the new copper coins, first minted by Maria II in 1837, was smaller than the earlier coinage, but the weight was unaltered. However, in 1882, Luis I reduced the size and weight of the copper currency.

3 REIS

COPPER

KM#	Date	Mintage	Fine	VF	XF	Unc
517 (Y1)	1868	.100	2.00	4.00	6.50	12.50
	1874	.280	2.00	4.00	6.50	12.50
	1875	1.200	2.00	4.00	8.00	15.00

5 REIS

COPPER

KM#	Date	Mintage	VG	Fine	VF	XF
480 (C99c)	1840	.174	2.00	4.00	8.00	18.00
	1843	—	5.00	8.00	15.00	40.00
	1848	.147	2.00	4.00	8.00	18.00
	1850	.130	2.00	4.00	8.00	18.00
	1852	.292	2.00	4.00	8.00	18.00
	1853	*.063	3.00	6.00	10.00	20.00

*NOTE: Struck for circulation primarily in Mozambique.

KM#	Date	Mintage	Fine	VF	XF	Unc
513 (Y2)	1867	.737	1.50	3.00	6.00	12.50
	1868	.740	1.50	3.00	6.00	12.50
	1871	.340	10.00	20.00	40.00	70.00

(Y2)	1872	.700	1.50	3.00	6.00	12.50
	1873	.600	8.00	15.00	27.50	50.00
	1874	1.080	.75	1.50	4.00	10.00
	1875	2.200	.75	1.50	4.00	10.00
	1876	.320	8.00	15.00	32.50	60.00
	1877	.620	8.00	15.00	27.50	50.00
	1878	Inc. Ab.	2.00	4.00	10.00	15.00
	1879	.332	2.00	4.00	10.00	15.00
	1882	—	—	Reported, not confirmed		

BRONZE

525 (Y5)	1882	5.200	.50	1.00	2.50	6.00
	1883	4.700	.50	1.00	2.50	7.00
	1884	1.730	.75	1.50	3.25	8.00
	1885	3.200	.50	1.25	2.75	7.00
	1886	4.170	1.00	2.25	5.00	10.00

530 (Y15)	1890	.430	.75	1.50	2.00	4.00
	1891	Inc. Ab.	.50	1.00	2.00	4.00
	1892/1	1.510	.50	1.50	3.00	9.00
	1892	Inc. Ab.	.25	.75	1.50	4.00
	1893	.280	.25	.75	1.50	4.50
	1897	1.120	1.00	3.00	5.00	10.00
	1898	.790	.25	.75	1.50	4.50
	1899	1.220	.25	.75	1.50	4.00
	1900	1.110	1.00	3.00	5.00	10.00
	1901	1.070	1.00	3.00	5.00	10.00
	1904	.720	.50	1.00	2.50	5.00
	1905	1.340	.25	.75	1.50	4.00
	1906/0	1.260	.30	1.00	2.00	5.00
	1906/9	Inc. Ab.	.30	1.00	2.00	5.00
	1906	Inc. Ab.	.25	.75	1.50	4.00

555 (Y28)	1910	1.000	.25	.75	1.25	3.50

10 REIS

COPPER
Obv: Plain shield, struck in collared dies.

KM#	Date	Mintage	VG	Fine	VF	XF
470 (C100c)	1837	—	2.00	5.00	8.00	18.00
	1838	—	2.00	5.00	8.00	18.00
	1839	—	2.00	5.00	8.00	18.00

Obv: Ornate shield.

481 (C100d)	1840	.392	2.00	3.00	6.00	15.00
	1841	.476	2.00	3.00	6.00	15.00
	1842	1.131	2.00	3.00	6.00	15.00
	1843	.837	2.00	3.00	6.00	15.00
	1844	.620	2.00	3.00	6.00	15.00
	1845	.545	2.00	3.00	6.00	15.00
	1846	1.166	2.00	3.00	6.00	15.00
	1847	.057	5.00	10.00	20.00	45.00
	1850	.443	2.00	3.00	6.00	15.00
	1851	1.236	2.00	3.00	6.00	15.00
	1852	.558	2.00	3.00	6.00	15.00
	1853	*.046	2.00	3.00	6.00	15.00

NOTE: Struck for circulation primarily in Mozambique.

KM#	Date	Mintage	VG	Fine	VF	XF
514 (Y3)	1867	.300	1.00	2.00	4.00	8.00
	1868	.450	2.50	5.00	10.00	20.00
	1870	Inc. Ab.	15.00	25.00	50.00	100.00
	1871	.360	2.50	5.00	10.00	20.00
	1873	2.000	.75	1.50	3.50	8.00
	1874	.220	5.00	10.00	20.00	40.00
	1878	—	—	Reported, not confirmed		

BRONZE

KM#	Date	Mintage	Fine	VF	XF	Unc
526 (Y6)	1882	14.795	1.00	2.00	4.50	10.00
	1883	Inc. Ab.	1.00	2.00	4.50	10.00
	1884	10.190	1.00	2.00	4.50	10.00
	1885	8.100	1.00	2.00	4.50	10.00
	1886	3.915	1.25	2.50	7.50	15.00

532 (Y16)	1891	3.445	1.00	2.00	4.50	10.00
	1891A	.895	2.50	6.00	15.00	35.00
	1892	10.300	1.00	2.00	4.50	10.00
	1892A	5.769	1.00	2.00	4.50	10.00

20 REIS

COPPER

KM#	Date	Mintage	VG	Fine	VF	XF
482 (C101)	1847	2.484	2.00	3.00	5.00	15.00
	1848	.861	2.00	3.00	5.00	15.00
	1849	2.269	2.00	3.00	5.00	15.00
	1850	1.803	2.00	3.00	5.00	15.00
	1851	.850	2.00	3.00	5.00	15.00
	1852	1.215	2.00	3.00	5.00	15.00
	1853	*.791	2.00	3.00	5.00	15.00

*NOTE: Struck for circulation primarily in Mozambique.

515 (Y4)	1867	.745	1.25	2.50	5.00	10.00
	1870	—	15.00	30.00	50.00	100.00
	1871	.310	3.00	6.00	10.00	20.00
	1872	.050	—	Reported, not confirmed		
	1873	2.500	1.00	2.00	3.00	8.00
	1874	1.575	1.00	2.00	4.00	10.00

PORTUGAL 1447

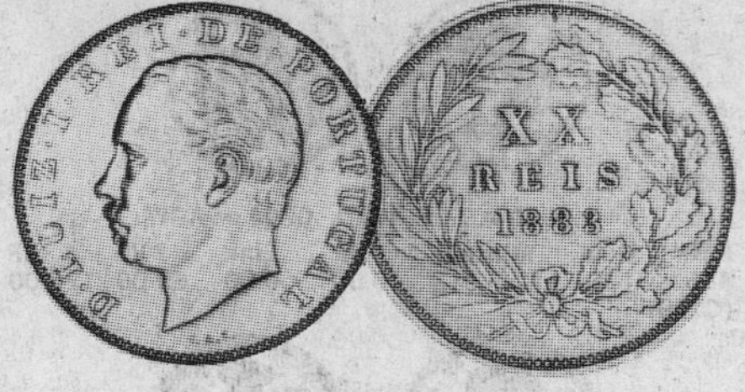

BRONZE

KM#	Date	Mintage	Fine	VF	XF	Unc
527	1882	17.735	.75	1.75	5.00	15.00
(Y7)	1883	Inc. Ab.	.75	1.75	5.00	15.00
	1884	17.200	.75	1.75	5.00	15.00
	1885	18.492	.75	1.75	5.00	15.00
	1886	4.572	.75	2.00	6.00	20.00

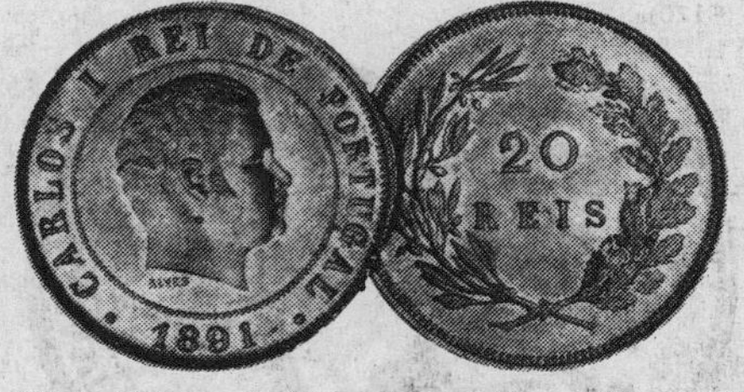

533	1891	3.282	.75	1.75	4.00	14.00
(Y17)	1891A	6.016	.75	1.75	5.00	15.00
	1892/1	15.411	1.00	2.00	4.50	17.50
	1892	Inc. Ab.	.75	1.75	4.00	14.00
	1892A	.658	1.50	4.00	10.00	30.00

50 REIS

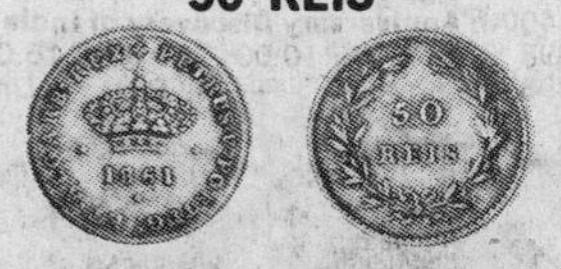

1.2500 g, .917 SILVER, .0368 oz ASW

KM#	Date	Mintage	VG	Fine	VF	XF
493	1855	.041	4.00	10.00	15.00	30.00
(C116)	1861	.800	1.00	2.00	4.00	7.50

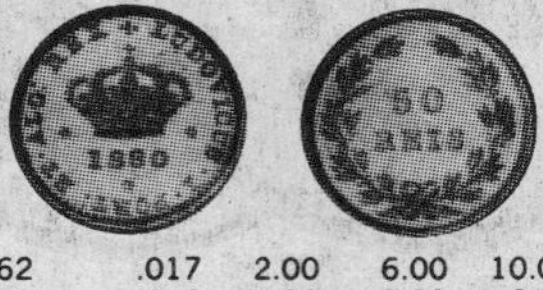

506	1862	.017	2.00	6.00	10.00	20.00
(Y8)	1863	.215	1.00	3.00	6.00	12.00
	1864	.050	4.00	7.00	12.00	30.00
	1868	—	—	Reported, not confirmed		
	1874	.060	2.00	6.00	10.00	20.00
	1875	Inc. Ab.	10.00	20.00	30.00	65.00
	1876	.100	1.00	3.00	5.00	10.00
	1877	.100	1.00	3.00	5.00	10.00
	1879	.080	1.00	3.00	5.00	10.00
	1880	.320	1.00	3.00	5.00	10.00
	1886	.100	3.00	7.00	16.00	50.00
	1887	Inc. Ab.	10.00	25.00	60.00	175.00
	1888	Inc. Be.	—	—	Rare	—
	1889	1.000	1.00	1.50	2.50	6.50

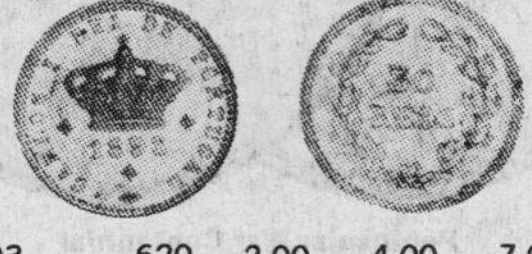

536	1893	.620	2.00	4.00	7.00	10.00
(Y20)						

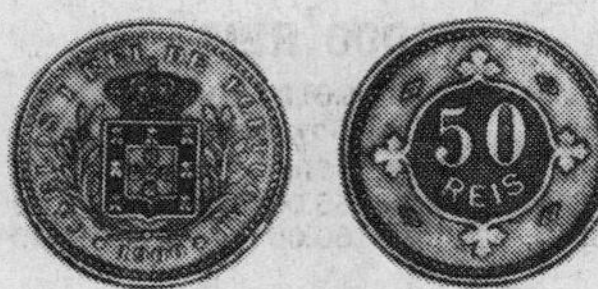

COPPER-NICKEL

KM#	Date	Mintage	Fine	VF	XF	Unc
545	1900	8.000	.50	1.00	2.00	6.00
(Y18)						

100 REIS

2.5000 g, .917 SILVER, .0737 oz ASW

Obv: Young head

KM#	Date	Mintage	VG	Fine	VF	XF
473	1838	1,544	20.00	40.00	80.00	180.00
(C104a)	1842	—	—	Reported, not confirmed		
	1843	—	5.00	9.00	16.00	35.00
	1848	—	—	Reported, not confirmed		

Obv: Mature head.

485	1851	—	2.50	5.00	12.50	27.50
(C104b)						

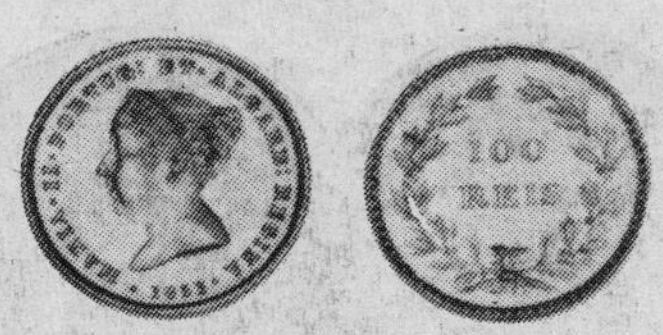

Obv: Older head.

KM#	Date	Mintage	VG	Fine	VF	XF
488	1853	—	2.50	5.00	10.00	20.00
(C104c)						

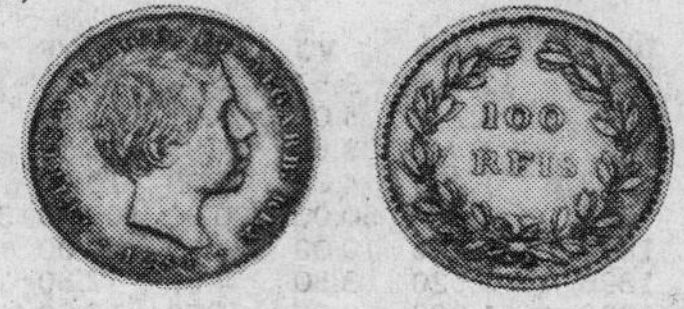

490	1854	.422	2.50	5.50	12.50	25.00
(C117)						

Obv: Young head.

497	1857	.043	20.00	40.00	80.00	160.00
(C117a)	1858	—	20.00	40.00	80.00	160.00
	1859	.455	2.00	4.00	10.00	20.00
	1860	—	—	Reported, not confirmed		
	1861	.762	2.00	3.50	7.00	15.00

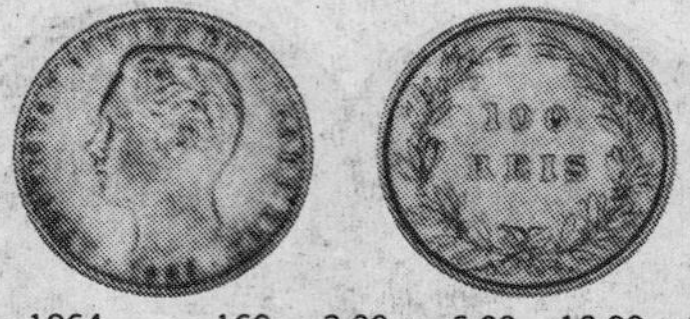

510	1864	.160	3.00	6.00	12.00	25.00
(Y9)	1865	.100	3.00	6.00	12.00	25.00
	1866	.010	25.00	40.00	90.00	180.00
	1869	.010	25.00	40.00	75.00	160.00
	1871	.060	4.50	9.00	18.00	37.50
	1872	.060	4.00	8.00	16.00	30.00
	1873	—	—	Reported, not confirmed		
	1874	.170	2.50	5.00	10.00	25.00
	1875	.130	2.25	4.50	9.00	22.50
	1876	.220	1.50	3.00	5.00	10.00
	1877	.120	2.00	4.00	10.00	22.50
	1878	.030	5.00	10.00	20.00	40.00
	1879	.560	1.50	2.00	4.00	8.00
	1880	.440	1.50	2.00	4.00	8.00
	1881	Inc. Ab.	17.50	37.50	75.00	150.00
	1886	.360	1.50	2.00	4.00	8.00
	1888	.500	1.50	2.00	4.00	8.00
	1889	1.500	1.00	1.50	3.00	6.00

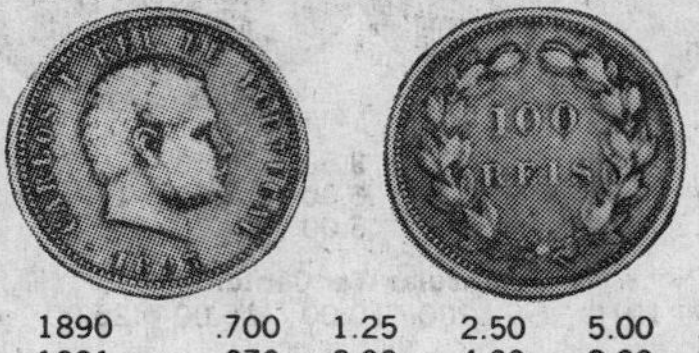

531	1890	.700	1.25	2.50	5.00	10.00
(Y21)	1891	.270	2.00	4.00	8.00	17.50
	1893	11.050	1.00	2.00	4.00	8.00
	1894	Inc. Ab.	15.00	30.00	60.00	120.00
	1895	—	—	Reported, not confirmed		
	1898	.930	1.00	2.00	4.00	9.00

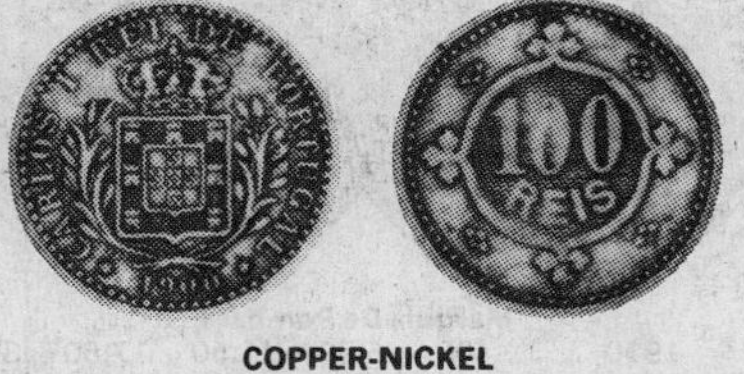

COPPER-NICKEL

KM#	Date	Mintage	Fine	VF	XF	Unc
546	1900	16.000	.25	.75	2.00	6.00
(Y19)						

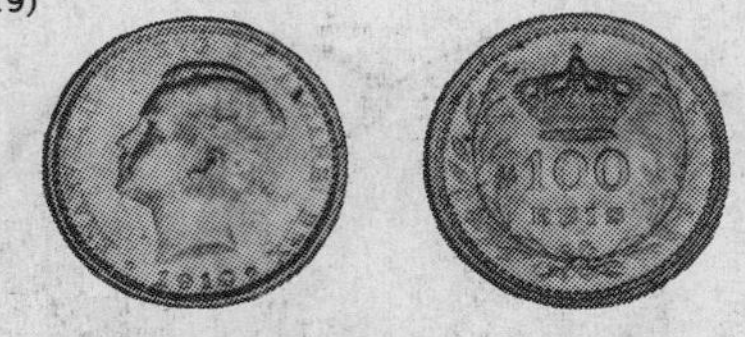

2.5000 g, .835 SILVER, .0671 oz ASW

548	1909	6.363	1.25	2.50	4.50	9.00
(Y29)	1910	Inc. Ab.	1.25	2.00	3.00	5.00

200 REIS

5.0000 g, .917 SILVER, .1474 oz ASW

Obv: Young head.

KM#	Date	Mintage	VG	Fine	VF	XF
474	1838	2,177	10.00	20.00	50.00	120.00
(C105a)	1841	272 pcs.	20.00	40.00	80.00	170.00
	1842	—	—	Reported, not confirmed		
	1843	1,181	7.50	12.50	25.00	65.00
	1846	—	—	Reported, not confirmed		
	1848	—	—	Reported, not confirmed		

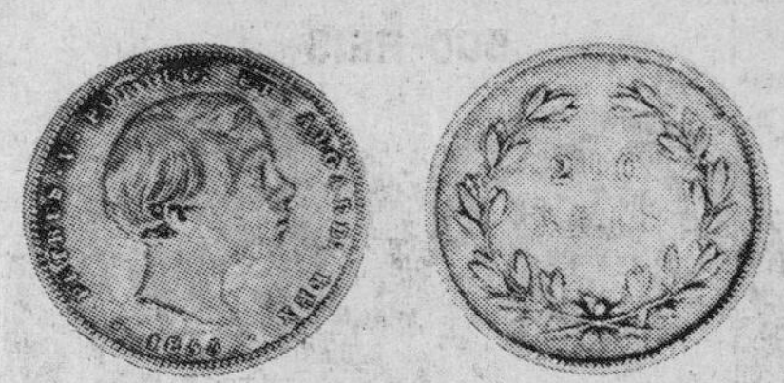

KM#	Date	Mintage	VG	Fine	VF	XF
491	1854	.292	2.00	4.00	8.00	25.00
(C118)	1855	.056	2.00	4.00	8.00	25.00

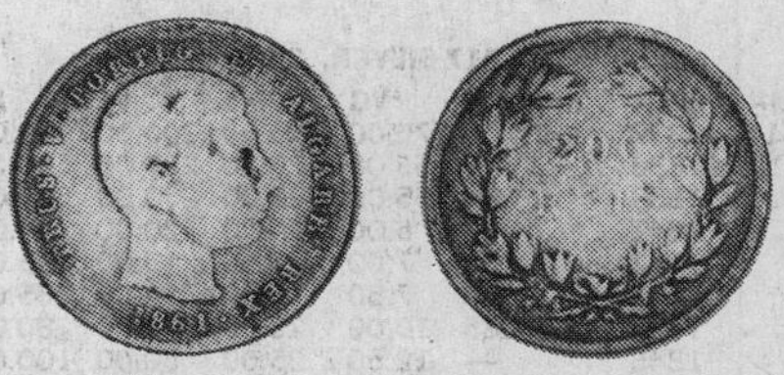

499	1858	.280	2.00	4.00	8.00	25.00
(C118a)	1859	—	—	Reported, not confirmed		
	1860	—	2.00	4.00	8.00	25.00
	1861	.202	20.00	40.00	80.00	160.00

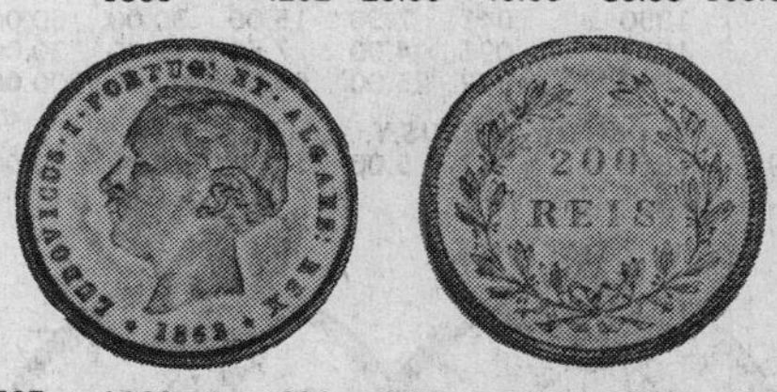

507	1862	.694	3.00	6.00	10.00	25.00
(Y10)	1863	.345	3.00	7.50	15.00	35.00
	1865	.050	6.50	12.50	25.00	60.00

Second bust

Similar to 100 Reis, KM#510.

512	1866	.010	35.00	70.00	150.00	300.00
(Y10a)	1867	.010	25.00	55.00	110.00	225.00
	1868	5,000	25.00	50.00	100.00	225.00
	1871	.075	8.50	17.50	35.00	75.00
	1872	.070	10.00	20.00	40.00	80.00
	1875	.070	5.00	10.00	20.00	45.00
	1876	.080	30.00	60.00	120.00	250.00
	1877	.030	8.50	17.50	35.00	75.00
	1878	.020	20.00	45.00	90.00	180.00
	1879	5,000	37.50	75.00	150.00	350.00
	1880	.150	2.50	5.00	10.00	22.50
	1886	.340	2.00	4.00	7.50	17.50
	1887	3.600	1.75	3.00	6.00	12.50
	1888	.700	2.00	4.00	7.50	17.50

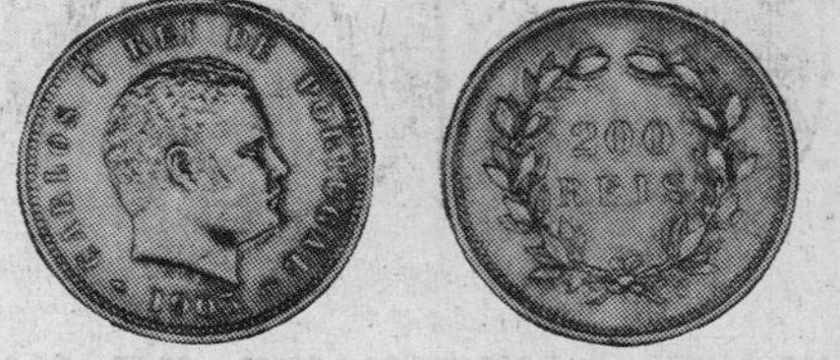

534	1891	2.365	1.50	2.50	4.00	10.00
(Y22)	1892	2.450	1.50	2.50	5.00	12.00
	1893/2	1.220	3.00	5.00	10.00	25.00
	1893	Inc. Ab.	2.50	4.50	8.00	20.00
	1901	.205	15.00	30.00	60.00	150.00
	1903	.200	4.00	7.50	15.00	30.00

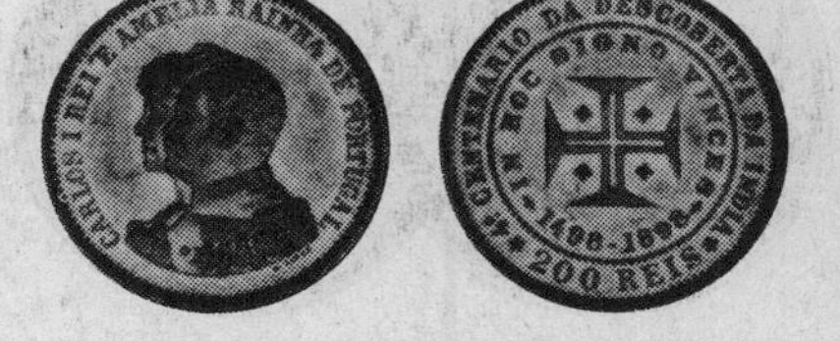

400th Anniversary Discovery of India

537	1898	.250	2.00	4.00	6.00	12.50
(Y25)	1898	—	—	P/L	Unc	25.00

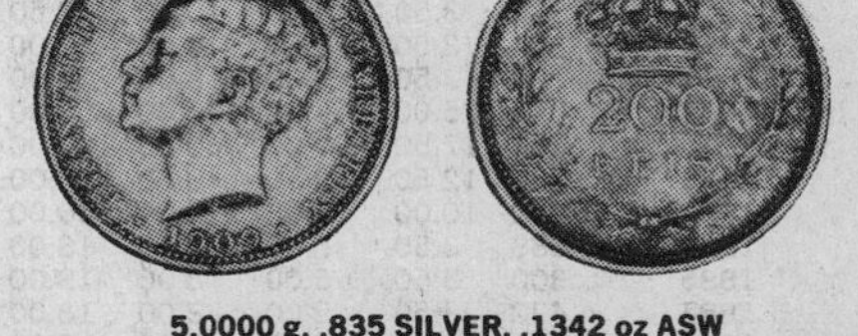

5.0000 g, .835 SILVER, .1342 oz ASW

549	1909	7.650	1.50	2.50	3.50	8.00
(Y30)						

500 REIS

12.5000 g, .917 SILVER, .3684 oz ASW

KM#	Date	Mintage	VG	Fine	VF	XF
471	1837	1.266	75.00	150.00	300.00	600.00
(C107a)	1838	2.645	65.00	125.00	250.00	500.00
	1839	2.084	65.00	125.00	250.00	500.00
	1841	.022	5.00	10.00	20.00	45.00
	1842	.135	7.00	7.50	15.00	35.00
	1843	.105	7.50	15.00	30.00	65.00
	1844	4.265	10.00	20.00	40.00	80.00
	1845	—	12.50	25.00	50.00	100.00
	1846	.074	5.00	10.00	20.00	40.00
	1847	.775	4.00	7.50	15.00	30.00
	1848	.024	7.50	15.00	30.00	60.00
	1849	.059	5.00	10.00	20.00	40.00
	1850	.041	7.50	15.00	30.00	60.00
	1851	.091	4.00	7.50	15.00	30.00
	1853	.022	25.00	50.00	100.00	200.00

Obv. leg: PETRUS.V.., young head.

| 492 | 1854 | .592 | 5.00 | 10.00 | 20.00 | 50.00 |
| (C119) | | | | | | |

| 494 | 1855 | 1.210 | 3.50 | 6.25 | 12.50 | 30.00 |
| (C119a) | 1856 | 1.478 | 3.50 | 6.25 | 10.00 | 25.00 |

498	1857	1.950	6.00	10.00	22.50	35.00
(C119b)	1858	3.091	3.25	6.25	12.50	27.50
	1859	2.660	3.25	6.25	12.50	27.50

509	1863	.148	4.00	6.50	15.00	45.00
(Y11)	1864	.341	3.50	5.50	10.00	30.00
	1865	.406	3.50	5.50	10.00	30.00
	1866	.378	3.50	5.50	10.00	22.50
	1867	.458	3.50	5.50	10.00	22.50
	1868	.388	3.50	5.50	10.00	22.50
	1870	.314	3.50	—	8.00	20.00
	1871	.228	3.50	5.00	8.00	20.00
	1872	.576	25.00	45.00	100.00	250.00
	1875	.140	17.50	30.00	60.00	140.00
	1876	.280	12.50	22.50	40.00	100.00
	1877	.050	10.00	15.00	25.00	60.00
	1879	.688	3.50	5.00	8.00	18.00
	1886	.300	3.50	5.00	8.00	18.00
	1887	.432	3.50	5.00	8.00	18.00
	1888	2.740	3.50	5.00	9.00	16.00
	1889	.960	3.50	5.00	8.00	16.00

KM#	Date	Mintage	VG	Fine	VF	XF
535	1891	12.476	3.50	4.50	6.50	12.50
(Y23)	1892/1	4.716	5.00	8.00	12.00	20.00
	1892	Inc. Ab.	3.50	4.50	6.50	12.50
	1893	1.494	4.00	6.00	10.00	17.50
	1894	.254	50.00	100.00	150.00	350.00
	1895	.216	10.00	20.00	45.00	90.00
	1896	3.520	3.50	4.50	7.50	15.00
	1898	1.000	3.50	4.50	7.50	15.00
	1899	3.100	3.50	4.50	7.50	15.00
	1900	.200	25.00	50.00	100.00	200.00
	1901	1.050	5.00	10.00	20.00	40.00
	1903	.920	4.00	6.00	10.00	17.50
	1904	—	Reported, not confirmed			
	1906	—	5.00	10.00	20.00	40.00
	1907	.384	4.00	6.00	10.00	17.50
	1908	1.840	4.00	6.00	10.00	17.50

400th Anniversary Discovery of India

| 538 | 1898 | .300 | 5.00 | 7.50 | 10.00 | 17.50 |
| (Y26) | 1898 | — | — | P/L | Unc | 35.00 |

547	1908	2.500	3.50	4.50	6.00	12.50
(Y31)	1909/8	1.513	6.00	12.50	17.50	35.00
	1909	Inc. Ab.	5.00	10.00	15.00	30.00

Peninsular War Centennial

| 556 | 1910 | .200 | 10.00 | 15.00 | 25.00 | 40.00 |
| (Y32) | | | | | | |

Marquis De Pombal

| 557 | 1910 | .400 | 6.50 | 11.50 | 17.50 | 32.50 |
| (Y34) | 1910 | — | — | — | Proof | 600.00 |

1000 REIS

29.6000 g, .917 SILVER, .8727 oz ASW

472	1837	2.295	80.00	100.00	200.00	450.00
(C108a)	1838	3.959	35.00	60.00	100.00	300.00
	1842	—	—	—	Rare	
	1843	—	Reported, not confirmed			
	1844	—	20.00	40.00	75.00	150.00
	1845	10.724	20.00	40.00	75.00	150.00

2.3900 g, .917 GOLD, .0704 oz AGW

KM#	Date	Mintage	VG	Fine	VF	XF
486	1851	.012	40.00	50.00	65.00	125.00
(C109)						

1.7735 g, .917 GOLD, .0523 oz AGW

| 495 | 1855 | 6.100 | 35.00 | 40.00 | 55.00 | 100.00 |
| (C120) | | | | | | |

25.0000 g, .917 SILVER, .7368 oz ASW
400th Anniversary Discovery of India

| 539 | 1898 | .300 | 10.00 | 12.00 | 15.00 | 35.00 |
| (Y27) | 1898 | — | — | P/L | Unc | 75.00 |

| 540 | 1899 | 1.500 | 10.00 | 12.00 | 15.00 | 30.00 |
| (Y24) | 1900 | 3 known | — | — | Proof | 7500. |

Peninsular War Centennial

| 558 | 1910 | .200 | 15.00 | 25.00 | 40.00 | 80.00 |
| (Y33) | 1910 | — | — | — | Proof | 900.00 |

2000 REIS

3.5470 g, .917 GOLD, .1045 oz AGW
Obv: Boy head.

KM#	Date	Mintage	Fine	VF	XF	Unc
496	1856	.038	65.00	100.00	200.00	300.00
(C121)	1857	.044	60.00	90.00	150.00	250.00

Obv: Young head.

500	1858	.013	60.00	90.00	150.00	275.00
(C121a)	1859	.016	60.00	90.00	150.00	275.00
	1860	.053	60.00	90.00	150.00	250.00

Rev: Arms in spray.

511	1864	.101	60.00	100.00	150.00	250.00
(Y-A12)	1865	.095	60.00	100.00	150.00	250.00
	1866	.086	60.00	100.00	150.00	250.00

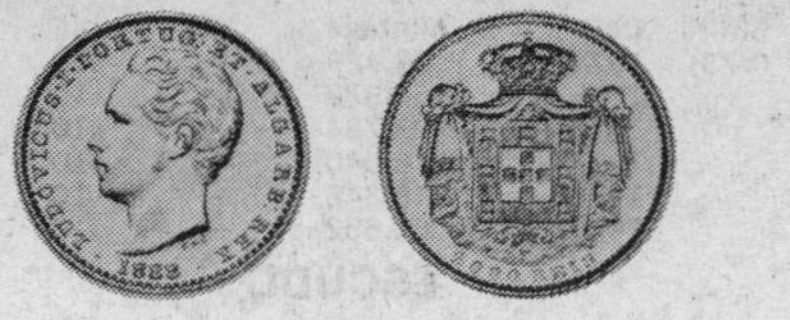

Rev: Mantled arms.

KM#	Date	Mintage	Fine	VF	XF	Unc
518	1868	.024	65.00	125.00	200.00	300.00
(Y12)	1869	.011	65.00	125.00	200.00	300.00
	1870	500 pcs.	300.00	600.00	1000.	1500.
	1871	500 pcs.	200.00	400.00	700.00	1000.
	1872	1,000	125.00	200.00	375.00	550.00
	1874	5,000	75.00	150.00	250.00	350.00
	1875	2,000	100.00	175.00	275.00	350.00
	1876	3,000	75.00	150.00	250.00	350.00
	1877	2,250	100.00	175.00	275.00	400.00
	1878	.022	65.00	125.00	200.00	300.00
	1881	1,000	150.00	200.00	400.00	600.00
	1888	500 pcs.	200.00	400.00	750.00	1200.

2500 REIS

4.7800 g, .917 GOLD, .1409 oz AGW
Obv: Young head.

KM#	Date	Mintage	Fine	VF	XF	Unc
475	1838	1,114	300.00	500.00	800.00	1200.
(C110a)						

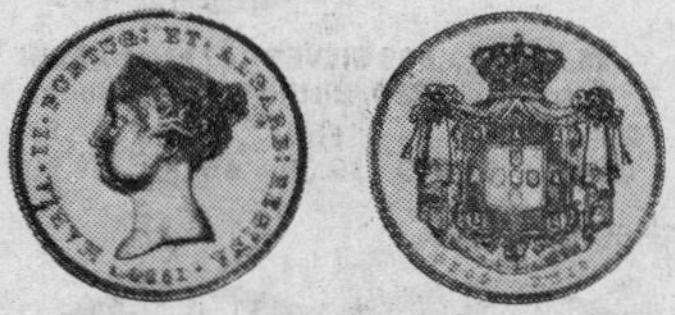

KM#	Date	Mintage	Fine	VF	XF	Unc
487	1851	.058	100.00	175.00	275.00	400.00
(C110b)						

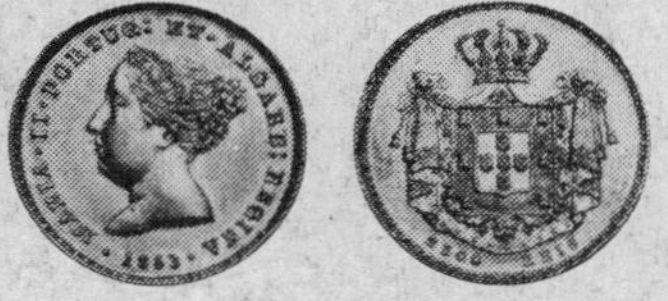

KM#	Date	Mintage	Fine	VF	XF	Unc
489	1853	1,010	250.00	450.00	650.00	1000.
(C110c)						

5000 REIS

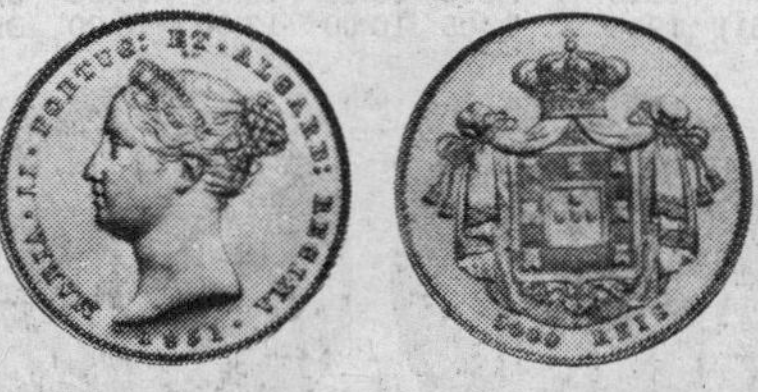

9.5600 g, .917 GOLD, .2818 oz AGW
Obv: Young head.

KM#	Date	Mintage	Fine	VF	XF	Unc
476	1838	2,410	200.00	250.00	500.00	800.00
(C111a)	1845	401 pcs.	500.00	1000.	2000.	3000.
	1851	.057	175.00	225.00	325.00	500.00

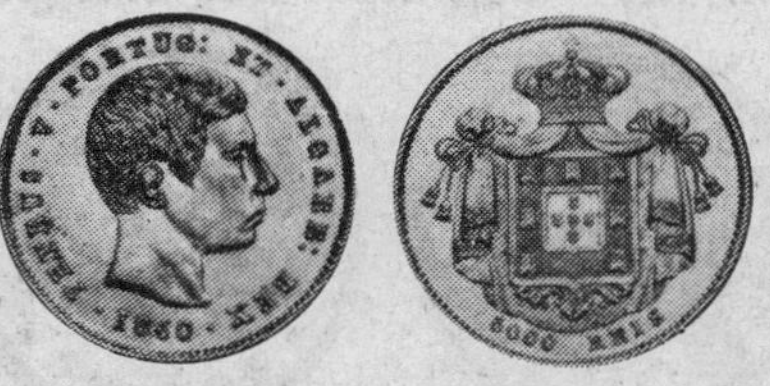

8.8675 g, .917 GOLD, .2613 oz AGW
Obv: Young head.

KM#	Date	Mintage	Fine	VF	XF	Unc
505	1860	.052	150.00	175.00	250.00	350.00
(C122)	1861	.081	150.00	175.00	250.00	350.00

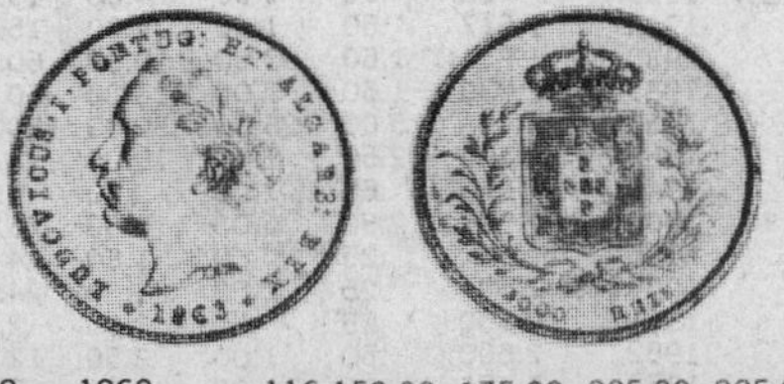

KM#	Date	Mintage	Fine	VF	XF	Unc
508	1862	.116	150.00	175.00	225.00	325.00
(Y-A13)	1863	.038	150.00	175.00	250.00	350.00

Rev: Mantled arms.

KM#	Date	Mintage	Fine	VF	XF	Unc
516	1867	.045	150.00	175.00	250.00	400.00
(Y13)	1868	.064	150.00	175.00	250.00	400.00
	1869	.077	150.00	175.00	250.00	400.00
	1870	.061	150.00	175.00	250.00	400.00
	1871	.047	150.00	175.00	250.00	400.00
	1872	.028	150.00	175.00	250.00	400.00
	1874	6,800	150.00	175.00	250.00	400.00
	1875	.010	150.00	175.00	250.00	400.00
	1876	.015	150.00	175.00	250.00	400.00
	1877	9,400	175.00	200.00	350.00	600.00
	1878	8,400	150.00	175.00	250.00	400.00
	1880	—	350.00	500.00	800.00	1200.
	1883	.023	150.00	175.00	250.00	400.00
	1886	.027	150.00	175.00	250.00	400.00
	1887	.044	150.00	175.00	250.00	400.00
	1888	4,800	150.00	175.00	250.00	400.00
	1889	9,000	150.00	175.00	250.00	400.00

10,000 REIS

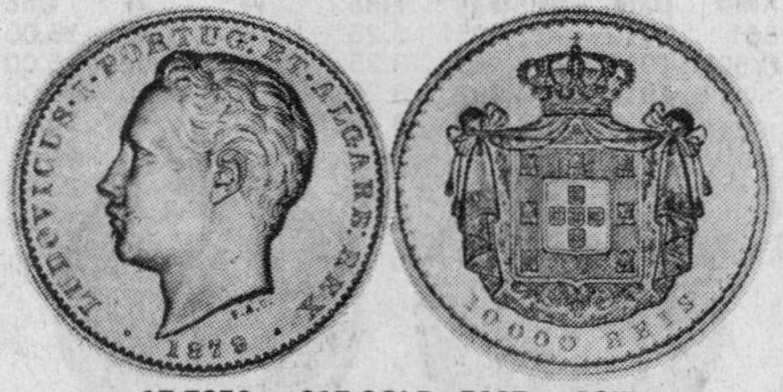

17.7350 g, .917 GOLD, .5227 oz AGW

KM#	Date	Mintage	Fine	VF	XF	Unc
520	1878	.023	275.00	300.00	400.00	700.00
(Y14)	1879	.036	275.00	300.00	400.00	700.00
	1880	.030	275.00	300.00	400.00	700.00
	1881	.019	275.00	300.00	425.00	750.00
	1882	.015	275.00	350.00	425.00	750.00
	1883	8,500	275.00	300.00	425.00	750.00
	1884	.013	275.00	300.00	425.00	750.00
	1885	.021	275.00	300.00	425.00	950.00
	1886	1,800	300.00	400.00	600.00	1000.
	1888	7,000	350.00	500.00	700.00	1250.
	1889	4,400	350.00	500.00	700.00	1250.

REPUBLIC

100 Centavos = 1 Escudo

CENTAVO

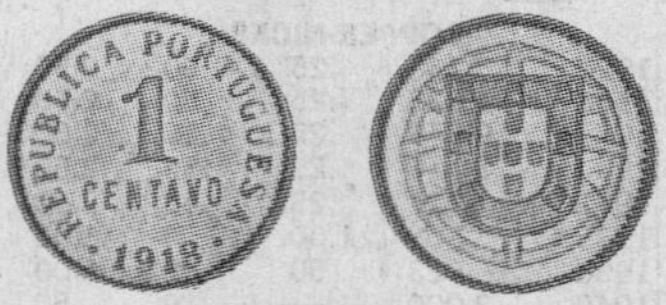

BRONZE

KM#	Date	Mintage	Fine	VF	XF	Unc
565	1917	12.260	.15	.30	.50	1.00
(Y36)	1918	13.280	.15	.30	.50	1.00
	1920	—	.20	.35	.75	1.50
	1921	4.949	.75	1.50	2.00	5.00
	1922	Inc. Ab.	—	—	Rare	—

2 CENTAVOS

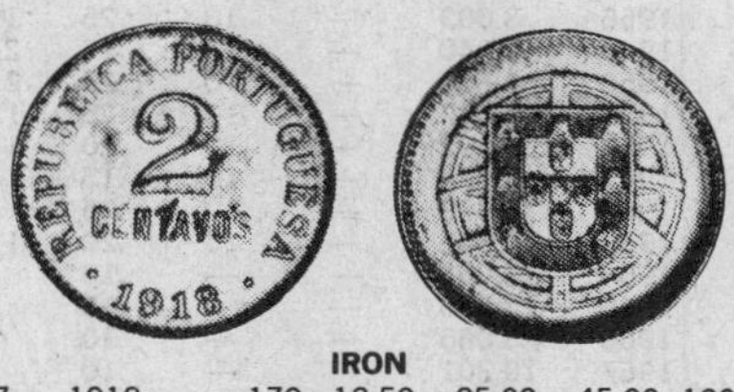

IRON

KM#	Date	Mintage	Fine	VF	XF	Unc
567	1918	.170	12.50	25.00	45.00	100.00
(Y35)						

BRONZE

KM#	Date	Mintage	Fine	VF	XF	Unc
568	1918	4.295	.10	.25	.50	1.00
(Y37)	1920	10.103	.10	.25	.50	1.00
	1921	.679	2.00	3.00	5.00	10.00

4 CENTAVOS

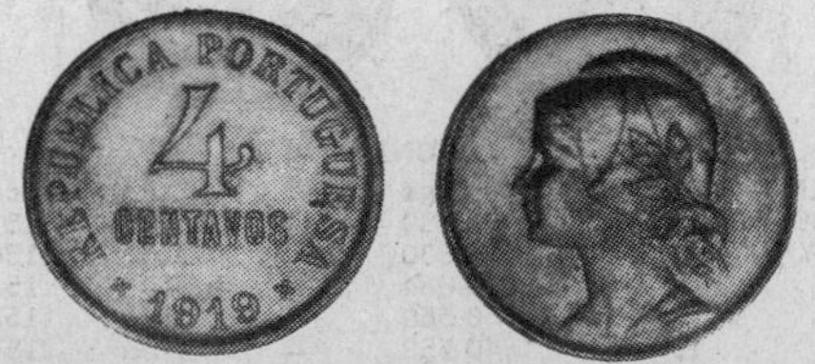

COPPER NICKEL

KM#	Date	Mintage	Fine	VF	XF	Unc
566	1917	4.961	.15	.25	.60	2.00
(Y42)	1919	10.067	.15	.25	.60	2.00

5 CENTAVOS

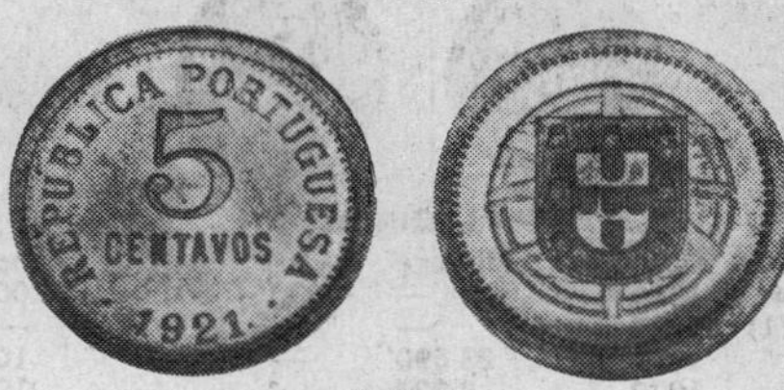

BRONZE

KM#	Date	Mintage	Fine	VF	XF	Unc
569	1920	.114	2.50	5.00	7.50	12.50
(Y38)	1921	5.916	.20	.90	2.50	3.00
	1922	Inc. Ab.	20.00	35.00	50.00	85.00

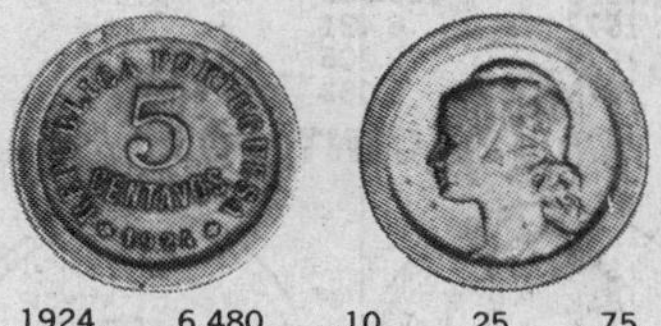

KM#	Date	Mintage	Fine	VF	XF	Unc
572	1924	6.480	.10	.25	.75	3.00
(Y39)	1925	7.260	.25	.75	1.75	5.00
	1927	26.320	.10	.20	.50	2.00

10 CENTAVOS

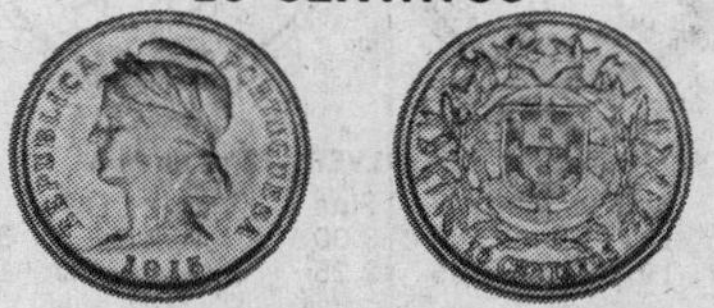

2.5000 g, .835 SILVER, .0671 oz ASW

KM#	Date	Mintage	Fine	VF	XF	Unc
563	1915	3.418	1.00	1.50	2.50	4.00
(Y48)						

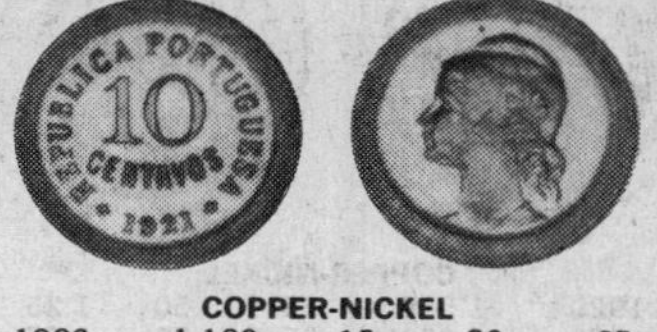

COPPER-NICKEL

KM#	Date	Mintage	Fine	VF	XF	Unc
570	1920	1.120	.15	.30	.65	2.50
(Y43)	1921	1.285	.15	.30	.65	2.50

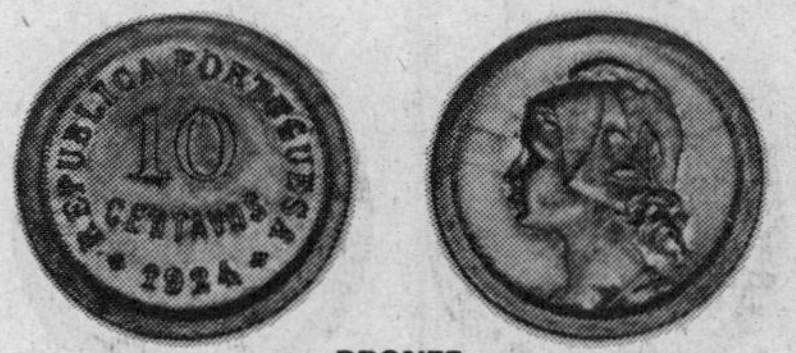

BRONZE

KM#	Date	Mintage	Fine	VF	XF	Unc
573	1924	1.210	1.00	2.00	3.50	6.00
(Y40)	1925	9.090	.15	.30	.75	3.00
	1926	26.250	.15	.25	.50	2.50
	1930	1.730	5.00	10.00	20.00	35.00
	1938	2.000	2.50	4.00	10.00	25.00
	1940	3.384	.75	1.50	2.25	4.00

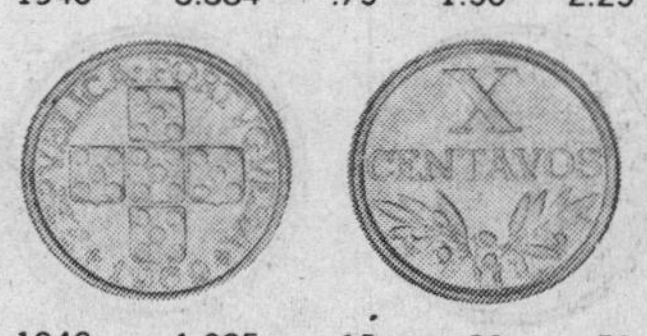

KM#	Date	Mintage	Fine	VF	XF	Unc
583	1942	1.035	.15	.30	.50	3.00
(Y60)	1943	18.765	.10	.15	.25	3.00
	1944	5.090	.15	.30	.50	3.00
	1945	8.090	.15	.30	.50	4.00
	1946	7.740	.15	.30	.50	7.50
	1947	9.283	.15	.30	.50	2.50
	1948	5.900	.25	.50	1.50	25.00
	1949	15.240	.10	.15	.25	1.50
	1950	8.860	.10	.20	.50	5.00
	1951	5.040	.10	.20	.50	6.00
	1952	4.960	.10	.20	.50	10.00
	1953	7.548	.10	.20	.50	6.00
	1954	2.452	.10	.15	.25	3.00
	1955	10.000	—	.10	.15	1.25
	1956	3.336	—	.10	.15	1.50
	1957	6.654	—	.10	.15	1.25
	1958	7.320	—	.10	.15	1.25
	1959	7.140	—	.10	.15	2.00
	1960	15.055	—	.10	.15	1.25
	1961	5.020	—	.10	.15	.70
	1962	14.980	—	.10	.15	.45
	1963	5.393	—	.10	.15	.80
	1964	10.257	—	.10	.15	.45
	1965	15.550	—	.10	.15	.70
	1966	8.864	—	.10	.15	.45

PORTUGAL 1450

KM#	Date	Mintage	Fine	VF	XF	Unc
(Y60)	1967	13.549	—	.10	.15	.45
	1968	22.515	—	.10	.15	.45
	1969	3.871	—	.10	.15	.60

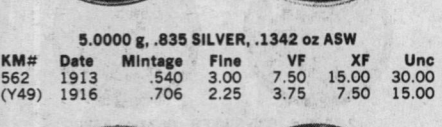

ALUMINUM

KM#	Date	Mintage	VF	XF	Unc
594	1969	—	40.00	60.00	100.00
(Y71)	1970	—	—	Rare	
	1971	23.590	—	—	.10
	1972	3.227	—	—	.10
	1973	4.239	—	—	.10
	1974	17.043	—	—	.10
	1975	Inc. Ab.	—	—	.10
	1976	19.906	—	—	.10
	1977	8.431	—	—	.10
	1978	2.205	—	—	.10
	1979	9.083	—	—	.10

20 CENTAVOS

5.0000 g, .835 SILVER, .1342 oz ASW

KM#	Date	Mintage	Fine	VF	XF	Unc
562	1913	.540	3.00	7.50	15.00	30.00
(Y49)	1916	.706	2.25	3.75	7.50	15.00

COPPER-NICKEL

KM#	Date	Mintage	Fine	VF	XF	Unc
571	1920	1.568	.25	.50	1.25	3.00
(Y44)	1921	3.030	.25	.50	1.25	3.00
	1922	.580	75.00	100.00	150.00	250.00

BRONZE

KM#	Date	Mintage	Fine	VF	XF	Unc
574	1924	6.220	.25	.75	2.25	5.00
(Y41)	1925	10.560	.25	.75	2.25	5.00

KM#	Date	Mintage	Fine	VF	XF	Unc
584	1942	Inc. Bl.	.10	.20	.50	2.75
(Y61)	1943	1.170	.10	.20	.50	4.00
	1944	7.290	.10	.20	.50	4.00
	1945	7.553	.10	.20	.50	4.00
	1948	2.750	.15	.30	1.00	7.00
	1949	12.250	.10	.15	.30	1.50
	1951	3.185	.10	.20	.50	5.00
	1952	1.815	.50	1.00	4.00	15.00
	1953	9.426	—	.10	.30	2.00
	1955	5.574	—	.10	.30	1.25
	1956	5.000	—	.10	.30	1.50
	1957	1.450	—	.10	.30	1.50
	1958	7.470	—	.10	.30	1.50
	1959	4.780	—	.10	.30	2.00
	1960	4.790	—	.10	.30	2.00
	1961	5.180	—	.10	.30	1.50
	1962	2.500	—	.10	.50	4.00
	1963	7.990	—	.10	.30	1.25
	1964	7.010	—	—	.15	.70
	1965	7.365	—	—	.15	.80
	1966	8.075	—	—	.15	.50
	1967	9.220	—	—	.15	.50
	1968	10.372	—	—	.15	.50
	1969	8.657	—	—	.15	.60

KM#	Date	Mintage	VF	XF	Unc
595	1969	5.000	—	.10	.15
(Y72)	1970	20.000	—	.10	.15
	1971	1.973	—	.10	.30
	1972	3.274	—	.10	.15
	1973	10.787	—	.10	.15
	1974	26.975	—	.10	.15

50 CENTAVOS

12.5000 g, .835 SILVER, .3356 oz ASW

KM#	Date	Mintage	Fine	VF	XF	Unc
561	1912	1.695	3.25	5.00	7.50	15.00
(Y50)	1913	4.443	3.25	5.00	7.50	15.00
	1914	4.992	3.25	5.00	7.50	15.00
	1916	5.080	3.25	5.00	7.50	15.00

ALUMINUM-BRONZE

KM#	Date	Mintage	Fine	VF	XF	Unc
575	1924	.810	10.00	17.50	25.00	45.00
(Y45)	1925	—	150.00	300.00	500.00	800.00
	1926	11.340	.15	.50	2.00	5.00

COPPER-NICKEL

KM#	Date	Mintage	Fine	VF	XF	Unc
577	1927	3.330	.25	.50	2.50	15.00
(Y54)	1928	6.823	.25	.50	2.50	15.00
	1929	9.779	.25	.50	2.50	15.00
	1930	1.116	.25	.50	2.50	15.00
	1931	7.127	.25	.50	2.50	15.00
	1935*	.902	1.00	2.00	8.00	20.00
	1938	.923	.50	1.00	5.00	18.00
	1940	2.000	—	.10	.50	4.00
	1944	2.974	—	.10	.25	2.00
	1945	5.700	—	.10	.25	2.00
	1946	4.334	—	.10	.35	3.50
	1947	6.998	—	.10	.35	3.50
	1951	4.610	—	.10	.25	1.75
	1952	2.421	—	.10	.25	5.00
	1953	2.369	.10	.25	.50	4.00
	1955	3.057	—	.10	.25	1.75
	1956	3.003	—	.10	.25	1.75
	1957	3.940	—	.10	.25	2.00
	1958	2.687	—	.10	.25	2.00
	1959	4.027	—	.10	.25	1.50
	1960	2.592	—	.10	.20	1.00
	1961	3.324	—	.10	.15	.50
	1962	6.678	—	.10	.15	.50
	1963	2.346	—	.10	.20	1.00
	1964	7.654	—	—	.10	.35
	1965	3.366	—	—	.10	.35
	1966	5.085	—	—	.10	.35
	1967	10.301	—	—	.10	.35
	1968	11.248	—	—	.10	.35

*NOTE: For exclusive use in Azores.

BRONZE

KM#	Date	Mintage	VF	XF	Unc
596	1969	3.480	—	.10	.15
(Y73)	1970	18.800	—	.10	.15
	1971	14.684	—	.10	.15
	1972	6.559	—	.10	.15
	1973	40.558	—	.10	.15

KM#	Date	Mintage	VF	XF	Unc
(Y73)	1974	37.429	—	.10	.15
	1975	2.372	—	.10	.15
	1976	23.734	—	.10	.15
	1977	16.340	—	.10	.15
	1978	48.348	—	.10	.15
	1979	61.652	—	.10	.15

ESCUDO

25.0000 g, .835 SILVER, .6711 oz ASW
October 5, 1910, Birth of the Republic

KM#	Date	Mintage	Fine	VF	XF	Unc
560	1910	*1.000	12.00	16.00	22.50	45.00
(Y47)						

*NOTE: Struck in 1914.

KM#	Date	Mintage	Fine	VF	XF	Unc
564	1915	1.818	10.00	12.00	16.00	35.00
(Y51)	1916	1.405	10.00	12.00	16.00	35.00

ALUMINUM-BRONZE

KM#	Date	Mintage	Fine	VF	XF	Unc
576	1924	2.709	.50	1.50	4.00	8.00
(Y46)	1926	2.346	10.00	20.00	30.00	50.00

COPPER-NICKEL

KM#	Date	Mintage	Fine	VF	XF	Unc
578	1927	1.917	.50	1.00	4.00	15.00
(Y55)	1928	7.462	.50	1.00	4.00	15.00
	1929	1.617	.50	1.00	4.00	15.00
	1930	1.911	1.50	3.00	10.00	60.00
	1931	2.039	1.50	3.00	10.00	60.00
	1935*	—	15.00	25.00	50.00	150.00
	1939	.304	2.50	5.00	10.00	75.00
	1940	1.259	.50	1.00	2.50	6.00
	1944	.993	2.50	5.00	10.00	75.00
	1945	Inc. Ab.	.25	.50	1.50	4.00
	1946	2.507	.25	.50	1.50	4.00
	1951	2.500	.25	.50	1.00	2.25
	1952	2.500	.50	1.00	3.50	12.50
	1957	1.656	.10	.25	1.00	3.00
	1958	1.447	—	.25	1.00	3.00

KM#	Date	Mintage	Fine	VF	XF	Unc
(Y55)	1959	1.908	.10	.25	.75	2.00
	1961	2.505	.10	.25	.50	1.50
	1962	2.757	.10	.20	.40	1.00
	1964	1.611	.10	.20	.40	1.00
	1965	1.683	.10	.20	.40	1.00
	1966	2.607	.10	.15	.30	.75
	1968	4.099	.10	.15	.30	.75

*NOTE: For exclusive use in Azores.

BRONZE

KM#	Date	Mintage	VF	XF	Unc
597	1969	3.020	.10	.15	.25
(Y74)	1970	10.032	.10	.15	.20
	1971	9.246	.10	.15	.20
	1972	1.277	.10	.15	.30
	1973	12.452	.10	.15	.20
	1974	21.023	.10	.15	.20
	1975	1.121	.10	.15	.30
	1976	7.353	.10	.15	.20
	1977	6.278	.10	.15	.20
	1978	7.061	.10	.15	.20
	1979	14.241	.10	.15	.20
	1980	16.780	.10	.15	.20

NICKEL-BRASS

KM#	Date	Mintage	VF	XF	Unc
611	1981	30.165	—	.10	.20
(Y85)	1982	53.018	—	.10	.20
	1983	53.165	—	.10	.20
	1984	59.463	—	.10	.20
	1985	46.832	—	.10	.20
	1986	8.030	—	.10	.20

World Hockey Games

612	ND(1983)	1.990	—	.10	.20
(Y90)					

631	1986	14.882	—	.10	.20
(Y105)	1987	21.922	—	.10	.20
	1988	17.168	—	.10	.20
	1989	—	—	.10	.20

2-1/2 ESCUDOS

3.5000 g, .650 SILVER, .0731 oz ASW

KM#	Date	Mintage	Fine	VF	XF	Unc
580	1932	2.592	1.25	2.50	5.00	14.00
(Y57)	1933	2.457	1.25	2.50	6.50	17.50
	1937	1.000	30.00	50.00	120.00	220.00
	1940	2.763	BV	1.00	4.00	7.50
	1942	3.847	BV	1.00	1.50	3.00
	1943	8.302	BV	1.00	1.50	2.50
	1944	9.134	BV	1.00	1.50	2.50
	1945	6.316	BV	1.00	1.50	3.50
	1946	3.208	BV	1.00	1.50	3.50
	1947	2.610	BV	1.00	1.50	3.50
	1948	1.818	1.25	2.50	5.00	10.00
	1951	4.000	BV	1.00	1.50	2.00

COPPER-NICKEL

KM#	Date	Mintage	VF	XF	Unc
590	1963	12.711	.10	.20	.50
(Y67)	1964	17.948	.10	.20	.50
	1965	19.512	.10	.20	.50
	1966	3.829	.30	.50	1.50
	1967	5.545	.10	.20	.50
	1968	6.087	.10	.20	.50
	1969	10.368	.10	.20	.50
	1970	2.400	.10	.20	.35
	1971	6.791	.10	.20	.35
	1972	2.316	.10	.20	.35
	1973	9.489	.10	.20	.35
	1974	22.913	.10	.20	.35
	1975	15.284	.10	.20	.35
	1976	68.582	.10	.20	.40
	1977	Inc. Ab.	.10	.20	.40
	1978	26.953	.10	.20	.40
	1979	28.402	.10	.20	.40
	1980	44.804	.10	.20	.40
	1981	25.420	.10	.20	.40
	1982	45.910	.10	.20	.40
	1983	62.946	.10	.20	.40
	1984	58.210	.10	.20	.40
	1985	60.142	.10	.20	.40

100th Anniversary Death of Alexandre Herculano

605	1977	5.990	.10	.15	.50
(Y82)	1977	.013	—	Proof	2.00

World Hockey Games

613	ND(1983)	1.990		.10	.50
(Y91)					

F.A.O. Issue

617	1983	.995		.10	.50
(Y98)					

5 ESCUDOS

7.0000 g, .650 SILVER, .1463 oz ASW

KM#	Date	Mintage	Fine	VF	XF	Unc
581	1932	.800	3.00	6.00	12.50	35.00
(Y58)	1933	6.717	BV	1.50	3.00	7.50
	1934	1.012	BV	2.50	5.00	7.50
	1937	1.500	4.00	10.00	40.00	60.00
	1940	1.500	BV	2.50	5.00	7.50
	1942	2.051	BV	2.00	3.00	5.00
	1943	1.354	BV	2.50	4.00	10.00
	1946	.404	2.50	3.50	5.00	7.50
	1947	2.420	BV	2.00	2.50	5.00
	1948	2.018	BV	2.00	2.50	5.00
	1951	.966	BV	2.00	2.50	5.00

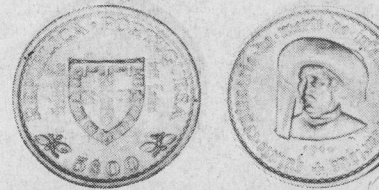

500th Anniversary Death of Prince Henry the Navigator

587	1960	.800	—	2.00	2.50	4.50
(Y64)	1960	—		—	Matte	—

PORTUGAL 1451

COPPER-NICKEL

KM#	Date	Mintage	VF	XF	Unc
591	1963	2.200	.10	.25	.60
(Y68)	1964	4.268	.10	.25	.60
	1965	7.294	.10	.25	.50
	1966	8.120	.10	.25	.50
	1967	8.118	.10	.25	.50
	1968	5.023	.10	.25	.50
	1969	4.977	.10	.25	.50
	1970	1.200	.10	.25	.75
	1971	3.380	.10	.25	.50
	1972	1.880	.10	.25	.75
	1973	2.836	.10	.25	.50
	1974	4.810	.10	.25	.50
	1975	Inc. Ab.	.10	.25	.50
	1976	4.962	.10	.25	.50
	1977	Inc. Ab.	.10	.25	.60
	1978	.672	.30	.50	1.50
	1979	19.546	.10	.25	.60
	1980	46.244	.10	.25	.60
	1981	20.565	.10	.25	.60
	1982	31.318	.10	.25	.60
	1983	51.056	.10	.25	.60
	1984	46.794	.10	.25	.60
	1985	45.441	.10	.25	.60
	1986	18.753	.10	.25	.60

100th Anniversary Death of Alexandre Herculano

606	1977	9.176	.25	.50	1.00
(Y83)	1977	.010	—	Proof	5.00

World Hockey Games

615	ND(1983)	1.990	.25	.50	1.00
(Y92)					

F.A.O. Issue

618	1983	.995	.25	.50	1.00
(Y99)					

NICKEL-BRASS

632	1986	21.426	.10	.25	.50
(Y106)	1987	40.548	.10	.25	.50
	1988	19.382	.10	.25	.50
	1989	—	.10	.25	.50

10 ESCUDOS

PORTUGAL 1452

12.5000 g, .835 SILVER, .3356 oz ASW
Battle of Ourique

KM#	Date	Mintage	Fine	VF	XF	Unc
579 (Y56)	1928	.200	6.00	12.00	18.00	32.50

582 (Y59)	1932	3.220	3.00	6.00	9.00	15.00
	1933	1.780	6.00	12.50	22.50	45.00
	1934	.400	5.00	7.50	12.50	25.00
	1937	.500	10.00	20.00	40.00	80.00
	1940	1.200	3.00	6.00	9.00	15.00
	1942	.186	25.00	50.00	100.00	150.00
	1948	.507	5.00	7.50	12.50	25.00

12.5000 g, .680 SILVER, .2732 oz ASW

586 (Y63)	1954	5.764	BV	2.50	4.00	6.00
	1955	4.056	BV	2.50	4.00	6.00

500th Anniversary Death of Prince Henry the Navigator

588 (Y65)	1960	.200	—	4.00	7.00	10.00
	1960	—	—	Matte	—	—

COPPER-NICKEL-CLAD-NICKEL

KM#	Date	Mintage	VF	XF	Unc
600 (Y-A68)	1971	3.049	.20	.40	1.00
	1972	3.520	.20	.40	1.00
	1973	3.427	.20	.40	1.00
	1974	4.043	.20	.40	1.00

NICKEL-BRASS

633 (Y107)	1986	12.818	.20	.40	1.00
	1987	32.815	.20	.40	1.00
	1988	32.579	.20	.40	1.00
	1989	—	.20	.40	1.00

Rural World

638 (Y113)	1987	2.000	.40	.60	2.00

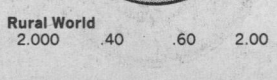

20 ESCUDOS

21.0000 g, .800 SILVER, .5401 oz ASW
25th Anniversary of Financial Reform

KM#	Date	Mintage	VF	XF	Unc
585 (Y62)	1953	1.000	5.00	7.50	10.00
	1953	—	—	Matte	—

500th Anniversary Death of Prince Henry the Navigator

589 (Y66)	1960	.200	10.00	16.00	22.00
	1960	—	—	Matte	—

10.0000 g, .650 SILVER, .2090 oz ASW
Salazar Bridge

592 (Y69)	1966	.200	2.00	3.00	4.50

COPPER-NICKEL

634 (Y108)	1986	45.361	.15	.25	1.00
	1987	68.216	.15	.25	1.00
	1988	57.482	.15	.25	1.00
	1989	—	.15	.25	1.00

25 ESCUDOS

COPPER-NICKEL

607 (Y81)	1977	7.657	.40	.75	1.25
	1978	12.278	.40	.75	1.25

100th Anniversary Death of Alexandre Herculano

608 (Y84)	1977	5.990	.50	.90	1.50
	1977	.013	—	Proof	7.00

International Year of the Child

KM#	Date	Mintage	VF	XF	Unc
609 (Y101)	1979	.990	.50	.90	1.50
	1979	.010	—	Proof	—

Increased size, 28mm.

610 (Y81a)	1980	.750	.40	.80	1.50
	1981	19.924	.40	.80	1.50
	1982	12.158	.40	.80	1.50
	1983	5.622	.40	.80	1.50
	1984	3.453	.40	.80	1.50
	1985	25.027	.40	.80	1.50

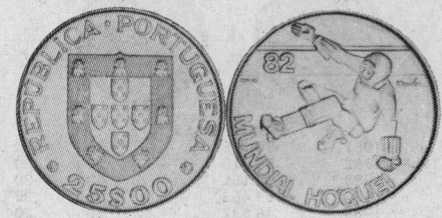

World Hockey Games

616 (Y93)	ND(1983)	1.990	.50	1.00	2.00

F.A.O. Issue

619 (Y100)	1983	.995	.50	1.00	2.00

10th Anniversary of Revolution
Obv: Waves breaking over arms. Rev: Stylized 25.

623 (Y95)	1984	1.980	.50	1.00	2.00

International Year of Disabled Persons

624 (Y96)	ND(1984)	1.990	.40	.75	1.50

King John I

627 (Y111)	1985	.500	.40	.60	1.00

10.8300 g, .925 SILVER, .3270 oz ASW

PORTUGAL 1453

KM#	Date	Mintage	VF	XF	Unc
627a	1985	.020	—	—	15.00
(Y111a)	1985	5,000	—	Proof	40.00

COPPER-NICKEL
Admission to European Common Market

635	1986	4.990	.40	.60	1.00
(Y103)					

11.0000 g, .925 SILVER, .3272 oz ASW

635a	1986	5,000	—	Proof	40.00
(Y103a)					

50 ESCUDOS

18.0000 g, .650 SILVER, .3761 oz ASW
500th Anniversary Cabral's Birth

593	1968	1.000	—	—	6.00
(Y70)					

500th Anniversary Vasco Da Gama's Birth

598	1969	1.000	—	—	6.00
(Y75)					

Centennial Marshal Carmona's Birth

599	1969	.500	—	—	6.00
(Y76)	1969	—	—	Matte	—

125th Anniversary Bank of Portugal

601	1971	.500	—	—	7.50
(Y77)					

400th Anniversary of Publication 'Os Lusíadas'

KM#	Date	Mintage	VF	XF	Unc
602	1972	1.000	—	—	7.50
(Y78)					

COPPER-NICKEL

636	1986	51.110	—	—	3.00
(Y109)	1987	28.248	—	—	3.00
	1988	41.905	—	—	3.00
	1989	—	—	—	3.00

100 ESCUDOS

18.0000 g, .650 SILVER, .3762 oz ASW
1974 Revolution

603	1974(76)	.950	.75	1.50	4.50
(Y79)	1974(76)	.010	—	Proof	7.50

COPPER-NICKEL
International Year of Disabled Persons

625	ND(1984)	.990	.75	1.00	3.25
(Y97)					

Fernando Pessoa - Poet

628	1985	.480	.75	1.00	5.00
(Y104)					

16.5000 g, .925 SILVER, .4907 oz ASW

628a	1985	5,000	—	Proof	6.00
(Y104a)					

COPPER-NICKEL
800th Anniversary of Death of King Alfonso Henriques

KM#	Date	Mintage	VF	XF	Unc
629	1985	.500	.75	1.00	3.25
(Y110)					

16.5000 g, .925 SILVER, .4907 oz ASW

629a	1985	.020	—	—	25.00
(Y110a)	1985	5,000	—	Proof	35.00

COPPER-NICKEL
D. Nuno Alvares Pereira

630	1985	.500	—	—	3.25
(Y112)					

16.5000 g, .925 SILVER, .4907 oz ASW

630a	1985	.020	—	—	25.00
(Y112a)	1985	5,000	—	Proof	50.00

COPPER-NICKEL
World Cup Soccer - Mexico

637	1986	.500	.75	1.00	3.25
(Y102)					

16.5000 g, .925 SILVER, .4907 oz ASW

637a	1986	.050	—	—	22.50
(Y102a)	1986	.020	—	Proof	35.00

COPPER-NICKEL
Golden Age of Portuguese Discoveries
Gil Eanes

639	1987	1.000	—	—	3.25
(Y103)					

16.5000 g, .925 SILVER, .4907 oz ASW

639a	1987	.050	—	—	20.00
	1987	.022	—	Proof	35.00

24.0000 g, .917 GOLD, .7075 oz AGW

639b	1987	5,585	—	—	550.00

PORTUGAL 1454

COPPER-NICKEL
Golden Age of Portuguese Discoveries
Nuno Tristao

KM#	Date	Mintage	VF	XF	Unc
640	1987	1,000	—	—	3.25

16.5000 g, .925 SILVER, .4907 oz ASW
| 640a | 1987 | .050 | — | — | 20.00 |
| | 1987 | .020 | — | Proof | 35.00 |

24.0000 g, .917 GOLD, .7075 oz AGW
| 640b | 1987 | 5,261 | — | — | 550.00 |

31.1190 g, .999 PALLADIUM, 1.0000 oz APW
| 640c | 1987 | 323 pcs. | — | — | 400.00 |
| | 1987 | 2,000 | — | Proof | 500.00 |

COPPER-NICKEL
Golden Age of Portuguese Discoveries
Diogo Cao
| 641 | 1987 | 1,000 | — | — | 3.25 |

16.5000 g, .925 SILVER, .4907 oz ASW
| 641a | 1987 | .050 | — | — | 20.00 |
| | 1987 | .020 | — | Proof | 35.00 |

24.0000 g, .917 GOLD, .7075 oz AGW
| 641b | 1987 | 5,256 | — | — | 550.00 |
| | 1987 | 2,000 | — | Proof | 800.00 |

COPPER-NICKEL
Amadeo De Souza Cardoso
| 644 | 1987 | .800 | — | — | 3.25 |

21.0000 g, .925 SILVER, .6246 oz ASW
| 644a | 1987 | .030 | — | — | 20.00 |
| | 1987 | .015 | — | Proof | 40.00 |

COPPER-NICKEL
Golden Age of Portuguese Discoveries
Bartolomeu Dias
| 642 | 1988 | 1,000 | — | — | 3.25 |

16.5000 g, .925 SILVER, .4907 oz ASW
| 642a | 1988 | .050 | — | — | 20.00 |
| | 1988 | .020 | — | Proof | 35.00 |

24.0000 g, .917 GOLD, .7077 oz AGW
| 642b | 1988 | 5,355 | — | — | 550.00 |

31.1190 g, .999 PLATINUM, 1.0000 oz APW
| 642c | 1988 | 907 pcs. | — | — | 725.00 |
| | 1988 | 2,000 | — | Proof | 1150.00 |

250 ESCUDOS

25.0000 g, .680 SILVER, .5466 oz ASW

1974 Revolution

KM#	Date	Mintage	VF	XF	Unc
604	1974(76)	.950	—	—	7.50
(Y80)	1974(76)	.010	—	Proof	10.00

COPPER-NICKEL
FAO Fisheries Conference
| 626 (Y94) | 1984 | .024 | 2.00 | 2.50 | 5.50 |

23.0000 g, .925 SILVER, .6841 oz ASW
| 626a (Y94a) | 1984 | 8,000 | — | Proof | 10.00 |

COPPER-NICKEL
Seoul Olympics - Runners
| 643 | 1988 | *.850 | — | — | 5.50 |

28.0000 g, .925 SILVER, .8327 oz ASW
| 643a | 1988 | .070 | — | Proof | 20.00 |
| | 1988 | .030 | — | Proof | 20.00 |

500 ESCUDOS

7.0000 g, .835 SILVER, .1879 oz ASW
XVII European Art Exhibition
| 620 (Y86) | 1983 | .200 | — | — | 10.00 |
| | 1983 | 8,500 | — | Proof | 30.00 |

750 ESCUDOS

12.5000 g, .835 SILVER, .3356 oz ASW
XVII European Art Exhibition
| 621 (Y87) | 1983 | .200 | — | — | 10.00 |
| | 1983 | 8,500 | — | Proof | 30.00 |

1000 ESCUDOS

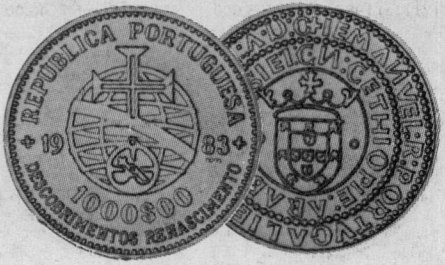

21.0000 g, .835 SILVER, .5638 oz ASW
XVII European Art Exhibition
KM#	Date	Mintage	VF	XF	Unc
622 (Y88)	1983	.200	—	—	10.00
	1983	8,500	—	Proof	30.00

17.0000 g, .925 SILVER, .5056 oz ASW
Louis de Camoes
| 611 (Y89) | 1980(1983) | .150 | — | — | 10.00 |
| | 1980(1983) | .010 | — | Proof | 30.00 |

MINT SETS (MS)

KM#	Date	Mintage	Identification	Issue Price	Mkt. Val.
MS1	1960(3)	—	KM587-589	—	35.00
MS2	1983(4)	10,000	KM612-613,615-616	3.00	5.00
MS3	1983(3)	50,000	KM620-622	30.00	50.00
MS4	1983(3)	5,000	KM617-619	4.00	6.00
MS5	1984(2)	10,000	KM624-625	3.00	5.00
MS6	1985(2)	20,000	KM627a,630a	22.00	30.00
MS7	1986(5)	50,000	KM631-634,636	6.00	6.00
MS8	1987/88(4)	50,000	KM639a-642a	78.00	80.00
MS9	1987/88(4)	5,000	KM639b-642b	2080.	2200.
MS10	1987(6)	50,000	KM631-634,636,638	10.00	10.00

PROOF SETS (PS)

PS1	1960(3)	—	KM587-589, matte finish	—	—
PS2	1974(2)	10,000	KM603-604	6.00	17.50
PS3	1977(3)	10,000	KM605-606,608	2.50	7.00
PS4	1983(3)	8,500	KM620-622	60.00	90.00
PS5	1985(2)	5,000	KM627a,630a	50.00	90.00
PS6	1987(4)	20,000	KM639a-642a	128.00	160.00
PS7	1987/88(4)	2,000	KM639a,640c,641b,642d		
			Prestige	2200.	2500.

Listings For
PORTUGUESE GUINEA: refer to Guinea-Bissau
PORTUGUESE INDIA: refer to Indian Enclaves
PRINCE EDWARD ISLAND: refer to Canada

PUERTO RICO

The Commonwealth of Puerto Rico, the easternmost island of the Greater Antilles in the West Indies, has an area of 3,435 sq. mi. (8,896 sq. km.) and a population of 3.3 million. Capital: San Juan. The commonwealth has its own constitution and elects its own governor. Its people are citizens of the United States, liable to the draft - but not to federal taxation. The chief industries of Puerto Rico are manufacturing, agriculture, and tourism. Manufactured goods, cement, dairy and livestock products, sugar, rum and coffee are exported, mainly to the United States.

Puerto Rico ('Rich Port') was discovered by Columbus who landed on the island and took possession for Spain on Oct. 19, 1493 - the only time Columbus set foot on the soil of what is now a possession of the United States. The first settlement, Caparra, was established by Ponce de Leon in 1508. The early years of the colony were not promising. Considerable gold was found, but the supply was soon exhausted. Efforts to enslave the Indians caused violent reprisals. Hurricanes destroyed crops and homes. French, Dutch, and English freebooters burned the towns. Puerto Rico remained a Spanish possession until 1898, when it was ceded to the United States following the Spanish-American War. Puerto Ricans were granted a measure of self-government and U.S. citizenship in 1917. Effective July 25, 1952, a Congressional resolution elevated Puerto Rico to the status of a free commonwealth associated with the United States.

RULERS
Spanish until 1898

MONETARY SYSTEM
100 Centavos = 1 Peso

COUNTERMARKED COINAGE

In 1884 a large number of holed coins were countermarked at Puerto Rico's seven customs houses to legitimatize them with a device very similar to a fleur-de-lys. These coins were redeemed in 1894.

5 CENTIMOS
BRONZE
c/m: Lys on Spanish 5 Centimos, Y#69.

KM#	Date	Year	Good	VG	Fine	VF
1	ND	(1877-79)	75.00	125.00	175.00	250.00

10 CENTIMOS

BRONZE
c/m: Lys on Spanish 5 Centimos, Y#69.

2	ND	(1877-79)	75.00	125.00	175.00	250.00

1/5 DOLLAR

SILVER
c/m: Lys on U.S. 20 Cent piece, Y#28.

3	ND	(1875-78)	225.00	350.00	500.00	700.00

1/4 DOLLAR

SILVER
c/m: Lys on U.S. Quarter, Y#31.

4	ND	(1866-91)	75.00	125.00	150.00	200.00

c/m: Lys on Spanish or Colonial 2 Reales, C#33.

5	ND	(1759-71)	75.00	125.00	175.00	250.00

1/2 DOLLAR

SILVER
c/m: Lys on U.S. Half Dollar, Y#37.

KM#	Date	Year	Good	VG	Fine	VF
6	ND	(1839-66)	75.00	125.00	175.00	250.00

c/m: Lys on Spanish or Colonial 4 Reales, C#36.

7	ND	(1791-1808)	200.00	300.00	350.00	500.00

DOLLAR
SILVER
c/m: Lys on U.S. bust type Dollar, C#34a.

8	ND	(1798-1803)	125.00	175.00	225.00	325.00

c/m: Lys on U.S. Trade Dollar, Y#44.

9	ND	(1873-85)	150.00	225.00	275.00	400.00

c/m: Lys on Spanish or Colonial 8 Reales, C#45.

10	ND	(1772-89)	125.00	200.00	275.00	400.00

REGULAR COINAGE
5 CENTAVOS

1.2500 g, .900 SILVER, .0361 oz ASW

KM#	Date	Mintage	Fine	VF	XF	Unc
15	1896	.600	8.00	12.50	20.00	75.00

10 CENTAVOS

2.5000 g, .900 SILVER, .0723 oz ASW

16	1896	.700	10.00	15.00	22.50	125.00

20 CENTAVOS

5.0000 g, .900 SILVER, .1446 oz ASW

13	1895	3.350	25.00	35.00	45.00	135.00

40 CENTAVOS

10.0000 g, .900 SILVER, .2893 oz ASW

KM#	Date	Mintage	Fine	VF	XF	Unc
17	1896	.725	115.00	225.00	375.00	2000.

PESO

25.0000 g, .900 SILVER, .7234 oz ASW

14	1895	8.500	125.00	250.00	450.00	900.00

VIEQUE
(Crab Island)

Vieques (Crab Island), located to the east of Puerto Rico is the largest of the Commonwealth's offshore islands. Two-thirds of the island are leased to the U.S. navy. The neighboring island to the north, Culebra, was leased to the navy until 1974, when the naval station was closed and bombardment exercises ceased. Puerto Rico's offshore island to the west, Mona, situated between the main island and the Dominican Republic, has been unpopulated since the late 16th century, and is of no numismatic significance.

COUNTERMARKED COINAGE
Type I: c/m: 12 Rayed Sunburst

COPPER
c/m: On Nova Constellatio Cent

KM#	Date	Good	VG	Fine	VF
1	ND(1783-5)	50.00	75.00	125.00	200.00

SILVER
c/m: On Danish West Indies 2 Skilling, C#12.

2	ND(1837)	40.00	55.00	85.00	125.00

c/m: On Danish West Indies 2 Skilling, C#18.

3	ND(1848)	40.00	55.00	85.00	125.00

c/m: On Danish West Indies 10 Skilling, C#16.

4	ND(1845)	45.00	65.00	100.00	140.00

c/m: On Danish West Indies 20 Skilling, C#17.

5	ND(1840)	50.00	75.00	125.00	200.00

c/m: On Danish 18th century silver coin.

6	ND	50.00	85.00	110.00	175.00

c/m: On Spain 2 Reales, C#134.

KM#	Date	Good	VG	Fine	VF
7	ND(1825)	85.00	125.00	150.00	225.00

Type II: c/s: V in 12 Rayed Sunburst

c/m: On 1/2 cut of Spanish-American 2 Reales

8	ND	100.00	135.00	175.00	250.00

QATAR

The State of Qatar, an emirate in the Persian Gulf between Bahrain and Trucial Oman, has an area of 4,247 sq. mi. (11,000 sq. km.) and a population of *342,000. Capital: Doha. Oil is the chief industry and export.

Qatar was under Turkish control from 1872 until the beginning of World War I when the Ottoman Turks evacuated the Qatar Peninsula. In 1916 Sheikh Abdullah placed Qatar under the protection of Great Britain and gave Britain responsibility for its defense and foreign relations. Qatar joined with Dubai in a Monetary Union and issued coins and paper money in 1966 and 1969. When Britain announced in 1968 that it would end treaty relationships with the Persian Gulf sheikhdoms in 1971, this union was dissolved. Qatar joined Bahrain and the seven trucial sheikhdoms (the latter now called the United Arab Emirates) in an effort to form a union of Arab Emirates. However the nine sheikhdoms were unable to agree on terms of union, and Qatar declared its independence as the State of Qatar on Sept. 3, 1971.

TITLES

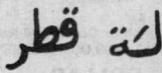

Daulat Qatar

RULERS
Khalifa, 1972—

MONETARY SYSTEM
100 Dirhem = 1 Riyal

DIRHEM

BRONZE

KM#	Date	Year	Mintage	VF	XF	Unc
2	AH1393	1973	.500	.10	.20	.50

5 DIRHEMS

BRONZE

3	AH1393	1973	1.000	.10	.20	.60
	1398	1978	1.000	.10	.20	.60

10 DIRHEMS

BRONZE

1	AH1392	1972	1.500	.20	.35	.80
	1393	1973	1.500	.20	.35	.80

25 DIRHEMS

COPPER-NICKEL

4	AH1393	1973	1.500	.25	.45	1.00
	1396	1976	2.000	.25	.45	1.00
	1401	1981	—	.25	.45	1.00

50 DIRHEMS

COPPER-NICKEL

KM#	Date	Year	Mintage	VF	XF	Unc
5	AH1393	1973	1.500	.40	.80	1.50
	1398	1978	2.000	.40	.80	1.50
	1401	1981	—	.40	.80	1.50

QATAR & DUBAI

The State of Qatar, which occupies the Qatar Peninsula jutting into the Persian Gulf from eastern Saudi Arabia, has an area of 4,247 sq. mi. (11,000 sq. km.) and a population of *342,000. Capital: Doha. The traditional occupations of pearling, fishing, and herding have been replaced in economic by petroleum-related industries. Crude oil, petroleum products, and tomatoes are exported.

Dubai is one of the seven sheikhdoms comprising the United Arab Emirates (formerly Trucial States) located along the southern shore of the Persian Gulf. It has a population of about 60,000. Capital (of the United Arab Emirates): Abu Dhabi.

Qatar, which initiated protective treaty relations with Great Britain in 1820, achieved independence on Sept. 3, 1971, upon withdrawal of the British military presence from the Persian Gulf, and replaced its special treaty arrangement with Britain with a treaty of general friendship. Dubai attained independence on Dec. 1, 1971, upon termination of Britain's protective treaty with the trucial Sheikhdoms, and on Dec. 2, 1971, entered into the union of the United Arab Emirates.

Despite the fact that the Emirate of Qatar and the Sheikhdom of Dubai were merged under a monetary union, the two territories were governed independently from each other. Qatar now uses its own currency while Dubai uses the United Arab Emirates currency and coins.

TITLES

قطر ودبي

Qatar Wa Dubai

RULERS
Ahmad II, 1960-1972

MONETARY SYSTEM
100 Dirhem = 1 Riyal

DIRHEM

BRONZE

KM#	Date	Year	Mintage	VF	XF	Unc
1	AH1386	1966	1.000	.10	.20	.50

5 DIRHEMS

BRONZE

2	AH1386	1966	2.000	.10	.20	.60
	1389	1969	2.000	.10	.20	.60

10 DIRHEMS

BRONZE

3	AH1386	1966	2.000	.20	.35	.80

25 DIRHEMS

COPPER-NICKEL

4	AH1386	1966	2.000	.25	.45	1.00
	1389	1969	2.000	.25	.45	1.00

50 DIRHEMS

COPPER-NICKEL

KM#	Date	Year	Mintage	VF	XF	Unc
5	AH1386	1966	2.000	.40	.80	1.50

Listings For

QUAITI: refer to Yemen Democratic Republic

RAS AL KHAIMA: refer to United Arab Emirates

REUNION

The Department of Reunion, an overseas department of France located in the Indian Ocean 400 miles (640 km.) east of Madagascar, has an area of 969 sq. mi. (2,510 sq. km.) and a population of *565,000. Capital: Saint-Denis. The island's volcanic soil is extremely fertile. Sugar, vanilla, coffee and rum are exported.

Although first visited by Portuguese navigators in the 16th century, Reunion was uninhabited when claimed for France by Capt. Goubert in 1638. It was first colonized as Isle de Bourbon by the French in 1662 as a layover station for ships rounding the Cape of Good Hope to India. It was renamed Reunion in 1793. The island remained in French possession except for the period of 1810-15, when it was occupied by the British. Reunion became an overseas department of France in 1946, and in 1958 voted to continue that status within the new French Union.

During the first half of the 19th century, Reunion was officially known as Isle de Bonaparte (1801-14) and Isle de Bourbon (1814-48). Reunion coinage of those periods is so designated.

ISLE DE BOURBON

The Restoration of the House of Bourbon in France caused the name of the Reunion Island to be changed to Isle de Bourbon from 1814-1848.

RULERS
Louis XVIII, 1814-1828

MONETARY SYSTEM
100 Centimes = 1 Franc

10 CENTIMES

BILLON

KM#	Date	Mintage	VG	Fine	VF	XF
1	1816A	.150	12.50	35.00	75.00	165.00

REUNION

MINT MARKS
(a) - Paris, privy marks only

MONETARY SYSTEM
100 Centimes = 1 Franc

50 CENTIMES

COPPER-NICKEL

KM#	Date	Mintage	Fine	VF	XF	Unc
4	1896	1.000	15.00	35.00	100.00	250.00

FRANC

COPPER-NICKEL

5	1896	.500	35.00	60.00	150.00	350.00

REUNION 1458

ALUMINUM

KM#	Date	Mintage	VF	XF	Unc
6.1	1948(a)	3.000	.15	.35	1.50
	1964(a)	1.000	.25	.50	1.75
	1968(a)	.450	.50	.75	3.50
	1969(a)	.500	.50	.75	2.50
	1971(a)	.800	.50	.75	2.00
	1973(a)	.500	.50	.75	2.50

Thinner Planchet
6.2	1969(a)	Inc. Ab.	.65	1.25	4.00

Mule. Obv: French Colonial. Rev: KM#6.1.

7	1948(a)	Inc. Ab.	—	—	—

2 FRANCS

ALUMINUM
8	1948(a)	2.000	.25	.50	2.00
	1968(a)	.100	2.50	4.50	8.00
	1969(a)	.150	1.50	2.50	5.00
	1970(a)	.300	.75	1.50	3.00
	1971(a)	.300	.75	1.50	3.00
	1973(a)	.500	.75	1.50	3.00

5 FRANCS

ALUMINUM
9	1955(a)	3.000	.50	.75	2.00
	1969(a)	.100	2.50	5.00	8.00
	1970(a)	.200	1.50	3.00	6.00
	1971(a)	.100	1.50	3.00	6.00
	1972(a)	.300	.75	1.50	2.50
	1973(a)	.250	.75	1.50	2.50

10 FRANCS

ALUMINUM-BRONZE
10	1955(a)	1.500	.45	.65	2.00
	1962(a)	.700	1.50	3.00	6.00
	1964(a)	1.000	.45	.65	1.50
	1969(a)	.300	1.00	2.00	5.00
	1970(a)	.300	1.00	2.00	4.00
	1971(a)	.200	1.50	3.50	7.00
	1972(a)	.400	1.00	2.00	5.00
	1973(a)	.700	.75	1.50	2.50

20 FRANCS

ALUMINUM-BRONZE
11	1955(a)	1.250	.65	1.00	3.00
	1960(a)	.100	2.75	5.50	9.00
	1961(a)	.300	2.25	4.50	7.00
	1962(a)	.190	2.75	5.00	8.00
	1964(a)	.750	.75	1.50	2.50
	1969(a)	.200	2.75	5.00	8.00
	1970(a)	.200	2.75	5.00	8.00

KM#	Date	Mintage	VF	XF	Unc
11	1971(a)	.200	2.75	5.00	8.00
	1972(a)	.300	2.00	3.00	3.00
	1973(a)	.550	.75	1.50	2.50

50 FRANCS

NICKEL
12	1962(a)	1.000	1.25	2.25	4.00
	1964(a)	.500	2.00	3.00	5.00
	1969(a)	.100	2.75	5.00	8.00
	1970(a)	.100	2.75	5.00	8.00
	1973(a)	.350	2.00	3.00	3.50

100 FRANCS

NICKEL
13	1964(a)	2.000	1.00	1.50	2.50
	1969(a)	.200	2.25	4.00	6.00
	1970(a)	.150	2.25	4.00	6.00
	1971(a)	.100	2.75	6.00	12.50
	1972(a)	.400	2.00	3.00	4.00
	1973(a)	.200	2.25	4.00	6.00

FLEUR DE COIN SETS (SS)

KM#	Date	Mintage	Identification	Issue Price	Mkt. Val.
SS1	1964(5)	—	KM6.1,10-13	—	10.00

NOTE: This set issued with Comoros set.

Listings For

RHODESIA: refer to Zimbabwe
RHODESIA & NYASALAND: refer to Zimbabwe
RIAU ARCHIPELAGO: refer to Indonesia

ROMANIA

The Socialist Republic of Romania, a Balkan country in southeast Europe, has an area of 91,699 sq. mi. (237,500 sq. km.) and a population of *23.2 million. Capital: Bucharest. The economy is predominantly agricultural; heavy industry and oil have become increasingly important since 1959. Machinery, foodstuffs, raw minerals and petroleum products are exported.

The area of Romania, generally referred to as Dacia by the ancient Romans, was subjected to wave after wave of barbarian conquest and foreign domination before its independence (of Turkey) was declared in 1877. In 1881 it became a monarchy under Carol I, changing to a constitutional monarchy with a bicameral legislature in 1888. The government was reorganized along Fascist lines in 1940, and in the following year Romania joined Germany's attack on the Soviet Union for recovering the region of Bessarabia annexed by Stalin in 1940. The country was subsequently occupied by the Russian Army which actively supported the program and goals of the Romanian Communists. On Nov. 19, 1946, a Communist-dominated government was installed and prompted the abdication of King Michael. Romania became a 'People's Republic' on Dec. 30, 1947.

RULERS
Carol I (as Prince), 1866-81 (as King), 1881-1914
Ferdinand I, 1914-1927
Mihai I, 1927-1930
Carol II, 1930-1940
Mihai I, 1940-1947

MINT MARKS
(a) - Paris, privy marks only
(b) - Brussels, privy marks only
B - Bucharest (1879-1900)
C - Bucharest
F - Feres
FM - Franklin Mint
H - Heaton
J - Hamburg
KN - Kings Norton
(p) - Thunderbolt - Poissy
V - Vienna
W - Watt (James Watt & Co.)
Huguenin - Le Locle

MONETARY SYSTEM
100 Bani = 1 Leu

BANU

COPPER
KM#	Date	Mintage	Fine	VF	XF	Unc
1	1867H	5.000	3.50	7.50	22.00	55.00
	1867H	Inc. Ab.	—	—	Proof	70.00
	1867WATT & CO. Inc. Ab.	6.00	12.00	25.00	65.00
	1867HEATON	—	—	—	Proof	85.00

GILT BRONZE
1a	1883	500 pcs.	—	—	—	1500.

BRONZE
1b	1888	500 pcs.	—	—	—	1000.

BAN

COPPER
26	1900B	20.007	1.50	2.25	5.50	16.00
	1900B	—	—	—	Proof	50.00

NOTE: Varieties exist.

2 BANI

COPPER

KM#	Date	Mintage	Fine	VF	XF	Unc
2	1867HEATON	10.000	2.50	6.00	12.00	30.00
	1867HEATON Inc. Ab.	—	—	Proof	55.00	
	1867WATT & CO. Inc. Ab.	3.00	7.50	14.00	35.00	
	1867WATT & CO. Inc. Ab.	—	—	Proof	80.00	

19.5mm
Obv leg: CAROL I DOMNUL (Prince)

| 11.1 | 1879B | .500 | 5.00 | 10.00 | 22.00 | 45.00 |

20mm

11.2	1879B Inc. Ab.	4.00	8.00	18.00	32.00
	1880/79B	10.500	3.00	5.00	10.00	22.50
	1880B Inc. Ab.	2.50	5.00	7.00	15.00
	1881B	1.250	15.00	20.00	35.00	85.00

Obv. leg: CAROL I REGE (King)

| 18 | 1882B | 5.000 | 4.00 | 8.00 | 16.00 | 40.00 |

Rev: ROMANIA added above shield.

| 27 | 1900B | 20.000 | 1.00 | 2.00 | 5.00 | 12.00 |

NOTE: Varieties exist.

5 BANI

COPPER

3	1867HEATON	25.000	2.00	4.00	8.00	24.00
	1867HEATON	—	—	Proof	75.00	
	1867WATT & CO. Inc. Ab.	3.00	5.00	10.00	32.00
	1867WATT & CO.	—	—	Proof	100.00	

Obv. leg: CAROL I REGE (King)

19	1882B	5.000	1.00	2.50	12.00	28.00
	1883B	3.000	1.00	2.00	10.00	26.00
	1884B	8.400	1.00	2.00	8.00	24.00
	1885B	3.600	2.00	4.00	15.00	36.00

COPPER-NICKEL

| 28 | 1900 | 20.000 | 1.00 | 2.50 | 6.00 | 14.00 |

KM#	Date	Mintage	Fine	VF	XF	Unc
31	1905	25.000	.50	1.00	3.00	8.00
	1905	—	—	—	Proof	25.00
	1906	24.000	.25	.50	2.00	7.00
	1906J	25.000	.25	.50	1.50	5.00

10 BANI

COPPER

4	1867HEATON	25.000	2.00	6.00	12.00	25.00
	1867HEATON Inc. Ab.	—	—	Proof	65.00	
	1867WATT & CO. Inc. Ab.	2.00	5.00	10.00	28.00
	1867WATT & CO.	—	—	Proof	100.00	

COPPER-NICKEL

| 29 | 1900 | 15.000 | .75 | 2.00 | 5.00 | 15.00 |
| | 1900 | — | — | — | Proof | 50.00 |

32	1905	17.500	.50	1.00	3.50	9.00
	1906	17.000	.25	.75	2.50	8.00
	1906J	17.500	.25	.75	1.50	6.00

20 BANI

COPPER-NICKEL

| 30 | 1900 | 2.500 | 3.00 | 8.00 | 22.00 | 65.00 |

33	1905	2.500	.50	2.50	8.00	25.00
	1906	3.000	.50	2.00	6.00	20.00
	1906J	2.500	.50	2.00	5.00	18.00

25 BANI

ALUMINUM

| 44 | 1921(H) | 30.000 | .50 | 1.00 | 3.00 | 8.00 |

NOTE: Sizes of hole vary from 3.8-4.3mm.

50 BANI

2.5000 g, .835 SILVER, .0671 oz ASW

KM#	Date	Mintage	Fine	VF	XF	Unc
9	1873	4.800	2.50	7.50	18.00	40.00
	1876	2.117	3.00	9.00	24.00	60.00

| 13 | 1881V | 1.000 | 5.00 | 10.00 | 25.00 | 80.00 |

Rev: Large letters.

| 21.1 | 1884B | 1.000 | 3.00 | 7.00 | 22.00 | 65.00 |

Obv: Different head.

| 21.2 | 1885B | .200 | 6.00 | 18.00 | 35.00 | 100.00 |

Rev: Small letters.

23	1894	.600	4.00	8.00	16.00	45.00
	1900	3.838	2.50	5.00	10.00	25.00
	1901	.194	6.00	14.00	32.50	90.00

41	1910	3.600	1.50	3.00	8.00	12.00
	1910	—	—	—	Proof	150.00
	1911	3.000	2.00	4.00	10.00	15.00
	1912	1.800	1.50	3.00	8.00	14.00
	1914	1.600	1.25	2.00	4.00	10.00
	1914	—	—	—	Proof	85.00

NOTE: Edge varieties exist.

ALUMINUM

| 45 | 1921(H) | 20.000 | .50 | 1.00 | 3.00 | 8.00 |

NOTE: Sizes of hole vary from 3.8-4.2mm.

LEU

5.0000 g, .835 SILVER, .1342 oz ASW

6	1870C	.400	20.00	45.00	110.00	340.00
	1870C medal strike Inc. Ab.					
	1870B Inc. Ab.	100.00	200.00	300.00	600.00
	1870 B medal strike Inc. Ab.	—	—	—	—

ROMANIA 1460

KM#	Date	Mintage	Fine	VF	XF	Unc
10	1873(b)	4.443	4.00	8.00	17.50	60.00
	1874(b)	4.511	5.00	12.00	25.00	80.00
	1876(b)	.225	35.00	75.00	150.00	320.00

NOTE: Varieties exist.

Obv. leg: CAROL I DOMNUL (Prince).

14	1881V	1.800	6.00	14.00	40.00	120.00
	1881V	—	—	—	Proof	—

Obv. leg: CAROL I REGE (King).

22	1884B	1.000	5.00	12.00	32.00	100.00
	1885B	.400	9.00	25.00	40.00	150.00
	1885B	—	—	—	Proof	—

24	1894	1.500	4.00	7.50	16.00	55.00
	1894	—	—	—	Proof	—
	1900	.799	5.00	10.00	22.00	65.00
	1901	.370	6.00	15.00	35.00	85.00
	1901	—	—	—	Proof	—

40th Anniversary of Reign

34	1906	2.500	4.00	8.00	15.00	35.00
	1906	—	—	—	Proof	85.00

42	1910	4.600	3.00	6.00	8.00	16.00
	1910	—	—	—	Proof	180.00
	1911	2.573	4.00	8.00	12.00	22.00
	1912	3.540	3.00	5.00	7.00	14.00
	1914	4.283	2.00	3.00	6.00	12.00
	1914	—	—	—	Proof	—

NOTE: Edge varieties exist.

COPPER-NICKEL

46	1924	100.000	.30	1.00	3.00	8.00
	1924(p)	100.006	.30	1.00	3.00	8.00

NICKEL-BRASS

56	1938	27.900	.10	.50	1.00	2.50
	1939	Inc. Ab.	.10	.50	1.50	3.00
	1940	Inc. Ab.	.10	.50	1.00	2.50
	1941	Inc. Ab.	.10	.50	1.00	2.50

2 LEI

10.0000 g, .835 SILVER, .2684 oz ASW

KM#	Date	Mintage	Fine	VF	XF	Unc
8	1872(b)	.262	6.00	15.00	50.00	165.00
	1872	—	—	—	Proof	450.00
	1873(b)	1.745	4.00	10.00	25.00	75.00
	1875(b)	3.092	4.00	9.00	22.00	65.00
	1876(b)	.653	5.00	12.00	40.00	135.00

15	1881V	1.150	12.00	25.00	65.00	200.00

25	1894	.600	8.00	16.00	40.00	140.00
	1894	—	—	—	Proof	—
	1900	.087	12.50	32.50	85.00	220.00
	1901	.012	350.00	500.00	700.00	1200.

43	1910	1.800	4.00	8.00	12.00	24.00
	1910	—	—	—	Proof	200.00
	1911	1.000	6.00	12.00	25.00	32.50
	1912	1.500	4.00	7.00	12.00	20.00
	1914	2.452	3.00	5.00	8.00	15.00
	1914	—	—	—	Proof	—

NOTE: Edge varieties exist.

COPPER-NICKEL

47	1924	50.000	.40	1.00	3.50	9.00
	1924(p)	50.008	.40	1.00	3.50	9.00

ZINC

58	1941	99.592	.35	.75	1.50	4.50

5 LEI

25.0000 g, .900 SILVER, .7234 oz ASW

KM#	Date	Mintage	Fine	VF	XF	Unc
12	1880B name near rim					
		1.800	17.50	35.00	70.00	160.00
	1880B name near truncation					
	Inc. Ab.	—	20.00	37.50	80.00	175.00
	1881B	2.200	15.00	30.00	50.00	150.00

16	1881B	.570	20.00	40.00	90.00	200.00

Lettered Edge
Obv: Similar to Y#27.

17.1	1881B	1.230	15.00	32.00	75.00	240.00
	1882B	1.100	15.00	35.00	80.00	250.00
	1883B	*2.300	15.00	30.00	55.00	160.00
	1884B	.300	25.00	60.00	120.00	300.00
	1885B	.040	90.00	150.00	300.00	750.00

***NOTE:** Varieties in crown on mantle exist.

Ornamented Edge

17.2	1901B	.082	40.00	80.00	150.00	260.00
	1901B	—	—	—	Proof	—

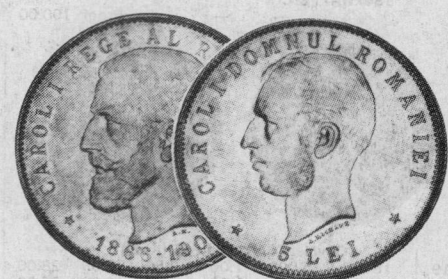

40th Anniversary of Reign

35	1906	.200	40.00	65.00	170.00	320.00
	1906	—	—	—	Proof	1200.

ROMANIA 1461

NICKEL-BRASS

KM#	Date	Mintage	Fine	VF	XF	Unc
48	1930H	15.000	1.00	2.50	5.00	15.00
	1930KN	15.000	1.00	3.00	6.50	18.00
	1930(a)	30.000	.50	2.00	4.00	10.00

ZINC

61	1942	140.000	.50	1.00	1.50	3.50

10 LEI

NICKEL-BRASS

49	1930	15.000	1.00	3.00	7.00	22.00
	1930	—	—	—	Proof	—
	1930(a)	30.000	1.00	2.50	6.00	18.00
	1930H	7.500	2.00	4.00	9.00	26.00
	1930KN	7.500	3.00	6.00	12.50	32.00

12-1/2 LEI

4.0323 g, .900 GOLD, .1167 oz AGW
Carol I - 40th Anniversary of Reign

36	1906	.032	75.00	95.00	125.00	260.00

20 LEI

6.4516 g, .900 GOLD, .1867 oz AGW
Obv. leg: CAROL I DOMNULU (Prince), light beard.
Reeded edge.

5	1868(b)	200 pcs.	—	4000.	5000.	7500.

Obv. leg: CAROL I DOMNUL (Prince), heavy beard.

7	1870C	5.000	500.00	750.00	1250.	2200.

Obv. leg: CAROL I REGE (King).

20	1883B	.150	95.00	125.00	150.00	220.00
	1884	.035	200.00	300.00	550.00	900.00
	1890B	.196	100.00	150.00	175.00	240.00

40th Anniversary of Reign

37	1906(b)	.015	125.00	150.00	200.00	325.00

NICKEL-BRASS

KM#	Date	Mintage	Fine	VF	XF	Unc
50	1930 London	42.000	2.00	6.00	12.00	26.00
	1930	—	—	—	Proof	—
	1930H	5.000	3.00	8.00	22.00	42.50
	1930KN	5.000	3.00	9.00	24.00	45.00

51	1930	6.750	1.00	3.00	8.00	16.50
	1930	—	—	—	Proof	—
	1930(a)	17.500	1.00	2.00	6.00	14.50
	1930H	4.370	1.50	5.00	12.00	28.00
	1930KN	4.380	2.00	6.00	15.00	36.00

ZINC

62	1942	30.500	.75	1.50	3.00	6.00
	1943	26.925	1.00	2.25	4.00	8.00
	1944	18.213	1.50	3.00	4.50	10.00

25 LEI

8.0645 g, .900 GOLD, .2333 oz AGW
Carol I 40th Anniversary of Reign

38	1906(b)	.024	150.00	200.00	250.00	500.00

50 LEI

16.1290 g, .900 GOLD, .4667 oz AGW
Carol I 40th Anniversary of Reign

39	1906(b)	.028	250.00	300.00	450.00	750.00

NICKEL

55	1937	*12.000	1.25	2.50	4.50	7.50
	1938	*8.000	3.75	7.50	15.00	27.50

*NOTE: 16.731 melted.

100 LEI

32.2580 g, .900 GOLD, .9335 oz AGW
Carol I 40th Anniversary of Reign

KM#	Date	Mintage	Fine	VF	XF	Unc
40	1906(b)	3.000	600.00	800.00	1200.	2000.

12.0000 g, .500 SILVER, .1929 oz ASW

52	1932(a)	2.000	9.00	16.00	35.00	90.00
	1932	16.400	5.00	10.00	20.00	45.00
	1932	—	—	—	Proof	225.00

			NICKEL			
54	1936	20.230	1.00	2.00	5.00	8.50
	1938	*3.250	7.50	10.00	22.50	60.00

*NOTE: 17.030 melted.

NICKEL-CLAD STEEL

64	1943	40.590	.50	1.00	1.50	5.00
	1944	21.289	.50	1.50	2.50	7.00

200 LEI

6.0000 g, .835 SILVER, .1611 oz ASW

63	1942	30.025	1.50	3.00	5.00	10.00

BRASS

66	1945	1.399	1.50	3.00	5.00	12.00

ROMANIA 1462

250 LEI

13.5000 g, .750 SILVER, .3255 oz ASW

KM#	Date	Mintage	Fine	VF	XF	Unc
53	1935	4.500	10.00	20.00	40.00	120.00

12.0000 g, .835 SILVER, .3222 oz ASW

57	1939	10.000	5.00	7.50	12.50	25.00
	1940	8.000	10.00	22.50	50.00	120.00

Lettered edge: NIHIL SINE DEO

59.1	1940	—	—	—	Rare	—
	1941(p)	13.750	6.00	9.00	12.00	20.00

Lettered edge: TOTUL PENTRU TARA

59.2	1941	2.250	18.00	27.50	47.50	100.00

500 LEI

25.0000 g, .835 SILVER, .6711 oz ASW

60	1941	.775	8.00	12.00	18.00	30.00

12.0000 g, .700 SILVER, .2701 oz ASW

65	1944	9.737	2.50	3.50	5.00	8.00

BRASS

67	1945	3.422	2.00	3.50	4.50	7.50

ALUMINUM
Obv: Designer's signature below neck.

KM#	Date	Mintage	Fine	VF	XF	Unc
68.1	1946	5.823	1.50	2.50	4.00	8.00

Obv: W/o designer's signature.

68.2	1946	Inc. Ab.	—	—	—	—

2000 LEI

BRASS

69	1946	24.619	2.00	2.50	3.50	6.00

NOTE: Many of these coins were privately silver plated.

25000 LEI

12.0000 g, .700 SILVER, .2701 oz ASW

70	1946	2.372	2.00	4.00	6.00	12.00

100000 LEI

25.0000 g, .700 SILVER, .5626 oz ASW

71	1946	2.002	6.00	8.00	12.50	22.00

MONETARY REFORM
100 Bani = 1 Leu

50 BANI

BRASS
August 1947 Coinage Reform

72	1947	13.266	1.00	2.00	3.00	8.00

LEU

BRASS
August 1947 Coinage Reform

73	1947	88.341	.75	2.00	3.00	7.00

2 LEI

BRONZE
August 1947 Coinage Reform

KM#	Date	Mintage	Fine	VF	XF	Unc
74	1947	40.000	1.00	2.50	4.00	9.00

5 LEI

ALUMINUM
August 1947 Coinage Reform

75	1947	56.026	1.00	2.00	5.00	13.50

10000 LEI

BRASS

76	1947	11.850	2.00	4.00	6.00	13.00

PEOPLE'S REPUBLIC
1947-1965

BAN

ALUMINUM-BRONZE
Currency Revaluation
Obv: W/o star at top of arms.

81.1	1952	—	.15	.25	1.00

Obv: Star at top of arms.

81.2	1953	—	.50	1.50	5.00	12.50
	1954	—	2.50	5.00	12.00	25.00

3 BANI

ALUMINUM-BRONZE
Obv: W/o star at top of arms.

82.1	1952	—	1.00	1.50	4.00	12.00

Obv: Star at top of arms.

82.2	1953	—	.50	1.00	2.00	5.00
	1954	—	2.00	4.00	10.00	22.00

5 BANI

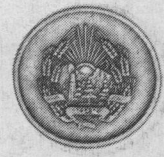 

ALUMINUM-BRONZE
Currency Revaluation

ROMANIA

Obv: W/o star at top of arms.

KM#	Date	Mintage	Fine	VF	XF	Unc
83.1	1952	—	.50	1.00	2.00	4.00

Obv: Star at top of arms.

83.2	1953	—	.25	.50	1.50	3.00
	1954	—	.25	.50	1.50	3.00
	1955	—	.25	.50	1.50	3.00
	1956	—	.20	.45	.80	2.00
	1957	—	.30	.60	1.20	3.50

NICKEL-CLAD STEEL
Obv: RPR on ribbon in arms.

89	1963	—	.20	.50	1.00	2.00

10 BANI

COPPER-NICKEL
Currency Revaluation
Obv: W/o star at top of arms.

84.1	1952	—	1.00	3.00	7.50	18.00

Obv: Star at top of arms, leg: ROMANA.

84.2	1954	—	.20	.80	2.00	5.00

Obv. leg: ROMINA

84.3	1955	—	.10	.20	.50	1.25
	1956	—	.10	.20	.50	1.25

15 BANI

NICKEL-CLAD STEEL

87	1960	—	.10	.20	.40	.80

25 BANI

COPPER-NICKEL
Currency Revaluation
Obv: W/o star at top of arms.

85.1	1952	—	.50	1.00	3.00	8.00

Obv: Star at top of arms, leg: ROMANA.

85.2	1953	—	.20	.60	1.50	3.50
	1954	—	.20	.50	1.00	2.50

Obv. leg: ROMINA.

KM#	Date	Mintage	Fine	VF	XF	Unc
85.3	1955	—	.15	.35	.80	2.50

NICKEL-CLAD STEEL

88	1960	—	.15	.25	.35	.75

50 BANI

COPPER-NICKEL

86	1955	—	1.00	2.00	3.50	6.00
	1956	—	1.50	3.00	5.50	12.00

LEU

COPPER-NICKEL-ZINC
People's Republic

78	1949	—	.70	1.35	2.00	5.00
	1950	—	.70	1.35	2.50	6.00
	1951	—	1.00	2.00	6.00	15.00

ALUMINUM

78a	1951	—	1.00	2.00	2.50	4.00
	1952	—	5.00	12.00	25.00	45.00

NICKEL-CLAD STEEL

90	1963	—	.25	.50	.75	1.50

2 LEI

ALUMINUM-BRONZE
People's Republic

79	1950	—	1.00	2.00	4.00	8.00
	1951	—	2.00	6.00	12.00	25.00

ALUMINUM

79a	1951	—	1.25	2.50	3.00	5.00
	1952	—	6.00	14.00	27.50	48.00

3 LEI

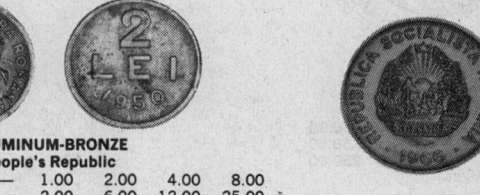

NICKEL-CLAD STEEL

91	1963	—	.25	.50	1.00	2.00

5 LEI

ALUMINUM
People's Republic

KM#	Date	Mintage	Fine	VF	XF	Unc
77	1948	—	1.00	1.50	3.00	7.00
	1949	—	1.00	1.50	2.50	5.00
	1950	—	1.00	1.50	2.50	5.00
	1951	—	1.00	2.00	4.00	8.00

20 LEI

ALUMINUM
People's Republic

80	1951	—	7.50	15.00	25.00	60.00

SOCIALIST REPUBLIC
1965-

5 BANI

NICKEL-CLAD STEEL
Obv: ROMANIA on ribbon in arms.

92	1966	—	.10	.20	.30	.60

ALUMINUM

92a	1975	—	—	—	.10	.20

15 BANI

NICKEL-CLAD STEEL

93	1966	—	—	.10	.20	.50

ALUMINUM

93a	1975	—	—	—	.10	.25

25 BANI

NICKEL-CLAD STEEL

94	1966	—	—	.15	.25	.60

ALUMINUM

94a	1982	—	—	.10	.20	.50

LEU

NICKEL-CLAD STEEL

95	1966	—	—	.25	.50	.75

1463

ROMANIA 1464

3 LEI

NICKEL-CLAD STEEL

KM#	Date	Mintage	Fine	VF	XF	Unc
96	1966	—	.25	.50	1.00	2.00

5 LEI

ALUMINUM

| 97 | 1978 | — | — | .50 | 1.00 | 2.00 |

50 LEI

13.8800 g, .925 SILVER, .4128 oz ASW
2050th Anniversary of First Independent State
Obv: Similar to 100 Lei, Y#98.

| 110 | 1983FM | 7,000 | — | — | Proof | 40.00 |
| | 1983FM | 1,000 | — | — | Proof | 150.00 |

*NOTE: Serially numbered on the edges.

100 LEI

27.7500 g, .925 SILVER, .8253 oz ASW
2050th Anniversary of First Independent State

98	1982FM	7,500	—	—	Proof	50.00
	1983FM	7,000	—	—	Proof	50.00
	1983FM	1,000	—	—	Proof	250.00

*NOTE: Serially numbered on the edges.

500 LEI

.900 GOLD
2050th Anniversary of First Independent State

99	1982FM	7,500	—	—	Proof	400.00
	1983FM	7,000	—	—	Proof	400.00
	1983FM	1,000	—	—	Proof	400.00

*NOTE: Serially numbered on the edges.

1000 LEI

14.4000 g, .900 GOLD, .4167 oz AGW
2050th Anniversary of First Independent State
Obv: Similar to 500 Lei, Y#99.

KM#	Date	Mintage	Fine	VF	XF	Unc
101	1983FM	7,000	—	—	Proof	525.00
	1983FM	1,000	—	—	Proof	850.00

*NOTE: Serially numbered on the edges.

PROOF SETS (PS)

KM#	Date	Mintage	Identification	Issue Price	Mkt. Val.
PS1	1982(2)	7,000	KM98-99	429.00	450.00
PS2	1983(4)	1,000	KM98-99,101,110 edge numbering	850.00	2000.

Listings For
RUANDA & URUNDI: refer to Rwanda-Burundi and Zaire

RWANDA

The Republic of Rwanda, located in central Africa between the Republic of the Congo and Tanzania, has an area of 10,169 sq. mi. (26,338 sq. km.) and a population of 7.3 million. Capital: Kigali. The economy is based on agriculture and mining. Coffee and tin are exported.

German Lieutenant Count von Goetzen was the first European to visit Rwanda, 1894. Four years later the court of the Mwami (the Tutsi king of Rwanda) willingly permitted the kingdom to become a protectorate of Germany. In 1916, during the African campaigns of World War I, Belgian troops from Congo occupied Rwanda. After the war it, together with Burundi, became a Belgian League of Nations mandate under the name of the Territory of Ruanda-Urundi. Following World War II, Ruanda-Urundi became a Belgian administered U.N. trust territory. The Tutsi monarchy was deposed by the U.N. supervised election of 1961, after which Belgium granted Rwanda internal autonomy. On July 1, 1962, the U.N. terminated the Belgian trusteeship and granted full independence to both Rwanda and Burundi.

For earlier coinage see Belgian Congo, and Rwanda and Burundi.

MINT MARKS
(a) - Paris, privy marks only
(b) - Brussels, privy marks only

MONETARY SYSTEM
100 Centimes = 1 Franc

1/2 FRANC

ALUMINUM

KM#	Date	Mintage	VF	XF	Unc
9	1970	5.000	.25	.50	1.50

FRANC

COPPER-NICKEL

| 5 | 1964(b) | 3.000 | 5.00 | 10.00 | 20.00 |
| | 1965(b) | 4.500 | .50 | 1.25 | 2.75 |

ALUMINUM

| 8 | 1969 | 5.000 | 2.50 | 5.00 | 7.50 |

12	1974	13.000	.15	.40	.75
	1977(a)	15.000	.15	.40	.75
	1985	—	.10	.15	.35

2 FRANCS

ALUMINUM
F.A.O. Issue

| 10 | 1970 | 5.000 | .10 | .20 | .50 |

5 FRANCS

BRONZE

KM#	Date	Mintage	VF	XF	Unc
6	1964(b)	4,000	.25	.80	1.75
	1965(b)	3,000	5.00	10.00	20.00

13	1974	7,000	1.00	3.00	5.00
	1977(a)	7,002	1.00	2.00	4.00
	1987	—	—	.15	.25	.70

10 FRANCS

3.7000 g, .900 GOLD, .1085 oz AGW

1	1961	10,000	—	—	60.00
	1961	—	Proof		65.00

COPPER-NICKEL

7	1964(b)	6,000	1.00	2.25	4.50

14.1	1974	6,000	2.50	4.00	7.00

Reduced size.

14.2	1985	—	.30	.75	1.75

20 FRANCS

BRASS

15	1977(a)	22,000	.75	1.75	4.00

25 FRANCS

7.5000 g, .900 GOLD, .2170 oz AGW
Similar to 10 Francs, KM#1.

KM#	Date	Mintage	VF	XF	Unc
2	1961	4,000	—	Proof	110.00

50 FRANCS

15.0000 g, .900 GOLD, .4340 oz AGW
Similar to 10 Francs, KM#1.

3	1961	3,000	—	Proof	225.00

BRASS

16	1977(a)	9,000	2.25	3.50	6.50

100 FRANCS

30.0000 g, .900 GOLD, .8681 oz AGW

4	1961	3,000	—	Proof	450.00

200 FRANCS

18.6200 g, .800 SILVER, .4789 oz ASW
F.A.O. Issue

11	1972	.030	—	7.50	12.50

PROOF SETS (PS)

KM#	Date	Mintage	Identification	Issue Price	Mkt. Val.
PS1	1961(4)	3,000	KM#1-4	—	850.00

RWANDA-BURUNDI

Rwanda-Burundi, a Belgian League of Nations mandate and United Nations trust territory comprising the provinces of Rwanda and Burundi of the former colony of German East Africa, was located in central Africa between the present Republic of the Congo, Uganda and mainland Tanzania. The mandate-trust territory had an area of 20,916 sq. mi. (54,272 sq. km.) and a population of 4.3 million.

For specific statistics and history of Rwanda and of Burundi see individual entries.

When Rwanda and Burundi were formed into a mandate for administration by Belgium, their names were changed to Ruanda and Urundi and they were organized as an integral part of the Belgian Congo. During the mandate-trust territory period, they utilized the coinage of the Belgian Congo, which from 1954 through 1960 carried the appropriate dual identification. After the Belgian Congo acquired independence as the Republic of the Congo, the provinces of Ruanda and Urundi reverted to their former names of Rwanda and Burundi and utilized a common currency issued by a Central Bank (B.E.R.B.) established for that purpose until the time when, as independent republics, each issued its own national coinage.

For earlier coinage see Belgian Congo.

FRANC

BRASS

KM#	Date	Mintage	VF	XF	Unc
1	1960	2,000	.50	1.25	2.00
	1961	16,000	.35	.75	1.25
	1964	3,000	.50	1.00	1.75

NOTE: For later coinage see individual listings under Rwanda and Burundi.

COPPER-NICKEL
Mule. Obv: Rwanda-Burundi, KM#1.
Rev: Belgium, 1 Franc Y#57.

2	1961	50 pcs.	—	—	—

Listings For
SAARLAND: refer to Germany/West

ST. BARTHOLOMEW

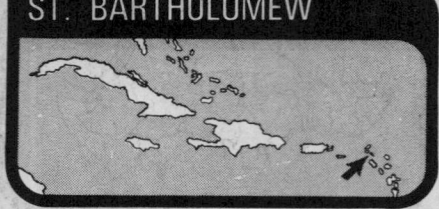

St. Bartholomew (St. Barthelemy, St. Barts), a French island possession located in the Leeward Islands of the West Indies about 15 miles northwest of Guadeloupe, of which it is a dependency, has an area of 10 sq. mi. (26 sq. km.) and a population of about 3,000. Capital: Basse-Terre, on the island of that name. The treeless island produces sugar, bananas, and rum.

St. Bartholomew was occupied by France in 1648 and sold to Sweden in 1784. In 1877 it was reacquired, by purchase, by France.

The coins issued under Sweden for St. Bartholomew -- crown-countermarked U.S. coins, Cayenne sous, Swedish and Polish billon -- have been extensively counterfeited.

RULERS
French, until 1784, 1877—
Swedish, 1784-1877

MONETARY SYSTEM
6 Stivers = 1 Real
11 Reales = 1 Dollar

COUNTERMARKED COINAGE
CENT

COPPER
c/m: Crown on U.S. Large Cent, C#16.

KM#	Date	Mintage	Good	VG	Fine	VF
1	ND	—	125.00	175.00	250.00	400.00

2 SOU

BILLON
c/m: Crown on Cayenne 2 Sou, C#1.

| 2 | ND | — | 100.00 | 150.00 | 250.00 | 350.00 |

STIVER

SILVER
c/m: Crown on Curacao Stiver, C#8.

| 3 | ND | — | 75.00 | 125.00 | 175.00 | 250.00 |

3 STIVERS
SILVER
c/m: Crowned 3/M on Spanish Colonial 1/2 Real.

| 4 | ND(1808) | — | 125.00 | 175.00 | 225.00 | 300.00 |

4 STIVERS
SILVER
c/m: Crowned 4/M on Spanish Colonial 1/2 Real.

| 5 | ND(1808) | — | 125.00 | 175.00 | 225.00 | 300.00 |

REAL

SILVER
c/m: Crown on Spanish Colonial 1 Real.

| 6 | ND | — | 75.00 | 125.00 | 200.00 | 300.00 |

7 STIVERS

SILVER
c/m: Crowned 7/M on Spanish Colonial 1 Real.

KM#	Date	Mintage	Good	VG	Fine	VF
7	ND(1808)	—	125.00	175.00	225.00	300.00

9 STIVERS
SILVER
c/m: Crowned 9/M on Spanish Colonial 1 Real.

| 8 | ND(1808) | — | 150.00 | 200.00 | 250.00 | 325.00 |

c/m: Crowned 9/M on Spanish 2 Reales.

| 9 | ND(1808) | — | 150.00 | 200.00 | 250.00 | 325.00 |

c/m: Crowned 9/M on France 1/10 Ecu, C#39.

| 10 | ND(1808) | — | 150.00 | 200.00 | 250.00 | 325.00 |

14 STIVERS
SILVER
c/m: Crowned 14/M on Spanish Colonial 2 Reales.

| 11 | ND(1808) | — | 150.00 | 200.00 | 250.00 | 325.00 |

2 REALES
SILVER
c/m: Crown on Spanish Colonial 2 Reales.

| 12 | ND | — | 125.00 | 175.00 | 225.00 | 300.00 |

18 STIVERS
SILVER
c/m: Crowned 18/M on Spanish Colonial 2 Reales.

| 13 | ND(1808) | — | 150.00 | 200.00 | 250.00 | 325.00 |

ST. CROIX

St. Croix, which has an area of 82 sq. mi. (212 sq. km.), is with St. Thomas and St. John one of the three principal islands of the more than 50 islands comprising the Virgin Islands of the United States, which are located in the western part of the Virgin Islands east of Puerto Rico and at the western end of the Lesser Antilles. Capital: Charlotte Amalie, on St. Thomas. Politically, the Virgin Islands of the United States are an unincorporated territory administered by the Interior Dept. The inhabitants, who have been citizens of the United States since 1927, have an elected governor, and one delegate to the U.S. House of Representatives who may vote in committee but not on the House floor. Tourism is the largest industry. Watch movements, jewelry, rum, wool, textiles, thermometers, and bay rum are exported.

The Virgin Islands were discovered by Columbus during his second voyage to America in 1493. St. Thomas was colonized by Denmark in 1666, and the entire Danish island group was under the control of the Danish West Indies Company until 1755, when the group was purchased by Frederick V of Denmark and made a royal colony. England occupied the Danish West Indies, during the Napoleonic Wars, in 1801 and again from 1807 to 1815, after which they were restored to Denmark. The United States purchased the Danish West Indies for defense purposes on March 31, 1917, for $25,000,000.

RULERS
Danish, until 1800,
1802-06, 1816-1917
British 1801, 1807-1815

COUNTERMARKED COINAGE
1798-1813
1/4 DOLLAR

.903 SILVER
c/m: StC on Mexico City 2 Reales, KM#90.

KM#	Date	Good	VG	Fine	VF
1	ND(1790)	125.00	175.00	225.00	325.00

c/m: StC on Mexico City 2 Reales, KM#91.

| 2 | ND(1792-1808) | 125.00 | 175.00 | 225.00 | 325.00 |

1/2 DOLLAR

.903 SILVER
c/m: StC on Bolivia (Potosi) 4 Reales, KM#72.

| 3 | ND(1791-1809) | 125.00 | 175.00 | 275.00 | 375.00 |

DOLLAR

.903 SILVER
c/m: StC on Mexico City 8 Reales, KM#107.

KM#	Date	Good	VG	Fine	VF
6	ND(1789-90)	125.00	175.00	275.00	375.00

c/m: StC on Mexico City 8 Reales, KM#109.

| 4 | ND(1791-1808) | 125.00 | 175.00 | 275.00 | 375.00 |

c/m: StC on Mexico City 8 Reales, KM#110.

| 5 | ND(1808-11) | 125.00 | 175.00 | 275.00 | 375.00 |

Listings For
ST. EUSTATIUS: refer to Netherlands Antilles

ST. HELENA & ASCENSION

The colony of St. Helena, a British colony located about 1,150 miles (1,850 km.) from the west coast of Africa, has an area of 47 sq. mi. (122 sq. km.) and a population of *5,000. Capital: Jamestown. Flax, lace, and rope are produced for export. Ascension and Tristan da Cunha are dependencies of St. Helena.

The island was discovered and named by the Portuguese navigator Joao de Nova Castella in 1502. The Portuguese imported livestock, fruit trees, and vegetables but established no permanent settlement. The Dutch occupied the island temporarily, 1645-51. The original European settlement was founded by representatives of the British East India Company sent to annex the island after the departure of the Dutch. The Dutch returned and captured St. Helena from the British on New Year's Day, 1673, but were in turn ejected by a British force under Sir Richard Munden. Thereafter St. Helena was the undisputed possession of Great Britain. The island served as the place of exile for Napoleon, several Zulu chiefs, and an ex-sultan of Zanzibar.

RULERS
British

MINT MARKS
PM - Pobjoy Mint

MONETARY SYSTEM
12 Pence = 1 Shilling

BRITISH EAST INDIA COMPANY
(1651-1834)
HALF PENNY

COPPER

KM#	Date	Mintage	Fine	VF	XF	Unc
4	1821	—	6.00	12.00	35.00	80.00
(1)	1821				Proof	125.00

BRONZE

| 4a | 1821 | | | | Proof | 125.00 |
| (1a) | | | | | | |

GILT BRONZE

| 4b | 1821 | | | | Proof | Rare |
| (1b) | | | | | | |

DECIMAL COINAGE
100 Pence = 1 Pound
25 PENCE

COPPER-NICKEL
St. Helena Tercentenary

KM#	Date	Mintage	Fine	VF	XF	Unc
5	1973	.100	—	—	—	3.00

28.2800 g, .925 SILVER, .8411 oz ASW

| 5a | 1973 | .010 | — | — | Proof | 20.00 |

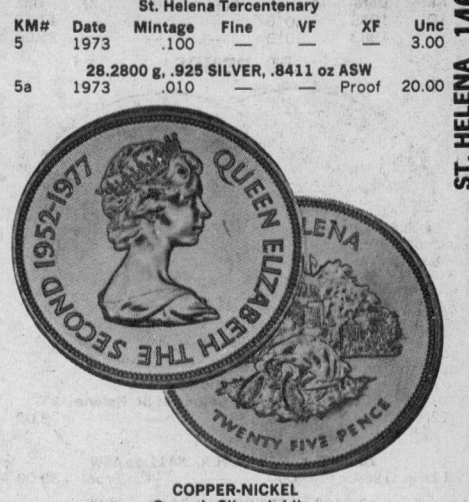

COPPER-NICKEL
Queen's Silver Jubilee

| 6 | 1977 | .050 | — | — | — | 3.00 |

28.2800 g, .925 SILVER, .8411 oz ASW

| 6a | 1977 | .025 | — | — | Proof | 22.00 |

COPPER-NICKEL
80th Birthday of Queen Mother

| 8 | 1980 | .100 | — | — | — | 3.00 |

28.2800 g, .925 SILVER, .8411 oz ASW

| 8a | 1980 | .025 | — | — | Proof | 20.00 |

COPPER-NICKEL
Wedding of Prince Charles and Lady Diana

| 9 | 1981 | .050 | — | — | — | 3.00 |

28.2800 g, .925 SILVER, .8411 oz ASW

| 9a | 1981 | .030 | — | — | Proof | 25.00 |

International Year of the Scout

ST. HELENA

KM# 1468

Obv: Portrait of Queen.

KM#	Date	Mintage	Fine	VF	XF	Unc
10	1983	.010	—	—	—	17.50
	1983	.010	—	—	Proof	25.00

50 PENCE

COPPER-NICKEL
150th Anniversary of Colony of St. Helena

| 12 | 1984 | .010 | — | — | — | 3.00 |

28.2800 g, .925 SILVER, .8411 oz ASW

| 12a | 1984 | 5,000 | — | — | Proof | 30.00 |

47.5400 g, .917 GOLD, 1.4017 oz AGW

| 12b | 1984 | 150 pcs. | — | — | Proof | 875.00 |

COPPER-NICKEL
Royal Visit of Prince Andrew

| 13 | 1984 | .125 | — | — | — | 3.00 |

28.2800 g, .925 SILVER, .8411 oz ASW

| 13a | 1984 | 5,000 | — | — | Proof | 35.00 |

CROWN

COPPER-NICKEL
25th Anniversary of Coronation

| 7 | 1978PM | — | — | — | — | 3.00 |

28.2800 g, .925 SILVER, .8411 oz ASW

| 7a | 1978PM | .070 | — | — | — | 15.00 |
| | 1978PM | .025 | — | — | Proof | 22.00 |

2 POUNDS

15.9800 g, .917 GOLD, .4712 oz AGW

International Year of the Scout

KM#	Date	Mintage	Fine	VF	XF	Unc
11	1983	2,000	—	—	—	400.00
	1983	2,000	—	—	Proof	450.00

ASCENSION ISLAND

An island of volcanic origin, Ascension Island lies in the south Atlantic 700 miles (1,100 km.) northwest of St. Helena. It has an area of 34 sq. mi. (88 sq. km.) on an island 9 miles (14 km.) long and 6 miles (10 km.) wide. Approximate population: 1,146. Although having little vegetation and scant rainfall, the island has a very healthy climate. The island is the nesting place for large numbers of sea turtles and sooty terns. Phosphates and guano are the chief natural sources of income.

The island was discovered on Ascension Day, 1501, by Joao da Nova, a Portuguese navigator. It lay unoccupied until 1815 when occupied by the British. It was under Admiralty rule until 1922 when it was annexed as a dependency of St. Helena. During World War II an airfield was built that has been used as a fueling stop for transatlantic flights to Southern Europe, North Africa and the Near East.

RULERS
British

MINT MARKS
PM - Pobjoy Mint

25 PENCE

COPPER-NICKEL
Wedding of Prince Charles and Lady Diana

| 3 | 1981PM | .050 | — | — | — | 3.00 |

28.2800 g, .925 SILVER, .8411 oz ASW

| 3a | 1981PM | 500 pcs. | — | — | Proof | 50.00 |

International Year of the Scout

| 4 | 1983 | .010 | — | — | — | 20.00 |
| | 1983 | .010 | — | — | Proof | 30.00 |

50 PENCE

COPPER-NICKEL

Royal Visit of Prince Andrew

KM#	Date	Mintage	Fine	VF	XF	Unc
6	1984	.125	—	—	—	3.00

28.2800 g, .925 SILVER, .8411 oz ASW

| 6a | 1984 | 5,000 | — | — | Proof | 30.00 |

CROWN

COPPER-NICKEL
25th Anniversary of Coronation

| 1 | 1978PM | — | — | — | — | 3.00 |

28.2800 g, .925 SILVER, .8411 oz ASW

| 1a | 1978PM | .070 | — | — | — | 15.00 |
| | 1978PM | .025 | — | — | Proof | 25.00 |

Mule. Obv: Isle of Man crown. Rev: Ascension KM#1.

| 2 | 1978PM (error) 367 pcs. | — | — | — | 200.00 | 250.00 |

2 POUNDS

15.9800 g, .917 GOLD, .4712 oz AGW
International Year of the Scout
Obv: Portrait of Queen Elizabeth.
Rev: Boy Scout viewing landscape.

| 5 | 1983 | 2,000 | — | — | — | 400.00 |
| | 1983 | 2,000 | — | — | Proof | 500.00 |

ST. HELENA-ASCENSION

PENNY

BRONZE

| 1 | 1984 | — | — | — | — | .15 |
| | 1984 | *.010 | — | — | Proof | 1.25 |

2 PENCE

BRONZE

| 2 | 1984 | — | — | — | — | .25 |
| | 1984 | *.010 | — | — | Proof | 1.50 |

5 PENCE

COPPER-NICKEL

KM#	Date	Mintage	Fine	VF	XF	Unc
3	1984	—	—	—	.10	.35
	1984	—	—	—	Proof	1.75

10 PENCE

COPPER-NICKEL

4	1984	—	—	—	.20	.50
	1984	—	—	—	Proof	2.00

50 PENCE

COPPER-NICKEL

5	1984	—	—	—	1.00	1.50
	1984	—	—	—	Proof	2.50

Prince Andrew's Marriage

7	1986	.013	—	—	—	4.00

28.2800 g, .925 SILVER, .8411 oz ASW

7a	1986	2,500	—	—	Proof	35.00

47.5400 g, .917 GOLD, 1.4017 oz AGW

7b	1986	50 pcs.	—	—	Proof	1200.

COPPER-NICKEL
Anniversary of Napoleon's Death

8	1986	.050	—	—	—	5.00

POUND

NICKEL-BRASS

KM#	Date	Mintage	Fine	VF	XF	Unc
6	1984	—	—	—	1.75	2.25
	1984	—	—	—	Proof	3.50

9.5000 g, .925 SILVER, .2826 oz ASW

6a	1984	.010	—	—	Proof	25.00

25 POUNDS

155.0000 g, .999 SILVER, 4.9839 oz ASW
Anniversary of Napoleon's Death
Reduced. Actual size: 65mm
Obv: Similar to 50 Pence, KM#7.

9	1986	.015	—	—	Proof	110.00

50 POUNDS

32.2600 g, .999 PLATINUM, 1.0051 oz APW
Anniversary of Napoleon's Death

10	1986	5,000	—	—	Proof	850.00

MINT SETS (MS)

KM#	Date	Mintage	Identification	Mkt.Val.
MS1	1984	—	KM1-6	5.50

ST. KITTS & NEVIS

St. Kitts (St. Christopher), a West Indian island located in the Leeward Islands southeast of Puerto Rico, is the principal component of a British associated state composed of the islands of St. Kitts, Nevis, and Anguilla. The associated state has an area of 104 sq. mi. (269 sq. km.) and a population of *40,000. Capital: Basseterre, on St. Kitts. The islands export sugar, molasses, rum, cotton, and coconuts.

St. Kitts was discovered by Columbus in 1493 and was settled by Thomas Warner, an Englishman, in 1623. The island was ceded to the British by the Treaty of Utrecht, 1713. France protested British occupancy, and on three occasions between 1616 and 1782 seized the island and held it for short periods. In early 1967 St. Kitts was united politically with Nevis and Anguilla to form a self-governing British associated state. In June 1967 Anguilla declared its independence of the federated state, and in Feb. 1969 unilaterally severed all ties with Britain and established the Republic of Anguilla. Britain refused to accept the unilateral movement and installed a commissioner to govern Anguilla, which remains a nominal part of the associated state. The political status of the three islands will be decided in the near future by a referendum.

From approximately 1750-1830, billon 2 sous of the French colony of Cayenne were countermarked 'SK' and used on St. Kitts. They were valued at 1-1/3 Pence.

RULERS
British

MONETARY SYSTEM
19th Century
108 Pence = 9 Shillings =
12 Bits = 1 Dollar
20th Century
100 Cents = 1 Dollar

NOTE: The grades shown describe the condition of the countermark, not the host coin itself, which is typically well worn.

SAINT KITTS

COUNTERMARKED COINAGE
1-1/2 PENCE
Black Dog

BILLON
c/m: S on French Colonies 24 Deniers, C#6.

KM#	Date	Mintage	Good	VG	Fine	VF
1	(1801)	—	50.00	75.00	100.00	125.00

2-1/4 PENCE

BILLON
c/m: S.K. on French Guyana 2 Sous, C#1.

2	(1809-1812)	—	50.00	75.00	100.00	125.00

1/8 DOLLAR

SILVER
c/m: S on cut 1/8 section of Spanish 8 Reales.

3	(1801)	—	175.00	300.00	400.00	500.00

1/4 DOLLAR

SILVER
c/m: S on 1/4 section of Spanish 8 Reales.

4	(1801)	—	175.00	300.00	400.00	500.00

SAINT KITTS 1470

1/2 DOLLAR

SILVER
c/m: S on 1/2 section of Spanish 8 Reales.

KM#	Date	Mintage	Good	VG	Fine	VF
5	(1801)	—	175.00	300.00	400.00	500.00

NEVIS

Nevis, a component of one of the West Indies Associated States, is located in the Leeward Islands and has an area of 50 sq. mi. (105 sq. km.) and a population of about 12,000. Charleston is the chief town and port. Sea-island cotton is the chief crop, and some sugar is produced.

Nevis was discovered by Columbus in 1493. It was first colonized by the English in 1628. Admiral De Grasse captured the island for France in 1782, but it was restored to Britain the following year. Alexander Hamilton, first Secretary of the Treasury, was born on Nevis in 1757.

RULERS
British

MONETARY SYSTEM
72 Black Dogs = 1 Dollar

COUNTERMARKED COINAGE
BLACK DOG

BILLON
c/m: NEVIS on French Guiana 2 Sous.

KM#	Date	Mintage	Good	VG	Fine
1	ND(1801)	—	75.00	100.00	175.00

4 BLACK DOGS
SILVER
c/m: NEVIS over incuse 4.

2	ND	—	125.00	200.00	325.00

6 BLACK DOGS
SILVER
c/m: NEVIS over incuse 6.

3	ND	—	135.00	210.00	335.00

7 BLACK DOGS
SILVER
c/m: NEVIS over incuse 7.

4	ND	—	125.00	200.00	325.00

9 BLACK DOGS

SILVER
c/m: NEVIS over incuse 9.

5	ND	—	100.00	200.00	300.00

ST. CHRISTOPHER & NEVIS

4 DOLLARS

COPPER-NICKEL
F.A.O. Issue

KM#	Date	Mintage	Fine	VF	XF	Unc
1	1970	.013	—	—	3.00	9.00
	1970	2,000	—	—	Proof	20.00

10 DOLLARS

COPPER-NICKEL
Royal Visit

3	1985	.100	—	—	7.50

28.2800 g, .925 SILVER, .8411 oz ASW
3a	1985	5,000	—	Proof	35.00

47.5400 g, .917 GOLD, 1.4013 oz AGW
3b	1985	250 pcs.	—	Proof	1200.

20 DOLLARS

COPPER-NICKEL
Independence

2	1983	—	—	—	15.00

28.2800 g, .925 SILVER, .8411 oz ASW
2a	1983	5,000	—	Proof	35.00

ST. KITTS & NEVIS

MONETARY SYSTEM
100 Cents = 1 Dollar

20 DOLLARS

COPPER-NICKEL
200th Anniversary of Battle of the Saints

KM#	Date	Mintage	VF	XF	Unc
1	1982	—	—	—	10.00

28.2800 g, .925 SILVER, .8411 oz ASW
1a	1982	2,500	—	Proof	40.00

100 DOLLARS

7.9900 g, .917 GOLD, .2356 oz AGW
Siege of Brimstone Hill
2	1982	15 pcs.	—	Proof	500.00

ST. LUCIA

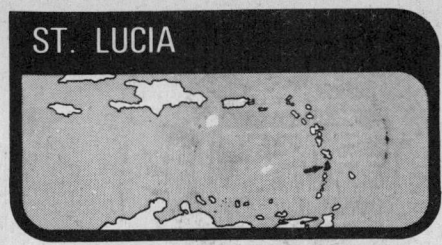

Saint Lucia, an independent island nation located in the Windward Islands of the West Indies between St. Vincent and Martinique, has an area of 238 sq. mi. (616 sq. km.) and a population of *128,000. Capital: Castries. The economy is agricultural. Bananas, copra, cocoa, sugar and logwood are exported.

Saint Lucia was discovered by Columbus in 1502. The first attempts at settlement undertaken by the British in 1605 and 1638 were frustrated by sickness and the determined hostility of the fierce Carib inhabitants. The French settled it in 1650 and made a treaty with the natives. Until 1814, when the island became a definite British possession, it was the scene of a continuous conflict between the British and French which saw the island change hands on at least 14 occasions. In 1967, under the West Indies Act, Saint Lucia was established as a British associated state, self-governing in internal affairs. Complete independence was attained on February 22, 1979. Saint Lucia is a member of the Commonwealth of Nations. The Queen of England is Chief of State.

RULERS
British

MONETARY SYSTEM
12 Deniers = 1 Sou
15 Sous = 1 Escalin
20 Sous = 1 Livre
6 Black Dogs = 4 Stampees
= 1 Bit = 9 Pence

COUNTERMARKED COLONIAL COINAGE

1811
3 STAMPEES
SILVER
c/m: Circle w/crenalated edges on 1/4 cut of Spanish or Spanish Colonial 2 Reales.

KM#	Date	Mintage	Good	VG	Fine	VF
5	ND(1811)	—	20.00	30.00	50.00	100.00

ESCALIN

SILVER, 2.00 G
c/m: Circle on 1/3 cut of Spanish or Spanish Colonial 2 Reales.

| 6 | ND(1811) | — | 20.00 | 30.00 | 45.00 | 75.00 |

1-1/2 ESCALINS
SILVER
c/m: Two circles on 1/4 cut of Spanish or Spanish Colonial 4 Reales.

| 7 | ND(1811) | — | 25.00 | 40.00 | 60.00 | 100.00 |

2 ESCALINS
SILVER, 4.00 g
c/m: Three circles on 1/3 cut of Spanish or Spanish Colonial 4 Reales.

| 8 | ND(1811) | — | 25.00 | 40.00 | 60.00 | 100.00 |

1813
2 LIVRES, 5 SOUS

SILVER, 5.30 g
c/m: S:Lucie on 1/3 outer cut of Spanish or Spanish Colonial 8 Reales.

| 9 | ND(1813) | — | 30.00 | 50.00 | 70.00 | 115.00 |

6 LIVRES, 15 SOUS

SILVER, 15.00 g
c/m: S:Lucie on 1/3 center cut of Spanish or Spanish Colonial 8 Reales.

| 10 | ND(1813) | — | 60.00 | 110.00 | 160.00 | 200.00 |

NOTE: There are no known genuine examples existing today of any other similar varieties cut from Spanish or Spanish Colonial 2 and 4 Reales with this countermark.

MODERN COINAGE
MONETARY SYSTEM
100 Cents = 1 Dollar

4 DOLLARS

COPPER-NICKEL
F.A.O. Issue

KM#	Date	Mintage	VF	XF	Unc
11	1970	.013	—	3.00	9.00
	1970	2,000	—	Proof	20.00

5 DOLLARS

COPPER-NICKEL
Papal Visit
Obv: Similar to 10 Dollars, KM#12.

| 14 | 1986 | — | — | — | 5.00 |

28.2800 g, .925 SILVER, .8411 oz ASW

| 14a | 1986 | 2,500 | — | Proof | 40.00 |

10 DOLLARS

COPPER-NICKEL
200th Anniversary of Battle of the Saints

| 12 | 1982 | — | — | — | 10.00 |

28.2800 g, .925 SILVER, .8411 oz ASW

KM#	Date	Mintage	VF	XF	Unc
12a	1982	2,500	—	Proof	35.00

COPPER-NICKEL
Royal Visit

| 13 | 1985 | .100 | — | — | 7.50 |

28.2800 g, .925 SILVER, .8411 oz ASW

| 13a | 1985 | 5,000 | — | Proof | 35.00 |

47.5400 g, .917 GOLD, 1.4013 oz AGW

| 13b | 1985 | 250 pcs. | — | Proof | 1200. |

28.2800 g, .925 SILVER, .8411 oz ASW
Commonwealth Finance Ministers Meeting

| 16 | 1986 | 1,000 | — | Proof | 30.00 |

500 DOLLARS

15.9800 g, .917 GOLD, .4709 oz AGW
Papal Visit

| 15 | 1986 | 100 pcs. | — | Proof | 750.00 |

ST. PIERRE & MIQUELON

The Territory of St. Pierre and Miquelon, a French overseas territory located 10 miles (16 km.) off the south coast of Newfoundland, has an area of 93 sq. mi. (242 sq. km.) and a population of *6,041. Capital: St. Pierre. The economy of the barren archipelago is based on cod fishing and fur farming. Fish and fish products, and mink and silver fox pelts are exported.

The islands, occupied by the French in 1604, were captured by the British in 1702 and held until 1763 when they were returned to the possession of France and employed as a fishing station. They passed between France and England on six more occasions between 1778 and 1814 when they were awarded permanently to France by the Treaty of Paris. The rugged, soil-poor granite islands, which will support only evergreen shrubs, are all that remain to France of her extensive colonies in North America. In 1958 St. Pierre and Miquelon voted in favor of the new constitution of the Fifth Republic of France, thereby choosing to remain within the new French Community.

RULERS
French

MINT MARKS
(a) - Paris, privy marks only

MONETARY SYSTEM
100 Centimes = 1 Franc

FRANC

ALUMINUM

KM#	Date	Mintage	Fine	VF	XF	Unc
1	1948(a)	.600	.50	.75	1.25	3.50

2 FRANCS

ALUMINUM

2	1948(a)	.300	.75	1.00	2.00	4.50

ST. THOMAS & PRINCE

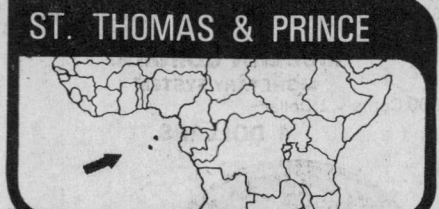

The Democratic Republic of Sao Tome and Principe (formerly the Portuguese overseas province of St. Thomas and Prince Islands) is located in the Gulf of Guinea 150 miles (241 km.) off the west African coast. It has an area of 372 sq. mi. (964 sq. km.) and a population of *114,000. Capital: Sao Tome. The economy of the islands is based on cocoa, copra and coffee.

St. Thomas and St. Prince were uninhabited when discovered by Portuguese navigators Joao de Santarem and Pedro de Escobar in 1470. After the failure of their initial settlement, 1485, the Portuguese successfully colonized St. Thomas with a colony of prisoners and exiled Jews, 1493. An initial prosperity based on the sugar trade gave way to a time of misfortune, 1567-1709, that saw the colony attacked and occupied or plundered by the French and Dutch; ravaged by the slave revolt of 1595; and finally rendered destitute by the transfer of the world sugar trade to Brazil. In the late 1800s, the colony turned from the production of sugar to cocoa, the basis of its present prosperity.

The islands were designated a Portuguese overseas province in 1951. On April 25, 1974, the government of Portugal was seized by a military junta which reached agreements providing for independence for the Portuguese overseas provinces of Portuguese Guinea (Guinea-Bissau), Mozambique, Cape Verde Islands, Angola, and St. Thomas and Prince Islands. The Democratic Republic of Sao Tome and Principe was declared on July 12, 1975.

RULERS
Portuguese, until 1975

20 REIS

COPPER

KM#	Date	Mintage	VG	Fine	VF	XF
A1	1813R	—	10.00	15.00	25.00	40.00
(15)	1815R	—	10.00	15.00	25.00	40.00

| D1 | 1819 Rio | — | 2.00 | 4.50 | 10.00 | 18.00 |
| (18) | 1825 | — | 3.00 | 5.00 | 11.50 | 20.00 |

NOTE: Previously listed in Mozambique.

40 REIS

COPPER

B1	1813 Rio	—	12.00	20.00	30.00	50.00
(16)	1815 Rio	—	20.00	30.00	45.00	60.00
E1	1819 Rio	—	3.75	7.50	15.00	25.00
(19)	1821 Bahia	—	3.50	7.50	15.00	25.00
	1821 Lisbon	—	2.00	4.50	9.00	13.50
	1822	—	20.00	30.00	45.00	60.00
	1825	—	4.00	6.00	11.50	16.50

NOTE: The difference between the Bahia and Lisbon coins is slight. The crown on the Bahia issue being rounder, approximately 2mm between the crown and rim.
NOTE: Previously listed in Mozambique.

80 REIS

COPPER

KM#	Date	Mintage	VG	Fine	VF	XF
C1 (17)	1813R	—	10.00	15.00	22.50	40.00
F1 (20)	1819 Rio	—	7.50	12.50	20.00	35.00
	1825	—	5.00	8.00	12.50	20.00

NOTE: Previously listed in Mozambique.

MONETARY REFORM
MONETARY SYSTEM
100 Centavos = 1 Escudo
100 Centimos = 1 Dobra

10 CENTAVOS

NICKEL-BRONZE

KM#	Date	Mintage	Fine	VF	XF	Unc
2	1929	.500	1.00	2.00	5.00	12.50

BRONZE

KM#	Date	Mintage	VF	XF	Unc
15	1962	.500	.10	.25	1.75

ALUMINUM

| 15a | 1971 | 1.000 | .10 | .15 | .25 |

20 CENTAVOS

NICKEL-BRONZE

KM#	Date	Mintage	Fine	VF	XF	Unc
3	1929	.250	1.25	2.50	5.00	12.50

BRONZE
18mm

KM#	Date	Mintage	VF	XF	Unc
16.1	1962	.250	.25	.50	3.00

ST. THOMAS & PRINCE ISLANDS

50 CENTAVOS

KM#	Date	Mintage	VF	XF	Unc
16.2	1971	.750	.10	.15	.25

16mm

NICKEL-BRONZE

KM#	Date	Mintage	Fine	VF	XF	Unc
1	1928	—	7.50	12.50	35.00	250.00
	1929	.400	2.50	5.00	15.00	200.00

KM#	Date	Mintage	VF	XF	Unc
8	1948	.080	2.00	10.00	40.00

COPPER-NICKEL

| 10 | 1951 | .050 | 2.00 | 10.00 | 40.00 |

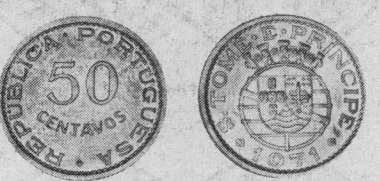

BRONZE
20mm

| 17.1 | 1962 | .480 | .25 | .50 | 1.75 |

22mm

| 17.2 | 1971 | .600 | .10 | .15 | .35 |

ESCUDO

COPPER-NICKEL

KM#	Date	Mintage	Fine	VF	XF	Unc
4	1939	.100	2.00	5.00	15.00	85.00

NICKEL-BRONZE

KM#	Date	Mintage	VF	XF	Unc
9	1948	.060	2.00	7.00	35.00

COPPER-NICKEL

KM#	Date	Mintage	VF	XF	Unc
11	1951	.018	7.50	18.50	65.00

BRONZE

| 18 | 1962 | .160 | .25 | .75 | 2.00 |
| | 1971 | .350 | .15 | .25 | .50 |

2-1/2 ESCUDOS

3.5000 g, .650 SILVER, .0732 oz ASW

KM#	Date	Mintage	Fine	VF	XF	Unc
5	1939	.080	4.00	8.00	22.00	55.00
	1948	.120	4.00	4.00	9.00	30.00

KM#	Date	Mintage	VF	XF	Unc
12	1951	.060	5.00	8.00	25.00

COPPER-NICKEL

| 19 | 1962 | .140 | .50 | 1.00 | 2.25 |
| | 1971 | .250 | .15 | .25 | .50 |

5 ESCUDOS

7.0000 g, .650 SILVER, .1462 oz ASW

KM#	Date	Mintage	Fine	VF	XF	Unc
6	1939	.060	5.00	10.00	25.00	65.00
	1948	.100	4.00	6.00	15.00	35.00

25mm

KM#	Date	Mintage	VF	XF	Unc
13	1951	.070	5.00	15.00	30.00

4.0000 g, .600 SILVER, .0771 oz ASW
22mm

KM#	Date	Mintage	VF	XF	Unc
20	1962	.090	1.25	2.50	5.00

COPPER-NICKEL

| 22 | 1971 | .160 | .50 | 1.00 | 2.25 |

10 ESCUDOS

12.5000 g, .835 SILVER, .3356 oz ASW

| 7 | 1939 | .040 | 15.00 | 30.00 | 100.00 |

12.5000 g, .720 SILVER, .2894 oz ASW

| 14 | 1951 | .040 | 4.00 | 12.00 | 25.00 |

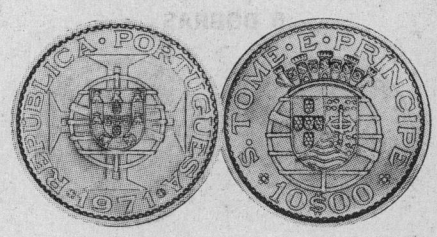

COPPER-NICKEL

| 23 | 1971 | .100 | .75 | 1.25 | 5.00 |

20 ESCUDOS

NICKEL

| 24 | 1971 | .060 | 1.50 | 3.00 | 8.00 |

1473

ST. THOMAS & PRINCE ISLANDS 1474

50 ESCUDOS

18.0000 g, .650 SILVER, .3762 oz ASW
500th Anniversary of Discovery

KM#	Date	Mintage	VF	XF	Unc
21	1970	1,000	—	—	10.00

DECIMAL COINAGE
100 Centimos = 1 Dobra

50 CENTIMOS

BRASS
F.A.O. Issue

25	1977	2,000	.10	.15	.30
	1977	2,500	—	Proof	3.00

DOBRA

BRASS
F.A.O. Issue

26	1977	1,500	.10	.15	.50
	1977	2,500	—	Proof	3.00

2 DOBRAS

COPPER-NICKEL
F.A.O. Issue

27	1977	1,000	.20	.30	.80
	1977	2,500	—	Proof	3.50

5 DOBRAS

COPPER-NICKEL
F.A.O. Issue

28	1977	750	.30	.50	1.20
	1977	2,500	—	Proof	5.00

10 DOBRAS

COPPER-NICKEL
F.A.O. Issue

29	1977	300	.60	1.00	2.25
	1977	2,500	—	Proof	5.00

20 DOBRAS

COPPER-NICKEL
F.A.O. Issue

KM#	Date	Mintage	VF	XF	Unc
30	1977	500	1.00	1.50	3.00
	1977	2,500	—	Proof	7.50

International Games - Gymnast

43	1984	—	—	Proof	20.00

100 DOBRAS

COPPER-NICKEL
World Fisheries Conference

41	ND(1984)	1,000	—	—	5.00

28.2800 g, .925 SILVER, .8411 oz ASW

41a	ND(1984)	.020	—	Proof	17.50

47.5400 g, .917 GOLD, 1.4017 oz AGW

41b	ND(1984)	100 pcs.	—	Proof	1450.

COPPER-NICKEL
10th Anniversary of Independence

KM#	Date	Mintage	VF	XF	Unc
42	ND(1985)	—	—	—	4.00

28.2800 g, .925 SILVER, .8411 oz ASW

42a	ND(1985)	1,000	—	Proof	35.00

47.5400 g, .917 GOLD, 1.4017 oz AGW

42b	ND(1985)	50 pcs.	—	Proof	1500.

250 DOBRAS

17.4000 g, .925 SILVER, .5175 oz ASW
World Population

31	1977	450 pcs.	—	—	55.00
	1977	750 pcs.	—	Proof	50.00

World Friendship

32	1977	450 pcs.	—	—	55.00
	1977	800 pcs.	—	Proof	50.00

Folklore

33	1977	300 pcs.	—	—	55.00
	1977	600 pcs.	—	Proof	50.00

World Unity

34	1977	400 pcs.	—	—	55.00
	1977	700 pcs.	—	Proof	50.00

Mother and Child

KM#	Date	Mintage	VF	XF	Unc
35	1977	350 pcs.	—	—	55.00
	1977	700 pcs.	—	Proof	50.00

2500 DOBRAS

6.4800 g, .900 GOLD, .1875 oz AGW
World Friendship

36	1977	100 pcs.	—	—	185.00
	1977	170 pcs.	—	Proof	175.00

World Population

37	1977	100 pcs.	—	—	185.00
	1977	170 pcs.	—	Proof	175.00

Folklore

38	1977	100 pcs.	—	—	185.00
	1977	170 pcs.	—	Proof	175.00

World Unity

39	1977	100 pcs.	—	—	185.00
	1977	170 pcs.	—	Proof	175.00

Mother and Child

40	1977	100 pcs.	—	—	185.00
	1977	170 pcs.	—	Proof	175.00

MINT SETS (MS)

KM#	Date	Mintage	Identification	Issue Price	Mkt. Val.
MS1	1977(5)	—	KM31-35	71.00	275.00
MS2	1977(5)	—	KM36-40	655.00	750.00

PROOF SETS (PS)

PS1	1977(5)	—	KM31-35	93.50	250.00
PS2	1977(5)	—	KM36-40	805.00	875.00

ST. VINCENT

St. Vincent and the Grenadines, consisting of the island of St. Vincent and the northern Grenadines (a string of islets stretching southward from St. Vincent), is located in the Windward Islands of the West Indies, West of Barbados and south of St. Lucia. The tiny nation has an area of 150 sq. mi. (388 sq. km.) and a population of *112,000. Capital: Kingstown. Arrowroot, cotton, sugar, molasses, rum, and cocoa are exported. Tourism is a principal industry.

St. Vincent was discovered by Columbus on Jan. 22, 1498, but was left undisturbed for more than a century. The British began colonization early in the 18th century against bitter and prolonged Carib resistance. The island was taken by the French in 1779, but was restored to the British in 1783, at the end of the American Revolution. St. Vincent and the northern Grenadines became a British associated state in Oct. 1969. Independence under the name of St. Vincent and the Grenadines was attained at midnight of Oct. 26, 1979. The new nation chose to become a member of the Commonwealth of Nations with the Queen of England as Chief of State.

RULERS
British

MONETARY SYSTEM
1797-1811
8 Shillings, 3 Pence = 11 Bits
= 1 Dollar
Commencing 1811
9 Shillings = 12 Bits = 1 Dollar
Commencing 1979
100 Cents = 1 Dollar

COUNTERMARKED COINAGE
BLACK DOG

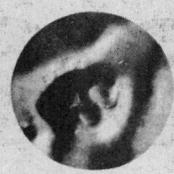

BILLON
c/m: Intaglio S.

KM#	Date	Mintage	Good	VG	Fine	VF
7	ND(1814)	—	25.00	50.00	75.00	100.00

STAMPEE

BILLON
c/m: Intaglio S on French Colonial coin bearing a crowned C c/m.

8	ND(1814)	—	25.00	50.00	75.00	100.00

IV - 1/2 BITS

SILVER
c/m: S/IV 1/2/B on Spanish or Spanish Colonial 2 Reales.

9	ND(1811-14)	—	100.00	200.00	300.00	350.00

VI BITS

SILVER
c/m: S/VI on 23mm center disk cut from Spanish or Spanish Colonial 8 Reales.

10	ND(1811-14)	—	100.00	150.00	200.00	300.00

IX BITS

SILVER
c/m: S/IX on Spanish or Spanish American 4 Reales.

KM#	Date	Mintage	Good	VG	Fine	VF
11	ND(1811-14)	—	750.00	1000.	1300.	1500.

XII BITS

SILVER
c/m: S/XII on holed Spanish or Spanish Colonial 8 Reales.

12	ND(1811-14)	—	500.00	750.00	1000.	1200.

NOTE: Refer to VI Bits, KM#10.

MODERN COINAGE
4 DOLLARS

COPPER-NICKEL
F.A.O. Issue

KM#	Date	Mintage	VF	XF	Unc
13	1970	.013	—	3.00	9.00
	1970	2,000	—	Proof	20.00

10 DOLLARS

COPPER-NICKEL
Royal Visit

14	1985	.100	—	—	7.50

28.2800 g, .925 SILVER, .8411 oz ASW

14a	1985	5,000	—	Proof	40.00

47.5400 g, .917 GOLD, 1.4013 oz AGW

14b	1985	250 pcs.	—	Proof	1200.

Listings For
SAMOA: refer to Western Samoa

SAN MARINO

The Republic of San Marino, the oldest and smallest republic in the world is located in north central Italy entirely surrounded by the Province of Emilia-Romagna. It has an area of 24 sq. mi. (61 sq. km.) and a population of *23,000. Capital: San Marino. The principal economic activities are farming, livestock raising, cheesemaking, tourism and light manufacturing. Building stone, lime, wheat, hides and baked goods are exported. The government derives most of its revenue from the sale of postage stamps for philatelic purposes.

According to tradition, San Marino was founded about 350 AD by a Christian stonecutter as a refuge against religious persecution. While gradually acquiring the institutions of an independent state, it avoided the factional fights of the Middle Ages and, except for a brief period in fief to Cesare Borgia, retained its freedom despite attacks on its sovereignty by the Papacy, the lords of Rimini, Napoleon and Mussolini. In 1862 San Marino established a customs union with, and put itself under the protection of, Italy. A Communist-Socialist coalition controlled the Government for 12 years after World War II. The Christian Democratic Party has been the core of Government since 1957.

San Marino has its own coinage, but Italian and Vatican City coins and currency are also in circulation.

MINT MARKS
M - Milan
R - Rome

MONETARY SYSTEM
100 Centesimi = 1 Lira

5 CENTESIMI

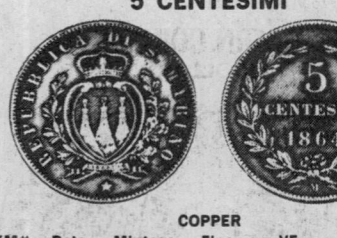

COPPER

KM#	Date	Mintage	Fine	VF	XF	Unc
1	1864M	.280	4.00	7.00	20.00	100.00
	1869M	.600	3.00	6.00	12.00	30.00
	1894R	.600	3.00	5.00	10.00	25.00

BRONZE

12	1935R	.400	1.25	2.00	3.00	6.00
	1936R	.400	1.25	2.00	3.00	6.00
	1937R	.400	1.25	2.00	3.00	6.00
	1938R	.200	1.50	2.50	3.75	7.50

10 CENTESIMI

COPPER

2	1875(m)	.150	4.00	8.00	25.00	60.00
	1893R	.150	4.00	7.50	22.00	45.00
	1894R	.150	4.00	7.50	22.00	45.00

BRONZE

13	1935R	.300	1.50	2.50	4.00	7.50
	1936R	.300	1.50	2.50	4.00	7.50
	1937R	.300	1.50	2.50	4.00	7.50
	1938R	.400	1.50	2.50	4.00	7.50

50 CENTESIMI

2.5000 g, .835 SILVER, .0671 oz ASW

3	1898R	.040	10.00	17.50	25.00	45.00

LIRA

5.0000 g, .835 SILVER, .1342 oz ASW

4	1898R	.020	17.50	27.50	37.50	75.00
	1906R	.030	15.00	22.50	35.00	65.00

ALUMINUM

KM#	Date	Mintage	VF	XF	Unc
14	1972	.291	—	.10	.20
22	1973	.291	—	.10	.20
30	1974	.276	—	.10	.20
40	1975	.291	—	.10	.20
51	1976	.195	—	.10	.20

F.A.O. Issue

63	1977	1.180	—	.10	.20
76	1978	.130	—	.15	.30
89	1979	.125	—	.15	.30

1980 Olympics

KM#	Date	Mintage	VF	XF	Unc
102	1980	.125	—	.15	.30

World Food Day

116	1981	.100	—	.15	.30

Social Conquest

131	1982	.100	—	.15	.30

Nuclear War Threat - Beast of War

145	1983	.072	—	.20	.40

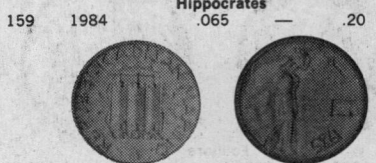

Hippocrates

159	1984	.065	—	.20	.40

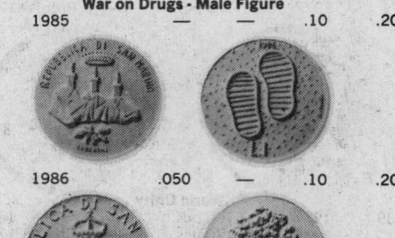

War on Drugs - Male Figure

173	1985		—	.10	.20
187	1986	.050	—	.10	.20
201	1987	.080	—	.10	.20

Fortifications - Corner Tower

218	1988	*.080	—	.10	.20

2 LIRE

10.0000 g, .835 SILVER, .2684 oz ASW

KM#	Date	Mintage	Fine	VF	XF	Unc
5	1898R	.010	20.00	37.50	55.00	175.00
	1906R	.015	20.00	37.50	55.00	155.00

SAN MARINO 1477

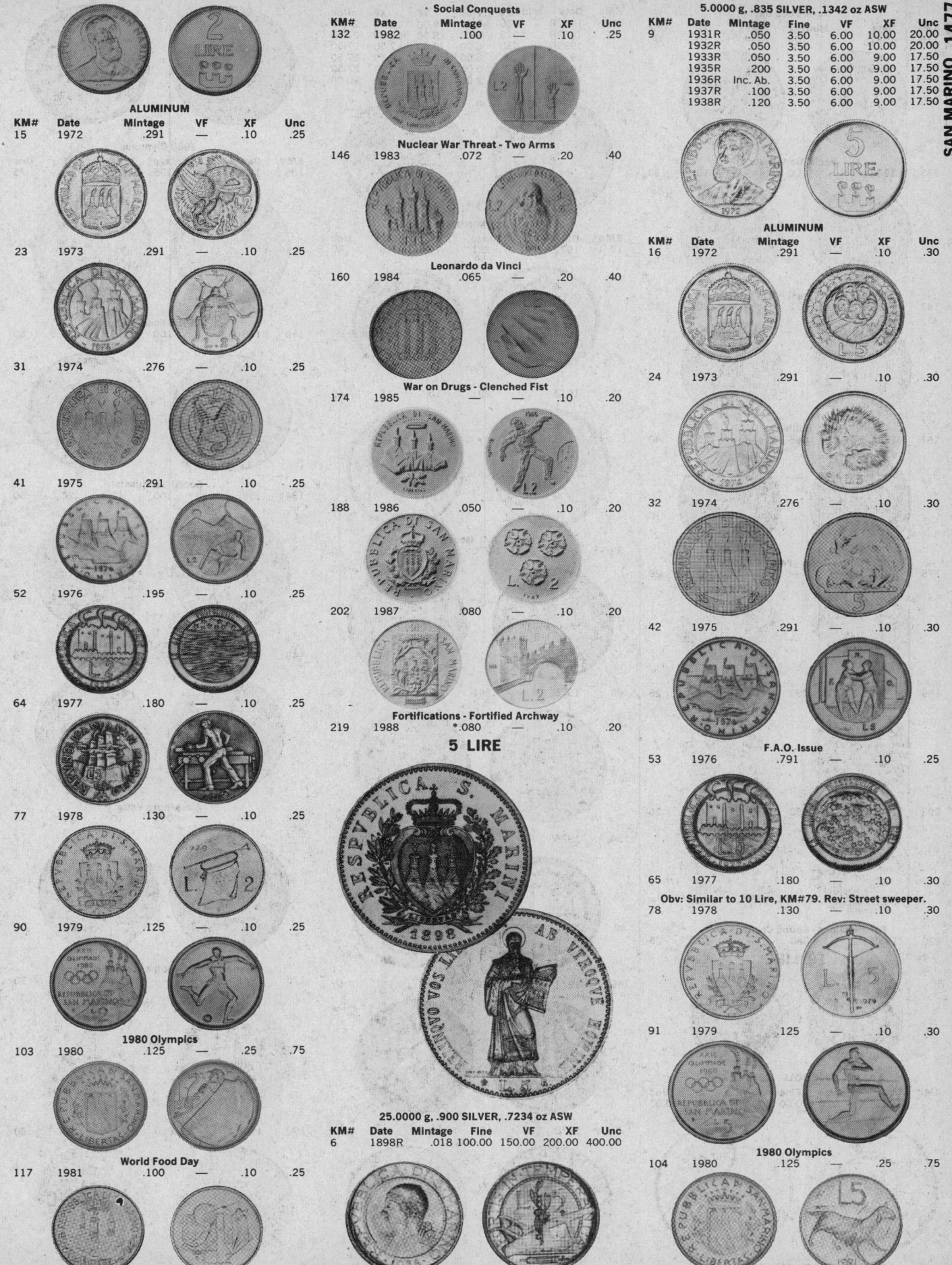

ALUMINUM

KM#	Date	Mintage	VF	XF	Unc
15	1972	.291	—	.10	.25
23	1973	.291	—	.10	.25
31	1974	.276	—	.10	.25
41	1975	.291	—	.10	.25
52	1976	.195	—	.10	.25
64	1977	.180	—	.10	.25
77	1978	.130	—	.10	.25
90	1979	.125	—	.10	.25

1980 Olympics
KM#	Date	Mintage	VF	XF	Unc
103	1980	.125	—	.25	.75

World Food Day
| 117 | 1981 | .100 | — | .10 | .25 |

Social Conquests
KM#	Date	Mintage	VF	XF	Unc
132	1982	.100	—	.10	.25

Nuclear War Threat - Two Arms
| 146 | 1983 | .072 | — | .20 | .40 |

Leonardo da Vinci
| 160 | 1984 | .065 | — | .20 | .40 |

War on Drugs - Clenched Fist
174	1985	—	—	.10	.20
188	1986	.050	—	.10	.20
202	1987	.080	—	.10	.20

Fortifications - Fortified Archway
| 219 | 1988 | *.080 | — | .10 | .20 |

5 LIRE

25.0000 g, .900 SILVER, .7234 oz ASW
KM#	Date	Mintage	Fine	VF	XF	Unc
6	1898R	.018	100.00	150.00	200.00	400.00

5.0000 g, .835 SILVER, .1342 oz ASW
KM#	Date	Mintage	Fine	VF	XF	Unc
9	1931R	.050	3.50	6.00	10.00	20.00
	1932R	.050	3.50	6.00	10.00	20.00
	1933R	.050	3.50	6.00	9.00	17.50
	1935R	.200	3.50	6.00	9.00	17.50
	1936R	Inc. Ab.	3.50	6.00	9.00	17.50
	1937R	.100	3.50	6.00	9.00	17.50
	1938R	.120	3.50	6.00	9.00	17.50

ALUMINUM
KM#	Date	Mintage	VF	XF	Unc
16	1972	.291	—	.10	.30
24	1973	.291	—	.10	.30
32	1974	.276	—	.10	.30
42	1975	.291	—	.10	.30

F.A.O. Issue
| 53 | 1976 | .791 | — | .10 | .25 |
| 65 | 1977 | .180 | — | .10 | .30 |

Obv: Similar to 10 Lire, KM#79. Rev: Street sweeper.
| 78 | 1978 | .130 | — | .10 | .30 |
| 91 | 1979 | .125 | — | .10 | .30 |

1980 Olympics
| 104 | 1980 | .125 | — | .25 | .75 |

SAN MARINO 1479

Fortifications - Sloping Fortress Wall

KM#	Date	Mintage	VF	XF	Unc
221	1988	*.080	—	.10	.30

20 LIRE

6.4516 g, .900 GOLD, .1867 oz AGW

KM#	Date	Mintage	Fine	VF	XF	Unc
8	1925R	9,334	300.00	600.00	1000.	2200.

15.0000 g, .800 SILVER, .3858 oz ASW

11	1931R	.010	20.00	40.00	80.00	175.00
	1932R	.010	35.00	70.00	120.00	250.00
	1933R	.010	25.00	45.00	90.00	180.00
	1935R	.010	30.00	50.00	100.00	200.00
	1936R	Inc. Ab.	30.00	50.00	100.00	200.00

20.0000 g, .600 SILVER, .3858 oz ASW

11a	1935R	Inc. Ab.	—	—	Rare	—
	1937R	5,100	100.00	150.00	250.00	400.00
	1938R	2,500	150.00	200.00	350.00	600.00

ALUMINUM-BRONZE

KM#	Date	Mintage	VF	XF	Unc
18	1972	.291	.10	.25	.50

26	1973	.291	.10	.25	.50

34	1974	.276	.10	.25	.50

F.A.O. Issue

44	1975	1.291	.10	.25	.50

KM#	Date	Mintage	VF	XF	Unc
55	1976	.195	.10	.25	.50

67	1977	.180	.10	.25	.50

80	1978	.130	.10	.25	.50

93	1979	.125	.10	.30	.50

1980 Olympics

106	1980	.125	.25	.50	1.00

World Food Day

120	1981	.100	.10	.30	.60

Social Conquests

135	1982	.200	.10	.25	.50

Nuclear War Threat - Torch Above Man

149	1983	.072	.10	.30	.75

Louis Pasteur

163	1984	.065	.10	.30	.75

War on Drugs - Open Hand

KM#	Date	Mintage	VF	XF	Unc
177	1985	—	—	.10	.50
191	1986	.050	—	.10	.50
205	1987	.080	—	.10	.50

Fortifications - Small Fortified Gate

222	1988	*.080	—	.10	.50

50 LIRE

STEEL

KM#	Date	Mintage	Fine	VF	XF	Unc
19	1972	.291	.15	.25	.50	1.00

27	1973	.291	.15	.25	.50	1.00

35	1974	.276	.15	.25	.50	1.00

45	1975	.831	.15	.25	.50	1.00

SAN MARINO

KM#	Date	Mintage	Fine	VF	XF	Unc
56	1976	.195	.15	.25	.50	1.00
68	1977	.180	.15	.25	.50	1.00
81	1978	.130	.15	.25	.50	1.00
94	1979	.125	.15	.25	.50	1.00

1980 Olympics

KM#	Date	Mintage	Fine	VF	XF	Unc
107	1980	.125	.25	.50	1.00	2.00

World Food Day

| 121 | 1981 | .100 | .15 | .25 | .50 | 1.00 |

Social Conquests

| 136 | 1982 | .200 | .15 | .25 | .50 | 1.00 |

Nuclear War Threat - Beast Above Woman

| 150 | 1983 | .072 | .20 | .40 | .80 | 1.50 |

Pierre and Marie Curie

KM#	Date	Mintage	Fine	VF	XF	Unc
164	1984	.065	.20	.40	.80	1.50

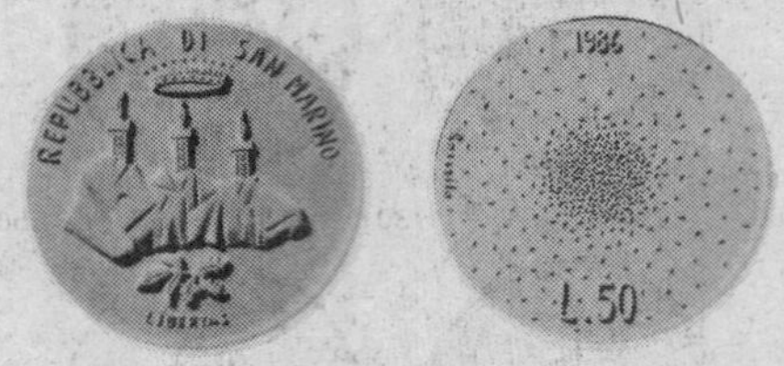

War on Drugs - Stylized Figures

178	1985	—	—	.10	.15	.75
192	1986	.050	—	.10	.15	.75
206	1987	.080	—	.10	.15	.75

Fortifications - Ramp Leading to Gate House

| 223 | 1988 | *.080 | — | .10 | .15 | .75 |

100 LIRE

STEEL

20	1972	.291	.15	.30	.60	1.25
28	1973	.291	.15	.30	.60	1.25
36	1974	.276	.15	.30	.60	1.25

KM#	Date	Mintage	Fine	VF	XF	Unc
46	1975	.821	.15	.30	.60	1.25
57	1976	1.853	.15	.30	.60	1.25
69	1977	.566	.15	.30	.60	1.25
70	1977	.566	.15	.30	.60	1.25

F.A.O. Issue

| 82 | 1978 | .875 | .15 | .30 | .60 | 1.25 |
| 95 | 1979 | .665 | .15 | .30 | .60 | 1.25 |

1980 Olympics

| 108 | 1980 | .665 | .25 | .50 | 1.00 | 2.00 |

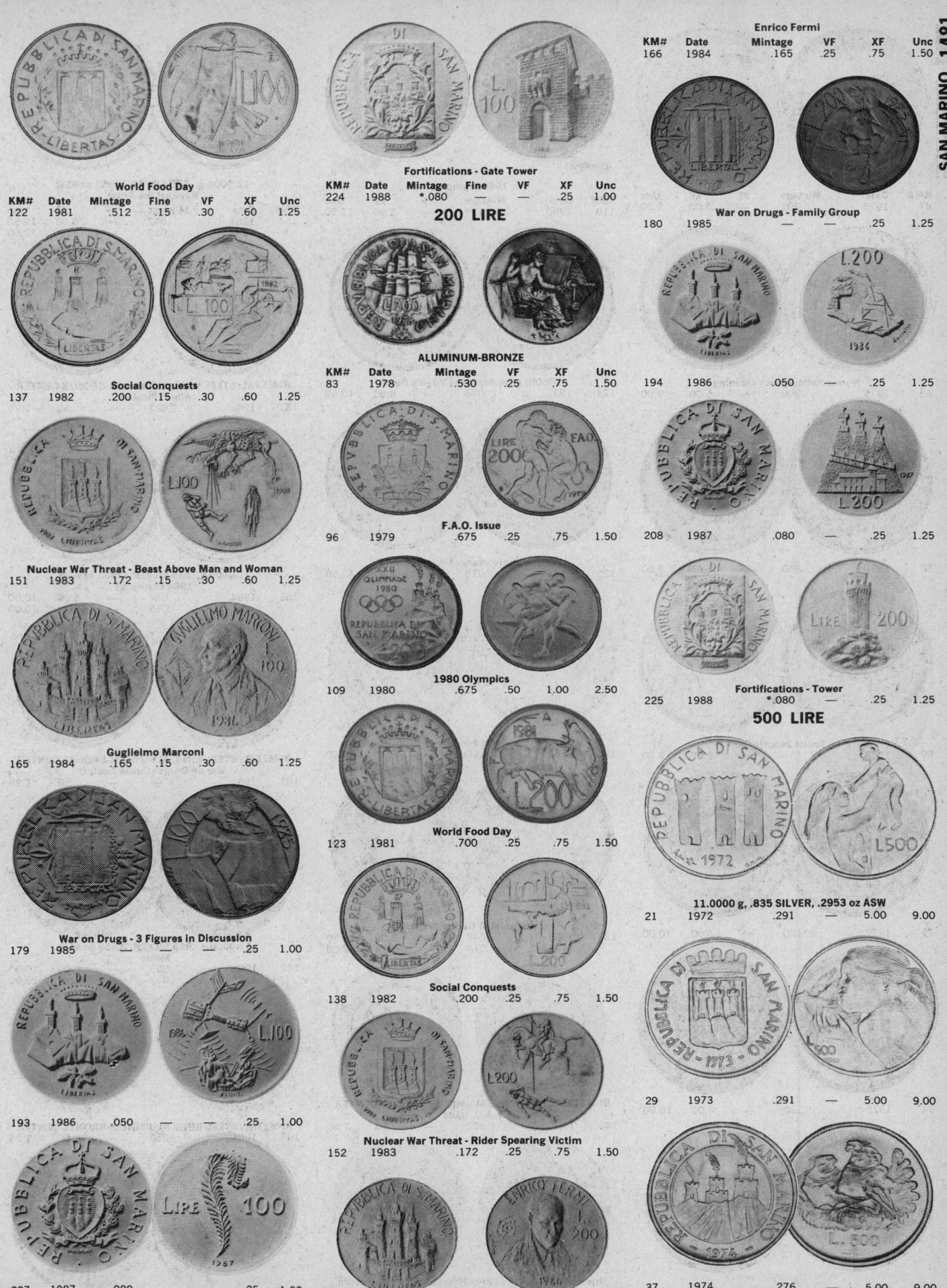

SAN MARINO

KM#	Date	Mintage	VF	XF	Unc
47	1975	.291	—	5.00	9.00

Numismatic Agency Opening

| 48 | 1975 | .200 | — | 5.00 | 9.00 |
| 58 | 1976 | .390 | — | 5.00 | 9.00 |

Social Security

59	1976	—	—	5.00	9.00
71	1977	.180	—	6.00	10.00
84	1978	.130	—	6.00	10.00
97	1979	.125	—	8.00	12.50

1980 Olympics

KM#	Date	Mintage	VF	XF	Unc
110	1980	.125	—	8.00	12.50

2000th Anniversary of Virgil's Death

| 124 | 1981 | .075 | — | 8.00 | 12.50 |

2000th Anniversary of Virgil's Death

| 125 | 1981 | .075 | — | 8.00 | 12.50 |

World Food Day

| 126 | 1981 | .100 | — | 8.00 | 12.50 |

Centennial of Garibaldi Death

| 139 | 1982 | .048 | — | 8.00 | 12.50 |
| | 1982 | .014 | — | Proof | 22.50 |

BI-METAL: STEEL RING, ALUMINUM-BRONZE CENTER
F.A.O. Issue

| 140 | 1982 | 1.852 | — | .50 | 1.50 |

Nuclear War Threat - Three Horses Above Two People

| 153 | 1983 | 1.922 | — | .50 | 1.50 |

11.0000 g, .835 SILVER, .2953 oz ASW
Raphael the Artist

KM#	Date	Mintage	VF	XF	Unc
154	1983	.042	—	8.00	12.50
	1983	.012	—	Proof	22.50

BI-METAL: STEEL RING, ALUMINUM-BRONZE CENTER
Albert Einstein

| 167 | 1984 | 2.633 | — | .50 | 1.25 |

11.0000 g, .835 SILVER, .2953 oz ASW
1984 Olympiad

| 168 | 1984 | .052 | — | 6.00 | 10.00 |
| | 1984 | .015 | — | Proof | 15.00 |

BI-METAL: STEEL RING, ALUMINUM-BRONZE CENTER
War on Drugs - Cured Addict

| 181 | 1985 | — | — | .50 | 1.25 |

11.0000 g, .835 SILVER, .2953 oz ASW
Music

| 182 | 1985 | .053 | — | 6.00 | 10.00 |
| | 1985 | .013 | — | Proof | 15.00 |

BI-METAL: STEEL RING, ALUMINUM-BRONZE CENTER

| 195 | 1986 | .050 | — | .50 | 1.25 |

SAN MARINO 1483

11.0000 g, .835 SILVER, .2953 oz ASW
Soccer - Field

KM#	Date	Mintage	VF	XF	Unc
196	1986	.045	—	—	6.00
	1986	.012	—	Proof	15.00

BI-METAL: STEEL RING, ALUMINUM-BRONZE CENTER

| 209 | 1987 | .080 | — | .50 | 1.50 |

11.0000 g, .835 SILVER, .2953 oz ASW
Zagreb University Games - Runner

| 213 | 1987 | .035 | — | — | 6.00 |
| | 1987 | .010 | — | Proof | 15.00 |

Winter Olympics - Downhill Skier

| 216 | 1988 | *.100 | — | — | 10.00 |

BI-METAL: STEEL RING, ALUMINUM-BRONZE CENTER
Fortifications - Hilltop Fortification

| 226 | 1988 | *.080 | — | .50 | 1.50 |

1000 LIRE

14.6000 g, .835 SILVER, .3919 oz ASW
Brunelleschi

| 72 | 1977 | .180 | — | — | 12.50 |

Tolstoy

| 85 | 1978 | .130 | — | — | 12.50 |

European Unity

KM#	Date	Mintage	VF	XF	Unc
98	1979	.125	—	—	12.50

1500th Anniversary of Birth of St. Benedict

| 112 | 1980 | .125 | — | — | 15.00 |

2000th Anniversary of Virgil's Death

| 127 | 1981 | .075 | — | — | 15.00 |

Centennial of Garibaldi Death

| 141 | 1982 | .048 | — | — | 15.00 |
| | 1982 | .014 | — | Proof | 22.50 |

Raphael the Artist

| 155 | 1983 | .042 | — | — | 15.00 |
| | 1983 | .012 | — | Proof | 22.50 |

1984 Olympiad

| 169 | 1984 | .052 | — | — | 12.00 |
| | 1984 | .015 | — | Proof | 22.50 |

Music - J.S. Bach

KM#	Date	Mintage	VF	XF	Unc
183	1985	.040	—	—	12.00
	1985	.012	—	Proof	22.50

Soccer - Flags

| 197 | 1986 | .045 | — | — | 18.00 |
| | 1986 | .012 | — | Proof | 30.00 |

| 210 | 1987 | .080 | — | — | 18.00 |

Zagreb University Games - Pole Vaulter

| 214 | 1987 | .035 | — | — | 18.00 |
| | 1987 | .010 | — | Proof | 30.00 |

Summer Olympics - Diver

| 217 | 1988 | *.100 | — | — | 20.00 |

Fortifications - Walls and Towers

| 227 | 1988 | *.080 | — | — | 20.00 |

SCUDO

3.0000 g, .917 GOLD, .0883 oz AGW

| 38 | 1974 | .060 | — | — | 75.00 |

SAN MARINO 1484

KM#	Date	Mintage	VF	XF	Unc
49	1975	.087	—	—	75.00
60	1976	.090	—	—	75.00
73	1977	.070	—	—	75.00

Democrazia

KM#	Date	Mintage	VF	XF	Unc
86	1978	.038	—	—	75.00

Miss Liberta

KM#	Date	Mintage	VF	XF	Unc
99	1979	.038	—	—	75.00

Peace

KM#	Date	Mintage	VF	XF	Unc
113	1980	.038	—	—	75.00
128	1981	.031	—	—	75.00

World Food Day

KM#	Date	Mintage	VF	XF	Unc
142	1982	.017	—	—	75.00

2.0000 g, .917 GOLD, .0590 oz AGW
Perpetual Liberty

KM#	Date	Mintage	VF	XF	Unc
156	1983	.014	—	—	75.00

Peace
Obv: Similar to 2 Scudi, KM#171.

KM#	Date	Mintage	VF	XF	Unc
170	1984	.011	—	—	75.00

International Year For Youth

KM#	Date	Mintage	VF	XF	Unc
184	1985	1,000	—	—	90.00

3.3920 g, .917 GOLD, .1000 oz AGW
Insects at Work

KM#	Date	Mintage	VF	XF	Unc
198	1986	8,000	—	—	75.00
211	1987	7,000	—	—	75.00

Disarmament

KM#	Date	Mintage	VF	XF	Unc
228	1988	.011	—	—	75.00

2 SCUDI

6.0000 g, .917 GOLD, .1769 oz AGW

KM#	Date	Mintage	VF	XF	Unc
39	1974	.060	—	—	125.00
50	1975	.080	—	—	125.00
61	1976	.118	—	—	125.00
74	1977	.068	—	—	125.00

Miss Liberta

KM#	Date	Mintage	VF	XF	Unc
87	1978	.029	—	—	125.00

Peace

KM#	Date	Mintage	VF	XF	Unc
100	1979	.037	—	—	125.00
114	1980	.037	—	—	125.00

World Food Day

KM#	Date	Mintage	VF	XF	Unc
129	1981	.030	—	—	125.00
143	1982	.016	—	—	125.00

4.0000 g, .917 GOLD, .1179 oz AGW
Perpetual Liberty

KM#	Date	Mintage	VF	XF	Unc
157	1983	.013	—	—	125.00

Liberty

KM#	Date	Mintage	VF	XF	Unc
171	1984	.010	—	—	125.00

International Year For Youth

KM#	Date	Mintage	VF	XF	Unc
185	1985	9,000	—	—	125.00

6.7840 g, .917 GOLD, .2000 oz AGW
Insects at Work

KM#	Date	Mintage	VF	XF	Unc
199	1986	8,000	—	—	125.00
212	1987	7,000	—	—	125.00

Disarmament

KM#	Date	Mintage	VF	XF	Unc
229	1988	.010	—	—	125.00

5 SCUDI

15.0000 g, .917 GOLD, .4422 oz AGW

KM#	Date	Mintage	VF	XF	Unc
62	1976	.015	—	—	625.00

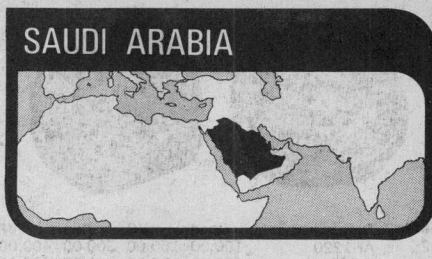

SAUDI ARABIA

The Kingdom of Saudi Arabia, an independent and absolute hereditary monarchy comprising the former sultanate of Nejd, the old kingdom of Hejaz, Asir and El Jasa, occupies four-fifths of the Arabian peninsula. The kingdom has an area of 830,000 sq. mi. (2,149,690 sq. km.) and a population of *12.7 million. Capital: Riyadh. The economy is based on oil, which provides 85 percent of Saudi Arabia's revenue.

Mohammed united the Arabs in the 7th century and his followers founded a great empire with its capital at Medina. The Turks established nominal rule over much of Arabia in the 16th and 17th centuries, and in the 18th century divided it into principalities.

The Kingdom of Saudi Arabia was created by King Ibn-Saud (1882-1953), a descendant of earlier Wahabi rulers of the Arabian peninsula. In 1901 he seized Riyadh, capital of the Sultanate of Nejd, and in 1905 established himself as Sultan. In 1913 he captured the Turkish province of Hasa; took the Hejaz in 1925 and by 1926 most of Asir. In 1932 he combined Nejd and Hejaz into the single kingdom of Saudi Arabia. Asir was incorporated into the kingdom a year later.

The following areas of Saudi Arabia were coin-issuing entities of interest to numismatics.

TITLES

العربية السعودية

El-Arabiyat El-Sa'udiyat

المملكة العربية السعودية

El-Mamlakat El-Arabiyat El-Sa'udiyat

MECCA

Mecca, the metropolis of Islam and the capital of Hejaz, is located inland from the Red Sea due east of the port of Jidda. A center of non-political commercial, cultural and religious activities, Mecca remained virtually independent until 1259. Two centuries of Egyptian rule were followed by four centuries of Turkish rule which lasted until the Arab revolts which extinguished all Turkish pretensions to sovereignty over any part of the Arabian peninsula.

MINTNAME

مكة

Mekha, Mecca

RULERS
Sharifs of Mecca
Ghalib b. Ma'Sud, AH1219-1229
Yahya b. Surer, AH1230-1240
Abdul Muttalib and Ibn Awn, AH1240-1248

1/2 MAHMUDI

COPPER
Mintname: *Mecca*

KM#	Date	Good	VG	Fine	VF
5	AH1240	200.00	300.00	400.00	600.00

NOTE: 1 known.

MAHMUDI

COPPER
Mintname: *Mecca*

	AH1219	100.00	150.00	300.00	400.00
1					

Mecca / SAUDI ARABIA 1486

KM#	Date	Good	VG	Fine	VF
2	AH1220	100.00	150.00	300.00	400.00
	1221	100.00	150.00	300.00	400.00
	1222	100.00	150.00	300.00	400.00

Mintname: *Mecca*
Obv: Bird. Rev: Fish.

| 3 | AH1223 | 125.00 | 175.00 | 300.00 | 450.00 |

| 4 | AH1230 | 125.00 | 175.00 | 300.00 | 450.00 |

HEJAZ

Hejaz, a province of Saudi Arabia and a former vilayet of the Ottoman empire, occupies an 800-mile long (1,287 km.) coastal strip between Nejd and the Red Sea. The province was a Turkish dependency until freed in World War I. Husain Ibn Ali, Amir of Mecca, opposed the Turkish control and, with the aid of Lawrence of Arabia, wrested much of Hejaz from the Turks and in 1916 assumed the title of King of Hejaz. Ibn Saud of Nejd conquered Hejaz in 1925, and in 1926 combined it and Nejd into a single kingdom.

TITLES

الحجاز

Al-Hejaz

RULERS

Al Husain Ibn Ali
AH1334-42/AD1916-24
Ibn Saud (of Nejd)
AH1342/AD1924

MONETARY SYSTEM

40 Para = 1 Piastre (Ghirsh)
20 Piastres = 1 Riyal
100 Piastres = 1 Dinar

COUNTERMARKED COINAGE

Maria Theresa Thalers, as well as many Turkish and Egyptian coins, are found countermarked *Al-Hijaz*. The countermark occurs in various sizes and styles of lettering. The mark may have been applied during 1916, and is reckoned by some authorities to have been used as late as 1923 although there is no evidence that it was ever applied officially.

NOTE: Caution should be excercised in the purchase of any of the Hejaz countermarked coins. The authenticity of most of the pieces on the market today is the subject of controversy, particularly pieces other than the Maria Theresa Thalers from the Vienna Mint, the Turkish 20 Piastres and 10 Piastres of AH1327, and the Turkish 20 and 40 Para nickel pieces (#'s 2,3,10,11, and 12 below). Also, the small 6mm size countermark is not believed to be original. Any coin dating after 1923 with the countermark is most doubtful. The following coins show the types which may be found with the countermark.

10 PARA
NICKEL
Accession Date: AH1327
c/m: *Hejaz* on Turkey 10 Para, KM#760.
Obv: Reshat.

KM#	Year	Good	VG	Fine	VF
1	2	5.00	10.00	20.00	40.00
	3	5.00	10.00	20.00	40.00
	4	5.00	10.00	20.00	40.00
	5	5.00	10.00	20.00	40.00
	6	5.00	10.00	20.00	40.00
	7	5.00	10.00	20.00	40.00
	8	5.00	10.00	20.00	40.00

Obv: El Ghazi.

| 2 | 7 | 5.00 | 10.00 | 20.00 | 40.00 |
| | 8 | 5.00 | 10.00 | 20.00 | 40.00 |

20 PARA

NICKEL
Accession Date: AH1327
c/m: *Hejaz* on Turkey 20 Para, KM#761.

KM#	Year	Good	VG	Fine	VF
3	2	5.00	7.00	9.00	15.00
	3	4.00	6.00	8.00	12.00
	4	2.00	4.00	8.00	10.00
	5	2.00	4.00	8.00	10.00
	6	2.00	4.00	8.00	12.00

40 PARA
NICKEL
c/m: *Hejaz* on Turkey 40 Para, KM#766.

4	3	4.00	6.00	12.00	25.00
	4	5.00	12.00	15.00	25.00
	5	2.00	5.00	10.00	15.00

COPPER-NICKEL
c/m: *Hejaz* on Turkey 40 Para, KM#779.

| 5 | 8 | 4.00 | 6.00 | 8.00 | 12.00 |
| | 9 | 6.00 | 10.00 | 18.00 | 35.00 |

Accession Date: AH1336
c/m: *Hejaz* on Turkey 40 Para, KM#828.

| 6 | 4 | 10.00 | 20.00 | 40.00 | 75.00 |

2 PIASTRES
SILVER
Accession Date: AH1327
c/m: *Hejaz* on Turkey 2 Piastres, KM#749.

7	1	12.50	20.00	40.00	75.00
	2	12.50	20.00	40.00	75.00
	3	12.50	20.00	40.00	75.00
	4	12.50	20.00	40.00	75.00
	5	12.50	20.00	40.00	75.00
	6	12.50	20.00	40.00	75.00

c/m: *Hejaz* on Turkey 2 Piastres, KM#770.

8	7	12.50	20.00	40.00	75.00
	8	12.50	20.00	40.00	75.00
	9	12.50	20.00	40.00	75.00

c/m: *Hejaz* on Egypt 2 Guerche, KM#307.

| 9 | 2H | 12.50 | 20.00 | 40.00 | 75.00 |
| | 3H | 12.50 | 20.00 | 40.00 | 75.00 |

NOTE: The above coins are all controversial.

5 PIASTRES

SILVER
Accession Date: AH1327
c/m: *Hejaz* on Turkey 5 Piastres, KM#750.

10	1	12.50	20.00	40.00	75.00
	2	12.50	20.00	40.00	75.00
	3	12.50	20.00	40.00	75.00
	4	12.50	20.00	40.00	75.00
	5	12.50	20.00	40.00	75.00
	6	12.50	20.00	40.00	75.00
	7	12.50	20.00	40.00	75.00

c/m: *Hejaz* on Turkey 5 Piastres, KM#771.

11	7	12.50	20.00	40.00	75.00
	8	12.50	20.00	40.00	75.00
	9	12.50	20.00	40.00	75.00

c/m: *Hejaz* on Egypt 5 Guerche, KM#308.

12	2H	12.50	20.00	40.00	75.00
	3H	12.50	20.00	40.00	75.00
	4H	12.50	20.00	40.00	75.00
	6H	12.50	20.00	40.00	75.00

10 PIASTRES
SILVER
Accession Date: AH1327
c/m: *Hejaz* on Turkey 10 Piastres, KM#751.

| 13 | 1 | 20.00 | 30.00 | 60.00 | 100.00 |
| | 2 | 20.00 | 30.00 | 60.00 | 100.00 |

KM#	Year	Good	VG	Fine	VF
13	3	20.00	30.00	60.00	100.00
	4	20.00	30.00	60.00	100.00
	5	20.00	30.00	60.00	100.00
	6	20.00	30.00	60.00	100.00
	7	20.00	30.00	60.00	100.00

c/m: *Hejaz* on Turkey 10 Piastres, KM#772.

14	7	20.00	30.00	60.00	100.00
	8	20.00	30.00	60.00	100.00
	9	20.00	30.00	60.00	100.00
	10	20.00	30.00	60.00	100.00

c/m: *Hejaz* on Egypt 10 Guerche, KM#309.

15	2H	20.00	30.00	60.00	100.00
	3H	20.00	30.00	60.00	100.00
	4H	20.00	30.00	60.00	100.00
	6H	20.00	30.00	60.00	100.00

20 PIASTRES

SILVER
Accession Date: AH1327
c/m: *Hejaz* on Egypt 20 Guerche, KM#310.

16	2H	35.00	60.00	100.00	150.00
	3H	35.00	60.00	100.00	150.00
	4H	35.00	60.00	100.00	150.00
	6H	35.00	60.00	100.00	150.00

c/m: *Hejaz* on Turkey 20 Piastres, KM#780.

17	8	35.00	60.00	100.00	150.00
	9	35.00	60.00	100.00	150.00
	10	35.00	60.00	100.00	150.00

c/m: *Hejaz* on Austria M.T. Thaler, Y#55.

| 18 | 1780 (restrike) | 15.00 | 30.00 | 60.00 | 125.00 |

REGULAR COINAGE

NOTE: All the regular coins of Hejaz bear the accessional date 1334 of Al-Husain Ibn Ali, plus the regnal year. Many of the bronze coins occur with a light silver wash.

1/8 PIASTRE

BRONZE

KM#	Date	Year	VG	Fine	VF	XF
21	AH1334	5	15.00	25.00	35.00	50.00

1/4 PIASTRE

BRONZE, 1.14 g

22	AH1334	5	4.00	8.00	15.00	25.00
	1334	5/6	125.00	200.00	275.00	400.00
	1334	6	75.00	125.00	200.00	300.00

| 25 | AH1334 | 8 | 5.00 | 10.00 | 15.00 | 22.00 |

1/2 PIASTRE

BRONZE

KM#	Date	Year	VG	Fine	VF	XF
23	AH1334	5	3.00	7.50	15.00	30.00

Similar to 1/4 Piastre, KM#25.

| 26 | AH1334 | 8 | — | — | Rare | |

NOTE: All known specimens are overstruck by Saudi Arabia KM#1 or KM#3.

PIASTRE

BRONZE

| 24 | AH1334 | 5 | 6.00 | 10.00 | 15.00 | 30.00 |

| 27 | AH1334 | 8 | 6.00 | 10.00 | 15.00 | 30.00 |

5 PIASTRES

6.1000 g, .917 SILVER, .1798 oz ASW

| 28 | AH1334 | 8 | 15.00 | 40.00 | 70.00 | 110.00 |

10 PIASTRES

12.0500 g, .917 SILVER, .3552 oz ASW

| 29 | AH1334 | 8 | 100.00 | 170.00 | 300.00 | 575.00 |

20 PIASTRES
(1 Ryal)

24.1000 g, .917 SILVER, .7105 oz ASW

KM#	Date	Year	VG	Fine	VF	XF
30	AH1334	8	20.00	40.00	60.00	85.00
		9	30.00	50.00	75.00	100.00

DINAR HASHIMI

GOLD

KM#	Date	Mintage	Fine	VF	XF	Unc
31	AH1334	8	—	BV	300.00	450.00

NOTE: Beware of counterfeits.

NEJD

Nejd, a province of Saudi Arabia which may be described as an open steppe, occupies the core of the Arabian peninsula. The province became a nominal dependency of the Turkish empire in 1871 and a sultanate of King Ibn-Saud in 1906.

TITLES
نجد
Nejd

RULERS
Ibn Sa'ud,
AH1322-1373/1905-1953AD
(In all of Hejaz after 1926, in all Saudi Arabia after 1932).

MONETARY SYSTEM
40 Para = 1 Piastre (Ghirsh)
20 Piastres = 1 Riyal
100 Piastres = 1 Dinar

COUNTERMARKED COINAGE
Maria Theresa Thalers were countermarked *Nejd* between 1916-1923 and after 1935.

NOTE: Other Turkish and Egyptian coins are reported with the Nejd cmk., but their legitimacy remains a matter of controversy. They are listed here, but should be regarded with caution. Only the large countermark is currently considered to be authentic. Indian Rupees cmk.'d *Nejd* are rather dubious. Coins bearing both the Nejd and Hejaz countermarks are of very questionable legitimacy as are all countermarked modern Maria Theresa Thalers from mints other than the Vienna Mint.

5 PIASTRES

SILVER
Accession Date: AH1327
c/m: *Nejd* on Egypt 5 Guerche, KM#308.

KM#	Year	Good	VG	Fine	VF
1	2H	25.00	50.00	100.00	150.00
	3H	25.00	50.00	100.00	150.00
	4H	25.00	50.00	100.00	150.00
	6H	25.00	50.00	100.00	150.00

c/m: *Nejd* on Egypt 5 Guerche, KM#321.

KM#	Date	Year	Good	VG	Fine	VF
2	AH1335	1916	25.00	50.00	100.00	150.00
		1917	25.00	50.00	100.00	150.00
		1917H	25.00	50.00	100.00	150.00

c/m: *Nejd* on Turkey 5 Piastres, KM#750.

KM#	Year	Good	VG	Fine	VF
3	1	25.00	50.00	100.00	150.00
	2	25.00	50.00	100.00	150.00
	3	25.00	50.00	100.00	150.00
	4	25.00	50.00	100.00	150.00
	5	25.00	50.00	100.00	150.00
	6	25.00	50.00	100.00	150.00
	7	25.00	50.00	100.00	150.00

c/m: *Nejd* on Turkey 5 Piastres, KM#771.

4	7	25.00	50.00	100.00	150.00
	8	25.00	50.00	100.00	150.00
	9	25.00	50.00	100.00	150.00

RUPEE

SILVER
c/m: *Nejd* on India Rupee, KM#450.

KM#	Date	Year	Good	VG	Fine	VF
5	1835	—	25.00	50.00	100.00	150.00

c/m: *Nejd* on India Rupee, KM#457.

| 6 | 1840 | — | 25.00 | 50.00 | 100.00 | 150.00 |

c/m: *Nejd* on India Rupee, KM#458.

| 7 | 1840 | — | 25.00 | 50.00 | 100.00 | 150.00 |

c/m: *Nejd* on India Rupee, KM#473.

| 8 | 1862-76 | — | 25.00 | 50.00 | 100.00 | 150.00 |

10 PIASTRES

SILVER
Accession Date: AH1293
c/m: *Nejd* on Egypt 10 Guerche, KM#289.

KM#	Year	Good	VG	Fine	VF
9	27	50.00	70.00	125.00	200.00
	29	50.00	70.00	125.00	200.00
	29H	50.00	70.00	125.00	200.00
	30H	50.00	70.00	125.00	200.00
	31H	50.00	70.00	125.00	200.00
	32H	50.00	70.00	125.00	200.00
	33H	50.00	70.00	125.00	200.00

c/m: *Nejd* on Turkey 10 Piastres, KM#751.

10	1	50.00	70.00	125.00	200.00
	2	50.00	70.00	125.00	200.00
	3	50.00	70.00	125.00	200.00
	4	50.00	70.00	125.00	200.00
	5	50.00	70.00	125.00	200.00
	6	50.00	70.00	125.00	200.00
	7	50.00	70.00	125.00	200.00

c/m: *Nejd* on Turkey 10 Piastres, KM#772.

11	7	50.00	70.00	125.00	200.00
	8	50.00	70.00	125.00	200.00
	9	50.00	70.00	125.00	200.00
	10	50.00	70.00	125.00	200.00

20 PIASTRES

SILVER
Accession Date: AH1327
c/m: *Nejd* on Egypt 20 Guerche, KM#310.

12	2H	75.00	125.00	200.00	350.00
	3H	75.00	125.00	200.00	350.00
	4H	75.00	125.00	200.00	350.00
	6H	75.00	125.00	200.00	350.00

c/m: *Nejd* on Turkey 20 Piastres, KM#780.

13	8	75.00	125.00	200.00	350.00
	9	75.00	125.00	200.00	350.00
	10	75.00	125.00	200.00	350.00

Nejd / SAUDI ARABIA 1488

c/m: *Nejd* on Austria M.T. Thaler, Y#55.

KM#	Date	Year	Good	VG	Fine	VF
14	1780	—	40.00	80.00	180.00	300.00

REGULAR COINAGE

Struck at occupied Mecca, Hejaz Mint by Ibn Sa'ud while establishing his kingdom.

1/4 GHIRSH

COPPER

KM#	Date	Mintage	VG	Fine	VF	XF
1	AH1343	—	15.00	22.00	30.00	50.00

NOTE: Several varieties exist.

1/2 GHIRSH

COPPER

2	AH1343	—	6.00	12.50	20.00	32.50

NOTE: Several varieties exist.

3	AH1344, yr. 2	—	3.00	8.00	16.00	25.00

HEJAZ and NEJD

NOTE: Copper-nickel, reeded-edge coins dated 1356 and silver coins dated AH1354 were struck at Philadelphia between 1944-1949.

ROYAL TITLES
Appearing on Coins

AH1344 (1926AD)
King of Hejaz and Sultan of Nejd

1/4 GHIRSH

COPPER-NICKEL

4	AH1344	—	1.25	2.50	5.00	15.00
	1344	—	—	—	Proof	—

1/2 GHIRSH

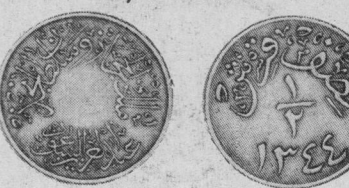

COPPER-NICKEL

KM#	Date	Mintage	VG	Fine	VF	XF
5	AH1344	—	2.50	4.00	7.00	15.00
	1344	—	—	—	Proof	—

GHIRSH

COPPER-NICKEL

6	AH1344	—	2.00	3.50	8.50	22.50
	1344	—	—	—	Proof	—

HEJAZ and NEJD and DEPENDENCIES

ROYAL TITLES
Appearing on Coins

AH1346-1348 (1928-1930AD)
King of Hejaz and Nejd and Dependencies

1/4 GHIRSH

COPPER-NICKEL

7	AH1346	3.000	3.00	5.00	10.00	20.00

13	AH1348	—	3.00	5.00	10.00	20.00
	1348	—	—	—	Proof	—

1/2 GHIRSH

COPPER-NICKEL

8	AH1346	3.000	3.00	5.00	10.00	25.00

14	AH1348	—	—	3.00	10.00	25.00
	1348	—	—	—	Proof	—

1/2 GHIRSH

COPPER-NICKEL

KM#	Date	Mintage	VG	Fine	VF	XF
9	AH1346	3.000	3.00	5.00	12.00	25.00

15	AH1348	—	—	3.00	5.00	12.00	25.00
	1348	—	—	—	Proof	—

1/4 RIYAL

6.0500 g, .917 SILVER, .1783 oz ASW

10	AH1346	.400	12.50	20.00	45.00	75.00
	1346	—	—	—	Proof	—
	1348	.200	17.50	30.00	60.00	100.00
	1348	—	—	—	Proof	—

1/2 RIYAL

12.1000 g, .917 SILVER, .3567 oz ASW

11	AH1346	.200	55.00	100.00	165.00	250.00
	1346	—	—	—	Proof	200.00
	1348	.100	55.00	100.00	165.00	250.00
	1348	—	—	—	Proof	—

RIYAL

24.1000 g, .917 SILVER, .7105 oz ASW

12	AH1346	.800	15.00	25.00	60.00	100.00
	1346	—	—	—	Proof	350.00
	1348	.400	20.00	30.00	85.00	115.00
	1348	—	—	—	Proof	—

SAUDI ARABIA

RULERS

Abd Al-Aziz Ibn Sa'ud
  AH1344-1373/1926-1953AD
Sa'ud Ibn Abdul Aziz
  AH1373-1383/1953-1964AD
Faisal, AH1383-1395/1964-1975AD
Khalid, AH1395-1403/1975-1982AD
Fhad ibn Abdul Aziz, AH1403- /1982-AD

MONETARY SYSTEM
Until 1960

22 Ghirsh = 1 Riyal
40 Riyals = 1 Guinea
20 Ghirsh = 1 Riyal

ROYAL TITLES
Appearing on coins

AH1356 (1937AD) and later
King of the Kingdom of Saudi Arabia

1/4 GHIRSH

COPPER-NICKEL
Plain edge

KM#	Date	Mintage	VG	Fine	VF	XF
19.1	AH1356	1.000	1.00	2.00	4.00	15.00

Reeded edge

| 19.2 | AH1356 | 21.500 | .10 | .25 | .50 | 1.00 |

Struck in 1947 (AH1366-67) at Philadelphia.

1/2 GHIRSH

COPPER-NICKEL
Plain edge

| 20.1 | AH1356 | 1.000 | 1.25 | 2.00 | 6.00 | 15.00 |

Reeded edge

| 20.2 | AH1356 | 10.850 | .15 | .25 | 1.00 | 3.00 |

Struck in 1947 (AH1366-67) at Philadelphia.

GHIRSH

COPPER-NICKEL
Plain edge

| 21.1 | AH1356 | 4.000 | 1.00 | 2.50 | 7.00 | 15.00 |

Reeded edge

| 21.2 | AH1356 | 7.150 | .50 | .75 | 1.50 | 3.00 |

Struck in 1947 (AH1366-67) at Philadelphia.

KM#	Date	Mintage	Fine	VF	XF	Unc
40	AH1376	10.000	.15	.25	.50	1.00
	1378	50.000	.15	.25	.50	1.00

2 GHIRSH

COPPER-NICKEL

| 41 | AH1376 | 50.000 | .10 | .35 | .75 | 2.00 |
| | 1379 | 28.110 | .10 | .35 | .70 | 1.50 |

4 GHIRSH

COPPER-NICKEL

KM#	Date	Mintage	Fine	VF	XF	Unc
42	AH1376	49.100	.25	.50	1.00	4.00
	1378	10.000	.25	.50	1.00	4.00

1/4 RIYAL

3.1000 g, .917 SILVER, .0913 oz ASW

| 16 | AH1354 | .900 | 1.75 | 2.50 | 3.00 | 5.00 |
| | 1354 | — | — | — | Proof | 150.00 |

2.9500 g, .917 SILVER, .0869 oz ASW

| 37 | AH1374 | — | — | BV | 3.00 | 5.00 |

1/2 RIYAL

5.8500 g, .917 SILVER, .1724 oz ASW

| 17 | AH1354 | .950 | 2.50 | 4.00 | 6.00 | 9.00 |

5.9500 g, .917 SILVER, .1754 oz ASW

| 38 | AH1374 | 2.000 | 2.50 | 3.00 | 4.50 | 6.50 |

RIYAL

11.6000 g, .917 SILVER, .3419 oz ASW

18	AH1354	60.000	BV	5.00	8.00	12.00
	1354	20.000	—	—	Proof	—
	1367	Inc. Ab.	—	BV	8.50	13.00
	1370	—	—	BV	8.00	12.00

| 39 | AH1374 | 48.000 | — | BV | 5.00 | 8.50 | 12.50 |

COUNTERMARKED COINAGE
70 – '65'/COUNTERMARK

The following pieces are countermarked examples of earlier types bearing the Arabic numerals "65". They were countermarked in a move to break money changers' monopoly on small coins in 1365AH (1946AD). These countermarks vary and are found with the Arabic numbers raised in a circle and incuse, the latter being scarcer.

1/4 GHIRSH

c/m: '65' on 1/4 Ghirsh, KM#4.

KM#	Date	Mintage	Good	VG	Fine	VF
22	AH1344	—	2.50	4.00	10.00	20.00

c/m: '65' on 1/4 Ghirsh, KM#7.

| 23 | AH1346 | — | 2.50 | 4.00 | 10.00 | 20.00 |

c/m: '65' on 1/4 Ghirsh, KM#13.

| 24 | AH1348 | — | 2.50 | 4.00 | 10.00 | 20.00 |

Plain edge
c/m: '65' on 1/4 Ghirsh, KM#19.

| 25 | AH1356 | — | 2.50 | 4.00 | 8.50 | 18.00 |

1/2 GHIRSH

c/m: '65' on 1/2 Ghirsh, KM#5.

| 26 | AH1344 | — | 2.50 | 4.00 | 7.50 | 25.00 |

 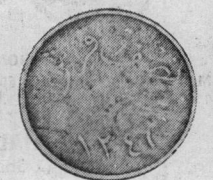

c/m: '65' on 1/2 Ghirsh, KM#8.

| 27 | AH1346 | — | 2.50 | 4.00 | 7.50 | 25.00 |

c/m: '65' on 1/2 Ghirsh, KM#14.

| 28 | AH1348 | — | 2.50 | 4.00 | 7.50 | 25.00 |

Plain edge
c/m: '65' on 1/2 Ghirsh, KM#20.1.

| 29 | AH1356 | — | 1.25 | 2.25 | 5.00 | 20.00 |

GHIRSH

c/m: '65' on 1 Ghirsh, KM#6.

| 30 | AH1344 | — | 2.50 | 4.00 | 10.00 | 25.00 |

SAUDI ARABIA 1490

c/m: '65' on 1 Ghirsh, KM#9.

KM#	Date	Mintage	Good	VG	Fine	VF
31	AH1346	—	2.50	4.00	10.00	25.00

c/m: '65' on 1 Ghirsh, KM#15.

| 32 | AH1348 | — | 2.50 | 4.00 | 10.00 | 25.00 |

Plain edge
c/m: '65' on 1 Ghirsh, KM#21.

| 33 | AH1356 | — | 2.00 | 3.00 | 8.00 | 20.00 |

MONETARY REFORM
5 Halala = 1 Ghirsh
HALALA

BRONZE

KM#	Date	Mintage	Fine	VF	XF	Unc
44	AH1383	5.000	.50	.60	.75	1.00
	1392	5.000	.50	.75	1.00	1.50

5 HALALA
(1 Ghirsh)

COPPER-NICKEL

| 45 | AH1392 | 130.000 | .10 | .15 | .30 | .50 |

| 53 | AH1397 | 20.000 | .15 | .25 | .50 | 1.75 |
| | 1400 | — | .15 | .25 | .50 | 1.50 |

F.A.O. Issue

KM#	Date	Year	Mintage	VF	XF	Unc
57	AH1398	1978	1.500	.30	.50	1.00

KM#	Date	Mintage	Fine	VF	XF	Unc
61	AH1408	—		.30	.50	1.00

10 HALALA

COPPER-NICKEL

| 46 | AH1392 | 55.000 | .10 | .20 | .35 | .50 |

| 54 | AH1397 | 50.000 | .15 | .25 | .75 | 1.50 |
| | 1400 | 29.500 | .25 | .75 | 1.00 | 2.00 |

F.A.O. Issue

KM#	Date	Year	Mintage	VF	XF	Unc
58	AH1398	1978	1.000	.25	.50	1.00

KM#	Date	Mintage	Fine	VF	XF	Unc
62	AH1408	—		.25	.50	1.00

25 HALALA

COPPER-NICKEL
Error. Denomination in masculine gender.

| 47 | AH1392 | 48.465 | .75 | 1.50 | 6.00 | 12.00 |

Denomination in feminine gender

| 48 | AH1392 | Inc. Ab. | .25 | .40 | 1.00 | 2.00 |

F.A.O. Issue

KM#	Date	Year	Mintage	VF	XF	Unc
49	AH1392	1973	.200	.15	.50	1.00

KM#	Date	Mintage	Fine	VF	XF	Unc
55	AH1397	20.000	.10	.35	.50	1.00
	1400	57.000	.35	.50	.75	1.50

| 63 | AH1408 | — | .10 | .35 | .50 | 1.00 |

50 HALALA

COPPER-NICKEL
F.A.O. Issue

KM#	Date	Year	Mintage	VF	XF	Unc
50	AH1392	1972	.500	.40	.75	1.25

| 51 | AH1392 | 16.000 | .20 | .35 | .60 | 1.25 |

| 56 | AH1397 | 20.000 | .25 | .35 | 1.00 | 3.00 |
| | 1400 | 21.600 | .75 | 1.00 | 1.50 | 3.50 |

| 64 | AH1408 | — | .75 | 1.00 | 2.00 | 4.00 |

100 HALALA

COPPER-NICKEL

| 52 | AH1396 | (1976) | 10.000 | .65 | 1.00 | 3.00 |
| | 1400 | (1980) | 4.950 | 1.75 | 3.00 | 4.50 |

F.A.O. Issue

KM#	Date	Year	Mintage	VF	XF	Unc
59	AH1397	1977	—	1.75	3.00	5.00
	1398	1978	.250	.75	1.50	2.50

KM#	Date	Mintage	Fine	VF	XF	Unc
65	AH1408	—	1.00	2.00	3.00

TRADE COINAGE
GUINEA

 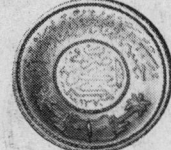

7.9881 g, .917 GOLD, .2354 oz AGW

36	AH1370	—	—	BV	120.00	135.00

43	AH1377	1.579	—	BV	120.00	145.00

SENEGAL

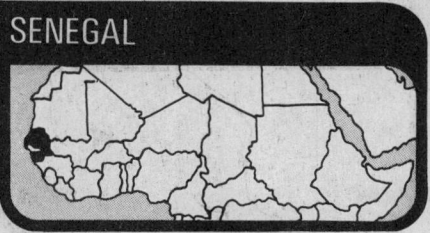

The Republic of Senegal, located on the bulge of West Africa between Mauritania and Guinea-Bissau, has an area of 75,750 sq. mi. (196,192 sq. km.) and a population of *7.7 million. Capital: Dakar. The economy is primarily agricultural. Peanuts and products, phosphates, and canned fish are exported.

An abundance of megalithic remains indicates that Senegal was inhabited in prehistoric times. The Portuguese had some trading stations on the banks of the Senegal River in the 15th century. French commercial establishments date from the 17th century. The French gradually acquired control over the interior regions, which were administered as a protectorate until 1920, and as a colony thereafter. After the 1958 French constitutional referendum, Senegal became a member of the French Community with virtual autonomy. In 1959 Senegal and the French Soudan merged to form the Mali Federation, which became fully independent on June 20, 1960. (April 4, the date the transfer of power agreement was signed with France, is celebrated as Senegal's independence day). The Federation broke up on Aug. 20, 1960, when Senegal seceded and proclaimed the Republic of Senegal. Soudan became the Republic of Mali a month later.

Senegal is a member of a monetary union of autonomous republics called the Monetary Union of West African States (Union Monetaire Ouest-Africaine). The other members are Ivory Coast, Benin, Burkina Faso (Upper Volta), Niger, Mauritania and Togo. Mali was a member, but seceded in 1962. Some of the member countries have issued coinage in addition to the common currency issued by the Monetary Union of West African States.

10 FRANCS

3.2000 g, .900 GOLD, .0926 oz AGW
Anniversary of Independence

KM#	Date	Mintage	VF	XF	Unc
1	1968	—	—	Proof	75.00

25 FRANCS

8.0000 g, .900 GOLD, .2315 oz AGW
Anniversary of Independence

2	1968	—	—	Proof	150.00

50 FRANCS

16.0000 g, .900 GOLD, .4630 oz AGW
Anniversary of Independence

3	1968	—	—	Proof	275.00

SENEGAL 1491

28.2800 g, .925 SILVER, .8411 oz ASW
25th Anniversary of Eurafrique Program

KM#	Date	Mintage	VF	XF	Unc
5	1975	1,968	—	—	85.00
	1975	.010	—	Proof	100.00

100 FRANCS

32.0000 g, .900 GOLD, .9260 oz AGW
Anniversary of Independence

4	1968	—	—	Proof	550.00

150 FRANCS

79.9400 g, .925 SILVER, 2.3776 oz ASW
25th Anniversary of Eurafrique Program
Rev: Similar to 50 Francs, KM#5.

6	1975	1,075	—	—	140.00
	1975	.010	—	Proof	160.00

250 FRANCS

3.9800 g, .917 GOLD, .1172 oz AGW
25th Anniversary of Eurafrique Program

7	1975	1,000	—	—	100.00
	1975	1,250	—	Proof	100.00

SENEGAL

500 FRANCS

7.9600 g, .917 GOLD, .2344 oz AGW
25th Anniversary of Eurafrique Program

KM#	Date	Mintage	VF	XF	Unc
8	1975	500 pcs.	—	—	150.00
	1975	1,250	—	Proof	150.00

1000 FRANCS

15.9500 g, .916 GOLD, .4697 oz AGW
25th Anniversary of Eurafrique Program

9	1975	217 pcs.	—	—	350.00
	1975	1,250	—	Proof	275.00

2500 FRANCS

39.9300 g, .916 GOLD, 1.1760 oz AGW
25th Anniversary of Eurafrique Program

10	1975	195 pcs.	—	—	800.00
	1975	1,250	—	Proof	700.00

MINT SETS (MS)

KM#	Date	Mintage	Identification	Issue Price	Mkt. Val.
MS1	1975(4)	195	KM7-10	—	1400.

PROOF SETS (PS)

PS1	1968(4)	—	KM1-4	—	1050.
PS2	1975(2)	—	KM5-6	—	260.

Listings For
SERBIA: refer to Yugoslavia

SEYCHELLES

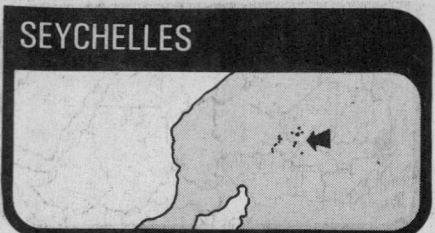

The Republic of Seychelles, an archipelago of 85 granite and coral islands situated in the Indian Ocean 600 miles (965 km.) northeast of Madagascar, has an area of 156 sq. mi. (404 sq. km.) and a population of *70,000. Among these islands are the Aldabra Islands, the Farquhar Group, and Ile Desroches, which the United Kingdom ceded to the Seychelles upon its independence. Capital: Victoria, on Mahe. The economy is based on fishing, a plantation system of agriculture, and tourism. Copra, cinnamon and vanilla are exported.

Although the Seychelles are marked on Portuguese charts of the early 16th century, the first recorded visit to the islands, by an English ship, occurred in 1609. The Seychelles were annexed to France by Captain Lazare Picault in 1743 and permanently settled in 1768, with the intention of establishing spice plantations to compete with the Dutch monopoly of the spice trade. British troops seized the islands in 1810, during the Napoleonic Wars; they were formally ceded to Britain by the Treaty of Paris, 1814. The Seychelles were a dependency of Mauritius until Aug. 31, 1903, when they became a separate British Crown Colony. The colony was granted limited internal self-government in 1970, and attained independence on June 28, 1976, becoming Britain's last African possession to do so. Seychelles is a member of the Commonwealth of Nations. The president is the Head of State and of Government.

RULERS
British, until 1976

MONETARY SYSTEM
100 Cents = 1 Rupee

CENT

BRONZE

KM#	Date	Mintage	VF	XF	Unc
5	1948	.300	.25	.50	1.25
	1948	—	—	Proof	100.00

14	1959	.030	1.00	2.00	3.00
	1959	—	—	Proof	—
	1961	.030	.50	1.00	2.50
	1961	—	—	Proof	—
	1963	.040	.50	1.00	1.50
	1963	—	—	Proof	—
	1965	.020	2.00	3.00	5.00
	1969	*5,000	15.00	25.00	60.00
	1969	—	—	Proof	5.00

*Latest reports indicate only 5,000 circulation strikes have been released to date in addition to proof issues.

ALUMINUM
F.A.O. Issue

17	1972	2.350	—	.10	.25

2 CENTS

BRONZE

6	1948	.350	.35	.60	1.50
	1948	—	—	Proof	125.00

15	1959	.030	.50	1.00	2.00
	1959	—	—	Proof	—
	1961	.030	.50	1.00	2.25
	1961	—	—	Proof	—
	1963	.040	.75	1.25	2.00
	1963	—	—	Proof	—
	1965	.020	2.00	3.00	4.00
	1968	.020	2.00	3.00	5.50
	1969	5,000	—	Proof	4.00

5 CENTS

BRONZE

7	1948	.300	.40	.80	2.00
	1948	—	—	Proof	150.00

16	1964	.020	1.00	1.75	4.50
	1964	—	—	Proof	—
	1965	.040	1.50	2.50	5.50
	1967	.020	1.50	3.00	5.00
	1968	.040	1.00	2.00	7.00
	1969	.100	.50	1.00	5.00
	1969	—	—	Proof	4.00
	1971	.025	.50	1.50	2.50

ALUMINUM
F.A.O. Issue

18	1972	2.200	—	.10	.25
	1975	1.200	—	.10	.25

10 CENTS

COPPER-NICKEL

1	1939	.036	8.00	20.00	70.00
	1939	—	—	Proof	175.00
	1943	.036	4.00	10.00	50.00
	1944	.036	4.00	10.00	50.00
	1944	—	—	Proof	175.00

8	1951	.036	2.00	5.00	9.00
	1951	—	—	Proof	150.00

KM#	Date	Mintage	VF	XF	Unc
12	1968	.020	3.00	8.00	30.00
	1969	.060	.75	1.00	12.00
	1969	—	—	Proof	3.00
	1970	.050	.75	1.00	8.00
	1971	.100	.75	1.00	3.00
	1972	.120	.50	.75	1.00
	1974	.100	.50	.75	1.00

RUPEE

11.6600 g, .500 SILVER, .1874 oz ASW

4	1939	.090	12.50	40.00	150.00
	1939	—	—	Proof	450.00

COPPER-NICKEL

13	1954	.150	.50	1.00	3.00
	1954	—	—	Proof	250.00
	1960	.060	.90	1.50	3.00
	1960	—	—	Proof	—
	1966	.045	1.25	2.25	7.50
	1967	.010	3.50	7.50	30.00
	1968	.040	2.50	5.00	20.00
	1969	.050	1.50	3.00	12.50
	1969	—	—	Proof	5.00
	1970	.050	1.50	2.50	10.00
	1971	.100	.75	1.50	5.00
	1972	.120	.75	1.50	2.00
	1974	.100	—	—	1.50

5 RUPEES

COPPER-NICKEL

19	1972	.220	1.50	2.00	3.00

15.5000 g, .925 SILVER, .4609 oz ASW

19a	1972	2,500	—	Proof	40.00
	1974	4,581	—	Proof	17.50

10 RUPEES

COPPER-NICKEL

20	1974	—	2.00	2.50	4.00

28.2800 g, .925 SILVER, .8411 oz ASW

20a	1974	.025	—	Proof	17.50

REPUBLIC
CENT

NICKEL-BRASS

KM#	Date	Mintage	VF	XF	Unc
10	1953	.130	.50	1.00	2.00
	1953	—	—	Proof	150.00
	1965	.040	1.00	1.50	5.00
	1967	.020	4.00	7.50	15.00
	1968	.050	1.00	4.00	12.50
	1969	.060	1.00	2.00	8.00
	1969	—	—	Proof	2.00
	1970	.075	.50	1.00	4.50
	1971	.100	.50	1.00	1.75
	1972	.120	.30	.50	1.00
	1973	.100	.15	.25	1.00
	1974	.100	.15	.25	.75

25 CENTS

2.9200 g, .500 SILVER .0469 oz ASW

2	1939	.036	7.50	35.00	125.00
	1939	—	—	Proof	250.00
	1943	.036	5.00	25.00	100.00
	1944	.036	3.50	20.00	85.00
	1944	—	—	Proof	—

COPPER-NICKEL

9	1951	.036	2.00	7.50	28.00
	1951	—	—	Proof	175.00

11	1954	.124	.75	1.00	2.00
	1954	—	—	Proof	150.00
	1960	.040	.75	1.25	2.00
	1960	—	—	Proof	—
	1964	.040	1.00	2.00	5.00
	1965	.040	1.00	2.00	5.00
	1966	.010	3.50	10.00	20.00
	1967	.020	2.50	4.00	15.00
	1968	.020	2.50	4.00	15.00
	1969	.100	1.00	2.00	4.00
	1969	—	—	Proof	2.00
	1970	.040	1.50	3.00	10.00
	1972	.120	.50	.75	1.00
	1973	.100	.50	.75	1.00
	1974	.100	.50	.75	1.00

1/2 RUPEE

5.8300 g, .500 SILVER, .0937 oz ASW

3	1939	.036	10.00	35.00	150.00
	1939	—	—	Proof	300.00

COPPER-NICKEL

12	1954	.072	.50	1.25	3.75
	1954	—	—	Proof	175.00
	1960	.060	.50	1.00	2.50
	1960	—	—	Proof	175.00
	1966	.015	1.50	5.00	15.00
	1967	.020	3.00	8.00	25.00

SEYCHELLES 1493

ALUMINUM
Declaration of Independence

KM#	Date	Mintage	VF	XF	Unc
21	1976	.109	.10	.25	.75
	1976	8,500	—	Proof	1.50

30	1977	—	—	.10	.15

46	1982	.500	—	.10	.20
	1982	—	—	Proof	2.25

5 CENTS

ALUMINUM
Declaration of Independence

22	1976	.209	.10	.25	.75
	1976	8,500	—	Proof	1.50

F.A.O. Issue

31	1977	.300	—	.10	.45

BRASS
World Food Day

43	1981	.720	—	.10	.50

47	1982	1.500	—	.10	.30
	1982	Inc. Ab.	—	Proof	2.50

10 CENTS

NICKEL-BRASS
Declaration of Independence

23	1976	.209	.25	.50	1.00
	1976	8,500	—	Proof	2.00

F.A.O. Issue

32	1977	.125	—	.10	.45

BRASS

SEYCHELLES 1494

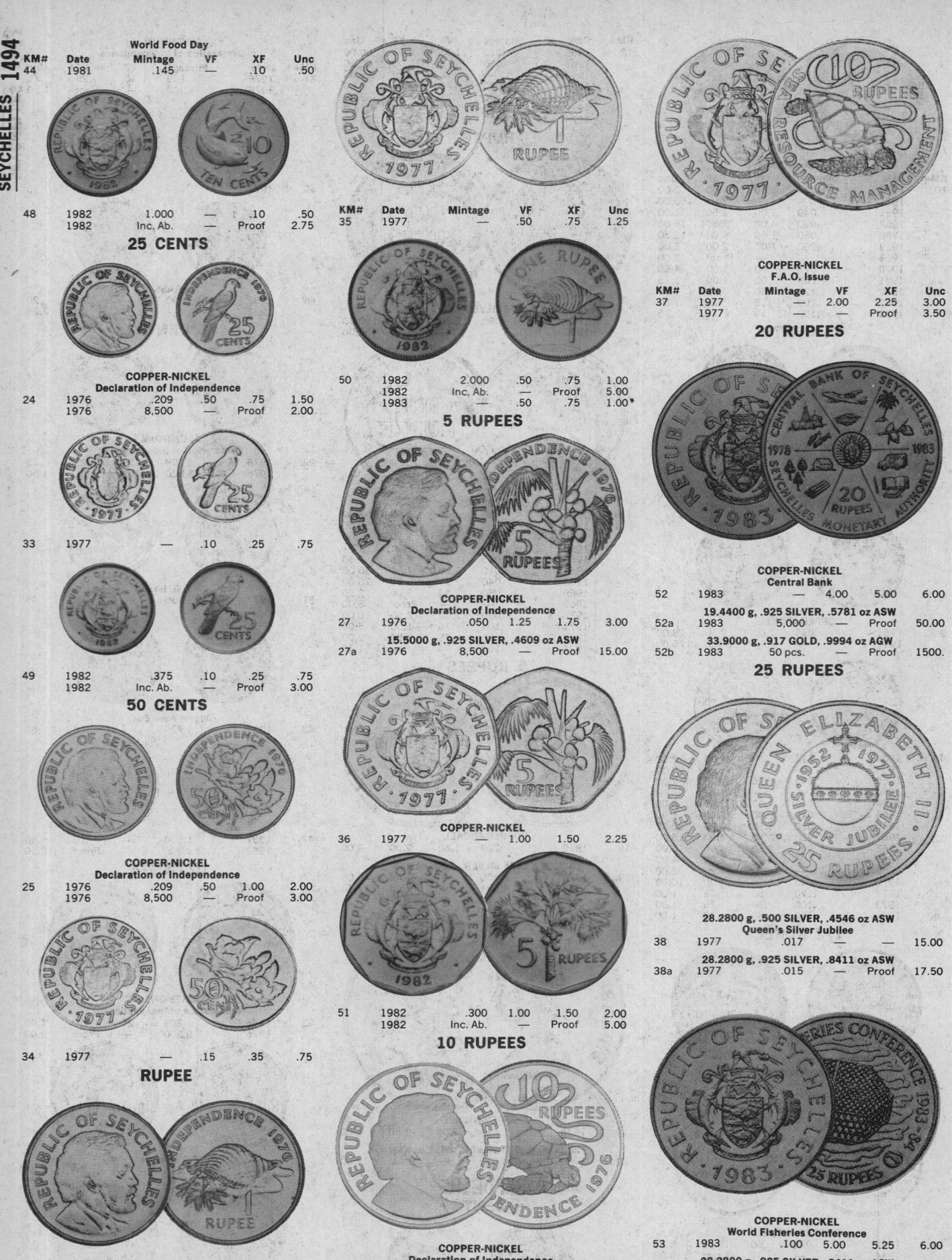

World Food Day

KM#	Date	Mintage	VF	XF	Unc
44	1981	.145	—	.10	.50

| | 1982 | 1.000 | — | .10 | .50 |
| 48 | 1982 | Inc. Ab. | — | Proof | 2.75 |

25 CENTS

COPPER-NICKEL
Declaration of Independence

| 24 | 1976 | .209 | .50 | .75 | 1.50 |
| | 1976 | 8,500 | — | Proof | 2.00 |

| 33 | 1977 | — | .10 | .25 | .75 |

| 49 | 1982 | .375 | .10 | .25 | .75 |
| | 1982 | Inc. Ab. | — | Proof | 3.00 |

50 CENTS

COPPER-NICKEL
Declaration of Independence

| 25 | 1976 | .209 | .50 | 1.00 | 2.00 |
| | 1976 | 8,500 | — | Proof | 3.00 |

| 34 | 1977 | — | .15 | .35 | .75 |

RUPEE

COPPER-NICKEL
Declaration of Independence

| 26 | 1976 | .259 | .75 | 1.00 | 1.50 |
| | 1976 | 8,500 | — | Proof | 2.50 |

KM#	Date	Mintage	VF	XF	Unc
35	1977	—	.50	.75	1.25

50	1982	2.000	.50	.75	1.00
	1982	Inc. Ab.	—	Proof	5.00
	1983	—	.50	.75	1.00*

5 RUPEES

COPPER-NICKEL
Declaration of Independence

| 27 | 1976 | .050 | 1.25 | 1.75 | 3.00 |

15.5000 g, .925 SILVER, .4609 oz ASW

| 27a | 1976 | 8,500 | — | Proof | 15.00 |

COPPER-NICKEL

| 36 | 1977 | — | 1.00 | 1.50 | 2.25 |

| 51 | 1982 | .300 | 1.00 | 1.50 | 2.00 |
| | 1982 | Inc. Ab. | — | Proof | 5.00 |

10 RUPEES

COPPER-NICKEL
Declaration of Independence

| 28 | 1976 | .050 | 2.00 | 2.25 | 3.00 |

28.2800 g, .925 SILVER, .8411 oz ASW

| 28a | 1976 | .029 | — | Proof | 15.00 |

COPPER-NICKEL
F.A.O. Issue

KM#	Date	Mintage	VF	XF	Unc
37	1977	—	2.00	2.25	3.00
	1977	—	—	Proof	3.50

20 RUPEES

COPPER-NICKEL
Central Bank

| 52 | 1983 | — | 4.00 | 5.00 | 6.00 |

19.4400 g, .925 SILVER, .5781 oz ASW

| 52a | 1983 | 5,000 | — | Proof | 50.00 |

33.9000 g, .917 GOLD, .9994 oz AGW

| 52b | 1983 | 50 pcs. | — | Proof | 1500. |

25 RUPEES

28.2800 g, .500 SILVER, .4546 oz ASW
Queen's Silver Jubilee

| 38 | 1977 | .017 | — | — | 15.00 |

28.2800 g, .925 SILVER, .8411 oz ASW

| 38a | 1977 | .015 | — | Proof | 17.50 |

COPPER-NICKEL
World Fisheries Conference

| 53 | 1983 | .100 | 5.00 | 5.25 | 6.00 |

28.2800 g, .925 SILVER, .8411 oz ASW

| 53a | 1983 | .020 | — | Proof | 25.00 |

47.5400 g, .917 GOLD, 1.4015 oz AGW

| 53b | 1983 | 100 pcs. | — | Proof | 1500. |

50 RUPEES

28.2800 g, .925 SILVER, .8411 oz ASW
Conservation Series
Rev: Squirrel Fish.

KM#	Date	Mintage	VF	XF	Unc
39	1978	4,453	—	—	20.00
	1978	4,281	—	Proof	30.00

19.4400 g, .925 SILVER, .5781 oz ASW
UNICEF and International Year of the Child

| 42 | 1980 | .010 | — | Proof | 20.00 |

Decade For Women
| 54 | 1985 | 500 pcs. | — | Proof | 37.50 |

100 RUPEES

31.6500 g, .925 SILVER, .9413 oz ASW
Conservation Series
Rev: White-tailed Tropicbird.

| 40 | 1978 | 4,453 | — | — | 30.00 |
| | 1978 | 4,075 | — | Proof | 35.00 |

35.0000 g, .500 SILVER, .5627 oz ASW

KM#	Date	Mintage	VF	XF	Unc
45a	1981	.010	—	Proof	27.50

World Food Day
| 45 | 1981 | 6,000 | — | — | 25.00 |
| | 1981 | 5,000 | — | Proof | 27.50 |

19.4400 g, .925 SILVER, .5781 oz ASW
10th Anniversary of Independence
| 55 | 1986 | 1,000 | — | Proof | 35.00 |

10th Anniversary of Liberation
| 57 | 1987 | 1,000 | — | Proof | 35.00 |

10th Anniversary of Central Bank
| 59 | 1988 | | | | 25.00 |

1.7000 g, .917 GOLD, .0501 oz AGW
10th Anniversary of Central Bank
Similar to KM#59.
| 60 | 1988 | | | | 35.00 |

1000 RUPEES

15.9800 g, .917 GOLD, .4707 oz AGW
Obv: President Mancham. Rev: Tortoise, date, value.
| 29 | 1976 | 5,000 | — | — | 250.00 |
| | 1976 | 1,000 | — | Proof | 350.00 |

10th Anniversary of Independence
Similar to 100 Rupees, KM#55.
| 56 | 1986 | 100 pcs. | — | Proof | 500.00 |

10th Anniversary of Liberation
KM#	Date	Mintage	VF	XF	Unc
58	1987	100 pcs.	—	Proof	450.00

15.9400 g, .917 GOLD, .4698 oz AGW
10th Anniversary of Central Bank
Similar to 100 Rupees, KM#59.
| 61 | 1988 | *5,000 | — | Proof | 250.00 |

1500 RUPEES

33.4370 g, .900 GOLD, .9676 oz AGW
Conservation Series
Rev: Black Paradise Flycatcher.
| 41 | 1978 | 683 pcs. | — | — | 600.00 |
| | 1978 | 201 pcs. | — | Proof | 900.00 |

MINT SETS (MS)

KM#	Date	Mintage	Identification	Issue Price	Mkt. Val.
MS1	1972(7)	—	KM10-13,17-19	—	9.00
MS2	1974(5)	—	KM10-13,20	—	9.00
MS3	1976(8)	—	KM21-28	—	16.00
MS4	1982(6)	—	KM46-51	—	5.00

PROOF SETS (PS)

PS1	1939(4)	—	KM1-4	—	1200.
PS2	1969(7)	5,000	KM10-16	8.40	25.00
PS3	1974(2)	5,000	KM19a,20a	37.00	35.00
PS4	1976(9)	1,000	KM21-26,27a,28a,29	375.00	400.00
PS5	1976(8)	7,500	KM21-26,27a,28a	42.50	45.00
PS6	1982(6)	5,000	KM46-51	29.95	20.00

Listings For
SHARJAH: refer to United Arab Emirates

SIERRA LEONE

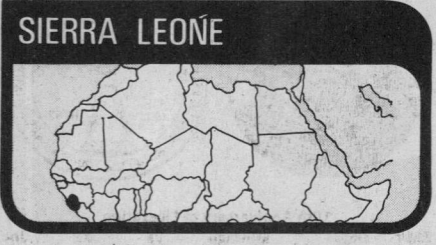

The Republic of Sierra Leone, a British Commonwealth nation located in western Africa between Guinea and Liberia, has an area of 27,699 sq. mi. (71,740 sq. km.) and a population of *4.3 million. Capital: Freetown. The economy is predominantly agricultural but mining contributes significantly to export revenues. Diamonds, iron ore, palm kernels, cocoa, and coffee are exported.

The coast of Sierra Leone was first visited by Portuguese and British slavers in the 15th and 16th centuries. The first settlement, at Freetown, 1787, was established as a refuge for freed slaves within the British Empire, runaway slaves from the United States and Negroes discharged from the British armed forces. The first settlers were virtually wiped out by tribal attacks and disease. The colony was re-established under the auspices of the Sierra Leone Company and transferred to the British Crown in 1807. The interior region was secured and established as a protectorate in 1896. Sierra Leone became independent within the Commonwealth on April 27, 1961, and adopted a republican constitution ten years later. It is a member of the Commonwealth of Nations. The president is Chief of State and Head of Government.

For similar coinage refer to British West Africa.

RULERS
British, until 1971

MONETARY SYSTEM
Until 1906
100 Cents = 50 Pence = 1 Dollar
Until 1960
12 Pence = 1 Shilling
Commencing 1960
100 Cents = 1 Leone

SIERRA LEONE COMPANY
10 CENTS
.902 SILVER

KM#	Date	Mintage	Fine	VF	XF	Unc
3	1805	6,100	30.00	80.00	150.00	275.00

COUNTERMARKED COINAGE
1/4 DOLLAR

.903 SILVER
c/m: Crowned WR on one quarter cut of a Spanish or Colonial 8 Reales.

KM#	Date	Mintage	VG	Fine	VF	XF
10	ND(1832)	—	75.00	125.00	200.00	300.00

1/2 DOLLAR

.903 SILVER
c/m: Crowned WR on Spanish or Spanish Colonial 4 Reales.

| 13 | ND(1832) | — | 60.00 | 100.00 | 150.00 | 225.00 |

SIERRA LEONE
1/2 CENT

BRONZE

KM#	Date	Mintage	VF	XF	Unc
16	1964	.600	—	.10	.15
	1964	.010	—	Proof	.50

2.8300 g, .925 SILVER, .0841 oz ASW
| 16a | 1964 | 22 pcs. | — | Proof | 650.00 |

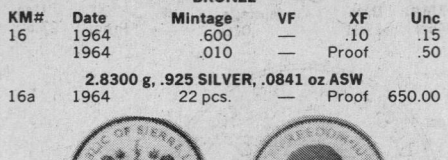

BRONZE
| 31 | 1980 | — | — | .10 | .15 |
| | 1980 | .010 | — | Proof | 1.00 |

CENT

BRONZE
| 17 | 1964 | 35.000 | — | .10 | .15 |
| | 1964 | .010 | — | Proof | .75 |

5.6700 g, .925 SILVER, .1686 oz ASW
| 17a | 1964 | 22 pcs. | — | Proof | 650.00 |

BRONZE
| 32 | 1980 | — | — | .10 | .15 | .20 |
| | 1980 | .010 | — | Proof | 1.00 |

5 CENTS

COPPER-NICKEL
| 18 | 1964 | .900 | .15 | .25 | .50 |
| | 1964 | .010 | — | Proof | .75 |

2.4900 g, .925 SILVER, .0740 oz ASW
| 18a | 1964 | 22 pcs. | — | Proof | 650.00 |

COPPER-NICKEL
33	1980	—	—	.10	.25	.35
	1980	.010	—	Proof	1.50
	1984	—	—	.10	.25	.35

10 CENTS

COPPER-NICKEL
| 19 | 1964 | 24.000 | .25 | .40 | .60 |
| | 1964 | .010 | — | Proof | 1.00 |

4.9200 g, .925 SILVER, .1463 oz ASW
| 19a | 1964 | 22 pcs. | — | Proof | 650.00 |

COPPER-NICKEL
KM#	Date	Mintage	VF	XF	Unc
34	1978	.200	.25	.40	.60
	1980	—	.20	.30	.50
	1980	.010	—	Proof	3.00
	1984	—	.20	.30	.50

20 CENTS

COPPER-NICKEL
| 20 | 1964 | 11.000 | .35 | .55 | .85 |
| | 1964 | .010 | — | Proof | 1.00 |

8.2200 g, .925 SILVER, .2444 oz ASW
| 20a | 1964 | 22 pcs. | — | Proof | 650.00 |

COPPER-NICKEL
30	1978	2.375	.35	.55	.85
	1980	—	.35	.50	.75
	1980	.010	—	Proof	4.75
	1984	—	.35	.55	.75

50 CENTS

COPPER-NICKEL
| 25 | 1972 | 1.000 | 1.00 | 1.50 | 2.50 |
| | 1972 | 2.000 | — | Proof | 5.00 |

COPPER-NICKEL
35	1980	—	1.00	1.25	2.00
	1980	.010	—	Proof	5.50
	1984	—	1.00	1.25	2.00

LEONE

COPPER-NICKEL
Sir Milton Marcai
| 21 | 1964 | .010 | — | Proof | 10.00 |

22.6220 g, .925 SILVER, .6738 oz ASW
| 21a | 1964 | 12 pcs. | — | Proof | 1000. |
| | 1976 | 962 pcs. | — | Proof | 100.00 |

.917 GOLD
| 21b | 1964 | 10 pcs. | — | Proof | 2500. |

SIERRA LEONE

COPPER NICKEL
10th Anniversary of Bank

KM#	Date	Mintage	VF	XF	Unc
26	1974	.103	1.00	1.50	3.00

28.2800 g, .925 SILVER, .8411 oz ASW

| 26a | 1974 | .022 | — | Proof | 15.00 |

GOLD
10th Anniversary of Bank

| 26b | 1974 | 100 pcs. | — | — | 1200. |

28.2800 g, .925 SILVER, .8411 oz ASW
70th Birthday of Dr. Siaka Stevens

| 27 | 1975 | .140 | — | — | 12.50 |
| | 1975 | .041 | — | Proof | 15.00 |

57.6050 g, .917 GOLD, 1.6985 oz AGW

| 27a | 1975 | 100 pcs. | — | Proof | 1200. |

COPPER-NICKEL
O.A.U. Summit Conference

| 36 | 1980 | .075 | 1.00 | 2.00 | 3.00 |

28.2800 g, .925 SILVER, .8411 oz ASW

| 36a | 1980 | .015 | — | Proof | 32.50 |

9.5000 g, .925 SILVER, .2825 oz ASW
Freetown Bicentennial

| 40 | 1987 | 3,000 | — | Proof | 35.00 |

16.0000 g, .917 GOLD, .4716 oz AGW

| 40a | 1987 | 1,250 | — | Proof | 300.00 |

NICKEL BRONZE

| 43 | 1987 | — | .50 | .75 | 1.50 |

2 LEONES

COPPER-NICKEL
F.A.O. Issue

| 29 | 1976 | .020 | 1.00 | 2.00 | 4.00 |

10 LEONES

28.2800 g, .925 SILVER, .8411 oz ASW
Year of the Scout

KM#	Date	Mintage	VF	XF	Unc
38	1983	.010	—	—	25.00
	1983	.010	—	Proof	32.50

World Wildlife Fund - Pygmy Hippopotamus

| 41 | 1987 | .025 | — | Proof | 35.00 |

100 LEONES

15.9800 g, .917 GOLD, .4711 oz AGW
Year of the Scout

| 39 | 1983 | 2,000 | — | — | 400.00 |
| | 1983 | 2,000 | — | Proof | 500.00 |

1/4 GOLDE

13.6360 g, .900 GOLD, .3946 oz AGW
5th Anniversary of Independence

| 22 | 1966 | 5,000 | — | — | 225.00 |

15.0000 g, .916 GOLD, .4418 oz AGW

| 22a | 1966 | 600 pcs. | — | Proof | 300.00 |

10.3150 g, PALLADIUM

| 22b | 1966 | 100 pcs. | — | Proof | 125.00 |

1/2 GOLDE

27.2730 g, .900 GOLD, .7891 oz AGW
5th Anniversary of Independence

KM#	Date	Mintage	VF	XF	Unc
23	1966	2,500	—	—	475.00

30.0000 g, .916 GOLD, .8836 oz AGW

| 23a | 1966 | 600 pcs. | — | Proof | 600.00 |

20.6290 g, PALLADIUM

| 23b | 1966 | — | — | Proof | 200.00 |

GOLDE

54.5450 g, .900 GOLD, 1.5783 oz AGW
5th Anniversary of Independence

| 24 | 1966 | 1,500 | — | — | 950.00 |

60.0000 g, .916 GOLD, 1.7672 oz AGW

| 24a | 1966 | 400 pcs. | — | Proof | 1200. |

41.2590 g, PALLADIUM

| 24b | 1966 | 100 pcs. | — | Proof | 400.00 |

41.2590 g, PLATINUM

| 24c | 1966 | — | — | Proof | 1000. |

5 GOLDE

15.9800 g, .917 GOLD, .4711 oz AGW
O.A.U. Summit Conference

| 37 | 1980 | 457 pcs. | — | — | 300.00 |
| | 1980 | 325 pcs. | — | Proof | 330.00 |

World Wildlife Fund - Duiker Zebra

| 42 | 1987 | 5,000 | — | Proof | 475.00 |

10 GOLDE

57.6000 g, .916 GOLD, 1.6965 oz AGW
70th Birthday Dr. Siaka Stevens

| 28 | 1975 | 727 pcs. | — | — | 950.00 |
| | 1975 | 307 pcs. | — | Proof | 1150. |

MINT SETS (MS)

KM#	Date	Mintage	Identification	Issue Price	Mkt. Val.
MS1	1966(3)	—	KM22-24	—	1650.

PROOF SETS (PS)

PS1	1964(6)	10,000	KM16-21	—	14.00
PS2	1964(6)	12	KM16a-20a,21b		5750.
PS3	1964(6)	10	KM16a-21a		4250.
PS4	1966(3)	400	KM22a-24a		2100.
PS5	1972(2)	1,000	KM25 (2 pcs. with 50 cent banknote (0 serials) in plush case.	—	15.00
PS6	1980(6)	10,000	KM30-35	34.00	40.00

SINGAPORE

The Republic of Singapore, a British Commonwealth nation situated at the southern tip of the Malay peninsula, has an area of 224 sq. mi. (581 sq. km.) and a population of *2.7 million. Capital: Singapore. The economy is based on entrepot trade, manufacturing and oil. Rubber, petroleum products, machinery and spices are exported.

Singapore's modern history - it was an important shipping center in the 14th century before the rise of Malacca and Penang - began in 1819 when Sir Thomas Stamford Raffles, an agent for the British East India Company, founded the town of Singapore. By 1825 its trade exceeded that of Malacca and Penang combined. The opening of the Suez Canal (1869) and the demand for rubber and tin created by the automobile and packaging industries combined to make Singapore one of the major ports of the world. In 1826 Singapore, Penang and Malacca were combined to form the Straits Settlements, which was made a Crown Colony in 1867. Singapore became a separate Crown Colony in 1946 when the Straits Settlements was dissolved. It joined in the formation of Malaysia in 1963, but broke away on Aug. 9, 1965, to become an independent republic. Singapore is a member of the Commonwealth of Nations. The president is Chief of State. The prime minister is Head of Government.

For earlier coinage see Straits Settlements, Malaya, Malaya and British Borneo, and Malaysia

MINT MARKS
sm - Singapore Mint monogram

MONETARY SYSTEM
100 Cents = 1 Dollar

CENT

BRONZE

KM#	Date	Mintage	VF	XF	Unc
1	1967	7.500	—	.20	.40
	1967	2,000	—	Proof	2.25
	1968	2.696	—	.25	.50
	1968	5,000	—	Proof	2.00
	1969	7.220	—	.20	.30
	1969	3,000	—	Proof	10.00
	1970	1.402	—	.40	.70
	1971	9.731	—	.20	.25
	1972	1.655	—	.20	.25
	1972	749 pcs.	—	Proof	40.00
	1973	6.377	—	.10	.20
	1973	1,000	—	Proof	5.00
	1974	9.421	—	—	.10
	1974	1,500	—	Proof	4.00
	1975	24.226	—	—	.10
	1975	3,000	—	Proof	1.50
	1976	2.500	—	.10	.20
	1976 *sm*	3,500	—	Proof	1.25
	1977 *sm*	3,500	—	Proof	1.25
	1978 *sm*	4,000	—	Proof	1.25
	1979 *sm*	3,500	—	Proof	1.25
	1980 *sm*	.014	—	Proof	1.00
	1982 *sm*	.020	—	Proof	1.00
	1983 *sm*	.015	—	Proof	1.00
	1984 *sm*	—	—	Proof	1.00

COPPER-CLAD STEEL

1a	1976	13.665	—	—	.25
	1977	13.940	—	—	.25
	1978	5.931	—	—	.25
	1979	11.986	—	—	.15
	1980	19.922	—	—	.15
	1981	38.084	—	—	.10
	1982	24.105	—	—	.10
	1983	2.204	—	—	.10
	1984	5.695	—	—	.10
	1985	.148	—	—	.35

2.9200 g, .925 SILVER, .0869 oz ASW

| 1b | 1981 *sm* | .030 | — | Proof | 5.00 |

BRONZE
Rev: Vanda Miss Joaquim plants.

49	1986	.120	—	—	.10
	1987	—	—	—	.10
	1988	—	—	—	.10

1.8100 g, .925 SILVER, .0538 oz ASW

KM#	Date	Mintage	VF	XF	Unc
49a	1985 *sm*	.020	—	Proof	2.25
	1986 *sm*	.015	—	Proof	2.25
	1987	—	—	Proof	2.25

COPPER CLAD STEEL
| 49b | 1986 | 20.000 | — | — | .10 |

5 CENTS

COPPER-NICKEL

2	1967	28.000	—	.15	.30
	1967	2,000	—	Proof	3.25
	1968	4.217	—	.20	.40
	1968	5,000	—	Proof	3.00
	1969	14.778	—	.10	.30
	1969	3,000	—	Proof	15.00
	1970	3.065	—	.20	.40
	1971	13.202	—	.10	.15
	1972	9.817	—	.10	.15
	1972	749 pcs.	—	Proof	50.00
	1973	2.980	—	.30	.50
	1973	1,000	—	Proof	7.50
	1974	10.868	—	.10	.15
	1974	1,500	—	Proof	6.50
	1975	1.729	—	.30	.50
	1975	3,000	—	Proof	2.50
	1976	15.541	—	.10	.15
	1976 *sm*	3,500	—	Proof	2.25
	1977	9.957	—	.10	.15
	1977 *sm*	3,500	—	Proof	2.25
	1978	5.956	—	.10	.20
	1978 *sm*	4,000	—	Proof	2.25
	1979	9.974	—	—	.10
	1979 *sm*	3,500	—	Proof	2.25
	1980	20.534	—	—	.15
	1980 *sm*	.014	—	Proof	2.00
	1981	.110	—	—	.10
	1982	.160	—	—	.10
	1982 *sm*	.020	—	Proof	2.00
	1983	.040	—	—	.10
	1983 *sm*	.015	—	Proof	2.00
	1984	18.880	—	—	.10
	1984 *sm*	.015	—	Proof	2.00
	1985	.148	—	—	.10

ALUMINUM
F.A.O. Issue

| 8 | 1971 | 3.049 | — | .10 | .35 |

COPPER-NICKEL CLAD STEEL

2a	1980	12.001	—	—	.10
	1981	23.866	—	—	.10
	1982	24.413	—	—	.10
	1983	4.016	—	—	.10
	1984	3.200	—	—	.10

1.6500 g, .925 SILVER, .0491 oz ASW

| 2b | 1981 *sm* | .030 | — | Proof | 5.00 |

ALUMINUM-BRONZE
Rev: Fruit salad plant.

50	1985	14.840	—	—	.10
	1986	—	—	—	.10
	1987	—	—	—	.10
	1988	—	—	—	.10

2.0000 g, .925 SILVER, .0595 oz ASW

50a	1985 *sm*	.020	—	Proof	2.50
	1986 *sm*	.015	—	Proof	2.50
	1987	.015	—	Proof	2.50

10 CENTS

COPPER-NICKEL

3	1967	40.000	—	.15	.30
	1967	2,000	—	Proof	4.50
	1968	36.261	—	.20	.40
	1968	5,000	—	Proof	4.25
	1969	25.000	—	.10	.20
	1969	3,000	—	Proof	20.00
	1970	21.304	—	.20	.50
	1971	33.041	—	.10	.20
	1972	2.675	—	.10	.25

KM#	Date	Mintage	VF	XF	Unc
3	1972	749 pcs.	—	Proof	60.00
	1973	14.290	—	.10	.20
	1973	1,000	—	Proof	10.00
	1974	13.450	—	.10	.20
	1974	1,500	—	Proof	7.50
	1975	.828	.10	.40	.80
	1975	3,000	—	Proof	4.00
	1976	29.718	—	.10	.20
	1976 *sm*	3,500	—	Proof	3.50
	1977	11.776	—	.10	.15
	1977 *sm*	3,500	—	Proof	3.50
	1978	5.936	—	.10	.30
	1978 *sm*	4,000	—	Proof	3.50
	1979	12.001	—	.10	.15
	1979 *sm*	3,500	—	Proof	3.50
	1980	40.299	—	.10	.15
	1980 *sm*	.014	—	Proof	3.00
	1981	58.600	—	.10	.15
	1982	48.514	—	.10	.15
	1982 *sm*	.020	—	Proof	3.00
	1983	10.415	—	.10	.15
	1983 *sm*	.015	—	Proof	3.00
	1984	29.700	—	.10	.15
	1984 *sm*	.015	—	Proof	3.00
	1985	.148	—	—	.15

3.3500 g, .925 SILVER, .0996 oz ASW

| 3a | 1981 *sm* | .030 | — | Proof | 7.50 |

COPPER-NICKEL
Rev: Star Jasmine plant.

51	1985	34.200	—	—	.15
	1986	—	—	—	.15
	1987	—	—	—	.15
	1988	—	—	—	.15

3.0500 g, .925 SILVER, .0907 oz ASW

51a	1985 *sm*	.020	—	Proof	4.00
	1986 *sm*	.015	—	Proof	4.00
	1987	.015	—	Proof	4.00

20 CENTS

COPPER-NICKEL

4	1967	36.500	.15	.30	.50
	1967	2,000	—	Proof	7.00
	1968	10.934	.15	.30	.50
	1968	5,000	—	Proof	6.00
	1969	8.460	.15	.30	1.20
	1969	3,000	—	Proof	30.00
	1970	3.250	.15	.30	.60
	1971	1.732	—	.50	.80
	1972	9.107	.15	.20	.50
	1972	749 pcs.	—	Proof	70.00
	1973	8.838	.15	.20	.40
	1973	1,000	—	Proof	17.50
	1974	4.567	.15	.20	.40
	1974	1,500	—	Proof	12.50
	1975	1.546	.15	.20	.40
	1975	3,000	—	Proof	6.50
	1976	19.760	.15	.20	.40
	1976 *sm*	3,500	—	Proof	6.00
	1977	7.074	.15	.20	.40
	1977 *sm*	3,500	—	Proof	6.00
	1978	4.450	.15	.20	.40
	1978 *sm*	4,000	—	Proof	6.00
	1979	14.865	—	.15	.25
	1979 *sm*	3,500	—	Proof	6.00
	1980	27.903	—	.15	.25
	1980 *sm*	.014	—	Proof	5.00
	1981	46.997	—	.15	.25
	1982	25.234	—	.15	.25
	1982 *sm*	.020	—	Proof	4.00
	1983	6.424	—	.15	.25
	1983 *sm*	.015	—	Proof	4.00
	1984	9.290	—	.15	.25
	1984 *sm*	.015	—	Proof	4.00
	1985	.148	—	—	.25

6.5100 g, .925 SILVER, .1936 oz ASW

| 4a | 1981 *sm* | .030 | — | Proof | 12.50 |

COPPER-NICKEL
Rev: Powder-puff plant.

| 52 | 1985 | 22.020 | — | .15 | .25 |
| | 1986 | — | — | .15 | .25 |

KM#	Date	Mintage	VF	XF	Unc
52	1987	—	—	.15	.25
	1988	—	—	.15	.25

5.2400 g, .925 SILVER, .1559 oz ASW

52a	1985 sm	.020	—	Proof	6.50
	1986 sm	.015	—	Proof	6.50
	1987	.015	—	Proof	6.50

50 CENTS

COPPER-NICKEL

5	1967	11.000	.30	.40	.80
	1967	2.000	—	Proof	10.00
	1968	3.189	.30	.40	.90
	1968	5.000	—	Proof	8.50
	1969	2.008	.30	.40	.90
	1969	3.000	—	Proof	35.00
	1970	3.102	.30	.40	.90
	1971	3.933	.30	.40	.90
	1972	5.427	.30	.40	.90
	1972	749 pcs.	—	Proof	90.00
	1973	4.474	.30	.40	.90
	1973	1.000	—	Proof	30.00
	1974	11.550	—	.35	.75
	1974	1.500	—	Proof	22.50
	1975	1.432	.35	.75	1.25
	1975	3.000	—	Proof	10.00
	1976	5.728	.30	.40	.90
	1976 sm	3.500	—	Proof	8.50
	1977	6.953	—	.35	.75
	1977 sm	3.500	—	Proof	8.50
	1978	3.934	—	.35	.75
	1978 sm	4.000	—	Proof	8.50
	1979	8.461	—	.30	.70
	1979 sm	3.500	—	Proof	8.50
	1980	14.717	—	.30	.50
	1980 sm	.014	—	Proof	7.00
	1981	29.542	—	.30	.50
	1982	13.756	—	.30	.50
	1982 sm	.020	—	Proof	5.00
	1983	4.482	—	.30	.50
	1983 sm	.015	—	Proof	5.00
	1984	4.210	—	.30	.50
	1984 sm	.015	—	Proof	5.00
	1985	.148	—	.30	.50

10.8200 g, .925 SILVER, .3218 oz ASW

| 5a | 1981 sm | .030 | — | Proof | 15.00 |

COPPER-NICKEL
Rev: Yellow Allamanda plant.

53	1985	11.384	—	.30	.50
	1986	—	—	.30	.50
	1987	—	—	.30	.50
	1988	—	—	.30	.50

8.5600 g, .925 SILVER, .2546 oz ASW

53a	1985 sm	.020	—	Proof	12.00
	1986 sm	.015	—	Proof	12.00
	1987	.015	—	Proof	12.00

DOLLAR

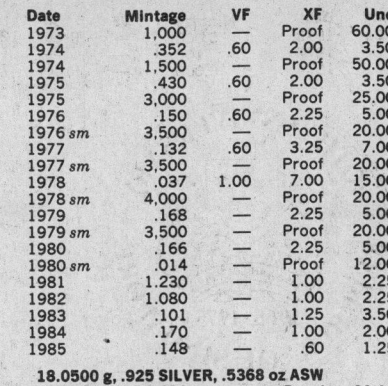

COPPER-NICKEL

6	1967	3.000	.60	1.20	2.50
	1967	2.000	—	Proof	27.50
	1968	2.194	.60	1.20	2.50
	1968	5.000	—	Proof	22.50
	1969	1.871	.60	1.25	3.00
	1969	3.000	—	Proof	100.00
	1970	.560	.75	1.50	3.75
	1971	.900	.60	1.20	2.50
	1972	.458	.75	2.00	5.00
	1972	749 pcs.	—	Proof	160.00
	1973	.341	.75	2.00	3.50

KM#	Date	Mintage	VF	XF	Unc
6	1973	1.000	—	Proof	60.00
	1974	.352	.60	2.00	3.50
	1974	1.500	—	Proof	50.00
	1975	.430	.60	2.00	3.50
	1975	3.000	—	Proof	25.00
	1976	.150	.60	2.25	5.00
	1976 sm	3.500	—	Proof	20.00
	1977	.132	.60	3.25	7.00
	1977 sm	3.500	—	Proof	20.00
	1978	.037	1.00	7.00	15.00
	1978 sm	4.000	—	Proof	20.00
	1979	.168	—	2.25	5.00
	1979 sm	3.500	—	Proof	20.00
	1980	.166	—	2.25	5.00
	1980 sm	.014	—	Proof	12.00
	1981	1.230	—	1.00	2.25
	1982	1.080	—	1.00	2.25
	1983	.101	—	1.25	3.50
	1984	.170	—	1.00	2.00
	1985	.148	—	.60	1.25

18.0500 g, .925 SILVER, .5368 oz ASW

6a	1975	3.000	—	Proof	80.00
	1976 sm	.010	—	Proof	27.50
	1977 sm	.010	—	Proof	27.50
	1978 sm	.010	—	Proof	30.00
	1979 sm	8.000	—	Proof	30.00
	1980 sm	.015	—	Proof	27.50
	1981 sm	.030	—	Proof	15.00
	1982 sm	.020	—	Proof	17.50
	1983 sm	.015	—	Proof	20.00
	1984 sm	.015	—	Proof	20.00

COPPER-NICKEL
Rev: Periwinkle.

54	1986	—	—	.75	1.50
	1987	—	—	.75	1.50

9.9700 g, .925 SILVER, .2965 oz ASW

54a	1985 sm	.020	—	Proof	15.00
	1986 sm	.015	—	Proof	15.00

NICKEL-BRONZE

54b	1987	—	—	—	.75
	1988	—	—	—	.75

8.4273 g, .925 SILVER, .2507 oz ASW

54c	1987	.015	—	Proof	15.00
	1988	.015	—	Proof	15.00

5 DOLLARS

25.0000 g, .500 SILVER, .4019 oz ASW
7th South East Asia Peninsular Games

10	1973	.250	—	—	12.00
	1973	5.000	—	Proof	120.00

NOTE: 15,000 PNC were issued. Current retail is $20.00.

COPPER-NICKEL
Changi Airport

| 19 | 1981 | .220 | — | 3.00 | 6.00 |

18.0500 g, .925 SILVER, .5368 oz ASW

KM#	Date	Mintage	VF	XF	Unc
19a	1981 sm	.020	—	Proof	40.00

COPPER-NICKEL
Benjamin Shears Bridge

| 22 | 1982 | .260 | — | 3.00 | 6.00 |

18.0500 g, .925 SILVER, .5368 oz ASW

| 22a | 1982 sm | .020 | — | Proof | 40.00 |

COPPER-NICKEL
Twelfth SEA Games

| 25 | 1983 | .270 | — | 3.00 | 6.00 |

20.0000 g, .925 SILVER, .5949 oz ASW

| 25a | 1983 sm | .020 | — | Proof | 40.00 |

COPPER-NICKEL
25 Years of Nation Building

| 32 | 1984 | .270 | — | 3.00 | 5.50 |

20.0000 g, .925 SILVER, .5949 oz ASW

| 32a | 1984 sm | .020 | — | Proof | 38.00 |

COPPER-NICKEL
25 Years of Public Housing
Obv: Coat of arms & legend.

| 48 | 1985 | .117 | — | 3.00 | 5.00 |

20.0000 g, .925 SILVER, .5949 oz ASW

| 48a | 1985 sm | .020 | — | Proof | 30.00 |

SINGAPORE 1500

COPPER-NICKEL
National Museum

KM#	Date	Mintage	VF	XF	Unc
68	1987	.070	—	—	5.00

20.0000 g, .925 SILVER, .5949 oz ASW
| 68a | 1987 | .025 | — | — | Proof 30.00 |

COPPER-NICKEL
Singapore Fire Brigade

| 70 | 1988 | .050 | — | — | 5.00 |

20.0000 g, .925 SILVER, .5949 oz ASW
| 70a | 1988 | .025 | — | — | Proof 30.00 |

10 DOLLARS

31.1000 g, .900 SILVER, .8999 oz ASW
Obv. leg: SINGAPORE inverted.
| 9.1 | 1972 | .080 | — | — | 40.00 |
| | 1972 | 3,000 | — | — | Proof 160.00 |

| 9.2 | 1973 | .080 | — | — | 25.00 |

31.1000 g, .500 SILVER, .5000 oz ASW

KM#	Date	Mintage	VF	XF	Unc
9.2a	1973	5,000	—	—	Proof 125.00
	1974	.100	—	—	17.50
	1974	6,000	—	—	Proof 75.00

10th Anniversary of Independence
| 11 | 1975 | .200 | — | — | 12.50 |
| | 1975 | .010 | — | — | Proof 65.00 |

15	1976	.150	—	—	12.50
	1976 sm	.010	—	—	Proof 50.00
	1977	.150	—	—	12.50
	1977 sm	.010	—	—	Proof 50.00

ASEAN 10th Anniversary
| 16 | 1977 | .200 | — | — | 12.50 |
| | 1977 sm | .010 | — | — | Proof 50.00 |

Communications Satellites
17.1	1978	.167	—	—	12.50
	1978 sm	.010	—	—	Proof 50.00
	1979	.168	—	—	12.50

KM#	Date	Mintage	VF	XF	Unc
17.1	1979 sm	9,000	—	—	Proof 50.00
	1980 sm	.014	—	—	Proof 30.00

NICKEL
| 17.1a | 1980 | .120 | — | 6.00 | 9.00 |

Obv: Raised stars and moon in arms.
| 17.2 | 1980 sm | .015 | — | — | Proof 25.00 |

Year of the Rooster
| 20 | 1981 | .180 | — | 6.00 | 12.50 |

31.1000 g, .500 SILVER, .5000 oz ASW
| 20a | 1981 sm | .020 | — | — | Proof 120.00 |

NICKEL
Year of the Dog
| 23 | 1982 | .210 | — | 6.00 | 12.50 |

31.1000 g, .500 SILVER, .5000 oz ASW
| 23a | 1982 sm | .020 | — | — | Proof 65.00 |

NICKEL
Year of the Pig
| 26 (Y25) | 1983 | .307 | — | 5.50 | 10.00 |

31.1000 g, .500 SILVER, .5000 oz ASW
| 26a | 1983 sm | .020 | — | — | Proof 50.00 |

NICKEL
Year of the Rat
| 33 | 1984 | .300 | — | 6.00 | 12.50 |

31.1000 g, .500 SILVER, .5000 oz ASW
| 33a | 1984 sm | .020 | — | — | Proof 50.00 |

SINGAPORE 1501

500 DOLLARS

NICKEL
Year of the Ox

KM#	Date	Mintage	VF	XF	Unc
44	1985	.307	—	5.50	10.00

31.1000 g, .500 SILVER, .5000 oz ASW

| 44a | 1985 sm | .020 | — | Proof | 40.00 |

NICKEL
Year of the Snake

KM#	Date	Mintage	VF	XF	Unc
71	1989	.250	—	6.00	10.00

31.1030 g, .925 SILVER, .9250 oz ASW

| 71a | 1989 | .025 | — | Proof | 35.00 |

50 DOLLARS

34.5594 g, .900 GOLD, 1.0000 oz AGW
10th Anniversary of Independence

KM#	Date	Mintage	VF	XF	Unc
14	1975	.030	—	—	500.00
	1975	2,000	—	Proof	900.00

NICKEL
Year of the Tiger

| 59 | 1986 | .300 | — | 6.00 | 10.00 |

31.1000 g, .500 SILVER, .5000 oz ASW

| 59a | 1986 | .020 | — | Proof | 40.00 |

31.1000 g, .500 SILVER, .5000 oz ASW
Financial Center

18	1980	.025	—	—	30.00
	1980 sm	.015	—	Proof	50.00
	1981	.050	—	—	30.00
	1981 sm	.020	—	Proof	50.00

100 DOLLARS

16.9650 g, .917 GOLD, .5000 oz AGW
Year of the Rooster

| 21 | 1981 sm | .012 | — | Proof | 500.00 |

NICKEL
Year of the Rabbit

| 66 | 1987 | — | — | 6.00 | 10.00 |

31.1000 g, .500 SILVER, .5000 oz ASW

| 66a | 1987 sm | .020 | — | Proof | 40.00 |

COPPER-NICKEL
Association of South East Asian Nations
Obv: Coat of arms above 1967-1987.
Rev: ASEAN logo within legend, value below.

| 68 (67) | 1987 | .100 | — | 6.00 | 10.00 |

31.1030 g, .500 SILVER, .5000 oz ASW

| 68a (67a) | 1987 sm | .025 | — | Proof | 40.00 |

6.9119 g, .900 GOLD, .2000 oz AGW
10th Anniversary of Independence

| 12 | 1975 | .100 | — | — | 120.00 |
| | 1975 | 3,000 | — | Proof | 180.00 |

150 DOLLARS

150th Anniversary of Founding of Singapore
24.8830 g, .920 GOLD, .7360 oz AGW

| 7 | 1969 | .198 | — | — | 400.00 |
| | 1969 | 500 pcs. | — | Proof | 2000. |

250 DOLLARS

Year of the Dog

| 24 | 1982 sm | 5,500 | — | Proof | 450.00 |

Year of the Pig

| 27 | 1983 sm | 5,000 | — | Proof | 450.00 |

Year of the Rat

| 34 | 1984 sm | 4,000 | — | Proof | 500.00 |

NICKEL
Year of the Dragon

| 69 (68) | 1988 | — | — | 6.00 | 15.00 |

31.1030 g, .500 SILVER, .5000 oz ASW

| 69a | 1988 | — | — | Proof | 50.00 |

17.2797 g, .900 GOLD, .5000 oz AGW
10th Anniversary of Independence

| 13 | 1975 | .030 | — | — | 250.00 |
| | 1975 | 2,000 | — | Proof | 500.00 |

Year of the Ox

| 45 | 1985 sm | 4,000 | — | Proof | 500.00 |

SINGAPORE 1502

KM#	Date	Mintage	VF	XF	Unc
		Year of the Tiger			
60	1986 sm	3,000	—	Proof	450.00
		Year of the Rabbit			
67	1987 sm	—	—	Proof	450.00
		Year of the Dragon			
70 (69)	1988 sm	—	—	Proof	450.00
		Year of the Snake			
		Similar to 10 Dollars, KM#71.			
72	1989	2,500	—	Proof	450.00

GOLD BULLION ISSUES

1 DOLLAR
(1/10 Ounce)

3.1100 g, .999 GOLD, .1000 oz AGW
Rev: Carp and lotus flower.

| 28 | 1983 | .020 | — | — | BV + 15% |
| | 1984 | .010 | — | — | BV + 15% |

2 DOLLARS
(1/4 Ounce)

7.7750 g, .999 GOLD, .2500 oz AGW
Rev: Qilin.

| 29 | 1983 | .020 | — | — | BV + 12% |
| | 1984 | .010 | — | — | BV + 12% |

5 DOLLARS
(1/2 Ounce)

15.5500 g, .999 GOLD, .5000 oz AGW
Rev: Phoenix.

| 30 | 1983 | .010 | — | — | BV + 9% |
| | 1984 | .010 | — | — | BV + 9% |

10 DOLLARS
(1 Ounce)

31.1000 g, .999 GOLD, 1.0000 oz AGW
Rev: Dragon.

| 31 | 1983 | .010 | — | — | BV + 7% |
| | 1984 | .010 | — | Proof | BV + 7% |

MINT SETS (MS)

KM#	Date	Mintage	Identification	Issue Price	Mkt. Val.
MS1	1967(6)	8,000	KM1-6	1.50	15.00
MS2	1968(6)	16,000	KM1-6	1.50	12.00
MS3	1969(6)	14,000	KM1-6	1.50	12.00
MS4	1970(6)	13,000	KM1-6	1.50	20.00
MS5	1970(6)*	27,000	KM1-6	1.75	20.00
MS7	1972(6)	11,000	KM1-6	3.00	15.00
MS8	1973(6)	15,000	KM1-6	2.00	8.50
MS9	1974(6)	20,000	KM1-6	2.00	8.50
MS10	1975(6)	30,000	KM1-6	*12.00	9.50
MS11	1975(3)	30,000	KM12-14	—	875.00
MS12	1976(6)	35,000	KM1a,2-6	2.00	10.00
MS13	1977(6)	40,000	KM1a,2-6	2.00	10.00
MS14	1978(6)	55,000	KM1a,2-6	—	20.00
MS15	1979(6)	65,000	KM1a,2-6	—	8.00
MS16	1980(6)	70,000	KM1a,2-6	—	8.00
MS17	1981(6)	110,000	KM1a,2-6	5.00	6.50
MS18	1982(6)	160,000	KM1a,2-6	5.00	6.50
MS19	1983(6)	40,000	KM1a,2-6 w/medallion, I.A.P.N.	—	9.00
MS20	1983(6)	150,000	KM1a,2-6	5.00	6.50
MS21	1984(6)	160,000	KM1a,2-6	3.75	7.50
MS22	1985(6)	148,424	KM1a,2-6	—	5.50
MS23	1986(6)	120,000	KM49-54	—	5.50
MS24	1987(6)	—	KM49-54	—	5.50
MS25	1988(6)	—	KM49-53,54b	—	5.50

*NOTE: Issued only in package of 3 sets plus KM#11, each set in plastic wallet for Expo '70 Osaka Japan.

PROOF SETS (PS)

KM#	Date	Mintage	Identification	Issue Price	Mkt. Val.
PS1	1967(6)	2,000	KM1-6	25.00	60.00
PS2	1968(6)	5,000	KM1-6	25.00	55.00
PS3	1969(6)	3,000	KM1-6	25.00	220.00
PS4	1972(6)	749	KM1-6	25.00	475.00
PS5	1973(6)	1,000	KM1-6	32.00	140.00
PS6	1974(6)	1,500	KM1-6	34.00	115.00
PS7	1975(6)	3,000	KM1-6	35.00	60.00
PS8	1975(3)	2,000	KM12-14	—	2680.
PS9	1976(6)	3,500	KM1-6	37.00	50.00
PS10	1977(6)	3,500	KM1-6	—	50.00
PS11	1978(6)	4,000	KM1-6	—	50.00
PS12	1979(7)	3,500	KM1-6,17.1	—	120.00
PS13	1980(7)	14,000	KM1-6,17.1	64.00	75.00
PS14	1981(6)	30,000	KM1b-2b,3a-6a, .925 Silver	82.00	80.00
PS15	1982(6)	20,000	KM1-5,6a	52.00	42.00
PS16	1983(6)	15,000	KM1-5,6a	52.00	45.00
PS17	1984(6)	15,000	KM1-5,6a	52.00	45.00
PS18	1985(6)	20,000	KM49a-54a	40.00	48.00
PS19	1986(6)	15,000	KM49a-54a	—	48.00
PS20	1987(6)	15,000	KM49a-54c	42.00	48.00

SOLOMON ISLANDS

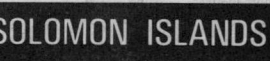

The Solomon Islands, located in the southwest Pacific east of Papua New Guinea, has an area of 10,983 sq. mi. (28,446 sq. km.) and a population of *314,000. Capital: Honiara. The most important islands of the Solomon chain are Guadalcanal (scene of some of the fiercest fighting of World War II), Malaitia, New Georgia, Florida, Vella Lavella, Choiseul, Rendova, San Cristobal, the Lord Howe group, the Santa Cruz islands, and the Duff group. Copra is the only important cash crop but it is hoped that timber will become an economic factor.

The Solomon Islands were discovered by Spanish navigator Alvaro de Mendana in 1567, and in 1569 he made an unsuccessful attempt to colonize them. European knowledge of the group would not be completed until the end of the 18th century. Germany declared a protectorate over the northern Solomons in 1885. The British protectorate over the southern Solomons was established in 1893. In 1899 Germany transferred its claim to all Solomon Islands except Buka and Bougainville to Great Britain in exchange for recognition of German claims in Western Samoa. Australia occupied the two German islands in 1914, and administered them after 1920.

The Japanese invaded the Solomons during 1942-43, but were driven out by an American counteroffensive after a series of bloody clashes.

Following World War II, the islands returned to the status of a British protectorate. In 1976 the protectorate was abolished, and the Solomons became a self-governing dependency. Full independence was achieved on July 7, 1978. Solomon Islands is a member of the Commonwealth of Nations. The Queen of England is Chief of State.

RULERS
British

MINT MARKS
FM - Franklin Mint, U.S.A.*

NOTE: From 1977 the Franklin Mint has produced coinage in up to 3 different qualities. Qualities of issue are designated in ( ) after each date and are defined as follows:

(M) MATTE - Normal circulation strike or a dull finish produced by sandblasting special uncirculated (polish finish) or proof quality dies.

(U) - SPECIAL UNCIRCULATED - Polished or proof-like in appearance without any frosted features.

(P) PROOF - The highest quality obtainable having mirror-like fields and frosted features.

MONETARY SYSTEM
100 Cents = 1 Dollar

CENT

BRONZE
F.A.O. Issue

KM#	Date	Mintage	VF	XF	Unc
1	1977	1.828	—	.10	.20
	1977FM(M)	6,000	—	—	.50
	1977FM(U)	—	—	—	2.00
	1977FM(P)	.014	—	Proof	1.00
	1978FM(M)	6,000	—	—	.50
	1978FM(U)	544 pcs.	—	—	2.00
	1978FM(P)	5,122	—	Proof	1.00
	1979FM(M)	6,000	—	—	.50
	1979FM(U)	677 pcs.	—	—	2.00
	1979FM(P)	2,845	—	Proof	1.50
	1980FM(M)	6,000	—	—	.50
	1980FM(U)	624 pcs.	—	—	2.00
	1980FM(P)	1,031	—	Proof	1.50
	1981FM(M)	6,000	—	—	.50
	1981FM(U)	212 pcs.	—	—	2.00
	1981FM(P)	448 pcs.	—	Proof	1.50
	1982FM(U)	—	—	—	2.00
	1982FM(P)	—	—	Proof	1.50
	1983FM(M)	—	—	—	.50
	1983FM(U)	200 pcs.	—	—	3.00
	1983FM(P)	—	—	Proof	1.50
	1985	—	—	—	.20

2 CENTS

SOLOMON ISLANDS

BRONZE

KM#	Date	Mintage	VF	XF	Unc
2	1977	2,400	—	.10	.25
	1977FM(M)	6,000	—	—	.75
	1977FM(U)	—	—	—	3.00
	1977FM(P)	.014	—	Proof	1.50
	1978FM(M)	6,000	—	—	.75
	1978FM(U)	544 pcs.	—	—	3.00
	1978FM(P)	5,122	—	Proof	1.50
	1979FM(M)	6,000	—	—	.75
	1979FM(U)	677 pcs.	—	—	3.00
	1979FM(P)	2,845	—	Proof	2.00
	1980FM(M)	6,000	—	—	.75
	1980FM(U)	624 pcs.	—	—	3.00
	1980FM(P)	1,031	—	Proof	2.00
	1981FM(M)	6,000	—	—	.75
	1981FM(U)	212 pcs.	—	—	3.00
	1981FM(P)	448 pcs.	—	Proof	2.00
	1982FM(U)	—	—	—	3.00
	1982FM(P)	—	—	Proof	2.00
	1983FM(M)	—	—	—	.75
	1983FM(U)	200 pcs.	—	—	3.00
	1983FM(P)	—	—	Proof	2.00
	1985	—	—	—	.25

5 CENTS

COPPER-NICKEL

KM#	Date	Mintage	VF	XF	Unc
3	1977	1,200	.10	.15	.30
	1977FM(U)	—	—	—	3.00
	1977FM(M)	6,000	—	—	1.50
	1977FM(P)	.014	—	Proof	2.00
	1978FM(M)	6,000	—	—	1.50
	1978FM(U)	544 pcs.	—	—	3.00
	1978FM(P)	5,122	—	Proof	2.00
	1979FM(M)	6,000	—	—	1.50
	1979FM(U)	677 pcs.	—	—	3.00
	1979FM(P)	2,845	—	Proof	2.50
	1980FM(M)	6,000	—	—	1.50
	1980FM(U)	624 pcs.	—	—	3.00
	1980FM(P)	1,031	—	Proof	2.50
	1981	—	—	—	—
	1981FM(M)	6,000	—	—	1.50
	1981FM(U)	212 pcs.	—	—	3.00
	1981FM(P)	448 pcs.	—	Proof	2.50
	1982FM(U)	—	—	—	3.00
	1982FM(P)	—	—	Proof	2.50
	1983FM(M)	—	—	—	1.50
	1983FM(U)	200 pcs.	—	—	4.00
	1983FM(P)	—	—	Proof	2.50
	1985	—	—	—	.30

10 CENTS

COPPER-NICKEL

KM#	Date	Mintage	VF	XF	Unc
4	1977	3,600	.15	.20	.35
	1977FM(M)	6,000	—	—	2.00
	1977FM(U)	—	—	—	5.00
	1977FM(P)	.014	—	Proof	3.00
	1978FM(M)	6,000	—	—	2.00
	1978FM(U)	544 pcs.	—	—	5.00
	1978FM(P)	5,122	—	Proof	3.00
	1979FM(M)	6,000	—	—	2.00
	1979FM(U)	677 pcs.	—	—	5.00
	1979FM(P)	2,845	—	Proof	4.00
	1980FM(M)	6,000	—	—	2.00
	1980FM(U)	624 pcs.	—	—	5.00
	1980FM(P)	1,031	—	Proof	4.00
	1981FM(M)	6,000	—	—	2.00
	1981FM(U)	212 pcs.	—	—	5.00
	1981FM(P)	448 pcs.	—	Proof	4.00
	1982FM(U)	—	—	—	5.00
	1982FM(P)	—	—	Proof	4.00
	1983FM(M)	—	—	—	2.00
	1983FM(U)	200 pcs.	—	—	6.00
	1983FM(P)	—	—	Proof	4.00

20 CENTS

COPPER-NICKEL

KM#	Date	Mintage	VF	XF	Unc
5	1977	3,000	.15	.30	.40
	1977FM(M)	5,000	—	—	3.00
	1977FM(P)	.014	—	Proof	4.00
	1978	.293	.25	.40	.75
	1978FM(M)	5,000	—	—	3.00
	1978FM(U)	544 pcs.	—	—	6.00
	1978FM(P)	5,122	—	Proof	4.00
	1979FM(M)	5,000	—	—	3.00
	1979FM(U)	677 pcs.	—	—	6.00
	1979FM(P)	2,845	—	Proof	4.00
	1980FM(M)	5,000	—	—	3.00
	1980FM(U)	624 pcs.	—	—	6.00
	1980FM(P)	1,031	—	Proof	4.00
	1981FM(M)	5,000	—	—	3.00
	1981FM(U)	212 pcs.	—	—	6.00
	1981FM(P)	448 pcs.	—	Proof	4.00
	1982FM(U)	—	—	—	6.00
	1982FM(P)	—	—	Proof	4.00
	1983FM(M)	—	—	—	3.00
	1983FM(U)	200 pcs.	—	—	7.00
	1983FM(P)	—	—	Proof	4.00

DOLLAR

COPPER-NICKEL

KM#	Date	Mintage	VF	XF	Unc
6	1977	1,500	1.00	1.50	2.00
	1977FM(M)	3,000	—	—	5.00
	1977FM(P)	.014	—	Proof	6.00
	1978FM(M)	3,000	—	—	5.00
	1978FM(U)	544 pcs.	—	—	10.00
	1978FM(P)	5,122	—	Proof	6.00
	1979FM(M)	3,000	—	—	5.00
	1979FM(U)	677 pcs.	—	—	10.00
	1979FM(P)	2,845	—	Proof	7.00
	1980FM(M)	3,000	—	—	5.00
	1980FM(U)	624 pcs.	—	—	10.00
	1980FM(P)	1,031	—	Proof	8.00
	1981FM(M)	3,000	—	—	5.00
	1981FM(U)	212 pcs.	—	—	10.00
	1981FM(P)	448 pcs.	—	Proof	8.00
	1982FM(U)	—	—	—	10.00
	1982FM(P)	—	—	Proof	8.00
	1983FM(M)	—	—	—	5.00
	1983FM(U)	200 pcs.	—	—	12.00
	1983FM(P)	—	—	Proof	8.00

1984 Olympics

19	1984	5,000	—	—	5.00

5 DOLLARS

28.2800 g, .925 SILVER, .8411 oz ASW

KM#	Date	Mintage	VF	XF	Unc
7	1977FM(M)	200 pcs.	—	—	65.00
	1977FM(P)	.015	—	Proof	12.50
	1978FM(P)	5,148	—	Proof	15.00
	1979FM(P)	2,845	—	Proof	20.00
	1980FM(P)	1,031	—	Proof	25.00
	1981FM(P)	448 pcs.	—	Proof	35.00
	1983FM(P)	339 pcs.	—	Proof	35.00

COPPER-NICKEL

7a	1978FM(P)	—	—	—	40.00
	1978FM(U)	544 pcs.	—	—	20.00
	1979FM(M)	200 pcs.	—	—	40.00
	1979FM(U)	677 pcs.	—	—	20.00
	1980FM(M)	200 pcs.	—	—	40.00
	1980FM(U)	624 pcs.	—	—	20.00
	1981FM(M)	200 pcs.	—	—	40.00
	1981FM(U)	212 pcs.	—	—	35.00
	1983FM(M)	202 pcs.	—	—	35.00

28.2800 g, .925 SILVER, .8411 oz ASW
Coronation Jubilee
Obv: Similar to 20 Cents, KM#5.

8	1978FM(P)	8,886	—	Proof	25.00

COPPER-NICKEL
Battle of Guadalcanal
Obv: Similar to 20 Cents, KM#5.

13	1982FM(U)	—	—	—	25.00

28.2800 g, .925 SILVER, .8411 oz ASW

13a	1982FM(P)	1,368	—	Proof	45.00

30.2800 g, .500 SILVER, .4868 oz ASW
30th Anniversary of Coronation

15	1983FM(P)	2,944	—	Proof	25.00

28.2800 g, .925 SILVER, .8411 oz ASW
International Year of the Child

16	1983	5,775	—	Proof	25.00

SOLOMON ISLANDS 1504

28.8800 g, .925 SILVER, .8589 oz ASW
Decade For Women
Obv: Portrait of Queen Elizabeth II.
Rev: Logo and woman and child in center.

KM#	Date	Mintage	VF	XF	Unc
22	1985	1,050	—	Proof	35.00

10 DOLLARS

COPPER-NICKEL
Obv: Similar to 20 Cents, KM#5.

10	1979FM(M)	100 pcs.	—	—	65.00
	1979FM(U)	777 pcs.	—	—	20.00
	1980FM(M)	100 pcs.	—	—	65.00
	1980FM(U)	624 pcs.	—	—	20.00
	1981FM(M)	100 pcs.	—	—	65.00
	1981FM(U)	212 pcs.	—	—	25.00
	1982FM(U)		—	—	20.00

42.2700 g, .925 SILVER, 1.2571 oz ASW

10a	1979FM(P)	4,670	—	Proof	27.50
	1980FM(P)	1,569	—	Proof	30.00
	1981FM(P)	593 pcs.	—	Proof	40.00
	1982FM(P)	579 pcs.	—	Proof	40.00

COPPER-NICKEL
Fifth Anniversary of Independence

17	1983FM(M)	202 pcs.	—	—	22.50

40.5000 g, .925 SILVER, 1.2045 oz ASW

17a	1983FM(P)	425 pcs.	—	Proof	55.00

33.4400 g, .925 SILVER, .9946 oz ASW
1984 Olympics

20	1984	2,500	—	Proof	40.00

100 DOLLARS

9.3700 g, .900 GOLD, .2711 oz AGW
Attainment of Sovereignty

9	1978FM	50 pcs.	—	—	275.00
	1978FM(U)	213 pcs.	—	—	225.00
	1978FM(P)	3,159	—	Proof	225.00

7.6400 g, .500 GOLD, .1228 oz AGW
Native Art

KM#	Date	Mintage	VF	XF	Unc
11	1980FM(U)	50 pcs.	—	—	200.00
	1980FM(P)	7,500	—	Proof	125.00

Shark

12	1981FM(P)	675 pcs.	—	Proof	350.00

9.3700 g, .900 GOLD, .2711 oz AGW
Battle of Guadalcanal

14	1982FM(P)	311 pcs.	—	Proof	350.00

5th Anniversary of Independence

18	1983FM(P)	268 pcs.	—	Proof	300.00

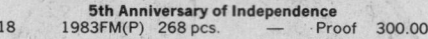

7.5000 g, .917 GOLD, .2211 oz AGW
1984 Olympics

21	1984	500 pcs.	—	Proof	250.00

MINT SETS (MS)

KM#	Date	Mintage	Identification	Issue Price	Mkt. Val.
MS1	1978(7)	544	KM1-6,7a	22.00	35.00
MS2	1979(8)	677	KM1-6,7a,10	31.00	45.00
MS3	1980(8)	624	KM1-6,7a,10	35.00	55.00
MS4	1981(8)	212	KM1-6,7a,10	36.00	60.00
MS5	1982(8)	—	KM1-6,10,13	36.00	60.00
MS6	1983(8)	192	KM1-6,7a,17	36.00	70.00

PROOF SETS (PS)

PS1	1977(7)	72,748	KM1-7	40.00	20.00
PS2	1978(7)	5,122	KM1-7	45.00	35.00
PS3	1979(8)	2,845	KM1-7,10a	77.00	70.00
PS4	1980(8)	1,031	KM1-7,10a	135.00	80.00
PS5	1981(8)	448	KM1-7,10a	137.00	100.00
PS6	1982(8)	—	KM1-6,10a,13a	87.00	110.00
PS7	1983(8)	334	KM1-7,17a	137.00	90.00

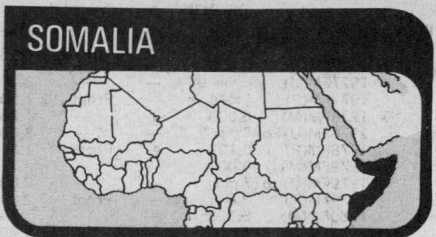

The Somali Democratic Republic, comprising the former British Somaliland Protectorate and Italian Somaliland, is located on the coast of the eastern projection of the African continent commonly referred to as the Horn. It has an area of 246,201 sq. mi. (637,657 sq. km.) and a population of *8.6 million. Capital: Mogadishu. The economy is pastoral and agricultural. Livestock, bananas and hides are exported.

The area of the British Somaliland Protectorate was known to the Egyptians at least 1,500 years B.C., and was occupied by the Arabs and Portuguese before British sea captains obtained trading and anchorage rights in 1827. The land of sandy clay and sporadic rainfall acquired a strategic importance with the opening of the Suez Canal in 1869. After negotiating treaties with the tribes, Britain declared the area a protectorate in 1888. Italy acquired Italian Somaliland in 1895 by purchase from the Sultan of Zanzibar. Britain occupied Italian Somaliland in 1941 and administered it until April 1, 1950, when it was returned to Italy as a U.N. trusteeship. The British Somaliland protectorate became independent on July 1, 1960. Five days later it joined with Italian Somaliland to form the Somali Republic. The country is presently under a revolutionary military regime installed Oct. 21, 1969.

MONETARY SYSTEM
100 Senti = 1 Shilin

ITALIAN SOMALILAND

TITLES

الصومال الايطاليانية

Al-Somal Al-Italianiah

RULERS
Vittorio Emanuele III, 1900-1946

MINT MARKS
R- Rome

MONETARY SYSTEM
100 Bese = 1 Rupia

BESA

BRONZE

KM#	Date	Mintage	Fine	VF	XF	Unc
1	1909R	2.000	10.00	17.50	30.00	100.00
	1910R	.500	10.00	17.50	30.00	100.00
	1913R	.200	12.50	20.00	35.00	160.00
	1921R	.500	12.50	20.00	35.00	160.00

2 BESE

BRONZE

2	1909R	.500	12.50	20.00	37.50	130.00
	1910R	.250	12.50	20.00	37.50	130.00
	1913R	.300	12.50	20.00	47.50	145.00
	1921R	.600	12.50	20.00	47.50	145.00
	1923R	1.500	12.50	20.00	47.50	145.00
	1924R	Inc. Ab.	12.50	20.00	47.50	145.00

4 BESE

BRONZE

KM#	Date	Mintage	Fine	VF	XF	Unc
3	1909R	.250	18.00	35.00	75.00	150.00
	1910R	.250	18.00	35.00	75.00	150.00
	1913R	.050	25.00	60.00	125.00	200.00
	1921R	.200	18.00	35.00	75.00	150.00
	1923R	.250	18.00	35.00	75.00	150.00
	1924R	Inc. Ab.	18.00	50.00	100.00	175.00

1/4 RUPIA

2.9160 g, .917 SILVER, .0859 oz ASW

KM#	Date	Mintage	Fine	VF	XF	Unc
4	1910R	.400	12.50	25.00	60.00	120.00
	1913R	.100	30.00	50.00	120.00	225.00

1/2 RUPIA

5.8319 g, .917 SILVER, .1719 oz ASW

KM#	Date	Mintage	Fine	VF	XF	Unc
5	1910R	.400	20.00	37.50	70.00	125.00
	1912R	.100	20.00	40.00	75.00	135.00
	1913R	.100	20.00	40.00	75.00	135.00
	1915R	.050	25.00	50.00	120.00	235.00
	1919R	.200	20.00	37.50	70.00	125.00

RUPIA

11.6638 g, .917 SILVER, .3437 oz ASW

KM#	Date	Mintage	Fine	VF	XF	Unc
6	1910R	.300	25.00	50.00	90.00	150.00
	1912R	.600	25.00	50.00	90.00	150.00
	1913R	.300	25.00	50.00	90.00	150.00
	1914R	.300	25.00	50.00	90.00	150.00
	1915R	.250	25.00	50.00	90.00	150.00
	1919R	.400	25.00	50.00	90.00	150.00
	1920R	1.300	500.00	900.00	2000.	3250.
	1921	.940	950.00	2150.	3350.	5500.

MONETARY REFORM
100 Centesimi = 1 Lira

5 LIRE

6.0000 g, .835 SILVER, .1611 oz ASW

KM#	Date	Mintage	Fine	VF	XF	Unc
7	1925	.400	50.00	100.00	175.00	300.00

10 LIRE

12.0000 g, .835 SILVER, .3221 oz ASW

KM#	Date	Mintage	Fine	VF	XF	Unc
8	1925	.100	75.00	150.00	250.00	400.00

SOMALIA
MONETARY SYSTEM
100 Centesimi = 1 Somalo =
1 Scellino = 1 Shilling

CENTESIMO

COPPER

KM#	Date	Year	Mintage	VF	XF	Unc
1	AH1369	1950	4.000	.15	.25	.75

5 CENTESIMI

COPPER

KM#	Date	Year	Mintage	VF	XF	Unc
2	AH1369	1950	6.800	.20	.50	1.00

BRASS

KM#	Date	Mintage	VF	XF	Unc
6	1967	10.000	.10	.15
	1975	—	.10	.15	.20

10 CENTESIMI

COPPER

KM#	Date	Year	Mintage	VF	XF	Unc
3	AH1369	1950	7.400	.30	.75	1.50

BRASS

KM#	Date	Mintage	VF	XF	Unc
7	1967	15.000	.10	.20	.30
	1975	—	.10	.20	.35

50 CENTESIMI

3.8000 g, .250 SILVER, .0305 oz ASW

KM#	Date	Year	Mintage	VF	XF	Unc
4	AH1369	1950	1.800	1.00	3.50	7.50

COPPER-NICKEL

KM#	Date	Mintage	VF	XF	Unc
8	1967	5.100	.25	.35	.75
	1975	—	.25	.35	.75

SOMALO

7.6000 g, .250 SILVER, .0610 oz ASW

KM#	Date	Year	Mintage	VF	XF	Unc
5	AH1369	1950	11.480	2.00	4.00	8.50

SCELLINO
(Schilling)

COPPER-NICKEL

KM#	Date	Mintage	VF	XF	Unc
9	1967	8.150	.75	2.50	4.00

5 SHILLINGS

COPPER-NICKEL
F.A.O. Issue

KM#	Date	Mintage	VF	XF	Unc
15	1970	.100	1.50	2.00	3.50
	1970	1,000	—	Proof	30.00

20 SHILLINGS

2.8000 g, .900 GOLD, .0810 oz AGW
5th Anniversary of Independence

KM#	Date	Mintage	VF	XF	Unc
10	1965	6,325	—	Proof	65.00

10th Anniversary of Independence

KM#	Date	Mintage	VF	XF	Unc
16	1970	8,000	—	Proof	65.00

50 SHILLINGS

7.0000 g, .900 GOLD, .2025 oz AGW

SOMALIA 1506

5th Anniversary of Independence

KM#	Date	Mintage	VF	XF	Unc
11	1965	6,325	—	Proof	125.00

10th Anniversary of Independence

| 17 | 1970 | 8,000 | — | Proof | 125.00 |

1st Anniversary of the 1969 Revolution

| 18 | 1970 | — | — | Proof | 125.00 |

100 SHILLINGS

14.0000 g, .900 GOLD, .4051 oz AGW
5th Anniversary of Independence

| 12 | 1965 | 6,325 | — | Proof | 250.00 |

10th Anniversary of Independence

| 19 | 1970 | 8,000 | — | Proof | 250.00 |

1st Anniversary of the 1969 Revolution

| 20 | 1970 | — | — | Proof | 250.00 |

200 SHILLINGS

28.0000 g, .900 GOLD, .8102 oz AGW
5th Anniversary of Independence

| 13 | 1965 | 6,325 | — | Proof | 480.00 |

10th Anniversary of Independence

KM#	Date	Mintage	VF	XF	Unc
21	1970	8,000	—	Proof	600.00

1st Anniversary of the 1969 Revolution

| 22 | 1970 | — | — | Proof | 480.00 |

500 SHILLINGS

70.0000 g, .900 GOLD, 2.0257 oz AGW
5th Anniversary of Independence
Obv: Similar to 20 Shillings, KM#10.

| 14 | 1965 | 6,325 | — | Proof | 1150. |

10th Anniversary of Independence
Obv: Similar to 200 Shillings, KM#22.

| 23 | 1970 | 8,000 | — | Proof | 1150. |

MONETARY REFORM
100 Senti = 1 Shilin

5 SENTI

ALUMINUM
F.A.O. Issue

KM#	Date	Mintage	VF	XF	Unc
A24	1976	—	—	—	—

F.A.O. Issue

| 24 | 1976 | 18.500 | .10 | .15 | .20 |

10 SENTI

ALUMINUM
F.A.O. Issue

| 25 | 1976 | 40.500 | .10 | .15 | .25 |

50 SENTI

COPPER-NICKEL
F.A.O. Issue

| 26 | 1976 | 10.080 | .10 | .15 | .50 |

SHILIN

COPPER-NICKEL
F.A.O. Issue

| 27 | 1976 | 20.040 | .25 | .50 | 1.50 |

10 SHILLINGS

COPPER-NICKEL
10th Anniversary of Republic

| 28 | 1979 | — | — | 2.00 | 4.00 |

28.2800 g, .925 SILVER, .8411 oz ASW

| 28a | 1979 | *5,000 | — | Proof | 30.00 |

COPPER-NICKEL
10th Anniversary of Republic

KM#	Date	Mintage	VF	XF	Unc
29	1979	—	—	2.00	4.00

28.2800 g, .925 SILVER, .8411 oz ASW

| 29a | 1979 | *5,000 | — | Proof | 30.00 |

COPPER-NICKEL
10th Anniversary of Republic

| 30 | 1979 | — | — | 2.00 | 4.00 |

28.2800 g, .925 SILVER, .8411 oz ASW

| 30a | 1979 | *5,000 | — | Proof | 30.00 |

COPPER-NICKEL
10th Anniversary of Republic

| 31 | 1979 | — | — | 2.00 | 4.00 |

28.2800 g, .925 SILVER, .8411 oz ASW

| 31a | 1979 | *5,000 | — | Proof | 30.00 |

COPPER-NICKEL
10th Anniversary of Republic

| 32 | 1979 | — | — | 2.00 | 4.00 |

28.2800 g, .925 SILVER, .8411 oz ASW

| 32a | 1979 | *5,000 | — | Proof | 30.00 |

25 SHILLINGS

COPPER-NICKEL
World Fisheries Conference

KM#	Date	Mintage	VF	XF	Unc
40	ND(1984)	.100	—	2.50	5.00

28.2800 g, .925 SILVER, .8411 oz ASW

| 40a | ND(1984) | .020 | — | Proof | 30.00 |

47.5400 g, .917 GOLD, 1.4011 oz AGW

| 40b | ND(1984) | 200 pcs. | — | Proof | 1250. |

150 SHILLINGS

28.2800 g, .925 SILVER, .8411 oz ASW
International Year of Disabled Persons
Obv: Coat of arms, date.

| 38 | 1983 | 5,500 | — | — | 25.00 |
| | 1983 | 5,500 | — | Proof | 32.50 |

1500 SHILLINGS

15.9800 g, .917 GOLD, .4711 oz AGW
10th Anniversary of Republic
Obv: Similar to KM#35.

| 33 | 1979 | 500 pcs. | — | — | 300.00 |
| | 1979 | 500 pcs. | — | Proof | 350.00 |

10th Anniversary of Republic
Obv: Similar to KM#35.

| 34 | 1979 | 500 pcs. | — | — | 300.00 |
| | 1979 | 500 pcs. | — | Proof | 350.00 |

10th Anniversary of Republic

| 35 | 1979 | 500 pcs. | — | — | 300.00 |
| | 1979 | 500 pcs. | — | Proof | 350.00 |

10th Anniversary of Republic

KM#	Date	Mintage	VF	XF	Unc
36	1979	500 pcs.	—	—	300.00
	1979	500 pcs.	—	Proof	350.00

10th Anniversary of Republic
Obv: Similar to KM#35.

| 37 | 1979 | 500 pcs. | — | — | 300.00 |
| | 1979 | 500 pcs. | — | Proof | 350.00 |

International Year of Disabled Persons
Obv: Similar to KM#35. Rev: Children holding a Koran.

| 39 | 1983 | — | — | — | 400.00 |
| | 1983 | — | — | Proof | 500.00 |

MINT SETS (MS)

KM#	Date	Mintage	Identification	Issue Price	Mkt. Val.
MS1	1979(5)	—	KM33-37	2375.	1500.

PROOF SETS (PS)

PS1	1965(5)	6,325	KM10-14	—	2100.
PS2	1965(5)	—	KM10-14, Gilt Copper Nickel		
PS3	1970(5)	8,000	KM16-17,19,21,23	334.95	2200.
PS4	1970(3)	14,500	KM18,20,22	—	850.00
PS5	1979(5)	5,000	KM28a-32a	325.00	150.00
PS6	1979(5)	—	KM33-37	3125.	1750.

Listings For
SOMALILAND: refer to Djibouti

SOUTH AFRICA

The Republic of South Africa, located at the southern tip of Africa, has an area, including the enclave of Walvis Bay, of 472,359 sq. mi. (1,233,404 sq. km.) and a population of *35.6 million. Capitals: Administrative, Pretoria; Legislative, Cape Town; Judicial, Bloemfontein. Manufacturing, mining and agriculture are the principal industries. Exports include wool, diamonds, gold, and metallic ores.

Portuguese navigator Bartholomew Diaz became the first European to sight the region of South Africa when he rounded the Cape of Good Hope in 1488, but throughout the 16th century the only white men to come ashore were the survivors of ships wrecked while attempting the stormy Cape passage. The first permanent settlement was established by Jan van Riebeeck of the Dutch East India Company in 1652. In subsequent decades additional Dutch and Germans and Huguenot refugees from France settled in the Cape area to form the Afrikaner segment of today's population.

Great Britain captured the Cape colony in 1795, and again in 1806, receiving permanent title in 1814. To escape British political rule and cultural dominance, many Afrikaner farmers (Boers) migrated northward (the Great Trek) beginning in 1836, and established the independent Boer Republics of the Transvaal (the South African Republic, Zuid Afrikaansche Republic) in 1852, and the Orange Free State in 1854. British political intrigues against the two republics, coupled with the discovery of diamonds and gold in the Boer-settled regions, led to the bitter Boer Wars (1880-81, 1899-1902) and the incorporation of the Boer republics into the British Empire.

On May 31, 1910, the two former Boer Republics (Transvaal and Orange Free State) were joined with the British colonies of Cape of Good Hope and Natal to form the Union of South Africa, a dominion of the British Empire. In 1934 the Union achieved status as a sovereign state within the British Empire.

Political integration of the various colonies did not still the conflict between the Afrikaners and the English-speaking groups, which continued to have a significant impact on political developments. A resurgence of Afrikaner nationalism in the 1940's and 1950's led to a referendum in the white community authorizing the relinquishment of dominion status and the establishment of a republic. The decision took effect on May 31, 1961. The Republic of South Africa withdrew from the British Commonwealth in Oct. 1961.

South African coins and currency bear inscriptions in both Afrikaans and English.

RULERS
British until 1961

MONETARY SYSTEM
Until 1961
- 12 Pence = 1 Shilling
- 2 Shillings = 1 Florin
- 20 Shillings = 1 Pound

Commencing 1961
- 100 Cents = 1 Rand

ZUID AFRIKAANSCHE REPUBLIC
MONETARY SYSTEM
- 12 Pence = 1 Shilling
- 20 Shillings = 1 Pond

PENNY

BRONZE

KM#	Date	Mintage	Fine	VF	XF	Unc
2	1892	.028	3.00	6.00	20.00	40.00
	1892	*8-10 pcs.	—	—	Proof	4000.
	1893	.055	30.00	45.00	110.00	200.00
	1894	.011	5.00	10.00	30.00	120.00
	1898	.263	1.00	2.00	5.00	15.00

3 PENCE

1.4138 g, .925 SILVER, .0420 oz ASW

KM#	Date	Mintage	Fine	VF	XF	Unc
3	1892	.024	3.00	6.00	20.00	100.00
	1892	*35-40 pcs.	—	—	Proof	1150.
	1893	.135	3.00	10.00	75.00	125.00
	1894	.104	4.00	12.50	65.00	175.00
	1895	.113	3.00	20.00	100.00	300.00
	1896	.166	2.00	4.00	8.00	40.00
	1897	.201	2.00	4.00	8.00	35.00

6 PENCE

2.8276 g, .925 SILVER, .0841 oz ASW

KM#	Date	Mintage	Fine	VF	XF	Unc
4	1892	.028	4.00	7.50	50.00	100.00
	1892	*40-50 pcs.	—	—	Proof	500.00
	1893	.096	3.00	6.00	65.00	140.00
	1894	.168	3.00	6.00	65.00	250.00
	1895	.179	3.00	6.00	65.00	250.00
	1896	.205	2.00	4.00	8.00	30.00
	1896	1 known	—	—	—	Proof
	1897	.220	1.50	3.00	6.00	35.00
	1897	1 known	—	—	—	Proof

SHILLING

5.6555 g, .925 SILVER, .1682 oz ASW

KM#	Date	Mintage	Fine	VF	XF	Unc
5	1892	.130	7.50	15.00	60.00	150.00
	1892	*40-50 pcs.	—	—	Proof	500.00
	1893	.137	10.00	50.00	250.00	1000.
	1894	.366	4.00	6.00	150.00	350.00
	1895	.327	4.00	10.00	250.00	500.00
	1896	.437	4.00	10.00	125.00	500.00
	1897	.397	2.00	4.00	10.00	45.00

2 SHILLINGS

11.3100 g, .925 SILVER, .3364 oz ASW

KM#	Date	Mintage	Fine	VF	XF	Unc
6	1892	.055	10.00	25.00	75.00	150.00
	1892	*50-60 pcs.	—	—	Proof	500.00
	1893	.106	15.00	50.00	350.00	950.00
	1894	.173	5.00	25.00	275.00	600.00
	1895	.150	7.50	35.00	300.00	850.00
	1896	.353	4.00	8.00	25.00	70.00
	1897	.148	3.00	6.00	20.00	70.00

2-1/2 SHILLINGS

14.1380 g, .925 SILVER, .4205 oz ASW

KM#	Date	Mintage	Fine	VF	XF	Unc
7	1892	.163	15.00	30.00	100.00	225.00
	1892	*50-60 pcs.	—	—	Proof	510.00
	1893	.135	20.00	80.00	400.00	700.00
	1894	.135	10.00	30.00	150.00	500.00
	1895	.182	10.00	60.00	400.00	700.00
	1896	.285	5.00	10.00	30.00	100.00
	1897	.149	5.00	10.00	30.00	100.00

5 SHILLINGS

28.2759 g, .925 SILVER, .8410 oz ASW
Single shaft wagon tongue

KM#	Date	Mintage	Fine	VF	XF	Unc
8.1	1892	.014	60.00	85.00	225.00	900.00

Double shaft wagon tongue

| 8.2 | 1892 | 4,327 | 75.00 | 100.00 | 250.00 | 1100. |
| | 1892 | *25-30 pcs. | — | — | Proof | 3500. |

Beware of counterfeit double shafts. Aside from there being two shafts on the wagon in the coat of arms (reverse), the two wheels of the wagon must be the same size. On single shaft crowns, the rear wheel is noticeably larger than the front wheel.

Single shaft wagon tongue

Double shaft wagon tongue

1/2 POND

3.9940 g, .916 GOLD, .1176 oz AGW
Rev: Double shaft wagon tongue

| 9.1 | 1892 | .010 | 100.00 | 150.00 | 250.00 | 500.00 |
| | 1892 | *20-25 pcs. | — | — | Proof | 7500. |

Rev: Single shaft wagon tongue

9.2	1892	—	—	—	Unique	—
	1893	Inc. Be.	500.00	1000.	2000.	3000.
	1894	.039	75.00	90.00	200.00	800.00
	1895	.135	75.00	90.00	150.00	400.00
	1896	.104	75.00	90.00	150.00	400.00
	1897	.075	75.00	90.00	150.00	400.00

EEN (1) POND

7.9880 g, .916 GOLD, .2353 oz AGW
Coarse beard

| 1.1 | 1874 | 142 | 2250. | 3000. | 4000. | 9000. |

Fine beard

| 1.2 | 1874 | 695 | 1500. | 2000. | 3000. | 6500. |

Rev: Double shaft wagon tongue

| 10.1 | 1892 | .016 | 120.00 | 150.00 | 200.00 | 350.00 |
| | 1892 | *12-15 pcs. | — | — | Proof | 12,500. |

Rev: Single shaft wagon tongue

KM#	Date	Mintage	Fine	VF	XF	Unc
10.2	1892	Inc. Bl.	300.00	500.00	1750.	4500.
	1893	.062	120.00	150.00	300.00	800.00
	1894	.318	120.00	150.00	350.00	1000.
	1895	.336	120.00	150.00	350.00	1000.
	1896	.235	120.00	135.00	250.00	900.00
	1897	.311	120.00	135.00	175.00	375.00
	1898	.137	120.00	135.00	150.00	300.00
	1898/stamped 99					
		130 pcs.	3500.	5000.	7000.00	10,000.
	1898/stamped 9		—	—	Unique	—
	1900	.788	120.00	135.00	175.00	300.00

KM#	Date	Mintage	Fine	VF	XF	Unc
23	1937	.038	1.50	3.00	6.00	12.50
	1937	116 pcs.	—	—	Proof	50.00
	1938	.051	1.00	2.00	4.00	8.00
	1938	44 pcs.	—	—	Proof	100.00
	1939	.102	.50	1.50	3.00	7.50
	1939	30 pcs.	—	—	Proof	—
	1941	.091	.50	1.50	3.00	7.50
	1942	3.756	.25	.50	1.00	2.00
	1943	9.918	.25	.50	.75	1.50
	1943	104 pcs.	—	—	Proof	50.00
	1944	4.468	.25	.50	.75	2.00
	1944	150 pcs.	—	—	Proof	35.00
	1945	5.297	.25	.50	1.50	3.00
	1945	150 pcs.	—	—	Proof	35.00
	1946	4.378	.25	.50	1.50	4.00
	1946	150 pcs.	—	—	Proof	35.00
	1947	3.895	.25	.50	1.50	4.00
	1947	2,600	—	—	Proof	4.00

Rev. denomination: 1/2 PENNY

KM#	Date	Mintage	Fine	VF	XF	Unc
13.2	1928	.105	5.00	12.50	35.00	75.00
	1929	.272	2.50	5.00	15.00	35.00
	1930	.147	3.50	7.00	20.00	40.00
	1930	14 pcs.	—	—	Proof	—
	1930 w/o star after date					
		Inc. Ab.	4.00	8.00	25.00	50.00
	1931	.145	3.50	7.00	25.00	50.00

.999 GOLD
Veld Boer War Siege Issue

11	1902	986 pcs.	825.00	1750.	3100.	5600.

PROOF SETS (PS)

KM#	Date	Mintage	Identification	Issue Price	Mkt. Val.
PS101	1892(9)	—	KM2-10	—	30,000.

UNION

MONETARY SYSTEM
12 Pence = 1 Shilling
2 Shillings = 1 Florin
20 Shillings = 1 Pound

1/4 PENNY FARTHING

BRONZE
Rev. denomination: 1/4 PENNY 1/4

KM#	Date	Mintage	Fine	VF	XF	Unc
12.1	1923	.033	2.00	4.00	8.00	15.00
	1923	1,402	—	—	Proof	30.00
	1924	.095	1.50	2.50	5.00	10.00

Rev. denomination: 1/4 PENNY

12.2	1926	16 pcs.	—	—	Proof	7000.
	1928	.064	1.50	3.00	5.00	12.50
	1928	14 pcs.	—	—	Proof	—
	1930	6,560	45.00	90.00	175.00	275.00
	1930	14 pcs.	—	—	Proof	—
	1931	.154	1.00	1.50	4.00	6.00

Rev. denomination: 1/4 D

12.3	1931	Inc. Ab.	5.00	10.00	15.00	35.00
	1931	62 pcs.	—	—	Proof	—
	1932	.105	1.00	1.50	3.50	7.00
	1932	12 pcs.	—	—	Proof	—
	1933	76 pcs.	—	—	—	—
	1933	20 pcs.	—	—	Proof	—
	1934	52 pcs.	—	—	—	—
	1934	24 pcs.	—	—	Proof	—
	1935	.061	1.00	1.50	3.50	8.00
	1935	20 pcs.	—	—	Proof	—
	1936	43 pcs.	—	—	—	—
	1936	40 pcs.	—	—	Proof	3000.

32.1	1948	2.415	.25	.50	1.00	2.00
	1948	1,120	—	—	Proof	3.00
	1949	3.568	.25	.50	1.00	2.50
	1949	800 pcs.	—	—	Proof	5.00
	1950	8.694	.25	.50	.75	1.50
	1950	500 pcs.	—	—	Proof	8.00

Rev. leg. reversed: SUID AFRIKA-SOUTH AFRICA

32.2	1951	3.511	.15	.35	.75	2.50
	1951	2,000	—	—	Proof	2.00
	1952	2.804	.15	.35	.75	2.00
	1952	15,500	—	—	Proof	2.00

44	1953	9.633	.15	.25	.50	1.50
	1953	5,000	—	—	Proof	2.00
	1954	6.568	.15	.25	.50	1.50
	1954	3.150	—	—	Proof	2.00
	1955	11.798	.15	.25	.50	1.50
	1955	2,850	—	—	Proof	2.00
	1956	1.287	.15	.25	.50	2.50
	1956	1,700	—	—	Proof	3.00
	1957	3.056	.15	.25	.50	1.50
	1957	1,130	—	—	Proof	4.00
	1958	5.452	.15	.25	.50	1.50
	1958	985 pcs.	—	—	Proof	5.00
	1959	1.567	.15	.25	.50	1.50
	1959	950 pcs.	—	—	Proof	6.00
	1960	1.023	.15	.25	.50	2.00
	1960	3.360	—	—	Proof	1.50

1/2 PENNY

BRONZE
Rev. denomination: 1/2 PENNY 1/2

13.1	1923	.012	35.00	50.00	90.00	125.00
	1923	1,402	—	—	Proof	100.00
	1924	.064	7.50	12.50	30.00	50.00
	1925	.069	7.50	12.50	35.00	100.00
	1926	.065	10.00	15.00	40.00	125.00

Rev. denomination: 1/2 D

13.3	1931	62 pcs.	—	—	Proof	—
	1932	.106	5.00	10.00	30.00	85.00
	1932	12 pcs.	—	—	Proof	—
	1933	.063	8.00	25.00	60.00	150.00
	1933	20 pcs.	—	—	Proof	—
	1934	.326	1.50	5.00	15.00	35.00
	1934	24 pcs.	—	—	Proof	—
	1935	.405	1.50	5.00	15.00	30.00
	1935	20 pcs.	—	—	Proof	—
	1936	.407	1.50	5.00	15.00	27.50
	1936	40 pcs.	—	—	Proof	300.00

24	1937	.638	1.00	2.00	9.00	15.00
	1937	116 pcs.	—	—	Proof	60.00
	1938	.560	1.00	2.00	6.00	15.00
	1938	44 pcs.	—	—	Proof	150.00
	1939	.271	2.50	5.00	10.00	20.00
	1939	30 pcs.	—	—	Proof	—
	1940	1.535	.30	.75	3.00	8.00
	1941	2.053	.30	.75	3.00	8.00
	1942	8.382	.25	.60	2.00	6.00
	1943	5.135	.25	.60	2.00	6.00
	1943	104 pcs.	—	—	Proof	60.00
	1944	3.920	.25	.75	3.00	8.00
	1944	150 pcs.	—	—	Proof	35.00
	1945	2.357	.25	.60	2.50	7.00
	1945	150 pcs.	—	—	Proof	35.00
	1946	1.022	.25	.75	3.00	9.00
	1946	150 pcs.	—	—	Proof	35.00
	1947	.258	1.00	3.00	6.00	17.50
	1947	2,600	—	—	Proof	6.00

33	1948	.685	.50	1.00	4.00	9.00
	1948	1,120	—	—	Proof	3.00
	1949	1.850	.25	.50	1.75	4.00
	1949	800 pcs.	—	—	Proof	3.00
	1950	2.186	.25	.50	1.50	3.00
	1950	500 pcs.	—	—	Proof	6.00
	1951	3.746	.25	.50	1.25	3.00
	1951	2,000	—	—	Proof	2.00
	1952	4.174	.25	.50	1.00	2.50
	1952	.016	—	—	Proof	2.00

Union of / SOUTH AFRICA 1509

Union of / SOUTH AFRICA 1510

KM#	Date	Mintage	Fine	VF	XF	Unc
45	1953	5.572	.15	.35	1.00	3.00
	1953	5,000	—	—	Proof	2.00
	1954	.101	2.00	4.00	7.50	12.50
	1954	3,150	—	—	Proof	12.50
	1955	3.774	.15	.35	1.00	3.00
	1955	2,850	—	—	Proof	2.00
	1956	1.305	.15	.35	1.00	3.00
	1956	1,700	—	—	Proof	3.00
	1957	2.025	.15	.35	1.00	3.00
	1957	1,130	—	—	Proof	4.00
	1958	2.171	.15	.35	1.00	2.50
	1958	985 pcs.	—	—	Proof	5.00
	1959	2.397	.15	.25	.75	2.00
	1959	900 pcs.	—	—	Proof	6.00
	1960	2.552	.15	.25	.75	2.00
	1960	3.360	—	—	Proof	1.50

PENNY

BRONZE
Rev. denomination: 1 PENNY 1

KM#	Date	Mintage	Fine	VF	XF	Unc
14.1	1923	.091	3.00	7.00	17.50	35.00
	1923	1,402	—	—	Proof	50.00
	1924	.134	4.00	10.00	25.00	50.00

Rev. denomination: PENNY

14.2	1926	.393	3.00	10.00	35.00	75.00
	1926	16 pcs.	—	—	Proof	—
	1927	.285	3.00	10.00	35.00	70.00
	1928	.386	3.00	10.00	35.00	70.00
	1929	1.093	1.00	4.00	12.50	20.00
	1930	.754	1.00	4.00	15.00	40.00
	1930	14 pcs.	—	—	Proof	—

Rev. denomination: 1 D.

14.3	1931	.248	1.00	5.00	17.50	40.00
	1931	62 pcs.	—	—	Proof	—
	1932	.260	1.00	5.00	20.00	50.00
	1932	12 pcs.	—	—	Proof	—
	1933	.225	2.00	10.00	30.00	45.00
	1933	20 pcs.	—	—	Proof	—
	1933 w/o star after date					
	Inc. Ab.	4.00	10.00	30.00	50.00
	1934	2.090	.50	1.50	8.00	22.50
	1934	24 pcs.	—	—	Proof	—
	1935	2.295	.50	1.50	8.00	22.50
	1935	20 pcs.	—	—	Proof	—
	1936	1.819	.35	1.00	5.00	20.00
	1936	40 pcs.	—	—	Proof	400.00

KM#	Date	Mintage	Fine	VF	XF	Unc
25	1937	3.281	.50	1.50	5.00	10.00
	1937	116 pcs.	—	—	Proof	75.00
	1938	1.840	.50	1.50	8.00	30.00
	1938	44 pcs.	—	—	Proof	100.00
	1939	1.506	.50	1.50	8.00	17.50
	1939	30 pcs.	—	—	Proof	—
	1940	3.592	.35	1.00	4.00	10.00
	1940 w/o star after date					
	Inc. Ab.	1.50	3.00	6.00	15.00
	1941	7.871	.25	.75	2.50	7.00
	1942	14.428	.25	.75	2.00	6.00
	1942 w/o star after date					
	Inc. Ab.	3.00	6.00	12.50	30.00
	1943	4.010	.25	.75	2.50	6.00
	1943	104 pcs.	—	—	Proof	70.00
	1944	6.425	.25	.75	2.50	7.00
	1944	150 pcs.	—	—	Proof	45.00
	1945	4.810	.25	.75	2.50	7.00
	1945	150 pcs.	—	—	Proof	45.00
	1946	2.605	.25	.75	3.00	8.00
	1946	150 pcs.	—	—	Proof	45.00
	1947	.135	2.50	4.00	7.50	17.50
	1947	2,600	—	—	Proof	7.00

34.1	1948	2.398	.25	.75	2.00	5.00
	1948	1,120	—	—	Proof	4.00
	1948 w/o star after date					
	Inc. Ab.	1.00	2.00	5.00	10.00
	1949	3.634	.25	.75	1.50	4.00
	1949	800 pcs.	—	—	Proof	4.00
	1950	4.890	.25	.75	1.50	4.00
	1950	500 pcs.	—	—	Proof	7.00

Rev. leg: SUID AFRIKA-SOUTH AFRICA

34.2	1951	3.787	.25	.75	1.50	4.00
	1951	2,000	—	—	Proof	2.00
	1952	12.674	.25	.50	1.00	2.50
	1952	.016	—	—	Proof	2.00

46	1953	5.491	.20	.35	.75	2.00
	1953	5,000	—	—	Proof	2.00
	1954	6.665	.20	.35	.75	3.00
	1954	3,150	—	—	Proof	3.00
	1955	6.508	.20	.35	.75	3.00
	1955	2,850	—	—	Proof	3.00
	1956	4.390	.20	.35	1.00	4.00
	1956	1,700	—	—	Proof	3.00
	1957	3.973	.20	.35	.75	3.00
	1957	1,130	—	—	Proof	5.00
	1958	5.311	.20	.35	.75	3.00
	1958	985 pcs.	—	—	Proof	6.00
	1959	5.066	.20	.35	.75	2.00
	1959	900 pcs.	—	—	Proof	7.00
	1960	5.106	.20	.35	.75	2.00
	1960	3.360	—	—	Proof	2.00

3 PENCE

1.4100 g, .800 SILVER, .0362 oz ASW

KM#	Date	Mintage	Fine	VF	XF	Unc
15.1	1923	.303	4.00	8.00	20.00	55.00
	1923	1,402	—	—	Proof	60.00
	1924	.501	4.00	10.00	25.00	65.00
	1925	Inc. Bl	10.00	35.00	150.00	750.00

Rev. denomination: 3 PENCE

15.2	1925	.358	5.00	25.00	80.00	150.00
	1925	—	—	—	Proof	—
	1926	1.572	1.00	3.50	20.00	50.00
	1926	16 pcs.	—	—	Proof	—
	1927	2.285	1.00	2.50	15.00	100.00
	1928	.919	1.50	5.00	35.00	125.00
	1929	1.948	1.00	3.50	12.50	50.00
	1930	.981	1.00	3.50	25.00	65.00
	1930	14 pcs.	—	—	Proof	—

Rev. denomination: 3D

15.3	1931	128 pcs.	—	—	Rare	5000.
	1931	62 pcs.	—	—	Proof	3500.
	1932	2.622	1.00	2.50	15.00	30.00
	1932	12 pcs.	—	—	Proof	—
	1933	5.135	1.00	2.50	15.00	30.00
	1933	20 pcs.	—	—	Proof	—
	1934	2.357	1.00	2.50	15.00	30.00
	1934	24 pcs.	—	—	Proof	—
	1935	1.655	1.00	2.50	15.00	35.00
	1935	20 pcs.	—	—	Proof	—
	1936	1.095	.75	3.50	17.50	40.00
	1936	40 pcs.	—	—	Proof	250.00

26	1937	3.576	.50	1.00	3.00	10.00
	1937	116 pcs.	—	—	Proof	80.00
	1938	2.394	.50	1.50	7.00	15.00
	1938	44 pcs.	—	—	Proof	100.00
	1939	3.224	.50	1.50	5.00	12.50
	1939	30 pcs.	—	—	Proof	—
	1940	4.887	.50	1.00	3.00	12.50
	1941	8.968	.50	1.00	3.00	8.00
	1942	8.056	.50	1.00	3.00	8.00
	1943	14.828	.50	1.00	2.00	5.00
	1943	104 pcs.	—	—	Proof	80.00
	1944	3.331	.50	1.00	2.00	6.00
	1944	150 pcs.	—	—	Proof	60.00
	1945/3	4.094	1.00	3.00	10.00	20.00
	1945	Inc. Ab.	.50	1.00	3.00	8.00
	1945	150 pcs.	—	—	Proof	60.00
	1946	2.219	.50	1.00	3.00	9.00
	1946	150 pcs.	—	—	Proof	65.00
	1947	1.130	.50	1.00	2.50	8.00
	1947	2,600	—	—	—	8.00

35.1	1948	2.721	.50	1.00	3.00	7.00
	1948	1,120	—	—	Proof	5.00
	1949	1.905	.50	1.00	3.00	7.00
	1949	800 pcs.	—	—	Proof	5.00
	1950	4.096	.50	1.00	2.50	5.00
	1950	500 pcs.	—	—	Proof	7.00

1.4100 g, .500 SILVER, .0226 oz ASW
Rev: Modified design.

35.2	1951	6.325	.25	.50	1.00	3.00
	1951	2,000	—	—	Proof	4.00
	1952	13.072	.25	.50	1.00	2.00
	1952	.016	—	—	Proof	2.00

NOTE: Many varieties exist of George VI threepence.

47	1953	5.488	.25	.50	1.00	3.00
	1953	5,000	—	—	Proof	3.00
	1954	3.901	.25	.50	1.00	3.50

Union of / SOUTH AFRICA 1511

KM#	Date	Mintage	Fine	VF	XF	Unc
47	1954	3,150	—	—	Proof	4.00
	1955	4.723	.25	.50	1.00	3.00
	1955	2,850	—	—	Proof	3.00
	1956	6.191	.25	.50	1.00	3.00
	1956	1,700	—	—	Proof	4.00
	1957	1.894	.25	.50	1.00	3.00
	1957	1,130	—	—	Proof	5.00
	1958	3.228	.25	.50	1.00	3.00
	1958	985 pcs.	—	—	Proof	6.00
	1959	2.553	.25	.50	1.00	2.00
	1959 no K-G on reverse					
		Inc. Ab.	2.00	3.00	5.00	10.00
	1959	900 pcs.	—	—	Proof	7.00
	1960	.021	1.00	2.50	4.00	7.00
	1960	3,360	—	—	Proof	2.00

6 PENCE

2.8300 g, .800 SILVER, .0727 oz ASW

KM#	Date	Mintage	Fine	VF	XF	Unc
16.1	1923	.209	4.00	15.00	45.00	90.00
	1923	1,402	—	—	Proof	90.00
	1924	.326	3.50	12.50	35.00	80.00

Rev. denomination: 6 PENCE

KM#	Date	Mintage	Fine	VF	XF	Unc
16.2	1925	.079	5.00	20.00	90.00	200.00
	1925	—	—	—	Proof	—
	1926	.722	2.00	10.00	55.00	125.00
	1926	16 pcs.	—	—	Proof	—
	1927	1.548	1.50	4.00	25.00	100.00
	1929	.784	2.00	8.00	30.00	60.00
	1930	.448	2.00	10.00	40.00	70.00
	1930	14 pcs.	—	—	Proof	—

Rev. denomination: 6 D

KM#	Date	Mintage	Fine	VF	XF	Unc
16.3	1931	4,805	75.00	150.00	250.00	550.00
	1931	62 pcs.	—	—	Proof	1000.
	1932	1.525	1.00	5.00	17.50	35.00
	1932	12 pcs.	—	—	Proof	—
	1933	2.819	1.00	5.00	17.50	50.00
	1933	20 pcs.	—	—	Proof	—
	1934	1.519	1.00	7.00	20.00	40.00
	1934	24 pcs.	—	—	Proof	—
	1935	.573	2.00	8.00	35.00	90.00
	1935	20 pcs.	—	—	Proof	—
	1936	.627	1.00	7.00	20.00	40.00
	1936	40 pcs.	—	—	Proof	275.00

KM#	Date	Mintage	Fine	VF	XF	Unc
27	1937	1.696	1.00	2.00	7.00	17.50
	1937	116 pcs.	—	—	Proof	90.00
	1938	1.725	1.00	2.00	7.00	17.50
	1938	44 pcs.	—	—	Proof	125.00
	1939	30 pcs.	—	—	Proof	—
	1940	1.629	1.00	1.50	5.00	10.00
	1941	2.263	1.00	1.50	5.00	10.00
	1942	4.936	.75	1.25	3.00	8.00
	1943	3.776	.75	1.25	3.00	8.00
	1943	104 pcs.	—	—	Proof	90.00
	1944	.228	2.00	7.00	15.00	30.00
	1944	150 pcs.	—	—	Proof	75.00
	1945	.420	1.00	5.00	10.00	25.00
	1945	150 pcs.	—	—	Proof	75.00
	1946	.291	1.00	6.00	15.00	30.00
	1946	150 pcs.	—	—	Proof	80.00
	1947	.579	1.00	1.50	5.00	10.00
	1947	2,600	—	—	Proof	10.00

KM#	Date	Mintage	Fine	VF	XF	Unc
36.1	1948	2.267	.75	1.25	2.50	6.00
	1948	1,120	—	—	Proof	10.00
	1949	.197	3.00	7.50	15.00	30.00
	1949	800 pcs.	—	—	Proof	15.00

KM#	Date	Mintage	Fine	VF	XF	Unc
36.1	1950	2.122	.75	1.00	2.00	5.00
	1950	500 pcs.	—	—	Proof	15.00

2.8300 g, .500 SILVER, .0454 oz ASW

KM#	Date	Mintage	Fine	VF	XF	Unc
36.2	1951	2.604	.50	1.00	2.00	4.00
	1951	2,000	—	—	Proof	4.00
	1952	4.281	.50	.75	1.25	3.00
	1952	.016	—	—	Proof	2.00

KM#	Date	Mintage	Fine	VF	XF	Unc
48	1953	2.501	.50	.75	1.75	4.50
	1953	5,000	—	—	Proof	3.00
	1954	2.200	.50	1.00	2.00	4.50
	1954	3,150	—	—	Proof	4.00
	1955	1.972	.50	1.00	2.00	4.50
	1955	2,850	—	—	Proof	3.00
	1956	1.774	.50	1.00	2.00	5.00
	1956	1,700	—	—	Proof	4.00
	1957	3.290	.50	.75	1.75	4.50
	1957	1,130	—	—	Proof	6.00
	1958	1.174	.50	1.00	2.00	4.50
	1958	985 pcs.	—	—	Proof	6.00
	1959	.262	1.00	2.00	4.00	12.00
	1959	900 pcs.	—	—	Proof	8.00
	1960	1.590	.50	.75	1.25	2.50
	1960	3,360	—	—	Proof	2.50

SHILLING

5.6600 g, .800 SILVER, .1455 oz ASW
Rev. denomination: 1 SHILLING 1

KM#	Date	Mintage	Fine	VF	XF	Unc
17.1	1923	.809	4.00	15.00	40.00	85.00
	1923	1,402	—	—	Proof	90.00
	1924	1.269	3.50	12.50	30.00	85.00

Rev. denomination: SHILLING

KM#	Date	Mintage	Fine	VF	XF	Unc
17.2	1926	.238	15.00	125.00	900.00	1750.
	1926	16 pcs.	—	—	Proof	—
	1927	.488	10.00	30.00	200.00	750.00
	1928	.889	8.00	30.00	125.00	400.00
	1929	.926	5.00	15.00	40.00	100.00
	1930	.422	6.00	20.00	100.00	225.00
	1930	14 pcs.	—	—	Proof	—

KM#	Date	Mintage	Fine	VF	XF	Unc
17.3	1931	6,603	100.00	200.00	500.00	1250.
	1931	62 pcs.	—	—	Proof	—
	1932	2.537	2.50	5.00	15.00	30.00
	1932	12 pcs.	—	—	Proof	—
	1933	1.463	3.50	7.00	30.00	70.00
	1933	20 pcs.	—	—	Proof	—
	1934	.821	3.50	7.00	35.00	100.00
	1934	24 pcs.	—	—	Proof	—
	1935	.685	4.00	8.50	45.00	125.00
	1935	20 pcs.	—	—	Proof	—
	1936	.693	3.50	7.00	25.00	60.00
	1936	40 pcs.	—	—	Proof	650.00

KM#	Date	Mintage	Fine	VF	XF	Unc
28	1937	1.194	1.50	3.00	10.00	20.00
	1937	116 pcs.	—	—	Proof	120.00
	1938	1.160	1.50	3.00	10.00	20.00
	1938	44 pcs.	—	—	Proof	250.00
	1939	30 pcs.	—	—	Proof	—
	1940	1.365	1.50	2.50	7.50	17.50
	1941	1.826	1.50	2.50	7.50	17.50
	1942	3.867	1.50	2.50	7.50	17.50
	1943	4.188	1.00	2.00	5.00	10.00
	1943	104 pcs.	—	—	Proof	175.00
	1944	.049	8.00	20.00	55.00	125.00
	1944	150 pcs.	—	—	Proof	150.00
	1945	.054	8.00	20.00	50.00	125.00
	1945	150 pcs.	—	—	Proof	150.00
	1946	.027	10.00	30.00	60.00	130.00
	1946	150 pcs.	—	—	Proof	200.00
	1947	9,784	15.00	35.00	60.00	100.00
	1947	2,600	—	—	Proof	125.00

KM#	Date	Mintage	Fine	VF	XF	Unc
37.1	1948	6,094	15.00	35.00	60.00	100.00
	1948	1,120	—	—	Proof	125.00
	1949	800 pcs.	—	—	Proof	250.00
	1950	1.704	1.50	2.50	4.00	8.00
	1950	500 pcs.	—	—	Proof	125.00

5.6600 g, .500 SILVER, .0909 oz ASW
Rev. denomination: 1 S.

KM#	Date	Mintage	Fine	VF	XF	Unc
37.2	1951	2.407	1.00	1.50	4.00	8.00
	1951	2,000	—	—	Proof	4.00
	1952	1.935	1.00	1.50	3.50	7.00
	1952	.016	—	—	Proof	3.00

KM#	Date	Mintage	Fine	VF	XF	Unc
49	1953	2.677	.75	1.25	2.50	5.50
	1953	5,000	—	—	Proof	4.00
	1954	3.579	.75	1.25	2.00	5.50
	1954	3,150	—	—	Proof	4.00
	1955	2.209	.75	1.25	2.50	5.50
	1955	2,850	—	—	Proof	5.50
	1956	2.143	.75	1.25	2.50	6.00
	1956	1,700	—	—	Proof	6.00
	1957	.792	1.00	2.00	5.00	10.00
	1957	1,130	—	—	Proof	6.00
	1958	4.068	.75	1.25	2.00	5.50
	1958	985 pcs.	—	—	Proof	8.00
	1959	.205	1.50	3.00	5.00	10.00
	1959	900 pcs.	—	—	Proof	10.00
	1960	2.190	.75	1.25	2.00	5.50
	1960	3,360	—	—	Proof	3.00

FLORIN

11.3100 g, .800 SILVER, .2909 oz ASW

KM#	Date	Mintage	Fine	VF	XF	Unc
18	1923	.696	5.00	20.00	40.00	100.00
	1923	1,402	—	—	Proof	125.00
	1924	1.513	4.00	15.00	30.00	80.00
	1925	.050	250.00	500.00	2000.	3000.

Union of SOUTH AFRICA 1512

KM#	Date	Mintage	Fine	VF	XF	Unc
18	1926	.324	7.50	40.00	300.00	750.00
	1927	.399	7.50	35.00	200.00	600.00
	1928	1.092	4.00	10.00	100.00	250.00
	1929	.648	5.00	15.00	125.00	300.00
	1930	.267	5.00	15.00	100.00	225.00
	1930	14 pcs.	—	—	Proof	1200.

2 SHILLINGS

11.3100 g, .800 SILVER, .2909 oz ASW
Rev. denomination: 2 SHILLINGS

22	1931	445 pcs.	—	—	Rare	3500.
	1931	62 pcs.	—	—	Proof	—
	1932	1.315	3.00	6.00	15.00	40.00
	1932	12 pcs.	—	—	Proof	—
	1933	.891	4.00	8.00	40.00	120.00
	1933	20 pcs.	—	—	Proof	—
	1934	.559	4.00	8.00	40.00	100.00
	1934	24 pcs.	—	—	Proof	—
	1935	.554	5.00	9.00	45.00	125.00
	1935	20 pcs.	—	—	Proof	—
	1936	.669	4.00	8.00	40.00	100.00
	1936	40 pcs.	—	—	Proof	750.00

29	1937	1.495	2.50	5.00	10.00	30.00
	1937	116 pcs.	—	—	Proof	150.00
	1938	.214	5.00	10.00	50.00	100.00
	1938	44 pcs.	—	—	Proof	325.00
	1939	.279	5.00	10.00	35.00	65.00
	1939	30 pcs.	—	—	Proof	1000.
	1940	2.600	2.50	3.50	6.00	17.50
	1941	1.764	2.50	3.50	6.00	17.50
	1942	2.847	2.00	3.00	5.00	10.00
	1943	3.124	2.00	3.00	5.00	10.00
	1943	104 pcs.	—	—	Proof	150.00
	1944	.225	3.50	7.00	17.50	40.00
	1944	150 pcs.	—	—	Proof	120.00
	1945	.473	3.00	6.00	15.00	35.00
	1945	150 pcs.	—	—	Proof	120.00
	1946	.014	7.50	20.00	40.00	200.00
	1946	150 pcs.	—	—	Proof	200.00
	1947	5.492	15.00	25.00	50.00	125.00
	1947	2,600	—	—	Proof	150.00

38.1	1948	7,893	15.00	20.00	50.00	90.00
	1948	1,120	—	—	Proof	125.00
	1949	.204	5.00	10.00	15.00	35.00
	1949	800 pcs.	—	—	Proof	125.00
	1950	5,445	20.00	60.00	100.00	175.00
	1950	500 pcs.	—	—	Proof	200.00

11.3100 g, .500 SILVER, .1818 oz ASW
Rev. denomination: 2 S

38.2	1951	.732	2.00	3.00	5.00	10.00
	1951	2,000	—	—	Proof	6.00
	1952	3,585	1.50	2.00	3.00	6.50
	1952	.016	—	—	Proof	4.00

KM#	Date	Mintage	Fine	VF	XF	Unc
50	1953	3.279	1.50	2.25	4.00	8.50
	1953	5,000	—	—	Proof	9.00
	1954	5.869	1.50	2.25	3.00	7.00
	1954	3,150	—	—	Proof	6.00
	1955	3.748	1.50	2.25	3.00	7.50
	1955	2,850	—	—	Proof	6.00
	1956	2.551	1.50	2.25	4.00	9.00
	1956	1,700	—	—	Proof	9.00
	1957	2.508	1.50	2.25	4.00	10.00
	1957	1,130	—	—	Proof	11.00
	1958	2.821	1.50	2.25	4.00	10.00
	1958	985 pcs.	—	—	Proof	11.00
	1959	1.220	1.50	2.25	4.00	10.00
	1959	900 pcs.	—	—	Proof	14.00
	1960	1.954	1.50	2.25	3.00	5.00
	1960	3,360	—	—	Proof	4.00

2-1/2 SHILLINGS

14.1400 g, .800 SILVER, .3637 oz ASW
Rev. leg: ZUID-AFRICA,
denomination: 2-1/2 SHILLINGS 2-1/2

19.1	1923	1.228	4.00	15.00	40.00	100.00
	1923	1,402	—	—	Proof	125.00
	1924	2.556	3.50	10.00	40.00	115.00
	1925	.460	15.00	35.00	300.00	1000.

Rev. denomination: 2-1/2 SHILLINGS

19.2	1926	.205	20.00	40.00	400.00	1200.
	1926	16 pcs.	—	—	Proof	—
	1927	.194	10.00	40.00	400.00	1200.
	1928	.984	5.00	25.00	125.00	375.00
	1929	.617	5.00	25.00	175.00	600.00
	1930	.324	5.00	15.00	100.00	250.00
	1930	14 pcs.	—	—	Proof	—

Rev. leg: SUID. AFRICA

19.3	1931	852 pcs.	500.00	1000.	1500.	3500.
	1931	62 pcs.	—	—	Proof	—
	1932	1.029	4.00	6.00	22.50	60.00
	1932	12 pcs.	—	—	Proof	—
	1933	.136	8.00	40.00	185.00	300.00
	1933	20 pcs.	—	—	Proof	—
	1934	.416	4.00	8.00	30.00	115.00
	1934	24 pcs.	—	—	Proof	—
	1935	.345	6.00	12.50	32.50	115.00
	1935	20 pcs.	—	—	Proof	—
	1936	.553	4.00	8.00	25.00	95.00
	1936	40 pcs.	—	—	Proof	850.00

30	1937	1.154	3.00	5.00	15.00	32.50
	1937	116 pcs.	—	—	Proof	175.00
	1938	.534	4.00	8.00	20.00	55.00
	1938	44 pcs.	—	—	Proof	400.00
	1939	.133	6.00	15.00	50.00	100.00
	1939	30 pcs.	—	—	Proof	—
	1940	2.976	2.00	4.50	8.00	20.00
	1941	1.988	3.00	4.50	8.00	20.00

KM#	Date	Mintage	Fine	VF	XF	Unc
30	1942	3.180	3.00	4.50	8.00	20.00
	1943	2.098	3.00	4.50	8.00	20.00
	1943	104 pcs.	—	—	Proof	175.00
	1944	1.361	3.00	5.00	10.00	25.00
	1944	150 pcs.	—	—	Proof	130.00
	1945	.183	3.50	7.00	25.00	60.00
	1945	150 pcs.	—	—	Proof	130.00
	1946	.011	15.00	30.00	60.00	120.00
	1946	150 pcs.	—	—	Proof	180.00
	1947	6,182	20.00	35.00	75.00	125.00
	1947	2,600	—	—	Proof	150.00

39.1	1948	2,720	70.00	125.00	150.00	200.00
	1948	1,120	—	—	Proof	150.00
	1949	2,691	70.00	125.00	150.00	275.00
	1949	800 pcs.	—	—	Proof	175.00
	1950	5,576	70.00	125.00	150.00	200.00
	1950	500 pcs.	—	—	Proof	200.00

14.1400 g, .500 SILVER, .2273 oz ASW
Rev. denomination: 2-1/2 S

39.2	1951	.785	3.00	4.50	6.00	15.00
	1951	2,000	—	—	Proof	9.00
	1952	2.011	2.00	3.00	4.00	8.50
	1952	.016	—	—	Proof	5.00

51	1953	2.519	2.00	3.00	4.00	8.50
	1953	5,000	—	—	Proof	6.00
	1954	4.252	2.00	3.00	4.00	8.50
	1954	3,150	—	—	Proof	9.00
	1955	3.866	2.00	3.00	4.00	8.50
	1955	2,850	—	—	Proof	8.00
	1956	2.438	2.00	3.00	4.00	8.50
	1956	1,700	—	—	Proof	13.00
	1957	2.138	2.00	3.00	4.00	8.50
	1957	1,130	—	—	Proof	14.00
	1958	2.261	2.00	3.00	4.50	9.00
	1958	985 pcs.	—	—	Proof	14.00
	1959	.047	2.50	4.00	6.00	12.00
	1959	900 pcs.	—	—	Proof	18.00
	1960	.016	3.00	5.00	7.50	12.50
	1960	3,360	—	—	Proof	5.00

5 SHILLINGS

28.2800 g, .800 SILVER, .7274 oz ASW
Royal Visit

31	1947	.306	BV	7.00	7.50	10.00
	1947	3,000	—	—	Proof	30.00

SOUTH AFRICA 1513

KM#	Date	Mintage	Fine	VF	XF	Unc
40.1	1948	.782	BV	6.00	7.50	10.00
	1948	.010	—	—	Proof	20.00
	1949	.538	BV	6.00	7.50	10.00
	1949	2,000	—	—	Proof	50.00
	1950	.084	BV	10.00	15.00	35.00
	1950	1,200	—	—	Proof	70.00

28.2800 g, .500 SILVER, .4546 oz ASW
Rev. denomination: 5 S.

40.2	1951	.367	BV	5.00	7.00	10.00
	1951	2,000	—	—	Proof	22.00

300th Anniversary Founding of Capetown

41	1952	1.726	BV	4.50	5.50	7.50
	1952	.016	—	—	Proof	13.00

52	1953	.263	BV	5.00	7.00	10.00
	1953	8,000	—	—	Proof	12.00
	1953	—	—	Matte Proof		700.00
	1954	.017	BV	10.00	15.00	25.00
	1954	3,890	—	—	Proof	40.00
	1955	.045	BV	7.50	10.00	20.00
	1955	2,250	—	—	Proof	20.00
	1956	.104	BV	5.00	7.00	10.00
	1956	2,200	—	—	Proof	25.00
	1957	.157	BV	5.00	7.00	10.00
	1957	1,600	—	—	Proof	25.00
	1958	.236	BV	5.00	7.00	10.00
	1958	1,500	—	—	Proof	35.00
	1959	6,139	35.00	65.00	125.00	200.00
	1959	2,200	—	—	Proof	200.00

50th Anniversary

KM#	Date	Mintage	Fine	VF	XF	Unc
55	1960	.422	BV	4.50	5.50	6.50
	1960	.022	—	—	Proof	8.00

NOTE: Many varieties exist of letters HM below building.

1/2 SOVEREIGN

3.9940 g, .917 GOLD, .1177 oz AGW
British type w/Pretoria mint mark: SA

20	1923	655 pcs.	—	—	Proof	500.00
	1925	.947	65.00	80.00	90.00	110.00
	1926	.808	65.00	80.00	90.00	110.00

1/2 POUND

3.9940 g, .917 GOLD, .1177 oz AGW
Similar to 1 Pound, KM#43.

42	1952	.016	—	—	—	65.00
	1952	.012	—	—	Proof	70.00

53	1953	4,000	—	—	Proof	75.00
	1954	1,225	—	—	Proof	85.00
	1955	900 pcs.	—	—	Proof	100.00
	1956	508 pcs.	—	—	Proof	200.00
	1957	560 pcs.	—	—	Proof	160.00
	1958	515 pcs.	—	—	Proof	175.00
	1959	1,130	—	—	—	90.00
	1959	630 pcs.	—	—	Proof	150.00
	1960	3,002	—	—	—	65.00
	1960	1,950	—	—	Proof	75.00

SOVEREIGN

7.9881 g, .917 GOLD, .2354 oz AGW
British type w/Pretoria mint mark: SA

21	1923	719 pcs.	200.00	300.00	400.00	500.00
	1923	655 pcs.	—	—	Proof	550.00
	1924	3,184	1000.	2000.	3500.	5000.
	1925	6,086	—	—	BV	120.00	135.00
	1926	11.108	—	—	BV	120.00	135.00
	1927	16.380	—	—	BV	120.00	135.00
	1928	18.235	—	—	BV	120.00	135.00
	1929	12.024	—	—	BV	120.00	135.00
	1930	10.028	—	—	BV	120.00	135.00
	1931	8.512	—	—	BV	120.00	135.00
	1932	1.067	—	—	BV	120.00	145.00

POUND

7.9881 g, .917 GOLD, .2354 oz AGW

43	1952	.017	—	—	—	125.00
	1952	.012	—	—	Proof	135.00

KM#	Date	Mintage	Fine	VF	XF	Unc
54	1953	4,000	—	—	Proof	135.00
	1954	1,225	—	—	Proof	150.00
	1955	900 pcs.	—	—	Proof	170.00
	1956	508 pcs.	—	—	Proof	275.00
	1957	560 pcs.	—	—	Proof	265.00
	1958	515 pcs.	—	—	Proof	275.00
	1959	1,132	—	—	—	175.00
	1959	630 pcs.	—	—	Proof	225.00
	1960	3,111	—	—	—	125.00
	1960	1,950	—	—	Proof	135.00

REPUBLIC

MONETARY SYSTEM
100 Cents = 1 Rand

1/2 CENT

BRASS

KM#	Date	Mintage	VF	XF	Unc
56	1961	39.196	.15	.25	1.00
	1961	7,530	—	Proof	.50
	1962	17.899	.15	.25	1.00
	1962	3,844	—	Proof	.75
	1963	11.615	.15	.25	2.00
	1963	4,025	—	Proof	.50
	1964	9.274	.15	.25	1.00
	1964	.016	—	Proof	.50

BRONZE
Bilingual

81	1970	*57.721	.10	.25	.50
	1970	.010	—	Proof	2.50
	1971	.020	—	—	2.50
	1971	.012	—	Proof	2.50
	1972	.020	—	—	2.50
	1972	.010	—	Proof	2.50
	1973	17.464	.10	.20	2.50
	1973	.011	—	Proof	2.50
	1974	.509	.20	.40	2.50
	1974	.015	—	—	2.50
	1975	10.760	.10	.20	2.50
	1975	.018	—	—	2.50
	1977	10.020	.10	.20	2.50
	1977	.019	—	Proof	2.50
	1978	10.016	.10	.20	2.50
	1978	.017	—	Proof	2.50
	1980	.015	—	Proof	2.50
	1981	.010	—	Proof	2.50
	1983	.014	—	Proof	2.50

*NOTE: Coins dated 1970 were also minted in 1971, 1972 and 1973.

President Fouche
Similar to 1 Cent, KM#91.

90	1976	9.762	.10	.20	.50
	1976	.021	—	Proof	.50

President Diederichs

97	1979	.020	—	—	.50
	1979	.015	—	Proof	.50

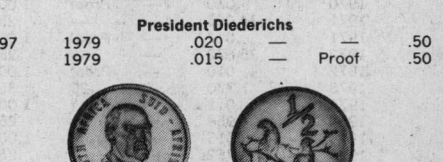

President Vorster

108	1982	.012	—	Proof	.50

SOUTH AFRICA 1514

CENT

BRASS

KM#	Date	Mintage	VF	XF	Unc
57	1961	52.274	.15	.40	1.50
	1961	7,530	—	Proof	.75
	1962	21.933	.15	.40	1.50
	1962	3,844	—	Proof	1.00
	1963	9.085	.15	.50	3.00
	1963	4,025	—	Proof	1.00
	1964	14.281	.15	.40	1.50
	1964	.016	—	Proof	2.00

BRONZE
English legend

KM#	Date	Mintage	VF	XF	Unc
65.1	1965	.026	—	—	2.00
	1965	.025	—	Proof	1.75
	1966	50.157	—	.10	.50
	1967	21.114	—	.10	.50
	1969	10.196	—	.10	.50

Afrikaans legend

KM#	Date	Mintage	VF	XF	Unc
65.2	1965	1,031	100.00	150.00	200.00
	1965	185 pcs.	—	Proof	250.00
	1966	50.182	—	.10	.50
	1966	.025	—	Proof	1.00
	1967	21.139	—	.10	.50
	1967	.025	—	Proof	1.00
	1969	10.208	—	.10	.50
	1969	.012	—	—	1.50

Charles Swart
English legend

KM#	Date	Mintage	VF	XF	Unc
74.1	1968	6.025	—	.10	.25
	1968	.025	—	Proof	1.00

Afrikaans legend

KM#	Date	Mintage	VF	XF	Unc
74.2	1968	6.000	—	.10	.25
	1968	.010	—	Proof	1.00

Bilingual

KM#	Date	Mintage	VF	XF	Unc
82	1970	37.082	—	—	.25
	1970	.010	—	Proof	1.00
	1971	34.065	—	—	.25
	1971	.012	—	Proof	1.00
	1972	35.672	—	—	.25
	1972	.010	—	Proof	1.00
	1973	1.770	.10	.20	.35
	1973	.011	—	Proof	1.00
	1974	54.954	—	—	.25
	1974	.015	—	Proof	1.00
	1975	63.752	—	—	.25
	1975	.018	—	Proof	1.00
	1977	72.444	—	—	.25
	1977	.019	—	Proof	1.00
	1978	70.152	—	—	.10
	1978	.017	—	Proof	.50

KM#	Date	Mintage	VF	XF	Unc
82	1980	63.432	—	—	.10
	1980	.015	—	Proof	.50
	1981	63.464	—	—	.10
	1981	.010	—	Proof	.50
	1983	182.131	—	—	.10
	1983	.014	—	Proof	.50
	1984	107.155	—	—	.10
	1984	.011	—	Proof	.50
	1985	186.042	—	—	.10
	1985	—	—	Proof	.50
	1986	—	—	—	.10
	1986	—	—	Proof	.50
	1987	—	—	—	.10
	1987	—	—	Proof	.50

President Fouche

KM#	Date	Mintage	VF	XF	Unc
91	1976	91.860	—	—	.10
	1976	.021	—	Proof	.50

President Diederichs

KM#	Date	Mintage	VF	XF	Unc
98	1979	63.432	—	—	.10
	1979	.015	—	Proof	.50

President Vorster

KM#	Date	Mintage	VF	XF	Unc
109	1982	145.976	—	—	.10
	1982	.012	—	Proof	.50

2 CENTS

BRONZE
English legend

KM#	Date	Mintage	VF	XF	Unc
66.1	1965	29.887	—	.10	.15
	1966	9.292	—	.10	.15
	1966	.025	—	Proof	.50
	1967	11.887	—	.10	.15
	1967	.025	—	Proof	.50
	1969	5.829	—	.10	.20
	1969	.012	—	Proof	.50

Afrikaans legend

KM#	Date	Mintage	VF	XF	Unc
66.2	1965	29.912	—	.10	.15
	1965	.025	—	Proof	.50
	1966	9.267	—	.10	.15
	1967	11.862	—	.10	.15
	1969	5.817	—	.10	.20

Charles Swart
English legend

KM#	Date	Mintage	VF	XF	Unc
75.1	1968	5.500	—	.10	.20
	1968	.010	—	Proof	.50

Afrikaans legend

KM#	Date	Mintage	VF	XF	Unc
75.2	1968	5.525	—	.10	.20
	1968	.025	—	Proof	.50

Bilingual

KM#	Date	Mintage	VF	XF	Unc
83	1970	35.227	—	—	.10
	1970	.010	—	Proof	.50
	1971	24.105	—	—	.10
	1971	.012	—	Proof	.50
	1972	7.314	—	—	.15
	1972	.010	—	Proof	.50
	1973	18.696	—	—	.10
	1973	.011	—	Proof	.50
	1974	25.315	—	—	.10
	1974	.015	—	Proof	.50
	1975	25.000	—	—	.10
	1975	.018	—	Proof	.50
	1977	45.116	—	—	.10
	1977	.019	—	Proof	.50
	1978	50.527	—	—	.10
	1978	.017	—	Proof	.50
	1980	37.795	—	—	.10
	1980	.015	—	Proof	.50
	1981	79.370	—	—	.10
	1981	.010	—	Proof	.50
	1983	112.575	—	—	.10
	1983	.014	—	Proof	.50
	1984	101.497	—	—	.10
	1984	.011	—	Proof	.50
	1985	102.708	—	—	.10
	1985	.011	—	Proof	.50
	1986	—	—	—	.10
	1986	—	—	Proof	.50
	1987	—	—	—	.10
	1987	—	—	Proof	.50

President Fouche

KM#	Date	Mintage	VF	XF	Unc
92	1976	51.474	—	—	.10
	1976	.021	—	Proof	.50

President Diederichs

KM#	Date	Mintage	VF	XF	Unc
99	1979	40.043	—	—	.10
	1979	.015	—	Proof	.50

President Vorster

KM#	Date	Mintage	VF	XF	Unc
110	1982	53.984	—	—	.10
	1982	.012	—	Proof	.50

2-1/2 CENTS

1.4100 g, .500 SILVER, .0226 oz ASW

KM#	Date	Mintage	VF	XF	Unc
58	1961	.299	.50	1.00	2.00
	1961	7,530	—	Proof	2.50

KM#	Date	Mintage	VF	XF	Unc
58	1962	.013	2.00	4.00	8.00
	1962	3,844	—	Proof	4.00
	1963	.037	1.50	2.50	4.00
	1963	4,025	—	Proof	4.00
	1964	.030	1.50	2.50	4.00
	1964	.016	—	Proof	1.00

5 CENTS

2.8300 g, .500 SILVER, .0454 oz ASW

KM#	Date	Mintage	VF	XF	Unc
59	1961	1.486	.50	.75	2.50
	1961	7,530	—	Proof	2.50
	1962	4.192	.50	.75	2.00
	1962	3,844	—	Proof	3.00
	1963	8.058	.50	.75	1.50
	1963	4,025	—	Proof	3.00
	1964	3.583	.50	.75	1.50
	1964	.016	—	Proof	1.50

NICKEL
English legend

KM#	Date	Mintage	VF	XF	Unc
67.1	1965	32.715	—	.10	.20
	1965	.025	—	Proof	.50
	1966	4.101	—	.10	.30
	1967	4.590	—	.10	.30
	1969	5.020	—	.10	.30

Afrikaans legend

67.2	1965	32.690	—	.10	.20
	1966	4.126	—	.10	.30
	1966	.025	—	Proof	.50
	1967	4.615	—	.10	.30
	1967	.025	—	Proof	.50
	1969	5.020	—	.10	.30
	1969	.012	—	Proof	.50

Charles Swart
English legend

76.1	1968	6.025	—	.10	.30
	1968	.025	—	Proof	.50

Afrikaans legend

76.2	1968	6.000	—	.10	.30
	1968	.010	—	Proof	.50

Bilingual

84	1970	6.662	—	.10	.20
	1970	.010	—	Proof	.50
	1971	20.341	—	.10	.20
	1971	.012	—	Proof	.50
	1972	3.126	—	.10	.25
	1972	.010	—	Proof	.50
	1973	17.103	—	.10	.20
	1973	.011	—	Proof	.50
	1974	19.993	—	.10	.20
	1974	.015	—	Proof	.50
	1975	22.000	—	.10	.15
	1975	.018	—	Proof	.50
	1977	56.139	—	.10	.15
	1977	.019	—	Proof	.50
	1978	25.642	—	.10	.15
	1978	.017	—	Proof	.50
	1980	46.665	—	.10	.15
	1980	.015	—	Proof	.50

KM#	Date	Mintage	VF	XF	Unc
84	1981	40.371	—	.10	.15
	1981	.010	—	Proof	.50
	1983	57.487	—	.10	.15
	1983	.014	—	Proof	.50
	1984	67.345	—	.10	.15
	1984	.011	—	Proof	.50
	1985	57.167	—	.10	.15
	1985	—	—	Proof	.50
	1986	—	—	.10	.15
	1986	—	—	Proof	.50
	1987	—	—	.10	.15
	1987	—	—	Proof	.50

President Fouche

93	1976	48.991	—	.10	.15
	1976	.021	—	Proof	.50

President Diederichs

100	1979	17.534	—	.10	.15
	1979	.015	—	Proof	.50

President Vorster

111	1982	47.258	—	.10	.15
	1982	.012	—	Proof	.50

10 CENTS

5.6600 g, .500 SILVER, .0909 oz ASW

60	1961	1.143	.75	1.25	2.50
	1961	7,530	—	Proof	2.50
	1962	2.451	.75	1.25	2.50
	1962	3,844	—	Proof	3.50
	1963	3.331	.75	1.25	2.50
	1963	4,025	—	Proof	3.50
	1964	4.169	.75	1.00	1.50
	1964	.016	—	Proof	1.50

NICKEL
English legend

68.1	1965	29.210	—	.10	.20
	1966	3.710	—	.10	.30
	1966	.025	—	Proof	.50
	1967	.075	—	—	1.00
	1967	.025	—	Proof	.50
	1969	.558	—	.10	.40
	1969	.012	—	Proof	.50

Afrikaans legend

68.2	1965	29.235	—	.10	.20
	1965	.025	—	Proof	.50
	1966	3.685	—	.10	.30
	1967	.050	—	—	1.00
	1969	.558	—	.10	.40

SOUTH AFRICA 1515

Charles Swart
English legend

KM#	Date	Mintage	VF	XF	Unc
77.1	1968	.050	—	—	2.00
	1968	.010	—	Proof	.50

Afrikaans legend

77.2	1968	.075	—	—	1.50
	1968	.025	—	Proof	.50

Bilingual

85	1970	7.608	—	.10	.20
	1970	.010	—	Proof	.50
	1971	6.452	—	.10	.20
	1971	.012	—	Proof	.50
	1972	10.038	—	.10	.20
	1972	.010	—	Proof	.50
	1973	1.770	—	.10	.20
	1973	.011	—	Proof	.50
	1974	9.912	—	.10	.20
	1974	.015	—	Proof	.50
	1975	13.006	—	.10	.20
	1975	.018	—	Proof	.50
	1977	28.851	—	.10	.20
	1977	.019	—	Proof	.50
	1978	25.009	—	.10	.20
	1978	.017	—	Proof	.50
	1980	5.040	—	.10	.20
	1980	.015	—	Proof	.50
	1981	9.624	—	.10	.20
	1981	.010	—	Proof	.50
	1983	26.495	—	.10	.20
	1983	.014	—	Proof	.50
	1984	35.465	—	.10	.20
	1984	.011	—	Proof	.50
	1985	29.270	—	.10	.20
	1985	—	—	Proof	.50
	1986	—	—	.10	.20
	1986	—	—	Proof	.50
	1987	—	—	.10	.20
	1987	—	—	Proof	.50

President Fouche

94	1976	30.986	—	.10	.20
	1976	.021	—	Proof	.50

President Diederichs

101	1979	5.044	—	.10	.25
	1979	.015	—	Proof	.50

President Vorster

112	1982	15.828	—	.10	.20
	1982	.012	—	Proof	.50

SOUTH AFRICA 1516

20 CENTS

11.3100 g, .500 SILVER, .1818 oz ASW

KM#	Date	Mintage	VF	XF	Unc
61	1961	2.962	1.00	1.50	3.00
	1961	7.530	—	Proof	3.50
	1962 sm.2	3.572	1.00	1.50	3.00
	1962 lg.2	I.A.	—	—	—
	1962	3.844	—	Proof	4.00
	1963	4.384	1.00	1.50	3.00
	1963	4.025	—	Proof	4.00
	1964	4.351	1.00	1.50	3.00
	1964	.016	—	Proof	2.50

NICKEL
English legend

KM#	Date	Mintage	VF	XF	Unc
69.1	1965	29.235	.15	.20	.30
	1965	.025	—	Proof	.50
	1966	4.049	.15	.20	.40
	1967	.058	—	—	1.00
	1969	9.952	—	—	7.50

Afrikaans legend

69.2	1965	29.210	.15	.20	.30
	1966	4.074	.15	.20	.40
	1966	.025	—	Proof	.50
	1967	.083	—	—	1.00
	1967	.025	—	Proof	.50
	1969	.021	—	—	5.00
	1969	.012	—	Proof	1.00

Charles Swart
English legend

78.1	1968	.075	—	—	2.00
	1968	.025	—	Proof	.50

Afrikaans legend

78.2	1968	.050	—	—	2.50
	1968	.010	—	Proof	.50

Bilingual

86	1970	.024	—	—	10.00
	1970	.010	—	Proof	1.50
	1971	5.905	.15	.20	.30

KM#	Date	Mintage	VF	XF	Unc
86	1971	.012	—	Proof	1.50
	1972	9.079	.15	.20	.30
	1972	.010	—	Proof	1.50
	1973	.031	—	—	5.00
	1973	.011	—	Proof	1.50
	1974	2.451	.15	.30	.50
	1974	.015	—	Proof	1.50
	1975	13.000	—	.15	.25
	1975	.018	—	Proof	1.00
	1977	30.650	—	.15	.25
	1977	.019	—	Proof	.50
	1978	10.051	—	.15	.25
	1978	.017	—	Proof	.50
	1980	13.335	—	.15	.25
	1980	.015	—	Proof	.50
	1981	8.554	—	.15	.25
	1981	.010	—	Proof	.50
	1983	25.668	—	.15	.25
	1983	.014	—	Proof	.50
	1984	31.607	—	.15	.25
	1984	.011	—	Proof	.50
	1985	29.329	—	.15	.25
	1985	—	—	Proof	.50
	1986	—	—	.15	.25
	1986	—	—	Proof	.50
	1987	—	—	.15	.25
	1987	—	—	Proof	.50

President Fouche

95	1976	18.826	—	.15	.25
	1976	.021	—	Proof	1.00

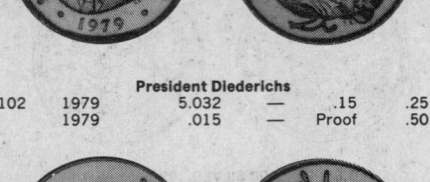

President Diederichs

102	1979	5.032	—	.15	.25
	1979	.015	—	Proof	.50

President Vorster

113	1982	18.105	—	.15	.25
	1982	.012	—	Proof	.50

50 CENTS

28.2800 g, .500 SILVER, .4546 oz ASW

62	1961	.055	BV	12.50	15.00
	1961	.020	—	Proof	20.00
	1962	.024	BV	15.00	20.00
	1962	6.024	—	Proof	25.00
	1963*	.158	BV	7.50	12.50
	1963	.010	—	Proof	15.00
	1964	.127	BV	7.50	12.50
	1964	.025	—	Proof	15.00

NOTE: Varieties exist w/narrow, high relief and wide, low letters.

NICKEL
English legend

KM#	Date	Mintage	VF	XF	Unc
70.1	1965	30 to 50 pcs.	—	Proof	4000.
	1966	8.081	—	.50	2.50
	1966	.025	—	Proof	3.50
	1967	.077	In sets only		1.50
	1967	.025	—	Proof	3.50
	1969	7.968	In sets only		10.00
	1969	.012	—	Proof	4.50

Afrikaans legend

70.2	1965	.028	—	—	3.50
	1965	.025	—	Proof	5.00
	1966	8.056	—	.50	2.50
	1967	.052	In sets only		2.00
	1969	7.968	In sets only		12.50

Charles Swart
English legend

79.1	1968	.750	—	.50	1.00

Afrikaans legend

79.2	1968	.775	—	.50	1.00
	1968	.025	—	Proof	3.50

Bilingual

87	1970	4.108	—	.50	1.00
	1970	.010	—	Proof	2.00
	1971	5.074	—	.50	1.00
	1971	.012	—	Proof	2.00
	1972	.781	—	.50	1.00
	1972	.010	—	Proof	2.00
	1973	1.054	—	.50	1.00
	1973	.011	—	Proof	2.00
	1974	1.957	—	.50	1.00
	1974	.015	—	Proof	2.00
	1975	4.906	—	.50	1.00
	1975	.018	—	Proof	1.50
	1977	10.196	—	.50	1.00
	1977	.019	—	Proof	1.50
	1978	5.071	—	.50	1.00
	1978	.017	—	Proof	1.50
	1980	4.268	—	.50	1.00
	1980	.015	—	Proof	1.50
	1981	5.701	—	.50	1.00
	1981	.010	—	Proof	1.50
	1983	5.150	—	.40	.75
	1983	.014	—	Proof	1.50
	1984	9.687	—	.40	.75
	1984	.011	—	Proof	1.50

SOUTH AFRICA 1517

KM#	Date	Mintage	VF	XF	Unc
87	1985	13.339	—	.40	.75
	1985	—	—	Proof	1.50
	1986	—	—	.40	.75
	1986	—	—	Proof	1.50
	1987	—	—	.40	.75
	1987	—	—	Proof	1.50

NOTE: Varieties exist.

President Fouche

96	1976	9.653	.30	.50	1.00
	1976	.021	—	Proof	2.50

President Diederichs

103	1979	5.051	.30	.50	1.00
	1979	.015	—	Proof	2.50

President Vorster

114	1982	2.092	.30	.50	1.00
	1982	.012	—	Proof	2.50

RAND

3.9940 g, .917 GOLD, .1177 oz AGW

KM#	Date	Mintage	VF	XF	Unc
63	1961	8,178	—	—	BV + 15%
	1961	3,932	—	—	BV + 20%
	1962	6,299	—	—	BV + 15%
	1962	2,344	—	—	BV + 20%
	1963	6,531	—	—	BV + 15%
	1963	2,508	—	—	BV + 20%
	1964	9,866	—	—	BV + 15%
	1964	4,000	—	—	BV + 20%
	1965	.016	—	—	BV + 15%
	1965	6,024	—	—	BV + 15%
	1966	.021	—	—	BV + 15%
	1966	.011	—	—	BV + 20%
	1967	.021	—	—	BV + 15%
	1967	.011	—	—	BV + 20%
	1968	9,375	—	—	BV + 15%
	1968	.011	—	—	BV + 20%
	1969	.110	—	—	BV + 15%
	1969	8,000	—	—	BV + 20%
	1970	.017	—	—	BV + 15%
	1970	6,000	—	—	BV + 20%
	1971	.018	—	—	BV + 15%
	1971	7,650	—	—	BV + 20%
	1972	.022	—	—	BV + 15%
	1972	7,500	—	—	BV + 20%
	1973	.022	—	—	BV + 15%
	1973	.013	—	—	BV + 20%
	1974	.022	—	—	BV + 15%
	1974	.017	—	—	BV + 20%
	1975	.022	—	—	BV + 15%
	1975	.020	—	—	BV + 20%
	1976	.027	—	—	BV + 15%
	1976	.022	—	—	BV + 20%
	1977	.027	—	—	BV + 15%
	1977	.020	—	—	BV + 20%
	1978	.032	—	—	BV + 15%
	1978	.019	—	—	BV + 20%
	1979	.034	—	—	BV + 15%
	1979	.020	—	—	BV + 20%
	1980	.190	—	—	BV + 15%
	1980	.018	—	—	BV + 20%
	1981	7,036	—	—	BV + 15%
	1981	.012	—	—	BV + 20%

KM#	Date	Mintage	VF	XF	Unc
63	1982	.014	—	—	BV + 20%
	1983	.015	—	—	BV + 20%

15.0000 g, .800 SILVER, .3858 oz ASW
English legend

71.1	1965	.027	—	BV	6.00
	1965	.025	—	Proof	5.00
	1966	1.434	—	BV	5.00
	1966	20 pcs.	—	Proof	1250.
	1968	.075	—	In sets only	7.50
	1968	.025	—	Proof	5.00

Afrikaans legend

71.2	1965	85 to 120 pcs.	—	V.I.P. Proof	1000.
	1966	1.459	—	BV	4.00
	1966	.025	—	Proof	5.00
	1968	.050	—	In sets only	7.50
	1968	20 pcs.	—	Proof	1250.

Verwoerd
English legend

72.1	1967	1.544	—	BV	4.00
	1967	20 pcs.	—	Proof	1250.

Afrikaans legend

72.2	1967	1.569	—	BV	4.00
	1967	.025	—	Proof	5.00

Dr. T. E. Donges
English legend

80.1	1969	.506	—	BV	4.00
	1969	20 pcs.	—	Proof	1250.

NOTE: The South African mint does not acknowledge the existence of the 1 Rand pieces above with mintages of 20 pieces each.

Afrikaans legend

KM#	Date	Mintage	VF	XF	Unc
80.2	1969	.517	—	BV	4.00
	1969	.012	—	Proof	6.00

Bilingual

88	1970	.024	—	BV	5.00
	1970	.010	—	Proof	8.00
	1971	.032	—	BV	5.00
	1971	.012	—	Proof	8.00
	1972	.030	—	BV	5.00
	1972	.010	—	Proof	8.00
	1973	.031	—	BV	5.00
	1973	.011	—	Proof	8.00
	1975	.038	—	BV	5.00
	1975	.018	—	Proof	8.00
	1976	.041	—	BV	5.00
	1976	.021	—	Proof	8.00
	1977	.019	—	Proof	8.00
	1978	.017	—	Proof	8.00
	1979	—	—	Proof	8.00
	1980	.015	—	Proof	8.00
	1981	.010	—	Proof	8.00
	1982	—	—	Proof	8.00
	1983	.014	—	Proof	8.00
	1984	.011	—	Proof	8.00
	1987	—	—	Proof	8.00

NICKEL

88a	1977	29.871	—	.75	2.00
	1978	12.021	—	.75	2.00
	1980	2.690	—	.75	2.00
	1981	2.055	—	.75	2.00
	1983	7.181	—	.75	2.00
	1984	5.747	—	.75	2.00
	1984	—	—	Proof	3.00
	1986	—	—	.75	2.00
	1986	—	—	Proof	2.00
	1987	—	—	.75	2.00
	1987	—	—	Proof	2.00
	1988	—	—	.75	2.00

.800 SILVER

89	1974	.035	—	—	12.50
	1974	.015	—	Proof	8.00

SOUTH AFRICA 1518

NICKEL
President Diederichs

KM#	Date	Mintage	VF	XF	Unc
104	1979	10.006	—	.75	2.00

14.9700 g, .800 SILVER, .3858 oz ASW

| 104a | 1979 | .015 | — | Proof | 8.00 |

NICKEL
President Vorster

| 115 | 1982 | 7.695 | — | .75 | 2.00 |

14.9700 g, .800 SILVER, .3858 oz ASW

| 115a | 1982 | .012 | — | Proof | 8.00 |

75th Anniversary of Parliament

| 116 | 1985 | .032 | — | — | 10.00 |
| | 1985 | .024 | — | Proof | 15.00 |

NICKEL
President Marais Viljoen

| 117 | 1985 | 3.983 | — | — | 1.00 |
| | 1985 | — | — | Proof | 5.00 |

14.9700 g, .800 SILVER, .3858 oz ASW
100th Anniversary of Johannesburg

119	1986	—	—	—	10.00
	1986	—	—	P/L	15.00
	1986	—	—	Proof	15.00

Year of the Disabled

KM#	Date	Mintage	VF	XF	Unc
120	1986	5,000	—	Proof	60.00

Bartolomeu Dias

| 122 | 1988 | — | — | — | 12.00 |
| | 1988 | — | — | Proof | 22.50 |

Huguenots

| 125 | 1988 | — | — | — | 12.00 |
| | 1988 | — | — | Proof | 22.50 |

The Great Trek

| 128 | 1988 | — | — | — | 12.00 |
| | 1988 | — | — | Proof | 22.50 |

2 RAND

7.9881 g, .917 GOLD, .2354 oz AGW

64	1961	6,946	—	—	BV + 10%
	1961	3,932	—	—	BV + 15%
	1962	.012	—	—	BV + 10%
	1962	2,344	—	—	BV + 15%
	1963	5,687	—	—	BV + 10%
	1963	2,508	—	—	BV + 15%
	1964	7,994	—	—	BV + 10%
	1964	4,000	—	—	BV + 15%
	1965	.016	—	—	BV + 10%
	1965	6,024	—	—	BV + 15%
	1966	.021	—	—	BV + 10%
	1966	.011	—	—	BV + 15%
	1967	.021	—	—	BV + 10%
	1967	.011	—	—	BV + 15%
	1968	.021	—	—	BV + 10%
	1968	.011	—	—	BV + 15%
	1969	.011	—	—	BV + 10%
	1969	8,000	—	—	BV + 15%
	1970	.017	—	—	BV + 10%
	1970	7,000	—	—	BV + 15%
	1971	.018	—	—	BV + 10%
	1971	7,650	—	—	BV + 15%
	1972	.025	—	—	BV + 10%
	1972	7,500	—	—	BV + 15%
	1973	.027	—	—	BV + 10%
	1973	.013	—	—	BV + 15%
	1974	.029	—	—	BV + 10%
	1974	.017	—	—	BV + 15%
	1975	.030	—	—	BV + 10%
	1975	.018	—	—	BV + 15%
	1976	.033	—	—	BV + 10%
	1976	.021	—	—	BV + 15%
	1977	.032	—	—	BV + 10%
	1977	.020	—	—	BV + 15%
	1978	.030	—	—	BV + 10%
	1978	.019	—	—	BV + 15%
	1979	.032	—	—	BV + 10%
	1979	.020	—	—	BV + 15%
	1980	.105	—	—	BV + 10%
	1980	.018	—	—	BV + 15%

KM#	Date	Mintage	VF	XF	Unc
64	1981	6,300	—	—	BV + 10%
	1981	.013	—	—	BV + 15%
	1982	.014	—	—	BV + 15%
	1983	.015	—	—	BV + 15%

BULLION ISSUES
1/10 KRUGERRAND

3.3900 g, .917 GOLD, .1000 oz AGW

105	1980	.857	—	—	BV + 15%
	1980	60 pcs.	—	Proof	2500.
	1981	1.310	—	—	BV + 15%
	1981	7,500	—	Proof	90.00
	1982	1.054	—	—	BV + 15%
	1982	.011	—	Proof	90.00
	1983	.141	—	—	BV + 15%
	1983	.015	—	Proof	90.00
	1984	.898	—	—	BV + 15%
	1984	.013	—	Proof	90.00
	1985	.276	—	—	BV + 15%
	1985	6,700	—	Proof	90.00
	1987 GRC	7,000	—	Proof	90.00

1/4 KRUGERRAND

8.4800 g, .917 GOLD, .2500 oz AGW

106	1980	.534	—	—	BV + 10%
	1980	60 pcs.	—	Proof	3000.
	1981	.719	—	—	BV + 10%
	1981	7,500	—	Proof	175.00
	1982	1.258	—	—	BV + 10%
	1982	.011	—	Proof	175.00
	1983	.062	—	—	BV + 10%
	1983	.015	—	Proof	175.00
	1984	.503	—	—	BV + 10%
	1984	.013	—	Proof	175.00
	1985	.587	—	—	BV + 10%
	1985	6,700	—	Proof	175.00
	1987 GRC	7,000	—	Proof	175.00

1/2 KRUGERRAND

16.9700 g, .917 GOLD, .5000 oz AGW

107	1980	.374	—	—	BV + 8%
	1980	60 pcs.	—	Proof	3500.
	1981	.169	—	—	BV + 8%
	1981	9,000	—	Proof	300.00
	1982	.416	—	—	BV + 8%
	1982	.013	—	Proof	300.00
	1983	.061	—	—	BV + 8%
	1983	.015	—	Proof	300.00
	1984	.184	—	—	BV + 8%
	1984	9,900	—	Proof	300.00
	1985	.098	—	—	BV + 8%
	1985	5,945	—	Proof	300.00
	1987 GRC	7,000	—	Proof	300.00

KRUGERRAND

33.9305 g, .917 GOLD, 1.0000 oz AGW

73	1967	.040	—	—	BV + 5%
	1967	.010	—	Proof	BV + 20%
	1968	.020	—	—	BV + 5%
	1968 frosted bust and frosted reverse				
		*5,000	—	Proof	1000.
	1968	9,000	—	Proof	BV + 25%
	1969	.020	—	—	BV + 5%
	1969	—	—	Proof	BV + 20%

*NOTE: In 1967-1969 superior quality specimens exhibiting proof-like surfaces are known. In addition, the following varieties are known: 1968 with normal mirror like obverse and reverse; 1968 with mirror like obverse and frosted reverse; 1969 with normal mirror like obverse and reverse; and 1969 with frosted bust and reverse frosted.

	1970	.211	—	—	BV + 5%
	1970	.010	—	—	BV + 5%
	1971	.550	—	—	BV + 5%
	1971	6,000	—	Proof	BV + 15%
	1972	.544	—	—	BV + 5%

KM#	Date	Mintage	VF	XF	Unc
73	1972	6,625	—	Proof	BV + 15%
	1973	.859	—		BV + 5%
	1973	.010	—	Proof	BV + 15%
	1974	3.203	—		BV + 5%
	1974	6,352	—	Proof	BV + 15%
	1975	4.804	—		BV + 5%
	1975	5,600	—	Proof	BV + 15%
	1976	2.893	—		BV + 5%
	1976	6,600	—	Proof	BV + 15%
	1977 188 serrations on edge				
		3.331	—		BV + 5%
	1977 188 serrations on edge				
		8,500	—	Proof	BV + 15%
	1977 220 serrations on edge				
		—	—		BV + 5%
	1977 220 serrations on edge				
		Inc. Ab.	—	Proof	BV + 15%
	1978	6.013	—		BV + 5%
	1978	.010	—	Proof	BV + 15%
	1979	4.941	—		BV + 5%
	1979	.012	—	Proof	BV + 15%
	1980	3.049	—		BV + 5%
	1980	.012	—	Proof	BV + 15%
	1981	3.186	—		BV + 5%
	1981	.013	—	Proof	BV + 15%
	1982	2.659	—		BV + 5%
	1982	.017	—	Proof	BV + 15%
	1983	3.369	—		BV + 5%
	1983	.019	—	Proof	BV + 15%
	1984	2.050	—		BV + 5%
	1985	.010	—	Proof	BV + 15%
	1985	.865	—		BV + 5%
	1985	.010	—	Proof	BV + 15%
	1987 GRC	.010	—	Proof	BV + 15%

OUNCE

75th Anniversary of Parliament
33.9305 g, .917 GOLD, 1.0000 oz AGW

| 118 | 1985 | 3,019 | — | Proof | 850.00 |

1/10 PROTEA

3.3900 g, .917 GOLD, .1000 oz AGW

| 131 | 1986 | *5,212 | — | Proof | 125.00 |

Bartolomew Dias
| 123 | 1988 | *7,500 | — | Proof | 100.00 |

Huguenots
| 126 | 1988 | *7,500 | — | Proof | 100.00 |

The Great Trek
| 129 | 1988 | *7,500 | — | Proof | 100.00 |

PROTEA

33.9300 g, .917 GOLD, 1.0000 oz AGW

| 121 | 1986 | *5,000 | — | Proof | 850.00 |

Bartolomeu Dias
| 124 | 1988 | *7,500 | — | Proof | 800.00 |

Huguenots
KM#	Date	Mintage	VF	XF	Unc
127	1988	*7,500	—	Proof	800.00

The Great Trek
| 130 | 1988 | *7,500 | — | — | Proof 800.00 |

SPECIAL SELECTS (S/S)

"Special selects" are of proof-like quality.

KM#	Date	Mintage	Identification	Issue Price	Mkt. Val.
SS1	1948	10,000	5 Shillings, KGVI	—	20.00
SS2	1949	2,000	5 Shillings, KGVI	—	40.00
SS3	1950	1,200	5 Shillings, KGVI	—	70.00
SS4	1951	1,483	5 Shillings, KGVI	—	40.00
SS5	1952	12,000	5 Shillings, Capetown	—	12.50
SS6	1953	8,000	5 Shillings, QEII	—	15.00
SS7	1954	3,890	5 Shillings, QEII	—	40.00
SS8	1955	2,230	5 Shillings, QEII	—	22.50
SS9	1956	2,200	5 Shillings, QEII	—	22.50
SS10	1957	1,600	5 Shillings, QEII	—	30.00
SS11	1958	1,500	5 Shillings, QEII	—	30.00
SS12	1959	2,200	5 Shillings, QEII	—	225.00
SS13	1960	22,367	5 Shillings, 50th Anniversary	—	10.00
SS14	1961	19,956	50 Cents, van Riebeeck	—	9.00
SS15	1962	6,024	50 Cents, van Riebeeck	—	12.00
SS16	1963	10,227	50 Cents, van Riebeeck	—	9.00
SS17	1964	25,000	50 Cents, van Riebeeck	—	8.00

MINT SETS (MS)

KM#	Date	Mintage	Identification	Issue Price	Mkt. Val.
MS1	1967(7)	50,000	KM65.1-70.1,72.1	7.50	7.00
MS2	1967(7)	50,000	KM65.2-70.2,72.2	7.50	7.00
MS3	1968(7)	50,000	KM71.1,74.1-79.1	7.50	10.00
MS4	1968(7)	50,000	KM71.2,74.2-79.2	7.50	10.00
MS5	1969(7)	5,000	KM65.1-70.1,80.1	7.50	22.50
MS6	1969(7)	5,000	KM65.2-70.2,80.2	7.50	22.50
MS7	1970(8)	14,000	KM81-88	7.50	11.00
MS8	1971(8)	20,000	KM81-88	7.50	10.00
MS9	1972(8)	20,000	KM81-88	7.50	10.00
MS10	1973(8)	20,000	KM81-88	7.50	10.00
MS11	1974(8)	20,000	KM81-87,89	7.50	17.50
MS12	1975(8)	20,000	KM81-88	7.50	10.00
MS13	1976(8)	20,000	KM88,90-96	5.65	10.00
MS14	1977(8)	20,000	KM81-87,88a	—	5.00
MS15	1978(8)	20,000	KM81-87,88a	—	5.00
MS16	1979(8)	20,000	KM97-103,104	—	5.00
MS17	1980(7)	20,000	KM82-87,88a	—	5.00
MS18	1981(7)	10,000	KM82-87,88a	—	5.00
MS19	1982(7)	10,000	KM82-87,115	—	5.00
MS20	1983(7)	13,000	KM82-87,88a	—	5.00
MS21	1984(7)	13,875	KM82-87,88a	—	5.00
MS22	1985(7)	10,200	KM82-87,117	—	6.00
MS23	1986(7)	—	KM82-87,88a	—	5.00
MS24	1987(7)	—	KM82-87,88a	—	5.00

PROOF SETS (PS)

KM#	Date	Mintage	Identification	Issue Price	Mkt. Val.
PS1	1923(10)	655	KM12.1-17.1,18,19.1,20-21	—	1250.
PS2	1923(8)	747	KM12.1-17.1,18,19.1	—	500.00
PS3	1926(6)	3 known	KM12.2,14.2-17.2,19.2	—	20,000.
PS4	1930(8)	14	KM12.2-17.2,18,19.2	—	12,000.
PS5	1930(8)	Inc. Ab.	KM12.2 (dated 1928), 13.2-17.2, 18,19.2	—	20,000.
PS6	1931(8)	62	KM12.3-17.3,19.3,22	—	15,000.
PS7	1932(8)	12	KM12.3-17.3,19.3,22	—	15,000.
PS8	1933(8)	20	KM12.3-17.3,19.3,22	—	7000.
PS9	1934(8)	24	KM12.3-17.3,19.3,22	—	7000.
PS10	1935(8)	20	KM12.3-17.3,19.3,22	—	7000.
PS11	1936(8)	40	KM12.3-17.3,19.3,22	—	7000.
PS12	1937(8)	116	KM23-30	—	800.00
PS13	1938(8)	44	KM23-30	—	1500.
PS14	1939(8)	30	KM23-30	—	15,000.
PS15	1943(8)	104	KM23-30	—	800.00
PS16	1944(8)	150	KM23-30	—	600.00
PS17	1945(8)	150	KM23-30	—	600.00
PS18	1946(8)	150	KM23-30	—	700.00
PS19	1947(8)	2,600	KM23-30	—	200.00
PS20	1948(9)	1,120	KM32.1,33,34.1-40.1	—	300.00
PS21	1949(9)	800	KM32.1,33,34.1-40.1	—	450.00
PS22	1950(9)	500	KM32.1,33,34.1-40.1	—	475.00
PS23	1951(9)	800	KM32.2,33,34.2-40.2	—	55.00
PS24	1952(11)	12,000	KM32.2,33,34.2-39.2,41-43	—	225.00
PS25	1952(9)	3,500	KM32.2,33,34.2-39.2,41	—	35.00
PS26	1953(11)	3,000	KM44-54	29.40	240.00
PS27	1953(9)	2,000	KM44-52	4.35	40.00
PS28	1953(2)	1,000	KM53-54	25.20	210.00
PS29	1954(11)	875	KM44-54	29.40	300.00
PS30	1954(9)	2,275	KM44-52	4.35	75.00
PS31	1954(2)	350	KM53-54	25.20	235.00
PS32	1955(11)	600	KM44-54	29.40	310.00
PS33	1955(9)	2,250	KM44-52	4.35	50.00
PS34	1955(2)	300	KM53-54	25.20	260.00
PS35	1956(11)	350	KM44-54	29.40	520.00
PS36	1956(9)	1,350	KM44-52	4.35	70.00
PS37	1956(2)	158	KM53-54	25.20	450.00
PS38	1957(11)	380	KM44-54	29.40	505.00
PS39	1957(9)	750	KM44-52	4.35	80.00
PS40	1957(2)	180	KM53-54	25.20	425.00
PS41	1958(11)	360	KM44-54	29.40	545.00
PS42	1958(9)	625	KM44-52	4.35	95.00
PS43	1958(2)	155	KM53-54	25.20	450.00
PS44	1959(11)	390	KM44-54	29.40	725.00
PS45	1959(9)	560	KM44-52	4.35	350.00
PS46	1959(2)	240	KM53-54	25.20	375.00
PS47	1960(11)	1,500	KM44-51,53-55	29.40	230.00
PS48	1960(9)	1,860	KM44-51,55	4.35	30.00
PS49	1960(2)	450	KM53-54	25.20	210.00
PS50	1961(9)	3,139	KM56-64	—	200.00
PS51	1961(7)	4,391	KM56-62	—	20.00
PS52	1961(2)	793	KM63-64	BV + 20%	
PS53	1962(9)	1,544	KM56-64	—	210.00
PS54	1962(7)	2,300	KM56-62	—	30.00
PS55	1962(2)	800	KM63-64	BV + 20%	
PS56	1963(9)	1,500	KM56-64	—	200.00
PS57	1963(7)	2,525	KM56-62	—	20.00
PS58	1963(2)	1,008	KM63-64	BV + 20%	
PS59	1964(9)	2,000	KM56-64	—	190.00
PS60	1964(7)	16,948	KM56-62	—	12.50
PS61	1964(2)	1,000	KM63-64	BV + 20%	
PS62	1965(9)	5,099	KM63-64,65.1,66.2,67.1,68.2, 69.1,70.2,71.1	23.50	185.00
PS63	1965(9)	85	KM63-64,65.1-66.2,67.1,68.2, 69.1,70.2,71.2 V.I.P.	—	925.00
PS64	1965(7)	19,889	KM65.1,66.2,67.1,68.2,69.1, 70.2,71.1	5.00	12.50
PS65	1965(2)	925	KM63-64	18.15	BV + 20%
PS66	1966(9)	10,000	KM63-64,65.2,66.1,67.2,68.1, 69.2,70.1,71.2	24.10	185.00
PS67	1966(7)	15,000	KM65.2,66.1,67.2,68.1,69.2, 70.1,71.2	5.00	8.00
PS68	1966(2)	1,000	KM63-64	18.15	BV + 20%
PS69	1967(9)	10,000	KM63-64,65.2,66.1,67.2,68.1, 69.2,70.1,72.2	24.10	185.00
PS70	1967(7)	15,000	KM65.2,66.1,67.2,68.1,69.2, 70.1,72.2	5.00	8.00
PS71	1967(2)	1,000	KM63-64	18.15	BV + 20%
PS72	1968(9)	10,000	KM63-64,71.1,74.2,75.1,76.2, 77.1,78.2,79.1	35.00	185.00
PS73	1968(7)	15,000	KM71.1,74.1,75.2,76.1,77.2, 78.1,79.2	16.00	8.00
PS74	1968(2)	1,000	KM63-64	28.00	BV + 20%
PS75	1969(9)	7,000	KM63-64,65.2,66.1,67.2,68.1, 69.2,70.1,80.2	34.85	190.00
PS76	1969(7)	5,000	KM65.2,66.1,67.2,68.1,69.2, 70.1,80.2	13.95	10.00
PS77	1969(2)	1,000	KM63-64	27.85	BV + 20%
PS78	1970(10)	6,000	KM63-64,81-88	35.05	195.00
PS79	1970(8)	4,000	KM81-88	14.00	15.00
PS80	1970(2)	1,000	KM63-64	28.05	BV + 20%
PS81	1971(10)	7,000	KM63-64,81-88	35.00	195.00
PS82	1971(8)	5,000	KM81-88	14.00	15.00
PS83	1971(2)	650	KM63-64	28.00	BV + 20%
PS84	1972(10)	6,000	KM63-64,81-88	32.80	195.00
PS85	1972(8)	4,000	KM81-88	13.10	15.00
PS86	1972(2)	1,500	KM63-64	26.25	BV + 20%
PS87	1973(10)	6,850	KM63-64,81-88	32.00	195.00
PS88	1973(8)	4,000	KM81-88	12.80	15.00
PS89	1973(2)	6,088	KM63-64	25.60	BV + 20%
PS90	1974(10)	11,000	KM63-64,81-87,89	52.50	195.00
PS91	1974(8)	4,000	KM81-87,89	15.00	15.00
PS92	1974(2)	5,600	KM63-64	45.00	BV + 20%
PS93	1975(10)	12,500	KM63-64,81-87,89	116.40	195.00
PS94	1975(8)	5,512	KM81-88	14.55	15.00
PS95	1975(2)	7,000	KM63-64	101.85	BV + 20%
PS96	1976(10)	14,000	KM63-64,88,90-96	92.00	195.00
PS97	1976(8)	7,000	KM88,90-96	11.50	15.00
PS98	1976(2)	12,000	KM63-64	80.50	BV + 20%
PS99	1977(10)	12,000	KM63-64,81-88	92.00	195.00
PS100	1977(8)	7,000	KM81-88	11.50	15.00
PS101	1977(2)	8,500	KM63-64	80.50	BV + 20%
PS102	1978(10)	10,000	KM63-64,81-88	—	195.00
PS103	1978(8)	7,000	KM81-88	—	15.00
PS104	1978(2)	9,000	KM63-64	BV + 20%	
PS105	1979(10)	10,000	KM63-64,97-103,104a	—	195.00
PS106	1979(8)	5,000	KM88,97-103,104a	—	15.00
PS107	1979(2)	10,000	KM63-64	BV + 20%	
PS108	1980(10)	10,000	KM63-64,81-88	—	195.00
PS109	1980(8)	5,000	KM81-88	—	15.00
PS110	1980(2)	8,000	KM63-64	BV + 20%	
PS111	1981(10)	6,000	KM63-64,81-88	—	195.00

SOUTH AFRICA 1520

KM#	Date	Mintage	Identification	Issue Price	Mkt. Val.
PS112	1981(8)	4,000	KM81-88	—	25.00
PS113	1981(2)	6,238	KM63-64	BV + 20%	
PS114	1982(10)	7,100	KM63-64,108-115	—	200.00
PS115	1982(8)	4,900	KM88,108-115	—	15.00
PS116	1982(2)	6,930	KM63-64	BV + 20%	
PS117	1983(10)	7,300	KM63-64,81-88	—	195.00
PS118	1983(8)	6,835	KM81-88	—	15.00
PS119	1983(2)	7,300	KM63-64	BV + 20%	
PS120	1984(8)	11,250	KM82-88,88a	—	15.00
PS121	1985(8)	9,859	KM82-87,116,117	—	22.50
PS122	1986(8)	—	KM82-87,88a,119	—	21.50
PS123	1987(8)	—	KM82-88,88a	—	15.00

Listings For

SOUTH ARABIA: refer to Yemen Democratic Republic
SOUTH KOREA: refer to Korea/South
SOUTH VIETNAM: refer to Vietnam/South
SOUTHERN RHODESIA: refer to Zimbabwe

SPAIN

The Spanish State, forming the greater part of the Iberian Peninsula of southwest Europe, has an area of 195,988 sq. mi. (507,606 sq. km.) and a population of 39.8 million including the Balearic and the Canary Islands. Capital: Madrid. The economy is based on agriculture, industry and tourism. Machinery, fruit, vegetables and chemicals are exported.

It isn't known when man first came to the Iberian Peninsula - the Altamira caves off the Cantabrian coast approximately 50 miles west of Santander were fashioned in Palaeolithic times. Spain was a battleground for centuries before it became a united nation, fought for by Phoenicians, Carthaginians, Greeks, Celts, Romans, Vandals, Visigoths and Moors. Ferdinand and Isabella destroyed the last Moorish stronghold in 1492, freeing the national energy and resources for the era of discovery and colonization that would make Spain the most powerful country in Europe during the 16th century. After the destruction of the Spanish Armada, 1588, Spain never again played a major role in European politics. Napoleonic France ruled Spain between 1808 and 1814. The monarchy was restored in 1814 and continued, interrupted by the short-lived republic of 1873-74, until the exile of Alfonso XIII in 1931 when the Second Republic was established.

The monarchy was reconstituted in 1947 under the regency of General Francisco Franco; the king designate to be crowned after Franco's death. Franco died on Nov. 20, 1975. Two days after his passing, Juan Carlos de Borbon, the grandson of Alfonso XIII, was proclaimed King of Spain.

RULERS

Carlos IV, 1788-1808
Jose Napoleon, 1808-1813
Ferdinand VII, 1808-1833 (in exile until 1814)
Isabel II, 1833-1868
Provisional Government, 1868-1871
Amadeo I, 1871-1873
 1st Republic, 1873-1874
Alfonso XII, 1874-1885
 Regency, 1885-1886
Alfonso XIII, 1886-1931
 2nd Republic and Civil War, 1931-1939
Francisco Franco, 1939-1975
Juan Carlos I, 1975 —

NOTE: From 1868 to 1982, two dates may be found on most Spanish coinage. The larger date is the year of authorization and the smaller date incused on the two six pointed-stars found on most types is the year of issue. The latter appears in parentheses in these listings.

HOMELAND MINT MARKS
Until 1851

(b) Brussels, privy marks only
B - Burgos
B, BA - Barcelona
BGA - Berga
Bo - Bilbao
C - Catalonia
NOTE: The Catalonia Mint was located at Reus between February 1-25, 1809 and March 31, 1809 to May 20, 1810 and again from April 14 to August 15, 1810. It was then temporarily located at Tarragonia until May 9, 1811 and finally located at Palma de Mallorca from June 2, 1811 to June 20, 1814.
CA - Cuenca
J, JA - Jubia
M, MD - Madrid
P,p,P., P.L., PA - Pamplona
S, S/L - Seville
Sr - Santander
T, To, Tole - Toledo
V, VA, VAL - Valencia
Crowned C - Cadiz
Crowned M - Madrid

Aqueduct - Segovia, until 1864

After 1848

3-Pointed star - Segovia after 1868
4-Pointed star - Jubia
6-Pointed star - Madrid
7-Pointed star - Seville
8-Pointed star - Barcelona
Other letters after date are initials of mint officials.

After 1982
Crowned M - Madrid

COLONIAL MINT MARKS

Many Spanish Colonial mints struck coins similar to regular Spanish issues until the 1820's. These issues are easily distinguished from regular Spanish issues by the following mint marks.

C, CH, Ch - Chihuahua, Mexico
D, DO, Do - Durango, Mexico
Ga - Guadalajara, Mexico
G, GG - Guatemala
G, Go - Guanajuato, Mexico
L, LIMAE, LIMA - Lima, Peru
M, Mo - Mexico City, Mexico
NG - Nueva Grenada, Guatemala
NR - Nuevo Reino, Colombia
PDV - Valladolid Michoacan, Mexico
P, PN, Pn - Popayan, Colombia
P, POTOSI - Potosi, Bolivia
So - Santiago, Chile
Z, Zs - Zacatecas, Mexico

MINTMASTER'S INITIALS
BARCELONA MINT

Letter	Date	Name
CC	1842-1843	
PS	1836-1841, 1843-1848	Francisco Paradaltas and Simeon Sola y Roca
SM	1850	Simeon Sola y Roca and Francisco Miro
SP	1822-1823	Pablo Sala and Francisco Paradaltas

MADRID MINT

AF	1808	Antonio de Goycoechea
AI	1807-1808	Antonio de Goycoechea and Ildefonso de Urquiza
AI	1808-1812	Antonio Rafael Narvaez and Isidoro Ramos del Manzano
FA	1799-1808	Francisco Herrera and Antonio Goicoechea
FM	1801	Francisco Herrera and Manuel de Lamas
IA	1808	Ildefonso de Urquiza and Antonio Goycoechea
IA	1810	Isidoro Ramos del Manzano and Antonio Rafael Narvaez
IG	1808-1810	Ildefonso de Urquiza and Gregorio Lazaro Labrandero
MF	1788-1802	Manuel de Lamas and Francisco Herrera
RN	1812-1813	Antonio Rafael Narvaez
RS	1810-1812	Antonio Rafael Narvaez and Jose Sanchez Delgado

SEVILLA MINT

C	1790-1791, 1801-1808	Carlos Tiburcio de Roxas
CJ	1815-1821	Carlos Tiburcio de Roxas and Joaquin Delgado Diaz
CN	1791-1810, 1812	Carlos Tiburcio de Roxas and Nicolas Lamas
DR	1835-1838	Joaquin Delgado Diaz and Benito de Roxas
J	1823	Jose Sanchez Delgado o Joaquin Delgado
JB	1824-1833	Joaquin Delgado Diaz and Benito de Roxas
LA	1810, 1812	Leonardo Carrero and Antonio de Larra
RD	1821-1823	Carlos Tiburcio de Roxas and Joaquin Delgado Diaz
RD	1835	Benito de Roxas and Joaquin Delgado Diaz
RD	1838-1852	Benito de Roxas and Vicente Delgado

VALENCIA MINT

GS	1811	Gregorio Lazaro Labrandero and Sixto Giber Polo
R	1821	
SG	1809-1814	Sixto Giber Polo

MONETARY SYSTEM

34 Maravedi = 1 Real (of Silver)
16 Reales = 1 Escudo

NOTE: The early coinage of Spain is listed by denomination based on a system of 16 Reales de Plata (silver) = 1 Escudo (gold). However, in the Constitutional period from 1808-1850, a concurrent system was introduced in which 20 Reales de Vellon (billon) = 8 Reales de Plata. This system does not necessarily refer to the composition of the coin itself. To avoid confusion we have listed the coins using the value as it appears on each coin, ignoring the monetary base.

MARAVEDI
COPPER
Mint mark: Aqueduct

Similar to 4 Maravedis, C#61.

C#	Date	Mintage	VG	Fine	VF	XF
59	1802	—	15.00	30.00	50.00	70.00

Mint mark: J, JA
Obv: Head of Ferdinand right.
Rev: Arms in angles of cross.

112	1824	—	10.00	17.50	25.00	40.00

167.1	1842	—	10.00	20.00	40.00	80.00
	1843	—	75.00	150.00	300.00	425.00

Mint mark: Crowned M

167.2	1842 DG	—	100.00	200.00	300.00	400.00

Mint mark: Aqueduct

167.3	1842	—	7.50	15.00	30.00	60.00

2 MARAVEDIS
COPPER
Mint mark: Aqueduct
Similar to 4 Maravedis, C#61.

60	1801	—	3.00	6.00	10.00	20.00
	1802	—	3.00	7.00	12.00	24.00
	1803	—	3.00	6.00	10.00	20.00
	1804	—	6.00	12.50	20.00	35.00
	1805	—	3.00	6.00	10.00	20.00
	1806	—	6.00	12.50	22.50	37.00
	1807	—	3.00	6.00	10.00	20.00
	1808	—	3.00	6.00	10.00	20.00

Mint mark: J, JA

106	1812	—	10.00	15.00	30.00	45.00
	1813	—	5.00	11.00	20.00	30.00
	1814	—	5.00	11.00	20.00	28.00
	1815	—	5.00	11.00	20.00	28.00
	1816	—	5.00	10.00	18.00	22.00
	1817	—	5.00	11.00	20.00	35.00

Mint mark: Aqueduct

116	1816	—	4.00	8.00	12.00	25.00
	1817	—	3.00	6.00	10.00	15.00
	1818	—	3.00	6.00	10.00	15.00
	1819	—	3.00	6.00	10.00	15.00
	1820	—	3.00	6.00	10.00	15.00
	1824	—	2.00	4.00	6.00	12.00
	1825	—	2.00	4.00	6.00	12.00
	1826	—	2.00	4.00	6.00	12.00
	1827	—	2.00	4.00	6.00	12.00
	1828	—	2.00	4.00	6.00	12.00
	1829	—	2.00	4.00	6.00	12.00
	1830	—	2.00	4.00	6.00	12.00
	1831	—	2.00	4.00	6.00	12.00
	1832	—	2.00	4.00	6.00	12.00
	1833	—	2.00	4.00	6.00	12.00

Obv. leg: FERDIN. IIV. (error)

116a	1832	—	10.00	15.00	25.00	45.00

Mint mark: J, JA
Thin laureate bust

109	1817	—	4.00	7.00	18.00	30.00
	1818	—	4.00	7.00	15.00	28.00
	1819	—	4.00	7.00	15.00	28.00
	1820	—	4.00	7.00	15.00	28.00
	1821	—	18.00	35.00	65.00	95.00

Large bare head

113	1824	—	5.00	12.00	20.00	30.00
	1826	—	4.00	10.00	18.00	28.00
	1827	—	6.00	15.00	23.00	35.00

Mint mark: B, BA

168.1	1855	—	12.50	20.00	40.00	80.00
	1858	—	10.00	15.00	25.00	50.00

Mint mark: J, JA

168.2	1838	—	15.00	35.00	70.00	100.00
	1840	—	40.00	80.00	150.00	225.00
	1841	—	45.00	110.00	200.00	275.00
	1842	—	45.00	110.00	200.00	300.00
	1844	—	40.00	80.00	175.00	250.00
	1848	—	7.00	15.00	25.00	45.00
	1849	—	5.00	9.00	20.00	30.00

Mint mark: Crowned M

C#	Date	Mintage	VG	Fine	VF	XF
168.3	1837 DG	—	75.00	150.00	275.00	500.00

Mint mark: Aqueduct

168.4	1836	—	12.00	30.00	75.00	125.00
	1837	—	12.00	25.00	70.00	110.00
	1838	—	3.00	5.00	10.00	17.50
	1839	—	3.00	5.00	10.00	17.50
	1840	—	3.00	5.00	10.00	17.50
	1841	—	3.00	5.00	10.00	17.50
	1842	—	3.00	5.00	10.00	17.50
	1843	—	3.00	5.00	10.00	17.50
	1844	—	3.00	5.00	10.00	17.50
	1845	—	3.00	5.00	10.00	17.50
	1846	—	3.00	5.00	10.00	17.50
	1847	—	3.00	5.00	10.00	17.50
	1848	—	3.00	5.00	10.00	17.50
	1849	—	3.00	5.00	10.00	17.50
	1850	—	3.00	5.00	10.00	17.50

4 MARAVEDIS

COPPER
Mint mark: Aqueduct

61	1801	—	3.00	6.00	8.00	12.50
	1802	—	3.00	6.00	8.00	12.50
	1803	—	3.00	6.00	8.00	12.50
	1804	—	5.00	10.00	14.00	25.00
	1805	—	5.00	10.00	14.00	25.00
	1806	—	5.00	10.00	14.00	25.00
	1807	—	5.00	9.00	12.50	20.00
	1808	—	3.00	6.00	8.00	12.50

Mint mark: J, JA
Similar to 2 Maravedis, C#106.

107	1812	—	4.50	11.00	25.00	35.00
	1813	—	4.50	11.00	20.00	30.00
	1814	—	4.00	10.00	20.00	30.00
	1815	—	4.50	11.00	20.00	30.00
	1816	—	4.00	10.00	20.00	30.00

117.1	1817	—	4.50	11.00	20.00	35.00
	1818	—	8.00	16.00	22.50	40.00

Mint mark: Aqueduct

117.2	1816	—	4.00	7.00	10.00	20.00
	1818	—	5.00	10.00	16.00	30.00
	1819	—	4.00	7.00	14.00	25.00
	1820	—	4.00	7.00	10.00	20.00
	1823	—	3.00	6.00	10.00	19.00
	1824	—	3.00	6.00	10.00	17.00
	1825	—	3.00	6.00	10.00	19.00
	1826	—	3.00	6.00	10.00	19.00
	1827	—	3.00	6.00	10.00	19.00
	1828	—	3.00	6.00	9.00	18.00
	1829	—	3.00	6.00	9.00	16.00
	1830	—	3.00	6.00	8.00	15.00
	1831	—	3.00	6.00	9.00	16.00
	1832	—	3.00	6.00	10.00	17.00
	1833	—	3.00	6.00	9.00	16.00

Mint mark: J, JA
Small head
Similar to 2 Maravedis, C#106 but w/thin laureate bust.

110.1	1817	—	5.00	9.00	14.00	25.00
	1818	—	5.00	9.00	17.50	27.50
	1819	—	5.00	10.00	18.00	28.00
	1820	—	5.00	9.00	14.00	30.00

Mint mark: Aqueduct

110.2	1817	—	5.00	9.00	14.00	30.00

Mint mark: J, JA
Large head

114	1824	—	4.00	8.00	12.00	25.00
	1825	—	6.00	12.00	30.00	55.00
	1826	—	4.00	8.00	12.00	20.00
	1827	—	5.00	10.00	14.00	18.00

161.1	1835	—	7.50	15.00	27.50	50.00
	1836	—	5.00	10.00	20.00	45.00

Mint mark: Crowned M

161.2	1836 DG	—	125.00	225.00	375.00	500.00

Mint mark: Aqueduct

C#	Date	Mintage	VG	Fine	VF	XF
161.3	1835	—	10.00	20.00	45.00	60.00
	1836	—	6.00	12.00	25.00	35.00

Mint mark: B, BA

169.1	1853	—	50.00	100.00	200.00	275.00
	1855	—	5.00	10.00	20.00	40.00

Mint mark: J, JA

169.2	1837	—	7.00	14.00	30.00	45.00
	1840	—	30.00	50.00	125.00	180.00
	1841	—	7.00	14.00	40.00	50.00
	1842	—	7.00	14.00	65.00	90.00
	1843	—	7.00	14.00	60.00	85.00
	1844	—	7.00	14.00	75.00	125.00
	1845	—	7.00	13.00	25.00	35.00
	1846	—	7.00	14.00	60.00	80.00
	1847	—	5.00	10.00	18.00	25.00
	1848	—	7.00	13.00	25.00	35.00
	1849	—	7.00	14.00	35.00	50.00
	1850	—	5.00	10.00	18.00	25.00

Mint mark: Aqueduct

169.3	1837	—	5.00	9.00	20.00	30.00
	1838	—	5.00	9.00	20.00	30.00
	1839	—	10.00	20.00	35.00	50.00
	1840	—	5.00	9.00	25.00	35.00
	1841	—	5.00	9.00	18.00	30.00
	1842	—	5.00	9.00	15.00	25.00
	1843	—	8.00	15.00	35.00	55.00
	1844	—	5.00	9.00	18.00	30.00
	1845	—	5.00	9.00	18.00	30.00
	1846	—	5.00	9.00	18.00	35.00
	1847	—	5.00	10.00	15.00	30.00
	1848	—	5.00	9.00	20.00	30.00
	1849	—	4.00	8.00	20.00	30.00
	1850	—	8.00	15.00	35.00	50.00

8 MARAVEDIS

COPPER
Mint mark: Aqueduct

62	1801	—	4.00	8.00	12.00	18.50
	1802	—	4.00	8.00	12.00	18.50
	1803	—	4.00	8.00	12.00	18.50
	1804	—	5.00	9.00	14.00	20.00
	1805	—	4.00	8.00	12.00	18.50
	1806	—	5.00	9.00	14.00	20.00
	1807	—	4.00	8.00	12.00	18.50
	1808	—	3.00	7.00	9.00	15.00

82	1809	—	25.00	50.00	75.00	100.00
	1810	—	20.00	40.00	65.00	80.00
	1811	—	14.00	28.00	45.00	55.00
	1812	—	10.00	20.00	35.00	40.00
	1813	—	16.00	32.50	50.00	60.00

SPAIN 1522

Mint mark: J, JA

C#	Date	Mintage	VG	Fine	VF	XF
108	1811	—	20.00	40.00	85.00	125.00
	1812	—	15.00	35.00	65.00	80.00
	1813	—	7.00	14.00	30.00	40.00
	1814	—	7.00	14.00	30.00	40.00
	1815	—	7.00	14.00	30.00	40.00
	1816	—	5.00	10.00	25.00	35.00
	1817	—	6.00	12.00	20.00	30.00

Mint mark: Aqueduct

118	1815	—	9.00	18.00	30.00	45.00
	1816	—	5.00	10.00	25.00	30.00
	1817	—	5.00	10.00	20.00	30.00
	1818	—	5.00	10.00	20.00	30.00
	1819	—	6.00	12.00	12.50	25.00
	1820	—	5.00	10.00	20.00	25.00
	1821	—	10.00	25.00	40.00	55.00
	1822	—	9.00	18.00	40.00	55.00
	1823	—	5.00	10.00	20.00	25.00
	1824	—	5.00	9.00	15.00	17.50
	1825	—	5.00	9.00	15.00	17.50
	1826	—	5.00	9.00	15.00	17.50
	1827	—	5.00	10.00	17.00	18.50
	1828	—	8.00	15.00	25.00	40.00
	1829	—	4.00	7.00	10.00	15.00
	1830	—	5.00	10.00	12.00	15.00
	1831	—	4.00	7.00	9.00	12.50
	1832	—	4.00	7.00	9.00	11.50
	1833	—	4.00	7.00	9.00	11.50

Mint mark: J, JA

111	1817	—	4.00	8.00	10.00	25.00
	1818	—	4.00	7.00	10.00	15.00
	1819	—	4.00	7.00	10.00	15.00
	1820	—	4.00	7.00	10.00	15.00
	1821	—	3.00	6.00	10.00	15.00

Obv: Bust, leg: FERN 7o POR LA. . . .

115	1822	—	6.00	12.00	20.00	35.00
	1823	—	5.00	10.00	17.50	30.00

Obv: Value omitted.

115a	1823	—	6.00	12.00	20.00	35.00

Obv: Bust, leg: FERDIN.VII D.G.HISP.REX.

114.5	1823	—	6.00	11.00	18.00	30.00
	1824	—	6.00	11.00	18.00	25.00
	1825	—	6.00	11.00	18.00	25.00
	1826	—	5.00	9.00	15.00	20.00
	1827	—	5.00	9.00	16.00	22.50

Mint mark: Aqueduct

114.7	1823	—	5.00	9.00	15.00	25.00

Mint mark: P, P.P., P.L., PA
Obv: Bust, leg: FERDIN.VII.D.G. HISP.REX.

118a	1823	—	12.00	25.00	45.00	65.00

Mint mark: J, JA

162.1	1835	—	6.00	15.00	30.00	45.00
	1836	—	8.00	18.00	35.00	55.00

Mint mark: Crowned M

162.2	1835 DG	—	125.00	225.00	300.00	400.00

Mint mark: Aqueduct

C#	Date	Mintage	VG	Fine	VF	XF
162.3	1835	—	4.00	10.00	20.00	35.00
	1836	—	3.00	8.00	16.00	30.00

154	1837	—	175.00	300.00	475.00	600.00

CAST BELL METAL
Mint mark: P, P.P., P.L., PA

C#	Date	Mintage	Good	VG	Fine	VF
170a.1	1837	—	50.00	75.00	100.00	175.00

Mint mark within oval

170a.2	1837	—	50.00	75.00	100.00	175.00

COPPER
Mint mark: B, BA

C#	Date	Mintage	VG	Fine	VF	XF
170.1	1853	—	25.00	45.00	65.00	115.00
	1854	*				
	1855	—	40.00	60.00	90.00	125.00
	1858	—	20.00	40.00	60.00	100.00

*NOTE: Only counterfeits seen.

Mint mark: J, JA

170.2	1837	—	5.00	10.00	22.00	30.00
	1838	—	6.00	12.00	25.00	35.00
	1839	—	10.00	25.00	55.00	70.00
	1840	—	12.00	20.00	32.50	40.00
	1841	—	6.00	12.00	20.00	30.00
	1842	—	5.00	10.00	18.00	25.00
	1843	—	5.00	10.00	18.00	25.00
	1844	—	5.00	12.00	20.00	32.50
	1845	—	5.00	10.00	15.00	20.00
	1846	—	5.00	10.00	18.00	25.00
	1847	—	5.00	10.00	18.00	25.00
	1848	—	5.00	10.00	15.00	20.00
	1849	—	10.00	15.00	20.00	30.00
	1850	—	5.00	10.00	18.00	25.00

Mint mark: Aqueduct

170.3	1837	—	5.00	10.00	20.00	35.00
	1838	—	5.00	10.00	20.00	30.00
	1839	—	5.00	9.00	17.00	25.00
	1840	—	5.00	9.00	20.00	27.50
	1841	—	5.00	9.00	17.00	25.00
	1842	—	5.00	9.00	17.00	25.00
	1843	—	5.00	9.00	17.00	25.00
	1844	—	4.00	8.00	13.00	17.50
	1845	—	4.00	8.00	15.00	22.50
	1846	—	5.00	9.00	17.00	25.00
	1847	—	5.00	11.00	17.50	25.00
	1848	—	6.00	12.50	18.50	25.00
	1849	—	5.00	10.00	12.50	25.00
	1850	—	7.00	15.00	30.00	40.00

1/2 REAL
1.6900 g, .903 SILVER, .0490 oz ASW
Mint mark: Crowned M
Obv: Bust of Charles IV right.

Rev: Crowned arms.

C#	Date	Mintage	VG	Fine	VF	XF
66.1	1802 FA	—	8.00	15.00	27.50	35.00
	1803 FA	—	5.00	10.00	18.50	30.00
	1804 FA	—	7.00	13.00	22.50	30.00
	1808 AI	—	7.00	14.00	25.00	35.00
	1808 FA	—	8.00	16.00	27.50	40.00

Mint mark: S, S/L

66.2	1802 CN	—	8.00	16.00	32.50	40.00
	1805 CN	—	8.00	16.00	32.50	40.00
	1807 CN	—	7.00	13.00	25.00	30.00

Mint mark: Crowned C
Obv: Laureate bust right. Rev: Crowned arms.

132.1	1814 CI	—	5.00	10.00	22.50	35.00
	1814 CJ	—	5.00	10.00	25.00	40.00

Mint mark: Crowned M

132.2	1815 GJ	—	6.00	12.50	27.50	40.00
	1816 GJ	—	6.00	12.00	18.00	30.00
	1817 GJ	—	6.00	12.00	18.00	35.00
	1818 GJ	—	6.00	12.00	16.00	30.00
	1819 GJ	—	6.00	12.00	18.00	35.00
	1820 GJ	—	6.00	12.50	18.00	30.00
	1824 AJ	—	8.00	15.00	25.00	35.00
	1826 AJ	—	6.00	12.50	25.00	35.00
	1828 AJ	—	8.00	15.00	25.00	30.00
	1830 AJ	—	6.00	12.00	17.50	35.00
	1831 AJ	—	9.00	17.50	25.00	35.00
	1832 AJ	—	6.00	12.00	20.00	30.00
	1833 AJ	—	6.00	12.00	25.00	35.00
	1833 JI	—	11.00	22.00	40.00	65.00

Mint mark: S, S/L

132.3	1825 JB	—	4.00	7.00	15.00	25.00
	1831 JB	—	4.00	7.00	15.00	25.00
	1832 JB	—	6.00	12.00	20.00	35.00
	1833 JB	—	7.00	13.00	20.00	35.00

Mint mark: C
Obv: Small draped bust.

132a.1	1812 SF	—	15.00	30.00	50.00	70.00
	1813 SF	—	15.00	30.00	50.00	70.00
	1814 SF	—	20.00	35.00	55.00	75.00

Mint mark: Crowned M

132a.2	1813 IJ	—	9.00	18.00	30.00	45.00
	1813 GJ	—	7.50	15.00	25.00	35.00
	1814 GJ	—	10.00	20.00	35.00	50.00

REAL
3.3800 g, .917 SILVER, .0995 oz ASW
Mint mark: Crowned M
Obv: Bust of Charles IV right.

68.1	1801 FA	—	5.00	10.00	16.00	25.00
	1802 FA	—	5.00	10.00	20.00	35.00
	1803 FA	—	6.00	12.00	18.00	25.00
	1805 FA	—	6.00	12.00	19.00	30.00
	1807 FA	—	6.00	12.00	18.00	25.00
	1807 AI	—	7.00	14.00	20.00	40.00
	1808 AI	—	7.00	14.00	19.00	30.00

Mint mark: S, S/L

68.2	1802 CN	—	10.00	20.00	45.00	65.00
	1807 CN	—	9.00	18.00	35.00	50.00

Mint mark: C
Obv: Large laureate bust.
Rev: Crowned arms.

133.1	1811 SF	—	12.50	22.50	40.00	55.00

Mint mark: Crowned C

133.2	1813 CJ	—	10.00	20.00	30.00	45.00

Mint mark: Crowned M

133.3	1815 GJ	—	8.00	16.50	32.50	50.00
	1816 GJ	—	8.00	16.50	30.00	50.00
	1817 GJ	—	8.00	16.50	25.00	45.00
	1819 GJ	—	10.00	20.00	27.50	45.00
	1820 GJ	—	9.00	18.50	25.00	55.00
	1824 AJ	—	15.00	30.00	55.00	80.00
	1826 AJ	—	10.00	20.00	40.00	60.00
	1828 AJ	—	10.00	20.00	40.00	60.00
	1830 AJ	—	7.00	15.00	22.00	35.00
	1831 AJ	—	8.00	17.00	30.00	45.00
	1832 AJ	—	7.00	15.00	20.00	30.00
	1833 AJ	—	10.00	20.00	30.00	50.00
	1833 JI	—	11.00	22.50	38.50	60.00
	1833 JJ	—	9.00	18.00	30.00	40.00

Mint mark: S, S/L

133.4	1830 JB	—	10.00	19.00	32.00	50.00
	1831 JB	—	6.00	12.00	25.00	35.00
	1832 JB	—	7.00	14.00	25.00	35.00
	1833 JB	—	7.00	14.00	20.00	30.00

Mint mark: C
Obv: Small draped bust.

133a.1	1811 SF	—	13.50	25.00	45.00	65.00
	1814 SF	—	22.50	40.00	80.00	130.00

Mint mark: Crowned M

C#	Date	Mintage	VG	Fine	VF	XF
133a.2	1813 IJ	—	22.50	40.00	60.00	85.00
	1814 IJ	—	15.00	30.00	45.00	75.00
	1814 GJ	—	9.00	18.50	30.00	50.00

171.1	1837 CL	—	30.00	60.00	110.00	150.00
	1838 CL	—	9.00	18.00	22.00	30.00
	1838 DG	—	50.00	90.00	170.00	230.00
	1839 CL	—	8.00	16.50	35.00	65.00
	1840 CL	—	15.00	30.00	60.00	115.00
	1841 CL	—	30.00	60.00	115.00	225.00
	1842 CL	—	35.00	70.00	140.00	180.00
	1843 CL	—	16.00	32.50	60.00	115.00
	1844 CL	—	7.00	15.00	30.00	60.00
	1845 CL	—	4.00	8.00	15.00	25.00
	1847 CL	—	4.00	8.00	15.00	25.00
	1848 CL	—	4.00	8.00	15.00	25.00
	1849 CL	—	4.00	8.00	15.00	25.00

Mint mark: S, S/L

171.2	1840 RD	—	20.00	45.00	100.00	130.00
	1844 RD	—	10.00	20.00	45.00	70.00
	1845 RD	—	15.00	30.00	70.00	100.00
	1850 RD	—	7.00	14.00	25.00	40.00
	1851 RD	—	7.00	14.00	25.00	40.00
	1852 RD	—	6.00	12.00	20.00	30.00

2 REALES
6.7700 g, .903 SILVER, .1965 oz ASW
Mint mark: Crowned M
Obv: Bust of Charles IV right.

69.1	1801 FA	—	7.00	15.00	22.00	35.00
	1802 FA	—	7.00	15.00	22.00	35.00
	1803 FA	—	7.00	15.00	22.00	35.00
	1804 FA	—	7.00	15.00	22.00	35.00
	1805 FA	—	7.00	15.00	22.00	35.00
	1806 FA	—	7.00	15.00	22.00	35.00
	1807 FA	—	7.00	15.00	22.00	35.00
	1807 AI	—	8.00	17.00	30.00	50.00
	1808 FA	—	7.00	15.00	22.00	35.00
	1808 IG	—	8.00	17.00	30.00	50.00
	1808 AI	—	7.00	15.00	25.00	40.00

Mint mark: S, S/L

69.2	1801 CN	—	8.00	16.00	25.00	40.00
	1802 CN	—	8.00	16.00	25.00	40.00
	1803 CN	—	8.00	16.00	25.00	40.00
	1804 CN	—	8.00	16.00	25.00	40.00
	1805 CN	—	8.00	16.00	25.00	40.00
	1806 CN	—	8.00	16.00	25.00	40.00
	1807 CN	—	8.00	16.00	25.00	40.00
	1808 CN	—	8.00	16.00	25.00	40.00

Mint mark: C

134.1	1811 SF	—	8.00	17.00	30.00	50.00
	1812 SF	—	40.00	70.00	125.00	175.00
	1813 SF	—	8.00	17.00	30.00	50.00
	1814 SF	—	14.00	27.50	35.00	55.00

Mint mark: Crowned C

134.2	1810 CI	—	9.00	18.00	25.00	40.00
	1810 CI w/small crowned C	—	11.00	21.00	35.00	60.00
	1811 CI	—	9.00	18.00	25.00	40.00
	1812 CI	—	9.00	18.00	25.00	40.00

Mint mark: Crowned M

134.3	1814 GJ	—	8.00	16.00	23.00	35.00
	1815 GJ	—	8.00	16.00	23.00	35.00
	1816 IJ	—	8.00	16.00	25.00	40.00

C#	Date	Mintage	VG	Fine	VF	XF
134.3	1817 GJ	—	8.00	16.00	23.00	35.00
	1818 GJ	—	9.00	19.00	25.00	40.00
	1819 GJ	—	9.00	19.00	25.00	45.00
	1820 GJ	—	8.00	16.00	23.00	35.00
	1821 AJ	—	7.00	15.00	30.00	50.00
	1822 AJ	—	16.00	32.50	40.00	65.00
	1823 AJ	—	8.00	16.00	25.00	40.00
	1824 AJ	—	8.00	16.00	25.00	40.00
	1825 AJ	—	8.00	16.00	25.00	40.00
	1826 AJ	—	8.00	16.00	23.00	35.00
	1827 AJ	—	8.00	16.00	25.00	40.00
	1828 AJ	—	8.00	16.00	23.00	35.00
	1829 AJ	—	8.00	16.00	23.00	35.00
	1830 AJ	—	8.00	16.00	23.00	30.00
	1831 AJ	—	8.00	16.00	25.00	40.00
	1832 AJ	—	8.00	16.00	23.00	35.00
	1833 AJ	—	9.00	18.00	25.00	40.00

Mint mark: S, S/L

134.4	1815 CJ	—	10.00	20.00	30.00	50.00
	1820 CJ	—	8.00	16.00	25.00	40.00
	1821 CJ	—	7.00	14.00	20.00	30.00
	1823 CJ	—	8.00	16.00	25.00	40.00
	1824 J	—	15.00	30.00	40.00	65.00
	1824 JB	—	8.00	16.00	25.00	40.00
	1825 JB	—	8.00	16.00	25.00	40.00
	1826 JB	—	8.00	16.00	25.00	40.00
	1827 JB	—	8.00	16.00	25.00	40.00
	1828 JB	—	8.00	16.00	25.00	40.00
	1829 JB	—	8.00	16.00	25.00	40.00
	1830 JB	—	8.00	16.00	25.00	40.00
	1831 JB	—	8.00	16.00	25.00	40.00
	1832 JB	—	8.00	16.00	25.00	45.00
	1833 JB	—	9.00	18.00	27.00	50.00

Mint mark: B, BA
Obv: Bare head of Ferdinand right.
Rev: Crowned arms.

134a.1	1812 SF	—	80.00	150.00	275.00	400.00

Mint mark: C

134a.2	1810 FS	—	14.00	27.50	45.00	60.00
	1810 SF	—	30.00	55.00	80.00	140.00
	1811 SF	—	11.00	22.50	35.00	50.00
	1811 FS	—	15.00	30.00	45.00	60.00

Mint mark: Crowned M

134a.3	1812 IJ	—	9.00	17.50	25.00	40.00
	1813 IJ	—	7.00	15.00	20.00	30.00
	1813 IG	—	12.00	25.00	40.00	60.00
	1813 GJ	—	7.00	15.00	20.00	30.00
	1814 GJ	—	12.00	25.00	40.00	60.00

Mint mark: V, VAL.

134a.4	1811 GS	—	70.00	140.00	200.00	250.00
	1812 GS	—	65.00	125.00	160.00	200.00

Mint mark: Crowned M
Obv: Young head of Isabella right.
Rev: Crowned arms in collar of The Golden Fleece.

163.1	1836 CR	—	20.00	40.00	80.00	110.00
	1836 DG	—	55.00	110.00	225.00	300.00
	1837 CR	—	60.00	125.00	250.00	350.00
	1838 CR	—	60.00	115.00	230.00	300.00
	1839 CL	—	45.00	90.00	200.00	300.00
	1841 CL	—	15.00	30.00	45.00	75.00
	1842 CL	—	45.00	90.00	200.00	325.00
	1843 CL	—	17.50	35.00	75.00	110.00

Mint mark: S, S/L

163.2	1836 DR	—	20.00	40.00	95.00	150.00
	1839 RD	—	17.00	35.00	60.00	100.00
	1840 RD	—	22.00	45.00	90.00	140.00

2.6291 g, .903 SILVER, .0761 oz ASW
Charles V - Pretender Issue

C#	Date	Mintage	Good	VG	Fine	VF
157	1837	—	225.00	375.00	450.00	600.00

Charles V - Pretender Issue

156	1838	—	225.00	375.00	450.00	600.00

6.7700 g, .903 SILVER, .1965 oz ASW

Mint mark: Crowned M

C#	Date	Mintage	VG	Fine	VF	XF
172.1	1844 CL	—	11.00	22.50	35.00	60.00
	1845 CL	—	11.00	22.50	35.00	50.00
	1847 CL	—	10.00	20.00	30.00	45.00
	1848 CL	—	11.00	22.50	35.00	55.00
	1849 CL	—	10.00	20.00	30.00	45.00

Mint mark: S, S/L

172.2	1845 RD	—	22.00	45.00	100.00	165.00
	1848 RD	—	17.00	35.00	65.00	80.00
	1850/45 RD	—	30.00	60.00	100.00	150.00
	1850 RD	—	20.00	40.00	70.00	100.00
	1851 RD	—	10.00	20.00	30.00	40.00

4 REALES
13.5400 g, .917 SILVER, .3931 oz ASW
Mint mark: Crowned M
Similar to 2 Reales, C#69.2.

70.1	1804 FA	—	20.00	30.00	55.00	80.00
	1805 FA	—	20.00	30.00	55.00	70.00
	1806 FA	—	25.00	40.00	80.00	125.00
	1808 AI	—	30.00	50.00	70.00	100.00
	1808 FA	—	30.00	50.00	70.00	100.00

Mint mark: S, S/L

70.2	1803 CN	—	20.00	40.00	60.00	85.00
	1807 CN	—	22.00	45.00	65.00	100.00

Mint mark: C

135a.1	1809 MP	—	65.00	125.00	225.00	600.00
	1809 SF	—	75.00	150.00	250.00	650.00
	1810 SF	—	100.00	200.00	325.00	775.00
	1814 SF	—	175.00	325.00	525.00	850.00

Mint mark: V, VAL.

135a.2	1809 SG	—	90.00	175.00	240.00	300.00
	1810 SG	—	35.00	65.00	110.00	150.00
	1811 SG	—	40.00	70.00	125.00	175.00

Mint mark: C
Obv: Armored bust.

135c	1811 SF	—	60.00	150.00	300.00	425.00

Obv: Laureate bust.

135.1	1812 SF	—	100.00	225.00	450.00	600.00
	1813 SF	—	275.00	550.00	800.00	1000.

SPAIN 1524

Mint mark: Crowned C

C#	Date	Mintage	VG	Fine	VF	XF
135.2	1812 CJ	—	25.00	45.00	70.00	100.00
	1812 CI	—	35.00	65.00	100.00	150.00

Mint mark: Crowned M

C#	Date	Mintage	VG	Fine	VF	XF
135.3	1814 GJ	—	90.00	175.00	300.00	400.00
	1815 GJ	—	12.00	25.00	40.00	65.00
	1816 GJ	—	20.00	40.00	65.00	100.00
	1817 GJ	—	18.00	35.00	60.00	90.00
	1818 GJ	—	18.00	35.00	60.00	100.00
	1819 GJ	—	70.00	125.00	200.00	300.00
	1822 SR	—	30.00	55.00	90.00	160.00
	1824 AJ	—	16.00	32.50	40.00	70.00
	1830 AJ	—	15.00	30.00	40.00	70.00

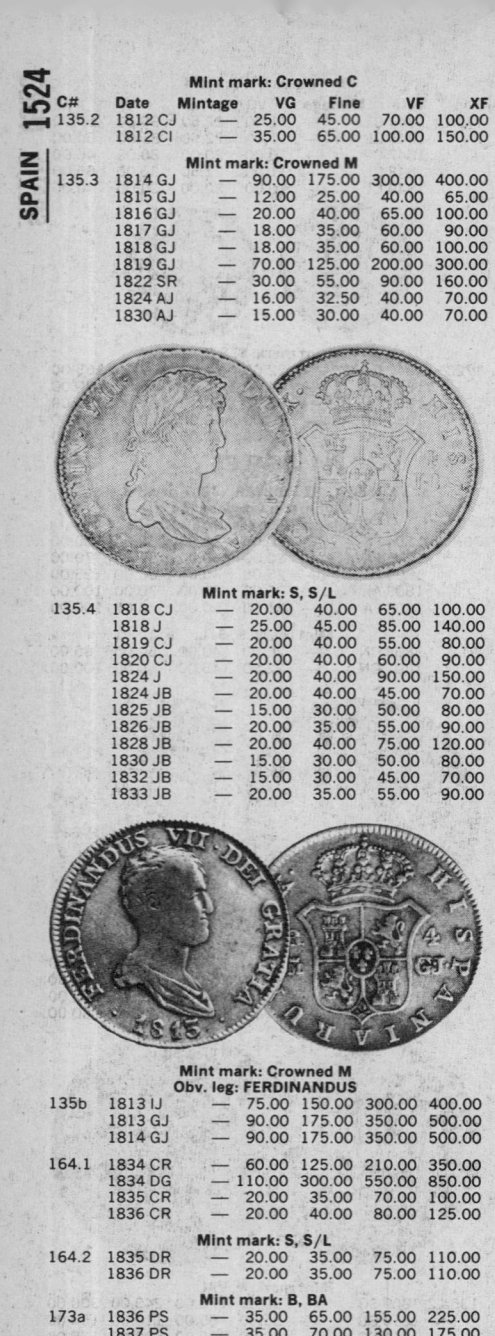

Mint mark: S, S/L

C#	Date	Mintage	VG	Fine	VF	XF
135.4	1818 CJ	—	20.00	40.00	65.00	100.00
	1818 J	—	25.00	45.00	85.00	140.00
	1819 CJ	—	20.00	40.00	55.00	80.00
	1820 CJ	—	20.00	40.00	60.00	90.00
	1824 J	—	20.00	40.00	90.00	150.00
	1824 JB	—	20.00	40.00	45.00	70.00
	1825 JB	—	15.00	30.00	50.00	80.00
	1826 JB	—	20.00	35.00	55.00	90.00
	1828 JB	—	20.00	40.00	75.00	120.00
	1830 JB	—	15.00	30.00	50.00	80.00
	1832 JB	—	15.00	30.00	45.00	70.00
	1833 JB	—	20.00	35.00	55.00	90.00

Mint mark: Crowned M
Obv. leg: FERDINANDUS

C#	Date	Mintage	VG	Fine	VF	XF
135b	1813 IJ	—	75.00	150.00	300.00	400.00
	1813 GJ	—	90.00	175.00	350.00	500.00
	1814 GJ	—	90.00	175.00	350.00	500.00
164.1	1834 CR	—	60.00	125.00	210.00	350.00
	1834 DG	—	110.00	300.00	550.00	850.00
	1835 CR	—	20.00	35.00	70.00	100.00
	1836 CR	—	20.00	40.00	80.00	125.00

Mint mark: S, S/L

C#	Date	Mintage	VG	Fine	VF	XF
164.2	1835 DR	—	20.00	35.00	75.00	110.00
	1836 DR	—	20.00	35.00	75.00	110.00

Mint mark: B, BA

C#	Date	Mintage	VG	Fine	VF	XF
173a	1836 PS	—	35.00	65.00	155.00	225.00
	1837 PS	—	35.00	70.00	130.00	175.00
	1837 RS	—	20.00	40.00	85.00	125.00

C#	Date	Mintage	VG	Fine	VF	XF
173.1	1837 PJ	—	15.00	30.00	50.00	70.00
	1838 PS	—	25.00	50.00	80.00	110.00
	1839 PS	—	80.00	175.00	375.00	525.00
	1840 PS	—	25.00	50.00	85.00	120.00
	1841 PS	—	15.00	30.00	50.00	65.00
	1842 CC	—	20.00	40.00	60.00	85.00
	1843 CC	—	75.00	150.00	350.00	425.00
	1843 PS	—	75.00	150.00	350.00	450.00
	1844 PS	—	20.00	40.00	70.00	100.00
	1845 PS	—	35.00	70.00	135.00	200.00
	1846 PS	—	80.00	175.00	300.00	450.00
	1847 PS	—	35.00	70.00	120.00	175.00

Mint mark: Crowned M

C#	Date	Mintage	VG	Fine	VF	XF
173.2	1837 CR	—	25.00	45.00	65.00	90.00
	1838 CL	—	45.00	90.00	150.00	225.00
	1839 CL	—	25.00	60.00	100.00	150.00
	1840 CL	—	20.00	35.00	70.00	100.00
	1841 CL	—	20.00	35.00	70.00	100.00
	1842 CL	—	40.00	80.00	140.00	250.00
	1843 CL	—	40.00	80.00	140.00	200.00
	1844 CL	—	45.00	90.00	175.00	275.00
	1845 CL	—	40.00	80.00	160.00	250.00
	1846 CL	—	35.00	65.00	110.00	175.00
	1847 CL	—	25.00	65.00	110.00	175.00

C#	Date	Mintage	VG	Fine	VF	XF
173.2	1848 CL	—	15.00	30.00	35.00	45.00
	1848 DG	—	125.00	200.00	475.00	750.00
	1849 CL	—	15.00	30.00	35.00	45.00

Mint mark: S, S/L

C#	Date	Mintage	VG	Fine	VF	XF
173.3	1837 DR	—	20.00	40.00	70.00	100.00
	1838 DR	—	25.00	50.00	100.00	200.00
	1838 RD	—	25.00	45.00	85.00	160.00
	1839 DR	—	35.00	70.00	180.00	300.00
	1839 RD	—	35.00	70.00	140.00	250.00
	1840 RD	—	50.00	100.00	210.00	400.00
	1841 RD	—	20.00	40.00	75.00	150.00
	1842 RD	—	20.00	40.00	70.00	150.00
	1843 RD	—	15.00	30.00	50.00	80.00
	1844 RD	—	40.00	80.00	185.00	375.00
	1845 RD	—	40.00	80.00	160.00	350.00

8 REALES
27.0700 g, .903 SILVER, .7859 oz ASW
Mint mark: Crowned M
Similar to 2 Reales, C#69.2.

C#	Date	Mintage	VG	Fine	VF	XF
71.1	1802 MF	—	200.00	375.00	500.00	700.00
	1802 FA	—	100.00	200.00	275.00	400.00
	1803 FA	—	150.00	300.00	450.00	550.00
	1805 FA	—	100.00	210.00	275.00	350.00
	1808 FA	—	150.00	300.00	500.00	600.00
	1808 AI	—	140.00	280.00	425.00	650.00
	1808 IG	—	200.00	375.00	475.00	750.00

Mint mark: S, S/L

C#	Date	Mintage	VG	Fine	VF	XF
71.2	1802 CN	—	125.00	250.00	375.00	500.00
	1803 CN	—	150.00	300.00	500.00	650.00

Mint mark: Crowned M

C#	Date	Mintage	VG	Fine	VF	XF
93	1809 IG	—	40.00	80.00	200.00	350.00
	1810 JG	—	550.00	1100.	2500.	3250.

Mint mark: S, S/L

C#	Date	Mintage	VG	Fine	VF	XF
136b	1808 CN	—	50.00	100.00	185.00	275.00
	1809 CN	—	50.00	100.00	185.00	275.00

Mint mark: Crowned M

Rev: Similar to C#136b.

C#	Date	Mintage	VG	Fine	VF	XF
136c	1812 IJ	—	225.00	450.00	600.00	800.00
	1813 IJ	—	200.00	400.00	550.00	750.00
	1813 IG	—	225.00	450.00	600.00	800.00
	1813 GJ	—	250.00	500.00	700.00	900.00

Mint mark: C

C#	Date	Mintage	VG	Fine	VF	XF
136a.1	1809 MP	—	450.00	875.00	1200.	1500.
	1809 SF	—	400.00	800.00	1100.	1300.
	1810 SF	—	425.00	850.00	1200.	1500.

Mint mark: V, VAL

C#	Date	Mintage	VG	Fine	VF	XF
136a.2	1811 GS	—	350.00	700.00	1100.	1500.
	1811 SG	—	300.00	600.00	1000.	1200.

Mint mark: C

C#	Date	Mintage	VG	Fine	VF	XF
136.1	1811 SF	—	625.00	1250.	—	—
	1812 SF	—	475.00	950.00	1800.	—
	1813 SF	—	475.00	950.00	1650.	1950.
	1814 SF	—	625.00	1250.	—	—

Mint mark: Crowned C

C#	Date	Mintage	VG	Fine	VF	XF
136.2	1810 CI	—	300.00	600.00	900.00	1300.
	1811 CI	—	175.00	325.00	575.00	850.00
	1811 CJ	—	190.00	425.00	700.00	950.00
	1812 CJ	—	175.00	400.00	650.00	900.00
	1813 CJ	—	75.00	125.00	200.00	300.00
	1814 CJ	—	75.00	125.00	200.00	300.00
	1815 CJ	—	500.00	1000.	1900.	2600.

Mint mark: Crowned M

C#	Date	Mintage	VG	Fine	VF	XF
136.3	1814 GJ	—	50.00	100.00	150.00	250.00
	1815 GJ	—	50.00	100.00	150.00	250.00
	1816 GJ	—	50.00	100.00	150.00	200.00
	1817 GJ	—	65.00	125.00	200.00	300.00
	1818 GJ	—	50.00	100.00	175.00	300.00
	1823 AJ	—	425.00	850.00	1400.	1700.
	1824 AJ	—	275.00	550.00	900.00	1250.
	1825 AJ	—	300.00	600.00	1100.	1600.
	1830 AJ	—	400.00	800.00	1600.	2000.

Mint mark: S, S/L

C#	Date	Mintage	VG	Fine	VF	XF
136.4	1809 CN	—	75.00	125.00	200.00	350.00
	1810 CN	—	450.00	900.00	1350.	2000.
	1812 CN	—	825.00	1650.	2400.	3600.
	1814 CN	—	250.00	500.00	1150.	1600.
	1815 CJ	—	65.00	125.00	175.00	250.00
	1816 CJ	—	50.00	100.00	150.00	200.00
	1817 CJ	—	50.00	100.00	150.00	200.00
	1818 CJ	—	50.00	100.00	150.00	200.00
	1819 CJ	—	65.00	125.00	200.00	300.00
	1820 CJ	—	50.00	100.00	150.00	200.00

1/2 ESCUDO

1.6900 g, .875 GOLD, .0475 oz AGW
Obv: Laureate head of Ferdinand right.
Rev: Crowned oval arms.

C#	Date	Mintage	VG	Fine	VF	XF
141	1817 GJ	—	50.00	90.00	150.00	175.00

ESCUDO

3.3800 g, .875 GOLD, .0951 oz AGW
Mint mark: Crowned M
Obv: Bust of Charles IV right.
Rev: Crowned shield in order chain.

73	1801 FA	—	65.00	80.00	100.00	150.00
	1807 FA	—	65.00	80.00	100.00	150.00

Similar to 1/2 Escudo, C#141.

142	1817 GJ	—	150.00	300.00	500.00	800.00

2 ESCUDOS

6.7700 g, .875 GOLD, .1905 oz AGW
Mint mark: Crowned M

74.1	1801 MF	—	125.00	150.00	175.00	225.00
	1801 FM	—	150.00	200.00	350.00	500.00
	1801 FA	—	125.00	150.00	175.00	225.00
	1802 FA	—	125.00	150.00	175.00	225.00
	1803 FA	—	125.00	150.00	175.00	225.00
	1804 FA	—	125.00	150.00	175.00	225.00
	1805 FA	—	125.00	150.00	175.00	225.00
	1806 FA	—	125.00	150.00	175.00	225.00
	1807 FA	—	125.00	150.00	175.00	225.00
	1807 AI	—	125.00	150.00	175.00	225.00
	1808 AI	—	125.00	150.00	175.00	225.00
	1808 FA	—	300.00	600.00	1000.	1500.

Mint mark: S, S/L

74.2	1801 CN	—	125.00	150.00	175.00	250.00
	1802 CN	—	125.00	150.00	175.00	250.00
	1803 CN	—	125.00	150.00	175.00	250.00
	1804 CN	—	125.00	150.00	175.00	250.00
	1805 CN	—	150.00	200.00	350.00	500.00
	1806 CN	—	125.00	150.00	175.00	250.00
	1807 CN	—	125.00	150.00	175.00	250.00
	1808 CN	—	125.00	150.00	175.00	250.00

Mint mark: Crowned C
Obv: Laureate uniformed bust of Ferdinand right.
Rev: Crowned arms in collar of The Golden Fleece.

143.1	1811 CI	—	125.00	200.00	300.00	450.00

Mint mark: Crowned M

143.2	1813 IG	—	250.00	500.00	900.00	1400.
	1813 IJ	—	150.00	275.00	400.00	600.00
	1813 GJ	—	125.00	150.00	200.00	300.00
	1814 GJ	—	150.00	275.00	400.00	600.00

Mint mark: S, S/L

143.3	1808 CN	—	125.00	150.00	200.00	300.00
	1809 CN	—	135.00	175.00	250.00	350.00

Mint mark: C
Obv: Laureate head of Ferdinand right.

143a.1	1811 SF	—	450.00	900.00	1400.	2000.
	1812 SF	—	400.00	800.00	1100.	1700.
	1813 SF	—	350.00	700.00	1000.	1500.

Mint mark: Crowned C

143a.2	1812 CI	—	125.00	150.00	200.00	300.00
	1813 CI	—	135.00	175.00	250.00	350.00

Mint mark: Crowned M

143a.3	1812 IJ	—	150.00	300.00	500.00	750.00
	1813 IJ	—	135.00	225.00	350.00	500.00
	1814 GJ	—	125.00	175.00	225.00	300.00
	1815 GJ	—	135.00	225.00	350.00	500.00
	1816 GJ	—	150.00	275.00	475.00	600.00
	1817 GJ	—	150.00	275.00	475.00	600.00
	1818 GJ	—	125.00	150.00	200.00	300.00
	1819 GJ	—	125.00	150.00	200.00	300.00
	1820 CJ	—	125.00	125.00	175.00	250.00
	1822 AJ	—	150.00	275.00	475.00	600.00
	1823 AJ	—	150.00	300.00	500.00	750.00
	1824 AJ	—	125.00	125.00	175.00	250.00
	1825 AJ	—	125.00	125.00	175.00	250.00
	1826 AJ	—	135.00	175.00	250.00	350.00
	1827 AJ	—	135.00	200.00	300.00	450.00
	1828 AJ	—	135.00	225.00	350.00	500.00
	1829 AJ	—	125.00	125.00	175.00	250.00
	1830 AJ	—	125.00	125.00	175.00	250.00
	1831 AJ	—	125.00	125.00	175.00	250.00
	1832 AJ	—	125.00	125.00	175.00	250.00
	1833 AJ	—	125.00	125.00	175.00	250.00

Mint mark: S, S/L

C#	Date	Mintage	VG	Fine	VF	XF
143a.4	1815 CJ	—	125.00	125.00	175.00	225.00
	1816 CJ	—	125.00	125.00	175.00	225.00
	1817 CJ	—	135.00	175.00	250.00	350.00
	1818 CJ	—	125.00	125.00	175.00	225.00
	1819 CJ	—	125.00	125.00	175.00	225.00
	1820 CJ	—	125.00	125.00	175.00	225.00
	1821 CJ	—	125.00	150.00	200.00	300.00
	1824 JB	—	135.00	175.00	275.00	400.00
	1825 JB	—	125.00	125.00	175.00	225.00
	1826 JB	—	125.00	125.00	175.00	225.00
	1827 JB	—	125.00	125.00	175.00	225.00
	1828 JB	—	135.00	175.00	275.00	400.00
	1829 JB	—	135.00	175.00	275.00	400.00
	1830 JB	—	135.00	225.00	350.00	500.00
	1831 JB	—	125.00	125.00	175.00	225.00
	1832 JB	—	125.00	125.00	175.00	225.00
	1833 JB	—	125.00	125.00	175.00	225.00

Mint mark: Crowned C
Obv: Bare head

143a.5	1811 CI	—	175.00	350.00	500.00	800.00

Mint mark: S, S/L

143a.6	1809 CN	—	135.00	150.00	200.00	375.00

Mint mark: C
Obv: Bare head, military bust.

143a.7	1814 SF	—	450.00	900.00	1400.	2000.

Mint mark: Crowned C

143a.8	1811 CI	—	125.00	140.00	180.00	275.00
	1812 CJ	—	125.00	140.00	180.00	275.00
	1813 CJ	—	125.00	140.00	180.00	275.00
	1814 CJ	—	125.00	140.00	180.00	275.00

4 ESCUDOS

13.5400 g, .875 GOLD, .3809 oz AGW
Mint mark: Crowned M
Obv: Bust of Charles IV right.
Rev: Crowned arms in collar of The Golden Fleece.

75.1	1801 MF	—	300.00	600.00	850.00	1250.
	1801 FA	—	200.00	250.00	350.00	500.00
	1803 FA	—	225.00	300.00	425.00	600.00

Mint mark: S, S/L

75.2	1801 C	—	1000.	2200.	3000.	4500.
	1808 C	—	1000.	2200.	3000.	4500.

Mint mark: Crowned M

144	1814 GJ	—	225.00	400.00	550.00	800.00
	1815 GJ	—	225.00	350.00	500.00	700.00
	1816 GJ	—	300.00	600.00	800.00	1200.
	1818 GJ	—	225.00	400.00	550.00	800.00
	1819 GJ	—	225.00	350.00	500.00	700.00
	1820 GJ	—	200.00	250.00	350.00	500.00
	1824 AI	—	750.00	1500.	2100.	3000.

8 ESCUDOS

27.0700 g, .875 GOLD, .7616 oz AGW
Mint mark: Crowned M
Obv: Bust of Charles IV right.

76.1	1802 FA	—	450.00	700.00	1100.	1700.
	1803 FA	—	900.00	1700.	2500.	4000.
	1805 FA	—	550.00	1100.	1600.	2600.

Mint mark: Crowned C
Obv: Laureate uniformed bust of Ferdinand right.
Rev: Crowned arms.

C#	Date	Mintage	VG	Fine	VF	XF
145	1811 CI	—	750.00	1250.	3600.	6000.

Mint mark: C
Obv: Laureate head.

145a.1	1813 SF	—	2500.	5000.	7000.	10,000.
	1814 SF	—	3000.	6000.	8000.*	16,500.

*NOTE: Stack's CICF Sale 4-89, XF realized $16,500.

Mint mark: Crowned M

145a.2	1814 GJ	—	1000.	2000.	2800.	4000.
	1816 GJ	—	1500.	3000.	4200.	6000.
	1817 GJ	—	1100.	2250.	3100.	4500.
	1819 GJ	—	1800.	3500.	5000.	7500.
	1820 GJ	—	450.00	750.00	1540.	1870.

DE VELLON COINAGE

REAL

1.3500 g, .875 SILVER, .0392 oz ASW
Mint mark: Crowned M

88	1812 AI	—	17.50	45.00	95.00	145.00
	1813 RN	—	25.00	60.00	120.00	180.00

2 REALES

2.7050 g, .903 SILVER, .0787 oz ASW
Mint mark: Crowned M

89	1811 AI	—	40.00	100.00	200.00	300.00
	1812 AI	—	35.00	80.00	160.00	240.00
	1812 RN	—	25.00	60.00	120.00	180.00
	1813 RN	—	60.00	150.00	300.00	450.00

4 REALES

5.4100 g, .903 SILVER, .1573 oz ASW
Mint mark: Crowned M

90.1	1808 AI	—	25.00	65.00	130.	200.
	1809 AI	—	10.00	17.50	30.00	45.00
	1810 AI	—	7.50	12.50	22.50	35.00
	1811 AI	—	6.50	10.00	20.00	30.00
	1811 RS	—	20.00	50.00	100.00	150.00
	1812 AI	—	10.00	17.50	30.00	45.00
	1812 RS	—	25.00	40.00	80.00	120.00
	1812 RN	—	10.00	17.50	30.00	45.00
	1813 RN	—	12.50	25.00	47.50	70.00

SPAIN 1526

Mint mark: S, S/L

C#	Date	Mintage	VG	Fine	VF	XF
90.2	1810 LA	—	30.00	70.00	140.00	210.00
	1812 LA	—	12.50	30.00	60.00	90.00

Mint mark: B, BA

137.5	1822 SP	—	10.00	20.00	32.50	50.00
	1823 SP	—	12.50	30.00	60.00	90.00

Mint mark: Crowned M

137.6	1822 SR	—	12.50	27.50	55.00	85.00
	1823 SR	—	15.00	35.00	65.00	100.00

Mint mark: S, S/L

137.7	1823 RD	—	12.50	27.50	55.00	85.00

Mint mark: V, VAL.
Obv: Small bare head bust of Ferdinand right.

137.1	1823 R Spanish arms	—	10.00	20.00	35.00	55.00

10 REALES

13.5400 g, .903 SILVER, .3931 oz ASW
Mint mark: Crowned M

91	1809 AI	—	200.00	500.00	1000.	1500.
	1810 AI	—	120.00	300.00	600.00	900.00
	1811 AI	.058	60.00	150.00	300.00	475.00
	1812 AI	.490	35.00	80.00	160.00	250.00
	1812 RN Inc. Ab.	35.00	80.00	160.00	250.00
	1813 RN	.135	70.00	175.00	350.00	525.00

Mint mark: Bo

138.1	1821 UG	—	15.00	35.00	70.00	100.00

Mint mark: Crowned M

138.2	1821 SR	—	10.00	17.50	30.00	45.00

Mint mark: Sr

138.3	1821 LT	—	15.00	35.00	70.00	100.00

Mint mark: S, S/L

138.4	1821 RD	—	17.50	40.00	80.00	125.00

Mint mark: Crowned M

174.1	1840 CL	—	70.00	175.00	350.00	525.00
	1840 DG	—	225.00	600.00	1200.	1800.
	1841 CL	—	65.00	165.00	325.00	500.00
	1842 CL	—	70.00	175.00	350.00	525.00
	1843 CL	—	55.00	140.00	275.00	425.00
	1844 CL	—	70.00	175.00	350.00	525.00
	1845 CL	—	100.00	250.00	500.00	750.00

Mint mark: S, S/L

174.2	1841 RD	—	75.00	150.00	300.00	600.00
	1842 RD	—	75.00	150.00	300.00	600.00
	1843 RD	—	75.00	150.00	300.00	600.00

20 REALES

27.0800 g, .903 SILVER, .7863 oz ASW

Mint mark: B, BA

C#	Date	Mintage	VG	Fine	VF	XF
92.1	1811	—	75.00	180.00	360.00	550.00
	1812	—	110.00	275.00	550.00	850.00

Mint mark: Crowned M

92.2	1808 AI	.017	100.00	250.00	500.00	750.00
	1809 AI	.700	35.00	80.00	160.00	250.00
	1810 IA	.993	400.00	1000.	2000.	3000.
	1810 AI Inc. Ab.	30.00	75.00	150.00	225.00
	1811 AI	.460	30.00	75.00	150.00	225.00
	1812 AI	.250	65.00	140.00	275.00	425.00
	1813 RN	.068	100.00	240.00	480.00	725.00

Mint mark: S, S/L

92.3	1812 LA	.013	120.00	300.00	600.00	900.00

Mint mark: B, BA

139.1	1822 SP	—	120.00	300.00	1150.	1750.
	1823 SP	—	40.00	80.00	150.00	300.00

Mint mark: S, S/L

139.2	1822 RD	—	40.00	100.00	150.00	300.00
(139.3)	1823 RD	—	50.00	125.00	225.00	400.00

139a	1821 SR	—	400.00	1000.	2000.	3000.
(139.2)	1822 SR	—	25.00	50.00	100.00	175.00
	1823 SR	—	60.00	125.00	200.00	300.00

140	1833 DG	—	400.00	1000.	2000.	3000.

Obv. leg. ends: DIOS
Rev: Similar to C#175.1.

165	1834 DG	—	325.00	825.00	1650.	2500.
	1834 NC	4,769	200.00	500.00	1000.	1500.
	1835 CR	.013	160.00	400.00	800.00	1200.
	1836 CR	.048	125.00	325.00	650.00	1200.

C#	Date	Mintage	VG	Fine	VF	XF
175.1	1837 CR	.115	70.00	175.00	350.00	525.00
	1838 CL	.231	65.00	165.00	325.00	500.00
	1839 CL	.074	400.00	1000.	2000.	3000.
	1840 CL	6,012	650.00	1625.	3250.	5000.
	1847 DG	—	500.00	1250.	2500.	3750.
	1848 CL	.067	50.00	125.00	250.00	400.00
	1849 CL	.120	70.00	175.00	350.00	525.00
	1850 DG	—	500.00	1250.	2500.	3750.

Mint mark: S, S/L

175.2	1842 RD	.012	225.00	—	1000.	1500.

80 REALES

6.7700 g, .875 GOLD, .1905 oz AGW
Mint mark: Crowned M

94	1809 AI	—	100.00	150.00	250.00	375.00
	1810 AI	—	200.00	500.00	1000.	1500.

94a	1811 AI	.440	100.00	150.00	275.00	450.00
	1812 AI	.238	100.00	200.00	400.00	650.00
	1813 RN	.161	125.00	250.00	450.00	750.00

Mint mark: B, BA

146.1	1822 SP	—	125.00	250.00	500.00	800.00
	1823 SP	—	100.00	125.00	200.00	300.00

Mint mark: Crowned M

146.2	1822 SR	—	100.00	125.00	160.00	225.00
	1823 SR	—	100.00	135.00	225.00	350.00

Mint mark: S, S/L

146.3	1823 RD	—	140.00	300.00	600.00	900.00

Mint mark: B, BA
Obv. leg. ends: DIOS

166.1	1836 PS	—	400.00	1000.	2000.	3000.

Mint mark: Crowned M

166.2	1834 CR	—	100.00	125.00	175.00	275.00
	1835 CR	—	100.00	125.00	160.00	250.00
	1836 CL	—	100.00	125.00	200.00	325.00
	1836 CR	—	110.00	200.00	400.00	600.00

Mint mark: S, S/L

166.3	1835 DR	—	125.00	215.00	425.00	650.00
	1835 RD	—	110.00	175.00	350.00	525.00
	1836 DR	—	110.00	175.00	350.00	525.00
	1837 DR	—	110.00	175.00	350.00	525.00

Mint mark: B, BA

C#	Date	Mintage	VG	Fine	VF	XF
176.1	1836 PS	—	400.00	1000.	2000.	3000.
	1838 PS CONSTITUCION					
		—	100.00	125.00	225.00	350.00
	1838 PS CONST					
		—	110.00	200.00	400.00	600.00
	1839 PS CONSTITUCION					
		—	170.00	400.00	800.00	1200.
	1839 PS CONST					
		—	100.00	125.00	225.00	350.00
	1840 PS	—	100.00	125.00	150.00	225.00
	1841 PS	—	100.00	125.00	150.00	225.00
	1842 CC	—	100.00	125.00	200.00	300.00
	1842 PS	—	600.00	1500.	3000.	4500.
	1843 CC	—	450.00	1000.	2100.	3250.
	1843 PS	—	325.00	800.00	1600.	2400.
	1844 PS	—	100.00	125.00	200.00	300.00
	1845 PS	—	100.00	125.00	200.00	300.00
	1846 PS	—	100.00	125.00	180.00	275.00
	1847 PS	—	100.00	125.00	210.00	325.00
	1848 PS	—	150.00	325.00	625.00	950.00

Mint mark: Crowned M

176.2	1834 CR	—	100.00	125.00	180.00	275.00
	1835 CR	—	100.00	125.00	160.00	250.00
	1836 CL	—	100.00	125.00	250.00	400.00
	1836 CR	—	120.00	265.00	525.00	800.00
	1837 CR	—	135.00	320.00	625.00	950.00
	1838 CL	—	130.00	300.00	600.00	900.00
	1839 CL	—	135.00	325.00	650.00	1000.
	1840 CL	—	110.00	200.00	400.00	600.00
	1841 CL	—	100.00	165.00	325.00	500.00
	1842 CL	—	175.00	400.00	800.00	1200.
	1843 CL	—	100.00	125.00	180.00	275.00
	1844 CL	—	100.00	125.00	200.00	300.00
	1845 CL	—	100.00	125.00	160.00	250.00
	1846 CL	—	100.00	150.00	300.00	450.00
	1847 CL	—	110.00	200.00	400.00	600.00
	1848 CL	—	100.00	150.00	300.00	450.00
	1849 CL	—	200.00	500.00	1000.	1500.

Mint mark: S, S/L

176.3	1835 DR	—	110.00	220.00	425.00	650.00
	1835 RD	—	100.00	125.00	250.00	375.00
	1836 DR	—	100.00	175.00	350.00	500.00
	1837 DR	—	100.00	170.00	375.00	550.00
	1838 DR	—	130.00	300.00	600.00	900.00
	1838 RD	—	165.00	400.00	800.00	1200.
	1839 RD	—	100.00	150.00	300.00	475.00
	1840 RD	—	100.00	140.00	275.00	425.00
	1841 RD	—	100.00	150.00	300.00	450.00
	1842 RD	—	100.00	140.00	275.00	425.00
	1843 RD	—	100.00	150.00	300.00	450.00
	1844 RD	—	100.00	150.00	300.00	450.00
	1845 RD	—	100.00	125.00	225.00	350.00
	1846 RD	—	100.00	175.00	350.00	525.00
	1847 RD	—	100.00	165.00	325.00	500.00
	1848 RD	—	200.00	500.00	1000.	1600.

Mint mark: B, BA
Obv. leg. ends: CONSTITUCION

176a	1837 PS	—	110.00	250.00	500.00	750.00
	1838 PS	—	100.00	125.00	225.00	350.00

160 REALES

13.5400 g, .875 GOLD, .3809 oz AGW
Mint mark: Crowned M

147	1822 SR	—	250.00	400.00	650.00	1000.

320 REALES

27.0700 g, .875 GOLD, .7616 oz AGW

Mint mark: Crowned M

C#	Date	Mintage	VG	Fine	VF	XF
95	1810 AI	.064	1500.	3250.	6500.	10,000.
	1810 RS Inc. Ab.	1750.	4500.	9000.	13,750.	
	1812 RS	.060	1500.	3000.	6500.	9500.

148	1822 SR	—	600.00	1300.	2750.	4250.
	1823 SR	—	1100.	2400.	5000.	7500.

DECIMAL COINAGE
10 Decimos = 1 Real
100 Centimos = 1 Real

1/20 REAL

COPPER
Mint mark: Aqueduct

Y#	Date	Mintage	VG	Fine	VF	XF
15	1852	—	5.00	12.50	22.50	35.00
	1853	—	2.50	5.00	10.00	20.00

5 CENTIMOS

COPPER
Mint mark: Aqueduct

24	1854	—	90.00	225.00	400.00	650.00
	1855	—	5.00	12.50	22.50	35.00
	1856	—	2.00	4.50	7.50	12.50
	1857	—	2.25	5.50	9.00	15.00
	1858	—	10.00	25.00	40.00	70.00
	1859	—	2.00	4.50	7.50	12.50
	1860	—	2.50	6.50	11.00	18.00
	1861	—	3.50	9.00	15.00	25.00
	1862	—	3.50	9.00	15.00	25.00
	1863	—	2.50	6.50	11.00	18.00
	1864	—	5.00	12.50	22.50	35.00

1/10 REAL

COPPER
Mint mark: Aqueduct

16	1850	—	3.00	7.50	12.50	25.00
	1851	—	10.00	22.50	40.00	65.00
	1852	—	3.00	7.50	12.50	25.00
	1853	—	2.50	5.00	10.00	20.00

10 CENTIMOS

COPPER
Mint mark: Aqueduct

25	1854	—	100.00	250.00	450.00	750.00
	1855	—	5.00	12.50	21.00	35.00
	1856	—	2.75	7.00	12.00	20.00
	1857	—	2.00	4.50	7.50	12.50
	1858	—	5.00	12.50	21.00	35.00
	1859	—	2.00	4.50	7.50	12.50
	1860	—	2.00	4.50	7.50	12.50
	1861	—	2.50	6.50	11.00	18.00
	1862	—	2.75	7.00	12.00	20.00
	1863	—	3.50	9.00	15.00	25.00
	1864	—	8.50	21.00	35.00	60.00

1/5 REAL

COPPER
Mint mark: Aqueduct

Y#	Date	Mintage	VG	Fine	VF	XF
17	1853	—	10.00	22.50	35.00	60.00

25 CENTIMOS

COPPER
Mint mark: BA

26.1	1863	—	50.00	125.00	200.00	350.00
	1864	—	17.50	40.00	70.00	120.00

Mint mark: Aqueduct

26.2	1854	—	2.75	7.00	12.00	20.00
	1855	—	2.00	4.50	7.50	12.50
	1856	—	2.00	4.50	7.50	12.50
	1857	—	2.25	5.50	9.00	15.00
	1858	—	2.00	4.50	7.50	12.50
	1859	—	2.00	4.50	7.50	12.50
	1860	—	2.00	4.50	7.50	12.50
	1861	—	2.00	4.50	7.50	12.50
	1862	—	2.00	4.50	7.50	12.50
	1863	—	2.00	4.50	7.50	12.50
	1864	—	2.50	6.50	11.00	18.00

1/2 REAL

COPPER
Mint mark: 4-pointed star
Similar to 1/5 Real, Y#17.

18.1	1850	—	17.50	40.00	70.00	120.00

Mint mark: 6-pointed star

18.2	1848 DG	—	50.00	125.00	225.00	400.00
	1848	—	5.00	10.00	20.00	45.00

Mint mark: Aqueduct

18.3	1848	—	35.00	90.00	150.00	250.00
	1849	—	25.00	70.00	120.00	200.00
	1850	—	5.00	10.00	20.00	40.00
	1851	—	5.00	10.00	20.00	40.00
	1852	—	5.00	10.00	20.00	40.00
	1853	—	5.00	10.00	20.00	40.00

REAL

1.3146 g, .900 SILVER, .0380 oz ASW
Mint mark: 8-pointed star

19.1	1852	—	7.00	16.00	27.50	40.00
	1853	—	3.00	7.50	12.50	18.00
	1854	—	5.00	12.50	21.00	30.00
	1855	—	4.25	10.00	17.50	25.00

Mint mark: 6-pointed star

19.2	1852	—	2.00	5.00	8.00	14.00
	1853	—	5.00	12.50	21.00	30.00
	1854	—	14.00	35.00	60.00	85.00
	1855	—	14.00	35.00	60.00	85.00

Mint mark: 7-pointed star

19.3	1850	—	5.00	12.50	21.00	30.00
	1851	—	32.50	85.00	140.00	200.00
	1852	—	2.00	5.25	8.75	12.50
	1853	—	2.50	6.25	10.00	15.00
	1854	—	7.00	16.00	27.50	40.00
	1855	—	5.00	12.50	21.00	30.00

Mint mark: 8-pointed star

27.1	1857	—	4.25	10.00	17.50	25.00
	1858	—	5.00	12.50	21.00	30.00
	1859	—	10.00	25.00	40.00	60.00
	1860/59	—	3.25	8.50	14.00	20.00
	1860	—	3.25	8.50	14.00	20.00
	1861	—	3.25	8.50	14.00	20.00
	1862	—	6.00	15.00	25.00	35.00
	1863	—	7.00	16.00	27.50	40.00
	1864	—	10.00	25.00	40.00	60.00

Mint mark: 6-pointed star

SPAIN 1528

Y#	Date	Mintage	VG	Fine	VF	XF
27.2	1857	—	4.25	10.00	17.50	25.00
	1858	—	9.25	22.50	37.50	55.00
	1859	—	3.00	6.00	10.00	18.00
	1860	—	3.25	8.50	14.00	20.00
	1861	—	9.25	22.50	37.50	55.00
	1862	—	4.00	8.00	15.00	30.00
	1863	—	5.00	12.50	20.00	30.00
	1864	—	7.00	16.00	27.50	40.00

Mint mark: 7-pointed star

Y#	Date	Mintage	VG	Fine	VF	XF
27.3	1857	—	20.00	50.00	85.00	120.00
	1858	—	7.50	19.00	30.00	45.00
	1859	—	10.00	25.00	40.00	60.00
	1860	—	3.25	8.50	14.00	22.50
	1861	—	18.00	45.00	75.00	110.00
	1862	—	9.25	22.50	37.50	55.00
	1863	—	3.25	8.50	14.00	22.50
	1864	—	7.00	16.00	27.50	40.00

2 REALES

2.6291 g, .900 SILVER, .0761 oz ASW
Mint mark: 8-pointed star

Y#	Date	Mintage	VG	Fine	VF	XF
20.1	1852	—	12.50	21.00	35.00	50.00
	1853	—	5.00	12.50	17.50	30.00
	1854	—	18.00	45.00	75.00	110.00
	1855	—	12.50	21.00	35.00	50.00

Mint mark: 6-pointed star

Y#	Date	Mintage	VG	Fine	VF	XF
20.2	1851	—	50.00	125.00	200.00	300.00
	1852	—	10.00	25.00	40.00	60.00
	1853	—	6.00	15.00	25.00	35.00
	1854	—	6.00	15.00	25.00	35.00
	1855	—	5.00	12.50	21.00	30.00

Mint mark: 7-pointed star

Y#	Date	Mintage	VG	Fine	VF	XF
20.3	1850	—	12.50	30.00	50.00	75.00
	1851	—	55.00	135.00	225.00	325.00
	1852	—	5.00	12.50	21.00	30.00
	1853	—	3.00	7.50	12.50	18.00
	1854	—	5.00	12.50	21.00	30.00
	1855	—	5.00	12.50	21.00	30.00

Mint mark: 8-pointed star

Y#	Date	Mintage	VG	Fine	VF	XF
28.1	1857	—	4.25	10.00	17.50	25.00
	1858	—	10.00	25.00	60.00	120.00
	1860	—	7.50	19.00	30.00	45.00
	1861	—	7.50	19.00	30.00	45.00
	1862	—	22.50	55.00	95.00	140.00
	1863	—	40.00	100.00	175.00	250.00
	1864	—	65.00	165.00	275.00	400.00

Mint mark: 6-pointed star

Y#	Date	Mintage	VG	Fine	VF	XF
28.2	1857	—	10.00	25.00	40.00	60.00
	1859	—	4.50	8.50	14.00	20.00
	1860	—	16.00	40.00	70.00	100.00
	1861	—	4.25	10.00	17.50	25.00
	1862	—	4.50	8.50	14.00	20.00
	1863	—	16.00	40.00	70.00	100.00
	1864	—	30.00	70.00	120.00	175.00

Mint mark: 7-pointed star

Y#	Date	Mintage	VG	Fine	VF	XF
28.3	1857	—	20.00	40.00	80.00	120.00
	1858	—	13.00	32.50	55.00	80.00
	1859	—	15.00	37.50	60.00	90.00
	1860	—	7.50	19.00	30.00	45.00
	1861	—	5.00	12.50	21.00	30.00
	1862	—	12.50	21.00	35.00	50.00
	1863	—	5.00	12.50	21.00	30.00
	1864	—	10.00	25.00	40.00	60.00

4 REALES

5.2582 g, .900 SILVER, .1521 oz ASW
Mint mark: 8-pointed star

Y#	Date	Mintage	VG	Fine	VF	XF
21.1	1852	—	7.50	15.00	35.00	55.00
	1853	—	10.00	25.00	40.00	60.00
	1854	—	9.25	22.50	37.50	55.00
	1855	—	60.00	150.00	250.00	350.00

Mint mark: 6-pointed star

Y#	Date	Mintage	VG	Fine	VF	XF
21.2	1852	—	5.00	10.00	20.00	30.00
	1853	—	16.00	40.00	65.00	95.00
	1854	—	7.50	19.00	30.00	45.00
	1855	—	15.00	37.50	60.00	90.00

Mint mark: 7-pointed star

Y#	Date	Mintage	VG	Fine	VF	XF
21.3	1852	—	5.00	12.50	21.00	30.00
	1853	—	5.00	12.50	21.00	30.00
	1854	—	4.25	10.00	17.50	25.00
	1855	—	12.50	21.00	35.00	50.00

Mint mark: 8-pointed star

Y#	Date	Mintage	VG	Fine	VF	XF
29.1	1857	—	65.00	160.00	275.00	400.00
	1858	—	15.00	37.50	60.00	90.00
	1859	—	10.00	25.00	40.00	60.00
	1860	—	10.00	25.00	40.00	60.00
	1861	—	7.50	15.00	30.00	50.00
	1862	—	60.00	150.00	250.00	350.00
	1864	—	65.00	155.00	260.00	375.00

Mint mark: 6-pointed star

Y#	Date	Mintage	VG	Fine	VF	XF
29.2	1856	—	12.50	25.00	50.00	75.00
	1857	—	7.50	15.00	30.00	45.00
	1858	—	6.00	12.50	25.00	35.00
	1859	—	5.00	10.00	21.00	30.00
	1860	—	32.50	85.00	140.00	200.00
	1861	—	7.50	15.00	30.00	45.00
	1862	—	5.00	10.00	20.00	30.00
	1863	—	5.00	10.00	20.00	30.00
	1864	—	20.00	50.00	85.00	120.00

Mint mark: 7-pointed star

Y#	Date	Mintage	VG	Fine	VF	XF
29.3	1857	—	30.00	70.00	120.00	175.00
	1858	—	40.00	100.00	175.00	250.00
	1859	—	30.00	70.00	120.00	175.00
	1860	—	10.00	25.00	40.00	60.00
	1861	—	12.50	30.00	50.00	75.00
	1862	—	15.00	37.50	60.00	90.00
	1863	—	12.50	21.00	35.00	50.00
	1864	—	10.00	25.00	40.00	60.00

10 REALES

13.1455 g, .900 SILVER, .3804 oz ASW
Mint mark: 8-pointed star
Similar to 4 Reales, Y#21.

Y#	Date	Mintage	VG	Fine	VF	XF
22.1	1851	—	150.00	375.00	625.00	900.00
	1852	—	25.00	60.00	100.00	150.00
	1853	—	10.00	25.00	40.00	60.00
	1854	—	15.00	37.50	60.00	90.00
	1855	—	30.00	70.00	120.00	175.00

Mint mark: 6-pointed star

Y#	Date	Mintage	VG	Fine	VF	XF
22.2	1851	—	25.00	60.00	100.00	150.00
	1852	—	10.00	20.00	40.00	60.00
	1853	—	10.00	20.00	40.00	60.00
	1854	—	14.00	35.00	60.00	85.00
	1855	—	50.00	125.00	200.00	300.00

Mint mark: 7-pointed star

Y#	Date	Mintage	VG	Fine	VF	XF
22.3	1851	—	75.00	180.00	300.00	450.00
	1852	—	7.50	20.00	35.00	50.00
	1853	—	10.00	25.00	40.00	60.00
	1854	—	10.00	25.00	40.00	60.00
	1855	—	16.00	40.00	70.00	100.00
	1856	—	150.00	400.00	700.00	1000.

Mint mark: 8-pointed star

Y#	Date	Mintage	VG	Fine	VF	XF
30.1	1859	—	60.00	150.00	250.00	350.00
	1860	—	60.00	150.00	250.00	350.00
	1861	—	37.50	90.00	150.00	225.00
	1862	—	50.00	125.00	200.00	300.00
	1863	—	100.00	275.00	450.00	650.00
	1864	—	55.00	135.00	225.00	325.00

Mint mark: 6-pointed star

Y#	Date	Mintage	VG	Fine	VF	XF
30.2	1857	—	32.50	85.00	140.00	200.00
	1858	—	20.00	50.00	85.00	120.00
	1859	—	20.00	50.00	85.00	120.00
	1860	—	15.00	30.00	45.00	90.00
	1861	—	20.00	50.00	85.00	120.00
	1862	—	12.50	21.00	35.00	50.00
	1863	—	7.50	15.00	25.00	45.00
	1864	—	20.00	50.00	85.00	120.00
	1865	—	45.00	115.00	190.00	275.00

Mint mark: 7-pointed star

Y#	Date	Mintage	VG	Fine	VF	XF
30.3	1857	—	65.00	165.00	275.00	400.00
	1858	—	55.00	135.00	225.00	325.00
	1859	—	60.00	150.00	250.00	350.00
	1860	—	100.00	250.00	425.00	600.00
	1861	—	25.00	60.00	100.00	150.00
	1863	—	40.00	100.00	175.00	250.00
	1864	—	125.00	325.00	550.00	800.00

20 REALES

26.2910 g, .900 SILVER, .7607 oz ASW
Mint mark: Crowned M
Rev: Similar to C#140.

Y#	Date	Mintage	VG	Fine	VF	XF
13.1	1850 CL	.126	35.00	65.00	95.00	135.00
	1850 DG	—	400.00	1000.	1750.	2500.

Mint mark: 7-pointed star

Y#	Date	Mintage	VG	Fine	VF	XF
13.2	1850 RD	—	200.00	500.00	750.00	1000.

Mint mark: 8-pointed star

Y#	Date	Mintage	VG	Fine	VF	XF
23.1	1850	—	325.00	850.00	1400.	2000.
	1851	1.055	150.00	300.00	400.00	600.00
	1852	1.053	250.00	625.00	1000.	1500.

Mint mark: 6-pointed star

Y#	Date	Mintage	VG	Fine	VF	XF
23.2	1850	.500	20.00	40.00	70.00	115.00
	1851	Inc. Ab.	15.00	30.00	50.00	80.00
	1852	Inc. Ab.	30.00	70.00	110.00	165.00
	1854	1.355	17.50	35.00	65.00	100.00
	1855	1.229	17.50	35.00	65.00	100.00

Mint mark: 7-pointed star

Y#	Date	Mintage	VG	Fine	VF	XF
23.3	1850	—	325.00	850.00	1400.	2000.
	1851	Inc. Ab.	25.00	60.00	100.00	150.00
	1852	Inc. Ab.	25.00	60.00	100.00	150.00
	1853	—	400.00	1000.	1900.	2750.
	1854	Inc. Ab.	20.00	40.00	80.00	120.00
	1855	Inc. Ab.	20.00	40.00	90.00	150.00

Mint mark: 8-pointed star
Rev: Similar to Y#23.1.

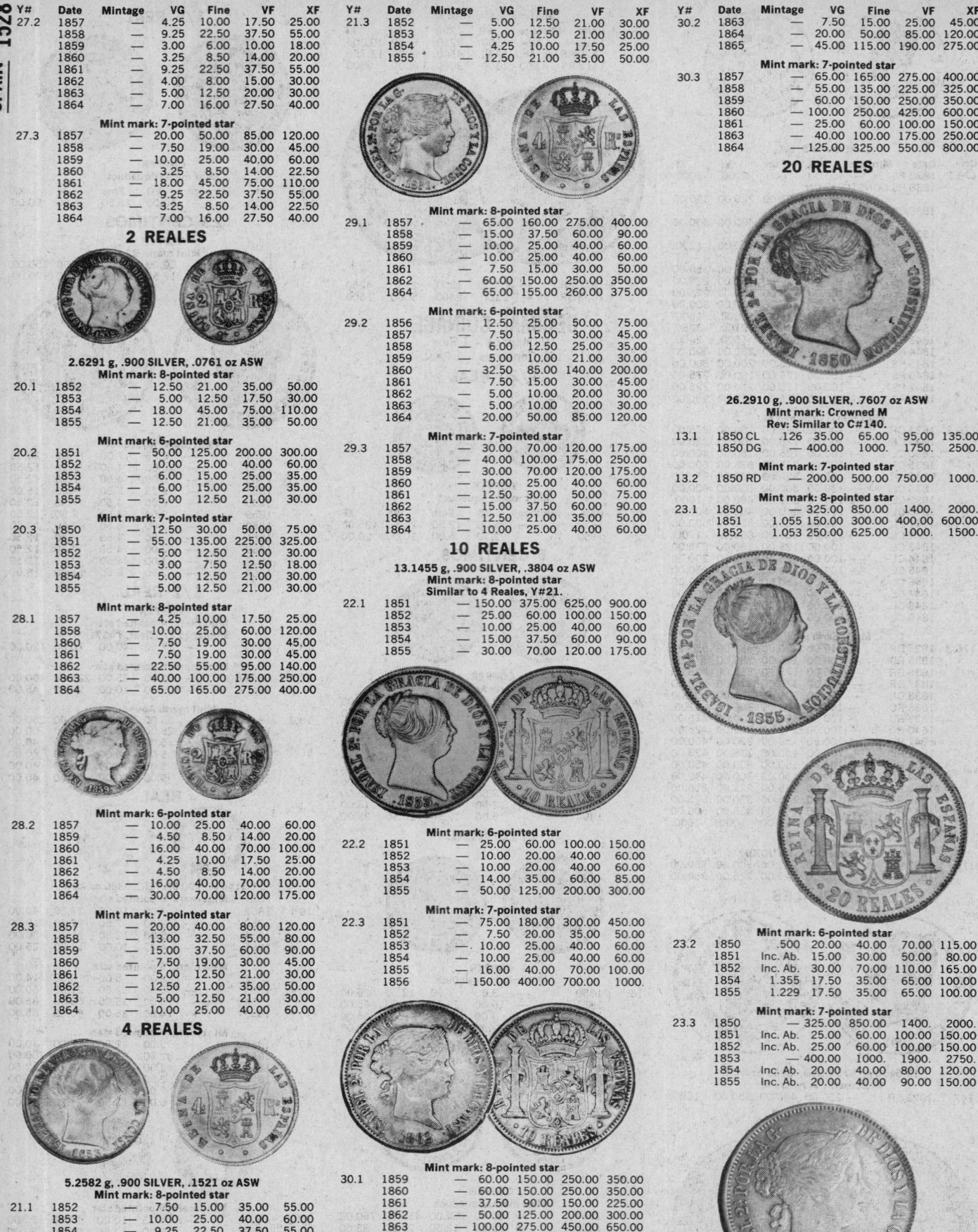

SPAIN 1529

Y#	Date	Mintage	VG	Fine	VF	XF
31.1	1857	.713	200.00	475.00	850.00	1250.
	1859	.880	240.00	600.00	1000.	1450.
	1862	1.594	400.00	1000.	1750.	2500.
	1863	.520	400.00	1000.	1750.	2500.

Mint mark: 6-pointed star

Y#	Date	Mintage	VG	Fine	VF	XF
31.2	1856	1.021	15.00	25.00	40.00	60.00
	1857	Inc. Ab.	12.50	20.00	40.00	60.00
	1858	1.626	15.00	30.00	50.00	75.00
	1859	Inc. Ab.	17.50	37.50	60.00	90.00
	1860	.941	17.50	40.00	70.00	100.00
	1861	1.352	12.50	20.00	40.00	60.00
	1862	Inc. Ab.	25.00	60.00	100.00	150.00
	1863	Inc. Ab.	60.00	140.00	250.00	350.00
	1864	2.776	20.00	50.00	85.00	120.00

Mint mark: 7-pointed star

Y#	Date	Mintage	VG	Fine	VF	XF
31.3	1856	Inc. Ab.	70.00	175.00	300.00	425.00
	1857	Inc. Ab.	30.00	70.00	120.00	175.00
	1858	Inc. Ab.	30.00	70.00	120.00	175.00
	1859	Inc. Ab.	70.00	175.00	300.00	425.00
	1860	Inc. Ab.	45.00	115.00	190.00	275.00
	1861	Inc. Ab.	75.00	190.00	300.00	450.00
	1862	Inc. Ab.	85.00	200.00	350.00	500.00
	1863	Inc. Ab.	85.00	200.00	325.00	475.00

1.6674 g, .900 GOLD, .0482 oz AGW
Mint mark: 6-pointed star
Similar to 40 Reales, Y#33.

Y#	Date	Mintage	VG	Fine	VF	XF
32	1857	—	200.00	500.00	825.00	1200.
	1861	—	40.00	85.00	140.00	200.00
	1862	—	175.00	400.00	700.00	1000.
	1863	—	425.00	1000.	1750.	2500.

40 REALES

3.3349 g, .900 GOLD, .0965 oz AGW
Mint mark: 8-pointed star

Y#	Date	Mintage	VG	Fine	VF	XF
33.1	1863	—	60.00	75.00	100.00	150.00
	1864	—	400.00	900.00	1500.	2200.

Mint mark: 6-pointed star

Y#	Date	Mintage	VG	Fine	VF	XF
33.2	1861	—	100.00	225.00	400.00	600.00
	1862	—	55.00	65.00	100.00	150.00
	1863	—	55.00	65.00	80.00	120.00

Obv: Draped bust of Isabel II left.
Rev: Crowned draped arms.

Y#	Date	Mintage	VG	Fine	VF	XF
A35.1	1864	—	55.00	65.00	75.00	120.00

Mint mark: 7-pointed star

Y#	Date	Mintage	VG	Fine	VF	XF
A35.2	1864	—	175.00	375.00	625.00	900.00

100 REALES

8.3371 g, .900 GOLD, .2412 oz AGW
Mint mark: 8-pointed star

Y#	Date	Mintage	VG	Fine	VF	XF
A23.1	1850 SM	—	400.00	850.00	1400.	2100.

Mint mark: 6-pointed star

Y#	Date	Mintage	VG	Fine	VF	XF
A23.2	1850 CL	—	125.00	150.00	200.00	300.00
	1850 DG	—	1500.	4000.	7000.	10,000
	1851 CL	—	200.00	500.00	825.00	1200.

Mint mark: 7-pointed star

Y#	Date	Mintage	VG	Fine	VF	XF
A23.3	1850 RD	—	400.00	900.00	1500.	2200.

Mint mark: 8-pointed star

Y#	Date	Mintage	VG	Fine	VF	XF
B23.1	1851	—	700.00	1500.	2750.	4000.
	1854	—	125.00	175.00	250.00	350.00
	1855	—	125.00	150.00	200.00	300.00

Mint mark: 6-pointed star

Y#	Date	Mintage	VG	Fine	VF	XF
B23.2	1851	—	700.00	1500.	2500.	3750.
	1852	—	550.00	1200.	2000.	3000.
	1854	—	125.00	150.00	250.00	375.00
	1855	—	125.00	150.00	175.00	275.00

Mint mark: 7-pointed star

Y#	Date	Mintage	VG	Fine	VF	XF
B23.3	1851	—	1250.	3000.	5000.	7500.
	1852	—	600.00	1400.	2500.	3500.
	1854	—	125.00	150.00	200.00	300.00
	1855	—	125.00	140.00	160.00	225.00

Mint mark: 8-pointed star
Similar to 2 Reales, C#33.

Y#	Date	Mintage	VG	Fine	VF	XF
35.1	1856	—	250.00	600.00	1100.	1650.
	1857	—	125.00	145.00	175.00	275.00
	1858	—	125.00	165.00	275.00	400.00
	1859	—	125.00	140.00	150.00	200.00
	1860	—	125.00	140.00	150.00	200.00
	1861	—	250.00	525.00	900.00	1350.
	1862	—	175.00	350.00	475.00	350.00

Mint mark: 6-pointed star

Y#	Date	Mintage	VG	Fine	VF	XF
35.2	1856	—	125.00	140.00	150.00	175.00
	1857	—	175.00	400.00	650.00	950.00
	1858	—	125.00	175.00	300.00	450.00
	1859	—	125.00	140.00	160.00	225.00
	1860	—	125.00	135.00	145.00	175.00
	1861	—	125.00	135.00	145.00	175.00
	1862	—	125.00	135.00	145.00	175.00

Mint mark: 7-pointed star

Y#	Date	Mintage	VG	Fine	VF	XF
35.3	1856	—	250.00	600.00	1100.	1650.
	1857	—	125.00	135.00	150.00	225.00
	1858	—	125.00	150.00	250.00	375.00
	1859	—	125.00	135.00	150.00	200.00
	1860	—	125.00	135.00	150.00	200.00
	1861	—	125.00	135.00	150.00	175.00
	1862	—	125.00	135.00	150.00	175.00

Mint mark: 6-pointed star
Rev: Crowned and mantled rectangluar arms.

Y#	Date	Mintage	VG	Fine	VF	XF
B35.1	1863	—	125.00	135.00	160.00	200.00
	1864	—	125.00	135.00	145.00	175.00

Mint mark: 7-pointed star

Y#	Date	Mintage	VG	Fine	VF	XF
B35.2	1863	—	175.00	375.00	625.00	900.00
	1864	—	175.00	400.00	700.00	1000.

SECOND DECIMAL COINAGE

100 Centimos = 1 Escudo

NOTE: For similar coins, with denominations expressed Cs. de Peso, see Philippines.

1/2 CENTIMO

COPPER
Mint mark: 8-pointed star

Y#	Date	Mintage	VG	Fine	VF	XF
36.1	1866 OM	—	5.00	12.50	21.00	35.00
	1867 OM	—	2.25	5.50	9.00	15.00
	1868 OM	—	2.25	5.50	9.00	15.00

Mint mark: 4-pointed star

Y#	Date	Mintage	VG	Fine	VF	XF
36.2	1866 OM	—	3.50	9.00	15.00	25.00
	1867 OM	—	2.25	5.50	9.00	15.00
	1868 OM	—	1.50	3.50	6.00	10.00

Mint mark: 6-pointed star

Y#	Date	Mintage	VG	Fine	VF	XF
36.3	1865	—	45.00	115.00	200.00	325.00
	1867 OM	—	18.00	45.00	75.00	125.00

Mint mark: 3-pointed star

Y#	Date	Mintage	VG	Fine	VF	XF
36.4	1866 OM	—	2.25	5.50	9.00	15.00
	1867 OM	—	2.00	4.00	7.00	12.50
	1868 OM	—	4.00	9.00	12.50	20.00

Mint mark: 7-pointed star

Y#	Date	Mintage	VG	Fine	VF	XF
36.5	1867 OM	—	6.00	14.00	25.00	40.00
	1868 OM	—	3.50	9.00	15.00	25.00

CENTIMO

COPPER
Mint mark: 8-pointed star

Y#	Date	Mintage	VG	Fine	VF	XF
37.1	1866	—	6.00	14.00	25.00	40.00
	1866 OM	—	3.50	7.00	10.00	15.00
	1867 OM	—	3.50	7.00	10.00	15.00
	1868 OM	—	2.00	4.00	7.00	12.50

Mint mark: 4-pointed star

Y#	Date	Mintage	VG	Fine	VF	XF
37.2	1866	—	8.50	21.00	35.00	60.00
	1866 OM	—	6.00	14.00	25.00	40.00
	1867 OM	—	4.50	11.00	18.00	30.00
	1868 OM	—	1.50	3.50	6.00	10.00

Mint mark: 6-pointed star

Y#	Date	Mintage	VG	Fine	VF	XF
37.3	1865	—	55.00	150.00	250.00	400.00

Mint mark: 3-pointed star

Y#	Date	Mintage	VG	Fine	VF	XF
37.4	1866	—	6.00	14.00	25.00	40.00
	1866 OM	—	4.00	8.00	16.00	30.00
	1867	—	20.00	50.00	90.00	150.00
	1867 OM	—	2.25	5.50	9.00	15.00
	1868 OM	—	2.25	5.50	9.00	15.00

Mint mark: 7-pointed star

Y#	Date	Mintage	VG	Fine	VF	XF
37.5	1867 OM	—	2.00	5.00	9.00	15.00
	1868 OM	—	2.00	5.00	9.00	15.00

2-1/2 CENTIMOS

COPPER
Mint mark: 8-pointed star

Y#	Date	Mintage	VG	Fine	VF	XF
38.1	1866	—	2.75	7.00	12.00	20.00
	1866 OM	—	2.75	7.00	12.00	20.00
	1867 OM	—	2.00	5.00	8.00	12.50
	1868 OM	—	2.00	5.00	8.00	12.50

Mint mark: 4-pointed star

Y#	Date	Mintage	VG	Fine	VF	XF
38.2	1866 OM	—	10.00	25.00	45.00	75.00
	1867 OM	—	2.00	4.50	7.50	12.50
	1868 OM	—	2.00	4.50	7.50	12.50

Mint mark: 6-pointed star

Y#	Date	Mintage	VG	Fine	VF	XF
38.3	1865	—	65.00	175.00	275.00	475.00
	1867 OM	—	17.50	40.00	70.00	120.00

Mint mark: 3-pointed star

Y#	Date	Mintage	VG	Fine	VF	XF
38.4	1866 OM	—	25.00	60.00	100.00	175.00
	1867 OM	—	2.50	6.50	11.00	18.00
	1868 OM	—	2.00	4.50	7.50	12.50

Mint mark: 7-pointed star

Y#	Date	Mintage	VG	Fine	VF	XF
38.5	1867 OM	—	2.00	4.50	7.50	12.50
	1868 OM	—	2.75	7.00	12.00	20.00

5 CENTIMOS

COPPER
Mint mark: 8-pointed star

Y#	Date	Mintage	VG	Fine	VF	XF
39.1	1866	—	10.00	25.00	40.00	70.00
	1866 OM	—	7.00	18.00	30.00	50.00
	1867	—	75.00	175.00	300.00	525.00
	1867 OM	—	2.00	4.50	7.50	12.50
	1868 OM	—	2.00	4.50	7.50	12.50

Mint mark: 4-pointed star

Y#	Date	Mintage	VG	Fine	VF	XF
39.2	1866	—	8.50	21.00	35.00	60.00
	1867 OM	—	2.00	4.50	7.50	12.50
	1868 OM	—	3.50	9.00	15.00	25.00

Mint mark: 6-pointed star

Y#	Date	Mintage	VG	Fine	VF	XF
39.3	1865	—	80.00	200.00	325.00	550.00

Mint mark: 3-pointed star

Y#	Date	Mintage	VG	Fine	VF	XF
39.4	1866 OM	—	3.50	9.00	15.00	25.00
	1867 OM	—	3.50	9.00	15.00	25.00
	1868 OM	—	2.50	6.50	11.00	18.00

Mint mark: 7-pointed star

Y#	Date	Mintage	VG	Fine	VF	XF
39.5	1867 OM	—	4.50	11.00	18.00	30.00
	1868 OM	—	2.00	4.50	7.50	12.50

SPAIN

10 CENTIMOS
1.2980 g, .810 SILVER, .0338 oz ASW
Mint mark: 6-pointed star
Similar to 20 Centimos, Y#41.

Y#	Date	Mintage	VG	Fine	VF	XF
40.1	1865	—	5.00	12.50	21.00	30.00
	1866	—	12.00	30.00	50.00	70.00
	1867	—	100.00	250.00	425.00	600.00
	1868 (68)	—	5.00	12.50	21.00	30.00

Mint mark: 7-pointed star

40.2	1864	—	16.00	40.00	65.00	95.00
	1865	—	5.00	12.50	20.00	30.00
	1866	—	12.50	21.00	35.00	50.00
	1868	—	60.00	150.00	275.00	400.00

20 CENTIMOS

2.5960 g, .810 SILVER, .0676 oz ASW
Mint mark: 6-pointed star

41.1	1864	—	25.00	60.00	100.00	150.00
	1865	—	7.00	16.00	27.50	40.00
	1866	—	50.00	125.00	200.00	300.00
	1867	—	75.00	175.00	300.00	450.00
	1868 (68)	—	3.50	8.50	14.00	20.00

Mint mark: 7-pointed star

41.2	1864	—	9.00	22.50	37.50	55.00
	1865	—	10.00	25.00	40.00	60.00
	1866	—	12.00	30.00	50.00	70.00

40 CENTIMOS

5.1920 g, .810 SILVER, .1352 oz ASW
Mint mark: 8-pointed star

42.1	1865	—	80.00	200.00	350.00	500.00

Mint mark: 6-pointed star

42.2	1864	—	12.50	21.00	35.00	50.00
	1865	—	5.00	10.00	12.50	25.00
	1866	—	3.50	7.50	12.50	25.00
	1867	—	3.50	7.50	12.50	20.00
	1868 (68)	—	3.50	7.50	12.50	20.00

Mint mark: 7-pointed star

42.3	1864	—	60.00	150.00	250.00	350.00
	1865	—	7.50	19.00	30.00	45.00
	1866	—	6.00	12.50	22.50	35.00

ESCUDO

12.9800 g, .900 SILVER, .3756 oz ASW
Mint mark: 6-pointed star

43.1	1864	—	20.00	50.00	85.00	120.00
	1865	—	16.00	40.00	65.00	95.00
	1866	—	16.00	40.00	65.00	95.00
	1867	—	6.50	12.50	22.50	35.00
	1868 (68)	—	6.00	10.00	15.00	25.00

Mint mark: 7-pointed star

43.2	1864	—	100.00	250.00	425.00	600.00
	1866	—	75.00	175.00	300.00	450.00

2 ESCUDOS
25.9600 g, .900 SILVER, .7512 oz ASW
Mint mark: 6-pointed star
Obv: Head of Isabel II right.
Rev: Crowned arms between pillars.

44	1865	—	800.00	2000.	3750.	5500.
	1866	—	1000.	2250.	4000.	6000.
	1867	4.234	12.50	25.00	40.00	70.00
	1868(68)	2.225	25.00	60.00	100.00	150.00

1.6774 g, .900 GOLD, .0485 oz AGW

Y#	Date	Mintage	Fine	VF	XF	Unc
45	1865	—	35.00	60.00	100.00	175.00
	1867	—	400.00	800.00	1350.	2000.00
	1868 (68)	—	300.00	600.00	1000.	1500.

4 ESCUDOS

3.3548 g, .900 GOLD, .0971 oz AGW
Mint mark: 6-pointed star

46.1	1865	—	55.00	70.00	90.00	140.00
	1866	—	55.00	70.00	90.00	140.00
	1867	—	55.00	65.00	80.00	120.00
	1868 (68)	—	75.00	100.00	140.00	225.00

Mint mark: 7-pointed star

46.2	1865	—	275.00	550.00	950.00	1300.
	1866	—	250.00	500.00	900.00	1200.

10 ESCUDOS

8.3870 g, .900 GOLD, .2427 oz AGW
Mint mark: 6-pointed star

47.1	1866	—	250.00	400.00	650.00	950.00
	1867	—	125.00	200.00	325.00	450.00
	1868 (68)	—	125.00	150.00	175.00	250.00

PLATINUM (OMS)

| 47.1a | 1868(68) | | | | | |

8.3870 g, .900 GOLD, .2427 oz AGW
Mint mark: 7-pointed star

| 47.2 | 1865 | — | 1500. | 3500. | 6000. | 8500. |

Mint mark: 6-pointed star

| 47.3 | 1868 (73) | — | 125.00 | 160.00 | 200.00 | 300.00 |

NOTE: This coin issued during the First Republic.

PROVISIONAL COINAGE
25 MILESIMAS DE ESCUDO

BRONZE
Battle of Alcolea Bridge.
Mint mark: 3-pointed star

| A50 | 1868 | .010 | 60.00 | 120.00 | 250.00 | 500.00 |

THIRD DECIMAL COINAGE
10 Milesimas = 1 Centimo
100 Centimos = 1 Peseta

CENTIMO

COPPER
Mint mark: 8-pointed star

| 51 | 1870 OM | 169.891 | .35 | .50 | 1.50 | 8.50 |

BRONZE
Mint mark: 6-pointed star

96	1906(6) SLV					
		7.500	.35	.75	1.50	4.00
	1906(6) SMV I.A.	75.00	150.00	250.00	500.00	

98	1911(1) PCV					
		1.462	3.50	7.00	20.00	50.00
	1912(2) PCV					
		2.109	.75	1.00	1.50	6.50

Y#	Date	Mintage	Fine	VF	XF	Unc
98	1913(3) PCV					
		1.429	1.00	1.75	4.00	10.00

2 CENTIMOS

COPPER
Mint mark: 8-pointed star

| 52 | 1870 OM | 115.869 | .35 | .75 | 2.50 | 9.00 |

BRONZE
Mint mark: 6-pointed star

97	1904(04) SMV					
		10.000	.35	.75	2.00	8.00
	1905(05) SMV					
		5.000	.35	.75	2.00	8.00

99	1911(11) PCV					
		2.284	.35	.75	2.00	5.00
	1912(12) PCV					
		5.216	.35	.50	1.50	4.50

5 CENTIMOS

COPPER
Mint mark: 8-pointed star

| 53 | 1870 OM | 287.381 | 2.00 | 7.50 | 15.00 | 75.00 |

Charles VII - Pretender Issue

| 66 | 1875(b) | .050 | 18.00 | 30.00 | 50.00 | 75.00 |

BRONZE

69	1877 OM	34.376	.75	3.50	12.00	60.00
	1878 OM	67.954	.75	3.50	12.00	60.00
	1879 OM	54.994	.75	3.50	12.00	60.00

IRON
Mint mark: 6-pointed star

| 103 | 1937 | 10.000 | .35 | 1.00 | 3.00 | 25.00 |

1530

ALUMINUM

Y#	Date	Mintage	Fine	VF	XF	Unc
110	1940	175.000	.10	.15	.75	10.00
	1941	202.107	.10	.15	.25	7.50
	1945	221.500	.10	.15	.25	3.00
	1953	31.573	.15	.25	.90	12.50

10 CENTIMOS

COPPER
Mint mark: 8-pointed star

54.1	1869	—			Rare	—
54.2	1870 OM	170.088	2.00	7.50	20.00	100.00

Charles VII - Pretender Issue

| 67 | 1875(b) | .100 | 15.00 | 25.00 | 50.00 | 75.00 |

BRONZE

70	1877 OM	29.567	.35	3.50	17.50	75.00
	1878 OM	68.740	.35	3.50	17.50	70.00
	1879 OM	56.313	.35	5.00	25.00	95.00

IRON

| A103 | 1938 | 1.000 | 350.00 | 550.00 | 800.00 | 2000. |

ALUMINUM
Mint mark: 6-pointed star

111	1940	225.000	.15	.50	1.00	12.50
	1941	247.981	.10	.20	.75	7.00
	1945	250.000	.10	.40	.90	4.00
	1953	865.850	.10	.40	.90	3.00

NOTE: Varieties exist.

| 121 | 1959 | 900.000 | — | — | — | .10 |
| | 1959 | .101 | | | Proof | 1.50 |

20 CENTIMOS
1.0000 g, .835 SILVER, .0268 oz ASW
Mint mark: 6-pointed star
Similar to 50 Centimos, Y#56.

Y#	Date	Mintage	Fine	VF	XF	Unc
55	1869(69) SNM	91 pcs.	1100.	1800.	2750.	6000.
	1870(70) SNM	5,000	100.00	200.00	400.00	800.00

25 CENTIMOS

NICKEL-BRASS
Mint mark: 6-pointed star

| 100 | 1925 PCS | 8.001 | .35 | .75 | 2.50 | 12.00 |

COPPER-NICKEL

| 101 | 1927 PCS | 12.000 | .20 | .50 | 1.75 | 7.50 |

| 107 | 1934 | 12.272 | .20 | .50 | 1.75 | 6.00 |

Vienna Mint

| 109 | 1937 | 42.000 | .20 | .40 | 1.50 | 6.00 |

COPPER

| 104 | 1938 | 45.500 | .75 | 2.00 | 5.00 | 15.00 |

50 CENTIMOS

2.5000 g, .835 SILVER, .0671 oz ASW
Mintmark: 6-pointed star

| 56 | 1869(69) SNM | .453 | 10.00 | 20.00 | 100.00 | 325.00 |
| | 1870(70) SNM | .540 | 20.00 | 40.00 | 250.00 | 900.00 |

| A76 | 1880(80) MSM | 2.787 | 1.50 | 3.00 | 15.00 | 75.00 |
| | 1881(81) MSM | 5.647 | 1.50 | 3.00 | 20.00 | 100.00 |

Y#	Date	Mintage	Fine	VF	XF	Unc
A76	1885(85) MSM	—	7.50	15.00	40.00	120.00
	1885/1(86) MSM	1.468	3.50	8.00	25.00	120.00
	1885(86) MSM Inc. Ab.		1.50	4.00	15.00	80.00

79	1889(89) MPM	.537	5.00	10.00	35.00	100.00
	1892/89(92) PGM	3.954	2.00	5.00	15.00	50.00
	1892(92) PGM Inc. Ab.		1.00	2.50	10.00	40.00
	1892(22) PGM	—	8.00	17.50	32.50	80.00
	1892/82(82) PGM	—	10.00	20.00	50.00	120.00
	1892(82) PGM	—	10.00	20.00	50.00	120.00
	1892(92) PGM	—	15.00	27.50	65.00	150.00
	1892(62) PGM	—	17.50	35.00	100.00	200.00
	1892(62) PGM/MPM	—	—	—	—	—

NOTE: Varieties exist.

| 83 | 1894(94) PGV | 1.109 | 3.00 | 9.00 | 35.00 | 110.00 |

| 87 | 1896(96) PGV | .297 | 15.00 | 32.50 | 100.00 | 250.00 |
| | 1900(00) SMV | 2.128 | 1.00 | 3.00 | 10.00 | 30.00 |

| 92 | 1904(04) SMV | 4.851 | .75 | 2.25 | 5.00 | 20.00 |
| | 1904(10) PCV | 1.303 | .75 | 2.25 | 5.00 | 25.00 |

| 93 | 1910(10) PCV | 4.526 | .75 | 2.25 | 5.00 | 25.00 |

| 102 | 1926 PCS | 4.000 | .75 | 2.25 | 5.00 | 15.00 |

COPPER

105	1937(34)	50.000	.35	1.00	2.00	7.50
	1937(36)	1.000	.35	1.50	3.50	10.00
	1937 w/o dates in stars Inc. Ab.		—	—	—	—
	1937 w/o stars Inc. Ab.		2.00	3.50	7.50	20.00

NOTE: Several varieties exist.

SPAIN 1532

COPPER-NICKEL
Rev: Arrows pointing down.

Y#	Date	Mintage	Fine	VF	XF	Unc
115	1949(51)	.990	1.00	2.00	3.00	12.50

Rev: Arrows pointing up.

Y#	Date	Mintage	Fine	VF	XF	Unc
116	1949(51)	8.010	.10	.25	1.00	5.00
	1949(E51)	5.000	75.00	150.00	325.00	700.00
	1949(52)	18.567	.10	.15	1.00	5.00
	1949(53)	17.500	.10	.15	1.00	5.00
	1949(54)	37.000	.10	.15	.75	4.00
	1949(56)	38.000	.10	.15	.75	4.00
	1949(62)	31.000	—	.15	.50	1.00
	1963(63)	4.000	.10	.15	1.50	6.00
	1963(64)	20.000	—	.10	.15	.50
	1963(65)	14.000	—	.10	.15	.50

NOTE: Issued to commemorate a numismatic exposition December 2, 1951. An E replaces the 19 on the lower star.

ALUMINUM

Y#	Date	Mintage	Fine	VF	XF	Unc
124	1966(67)	80.000	—	—	.10	.50
	1966(68)	100.000	—	—	.10	.50
	1966(69)	50.000	—	—	.10	.50
	1966(70)	.023	—	—	6.00	14.00
	1966(71)	99.000	—	—	.10	.50
	1966(72)	2.283	—	—	.10	1.00
	1966(72)	.023	—	—	Proof	4.00
	1966(73)	10.000	—	—	.10	.50
	1966(73)	.028	—	—	Proof	5.00
	1966(74)	—	—	—	.10	.50
	1966(74)	.025	—	—	Proof	6.50
	1966(75)	.075	—	—	Proof	2.00

Y#	Date	Mintage	Fine	VF	XF	Unc
126	1975(76)	4.060	—	—	—	—
	1975(76)	—	—	—	Proof	2.00

NOTE: Recalled from circulation.

World Cup Soccer Games

Y#	Date	Mintage	Fine	VF	XF	Unc
132	1980(80)	15.000	—	—	.10	.50

PESETA

5.0000 g, .835 SILVER, .1342 oz ASW
Mint mark: 6-pointed star
Obv. leg: GOBIERNO PROVISIONAL

Y#	Date	Mintage	Fine	VF	XF	Unc
A55	1869(69) SNM	7.000	3.50	15.00	90.00	300.00

Obv. leg: ESPANA

Y#	Date	Mintage	Fine	VF	XF	Unc
58	1869(69) SNM	.367	30.00	220.00	850.00	2250.
	1870(70) SNM	3.865	7.50	30.00	160.00	450.00
	1870(73) DEM	5.165	4.00	25.00	145.00	350.00

Y#	Date	Mintage	Fine	VF	XF	Unc
B75	1876(76) DEM	4.427	3.50	30.00	160.00	450.00

Y#	Date	Mintage	Fine	VF	XF	Unc
B76	1881(81) MSM	.799	18.00	100.00	525.00	1250.
	1882/81(82) MSM	—	10.00	75.00	325.00	750.00
	1882(82) MSM	3.506	3.50	15.00	185.00	500.00
	1883(83) MSM	8.440	3.00	15.00	120.00	350.00
	1884/3(84) MSM	5,839	250.00	525.00	1650.	4500.
	1885(85) MSM	3.336	3.50	15.00	185.00	500.00
	1885(86) MSM	3.954	3.50	12.50	145.00	450.00

Y#	Date	Mintage	Fine	VF	XF	Unc
80	1889(89) MPM	.760	35.00	85.00	265.00	1250.
	1891(91) PGM	4.948	3.00	15.00	60.00	250.00

Y#	Date	Mintage	Fine	VF	XF	Unc
84	1893(93) PGL	1.958	5.50	18.00	145.00	450.00
	1894(94) PGV	1.044	18.00	65.00	200.00	800.00

Y#	Date	Mintage	Fine	VF	XF	Unc
88	1896(96) PGV	6.412	2.50	7.00	20.00	90.00
	1899(99) SGV	7.472	2.50	7.00	20.00	80.00
	1900(00) SMV	18.650	2.00	5.00	15.00	70.00
	1901(01) SMV	8.449	2.00	6.00	20.00	80.00
	1902(02) SMV	2.599	7.50	15.00	40.00	150.00

Y#	Date	Mintage	Fine	VF	XF	Unc
94	1903(03) SMV	10.602	2.00	5.50	20.00	65.00
	1904(04) SMV	5.294	2.00	6.00	30.00	90.00
	1904(05) SMV	—	—	—	—	—
	1905(05) SMV	.492	30.00	70.00	280.00	800.00

Y#	Date	Mintage	Fine	VF	XF	Unc
108	1933(3-4)	2.000	2.00	3.50	7.50	20.00

NOTE: Several varieties exist.

BRASS

Y#	Date	Mintage	Fine	VF	XF	Unc
106	1937	50.000	.50	1.00	2.00	5.00

ALUMINUM-BRONZE

Y#	Date	Mintage	Fine	VF	XF	Unc
112	1944	150.000	.15	.65	2.00	10.00
	1946(48)	—	50.00	75.00	165.00	350.00

Y#	Date	Mintage	Fine	VF	XF	Unc
113	1947(48)	15.000	.15	.50	2.00	12.50
	1947(49)	27.600	.15	.40	1.00	15.00
	1947(50)	4.000	.25	1.00	4.00	25.00
	1947(51)	9.185	.15	.75	3.00	10.00
	1947(E51)	5,000	75.00	150.00	325.00	700.00
	1947(52)	19.195	.10	.20	.50	4.00
	1947(53)	34.000	.10	.20	.50	4.00
	1947(54)	50.000	.10	.20	.50	4.00
	1947(56)	—	1.50	4.50	12.50	100.00
	1953(54)	40.272	.10	.20	.50	4.00
	1953(56)	118.000	—	.10	.25	2.00
	1953(60)	45.160	—	.10	.20	4.00
	1953(61)	25.830	—	.10	.25	3.00
	1953(62)	66.252	—	.10	.20	1.50
	1953(63)	37.000	—	.10	.25	3.00
	1963(63)	36.000	—	.10	.25	1.50
	1963(64)	80.000	—	.10	.20	.75
	1963(65)	70.000	—	.10	.35	.75
	1963(66)	63.000	—	.10	.20	.75
	1963(67)	11.300	—	.10	.25	6.00

NOTE: Issued to commemorate a numismatic exposition December 2, 1951. An E replaces 19 on the lower star.

Y#	Date	Mintage	Fine	VF	XF	Unc
125	1966(67)	59.000	—	.10	.20	.50
	1966(68)	120.000	—	.10	.20	.50
	1966(69)	120.000	—	.10	.20	.50
	1966(70)	75.000	—	.10	.20	.50
	1966(71)	115.270	—	.10	.20	.50
	1966(72)	106.000	—	.10	.20	.50
	1966(72)	.023	—	—	Proof	6.00
	1966(73)	152.000	—	.10	.20	.50

Y#	Date	Mintage	Fine	VF	XF	Unc
125	1966(73)	.028	—	—	Proof	7.00
	1966(74)	181.000	—	—	.10	.20
	1966(74)	.025	—	—	Proof	8.50
	1966(75)	227.580	—	—	.10	.20
	1966(75)	.025	—	—	Proof	2.50

127	1975(76)	170.380	—	—	.10	.25
	1975(76)	—	—	—	Proof	2.00
	1975(77)	247.370	—	—	.10	.25
	1975(77)	Inc. Ab.	—	—	Proof	2.00
	1975(78)	*604.000	—	—	.10	.25
	1975(79)	507.000	—	—	.10	.25
	1975(79)	—	—	—	Proof	1.00
	1975(80)	545.000	—	—	.10	.25

*NOTE: Two varieties exist of this date.

World Cup Soccer Games

133	1980(80)	200.000	—	—	.10	.25
	1980(81)	200.000	—	—	.10	.25
	1980(82)	—	—	—	.10	.25

ALUMINUM
Mint mark: Crowned M
Circulation Coins

140.1	1982	—	—	—	.10	.20
(140)	1983	—	—	—	.10	.20
	1984	—	—	—	.10	.20
	1985	—	—	—	.10	.15
	1986	—	—	—	—	.10
	1987	50.000	—	—	—	.10
	1988	—	—	—	—	.10

Madrid Numismatic Exposition

| 140.2 | 1987 | .060 | — | — | Proof | 15.00 |

2 PESETAS

10.0000 g, .835 SILVER, .2685 oz ASW
Mint mark: 6-pointed star

59	1869(68) SNM	—	17.50	50.00	165.00	600.00
	1869(69) SNM	3.270	5.00	10.00	30.00	250.00
	1870(70) SNM	1.504	6.50	12.50	65.00	300.00
	1870(73) DEM	11.880	5.00	8.00	27.50	200.00
	1870(74) DEM	14.893	5.00	8.00	27.50	175.00
	1870(75) DEM	4.997	7.00	10.00	40.00	275.00

Y#	Date	Mintage	Fine	VF	XF	Unc
C76	1879(79) EMM	5.578	5.50	9.00	32.50	250.00
	1881(81) MSM	3.639	5.50	9.00	32.50	250.00
	1882/1(82) MSM	20.343	4.50	7.50	25.00	200.00
	1882(82) MSM	Inc. Ab.	4.50	7.50	25.00	175.00
	1883(83) MSM	3.318	5.00	9.00	28.00	200.00
	1884(84) MSM	2.839	5.50	10.00	30.00	225.00

81	1889(89) MPM	.559	10.00	20.00	125.00	350.00
	1891(91) PGM	.093	75.00	150.00	475.00	1200.
	1892(92) PGM	1.379	7.00	15.00	50.00	175.00

| 85 | 1894(94) PGV | .279 | 35.00 | 125.00 | 365.00 | 1000. |

| 95 | 1905(05) SMV | 3.589 | 4.50 | 8.00 | 16.00 | 50.00 |

ALUMINUM
Mint mark: Crowned M
Circulation Coinage

141	1982	—	—	—	.10	.15
	1984	—	—	—	.10	.15

2-1/2 PESETAS

ALUMINUM-BRONZE
Mint mark: 6-pointed star

114	1953(54)	22.729	.10	.25	1.25	2.00
	1953(56)	30.322	.10	.25	1.00	1.50
	1953(68)	1.000	—	—	350.00	600.00
	1953(69)	2.000	—	—	400.00	700.00
	1953(70)	6.800	—	—	65.00	125.00
	1953(71)	10.000	—	—	45.00	100.00

5 PESETAS

25.0000 g, .900 SILVER, .7234 oz ASW
Mint mark: 6-pointed star

Y#	Date	Mintage	Fine	VF	XF	Unc
60	1869(69) SNM	100 pcs.	3500.	5500.	7500.	12,000.
	1870(70) SNM	5.923	10.00	20.00	45.00	200.00

61	1871(71) SDM	13.641	10.00	20.00	45.00	200.00
	1871(73) SDM	Inc. Ab.	20.00	40.00	135.00	250.00
	1871(73) DEM	2.870	100.00	225.00	550.00	1500.
	1871(74) DEM	5.075	10.00	20.00	80.00	200.00
	1871(75) DEM	3.000	10.00	20.00	80.00	175.00

Mint mark: 6-pointed star

74	1875(75) DEM	8.641	10.00	20.00	65.00	175.00
	1876(76) DEM	8.548	10.00	20.00	65.00	250.00

SPAIN 1534

NOTE: Issued to commemorate the 1958 Barcelona Exposition w/BA replacing the star on left side of rev.

Y#	Date	Mintage	Fine	VF	XF	Unc
128	1975(76)	156.658	—	—	.10	.50
	1975(76)	—	—	—	Proof	2.50
	1975(77)	154.327	—	—	.10	.50
	1975(77) Inc. Ab.	—	—	—	Proof	2.00
	1975(78)	414.000	—	—	.10	.25
	1975(79)	436.000	—	—	.10	.25
	1975(79)	—	—	—	Proof	1.75
	1975(80)	298.000	—	—	.10	.25

World Cup Soccer Games

134	1980(80)	75.000	—	—	.10	.25
	1980(81)	200.000	—	—	.10	.25
	1980(82)	—	—	—	.10	.25

Mule. Obv: Y#128. Rev: Y#134 w/(80) star.

138	1975(80)	.030	—	—	40.00	60.00

Mint mark: Crowned M

128a	1982	—	—	—	.10	.25
	1983	—	—	—	.10	.25
	1984	—	—	—	.10	.25

10 PESETAS

3.2258 g, .900 GOLD, .0933 oz AGW
Mint mark: 6-pointed star
Similar to 25 Pesetas, Y#78.

77	1878(78) EMM					
		.091	125.00	200.00	300.00	400.00
	1879(79) EMM					
		.033	400.00	800.00	1250.	1750.
	1878(61) DEM					
		496 pcs.	—	—	750.00	1000.
	1878(62) DEM					
		.018	—	—	75.00	85.00

NOTE: The above two coins were restruck by the Spanish Mint from original dies in 1961 and 1962 and are considered official restrike issues.

COPPER-NICKEL
Mint mark: Crowned M

143	1983	—	—	.10	.15	.25
	1984	—	—	.10	.15	.25
	1985	—	—	.10	.15	.25

20 PESETAS

6.4516 g, .900 GOLD, .1867 oz AGW
Mint mark: 6-pointed star

A82	1889(89) MPM					
		.875	125.00	200.00	300.00	425.00
	1890(90) MPM					
		2.344	100.00	115.00	150.00	250.00
	1887(61) PGV					
		800 pcs.	—	—	600.00	900.00
	1887(62) PGV					
		.011	—	—	100.00	150.00

NOTE: For above two coins dated (61) & (62) see note after 10 Pesetas, Y#77.

Rev: Similar to Y#75.

Y#	Date	Mintage	Fine	VF	XF	Unc
86	1892(92) PGM					
		7.000	10.00	20.00	70.00	275.00
	1893(93) PGL					
		2.500	12.00	20.00	70.00	325.00
	1893(93) PGV					
		.518	25.00	75.00	275.00	600.00
	1894(94) PGV					
		3.871	12.00	20.00	70.00	300.00

Rev: Similar to Y#75.

89	1896(96) PGV					
		4.272	10.00	15.00	55.00	125.00
	1897(97) SGV					
		6.733	8.00	12.00	45.00	100.00
	1898(98) SGV					
		39.977	8.00	15.00	30.00	70.00
	1899(99) SGV					
		13.930	20.00	35.00	65.00	250.00

NOTE: All other date and mintmaster's or assayer's initial combinations on crowns of this era are contemporary counterfeits.

NICKEL

117	1949(49)	.612	.50	1.00	2.00	6.00
	1949(50)	21.000	.25	.50	1.00	3.00
	1949(51)	.145	45.00	120.00	225.00	500.00
	1949(E51)	6.000	175.00	450.00	725.00	1250.

NOTE: Issued to commemorate a numismatic exposition December 2, 1951. An E replaces the 19 on the lower star.

COPPER-NICKEL

118	1957(58)	13.000	.10	.20	.50	5.00
	1957(BA)	.043	15.00	35.00	75.00	125.00
	1957(59)	107.000	—	.10	.20	1.00
	1957(60)	26.000	—	.10	.25	2.00
	1957(61)	78.992	—	.10	.25	4.00
	1957(62)	40.963	—	.10	.25	1.50
	1957(63)	50.000	—	.50	2.00	20.00
	1957(64)	51.000	—	.10	.25	1.50
	1957(65)	25.000	—	.10	.25	1.50
	1957(66)	28.000	—	.10	.25	2.50
	1957(67)	30.000	—	.10	.25	1.50
	1957(68)	60.000	—	.10	.25	1.00
	1957(69)	40.000	—	.10	.25	1.25
	1957(70)	43.000	—	.10	.25	1.25
	1957(71)	77.000	—	.10	.25	1.50
	1957(72)	70.000	—	—	.10	.50
	1957(72)	.023	—	—	Proof	7.00
	1957(73)	78.000	—	—	.10	1.50
	1957(73)	.028	—	—	Proof	9.00
	1957(74)	100.000	—	—	.10	.25
	1957(74)	.025	—	—	Proof	11.00
	1957(75)	139.047	—	—	.10	.25
	1957(75)	.025	—	—	Proof	3.50

	Y#	Date	Mintage	Fine	VF	XF	Unc
75	1877(77) DEM						
		6.987	10.00	20.00	65.00	250.00	
	1878(78) DEM						
		5.000	10.00	20.00	65.00	250.00	
	1878(78) EMM						
		4.147	10.00	20.00	65.00	250.00	
	1879(79) EMM						
		1.634	15.00	35.00	140.00	300.00	
	1881(81) MSM						
		.699	25.00	75.00	280.00	600.00	

76	1882/1 MSM	—	30.00	60.00	250.00	800.00
	1882(81) MSM	—	10.00	22.00	100.00	375.00
	1882(82) MSM					
		1.662	10.00	22.00	100.00	250.00
	1883(83) MSM					
		5.507	8.00	12.00	45.00	150.00
	1884(84) MSM					
		5.848	8.00	12.00	45.00	150.00
	1885(85) MSM					
		3.144	8.00	12.00	45.00	150.00
	1885(86) MSM					
		1.951	10.00	20.00	160.00	300.00
	1885(87) MSM					
		9.000	8.00	12.00	45.00	150.00
	1885(87) MPM					
		2.803	15.00	25.00	135.00	275.00

82	1888(88) MSM					
		—	165.00	350.00	725.00	1600.
	1888(88) MPM					
		10.644	8.00	12.00	45.00	175.00
	1889(89) MPM					
		4.681	10.00	15.00	45.00	175.00
	1890(90) MPM					
		4.275	10.00	15.00	45.00	175.00
	1890(90) PGM					
		3.000	10.00	15.00	45.00	175.00
	1891(91) PGM					
		11.660	8.00	12.00	45.00	175.00
	1892(92) PGM					
		1.294	12.50	20.00	85.00	250.00

Y#	Date	Mintage	Fine	VF	XF	Unc
A86	1892(92) PGM	2.430	800.00	1400.	2000.	2750.

A89	1899(99) SMV	2.086	125.00	175.00	250.00	350.00
	1896(61) MPM	900 pcs.	—	—	600.00	750.00
	1896(62) MPM	.012	—	—	110.00	160.00

NOTE: For above two coins dated (61) & (62) see note after 10 Pesetas, Y#77.

91	1904(04) SMV	3.814	1000.	2200.	3250.	4500.

25 PESETAS

8.0645 g, .900 GOLD, .2333 oz AGW
Mint mark: 6-pointed star

A62	1871(75)SDM	25 pcs.	—	—	Rare	—

78	1876(76) DEM	1.281	120.00	135.00	150.00	200.00
	1877(77) DEM	10.048	120.00	135.00	150.00	200.00
	1878(78) DEM	5.192	120.00	135.00	150.00	200.00
	1878(78) EMM	3.000	120.00	135.00	150.00	200.00
	1879(79) EMM	3.478	120.00	135.00	150.00	200.00
	1880(80) MSM	6.863	120.00	135.00	150.00	200.00
	1876(61) DEM	300 pcs.	—	—	1800.	2500.
	1876(62) DEM	6.000	—	—	300.00	400.00

NOTE: For above two coins dated (61) & (62) see note after 10 Pesetas, Y#77.

A78	1881(81) MSM	4.366	120.00	135.00	150.00	200.00
	1882(82) MSM	.414	200.00	400.00	600.00	800.00
	1883(83) MSM	.669	200.00	425.00	650.00	900.00
	1884(84) MSM	1.033	150.00	250.00	450.00	600.00
	1885(85) MSM					

Y#	Date	Mintage	Fine	VF	XF	Unc
A78	1885(86) MSM	.503	500.00	900.00	1200.	1600.
		.491	750.00	1500.	2000.	2500.

COPPER-NICKEL

119	1957(58)	8.635	—	.20	.50	8.00
	1957(BA)	.043	15.00	35.00	70.00	125.00
	1957(59)	42.185	—	.20	.40	2.00
	1957(61)	24.120	—	8.00	20.00	50.00
	1957(64)	42.200	—	.20	.30	1.25
	1957(65)	20.000	—	.20	.30	1.50
	1957(66)	15.000	—	.20	.30	1.75
	1957(67)	20.000	—	.20	.30	1.50
	1957(68)	30.000	—	.20	.30	1.25
	1957(69)	24.000	—	.20	.30	1.25
	1957(70)	25.000	—	.20	.30	.75
	1957(71)	7.800	—	1.00	5.00	20.00
	1957(72)	4.733	—	.20	.30	1.75
	1957(72)	.023	—	—	Proof	10.00
	1957(73)	.028	—	—	Proof	15.00
	1957(74)	5.000	—	.20	.30	.75
	1957(74)	.025	—	—	Proof	15.00
	1957(75)	10.270	—	.20	.30	.75
	1957(75)	.025	—	—	Proof	5.00

NOTE: Issued to commemorate the 1958 Barcelona Exposition w/BA replacing the star on left side of rev.

129	1975(76)	35.333	—	.20	.25	1.00
	1975(76)	—	—	—	Proof	2.00
	1975(77)	44.990	—	.20	.25	1.00
	1975(77)	Inc. Ab.	—	—	Proof	2.00
	1975(78)	98.000	—	.20	.25	.50
	1975(79)	172.000	—	.20	.25	.50
	1975(79)	—	—	—	Proof	2.00
	1975(80)	136.000	—	.20	.25	.50

World Cup Soccer Games

135	1980(80)	35.000	—	.20	.30	.60
	1980(81)	80.000	—	.20	.30	.60
	1980(82)	—	—	.20	.30	.60

Mint mark: Crowned M

129a	1982	—	—	.20	.25	.50
	1983	—	—	.20	.25	.50
	1984	—	—	.20	.25	.50

50 PESETAS

COPPER-NICKEL
Mint mark: 6-pointed star

120	1957(58)	21.471	—	.50	1.00	3.00
	1957(BA)	.043	15.00	35.00	70.00	125.00

NOTE: Issued to commemorate the 1958 Barcelona Exposition w/BA replacing the star on left side of rev.

	1957(59)	28.000	—	.50	1.00	3.00
	1957(60)	24.800	—	.50	1.00	3.00
	1957(67)	.850	.50	1.00	2.00	5.00
	1957(68)	1.000	—	—	425.00	650.00
	1957(69)	1.200	—	—	350.00	500.00
	1957(70)	.019	—	—	55.00	125.00
	1957(71)	4.400	—	.50	.75	3.00

Y#	Date	Mintage	Fine	VF	XF	Unc
120	1957(72)	.023	—	—	Proof	14.00
	1957(73)	.028	—	—	Proof	17.50
	1957(74)	.025	—	—	Proof	21.00
	1957(75)	.025	—	—	Proof	7.00

NOTE: Edge varieties exist.

130	1975(76)	4.000	—	—	.50	.60	1.50
	1975(76)	—	—	—	—	Proof	3.00
	1975(78)	17.000	—	—	.50	.60	1.25
	1975(79)	33.000	—	—	.50	.60	1.00
	1975(79)	—	—	—	—	Proof	3.00
	1975(80)	30.000	—	—	.50	.60	1.00

World Cup Soccer Games

136	1980(80)	15.000	—	.50	.60	1.00
	1980(81)	20.000	—	.50	.60	1.00
	1980(82)	—	—	.50	.60	1.00

Mint mark: Crowned M

130a	1982	—	—	.50	.60	.80
	1983	—	—	.50	.60	.80
	1984	—	—	.50	.60	.80

100 PESETAS

32.2581 g, .900 GOLD, .9334 oz AGW
Mint mark: 6-pointed star
Provisional Government

B62	1870(70) SD-M	12 pcs.	—	—	Rare	—

SPAIN 1536

.900 YELLOW GOLD

Y#	Date	Mintage	Fine	VF	XF	Unc
C62	1871(71) SD-M	25 pcs.	—	—	Rare	—

.900 RED GOLD

| C62a | 1871(71) SD-M | 50 pcs. | — | — | Rare | — |

90	1897(97)SGV	.150	600.00	900.00	1250.	2000.
	1897(61)SGV	810 pcs.	—	—	1500.	2000.
	1897(62)SGV	6,000	—	—	550.00	750.00

NOTE: The above two coins were restruck by the Spanish Mint from original dies in 1961 and 1962 and are considered official restrike issues.

19.0000 g, .800 SILVER, .4887 oz ASW

122	1966(66)	35.000	—	BV	4.00	6.00
	1966(67)	15.000	—	BV	4.00	8.00
	1966(68)	24.000	—	BV	4.00	8.00
	1966(69) 69 w/straight 9 in star					
		1.000	—	—	60.00	120.00
	1966(69) 69 w/curved 9 in star					
		Inc. Ab.	—	—	50.00	100.00
	1966(70)	.995	—	BV	6.00	8.00	12.00

COPPER-NICKEL

Y#	Date	Mintage	Fine	VF	XF	Unc
131	1975(76)	4.000	—	1.00	1.50	2.00
	1975(76)	—	—	—	Proof	4.00

World Cup Soccer Games

| 137 | 1980(80) | 20.000 | — | 1.00 | 1.50 | 2.00 |

ALUMINUM-BRONZE

139	1982	—	—	1.00	1.25	1.75
	1982	—	—	—	Proof	10.00
	1983	—	—	1.00	1.25	1.75
	1984	—	—	1.00	1.25	1.75
	1985	—	—	1.00	1.25	1.75
	1986	—	—	1.00	1.25	1.75
	1987	—	—	1.00	1.25	1.75
	1988	—	—	1.00	1.25	1.75

NOTE: Edge varieties exist.

200 PESETAS

COPPER-NICKEL

146.1	1986	—	—	2.00	2.50	3.00
(146)	1987	10.000	—	2.00	2.50	3.00
	1988	—	—	2.00	2.50	3.00

Madrid Numismatic Exposition

| 146.2 | 1987 | .060 | — | — | Proof | 25.00 |

500 PESETAS

COPPER-ALUMINUM-NICKEL
King and Queen of Spain

| 147 | 1987 | 10.000 | — | — | 5.00 | 7.00 |
| | 1988 | — | — | — | 5.00 | 7.00 |

REVOLUTIONARY COINAGE

NOTE: Former Y#62, 2 Pesetas, 1873 Cartagena Mint, Cantonal issue similar to Y#64, 10 Reales and Y#63, 5 Pesetas is considered a fantasy struck later for collectors. Refer to *Unusual World Coins*, 2nd edition, Krause Publications, Inc., 1989.

10 REALES
(2-1/2 Pesetas)

13.5000 g, .900 SILVER, .3907 oz ASW
Cartagena Mint

Y#	Date	Mintage	Fine	VF	XF	Unc
64	1873	—	150.00	350.00	650.00	1200.

5 PESETAS

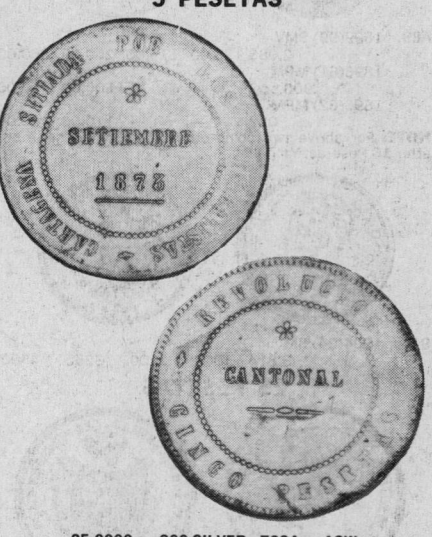

25.0000 g, .900 SILVER, .7234 oz ASW
Cartagena Mint

| 63 | 1873 | — | 100.00 | 175.00 | 250.00 | 450.00 |

NOTE: Several varieties exist.

MINT SETS (MS)

KM#	Date	Mintage	Identification	Issue Price	Mkt. Val.
MS1	1949(E51) (3)	5,000	Y113,116,117	—	2500.
MS2	1958Ba(3)	—	Y118-120	—	375.00

NOTE: The following sets contain 10 Centimos, Y121 dated 1959. Other denominations have the date in the stars.

MS3	1966(8)	—	Y113,114,116,118-122	—	1250.
MS4	1968(8)	1,000	Y114,118-122,124,125	3.60	1250.
MS5	1969(8)	1,200	Y114,118-122,124,125	3.60	1250.
MS6	1970(8)	6,000	Y114,118-122,124,125	3.60	250.00
MS7	1971(8)	10,000	Y114,118-122,124,125 (100 Peseta coin has star date of 70)	3.60	125.00
MS8	1980(80) (6)	—	Y132-137	—	10.00

PROOF SETS (PS)

PS1	1972(6)	30,000	Y118-121,124,125	10.00	25.00
PS2	1973(6)	25,000	Y118-121,124,125	10.00	45.00
PS3	1974(6)	23,000	Y118-121,124,125	10.00	25.00
PS4	1975(6)	75,000	Y118-121,124,125	10.00	17.50
PS5	1976(6)	.400	Y126-131	7.50	10.00
PS6	1977(3)	.300	Y127-129	—	5.00
PS7	1979(4)	.300	Y127-130	—	7.50
PS8	1987(6)	—	Y147,Pn4,4a,5-6,Mint Medal	55.00	55.00
PS9	1987(2)	—	Y140.2,146.2	—	40.00

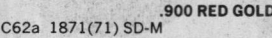

SPAIN-Local

The following cities and provinces of Spain were coin-issuing entities.

BALEARIC ISLANDS
Majorca

The Balearic Islands, an archipelago located in the Mediterranean Sea off the east coast of Spain including Majorca, Minorca, Cabrera, Ibiza, Formentera and a number of islets.

Majorca, largest of the Balearic Islands is famous for its 1,000-year-old olive trees.

RULERS
Ferdinand (Fernando) VII, 1808-1833

MONETARY SYSTEM
12 Dineros = 6 Doblers = 1 Sueldo (Sou)
30 Sueldos = 1 Duro

12 DINEROS

COPPER

C#	Date	Mintage	VG	Fine	VF	XF
L51	1811	—	40.00	75.00	125.00	275.00
	1812 DEI GRATIA, small date					
		5.00	8.00	15.00	35.00	
	1812 DEI GRATIA, large date					
		5.00	8.00	15.00	35.00	
	1812 DEI GRAT					
		12.50	20.00	35.00	85.00	

30 SUELDOS
(Sous)

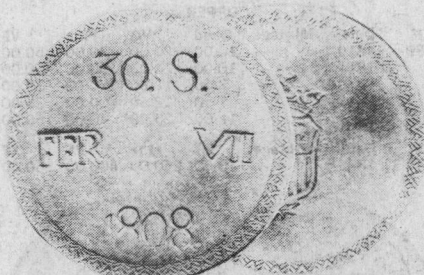

SILVER
Obv. and rev: Ornate rim.

L7.1	1808	—	50.00	90.00	130.00	250.00

Obv: FER.VII, value and date in depression.

L7.2	1808	—	40.00	80.00	120.00	200.00

Rev: Similar to C#L52.2.

C#	Date	Mintage	VG	Fine	VF	XF
L52.1	1808 FER. VII	100.00	175.00	250.00	350.00	

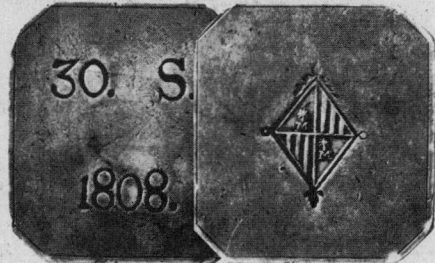

Obv: W/o FER VII.

L52.2	1808	—	150.00	300.00	700.00	1250.

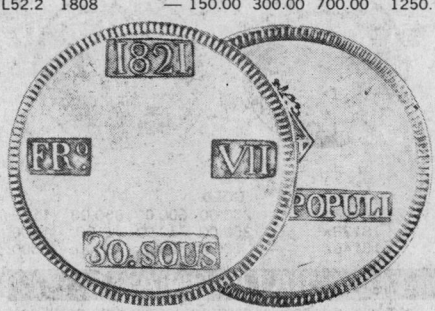

L53.1	1821 FRo. VII	40.00	75.00	125.00	200.00	

Obv: (error) FRo.VII inverted.

L53.2	1821 FRo. VII	300.00	600.00	1000.	1500.	

5 PESETAS

SILVER
Obv. leg. ends: CONST.

C#	Date	Mintage	VG	Fine	VF	XF
L9.1	1823	—	40.00	75.00	125.00	200.00

Obv. leg. ends: EYND.

L9.2	1823	—	80.00	120.00	180.00	275.00

BARCELONA

Barcelona was a maritime province located in north-east Spain. The city was the provincial capital of Barcelona. Barcelona is a major port and commercial center.

RULERS
Joseph (Jose) Napoleon, 1808-1814
Ferdinand (Fernando) VII, restored 1814-1833

MINT MARKS
Ba - Barcelona

MONETARY SYSTEM
4 Quartos = 1 Sueldo
6 Sueldos = 1 Peseta

1/2 QUARTO

COPPER
Similar to 4 Quartos, C#L14.

C#	Date	Mintage	Good	VG	Fine	VF
L11	ND(1811)	—	20.00	40.00	60.00	80.00

QUARTO

COPPER
Similar to 4 Quartos, C#L14.

L12	1808	—	17.50	35.00	70.00	100.00
	1809	—	10.00	20.00	35.00	50.00
	1810	—	10.00	20.00	35.00	50.00
	1811	—	20.00	40.00	80.00	120.00
	1812	—	10.00	20.00	35.00	50.00
	1813	—	20.00	40.00	75.00	150.00

2 QUARTOS

COPPER
Similar to 4 Quartos, C#L14.

L13	1808	—	10.00	25.00	50.00	80.00
	1809	—	10.00	20.00	30.00	40.00
	1810	—	20.00	40.00	80.00	125.00
	1813	—	10.00	25.00	50.00	70.00
	1814	—	20.00	60.00	125.00	200.00

3 QUARTOS

COPPER

L21	1823	—	2.00	5.00	15.00	20.00

4 QUARTOS

COPPER

C#	Date	Mintage	Good	VG	Fine	VF
L14	1808	—	10.00	30.00	60.00	90.00
	1809	—	5.00	10.00	20.00	30.00
	1810	—	3.00	10.00	15.00	20.00
	1811	—	4.00	10.00	15.00	20.00
	1812	—	3.00	10.00	15.00	20.00

Obv. leg: Widely spaced.

C#	Date	Mintage	Good	VG	Fine	VF
L14b	1813	—	5.00	12.50	25.00	30.00
	1814	—	7.50	15.00	30.00	40.00

CAST COPPER

C#	Date	Mintage	Good	VG	Fine	VF
L14a	1808	—	5.00	11.50	15.00	20.00
	1809	—	3.00	9.50	15.00	20.00
	1810	—	2.00	9.50	15.00	20.00
	1811	—	4.00	10.00	15.00	25.00
	1812	—	3.00	9.50	15.00	20.00
L14c	1813	—	5.00	11.50	15.00	20.00
	1814	—	5.00	11.50	15.00	20.00

6 QUARTOS

COPPER

C#	Date	Mintage	Good	VG	Fine	VF
L22	1823	—	10.00	20.00	30.00	40.00

PESETA

SILVER

C#	Date	Mintage	VG	Fine	VF	XF
L15	1809	—	20.00	40.00	55.00	80.00
	1810	—	15.00	25.00	30.00	40.00
	1811	—	15.00	25.00	30.00	40.00
	1812	—	18.00	35.00	45.00	65.00
	1813	—	20.00	40.00	50.00	70.00
	1814	—	35.00	60.00	85.00	120.00

2-1/2 PESETAS

SILVER

C#	Date	Mintage	VG	Fine	VF	XF
L16	1808	—	150.00	275.00	325.00	400.00
	1809	—	125.00	200.00	250.00	300.00
	1810	—	200.00	400.00	500.00	650.00
	1814	—	300.00	575.00	725.00	975.00

5 PESETAS

SILVER

C#	Date	Mintage	VG	Fine	VF	XF
L17	1808	—	125.00	250.00	400.00	600.00
	1809	—	125.00	250.00	400.00	600.00
	1810	—	125.00	250.00	400.00	600.00
	1811	—	125.00	250.00	325.00	450.00
	1812	—	125.00	250.00	400.00	700.00
	1813	—	300.00	600.00	900.00	1250.
	1814	—	1000.	2100.	2800.	3500.

20 PESETAS

GOLD

C#	Date	Mintage	VG	Fine	VF	XF
L18	1812Ba	—	250.00	600.00	850.00	1100.
	1813Ba	—	350.00	750.00	1100.	1500.
	1814Ba	—	1000.	2500.	3500.	5000.

CATALONIA

Catalonia, a triangular territory forming the north-east corner of the Iberian Peninsula, was formerly a province of Spain and also formerly a principality of Aragon. In 1833 the region was divided into four provinces, Barcelona, Gerona, Lerida and Tarragona.

RULERS
Ferdinand (Fernando) VII, 1808-1833
Isabel II, 1833-1868

MINT MARKS
C - Catalonia

MONETARY SYSTEM
12 Ardites (Dineros) = 8 Ochavos =
  4 Quartos = 1 Sueldo
6 Sueldos = 1 Peseta
5 Pesetas = 1 Duro

OCHAVO

COPPER

C#	Date	Mintage	Good	VG	Fine	VF
L34	1813	—	10.00	20.00	30.00	40.00

QUARTO

COPPER
Obv: Crowned spade Catalonian arms.
Rev: Crowned Spanish arms.

L35	1813	—	10.00	15.00	25.00	35.00

QUARTO/Y MEDIO
(1-1/2 Quartos)

COPPER
Obv: Crowned round Catalonian arms.
Rev: Crowned oval Spanish arms.

L36	1811	—	10.00	20.00	40.00	65.00
	1812	—	25.00	65.00	100.00	125.00
	1813	—	10.00	20.00	27.50	35.00

II QUARTOS

COPPER
Obv: Crowned lozenge Catalonian arms in branches.
Rev: Crowned Spanish arms.

L37	1813	—	7.50	15.00	25.00	35.00
	1814	—	10.00	22.50	32.50	40.00

III QUARTOS

COPPER

C#	Date	Mintage	Good	VG	Fine	VF
L38	1810	—	9.00	17.50	22.50	35.00
	1811	—	7.00	12.50	17.50	25.00
	1812	—	5.00	7.50	10.00	20.00
	1813	—	5.00	7.50	10.00	20.00
	1814	—	5.00	7.50	10.00	20.00

C#	Date	Mintage	VG	Fine	VF	XF
L40	1836 CATHAL		50.00	125.00	225.00	300.00
	1836 CATALUNA		40.00	80.00	120.00	150.00

C#	Date	Mintage	VG	Fine	VF	XF
L40a	1836	—	12.50	25.00	32.50	40.00
	1837	—	5.00	7.50	12.50	25.00
	1838	—	6.00	10.00	15.00	30.00
	1839	—	6.00	10.00	15.00	30.00
	1840	—	12.00	25.00	40.00	65.00
	1841	—	5.00	7.50	12.50	25.00
	1842	—	20.00	40.00	80.00	110.00
	1843	—	22.00	45.00	65.00	80.00
	1844	—	10.00	15.00	20.00	30.00
	1845	—	20.00	40.00	75.00	100.00
	1846	—	10.00	20.00	25.00	35.00

VI QUARTOS

COPPER

C#	Date	Mintage	Good	VG	Fine	VF
L39	1810	—	10.00	20.00	30.00	50.00
	1811	—	10.00	20.00	30.00	50.00
	1812	—	7.50	12.50	20.00	35.00
	1813	—	7.50	12.50	20.00	35.00
	1814	—	12.00	25.00	40.00	50.00

C#	Date	Mintage	VG	Fine	VF	XF
L40.3	1836	—	110.00	250.00	400.00	500.00

C#	Date	Mintage	VG	Fine	VF	XF
L40.3a	1836	—	12.00	25.00	40.00	55.00
	1837	—	7.50	12.50	22.50	45.00
	1838	—	7.50	12.50	20.00	40.00
	1839	—	7.50	12.50	20.00	40.00
	1840	—	7.50	12.50	20.00	40.00
	1841	—	12.50	20.00	30.00	45.00
	1842	—	100.00	225.00	375.00	625.00
	1843	—	30.00	70.00	125.00	300.00
	1844	—	7.50	12.50	20.00	40.00
	1845	—	7.50	12.50	20.00	40.00
	1846	—	7.50	12.50	20.00	40.00
	1847	—	45.00	125.00	200.00	250.00
	1848	—	45.00	125.00	200.00	250.00

Charles V - Pretender Issue
Mint mark: BGA
Rev: Crowned Catalonian arms within legend.

C#	Date	Mintage	Good	VG	Fine	VF
A155	1840	—	250.00	400.00	550.00	600.00

Rev: Crowned Spanish arms within legend.

| 155 | 1840 | — | 300.00 | 500.00 | 575.00 | 650.00 |

PESETA

SILVER
Mint mark: B

C#	Date	Mintage	VG	Fine	VF	XF
L40.7	1836 PS	—	20.00	50.00	80.00	125.00
	1837 PS	—	25.00	65.00	110.00	140.00

GERONA

Gerona, a maritime frontier province in the extreme north-east corner of Spain and the provincal capital city of Gerona. The city of Gerona is the ancient city of Gerunda where St. Paul and St. James known as Santiago, patron saint of Spain and one of the twelve apostles, first rested when they came to Spain.

RULERS
Ferdinand (Fernando) VII, 1808-1833

MONETARY SYSTEM
12 Ardites (Dineros) = 8 Ochavos =
 4 Quartos = 1 Sueldo
6 Sueldos = 1 Peseta
5 Pesetas = 1 Duro

DURO

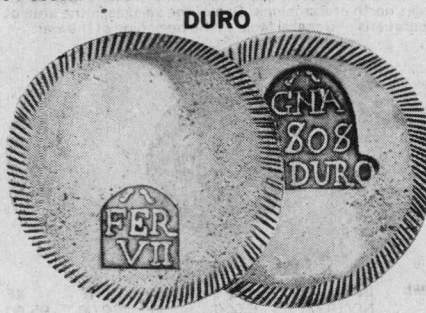

SILVER

| L41 | 1808 | — | 50.00 | 80.00 | 125.00 | 200.00 |

COPPER

| L41a | 1809 | — | 60.00 | 90.00 | 150.00 | 200.00 |

5 PESETAS

SILVER
Obv: Crude bust of Ferdinand right.

Rev: Crowned arms divide value.

C#	Date	Mintage	VG	Fine	VF	XF
L42	1809	—	1250.	2300.	3800.	4500.

LERIDA

Lerida, a frontier province of northern Spain and the provincal capital city of Lerida. The province is bounded on the north by France and on the east by Barcelona and Gerona.

RULERS
Ferdinand VII, 1808-1833

MONETARY SYSTEM
12 Ardites (Dineros) = 8 Ochavos =
 4 Quartos = 1 Sueldo
6 Sueldos = 1 Peseta
5 Pesetas = 1 Duro

5 PESETAS

SILVER

| L45 | 1809 | — | 1800. | 2500. | 4000. | 5000. |

| L46 | 1809 | — | 1500. | 2300. | 3750. | 4500. |

NAVARRE

Navarre, a frontier province of northern Spain and a former kingdom which included part of the south-west corner of France. The Kingdom of Navarre was ultimately divided and absorbed by France and Spain.

RULERS
Carlos VII (IV in Spain), 1788-1808
Ferdinand (Fernando) III
 (VII in Spain), 1808-1833

1/2 MARAVEDI

COPPER
Similar to 6 Maravedi, C#L92.

| L81 | 1818PP | — | 15.00 | 27.50 | 35.00 | 40.00 |
| | 1819PP | — | 20.00 | 40.00 | 50.00 | 60.00 |

L82	1831PP	—	12.00	25.00	35.00	45.00
	1381PP (error)	—	90.00	165.00	200.00	250.00
	1832PP	—	90.00	165.00	200.00	250.00

MARAVEDI

COPPER

C#	Date	Mintage	VG	Fine	VF	XF
L83	1818PP	—	10.00	20.00	30.00	40.00
	1824Ja	—	10.00	20.00	27.50	35.00
	1825PP	—	8.00	12.50	22.50	30.00
	1826PP	—	8.00	12.50	22.50	30.00

Obv: Laureate bust. Rev: Arms.

L83a	1818PP	—	9.00	17.50	22.50	30.00
	1819PP	—	9.00	17.50	22.50	30.00
	1820PP	—	10.00	27.50	27.50	35.00

Similar to 1/2 Maravedi, C#L82.

L84	1829PP	—	7.50	15.00	20.00	25.00
	1830PP	—	7.50	15.00	20.00	25.00
	1831PP	—	9.00	17.50	22.50	30.00
	1832PP	—	9.00	17.50	22.50	30.00
	1833PP	—	15.00	30.00	45.00	50.00

3 MARAVEDIS

COPPER
Similar to 6 Maravedi, C#L92a.

L89	1818PP	—	25.00	45.00	65.00	85.00
	1819PP	—	20.00	35.00	55.00	70.00
	1820PP	—	20.00	35.00	55.00	70.00
	1825PP	—	20.00	35.00	55.00	70.00
	1826PP	—	20.00	35.00	55.00	70.00

Similar to 6 Maravedi, C#L92b.

| L89a | 1818PP | — | 15.00 | 30.00 | 45.00 | 65.00 |
| | 1819PP | — | 15.00 | 30.00 | 45.00 | 65.00 |

Similar to 1/2 Maravedi, C#L82.

L90	1829PP	—	12.50	25.00	40.00	60.00
	1830PP	—	10.00	15.00	20.00	40.00
	1831PP	—	15.00	30.00	45.00	65.00
	1832PP	—	12.50	25.00	40.00	60.00
	1833PP	—	12.50	25.00	40.00	60.00

6 MARAVEDIS

COPPER
Obv: Young bust, bare head. Rev: Arms.

| L92 | 1818PP | — | 25.00 | 50.00 | 80.00 | 100.00 |

Obv: Laureate bust.

L92a	1818PP	—	35.00	70.00	120.00	150.00
	1819PP	—	25.00	50.00	80.00	100.00
	1820PP	—	30.00	55.00	90.00	125.00

TARRAGONA

Tarragona, a maritime province in north east Spain, south of Barcelona and Lerida, and the provincal capital city of Tarragona. The province produces excellent wines; the city is a flourishing seaport.

RULERS
Ferdinand (Fernando) III,
 (VII in Spain) 1808-1833

5 PESETAS

SILVER
Obv. leg: FER· VII· (raised periods).
Rev: Curved base crown/shield.

| L96.1 | 1809. small 0 | — | 60.00 | 90.00 | 140.00 | 200.00 |

Tarragona / SPAIN 1540

Obv. leg: FER VII (raised periods).
Rev: Curved base crown/shield.

C#	Date	Mintage	VG	Fine	VF	XF
L96.2	1809. large 0	—	60.00	90.00	140.00	200.00

Obv. leg: FER VII.
Rev: Straight base crown/shield.
L96.3 1809. small 0 — 60.00 90.00 140.00 200.00

Obv. leg: FER VII. Rev: Similar to C#L96.1.
L96.4 1809. small 0 — 60.00 90.00 140.00 200.00

Obv. leg: FER VII.
Rev: Similar to C#L96.3.
L96.5 1809. small 0, lazy 9
— 60.00 90.00 140.00 200.00
Obv. leg: FER./F.o.
L96.6 1809. — — Rare —

TORTOSA
Tortosa, a fortified city of Spain, is in Tarragona province.
RULERS
Fernando VII, 1808-1833

DURO
(5 Pesetas)

SILVER, uniface
4 c/m: Tower, 1, DURO & TOR. SA.

C#	Date	Mintage	VG	Fine	VF	XF
L100	ND (1808-9)	—	350.00	750.00	1250.	2000.

VALENCIA
Valencia, a maritime province of eastern Spain and the capital city of Valencia. Once a former kingdom, Valencia included the present provinces of Castellon de la Plana and Alicante.

RULERS
Ferdinand (Fernando) VII, 1808-1833

2 REALES DE VELLON
(1 Real)

SILVER
L103	1809LL	—	17.50	32.50	55.00	90.00

4 REALES DE VELLON
(2 Reales)

SILVER
L106	1823LL	—	12.50	22.50	37.50	65.00

NOTE: The 4 Reales de Vellon circulated as a regular issue 2 Reales while the 2 Reales de Vellon circulated as a regular 1 Real.

SPAIN-Civil War

With the loss of her American empire, Spain drifted into chaotic times. Stung by their defeats in Cuba, the army blamed the Socialists for what they considered to be mismanagement at home. Additional political complications were derived from the successful Russian Revolution which gave impetus to an already thriving Socialist party and trade union movement. Finally, King Alphonso XIII committed the fatal mistake of encouraging a reckless general to start a campaign in Morocco that ended in the virtual extermination of the Spanish army. Fearing that the inevitable parliamentary investigation would incriminate the crown, he offered no objection when General Primo de Rivera seized the government and established himself as dictator in 1926. Rivera fell from power in 1930, and the government was taken over by an alliance of Liberals and Socialists who tried to separate the Church and State, take the army out of politics, and introduce effective labor and agrarian reforms despite numerous strikes and street riots. The election of 1936 brought to power a coalition of Socialists, Liberals and Communists, to the dismay of the traditionalists and landowners.

A number of right-wing generals, including the young and clever Francisco Franco, began preparations for a military coup which erupted into a civil war in July of 1936. The destructive conflict, in which more than a million died, lasted three years. During the struggle, areas under control of both the Nationalist (rebels) and the Republican (Loyalists) issued coinages that circulated to whatever extent the political and military situation permitted. The war ended in defeat for the Loyalists when Madrid fell to Franco on March 28, 1939.

During the Spanish Civil War (1936-1939) a great many coins and tokens were minted in the provincial districts. The coins are grouped here under the heading of the district in which they most commonly circulated.

REPUBLICAN ZONE
ARENYS DE MAR
A resort village on the Mediterranean shore that is 20 miles north of Barcelona. One of the villages in the area of operations of General Mola at the beginning of the war.

50 CENTIMOS

ALUMINUM, uniface
KM#	Date	Mintage	Fine	VF	XF
1	ND(1937)	6,000	50.00	70.00	95.00

PESETA

ALUMINUM, uniface
2	ND(1937)	3,500	70.00	95.00	125.00

ASTURIAS AND LEON
Asturias is a province on the northern coast of Spain with the province of Leon just to its south. The councils of these adjoining provinces decided to mint coins in 1937 for use in the area due to lack of other circulating coins in the north.

50 CENTIMOS

COPPER-NICKEL
Gijon Mint

KM#	Date	Mintage	Fine	VF	XF	Unc
1	1937	.200	15.00	20.00	25.00	35.00

PESETA

COPPER
Guernica Mint

| 2 | 1937 | .100 | 10.00 | 12.50 | 15.00 | 30.00 |

2 PESETAS

COPPER-NICKEL
Gijon Mint

| 3 | 1937 | .400 | 5.00 | 7.50 | 10.00 | 25.00 |

NOTE: Varieties exist with differences in the leaves.

EUZKADI
Viscayan Republic

Euzkadi or the Viscayan Republic was located in north central Spain adjoining the southeast corner of France. It was made up of 4 provinces - Bilbao, Guipuzcoa, Navarre, and Victoria. These Basque provinces declared autonomy on October 8, 1936. The 2 nickel coins were made in Brussels, Belgium and saw some circulation before the end of the Republic on June 18, 1937.

PESETA

NICKEL
Brussels Mint

| 1 | 1937 | 7.000 | 2.50 | 4.50 | 7.50 | 18.00 |

2 PESETAS

NICKEL
Brussels Mint

| 2 | 1937 | 6.000 | 3.00 | 5.00 | 10.00 | 20.00 |

IBI

A village north and west of Alicante on the east coast of Spain. The isolation of the area in comparison with other contending areas made the maintaining of this area during the war very difficult.

25 CENTIMOS

COPPER

KM#	Date	Mintage	Fine	VF	XF	Unc
1.1 (1)	1937	.030	10.00	20.00	25.00	40.00

NOTE: Varieties exist.

Obv: Map in field.

| 1.2 (1a) | 1937 | 7,000 | 40.00 | 50.00 | 65.00 | 90.00 |

PESETA

NICKEL-BRASS

| 2 | 1937 | 5,000 | 25.00 | 35.00 | 50.00 | 80.00 |

L'AMETLLA DEL VALLES

A town in the province of Tarragona in northeastern Spain. The town adopted the name L'Ametlla del Valles in 1933. Before that the name was La Ametlla.

25 CENTIMOS

BRASS

| 1 | ND(1937) | .050 | 10.00 | 15.00 | 25.00 | 35.00 |

50 CENTIMOS

ALUMINUM

| 2.1 (2) | ND(1937) | 3,000 | 30.00 | 40.00 | 60.00 | 100.00 |

Obv: W/o legend.

| 2.2 (2a) | ND(1937) | .030 | 10.00 | 15.00 | 30.00 | 50.00 |

PESETA

ALUMINUM

| 3.1 (3) | ND(1937) | 3,000 | 25.00 | 45.00 | 60.00 | 90.00 |

 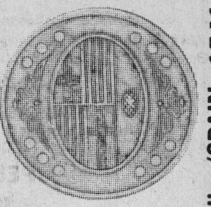

Obv: W/o legend.

KM#	Date	Mintage	Fine	VF	XF	Unc
3.2 (3a)	ND(1937)	.030	10.00	15.00	30.00	50.00

MENORCA

Menorca is the smaller of the 2 major islands in the Balearic Islands. A serious coin and supply shortage developed during the war because of the isolation of the island from the mainland.

5 CENTIMOS

BRASS

| 1 | 1937 | .042 | — | 15.00 | 20.00 | 25.00 |

10 CENTIMOS

BRASS

| 2 | 1937 | .032 | — | 15.00 | 20.00 | 30.00 |

25 CENTIMOS

BRASS

| 3 | 1937 | .038 | — | 15.00 | 20.00 | 30.00 |

PESETA

BRASS

| 4 | 1937 | .037 | — | 15.00 | 20.00 | 30.00 |

2-1/2 PESETAS

BRASS

| 5 | 1937 | .024 | — | 20.00 | 30.00 | 35.00 |

NULLES

Nulles is a mountain village in the province of Tarragona. The mountainous terrain of the area isolated the village from friendly forces and normal commerce. Therefore, in 1937, an undated series of 5 denominations were issued.

5 CENTIMOS

ZINC, octagonal, 23mm
Uniface, similar to 10 Centimos, KM#2.

KM#	Date	Mintage	Fine	VF	XF
1	ND(1937)	5,000	45.00	75.00	110.00

10 CENTIMOS

ZINC, uniface

| 2 | ND(1937) | 3,000 | 80.00 | 130.00 | 165.00 |

25 CENTIMOS

BRASS, square, 20mm

Uniface, similar to 10 Centimos, KM#2.

KM#	Date	Mintage	Fine	VF	XF
3	ND(1937)	5,000	70.00	95.00	110.00

50 CENTIMOS
BRASS, octagonal, 22mm
Uniface, similar to 10 Centimos, KM#2.

| 4 | ND(1937) | 1,000 | 70.00 | 115.00 | 140.00 |

PESETA

BRASS, uniface

| 5 | ND(1937) | 5,000 | 75.00 | 95.00 | 110.00 |

OLOT
A village in the province of Gerona in northeastern Spain near the French border. The village council authorized 2 denominations of coins on September 24, 1937.

10 CENTIMOS

IRON

KM#	Date	Mintage	Good	VG	Fine	VF
1	1937	.025	80.00	90.00	100.00	175.00

15 CENTIMOS

IRON

| 2 | 1937 | 100 pcs. | 1000. | 1500. | 2000. | Rare |

NOTE: The above is considered a pattern.

SANTANDER, PALENCIA & BURGOS
Three provinces in northern Spain with Santander being the northern-most on the Spanish coast. The three provinces met in council and issued two denominations of coins for use in the provinces.

50 CENTIMOS

COPPER-NICKEL, 20mm

KM#	Date	Mintage	Fine	VF	XF	Unc
1.1 (1)	1937	.100	—	7.50	10.00	25.00

Rev: Letters PR or PJR below CTS.

| 1.2 (1a) | 1937 | .010 | 20.00 | 30.00 | 40.00 | 50.00 |

PESETA

COPPER-NICKEL

| 2 | 1937 | .300 | — | 7.50 | 10.00 | 25.00 |

SEGARRA DE GAIA
A village in the southern part of the province of Tarragona. A single denomination of coin was authorized in 1937.

PESETA

COPPER-NICKEL
Uniface, value over bars of Aragon in circle.

KM#	Date	Mintage	Fine	VF	XF	Unc
1	ND(1937)	5,000	15.00	25.00	40.00	65.00

COPPER, 23mm
Uniface

| 1a | ND(1937) | .020 | 15.00 | 25.00 | 40.00 | 50.00 |

ALUMINUM, stamped
Uniface, 5 line inscription

| 2 | ND(1937) | .030 | — | Reported, not confirmed |

BRASS

| 2a | ND(1937) | — | 30.00 | 40.00 | 70.00 | 85.00 |

NATIONALIST ZONE

CAZALLA DE SIERRA
A town 43 miles north of Seville that issued a 10 Centimos in brass in 1936 (undated).

10 CENTIMOS

BRASS

| 1 | ND(1936) | .010 | 25.00 | 30.00 | 40.00 | — |

EL ARAHAL
A town 30 miles east of Seville. Issued three undated types of coins in 1936.

50 CENTIMOS

BRASS, uniface

| 1 | ND(1936) | 3,000 | 25.00 | 40.00 | 50.00 | 70.00 |

PESETA

BRASS, uniface

| 2 | ND(1936) | .010 | 20.00 | 30.00 | 40.00 | 50.00 |

2 PESETAS

BRASS, uniface

| 3 | ND(1936) | .010 | 20.00 | 30.00 | 40.00 | 50.00 |

LORA DEL RIO
A town 35 miles northeast of Seville. Issued an undated 25 Centimos in 1936.

25 CENTIMOS

BRASS
Obv: 5 line inscription, wheat ear to right.
Rev: Crowned arms of Lora del Rio on cross.

KM#	Date	Mintage	Fine	VF	XF	Unc
1	ND(1936)	1,500	80.00	115.00	165.00	215.00

MARCHENA
A village 30 miles east of Seville. It was the last issuer in Seville province. Two varieties of undated coins were produced in 1936.

25 CENTIMOS

BRASS, Uniface

| 1.1 (1) | ND(1936) | 5,000 | 30.00 | 65.00 | 85.00 | — |

Value as 0.25C, uniface.

| 1.2 (1a) | ND(1936) 500 pcs. | 75.00 | 100.00 | 200.00 |

NOTE: Counstermarked varieties exist.

LA PUEBLA DE CAZALLA
A village only a few miles east of El Arahal and some 40 miles from Sevilla. Undated coins of two values were issued in 1936.

10 CENTIMOS

BRASS, 23mm

| 1 | ND(1936) | 1,500 | 55.00 | 70.00 | 90.00 | 150.00 |

NOTE: Counterstamped varieties exist.

25 CENTIMOS

BRASS, 25mm

| 2 | ND(1936) | 5,000 | 45.00 | 65.00 | 85.00 | 140.00 |

NOTE: Counterstamped varieties exist.

SRI LANKA

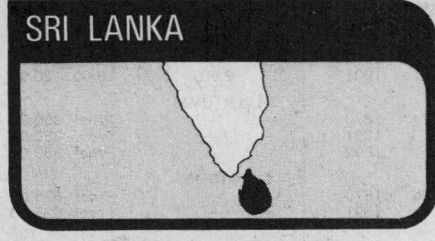

The Democratic Socialist Republic of Sri Lanka (formerly Ceylon) situated in the Indian Ocean 18 miles (29 km.) southeast of India, has an area of 25,332 sq. mi. (65,610 sq. km.) and a population of *17.5 million. Capital: Colombo. The economy is chiefly agricultural. Tea, coconut products and rubber are exported.

The earliest known inhabitants of Ceylon, the Veddahs, were subjugated by the Sinhalese from northern India in the 6th century B.C. Sinhalese rule was maintained until 1408, after which the island was controlled by China for 30 years. The Portuguese came to Ceylon in 1505 and maintained control of the coastal area for 150 years. They were supplanted by the Dutch in 1658, who were in turn supplanted by the British who seized the Dutch colonies in 1796, and made them a Crown Colony in 1802. In 1815, the British conquered the independent Kingdom of Kandy in the central part of the island. Constitutional changes in 1931 and 1946 granted the Ceylonese a measure of autonomy and a parliamentary form of government. Britain granted Ceylon independence as a self-governing republic within the British Commonwealth on Feb. 4, 1948. On May 22, 1972, the Ceylonese adopted a new Constitution which declared Ceylon to be the Republic of Sri Lanka - 'Resplendent Island'. Sri Lanka is a member of the Commonwealth of Nations. The president is Chief of State. The prime minister is Head of Government.

RULERS
British, 1796-1972

CEYLON

British Colonial Coinage

MINT MARKS
H - Heaton, Birmingham
B - Bombay

MONETARY SYSTEM
4 Pies = 1 Stiver
4 Stivers = 1 Fanam
12 Fanams = 1 Rixdollar = 1 Rupee = 1-1/2 Shillings
2 Rupees = 3 Shillings

DUMP COINAGE
1/4 PICE
(1/256 Rixdaler)

COPPER, dump
Obv: C.G., date. Rev: Value.

KM#	Date	Mintage	Good	VG	Fine	VF
72	1813	—	—	—	—	—

1/48 RIXDOLLAR

COPPER, dump
Rev: Elephant faces left.

63	1801	—	5.00	10.00	17.50	25.00
	1802	—	5.00	10.00	17.50	25.00
	1803	—	5.00	10.00	17.50	25.00
	1811	—	6.50	12.00	22.50	35.00
	1812	—	6.50	12.00	20.00	30.00
	1813	—	8.50	15.00	22.50	35.00
	1814	—	8.50	15.00	22.50	35.00
	1815	—	8.50	15.00	22.50	35.00
	1816	—	75.00	125.00	175.00	225.00

Obv: Two parallel lines under 48.

| 66 | 1802 | — | 15.00 | 20.00 | 30.00 | 60.00 |

Rev: Elephant faces right.

| 69 | 1803 | — | — | — | Unique | — |

1/24 RIXDOLLAR

COPPER, dump

64	1801	—	10.00	22.50	35.00	50.00
	1802	—	7.00	18.50	40.00	50.00
	1803	—	6.00	17.50	30.00	40.00
	1805	—	10.00	18.50	45.00	55.00
	1811	—	7.00	16.50	30.00	40.00
	1812	—	7.00	18.50	30.00	40.00
	1813	—	7.00	18.50	35.00	45.00
	1814	—	12.50	23.50	32.50	45.00
	1815	—	12.50	21.50	45.00	55.00
	1816	—	20.00	55.00	85.00	110.00

Obv: Two parallel lines under 24.

| 67 | 1802 | — | 55.00 | 125.00 | 300.00 | 350.00 |

Rev: Elephant faces right.

| 70 | 1803 | — | 50.00 | 125.00 | 175.00 | 250.00 |
| | 1805 | — | 50.00 | 125.00 | 175.00 | 250.00 |

1/12 RIXDOLLAR

COPPER, dump
Rev: Elephant faces left.

65	1801	—	10.00	25.00	32.50	45.00
	1802	—	8.00	16.50	25.00	35.00
	1803	—	8.00	16.50	25.00	35.00
	1804	—	12.50	25.00	35.00	55.00
	1805	—	12.50	25.00	35.00	55.00
	1811	—	9.00	22.50	35.00	45.00
	1812	—	9.00	22.50	35.00	45.00
	1813	—	9.00	30.00	45.00	60.00
	1814	—	9.00	27.50	45.00	60.00
	1815	—	9.00	22.50	35.00	55.00

Obv: Two parallel lines under 12.

| 68 | 1802 | 3 known | | | Rare | |

Rev: Elephant faces right.

| 71 | 1803 | — | 85.00 | 170.00 | 300.00 | 400.00 |

MILLED COINAGE
1/2 STIVER

COPPER

KM#	Date	Mintage	Fine	VF	XF	Unc
80	1815	2.400	4.00	12.00	25.00	100.00
	1815	—	—	—	Proof	225.00

STIVER

COPPER

| 81 | 1815 | 2.800 | 3.50 | 10.00 | 30.00 | 100.00 |
| | 1815 | — | — | — | Proof | 250.00 |

2 STIVERS

COPPER
Obv: W/o rose below bust.

| 82.1 | 1815 | 1.920 | 5.00 | 15.00 | 50.00 | 150.00 |
| | 1815 | — | — | — | Proof | 275.00 |

Obv: Rose below bust.

| 82.2 | 1815 | — | — | — | Proof | 200.00 |

24 STIVERS

.892 SILVER

KM#	Date	Mintage	VG	Fine	VF	XF
76	1803	—	17.50	35.00	65.00	100.00
	1804	—	20.00	40.00	70.00	100.00
	1805	—	35.00	70.00	120.00	150.00
	1808	—	25.00	55.00	100.00	150.00
	1809	—	35.00	70.00	115.00	150.00

48 STIVERS

.892 SILVER

77	1803	—	30.00	60.00	125.00	150.00
	1804	—	30.00	60.00	125.00	150.00
	1805	—	30.00	60.00	125.00	150.00
	1808	—	30.00	60.00	125.00	150.00
	1809	—	25.00	50.00	100.00	125.00

Rev: Elephant faces right.

| 78 | 1803 | — | 75.00 | 125.00 | 175.00 | 225.00 |

96 STIVERS

.833 SILVER

79	1803	—	40.00	80.00	125.00	175.00
	1808	—	—	—	—	—
	1809	—	45.00	90.00	150.00	200.00

1/192 RIXDOLLAR

COPPER

KM#	Date	Mintage	Fine	VF	XF	Unc
73	1802	3.600	2.50	7.50	20.00	60.00
	1802	—	—	—	Proof	100.00
	1802	—	—	—	Gilt Proof	75.00
	1804	—	—	—	Proof	175.00
	1804	—	—	—	Gilt Proof	175.00

1/96 RIXDOLLAR

COPPER

74	1802	1.800	4.00	8.00	22.50	75.00
	1802	—	—	—	Proof	125.00
	1802	—	—	—	Gilt Proof	100.00

1/48 RIXDOLLAR

COPPER

75	1802	2.700	5.00	10.00	25.00	80.00
	1802	—	—	—	Proof	150.00
	1802	—	—	—	Gilt Proof	120.00
	1804	—	—	—	Proof	225.00
	1804	—	—	—	Gilt Proof	225.00

RIX DOLLAR

.892 SILVER

KM#	Date	Mintage	Fine	VF	XF	Unc
84	1821	.400	12.00	28.00	80.00	220.00
	1821	—	—	—	Proof	250.00

COUNTERMARKED COINAGE
1/3 RIXDOLLAR
SILVER, dump
c/m: Crown on Madras Arcot 1/4 Rupee.

KM#	Date	Mintage	VG	Fine	VF	XF
85	ND(1823)	.260	22.50	50.00	90.00	150.00

1-1/3 RIXDOLLAR
(16 Fanams)
SILVER, dump
c/m: Crown on Madras Arcot Rupee.

| 86 | ND(1823) | .282 | 80.00 | 160.00 | 240.00 | 360.00 |

HOMELAND COINAGE
4 Farthings = 1 Penny
1/4 FARTHING

COPPER and BRONZE
NOTE: From 1839 through 1868 homeland type 1/4 Farthings were issued by Great Britain for circulation in Ceylon. These are listed under Great Britain.

1/2 FARTHING

COPPER and BRONZE
NOTE: From 1828 through 1868 homeland type 1/2 Farthings were issued by Great Britain for circulation in Ceylon. These are listed under Great Britain.

1-1/2 PENCE

SILVER
NOTE: From 1834 through 1870 homeland type 1 1/2 Pence were issued by Great Britain for circulation in Ceylon and Jamaica. These are listed under Great Britain.

DECIMAL COINAGE
100 Cents = 1 Rupee
1/4 CENT

COPPER

KM#	Date	Mintage	Fine	VF	XF	Unc
90	1870	.200	1.50	3.00	5.00	10.00
	1870	—	—	—	Proof	70.00
	1890	.200	1.50	3.00	5.00	10.00
	1890	—	—	—	Proof	70.00
	1891	—	—	—	Proof	100.00
	1892	—	—	—	Proof	100.00
	1898	.160	2.50	5.00	8.00	15.00
	1898	—	—	—	Proof	70.00
	1901	.216	1.50	3.00	5.00	10.00
	1901	—	—	—	Proof	70.00

SILVER (OMS)

90a	1870	—	—	—	Proof	200.00
	1890	—	—	—	Proof	200.00
	1891	—	—	—	Proof	200.00
	1898	—	—	—	Proof	200.00

GOLD (OMS)

90b	1870	—	—	—	Proof	450.00
	1891	—	—	—	Proof	450.00
	1904	—	—	—	Proof	450.00

COPPER

KM#	Date	Mintage	Fine	VF	XF	Unc
100	1904	.103	2.50	5.00	10.00	20.00
	1904	—	—	—	Proof	100.00

1/2 CENT

COPPER

91	1870	3.040	1.00	1.50	3.00	8.00
	1870	—	—	—	Proof	75.00
	1890	.400	1.50	3.50	8.00	16.00
	1890	—	—	—	Proof	80.00
	1891	1.000	1.25	2.75	4.00	12.00
	1891	—	—	—	Proof	75.00
	1892	—	—	—	Proof	150.00
	1895	4.040	1.00	1.75	3.00	8.00
	1895	—	—	—	Proof	75.00
	1898	4.000	1.25	2.50	4.00	10.00
	1898	—	—	—	Proof	75.00
	1901	2.020	1.25	2.50	4.00	10.00

SILVER (OMS)

91a	1870	—	—	—	Proof	250.00
	1890	—	—	—	Proof	250.00
	1891	—	—	—	Proof	250.00
	1895	—	—	—	Proof	250.00
	1898	—	—	—	Proof	250.00

GOLD (OMS)

91b	1870	—	—	—	Proof	550.00
	1891	—	—	—	Proof	550.00
	1895	—	—	—	Proof	550.00

COPPER

101	1904	2.012	1.00	2.00	5.00	12.00
	1904	—	—	—	Proof	75.00
	1905	1.000	1.50	3.00	6.00	15.00
	1905	—	—	—	Proof	75.00
	1906	3.056	1.00	2.00	5.00	12.00
	1906	—	—	—	Proof	75.00
	1908	1.000	1.50	3.00	6.00	15.00
	1908	—	—	—	Proof	75.00
	1909	3.000	1.00	2.00	5.00	12.00
	1909	—	—	—	Proof	75.00

106	1912	5.008	1.25	2.75	4.00	10.00
	1912	—	—	—	Proof	75.00
	1914	2.000	1.25	2.75	6.00	12.00
	1914	—	—	—	Proof	75.00
	1917	2.000	1.50	3.00	6.00	12.00
	1917	—	—	—	Proof	75.00
	1926	5.000	.50	1.00	2.00	5.00

110	1937	3.026	.30	.85	1.50	3.50
	1937	—	—	—	Proof	125.00
	1940	5.080	.25	.65	1.25	3.00

CENT

COPPER

92	1870	7.055	1.50	3.00	6.00	15.00
	1870	—	—	—	Proof	75.00
	1890	4.940	1.50	3.00	5.00	12.00
	1890	—	—	—	Proof	75.00
	1891	1.328	2.00	4.00	8.00	20.00
	1891	—	—	—	Proof	75.00
	1892	5.000	1.50	3.00	6.00	15.00

KM#	Date	Mintage	Fine	VF	XF	Unc
92	1892	—	—	—	Proof	75.00
	1900	1.000	2.50	5.00	10.00	20.00
	1900	—	—	—	Proof	175.00
	1901	1.014	2.50	5.00	10.00	20.00

SILVER (OMS)

92a	1870	—	—	—	Proof	350.00
	1891	—	—	—	Proof	350.00
	1892	—	—	—	Proof	350.00

GOLD (OMS)

| 92b | 1870 | — | — | — | Proof | 625.00 |
| | 1891 | — | — | — | Proof | 625.00 |

COPPER

102	1904	2.529	1.00	2.00	4.00	8.00
	1904	—	—	—	Proof	75.00
	1905	1.509	1.25	2.25	5.00	10.00
	1905	—	—	—	Proof	75.00
	1906	1.751	1.25	2.25	5.00	10.00
	1906	—	—	—	Proof	75.00
	1908	—	1.00	2.00	4.00	8.00
	1908	—	—	—	Proof	75.00
	1909	2.500	1.00	2.00	4.00	8.00
	1909	—	—	—	Proof	75.00
	1910	8.236	.50	1.00	2.50	5.00
	1910	—	—	—	Proof	75.00

107	1912	5.855	.50	1.00	2.00	4.00
	1912	—	—	—	Proof	75.00
	1914	6.000	.50	1.00	2.25	5.00
	1914	—	—	—	Proof	75.00
	1917	1.000	1.00	1.75	3.00	8.00
	1917	—	—	—	Proof	75.00
	1920	2.000	.50	1.00	2.25	5.00
	1920	—	—	—	Proof	75.00
	1922	2.930	.50	1.00	2.25	5.00
	1922	—	—	—	Proof	75.00
	1923	2.500	.50	1.00	2.25	5.00
	1923	—	—	—	Proof	75.00
	1925	7.490	.35	.75	1.50	3.50
	1925	—	—	—	Proof	75.00
	1926	3.750	.35	.75	1.50	3.50
	1926	—	—	—	Proof	75.00
	1928	2.500	.35	.75	1.50	4.00
	1928	—	—	—	Proof	75.00
	1929	5.000	.35	.75	1.50	3.50
	1929	—	—	—	Proof	75.00

111	1937	4.538	.25	.50	1.25	3.00
	1937	—	—	—	Proof	—
	1940	10.190	.15	.30	1.00	2.00
	1940	—	—	—	Proof	75.00
	1942	20.780	.15	.30	1.00	2.00

BRONZE

111a	1942	Inc. Ab.	.15	.30	.75	1.75
	1942	—	—	—	Proof	75.00
	1943	43.705	.15	.30	.50	1.25
	1945	34.100	.15	.35	.60	1.20
	1945*	—	—	—	Proof	20.00

*NOTE: These were restruck in quantity.

ALUMINUM

| 127 | 1963 | 33.000 | — | — | — | .10 |

KM#	Date	Mintage	Fine	VF	XF	Unc
127	1963	—	—	—	Proof	—
	1965	12.000	—	—	.10	.15
	1967	10.000	—	—	.10	.15
	1968	22.505	—	—	—	.10
	1969	10.000	—	—	—	.10
	1970	15.000	—	—	—	.10
	1971	55.000	—	—	—	.10
	1971	—	—	—	Proof	.50

2 CENTS

NICKEL-BRASS
117	1944	30.165	.10	.25	.50	1.00

Obv. leg: W/o EMPEROR OF INDIA.
| 119 | 1951 | 15.000 | .10 | .25 | .75 | 1.50 |
| | 1951 | — | — | — | Proof | 20.00 |

124	1955	37.131	.10	.15	.25	.50
	1957	38.200	.10	.15	.25	.50
	1957	—	—	—	—	75.00

ALUMINUM
128	1963	26.000	—	—	.10	.15
	1963	—	—	—	Proof	—
	1965	7.000	—	—	.10	.15
	1967	15.000	—	—	.10	.15
	1968	15.000	—	—	.10	.15
	1969	—	—	—	.10	.15
	1970	13.000	—	—	.10	.15
	1971	45.000	—	—	.10	.15
	1971	—	—	—	Proof	1.00

5 CENTS

COPPER
93	1870	7.009	5.00	10.00	30.00	80.00
	1870	—	—	—	Proof	125.00
	1890	1.001	7.50	20.00	50.00	110.00
	1890	—	—	—	Proof	135.00
	1891	—	—	—	Proof	225.00
	1892	1.000	7.50	20.00	50.00	110.00
	1892	—	—	—	Proof	135.00

SILVER (OMS)
93a	1890	—	—	—	Proof	400.00
	1891	—	—	—	Proof	400.00
	1892	—	—	—	Proof	400.00

GOLD (OMS)
| 93b | 1891 | — | — | — | Proof | 1000. |

COPPER-NICKEL
| 103 | 1909 | 2.000 | 1.50 | 3.00 | 5.00 | 15.00 |
| | 1910 | 4.000 | 1.00 | 2.00 | 3.50 | 10.00 |

KM#	Date	Mintage	Fine	VF	XF	Unc
108	1912H	4.000	.75	1.50	3.00	8.00
	1920	6.000	.50	1.00	2.00	6.00
	1926	3.000	.75	1.50	4.00	10.00

NICKEL-BRASS
113.1	1942	12.752	.35	.75	1.50	4.00
	1942	—	—	—	Proof	50.00
	1943	Inc. Ab.	.35	.75	1.50	4.00
	1943	—	—	—	Proof	50.00

Thin Planchet
113.2	1944	18.064	.20	.35	.70	1.75
	1945	31.192	.15	.30	.60	1.50
	1945	—	—	—	Proof	60.00

NOTE: Varieties exist in bust, denomination and legend placement for 1945.

Obv. leg: W/o EMPEROR OF INDIA.
| 120 | 1951 | — | — | — | Proof | 20.00 |

129	1963	16.000	—	.10	.15	.25
	1963	—	—	—	Proof	—
	1965	9.000	—	.10	.15	.25
	1968	12.000	—	.10	.15	.25
	1968	—	—	—	Proof	3.00
	1969	2.500	—	.10	.20	.40
	1970	7.000	—	.10	.15	.25
	1971	32.000	—	.10	.15	.25
	1971	—	—	—	Proof	1.50

10 CENTS

1.1664 g, .800 SILVER, .0300 oz ASW
94	1892	2.500	1.50	3.50	7.00	15.00
	1892	—	—	—	Proof	100.00
	1893	2.500	1.50	3.50	7.00	15.00
	1893	—	—	—	Proof	100.00
	1894	3.000	1.50	3.50	7.00	15.00
	1894	—	—	—	Proof	100.00
	1897	1.500	1.50	3.50	9.00	20.00
	1899	1.000	1.75	4.00	10.00	25.00
	1900	1.000	1.75	4.00	10.00	25.00

97	1902	1.000	1.00	2.50	6.00	20.00
	1902	—	—	—	Proof	100.00
	1903	1.000	1.00	2.50	6.00	20.00
	1903	—	—	—	Proof	100.00
	1907	.500	2.50	5.00	15.00	25.00
	1908	1.500	1.00	2.50	6.00	15.00
	1909	1.000	1.00	2.50	6.00	15.00
	1910	2.000	1.00	2.50	6.00	15.00

104	1911	1.000	1.00	1.75	5.00	12.00
	1912	1.000	1.25	2.00	6.00	15.00
	1913	2.000	1.00	1.50	4.00	10.00
	1914	2.000	1.00	1.50	4.00	10.00
	1914	—	—	—	Proof	100.00
	1917	.879	1.00	2.50	7.50	17.50
	1917	—	—	—	Proof	100.00

1.1664 g, .550 SILVER, .0206 oz ASW
| 104a | 1919B | .750 | 1.50 | 3.50 | 10.00 | 20.00 |
| | 1919B | — | — | — | Proof | 100.00 |

KM#	Date	Mintage	Fine	VF	XF	Unc
104a	1920B	3.059	1.00	2.50	6.00	15.00
	1920B	—	—	—	Proof	100.00
	1921B	1.583	.75	1.75	5.00	10.00
	1921B	—	—	—	Proof	100.00
	1922	.282	1.75	3.50	10.00	25.00
	1922	—	—	—	Proof	100.00
	1924	1.508	.75	1.75	4.00	10.00
	1924	—	—	—	Proof	100.00
	1925	1.500	.75	1.75	4.00	10.00
	1925	—	—	—	Proof	100.00
	1926	1.500	.75	1.75	4.00	10.00
	1926	—	—	—	Proof	100.00
	1927	1.500	.75	1.75	4.00	10.00
	1927	—	—	—	Proof	100.00
	1928	1.500	.75	1.75	4.00	10.00
	1928	—	—	—	Proof	100.00

1.1664 g, .800 SILVER, .0300 oz ASW
| 112 | 1941 | 16.271 | .65 | 1.00 | 2.50 | 6.00 |

NICKEL-BRASS
| 118 | 1944 | 30.500 | .25 | .50 | 1.00 | 2.00 |

Obv. leg: W/o EMPEROR OF INDIA.
121	1951	34.760	.10	.20	.40	1.00
	1951	—	—	—	Proof	15.00
	1951	*3.000	—	Proof restrike		4.00

***NOTE:** Restrikes differ in the formation of native characters.

130	1963	14.000	—	.10	.15	.25
	1963	—	—	—	Proof	—
	1965	3.000	—	.10	.15	.35
	1969	6.000	—	.10	.15	.25
	1970	—	—	—	.10	.15	.25
	1971	29.000	—	.10	.15	.20
	1971	—	—	—	Proof	1.25

25 CENTS

2.9160 g, .800 SILVER, .0750 oz ASW
95	1892	.500	5.00	10.00	22.00	50.00
	1892	—	—	—	Proof	100.00
	1893	1.500	3.00	7.00	15.00	35.00
	1893	—	—	—	Proof	100.00
	1895	1.200	3.00	7.00	15.00	35.00
	1899	.600	5.00	10.00	22.00	50.00
	1900	.400	6.00	12.00	25.00	60.00

98	1902	.400	4.00	8.00	20.00	40.00
	1902	—	—	—	Proof	100.00
	1903	.400	4.00	8.00	20.00	40.00
	1903	—	—	—	Proof	100.00
	1907	.120	7.50	20.00	30.00	50.00
	1908	.400	4.00	8.00	15.00	35.00
	1909	.400	4.00	8.00	15.00	35.00
	1910	.800	2.00	5.00	10.00	20.00
	1911	.400	3.00	6.00	12.00	30.00

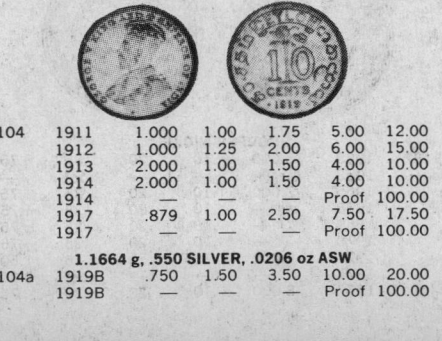

Ceylon / SRI LANKA 1546

KM#	Date	Mintage	Fine	VF	XF	Unc
105	1911	—	—	—	Proof	125.00
	1913	1.200	1.50	2.50	7.50	17.50
	1913	—	—	—	Proof	125.00
	1914	.400	3.00	6.00	12.00	25.00
	1914	—	—	—	Proof	125.00
	1917	.300	4.00	8.00	15.00	35.00
	1917	—	—	—	Proof	125.00

2.9160 g, .550 SILVER, .0516 oz ASW

105a	1919B	1.400	1.25	3.00	7.50	15.00
	1919B	—	—	—	Proof	100.00
	1920B	1.600	1.25	3.00	7.50	15.00
	1920B	—	—	—	Proof	100.00
	1921B	.600	3.50	7.50	15.00	30.00
	1921B	—	—	—	Proof	100.00
	1922	1.211	1.25	3.25	7.50	15.00
	1922	—	—	—	Proof	100.00
	1925	1.004	1.25	3.50	7.50	15.00
	1925	—	—	—	Proof	100.00
	1926	1.000	1.25	3.50	7.50	15.00
	1926	—	—	—	Proof	100.00

NICKEL-BRASS

| 115 | 1943 | 13.920 | .25 | .50 | 1.00 | 2.00 |

Obv. leg: W/o EMPEROR OF INDIA.

122	1951	25.940	.10	.30	—	1.50
	1951	—	—	—	Proof	20.00
	1951	*2.500	—	Proof restrike	—	4.00

*NOTE: Numerals 9 and 5 differ on restrikes.

COPPER-NICKEL

131	1963	30.000	—	.10	.20	.40
	1963	—	—	—	Proof	—
	1965	8.000	—	.10	.25	.50
	1968	—	—	.10	.25	.50
	1969	—	—	.10	.25	.50
	1970	—	—	.10	.25	.50
	1971	24.000	—	.10	.15	.30
	1971	—	—	—	Proof	1.50

50 CENTS

5.8319 g, .800 SILVER, .1500 oz ASW

96	1892	.250	10.00	20.00	40.00	80.00
	1892	—	—	—	Proof	150.00
	1893	.750	6.00	12.00	27.50	45.00
	1893	—	—	—	Proof	125.00
	1895	.450	5.00	8.00	30.00	60.00
	1899	.100	12.50	30.00	50.00	100.00
	1900	.200	5.00	10.00	30.00	70.00

99	1902	.200	5.00	10.00	30.00	70.00
	1902	—	—	—	Proof	125.00
	1903	.800	3.00	8.00	18.00	35.00
	1903	—	—	—	Proof	125.00
	1910	.200	7.00	13.00	30.00	60.00
109	1913	.400	7.00	13.00	30.00	60.00

KM#	Date	Mintage	Fine	VF	XF	Unc
109	1913	—	—	—	Proof	125.00
	1914	.200	5.00	15.00	30.00	60.00
	1914	—	—	—	Proof	125.00
	1917	1.073	2.50	5.00	10.00	20.00
	1917	—	—	—	Proof	125.00

5.8319 g, .550 SILVER, .1031 oz ASW

109a	1919B	.750	1.00	3.00	7.50	16.00
	1919B	—	—	—	Proof	90.00
	1920B	.800	1.00	3.00	7.00	16.00
	1920B	—	—	—	Proof	90.00
	1921B	.800	1.00	3.00	7.00	16.00
	1921B	—	—	—	Proof	90.00
	1922	1.040	1.00	3.00	7.00	16.00
	1922	—	—	—	Proof	90.00
	1924	1.010	1.00	3.00	7.00	16.00
	1924	—	—	—	Proof	90.00
	1925	.500	2.00	5.00	10.00	20.00
	1925	—	—	—	Proof	90.00
	1926	.500	2.00	5.00	10.00	20.00
	1926	—	—	—	Proof	90.00
	1927	.500	2.00	5.00	10.00	20.00
	1927	—	—	—	Proof	90.00
	1928	.500	2.00	5.00	10.00	20.00
	1928	—	—	—	Proof	90.00
	1929	.500	2.00	5.00	10.00	20.00
	1929	—	—	—	Proof	90.00

| 114 | 1942 | .662 | 2.00 | 4.00 | 8.00 | 17.50 |

BRASS

| 114a | 1943 | 6 known | — | — | Proof | 500.00 |

NICKEL-BRASS

| 116 | 1943 | 8.600 | .35 | .75 | 1.50 | 3.00 |

Obv. leg: W/o EMPEROR OF INDIA.

123	1951	19.980	.20	.35	.75	1.50
	1951	—	—	—	Proof	20.00
	1951	*1.500	—	Proof restrike	—	5.00

*NOTE: Restrikes differ slightly in the formation of native inscriptions.

COPPER-NICKEL

132	1963	15.000	.10	.20	.35	.75
	1963	—	—	—	Proof	—
	1965	7.000	.10	.20	.35	.75
	1968	—	.10	.20	.35	.75
	1969	—	.10	.20	.35	.75
	1970	—	.10	.20	.35	.75
	1971	4.000	.25	.50	.75	1.50
	1971	—	—	—	Proof	2.00
	1972	8.000	.10	.20	.35	.75

RUPEE

COPPER-NICKEL
2500 Years of Buddhism

KM#	Date	Mintage	Fine	VF	XF	Unc
125	1957	2.000	.50	1.00	2.00	3.00
	1957	1,800	—	—	Proof	15.00

133	1963	20.000	.10	.20	.40	1.00
	1963	—	—	—	Proof	—
	1965	5.000	.15	.25	.50	1.50
	1969	2.500	.15	.25	.50	1.50
	1970	—	.15	.25	.50	1.50
	1971	5.000	.15	.25	.50	1.25
	1971	—	—	—	Proof	3.00
	1972	7.000	.15	.25	.50	1.00

2 RUPEES

COPPER-NICKEL
F.A.O. Issue

| 134 | 1968 | — | .50 | 1.50 | 2.25 | 3.00 |

5 RUPEES

28.2757 g, .925 SILVER, .8409 oz ASW
2500 Years of Buddhism

126	1957	.500	8.00	12.50	17.50	30.00
	1957	1,800	—	—	Proof	65.00

PROOF SETS (PS)

KM#	Date	Mintage	Identification	Issue Price	Mkt. Val.
PS1	1951(6)	150*	KM111a,119-123	—	40.00

*NOTE: Restrikes exist.

PS2	1957(2)	400	KM125-126	—	90.00
PS3	1957(4)	700	KM125-126 (2 each)	—	160.00
PS4	1971(7)	20,000	KM127-133	—	10.00

SRI LANKA
100 Cents = 1 Rupee

CENT

ALUMINUM

KM#	Date	Mintage	VF	XF	Unc
137	1975	52.778	—	.10	.25
	1975	1,431	—	Proof	2.00
	1978	34.006	—	.10	.25
	1978	Inc. Ab.	—	Proof	2.00

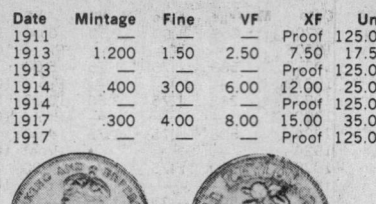

2 CENTS

ALUMINUM

KM#	Date	Mintage	VF	XF	Unc
138	1975	62.503	—	.10	.25
	1975	1,431	—	Proof	2.50
	1977	2.500	—	.10	.25
	1978	23.425	—	.10	.25
	1978	Inc. Ab.	—	Proof	3.00

5 CENTS

NICKEL-BRASS

139	1975	19.584	—	.10	.25
	1975	1,431	—	Proof	2.50

ALUMINUM

139a	1978	272.308	—	.10	.25
	1978	Inc. Ab.	—	Proof	3.00

10 CENTS

NICKEL-BRASS

140	1975	10.800	—	.10	.25
	1975	1,431	—	Proof	4.25

ALUMINUM

140a	1978	188.820	—	.10	.25
	1978	Inc. Ab.	—	Proof	3.00

25 CENTS

COPPER-NICKEL
Security edge

141.1	1975	39.600	—	.10	.25
	1975	1,431	—	Proof	3.00
	1978	65.009	—	.10	.25
	1978	Inc. Ab.	—	Proof	3.00

Reeded edge

141.2	1982	90.000	—	.10	.25
	1982	Inc. Ab.	—	Proof	3.00

50 CENTS

COPPER-NICKEL
Security edge

135.1	1972	11.000	.15	.30	.60
	1975	34.000	.15	.30	.60
	1975	1,431	—	Proof	4.00
	1978	66.010	.15	.30	.60
	1978	Inc. Ab.	—	Proof	4.00

Reeded edge

135.2	1982	65.000	.10	.20	.50
	1982	Inc. Ab.	—	Proof	4.00

RUPEE

COPPER-NICKEL
Security edge

KM#	Date	Mintage	VF	XF	Unc
136.1	1972	5.000	.30	.60	1.25
	1975	31.500	.25	.50	1.00
	1975	1,431	—	Proof	6.50
	1978	37.018	.25	.50	1.00
	1978	Inc. Ab.	—	Proof	6.50

Reeded edge

136.2	1982	75.000	.25	.50	1.00
	1982	Inc. Ab.	—	Proof	5.00

Inauguration of President

144	1978	2.000	.30	.60	1.50
	1978	—	—	Proof	8.00

2 RUPEES

COPPER-NICKEL
Non-Aligned Nations Conference

142	1976	2.000	.50	1.00	1.50
	1976	1,000	—	Proof	7.50

Mahaweli Dam

145	1981	45.000	.25	.50	1.25

Circulation Coinage

147	1984	25.000	.25	.50	1.00

5 RUPEES

NICKEL
Non-Aligned Nations Conference

143	1976	1.000	.75	1.25	2.50
	1976	1,000	—	Proof	12.00

COPPER-NICKEL

Universal Adult Franchise

KM#	Date	Mintage	VF	XF	Unc
146	1981	2.000	.50	1.00	1.50

ALUMINUM-BRONZE
Circulation Coinage

148	1984	25.000	.25	.50	1:25
	1986	—	.25	.50	1.25

NOTE: Varieties in edge inscriptions exist.

10 RUPEES

COPPER-NICKEL
I.Y.S.H.

149	1987				3.00

PROOF SETS (PS)

KM#	Date	Mintage	Identification	Issue Price	Mkt. Val.
PS1	1978 (7)	20,000	KM135-138,139a-140a,141	26.00	20.00

Listings For
STRAITS SETTLEMENTS: refer to Malaysia

SUDAN

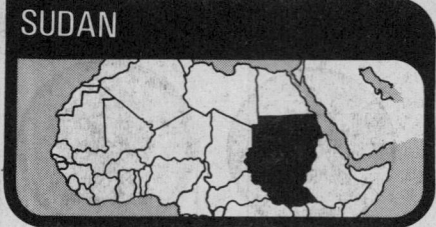

The Republic of the Sudan, located in northeast Africa on the Red Sea between Egypt and Ethiopia, has an area of 967,500 sq. mi. (2,505,813 sq. km.) and a population of *25 million. Capital: Khartoum. Agriculture and livestock raising are the chief occupations. Cotton, gum arabic and peanuts are exported.

The Sudan, site of the powerful Nubian kingdom of Roman times, was a collection of small independent states from the 14th century until 1820-22 when it was conquered and united by Mohammed Ali, Pasha of Egypt. Egyptian forces were driven from the area during the Mahdist revolt, 1881-98, but the Sudan was retaken by Anglo-Egyptian expeditions, 1896-98, and established as an Anglo-Egyptian condominium in 1899. Britain supplied the administrative apparatus and personnel, but the appearance of joint Anglo-Egyptian administration was continued until Jan. 9, 1954, when the first Sudanese self-government parliament was inaugurated. The Sudan achieved independence on Jan. 1, 1956 with the consent of the British and Egyptian government.

TITLES

El-Jomhuriyat Es-Sudan

MINTNAME

ام درمان

Omdurman

RULERS
Mohammed Ahmed (the Mahdi),
AH1298-1302/1881-1885AD
Abdullah Ibn Mohammed (the Khalifa)
AH1302-1316/1885-1898AD

MONETARY SYSTEM
40 Para = 1 Ghirsh = Piastre

MOHAMMED AHMED (the Mahdi)
Khartoum Mint
Translation of Arabic legends on Mahdi coinage:

با أمر المهدى - by order of the Mahdi (in Tughra)

ضرب - Struck (Dar)

في - In (El)

الهجرة - Hejira

١٣٠٢ - 1302

سنة - Sanat(year)

10 PIASTRES

SILVER

KM#	Date	Year	VG	Fine	VF	XF
1	AH1302	5	—	—	Rare	—

20 PIASTRES

SILVER

KM#	Date	Year	VG	Fine	VF	XF
2	AH1302	5	225.00	325.00	500.00	700.00

100 PIASTRES

GOLD

3	AH1255	2	—	—	Rare	—

NOTE: Struck by the Mahdi which is a copy of Egyptian coin under Turkish Sultan. This issue is more crude than the Egyptian type and has crude edge milling. Reverse Arabic legend "Struck in Misr" (Egypt); however they were struck in the Sudan about AH1302.

ABDULLAH IBN MOHAMMED
(the Khalifa)
Omdurman Mint

مقبول - Accepted (money) i.e., legal (Tughra) - 'Maqbul'

سنة ٥ - Sanat (year) 5

سنة ٤ - Sanat (year) 4

سنة ١١ - Sanat 11 (year)

ضرب - Struck - 'Duriba'

في - At

ام درمان - Omdurman

١٣٠٤ - 1304 (A.H.)

١٣٠٩ - 1309 (A.H.)

٢٠ - 20

قرش - ش - Guresh - Piastres

عملة جديدة - New coinage (in tughra) - 'Umla Jadida'

جيد - Good - 'Jayyid'

عز نصره - May his victory be glorified- 'Azza Nasruhu'

ش ٢٠ - 20 Piastres

NOTE: The coins of the Khalifa have been reordered in this edition by Yeoman #'s rather than by metallic composition. Except for the 10 Para (Y#4), which is of copper (more or less pure), the remaining coins (Y#6-32a) show the following progressive debasement:

AH Year Metallic Composition
1304 - Silver
1309 - Debased Silver
1310 - Debased Silver, Silver—Washed Copper, Billon
1311 - Billon, Silver-Washed Copper, Copper
1312 - Billon, Silver-Washed Copper, Copper
1315 - Copper, Sometimes Silver-Washed.

NOTE: The metal is not indicated beneath the photos, as usual, because each type occurs in a range of debasements. Different degrees of debasement do not constitute definable subtypes.

10 PARA
25mm

KM#	Date	Year	VG	Fine	VF	XF
8	AH1308	6				

NOTE: Probably a pattern.

PIASTRE
(Ghirsh)

Plain borders, 18mm

4	AH1304	1	60.00	100.00	150.00	250.00
	1311	9	40.00	65.00	100.00	175.00
	1311	11	40.00	65.00	100.00	175.00

2 PIASTRES

Plain borders, 18mm

9	AH1310	8	65.00	100.00	250.00	250.00
	1311	9	65.00	100.00	250.00	250.00
	1311	11	65.00	100.00	250.00	250.00

Wreath borders

18	AH1311	11	20.00	35.00	75.00	75.00

Borders of crescents, stars and roses.

22	AH1312	—	25.00	40.00	125.00	125.00

2-1/2 PIASTRES

Obv: *Umla Jadida* below toughra.
Border of crescents, stars, circles.

23.1	AH1312	—	20.00	35.00	90.00	90.00

NOTE: KM#23.1 differs from KM#22 by the presence of the *Shadda* which looks like the letter W, after the numeral "2" on the reverse.

Obv: *Maqbul* below toughra.
Border of crescents, stars, circles.

23.2	AH1312	—	30.00	50.00	140.00	140.00

Border of crescents only.

24	AH1312	—	25.00	45.00	125.00	125.00

4 PIASTRES
Plain borders, 25mm

10	AH1310	8	175.00	250.00	500.00	500.00

5 PIASTRES

Border of double crescents.

5	AH1304	4	35.00	55.00	150.00	150.00
	1304	5	20.00	40.00	125.00	125.00
	1311	11	15.00	27.50	75.00	100.00

NOTE: Coins of AH1304/yr. 4 come in two varieties, one with numeral 1 at top on reverse and one with 4.

Plain borders, 21-22mm

11	AH1310	8	45.00	75.00	250.00	300.00

Borders of crescents and stars.

19	AH1311	—	20.00	40.00	80.00	100.00

Borders of crescents only

20	AH1311	—	40.00	60.00	100.00	175.00

10 PIASTRES

Borders of double crescents.

KM#	Date	Year	VG	Fine	VF	XF
6	AH1304	4	75.00	150.00	250.00	350.00
	1311	11	50.00	100.00	200.00	300.00

Plain borders

| 12 | AH1310 | 8 | 50.00 | 150.00 | 300.00 | 400.00 |

Wreath borders

| 13 | AH1310 | 8 | 65.00 | 110.00 | 150.00 | 250.00 |

20 PIASTRES

Borders of double crescents.

7	AH1304	4	10.00	25.00	40.00	75.00
1304 on obv. w/1 on rev.		5	10.00	25.00	40.00	75.00
1309 on obv. w/1 on rev., normal date		5	10.00	22.50	35.00	60.00
1309 on obv. w/1 on rev., 9 of date retrograde		5	20.00	37.50	60.00	100.00

Borders of crescents, stars and roses.

14	AH1310	10	10.00	15.00	25.00	40.00
	1311	—	10.00	15.00	25.00	40.00
	1311	9	10.00	15.00	25.00	40.00
	1311	11	10.00	15.00	25.00	40.00
	1312	11	10.00	15.00	25.00	40.00
	1312	12	10.00	15.00	25.00	40.00
	1312	—	10.00	15.00	25.00	40.00

Borders of crescents only.
Rev: W/o *Azza Nasruhu.*

21	AH1311	11	12.50	25.00	40.00	75.00
	1312	12	12.50	25.00	40.00	75.00

Borders of crescents only.
Rev: *Azza Nasruhu.*

KM#	Date	Year	VG	Fine	VF	XF
25	AH1302	9	15.00	30.00	50.00	100.00
	1312	12	10.00	20.00	30.00	55.00

NOTE: The date 1302 on the year 9 is in error for 1312, and is not to be confused with the Mahdi crown, KM#2.

AH1315, R.Y. 8

AH1312, R.Y. 12
Rev: Wreath borders w/spears below.

15	AH1310	8	10.00	17.50	27.50	55.00
	1311	11	12.00	25.00	40.00	75.00
	1312	12	7.00	12.50	20.00	40.00
	1315	8	6.00	11.50	18.50	35.00

NOTE: Many minor die varieties of this type exist.

Obv. and rev: Wreath w/spears below.

| 16 | AH1310 | 8 | 20.00 | 35.00 | 50.00 | 100.00 |

Wreath borders. W/o spears on either side.

17	AH1310	8	8.00	15.00	25.00	40.00
	1315	12	8.00	15.00	25.00	40.00

AH1312, R.Y. 12
Wreath borders. Obv: Spears below.

26	AH1312	12	4.00	6.50	10.00	20.00
	1313	13	7.00	14.00	20.00	35.00
	1315	8	7.00	12.50	17.50	30.00
	1315	12	7.00	12.50	17.50	30.00

REPUBLIC
10 Millim (Milliemes) = 1 Ghirsh (Piastre)

MILLIM

BRONZE

KM#	Date	Year	Mintage	VF	XF	Unc
29	AH1376	1956	5.000	—	.10	.20
	1379	1960	1.300	—	.10	.25
	1387	1967	—	—	.10	.20
	1387	1967	7,834	—	Proof	.25
	1388	1968	—	—	.10	.20
	1388	1968	5,251	—	Proof	.50
	1389	1969	—	—	.10	.20
	1389	1969	2,149	—	Proof	1.00

NOTE: Except for the proof sets, mintage figures have not generally been made available since 1967. Existence of circulation strikes of KM#29-36 of years 1967, 68, 69 are uncertain.

Rev: New Arabic legends.

39	AH1390	1970	1,646	—	Proof	1.00
	1391	1971	1,772	—	Proof	1.00

NOTE: Existence of circulation strikes of KM#39-45 dated 1970 or 1971 is uncertain, despite unconfirmed reports of their existence.

2 MILLIM

BRONZE

30	AH1376	1956	5.000	—	.10	.35
	1387	1967	—	—	.10	.20
	1387	1967	7,834	—	Proof	.50
	1388	1968	—	—	.10	.20
	1388	1968	5,251	—	Proof	.75
	1389	1969	—	—	.10	.20
	1389	1969	2,149	—	Proof	1.00

40	AH1390	1970	1,646	—	Proof	1.25
	1391	1971	1,772	—	Proof	1.25

5 MILLIM

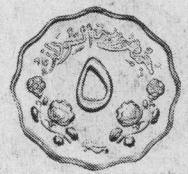

BRONZE

31	AH1376	1956	30.000	.10	.20	.40
	1382	1962	6.000	.10	.20	.40
	1386	1966	4.000	.10	.15	.30
	1387	1967	4.000	.10	.15	.30
	1387	1967	7,834	—	Proof	.75
	1388	1968	—	.10	.15	.30
	1388	1968	5,251	—	Proof	1.00
	1389	1969	—	.10	.15	.30
	1389	1969	2,149	—	Proof	1.25

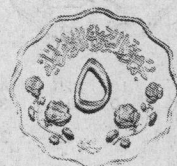

41	AH1390	1970	—	.20	.40	.80
	1390	1970	1,646	—	Proof	1.25
	1391	1971	3.000	.20	.40	.80
	1391	1971	1,772	—	Proof	1.25

SUDAN 1550

Anniversary of Revolution

KM#	Date	Year	Mintage	VF	XF	Unc
47	AH1391	1971	.500	.10	.15	.35

F.A.O. Issue

53	AH1392	1972	6.000	—	.10	.20
	1393	1973	9.000	—	.10	.15
54	AH1392	1972	—	—	.10	.30

BRASS
Rev: Ribbon above bird w/3 equal sections.

54a.1	AH1395	1975	4.132	—	.10	.25
	1398	1978	—	—	.10	.25
	1400	1980	—	—	Proof	1.00
	1403	1983	—	—	.10	.25

Rev: Ribbon w/long center section.

54a.2	AH1398	1978	—	—	.10	.25
	1403	1983	—	—	.10	.25

F.A.O. Issue

60	AH1396	1976	7.868	—	.10	.20
	1398	1978	7.000	—	.10	.20

20th Anniversary of Independence

94	AH1396	1976	—	.15	.20	.25

10 MILLIM

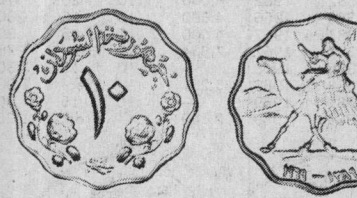

BRONZE

32	AH1376	1956	15.00	.10	.20	.40
	1380	1960	12.250	.10	.15	.30
	1381	1962 high date	—	.10	.15	.30
	1381	1962 low date	—	.10	.15	.30
	1386	1966	1.000	.10	.15	.40
	1387	1967	1.000	.10	.15	.30
	1387	1967	7.834	—	Proof	1.00
	1388	1968	—	.10	.15	.30
	1388	1968	5.251	—	Proof	1.25

KM#	Date	Year	Mintage	VF	XF	Unc
32	1389	1969	—	.10	.15	.30
	1389	1969	2,149	—	Proof	1.50

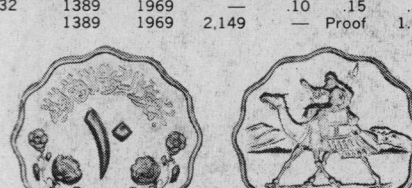

42	AH1390	1970	—	.20	.40	.90
	1390	1970	1.646	—	Proof	1.25
	1391	1971	3.000	.20	.40	.90
	1391	1971	1.772	—	Proof	1.25

Anniversary of Revolution

48	AH1391	1971	.500	.15	.30	.70

55	AH1392	1972	6.500	.10	.15	.40

BRASS

55a	AH1395	1975	12.000	.10	.15	.35
	1398	1978	9.410	.10	.20	.45
	1400	1980	2.490	—	Proof	1.50

F.A.O. Issue

61	AH1396	1976	3.000	.10	.15	.25
	1398	1978	—	.10	.15	.25

20th Anniversary of Independence

62	AH1396	1976	3.610	.10	.15	.35

GHIRSH

BRONZE
Rev: Ribbon above bird w/3 equal sections.

97	AH1403	1983	—	—	—	—

2 GHIRSH

COPPER-NICKEL

33	AH1376	1956	5.000	.15	.35	.50
	1381	1962	—	.15	.35	.50

KM#	Date	Year	Mintage	VF	XF	Unc
36	AH1382	1963	1.250	.15	.35	.75
	1387	1967	—	.15	.35	.75
	1387	1967	7,834	—	Proof	1.25
	1388	1968	—	.15	.35	.75
	1388	1968	5,251	—	Proof	1.50
	1389	1969	—	.15	.35	.75
	1389	1969	2,149	—	Proof	1.75

43	AH1390	1970	—	.30	.60	1.25
	1390	1970	1,646	—	Proof	1.25
	1391	1971	1,772	—	Proof	1.25

Anniversary of Revolution

49	AH1391	1971	.500	.15	.30	.50

Mule. Obv: KM#49. Rev: KM#43.

50	AH1390	1970	—	—	—	—

Rev: Ribbon above bird w/3 equal sections.

57.1	AH1395	1975	1.000	.10	.20	.40
	1398	1978	1.250	.10	.20	.40
	1399	1979	2.000	.10	.20	.40
	1400	1980	6.825	.10	.20	.40
	1400	1980	Inc. Ab.	—	Proof	2.00

Rev: Ribbon above bird w/long center section.

57.2	AH1400	1980	—	.10	.20	.40
	1403	1983	—	.10	.20	.40

F.A.O. Issue

63	AH1396	1976	.500	.10	.20	.40
	1398	1978	Inc. Ab.	.10	.20	.40

20th Anniversary of Independence

64	AH1396	1976	1.750	.10	.20	.50

5 GHIRSH

COPPER-NICKEL

KM#	Date	Year	Mintage	VF	XF	Unc
34	AH1376	1956	40.000	.15	.30	.75
	1386	1966	—	—	Proof	1.50
	1387	1967	—	.20	.30	.60
	1387	1967	7,834	—	Proof	1.50
	1388	1968	—	.20	.30	.60
	1388	1968	5,251	—	Proof	1.75
	1389	1969	—	.20	.30	.60
	1389	1969	2,149	—	Proof	2.00

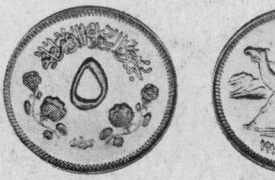

44	AH1390	1970	1,646	—	Proof	2.00
	1391	1971	1,772	—	Proof	2.00

Anniversary of Revolution

51	AH1391	1971	.500	.20	.30	.75

Rev: Ribbon above bird w/3 equal sections.

58.1	AH1395	1975	1.600	.20	.30	.65
	1397	1977	2.000	.20	.30	.65
	1398	1978	1.000	.20	.30	.65
	1400	1980	1.000	.20	.30	.65
	1400	1980	Inc. Ab.	—	Proof	3.00
	1403	1983	4.200	.20	.30	.65

Rev: Ribbon above bird w/long center section.

58.2	AH1400	1980	Inc. KM58.1	.20	.30	.65
	1403	1983	Inc. KM58.1	.20	.30	.65

F.A.O. Issue

65	AH1396	1976	.500	.20	.30	.65
	1398	1978	—	.20	.30	.65

20th Anniversary of Independence

66	AH1396	1976	3.940	.25	.50	1.00

Arab Economic Unity

KM#	Date	Year	Mintage	VF	XF	Unc
74	AH1398	1978	5.040	.15	.25	.50

F.A.O. Issue

84	AH1401	1981	1.000	.20	.40	.65

10 GHIRSH

COPPER-NICKEL

35	AH1376	1956	15.000	.35	.75	1.25
	1387	1967	—	.30	.60	1.00
	1387	1967	7,834	—	Proof	1.75
	1388	1968	—	.30	.60	1.00
	1388	1968	5,251	—	Proof	2.25
	1389	1969	—	.30	.60	1.00
	1389	1969	2,149	—	Proof	2.50

45	AH1390	1970	—	.60	1.25	2.00
	1390	1970	1,646	—	Proof	3.00
	1391	1971	.385	.60	1.25	2.00
	1391	1971	1,772	—	Proof	3.00

Anniversary of Revolution

52	AH1391	1971	.500	.40	.75	1.25

Rev: Ribbon above bird w/3 equal sections.

59.1	AH1395	1975	1.000	.35	.75	1.25
	1397	1977	1.000	.35	.75	1.25
	1400	1980	2.965	.35	.75	1.25
	1400	1980	—	—	Proof	4.50
	1403	1983	1.100	.35	.75	1.25

Rev: Ribbon above bird w/long center section.

59.2	AH1400	1980	—	.35	.75	1.25

Reduced size.

KM#	Date	Year	Mintage	VF	XF	Unc
59.3	AH1403	1983	—	.35	.75	1.25

F.A.O. Issue

67	AH1396	1976	.500	.30	.60	1.00

20th Anniversary of Independence

68	AH1396	1976	5.540	.25	.50	1.00

F.A.O. Issue

85	AH1401	1981	1.000	.40	.80	1.25

Council of Arab Economic Unity

95	AH1398	1978	1.000	.40	.80	1.25

20 GHIRSH

COPPER-NICKEL

37	AH1387	1967	7,834	—	Proof	3.00
	1388	1968	5,251	—	Proof	3.50
	1389	1969	2,149	—	Proof	7.00

SUDAN 1552

KM#	Date	Year	Mintage	VF	XF	Unc
46	AH1390	1970	1,646	—	Proof	9.00
	1391	1971	1,772	—	Proof	9.00

F.A.O. Issue
Obv: Legend & denomination.
Rev: National emblem, dates.

96	AH1405	1985	—	—	—	3.00
98	AH1403	1983	—	—	—	2.00

25 GHIRSH

COPPER-NICKEL
F.A.O. Issue

38	AH1388	1968	—	—	—	8.00
	1388	1968	.224	—	Proof	16.00

50 GHIRSH

COPPER-NICKEL
F.A.O. Issue

| 56 | AH1392 | 1972 | 1.000 | 1.00 | 2.00 | 4.00 |

NOTE: An additional 30,000 specimens, dated 1976, are reported to have been struck.

Establishment of Arab Cooperative

| 69 | AH1396 | 1976 | — | 1.00 | 2.00 | 4.00 |

8th Anniversary of 1969 Revolt
F.A.O. Issue

| 73 | AH1397 | 1977 | .100 | 1.00 | 2.00 | 4.00 |

POUND

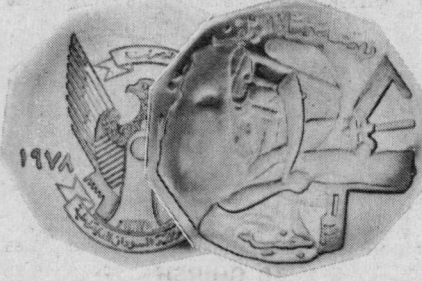

COPPER-NICKEL
Rural Women and F.A.O. Issue

KM#	Date	Year	Mintage	VF	XF	Unc
75	AH1398	1978	.456	2.00	3.00	5.00

2-1/2 POUNDS

28.2800 g, .925 SILVER, .8410 oz ASW
Conservation Series
Rev: Shoebill Stork.

70	AH1396	1976	5,183	—	—	20.00
	1396	1976	5,590	—	Proof	25.00

5 POUNDS

35.0000 g, .925 SILVER, 1.0409 oz ASW
Conservation Series
Rev: Hippopotamus.

71	AH1396	1976	5,087	—	—	30.00
	1396	1976	5,393	—	Proof	35.00

17.5000 g, .925 SILVER, .5205 oz ASW
Khartoum Meeting of O.A.U.

76	AH1398	1978	21 pcs.	—	—	—
	1398	1978	1,423	—	Proof	25.00

1400th Anniversary of Islam

80	AH1400	1980	7,500	—	—	20.00
	1400	1980	5,500	—	Proof	25.00

28.2800 g, .925 SILVER, .8410 oz ASW
25th Anniversary of Independence

KM#	Date	Year	Mintage	VF	XF	Unc
86	AH1401	1981	.020	—	—	35.00
	AH1401	1981	.020	—	Proof	45.00

19.4400 g, .925 SILVER, .5781 oz ASW
UNICEF and I.Y.C.

| 87 | AH1401 | 1981 | .035 | — | Proof | 25.00 |

Decade For Women

| 92 | AH1404 | 1984 | .020 | — | Proof | 20.00 |

10 POUNDS

35.0000 g, .925 SILVER, 1.0409 oz ASW
Khartoum Meeting of O.A.U.

77	AH1398	1978	21 pcs.	—	—	150.00
	1398	1978	1,417	—	Proof	35.00

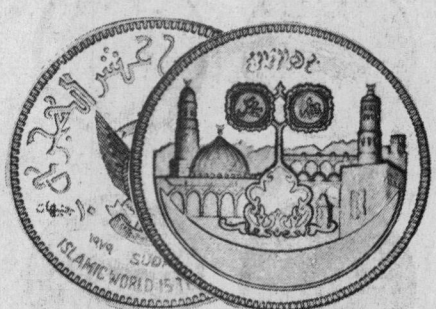

1400th Anniversary of Islam

81	AH1400	1980	3,000	—	—	25.00
	1400	1980	2,000	—	Proof	35.00

28.2800 g, .925 SILVER, .8411 oz ASW
Year of the Disabled Persons

KM#	Date	Year	Mintage	VF	XF	Unc
88	AH1401	1981	.010	—	—	20.00
	1401	1981	.010	—	Proof	30.00

25 POUNDS

8.2500 g, .917 GOLD, .2432 oz AGW
Khartoum Meeting of O.A.U.

78	AH1398	1978	15 pcs.	—	—	600.00
	1398	1978	467 pcs.	—	Proof	225.00
	1398*	1978	—	Restrike Proof		150.00

*NOTE: CS with counterstamp between dates.

1400th Anniversary of Islam

82	AH1400	1980	7,500	—	—	135.00
	1400	1980	5,500	—	Proof	150.00

50 POUNDS

17.5000 g, .917 GOLD, .5160 oz AGW
Khartoum Meeting of O.A.U.

79	AH1398	1978	11 pcs.	—	—	1500.
	1398	1978	211 pcs.	—	Proof	375.00
	1398*	1978	—	Restrike Proof		275.00

*NOTE: With counterstamp between dates.

1400th Anniversary of Islam

83	AH1400	1980	3,000	—	—	285.00
	1400	1980	—	—	Proof	325.00

7.9900 g, .917 GOLD, .2353 oz AGW
25th Anniversary of Independence

89	AH1401	1981	5,000	—	—	130.00
	AH1401	1981	5,000	—	Proof	140.00

100 POUNDS

33.4370 g, .900 GOLD, .9676 oz AGW
Conservation Series
Rev: Scimitar-horned Onyx.

KM#	Date	Year	Mintage	VF	XF	Unc
72	AH1396	1976	872 pcs.	—	—	600.00
	1396	1976	251 pcs.	—	Proof	850.00

15.9800 g, .917 GOLD, .4706 oz AGW
25th Anniversary of Independence

90	AH1401	1981	2,500	—	—	275.00
	AH1401	1981	2,500	—	Proof	300.00

Year of the Disabled Persons

91	AH1401	1981	2,000	—	—	300.00
	1401	1981	2,000	—	Proof	400.00

8.1000 g, .917 GOLD, .2388 oz AGW
Decade For Women

93	AH1404	1984	500 pcs.	—	Proof	250.00

MINT SETS (MS)

KM#	Date	Mintage	Identification	Issue Price	Mkt. Val.
MS1	1976(2)	—	KM70-71	—	60.00

PROOF SETS (PS)

PS1	1967(8)	7,834	KM29-32,34-37	15.25	6.00
PS2	1968(8)	5,251	KM29-32,34-37	15.25	7.50
PS3	1969(8)	2,149	KM29-32,34-37	15.25	10.00
PS4	1970(8)	1,646	KM39-46	15.25	15.00
PS5	1971(8)	1,772	KM39-46	15.25	15.00
PS6	1976(2)	—	KM70a-71a	—	60.00
PS7	1978(4)	—	KM76-79	—	660.00
PS8	1980(5)	—	KM54,55a,57-59	—	12.00
PS9	1980(4)	—	KM80-83	—	535.00

DARFUR

The province of Darfur makes up most of the western border of the Republic of Sudan. Darfur had been an independent kingdom until taken over by Egypt in 1874. While the British were involved in subduing the eastern Sudan, Ali Dinar established the sultanate of Darfur. His coins copied the type of 20 Para of Mohammed II of Egypt. The mint was located at Al Fasher (the capitol of the province) and was active from 1908 to 1914 with most of the coins bearing a 1327 (1909AD) date.

TITLES

Al-Fasher الفشير

RULERS
Ali Dinar, 1896-1916

PIASTRE

BILLON
Al-Fasher Mint

KM#	Date	Good	VG	Fine	VF
1	AH1327	15.00	30.00	45.00	60.00

NOTE: Very crudely struck.

SURINAM

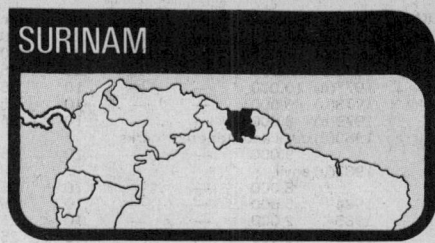

The Republic of Surinam also known as Dutch Guiana, located on the north central coast of South America between Guyana and French Guiana has an area of 63,037 sq. mi. (163,265 sq. km.) and a population of *400,000. Capital: Paramaribo. The country is rich in minerals and forests, and self-sufficient in rice, the staple food crop. The mining, processing and exporting of bauxite is the principal economic activity.

Lieutenants of Amerigo Vespucci sighted the Guiana coast in 1499. Spanish explorers of the 16th century, disappointed at finding no gold, departed leaving the area to be settled by the British in 1652. The colony prospered and the Netherlands acquired it in 1667 in exchange for the Dutch rights in Nieuw Nederland (state of New York). During the European wars of the 18th and 19th centuries, which were fought in part in the new world, Surinam was occupied by the British from 1781-1784 and 1796-1814. Surinam became an autonomous part of the Kingdom of the Netherlands on Dec. 15, 1954. Full independence was achieved on Nov. 25, 1975. In 1980, a revolution installed a military government.

RULERS
Dutch, until 1975

MINT MARKS
FM - Franklin Mint, U.S.A.**
P - Philadelphia, U.S.A.
S - Sydney
(u) - Utrecht (privy marks only)

**NOTE: From 1975 the Franklin Mint has produced coinage in up to 3 different qualities. Qualities of issue are designated in ( ) after each date and are defined as follows:

(M) MATTE - Normal circulation strike or a dull finish produced by sandblasting special uncirculated (polish finish) or proof quality dies.

(U) SPECIAL UNCIRCULATED - Polished or proof-like in appearance without any frosted features.

(P) PROOF - The highest quality obtainable having mirror-like fields and frosted features.

MONETARY SYSTEM
100 Cents = 1 Gulden

World War II Coinage

The 1942-43 issues following are homeland coinage types of the Netherlands - Y#36, Y#43 and Y#44 - were executed expressly for use in Surinam. Related issues produced for use in both Curacao and Surinam are listed under Curacao. They are distinguished by the presence of a palm tree (acorn on Homeland issues) and a mint mark (P-Philadelphia, D-Denver, S-San Francisco) flanking the date. Also see the Netherlands for similar issues.

CENT

BRASS

KM#	Date	Mintage	Fine	VF	XF	Unc
2	1943P palm					
		4.000	2.50	5.00	10.00	20.00

BRONZE

2a	1957(u)	1.200	.50	1.25	2.50	5.50
	1957(u)	—	—	—	Proof	30.00
	1959(u)	1.800	.50	1.25	2.50	5.50
	1959(u)	—	—	—	Proof	30.00
	1960(u)	1.200	.50	1.25	2.50	5.50
	1960(u)	—	—	—	Proof	30.00

NOTE: For similar coins dated 1942P see Netherlands Antilles (Curacao).

3	1962(u) fish					
		6.000	—	.10	.25	1.00
	1962(u)S					
		650 pcs.	—	—	Proof	15.00
	1966(u)	9.500	—	.10	.25	.50
	1966(u)	—	—	—	Proof	45.00
	1970(u) cock					
		5.000	—	.10	.25	.85
	1972(u)	6.000	—	.10	.25	.75

ALUMINUM

SURINAM 1554

KM#	Date	Mintage	Fine	VF	XF	Unc
3a	1974(u)	1.000	—	.10	.25	.50
	1975(u)	1.000	—	.10	.25	.50
	1976(u)	3.000	—	.10	.25	.35
	1977(u)	10.000	—	—	.10	.35
	1978(u)	6.000	—	—	.10	.35
	1979(u)	8.000	—	—	.10	.35
	1980(u) cock and star privy marks					
		9.000	—	—	.10	.35
	1982(u) anvil					
		8.000	—	—	.10	.35
	1984	5.000	—	—	.10	.25
	1985	2.000	—	—	.10	.25
	1986	3.000	—	—	.10	.25

COPPER PLATED STEEL

| 3b | 1987 | — | — | — | — | .10 |
| | 1988 | *1,500 | — | — | Proof | 2.00 |

5 CENT
For a 5 cent coin dated 1943 see Netherlands Antilles (Curacao).

NICKEL-BRASS

4.1	1962(u) fish					
		2.200	.20	.50	1.00	2.50
	1962(u)S					
		650 pcs.	—	—	Proof	20.00
	1966(u) privy marks					
		1.800	.20	.50	1.00	2.50
	1966(u)	—	—	—	Proof	45.00
	1966 w/o privy marks					
		.400	.50	1.00	2.50	5.00
	1971(u) cock					
		.500	.30	.60	1.25	3.25
	1972(u)	1.500	.25	.50	1.00	2.50

Medal struck

| 4.2 | 1966(u) | — | 5.50 | 11.00 | 17.50 | 30.00 |

ALUMINUM

4.1a	1976(u)	5.500	—	.10	.25	.75
	1978(u)	3.000	—	.10	.25	.75
	1979(u)	2.000	—	.10	.25	.75
	1980(u) cock and star privy marks					
		1.000	—	.10	.25	.75
	1982(u) anvil					
		1.000	—	.10	.25	.75
	1985	1.000	—	.10	.25	.75
	1986	1.500	—	.10	.25	.75

COPPER PLATED STEEL

| 4.1b | 1987 | — | — | — | — | .10 |
| | 1988 | *1,500 | — | — | Proof | 2.00 |

10 CENT

1.4000 g, .640 SILVER, .0288 oz ASW

| 1 | 1942P palm | | | | | |
| | | 1.500 | 5.00 | 12.00 | 17.50 | 30.00 |

For similar coins dated 1941P and 1943P see Netherlands Antilles (Curacao).

COPPER-NICKEL

5	1962(u) fish					
		3.000	—	.10	.50	2.25
	1962(u)S					
		650 pcs.	—	—	Proof	20.00
	1966(u)	2.500	—	.10	.50	2.25
	1966(u)	—	—	—	Proof	55.00
	1971(u) cock					
		.500	—	.50	2.50	6.00
	1972(u)	1.500	—	.10	.50	2.00
	1974(u)	1.500	—	.10	.50	2.00
	1976(u)	5.000	—	.10	.20	.50
	1978(u)	2.000	—	.10	.20	.50
	1979(u)	2.000	—	.10	.20	.50
	1982(u) anvil					
		1.000	—	.10	.20	.50
	1985	1.000	—	.10	.20	.50
	1986	1.500	—	.10	.20	.50
	1987	—	—	.10	.20	.50
	1988	*1,500	—	—	Proof	3.00

25 CENT

COPPER-NICKEL

6	1962(u) fish					
		2.300	.20	.50	1.75	2.75
	1962(u)S					
		650 pcs.	—	—	Proof	20.00

KM#	Date	Mintage	Fine	VF	XF	Unc
6	1966(u)	2.300	.20	.50	1.75	2.75
	1966(u)	—	—	—	Proof	55.00
	1972(u) cock					
		1.800	.20	.50	1.75	2.75
	1974(u)	1.500	.20	.50	1.75	2.75
	1976(u)	5.000	—	.20	.30	.75
	1979(u)	2.000	—	.20	.30	.75
	1982(u) anvil					
		2.000	—	.20	.30	.75
	1985	1.000	—	.20	.30	.75
	1986	1.500	—	.20	.30	.75
	1987	—	—	.20	.30	.75
	1988	*1,500	—	—	Proof	5.00

100 CENT

COPPER-NICKEL

| 15 | 1987 | — | — | — | — | .75 |
| | 1988 | *1,500 | — | — | Proof | 12.00 |

250 CENT

COPPER-NICKEL

| 16 | 1987 | — | — | — | — | 1.75 |
| | 1988 | *1,500 | — | — | Proof | 17.50 |

GULDEN

10.0000 g, .720 SILVER, .2315 oz ASW

7	1962(u)	.150	—	3.00	5.00	10.00
	1962(u)S					
		650 pcs.	—	—	Proof	50.00
	1966(u)	*.100	—	—	55.00	95.00
	1966(u)	—	—	—	Proof	175.00

*Never officially released to circulation.

10 GULDEN

15.9500 g, .925 SILVER, .4743 oz ASW
1st Anniversary of Independence

| 8 | 1976(u) | .100 | — | — | 8.00 | 15.00 |
| | 1976(u)F | 5,711 | — | — | Proof | 30.00 |

25 GULDEN

25.8500 g, .925 SILVER, .7687 oz ASW
1st Anniversary of Independence

Rev: Similar to 10 Gulden, KM#8.

KM#	Date	Mintage	Fine	VF	XF	Unc
9	1976(u)	.075	—	—	20.00	28.00
	1976(u)F	5,503	—	—	Proof	40.00

15.5000 g, .925 SILVER, .4610 oz ASW
1st Anniversary of Revolution

11	1981FM(U)	.010	—	—	18.00	25.00
	1981FM(P)					
		800 pcs.	—	—	Proof	40.00

25.1000 g, .925 SILVER, .7435 oz ASW
5th Anniversary of Revolution

| 13 | 1985(u) | 4,800 | — | — | — | 30.00 |
| | 1985(u) | 200 pcs. | — | — | Proof | 50.00 |

30 GULDEN

14.0200 g, .925 SILVER, .4170 oz ASW
30th Anniversary of Central Bank

| 19 | 1987(u) | — | — | — | — | 40.00 |

100 GULDEN

6.7200 g, .900 GOLD, .1945 oz ASW
1st Anniversary of Independence

| 10 | 1976(u) | .020 | — | — | — | 125.00 |
| | 1976(u) | 4,749 | — | — | Proof | 150.00 |

NOTE: 900 pieces have been reported struck in 'rose' gold.

200 GULDEN

7.1200 g, .500 GOLD, .1144 oz AGW
1st Anniversary of Revolution

KM#	Date	Mintage	Fine	VF	XF	Unc
12	1981FM(U)	.011	—	—	—	125.00
	1981FM(P) 1.363		—	—	Proof	165.00

250 GULDEN

6.7200 g, .900 GOLD, .1944 oz AGW
5th Anniversary of Revolution
Similar to 25 Gulden, KM#13.

14	1985(u)	5.000	—	—	—	150.00
	1985(u)	200 pcs.	—	—	Proof	200.00

500 GUILDERS

7.9800 g, .917 GOLD, .2354 oz AGW
40th Anniversary of Military Sports Organization
Obv: Similar to 1,000 Guilders, KM#18.

17	1988	2,500	—	—	Proof	250.00

1000 GUILDERS

15.9800 g, .917 GOLD, .4708 oz AGW
40th Anniversary of Military Sports Organization

18	1988	1,250	—	—	Proof	500.00

PROOF SETS (PS)

KM#	Date	Mintage	Identification	Issue Price	Mkt. Val.
PS1	1962(5)	650	KM3-7	—	125.00
PS2	1966(5)	—	KM3-7	—	375.00
PS3	1976(3)	—	KM8-10	145.00	220.00
PS4	1976(2)	—	KM8-9	50.00	70.00
PS5	1988(6)	*1,500	KM3b,4.1b,5-6,15-16	42.00	42.00

SWAZILAND

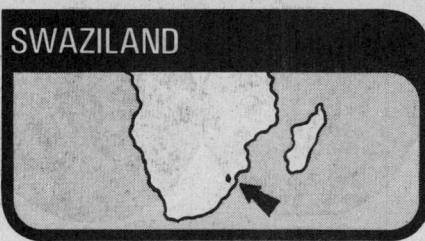

The Kingdom of Swaziland, located in south-eastern Africa, has an area of 6,704 sq. mi. (17,363 sq. km.) and a population of *757,000. Capital: Mbabane (administrative); Lobamba (legislative). The diversified economy includes mining, agriculture, and light industry. Asbestos, iron ore, wood pulp, and sugar are exported.

The people of the present Swazi nation established themselves in an area including what is now Swaziland in the early 1800s. The first Swazi contact with the British came early in the reign of the extremely able Swazi leader Mswati when he asked the British for aid against Zulu raids into Swaziland. The British and Transvaal responded by guaranteeing the independence of Swaziland, 1881. South Africa assumed the power of protection and administration in 1894 and Swaziland continued under this administration until the conquest of the Transvaal during the Anglo-Boer War, when administration was transferred to the British government. After World War II, Britain began to prepare Swaziland for independence, which was achieved on Sept. 6, 1968. The Kingdom is a member of the Commonwealth of Nations. The king of Swaziland is normally Chief of State. The prime minister is Head of Government.

RULERS

Sobhuza II, 1968-1982
Queen Ntombi, Regent for
 Prince Makhosetive, 1982-1986
King Makhosetive, 1986-

MONETARY SYSTEM

100 Cents = 1 Luhlanga
25 Luhlanga = 1 Lilangeni
 (plural - Emalangeni)

CENT

BRONZE

KM#	Date	Mintage	VF	XF	Unc
7	1974	6.002	—	—	.10
	1974	.013	—	Proof	.75
	1979	.500	—	.10	.15
	1979	.010	—	Proof	.75
	1982	—	—	.10	.15
	1983	.100	—	.10	.15
	1984	1.000	—	.10	.15

F.A.O. Issue

21	1975	2.500	—	.10	.15

39	1986	—	—	—	.15

2 CENTS

BRONZE

8	1974	2.252	—	.10	.15
	1974	.013	—	Proof	.75
	1979	1.000	—	.10	.20
	1979	.010	—	Proof	1.00
	1982	—	—	.10	.20
	1984	.500	—	.10	.20

F.A.O. Issue

KM#	Date	Mintage	VF	XF	Unc
22	1975	1.500	—	.10	.20

5 CENTS

2.7500 g, .800 SILVER, .0707 oz ASW

1	1968	.010	—	Proof	4.00

COPPER-NICKEL

9	1974	1.252	.10	.15	.30
	1974	.013	—	Proof	1.00
	1975	1.500	.10	.15	.30
	1979	1.000	.10	.15	.30
	1979	.010	—	Proof	1.75
	1984	.680	.10	.15	.30

40	1986	—	—	—	.30

10 CENTS

4.3800 g, .800 SILVER, .1126 oz ASW

2	1968	.010	—	Proof	6.00

COPPER-NICKEL

10	1974	.752	.15	.25	.50
	1974	.013	—	Proof	1.00
	1979	.500	.15	.25	.50
	1979	3,231	—	Proof	2.50
	1984	1.000	.15	.25	.50

F.A.O. Issue

23	1975	1.500	.20	.30	.60

41	1986	—	—	—	.50

SWAZILAND 1556

20 CENTS

6.6300 g, .800 SILVER, .1705 oz ASW

KM#	Date	Mintage	VF	XF	Unc
3	1968	.010	—	Proof	7.00

COPPER-NICKEL

11	1974	.502	.25	.50	1.00
	1974	.013	—	Proof	1.50
	1975	1.000	.25	.50	1.00
	1979	—	.25	.50	1.00
	1979	.010	—	Proof	3.00

F.A.O. Issue

31	1981	.150	.25	.50	1.50

42	1986	—	—	—	1.00

50 CENTS

10.3900 g, .800 SILVER, .2672 oz ASW

4	1968	.010	—	Proof	8.00

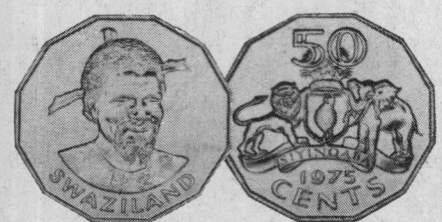

COPPER-NICKEL

12	1974	.252	1.00	1.50	2.50
	1974	.013	—	Proof	3.00
	1975	.500	1.00	1.50	2.50
	1979	—	.50	1.00	2.00
	1979	.010	—	Proof	5.00
	1981	.150	.50	1.00	2.00
	1984	1.000	.50	1.00	2.00

KM#	Date	Mintage	VF	XF	Unc
43	1986	—	—	—	2.00

LUHLANGA

15.0000 g, .800 SILVER .3858 oz ASW

5	1968	.010	—	Proof	10.00

LILANGENI

33.9305 g, .917 GOLD, 1.0000 oz AGW

6	1968	*2,000	—	Proof	700.00

*NOTE: Approximately 1,450 melted.

COPPER-NICKEL

13	1974	.127	1.50	2.50	4.00
	1974	.013	—	Proof	5.00
	1979	—	1.00	2.00	4.00
	1979	.010	—	Proof	6.00
	1984	.100	1.00	2.00	4.00

F.A.O. Issue And International Women's Year

24	1975	.100	1.50	2.50	4.50

F.A.O. Issue

28	1976	.100	1.50	2.50	4.50

15.5500 g, .999 GOLD, .5000 oz AGW
Rev: Dates 1921-1979.

KM#	Date	Mintage	VF	XF	Unc
29.1	1979	1,250	—	—	275.00
	1979	Inc. Ab.	—	Proof	325.00

Rev: Dates 1923-1979.

29.2	1979	—	—	—	350.00

COPPER-NICKEL
F.A.O. Issue

32	1981	.871	1.50	2.50	4.00

11.6600 g, .925 SILVER, .3468 oz ASW

32a	1981	5,000	—	—	15.00
	1981	5,000	—	Proof	20.00

COPPER-NICKEL

44	1986	—	—	—	4.00

2 EMALANGENI

31.1000 g, .999 GOLD, 1.0000 oz AGW

30	1979	1,250	—	—	550.00
	1979	Inc. Ab.	—	Proof	600.00

17.0000 g, .925 SILVER, .5056 oz ASW
Diamond Jubilee

33	1981	—	—	Proof	12.50

SWAZILAND 1557

KM#	Date	Mintage	VF	XF	Unc
33a	1981	.050	2.00	4.00	6.00

COPPER-NICKEL

5 EMALANGENI

10.3000 g, .925 SILVER, .3063 oz ASW
H. M. 75th Anniversary

| 14 | 1974 | — | — | Proof | 17.50 |

5.5600 g, .900 GOLD, .1609 oz AGW
H. M. 75th Anniversary
| 15 | 1974 | .060 | — | Proof | 125.00 |

7-1/2 EMALANGENI

16.2000 g, .925 SILVER, .4818 oz ASW
H. M. 75th Anniversary
| 16 | 1974 | — | — | Proof | 45.00 |

10 EMALANGENI

11.1200 g, .900 GOLD, .3218 oz AGW
H. M. 75th Anniversary
| 17 | 1974 | .040 | — | Proof | 250.00 |

25.5000 g, .925 SILVER, .7584 oz ASW
H. M. 75th Birthday
| 25 | 1975 | 1,000 | — | — | 40.00 |
| | 1975 | 1,500 | — | Proof | 50.00 |

15 EMALANGENI

32.6000 g, .925 SILVER, .9696 oz ASW
H.M. 75th Anniversary and Independence
Obv: Similar to 25 Emalangeni, KM#20.

KM#	Date	Mintage	VF	XF	Unc
18	1974	—	—	Proof	55.00

NOTE: Stamped serial number of issue on reverse.

20 EMALANGENI

22.2300 g, .900 GOLD, .6433 oz AGW
H. M. 75th Anniversary and UNICEF
| 19 | 1974 | .025 | — | Proof | 425.00 |

25 EMALANGENI

27.7800 g, .900 GOLD, .8039 oz AGW
H. M. 75th Anniversary
| 20 | 1974 | .015 | — | — | 525.00 |

28.2800 g, .925 SILVER, .8411 oz ASW
Diamond Jubilee
| 34 | 1981 | .010 | — | — | 20.00 |
| | 1981 | .010 | — | Proof | 25.00 |

Accession of King Makhosetive
Similar to 250 Emalangeni, KM#38.
| 37 | 1986 | 2,500 | — | Proof | 35.00 |

50 EMALANGENI

4.3100 g, .900 GOLD, .1247 oz AGW
H. M. 75th Birthday

KM#	Date	Mintage	VF	XF	Unc
26	1975	3,510	—	—	75.00
	1975	3,262	—	Proof	90.00

100 EMALANGENI

8.6400 g, .900 GOLD, .2500 oz AGW
H. M. 75th Birthday
| 27 | 1975 | 1,000 | — | — | 150.00 |
| | 1975 | 1,000 | — | Proof | 225.00 |

250 EMALANGENI

15.9800 g, .917 GOLD, .4711 oz AGW
Diamond Jubilee
| 35 | 1981 | 2,000 | — | — | 300.00 |
| | 1981 | 2,000 | — | Proof | 425.00 |

Accession of King Makhosetive
| 38 | 1986 | 250 pcs. | — | — | 350.00 |
| | 1986 | 250 pcs. | — | Proof | 400.00 |

BULLION ISSUES
5 GOLD EMALANGENI

31.1000 g, .999 GOLD, 1.0000 oz AGW
Queen Elizabeth II Silver Jubilee
| 36 | 1978 | — | — | — | 600.00 |

MINT SETS (MS)

KM#	Date	Mintage	Identification	Issue Price	Mkt. Val.
MS1	1974(7)	—	KM7-13	10.00	9.00
MS2	1975(3)	1,000	KM25-27	—	265.00
MS3	1986(6)	—	KM39-44	—	8.00

PROOF SETS (PS)

PS1	1968(5)	10,000	KM1-5	25.80	35.00
PS2	1974(7)	20,000	KM7-13	18.00	13.00
PS3	1974(4)	—	KM15,17,19,20	745.00	1300.
PS4	1974(3)	—	KM14,16,17	70.00	290.00
PS5	1975(3)	1,000	KM25-27	—	365.00
PS6	1975(2)	25,000	KM26-27	252.00	315.00
PS7	1979(7)	3,231	KM7-13	34.00	20.00
PS8	1979(2)	1,250	KM29.1,30	1172.	925.00

SWEDEN 1558

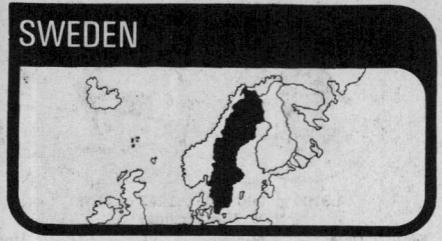

The Kingdom of Sweden, a limited constitutional monarchy located in northern Europe between Norway and Finland, has an area of 173,732 sq. mi. (449,964 sq. km.) and a population of *8.4 million. Capital: Stockholm. Mining, lumbering and a specialized machine industry dominate the economy. Machinery, paper, iron and steel, motor vehicles and wood pulp are exported.

Sweden was founded as a Christian stronghold by Olaf Skottkonung late in the 10th century. After conquering Finland late in the 13th century, Sweden, together with Norway, came under the rule of Denmark, 1397-1523, in an association known as the Union of Kalmar. Modern Sweden had its beginning in 1523 when Gustavus Vasa drove the Danes out of Sweden and was himself chosen king. Under Gustavus Adolphus II and Charles XII, Sweden was one of the great powers of 17th century Europe - until Charles invaded Russia in 1708, and was defeated at the Battle of Pultowa in June, 1709. Early in the 18th century, a coalition of Russia, Poland and Denmark took away Sweden's Baltic empire and in 1809 Sweden was forced to cede Finland to Russia. Norway was ceded to Sweden by the Treaty of Kiel in January, 1814. The Norwegians resisted for a time but later signed the Act of Union at the Convention of Moss in August, 1814. The Union was dissolved in 1905 and Norway became independent. A new constitution which took effect on Jan. 1, 1975, restricts the function of the king largely to a ceremonial role.

RULERS
Gustaf IV Adolph, 1792-1809
Carl XIII, 1809-1818
Carl XIV Johan, 1818-1844
Oscar I, 1844-1859
Carl XV, 1859-1872
Oscar II, 1872-1907
Gustaf V, 1907-1950
Gustaf VI, 1950-1973
Carl XVI Gustaf, 1973 -

MINTMASTER'S INITIALS

Letter	Date	Name
AG,G	1838-1855	Alexander Grandinson
AL	1897-1916	Adolf Lindberg
CB	1821-1837	Christopher Borg
EB	1875-1908	Emil Brusewitz
EL	1916-1944	Erik Lindberg, engraver
G	1799-1830	Lars Grandel, engraver
G	1927-1945	Alf Grabe
LA	1853-1897	Lea Ahlborn, engraver
LB	1819-1821	Lars Bergencreutz
LH	1944—	Leon Holmgren
OL	1773-1819	Olof Lidijn
ST,T	1855-1875	Sebastian Tham
TS	1945-1961	Torsten Swensson
U	1961—	Benkt Ulvfot
W	1908-1927	Karl-August Wallroth

MONETARY SYSTEM
1798-1830
48 Skilling = 1 Riksdaler Species
2 Riksdaler (Speciesdaler) = 1 Ducat
1830-1855
32 Skilling Banco = 1 Riksdaler Riksgalds
12 Riksdaler Riksgalds = 3 Riksdaler Species
1855-1873
100 Ore = 4 Riksdaler Riksmynt
4 Riksdaler Riksmynt = 1 Riksdaler Species
Commencing 1873
100 Ore = 1 Riksdaler Riksmynt = 1 Krona

MONETARY REFORM
1/12 SKILLING

COPPER

C#	Date	Mintage	VG	Fine	VF	XF
78	1802	2.039	.50	1.00	2.00	6.00
	1803	1.008	.75	1.50	3.00	9.00
	1805	2.526	.50	1.00	2.00	6.00
	1808	3.476	.50	1.00	2.00	6.00

C#	Date	Mintage	VG	Fine	VF	XF
100	1812	2.880	.75	2.00	6.00	12.00

120	1825 reeded edge	.576	1.50	3.00	7.00	15.00
	1825 plain edge	—	4.00	8.00	15.00	35.00

1/6 SKILLING

COPPER

121	1830 reeded edge	2.544	.50	1.50	4.00	10.00
	1830 plain edge	Inc. Ab.	1.00	3.00	7.00	15.00
	1831	Inc. Ab.	2.50	5.00	10.00	20.00

Draped bust w/pearl border.

125	1832	.912	6.50	12.50	25.00	50.00

Plain border

| 125.1 | 1832 | Inc. Ab. | 1.50 | 3.00 | 6.00 | 12.00 |

Obv: Naked bust w/pearl border.

125a	1832	Inc. Ab.	5.00	10.00	20.00	40.00

129	1835	.538	.50	1.00	3.00	8.00
	1836/5	1.498	.50	1.00	2.50	7.50
	1836	Inc. Ab.	.50	1.00	2.50	7.50
	1838	.427	1.25	3.50	6.00	17.50
	1839	.827	.50	1.00	3.00	8.00
	1840/35	.860	.60	1.30	4.00	10.00
	1840	Inc. Ab.	.50	1.00	3.00	8.00
	1843/35	.865	1.75	3.50	8.50	21.50
	1843	Inc. Ab.	1.25	2.50	6.00	15.00
	1844	.071	30.00	60.00	120.00	180.00

160	1844/35	.291	5.00	10.00	20.00	40.00
	1844	Inc. Ab.	.50	1.25	3.00	9.00
	1845	.092	2.00	4.00	10.00	30.00
	1846	.067	2.00	4.00	10.00	30.00
	1847	.823	.50	1.00	2.50	7.50
	1849	.537	.50	1.00	2.50	7.50
	1850	.407	.50	2.00	5.00	15.00
	1851	.486	.50	1.00	2.50	7.50
	1852	.462	.50	1.00	2.50	7.50
	1853	.126	1.50	3.00	7.50	22.50
	1854	.422	.50	1.00	2.50	7.50
	1855	.311	.50	1.00	2.50	7.50

1/4 SKILLING

COPPER

C#	Date	Mintage	VG	Fine	VF	XF
79	1802	3.383	.75	1.50	4.00	12.00
	1803	3.217	.75	1.50	4.00	12.00
	1805	5.189	.75	1.50	4.00	12.00
	1806	8.141	.75	1.50	4.00	12.00
	1807	.641	.75	1.50	4.00	12.00
	1808 narrow crown	7.480	1.00	2.00	5.00	15.00
	1808 wider crown	Inc. Ab.	.75	1.50	4.00	12.00

101	1817	1.152	10.00	25.00	50.00	100.00

122	1819	2.500	.50	1.50	5.00	25.00
	1820	2.652	.50	1.50	5.00	25.00
	1821	.768	.50	1.50	5.00	25.00
	1824 space between crown & monogram	2.496	1.00	3.00	10.00	40.00
	1824 crown touches monogram	Inc. Ab.	1.00	3.00	10.00	40.00
	1825 open 4 in denomination	3.200	.50	1.50	5.00	25.00
	1825 closed 4 in denomination	Inc. Ab.	.50	1.50	5.00	25.00
	1827 open 4 in denomination	4.320	.50	1.50	5.00	25.00
	1827 closed 4 in denomination	Inc. Ab.	.50	1.50	5.00	25.00
	1828	.905	.50	1.50	5.00	25.00
	1829	1.080	.50	1.50	5.00	25.00
	1830	2.560	1.00	3.00	10.00	40.00

126	1832	.160	5.00	10.00	35.00	70.00
	1833/2	.096	3.50	7.00	20.00	40.00

1/3 SKILLING

COPPER

130	1835	.483	2.50	5.00	15.00	35.00
	1836	.985	1.00	2.00	6.00	17.50
	1837	1.096	1.00	2.00	6.00	17.50
	1839	.921	1.00	2.00	6.00	17.50
	1840	.692	1.00	2.00	6.00	17.50
	1841	.013	25.00	50.00	100.00	150.00
	1842	.612	1.00	2.00	6.00	17.50
	1843	.593	1.00	2.00	6.00	17.50

161	1844	.226	1.00	2.00	5.00	15.00

SWEDEN 1559

C#	Date	Mintage	VG	Fine	VF	XF
161	1845	.192	1.00	2.00	5.00	15.00
	1846	.079	2.50	5.00	10.00	30.00
	1847	.783	1.00	2.00	5.00	15.00
	1848/7	.933	1.50	2.75	7.00	21.50
	1848	Inc. Ab.	1.00	2.00	5.00	15.00
	1850 BANCO	.537	1.00	2.00	5.00	15.00
	1850 BANCO w/two dots above A (error)					
		Inc. Ab.	4.00	8.00	20.00	60.00
	1851	.538	1.00	2.00	5.00	15.00
	1852	.489	1.00	2.00	5.00	15.00
	1853	.070	2.50	5.00	10.00	30.00
	1854	.495	1.00	2.00	5.00	15.00
	1855	.377	1.00	2.00	5.00	15.00

1/2 SKILLING
COPPER
Obv: 3 crowns on orb. Rev: Value, date.

76	1801	3.203	1.00	2.50	5.00	20.00
	1802	1.188	1.00	2.50	5.00	20.00

81	1802	*2.340	1.00	3.00	7.00	20.00
	1803	*5.048	1.00	3.00	7.00	20.00
	1804	(.595)	35.00	100.00	225.00	500.00
	1805	*.173	1.25	3.00	7.00	20.00
	1807	1.950	1.25	4.00	8.00	25.00
	1809	4.845	1.25	4.00	8.00	25.00

*NOTE: Struck over 18th century 1 ore - worth 50 per cent to 100 per cent more if earlier date visible.

102	1815	1.421	2.00	6.00	15.00	30.00
	1816	.566	2.50	9.00	18.00	37.50
	1817	Inc. Ab.	3.00	12.50	25.00	50.00

123	1819	1.264	1.00	2.50	7.50	30.00
	1820	1.296	1.00	2.50	7.50	30.00
	1821	1.840	1.00	2.50	7.50	30.00
	1822	.944	1.00	2.50	7.50	30.00
	1824	.640	1.00	2.50	7.50	30.00
	1825	.816	2.00	4.00	15.00	60.00
	1827 SKIL--LING	.800	1.00	2.50	7.50	30.00
	1827 SKIL LING	Inc. Ab.	5.00	10.00	25.00	75.00
	1828	1.872	1.00	2.50	7.50	30.00
	1829	.822	1.00	2.50	7.50	30.00
	1830	.394	1.50	3.50	10.00	35.00

127	1832	.288	3.50	7.00	20.00	40.00
	1833	3 pcs.	—	—	Rare	

2/3 SKILLING

COPPER

C#	Date	Mintage	VG	Fine	VF	XF
131	1835	.198	3.00	6.00	20.00	60.00
	1836	.928	1.50	3.00	10.00	30.00
	1837	1.026	1.50	3.00	10.00	35.00
	1839	.654	1.50	3.00	10.00	35.00
	1840	.646	1.50	3.00	10.00	35.00
	1842	.526	1.50	3.00	10.00	35.00
	1843	.626	1.50	3.00	10.00	35.00

162	1844	.266	3.50	7.00	20.00	60.00
	1845/4	.495	4.00	8.50	25.00	70.00
	1845	Inc. Ab.	3.50	7.00	20.00	60.00

Redesigned smaller head

165	1845/4	Inc. C162	3.00	6.50	18.50	55.00
	1845	Inc. C162	2.50	5.00	15.00	45.00
	1846/4	.123	1.90	3.75	12.50	37.50
	1846	Inc. Ab.	1.50	3.00	10.00	30.00
	1847	.089	1.50	3.00	10.00	30.00
	1849/4	.219	2.00	4.00	13.50	40.00
	1849	Inc. Ab.	1.50	3.00	10.00	30.00
	1850	.329	1.50	3.00	10.00	30.00
	1851	.467	1.50	3.00	10.00	30.00
	1852	.297	1.50	3.00	10.00	30.00
	1853	.052	4.00	8.00	25.00	75.00
	1854	.408	1.50	3.00	10.00	30.00
	1855	.506	1.50	3.00	10.00	30.00

SKILLING

COPPER

82	1802	—	3.00	7.00	15.00	60.00
	1803	—	6.00	14.00	30.00	100.00
	1805	—	3.00	7.00	15.00	60.00

NOTE: Struck over 18th century 2 Ore - worth 50 percent to 100 percent more if earlier date visible.

103	1812	.480	4.00	10.00	27.50	55.00
	1814	.730	4.00	12.00	30.00	60.00
	1815	Inc. Ab.	4.00	10.00	27.50	55.00
	1816	.230	4.00	10.00	27.50	55.00
	1817	.202	6.00	15.00	35.00	75.00

C#	Date	Mintage	VG	Fine	VF	XF
124	1819	1.176	1.50	5.00	15.00	60.00
	1820 oblique milling	1.376	1.50	5.00	15.00	60.00
	1820 square milling					
		Inc. Ab.	6.00	12.50	40.00	100.00
	1821	.704	1.50	5.00	15.00	60.00
	1822	.520	2.00	6.00	17.50	70.00
	1825	.472	1.50	5.00	15.00	50.00
	1827	.504	1.50	5.00	15.00	60.00
	1828	.664	1.50	5.00	15.00	60.00
	1829	.816	1.50	4.00	15.00	60.00
	1830	.220	2.50	6.00	17.50	70.00

128	1832	8,000	50.00	100.00	250.00	450.00

132	1835 wide wreath	.186	50.00	100.00	250.00	500.00
	1835 narrow wreath					
		Inc. Ab.	3.00	6.00	15.00	45.00
	1836/5	.651	4.00	8.00	20.00	60.00
	1836	Inc. Ab.	3.00	6.00	15.00	45.00
	1837	.628	5.00	10.00	25.00	60.00
	1838	.140	5.00	10.00	25.00	60.00
	1839	.360	5.00	10.00	25.00	60.00
	1840	.278	5.00	10.00	25.00	60.00
	1842	.499	5.00	10.00	25.00	60.00
	1843	.361	5.00	10.00	25.00	60.00

Large head of Oscar I.

163	1844	.093	6.00	12.00	30.00	90.00
	1845/4	.097	6.00	12.00	30.00	90.00

Redesigned, smaller head.

166	1847	.150	3.00	6.00	15.00	45.00
	1849	.306	3.00	6.00	15.00	45.00
	1850	.137	3.00	6.00	15.00	45.00
	1851	.151	3.00	6.00	15.00	45.00
	1852	.154	3.00	6.00	15.00	45.00
	1853	.031	6.00	12.00	30.00	90.00
	1854	.064	3.00	6.00	15.00	45.00
	1855	.040	5.00	10.00	25.00	75.00

2 SKILLING

COPPER

C#	Date	Mintage	VG	Fine	VF	XF
133	1835	.079	10.00	20.00	60.00	200.00
	1836 wide wreath					
		.583	120.00	250.00	500.00	1000.
	1836 narrow wreath					
		Inc. Ab.	3.50	7.50	22.50	75.00
	1837	.388	4.00	8.00	25.00	80.00
	1839	.270	4.00	8.00	25.00	80.00
	1840	.069	5.00	10.00	30.00	90.00
	1841	.093	5.00	10.00	30.00	90.00
	1842	.123	5.00	10.00	30.00	90.00
	1843	.162	5.00	10.00	30.00	100.00

Rev: Similar to C#133.

C#	Date	Mintage	VG	Fine	VF	XF
164	1844	.089	7.50	15.00	50.00	150.00
	1845	.120	7.50	15.00	50.00	150.00

Obv: Smaller head. Rev: Similar to C#133.

167	1845	Inc.C164	7.50	15.00	45.00	135.00
	1846	.056	6.00	12.00	35.00	100.00
	1847	.115	5.00	12.00	35.00	100.00
	1849	.138	5.00	12.00	35.00	100.00
	1850	.081	5.00	12.00	35.00	100.00
	1851	.083	5.00	12.00	35.00	100.00
	1852	.061	5.00	12.00	35.00	100.00
	1853	.023	8.00	15.00	50.00	150.00
	1854	.038	5.00	12.00	35.00	100.00
	1855	.011	8.00	15.00	50.00	150.00

4 SKILLING

COPPER

168	1849	.444	4.00	8.00	30.00	90.00
	1850	.170	6.00	12.00	40.00	120.00
	1851	.038	7.50	15.00	50.00	150.00
	1852	.038	7.50	15.00	50.00	150.00
	1855	.074	6.00	12.00	40.00	120.00
	1855 denomination and BANCO larger					
		Inc. Ab.	10.00	20.00	70.00	200.00

1/32 RIKSDALER

1.0600 g, .750 SILVER, .0255 oz ASW

C#	Date	Mintage	VG	Fine	VF	XF
171	1851 AG	—	—	—	Rare	
	1852/1 AG	.480	1.50	3.50	7.00	25.00
	1852 AG	I.A.	1.00	2.50	5.00	15.00
	1853 AG small AG					
		.775	1.00	2.50	5.00	15.00
	1853 AG large AG					
		Inc. Ab.	1.00	2.50	5.00	15.00

1/24 RIKSDALER

.382 SILVER

105	1810 OL	.742	3.50	7.00	20.00	60.00
	1811 OL	.378	4.00	8.00	20.00	60.00
	1812 OL	.537	4.00	8.00	20.00	60.00
	1813 OL	.444	4.00	8.00	20.00	60.00
	1814 OL	.101	5.00	10.00	30.00	75.00
	1816 OL	.160	5.00	10.00	30.00	75.00

1/16 RIKSDALER

2.1300 g, .750 SILVER, .0513 oz ASW

144	1835 CB	.433	4.00	8.00	15.00	40.00
	1836/5 CB	.088	6.00	15.00	25.00	60.00
	1836 CB	I.A.	5.00	10.00	20.00	50.00

173	1845 AG	4.185	12.50	25.00	50.00	100.00
	1846/5 AG	.034	11.50	22.50	45.00	90.00
	1846 AG	I.A.	10.00	20.00	40.00	80.00
	1848 AG	4.173	1.50	4.00	8.00	25.00
	1849 AG	1.006	—	—	Rare	—
	1850 AG	I.A.	2.00	5.00	10.00	30.00
	1851 AG	.847	2.00	5.00	10.00	30.00
	1852 AG	.934	2.00	5.00	10.00	30.00
	1855 AG	.830	2.00	5.00	10.00	30.00

1/12 RIKSDALER

.507 SILVER

106	1811 OL	.735	12.00	30.00	65.00	150.00

2.8300 g, .750 SILVER, .0682 oz ASW

145	1831 CB	.212	6.50	12.00	25.00	50.00
	1832/1 CB					
		1.463	6.50	13.50	25.00	40.00
	1832 CB	I.A.	5.00	10.00	20.00	40.00
	1833/1 CB	.157	7.50	15.00	32.50	60.00
	1833 CB	I.A.	6.00	12.00	25.00	50.00

1/8 RIKSDALER

4.2500 g, .750 SILVER, .1024 oz ASW

146	1830 CB reeded edge					
		1.796	12.50	25.00	50.00	100.00
	1830 CB stars & flowers on edge					
		Inc. Ab.	37.50	75.00	150.00	300.00
	1831 CB	1.324	3.50	7.00	15.00	40.00
	1832 CB	2.829	3.00	6.00	12.00	35.00

C#	Date	Mintage	VG	Fine	VF	XF
146	1833 CB	1.032	3.50	7.00	15.00	40.00
	1834 CB	.103	6.00	12.00	25.00	60.00
	1835 CB	.103	6.00	12.00	25.00	60.00
	1836 CB	2,026	15.00	30.00	60.00	100.00
	1837 CB	7,000	17.50	35.00	70.00	120.00

175	1852 AG	.046	40.00	80.00	175.00	350.00

1/6 RIKSDALER

6.2500 g, .691 SILVER, .1388 oz ASW

86	1801 OL	.420	10.00	25.00	50.00	100.00
	1802 OL	1.254	7.00	17.50	40.00	75.00
	1803 OL	2.341	7.00	17.50	40.00	75.00
	1804 OL	2.156	7.00	17.50	40.00	75.00
	1805 OL	.978	7.00	17.50	40.00	75.00
	1806 OL	.341	8.00	20.00	45.00	85.00
	1807 OL	.909	7.00	17.50	40.00	75.00
	1808 OL	.943	7.00	17.50	40.00	75.00
	1809 OL	.707	8.00	20.00	45.00	85.00

107	1809 OL	—	50.00	120.00	225.00	450.00
	1810 OL	.297	15.00	30.00	80.00	225.00
	1814/0 OL	.199	20.00	45.00	90.00	225.00
	1814 OL	Inc. Ab.	20.00	45.00	90.00	225.00

Obv: NORR in legends.

107a	1815 OL	.059	60.00	135.00	300.00	550.00
	1817 OL	.091	60.00	125.00	275.00	500.00

135	1819 OL	.052	30.00	60.00	125.00	300.00
	1826 CB	1.974	45.00	90.00	180.00	400.00

6.1900 g, .691 SILVER, .1375 oz ASW

140	1828 CB edge inscription					
		1.024	—	—	Rare	—
	1828 CB w/o edge inscription					
		Inc. Ab.	—	—	Rare	—
	1829 CB	2.039	20.00	40.00	80.00	175.00

1/4 RIKSDALER

8.500 g, .750 SILVER, .2049 oz ASW

C#	Date	Mintage	VG	Fine	VF	XF
147	1830 CB	.704	10.00	25.00	50.00	100.00
	1830 CB plain edge					
	Inc. Ab.		20.00	45.00	90.00	175.00
	1831 CB	2.470	8.00	20.00	40.00	90.00
	1832 CB	.522	10.00	25.00	50.00	100.00
	1833 CB	.063	18.00	35.00	75.00	150.00
	1834/3 CB	.953	9.00	20.00	45.00	95.00
	1834 CB	I.A.	8.00	20.00	40.00	90.00
	1836 CB	2,766	50.00	100.00	225.00	450.00

177	1846/4 AG	.221	20.00	45.00	90.00	200.00
	1848/4 AG	.130	20.00	45.00	90.00	200.00
	1852 AG		—	—	Rare	—

1/3 RIKSDALER

.878 SILVER

108	1813 OL	.063	60.00	125.00	250.00	475.00
	1814 OL	.033	60.00	125.00	275.00	525.00

9.7500 g, .878 SILVER, .2752 oz ASW

141	1827 CB	—	—	Rare	—	
	1828 CB edge inscription					
		.061	40.00	80.00	160.00	250.00
	1828 CB w/o edge inscription					
	Inc. Ab.		50.00	100.00	200.00	300.00
	1829 CB edge inscription					
		.109	40.00	80.00	160.00	250.00
	1829 CB w/o edge inscription					
	Inc. Ab.		50.00	100.00	200.00	300.00

1/2 RIKSDALER

17.0000 g, .750 SILVER, .4099 oz ASW

148	1831 CB	.270	25.00	50.00	100.00	250.00
	1831 CB plain edge					
	Inc. Ab.		40.00	80.00	160.00	400.00
	1832 CB	.142	27.50	55.00	110.00	300.00
	1833/1 CB					
		.191	27.50	55.00	110.00	300.00
	1833 CB	I.A.	25.00	50.00	100.00	275.00
	1836/1 CB					
		2,482	55.00	110.00	225.00	550.00
	1836 CB	I.A.	50.00	100.00	200.00	500.00
	1838 CB	—	—	—	Rare	—

C#	Date	Mintage	VG	Fine	VF	XF
179	1845 AG	.022	25.00	60.00	150.00	300.00
	1846/5 AG	.082	25.00	60.00	150.00	300.00
	1846 AG	I.A.	25.00	60.00	150.00	300.00
	1848/7 AG	.074	25.00	60.00	150.00	300.00
	1848 AG	I.A.	25.00	60.00	150.00	300.00
	1852 AG	1,104	—	—	Rare	—

RIKSDALER

29.3600 g, .878 SILVER, .8287 oz ASW

90	1801 OL	.091	80.00	175.00	375.00	700.00
	1805 OL	.150	80.00	175.00	350.00	650.00
	1806 OL	.205	70.00	150.00	300.00	550.00
	1807 OL	.037	80.00	175.00	350.00	650.00

110	1812 OL	.043	100.00	200.00	400.00	750.00
	1814/2 OL					
		6,600	125.00	250.00	450.00	800.00
	1814 OL	I.A.	125.00	250.00	450.00	800.00

Obv: NORR added to legend

110a	1814 OL	I.A.	250.00	600.00	1100.	2000.
	1815 OL	.066	100.00	200.00	350.00	700.00
	1816/5 OL	.012	100.00	200.00	400.00	800.00
	1816 OL	I.A.	100.00	200.00	400.00	800.00
	1817 OL	9,895	125.00	250.00	500.00	1000.
	1818 OL	.015	150.00	300.00	600.00	1200.

SWEDEN 1561

29.2500 g, .878 SILVER, .8256 oz ASW

C#	Date	Mintage	VG	Fine	VF	XF
138	1818 OL					
	Inc. C110a		65.00	125.00	300.00	600.00
	1819 OL	.014	75.00	175.00	400.00	800.00
	1819 LB	I.A.	75.00	175.00	400.00	800.00
	1820 LB	.011	75.00	175.00	400.00	800.00
	1820 LB bust of Karl XIII					
	Inc. Ab.		—	—	Rare	—
	1821 LB	.029	50.00	100.00	300.00	550.00
	1822 CB	.034	40.00	80.00	200.00	500.00
	1823 CB large bust					
		.026	40.00	80.00	200.00	500.00
	1823 CB small bust					
	Inc. Ab.		40.00	80.00	200.00	500.00
	1824 CB	.053	40.00	80.00	200.00	500.00
	1825 CB	.020	40.00	80.00	200.00	500.00
	1826 CB	7,538	65.00	125.00	300.00	600.00
	1827 CB	.017	40.00	80.00	200.00	500.00

300 Years of Political and Religious Freedom

139	1821 CB	7,339	60.00	125.00	250.00	450.00

Obv: Similar to C#143a.
Rev: 7 angel heads around arms.

143 (C143.1)	1827 CB	—	200.00	400.00	800.00	1200.

Rev: 9 angel heads around arms.

143a (C143.2)	1827 CB					
		610 pcs.	250.00	500.00	1000.	1500.
	1829 CB					
		409 pcs.	250.00	500.00	1000.	1500.

SWEDEN

34.0000 g, .750 SILVER, .8198 oz ASW

C#	Date	Mintage	VG	Fine	VF	XF
149	1831 CB	.047	35.00	70.00	175.00	350.00
	1832/1 CB	2.100	165.00	325.00	700.00	1200.
	1832 CB Inc. Ab.		150.00	300.00	650.00	1100.
	1833/1 CB	.039	40.00	80.00	200.00	400.00
	1833 CB Inc. Ab.		35.00	70.00	175.00	350.00
	1834/1 CB	.068	30.00	60.00	150.00	325.00
	1834 CB Inc. Ab.		30.00	60.00	150.00	300.00
	1834 CB plain edge Inc. Ab.		40.00	80.00	200.00	400.00
	1835 CB	.331	30.00	60.00	150.00	300.00
	1836 CB	.093	35.00	70.00	175.00	350.00
	1837 CB	.177	30.00	60.00	150.00	300.00
	1838 AG	.834	30.00	60.00	150.00	300.00
	1839 AG	.212	30.00	60.00	150.00	300.00
	1840 AG	.068	45.00	90.00	225.00	500.00
	1841 AG	.549	30.00	60.00	150.00	300.00
	1842 AG	.288	35.00	70.00	175.00	350.00

Rev: Arms w/3 crowns.

149a	1842 AG	I.A.	35.00	70.00	175.00	350.00
(C149.1)	1843/2AG		—	—	Rare	

C#	Date	Mintage	Fine	VF	XF	Unc
180	1844 AG	.088	60.00	125.00	350.00	500.00
	1845 AG large head	.043	65.00	130.00	400.00	650.00

181	1845 AG small head Inc. C180		75.00	150.00	400.00	700.00
	1846 AG obv. GOTH	.111	45.00	100.00	300.00	500.00
	1846 AG obv. GOTH w/o period Inc. Ab.		45.00	100.00	300.00	550.00
	1847 AG	.060	60.00	125.00	350.00	600.00
	1848 AG	.185	45.00	90.00	275.00	500.00
	1850 AG	.070	50.00	100.00	325.00	550.00

C#	Date	Mintage	Fine	VF	XF	Unc
181	1851 AG	.122	45.00	90.00	275.00	500.00
	1852 AG	.054	60.00	125.00	350.00	600.00
	1853AG GOTH, small date	.109	45.00	90.00	275.00	500.00
	1853 AG GOTH w/o period, small date Inc. Ab.		45.00	90.00	275.00	500.00
	1853 large date Inc. Ab.		50.00	100.00	300.00	575.00
	1854 AG	.034	60.00	125.00	350.00	600.00
	1855 AG small date	.161	45.00	90.00	275.00	500.00
	1855 AG large date Inc. Ab.		45.00	90.00	275.00	500.00

MONETARY REFORM

100 Ore = 1 Riksdaler Riksmynt
4 Riksdaler Riksmynt = 1 Riksdaler Specie

1/2 ORE

BRONZE

C#	Date	Mintage	VG	Fine	VF	XF
185	1856	.026	15.00	30.00	60.00	125.00
	1857	1.312	.50	1.00	1.50	5.00
	1858/7	1.849	.75	1.50	3.00	10.00
	1858	Inc. Ab.	.50	1.00	1.50	5.00

Y#	Date	Mintage	VG	Fine	VF	XF
1	1867 lg.dt.	.064	2.50	5.00	10.00	20.00
	1867 small date Inc. Ab.		4.00	8.00	15.00	30.00

ORE

BRONZE

C#	Date	Mintage	Fine	VF	XF	Unc
186	1856	.024	35.00	70.00	140.00	300.00
	1857	1.596	1.50	3.00	9.00	20.00
	1858/7	6.290	2.50	5.00	15.00	30.00
	1858 L.A.	I.A.	1.00	2.50	7.50	17.50
	1858 L.A	Inc. Ab.	1.00	2.50	7.50	17.50
	1858 LA	Inc.Ab.	1.00	2.50	7.50	17.50

Y#	Date	Mintage	Fine	VF	XF	Unc
2	1860	.046	15.00	30.00	60.00	125.00
	1861	.300	3.00	8.00	15.00	30.00
	1862	.079	5.00	12.00	25.00	50.00
	1863	.450	5.00	12.00	25.00	50.00
	1864 L.A.	1.848	1.25	3.00	6.00	15.00
	1864 LA	Inc. Ab.	1.25	3.00	6.00	15.00
	1865/4	.561	7.00	15.00	30.00	60.00
	1865	Inc. Ab.	2.50	6.00	12.00	27.50
	1866	.327	1.25	3.00	6.00	15.00
	1867	.956	1.25	3.00	6.00	15.00
	1870	1.079	1.25	3.00	6.00	15.00
	1871/61	1.063	2.50	6.00	12.00	25.00
	1871 L.A.	Inc. Ab.	1.25	3.00	6.00	15.00
	1871 LA	Inc. Ab.	1.25	3.00	6.00	15.00
	1872 L.A.	1.897	1.00	3.00	6.00	12.00
	1872 L.A.	Inc. Ab.	1.00	3.00	6.00	12.00
	1872 LA	Inc. Ab.	1.00	2.50	5.00	10.00

11	1873 LA	1.867	3.00	6.00	12.00	25.00
	1873 L.A.	Inc. Ab.	3.00	6.00	12.00	25.00
	1873 L.A.	Inc. Ab.	3.00	6.00	12.00	25.00
	1873 SVFRIGES (error) Inc. Ab.		20.00	40.00	60.00	125.00

2 ORE

BRONZE

C#	Date	Mintage	Fine	VF	XF	Unc
187	1856	.022	40.00	80.00	150.00	350.00
	1857 long beard	1.121	3.00	7.50	20.00	45.00
	1857 short beard Inc. Ab.		3.00	7.50	20.00	45.00
	1858/7	2.831	5.00	10.00	30.00	60.00
	1858	Inc. Ab.	3.00	7.50	20.00	40.00

Y#	Date	Mintage	Fine	VF	XF	Unc
3	1860	.197	10.00	25.00	50.00	100.00
	1861	1.626	2.50	6.00	12.00	25.00
	1862	.213	6.00	15.00	30.00	60.00
	1863/2	1.621	3.00	7.50	15.00	35.00
	1863	Inc. Ab.	2.50	6.00	12.00	25.00
	1864	.600	2.50	6.00	12.00	25.00
	1865	.629	4.00	10.00	20.00	40.00
	1866/5	.400	6.00	15.00	30.00	60.00
	1866	Inc. Ab.	3.00	7.50	15.00	30.00
	1867 L.A.	.428	2.50	6.00	12.00	25.00
	1867 LA	Inc. Ab.	2.50	6.00	12.00	25.00
	1871/61	.718	3.00	7.00	13.50	25.00
	1871	Inc. Ab.	2.50	6.00	12.00	25.00
	1872	1.646	2.00	5.00	10.00	20.00

12	1873	1.294	7.50	15.00	30.00	60.00

5 ORE

BRONZE

C#	Date	Mintage	Fine	VF	XF	Unc
188	1857 small L.A	.731	4.00	10.00	35.00	70.00
	1857 large L.A Inc. Ab.		4.00	10.00	35.00	70.00
	1857 curved top 5 Inc. Ab.		20.00	60.00	125.00	250.00
	1858/7	1.193	4.00	10.00	35.00	75.00
	1858	Inc. Ab.	10.00	20.00	60.00	125.00

Y#	Date	Mintage	Fine	VF	XF	Unc
4	1860/57	.068	25.00	60.00	120.00	250.00
	1860	Inc. Ab.	20.00	50.00	100.00	200.00
	1861/57	.343	8.00	25.00	50.00	100.00
	1861	Inc. Ab.	6.00	15.00	30.00	60.00
	1862 star	.136	7.00	17.50	35.00	75.00
	1862 rose	I.A.	30.00	75.00	150.00	300.00
	1863/2	.633	6.50	16.50	32.50	85.00
	1863	Inc. Ab.	6.00	15.00	30.00	75.00

Y#	Date	Mintage	Fine	VF	XF	Unc
4	1864/2	.264	6.50	16.50	32.50	85.00
	1864	Inc. Ab.	6.00	15.00	35.00	75.00
	1865	.104	7.00	17.50	35.00	75.00
	1866/5	.120	20.00	50.00	100.00	200.00
	1866	Inc. Ab.	7.00	17.50	35.00	75.00
	1867/6	.741	3.50	11.00	27.50	55.00
	1867	Inc. Ab.	3.00	10.00	25.00	50.00
	1872/66	.620	8.00	20.00	50.00	100.00
	1872	Inc. Ab.	3.00	10.00	25.00	50.00

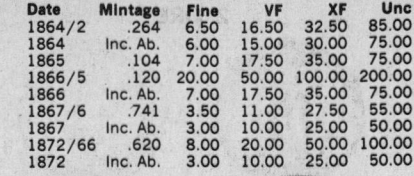

13	1873/2	.783	25.00	40.00	75.00	150.00
	1873 w/o dots above "O" in GOTH					
		Inc. Ab.	17.50	27.50	55.00	110.00
	1873 dots above "O" in GOTH					
		Inc. Ab.	17.50	27.50	55.00	110.00

10 ORE

.8500 g, .750 SILVER, .0204 oz ASW

C#	Date	Mintage	Fine	VF	XF	Unc
192	1855 AG small AG					
		1.359	10.00	25.00	60.00	125.00
	1855 AG larger AG					
		Inc. Ab.	10.00	25.00	60.00	125.00
	1855 G long beard					
		Inc. Ab.	3.00	7.50	20.00	45.00
	1855 G shorter beard					
		Inc. Ab.	3.00	7.50	20.00	45.00
	1855 T	Inc. Ab.	3.00	7.50	20.00	45.00
	1857 ST	1.007	3.00	7.50	20.00	45.00
	1858/7 ST	.354	5.00	12.00	30.00	65.00
	1858 ST	I.A.	4.00	10.00	25.00	50.00
	1859/7 ST					
		1.684	4.00	10.00	25.00	50.00
	1859/8 ST	I.A.	4.00	10.00	25.00	50.00
	1859 ST	I.A.	3.00	7.50	20.00	45.00

Y#	Date	Mintage	Fine	VF	XF	Unc
5	1861 ST	.579	4.00	10.00	25.00	55.00
	1862 ST	I.A.	300.00	600.00	900.00	1900.
	1863 ST	.449	6.00	15.00	35.00	75.00
	1864 ST	I.A.	4.00	10.00	25.00	50.00
	1865 ST	.560	4.00	10.00	25.00	50.00
	1867 ST	.609	4.00	10.00	25.00	50.00
	1869 ST	.210	5.00	12.50	30.00	65.00
	1870 ST	.384	4.00	10.00	25.00	50.00
	1871 ST	1.162	2.00	6.00	15.00	35.00

17	1872 ST	.120	60.00	85.00	125.00	180.00
	1873 ST	.635	50.00	75.00	100.00	160.00
	1873 ST inverted V in SVERIGES (error)					
		Inc. Ab.	65.00	130.00	200.00	300.00
	1873 ST SVF.RIGES (error)					
		Inc. Ab.	50.00	100.00	200.00	450.00

25 ORE

2.1300 g, .750 SILVER, .0513 oz ASW

C#	Date	Mintage	Fine	VF	XF	Unc
193	1855 ST	.437	6.00	15.00	40.00	80.00
	1856 ST	1.763	5.00	12.00	30.00	65.00
	1857/6 ST	.434	12.00	30.00	70.00	140.00
	1857 ST	I.A.	10.00	25.00	65.00	125.00
	1858/7 ST					
		1.183	10.00	25.00	65.00	140.00
	1858 ST	I.A.	10.00	25.00	65.00	140.00
	1859/7 ST	—	6.50	16.50	45.00	90.00
	1859/8 ST	—	6.50	16.50	45.00	90.00
	1859 ST	—	6.00	15.00	40.00	80.00

Y#	Date	Mintage	Fine	VF	XF	Unc
6	1862 ST	1,762	450.00	800.00	1200.	3000.
	1864/2 ST	.266	16.50	32.50	65.00	140.00
	1864 ST	I.A.	15.00	30.00	60.00	125.00
	1865 ST	.400	15.00	30.00	60.00	125.00
	1866 ST	.039	17.50	35.00	70.00	140.00
	1867/6 ST	.198	18.00	37.50	75.00	150.00
	1867 ST	I.A.	15.00	30.00	70.00	125.00
	1871/61 ST	.660	12.00	22.50	50.00	100.00
	1871 ST	I.A.	11.00	20.00	45.00	90.00

50 ORE

4.2500 g, .750 SILVER, .1024 oz ASW

C#	Date	Mintage	Fine	VF	XF	Unc
194	1857 ST	.492	50.00	100.00	200.00	400.00

Y#	Date	Mintage	Fine	VF	XF	Unc
7	1862 ST	2,319	500.00	800.00	1250.	3000.

RIKSDALER RIKSMYNT

8.5000 g, .750 SILVER, .2049 oz ASW
Obv: Short goatee.

C#	Date	Mintage	Fine	VF	XF	Unc
195	1857 ST	.645	40.00	80.00	150.00	350.00

Obv: Long goatee.

195a	1857 ST	Inc. Ab.	40.00	80.00	150.00	350.00

Y#	Date	Mintage	Fine	VF	XF	Unc
8	1860 ST	.125	40.00	80.00	165.00	350.00
	1861/0 ST	.158	45.00	90.00	180.00	375.00
	1861 ST	Inc. Ab.	40.00	80.00	165.00	350.00
	1862 ST	—	600.00	800.00	1250.	2750.
	1864 ST	.085	45.00	90.00	175.00	400.00
	1864 ST w/o edge lettering					
		Inc. Ab.	50.00	100.00	200.00	450.00
	1865 ST	.059	75.00	150.00	300.00	600.00
	1867/6 ST	.106	45.00	90.00	180.00	450.00
	1867 ST	Inc. Ab.	40.00	80.00	165.00	375.00
	1871/61 ST	.208	38.50	75.00	155.00	300.00
	1871 ST	Inc. Ab.	35.00	70.00	140.00	300.00

Obv: Deepened hairlines.

18	1873	Inc. Ab.	200.00	400.00	650.00	1000.

2 RIKSDALER RIKSMYNT

17.0000 g, .750 SILVER, .4099 oz ASW

C#	Date	Mintage	Fine	VF	XF	Unc
196	1857 ST	.288	80.00	165.00	325.00	700.00

Y#	Date	Mintage	Fine	VF	XF	Unc
9	1862 ST	640 pcs.	350.00	700.00	1200.	2750.
	1864/2 ST	.038	135.00	275.00	550.00	1100.
	1864 ST	Inc. Ab.	125.00	250.00	500.00	1000.
	1871 ST small date and large head					
		.019	125.00	250.00	500.00	1000.

Obv: Small head. Rev: Large date.

9.1	1871 ST	Inc. Ab.	125.00	250.00	500.00	1000.

RIKSDALER SPECIES
(4 Riksdaler Riksmynt)

34.0000 g, .750 SILVER, .8198 oz ASW
Obv: Bust right w/short goatee.
Rev: Crowned, supported arms.

C#	Date	Mintage	Fine	VF	XF	Unc
197	1855 ST	2,117	—	—	Rare	—
	1856/5 ST	.776	225.00	450.00	650.00	1300.
	1856 ST	Inc. Ab.	200.00	400.00	600.00	1200.
	1857 ST	.483	55.00	100.00	325.00	675.00

197a	1856 ST	Inc. Ab.	55.00	100.00	275.00	550.00
	1857 ST	Inc. Ab.	100.00	200.00	400.00	800.00
	1859 ST	.101	60.00	125.00	350.00	750.00

Y#	Date	Mintage	Fine	VF	XF	Unc
10	1861 ST	.207	60.00	125.00	275.00	550.00
	1862 ST L.A., edge lettering large and small					

SWEDEN

SWEDEN 1564

Y#	Date	Mintage	Fine	VF	XF	Unc
10		.943	40.00	80.00	250.00	475.00
	1862 ST L A					
		Inc. Ab.	40.00	80.00	250.00	475.00
	1862 ST w/o engraver's initials					
		Inc. Ab.	80.00	150.00	350.00	700.00
	1862 ST w/o edge lettering					
		Inc. Ab.	125.00	250.00	500.00	1000.
	1863 ST	.268	60.00	125.00	300.00	600.00
	1864 ST	.535	40.00	80.00	240.00	500.00
	1865 ST	.107	60.00	125.00	300.00	600.00
	1866/5 ST	.041	75.00	155.00	350.00	750.00
	1866 ST	Inc. Ab.	70.00	140.00	325.00	675.00
	1866 ST w/o edge lettering					
		Inc. Ab.	125.00	250.00	500.00	1000.
	1867 ST	.064	60.00	125.00	300.00	600.00
	1868 ST	.120	60.00	125.00	300.00	600.00
	1869 ST	.314	35.00	70.00	200.00	400.00
	1870 ST	.161	60.00	125.00	300.00	600.00
	1871 ST	.260	40.00	80.00	250.00	500.00

MONETARY REFORM

100 Ore = 1 Krona

DATE VARIETIES

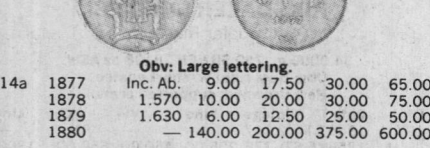

1916 short tailed 6

1936 long tailed 6

ORE

BRONZE
Obv: Small lettering.

Y#	Date	Mintage	Fine	VF	XF	Unc
14	1874	2.370	4.00	9.00	17.50	35.00
	1875	2.829	4.00	9.00	17.50	35.00
	1876	1.889	17.50	25.00	40.00	75.00
	1877	1.590	9.00	17.50	30.00	65.00

Obv: Large lettering.

Y#	Date	Mintage	Fine	VF	XF	Unc
14a	1877	Inc. Ab.	9.00	17.50	30.00	65.00
	1878	1.570	10.00	20.00	30.00	75.00
	1879	1.630	6.00	12.50	25.00	50.00
	1880	—	140.00	200.00	375.00	600.00

Obv: Legend lengthened.

Y#	Date	Mintage	Fine	VF	XF	Unc
14b	1879	Inc. Ab.	125.00	180.00	325.00	500.00
	1880	1.713	12.50	20.00	35.00	70.00
	1881	1.984	5.00	10.00	20.00	40.00
	1882	2.587	3.00	6.00	12.00	25.00
	1883	2.587	3.00	6.00	12.00	25.00
	1884	2.626	3.00	6.00	12.00	25.00
	1885	2.464	3.00	6.00	12.00	25.00
	1886	1.234	4.00	8.00	15.00	35.00
	1888	1.738	4.00	8.00	15.00	35.00
	1889	1.189	4.00	8.00	15.00	35.00
	1890	1.949	2.00	5.00	12.00	25.00
	1891	2.723	2.00	5.00	12.00	25.00
	1892	.280	45.00	65.00	110.00	225.00
	1893	2.145	2.00	5.00	12.00	25.00
	1894	.590	20.00	30.00	45.00	100.00
	1895	2.012	1.00	3.00	7.00	15.00
	1896	1.463	1.00	3.00	7.00	15.00
	1897	2.544	.50	2.00	4.00	10.00
	1898	2.959	.50	2.00	4.00	10.00
	1899	2.821	.50	2.00	4.00	10.00
	1900	2.929	.50	2.00	4.00	10.00
	1901	3.075	.50	2.00	4.00	10.00
	1902	2.685	.50	2.00	4.00	10.00
	1903	2.666	.50	2.00	4.00	10.00
	1904	2.033	.50	1.00	4.00	10.00
	1905	3.556	.50	1.00	3.00	8.00

Y#	Date	Mintage	Fine	VF	XF	Unc
32	1906	1.783	4.00	10.00	20.00	40.00
	1907	8.251	.20	.75	3.00	6.00

Obv: Small cross.

Y#	Date	Mintage	Fine	VF	XF	Unc
44.1	1909	3.810	7.50	12.50	25.00	120.00
(44)						

Obv: Large cross.

Y#	Date	Mintage	Fine	VF	XF	Unc
44.2	1909	Inc. Ab.	2.50	5.00	10.00	40.00
(44.1)	1910	1.583	4.00	9.00	15.00	60.00
	1911	3.150	.50	1.50	4.00	18.00
	1912	3.170	.50	1.50	4.00	18.00
	1913/12	3.197	.50	1.50	4.00	18.00
	1913	Inc. Ab.	.50	1.50	4.00	18.00
	1914 open 4					
		2.214	35.00	60.00	125.00	250.00
	1914 closed 4					
		Inc. Ab.	.75	2.50	9.00	40.00
	1915	4.471	.25	.75	2.00	8.00
	1916 short 6					
		7.620	.25	.75	2.00	7.50
	1916 long 6					
		Inc. Ab.	.30	1.00	2.50	12.00
	1920	5.548	.25	.50	1.25	5.00
	1921	7.442	.25	.50	1.25	5.00
	1922	1.165	2.50	5.00	7.50	30.00
	1923	4.512	.35	1.00	2.00	8.00
	1924	2.579	.25	1.00	2.00	9.00
	1925	4.715	.20	.50	1.00	5.00
	1926	6.739	.20	.50	1.00	5.00
	1927	3.601	.20	.50	1.00	5.00
	1928	2.381	.50	1.00	3.00	12.00
	1929	6.091	.20	.50	1.00	5.00
	1930	5.477	.20	.50	1.00	5.00
	1931	5.680	.20	.50	1.00	5.00
	1932	3.339	.30	.75	2.00	8.00
	1933	3.427	.30	.75	1.25	6.00
	1934	6.121	.20	.40	.75	4.00
	1935	4.600	.20	.40	.75	4.00
	1936 long 6					
		6.116	.30	.75	1.50	5.00
	1936 short 6					
		Inc. Ab.	.20	.40	.75	4.00
	1937	7.738	.20	.30	.75	3.00
	1938	6.993	.20	.30	.75	3.00
	1939	6.562	.20	.30	.75	3.00
	1940	4.060	.20	.30	.50	2.00
	1941	11.599	.20	.30	.50	2.00
	1942	3.992	.20	.30	.75	3.00
	1950	22.421	—	.10	.40	2.00

IRON
World War I Issues
Similar to Y#44.

Y#	Date	Mintage	Fine	VF	XF	Unc
52	1917	8.128	1.00	2.00	4.00	8.00
	1918	9.706	1.25	2.50	5.00	10.00
	1919	7.170	2.00	4.00	8.00	15.00

World War II Issues
Similar to Y#44.

Y#	Date	Mintage	Fine	VF	XF	Unc
69	1942	10.053	.15	.30	1.00	4.00
	1943	10.714	.15	.30	1.25	6.00
	1944	8.699	.15	.30	1.00	6.00
	1945	9.527	.15	.30	1.00	6.00
	1946	6.611	.15	.50	2.00	8.00
	1947	14.245	.10	.20	.75	3.00
	1948	15.442	.10	.20	.75	3.00
	1949	11.779	.10	.20	.75	3.00
	1950	14.432	.10	.20	.75	3.00

BRONZE

Y#	Date	Mintage	Fine	VF	XF	Unc
72	1952 TS	3.819	.10	.30	.75	4.00
	1953 TS	22.636	—	.10	.50	3.00
	1954 TS	15.492	—	.10	.50	3.00
	1955 TS	24.008	—	.10	.50	3.00
	1956 TS	20.792	—	.10	.50	3.00
	1957 TS	21.019	—	.10	.50	3.00
	1958 TS	20.220	—	.10	.50	3.00
	1959 TS	14.028	—	.10	.50	3.00
	1960 TS	21.840	—	.10	.40	2.00
	1961 TS	11.458	—	.10	.60	3.00
	1961 U	4.928	.10	.30	.75	4.00
	1962 U	19.698	—	.10	.50	3.00
	1963 U	26.070	—	.10	.20	.60
	1964 U	19.290	—	.10	.20	.60
	1965 U	22.335	—	.10	.20	.60
	1966 U	24.093	—	—	.10	.40
	1967 U	30.420	—	—	.10	.40
	1968 U	20.760	—	—	.10	.40
	1969 U	20.198	—	—	.10	.40
	1970 U	44.400	—	—	.10	.40
	1971 U	16.490	—	—	.10	.40

2 ORE

BRONZE
Obv: Small lettering

Y#	Date	Mintage	Fine	VF	XF	Unc
15	1874	1.914	2.00	7.00	20.00	50.00
	1875/74	2.441	30.00	55.00	100.00	225.00
	1875	Inc. Ab.	1.00	7.00	25.00	50.00
	1876/5	1.402	30.00	60.00	120.00	225.00
	1876	Inc. Ab.	3.00	12.50	35.00	90.00
	1877	1.015	3.00	12.50	35.00	90.00
	1878	.865	50.00	75.00	150.00	300.00

Obv: Large lettering

Y#	Date	Mintage	Fine	VF	XF	Unc
15a	1877	Inc. Ab.	3.00	12.50	35.00	90.00
	1878	Inc. Ab.	4.00	15.00	40.00	100.00
	1879	.935	2.00	10.00	30.00	70.00
	1880	.825	3.00	15.00	40.00	90.00
	1881	1.244	1.00	4.00	12.00	50.00
	1882	1.777	1.00	4.00	12.00	50.00
	1883	1.483	1.00	4.00	12.00	50.00
	1884 open 4					
		1.316	1.00	4.00	12.00	50.00
	1884 closed 4					
		Inc. Ab.	8.00	17.50	35.00	100.00
	1885	.615	2.00	7.00	20.00	60.00
	1886	1.241	1.00	4.00	12.00	45.00
	1888	.865	1.00	4.00	12.00	45.00
	1889	.589	1.00	4.00	12.00	45.00
	1890	.912	.75	2.00	7.50	30.00
	1891	.942	.75	2.00	7.50	30.00
	1892	.688	.75	2.00	7.50	30.00
	1893	.558	.75	2.00	7.50	30.00
	1894 open 4					
		.586	.75	2.00	10.00	35.00
	1894 closed 4					
		Inc. Ab.	8.50	17.50	40.00	100.00
	1895	.781	.75	2.00	8.00	30.00
	1896	.908	.75	2.00	8.00	30.00
	1897	1.300	.50	2.00	8.00	30.00
	1898	1.527	.50	2.00	8.00	30.00
	1899	2.172	.50	2.00	8.00	30.00
	1900 oval OO					
		.688	1.00	3.00	10.00	40.00
	1900 round OO					
		Inc. Ab.	30.00	60.00	100.00	225.00
	1901	1.420	.50	2.00	6.00	25.00
	1902	2.040	.50	2.00	6.00	25.00
	1904	.698	.50	2.00	8.00	30.00
	1905	1.430	.50	2.00	6.00	25.00

Y#	Date	Mintage	Fine	VF	XF	Unc
33	1906/5	.994	25.00	45.00	75.00	200.00
	1906	Inc. Ab.	5.00	12.00	25.00	70.00
	1907	3.810	.25	1.00	4.00	15.00

Y#	Date	Mintage	Fine	VF	XF	Unc
45	1909	1.580	.75	3.00	12.50	40.00
	1910	.809	2.00	7.00	25.00	80.00
	1912	.446	2.00	9.00	30.00	100.00
	1913	.806	.50	3.00	17.50	50.00
	1914	1.200	.50	3.00	17.50	50.00
	1915	.814	.50	3.00	17.50	50.00
	1916/5	2.820	4.00	8.00	25.00	80.00
	1916 short 6					
		Inc. Ab.	.25	1.00	8.00	35.00
	1916 long 6					
		Inc. Ab.	.25	1.00	8.00	35.00
	1919	1.203	.25	1.00	7.00	30.00
	1920	3.465	.30	.75	3.00	15.00
	1921	2.958	.30	.75	3.00	15.00
	1922	.932	1.00	3.00	10.00	40.00
	1923	.769	2.00	4.00	10.00	50.00
	1924	1.283	.50	1.25	7.00	35.00
	1925	3.903	.20	.75	3.00	15.00
	1926	3.579	.20	.75	3.00	15.00
	1927	2.190	.20	.75	3.00	15.00

SWEDEN 1565

Y#	Date	Mintage	Fine	VF	XF	Unc
45	1928	.832	.50	1.50	8.00	35.00
	1929	2.384	.20	.60	3.00	14.00
	1930	2.590	.20	.60	3.00	14.00
	1931	2.296	.20	.60	3.00	14.00
	1932	1.179	.50	1.25	8.00	35.00
	1933	1.721	.20	.75	3.00	14.00
	1934	1.795	.20	.75	3.00	14.00
	1935	3.678	.20	.40	1.50	8.00
	1936 short 6	2.244	.10	.40	1.50	10.00
	1936 long 6	Inc. Ab.	1.00	1.50	5.00	20.00
	1937	2.981	.15	.40	1.50	8.00
	1938	3.225	.15	.40	1.50	8.00
	1939	4.014	.10	.40	1.00	7.50
	1940	3.305	.10	.40	1.00	7.50
	1941	7.337	.10	.40	1.00	7.50
	1942	1.614	.50	1.00	2.00	15.00
	1950	5.823	.10	.25	.75	5.00

IRON
World War I Issues
Similar to Y#45.

Y#	Date	Mintage	Fine	VF	XF	Unc
53	1917	4.576	2.00	3.00	7.00	15.00
	1918	4.982	3.00	5.00	12.00	25.00
	1919	2.923	6.00	10.00	25.00	50.00
	1920	1 pc.	—	—	—	—

World War II Issues
Similar to Y#45.

Y#	Date	Mintage	Fine	VF	XF	Unc
70	1942	9.344	.15	.30	3.00	12.00
	1943	6.999	.15	.30	3.00	12.00
	1944	6.126	.15	.30	3.00	12.00
	1945	4.773	.20	.40	3.50	15.00
	1946	5.854	.15	.30	3.00	12.00
	1947	9.536	.15	.30	2.00	8.00
	1948	11.424	.15	.30	2.00	8.00
	1949 long 9	10.600	.15	.30	2.00	8.00
	1949 short 9	I.A.	.15	.30	2.00	8.00
	1950	13.323	.15	.30	2.00	8.00

BRONZE

Y#	Date	Mintage	Fine	VF	XF	Unc
73	1952 TS	3.011	.20	.50	1.50	7.50
	1953 TS	15.620	.10	.20	1.00	5.00
	1954 TS	10.086	.10	.20	1.00	5.00
	1955 TS	12.963	.10	.20	1.00	5.00
	1956 TS	13.890	.10	.20	1.00	5.00
	1957 TS	9.997	.10	.20	1.00	5.00
	1958 TS	10.106	.10	.20	1.00	5.00
	1959 TS	11.572	.10	.20	1.00	5.00
	1960 TS	11.093	.10	.20	1.00	5.00
	1961 TS	9.673	.10	.20	1.00	5.00
	1961 U	1.075	1.50	3.00	5.00	17.50
	1962 U	9.569	—	.10	.50	2.50
	1963 U	13.338	—	.10	.50	2.50
	1964 U	19.346	—	.10	.20	1.00
	1965 U	23.356	—	.10	.20	1.00
	1966 U	18.278	—	.10	.20	1.00
	1967 U	23.931	—	—	.10	.50
	1968 U	26.238	—	—	.10	.50
	1969 U	16.843	—	—	.10	.50
	1970 U	31.254	—	—	.10	.50
	1971 U	19.179	—	—	.10	.50

5 ORE

BRONZE
Obv: Small lettering.

Y#	Date	Mintage	Fine	VF	XF	Unc
16	1874	.866	4.00	20.00	50.00	100.00
	1875/4	1.234	6.00	30.00	75.00	150.00
	1875	Inc. Ab.	4.00	20.00	50.00	100.00
	1876	.609	4.00	20.00	50.00	100.00
	1877	.514	15.00	60.00	150.00	300.00
	1878	.364	4.00	20.00	50.00	100.00
	1879	.350	20.00	75.00	150.00	300.00
	1880/70	.403	15.00	50.00	125.00	250.00
	1880	Inc. Ab.	15.00	50.00	125.00	250.00
	1881	.625	4.00	20.00	50.00	100.00
	1882/1	.825	15.00	60.00	120.00	240.00
	1882	Inc. Ab.	4.00	20.00	60.00	120.00
	1883	.578	4.00	20.00	50.00	100.00
	1884	.784	4.00	20.00	50.00	100.00
	1885	.282	4.00	20.00	50.00	100.00
	1886	.269	4.50	20.00	60.00	120.00
	1887	.251	5.00	25.00	70.00	140.00
	1888	.214	5.00	25.00	70.00	140.00
	1889	.220	3.00	15.00	45.00	90.00

Obv: Large lettering.

Y#	Date	Mintage	Fine	VF	XF	Unc
16a	1888	Inc. Ab.	75.00	120.00	175.00	400.00
	1889	Inc. Ab.	3.00	15.00	45.00	90.00
	1890	.339	3.00	15.00	60.00	120.00
	1891/81	.374	2.00	10.00	35.00	100.00
	1891	Inc. Ab.	2.00	10.00	35.00	100.00
	1892	.586	1.00	7.00	30.00	80.00
	1895	.529	1.00	7.00	30.00	80.00
	1896	.309	2.00	10.00	35.00	95.00
	1897	.570	1.00	6.00	20.00	60.00
	1898	.721	1.00	6.00	20.00	60.00
	1899	1.225	1.00	6.00	20.00	60.00
	1900	.365	1.00	6.00	20.00	60.00
	1901	.442	1.00	6.00	20.00	60.00
	1902	.652	1.00	6.00	20.00	60.00
	1903	.243	2.00	9.00	30.00	80.00
	1904	.414	1.00	6.00	20.00	50.00
	1905	.545	1.00	6.00	25.00	55.00

Y#	Date	Mintage	Fine	VF	XF	Unc
34	1906	.565	.75	5.00	20.00	50.00
	1907	1.953	.50	2.00	10.00	30.00

Obv: Small cross.

Y#	Date	Mintage	Fine	VF	XF	Unc
46.1	1909	.917	1.00	5.00	35.00	100.00

Obv: Large cross.

Y#	Date	Mintage	Fine	VF	XF	Unc
46.2	1909	Inc. Ab.	10.00	40.00	125.00	450.00
	1910	.031	100.00	200.00	400.00	800.00
	1911	.778	1.00	5.00	40.00	140.00
	1912	.547	1.50	6.00	50.00	190.00
	1913	.762	1.00	4.00	40.00	135.00
	1914	.400	3.00	9.00	60.00	225.00
	1915	1.222	.50	4.00	20.00	70.00
	1916/5	.955	15.00	30.00	60.00	175.00
	1916 short 6	Inc. Ab.	.50	4.00	20.00	70.00
	1916 long 6	Inc. Ab.	.50	4.00	20.00	70.00
	1919	1.129	.50	2.00	12.00	50.00
	1920	2.361	.50	2.00	8.00	30.00
	1921	1.879	.30	1.00	10.00	40.00
	1922	.763	.50	5.00	25.00	95.00
	1923	.506	2.00	9.00	60.00	195.00
	1924	.900	.40	3.00	17.50	70.00
	1925	1.944	.30	1.50	9.00	40.00
	1926	1.742	.30	1.50	9.00	40.00
	1927	.036	100.00	150.00	350.00	700.00
	1928	.987	.30	2.00	10.00	50.00
	1929	1.670	.30	1.00	9.00	40.00
	1930	1.716	.30	1.00	9.00	40.00
	1931	1.131	.20	1.00	9.00	40.00
	1932	1.165	.20	1.00	9.00	40.00
	1933	.574	2.00	5.00	25.00	100.00
	1934	1.710	.20	.75	5.00	30.00
	1935	1.682	.20	.75	5.00	30.00
	1936 short 6	1.626	.20	.75	6.00	30.00
	1936 long 6	Inc. Ab.	.40	1.00	7.00	35.00
	1937	2.637	.20	.50	4.00	20.00
	1938	2.354	.20	.50	4.00	20.00
	1939	2.592	.20	.75	6.00	25.00
	1940	2.730	.20	.50	3.00	15.00
	1940 serif 4	Inc. Ab.	.20	.50	3.00	15.00
	1941	2.055	.20	.50	3.00	15.00
	1942	.395	2.50	6.00	25.00	95.00
	1950	12.559	.10	.20	.75	5.00

IRON
World War I Issues
Similar to Y#46.

Y#	Date	Mintage	Fine	VF	XF	Unc
54	1917	2.953	5.00	10.00	20.00	40.00
	1918	2.458	10.00	20.00	35.00	70.00
	1919	2.302	10.00	20.00	30.00	60.00

World War II Issues
Similar to Y#46.

Y#	Date	Mintage	Fine	VF	XF	Unc
71	1942	4.343	.20	.75	7.00	30.00
	1943	5.570	.20	.75	7.00	30.00
	1944	4.562	.20	.75	7.00	30.00
	1945	3.771	.20	.75	7.00	30.00
	1946	2.575	—	.50	5.00	20.00
	1947	6.035	—	.50	5.00	20.00
	1948	6.250	—	.50	5.00	20.00
	1949	7.840	—	.50	4.00	17.50
	1950	5.290	—	.50	4.00	17.50

BRONZE

Y#	Date	Mintage	Fine	VF	XF	Unc
74	1952 TS	3.065	.20	.50	2.50	11.00
	1953 TS	12.329	.20	.50	2.50	11.00
	1954 TS	7.232	.20	.50	2.50	11.00
	1955 TS	8.465	.20	.50	2.50	11.00
	1956 TS	7.997	.20	.50	2.50	11.00
	1957 TS	6.276	.20	.50	2.50	11.00
	1958 TS	9.498	.20	.50	2.50	11.00
	1959 TS	8.370	.20	.50	2.50	11.00
	1960 TS	10.542	.20	.40	2.00	8.00
	1961 TS	3.909	.20	.40	2.00	8.00
	1961 U	2.452	.20	.50	2.50	10.00
	1962 U	22.306	—	.10	.50	3.00
	1963 U	17.156	—	.10	.50	3.00
	1964 U	10.923	—	.10	.75	7.00
	1964 U 50 in crown	Inc. Ab.	2.50	5.00	10.00	25.00
	1965 U	22.635	—	.10	.20	1.00
	1966 U	18.213	—	.10	.20	1.00
	1967 U	20.776	—	.10	.20	1.00
	1968 U	27.094	—	.10	.20	1.00
	1969 U	26.887	—	.10	.20	1.00
	1970 U	29.420	—	.10	.20	1.00
	1971 U	15.749	—	.10	.20	1.00

Y#	Date	Mintage	Fine	VF	XF	Unc
88	1972 U	107.894	—	—	.10	.20
	1973 U	193.038	—	—	.10	.20

Y#	Date	Mintage	Fine	VF	XF	Unc
91	1976 U	4.672	—	—	.10	.35
	1977 U	31.037	—	—	.10	.25
	1978 U	46.022	—	—	.10	.25
	1979 U	65.833	—	—	.10	.25
	1980 U	60.997	—	—	.10	.20
	1981 U	19.791	—	—	.10	.20

BRASS

Y#	Date	Mintage	Fine	VF	XF	Unc
91a	1981 U	35.170	—	—	.10	.15
	1982 U	40.471	—	—	.10	.15
	1983 U	36.471	—	—	.10	.15
	1984 U	13.455	—	—	.10	.15

10 ORE

1.4500 g, .400 SILVER, .0186 oz ASW
Obv: Small lettering.

Y#	Date	Mintage	Fine	VF	XF	Unc
19	1874 ST	2.875	12.00	20.00	45.00	100.00
	1875/4 ST	1.503	55.00	80.00	135.00	275.00
	1875 ST	Inc. Ab.	50.00	75.00	125.00	250.00
	1876/5 ST	1.814	15.00	30.00	60.00	120.00
	1876 ST	Inc. Ab.	12.50	25.00	50.00	100.00

Obv: Large lettering.

Y#	Date	Mintage	Fine	VF	XF	Unc
27	1880 EB	.851	30.00	45.00	65.00	130.00
	1881 EB	.763	30.00	45.00	65.00	130.00
	1882/1 EB	.735	65.00	100.00	150.00	300.00
	1882 EB	Inc. Ab.	30.00	45.00	65.00	130.00
	1883 EB	.694	20.00	35.00	55.00	100.00
	1884 EB	1.560	12.00	25.00	50.00	100.00

SWEDEN 1566

Y#	Date	Mintage	Fine	VF	XF	Unc
27	1887 EB	1.513	12.00	25.00	50.00	100.00
	1890 EB	.922	12.00	25.00	50.00	100.00
	1891 EB	.827	12.00	25.00	50.00	100.00
	1892 EB	1.215	4.00	10.00	35.00	70.00
	1894 EB	1.733	2.50	7.50	25.00	45.00
	1896 EB	2.084	2.00	6.00	20.00	35.00
	1897 EB	.819	2.50	7.50	25.00	45.00
	1898 EB	2.087	1.00	4.50	20.00	35.00
	1899 EB	2.041	1.00	4.50	20.00	35.00
	1900 EB	1.173	1.50	6.00	20.00	35.00
	1902 EB	1.946	1.00	4.50	20.00	35.00
	1903 EB	1.509	1.00	4.50	20.00	35.00
	1904 EB	3.280	.75	2.50	12.50	25.00

Y#	Date	Mintage	Fine	VF	XF	Unc
35	1907 EB	7.320	.60	2.00	9.00	17.50

Y#	Date	Mintage	Fine	VF	XF	Unc
47	1909 W	1.610	2.50	7.00	22.50	65.00
	1911 W	3.180	.75	3.00	10.00	30.00
	1913 W	1.581	1.50	5.00	17.50	50.00
	1914 W	1.571	1.00	3.50	10.00	30.00
	1915 W	1.547	1.00	5.00	15.00	45.00
	1916/5 W	3.035	5.00	10.00	30.00	100.00
	1916 W	Inc. Ab.	1.00	3.00	10.00	30.00
	1917 W	4.996	.75	1.50	5.00	17.50
	1918 W	4.114	.75	1.50	5.00	17.50
	1919 W	5.740	.75	1.50	5.00	17.50
	1927 W	2.510	.40	1.00	5.00	20.00
	1928 G	2.901	.40	1.00	5.00	20.00
	1929 G	5.505	.40	1.00	3.00	15.00
	1930 G	3.223	.40	1.00	3.00	15.00
	1931 G	4.272	.40	1.00	3.00	15.00
	1933 G	1.948	1.00	2.00	7.00	25.00
	1934 G	4.059	.40	.60	1.25	7.50
	1935 G	2.426	.40	.60	1.25	7.50
	1936 G short 6	5.097	2.50	7.00	20.00	60.00
	1936 G long 6	Inc. Ab.	.30	.50	1.50	7.50
	1937 G	5.117	.30	.40	1.00	6.00
	1938 G	7.428	.30	.40	1.00	6.00
	1938 G	—	—	—	Proof	15.00
	1939 G	2.021	.30	.75	2.50	12.00
	1939 G	—	—	—	Proof	20.00
	1940 G	3.017	.30	.50	1.00	6.00
	1941 G	9.106	.30	.60	1.00	6.00
	1942 G	3.692	.30	.60	1.00	6.00

NICKEL-BRONZE

Y#	Date	Mintage	Fine	VF	XF	Unc
55	1920 W	3.612	.50	2.00	9.00	40.00
	1921 W	2.270	.50	2.00	9.00	40.00
	1923 W	2.144	.50	2.00	10.00	50.00
	1924 W	1.600	.75	3.00	15.00	60.00
	1925 W	1.472	1.00	5.00	20.00	80.00
	1940 G	3.374	.20	.50	3.00	17.50
	1941	.816	.75	2.00	7.50	30.00
	1946 TS	4.117	.10	.30	1.50	8.00
	1947 TS	4.133	.10	.30	1.50	8.00

1.4400 g, .400 SILVER, .0185 oz ASW

Y#	Date	Mintage	Fine	VF	XF	Unc
64	1942 G	1.600	.30	.50	1.50	8.00
	1942 G	—	—	—	Proof	35.00
	1943 G	7.661	.30	.50	1.50	8.00
	1944 G	12.277	.30	.40	1.00	5.00
	1945 G	11.703	.30	.40	1.00	5.00
	1945 TS	Inc. Ab.	.30	.60	1.50	8.00
	1945 TS/G	I.A.	.50	.75	2.50	10.00
	1946/5 TS open 6	3.576	6.00	12.00	25.00	50.00
	1946 TS open 6	Inc. Ab.	.30	.75	4.00	15.00
	1946 TS closed 6	Inc. Ab.	.30	.75	4.00	15.00
	1947 TS	7.293	.20	.40	1.00	5.00
	1948 TS	10.419	.20	.40	.75	5.00
	1949 TS	12.044	.20	.30	.75	5.00
	1950 TS	31.824	.20	.30	.75	4.00

Y#	Date	Mintage	Fine	VF	XF	Unc
75	1952 TS	4.660	BV	.40	1.00	5.00
	1953 TS	28.484	BV	.30	.75	4.00
	1954 TS	15.913	BV	.30	.75	4.00
	1955 TS	16.687	BV	.30	.75	4.00
	1956 TS	21.986	BV	.25	.50	3.00
	1957 TS	21.294	BV	.25	.50	3.00
	1958 TS	19.605	BV	.25	.50	3.00
	1959 TS	18.523	BV	.25	.50	3.00
	1960 TS	16.605	BV	.25	.50	3.00
	1961 TS	8.284	BV	.25	.50	3.00
	1961 U	7.843	BV	.25	.50	3.00
	1962 U	8.619	BV	.25	.50	3.00

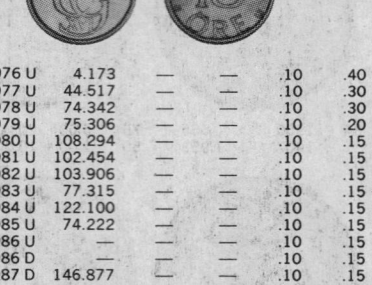

COPPER-NICKEL

Y#	Date	Mintage	Fine	VF	XF	Unc
83	1962 U	8.814	.10	.25	.50	3.00
	1963 U	28.170	—	—	.10	.50
	1964 U	36.895	—	—	.10	.50
	1965 U	29.870	—	—	.10	.50
	1966 U	20.435	—	—	.10	.50
	1967 U	18.245	—	—	.10	.50
	1968 U	51.490	—	—	.10	.40
	1969 U	55.880	—	—	.10	.40
	1970 U	60.910	—	—	.10	.40
	1971 U	27.075	—	—	.10	.40
	1972 U	36.750	—	—	.10	.20
	1973 U	160.740	—	—	.10	.20

Y#	Date	Mintage	Fine	VF	XF	Unc
92	1976 U	4.173	—	—	.10	.40
	1977 U	44.517	—	—	.10	.30
	1978 U	74.342	—	—	.10	.30
	1979 U	75.306	—	—	.10	.20
	1980 U	108.294	—	—	.10	.15
	1981 U	102.454	—	—	.10	.15
	1982 U	103.906	—	—	.10	.15
	1983 U	77.315	—	—	.10	.15
	1984 U	122.100	—	—	.10	.15
	1985 U	74.222	—	—	.10	.15
	1986 U	—	—	—	.10	.15
	1986 D	—	—	—	.10	.15
	1987 D	146.877	—	—	.10	.15
	1988 D	—	—	—	.10	.15

25 ORE

2.4200 g, .600 SILVER, .0467 oz ASW
Obv: Small lettering

Y#	Date	Mintage	Fine	VF	XF	Unc
20	1874 ST	2.100	12.00	25.00	60.00	150.00
	1875/4 ST	1.131	50.00	95.00	180.00	350.00
	1875 ST	Inc. Ab.	40.00	75.00	140.00	275.00
	1876/5 ST	2.125	15.00	30.00	75.00	175.00
	1876 ST	Inc. Ab.	12.00	25.00	60.00	150.00
	1877 FB	.894	15.00	30.00	75.00	175.00
	1878/7 EB	.859	60.00	125.00	250.00	500.00
	1878 EB	Inc. Ab.	50.00	100.00	200.00	400.00

Obv: Large lettering

Y#	Date	Mintage	Fine	VF	XF	Unc
28	1880 EB	1.180	6.00	17.50	50.00	150.00
	1881 EB	1.392	5.00	15.00	40.00	120.00
	1883 EB	1.100	3.00	10.00	30.00	90.00
	1885 EB	1.168	4.50	12.00	37.50	110.00
	1889 EB	.422	4.50	12.00	37.50	110.00
	1890 EB	.469	3.00	10.00	30.00	90.00
	1896 EB	.794	2.50	8.00	25.00	80.00
	1897 EB	1.097	1.50	6.00	20.00	75.00
	1898 EB	1.458	1.50	6.00	20.00	75.00
	1899 EB	1.458	1.50	6.00	20.00	75.00
	1902 EB	1.259	1.50	6.00	20.00	75.00
	1904 EB	.692	1.50	6.00	20.00	75.00
	1905 EB	.732	1.50	6.00	20.00	75.00

Y#	Date	Mintage	Fine	VF	XF	Unc
36	1907 EB	3.223	1.00	3.50	15.00	40.00

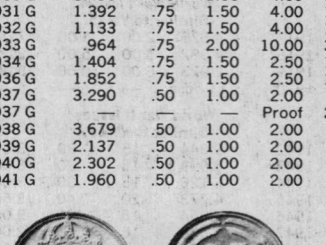

Y#	Date	Mintage	Fine	VF	XF	Unc
48	1910 W	2.044	1.00	4.00	10.00	50.00
	1912 W	1.014	1.00	4.00	20.00	60.00
	1914 W	3.719	1.00	2.50	10.00	35.00
	1916 W	1.270	1.00	4.00	20.00	55.00
	1917 W	1.657	1.00	2.00	10.00	35.00
	1918 W	2.365	1.00	3.00	12.00	45.00
	1919 W	3.205	1.00	2.00	8.00	30.00
	1927 W	1.688	1.00	2.50	8.00	30.00
	1928 G	.837	1.00	4.00	15.00	50.00
	1929 G	1.125	.75	2.00	8.00	20.00
	1930 G	3.490	.75	1.50	4.00	15.00
	1931 G	1.392	.75	1.50	4.00	15.00
	1932 G	1.133	.75	1.50	4.00	15.00
	1933 G	.964	.75	2.00	10.00	30.00
	1934 G	1.404	.75	1.50	2.50	10.00
	1936 G	1.852	.75	1.50	2.50	10.00
	1937 G	3.290	.50	1.00	2.00	6.00
	1937 G	—	—	—	Proof	20.00
	1938 G	3.679	.50	1.00	2.00	6.00
	1939 G	2.137	.50	1.00	2.00	6.00
	1940 G	2.302	.50	1.00	2.00	6.00
	1941 G	1.960	.50	1.00	2.00	6.00

NICKEL-BRONZE

Y#	Date	Mintage	Fine	VF	XF	Unc
56	1921 W	1.355	2.00	5.00	20.00	75.00
	1940 G	2.333	.25	1.00	5.00	20.00
	1941 G	1.057	.25	1.00	5.00	25.00
	1946 TS	2.066	.20	.40	2.00	10.00
	1947 TS	1.594	.20	.50	2.00	10.00

2.3200 g, .400 SILVER, .0298 oz ASW

Y#	Date	Mintage	Fine	VF	XF	Unc
65	1943 G	9.855	BV	.75	2.00	10.00
	1944 G	9.532	BV	.75	2.00	10.00
	1945 G	5.363	BV	.75	2.00	10.00
	1945 TS	Inc. Ab.	.50	1.50	3.00	15.00
	1945 G/TS	I.A.	BV	1.00	5.00	20.00
	1946 TS	2.250	BV	.60	3.00	15.00
	1947 TS	5.633	BV	.50	1.50	6.00
	1948 TS	3.191	BV	.60	1.50	6.00
	1949 TS	5.812	BV	.60	1.50	6.00
	1950 TS	12.059	BV	.60	1.00	4.00

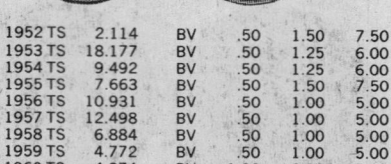

Y#	Date	Mintage	Fine	VF	XF	Unc
76	1952 TS	2.114	BV	.50	1.50	7.50
	1953 TS	18.177	BV	.50	1.25	6.00
	1954 TS	9.492	BV	.50	1.25	6.00
	1955 TS	7.663	BV	.50	1.50	7.50
	1956 TS	10.931	BV	.50	1.00	5.00
	1957 TS	12.498	BV	.50	1.00	5.00
	1958 TS	6.884	BV	.50	1.00	5.00
	1959 TS	4.772	BV	.50	1.00	5.00
	1960 TS	4.374	BV	1.00	3.00	15.00
	1961 TS	8.380	BV	.50	1.00	5.00

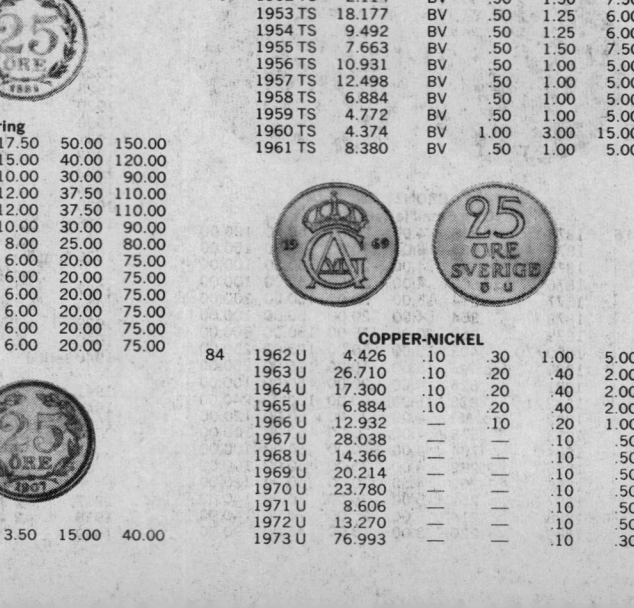

COPPER-NICKEL

Y#	Date	Mintage	Fine	VF	XF	Unc
84	1962 U	4.426	.10	.30	1.00	5.00
	1963 U	26.710	.10	.20	.40	2.00
	1964 U	17.300	.10	.20	.40	2.00
	1965 U	6.884	.10	.20	.40	2.00
	1966 U	12.932	—	.10	.20	1.00
	1967 U	28.038	—	—	.10	.50
	1968 U	14.366	—	—	.10	.50
	1969 U	20.214	—	—	.10	.50
	1970 U	23.780	—	—	.10	.50
	1971 U	8.606	—	—	.10	.50
	1972 U	13.270	—	—	.10	.50
	1973 U	76.993	—	—	.10	.30

Y#	Date	Mintage	Fine	VF	XF	Unc
93	1976 U	2.815	—	—	.10	.50
	1977 U	5.509	—	—	.10	.40
	1978 U	54.593	—	—	.10	.20
	1979 U	48.423	—	—	.10	.20
	1980 U	38.889	—	—	.10	.20
	1981 U	46.371	—	—	.10	.15
	1982 U	43.218	—	—	.10	.15
	1983 U	28.954	—	—	.10	.15
	1984 U	7.302	—	—	.10	.15

50 ORE

5.0000 g, .600 SILVER, .0965 oz ASW

Y#	Date	Mintage	Fine	VF	XF	Unc
21	1875 ST	1.908	7.50	35.00	120.00	325.00
	1877 EB	.149	60.00	120.00	300.00	800.00
	1878 EB	.319	10.00	50.00	150.00	450.00
	1880 EB	.188	20.00	60.00	175.00	500.00
	1881 EB	.268	15.00	50.00	150.00	450.00
	1883 EB	.770	6.00	30.00	100.00	250.00
	1898 EB	.505	6.00	30.00	100.00	250.00
	1899 EB	.720	6.00	30.00	100.00	250.00

Y#	Date	Mintage	Fine	VF	XF	Unc
37	1906 EB	.319	3.00	15.00	60.00	175.00
	1907 EB	.803	2.50	10.00	50.00	125.00

Y#	Date	Mintage	Fine	VF	XF	Unc
49	1911 W	.472	4.00	15.00	45.00	150.00
	1912 W	.482	5.00	17.00	50.00	170.00
	1914 W	.378	5.00	17.00	50.00	170.00
	1916/5 W	.537	5.00	18.50	50.00	180.00
	1916 W	Inc. Ab.	4.00	15.00	40.00	150.00
	1919 W	.458	4.00	15.00	45.00	125.00
	1927 W	.672	1.50	6.00	25.00	70.00
	1928 G	1.135	1.50	4.00	12.00	45.00
	1929 G	.471	2.00	6.00	25.00	70.00
	1930 G	.548	2.00	6.00	20.00	65.00
	1931 G	.671	1.50	4.00	15.00	45.00
	1933 G	.548	1.50	4.00	15.00	45.00
	1934 G	.613	1.50	4.00	12.00	40.00
	1935 G	.691	1.50	4.00	12.00	40.00
	1936 G short 6	.823	1.50	4.00	12.00	40.00
	1936 G long 6	Inc. Ab.	2.00	7.00	20.00	65.00
	1938 G	.442	1.00	2.50	7.50	25.00
	1939 G	.922	1.00	2.00	5.00	15.00
	1939 G	—	—	—	Proof	50.00

NICKEL-BRONZE
Similar to 10 Ore, Y#55.

Y#	Date	Mintage	Fine	VF	XF	Unc
57	1920 W	.480	2.00	8.00	40.00	175.00
	1921 W	.215	5.00	20.00	70.00	300.00
	1924 W	.645	2.00	8.00	60.00	225.00
	1940 G	1.341	.50	1.50	7.50	30.00
	1946 TS	1.426	.50	1.50	5.00	20.00
	1947 TS	1.032	.50	1.00	5.00	20.00

4.8000 g, .400 SILVER, .0617 oz ASW

Y#	Date	Mintage	Fine	VF	XF	Unc
66	1943 G	.785	2.00	5.00	15.00	60.00
	1944 G	1.540	.75	1.50	4.00	15.00
	1945 G	2.585	.75	1.50	4.00	15.00
	1946 TS	1.091	.75	1.50	4.00	15.00
	1947 TS	1.771	.75	1.50	4.00	15.00
	1948 TS	1.731	.75	1.50	4.00	15.00
	1949 TS	1.883	.75	1.50	4.00	15.00
	1950 TS	3.354	.65	1.00	3.00	12.00

Y#	Date	Mintage	Fine	VF	XF	Unc
77	1952 TS	1.198	.75	1.50	6.00	25.00
	1953 TS	4.396	.65	1.25	5.00	22.50
	1954 TS	5.779	.65	1.25	5.00	22.50
	1955 TS	2.700	1.00	2.00	7.50	27.50
	1956 TS	7.057	.50	1.00	4.00	12.50
	1957 TS	2.405	.65	1.25	5.00	20.00
	1958 TS	1.660	.65	1.25	5.00	20.00
	1961 TS	2.775	.50	1.00	4.50	15.00

COPPER-NICKEL

Y#	Date	Mintage	Fine	VF	XF	Unc
85	1962 U	1.400	.50	1.00	5.00	25.00
	1963 U	5.808	.15	.25	1.00	6.00
	1964 U	5.325	.15	.25	1.00	6.00
	1965 U	6.453	.15	.25	.50	3.00
	1966 U	6.309	.15	.25	.40	2.00
	1967 U	7.890	.15	.25	.40	2.00
	1968 U	9.198	—	.15	.25	1.00
	1969 U	7.265	—	.15	.25	1.00
	1970 U	9.426	—	.15	.25	1.00
	1971 U	7.218	—	.15	.25	1.00
	1972 U	7.388	—	.15	.25	1.00
	1973 U	52.467	—	.15	.20	.60

Y#	Date	Mintage	Fine	VF	XF	Unc
94	1976 U	2.589	—	.15	.25	.70
	1977 U	10.360	—	—	.15	.30
	1978 U	33.282	—	—	.15	.30
	1979 U	30.274	—	—	.15	.25
	1980 U	28.666	—	—	.15	.25
	1981 U	15.516	—	—	.15	.25
	1982 U	14.778	—	—	.15	.25
	1983 U	17.530	—	—	.15	.25
	1984 U	27.541	—	—	.15	.25
	1985 U	14.062	—	—	.15	.25
	1986 U	—	—	—	.15	.25
	1987 D	1.077	—	—	.15	.25
	1988 D	—	—	—	.15	.25

KRONA

7.5000 g, .800 SILVER, .1929 oz ASW

Y#	Date	Mintage	Fine	VF	XF	Unc
22	1875 ST	3.531	10.00	40.00	120.00	325.00
	1876/5 ST	2.510	15.00	50.00	175.00	450.00
	1876 ST	Inc. Ab.	12.00	40.00	135.00	350.00

Obv: OCH replaces O in royal title.

Y#	Date	Mintage	Fine	VF	XF	Unc
22a	1877 EB	.554	15.00	75.00	225.00	600.00
	1879 EB	.077	40.00	120.00	300.00	800.00
	1880 EB	.177	15.00	75.00	225.00	600.00
	1881 EB	.619	15.00	75.00	225.00	600.00
	1883 EB	.205	15.00	75.00	225.00	600.00
	1884 EB	.382	15.00	75.00	225.00	600.00
	1887 EB	.058	40.00	120.00	300.00	800.00
	1888 EB	.062	40.00	120.00	300.00	800.00
	1889 EB	.425	12.00	60.00	175.00	500.00

Obv: W/o initials below bust.

Y#	Date	Mintage	Fine	VF	XF	Unc
29	1890 EB	.594	10.00	50.00	150.00	350.00
	1897 EB	.735	5.00	30.00	80.00	220.00
	1898 EB	1.860	4.(	25.00	70.00	175.00
	1901/898 EB	.271	6.50	40.00	100.00	300.00
	1901 EB	Inc. Ab.	5.00	30.00	75.00	230.00
	1903 EB	.473	5.00	30.00	80.00	225.00
	1904 EB	.564	4.00	25.00	70.00	200.00

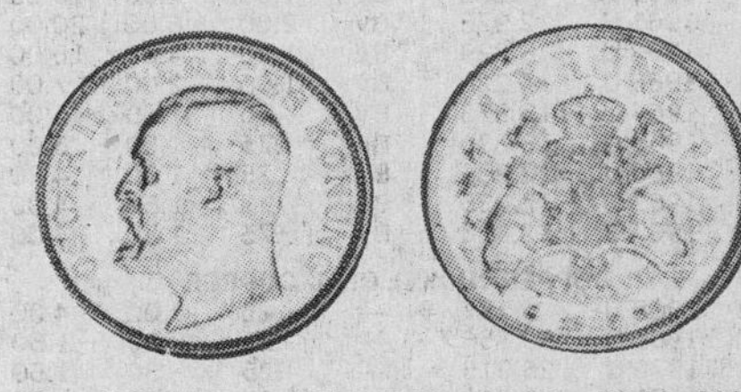

Y#	Date	Mintage	Fine	VF	XF	Unc
38	1906 EB	.427	5.00	25.00	70.00	200.00
	1907 EB	1.058	3.50	12.50	60.00	160.00

Obv: W/dots in date.

Y#	Date	Mintage	Fine	VF	XF	Unc
50.1	1.9.1.0 W	.643	4.00	20.00	60.00	175.00
	1.9.1.2 W	.303	6.00	25.00	100.00	250.00
	1.9.1.3 W	.353	5.00	20.00	65.00	175.00
	1.9.1.4 W	.622	4.00	20.00	60.00	175.00
	1.9.1.5. W	1.416	4.00	15.00	45.00	125.00
	1.9.1.6./5 W	1.139	6.00	25.00	75.00	225.00
	1.9.1.6 W	Inc. Ab.	4.00	20.00	60.00	175.00
	1.9.1.8 W	.258	4.00	8.00	45.00	225.00
	1.9.2.3 W	.746	3.00	12.00	40.00	120.00
	1.9.2.4 W	2.066	2.50	10.00	30.00	80.00

Obv: W/o dots in date.

Y#	Date	Mintage	Fine	VF	XF	Unc
50.2	1924 W	Inc. Ab.	3.00	12.50	35.00	100.00
	1925 W	.370	4.00	17.50	70.00	220.00
	1926 W	.465	3.00	15.00	45.00	125.00
	1927 G	.401	4.00	17.50	60.00	175.00
	1928 G	.739	3.00	8.00	35.00	100.00
	1929 G	1.346	2.50	6.00	15.00	50.00
	1930 G	1.744	2.50	5.00	10.00	35.00
	1931 G	1.008	2.50	5.00	10.00	35.00
	1932 G	1.036	2.50	5.00	10.00	35.00
	1933 G	1.045	2.50	5.00	10.00	35.00
	1934 G	.586	2.50	5.00	15.00	50.00
	1935 G	1.604	2.00	3.00	5.00	15.00
	1936/5 G	3.223	1.50	2.00	3.50	12.50
	1936 G	Inc. Ab.	1.50	2.00	3.00	10.00
	1937 G	2.667	1.50	2.00	3.00	10.00
	1938 G	1.911	1.50	2.00	3.00	10.00
	1938 G	—	—	—	Proof	30.00
	1939 G	7.589	1.50	2.00	3.00	5.00
	1940 G	6.917	1.50	2.00	3.00	5.00
	1941/4 G	2.183	4.00	6.00	15.00	40.00
	1941 G	Inc. Ab.	1.50	2.00	3.50	10.00
	1942 G	.240	40.00	60.00	125.00	250.00

7.0000 g .400 SILVER, .0900 oz ASW

Y#	Date	Mintage	Fine	VF	XF	Unc
67	1942 G	5.650	1.00	1.50	5.00	20.00
	1943 G	7.916	1.00	1.50	5.00	20.00
	1944 G	7.423	1.00	1.50	3.00	12.00
	1945 G	7.359	1.00	1.50	3.00	12.00
	1945 TS	Inc. Ab.	1.50	2.00	4.50	17.50
	1945 TS/G	I.A.	2.00	3.00	6.00	25.00
	1946 TS	19.170	1.00	1.50	2.00	9.00
	1947 TS	9.124	1.00	1.50	2.00	9.00
	1948 TS	10.447	1.00	1.50	2.00	9.00
	1949 TS	7.981	1.00	1.50	2.00	9.00
	1950 TS	5.310	1.00	1.50	3.00	12.00

SWEDEN 1568

Y#	Date	Mintage	Fine	VF	XF	Unc
78	1952 TS	1.102	BV	1.50	5.00	20.00
	1953 TS	3.306	BV	1.50	5.00	20.00
	1954 TS	6.461	BV	1.50	5.00	20.00
	1955 TS	4.141	BV	1.50	5.00	20.00
	1956 TS	6.227	BV	1.50	4.50	18.00
	1957 TS	3.544	BV	1.50	5.00	20.00
	1958 TS	1.439	1.00	2.50	7.50	30.00
	1959 TS	1.187	2.50	5.00	15.00	60.00
	1960 TS	4.085	BV	1.50	4.00	15.00
	1961 TS	4.283	BV	1.50	4.00	15.00
	1961 U	2.973	BV	2.00	6.00	20.00
	1962 U	6.839	BV	1.50	4.00	15.00
	1963 U	14.228	BV	1.00	2.00	7.00
	1964 U	15.973	BV	.75	1.50	5.00
	1965 U	18.639	BV	.75	1.50	5.00
	1966 U	22.396	BV	.75	1.50	4.00
	1967 U	17.235	BV	.75	1.50	4.00
	1968 U	12.326	BV	.75	1.50	4.00

COPPER-NICKEL CLAD COPPER

78a	1968 U	5.177	—	.25	1.00	4.00
	1969 U	30.856	—	.25	.30	1.50
	1970 U	25.315	—	.25	.30	1.50
	1971 U	18.342	—	.25	.30	1.50
	1972 U	21.941	—	.25	.30	1.50
	1973 U	142.000	—	.25	.30	1.00

95	1976 U	4.321	—	.25	.40	1.25
	1977 U	80.478	—	.25	.30	.50
	1978 U	81.408	—	.25	.30	.50
	1979 U	47.450	—	.25	.30	.40
	1980 U	51.694	—	.25	.30	.40
	1981 U	62.079	—	.25	.30	.40

COPPER-NICKEL

95a	1982 U	24.837	—	—	.25	.40
	1983 U	23.530	—	—	.25	.40
	1984 U	37.805	—	—	.25	.40
	1985 U	4.893	—	—	.25	.40
	1986 U	—	—	—	.25	.40
	1987 D	21.543	—	—	.25	.40
	1988 D	—	—	—	.25	.40

2 KRONOR

15.0000 g, .800 SILVER, .3858 oz ASW

23	1876 EB wide date, 6mm wide, large E.B.
	.370 500.00 1000. 1800. 3750.
	1876 EB wide date, small E.B.
	Inc. Ab. 200.00 400.00 750.00 2250.
	1876 EB smaller date, 5mm wide
	Inc. Ab. 15.00 75.00 325.00 650.00
	1877 EB .168 22.00 90.00 325.00 750.00
	1878 EB .193 16.50 80.00 325.00 750.00
	1880/76 EB .128 50.00 160.00 500.00 1150.
	1880 EB Inc. Ab. 40.00 125.00 400.00 900.00

Obv: OCH replaces O in royal title.

23a	1878 EB	.022	500.00	900.00	1500.	3000.
	1880 EB	.065	30.00	110.00	350.00	1100.

Obv: W/o initials below bust.

Y#	Date	Mintage	Fine	VF	XF	Unc
30	1890 EB	.072	22.00	90.00	325.00	725.00
	1892 EB	.087	25.00	80.00	325.00	700.00
	1893 EB	.049	40.00	110.00	350.00	825.00
	1897 EB	.207	10.00	40.00	150.00	325.00
	1898 EB	.141	12.00	45.00	150.00	325.00
	1900 EB	.131	12.00	50.00	160.00	375.00
	1903 EB	.064	40.00	100.00	325.00	625.00
	1904 EB	.175	12.00	30.00	125.00	300.00

15.0000 g, .800 SILVER, .3858 oz ASW
Silver Jubilee

31	1897 EB	.246	6.00	8.00	10.00	20.00

39	1906 EB	.112	10.00	30.00	95.00	225.00
	1907 EB	.301	7.50	20.00	75.00	180.00

Golden Wedding Anniversary

40	1907 EB	.251	7.00	9.00	11.00	22.00

51	1910 W	.375	6.50	12.50	55.00	125.00
	1910 W mintmaster's initial further away from
	date	Inc. Ab.	40.00	100.00	300.00	650.00
	1912 W	.157	10.00	30.00	100.00	275.00
	1913 W	.305	6.50	12.50	55.00	125.00
	1914 W	.192	6.00	17.50	60.00	175.00
	1915 W	.156	9.00	22.50	70.00	190.00
	1922 W	.202	6.00	10.00	25.00	90.00
	1924 W	.199	6.00	10.00	25.00	90.00
	1926 W	.222	6.00	10.00	25.00	90.00
	1928 G	.160	6.00	12.50	35.00	125.00
	1929 G	.184	6.00	10.00	25.00	90.00
	1930 G	.178	6.00	9.00	22.50	75.00
	1931 G	.211	5.00	6.50	12.50	40.00
	1934 G	.273	5.00	6.50	7.50	40.00
	1935 G	.211	5.00	6.50	7.50	40.00
	1936 G	.491	5.00	6.50	7.00	17.50
	1937 G	.130	6.00	11.00	25.00	65.00
	1937 G	—	—	—	Proof	250.00
	1938 G	.639	4.50	6.00	7.00	12.50
	1938 G	—	—	—	Proof	40.00
	1939 G	1.200	4.50	6.00	7.00	12.50
	1939 G	—	—	—	Proof	40.00
	1940 G	.518	4.50	6.00	7.00	12.50

Y#	Date	Mintage	Fine	VF	XF	Unc
51	1940 G serif 4
		Inc. Ab.	5.00	7.00	10.00	25.00

400th Anniversary of Political Liberty

58	1921 W	.265	4.00	6.00	8.00	15.00

300th Anniversary Death of Gustaf II Adolf

59	1932 G	.254	5.00	7.50	10.00	16.00

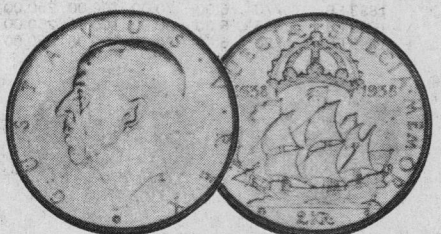

300th Anniversary Settlement of Delaware

61	1938 G	.509	4.00	5.00	6.50	10.00

14.0000 g, .400 SILVER, .1800 oz ASW

68	1942 G	.200	1.50	3.50	6.00	18.00
	1943 G	.272	4.00	6.00	10.00	50.00
	1944 G	.627	1.50	2.00	3.50	10.00
	1945 G	.970	1.50	2.00	3.00	8.00
	1945 G w/o dots in motto
		Inc. Ab.	3.50	6.00	10.00	24.00
	1945 TS	Inc. Ab.	1.50	3.50	5.00	15.00
	1945 TS/G	I.A.	3.00	5.00	8.00	20.00
	1946 TS	.978	1.50	2.00	3.00	8.00
	1947 TS	1.466	1.50	2.00	3.00	8.00
	1948 TS	.282	1.50	3.00	5.00	16.00
	1949 TS	.332	1.50	3.00	5.00	16.00
	1950/1 TS	3.727	1.50	2.00	5.00	12.50
	1950 TS	Inc. Ab.	1.50	2.00	4.00	10.00

79	1952 TS	.315	2.00	2.50	5.00	12.00
	1953 TS	1.009	—	BV	2.50	6.50
	1954 TS	2.301	—	BV	2.50	6.50
	1955 TS	1.138	—	BV	2.50	6.50
	1956 TS	1.709	—	BV	2.50	6.50
	1957 TS	.689	—	BV	3.00	9.00
	1958 TS	1.104	—	BV	2.50	6.50
	1959 TS	.581	—	BV	3.00	9.00
	1961 TS	.534	—	BV	2.50	6.50
	1963 U	1.469	—	BV	2.50	4.50
	1964 U	1.213	—	BV	2.50	4.50
	1965 U	1.190	—	BV	2.50	4.50
	1966 U	.989	—	BV	2.50	4.50

COPPER-NICKEL

79a	1968 U	1.171	.45	.65	1.50	2.50

Y#	Date	Mintage	Fine	VF	XF	Unc
79a	1969 U	1.148	.45	.65	1.00	2.00
	1970 U	1.159	.45	.65	1.00	2.00
	1971 U	1.213	.45	.65	1.00	2.00

5 KRONOR

2.2402 g, .900 GOLD, .0648 oz AGW

24	1881 EB	.065	40.00	60.00	80.00	100.00
	1882 EB	.030	50.00	70.00	100.00	125.00
	1883 EB	.028	60.00	90.00	120.00	150.00
	1886/3 EB	.042	40.00	60.00	80.00	100.00
	1886 EB	Inc. Ab.	40.00	60.00	80.00	100.00
	1894 EB	.051	40.00	60.00	80.00	100.00
	1899 EB	.104	40.00	50.00	70.00	90.00

| 24a | 1901 EB | .109 | 40.00 | 50.00 | 70.00 | 100.00 |

| 62 | 1920 W | .103 | 40.00 | 50.00 | 80.00 | 110.00 |

25.0000 g, .900 SILVER, .7234 oz ASW
500th Anniversary of Riksdag

| 60 | 1935 G | .664 | 7.50 | 10.00 | 12.50 | 22.00 |

18.0000 g, .400 SILVER, .2315 oz ASW
70th Birthday of Gustaf VI Adolf

| 81 | 1952 TS | .242 | 7.50 | 12.50 | 17.50 | 30.00 |

Regular Issue

80	1954 TS	1.510	—	BV	4.00	10.00
	1955 TS	3.569	—	BV	3.50	9.00
	1971 U	.713	—	BV	3.50	5.50

Constitution Sesquincentennial

Y#	Date	Mintage	Fine	VF	XF	Unc
82	1959 TS	.504	—	BV	5.00	10.00

80th Birthday of Gustaf VI Adolf

| 86 | 1962 U | .256 | — | 10.00 | 17.50 | 35.00 |

Parliament Reform

| 87 | 1966 U | 1.024 | — | BV | 3.50 | 5.00 |

COPPER-NICKEL CLAD NICKEL

89	1972 U	23.947	—	1.00	1.25	2.00
	1973 U	1.139	—	1.00	1.50	3.50

COPPER-NICKEL

96	1976 U	2.253	—	—	1.00	2.00
	1977 U	3.985	—	—	1.00	2.00
	1978 U	3.952	—	—	1.00	2.00
	1979 U	3.164	—	—	1.00	2.00
	1980 U	2.222	—	—	1.00	2.00
	1981 U	5.507	—	—	1.00	1.25
	1982 U	36.604	—	—	1.00	1.25
	1983 U	31.364	—	—	1.00	1.25
	1984 U	27.687	—	—	1.00	1.25
	1985 U	10.375	—	—	1.00	1.25
	1986 U	—	—	—	1.00	1.25
	1987 D	15.117	—	—	1.00	1.25
	1988 D	—	—	—	1.00	1.25

10 KRONOR

4.4803 g, .900 GOLD, .1296 oz AGW

Y#	Date	Mintage	Fine	VF	XF	Unc
25	1873 ST	.200	70.00	85.00	125.00	250.00
	1874/3 ST	.261	70.00	85.00	100.00	150.00
	1874 ST	Inc. Ab.	70.00	85.00	100.00	135.00
	1874 ST	—	—	—	Proof	1300.
	1876 ST	.102	70.00	85.00	110.00	150.00

Obv: OCH substituted for O. in royal title.

25a	1876 EB	.068	70.00	90.00	175.00	300.00
	1877 EB	.055	75.00	150.00	250.00	375.00
	1880 EB	.027	75.00	150.00	250.00	375.00
	1883 EB L.A.	.149	70.00	80.00	90.00	120.00
	1883 LA	Inc. Ab.	70.00	80.00	90.00	120.00
	1883 L.A. larger L.A.					
		Inc. Ab.	70.00	80.00	90.00	120.00
	1894 EB	.036	70.00	80.00	110.00	160.00
	1895 EB	.065	70.00	80.00	110.00	160.00

Obv: Larger head.

25b	1901 EB	.213	70.00	80.00	90.00	100.00
	1901 EB	Inc. Ab.	—	—	Proof	525.00

18.0000 g, .830 SILVER, .4803 oz ASW
90th Birthday of Gustaf VI Adolf

| 90 | 1972 U | 2.000 | — | 3.00 | 6.00 | 9.00 |

20 KRONOR

8.9606 g, .900 GOLD, .2593 oz AGW

26	1873 ST	.115	150.00	200.00	300.00	500.00
	1874 ST	.240	150.00	200.00	300.00	400.00
	1875 ST	.359	150.00	200.00	300.00	400.00
	1876/5 ST	.026	200.00	350.00	600.00	1200.
	1876 ST	Inc. Ab.	200.00	350.00	600.00	1200.

Rev: Arms wider

26c	1876 EB	.173	150.00	200.00	300.00	400.00
	1877 EB	.103	150.00	200.00	300.00	400.00

Obv: OCH substituted for O. in royal title.

26a	1877 EB	.083	150.00	200.00	300.00	400.00
	1878/7 EB	.245	150.00	200.00	300.00	400.00
	1878 EB	Inc. Ab.	150.00	200.00	300.00	400.00
	1879 EB	.075	150.00	200.00	400.00	600.00
	1879 EB	Unique	—	—	Proof	10,000.
	1880 EB	.127	150.00	200.00	300.00	400.00
	1881 EB	.047	175.00	350.00	600.00	1000.
	1884 EB	.191	150.00	200.00	300.00	400.00
	1885 EB	6,250	400.00	800.00	1700.	2500.
	1886 EB	.173	150.00	200.00	300.00	400.00
	1887 EB	.059	175.00	350.00	600.00	1000.

SWEDEN 1570

Y#	Date	Mintage	Fine	VF	XF	Unc
26a	1889 EB	.202	150.00	200.00	300.00	400.00
	1890 EB	.155	150.00	200.00	300.00	400.00
	1895 EB	.135	150.00	200.00	250.00	350.00
	1898 EB	.313	150.00	200.00	250.00	350.00
	1899 EB	.261	150.00	200.00	250.00	325.00

Obv: Larger head.

26b	1900 EB	.104	140.00	200.00	350.00	550.00
	1901 EB	.227	140.00	160.00	250.00	350.00
	1902 EB	.114	140.00	160.00	300.00	400.00

| 63 | 1925 W | .387 | 150.00 | 300.00 | 400.00 | 600.00 |

50 KRONOR

27.0000 g, .925 SILVER, .8029 oz ASW
Constitutional Reform

| 97 | 1975 U | .500 | — | — | 16.50 |

Wedding Commemorative

| 98 | 1976 U | 2.000 | — | — | 12.50 |

100 KRONOR

16.0000 g, .925 SILVER, .4759 oz ASW
Parliament

| 101 | 1983 | .400 | — | — | 22.50 |

Stockholm Conference

| 102 | 1984 | .300 | — | — | 22.50 |

International Youth Year

Y#	Date	Mintage	Fine	VF	XF	Unc
103	1985	.120	—	—	—	22.50

European Music Year

| 104 | 1985 | .120 | — | — | — | 22.50 |

International Year of the Forest

| 105 | 1985 | .120 | — | — | — | 22.50 |

Swedish Colony in Delaware

| 106 | 1988 | .150 | — | — | — | 25.00 |

200 KRONOR

27.0000 g, .925 SILVER, .8029 oz ASW
Swedish Royal Succession Law

| 99 | 1980 U | .500 | — | — | — | 40.00 |

10th Anniversary of Reign

| 100 | 1983 | .100 | — | — | — | 40.00 |

Ice Hockey

Y#	Date	Mintage	Fine	VF	XF	Unc
108	1989	*.080	—	—	—	40.00

1000 KRONOR

5.8000 g, .900 GOLD, .1678 oz AGW
Swedish Colony in Delaware
Similar to 100 Kronor, Y#106.

| 107 | 1988 | *.010 | — | — | — | 500.00 |

Ice Hockey
Similar to 200 Kronor, Y#108.

| 109 | 1989 | — | — | — | — | 250.00 |

TRADE COINAGE
DUCAT

3.5000 g, .986 GOLD, .1109 oz AGW

C#	Date	Mintage	VG	Fine	VF	XF
93	1801 OL	3,100	225.00	550.00	1100.	1800.
	1802 OL	4,827	175.00	375.00	750.00	1500.
	1803 OL	7,300	150.00	350.00	700.00	1200.
	1804 OL	8,700	175.00	375.00	750.00	1500.
	1805 OL	.013	150.00	350.00	700.00	1200.
	1806 OL	.014	150.00	350.00	700.00	1200.
	1807 OL	.011	150.00	350.00	700.00	1200.
	1808 OL	.033	150.00	350.00	700.00	1200.
	1809 OL	.021	150.00	350.00	700.00	1200.

| 94 | 1801 OL | 900 pcs. | 500.00 | 1100. | 2250. | 3750. |

| 95 | 1804 OL | 1,254 | 400.00 | 900.00 | 1800. | 3000. |

111	1810 OL	.014	150.00	350.00	700.00	1200.
	1811 OL	9,750	150.00	400.00	800.00	1300.
	1812 OL	.016	150.00	350.00	700.00	1200.
	1813 OL	.026	150.00	350.00	700.00	1200.
	1814 OL	.022	150.00	350.00	700.00	1200.

C#	Date	Mintage	VG	Fine	VF	XF
111a	1815 OL	8,060	185.00	400.00	800.00	1300.
	1816 OL	6,130	200.00	450.00	900.00	1400.
	1817 OL	5,673	225.00	450.00	1000.	1500.

Dalarna Mines Commemorative

| 112 | 1810 OL | 1,322 | 250.00 | 550.00 | 1100. | 1800. |

150	1818 OL	6,389	100.00	225.00	450.00	800.00
	1819 OL	1,828	—	—	Rare	—
	1820 LB	7,248	110.00	250.00	500.00	900.00

Obv: Bust right. Rev: Shield.

150	1821 LB	.019	100.00	225.00	450.00	800.00
	1822 CB	5,222	100.00	225.00	500.00	900.00
	1823 AG	3,155	100.00	225.00	500.00	900.00
	1824 CB	3,370	100.00	225.00	500.00	900.00
	1825 CB	8,127	100.00	225.00	450.00	800.00
	1826 CB	4,126	100.00	225.00	500.00	800.00
	1827/6 CB	4,579	110.00	250.00	500.00	875.00
	1827 CB	I.A.	100.00	225.00	450.00	800.00
	1828 CB	5,150	100.00	225.00	450.00	800.00
	1829 CB	5,642	100.00	225.00	450.00	800.00

151	1830 CB	5,269	85.00	200.00	375.00	750.00
	1831 CB	3,917	85.00	200.00	375.00	750.00
	1832 CB	2,082	85.00	200.00	375.00	750.00
	1833 CB	2,310	85.00	200.00	375.00	750.00
	1834 CB	3,142	85.00	200.00	375.00	750.00
	1835 CB	7,622	85.00	200.00	375.00	750.00
	1836 CB	1,947	—	—	Rare	—
	1837 CB	.013	75.00	175.00	350.00	700.00
	1838 AG	.015	75.00	175.00	350.00	700.00
	1839 AG	.010	75.00	175.00	350.00	700.00
	1840 AG	1,840	125.00	300.00	600.00	1200.
	1841 AG	.013	75.00	175.00	350.00	700.00
	1842 AG	.030	75.00	175.00	350.00	700.00
	1843 AG	.074	70.00	160.00	325.00	650.00

Obv: Large head of Oscar I right.

| 198 | 1844 AG | 946 pcs. | — | — | Rare | — |
| | 1845/4 AG | .046 | 125.00 | 300.00 | 600.00 | 900.00 |

Obv: Smaller head.

198a	1845/4 AG	I.A.	75.00	165.00	325.00	650.00
	1845 AG	I.A.	65.00	150.00	300.00	600.00
	1846 AG	.022	65.00	150.00	300.00	600.00
	1847/4 AG	.018	75.00	165.00	350.00	675.00
	1847 AG	I.A.	65.00	150.00	300.00	600.00
	1848 AG	.037	65.00	150.00	300.00	600.00
	1849/4 AG	.014	75.00	165.00	350.00	675.00
	1849 AG	I.A.	65.00	150.00	300.00	600.00
	1850 AG	.020	65.00	150.00	300.00	600.00
	1851 AG	.016	65.00	150.00	300.00	600.00
	1852 AG	.027	65.00	150.00	300.00	600.00
	1853 AG	.013	65.00	150.00	300.00	600.00
	1854 AG small AG					

C#	Date	Mintage	VG	Fine	VF	XF
198a		.020	65.00	150.00	300.00	600.00
	1854 AG large AG	Inc. Ab.	65.00	150.00	300.00	600.00
	1855 AG	.018	65.00	150.00	300.00	600.00
	1856 ST	.012	65.00	150.00	300.00	600.00
	1857 ST small ST	.027	65.00	150.00	300.00	600.00
	1857 ST large ST	Inc. Ab.	65.00	150.00	300.00	600.00
	1858 AG	.041	65.00	150.00	300.00	600.00
	1859 ST	.031	65.00	150.00	300.00	600.00

B10	1860 ST	.058	60.00	125.00	275.00	550.00
	1861/0 ST	.038	70.00	140.00	325.00	625.00
	1861 ST	I.A.	60.00	125.00	275.00	550.00
	1862 ST	.042	60.00	125.00	275.00	550.00
	1863 ST	.037	50.00	100.00	250.00	450.00
	1864/3 ST	.038	70.00	140.00	325.00	625.00
	1864 ST small L.A.	Inc. Ab.	60.00	125.00	275.00	550.00
	1864 ST larger L.A.	Inc. Ab.	60.00	125.00	275.00	550.00
	1865 ST large year and ST	.039	60.00	125.00	275.00	550.00
	1865 ST smaller year and ST	Inc. Ab.	60.00	125.00	275.00	550.00
	1866 ST large ST	.032	60.00	125.00	275.00	550.00
	1866 ST smaller ST	Inc. Ab.	60.00	125.00	275.00	550.00
	1867 ST	.011	60.00	125.00	275.00	550.00
	1867 TS	I.A.	125.00	300.00	600.00	1000.
	1868 ST small ST	9,398	65.00	150.00	300.00	600.00
	1868 ST larger ST	Inc. Ab.	65.00	150.00	300.00	600.00

2 DUCATS

7.0000 g, .986 GOLD, .2219 oz AGW

152	1830 CB	2 pcs.	—	—	Rare	—
	1836 CB	1,500	250.00	650.00	1300.	2000.
	1837 CB	1,989	250.00	650.00	1300.	2000.
	1838 AG	1,000	300.00	700.00	1500.	2400.
	1839 AG	2,200	250.00	650.00	1300.	2000.
	1842 AG	1,546	300.00	700.00	1500.	2400.
	1843 AG	2,159	250.00	650.00	1300.	2000.

199	1850 AG	819 pcs.	400.00	900.00	1900.	2800.
	1852 AG	386 pcs.	—	—	Rare	—
	1857 ST	763 pcs.	350.00	800.00	1600.	2500.

4 DUCATS

14.0000 g, .986 GOLD, .4438 oz AGW

153	1837 CB	1,625	400.00	900.00	1900.	2800.
	1838 AG	625 pcs.	450.00	1000.	2000.	3000.
	1839 AG	2,000	400.00	900.00	1900.	2800.
	1841 AG	2,084	450.00	1000.	2100.	3300.
	1843 AG	4,405	350.00	800.00	1600.	2500.

C#	Date	Mintage	VG	Fine	VF	XF
200	1846 AG	400 pcs.	600.00	1300.	2600.	3800.
	1850 AG	507 pcs.	500.00	1000.	2100.	3200.
	1852 AG	2 pcs.	—	—	Rare	—

CAROLIN-10 FRANCS

3.2258 g, .900 GOLD, .0933 oz AGW

Y#	Date	Mintage	Fine	VF	XF	Unc
A10	1868	.033	75.00	150.00	300.00	400.00
	1869	.031	75.00	150.00	300.00	425.00
	1871	5,153	125.00	250.00	500.00	750.00
	1871 larger ear	Inc. Ab.	175.00	350.00	700.00	1000.
	1872	.012	125.00	250.00	500.00	750.00
	1872 larger ear	Inc. Ab.	275.00	550.00	800.00	1250.

MINT SETS (MS)

KM#	Date	Mintage	Identification	Issue Price	Mkt. Val.
MS-A1	1973(6)	—	Y78a,83-85,88-89	—	6.00
MS1	1976(6)	—	Y91-96	7.50	7.00
MS2	1977(6)	—	Y91-96	—	5.00
MS3	1978(6)	—	Y91-96	—	5.00
MS4	1979(6)	—	Y91-96	—	5.00
MS5	1980(6)	—	Y91-96	—	5.00
MS6	1981(6)	—	Y91-96	—	5.00
MS7	1981(6)	—	Y91a,92-96	—	5.00
MS8	1982(6)	—	Y91a,92-94,95a,96	—	5.00
MS9	1983(6)	—	Y91a,92-94,95a,96 soft plastic case	5.25	5.00
MS10	1983(6)	—	Y91a,92-94,95a,96 hard plastic case	6.20	5.00
MS11	1985(4)	—	Y92,94,95a,96 hard plastic case	—	5.00
MS-A12	1985(4)	—	Y92,94,95a,96 soft plastic case	—	5.00
MS12	1986(4)	—	Y92,94,95a,96 hard plastic case	—	5.00
MS13	1986(4)	—	Y92,94,95a,96 soft plastic case	—	5.00

SWEDEN 1571

SWISS CANTONS 1572

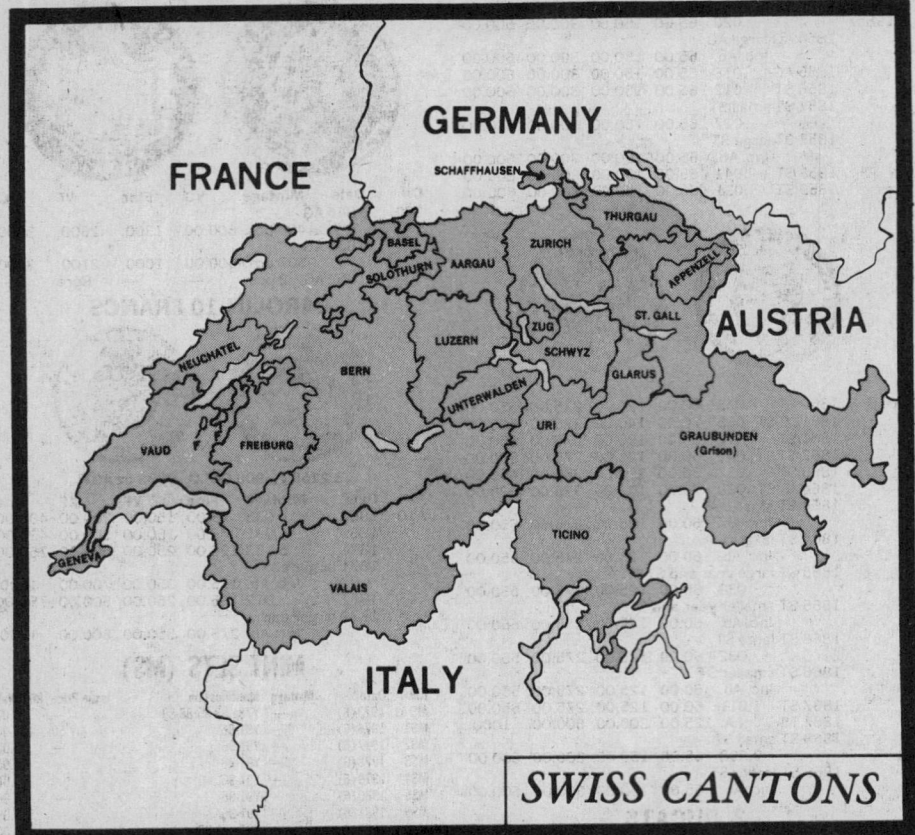

In Switzerland, canton is the name given to each of the 23 states comprising the Swiss Federation. The origin of the cantons is rooted in the liberty-loving instincts of the peasants of Helvetia.

After the Romans departed Switzerland to defend Rome against the barbarians, Switzerland became, in the Middle Ages, a federation of fiefs of the Holy Roman Empire. In 888 it was again united by Rudolf of Burgundy, a minor despot, and for 150 years Switzerland had a king. Upon the death of the last Burgundian king, the kingdom crumbled into a loose collection of feudal fiefs ruled by bishops and ducal families who made their own laws and levied their own taxes. Eventually this division of rule by arbitrary despots became more than the freedom-loving and resourceful peasants could bear. The citizens living in the remote valleys of Uri, Schwyz (from which Switzerland received its name) and Unterwalden decided to liberate themselves from all feudal obligations and become free men.

On Aug. 1, 1291, the elders of these three small states met on a tiny heath known as the Rutli on the shores of the Lake of Lucerne and negotiated an 'eternal pact' which recognized their right to local self-government, and pledged one another assistance against any encroachment upon these rights. The pact was the beginning of the 'Everlasting League' and the foundation of the Swiss Confederation.

CANTONAL MINT MARKS OF SWITZERLAND

Mint mark	Canton	Mint
A.-B.	Geneva	Geneva 1847 (Auguste Bovet)
A.B.	Graubunden	Geneva 1842 (Antoine Bovy)
A-B	Graubunden	Private coiner 1836 (Antoine Bovy)
A-B	Graubunden	Geneva 1842 (Antoine Bovy)
B	Basel	Basel 1826 (Bel-Bessiere)
B	Freiburg	Freiburg 1830 (Bel-Bessiere)
B	Glarus	Unknown site 1806-1814
B	Graubunden	Bern 1820
B	Graubunden	Private coiner 1826
B	Luzern	Luzern 1807-1814 (Bruppacher)
B	Schwyz	Schwyz or Aargau 1810
B	Zurich	Zurich 1806-1813 (Bruckmann)
BEL	Basel	Basel 1826 (Bel-Bessiere)
BEL	Freiburg	Freiburg 1830-1846 (Bel-Bessiere)
BEL	Vaud	Lausanne 1826-1834 (Bel-Bessiere)
D	Zurich	Stuttgart 1842-1848
DB	Schwyz	Schwyz 1843-1846
F	Glarus	Unknown site 1806-1807
G	Geneva	Geneva An 8-13
H	Geneva	Geneva 1817 (Hoyer)
H	Schwyz	Schwyz or Aargau 1810-1811
HB	Graubunden	Private coiner 1836 (Bruppacher)
K	St. Gall	St. Gall 1807-1817 (Kukler)
M	Aargau	Aargau 1807-1808 (Meyer)
M	Schwyz	Aargau or Schwyz 1844
N	Graubunden	Bern 1825 (Nett)
SIBER	Vaud	Lausanne 1845 (Siber)
Star	Ticino	Luzern 1813

AARGAU
Argau, Argovie

Located in north central Switzerland. Was named after the river Aar. Was admitted to the Swiss Confederation in 1803.

MONETARY SYSTEM
10 Rappen = 4 Kreuzer = 1 Batzen
10 Batzen = 1 Frank

RAPPEN

KM#	Date	Mintage	VG	Fine	VF	XF
15 (C1)	1809	.044	12.50	25.00	45.00	80.00
	1811	.039	4.00	10.00	17.50	25.00
	1816	—	4.00	10.00	17.50	25.00

Rev: Wreath of stars and flowers.

| 18 (C1) | 1810 | .020 | 12.50 | 25.00 | 45.00 | 80.00 |

2 RAPPEN

11 (C2)	1808	.092	3.00	6.00	12.50	17.50
	1811	—	7.50	15.00	30.00	40.00
	1812	—	3.00	6.00	12.50	20.00
	1813	—	3.00	6.00	12.50	20.00
	1814	—	3.00	6.00	12.50	20.00
	1816	—	3.00	6.00	12.50	22.50

2-1/2 RAPPEN
(Ein (1) Kreuzer)

BILLON

KM#	Date	Mintage	VG	Fine	VF	XF
25 (C11)	1831	—	4.00	8.00	17.50	30.00

5 RAPPEN

BILLON

| 24 (C12) | 1829 | 1,000 | 6.00 | 12.50 | 22.50 | 60.00 |
| | 1831 | — | 6.00 | 12.50 | 22.50 | 60.00 |

1/2 BATZEN

BILLON

8 (C3)	1807	—	7.50	15.00	50.00	80.00
	1808	—	7.50	15.00	50.00	80.00
	1809	—	6.00	12.50	22.50	60.00
	1811	—	6.00	12.50	22.50	60.00
	1815	—	6.00	12.50	22.50	60.00

BATZEN

BILLON
Obv: Oval arms, leg: AARGAU. Rev: Oak branches.

| 5 (C4) | 1805 | 1,000 | 20.00 | 45.00 | 90.00 | 150.00 |

Obv. leg: ARGAU.

| 6 (C4) | 1806 | — | 20.00 | 45.00 | 125.00 | 180.00 |

Obv: Pointed arms w/garlands.

| 7 (C4b) | 1806 | — | 20.00 | 45.00 | 125.00 | 180.00 |

9 (5)	1807	.132	7.50	15.00	30.00	50.00
	1808	.184	7.50	15.00	27.50	55.00
	1809	.350	7.50	15.00	27.50	55.00
	1810	.215	7.50	15.00	27.50	55.00
	1811	.060	7.50	15.00	27.50	55.00
	1816	—	10.00	20.00	45.00	125.00

Obv. leg: ARGAU. Rev: Palm branches.

| 12 (C4a) | 1808 | — | 35.00 | 80.00 | 110.00 | 160.00 |

KM#	Date	Mintage	VG	Fine	VF	XF
21 (C13)	1826	—	5.00	10.00	25.00	37.50

Rev: W/o inner circle.

| 22 (C13a) | 1826 | — | 12.50 | 30.00 | 60.00 | 110.00 |

5 BATZEN
SILVER

10 (C5)	1807 M	250 pcs.	100.00	200.00	250.00	375.00
	1808 M	.114	12.50	25.00	45.00	80.00

13.1 (C5a)	1808	—	60.00	125.00	180.00	235.00
	1809	.084	12.50	25.00	60.00	80.00
	1810	.171	12.50	25.00	60.00	80.00

13.2 (C5a)	1812	.073	70.00	150.00	300.00	500.00
	1814	—	70.00	150.00	300.00	500.00
	1815	—	12.50	25.00	60.00	80.00

| 19 (C5b) | *1811* | .065 | 12.50 | 25.00 | 60.00 | 80.00 |

| 23 (C14) | 1826 | .508 | 10.00 | 20.00 | 45.00 | 80.00 |

10 BATZEN

SILVER

Obv: Palm and laurel wreath flanking arms.

KM#	Date	Mintage	VG	Fine	VF	XF
14 (C8)	1808	3,884	55.00	120.00	150.00	420.00
	1809	9,842	40.00	90.00	150.00	420.00
	1818	3,223	50.00	100.00	200.00	480.00

Obv: Laurel branches both sides of arms.

| 16 (C8a) | 1809 | Inc. Ab. | 50.00 | 100.00 | 200.00 | 480.00 |

20 BATZEN

SILVER

| 17 (C9) | 1809 | .014 | 60.00 | 125.00 | 200.00 | 480.00 |

4 FRANK

SILVER

| 20 (C10) | 1812 | 2,527 | 150.00 | 275.00 | 400.00 | 1100. |

APPENZELL

Located in northeast Switzerland, completely surrounded by the canton of St. Gall. The name was derived from "Abbot's Cell". Achieved independence from the abbots of St. Gall in the period 1377/1411. Divided by religious differences in to two half cantons, Ausser-Rhoden (Protestant) and Inner-Rhoden (Catholic). Both were joined to the Canton to Santis 1797-1803, but regained their independent status in 1803.

MONETARY SYSTEM
4 Pfenning = 1 Kreuzer
10 Rappen = 4 Kreuzer = 1 Batzen
10 Batzen = 1 Franken

AUSSER RHODEN
PFENNIG

COPPER

| 11 (C1) | 1816 | .066 | 40.00 | 90.00 | 150.00 | 210.00 |

KREUZER

BILLON

| 10 (C2) | 1813 | .086 | 10.00 | 22.50 | 30.00 | 50.00 |

1/2 BATZEN

BILLON

KM#	Date	Mintage	VG	Fine	VF	XF
5 (C3)	1808	.073	12.50	25.00	70.00	110.00
	1809	.060	8.50	17.50	30.00	60.00
	1816	.081	10.00	20.00	45.00	110.00

BATZEN

BILLON

6 (C4)	1808	.266	10.00	20.00	45.00	110.00
	1816	.203	10.00	20.00	45.00	110.00

1/2 FRANKEN

SILVER

| 7 (C5) | 1809 | 6,534 | 50.00 | 90.00 | 200.00 | 275.00 |

2 FRANKEN

SILVER

| 8 (C6) | 1812 | 1,861 | 85.00 | 180.00 | 265.00 | 550.00 |

4 FRANKEN

SILVER

| 9 (C7) | 1812 | 2,357 | 110.00 | 200.00 | 325.00 | 750.00 |

Appenzell / SWITZERLAND 1574

KM#	Date	Mintage	VG	Fine	VF	XF
12 (C8)	1816	1,850	150.00	300.00	450.00	900.00

BASEL
Basilea

A bishopric in northwest Switzerland, founded in the 5th century. The first coinage was c.1000AD. During the Reformation Basel became Protestant and the bishop resided henceforth in the town of Porrentruy. The Congress of Vienna gave the territories of the Bishopric to Bern. Today they form the Canton Jura and the French speaking part of Bern.

CANTON
MONETARY SYSTEM
After 1803
10 Rappen = 1 Batzen
10 Batzen = 1 Frank

RAPPEN

BILLON

KM#	Date	Mintage	VG	Fine	VF	XF
201 (C101)	1810	—	3.00	6.00	10.00	15.00
	1818	—	3.00	6.00	10.00	15.00

2 RAPPEN

BILLON

| 202 (C102) | 1810 | — | 3.00 | 6.00 | 10.00 | 25.00 |
| | 1818 | — | 3.00 | 6.00 | 10.00 | 25.00 |

5 RAPPEN

BILLON

| 204 (C108) | 1826B | — | 5.00 | 10.00 | 15.00 | 30.00 |

| 205 (C108a) | 1826 | — | 25.00 | 50.00 | 125.00 | 180.00 |

Obv: Value in exergue.

| 206 (C108b) | 1826 | — | 25.00 | 50.00 | 125.00 | 180.00 |

1/2 BATZEN

BILLON

KM#	Date	Mintage	VG	Fine	VF	XF
197 (C103)	1809	—	6.00	12.50	20.00	40.00

BATZEN

BILLON
Under the Republic

| 195 (C104) | 1805 | — | 15.00 | 30.00 | 55.00 | 85.00 |

As a Canton

196 (C104a)	1805	—	17.50	37.50	80.00	125.00
	1806	—	8.50	17.50	40.00	85.00
	1809	—	5.00	9.00	17.50	40.00
	1810	—	5.00	12.00	25.00	35.00

| 207 (C109a) | 1826 | — | 25.00 | 50.00 | 90.00 | 150.00 |

| 208 (C109) | 1826B | — | 5.00 | 10.00 | 15.00 | 27.50 |

3 BATZEN

SILVER

| 198 (C105) | 1809 | — | 10.00 | 20.00 | 30.00 | 60.00 |
| | 1810 | — | 15.00 | 22.50 | 35.00 | 70.00 |

5 BATZEN

SILVER

| 199 (C106) | 1809 | — | 25.00 | 50.00 | 125.00 | 165.00 |
| | 1810 | — | 12.50 | 25.00 | 50.00 | 110.00 |

Obv: BATZEN

KM#	Date	Mintage	VG	Fine	VF	XF
209 (C110)	1826	—	12.50	25.00	45.00	90.00

Obv: BATZn

| 210 (C110a) | 1826 | — | 25.00 | 50.00 | 125.00 | 210.00 |

BERN

A city and canton in west central Switzerland. It was founded as a military post in 1191 and became an imperial city with the mint right in 1218. It was admitted to the Swiss Confederation as a canton in 1353.

MINTMASTER'S INITIALS
D-B - J. De Beyer

DUPLONE
7.6400 g, .900 GOLD, .2210 oz AGW
Obv: Crowned pointed shield. Rev: Standing Swiss.

| 163 (C61a) | 1819 | — | 250.00 | 600.00 | 1250. | 2200. |
| | 1829 | — | 300.00 | 750.00 | 1500. | 2400. |

4 DUCATS
14.0000 g, .986 GOLD, .4438 oz AGW

| 155 (C55) | 1825 | — | — | — | Rare | — |

*NOTE: Stack's International sale 3-88 BU realized $12,100.

MONETARY REFORM
MONETARY SYSTEM
Commencing 1803
10 Rappen = 1 Batzen
10 Batzen = 1 Frank

RAPPEN

BILLON
Obv. leg: CANTON BERN

| 172 (C71) | 1811 | — | 3.50 | 6.00 | 12.50 | 18.00 |
| | 1829 | — | 6.00 | 12.50 | 22.50 | 37.50 |

Obv. leg: REPUBL. BERN

175 (C71a)	1818	—	3.50	6.00	12.50	18.00
	1819	—	3.50	6.00	12.50	18.00
	1836	—	3.50	6.00	12.50	18.00

2 RAPPEN

BILLON

| 171 (C73) | 1809 | — | 5.00 | 10.00 | 20.00 | 50.00 |

2-1/2 RAPPEN

BILLON

KM#	Date	Mintage	VG	Fine	VF	XF
173	1811	.114	3.50	6.00	12.50	18.00
(C75)	1829	—	3.50	6.00	12.50	18.00

5 RAPPEN

BILLON
Rev: W/inner beaded circle.

192	1826	—	3.00	6.00	9.00	18.00
(C87)						

Rev: W/o inner beaded circle.

193	1826	—	6.00	15.00	22.50	32.50
(C87a)						

1/2 BATZEN

BILLON

176	1818	—	5.00	10.00	20.00	30.00
(C77)	1824	—	5.00	10.00	20.00	30.00

BATZEN

BILLON

177	1818	—	5.00	9.00	15.00	32.50
(C79)	1824	—	5.00	9.00	15.00	32.50

Obv. leg: BATZ

194.1	1826	—	2.50	5.00	10.00	22.50
(C88)						

Obv. leg: BAZ

194.2	1826	—	5.00	8.00	13.50	32.50
(C88a)						

NOTE: These are found overstruck on 1/2 Batzen, KM#91.

2-1/2 BATZEN

SILVER
Obv. leg: BATZ

195.1	1826	—	5.00	10.00	20.00	45.00
(C89)						

Obv. leg: BAZ

195.2	1826	—	10.00	20.00	40.00	60.00
(C89a)						

5 BATZEN

SILVER

KM#	Date	Mintage	VG	Fine	VF	XF
170	1808	—	17.50	40.00	60.00	110.00
(C81)	1810	—	17.50	40.00	60.00	110.00
	1811	—	35.00	100.00	150.00	300.00
	1818	—	20.00	45.00	75.00	150.00

Obv. leg: BATZ

196.1	1826	—	12.50	25.00	35.00	60.00
(C90)						

Obv. leg: BAZ

196.2	1826	—	17.50	40.00	65.00	125.00
(C90a)						

196.3	1826	—	20.00	50.00	100.00	180.00
(C90b)						

FRANK

SILVER

174	1811	.011	37.50	80.00	140.00	300.00
(C82)						

2 FRANKEN

SILVER

198	1835	—	90.00	150.00	320.00	600.00
(C83)						

4 FRANKEN

SILVER

KM#	Date	Mintage	VG	Fine	VF	XF
190	1823	—	200.00	450.00	625.00	1350.
(C85)						

199	1835	—	150.00	300.00	450.00	875.00
(C85a)						

COUNTERSTAMPED COINAGE
40 BATZEN (BZ)

NOTE: During the period 1816-1819 an estimated 660,000 French Ecus of Louis XV and Louis XVI 1726-1793 and 6 Livres dated 1793-1794 along with 40 Batzen and 4 Franken of the Helvetian Republic were counterstamped with a bear and 40 BZ. on shields.
Approximately ninety percent of the counterstamped pieces were melted by 1851. It is estimated some 5,000 pieces or less still exist.

SILVER
c/s: On France Louis XV Ecu, C#42.

KM#	Date	Year	VG	Fine	VF	XF
178	ND	(1726-41)	200.00	250.00	350.00	750.00
(C34.1)						

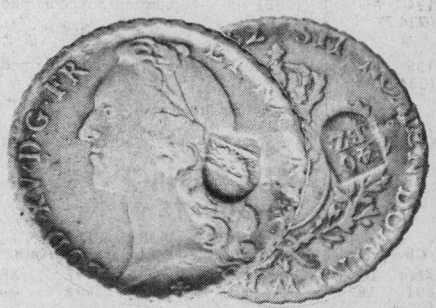

c/s: On France Louis XV Ecu, C#47.

179	ND	(1740-71)	200.00	250.00	350.00	750.00
(C34.2)						

Bern / SWITZERLAND 1575

Bern / SWITZERLAND 1576

c/s: On France Louis XV Ecu, C#47a.

KM#	Date	Year	VG	Fine	VF	XF
180 (C34.3)	ND	(1770-74)	175.00	225.00	300.00	700.00

c/s: On France Louis XVI Ecu, C#78.

KM#	Date	Year	VG	Fine	VF	XF
181 (C34.4)	ND	(1774-92)	175.00	225.00	300.00	700.00

c/s: On France Louis XVI Constitutional Ecu, C#93.

KM#	Date	Year	VG	Fine	VF	XF
182 (C34.5)	ND	(1792-93)	225.00	300.00	500.00	1000.

c/s: On France 6 Livres, C#123.

KM#	Date	Year	VG	Fine	VF	XF
183 (C34.6)	ND	(1793-94)	400.00	650.00	925.00	1500.

c/s: On Helvetia 40 Batzen, KM#4.1.

| 184 (C34.7) | ND | (1798) | — | Reported, not confirmed | | |

c/s: On Helvetia 40 Batzen, KM#4.2.

| 185 (C34.8) | ND | (1798) | — | Reported, not confirmed | | |

c/s: On Helvetia 4 Franken, KM#10.

| 186 (C34.9) | ND | (1799-1801) | — | Reported, not confirmed | | |

TRADE COINAGE
4 DUCATS
14.0000 g, .986 GOLD, .4438 oz AGW
Obv: Crowned pointed arms. Rev: Date, value in wreath.

KM#	Date	Mintage	VG	Fine	VF	XF
191 (C55)	1825	—			Rare	

FREIBURG
Friburg, Fribourg, Freyburg

A canton and city located in western Switzerland. The city was founded in 1178 and obtained the mint right in 1422. It joined the Swiss Confederation in 1481. During the Helvetian Republic period it was known as Sarine Et Broye but changed the name back to Freiburg in 1803.

MONETARY SYSTEM
After 1798

10 Rappen = 1 Batzen
10 Batzen = 1 Frank

2-1/2 RAPPEN

BILLON
Obv: Arms, value below.

KM#	Date	Mintage	VG	Fine	VF	XF
81 (C41)	1827	—	3.50	6.00	9.00	16.00

Obv: Pointed arms.

| 91 (C41.5) | 1846BEL | — | 3.50 | 6.00 | 9.00 | 16.00 |

5 RAPPEN

BILLON

| 70 (C31) | 1806 | — | 6.00 | 15.00 | 22.50 | 32.50 |

Obv: Date.

| 82 (C42) | 1827 | — | 6.00 | 15.00 | 22.50 | 32.50 |
| | 1828 | — | 6.00 | 15.00 | 22.50 | 32.50 |

Rev: Date.

| 87 (C42a) | 1830BEL | — | 3.00 | 6.00 | 12.50 | 20.00 |
| | 1831BEL | — | 4.00 | 8.00 | 15.00 | 27.50 |

1/2 BATZEN

BILLON

| 73 (C32) | 1810 | — | 7.50 | 17.50 | 25.00 | 32.50 |
| | 1811 | — | 3.75 | 8.00 | 15.00 | 27.50 |

BATZEN

BILLON

KM#	Date	Mintage	VG	Fine	VF	XF
71 (C33)	1806	—	5.00	12.00	18.00	65.00

| 74 (C34) | 1810 | — | 5.00 | 12.00 | 18.00 | 65.00 |

| 75 (C34a) | 1811 | — | 4.00 | 8.00 | 14.00 | 27.50 |

SILVER (OMS)

| 75a (C34b) | 1811 | — | — | — | — | — |

BILLON
Obv. value: BAZ

| 83 (C43) | 1827 | — | 4.00 | 8.00 | 14.00 | 27.50 |
| | 1828 | — | 4.00 | 8.00 | 14.00 | 27.50 |

Obv. value: BATZ.

| 85 (C43b) | 1829 | — | 4.00 | 8.00 | 14.00 | 27.50 |

| 88 (C43a) | 1830B | — | 4.00 | 8.00 | 14.00 | 27.50 |

5 BATZEN

SILVER

| 76 (C35) | 1811 | — | 15.00 | 35.00 | 50.00 | 90.00 |
| | 1814 | — | 15.00 | 35.00 | 50.00 | 90.00 |

84 (C44)	1827	—	15.00	35.00	50.00	90.00
	1828	—	15.00	35.00	70.00	100.00
	1829	—	12.50	25.00	55.00	125.00

KM#	Date	Mintage	VG	Fine	VF	XF
89 (C44a)	1830	—	12.50	25.00	55.00	125.00

10 BATZEN

SILVER

| 77 (C37) | 1811 | 4,907 | 30.00 | 75.00 | 125.00 | 250.00 |

| 78 (C37a) | 1812 | Inc. Ab. | 30.00 | 75.00 | 125.00 | 250.00 |

4 FRANKEN

SILVER

| 79 (C39) | 1813 | 2,429 | 175.00 | 300.00 | 500.00 | 950.00 |

GENEVA

A canton and city in southwestern Switzerland. The city became a bishopric c.400 AD and was part of the Burgundian Kingdom for 500 years. They became completely independent in 1530. In 1798 they were occupied by France but became independent again in 1813. They joined the Swiss Confederation in 1815.

MONETARY SYSTEM
1814-1838
12 Deniers = 4 Quarts = 1 Sol
12 Sols = 1 Florin
12 Florins, 9 Sols = 1 Thaler
35 Florins = 1 Pistole

6 DENIERS

BILLON

| 115 (C51) | 1817 | — | 2.50 | 5.00 | 8.00 | 15.00 |

SILVER

| 115a (C51b) | 1817 | — | — | — | Rare | — |

BILLON

KM#	Date	Mintage	VG	Fine	VF	XF
118 (C51a)	1819	—	2.50	5.00	8.00	15.00
	1825	—	4.00	7.00	10.00	22.50
	1833	—	2.50	5.00	8.00	15.00

SILVER

118a (C51c)	1819	—	—	—	Rare	—
	1825	—	—	—	Rare	—
	1833	—	—	—	Rare	—

SOL

BILLON

| 116 (C52.1) | 1817 H | — | 2.00 | 3.50 | 7.50 | 12.00 |

SILVER

| 116a (C52.1a) | 1817 H | — | — | — | Rare | — |

BILLON

| 119 (C52.2) | 1819 | — | 2.00 | 3.50 | 7.50 | 12.00 |

SILVER

| 119a (C52.2a) | 1819 | — | — | — | Rare | — |

BILLON

| 120 (C52.3) | 1825 | — | 2.00 | 3.00 | 6.00 | 9.00 |
| | 1833 | — | 2.00 | 3.00 | 6.00 | 9.00 |

SILVER

| 120a (C52.3a) | 1825 | — | — | — | Rare | — |
| | 1833 | — | — | — | Rare | — |

1-1/2 SOL

BILLON

| 117 (C53) | 1817 H | — | 2.50 | 4.50 | 9.00 | 18.00 |

| 121 (C53a) | 1825 | — | 2.50 | 4.50 | 9.00 | 18.00 |

SILVER

| 121a (C53b) | 1825 | — | — | — | Rare | — |

NOTE: Types KM#115a, 118a, 116a, 120, 120a and 121a struck in fine silver are presentation pieces.

DECIMAL COINAGE
100 Centimes = 1 Franc

CENTIME

BILLON

KM#	Date	Mintage	VG	Fine	VF	XF
125 (C63)	1839	.325	2.50	4.50	6.50	12.50

SILVER

| 125a (C63a) | 1839 | — | — | — | Rare | — |

COPPER

130 (C61)	1840	—	2.50	4.50	6.50	12.50
	1844	—	2.50	4.50	6.50	12.50
	1846	—	3.50	6.00	9.00	15.00

| 132 (C62) | 1847 | — | 2.50 | 4.50 | 6.50 | 12.50 |

SILVER

| 132a (C62a) | 1847 | — | — | — | Rare | — |

2 CENTIMES

BILLON

| 126 (C64) | 1839 | .078 | 4.00 | 8.00 | 18.00 | 27.50 |

SILVER

| 126a (C64a) | 1839 | — | — | — | Rare | — |

4 CENTIMES

BILLON

| 127 (C65) | 1839 | .331 | 3.75 | 5.50 | 11.00 | 22.50 |

SILVER

| 127a (C65a) | 1839 | — | — | — | Rare | — |

5 CENTIMES

BILLON

| 131 (C66) | 1840 | .699 | 3.00 | 5.00 | 9.00 | 15.00 |

SILVER

| 131a (C66a) | 1840 | — | — | — | Rare | — |

BILLON
Rev: Arms on shield.

| 133 (C69) | 1847 A.-B. | I.A. | 3.00 | 5.00 | 9.00 | 15.00 |

SILVER

| 133a (C69a) | 1847 | — | — | — | Rare | — |

10 CENTIMES

BILLON

KM#	Date	Mintage	VG	Fine	VF	XF
128 (C67)	1839	—	3.00	5.00	9.00	17.50
	1844	—	3.00	5.00	8.00	14.00

SILVER

| 128a (C67a) | 1839 | — | — | Rare | — | |

BILLON

| 134 (C70) | 1847 A.-B. | — | 3.00 | 5.00 | 9.00 | 14.00 |

SILVER

| 134a (C70a) | 1847 | — | — | Rare | — | |

25 CENTIMES

BILLON

| 129 (C68) | 1839 | — | 2.50 | 6.00 | 10.00 | 18.00 |
| | 1844 | — | 2.50 | 6.00 | 10.00 | 18.00 |

SILVER

| 129a (C68a) | 1839 | — | — | Rare | — | |

BILLON

| 135 (C71) | 1847 A.-B. | — | 3.75 | 8.00 | 12.50 | 20.00 |

SILVER

| 136 (C71a) | 1847 | — | — | Rare | — | |

5 FRANCS

SILVER

KM#	Date	Mintage	VG	Fine	VF	XF
137 (C72)	1848	1,176	150.00	210.00	275.00	500.00

10 FRANCS

SILVER
Obv: Similar to 5 Francs, KM#137.

| 138 (C73) | 1848 | 385 pcs. | 125.00 | 275.00 | 500.00 | 900.00 |
| | 1851 | 678 pcs. | 100.00 | 250.00 | 425.00 | 825.00 |

3.8000 g, .750 GOLD, .0916 oz AGW
| 139 (C74) | 1848 | 336 pcs. | 600.00 | 1250. | 1750. | 2500. |

20 FRANCS

7.6000 g, .750 GOLD, .1833 oz AGW
| 140 (C75) | 1848 | 3,421 | 300.00 | 650.00 | 1100. | 1650. |

NOTE: Types KM#125a-129a, 131a-134a and 136 struck in fine silver are presentation pieces.

GLARUS

A canton in eastern Switzerland. Independence was gained in c.1390 but from 1798-1803 it was occupied by the French. They rejoined the Swiss Confederation in 1803.

MONETARY SYSTEM
3 Rappen = 1 Schilling
100 Rappen = 1 Frank

SCHILLING

BILLON

BILLON

| 10 (C1) | 1806 F | — | 8.00 | 15.00 | 30.00 | 100.00 |
| | 1807 F | — | 10.00 | 20.00 | 40.00 | 80.00 |

Obv: Shield w/garlands.

KM#	Date	Mintage	VG	Fine	VF	XF
13 (C1a)	1808	—	10.00	20.00	45.00	80.00
	1809	—	8.00	15.00	40.00	100.00
	1811	—	8.00	15.00	40.00	90.00
	1812	—	8.00	15.00	40.00	90.00
	1813	—	8.00	15.00	40.00	90.00

Obv: Shield in branches.

| 15 (C1b) | 1809 | — | 8.00 | 15.00 | 30.00 | 80.00 |
| | 1810 | — | 150.00 | 250.00 | 500.00 | 1000. |

3 SCHILLING

BILLON

| 11 (C2) | 1806 | .134 | 35.00 | 70.00 | 125.00 | 260.00 |

| 14 (C2a) | 1808 | — | 35.00 | 70.00 | 125.00 | 260.00 |
| | 1812 | — | 35.00 | 70.00 | 125.00 | 260.00 |

16 (C2b)	1809	—	35.00	70.00	125.00	260.00
	1810	—	35.00	70.00	125.00	260.00
	1814	—	35.00	70.00	125.00	260.00

15 SCHILLING

SILVER

12 (C3)	1806 B	7,067	70.00	125.00	250.00	600.00
	1807 B	Inc. Ab.	70.00	125.00	250.00	600.00
	1811 B	Inc. Ab.	90.00	180.00	325.00	1000.
	1813 B	Inc. Ab.	70.00	125.00	250.00	600.00
	1814 B	Inc. Ab.	90.00	180.00	375.00	900.00

40 BATZEN

.900 SILVER
Glarus Shooting Festival

KM#	Date	Mintage	Fine	VF	XF	Unc
20 (2)	1847	3,200	850.00	1500.	3000.	5500.

GRAUBUNDEN

The largest and most easterly of the Swiss cantons. The district was set up in the reign of Roman Emperor Augustus and was one of the various factions sparring for power in the 14th and 15th centuries. The name is derived from "Grey League". The first coins were issued in c.

1600. They joined the Swiss Confederation in 1803.

MINTMASTER'S INITIALS
A-B - Bouey
H.B. - Bruppacher

MONETARY SYSTEM
15 Rappen = 6 Bluzger = 1 Schweizer Batzen
10 Schweizer Batzen = 1 Frank
16 Franken = 1 Duplone

1/6 BATZEN

BILLON
Rev. value: 1/6 BATZEN

KM#	Date	Mintage	VG	Fine	VF	XF
5 (C1)	1807	.058	3.00	7.50	15.00	30.00
	1820	.480	10.00	20.00	32.50	55.00

Rev. value: 1/6 BAZEN

| 16 (C1a) | 1842 A.B. | .172 | 2.50 | 6.00 | 12.50 | 30.00 |

1/2 BATZEN

BILLON

6 (C2)	1807	.075	10.00	25.00	50.00	100.00
	1820 B	.060	7.50	17.50	40.00	80.00

| 9 (C2a) | 1812 | .100 | 12.50 | 30.00 | 75.00 | 200.00 |

13 (C3)	1836 A-B	.212	6.00	15.00	30.00	60.00
	1842 A-B	.162	5.00	10.00	25.00	40.00

BATZEN

BILLON

| 7 (C4) | 1807 | .056 | 5.00 | 10.00 | 30.00 | 60.00 |

11 (C4a)	1820 B	.050	5.00	10.00	30.00	60.00
	1826 B	.050	6.00	15.00	37.50	90.00

Rev: Value w/short "1".

KM#	Date	Mintage	VG	Fine	VF	XF
14 (C5)	1836 HB Inc. Ab.		20.00	60.00	125.00	275.00

Rev: Value w/tall "1".

15 (C5a)	1836	.099	6.00	15.00	25.00	50.00
	1842 A-B	.100	5.00	10.00	22.50	40.00

5 BATZEN

SILVER

8 (C6)	1807	6.398	25.00	50.00	100.00	150.00
	1820	.016	25.00	50.00	100.00	150.00
	1826	—	32.50	80.00	170.00	210.00

10 BATZEN

SILVER

| 12 (C7) | 1825N | 2,000 | 100.00 | 200.00 | 320.00 | 600.00 |

4 FRANCS

.880 SILVER
Chur in Graubunden Shooting Festival

KM#	Date	Mintage	Fine	VF	XF	Unc
17 (1)	1842	6,000	350.00	600.00	1150.	2000.

16 FRANKEN

7.6400 g, .900 GOLD, .2211 oz AGW

KM#	Date	Mintage	VG	Fine	VF	XF
10 (C8)	1813	100 pcs.	—	3000.	6000.	9000.

LUZERN
Lucerne

A canton and city in central Switzerland. The city grew around the Benedictine Monastery which was founded in 750. They joined the Swiss Confederation as the 4th member in 1332. Few coins were issued before the 1500s.

MINTMASTER'S INITIALS
B, Br - Bruppacher
HL - Hedlinger
M - Meyer

ANGSTER
COPPER
Similar to 1 Rappen, KM#96.

KM#	Date	Mintage	VG	Fine	VF	XF
76 (C3)	1804	—	6.00	12.50	25.00	50.00
	1811	—	5.00	10.00	20.00	30.00
	1823	—	2.50	5.00	10.00	15.00
	1832	—	2.50	5.00	10.00	15.00
	1834	—	2.50	5.00	10.00	15.00

Obv. leg: CANTON LUZERN

117 (C6)	1839	—	2.50	5.00	10.00	15.00
	1843	—	2.50	5.00	10.00	15.00

RAPPEN
COPPER
Similar to KM#96.

| 75 (C4) | 1804 | — | 2.50 | 5.00 | 10.00 | 15.00 |

| 96 (C4.1) | 1804 | — | 2.50 | 5.00 | 7.50 | 12.50 |

Rev. value: 1 RAPPEN or RAPEN

115 (C5)	1831	—	2.50	5.00	7.50	12.50
116 (C5a)	1834	—	2.50	5.00	7.50	12.50

Obv. leg: CANTON LUZERN, oak circle.

| 118 (C6) | 1839 | — | 2.50 | 5.00 | 7.50 | 12.50 |

Obv. leg: CANTON LUZERN, oak wreath.

119 (C7)	1839	—	2.50	5.00	7.50	12.50
	1843	—	2.50	5.00	7.50	12.50
	1844	—	2.50	5.00	7.50	12.50
	1845	—	2.50	5.00	7.50	12.50
	1846	—	2.50	5.00	7.50	12.50

1/2 BATZEN

BILLON

| 106 (C28) | 1813 | — | 5.00 | 10.00 | 27.50 | 50.00 |

BATZEN

Luzern / SWITZERLAND 1580

BILLON
Obv. value: 1 BAZ. Rev: X RAPPEN.

KM#	Date	Mintage	VG	Fine	VF	XF
95 (C30)	1803	—	7.50	15.00	35.00	50.00

97 (C30a)	1804	—	6.00	9.00	15.00	25.00
	1805	—	—	—	—	—
	1806	—	7.50	17.50	37.50	65.00

Obv. leg: MONETA REIPUB.LUCERNENCIS.

| 99 (C30b) | 1805 | — | 6.00 | 12.50 | 20.00 | 30.00 |

101 (C31)	1807	—	3.00	6.00	12.50	25.00
	1808	—	3.00	6.00	12.50	25.00
	1809	—	3.00	6.00	12.50	25.00
	1810	—	3.00	6.00	12.50	25.00
	1811	—	3.00	6.00	12.50	25.00

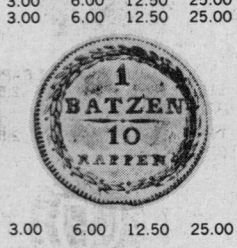

| 107 (C31b) | 1813 | — | 3.00 | 6.00 | 12.50 | 25.00 |

2-1/2 BATZEN

SILVER
| 110 (C33a) | 1815 | — | 15.00 | 30.00 | 60.00 | 90.00 |

Rev: Date (Canton).
| 111 (C33) | 1815 | — | 7.50 | 12.50 | 20.00 | 32.50 |

5 BATZEN

SILVER

KM#	Date	Mintage	VG	Fine	VF	XF
100 (C34)	1806	—	12.50	30.00	60.00	90.00

(Luzern 5 Batz coins)

| 104 (C34a) | 1810 | — | 12.50 | 25.00 | 45.00 | 80.00 |

| 108 (C34c) | 1813 | — | 12.50 | 25.00 | 45.00 | 80.00 |
| | 1814 | — | 12.50 | 25.00 | 45.00 | 80.00 |

| 112 (C34b) | 1815 | — | 12.50 | 25.00 | 45.00 | 80.00 |
| | 1816 | — | 12.50 | 25.00 | 45.00 | 80.00 |

10 BATZEN

SILVER
| 105 (C35) | 1811 | — | 90.00 | 225.00 | 425.00 | 650.00 |
| | 1812 | — | 25.00 | 50.00 | 120.00 | 200.00 |

40 BATZEN

| 113 (C37) | 1816 | 3,107 | 175.00 | 350.00 | 500.00 | 950.00 |
| | 1817 | 3,989 | 200.00 | 400.00 | 550.00 | 1100. |

4 FRANKEN

SILVER
| 109 (C36) | 1813 | — | 100.00 | 200.00 | 300.00 | 550.00 |
| | 1814 | .044 | 50.00 | 90.00 | 140.00 | 300.00 |

10 FRANKS

3.2258 g, .900 GOLD, .0933 oz AGW

KM#	Date	Mintage	VG	Fine	VF	XF
98 (C43)	1804	—	325.00	700.00	1500.	2150.

20 FRANKS

6.4516 g, .900 GOLD, .1867 oz AGW

| 102 (C44) | 1807 B | — | 700.00 | 1400. | 2500. | 4250. |

NEUCHATEL

A canton on the west central border of Switzerland. The first coins (bracteates) were struck in the 11th century. They were under Prussian rule from 1707 to 1806. France occupied the canton from 1806-1815. They reverted to Prussia until 1857, when they became a full member of the Swiss Confederation.

RULERS
Friedrich Wilhelm III, of Prussia,
 1797-1806
Alexandre Berthier, Prince,
 1806-1814
Friedrich Wilhelm III,
 1814-1840

MINTMASTER'S INITIALS
Letter	Date	Name
IP		Jean Party

MONETARY SYSTEM
4 Kreuzer = 1 Batzen
7 Kreuzer = 1 Piecette
21 Batzen = 1 Gulden
2 Gulden = 1 Thaler

1/2 KREUZER

BILLON
KM#	Date	Mintage	VG	Fine	VF	XF
64 (C25)	1802	—	15.00	30.00	70.00	100.00

KREUZER

BILLON
| 62 (C27) | 1802 | — | 3.75 | 7.50 | 15.00 | 40.00 |
| | 1803 | — | 2.50 | 5.00 | 9.00 | 15.00 |

| 66 (C35) | 1807 | — | 2.50 | 5.00 | 9.00 | 18.00 |
| | 1808 | — | 2.50 | 5.00 | 9.00 | 18.00 |

| 71 (C40) | 1817 | .303 | 2.50 | 5.00 | 9.00 | 15.00 |
| | 1818 | Inc. Ab. | 3.75 | 7.50 | 10.00 | 15.00 |

1/2 BATZEN
BILLON
Obv: Crowned arms, leg: F.G.BOR.REX.PR. . . . . .
Rev: Cross.

KM#	Date	Mintage	VG	Fine	VF	XF
55 (C28)	1803	—	3.75	5.00	9.00	18.00

Obv. leg: F.W.III.BOR.REX.P. . . . . . .,

| 57 (C28a) | 1803 | — | 3.75 | 5.00 | 9.00 | 18.00 |

BILLON
Rev. value: DEMI BATZ

| 67 (C36a) | 1807 | — | 4.50 | 9.00 | 12.50 | 22.50 |

Rev. value: 1/2 BATZ

68 (C36)	1807	—	2.50	4.50	7.50	15.00
	1808	—	2.50	4.50	7.50	20.00
	1809	—	3.00	6.00	10.00	22.50

BATZEN

65 (C37)	1806	—	7.50	15.00	22.50	32.50
	1807	—	2.50	5.00	8.00	15.00
	1808	—	2.50	5.00	8.00	15.00
	1809	—	3.75	7.50	10.00	25.00
	1810	—	5.00	10.00	18.00	35.00

| 69 (C37a) | 1807 | — | 2.50 | 5.00 | 7.50 | 15.00 |
| | 1808 | — | 2.50 | 5.00 | 7.50 | 15.00 |

ST. GALL
St. Gallen

A canton in northeast Switzerland which completely surrounds the canton of Appenzell. It joined the Swiss Confederation in 1803.

PFENNIG

BILLON
Uniface, arms on concave planchet.

| 100 (C51) | ND | .151 | 4.00 | 8.00 | 12.50 | 20.00 |

2 PFENNIG

BILLON

| 108 (C52) | 1808 | — | 50.00 | 100.00 | 180.00 | 230.00 |

1/2 KREUZER

BILLON

KM#	Date	Mintage	VG	Fine	VF	XF
109 (C53)	1808 K	.111	5.00	10.00	17.50	27.50
	1809 K	.118	5.00	10.00	17.50	27.50
	1810 K	.101	5.00	10.00	17.50	27.50
	1811 K	.099	5.00	10.00	17.50	27.50
	1812 K	.175	5.00	10.00	17.50	27.50
	1813 K	.149	5.00	10.00	17.50	27.50
	1814 K	.114	5.00	10.00	17.50	27.50
	1815 K	.136	5.00	10.00	17.50	27.50
	1816 K	.238	5.00	10.00	17.50	27.50
	1817 K	—	5.00	10.00	17.50	27.50

KREUZER

BILLON

| 101 (C54) | 1807 K | .162 | 5.00 | 10.00 | 20.00 | 45.00 |
| | 1808 K | .202 | 5.00 | 10.00 | 20.00 | 45.00 |

102 (C55)	1807	Inc. C54	50.00	100.00	180.00	230.00
	1809 K	.160	2.50	6.00	9.00	15.00
	1810 K	.146	2.50	6.00	9.00	15.00
	1811 K	.106	2.50	6.00	9.00	15.00
	1812 K	.135	2.50	6.00	9.00	15.00
	1813 K	.102	2.50	6.00	9.00	15.00
	1815 K	1.116	2.50	6.00	9.00	15.00
	1816 K	.135	2.50	6.00	9.00	15.00

1/2 BATZEN

BILLON

103 (C57)	1807	.110	5.00	10.00	15.00	30.00
	1808 K	.209	2.50	5.00	10.00	25.00
	1809 K	.267	2.50	5.00	10.00	25.00
	1810 K	.290	2.50	5.00	10.00	27.50
	1811 K	.349	2.50	5.00	10.00	45.00
	1812 K	.252	2.50	5.00	10.00	45.00
	1813 K	.154	2.50	5.00	10.00	45.00
	1814 K	.140	2.50	5.00	10.00	45.00
	1815 K	.181	2.50	5.00	10.00	45.00
	1816 K	.134	2.50	5.00	10.00	45.00
	1817 K	—	7.50	15.00	22.50	60.00

104 (C56)	1807 K	Inc. C57	5.00	10.00	15.00	30.00
	1808 K	Inc. C57	2.50	5.00	10.00	25.00
	1809 K	Inc. C57	5.00	10.00	15.00	25.00
	1810 K	Inc. C57	5.00	10.00	15.00	30.00

NOTE: Some varieties of KM#104 do not have the K mint mark.

BATZEN

BILLON

105 (C59)	1807 K	.063	5.00	12.50	20.00	45.00
	1808 K	.133	3.00	6.00	10.00	25.00
	1809 K	.187	5.00	10.00	20.00	40.00

KM#	Date	Mintage	VG	Fine	VF	XF
106 (C58)	1807	Inc. C59	7.50	15.00	27.50	45.00

Obv: Date. Rev. value: 1 BATZEN.

110 (C60)	1810 K	.259	2.50	5.00	12.50	40.00
	1811 K	.319	2.50	5.00	12.50	40.00
	1812 K	.341	2.50	5.00	12.50	40.00
	1813 K	—	2.50	5.00	12.50	40.00
	1814 K	.229	2.50	5.00	12.50	40.00
	1815 K	1.008	2.50	5.00	12.50	40.00
	1816 K	.068	2.50	5.00	12.50	40.00
	1817 K	—	7.50	15.00	22.50	70.00

Many varieties of KM#110 are known, including some w/o the K mint mark.

6 KREUZER

BILLON
Obv: Arms in oak branches.
Rev: Value and date in oak branches.

| 107 (C61) | 1807 | 4,510 | 30.00 | 55.00 | 80.00 | 150.00 |

5 BATZEN

SILVER
Obv: Date in exergue.

111 (C63)	1810 K	—	12.50	27.50	40.00	65.00
	1811 K	—	20.00	40.00	60.00	90.00
	1812 K	—	25.00	55.00	120.00	160.00
	1813 K	—	17.50	35.00	55.00	90.00

113 (C63a)	1813 K	—	12.50	27.50	50.00	80.00
	1814 K	—	12.50	27.50	50.00	80.00
	1817 K	—	20.00	40.00	60.00	90.00

| 114 (C63b) | 1817 K | — | 20.00 | 40.00 | 60.00 | 90.00 |

1/2 FRANKEN

SILVER

KM#	Date	Mintage	VG	Fine	VF	XF
112 (C62)	1810 K	759 pcs.	150.00	300.00	725.00	1200.

SCHAFFHAUSEN

A canton located on the north central border of Switzerland. The first coins, which were issued in the 13th century were known as "Ram Bracteates". It joined the Swiss Confederation in 1501.

MONETARY SYSTEM
4 Kreuzer = 1 Batzen

KREUZER

BILLON

KM#	Date	Mintage	VG	Fine	VF	XF
65 (C1)	1808	.216	20.00	40.00	80.00	120.00

1/2 BATZEN

BILLON

66 (C2)	1808	.080	10.00	20.00	30.00	55.00

68 (C2a)	1809	.030	12.00	22.00	35.00	65.00

BATZEN

BILLON

67 (C3)	1808	.064	25.00	55.00	80.00	150.00

Rev. value: 1 BATZEN

69 (C3a)	1809	.015	12.50	27.50	45.00	90.00

SCHWYZ
Schwytz, Suitensis

A canton in central Switzerland. In 1291 it became one of the three cantons that would ultimately become the Swiss Confederation and were known as the "Everlasting League". The first coinage was issued in 1624.

MINTMASTER'S INITIALS
S - Stedelin

MONETARY SYSTEM
2 Angster = 1 Rappen
10 Rappen = 1 Batzen
10 Batzen = 1 Frank
4 Franken = 1 Thaler

ANGSTER

COPPER

KM#	Date	Mintage	VG	Fine	VF	XF
55 (C31)	1810	—	2.50	5.00	9.00	18.00
	1811	—	2.50	5.00	9.00	18.00
	1812	—	2.50	5.00	9.00	18.00
	1813	—	5.00	12.50	20.00	30.00
	1814	—	3.75	7.50	15.00	25.00
	1815	—	5.00	12.50	20.00	30.00
	1816	—	2.50	5.00	9.00	18.00
	1821	—	5.00	12.50	20.00	30.00
	1827	—	5.00	12.50	20.00	30.00
	1838	—	5.00	12.50	20.00	30.00
	1843	—	2.50	5.00	9.00	15.00
	1845	—	2.50	5.00	9.00	15.00
	1846	—	2.50	5.00	9.00	15.00

RAPPEN

COPPER

59 (C32)	1811	—	2.50	5.00	12.50	20.00
	1812	—	2.00	3.50	7.50	10.00
	1815	—	2.00	3.50	7.50	10.00
	1845	—	2.50	3.75	5.00	8.00
	1846	—	3.00	6.00	12.00	18.00

NOTE: Many varieties exist, including some w/value 1 RAPEN and mint mark B.

60 (C33)	1811	—	2.50	5.00	12.00	18.00
	1812	—	2.00	3.00	7.00	9.00

65 (C33a)	1815	—	2.00	3.00	7.00	9.00
	1816	—	3.75	7.50	12.00	18.00
	1843	—	2.00	3.75	5.00	9.00
	1844	—	3.75	7.50	12.00	18.00
	1845	—	2.00	3.00	5.00	9.00
	1846	—	2.50	6.00	12.00	18.00

2 RAPPEN

BILLON

61 (C35)	1811	—	2.50	6.00	10.00	16.00
	1812	—	2.50	6.00	10.00	16.00
	1813	—	2.50	6.00	10.00	16.00

NOTE: Varieties of these coins are known with value as 2 RAPEN.

62 (C35a)	1811	—	3.00	6.00	12.00	18.00
	1812	—	2.50	3.75	7.50	12.50
	1813	—	5.00	12.00	18.00	—
	1814	—	2.50	3.75	7.50	12.50
	1815	—	2.50	3.75	7.50	12.50
	1842	—	7.00	15.00	30.00	40.00
	1843	—	2.50	3.75	7.50	12.50
	1843 DB	—	2.50	3.75	7.50	12.50
	1844 DB	—	5.00	10.00	15.00	27.50
	1845 DB	—	2.50	3.75	7.50	12.50
	1846 DB	—	2.50	3.75	7.50	12.50

NOTE: Many varieties exist, including some w/value 2 RAPEN and mint mark B.

2/3 BATZEN

BILLON

KM#	Date	Mintage	VG	Fine	VF	XF
56 (C36)	1810	—	7.50	15.00	37.50	60.00
	1811	—	7.50	15.00	37.50	60.00

Rev. value: 2/3 BATZEN

63 (C36a)	1812	—	25.00	55.00	90.00	130.00

Rev. value: 2/3 BATZ

64 (C36b)	1812	—	30.00	60.00	150.00	180.00

2 BATZEN

BILLON

57 (C38)	1810B	—	27.50	60.00	130.00	210.00

4 BATZEN

SILVER
Obv: Arms in laurel branches.
Rev: Value and date in wreath, leg. around border.

58 (C40)	1810 H	—	60.00	200.00	350.00	450.00
	1811 H	—	50.00	80.00	150.00	275.00

NOTE: Varieties exist with value 4 BATZ.
NOTE: For pattern issues struck under joint coinage of Uri, Schwyz and Unterwalden - see Uri.

TRADE COINAGE
DUCAT

3.5000 g, .986 GOLD, .1109 oz AGW

66 (C45)	1844 M	50 pcs.	—	—	Rare	—

SOLOTHURN
Solodornensis, Soleure

A canton in northwest Switzerland. Bracteates were struck in the 1300s even though the mint right was not officially granted until 1381. They joined the Swiss Confederation in 1481.

MONETARY SYSTEM
Commencing 1804
10 Rappen = 4 Kreuzer = 1 Batzen
10 Batzen = 1 Frank

RAPPEN

BILLON

71 (C41)	1813	—	9.00	18.00	30.00	50.00

2-1/2 RAPPEN

BILLON

85 (C52)	1830	—	2.50	5.00	10.00	25.00

5 RAPPEN

BILLON

KM#	Date	Mintage	VG	Fine	VF	XF
78 (C53)	1826	—	10.00	20.00	35.00	50.00

KREUZER

BILLON

72 (C42)	1813	—	3.75	7.50	12.50	25.00

BATZEN

BILLON

65 (C44)	1805	—	7.50	15.00	30.00	50.00

66 (C45)	1807	—	27.50	60.00	100.00	200.00
	1808	—	7.50	15.00	30.00	50.00
	1809	—	7.50	15.00	30.00	50.00

67 (C45a)	1809	—	7.50	15.00	30.00	50.00
	1810	—	3.00	6.00	12.50	30.00
	1811	—	3.00	6.00	12.50	30.00

79 (C54a)	1826	—	6.00	12.00	18.00	37.50

80 (C54b)	1826	—	2.50	6.00	12.50	27.50

2-1/2 BATZEN

SILVER
Obv: Crowned oval arms in laurel branches, value below.
Rev: Cross in quatrefoil.

KM#	Date	Mintage	VG	Fine	VF	XF
81 (C55)	1826	—	10.00	20.00	40.00	80.00

5 BATZEN

SILVER

68 (C46)	1809	—	45.00	90.00	200.00	300.00
	1811	—	20.00	40.00	80.00	135.00

Obv. value: 5 BATZ

82 (C56)	1826	—	15.00	30.00	50.00	90.00

Obv. value: 5 BAZ.

83 (C56a)	1826	—	17.50	37.50	75.00	125.00

FRANK

SILVER

70 (C47)	1812	2,000	100.00	200.00	450.00	600.00

4 FRANKEN

SILVER

73 (C48)	1813	250 pcs.	200.00	400.00	550.00	1000.

8 FRANKEN

3.8200 g, .900 GOLD, .2211 oz AGW

74 (C49)	1813	106 pcs.	—	2750.	5000.	8250.

16 FRANKEN

7.6400 g, .900 GOLD, .2211 oz AGW

KM#	Date	Mintage	VG	Fine	VF	XF
75 (C50)	1813	150 pcs.	—	2750.	5000.	8250.

32 FRANKEN

15.2800 g, .900 GOLD, .4421 oz AGW
Obv: Crowned oval arms on spade shield in branches, date below.
Rev: Standing knight holding shield, value below.

76 (C51) (C32)	1813	—	—	Rare	—

THURGAU
Thurgovie

A canton in northeast Switzerland. They were ruled by the Swiss Confederates beginning c. 1460 until 1798. In 1803 they joined the Swiss Confederation.

MONETARY SYSTEM
4 Kreuzer = 1 Schweizer Batzen
10 Batzen = 1 Frank

1/2 KREUZER

BILLON

1 (C1)	1808	.100	40.00	90.00	180.00	240.00

KREUZER

BILLON

2 (C2)	1808	.099	7.50	17.50	37.50	55.00

1/2 BATZEN

BILLON

3 (C3)	1808	.149	10.00	22.50	45.00	80.00

BATZEN

BILLON

4 (C4)	1808	.232	11.00	25.00	40.00	95.00
	1809	Inc. Ab.	11.00	25.00	40.00	95.00

5 BATZEN

SILVER

5 (C5)	1808	2,580	175.00	275.00	450.00	600.00

TICINO
Tessin

A canton in southeast Switzerland. They were previously known as the Lombard vassal state of Bellinzona. They joined the Swiss Confederation in 1803.

MONETARY SYSTEM
12 Denari = 1 Soldo
20 Soldi = 1 Franco

TRE (3) DENARI

COPPER
Obv: Arms. Rev: Value above branches.

KM#	Date	Mintage	VG	Fine	VF	XF
5 (C1)	1814	.417	5.00	9.00	15.00	27.50
	1835	.598	5.00	9.00	15.00	27.50

| 9 (C1a) | 1841 | .322 | 5.00 | 9.00 | 15.00 | 27.50 |

SEI (6) DENARI

COPPER
Obv: Arms. Rev: Value and date within wreath.

1 (C2)	1813	.280	5.00	9.00	15.00	32.50
	1835	.364	7.50	15.00	27.50	40.00
	1841	.241	5.00	9.00	15.00	32.50

TRE (3) SOLDI

BILLON

2 (C3)	1813 star	1.405	5.00	10.00	27.50	60.00
	1813 w/o star Inc. Ab.		5.00	10.00	22.50	50.00
	1835	.323	3.75	5.00	12.50	32.50
	1838	.514	3.75	5.00	12.50	32.50
	1841	.243	2.00	4.00	10.00	30.00

1/4 FRANCO

SILVER

| 7 (C4) | 1835 | .058 | 20.00 | 40.00 | 60.00 | 125.00 |

1/2 FRANCO

SILVER

| 8 (C5) | 1835 | .044 | 20.00 | 45.00 | 80.00 | 160.00 |

FRANCO

SILVER

KM#	Date	Mintage	VG	Fine	VF	XF
3 (C6)	1813 star	5,920	95.00	200.00	275.00	600.00
	1813 w/o star Inc. Ab.		70.00	150.00	225.00	475.00

2 FRANCHI

SILVER

4 (C7)	1813 star	4,150	140.00	300.00	550.00	1000.
	1813 w/o star Inc. Ab.		120.00	250.00	450.00	850.00

4 FRANCHI

SILVER

6 (C8)	1814 star	7,921	140.00	300.00	550.00	1000.
	1814 w/o star Inc. Ab.		120.00	250.00	450.00	850.00

NOTE: Coins of 3 Soldi, Franco, 2 Franchi and 4 Franchi with star mint mark were struck at Luzern. Those without star were coined at Bern.

UNTERWALDEN
Subsilvania

A canton in central Switzerland which was one of the three original cantons which became the Swiss Confederation in 1291. It is made up of two half cantons - Nidwalden and Obwalden. They had their own coinage beginning in the 1500s.

MINTMASTER'S INITIALS
S - Samson

MONETARY SYSTEM
4 Kreuzer = 1 Batzen
10 Batzen = 1 Frank

NIDWALDEN
1/2 BATZEN

BILLON

| 11 (C11) | 1811 | .012 | 18.00 | 45.00 | 90.00 | 135.00 |

BATZEN

BILLON

KM#	Date	Mintage	VG	Fine	VF	XF
12 (C12)	1811	.012	18.00	45.00	90.00	135.00

5 BATZEN

SILVER

| 13 (C13) | 1811 | 3,600 | 80.00 | 150.00 | 300.00 | 425.00 |

OBWALDEN
1/2 BATZEN

BILLON

| 21 (C21) | 1812 | — | 18.00 | 45.00 | 75.00 | 115.00 |

BATZEN

BILLON

| 22 (C22) | 1812 | — | 20.00 | 45.00 | 75.00 | 135.00 |

5 BATZEN

SILVER

| 23 (C23) | 1812 | — | 60.00 | 100.00 | 260.00 | 425.00 |

URI
Uranie

A canton in central Switzerland. It is one of the three original cantons which became the Swiss Confederation in 1291. They had their own coinage from the early 1600s until 1811.

MONETARY SYSTEM
10 Rappen = 1 Batzen
10 Batzen = 1 Frank

RAPPEN

BILLON

| 40 (C11) | 1811 | .019 | 45.00 | 100.00 | 175.00 | 210.00 |

1/2 BATZEN

BILLON

KM#	Date	Mintage	VG	Fine	VF	XF
41 (C12)	1811	.015	27.50	60.00	95.00	200.00

BATZEN

BILLON

| 42 (C13) | 1811 | .020 | 27.50 | 60.00 | 95.00 | 200.00 |

2 BATZEN

SILVER

| 43 (C14) | 1811 | 4,995 | 60.00 | 120.00 | 180.00 | 300.00 |

4 BATZEN

SILVER

| 44 (C15) | 1811 | 3,510 | 70.00 | 150.00 | 275.00 | 450.00 |

VAUD
Waadt

A canton in southwest Switzerland. They had possession of Bern from 1536 until 1798. They joined the Swiss Confederation in 1803.

MINTMASTER'S INITIALS
BEL - Bel Bessiere

MONETARY SYSTEM
10 Rappen = 1 Batz
10 Batz = 1 Franc
4 Francs = 1 Thaler

RAPPEN

BILLON

| 5 (C1) | 1804 | .211 | 12.50 | 30.00 | 80.00 | 150.00 |

| 12 (C1a) | 1807 | Inc. Ab. | 10.00 | 20.00 | 60.00 | 100.00 |

2-1/2 RAPPEN

BILLON

| 14 (C2) | 1809 | .230 | 5.00 | 10.00 | 15.00 | 27.50 |

KM#	Date	Mintage	VG	Fine	VF	XF
18 (C2a)	1816	—	5.00	10.00	15.00	27.50

1/2 BATZEN

BILLON

6 (C3)	1804	2,962	3.00	6.00	10.00	15.00
	1805	Inc. Ab.	2.50	5.00	8.00	12.50
	1806	Inc. Ab.	2.50	5.00	8.00	12.50
	1807	Inc. Ab.	2.50	5.00	8.00	12.50
	1808	Inc. Ab.	5.00	12.00	20.00	37.50
	1809	—	2.50	5.00	8.00	12.50
	1810	—	2.50	5.00	8.00	12.50
	1811	—	2.00	4.00	7.50	12.50
	1813	—	2.50	5.00	8.00	12.50
	1814	—	2.50	5.00	8.00	12.50
	1816	—	2.50	5.00	8.00	12.50
	1817	—	4.00	9.00	15.00	25.00
	1818	—	2.00	4.00	7.50	12.50
	1819	—	2.50	5.00	8.00	12.50

BATZEN

BILLON
Obv: W/o branches around arms.

| 7 (C4) | 1804 | — | 20.00 | 45.00 | 100.00 | 180.00 |

8 (C4a)	1804	—	4.00	8.00	27.50	40.00
	1805	—	2.50	5.50	10.00	30.00
	1806	—	3.00	6.00	12.50	25.00
	1807	—	3.00	6.00	12.50	25.00
	1808	—	—	—	Rare	—
	1809	—	8.50	17.50	35.00	50.00
	1810	—	3.00	6.00	12.50	25.00
	1811	—	3.00	6.00	12.50	25.00
	1812	—	3.00	6.00	12.50	25.00
	1813	—	3.00	6.00	12.50	25.00
	1814	—	3.00	6.00	12.50	25.00
	1815	—	3.00	6.00	12.50	25.00
	1816	—	3.00	6.00	12.50	25.00
	1817	—	3.00	6.00	12.50	25.00
	1818	—	3.00	5.50	10.00	18.00
	1819	—	3.00	5.00	9.00	16.00
	1820	—	4.00	9.00	15.00	27.50

20 (C11)	1826BEL	—	12.50	27.50	60.00	100.00
	1827BEL	—	2.50	5.50	10.00	17.00
	1828BEL	—	2.50	5.50	8.00	15.00
	1829BEL	—	2.50	5.50	8.00	15.00
	1830BEL	—	2.50	5.50	8.00	15.00
	1831BEL	—	2.50	5.50	8.00	15.00
	1832BEL	—	2.50	6.00	12.00	17.50
	1834BEL	—	6.00	12.50	37.50	60.00

5 BATZEN

SILVER

KM#	Date	Mintage	VG	Fine	VF	XF
9 (C5)	1804	1,692	70.00	150.00	350.00	500.00

| 11 (C5a) | 1805 | — | 40.00 | 90.00 | 200.00 | 260.00 |
| | 1806 | — | 40.00 | 90.00 | 200.00 | 260.00 |

13 (C5b)	1807	—	12.50	27.50	80.00	100.00
	1810	—	12.50	27.50	80.00	100.00
	1811	—	12.50	27.50	80.00	100.00
	1812	—	12.50	27.50	70.00	95.00
	1813	—	12.50	27.50	70.00	95.00
	1814	—	15.00	30.00	90.00	135.00

21 (C12)	1826	—	12.50	27.50	80.00	100.00
	1827BEL	—	10.00	20.00	45.00	80.00
	1828BEL	—	10.00	20.00	45.00	80.00
	1829BEL	—	12.50	27.50	80.00	100.00
	1830BEL	—	10.00	20.00	45.00	80.00
	1831BEL	—	10.00	20.00	45.00	80.00

10 BATZEN

SILVER

| 10 (C6) | 1804 | 1,234 | 150.00 | 300.00 | 600.00 | 950.00 |

| 15 (C7) | 1810 | 1,234 | 45.00 | 100.00 | 160.00 | 300.00 |
| | 1811 | 2,963 | 45.00 | 100.00 | 160.00 | 300.00 |

Vaud / SWITZERLAND 1585

Vaud / SWITZERLAND 1586

KM#	Date	Mintage	VG	Fine	VF	XF
19 (C7a)	1823	6,198	45.00	100.00	160.00	300.00

20 BATZEN

SILVER

16 (C8)	1810	6,590	35.00	85.00	220.00	450.00
	1811	Inc. Ab.	35.00	85.00	220.00	450.00

40 BATZEN

SILVER

| 17 (C10) | 1812 | 2,485 | 85.00 | 200.00 | 420.00 | 850.00 |

NOTE: 616 pieces were melted in 1851.

FRANC

SILVER

| 22 (C13) | 1845 | 8,626 | 20.00 | 40.00 | 75.00 | 100.00 |

NOTE: This coin was struck to commemorate a Shooting Festival held on August 10, 1845. It had legal tender status.

COUNTERSTAMPED COINAGE
39 BATZEN (BZ)

As in the canton of Bern, French Ecus dated 1726 to 1793 along with 6 Livres dated 1793-1794 were counterstamped and freely circulated. In Vaud, the counterstamp consisted of the arms of Vaud on one side and the new value 39 BZ on the other.

SILVER
c/s: On France Louis XV Ecu, C#42.

KM#	Date	Year	VG	Fine	VF	XF
23	ND	(1726-41)	600.00	1000.	1500.	2000.

(C9.1)

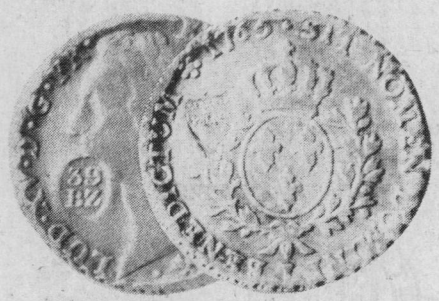

c/s: On France Louis XV Ecu, C#47.
24 (C9.2)	ND	(1740-71)	600.00	1000.	1500.	2000.

c/s: On France Louis XV Ecu, C#47a.
| 25 (C9.3) | ND | (1770-74) | 600.00 | 1000. | 1500. | 2000. |

c/s: On France Louis XVI Ecu, C#78.
| 26 (C9.4) | ND | (1774-92) | 600.00 | 1000. | 1500. | 2000. |

c/s: On France Louis XVI Constitutional Ecu, C#93.
| 27 (C9.5) | ND | (1792-93) | 750.00 | 1600. | 2400. | 3200. |

c/s: On France 6 Livres, C#123.
| 28 (C9.6) | ND | (1793-94) | 900.00 | 2000. | 2750. | 3750. |

ZUG
Tugium, Tugiensis

A canton in central Switzerland. They joined the Swiss Confederation in 1352 and had their own coinage from 1564 to 1805.

MONETARY SYSTEM
12 Haller = 12 Angster = 3 Rappen = 1 Schilling
2 Schilling = 1 Assis

ANGSTER
COPPER
Obv: Arms in branches. Rev: Date, value in cartouche.

KM#	Date	Mintage	VG	Fine	VF	XF
61 (C1)	1804	—	20.00	40.00	60.00	120.00

RAPPEN
COPPER
Obv: Arms in branches. Rev: Date, value in cartouche.

63 (C2)	1805	—	3.75	7.50	10.00	18.00

ZURICH
Thicurinae, Thuricensis
Ticurinae, Turicensis

A canton in north central Switzerland. It was the mint for the dukes of Swabia in the 10th and 11th centuries. The mint right was obtained in 1238. The first coinage struck were bracteates and the last coins were struck in 1848. It joined the Swiss Confederation in 1351.

MINTMASTER'S INITIALS
B - Bruckmann
V - Vorster

MONETARY SYSTEM
Commencing 1803
3 Haller = 1 Rappen
4 Rappen = 1 Schilling
10 Schilling = 4 Batzen
160 Batzen = 1 Ducat

3 HALLER

BILLON
180 (C4)	ND	3,518	2.50	4.50	6.00	10.00

Error: HALER
| 181 (C4a) | ND | Inc. Ab. | 4.00 | 9.00 | 15.00 | 25.00 |

NOTE: These were struck from 1827-1841.

RAPPEN

KM#	Date	Mintage	VG	Fine	VF	XF
194 (C51)	1842	—	2.50	4.50	9.00	20.00
	1844	—	5.00	12.00	20.00	30.00
	1845	—	2.50	4.50	9.00	16.00
	1846	—	30.00	60.00	120.00	300.00
	1848	—	2.50	4.50	9.00	16.00

2 RAPPEN

BILLON
195 (C52)	1842D	.460	4.00	9.00	15.00	22.50

10 SCHILLING

SILVER
182 (C55)	ND(1806)	—	8.50	15.00	37.50	60.00
	1807 B	—	12.50	27.50	45.00	80.00
	1808 B	—	6.00	12.50	27.50	50.00
	1809 B	—	6.00	12.50	27.50	50.00
	1810 B	—	6.00	12.50	27.50	50.00
	1811 B	—	6.00	12.50	27.50	50.00

8 BATZEN

SILVER
184 (C56)	1810 B	.108	25.00	45.00	75.00	150.00
	1814 B	Inc. Ab.	30.00	60.00	100.00	180.00

10 BATZEN

SILVER
185 (C57)	1812 B	.028	32.50	70.00	100.00	175.00

20 BATZEN

SILVER
Rev: Large date, thick stems.
186 (C58)	1813 B	—	40.00	90.00	165.00	270.00

Rev: Small date, thin stems.

KM#	Date	Mintage	VG	Fine	VF	XF
187 (C58b)	1813	—	40.00	90.00	165.00	270.00

Obv: Longer garlands. Rev: Small date, thin stems.

188 (C58c)	1813	—	50.00	100.00	175.00	280.00

192 (C58a)	1826	—	55.00	120.00	200.00	350.00

40 BATZEN

SILVER
Obv: Shield 18mm wide, short right hand garland.
Rev: Large date.

189 (C59)	1813	—	60.00	80.00	120.00	250.00

Obv: Shield 19mm wide, long right hand garland.
Rev: Small date.

KM#	Date	Mintage	VG	Fine	VF	XF
190 (C59a)	1813 B	—	60.00	80.00	120.00	250.00

Obv: Shield 18mm wide, short right hand garland, small wreath. Rev: Small date.

191	1813 B	—	60.00	80.00	120.00	250.00

TRADE COINAGE
DUCAT

3.5000 g, .986 GOLD, .1109 oz AGW

185 (C60)	1810 B	—	300.00	900.00	1450.	2500.

SWITZERLAND

The Swiss Federation, located in central Europe north of Italy and south of Germany, has an area of 15,941 sq. mi. (41,288 sq. km.) and a population of *6.5 million. Capital: Bern. The economy centers about a well-developed manufacturing industry. Machinery, chemicals, watches and clocks, and textiles are exported.

Switzerland, the habitat of lake dwellers in prehistoric times, was peopled by the Celtic Helvetians when Julius Caesar made it a part of the Roman Empire in 58 B.C. After the decline of Rome, Switzerland was invaded by Teutonic tribes, who established small temporal holdings which in the Middle Ages, became a federation of fiefs of the Holy Roman Empire. As a nation, Switzerland originated in 1291 when the districts of Nidwalden, Schwyz and Uri united to defeat Austria and attain independence as the Swiss Confederation. After acquiring new cantons in the 14th century, Switzerland was made independent from the Holy Roman Empire by the 1648 Treaty of Westphalia. The revolutionary armies of Napoleonic France occupied Switzerland and set up the Helvetian Republic, 1798-1803. After the fall of Napoleon, the Congress of Vienna, 1815, recognized the independence of Switzerland and guaranteed its neutrality. The Swiss Constitutions of 1848 and 1874 established a union modeled upon that of the United States.

MINT MARKS
A - Paris
AB - Strasbourg
B - Bern
B. - Brussels 1874
BA - Basel
BB - Strasbourg
S - Solothurn

NOTE: The coinage of Switzerland has been struck at the Bern Mint since 1853 with but a few exceptions. All coins minted there carry a 'B' mint mark through 1969, except for the 2- Centime and 2-Franc values where the mint mark was discontinued after 1968. In 1968 and 1969 some issues were struck at both Bern (B) and in London (no mint mark).

Up through 1981 all circulation coinage was struck with normal coin die alignment. Commencing with 1982 all pieces are struck with medallic die alignment.

MONETARY SYSTEM
10 Rappen = 1 Batzen
10 Batzen = 1 Franc
16 Franken = 1 Duplone

HELVETIAN REPUBLIC
RAPPEN

BILLON

KM#	Date	Mintage	VG	Fine	VF	XF
11	1800	—	3.00	7.50	15.00	25.00
	1801	—	2.50	5.00	10.00	20.00
	1802	—	3.00	7.50	15.00	25.00

1/2 BATZEN

BILLON

6	1802	—	3.00	10.00	16.00	28.00
	1803	—	5.00	12.50	25.00	45.00

BATZEN
BILLON
Obv: HELVET.REPUBL. in wreath.
Rev: Similar to 1 Rappen, KM#11.

8	1801B	—	5.00	12.50	22.50	37.50
	1802B	—	5.00	12.50	22.50	37.50
	1803B	—	5.00	12.50	22.50	37.50

5 BATZEN
SILVER
Obv: Standing Swiss holding flag.
Rev: Value within wreath.

9	1802B	—	90.00	200.00	275.00	425.00

10 BATZEN

SILVER

Obv: Standing Swiss holding flag.
Rev: Value within wreath.

KM#	Date	Mintage	VG	Fine	VF	XF
1	1801B	—	30.00	75.00	160.00	300.00

4 FRANKEN

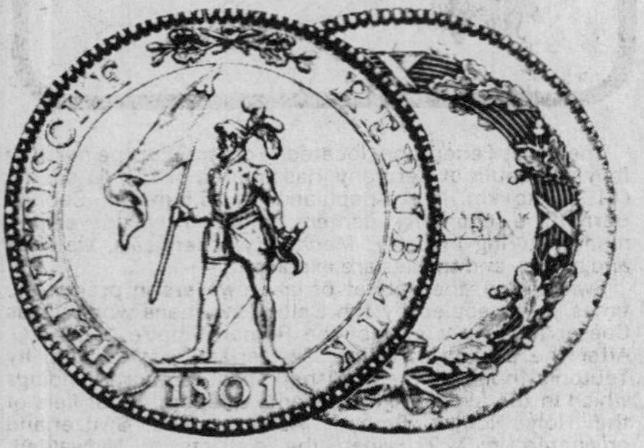

SILVER

10	1801B	—	175.00	375.00	650.00	1000.

SWITZERLAND

Confoederatio Helvetica

MONETARY SYSTEM

100 Rappen (Centimes) = 1 Franc

RAPPEN

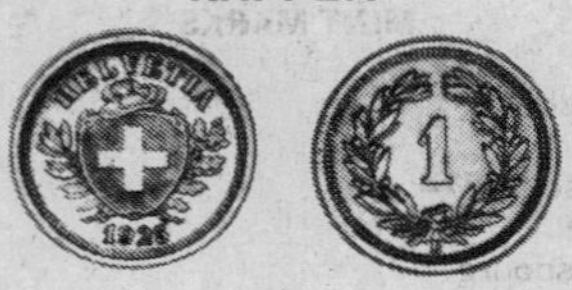

BRONZE

KM#	Date	Mintage	Fine	VF	XF	Unc
3	1850A	2.270	28.00	50.00	80.00	175.00
	1851A	2.730	20.00	40.00	70.00	120.00
	1853B thick cross					
		2.008	28.00	50.00	75.00	165.00
	1853B thin cross					
		Inc. Ab.	1000.	2000.	3000.	3500.
	1855B	.500	250.00	375.00	600.00	1000.
	1856B	2.500	20.00	37.50	60.00	125.00
	1857B	1.587	25.00	40.00	60.00	100.00
	1863B	.501	120.00	190.00	260.00	475.00
	1864B	.501	125.00	200.00	280.00	550.00
	1866B	1.000	50.00	75.00	120.00	265.00
	1868B	2.000	12.00	20.00	32.50	70.00
	1870B	.500	50.00	75.00	180.00	380.00
	1872B	2.080	10.00	17.50	27.50	60.00
	1875B	.975	22.50	35.00	45.00	75.00
	1876B	1.000	22.50	35.00	45.00	75.00
	1877B	.923	22.50	35.00	45.00	75.00
	1878B	.981	22.50	35.00	45.00	75.00
	1879B	.998	22.50	35.00	45.00	75.00
	1880B	.992	22.50	35.00	45.00	75.00
	1882B	1.000	12.00	17.50	25.00	55.00
	1883B	1.000	12.00	17.50	25.00	55.00
	1884B	1.000	12.00	17.50	25.00	55.00
	1887B	1.504	7.00	11.00	20.00	35.00
	1889B	.500	27.50	35.00	65.00	190.00
	1890B	1.000	10.00	16.00	20.00	35.00
	1891B thick cross					
		2.000	10.00	16.00	20.00	35.00
	1891B thin cross					
		Inc. Ab.	10.00	16.00	20.00	35.00
	1892B	1.000	10.00	16.00	20.00	35.00
	1894B	1.000	10.00	16.00	20.00	45.00
	1895B	2.000	1.75	3.75	7.50	20.00
	1896B	36 pcs.	—	—	Rare	—
	1897B	.500	16.00	28.00	35.00	65.00
	1898B	1.500	4.25	7.00	10.00	20.00
	1899B	1.500	4.25	7.00	10.00	20.00
	1900B	2.000	4.25	7.00	10.00	20.00
	1902B	.950	40.00	60.00	85.00	190.00
	1903B	1.000	18.00	22.50	27.50	60.00
	1904B	1.000	18.00	22.50	27.50	50.00
	1905B	2.000	5.00	8.00	12.00	20.00
	1906B	1.000	10.00	20.00	27.50	60.00
	1907B	2.000	5.00	8.00	12.00	22.50
	1908B	3.000	1.00	2.00	4.00	12.00
	1909B	1.000	15.00	17.50	20.00	32.50
	1910B	.500	4.00	8.00	12.50	20.00
	1911B	.500	4.00	8.00	12.50	20.00
	1912B	2.000	.25	1.00	3.50	12.00
	1913B	3.000	.25	.50	1.25	6.00
	1914B	3.500	.25	.75	2.50	9.00
	1915B	3.000	.25	.75	2.50	9.00
	1917B	2.000	.25	1.00	5.00	15.00
	1918B	3.000	.25	.75	2.50	6.00
	1919B	3.000	.25	.75	2.50	6.00
	1920B	1.000	.25	1.00	5.00	12.00
	1921B	3.000	.25	.75	2.50	7.00
	1924B	2.000	.25	.75	2.50	9.00
	1925/4B	2.500	.25	1.00	6.00	12.00
	1925B	Inc. Ab.	.25	1.00	6.00	12.00
	1926B	2.000	.25	1.00	5.00	12.00
	1927B	1.500	.25	1.00	6.00	12.00

KM#	Date	Mintage	Fine	VF	XF	Unc
3	1928B	2.000	.25	.75	2.50	9.00
	1929B	4.000	.25	.50	1.25	6.00
	1930B	2.500	.25	.50	1.25	7.00
	1931B	5.000	.25	.50	1.25	3.50
	1932B	5.000	.25	.50	1.25	5.00
	1933B	3.000	.25	1.00	3.75	9.00
	1934B	3.000	.25	.50	1.25	5.00
	1936B	2.000	.25	.50	1.25	9.00
	1937B	2.400	.25	.50	1.25	5.00
	1938B	5.300	.25	.50	1.25	5.00
	1939B	.010	15.00	18.00	25.00	45.00
	1940B	3.027	.25	.50	1.25	6.00
	1941B	12.794	.20	.30	.60	4.00

ZINC

3a	1942B	17.969	.25	.50	1.25	5.25
	1943B	8.647	.25	.50	1.25	7.25
	1944B	11.825	.25	.50	1.25	5.25
	1945B	2.800	2.00	4.00	6.00	20.00
	1946B	12.063	.25	.50	1.25	5.25

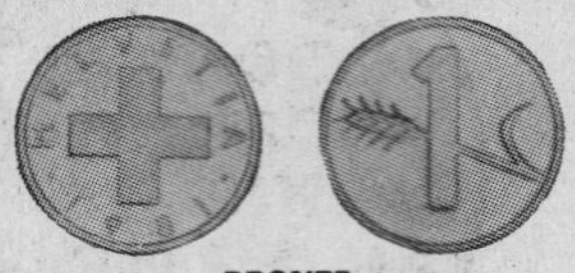

BRONZE

46	1948B	10.500	—	.10	.50	1.25
	1949B	11.100	—	.10	.50	1.25
	1950B	3.610	.10	.25	1.25	4.25
	1951B	22.624	—	.10	.50	1.25
	1952B	11.520	—	.10	.30	1.25
	1953B	5.947	—	.10	.50	1.75
	1954B	5.175	—	.10	.50	1.75
	1955B	5.282	—	.10	.60	2.50
	1956B	4.960	—	.10	.50	1.75
	1957B	15.226	—	.10	.20	.60
	1958B	20.142	—	.10	.20	.60
	1959B	5.582	—	.10	.25	1.25
	1962B	5.010	—	.10	.25	1.25
	1963B	15.920	—	—	.10	.35
	1966B	5.030	—	—	.10	.35
	1967B	3.020	—	—	.10	.35
	1968B	4.920	—	—	.10	.35
	1969B	4.810	—	—	.10	.35
	1970	7.810	—	—	.10	.35
	1971	5.030	—	—	.10	.35
	1973	3.000	—	—	.10	.35
	1974	3.007	—	—	.10	.25
	1974	2,400	—	—	Proof	10.00
	1975	3.010	—	—	.10	.25
	1975	.010	—	—	Proof	1.00
	1976	3.005	—	—	.10	.25
	1976	5,130	—	—	Proof	1.50
	1977	2.007	—	—	.10	.25
	1977	7,030	—	—	Proof	1.00
	1978	2.010	—	—	.10	.25
	1978	.010	—	—	Proof	1.00
	1979	1.030	—	—	.10	.25
	1979	.010	—	—	Proof	1.00
	1980	1.030	—	—	.10	.25
	1980	.010	—	—	Proof	1.00
	1981	4.935	—	—	.10	.15
	1981	.010	—	—	Proof	1.00
	1982	6.655	—	—	.10	.15
	1982	.010	—	—	Proof	1.00
	1983	4.031	—	—	.10	.15
	1983	.011	—	—	Proof	1.00
	1984	3.995	—	—	.10	.15
	1984	.014	—	—	Proof	1.00
	1985	3.027	—	—	.10	.15
	1985	.012	—	—	Proof	1.00
	1986B	2.031	—	—	.10	.15
	1986B	.010	—	—	Proof	1.00
	1987B	1.000	—	—	.10	.15
	1987B	8,800	—	—	Proof	1.00
	1988B	—	—	—	.10	.15
	1988B	—	—	—	Proof	1.00

2 RAPPEN

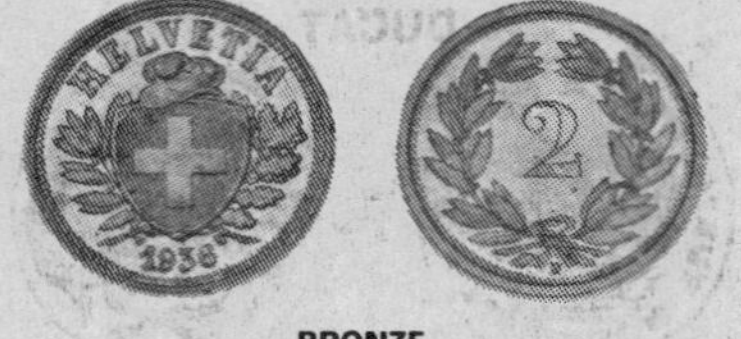

BRONZE

KM#	Date	Mintage	Fine	VF	XF	Unc
4	1850A	7.290	1.00	3.00	10.00	35.00
	1851A	3.720	1.00	3.00	10.00	35.00
	1866B	1.000	5.50	12.50	20.00	45.00
	1870B	.540	20.00	35.00	50.00	120.00
	1875B	.984	5.00	10.00	17.00	35.00
	1879B	.990	5.00	10.00	17.00	35.00
	1883B	1.000	3.00	4.00	8.50	20.00
	1886B	1.000	3.00	4.00	8.50	20.00
	1888B	.500	17.50	28.00	40.00	110.00
	1890B	1.000	1.50	3.75	8.00	20.00
	1893B	2.000	1.50	3.00	5.75	15.00
	1896B	20 pcs.	—	—	Rare	—
	1897B	.487	12.00	17.50	28.00	60.00
	1898B	.500	12.00	17.50	28.00	60.00
	1899B	1.000	3.00	4.00	8.00	20.00
	1900B	1.000	3.00	4.00	8.00	20.00
	1902B	.500	15.00	22.50	28.00	75.00
	1903B	.500	15.00	22.50	28.00	60.00
	1904B	.500	15.00	22.50	28.00	60.00

KM#	Date	Mintage	Fine	VF	XF	Unc
4	1906B	.500	15.00	22.50	28.00	60.00
	1907B	1.000	1.00	3.75	5.75	20.00
	1908B	1.000	1.00	3.50	5.50	17.00
	1909B	1.000	1.00	3.50	5.50	17.00
	1910B	.500	7.50	14.00	20.00	60.00
	1912B	1.000	.50	3.50	5.50	12.00
	1913B	1.000	.50	3.50	5.50	18.00
	1914B	1.000	.50	3.50	5.50	15.00
	1915B	1.000	.50	3.50	5.50	15.00
	1918B	1.000	.50	3.50	5.50	15.00
	1919B	2.000	.25	.60	1.50	6.00
	1920B	.500	15.00	22.50	28.00	70.00
	1925B	1.250	.25	.60	1.50	9.00
	1926B	.750	3.75	6.50	10.00	37.50
	1927B	.500	15.00	22.50	28.00	65.00
	1928B	.500	15.00	22.50	28.00	65.00
	1929B	.750	1.75	5.00	8.00	22.00
	1930B	1.000	.25	.60	1.50	10.00
	1931B	1.288	.25	.60	1.50	10.00
	1932B	1.500	.25	.60	1.50	7.50
	1933B	1.000	.25	.60	1.50	10.00
	1934B	.500	6.00	10.00	15.00	35.00
	1936B	.500	4.25	7.25	10.00	30.00
	1937B	1.200	.25	.50	.90	6.00
	1938B	1.369	.25	.50	.90	9.50
	1941B	3.448	.25	.50	.90	3.75

ZINC

4a	1942B	8.954	.25	.50	.90	6.00
	1943B	4.499	.25	.50	.90	8.00
	1944B	8.086	.25	.50	.90	6.00
	1945B	3.640	1.00	2.00	3.00	12.00
	1946B	1.393	4.00	9.00	15.00	35.00

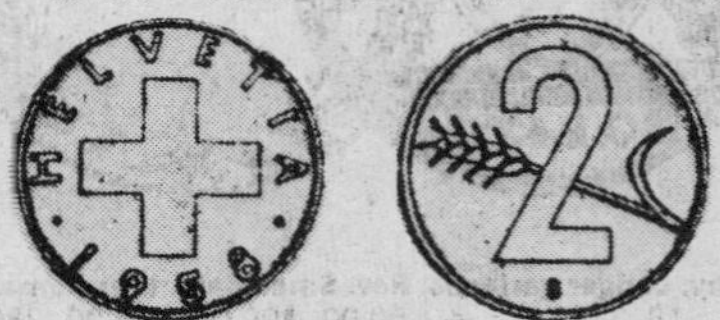

BRONZE

47	1948B	10.197	.10	.25	.60	3.00
	1951B	9.622	.10	.25	.60	3.00
	1952B	1.915	.10	.25	1.50	3.00
	1953B	2.006	.10	.25	1.25	3.00
	1954B	2.539	.10	.15	.60	2.50
	1955B	2.493	.10	.15	.60	2.50
	1957B	8.099	.10	.15	.60	1.75
	1958B	6.078	.10	.15	.60	1.75
	1963B	10.065	—	.10	.15	.60
	1966B	2.510	—	.10	.20	.60
	1967B	1.510	—	.10	.25	.60
	1968B	2.860	—	.10	.15	.45
	1969	6.200	—	.10	.15	.35
	1970	3.115	—	.10	.15	.30
	1974	3.540	—	.10	.15	.30
	1974	2,400	—	—	Proof	20.00

5 RAPPEN

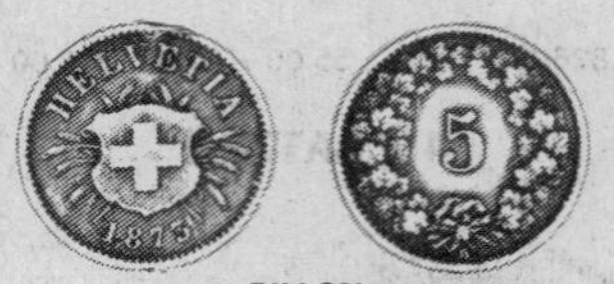

BILLON

5	1850BB	7.970	5.00	12.00	30 00	90.00
	1850AB	Inc. Ab.	40.00	70.00	425.00	950.00
	1850	Inc. Ab.	300.00	500.00	1250.	2100.
	1851BB	12.042	200.00	400.00	850.00	1750.
	1872B	1.213	16.00	22.50	35.00	90.00
	1873B	1.622	16.00	22.50	35.00	90.00
	1874B	1.700	16.00	22.50	35.00	90.00
	1876B	.989	22.50	40.00	55.00	120.00
	1877B	.978	22.50	40.00	55.00	120.00

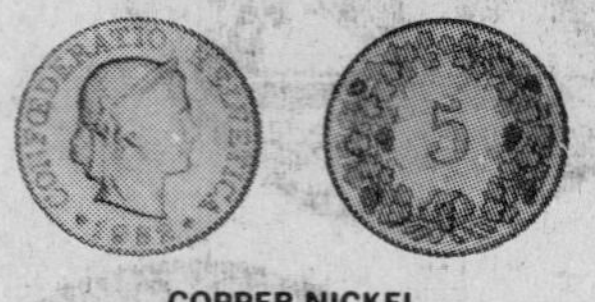

COPPER-NICKEL

26	1879B	1.000	10.00	25.00	55.00	140.000
	1880B	2.000	1.00	2.50	16.50	65.00
	1881B	2.000	1.00	2.50	16.50	60.00
	1882B	3.000	.75	2.00	15.00	45.00
	1883B	3.000	.75	2.00	15.00	45.00
	1884B	2.000	1.00	2.50	16.50	70.00
	1885B	3.000	.75	2.00	15.00	45.00
	1887B	.500	22.00	45.00	90.00	325.00
	1888B	1.500	1.00	2.50	16.50	55.00
	1889B	.500	22.00	45.00	90.00	320.00
	1890B	1.000	5.00	10.00	35.00	90.00
	1891B	1.000	5.00	10.00	35.00	100.00
	1892B	1.000	5.00	10.00	35.00	100.00
	1893B	2.000	.75	2.50	12.50	35.00
	1894B	2.000	.75	2.50	12.50	35.00
	1895B	2.000	.75	2.50	12.50	35.00
	1896B	16 pcs.	—	—	Rare	—
	1897B	.500	6.50	12.50	35.00	120.00
	1898B	2.500	.50	1.50	7.00	35.00
	1899B	1.500	.75	2.50	22.50	70.00
	1900B	2.000	.50	1.00	15.00	40.00
	1901B	3.000	.50	1.00	15.00	40.00
	1902B	1.000	6.50	15.00	45.00	120.00

SWITZERLAND 1589

KM#	Date	Mintage	Fine	VF	XF	Unc
26	1903B	2.000	.50	1.50	16.00	60.00
	1904B	1.000	6.50	15.00	45.00	120.00
	1905B	1.000	3.50	8.50	27.50	80.00
	1906B	3.000	.50	1.00	7.50	30.00
	1907B	5.000	.50	1.00	7.50	18.50
	1908B	3.000	.50	1.00	7.50	25.00
	1909B	2.000	.50	1.00	7.50	30.00
	1910B	1.000	1.50	3.50	10.00	60.00
	1911B	2.000	.50	1.00	3.00	18.00
	1912B	3.000	.50	1.00	3.00	18.00
	1913B	3.000	.50	1.00	3.00	18.00
	1914B	3.000	.50	1.00	3.00	45.00
	1915B	3.000	.50	1.00	3.00	70.00
	1917B	1.000	1.50	2.50	6.00	50.00
	1919B	6.000	.15	.50	3.00	18.00
	1920B	5.000	.15	.50	3.00	22.00
	1921B	3.000	.15	.50	3.00	20.00
	1922B	4.000	.15	.50	1.25	18.00
	1925B	3.000	.15	.50	1.25	20.00
	1926B	3.000	.15	.50	1.25	20.00
	1927B	2.000	.15	.50	1.50	25.00
	1928B	2.000	.15	.50	1.50	25.00
	1929B	2.000	.15	.30	.80	17.50
	1930B	3.000	.15	.30	.80	17.50
	1931B	5.037	.15	.30	.80	11.00
	1940B	1.416	.20	.35	2.50	40.00
	1942B	5.078	.15	.30	.90	18.00
	1943B	6.591	.15	.30	.90	18.00
	1944B	9.981	.15	.30	.90	18.00
	1945B	.985	.25	.50	4.00	45.00
	1946B	6.179	.10	.15	.60	7.25
	1947B	5.125	.10	.15	.60	9.50
	1948B	4.710	.10	.15	.60	5.00
	1949B	4.589	.10	.15	.60	5.00
	1950B	.920	.25	.50	1.75	5.00
	1951B	2.141	.10	.25	1.75	20.00
	1952B	4.690	—	.10	.30	3.50
	1953B	9.131	—	.10	.30	3.00
	1954B	8.038	—	.10	.30	3.00
	1955B	19.943	—	.10	.20	1.75
	1957B	10.147	—	.10	.20	1.75
	1958B	10.217	—	.10	.20	1.75
	1959B	11.086	—	.10	.20	1.75
	1962B	23.840	—	.10	.15	.60
	1963B	29.730	—	.10	.15	.50
	1964B	17.080	—	.10	.15	.50
	1965B	1.430	.10	.30	.90	1.25
	1966B	10.010	—	.10	.15	.35
	1967B	13.010	—	.10	.25	.90
	1968B	10.020	—	.10	.15	.35
	1969B	32.990	—	—	.10	.25
	1970	34.800	—	—	.10	.25
	1971	40.020	—	—	.10	.25
	1974	30.002	—	—	.10	.25
	1974	2,400	—	—	Proof	15.00
	1975	34.005	—	—	.10	.25
	1975	.010	—	—	Proof	1.25
	1976	12.005	—	—	.10	.25
	1976	5,130	—	—	Proof	2.25
	1977	14.012	—	—	.10	.20
	1977	7,030	—	—	Proof	1.25
	1978	16.415	—	—	.10	.20
	1978	.010	—	—	Proof	1.00
	1979	27.010	—	—	.10	.20
	1979	.010	—	—	Proof	1.00
	1980	15.500	—	—	.10	.20
	1980	.010	—	—	Proof	1.00

BRASS

KM#	Date	Mintage	Fine	VF	XF	Unc
26a	1918B	6.000	10.00	15.00	25.00	35.00

NICKEL

KM#	Date	Mintage	Fine	VF	XF	Unc
26b	1932B	6.000	.15	.25	.60	5.50
	1933B	3.000	.15	.25	.60	7.25
	1934B	4.000	.15	.25	.60	5.50
	1936B	1.000	.15	.25	1.50	8.50
	1937B	2.000	.15	.25	.60	9.50
	1938B	1.000	.15	.25	1.50	7.25
	1939B	10.048	.15	.25	.60	5.50
	1940B	1.410	.15	.25	1.25	30.00
	1941B	3.030	1.25	2.00	6.00	20.00

ALUMINUM-BRASS

KM#	Date	Mintage	Fine	VF	XF	Unc
26c	1981	79.020	—	—	.10	.20
	1981	.010	—	—	Proof	1.00
	1982	75.340	—	—	.10	.20
	1982	.010	—	—	Proof	1.00
	1983	92.746	—	—	.10	.20
	1983	.011	—	—	Proof	1.00
	1984	69.960	—	—	.10	.20
	1984	.014	—	—	Proof	1.00
	1985	60.032	—	—	.10	.20
	1985	.012	—	—	Proof	1.00
	1986B	55.041	—	—	.10	.20
	1986B	.010	—	—	Proof	1.00
	1987B	39.800	—	—	.10	.20
	1987B	8,800	—	—	Proof	1.00
	1988B	—	—	—	.10	.20
	1988B	—	—	—	Proof	1.00

10 RAPPEN

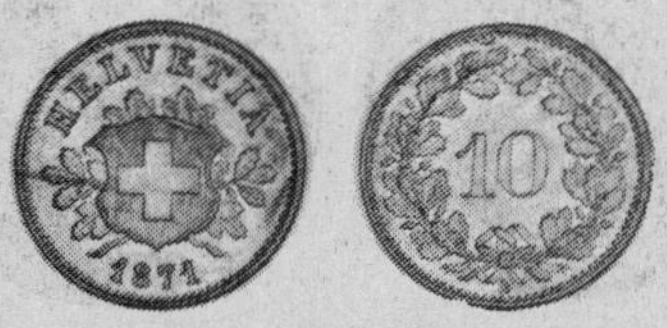

BILLON

KM#	Date	Mintage	Fine	VF	XF	Unc
6	1850BB	8.780	5.00	15.00	40.00	120.00
6	1851BB	4.530	22.50	50.00	120.00	275.00
	1871B	.844	22.50	35.00	65.00	120.00
	1873B	1.398	15.00	25.00	35.00	80.00
	1875B	.174	275.00	520.00	650.00	1200.
	1876B	1.962	15.00	25.00	35.00	70.00

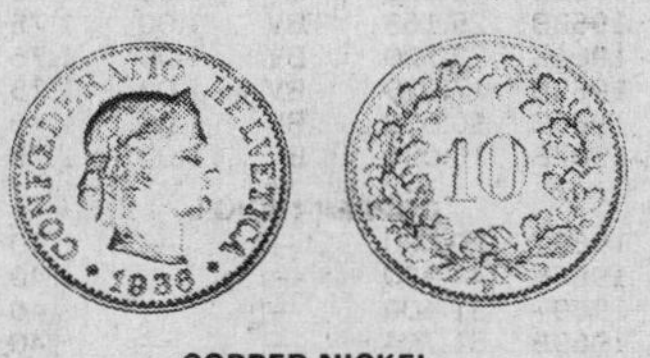

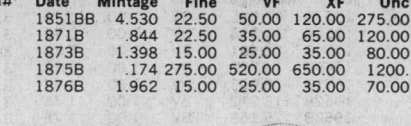

COPPER-NICKEL

KM#	Date	Mintage	Fine	VF	XF	Unc
27	1879B	1.000	6.00	15.00	50.00	130.00
	1880B	2.000	.75	2.00	15.00	70.00
	1881B	3.000	.75	2.00	15.00	60.00
	1882B	3.000	.75	2.00	15.00	60.00
	1883B	2.000	.75	2.00	15.00	65.00
	1884B	3.000	.75	2.00	15.00	50.00
	1885B	3.000	.75	2.00	15.00	50.00
	1894B	1.000	1.00	3.00	18.00	70.00
	1895B	2.000	.75	2.00	15.00	50.00
	1896B	16 pcs.	—	—	Rare	—
	1897B	.500	2.00	5.00	35.00	90.00
	1898B	1.000	2.50	5.50	40.00	120.00
	1899B	.500	2.50	5.50	40.00	120.00
	1900B	1.500	1.00	2.50	15.00	55.00
	1901B	1.000	1.00	2.50	15.00	55.00
	1902B	1.000	1.00	2.50	15.00	60.00
	1903B	1.000	1.00	2.50	15.00	60.00
	1904B	1.000	1.00	2.50	15.00	60.00
	1906B	1.000	1.00	2.50	15.00	50.00
	1907B	2.000	.25	.50	7.00	30.00
	1908B	2.000	.25	.50	7.00	30.00
	1909B	2.000	.25	.50	7.00	30.00
	1911B	1.000	1.00	2.50	10.00	45.00
	1912B	1.500	.25	.50	7.00	40.00
	1913B	2.000	.25	.50	7.00	40.00
	1914B	2.000	.25	.50	7.00	55.00
	1915B	1.200	1.00	3.00	20.00	100.00
	1919B	3.000	.15	.25	1.25	18.50
	1920B	3.500	.15	.25	1.25	18.50
	1921B	3.000	.15	.25	1.25	18.50
	1922B	2.000	.20	.50	2.50	30.00
	1924B	2.000	.20	.50	2.50	25.00
	1925B	3.000	.15	.25	1.25	18.50
	1926B	3.000	.15	.25	1.25	18.50
	1927B	2.000	.15	.25	1.25	18.50
	1928B	2.000	.15	.25	1.25	18.50
	1929B	2.000	.15	.25	1.25	18.50
	1930B	2.000	.20	.50	2.50	35.00
	1931B	2.244	.20	.50	2.50	35.00
	1940B	2.000	.20	.50	2.50	35.00
	1942B	2.110	.20	.50	2.50	35.00
	1943B	3.176	.20	.50	2.50	30.00
	1944B	6.133	.10	.20	.75	8.50
	1945B	.993	.20	.50	3.00	50.00
	1946B	4.010	.10	.20	.75	30.00
	1947B	3.152	.10	.20	.75	30.00
	1948B	1.000	.20	.50	1.25	35.00
	1949B	2.269	.15	.25	.75	30.00
	1950B	3.200	.10	.15	.30	3.50
	1951B	3.430	.10	.15	.30	6.00
	1952B	4.452	.10	.15	.30	6.00
	1953B	6.149	.10	.15	.30	6.00
	1954B	3.200	.10	.15	.30	11.00
	1955B	11.795	.10	.15	.30	3.50
	1957B	10.092	.10	.15	.30	3.50
	1958B	10.040	.10	.15	.30	3.50
	1959B	13.053	.10	.15	.30	3.50
	1960B	4.040	.10	.15	.30	3.50
	1961B	7.949	—	.10	.25	1.25
	1962B	34.965	—	.10	.25	.90
	1964B	16.340	—	.10	.25	.90
	1965B	14.190	—	.10	.25	.90
	1966B	4.025	—	.10	.25	.90
	1967B	10.000	—	.10	.25	.90
	1968B	14.065	—	.10	.15	.35
	1969B	28.855	—	.10	.15	.35
	1970	40.020	—	.10	.15	.35
	1972	7.877	—	.10	.15	.35
	1973	30.350	—	.10	.15	.35
	1974	30.007	—	—	.10	.30
	1974	2,400	—	—	Proof	15.00
	1975	25.003	—	—	.10	.30
	1975	.010	—	—	Proof	1.75
	1976	19.013	—	—	.10	.30
	1976	5,130	—	—	Proof	3.00
	1977	10.007	—	—	.10	.30
	1977	7,030	—	—	Proof	1.75
	1978	19.958	—	—	.10	.30
	1978	.010	—	—	Proof	.010
	1979	18.010	—	—	.10	.30
	1979	.010	—	—	Proof	.010
	1980	18.005	—	—	.10	.30
	1980	.010	—	—	Proof	1.50
	1981	30.140	—	—	.10	.30
	1981	.010	—	—	Proof	1.50
	1982	50.110	—	—	.10	.30
	1982	.010	—	—	Proof	1.50
	1983	40.033	—	—	.10	.30
	1983	.011	—	—	Proof	1.50
	1984	22.022	—	—	.10	.30
	1984	.014	—	—	Proof	1.50
	1985	3.032	—	—	.10	.30
	1985	.012	—	—	Proof	1.50
	1986B	2.324	—	—	.10	.30
	1986B	.010	—	—	Proof	1.50
27	1987B	5.000	—	—	.10	.30
	1987B	8,800	—	—	Proof	1.50
	1988B	—	—	—	.10	.30
	1988B	—	—	—	Proof	1.50

BRASS

KM#	Date	Mintage	Fine	VF	XF	Unc
27a	1918B	6.000	15.00	17.50	30.00	60.00
	1919B	3.000	50.00	70.00	85.00	150.00

NICKEL

KM#	Date	Mintage	Fine	VF	XF	Unc
27b	1932B	3.500	.10	.25	.75	11.50
	1933B	2.000	.10	.25	.75	12.00
	1934B	3.000	.10	.25	.75	11.50
	1936B	1.500	.15	.30	.90	12.00
	1937B	1.000	.15	.30	.90	11.50
	1938B	1.000	.15	.30	.90	11.50
	1939B	10.022	.15	.30	.90	11.50

20 RAPPEN

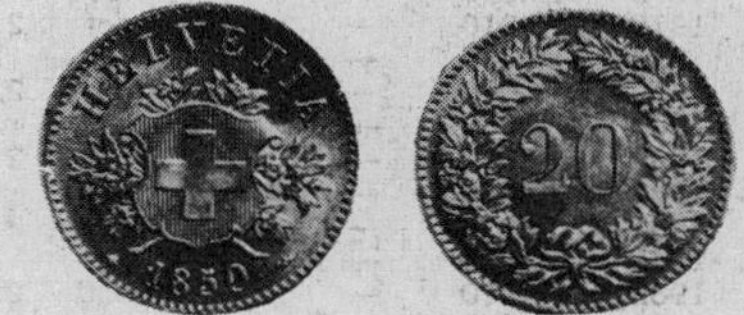

BILLON

KM#	Date	Mintage	Fine	VF	XF	Unc
7	1850BB	5.390	5.00	15.00	37.50	120.00
	1851BB	6.160	50.00	150.00	375.00	850.00
	1858B	1.548	15.00	25.00	50.00	150.00
	1859B	2.776	7.50	16.00	30.00	80.00

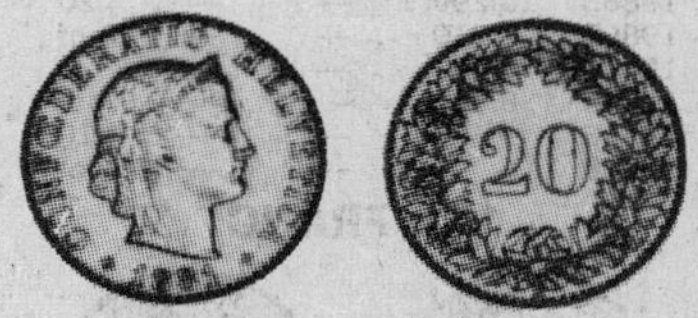

NICKEL

KM#	Date	Mintage	Fine	VF	XF	Unc
29	1881B	1.000	.75	1.50	16.50	60.00
	1883B	2.500	.50	1.00	10.00	40.00
	1884B	4.000	.50	1.00	10.00	30.00
	1885B	3.000	.50	1.00	10.00	35.00
	1887B	.500	4.00	6.00	40.00	100.00
	1891B	1.000	.50	1.00	16.00	45.00
	1893B	1.000	.50	1.00	16.00	45.00
	1894B	1.000	.50	1.00	16.00	45.00
	1896B	1.000	.50	1.00	16.00	45.00
	1897B	.500	1.50	3.00	18.00	75.00
	1898B	.500	2.50	5.00	22.00	100.00
	1899B	.500	2.50	5.00	22.00	100.00
	1900B	1.000	.50	1.00	10.00	45.00
	1901B	1.000	.50	1.00	10.00	45.00
	1902B	1.000	.50	1.00	10.00	45.00
	1903B	1.000	.50	1.00	10.00	45.00
	1906B	1.000	.50	1.00	10.00	45.00
	1907B	1.000	.50	1.00	7.50	35.00
	1908B	1.500	.25	.50	7.00	32.00
	1909B	2.000	.25	.50	7.00	30.00
	1911B	1.000	.25	.50	7.00	35.00
	1912B	2.000	.25	.50	7.00	30.00
	1913B	1.500	.25	.50	7.00	30.00
	1919B	1.500	.25	.50	7.00	30.00
	1920B	3.100	.25	.50	7.00	15.00
	1921B	2.500	.25	.50	7.00	15.00
	1924B	1.100	.25	.50	7.00	20.00
	1925B	1.500	.25	.50	7.00	15.00
	1926B	1.500	.25	.50	7.00	15.00
	1927B	.500	1.00	2.50	20.00	100.00
	1929B	2.000	.20	.30	.90	12.50
	1930B	2.000	.20	.30	.90	12.50
	1931B	2.250	.20	.30	.90	12.00
	1932B	2.000	.20	.30	.90	12.00
	1933B	1.500	.20	.30	.90	12.00
	1934B	2.000	.20	.30	.90	12.00
	1936B	1.000	.20	.30	.90	15.00
	1938B	2.805	.20	.30	.90	12.00

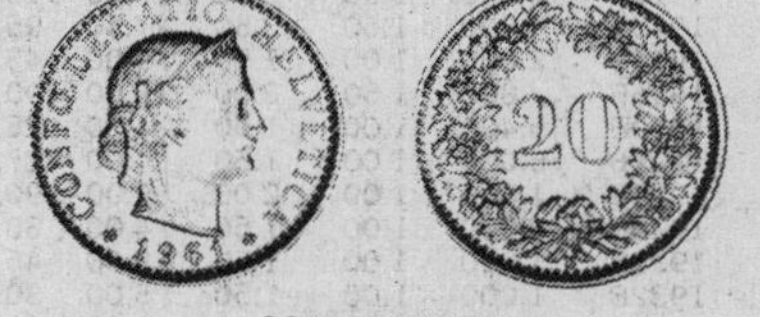

COPPER-NICKEL

KM#	Date	Mintage	Fine	VF	XF	Unc
29a	1939B	8.100	—	.20	.60	35.00
	1943B	10.173	—	.20	.40	25.00
	1944B	7.139	—	.20	.40	10.00
	1945B	1.992	.20	.50	1.75	38.00
	1947B	5.131	—	.20	.40	12.00
	1950B	5.970	—	.20	.40	5.00
	1951B	3.640	—	.20	.40	8.00
	1952B	3.070	—	.20	.40	8.00
	1953B	6.958	—	.20	.40	5.00
	1954B	1.504	.20	.30	.90	17.00
	1955B	9.104	—	.20	.40	6.00
	1956B	5.111	—	.20	.40	7.00
	1957B	2.535	—	.20	.40	15.00
	1958B	5.037	—	.20	.40	6.00
	1959B	10.136	—	.20	.35	3.00
	1960B	15.467	—	.20	.35	3.00
	1961B	8.234	—	.20	.35	3.00

SWITZERLAND 1590

KM#	Date	Mintage	Fine	VF	XF	Unc
29a	1962B	30.145	—	.20	.35	2.00
	1963B	9.020	—	.20	.35	2.00
	1964B	14.370	—	—	.20	1.50
	1965B	15.005	—	—	.20	1.50
	1966B	10.785	—	—	.20	.60
	1967B	8.995	—	—	.20	.60
	1968B	10.540	—	—	.20	.50
	1969B	39.875	—	—	.20	.50
	1970	45.605	—	—	.20	.50
	1971	25.160	—	—	.20	.50
	1974	30.025	—	—	.20	.40
	1974	2,400	—	—	Proof	25.00
	1975	50.060	—	—	.20	.40
	1975	.010	—	—	Proof	2.25
	1976	23.150	—	—	.20	.40
	1976	5,130	—	—	Proof	3.75
	1977	14.012	—	—	.20	.40
	1977	7,030	—	—	Proof	2.25
	1978	14.815	—	—	.20	.40
	1978	.010	—	—	Proof	2.00
	1979	18.380	—	—	.20	.40
	1979	.010	—	—	Proof	2.00
	1980	24.560	—	—	.20	.40
	1980	.010	—	—	Proof	2.00
	1981	22.020	—	—	.20	.40
	1981	.010	—	—	Proof	2.00
	1982	25.035	—	—	.20	.40
	1982	.010	—	—	Proof	2.00
	1983	10.026	—	—	.20	.40
	1983	.011	—	—	Proof	2.00
	1984	22.055	—	—	.20	.40
	1984	.014	—	—	Proof	2.00
	1985	40.027	—	—	.20	.40
	1985	.012	—	—	Proof	2.00
	1986B	10.299	—	—	.20	.40
	1986B	.010	—	—	Proof	2.00
	1987B	10.000	—	—	.20	.40
	1987B	8,800	—	—	Proof	2.00
	1988B	—	—	—	.20	.40
	1988B	—	—	—	Proof	2.00

1/2 FRANC

2.5000 g, .900 SILVER, .0723 oz ASW

8	1850A	4.500	60.00	120.00	225.00	575.00
	1851A	Inc. Ab.	60.00	120.00	225.00	550.00

2.5000 g, .835 SILVER, .0671 oz ASW

23	1875B	1.000	22.00	65.00	200.00	575.00
	1877B	1.000	25.00	100.00	275.00	700.00
	1878B	1.000	25.00	100.00	300.00	725.00
	1879B	1.000	15.00	35.00	100.00	400.00
	1881B	1.000	8.00	20.00	80.00	350.00
	1882B	1.000	8.00	22.50	100.00	400.00
	1894A	.800	20.00	75.00	150.00	350.00
	1896B	28 pcs.	—	—	Rare	—
	1898B	1.600	2.00	5.00	25.00	100.00
	1899B	.400	5.00	10.00	95.00	350.00
	1900B	.400	5.00	10.00	95.00	350.00
	1901B	.200	22.00	80.00	300.00	900.00
	1903B	.800	2.00	5.00	30.00	120.00
	1904B	.400	4.00	15.00	170.00	900.00
	1905B	.600	2.00	5.00	55.00	190.00
	1906B	1.000	1.00	3.00	50.00	210.00
	1907B	1.200	1.00	2.50	50.00	190.00
	1908B	.800	1.50	2.50	30.00	125.00
	1909B	1.000	1.00	2.00	27.50	110.00
	1910B	1.000	1.00	2.00	27.50	110.00
	1913B	.800	1.50	2.50	27.50	95.00
	1914B	2.000	1.00	1.50	9.00	45.00
	1916B	.800	1.50	2.50	18.00	100.00
	1920B	5.400	1.00	1.50	4.00	25.00
	1921B	6.000	1.00	1.50	4.00	27.50
	1928B	1.000	1.00	2.00	9.00	90.00
	1929B	2.000	1.00	1.50	4.00	30.00
	1931B	1.000	1.00	1.50	5.00	45.00
	1932B	1.000	1.00	1.50	5.00	30.00
	1934B	2.000	1.00	2.00	9.00	25.00
	1936B	.400	1.50	3.00	6.00	40.00
	1937B	1.000	1.00	1.50	3.50	18.00
	1939B	1.001	1.00	1.50	3.50	22.00
	1940B	2.002	1.00	1.50	3.50	18.00
	1941B	.200	1.50	2.50	3.50	25.00
	1942B	2.969	1.00	1.50	3.00	10.00
	1943B	4.572	1.00	1.50	3.00	10.00
	1944B	7.456	1.00	1.50	3.00	10.00
	1945B	4.928	1.00	1.50	2.50	6.00
	1946B	6.817	1.00	1.50	2.50	6.00
	1948B	6.113	1.00	1.50	2.50	6.00
	1950B	7.148	1.00	1.50	2.50	6.00
	1951B	8.530	BV	1.00	1.75	5.00
	1952B	14.023	BV	1.00	1.75	3.75
	1953B	3.567	BV	1.00	1.75	6.00
	1955B	1.320	1.00	1.50	2.00	12.00
	1956B	4.250	BV	1.00	1.75	5.00

KM#	Date	Mintage	Fine	VF	XF	Unc
23	1957B	12.085	BV	1.00	1.75	3.50
	1958B	11.558	BV	1.00	1.75	3.50
	1959B	12.581	BV	1.00	1.75	3.50
	1960B	14.528	BV	1.00	1.75	3.50
	1961B	6.906	BV	1.00	1.75	3.50
	1962B	18.272	BV	1.00	1.75	3.50
	1963B	25.168	BV	1.00	1.75	3.50
	1964B	22.720	BV	1.00	1.75	3.50
	1965B	17.920	BV	1.00	1.75	3.50
	1966B	10.008	BV	1.00	1.75	3.50
	1967B	16.096	BV	1.00	1.75	3.50

COPPER-NICKEL

23a.1	1968	20.000	—	—	.40	.60
	1968B	44.920	—	—	.40	.60
	1969	31.400	—	—	.40	.60
	1969B	51.704	—	—	.40	.60
	1970	52.620	—	—	.40	.60
	1971	34.472	—	—	.40	.60
	1972	9.996	—	—	.40	.60
	1973	5.000	—	—	.40	.60
	1974	45.006	—	—	.40	.60
	1974	2,400	—	—	Proof	35.00
	1975	27.234	—	—	.40	.60
	1975	.010	—	—	Proof	3.25
	1976	10.009	—	—	.40	.60
	1976	5,130	—	—	Proof	5.00
	1977	19.011	—	—	.40	.60
	1977	7,030	—	—	Proof	3.25
	1978	20.818	—	—	.40	.60
	1978	.010	—	—	Proof	2.50
	1979	27.010	—	—	.40	.60
	1979	.010	—	—	Proof	2.50
	1980	31.064	—	—	.40	.60
	1980	.010	—	—	Proof	2.50
	1981	30.155	—	—	.40	.60
	1981	.010	—	—	Proof	2.50

Obv. and rev: Medallic alignment. Obv: 22 stars.

23a.2	1982	30.151	—	—	.40	.60
	1982	.010	—	—	Proof	8.50

Obv: 23 stars.

23a.3	1983	22.020	—	—	.40	.60
	1983	.011	—	—	Proof	2.50
	1984	22.036	—	—	.40	.60
	1984	.014	—	—	Proof	2.50
	1985	6.026	—	—	.40	.60
	1985	.012	—	—	Proof	2.50
	1986B	5.031	—	—	.40	.60
	1986B	.010	—	—	Proof	2.50
	1987B	10.000	—	—	.40	.60
	1987B	8,800	—	—	Proof	2.50
	1988B	—	—	—	.40	.60
	1988B	—	—	—	Proof	2.50

FRANC

5.0000 g, .900 SILVER, .1447 oz ASW

9	1850A	5.750	65.00	120.00	250.00	600.00
	1851A	Inc. Ab.	65.00	125.00	270.00	625.00
	1857B	526 pcs.	—	—	Rare	—

5.0000 g, .800 SILVER, .1286 oz ASW

9a	1860B	.515	120.00	250.00	425.00	2100.
	1861B	3.002	30.00	60.00	120.00	425.00

5.0000 g, .835 SILVER, .1342 oz ASW

24	1875B	1.036	30.00	70.00	270.00	900.00
	1876B	2.500	5.00	15.00	130.00	450.00
	1877B	2.520	5.00	15.00	150.00	550.00
	1880B	.944	10.00	35.00	325.00	1150.
	1886B	1.000	4.00	12.50	110.00	350.00
	1887B	1.000	4.00	12.50	110.00	325.00
	1894A	1.200	4.00	12.50	110.00	350.00
	1896B	28 pcs.	—	—	Rare	—
	1898B	.400	4.00	12.50	95.00	350.00
	1899B	.400	4.00	12.50	110.00	350.00
	1900B	.400	4.00	12.50	130.00	550.00
	1901B	.400	5.00	25.00	250.00	750.00
	1903B	1.000	3.00	6.00	50.00	250.00
	1904B	.400	8.00	25.00	300.00	1200.
	1905B	.700	3.00	6.00	50.00	300.00
	1906B	.700	3.00	6.00	70.00	500.00
	1907B	.800	3.00	6.00	60.00	450.00
	1908B	1.200	3.00	6.00	35.00	250.00
	1909B	.900	3.00	6.00	35.00	210.00
	1910B	1.000	3.00	6.00	25.00	180.00
	1911B	1.200	3.00	5.00	25.00	150.00
	1912B	1.200	3.00	5.00	25.00	150.00
	1913B	1.200	3.00	5.00	25.00	120.00
	1914B	4.200	3.00	5.00	25.00	100.00

KM#	Date	Mintage	Fine	VF	XF	Unc
24	1916B	1.000	3.00	5.00	25.00	125.00
	1920B	3.300	3.00	5.00	6.00	35.00
	1920B	—	—	—	Proof	150.00
	1921B	3.800	3.00	5.00	6.00	35.00
	1928B	1.500	3.00	5.00	6.00	27.50
	1931B	1.000	3.00	5.00	6.00	40.00
	1932B	.500	3.00	5.00	25.00	100.00
	1934B	.500	3.00	5.00	25.00	90.00
	1936B	.500	3.00	5.00	22.50	70.00
	1937B	1.000	1.50	2.50	5.00	35.00
	1939B	2.106	1.50	2.50	5.00	18.00
	1940B	2.003	1.50	2.50	5.00	15.00
	1943B	3.526	1.50	2.00	3.75	11.00
	1943B	—	—	—	Proof	150.00
	1944B	6.225	1.50	2.00	3.75	11.00
	1945B	7.794	1.50	2.00	3.00	9.00
	1946B	2.539	1.50	2.00	3.00	12.00
	1947B	.624	2.00	2.50	3.00	15.00
	1952B	2.853	1.50	2.00	3.00	7.00
	1953B	.786	1.50	2.50	4.50	30.00
	1955B	.194	2.50	5.00	11.00	30.00
	1956B	2.500	1.50	2.00	3.00	8.00
	1957B	6.420	1.50	2.00	3.00	6.00
	1958B	3.580	1.50	2.00	3.00	7.00
	1959B	1.859	1.50	2.00	3.00	7.00
	1960B	3.523	BV	2.00	3.00	7.00
	1961B	6.549	BV	2.00	3.00	7.00
	1962B	6.220	BV	2.00	3.00	7.00
	1963B	13.476	BV	2.00	3.00	5.00
	1964B	12.560	BV	2.00	3.00	5.00
	1965B	5.032	BV	2.00	3.00	7.00
	1966B	3.032	BV	2.00	3.00	7.00
	1967B	2.088	BV	2.00	3.00	8.00

COPPER-NICKEL

24a.1	1968	15.000	—	—	.85	1.25
	1968B	40.864	—	—	.85	1.25
	1969B	37.598	—	—	.85	1.25
	1970	24.240	—	—	.85	1.25
	1971	11.496	—	—	.85	1.25
	1973	5.000	—	—	.85	1.75
	1974	15.012	—	—	.85	1.25
	1974	2,400	—	—	Proof	50.00
	1975	13.012	—	—	.85	1.25
	1975	.010	—	—	Proof	4.50
	1976	5.009	—	—	.85	1.25
	1976	5,130	—	—	Proof	7.50
	1977	6.019	—	—	.85	1.25
	1977	7,030	—	—	Proof	4.50
	1978	13.548	—	—	.85	1.25
	1978	.010	—	—	Proof	3.50
	1979	10.800	—	—	.85	1.25
	1979	.010	—	—	Proof	3.50
	1980	11.002	—	—	.85	1.25
	1980	.010	—	—	Proof	4.00
	1981	18.013	—	—	.85	1.25
	1981	.010	—	—	Proof	4.00

Obv. and rev: Medallic alignment. Obv: 22 stars.

24a.2	1982	15.039	—	—	.80	1.00
	1982	.010	—	—	Proof	12.00

Obv: 23 stars.

24a.3	1983	7.018	—	—	.80	1.00
	1983	.011	—	—	Proof	4.00
	1984	3.028	—	—	.80	1.00
	1984	.014	—	—	Proof	4.00
	1985	20.042	—	—	.80	1.00
	1985	.012	—	—	Proof	4.00
	1986B	17.997	—	—	.80	1.00
	1986B	.010	—	—	Proof	4.00
	1987B	17.000	—	—	.80	1.00
	1987B	8,800	—	—	Proof	4.00
	1988B	—	—	—	.80	1.00
	1988B	—	—	—	Proof	4.00

2 FRANCS

10.0000 g, .900 SILVER, .2894 oz ASW

10	1850A	2.500	175.00	350.00	550.00	1200.
	1857B	622 pcs.	3000.	5500.	9000.	14,500.

10.0000 g, .800 SILVER, .2572 oz ASW

10a	1860B	2.001	50.00	100.00	240.00	900.00
	1862B	1.000	60.00	120.00	270.00	1100.
	1863B	.500	200.00	300.00	750.00	2400.

10.0000 g, .835 SILVER, .2685 oz ASW

21	1874B	1.000	12.50	30.00	275.00	1100.

SWITZERLAND 1591

KM#	Date	Mintage	Fine	VF	XF	Unc
21	1875B	.982	15.00	35.00	325.00	1300.
	1878B	1.500	10.00	20.00	200.00	725.00
	1879B	.518	20.00	60.00	550.00	2700.
	1886B	1.000	5.00	12.50	140.00	475.00
	1894A	.700	6.00	15.00	180.00	725.00
	1896B	20 pcs.				Rare
	1901B	.050	160.00	300.00	1500.	6000.
	1903B	.300	4.00	10.00	140.00	575.00
	1904B	.200	10.00	30.00	375.00	1200.
	1905B	.300	4.00	10.00	135.00	600.00
	1906B	.400	4.00	10.00	145.00	725.00
	1907B	.300	4.00	10.00	175.00	850.00
	1908B	.200	10.00	30.00	375.00	1200.
	1909B	.300	4.00	8.00	110.00	375.00
	1910B	.250	7.50	20.00	210.00	900.00
	1911B	.400	4.00	7.00	65.00	275.00
	1912B	.400	4.00	7.00	65.00	275.00
	1913B	.300	4.00	7.00	65.00	275.00
	1914B	1.000	4.00	6.00	25.00	145.00
	1916B	.250	6.00	12.00	120.00	600.00
	1920B	2.300	4.00	5.00	7.00	40.00
	1920B	—	—	—	Proof	225.00
	1921B	2.000	4.00	5.00	7.00	40.00
	1922B	.400	4.00	7.00	45.00	275.00
	1928B	.750	4.00	5.00	8.00	55.00
	1931B	.500	4.00	5.00	10.00	65.00
	1932B	.250	4.00	8.00	40.00	275.00
	1936B	.250	4.00	7.00	35.00	165.00
	1937B	.250	4.00	6.00	18.00	90.00
	1939B	1.455	2.50	3.50	5.50	15.00
	1940B	2.502	2.50	3.50	5.50	15.00
	1940B	—	—	—	Proof	175.00
	1941B	1.192	2.50	3.50	5.50	18.00
	1943B	2.089	2.50	3.50	5.50	18.00
	1943B	—	—	—	Proof	175.00
	1944B	6.276	2.50	3.50	5.50	15.00
	1944B	—	—	—	Proof	175.00
	1945B	1.134	2.50	3.50	6.00	30.00
	1946B	1.629	2.50	3.50	6.00	20.00
	1947B	.500	3.00	4.00	6.00	35.00
	1948B	.920	3.00	4.00	6.00	18.00
	1953B	.438	3.00	4.00	6.00	35.00
	1955B	1.032	2.50	3.50	5.50	20.00
	1957B	2.298	2.50	3.50	5.00	15.00
	1958B	.650	3.00	4.00	5.00	15.00
	1958B	—	—	—	Proof	175.00
	1959B	2.905	BV	2.50	5.00	17.00
	1960B	1.980	BV	2.50	5.00	12.00
	1961B	4.653	BV	2.50	5.00	10.00
	1963B	8.030	BV	2.50	5.00	10.00
	1964B	4.558	BV	2.50	5.00	10.00
	1965B	8.526	BV	2.50	5.00	10.00
	1967B	4.132	BV	2.50	5.00	10.00

COPPER-NICKEL

KM#	Date	Mintage	Fine	VF	XF	Unc
21a.1	1968	10.00	—	—	1.60	3.50
	1968	31.588	—	—	1.60	2.75
	1969B	17.296	—	—	1.60	3.00
	1970	10.350	—	—	1.60	2.75
	1972	5.003	—	—	1.60	2.75
	1973	5.996	—	—	1.60	2.75
	1974	15.009	—	—	1.60	2.25
	1974	2.400	—	—	Proof	70.00
	1975	7.061	—	—	1.60	2.25
	1975	.010	—	—	Proof	6.00
	1976	5.011	—	—	1.60	2.25
	1976	5.130	—	—	Proof	11.00
	1977	2.010	—	—	1.60	2.00
	1977	7.030	—	—	Proof	6.00
	1978	12.812	—	—	1.60	2.00
	1978	.010	—	—	Proof	5.00
	1979	10.990	—	—	1.60	2.00
	1979	.010	—	—	Proof	5.00
	1980	10.001	—	—	1.60	2.00
	1980	.010	—	—	Proof	5.50
	1981	13.852	—	—	1.60	2.00
	1981	.010	—	—	Proof	5.50

Obv. and rev: Medallic alignment. Obv: 22 stars.

21a.2	1982	5.912	—	—	1.60	2.00
	1982	.010	—	—	Proof	14.00

Obv: 23 stars.

21a.3	1983	3.023	—	—	1.60	2.00
	1983	.011	—	—	Proof	5.50
	1984	2.029	—	—	1.60	2.00
	1984	.014	—	—	Proof	5.50
	1985	3.022	—	—	1.60	2.00
	1985	.012	—	—	Proof	5.50
	1986B	3.032	—	—	1.60	2.00
	1986B	.010	—	—	Proof	5.50
	1987B	8.000	—	—	1.60	2.00
	1987B	8.800	—	—	Proof	5.50
	1988B	—	—	—	1.60	2.00
	1988B	—	—	—	Proof	5.50

5 FRANCS

25.0000 g, .900 SILVER, .7234 oz ASW

KM#	Date	Mintage	Fine	VF	XF	Unc
11	1850A	.140	175.00	250.00	425.00	1200.
	1851A	.360	140.00	220.00	350.00	1100.
	1873B	.030	600.00	950.00	1550.	3600.
	1874B	1.400	120.00	180.00	270.00	725.00
	1874B	.196	130.00	190.00	325.00	900.00

NOTE: The dot after the B is for Brussels. For coins dated 1855 see Shooting Talers.

34	1888B	.025	400.00	600.00	1350.	3250.
	1889B	.225	120.00	200.00	420.00	1250.
	1890B	.305	120.00	200.00	400.00	1200.
	1891B	.150	125.00	200.00	420.00	1250.
	1892B	.190	120.00	200.00	400.00	1200.
	1894B	.034	450.00	1200.	2000.	5000.
	1895B	.046	375.00	650.00	1500.	3600.
	1896B	2.000	—	—	Rare	42,000.
	1900B	.033	425.00	725.00	1200.	2800.
	1904B	.040	360.00	600.00	1100.	2800.
	1907B	.277	120.00	190.00	300.00	900.00
	1908B	.200	130.00	200.00	350.00	1100.
	1909B	.120	145.00	250.00	390.00	1100.
	1912B	.011	1800.	2750.	4000.	7000.
	1916B	.022	650.00	1000.	1500.	3250.

Obv: Similar to KM#38.

37	1922B	2.400	70.00	100.00	175.00	425.00
	1923B	11.300	50.00	70.00	120.00	250.00
	1923B	—	—	—	Proof	900.00

38	1924B	.182	200.00	400.00	625.00	1450.
	1925B	2.830	60.00	110.00	170.00	375.00
	1926B	2.000	60.00	110.00	190.00	420.00
	1928B	.024	2750.	6000.	8500.	12,500.

15.0000 g, .835 SILVER, .4027 oz ASW

NOTE: The several varieties of number KM#40, the 1931 and 1967 5 Francs, are distinguished by the relation of the edge lettering to the head of William Tell and in the amount of rotation of the reverse in relation to the obverse. Beginning above the head the normal sequence is:

a) **PROVIDEBIT ********** *** DOMINUS**

A fairly common variety shows the lettering:
b) ********** *** **DOMINUS PROVIDEBIT**

A somewhat rarer variety shows:
c) ********** **PROVIDEBIT *** DOMINUS**

The reverse of the regular issue is upset 180 degrees. There are varieties with:

d) The reverse rotated about 15 degrees to the left of the normal upset position.

e) The reverse rotated about 15 degrees to the right of the normal position.

Raised edge lettering.

KM#	Date	Mintage	Fine	VF	XF	Unc
40	1931B(a)	3.520	4.50	9.00	25.00	85.00
	1931B(b)	I.A.	15.00	45.00	100.00	275.00
	1931B(c)	I.A.	150.00	400.00	625.00	1200.
	1932B	10.580	4.50	6.00	10.00	25.00
	1933B	5.900	4.50	6.00	10.00	25.00
	1935B	3.000	4.50	6.00	12.00	32.50
	1937B	.645	5.00	7.00	12.00	55.00
	1939B	2.197	4.50	6.00	14.00	30.00
	1940B	1.601	4.50	6.00	15.00	32.50
	1948B	.416	5.00	7.00	15.00	55.00
	1949B	.407	5.00	7.00	15.00	60.00
	1950B	.482	5.00	7.00	15.00	50.00
	1951B	1.196	4.50	6.00	14.00	30.00
	1951B	—	—	—	Proof	200.00
	1952B	.155	30.00	60.00	90.00	220.00
	1953B	3.403	BV	5.00	10.00	18.00
	1954B	6.600	BV	5.00	10.00	16.00
	1965B	5.021	BV	5.00	9.00	12.00
	1966B	9.016	BV	5.00	9.00	12.00
	1967B(a)	13.817	BV	5.00	9.00	12.00
	1967B(b)	—	10.00	30.00	70.00	150.00
	1967B(c)	—	20.00	70.00	250.00	600.00
	1968B	—	—	—	Rare	
	1969B	8.637	BV	5.00	9.00	12.00

COPPER-NICKEL

40a.1	1968B	33.871	—	—	3.75	6.50
	1970	6.306	—	—	3.75	6.50
	1973	5.002	—	—	3.75	4.50
	1974	6.007	—	—	3.75	4.50
	1974	2.400	—	—	Proof	110.00
	1975	2.500	—	—	3.75	4.50
	1975	.010	—	—	Proof	10.00
	1976	1.500	—	—	3.75	4.50
	1976	5.130	—	—	Proof	16.00
	1977	—	—	—	3.75	4.50
	1977	7.030	—	—	Proof	10.00
	1978	.900	—	—	3.75	4.50
	1978	.010	—	—	Proof	8.50
	1979	—	—	—	3.75	4.50
	1979	.010	—	—	Proof	8.50
	1980	4.016	—	—	3.75	4.50
	1980	.010	—	—	Proof	10.00
	1981	6.008	—	—	3.75	4.50
	1981	.010	—	—	Proof	10.00

Obv. and rev: Medallic alignment.

40a.2	1982	5.040	—	—	3.75	4.50
	1982	.010	—	—	Proof	20.00
	1983	4.022	—	—	3.75	4.50
	1983	.011	—	—	Proof	10.00
	1984	3.939	—	—	3.75	4.50
	1984	.014	—	—	Proof	10.00

Incuse edge lettering.

40a.3	1985	4.038	—	—	3.75	4.50
	1985	.012	—	—	Proof	10.00
	1986B	7.083	—	—	3.75	4.50
	1986B	.010	—	—	Proof	10.00
	1987B	7.000	—	—	3.75	4.50
	1987B	8.800	—	—	Proof	10.00
	1988B	—	—	—	3.75	4.50
	1988B	—	—	—	Proof	10.00

SWITZERLAND 1592

COMMEMORATIVE COINAGE
5 FRANCS

15.0000 g, .835 SILVER, .4027 oz ASW
Armament Fund

KM#	Date	Mintage	Fine	VF	XF	Unc
41	1936B	.200	—	20.00	30.00	50.00

600th Anniversary Battle of Laupen

| 42 | 1939B | .031 | — | 475.00 | 575.00 | 850.00 |

Zurich Exposition

| 43 | 1939* | .060 | — | 50.00 | 90.00 | 150.00 |
| | 1939 | — | — | — | Matte Proof | 300.00 |

*Minted at Huguenin, Le Locle.

650th Anniversary of Confederation

| 44 | 1941B | .100 | — | 35.00 | 50.00 | 85.00 |

500th Anniversary Battle of St. Jakob An Der Birs

| 45 | 1944B | .102 | — | 35.00 | 50.00 | 85.00 |

Swiss Constitution Centennial

| 48 | 1948B | .500 | — | 10.00 | 12.50 | 20.00 |

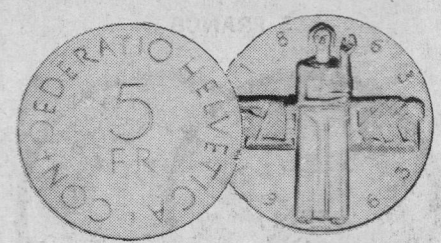

Red Cross Centennial

KM#	Date	Mintage	Fine	VF	XF	Unc
51	1963B	.623	—	5.00	7.00	14.00

COPPER-NICKEL
100th Anniversary of Constitution

| 52 | 1974 | 3.700 | — | — | 4.00 | 5.50 |
| | 1974 | .130 | — | — | Proof | 12.00 |

European Monument Protection

| 53 | 1975 | 2.500 | — | — | 4.00 | 6.00 |
| | 1975 | .060 | — | — | Proof | 22.50 |

Battle of Murten

| 54 | 1976 | 1.500 | — | — | 4.00 | 5.50 |
| | 1976 | .100 | — | — | Proof | 12.00 |

Johann Heinrich Pestalozzi

| 55 | 1977 | .800 | — | — | 4.00 | 7.00 |
| | 1977 | .050 | — | — | Proof | 25.00 |

Henry Dunant

| 56 | 1978 | .900 | — | — | 4.00 | 6.00 |
| | 1978 | .060 | — | — | Proof | 12.00 |

Centennial of Birth of Albert Einstein

KM#	Date	Mintage	Fine	VF	XF	Unc
57	1979	.900	—	—	4.00	7.50
	1979	.035	—	—	Proof	120.00

Centennial of Birth of Albert Einstein

| 58 | 1979 | .900 | — | — | 4.00 | 6.00 |
| | 1979 | .035 | — | — | Proof | 50.00 |

Ferdinand Hodler

| 59 | 1980 | .950 | — | — | 4.00 | 6.00 |
| | 1980 | .050 | — | — | Proof | 20.00 |

Stans Convention of 1481

| 60 | 1981 | .900 | — | — | 4.00 | 6.00 |
| | 1981 | .050 | — | — | Proof | 16.00 |

Gotthard Railway

| 61 | 1982 | 1.100 | — | — | 4.00 | 5.50 |
| | 1982 | .065 | — | — | Proof | 22.50 |

Ernest Ansermet

| 62 | 1983 | .951 | — | — | 4.00 | 6.00 |
| | 1983 | .060 | — | — | Proof | 16.00 |

Centennial of Birth of Auguste Piccard

KM#	Date	Mintage	Fine	VF	XF	Unc
63	1984	1.000	—	—	4.00	5.50
	1984	.075	—	—	Proof	16.00

European Year of Music

KM#	Date	Mintage	Fine	VF	XF	Unc
64	1985	1.156	—	—	4.00	5.50
	1985	.084	—	—	Proof	13.00

500th Anniversary of the Battle of Sempach

KM#	Date	Mintage	Fine	VF	XF	Unc
65	1986B	1.080	—	—	4.00	5.50
	1986B	.076	—	—	Proof	13.00

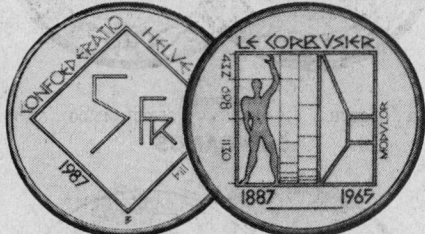

Corbusier

KM#	Date	Mintage	Fine	VF	XF	Unc
66	1987B	.960	—	—	4.00	7.00
	1987B	.062	—	—	Proof	22.00

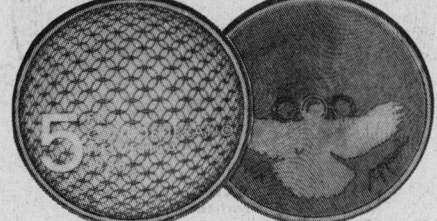

Olympics - Dove and Rings

KM#	Date	Mintage	Fine	VF	XF	Unc
67	1988B	1.026	—	—	4.00	6.00
	1988B	.069	—	—	Proof	20.00

10 FRANCS

3.2258 g, .900 GOLD, .0933 oz AGW

KM#	Date	Mintage	Fine	VF	XF	Unc
36	1911B	.100	75.00	150.00	250.00	425.00
	1912B	.200	65.00	100.00	125.00	175.00
	1913B	.600	65.00	100.00	125.00	175.00
	1914B	.200	65.00	100.00	125.00	175.00
	1915B	.400	65.00	100.00	125.00	175.00
	1916B	.130	65.00	100.00	125.00	175.00
	1922B	1.020	65.00	100.00	125.00	165.00

20 FRANCS

6.4516 g, .900 GOLD, .1867 oz AGW
Reeded edge.

KM#	Date	Mintage	Fine	VF	XF	Unc
31.1	1883	.250	100.00	110.00	140.00	155.00

Edge: DOMINUS XXX PROVIDEBIT XXXXXXXXXX

31.1	1886	.250	100.00	110.00	120.00	145.00
(31.1)	1887B	176 pcs.	—	15,000.	17,500.	20,000.
	1888B	4.224	4500.	6500.	8500.	11,000.
	1889B	.100	100.00	110.00	135.00	190.00
	1890B	.125	100.00	110.00	120.00	145.00
	1891B	.100	100.00	110.00	125.00	180.00
	1892B	.100	100.00	110.00	125.00	165.00
	1893B	.100	100.00	110.00	125.00	165.00
	1893B*	25 pcs.	—	—	Rare	—
	1894B	.121	100.00	110.00	125.00	165.00
	1895B	.200	100.00	110.00	125.00	150.00
	1895B*	19 pcs.	—	—	Rare	—
	1896B	.400	100.00	110.00	125.00	145.00

*NOTE: Struck of bright Valaisan gold from Gondo with a small cross punched in the center of the Swiss cross.

Edge: DOMINUS XXX/XXXXXXXXXX PROVIDEBIT

31.2	1896B	Inc. Ab.	125.00	145.00	160.00	190.00

35.1	1897B	.400	BV	95.00	100.00	120.00
	1897B*	29 pcs.	—	—	Rare	—
	1898B	.400	BV	95.00	100.00	120.00
	1899B	.300	BV	95.00	100.00	120.00
	1900B	.400	BV	95.00	100.00	120.00
	1901B	.500	BV	95.00	100.00	120.00
	1902B	.600	BV	95.00	100.00	120.00
	1903B	.200	BV	95.00	120.00	150.00
	1904B	.100	BV	95.00	115.00	175.00
	1905B	.100	BV	95.00	115.00	170.00
	1906B	.100	BV	95.00	100.00	155.00
	1907B	.150	BV	95.00	100.00	125.00
	1908B	.355	BV	95.00	100.00	120.00
	1909B	.400	BV	95.00	100.00	120.00
	1910B	.375	BV	95.00	100.00	120.00
	1911B	.350	BV	95.00	100.00	120.00
	1912B	.450	BV	95.00	100.00	120.00
	1913B	.700	BV	95.00	100.00	120.00
	1914B	.700	BV	95.00	100.00	120.00
	1915B	.750	BV	95.00	100.00	120.00
	1916B	.300	BV	95.00	100.00	120.00
	1922B	2.784	BV	95.00	100.00	115.00
	1925B	.400	BV	95.00	100.00	120.00
	1926B	.050	120.00	150.00	200.00	325.00
	1927B	5.015	BV	95.00	100.00	115.00
	1930B	3.372	BV	95.00	100.00	115.00
	1935B	.175	BV	95.00	100.00	120.00
	1935L-B**	20.009	BV	95.00	100.00	115.00

*NOTE: Struck of bright Valaisan gold from Gondo with a small cross punched in the center of the Swiss cross.

**NOTE: The 1935L-B coin was struck in 1945, 1946 and 1947.

Edge: AD LEGEM ANNI MCMXXXI

35.2	1947B	9.200	BV	95.00	100.00	115.00
	1949B	10.000	BV	95.00	100.00	115.00

25 FRANCS

5.6450 g, .900 GOLD, .1634 oz AGW

KM#	Date	Mintage	Fine	VF	XF	Unc
49	1955	5.000	—	—	—	—
	1958	5.000	—	—	—	—
	1959B	5.000	—	—	—	—

50 FRANCS

11.2900 g, .900 GOLD, .3267 oz AGW

KM#	Date	Mintage	Fine	VF	XF	Unc
50	1955	2.000	—	—	—	—
	1958	2.000	—	—	—	—
	1959B	2.000	—	—	—	—

NOTE: KM#49 and 50 are not available in commercial channels.

100 FRANCS

32.2581 g, .900 GOLD, .9334 oz AGW

KM#	Date	Mintage	Fine	VF	XF	Unc
39	1925B	5.000	—	7000.	9000.	12,500.

SHOOTING FESTIVAL COMMEMORATIVES

The listings which follow have traditionally been categorized as "Swiss Shooting Thalers" in many catalogs. Technically, all are medallic issues, rather than "coins", excepting the Solothurn issue of 1855, which according to the Swiss Federal Finance Department was "legally equal" to the then current silver 5 Francs issue to which it was identical in design, aside from bearing an edge inscription which read; EIDGEN FREISCHIESSEN SOLOTHURN (National Shooting Fest (in) Solothurn). For subsequent issues, denominations have been indicated "with government consent (though they) were not given legal tender status". The presence of the denomination was intended to indicate these "talers were of the same weight and fineness as (prescribed for) legal tender coins". Two generally associated "Shooting Festival" coins of earlier dates -- 1842 Graubunden and 1847 Glarus -- will be found incorporated in the listings for those cantons, as they were issued prior to the Swiss confederation of 1848.

5 FRANCS

.835 SILVER
Solothurn
Similar to KM#11 but edge is lettered:
EIDGEN FREISCHIESEN SOLOTHURN 1855*

KM#	Date	Mintage	Fine	VF	XF	Unc
S3	1855	3.000	—	1500.	2200.	3600.

Bern

S4	1857	5.195	—	325.00	475.00	900.00

Zurich

S5	1859	6.000	—	200.00	300.00	650.00

SWITZERLAND 1594

Stans in Nidwalden

KM#	Date	Mintage	Fine	VF	XF	Unc
S6	1861	6,000	—	175.00	300.00	450.00

Zurich

KM#	Date	Mintage	Fine	VF	XF	Unc
S11	1872	.010	—	85.00	110.00	325.00

Bern

KM#	Date	Mintage	Fine	VF	XF	Unc
S17	1885	.025	—	75.00	100.00	250.00

Fribourg

S18	1934B	.040	—	35.00	45.00	65.00
	1934B	—			Matte Proof	300.00

La Chaux-De-Fonds in Neuchatel

| S7 | 1863 | 6,000 | — | 175.00 | 250.00 | 600.00 |

St. Gallen

| S12 | 1874 | .015 | — | 85.00 | 110.00 | 225.00 |

Lucerne

| S20 | 1939B | .040 | — | 35.00 | 45.00 | 65.00 |

50 FRANCS

Lausanne

| S13 | 1876 | .020 | — | 75.00 | 100.00 | 300.00 |

Basel

| S14 | 1879 | .030 | — | 75.00 | 100.00 | 250.00 |

Schaffhausen

| S8 | 1865 | .010 | — | 100.00 | 175.00 | 350.00 |

25.0000 g, .900 SILVER, .7235 oz ASW

Oberhasli

| S22 | 1984 | 6,000 | — | — | — | 50.00 |
| | 1984 | 200 pcs. | — | — | Proof | 250.00 |

Schwyz

| S9 | 1867 | 8,000 | — | 100.00 | 200.00 | 350.00 |

Fribourg

| S15 | 1881 | .030 | — | 75.00 | 100.00 | 250.00 |

Zug

| S10 | 1869 | 6,000 | — | 125.00 | 225.00 | 500.00 |

Lugano

| S16 | 1883 | .030 | — | 75.00 | 100.00 | 250.00 |

Altdorf

| S24 | 1985 | 3,500 | — | — | Proof | 55.00 |

Altdorf
KM#	Date	Mintage	Fine	VF	XF	Unc
S25	1985	300 pcs.	—	—	Proof	1000.

Appenzell
Similar to 50 Francs, KM#S26.
S27	1986	350 pcs.	—	—	Proof	800.00

Glarus
Similar to 50 Francs, KM#S28.
S29	1987	300 pcs.	—	—	Proof	800.00

Aargau
Similar to 50 Francs, KM#S30.
S31	1988	400 pcs.	—	—	Proof	800.00

Appenzell
KM#	Date	Mintage	Fine	VF	XF	Unc
S26	1986	3,700	—	—	Proof	50.00

Glarus
S28	1987	3,200	—	—	Proof	50.00

Aargau
S30	1988	3,000	—	—	Proof	50.00

100 FRANCS

25.9000 g, .900 GOLD, .7494 oz AGW
Fribourg
S19	1934	2,000	—	1800.	2200.	3000.

17.5000 g, .900 GOLD, .5064 oz AGW
Lucerne
S21	1939	6,000	—	500.00	625.00	1000.

1000 FRANCS

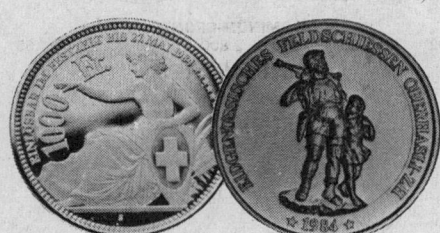

26.0000 g, .900 GOLD, .7524 oz AGW
Oberhasli
S23	1984	300 pcs.	—	—	Proof	1200.

MINT SETS (MS)

KM#	Date	Mintage	Identification	Issue Price	Mkt. Val.
MS1	1896(9)		KM3-4,21,23-24,26-27,29,34		Rare
MS2	1970(9)	10,000	KM21a,23a-24a,26-27,29a,40a,46-47	6.40	15.00
MS3	1971(5)	5,000	KM23a-24a,26,29a,46	2.40	18.00
MS4	1972(3)	5,000	KM21a,23a,27	2.40	12.00
MS5	1973(6)	10,000	KM21a,23a-24a,27,40a,46	6.40	13.00
MS6	1974(7)	10,000	KM21a,23a-24a,26-27,29a,40a,46-47		15.00
MS7	1975(8)	10,000	KM21a,23a-24a,26-27,29a,40a,46	6.40	15.00
MS8	1976(8)	10,000	KM21a,23a-24a,26-27,29a,40a,46	9.00	15.00
MS9	1977(8)	10,000	KM21a,23a-24a,26-27,29a,40a,46	9.00	17.00
MS10	1978(8)	10,000	KM21a,23a-24a,26-27,29a,40a,46	9.00	15.00
MS11	1979(8)	10,000	KM21a,23a-24a,26-27,29a,40a,46	9.00	15.00
MS12	1980(8)	15,000	KM21a,23a-24a,26-27,29a,40a,46	9.00	15.00
MS13	1981(8)	15,000	KM21a,23a-24a,26c,27,29a,40a,46	9.00	12.00
MS14	1982(8)	15,000	KM21a,23a-24a,26c,27,29a,40a,46	9.00	18.00
MS15	1983(8)	15,740	KM21a,23a-24a,26c,27,29a,40a,46	9.00	15.00
MS16	1984(8)	20,000	KM21a.3,23a.3-24a.3,26c,27,29a,40a.2,46	9.00	15.00
MS17	1985(8)	22,140	KM21a.3,23a.3-24a.3,26c,27,29a,40a.3,46	9.00	15.00
MS18	1986(8)	21,400	KM21a.3,23a.3-24a.3,26c,27,29a,40a.3,46	9.00	12.50
MS19	1987(8)	19,100	KM21a.3,23a.3-24a.3,26c,27,29a,40a.3,46	9.00	12.50
MS20	1988(8)	—	KM21a.3,23a.3-24a.3,26c,27,29a,40a.3,46	—	12.50

PROOF SETS (PS)

PS1	1974(9)	2,400	KM21a,23a-24a,26-27,29a,40a,46-47	12.80	500.00
PS2	1975(8)	10,000	KM21a,23a-24a,26-27,29a,40a,46	16.75	45.00
PS3	1976(8)	5,130	KM21a,23a-24a,26-27,29a,40a,46	16.75	80.00
PS4	1977(8)	7,030	KM21a,23a-24a,26-27,29a,40a,46	16.75	45.00
PS5	1978(8)	10,090	KM21a,23a-24a,26-27,29a,40a,46	28.00	40.00
PS6	1979(8)	10,150	KM21a,23a-24a,26-27,29a,40a,46	28.00	40.00
PS7	1980(8)	10,010	KM21a,23a-24a,26-27,29a,40a,46	30.00	45.00
PS8	1981(8)	10,280	KM21,23b-24a,26a,27,29a,40,46	30.00	40.00
PS9	1982(8)	10,090	KM21b,23b-24a,26a,27,29a,40,46	30.00	90.00
PS10	1983(8)	11,390	KM21b,23b-24a,26a-27a,29a,40,46	30.00	40.00
PS11	1984(8)	14,100	KM21b,23b-24a,26a-27a,29a,40,46	30.00	40.00
PS12	1985(8)	12,060	KM21a.3,23a.3-24a.3,26c,27,29a,40a.3,46	30.00	40.00
PS13	1986(8)	10,000	KM21a.3,23a.3-24a.3,26c,27,29a,40a.3,46	30.00	32.50
PS14	1987(8)	8,800	KM21a.3,23a.3-24a.3,26c,27,29a,40a.3,46	30.00	32.50
PS15	1988(8)	—	KM21a.3,23a.3-24a.3,26c,27,29a,40a.3,46	—	32.50

SYRIA

The Syrian Arab Republic, located in the Near East at the eastern end of the Mediterranean Sea, has an area of 71,498 sq. mi. (185,180 sq. km.) and a population of *12.2 million. Capital: Greater Damascus. Agriculture and animal breeding are the chief industries. Cotton, crude oil and livestock are exported.

Ancient Syria, a land bridge connecting Europe, Africa and Asia, has spent much of its history in thrall to the conqueror's whim. Its subjection by Egypt about 1500 B.C. was followed by successive conquests by the Hebrews, Phoenicians, Babylonians, Assyrians, Persians, Macedonians, Romans, Byzantines and finally, in 636 A.D., by the Moslems. The Arabs made Damascus, one of the oldest continuously inhabited cities of the world, the trade center and capital of an empire stretching from India to Spain. In 1516, following the total destruction of Damascus by the Mongols of Tamerlane, Syria fell to the Ottoman Turks and remained a part of Turkey until the end of World War I. The League of Nations gave France a mandate to the Levant states of Syria and Lebanon in 1920. In 1930, following a series of uprisings, France recognized Syria as an independent republic, but still subject to the mandate. Lebanon became fully independent on Nov. 22, 1943, and Syria on Jan. 1, 1944.

TITLES
الجمهورية السورية
Al-Jumhuriya Al-Suriya

الجمهورية السعودية السورية
Al-Jumhuriya Al-Arabiya Al-Suriya

RULERS
Ottoman, until 1918

MINT MARKS
(a) - Paris, privy marks only

MINTNAME
Damascus دمشق

Haleb حلب

MONETARY SYSTEM
100 Piastres = 1 Pound (Lira)

FRENCH PROTECTORATE
1/2 PIASTRE

COPPER-NICKEL
KM#	Date	Mintage	Fine	VF	XF	Unc
68	1921(a)	4.000	.50	1.50	4.00	15.00

NICKEL-BRASS
75	1935(a)	.600	1.00	3.50	10.00	40.00
	1936(a)	.800	1.00	3.00	8.00	25.00

PIASTRE

NICKEL-BRASS

SYRIA 1596

KM#	Date	Mintage	Fine	VF	XF	Unc
71	1929(a)	.750	.50	2.00	7.00	32.50
	1933(a)	.600	1.00	3.00	10.00	40.00
	1935(a)	1.950	.35	1.00	3.50	22.50
	1936(a)	1.400	.50	1.50	5.50	25.00

ZINC

| 71a | 1940(a) | 2.060 | 1.00 | 5.00 | 25.00 | 85.00 |

2 PIASTRES

ALUMINUM-BRONZE

| 69 | 1926(a) | .600 | 5.00 | 10.00 | 25.00 | 75.00 |
| | 1926 w/o privy marks | | | | | |

2-1/2 PIASTRES

ALUMINUM-BRONZE

| 76 | 1940(a) | 2.000 | 1.00 | 2.00 | 5.00 | 12.50 |

5 PIASTRES

ALUMINUM-BRONZE

70	1926(a)	.300	.75	2.00	8.00	25.00
	1926 w/o privy marks	.400	.75	3.00	12.00	35.00
	1933(a)	1.200	.40	2.00	12.50	40.00
	1935(a)	2.000	.30	1.25	8.00	25.00
	1936(a)	.900	.50	2.00	10.00	30.00
	1940(a)	.500	.50	1.50	4.00	15.00

10 PIASTRES

2.0000 g, .680 SILVER .0437 oz ASW

| 72 | 1929 | 1.000 | 3.00 | 7.50 | 25.00 | 75.00 |

25 PIASTRES

5.0000 g, .680 SILVER .1093 oz ASW

73	1929	1.000	3.00	5.00	22.50	85.00
	1933(a)	.500	5.00	15.00	40.00	150.00
	1936(a)	.897	3.50	7.50	25.00	95.00
	1937(a)	.393	5.00	10.00	32.50	125.00

50 PIASTRES

10.0000 g, .680 SILVER .2186 oz ASW

74	1929	.880	5.00	10.00	30.00	125.00
	1933(a)	.250	7.50	12.50	45.00	200.00
	1936(a)	.400	6.00	12.00	35.00	150.00
	1937(a)	Inc. Ab.	7.50	15.00	50.00	175.00

WORLD WAR II COINAGE
PIASTRE

BRASS

KM#	Date	Mintage	Fine	VF	XF	Unc
77	ND	—	.75	1.00	3.00	6.00

2-1/2 PIASTRES

ALUMINUM

| 78 | ND | — | 10.00 | 15.00 | 25.00 | 50.00 |

REPUBLIC
1944-1958
2-1/2 PIASTRES

COPPER-NICKEL

KM#	Date	Year	Mintage	VF	XF	Unc
81	AH1367	1948	2.500	.30	.50	2.00
	1375	1956	5.000	.25	.40	.75

5 PIASTRES

COPPER-NICKEL

| 82 | AH1367 | 1948 | 8.000 | .50 | 1.00 | 2.50 |
| | 1375 | 1956 | 4.000 | .35 | .60 | 1.00 |

10 PIASTRES

COPPER-NICKEL

| 83 | AH1367 | 1948 | — | .60 | 1.00 | 2.50 |
| | 1375 | 1956 | 4.000 | .40 | .85 | 1.50 |

25 PIASTRES

2.5000 g, .600 SILVER .0482 oz ASW

| 79 | AH1366 | 1947 | 6.300 | 2.50 | 5.00 | 17.50 |

50 PIASTRES

5.0000 g, .600 SILVER .0965 oz ASW

| 80 | AH1366 | 1947 | 4.500 | 3.50 | 7.00 | 20.00 |

1/2 POUND

3.3793 g, .900 GOLD, .0978 oz AGW

KM#	Date	Year	Mintage	VF	XF	Unc
84	AH1369	1950	.100	60.00	65.00	100.00

LIRA

10.0000 g, .680 SILVER, .2186 oz ASW

| 85 | AH1369 | 1950 | 7.000 | 5.00 | 7.50 | 15.00 |

POUND

6.7586 g, .900 GOLD .1956 oz AGW

| 86 | AH1369 | 1950 | .250 | 100.00 | 110.00 | 150.00 |

UNITED ARAB REPUBLIC
1958-1961
2-1/2 PIASTRES

ALUMINUM-BRONZE

| 90 | AH1380 | 1960 | 1.100 | .10 | .15 | .50 |

5 PIASTRES

ALUMINUM-BRONZE

| 91 | AH1380 | 1960 | 4.240 | .10 | .15 | .40 |

10 PIASTRES

ALUMINUM-BRONZE

| 92 | AH1380 | 1960 | 2.800 | .10 | .20 | .65 |

25 PIASTRES

2.5000 g, .600 SILVER, .0482 oz ASW

| 87 | AH1377 | 1958 | 2.300 | 1.50 | 2.00 | 6.00 |

50 PIASTRES

5.000 g, .600 SILVER, .0965 oz ASW

KM#	Date	Year	Mintage	VF	XF	Unc
88	AH1377	1958	.120	3.00	6.50	15.00

| 89 | AH1378 | 1959 | 1.500 | 3.00 | 4.50 | 9.00 |

SYRIAN ARAB REPUBLIC
1961—
2-1/2 PIASTRES

ALUMINUM-BRONZE

| 93 | AH1382 | 1962 | 8.000 | .10 | .20 | .50 |
| | 1385 | 1965 | 8.000 | .10 | .20 | .50 |

| 104 | AH1393 | 1973 | 10.000 | .10 | .15 | .25 |

5 PIASTRES

ALUMINUM-BRONZE

| 94 | AH1382 | 1962 | 7.000 | .10 | .15 | .30 |
| | 1385 | 1965 | 18.000 | .10 | .15 | .30 |

F.A.O. Issue

| 100 | AH1391 | 1971 | 15.000 | — | .15 | .25 |

| 105 | AH1394 | 1974 | — | .10 | .15 | .25 |

F.A.O. Issue

| 110 | AH1396 | 1976 | 2.000 | .10 | .15 | .25 |

Similar to KM#94 but heavier neck feathers.

| 116 | AH1399 | 1979 | — | .10 | .15 | .30 |

10 PIASTRES

ALUMINUM-BRONZE

KM#	Date	Year	Mintage	VF	XF	Unc
95	AH1382	1962	6.000	.10	.15	.40
	1385	1965	22.000	.10	.15	.40

| 106 | AH1394 | 1974 | — | .10 | .15 | .30 |

BRASS
F.A.O. Issue
Similar to 5 Piastres, KM#110.

| 111 | AH1396 | 1976 | .500 | .10 | .15 | .25 |

ALUMINUM-BRONZE
Similar to KM#95 but heavier neck feathers.

| 117 | AH1399 | 1979 | — | .10 | .15 | .40 |

25 PIASTRES

NICKEL

| 96 | AH1387 | 1968 | 15.000 | .20 | .30 | .60 |

25th Anniversary Al-Ba'ath Party

| 101 | AH1392 | 1972 | — | .15 | .25 | .60 |

| 107 | AH1394 | 1974 | — | .10 | .25 | .50 |

F.A.O. Issue
Similar to 5 Piastres, KM#110.

| 112 | AH1396 | 1976 | 1.000 | .10 | .25 | .50 |

COPPER-NICKEL

| 118 | AH1399 | 1979 | — | .10 | .25 | .50 |

50 PIASTRES

NICKEL

| 97 | AH1387 | 1968 | 10.000 | .25 | .50 | .85 |

25th Anniversary Al-Ba'ath Party

KM#	Date	Year	Mintage	VF	XF	Unc
102	AH1392	1972	—	.20	.30	1.00

| 108 | AH1394 | 1974 | — | .20 | .30 | 1.00 |

F.A.O. Issue
Similar to 5 Piastres, KM#110.

| 113 | AH1396 | 1976 | 1.000 | .10 | .20 | .40 |

COPPER-NICKEL

| 119 | AH1399 | 1979 | — | .20 | .40 | 1.00 |

POUND

NICKEL

| 98 | AH1387 | 1968 | 10.000 | .30 | .75 | 1.25 |
| | 1391 | 1971 | 10.000 | .30 | .75 | 1.25 |

F.A.O. Issue

| 99 | AH1388 | 1968 | .500 | .50 | 1.00 | 1.50 |

25th Anniversary Al-Ba'ath Party

| 103 | AH1392 | 1972 | 10.000 | .30 | .75 | 1.25 |

| 109 | AH1394 | 1974 | — | .40 | .70 | 1.25 |

SYRIA 1598

F.A.O. Issue

KM#	Date	Year	Mintage	VF	XF	Unc
114	AH1396	1976	.500	.40	.70	1.25

Re-Election of President

| 115 | AH1398 | 1978 | — | .50 | 1.00 | 4.00 |

COPPER-NICKEL

| 120 | AH1399 | 1979 | — | .40 | .70 | 1.25 |

TANZANIA

The United Republic of Tanzania, located on the east coast of Africa between Kenya and Mozambique, consists of Tanganyika and the islands of Zanzibar and Pemba. It has an area of 364,900 sq. mi. (945,087 sq. km.) and a population of *24.7 million. Capital: Dar es Salaam (Haven of Peace). The chief exports are cotton, coffee, diamonds, sisal, cloves, petroleum products, and cashew nuts.
Tanzania is a member of the Commonwealth of Nations. The President is Chief of State.

GERMAN EAST AFRICA

German East Africa (Tanganyika), located on the coast of east-central Africa between British East Africa (now Kenya) and Portuguese East Africa (now Mozambique), had an area of 362,284 sq. mi. (938,216 sq. km.) and a population of about 6 million. Capital: Dar es Salaam. Chief products prior to German control were ivory and slaves; after German control, sisal, coffee, and rubber. Germany acquired control of the area by treaties with coastal chiefs in 1884, established it as a protectorate in 1891, and proclaimed it the Colony of German East Africa in 1897. After World War I, Tanganyika was entrusted to Great Britain as a League of Nations mandate, and after World War II as a United Nations trust territory. Tanganyika became an independent nation within the British Commonwealth on Dec. 9, 1961.

TITLES
شراكتة المانيا
Sharakat Almaniyah

RULERS
Wilhelm II, 1888-1918

MINT MARKS
A - Berlin
J - Hamburg
T - Tabora

MONETARY SYSTEM
Until 1904
64 Pesa = 1 Rupie
Commencing 1904
100 Heller = 1 Rupie

PESA

COPPER

KM#	Date	Mintage	Fine	VF	XF	Unc
1	1890	1.000	.75	3.00	6.00	17.50
	1890	—	—	—	Proof	110.00
	1891	12.551	1.00	3.75	7.50	20.00
	1892	27.541	1.00	3.75	7.50	20.00

1/2 HELLER

BRONZE

6	1904A	1.201	1.25	4.00	6.50	17.50
	1905A	7.192	2.25	5.25	9.00	20.00
	1905J	4.000	2.25	5.25	9.00	20.00
	1906J	6.000	1.25	4.00	6.50	17.50
	1906J	—	—	—	Proof	150.00

HELLER

BRONZE

| 7 | 1904A | 10.256 | .75 | 2.25 | 3.75 | 15.00 |

KM#	Date	Mintage	Fine	VF	XF	Unc
7	1904A	—	—	—	Proof	65.00
	1904J	2.500	.75	2.25	7.00	18.00
	1905A	3.760	.75	2.25	7.00	18.00
	1905A	—	—	—	Proof	65.00
	1905J	7.556	.75	2.25	3.75	15.00
	1906A	3.004	.75	2.25	7.00	18.00
	1906A	—	—	—	Proof	65.00
	1906J	1.962	.75	2.25	7.00	18.00
	1907J	17.790	.75	1.25	3.75	15.00
	1908J	12.205	.75	1.25	3.75	15.00
	1908J	—	—	—	Proof	85.00
	1909J	1.698	1.50	4.00	12.00	20.00
	1909J	—	—	—	Proof	85.00
	1910J	5.096	.75	1.25	3.75	15.00
	1910J	—	—	—	Proof	75.00
	1911J	6.420	.75	1.25	3.75	15.00
	1911J	—	—	—	Proof	75.00
	1912J	7.012	.75	1.25	3.75	15.00
	1912J	—	—	—	Proof	75.00
	1913J	—	.75	1.25	3.75	15.00
	1913A	—	—	—	Proof	75.00
	1913A	5.186	.75	1.25	3.75	15.00
	1913J	—	—	—	Proof	100.00

5 HELLER

BRONZE

11	1908J	.600	10.00	20.00	40.00	250.00
	1908J	—	—	—	Proof	450.00
	1909J	.756	10.00	20.00	40.00	250.00
	1909J	60 pcs.	—	—	Proof	500.00

COPPER-NICKEL

13	1913A	1.000	5.00	10.00	20.00	60.00
	1913A	—	—	—	Proof	110.00
	1913J	1.000	5.00	10.00	20.00	50.00
	1913J	—	—	—	Proof	110.00
	1914J	1.000	4.00	9.00	15.00	50.00
	1914J	—	—	—	Proof	110.00

BRASS, 1 1/2-2mm thick
Obv: Oval opening on crown.

| 14.1 | 1916T | .030 | 2.50 | 6.00 | 10.00 | 40.00 |

Obv: Horizontal opening on crown, 1mm or less thick.

| 14.2 | 1916T | Inc. Ab. | 2.50 | 5.00 | 8.00 | 27.50 |

10 HELLER

COPPER-NICKEL

12	1908J	—	2.50	9.00	15.00	60.00
	1908J	—	—	—	Proof	170.00
	1909J	1.990	2.50	9.00	15.00	60.00
	1909J	—	—	—	Proof	120.00

Listings For
TANNA-TUVA: refer to Union of Soviet Socialist Republics

KM#	Date	Mintage	Fine	VF	XF	Unc
12	1910J	.500	2.50	9.00	15.00	60.00
	1910J	—	—	—	Proof	120.00
	1911A	.500	3.00	12.00	22.50	75.00
	1911A	—	—	—	Proof	120.00
	1914J	.200	3.00	12.00	22.50	75.00
	1914J	—	—	—	Proof	170.00

20 HELLER

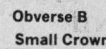

Obverse A Large Crown

Obverse B Small Crown

Reverse A Curled Tip On Second L

Reverse B Pointed Tips On L's

Reverse C Curled Tips On L's

KM#	Date	Mintage	Good	VG	Fine	VF
		COPPER				
15	1916T Obv. A Rev. A	.300	1.50	3.00	5.00	7.50
	1916T Obv. A Rev. B					
	Inc. Ab.	40.00	70.00	125.00	175.00	
	1916T Obv. B Rev. A					
	Inc. Ab.	18.00	40.00	60.00	85.00	
	1916T Obv. B Rev. B					
	Inc. Ab.	1.50	3.00	5.00	7.50	
	1916T Obv. A Rev. C					
	Inc. Ab.	—	—	Rare	—	
	1916T Obv. B Rev. C					
	Inc. Ab.	—	—	Rare	—	
		BRASS				
15a	1916T Obv. A Rev. A	1.600	1.50	3.00	5.00	7.50
	1916T Obv. A Rev. B					
	Inc. Ab.	1.75	3.50	6.00	12.50	
	1916T Obv. B Rev. A					
	Inc. Ab.	1.75	3.50	6.00	12.50	
	1916T Obv. B Rev. B					
	Inc. Ab.	1.50	3.00	5.00	7.50	
	1916T Obv. A Rev. C					
	Inc. Ab.	2.00	4.00	10.00	30.00	
	1916T Obv. B Rev. C					
	Inc. Ab.	2.50	5.00	12.00	35.00	

1/4 RUPIE

2.9160 g, .917 SILVER, .0859 oz ASW

KM#	Date	Mintage	Fine	VF	XF	Unc
3	1891	.077	5.00	12.00	25.00	85.00
	1891	—	—	—	Proof	175.00
	1898	.100	6.00	18.00	40.00	135.00
	1901	.350	5.00	12.00	25.00	85.00

8	1904A	.300	5.00	12.00	25.00	110.00
	1904A	—	—	—	Proof	175.00
	1906A	.300	5.00	12.00	25.00	110.00
	1906A	—	—	—	Proof	175.00
	1906J	.100	8.00	20.00	50.00	135.00
	1907J	.200	7.00	18.00	45.00	135.00

KM#	Date	Mintage	Fine	VF	XF	Unc
8	1909A	.300	6.00	13.50	30.00	120.00
	1910A	.600	5.00	12.00	25.00	110.00
	1910J	—	—	—	Proof	175.00
	1912J	.400	6.00	13.50	30.00	120.00
	1912J	—	—	—	Proof	175.00
	1913A	.200	6.00	13.50	30.00	120.00
	1913A	—	—	—	Proof	175.00
	1913J	.400	5.00	12.00	30.00	110.00
	1913J	—	—	—	Proof	175.00
	1914J	.200	6.00	13.50	30.00	120.00
	1914J	—	—	—	Proof	175.00

1/2 RUPIE

5.8319 g, .917 SILVER, .1719 oz ASW

4	1891	.068	12.50	25.00	50.00	120.00
	1891	—	—	—	Proof	175.00
	1897	.075	14.00	40.00	65.00	170.00
	1901	.215	12.50	25.00	50.00	145.00

9	1904A	.400	12.50	25.00	50.00	140.00
	1904A	—	—	—	Proof	175.00
	1906A	.050	20.00	65.00	85.00	200.00
	1906A	—	—	—	Proof	250.00
	1906J	.050	20.00	65.00	85.00	200.00
	1907J	.140	14.00	40.00	60.00	140.00
	1907J	—	—	—	Proof	175.00
	1909A	.100	14.00	35.00	55.00	140.00
	1910A	.300	14.00	35.00	55.00	140.00
	1910J	—	—	—	Proof	300.00
	1912A	.200	12.50	25.00	50.00	140.00
	1913A	.100	12.50	25.00	50.00	140.00
	1913J	.200	14.00	35.00	55.00	140.00
	1914J	.100	14.00	35.00	60.00	140.00

RUPIE

11.6638 g, .917 SILVER, .3437 oz ASW

2	1890	.154	9.00	17.50	40.00	90.00
	1890	—	—	—	Proof	300.00
	1891	.126	9.00	17.50	40.00	90.00
	1891	—	—	—	Proof	300.00
	1892	.360	9.00	17.50	40.00	90.00
	1892	—	—	—	Proof	300.00
	1893	.142	12.50	27.50	60.00	225.00
	1894	.048	17.50	75.00	185.00	375.00
	1897	.244	12.50	27.50	60.00	200.00
	1898	.357	12.50	27.50	60.00	200.00
	1899	.227	15.00	32.50	75.00	240.00
	1900	.209	12.50	27.50	60.00	200.00
	1901	.319	12.50	22.50	55.00	180.00
	1902	.151	15.00	35.00	80.00	250.00

10	1904A	1.000	11.50	20.00	45.00	120.00
	1904A	—	—	—	Proof	200.00
	1905A	.300	15.00	27.50	60.00	135.00
	1905A	—	—	—	Proof	200.00
	1905J	1.000	11.50	20.00	45.00	120.00
	1905J	—	—	—	Proof	200.00
	1906J	.950	11.50	20.00	45.00	120.00
	1906J	.700	15.00	27.50	65.00	140.00
	1907J	.880	9.00	15.00	35.00	115.00
	1908J	.500	12.50	22.50	55.00	125.00

KM#	Date	Mintage	Fine	VF	XF	Unc
10	1908J	—	—	—	Proof	200.00
	1909A	.200	15.00	27.50	60.00	135.00
	1910A	.270	9.00	15.00	35.00	115.00
	1911A	.300	12.50	22.50	55.00	125.00
	1911A	—	—	—	Proof	200.00
	1911J	1.400	9.00	15.00	35.00	115.00
	1911J	—	—	—	Proof	250.00
	1912J	.300	12.50	22.50	55.00	125.00
	1912J	—	—	—	Proof	200.00
	1913A	.400	12.50	22.50	55.00	125.00
	1913J	1.400	9.00	15.00	35.00	115.00
	1913J	—	—	—	Proof	250.00
	1914J	.500	12.50	22.50	50.00	125.00

2 RUPIEN

23.3200 g, .917 SILVER, .6872 oz ASW

5	1893	.033	125.00	230.00	475.00	1000.
	1893	—	—	—	Proof	2000.
	1894	.018	175.00	330.00	700.00	1200.

15 RUPIEN

7.1680 g, .750 GOLD, .1728 oz AGW
Obv: Right arabesque ends under T of OSTAFRIKA.

16.1	1916T	9,803	400.00	675.00	925.00	1100.

Obv: Right arabesque ends under first A of OSTAFRIKA.

16.2	1916T	6,395	400.00	700.00	950.00	1150.

ZANZIBAR

The British protectorate of Zanzibar and adjacent small islands, located in the Indian Ocean 22 miles (35 km.) off the coast of Tanganyika, comprised a portion of British East Africa. Zanzibar was also the name of a sultanate which included the Zanzibar and Kenya protectorates. Zanzibar has an area of 637 sq. mi. (1,651 sq. km.). Chief city: Zanzibar. The islands are noted for their cloves, of which Zanzibar is the world's foremost producer.

Zanzibar came under Portuguese control in 1503, was conquered by the Omani Arabs in 1698, became independent of Oman in 1860, and (with Pemba) came under British control in 1890. Britain granted the protectorate self-government in 1961, and independence within the British Commonwealth on Dec. 19, 1963. On April 26, 1964, Tanganyika and Zanzibar (with Pemba) united to form the United Republic of Tanganyika and Zanzibar. The name of the country, which remained within the British Commonwealth, was changed to Tanzania on Oct. 29, 1964.

TITLES

زنجباراه

Zanjibara

RULERS
Sultan Barghash Ibn Sa' Id,
1870-1888AD
Sultan Ali Bun Hamud, 1902-1911AD

MONETARY SYSTEM
64 Pysa (Pice) = 1 Rupee
136 Pysa = 1 Ryal (to 1908)
100 Cents = 1 Rupee (to 1909)

PYSA

5 RYALS

10 SENTI

COPPER

KM#	Date	Mintage	Fine	VF	XF	Unc
1	AH1299	4.640	1.00	1.50	3.00	25.00
	1299	—	—	—	Proof	150.00

GOLD

KM#	Date	Mintage	Fine	VF	XF	Unc
6	AH1299	2,000	—	—	Rare	11,000.

DECIMAL COINAGE
100 Cents = 1 Rupee

CENT

NICKEL-BRASS

KM#	Date	Mintage	VF	XF	Unc
11	1977	19.505	.50	1.50	3.50
	1979	8.000	.50	1.50	3.50
	1980	10.000	.50	1.50	3.50
	1981	10.000	.50	1.50	3.50

20 SENTI

7	AH1304	18.680	1.25	1.75	4.00	35.00
	1304	—	—	—	Proof	175.00

1/4 RYAL

BRONZE

| 8 | 1908 | 1.000 | 25.00 | 50.00 | 135.00 | 250.00 |

10 CENTS

NICKEL-BRASS

2	1966	26.500	.10	—	.20	.50
	1966	5,500	—	Proof		1.50
	1970	5.000	.10	—	.20	.50
	1973	20.100	.10	—	.20	.50
	1975	—	.10	—	.20	.50
	1976	10.000	.10	—	.20	.50
	1977	10.000	.10	—	.20	.50
	1979	10.000	.10	—	.20	.50
	1980	10.000	.10	—	.20	.50
	1981	10.000	.10	—	.20	.50
	1982	—	.10	—	.20	.50
	1983	.050	.10	—	.20	.50

50 SENTI

SILVER

| 2 | AH1299 | — | — | Rare | — |

1/2 RYAL

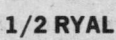

BRONZE

| 9 | 1908 | .100 | 75.00 | 125.00 | 175.00 | 400.00 |

20 CENTS

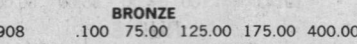

COPPER-NICKEL

3	1966	6.250	.15	.25	.50
	1966	5,500	—	Proof	2.00
	1970	10.000	.15	.25	.50
	1973	10.000	.15	.25	.50
	1980	10.000	.15	.25	.50
	1981	—	.15	.25	.50
	1982	10.000	.15	.25	.50
	1983	—	.15	.25	.50
	1984	10.000	.15	.25	.50

SHILINGI

SILVER

| 3 | AH1299 | — | — | Rare | — |

RYAL

NICKEL

| 10 | 1908 | .100 | 100.00 | 200.00 | 350.00 | 650.00 |

TANZANIA

MONETARY SYSTEM
100 Senti = 1 Shilingi

5 SENTI

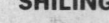

SILVER

4	AH1299	.060	125.00	150.00	225.00	400.00
4a	AH1299	**COPPER (OMS)** —	—	—	Unique	—

2-1/2 RYALS

BRONZE

KM#	Date	Mintage	VF	XF	Unc
1	1966	55.250	—	.10	.25
	1966	5.500	—	Proof	1.00
	1971	5.000	—	.10	.20
	1972	—	—	.10	.20
	1973	20.000	—	.10	.20
	1974	12.500	—	.10	.20
	1975	—	—	.10	.20
	1976	37.500	—	.10	.20
	1977	10.000	—	.10	.20
	1979	7.200	—	.10	.20
	1980	10.000	—	.10	.20
	1981	13.650	—	.10	.20
	1982	—	—	.10	.20
	1983	.018	—	.10	.20
	1984	—	—	.10	.20

COPPER-NICKEL

4	1966	48.000	.40	.60	1.25
	1966	5,500	—	Proof	3.00
	1972	10.000	.25	.50	1.00
	1974	15.000	.25	.50	1.00
	1975	—	.25	.50	1.00
	1977	5,000	.25	.50	1.00
	1980	10.000	.25	.50	1.00
	1981	—	.25	.50	1.00
	1982	10.000	.25	.50	1.00
	1983	10.000	.25	.50	1.00
	1984	10.000	.25	.50	1.00

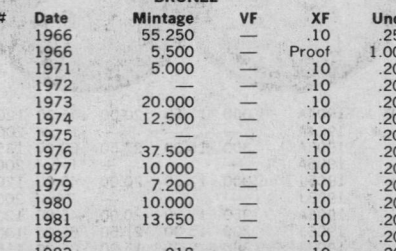

GOLD

| 5 | AH1299 | — | — | Rare | 17,000. |

NICKEL CLAD STEEL

| 22 | 1987 | — | — | .25 | .50 | 1.00 |

5 SHILINGI

COPPER-NICKEL
F.A.O. Issue
10th Anniversary of Independence

KM#	Date	Mintage	VF	XF	Unc
5	1971	1,000	1.00	1.50	2.25

F.A.O. Issue
Rev: Similar to KM#5.

6	1972	8,000	1.00	1.50	2.00
	1973	5,000	1.00	1.50	2.00
	1980	5,000	1.00	1.50	2.00

10th Anniversary Bank of Tanzania

10	1976	1,000	1.00	1.50	2.25
	1976	200 pcs.	—	Proof	40.00

F.A.O. Issue

12	1978	.050	—	1.50	2.00
	1978	2,000	—	Proof	15.00

23	1987	—	1.00	1.50	2.00

10 SHILINGI

COPPER-NICKEL

KM#	Date	Mintage	VF	XF	Unc
20	1987	—	—	—	1.00

20 SHILINGI

COPPER-NICKEL
20th Anniversary of Independence

13	1981	.997	3.00	5.00	9.00

16.0000 g, .925 SILVER, .4759 oz ASW

13a	1981	.020	—	Proof	35.00

20th Anniversary
Obv: Portrait right.
Rev: Torch & inscription within wreath.

21	1986	—	3.50	6.00	10.00

25 SHILINGI

25.4000 g, .500 SILVER, .4083 oz ASW
Conservation Series
Obv: Similar to 1500 Shilingi, KM#9.
Rev: Southern Giraffe.

7	1974	8,848	—	—	25.00

28.2800 g, .925 SILVER, .8411 oz ASW

7a	1974	.013	—	Proof	30.00

50 SHILINGI

31.8500 g, .500 SILVER, .5120 oz ASW
Conservation Series
Obv: Similar to 1500 Shilingi, KM#9.
Rev: Black Rhinoceros.

8	1974	8,826	—	—	26.50

35.0000 g, .925 SILVER, 1.0409 oz ASW

8a	1974	.012	—	Proof	32.50

100 SHILINGI

23.3300 g, .925 SILVER, .6938 oz ASW
Decade For Women
Obv: President Nyerere. Rev: Nurse lifting baby.

16	1984	1,000	—	Proof	35.00

COPPER-NICKEL
Wildlife - Elephant Mother and Calf

KM#	Date	Mintage	VF	XF	Unc
18	1986	—	—	—	4.00

19.4400 g, .925 SILVER, .5782 oz ASW

18a	1986	.025	—	Proof	35.00

200 SHILINGI

28.2800 g, .925 SILVER, .8411 oz ASW
20th Anniversary of Independence
Obv: Similar to 20 Shilingi, KM#13.

14	1981	110 pcs.	—	—	—
	1981	Inc. Ab.	—	Proof	—

1000 SHILINGI

8.1000 g, .900 GOLD, .2344 oz AGW
Decade For Women

17	1984	500 pcs.	—	Proof	225.00

1500 SHILINGI

33.4370 g, .900 GOLD, .9676 oz AGW
Conservation Series
Rev: Cheetah.

9	1974	2,779	—	—	600.00
	1974	866 pcs.	—	Proof	725.00

2000 SHILINGI

15.9800 g, .917 GOLD, .4712 oz AGW
20th Anniversary of Independence
Rev: Similar to 20 Shilingi, KM#13.

15	1981	110 pcs.	—	—	325.00
	1981	Inc. Ab.	—	Proof	325.00

TANZANIA 1602

Wildlife - Banded Green Sunbird

KM#	Date	Mintage	VF	XF	Unc
19	1986	5,000	—	Proof	425.00

PROOF SETS (PS)

KM#	Date	Mintage	Identification	Issue Price	Mkt. Val.
PS1	1966(4)	5,500	KM1-4	10.50	7.50
PS2	1974(2)	30,000	KM7a-8a	50.00	62.50

THAILAND

The Kingdom of Thailand (formerly Siam), a constitutional monarchy located in the center of mainland southeast Asia between Burma and Laos, has an area of 198,457 sq. mi. (514,000 sq. km.) and a population of *53.9 million. Capital: Bangkok. The economy is based on agriculture and mining. Rubber, rice, teakwood, tin and tungsten are exported.

The history of Thailand, the only country in south and southeast Asia that was never colonized by an European power, dates from the 6th century A.D. when tribes of the Thai stock migrated into the area from the Asiatic continent, a process that accelerated with the Mongol invasion of China in the 13th century. After 400 years of sporadic warfare with the neighboring Burmese, King Taskin won the last battle in 1767. He founded a new capital, Dhonburi, on the west bank of the Chao Praya River. King Rama I moved the capital to Bangkok in 1782, thus initiating the so-called Bangkok Period of Siamese coinage characterized by Pot Duang money (bullet coins) stamped with regal symbols.

The Thai were introduced to the Western world by the Portuguese, who were followed by the Dutch, British and French. Rama III of the present ruling dynasty negotiated a treaty of friendship and commerce with Britain in 1826, and in 1896 the independence of the kingdom was guaranteed by an Anglo-French accord. The absolute monarchy was changed into a constitutional monarchy in 1932.

RULERS

Rama I (Phra Buddha Yot Fa Chulaloke Maharaj), 1782-1809
Rama II (Phra Buddha Lert La Napali), 1809-1824
Rama III (Phra Nang Klao), 1824-1851
Rama IV (Phra Chom Klao 'Mongkut'), 1851-1868
Rama V (Phra Maha Chulalongkorn), 1868-1910
Rama VI (Phra Maha Vajiravudh), 1910-1925
Rama VII (Phra Maha Prajadhipok), 1925-1935
Rama VIII (Phra Maha Ananda Mahidol), 1935-1946
Rama IX (Phra Maha Bhumifhol Adulyadej), 1946-

MONETARY SYSTEM
Old currency system

2 Solos = 1 Att
2 Att = 1 Sio (Pai)
2 Sio = 1 Sik
2 Sik = 1 Fuang
2 Fuang = 1 Salung (not Sal'ung)
4 Salung = 1 Baht
4 Baht = 1 Tamlung
20 Tamlung = 1 Chang

UNITS OF OLD THAI CURRENCY

Chang -	ชั่ง	Sik -	ชีก
Tamlung -	ตำลึง	Sio (Pai) -	เสี้ยว
Baht -	บาท	Att -	อัฐ
Salung -	สลึง	Solos -	โสฬส
Fuang -	เฟื้อง		

MINT MARKS
H-Heaton Birmingham

DATING

Typical BE Dating

Typical CS Dating

Denomination

2-1/2 (Satang)   RS Dating

DATE CONVERSION TABLES
B.E. date - 543 = A.D. date
Ex: 2516 - 543 = 1973

R.S. date + 1781 = A.D. date
Ex: 127 + 1781 = 1908

C.S. date + 638 = A.D. date
Ex 1238 + 638 = 1876

Primary denominations used were 1 Baht, 1/4 and 1/8 Baht up to the reign of Rama IV. Other denominations are

Listings For
TARIM: refer to Yemen Democratic Republic
TCHAD: refer to Chad

much scarcer.

BULLET COINAGE

Gold and silver "bullet" coins have been a medium of exchange since medieval times. Interesting enough is the fact that a one Baht bullet made of gold will weigh the same as a one Baht bullet in silver. The reason for this is that Baht originally was a weight not a denomination. It was a coinage weight only until the time of Rama VII, (1925-1935) and now it is a weight and also a denomination (as far as standard weight coins are concerned). Usually one gold Baht was equal to 16 silver Baht on an exchange basis.

Bullet Weights

Grams

BAHT	1/2 BAHT	1/4 BAHT	1/8 BAHT
15.40	7.70	3.85	1.92

1/16 BAHT	1/32 BAHT	1/64 BAHT
0.96	0.48	0.24

Chopmarks exist on bullet coins as they do on many other coins that have traveled on their way through the Orient. One must be careful not to mistake a money changer's chopmark for the regular dynastic marks on the bullet. Some chopmarks are rather simple in design while others appear to be rather elaborate.

DYNASTIC MARKS

Chakra

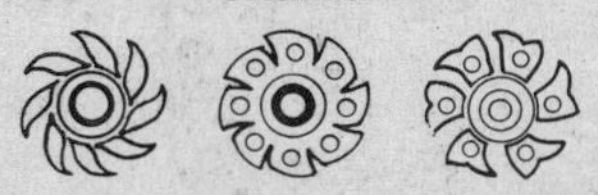

The Chakra, symbol of the God Vishnu, is the mark of the Bangkok Dynasty. It varies slightly in design between issues, being very ornate on ceremonial issues.

RAMA I

1782-1809

Tri Unalom

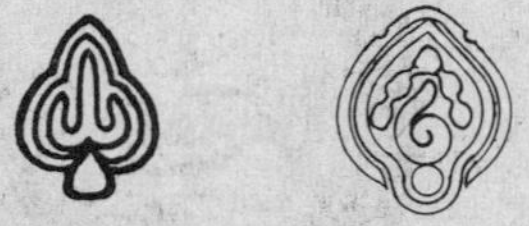

The trident, the symbol of the Hindu God, Siva, used as the first mark of Rama I. The unalom is an ornamented conch shell, used as the second mark of Rama I.

RAMA II

1809-1824

Krut

A facing Krut, half man - half bird, used as the mark of Rama II.

RAMA III

1824-1851

Krut Sio Prasat Dok Mai

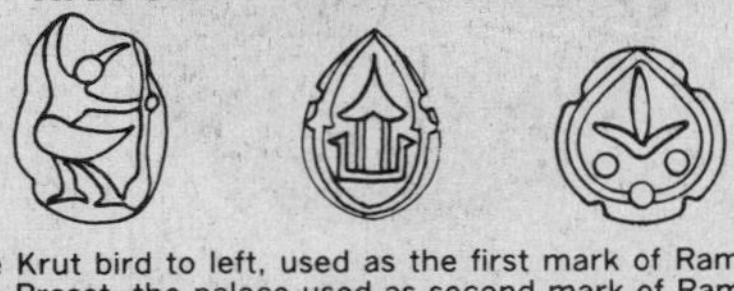

The Krut bird to left, used as the first mark of Rama III. The Prasat, the palace used as second mark of Rama III. The Dok Mai was a flower used as third mark of Rama III.

Bai Matum Ruang Puang Arrow Head

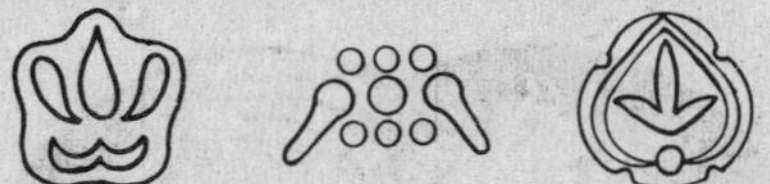

The Bai Matum is a bale-fruit tree used as the fourth mark of Rama III. The Ruang Puang is a beehive used as the fifth mark of Rama III. Very similar to Dok Mai, having only one dot below the point used as the sixth mark of Rama III.

Chaleo

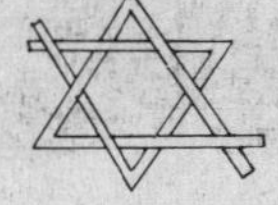

A symbol of varied meanings. In this instance it is believed to represent a charm to ward off evil spirits, found as a seventh mark on bullet coinage of Rama III.

RAMA IV

1851-1868

P'ra Tao Mongkut

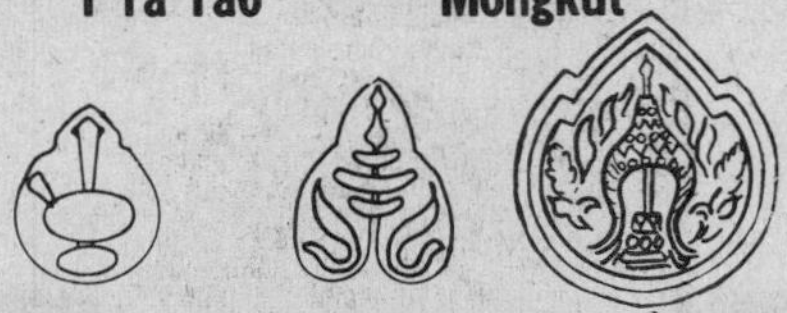

The P'ra Tao or royal water pot was used as the first mark of Rama IV. The Royal Siamese Crown was used as the second mark of Rama IV.

RAMA V

1868-1910

P'ra Kieo 1876 Cho Rampeuy 1880

The Royal Coronet worn on the top knot of the Royal Princess on ceremonial occasions. First used on the occasion of the funeral of Princess Charoenkamol Suksawadi who died in 1874. The Thai flower was on a ceremonial issue along with an ornate crown of two vessels in memory of Somdet Pira Deb Sirindhra, the mother of Rama V and commemorating his age, dated CS1242.

MARKET VALUATIONS

Market valuations are primarily based on the quality and condition of the countermarks found on bullet coinage.

SILVER POT DUANG

(Bullet Coins)

1/128 BAHT

SILVER, 0.12 g

C#	King	Mark	Good	VG	Fine	VF
120	Rama IV	P'ra Tao	—	—	—	—

ATT

(1/64 Baht)

SILVER, 0.24 g

C#	King	Mark	Good	VG	Fine	VF
121	Rama IV	P'ra Tao	12.00	20.00	30.00	45.00

SIO

(Pai) (1/32 Baht)

SILVER, 0.48 g

C#	King	Mark	Good	VG	Fine	VF
1	Rama I	Tri	6.00	10.00	15.00	22.50
8	Rama I	Unalom	6.00	10.00	15.00	22.50
42	Rama III	Prasat	6.00	10.00	15.00	22.50
51	Rama III	Dok Mai	6.00	10.00	15.00	22.50
61	Rama III	Bai Matum	6.00	10.00	15.00	22.50
71	Rama III	Ruang Puang	6.00	10.00	15.00	22.50
81	Rama III	Arrow Head	6.00	10.00	15.00	22.50
122	Rama IV	P'ra Tao	6.00	10.00	15.00	22.50

SIK

(1/16 Baht)

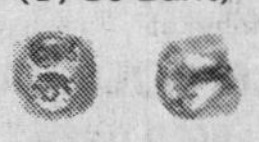

SILVER, 0.96 g

C#	King	Mark	Good	VG	Fine	VF
2	Rama I	Tri	6.00	12.50	20.00	30.00
9	Rama I	Unalom	8.00	16.50	27.50	40.00
16	Rama II	Krut	10.00	20.00	35.00	50.00
43	Rama III	Prasat	3.00	6.00	10.00	15.00
52	Rama III	Dok Mai	2.50	5.00	6.00	10.00
62	Rama III	Bai Matum	2.50	5.00	8.00	12.00
72	Rama III	Ruang Puang	2.50	5.00	8.00	12.00
82	Rama III	Arrow Head	2.50	5.00	8.00	12.00
123	Rama IV	P'ra Tao	2.00	3.00	5.00	6.00
133	Rama IV	Mongkut	2.75	5.50	9.00	13.50

FUANG

(1/8 Baht)

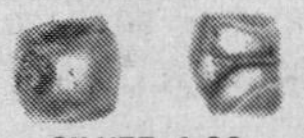

SILVER, 1.92 g

C#	King	Mark	Good	VG	Fine	VF
3	Rama I	Tri	7.50	15.00	25.00	37.50
10	Rama I	Unalom	7.50	15.00	25.00	37.50
17	Rama II	Krut	10.00	20.00	35.00	50.00
44	Rama III	Prasat	3.00	6.00	10.00	15.00
44.1	Rama III	Prasat and Unalom	12.50	25.00	40.00	60.00
44.2	Rama III	Prasat and Krut	12.50	25.00	40.00	60.00
53	Rama III	Dok Mai	2.50	5.00	8.00	12.00
63	Rama III	Bai Matum	2.00	4.00	7.00	10.00
73	Rama III	Ruang Puang	2.50	5.00	7.50	11.00
83	Rama III	Arrow Head	2.50	5.00	7.50	11.00
124	Rama IV	P'ra Tao	2.00	3.00	5.00	7.50
134	Rama IV	Mongkut	2.00	3.00	5.00	7.50

SALU'NG

(1/4 Baht)

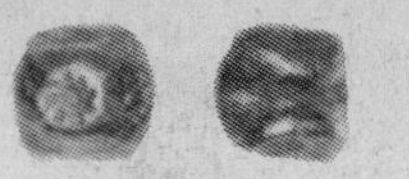

SILVER, 3.85 g

C#	King	Mark	Good	VG	Fine	VF
4	Rama I	Tri	6.50	11.50	18.50	27.50
11	Rama I	Unalom	7.50	15.00	25.00	37.50
18	Rama II	Krut	12.50	20.00	25.00	40.00
45	Rama III	Prasat	3.00	6.00	10.00	15.00
54	Rama III	Dok Mai	3.00	6.00	10.00	15.00
64	Rama III	Bai Matum	2.50	5.00	8.00	12.00
74	Rama III	Ruang Puang	2.75	5.50	9.00	13.50
84	Rama III	Arrow Head	2.75	5.50	9.00	13.50
125	Rama IV	P'ra Tao	2.50	4.00	7.00	10.00
135	Rama IV	Mongkut	2.50	4.00	7.00	10.00

2 SALU'NG

(1/2 Baht)

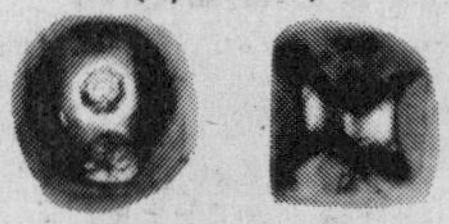

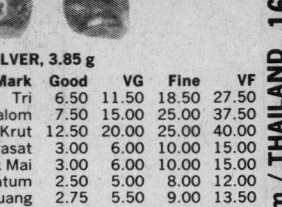

SILVER, 7.70 g

C#	King	Mark	Good	VG	Fine	VF
5	Rama I	Tri	6.00	12.50	22.50	35.00
12	Rama I	Unalom	7.50	15.00	25.00	37.50
19	Rama II	Krut	15.00	25.00	35.00	50.00
46	Rama III	Prasat	5.00	7.50	12.50	18.50
55	Rama III	Dok Mai	10.00	18.50	30.00	45.00
65	Rama III	Bai Matum	7.50	12.50	20.00	30.00

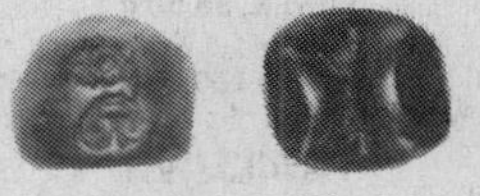

C#	King	Mark	Good	VG	Fine	VF
136	Rama IV	Mongkut	4.50	7.50	13.50	20.00
136.1	Rama IV	Mongkut and Prasat	12.50	20.00	35.00	50.00

BAHT

SILVER, 15.40 g

C#	King	Mark	Good	VG	Fine	VF
1	Rama I	Tri	10.00	15.00	20.00	25.00

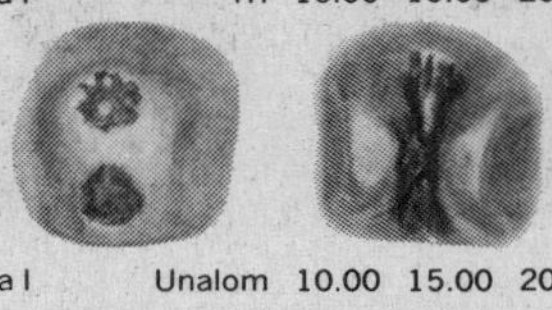

C#	King	Mark	Good	VG	Fine	VF
13	Rama I	Unalom	10.00	15.00	20.00	25.00

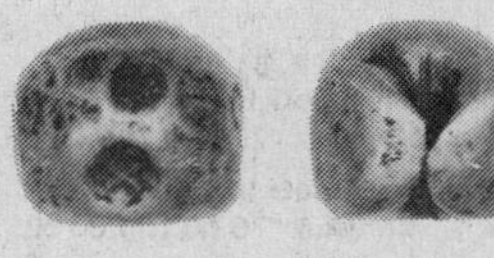

C#	King	Mark	Good	VG	Fine	VF
20	Rama II	Krut	10.00	15.00	20.00	25.00
39	Rama III	Chaleo	—	—	Rare	—
47	Rama III	Prasat	10.00	15.00	20.00	25.00
56	Rama III	Dok Mai	20.00	30.00	50.00	75.00
66	Rama III	Bai Matum	17.50	27.50	45.00	65.00
127	Rama IV	P'ra Tao	Reported, not confirmed			

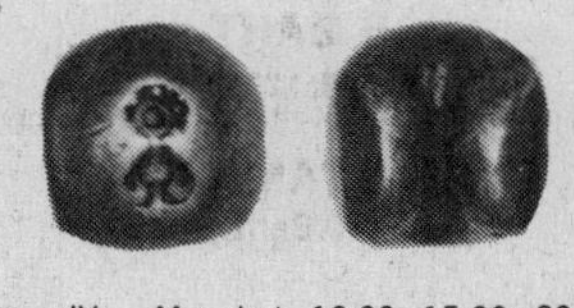

C#	King	Mark	Good	VG	Fine	VF
137	Rama IV	Mongkut	10.00	15.00	20.00	25.00
137.1	Rama IV	Mongkut and Prasat	25.00	50.00	80.00	120.00

Death of Princess Charoenkamol Suksawadi

C#	King	Mark	Good	VG	Fine	VF
177	Rama V	P'ra Kieo	—	—	Rare	—

1-1/2 BAHT

SILVER, 23.10 g

C#	King	Mark	Good	VG	Fine	VF
48	Rama III	Prasat	—	—	Rare	—

2 BAHT

SILVER, 30.80 g

C#	King	Mark	Good	VG	Fine	VF
14	Rama I	Unalom	—	—	Rare	—

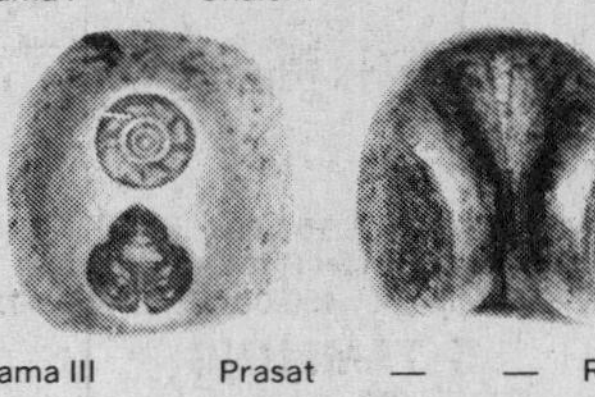

C#	King	Mark	Good	VG	Fine	VF
49	Rama III	Prasat	—	—	Rare	—

c/m: 8 dots in Chakra

C#	King	Mark	Good	VG	Fine	VF
138	Rama IV	Mongkut	45.00	75.00	125.00	185.00

c/m: 6 blades in Chakra

C#	King	Mark	Good	VG	Fine	VF
138.1	Rama IV	Mongkut	100.00	200.00	350.00	475.00

c/m: 8 blades in Chakra, elaborate design.

C#	King	Mark	Good	VG	Fine	VF
138.2	Rama IV	Mongkut	50.00	90.00	150.00	225.00

Siam / THAILAND 1604

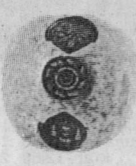

Somdet P'ra Deb Sirindhra

C#	King	Mark	Good	VG	Fine	VF
188	Rama V	Cho Rampeuy	250.00	350.00	425.00	500.00

2-1/2 BAHT

SILVER, 38.50 g

C#	King	Mark	VG	Fine	VF	XF
31	Rama III	Krut Sio	150.00	300.00	500.00	750.00

NOTE: Three varieties exist.

TAMLUNG
(4 Baht)

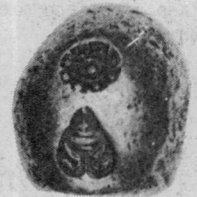 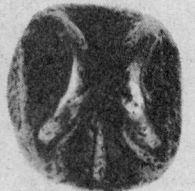

SILVER, 61.60 g
c/m: 8 dots in Chakra

139	Rama IV	Mongkut	75.00	135.00	225.00	335.00

c/m: 7 dots in Chakra

139.1	Rama IV	Mongkut	75.00	135.00	225.00	325.00

Cremation of Somdet P'ra Deb Sirindhra

189	Rama V	Cho Rampeuy	250.00	350.00	450.00	550.00

4-1/2 BAHT
SILVER

32	Rama III	Krut Sio	750.00	950.00	1000.	1150.

8 BAHT
SILVER, 123.20 g

33	Rama III	Krut Sio	750.00	950.00	1000.	1200.

2-1/2 TAMLUNG
(10 Baht)

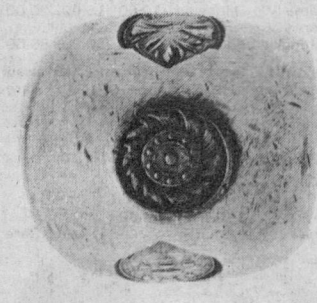

SILVER, 154.00 g
Cremation of Somdet P'ra Deb Sirindhra

190	Rama V	Cho Rampeuy	450.00	600.00	750.00	900.00

5 TAMLUNG
(20 Baht)

SILVER, 308.00 g
Cremation of Somdet P'ra Deb Sirindhra

191	Rama V	Cho Rampeuy	1200.	1500.	1850.	2250.

10 TAMLUNG
(40 Baht)

SILVER, 616.00 g
Cremation of Somdet P'ra Deb Sirindhra

C#	King	Mark	VG	Fine	VF	XF
192	Rama V	Cho Rampeuy	2250.	3000.	3750.	4500.

20 TAMLUNG
(80 Baht)

SILVER, 1,232.00 g
Cremation of Somdet P'ra Deb Sirindhra

193	Rama V	Cho Rampeuy	4500.	6000.	7500.	9000.

140	Rama IV	Mongkut	4500.	6000.	7500.	9000.

GOLD POT DUANG
(Bullet Coins)

1/32 GOLD BAHT
GOLD, 0.48 g

152	Rama IV	P'ra Tao	60.00	80.00	100.00	120.00
162	Rama IV	Mongkut	—	—	—	—

1/16 GOLD BAHT
GOLD, 0.96 g

92	Rama III	Prasat	75.00	100.00	125.00	150.00
153	Rama IV	P'ra Tao	90.00	130.00	165.00	200.00
163	Rama IV	Mongkut	70.00	90.00	100.00	120.00

1/8 GOLD BAHT

GOLD, 1.96 g

93	Rama III	Prasat	100.00	150.00	200.00	250.00
103	Rama III	Dok Mai	150.00	200.00	250.00	300.00
113	Rama III	Bai Matum	150.00	200.00	250.00	300.00
154	Rama IV	P'ra Tao	90.00	120.00	160.00	180.00

1/4 GOLD BAHT

GOLD, 3.85 g

155	Rama IV	P'ra Tao	100.00	140.00	170.00	200.00
165	Rama IV	Mongkut	250.00	325.00	400.00	475.00

1/2 GOLD BAHT
GOLD, 7.70 g

105	Rama III	Dok Mai	—	—	Rare	—
166	Rama IV	Mongkut	175.00	250.00	325.00	400.00

GOLD BAHT
GOLD, 15.40 g

96	Rama III	Prasat	600.00	850.00	1100.	1350.
167	Rama IV	Mongkut	500.00	700.00	900.00	1150.

1-1/2 GOLD BAHT
GOLD, 23.10 g

C#	King	Mark	VG	Fine	VF	XF
167.5	Rama IV	Mongkut	—	—	Rare	—

2 GOLD BAHT
GOLD, 30.80 g

168	Rama IV	Mongkut	650.00	700.00	850.00	1000.

4 GOLD BAHT
GOLD, 61.60 g

169	Rama IV	Mongkut	1200.	1500.	1700.	2000.

COUNTERMARKED TRADE COINAGE

Foreign trade brought in quantities of silver 8 Reales which were not widely accepted by the public. As a result many were countermarked with the royal marks "Chakra" and "Mongkut" in the period 1858-1860 to guarantee their value.

DOLLAR

.903 SILVER
c/m: Chakra and Mongkut on Chihuahua 8 Reales, KM#377.2.

C#	Date	Year	Good	VG	Fine	VF
141.1	ND	(1831-57)	275.00	450.00	800.00	1200.

c/m: Chakra and Mongkut on Durango 8 Reales, KM#377.4.

141.4	ND	(1825-57)	275.00	450.00	800.00	1200.

c/m: Chakra and Mongkut on Guanajanto 8 Reales, KM#377.8.

141.6	ND	(1825-57)	200.00	325.00	550.00	800.00

c/m: Chakra and Mongkut on Mexico City 8 Reales, KM#377.10.

C#	Date	Year	Good	VG	Fine	VF
141.8	ND	(1824-57)	200.00	325.00	550.00	800.00

c/m: Chakra and Mongkut on Zacatecas 8 Reales, KM#377.13.

141.11ND	(1825-57)	275.00	450.00	800.00	1200.

c/m: Chakra and Mongkut on Cuzco 8 Reales, KM#142.4.

141.14ND	(1830-34)	350.00	600.00	1000.	1500.

c/m: Chakra and Mongkut on Lima 8 Reales, KM#142.10.

141.17ND	(1841-55)	350.00	600.00	1000.	1500.

c/m: Chakra and Mongkut on Philippines 8 Reales, KM#129.

C#	Date	Year	Good	VG	Fine	VF
141.20ND	(1825-57)	600.00	1000.	1750.	2500.

LOCAL COINAGE

The following tin coins were struck in 5 of the 7 districts formerly comprising the Kingdom of Patani, during the period of Thai Suzerainty (1832-1902).

JARING
(Jering)

All coins of Jaring are uniface

One of the 7 provinces cut out of Patani State after the uprising of 1830/31. It lies on the east coast of the Malay peninsula. The uniface tin coins were made from 1845 to 1894.

TITLES

Jering   جريج

PITIS

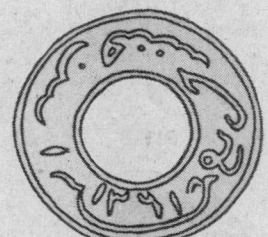

TIN
Arabic leg: *Ini Pitis Jering Sanat 1261*

KM#	Date	Good	VG	Fine	VF
1	AH1261	10.00	15.00	30.00	65.00

Arabic leg: *Ini Pitis Balad Jarin Sanat 1297*

2	AH1297	10.00	15.00	30.00	65.00

Arabic leg: *Hadha al-Diwan al-Raj al-Adil Fi Balad al-Jarin 1302*

3	AH1302	11.50	17.50	35.00	70.00
	1312	11.50	17.50	35.00	70.00

Crude imitation of KM#3

3a	ND	6.00	10.00	15.00	30.00

LEGEH
Ligeh, Ligor, Langkat

One of the inland provinces cut out of Patani State. Coins attributable to Legeh run from 1840 to 1893. Siam again assumed control in 1902.

TITLES

Dar Es-Salam   دار السلام

Negri Ligkeh   نكري لغكه

PITIS

TIN
Obv. leg: Arabic *Pitis Negeri Langkat Dar al-Salam.* Rev. leg: Arabic *Malik al Adil Khalifat al-Mu'minin.*

KM#	Date	Good	VG	Fine	VF
1	ND	13.50	20.00	40.00	70.00

NOTE: For a piece dated 1256, sometimes attributed to Legeh, see KM#4 of Kelantan (Malaysia).

Obv. leg: Arabic *Al-Sultan al-Muzaffar Daulat Langkat Khalifat.*
Rev. leg: Arabic *Al-Shamar Wal-Qamar Fi Rabi al-Awal Sanat 1307*

2	AH1307	7.50	15.00	30.00	55.00
	1313	—	Reported, not confirmed		

PATANI
Pattani

Patani (Pattani), a former Malay state in the Malay peninsula, is a small province or 'changwat' of Thailand (Siam) on the eastern side of peninsular Thailand near the border of Malaya, has an area of 777 sq. mi. (2,012 sq. km.) and a population of about 275,000. After the 1830/31 uprising it was one of 7 provinces administered by Siam through Malayan governors. Patani was the most prolific coin issuer of the Siamese period having made coins periodically from 1845 to 1891. Formerly ruled by a Moslem Rajah subject to Siam.

TITLES

Khalifat Al-Karam   خليفة الكرم

Al-Patani   الفطاني

PITIS

Patani / THAILAND 1606

TIN
Obv. leg: Arabic *Ini Pitis Belanja Raja Patani.*
Rev. leg: Arabic *Khalifat al-Mu'minin Sanat 1261.*

KM#	Date	Good	VG	Fine	VF
1	AH1261	7.50	12.50	17.50	25.00

Obv. leg: Arabic *Al-Sultan al-Azam Wa Khalifat al-Karam.* Rev. leg: Arabic *Al-Malik al-Balad al-Patani al-Imami 1284*

| 2 | AH1284 | 7.50 | 12.50 | 17.50 | 25.00 |

Obv. leg: Arabic *Al-Sultan al-Patani Sanat 1297.*
Rev. leg: Arabic *Wa Khalifat al-Karam.*

| 3 | AH1297 | 7.50 | 12.50 | 17.50 | 25.00 |

Obv. leg: Arabic *Al-Matsaraf Fi Balad al-Patania Sanat 1301.* Rev. leg: Arabic *Zarb Fi Harat al-Daulat Azza Nasrahu*

| 4 | AH1301 | 12.50 | 17.50 | 25.00 | 35.00 |

Obv. leg: Arabic *Al-Matsaraf Fi Balad al-Patani Sanat 1309.* Rev. leg: Arabic *Ini Pitis Belanja di-Dalam Negri Patani*

| 5 | AH1309 | 7.50 | 12.50 | 17.50 | 25.00 |

KUPANG

GOLD
Obv: Bull standing to left.
Rev. leg: Arabic *Malik al-Adil* in 2 lines.

KM#	Date	Year	Fine	VF	XF	Unc
50	ND	(1800-50)	45.00	50.00	60.00	80.00

Obv: Bull standing to left.
Rev. leg: Arabic *Al-Adil.*

| 51 | ND | (1800-50) | 45.00 | 50.00 | 60.00 | 80.00 |

Obv: Bull standing to left.
Rev. leg: Arabic *Malik al-Adil* in 3 lines.

| 52 | ND | (1800-50) | 45.00 | 50.00 | 60.00 | 80.00 |

Obv: Bull standing to left.
Rev. leg: Arabic *Asma Adil.*

| 53 | ND | (1800-50) | 45.00 | 50.00 | 60.00 | 80.00 |

Obv: Bull standing to right.
Rev. leg: Arabic *Malik al-Adil* in 2 lines.

| 54 | ND | (1800-50) | 80.00 | 85.00 | 110.00 | 140.00 |

Obv: 8-pointed star.
Rev. leg: Arabic *Malik al-Adil.*

| 55 | ND | (1800-50) | 50.00 | 60.00 | 75.00 | 100.00 |

Obv: 6-pointed star.
Rev. leg: Arabic *Malik al-Adil.*

| 56 | ND | (1800-50) | 45.00 | 50.00 | 60.00 | 80.00 |

Obv: 4-petalled flower.
Rev. leg: Arabic *Malik al-Adil.*

| 57 | ND | (1800-50) | 50.00 | 60.00 | 70.00 | 90.00 |

Obv. leg: Arabic *Dama Shah.*
Rev. leg: Arabic *Binaqdi Sahibi.*

KM#	Date	Year	Fine	VF	XF	Unc
58	ND	(1800-50)	50.00	60.00	70.00	90.00

Obv. leg: Arabic *Shah Adil.*
Rev. leg: Arabic *Malik al-Adil.*

| 59 | ND | (1800-50) | 50.00 | 60.00 | 70.00 | 90.00 |

Obv. leg: Arabic *Al-Julus Kelantan.*
Rev. leg: Arabic *Al-Mutawakkilu Ala Liah.*

| 60 | ND | (1800-50) | 50.00 | 60.00 | 70.00 | 90.00 |

Obv. leg: Arabic *Aqam'u'd-Din.*
Rev. leg: Arabic *Malik al-Adil.*

| 61 | ND | (1800-50) | 50.00 | 60.00 | 70.00 | 90.00 |

Obv. leg: Arabic *Shah Alam.*
Rev. leg: Arabic *Malik al-Adil.*

| 62 | ND | (1800-50) | 50.00 | 60.00 | 70.00 | 90.00 |

Obv. leg: Arabic *Sultan.*
Rev. leg: Arabic *Mu'azzam Shah.*

| 63 | ND | (1800-50) | 60.00 | 70.00 | 85.00 | 110.00 |

Obv. leg: Arabic *Sultan Muhammad.*
Rev. leg: Arabic *Mu'azzam Shah.*

| 64 | ND | (1800-50) | 60.00 | 70.00 | 85.00 | 110.00 |

Obv. leg: Arabic *Al-Julus Kelantan.*
Rev. leg: Arabic *Khalifata'r-Rahman.*

| 65 | ND(1800-50) | — | 40.00 | 50.00 | 60.00 | 90.00 |

REMAN
Rhaman

Another of the inland provinces cut from Patani State. Only a single type tin coin is presently known from Reman. This piece was minted about 1890.

TITLES

Rehman

PITIS

TIN
Uniface. Retrograde Arabic leg: *Ini Pitis Rahman Raja Melayu*

KM#	Date	Good	VG	Fine	VF
1	ND	12.50	20.00	40.00	70.00

SAI
Saiburi, Teluban

Sai is one of the provinces on the east coast of Malaya cut from the state of Patani. The tin Pitis of this province were made from c.1870 to 1891 and are distinctive in that they have a reverse that bears no legend. It carries only a decorative motif.

TITLES

Al-Saiwi

PITIS

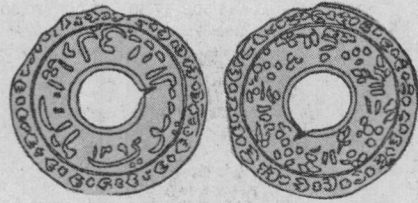

TIN
Obv. leg: Arabic *Malik al-Adil Fi Balad al-Saiwi 1290*

| 1 | AH1290 | 12.50 | 17.50 | 25.00 | 50.00 |

Obv. leg: Arabic *Al-Dawlat al-Khairiyat Fi Balad al-Saiwi 1307*

KM#	Date	Good	VG	Fine	VF
2	AH1307	12.50	17.50	25.00	50.00

NOTE: A number of Chinese token issues are tentatively assigned to the Patani state of Jala (Jalor).

THAILAND

REGULAR COINAGE

1/16 FUANG
(1 Solot)

TIN
Dark color and crude rims. Usually plain edge.

Y#	Date	Year	VG	Fine	VF	XF
5	ND	(1862)	1.00	2.00	4.00	6.00

NOTE: Rotated dies are common.

| 16 | ND | (1868) | 4.00 | 9.50 | 17.50 | 30.00 |

1/2 ATT
(1 Solot)

COPPER

Y#	Date	Mintage	Fine	VF	XF	Unc
17	CS1236(1874)	—	.75	1.50	4.50	11.00
	1244(1882)	2.560	.75	1.50	4.50	11.00

COPPER-NICKEL (OMS)

| 17a | CS1244(1882) | — | 75.00 | 125.00 | 150.00 | 225.00 |

BRONZE

21	(CS)1249(1887)					
		—	1.50	3.00	5.00	12.00
	(RS)109(1890)					
		10.240	.75	1.50	4.50	9.00
	118(1899)	—	.75	1.50	4.50	9.00
	124(1905)	—	.75	1.50	4.50	9.00

NOTE: These coins were also minted in RS114, RS115, RS121, and RS122. The last year had a mintage of 5,120,000. Coins with these dates have not been observed and were probably additional mintings of coins dated RS109 and RS118. Varieties in numeral size and rotated dies exist.

1/8 FUANG
(1 Att)

TIN
Dark color, reeded edge.

Y#	Date	Year	VG	Fine	VF	XF
6	ND	(1862)	1.00	2.00	4.00	9.00

NOTE: Rotated dies are common. At least three die varieties are known. Contemporary counterfeits from Hong Kong were also widely distributed. They are somewhat more common in the higher grades.

ATT
(1/64 Baht)

COPPER

Y#	Date	Mintage	Fine	VF	XF	Unc
18	CS1236(1874)	—	1.00	2.00	4.00	8.00
	1238(1876)	—	1.00	2.00	4.00	8.00
	(CS)1244(1882) 15.300		1.00	2.00	4.00	8.00

BRONZE

Y#	Date	Mintage	Fine	VF	XF	Unc
22	(CS)1249(1887)	—	1.75	3.50	6.00	12.00
	RS109(1890) 10.240		1.00	2.00	4.00	8.50
	114*(1895) 5.120		1.00	2.00	4.00	8.50
	115(1896)	—	1.00	2.00	4.00	8.50
	(CS)118(1899)	—	1.00	2.00	4.00	8.50
	121(1902) 11.251		1.00	2.00	4.00	8.50
	RS122*(1903) 4.109		1.00	2.00	4.00	8.50
	(CS)124(1905)	—	1.00	2.00	4.00	8.50

*NOTE: RS114 and RS122 exist with large and small numerals.

1/4 FUANG
(1/32 Baht = 1 Sio)

COPPER
Thick (2.5mm) planchet, crude with plain edge.

Y#	Date	Year	VG	Fine	VF	XF
1	ND	(1865)	12.00	25.00	40.00	65.00

NOTE: Rotated dies are common.

BRASS

| 1a | ND | (1865) | 12.00 | 30.00 | 45.00 | 75.00 |

COPPER
Thin (1.5mm) planchet

| 3 | ND | (1865) | 11.00 | 25.00 | 40.00 | 65.00 |

BRASS

| 3a | ND | (1865) | — | | | |

2 ATT
(1/32 Baht = 1 Sio)

COPPER

Y#	Date	Mintage	Fine	VF	XF	Unc
19	CS1236(1874)	—	1.75	3.50	6.00	13.00
	1238(1876)	—	1.75	3.50	6.00	13.00
	1244(1882) 10.200		1.75	3.50	6.00	13.00

BRONZE

23	CS1249(1887)	—	3.00	6.00	10.00	20.00
	RS109(1890) 5.120		1.25	2.50	5.00	12.00
	(RS)114(1895)	—	1.25	2.50	5.00	12.00
	115(1896)	—	1.25	2.50	5.00	12.00
	118(1899)	—	1.25	2.50	5.00	12.00
	119(1900) .735		2.00	4.00	10.00	20.00
	121(1902)	—	1.25	2.50	5.00	12.00
	2.797		1.25	2.50	5.00	12.00
	(RS)122(1903) 2.323		1.25	2.50	5.00	12.00
	(RS)124(1905)	—	1.25	2.50	5.00	12.00

NOTE: Varieties in numeral size and rotated dies exist.

1/2 FUANG
(1/16 Baht = 1 Sik)

COPPER
Thick (3mm) planchet. Crude, plain edges.

Y#	Date	Year	VG	Fine	VF	XF
2	ND	(1865)	7.50	15.00	25.00	55.00

BRASS

| 2a | ND | (1865) | 10.00 | 20.00 | 35.00 | 65.00 |

COPPER
Thin (1.5mm) planchet.

| 4 | ND | (1865) | 10.00 | 20.00 | 40.00 | 90.00 |

BRASS

| 4a | ND | (1865) | 15.00 | 30.00 | 50.00 | 100.00 |

NOTE: Rotated dies are common.

1/16 BAHT
(1 Sik)

SILVER
Thick Flan

Y#	Date	Mintage	Fine	VF	XF	Unc
7.1 (Y7)	ND(1860)	—	20.00	30.00	50.00	70.00

Obv: Smaller crown, Rev: Larger elephant.

| 7.2 (Y7.1) | ND(1860) | — | 40.00 | 60.00 | 85.00 | 130.00 |

.900 GOLD
Reeded edge
Similar to 1/16 Baht, Y#7, but thinner planchet.

| 7a | ND(1864) | — | 275.00 | 350.00 | 400.00 | 600.00 |

4 ATT
(1/16 Baht = 1 Sik)

COPPER

Y#	Date	Mintage	Fine	VF	XF	Unc
20	(CS)1238(1876)	—	15.00	30.00	50.00	75.00

NOTE: Beware of high quality fakes which rock when placed on a flat surface.

FUANG
(1/8 Baht)

SILVER
Thick flan
Denomination indicated by number of stars on plain edge; 8 stars = 1 Baht.

| 8 | ND(1860) | — | 6.00 | 12.00 | 20.00 | |

.900 GOLD
Reeded edge
Similar to 1 Fuang, Y#8, but thinner planchet.

| 8a | ND(1864) | — | 250.00 | 400.00 | 550.00 | 750.00 |

SILVER

| 28 | ND(1868) | — | 3.00 | 6.00 | 12.00 | 20.00 |

| 32.1 (Y32) | ND(1876-1902) | — | 2.50 | 3.50 | 5.00 | 8.00 |

GOLD

| 32.1a (Y32a) | ND(1876) | — | 150.00 | 200.00 | 250.00 | 300.00 |

SILVER

32.2 (Y32.1)	RS120(1901)	—	2.00	3.00	5.00	8.00
	121(1902) .380		2.00	3.00	5.00	8.00
	122(1903) .460		2.00	3.00	5.00	8.00
	123(1904) .310		2.00	3.00	5.00	8.00
	124(1905) .410		2.00	3.00	5.00	8.00
	125(1906)	—	2.00	3.00	5.00	8.00
	(RS)126(1907)	—	2.00	3.00	5.00	8.00
	127(1908) .480		2.00	3.00	5.00	8.00

GOLD

32.2a (Y32.1a)	RS122 (1903)	300.00	400.00	500.00	650.00
	RS123 (1904)	300.00	400.00	500.00	650.00
	RS124 (1905)	300.00	400.00	500.00	650.00
	RS125 (1906)	300.00	400.00	500.00	650.00
	RS126 (1907)	300.00	400.00	500.00	650.00
	RS127 (1908)	300.00	400.00	500.00	650.00
	RS128 (1909)	300.00	400.00	500.00	650.00
	RS129 (1910)	300.00	400.00	500.00	650.00

SALUNG
(1/4 Baht)

SILVER
Thick flan
Denomination indicated by number of stars on plain

THAILAND 1608

edge; 8 stars = 1 Baht.

Y#	Date	Mintage	Fine	VF	XF	Unc
9	ND(1860)	—	10.00	25.00	50.00	80.00

GOLD

| 9a | ND(1864) | — | 500.00 | 600.00 | 700.00 | 800.00 |

SILVER

| 29 | ND(1868) | — | 7.50 | 15.00 | 25.00 | 50.00 |

| 33 | ND(1876-1902) | — | 5.00 | 8.00 | 13.00 | 18.00 |
| | ND(1876-1902) | — | — | — | Proof | 100.00 |

33a	RS120(1901)	—	3.50	5.00	8.00	15.00
	121(1902)	.560	2.50	4.00	7.00	15.00
	122(1903)	.340	2.50	4.00	7.00	15.00
	123(1904)	.190	3.50	5.00	8.00	15.00
	125(1906)		2.50	4.00	7.00	15.00
	126(1907)	—	3.50	5.00	8.00	15.00
	(RS)127(1908)	.270	2.50	4.00	7.00	15.00

2 SALUNG
(1/2 Baht)

SILVER
Thick flan
Denomination indicated by number of stars on the edge; 8 stars = 1 Baht.

| 10.1 (Y10) | ND(1860) | — | 30.00 | 60.00 | 100.00 | 150.00 |

Thin flan

| 10.2 (Y10.1) | ND(1864) | — | 950.00 | 1350.00 | 1650. | 2200. |

GOLD

| 10.2a (Y10.1a) | ND(1864) | — | 700.00 | 900.00 | 1400. | 1800. |

Reeded edge.

| 15.5 | ND(1895) | — | 700.00 | 1100. | 1500. | 2000. |

BAHT

15.4500 g, .900 SILVER, .4470 oz ASW
Thick flan
Denomination indicated by number of stars on plain edge; 8 stars = 1 Baht.

| 11 | ND(1860) | — | 12.00 | 20.00 | 45.00 | 100.00 |

GOLD

| 11a | ND(1864) | — | 1400. | 1700. | 2000. | 3000. |

SILVER

Y#	Date	Mintage	Fine	VF	XF	Unc
31	ND(1868)	—	12.00	20.00	45.00	100.00

| 34 | ND(1876-1902) | — | 6.00 | 15.00 | 25.00 | 40.00 |

34a	RS120(1901)	—	60.00	100.00	135.00	225.00
	121(1902)	*4.070	6.00	15.00	20.00	50.00
	122(1903)	19.150	5.00	12.00	15.00	40.00
	123(1904)	4.790	5.00	12.00	17.50	45.00
	(RS)124(1905)	6.770	5.00	12.00	17.50	45.00
	125(1906)	—	5.00	12.00	17.50	45.00
	126(1907)	12.00	12.00	25.00	35.00	60.00

*NOTE: Because of a faulty die used the second 1 appears to be a 0 in some examples of this date.

2 BAHT

30.2000 g, .900 SILVER, .8738 oz ASW
Denomination indicated by number of stars on plain edge; 16 stars = 2 Baht.

| 12 | ND(1860) | — | 150.00 | 250.00 | 375.00 | 600.00 |

GOLD

| 12a | ND(1864) | — | 3500. | 4000. | 4650. | 5500. |

2-1/2 BAHT

GOLD
Rev: Small elephant.

| 13 | ND(1863) | — | 250.00 | 400.00 | 550.00 | 750.00 |

Rev: Large elephant.

Y#	Date	Mintage	Fine	VF	XF	Unc
13.5	ND(1895)	—	250.00	400.00	650.00	850.00

4 BAHT

60.4000 g, .900 SILVER, 1.7477 oz ASW
Plain edge

| A12 | ND(1860) | — | 1750. | 2750. | 4250. | 6000. |

GOLD, 60.77 g

| A12a | ND(1864) | — | — | — | Rare | — |

NOTE: Spink-Taisei Auction, Feb. 1988, XF specimen realized $74,800.

Reeded edge, 3.40 g.
Obv: Small elephant.

| 14 | ND(1863) | — | 300.00 | 450.00 | 600.00 | 800.00 |

3.80 g
Obv: Large elephant.

| 14.5 | ND(1895) | — | 300.00 | 400.00 | 550.00 | 750.00 |

8 BAHT

GOLD, 6.80 g
Reeded edge.
Obv: Small elephant.

| 15 | ND(1863) | — | 500.00 | 900.00 | 1200. | 1800. |

7.60 g
Obv: Large elephant.

| 15.6 | ND(1895) | — | 700.00 | 1000. | 1300. | 2000. |

DECIMAL COINAGE
100 Satang = 1 Baht
25 Satang = 1 Salung

THAILAND 1609

1/2 SATANG

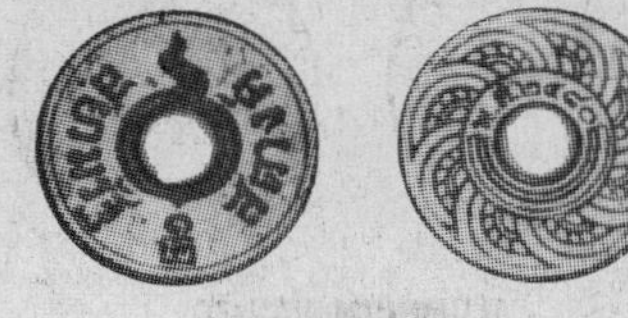

BRONZE

Y#	Date	Year	Mintage	VF	XF	Unc
50	(BE)2480	(1937)	—	.50	1.50	2.50

SATANG

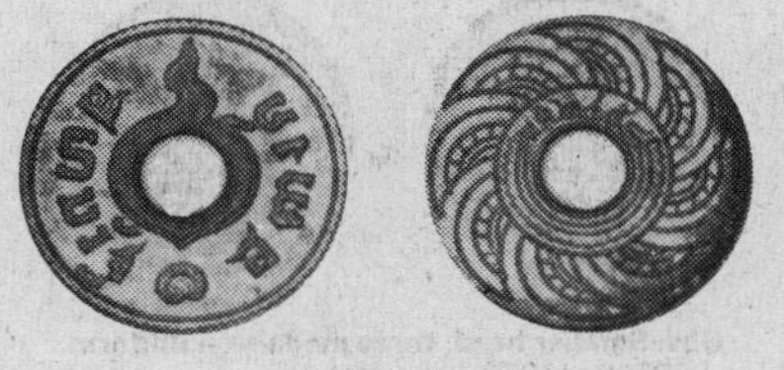

BRONZE

Y#	Date	Year	Mintage	VF	XF	Unc
35	RS127	(1908)	17.000	2.50	5.00	15.00
	128	(1909)	.150	3.50	7.00	20.00
	(RS)129	(1910)	9.000	1.50	3.50	15.00
	130	(1911)	30.000	1.50	3.50	10.00
	BE2456	(1913)	10.000	1.00	1.50	3.50
	2457	(1914)	1.000	2.00	4.00	10.00
	2458	(1915)	5.000	.75	1.00	2.25
	2461	(1918)	18.880	.65	1.25	2.50
	2462	(1919)	6.400	.65	1.00	2.25
	2463	(1920)	17.240	1.00	1.50	3.00
	2464	(1921)	6.360	15.00	25.00	35.00
	2466	(1923)	14.000	.75	1.00	2.25
	2467	(1924)	Inc. Ab.	1.00	1.50	3.00
	2469	(1926)	20.000	.50	.75	2.00
	2470	(1927)	—	.50	.75	2.00
	2472	(1929)	—	.50	1.00	2.25
	2478	(1935)	—	.50	.70	1.50
	2480	(1937)	—	.50	.70	1.50

NOTE: Variations in lettering exist.

GOLD (OMS)

Y#	Date	Year	Mintage	VF	XF	Unc
35a	RS127	(1908)	—	—	Rare	—

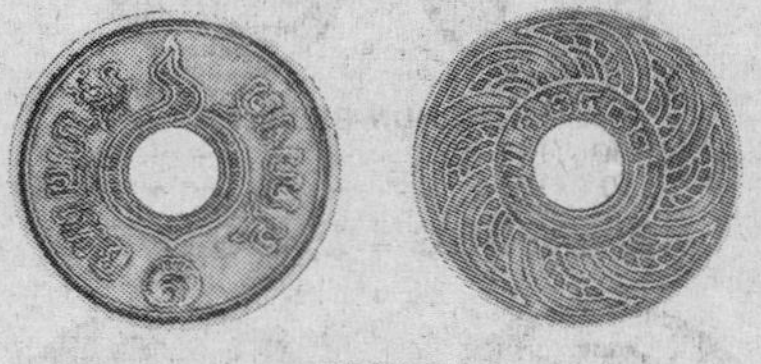

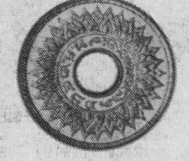

BRONZE

Y#	Date	Year	Mintage	VF	XF	Unc
51	BE2482	(1939)	24.400	1.50	3.00	6.00

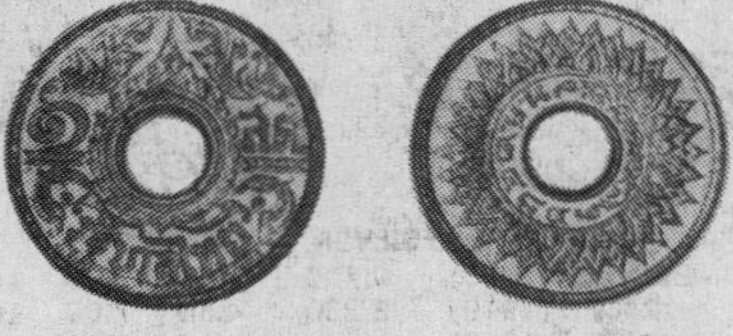

Y#	Date	Year	Mintage	VF	XF	Unc
54	BE2484	(1941)	—	.50	1.50	3.00

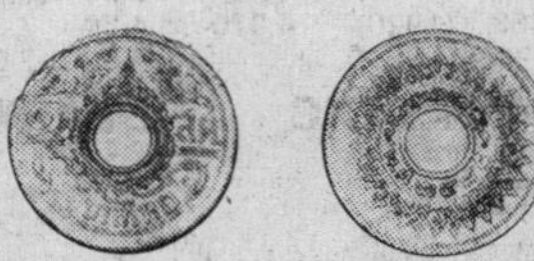

TIN
BE date & denomination in Thai numerals, w/o hole.

Y#	Date	Year	Mintage	VF	XF	Unc
57	BE2485	(1942)	20.700	.30	.50	1.00

NOTE: Approximately 790,000 coins were restruck for circulation 1967-73.

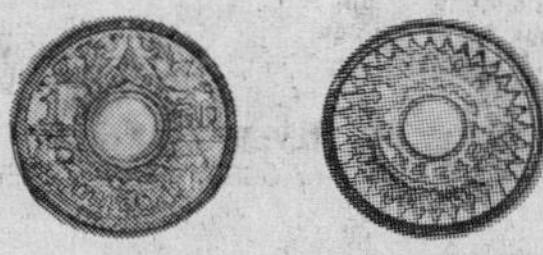

BE date and denomination in Western numerals, w/o hole.

Y#	Date	Year	Mintage	VF	XF	Unc
60	BE2487	—	.500	.10	.20	.50

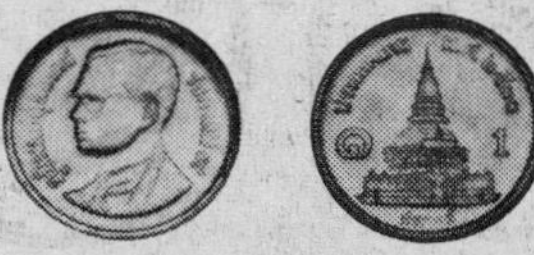

ALUMINUM

Y#	Date	Year	Mintage	VF	XF	Unc
186	BE2530	(1987)	—	—	—	.10
	2531	(1988)	—	—	—	.10

2-1/2 SATANG

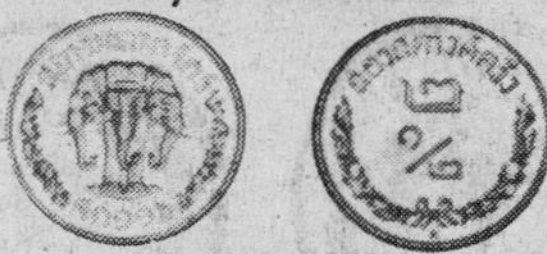

COPPER-NICKEL

Y#	Date	Year	Mintage	VF	XF	Unc
24	RS116H	(1897)	5.080	3.00	4.00	6.00

NOTE: Issued in 1898 although dated RS116 (1897).

5 SATANG

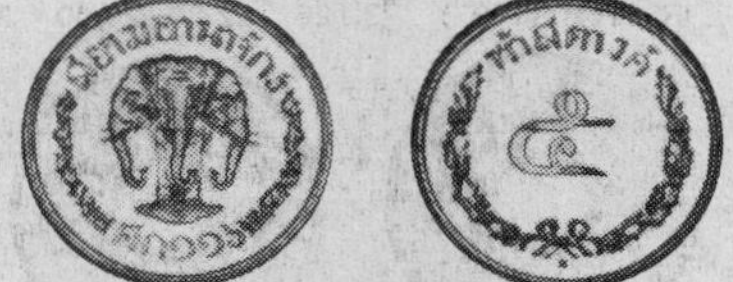

COPPER-NICKEL

Y#	Date	Year	Mintage	VF	XF	Unc
25	RS116H	(1897)	5.080	10.00	14.00	20.00

NOTE: Issued in 1898 although dated RS116 (1897).

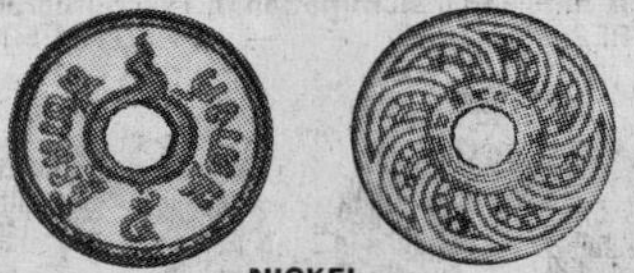

NICKEL

Y#	Date	Year	Mintage	VF	XF	Unc
36	RS127	(1908)	7.000	3.00	4.00	6.00
	128	(1909)	4.000	3.50	4.50	7.00
	129	(1910)	4.000	1.50	2.00	5.00
	131	(1912)	2.000	1.50	2.50	6.00
	BE2456	(1913)	2.000	1.50	2.50	4.00
	2457	(1914)	2.000	1.50	2.50	4.00
	2461	(1918)	2.000	1.50	2.50	4.00
	2462	(1919)	2.000	1.00	2.00	4.00
	2463	(1920)	9.900	1.00	1.50	3.00
	2464	(1921)	13.000	.60	1.00	2.00
	2469	(1926)	20.000	.60	1.00	2.00
	2478	(1935)	10.000	.50	1.00	2.00
	2480	(1937)	20.000	.60	1.25	2.00
	2482	(1939)	—Reported, not confirmed			

NOTE: Variations in lettering exist.

GOLD (OMS)

Y#	Date	Year	Mintage	VF	XF	Unc
36a	RS127	(1908)	—	—	Rare	—

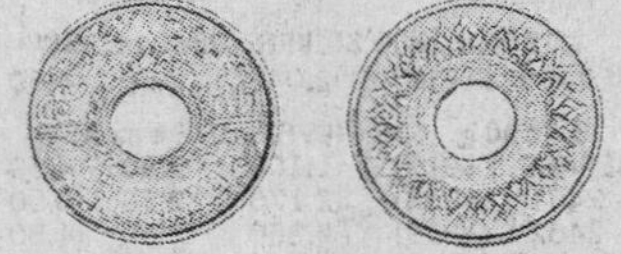

1.5000 g, .650 SILVER, .0313 oz ASW

Y#	Date	Year	Mintage	VF	XF	Unc
55	(BE)2484	(1941)	—	2.00	3.00	4.50

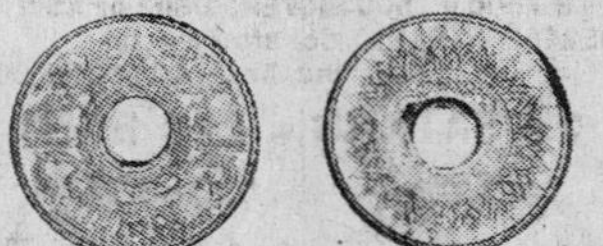

TIN
BE date and denomination in Thai numerals.

Y#	Date	Year	Mintage	VF	XF	Unc
58	(BE)2485	(1942)	—	.50	1.50	3.00

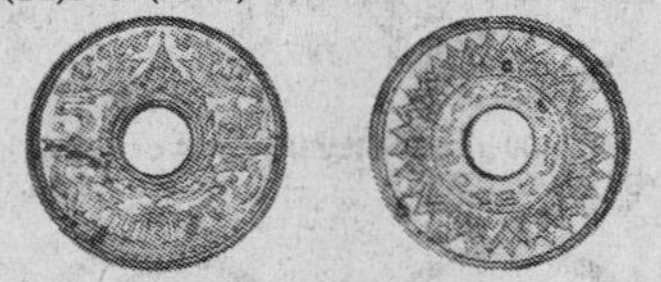

Thick (2.2mm) planchet.
BE date and denomination in Western numerals.

Y#	Date	Year	Mintage	VF	XF	Unc
61	BE2487	(1944)	—	.50	1.25	3.00
	2488	(1945)	—	.50	1.25	3.00

Medium planchet

Y#	Date	Year	Mintage	VF	XF	Unc
61b	BE2488	(1945)	—	.50	1.25	3.00

Thin (2.0mm) planchet.

Y#	Date	Year	Mintage	VF	XF	Unc
61a	BE2488	(1945)	—	.50	1.25	3.00

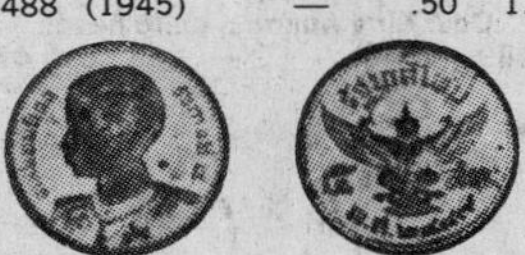

Obv: King Ananda, child head.

Y#	Date	Year	Mintage	VF	XF	Unc
64	BE2489	(1946)	—	.50	1.00	2.00

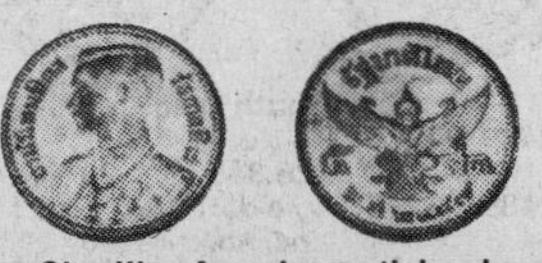

Obv: King Ananda, youth head.

Y#	Date	Year	Mintage	VF	XF	Unc
68	BE2489	(1946)	24.480	.15	.50	1.00

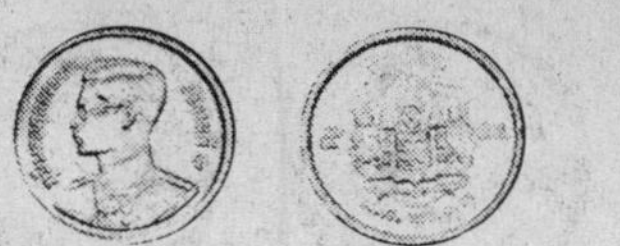

Obv: King Bhumiphol, one medal on uniform.

Y#	Date	Year	Mintage	VF	XF	Unc
72	BE2493	(1950)	*6.480	.50	1.00	1.50

*Coins bearing this date were also struck in 1954, 58, 59, and 73. Mintages are included here.

ALUMINUM-BRONZE

Y#	Date	Year	Mintage	VF	XF	Unc
72a	BE2493	(1950)	15.500	.25	1.00	2.00

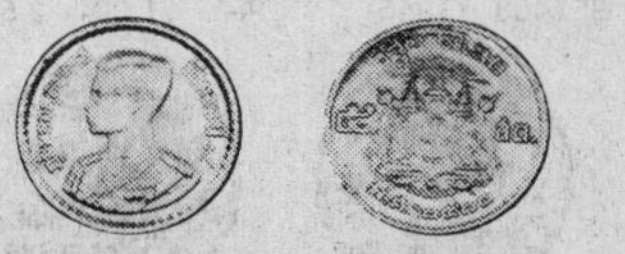

Obv: Smaller head, three medals on uniform.

Y#	Date	Year	Mintage	VF	XF	Unc
78	BE2500	(1957)	*46.440	—	.10	.25

*Current issues are minted without date change.

BRONZE

Y#	Date	Year	Mintage	VF	XF	Unc
78a	BE2500	(1957)	*6.240	.50	1.50	2.00

TIN

Y#	Date	Year	Mintage	VF	XF	Unc
78b	BE2500	(1957)	—	1.75	3.00	5.00

NOTE: The above coins were struck to replace Y#72 in mint sets.

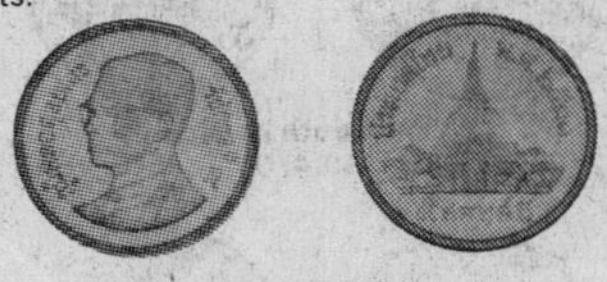

ALUMINUM

Y#	Date	Year	Mintage	VF	XF	Unc
208	BE2531	(1988)	—	—	—	.10

10 SATANG

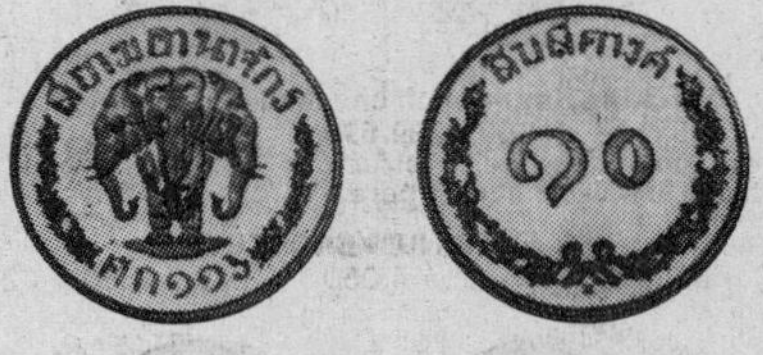

COPPER-NICKEL

Y#	Date	Year	Mintage	VF	XF	Unc
26	RS116H	(1897)	3.810	20.00	30.00	40.00

NICKEL

Y#	Date	Year	Mintage	VF	XF	Unc
37	RS127	(1908)	7.000	1.50	3.00	6.00
	(RS)129	(1910)	5.000	1.50	3.00	6.00
	130	(1911)	.500	2.00	5.00	8.00
	131	(1912)	1.500	1.50	3.00	7.00
	BE2456	(1913)	1.000	1.25	2.00	4.00
	2457	(1914)	1.000	1.25	2.00	4.00
	2461	(1918)	.770	2.50	3.50	6.00
	2462	(1919)	.774	1.25	1.50	2.00
	(BE)2463	(1920)	Inc. Ab.	1.25	1.50	2.00
	2464	(1921)	21.727	1.00	1.25	1.50
	2478	(1935)	5.000	1.00	1.25	1.50
	2480	(1937)	5.000	.75	1.00	1.25
	2482	(1939)	—Reported, not confirmed			

NOTE: Variations in lettering exist.

GOLD (OMS)

Y#	Date	Year	Mintage	VF	XF	Unc
37a	RS127	(1908)	—	—	Rare	—

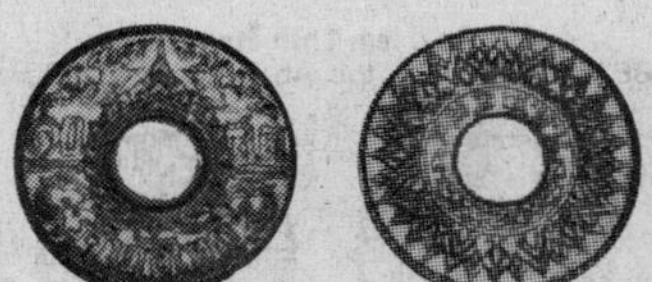

2.5000 g, .650 SILVER, .0522 oz ASW

Y#	Date	Year	Mintage	VF	XF	Unc
56	BE2484	(1941)	—	4.00	6.00	9.00

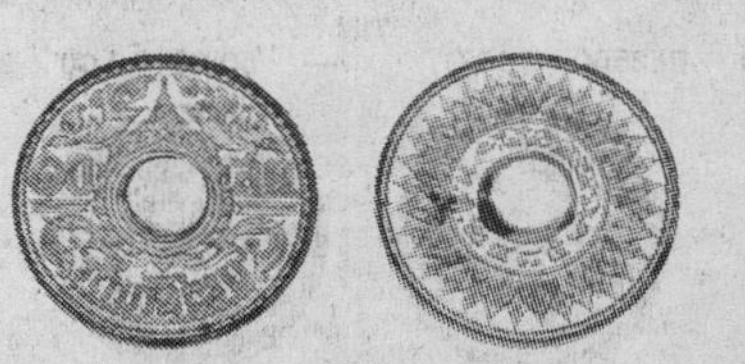

TIN
BE date and denomination in Thai numerals.

Y#	Date	Year	Mintage	VF	XF	Unc
59	BE2485	(1942)	.230	1.00	2.00	3.50

THAILAND 1610

Thick (2.5mm) planchet.
BE date and denomination in Western numerals.

Y#	Date	Year	Mintage	VF	XF	Unc
62	BE2487	(1944)	—	1.00	2.00	3.50

Thin (2.0mm) planchet.

| 62a | BE2488 | (1945) | — | 1.00 | 2.50 | 4.00 |

Obv: King Ananda, child head.

| 65 | BE2489 | (1946) | — | .50 | 1.25 | 2.25 |

Obv: Youth head.

| 69 | BE2489 | (1946) | 40.470 | .50 | 1.25 | 2.00 |

Obv: King Bhumiphol, one medal on uniform.

| 73 | BE2493 | (1950) | *139.695 | .40 | 1.00 | 1.50 |

*These coins were also struck in 1954-1973 and the mintages are also included here.

ALUMINUM-BRONZE

| 73a | BE2493 | (1950) | 4.060 | .75 | 1.50 | 2.50 |

Obv: Smaller head. Three medals on uniform.

| 79 | BE2500 | (1957) | *55.410 | .10 | .25 | .50 |

*Current issues are minted without date change.

BRONZE
Rev. leg: Thick style.

| 79a | BE2500 | (1957) | *13.365 | .25 | .75 | 1.25 |

Rev. leg: Thin style.

| 79c | BE2500 | (1957) | Inc. Ab. | 2.50 | 5.00 | 10.00 |

TIN

| 79b | BE2500 | (1957) | — | 50.00 | 70.00 | 90.00 |

ALUMINUM

| 209 | BE2531 | (1988) | — | — | — | .10 |

20 SATANG

COPPER-NICKEL

Y#	Date	Year	Mintage	VF	XF	Unc
27	RS116H	(1897)	3.126	12.00	20.00	30.00

 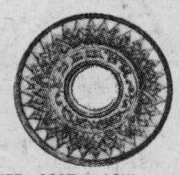

3.0000 g, .650 SILVER, .0627 oz ASW
BE date and denomination in Thai numerals.

| A56 | BE2485 | (1942) | — | 7.50 | 11.50 | 15.00 |

TIN
BE date and denomination in Western numerals.

| 63 | BE2488 | (1945) | — | 1.00 | 2.50 | 4.00 |

SALUNG = 1/4 BAHT

3.7500 g, .800 SILVER, .0965 oz ASW

| 43 | BE2458 | (1915) | 2.040 | 2.50 | 4.50 | 6.00 |

3.7500 g, .650 SILVER, .0784 oz ASW

43a	BE2460	(1917)	1.100	2.50	4.50	6.00
	2461	(1918)	2.170	2.50	4.50	6.00
	2462	(1919)	7.860	2.50	4.50	6.00
	(BE)2467	(1924)	2.100	2.50	4.50	6.00
	2468	(1925)		2.50	4.50	6.00

3.7500 g, .500 SILVER, .0603 oz ASW

| 43b | BE2462 | (1919) | dot after legend | | | |
| | | | Inc. Ab. | 40.00 | 55.00 | 75.00 |

25 SATANG = 1/4 BAHT

3.7500 g, .650 SILVER, .0784 oz ASW

| 48 | (BE)2472 | (1929) | — | 4.00 | 8.00 | 14.00 |

TIN
Obv: King Ananda, child head.

| 66 | BE2489 | (1946) | — | 3.00 | 4.00 | 6.00 |

Obv: Youth head.

70	BE2489	(1946)	dot			
			*226.348	.20	.40	.75
	BE2489	(1946)	w/o dot			
			Inc. Ab.	.20	.40	.75

*NOTE: These coins were also struck 1954-64 and mintage figure is a total.

ALUMINUM-BRONZE
Obv: King Bhumiphol, one medal on uniform.

Y#	Date	Year	Mintage	VF	XF	Unc
76	BE2493	(1950)	23.170	.75	1.75	3.00

Obv: Smaller head; three medals on uniform.

80	BE2500	(1957)	dot			
			620.480	.10	.15	.25
	BE2500	(1957)	w/o dot			
			Inc. Ab. Reported, not confirmed			

*NOTE: Current issues are minted without date change and with and without reeded edges.

BRASS

| 109 | BE2520 | (1977) | 183.356 | — | .10 | .15 |

ALUMINUM-BRONZE

| 187 | BE2530 | (1987) | — | — | — | .10 |
| | 2530 | (1988) | — | — | — | .10 |

2 SALUNG = 1/2 BAHT

7.5000 g, .800 SILVER, .1929 oz ASW

44	BE2458	(1915)	2.740	4.50	7.00	10.00
	2462	(1919)	3.230	4.50	7.00	10.00
	2462	(1919)	dot after legend			
			Inc. Ab.	6.50	10.00	20.00
	2463	(1920)	4.970	4.50	7.00	10.00
	(BE)2464	(1921)	—	4.50	7.00	10.00

50 SATANG = 1/2 BAHT

7.5000 g, .650 SILVER, .1567 oz ASW

| 49 | (BE)2472 | (1929) | 17.008 | 7.50 | 12.50 | 20.00 |

TIN
Obv: King Ananda, child head.

| 67 | BE2489 | (1946) | — | 15.00 | 40.00 | 90.00 |

THAILAND 1611

Obv: Youth head.

Y#	Date	Year	Mintage	VF	XF	Unc
71	BE2489	(1946)	*17.008	.75	1.00	1.50

*Coins bearing this date were also minted in 1954-57 and mintage figure is a total.

ALUMINUM-BRONZE
Obv: King Bhumiphol, one medal on uniform.

| 77 | BE2493 | (1950) | 20.710 | .75 | 1.75 | 3.50 |

Obv: Smaller head; three medals on uniform.

| 81 | BE2500 | (1957) | *439.874 | .10 | .15 | .25 |

*Current issues are minted without date change.

| 168 | BE2523 | (1980) | 122.260 | .10 | .15 | .25 |

BRASS

| 203 | BE2531 | (1988) | — | — | — | .10 |

BAHT

15.0000 g, .900 SILVER, .4340 oz ASW

| 39 | RS127 | (1908) | 1.037 | 200.00 | 300.00 | 400.00 |

45	BE2456	(1913)	2.690	10.00	15.00	20.00
	2457	(1914)	.490	12.50	18.50	30.00
	(BE)2458	(1915)	5.000	10.00	15.00	20.00
	(BE)2459	(1916)	9.080	10.00	15.00	20.00
	(BE)2460	(1917)	14.340	10.00	15.00	20.00
	2461	(1918)	3.840	10.00	15.00	20.00

NOTE: BE2456 is often found weakly struck so it does appear similar to a counterfeit.

COPPER-NICKEL-SILVER-ZINC

Y#	Date	Year	Mintage	VF	XF	Unc
82	BE2500	(1957)	*3.143	.75	1.50	3.00

*These coins were minted in years 1958-60 and mintage figure is a total.

SILVER (OMS)

| 82a | BE2500 | (1957) | — | — | — | 30.00 |

COPPER-NICKEL
King Bhumiphol & Queen Sirikit

| 83 | BE2504 | (1961) | 4.430 | .40 | .75 | 1.50 |

| 84 | BE2505 | (1962) | *883.086 | .10 | .15 | .30 |

*These coins were minted from 1962-82 and mintage figure is a total.

King's 36th Birthday

| 85 | ND | (1963) | 3.000 | .25 | .75 | 1.50 |

Fifth Asian Games

| 87 | BE2509 | 1966 | 9.000 | .25 | .75 | 1.50 |

Sixth Asian Games

| 91 | BE2513 | 1970 | 9.000 | .25 | .75 | 1.50 |

F.A.O. Issue

| 96 | BE2515 | (1972) | 9.000 | .10 | .25 | .75 |

Prince Vajiralongkorn Investiture

Y#	Date	Year	Mintage	VF	XF	Unc
97	BE2515	(1972)	9.000	.15	.40	1.00

25th Anniversary World Health Organization

| 99 | BE2516 | 1973 | 1.000 | .25 | .65 | 1.25 |

| 100 | BE2517 | (1974) | 248.978 | .15 | .40 | 1.00 |

Eighth SEAP Games

| 105 | BE2518 | 1975 | 3.000 | .25 | .65 | 1.25 |

75th Birthday of Princess Mother

| 107 | BE2518 | (1975) | 9.000 | .15 | .40 | 1.00 |

| 110 | BE2520 | (1977) | 506.460 | .10 | .20 | .50 |

F.A.O. Issue

| 112 | BE2520 | (1977) | 2.000 | .10 | .20 | .50 |

THAILAND 1612

Princess' Graduation

Y#	Date	Year	Mintage	VF	XF	Unc
114	BE2520	(1977)	8.998	.10	.20	.50

Investiture of Princess Sirindhorn
| 124 | BE2520 | (1977) | 5.000 | .10 | .20 | .50 |

Graduation of Crown Prince
| 127 | BE2521 | (1978) | 5.000 | .10 | .20 | .50 |

Eighth Asian Games
| 130 | BE2521 | 1978 | 5.000 | .10 | .20 | .50 |

F.A.O. Issue
| 157 | BE2525 | (1982) | 1.500 | .10 | .20 | .50 |

Obv: Large portrait w/collar touching hairline.
159.1	BE2525	(1982)	123.585	.10	.20	.50
	2527	(1984)	—	.10	.20	.50
	2528	(1985)	—	.10	.20	.50

Obv: Small portrait w/space between collar and hairline.
| 159.2 | BE2525 | (1982) | Inc. Ab. | 2.50 | 5.00 | 10.00 |

Circulation Coinage
183	BE2529	(1986)	—	—	—	.10
	2530	(1987)	—	—	—	.10
	2531	(1988)	—	—	—	.10

2 BAHT
COPPER-NICKEL
Graduation of Princess Chulabhorn
| 134 | BE2522 | (1979) | 5.000 | .20 | .40 | 1.00 |

COPPER-NICKEL CLAD COPPER
International Youth Year
| 176 | BE2528 | 1985 | 5.000 | .20 | .40 | 1.00 |

XIII SEA Games

Y#	Date	Year	Mintage	VF	XF	Unc
177	BE2528	1985	5.000	.20	.40	1.00

National Years of the Trees
| 178 | ND | (1986) | 3.000 | .50 | 1.00 | 3.50 |

Year of Peace
| 180 | BE2529 | 1986 | 5.000 | — | — | .50 |

Chulachomklao Royal Military Academy
| 188 | BE2530 | (1987) | — | — | — | .50 |

Princess Chulabhorn Awarded Einstein Medal
| 191 | BE2530 | (1987) | — | — | — | .50 |

King's 60th Birthday
| 194 | BE2530 | (1987) | — | — | — | .50 |

72nd Anniversary of Thai Cooperatives
| 204 | BE2531 | (1988) | — | — | — | .50 |

42nd Anniversary of Reign
| 210 | BE2531 | (1988) | — | — | — | .50 |

100th Anniversary of Siriraj Hospital
| 220 | BE2531 | (1988) | — | — | — | .50 |

Crown Prince's Birthday

Y#	Date	Year	Mintage	VF	XF	Unc
222	BE2531	(1988)	—	—	—	.50

5 BAHT

COPPER-NICKEL
| 98 | BE2515 | (1972) | 30.016 | .30 | .60 | 1.20 |

COPPER-NICKEL CLAD COPPER
| 111 | BE2520 | (1977) | 27.257 | .30 | .60 | 1.20 |
| | 2522 | (1979) | 72.740 | .30 | .60 | 1.20 |

King's 50th Birthday
Obv. leg: *Prathet Thai.*
| 120 | BE2520 | (1977) | 5.000 | .35 | .75 | 1.50 |

Error: Obv. leg. *Siam Minta.*
| 121 | BE2520 | (1977) | — | 1.00 | 2.00 | 4.50 |

Eighth Asian Games
| 131 | BE2521 | 1978 | .500 | .35 | .75 | 1.50 |

THAILAND 1613

Royal Cradle Ceremony

Y#	Date	Year	Mintage	VF	XF	Unc
132	BE2522	(1979)	1.000	.35	.75	1.50

Queen's Anniversary and F.A.O. Ceres Medal
| 137 | BE2523 | (1980) | 9.000 | .25 | .50 | 1.25 |

80th Birthday of King's Mother
| 140 | BE2523 | (1980) | 3.504 | .25 | .50 | 1.25 |

King Rama VI Birth Centennial
| 142 | BE2524 | (1981) | 2.222 | .25 | .50 | 1.25 |

Rama VII Constitutional Monarchy
| 144 | BE2523 | (1980) | 2.113 | .25 | .50 | 1.25 |

Bicentennial of Bangkok
| 149 | BE2525 | (1982) | 5.000 | .25 | .50 | 1.25 |

F.A.O. Issue
| 158 | BE2525 | (1982) | .400 | .35 | .75 | 1.50 |

Y#	Date	Year	Mintage	VF	XF	Unc
160	BE2525	(1982)	.200	.50	1.00	1.75
	2528	(1985)	—	.50	1.00	1.75
	2529	(1986)	—	.50	1.00	1.75

75th Anniversary of Boy Scouts
| 161 | BE2525 | (1982) | .200 | .50 | 1.00 | 1.75 |

84th Birthday of Princess Mother
| 171 | BE2527 | (1984) | .480 | .35 | .75 | 1.50 |

200th Anniversary of Rama III
| 184 | BE2530 | (1987) | — | — | — | .60 |

Circulation Coinage
| 185 | BE2530 | (1987) | 14.000 | — | — | .60 |
| | 2531 | (1988) | — | — | — | .60 |

King's 60th Birthday
| 195 | BE2530 | (1987) | — | — | — | .60 |

42nd Year of Reign
| 211 | BE2531 | (1988) | — | — | — | .60 |

Circulation Coinage
Y#	Date	Year	Mintage	VF	XF	Unc
219	BE2531	(1988)	—	—	—	.50

10 BAHT

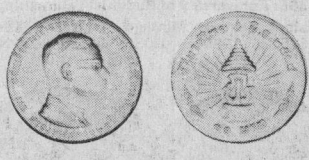

5.0000 g, .800 SILVER, .1286 oz ASW
King Bhumiphol 25th Anniversary of Reign
| 92 | BE2514 | (1971) | 2.000 | BV | 1.50 | 2.50 |

NICKEL
Crown Prince Vajiralongkorn and Princess Soamsawali Wedding
| 117 | BE2520 | (1977) | 1.890 | .50 | 1.00 | 1.75 |

Princess' Graduation
| 115 | BE2520 | (1977) | 2.095 | .50 | 1.00 | 1.75 |
BRONZE (OMS)
| 115a | BE2520 | (1977) | — | — | — | 20.00 |

COPPER-NICKEL
Graduation of Princess Chulabhorn
| 135 | BE2522 | (1979) | 1.196 | .50 | 1.00 | 1.75 |

NICKEL
80th Birthday of King's Mother
| 141 | BE2523 | (1980) | 1.288 | .50 | 1.00 | 1.75 |

THAILAND

30th Anniversary of Buddhist Fellowship

Y#	Date	Year	Mintage	VF	XF	Unc
145	BE2523	(1980)	1.035	.50	1.00	1.75

King Rama IX Anniversary of Reign

| 146 | BE2524 | (1981) | 2.039 | .50 | 1.00 | 1.75 |

50th Birthday of Queen Sirikit

| 154 | BE2525 | (1982) | .500 | .75 | 1.25 | 2.25 |
| | 2525 | (1982) | 9,999 | — | Proof | 4.00 |

75th Anniversary of Boy Scouts
Similar to 5 Baht, Y#161.

| 162 | BE2525 | (1982) | .100 | 1.00 | 1.50 | 2.50 |
| | 2525 | (1982) | 1,500 | — | Proof | 15.00 |

100th Anniversary of Postal Service

| 163 | BE2526 | (1983) | .300 | .50 | 1.00 | 1.75 |
| | 2526 | (1983) | 5,000 | — | Proof | 6.50 |

700th Anniversary of Thai Alphabet

| 165 | BE2526 | (1983) | .500 | .50 | 1.00 | 1.75 |
| | 2526 | (1983) | 4,667 | — | Proof | 6.50 |

84th Birthday of Princess Mother
Similar to 5 Baht, Y#171.

| 172 | BE2527 | (1984) | .180 | .75 | 1.25 | 2.25 |
| | 2527 | (1984) | 3,192 | — | Proof | 15.00 |

72nd Anniversary of Government Savings Bank

Y#	Date	Year	Mintage	VF	XF	Unc
175	BE2528	(1985)	.500	.50	1.00	1.75
	2528	(1985)	2,600	—	Proof	12.50

National Years of the Trees

| 179 | ND | (1986) | .100 | .75 | 1.50 | 4.00 |

SILVER

| 179a | ND | (1986) | 5,000 | — | Proof | 14.00 |

NICKEL
6th Asean Orchid Congress

| 181 | BE2529 | 1986 | — | — | — | 1.25 |
| | 2529 | 1986 | — | — | Proof | 5.00 |

Military Academy

| 189 | BE2530 | (1987) | — | — | — | 1.25 |

Asian Institute of Technology

| 190 | BE2530 | (1987) | — | — | — | 1.25 |

Princess Chulabhorn Awarded Einstein Medal

| 192 | BE2530 | (1987) | — | — | — | 1.25 |
| | 2530 | (1987) | — | — | Proof | 5.00 |

King's 60th Birthday

Y#	Date	Year	Mintage	VF	XF	Unc
196	BE2530	(1987)	—	—	—	1.25
	2530	(1987)	—	—	Proof	5.00

72nd Anniversary of Thai Cooperatives

| 205 | BE2531 | (1988) | — | — | — | 1.25 |

42nd Year of Reign

| 212 | BE2531 | (1988) | — | — | — | 1.25 |

100th Anniversary of Siriraj Hospital

| 221 | BE2531 | (1988) | — | — | — | 1.25 |
| | 2531 | (1988) | — | — | Proof | 5.00 |

Crown Prince's Birthday

| 223 | BE2531 | (1988) | — | — | — | 1.25 |
| | 2531 | (1988) | — | — | Proof | 5.00 |

STAINLESS STEEL RING, ALUMINUM-BRONZE CORE

| 225 | BE2531 | (1988) | .100 | — | — | 4.00 |

20 BAHT

19.6000 g, .750 SILVER, .4726 oz ASW
King Bhumiphol 36th Birthday

Y#	Date	Year	Mintage	VF	XF	Unc
86	ND	(1963)	1.000	—	7.50	12.50

50 BAHT

24.7000 g, .900 SILVER, .7147 oz ASW
20th Year Buddhist Fellowship

95	BE2514	(1971)	.200	—	9.00	15.00
	2514	(1971)	.060	—	P/L	18.00

24.8500 g, .400 SILVER, .3195 oz ASW
National Museum Centennial

101	BE2517	(1974)	.200	—	6.00	10.00

25.5500 g, .500 SILVER, .4173 oz ASW
Conservation Series
Rev: Sumatran Rhinoceros.

Y#	Date	Year	Mintage	VF	XF	Unc
102	BE2517	(1974)	.020	—	—	20.00

28.2800 g, .925 SILVER, .8411 oz ASW

102a	BE2517	(1974)	9,885	—	Proof	30.00

100 BAHT

31.9000 g, .500 SILVER, .5128 oz ASW
Conservation Series
Rev: Brown-antlered deer.

103	BE2517	(1974)	.020	—	—	25.00

35.0000 g, .925 SILVER, 1.0409 oz ASW

103a	BE2517	(1974)	9,294	—	Proof	35.00

25.0000 g, .900 SILVER, .7234 oz AGW
Ministry of Finance

106	BE2518	(1975)	.030	—	8.00	12.50

150 BAHT

3.7500 g, .900 GOLD, .1085 oz AGW
Queen Sirikit 36th Birthday

88	BE2511	(1968)	.200	—	—	75.00

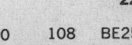

22.0000 g, .925 SILVER, .6543 oz ASW
75th Birthday of Princess Mother

108	BE2518	(1975)	.200	—	8.00	15.00

F.A.O. Issue

Y#	Date	Year	Mintage	VF	XF	Unc
113	BE2520	(1977)	.050	—	8.00	15.00

Crown Prince Vajiralongkorn and Princess Soamsawali Wedding

118	BE2520	(1977)	.200	—	8.00	15.00

Princess' Graduation

116	BE2520	(1977)	.100	—	8.00	15.00

Investiture of Princess Sirindhorn

125	BE2520	(1977)	.050	—	8.00	15.00

9th World Orchid Conference

123	BE2521	1978	.030	—	8.00	15.00

THAILAND 1616

Graduation of Crown Prince

Y#	Date	Year	Mintage	VF	XF	Unc
128	BE2521	(1978)	.050	—	8.00	15.00

7.5000 g, .925 SILVER, .2230 oz ASW
King's 60th Birthday
Similar to 6000 Baht, Y#202.

| 197 | BE2530 | (1987) | — | — | — | 8.00 |
| | 2530 | (1987) | — | — | Proof | 15.00 |

42nd Year of Reign
Similar to 10 Baht, Y#212.

| 213 | BE2531 | (1988) | — | — | — | 15.00 |
| | 2531 | (1988) | — | — | Proof | 30.00 |

200 BAHT

22.3500 g, .925 SILVER, .6646 oz ASW
Royal Cradle Ceremony

| 133 | BE2522 | (1979) | .050 | — | 10.00 | 17.50 |

23.3200 g, .925 SILVER, .6935 oz ASW
International Year of the Child

| 152 | BE2524 | 1981 | 9,525 | — | — | 35.00 Proof |

23.1800 g, .925 SILVER, .6894 oz ASW
25th Anniversary of World Wildlife Fund
Rev: Siamese Fireback Pheasant.

| 206 | BE2530 | 1987 | *.025 | — | Proof | — |

250 BAHT

28.2800 g, .925 SILVER, .8411 oz ASW
International Year of Disabled Persons
Obv: King Rama IX.

| 169 | BE2526 | 1983 | 307 pcs. | — | — | 25.00 |
| | 2526 | 1983 | 233 pcs. | — | Proof | 35.00 |

300 BAHT

7.5000 g, .900 GOLD, .2170 oz AGW
Queen Sirikit 36th Birthday

Y#	Date	Year	Mintage	VF	XF	Unc
89	BE2511	(1968)	.100	—	—	150.00

22.0000 g, .925 SILVER, .6543 oz ASW
Graduation of Princess Chulabhorn

| 136 | BE2522 | (1979) | .020 | — | 15.00 | 20.00 |

15.0000 g, .925 SILVER, .4461 oz ASW
King's 60th Birthday
Similar to 6000 Baht, Y#202.

| 198 | BE2530 | (1987) | — | — | — | 18.00 |
| | 2530 | (1987) | — | — | Proof | 25.00 |

42nd Year of Reign
Similar to 10 Baht, Y#212.

| 214 | BE2531 | (1988) | — | — | — | 20.00 |
| | 2531 | (1988) | — | — | Proof | 35.00 |

400 BAHT

10.0000 g, .900 GOLD, .2893 oz AGW
King Bhumiphol 25th Anniversary of Reign

| 93 | BE2514 | (1971) | .040 | — | — | 200.00 |

600 BAHT

15.0000 g, .900 GOLD, .4340 oz AGW
Queen Sirikit 36th Birthday

| 90 | BE2511 | (1968) | .040 | — | — | 250.00 |

14.9000 g, .925 SILVER, .4432 oz ASW
Queen's Anniversary and F.A.O. Ceres Medal

| 138 | BE2523 | (1980) | .023 | — | 27.50 | 30.00 |

Rama VI Birth Centennial

| 143 | BE2524 | (1981) | .019 | — | 27.50 | 30.00 |

King Rama IX Anniversary of Reign

Y#	Date	Year	Mintage	VF	XF	Unc
147	BE2524	(1981)	.015	—	27.50	30.00

Bicentennial of Bangkok

| 150 | BE2525 | (1982) | .015 | — | 27.50 | 30.00 |

22.0000 g, .925 SILVER, .6543 oz ASW
50th Birthday of Queen Sirikit

| 155 | BE2525 | (1982) | 3,895 | — | 27.50 | 30.00 |
| | 2525 | (1982) | 1,011 | — | Proof | 35.00 |

100th Anniversary of Postage Stamps

| 164 | BE2526 | 1983 | 5,000 | — | 27.50 | 30.00 |
| | 2526 | 1983 | 1,400 | — | Proof | 35.00 |

700th Anniversary of Thai Alphabet

| 166 | BE2526 | (1983) | 4,300 | — | 27.50 | 30.00 |
| | 2526 | (1983) | 780 pcs. | — | Proof | 45.00 |

84th Birthday of Princess Mother

| 173 | BE2527 | (1984) | 3,530 | — | 27.50 | 30.00 |
| | 2527 | (1984) | 497 pcs. | — | Proof | 60.00 |

6th Asean Orchid Congress
Similar to 10 Baht, Y#181.

| 182 | BE2529 | 1986 | — | — | — | 30.00 |
| | 2529 | 1986 | — | — | Proof | 50.00 |

Princess Chulabhorn Awarded Einstein Medal
Similar to 10 Baht, Y#192.

| 193 | BE2530 | (1987) | — | — | — | 30.00 |
| | 2530 | (1987) | — | — | Proof | 50.00 |

30.0000 g, .925 SILVER, .8922 oz ASW
King's 60th Birthday
Similar to 6000 Baht, Y#202.

THAILAND 1617

Y#	Date	Year	Mintage	VF	XF	Unc
199	BE2530	(1987)	—	—	—	30.00
	2530	(1987)	—	—	Proof	50.00

42nd Year of Reign
Similar to 10 Baht, Y#212.

| 215 | BE2531 | (1988) | — | — | — | 30.00 |
| | 2531 | (1988) | — | — | Proof | 60.00 |

Crown Prince's Birthday
Similar to 10 Baht, Y#223.

| 224 | BE2531 | (1988) | — | — | — | 35.00 |
| | 2531 | (1988) | — | — | Proof | 75.00 |

800 BAHT

20.0000 g, .900 GOLD, .5787 oz AGW
King Bhumiphol 25th Anniversary of Reign
| 94 | BE2514 | (1971) | .020 | — | — | 350.00 |

1500 BAHT

3.7500 g, .900 GOLD, .1085 oz AGW
King's 60th Birthday
Similar to 6000 Baht, Y#202.
| 200 | BE2530 | (1987) | — | — | — | 80.00 |
| | 2530 | (1987) | — | — | Proof | 120.00 |

42nd Year of Reign
Similar to 10 Baht, Y#212.
| 216 | BE2531 | (1988) | — | — | — | 75.00 |
| | 2531 | (1988) | — | — | Proof | 150.00 |

2500 BAHT

15.0000 g, .900 GOLD, .4340 oz AGW
Crown Prince Vajiralongkorn and Princess Soamsawali
Wedding
| 119 | BE2520 | (1977) | .020 | — | — | 250.00 |

Investiture of Princess Sirindhorn
| 126 | BE2520 | (1977) | 5,000 | — | — | 250.00 |

International Year of Disabled Persons
Obv: King Rama IX. Rev: Similar to 250 Baht, Y#169.
| 170 | BE2526 | (1983) | 92 pcs. | — | — | 450.00 |
| | 2526 | (1983) | 793 pcs. | — | Proof | 500.00 |

15.9800 g, .900 GOLD, .4625 oz AGW
15th Anniversary of World Wildlife Fund
Rev: Asian Elephant.
| 207 | BE2530 | 1987 | *5,000 | — | Proof | 250.00 |

3000 BAHT

15.0000 g, .900 GOLD, .4340 oz AGW
Graduation of Crown Prince
| 129 | BE2521 | (1978) | .010 | — | — | 250.00 |

7.5000 g, .900 GOLD, .2170 oz AGW
King's 60th Birthday
Similar to 6000 Baht, Y#202.

Y#	Date	Year	Mintage	VF	XF	Unc
201	BE2530	(1987)	—	—	—	150.00
	2530	(1987)	—	—	Proof	240.00

42nd Year of Reign
Similar to 10 Baht, Y#212.
| 217 | BE2531 | (1988) | — | — | — | 150.00 |
| | 2531 | (1988) | — | — | Proof | 300.00 |

4000 BAHT

17.1700 g, .900 GOLD, .4969 oz AGW
International Year of the Child
| 153 | BE2524 | (1981) | 3,963 | — | Proof | 375.00 |

5000 BAHT

33.4370 g, .900 GOLD, .9676 oz AGW
Conservation Series
Rev: White-Eyed River Martin.
| 104 | BE2517 | (1974) | 2,602 | — | — | 950.00 |
| | BE2517 | (1974) | 623 pcs. | — | Proof | 2000. |

30.0000 g, .900 GOLD, .8681 oz AGW
King's 50th Birthday
| 122 | BE2520 | (1977) | 6,400 | — | — | 500.00 |

6000 BAHT

15.0000 g, .900 GOLD, .4341 oz AGW
50th Birthday of Queen Sirikit
Similar to 10 Baht, Y#154.
| 156 | BE2525 | (1982) | 1,471 | — | — | 325.00 |
| | 2525 | (1982) | 99 pcs. | — | Proof | 800.00 |

700th Anniversary of Thai Alphabet
Similar to 10 Baht, Y#165.
| 167 | BE2526 | (1983) | 700 pcs. | — | — | 350.00 |
| | 2526 | (1983) | 235 pcs. | — | Proof | 650.00 |

84th Birthday of Princess Mother
Similar to 5 Baht, Y#171.
| 174 | BE2526 | (1984) | 835 pcs. | — | — | 350.00 |
| | 2526 | (1984) | 246 pcs. | — | Proof | 650.00 |

King's 60th Birthday
| 202 | BE2530 | (1987) | — | — | — | 300.00 |
| | 2530 | (1987) | — | — | Proof | 480.00 |

42nd Year of Reign
Similar to 10 Baht, Y#212.
| 218 | BE2531 | (1988) | — | — | — | 300.00 |
| | 2531 | (1988) | — | — | Proof | 600.00 |

9000 BAHT

12.0000 g, .900 GOLD, .3472 oz AGW
Queen's Anniversary and F.A.O.
Similar to 5 Baht, Y#137.

Y#	Date	Year	Mintage	VF	XF	Unc
139	BE2523	(1980)	3,900	—	—	400.00

King Rama VI Birth Centennial
| A143 | BE2524 | (1981) | 2,600 | — | — | 400.00 |

15.0000 g, .900 GOLD, .4340 oz AGW
King Rama IX Anniversary of Reign
| 148 | BE2524 | (1981) | 4,000 | — | — | 400.00 |

Bicentennial of Bangkok
Similar to 5 Baht, Y#149.
| 151 | BE2525 | (1982) | 3,290 | — | — | 400.00 |

700th Anniversary of Thai Alphabet
Similar to 10 Baht, Y#165.
| 167 | BE2526 | (1983) | — | — | — | 400.00 |
| | 2526 | (1983) | — | — | Proof | 400.00 |

OCCUPATION COINAGE

These coins were to be circulated in the four occupied provinces of Malaya during World War II. They were not put into circulation there but were later used in Japanese military service clubs in Bangkok before Japan's surrender in 1945.

SEN

TIN

KM#	Date	Mintage	VF	XF	Unc
5	BE2486	(1943)			

5 SEN

TIN
| 10 | BE2486 | (1943) | | | |

10 SEN

TIN
| 15 | BE2486 | (1943) | — | — | 350.00 | 500.00 |

BULLION ISSUES

In 1943, the government of Thailand made an internal loan by virtue of the Royal Act of Internal Loan related regulation of the Ministry of Finance, both dated 17th May, 1943.

Eight years later another Regulation of the Ministry of Finance dated 11th June, 1951 related to the actual redemption of the loan above mentioned was proclaimed with the following effect:

Bond holders have the choice to be paid either in gold coins or gold bars or in other forms, all of which should bear the Garuda emblem and the specific inscription as to its weight and gold purity.

50 BAHT

8.6930 g, .995 GOLD, .2781 oz AGW
| 1 | ND(1951) | — | 200.00 | 250.00 | 300.00 |

100 BAHT

17.3870 g, .995 GOLD, .5562 oz AGW
| 2 | ND(1951) | — | 450.00 | 500.00 | 600.00 |

THAILAND 1618

1000 BAHT

173.8790 g, .995 GOLD, 5.5620 oz AGW

KM#	Date	Mintage	VF	XF	Unc
3	ND(1951)	—	4000.	5000.	6000.

MINT SETS (MS)

KM#	Date	Mintage	Identification	Issue Price	Mkt. Val.
MS1	ND(1895)(3)	—	Y13-15	—	—
MS2	Mixed(32)	—	Two each Y57,70,72,73 78a,78-87,91	22.00	60.00
MS3	Mixed(30)	—	Two each Y60,70,72,73, 78,78a,79,79a,80-86	—	30.00
MS4	Mixed(10)	—	Y70,72,73,78,78a,79,79a,80-82	—	12.00
MS5	Mixed(8)	—	Y83,85-87,91,92,95,97	11.00	40.00
MS6	1975(2)	—	Y102-103	32.50	45.00
MS7	1988(7)	—	Y183,185-187,203,208-209	—	3.50

PROOF SETS (PS)

| PS1 | 1975(2) | 30,000 | Y102a-103a | 50.00 | 65.00 |

Listings For
TIMOR: refer to Indonesia

TIBET

Tibet, an autonomous region of China located in central Asia between the Himalayan and Kunlun Mts. has an area of 471,660 sq. mi. (1,221,599 sq. km.) and a population of *1.9 million. Capital: Lhasa. The economy is based on agriculture and livestock raising. Wool, livestock, salt and hides are exported.

Lamaism, a form of Buddhism, developed in Tibet in the 8th century. From that time until the 1900s, the Dalai Lama virtually isolated the country from the outside world. The British in India achieved some influence in the early 20th century, and encouraged Tibet to declare its independence from China in 1913. The Communist revolution in China marked a new era in Tibetan history. Chinese Communist troops invaded Tibet in Oct., 1950. After a token resistance, Tibet signed an agreement with China in which China recognized the spiritual and temporal leadership of the Dalai Lama, and Tibet recognized the suzerainty of China. In 1959, a nationwide revolt triggered by Communist-initiated land reform broke out. The revolt was ruthlessly crushed. The Dalai Lama fled to India, and on Sept. 1, 1965, the Chinese made Tibet an autonomous region of China.

The first coins to circulate in Tibet were those of neighboring Nepal about 1570. Shortly after 1720, the Nepalese government began striking specific issues for use in Tibet; they were exchanged with the Tibetans for an equal weight in silver bullion. The first Tibetan government mint opened in 1791, but operations were suspended two years later. The Chinese opened a second mint in Lhasa in 1792. It produced a coinage until 1836. Shortly thereafter, the Tibetan mint was reopened and the government of Tibet continued to strike coins until 1953.

DATING
Based on the Tibetan calendar, Tibetan coins are dated by the cycle which contains 60 years. Example 15th cycle 25th year = 1891 AD.

13/40 - 1786	14/40 - 1846	15/40 - 1906
13/60 - 1806	14/60 - 1866	15/60 - 1926
14/20 - 1826	15/20 - 1886	16/20 - 1946

Certain Sino-Tibetan issues are dated in the year of reign of the Emperor of China.

MONETARY SYSTEM
15 Skar = 1-1/2 Sho = 1 Tangka
10 Sho = 1 Srang

TANGKA

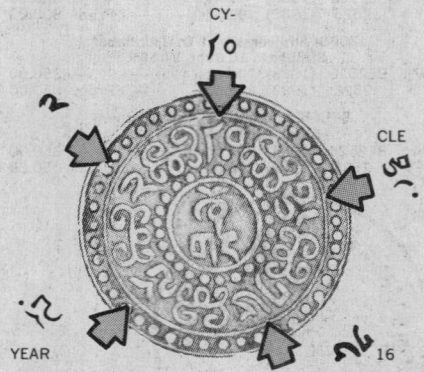

16(th) CYCLE 2(nd) YEAR = 1928AD

16(th) CYCLE 7(th) YEAR = 1933AD

NUMERALS

1	༡	གཅིག
2	༢	གཉིས
3	༣	གསུམ
4	༤	བཞི
5	༥	ལྔ
6	༦	དྲུག
7	༧	བདུན
8	༨	བརྒྱད
9	༩	དགུ
10	༡༠	བཅུ or བཅུ་ཐམ་པ
11	༡༡	བཅུ་གཅིག
12	༡༢	བཅུ་གཉིས
13	༡༣	བཅུ་གསུམ
14	༡༤	བཅུ་བཞི
15	༡༥	བཅོ་ལྔ
16	༡༦	བཅུ་དྲུག
17	༡༧	བཅུ་བདུན
18	༡༨	བཅོ་བརྒྱད
19	༡༩	བཅུ་དགུ
20	༢༠	ཉི་ཤུ
21	༢༡	ཉི་ཤུ་རྩ་གཅིག or ཉེར་གཅིག
22	༢༢	ཉེར་གཉིས
23	༢༣	ཉེར་གསུམ
24	༢༤	ཉེར་བཞི
25	༢༥	ཉེར་ལྔ
26	༢༦	ཉེར་དྲུག
27	༢༧	ཉེར་བདུན
28	༢༨	ཉེར་བརྒྱད

SINO-TIBETAN COINAGE

RULERS
Chia Ch'ing, 1796-1820
Tao Kuang, 1820-1851
Hsuan T'ung, 1909-1911

Early Period: 1792-1836
SHO

TIBET 1619

SILVER, 3.40-3.80 g
25-29mm

C#	Date	Year	Good	VG	Fine	VF
83	8	(1803)	12.50	30.00	45.00	65.00
	9	(1804)	12.50	30.00	45.00	65.00
	24	(1819)	12.50	25.00	35.00	50.00
	25	(1820)	10.00	20.00	27.50	37.50

One Miscal in Manchu script added, 30mm.

| 85 | 6 | (1801) | — | — | Rare | — |

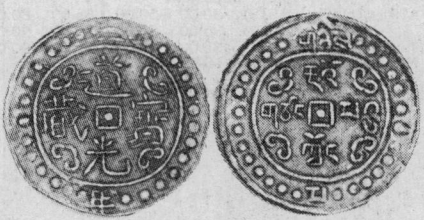

26-28mm

93	1	(1821)	25.00	40.00	55.00	80.00
	2	(1822)	10.00	15.00	25.00	40.00
	3	(1823)	10.00	15.00	25.00	40.00
	4	(1824)	15.00	30.00	40.00	60.00
	15	(1835)	15.00	30.00	40.00	60.00
	16	(1836)	15.00	30.00	40.00	60.00

In the name of Hsuan Tung:

1/2 SKAR

COPPER, 3.10-3.60 g

Y#	Date	Mintage	Good	VG	Fine	VF
A4	(1910)	—	45.00	60.00	90.00	150.00

SKAR

COPPER, 5.40-6.60 g

| 4 | (1910) | — | 40.00 | 50.00 | 80.00 | 160.00 |

SHO

SILVER, 3.30-4.10 g

| 5 | (1910) | — | 20.00 | 30.00 | 40.00 | 60.00 |

NOTE: A variety exists, having the inner circle of dots, on the Chinese side, connected by lines.

2 SHO

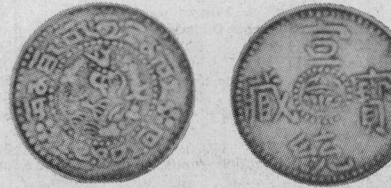

SILVER, 5.20-8.40 g

| 6 | (1910) | — | 25.00 | 40.00 | 80.00 | 150.00 |

TIBETAN COINAGE
'Kong-par' TANGKA

BILLON, 5.00-5.60 g
Rev: Sun and moon above date arch.

C#	Date	Year	Good	VG	Fine	VF
60.2	13-46		8.50	12.00	20.00	30.00

NOTE: It is believed that this type was struck in the 1820's.

4.20-5.60 g
Obv: Similar to C#60.1 but larger Buddhist characters.
Rev: Crescent and 3 dots above date arch.

| 60.3 | 13-46 | | 3.00 | 4.50 | 7.00 | 10.00 |

NOTE: It is believed that this type was struck in the 1860's. Numerous minor varieties exist.

3.60-5.20 g
Giamda Mint

A13	15-24	(1890)	3.00	4.00	6.00	9.00
	15-25	(1891)	4.00	5.50	9.00	14.00

Miscellaneous TANGKAS

SILVER, ca. 5.40 g

C#	Date	Good	VG	Fine	VF
15	ND(ca.1840)	—	—	Rare	—

4.60-4.80 g

C#	Date	Year	Good	VG	Fine	VF
27	15-28	(1894)	4.00	8.00	13.00	20.00
	15-30	(1896)	15.00	23.00	30.00	40.00
	15-40	(1906)	4.00	8.00	13.00	20.00
	15-46	(1912)	25.00	35.00	45.00	60.00

NOTE: In addition to the above meaningful (probably) dates, the following meaningless ones exist: 13-16, 13-31, 13-92, 16-16, 16-61, 16-69, 16-92, 92-39, 96-61 (sixes may be reversed threes and nines reversed ones). These are of billon, varying from 3.9 to 4.7 g.

NOTE: The legend appears to be in ornamental Lansa script and has yet to be deciphered. The type is a copy of the Nepalese issue: 'Cho-Tang'. Although struck unofficially, it was legal tender, due to an edict issued in 1881 ordering that no distinction be made between false and genuine coins!

NOTE: This type was cut to make change and the resulting fractions are occasionally encountered.

'Ga-den' TANGKA

SILVER, 5.00-5.50 g
Obv: Five petals around lotus center.

Y#	Date	Mintage	Good	VG	Fine	VF
13	ND(ca.1850)	—	5.00	10.00	15.00	25.00

NOTE: Two major and numerous minor die varieties exist.

4.0000-5.2000 g
Dodpal Mint
Obv: Five dots around lotus center, North symbol.

Y#	Date	Mintage	VG	Fine	VF	XF
13.1	ND(ca.1875-95)	—	1.00	2.00	3.00	4.50

NOTE: Five major varieties exist.

Tip Arsenal Mint
3.90-5.20 g
Obv: Three elongated dots on either side of lotus center and new arrangement of 8 symbols.

| 13.2 | ND(ca.1895-1901) | — | 1.00 | 2.25 | 3.75 | 5.00 |

NOTE: Five major varieties exist.

BILLON, 4.70-5.30 g
Obv: Seven dots around lotus center, uniform edge and thickness.

| 13.3 | ND(ca.1900) | — | 20.00 | 25.00 | 40.00 | 50.00 |

3.80-5.70 g
Similar to Y#13.3, but not uniform.

| 13.4 | ND(ca.1901-06) | — | 1.00 | 2.00 | 3.00 | 4.50 |

NOTE: Eight major varieties exist, including an error having the eight symbols rotated one position clockwise.

3.80 g
Obv: 8mm circle around lotus, North and West symbols are similar.

| 13.5 | ND(ca.1905) | — | 20.00 | 25.00 | 40.00 | 50.00 |

TIBET

3.00-5.60 g
Dode Mint
Obv: Nine dots within lotus circle.

Y#	Date	Mintage	VG	Fine	VF	XF
13.6	ND(ca.1906-12)	—	1.00	2.00	3.00	4.50

NOTE: Eight major varieties exist. See Y#13.9, 13.10 and 13.11 for other types, having nine dots within lotus circle.

SILVER, 2.70-5.00 g

| 14 | ND(ca.1909) | — | 3.00 | 4.00 | 6.50 | 9.00 |

NOTE: This Tangka was struck for presentation to monks.

BILLON, 3.30-4.50 g
Obv: Eleven dots within lotus circle.

| 13.7 | ND(ca.1912-23) | — | 1.00 | 2.00 | 3.00 | 4.50 |

NOTE: Four major varieties and numerous minor ones exist (40 to 78 dots compose outer circles).

3.00-5.00 g
Obv: Nine dots within lotus circle, northeast symbol.

| 13.8 | ND(ca.1914-23) | — | 1.00 | 2.00 | 2.75 | 3.50 |

NOTE: Five major and numerous minor varieties exist (35 to 68 dots compose outer circles).

Ser-Khang Mint
3.30-4.60 g
Northeast symbol

| 13.9 | ND(ca.1920) | — | 4.00 | 7.00 | 11.00 | 15.00 |

NOTE: Several other features are unique to this type.

Dode Mint
3.80-4.30 g
Obv: Nine dots within lotus circle,
uniform thickness (1.mm).

| 13.10 | 1929-30 | — | 7.00 | 10.00 | 15.00 | 25.00 |

NOTE: Two minor die varieties exist.

SILVER, 3.10-5.30 g
Tapchi Mint

Y#	Date	Mintage	VG	Fine	VF	XF
31	1946-48	—	3.00	4.00	5.00	8.00

NOTE: This type was struck for presentation to monks.

2 TANGKA

BILLON, 7.80-10.50 g
Dode Mint

| 15 | ND(ca.1912) | — | 100.00 | 150.00 | 200.00 | 275.00 |

NOTE: Counterfeits exist. This type is similar to Y#13.6 except for its uniform edge and its weight.

SHO-SRANG COINAGE
Size same as 'Kong-par' Tangka

1/8 SHO

COPPER
Dode Mint

Y#	Date	Year	Good	VG	Fine	VF
A7	1	(1909)	35.00	50.00	80.00	125.00

NOTE: A silver striking of this type exists (rare).

1/4 SHO

COPPER

| B7 | 1 | (1909) | 35.00 | 50.00 | 80.00 | 125.00 |

NOTE: The above coin struck in silver is a forgery.

2 1/2 SKAR

COPPER
Dode Mint

| 10 | 15-43 | (1909) | — | — | Rare | — |

23.5mm, 3.69-6.09 g
Obv: Lion looking upwards.

16	15-47	(1913)	4.00	8.00	12.00	20.00
	15-48	(1914)	4.00	8.00	12.00	20.00
	15-49	(1915)	10.00	20.00	25.00	35.00
	15-50	(1916)	8.00	15.00	20.00	30.00
	15-51	(1917)	6.00	12.00	17.50	25.00
	15-52	(1918)	4.00	8.00	12.50	20.00

Mekyi Mint
Obv: Lion looking backwards.

Y#	Date	Year	Good	VG	Fine	VF
16.1	15-48	(1914)	4.00	10.00	16.50	25.00

Dode Mint

A19	15-52	(1918)	30.00	50.00	65.00	80.00
	15-53	(1919)	35.00	60.00	75.00	90.00
	15-55	(1921)	35.00	60.00	75.00	90.00

NOTE: Counterfeits dated 15-55 exist.

5 SKAR

COPPER
Dode Mint

| A10 | 15-43 | (1909) | — | — | Rare | — |

27mm
Obv: Lion looking upwards.

17	15-47	(1913)	.80	2.00	5.00	12.00
	15-48	(1914)	.50	1.25	4.00	9.00
	15-49	(1915)	.50	1.25	4.00	9.00
	15-50	(1916)	.50	1.25	4.00	9.00
	15-51	(1917)	.50	1.25	4.00	9.00
	15-52	(1918)	.80	2.00	5.00	12.00

Mekyi Mint
Obv: Lion looking backwards.

17.1	15-48	(1914)	.60	1.50	4.00	10.00
	15-49	(1915)	.40	1.00	3.50	8.00
	15-50	(1916)	.40	1.00	3.50	8.00
	15-51	(1917)	.40	1.00	3.50	8.00
	15-52	(1918)	.40	1.00	3.50	8.00

NOTE: The appearance of the lion on all 15-48 specimens and a few 15-49 specimens varies from those on all others.

21mm
Lower Dode Mint

19	15-52	(1918)	.80	2.00	3.00	4.50
	15-53	(1919)	.60	1.50	2.50	4.00
	15-54	(1920)	.50	1.25	2.00	3.50
	15-55	(1921)	.50	1.25	2.00	3.50
	15-56	(1922)	.50	1.25	2.00	3.50
56-15 (error)		(1922)	10.00	15.00	20.00	30.00

NOTE: Reverse inscription reads counterclockwise on error date coin.

Upper Dode Mint
Rev: Dot added above center.

Y#	Date	Year	Good	VG	Fine	VF
19.1	15-55	(1921)	5.00	7.50	12.00	18.00
	15-56	(1922)	2.00	3.50	5.00	8.00

7 1/2 SKAR

COPPER
Dode Mint

11	15-43	(1909)	—		Rare	—

 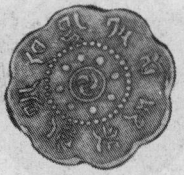

20	15-52	(1918)	.60	1.50	2.50	4.50
	15-53	(1919)	.50	1.25	2.00	3.50
	15-54	(1920)	.50	1.25	2.00	3.50
	15-55	(1921)	.50	1.25	2.00	3.50
	15-56	(1922)	.50	1.25	2.00	3.50
	15-60	(1926)	10.00	15.00	20.00	30.00

NOTE: Some 15-52, 15-53 and 15-55 specimens have the reverse central 'whirlwind' in a counterclockwise direction.

SHO

COPPER, 25.6mm
Dode Mint
Rev: Central leg. horizontal.

21	15-52	(1918)	15.00	20.00	30.00	50.00

NOTE: Two varieties exist (lion's head).

Mekyi Mint
24mm, 3.95-7.13 g
Obv: Lion looking up, w/o dot.

21.1	15-52	(1918)	.50	1.25	1.75	4.00
	15-53	(1919)	.30	.75	1.25	3.00
	15-54	(1920)	.30	.75	1.25	3.00
	15-55	(1921)	.30	.75	1.25	3.00
	15-56	(1922)	.30	.75	1.25	3.00
	15-57	(1923)	.50	1.25	1.75	4.00
	15-58	(1924)	.30	.75	1.25	3.00
	15-59	(1925)	.30	.75	1.25	3.00
	15-60	(1926)	.30	.75	1.25	3.00
	16-1	(1927)	.30	.75	1.25	3.00
	16-2	(1928)	.30	.75	1.25	3.00

Ser-Khang Mint
3.01-7.27 g
Obv: Lion looking up, w/dot.

21.2	15-54	(1920)	.50	1.25	2.00	3.50
	54-15 (error)	(1920)	10.00	15.00	20.00	30.00
	15/51-54(error)	(1920)	10.00	15.00	20.00	30.00
	15-55	(1921)	.40	1.00	1.50	3.00
	15-55 (error) 'year' and '55' transposed	(1921)	10.00	15.00	20.00	30.00

Obv: Lion looking diagonally upwards, with dot.

Y#	Date	Year	Good	VG	Fine	VF
21.3	15-54	(1920)	2.00	3.00	5.00	8.00
	15-55	(1921)	.30	.75	1.25	2.50
	15-56	(1922)	.30	.75	1.25	2.50
	15-57	(1923)	.40	1.00	1.75	3.50
	15-58	(1924)	.30	.75	1.25	2.50
	15-59	(1925)	.30	.75	1.25	2.50
	15-60	(1926)	.30	.75	1.25	2.50
	16-1/15-60	(1927)	4.00	7.00	10.00	15.00
	16-1	(1927)	.30	.75	1.25	2.00
	16-2	(1928)	.30	.75	1.25	2.00

NOTE: Specimens dated 15-54 may all be contemporary forgeries.

Dode Mint
24mm, 3.43-4.73 g
Rev: Central leg. vertical.

Y#	Date	Year	VG	Fine	VF	XF
21a	15-56	(1922)	5.00	7.00	10.00	17.50
	15-57	(1923)	.60	1.50	2.50	5.00
	15-58	(1924)	.60	1.50	2.50	5.00
	15-59/8	(1925)	.50	1.25	2.00	4.00
	15-60/59	(1926)	.50	1.25	2.00	4.00
	16-1	(1927)	.50	1.25	2.00	4.00
	16-1 dot below O above denomination	(1927)	.50	1.25	2.00	4.00
	(16-2/1)	(1927/8)	—	Reported, not confirmed		
	16-2	(1928)	.60	1.50	2.50	5.00

NOTE: Two varieties (lion) exist for each of the following dates: 15-56, 15-57, 15-58 & 16-2.

Tapchi Mint
24mm, 4.02-6.09 g
The following marks are located in the position indicated by the arrow:

a: b: c: d: e: f: g:

23	16-6 (a)	(1932)	1.00	1.75	3.00	5.00	
	16-7 (a)	(1933)	1.25	2.00	3.25	5.50	
	16-8 (a)	(1934)	1.50	2.50	4.00	7.00	
	16-9 (a)	(1935)	.75	1.50	2.50	4.00	
	16-9 (b)	(1935)	.75	1.25	2.00	3.00	
	16-10 (a)	(1936)	2.00	3.50	6.00	10.00	
	16-10 (b)	(1936)	2.00	3.50	6.00	10.00	
	16-10 (c)	(1936)	.75	1.25	2.00	3.00	
	16-11 (a)	(1937)	1.50	2.50	4.00	7.00	
	16-11 (b)	(1937)	2.00	3.50	6.00	10.00	
	16-11 (c)	(1937)	1.50	2.50	4.00	7.00	
	16-11 (d)	(1937)	1.50	2.50	4.00	7.00	
	16-11 (e)	(1937)	.75	1.25	2.00	3.00	
	16-11 (f)	(1937)	2.00	3.50	6.00	10.00	
	16-11 (g)	(1937)	—	Reported, not confirmed			
	16-12 (d)	(1938)	2.00	3.50	6.00	10.00	
	16-12 (f)	(1938)	1.50	2.50	4.00	7.00	
	16-12 (g)	(1938)	1.50	2.50	4.00	7.00	

3 SHO

COPPER
Single cloud line

27	16-20	(1946)	5.00	10.00	15.00	25.00

NOTE: Three varieties of conch-shell on reverse.

Double cloud-line

Y#	Date	Year	VG	Fine	VF	XF
27.1	16-20	(1946)	10.00	20.00	35.00	50.00

5 SHO

SILVER

8	1	(1909)	—		Rare	—

Dode Mint
10.30 g
Obv: Lion looking upwards.

18	15-47	(1913)	27.50	35.00	50.00	75.00
	15-48	(1914)	22.50	30.00	42.50	60.00
	15-49	(1915)	22.50	30.00	42.50	60.00
	15-50	(1916)	22.50	30.00	42.50	60.00
	15-58	(1924)	30.00	50.00	80.00	110.00
	15-59	(1925)	30.00	50.00	80.00	110.00
	15-60	(1926)	30.00	50.00	80.00	110.00

NOTE: Two 15-50 varieties exist; small and large lions, or 14mm vs. 15mm lion-circle.

Mekyi Mint
Obv: Lion looking backwards.

18.1	15-49	(1915)	22.50	30.00	40.00	55.00
	15-50	(1916)	22.50	30.00	42.50	60.00
	15-51	(1917)	22.50	30.00	42.50	60.00
	15-52	(1918)	22.50	30.00	42.50	60.00
	15-53	(1919)	30.00	50.00	80.00	110.00
	15-56	(1922)	30.00	50.00	80.00	110.00
	15-59	(1925)	30.00	50.00	80.00	110.00
	15-60	(1926)	30.00	50.00	80.00	110.00
	16-1	(1927)	30.00	50.00	80.00	110.00

Dode Mint

18.2	15-52	(1918)	40.00	50.00	80.00	110.00

32	—	(1928-29)			Rare	

TIBET 1622

24mm, 5.00 g

Y#	Date	Year	VG	Fine	VF	XF
32a	16-4	(1930)	—	—	Rare	—

COPPER, 29mm
Tapchi Mint
Obv: Two mountains w/two suns.

28	16-21	(1947)	1.40	3.50	6.00	10.00

Obv: Three mountains w/two suns.

28.1	16-21	(1947)	.80	2.00	2.75	4.00
	16-22	(1948)	.40	1.00	1.75	3.00
	16-22 dot after 16					
		(1948)	1.00	2.50	3.50	5.00
	16-23 12 rays in right sun					
		(1949)	.40	1.00	1.75	3.00
	16-23 dot after 16, 10 rays in right sun					
		(1949)	1.00	2.50	3.50	5.00
	16-24	(1950)	3.25	8.00	13.00	20.00
	16-24/23	(1950)	3.25	8.00	13.00	20.00

Y#	Date	Year	Mintage	VF	XF	Unc
28.1a	16-21	(1947)	2,000		(restrike)	22.50

.925 SILVER
| 28.1b | 16-21 | (1947) | 1,000 | | (restrike) | 37.50 |

.500 GOLD
| 28.1c | 16-21 | (1947) | 250 pcs. | | (restrike) | 200.00 |

NOTE: The above medallic restrikes were authorized by the Dalai Lama in exile.

COPPER
Obv: Cloud over middle mountain missing.

Y#	Date	Year	VG	Fine	VF	XF
28.2	16-22	(1948)	4.00	10.00	15.00	25.00

Obv: Moon and sun over mountains.

28a	16-23	(1949)	2.50	6.00	10.00	17.50
	16-24		3.25	8.00	13.00	20.00
	16-24	(1950)	.40	1.00	2.25	4.00
	16-24 moon cut over sun					
			2.00	5.00	8.00	14.00
	16-25	(1951)	.40	1.00	2.25	4.00
	16-25/24		.80	2.00	4.00	7.00
	16-26	(1952)	1.20	3.00	5.00	9.00
	dot before 26		.70	1.75	3.50	6.00
	16-27	(1953)	.90	2.25	4.25	7.50
	dot before 27		1.10	2.75	4.75	8.50

NOTE: Edge varieties exist.

SRANG

SILVER, 18.50 g
Dode Mint

Y#	Date	Year	VG	Fine	VF	XF
9		1	(1909)	100.00	175.00	250.00	350.00

Plain edge.
| 12 | 15-43 | (1909) | 100.00 | 150.00 | 275.00 | 375.00 |

NOTE: Varieties exist.

Obv: Lion looking upwards, reeded edge.
| A18 | 15-48 | (1914) | 250.00 | 450.00 | 650.00 | 800.00 |

Obv: Lion looking backwards.
| A18.1 | 15-52 | (1918) | 100.00 | 200.00 | 350.00 | 500.00 |
| | 15-53 | (1919) | 125.00 | 250.00 | 400.00 | 550.00 |

Similar to 5 Sho, Y#32.
| — | — | (1928-29) | — | — | Rare | — |

1 1/2 SRANG

SILVER, 5.00 g
Tapchi Mint

24	16-10	(1936)	2.50	5.00	6.50	9.00
	16-11	(1937)	2.50	5.00	6.50	9.00
	16-12	(1938)	2.50	5.00	6.50	9.00
	16-20	(1946)	6.00	10.00	14.00	20.00

3 SRANG

SILVER, 11.30 g
Tapchi Mint

Y#	Date	Year	VG	Fine	VF	XF
25	16-7	(1933)	4.00	8.50	12.00	18.00
	16-8	(1934)	4.00	8.50	12.00	18.00

26	16-9	(1935)	BV	5.00	10.00	15.00
	16-10	(1936)	BV	5.00	8.00	12.00
	16-11	(1937)	BV	5.00	8.00	12.00
	16-12	(1938)	BV	5.00	8.00	12.00
	16-20	(1946)	5.00	8.50	11.00	14.00

NOTE: Dates for Y#25 and 26 are written in words, not numerals.

5 SRANG

NOTE: No coins of this denomination are known to have been struck. Two Tanka types (Y#14 & 31, see under 'ga-den' Tangkas) circulated briefly with this value and later with a value of 10 Srang.

10 SRANG

BILLON
Tapchi Mint
Obv: Two suns. Rev: Numerals for denomination.
| 29 | 16-22 | (1948) | 3.00 | 4.50 | 7.00 | 12.50 |

Rev: Word for denomination.
29.1	16-23 w/dot					
		(1949)	3.50	6.00	8.50	14.00
	16-23 w/o dot					
		(1949)	3.50	6.00	8.50	14.00

Obv: Moon and sun.
29a	16-23	(1949)	12.00	20.00	30.00	45.00
	16-24/23		4.00	8.00	11.00	20.00
	16-24/22	(1950)	3.00	6.00	9.00	18.00
	16-24 moon cut over sun					
		(1950)	5.00	10.00	15.00	25.00
	16-25 w/o dot					
		(1951)	3.00	6.00	9.00	18.00
	16-25 w/dot					
			4.00	8.00	11.00	20.00

Y#	Date	Year	VG	Fine	VF	XF
29a	16-26 w/o dot	(1952)	4.00	8.00	11.00	20.00
	16-26 w/dot		4.00	8.00	11.00	20.00

*NOTE: The 'dot' is after the denomination.

COPPER-NICKEL
Obv: Moon and sun.

Y#	Date	Year	Mintage	VF	XF	Unc
29b	16-24	(1950)	5,000	(restrike)		10.00

.925 SILVER
| 29c | 16-24 | (1950) | 2,000 | (restrike) Proof | | 45.00 |

.500 GOLD
| 29d | 16-24 | (1950) | 500 pcs. (restrike) Proof | | | 250.00 |

NOTE: The above medallic restrikes were authorized by the Dalai Lama in exile.

BILLON
Dogu Mint

Y#	Date	Year	VG	Fine	VF	XF
30	16-24	(1950)	2.50	5.00	9.00	20.00
	16-25	(1951)	2.50	5.00	9.00	20.00

20 SRANG

GOLD
Ser-Khang Mint

Y#	Date	Year	Fine	VF	XF	Unc
22	15-52	(1918)	300.00	400.00	500.00	700.00
	15-53	(1919)	300.00	450.00	550.00	800.00
	15-54	(1920)	300.00	500.00	650.00	850.00
	15-55	(1921)	400.00	700.00	1000.	1500.

TRADE COINAGE
MONETARY SYSTEM
1 Rupee = 3 Tangka

1/4 RUPEE

.935 SILVER, 2.80 g
Szechuan (China) Mint

Y#	Date	Mintage	Fine	VF	XF	Unc
1	ND(1905-12)	*.823	30.00	50.00	75.00	150.00

NOTE: Varieties exist.

GOLD (OMS)
| 1a | ND(1905) | — | — | — | Rare | — |

1/2 RUPEE

.935 SILVER, 5.60 g

Y#	Date	Mintage	Fine	VF	XF	Unc
2	ND(1905-12)	*.136	35.00	60.00	90.00	170.00

NOTE: Varieties exist.

GOLD (OMS)
| 2a | ND(1905) | — | — | — | Rare | — |

RUPEE

.935 SILVER, 11.40 g
Obv: Small bust w/o collar.

| 3 | ND(1903-05) | *14.127 | 15.00 | 22.50 | 32.50 | 65.00 |

Rev: Horizontal rosette.
| 3.1 | ND(1903-05) | — | 25.00 | 35.00 | 50.00 | 90.00 |

Obv: Small bust w/collar.
| 3.2 | ND(1905-12) | *14.127 | 8.00 | 14.00 | 28.00 | 50.00 |

BILLON
| 3a | ND(1912-38) | — | 6.50 | 13.00 | 25.00 | 50.00 |

GOLD (OMS)
| 3b | ND(1905) | — | — | — | Rare | — |

SILVER
Obv: Large bust.
| 3.3 | ND(1910) | — | 26.00 | 40.00 | 65.00 | 110.00 |

*NOTE: Mintage figures are for 1900-1928 and do not include pieces struck between 1929-1938. In addition to the types illustrated above, large quantities of the following coins also circulated in Tibet; China Dollar Y#329 and India Rupees, Y#12 and 23. Similar crown size pieces struck in silver and gold are fantasies. Refer to *Unusual World Coins*, 2nd edition.

TOGO 1623

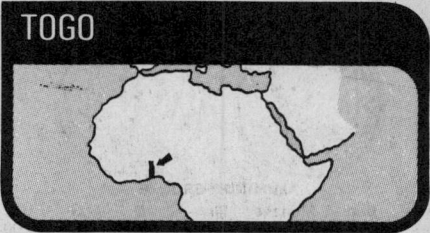

The Republic of Togo (formerly part of German Togoland), situated on the Gulf of Guinea in West Africa between Ghana and Dahomey, has an area of 21,622 sq. mi. (56,000 sq. km.) and a population of *3.4 million. Capital: Lome. Agriculture and herding, the production of dye-woods, and the mining of phosphates and iron ore are the chief industries. Copra, phosphates and coffee are exported.

Although Brazilians were the first traders to settle in Togo, Germany achieved possession, in 1884, by inducing coastal chiefs to place their territories under German protection. The German protectorate was extended international recognition at the Berlin conference of 1885 and its ultimate boundaries delimited by treaties with France in 1897 and with Britain in 1904. Togoland was occupied by Anglo-French forces in 1914, subsequently becoming a League of Nations mandate and a U.N. trusteeship divided, for administrative purpose, between Great Britain and France. The British portion voted in 1957 for incorporation with Ghana. The French portion became the independent Republic of Togo on April 27, 1960.

RULERS
German, 1884-1914
Anglo - French, 1914-1957
French, 1957-1960

MINT MARKS
(a) - Paris, privy marks only

MONETARY SYSTEM
100 Centimes = 1 Franc

50 CENTIMES

ALUMINUM-BRONZE

KM#	Date	Mintage	Fine	VF	XF	Unc
1	1924(a)	3.691	1.50	5.00	10.00	55.00
	1925(a)	2.064	2.00	6.00	12.00	60.00
	1926(a)	.445	4.00	10.00	35.00	110.00

FRANC

ALUMINUM-BRONZE

| 2 | 1924(a) | 3.472 | 2.50 | 5.00 | 15.00 | 65.00 |
| | 1925(a) | 2.768 | 3.00 | 6.00 | 25.00 | 80.00 |

ALUMINUM
| 4 | 1948(a) | 5.000 | 2.00 | 4.00 | 10.00 | 20.00 |

2 FRANCS

ALUMINUM-BRONZE

| 3 | 1924(a) | .750 | 4.50 | 13.50 | 40.00 | 150.00 |
| | 1925(a) | .580 | 5.50 | 16.00 | 55.00 | 200.00 |

ALUMINUM
Similar to 1 Franc, KM#4.
| 5 | 1948(a) | 5.000 | 2.50 | 5.00 | 12.00 | 25.00 |

TOGO 1624

5 FRANCS

ALUMINUM-BRONZE

KM#	Date	Mintage	Fine	VF	XF	Unc
6	1956(a)	10,000	1.00	2.00	4.00	10.00

REPUBLIC
2500 FRANCS
.925 SILVER
Similar to 5000 Francs, KM#8.

| 7 | 1977 | — | — | Proof | 30.00 |

5000 FRANCS

24.3600 g, .925 SILVER, .7245 oz ASW

| 8 | 1977 | — | — | Proof | 50.00 |

10000 FRANCS

49.3200 g, .925 SILVER, 1.4669 oz ASW
Rev: Similar to 5000 Francs, KM#8.

| 9 | 1977 | — | — | Proof | 65.00 |

15000 FRANCS

4.4800 g, .917 GOLD, .1320 oz AGW

| 10 | 1977 | — | — | Proof | 120.00 |

25000 FRANCS

9.0000 g, .917 GOLD, .2653 oz AGW

| 11 | 1977 | — | — | Proof | 200.00 |

50000 FRANCS

18.0000 g, .917 GOLD, .5306 oz AGW
Similar to 25,000 Francs, KM#11.

| 12 | 1977 | — | — | Proof | 350.00 |

TOKELAU ISLANDS

Tokelau or Union Islands, a New Zealand Territory located in the South Pacific 2,100 miles (3,379 km.) northeast of New Zealand and 300 miles (483 km.) north of Samoa, has an area of 4 sq. mi. (10 sq. km.) and a population of *1,600. Geographically, the group consists of four atolls - Atafu, Nukunono, Fakaofo and Swains - but the last belongs to American Samoa (and the United States claims the other three). The people are of Polynesian origin; Samoan is the official language. The islands are administered by the New Zealand Minister for Foreign Affairs; councils of family elders handle local government at the village level. The chief settlement is Fenuafala, on Fakaofo. It is connected by wireless with the offices of the New Zealand Administrative Center, located at Apia, Western Samoa. Subsistence farming and the production of copra for export are the main occupations. Revenue is also derived from the sale of postage stamps and, since 1978, coins.

Great Britain annexed the group of islands in 1889. They were added to the Gilbert and Ellice Islands colony in 1916. In 1926, they were brought under the jurisdiction of Western Samoa, which was held as a mandate of the League of Nations by New Zealand. They were declared a part of New Zealand in 1948.

Tokelau Islands issued its first coin in 1978, a "$1 Tahi Tala," Tokelauan for "One Dollar." The coin has a number of unusual features. The edge is inscribed, "Tokelau's First Coin." The obverse portrait of Queen Elizabeth II is identified by neither name nor title. The three dots of each such group comprising the obverse border symbolize the three principal atolls.

RULERS
British

TALA

COPPER-NICKEL

KM#	Date	Mintage	VF	XF	Unc
1	1978	.010	1.00	2.00	7.50

27.2500 g, .925 SILVER, .8104 oz ASW

| 1a | 1978 | 5,000 | — | Proof | 35.00 |

COPPER-NICKEL

| 2 | 1979 | .011 | 1.00 | 2.00 | 5.50 |

27.2500 g, .925 SILVER, .8104 oz ASW

| 2a | 1979 | — | — | Proof | 30.00 |

COPPER-NICKEL
Coconut Crab

KM#	Date	Mintage	VF	XF	Unc
3	1980	.010	1.00	2.00	3.50

27.2500 g, .925 SILVER, .8104 oz ASW

| 3a | 1980 | 6,004 | — | Proof | 30.00 |

COPPER-NICKEL
Frigate Bird

| 4 | 1981 | 6,500 | 1.00 | 2.00 | 3.50 |

27.2500 g, .925 SILVER, .8104 oz ASW

| 4a | 1981 | 6,500 | — | Proof | 30.00 |

COPPER-NICKEL
Outrigger Canoe

| 5 | 1982 | .010 | 1.00 | 2.00 | 3.50 |

27.2500 g, .925 SILVER, .8104 oz ASW

| 5a | 1982 | 5,000 | — | Proof | 30.00 |

COPPER-NICKEL
Water Conservation

| 6 | 1983 | 2,000 | 1.00 | 2.50 | 6.00 |

5 TALA

28.2800 g, .925 SILVER, .8411 oz ASW
Water Conservation
Obv: Similar to 1 Tala, KM#6.

KM#	Date	Mintage	VF	XF	Unc
7	1983	1,000	—	Proof	40.00

27.0500 g, .925 SILVER, .8045 oz ASW
Fishermen in Sailboat
Plain edge.

8.1	1984	1,500	—	—	25.00

Reeded edge.

8.2	1984	500 pcs.	—	Proof	45.00

TONGA

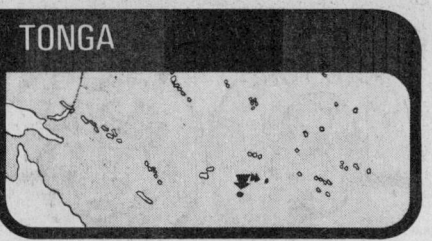

The Kingdom of Tonga (or Friendly Islands), a member of the British Commonwealth, is an archipelago situated in the southern Pacific Ocean south of Western Samoa and east of Fiji comprising 150 islands. Tonga has an area of 270 sq. mi. (699 sq. km.) and a population of *108,000. Capital: Nuku'alofa. Primarily agricultural, the kingdom exports bananas and copra.

Dutch navigators Willem Schouten and Jacob Lemaire were the first Europeans to visit Tonga in 1616. They were followed by the noted Dutch explorer Abel Tasman who visited the Tongatapu group in 1643. No further European contact was made until 1773 when British navigator Capt. James Cook arrived and, impressed by the peaceful deportment of the natives, named the islands the Friendly Islands. Within a few years of Cook's visit, Tonga was embroiled in a civil war that lasted until the great chief Tauffahau, who reigned as Siasoi Tupou I (1845-93), was converted to Christianity and brought unity and peace to the islands. Tonga became a self-governing protectorate of Great Britain in 1900 and a fully independent state on June 4, 1970. The monarchy is a member of the Commonwealth of Nations. The monarch is Chief of State and Head of Government.

RULERS
Queen Salote, 1918-1965
King Taufa'ahau, 1965—

MONETARY SYSTEM
16 Pounds = 1 Koula

1/4 KOULA

8.1250 g, .916 GOLD, .2395 oz AGW

KM#	Date	Mintage	VF	XF	Unc
1	1962	—	—	—	115.00
	1962	6,300	—	Proof	135.00

PLATINUM

1a	1962	—	—	Proof	350.00

1/2 KOULA

16.2500 g, .916 GOLD, .4789 oz AGW

2	1962	—	—	—	220.00
	1962	3,000	—	Proof	260.00

PLATINUM

2a	1962	—	—	Proof	600.00

KOULA

32.5000 g, .916 GOLD, .9278 oz AGW

3	1962	—	—	—	450.00
	1962	—	—	Proof	600.00

PLATINUM

3a	1962	—	—	Proof	900.00

DECIMAL COINAGE
100 Seniti = 1 Pa'anga
100 Pa'anga = 1 Hau

SENITI

BRONZE

KM#	Date	Mintage	VF	XF	Unc
4	1967	.500	—	.10	.15 1.00
	1967	—	—	Proof	2.00

27	1968	.500	.10	.15	1.00
	1968	—	—	Proof	2.00

BRASS

27a	1974	.500	.10	.15	1.00

BRONZE
F.A.O. Issue

42	1975	1.000	—	.10	.15
	1979	1.000	—	.10	.15

F.A.O. Issue

66	1981	1.544	—	.10	.15

2 SENITI

BRONZE

5	1967	.500	—	.10	.75
	1967	—	—	Proof	2.00

28	1968	.200	—	.10	.75
	1968	—	—	Proof	2.00
	1974	.025	—	.10	.75

F.A.O. Issue

43	1975	.400	—	.10	.15
	1979	.500	—	.10	.20

F.A.O. Issue

67	1981	1.102	—	.10	.20

TONGA

5 SENITI

COPPER-NICKEL

KM#	Date	Mintage	VF	XF	Unc
6	1967	.300	.10	.15	.40
	1967	—		Proof	2.50
29	1968	.100	.10	.15	.25
	1968	—	—	Proof	2.50
	1974	.075	.10	.15	.35

F.A.O. Issue

44	1975	.100	.10	.15	.40
	1977	.110	.10	.15	.40
	1979	.100	.10	.15	.40

F.A.O. Issue

68	1981	.941	.10	.15	.40

10 SENITI

COPPER-NICKEL

7	1967	.300	.20	.35	.75
	1967	—		Proof	3.00
30	1968	.100	.20	.40	.75
	1968	—	—	Proof	3.00
	1974	.050	.25	.50	1.00

F.A.O. Issue

45	1975	.075	.20	.35	.50
(48)	1977	.025	.20	.30	.50
	1979	.100	.20	.30	.50

F.A.O. Issue

69	1981	.712	.20	.30	.50

20 SENITI

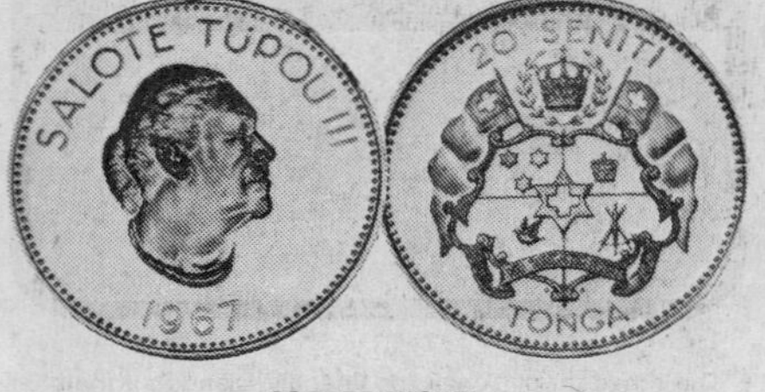

COPPER-NICKEL

KM#	Date	Mintage	VF	XF	Unc
8	1967	.150	.35	.60	1.00
	1967	—		Proof	3.50
13	1967	.015	.75	1.25	2.00
	1967	—	—	Proof	2.50
31	1968	.035	.40	.70	1.00
	1968	—	—	Proof	3.00
	1974	.050	.35	.60	.85

F.A.O. Issue

46	1975	.075	.35	.60	1.00
	1977	.025	.35	.60	1.00
	1979	.050	.35	.60	1.00

F.A.O. Issue

70	1981	.610	.30	.50	.75

50 SENITI

COPPER-NICKEL

9	1967	.075	.85	1.25	2.00
	1967	—		Proof	3.50

KM#	Date	Mintage	VF	XF	Unc
15	1967	.015	1.00	2.00	3.00
	1967	—	—	Proof	4.00
32	1968	.025	.75	1.50	2.50
	1968	—	—	Proof	4.00
41	1974	.050	.75	1.25	2.00

F.A.O. Issue

47	1975	.040	.50	1.00	1.50
	1977	.020	.75	1.25	2.00
	1978	.060	.50	1.00	1.50

F.A.O. Issue

71	1981	.555	.50	1.00	1.50

PA'ANGA   TONGA 1627

100th Anniversary of Automobile Industry
Rolls-Royce and Silver Ghost

85th Birthday of Queen Mother
Queen Mother as a Young Girl

COPPER-NICKEL

KM#	Date	Mintage	VF	XF	Unc
82	1985	—	—	—	3.00

KM#	Date	Mintage	VF	XF	Unc
98	1985	—	—	—	3.00

KM#	Date	Mintage	VF	XF	Unc
11	1967	.078	1.00	1.50	3.00
	1967	—	—	Proof	4.00

100th Anniversary of Automobile Industry
Range Rover and Land Rover

| 83 | 1985 | — | — | — | 3.00 |

85th Birthday of Queen Mother
Wedding Portrait of King George VI and Elizabeth

| 99 | 1985 | — | — | — | 3.00 |

Rev: Similar to KM#11.

| 17 | 1967 | .013 | 1.50 | 2.00 | 4.00 |
| | 1967 | 1,923 | — | Proof | 5.00 |

100th Anniversary of Automobile Industry
Mini Morris Cowley and Touring Car

| 84 | 1985 | — | — | — | 3.00 |

85th Birthday of Queen Mother
Portrait of King George VI and Elizabeth

| 100 | 1985 | — | — | — | 3.00 |

33	1968	.014	1.50	2.00	3.50
	1968	—	—	Proof	6.00
	1974	.010	1.50	2.00	4.00

100th Anniversary of Automobile Industry
MGB GT and MGTA

| 85 | 1985 | — | — | — | 3.00 |

85th Birthday of Queen Mother
Queen Mother holding Queen Elizabeth II

| 101 | 1985 | — | — | — | 3.00 |

F.A.O. Issue

| 48 | 1975 | .013 | 1.00 | 2.00 | 3.50 |

85th Birthday of Queen Mother
Portrait of Queen Mother

| 102 | 1985 | — | — | — | 3.00 |

F.A.O. Issue

| 57 | 1977 | .025 | 1.00 | 1.50 | 3.00 |

TONGA 1628

60th Birthday and F.A.O. Issue
Rev: Similar to KM#57.

KM#	Date	Mintage	VF	XF	Unc
58	1978	.010	1.00	2.00	4.00

24.5000 g, .999 SILVER, .7869 oz ASW
| 58a | 1978 | 750 pcs. | — | Proof | 35.00 |

COPPER-NICKEL
F.A.O. Technical Cooperation Program
| 60 | 1979 | .026 | 1.00 | — | 3.00 |

24.5000 g, .999 SILVER, .7869 oz ASW
| 60a | 1979 | 850 pcs. | — | Proof | 35.00 |

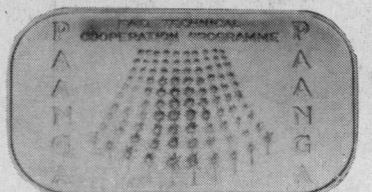

COPPER-NICKEL
F.A.O. and Rural Women's Advancement
| 62 | 1980 | 8,000 | 1.00 | 3.50 | 5.00 |

24.5000 g, .999 SILVER, .7869 oz ASW
| 62a | 1980 | 2,200 | — | Proof | 30.00 |

COPPER-NICKEL
F.A.O. World Food Day
Obv: Similar to KM#57.
| 72 | 1981 | .485 | 1.00 | 1.50 | 3.50 |

24.5000 g, .999 SILVER, .7869 oz ASW
| 72a | 1981 | 3,500 | — | Proof | 30.00 |

COPPER-NICKEL
Christmas
KM#	Date	Mintage	VF	XF	Unc
77	1982	5,000	1.00	2.00	4.00

15.5000 g, .925 SILVER, .4610 oz ASW
| 77a | 1982 | 2,500 | — | Proof | 17.50 |

26.0000 g, .917 GOLD, .7666 oz AGW
Christmas
| 77b | 1982 | 250 pcs. | — | Proof | 500.00 |

30.4000 g, .950 PLATINUM, .9286 oz APW
| 77c | 1982 | 25 pcs. | — | Proof | 800.00 |

COPPER-NICKEL
Christmas
| 80 | 1983 | — | 1.00 | 1.50 | 3.50 |

15.5000 g, .925 SILVER, .4610 oz ASW
| 80a | 1983 | 2,500 | — | Proof | 17.50 |

26.0000 g, .917 GOLD, .7666 oz AGW
Christmas
| 80b | 1983 | 250 pcs. | — | Proof | 500.00 |

30.4000 g, .950 PLATINUM, .9286 oz APW
| 80c | 1983 | 25 pcs. | — | Proof | 800.00 |

COPPER-NICKEL
Christmas
| 81 | 1984 | 5,000 | 1.00 | 1.50 | 3.50 |

15.5000 g, .925 SILVER, .4610 oz ASW
| 81a | 1984 | 2,500 | — | Proof | 17.50 |

26.0000 g, .917 GOLD, .7666 oz AGW
Christmas
| 81b | 1984 | 250 pcs. | — | Proof | 500.00 |

30.4000 g, .950 PLATINUM, .9286 oz APW
| 81c | 1984 | 25 pcs. | — | Proof | 800.00 |

SILVER-CLAD COPPER-NICKEL
100th Anniversary of Automobile Industry
Rolls-Royce and Silver Ghost
Similar to 50 Seniti, KM#82.
| 86 | 1985 | | | | 8.00 |

28.2800 g, .925 SILVER, .8411 oz ASW
| 86a | 1985 | 5,000 | — | Proof | 30.00 |

SILVER-CLAD COPPER-NICKEL
100th Anniversary of Automobile Industry
Range Rover and Land Rover
Similar to 50 Seniti, KM#83.
| 87 | 1985 | | | | 8.00 |

28.2800 g, .925 SILVER, .8411 oz ASW
| 87a | 1985 | 5,000 | — | Proof | 30.00 |

SILVER-CLAD COPPER-NICKEL
100th Anniversary of Automobile Industry
Mini Morris Cowley and Touring Car
Similar to 50 Seniti, KM#84.
| 88 | 1985 | | | | 8.00 |

28.2800 g, .925 SILVER, .8411 oz ASW
| 88a | 1985 | 5,000 | — | Proof | 30.00 |

SILVER-CLAD COPPER-NICKEL
100th Anniversary of Automobile Industry
MGB GT and MG TA
Similar to 50 Seniti, KM#85.
| 89 | 1985 | | | | 8.00 |

28.2800 g, .925 SILVER, .8411 oz ASW
| 89a | 1985 | 5,000 | — | Proof | 30.00 |

SILVER-CLAD COPPER-NICKEL
85th Birthday of Queen Mother
Queen Mother as a Young Girl
Similar to 50 Seniti, KM#98.
| 103 | 1985 | | | | 8.00 |

28.2800 g, .925 SILVER, .8411 oz ASW
| 103a | 1985 | 5,000 | — | Proof | 30.00 |

SILVER-CLAD COPPER-NICKEL
85th Birthday of Queen Mother
Wedding Portrait of King George VI and Elizabeth
Similar to 50 Seniti, KM#99.
| 104 | 1985 | | | | 8.00 |

28.2800 g, .925 SILVER, .8411 oz ASW
KM#	Date	Mintage	VF	XF	Unc
104a	1985	5,000	—	Proof	30.00

SILVER-CLAD COPPER-NICKEL
85th Birthday of Queen Mother
Portrait of King George VI and Elizabeth
Similar to 50 Seniti, KM#100.
| 105 | 1985 | | | | 8.00 |

28.2800 g, .925 SILVER, .8411 oz ASW
| 105a | 1985 | 5,000 | — | Proof | 30.00 |

SILVER-CLAD COPPER-NICKEL
85th Birthday of Queen Mother
Queen Mother holding Queen Elizabeth II
Similar to 50 Seniti, KM#101.
| 106 | 1985 | | | | 8.00 |

28.2800 g, .925 SILVER, .8411 oz ASW
| 106a | 1985 | 5,000 | — | Proof | 30.00 |

SILVER-CLAD COPPER-NICKEL
85th Birthday of Queen Mother
Portrait of Queen Mother
Similar to 50 Seniti, KM#102.
| 107 | 1985 | | | | 8.00 |

28.2800 g, .925 SILVER, .8411 oz ASW
| 107a | 1985 | 5,000 | — | Proof | 30.00 |

COPPER-NICKEL
Christmas
| 118 | 1985 | — | 1.00 | 1.50 | 3.50 |

15.5000 g, .925 SILVER, .4610 oz ASW
| 118a | 1985 | 250 pcs. | — | Proof | 50.00 |

26.0000 g, .917 GOLD, .7666 oz AGW
| 118b | 1985 | 250 pcs. | — | Proof | 500.00 |

30.4000 g, .950 PLATINUM, .9286 oz APW
| 118c | 1985 | | — | Proof | 800.00 |

COPPER-NICKEL
Christmas
Obv: Taufa'ahan Tupou IV. Rev: Three Wise Men.
| 123 | 1986 | | | | 3.50 |

15.5000 g, .925 SILVER, .4610 oz ASW
| 123a | 1986 | | — | Proof | 50.00 |

26.0000 g, .917 GOLD, .7666 oz AGW
| 123b | 1986 | | — | Proof | 500.00 |

30.4000 g, .950 PLATINUM, .9286 oz APW
| 123c | 1986 | | — | Proof | 800.00 |

COPPER-NICKEL
Christmas
| 127 | 1988 | — | — | — | 3.50 |
| | 1988 | — | — | Proof | 6.00 |

15.5000 g, .925 SILVER, .4610 oz ASW
| 127a | 1988 | | — | Proof | 50.00 |

26.0000 g, .917 GOLD, .7666 oz AGW
| 127b | 1988 | | — | Proof | 500.00 |

30.4000 g, .950 PLATINUM, .9286 oz APW
| 127c | 1988 | | — | Proof | 800.00 |

2 PA'ANGA

TONGA 1629

60th Birthday and F.A.O. Issue
Rev: Similar to KM#49.

COPPER-NICKEL

KM#	Date	Mintage	VF	XF	Unc
19	1967	.010	2.00	3.00	5.00
	1967	—	—	Proof	8.00

KM#	Date	Mintage	VF	XF	Unc
59	1978	.010	—	3.00	5.00

42.1000 g, .999 SILVER, 1.3523 oz ASW
| 59a | 1978 | 750 pcs. | — | Proof | 40.00 |

28.2800 g, .500 SILVER, .4546 oz ASW
Commonwealth Games
KM#	Date	Mintage	VF	XF	Unc
120	1986	.050	2.00	4.00	8.00

28.2800 g, .925 SILVER, .8411 oz ASW
| 120a | 1986 | .020 | — | Proof | 15.00 |

COPPER-NICKEL
F.A.O. - SEA Resource Management
| 61 | 1979 | 8,000 | 2.50 | 3.50 | 7.00 |

42.1000 g, .999 SILVER, 1.3523 oz ASW
| 61a | 1979 | 850 pcs. | — | Proof | 50.00 |

Wildlife - Whales
| 121 | 1986 | .025 | — | Proof | 15.00 |

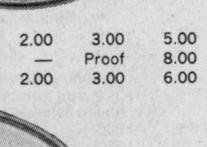

37	1968	.014	2.00	3.00	5.00
	1968	—	—	Proof	8.00
	1974	.010	2.00	3.00	6.00

COPPER-NICKEL
F.A.O. and SEA Resource Management
Rev: Similar to KM#61.
| 63 | 1980 | 8,000 | 2.50 | 3.50 | 7.00 |

42.1000 g, .999 SILVER, 1.3523 oz ASW
| 63a | 1980 | 2,200 | — | Proof | 45.00 |

155.5200 g, .999 SILVER, 5.0000 oz ASW
America's Cup
Reduced. Actual size: 65mm.
| 124 | 1987 | 7,500 | — | Proof | 140.00 |

5 PA'ANGA

F.A.O. Issue
| 49 | 1975 | .013 | 2.00 | 3.00 | 5.00 |
| | 1977 | .012 | 2.00 | 3.00 | 5.00 |

COPPER-NICKEL
F.A.O. World Food Day
Obv: Similar to KM#63.
| 73 | 1981 | .485 | 2.00 | 2.50 | 4.00 |

42.1000 g, .999 SILVER, 1.3523 oz ASW
| 73a | 1981 | 3,500 | — | Proof | 32.50 |

TONGA

31.0000 g, .999 SILVER, .9957 oz ASW
Constitution Centennial

KM#	Date	Mintage	VF	XF	Unc
50	1975	2,118	—	—	25.00
	1975	418 pcs.	—	Proof	35.00

COPPER-NICKEL
International Games - Judo

| 119 | 1986 | — | — | Proof | 20.00 |

10 PA'ANGA

62.0000 g, .999 SILVER, 1.9915 oz ASW
Constitution Centennial
Rev: Similar to 5 Pa'anga, KM#50.

51	1975	1,116	—	—	45.00
	1975	420 pcs.	—	Proof	55.00

0.4000 g, .917 GOLD, .0117 oz AGW
F.A.O. and Rural Women's Advancement
Obv: Queen Salote. Rev: Female symbol on dove.

64	1980	750 pcs.	—	—	25.00
	1980	2,000	—	Proof	25.00

28.2800 g, .925 SILVER, .8411 oz ASW
Commonwealth Games

KM#	Date	Mintage	VF	XF	Unc
78	1982	500 pcs.	—	—	30.00
	1982	1,000	—	Proof	27.50

5.1000 g, .375 GOLD, .0615 oz AGW
100th Anniversary of Automobile Industry
Rolls-Royce and Silver Ghost
Similar to 50 Seniti, KM#82.

| 90 | 1985 | 1,000 | — | Proof | 50.00 |

7.9600 g, .917 GOLD, .2347 oz AGW

| 90a | 1985 | 500 pcs. | — | Proof | 150.00 |

5.1000 g, .375 GOLD, .0615 oz AGW
100th Anniversary of Automobile Industry
Range Rover and Land Rover
Similar to 50 Seniti, KM#83.

| 91 | 1985 | 1,000 | — | Proof | 50.00 |

7.9600 g, .917 GOLD, .2347 oz AGW

| 91a | 1985 | 500 pcs. | — | Proof | 150.00 |

5.1000 g, .375 GOLD, .0615 oz AGW
100th Anniversary of Automobile Industry
Mini Morris Cowley and Touring Car
Similar to 50 Seniti, KM#84.

| 92 | 1985 | 1,000 | — | Proof | 50.00 |

7.9600 g, .917 GOLD, .2347 oz AGW

| 92a | 1985 | 500 pcs. | — | Proof | 150.00 |

5.1000 g, .375 GOLD, .0615 oz AGW
100th Anniversary of Automobile Industry
MGB GT and MG TA
Similar to 50 Seniti, KM#85.

| 93 | 1985 | 1,000 | — | Proof | 50.00 |

7.9600 g, .917 GOLD, .2347 oz AGW

| 93a | 1985 | 500 pcs. | — | Proof | 150.00 |

5.1000 g, .375 GOLD, .0615 oz AGW
85th Birthday of Queen Mother
Queen Mother as a Young Girl
Similar to 50 Seniti, KM#98.

| 108 | 1985 | 1,000 | — | Proof | 50.00 |

7.9600 g, .917 GOLD, .2347 oz AGW

| 108a | 1985 | 500 pcs. | — | Proof | 150.00 |

5.1000 g, .375 GOLD, .0615 oz AGW
85th Birthday of Queen Mother
Wedding Portrait of King George VI and Elizabeth
Similar to 50 Seniti, KM#99.

| 109 | 1985 | 1,000 | — | Proof | 50.00 |

7.9600 g, .917 GOLD, .2347 oz AGW

| 109a | 1985 | 500 pcs. | — | Proof | 150.00 |

5.1000 g, .375 GOLD, .0615 oz AGW
85th Birthday of Queen Mother
Portrait of King George VI and Elizabeth
Similar to 50 Seniti, KM#100.

| 110 | 1985 | 1,000 | — | Proof | 50.00 |

7.9600 g, .917 GOLD, .2347 oz AGW

| 110a | 1985 | 500 pcs. | — | Proof | 150.00 |

5.1000 g, .375 GOLD, .0615 oz AGW
85th Birthday of Queen Mother
Queen Mother holding Queen Elizabeth II
Similar to 50 Seniti, KM#101.

| 111 | 1985 | 1,000 | — | Proof | 50.00 |

7.9600 g, .917 GOLD, .2347 oz AGW

| 111a | 1985 | 500 pcs. | — | Proof | 150.00 |

5.1000 g, .375 GOLD, .0615 oz AGW
85th Birthday of Queen Mother
Portrait of Queen Mother
Similar to 50 Seniti, KM#102.

| 112 | 1985 | 1,000 | — | Proof | 50.00 |

7.9600 g, .917 GOLD, .2347 oz AGW

| 112a | 1985 | 500 pcs. | — | Proof | 150.00 |

COPPER-NICKEL
America's Cup - National Flags
Obv: Taufa'ahau Tupou IV.

| 126 | 1987 | — | — | — | 7.00 |

31.1030 g, .999 PALLADIUM, 1.0000 oz APDW

| 126a | 1987 | .025 | — | Proof | 175.00 |

311.0400 g, .999 SILVER, 10.0000 oz ASW
America's Cup - Sailboat and Map
Reduced. Actual size: 75mm
Obv: Taufa'ahau Tupou IV.

KM#	Date	Mintage	VF	XF	Unc
125	1987	5,000	—	Proof	250.00

20 PA'ANGA

140.0000 g, .999 SILVER, 4.4971 oz ASW
Constitution Centennial
Rev: Similar to 5 Pa'anga, KM#50.

52	1975	.011	—	—	100.00
	1975	4,000	—	Proof	125.00

0.8000 g, .917 GOLD, .0235 oz AGW
F.A.O. and Rural Women's Advancement
Obv: Queen Salote. Rev: Female symbol on dove.

65	1980	750 pcs.	—	—	35.00
	1980	2,000	—	Proof	35.00

25 PA'ANGA

5.0000 g, .917 GOLD, .1474 oz AGW
Constitution Centennial
Obv: King George Tupou I. Rev: Arms.

53	1975	405 pcs.	—	—	100.00
	1975	105 pcs.	—	Proof	150.00

50 PA'ANGA

10.0000 g, .917 GOLD, .2948 oz AGW
Constitution Centennial
Obv: King George Tupou II. Rev: Arms.

54	1975	205 pcs.	—	—	200.00
	1975	105 pcs.	—	Proof	250.00

75 PA'ANGA

15.0000 g, .917 GOLD, .4423 oz AGW
Constitution Centennial
Obv: Queen Salote Tupou III. Rev: Arms.

55	1975	204 pcs.	—	—	250.00
	1975	105 pcs.	—	Proof	400.00

100 PA'ANGA

20.0000 g, .917 GOLD, .5897 oz AGW
Constitution Centennial

KM#	Date	Mintage	VF	XF	Unc
56	1975	205 pcs.	—	—	350.00
	1975	105 pcs.	—	Proof	500.00

1/4 HAU

16.0000 g, .980 PALLADIUM, .5041 oz APW
| 21 | 1967 | 1,700 | — | — | 90.00 |

1/2 HAU

32.0000 g, .980 PALLADIUM, 1.0082 oz APW
| 23 | 1967 | 1,650 | — | — | 160.00 |

28.2800 g, .925 SILVER, .8411 oz ASW
Wedding and Treaty of Friendship
| 74 | 1981 | 1,000 | — | — | 30.00 |
| | 1981 | .015 | — | Proof | 25.00 |

10.0000 g, .917 GOLD, .2948 oz AGW
Wildlife - Ground Dwelling Birds
| 122 | 1986 | 5,000 | — | Proof | 475.00 |

HAU

64.0000 g, .980 PALLADIUM, 2.0164 oz APW
| 25 | 1967 | 1,500 | — | — | 300.00 |

7.9900 g, .917 GOLD, .2356 oz AGW
Wedding and Treaty of Friendship
| 75 | 1981 | 500 pcs. | — | — | 150.00 |
| | 1981 | 2,500 | — | Proof | 150.00 |

Commonwealth Games
Obv: Similar to 10 Pa'anga, KM#78.
| 79 | 1982 | 500 pcs. | — | — | 150.00 |
| | 1982 | 500 pcs. | — | Proof | 150.00 |

52.0000 g, .950 PLATINUM, 1.5884 oz APW

100th Anniversary of Automobile Industry
Rolls Royce and Silver Ghost
Similar to 50 Seniti, KM#82.
KM#	Date	Mintage	VF	XF	Unc
94	1985	—	—	Proof	BV + 15%

100th Anniversary of Automobile Industry
Range Rover and Land Rover
Similar to 50 Seniti, KM#83.
| 95 | 1985 | — | — | Proof | BV + 15% |

100th Anniversary of Automobile Industry
Mini Morris Cowley and Touring Car
Similar to 50 Seniti, KM#84.
| 96 | 1985 | — | — | Proof | BV + 15% |

100th Anniversary of Automobile Industry
MGA GT and MG TA
Similar to 50 Seniti, KM#85.
| 97 | 1985 | — | — | Proof | BV + 15% |

85th Birthday of Queen Mother
Queen Mother as a Young Girl
Similar to 50 Seniti, KM#98.
| 113 | 1985 | — | — | Proof | BV + 15% |

85th Birthday of Queen Mother
Wedding Portrait of King George VI and Elizabeth
Similar to 50 Seniti, KM#99.
| 114 | 1985 | — | — | Proof | BV + 15% |

85th Birthday of Queen Mother
Portrait of King George VI and Elizabeth
Similar to 50 Seniti, KM#100.
| 115 | 1985 | — | — | Proof | BV + 15% |

85th Birthday of Queen Mother
Queen Mother holding Queen Elizabeth II
Similar to 50 Seniti, KM#101.
| 116 | 1985 | — | — | Proof | BV + 15% |

85th Birthday of Queen Mother
Portrait of Queen Mother
Similar to 50 Seniti, KM#102.
| 117 | 1985 | — | — | Proof | BV + 15% |

5 HAU

15.9800 g, .917 GOLD, .4711 oz AGW
Wedding and Treaty of Friendship
| 76 | 1981 | 250 pcs. | — | — | 275.00 |
| | 1981 | 1,000 | — | Proof | 275.00 |

COUNTERMARKED COINAGE
20 SENITI

COPPER-NICKEL
c/m: 1918/TTIV/1968 on KM#13.
| 14 | 1967 | 1,577 | — | Proof | 4.00 |

50 SENITI

GILT COPPER-NICKEL
c/m: IN MEMORIAM/1965-1970 on KM#9.
| 10 | 1967 | Inc. Ab. | — | — | 2.00 |

COPPER-NICKEL
c/m: 1918/TTIV/1968 on KM#15.
KM#	Date	Mintage	VF	XF	Unc
16	1967	1,577	—	Proof	5.00

PA'ANGA

GILT COPPER-NICKEL
c/m: IN MEMORIAM/1965-1970 on KM#11.
| 12 | 1967 | Inc. Ab. | — | — | 4.00 |

COPPER-NICKEL
c/m: 1918/TTIV/1968 on KM#17.
| 18 | 1967 | 1,577 | — | Proof | 5.00 |

GILT COPPER-NICKEL
c/m: Oil Rig 1969 OIL SEARCH on KM#17.
| 34 | 1968 | 5,017 | 1.25 | 2.50 | 3.50 |

c/m: COMMONWEALTH MEMBER/1970 on KM#17.
| 35 | 1968 | 3,000 | 2.00 | 3.00 | 4.00 |

c/m: INVESTITURE/1971 on KM#17.
| 36 | 1968 | 3,000 | 2.00 | 3.00 | 4.00 |
| | 1968 | 1,000 | — | Proof | 6.00 |

TONGA 1632

2 PA'ANGA

COPPER-NICKEL
c/m: 1918/TTIV/1968 on KM#19.

KM#	Date	Mintage	VF	XF	Unc
20	1967	1,577	—	Proof	8.00

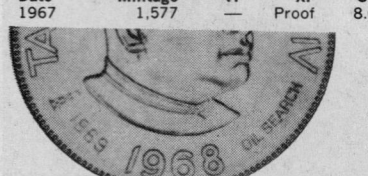

GILT COPPER-NICKEL
c/m: Oil Rig 1969 OIL SEARCH on KM#37.

38	1968	5,039	2.00	4.00	6.00

c/m: COMMONWEALTH MEMBER/1970 on KM#37.

39	1968	3,006	3.00	5.00	8.00

c/m: INVESTITURE/1971 on KM#37.

40	1968	3,000	3.00	5.00	8.00
	1968	1,000	—	Proof	9.00

1/4 HAU
16.0000 g, .980 PALLADIUM, .5040 oz APW
c/m: 1918/TTIV/1968 on Y#15.

22	1967	400 pcs.	—	—	95.00

1/2 HAU

32.0000 g, .980 PALLADIUM, 1.0082 oz APW
c/m: 1918/TTIV/1968 on Y#16a.

24	1967	513 pcs.	—	—	165.00

HAU
64.0000 g, .980 PALLADIUM, 2.0164 oz APW
c/m: 1918/TTIV/1968 on Y#17.

26	1967	400 pcs.	—	—	320.00

MINT SETS (MS)

KM#	Date	Mintage	Identification	Issue Price	Mkt. Val.
MS1	1962(3)	—	KM1-3	—	800.00
MS2	1967(3)	1,500	KM21,23,25	207.00	550.00
MS3	1968(3)	400	KM22,24,26	—	580.00
MS4	1970(2)	10,000	KM10,12	2.30	8.00
MS5	1969(3)	10,000	KM34,38	13.68	12.00
MS6	1970(2)	3,000	KM35,39	13.68	15.00
MS7	1971(2)	3,000	KM36,40	4.80	15.00
MS8	1974(8)	10,000	KM27-33,37	7.60	15.00
MS9	1975(8)	—	KM42-49	7.75	12.00
MS10	1975(4)	—	KM53-56	384.50	900.00
MS11	1975(3)	—	KM50-52	59.60	170.00
MS12	1977(5)	—	KM44-47	.85	4.00
MS13	1977(2)	—	KM49,57	3.00	8.00
MS14	1978(2)	—	KM58-59	3.00	9.00
MS15	1978(5)	—	KM42-46	—	2.00
MS16	1979(2)	8,008	KM60-61	3.00	10.00
MS17	1980(2)	8,000	KM62-63	3.00	12.00
MS18	1980(2)	750	KM64-65, Gold	30.00	60.00
MS19	1981(8)	15,000	KM66-73	5.38	10.00
MS20	1985(4)	20,000	KM82-85, auto industry	21.00	12.50

PROOF SETS (PS)

KM#	Date	Mintage	Identification	Issue Price	Mkt. Val.
PS1	1962(3)	250	KM1-3	—	975.00
PS2	1962(3)	25	KM1a-3a, Platinum	—	1850.
PS3	1967(7)	5,000	KM4-9,11	15.00	12.00
PS4	1967(4)	1,923	KM13,15,17,19	17.25	20.00
PS5	1968(2)	2,500	KM27-33,37	22.50	25.00
PS6	1968(4)	1,577	KM14,16,18,20	22.80	25.00
PS8	1971(2)	1,000	KM36,40	13.40	20.00
PS9	1975(7)	—	KM50-56	—	1500.
PS10	1975(4)	975	KM53-56	537.89	1300.
PS11	1978(2)	750	KM58a-59a	—	75.00
PS12	1979(2)	854	KM60a-61a	45.00	90.00
PS13	1980(2)	400	KM62a-63a	80.00	75.00
PS14	1980(2)	200	KM64-65	60.00	60.00
PS15	1981(2)	3,500	KM72a-73a	88.00	60.00
PS16	1985(5)	20,000*	KM98-102, Copper-Nickel	26.25	20.00
PS17	1985(5)	10,000*	KM103-107, Silver-clad Copper-Nickel	55.00	40.00
PS18	1985(5)	5,000*	KM103a-107a, .925 Silver	180.00	150.00
PS19	1985(5)	1,000*	KM108-112, .374 Gold	315.00	250.00
PS20	1985(5)	500*	KM108a-112a, .917 Gold	775.00	750.00
PS21	1985(5)	50*	KM113-117, .950 Platinum	5850.	BV + 15%
PS22	1985(4)	10,000*	KM86-89	44.00	32.50
PS23	1985(4)	5,000*	KM86a-89a, .925 Silver	144.00	120.00
PS24	1985(4)	1,000*	KM90-93, .374 Gold	252.00	200.00
PS25	1985(4)	500*	KM90a-93a, .917 Gold	620.00	600.00
PS26	1985(4)	50*	KM94-97, .950 Platinum	4680.	BV + 15%

Listings For
TONKIN: refer to Vietnam

TRINIDAD & TOBAGO

The Republic of Trinidad and Tobago, a member of the British Commonwealth situated 7 miles (11 km.) off the coast of Venezuela, has an area of 1,981 sq. mi. (5,130 sq. km.) and a population of *1.3 million. Capital: Port—of-Spain. The island of Trinidad contains the world's largest natural asphalt bog. Birds of Paradise live on little Tobago, the only place outside of their native New Guinea where they can be found in a wild state. Petroleum and petroleum products are the mainstay of the economy. Petroleum products, crude oil and sugar are exported.

Trinidad and Tobago were discovered by Columbus in 1498. Trinidad remained under Spanish rule from the time of its settlement in 1592 until its capture by the British in 1797. It was ceded to the British in 1802. Tobago was occupied at various times by the French, Dutch and English before being ceded to Britain in 1814. Trinidad and Tobago were merged into a single colony in 1888. The colony was part of the Federation of the West Indies until Aug. 31, 1962, when it became an independent member of the Commonwealth of Nations. A new constitution establishing a republican form of government was adopted on Aug. 1, 1976. Trinidad and Tobago is a member of the Commonwealth of Nations. The President is Chief of State. The Prime Minister is Head of Government.

RULERS
British, until 1976

TRINIDAD

Trinidad was discovered by Columbus in 1498. It remained under Spanish rule from the time of its settlement in 1592 until its capture by the British in 1797. It was ceded to the British in 1802.

MONETARY SYSTEM
9 Bits or Shillings = 8 Reales

CUT & COUNTERMARKED COINAGE

3 PENCE
SILVER
Cut quarter segment from Spanish Colonial Real.

KM#	Date	Mintage	VG	Fine	VF
3	ND(1804)	—	25.00	50.00	75.00

6 PENCE
SILVER
Cut half segment from Spanish Colonial Real.

6	ND(1804)	—	25.00	50.00	75.00

SHILLING

SILVER, 2.98 g
c/m: T on center plug cut from Spanish or Spanish Colonial 8 Reales, C#26.

10	ND(1811)	.025	75.00	100.00	125.00

9 SHILLINGS

SILVER
c/m: T on holed Spanish or Spanish Colonial 8 Reales

13	ND(1811)	.025	300.00	400.00	500.00

Similar to KM#13 but w/o T c/m.

14	ND(1811)	Inc. Ab.	300.00	400.00	500.00

TRINIDAD AND TOBAGO
MINT MARKS
FM - Franklin Mint, U.S.A.*

*NOTE: From 1975 the Franklin Mint has produced coinage in up to 3 different qualities. Qualities of issue are designated in ( ) after each date and are defined as follows:

(M) MATTE - Normal circulation strike or a dull finish produced by sandblasting special uncirculated (polish finish) or proof quality dies.

(U) SPECIAL UNCIRCULATED - Polished or proof-like in appearance without any frosted features.

(P) PROOF - The highest quality obtainable having mirror-like fields and frosted features.

MONETARY SYSTEM
100 Cents = 1 Dollar

CENT

BRONZE

KM#	Date	Mintage	VF	XF	Unc
1	1966	24.500	—	—	.15
	1966	8,000	—	Proof	1.00
	1967	4.000	—	—	.15
	1968	5.000	—	—	.15
	1970	5.000	—	—	.15
	1970	2,104	—	Proof	1.50
	1971	10.600	—	—	.15
	1971FM(M)	.286	—	—	.20
	1971FM(P)	.012	—	Proof	.50
	1972	16.500	—	—	.15
	1973	10.000	—	—	.15

10th Anniversary of Independence

9	1972	5.000	—	.10	.15
	1972FM(M)	.125	—	—	.25
	1972FM(P)	.016	—	Proof	.50

17	1973FM(M)	.127	—	—	.75
	1973FM(P)	.020	—	Proof	1.50

Similar to KM#1 but obv. & rev. leg: TRINIDAD AND TOBAGO.

18	1973FM(M)	Inc. Ab.	—	—	.50
	1973FM(P)	Inc. Ab.	—	Proof	1.00

25	1974FM(M)	.128	—	—	.25
	1974FM(P)	.014	—	Proof	.50
	1975	10.000	—	—	.15
	1975FM(M)	.125	—	—	.15
	1975FM(U)	1,111	—	—	1.25
	1975FM(P)	.024	—	Proof	.50
	1976	15.050	—	—	.15

29	1976FM(M)	.150	—	—	.15
	1976FM(U)	582 pcs.	—	—	1.50
	1976FM(P)	.010	—	Proof	.50
	1977	25.000	—	—	.15
	1977FM(M)	.150	—	—	.15
	1977FM(U)	633 pcs.	—	—	1.50
	1977FM(P)	5,337	—	Proof	.50
	1978	12.500	—	—	.15
	1978FM(M)	.150	—	—	.15
	1978FM(U)	472 pcs.	—	—	1.50
	1978FM(P)	4,845	—	Proof	1.00
	1979	30.200	—	—	.15
	1979FM(M)	.150	—	—	.15
	1979FM(U)	518 pcs.	—	—	1.50
	1979FM(P)	3,270	—	Proof	.15
	1980	12.500	—	—	.10
	1980FM(M)	.075	—	—	.15
	1980FM(U)	796 pcs.	—	—	1.50
	1980FM(P)	2,393	—	Proof	1.00
	1981	—	—	—	.15
	1981FM(M)	—	—	—	.15
	1981FM(U)	—	—	—	1.50
	1981FM(P)	—	—	Proof	1.00
	1982	—	—	—	.15
	1983	—	—	—	.15

KM#	Date	Mintage	VF	XF	Unc
29	1984	—	—	—	.15
	1986	—	—	—	.15

2.0000 g, .925 SILVER, .0594 oz ASW
| 29a | 1981FM(P) | 898 pcs. | — | Proof | 7.50 |

BRONZE
20th Anniversary of Independence
Obv: Coat of Arms.

42	1982FM(M)	—	—	—	.15
	1982FM(U)	—	—	—	1.50
	1982FM(P)	—	—	Proof	1.00

2.0000 g, .925 SILVER, .0594 oz ASW
| 42a | 1982FM(P) | 699 pcs. | — | Proof | 7.50 |

BRONZE

51	1983FM(M)	—	—	—	.15
	1983FM(P)	—	—	Proof	1.00
	1984FM(P)	—	—	Proof	1.00

2.0000 g, .925 SILVER, .0594 oz ASW
51a	1983FM(P)	1,344	—	Proof	7.50
	1984FM(P)	—	—	Proof	7.50

5 CENTS

BRONZE

2	1966	7.500	—	.10	.25
	1966	8,000	—	Proof	1.25
	1967	3.000	—	.10	.25
	1970	2,104	—	Proof	1.75
	1971	2.400	—	.10	.25
	1971FM(M)	.057	—	—	.15
	1971FM(P)	.012	—	Proof	.75
	1972	2.250	—	.10	.20

10th Anniversary of Independence
10	1972	.015	—	—	.35
	1972FM(M)	.025	—	—	.25
	1972FM(P)	.016	—	Proof	.75

Similar to KM#2 but obv. & rev. leg: TRINIDAD AND TOBAGO.
19	1973FM(M)	.027	—	—	.50
	1973FM(P)	.020	—	Proof	.75

Similar to 1 Cent, KM#17.
57	1973FM(M)	—	—	—	—
	1973FM(P)	—	—	—	—

26	1974FM(M)	.028	—	—	.50
	1974FM(P)	.014	—	Proof	.75
	1975	1.500	—	.10	.20
	1975FM(M)	.025	—	—	.20
	1975FM(U)	1,111	—	—	1.50
	1975FM(P)	.024	—	Proof	.75
	1976	7.500	—	.10	.20

30	1976FM(M)	.030	—	—	.20
	1976FM(U)	582 pcs.	—	—	1.75

KM#	Date	Mintage	VF	XF	Unc
30	1976FM(P)	.010	—	Proof	.75
	1977	12.000	—	.10	.20
	1977FM(M)	.030	—	—	.20
	1977FM(U)	633 pcs.	—	—	1.75
	1977FM(P)	5,337	—	Proof	.75
	1978	1.500	—	.10	.20
	1978FM(M)	.030	—	—	.20
	1978FM(U)	472 pcs.	—	—	1.75
	1978FM(P)	4,845	—	Proof	1.25
	1979	—	—	.10	.20
	1979FM(M)	.030	—	—	.20
	1979FM(U)	518 pcs.	—	—	1.75
	1979FM(P)	3,270	—	Proof	1.25
	1980	15.000	—	.10	.20
	1980FM(M)	.015	—	—	.20
	1980FM(U)	796 pcs.	—	—	1.75
	1980FM(P)	2,393	—	Proof	1.25
	1981	—	—	.10	.20
	1981FM(M)	—	—	—	.20
	1981FM(U)	—	—	—	1.75
	1981FM(P)	—	—	Proof	1.25

3.5000 g, .925 SILVER, .1040 oz ASW
| 30a | 1981FM(P) | 898 pcs. | — | Proof | 10.00 |

BRONZE
20th Anniversary of Independence
Obv: Coat of Arms.

43	1982FM(M)	—	—	—	.20
	1982FM(U)	—	—	—	1.75
	1982FM(P)	—	—	Proof	1.25

3.5000 g, .925 SILVER, .1040 oz ASW
| 43a | 1982FM(P) | 699 pcs. | — | Proof | 10.00 |

BRONZE
Obv: Coat of arms.

52	1983FM(M)	—	—	—	.20
	1983FM(P)	—	—	Proof	1.25
	1984FM(P)	—	—	Proof	1.25

3.5000 g, .925 SILVER, .1040 oz ASW
52a	1983FM(P)	1,324	—	Proof	10.00
	1984FM(P)	—	—	Proof	10.00

10 CENTS

COPPER-NICKEL

3	1966	7.800	—	.10	.30
	1966	8,000	—	Proof	1.50
	1967	4.000	—	.10	.30
	1970	2,104	—	Proof	2.00
	1971	—	—	.10	.30
	1971FM(M)	.029	—	—	.35
	1971FM(P)	.012	—	Proof	1.00
	1972	4.000	—	.10	.30

10th Anniversary of Independence
11	1972	.041	—	—	.40
	1972FM(M)	.013	—	—	.60
	1972FM(P)	.016	—	Proof	1.00

Similar to KM#3 but obv. and rev leg: TRINIDAD AND TOBAGO.
20	1973FM(M)	.014	—	—	1.00
	1973FM(P)	.020	—	Proof	1.00

Similar to 1 Cent, KM#17.
58	1973FM(M)	—	—	—	—
	1973FM(P)	—	—	—	—

27	1974FM(M)	.016	—	—	1.00
	1974FM(P)	.014	—	Proof	1.00
	1975	4.000	—	.10	.25

TRINIDAD and TOBAGO 1633

TRINIDAD and TOBAGO

KM#	Date	Mintage	VF	XF	Unc
27	1975FM(M)	.013	—	—	.50
	1975FM(U)	1,111	—	—	1.75
	1975FM(P)	.024	—	Proof	1.00
	1976	14.720	—	.10	.20
31	1976FM(M)	.015	—	—	.50
	1976FM(U)	582 pcs.	—	—	2.00
	1976FM(P)	.010	—	Proof	1.00
	1977	17.280	—	.10	.20
	1977FM(M)	.015	—	—	.50
	1977FM(U)	633 pcs.	—	—	2.00
	1977FM(P)	5,337	—	Proof	1.00
	1978	10.000	—	.10	.20
	1978FM(M)	.015	—	—	.50
	1978FM(U)	472 pcs.	—	—	2.00
	1978FM(P)	4,845	—	Proof	1.50
	1979	1.970	—	.10	.30
	1979FM(M)	.015	—	—	.50
	1979FM(U)	518 pcs.	—	—	2.00
	1979FM(P)	3,270	—	Proof	1.50
	1980	20.000	—	.10	.30
	1980FM(M)	7,500	—	—	.50
	1980FM(U)	796 pcs.	—	—	2.00
	1980FM(P)	2,393	—	Proof	1.50
	1981	—	—	.10	.30
	1981FM(M)	—	—	—	.50
	1981FM(U)	—	—	—	2.00
	1981FM(P)	—	—	Proof	1.50

1.5000 g, .925 SILVER, .0446 oz ASW

| 31a | 1981FM(P) | 898 pcs. | — | Proof | 10.00 |

COPPER-NICKEL
20th Anniversary of Independence
Obv: Coat of Arms.

44	1982FM(M)	—	—	—	.50
	1982FM(U)	—	—	—	2.00
	1982FM(P)	—	—	Proof	1.50

1.5000 g, .925 SILVER, .0446 oz ASW

| 44a | 1982FM(P) | 699 pcs. | — | Proof | 10.00 |

COPPER-NICKEL
Obv: Coat of arms.

53	1983FM(M)	—	—	—	.50
	1983FM(P)	—	—	Proof	1.50
	1984FM(P)	—	—	Proof	1.50

1.5000 g, .925 SILVER, .0446 oz ASW

| 53a | 1983FM(P) | — | — | Proof | 10.00 |
| | 1984FM(P) | — | — | Proof | 10.00 |

25 CENTS

COPPER-NICKEL

4	1966	7.200	.10	.15	.35
	1966	8.000	—	Proof	1.75
	1967	1.800	.10	.15	.50
	1970	2,014	—	Proof	2.25
	1971	1.500	.10	.15	.50
	1971FM(M)	.011	—	—	.65
	1971FM(P)	.012	—	Proof	1.25
	1972	3.000	.10	.15	.35

10th Anniversary of Independence

12	1972	.014	—	—	.60
	1972FM(M)	5,000	—	—	1.50
	1972FM(P)	.016	—	Proof	1.25

Similar to KM#4 but obv. and rev. leg: TRINIDAD AND TOBAGO.

| 21 | 1973FM(M) | 6,575 | — | — | 2.25 |
| | 1973FM(P) | .020 | — | Proof | 1.25 |

Similar to 1 Cent, KM#17.

KM#	Date	Mintage	VF	XF	Unc
59	1973FM(M)	—	—	—	—
	1973FM(P)	—	—	—	—
28	1974FM(M)	8,258	—	—	1.75
	1974FM(P)	.014	—	Proof	1.25
	1975	3.000	.10	.15	.30
	1975FM(M)	5,000	—	—	1.50
	1975FM(U)	1,111	—	—	2.00
	1975FM(P)	.024	—	Proof	1.25
	1976	9.000	.10	.15	.30
32	1976FM(M)	6,000	—	—	1.00
	1976FM(U)	582 pcs.	—	—	2.25
	1976FM(P)	.010	—	Proof	1.25
	1977	9.000	.10	.15	.30
	1977FM(M)	6,000	—	—	1.00
	1977FM(U)	633 pcs.	—	—	2.25
	1977FM(P)	5,337	—	Proof	1.25
	1978	5.470	.10	.15	.30
	1978FM(M)	6,000	—	—	1.00
	1978FM(U)	472 pcs.	—	—	2.25
	1978FM(P)	4,845	—	Proof	1.75
	1979	—	.10	.15	.40
	1979FM(M)	6,000	—	—	1.00
	1979FM(U)	518 pcs.	—	—	2.25
	1979FM(P)	3,270	—	Proof	1.75
	1980	15.000	.10	.15	.40
	1980FM(M)	3,000	—	—	1.00
	1980FM(U)	796 pcs.	—	—	2.25
	1980FM(P)	2,393	—	Proof	1.75
	1981	—	.10	.15	.40
	1981FM(M)	—	—	—	1.00
	1981FM(U)	—	—	—	2.25
	1981FM(P)	—	—	Proof	1.75
	1983	—	.10	.15	.40
	1983FM(M)	—	—	—	1.00
	1983FM(P)	—	—	Proof	1.75
	1984FM(P)	—	—	Proof	1.75

3.6000 g, .925 SILVER, .1070 oz ASW

32a	1981FM(P)	898 pcs.	—	Proof	10.00
	1983FM(P)	—	—	Proof	10.00
	1984FM(P)	—	—	Proof	10.00

COPPER-NICKEL
20th Anniversary of Independence
Obv: Coat of Arms.

45	1982FM(M)	—	—	—	1.00
	1982FM(U)	—	—	—	2.25
	1982FM(P)	—	—	Proof	1.75

3.6000 g, .925 SILVER, .1070 oz ASW

| 45a | 1982FM(P) | 699 pcs. | — | Proof | 10.00 |

50 CENTS

COPPER-NICKEL

5	1966	.975	.25	.50	1.25
	1966	8.000	—	Proof	2.00
	1967	.750	.25	.50	1.25
	1970	2,104	—	Proof	2.50
	1971FM(M)	5,714	—	—	2.00
	1971FM(P)	.012	—	Proof	1.50

10th Anniversary of Independence

KM#	Date	Mintage	VF	XF	Unc
13	1972	.375	.50	.75	1.50
	1972FM(M)	2,500	—	—	5.00
	1972FM(P)	.016	—	Proof	1.50
22	1973FM(M)	4,075	—	—	2.50
	1973FM(P)	.020	—	Proof	1.50
	1974FM(M)	5,758	—	—	2.00
	1974FM(P)	.014	—	Proof	1.50
	1975FM(M)	2,500	—	—	3.75
	1975FM(U)	1,111	—	—	2.25
	1975FM(P)	.024	—	Proof	1.50
	1976	.750	—	.75	1.50
33	1976FM(M)	3,000	—	—	3.25
	1976FM(U)	582 pcs.	—	—	2.50
	1976FM(P)	.010	—	Proof	1.50
	1977	1.500	.25	.50	1.00
	1977FM(M)	3,000	—	—	3.00
	1977FM(U)	633 pcs.	—	—	2.50
	1977FM(P)	5,337	—	Proof	1.50
	1978	.563	.50	.75	1.50
	1978FM(M)	3,000	—	—	3.00
	1978FM(U)	472 pcs.	—	—	2.50
	1978FM(P)	4,845	—	Proof	2.00
	1979	.750	.50	.75	1.50
	1979FM(M)	3,000	—	—	3.25
	1979FM(U)	518 pcs.	—	—	2.50
	1979FM(P)	3,270	—	Proof	2.00
	1980	3.750	.25	.50	1.00
	1980FM(M)	1,500	—	—	3.00
	1980FM(U)	796 pcs.	—	—	2.50
	1980FM(P)	2,393	—	Proof	2.00
	1981FM(M)	—	—	—	3.00
	1981FM(U)	—	—	—	2.50
	1981FM(P)	—	—	Proof	2.00

7.2500 g, .925 SILVER, .2156 oz ASW

| 33a | 1981FM(P) | 898 pcs. | — | Proof | 12.50 |

COPPER-NICKEL
20th Anniversary of Independence
Obv: Coat of Arms.

46	1982FM(M)	—	—	—	3.00
	1982FM(U)	—	—	—	2.50
	1982FM(P)	—	—	Proof	2.00

7.2500 g, .925 SILVER, .2156 oz ASW

| 46a | 1982FM(P) | 699 pcs. | — | Proof | 12.50 |

COPPER-NICKEL
Obv: Coat of arms.

54	1983FM(M)	—	—	—	3.00
	1983FM(P)	—	—	Proof	2.00
	1984FM(P)	—	—	Proof	2.00

7.2500 g, .925 SILVER, .2156 oz ASW

| 54a | 1983FM(P) | 1,325 | — | Proof | 12.50 |
| | 1984FM(P) | — | — | Proof | 12.50 |

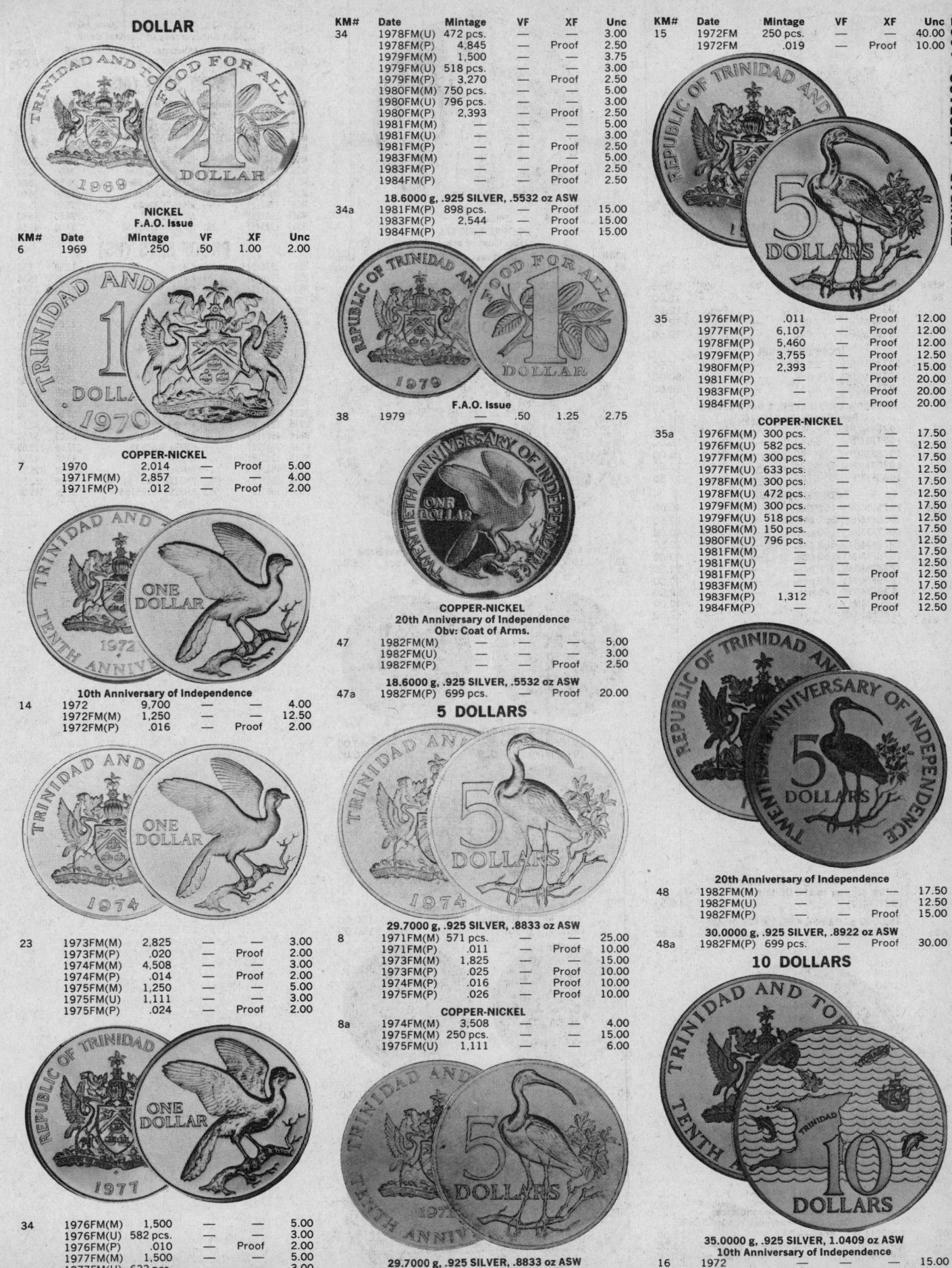

TRINIDAD and TOBAGO 1635

TRINIDAD and TOBAGO

KM#	Date	Mintage	VF	XF	Unc
24	1973FM(M)	1,700	—	—	15.00
	1973FM(P)	.024	—	Proof	12.50
	1974FM(P)	.021	—	Proof	12.50
	1975FM(P)	.028	—	Proof	12.50

COPPER-NICKEL

24a	1974FM(M)	3,632	—	—	7.50
	1975FM(P)	125 pcs.	—	—	50.00
	1975FM(U)	1,111	—	—	10.00

35.0000 g, .925 SILVER, 1.0409 oz ASW
Rev: Similar to KM#16.

36	1976FM(P)	.013	—	Proof	12.50
	1977FM(P)	6,643	—	Proof	15.00
	1978FM(P)	7,449	—	Proof	15.00
	1979FM(P)	4,994	—	Proof	17.50
	1980FM(P)	3,726	—	Proof	17.50

COPPER-NICKEL

36a	1976FM(M)	150 pcs.	—	—	40.00
	1976FM(U)	582 pcs.	—	—	12.50
	1977FM(M)	150 pcs.	—	—	40.00
	1977FM(U)	633 pcs.	—	—	12.50
	1978FM(M)	150 pcs.	—	—	40.00
	1978FM(U)	472 pcs.	—	—	12.50
	1979FM(M)	150 pcs.	—	—	40.00
	1979FM(U)	796 pcs.	—	—	12.50
	1980FM(M)	—	—	—	40.00
	1980FM(U)	—	—	—	12.50

5th Anniversary of the Republic
Obv: Similar to 100 Dollars, KM#41.

40	1981FM(U)	—	—	—	15.00

35.0000 g, .925 SILVER, 1.0409 oz ASW

40a	1981FM(P)	2,374	—	Proof	35.00

COPPER-NICKEL
20th Anniversary of Independence
Obv: Coat of Arms.

49	1982FM(M)	—	—	—	15.00
	1982FM(U)	—	—	—	20.00
	1982FM(P)	—	—	Proof	22.50

35.0000 g, .925 SILVER, 1.0409 oz ASW

49a	1982FM(P)	1,682	—	Proof	25.00

COPPER-NICKEL
Obv: Coat of arms.

KM#	Date	Mintage	VF	XF	Unc
55	1983FM(U)	288 pcs.	—	—	20.00

35.0000 g, .925 SILVER, 1.0409 oz ASW

55a	1983FM(P)	1,565	—	Proof	30.00
	1984FM(P)	—	—	Proof	30.00

25 DOLLARS

30.2800 g, .500 SILVER, .4868 oz ASW
10th Anniversary of Caribbean Development Bank

39	1980FM(P)	3,039	—	Proof	25.00

100 DOLLARS

6.2100 g, .500 GOLD, .0998 oz AGW

37	1976FM(M)	200 pcs.	—	—	80.00
	1976FM(P)	.029	—	Proof	70.00

5th Anniversary of the Republic

41	1981FM(U)	100 pcs.	—	—	150.00
	1981FM(P)	400 pcs.	—	Proof	150.00

20th Anniversary of Independence

50	1982FM(P)	1,380	—	Proof	110.00

200 DOLLARS

11.1700 g, .500 GOLD, .1796 oz AGW
20th Anniversary of Central Bank

KM#	Date	Mintage	VF	XF	Unc
56	1984FM(P)	1,200	—	Proof	150.00

MINT SETS (MS)

KM#	Date	Mintage	Identification	Issue Price	Mkt. Val.
MS1	1973(8)	1,575	KM8,18-24	24.00	20.00
MS2	1974(8)	3,258	KM8a,22-23,24a,25-28	25.00	15.00
MS3	1975(8)	1,111	KM8a,22-23,24a,25-28	27.50	20.00
MS4	1976(8)	582	KM29-34,35a-36a	27.50	30.00
MS5	1977(8)	632	KM29-34,35a-36a	27.50	30.00
MS6	1978(8)	472	KM29-34,35a-36a	27.50	30.00
MS7	1979(8)	518	KM29-34,35a-36a	28.50	30.00
MS8	1980(8)	796	KM29-34,35a-36a	28.50	30.00
MS9	1981(8)	—	KM29-34,35a,40	28.50	45.50
MS10	1982(8)	—	KM42-49	28.50	45.50
MS11	1983(8)	281	KM32,34,35a,51-55	37.00	45.50

PROOF SETS (PS)

PS1	1966(5)	8,000	KM1-5	12.50	7.50
PS2	1970(6)	2,104	KM1-5,6	15.25	15.00
PS3	1971(7)	11,039	KM1-5,6,8	21.00	17.50
PS4	1971(6)	488	KM1-5,6	15.00	12.50
PS5	1972(9)	13,874	KM9-16	35.00	30.00
PS6	1972(9)	15,957	KM9-15	22.00	17.50
PS7	1973(9)	14,615	KM8,17,19-24	35.00	30.00
PS8	1973(7)	5,050	KM,8,17,19-23	22.00	17.50
PS9	1974(8)	13,991	KM8,22-28	50.00	30.00
PS10	1975(8)	24,472	KM8,22-28	55.00	30.00
PS11	1976(8)	10,099	KM29-36	55.00	32.50
PS12	1977(8)	5,337	KM29-36	55.00	34.00
PS13	1978(8)	4,845	KM29-36	55.00	37.50
PS14	1979(8)	3,270	KM29-36	57.00	40.00
PS15	1980(8)	2,393	KM29-36	66.00	42.50
PS16	1981(8)	—	KM29-34,35a,40a	87.00	57.50
PS17	1981(8)	—	KM29a-34a,35a,40a	222.00	120.00
PS18	1982(8)	—	KM42-49	87.00	47.50
PS19	1982(8)	—	KM42a-49a	222.00	125.00
PS20	1983(8)	461	KM32,34,35a,51-54,55a	87.00	52.50
PS21	1983(8)	753	KM32a,34a,35,51a-55a	197.00	115.00

TRISTAN DA CUNHA

Tristan da Cunha is the principal island and group name of a small cluster of volcanic islands located in the South Atlantic midway between the Cape of Good Hope and South America, and 1,500 miles (2,414 km.) south-southwest of the British colony of St. Helena. The other islands are Inaccessible, Gough, and the three Nightingale Islands. The group, which comprises a dependency of St. Helena, has a total area of 40 sq. mi. (104 sq. km.) and a population of less than 300. There is a village of 60 houses called Edinburgh. Potatoes are the staple subsistence crop.

Tristan da Cunha was discovered in 1506 by Portuguese admiral Tristao da Cunha. Unsuccessful attempts to colonize the islands were made by the Dutch in 1656, but the first permanent inhabitant didn't arrive until 1810. During the exile of Napoleon on St. Helena, Britain placed a temporary garrison on Tristan da Cunha to prevent any attempt to rescue Napoleon from his island prison. The islands were formally annexed to Britain in 1816 and became a dependency of St. Helena in 1938.

RULERS
British

MINT MARKS
PM - Pobjoy Mint

MONETARY SYSTEM
25 Pence = 1 Crown
4 Crowns = 1 Pound

25 PENCE

COPPER-NICKEL
Queen's Silver Jubilee

KM#	Date	Mintage	Fine	VF	XF	Unc
1	1977	.050	—	1.00	1.75	3.00

28.2800 g, .925 SILVER, .8411 oz ASW

| 1a | 1977 | .025 | — | — | Proof | 22.50 |

80th Birthday of Queen Mother

KM#	Date	Mintage	Fine	VF	XF	Unc
3	1980	.065	—	1.00	1.75	3.00

28.2800 g, .925 SILVER, .8411 oz ASW (OMS)

| 3a | 1980 | .025 | — | — | Proof | 20.00 |

COPPER-NICKEL
Wedding of Prince Charles and Lady Diana

| 4 | 1981PM | — | — | 1.00 | 1.75 | 3.00 |

28.2800 g, .925 SILVER, .8411 oz ASW

| 4a | 1981PM | .030 | — | — | Proof | 22.50 |

50 PENCE

28.2800 g, .925 SILVER, .8411 oz ASW
40th Wedding Anniversary of Queen Elizabeth and Prince Philip

| 7 | 1987 | 2,000 | — | — | Proof | 40.00 |

47.5400 g, .917 GOLD, 1.4001 oz AGW

| 7a | 1987 | 75 pcs. | — | — | Proof | 1500. |

COPPER-NICKEL

| 7b | 1987 | — | — | — | — | 3.00 |

CROWN

COPPER-NICKEL
25th Anniversary of Coronation

KM#	Date	Mintage	Fine	VF	XF	Unc
2	1978PM	—	—	1.00	1.75	3.00

28.2800 g, .925 SILVER, .8411 oz ASW

| 2a | 1978PM | .070 | — | — | — | 15.00 |
| | 1978PM | .025 | — | — | Proof | 22.50 |

International Year of the Scout
Obv: Portrait of Queen Elizabeth II.

| 5 | 1983 | .010 | — | — | — | 15.00 |
| | 1983 | .010 | — | — | Proof | 22.50 |

2 POUNDS

15.9800 g, .917 GOLD, .4712 oz AGW
International Year of the Scout
Obv: Portrait of Queen Elizabeth II.
Rev: Scout emblem.
Similar to 1 Crown, KM#5.

| 6 | 1983 | 2,000 | — | — | — | 400.00 |
| | 1983 | 2,000 | — | — | Proof | 500.00 |

Tunis / TUNISIA 1638

TUNISIA-TUNIS

The Republic of Tunisia, located on the northern coast of Africa between Algeria and Libya, has an area of 63,170 sq. mi. (163,610 sq. km.) and a population of *7.9 million. Capital: Tunis. Agriculture is the backbone of the economy. Crude oil, phosphates, olive oil, and wine are exported.

Tunisia, settled by the Phoenicians in the 12th century B.C., was the center of the seafaring Carthaginian empire. After the total destruction of Carthage, Tunisia became part of Rome's African province. It remained a part of the Roman Empire (except for the 439-533 interval of Vandal conquest) until taken by the Arabs, 648, who administered it until the Turkish invasion of 1570. Under Turkish control, the public revenue was heavily dependent upon the piracy of Mediterranean shipping, an endeavor that wasn't abandoned until 1819 when a coalition of powers threatened appropriate reprisal. Deprived of its major source of income, Tunisia underwent a financial regression that ended in bankruptcy, enabling France to establish a protectorate over the country in 1881. National agitation and guerrilla fighting forced France to grant Tunisia internal autonomy in 1955 and to recognize Tunisian independence on March 20, 1956. Tunisia abolished the monarchy and established a republic on July 25, 1957.

TITLES

المملكة التونسية
Al-Mamlaka Al-Tunisiya

الجمهورية التونسية
Al-Jumhuriya Al-Tunisiya

TUNIS

Tunis, the capital and major seaport of Tunisia, existed in the Carthaginian era, but its importance dates only from the Moslem conquest, following which it became a major center of Arab power and prosperity. Spain seized it in 1535, lost it in 1564, retook it in 1573 and ceded it to the Turks in 1574. Thereafter the history of Tunis merged with that of Tunisia.

RULERS
Ottoman, until 1881

LOCAL RULERS
Muhammad Bey
  AH1271-1276/1855-1859AD
Muhammad Al-Sadiq Bey
  AH1276-1299/1859-1882AD
Ali Bey
  AH1299-1320/1882-1902AD
Muhammad Al-Hadi Bey
  AH1320-1324/1902-1906AD
Muhammad Al-Nasir Bey
  AH1324-1340/1906-1922AD
Muhammad Al-Habib Bey
  AH1340-1348/1922-1929AD
Ahmad Pasha Bey
  AH1348-1361/1929-1942AD
Muhammad Al-Munsif Bey
  AH1361-1362/1942-1943AD
Muhammad Al-Amin Bey
  AH1362-1376/1943-1957AD

NOTE: All coins struck until AH1298/1881AD bear the name of the Ottoman Sultan; the name of the Bey of Tunis was added in AH1272/1855AD. After AH1298, when the French established their protectorate, only the Bey's name appears on the coin until AH1376/1956AD.

MINT

تونس

TUNIS

With exceptions noted in their proper place, all coins were struck at Tunis prior to AH1308/1891AD. Thereafter, all coins were struck at Paris with mint mark A until 1928, symbols of the mint from 1929-1957.

MONETARY SYSTEM
Until 1891
6 Burben (Bourbine) = 1 Burbe (Bourbe)
2 Burbe (Bourbe) = 1 Asper
13 Burbe = 1 Kharub (Caroub)
16 Kharub (Caroub) = 1 Piastre (Sebili)

Arabic name	French name	Value
Qafsi of Falls Raqiq	Bourbine	1/12 Nasri
Fals	Bourbe	6 Qafsi or 1/2 Nasri
Nasri	Asper	1/52 Riyal
Kharub	Caroub	1/16 Riyal
1/8 Riyal	1/8 Piastre	1 Kharub
1/4 Riyal	1/4 Piastre	4 Kharub
1/2 Riyal	1/2 Piastre	8 Kharub
Riyal	Piastre	16 Kharub

OTTOMAN ISSUES
SELIM III
AH1203-1222/1789-1807AD

ASPER
BILLON, 9x9mm, square
Obv. leg: *Sultan Selim.* Rev: Date and mint.

KM#	Date	Mintage	Good	VG	Fine	VF
75	AH1216	—	30.00	60.00	100.00	150.00

4 KHARUB
BILLON, 21mm, 4.00 g

74	AH1215	—	—	—	—	—
	1217	—	—	—	—	—

8 KHARUB
BILLON, 27-28mm, 7.10-7.70 g
Similar to 1 Piastre, KM#72.

73	AH1216	—	15.00	25.00	40.00	75.00
	1217	—	15.00	25.00	40.00	75.00
	1218	—	15.00	25.00	40.00	75.00
	1219	—	15.00	25.00	40.00	75.00
	1220	—	15.00	25.00	40.00	75.00
	1221	—	15.00	25.00	40.00	75.00
	1222	—	15.00	25.00	40.00	75.00

NOTE: Varieties of ornamentation exist.

PIASTRE

BILLON, 14.90-16.00 g

72.2	AH1216	—	18.00	30.00	50.00	85.00
	1217	—	18.00	30.00	50.00	85.00
	1218	—	18.00	30.00	50.00	85.00
	1219	—	18.00	30.00	50.00	85.00
	1220	—	18.00	30.00	50.00	85.00
	1221	—	18.00	30.00	50.00	85.00
	1222	—	18.00	30.00	50.00	85.00

NOTE: Varieties of ornamentation exist.

MUSTAFA IV
AH1222-1223/1807/1808AD

4 KHARUB
BILLON, 21mm, 3.50 g
Similar To 1 Piastre, KM#72.

| 78 | AH1223 | — | 100.00 | 150.00 | 300.00 | 400.00 |

8 KHARUB
BILLON, 27mm, 7.50 g

| 76 | AH1222 | — | 125.00 | 200.00 | 350.00 | 600.00 |
| | 1223 | — | 125.00 | 200.00 | 350.00 | 600.00 |

PIASTRE

BILLON, 35mm, 16.00 g

| 77 | AH1222 | — | 100.00 | 175.00 | 300.00 | 500.00 |
| | 1223 | — | 100.00 | 175.00 | 300.00 | 500.00 |

MAHMUD II
AH1223-1255/1808-1839AD

BURBEN
COPPER, 0.80 g

KM#	Date	Mintage	Good	VG	Fine	VF
85	AH1230	—	15.00	27.50	50.00	80.00

ASPER
BILLON, 8mm square, 0.20 g

| 83 | AH1228 | — | — | — | — | — |

KHARUB

BILLON, 0.60-0.70 g

91	AH1241	—	6.00	10.00	17.50	30.00
	1242	—	6.00	10.00	17.50	30.00
	1249	—	3.00	5.00	10.00	20.00
	1250	—	3.00	5.00	10.00	20.00
	1251	—	3.00	5.00	10.00	20.00
	1252	—	3.00	5.00	10.00	20.00
	1253	—	3.00	5.00	10.00	20.00
	1254	—	3.00	5.00	10.00	20.00
	1255	—	3.00	5.00	10.00	20.00

2 KHARUB
BILLON, 16mm, 1.30 g

| 92 | AH1243 | — | 9.00 | 15.00 | 35.00 | 60.00 |
| | 1244 | — | 9.00 | 15.00 | 35.00 | 60.00 |

4 KHARUB
BILLON, 21mm, 3.50 g

81	AH1223	—	30.00	60.00	100.00	150.00
	1228	—	30.00	60.00	100.00	150.00
	1231	—	30.00	60.00	100.00	150.00

20mm, 2.50 g

88	AH1240	—	6.00	10.00	30.00	60.00
	1241	—	6.00	10.00	30.00	60.00
	1242	—	6.00	10.00	30.00	60.00
	1243	—	6.00	10.00	30.00	60.00
	1245	—	6.00	10.00	30.00	60.00
	1246	—	6.00	10.00	30.00	60.00
	1249	—	6.00	10.00	30.00	60.00
	1250	—	6.00	10.00	30.00	60.00
	1252	—	6.00	10.00	30.00	60.00
	1253	—	6.00	10.00	30.00	60.00
	1254	—	6.00	10.00	30.00	60.00
	1255	—	6.00	10.00	30.00	60.00

8 KHARUB
BILLON, 27mm, 7.50 g

84	AH1228	—	30.00	60.00	100.00	150.00
	1231	—	30.00	60.00	100.00	150.00
	1232	—	30.00	60.00	100.00	150.00
	1233	—	30.00	60.00	100.00	150.00

26mm, 5.00 g

89	AH1240	—	6.00	10.00	20.00	40.00
	1241	—	6.00	10.00	20.00	40.00
	1242	—	6.00	10.00	20.00	40.00
	1243	—	6.00	10.00	20.00	40.00
	1244	—	6.00	10.00	20.00	40.00
	1245	—	6.00	10.00	20.00	40.00
	1246	—	6.00	10.00	20.00	40.00
	1247	—	6.00	10.00	20.00	40.00
	1248	—	6.00	10.00	20.00	40.00
	1251	—	8.00	12.00	30.00	60.00
	1252	—	6.00	10.00	20.00	40.00
	1253	—	6.00	10.00	20.00	40.00
	1254	—	6.00	10.00	20.00	40.00

PIASTRE

BILLON, 16.00 g

KM#	Date	Mintage	Good	VG	Fine	VF
82	AH1225	—	20.00	40.00	70.00	125.00
	1226	—	20.00	40.00	70.00	125.00
	1227	—	20.00	40.00	70.00	125.00
	1228	—	20.00	40.00	70.00	125.00
	1229	—	20.00	40.00	70.00	125.00
	1230	—	20.00	40.00	70.00	125.00
	1231	—	20.00	40.00	70.00	125.00
	1232	—	20.00	40.00	70.00	125.00
	1233	—	25.00	50.00	80.00	150.00
	1234	—	40.00	75.00	125.00	200.00

11.00-11.50 g

90	AH1240	—	5.50	9.00	15.00	30.00
	1241	—	5.50	9.00	15.00	30.00
	1242	—	5.50	9.00	15.00	30.00
	1243	—	5.50	9.00	15.00	30.00
	1244	—	5.50	9.00	15.00	30.00
	1245	—	5.50	9.00	15.00	30.00
	1246	—	5.50	9.00	15.00	30.00
	1247	—	5.50	9.00	15.00	30.00
	1248	—	5.50	9.00	15.00	30.00
	1249	—	5.50	9.00	15.00	30.00
	1250	—	5.50	9.00	15.00	30.00
	1251	—	5.50	9.00	15.00	30.00
	1252	—	5.50	9.00	15.00	30.00
	1253	—	5.50	9.00	15.00	30.00
	1254	—	5.50	9.00	15.00	30.00
	1255	—	5.50	9.00	15.00	30.00

2 PIASTRES

BILLON, 39mm, 27.40 g

86	AH1232	—	—	Reported, not confirmed

38mm, 23.00 g

93	AH1244	—	35.00	60.00	100.00	150.00
	1245	—	35.00	60.00	100.00	150.00
	1246	—	35.00	60.00	100.00	175.00
	1248	—	75.00	125.00	175.00	350.00

SULTANI

.986 GOLD, 20mm, 2.50-3.20 g

KM#	Date	Mintage	Fine	VF	XF	Unc
87	AH1236	—	200.00	300.00	400.00	550.00

SULTAN ABDUL MEJID
AH1255-1277 / 1839-1861AD
Without the name of the Bey of Tunis

PRE-REFORM COINAGE
4 KHARUB

BILLON, 20mm, 2.77 g

KM#	Date	Mintage	Good	VG	Fine	VF
97	AH1256	—	35.00	65.00	125.00	200.00

8 KHARUB

BILLON, 26mm, 5.00 g

98	AH1256	—	35.00	65.00	130.00	225.00

PIASTRE

BILLON, 32mm, 11.00 g

96	AH1255	—	35.00	60.00	100.00	150.00

REFORM COINAGE
After AH1263/1847AD

BURBE

COPPER, 1.00 g

101	AH1263	—	2.00	4.00	10.00	20.00
	1264	—	2.00	4.00	10.00	20.00
	1265	—	2.00	4.00	10.00	20.00
	1266	—	2.00	4.00	10.00	20.00

ASPER

COPPER, 2.00 g

102	AH1263	—	2.00	4.00	7.00	15.00
	1264	—	2.00	4.00	7.00	15.00
	1265	—	2.00	4.00	7.00	15.00
	1266	—	2.00	4.00	7.00	15.00
	1267	—	2.00	4.00	7.00	15.00

1/2 KHARUB
(3-1/4 Asper)

COPPER, 5.50 g
Reeded edge.

103.1	AH1263	—	4.00	8.00	15.00	30.00

Plain edge.

103.2	AH1264	—	2.50	4.00	7.50	15.00
	1265	—	2.50	4.00	7.50	15.00
	1266	—	2.50	4.00	7.50	15.00
	1267	—	2.50	4.00	7.50	15.00
	1268	—	2.50	4.00	7.50	15.00
	1269	—	2.50	4.00	7.50	15.00

KHARUB

COPPER, 11.50 g

104	AH1263	—	4.00	8.00	15.00	25.00
	1264	—	2.00	4.00	10.00	15.00
	1265	—	2.00	4.00	10.00	15.00
	1266	—	2.00	4.00	10.00	15.00
	1267	—	2.00	4.00	10.00	15.00
	1268	—	2.00	4.00	10.00	15.00
	1269	—	1.00	2.00	5.00	10.00

KM#	Date	Mintage	Good	VG	Fine	VF
104	1270	—	6.00	10.00	20.00	30.00
	1271	—	6.00	10.00	20.00	30.00

c/m: Arabic '1' on KM#104.

105	AH1263-71	—	3.00	6.00	12.00	25.00

2 PIASTRES

SILVER, 28mm, 6.50 g

106	AH1263	—	15.00	22.00	60.00	125.00
	1264	—	15.00	22.00	60.00	125.00

Modified design

109	AH1267	—	15.00	22.00	60.00	125.00

5 PIASTRES

SILVER, 33mm, 16.00 g

107	AH1263	—	75.00	150.00	300.00	600.00
	1264	—	75.00	150.00	300.00	600.00

Modified design

108	AH1265	—	35.00	60.00	125.00	200.00
	1266	—	11.00	18.00	35.00	65.00
	1267	—	11.00	18.00	35.00	65.00
	1268	—	11.00	18.00	35.00	65.00
	1269	—	11.00	18.00	35.00	65.00
	1270	—	11.00	18.00	35.00	65.00
	1271	—	11.00	18.00	35.00	65.00

SULTAN ABDUL MEJID
With Muhammad Bey
AH1272-1276 / 1856-1859AD

NOTE: The copper coins of this series exhibit two major varieties of calligraphy, the first having thin, crude lettering, the second having thicker, more elegant lettering.

3 ASPER

COPPER, 5.80 g

112.1	AH1272	—	4.50	7.50	15.00	30.00
	1273	—	4.50	7.50	15.00	30.00

Thick legend.

112.2	AH1272	—	4.50	7.50	15.00	30.00
	1274	—	4.50	7.50	15.00	30.00

6 ASPER

COPPER, 11.60 g

KM#	Date	Mintage	Good	VG	Fine	VF
113.1	AH1272	—	2.75	4.50	10.00	20.00
	1273	—	2.75	4.50	10.00	20.00
		Thick legend.				
113.2	AH1272	—	2.75	4.50	10.00	20.00
	1273	—	2.75	4.50	10.00	20.00
	1274	—	2.75	4.50	10.00	20.00

KHARUB

COPPER
c/m: Arabic '1' on 6 Asper, KM#113.1 and 113.2.

| 114 | AH1272-4 | — | 3.00 | 6.00 | 12.00 | 20.00 |

13 ASPER

COPPER, 23.00 g

| 115.1 | AH1272 | — | 5.00 | 8.50 | 12.50 | 25.00 |
| | 1273 | — | 5.00 | 8.50 | 12.50 | 25.00 |

		Thick legend.				
115.2	AH1273	—	5.00	8.50	12.50	25.00
	1274	—	5.00	8.50	12.50	25.00
	1275	—	6.00	10.00	15.00	30.00

2 KHARUB

COPPER
c/m: Arabic '2' on 13 Asper, KM#115.1.

| 116 | AH1272 | — | 3.50 | 6.00 | 10.00 | 25.00 |
| | 1273 | — | 3.50 | 6.00 | 10.00 | 25.00 |

c/m: Arabic '21' on 13 Asper, KM#115.2.

131	AH1273	—	3.50	6.00	10.00	25.00
	1274	—	3.50	6.00	10.00	25.00
	1275	—	3.50	6.00	10.00	25.00

Thick legend. 23.00 g

KM#	Date	Mintage	Good	VG	Fine	VF
134.1	AH1273	—	6.00	10.00	20.00	40.00
	1274	—	6.00	10.00	20.00	40.00
	1275	—	3.00	6.00	12.00	25.00
	1276	—	5.00	8.00	15.00	30.00
		Thin legend.				
134.2	AH1276	—	12.00	18.00	28.00	45.00

SILVER, 0.40 g

132	AH1273	—	5.00	12.00	25.00	40.00
	1274	—	5.00	12.00	25.00	40.00
	1275	—	5.00	12.00	25.00	40.00
	1276	—	5.00	12.00	30.00	50.00

4 KHARUB

SILVER, 0.80 g

KM#	Date	Mintage	VG	Fine	VF	XF
135	AH1274	—	15.00	30.00	70.00	125.00
	1275	—	15.00	30.00	70.00	125.00

8 KHARUB

SILVER, 1.60 g

| 136 | AH1274 | — | 15.00 | 40.00 | 75.00 | 150.00 |
| | 1275 | — | 15.00 | 40.00 | 75.00 | 150.00 |

PIASTRE

SILVER, 3.20 g
Thick legend.

117.1	AH1272	—	15.00	30.00	70.00	125.00
	1273	—	15.00	30.00	70.00	125.00
		Thin legend.				
117.2	AH1272	—	20.00	35.00	65.00	125.00

2 PIASTRES

SILVER, 6.40 g
Thick legend.

118.1	AH1272	—	20.00	50.00	100.00	180.00
		Thin legend.				
118.2	AH1272	—	25.00	55.00	110.00	190.00

3 PIASTRES

SILVER, 9.60 g

| 119 | AH1272 | — | 50.00 | 125.00 | 200.00 | 300.00 |

---

4 PIASTRES

SILVER, 31mm, 12.80 g

KM#	Date	Mintage	VG	Fine	VF	XF
120	AH1272	—	75.00	150.00	300.00	400.00

5 PIASTRES

SILVER, 33mm, 16.00 g

121	AH1272	—	150.00	300.00	600.00	1000.
	1273	—	150.00	300.00	600.00	1000.
	1274	—	150.00	300.00	600.00	1000.

.9800 g, .900 GOLD, 12mm, .0284 oz AGW

122	AH1272	—	22.50	30.00	75.00	130.00
	1273	—	22.50	30.00	75.00	130.00
	1274	—	22.50	30.00	75.00	130.00
	1275	—	22.50	30.00	75.00	130.00

10 PIASTRES

1.7700 g, 1.000 GOLD, .0569 oz AGW

| 123 | AH1272 | — | 40.00 | 60.00 | 100.00 | 160.00 |

1.9700 g, .900 GOLD, .0570 oz AGW

| 124 | AH1272 | — | 40.00 | 60.00 | 100.00 | 160.00 |
| | 1274 | — | 40.00 | 60.00 | 100.00 | 160.00 |

20 PIASTRES

3.5500 g, 1.000 GOLD, 21mm, .1141 oz AGW

| 125 | AH1272 | — | 100.00 | 125.00 | 200.00 | 425.00 |

25 PIASTRES

4.9200 g, .900 GOLD, 20mm, .1424 oz AGW

133	AH1273	—	125.00	150.00	250.00	425.00
	1274	—	125.00	150.00	250.00	425.00
	1275	—	125.00	150.00	250.00	425.00

40 PIASTRES

7.1000 g, 1.000 GOLD, 26mm, .2283 oz AGW

| 126 | AH1272 | — | 135.00 | 175.00 | 300.00 | 550.00 |

50 PIASTRES

9.8400 g, .900 GOLD, .2847 oz AGW

127	AH1272	—	175.00	200.00	300.00	500.00
	1273	—	175.00	200.00	300.00	500.00
	1274	—	175.00	200.00	300.00	500.00
	1275	—	175.00	200.00	300.00	500.00

80 PIASTRES

14.2100 g, 1.000 GOLD, 31mm, .4569 oz AGW

| 128 | AH1272 | — | 325.00 | 450.00 | 800.00 | 1100. |

100 PIASTRES

17.7100 g, 1.000 GOLD, 33mm, .5694 oz AGW

| 129 | AH1272 | — | 400.00 | 600.00 | 800.00 | 1250. |

19.6800 g, .900 GOLD, .5695 oz AGW

KM#	Date	Mintage	VG	Fine	VF	XF
130	AH1272	—	375.00	500.00	750.00	1250.
	1273	—	375.00	500.00	750.00	1250.
	1274	—	375.00	500.00	750.00	1250.

SULTAN ABDUL MEJID
With Muhammad al-Sadiq Bey
AH1276-1277 / 1859-1860AD
2 KHARUB

COPPER, 23.00 g
Thin legend.
| 137.1 | AH1276 | — | 10.00 | 20.00 | 35.00 | 80.00 |

Thick legend.
| 137.2 | AH1276 | — | 10.00 | 20.00 | 35.00 | 80.00 |

8 KHARUB
SILVER, 18mm, 1.60 g
| 142 | AH1277 | — | 60.00 | 100.00 | 250.00 | 450.00 |

PIASTRE
SILVER, 22mm, 3.20 g
| 143 | AH1278 (sic) | — | 75.00 | 150.00 | 300.00 | 500.00 |

2 PIASTRES

SILVER, 6.40 g
| 138 | AH1276 | — | — | — | Rare | — |

25 PIASTRES
GOLD, 20mm, 4.90 g
| 139 | AH1276 | — | 125.00 | 200.00 | 400.00 | 650.00 |

50 PIASTRES
GOLD, 26mm, 9.80 g
| 140 | AH1276 | — | 150.00 | 300.00 | 500.00 | 750.00 |

100 PIASTRES

GOLD, 33mm, 19.70 g
| 141 | AH1276 | — | 1000. | 1250. | 1500. | 2000. |

SULTAN ABDUL AZIZ
With Muhammad al-Sadiq Bey
AH1277-1293 / 1860-1876AD

1/4 KHARUB

COPPER, 1.00 g
KM#	Date	Mintage	VG	Fine	VF	XF
153	AH1281	3.200	2.00	3.00	5.00	12.00

1.50 g
| 171 | AH1289 | — | 4.50 | 7.50 | 20.00 | 45.00 |

1/2 KHARUB

COPPER, 1.80 g
| 154 | AH1281 | 3.200 | .60 | 1.00 | 2.00 | 6.00 |

3.20 g
| 172 | AH1289 | — | 2.50 | 8.00 | 20.00 | 40.00 |

KHARUB

COPPER, 3.50 g
| 155 | AH1281 | 5.600 | .60 | 1.00 | 3.00 | 6.00 |

6.20 g
| 173 | AH1289 | — | 1.50 | 2.25 | 8.00 | 20.00 |
| | 1290 | — | 2.25 | 3.50 | 10.00 | 25.00 |

2 KHARUB

COPPER, 7.50 g
| 156 | AH1281 | 12.000 | .75 | 1.25 | 4.00 | 10.00 |

12.90 g
| 157 | AH1281 | — | 10.00 | 15.00 | 20.00 | 40.00 |

KM#	Date	Mintage	VG	Fine	VF	XF
157	1283	—	2.50	6.00	15.00	25.00
	1284	—	2.50	6.00	15.00	25.00

NOTE: 3 varieties of inscription exist for AH1283.

12.00-12.50 g
| 174 | AH1289 | — | 1.75 | 3.00 | 6.00 | 12.50 |
| | 1290 | — | 3.50 | 6.00 | 12.50 | 30.00 |

4 KHARUB

COPPER, 15.00 g
| 158 | AH1281 | 12.000 | 1.50 | 2.50 | 6.00 | 10.00 |
| | 1283 | — | 25.00 | 40.00 | 60.00 | 125.00 |

8 KHARUB

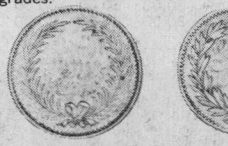

COPPER, 30.00 g
| 159 | AH1281 | 10.000 | 2.00 | 5.00 | 10.00 | 20.00 |

NOTE: KM#153-156, 158 and 159 were struck at the Heaton Mint, Birmingham, and are relatively common in higher grades.

SILVER, 1.80 g
160	AH1281	—	30.00	50.00	100.00	150.00
	1282	—	30.00	50.00	100.00	150.00
	1283	—	30.00	50.00	100.00	150.00
	1284	—	30.00	50.00	100.00	150.00
	1285	—	30.00	50.00	100.00	150.00
	1286	—	30.00	50.00	100.00	150.00
	1287	—	30.00	50.00	100.00	150.00
	1288	—	30.00	50.00	100.00	150.00
	1289	—	15.00	25.00	50.00	100.00
	1290	—	30.00	50.00	100.00	150.00
	1291	—	30.00	50.00	100.00	150.00
	1292	—	30.00	50.00	100.00	150.00
	1293	—	30.00	50.00	100.00	150.00

PIASTRE

SILVER, 3.20 g
145	AH1279	—	20.00	35.00	60.00	100.00
	1280	—	20.00	35.00	60.00	100.00
	1281	—	20.00	35.00	60.00	100.00
	1282	—	20.00	35.00	60.00	100.00
	1284	—	20.00	35.00	60.00	100.00
	1287	—	20.00	35.00	60.00	100.00
	1288	—	20.00	35.00	60.00	100.00
	1289	—	5.00	9.00	20.00	50.00
	1290	—	6.00	10.00	25.00	60.00
	1291	—	20.00	35.00	60.00	100.00
	1292	—	20.00	35.00	60.00	100.00
	1293	—	20.00	35.00	60.00	100.00

Tunis / TUNISIA 1642

c/m: Star on Piastre, KM#145.

KM#	Date	Mintage	VG	Fine	VF	XF
146	AH1279-93	—	6.00	10.00	20.00	45.00

2 PIASTRES

SILVER, 6.27 g

| 161 | AH1281 Paris | — | — | — | Proof | 325.00 |

NOTE: Without name of the Bey of Tunis - possibly a pattern.

6.40 g

147	AH1279	—	30.00	60.00	100.00	150.00
	1280	—	30.00	60.00	100.00	150.00
	1282	—	30.00	60.00	100.00	150.00
	1283	—	30.00	60.00	100.00	150.00
	1284	—	30.00	60.00	100.00	150.00
	1287	—	30.00	60.00	100.00	150.00
	1288	—	30.00	60.00	100.00	150.00
	1289	—	10.00	15.00	30.00	60.00
	1290	—	10.00	15.00	30.00	60.00
	1291	—	30.00	60.00	100.00	150.00
	1292	—	30.00	60.00	100.00	150.00
	1293	—	30.00	60.00	100.00	150.00

c/m: Star on 2 Piastres, KM#147.

| 165 | AH1287-93 | — | 6.00 | 10.00 | 25.00 | 55.00 |

3 PIASTRES

SILVER, 30mm, 9.60 g

| 166 | AH1288 | — | 100.00 | 150.00 | 250.00 | 400.00 |

4 PIASTRES

SILVER, 12.80 g

167	AH1288	—	20.00	40.00	95.00	180.00
	1290	—	12.00	25.00	50.00	100.00
	1291	—	12.00	25.00	50.00	100.00
	1292	—	15.00	30.00	80.00	150.00
	1293	—	15.00	30.00	80.00	150.00

c/m: Star on KM#167.

KM#	Date	Mintage	VG	Fine	VF	XF
168	AH1288-93	—	15.00	40.00	80.00	110.00

Mule. Obv: KM#186. Rev: KM#167.

| 175 | AH1292 | — | 35.00 | 50.00 | 100.00 | 210.00 |

5 PIASTRES

.9800 g, .900 GOLD, .0284 oz AGW

| 162 | AH1281 | — | 20.00 | 30.00 | 50.00 | 110.00 |
| | 1281 | — | — | — | Proof | 150.00 |

c/m: Star on KM#162.

| 163 | AH1281 | — | 20.00 | 30.00 | 50.00 | 110.00 |

169	AH1288	—	20.00	30.00	50.00	100.00
	1289	—	20.00	30.00	50.00	100.00
	1290	—	20.00	30.00	50.00	100.00
	1291	—	20.00	30.00	50.00	100.00
	1292	—	25.00	40.00	60.00	110.00

NOTE: Varieties exist for AH1290 dated coins.

c/m: Star on KM#169.

170	AH1288	—	20.00	35.00	60.00	100.00
	1289	—	20.00	35.00	60.00	100.00
	1290	—	20.00	35.00	60.00	100.00
	1291	—	20.00	35.00	60.00	100.00
	1292	—	20.00	35.00	60.00	100.00

16.0000 g, .900 SILVER, 33mm, .4630 oz ASW

164	AH1281	—	100.00	150.00	250.00	350.00
	1282	—	100.00	150.00	250.00	350.00
	1288	—	100.00	150.00	250.00	350.00
	1290	—	100.00	150.00	250.00	350.00
	1291	—	100.00	150.00	250.00	350.00
	1293	—	100.00	150.00	250.00	350.00

10 PIASTRES

1.9700 g, .900 GOLD, .0570 oz AGW

150	AH1280	—	40.00	60.00	80.00	180.00
	1281	—	40.00	60.00	80.00	180.00
	1281	—	—	—	Proof	275.00
	1284	—	40.00	60.00	80.00	180.00
	1287	—	40.00	60.00	80.00	180.00
	1288	—	40.00	60.00	80.00	180.00

c/m: Star on KM#150.

| 151 | AH1280-8 | — | 45.00 | 70.00 | 85.00 | 135.00 |

25 PIASTRES

4.9200 g, .900 GOLD, .1424 oz AGW

148	AH1279	—	100.00	150.00	225.00	300.00
	1280	—	100.00	150.00	225.00	300.00
	1281	—	100.00	150.00	225.00	300.00
	1281	—	—	—	Proof	400.00
	1283	—	100.00	150.00	225.00	300.00
	1285	—	100.00	150.00	225.00	300.00
	1287	—	100.00	150.00	225.00	300.00
	1288	—	100.00	150.00	225.00	300.00
	1289	—	100.00	125.00	165.00	250.00
	1290	—	100.00	125.00	165.00	250.00
	1291	—	100.00	125.00	165.00	250.00

50 PIASTRES

9.8400 g., .900 GOLD, .2847 oz AGW

KM#	Date	Mintage	VG	Fine	VF	XF
152	AH1280	—	200.00	225.00	285.00	500.00
	1281	—	200.00	225.00	275.00	350.00
	1281	—	—	—	Proof	550.00
	1286	—	200.00	225.00	275.00	350.00
	1288	—	200.00	225.00	275.00	350.00
	1293	—	250.00	275.00	350.00	450.00

100 PIASTRES

19.6800 g, .900 GOLD, .5695 oz AGW

149	AH1279	—	375.00	575.00	950.00	2000.
	1280	—	375.00	575.00	950.00	2000.
	1281	—	375.00	575.00	950.00	2000.
	1281	—	—	—	Proof	3000.
	1283	—	375.00	575.00	950.00	2000.
	1285	—	375.00	575.00	950.00	2000.
	1286	—	375.00	575.00	950.00	2000.

NOTE: KM#148-150, 152, 161, 162, 164 and 166, dated AH1281, were all struck at Tunis, from dies produced at the Heaton Mint in Birmingham, hence their obvious superiority.

SULTAN MURAD V
With Muhammad al-Sadiq Bey
AH1293/1876AD

25 PIASTRES

4.9200 g, .900 GOLD, 20mm, .1424 oz AGW

| 177 | AH1293 | — | 300.00 | 500.00 | 750.00 | 1500. |

SULTAN ABDUL HAMID II
With Muhammad al-Sadiq Bey
AH1293-1299/1876-1882AD

2 KHARUB

COPPER, 31mm, 12.50 g

| 180 | AH1293 | — | 12.50 | 20.00 | 45.00 | 85.00 |

8 KHARUB

SILVER, 1.50 g
Obv: Al-Ghazi

181	AH1293	—	37.50	75.00	150.00	275.00
	1295	—	30.00	60.00	125.00	225.00
	1296	—	37.50	75.00	150.00	275.00
	1297	—	37.50	75.00	150.00	275.00
	1298	—	37.50	75.00	150.00	275.00

Obv: W/o Al-Ghazi

| 188 | AH1293 | — | 60.00 | 125.00 | 250.00 | 400.00 |
| | 1294 | — | 60.00 | 125.00 | 250.00 | 400.00 |

PIASTRE

SILVER, 22.5mm, 3.20 g
Obv: W/o Al-Ghazi

| 182 | AH1293 | — | 35.00 | 75.00 | 150.00 | 300.00 |
| | 1294 | — | 35.00 | 75.00 | 150.00 | 300.00 |

Obv: Al-Ghazi added.

189	AH1294	—	35.00	75.00	150.00	300.00
	1295	—	35.00	75.00	150.00	300.00
	1296	—	35.00	75.00	150.00	300.00
	1297	—	35.00	75.00	150.00	300.00
	1298	—	35.00	75.00	150.00	300.00

c/m: Star on KM#182.

| 183 | AH1293-4 | — | 35.00 | 60.00 | 100.00 | 150.00 |

c/m: Star on KM#189.

| 190 | AH1294-8 | — | 35.00 | 60.00 | 100.00 | 150.00 |

2 PIASTRES

SILVER, 26.5mm, 6.40 g

| 184 | AH1293 | — | 40.00 | 70.00 | 150.00 | 300.00 |
| | 1294 | — | 40.00 | 70.00 | 150.00 | 300.00 |

Obv: Al-Ghazi added.

KM#	Date	Mintage	VG	Fine	VF	XF
191	AH1294	—	40.00	70.00	150.00	300.00
	1297	—	60.00	100.00	175.00	350.00

c/m: Star on KM#184.

185	AH1293	—	35.00	75.00	150.00	300.00
	1294	—	35.00	75.00	150.00	300.00

c/m: Star on KM#191.

192	AH1294	—	35.00	75.00	150.00	300.00

4 PIASTRES
SILVER, 12.8 g, 31mm
Obv: W/o Al-Ghazi

186	AH1293	—	20.00	60.00	125.00	250.00
	1294	—	20.00	60.00	125.00	250.00

Obv: Al-Ghazi added.

193	AH1294	—	20.00	60.00	125.00	250.00
	1296	—	20.00	60.00	125.00	250.00

c/m: Star on KM#186.

187	AH1292	—	20.00	35.00	75.00	150.00
	1293	—	20.00	35.00	75.00	150.00
	1294	—	20.00	35.00	75.00	150.00

c/m: Star on KM#193.

194	AH1294	—	20.00	35.00	75.00	150.00
	1295	—	20.00	35.00	75.00	150.00
	1296	—	20.00	35.00	75.00	150.00
	1297	—	20.00	35.00	75.00	150.00

5 PIASTRES
0.9800 g, .900 GOLD, 12.5mm, .0284 oz AGW

195	AH1294	—	40.00	75.00	150.00	250.00

25 PIASTRES

4.9200 g, .900 GOLD, .1424 oz AGW

196	AH1294	—	85.00	110.00	175.00	250.00
	1295	—	85.00	110.00	175.00	250.00
	1296	—	85.00	110.00	175.00	250.00
	1297	—	85.00	110.00	175.00	250.00
	1298	—	—	—	Rare	—

50 PIASTRES
9.8400 g, .900 GOLD, 26mm, .2847 oz AGW

197	AH1294	—	—	—	Rare	—
	1295	—	—	—	Rare	—
	1297	—	150.00	200.00	250.00	350.00

PROOF SETS (PS)

KM#	Date	Mintage	Identification	Issue Price	Mkt. Val.
PS1	1864(AH1281)	(5)	KM148-150,152,162	—	4375.

TUNISIA

FRENCH PROTECTORATE
MINT MARKS
(a) - Paris, privy marks only
A - Paris

MUHAMMAD AL-SADIQ BEY
Alone: AH1298-1299 / 1881-1882AD

8 KHARUB
SILVER, 18.5mm, 1.60 g

KM#	Date	Mintage	Fine	VF	XF	Unc
201	AH1299	—	200.00	400.00	750.00	1250.

PIASTRE

SILVER, 3.20 g

202	AH1299	—	200.00	400.00	750.00	1250.

2 PIASTRES
SILVER, 26.5mm, 6.40 g

KM#	Date	Mintage	Fine	VF	XF	Unc
203	AH1299	—	200.00	400.00	750.00	1250.

25 PIASTRES
4.9200 g, .900 GOLD, 20mm, .1424 oz AGW

200	AH1298	—	100.00	250.00	500.00	750.00
	1300	—	100.00	250.00	500.00	750.00

50 PIASTRES
9.8400 g, .900 GOLD, 26mm, .2847 oz AGW

204	AH1299	—	300.00	400.00	650.00	1000.

ALI BEY
AH1299-1320 / AD1882-1902

8 KHARUB

SILVER, 1.60 g

205	AH1300	—	15.00	25.00	55.00	115.00
	1301	—	15.00	25.00	55.00	115.00
	1302	—	15.00	25.00	55.00	115.00
	1303	—	15.00	25.00	55.00	115.00
	1304	—	15.00	25.00	55.00	115.00
	1305	—	15.00	25.00	55.00	115.00
	1306	—	15.00	25.00	55.00	115.00
	1307	—	15.00	25.00	55.00	115.00
	1308	—	15.00	25.00	55.00	115.00

PIASTRE

SILVER, 3.20 g

206	AH1300	—	18.00	30.00	75.00	155.00
	1301	—	18.00	30.00	75.00	155.00
	1302	—	18.00	30.00	75.00	155.00
	1303	—	18.00	30.00	75.00	155.00
	1304	—	18.00	30.00	75.00	155.00
	1305	—	18.00	30.00	75.00	155.00
	1306	—	18.00	30.00	75.00	155.00
	1307	—	18.00	30.00	75.00	155.00
	1308	—	18.00	30.00	75.00	155.00

Modified design.

215	AH1308	—	20.00	35.00	75.00	150.00

2 PIASTRES

SILVER, 6.40 g

207	AH1300	—	30.00	50.00	125.00	275.00
	1301	—	30.00	50.00	125.00	275.00
	1302	—	30.00	50.00	125.00	275.00
	1303	—	30.00	50.00	125.00	275.00
	1304	—	30.00	50.00	125.00	275.00
	1305	—	30.00	50.00	125.00	275.00
	1306	—	30.00	50.00	125.00	275.00
	1307	—	30.00	50.00	125.00	275.00
	1308	—	30.00	50.00	125.00	275.00

Modified design.

210	AH1308	—	40.00	70.00	125.00	275.00

4 PIASTRES

SILVER, 12.80 g

208	AH1300	—	30.00	50.00	150.00	325.00
	1301	—	30.00	50.00	150.00	325.00
	1302	—	30.00	50.00	150.00	325.00
	1303	—	30.00	50.00	150.00	325.00
	1304	—	30.00	50.00	150.00	325.00

KM#	Date	Mintage	Fine	VF	XF	Unc
208	1305	—	30.00	50.00	150.00	325.00
	1306	—	30.00	50.00	150.00	325.00
	1307	—	30.00	50.00	150.00	325.00
	1308	—	30.00	50.00	150.00	325.00

Modified design.

216	AH1308	—	40.00	70.00	180.00	350.00

25 PIASTRES

4.9200 g, .900 GOLD, .1424 oz AGW

209	AH1300	—	85.00	110.00	150.00	250.00
	1302	—	85.00	110.00	150.00	250.00

25 PIASTRES-15 FRANCS

4.8730 g, .900 GOLD, .1410 oz AGW

212	AH1304	.080	85.00	110.00	175.00	300.00
	1308	Inc. Ab.	85.00	110.00	175.00	300.00

Rev: Modified design.

214	AH1307A	.052	85.00	110.00	175.00	300.00
	1308A	.120	85.00	110.00	175.00	300.00
	1308A	—	—	—	Proof	1000.

50 PIASTRES
4.8730 g, .900 GOLD, .1410 oz AGW

213	AH1304	—	200.00	350.00	500.00	750.00

100 PIASTRES
9.7460 g, .900 GOLD, .2820 oz AGW

211	AH1303	—	300.00	600.00	1000.	1500.

DECIMAL SYSTEM
100 Centimes = 1 Franc

NOTE: The following coins all bear French inscriptions on one side, Arabic on the other, and usually have both AH and AD dates. They are struck in the name of the Tunisian Bey.

CENTIME

BRONZE
Obv. leg: Ali.

KM#	Date	Year	Mintage	VF	XF	Unc
219	AH1308	1891A	.500	6.00	10.00	20.00

2 CENTIMES

BRONZE
Obv. leg: Ali.

220	AH1308	1891A	1.000	2.25	5.00	12.00

5 CENTIMES

BRONZE
Obv. leg: Ali.

221	AH1308	1891A	4.300	2.00	6.00	20.00
	1308	1891A	—	—	Proof	50.00

TUNISIA

KM#	Date	Year	Mintage	VF	XF	Unc
221	1309	1892A	1.192	2.50	7.00	20.00
	1310	1893A	1.008	3.00	10.00	25.00

Obv. leg: *Muhammad al-Hadi.*

228	AH1321	1903A	.500	6.00	10.00	25.00
	1322	1904A	1.000	5.50	8.00	18.00

Obv. leg: *Muhammad al-Nasir.*

235	AH1325	1907A	1.000	2.00	4.00	15.00
	1326	1908A	1.000	2.00	4.00	15.00
	1330	1912A	1.000	2.00	4.00	15.00
	1332	1914A	1.000	2.00	4.00	15.00
	1334	1916A	2.000	1.50	3.00	10.00
	1336	1917A	2.021	1.50	3.00	10.00

NICKEL BRONZE
Obv. leg: *Mohammed al-Nasir.*

242	AH1337	1918(a)	1.549	1.00	2.50	10.00
	1337	1919(a)	4.451	.75	2.00	10.00
	1338/7					
		1920(a)	2.206	3.00	7.50	25.00
	1338	1920(a)	Inc. Ab.	2.00	5.00	20.00
	1339	1920(a)	Inc. Ab.	1.00	2.50	10.00

Reduced Size

| 245 | AH1339 | 1920(a) | 1.794 | 10.00 | 20.00 | 40.00 |

Obv. leg: *Ahmad.*

258	AH1350	1931(a)	2.000	3.00	10.00	20.00
	1352	1933(a)	1.000	3.00	12.00	25.00
	1357	1938(a)	1.200	1.00	3.00	5.00

10 CENTIMES

BRONZE
Obv. leg: *Ali.*

222	AH1308	1891A	2.600	4.00	8.00	20.00
	1309	1892A	1.374	4.00	10.00	25.00
	1310	1892A	—	75.00	125.00	200.00
	1310	1893A	.026	75.00	125.00	200.00

Obv. leg: *Muhammad al-Hadi.*

KM#	Date	Year	Mintage	VF	XF	Unc
229	AH1321	1903A	.250	6.00	15.00	30.00
	1322	1904A	.500	6.00	12.00	20.00

Obv. leg: *Muhammad al-Nasir.*

236	AH1325	1907A	.500	3.00	6.00	20.00
	1326	1908A	.500	3.00	6.00	20.00
	1329	1911A	.500	3.00	6.00	20.00
	1330	1912A	.500	3.00	6.00	20.00
	1332	1914A	.500	3.00	6.00	20.00
	1334	1916A	1.000	3.00	6.00	20.00
	1336	1917A	1.050	3.00	6.00	20.00

NICKEL-BRONZE
Obv. leg: *Muhammad al-Nasir.*

243	AH1337	1918(a)	1.288	2.00	4.00	12.00
	1337	1919(a)	2.712	1.25	3.00	10.00
	1338	1920(a)	3.000	1.25	3.00	10.00

Obv. leg: *Muhammad al-Habib.*

| 254 | AH1345 | 1926(a) | 1.000 | 10.00 | 20.00 | 75.00 |

Obv. leg: *Ahmad.*

259	AH1350	1931(a)	.750	4.00	12.00	30.00
	1352	1933(a)	1.000	4.00	12.00	30.00
	1357	1938(a)	1.200	1.50	4.00	10.00

ZINC
Obv. leg: *Ahmad.*

267	AH1360	1941(a)	5.000	2.50	6.00	25.00
	1361	1942(a)	10.000	1.50	4.00	20.00

Obv. leg: *Muhammad al Amin.*

| 271 | AH1364 | 1945(a) | 10.000 | 20.00 | 40.00 | 70.00 |

NOTE: Most were probably melted.

20 CENTIMES

ZINC
Obv. leg: *Ahmad.*

| 268 | AH1361 | 1942(a) | 5.000 | 8.00 | 20.00 | 35.00 |

Obv. leg: *Muhammad al-Amin.*

| 272 | AH1364 | 1945(a) | 5.205 | 30.00 | 60.00 | 90.00 |

NOTE: A large quantity was remelted.

25 CENTIMES

NICKEL-BRONZE
Obv. leg: *Muhammad al-Nasir.*

KM#	Date	Year	Mintage	VF	XF	Unc
244	AH1337	1918(a)	—	3.50	8.50	25.00
	1337	1919(a)	2.000	2.00	5.00	20.00
	1338	1920(a)	2.000	2.00	5.00	20.00

Obv. leg: *Ahmad.*

260	AH1350	1931(a)	.300	5.00	12.00	30.00
	1352	1933(a)	.400	5.00	12.00	30.00
	1357	1938(a)	.480	3.00	7.50	15.00

50 CENTIMES

2.5000 g, .835 SILVER, .0671 oz ASW
Obv. leg: *Ali.*

223	AH1308	1891A	1.470	8.00	18.00	35.00
	1309	1892A	1,000	—	100.00	175.00
	1310	1893A	1,000	—	100.00	175.00
	1311	1894A	1,000	—	100.00	175.00
	1313	1895A	1,000	—	100.00	175.00
	1314	1896A	1,000	—	100.00	175.00
	1315	1897A	1,000	—	100.00	175.00
	1316	1898A	1,000	—	100.00	175.00
	1317	1899A	1,000	—	100.00	175.00
	1318	1900A	1,000	—	100.00	175.00
	1319	1901A	1,000	—	100.00	175.00
	1320	1902A	1,000	—	100.00	175.00

Obv. leg: *Muhammad al-Hadi.*

230	AH1321	1903A	1,003	—	100.00	175.00
	1322	1904A	1,003	—	100.00	175.00
	1323	1905A	1,003	—	100.00	175.00
	1324	1906A	1,003	—	100.00	175.00

Obv. leg: *Muhammad al-Nasir.*

237	AH1325	1907A	.201	4.00	10.00	40.00
	1326	1908A	2,006	—	75.00	135.00
	1327	1909A	1,003	—	100.00	175.00
	1328	1910A	1,003	—	100.00	175.00
	1329	1911A	1,003	—	100.00	175.00
	1330	1912A	.201	4.00	10.00	35.00
	1331	1913A	1,003	—	100.00	175.00
	1332	1914A	.201	4.00	10.00	35.00
	1334	1915A	.707	2.00	6.00	18.00
	1334	1916A	3.614	1.50	4.00	15.00
	1335	1916A	Inc. Ab.	1.50	4.00	15.00
	1335	1917A	2.139	1.50	4.00	15.00
	1336	1917A	Inc. Ab.	1.50	4.00	15.00
	1337	1918A	1,003	—	100.00	175.00
	1338	1919A	1,003	—	100.00	175.00
	1339	1920A	1,003	—	100.00	175.00
	1340	1921A	1,003	—	100.00	175.00

ALUMINUM-BRONZE

246	AH1340	1921(a)	4.000	.50	1.50	15.00
	1345	1926(a)	1.000	1.00	2.50	25.00
	1352	1933(a)	.500	2.00	5.00	40.00
	1360	1941(a)	4.646	.35	1.25	10.00
	1364	1945(a)	11.180	.20	.60	10.00

2.5000 g, .835 SILVER, .0671 oz ASW
Obv. leg: *Muhammad al-Habib.*

249	AH1341	1922A	1,003	—	100.00	200.00
	1342	1923A	2,009	—	100.00	200.00
	1343	1924A	1,003	—	100.00	200.00

KM#	Date	Year	Mintage	VF	XF	Unc
249	1344	1925A	1,003	—	100.00	200.00
	1345	1926A	1,003	—	100.00	200.00
	1346	1927A	1,003	—	100.00	200.00
	1347	1928A	1,003	—	100.00	200.00

FRANC

5.0000 g, .835 SILVER, .1342 oz ASW
Obv. leg: *Ali.*

KM#	Date	Year	Mintage	VF	XF	Unc
224	AH1308	1891A	1.575	10.00	20.00	40.00
	1309	1892A	1.575	10.00	20.00	40.00
	1310	1893A	703 pcs.	—	135.00	225.00
	1311	1894A	703 pcs.	—	135.00	225.00
	1313	1895A	703 pcs.	—	135.00	225.00
	1314	1896A	703 pcs.	—	135.00	225.00
	1315	1897A	703 pcs.	—	135.00	225.00
	1316	1898A	703 pcs.	—	135.00	225.00
	1317	1899A	703 pcs.	—	135.00	225.00
	1318	1900A	703 pcs.	—	135.00	225.00
	1319	1901A	700 pcs.	—	135.00	225.00
	1320	1902A	703 pcs.	—	135.00	225.00

Obv. leg: *Muhammad al-Hadi.*

231	AH1321	1903A	703 pcs.	—	135.00	225.00
	1322	1904A	.500	30.00	50.00	110.00
	1323	1905A	703 pcs.	—	135.00	225.00
	1324	1906A	703 pcs.	—	135.00	225.00

Obv. leg: *Muhammad al-Nasir.*

238	AH1325	1907A	.301	4.00	10.00	35.00
	1326	1908A	.401	4.00	8.00	35.00
	1327	1909A	703 pcs.	—	135.00	225.00
	1328	1910A	703 pcs.	—	135.00	225.00
	1329	1911A	1.051	2.75	6.50	30.00
	1330	1912A	.501	3.25	8.00	30.00
	1331	1913A	703 pcs.	—	135.00	225.00
	1332	1914A	.201	3.50	9.00	30.00
	1333	1914A	I.A.	3.50	9.00	30.00
	1334	1915A	1.060	2.00	5.00	12.00
	1334	1916A	3.270	1.50	4.00	10.00
	1335	1916A	Inc. Ab.	1.50	4.00	10.00
	1335	1917A	1.628	2.00	5.00	12.00
	1336	1918A	.804	1.75	4.50	15.00
	1337	1918A	Inc. Ab.	1.75	4.50	15.00
	1338	1919A	703 pcs.	—	135.00	225.00
	1339	1920A	703 pcs.	—	135.00	225.00
	1340	1921A	703 pcs.	—	135.00	225.00

ALUMINUM-BRONZE

247	AH1340	1921(a)	5.000	1.00	2.50	15.00
	1344	1926(a)	1.000	1.50	4.00	25.00
	1345	1926(a)	1.000	1.50	4.00	25.00
	1360	1941(a)	6.612	.50	1.50	10.00
	1364	1945(a)	10.699	.35	1.00	10.00

5.0000 g, .835 SILVER, .1342 oz ASW
Obv. leg: *Muhammad al-Habib.*

250	AH1341	1922A	703 pcs.	—	135.00	275.00
	1342	1923A	1,409	—	100.00	250.00
	1343	1924A	703 pcs.	—	135.00	275.00
	1344	1925A	703 pcs.	—	135.00	275.00
	1345	1926A	703 pcs.	—	135.00	275.00
	1346	1927A	703 pcs.	—	135.00	275.00

5.5000 g, .835 SILVER, .1476 oz ASW

250a	AH1347	1928A	703 pcs.	—	135.00	275.00

2 FRANCS

10.0000 g, .835 SILVER, .2685 oz ASW

Obv. leg: *Ali.*

KM#	Date	Year	Mintage	VF	XF	Unc
225	AH1308	1891A	.595	12.00	25.00	60.00
	1309	1892A	.432	12.00	25.00	60.00
	1310	1893A	300 pcs.	—	150.00	250.00
	1311	1894A	300 pcs.	—	150.00	250.00
	1313	1895A	300 pcs.	—	150.00	250.00
	1314	1896A	300 pcs.	—	150.00	250.00
	1315	1897A	300 pcs.	—	150.00	250.00
	1316	1898A	300 pcs.	—	150.00	250.00
	1317	1899A	300 pcs.	—	150.00	250.00
	1318	1900A	300 pcs.	—	150.00	250.00
	1319	1901A	300 pcs.	—	150.00	250.00
	1320	1902A	300 pcs.	—	150.00	250.00

Obv. leg: *Muhammad al-Hadi.*

232	AH1321	1903A	303 pcs.	—	150.00	250.00
	1322	1904A	.150	40.00	75.00	200.00
	1323	1905A	303 pcs.	—	150.00	250.00
	1324	1906A	303 pcs.	—	150.00	250.00

Obv. leg: *Muhammad al-Nasir.*

239	AH1325	1907A	306 pcs.	—	150.00	250.00
	1326	1908A	.101	20.00	40.00	85.00
	1327	1909A	303 pcs.	—	150.00	250.00
	1328	1910A	303 pcs.	—	150.00	250.00
	1329	1911A	.475	7.50	15.00	40.00
	1330	1912A	.200	10.00	20.00	45.00
	1331	1913A	303 pcs.	—	150.00	250.00
	1332	1914A	.100	8.50	15.00	25.00
	1333	1914A	I.A.	8.50	15.00	25.00
	1334	1915A	.408	8.50	15.00	25.00
	1334	1916A	1.000	8.50	12.50	20.00
	1335	1916A	Inc. Ab.	8.50	15.00	35.00
	1336	1917A	303 pcs.	—	150.00	250.00
	1337	1918A	303 pcs.	—	150.00	250.00
	1338	1919A	303 pcs.	—	150.00	250.00
	1339	1920A	303 pcs.	—	150.00	250.00
	1340	1921A	303 pcs.	—	150.00	250.00

ALUMINUM-BRONZE

248	AH1340	1921(a)	1.500	2.00	5.00	25.00
	1343	1924(a)	.500	3.50	8.50	40.00
	1345	1926(a)	.500	3.50	8.50	40.00
	1360	1941(a)	1.976	1.50	4.00	15.00
	1364	1945(a)	6.464	.75	2.00	15.00

10.0000 g, .835 SILVER, .2685 oz ASW
Obv. leg: *Muhammad al-Habib.*

251	AH1341	1922A	303 pcs.	—	150.00	325.00
	1342	1923A	690 pcs.	—	135.00	275.00
	1343	1924A	303 pcs.	—	150.00	325.00
	1344	1925A	303 pcs.	—	150.00	325.00
	1345	1926A	303 pcs.	—	150.00	325.00
	1346	1927A	303 pcs.	—	150.00	325.00
	1347	1928A	303 pcs.	—	150.00	325.00

5 FRANCS

5.0000 g, .680 SILVER, .1093 oz ASW
Obv. leg: *Ahmad.*

Y#	Date	Mintage	VF	XF	Unc
261	AH1353(a)	2.000	3.50	5.00	17.50
	1355(a)	2.000	3.50	5.00	17.50

KM#	Date	Year	Mintage	VF	XF	Unc
264	AH1358(a)	1939	1.600	3.00	6.00	15.00

ALUMINUM-BRONZE
Obv. leg: *Muhammad al-Amin.*

KM#	Date	Year	Mintage	VF	XF	Unc
273	AH1365(a)	1946	10.000	1.50	10.00	10.00

COPPER-NICKEL

277	AH1373(a)	1954	18.000	.20	1.00	3.00
	1376(a)	1957	4.000	.50	1.00	2.50

10 FRANCS

3.2258 g, .900 GOLD, .0933 oz AGW
Obv. leg: *Ali.*

226	AH1308	1891A	.400	55.00	75.00	100.00
	1308	1891A	—	—	Proof	900.00
	1309	1892A	83 pcs.	—	300.00	500.00
	1310	1893A	83 pcs.	—	300.00	500.00
	1311	1894A	83 pcs.	—	300.00	500.00
	1313	1895A	83 pcs.	—	300.00	500.00
	1314	1896A	83 pcs.	—	300.00	500.00
	1315	1897A	83 pcs.	—	300.00	500.00
	1316	1898A	83 pcs.	—	300.00	500.00
	1317	1899A	83 pcs.	—	300.00	500.00
	1318	1900A	83 pcs.	—	300.00	500.00
	1319	1901A	80 pcs.	—	300.00	500.00
	1320	1902A	83 pcs.	—	300.00	500.00

Obv. leg: *Muhammad al-Hadi.*

233	AH1321	1903A	83 pcs.	—	300.00	475.00
	1322	1904A	83 pcs.	—	300.00	475.00
	1323	1905A	83 pcs.	—	300.00	475.00
	1324	1906A	83 pcs.	—	300.00	475.00

Obv. leg: *Muhammad al-Nasir.*

240	AH1325	1907A	36 pcs.	—	300.00	500.00
	1326	1908A	166 pcs.	—	300.00	500.00
	1327	1909A	83 pcs.	—	300.00	500.00
	1328	1910A	83 pcs.	—	300.00	500.00
	1329	1911A	83 pcs.	—	300.00	500.00
	1330	1912A	83 pcs.	—	300.00	500.00
	1331	1913A	83 pcs.	—	300.00	500.00
	1332	1914A	83 pcs.	—	300.00	500.00
	1334	1915A	83 pcs.	—	300.00	500.00
	1334	1916A	83 pcs.	—	300.00	500.00
	1336	1917A	83 pcs.	—	300.00	500.00
	1337	1918A	83 pcs.	—	300.00	500.00
	1338	1919A	83 pcs.	—	300.00	500.00
	1339	1920A	83 pcs.	—	300.00	500.00
	1340	1921A	83 pcs.	—	300.00	500.00

Obv. leg: *Muhammad al-Habib Bey.*

252	AH1341	1922A	83 pcs.	—	300.00	500.00
	1342	1923A	169 pcs.	—	250.00	425.00
	1343	1924A	83 pcs.	—	300.00	500.00
	1344	1925A	83 pcs.	—	300.00	500.00
	1345	1926A	83 pcs.	—	300.00	500.00
	1346	1927A	83 pcs.	—	300.00	500.00
	1347	1928A	83 pcs.	—	300.00	500.00

10.0000 g, .680 SILVER, .2186 oz ASW
Obv. leg: *Ahmad.*

255	AH1349	1930A	.060	35.00	60.00	110.00
	1350	1931A	1,103	150.00	250.00	350.00
	1351	1932A	.060	35.00	60.00	110.00
	1352	1933A	1,103	150.00	250.00	350.00
	1353	1934A	.030	30.00	50.00	90.00

TUNISIA 1646

KM#	Date	Mintage	VF	XF	Unc
262	AH1353(a)	1,501	4.50	9.00	15.00
	1354(a)	1,103	—	150.00	250.00
	1355(a)	2,006	—	135.00	225.00
	1356(a)	1,103	—	150.00	250.00

KM#	Date	Year	Mintage	VF	XF	Unc
265	AH1358	1939(a)	.501	6.00	15.00	35.00
	1359	1940(a)	—	—	135.00	225.00
	1360	1941(a)	1,103	—	135.00	225.00
	1361	1942(a)	1,103	—	135.00	225.00

Obv. leg: Muhammad al-Amin.

269	AH1363	1943	1,503	—	225.00	350.00
	1364	1944	2,206	—	200.00	300.00

20 FRANCS

6.4516 g, .900 GOLD, .1867 oz AGW
Obv. leg: Ali.

227	AH1308	1891A	.400	90.00	95.00	125.00
	1309	1892A	.937	90.00	95.00	125.00
	1310	1892A	Inc. Ab.	90.00	95.00	125.00
	1310	1893A	.035	90.00	95.00	125.00
	1311	1894A	20 pcs.	—	450.00	650.00
	1313	1895A	20 pcs.	—	450.00	650.00
	1314	1896A	20 pcs.	—	450.00	650.00
	1315	1897A	.164	90.00	95.00	140.00
	1316	1898A	.150	90.00	95.00	140.00
	1316	1899A	.150	90.00	95.00	140.00
	1318	1900A	.150	90.00	95.00	140.00
	1319	1901A	.150	90.00	95.00	140.00
	1320	1902A	20 pcs.	—	450.00	650.00

Obv. leg: Muhammad al-Hadi.

234	AH1321	1903A	.300	90.00	95.00	125.00
	1321	1904A	.600	90.00	95.00	140.00
	1322	1904A	Inc. Ab.	90.00	95.00	140.00
	1323	1905A	23 pcs.	—	450.00	650.00
	1324	1906A	23 pcs.	—	450.00	650.00

Obv. leg: Muhammad al-Nasir.

241	AH1325	1907A	26 pcs.	—	450.00	650.00
	1326	1908A	46 pcs.	—	400.00	600.00
	1327	1909A	23 pcs.	—	450.00	650.00
	1328	1910A	23 pcs.	—	450.00	650.00
	1329	1911A	23 pcs.	—	450.00	650.00
	1330	1912A	23 pcs.	—	450.00	650.00
	1331	1913A	23 pcs.	—	450.00	650.00
	1332	1914A	23 pcs.	—	450.00	650.00
	1334	1915A	23 pcs.	—	450.00	650.00
	1334	1916A	23 pcs.	—	450.00	650.00
	1336	1917A	23 pcs.	—	450.00	650.00
	1337	1918A	23 pcs.	—	450.00	650.00
	1338	1919A	23 pcs.	—	450.00	650.00
	1339	1920A	23 pcs.	—	450.00	650.00
	1340	1921A	23 pcs.	—	450.00	650.00

Obv. leg: Muhammad al-Habib.

253	AH1341	1922A	23 pcs.	—	450.00	750.00
	1342	1923A	49 pcs.	—	400.00	650.00
	1343	1924A	23 pcs.	—	450.00	750.00
	1344	1925A	23 pcs.	—	450.00	750.00
	1345	1926A	23 pcs.	—	450.00	750.00
	1346	1927A	23 pcs.	—	450.00	750.00
	1347	1928A	23 pcs.	—	450.00	750.00

20.0000 g, .680 SILVER, .4372 oz ASW
Obv. leg: Ahmad.

256	AH1349	1930(a)	.020	60.00	100.00	170.00
	1350	1931(a)	53 pcs.	200.00	300.00	500.00
	1351	1932(a)	.020	75.00	125.00	185.00
	1352	1933(a)	53 pcs.	200.00	300.00	500.00
	1353	1934(a)	9,500	60.00	100.00	170.00

NOTE: It is believed that an additional number of coins dated AH1353/1934(a) were struck and included in mintage figures of KM#263 of the same date.

KM#	Date	Mintage	VF	XF	Unc
263	AH1353(a)	1,250	12.50	25.00	55.00
	1354(a)	53 pcs.	—	275.00	450.00
	1355(a)	106 pcs.	—	225.00	375.00
	1356(a)	53 pcs.	—	275.00	450.00

KM#	Date	Year	Mintage	VF	XF	Unc
266	AH1358	1939(a)	.100	20.00	45.00	90.00
	1359	1940(a)	— Reported, not confirmed			
	1360	1941(a)	53 pcs.	—	275.00	450.00
	1361	1942(a)	53 pcs.	—	275.00	450.00

Obv. leg: Muhammad al-Amin.

270	AH1363	1943	103 pcs.	—	300.00	500.00
	1364	1944	106 pcs.	—	300.00	500.00

COPPER-NICKEL

274	AH1370	1950(a)	10,000	.50	2.00	6.00
	1376	1957(a)	4,000	.35	1.00	4.00

50 FRANCS

COPPER-NICKEL
Obv. leg: Muhammad al-Amin.

KM#	Date	Year	Mintage	VF	XF	Unc
275	AH1370	1950(a)	5,000	.50	2.00	6.00
	1376	1957(a)	.600	1.00	2.50	5.00

100 FRANCS

6.5500 g, .900 GOLD, .1895 oz AGW
Obv. leg: Ahmad.

257	AH1349	1930(a)	3,000	100.00	125.00	150.00
	1350	1931(a)	33 pcs.	—	550.00	900.00
	1351	1932(a)	3,000	100.00	125.00	150.00
	1352	1933(a)	33 pcs.	—	550.00	900.00
	1353	1934(a)	133 pcs.	—	400.00	400.00
	1354	1935(a)	3,000	100.00	130.00	160.00
	1355	1936(a)	33 pcs.	—	550.00	900.00
	1356	1937(a)	33 pcs.	—	550.00	900.00

COPPER-NICKEL
Obv. leg: Muhammad al-Amin.

276	AH1370	1950(a)	8,000	2.00	5.00	10.00
	1376	1957(a)	1,000	2.00	4.00	8.00

REPUBLIC
1000 Millim = 1 Dinar

NOTE: KM#280-282 and KM#306-309 were struck in Czechoslovakia, while the exact mint unknown. KM#291 and 303 were struck at Paris and have the usual privy marks of that mint. KM#280-282 and KM#306-309 have frozen dates and are being restruck as needed.

MILLIM

ALUMINUM

KM#	Date	Mintage	VF	XF	Unc
280	1960	—	—	.10	.25

2 MILLIM

ALUMINUM

281	1960	—	—	.10	.25

5 MILLIM

ALUMINUM

282	1960	—	—	.10	.25
	1983	—	—	.10	.25

10 MILLIM

BRASS

KM#	Date	Year	Mintage	VF	XF	Unc
306	AH1380	1960	—	.15	.25	.50

20 MILLIM

BRASS

KM#	Date	Year	Mintage	VF	XF	Unc
307	AH1380	1960	—	.30	.50	.80
	1403	1983	—	.30	.50	.80

50 MILLIM

BRASS

308	AH1380	1960	—	.65	.85	1.25
	1403	1983	—	.65	.85	1.25

100 MILLIM

BRASS

309	AH1380	1960	—	1.25	1.50	2.00
	1403	1983	—	1.25	1.50	2.00

1/2 DINAR

NICKEL

KM#	Date	Mintage	VF	XF	Unc
291	1968(a)	.500	1.00	2.00	3.00

COPPER-NICKEL
F.A.O. Issue

303	1976	—	1.50	3.00	6.00
	1983	—	1.50	3.00	6.00

DINAR

21.1840 g, .925 SILVER, .6300 oz ASW
Hannibal

KM#	Date	Mintage	VF	XF	Unc
292	1969FM-NI	.015	—	Proof	15.00
	1969NI	5,000	—	Proof	40.00

Masinissa
Obv: Similar to KM#292.

293	1969FM-NI	.015	—	Proof	15.00
	1969NI	5,000	—	Proof	40.00

Jugurtha
Obv: Similar to KM#292.

294	1969FM-NI	.015	—	Proof	15.00
	1969NI	5,000	—	Proof	40.00

Virgil
Obv: Similar to KM#292.

295	1969FM-NI	.015	—	Proof	15.00
	1969NI	5,000	—	Proof	40.00

St. Augustine
Obv: Similar to KM#292.

296	1969FM-NI	.015	—	Proof	15.00
	1969NI	5,000	—	Proof	40.00

Phoenician Ship
Obv: Similar to KM#292.

KM#	Date	Mintage	VF	XF	Unc
297	1969FM-NI	.015	—	Proof	35.00
	1969NI	5,000	—	Proof	75.00

Neptune
Obv: Similar to KM#292.

298	1969FM-NI	.015	—	Proof	15.00
	1969NI	5,000	—	Proof	40.00

Venus
Obv: Similar to KM#292.

299	1969FM-NI	.015	—	Proof	22.50
	1969NI	5,000	—	Proof	50.00

Thysdrus-El Djem
Obv: Similar to KM#292.

300	1969FM-NI	.015	—	Proof	15.00
	1969NI	5,000	—	Proof	40.00

Sbeitla-Sufetula
Obv: Similar to KM#292.

301	1969FM-NI	.015	—	Proof	15.00
	1969NI	5,000	—	Proof	40.00

TUNISIA 1648

18.0000 g, .680 SILVER, .3935 oz ASW
F.A.O. Issue

KM#	Date	Mintage	VF	XF	Unc
302	1970(a)	.100	—	5.00	10.00
	1970(a)	1,250	—	Proof	40.00

COPPER-NICKEL
F.A.O. Issue

304	1976	—	1.50	3.00	6.00
	1983	—	1.50	3.00	6.00

2 DINARS

3.8000 g, .900 GOLD, .1099 oz AGW
10th Anniversary of Republic

286	1967	7,259	—	Proof	70.00

5 DINARS

11.7900 g, .900 GOLD, .3412 oz AGW

283	1962	—	—	Proof	200.00

284	1963	—	—	Proof	200.00

9.5000 g, .900 GOLD, .2749 oz AGW
10th Anniversary of Republic

287	1967	7,259	—	Proof	165.00

24.0000 g, .680 SILVER, .5247 oz ASW

XX Anniversary of Independence

KM#	Date	Mintage	VF	XF	Unc
305	1976	.201	—	—	15.00
	1976	—	—	Proof	30.00

9.4120 g, .900 GOLD, .2723 oz AGW
Obv: Habib Bourguiba. Rev: President's return.

310	1981	1,450	—	Proof	175.00

27.2200 g, .925 SILVER, .8096 oz ASW
International Year of the Child
Obv: Similar to 1 Dinar, KM#302.

313	1982	7,575	—	—	20.00
	1982	1,108	—	Proof	35.00

10 DINARS

23.4800 g, .900 GOLD, .6795 oz AGW

285	1962	—	—	Proof	400.00
	1964	—	—	Proof	400.00

19.0000 g, .900 GOLD, .5498 oz AGW
10th Anniversary of Republic

288	1967	6,480	—	Proof	300.00

18.8240 g, .900 GOLD, .5447 oz AGW
Obv: Habib Bourguiba. Rev: President's return.

311	1981	2,000	—	Proof	325.00

18.8080 g, .900 GOLD, .5442 oz AGW
Obv: Habib Bourguiba. Rev: Silhouette of girl.

312	1981	2,000	—	Proof	325.00

38.0000 g, .900 SILVER, 1.0995 oz ASW
Gabes Bank

314	1982	2,500	—	Proof	30.00

Central Bank at Nabeul

315	1982	1,000	—	Proof	40.00

Sfax Branch Office

316	1982	1,000	—	Proof	40.00

20 DINARS

38.0000 g, .900 GOLD, 1.0996 oz AGW
10th Anniversary of Republic

KM#	Date	Mintage	VF	XF	Unc
289	1967	3,536	—	—	600.00

40 DINARS

76.0000 g, .900 GOLD, 2.1991 oz AGW
10th Anniversary of Republic

290	1967	3,031	—	Proof	1250.

75 DINARS

15.5500 g, .900 GOLD, .4500 oz AGW
International Year of the Child

317	1982	2,980	—	Proof	250.00

PROOF SETS (PS)

KM#	Date	Mintage	Identification	Issue Price	Mkt. Val.
PS2	1967(5)	3,031	KM286-290	—	2400.
PS3	1969FM-NI(10)	*15,202	KM292-301	77.00	175.00
PS4	1969NI(10)	5,000	KM292-301	—	445.00

*NOTE: Many sets were ruined while in storage.

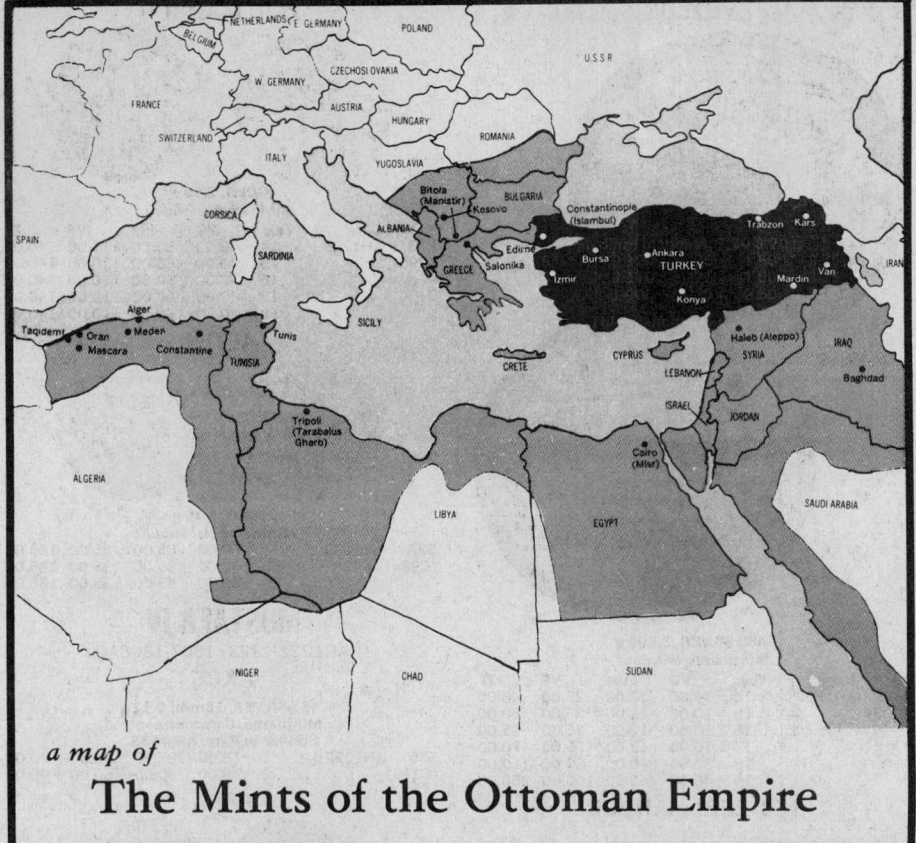

a map of
The Mints of the Ottoman Empire

The Republic of Turkey, a parliamentary democracy of the Near East located partially in Europe and partially in Asia between the Black and the Mediterranean Seas, has an area of 301,382 sq. mi. (780,576 sq. km.) and a population of *55.4 million. Capital: Ankara. Turkey exports cotton, hazelnuts, and tobacco, and enjoys a virtual monopoly in meerschaum.

The Ottoman Turks, a tribe from Central Asia, first appeared in the early 13th century, and by the 17th century had established the Ottoman Empire which stretched from the Persian Gulf to the southern frontier of Poland, and from the Caspian Sea to the Algerian plateau. The defeat of the Turkish navy by the Holy League in 1571, and of the Turkish forces besieging Vienna in 1683, began the steady decline of the Ottoman Empire which, accelerated by the rise of nationalism, contracted its European border, and by the end of World War I deprived it of its Arab lands. The present Turkish boundaries were largely fixed by the Treaty of Lausanne in 1923. The sultanate and caliphate, the political and spiritual ruling institutions of the old empire, were separated and the sultanate abolished in 1922. On Oct. 29, 1923, Turkey formally became a republic.

RULERS
Selim III, AH1203-1222/
  1789-1807AD
Mustafa IV, AH1222-1223/
  1807-1808AD
Mahmud II, AH1223-1255
  1808-1839AD
Abdul Mejid, AH1255-1277/
  1839-1861AD
Abdul Aziz, AH1277-1293/
  1861-1876AD
Murad V, AH1293/1876AD
Abdul Hamid II, AH1293-1327/
  1876-1909AD
Muhammad V, AH1327-1336/
  1909-1918AD
Muhammad VI, AH1336-1341/
  1918-1923AD
Republic, AH1341/AD1923—

MINTNAMES

Bursa   بروسة
(Brusah)

Constantinople   قسطنطنية
(Qustantiniyah)

Edirne   ادرنة
(Adrianople)

Islambul   اسلامبول (or) إسلامبول
Istanbul

Kara Amid   كارآمد
(Amid)

Kosova   قوصوه
Manistir   مناستر

Salonika   سلانيك
(Selanik, Saloniki)

MONETARY EQUIVALENTS
3 Akche = 1 Para
5 Para = Beshlik (Beshparalik)
10 Para = Onluk
20 Para = Yirmilik
30 Para = Zolta
40 Para = Piastre (Kurush)
1-1/2 Piastres (Kurush) = Altmishlik

MONETARY SYSTEM
Silver Coinage
40 Para = 1 Piastre
2 Piastres = 1 Ikilik
2-1/2 Piastres = Yuzluk
3 Piastres = Uechlik
5 Piastres = Beshlik
6 Piastres = Altilik

Gold Coinage
100 Piastres (Kurush) = 1 Turkish Pound (Lira)

This system has remained essentially unchanged since its introduction by Ahmad III in 1688, except that the Asper and Para have long since ceased to be coined. The Piastre, established as a crown-sized silver coin approximately equal to the French Ecu of Louis XIV, has shrunk to a tiny copper coin, worth about 1/15 of a U.S. cent. Since the establishment of the Republic in 1923, the Turkish terms, Kurus and Lira, have replaced the European names Piastres and Turkish Pounds.

MINT VISIT ISSUES
From time to time, certain cities of the Ottoman Empire, such as Bursa, Edirne, Kosova, Manistir and Salonika were honored by having special coins struck at Istanbul, but with inscriptions stating that they were struck in the city of honor. These were produced on the occasion of the Sultan's visit to that city. The coins were struck in limited, but not small quantities, and were probably intended for distribution to the notables of the city and the Sultan's own followers. Because they were of the same size and type as the regular circulation issues struck at Istanbul, many specimens found their way into circulation and worn or mounted specimens are found today, although some have been preserved in XF or better condition. Mintage statistics are not known.

MONNAIE DE LUXE
In the 23rd year of the reign of Abdul Hamid II, two parallel series of gold coins were produced, regular mint issues and 'monnaies de luxe', which were intended primarily for presentation and jewelry purposes. The 'monnaies de luxe' were struck to a slightly less weight and the same fineness as regular issues, but were broader and thinner, and from more ornate dies.

Coins are listed by type, followed by a list of reported years. Most of the reported years have never been confirmed and other years may also exist. Mintage figures are known for the AH1293 and 1327 series, but are unreliable and of little utility.

Although some years are undoubtedly much rarer than others, there is at present no date collecting of Ottoman gold and therefore little justification for higher prices for rare dates.

There is no change in design in the regular series. Only the toughra, accessional date and regnal year vary. The deluxe series show ornamental changes. The standard coins do not bear the denomination.

HONORIFIC TITLES

El Ghazi   *Reshat*

The first coinage of Abdul Hamid II has a flower to the right of the toughra while the second coinage has *El Ghazi* (The Victorious). The first coinage of Mohammad Reshat V has *Reshat* to the right of the toughra while his second coinage has *El Ghazi*.

SELIM III
AH1203-1222/1789-1807AD

THIRD COINAGE
Light coinage based on a Piastre weighing approximately 12.80 g with second Toughra.

PARA

.465 SILVER, 0.32 g
Mintname: *Islambul*

KM#	Date	Year	VG	Fine	VF	XF
486	AH1203	14	.75	1.25	6.00	12.00
(C86a)		15	.75	1.25	6.00	12.00
		16	.75	1.25	6.00	12.00
		17	.75	1.25	6.00	12.00
		18	.75	1.25	6.00	12.00
		19	2.00	4.00	12.00	30.00

5 PARA

.465 SILVER, 1.60 g
Mintname: *Islambul*

489	AH1203	14	6.50	10.00	25.00	40.00
(C87a)		15	6.50	10.00	25.00	40.00
		16	6.50	10.00	25.00	40.00
		17	6.50	10.00	25.00	40.00
		18	6.50	10.00	25.00	40.00
		19	10.00	15.00	35.00	75.00

TURKEY 1650

10 PARA

.465 SILVER, 3.05 g
Mintname: *Islambul*

KM#	Date	Year	VG	Fine	VF	XF
492	AH1203	14	4.00	8.00	17.50	35.00
(C88a)		15	4.00	8.00	17.50	35.00
		15	4.00	8.00	17.50	35.00
		16	4.00	8.00	17.50	35.00
		17	4.00	8.00	17.50	35.00
		18	4.00	8.00	17.50	35.00
		19	8.00	15.00	25.00	55.00

20 PARA

.465 SILVER, 6.45 g
Mintname: *Islambul*

KM#	Date	Year	VG	Fine	VF	XF
495	AH1203	15	40.00	80.00	150.00	275.00
(C89a)		16	40.00	80.00	150.00	275.00
		19	—	—	—	—

PIASTRE

.465 SILVER, 12.62 g
Mintname: *Islambul*

KM#	Date	Year	VG	Fine	VF	XF
498	AH1203	14	20.00	30.00	60.00	125.00
(C90a)		15	20.00	30.00	60.00	125.00
		16	20.00	30.00	60.00	125.00
		17	20.00	30.00	60.00	125.00
		18	20.00	30.00	60.00	125.00
		19	—	—	—	—

2 PIASTRES

.465 SILVER, 25.60 g
Mintname: *Islambul*

KM#	Date	Year	VG	Fine	VF	XF
504	AH1203	14	10.00	12.00	30.00	45.00
(C92a)		15	10.00	12.00	25.00	35.00
		15	10.00	12.00	25.00	35.00
		16	10.00	12.00	25.00	35.00
		17	10.00	12.00	25.00	35.00
		18	—	—	—	—
		19	—	—	—	—

YUZLUK

.465 SILVER, 32.00 g
Mintname: *Islambul*

KM#	Date	Year	VG	Fine	VF	XF
507	AH1203	14	10.00	12.00	25.00	40.00
(C93)		15	10.00	12.00	25.00	50.00
		16	10.00	12.00	25.00	55.00
		17	10.00	12.00	25.00	70.00
		18	30.00	40.00	60.00	110.00
		19	40.00	60.00	100.00	250.00

1/4 ZERI MAHBUB

GOLD, 0.60 g
Mintname: *Islambul*

KM#	Date	Year	VG	Fine	VF	XF
510	AH1203	14	22.50	35.00	50.00	75.00
(C93.5)		15	22.50	35.00	50.00	75.00
		16	22.50	35.00	50.00	75.00
		17	22.50	35.00	50.00	75.00

1/4 ALTIN

GOLD, 15mm, 0.90 g
Mintname: *Islambul*
Plain borders

KM#	Date	Year	VG	Fine	VF	XF
514	AH1203	14	22.50	35.00	50.00	70.00
(C96a)		15	22.50	35.00	50.00	70.00
		16	22.50	35.00	50.00	70.00
		17	22.50	35.00	50.00	70.00
		18	22.50	35.00	50.00	70.00
		19	22.50	35.00	50.00	70.00

1/2 ZERI MAHBUB

GOLD, 1.20 g
Mintname: *Islambul*

KM#	Date	Year	VG	Fine	VF	XF
517	AH1203	14	40.00	65.00	80.00	100.00
(C94)		15	40.00	65.00	80.00	100.00
		16	40.00	65.00	80.00	100.00
		17	40.00	65.00	80.00	100.00

1/2 ALTIN

GOLD, 1.65 g
Mintname: *Islambul*

KM#	Date	Year	VG	Fine	VF	XF
520	AH1203	18	60.00	90.00	135.00	185.00
(C97)						

ZERI MAHBUB

GOLD, 2.40 g
Mintname: *Islambul*

KM#	Date	Year	VG	Fine	VF	XF
523	AH1203	14	40.00	60.00	110.00	140.00
(C95)		15	40.00	60.00	110.00	140.00
		16	40.00	60.00	110.00	140.00
		17	40.00	60.00	110.00	140.00
		18	40.00	60.00	110.00	140.00

ALTIN

GOLD, 3.45 g
Mintname: *Islambul*

KM#	Date	Year	VG	Fine	VF	XF
527	AH1203	17	60.00	85.00	135.00	185.00
(C98a)		18	60.00	85.00	135.00	185.00
		19	60.00	85.00	135.00	185.00

MUSTAFA IV
AH1222-1223/1807-1808AD

AKCE

.465 SILVER, 12mm, 0.12 g
Mintname: *Constantinople*
Similar to Para, KM#536.

KM#	Date	Year	VG	Fine	VF	XF
535	AH1222	1	18.50	27.50	42.50	70.00
(C110)		2	30.00	50.00	60.00	90.00

PARA

.465 SILVER, 0.40 g
Mintname: *Constantinople*

KM#	Date	Year	VG	Fine	VF	XF
536	AH1222	1	15.00	17.50	35.00	50.00
(C111)		2	20.00	40.00	50.00	75.00

5 PARA

.465 SILVER, 1.50 g
Mintname: *Constantinople*

KM#	Date	Year	VG	Fine	VF	XF
537	AH1222	1	40.00	45.00	125.00	200.00
(C112)		2	60.00	90.00	200.00	300.00

10 PARA

.465 SILVER, 3.30 g
Mintname: *Constantinople*

KM#	Date	Year	VG	Fine	VF	XF
538	AH1222	1	35.00	50.00	100.00	150.00
(C113)		2	40.00	65.00	200.00	300.00

PIASTRE

.465 SILVER, 12.95 g
Mintname: *Constantinople*

KM#	Date	Year	VG	Fine	VF	XF
539	AH1222	1	200.00	350.00	500.00	700.00
(C115)		2	200.00	350.00	750.00	1000.

2 ZOLOTA

.465 SILVER, 19.45 g
Mintname: *Constantinople*

KM#	Date	Year	VG	Fine	VF	XF
540 (C116)	AH1222	1	400.00	600.00	1250.	2000.

2 PIASTRES

.465 SILVER, 26.10 g
Mintname: *Constantinople*

541 (C116.5)	AH1222	1	400.00	600.00	1250.	2000.

2-1/2 PIASTRES

.465 SILVER, 42mm, 32.80 g
Mintname: *Constantinople*
Similar to 1 Piastre, KM#548.

542 (C117)	AH1222	1	450.00	900.00	1500.	2250.

1/4 ALTIN

GOLD, 0.77 g
Mintname: *Constantinople*

KM#	Date	Year	VG	Fine	VF	XF
543 (C125)	AH1222	1	40.00	60.00	100.00	150.00
		2	45.00	65.00	120.00	175.00

1/2 ZERI MAHBUB

GOLD, 1.20 g
Mintname: *Constantinople*

544 (C121)	AH1222	1	60.00	90.00	135.00	200.00
		2	60.00	90.00	135.00	200.00

ZERI MAHBUB

GOLD, 2.35 g
Mintname: *Constantinople*

545 (C122)	AH1222	1	90.00	150.00	250.00	350.00
		2	125.00	200.00	300.00	450.00

ALTIN

GOLD, 3.20 g
Mintname: *Constantinople*

546 (C127)	AH1222	1	100.00	150.00	200.00	265.00
		2	130.00	180.00	250.00	325.00

MAHMUD II
AH1223-1255/1808-1839AD

Copper Coinage
PARA

COPPER
Mintname: *Van*

KM#	Date	Mintage	Good	VG	Fine	VF
547 (175)	AH1225	—	50.00	60.00	70.00	115.00
	1231		50.00	60.00	70.00	115.00

Silver Coinage

The silver currency of the reign of Mahmud II is characterized by frequent change of standard, so that the Piastre (Kurus), which began with 5.90 g of pure silver, had dropped to only 0.56 g in the lower denominations (token currency), and 0.94 g in the higher (actual currency). From time to time, the fineness, diameter, weight and type of the coins were changed, with the result that it is difficult, and not very meaningful, to attempt to trace individual denominations through the 32 years of his reign. For that reason, following Craig and others, the coins are grouped by standards of weight, fineness, or size. Changes in fineness, weight, and size are regularly indicated, as are distinguishing features whenever necessary for the proper identification of coins. The tolerance on Mahmud's silver coinage was considerable, particularly on the smaller denominations and the weights listed are approximate.

First Series
Years 1-2
AKCE

.465 SILVER, 9mm, 0.10-0.16 g
Mintname: *Constantinople*

KM#	Date	Year	VG	Fine	VF	XF
550 (C171)	AH1223	1	6.00	15.00	35.00	70.00
		2	6.00	15.00	35.00	70.00

PARA

.465 SILVER, 0.32 g
Mintname: *Constantinople*

KM#	Date	Year	VG	Fine	VF	XF
551 (C172)	AH1223	1	4.00	10.00	16.00	30.00
		2	4.00	10.00	16.00	30.00

5 PARA

.465 SILVER, 1.50-1.60 g
Mintname: *Constantinople*

552 (C173)	AH1223	1	6.00	15.00	35.00	70.00
		2	6.00	15.00	35.00	70.00

10 PARA

.465 SILVER, 2.80-3.20 g
Mintname: *Constantinople*

553 (C174)	AH1223	*1	7.00	15.00	35.00	70.00
		2	10.00	17.50	40.00	80.00

*NOTE: Two obverse varieties exist.

PIASTRE

.465 SILVER, 12.00-13.18 g
Mintname: *Constantinople*

554 (C176)	AH1223	1	50.00	150.00	300.00	450.00
		2	75.00	200.00	350.00	550.00

Second Series
Years 2-14
AKCE

.465 SILVER, 11mm, 0.10-0.12 g
Mintname: *Constantinople*

556 (C171a)	AH1223	5	1.50	3.00	15.00	25.00
		12	1.50	3.00	15.00	25.00
		15	10.00	25.00	50.00	90.00

PARA

.465 SILVER, 0.18-0.26 g
Mintname: *Constantinople*

557 (C172a)	AH1223	3	1.00	3.00	4.00	10.00
		4	1.00	3.00	4.00	10.00
		5	1.00	3.00	4.00	10.00
		6	1.00	3.00	4.00	10.00
		7	1.00	3.00	4.00	10.00
		8	1.00	3.00	4.00	10.00
		9	1.00	3.00	4.00	10.00
		10	1.00	3.00	4.00	10.00
		11	1.00	3.00	4.00	10.00
		12	1.00	3.00	4.00	10.00
		13	1.00	3.00	4.00	10.00
		14	1.00	3.00	4.00	10.00

5 PARA

.465 SILVER, 1.01-1.20 g
Mintname: *Constantinople*

KM#	Date	Year	VG	Fine	VF	XF
558 (C173a)	AH1223	3	3.00	6.00	20.00	35.00
		4	3.00	6.00	20.00	35.00
		5	3.00	6.00	20.00	35.00
		6	3.00	6.00	20.00	35.00
		7	3.00	6.00	20.00	35.00
		8	3.00	6.00	20.00	35.00
		9	3.00	6.00	20.00	35.00
		10	3.00	6.00	20.00	35.00
		11	3.00	6.00	20.00	35.00
		12	3.00	6.00	20.00	35.00
		13	3.00	6.00	20.00	35.00
		14	3.00	6.00	20.00	35.00

10 PARA

.465 SILVER, 2.10-2.50 g
Mintname: *Constantinople*

KM#	Date	Year	VG	Fine	VF	XF
559 (C174a)	AH1223	3	2.00	5.00	15.00	30.00
		4	2.00	5.00	15.00	30.00
		5	2.00	5.00	15.00	30.00
		6	2.00	5.00	15.00	30.00
		7	2.00	5.00	15.00	30.00
		8	2.00	5.00	15.00	30.00
		9	2.00	5.00	15.00	30.00
		10	2.00	5.00	15.00	30.00
		11	2.00	5.00	15.00	30.00
		12	2.00	5.00	15.00	30.00
		13	2.00	5.00	15.00	30.00
		14	2.00	5.00	15.00	30.00

PIASTRE

.465 SILVER, 33mm, 9.60 g
Mintname: *Constantinople*

KM#	Date	Year	VG	Fine	VF	XF
560 (C176a)	AH1223	3	12.00	18.00	32.00	100.00
		4	12.00	18.00	32.00	100.00
		5	12.00	18.00	32.00	100.00
		6	12.00	18.00	32.00	100.00
		7	12.00	18.00	32.00	100.00
		8	12.00	18.00	32.00	100.00
		9	12.00	18.00	32.00	100.00
		10	12.00	18.00	32.00	100.00
		11	12.00	18.00	32.00	100.00
		12	12.00	18.00	32.00	100.00
		13	12.00	18.00	32.00	100.00

Third Series - Cihadiye
(Jyhadiye)
Years 3-11

PIASTRE

.730 SILVER, 4.60-5.20 g
Mintname: *Constantinople*

KM#	Date	Year	VG	Fine	VF	XF
562 (C181)	AH1223	3	125.00	200.00	350.00	700.00

100 PARA
(2-1/2 Piastres)

.730 SILVER, 12.50-13.20 g
Mintname: *Constantinople*

KM#	Date	Year	VG	Fine	VF	XF
563 (C183)	AH1223	2	—	Reported, not confirmed		
		3	40.00	80.00	160.00	300.00
		4	40.00	80.00	160.00	300.00
		5	40.00	80.00	160.00	300.00
		6	40.00	80.00	160.00	300.00
		7	40.00	80.00	160.00	300.00
		8	40.00	80.00	160.00	300.00
		9	50.00	100.00	200.00	350.00
		10	75.00	150.00	275.00	450.00
		11	175.00	250.00	450.00	700.00

5 PIASTRES

.730 SILVER, 24.00-26.00 g
Mintname: *Constantinople*

KM#	Date	Year	VG	Fine	VF	XF
564 (C184)	AH1223	3	20.00	30.00	55.00	90.00
		4	20.00	30.00	50.00	85.00
		5	20.00	30.00	50.00	85.00
		6	20.00	30.00	50.00	85.00
		7	20.00	30.00	50.00	85.00
		8	20.00	30.00	75.00	110.00
		9	20.00	30.00	75.00	110.00
		10	100.00	150.00	225.00	350.00
		11	125.00	250.00	425.00	600.00

Fourth Series
Years 14-15

PARA

.465 SILVER, 0.15 g
Mintname: *Constantinople*

KM#	Date	Year	VG	Fine	VF	XF
566 (C172b)	AH1223	14	1.25	2.50	6.00	12.00
		15	1.25	2.50	6.00	12.00

5 PARA

.465 SILVER, 18mm, 0.85 g
Mintname: *Constantinople*

KM#	Date	Year	VG	Fine	VF	XF
567 (C173b)	AH1223	14	7.00	15.00	50.00	80.00

NOTE: Yr. 13 is reported.

10 PARA

.465 SILVER, 22mm, 1.60-1.80 g
Mintname: *Constantinople*

KM#	Date	Year	VG	Fine	VF	XF
568 (C174b)	AH1223	14	5.00	10.00	35.00	60.00
		15	10.00	20.00	50.00	100.00

PIASTRE

.465 SILVER, 32mm, 5.50 g
Mintname: *Constantinople*

KM#	Date	Year	VG	Fine	VF	XF
569 (C176b)	AH1223	14	25.00	35.00	75.00	150.00
		15	45.00	60.00	100.00	175.00

2 PIASTRES

.465 SILVER, 11.50-13.40 g
Mintname: *Constantinople*

KM#	Date	Year	VG	Fine	VF	XF
570 (C190)	AH1223	14	25.00	50.00	100.00	200.00
		15	30.00	60.00	120.00	225.00

NOTE: Some coins have stars above and below regnal year box.

Fifth Series
Years 15-16
Reeded edge on all but Para

PARA

.730 SILVER, 0.14-0.17 g
Mintname: *Constantinople*

KM#	Date	Year	VG	Fine	VF	XF
572 (C172c)	AH1223	15	1.50	3.00	6.00	15.00
		16	1.50	3.00	6.00	15.00

5 PARA

.730 SILVER, 0.80 g
Mintname: *Constantinople*

KM#	Date	Year	VG	Fine	VF	XF
573 (C186)	AH1223	15	8.00	17.50	40.00	60.00
		16	7.50	15.00	35.00	50.00
		18	15.00	30.00	70.00	125.00

10 PARA

.730 SILVER, 1.60 g
Mintname: *Constantinople*

KM#	Date	Year	VG	Fine	VF	XF
574 (C174c)	AH1223	15	7.50	15.00	20.00	35.00
		16	7.50	15.00	20.00	35.00
		18	7.50	15.00	20.00	35.00

PIASTRE

.730 SILVER, 6.15 g
Mintname: *Constantinople*

KM#	Date	Year	VG	Fine	VF	XF
575 (C176c)	AH1223	15	20.00	30.00	50.00	100.00
		16	20.00	30.00	50.00	100.00

2 PIASTRES

.730 SILVER, 12.00-13.00 g
Mintname: *Constantinople*

KM#	Date	Year	VG	Fine	VF	XF
576	AH1223	15	10.00	18.00	40.00	70.00
(C190a)		16	10.00	20.00	45.00	80.00

Sixth Series
Years 16-21

PARA

.600 SILVER, 12mm, 0.15-0.20 g
Mintname: *Constantinople*

KM#	Date	Year	VG	Fine	VF	XF
578	AH1223	17	1.50	3.00	10.00	17.50
(C172d)		18	1.50	3.00	10.00	17.50
		19	1.50	3.00	10.00	17.50
		20	1.50	3.00	10.00	17.50
		21	1.50	3.00	10.00	17.50

30 PARA

.600 SILVER, 3.00-3.40 g
Mintname: *Constantinople*

KM#	Date	Year	VG	Fine	VF	XF
579	AH1223	17	4.00	6.00	15.00	30.00
(C192)		18	4.00	6.00	15.00	30.00
		19	4.00	6.00	15.00	30.00
		20	4.00	6.00	15.00	30.00
		21	4.00	6.00	15.00	35.00

NOTE: This coin occurs frequently in high grade.

60 PARA

.600 SILVER, 5.60-6.25 g
Mintname: *Constantinople*

KM#	Date	Year	VG	Fine	VF	XF
580	AH1223	16	8.00	12.00	25.00	40.00
(C193)		17	5.00	8.00	16.00	25.00
		18	5.00	8.00	16.00	25.00
		19	5.00	8.00	16.00	25.00
		20	5.00	8.00	16.00	25.00
		21	5.00	8.00	16.00	25.00

NOTE: This coin occurs frequently in high grade.

Seventh Series
Years 21-22
Wavy borders

NOTE: A Para was struck in this series, in low grade silver .460, in the year 22, but is not distinguishable from yr. 22 pieces of the eighth series C#172e.

AKCE
SILVER
Mintname: *Constantinople*

KM#	Date	Year	VG	Fine	VF	XF
582	AH1223	21	3.00	5.00	7.00	15.00
(C171d)						

20 PARA

.833 SILVER, 0.80 g
Mintname: *Constantinople*

KM#	Date	Year	VG	Fine	VF	XF
583	AH1223	21	4.00	6.00	9.00	15.00
(C194)		22	10.00	15.00	25.00	40.00

NOTE: This coin occurs frequently in high grade, also with open and closed rosettes on obverse and reverse.

PIASTRE

.833 SILVER, 1.40-1.60 g
Mintname: *Constantinople*

KM#	Date	Year	VG	Fine	VF	XF
584	AH1223	21	5.00	6.50	11.00	20.00
(C195)		22	12.00	18.00	30.00	50.00

NOTE: This coin occurs frequently in high grade, also with open and closed rosettes on obverse and reverse.

10 PIASTRES
Two different designs exist dated year 22 and are considered patterns.

Eighth Series - Cedid
(Jadid)
Years 22-25

NOTE: Coins of the eighth series are readily distinguished from the ninth series, as they lack the large dot below the inner wreath that appears on the ninth series. In the eighth and ninth series, with the exception of the Para, all coins have the word *Adli* (the Just) at right of the toughra, sometimes with vertical mark below. The Para is distinguished only by date, however. Many coins are debased with a silver wash.

PARA

.220 SILVER, 0.10 g
Mintname: *Constantinople*

KM#	Date	Year	VG	Fine	VF	XF
586	AH1223	22	.65	1.60	2.50	8.00
(C172e)		23	.65	1.60	2.50	8.00
		24	.65	1.60	2.50	8.00
		25	.90	2.00	3.50	8.00

10 PARA

.220 SILVER, 17mm, 0.80 g
Mintname: *Constantinople*

KM#	Date	Year	VG	Fine	VF	XF
587	AH1223	22	2.00	6.00	15.00	35.00
(C197)		23	2.00	6.00	15.00	35.00
		24	2.00	6.00	15.00	35.00
		25	2.00	6.00	15.00	35.00

20 PARA

.220 SILVER, 1.40-1.80 g
Mintname: *Constantinople*

KM#	Date	Year	VG	Fine	VF	XF
588	AH1223	21	—	—	Rare	—
(C198)		22	1.00	2.00	5.00	12.00
		23	1.00	2.00	5.00	12.00
		24	1.00	2.00	5.00	12.00
		25	1.00	2.00	5.00	12.00

PIASTRE

.220 SILVER, 2.60-3.00 g
Mintname: *Constantinople*

KM#	Date	Year	VG	Fine	VF	XF
589	AH1223	22	2.75	3.00	6.25	15.00

KM#	Date	Year	VG	Fine	VF	XF
(C199)		23	2.75	3.00	6.25	15.00
		24	2.75	3.00	6.25	15.00
		25	2.75	3.00	6.25	15.00

100 PARA
(2-1/2 Piastres)

.220 SILVER, 7.20-7.80 g
Mintname: *Constantinople*

KM#	Date	Year	VG	Fine	VF	XF
590	AH1223	22	4.75	7.50	11.00	25.00
(C200)		23	3.50	5.00	8.00	15.00
		24	3.50	5.00	8.00	15.00
		25	3.50	5.00	8.00	15.00

5 PIASTRES

.220 SILVER, 15.00-16.00 g
Rev: Similar to 100 Para, KM#674.
Mintname: *Constantinople*

KM#	Date	Year	VG	Fine	VF	XF
591	AH1223	22	3.00	5.00	12.50	25.00
(C201)		23	3.00	5.00	12.50	25.00
		24	3.00	5.00	12.50	25.00
		25	3.00	5.00	15.00	30.00

Ninth Series
Years 25-32

Large dot added beneath inner wreath on obverse and reverse except on 1 Akce and 1 Para.

AKCE

.170 SILVER, 0.04-0.07 g
Mintname: *Constantinople*

KM#	Date	Year	VG	Fine	VF	XF
593	AH1223	25	5.00	10.00	25.00	55.00
(C171f)		26	2.50	4.00	15.00	40.00
		27	2.50	4.00	15.00	40.00

PARA

.170 SILVER, 0.08-0.15 g
Mintname: *Constantinople*

KM#	Date	Year	VG	Fine	VF	XF
594	AH1223	26	1.00	1.50	2.75	7.00
(C172f)		27	.75	1.25	2.00	5.00
		28	.75	1.25	2.00	5.00
		29	.75	1.25	2.00	5.00
		30	.75	1.25	2.00	5.00
		31	.75	1.25	2.00	5.00
		32	.75	1.25	2.00	5.00

10 PARA

.170 SILVER, 0.50-0.75 g
Mintname: *Constantinople*

KM#	Date	Year	VG	Fine	VF	XF
595	AH1223	25	2.00	3.00	5.00	12.50
(C197a)		26	5.00	7.50	10.00	18.50
		27	2.00	3.00	5.00	12.50
		28	2.00	3.00	5.00	12.50
		29	2.00	3.00	5.00	12.50
		30	2.00	3.00	5.00	12.50
		31	2.00	3.00	5.00	12.50
		32	2.00	3.00	5.00	12.50

20 PARA

.170 SILVER, 1.35-1.60 g
Mintname: *Constantinople*

KM#	Date	Year	VG	Fine	VF	XF
596	AH1223	25	2.00	2.50	4.00	10.00
(C198a)		26	2.00	2.50	4.00	10.00
		27	2.00	2.50	4.00	10.00
		28	2.00	2.50	4.00	10.00
		29	2.00	2.50	4.00	10.00
		30	2.00	2.50	4.00	10.00
		31	2.00	2.50	4.00	10.00
		32	2.00	2.50	4.00	10.00

NOTE: Years 26 and 31 are easily confused.

PIASTRE

.170 SILVER, 2.60-3.00 g
Mintname: *Constantinople*

KM#	Date	Year	VG	Fine	VF	XF
597	AH1223	25	3.50	5.00	8.00	17.50
(C199a)		26	3.50	5.00	8.00	17.50

100 PARA
(2-1/2 Piastres)

.170 SILVER, 6.40-7.80 g
Mintname: *Constantinople*

KM#	Date	Year	VG	Fine	VF	XF
598	AH1223	25	3.00	4.50	9.00	18.50
(C200a)		26	3.00	4.50	9.00	18.50

5 PIASTRES

.170 SILVER, 13.00-16.00 g
Mintname: *Constantinople*
Obv: Similar to KM#591.

KM#	Date	Year	VG	Fine	VF	XF
599	AH1223	25	4.00	7.00	12.50	25.00
(C201a)		26	4.00	7.00	12.50	25.00

Tenth Series
Years 26-32

1-1/2 PIASTRE

.435 SILVER, 2.60-3.00 g
Mintname: *Constantinople*

KM#	Date	Year	VG	Fine	VF	XF
601	AH1223	26	4.00	6.00	12.00	25.00

KM#	Date	Year	VG	Fine	VF	XF
(C206)		27	3.50	5.00	10.00	20.00
		28	3.50	5.00	10.00	20.00
		29	3.50	5.00	10.00	20.00
		30	3.50	5.00	10.00	20.00
		31	3.50	5.00	10.00	20.00
		32	3.50	5.00	10.00	20.00

3 PIASTRES

.435 SILVER, 5.60-6.20 g
Mintname: *Constantinople*

KM#	Date	Year	VG	Fine	VF	XF
602	AH1223	26	5.00	7.50	12.00	25.00
(C207)		27	4.50	6.00	10.00	20.00
		28	4.50	6.00	10.00	20.00
		29	4.50	6.00	10.00	20.00
		30	4.50	6.00	10.00	20.00
		31	4.50	6.00	10.00	20.00
		32	4.50	6.00	10.00	20.00

6 PIASTRES

.435 SILVER, 11.00-13.00 g
Mintname: *Constantinople*

KM#	Date	Year	VG	Fine	VF	XF
603	AH1223	26	6.00	8.00	15.00	40.00
(C208)		27	6.00	8.00	15.00	30.00
		28	6.00	8.00	15.00	30.00
		29	6.00	8.00	15.00	30.00
		30	6.00	8.00	15.00	30.00
		31	6.00	8.00	15.00	30.00
		32	6.50	9.00	17.50	32.50

Gold Coinage

The gold emissions of Mahmud II are characterized by several simultaneous series, each with its characteristic name. They are distinguished by weight and by special symbols, such as the ornament to right of the toughra, the border, and variations in design. These are indicated for each series, along with the weights and diameters of each denomination. Each series comprises several denominations, with the basic unit known as the Altin (Gold Coin) or Tak (Single); other denominations include the Double (Clifte), Half (Yarim, or Nisfiye), and Quarter (Ceyrek, or Rubiye). Not all denominations were struck in every series. Some series can be divided into several subvarieties, which are listed separately below. Finally, a few coins were struck that do not fit into any of the series.

Zeri Mahbub Series
"Beloved Gold Series"

The obverse of all denominations consists of a toughra, with mint name and date below on the 1 and 1/2 Zeri Mahbub only. The reverse of the 1 and 1/2 bears a four-line inscription; the reverse of the 1/4, the mint and date.

FIRST TYPE
Lily on 1 and 1/2 Zeri Mahbub, branch with one rose on the 1/4 Zeri Mahbub.

1/4 ZERI MAHBUB

GOLD, 0.70-0.80 g
Mintname: *Constantinople*

KM#	Date	Year	VG	Fine	VF	XF
605	AH1223	1	15.00	20.00	30.00	40.00
(C218)		2	15.00	20.00	30.00	40.00
		3	15.00	25.00	40.00	60.00
		4	15.00	20.00	30.00	40.00
		5	15.00	20.00	30.00	40.00

1/2 ZERI MAHBUB

GOLD, 1.10-1.20 g
Mintname: *Constantinople*

KM#	Date	Year	VG	Fine	VF	XF
606	AH1223	1	35.00	50.00	70.00	90.00
(C209)		2	35.00	50.00	70.00	90.00
		3	35.00	50.00	70.00	90.00
		4	35.00	50.00	70.00	90.00
		5	35.00	50.00	70.00	90.00

ZERI MAHBUB

GOLD, 2.30-2.40 g
Mintname: *Constantinople*

KM#	Date	Year	VG	Fine	VF	XF
607	AH1223	1	50.00	75.00	100.00	150.00
(C210)		2	50.00	75.00	100.00	150.00
		3	—	Reported, not confirmed		
		4	—	Reported, not confirmed		
		5	50.00	75.00	100.00	150.00

SECOND TYPE
Rose replaces lily on 1 and 1/2 Zeri Mahbub, branch with 2 roses replaces branch with one rose on the 1/4 Zeri Mahbub.

1/4 ZERI MAHBUB

GOLD, 0.75-0.79 g
Mintname: *Constantinople*

KM#	Date	Year	VG	Fine	VF	XF
608	AH1223	6	15.00	20.00	30.00	45.00
(C218b)		7	15.00	20.00	30.00	45.00
		8	15.00	20.00	30.00	45.00
		9	15.00	20.00	30.00	45.00
		10	15.00	20.00	30.00	45.00
		11	15.00	20.00	35.00	50.00
		12	15.00	20.00	35.00	50.00
		13	15.00	20.00	35.00	50.00
		14	15.00	20.00	35.00	50.00

1/2 ZERI MAHBUB

GOLD, 18mm, 1.10-1.20 g
Mintname: *Constantinople*

KM#	Date	Year	VG	Fine	VF	XF
609	AH1223	6	—	Reported, not confirmed		
(C209b)		7	—	Reported, not confirmed		
		8	40.00	60.00	80.00	100.00
		9	—	Reported, not confirmed		
		10	—	Reported, not confirmed		
		11	—	Reported, not confirmed		
		12	40.00	60.00	80.00	100.00

ZERI MAHBUB

GOLD, 2.30-2.40 g
Mintname: *Constantinople*

KM#	Date	Year	VG	Fine	VF	XF
610	AH1223	6	40.00	75.00	85.00	125.00
(C210b)		7	40.00	75.00	85.00	125.00
		8	40.00	75.00	85.00	125.00
		9	40.00	75.00	85.00	125.00
		10	40.00	75.00	85.00	125.00
		11	40.00	75.00	85.00	125.00
		12	40.00	75.00	85.00	125.00
		13	—	Reported, not confirmed		
		14	40.00	75.00	85.00	125.00
		15	40.00	75.00	85.00	125.00

Rumi Series

Characterized by a flower to right of tughra and an ornamental border, consisting of a wavy line hexagon, on both sides.

1/2 RUMI ALTIN

GOLD, 1.20 g

KM#	Date	Year	VG	Fine	VF	XF
612	AH1223	10	75.00	100.00	125.00	175.00
(C212)		11	75.00	100.00	125.00	175.00
		12	75.00	100.00	125.00	175.00
		13	75.00	100.00	125.00	175.00

Mintname: Constantinople

RUMI ALTIN

GOLD, 2.40 g
Mintname: Constantinople

613	AH1223	10	200.00	250.00	300.00	350.00
(C213)						

2 RUMI ALTIN

GOLD, 4.70-4.80 g
Mintname: Constantinople

614	AH1223	8	80.00	100.00	125.00	200.00
(C214)		9	80.00	100.00	125.00	200.00
		10	80.00	100.00	125.00	200.00
		11	80.00	100.00	125.00	200.00
		12	80.00	100.00	125.00	200.00
		13	80.00	100.00	125.00	200.00
		22	80.00	125.00	150.00	225.00

New Rumi Series

Similar to the Rumi series, except that the wavy borders are replaced by an inscription containing the name and titles of Mahmud II.

RUMI ALTIN

GOLD, 23mm, 2.40 g
Mintname: Constantinople

616	AH1223	9	—	Reported, not confirmed		
(C215)		10	40.00	50.00	90.00	120.00
		11	40.00	50.00	90.00	120.00
		12	40.00	50.00	90.00	120.00
		13	40.00	50.00	90.00	120.00
		14	40.00	50.00	90.00	120.00
		15	40.00	50.00	90.00	120.00

2 RUMI ALTIN

GOLD, 4.70-4.80 g
Mintname: Constantinople

617	AH1223	9	100.00	125.00	150.00	200.00
(C217)		10	100.00	125.00	150.00	200.00
		11	100.00	125.00	150.00	200.00
		12	100.00	125.00	150.00	200.00

Surre Series

'Surre' means a purse, the amount sent by the Sultan annually to the Hejaz for the holy cities. They were used by pilgrims to Mecca. They bear the mint name *Darulhilafe* in place of *Constantinople*, with either of two epithets, *El-Aliye* (the Lofty) or *Es-Seniye* (the Sublime) and are therefore known as Elaliye and Esseniye Altins, respectively.

El-Allye Surre Series

1/4 SURRE ALTIN

GOLD, 0.48 g
Mintname: Darulhilafe

619	AH1223	15	30.00	50.00	100.00	150.00
(C219a)		16	30.00	50.00	100.00	150.00

1/2 SURRE ALTIN

GOLD, 15-16mm, 0.78 g
Mintname: Darulhilafe

KM#	Date	Year	VG	Fine	VF	XF
620	AH1223	15	40.00	60.00	150.00	250.00
(C220a)		16	40.00	60.00	150.00	250.00

SURRE ALTIN

GOLD, 1.56 g
Mintname: Darulhilafe

621	AH1223	15	60.00	85.00	110.00	150.00
(C221a)		16	60.00	85.00	110.00	150.00

Esseniye Surre Series

1/4 SURRE ALTIN

GOLD, 0.48 g
Mintname: Darulhilafe

623	AH1223	15	30.00	45.00	100.00	150.00
(C219)						

1/2 SURRE ALTIN

GOLD, 0.78 g
Mintname: Darulhilafe

624	AH1223	15	50.00	75.00	200.00	300.00
(C220)						

SURRE ALTIN

GOLD, 1.50 g
Mintname: Darulhilafe

625	AH1223	15	60.00	90.00	150.00	225.00
(C221)						

Additional Series

The following type does not fit into any of the recognized series.

1/4 ALTIN

GOLD, 14mm, 0.58 g
Considered a 1/4 Zeri Mahbub.
Azze Nasaru above mint name: *Constantinople*.

627	AH1223	13	15.00	20.00	40.00	60.00
(C218a)		14	15.00	20.00	40.00	60.00
		15	15.00	20.00	40.00	60.00

Adli Series

Types as the Zeri Mahbub series, except that the word *Adli* replaces the flower to right of tughra.

1/4 ADLI ALTIN

GOLD, 0.40-0.45 g
Mintname: Constantinople

629	AH1223	16	20.00	30.00	75.00	125.00
(C219b)		17	20.00	30.00	75.00	125.00

1/2 ADLI ALTIN

GOLD, 0.75-0.85 g
Mintname: Constantinople

KM#	Date	Year	VG	Fine	VF	XF
630	AH1223	15	45.00	60.00	75.00	90.00
(C209a)		16	—	Reported, not confirmed		
		17	45.00	60.00	75.00	90.00
		18	45.00	60.00	75.00	90.00
		19	45.00	60.00	75.00	90.00
		20	45.00	60.00	75.00	90.00
		21	45.00	60.00	75.00	90.00
		22	45.00	60.00	75.00	90.00
		23	45.00	60.00	75.00	90.00
		24	—	Reported, not confirmed		
		25	45.00	60.00	75.00	90.00
		26	—	Reported, not confirmed		
		27	45.00	60.00	75.00	90.00
		28	—	Reported, not confirmed		
		29	45.00	60.00	75.00	90.00
		30	45.00	60.00	75.00	90.00
		31	45.00	60.00	75.00	90.00

ADLI ALTIN

GOLD, 1.50-1.60 g
Mintname: Constantinople

631	AH1223	15	30.00	40.00	100.00	130.00
(C210a)		17	30.00	40.00	100.00	130.00
		18	30.00	40.00	100.00	130.00
		19	30.00	40.00	100.00	130.00
		20	30.00	40.00	100.00	130.00

New Adli Series

Tughra on obverse, mint and date on reverse. Additional legends around, obverse and reverse.

1/4 NEW ADLI ALTIN

GOLD, 0.38-0.43 g
Mintname: Constantinople

633	AH1223	15	10.00	20.00	30.00	45.00
(C228)		17	10.00	20.00	30.00	45.00
		18	10.00	20.00	30.00	45.00
		19	10.00	20.00	30.00	45.00
		20	10.00	20.00	30.00	45.00
		21	10.00	20.00	30.00	45.00
		22	10.00	20.00	30.00	45.00
		23	10.00	20.00	30.00	45.00
		24	10.00	20.00	40.00	55.00

1/2 NEW ADLI ALTIN

GOLD, 0.78 g
Mintname: Constantinople

634	AH1223	16	30.00	40.00	50.00	75.00
(C229)		17	30.00	40.00	50.00	75.00
		18	30.00	40.00	50.00	75.00
		19	30.00	40.00	50.00	75.00
		20	30.00	40.00	50.00	75.00
		21	—	Reported, not confirmed		

NEW ADLI ALTIN

GOLD, 1.58 g
Mintname: Constantinople

635	AH1223	16	27.50	40.00	60.00	80.00
(C230)		17	27.50	40.00	60.00	80.00
		18	27.50	40.00	60.00	80.00
		19	27.50	40.00	60.00	80.00
		20	27.50	40.00	60.00	80.00
		21	—	Reported, not confirmed		
		22	—	Reported, not confirmed		

Hayriye Series

Similar to the New Adli, but in place of the ring of legend

TURKEY 1655

around the edge, there are alternating ovals of inscription and branches.

1/2 HAYRIYE ALTIN

GOLD, 0.86 g
Mintname: *Constantinople*

KM#	Date	Year	VG	Fine	VF	XF
637 (C232)	AH1223	21	25.00	35.00	45.00	65.00
		22	25.00	35.00	45.00	65.00
		23	25.00	35.00	45.00	65.00
		24	25.00	35.00	45.00	65.00
		25	25.00	35.00	45.00	65.00
		26	25.00	35.00	45.00	65.00

HAYRIYE ALTIN

GOLD, 1.73 g
Mintname: *Constantinople*

638 (C233)	AH1223	21	30.00	35.00	45.00	90.00
		22	30.00	35.00	45.00	90.00
		23	30.00	35.00	45.00	90.00
		24	30.00	35.00	45.00	90.00
		25	30.00	35.00	45.00	90.00
		26	— Reported, not confirmed			

2 HAYRIYE ALTIN

GOLD, 3.55 g
Mintname: *Constantinople*

639 (C234)	AH1223	21	100.00	125.00	150.00	200.00

New (Yeni) Series

The Yeni or new series comprises but one denomination, distinguished by starlike wavy pattern around edge.

1/4 NEW ALTIN
Yeni Rubiye

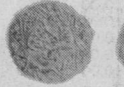

GOLD, 12mm, 0.26-0.31 g
Mintname: *Constantinople*

641 (C237)	AH1223	24	15.00	25.00	40.00	55.00
		25	15.00	25.00	40.00	55.00
		26	15.00	25.00	40.00	55.00
		27	15.00	25.00	40.00	55.00
		28	15.00	25.00	40.00	55.00
		29	— Reported, not confirmed			
		30	17.50	22.50	25.00	30.00

Cedid Mahmudiye Series

Like the Hayriye, but ovals of inscription and branches replaced by a wreath design.

1/4 CEDID MAHMUDIYE

GOLD, 0.38-0.40 g
Mintname: *Constantinople*

643 (C239)	AH1223	26	15.00	25.00	35.00	45.00
		27	15.00	25.00	35.00	45.00
		28	15.00	25.00	35.00	45.00
		29	15.00	25.00	35.00	45.00
		30	15.00	25.00	35.00	45.00
		31	15.00	25.00	35.00	45.00
		32	15.00	25.00	35.00	45.00

1/2 CEDID MAHMUDIYE

GOLD, 0.76-0.80 g
Mintname: *Constantinople*

KM#	Date	Year	VG	Fine	VF	XF
644 (C240)	AH1223	26	20.00	30.00	50.00	75.00
		27	20.00	30.00	50.00	75.00
		28	20.00	30.00	50.00	75.00
		29	20.00	30.00	50.00	75.00
		30	20.00	30.00	50.00	75.00
		31	20.00	30.00	50.00	75.00
		32	20.00	30.00	50.00	75.00

CEDID MAHMUDIYE

GOLD, 1.58-1.60 g
Mintname: *Constantinople*

645 (C241)	AH1223	26	30.00	40.00	70.00	85.00
		27	30.00	40.00	70.00	85.00
		28	30.00	40.00	70.00	85.00
		29	30.00	40.00	70.00	85.00
		30	30.00	40.00	70.00	85.00
		31	30.00	40.00	70.00	85.00
		32	30.00	40.00	70.00	85.00

Mint Visit Coinage

Mahmud II's visit to Edirne.

ادرنة

Edirne Mint mark:

1/2 HAYRIYE ALTIN

GOLD, 0.88 g
Mintname: *Edirne*

647 (C232a)	AH1223	24	60.00	100.00	150.00	250.00

1 HAYRIYE ALTIN

GOLD, 1.80 g
Mintname: *Edirne*

648 (C233a)	AH1223	24	100.00	120.00	150.00	200.00

2 HAYRIYE ALTIN

GOLD, 3.55 g
Mintname: *Edirne*

649 (C234a)	AH1223	24	175.00	225.00	275.00	350.00

ADBUL MEJID
AH1255-1277 / 1839-1861AD

Standard, fineness, and denominations of the silver coinage similar to the ninth (for the 1, 10, and 20 Para) and tenth (for the 1-1/2, 3, and 6 Piastres) series of Muhmud II (C#202-204, 206-208).

Pre-Reform Coinage
PARA

BILLON, 0.14-0.20 g
Mintname: *Constantinople*

651 (C265)	AH1255	1	1.50	2.25	3.00	5.00
		2	1.50	2.25	3.00	5.00
		3	2.50	4.00	5.00	7.50

KM# (C265)	Date	Year	VG	Fine	VF	XF
		4	1.50	2.25	3.00	5.00
		5	1.50	2.25	3.00	5.00
		6	7.50	10.00	15.00	20.00

10 PARA

BILLON, 0.60-0.80 g
Mintname: *Constantinople*

652 (C266)	AH1255	1	2.00	3.00	4.00	7.50
		2	2.00	3.00	4.00	7.50
		3	3.00	4.00	5.00	8.00
		4	2.00	3.00	4.00	7.50
		5	2.00	3.00	4.00	7.50

20 PARA

BILLON, 1.35-1.60 g
Mintname: *Constantinople*

653 (C267)	AH1255	1	.50	1.00	2.50	4.00
		2	1.50	2.50	4.00	7.50
		3	1.50	2.50	4.00	7.50
		4	1.00	2.00	3.50	5.00
		5	2.00	3.00	5.00	9.00

1-1/2 PIASTRES

SILVER, 2.60-3.00 g
Mintname: *Constantinople*

654 (C269)	AH1255	1	6.00	8.50	13.00	19.00
		2	5.00	6.50	12.00	18.00
		3	7.00	9.00	14.00	20.00
		4	5.00	6.50	12.00	18.00
		5	5.00	6.50	12.00	18.00

3 PIASTRES

SILVER, 5.60-6.20 g
Mintname: *Constantinople*

655 (C270)	AH1255	1	20.00	32.50	60.00	80.00
		2	45.00	75.00	100.00	150.00
		3	100.00	200.00	275.00	350.00
		4	100.00	200.00	275.00	350.00

6 PIASTRES

SILVER, 12.42-13.00 g
Mintname: *Constantinople*

656 (C271)	AH1255	1	40.00	50.00	75.00	150.00
		2	80.00	120.00	200.00	325.00

1/4 MEMDUHIYE ALTIN

GOLD, 0.38-0.40 g
Mintname: *Constantinople*

657 (C273)	AH1255	1	17.50	25.00	35.00	55.00
		2	17.50	25.00	35.00	55.00
		3	17.50	25.00	35.00	55.00
		4	17.50	25.00	35.00	55.00
		5	17.50	25.00	35.00	55.00

1/2 MEMDUHIYE ALTIN

GOLD, 0.78-0.80 g
Mintname: *Constantinople*

KM#	Date	Year	VG	Fine	VF	XF
658	AH1255	1	40.00	50.00	60.00	80.00
(C274)		2	40.00	50.00	60.00	80.00
		3	40.00	50.00	60.00	80.00
		4	40.00	50.00	60.00	80.00
		5	40.00	50.00	60.00	80.00

MEMDUHIYE ALTIN

GOLD, 1.58-1.60 g
Mintname: *Constantinople*

KM#	Date	Year	VG	Fine	VF	XF
659	AH1255	1	45.00	55.00	75.00	150.00
(C275)		2	45.00	55.00	75.00	150.00
		3	45.00	55.00	75.00	150.00
		4	45.00	55.00	75.00	150.00
		5	45.00	55.00	75.00	150.00

NOTE: The Memduhiye issue of Abdul Mejid was of the same fineness, weight and diameter as the Mahmudiye issue of Mahmud II. Although officially valued at 20 Piastres, the actual value of the Memduhiye Altin varied with the relative prices of gold and silver.

1/2 ZERI MAHBUB

GOLD, 0.80 g
Rev: Four-line inscription, mintname: *Constantinople*.

KM#	Date	Year	VG	Fine	VF	XF
660	AH1255	1	45.00	60.00	75.00	100.00
(C278)		2	45.00	60.00	75.00	100.00
		3	45.00	60.00	75.00	100.00
		4	45.00	60.00	75.00	100.00
		5	45.00	60.00	75.00	100.00
		6	75.00	100.00	120.00	200.00

Modern Coinage
MONETARY SYSTEM
1844-1923
40 Para = 1 Piastre (Kurus)
100 Piastres = 1 Pound (Lira)

NOTE: The 20 Piastre coin was known as a Mecidi, after the name of Abdul Mejid, who established the currency reform in 1844. The entire series is sometimes called Mejidiye coinage.

PARA

COPPER
Accession date: AH1255
Mintname: *Constantinople*
Thick planchet, 1.00-1.10 g

KM#	Year	Mintage	VG	Fine	VF	XF
665.1	8	1.000	2.00	4.00	10.00	20.00
(C282)	9	.375	5.00	10.00	30.00	50.00
	10	1.250	3.00	5.00	12.00	25.00
	11	.165	2.00	4.00	8.00	15.00
	12	1.600	2.00	4.00	8.00	15.00
	13	.800	2.00	3.00	6.00	12.00
	14	.300	4.00	6.00	15.00	25.00
	15	.700	3.00	6.00	12.00	20.00
	16	3.400	3.00	6.00	12.00	20.00

Medium planchet, 0.80-0.90 g

665.2	16	Inc. Ab.	.50	1.00	1.75	5.00
(C282a)	17	.800	1.00	3.00	6.00	10.00
	18	4.500	.75	1.50	2.50	5.00

Thin planchet, 0.50-0.60 g

665.3	18	Inc. Ab.	.50	1.00	2.50	5.00
(C282b)	19	2.500	.25	.50	1.25	2.50
	21	—	10.00	20.00	45.00	70.00

NOTE: The thin planchet coin of "year 16" is actually year 19 with broken 9.

5 PARA

COPPER
Accession date: AH1255
Mintname: *Constantinople*
Thick planchet, 4.90-6.80 g

KM#	Year	Mintage	VG	Fine	VF	XF
666.1	7	—	7.50	15.00	20.00	50.00
(C283)	8	1.000	1.00	2.00	7.50	15.00
	9	.300	10.00	20.00	50.00	100.00
	10	.800	1.50	3.00	6.00	15.00
	11	2.542	1.50	3.00	6.00	15.00
	12	3.680	.75	1.25	5.00	15.00
	13	4.640	.75	1.25	5.00	15.00
	14	3.400	.75	1.25	8.00	25.00
	15	5.060	.75	1.25	8.00	25.00

Medium planchet, 3.70-4.20 g

666.2	15	Inc. Ab.	2.00	4.00	20.00	40.00
(C283a)	16	6.300	.50	1.00	2.00	10.00
	17	6.500	.50	1.00	2.00	10.00

Thin planchet, 2.50-3.30 g

666.3	18	2.000	1.25	2.75	15.00	25.00
(C283b)	19	9.300	.50	1.00	2.00	10.00
	20	10.060	.50	1.00	2.00	10.00
	21	6.200	.50	1.00	2.00	10.00

10 PARA

COPPER
Accession date: AH1255
Mintname: *Constantinople*
Thick planchet, 9.00-12.80 g

667.1	15	.750	5.00	15.00	30.00	75.00
(C284)						

Medium planchet, 7.50-8.20 g

667.2	16	9.120	.75	1.50	3.75	12.00
(C284a)	17	9.110	.75	1.50	3.75	12.00
	18	1.900	1.25	2.50	5.00	15.00

Thin planchet, 4.90-5.70 g

667.3	17	Inc. Ab.	2.50	5.00	6.50	15.00
(C284b)	18	Inc. Ab.	1.25	2.50	5.00	15.00
	19	33.600	.35	.75	2.00	12.00
	20	20.800	.35	.75	2.00	12.00
	21	7.500	.35	.75	2.00	12.00

20 PARA

COPPER
Accession date: AH1255
Mintname: *Constantinople*
Thick planchet, 14.00-16.00 g

668.1	16	4.350	1.25	2.50	5.00	15.00
(C285)	17	2.050	2.00	4.00	7.50	20.00

Thin planchet, 10.00-11.00 g

668.2	17	Inc. Ab.	1.00	2.00	4.50	15.00
(C285a)	19	1.200	1.00	2.00	4.50	15.00
	20	3.000	1.00	2.00	4.50	15.00
	21	8.400	.50	1.00	3.00	15.00

0.6013 g, .830 SILVER, .0160 oz ASW
Mintname: *Constantinople*

669	9	.400	4.50	10.00	35.00	75.00
(C287)	10	.910	2.50	5.00	15.00	25.00
	11	.390	2.00	4.00	15.00	25.00
	12	.270	3.75	7.50	20.00	35.00
	13	.230	4.50	9.00	40.00	75.00
	14	.180	3.75	7.50	20.00	35.00
	15	.240	3.75	7.50	15.00	25.00

KM#	Year	Mintage	VG	Fine	VF	XF
(C287)	16	.270	2.50	5.00	15.00	25.00
	17	.170	2.50	5.00	20.00	35.00
	18	.260	2.00	4.00	15.00	35.00
	19	.900	2.00	4.25	20.00	35.00
	20	.150	2.00	4.25	15.00	25.00
	21	.250	4.25	8.50	15.00	25.00
	22	.190	4.25	8.50	15.00	25.00
	23	.620	25.00	50.00	150.00	250.00

40 PARA

COPPER
Accession date: AH1255
Mintname: *Constantinople*

670	17	1.450	2.50	5.00	7.50	25.00
(C286)	17	—	—	Proof	—	—
	18	3.950	1.50	3.25	8.00	25.00
	19	11.3000	1.25	2.50	6.50	25.00
	20	14.030	1.25	2.50	6.50	25.00
	21	9.300	1.25	2.50	6.50	25.00
	22	4.140	2.50	5.00	10.00	30.00
	23	—	50.00	75.00	100.00	150.00

PIASTRE

1.2027 g, .830 SILVER, .0321 oz ASW
Accession date: AH1255
Mintname: *Constantinople*

671	6	—	20.00	30.00	50.00	100.00
(C288)	7	.650	1.00	2.00	6.00	12.00
	8	1.420	1.00	2.00	6.00	12.00
	9	.910	1.00	2.00	6.00	12.00
	10	.970	1.00	2.50	7.00	15.00
	11	1.040	1.00	2.50	7.00	15.00
	12	1.100	1.00	2.50	7.00	15.00
	13	.820	1.00	2.50	7.00	15.00
	14	.790	1.00	2.50	7.00	15.00
	15	.960	1.00	3.00	8.00	20.00
	16	1.220	1.00	2.50	7.00	15.00
	17	.810	1.50	4.00	10.00	25.00
	18	.720	1.50	4.00	10.00	25.00
	19	2.270	1.00	3.00	8.00	20.00
	20	1.165	1.00	3.00	8.00	20.00
	21	1.405	1.00	3.00	7.00	15.00
	22	.825	1.00	3.00	8.00	20.00
	23	.755	5.00	10.00	20.00	50.00

2 PIASTRES

2.4055 g, .830 SILVER, .0642 oz ASW
Accession date: AH1255
Mintname: *Constantinople*

672	7	1.035	1.00	2.00	6.00	12.00
(C289)	8	1.150	1.00	2.00	6.00	12.00
	9	.530	1.00	3.00	8.00	20.00
	10	.543	1.50	4.00	10.00	25.00
	11	.695	1.50	4.00	10.00	20.00
	12	.685	1.50	5.00	12.00	25.00
	13	.540	1.50	5.00	12.00	25.00
	14	.280	2.00	7.00	15.00	30.00
	15	.300	1.50	5.00	12.00	25.00
	16	.510	1.50	5.00	12.00	25.00
	19	.275	15.00	30.00	50.00	100.00
	20	.105	12.00	25.00	40.00	85.00
	21	—	—	—	Rare	—

5 PIASTRES

6.0130 g, .830 SILVER, .1605 oz ASW
Accession date: AH1255
Mintname: *Constantinople*

673	6	1.347	2.00	4.00	10.00	20.00
(C290)	7	2.612	2.00	4.00	10.00	20.00

TURKEY 1657

TURKEY 1658

KM#	Year	Mintage	VG	Fine	VF	XF
(C290)	8	.362	2.00	4.00	10.00	20.00
	9	.240	2.00	4.00	10.00	20.00
	10	.252	3.00	6.00	15.00	35.00
	11	.314	2.50	4.50	12.00	30.00
	12	.452	2.50	4.50	12.00	30.00
	13	.498	2.50	4.50	12.00	30.00
	14	.354	2.50	4.50	12.00	30.00
	15	.680	2.00	4.00	10.00	20.00
	16	.972	2.00	4.00	10.00	20.00
	17	.206	2.50	4.50	12.00	30.00
	18	.218	2.50	4.50	12.00	30.00
	19	.384	2.50	4.50	12.00	30.00
	20	.310	2.50	4.50	12.00	30.00
	21	.324	2.50	4.50	12.00	30.00
	22	.214	2.50	4.50	12.00	30.00
	23	.120	5.00	10.00	20.00	45.00

10 PIASTRES

12.0270 g, .830 SILVER, .3210 oz ASW
Accession date: AH1255
Mintname: *Constantinople*

KM#	Year	Mintage	VG	Fine	VF	XF
674	6	.338	15.00	35.00	75.00	135.00
(C291)	7	.012	200.00	350.00	500.00	750.00
	9	—	—	—	Rare	7500.
	13	—	—	—	Rare	7500.

20 PIASTRES

24.0550 g, .830 SILVER, .6419 oz ASW
Accession date: AH1255
Mintname: *Constantinople*
Rev: Small inscription.

KM#	Year	Mintage	VG	Fine	VF	XF
675	6	2.013	6.00	12.00	20.00	45.00
(C292)	7	.740	6.00	12.00	20.00	45.00
	8	1.671	6.00	12.00	20.00	45.00
	9	3.125	6.00	10.00	18.00	40.00
	10	1.020	6.00	12.00	20.00	45.00
	11	.815	6.00	12.00	20.00	45.00
	12	.684	6.00	12.00	20.00	45.00
	13	.485	6.00	12.00	20.00	45.00
	14	.633	6.00	12.00	20.00	45.00
	15	.797	6.00	12.00	20.00	45.00

Rev: Large inscription.

676	8	Inc. Ab.	—	—	—	—
(C292a)	15	Inc. Ab.	6.00	12.00	20.00	45.00
	16	.320	6.00	12.00	20.00	45.00
	17	.410	8.00	15.00	30.00	55.00
	18	.340	10.00	20.00	35.00	70.00
	19	.201	40.00	75.00	125.00	200.00
	20	.103	10.00	20.00	35.00	75.00
	21	.513	8.00	15.00	30.00	60.00
	22	.624	8.00	15.00	30.00	60.00
	23	.317	10.00	20.00	40.00	75.00

25 PIASTRES

1.8040 g, .917 GOLD, .0532 oz AGW
Accession date: AH1255
Mintname: *Constantinople*

KM#	Year	Mintage	VG	Fine	VF	XF
677	17	—	30.00	40.00	75.00	125.00
(C295)	18	—	30.00	40.00	75.00	125.00
	19	—	30.00	40.00	75.00	125.00
	20	—	30.00	40.00	75.00	125.00
	21	—	30.00	40.00	75.00	125.00
	22	—	30.00	40.00	75.00	125.00
	23	—	30.00	40.00	75.00	125.00

50 PIASTRES

3.6080 g, .917 GOLD, .1064 oz AGW
Accession date: AH1255

Mintname: *Constantinople*

KM#	Year	Mintage	VG	Fine	VF	XF
678	6	—	BV	60.00	80.00	120.00
(C296)	7	—	BV	60.00	80.00	120.00
	8	—	BV	60.00	80.00	120.00
	9	—	BV	60.00	80.00	120.00
	10	—	BV	60.00	80.00	120.00
	11	—	BV	60.00	80.00	120.00
	12	—	BV	60.00	80.00	120.00
	13	—	BV	60.00	80.00	120.00
	15	—	BV	60.00	80.00	120.00
	16	—	BV	60.00	80.00	120.00
	17	—	BV	60.00	80.00	120.00
	20	—	BV	60.00	80.00	120.00
	22	—	BV	60.00	80.00	120.00

100 PIASTRES

7.2160 g, .917 GOLD, .2128 oz AGW
Accession date: AH1255
Mintname: *Constantinople*

679	5	—	—	BV	110.00	125.00
(C297)	6	—	—	BV	110.00	125.00
	7	—	—	BV	110.00	125.00
	8	—	—	BV	110.00	125.00
	9	—	—	BV	110.00	125.00
	10	—	—	BV	110.00	125.00
	11	—	—	BV	110.00	125.00
	12	—	—	BV	110.00	125.00
	13	—	—	BV	110.00	125.00
	14	—	—	BV	110.00	125.00
	15	—	—	BV	110.00	125.00
	16	—	—	BV	110.00	125.00
	17	—	—	BV	110.00	125.00
	18	—	—	BV	110.00	125.00
	19	—	—	BV	110.00	125.00
	20	—	—	BV	110.00	125.00
	21	—	—	BV	110.00	125.00
	22	—	—	BV	110.00	125.00
	23	—	—	BV	110.00	125.00

250 PIASTRES

18.0400 g, .917 GOLD, .5319 oz AGW
Accession date: AH1255
Mintname: *Constantinople*

680	7	—	250.00	275.00	450.00	650.00
(C298)	9	—	250.00	275.00	450.00	650.00
	18	—	250.00	275.00	450.00	650.00
	22	—	250.00	275.00	450.00	650.00

500 PIASTRES

36.0800 g, .917 GOLD, 1.0638 oz AGW
Accession date: AH1255
Mintname: *Constantinople*

681	6	—	BV	525.00	750.00	1100.
(C299)	18	—	BV	525.00	750.00	1100.
	20	—	BV	525.00	750.00	1100.
	22	—	BV	525.00	750.00	1100.

Mint Visit Coinage
Abdul Mejid's visit to Edirne.

ادرنة

Edirne Mint mark

50 PIASTRES

3.6080 g, .917 GOLD, .1064 oz AGW
Accession date: AH1255
Mintname: *Edirne*

KM#	Year	Mintage	Fine	VF	XF	Unc
682 (C300)	8	.010	250.00	400.00	650.00	1250.

100 PIASTRES

7.2160 g, .917 GOLD, .2128 oz AGW
Accession date: AH1255
Mintname: *Edirne*

683	8	.010	300.00	600.00	800.00	1500.
(C301)						

ABDUL AZIZ
AH1277-1293/1861-1876AD

5 PARA

COPPER
Accession date: AH1277
Mintname: *Constantinople*

KM#	Year	Mintage	VG	Fine	VF	XF
685 (Y1)	1	—	2.25	5.00	12.50	20.00

699 (Y4)	4	16.000	.50	1.00	3.00	10.00

10 PARA

COPPER
Accession date: AH1277
Mintname: *Constantinople*

686 (Y2)	1	—	3.00	4.00	10.00	20.00

700 (Y5)	4	8.000	.50	1.00	3.00	10.00
	4				Proof	125.00

20 PARA

COPPER
Accession date: AH1277
Mintname: *Constantinople*

687 (Y3)	1	—	4.00	5.00	12.00	22.50

701 (Y6)	4	4.000	.35	1.00	2.50	10.00
	4				Proof	150.00

TURKEY 1659

0.6013 g, .830 SILVER, .0160 oz ASW

KM#	Year	Mintage	VG	Fine	VF	XF
688	1	.420	3.00	5.00	10.00	20.00
(Y8)	2	.850	3.00	5.00	10.00	20.00
	3	1.570	3.00	5.00	10.00	20.00
	4	.930	20.00	40.00	75.00	125.00
	5	.740	3.00	5.00	10.00	20.00
	6	.520	4.00	8.00	15.00	35.00
	7	.350	6.00	12.00	25.00	50.00

40 PARA

COPPER
Accession date: AH1277
Mintname: *Constantinople*

702	4	2.000	2.00	3.00	10.00	25.00
(Y7)						

PIASTRE

1.2027 g, .830 SILVER, .0321 oz ASW
Accession date: AH1277
Mintname: *Constantinople*

689	1	.545	2.00	3.00	10.00	25.00
(Y9)	2	2.245	2.00	3.00	7.50	20.00
	3	1.370	2.00	3.00	7.50	20.00
	4	.900	2.00	3.00	7.50	20.00
	5	.685	2.00	3.00	7.50	20.00
	7	.535	20.00	40.00	75.00	150.00

2 PIASTRES

2.4055 g, .830 SILVER, .0642 oz ASW
Accession date: AH1277
Mintname: *Constantinople*

690	1	.055	25.00	50.00	100.00	200.00
(Y10)	2	.065	30.00	60.00	125.00	250.00
	3	.235	20.00	35.00	75.00	125.00
	5	.135	40.00	75.00	125.00	250.00
	5	—	—	—	Proof	1500.

5 PIASTRES

6.0130 g, .830 SILVER, .1605 oz ASW
Accession date: AH1277
Mintname: *Constantinople*

691	1	.016	2.50	4.00	8.50	20.00
(Y11)	2	.280	2.50	4.00	8.50	20.00
	3	.288	2.50	4.00	8.50	20.00
	4	.280	2.50	4.00	8.50	20.00
	5	.242	2.50	4.00	8.50	20.00
	6	.342	2.50	4.00	8.50	20.00
	7	.248	2.50	4.00	8.50	20.00
	8	.020	40.00	70.00	120.00	225.00
	9	.050	2.50	4.00	8.50	20.00
	10	.230	2.50	4.00	8.50	20.00
	11	.126	2.50	4.00	8.50	20.00
	12	.186	2.50	4.00	8.50	20.00
	13	.284	2.50	4.00	8.50	20.00
	14	.202	2.50	4.00	8.50	20.00
	15	.154	4.00	8.00	12.00	30.00

10 PIASTRES

12.0270 g, .830 SILVER, .3210 oz ASW
Accession date: AH1277
Mintname: *Constantinople*

692	1	—	17.50	35.00	75.00	150.00
(Y12)	2	.280	35.00	75.00	135.00	300.00
	5	—	—	—	Proof	6000.

20 PIASTRES

24.0550 g, .830 SILVER, .6419 oz ASW
Accession date: AH1277
Mintname: *Constantinople*
Rev: Similar to Y#22.

KM#	Year	Mintage	VG	Fine	VF	XF
693	1	1.055	6.00	10.00	20.00	40.00
(Y13)	2	3.106	6.00	10.00	20.00	40.00
	3	.257	6.00	10.00	20.00	40.00
	4	.234	12.00	25.00	50.00	100.00
	5	.387	6.00	10.00	20.00	40.00
	6	.314	6.00	10.00	20.00	40.00
	7	.640	6.00	10.00	20.00	40.00
	8	1.457	6.00	10.00	20.00	40.00
	9	.859	6.00	10.00	20.00	40.00
	10	.528	6.00	10.00	20.00	40.00
	11	.530	6.00	10.00	20.00	40.00
	12	.233	6.00	10.00	20.00	40.00
	12	—	—	—	Proof	1000.
	13	.514	6.00	10.00	20.00	40.00
	14	.584	6.00	10.00	20.00	40.00
	15	4.034	6.00	10.00	20.00	40.00

25 PIASTRES

1.8040 g, .917 GOLD, .0532 oz AGW
Accession date: AH1277
Mintname: *Constantinople*

694	1	.052	27.50	32.50	40.00	60.00
(Y16)	2	.086	27.50	32.50	40.00	60.00
	3	.089	27.50	32.50	40.00	60.00
	4	.069	27.50	32.50	40.00	60.00
	5	.067	27.50	32.50	40.00	60.00
	6	.073	27.50	32.50	40.00	60.00
	7	.080	27.50	32.50	40.00	60.00
	8	.036	27.50	32.50	40.00	60.00
	9	.113	27.50	32.50	40.00	60.00
	10	.064	27.50	32.50	40.00	60.00
	11	.065	27.50	32.50	40.00	60.00
	12	.122	27.50	32.50	40.00	60.00
	13	.094	27.50	32.50	40.00	60.00
	14	.058	27.50	32.50	40.00	60.00
	15	.017	32.50	45.00	60.00	100.00

50 PIASTRES

3.6080 g, .917 GOLD, .1064 oz AGW
Accession date: AH1277
Mintname: *Constantinople*

695	1	5,800	65.00	125.00	200.00	300.00
(Y-A16)	2	—	65.00	125.00	200.00	300.00
	3	—	65.00	125.00	200.00	300.00
	7	2.000	65.00	125.00	200.00	300.00
	8	2.000	65.00	125.00	200.00	300.00
	9	.025	60.00	85.00	150.00	250.00

100 PIASTRES

7.2160 g, .917 GOLD, .2128 oz AGW
Accession date: AH1277
Mintname: *Constantinople*

696	1	2.347	—	BV	110.00	125.00
(Y17)	2	3.129	—	BV	110.00	125.00
	3	.478	—	BV	110.00	125.00
	4	.628	—	BV	110.00	125.00
	5	.561	—	BV	110.00	125.00
	6	.330	—	BV	110.00	125.00
	7	1.491	—	BV	110.00	125.00
	8	.495	—	BV	110.00	125.00
	9	1.570	—	BV	110.00	125.00
	10	.304	—	BV	110.00	125.00
	11	.866	—	BV	110.00	125.00
	12	.372	—	BV	110.00	125.00
	13	.246	—	BV	110.00	125.00
	14	.286	—	BV	110.00	125.00
	15	3,600	110.00	120.00	160.00	200.00

250 PIASTRES

18.0400 g, .917 GOLD, .5319 oz AGW
Accession date: AH1277

Mintname: *Constantinople*

KM#	Year	Mintage	VG	Fine	VF	XF
697	1	3,040	325.00	425.00	800.00	1250.
(Y-A17)	2	360 pcs.	—	—	Rare	—
	4	480 pcs.	—	—	Rare	—
	5	—	325.00	425.00	800.00	1250.
	7	2,800	300.00	400.00	600.00	1000.
	8	.030	250.00	325.00	500.00	700.00
	9	8,000	250.00	350.00	500.00	700.00

500 PIASTRES

36.0800 g, .917 GOLD, 1.0638 oz AGW
Accession date: AH1277
Mintname: *Constantinople*

698	1	1,520	525.00	700.00	1000.	1400.
(Y-B17)	2	1,660	525.00	700.00	1000.	1400.
	3	680 pcs.	600.00	800.00	1250.	1750.
	4	900 pcs.	600.00	800.00	1250.	1750.
	5	—	600.00	800.00	1250.	1750.
	6	—	600.00	800.00	1250.	1750.
	7	.021	BV	525.00	650.00	950.00
	8	.071	BV	525.00	650.00	950.00
	9	.074	BV	525.00	650.00	950.00
	10	.030	BV	525.00	650.00	950.00
	11	.036	BV	525.00	650.00	950.00
	12	—	600.00	800.00	1250.	1750.
	13	.059	BV	525.00	650.00	950.00

Mint Visit Coinage

Abdul Aziz's visit to Bursa.

بروسة

Bursa Mint mark

PIASTRE

1.2027 g, .830 SILVER, .0321 oz ASW
Accession date: AH1277
Mintname: *Bursa*

KM#	Year	Mintage	Fine	VF	XF	Unc
703	1	.040	150.00	250.00	400.00	600.00
(Y9a)						

2 PIASTRES

2.4055 g, .830 SILVER, .0642 oz ASW
Accession date: AH1277
Mintname: *Bursa*

704	1	.040	100.00	175.00	300.00	500.00
(Y10a)						

5 PIASTRES

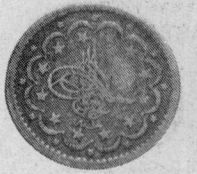 

6.0130 g, .830 SILVER, .1605 oz ASW
Accession date: AH1277
Mintname: *Bursa*

705	1	.018	125.00	200.00	350.00	600.00
(Y11a)						

25 PIASTRES

1.8040 g, .917 GOLD, .0532 oz AGW
Accession date: AH1277
Mintname: *Bursa*

706	1	4,800	150.00	300.00	450.00	650.00
(Y16a)						

50 PIASTRES

3.6080 g, .917 GOLD, .1064 oz AGW
Accession date: AH1277
Mintname: *Bursa*

TURKEY 1660

KM#	Year	Mintage	Fine	VF	XF	Unc
707 (Y-A16a)	1	2,476	200.00	400.00	650.00	1000.

100 PIASTRES

7.2160 g, .917 GOLD, .2128 oz AGW
Accession date: AH1277
Mintname: *Bursa*

| 708 (Y17a) | 1 | 9,737 | 200.00 | 350.00 | 550.00 | 900.00 |

MURAD V
AH1293/1876AD
PIASTRE

1.2027 g, .830 SILVER, .0321 oz ASW
Accession date: AH1293
Mintname: *Constantinople*
Obv: W/o flower to right of toughra.

KM#	Year	Mintage	VG	Fine	VF	XF
710 (Y18)	1	.280	75.00	125.00	175.00	275.00

5 PIASTRES

6.0130 g, .830 SILVER, .1605 oz ASW
Accession date: AH1293
Mintname: *Constantinople*
Obv: W/o flower to right of toughra.

| 711 (Y20) | 1 | .020 | 100.00 | 150.00 | 250.00 | 400.00 |

20 PIASTRES

24.0550 g, .830 SILVER, .6419 oz ASW
Accession date: AH1293
Mintname: *Constantinople*
Obv: W/o flower to right of toughra.

| 712 (Y22) | 1 | .128 | 30.00 | 50.00 | 75.00 | 125.00 |

NOTE: Beware of specimens of Y#31 altered to appear as a piece of Murad. The toughra is very different.

25 PIASTRES

1.8040 g, .917 GOLD, .0532 oz AGW
Accession date: AH1293
Mintname: *Constantinople*
Obv: W/crescent above toughra.

| 713 (Y-A22) | 1 | .014 | 100.00 | 175.00 | 300.00 | 450.00 |

50 PIASTRES

3.6080 g, .917 GOLD, .1064 oz AGW
Accession date: AH1293
Mintname: *Constantinople*

KM#	Year	Mintage	VG	Fine	VF	XF
714 (Y-B22)	1	4,500	300.00	500.00	750.00	1250.

100 PIASTRES

7.2160 g, .917 GOLD, .2128 oz AGW
Accession date: AH1293
Mintname: *Constantinople*
Obv: W/crescent above toughra.

| 715 (Y-C22) | 1 | 7,700 | BV | 110.00 | 175.00 | 250.00 |

ABDUL HAMID II
AH1293-1327/1876-1909AD
5 PARA

COPPER
Accession date: AH1293
Mintname: *Constantinople*

728 (Y23)	2	—	—	—	Rare	—
	3	—	.25	.50	3.00	10.00
	4	—	.25	.50	3.00	10.00

1.0023 g, .100 SILVER, .0032 oz ASW

743 (Y24)	25	3.336	.25	.50	1.25	4.00
	26	—	.25	.50	1.25	4.00
	27	—	.25	.50	1.25	4.00
	28	—	.50	1.00	3.00	12.00
	30	—	6.00	12.00	20.00	40.00

10 PARA

2.0046 g, .100 SILVER, .0064 oz ASW
Accession date: AH1293
Mintname: *Constantinople*

744 (Y25)	25	3.492	.15	.25	1.00	4.00
	26	—	.15	.25	1.00	4.00
	27	—	.15	.25	1.00	4.00
	28	—	.15	.25	1.50	6.00
	30	—	1.00	2.00	5.00	15.00

20 PARA

0.6013 g, .830 SILVER, .0160 oz ASW
Mintname: *Constantinople*
Accession date: AH1293

| 717 (Y26) | 1 | .110 | 25.00 | 50.00 | 100.00 | 175.00 |
| | 4 | .050 | 40.00 | 80.00 | 150.00 | 225.00 |

| 734 (Y-F31) | 8 | .350 | 5.00 | 7.50 | 15.00 | 35.00 |

PIASTRE

1.2027 g, .830 SILVER, .0321 oz ASW
Accession date: AH1293
Mintname: *Constantinople*
Obv: Flower to right of toughra.

718 (Y27)	1	.345	40.00	75.00	150.00	250.00
	2	.020	50.00	100.00	175.00	300.00
	4	.045	40.00	75.00	150.00	250.00

Obv: *El-Ghazi* to right of toughra.

KM#	Year	Mintage	VG	Fine	VF	XF
735 (Y32)	8	.210	1.00	1.75	3.50	7.00
	9	.600	.65	1.25	2.50	5.00
	11	8.830	.65	1.25	2.50	5.00
	13	.130	4.00	10.00	20.00	35.00
	16	4.000	.65	1.25	2.50	5.00
	17	6.440	.65	1.25	2.50	5.00
	18	.040	5.00	15.00	30.00	50.00
	19	3.070	.65	1.25	2.50	5.00
	20	4.122	.65	1.25	2.50	5.00
	21	.040	3.00	7.50	15.00	30.00
	22	3.979	.65	1.25	2.50	5.00
	23	3.760	.65	1.25	2.50	5.00
	24	2.041	.65	1.25	2.50	5.00
	25	.084	3.00	7.50	15.00	30.00
	26	.055	3.00	7.50	15.00	30.00
	27	9.945	.65	1.25	2.50	5.00
	28	16.139	.65	1.25	2.50	5.00
	29	7.076	.65	1.25	2.50	5.00
	30	.707	.65	1.25	2.50	5.00
	31	1.366	.65	1.25	2.50	5.00
	32	1.140	.65	1.25	2.50	5.00
	33	1.700	.65	1.25	2.50	5.00
	34	—	40.00	60.00	115.00	225.00

2 PIASTRES

2.4055 g, .830 SILVER, .0642 oz ASW
Accession date: AH1293
Mintname: *Constantinople*
Obv: Flower to right of toughra.

| 719 (Y28) | 1 | .010 | 150.00 | 300.00 | 500.00 | 800.00 |

Obv: *El-Ghazi* to right of toughra.

736 (Y33)	8	.103	2.00	2.50	5.00	10.00
	9	.605	1.75	2.75	4.50	6.50
	11	5.115	1.50	2.00	4.00	6.00
	12	.325	1.75	2.75	4.50	6.50
	13	.030	15.00	22.50	35.00	75.00
	16	.980	1.50	2.00	4.00	6.00
	17	3.736	1.50	2.00	4.00	6.00
	18	.023	15.00	25.00	35.00	75.00
	19	3.507	1.50	2.00	4.00	6.00
	20	3.370	1.50	2.00	4.00	6.00
	21	.021	15.00	25.00	35.00	75.00
	22	2.980	1.50	2.00	4.00	6.00
	23	3.139	1.50	2.00	4.00	6.00
	24	1.490	1.75	2.25	4.50	6.50
	25	.014	15.00	25.00	35.00	75.00
	26	.017	15.00	25.00	35.00	75.00
	27	4.689	1.50	2.00	4.00	6.00
	28	7.567	1.50	2.00	4.00	6.00
	29	7.775	1.50	2.00	4.00	6.00
	30	1.366	1.50	2.00	4.00	6.00
	31	3.014	1.50	2.00	4.00	6.00
	32	1.625	1.50	2.00	4.00	6.00
	33	2.173	1.50	2.00	4.00	6.00
	34	—	45.00	90.00	140.00	200.00

5 PIASTRES

6.0130 g, .830 SILVER, .1605 oz ASW
Accession date: AH1293
Mintname: *Constantinople*
Obv: Flower to right of toughra.

720 (Y29)	1	.042	50.00	100.00	150.00	250.00
	2	.014	30.00	60.00	100.00	200.00
	3	.016	10.00	20.00	35.00	75.00
	4	.269	7.50	15.00	30.00	60.00

Obv: *El-Ghazi* to right of toughra.

KM#	Year	Mintage	VG	Fine	VF	XF
737	8	.082	4.00	8.00	11.00	17.50
(Y34)	9	.614	BV	3.50	5.00	7.50
	11	1.788	BV	3.50	5.00	7.50
	12	1.880	BV	3.50	5.00	7.50
	13	2.182	BV	3.50	5.00	7.50
	14	.380	BV	3.50	5.00	7.50
	15	.194	BV	4.00	6.00	9.00
	16	.914	BV	3.50	5.00	7.50
	17	1.337	BV	3.50	5.00	7.50
	18	.012	20.00	35.00	55.00	85.00
	19	.031	10.00	20.00	35.00	60.00
	20	.162	4.00	7.50	12.00	20.00
	21	.018	15.00	30.00	45.00	75.00
	22	.008	15.00	30.00	45.00	75.00
	23	.007	15.00	30.00	45.00	75.00
	24	.126	BV	3.75	6.50	10.00
	25	.013	15.00	30.00	45.00	75.00
	26	.008	15.00	30.00	45.00	75.00
	27	.016	15.00	30.00	45.00	75.00
	28	.006	15.00	30.00	45.00	75.00
	29	.007	15.00	30.00	45.00	75.00
	30	.038	5.00	10.00	15.00	30.00
	31/30	3.175	6.00	13.00	25.00	35.00
	31	Inc. Ab.	3.50	4.50	7.00	15.00
	32	3.334	BV	3.25	4.50	7.00
	33	.907	BV	3.25	4.50	7.00
	34	—	50.00	80.00	110.00	200.00

10 PIASTRES

12.0270 g, .830 SILVER, .3210 oz ASW
Accession date: AH1293
Mintname: *Constantinople*

KM#	Year	Mintage	VG	Fine	VF	XF
721	1	.004	125.00	200.00	300.00	500.00
(Y30)	3	.005	12.50	25.00	37.50	80.00

Obv: *El Ghazi* to right of toughra.

KM#	Year	Mintage	VG	Fine	VF	XF
738	12	—	25.00	50.00	100.00	175.00
(Y35)	13	.161	5.00	10.00	20.00	40.00
	20	.034	25.00	50.00	100.00	175.00
	31	.051	20.00	40.00	75.00	125.00
	32	.575	7.50	12.50	15.00	20.00
	33	.273	6.00	10.00	12.50	15.00

12- 1/2 PIASTRES

0.8770 g, .917 GOLD, .0258 oz AGW
Accession date: AH1293
Mintname: *Constantinople*
Monnaie de Luxe

KM#	Year	Mintage	VG	Fine	VF	XF
745	25	—	40.00	70.00	100.00	125.00
(Y-A40)	26	720 pcs.	40.00	70.00	100.00	125.00
	27	—	40.00	70.00	100.00	125.00
	28	800 pcs.	40.00	70.00	100.00	125.00
	29	.012	20.00	30.00	45.00	75.00
	30	.013	20.00	30.00	45.00	75.00
	31	.024	20.00	30.00	45.00	75.00
	32	.014	20.00	30.00	45.00	75.00
	33	.013	20.00	30.00	45.00	75.00
	34	—	20.00	30.00	45.00	75.00

20 PIASTRES

24.0550 g, .830 SILVER, .6419 oz ASW
Accession date: AH1293
Mintname: *Constantinople*
Obv: Flower to right of toughra.
Rev: Similar to Y#22.

KM#	Year	Mintage	VG	Fine	VF	XF
722	1	1.402	BV	12.00	25.00	40.00
(Y31)	2	1.357	BV	12.00	20.00	35.00
	3	5.940	BV	12.00	20.00	35.00

25 PIASTRES

1.8040 g, .917 GOLD, .0532 oz AGW
Accession date: AH1293
Mintname: *Constantinople*
Obv: Flower to right of toughra.

KM#	Year	Mintage	VG	Fine	VF	XF
723	1	—	—	—	Rare	—
(Y-A31)	2	—	—		Rare	—
	3	5,000	50.00	100.00	150.00	200.00
	4	3,600	50.00	100.00	150.00	200.00
	5	—	50.00	100.00	125.00	175.00
	6	—	50.00	100.00	125.00	175.00

Obv: *El Ghazi* to right of toughra.

KM#	Year	Mintage	VG	Fine	VF	XF
729	6	—	—	—	Rare	—
(Y36)	7	—	BV	27.50	35.00	50.00
	8	—	BV	27.50	35.00	50.00
	9	—	BV	27.50	35.00	50.00
	10	—	BV	27.50	35.00	50.00
	11	—	BV	27.50	35.00	50.00
	12	—	BV	27.50	35.00	50.00
	13	—	BV	27.50	35.00	50.00
	14	—	BV	27.50	35.00	50.00
	15	—	BV	27.50	35.00	50.00
	16	—	BV	27.50	35.00	50.00
	17	—	BV	27.50	35.00	50.00
	18	—	BV	27.50	35.00	50.00
	19	—	BV	27.50	35.00	50.00
	20	—	BV	27.50	35.00	50.00
	21	—	BV	27.50	35.00	50.00
	22	—	BV	27.50	35.00	50.00
	23	—	BV	27.50	35.00	50.00
	24	—	BV	27.50	35.00	50.00
	25	.057	BV	27.50	35.00	50.00
	26	—	BV	27.50	35.00	50.00
	27	—	BV	27.50	35.00	50.00
	28	—	BV	27.50	35.00	50.00
	29	—	BV	27.50	35.00	50.00
	30	—	BV	27.50	35.00	50.00
	31	—	BV	27.50	35.00	50.00
	32	—	BV	27.50	35.00	50.00
	33	—	BV	27.50	35.00	50.00
	34	—	BV	27.50	35.00	50.00

1.7540 g, .917 GOLD, .0512 oz AGW
Monnaie de Luxe

KM#	Year	Mintage	VG	Fine	VF	XF
739	18	—	—	—	Rare	—
(Y-B40)	23	—	60.00	75.00	90.00	110.00
	24	—	60.00	75.00	90.00	110.00
	25	—	60.00	75.00	90.00	110.00
	26	—	60.00	75.00	90.00	110.00
	27	—	60.00	75.00	90.00	110.00
	28	—	60.00	75.00	90.00	110.00
	29	—	60.00	75.00	90.00	110.00
	30	—	60.00	75.00	90.00	110.00
	31	—	60.00	75.00	90.00	110.00
	32	—	60.00	75.00	90.00	110.00
	33	—	60.00	75.00	90.00	110.00
	34	—	60.00	75.00	90.00	110.00

50 PIASTRES

3.6080 g, .917 GOLD, .1064 oz AGW
Accession date: AH1293
Mintname: *Constantinople*
Obv: Flower to right of toughra.

KM#	Year	Mintage	VG	Fine	VF	XF
724	1	—	75.00	100.00	150.00	300.00
(Y-B31)	3	—	75.00	100.00	150.00	300.00
	6	—	100.00	200.00	350.00	750.00

Obv: *El Ghazi* to right of toughra.

KM#	Year	Mintage	VG	Fine	VF	XF
731	7	—	BV	60.00	70.00	100.00
(Y37)	8	—	BV	60.00	70.00	100.00
	9	—	BV	60.00	70.00	100.00
	10	—	BV	60.00	70.00	100.00
	11	—	BV	60.00	70.00	100.00
	12	—	BV	60.00	70.00	100.00
	13	—	BV	60.00	70.00	100.00
	14	—	BV	60.00	70.00	100.00
	15	—	BV	60.00	70.00	100.00
	16	—	BV	60.00	70.00	100.00
	17	—	BV	60.00	70.00	100.00
	18	—	BV	60.00	70.00	100.00
	19	—	BV	60.00	70.00	100.00
	20	—	BV	60.00	70.00	100.00
	21	—	BV	60.00	70.00	100.00
	22	—	BV	60.00	70.00	100.00
	23	—	BV	60.00	70.00	100.00
	24	—	BV	60.00	70.00	100.00
	25	.013	BV	60.00	70.00	100.00
	26	—	BV	60.00	70.00	100.00
	27	—	BV	60.00	70.00	100.00
	28	—	BV	60.00	70.00	100.00
	29	—	BV	60.00	70.00	100.00
	30	—	BV	60.00	70.00	100.00
	31	—	BV	60.00	70.00	100.00
	32	—	BV	60.00	70.00	100.00
	33	—	BV	60.00	70.00	100.00
	34	—	BV	60.00	70.00	100.00

3.5080 g, .917 GOLD, .1034 oz AGW
Monnaie de Luxe

KM#	Year	Mintage	VG	Fine	VF	XF
740	18	—	—	—	Rare	—
(Y-C40)	23	—	60.00	85.00	100.00	150.00
	24	—	60.00	85.00	100.00	150.00
	25	—	60.00	85.00	100.00	150.00
	26	—	60.00	85.00	100.00	150.00
	27	—	60.00	85.00	100.00	150.00
	28	—	60.00	85.00	100.00	150.00
	29	—	60.00	85.00	100.00	150.00
	30	—	60.00	85.00	100.00	150.00
	31	—	60.00	85.00	100.00	150.00
	32	—	60.00	85.00	100.00	150.00
	33	—	60.00	85.00	100.00	150.00
	34	—	60.00	85.00	100.00	150.00

100 PIASTRES

7.2160 g, .917 GOLD, .2128 oz AGW
Accession date: AH1293
Mintname: *Constantinople*
Obv: Flower to right of toughra.

KM#	Year	Mintage	VG	Fine	VF	XF
725	1	—	110.00	150.00	200.00	275.00
(Y-C31)	2	—	110.00	150.00	200.00	275.00
	3	—	110.00	150.00	200.00	275.00
	4	—	150.00	200.00	300.00	400.00
	6	—	110.00	150.00	200.00	275.00

Obv: *El Ghazi* to right of toughra.

KM#	Year	Mintage	VG	Fine	VF	XF
730	6	—	—	BV	110.00	125.00
(Y38)	7	—	—	BV	110.00	125.00
	8	—	—	BV	110.00	125.00
	9	—	—	BV	110.00	125.00
	10	—	—	BV	110.00	125.00
	11	—	—	BV	110.00	125.00
	12	—	—	BV	110.00	125.00
	13	—	—	BV	110.00	125.00
	14	—	—	BV	110.00	125.00
	15	—	—	BV	110.00	125.00
	16	—	—	BV	110.00	125.00
	17	—	—	BV	110.00	125.00
	18	—	—	BV	110.00	125.00
	19	—	—	BV	110.00	125.00
	20	—	—	BV	110.00	125.00
	21	—	—	BV	110.00	125.00
	22	—	—	BV	110.00	125.00
	23	—	—	BV	110.00	125.00
	24	—	—	BV	110.00	125.00
	25	3,000	—	BV	110.00	125.00
	26	—	—	BV	110.00	125.00
	27	—	—	BV	110.00	125.00

TURKEY 1662

KM#	Year	Mintage	VG	Fine	VF	XF
(Y38)	28	—	BV	110.00	125.00	
	29	—	BV	110.00	125.00	
	30	—	BV	110.00	125.00	
	31	—	BV	110.00	125.00	
	32	—	BV	110.00	125.00	
	33	—	BV	110.00	125.00	
	34	—	BV	110.00	125.00	

500 PIASTRES

7.0160 g, .917 GOLD, .2068 oz AGW
Monnaie de Luxe

KM#	Year	Mintage	VG	Fine	VF	XF
741	18	—	—	—	Rare	—
(Y-D40)	23	—	BV	110.00	150.00	200.00
	24	—	BV	110.00	150.00	200.00
	25	—	BV	110.00	150.00	200.00
	26	—	BV	110.00	150.00	200.00
	27	—	BV	110.00	150.00	200.00
	28	—	BV	110.00	150.00	200.00
	29	—	BV	110.00	150.00	200.00
	30	—	BV	110.00	150.00	200.00
	31	—	BV	110.00	150.00	200.00
	32	—	BV	110.00	150.00	200.00
	33	—	BV	110.00	150.00	200.00
	34	—	BV	110.00	150.00	200.00

36.0800 g, .917 GOLD, 1.0638 oz AGW
Accession date: AH1293
Mintname: *Constantinople*
Obv: Flower to right of toughra.

KM#	Year	Mintage	VG	Fine	VF	XF
727	1	—	BV	500.00	650.00	900.00
(Y-E31)	2	—	BV	500.00	650.00	900.00
	3	—	BV	500.00	650.00	900.00
	4	—	BV	500.00	650.00	900.00
	6	—	BV	500.00	650.00	900.00

Obv: *El Ghazi* **to right of toughra.**

KM#	Year	Mintage	VG	Fine	VF	XF
733	7	—	BV	500.00	550.00	750.00
(Y40)	8	—	BV	500.00	550.00	750.00
	9	—	BV	500.00	550.00	750.00
	10	—	BV	500.00	550.00	750.00
	11	—	BV	500.00	550.00	750.00
	12	—	BV	500.00	550.00	750.00
	13	—	BV	500.00	550.00	750.00
	14	—	BV	500.00	550.00	750.00
	15	—	BV	500.00	550.00	750.00
	16	—	BV	500.00	550.00	750.00
	17	—	BV	500.00	550.00	750.00
	18	—	BV	500.00	550.00	750.00
	19	—	BV	500.00	550.00	750.00
	20	—	BV	500.00	550.00	750.00
	21	—	BV	500.00	550.00	750.00
	22	—	BV	500.00	550.00	750.00
	23	—	BV	500.00	550.00	750.00
	24	—	BV	500.00	550.00	750.00
	25	.011	BV	500.00	550.00	750.00
	26	—	BV	500.00	550.00	750.00
	27	—	BV	500.00	550.00	750.00
	28	—	BV	500.00	550.00	750.00
	29	—	BV	500.00	550.00	750.00
	30	—	BV	500.00	550.00	750.00
	31	—	BV	500.00	550.00	750.00
	32	—	BV	500.00	550.00	750.00
	33	—	BV	500.00	550.00	750.00
	34	—	BV	500.00	550.00	750.00

250 PIASTRES

17.5400 g, .917 GOLD, .5169 oz AGW
Accession date: AH1293
Mintname: *Constantinople*
Obv: Flower to right of toughra.

KM#	Year	Mintage	VG	Fine	VF	XF
726 (Y-D31)	1	—	600.00	1000.	1600.	2000.

Obv: *El Ghazi* **at right of toughra.**

KM#	Year	Mintage	VG	Fine	VF	XF
732	7	—	BV	250.00	300.00	450.00
(Y39)	8	—	BV	250.00	300.00	450.00
	9	—	BV	250.00	300.00	450.00
	10	—	BV	250.00	300.00	450.00
	11	—	BV	250.00	300.00	450.00
	12	—	BV	250.00	300.00	450.00
	13	—	BV	250.00	300.00	450.00
	14	—	BV	250.00	300.00	450.00
	15	—	BV	250.00	300.00	450.00
	16	—	BV	250.00	300.00	450.00
	17	—	BV	250.00	300.00	450.00
	18	—	BV	250.00	300.00	450.00
	19	—	BV	250.00	300.00	450.00
	20	—	BV	250.00	300.00	450.00
	21	—	BV	250.00	300.00	450.00
	22	—	BV	250.00	300.00	450.00
	23	—	BV	250.00	300.00	450.00
	24	—	BV	250.00	300.00	450.00
	25	400 pcs.	BV	250.00	300.00	450.00
	26	—	BV	250.00	300.00	450.00
	27	—	BV	250.00	300.00	450.00
	28	—	BV	250.00	300.00	450.00
	29	—	BV	250.00	300.00	450.00
	30	—	BV	250.00	300.00	450.00
	31	—	BV	250.00	300.00	450.00
	32	—	BV	250.00	300.00	450.00

Monnaie de Luxe

KM#	Year	Mintage	VG	Fine	VF	XF
742	24	—	BV	275.00	400.00	600.00
(Y41)	25	—	BV	275.00	400.00	600.00
	26	—	BV	275.00	400.00	600.00
	27	—	BV	275.00	400.00	600.00
	28	—	BV	275.00	400.00	600.00
	29	—	BV	275.00	400.00	600.00
	30	—	BV	275.00	400.00	600.00
	31	—	BV	275.00	400.00	600.00
	32	—	BV	275.00	400.00	600.00
	33	—	BV	275.00	400.00	600.00
	34	—	—	—	Rare	—

Monnaie de Luxe

KM#	Year	Mintage	VG	Fine	VF	XF
746	26	—	600.00	750.00	900.00	1200.
(Y42)	27	—	600.00	750.00	900.00	1200.
	28	—	600.00	750.00	900.00	1200.
	29	—	600.00	750.00	900.00	1200.
	30	—	600.00	750.00	900.00	1200.
	31	—	600.00	750.00	900.00	1200.
	32	—	600.00	750.00	900.00	1200.
	33	—	600.00	750.00	900.00	1200.
	34	—	600.00	750.00	900.00	1200.

MUHAMMAD V
AH1327-1336/1909-1918AD

5 PARA

NICKEL
Accession date: AH1327
Mintname: *Constantinople*
Obv: *Reshat* **to right of toughra.**

KM#	Year	Mintage	VG	Fine	VF	XF
759	2	1.664	1.00	2.00	4.00	8.00
(Y43)	3	21.760	.50	1.00	2.00	4.00
	4	21.392	.50	1.00	2.00	4.00
	5	30.579	.50	1.00	2.00	4.00
	6	15.751	.50	1.00	2.00	4.00
	7	2.512	15.00	35.00	60.00	100.00

Obv: *El-Ghazi* **to right of toughra.**

KM#	Year	Mintage	VG	Fine	VF	XF
767 (Y43a)	7	.740	15.00	30.00	45.00	70.00

10 PARA

NICKEL
Accession date: AH1327
Mintname: *Constantinople*
Obv: *Reshat* **to right of toughra.**

KM#	Year	Mintage	VG	Fine	VF	XF
760	2	2.576	.25	.50	2.00	5.00
(Y44)	3	18.992	.15	.25	.50	2.00
	4	18.576	.15	.25	.50	2.00
	5	31.799	.15	.25	.50	2.00
	6	17.024	.15	.25	.50	2.00
	7	21.680	.30	.65	1.50	4.00

Obv: *El Ghazi* **to right of toughra.**

KM#	Year	Mintage	VG	Fine	VF	XF
768	7	Inc. KM760	.30	.60	1.50	4.00
(Y44a)	8	7.590	.50	1.00	4.00	10.00

20 PARA

NICKEL
Accession date: AH1327

Mintname: *Constantinople*
Obv: *Reshat* at right of toughra.

KM#	Year	Mintage	VG	Fine	VF	XF
761 (Y45)	2	1.524	.25	.50	2.00	8.00
	3	11.418	.15	.35	1.50	6.00
	4	10.848	.15	.25	1.00	5.00
	5	24.350	.15	.25	1.00	5.00
	6	20.663	.15	.25	1.00	5.00
	7	—	—	—	Rare	—
	W/o R.Y.	—	5.00	8.50	15.00	25.00

Obv: *El-Ghazi* at right of toughra.

KM#	Year	Mintage	VG	Fine	VF	XF
769 (Y45.1)	7	—	—	—	Rare	—

40 PARA

NICKEL
Accession date: AH1327
Mintname: *Constantinople*
Obv: *Reshat* to right of toughra.

KM#	Year	Mintage	VG	Fine	VF	XF
766 (Y46)	3	1.992	.50	1.00	3.00	10.00
	4	8.716	.15	.30	1.00	5.00
	5	9.248	.15	.30	1.00	5.00

COPPER-NICKEL
Obv: *El-Ghazi* at right of toughra.

KM#	Year	Mintage	VG	Fine	VF	XF
779 (Y46a)	8	16.339	.15	.30	1.00	5.00
	9	3.034	1.00	2.00	6.00	15.00

PIASTRE

1.2027 g, .830 SILVER, .0321 oz ASW
Accession date: AH1327
Mintname: *Constantinople*

KM#	Year	Mintage	VG	Fine	VF	XF
748 (Y47)	1	1.270	.75	1.50	3.00	6.00
	2	8.770	.65	1.25	2.50	5.00
	3	.840	1.50	3.00	6.00	12.50

2 PIASTRES

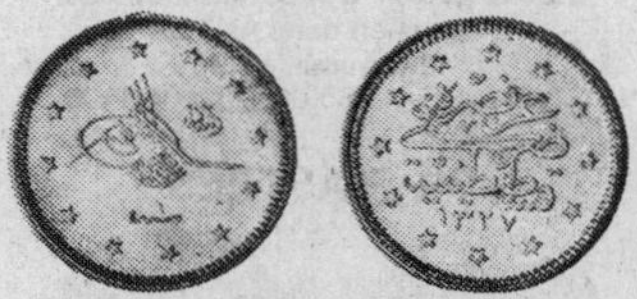

2.4055 g, .830 SILVER, .0642 oz ASW
Accession date: AH1327
Mintname: *Constantinople*
Obv: *Reshat* to right of toughra.

KM#	Year	Mintage	VG	Fine	VF	XF
749 (Y48)	1	5.157	1.75	2.25	3.50	7.50
	2	11.120	1.50	2.00	3.00	6.50
	3	6.110	1.50	2.00	3.00	6.50
	4	4.031	1.50	2.00	3.00	6.50
	5	.301	2.50	5.00	10.00	20.00
	6	1.884	2.00	2.50	4.00	8.00

Obv: *El Ghazi* to right of toughra.

KM#	Year	Mintage	VG	Fine	VF	XF
770 (Y-A50)	7	.017	12.50	25.00	40.00	75.00
	8	.398	20.00	30.00	50.00	100.00
	9	.008	60.00	100.00	200.00	350.00

5 PIASTRES

6.0130 g, .830 SILVER, .1605 oz ASW
Accession date: AH1327
Mintname: *Constantinople*
Obv: *Reshat* to right of toughra.

KM#	Year	Mintage	VG	Fine	VF	XF
750 (Y49)	1	1.558	BV	3.50	6.00	9.00
	2	1.886	BV	3.50	6.00	9.00
	3	1.273	BV	3.50	6.00	9.00
	4	1.635	BV	3.50	6.00	9.00
	5	.194	6.00	9.00	13.50	25.00
	6	.664	3.25	3.50	5.00	8.00
	7	.834	3.25	3.50	5.00	8.00

Obv: *El Ghazi* to right of toughra.

KM#	Year	Mintage	VG	Fine	VF	XF
771 (Y-B50)	7	Inc. KM750	3.50	4.50	7.00	10.00
	8	.648	4.00	7.00	10.00	20.00
	9	3.938	50.00	100.00	200.00	350.00

10 PIASTRES

12.0270 g, .830 SILVER, .3210 oz ASW
Accession date: AH1327
Mintname: *Constantinople*
Obv: *Reshat* to right of toughra.

KM#	Year	Mintage	VG	Fine	VF	XF
751 (Y50)	1	.110	12.50	25.00	50.00	100.00
	2	Inc. Ab.	10.00	20.00	50.00	100.00
	3	8,000	150.00	250.00	500.00	1000.
	4	.096	3.50	7.50	15.00	22.50
	5	.034	12.00	20.00	40.00	80.00
	6	.081	7.50	12.50	17.50	30.00
	7	.582	5.00	10.00	16.50	27.50

Obv: *El-Ghazi* to right of toughra.

KM#	Year	Mintage	VG	Fine	VF	XF
772 (Y-C50)	7	Inc. KM751	3.50	7.50	15.00	25.00
	8	.408	7.00	9.00	17.50	27.50
	9	.299	10.00	20.00	35.00	50.00
	10	.666	12.50	25.00	50.00	85.00

12-1/2 PIASTRES

.9020 g, .917 GOLD, .0266 oz AGW
Accession date: AH1327
Mintname: *Constantinople*
Monnaie de Luxe
Obv: *Reshat* to right of toughra.

KM#	Year	Mintage	VG	Fine	VF	XF
762 (Y-F51)	2	—	20.00	30.00	50.00	90.00
	3	—	20.00	30.00	50.00	90.00
	4	—	20.00	30.00	50.00	90.00
	5	—	20.00	30.00	50.00	90.00
	6	—	20.00	30.00	50.00	90.00

20 PIASTRES

24.0550 g, .830 SILVER, .6419 oz ASW
Accession date: AH1327
Mintname: *Constantinople*
Rev: Similar to KM#712.

KM#	Year	Mintage	VG	Fine	VF	XF
780 (Y51)	8	.713	BV	12.00	20.00	35.00
	9	5.962	BV	10.00	15.00	30.00
	10	11.025	BV	12.00	20.00	35.00

25 PIASTRES

1.8040 g, .917 GOLD, .0532 oz AGW
Accession date: AH1327
Mintname: *Constantinople*
Obv: *Reshat* to right of toughra.

KM#	Year	Mintage	VG	Fine	VF	XF
752 (Y-A51)	1	—	BV	30.00	40.00	50.00
	2	—	BV	30.00	40.00	50.00
	3	—	BV	30.00	40.00	50.00
	4	—	BV	30.00	40.00	50.00
	5	—	BV	30.00	40.00	50.00
	6	—	BV	30.00	40.00	50.00

Monnaie de Luxe

KM#	Year	Mintage	VG	Fine	VF	XF
763 (Y-G51)	2	—	35.00	50.00	60.00	70.00
	3	—	35.00	50.00	60.00	70.00
	4	—	35.00	50.00	60.00	70.00
	5	—	50.00	60.00	75.00	100.00
	6	—	50.00	60.00	75.00	100.00

Obv: *El Ghazi* to right of toughra.

KM#	Year	Mintage	VG	Fine	VF	XF
773 (Y53)	7	—	BV	35.00	45.00	55.00
	8	—	BV	35.00	45.00	55.00
	9	—	BV	35.00	45.00	55.00
	10	—	BV	40.00	50.00	60.00

Monnaie de Luxe

KM#	Year	Mintage	VG	Fine	VF	XF
774 (Y-A53)	8	—	60.00	80.00	100.00	120.00

50 PIASTRES

3.6080 g, .917 GOLD, .1064 oz AGW
Accession date: AH1327
Mintname: *Constantinople*
Obv: *Reshat* to right of toughra.

KM#	Year	Mintage	VG	Fine	VF	XF
753 (Y-B51)	1	—	BV	60.00	70.00	90.00
	2	—	BV	60.00	70.00	90.00
	3	—	BV	60.00	70.00	90.00
	4	—	BV	60.00	70.00	90.00
	5	—	BV	60.00	70.00	90.00
	6	—	BV	60.00	70.00	90.00

Monnaie de Luxe

KM#	Year	Mintage	VG	Fine	VF	XF
764 (Y-H51)	2	—	60.00	70.00	100.00	120.00
	3	—	60.00	70.00	100.00	120.00
	4	—	60.00	70.00	100.00	120.00
	5	—	60.00	70.00	100.00	120.00
	6	—	60.00	70.00	100.00	120.00

Obv: *El Ghazi* to right of toughra.

KM#	Year	Mintage	VG	Fine	VF	XF
775 (Y54)	7	—	60.00	75.00	150.00	250.00
	8	—	60.00	75.00	150.00	250.00
	9	—	60.00	75.00	150.00	250.00
	10	—	65.00	85.00	165.00	275.00

Monnaie de Luxe

KM#	Year	Mintage	VG	Fine	VF	XF
781 (Y-A54)	8	—	100.00	150.00	200.00	300.00

100 PIASTRES

7.2160 g, .917 GOLD, .2128 oz AGW
Accession date: AH1327
Obv: *Reshat* to right of toughra.
Mintname: *Constantinople*

KM#	Year	Mintage	VG	Fine	VF	XF
754 (Y-C51)	1	—	—	BV	110.00	145.00
	2	—	—	BV	110.00	145.00
	3	—	—	BV	110.00	145.00
	4	—	—	BV	110.00	145.00

TURKEY 1664

KM#	Year	Mintage	VG	Fine	VF	XF
(Y-C51)	5	—	—	BV	110.00	145.00
	6	—	—	BV	110.00	145.00
	7	—	—	BV	110.00	145.00

Monnaie de Luxe

755	1	—	BV	110.00	150.00	225.00
(Y-J51)	2	—	BV	110.00	150.00	225.00
	3	—	BV	110.00	150.00	225.00
	4	—	BV	110.00	150.00	225.00
	5	—	BV	110.00	150.00	225.00
	6	—	BV	110.00	150.00	225.00

Obv: *El Ghazi* to right of toughra.

776	7	—	—	BV	110.00	150.00
(Y55)	8	—	—	BV	110.00	150.00
	9	—	—	BV	110.00	150.00
	10	—	—	BV	110.00	150.00

Monnaie de Luxe

782	8	—	110.00	150.00	220.00	300.00
(Y-A55)						

250 PIASTRES
18.0400 g, .917 GOLD, .5319 oz AGW
Accession date: AH1327
Mintname: *Constantinople*
Obv: *Reshat* to right of toughra.

756	1	—	—	BV	350.00	425.00
(Y-D51)	2	—	—	BV	350.00	425.00
	3	—	—	BV	350.00	425.00
	4	—	—	BV	350.00	425.00
	5	—	—	BV	350.00	425.00
	6	—	—	BV	350.00	425.00

Monnaie de Luxe

757	1	—	BV	350.00	450.00	625.00
(Y-L51)	2	—	BV	350.00	450.00	625.00
	3	—	BV	350.00	450.00	625.00
	4	—	BV	350.00	450.00	625.00
	5	—	BV	350.00	450.00	625.00
	6	—	BV	350.00	450.00	625.00

Obv: *El Ghazi* to right of toughra.

777	7	—	1000.00	1250.00	1500.	1750.
(Y56)	8	—	—	—	Rare	—
	9	—	—	—	Rare	—

Monnaie de Luxe

783	8	—	350.00	425.00	500.00	850.00
(Y-A56)						

500 PIASTRES

36.0800 g, .917 GOLD, 1.0638 oz AGW
Accession date: AH1327
Mintname: *Constantinople*
Obv: *Reshat* to right of toughra.

KM#	Year	Mintage	VG	Fine	VF	XF
758	1	—	—	BV	525.00	650.00
(Y-E51)	2	—	—	BV	525.00	650.00
	3	—	—	BV	525.00	650.00
	4	—	—	BV	525.00	650.00
	5	—	—	BV	525.00	650.00
	6	—	—	BV	525.00	650.00

Monnaie de Luxe

765	2	—	600.00	750.00	900.00	1350.
(Y-M51)	3	—	600.00	750.00	900.00	1350.
	4	—	600.00	750.00	900.00	1350.
	5	—	600.00	750.00	900.00	1350.
	6	—	600.00	750.00	900.00	1350.
	7	484 pcs.	800.00	1100.	1600.	1900.
	8	19 pcs.	800.00	1000.	1400.	1700.

Obv: *El Ghazi* to right of toughra.

784	9	22 pcs.	750.00	850.00	1200.	1650.
(Y57)	10	—	750.00	850.00	1200.	1650.

Monnaie de Luxe

Obv: *El Ghazi* to right of toughra.

KM#	Year	Mintage	VG	Fine	VF	XF
778	7	295 pcs.	750.00	950.00	1500.	2000.
(Y-A57)	8	1,216	750.00	850.00	1300.	1800.

Mint Visit Coinage
Muhammad V's visit to Bursa

بروسة

Bursa Mint mark

2 PIASTRES

2.4055 g, .830 SILVER, .0642 oz ASW
Accession date: AH1327
Mintname: *Bursa*

KM#	Year	Mintage	Fine	VF	XF	Unc
785	1	—	15.00	25.00	40.00	80.00
(Y48a)						

5 PIASTRES

6.0130 g, .830 SILVER, .1605 oz ASW
Accession date: AH1327
Mintname: *Bursa*

786	1	—	20.00	35.00	60.00	100.00
(Y49a)						

25 PIASTRES

1.8040 g, .917 GOLD, .0532 oz AGW
Accession date: AH1327
Mintname: *Bursa*

787	1	—	185.00	275.00	400.00	800.00
(Y-A51a)						

50 PIASTRES

3.6080 g, .917 GOLD, .1064 oz AGW
Accession date: AH1327
Mintname: *Bursa*

788	1	—	165.00	275.00	350.00	600.00
(Y-B51a)						

100 PIASTRES

7.2160 g, .917 GOLD, .2128 oz AGW
Accession date: AH1327
Mintname: *Bursa*

788	1	—	225.00	350.00	450.00	650.00
(Y-C51a)						

Muhammad V's visit to Edirne

ادرنة

Edirne Mint mark

2 PIASTRES

2.4055 g, .830 SILVER, .0642 oz ASW
Accession date: AH1327
Mintname: *Edirne*

KM#	Year	Mintage	Fine	VF	XF	Unc
790 (Y48b)	2	—	15.00	25.00	40.00	80.00

5 PIASTRES

6.0130 g, .830 SILVER, .1605 oz ASW
Accession date: AH1327
Mintname: Edirne

| 791 (Y49b) | 2 | — | 20.00 | 35.00 | 60.00 | 100.00 |

10 PIASTRES

12.0270 g, .830 SILVER, .3210 oz ASW
Accession date: AH1327
Mintname: Edirne

| 792 (Y50b) | 2 | — | 90.00 | 150.00 | 250.00 | 425.00 |

50 PIASTRES

3.6080 g, .917 GOLD, .1064 oz AGW
Accession date: AH1327
Mintname: Edirne

| 793 (Y-B51b) | 2 | — | 200.00 | 275.00 | 350.00 | 500.00 |

100 PIASTRES

7.2160 g, .917 GOLD, .2128 oz AGW
Accession date: AH1327
Mintname: Edirne

| 794 (Y-C51b) | 2 | — | 250.00 | 350.00 | 500.00 | 650.00 |

500 PIASTRES

36.0800 g, .917 GOLD, 1.0638 oz AGW
Accession date: AH1327
Mintname: Edirne

| 795 (Y-E51b) | 2 | — | 1500. | 2500. | 3500. | 4000. |

Muhammad V's visit to Kosova

قوصوه

Kosova Mint mark

2 PIASTRES

2.4055 g, .830 SILVER, .0642 oz ASW
Accession date: AH1327
Mintname: Kosova

KM#	Year	Mintage	Fine	VF	XF	Unc
796 (Y48c)	3	.013	15.00	25.00	40.00	80.00

5 PIASTRES

6.0130 g, .830 SILVER, .1605 oz ASW
Accession date: AH1327
Mintname: Kosova

| 797 (Y49c) | 3 | 3,000 | 20.00 | 35.00 | 60.00 | 100.00 |

10 PIASTRES

12.0270 g, .830 SILVER, .3210 oz ASW
Accession date: AH1327
Mintname: Kosova

| 798 (Y50c) | 3 | 1,500 | 100.00 | 175.00 | 300.00 | 525.00 |

50 PIASTRES

3.6080 g, .917 GOLD, .1064 oz AGW
Accession date: AH1327
Mintname: Kosova

| 799 (Y-B51c) | 3 | 1,200 | 225.00 | 275.00 | 400.00 | 650.00 |

100 PIASTRES

7.2160 g, .917 GOLD, .2128 oz AGW
Accession date: AH1327
Mintname: Kosova

| 800 (Y-C51c) | 3 | 750 pcs. | 250.00 | 300.00 | 450.00 | 750.00 |

500 PIASTRES

36.0800 g, .917 GOLD, 1.0638 oz AGW
Accession date: AH1327
Mintname: Kosova

| 801 (Y-E51c) | 3 | 20 pcs. | 3000. | 4000. | 5000. | 6000. |

Muhammad V's visit to Manastir

مناستر

Manastir Mint mark

2 PIASTRES

2.4055 g, .830 SILVER, .0642 oz ASW
Accession date: AH1327
Mintname: Manastir

KM#	Year	Mintage	Fine	VF	XF	Unc
802 (Y48d)	3	.013	15.00	25.00	40.00	80.00

5 PIASTRES

6.0130 g, .830 SILVER, .1605 oz ASW
Accession date: AH1327
Mintname: Manastir

| 803 (Y49d) | 3 | 3,000 | 20.00 | 35.00 | 60.00 | 100.00 |

10 PIASTRES

12.0270 g, .830 SILVER, .3210 oz ASW
Accession date: AH1327
Mintname: Manastir

| 804 (Y50d) | 3 | 1,500 | 100.00 | 175.00 | 275.00 | 525.00 |

50 PIASTRES

3.6080 g, .917 GOLD, .1064 oz AGW
Accession date: AH1327
Mintname: Manastir

| 805 (Y-B51d) | 3 | 1,200 | 200.00 | 325.00 | 450.00 | 600.00 |

100 PIASTRES

7.2160 g, .917 GOLD, .2128 oz AGW
Accession date: AH1327
Mintname: Manastir

| 806 (Y-C51d) | 3 | 750 pcs. | 225.00 | 350.00 | 450.00 | 750.00 |

500 PIASTRES

36.0800 g, .917 GOLD, 1.0638 oz AGW
Accession date: AH1327
Mintname: Manastir

| 807 (Y-E51d) | 3 | 20 pcs. | 2500. | 4000. | 5000. | 6250. |

Muhammad V's visit to Salonika

Salonika Mintmark

2 PIASTRES

2.4055 g, .830 SILVER, .0642 oz ASW
Accession date: AH1327
Mintname: *Salonika*

KM#	Year	Mintage	Fine	VF	XF	Unc
808 (Y48e)	3	.013	15.00	25.00	40.00	80.00

5 PIASTRES

6.0130 g, .830 SILVER, .1605 oz ASW
Accession date: AH1327
Mintname: *Salonika*

KM#	Year	Mintage	Fine	VF	XF	Unc
809 (Y49e)	3	3,000	20.00	35.00	60.00	100.00

10 PIASTRES

12.0270 g, .830 SILVER, .3210 oz ASW
Accession date: AH1327
Mintname: *Salonika*

KM#	Year	Mintage	Fine	VF	XF	Unc
810 (Y50e)	3	1,500	100.00	175.00	275.00	525.00

50 PIASTRES

3.6080 g, .917 GOLD, .1064 oz AGW
Accession date: AH1327
Mintname: *Salonika*

KM#	Year	Mintage	Fine	VF	XF	Unc
811 (Y-B51e)	3	1,200	200.00	325.00	400.00	600.00

100 PIASTRES

7.2160 g, .917 GOLD, .2128 oz AGW
Accession date: AH1327
Mintname: *Salonika*

KM#	Year	Mintage	Fine	VF	XF	Unc
812 (Y-C51e)	3	750 pcs.	225.00	350.00	450.00	750.00

500 PIASTRES

36.0800 g, .917 GOLD, 1.0638 oz AGW
Accession date: AH1327
Mintname: *Salonika*

KM#	Year	Mintage	Fine	VF	XF	Unc
813 (Y-E51e)	3	20 pcs.	2500	4000	5250	6750

MUHAMMAD VI
AH1336-1341/1918-1923AD
40 PARA

COPPER-NICKEL
Accession date: AH1336
Mintname: *Constantinople*

KM#	Year	Mintage	VG	Fine	VF	XF
828 (Y58)	4	6,520	1.75	2.50	4.00	10.00

2 PIASTRES

2.4055 g, .830 SILVER, .0642 oz ASW
Accession date: AH1336
Mintname: *Constantinople*

KM#	Year	Mintage	VG	Fine	VF	XF
815 (Y59)	1	.025	50.00	100.00	150.00	220.00
	2	.003	75.00	125.00	200.00	350.00

5 PIASTRES

6.0130 g, .830 SILVER, .1605 oz ASW
Accession date: AH1336
Mintname: *Constantinople*

KM#	Year	Mintage	VG	Fine	VF	XF
816 (Y60)	1	.010	50.00	125.00	175.00	265.00
	2	2,000	75.00	150.00	225.00	385.00

10 PIASTRES

12.0270 g, .830 SILVER, .3210 oz ASW
Accession date: AH1336
Mintname: *Constantinople*

KM#	Year	Mintage	VG	Fine	VF	XF
817 (Y61)	1	—	120.00	400.00	400.00	600.00
	2	1,000	200.00	400.00	600.00	1000

20 PIASTRES

24.0550 g, .830 SILVER, .6419 oz ASW
Accession date: AH1336
Mintname: *Constantinople*

KM#	Year	Mintage	VG	Fine	VF	XF
818 (Y62)	1	—	30.00	60.00	125.00	185.00
	2	1,530	350.00	525.00	650.00	925.00

25 PIASTRES

1.8040 g, .917 GOLD, .0532 oz AGW
Accession date: AH1336
Mintname: *Constantinople*

KM#	Year	Mintage	VG	Fine	VF	XF
819 (Y63)	1	—	30.00	40.00	50.00	100.00
	2	—	30.00	40.00	50.00	100.00
	3	—	40.00	75.00	150.00	200.00
	4	—	50.00	90.00	200.00	300.00
	5	—	80.00	140.00	240.00	375.00

Monnaie de Luxe

KM#	Year	Mintage	VG	Fine	VF	XF
825 (Y63a)	2	—	60.00	80.00	100.00	150.00
	3	—	60.00	80.00	100.00	150.00

50 PIASTRES

3.6080 g, .917 GOLD, .1064 oz AGW
Accession date: AH1336
Mintname: *Constantinople*

KM#	Year	Mintage	VG	Fine	VF	XF
820 (Y64)	1	—	100.00	125.00	150.00	300.00
	2	—	100.00	125.00	150.00	300.00
	3	—	150.00	200.00	250.00	500.00
	4	—	250.00	450.00	750.00	1500.
	5	—	200.00	300.00	450.00	1000.

100 PIASTRES

7.2160 g, .917 GOLD, .2128 oz AGW
Accession date: AH1336
Mintname: *Constantinople*

KM#	Year	Mintage	VG	Fine	VF	XF
821 (Y65)	1	—	BV	110.00	140.00	180.00
	2	—	BV	110.00	140.00	180.00
	3	—	150.00	180.00	225.00	450.00
	4	—	—	Reported, not confirmed		
	5	—	400.00	600.00	800.00	1000.

Monnaie de Luxe

KM#	Year	Mintage	VG	Fine	VF	XF
826 (Y65a)	2	—	250.00	300.00	325.00	375.00
	3	—	250.00	300.00	325.00	375.00

250 PIASTRES

18.0400 g, .917 GOLD, .5319 oz AGW
Accession date: AH1336
Mintname: *Constantinople*

KM#	Year	Mintage	VG	Fine	VF	XF
822 (Y66)	1	—	1750	3000.	4500.	6500.
	2	26 pcs.	1750	3000.	4500.	6500.
	3	31 pcs.	1750	3000.	4500.	6500.
	4	—	—	Reported, not confirmed		
	5	—	—	Reported, not confirmed		

Monnaie de Luxe

KM#	Year	Mintage	VG	Fine	VF	XF
827 (Y66a)	2	.019	300.00	500.00	700.00	900.00
	3	Inc. Ab.	250.00	425.00	600.00	800.00

500 PIASTRES

TURKEY 1667

36.0800 g, .917 GOLD, 1.0638 oz AGW
Accession date: AH1336
Mintname: *Constantinople*

KM#	Year	Mintage	VG	Fine	VF	XF
823	1	—	1000.	1200.	1450.	1800.
(Y67)	2	—	1000.	1200.	1450.	1800.
	3	—	1000.	1200.	1450.	1800.
	4	23 pcs.	2000.	4000.	6000.	8000.
	5	22 pcs.	2000.	4000.	6000.	8000.

		Monnaie de Luxe				
824	1	—	1000.	1250.	1750.	2400.
(Y67a)	2	5,207	600.00	750.00	950.00	1300.
	3	Inc. Ab.	600.00	750.00	950.00	1300.
	4	88 pcs.	1500.	2000.	2500.	3200.

REPUBLIC
OLD MONETARY SYSTEM
100 PARA

ALUMINUM-BRONZE

KM#	Date	Mintage	Fine	VF	XF	Unc
830	AH1340	1.798	3.00	5.00	10.00	60.00
(Y68)	1341	5.583	1.00	2.50	5.00	20.00
834	1926	4.388	1.00	2.50	5.00	20.00
(Y68a)	1928	—	150.00	225.00	400.00	600.00

5 KURUS

ALUMINUM-BRONZE

831	AH1340	5.023	1.00	2.50	6.00	20.00
(Y69)	1341	23.545	1.00	2.50	6.00	20.00
835	1926	.356	1.00	2.50	6.00	20.00
(Y69a)	1928	—	175.00	250.00	500.00	700.00

10 KURUS

ALUMINUM-BRONZE

KM#	Date	Mintage	Fine	VF	XF	Unc
832	AH1340	4.836	1.50	3.00	8.00	30.00
(Y70)	1341	14.223	1.50	3.00	8.00	30.00
836	1926	.856	1.25	2.50	7.50	30.00
(Y70a)	1928	—	125.00	200.00	375.00	575.00

25 KURUS

NICKEL

833	AH1341	4.973	2.00	4.00	10.00	25.00
(Y71)						

837	1926	.027	175.00	250.00	450.00	650.00
(Y71a)	1928	5.794	1.50	3.00	6.00	18.00

Gold Coinage

The gold coins continued to be struck to the weights and finenesses of the old Ottoman system, but were tariffed at the going price of gold. The same continues to hold true today. Both regular and de luxe strikes were made.

25 PIASTRES

1.8040 g, .917 GOLD, .0532 oz AGW
Rev: AH Date: 23 Nisan 1336.

840	1926	4,539	40.00	75.00	140.00	175.00
(Y72)	1927	.014	40.00	75.00	120.00	150.00
	1928	8,424	40.00	75.00	130.00	165.00
	1929	—	40.00	75.00	120.00	150.00

1.7540 g, .917 GOLD, .0517 oz AGW
Monnaie de Luxe

844	1927	4,103	50.00	75.00	125.00	200.00
(Y77)	1928	4,549	50.00	75.00	125.00	200.00

50 PIASTRES

3.6080 g, .917 GOLD, .1064 oz AGW
Rev: AH Date: 23 Nisan 1336.

841	1926	2,168	60.00	100.00	165.00	225.00
(Y73)	1927	2,116	60.00	100.00	165.00	225.00
	1928	2,431	60.00	100.00	165.00	225.00
	1929	—	60.00	100.00	165.00	225.00

3.5080 g, .917 GOLD, .1034 oz AGW
Monnaie de Luxe

KM#	Date	Mintage	Fine	VF	XF	Unc
845	1927	3,903	75.00	150.00	250.00	375.00
(Y78)	1928	3,620	75.00	150.00	250.00	375.00

100 PIASTRES

7.2160 g, .917 GOLD, .2128 oz AGW
Rev: AH Date: 23 Nisan 1336.

842	1926	1,073	110.00	130.00	250.00	350.00
(Y74)	1927	—	110.00	130.00	250.00	350.00
	1928	920 pcs.	110.00	130.00	250.00	350.00
	1929	—	110.00	130.00	250.00	350.00

7.0160 g, .917 GOLD, .2069 oz AGW
Monnaie de Luxe

846	1927	8,676	125.00	150.00	250.00	350.00
(Y79)	1928	6,092	125.00	150.00	250.00	350.00

250 PIASTRES

18.0400 g, .917 GOLD, .5319 oz AGW
Rev: AH Date: 23 Nisan 1336.

843	1926	604 pcs.	250.00	275.00	350.00	500.00
(Y75)	1927	886 pcs.	250.00	275.00	350.00	500.00
	1928	110 pcs.	250.00	275.00	350.00	500.00
	1929	—	250.00	275.00	350.00	500.00

17.5400 g, .917 GOLD, .5172 oz AGW
Monnaie de Luxe

847	1927	7,411	BV	250.00	350.00	500.00
(Y80)	1928	5,045	BV	250.00	350.00	500.00

TURKEY 1668

500 PIASTRES

36.0800 g, .917 GOLD, 1.0638 oz AGW
Rev: AH Date: 23 Nisan 1336.

KM#	Date	Mintage	Fine	VF	XF	Unc
839	1925	226 pcs.	BV	500.00	550.00	750.00
(Y76)	1926	2,268	BV	500.00	550.00	750.00
	1927	4,011	BV	500.00	550.00	750.00
	1928	375 pcs.	BV	500.00	550.00	750.00
	1929	—	BV	500.00	550.00	750.00

35.0800 g, .917 GOLD, 1.0344 oz AGW
Monnaie de Luxe

848	1927	5,097	BV	500.00	600.00	800.00
(Y81)	1928	2,242	BV	500.00	600.00	800.00

DECIMAL COINAGE
Western numerals and Latin alphabet

40 Para = 1 Kurus
100 Kurus = 1 Lira

NOTE: Mintage figures of the 1930's and early 1940's may not be exact. It is suspected that in some cases, figures for a particular year may include quantities struck with the previous year's date.

10 PARA
(1/4 Kurus)

ALUMINUM-BRONZE

KM#	Date	Mintage	VG	Fine	VF	XF
868	1940	30.800	.25	.75	2.50	5.00
(Y91)	1941	22.400	.25	.75	2.50	5.00
	1942	26.800	.25	.75	2.50	5.00

1/2 KURUS
(20 Para)

BRASS

KM#	Date	Mintage	VG	Fine	VF	XF
884	1948	150 pcs.	—	—	300.00	350.00
(Y-A92)						

Not released to circulation.

KURUS

COPPER-NICKEL

861	1935	.784	2.00	4.00	6.00	15.00
(Y87)	1936	5.300	.25	1.00	2.50	7.00
	1937	4.500	.25	1.00	2.50	7.00

867	1938	16.400	.25	.50	1.50	4.00
(Y90)	1939	21.600	.25	.50	1.50	4.00
	1940	8.800	.50	1.00	2.00	8.00
	1941	6.700	.25	.75	1.75	5.00
	1942	10.800	.25	.50	1.50	4.00
	1943	4.000	.25	.75	1.75	5.00
	1944	6.000	.25	.75	1.75	5.00

BRASS

KM#	Date	Mintage	Fine	VF	XF	Unc
881	1947	.890	1.00	1.50	2.50	5.00
(Y93)	1948	35.470	.15	.25	.50	1.50
	1949	29.530	.15	.25	.50	1.25
	1950	32.800	.15	.25	.50	1.25
	1951	6.310	.15	.30	.75	2.25
895	1961	1.180	—	—	.10	.30
(Y154)	1962	3.620	—	—	.10	.25
	1963	1.085	—	—	.10	.30

BRONZE

895a	1963	1.180	—	—	.10	.30
(Y154a)	1964	2.520	—	—	.10	.20
	1965	1.860	—	—	.10	.20
	1966	1.820	—	—	.10	.20
	1967	2.410	—	—	.10	.20
	1968	1.040	—	—	.10	.20
	1969	.900	—	—	.10	.20
	1970	1.960	—	—	.10	.20
	1971	2.940	—	—	.10	.20
	1972	.720	—	—	.10	.30
	1973	.540	—	—	.10	.30
	1974	.510	—	—	.10	.30

ALUMINUM

895b	1975	.690	—	.10	.25	1.00
(Y154c)	1976	.200	—	.10	.25	1.50
	1977	.108	—	.10	.25	1.75

BRONZE
F.A.O. Issue

924	1979	.015	—	.25	1.00	3.00
(Y187)						

ALUMINUM

924a	1979	.015	—	.25	1.00	3.00
(Y187a)						

2-1/2 KURUS

BRASS

KM#	Date	Mintage	Fine	VF	XF	Unc
885	1948	24.720	.25	.50	1.00	3.00
(Y94)	1949	23.720	.25	.50	1.00	3.00
	1950	11.560	.35	.65	1.25	4.00
	1951	2.000	2.00	5.00	12.00	40.00

5 KURUS

COPPER-NICKEL

KM#	Date	Mintage	VG	Fine	VF	XF
862	1935	.100	2.00	5.00	8.00	20.00
(Y88)	1936	2.900	.50	1.00	2.00	8.00
	1937	4.060	.30	.75	1.50	8.00
	1938	13.380	.25	.50	1.00	5.00
	1939	12.520	.25	.50	1.00	5.00
	1940	4.340	.30	.75	1.50	5.00
	1942	10.160	.20	.40	1.00	5.00
	1943	15.360	.20	.40	1.00	5.00

BRASS

KM#	Date	Mintage	Fine	VF	XF	Unc
887	1949	4.500	.25	.50	1.00	4.00
(Y95)	1950	45.900	.15	.35	.75	3.00
	1951	29.600	.15	.35	.75	3.00
	1955	15.300	.15	.35	.75	3.00
	1956	21.380	.15	.35	.75	3.00
	1957	3.320	.25	.50	1.00	4.00

BRONZE, 2.50 g

890.1	1958	25.870	.10	.25	.50	1.50
(Y155)	1959	21.580	—	—	.10	.30
	1960	17.150	—	—	.10	.30
	1961	11.110	—	—	.10	.20
	1962	15.280	—	—	.10	.30
	1963	17.680	—	—	.10	.20
	1964	18.190	—	—	.10	.30
	1965	19.170	—	—	.10	.30
	1966	19.840	—	—	.10	.30
	1967	16.170	—	—	.10	.30
	1968	26.050	—	—	.10	.30

Reduced weight, 2.00 g

890.2	1969	33.630	—	—	.10	.30
(Y155a)	1970	29.360	—	—	.10	.30
	1971	17.440	—	—	.10	.30
	1972	22.670	—	—	.10	.20
	1973	17.370	—	—	.10	.20

1.35 g

890.3	1974	13.540	—	—	.10	.20
(Y155b)						

ALUMINUM

890a	1975	1.560	—	—	.10	.30
(Y155c)	1976	1.321	—	—	.10	.30
	1977	.190	—	.10	.20	1.00

F.A.O. Issue

906	1975	1.019	—	—	.50	1.50
(Y163)						

F.A.O. Issue

907	1976	.017	—	.50	1.50	4.00
(Y172)						

TURKEY 1669

BRONZE
F.A.O. Issue

KM#	Date	Mintage	Fine	VF	XF	Unc
934 (Y-A195)	1980	.013	—	.25	.75	2.00

10 KURUS

COPPER-NICKEL

KM#	Date	Mintage	VG	Fine	VF	XF
863 (Y89)	1935	.060	2.00	5.00	8.00	20.00
	1936	3.580	.75	2.00	5.00	12.50
	1937	3.020	.50	1.00	4.00	8.00
	1938	6.610	.50	1.00	4.00	8.00
	1939	4.610	.50	1.00	2.50	5.00
	1940	6.960	.50	1.00	2.50	5.00

BRASS

KM#	Date	Mintage	Fine	VF	XF	Unc
888 (Y96)	1949	27.000	.10	.25	.75	3.00
	1951	6.200	.10	.25	.75	3.00
	1955	10.090	.10	.25	.75	3.00
	1956	9.910	.10	.25	.75	3.00

BRONZE, 4.00 g

891.1 (Y156)	1958	14.770	—	.10	.25	1.50
	1959	11.160	—	.10	.10	.40
	1960	9.450	—	.10	.10	.40
	1961	5.370	—	.10	.10	.40
	1962	9.250	—	.10	.10	.40
	1963	10.390	—	.10	.10	.40
	1964	9.890	—	.10	.10	.40
	1965	10.480	—	.10	.10	.40
	1966	12.200	—	.10	.10	.40
	1967	11.410	—	.10	.10	.40
	1968	1.862	—	.10	.10	.40

Reduced weight, 3.50 g

891.2 (Y156a)	1969	21.190	—	—	.10	.20
	1970	19.930	—	—	.10	.20
	1971	14.780	—	—	.10	.20
	1972	17.960	—	—	.10	.20
	1973	11.930	—	—	.10	.20

2.50 g

891.3 (Y156c)	1974	9.280	—	—	.10	.20

ALUMINUM

891a (Y156b)	1975	2.165	—	—	.10	.30
	1976	.559	—	.10	.20	.60
	1977	.106	—	.10	.50	1.00

BRONZE
F.A.O. Issue, 3.50 g

898.1 (Y164)	1971	.630	—	.10	.15	.75
	1972	.500	—	.10	.50	2.00
	1973	.010	—	4.00	10.00	30.00

2.50 g

898.2 (Y164a)	1974	.605	—	.10	.50	1.00

ALUMINUM

898a (Y164b)	1975	.517	—	.10	.25	.75

F.A.O. Issue

KM#	Date	Mintage	Fine	VF	XF	Unc
908 (Y173)	1976	.017	—	.50	2.00	5.00

BRONZE
F.A.O. Issue

935 (Y195)	1980	.013	—	.25	1.00	2.50

25 KURUS

3.0000 g, .830 SILVER, .0801 oz ASW

KM#	Date	Mintage	VG	Fine	VF	XF
864 (Y83)	1935	.888	1.00	2.00	6.00	15.00
	1936	10.576	1.00	2.00	10.00	20.00
	1937	8.536	1.00	2.00	10.00	20.00

NICKEL-BRONZE

880 (Y92)	1944	20.000	.25	.50	1.00	2.50
	1945	5.328	1.00	1.50	3.00	
	1946	2.672	.50	1.25	2.00	4.00

BRASS

KM#	Date	Mintage	Fine	VF	XF	Unc
886 (Y97)	1948	18.000	.10	.20	.40	1.25
	1949	21.000	.10	.20	.40	1.25
	1951	2.000	.25	.50	2.50	10.00
	1955	9.624	.10	.20	.40	1.25
	1956	14.376	.10	.20	.40	1.25

STAINLESS STEEL
Obv: Smooth ground under woman's feet.

892.1 (Y157)	1959	21.864	.10	.15	.30	.75

Obv: Rough ground under woman's feet.

892.2 (Y157b)	1960	14.778	—	.10	.15	.70
	1961	7.248	—	.10	.15	1.00
	1962	10.722	—	.10	.15	.80
	1963	11.016	—	.10	.15	.80
	1964	13.962	—	.10	.15	.70
	1965	9.816	—	.10	.15	.70
	1966	2.424	—	.10	.15	.80

Reduced weight, 4.00 g

892.3 (Y157a)	1966	7.596	—	—	.10	.50
	1967	17.022	—	—	.10	.25
	1968	31.482	—	—	.10	.25
	1969	34.566	—	—	.10	.25
	1970	32.960	—	—	.10	.25
	1973	20.496	—	—	.10	.25
	1974	16.602	—	—	.10	.25
	1977	10.204	—	—	.10	.25
	1978	.185	.35	.75	1.25	2.00

50 KURUS

6.0000 g, .830 SILVER, .1601 oz ASW

KM#	Date	Mintage	VG	Fine	VF	XF
865 (Y84)	1935	.630	3.00	6.00	10.00	20.00
	1936	5.082	2.00	5.00	8.00	15.00
	1937	4.270	12.00	30.00	50.00	100.00

4.0000 g, .600 SILVER, .0772 oz ASW

KM#	Date	Mintage	Fine	VF	XF	Unc
882 (Y98)	1947	9.296	1.00	2.50	3.50	5.00
	1948	12.704	1.00	2.50	3.50	5.00

STAINLESS STEEL

899 (Y161)	1971	16.756	—	.10	.15	.25
	1972	22.152	—	.10	.15	.25
	1973	18.928	—	.10	.15	.25
	1974	14.480	—	.10	.15	.25
	1975	27.714	—	.10	.15	.25
	1976	27.476	—	.10	.15	.25
	1977	5.062	—	.10	.15	.30
	1979	3.714	—	.10	.15	.30

F.A.O. Issue

913 (Y178)	1978	.010	—	.20	.50	1.75

F.A.O. Issue

925 (Y188)	1979	.020	—	.20	.50	1.75

F.A.O. Issue

936 (Y196)	1980	.013	—	.10	.20	1.00

100 KURUS
(1 Lira)

12.0000 g, .830 SILVER, .3203 oz ASW
Obv: High star.

KM#	Date	Mintage	VG	Fine	VF	XF
860.1 (Y82.1)	1934	.718	15.00	30.00	40.00	70.00

TURKEY 1670

Obv: Low star.

KM#	Date	Mintage	VG	Fine	VF	XF
860.2 (Y82.2)	1934	Inc. Ab.	10.00	20.00	30.00	40.00

1/2 LIRA

7.8600 g, .925 SILVER, .2337 oz ASW
100th Anniversary of Ataturk's Birth

KM#	Date	Mintage	Fine	VF	XF	Unc
941 (Y203)	1981	.025	—	—	—	12.50

8.0000 g, .917 GOLD, .2358 oz AGW

| 941a (Y203a) | 1981 | .025 | — | — | — | 125.00 |

LIRA

12.0000 g, .830 SILVER, .3203 oz ASW
Kemal Ataturk

KM#	Date	Mintage	VG	Fine	VF	XF
866 (Y85)	1937	1.624	5.00	10.00	15.00	25.00
	1938	8.282	25.00	50.00	75.00	150.00
	1939	.376	5.00	10.00	15.00	25.00

Ismet Inonu

| 869 (Y86) | 1940 | .253 | 7.50 | 12.50 | 15.00 | 20.00 |
| | 1941 | 6.167 | 4.50 | 10.00 | 12.50 | 20.00 |

7.5000 g, .600 SILVER, .1447 oz ASW

KM#	Date	Mintage	Fine	VF	XF	Unc
883 (Y99)	1947	11.104	1.50	3.50	5.00	7.00
	1948	16.896	1.50	3.00	4.00	6.50

COPPER-NICKEL

| 889 (Y158) | 1957 | 25.000 | .25 | .50 | 1.00 | 2.50 |

STAINLESS STEEL

KM#	Date	Mintage	Fine	VF	XF	Unc
889a.1 (Y158a)	1959	7.452	—	.10	.20	.50
	1960	11.436	—	.10	.20	.50
	1961	2.100	—	.10	.20	1.00
	1962	4.228	—	.10	.20	.50
	1963	4.316	—	.10	.20	.50
	1964	4.976	—	.10	.20	.50
	1965	5.348	—	.10	.20	.50
	1966	8.040	—	.10	.20	.50

Reduced weight, 7.00 g

889a.2 (Y158b)	1967	10.444	—	.10	.20	.50
	1968	12.728	—	.10	.20	.50
	1969	6.612	—	.10	.20	.50
	1970	8.652	—	.10	.20	.50
	1971	10.504	—	.10	.20	.50
	1972	26.512	—	.10	.20	.50
	1973	12.596	—	.10	.20	.50
	1974	11.596	—	.10	.20	.50
	1975	20.348	—	.10	.20	.50
	1976	23.144	—	.10	.20	.50
	1977	30.244	—	.10	.20	.50
	1978	22.156	—	.10	.20	.50
	1979	9.289	—	.10	.20	.50
	1980	3.585	—	.10	.20	.50

F.A.O. Issue

| 914 (Y179) | 1978 | .020 | — | .50 | 1.00 | 2.00 |

F.A.O. Issue
Similar to 50 Kurus, KM#925.

| 926 (Y189) | 1979 | .020 | — | .50 | 1.00 | 2.00 |

F.A.O. Issue

| 937 (Y197) | 1980 | .013 | — | .40 | .75 | 1.50 |

16.0000 g, .925 SILVER, .4758 oz ASW
100th Anniversary of Ataturk's Birth

| 942 (Y202) | 1981 | — | — | — | — | 22.50 |

16.0000 g, .917 GOLD, .4716 oz AGW

| 942a (Y202a) | 1981 | .025 | — | — | — | 250.00 |

ALUMINUM

| 943 (Y207) | 1981 | .015 | — | — | .10 | .25 |
| | 1982 | .017 | — | — | .10 | .25 |

962 (Y231)	1983	.090	—	—	.10	.20
	1984	.024	—	—	.10	.20
	1985	.042	—	—	.10	.20

2-1/2 LIRA

STAINLESS STEEL, 12.00 g

KM#	Date	Mintage	Fine	VF	XF	Unc
893.1 (Y159)	1960	4.015	—	.25	1.00	6.00
	1961	1.222	—	.25	1.00	9.00
	1962	3.636	—	.25	1.00	6.00
	1963	3.108	—	.25	1.00	6.00
	1964	2.710	—	.25	1.00	6.00
	1965	1.246	—	.25	1.00	7.00
	1966	1.788	—	.25	1.00	6.00
	1967	5.333	—	.25	1.00	5.00
	1968	2.707	—	.25	1.00	5.00

Reduced weight, 9.00 g

893.2 (Y159b)	1969	1.378	—	.15	.75	3.50
	1970	3.777	—	.15	.75	3.50
	1971	2.170	—	.15	.75	3.50
	1972	9.147	—	.15	.50	3.50
	1973	4.348	—	.15	.50	4.00
	1974	3.816	—	.15	.50	4.00
	1975	9.811	—	.15	.50	3.00
	1976	3.952	—	.15	.50	3.00
	1977	21.473	—	.10	.25	.50
	1978	15.738	—	.10	.25	.50
	1979	6.074	—	.10	.25	.50
	1980	2.621	—	.10	.25	.75

F.A.O. Issue

| 896 (Y165) | 1970 | .200 | — | .10 | .25 | .75 |

F.A.O. Issue

| 910 (Y175) | 1977 | .025 | — | .25 | .50 | 1.25 |

F.A.O. Issue

| 915 (Y180) | 1978 | .010 | — | 1.00 | 2.00 | 4.00 |

F.A.O. Issue

| 927 (Y190) | 1979 | .020 | — | 1.00 | 2.00 | 4.00 |

F.A.O. Issue

KM#	Date	Mintage	Fine	VF	XF	Unc
938 (Y198)	1980	.013	—	.50	1.50	3.00

5 LIRA

STAINLESS STEEL

905 (Y162)	1974	2.842	—	.15	.75	3.00
	1975	10.855	—	.15	.25	2.00
	1976	17.532	—	.15	.25	2.00
	1977	1.617	—	.15	.75	3.00
	1978	.076	1.50	2.50	3.50	6.00
	1979	6.074	—	.15	.30	1.00

International Women's Year and F.A.O. Issue

909 (Y174)	1976	.017	—	1.50	2.50	5.00

F.A.O. Issue

911 (Y176)	1977	.025	—	.75	1.50	2.00

F.A.O. Issue

916 (Y181)	1978	.010	—	1.25	3.00	4.00

F.A.O. Issue

KM#	Date	Mintage	Fine	VF	XF	Unc
928 (Y191)	1979	.020	—	1.25	3.00	4.00

F.A.O. Issue

939 (Y199)	1980	.013	—	1.00	2.00	3.00

ALUMINUM
Rev: Crescent opens to left.

944 (Y214)	1981	62.355	—	—	.10	.30

Rev: Crescent opens to right.

949.1 (Y217)	1982	69.975	—	—	.10	.30

Rev: Bolder, larger 5.

949.2 (Y217)	1983	—	—	—	.10	.30

963 (Y227)	1984	17.316	—	—	.10	.30
	1985	9.405	—	—	.10	.30
	1986	.010	—	—	.20	.50
	1987	.500	—	—	.20	.50

10 LIRA

15.0000 g, .830 SILVER, .4003 oz ASW

894 (Y160)	1960	8.000	—	—	4.50	6.00	9.00

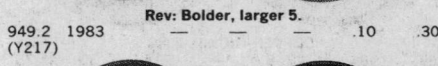

ALUMINUM
Rev: Crescent opens to left.

945 (Y215)	1981	25.520	—	—	.10	.25	.50

Rev: Crescent opens to right.

KM#	Date	Mintage	Fine	VF	XF	Unc
950.1 (Y218)	1982	17.092	—	—	.10	.25	.50

Obv: Similar to KM#950.1. Rev: Similar to KM#964.

950.2 (Y218)	1983	90.300	—	—	.10	.25	.60

964 (Y228)	1984	23.360	—	—	.10	.25	.50
	1985	41.736	—	—	—	.10	.25
	1986	79.780	—	—	—	.10	.25
	1987	62.340	—	—	—	.10	.25
	1988	—	—	—	—	.10	.25

20 LIRA

ALUMINUM
F.A.O. Issue

946 (Y205)	1981	.010	—	—	1.50	2.50

965 (Y232)	1984	1.644	—	.10	.25	1.00

25 LIRA

14.6000 g, .830 SILVER, .3896 oz ASW
50th Anniversary of National Assembly

897 (Y166)	1970	.023	—	—	10.00	20.00
	1970	Inc. Ab.	—	—	Proof	40.00

ALUMINUM

975 (Y236)	1985	37.014	—	—	.10	.35
	1986	50.820	—	—	.10	.35
	1987	61.335	—	—	.10	.35
	1988	—	—	—	.10	.35

TURKEY 1672

50 LIRA

19.0000 g, .830 SILVER, .5070 oz ASW
900th Anniversary of Battle of Malazgirt

KM#	Date	Mintage	Fine	VF	XF	Unc
900	1971	.033	—	—	12.00	22.50
(Y167)	1971	Inc. Ab.	—	—	Proof	30.00

20.1000 g, .830 SILVER, .5363 oz ASW
50th Anniversary of 30 August 1922 Victory

901	1972	.172	—	—	10.00	15.00
(Y168)	1972		—	—	Proof	20.00

13.0000 g, .900 SILVER, .3761 oz ASW
50th Anniversary of Republic

902	1973	.070	—	—	6.00	9.00
(Y169)	1973	Inc. Ab.	—	—	Proof	20.00

8.8500 g, .830 SILVER, .2361 oz ASW
F.A.O. Issue

912	1977	.025	—	—	7.00	10.00
(Y177)						

COPPER-NICKEL-ZINC

966	1984	14.731	—	.10	.20	.50
(Y233)	1985	52.658	—	.10	.20	.40
	1986	82.588	—	.10	.20	.40
	1987	32.078	—	.10	.20	.40

ALUMINUM-BRONZE

987	1988					.10

100 LIRA

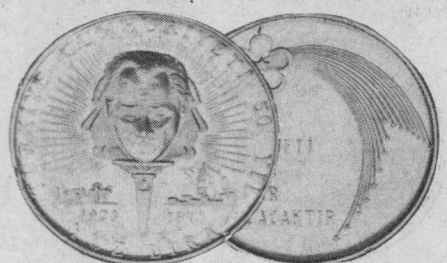

22.0000 g, .900 SILVER, .6367 oz ASW
50th Anniversary of Republic

KM#	Date	Mintage	Fine	VF	XF	Unc
903	1973	.065	—	—	10.00	15.00
(Y170)						

COPPER-NICKEL
Soccer-Madrid

951	1982	.100	.50	1.00	2.00	5.00
(Y210)						

COPPER-NICKEL-ZINC

967	1984	.758	—	.15	.30	.75
(Y234)	1985	.866	—	.15	.30	.75
	1986	12.064	—	.15	.30	.75
	1987	91.400	—	.10	.20	.60
	1988		—	.10	.20	.50

ALUMINUM-BRONZE

988	1988					.10

150 LIRA

9.0000 g, .800 SILVER, .2314 oz ASW
World Cup Soccer Championship

917	1978	5,000	—	—	—	25.00
(Y185)						

F.A.O. Issue

KM#	Date	Mintage	Fine	VF	XF	Unc
918	1978	.010	—	—	—	15.00
(Y182)	1978	2,500	—	—	Proof	25.00

F.A.O. Issue

929	1979	.010	—	—	—	12.50
(Y192)	1979	2,500	—	—	Proof	25.00

200 LIRA

9.0000 g, .830 SILVER, .2402 oz ASW
Mevlana Celaleddin I-Rumi

919	1978	.010	—	—	—	20.00
(Y186)	1978	1,000	—	—	Proof	35.00

500 LIRA

6.0000 g, .917 GOLD, .1769 oz AGW
50th Anniversary of Republic

904	1973	.030	—	—	—	150.00
(Y171)						

8.0000 g, .917 GOLD, .2358 oz AGW
F.A.O. Issue

920	1978	650 pcs.	—	—	Proof	200.00
(Y183)						

Mevlana Celaleddin I-Rumi

921	1978	900 pcs.	—	—	Proof	200.00
(Y-A186)						

F.A.O. Issue

930	1979	783 pcs.	—	—	Proof	200.00
(Y193)						

23.3300 g, .925 SILVER, .6938 oz ASW
UNICEF and I.Y.C.

931	1979(1981)	.010	—	—	—	20.00
(Y208)						

TURKEY 1673

9.0000 g, .900 SILVER, .2604 oz ASW
F.A.O. Issue

KM#	Date	Mintage	Fine	VF	XF	Unc
940	1980	.013	—	—	—	10.00
(Y200)	1980	4,000	—	—	Proof	25.00

23.3300 g, .925 SILVER, .6938 oz ASW
Soccer - Madrid

952	1982	.012	—	—	—	20.00
(Y211)						

Soccer - Madrid

953	1982	.012	—	—	—	20.00
(Y213)						

COPPER-NICKEL
Lidya - First Coin in the World

957	1983	3,542	—	—	3.50	7.00
(Y222)						

World Fisheries Conference

968	ND(1984)	3,000	—	—	2.50	6.00
(Y225)						

28.2800 g, .925 SILVER, .8411 oz ASW

968a	ND(1984)	.763	—	—	Proof	40.00
(Y225a)						

47.5400 g, .917 GOLD, 1.4009 oz AGW
World Fisheries Conference

968b	ND(1984)					
(Y225b)		74 pcs.	—	—	Proof	1550.

COPPER-NICKEL
40th Anniversary of F.A.O.

KM#	Date	Mintage	Fine	VF	XF	Unc
979	ND(1986)	3,000	—	—	Proof	10.00
(Y240)						

ALUMINUM-BRONZE

989	1989					.40

1000 LIRA

16.0000 g, .917 GOLD, .4717 oz AGW

922	1978	650 pcs.	—	—	Proof	400.00
(Y184)						

Mevlana Celaleddin I-Rumi

923	1978	450 pcs.	—	—	Proof	450.00
(Y-B186)						

F.A.O. Issue

932	1979	900 pcs.	—	—	Proof	400.00
(Y194)						

COPPER-NICKEL
Shelter For The Homeless

980	ND(1987)	—	—	—	Proof	7.00

NICKEL-BRONZE
Peace

985	1986	—	—	—	Proof	6.00

1500 LIRA

16.0000 g, .925 SILVER, .4758 oz ASW
F.A.O. Issue

947	1981	6,000	—	—	—	12.50
(Y206)	1982	500 pcs.	—	—	Proof	27.50
	1983	4,433	—	—	—	17.50

World Food Day

KM#	Date	Mintage	Fine	VF	XF	Unc
958	1983	1,552	—	—	Proof	30.00
(Y226)						

3000 LIRA

28.2800 g, .925 SILVER, .8411 oz ASW
International Year of Disabled Persons

948	1981	.014	—	—	—	25.00
(Y221)	1981	.016	—	—	Proof	22.50

International Year of the Scout

959	1983	.012	—	—	—	25.00
(Y219)	1983	.014	—	—	Proof	22.50

16.0000 g, .925 SILVER, .4758 oz ASW
60th Anniversary of the Republic

960	1983	4,000	—	—	Proof	30.00
(Y229)						

5000 LIRA

7.1300 g, .500 GOLD, .1146 oz AGW
Soccer - Madrid

954	1982	2,400	—	—	Proof	135.00
(Y212)						

TURKEY 1674

23.3300 g, .925 SILVER, .6939 oz ASW
Decode for Women

KM#	Date	Mintage	Fine	VF	XF	Unc
969 (Y223)	1984	.020	—	—	Proof	20.00

1984 Summer Olympics

| 970 (Y230) | ND(1984) | — | — | — | Proof | 40.00 |

Winter Olympics
Obv: Similar to KM#970.
Rev: Sporting figures within smoky torch.

| 971 (Y237) | 1984 | .010 | — | — | Proof | 40.00 |

50th Anniversary of Womans Suffrage

| 972 (Y238) | 1984 | 1,000 | — | — | Proof | 35.00 |

500th Anniversary of Turkish Navy

| 976 (Y239) | 1985 | 1,000 | — | — | Proof | 35.00 |

Forestry

| 977 (Y241) | 1985 | 2,000 | — | — | Proof | 30.00 |

Youth Year

KM#	Date	Mintage	Fine	VF	XF	Unc
978 (Y242)	1985	2,000	—	—	Proof	30.00

10000 LIRA

17.1700 g, .900 GOLD, .4900 oz AGW
UNICEF and I.Y.C.
Similar to 500 Lira, KM#931.

| 933 (Y209) | 1979(1981) | 4,450 | — | — | — | 300.00 |

22.9700 g, .925 SILVER, .6832 oz ASW
Shelter For The Homeless

| 981 | ND(1987) | — | — | — | Proof | 40.00 |

130 Years of Turkish Forestry

| 982 | 1987 | 5,000 | — | — | Proof | 40.00 |

23.3300 g, .925 SILVER, .6939 oz ASW
Winter Olympics - Bear Holding Torch

| 983 | 1988 | *.010 | — | — | Proof | 35.00 |

Summer Olympics - Torch

| 984 | 1988 | *.010 | — | — | Proof | 35.00 |

Soccer

KM#	Date	Mintage	Fine	VF	XF	Unc
986	1986	5,000	—	—	Proof	18.00

30000 LIRA

15.9800 g, .917 GOLD, .4712 oz AGW
International Year of Disabled Persons
Obv: Denomination within wreath.
Rev: Person on crutches, I.Y.D.P. logo.

| 955 (Y235) | 1982 | 4,000 | — | — | — | 400.00 |
| | 1982 | 3,000 | — | — | Proof | 450.00 |

International Year of the Scout
Obv: Denomination within sprays.

| 961 (Y220) | 1983 | 2,000 | — | — | — | 450.00 |
| | 1983 | 2,000 | — | — | Proof | 500.00 |

50000 LIRA

7.1300 g, .900 GOLD, .2063 oz AGW
Decade for Women

| 973 (Y224) | 1984 | 996 pcs. | — | — | Proof | 200.00 |

100000 LIRA

33.8200 g, .917 GOLD, .9972 oz AGW
Islamic World 15th Century

| 956 (Y216) | 1982 | .012 | — | — | Proof | 800.00 |

200000 LIRA

33.8200 g, .917 GOLD, .9972 oz AGW
Turkish Womens' Suffrage

| 974 (Y238) | 1984 | 58 pcs. | — | — | Proof | 1850. |

BULLION ISSUES

Since 1943, the Turkish government has issued regular and deluxe gold coins in five denominations corresponding to the old traditional 25, 50, 100, 250, and 500 Piastres of the Ottoman period. The regular coins are all dated 1923, plus the year of the republic (e.g. 1923/40 - 1963), deluxe coins bear actual AD dates. For a few years, 1944-1950, the bust of Ismet Inonu replaced that of Kemal Ataturk.

25 PIASTRES

1.8041 g, .917 GOLD, .0532 oz AGW
Ismet Inonu

850 (Y-A99)	1923/20	—	BV	50.00	65.00	90.00
	1923/22	3,228	BV	50.00	75.00	120.00
	1923/23	2,757	BV	50.00	75.00	120.00
	1923/24	.046	BV	50.00	65.00	90.00
	1923/25	.020	BV	50.00	70.00	110.00
	1923/26	.011	BV	50.00	70.00	110.00

TURKEY 1675

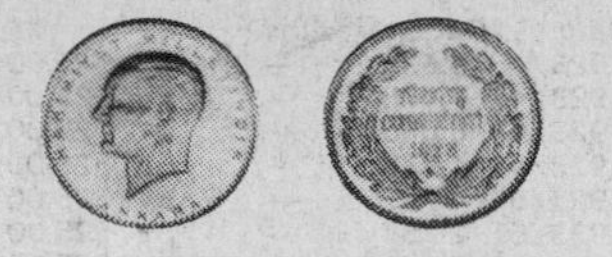

Kemal Ataturk

KM#	Date	Mintage	Fine	VF	XF	Unc
851	1923/20	.014	BV	30.00	35.00	50.00
(Y100)	1923/27	.018	BV	30.00	35.00	50.00
	1923/28	.015	BV	30.00	35.00	50.00
	1923/29	.015	BV	30.00	35.00	50.00
	1923/30	.017	BV	30.00	35.00	50.00
	1923/31	.019	BV	30.00	35.00	50.00
	1923/32	5,455	BV	30.00	35.00	50.00
	1923/33	.011	BV	30.00	35.00	50.00
	1923/34	.020	BV	30.00	35.00	50.00
	1923/35	.025	BV	30.00	35.00	50.00
	1923/36	.034	BV	30.00	35.00	50.00
	1923/37	.031	BV	30.00	35.00	50.00
	1923/38	.035	BV	30.00	35.00	50.00
	1923/39	.046	BV	30.00	35.00	50.00
	1923/40	.049	BV	30.00	35.00	50.00
	1923/41	.059	BV	30.00	35.00	50.00
	1923/42	.074	BV	30.00	35.00	50.00
	1923/43	.090	BV	30.00	35.00	50.00
	1923/44	.085	BV	30.00	35.00	50.00
	1923/45	.073	BV	30.00	35.00	50.00
	1923/46	.089	BV	30.00	35.00	50.00
	1923/47	.119	BV	30.00	35.00	50.00
	1923/48	.112	BV	30.00	35.00	50.00
	1923/49	.112	BV	30.00	35.00	50.00
	1923/50	.067	BV	30.00	35.00	50.00
	1923/51	.040	BV	30.00	35.00	50.00
	1923/52	.071	BV	30.00	35.00	50.00
	1923/53	.124	BV	30.00	35.00	50.00
	1923/54	196	BV	30.00	35.00	50.00
	1923/55	.112	BV	30.00	35.00	50.00
	1923/56	—	BV	30.00	35.00	50.00
	1923/57	—	BV	30.00	35.00	50.00

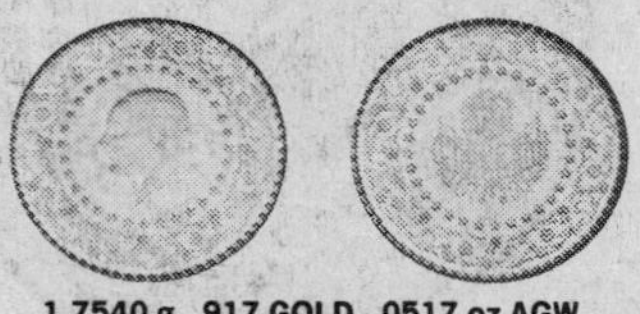

1.7540 g, .917 GOLD, .0517 oz AGW
Monnaie de Luxe
Kemal Ataturk

KM#	Date	Mintage	Fine	VF	XF	Unc
870	1942	138 pcs.	—	50.00	75.00	150.00
(Y144)	1943	386 pcs.	—	50.00	75.00	125.00
	1944	811 pcs.	—	50.00	75.00	125.00
	1946	235 pcs.	—	50.00	75.00	150.00
	1950	2,053	—	30.00	40.00	60.00
	1951	2,035	—	30.00	40.00	60.00
	1952	3,374	—	30.00	40.00	60.00
	1953	1,944	—	30.00	40.00	60.00
	1954	2,244	—	30.00	40.00	60.00
	1955	2,573	—	30.00	40.00	60.00
	1956	4,004	—	30.00	40.00	60.00
	1957	8,842	—	30.00	40.00	60.00
	1958	9,546	—	30.00	40.00	60.00
	1959	.017	—	30.00	40.00	60.00
	1960	.019	—	30.00	40.00	60.00
	1961	.035	—	30.00	40.00	60.00
	1962	.031	—	30.00	40.00	60.00
	1963	.047	—	30.00	40.00	60.00
	1964	.057	—	30.00	40.00	60.00
	1965	.078	—	30.00	40.00	60.00
	1966	.106	—	30.00	40.00	60.00
	1967	.114	—	30.00	40.00	60.00
	1968	.152	—	30.00	40.00	60.00
	1969	.163	—	30.00	40.00	60.00
	1970	.224	—	30.00	40.00	60.00
	1971	.306	—	30.00	40.00	60.00
	1972	.271	—	30.00	40.00	60.00
	1973	.162	—	30.00	40.00	60.00
	1974	.141	—	30.00	40.00	60.00
	1975	.202	—	30.00	40.00	60.00
	1976	.583	—	30.00	40.00	60.00
	1977	1.089	—	30.00	40.00	60.00
	1978	.238	—	30.00	40.00	60.00
	1980	—	—	30.00	40.00	60.00

Monnaie de Luxe
Ismet Inonu

KM#	Date	Mintage	Fine	VF	XF	Unc
875	1943					
(Y134)		Inc. KM870	80.00	100.00	150.00	200.00
	1944					
		Inc. KM870	80.00	100.00	150.00	200.00
	1945	592 pcs.	80.00	100.00	150.00	200.00
	1946					
		Inc. KM870	80.00	100.00	150.00	200.00
	1947	3,443	80.00	100.00	125.00	200.00
	1948	714 pcs.	80.00	100.00	150.00	200.00
	1949	552 pcs.	80.00	100.00	150.00	200.00

50 PIASTRES

3.6083 g, .917 GOLD, .1064 oz AGW
Ismet Inonu

KM#	Date	Mintage	Fine	VF	XF	Unc
852	1923/20	—	60.00	100.00	125.00	175.00
(Y-B99)	1923/22	1,093	60.00	100.00	125.00	175.00
	1923/23					
		897 pcs.	60.00	125.00	150.00	200.00
	1923/24	.011	60.00	100.00	125.00	175.00
	1923/25	3,004	60.00	100.00	125.00	175.00
	1923/26					
		817 pcs.	60.00	125.00	150.00	200.00
	1923/27	5,228	60.00	100.00	125.00	175.00

Kemal Ataturk

KM#	Date	Mintage	Fine	VF	XF	Unc
853	1923/20	.012	BV	50.00	60.00	80.00
(Y101)	1923/27	I.A.	BV	50.00	60.00	80.00
	1923/28	3,300	BV	50.00	60.00	80.00
	1923/29	6,384	BV	50.00	60.00	80.00
	1923/30	4,590	BV	50.00	60.00	80.00
	1923/31	9,068	BV	50.00	60.00	80.00
	1923/32	4,344	BV	50.00	60.00	80.00
	1923/33	3,958	BV	50.00	60.00	80.00
	1923/34	9,499	BV	50.00	60.00	80.00
	1923/35	9,307	BV	50.00	60.00	80.00
	1923/36	.012	BV	50.00	60.00	80.00
	1923/37	9,049	BV	50.00	60.00	80.00
	1923/38	9,854	BV	50.00	60.00	80.00
	1923/39	.011	BV	50.00	60.00	80.00
	1923/40	.013	BV	50.00	60.00	80.00
	1923/41	.013	BV	50.00	60.00	80.00
	1923/42	.018	BV	50.00	60.00	80.00
	1923/43	.026	BV	50.00	60.00	80.00
	1923/44	.026	BV	50.00	60.00	80.00
	1923/45	.025	BV	50.00	60.00	80.00
	1923/46	.028	BV	50.00	60.00	80.00
	1923/47	.038	BV	50.00	60.00	80.00
	1923/48	.035	BV	50.00	60.00	80.00
	1923/49	.028	BV	50.00	60.00	80.00
	1923/50	.016	BV	50.00	60.00	80.00
	1923/51	.008	BV	50.00	60.00	80.00
	1923/52	.014	BV	50.00	60.00	80.00
	1923/53	.028	BV	50.00	60.00	80.00
	1923/54	.054	BV	50.00	60.00	80.00
	1923/55	.016	BV	50.00	60.00	80.00
	1923/57	—	BV	50.00	60.00	80.00

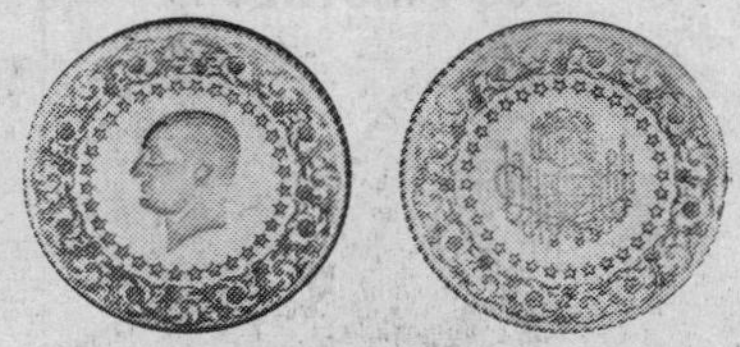

Monnaie de Luxe
Kemal Ataturk

KM#	Date	Mintage	Fine	VF	XF	Unc
871	1942	115 pcs.	100.00	150.00	200.00	250.00
(Y145)	1943	91 pcs.	100.00	150.00	200.00	250.00
	1944	950 pcs.	80.00	125.00	150.00	175.00
	1946	565 pcs.	80.00	125.00	150.00	175.00
	1950	1,971	—	50.00	80.00	150.00
	1951	1,780	—	50.00	80.00	150.00
	1952	2,557	—	50.00	80.00	150.00
	1953	2,392	—	50.00	80.00	150.00
	1954	1,714	—	50.00	80.00	150.00
	1955	4,143	—	50.00	70.00	125.00
	1956	2,956	—	50.00	70.00	125.00
	1957	6,855	—	50.00	70.00	125.00
	1958	6,381	—	50.00	70.00	125.00
	1959	.012	—	50.00	60.00	75.00
	1960	.012	—	50.00	60.00	75.00
	1961	.015	—	50.00	60.00	75.00
	1962	.022	—	50.00	60.00	75.00
	1963	.029	—	50.00	60.00	75.00
	1964	.034	—	50.00	60.00	75.00
	1965	.044	—	50.00	60.00	75.00
	1966	.058	—	50.00	60.00	75.00
	1967	.064	—	50.00	60.00	75.00
	1968	.082	—	50.00	60.00	75.00
	1969	.079	—	50.00	60.00	75.00
	1970	.109	—	50.00	60.00	75.00
	1971	.154	—	50.00	60.00	75.00
	1972	.110	—	50.00	60.00	75.00
	1973	.073	—	50.00	60.00	75.00
	1974	.045	—	50.00	60.00	75.00
	1975	.072	—	50.00	60.00	75.00
	1976	.196	—	50.00	60.00	75.00
	1977	.361	—	50.00	60.00	75.00
	1978	.161	—	50.00	60.00	75.00
	1980	—	—	50.00	60.00	75.00

Monnaie de Luxe
Ismet Inonu

KM#	Date	Mintage	Fine	VF	XF	Unc
876	1943					
(Y135)		Inc. KM871	—	150.00	200.00	250.00
	1944					
		Inc. KM871	—	125.00	175.00	225.00
	1945	515 pcs.	—	125.00	175.00	225.00
	1946					
		Inc. KM871	—	100.00	150.00	200.00
	1947	3,481	—	100.00	150.00	200.00
	1948	773 pcs.	—	100.00	150.00	200.00
	1949	582 pcs.	—	100.00	150.00	200.00

100 PIASTRES

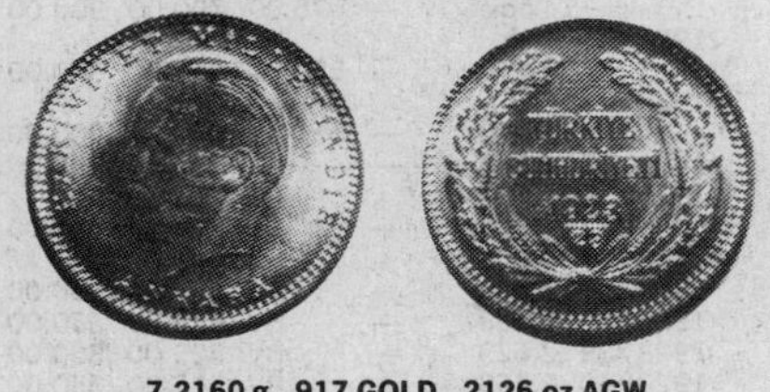

7.2160 g, .917 GOLD, .2126 oz AGW
Ismet Inonu

KM#	Date	Mintage	Fine	VF	XF	Unc
854	1923/20	—	—	BV	110.00	150.00
(Y-C99)	1923/22	3 pcs.	—	—	Rare	—
	1923/23	.381	—	BV	110.00	150.00
	1923/24	2,274	—	BV	110.00	160.00
(Y-C99)	1923/25	.028	—	BV	110.00	160.00
	1923/26	2,097	—	BV	110.00	160.00
	1923/27	.017	—	BV	110.00	160.00

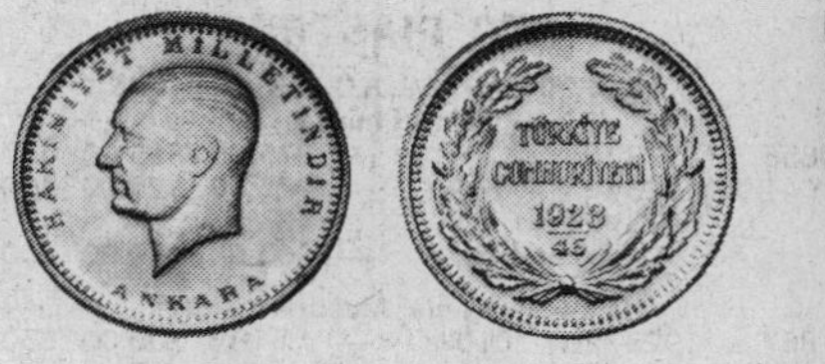

Kemal Ataturk

KM#	Date	Mintage	Fine	VF	XF	Unc
855	1923/20	.029	—	BV	110.00	125.00
(Y102)	1923/27	I.A.	—	BV	110.00	125.00
	1923/28	3 pcs.	—	—	Rare	—
	1923/29	2,111	—	BV	110.00	125.00
	1923/30	.013	—	BV	110.00	125.00
	1923/31	.109	—	BV	110.00	125.00
	1923/32	.134	—	BV	110.00	125.00
	1923/33	.216	—	BV	110.00	125.00
	1923/34	.463	—	BV	110.00	125.00
	1923/35	.405	—	BV	110.00	125.00
	1923/36	.025	—	BV	110.00	125.00
	1923/37	.131	—	BV	110.00	125.00
	1923/38	.159	—	BV	110.00	125.00
	1923/39	.085	—	BV	110.00	125.00
	1923/40	.010	—	BV	110.00	125.00
	1923/41	.164	—	BV	110.00	125.00
	1923/42	.063	—	BV	110.00	125.00
	1923/43	.056	—	BV	110.00	125.00
	1923/44	.198	—	BV	110.00	125.00
	1923/45	.176	—	BV	110.00	125.00
	1923/46	1.290	—	BV	110.00	125.00
	1923/47	.513	—	BV	110.00	125.00
	1923/48					
		600 pcs.	110.00	130.00	150.00	200.00
	1923/49	1,300	—	110.00	120.00	150.00
	1923/50	.047	—	BV	110.00	125.00
	1923/51	.240	—	BV	110.00	125.00
	1923/52	1.047	—	BV	110.00	125.00
	1923/53	.550	—	BV	110.00	125.00
	1923/54	.018	—	BV	110.00	125.00
	1923/55	.309	—	BV	110.00	125.00
	1923/57	—	—	BV	110.00	125.00
	1923/58	—	—	BV	110.00	125.00

7.0160 g, .917 GOLD, .2069 oz AGW
Monnaie de Luxe
Kemal Ataturk

KM#	Date	Mintage	Fine	VF	XF	Unc
872	1942	8,659	—	125.00	150.00	225.00
(Y146)	1943	6,594	—	125.00	150.00	225.00
	1944	7,160	—	125.00	150.00	225.00
	1948	.014	—	125.00	150.00	200.00
	1950	.025	—	125.00	150.00	200.00
	1951	.035	—	125.00	150.00	175.00
	1952	.041	—	125.00	150.00	175.00
	1953	.032	—	125.00	150.00	175.00
	1954	.024	—	125.00	150.00	175.00
	1955	4,881	—	125.00	150.00	200.00
	1956	.011	—	110.00	125.00	150.00
	1957	.049	—	110.00	125.00	150.00
	1958	.067	—	110.00	125.00	150.00
	1959	.089	—	110.00	125.00	150.00
	1960	.057	—	110.00	125.00	150.00
	1961	.077	—	110.00	125.00	150.00
	1962	.108	—	110.00	125.00	150.00
	1963	.146	—	110.00	125.00	150.00
	1964	.128	—	110.00	125.00	150.00
	1965	.157	—	110.00	125.00	150.00
	1966	.190	—	110.00	125.00	150.00
	1967	.177	—	110.00	125.00	150.00
	1968	.143	—	110.00	125.00	150.00
	1969	.206	—	110.00	125.00	150.00
	1970	.253	—	110.00	125.00	150.00
	1971	.293	—	110.00	125.00	150.00
	1972	.222	—	110.00	125.00	150.00
	1973	.140	—	110.00	125.00	150.00
	1974	.082	—	110.00	125.00	150.00
	1975	.142	—	110.00	125.00	150.00
	1976	.265	—	110.00	125.00	150.00
	1977	.277	—	110.00	125.00	150.00
	1978	.086	—	110.00	125.00	150.00
	1980	—	—	110.00	125.00	150.00

Monnaie de Luxe
Ismet Inonu

KM#	Date	Mintage	Fine	VF	XF	Unc
877	1943					
(Y136)		Inc. KM872	150.00	200.00	275.00	325.00
	1944					
		Inc. KM872	150.00	200.00	275.00	375.00
	1945	2,202	150.00	200.00	275.00	400.00
	1946	8,863	150.00	200.00	275.00	325.00
	1947	.028	150.00	200.00	275.00	325.00
	1948					

TURKEY 1676

KM#	Date	Mintage	Fine	VF	XF	Unc
(Y136)		Inc. KM872	150.00	200.00	275.00	325.00
	1949	6,578	150.00	200.00	275.00	325.00
	1950	Inc. KM872	150.00	200.00	275.00	325.00

250 PIASTRES
18.0400 g, .917 GOLD, .5319 oz AGW
Ismet Inonu

KM#	Date	Mintage	Fine	VF	XF	Unc
856	1923/20	—	—	275.00	325.00	400.00
(Y-D99)	1923/23	.014	—	275.00	325.00	400.00
	1923/24	60 pcs.	—	300.00	400.00	500.00

Kemal Ataturk

KM#	Date	Mintage	Fine	VF	XF	Unc
857	1923/20	.010	—	BV	300.00	350.00
(Y103)	1923/29	3 pcs.	—		Rare	
	1923/30	130 pcs.	—	500.00	700.00	900.00
	1923/31	—	—	500.00	700.00	900.00
	1923/38	245 pcs.	—	350.00	375.00	600.00
	1923/39	389 pcs.	—	350.00	375.00	600.00
	1923/40	435 pcs.	—	350.00	375.00	600.00
	1923/41	349 pcs.	—	350.00	375.00	600.00
	1923/42	460 pcs.	—	350.00	375.00	600.00
	1923/43	1,008	—	275.00	325.00	400.00
	1923/44	712 pcs.	—	275.00	325.00	400.00
	1923/45	1,034	—	275.00	325.00	400.00
	1923/46	1,035	—	275.00	325.00	400.00
	1923/47	1,408	—	275.00	325.00	400.00
	1923/48	904 pcs.	—	275.00	325.00	400.00
	1923/49	1,066	—	275.00	325.00	400.00
	1923/50	975 pcs.	—	275.00	325.00	400.00
	1923/51	298 pcs.	—	275.00	325.00	400.00
	1923/52	610 pcs.	—	275.00	325.00	400.00
	1923/53	586 pcs.	—	275.00	325.00	400.00
	1923/54	289 pcs.	—	275.00	325.00	400.00
	1923/55	267 pcs.	—	275.00	325.00	400.00
	1923/57		—	275.00	325.00	400.00

17.5400 g, .917 GOLD, .5172 oz AGW
Monnaie de Luxe
Kemal Ataturk

KM#	Date	Mintage	Fine	VF	XF	Unc
873	1942	.010	—	300.00	425.00	600.00
(Y147)	1943	.011	—	300.00	425.00	600.00
	1944	.015	—	350.00	700.00	900.00
	1946	.016	—	350.00	700.00	900.00
	1947	.042	—	300.00	425.00	600.00
	1948	.013	—	300.00	425.00	600.00
	1950	.045	—	300.00	425.00	600.00
	1951	.041	—	275.00	325.00	400.00
	1952	.059	—	275.00	325.00	400.00
	1953	.045	—	275.00	325.00	400.00
	1954	.040	—	275.00	325.00	400.00
	1955	7,067	—	275.00	325.00	400.00
	1956	.014	—	275.00	325.00	400.00
	1957	.047	—	275.00	325.00	400.00
	1958	.075	—	275.00	325.00	400.00
	1959	.093	—	275.00	325.00	400.00
	1960	.050	—	275.00	325.00	400.00
	1961	.065	—	275.00	325.00	400.00
	1962	.099	—	275.00	325.00	400.00
	1963	.137	—	275.00	325.00	400.00
	1964	.152	—	275.00	325.00	400.00
(Y147)	1965	.194	—	275.00	325.00	400.00
	1966	.218	—	275.00	325.00	400.00
	1967	.201	—	275.00	325.00	400.00
	1968	.150	—	275.00	325.00	400.00
	1969	.262	—	275.00	325.00	400.00
	1970	.301	—	275.00	325.00	400.00
	1971	.356	—	275.00	325.00	400.00
	1972	.305	—	275.00	325.00	400.00
	1973	.198	—	275.00	325.00	400.00
	1974	.142	—	275.00	325.00	400.00
	1975	.223	—	275.00	325.00	400.00
	1976	.345	—	275.00	325.00	400.00
	1977	.227	—	275.00	325.00	400.00
	1978	.311	—	275.00	325.00	400.00
	1980		—	275.00	325.00	400.00

Monnaie de Luxe
Ismet Inonu

KM#	Date	Mintage	Fine	VF	XF	Unc
878	1943	Inc. KM873	—	275.00	325.00	425.00
(Y137)	1944	Inc. KM873	—	275.00	325.00	425.00
	1945	4,135	—	300.00	400.00	550.00
	1946	Inc. KM873	—	275.00	325.00	425.00
	1947	Inc. KM873	—	275.00	325.00	425.00
	1948	Inc. KM873	—	275.00	325.00	425.00
	1949	.011	—	275.00	325.00	425.00
	1950	Inc. KM873	—	275.00	325.00	425.00

500 PIASTRES

36.0800 g, .917 GOLD, 1.0638 oz AGW
Ismet Inonu
Similar to 100 Piastres, KM#855.

KM#	Date	Mintage	Fine	VF	XF	Unc
858	1923/20	—	—	BV	550.00	700.00
(Y-E99)	1923/23	9,006	—	BV	550.00	700.00
	1923/24	7,923	—	650.00	800.00	900.00
	1923/25	272 pcs.	—	750.00	900.00	1000.

Kemal Ataturk

KM#	Date	Mintage	Fine	VF	XF	Unc
859	1923/20	.012	—	BV	550.00	700.00
(Y104)	1923/27	615 pcs.	—	650.00	800.00	1000.
	1923/28	34 pcs.	—	650.00	800.00	1000.
	1923/29	137 pcs.	—	575.00	700.00	900.00
	1923/30	45 pcs.	—	575.00	700.00	900.00
	1923/31	100 pcs.	—	575.00	700.00	900.00
	1923/32	74 pcs.	—	575.00	700.00	900.00
	1923/33	268 pcs.	—	550.00	650.00	800.00
	1923/34	758 pcs.	—	550.00	650.00	800.00
	1923/35	1,586	—	BV	525.00	550.00
	1923/36	765 pcs.	—	BV	525.00	550.00
	1923/37	983 pcs.	—	BV	525.00	550.00
	1923/38	1,738	—	BV	525.00	550.00
	1923/39	2,629	—	BV	525.00	550.00
	1923/40	2,763	—	BV	525.00	550.00
	1923/41	3,440	—	BV	525.00	550.00
	1923/42	3,335	—	BV	525.00	550.00
	1923/43	4,914	—	BV	525.00	550.00
	1923/44	4,308	—	BV	525.00	550.00
	1923/45	3,488	—	BV	525.00	550.00
(Y104)	1923/46	5,636	—	BV	525.00	550.00
	1923/47	7,588	—	BV	525.00	550.00
	1923/48	6,060	—	BV	525.00	550.00
	1923/49	4,235	—	BV	525.00	550.00
	1923/50	4,733	—	BV	525.00	550.00
	1923/51	2,757	—	BV	525.00	550.00
	1923/52	2,041	—	BV	525.00	550.00
	1923/53	4,819	—	BV	525.00	550.00
	1923/54	1,401	—	BV	525.00	550.00
	1923/55	1,484	—	BV	525.00	550.00
	1923/57		—	BV	525.00	550.00

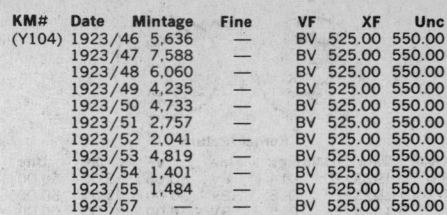

35.0800 g, .917 GOLD, 1.0344 oz AGW
Monnaie de Luxe
Kemal Ataturk

KM#	Date	Mintage	Fine	VF	XF	Unc
874	1942	2,949	—	525.00	550.00	575.00
(Y148)	1943	1,210	—	525.00	550.00	575.00
	1944	1,254	—	525.00	550.00	575.00
	1947	3,699	—	525.00	550.00	575.00
	1950	59 pcs.	—	525.00	550.00	575.00
	1951	21 pcs.	—	525.00	550.00	575.00
	1952	26 pcs.	—	525.00	550.00	575.00
	1953	35 pcs.	—	525.00	550.00	575.00
	1954	182 pcs.	—	525.00	550.00	575.00
	1955	14 pcs.	—	525.00	550.00	575.00
	1956	13 pcs.	—	525.00	550.00	575.00
	1957	68 pcs.	—	525.00	550.00	575.00
	1958	121 pcs.	—	525.00	550.00	575.00
	1959	294 pcs.	—	550.00	700.00	900.00
	1960	208 pcs.	—	550.00	700.00	900.00
	1961	619 pcs.	—	550.00	700.00	900.00
	1962	1,228	—	525.00	550.00	575.00
	1963	1,985	—	525.00	550.00	575.00
	1964	2,787	—	525.00	550.00	575.00
	1965	4,631	—	525.00	550.00	575.00
	1966	5,572	—	525.00	550.00	575.00
	1967	6,637	—	525.00	550.00	575.00
	1968	5,983	—	525.00	550.00	575.00
	1969	7,152	—	525.00	550.00	575.00
	1970	.011	—	525.00	550.00	575.00
	1971	.015	—	525.00	550.00	575.00
	1972	.015	—	525.00	550.00	575.00
	1973	7,939	—	525.00	550.00	575.00
	1974	5,412	—	525.00	550.00	575.00
	1975	6,205	—	525.00	550.00	575.00
	1976	.011	—	525.00	550.00	575.00
	1977	6,931	—	525.00	550.00	575.00
	1978	5,740	—	525.00	550.00	575.00
	1980	—	—	525.00	550.00	575.00

Monnaie de Luxe
Ismet Inonu

KM#	Date	Mintage	Fine	VF	XF	Unc
879	1943		—	525.00	550.00	600.00
(Y138)	1944	Inc. KM874	—	525.00	550.00	600.00
		Inc. KM874	—	525.00	550.00	600.00
	1945	115 pcs.	—	525.00	550.00	600.00
	1946	298 pcs.	—	525.00	550.00	600.00
	1947	Inc. KM874	—	525.00	550.00	600.00
	1948	40 pcs.	—	525.00	550.00	600.00

MINT SETS (MS)

KM#	Date	Mintage	Identification	Issue Price	Mkt. Val.
MS1	1962(6)	—	KM889a.1,890.1-891.1,892.2, 893.1,894	—	Rare
MS2	1964(6)		KM889a.1,890.1-891.1,892.2, 893.1,895a	—	7.50
MS3	1965(6)		KM889a.1,890.1-891.1,892.2, 893.1,895a	—	7.50
MS4	1966(6)		KM889a.1,890.1-891.1,892.2, 893.1,895a	—	7.50
MS5	1968(6)		KM889a.2,890.1-891.1,892.3, 893.1,895a	—	7.50
MS6	1969(6)		KM889a.2,890.2-891.2,892.3, 893.2,895a	—	6.00
MS7	1970(6)		KM889a.2,890.2-891.2,892.3, 893.2,895a	—	6.00
MS8	1971(6)		KM889a.2,890.2-891.2,893.2, 895a,899	—	6.00
MS9	1972(6)		KM889a.2,890.2-891.2,893.2, 895a,899	—	4.00
MS10	1973(7)		KM889a.2,890.2-891.2,893.2, 893.2,895a,899	—	4.00
MS11	1974(7)		KM889a.2,890.3-892.3,893.2, 895a,899	—	4.00
MS12	1975(7)		KM889a.2,890a-891a,893.2, 895c,899,905	—	4.00
MS13	1976(7)		KM889a.2,890a-891a,893.2, 895c,899,905	—	4.00
MS14	1977(8)		KM889a.2,890a-891a,892.3, 893.2,895c,899,905	—	3.50
MS15	1978(4)		KM889a.2,892.3,893.2,905	—	3.00
MS16	1979(4)		KM889a.2,893.2,899,905	—	3.00
MS17	1980(2)		KM889a.2,893.2	—	2.00
MS18	1981(3)		KM943-945	—	3.00
MS19	1982(3)		KM943,949,950	—	3.00
MS20	1983(2)		KM949,950	—	3.00
MS21	1984(6)		KM962-967	—	5.50
MS22	1985(6)		KM962-964,966,967,975	—	5.00
MS23	1986(5)		KM963-967	—	4.00

TURKS & CAICOS IS.

The Colony of the Turks and Caicos Islands, a British colony situated in the West Indies at the eastern end of the Bahama Islands, has an area of 166 sq. mi. (430 sq. km.) and a population of *9,000. Capital: Cockburn Town, on Grand Turk. The principal industry of the colony is the production of salt, which is gathered by raking. Salt, crayfish, and conch shells are exported.

The Turks and Caicos Islands were discovered by Juan Ponce de Leon in 1512, but were not settled until 1678 when Bermudians arrived to rake salt from the salt ponds. The British settlers were driven from the island by the Spanish in 1710, during the long War of the Spanish Succession. They returned and throughout the remaining years of the war repulsed repeated attacks by France and Spain. In 1799 the islands were granted representation in the Bahamian assembly, but in 1848, on petition of the inhabitants, they were made a separate colony under Jamaica. They were annexed by Jamaica in 1873 and remained a dependency until 1959 when they became a unit territory of the Federation of the West Indies. When the Federation was dissolved in 1962, the Turks and Caicos Islands became a separate Crown Colony.

RULERS
British

1/4 CROWN

COPPER-NICKEL

KM#	Date	Mintage	Fine	VF	XF	Unc
51	1981	—				.75

1/2 CROWN

COPPER-NICKEL

| 52 | 1981 | — | | | | 1.50 |

CROWN

COPPER-NICKEL

| 1 | 1969 | .050 | | | 1.50 | 3.50 |
| | 1969 | 6,000 | | | Proof | 5.00 |

KM#	Date	Mintage	Fine	VF	XF	Unc
5	1975	590 pcs.	—	—	—	10.00
	1975	1,370	—	—	Proof	7.50
	1976	1,960	—	—	—	5.00
	1976	2,270	—	—	Proof	7.50
	1977	1,420	—	—	Proof	7.50

Prince Andrew's Marriage

| 60 | 1986 | .020 | | | | 4.00 |

28.2800 g, .925 SILVER, .8411 oz ASW

| 60a | 1986 | 5,000 | — | — | Proof | 27.50 |

COPPER-NICKEL
World Wildlife Fund - Iguana

| 64 | 1988 | | | | | 4.00 |

28.2800 g, .925 SILVER, .8411 oz ASW

| 64a | 1988 | *.025 | — | — | Proof | 30.00 |

5 CROWNS

24.2400 g, .500 SILVER, .3897 oz ASW

6	1975	440 pcs.	—	—	—	20.00
	1975	1,320	—	—	Proof	15.00
	1976	1,760	—	—	—	12.50
	1976	2,220	—	—	Proof	12.50
	1977	1,370	—	—	Proof	15.00

14.5800 g, .500 SILVER, .2344 oz ASW
Lord Mountbatten

TURKS & CAICOS ISLANDS 1678

Obv: Similar to 10 Crowns, KM#45.

KM#	Date	Mintage	Fine	VF	XF	Unc
47	1980	—	—	—	Proof	8.00

10 CROWNS

29.9800 g, .925 SILVER, .8916 oz ASW
Age of Exploration

7	1975	1,250	—	—	—	27.50
	1975	2,935	—	—	Proof	27.50

Obv: Similar to KM#7.

12	1976	4,185	—	—	—	25.00
	1976	2,220	—	—	Proof	30.00
	1977	1,370	—	—	Proof	35.00

29.7000 g, .925 SILVER, .8832 oz ASW
10th Anniversary of Prince Charles' Investiture

45	1979	.025	—	—	Proof	17.50

23.3300 g, .500 SILVER, .3750 oz ASW
Lord Mountbatten
Obv: Similar to KM#45.

48	1980	—	—	—	Proof	16.50

29.7000 g, .925 SILVER, .8832 oz ASW
Wedding of Prince Charles and Lady Diana
Similar to 100 Crowns, KM#54.

KM#	Date	Mintage	Fine	VF	XF	Unc
53	1981	.040	—	—	Proof	27.50

23.2800 g, .925 SILVER, .6923 oz ASW
International Year of the Child

55	1982	7,928	—	—	Proof	30.00

World Football Championship

56	1982	7,865	—	—	Proof	30.00

World Football Championship

57	1982	7,165	—	—	Proof	30.00

Summer Olympics

KM#	Date	Mintage	Fine	VF	XF	Unc
58	1984	2,160	—	—	Proof	35.00

Decade For Women

63	1985	1,001	—	—	Proof	25.00

20 CROWNS

38.7000 g, .925 SILVER, 1.1509 oz ASW
Churchill Centenary

2	1974	.268	—	—	—	12.50
	1974	8,400*	—	—	Proof	17.50

NOTE: 4,100 issued individually while 4,300 were issued in binational sets along with Cayman Islands 25 Dollars, KM#10.

Christopher Columbus
Obv: Similar to 10 Crowns, KM#7.

8	1975	1,037	—	—	—	30.00
	1975	2,769	—	—	Proof	35.00

TURKS & CAICOS ISLANDS 1679

U.S. Bicentennial
Obv: Similar to 10 Crowns, KM#7.

KM#	Date	Mintage	Fine	VF	XF	Unc
13	1976	5,022	—	—	—	25.00
	1976	4,474	—	—	Proof	32.50

29.8100 g, .500 SILVER, .4792 oz ASW
Lord Mountbatten
Obv: Similar to 10 Crowns, KM#45.

KM#	Date	Mintage	Fine	VF	XF	Unc
49	1980	—	—	—	Proof	20.00

25 CROWNS

Griffin of Edward III
Obv: Similar to 50 Crowns, KM#39.

KM#	Date	Mintage	Fine	VF	XF	Unc
25	1978	—	—	—	Proof	50.00

4.5000 g, .500 GOLD, .0723 oz AGW

9.1	1975	1,272	—	—	—	45.00
	1975	2,096	—	—	Proof	45.00

19mm

9.2	1976	—	—	—	—	45.00
	1976	2,185	—	—	Proof	45.00
	1977	2,125	—	—	Proof	45.00

Red Dragon of Wales
Obv: Similar to 50 Crowns, KM#39.

26	1978	—	—	—	Proof	50.00

Victoria Portraits
Obv: Similar to 10 Crowns, KM#7.

14	1976	.025	—	—	—	17.50
	1976	.022	—	—	Proof	25.00
	1977	1,934	—	—	Proof	70.00

43.7500 g, .925 SILVER, 1.3012 oz ASW
Queen's Silver Jubilee
Obv: Similar to 10 Crowns, KM#7.

19	1977	—	—	—	—	25.00
	1977	.013	—	—	Proof	30.00

White Greyhound of Richmond
Obv: Similar to 50 Crowns, KM#39.

27	1978	—	—	—	Proof	50.00

George III Portraits
Obv: Similar to 1/2 Crown, KM#52.

18	1977	—	—	—	—	45.00
	1977	1,973	—	—	Proof	65.00

Unicorn of Scotland
Obv: Similar to 50 Crowns, KM#39.

28	1978	—	—	—	Proof	70.00

XI Commonwealth Games
Obv: Similar to 10 Crowns, KM#55.

23	1978	.010	—	—	Proof	30.00

**25th Anniversary of Coronation
Lion of England**
Obv: Similar to 50 Crowns, KM#39.

24	1978	—	—	—	Proof	50.00

White Horse of Hannover
Similar to 50 Crowns, KM#39.

29	1978	—	—	—	Proof	50.00

TURKS & CAICOS ISLANDS 1680

Black Bull of Clarence
Obv: Similar to 50 Crowns, KM#39.

KM#	Date	Mintage	Fine	VF	XF	Unc
30	1978	—	—	—	Proof	50.00

Yale of Beaufort
Obv: Similar to 50 Crowns, KM#39.

| 31 | 1978 | — | — | — | Proof | 50.00 |

Falcon of the Plantaganets
Obv: Similar to 50 Crowns, KM#39.

| 32 | 1978 | — | — | — | Proof | 50.00 |

White Lion of Mortimer
Obv: Similar to 50 Crowns, KM#39.

| 33 | 1978 | — | — | — | Proof | 50.00 |

50 CROWNS

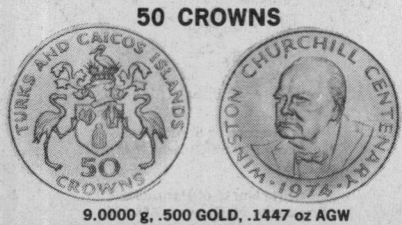

9.0000 g, .500 GOLD, .1447 oz AGW
Churchill Centenary

KM#	Date	Mintage	Fine	VF	XF	Unc
3	1974	.030	—	—	—	75.00
	1974	4,000	—	—	Proof	85.00

6.2200 g, .500 GOLD, .1000 oz AGW
Christopher Columbus

| 10 | 1975 | 2,863 | — | — | — | 90.00 |
| | 1975 | 1,577 | — | — | Proof | 100.00 |

U.S. Bicentennial

| 15 | 1976 | 905 pcs. | — | — | — | 100.00 |
| | 1976 | 2,421 | — | — | Proof | 100.00 |

55.1800 g, .925 SILVER, 1.6412 oz ASW
Queen Victoria
Obv: Similar to 10 Crowns, KM#7.

16	1976	3,500	—	—	—	50.00
	1976	2,908	—	—	Proof	55.00
	1977	940 pcs.	—	—	Proof	80.00

9.0000 g, .500 GOLD, .1447 oz AGW
Queen's Silver Jubilee

| 20 | 1977 | — | — | — | — | 85.00 |
| | 1977 | 2,903 | — | — | Proof | 100.00 |

55.1800 g, .925 SILVER, 1.6412 oz ASW
George III Portraits
Obv: Similar to 10 Crowns, KM#7.

| 21 | 1977 | — | — | — | — | 75.00 |
| | 1977 | 958 pcs. | — | — | Proof | 125.00 |

9.0000 g, .500 GOLD, .1447 oz AGW
25th Anniversary of Coronation
Lion of England

KM#	Date	Mintage	Fine	VF	XF	Unc
34	1978	261 pcs.	—	—	Proof	200.00

Griffin of Edward III

| 35 | 1978 | 266 pcs. | — | — | Proof | 200.00 |

Red Dragon of Wales

| 36 | 1978 | 266 pcs. | — | — | Proof | 200.00 |

White Greyhound of Richmond

| 37 | 1978 | 270 pcs. | — | — | Proof | 200.00 |

Unicorn of Scotland

| 38 | 1978 | 268 pcs. | — | — | Proof | 200.00 |

White Horse of Hannover

| 39 | 1978 | 266 pcs. | — | — | Proof | 200.00 |

Black Bull of Clarence

| 40 | 1978 | 269 pcs. | — | — | Proof | 200.00 |

Yale of Beaufort

| 41 | 1978 | 254 pcs. | — | — | Proof | 200.00 |

TURKS & CAICOS ISLANDS 1681

Falcon of the Plantagenets

KM#	Date	Mintage	Fine	VF	XF	Unc
42	1978	265 pcs.	—	—	—	Proof 200.00

White Lion of Mortimer

| 43 | 1978 | 265 pcs. | — | — | — | Proof 200.00 |

Reduced. Actual size: 63mm.
136.0800 g, .925 SILVER, 4.0699 oz ASW
Columbus Voyage Proposal to Ferdinand and Isabella

| 61 | 1986 | .020 | — | Proof 60.00 |

100 CROWNS

18.0150 g, .500 GOLD, .2896 oz AGW
Churchill Centenary

KM#	Date	Mintage	VF	XF	Unc
4	1974	4,500	—	—	150.00
	1974	5,100	—	Proof	150.00

12.4400 g, .500 GOLD, .2000 oz AGW
Age of Exploration

KM#	Date	Mintage	VF	XF	Unc
11	1975	756 pcs.	—	—	150.00
	1975	1,508	—	Proof	150.00

18.0150 g, .500 GOLD, .2896 oz AGW
Victoria Portraits

17	1976	250 pcs.	—	—	200.00
	1976	350 pcs.	—	Proof	200.00
	1977	1,655	—	—	175.00
	1977	2,648	—	Proof	190.00

George III Portraits

22	1977	—	—	—	180.00
	1977	844 pcs.	—	Proof	225.00

XI Commonwealth Games

| 44 | 1978 | 5,000 | — | — | 175.00 |

10th Anniversary of Prince Charles' Investiture

| 46 | 1979 | .010 | — | — | 175.00 |

12.9600 g, .500 GOLD, .2083 oz AGW
Lord Mountbatten
Obv: Similar to 10 Crowns, KM#45.

| 50 | 1980 | — | — | Proof | 150.00 |

6.4800 g, .900 GOLD, .1875 oz AGW
Wedding of Prince Charles and Lady Diana

| 54 | 1981 | 1,205 | — | Proof | 130.00 |

Soccer

KM#	Date	Mintage	VF	XF	Unc
59	1982	565 pcs.	—	Proof	200.00

7.1300 g, .900 GOLD, .2063 oz AGW
Decade For Women

| 62 | 1985 | 313 pcs. | — | — | Proof 250.00 |

10.0000 g, .917 GOLD, .2949 oz AGW
World Wildlife Fund - Crayfish

| 65 | 1988 | *5,000 | — | Proof | 175.00 |

MINT SETS (MS)

KM#	Date	Mintage	Identification	Issue Price	Mkt. Val.
MS1	1975(7)	440	KM5-11	214.00	375.00

PROOF SETS (PS)

PS1	1974(2)	1,600	KM2,4	—	170.00
PS2	1975(7)	1,270	KM5-8,9,1,10-11	313.00	385.00
PS3	1976(4)	2,185	KM5,6,9.2,12	78.00	100.00
PS4	1976(3)	—	KM14,16,17	280.00	280.00
PS5	1976(2)	1,951	KM13,15	108.00	135.00
PS6	1977(4)	1,370	KM5,6,9.2,12	87.50	100.00
PS7	1977(3)	—	KM18,21,22	280.00	415.00
PS8	1977(2)	—	KM14,18	62.00	135.00
PS9	1978(10)	—	KM24-33	560.00	520.00
PS10	1978(10)	—	KM34-43	1120.	2000.
PS11	1979(2)	—	KM45,46	227.50	190.00
PS12	1980(4)	—	KM47-50	457.50	195.00
PS13	1980(3)	—	KM47-49	107.50	45.00

TUVALU 1682

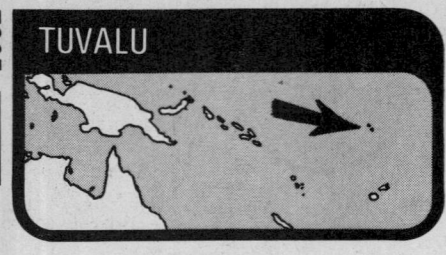

Tuvalu (formerly the Ellice or Lagoon Islands of the Gilbert and Ellice Islands), located in the South Pacific north of the Fiji Islands, has an area of 10 sq. mi. (26 sq. km.) and a population of *9,000. Capital: Funafuti. The independent state includes the islands of Nanumanga, Nanumea, Nui, Niutao, Viatupa, Funafuti, Nukufetau, Nukulailai and Nurakita. The latter four islands were claimed by the United States until relinquished by the Feb. 7, 1979, Treaty of Friendship signed by the United States and Tuvalu. The principal industries are copra production and phosphate mining.

The islands were discovered in 1764 by John Byron, a British navigator, and annexed by Britain in 1892. In 1915 they became part of the crown colony of the Gilbert and Ellice Islands. In 1974 the islanders voted to separate from the Gilberts, becoming on Jan. 1, 1976, the separate constitutional dependency of Tuvalu. Full independence was attained on Oct. 1, 1978. Tuvalu is a member of the Commonwealth of Nations. The Queen of England is Head of State.

RULERS
British

MONETARY SYSTEM
100 Cents = 1 Dollar

CENT

BRONZE

KM#	Date	Mintage	Fine	VF	XF	Unc
1	1976	.093	—	—	.10	.20
	1976	.020	—	—	Proof	1.00
	1981	—	—	—	.10	.20
	1985	—	—	—	.10	.20

2 CENTS

BRONZE

2	1976	.051	—	.10	.15	.30
	1976	.020	—	—	Proof	1.00
	1981	—	—	.10	.15	.30
	1985	—	—	.10	.15	.30

5 CENTS

COPPER-NICKEL

3	1976	.026	—	.10	.20	.40
	1976	.020	—	—	Proof	1.00
	1981	—	—	.10	.20	.40
	1985	—	—	.10	.20	.40

10 CENTS

COPPER-NICKEL

4	1976	.026	.15	.20	.30	.60
	1976	.020	—	—	Proof	2.00
	1981	—	.15	.20	.30	.60
	1985	—	.15	.20	.30	.60

20 CENTS

COPPER-NICKEL

KM#	Date	Mintage	Fine	VF	XF	Unc
5	1976	.036	.30	.40	.50	1.00
	1976	.020	—	—	Proof	2.50
	1981	—	.30	.40	.50	1.00
	1985	—	.30	.40	.50	1.00

50 CENTS

COPPER-NICKEL

6	1976	.019	.50	.75	1.00	2.00
	1976	.020	—	—	Proof	3.00
	1981	—	.50	.75	1.00	2.00
	1985	—	.50	.75	1.00	2.00

DOLLAR

COPPER-NICKEL

7	1976	.021	1.00	1.50	2.00	4.00
	1976	.020	—	—	Proof	4.50
	1981	—	1.00	1.50	2.00	4.00
	1985	—	1.00	1.50	2.00	4.00

5 DOLLARS

28.2800 g, .925 SILVER, .8411 oz ASW

KM#	Date	Mintage	VF	XF	Unc
8	1976	.020	—	Proof	18.00

COPPER-NICKEL
Wedding of Prince Charles and Lady Diana

12	1981	—	—	—	7.50

28.2800 g, .925 SILVER, .8411 oz ASW

12a	1981	.035	—	Proof	30.00

10 DOLLARS

35.0000 g, .500 SILVER, .5627 oz ASW
First Anniversary of Independence
Obv: Similar to 5 Dollars, KM#8.

KM#	Date	Mintage	VF	XF	Unc
10	1979	5,000	—	—	16.50

35.0000 g, .925 SILVER, 1.0409 oz ASW

10a	1979	2,500	—	Proof	45.00

35.0000 g, .500 SILVER, .5627 oz ASW
80th Birthday Of Queen Mother
Obv: Similar to 5 Dollars, KM#8.

11	1980	—	—	—	12.50

35.0000 g, .925 SILVER, 1.0409 oz ASW

11a	1980	—	—	Proof	22.50

35.0000 g, .500 SILVER, .5627 oz ASW
Duke of Edinburgh Award
Obv: Similar to 5 Dollars, KM#8.

13	1981	5,000	—	—	17.50

35.0000 g, .925 SILVER, 1.0409 oz ASW

13a	1981	5,000	—	Proof	27.50

35.0000 g, .500 SILVER, .5627 oz ASW
Royal Visit
Obv: Similar to 5 Dollars, KM#8.

15	1982	2,500	—	—	25.00

35.0000 g, .925 SILVER, 1.0409 oz ASW

15a	1982	2,500	—	Proof	30.00

50 DOLLARS

15.9800 g, .917 GOLD, .4710 oz AGW

KM#	Date	Mintage	VF	XF	Unc
9	1976	2,074	—	Proof	325.00

Wedding of Prince Charles and Lady Diana

| 14 | 1981 | 5,000 | — | Proof | 300.00 |

MINT SETS (MS)

KM#	Date	Mintage	Identification	Issue Price	Mkt. Val.
MS1	1985(7)	—	KM1-7	10.00	10.00

PROOF SETS (PS)

| PS1 | 1976(7) | 20,000 | KM1-7 | 13.00 | 15.00 |

UGANDA

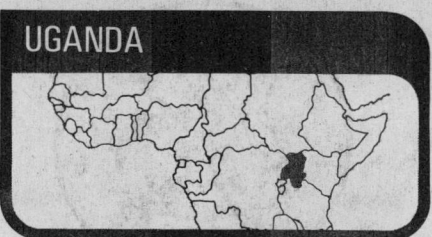

The Republic of Uganda, a former British protectorate located astride the equator in east-central Africa, has an area of 91,134 sq. mi. (236,036 sq. km.) and a population of *16.8 million. Capital: Kampala. Agriculture, including livestock, is the basis of the economy; there is some mining of copper, tin, gold and lead. Coffee, cotton, copper and tea are exported.

Uganda was first visited by Arab slavers in the 1830s. They were followed in the 1860s by British explorers searching for the headwaters of the Nile. The explorers, and the missionaries who followed them into the Lake Victoria region of south-central Africa in 1877-79, found well—developed African kingdoms dating back several centuries. In 1894 the local native Kingdom of Buganda was established as a British protectorate that was extended in 1896 to encompass an area substantially the same as the present Republic of Uganda. The protectorate was given a ministerial form of government in 1955, full internal self-government on March 1, 1962, and complete independence on Oct. 9, 1962. Uganda is a member of the Commonwealth of Nations. The president is Chief of State and Head of Government.

For earlier coinage refer to East Africa.

RULERS
British until 1962

MONETARY SYSTEM
100 Cents = 1 Shilling

5 CENTS

BRONZE

KM#	Date	Mintage	VF	XF	Unc
1	1966	41.000	.10	.15	.30
	1966	—	—	Proof	1.00
	1974	10.000	.10	.15	.35
	1975	14.784	.10	.15	.35
	1976	10.000	.10	.15	.35

10 CENTS

BRONZE

2	1966	19.100	.10	.15	.35
	1966	—	—	Proof	1.00
	1968	20.000	.10	.15	.35
	1970	6.000	.10	.20	.40
	1972	5.000	.10	.20	.50
	1974	5.000	.10	.20	.40
	1975	14.110	.10	.15	.30
	1976	10.000	.10	.15	.30

20 CENTS

BRONZE

3	1966	7.000	.10	.20	.40
	1966	—	—	Proof	1.00
	1974	2.000	.15	.30	.65

50 CENTS

COPPER-NICKEL

KM#	Date	Mintage	VF	XF	Unc
4	1966	16.000	.15	.30	.75
	1966	—	—	Proof	1.00
	1970	3.000	.15	.35	1.00
	1974	10.000	.15	.30	.75
	1976	10.000	.15	.30	.75

SHILLING

COPPER-NICKEL

5	1966	24.500	.25	.50	1.00
	1966	—	—	Proof	2.00
	1968	10.000	.25	.60	1.25
	1972	—	.25	.60	1.25
	1975	15.540	.25	.60	1.25
	1976	10.000	.25	.60	1.25

COPPER PLATED STEEL

27	1987	—	—	—	.25
	1987	—	—	Proof	2.00

2 SHILLINGS

COPPER-NICKEL

6	1966	4.000	.75	1.25	2.50
	1966	—	—	Proof	3.00

4.0000 g, .999 SILVER, .1284 oz ASW
Visit of Pope Paul VI

8	1969	8,170	—	Proof	10.00
	1970	Inc. Ab.	—	Proof	10.00

COPPER PLATED STEEL

28	1987	—	—	—	.50
	1987	—	—	Proof	4.00

5 SHILLINGS

COPPER-NICKEL
F.A.O. Issue

KM#	Date	Mintage	VF	XF	Unc
7	1968	.100	—	2.00	3.50
	1968	5,000	—	Proof	8.00

10.0000 g, .999 SILVER, .3212 oz ASW
Visit of Pope Paul VI

9	1969	7,670	—	Proof	15.00
	1970	Inc. Ab.	—	Proof	15.00

COPPER-NICKEL

18	1972	*8.000	—	75.00	135.00

NOTE: Withdrawn from circulation. Almost entire mintage was remelted.

STAINLESS STEEL

29	1987	—	—	—	1.50
	1987	—	—	Proof	6.00

10 SHILLINGS

20.0000 g, .999 SILVER, .6424 oz ASW
Martyrs' Shrine

KM#	Date	Mintage	VF	XF	Unc
10	1969	6,720	—	Proof	20.00
	1970	Inc. Ab.	—	Proof	20.00

COPPER-NICKEL
Wedding of Prince Charles and Lady Diana

21	1981	.010	—	—	7.50

STAINLESS STEEL

30	1987	—	—	—	2.50
	1987	—	—	Proof	12.00

20 SHILLINGS

40.0000 g, .999 SILVER, 1.2848 oz ASW
Visit of Pope Paul VI

11	1969	6,670	—	Proof	30.00
	1970	Inc. Ab.	—	Proof	30.00

25 SHILLINGS

50.0000 g, .999 SILVER, 1.6061 oz ASW
Visit of Pope Paul VI
Rev: Arms.

KM#	Date	Mintage	VF	XF	Unc
12	1969	6,070	—	Proof	40.00
	1970	Inc. Ab.	—	Proof	40.00

30 SHILLINGS

60.0000 g, .999 SILVER, 1.9273 oz ASW.
Illustration reduced, actual diameter - 60mm.
Visit of Pope Paul VI
Rev: Arms.

13	1969	6,720	—	Proof	50.00
	1970	Inc. Ab.	—	Proof	50.00

50 SHILLINGS

6.9100 g, .900 GOLD, .1999 oz AGW
Martyrs' Shrine

14	1969	4,390	—	Proof	125.00
	1970	Inc. Ab.	—	Proof	125.00

100 SHILLINGS

13.8200 g, .900 GOLD, .3999 oz AGW
Visit of Pope Paul VI

15	1969	4,190	—	Proof	260.00
	1970	Inc. Ab.	—	Proof	260.00

UGANDA 1685

31.4700 g, .925 SILVER, .9360 oz ASW
Wedding of Prince Charles and Lady Diana

KM#	Date	Mintage	VF	XF	Unc
22	1981	5,000	—	Proof	32.50

200 SHILLINGS

28.2800 g, .925 SILVER, .8411 oz ASW
International Year of Disabled Persons

26	1981	.010	—	—	20.00
	1981	.010	—	Proof	27.50

500 SHILLINGS

69.1200 g, .900 GOLD, 2.0002 oz AGW
Visit of Pope Paul VI

16	1969	1,680	—	Proof	1250.
	1970	Inc. Ab.	—	Proof	1250.

136.0000 g, .500 SILVER, 2.1864 oz ASW
Wildlife - Elephants

KM#	Date	Mintage	VF	XF	Unc
23	1981	700 pcs.	—	—	125.00

136.0000 g, .925 SILVER, 4.0450 oz ASW

23a	1981	700 pcs.	—	Proof	150.00

1000 SHILLINGS

138.2400 g, .900 GOLD, 4.0005 oz AGW
Visit of Pope Paul VI

17	1969	1,390	—	Proof	2400.
	1970	Inc. Ab.	—	Proof	2400.

10.0000 g, .500 GOLD, .1607 oz AGW
Wedding of Prince Charles and Lady Diana
Rev: Busts of Charles and Diana right.

24	1981	1,500	—	Proof	150.00

5000 SHILLINGS

33.9300 g, .917 GOLD, 1.0000 oz AGW
Crested Crane
Obv: Facing portrait of Dr. Milton Obote.

25	1981	500 pcs.	—	—	625.00
	1981	100 pcs.	—	Proof	750.00

POUND

GOLD
O.A.U. Kampala 1975
Obv: Idi Amin.

KM#	Date	Mintage	VF	XF	Unc
19	1975	—	—	Proof	675.00

9.8800 g, .917 GOLD, .2913 oz AGW
Idi Amin as Field Marshall

20	1975	2,000	—	—	300.00

MINT SETS (MS)

KM#	Date	Mintage	Identification	Issue Price	Mkt. Val.
MS1	1987(4)	—	KM27-30	10.50	12.50

PROOF SETS (PS)

PS1	1966(6)	8,250	KM1-6	7.75	9.00
PS2	1969(10)	1,390	KM8-17	790.00	4200.
PS3	1969(6)	6,070	KM8-13	78.50	165.00
PS4	1970(10)	Inc. KM-PS2	KM8-17	790.00	4200.
PS5	1970(6)	Inc. KM-PS3	KM8-13	78.50	165.00
PS6	1987(4)	2,500	KM27-30	25.00	25.00

Listings For
UMM AL QAIWAIN: refer to United Arab Emirates

a map of Union Of Soviet Socialist Republics

KEY
1 - Russian Soviet Federation Socialist Republic
2 - Estonian S.S.R.
3 - Latvian S.S.R.
4 - Lithuanian S.S.R.
5 - Byelorussian S.S.R.
6 - Ukrainian S.S.R.
7 - Moldavian S.S.R.
8 - Georgian S.S.R.
9 - Armenian S.S.R.
10 - Azerbaijan S.S.R.
11 - Turkmen S.S.R.
12 - Uzbek S.S.R.
13 - Tadzhik S.S.R.
14 - Kirgiz S.S.R.
15 - Kazakh S.S.R.

The Union of Soviet Socialist Republics, which occupies the northern part of Asia and the eastern half of Europe, has an area of 8,649,538 sq. mi. (22,402,200 sq. km.) and a population of *287 million. Capital: Moscow. The Soviet Union, the world's second ranking industrial power, exports machinery, iron and steel, crude oil, timber and nonferrous metals.

The first Russian dynasty was founded in Novgorod by the Viking Rurik in 862 A.D. Under Yaroslav the Wise (1019-54) the subsequent Kievan state became one of the great commercial and cultural centers of Europe before falling to the Mongols of the Batu Khan, 13th century, who ruled Russia until late in the 15th century when Ivan III threw off the Mongol yoke. The Russian Empire was enlarged, solidified and Westernized during the reigns of Ivan the Terrible, Peter the Great and Catherine the Great, and by 1881 extended to the Pacific and into Central Asia. Modern Russian history began in March of 1917 when Tsar Nicholas II abdicated under pressure and was replaced by a provisional government composed of both radical and conservative elements. This government rapidly lost ground to the Bolshevik wing of the Socialist Democratic Labor Party which attained power following the Bolshevik Revolution which began on Nov. 7, 1917. The Union of Soviet Socialist Republics was established as a federation under the premiership of Lenin on Dec. 30, 1922.

RUSSIA-EMPIRE

RULERS
Alexander I, 1801-1825
Nicholas I, 1825-1855
Alexander II, 1855-1881
Alexander III, 1881-1894
Nicholas II, 1894-1917

MINT MARKS
EM - Ekaterinburg, 1762-1877
ИМ - Ichora, 1811-1821
КМ - Kolpina (Ichora), 1810
КМ - Kolyvan, 1767-1830 (later Souzan)
СПБ - St. Petersburg, 1724-1915
СПМ - St. Petersburg (Ichora), 1840-1843
СМ - Souzan (Kolyvan), 1831-1847
ВМ - Warsaw, 1850-1864
МШ - Warsaw, 1842-1854
Star (on rim) - Paris, 1896-1899
2 Stars (on rim) - Brussels, 1897-1899

MINTMASTER'S INITIALS
EKATERINBURG MINT

Initials	Years	Mintmaster
НМ	1810-21	Nicholai Mundt
ИФ	1811	Ivan Felkner
ФГ	1811-23	Franz German
ПГ	1823-25	Peter Gramatchikov
ИШ	1825	Ivan Shevkunov
ИК	1825-30	Ivan Kolobov
ФХ	1830-37	Fedor Khvochinski
КТ	1837	Konstantin Tomson
НА	1837-39	Nicholai Alexeev

IZHORA and KOLPINA MINTS
МК	1810-11	Mikhail Kleiner
ПС	1811-14	Paul Stupitzyn
ЯБ	1820-21	Yakov Vilson

KOLYVAN and SOUZAN MINTS
ПБ	1810-11	Peter Berezowski
АМ	1812-17	Alexei Maleev
ДБ	1817-18	Dmitri Bikhto
АД	1818-21	Alexander Deichmann
АМ	1821-30	Andrei Mevius

LENINGRAD MINT
| АГ | 1921-1922 | A.F. Hartman |
| ПЛ | 1922-1927 | P.V. Latishev |

LONDON MINT
| Т.Р. | 1924 | Thomas Ross |
| ФР | 1924 | Thomas Ross |

ST. PETERSBURG MINT
АИ	1801-03	Alexie Ivanov
ФГ	1803-17	Fedor Gelman
ХЛ	1804-05	Khristopher Leo
МК	1808-09	Mikhail Kleiner
МФ	1812-22	Mikhail Fedorov
ПС	1811-25	Paul Stupitzyn
ПД	1820-38	Paul Danilov
НГ	1825-42	Nikolai Grachev
АЧ	1839-43	Alexei Chadov
КБ	1844-46	Constantine Butenev
АГ	1846-57	Alexander Gertov
ПА	1847-52	Paul Alexiev
НІ	1848-77	Nicholai Iossa
ФБ	1856-61	Fedor Blum
ПФ	1858-62	Paul Follendorf
МИ	1861-63	Mikhail Ivanov
АБ	1863	Alexander Belozerov
АС	1864-65	Aggei Svechin
НФ	1864-82	Nikolai Follendorf
СШ	1865-66	Sergei Shostak
ДС	1882-83	Dmitri Sabaneev
АГ	1883-99	Appolon Grasgov
ЭБ	1899-1913	Elikum Babayntz
ФЗ	1899-1901	Felix Zaleman
АР	1901-05	Alexander Redko
ВС	1913-17	Victor Smirnov

NOTE: St. Petersburg Mint became Petrograd in 1914 and Leningrad in 1924.

MONETARY SYSTEM
1/4 Kopek = Polushka ПОЛУШКА
1/2 Kopek = Denga, Denezhka
ДЕНГА, ДЕНЕЖКА
Kopek КОПѢИКА
(2, 3 & 4) Kopeks КОПѢИКИ
(5 and up) Kopeks КОПѢЕКЪ
3 Kopeks = Altyn, Altynnik
АЛТЫНЪ, АЛТЫННИКЪ
10 Kopeks = Grivna, Grivennik
ГРИВНА, ГРИВЕННИКЪ
25 Kopeks = Polupoltina, Polupoltinnik
ПОЛУПОЛТИНА
ПОЛУПОЛТИННИКЪ
50 Kopeks = Poltina, Poltinnik
ПОЛТИНА, ПОЛТИННИКЪ
100 Kopeks = Rouble, Ruble РУБЛЪ
10 Roubles = Imperial ИМПЕРІАЛЪ
10 Roubles = Chervonetz ЧЕРВОНЕЦ

NOTE: Mintage figures for years after 1885 are for fiscal years and may or may not reflect actual rarity, the commemorative and 1917 silver figures being exceptions.

NOTE: For silver coins with Zlotych and Kopek or Ruble denominations see Poland.

NOTE: For gold coins with Zlotych and Ruble denominations see Poland.

NOTE: Gold coins of 1 ducat denomination with both multiples and fractions are known before Peter I. Most Russian authorities agree that these pieces were not meant to be coins but were only made as awards for the military. The higher the rank of the individual the larger the gold piece. Thus the range was from a gold denga for a common soldier to a "Portugal" or 10 ducat size for a high ranking officer.

POLUSHKA
(1/4 Kopek)

COPPER, 3.00 g
Mint mark: EM

C#	Date	Mintage	VG	Fine	VF	XF
111.1	1803	.012	15.00	30.00	60.00	120.00
	1804	20 pcs.	—	Rare	—	
	1805	.025	15.00	30.00	60.00	120.00
	1808	—	25.00	50.00	100.00	200.00
	1810	—	25.00	50.00	100.00	200.00

Mint mark: КМ

111.2	1803	—	20.00	40.00	80.00	160.00
	1804	—	20.00	40.00	80.00	160.00
	1805	—	20.00	40.00	80.00	160.00
	1807	—	20.00	40.00	80.00	160.00

Mint mark: EM

142.1	1840	10.793	2.00	4.00	8.00	20.00
	1841	3.230	2.00	4.00	8.00	20.00
	1842	1.600	2.00	4.00	8.00	20.00
	1843	1.664	2.00	4.00	8.00	20.00

Mint mark: СПМ

142.2	1840	6.400	4.00	7.50	15.00	30.00
	1841	6.400	3.00	6.00	12.00	24.00
	1842	12.800	3.00	6.00	12.00	24.00

Mint mark: СМ

142.3	1839	.450	12.50	25.00	50.00	100.00
	1840	2.573	4.00	7.50	15.00	30.00
	1841	3.571	4.00	7.50	15.00	30.00
	1842	3.960	4.00	7.50	15.00	30.00
	1843	2.006	4.00	7.50	15.00	30.00
	1844	3.400	4.00	7.50	15.00	30.00
	1845	3.000	4.00	7.50	15.00	30.00
	1846	3.000	4.00	7.50	15.00	30.00

Mint mark: EM

147.1	1849	—	30.00	60.00	120.00	200.00
	1850	5.184	1.50	3.00	5.00	10.00
	1851	7.776	1.50	3.00	5.00	10.00
	1852	1.178	1.50	3.00	5.00	10.00
	1853	5.382	1.50	3.00	5.00	10.00
	1854	4.538	1.50	3.00	5.00	10.00
	1855	6.442	3.00	6.00	13.00	25.00

Mint mark: СПМ

| 147.2 | 1849 | — | — | — | Rare | — |

Mint mark: ВМ

147.3	1850	—	7.00	12.00	25.00	50.00
	1851	.080	7.00	12.00	25.00	50.00
	1852	.080	7.00	12.00	25.00	50.00
	1853	.040	7.00	12.00	25.00	50.00

Russia-Empire / USSR

Mint mark: EM
Plain border

Y#	Date	Mintage	Fine	VF	XF	Unc
1.1	1855	6.422	2.00	4.00	8.00	20.00
	1856	6.000	2.00	4.00	8.00	20.00
	1857	6.000	2.00	4.00	8.00	20.00
	1858	6.970	2.00	4.00	8.00	20.00
	1859	3.834	2.00	4.00	8.00	20.00

Mint mark: BM

1.2	1855	.040	7.00	15.00	30.00	60.00
	1860	—	7.00	15.00	30.00	60.00

Mint mark: EM
Toothed border

1.3	1858	—	—	—	Rare	—
	1859	—	2.00	4.00	8.00	20.00
	1860	—	60.00	120.00	200.00	300.00
	1861	.192	3.00	6.00	12.00	25.00
	1862	.992	2.00	4.00	8.00	20.00
	1863	.300	4.00	8.00	15.00	30.00
	1864	.403	4.00	8.00	15.00	30.00
	1865	.122	2.00	4.00	8.00	20.00
	1866	.326	2.00	4.00	8.00	20.00
	1867	.832	10.00	20.00	40.00	80.00

Mint mark: BM

1.4	1861	3.160	3.00	6.00	15.00	35.00

Mint mark: EM

7.1	1867	Inc.Y1.3	10.00	17.00	35.00	70.00
	1868	.700	2.00	5.00	10.00	20.00
	1869	.615	2.00	5.00	10.00	20.00
	1870	.435	2.00	5.00	10.00	20.00
	1871	.155	2.00	5.00	10.00	20.00
	1872	.540	2.00	5.00	10.00	20.00
	1873	.823	2.00	5.00	10.00	20.00
	1874	.340	2.00	5.00	10.00	20.00
	1875	.300	1.25	2.50	5.00	10.00
	1876	—	40.00	80.00	150.00	300.00

Mint mark: СПБ

7.2	1867	24 pcs.	3.00	6.00	12.00	25.00
	1868	.060	3.00	6.00	12.00	25.00
	1869	.092	3.00	6.00	12.00	25.00
	1870	.020	3.50	7.50	15.00	30.00
	1871	—	40.00	80.00	150.00	300.00
	1876	.800	1.25	2.50	5.00	15.00
	1877	.720	1.25	2.50	5.00	15.00
	1878	1.100	1.25	2.50	5.00	15.00
	1879	.280	1.50	3.00	6.00	15.00
	1880	.180	1.25	2.50	9.00	20.00
	1881	.060	3.00	5.00	9.00	20.00

29	1881	.200	2.50	5.00	10.00	20.00
	1882	.060	2.50	5.00	10.00	20.00
	1883	.240	1.50	3.00	6.00	12.00
	1884	.140	2.50	4.00	8.00	20.00
	1885	.480	1.50	3.00	6.00	12.00
	1886	1.060	1.25	2.50	5.00	10.00
	1887	1.000	1.25	2.50	5.00	10.00
	1888	.200	1.50	3.00	6.00	12.00
	1889	.181	2.50	4.00	8.00	20.00
	1890	Inc. Ab.	1.50	3.00	6.00	12.00
	1891	.400	1.50	3.00	6.00	12.00
	1892	.918	1.25	2.50	5.00	12.00
	1893	.740	1.25	2.50	5.00	12.00

47.1	1894	—	6.00	12.00	25.00	40.00
	1895	.060	2.50	5.00	10.00	20.00
	1896	5.960	.50	1.00	2.00	7.00
	1897	3.040	.50	1.00	2.00	7.00
	1898	8.000	.50	1.00	2.00	7.00
	1899	8.000	.50	1.00	2.00	7.00
	1900	4.000	.50	1.00	2.00	7.00
	1909	2.000	1.00	2.00	4.00	12.00
	1910	8.000	4.00	8.00	15.00	30.00
	Common date	—	—	—	Proof	35.00

Mint: Petrograd - w/o mint mark

47.2	1915	.500	2.00	5.00	10.00	20.00
	1916	1.200	40.00	80.00	150.00	300.00

DENGA
(1/2 Kopek)

COPPER, 6.50 g
Mint mark: EM

C#	Date	Mintage	VG	Fine	VF	XF
112.1	1804	20 pcs.	—	—	—	—
	1805	.040	50.00	100.00	175.00	225.00
	1808	—	—	—	Rare	—
	1810	—	—	—	Rare	—

Mint mark: KM

112.2	1804	—	40.00	80.00	150.00	300.00
	1805	—	40.00	80.00	150.00	300.00
	1807	—	40.00	80.00	150.00	300.00

Mint mark: EM
Obv: Type 1 eagle

116.1	1810 HM	.036	—	—	Rare	—

Mint mark: KM
Obv: Type 2 eagle

116.2	1811 ПБ	—	5.00	10.00	20.00	40.00

Mint mark: EM
Obv: Type 3 eagle

116.3	1811 HM plain edge	.099	3.75	7.50	15.00	30.00
	1811 HM reeded edge	Inc. Ab.	3.75	7.50	15.00	30.00
	1813 HM	.024	4.00	8.00	15.00	30.00
	1815 HM	.059	4.00	8.00	15.00	30.00
	1818 HM	23.410	2.00	4.00	8.00	15.00
	1819 HM	1.360	2.00	4.00	8.00	15.00
	1822 ФГ	—	25.00	50.00	100.00	200.00
	1825 ИК	.555	3.00	6.00	12.00	25.00

Mint mark: ИМ

116.4	1810 ФГ	.026	25.00	50.00	100.00	200.00
	1810 МК	I.A.	3.50	7.00	15.00	30.00
	1811 МК	.160	2.50	5.00	10.00	20.00
	1812 ПС	.510	2.50	5.00	10.00	20.00
	1813 ПС	1.220	2.50	5.00	10.00	20.00
	1814 ПС	2.250	2.50	5.00	10.00	20.00
	1814 СП	I.A.	2.50	5.00	10.00	20.00

Mint mark: KM

116.5	1812 АМ	—	4.00	8.00	15.00	30.00
	1813 АМ	—	4.00	8.00	15.00	30.00
	1814 АМ	—	4.00	8.00	15.00	30.00
	1815 АМ	—	4.00	8.00	15.00	30.00
	1816 АМ	—	4.00	8.00	15.00	30.00
	1817 АМ	—	4.00	8.00	15.00	30.00

Mint mark: СПБ

116.6	1810 ФГ	—	6.00	12.00	25.00	50.00
	1811 МК	.075	3.00	6.00	12.00	25.00
	1812 ПС	—	25.00	50.00	100.00	200.00

Mint mark: EM

135.1	1827 ИК	2.165	3.00	6.00	12.00	25.00
	1828 ИК	—	3.00	6.00	12.00	25.00

Mint mark: СПБ

135.2	1828	—	25.00	50.00	100.00	200.00

COPPER, 4.00 g
Mint mark: EM

143.1	1840	10.999	2.00	4.00	8.00	15.00
	1841	3.384	2.00	4.00	8.00	15.00
	1842	3.600	2.00	4.00	8.00	15.00
	1843	2.580	2.00	4.00	8.00	15.00

Mint mark: СПБ

143.2	1840	—	6.00	12.00	25.00	50.00

Mint mark: СПМ

C#	Date	Mintage	VG	Fine	VF	XF
143.3	1840	6.400	2.00	4.00	8.00	15.00
	1841	6.400	2.00	4.00	8.00	15.00
	1842	12.800	2.00	4.00	8.00	15.00

Mint mark: CM

143.4	1839	.454	4.00	8.00	15.00	30.00
	1840	2.560	2.00	4.00	8.00	15.00
	1841	3.542	2.00	4.00	8.00	15.00
	1842	3.960	2.00	4.00	8.00	15.00
	1843	2.006	2.00	4.00	8.00	15.00
	1844	3.400	2.00	4.00	8.00	15.00
	1845	3.000	2.00	4.00	8.00	15.00
	1846	3.000	2.00	4.00	8.00	15.00
	1847	2.532	2.00	4.00	8.00	15.00

Mint mark: МШ

143.5	1848	.087	15.00	30.00	60.00	110.00

Mint mark: EM

148.1	1849	—	25.00	50.00	100.00	200.00
	1850	3.562	1.00	2.00	4.00	8.00
	1851	6.426	1.00	2.00	4.00	8.00
	1852	14.672	1.00	2.00	4.00	8.00
	1853	12.243	1.00	2.00	4.00	8.00
	1854	13.754	1.00	2.00	4.00	8.00
	1855	20.510	1.50	3.00	6.00	12.00

Mint mark: СПМ

148.2	1849	50 pcs.	25.00	50.00	100.00	200.00

Mint mark: BM

148.3	1850	1.840	2.00	4.00	8.00	15.00
	1851	1.200	2.00	4.00	8.00	15.00
	1852	1.231	2.00	4.00	8.00	15.00
	1853	.804	2.00	4.00	8.00	15.00
	1854	.352	2.00	4.00	8.00	15.00
	1855	6.380	4.00	8.00	15.00	30.00

Mint mark: EM
Plain border

Y#	Date	Mintage	Fine	VF	XF	Unc
2.1	1855	Inc.C148.1	2.00	4.00	8.00	20.00
	1856	6.000	2.00	4.00	8.00	20.00
	1857	6.000	2.00	4.00	8.00	20.00
	1858	11.147	2.00	4.00	8.00	20.00
	1859	5.871	2.00	4.00	8.00	20.00

Mint mark: BM

2.2	1855	6.380	5.00	10.00	20.00	40.00
	1856	4.278	5.00	10.00	20.00	40.00
	1857	1.909	5.00	10.00	20.00	40.00
	1858	.311	5.00	10.00	20.00	40.00
	1859	3.719	5.00	10.00	20.00	40.00
	1860	1.861	4.00	8.00	16.00	35.00

Mint mark: EM
Toothed border

2.3	1859	—	2.00	4.00	10.00	20.00
	1860	2.838	2.00	5.00	10.00	20.00
	1861	2.277	2.00	5.00	10.00	20.00
	1862	3.072	2.00	5.00	10.00	20.00
	1863	1.011	2.00	5.00	10.00	20.00
	1864	1.116	3.00	6.00	12.00	30.00
	1865	.560	50.00	100.00	200.00	300.00
	1866	.333	4.00	8.00	15.00	40.00
	1867	.390	8.00	15.00	30.00	70.00

Mint mark: BM

2.4	1861	2.819	4.00	8.00	15.00	30.00
	1862	1.036	4.00	8.00	15.00	30.00
	1863	2.400	6.00	12.50	25.00	50.00

Y# 8.1 — Mint mark: ЕМ

Date	Mintage	Fine	VF	XF	Unc
1867	Inc.Y2.3	7.00	15.00	30.00	60.00
1868	1.190	1.50	3.00	6.00	12.00
1869	.593	1.50	3.00	6.00	12.00
1870	.510	2.00	4.00	8.00	15.00
1871	.223	1.50	3.00	6.00	12.00
1872	.365	1.50	3.00	6.00	12.00
1873	.963	1.50	3.00	6.00	12.00
1874	.300	1.50	3.00	6.00	12.00
1875	.321	3.00	6.00	12.00	25.00
1876	Inc. Ab.	50.00	100.00	200.00	300.00

8.2 — Mint mark: СПБ

Date	Mintage	Fine	VF	XF	Unc
1867	—	5.00	10.00	20.00	40.00
1868	.060	3.00	6.00	12.00	25.00
1869	.145	2.00	4.50	9.00	17.50
1870	.025	5.00	10.00	20.00	40.00
1871	—	50.00	100.00	200.00	300.00
1876	.770	1.00	2.25	4.50	9.00
1877	1.290	1.00	2.25	4.50	9.00
1878	1.120	1.00	2.25	4.50	9.00
1879	.740	1.00	2.25	4.50	9.00
1880	1.260	1.00	2.25	4.50	9.00
1881	.420	1.00	2.25	4.50	9.00

30

Date	Mintage	Fine	VF	XF	Unc
1881	.440	1.00	2.25	4.50	15.00
1882	.350	1.00	2.25	4.50	9.00
1883	.540	1.00	2.25	4.50	9.00
1884	.550	1.00	2.25	4.50	9.00
1885	.680	1.00	2.25	4.50	9.00
1886	.560	1.00	2.25	4.50	9.00
1887	.600	1.00	2.25	4.50	9.00
1888	.610	1.00	2.25	4.50	9.00
1889	4.650	1.00	2.00	4.00	7.50
1890	2.040	1.00	2.00	4.00	7.50
1892	2.271	1.00	2.00	4.00	7.50
1893	3.900	1.00	2.00	4.00	7.50
1894	—	1.00	2.00	4.00	7.50

48.1

Date	Mintage	Fine	VF	XF	Unc
1894	—	5.00	10.00	20.00	40.00
1895	2.992	1.00	2.00	4.00	8.00
1896	1.340	1.00	2.00	4.00	8.00
1897	60.000	.25	.50	1.00	5.00
1898	76.000	.25	.50	1.00	5.00
1899	76.000	.25	.50	1.00	5.00
1900	36.000	.25	.50	1.00	5.00
1908	8.000	.25	.50	1.00	5.00
1909	49.500	.25	.50	1.00	4.00
1910	24.000	.25	.50	1.00	5.00
1911	35.800	.25	.50	1.00	5.00
1912	28.000	.25	.50	1.00	5.00
1913	50.000	.25	.50	1.00	5.00
1914	14.000	.25	.50	1.00	5.00
Common date	—	—	—	Proof	35.00

Mint: Petrograd - w/o mint mark

| 48.2 | 1915 | 12.000 | .25 | .50 | 1.00 | 5.00 |
| | 1916 | 9.400 | .25 | .50 | 1.00 | 5.00 |

KOPEK

COPPER, reduced weight, 4.00 g
Mint mark: ЕМ

C#	Date	Mintage	VG	Fine	VF	XF
113.1	1804	200 pcs.	50.00	100.00	200.00	300.00
	1805	.114	20.00	40.00	80.00	150.00

Mint mark: КМ

113.2	1804	—	20.00	40.00	80.00	160.00
	1805	—	20.00	40.00	80.00	160.00
	1807	—	20.00	40.00	80.00	160.00

Mint mark: ЕМ
Obv: Type 1 eagle.

| 117.1 | 1810 HM | .510 | 20.00 | 40.00 | 80.00 | 150.00 |

Mint mark: КМ
Obv: Type 2 eagle.

C#	Date	Mintage	VG	Fine	VF	XF
117.2	1811 ПБ	—	—	—	Rare	—

Mint mark: ЕМ
Obv: Type 3 eagle.

117.3	1811 HM	1.420	1.50	3.00	6.00	12.00
	1811 HM reeded edge					
		—	—	—	Rare	—
	1813 HM	.030	25.00	50.00	100.00	200.00
	1815 HM	.031	25.00	50.00	100.00	200.00
	1818 HM					
		55.750	1.50	3.00	6.00	12.00
	1819 HM					
		35.030	1.50	3.00	6.00	12.00
	1821 HM	10.160	1.50	3.00	6.00	12.00
	1822 ФГ	10.265	1.50	3.00	6.00	12.00
	1823 ФГ	10.350	1.50	3.00	6.00	12.00
	1824 ПГ	—	1.50	3.00	6.00	12.00
	1825 ИК	—	1.50	3.00	6.00	12.00

NOTE: Varieties exist.

Mint mark: ИМ

117.4	1811 МК	.490	1.50	3.00	6.00	12.00
	1812 ПС	1.040	1.50	3.00	6.00	12.00
	1813 ПС	1.980	1.50	3.00	6.00	12.00
	1814 ПС	3.740	1.50	3.00	6.00	12.00
	1820 ЯБ	—	1.50	3.00	6.00	12.00
	1821 ЯБ	—	1.50	3.00	6.00	12.00

Mint mark: КМ

117.5	1810	—	25.00	50.00	100.00	200.00
	1811 ПБ	—	1.50	3.00	6.00	10.00
	1812 АМ	—	2.50	5.00	10.00	20.00
	1813 АМ	—	2.50	5.00	10.00	20.00
	1814 АМ	—	2.50	5.00	10.00	20.00
	1815 АМ	—	2.50	5.00	10.00	20.00
	1816 АМ	—	2.50	5.00	10.00	20.00
	1817 АМ	—	2.50	5.00	10.00	20.00
	1818 АД	—	2.50	5.00	10.00	20.00
	1818 ДБ	—	2.50	5.00	10.00	20.00
	1819 АД	—	2.50	5.00	10.00	20.00
	1820 АД	—	2.50	5.00	10.00	20.00
	1821 АМ	—	2.50	5.00	10.00	20.00
	1822 АМ	—	2.50	5.00	10.00	20.00
	1823 АМ	—	2.50	5.00	10.00	20.00
	1824 АМ	—	2.50	5.00	10.00	20.00
	1825 АМ	—	2.50	5.00	10.00	20.00

Mint mark: СПБ

117.6	1810 ФГ	.093	25.00	50.00	100.00	200.00
	1810 МК	I.A.	2.00	4.00	8.00	15.00
	1811 МК	.260	1.50	3.00	6.00	12.00

Mint mark: ЕМ

136.1	1827 ИК	2.646	1.50	3.00	6.00	12.00
	1828 ИК	43.015	1.50	3.00	6.00	12.00
	1829 ИК	48.215	1.50	3.00	6.00	12.00
	1830 ИК	2.100	1.50	3.00	6.00	12.00

Mint mark: КМ

136.2	1826 АМ	6.250	2.50	5.00	10.00	20.00
	1827 АМ	5.000	2.50	5.00	10.00	20.00
	1828 АМ	5.000	2.50	5.00	10.00	20.00
	1829 АМ	5.000	2.50	5.00	10.00	20.00
	1830 АМ	5.000	2.50	5.00	10.00	20.00

Mint mark: СПБ

| 136.3 | 1828 | — | 25.00 | 50.00 | 100.00 | 200.00 |

Mint mark: ЕМ

C#	Date	Mintage	VG	Fine	VF	XF
138.1	1830 ФХ	—	25.00	50.00	100.00	200.00
	1831 ФХ	13.050	1.50	3.00	6.00	12.00
	1832 ФХ	3.400	1.50	3.00	6.00	12.00
	1833 ФХ	2.883	1.50	3.00	6.00	12.00
	1834 ФХ	5.020	1.50	3.00	6.00	12.00
	1835 ФХ	6.570	1.50	3.00	6.00	12.00
	1836 ФХ	2.100	1.50	3.00	6.00	12.00
	1837 КТ	4.890	1.50	3.00	6.00	12.00
	1837 НА	I.A.	1.50	3.00	6.00	12.00
	1838 НА	1.043	25.00	50.00	100.00	200.00

Mint mark: СПБ

| 138.2 | 1830 | 29 pcs. | — | — | Rare | — |

Mint mark: СМ

138.3	1831	2.000	2.50	5.00	10.00	20.00
	1832	2.000	2.50	5.00	10.00	20.00
	1833	.045	2.50	5.00	10.00	20.00
	1834	2.000	2.50	5.00	10.00	20.00
	1835	2.000	2.50	5.00	10.00	20.00
	1836	.100	2.50	5.00	10.00	20.00
	1837	1.000	2.50	5.00	10.00	20.00
	1838	1.800	2.50	5.00	10.00	20.00
	1839	.020	20.00	40.00	80.00	120.00

Mint mark: ЕМ

144.1	1840	20.778	1.00	2.00	4.00	8.00
	1841	19.341	1.00	2.00	4.00	8.00
	1842	13.581	1.00	2.00	4.00	8.00
	1843	12.520	1.00	2.00	4.00	8.00
	1844	—	1.00	2.00	4.00	8.00

Mint mark: СПБ

| 144.2 | 1840 | 11.200 | 5.00 | 10.00 | 20.00 | 40.00 |

Mint mark: СПМ

144.3	1840	Inc. Ab.	1.00	2.00	4.00	8.00
	1841	11.200	1.00	2.00	4.00	8.00
	1842	11.200	1.00	2.00	4.00	8.00
	1843	11.200	1.00	2.00	4.00	8.00

Mint mark: СМ

144.4	1839	.795	2.00	4.00	8.00	15.00
	1840	4.500	1.50	3.00	6.00	12.00
	1841	6.120	1.50	3.00	6.00	12.00
	1842	7.002	1.50	3.00	6.00	12.00
	1843	3.498	1.50	3.00	6.00	12.00
	1844	5.250	1.50	3.00	6.00	12.00
	1845	5.250	1.50	3.00	6.00	12.00
	1846	5.250	1.50	3.00	6.00	12.00
	1847	2.368	3.00	6.00	12.00	25.00

Mint mark: ЕМ

149.1	1849	—	25.00	50.00	100.00	200.00
	1850	1.843	.50	1.00	3.00	7.00
	1851	4.790	.50	1.00	3.00	7.00
	1852	14.006	.50	1.00	3.00	7.00
	1853	21.328	.50	1.00	3.00	7.00
	1854	22.397	.50	1.00	3.00	7.00
	1855	—	2.00	4.00	6.00	10.00

Mint mark: СПМ

| 149.2 | 1849 | 50 pcs. | — | — | Rare | — |

Mint mark: ВМ

149.3	1850	—	2.00	4.00	8.00	15.00
	1851	.797	2.00	4.00	8.00	15.00
	1852	.311	2.00	4.00	8.00	15.00
	1853	.391	2.00	4.00	8.00	15.00
	1855	3.534	2.00	4.00	8.00	15.00

Mint mark: EM
Obv: Crowned small A. Plain border.

Y#	Date	Mintage	Fine	VF	XF	Unc
3.1	1855	24.594	1.00	2.00	6.00	15.00
	1856	10.641	1.00	2.00	6.00	15.00
	1857	5.659	1.00	2.00	6.00	15.00
	1858	13.751	1.00	2.00	6.00	15.00
	1859	11.059	1.00	2.00	6.00	15.00

Mint mark: BM
Obv: Crowned tall A. Rev: Large date.

3.2	1855	Inc.C149.3	2.00	4.00	12.00	25.00
	1856	3.337	2.00	4.00	12.00	25.00
	1858	1.528	2.00	4.00	12.00	25.00
	1859	3.109	2.00	4.00	12.00	25.00
	1860	3.766	2.00	4.00	12.00	25.00

Mint mark: EM
Obv: Crowned small A. Toothed border.

3.3	1859	—	1.00	2.00	4.00	10.00
	1860	8.306	1.00	2.00	4.00	10.00
	1861	10.130	1.00	2.00	4.00	10.00
	1862	10.165	1.00	2.00	4.00	10.00
	1863	6.544	1.00	2.00	4.00	10.00
	1864	4.400	1.00	2.00	4.00	10.00
	1865	14.230	1.00	2.00	4.00	10.00
	1866	12.304	1.00	2.00	4.00	10.00
	1867	5.851	5.00	10.00	20.00	40.00

Mint mark: BM
Obv: Crowned tall A

3.4	1861	1.800	2.50	5.00	10.00	20.00
	1862	2.100	2.50	5.00	10.00	20.00
	1863	2.854	2.50	5.00	10.00	20.00
	1864	1.046	2.50	5.00	10.00	20.00

Mint mark: EM

9.1	1867	Inc.У3.3	3.00	6.00	12.00	25.00
	1868	6.305	.50	1.00	3.00	10.00
	1869	10.230	.50	1.00	3.00	10.00
	1870	9.875	.50	1.00	3.00	10.00
	1871	2.880	.50	1.00	3.00	10.00
	1872	5.713	.50	1.00	3.00	10.00
	1873	5.213	.50	1.00	3.00	10.00
	1874	5.013	.50	1.00	3.00	10.00
	1875	6.438	.50	1.00	3.00	10.00
	1876	1.755	4.00	8.00	15.00	30.00

Mint mark: СПБ

9.2	1867	—	2.00	4.00	8.00	20.00
	1868	.750	1.00	2.00	4.00	10.00
	1869	.739	1.00	2.00	4.00	10.00
	1870	1.143	1.00	2.00	4.00	10.00
	1871	—	.50	100.00	200.00	300.00
	1876	2.930	.50	1.00	3.00	6.00
	1877	7.065	.50	1.00	3.00	6.00
	1878	8.241	.50	1.00	3.00	6.00
	1879	9.045	.50	1.00	3.00	6.00
	1880	7.730	.50	1.00	3.00	6.00
	1881	8.415	.50	1.00	3.00	6.00
	1882	5.685	.50	1.00	3.00	6.00
	1883	7.830	.50	1.00	3.00	6.00
9.2	1884	2.500	.50	1.00	2.00	6.00
	1885	3.400	.50	1.00	2.00	6.00
	1886	3.210	.50	1.00	2.00	6.00
	1887	6.000	.25	.50	1.00	5.00
	1888	6.000	.25	.50	1.00	5.00
	1889	9.000	.25	.50	1.00	5.00
	1890	6.905	.25	.50	1.00	5.00
	1891	10.875	.25	.50	1.00	5.00
	1892	5.640	.25	.50	1.00	5.00
	1893	13.395	.25	.50	1.00	5.00
	1894	15.490	.25	.50	1.00	5.00
	1895	18.200	.25	.50	1.00	4.50
	1896	22.960	.25	.50	1.00	4.50
	1897	30.000	.25	.50	1.00	4.50
	1898	50.000	.25	.50	1.00	4.50
	1899	50.000	.25	.50	1.00	4.50
	1900	30.000	.25	.50	1.00	4.50
	1901	30.000	.25	.50	1.00	4.50
	1902	20.000	2.50	5.00	10.00	20.00
	1903	74.400	.25	.50	1.00	4.50
	1904	30.600	.25	.50	1.00	4.50
	1905	23.000	.25	.50	1.00	4.50
	1906	20.000	.25	.50	1.00	4.50
	1907	20.000	.25	.50	1.00	4.50
	1908	40.000	.25	.50	1.00	4.50
	1909	27.500	.25	.50	1.00	4.50
	1910	36.500	.25	.50	1.00	4.50
	1911	38.150	.25	.50	1.00	4.50
	1912	31.850	.25	.50	1.00	4.50
	1913	61.500	.25	.50	1.00	4.50
	1914	32.500	.25	.50	1.00	4.50
	Common date				Proof	35.00

Mint: Petrograd - w/o mint mark

9.3	1915	58.000	.25	.50	1.00	4.50
	1916	46.500	.25	.50	1.00	4.50
	1917	—			Rare	—

2 KOPEKS

COPPER
Mint mark: EM

C#	Date	Mintage	VG	Fine	VF	XF
114.1	1802	45.798	10.00	20.00	40.00	100.00
	1803	.298	25.00	50.00	100.00	200.00
	1804	—	—	—	Rare	—

Mint mark: KM

114.2	1804	—	25.00	50.00	100.00	200.00
	1805	—	25.00	50.00	100.00	200.00
	1807	—	25.00	50.00	100.00	200.00

Mint mark: EM
Obv: Type 1 eagle.

118.1	1810 НМ	79.364	1.00	2.00	4.00	8.00

NOTE: Exists with large and small date.

Mint mark: KM
Obv: Type 2 eagle.

118.2	1810	—	4.00	8.00	15.00	30.00
	1810 ПБ	—	4.00	8.00	15.00	30.00
	1811 ПБ	—	4.00	8.00	15.00	30.00
	1812	—	4.00	8.00	15.00	30.00

Mint mark: EM
Obv: Type 3 eagle.

118.3	1810 НМ					
		129.000	1.00	2.00	4.00	8.00
	1811 НМ plain edge					
	Inc. Ab.	1.00	2.00	4.00	8.00
118.3	1811 НМ reeded edge					
	Inc. Ab.	1.00	2.00	4.00	8.00
	1812 НМ					
		132.085	1.00	2.00	4.00	8.00
	1812 НМ inverted 2					
	Inc. Ab.	1.00	2.00	4.00	8.00
	1813 НМ					
		64.980	1.00	2.00	4.00	8.00
	1814 НМ					
		110.000	1.00	2.00	4.00	8.00
	1815 НМ					
		44.970	1.00	2.00	4.00	8.00
	1816 НМ					
		64.150	1.00	2.00	4.00	8.00
	1817 НМ					
		75.000	1.00	2.00	4.00	8.00
	1818 НМ					
		60.625	1.00	2.00	4.00	8.00
	1818 ФГ	I.A.	1.00	2.00	4.00	8.00
	1819 НМ					
		100.468	1.00	2.00	4.00	8.00
	1820 НМ					
		75.180	1.00	2.00	4.00	8.00
	1821 НМ					
		55.170	1.00	2.00	4.00	8.00
	1821 ФГ	I.A.	1.00	2.00	4.00	8.00
	1822 ФГ	44.867	1.00	2.00	4.00	8.00
	1823 ФГ	44.935	1.00	2.00	4.00	8.00
	1823 ПГ	I.A.	—	—	Rare	—
	1824 ПГ	36.600	1.00	2.00	4.00	8.00
	1825 ПГ	73.856	1.00	2.00	4.00	8.00
	1825 ИШ	I.A.	1.00	2.00	4.00	8.00
	1825 ИК	I.A.	1.00	2.00	4.00	8.00
137.1	1826 ИК	50.450	2.50	5.00	10.00	20.00
	1827 ИК	34.065	2.50	5.00	10.00	20.00
	1828 ИК	14.475	2.50	5.00	10.00	20.00
	1829 ИК	13.790	2.50	5.00	10.00	20.00
	1830 ИК	15.450	2.50	5.00	10.00	20.00

NOTE: Varieties exist.

Mint mark: ИМ

118.4	1810 МК	—	1.00	2.00	4.00	8.00
	1811 ПС	I.A.	1.00	2.00	4.00	8.00
	1811 МК	—	1.00	2.00	4.00	8.00
	1812 ПС	—	1.00	2.00	4.00	8.00
	1813 ПС	—	1.00	2.00	4.00	8.00
	1814 ПС	—	1.00	2.00	4.00	8.00
	1814	—	1.00	2.00	4.00	8.00

Mint mark: KM

118.5	1812 АМ	—	1.00	2.00	4.00	8.00
	1813 АМ	—	1.00	2.00	4.00	8.00
	1814 АМ	—	1.00	2.00	4.00	8.00
	1815 АМ	—	1.00	2.00	4.00	8.00
	1816 АМ	—	1.00	2.00	4.00	8.00
	1817 АМ	—	1.00	2.00	4.00	8.00
	1817 АБ	—	1.00	2.00	4.00	8.00
	1818 ДБ	—	1.00	2.00	4.00	8.00
	1819 АД	—	1.00	2.00	4.00	8.00
	1820 АД	—	1.00	2.00	4.00	8.00
	1821 АД	—	1.00	2.00	4.00	8.00
	1821 АМ	—	1.00	2.00	4.00	8.00
	1822 АМ	—	1.00	2.00	4.00	8.00
	1823 АМ	—	1.00	2.00	4.00	8.00
	1824 АМ	—	1.00	2.00	4.00	8.00
	1825 АМ	—	1.00	2.00	4.00	8.00
137.2	1826 АМ	9.375	2.50	5.00	10.00	20.00
	1827 АМ	I.A.	2.50	5.00	10.00	20.00
	1828 АМ	15.000	2.50	5.00	10.00	20.00
	1829 АМ	15.000	2.50	5.00	10.00	20.00
	1830 АМ	15.000	2.50	5.00	10.00	20.00

Mint mark: СПБ

118.6	1810 ФГ	—	1.00	2.00	4.00	8.00
	1810 МК	—	1.00	2.00	4.00	8.00
	1810 ПС	—	1.00	2.00	4.00	8.00
	1811 МК	—	1.00	2.00	4.00	8.00
	1811 ПС	—	1.00	2.00	4.00	8.00
	1812 ПС	—	1.00	2.00	4.00	8.00
	1813 ПС	—	1.00	2.00	4.00	8.00
	1814 ПС	—	3.00	6.00	12.00	25.00
	1818	—	20.00	40.00	80.00	150.00
137.3	1828	—	25.00	50.00	100.00	200.00

Mint: Kolpino

118.7	1810 МК	—	20.00	40.00	80.00	150.00

Russia-Empire / USSR

Mint mark: EM

C#	Date	Mintage	VG	Fine	VF	XF
139.1	1830 ФХ	—	20.00	40.00	80.00	150.00
	1831 ФХ	—	20.00	40.00	80.00	150.00
	1833 ФХ	.261	3.00	6.00	12.00	25.00
	1837 НА	16.845	3.00	6.00	12.00	25.00
	1838 НА	6.623	3.00	6.00	12.00	25.00
	1839 НА	8.250	3.00	6.00	12.00	25.00

Mint mark: СПБ

139.2	1830	29 pcs.	—	—	Rare	—

Mint mark: СМ

C#	Date	Mintage	VG	Fine	VF	XF
139.3	1831	1.500	2.00	4.00	8.00	15.00
	1832	1.500	2.00	4.00	8.00	15.00
	1833	.539	2.00	4.00	8.00	15.00
	1834	1.500	2.00	4.00	8.00	15.00
	1835	1.500	2.00	4.00	8.00	15.00
	1836	1.350	2.00	4.00	8.00	15.00
	1837	1.000	2.00	4.00	8.00	15.00
	1838	10.500	2.00	4.00	8.00	15.00
	1839	7.073	2.00	4.00	8.00	15.00

Mint mark: EM

C#	Date	Mintage	VG	Fine	VF	XF
145.1	1840	20.778	1.50	3.00	6.00	12.00
	1841	14.999	1.50	3.00	6.00	12.00
	1842	12.446	1.50	3.00	6.00	12.00
	1843	11.020	1.50	3.00	6.00	12.00
	1844	5.500	1.50	3.00	6.00	12.00

Mint mark: СПБ

145.2	1840	—	6.00	12.00	25.00	50.00
	1841	—	25.00	50.00	100.00	200.00

Mint mark: СПМ

145.3	1840	4.800	1.00	2.00	4.00	8.00
	1841	Inc. Ab.	1.00	2.00	4.00	8.00
	1842	4.800	1.00	2.00	4.00	8.00
	1843	4.800	1.00	2.00	4.00	8.00

Mint mark: СМ

145.4	1839	.341	1.00	2.00	4.00	8.00
	1840	1.929	1.00	2.00	4.00	8.00
	1841	2.636	1.00	2.00	4.00	8.00
	1842	3.000	1.00	2.00	4.00	8.00
	1843	1.500	1.00	2.00	4.00	8.00
	1844	2.250	1.00	2.00	4.00	8.00
	1845	2.250	1.00	2.00	4.00	8.00
	1846	2.250	1.00	2.00	4.00	8.00
	1847	2.209	1.00	2.00	4.00	8.00

Mint mark: МШ

145.5	1848	.031	20.00	40.00	80.00	150.00

Mint mark: EM

C#	Date	Mintage	VG	Fine	VF	XF
150.1	1849	—	25.00	50.00	100.00	200.00
	1850	2.206	1.50	3.00	6.00	12.00
	1851	8.356	1.50	3.00	6.00	12.00
	1852	6.874	1.50	3.00	6.00	12.00
	1853	7.561	1.50	3.00	6.00	12.00
	1854	4.541	1.50	3.00	6.00	12.00
(Y4.1)	1855	8.587	.50	1.00	2.00	5.00
	1856	9.167	.50	1.00	2.00	5.00
	1857	3.359	.50	1.00	2.00	5.00
	1858	10.028	.50	1.00	2.00	5.00
	1859	14.772	.50	1.00	2.00	5.00

Mint mark: СПМ

150.2	1849	50 pcs.	—	—	Rare	—

Mint mark: ВМ

150.3	1850	—	10.00	20.00	40.00	80.00
	1851	.298	5.00	10.00	20.00	40.00
	1852	.202	5.00	10.00	20.00	40.00
	1853	2.642	25.00	50.00	100.00	200.00
	1854	.148	5.00	10.00	20.00	40.00

C#	Date	Mintage	VG	Fine	VF	XF
(Y4.2)	1855	1.347	1.00	2.00	6.00	12.00
	1856	1.190	1.00	2.00	6.00	12.00
	1858	.750	1.00	2.00	6.00	12.00
	1859	1.595	1.00	2.00	6.00	12.00
	1860	1.605	—	—	Rare	—

Mint mark: EM
Obv: Ribbons added to crown.

Y#	Date	Mintage	Fine	VF	XF	Unc
4a.1	1859	—	1.00	2.00	5.00	15.00
	1860	19.239	1.00	2.00	5.00	15.00
	1861	18.547	1.00	2.00	5.00	15.00
	1862	16.889	1.00	2.00	5.00	15.00
	1863	21.703	1.00	2.00	5.00	15.00
	1864	14.175	1.00	2.00	5.00	15.00
	1865	26.921	1.00	2.00	5.00	15.00
	1866	21.890	1.00	2.00	5.00	15.00
	1867	8.970	1.00	2.00	5.00	15.00

Mint mark: ВМ

4a.2	1860	—	3.00	6.00	12.00	25.00
	1861	.586	3.00	6.00	12.00	25.00
	1862	.966	3.00	6.00	12.00	25.00
	1863	1.739	3.00	6.00	12.00	25.00

Mint mark: EM

10.1	1867	.150	5.00	10.00	20.00	40.00
	1868	18.200	.50	1.00	2.00	10.00
	1869	22.174	.50	1.00	2.00	10.00
	1870	21.884	.50	1.00	2.00	10.00
	1871	7.058	.50	1.00	2.00	10.00
	1872	12.734	.50	1.00	2.00	10.00
	1873	7.364	.50	1.00	2.00	10.00
	1874	8.551	.50	1.00	2.00	10.00
	1875	10.451	.50	1.00	2.00	10.00
	1876	2.905	.50	1.00	2.00	10.00

Mint mark: СПБ

10.2	1867	—	3.00	6.00	12.00	25.00
	1868	.659	1.50	3.00	6.00	15.00
	1869	.643	1.50	3.00	6.00	15.00
	1870	.231	1.00	2.00	4.00	20.00
	1871	—	40.00	80.00	150.00	250.00
	1876	3.240	.50	1.00	2.00	8.00
	1877	5.010	.50	1.00	2.00	8.00
	1878	8.093	.50	1.00	2.00	8.00
	1879	7.380	.50	1.00	2.00	8.00
	1880	6.525	.50	1.00	2.00	8.00
	1881	7.299	.50	1.00	2.00	8.00
	1882	4.478	.50	1.00	2.00	8.00
	1883	6.230	.50	1.00	2.00	8.00
	1884	2.625	.50	1.00	2.00	8.00
	1885	3.070	.50	1.00	2.00	8.00
	1886	3.123	.50	1.00	2.00	8.00
	1887	1.725	.50	1.00	2.00	8.00
	1888	1.822	.50	1.00	2.00	8.00
	1889	2.812	.50	1.00	2.00	8.00
	1890	2.538	.50	1.00	2.00	8.00
	1891	2.788	.50	1.00	2.00	8.00
	1892	.918	2.00	4.00	8.00	20.00
	1893	10.295	.50	1.00	2.00	5.00
	1894	8.600	.50	1.00	2.00	5.00
	1895	9.122	.50	1.00	2.00	5.00
	1896	14.675	.50	1.00	2.00	5.00
	1897	9.500	.50	1.00	2.00	5.00
	1898	17.500	.50	1.00	2.00	5.00
	1899	17.500	.50	1.00	2.00	5.00
	1900	20.500	.50	1.00	2.00	5.00
	1901	20.000	.50	1.00	2.00	5.00
	1902	10.000	.50	1.00	2.00	5.00
	1903	29.200	.50	1.00	2.00	5.00
	1904	13.300	.50	1.00	2.00	5.00
	1905	15.000	.50	1.00	2.00	5.00
	1906	6.250	.50	1.00	2.00	5.00
	1907	7.500	.50	1.00	2.00	5.00
	1908	19.000	.50	1.00	2.00	5.00
	1909	16.250	.50	1.00	2.00	5.00
	1910	12.000	.50	1.00	2.00	5.00
	1911	17.200	.50	1.00	2.00	5.00
	1912	17.050	.50	1.00	2.00	5.00
	1913	26.000	.50	1.00	2.00	5.00
	1914	20.000	.50	1.00	2.00	5.00
Common date	—	—	—	Proof	35.00	

Mint: Petrograd - w/o mint mark

10.3	1915	33.750	.50	1.00	2.00	5.00
	1916	31.500	.50	1.00	2.00	5.00

3 KOPEKS

COPPER
Mint mark: EM

C#	Date	Mintage	VG	Fine	VF	XF
146.1	1840	5.230	3.00	6.00	12.00	25.00
	1841	13.417	3.00	6.00	12.00	25.00
	1842	13.700	3.00	6.00	12.00	25.00
	1843	14.578	3.00	6.00	12.00	25.00
	1844	4.840	3.00	6.00	12.00	25.00

Mint mark: СПБ

146.2	1840	—	20.00	40.00	80.00	150.00

Mint mark: СПМ

146.3	1840	2.133	5.00	10.00	20.00	40.00
	1841	2.133	5.00	10.00	20.00	40.00
	1842	2.133	5.00	10.00	20.00	40.00
	1843	2.133	5.00	10.00	20.00	40.00

Mint mark: СМ

146.4	1839	.142	10.00	20.00	50.00	100.00
	1840	.827	4.00	7.50	15.00	30.00
	1841	1.171	4.00	7.50	15.00	30.00
	1842	1.360	4.00	7.50	15.00	30.00
	1843	.669	4.00	7.50	15.00	30.00
	1844	1.000	4.00	7.50	15.00	30.00
	1845	1.000	4.00	7.50	15.00	30.00
	1846	1.000	4.00	7.50	15.00	30.00
	1847	1.000	4.00	7.50	15.00	30.00

Mint mark: МШ

146.5	1848	.017	—	—	Rare	—

Mint mark: EM
Obv: First variety - six coats of arms.

Y#	Date	Mintage	VG	Fine	VF	XF
151.1	1849	—	20.00	40.00	80.00	150.00
	1850	.184	2.00	4.00	7.50	15.00
	1851	3.448	2.00	4.00	7.50	15.00
	1852	5.444	2.00	4.00	7.50	15.00
	1853	3.719	2.00	4.00	7.50	15.00
	1854	1.351	2.00	4.00	7.50	15.00
(Y5.1)	1855	2.835	1.00	2.00	4.00	8.00
	1856	6.700	1.00	2.00	4.00	8.00
	1857	4.726	1.00	2.00	4.00	8.00
	1858	10.662	1.00	2.00	4.00	8.00
	1859	15.821	1.00	2.00	4.00	8.00
Common date			—	—	Proof	200.00

Mint mark: СПМ

151.2	1849	—	25.00	50.00	100.00	200.00

Mint mark: ВМ

151.3	1850	.050	4.00	7.50	15.00	30.00
	1851	.100	4.00	7.50	15.00	30.00
	1852	.100	4.00	7.50	15.00	30.00
	1853	.089	4.00	7.50	15.00	30.00
	1854	.161	4.00	7.50	15.00	30.00
(Y5.2)	1856	.417	5.00	10.00	20.00	40.00
	1857	.021	7.50	12.50	25.00	50.00
	1858	.712	2.50	5.00	10.00	20.00
	1859	.400	5.00	7.50	15.00	30.00

Mint mark: EM
Obv: Second variety - eight coats of arms.

Y#	Date	Mintage	Fine	VF	XF	Unc
5a.1	1859	—	2.00	4.00	8.00	25.00
	1860	14.010	2.00	4.00	8.00	25.00
	1861	7.738	2.00	4.00	8.00	25.00

Y#	Date	Mintage	Fine	VF	XF	Unc
5a.1	1862	10.377	2.00	4.00	8.00	25.00
	1863	3.939	2.00	4.00	8.00	25.00
	1864	6.121	4.00	8.00	15.00	30.00
	1865	5.740	40.00	80.00	150.00	250.00
	1866	6.611	2.00	4.00	8.00	25.00
	1867	1.786	4.00	8.00	15.00	30.00

Mint mark: ВМ

Y#	Date	Mintage	Fine	VF	XF	Unc
5a.2	1860	.283	7.50	15.00	30.00	75.00
	1861	.284	6.00	12.50	25.00	60.00
	1862	.200	6.00	12.50	25.00	60.00
	1863	.401	9.00	17.50	35.00	80.00

Mint mark: ЕМ

Y#	Date	Mintage	Fine	VF	XF	Unc
11.1	1867	.160	2.00	4.00	8.00	20.00
	1868	6.059	1.00	2.00	4.00	15.00
	1869	5.526	1.00	2.00	4.00	15.00
	1870	5.018	1.00	2.00	4.00	15.00
	1871	1.585	1.00	2.00	4.00	15.00
	1872	3.018	1.00	2.00	4.00	15.00
	1873	4.704	1.00	2.00	4.00	15.00
	1874	4.419	1.00	2.00	4.00	15.00
	1875	3.595	1.00	2.00	4.00	15.00
	1876	.890	1.00	2.00	4.00	15.00

Mint mark: СПБ

Y#	Date	Mintage	Fine	VF	XF	Unc
11.2	1867	54 pcs.	4.00	7.50	15.00	30.00
	1868	.910	2.00	4.00	8.00	20.00
	1869	.723	2.00	4.00	8.00	20.00
	1870	.080	6.00	12.00	25.00	50.00
	1871	—	40.00	80.00	150.00	250.00
	1876	4.863	.75	1.50	3.00	12.00
	1877	5.902	.75	1.50	3.00	12.00
	1878	6.355	.75	1.50	3.00	12.00
	1879	7.355	.75	1.50	3.00	12.00
	1880	6.773	.75	1.50	3.00	12.00
	1881	6.141	.75	1.50	3.00	12.00
	1882	4.280	.75	1.50	3.00	12.00
	1883	1.061	.75	1.50	3.00	12.00
	1884	2.975	.75	1.50	3.00	12.00
	1891	1.983	2.00	3.00	6.00	20.00
	1892	.648	2.00	3.00	6.00	20.00
	1893	6.365	.50	1.00	2.00	8.00
	1894	4.803	.50	1.00	2.00	8.00
	1895	5.417	.50	1.00	2.00	8.00
	1896	7.923	.50	1.00	2.00	8.00
	1897	6.667	.50	1.00	2.00	8.00
	1898	11.667	.50	1.00	2.00	8.00
	1899	11.667	.50	1.00	2.00	8.00
	1900	16.667	.50	1.00	2.00	8.00
	1901	10.000	.50	1.00	2.00	8.00
	1902	3.333	.50	1.00	2.00	8.00
	1903	11.400	.50	1.00	2.00	8.00
	1904	6.934	.50	1.00	2.00	8.00
	1905	3.333	.50	1.00	2.00	8.00
	1906	5.667	.50	1.00	2.00	8.00
	1907	2.500	.50	1.00	2.00	8.00
	1908	12.667	.50	1.00	2.00	8.00
	1909	6.733	.50	1.00	2.00	8.00
	1910	6.667	.50	1.00	2.00	8.00
	1911	9.467	.50	1.00	2.00	8.00
	1912	8.533	.50	1.00	2.00	8.00
	1913	15.333	.50	1.00	2.00	8.00
	1914	8.167	.50	1.00	2.00	8.00
	Common date	—	—	—	Proof	35.00

Mint: Petrograd - w/o mint mark

Y#	Date	Mintage	Fine	VF	XF	Unc
11.3	1915	19.833	.50	1.00	2.00	15.00
	1916	25.667	.50	1.00	2.00	15.00

5 KOPEKS

COPPER
Mint mark: ЕМ

C#	Date	Mintage	VG	Fine	VF	XF
115.1	1802	12.592	10.00	20.00	40.00	80.00
	1803	31.820	9.00	17.50	30.00	50.00
	1804	26.268	9.00	17.50	30.00	50.00
	1805	16.519	10.00	20.00	40.00	80.00
	1806	38.416	7.50	15.00	30.00	60.00
	1807	10.667	10.00	20.00	40.00	80.00
	1808	10.001	10.00	20.00	40.00	80.00
	1809	10.140	10.00	20.00	40.00	80.00
	1810	15.802	10.00	20.00	40.00	80.00

NOTE: Varieties exist.

Mint mark: КМ

C#	Date	Mintage	VG	Fine	VF	XF
115.2	1802	4.000	12.50	25.00	50.00	100.00
	1803	3.600	12.50	25.00	50.00	100.00
	1804	4.000	12.50	25.00	50.00	100.00
	1805	5.000	12.50	25.00	50.00	100.00
	1806	5.000	12.50	25.00	50.00	100.00
	1807	5.000	12.50	25.00	50.00	100.00
	1808	5.000	12.50	25.00	50.00	100.00
	1809	5.000	12.50	25.00	50.00	100.00
	1810	—	12.50	25.00	50.00	100.00

NOTE: Varieties exist.

1.0366 g, .868 SILVER, .0289 oz ASW
Mint mark: СПБ

C#	Date	Mintage	VG	Fine	VF	XF
126	1810 ФГ	—	50.00	100.00	200.00	300.00
	1811 ФГ	.080	10.00	20.00	40.00	80.00
	1811	Inc. Ab.	—	—	Rare	—
	1812 МФ	—	—	—	Rare	—
	1813 ПС	.620	3.00	6.00	12.00	25.00
	1814 ПС	1.300	3.00	6.00	12.00	25.00
	1814 МФ	I.A.	3.00	6.00	12.00	25.00
	1815 МФ	3.000	3.00	6.00	12.00	25.00
	1815	Inc. Ab.	—	—	Rare	—
	1816 МФ	1.040	3.00	6.00	12.00	25.00
	1816 ПС	I.A.	3.00	6.00	12.00	25.00
	1817 ПС	.120	3.00	6.00	12.00	25.00
	1818 ПС	.340	3.00	6.00	12.00	25.00
	1819 ПС	.920	3.00	6.00	12.00	25.00
	1820 ПС	.460	3.00	6.00	12.00	25.00
	1820 ПД	I.A.	3.00	6.00	12.00	25.00
	1821 ПД	2.000	3.00	6.00	12.00	25.00
	1822 ПД	1.060	3.00	6.00	12.00	25.00
	1823 ПД	2.300	3.00	6.00	12.00	25.00
	1824 ПД	1.740	3.00	6.00	12.00	25.00
	1825 ПД	1.160	3.00	6.00	12.00	25.00
	1825 НГ	Inc. Ab.	—	—	Rare	—
152.3	1826 НГ	1.340	3.00	6.00	12.00	25.00

C#	Date	Mintage	VG	Fine	VF	XF
156	1826 НГ	Inc. C152.3	3.00	6.00	12.00	25.00
	1827 НГ	1.769	3.00	6.00	12.00	25.00
	1828 НГ	.060	5.00	10.00	20.00	40.00
	1829 НГ	.080	5.00	10.00	20.00	40.00
	1830 НГ	1.500	3.00	6.00	12.00	25.00
	1831 НГ	.520	3.00	6.00	12.00	25.00

COPPER
Mint mark: ЕМ

C#	Date	Mintage	VG	Fine	VF	XF
140.1	1830 ФХ	—	25.00	50.00	100.00	200.00
140.1	1831 ФХ	41.120	3.50	6.50	12.50	25.00
	1831	—	4.00	8.00	15.00	30.00
	1832 ФХ	30.080	3.50	6.50	12.50	25.00
	1833 ФХ	14.332	3.50	6.50	12.50	25.00
	1834 ФХ	41.785	3.50	6.50	12.50	25.00
	1835 ФХ	41.763	3.50	6.50	12.50	25.00
	1836 ФХ	31.332	3.50	6.50	12.50	25.00
	1837 ФХ	19.745	4.00	8.00	15.00	30.00
	1837 КТ	I.A.	3.50	6.50	12.50	25.00
	1837 НА	I.A.	3.50	6.50	12.50	25.00
	1838 НА	24.430	3.50	6.50	12.50	25.00
	1839 НА	1.400	4.00	8.00	15.00	30.00

Mint mark: СПБ

C#	Date	Mintage	VG	Fine	VF	XF
140.2	1830	25 pcs.	—	—	Rare	—

Mint mark: СМ

C#	Date	Mintage	VG	Fine	VF	XF
140.3	1831	5.900	4.00	7.50	15.00	30.00
	1832	5.900	4.00	7.50	15.00	30.00
	1833	6.295	4.00	7.50	15.00	30.00
	1834	5.900	4.00	7.50	15.00	30.00
	1835	5.000	4.00	7.50	15.00	30.00
	1836	5.240	4.00	7.50	15.00	30.00
	1837	5.200	4.00	7.50	15.00	30.00
	1838	1.420	4.00	7.50	15.00	30.00
	1839	1.400	7.50	15.00	30.00	60.00

1.0366 g, .868 SILVER, .0289 oz ASW
Mint mark: СПБ

C#	Date	Mintage	VG	Fine	VF	XF
163	1832 НГ	.224	1.00	2.00	4.00	12.00
	1833 НГ	1.026	1.00	2.00	4.00	12.00
	1834 НГ	.780	1.00	2.00	4.00	12.00
	1835 НГ	1.010	1.00	2.00	4.00	12.00
	1836 НГ	.900	1.00	2.00	4.00	12.00
	1837 НГ	1.140	1.00	2.00	4.00	12.00
	1838 НГ	2.400	1.00	2.00	4.00	12.00
	1839 НГ	1,002	20.00	40.00	80.00	150.00
	1840 НГ	.420	1.50	3.00	6.00	15.00
	1841 НГ	.100	1.50	3.00	6.00	15.00
	1842 АЧ	.100	1.50	3.00	6.00	15.00
	1843 АЧ	.400	1.50	3.00	6.00	15.00
	1844 КБ	.401	1.50	3.00	6.00	15.00
	1845 КБ	1.740	1.00	2.00	4.00	10.00
	1846 ПА	.280	1.00	2.00	4.00	10.00
	1847 ПА	1.010	1.00	2.00	4.00	10.00
	1848 НI	1.000	1.00	2.00	4.00	10.00
	1849 ПА	1.020	1.00	2.00	4.00	10.00
	1850 ПА	1.300	1.00	2.00	4.00	10.00
	1851 ПА	1.000	1.00	2.00	4.00	10.00
	1852 ПА	.900	1.00	2.00	4.00	10.00
	1852 НI	Inc. Ab.	—	—	Rare	—
	1853 НI	.900	1.00	2.00	7.50	20.00
	1854 НI	.500	1.00	2.00	7.50	20.00
(Y13)	1855 НI	.640	1.00	2.00	4.00	10.00
	1856 ФБ	.680	1.00	2.00	4.00	10.00
	1857 ФБ	.080	2.00	4.00	8.00	15.00
	1858 ФБ	.040	2.50	5.00	10.00	20.00

COPPER
Mint mark: ЕМ
Obv: Six coats of arms.

C#	Date	Mintage	Fine	VF	XF	Unc
152.1	1849	—	50.00	100.00	200.00	350.00
	1850	.373	4.00	7.50	15.00	40.00
	1851	2.241	4.00	7.50	15.00	40.00
	1852	3.961	4.00	7.50	15.00	40.00
	1853	1.474	30.00	60.00	120.00	200.00
	1854	.356	4.00	7.50	15.00	40.00
(Y6.1)	1855	.740	3.00	6.00	12.00	25.00
	1856	5.146	2.00	4.00	8.00	20.00
	1857	8.675	2.00	4.00	8.00	20.00
	1858	19.561	2.00	4.00	8.00	20.00
	1859	19.441	2.00	4.00	8.00	20.00

Mint mark: СПМ

C#	Date	Mintage	Fine	VF	XF	Unc
152.2	1849	—	50.00	100.00	200.00	300.00

Mint mark: ВМ

C#	Date	Mintage	Fine	VF	XF	Unc
152.4	1850	—	15.00	25.00	50.00	120.00
	1851	.024	15.00	25.00	50.00	120.00
	1852	.016	15.00	25.00	50.00	120.00
	1853	.040	15.00	25.00	50.00	120.00
(Y6.2)	1856	.040	15.00	25.00	50.00	120.00

Mint mark: EM
Obv: Eight coats of arms.

Y#	Date	Mintage	Fine	VF	XF	Unc
6a	1858	—	—	—	Rare	
	1859	Inc. Ab.	2.00	4.00	8.00	20.00
	1860	25.260	2.00	4.00	8.00	20.00
	1861	28.022	2.00	4.00	8.00	20.00
	1862	22.055	2.00	4.00	8.00	20.00
	1863	22.511	2.00	4.00	8.00	20.00
	1864	26.042	2.00	4.00	8.00	20.00
	1865	38.943	2.00	4.00	8.00	20.00
	1866	24.767	2.00	4.00	8.00	20.00
	1867	11.697	4.00	8.00	16.00	40.00

1.0366 g, .750 SILVER, .0250 oz ASW
Mint mark: СПБ
Obv: Ribbons added to crown.

Y#	Date	Mintage	Fine	VF	XF	Unc
19.1	1859	.120	—	—	Rare	
	1859 ФБ	I.A.	4.00	8.00	16.00	40.00
	1860 ФБ	.020	4.00	8.00	16.00	40.00

Obv: Redesigned eagle, engrailed edge.

19.2	1860 ФБ	.180	2.00	4.00	10.00	25.00
	1861 ФБ	.360	2.00	4.00	10.00	25.00
	1861 МИ	I.A.	4.00	8.00	16.00	40.00
	1861	—	—	—	Rare	
	1862 МИ	.400	2.00	4.00	10.00	25.00
	1863 АБ	.200	2.00	4.00	10.00	25.00
	1864 НФ	.240	2.00	4.00	10.00	25.00
	1865 НФ	.240	2.00	4.00	10.00	25.00
	1866 НФ	.190	2.00	4.00	10.00	25.00
	1866	I.A.	10.00	20.00	45.00	100.00

.8998 g, .500 SILVER, .0144 oz ASW
Reeded edge

19a.1	1868 HI	.180	1.75	3.50	7.50	25.00
	1869 HI	.240	1.75	3.50	7.50	25.00
	1869 HI	.170	1.75	3.50	7.50	25.00
	1870 HI	.220	1.75	3.50	7.50	25.00
	1871 HI	.200	1.75	3.50	7.50	25.00
	1872 HI	.180	1.75	3.50	7.50	25.00
	1873 HI	.160	1.75	3.50	7.50	25.00
	1874 HI	.200	1.75	3.50	7.50	25.00
	1875 HI	.200	1.75	3.50	7.50	25.00
	1876 HI	.240	1.75	3.50	7.50	25.00
	1877 HI	.200	1.75	3.50	7.50	25.00
	1877 НФ	I.A.	5.00	10.00	20.00	50.00
	1878 НФ	.220	1.75	3.50	7.50	25.00
	1878 HI	I.A.	7.50	15.00	30.00	75.00
	1879 НФ	.140	1.75	3.50	7.50	25.00
	1880 НФ	.240	1.75	3.50	7.50	25.00
	1881 НФ	.200	1.75	3.50	7.50	25.00
	1882 НФ	1.760	1.00	2.00	4.00	10.00
	1883 ДС	1.000	1.00	2.00	4.00	10.00
	1883 АГ	I.A.	1.00	2.00	4.00	10.00
	1884 АГ	3.460	1.00	2.00	4.00	10.00
	1885 АГ	1.700	1.00	2.00	4.00	10.00
	1886 АГ	2.000	1.00	2.00	4.00	10.00
	1887 АГ	3.000	1.00	2.00	4.00	10.00
	1888 АГ	4.000	1.00	2.00	4.00	10.00
	1889 АГ	3.500	1.00	2.00	4.00	10.00
	1890 АГ	8.000	1.00	2.00	4.00	10.00
	1891 АГ	2.000	1.00	2.00	4.00	10.00
	1892 АГ	8.000	1.00	2.00	4.00	10.00
	1893 АГ	2.000	1.00	2.00	4.00	10.00
	1897 АГ	2.000	1.00	2.00	4.00	10.00
	1898 АГ	3.980	1.00	2.00	4.00	10.00
	1899 АГ	4.605	1.00	2.00	4.00	10.00
	1899 ЗБ	I.A.	1.00	2.00	4.00	10.00
	1900 ФЗ	5.205	1.00	2.00	4.00	10.00
	1901 ФЗ	5.790	1.00	2.00	4.00	10.00
	1901 АР	I.A.	1.00	2.00	4.00	10.00
	1902 АР	6.000	1.00	2.00	4.00	10.00
	1903 АР	9.000	1.00	2.00	4.00	10.00
	1904 АР	10 pcs.	—	—	Rare	
	1905 АР	10.000	1.00	2.00	4.00	10.00
	1906 ЗБ	4.000	1.00	2.00	4.00	10.00
	1908 ЗБ	.400	1.00	2.00	4.00	10.00
	1909 ЗБ	3.100	1.00	2.00	4.00	10.00
	1910 ЗБ	2.500	1.00	2.00	4.00	10.00

Y#	Date	Mintage	Fine	VF	XF	Unc
19a.1	1911 ЗБ	2.700	1.00	2.00	4.00	10.00
	1912 ЗБ	3.000	1.00	2.00	4.00	10.00
	1913 ЗБ	1.300	2.00	4.00	8.00	20.00
	1913 ВС	I.A.	1.00	2.00	4.00	10.00
	1914 ВС	I.A.	1.00	2.00	4.00	10.00

Mint: Petrograd - w/o mint mark

19a.2	1915 ВС	3.000	1.00	2.00	4.00	10.00

COPPER
Mint mark: EM

12.1	1867	1.459	3.00	6.00	12.00	25.00
	1868	23.019	1.00	3.00	6.00	20.00
	1869	20.277	1.00	3.00	6.00	20.00
	1870	21.158	1.00	3.00	6.00	20.00
	1871	6.304	1.00	3.00	6.00	20.00
	1872	11.890	1.00	3.00	6.00	20.00
	1873	13.052	1.00	3.00	6.00	20.00
	1874	12.879	1.00	3.00	6.00	20.00
	1875	19.624	1.00	3.00	6.00	20.00
	1876	5.329	1.00	3.00	6.00	20.00

Mint mark: СПБ

12.2	1867	44 pcs.	4.00	7.50	15.00	40.00
	1868	.821	2.00	4.00	8.00	30.00
	1869	.942	2.00	4.00	8.00	30.00
	1870	.028	5.00	10.00	20.00	40.00
	1871	—	40.00	80.00	150.00	250.00
	1876	4.655	1.00	3.00	6.00	20.00
	1877	7.184	1.00	3.00	6.00	20.00
	1878	12.542	1.00	3.00	6.00	20.00
	1879	14.652	1.00	3.00	6.00	20.00
	1880	6.773	1.00	3.00	6.00	20.00
	1881	13.824	1.00	3.00	6.00	20.00
	1911	3.800	6.00	12.50	25.00	50.00
	1912	2.700	10.00	17.50	35.00	70.00

Mint: Petrograd - w/o mint mark

12.3	1916	8.000	40.00	80.00	150.00	250.00
	1917	—	—	—	Rare	

10 KOPEKS
(Grivennik)

2.0732 g, .868 SILVER, .0578 oz ASW
Mint mark: СПБ

C#	Date	Mintage	VG	Fine	VF	XF
119	1802 АИ	.190	25.00	50.00	100.00	200.00
	1803 АИ	.040	35.00	70.00	130.00	250.00
	1804 ФГ	.380	25.00	50.00	100.00	200.00
	1805 ФГ	.112	25.00	50.00	100.00	200.00

119a	1808 ФГ	—	35.00	70.00	130.00	250.00
	1809 МК	.035	25.00	50.00	100.00	200.00
	1810 ФГ	.077	25.00	50.00	100.00	200.00

127	1810 ФГ	—	5.00	10.00	20.00	40.00
	1811 ФГ	.930	2.50	5.00	10.00	20.00
	1812 МФ	—	—	—	Rare	
	1813 ПС	1.010	2.50	5.00	10.00	20.00
	1814 ПС	2.120	2.50	5.00	10.00	20.00
	1814 СП	I.A.	—	—	Rare	
	1814 МФ	I.A.	2.50	5.00	10.00	20.00
	1815 МФ	2.000	2.50	5.00	10.00	20.00
	1816 МФ	.250	2.50	5.00	10.00	20.00
	1816 ПС	I.A.	2.50	5.00	10.00	20.00
	1817 ПС	.160	2.50	5.00	10.00	20.00
	1818 ПС	.630	2.50	5.00	10.00	20.00
	1819 ПС	1.520	2.50	5.00	10.00	20.00
	1820 ПС	.520	2.50	5.00	10.00	20.00
	1820 ПД	I.A.	2.50	5.00	10.00	20.00
	1821 ПД	2.250	2.50	5.00	10.00	20.00
	1822 ПД	2.070	2.50	5.00	10.00	20.00

C#	Date	Mintage	VG	Fine	VF	XF
127	1823 ПД	3.850	2.50	5.00	10.00	20.00
	1824 ПД	1.330	2.50	5.00	10.00	20.00
	1825 ПД	1.350	2.50	5.00	10.00	20.00
	1825 НГ	I.A.	5.00	10.00	20.00	40.00
152.7	1826 НГ	2.050	2.50	5.00	10.00	20.00

157	1826 НГ					
	Inc. C152.7		2.50	5.00	10.00	20.00
	1827 НГ	1.290	2.50	5.00	10.00	20.00
	1828 НГ	.370	2.50	5.00	10.00	20.00
	1829 НГ	.040	3.00	10.00	20.00	40.00
	1830 НГ	.500	2.50	5.00	10.00	20.00
	1831 НГ	.450	2.50	5.00	10.00	20.00

COPPER
Mint mark: EM

141.1	1830 ФХ	—	20.00	40.00	80.00	150.00
	1831 ФХ	2.640	7.50	15.00	30.00	60.00
	1832 ФХ	7.620	7.50	15.00	30.00	60.00
	1833 ФХ	6.968	7.50	15.00	30.00	60.00
	1834 ФХ	9.134	7.50	15.00	30.00	60.00
	1835 ФХ	5.175	7.50	15.00	30.00	60.00
	1836 ФХ	7.240	7.50	15.00	30.00	60.00
	1837 ФХ	9.728	7.50	15.00	30.00	60.00
	1837 КТ-ФХ	—	15.00	30.00	60.00	120.00
	1837 КТ	I.A.	7.50	15.00	30.00	60.00
	1837 НА	I.A.	7.50	15.00	30.00	60.00
	1838 НА	5.468	7.50	15.00	30.00	60.00
	1839 НА	.350	8.50	17.50	35.00	70.00

Mint mark: СПБ

141.2	1830	25 pcs.	—	—	Rare	

Mint mark: СМ

141.3	1831	.510	8.50	17.50	35.00	70.00
	1832	.510	8.50	17.50	35.00	70.00
	1833	.700	8.50	17.50	35.00	70.00
	1834	.510	8.50	17.50	35.00	70.00
	1835	.500	8.50	17.50	35.00	70.00
	1836	.600	8.50	17.50	35.00	70.00
	1837	.500	8.50	17.50	35.00	70.00
	1838	.350	8.50	17.50	35.00	70.00
	1839	.350	10.00	20.00	40.00	80.00

2.0700 g, .868 SILVER, .0577 oz ASW
Mint mark: СПБ

164.1	1832 НГ	.104	4.00	8.00	15.00	30.00
	1833 НГ	.880	2.00	4.00	8.00	15.00
	1834 НГ	.400	2.00	4.00	8.00	15.00
	1835 НГ	.940	2.00	4.00	8.00	15.00
	1836 НГ	.490	2.00	4.00	8.00	15.00
	1837 НГ	2.360	2.00	4.00	8.00	15.00
	1838 НГ	.500	2.00	4.00	8.00	15.00
	1839 НГ	2.411	2.00	4.00	8.00	15.00
	1840 НГ	.190	2.00	4.00	8.00	15.00
	1841 НГ	.500	2.00	4.00	8.00	15.00
	1842 НГ	—	—	—	Rare	
	1842 АЧ	.300	2.00	4.00	8.00	15.00

C#	Date	Mintage	VG	Fine	VF	XF
164.1	1843 АЧ	.180	2.00	4.00	8.00	15.00
	1844 КБ	.461	2.00	4.00	8.00	15.00
	1845 КБ	2.435	2.00	4.00	8.00	15.00
	1846 ПА	.810	2.00	4.00	8.00	15.00
	1847 ПА	3.180	2.00	4.00	8.00	15.00
	1848 НІ	1.860	2.00	4.00	8.00	15.00
	1849 ПА	3.110	2.00	4.00	8.00	15.00
	1850 ПА	2.450	2.00	4.00	8.00	15.00
	1851 ПА	1.500	2.00	4.00	8.00	15.00
	1852 ПА	1.350	2.00	4.00	8.00	15.00
	1852 НІ	I.A.	2.00	4.00	8.00	15.00
	1853 НІ	1.350	2.00	4.00	8.00	15.00
	1854 НІ	1.000	2.00	4.00	8.00	15.00
(Y14.1)	1855 НІ	3.201	2.00	4.00	8.00	15.00
	1856 ФБ	1.940	2.00	4.00	8.00	15.00
	1857 ФБ	3.110	2.00	4.00	8.00	15.00
	1858 ФБ	2.600	2.00	4.00	8.00	15.00

Mint mark: МШ

C#	Date	Mintage	VG	Fine	VF	XF
164.2	1854	—	—	—	Rare	—
(Y14.2)	1855	.103	25.00	50.00	100.00	200.00

2.0732 g, .750 SILVER, .0499 oz ASW
Mint mark: СПБ
Type 1, engrailed edge.

Y#	Date	Mintage	Fine	VF	XF	Unc
20.1	1859 ФБ	3.920	1.00	2.00	4.00	15.00
	1860 ФБ	.580	1.00	2.00	4.00	15.00

Type 2, eagle redesigned.

Y#	Date	Mintage	Fine	VF	XF	Unc
20.2	1860 ФБ	2.810	1.00	2.00	4.00	15.00
	1861 ФБ	5.660	1.00	2.00	4.00	15.00
	1861 МИ	I.A.	1.00	2.00	4.00	15.00
	1861	19.300	1.00	2.00	4.00	15.00
	1862 МИ	5.800	1.00	2.00	4.00	15.00
	1863 АБ	5.750	1.00	2.00	4.00	15.00
	1864 НФ	3.740	1.00	2.00	4.00	15.00
	1865 НФ	3.886	1.00	2.00	4.00	15.00
	1866 НФ	2.533	1.00	2.00	4.00	15.00
	1866 НІ	I.A.	1.00	2.00	4.00	15.00

1.7996 g, .500 SILVER, .0289 oz ASW
Mint mark: СПБ
Reeded edge

Y#	Date	Mintage	Fine	VF	XF	Unc
20a.2	1867 НІ	6.445	.50	1.00	3.00	10.00
	1868 НІ	4.740	.50	1.00	3.00	10.00
	1869 НІ	3.710	.50	1.00	3.00	10.00
	1870 НІ	3.310	.50	1.00	3.00	10.00
	1871 НІ	4.195	.50	1.00	3.00	10.00
	1872 НІ	2.130	.50	1.00	3.00	10.00
	1873 НІ	2.620	.50	1.00	3.00	10.00
	1874 НІ	2.520	.50	1.00	3.00	10.00
	1875 НІ	3.590	.50	1.00	3.00	10.00
	1876 НІ	4.900	.50	1.00	3.00	10.00
	1877 НІ	2.090	.50	1.00	3.00	10.00
	1877 НФ	I.A.	.50	1.00	3.00	12.00
	1878 НФ	6.920	.50	1.00	3.00	10.00
	1878 НІ	I.A.	5.00	10.00	20.00	50.00
	1879 НФ	6.890	.50	1.00	3.00	10.00
	1880 НФ	6.740	.50	1.00	3.00	10.00
	1881 НФ	2.950	.50	1.00	3.00	10.00
	1882 НФ	.920	.50	1.00	3.00	10.00
	1883 ДС	1.520	.50	1.00	3.00	10.00
	1883 АГ	I.A.	.50	1.00	3.00	10.00
	1884 АГ	1.710	.50	1.00	3.00	10.00
	1885 АГ	1.300	.50	1.00	3.00	10.00
	1886 АГ	2.000	.50	1.00	3.00	10.00
	1887 АГ	4.000	.50	1.00	3.00	10.00
	1888 АГ	2.000	.50	1.00	3.00	10.00
	1889 АГ	5.000	.50	1.00	3.00	10.00
	1890 АГ	3.750	.50	1.00	3.00	10.00
	1891 АГ	3.240	.50	1.00	3.00	10.00
	1893 АГ	4.250	.50	1.00	3.00	10.00
	1894 АГ	4.000	.50	1.00	3.00	10.00
	1895 АГ	1.000	.50	1.00	3.00	10.00
	1896 АГ	2.010	.50	1.00	3.00	10.00
	1897 АГ	3.150	.50	1.00	3.00	10.00
	1898 АГ	6.610	.50	1.00	2.00	5.00
	1899 АГ	14.000	.50	1.00	2.00	5.00
	1899 ЭБ	I.A.	.50	1.00	2.00	5.00
	1900 ФЗ	2.603	.50	1.00	2.00	5.00
	1901 ФЗ	15.000	.50	1.00	2.00	5.00
	1901 АР	I.A.	.50	1.00	2.00	5.00
	1902 АР	17.000	.50	1.00	2.00	5.00
	1903 АР	28.500	.50	1.00	2.00	5.00
	1904 АР	20.000	.50	1.00	2.00	5.00
	1905 АР	25.000	.50	1.00	2.00	5.00
	1906 ЭБ	17.500	.50	1.00	2.00	5.00
	1907 ЭБ	20.000	.50	1.00	2.00	5.00
	1908 ЭБ	8.210	.50	1.00	2.00	5.00
	1909 ЭБ	25.290	.50	1.00	2.00	5.00
	1910 ЭБ	20.000	.50	1.00	2.00	5.00
	1911 ЭБ	19.180	.50	1.00	2.00	5.00
	1912 ЭБ	20.000	.50	1.00	2.00	5.00
	1913 ЭБ	7.250	.50	1.00	2.00	5.00
	1913 ВС	I.A.	.50	1.00	2.00	5.00
	1914 ВС	51.250	.50	1.00	2.00	5.00
	Common date	—	—	—	Proof	100.00

Mint: Petrograd - w/o mint mark

Y#	Date	Mintage	Fine	VF	XF	Unc
20a.3	1915 ВС	82.500	.50	.75	1.00	3.00
	1916 ВС	121.500	.50	.75	1.00	3.00
	1917 ВС	17.600	—	25.00	35.00	75.00

Mint: Osaka, Japan-w/o mint mark

Y#	Date	Mintage	Fine	VF	XF	Unc
20a.1	1916	70.001	1.00	2.00	5.00	10.00

15 KOPEKS

For similar coins not listed here refer to Poland.

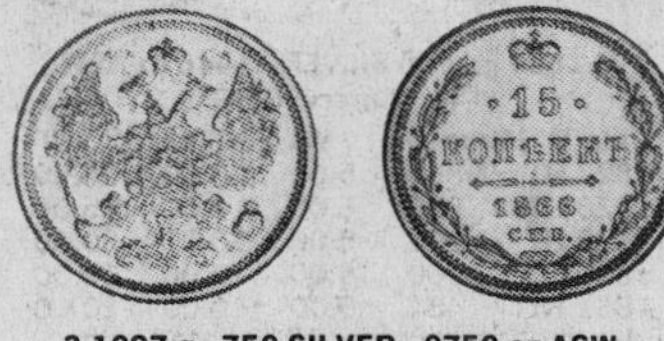

3.1097 g, .750 SILVER, .0750 oz ASW
Mint mark: СПБ
Engrailed edge

Y#	Date	Mintage	Fine	VF	XF	Unc
21	1860 ФБ	4.480	1.25	1.50	3.00	12.50
	1861 ФБ	10.120	1.25	1.50	3.00	12.50
	1861 МИ	I.A.	1.25	1.50	3.00	12.50
	1861	13.300	1.25	1.50	3.00	12.50
	1862 МИ	10.000	1.25	1.50	3.00	12.50
	1863 АБ	9.960	1.25	1.50	3.00	12.50
	1864 НФ	10.715	1.25	1.50	3.00	12.50
	1865 НФ	10.703	1.25	1.50	3.00	12.50
	1866 НФ	6.329	1.25	1.50	3.00	12.50
	1866 НІ	I.A.	1.25	1.50	3.00	12.50

2.6994 g, .500 SILVER, .0434 oz ASW

Y#	Date	Mintage	Fine	VF	XF	Unc
21a.2	1867 НІ	8.720	.75	1.00	3.00	10.00
	1868 НІ	7.460	.75	1.00	3.00	10.00
	1869 НІ	8.120	.75	1.00	3.00	10.00
	1870 НІ	9.380	.75	1.00	3.00	10.00
	1871 НІ	9.460	.75	1.00	3.00	10.00
	1872 НІ	5.880	.75	1.00	3.00	10.00
	1873 НІ	7.960	.75	1.00	3.00	10.00
	1874 НІ	6.960	.75	1.00	3.00	10.00
	1875 НІ	7.480	.75	1.00	3.00	10.00
	1876 НІ	9.760	.75	1.00	3.00	10.00
	1877 НІ	4.360	.75	1.00	3.00	10.00
	1877 НФ	I.A.	2.00	5.00	12.50	25.00
	1878 НФ	1.116	.75	1.00	3.00	10.00
	1879 НФ	12.504	.75	1.00	3.00	10.00
	1880 НФ	11.655	.75	1.00	3.00	10.00
	1881 НФ	4.900	.75	1.00	3.00	10.00
	1882 НФ	1.470	.75	1.00	3.00	10.00
	1882 ДС	Inc. Ab.	10.00	20.00	30.00	60.00
	1883 ДС	4.020	.75	1.00	3.00	10.00
	1883 АГ	I.A.	.75	1.00	3.00	10.00
	1884 АГ	2.520	.75	1.00	3.00	10.00
	1885 АГ	1.420	.75	1.00	3.00	10.00
	1886 АГ	1.840	.75	1.00	3.00	10.00
	1887 АГ	3.000	.75	1.00	3.00	10.00
	1888 АГ	—	5.00	10.00	20.00	40.00
	1889 АГ	2.835	.75	1.00	2.00	6.00
	1890 АГ	3.500	.75	1.00	2.00	6.00
	1891 АГ	4.710	.75	1.00	2.00	6.00
	1893 АГ	6.500	.75	1.00	2.00	6.00
	1896 АГ	3.160	.75	1.00	2.00	6.00
	1897 АГ	I.A.	.75	1.00	2.00	6.00
	1898 АГ	3.000	.75	1.00	2.00	6.00
	1899 АГ	12.665	.75	1.00	2.00	6.00
	1899 ЭБ	I.A.	.75	1.00	2.00	6.00
	1900 ФЗ	12.665	.75	1.00	2.00	5.00
	1901 ФЗ	6.670	.75	1.00	2.00	5.00
	1901 АР	I.A.	.75	1.00	2.00	5.00
	1902 АР	28.667	.75	1.00	2.00	5.00
	1903 АР	16.667	.75	1.00	2.00	5.00
	1904 АР	15.600	.75	1.00	2.00	5.00
	1905 АР	24.000	.75	1.00	2.00	5.00
	1906 ЭБ	23.333	.75	1.00	2.00	5.00
	1907 ЭБ	30.000	.75	1.00	2.00	5.00
	1908 ЭБ	29.000	.75	1.00	2.00	5.00
	1909 ЭБ	21.667	.75	1.00	2.00	5.00
	1911 ЭБ	6.313	.75	1.00	2.00	5.00
	1912 ЭБ	13.333	.75	1.00	2.00	5.00
	1912 ВС	Inc. Ab.	2.00	5.00	12.50	25.00
	1913 ЭБ	5.300	5.00	10.00	20.00	40.00
	1913 ВС	I.A.	.75	1.00	2.00	5.00
	1914 ВС	43.367	.75	1.00	2.00	5.00

Mint: Petrograd - w/o mint mark

Y#	Date	Mintage	Fine	VF	XF	Unc
21a.3	1915 ВС	59.333	.75	1.50	2.00	4.00
	1916 ВС	96.773	.75	1.50	2.00	4.00
	1917 ВС	14.320	—	25.00	35.00	75.00

Mint: Osaka, Japan-w/o mint mark
Reeded edge

Y#	Date	Mintage	Fine	VF	XF	Unc
21a.1	1916	96.666	BV	1.00	2.00	5.00

20 KOPEKS

4.1463 g, .868 SILVER, .1157 oz ASW
Mint mark: СПБ

C#	Date	Mintage	VG	Fine	VF	XF
128	1810 ФГ	.250	5.00	10.00	20.00	30.00
	1811 ФГ	1.969	2.50	5.00	10.00	20.00
	1813 ПС	1.900	2.50	5.00	10.00	20.00
	1814 ПС	1.850	2.50	5.00	10.00	20.00
	1814 МФ	I.A.	2.50	5.00	10.00	20.00
	1815 МФ	1.025	2.50	5.00	10.00	20.00
	1816 МФ	.115	6.00	12.50	25.00	50.00
	1816 ПС	I.A.	2.50	5.00	10.00	20.00
	1817 ПС	1.545	2.50	5.00	10.00	20.00
	1818 ПС	2.000	2.50	5.00	10.00	20.00
	1819 ПС	1.705	2.50	5.00	10.00	20.00
	1820 ПС	1.895	2.50	5.00	10.00	20.00
	1820 ПД	I.A.	2.50	5.00	10.00	20.00
	1821 ПД	3.025	2.50	5.00	10.00	20.00
	1822 ПД	2.100	2.50	5.00	10.00	20.00
	1823 ПД	7.075	2.50	5.00	10.00	20.00
	1823	—	—	—	Rare	—
	1824 ПД	1.750	2.50	5.00	10.00	20.00
	1825 ПД	1.375	2.50	5.00	10.00	20.00
	1825 НГ	I.A.	6.00	12.50	25.00	50.00

Similar to C#128.

C#	Date	Mintage	VG	Fine	VF	XF
153	1826 НГ	2.815	2.50	5.00	10.00	20.00

Obv: Eagle w/wings pointed down.

C#	Date	Mintage	VG	Fine	VF	XF
158	1826 НГ	Inc. C153	4.50	9.00	17.50	35.00
	1827 НГ	.465	4.50	9.00	17.50	35.00
	1828 НГ	.050	7.50	15.00	30.00	60.00
	1829 НГ	.250	4.50	9.00	17.50	35.00
	1830 НГ	1.175	4.50	9.00	17.50	35.00
	1831 НГ	.385	4.50	9.00	17.50	35.00

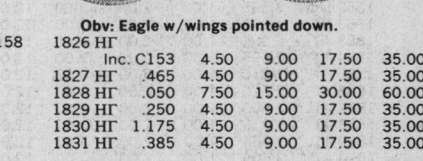

Obv: Variety I eagle.

C#	Date	Mintage	VG	Fine	VF	XF
165	1832 НГ	.097	3.00	6.00	10.00	25.00
	1833 НГ	.435	2.50	5.00	10.00	20.00
	1834 НГ	.320	2.50	5.00	10.00	20.00
	1835 НГ	.500	2.50	5.00	10.00	20.00
	1836 НГ	1.280	2.50	5.00	10.00	20.00
	1837 НГ	1.300	2.50	5.00	10.00	20.00
	1838 НГ	1.635	2.50	5.00	10.00	20.00
	1839 НГ	4.030	2.50	5.00	10.00	20.00
	1840 НГ	2.075	2.50	5.00	10.00	20.00
	1841 НГ	.025	6.00	12.00	20.00	40.00
	1842 АЧ	—	20.00	40.00	80.00	150.00
	1843 АЧ	—	20.00	40.00	80.00	150.00
	1844 КБ	—	20.00	40.00	80.00	150.00
	1845 КБ	.105	2.50	5.00	10.00	20.00
	1846 ПА	.630	2.50	5.00	10.00	20.00
	1847 ПА	3.923	2.50	5.00	10.00	20.00
	1848 НІ	2.636	2.50	5.00	10.00	20.00
	1849 ПА	3.250	2.50	5.00	10.00	20.00
	1850 ПА	3.075	2.50	5.00	10.00	20.00
	1851 ПА	2.000	2.50	5.00	10.00	20.00
	1852 НІ	1.800	—	—	Rare	—
	1852 ПА	I.A.	2.50	5.00	10.00	20.00
	1853 НІ	1.800	2.50	5.00	10.00	20.00
	1854 НІ	.990	2.50	5.00	10.00	20.00
(Y15)	1855 НІ	3.090	2.50	5.00	10.00	20.00
	1856 ФБ	3.240	2.50	5.00	10.00	20.00
	1857 ФБ	4.275	2.50	5.00	10.00	20.00
	1857 MW	—	6.00	12.50	25.00	50.00
	1858 ФБ	4.150	2.50	5.00	10.00	20.00

4.1463 g, .750 SILVER, .0999 oz ASW
Engrailed edge

Y#	Date	Mintage	Fine	VF	XF	Unc
22.1	1859 ФБ	3.960	1.50	3.00	5.00	15.00
	1860 ФБ	1.070	1.50	3.00	5.00	15.00

Obv: Eagle redesigned.

Y#	Date	Mintage	Fine	VF	XF	Unc
22.2	1860 ФБ	14.440	1.50	3.00	5.00	15.00
	1861 ФБ	19.500	1.50	3.00	5.00	15.00
	1861 МИ	I.A.	1.50	3.00	5.00	15.00
	1861	19.000	1.50	3.00	5.00	15.00
	1862 МИ	19.500	1.50	3.00	5.00	15.00
	1863 АБ	19.230	1.50	3.00	5.00	15.00
	1864 НФ	20.060	1.50	3.00	5.00	15.00
	1865 НФ	20.048	1.50	3.00	5.00	15.00
	1866 НФ	10.067	1.50	3.00	5.00	15.00
	1866 НІ	Inc. Ab.	1.50	3.00	5.00	15.00

NOTE: Varieties of eagle exist for 1860 dated coins.

3.5992 g, .500 SILVER, .0579 oz ASW
Reeded edge

Y#	Date	Mintage	Fine	VF	XF	Unc
22a.1	1867 НІ	15.355	1.00	2.00	3.00	12.00
	1868 НІ	11.975	1.00	2.00	3.00	12.00
	1869 НІ	17.017	1.00	2.00	3.00	12.00
	1870 НІ	16.255	1.00	2.00	3.00	12.00
	1871 НІ	18.860	1.00	2.00	3.00	12.00
	1872 НІ	11.980	1.00	2.00	3.00	12.00
	1873 НІ	15.185	1.00	2.00	3.00	12.00
	1874 НІ	14.850	1.00	2.00	3.00	12.00
	1875 НІ	15.545	1.00	2.00	3.00	12.00
	1876 НІ	16.255	1.00	2.00	3.00	12.00
	1877 НІ	6.950	1.00	2.00	3.00	12.00
	1877 НФ	I.A.	1.00	2.00	3.00	12.00
	1878 НФ	25.335	1.00	2.00	3.00	12.00
	1878 НІ	I.A.	5.00	10.00	20.00	50.00
	1879 НФ	23.070	1.00	2.00	3.00	12.00
	1880 НФ	22.605	1.00	2.00	3.00	12.00
	1881 НФ	9.350	1.00	2.00	3.00	12.00
	1882 НФ	3.535	1.00	2.00	3.00	12.00
	1883 ДС	4.270	1.00	2.00	3.00	12.00
	1883 АГ	I.A.	1.00	2.00	3.00	12.00
	1884 АГ	2.595	1.00	2.00	3.00	12.00
	1885 АГ	1.610	1.00	2.00	3.00	12.00
	1886 АГ	2.625	1.00	2.00	3.00	12.00
	1887 АГ	2.500	1.00	2.00	3.00	12.00
	1888 АГ	3.035	1.00	2.00	3.00	12.00
	1889 АГ	1.964	1.00	2.00	3.00	12.00
	1890 АГ	3.500	1.00	2.00	3.00	12.00
	1891 АГ	6.105	1.00	2.00	3.00	12.00
	1893 АГ	7.500	1.00	2.00	3.00	12.00
	1901 ФЗ	7.750	BV	1.00	2.00	5.00
	1901 АР	I.A.	10.00	20.00	40.00	80.00
	1902 АР	10.000	BV	1.00	2.00	5.00
	1903 АР	I.A.	BV	1.00	2.00	5.00
	1904 АР	13.000	BV	1.00	2.00	5.00
	1905 АР	11.000	BV	1.00	2.00	5.00
	1906 ЭБ	15.000	BV	1.00	2.00	5.00
	1907 ЭБ	20.000	BV	1.00	2.00	5.00
	1908 ЭБ	5.000	BV	1.00	2.00	5.00
	1909 ЭБ	18.875	BV	1.00	2.00	5.00
	1910 ЭБ	11.000	BV	1.00	2.00	5.00
	1911 ЭБ	7.100	BV	1.00	2.00	5.00
	1912 ЭБ	15.000	BV	1.00	2.00	5.00
	1912 ВС	I.A.	5.00	10.00	20.00	40.00
	1913 ЭБ	4.250	BV	1.00	2.00	5.00
	1913 ВС	I.A.	BV	1.00	2.00	5.00
	1914 ВС	52.750	BV	1.00	2.00	5.00

NOTE: Edge varieties exist for 1906 dated coins.

Mint: Petrograd - w/o mint mark

Y#	Date	Mintage	Fine	VF	XF	Unc
22a.2	1915 ВС	105.500	BV	1.00	2.00	4.00
	1916 ВС	131.670	BV	1.00	2.00	4.00
	1917 ВС	3.500	—	35.00	55.00	100.00
	Common date	—	—	—	Proof	125.00

POLUPOLTINNIK

4.1400 g, .868 SILVER, .1155 oz ASW
Mint mark: СПБ

C#	Date	Mintage	VG	Fine	VF	XF
121	1802 АИ	.324	50.00	100.00	175.00	250.00
	1803 АИ	.152	60.00	110.00	200.00	275.00
	1803 ФГ	I.A.	60.00	120.00	200.00	350.00
	1804 ФГ	.168	50.00	100.00	175.00	250.00
	1805 ФГ	.137	60.00	110.00	200.00	275.00

C#	Date	Mintage	VG	Fine	VF	XF
121a	1808 ФГ	—	—	—	Rare	—
	1809 МК	.040	60.00	120.00	200.00	275.00
	1809 ФГ	I.A.	—	—	Rare	—
	1810 ФГ	.066	60.00	120.00	200.00	275.00

25 KOPEKS

5.1830 g, .868 SILVER, .1446 oz ASW
Mint mark: СПБ

C#	Date	Mintage	VG	Fine	VF	XF
159	1827 НГ	1.860	5.00	10.00	25.00	50.00
	1828 НГ	.320	6.00	12.50	35.00	65.00
	1829 НГ	1.200	5.00	10.00	20.00	50.00
	1830 НГ	1.160	5.00	10.00	20.00	50.00
	1831 НГ	.484	5.00	10.00	20.00	50.00

NOTE: Edge varieties exist for 1828 dated coins.

For similar coins not listed here refer to Poland.

Obv: Variety I eagle.

C#	Date	Mintage	VG	Fine	VF	XF
166	1832 НГ	.308	3.50	8.00	15.00	30.00
	1833 НГ	.260	3.50	8.00	15.00	30.00
	1834 НГ	.260	3.50	8.00	15.00	30.00
	1835 НГ	.356	3.50	8.00	15.00	30.00
	1836 НГ	1.072	3.50	8.00	15.00	30.00
	1837 НГ	1.144	3.50	8.00	15.00	30.00
	1838 НГ	2.672	3.50	8.00	15.00	30.00
	1839 НГ	2.738	3.50	8.00	15.00	30.00
	1840 НГ	.604	3.50	8.00	15.00	30.00
	1841 НГ	.020	20.00	40.00	80.00	150.00
	1842 АЧ	—	20.00	40.00	80.00	150.00
	1843 АЧ	—	20.00	40.00	80.00	150.00
	1844 КБ	.021	3.50	8.00	15.00	30.00
	1845 КБ	.569	3.50	8.00	15.00	30.00
	1846 ПА	.576	3.50	8.00	15.00	30.00
	1847 ПА	4.824	2.50	6.00	12.50	25.00
	1848 НІ	2.636	2.50	6.00	12.50	25.00
	1849 ПА	3.440	2.50	6.00	12.50	25.00
	1850 ПА	3.740	2.50	6.00	12.50	25.00
	1851 ПА	2.400	2.50	6.00	12.50	25.00
	1852 ПА	2.160	2.50	6.00	12.50	25.00
	1852 НІ	I.A.	10.00	20.00	40.00	80.00
	1853 НІ	2.160	2.50	6.00	12.50	25.00
	1853	—	10.00	20.00	40.00	80.00
	1854 НІ	1.148	2.50	6.00	12.50	25.00
(Y16.1)	1855 НІ	10.396	2.50	5.00	7.50	12.50
	1856 ФБ	4.444	2.50	5.00	10.00	20.00
	1857 ФБ	5.420	2.50	5.00	10.00	20.00
	1858 ФБ	5.528	2.50	5.00	10.00	20.00
	1858	Inc. Ab.	5.00	10.00	20.00	40.00
	Common date	—	—	—	Proof	200.00

NOTE: Varieties of eagle and crown exist.

Mint mark: MW

Y#	Date	Mintage	Fine	VF	XF	Unc
16.2	1854	.033	10.00	20.00	40.00	80.00
	1857 MW	—	10.00	20.00	40.00	80.00

Mint mark: СПБ
Obv: Eagle redesigned.

Y#	Date	Mintage	Fine	VF	XF	Unc
23	1859 ФБ	4.400	5.00	10.00	20.00	60.00
	1860 ФБ	1.052	7.50	15.00	30.00	80.00
	1861 ФБ	.116	12.50	25.00	50.00	125.00
	1861 МИ	Inc. Ab.	12.50	25.00	50.00	125.00
	1862 МИ	.036	15.00	37.50	75.00	150.00
	1863 АБ	.036	15.00	37.50	75.00	150.00
	1864 НФ	.068	15.00	37.50	75.00	150.00
	1865 НФ	.016	15.00	37.50	75.00	150.00
	1866 НФ	.036	15.00	37.50	75.00	150.00
	1866 НІ	I.A.	15.00	37.50	75.00	150.00
	1867 НІ	.048	15.00	37.50	75.00	150.00
	1868 НІ	.040	15.00	37.50	75.00	150.00
	1869 НІ	.020	15.00	37.50	75.00	150.00
	1870 НІ	.044	15.00	37.50	75.00	150.00
	1871 НІ	.024	15.00	37.50	75.00	150.00
	1872 НІ	.044	15.00	37.50	75.00	150.00
	1873 НІ	.036	15.00	37.50	75.00	150.00
	1874 НІ	.032	15.00	37.50	75.00	150.00
	1875 НІ	.024	15.00	37.50	75.00	150.00
	1876 НІ	.040	15.00	37.50	75.00	150.00
	1877 НІ	1.776	7.50	15.00	30.00	80.00
	1877	Inc. Ab.	15.00	37.50	75.00	150.00
	1877 НФ	I.A.	7.50	15.00	30.00	80.00
	1878 НФ	1.768	5.00	10.00	20.00	40.00
	1879 НФ	.032	15.00	37.50	75.00	150.00

Y#	Date	Mintage	Fine	VF	XF	Unc
23	1880 НФ	.078	12.50	25.00	50.00	125.00
	1881 НФ	2,001	25.00	50.00	75.00	150.00
	1882 НФ	2,007	25.00	50.00	75.00	150.00
	1883 ДС	2,008	25.00	50.00	75.00	150.00
	1883 АГ	Inc. Ab.	25.00	50.00	75.00	200.00
	1884 АГ	2,004	25.00	50.00	75.00	175.00
	1885 АГ	1,001	25.00	50.00	75.00	200.00

4.9990 g, .900 SILVER, .1446 oz ASW
Mint: St. Petersburg-w/o mint mark

Y#	Date	Mintage	Fine	VF	XF	Unc
44	1886 АГ	4,058	25.00	50.00	90.00	175.00
	1887 АГ	.028	20.00	40.00	80.00	150.00
	1888 АГ	4,007	25.00	50.00	90.00	175.00
	1889 АГ	1,002	50.00	75.00	125.00	250.00
	1890 АГ	2,006	25.00	50.00	90.00	175.00
	1891 АГ	.024	25.00	50.00	90.00	175.00
	1892 АГ	4,006	25.00	50.00	90.00	175.00
	1893 АГ	8,008	25.00	50.00	90.00	175.00
	1894 АГ	—	15.00	30.00	60.00	100.00
	Common date	—	—	—	Proof	450.00

Y#	Date	Mintage	Fine	VF	XF	Unc
57	1895	1.000	8.00	15.00	40.00	80.00
	1896	27.212	5.00	10.00	20.00	35.00
	1900	.560	15.00	30.00	60.00	125.00
	1901	*150 pcs.	75.00	125.00	250.00	400.00

30 KOPEKS

Refer to Poland

POLTINA

(1/2 Rouble)

10.3600 g, .868 SILVER, .2892 oz ASW
Mint mark: СПБ

C#	Date	Mintage	VG	Fine	VF	XF
123	1802 АИ	.104	25.00	50.00	100.00	250.00
	1803 АИ	.242	25.00	50.00	100.00	250.00
	1804 ФГ	.230	25.00	50.00	100.00	250.00
	1805 ФГ	.315	25.00	50.00	100.00	250.00

C#	Date	Mintage	VG	Fine	VF	XF
123a	1809 МК	.011	—	—	Rare	—
	1810 ФГ	.079	50.00	75.00	150.00	300.00

C#	Date	Mintage	VG	Fine	VF	XF
129	1810 ФГ	Inc. C123a	6.00	12.00	30.00	70.00
	1811 ФГ	.090	6.00	12.00	30.00	70.00
	1812 МФ	.045	6.00	12.00	30.00	70.00
	1813 ПС	.580	6.00	12.00	30.00	70.00
	1814 ПС	.662	6.00	12.00	30.00	70.00
	1814 МФ	I.A.	6.00	12.00	30.00	70.00
	1815 МФ	1.700	6.00	12.00	30.00	70.00
	1816 МФ	.270	6.00	12.00	30.00	70.00

Russia-Empire / USSR

C#	Date	Mintage	VG	Fine	VF	XF
129	1816 ПС	I.A.	6.00	12.00	30.00	70.00
	1817 ПС	2.820	6.00	12.00	30.00	70.00
	1818 ПС	4.250	6.00	12.00	30.00	70.00
	1819 ПС	2.430	6.00	12.00	30.00	70.00
	1819	Inc. Ab.	—	—	—	Rare
	1820 ПС	1.356	—	—	—	Rare
	1820 ПД	I.A.	6.00	12.00	30.00	70.00
	1821 ПД	.480	6.00	12.00	30.00	70.00
	1822 ПД	.090	6.00	12.00	30.00	70.00
	1823 ПД	.200	6.00	12.00	30.00	70.00
	1824 ПД	.320	6.00	12.00	30.00	70.00
	1825 ПД	.152	6.00	12.00	30.00	70.00
	1826 НГ	.201	6.00	12.00	30.00	70.00

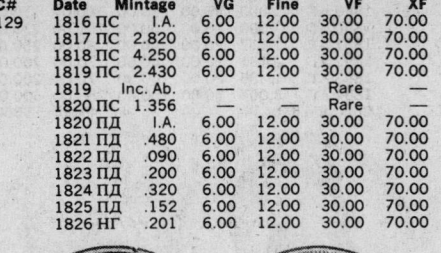

C#	Date	Mintage	VG	Fine	VF	XF
160	1826 НГ	I.C129	12.50	25.00	60.00	150.00
	1826 ПД		—	—	Rare	—
	1827 НГ	.164	12.50	25.00	60.00	150.00
	1828 НГ	.274	12.50	25.00	60.00	150.00
	1829 НГ	.880	12.50	25.00	60.00	150.00
	1830 НГ	.290	12.50	25.00	60.00	150.00
	1831 НГ	.140	12.50	25.00	60.00	150.00

Variety I eagle

C#	Date	Mintage	VG	Fine	VF	XF
167.1	1832 НГ	.050	10.00	20.00	40.00	100.00
	1833 НГ	.082	10.00	20.00	40.00	100.00
	1834 НГ	.046	10.00	20.00	40.00	100.00
	1835 НГ	.020	10.00	20.00	40.00	100.00
	1836 НГ	.140	7.50	15.00	30.00	60.00
	1837 НГ	.104	7.50	15.00	30.00	60.00
	1838 НГ	.004	—	—	Rare	—
	1839 НГ	1.830	5.00	10.00	25.00	45.00
	1840 НГ	.960	5.00	10.00	25.00	45.00
	1841 НГ	.010	15.00	30.00	60.00	125.00
	1842 НГ		—	—	Rare	—
	1842 АЧ	.214	5.00	10.00	25.00	40.00
	1843 АЧ		—	10.00	20.00	40.00	100.00
	1844 КБ	.348	5.00	10.00	25.00	45.00
	1845 КБ	2.009	5.00	10.00	25.00	45.00
	1846 ПА	.460	5.00	10.00	25.00	45.00
	1847 ПА	.615	5.00	10.00	25.00	45.00
	1848 НI	1.560	5.00	10.00	25.00	45.00
	1849 ПА	.450	5.00	10.00	25.00	45.00
	1850 ПА	.530	5.00	10.00	25.00	45.00
	1851 ПА	.800	5.00	10.00	25.00	45.00
	1852 ПА	.720	5.00	10.00	25.00	45.00
	1852 НI	I.A.	7.50	15.00	35.00	60.00
	1853 НI	.720	5.00	10.00	25.00	45.00
	1854 НI	.440	5.00	10.00	25.00	45.00
(Y17)	1855 НI	.714	5.00	10.00	25.00	45.00
	1856 ФБ	.450	5.00	10.00	25.00	45.00
	1857 ФБ	1.650	5.00	10.00	25.00	45.00
	1858 ФБ	1.112	5.00	15.00	25.00	50.00
	Common date				Proof	300.00

NOTE: Varieties of eagle and wreath exist.

Mint mark: МШ

C#	Date	Mintage	VG	Fine	VF	XF
167.2	1842	.076	7.50	15.00	30.00	60.00
	1843	.023	10.00	20.00	40.00	80.00
	1844	.116	7.50	15.00	30.00	60.00
	1845	.138	7.50	15.00	30.00	60.00
	1846	.308	7.50	15.00	30.00	60.00
	1847	.783	7.50	15.00	30.00	60.00

Mint mark: СПБ
Variety II eagle

Y#	Date	Mintage	Fine	VF	XF	Unc
24	1859 ФГ	1.392	10.00	20.00	40.00	100.00
	1860 ФГ	.192	20.00	40.00	85.00	175.00
	1861 ФГ	.064	25.00	50.00	100.00	200.00
	1861 МИ	I.A.	40.00	80.00	150.00	300.00
	1862 МИ	.024	30.00	60.00	125.00	250.00
	1863 АБ	.022	30.00	60.00	125.00	250.00
	1864 НФ	.034	30.00	60.00	125.00	250.00

Y#	Date	Mintage	Fine	VF	XF	Unc
24	1865 НФ	.024	30.00	60.00	125.00	250.00
	1866 НФ	.022	30.00	60.00	125.00	250.00
	1866 НI	I.A.	30.00	60.00	125.00	250.00
	1867 НI	.026	30.00	60.00	125.00	250.00
	1868 НI	.030	30.00	60.00	125.00	250.00
	1869 НI	.020	30.00	60.00	125.00	250.00
	1870 НI	6,000	40.00	80.00	150.00	300.00
	1871 НI	.020	30.00	60.00	125.00	250.00
	1872 НI	.022	30.00	60.00	125.00	250.00
	1873 НI	.036	30.00	60.00	125.00	250.00
	1874 НI	.016	30.00	60.00	125.00	250.00
	1875 НI	.014	30.00	60.00	125.00	250.00
	1876 НI	.024	30.00	60.00	125.00	250.00
	1876	Inc. Ab.	40.00	80.00	150.00	300.00
	1877 НI	1.034	10.00	20.00	40.00	100.00
	1877 НФ	I.A.	15.00	30.00	60.00	125.00
	1878 НФ	.778	10.00	20.00	40.00	100.00
	1879 НФ	.014	30.00	60.00	125.00	250.00
	1880 НФ	.042	25.00	50.00	100.00	200.00
	1881 НФ	1,011	40.00	80.00	150.00	300.00
	1882 НФ	1,007	40.00	80.00	150.00	300.00
	1883 ДС	1,008	40.00	80.00	150.00	300.00
	1883 АГ	I.A.	50.00	100.00	200.00	400.00
	1884 АГ	1,004	40.00	80.00	150.00	300.00
	1885 АГ	511 pcs.	50.00	100.00	200.00	400.00

NOTE: Edge varieties exist.

50 KOPEKS

9.9980 g, .900 SILVER, .2893 oz ASW
Mint: St. Petersburg-w/o mint mark

	Date	Mintage	Fine	VF	XF	Unc
45	1886 АГ	2,058	15.00	30.00	80.00	250.00
	1887 АГ	.026	20.00	40.00	80.00	250.00
	1888 АГ	2,007	15.00	30.00	80.00	250.00
	1889 НФ	1,002	20.00	40.00	80.00	250.00
	1890 АГ	2,006	15.00	30.00	80.00	250.00
	1891 АГ	.024	20.00	40.00	80.00	250.00
	1892 АГ	2,006	15.00	30.00	80.00	250.00
	1893 НФ	4,008	15.00	30.00	80.00	250.00
	1894 АГ		15.00	25.00	75.00	200.00
	Common date		—	—	Proof	750.00

Mint mark: Star on rim

	Date	Mintage	Fine	VF	XF	Unc
58.1	1896	.245	10.00	20.00	40.00	80.00
	1897	46.755	7.50	12.50	25.00	60.00
	1899	10.000	7.50	12.50	25.00	60.00

Mint: St. Petersburg-w/o mint mark

	Date	Mintage	Fine	VF	XF	Unc
58.2	1895 АГ	5.400	5.00	10.00	25.00	65.00
	1896 АГ	17.402	5.00	8.00	15.00	55.00
	1898 АГ		—	—	Rare	—
	1899 ЗБ	15.442	5.00	10.00	25.00	65.00
	1899 ФЗ	I.A.	5.00	10.00	25.00	65.00
	1899 АГ	I.A.	5.00	10.00	25.00	65.00
	1900 ФЗ	3.360	5.00	10.00	25.00	65.00
	1901 АР	.412	5.00	12.50	35.00	80.00
	1901 ФЗ	I.A.	5.00	12.50	35.00	80.00
	1902 АР	.036	10.00	20.00	40.00	100.00
	1903 АР	—	200.00	300.00	400.00	600.00
	1904 АР	4,010	25.00	50.00	100.00	200.00
	1906 ЗБ	.010	25.00	50.00	100.00	200.00
	1907 ЗБ	.200	10.00	20.00	40.00	100.00
	1908 ЗБ	.040	10.00	20.00	40.00	100.00
	1909 ЗБ	.050	10.00	20.00	40.00	100.00
	1910 ЗБ	.150	10.00	20.00	40.00	100.00
	1911 ЗБ	.800	10.00	20.00	40.00	80.00
	1912 ЗБ	7.085	5.00	8.00	15.00	45.00
	1913 ЗБ	6.420	7.50	15.00	35.00	70.00
	1913 ВС	I.A.	5.00	10.00	20.00	45.00
	1914 ВС	1.200	5.00	10.00	20.00	45.00
	Common date		—	—	Proof	400.00

75 KOPEKS

Refer to Poland

ROUBLE

20.7300 g, .868 SILVER, .5785 oz ASW
Mint mark: СПБ

C#	Date	Mintage	VG	Fine	VF	XF
125	1802 АИ	5.360	20.00	40.00	80.00	150.00
	1803 АИ	2.429	20.00	40.00	80.00	150.00
	1803 ФГ	I.A.	25.00	50.00	100.00	200.00
	1804 ФГ	4.355	20.00	40.00	80.00	150.00
	1805 ФГ	2.020	20.00	40.00	80.00	150.00

	Date	Mintage	VG	Fine	VF	XF
125a	1807 ФГ	.533	25.00	50.00	90.00	150.00
	1808 ФГ	1.701	25.00	50.00	90.00	150.00
	1808 МК	I.A.	25.00	50.00	90.00	150.00
	1809 МК	2.177	25.00	50.00	90.00	150.00
	1809 ФГ	I.A.	25.00	50.00	90.00	150.00
	1810 ФГ	1.682	25.00	50.00	100.00	200.00

	Date	Mintage	VG	Fine	VF	XF
130	1810 ФГ	Inc. C125a	—	—	Rare	—
	1811 ФГ	2.675	10.00	20.00	35.00	75.00
	1812 МФ	4.076	10.00	20.00	35.00	75.00
	1813 ПС	5.210	10.00	20.00	35.00	75.00
	1814 МФ	3.600	10.00	20.00	35.00	75.00
	1814 ПС	I.A.	10.00	20.00	35.00	75.00
	1814	Inc. Ab.	15.00	30.00	50.00	90.00
	1815 МФ	4.750	10.00	20.00	35.00	75.00
	1816 МФ	1.782	10.00	20.00	35.00	75.00
	1816 ПС		10.00	20.00	35.00	75.00
	1817 ПС	11.775	10.00	20.00	35.00	75.00
	1818 ПС	16.275	10.00	20.00	35.00	75.00
	1818 СП		10.00	20.00	35.00	75.00
	1818	Inc. Ab.	15.00	30.00	50.00	90.00
	1819 ПС	6.355	10.00	20.00	35.00	75.00
	1820 ПС	1.962	10.00	20.00	35.00	75.00
	1820 ПД	I.A.	10.00	20.00	35.00	75.00
	1821 ПД	.840	10.00	20.00	35.00	75.00
	1822 ПД	3.120	10.00	20.00	35.00	75.00
	1823 ПД	2.955	10.00	20.00	35.00	75.00
	1824 ПД	2.035	10.00	20.00	35.00	75.00
	1825 ПД	1.461	10.00	20.00	35.00	75.00
	1825 НГ		—	40.00	60.00	100.00
(155)	1826 НГ	.730	15.00	35.00	75.00	125.00

C#	Date	Mintage	Fine	VF	XF	Unc
161	1826 НГ	I.C155	75.00	125.00	200.00	275.00
	1827 НГ	.584	25.00	40.00	90.00	250.00
	1828 НГ	2.530	22.50	35.00	80.00	250.00
	1829 НГ	5.510	22.50	35.00	80.00	250.00

Russia-Empire / USSR 1696

C#	Date	Mintage	Fine	VF	XF	Unc
161	1830 HГ	6.010	22.50	35.00	80.00	250.00
	1831 HГ	3.670	22.50	35.00	80.00	250.00

NOTE: Edge varieties exist.

C#	Date	Mintage	Fine	VF	XF	Unc
168.1	1832 HГ	1.941	18.00	25.00	55.00	150.00
	1833 HГ	1.711	18.00	25.00	55.00	150.00
	1834 HГ	2.270	18.00	25.00	55.00	150.00
	1835 HГ	.244	25.00	40.00	75.00	175.00
	1836 HГ	1.102	18.00	25.00	55.00	150.00
	1837 HГ	1.478	18.00	25.00	55.00	150.00
	1838 HГ	.232	25.00	40.00	75.00	175.00
	1839 HГ	.036	125.00	250.00	400.00	—
	1840 HГ	2.627	18.00	25.00	55.00	150.00
	1841 HГ	6.155	18.00	25.00	55.00	150.00
	1842 AЧ	4.965	18.00	25.00	55.00	150.00
	1843 AЧ	5.320	18.00	25.00	55.00	150.00
	1844 KБ	2.933	18.00	25.00	55.00	150.00
	1845 KБ	.683	18.00	25.00	55.00	150.00
	1846 ПA	3.523	18.00	25.00	55.00	150.00
	1847 ПA	.563	20.00	30.00	70.00	165.00
	1848 HI	1.542	18.00	25.00	55.00	150.00
	1849 ПA	1.708	18.00	25.00	55.00	150.00
	1850 ПA	1.600	18.00	25.00	55.00	150.00
	1851 ПA	2.400	18.00	25.00	55.00	150.00
	1852 ПA	2.560	18.00	25.00	55.00	150.00
	1852 HI	I.A.	25.00	40.00	75.00	175.00
	1853 HI	2.160	18.00	25.00	55.00	150.00
	1854 HI	3.070	18.00	25.00	55.00	150.00
(Y18)	1855 HI	1.068	18.00	25.00	55.00	150.00
	1856 ФБ	1.388	18.00	25.00	55.00	150.00
	1857 ФБ	.250	25.00	40.00	75.00	200.00
	1858 ФБ	.570	25.00	40.00	75.00	200.00
	Common date	—	—	—	Proof	450.00

Mint mark: MW

168.2	1842	.257	22.50	35.00	75.00	135.00
	1843	.267	22.50	35.00	75.00	135.00
	1844	2.364	22.50	35.00	75.00	135.00
	1845	.345	25.00	45.00	95.00	150.00
	1846	.511	22.50	35.00	75.00	135.00
	1847	.987	22.50	35.00	75.00	135.00

Mint mark: СПБ
Alexander I Monument

| 169 | 1834 | .015 | 75.00 | 150.00 | 325.00 | 500.00 |

Battle of Borodino Memorial

C#	Date	Mintage	Fine	VF	XF	Unc
170	1839 HГ	.160	65.00	125.00	225.00	425.00

NOTE: The 1841 marriage Rouble is a medal.

Mint: St. Petersburg-w/o mint mark
Nicholas I Memorial

Y#	Date	Mintage	Fine	VF	XF	Unc
28	1859	.050	60.00	110.00	190.00	325.00

Mint mark: СПБ

25	1859 ФБ	.014	75.00	150.00	300.00	500.00
	1860 ФБ	—	50.00	100.00	150.00	350.00
	1861 ФБ	.076	50.00	100.00	150.00	350.00
	1861 МИ	I.A.	50.00	100.00	150.00	350.00
	1862 МИ	.022	50.00	100.00	150.00	350.00
	1863 AБ	.005	75.00	150.00	300.00	500.00
	1864 HФ	.114	25.00	50.00	100.00	225.00
	1865 HФ	.115	25.00	50.00	100.00	225.00
	1866 HI	.110	25.00	50.00	100.00	225.00
	1866 I.A.		25.00	50.00	100.00	225.00
	1867 HI	.425	17.50	25.00	50.00	135.00
	1868 HI	.775	17.50	25.00	50.00	135.00
	1869 HI	.285	17.50	25.00	50.00	135.00
	1870 HI	.386	17.50	25.00	50.00	135.00
	1871 HI	.884	17.50	25.00	50.00	135.00
	1872 HI	.978	17.50	25.00	50.00	135.00
	1873 HI	.673	17.50	25.00	50.00	135.00
	1874 HI	.648	17.50	25.00	50.00	135.00
	1875 HI	.687	17.50	25.00	50.00	135.00
	1876 HI	.778	17.50	25.00	50.00	135.00
	1877 HI	6.923	15.00	20.00	35.00	100.00
	1877 I.A.		17.50	25.00	50.00	135.00
	1878 HФ	8.087	15.00	20.00	35.00	100.00
	1879 HФ	.611	17.50	25.00	50.00	135.00
	1880 HФ	.521	17.50	25.00	50.00	135.00
	1881 HФ	.699	17.50	25.00	50.00	135.00
	1882 HФ	.434	17.50	25.00	50.00	135.00
	1883 ДС	.425	17.50	25.00	50.00	135.00
	1883 AГ	I.A.	50.00	100.00	150.00	400.00
	1884 AГ	.355	17.50	25.00	50.00	135.00
	1885 AГ	.500	17.50	25.00	50.00	135.00

Mint: St. Petersburg-w/o mint mark
Alexander III Coronation

| 43 | 1883 | .279 | 30.00 | 45.00 | 80.00 | 190.00 |

19.9960 g, .900 SILVER, .5786 oz ASW
Mintmaster's initials and stars found on edge.

46	1886 AГ	.488	20.00	40.00	75.00	225.00
	1887 AГ	.491	20.00	40.00	75.00	225.00
	1888 AГ	.498	20.00	40.00	75.00	225.00

Y#	Date	Mintage	Fine	VF	XF	Unc
46	1889 AГ	1.002	125.00	250.00	500.00	1000.
	1890 AГ	.090	25.00	50.00	100.00	275.00
	1891 AГ	1.117	20.00	40.00	80.00	250.00
	1892 AГ	2.131	20.00	40.00	70.00	200.00
	1893 AГ	1.485	20.00	40.00	70.00	200.00
	1894 AГ	3.007	50.00	100.00	250.00	500.00
	Common date		—	—	Proof	1500.

Mint mark: 2 stars on rim

59.1	1897	26.000	10.00	17.50	30.00	85.00
	1898	14.000	10.00	17.50	30.00	85.00
	1899	10.000	10.00	17.50	30.00	85.00

Mint mark: Star on rim

| 59.2 | 1896 | 12.000 | 10.00 | 17.50 | 30.00 | 85.00 |
| | 1898 | 5.000 | 10.00 | 17.50 | 30.00 | 85.00 |

Mint: St. Petersburg-w/o mint mark

59.3	1895 AГ	1.240	12.00	20.00	35.00	100.00
	1896 AГ	12.540	10.00	17.50	30.00	85.00
	1897 AГ	18.515	10.00	17.50	30.00	85.00
	1898 AГ	18.725	10.00	17.50	30.00	85.00
	1899 ЗБ	6.503	12.00	17.50	30.00	85.00
	1899 ФЗ	I.A.	10.00	17.50	30.00	85.00
	1900 ФЗ	3.484	10.00	17.50	35.00	100.00
	1901 ФЗ	2.608	10.00	17.50	35.00	90.00
	1901 AP	I.A.	12.00	20.00	40.00	100.00
	1902 AH	.140	20.00	30.00	50.00	150.00
	1903 AP	.056	40.00	80.00	180.00	400.00
	1904 AP	.012	40.00	80.00	180.00	400.00
	1905 AP	.021	40.00	80.00	180.00	400.00
	1906 ЗБ	.046	40.00	80.00	180.00	400.00
	1907 ЗБ	.400	20.00	30.00	50.00	150.00
	1908 ЗБ	.130	20.00	30.00	50.00	150.00
	1909 ЗБ	.051	40.00	80.00	180.00	400.00
	1910 ЗБ	.075	20.00	40.00	80.00	200.00
	1911 ЗБ	.129	25.00	40.00	80.00	200.00
	1912 ЗБ	2.111	15.00	25.00	50.00	125.00
	1913 ЗБ	.022	50.00	100.00	200.00	450.00
	1913 BC	I.A.	50.00	100.00	200.00	450.00
	1914 BC	.536	25.00	35.00	90.00	250.00
	1915 BC	*5,000	30.00	60.00	125.00	250.00
	Common date		—	—	Proof	900.00

NOTE: Varieties exist with plain edge. These are mint errors and rare.

Nicholas II Coronation

| 60 | 1896 AГ | .191 | 25.00 | 40.00 | 70.00 | 150.00 |
| | 1896 AГ | — | — | — | Proof | 375.00 |

Alexander II Memorial

| 61 | 1898 AГ | *5,000 | 125.00 | 225.00 | 350.00 | 850.00 |
| | 1898 AГ | — | — | — | Proof | 1000. |

Napoleon Defeat Centennial

Y#	Date	Mintage	Fine	VF	XF	Unc
68	1912 ЗБ	.027	60.00	110.00	160.00	300.00

Alexander III Memorial

69	1912 ЗБ	900 pcs.	200.00	400.00	750.00	1250.
	1912 ЗБ	—	—	—	Proof	1500.

Mint: St. Petersburg-w/o mint mark
300th Anniversary Romanov Dynasty

70	1913 ВС	1.472	12.50	17.50	30.00	65.00

200th Anniversary Battle of Gangut

71	1914 ВС	*.030	400.00	600.00	1200.	1800.

*NOTE: Only 317 pieces were issued.

1-1/2 ROUBLES/10 ZLOTYCH
For similar coins not listed here refer to Poland.

31.1000 g, .868 SILVER, .8679 oz ASW
Mint: St. Petersburg-w/o mint mark

C#	Date	Mintage	Fine	VF	XF	Unc
A172	1835	36 pcs.	—	—	5000.	10,000.

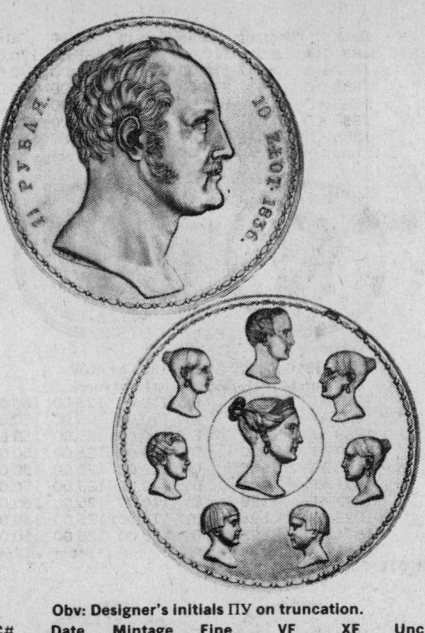

Obv: Designer's initials ПУ on truncation.

C#	Date	Mintage	Fine	VF	XF	Unc
172.1	1836	50 pcs.	—	—	5000.	7700.

Rev: Die break at rim lower right.
| 172.2 | 1836 | (restrike) | — | — | 2500. | 4000. |

Obv: Designer's name below bust.
| 172.3 | 1836 | Inc. Ab. | — | — | 5000. | 7500. |

Obv: W/o designer's name or initials.
| 172.4 | 1836 | Inc. Ab. | — | — | 5500. | 8500. |

NOTE: The above coins were struck as presentation pieces.

Mint mark: СПБ
Battle of Borodino Memorial

173	1839	6,000	400.00	800.00	1100.	1750.

3 ROUBLES

10.3500 g, PLATINUM, .3327 oz APW

NOTE: The low mintage figures incorporated in the following listings of Russian platinum issues are not necessarily reflective of relative scarcity as many of the issues were restruck at later dates, using original dies in unrecorded quantities.

Mint mark: СПБ

	Date	Mintage	Fine	VF	XF	Unc
177	1828	.020	250.00	425.00	650.00	900.00
	1829	.043	225.00	350.00	525.00	750.00
	1830	.106	225.00	350.00	525.00	750.00
	1831	.087	225.00	350.00	525.00	750.00
	1832	.066	225.00	350.00	525.00	750.00
	1833	.085	250.00	400.00	600.00	850.00
	1834	.091	225.00	300.00	500.00	750.00
	1835	.139	250.00	400.00	600.00	800.00
	1836	.044	275.00	350.00	550.00	750.00
	1837	.046	275.00	350.00	550.00	750.00
	1838	.049	275.00	350.00	550.00	750.00
	1839	6 pcs.	—	—	Proof	3200.
	1840	3 pcs.	—	—	Proof	2100.
	1841	.017	250.00	400.00	600.00	850.00
	1842	.146	225.00	350.00	500.00	650.00
	1843	.172	225.00	350.00	550.00	750.00
	1844	.215	225.00	375.00	600.00	850.00
	1845	.050	250.00	425.00	700.00	900.00
	Common date	—	—	—	Proof	1450.

For similar coins not listed here refer to Poland.

3.9260 g, .917 GOLD, .1157 oz AGW

Y#	Date	Mintage	Fine	VF	XF	Unc
26	1869 НІ	.143	175.00	225.00	300.00	400.00
	1870 НІ	.200	175.00	225.00	300.00	400.00
	1871 НІ	.200	175.00	225.00	300.00	400.00
	1872 НІ	.100	175.00	225.00	300.00	400.00
	1873 НІ	.077	175.00	225.00	300.00	400.00
	1874 НІ	.270	175.00	225.00	300.00	400.00
	1875 НІ	.100	175.00	225.00	300.00	400.00
	1876 НІ	.063	175.00	225.00	300.00	400.00
	1877 НІ	.050	175.00	225.00	300.00	400.00
	1877 НФ	I.A.	175.00	225.00	300.00	400.00
	1878 НФ	.194	175.00	225.00	300.00	400.00
	1879 НФ	5 pcs.	—	—	—	1650.
	1880 НФ	.100	175.00	225.00	300.00	400.00
	1881 НФ	.048	175.00	225.00	300.00	400.00
	1882 НФ	6 pcs.	—	—	Rare	
	1883 ДС	9,007	175.00	225.00	350.00	500.00
	1883 АГ	I.A.	—	—	Rare	
	1884 АГ	.047	175.00	225.00	350.00	500.00
	1885 АГ	.029	175.00	250.00	375.00	550.00
	Common date	—	—	—	Proof	1200.

5 ROUBLES

6.0800 g, .986 GOLD, .1928 oz AGW
Mint mark: СПБ

C#	Date	Mintage	Fine	VF	XF	Unc
131	1802 ХЛ	15 pcs.	—	—	Rare	
	1803 ХЛ	6 pcs.	—	—	Rare	
	1804 ХЛ	.037	250.00	400.00	800.00	1200.
	1805 ХЛ	8,109	250.00	400.00	800.00	1200.
	1806 ХЛ	2 pcs.	—	—	Rare	

6.5440 g, .917 GOLD, .1929 oz AGW

132	1817 ФГ	.710	130.00	180.00	300.00	500.00
	1818 МФ	1.520	130.00	200.00	325.00	550.00
	1819 МФ	.963	130.00	180.00	300.00	500.00
	1822 МФ	—	130.00	180.00	300.00	500.00
	1823 ПС	.440	130.00	180.00	300.00	500.00
	1824 ПС	.276	130.00	180.00	300.00	500.00
	1825 ПС	.101	400.00	700.00	1200.	2000.
	1825 ПС	—	—	—	Proof	3000.
	1825 ПД	I.A.	300.00	500.00	800.00	1400.

Similar to C#132.

174	1826 ПД	.212	130.00	180.00	300.00	500.00
	1827 ПД	—	300.00	500.00	900.00	1500.
	1828 ПД	.604	130.00	180.00	300.00	500.00
	1829 ПД	.733	130.00	180.00	300.00	500.00
	1830 ПД	.490	130.00	180.00	300.00	500.00
	1831 ПД	.846	150.00	300.00	400.00	650.00

Discovery of Gold at Kolyvan Mines

| 176 | 1832 ПД | 1,000 | 600.00 | 1200. | 2200. | 3500. |
| | 1832 | — | — | — | Proof | 4500. |

C#	Date	Mintage	Fine	VF	XF	Unc
175.1	1832 ПД	.481	110.00	130.00	150.00	225.00
	1833 ПД	.829	110.00	130.00	150.00	225.00
	1834 ПД	1.346	110.00	130.00	150.00	225.00
	1835 ПД	1.440	110.00	130.00	150.00	225.00
	1835	Inc. Ab.	—	—	Rare	—
	1836 ПД	.953	110.00	130.00	150.00	225.00
	1837 ПД	.048	150.00	200.00	250.00	400.00
	1838 ПД	.302	110.00	130.00	150.00	225.00
	1839 АЧ	1.609	110.00	130.00	150.00	225.00
	1840 АЧ	1.277	110.00	130.00	150.00	225.00
	1841 АЧ	1.668	110.00	130.00	150.00	225.00
	1842 АЧ	2.180	110.00	130.00	150.00	225.00
	1843 АЧ	1.852	110.00	130.00	150.00	225.00
	1844 КБ	2.365	110.00	130.00	150.00	225.00
	1845 КБ	2.842	110.00	130.00	150.00	225.00
	1846 АГ	3.442	110.00	130.00	150.00	225.00
	Common date	—	—	—	Proof	2000.

Mint mark: МШ

C#	Date	Mintage	Fine	VF	XF	Unc
175.2	1842	695 pcs.	700.00	1000.	1500.	2500.
	1846	62 pcs.	1000.	1500.	2000.	3000.
	1848	485 pcs.	700.00	1000.	1500.	2500.
	1849	133 pcs.	700.00	1000.	1500.	2500.
	Common date	—	—	—	Proof	3000.

Mint mark: СПБ
Different eagle

C#	Date	Mintage	Fine	VF	XF	Unc
175.3	1846 АГ	I.C175.1	110.00	120.00	140.00	200.00
	1847 АГ	3.900	110.00	150.00	200.00	275.00
	1848 АГ	2.900	110.00	120.00	140.00	200.00
	1849 АГ	3.100	110.00	120.00	140.00	200.00
	1850 АГ	3.900	110.00	120.00	140.00	200.00
	1851 АГ	3.400	110.00	120.00	140.00	200.00
	1852 АГ	3.900	110.00	120.00	140.00	200.00
	1853 АГ	3.900	110.00	120.00	140.00	200.00
	1854 АГ	3.900	110.00	120.00	140.00	200.00

Y#	Date	Mintage	Fine	VF	XF	Unc
A26	1855 АГ	3.400	110.00	120.00	135.00	200.00
	1856 АГ	3.800	110.00	120.00	135.00	200.00
	1857 АГ	4.500	110.00	120.00	135.00	200.00
	1858 АГ	3.500	110.00	120.00	135.00	200.00
	1858 ПФ	—	110.00	120.00	135.00	200.00
	Common date	—	—	—	Proof	2000.

Y#	Date	Mintage	Fine	VF	XF	Unc
B26	1859 ПФ	3.900	110.00	120.00	135.00	190.00
	1860 ПФ	3.600	110.00	120.00	135.00	190.00
	1861 ПФ	3.500	110.00	120.00	135.00	190.00
	1862 ПФ	6.354	110.00	120.00	135.00	190.00
	1863 МИ	7.200	110.00	120.00	135.00	190.00
	1864 АС	3.900	110.00	120.00	135.00	190.00
	1865 АС	3.902	110.00	120.00	135.00	190.00
	1865 СШ	I.A.	110.00	120.00	135.00	190.00
	1866 СШ	3.900	110.00	120.00	135.00	190.00
	1866 HI	I.A.	110.00	120.00	135.00	190.00
	1867 HI	3.494	110.00	120.00	135.00	190.00
	1868 HI	3.400	110.00	120.00	135.00	190.00
	1869 HI	3.900	110.00	120.00	135.00	190.00
	1870 HI	5.000	110.00	120.00	135.00	190.00
	1871 HI	.800	110.00	120.00	135.00	190.00
	1872 HI	2.400	110.00	120.00	135.00	190.00
	1873 HI	3.000	110.00	120.00	135.00	190.00
	1874 HI	4.800	110.00	120.00	135.00	190.00
	1875 HI	4.000	110.00	120.00	135.00	190.00
	1876 HI	6.000	110.00	120.00	135.00	170.00
	1877 HI	6.600	110.00	120.00	135.00	170.00
	1877 НФ	I.A.	110.00	120.00	135.00	170.00
	1878 НФ	6.800	110.00	120.00	135.00	170.00
	1879 НФ	7.225	110.00	120.00	135.00	170.00
	1880 НФ	6.200	110.00	120.00	135.00	170.00

Y#	Date	Mintage	Fine	VF	XF	Unc
B26	1881 НФ	5.500	110.00	120.00	135.00	170.00
	1882 НФ	4.547	110.00	120.00	135.00	170.00
	1883 ДС	5.632	110.00	120.00	135.00	170.00
	1883 АГ	I.A.	110.00	120.00	135.00	170.00
	1884 АГ	4.801	110.00	120.00	135.00	170.00
	1885 АГ	5.433	110.00	120.00	135.00	170.00
	Common date	—	—	—	Proof	1750.

6.4516 g, .900 GOLD, .1867 oz AGW
Mint: St. Petersburg-w/o mint mark

Y#	Date	Mintage	Fine	VF	XF	Unc
42	1886 АГ	.351	BV	110.00	125.00	160.00
	1887 АГ	3.261	BV	110.00	125.00	150.00
	1888 АГ	5.257	BV	110.00	125.00	150.00
	1889 АГ	4.200	BV	110.00	125.00	150.00
	1890 АГ	5.600	BV	110.00	125.00	150.00
	1891 АГ	.541	BV	110.00	125.00	150.00
	1892 АГ	.128	BV	110.00	125.00	160.00
	1893 АГ	.598	BV	110.00	125.00	150.00
	1894 АГ	.598	BV	110.00	125.00	150.00
	Common date	—	—	—	Proof	1350.

NOTE: Edge varieties exist.

Y#	Date	Mintage	Fine	VF	XF	Unc
A61	1895 АГ	36 pcs.	—	2250.	4500.	6000.
	1896 АГ	33 pcs.	—	2250.	4500.	6000.

4.3013 g, .900 GOLD, .1244 oz AGW

Y#	Date	Mintage	Fine	VF	XF	Unc
62	1897 АГ	5.372	—	BV	65.00	80.00
	1898 АГ	52.378	—	BV	65.00	75.00
	1899 ЗБ	20.400	—	BV	65.00	80.00
	1899 ФЗ	I.A.	—	BV	65.00	80.00
	1900 ФЗ	.031	—	BV	80.00	110.00
	1901 ФЗ	7.500	—	BV	70.00	90.00
	1901 АР	I.A.	—	BV	70.00	90.00
	1902 АР	6.240	—	BV	70.00	90.00
	1903 АР	5.148	—	BV	70.00	90.00
	1904 АР	2.016	—	BV	80.00	110.00
	1906 ЗБ	10 pcs.	—	—	2000.	2500.
	1907 ЗБ	109 pcs.	—	—	900.00	1250.
	1909 ЗБ	—	BV	65.00	80.00	90.00
	1910 ЗБ	.200	BV	65.00	80.00	100.00
	1911 ЗБ	.100	BV	65.00	80.00	100.00
	Common date	—	—	—	Proof	900.00

6 ROUBLES

20.7100 g, PLATINUM, .6655 oz APW
Mint mark: СПБ

C#	Date	Mintage	Fine	VF	XF	Unc
178	1829	828 pcs.	1000.	2000.	2750.	3500.
	1830	8,610	1000.	2000.	2500.	3250.
	1831	2,784	1000.	1750.	2750.	3500.
	1832	1,502	1000.	2000.	2750.	3500.
	1833	302 pcs.	1000.	2000.	2750.	3500.
	1834	11 pcs.	1250.	2500.	3200.	4200.
	1835	107 pcs.	1000.	2000.	2500.	3250.
	1836	11 pcs.	—	—	Proof	5500.
	1837	253 pcs.	1000.	2000.	2750.	3500.
	1838	12 pcs.	—	—	Rare	—
	1839	2 pcs.	—	—	Rare	—
	1840	1 pc.	—	—	Rare	—
	1841	170 pcs.	1000.	2000.	2750.	3500.
	1842	121 pcs.	1000.	2000.	2750.	3500.
	1843	127 pcs.	1000.	2000.	2750.	3500.
	1844	4 pcs.	—	—	Rare	—
	1845	2 pcs.	—	—	Rare	—
	Common date	—	—	—	Proof	5000.

7 ROUBLES 50 KOPEKS

6.4516 g, .900 GOLD, .1867 oz AGW
Mint: St. Petersburg-w/o mint mark

Y#	Date	Mintage	Fine	VF	XF	Unc
63	1897 АГ	16.829	BV	110.00	135.00	250.00

10 ROUBLES

12.1700 g, .986 GOLD, .3858 oz AGW
Mint mark: СПБ

C#	Date	Mintage	Fine	VF	XF	Unc
133	1802	.074	2500.	3000.	3500.	4500.
	1802 АИ	I.A.	2500.	3000.	3500.	4500.
	1804 ХЛ	.072	2500.	3000.	3500.	4500.
	1805 ХЛ	.055	1500.	2000.	2150.	4250.
	1806 ХЛ	126 pcs.	—	—	Rare	—

12.9039 g, .900 GOLD, .3734 oz AGW
Mint: St. Petersburg-w/o mint mark

Y#	Date	Mintage	Fine	VF	XF	Unc
A42	1886 АГ	.057	200.00	300.00	500.00	750.00
	1887 АГ	.475	200.00	250.00	350.00	600.00
	1888 АГ	.023	200.00	300.00	500.00	750.00
	1889 АГ	.343	200.00	250.00	350.00	600.00
	1890 АГ	.015	200.00	300.00	500.00	750.00
	1891 АГ	3,010	250.00	400.00	650.00	900.00
	1892 АГ	8,006	250.00	400.00	650.00	900.00
	1893 АГ	1,008	250.00	400.00	650.00	900.00
	1894 АГ	1,007	250.00	400.00	650.00	900.00
	Common date	—	—	—	Proof	2800.

Rev. leg: ИМПЕРІАЛЪ (IMPERIAL).

Y#	Date	Mintage	Fine	VF	XF	Unc
A63	1895 АГ	125 pcs.	—	3000.	3500.	4000.
	1896 АГ	125 pcs.	—	3000.	3500.	4000.
	1897 АГ	125 pcs.	—	3000.	3500.	4000.

8.6026 g, .900 GOLD, .2489 oz AGW

Y#	Date	Mintage	Fine	VF	XF	Unc
64	1898 АГ	.200	—	BV	130.00	175.00
	1899 АГ	27.600	—	BV	120.00	145.00
	1899 ФЗ	I.A.	—	BV	120.00	145.00
	1899 ЗБ	I.A.	—	BV	130.00	175.00
	1900 ФЗ	6.021	—	BV	130.00	175.00
	1901 ФЗ	2.377	—	BV	130.00	175.00
	1901 АР	I.A.	—	BV	130.00	175.00
	1902 АР	2.019	—	BV	130.00	175.00
	1903 АР	2.817	—	BV	130.00	175.00
	1904 АР	1.025	—	BV	130.00	175.00
	1906 ЗБ	10 pcs.	—	—	Proof	3200.
	1909 ЗБ	.050	BV	120.00	140.00	200.00
	1910 ЗБ	.100	BV	120.00	140.00	200.00
	1911 ЗБ	.050	BV	120.00	140.00	200.00
	Common date	—	—	—	Proof	1800.

12 ROUBLES

41.4100 g, PLATINUM, 1.3311 oz APW
Mint mark: СПБ

C#	Date	Mintage	Fine	VF	XF	Unc
179	1830	119 pcs.	2000.	3500.	4500.	9000.
	1831	1,463	1800.	3250.	4250.	6500.
	1832	1,102	1800.	3000.	4250.	6500.
	1833	255 pcs.	2000.	3250.	5000.	9000.
	1834	11 pcs.	—	—	Proof	8000.
	1835	127 pcs.	2000.	3500.	4500.	9000.
	1836	11 pcs.	—	—	Proof	8000.
	1837	53 pcs.	2000.	3500.	5500.	10,000.
	1838	12 pcs.	—	—	Rare	—
	1839	2 pcs.	—	—	Rare	—
	1840	1 pc.	—	—	Rare	—
	1841	75 pcs.	2000.	3500.	4750.	10,000.
	1842	115 pcs.	2000.	3300.	5500.	10,000.
	1843	122 pcs.	2000.	3500.	5500.	10,000.
	1844	4 pcs.	—	—	Proof	7000.
	1845	2 pcs.	—	—	Rare	—
	Common date	—	—	—	Proof	6500.

NOTE: Varieties exist.

15 ROUBLES

12.9039 g, .900 GOLD, .3734 oz AGW
Mint: St. Petersburg-w/o mint mark

Y#	Date	Mintage	Fine	BV	VF	XF	Unc
65	1897 АГ	11.900		BV	195.00	220.00	300.00

25 ROUBLES

32.7200 g, .917 GOLD, .9640 oz AGW
Mint mark: СПБ

27	1876	100 pcs.	—	—	Proof	17,600.

NOTE: Realized in Stack's International sale 3-88.

32.2500 g, .900 GOLD, .9332 oz AGW
Mint: St. Petersburg-w/o mint mark
Rev. leg: 2-1/2 ИМПЕРІАЛА (IMPERIALS).

Y#	Date	Mintage	Fine	VF	XF	Unc
A65	1896	300 pcs.	—	4000.	5000.	7000.
	1908	150 pcs.	—	4000.	5000.	7000.
	1908	25 pcs.	—	—	Proof	13,000.

37 ROUBLES 50 KOPEKS

32.2500 g, .900 GOLD, .9335 oz AGW
Mint: St. Petersburg-w/o mint mark
Rev. leg: 100 ФРАНКОВЪ (FRANCS).

B65	1902		—	4000.	5000.	9000.
	1902	225 pcs.	—	—	Proof	15,400.

РСФСР (R.S.F.S.R.)

РСФСР (Россиискои Социалистическои Федеративнои Советскои Респуълики) R.S.F.S.R. (Russian Socialist Federated Soviet Republic)

MONETARY SYSTEM
100 Kopeks = 1 Rouble

10 KOPEKS

1.8000 g, .500 SILVER, .0289 oz ASW

80	1921	.950	5.00	10.00	25.00	50.00
	1922	18.640	.50	1.00	2.00	6.00
	1923	33.424	.50	1.00	2.00	5.00
	Common date	—	—	—	Proof	55.00

15 KOPEKS

2.7000 g, .500 SILVER, .0434 oz ASW

81	1921	.933	6.00	12.00	30.00	60.00
	1922	13.633	1.00	1.50	4.00	10.00
	1923	28.503	.75	1.00	2.00	5.00
	Common date	—	—	—	Proof	60.00

20 KOPEKS

3.6000 g, .500 SILVER, .0578 oz ASW

Y#	Date	Mintage	Fine	VF	XF	Unc
82	1921	.825	6.00	12.00	30.00	60.00
	1922	14.220	1.00	2.00	4.00	12.00
	1923	27.580	1.00	1.75	3.00	6.00
	Common date	—	—	—	Proof	75.00

NOTE: Varieties exist.

50 KOPEKS

9.9980 g, .900 SILVER, .2893 oz ASW
Mintmaster's initials on edge.

83	1921 АГ	1.400	4.00	6.00	8.00	22.00
	1922 АГ	8.224	10.00	15.00	25.00	60.00
	1922 ПЛ	I.A.	4.00	6.00	8.00	22.00
	Common date	—	—	—	Proof	125.00

ROUBLE

19.9960 g, .900 SILVER, .5786 oz ASW
Mintmaster's initials on edge.

84	1921 АГ	1.000	6.00	12.00	20.00	65.00
	1922 АГ	2.050	9.00	15.00	35.00	90.00
	1922 ПЛ	I.A.	9.00	15.00	35.00	90.00
	Common date	—	—	—	Proof	150.00

СССР (U.S.S.R.)

СССР (Союз Советских Социалистических Республик) U.S.S.R. (Union of Soviet Socialist Republics).

MONETARY SYSTEM
100 Kopecks = 1 Rouble

1/2 KOPEK

COPPER

75	1925	45.380	3.50	7.50	14.50	30.00
	1927	—	3.50	7.50	14.50	30.00
	1928	—	4.50	8.00	16.50	35.00

KOPEK

BRONZE

76	1924 reeded edge					

USSR

Y#	Date	Mintage	Fine	VF	XF	Unc
76		176.511	1.00	2.00	6.00	16.00
	1924 plain edge					
		Inc. Ab.	25.00	50.00	100.00	200.00
	1925	Inc. Ab.	40.00	80.00	150.00	250.00

ALUMINUM-BRONZE

Y#	Date	Mintage	Fine	VF	XF	Unc
91	1926	87.915	.50	1.00	1.50	5.50
	1927	—	.50	1.00	1.50	5.00
	1928	—	.50	1.00	1.50	5.00
	1929	95.950	.50	1.00	1.50	5.00
	1930	85.351	.50	1.00	1.50	5.00
	1931	106.100	.50	1.00	1.50	5.00
	1932	56.900	.50	1.00	1.50	5.00
	1933	111.257	.50	1.00	1.50	5.00
	1934	100.245	.50	1.00	1.50	5.00
	1935	66.405	.50	1.00	2.00	6.00

NOTE: Varieties exist.

Y#	Date	Mintage	Fine	VF	XF	Unc
98	1935	Inc.Y91	.50	1.00	2.50	9.00
	1936	132.204	.50	1.00	2.00	7.50

Y#	Date	Mintage	Fine	VF	XF	Unc
105	1937	—	.25	.50	.75	1.50
	1938	—	.25	.50	.75	1.50
	1939	—	.25	.50	.75	1.50
	1940	—	.25	.50	.75	1.50
	1941	—	.25	.60	1.00	1.75
	1945	—	.50	1.00	2.00	6.00
	1946	—	.50	1.00	2.00	6.00

NOTE: Varieties exist.

Y#	Date	Mintage	Fine	VF	XF	Unc
112	1948	—	.50	1.00	2.00	5.00
	1949	—	.50	1.00	2.00	5.00
	1950	—	.50	1.00	2.50	8.00
	1951	—	.50	1.00	2.50	8.00
	1952	—	.30	.75	1.50	3.00
	1953	—	.30	.75	1.50	3.00
	1954	—	.30	.75	1.50	3.00
	1955	—	.30	.75	1.50	3.00
	1956	—	.30	.75	1.50	3.00

NOTE: Varieties exist.

Y#	Date	Mintage	Fine	VF	XF	Unc
119	1957	—	1.00	2.00	4.00	12.00

BRASS

Y#	Date	Mintage	Fine	VF	XF	Unc
126	1961	—	—	.10	.25	1.00
	1962	—	—	.10	.25	.50
	1963	—	—	.10	.25	.50
	1964	—	—	.10	.25	.50
	1965	—	—	.10	.25	.50
	1966	—	—	.10	.25	.50
	1967	—	—	.10	.25	.50
	1968	—	—	.10	.25	.50
	1969	—	—	.10	.25	.50
	1970	—	—	.10	.25	.50
	1971	—	—	.10	.25	.50
	1972	—	—	.10	.25	.50
	1973	—	—	.10	.25	.50
	1974	—	—	.10	.25	.50
	1975	—	—	.10	.25	.50
	1976	—	—	.10	.25	.50
	1977	—	—	.10	.25	.50
	1978	—	—	.10	.25	.50
	1979	—	—	.10	.25	.50
	1980	—	—	.10	.25	.50
	1981	—	—	.10	.25	.50
	1982	—	—	.10	.25	.50
	1983	—	—	.10	.25	.50
	1984	—	—	.10	.25	.50
	1985	—	—	.10	.25	.50
	1986	—	—	.10	.25	.50
	1987	—	—	.10	.25	.50
	1988	—	—	.10	.25	.50

NOTE: Varieties exist.

2 KOPEKS

BRONZE

Y#	Date	Mintage	Fine	VF	XF	Unc
77	1924 reeded edge					
		119.995	1.00	2.00	6.00	18.00
	1924 plain edge	25.00	50.00	100.00	200.00	
	1925	Inc. Ab.	40.00	80.00	150.00	250.00

NOTE: Varieties exist.

ALUMINUM-BRONZE

Y#	Date	Mintage	Fine	VF	XF	Unc
92	1926	105.052	.25	.50	1.00	3.00
	1927	—	40.00	70.00	130.00	200.00
	1928	—	.25	.50	1.00	3.00
	1929	80.000	.25	.50	1.00	4.00
	1930	134.186	.25	.50	1.00	3.00
	1931	99.523	.25	.50	1.00	3.00
	1932	39.573	.25	.50	1.00	3.00
	1933	54.874	.25	.50	1.00	3.00
	1934	61.574	.25	.50	1.00	3.00
	1935	81.121	.25	.50	1.50	4.00

NOTE: Varieties exist.

Y#	Date	Mintage	Fine	VF	XF	Unc
99	1935	—	.50	1.00	2.50	9.00
	1936	94.354	.25	.50	2.00	7.00

NOTE: Varieties exist.

Y#	Date	Mintage	Fine	VF	XF	Unc
106	1937	—	.25	.50	1.00	2.50
	1938	—	.25	.50	1.00	2.50
	1939	—	.25	.50	1.00	2.50
	1940	—	.25	.50	1.00	2.50
	1941	—	.25	.50	1.00	2.50
	1945	—	.50	1.00	2.00	5.00
	1946	—	.25	.50	1.00	4.00

Y#	Date	Mintage	Fine	VF	XF	Unc
113	1948	—	.25	.50	1.00	2.50
	1949	—	.25	.50	1.00	2.50
	1950	—	.25	.50	1.00	2.50
	1951	—	.50	1.00	2.00	6.00
	1952	—	.25	.50	1.00	3.00
	1953	—	.20	.50	1.00	2.00
	1954	—	.25	.50	1.00	2.00
	1955	—	.20	.50	1.00	2.00
	1956	—	.20	.50	1.00	2.00

NOTE: Varieties exist.

Y#	Date	Mintage	Fine	VF	XF	Unc
120	1957	—	.50	1.00	2.50	9.00

BRASS

Y#	Date	Mintage	Fine	VF	XF	Unc
127	1961	—	—	.10	.25	.50
	1962	—	—	.10	.25	.50
	1963	—	—	.10	.25	.50
	1964	—	—	.10	.25	.50
	1965	—	—	.10	.25	.50
	1966	—	—	.10	.25	.50
	1967	—	—	.10	.25	.50
	1968	—	—	.10	.25	.50
	1969	—	—	.10	.25	.50
	1970	—	—	.10	.25	.50
	1971	—	—	.10	.25	.50
	1972	—	—	.10	.25	.50
	1973	—	—	.10	.25	.50
	1974	—	—	.10	.25	.50
	1975	—	—	.10	.25	.50
	1976	—	—	.10	.25	.50
	1977	—	—	.10	.25	.50
	1978	—	—	.10	.25	.50
	1979	—	—	.10	.25	.50
	1980	—	—	.10	.25	.50
	1981	—	—	.10	.25	.50
	1982	—	—	.10	.25	.50
	1983	—	—	.10	.25	.50
	1984	—	—	.10	.25	.50
	1985	—	—	.10	.25	.50
	1986	—	—	.10	.25	.50
	1987	—	—	.10	.25	.50
	1988	—	—	.10	.25	.50

NOTE: Varieties exist.

3 KOPEKS

BRONZE

Y#	Date	Mintage	Fine	VF	XF	Unc
78	1924 reeded edge					
		101.283	50.00	75.00	150.00	250.00
	1924 plain edge					
		Inc. Ab.	2.00	4.00	8.00	20.00

NOTE: Varieties exist.

ALUMINUM-BRONZE

Y#	Date	Mintage	Fine	VF	XF	Unc
93	1926	19.940	1.25	2.00	4.00	7.00
	1926 obv. of Y#100	—	—	Rare	—	
	1927	—	5.00	10.00	20.00	40.00
	1928	—	1.00	2.00	4.00	7.00
	1929	50.150	1.00	2.00	4.00	8.00
	1930	74.159	.25	.50	1.00	4.00
	1931	121.168	.25	.50	1.00	4.00
	1931 w/o CCCP obv.	—	—	Rare	—	
	1932	37.718	.25	.50	1.00	4.00
	1933	44.764	.25	.50	2.00	6.00
	1934	44.529	.25	.50	2.00	6.00
	1935	58.303	.25	.50	2.50	7.00

NOTE: Varieties exist.

Y#	Date	Mintage	Fine	VF	XF	Unc
100	1935	—	.50	2.00	5.00	14.00
	1936	62.757	.25	1.00	4.00	10.00

NOTE: Varieties exist.

Y#	Date	Mintage	Fine	VF	XF	Unc
107	1937	—	.25	.50	1.00	4.00
	1938	—	.25	.50	1.00	4.00
	1939	—	.25	.50	1.00	4.00
	1940	—	.25	.50	1.00	3.00
	1941	—	.25	.50	1.00	4.00
	1943	—	.25	.50	1.00	4.00
	1945	—	.50	1.00	3.00	9.00
	1946	—	.25	.50	1.00	5.00

NOTE: Varieties exist.

Y#	Date	Mintage	Fine	VF	XF	Unc
94	1931	89.540	.50	1.00	1.50	5.00
	1932	65.100	.50	1.00	1.50	5.00
	1933	18.135	1.00	2.00	5.00	16.00
	1934	5.354	.50	1.00	2.00	5.00
	1935	11.735	.50	1.00	2.50	6.00

NOTE: Varieties exist.

Y#	Date	Mintage	Fine	VF	XF	Unc
129	1984	—	.10	.15	.30	.75
	1985	—	.10	.15	.30	.75
	1986	—	.10	.15	.30	.75
	1987	—	.10	.15	.30	.75
	1988	—	.10	.15	.30	.75

NOTE: Varieties exist.

10 KOPEKS

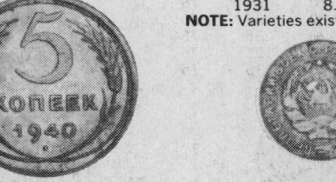

1.8000 g, .500 SILVER, .0289 oz ASW

Y#	Date	Mintage	Fine	VF	XF	Unc
86	1924	67.351	.50	1.00	2.50	6.00
	1925	101.013	.50	1.00	2.50	5.00
	1927	—	.50	1.00	2.50	6.00
	1928	—	.50	1.00	2.00	5.00
	1929	64.900	.50	1.00	2.50	6.00
	1930	163.424	.50	1.00	2.00	5.00
	1931	8.791	40.00	70.00	120.00	200.00

NOTE: Varieties exist.

Y#	Date	Mintage	Fine	VF	XF	Unc
114	1948	—	.25	.50	1.00	5.00
	1949	—	.25	.50	1.00	4.00
	1950	—	.25	.50	1.00	4.00
	1951	—	.50	1.00	2.00	7.00
	1952	—	.25	.50	1.00	4.00
	1953	—	.25	.50	1.00	3.00
	1954	—	.25	.50	1.00	3.00
	1955	—	.25	.50	1.00	3.00
	1956	—	.25	.50	1.00	3.00

NOTE: Varieties exist.

Y#	Date	Mintage	Fine	VF	XF	Unc
101	1935	—	2.00	4.00	9.00	26.00
	1936	5.242	2.00	4.00	9.00	28.00

NOTE: Varieties exist.

Y#	Date	Mintage	Fine	VF	XF	Unc
121	1957	—	.50	1.00	2.50	9.00

Y#	Date	Mintage	Fine	VF	XF	Unc
108	1937	—	.25	.50	1.00	4.00
	1938	—	.25	.50	1.00	4.00
	1939	—	.25	.50	1.00	4.00
	1940	—	.25	.50	1.00	3.00
	1941	—	.25	.50	1.00	4.00
	1943	—	.25	.50	1.00	4.00
	1945	—	1.00	2.00	5.00	12.00
	1946	—	.25	.50	1.00	6.00

NOTE: Varieties exist.

COPPER-NICKEL

Y#	Date	Mintage	Fine	VF	XF	Unc
95	1931	122.511	.25	.50	1.50	4.00
	1932	171.641	.25	.50	1.00	3.00
	1933	163.125	.25	.50	1.00	3.00
	1934	104.059	.25	.50	1.00	5.00

NOTE: Varieties exist.

Y#	Date	Mintage	Fine	VF	XF	Unc
102	1935	79.628	.25	.50	1.00	5.00
	1936	122.260	.25	.50	1.00	4.00

BRASS

Y#	Date	Mintage	Fine	VF	XF	Unc
128	1961	—	—	.10	.25	.60
	1962	—	—	.10	.25	.60
	1965	—	—	.10	.25	.60
	1966	—	—	.10	.25	.60
	1967	—	—	.10	.25	.60
	1968	—	—	.10	.25	.60
	1969	—	—	.10	.25	.60
	1970	—	—	.10	.25	.60
	1971	—	—	.10	.25	.60
	1972	—	—	.10	.25	.60
	1973	—	—	.10	.25	.60
	1974	—	—	.10	.25	.60
	1975	—	—	.10	.25	.60
	1976	—	—	.10	.25	.60
	1977	—	—	.10	.25	.60
	1978	—	—	.10	.25	.60
	1979	—	—	.10	.25	.60
	1980	—	—	.10	.25	.60
	1981	—	—	.10	.25	.60
	1982	—	—	.10	.25	.60
	1983	—	—	.10	.25	.60
	1984	—	—	.10	.25	.60
	1985	—	—	.10	.25	.60
	1986	—	—	.10	.25	.60
	1987	—	—	.10	.25	.60
	1988	—	—	.10	.25	.60

NOTE: Varieties exist.

Y#	Date	Mintage	Fine	VF	XF	Unc
115	1948	—	.25	.50	1.50	5.00
	1949	—	.25	.50	1.00	4.00
	1950	—	.25	.50	1.00	4.00
	1951	—	.50	1.00	2.00	5.00
	1952	—	.25	.50	1.00	4.00
	1953	—	.25	.50	1.00	4.00
	1954	—	.25	.50	1.00	4.00
	1955	—	.25	.50	1.00	4.00
	1956	—	.25	.50	1.00	4.00

Y#	Date	Mintage	Fine	VF	XF	Unc
109	1937	—	.30	.75	1.25	2.50
	1938	—	.30	.75	1.25	2.50
	1939	—	.30	.60	1.00	2.00
	1940	—	.30	.60	1.00	2.00
	1941	—	.30	.60	1.00	3.00
	1942	—	.50	1.00	3.00	8.00
	1943	—	.30	.60	1.00	2.00
	1944	—	.50	1.00	2.00	5.00
	1945	—	.30	.75	1.25	3.00
	1946	—	.30	.75	1.25	3.00
	1946 obv. of Y#102		—	—	Rare	—

NOTE: Varieties exist.

5 KOPEKS

BRONZE

Y#	Date	Mintage	Fine	VF	XF	Unc
79	1924 reeded edge	88.510	50.00	75.00	150.00	250.00
	1924 plain edge Inc. Ab.		3.00	6.00	12.00	32.00

NOTE: Varieties exist.

ALUMINUM-BRONZE

Y#	Date	Mintage	Fine	VF	XF	Unc
94	1926	14.697	.50	1.00	3.00	8.00
	1927	—	2.00	4.00	12.00	30.00
	1928	—	.50	1.00	2.00	6.00
	1929	20.220	.50	1.00	2.00	6.00
	1930	44.490	.50	1.00	1.50	5.00

Y#	Date	Mintage	Fine	VF	XF	Unc
122	1957	—	1.00	2.00	3.00	9.00

NOTE: Varieties exist.

Y#	Date	Mintage	Fine	VF	XF	Unc
129	1961	—	.10	.15	.30	.75
	1962	—	.10	.15	.30	.75
	1965	—	.10	.15	.30	.75
	1966	—	.10	.15	.30	.75
	1967	—	.10	.15	.30	.75
	1968	—	.10	.15	.30	.75
	1969	—	.10	.15	.30	.75
	1970	—	.10	.15	.30	.75
	1971	—	.10	.15	.30	.75
	1972	—	.10	.15	.30	.75
	1973	—	.10	.15	.30	.75
	1974	—	.10	.15	.30	.75
	1975	—	.10	.15	.30	.75
	1976	—	.10	.15	.30	.75
	1977	—	.10	.15	.30	.75
	1978	—	.10	.15	.30	.75
	1979	—	.10	.15	.30	.75
	1980	—	.10	.15	.30	.75
	1981	—	.10	.15	.30	.75
	1982	—	.10	.15	.30	.75
	1983	—	.10	.15	.30	.75

Obv: 8 and 7 ribbons on wreath.

Y#	Date	Mintage	Fine	VF	XF	Unc
116	1948	—	.25	.50	2.00	5.00
	1949	—	.25	.50	1.00	3.00
	1950	—	.25	.50	1.00	2.00
	1951	—	.25	.50	1.00	5.00
	1952	—	.25	.50	1.00	4.00
	1953	—	.25	.50	1.00	2.00
	1954	—	.25	.50	1.00	2.00
	1955	—	.25	.50	1.00	2.00
	1956	—	.25	.50	1.00	2.00
	1956 rev. of Y#123		50.00	75.00	150.00	250.00

NOTE: Varieties exist.

Obv: 7 and 7 ribbons on wreath.

Y#	Date	Mintage	Fine	VF	XF	Unc
123	1957 rev. of Y#116		50.00	75.00	150.00	250.00
	1957	—	.25	.50	2.00	6.00

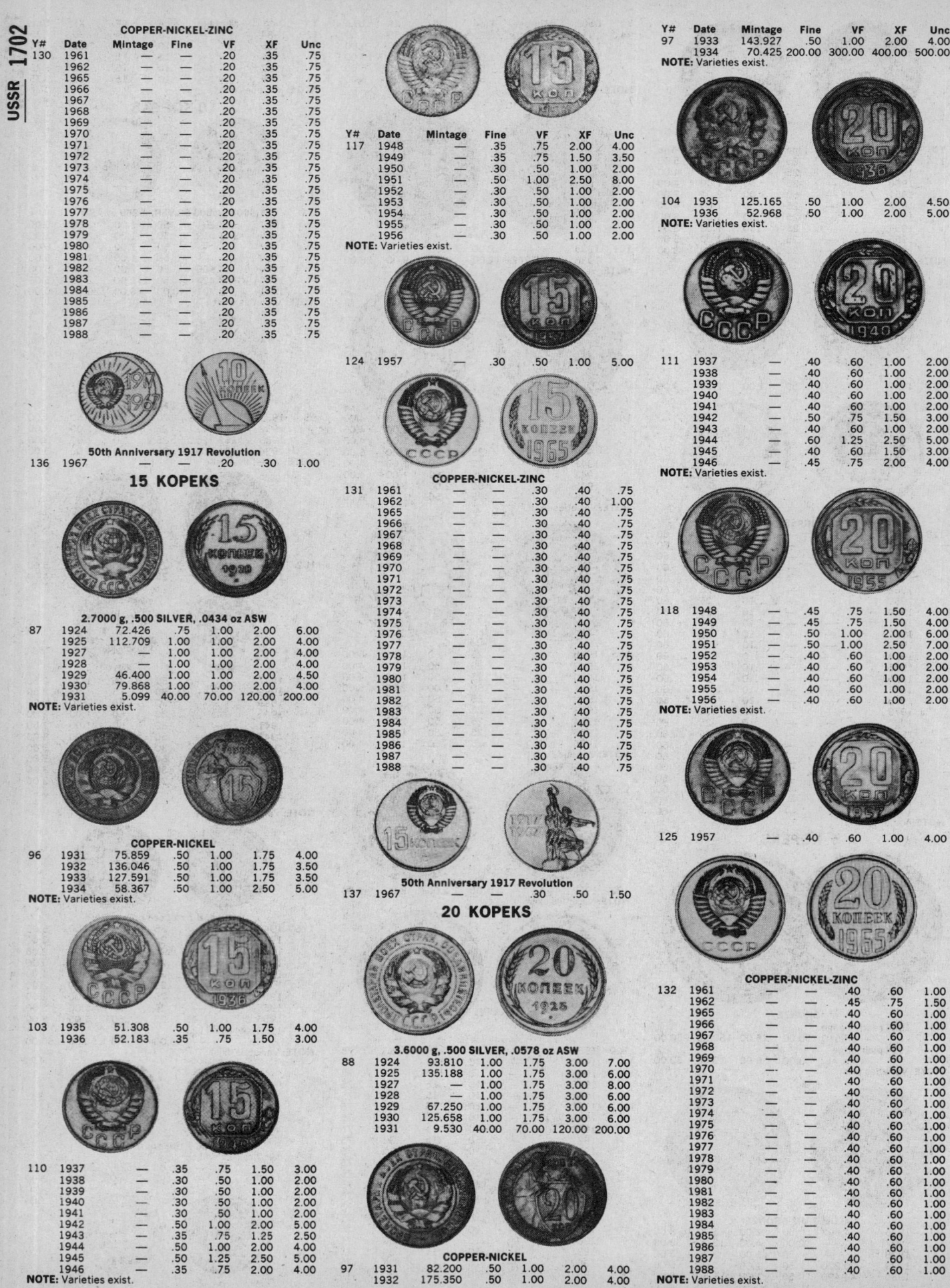

50th Anniversary 1917 Revolution

Y#	Date	Mintage	Fine	VF	XF	Unc
138	1967	—	.40	.60	.75	2.00

50 KOPEKS

9.9980 g, .900 SILVER, .2893 oz ASW
Edge: Weight shown in old Russian units.

Y#	Date	Mintage	Fine	VF	XF	Unc
89.1	1924 ПЛ	26.559	4.00	6.00	8.00	20.00
	1924 ТР	40.000	4.00	6.00	8.00	20.00

Edge: Weight shown in grams only.

89.2	1925 ПЛ	43.557	4.00	6.00	8.00	20.00
	1926 ПЛ	24.374	4.00	6.00	8.00	20.00
	1927 ПЛ	—	4.00	6.00	10.00	30.00
	Common date	—	—	—	Proof	150.00

NOTE: Varieties exist.

COPPER-NICKEL-ZINC
Plain edge

133.1	1961	—	1.00	2.00	5.00	12.00

NOTE: Varieties exist.

Lettered edge

133.2	1964	—	—	—	1.00	1.50
	1965	—	—	—	1.00	1.50
	1966	—	—	—	1.00	1.50
	1967	—	—	—	1.00	1.50
	1968	—	—	—	1.00	1.50
	1969	—	—	—	1.00	1.50
	1970	—	—	—	1.00	1.50
	1971	—	—	—	1.00	1.50
	1972	—	—	—	1.00	1.50
	1973	—	—	—	1.00	1.50
	1974	—	—	—	1.00	1.50
	1975	—	—	—	1.00	1.50
	1976	—	—	—	1.00	1.50
	1977	—	—	—	1.00	1.50
	1978	—	—	—	1.00	1.50
	1979	—	—	—	1.00	1.50
	1980	—	—	—	1.00	1.50
	1981	—	—	—	1.00	1.50
	1982	—	—	—	1.00	1.50
	1983	—	—	—	1.00	1.50
	1984	—	—	—	1.00	1.50
	1985	—	—	—	1.00	1.50
	1986	—	—	—	1.00	1.50
	1987	—	—	—	1.00	1.50
	1988	—	—	—	1.00	1.50

50th Anniversary 1917 Revolution

139	ND(1967)	—	—	1.00	1.50	2.50

ROUBLE

19.9960 g, .900 SILVER, .5786 oz ASW

Y#	Date	Mintage	Fine	VF	XF	Unc
90	1924 ПЛ	12.998	7.50	12.50	22.50	50.00
	1924 ПЛ	—	—	—	Proof	225.00

NOTE: Varieties exist.

COPPER-NICKEL-ZINC
Plain edge

134.1	1961	—	2.00	3.50	6.00	15.00

Lettered edge

134.2	1964	—	—	—	2.00	2.50
	1965	—	—	—	2.00	2.50
	1966	—	—	—	2.00	2.50
	1967	—	—	—	2.00	2.50
	1968	—	—	—	2.00	2.50
	1969	—	—	—	2.00	2.50
	1970	—	—	—	2.00	2.50
	1971	—	—	—	2.00	2.50
	1972	—	—	—	2.00	2.50
	1973	—	—	—	2.00	2.50
	1974	—	—	—	2.00	2.50
	1975	—	—	—	2.00	2.50
	1976	—	—	—	2.00	2.50
	1977	—	—	—	2.00	2.50
	1978	—	—	—	2.00	2.50
	1979	—	—	—	2.00	2.50
	1980	—	—	—	2.00	2.50
	1981	—	—	—	2.00	2.50
	1982	—	—	—	2.00	2.50
	1983	—	—	—	2.00	2.50
	1984	—	—	—	2.00	2.50
	1985	—	—	—	2.00	2.50
	1986	—	—	—	2.00	2.50
	1987	—	—	—	2.00	2.50
	1988	—	—	—	2.00	2.50

20th Anniversary End of World War II

135	1965	—	—	2.00	2.50	3.50

50th Anniversary of 1917 Revolution

140	1967	—	—	2.00	2.50	3.50

Lenin Birth Centennial

Y#	Date	Mintage	Fine	VF	XF	Unc
141	1970	—	—	2.00	2.50	3.50

30th Anniversary of World War II Victory

142	1975 date on edge	—	—	2.00	2.50	3.50

NOTE: Varieties exist.

60th Anniversary of Revolution

143	1977	—	—	2.00	2.50	3.50

1980 Olympics

144	1977	.500	—	2.00	2.50	4.00
	1977	Inc. Ab.	—	—	Proof	

1980 Olympics

153	1978	.500	—	2.00	2.50	4.00
	1978	Inc. Ab.	—	—	Proof	

1980 Olympics

164	1979	.500	—	2.00	2.50	4.00
	1979	Inc. Ab.	—	—	Proof	

USSR 1704

1980 Olympics

Y#	Date	Mintage	Fine	VF	XF	Unc
165	1979	.500	—	2.00	2.50	4.00
	1979	Inc. Ab.	—	—	Proof	—

COPPER-NICKEL
1980 Olympics

177	1980	.500	—	2.00	2.50	4.00
	1980	Inc. Ab.	—	—	Proof	—

1980 Olympics

178	1980	.500	—	2.00	2.50	4.00
	1980	Inc. Ab.	—	—	Proof	—

20th Anniversary of Manned Space Flights-Yuri Gagarin

188	1981	—	—	—	—	4.00

Russian-Bulgarian Friendship

189	1981	—	—	—	—	4.00

60th Anniversary of the Soviet State

190	ND(1982)	—	—	—	—	5.00

Karl Marks (Marx)

Y#	Date	Mintage	Fine	VF	XF	Unc
191	1983	—	—	—	—	4.00

20th Anniversary of First Woman in Space

192	1983	—	—	—	—	4.00
	1983	—	—	—	Proof	—

Ivan Fedorov - First Russian Printer

193	1983	—	—	—	—	4.50
	1983	—	—	—	Proof	—

150th Anniversary of Birth of Dimitri Ivanovich Mendelejev

194	1984	—	—	—	—	4.50
	1984	—	—	—	Proof	—

A.S. Popov

195	1984	—	—	—	—	5.00

185th Anniversary of Birth of Aleksander Sergeevich Pushkin

196	1984	—	—	—	—	5.00
	1984	—	—	—	Proof	—

Vladimir Ilich Lenin

Y#	Date	Mintage	Fine	VF	XF	Unc
197	1985	—	—	—	—	5.00

40th Anniversary Victory WWII

198	1985	—	—	—	—	5.00

Moscow Festival

199	1985	—	—	—	—	5.00

Friedrich Engels

200	1985	—	—	—	—	4.00

International Year of Peace

201	1986	—	—	—	—	4.00

M.V. Lomonosov

202	1986	—	—	—	Proof	6.00

USSR 1705

Battle of Borodino - Soldiers
Y#	Date	Mintage	Fine	VF	XF	Unc
203	1987	—	—	—	—	5.00

Battle of Borodino - Monument
| 204 | 1987 | — | — | — | — | Proof 5.00 |

Constantin - Eduardo Ziolkowskij
| 205 | 1987 | — | — | — | — | Proof 6.00 |

70th Anniversary of Bolshevik Revolution
| 206 | 1987 | — | — | — | — | Proof 6.00 |

Maxim Gorki
| 209 | 1988 | .020 | — | — | — | 6.00 |

Leo Tolstoi
| 216 | 1988 | — | — | — | — | — |
| | 1988 | .020 | — | — | — | Proof 6.00 |

3 ROUBLES

COPPER-NICKEL
70th Anniversary of Bolshevik Revolution
| 207 | 1987 | — | — | — | — | Proof 9.00 |

34.5580 g, .900 SILVER, 1.0000 oz ASW
Cathedral of St. Sophia in Kiev

Y#	Date	Mintage	Fine	VF	XF	Unc
210	1988	.035	—	—	Proof	40.00

Coin Design of St. Vladimir, 977-1015
| 211 | 1988 | .035 | — | — | Proof | 40.00 |

5 ROUBLES

16.6700 g, .900 SILVER, .4824 oz ASW
1980 Olympics
Rev: City view of Kiev.
| 145 | 1977 | .450 | — | — | — | 9.00 |
| | 1977 | Inc. Ab. | — | — | Proof | 10.00 |

1980 Olympics
Rev: City view of Leningrad.
| 146 | 1977 | .450 | — | — | — | 9.00 |
| | 1977 | Inc. Ab. | — | — | Proof | 10.00 |

1980 Olympics
Rev: City view of Minsk.
| 147 | 1977 | .450 | — | — | — | 9.00 |
| | 1977 | Inc. Ab. | — | — | Proof | 10.00 |

1980 Olympics
Rev: City view of Tallinn.
Y#	Date	Mintage	Fine	VF	XF	Unc
148	1977	.450	—	—	—	9.00
	1977	Inc. Ab.	—	—	Proof	10.00

1980 Olympics
| 154 | 1978 | .450 | — | — | — | 9.00 |
| | 1978 | Inc. Ab. | — | — | Proof | 10.00 |

1980 Olympics
| 155 | 1978 | .450 | — | — | — | 9.00 |
| | 1978 | Inc. Ab. | — | — | Proof | 10.00 |

1980 Olympics
| 156 | 1978 | .450 | — | — | — | 9.00 |
| | 1978 | Inc. Ab. | — | — | Proof | 10.00 |

1980 Olympics
| 157 | 1978 | .450 | — | — | — | 9.00 |
| | 1978 | Inc. Ab. | — | — | Proof | 10.00 |

1980 Olympics

USSR 1706

Y#	Date	Mintage	Fine	VF	XF	Unc
166	1979	.450	—	—	—	9.00
	1979	Inc. Ab.	—	—	Proof	10.00

1980 Olympics

167	1979	.450	—	—	—	9.00
	1979	Inc. Ab.	—	—	Proof	10.00

1980 Olympics

179	1980	.450	—	—	—	9.00
	1980	Inc. Ab.	—	—	Proof	10.00

1980 Olympics

180	1980	.450	—	—	—	9.00
	1980	Inc. Ab.	—	—	Proof	10.00

1980 Olympics

181	1980	.450	—	—	—	9.00
	1980	Inc. Ab.	—	—	Proof	10.00

1980 Olympics

182	1980	.450	—	—	—	9.00
	1980	Inc. Ab.	—	—	Proof	10.00

COPPER-NICKEL
70th Anniversary of Bolshevik Revolution

Y#	Date	Mintage	Fine	VF	XF	Unc
208	1987	—	—	—	Proof	15.00

Peter the Great

217	1988	—	—	—	Proof	25.00

1000 Years of Christianity in Russia

218	1988	—	—	—	Proof	25.00

St. Sophia Cathedral

219	1988	—	—	—	Proof	25.00

10 ROUBLES

33.3000 g, .900 SILVER, .9636 oz ASW
1980 Olympics
Rev: City view of Moscow.

Y#	Date	Mintage	Fine	VF	XF	Unc
149	1977	.450	—	—	—	18.50
	1977	Inc. Ab.	—	—	Proof	22.50

1980 Olympics
Obv: Similar to Y#149.
Rev: Map of Soviet Union.

150	1977	.450	—	—	—	18.50
	1977	Inc. Ab.	—	—	Proof	22.50

1980 Olympics
Obv: Similar to Y#149.

158.1	1978	.450	—	—	—	18.50
	1978	Inc. Ab.	—	—	Proof	22.50
		Rev: W/o mintmark.				
158.2	1978	*100 pcs.	—	—	—	110.00

1980 Olympics
Obv: Similar to Y#149.

159	1978	.450	—	—	—	18.50
	1978	Inc. Ab.	—	—	Proof	22.50

1980 Olympics
Obv: Similar to Y#149.

160	1978	.450	—	—	—	18.50
	1978	Inc. Ab.	—	—	Proof	22.50

1980 Olympics
Obv: Similar to Y#149.

Y#	Date	Mintage	Fine	VF	XF	Unc
161	1978	.450	—	—	—	18.50
	1978	Inc. Ab.	—	—	Proof	22.50

1980 Olympics
Obv: Similar to Y#149.

Y#	Date	Mintage	Fine	VF	XF	Unc
172	1979	.450	—	—	—	18.50
	1979	Inc. Ab.	—	—	Proof	22.50

1980 Olympics
Obv: Similar to Y#149.

| | 1979 | .450 | — | — | — | 18.50 |
| 168 | 1979 | Inc. Ab. | — | — | Proof | 22.50 |

1980 Olympics
Obv: Similar to Y#149.

| 183 | 1980 | .450 | — | — | — | 18.50 |
| | 1980 | Inc. Ab. | — | — | Proof | 22.50 |

1980 Olympics
Obv: Similar to Y#149.

| 169 | 1979 | .450 | — | — | — | 18.50 |
| | 1979 | Inc. Ab. | — | — | Proof | 22.50 |

1980 Olympics
Obv: Similar to Y#149.

| 184 | 1980 | .450 | — | — | — | 18.50 |
| | 1980 | Inc. Ab. | — | — | Proof | 22.50 |

1980 Olympics
Obv: Similar to Y#149.

| 170 | 1979 | .450 | — | — | — | 18.50 |
| | 1979 | Inc. Ab. | — | — | Proof | 22.50 |

1980 Olympics
Obv: Similar to Y#149.

| 185 | 1980 | .450 | — | — | — | 18.50 |
| | 1980 | Inc. Ab. | — | — | Proof | 22.50 |

25 ROUBLES

1980 Olympics
Obv: Similar to Y#149.

| 171 | 1979 | .450 | — | — | — | 18.50 |
| | 1979 | Inc. Ab. | — | — | Proof | 22.50 |

31.1000 g, .999 PALLADIUM, 1.0000 oz APW
St. Vladimir, Grand Duke of Kiev
Obv: Similar to 10 Roubles, Y#149.

| 212 | 1988 | 7,000 | — | — | — | 225.00 |

50 ROUBLES

7.7800 g, .900 GOLD, .2251 oz AGW
Cathedral of St. Sophia in Novgorod
Obv: Similar to 10 Roubles, Y#149.

Y#	Date	Mintage	Fine	VF	XF	Unc
213	1988	.025	—	—	—	125.00

100 ROUBLES

17.2800 g, .900 GOLD, .500 oz AGW
1980 Olympics

| A163 | 1977 | .130 | — | — | — | 265.00 |
| | 1977 | Inc. Ab. | — | — | Proof | 300.00 |

1980 Olympics

| 151 | 1978 | .130 | — | — | — | 265.00 |
| | 1978 | Inc. Ab. | — | — | Proof | 300.00 |

1980 Olympics

162	1978	.130	—	—	—	265.00
	1978	Inc. Ab.	—	—	Matte	—
	1978	Inc. Ab.	—	—	Proof	300.00

1980 Olympics

| 173 | 1979 | .130 | — | — | — | 265.00 |
| | 1979 | Inc. Ab. | — | — | Proof | 300.00 |

1980 Olympics

| 174 | 1979 | .130 | — | — | — | 265.00 |
| | 1979 | Inc. Ab. | — | — | Proof | 300.00 |

USSR 1708

1980 Olympics

Y#	Date	Mintage	Fine	VF	XF	Unc
186	1980	.130	—	—	—	265.00
	1980	Inc. Ab.			Proof	300.00

15.5500 g, .900 GOLD, .4500 oz AGW
Coin Design of St. Vladimir, 977-1015
Obv: Similar to Y#186.

| 214 | 1988 | .016 | — | — | — | 250.00 |

150 ROUBLES

15.5400 g, .999 PLATINUM, .4991 oz APW
1980 Olympics

| 152 | 1977 | .040 | — | — | — | BV + 10% |
| | 1977 | Inc. Ab. | | | Proof | 375.00 |

1980 Olympics

| 163 | 1978 | .040 | — | — | — | BV + 10% |
| | 1978 | Inc. Ab. | | | Proof | 375.00 |

1980 Olympics

| 175 | 1979 | .040 | — | — | — | BV + 10% |
| | 1979 | Inc. Ab. | | | — | 375.00 |

1980 Olympics

| 176 | 1979 | .040 | — | — | — | 375.00 |
| | 1979 | Inc. Ab. | | | Proof | 375.00 |

1980 Olympics

Y#	Date	Mintage	Fine	VF	XF	Unc
187	1980	.040	—	—	—	BV + 10%
	1980	Inc. Ab.			Proof	375.00

15.5500 g, .999 PLATINUM, .5000 oz APW
Grand Duke Igor Writing Poetry
Obv: Similar to Y#187.

| 215 | 1988 | .016 | — | — | — | 350.00 |

TRADE COINAGE
CHERVONETZ
(10 Roubles)

8.6026 g, .900 GOLD, .2489 oz AGW
Obv: РСФСР below arms.
Mintmaster's initials on edge

85	1923 ПЛ	2.751	130.00	160.00	200.00	250.00
	1923 ПЛ	—	—	—	Proof	1000.
	1975	.250	—	—	—	BV + 10%
	1976 ЛМД	1.000	—	—	—	BV + 10%
	1977 ММД	1.000	—	—	—	BV + 10%
	1977 ЛМД	1.000	—	—	—	BV + 10%
	1978 ММД	.350	—	—	—	BV + 10%
	1979 ММД	1.000	—	—	—	BV + 10%
	1980 ММД	.900	—	—	—	BV + 10%
	1980 ММД	.100	—	—	—	Proof 150.00
	1981	1.000	—	—	—	BV + 10%

Obv: CCCP below arms.

| A86 | 1925 | .600 | — | — | — | Unique |

MINT SETS (MS)

KM#	Date	Mintage	Identification	Issue Price	Mkt. Val.
MS1	1957(4)	—	Y122-125	2.25	30.00
MS2	1961(9)	—	Y126-132,133.1,134.1	4.50	28.00
MS3	1962(7)	—	Y126-132	2.25	4.50
MS4	1964(4)	—	Y126,127,133.2,134.2	2.55	4.00
MS5	1965(9)	—	Y126-132,133.2,134.2	4.50	7.50
MS6	1966(9)	—	Y126-132,133.2,134.2	4.50	7.50
MS7	1967(9)	—	Y126-132,133.2,134.2	4.50	7.50
MS8	1967(5)	—	Y136-140	6.00	10.00
MS9	1968(9)	—	Y126-132, 133a,134a and mint token.	6.00	7.50
MS10	1969(9)	—	Y126-132,133.2,134.2	7.00	7.50
MS11	1970(9)	—	Y126-132,133.2,134.2	11.00	7.50
MS12	1971(9)	—	Y126-132,133.2,134.2	6.00	7.50
MS13	1972(9)	10,000	Y126-132,133.2,134.2	7.00	7.50
MS14	1973(9)	8,000	Y126-132,133.2,134.2	11.00	7.50
MS15	1974(9)	27,500	Y126-132,133.2,134.2, square mint token.	11.00	7.50
MS16	1975(9)	27,500	Y126-132,133.2,134.2	11.00	7.50
MS17	1976(9)	55,000	Y126-132,133.2,134.2	11.00	7.50
MS18	1977(9)	58,750	Y126-132,133.2,134.2	11.00	7.50
MS19	1978(9)	60,000	Y126-132,133.2,134.2	11.00	7.50
MS20	1979(9)	—	Y126-132,133a,134a	19.00	7.50
MS21	1980(9)	—	Y126-132,133a,134a	19.00	7.50
MS22	1983(9)	—	Y126-132,133a,134a	—	7.50
MS23	1984(9)	—	Y126-132,133a,134a	—	7.50
MS24	1985(9)	—	Y126-132,133a,134a	—	7.50
MS25	Mixed date (9)	—	Y135,140-143,188-190	—	10.00
MS26	Mixed date (8)	—	Y135,140-143,188-189	—	6.00
MS27	1988(9)	—	Y126-133,134.2	—	15.00

PROOF SETS (PS)

| PS1 | Mixed date (5) | — | Y152,163,175-176,187 | — | 1650. |

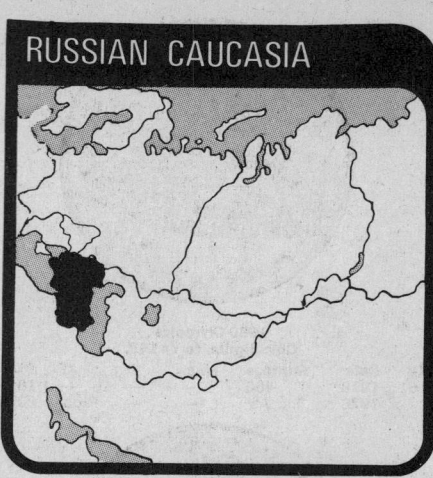

RUSSIAN CAUCASIA

Russian Caucasia, a natural area in Russia located between the Black and Caspian Seas, was a region of mystery and myth to the Ancient Greeks. It was there that Prometheus was bound for the eagle's torment and the Argonauts sought the Golden Fleece. For more than a thousand years Caucasia was the refuge for wave after wave of migrating peoples. Greeks, Romans, Persians, Turks, Huns, Mongols and finally the Russians invaded the treeless steppes and wooded highlands of this range-flanked granite bridge between Europe and Asia. Russian aggression, heroically resisted by the independent mountain races, began early in the 18th century and continued until the last opposition was stifled. The several states of Caucasia made a futile attempt to establish an independent federated republic during the Russian February Revolution of 1917, but were quickly reconquered after the triumph of Bolshevism over the Kerensky administration.

The following areas of Russian Caucasia were coin-issuing entities of interest to numismatics.

ARMAVIR

Armavir is a trading town located in the center of the province of Armavir in northern Russian Caucasia.

LOCAL CURRENCY UNDER THE WHITE RUSSIANS
ROUBLE

COPPER
Reeded edge, thin planchet, monogram below tail.

KM#	Date	Mintage	VG	Fine	VF	XF
1 (Y1)	1918	—	75.00	150.00	250.00	400.00

3 ROUBLES

COPPER
Monogram below tail, reeded edge.

| 2.1 (Y2.1) | 1918 | — | 50.00 | 100.00 | 175.00 | 275.00 |

Monogram below claw.

| 2.2 (Y2.2) | 1918 | — | 50.00 | 100.00 | 175.00 | 275.00 |

5 ROUBLES

COPPER

KM#	Date	Mintage	VG	Fine	VF	XF
3 (Y3)	1918	—	150.00	225.00	400.00	550.00

AZERBAIJAN S.S.R.

During the 18th century, a number of independent Khanates arose in what is now Soviet Azerbaijan. Three of these Khanates struck coins in the 19th century and are listed individually: Karabagh, Sheki and Shemakha. Coins of Iranian Azerbaijan (Maragheh, Tabriz, Khuy, Saujbulagh, Ardabil and Urumi) are of ordinary Iranian type, and are listed under Iran.

A 5 Ruble piece dated 1920 of the Azerbaijan Republic is believed to be a fantasy.

DAGHESTAN A.S.S.R.

Dagestan

Daghestan is a mountainous Autonomous Soviet Socialist Republic bounded on the north by Chechno-Ingush, on the south by Azerbaijan, on the east by the Caspian Sea, and on the west by Georgia. The republic was created in 1921 from the former province of Daghestan.

RULERS
Emir Uzun-Hayir (Uzun-Kheir)
AH1338-1339 / 1919-1920AD

2-1/2 TOMAN

A 2-1/2 Toman coin was reportedly struck, but no specimens are known.

5 TOMAN
BRASS

KM#	Date	Mintage	Fine	VF	XF
2 (Y2)	AH1338	—	—	—	—

10 TOMAN

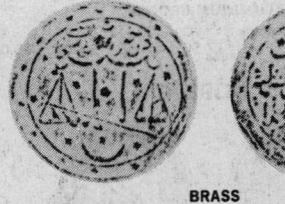 

BRASS
3 (Y3)	AH1338	—	—	—	—

COPPER
Struck over Russia 2 Kopek, Y#10.
4 (Y3a)	AH1338	—	—	—	—

GEORGIAN S.S.R.

The Georgian Soviet Socialist Republic, a former kingdom bounded on the north by the Russian Soviet Federated Socialist Republic, on the south by Armenia and Turkey, on the east by Azerbaijan, and on the west by the Black Sea. After centuries of rule by Turkey or Persia, Georgia became a vassal of Russia in 1783. It came under direct rule in September, 1801. Russia recognized Georgia's independence in 1920, invaded the country in 1921, and made it a direct member of the U.S.S.R. in 1936. Soviet dictator Joseph Stalin was a native son of Georgia.

RUSSIAN ISSUES

Struck under the authority of Alexander I (1801-25) and Nicholas I (1825-55) of Russia at the Tiflis (Tbilisi) Mint.

MINTMASTERS INITIALS
Letter	Date	Name
AT	1810-1831	A. Trifonov
BK	1831-1834	Vasilij Klejmenov

MONETARY SYSTEM
5 Dinars = 1 Puli
2 Puli = 1 Kopek
4 Puli = 1 Bisti
50 Bisti = 1 Abaze

DATING
The dates are shown in a quantitive manner ex. 1000 plus 800 plus 10 plus 9 = 1819.

NOTE: The fine style 1 and 2 Abaze coins of 1828 are patterns, struck at St. Petersburg.

PULI

COPPER
KM#	Date	Mintage	VG	Fine	VF	XF
70 (C81)	1804	4,000	—	—	Rare	—
	1805	Inc. Ab.	50.00	100.00	175.00	275.00
	1806	.015	50.00	100.00	175.00	275.00

2 PULI

COPPER
KM#	Date	Mintage	VG	Fine	VF	XF
71 (C82)	1804	3,000	—	—	Rare	—
	1805	Inc. Ab.	60.00	120.00	200.00	325.00
	1806	.034	30.00	60.00	100.00	150.00
	1808	.012	30.00	60.00	100.00	150.00
	1810	.050	30.00	60.00	100.00	150.00

BISTI

COPPER
KM#	Date	Mintage	VG	Fine	VF	XF
72 (C83)	1804	1,000	—	—	Rare	—
	1805	Inc. Ab.	65.00	125.00	175.00	275.00
	1806	.025	20.00	40.00	80.00	150.00
	1808	.020	20.00	40.00	80.00	150.00
	1810	.315	20.00	40.00	80.00	150.00

1/2 ABAZI

.917 SILVER
KM#	Date	Mintage	VG	Fine	VF	XF
73 (C84)	1804 ПЗ	5,000	—	—	Rare	—
	1805 ПЗ	I.A.	25.00	50.00	100.00	200.00
	1810 AT	398 pcs.	—	—	Rare	—
	1813 AT	2,000	—	—	Rare	—
	1820 AT	4,000	30.00	60.00	110.00	225.00
	1821 AT	Inc. Ab.	25.00	50.00	100.00	200.00
	1822 AK	1,000	25.00	50.00	100.00	200.00
	1823 AK	4,000	25.00	50.00	100.00	200.00
	1824 AK	4,000	25.00	50.00	100.00	200.00
	1826 AT	5,000	25.00	50.00	100.00	200.00
	1827 AT	7,000	25.00	50.00	100.00	200.00
	1828 AT	.016	15.00	30.00	60.00	100.00
	1831 AT	—	25.00	50.00	100.00	225.00
	1832 BK	—	25.00	50.00	100.00	200.00
	1833 BK	—	25.00	50.00	95.00	200.00

ABAZI

SILVER, 19mm
KM#	Date	Mintage	VG	Fine	VF	XF
74 (C85)	1804 ПЗ	—	—	—	Rare	—
	1805 ПЗ	.019	13.50	27.50	40.00	60.00
	1806 ПЗ	.023	12.50	25.00	50.00	75.00
	1806 AK	Inc. Ab.	13.50	27.50	40.00	60.00
	1807 AK	9,000	13.50	27.50	40.00	60.00
	1808 AK	.014	13.50	27.50	40.00	60.00
	1809 AK	.017	13.50	27.50	40.00	60.00
	1810 AT	4,000	25.00	50.00	75.00	110.00
	1811 AT	1,000	—	—	Rare	—
	1812 AT	9,000	12.50	25.00	50.00	75.00
	1813 AT	7,000	12.50	25.00	50.00	75.00
	1814 AT	3,000	13.50	27.50	40.00	60.00
	1815 AT	3,000	20.00	40.00	60.00	90.00
	1816 AT	.012	13.50	27.50	40.00	60.00
	1818 AT	8,000	13.50	27.50	40.00	60.00
	1819 AT	.010	13.50	27.50	40.00	60.00
	1820 AT	.012	13.50	27.50	40.00	60.00
	1821 AT	.014	13.50	27.50	40.00	60.00
(C85)	1822 AT	5,000	15.00	30.00	50.00	75.00
	1822 AK	Inc. Ab.	13.50	27.50	40.00	60.00
	1823 AK	5,000	13.50	27.50	40.00	60.00
	1824 AK	5,000	13.50	27.50	40.00	60.00
	1826 AK	5,000	13.50	27.50	40.00	60.00
	1828 AT	—	—	—	Rare	—
	1830 AT	—	13.50	27.50	40.00	60.00
	1831 AT	—	13.50	27.50	40.00	60.00

2 ABAZI

.917 SILVER, 23mm
KM#	Date	Mintage	VG	Fine	VF	XF
75 (C86)	1804 ПЗ	.033	—	—	Rare	—
	1805 ПЗ Inc. Ab.		15.00	30.00	50.00	75.00
	1806 AK	.042	15.00	30.00	50.00	75.00
	1807 AK	.071	15.00	30.00	50.00	75.00
	1807 AT Inc. Ab.		30.00	60.00	90.00	150.00
	1808 AK	.065	15.00	30.00	50.00	75.00
	1809 AK	.086	15.00	30.00	50.00	75.00
	1810 AK	.020	17.50	35.00	55.00	85.00
	1811 AT	.005	20.00	40.00	60.00	90.00
	1812 AT	.059	15.00	30.00	50.00	75.00
	1813 AT	.048	15.00	30.00	50.00	75.00
	1814 AT	.020	15.00	30.00	50.00	75.00
	1815 AT	.021	15.00	30.00	50.00	75.00
	1816 AT	.079	15.00	30.00	50.00	75.00
	1818 AT	.085	15.00	30.00	50.00	75.00
	1819 AT	.105	15.00	30.00	50.00	75.00
	1820 AT	.112	15.00	30.00	50.00	75.00
	1821 AT	.075	15.00	30.00	50.00	75.00
	1822 AT	.024	22.50	45.00	65.00	100.00
	1822 AK Inc. Ab.		15.00	30.00	50.00	75.00
	1823 AK	.039	15.00	30.00	50.00	75.00
	1824 AK	.032	15.00	30.00	50.00	75.00
	1826 AT	.075	15.00	30.00	50.00	75.00
	1827 AT	.172	15.00	30.00	50.00	75.00
	1828 AT	.126	15.00	30.00	50.00	75.00
	1829 AT	.213	10.00	20.00	35.00	60.00
	1830 AT	.273	10.00	20.00	35.00	60.00
	1831 AT	.338	10.00	20.00	35.00	60.00
	1831 BK Inc. Ab.		10.00	20.00	35.00	60.00
	1832 BK	.210	10.00	20.00	35.00	60.00
	1833 BK	.114	15.00	30.00	50.00	75.00

KARABAGH

Former Khanate in Azerbaijan. Principal Mint in modern town of Shusha (then Panahabad). Broke away from Persia in second half of 1700's. Absorbed by Russia in 1819.

RULERS
Ibrahim Khalil Khan, 1763-1806
Mahdi Quli Khan Muzatfar, 1806-1822

MINTNAME

بناه باد

Panahabad (Shusha)

MONETARY SYSTEM
Derived from the Safavid Persian System

1 Bisti = 20 Dinars
1 Abbasi = 200 Dinars

All coins are anonymous except KM#5, which is in the name of Fath'ali Shah of Iran.

The silver abbasi of Karabagh circulated widely in Iran, where it came to be known as a "Panabadi", a term later used for the half Kran in Iran.

ABBASI

SILVER
In the name of Fath'ali Shah
KM#	Date	Good	VG	Fine	VF
5	AH1216	10.00	20.00	35.00	50.00

Obv: Mintname. Rev: Russian crown and branches.

KM#	Date	Good	VG	Fine	VF
6	AH1222	10.00	20.00	37.50	55.00

Obv: Kalimah. Rev: Mintname and date.

7	AH1221	8.00	15.00	30.00	45.00

Obv: Date and unread Inscription. Rev: Mintname.
(Date sometimes also on reverse.)

8	AH1228-1237	—	10.00	25.00	35.00

NOTE: The above listing of types is incomplete. In addition, more dates of the listed type likely exist.

SCHAMAKHI

Schamakhi is a former khanate located in Azerbaijan. It was under Persian rule throughout much of its history until liberated by the Russians who annexed the khanate in 1813.

RULERS
Persian until annexed to Russia in 1813

MINTNAME

سماخه

Shamakha

شماخ

Shamakhi

MONETARY SYSTEM
20 Dinars = 1 Bisti
10 Bisti = 1 Abbasi

ABBASI
SILVER, 2.00-2.30 g

KM#	Date	Good	VG	Fine	VF
20 (C51)	AH1227-35	15.00	30.00	50.00	75.00

SHEKI

Sheki, a former khanate in Russian Caucasia, was occupied by Russia in 1807 and annexed in 1819.

RULERS
Ja'far Quli Khan, 1806
Ismail Khan, 1815-1819
Annexed to Russia in 1819.

MONETARY SYSTEM
200 Dinars = 1 Abbasi
20 Dinars = 1 Bisti

MINTNAME

نخوي

Nukha

BISTI
COPPER
Obv: Crowned date. Rev: Mint name.

10 (C5)	AH1221	25.00	45.00	80.00	150.00

KM#	Date	Good	VG	Fine	VF
11 (C7)	1223	25.00	45.00	80.00	150.00
	1226	25.00	45.00	80.00	150.00

12 (C10)	AH1228	25.00	45.00	80.00	150.00
	1233	25.00	45.00	80.00	150.00

1/2 ABBASI
SILVER, 1.10-1.20 g

15 (C21)	AH1231-32	25.00	55.00	110.00	175.00

ABBASI

SILVER, 2.10-2.30 g

5 (C22)	AH1218	25.00	55.00	110.00	175.00
16 (C23)	AH1232	25.00	55.00	110.00	175.00

TANNU TUVA

The Tannu-Tuva People's Republic (Tuva), an autonomous part of the Union of Soviet Socialist Republics located in central Asia on the northwest border of Outer Mongolia, has an area of 64,000 sq. mi. (165,760 sq. km.) and a population of about 175,000. Capital: Kyzyl. The economy is based on herding, forestry and mining.

As Urianghi, Tuva was part of Outer Mongolia of the Chinese Empire when tsarist Russia, after fomenting a separatist movement, extended its protection to the mountainous country in 1914. Tuva declared its independence as the Tannu-Tuva People's Republic in 1921 under the auspices of the Tuva People's Revolutionary Party. In 1926, following Russia's successful mediation of the resultant Tuvinian-Mongolian territorial dispute, Tannu—Tuva and Outer Mongolia formally recognized each other's independence. The Tannu-Tuva People's Republic became an autonomous region of the U.S.S.R. on Oct. 13, 1944.

MONETARY SYSTEM
100 Kopejek (Kopeks) = 1 Aksha

KOPEJEK

ALUMINUM-BRONZE

KM#	Date	Mintage	VG	Fine	VF	XF
1 (Y1)	1934	—	17.50	25.00	35.00	60.00

2 KOPEJEK

ALUMINUM-BRONZE

2 (Y2)	1933	—	—	—	—	—
	1934	—	20.00	27.50	40.00	65.00

3 KOPEJEK

ALUMINUM-BRONZE

3 (Y3)	1934	—	17.50	25.00	35.00	60.00

5 KOPEJEK

ALUMINUM-BRONZE

4 (Y4)	1934	—	20.00	27.50	40.00	65.00

10 KOPEJEK

COPPER-NICKEL

KM#	Date	Mintage	VG	Fine	VF	XF
5 (Y5)	1934	—	20.00	27.50	40.00	65.00

15 KOPEJEK

COPPER-NICKEL

| 6 (Y6) | 1934 | — | 20.00 | 27.50 | 40.00 | 65.00 |

20 KOPEJEK

COPPER-NICKEL

| 7 (Y7) | 1934 | — | 20.00 | 27.50 | 40.00 | 65.00 |

RUSSIAN TURKESTAN

Turkestan is the name conventionally used to designate the extensive area of desert plains and low plateaus in Central Asia lying between Siberia on the north, Chinese Sinkiang and Afghanistan on the south, the Caspian Sea on the west, and Mongolia and the Gobi desert on the east. The region was occupied by Turkic nomads as early as the 6th century. They were organized as tribal states for a time and, except for a few oasis cities, were relatively undisturbed by successive invasions by Mongols. Gradually, separate independent Islamic emirates developed around the cities of Bukhara, Khiva and Khoqand. The eastern part of Turkestan, (Chinese Sinkiang) fell to the Chinese Communists in Oct. of 1949. The domination of Russia over most of the Turkic peoples of Asia began late in the 15th century when Ivan III brought the Mongol occupation of Russia to an end. By 1900 the whole of Central Asia to the borders of China, Afghanistan and Persia had come under Russian suzerainty. Western Turkestan was established as an autonomous Soviet Socialist Republic in 1920. J. V. Stalin, then People's Commissar of Nationalities, objected to the formation of a single Turkish nation within the U.S.S.R. and effected the partition of the republic into the Soviet Socialist Republics of Uzbekistan, Turkmenistan, Kazakhstan, Kirghizstan and Tajikistan.

NOTE: The numerals '0' and '5' have variant forms in Russian Turkestan:

0   O   instead of   ◆

5   ʊ   or ʋ   instead of   ᴖ ᴐ

Note that the circle is used for 'zero', not for 'five' in Turkestan.

EMIRATE OF BUKHARA

Bukhara, a city and former emirate in southern Russian Turkestan, formed part (Sogdiana) of the Seleucid empire after the conquest of Alexander the Great and remained an important regional center, sometimes city state, until the 19th century. It became virtually a Russian vassal in 1868 as a consequence of the Czarist invasion of 1866, following which it gradually became a part of Russian Turkestan.

RULERS

Haidar Tora,
  AH1215-1242/1800-1826AD
Nasr Allah,
  AH1242-1277/1826-1860AD
Muzaffar al-Din,
  AH1277-1284/1860-1867AD
Russian Vassal,
  AH1284-1336/1868-1917AD
Independent, AH1336-1338/1917-1920AD

MINTNAME

بخارا

Bukhara

HAIDAR TORA
(Amir Said Mir Haidar)
AH1215-1242/1800-1826AD

FALUS

COPPER
Obv. and rev: Legends.

C#	Date	Good	VG	Fine	VF
48	AH1232	3.00	5.00	10.00	20.00

Obv. and rev: Legend within Greek border.

C#	Date	Good	VG	Fine	VF
51	AH1221	3.50	6.50	12.50	25.00
	1228	3.50	6.50	12.50	25.00
	1229	3.50	6.50	12.50	25.00
	1241	3.50	6.50	12.50	25.00
	1242	3.50	6.50	12.50	25.00

Obv: Fish.

| 52 | AH1241 | — | 7.50 | 15.00 | 30.00 |

2 FALUS

SILVER

C#	Date	VG	Fine	VF	XF
54	AH1227	—	15.00	25.00	50.00
	1228	—	15.00	25.00	50.00

TENGA

SILVER, 2.50-3.00 g

55	AH1216	8.00	15.00	25.00	45.00
	1217	8.00	15.00	25.00	45.00
	1223/1217	9.00	16.50	27.50	50.00
	1226	8.00	15.00	25.00	45.00
	1228/1215	9.00	16.50	27.50	50.00
	1230/1231	9.00	16.50	27.50	50.00
	1231/1216	9.00	16.50	27.50	50.00
	1232/1231	9.00	16.50	27.50	50.00
	1233/1218	9.00	16.50	27.50	50.00
	1234	8.00	15.00	25.00	45.00
	1235	8.00	15.00	25.00	45.00
	1236	8.00	15.00	25.00	45.00

TILLA

GOLD
In his own name
Obv: Teardrop and date. Rev: Circle.

61	AH1215	85.00	110.00	160.00	200.00
	1216	85.00	110.00	160.00	200.00
	1217/1216	95.00	120.00	175.00	225.00
	1218	85.00	110.00	160.00	200.00
	1219	85.00	110.00	160.00	200.00
	1220/1216	95.00	120.00	175.00	225.00

In his own name
Rev: Octagon.

62	AH1221	100.00	150.00	225.00	300.00
	1222	100.00	150.00	225.00	300.00
	1225	100.00	150.00	225.00	300.00
	1226	100.00	150.00	225.00	300.00
	1227	100.00	150.00	225.00	300.00
	1229	100.00	150.00	225.00	300.00

Obv: Teardrop. Rev: Circle.

| 63 (C61.1) | AH1225 | 75.00 | 100.00 | 150.00 | 175.00 |

In the name of Ma'sum Ibn Danyal
Obv: Teardrop border

65	AH1229	85.00	110.00	160.00	200.00
	1230/1229	95.00	120.00	175.00	225.00

Bukhara / RUSSIAN TURKESTAN / USSR

C#	Date	VG	Fine	VF	XF
65	1230	85.00	110.00	160.00	200.00
	1231	85.00	110.00	160.00	200.00
	1233/1033(sic)				
		95.00	120.00	175.00	225.00
	1233/1232				
		95.00	120.00	175.00	225.00
	1234	85.00	110.00	160.00	200.00

65a	AH1233	75.00	100.00	150.00	185.00
	1234	75.00	100.00	150.00	185.00
	1235	75.00	100.00	150.00	185.00
	1236/1235				
		85.00	110.00	165.00	200.00
	1236	75.00	100.00	150.00	185.00
	1239/1240				
		85.00	110.00	175.00	225.00
	1241	75.00	100.00	150.00	185.00

66	AH1236	75.00	100.00	150.00	185.00
(C65a.1)					

HUSSAIN SAYYID
AH1242/1826AD
TENGA
SILVER

70	AH1241/1242	20.00	50.00	75.00	100.00

NASRULLAH
AH1242-1277/1826-1860AD
FALUS
BRASS

71	AH1244	10.00	20.00	35.00	70.00

TENGA
SILVER
Legends of Haidar Tora

72	AH1244	50.00	70.00	100.00	135.00

ANONYMOUS COINAGE
FALUS
COPPER or BRASS

C#	Date	Good	VG	Fine	VF
90	AH1277	5.00	8.50	15.00	22.50
	1281	5.00	8.50	15.00	22.50
	1284	5.00	8.50	15.00	22.50
	1285	5.00	8.50	15.00	22.50

BRONZE or BRASS

Y#	Date	VG	Fine	VF	XF
(Y1)	AH1322	8.50	16.50	25.00	45.00
	1324	8.50	16.50	25.00	45.00

TENGA

SILVER, 3.20 g
In the name of Ma'sum

C#	Date	VG	Fine	VF	XF
75	AH1242	8.50	15.00	30.00	45.00
	1244	8.50	15.00	30.00	45.00
	1245	8.50	15.00	30.00	45.00
	1247	8.50	15.00	30.00	45.00
	1248	8.50	15.00	30.00	45.00
	1249	8.50	15.00	30.00	45.00
	1255	8.50	15.00	30.00	45.00
	1257	8.50	15.00	30.00	45.00
	1258	8.50	15.00	30.00	45.00
	1261	10.00	20.00	40.00	75.00
	1263	8.50	15.00	30.00	45.00
	1265	8.50	15.00	30.00	45.00

C#	Date	VG	Fine	VF	XF
75	1267	8.50	15.00	30.00	45.00
	1269	8.50	15.00	30.00	45.00
	1271	8.50	15.00	30.00	45.00
	1273	8.50	15.00	30.00	45.00
	1275	8.50	15.00	30.00	45.00
	1276	8.50	15.00	30.00	45.00
	1277	8.50	15.00	30.00	45.00

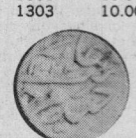 

(C91)	AH1278	10.00	16.50	25.00	40.00
	1279	10.00	16.50	25.00	40.00
	1281	10.00	16.50	25.00	40.00
	1282	10.00	16.50	25.00	40.00
	1283	10.00	16.50	25.00	40.00
	1284	10.00	16.50	25.00	40.00
	1285	10.00	16.50	25.00	40.00
	1293/1283				
		20.00	30.00	45.00	60.00
	1293/1284				
		20.00	30.00	45.00	60.00
	1293	10.00	16.50	25.00	40.00
	1294/1293				
		20.00	30.00	45.00	60.00
	1294/1296				
		20.00	30.00	45.00	60.00
	1294	10.00	16.50	25.00	40.00
	1295	10.00	16.50	25.00	40.00
	1296	10.00	16.50	25.00	40.00
	1297/1298				
		20.00	30.00	45.00	60.00
	1297	10.00	16.50	25.00	40.00
	1298	10.00	16.50	25.00	40.00
	1299/1298				
		20.00	30.00	45.00	60.00
	1299	10.00	16.50	25.00	40.00
	1300	10.00	16.50	25.00	40.00
	1301/1299				
		20.00	30.00	45.00	60.00
	1301	10.00	16.50	25.00	40.00
	1303	10.00	16.50	25.00	40.00

Thin and thick flan

Y#	Date	VG	Fine	VF	XF
(Y2)	1304	7.50	12.50	20.00	30.00
	1305/1304				
		10.00	16.50	27.50	40.00
	1305	7.50	12.50	20.00	30.00
	1306/1305				
		10.00	16.50	27.50	40.00
	1306/1307				
		10.00	16.50	27.50	40.00
	1306/1308				
		10.00	16.50	27.50	40.00
	1306	7.50	12.50	20.00	30.00
	1307	7.50	12.50	20.00	30.00
	1308/1309				
		10.00	16.50	27.50	40.00
	1308	7.50	12.50	20.00	30.00
	1309/1310				
		10.00	16.50	27.50	40.00
	1309	7.50	12.50	20.00	30.00
	1310/1315				
		10.00	16.50	27.50	40.00
	1310	7.50	12.50	20.00	30.00
	1311	7.50	12.50	20.00	30.00
	1315	7.50	12.50	20.00	30.00
	1316	7.50	12.50	20.00	30.00
	1319	7.50	12.50	20.00	30.00
	1320	7.50	12.50	20.00	30.00
	1322	7.50	12.50	20.00	30.00
	1323/1322				
		10.00	16.50	27.50	40.00
	1323	7.50	12.50	20.00	30.00

TILLA

GOLD

C#	Date	VG	Fine	VF	XF
85	AH1243/1242				
		85.00	110.00	165.00	200.00
	1243	75.00	100.00	150.00	185.00
	1244/1245				
		85.00	110.00	165.00	200.00
	1244	75.00	100.00	150.00	185.00
	1246	75.00	100.00	150.00	185.00
	1247/1244				
		85.00	110.00	165.00	200.00

C#	Date	VG	Fine	VF	XF
85	1248	75.00	100.00	150.00	185.00
	1254	75.00	100.00	150.00	185.00
	1255/1254				
		85.00	110.00	165.00	200.00
	1255	75.00	100.00	150.00	185.00
	1256/1254				
		85.00	110.00	165.00	200.00
	1256/1255				
		85.00	110.00	165.00	200.00
	1256	75.00	100.00	150.00	185.00
	1257/1258				
		85.00	110.00	165.00	200.00
	1257	75.00	100.00	150.00	185.00
	1264	75.00	100.00	150.00	185.00
	1265/1266				
		85.00	110.00	165.00	200.00
	1272/1275				
		85.00	110.00	165.00	200.00
	1273/1243				
		85.00	110.00	165.00	200.00
	1273	75.00	100.00	150.00	185.00

NOTE: The following date combinations for the above coin are reported: Obv: 1247-rev: 1246, Obv: 1257-rev: 1261, obv: 1273-rev: 1274 and obv: 1273-rev: 1275.

(C95)	AH1278	70.00	90.00	115.00	150.00
	1279	70.00	90.00	115.00	150.00
	1283	70.00	90.00	115.00	150.00
	1284	70.00	90.00	115.00	150.00
	1285	70.00	90.00	115.00	150.00
	1289	70.00	90.00	115.00	150.00
	1291	60.00	85.00	115.00	150.00
	1294	60.00	85.00	115.00	150.00
	1296/1300				
		75.00	100.00	125.00	175.00
	1296	60.00	85.00	115.00	150.00
	1297	60.00	85.00	115.00	150.00
	1299	60.00	85.00	115.00	150.00

NOTE: The date combination of obv: 1279 and rev: 1285 is reported for the above coin.

Y#	Date	VG	Fine	VF	XF
(Y3)	AH1303	75.00	100.00	125.00	165.00
	1306	75.00	100.00	125.00	165.00
	1309	75.00	100.00	125.00	165.00
	1315	75.00	100.00	125.00	165.00
	1316	75.00	100.00	125.00	165.00
	1319	75.00	100.00	125.00	165.00
	1325	75.00	100.00	125.00	165.00
	1327	75.00	100.00	125.00	165.00
	1328	75.00	100.00	125.00	165.00
	1329	75.00	100.00	125.00	165.00

ALIM IBN SAYYID MIR AMIN
AH1329-1338/1911-1920AD
Independent after AH1336/1917AD
FALUS

COPPER
Rev: "2" or "4" in circle.

4	AH1332	5.00	8.50	15.00	22.50
	1334	7.50	12.00	—	25.00

Date range 1331-36 reported, but unconfirmed.

Rev: 32 in a circle

4.1	AH1322	5.00	8.50	15.00	30.00
	1323	5.00	8.50	15.00	30.00
	1324	5.00	8.50	15.00	30.00
	1326	5.00	8.50	15.00	30.00
	1329	5.00	8.50	15.00	30.00
	1330	5.00	8.50	15.00	30.00
	1331	5.00	8.50	15.00	30.00
	1332	5.00	8.50	15.00	30.00
	1333	5.00	8.50	15.00	30.00
	1335	5.00	8.50	15.00	30.00
	(13)36	15.00	25.00	40.00	60.00

4 FALUS

COPPER

Y#	Date	VG	Fine	VF	XF
5	AH1334	8.00	12.50	20.00	35.00
	1335	8.00	12.50	20.00	35.00

8 FALUS

COPPER

A5	AH1335	8.00	12.50	20.00	35.00

TENGA

BRONZE

6	AH1336	15.00	25.00	37.50	65.00

6a	AH1336	15.00	25.00	35.00	60.00
	1337	15.00	25.00	35.00	60.00

2 TENGA

BRONZE or BRASS

7	AH1336	15.00	25.00	35.00	55.00
	1337	15.00	25.00	35.00	55.00

7.1	AH1336	20.00	30.00	50.00	75.00
	1337	20.00	30.00	50.00	75.00

3 TENGA

BRONZE or BRASS

8	AH1336	15.00	25.00	35.00	50.00
	1337	15.00	25.00	35.00	50.00

4 TENGA

BRONZE or BRASS

9	AH1336	25.00	45.00	65.00	90.00

5 TENGA

BRONZE or BRASS

Y#	Date	VG	Fine	VF	XF
10	AH1336	22.50	35.00	50.00	75.00
	1337	22.50	35.00	50.00	75.00

10 TENGA

BRONZE or BRASS

11	AH1337	10.00	17.50	30.00	50.00
	1338/1337	10.00	17.50	30.00	50.00

20 TENGA

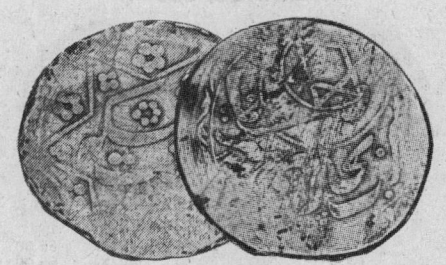

BRONZE or BRASS

12	AH1336	22.50	35.00	50.00	75.00
	1337	22.50	35.00	50.00	75.00

KHANATE OF KHIVA

Khiva, a present town once a great kingdom under the names of Chorasmia, Khwarezm and Urgenj, is located in Russian Turkestan east of the Caspian Sea and south of the Aral Sea. Russia established relations with Khiva in the 17th century, occupied it in 1873, and annexed it in 1875. In AH1338/1920AD it became Khwarezm Soviet People's Republic.

RULERS

Muhammad Rahim
  AH122x-1241/1825AD
Allah Quli
  AH1241-1258/1825-1842AD
Muhammad Amin
  AH1261-1271/1845-1855AD
Sayyid Muhammad Khan
  AH1272-1282/1856/1865AD
Sayyid Muhammad Rahim
  AH1282-1289/1865-1872AD
Russian
  AH1290-1337/1873-1918AD
Sayyid Abdullah Khan and Junaid Khan
  AH1337-1338/1918-1920AD

MINTNAME

خوارزم

Khwarezm

MUHAMMAD RAHIM
AH122x-1241/1825AD

TENGA

SILVER

C#	Date	VG	Fine	VF	XF
40	AH1232	12.50	25.00	40.00	75.00
	1235	12.50	25.00	40.00	75.00

ALLAH QULI
AH1241-1258/1825-1842AD

TENGA

SILVER

C#	Date	VG	Fine	VF	XF
50	AH1247	12.50	25.00	40.00	75.00
	1248	12.50	25.00	40.00	75.00
	1258	12.50	25.00	40.00	75.00

NOTE: Varieties exist.

MUHAMMAD AMIN
AH1261-1271/1845-1855AD

TENGA

SILVER

60	AH1262	12.50	25.00	40.00	75.00
	1263	12.50	25.00	40.00	75.00
	1264	12.50	25.00	40.00	75.00
	1265	12.50	25.00	40.00	75.00
	1266	12.50	25.00	40.00	75.00
	1267	12.50	25.00	40.00	75.00
	1268	12.50	25.00	40.00	75.00
	1269	12.50	25.00	40.00	75.00

1/2 TILLA

GOLD

65	AH1261	100.00	175.00	250.00	400.00
	1265	100.00	175.00	250.00	400.00
	1271	100.00	175.00	250.00	400.00

SAYYID MUHAMMAD KHAN
AH1272-1282/1856-1865AD

FALUS

COPPER

Y#	Date	VG	Fine	VF	XF
1	AH1272	20.00	35.00	50.00	75.00
	1274	20.00	35.00	50.00	75.00
	1275	20.00	35.00	50.00	75.00
	1277	20.00	35.00	50.00	75.00
	1278	20.00	35.00	50.00	75.00
	1279	20.00	35.00	50.00	75.00
	1280	20.00	35.00	50.00	75.00

TENGA

SILVER
Type I - Obv: Date in center. Rev: Ornamented.

2	AH1273	10.00	25.00	45.00	75.00
	1274	10.00	25.00	45.00	75.00
	1275	10.00	25.00	45.00	75.00
	1276	10.00	25.00	45.00	75.00
	1277	10.00	25.00	45.00	75.00
	1278	10.00	25.00	45.00	75.00
	1279	10.00	25.00	45.00	75.00
	1280	10.00	25.00	45.00	75.00
	1281	10.00	25.00	45.00	75.00

Type II - Plain posthumous issue.

2.1	AH1282	8.00	20.00	30.00	45.00
	1283	8.00	20.00	30.00	45.00
	1284/1283				
		10.00	26.50	40.00	60.00
	1284	8.00	20.00	30.00	45.00
	1285	8.00	20.00	30.00	45.00
	1287	8.00	20.00	30.00	45.00
	1288	8.00	20.00	30.00	45.00

Khiva

TILLA

GOLD

Y#	Date	VG	Fine	VF	XF
A3	AH1276			—	—
	1277			—	—

SAYYID MUHAMMAD RAHIM
AH1282-1289/1865-1872AD

FALUS

COPPER

3	AH1286	12.50	25.00	50.00	75.00
	1290	12.50	25.00	50.00	75.00
	1308	12.50	25.00	50.00	75.00
	1310	12.50	25.00	50.00	75.00
	1311	12.50	25.00	50.00	75.00

TENGA

SILVER

6	AH1287	10.00	21.50	42.50	70.00
	1294	10.00	21.50	42.50	70.00
	1301	10.00	21.50	42.50	70.00
	1303	10.00	21.50	42.50	70.00
	1305	10.00	21.50	42.50	70.00
	1306	10.00	21.50	42.50	70.00
	1307	10.00	21.50	42.50	70.00
	1308	10.00	21.50	42.50	70.00
	1311	10.00	21.50	42.50	70.00
	1312	10.00	21.50	42.50	70.00

2-1/2 TENGA

COPPER, 26mm

4	AH1303	13.50	25.00	32.50	—

5 TENGA

COPPER, 30mm

5	AH1303	13.50	30.00	37.50	—

TILLA

GOLD

7	AH1277	100.00	150.00	250.00	400.00

SAYYID ABDULLAH KHAN and JUNAID KHAN
AH1337-1338/1918-1920AD

TENGA

SILVER

8	AH1337	—	—	Rare	—

2-1/2 TENGA

COPPER

9	AH1337	27.50	37.50	50.00	90.00

5 TENGA

COPPER
Obv: Sun w/13 rays, date below line.
Rev: Leg. in small circle.

Y#	Date	VG	Fine	VF	XF
10	AH1337	37.50	52.50	70.00	110.00

NOTE: Many die varieties exist.

KHWAREZM SOVIET PEOPLE'S REPUELIC
AH1338-1343/1920-1924AD

20 ROUBLES

BRONZE or BRASS

1	AH1338	22.50	30.00	40.00	65.00
	1339	20.00	30.00	40.00	65.00
	1340	20.00	30.00	40.00	65.00

25 ROUBLES

BRONZE or BRASS

2	AH1339	17.50	30.00	40.00	65.00

Obv: 12 rayed sunburst.

2.1	AH1339	17.50	30.00	40.00	65.00

100 ROUBLES

BRONZE or BRASS

3	AH1339	17.50	25.00	32.50	55.00

500 ROUBLES

BRONZE or BRASS

4	AH1339	50.00	75.00	200.00	275.00

4a	AH1339	20.00	30.00	40.00	65.00
	1340	20.00	30.00	40.00	65.00

KHOQAND

Khoqand, a town and former khanate in eastern Turkestan, was a powerful state in the 18th century. Russian superiority in the area was recognized following the holy war of 1875 and was annexed in 1875. It regained its independence briefly during 1918-1920 and became a Soviet People's Republic briefly between 1920-1924, and finally was absorbed into Uzbekistan S.S.R.

RULERS
Muhammad Ali Khan
 AH1238-1256/1822-1840AD
Sher Ali
 AH1258-1261/1842-1845AD
Muhammad Khudayar Khan
 AH1261-1275/1845-1858AD
Muhammad Fuland, Rebel
 AH1275-1290/1858-1873AD
Malla Khan
 AH1275-1275/1858-1862AD
Shah Murad
 AH1278-1279/1862AD
Muhammad Khudayar Khan
 AH1279-1280/1862-1863AD
Sayyid Sultan
 AH1280-1282/1863-1864AD
Muhammad Khudayer Khan
 AH1282-1292/1865-1875AD
 Independent until AH1283/1866AD
 Russian Vassal AH1283-1293/
  1866-1876AD
Nasir al-Din
 AH1292-1293/1875-1876AD
Annexed To Russia, 1875-1876AD

MINTNAMES
Until AH1257, the coinage of Khoqand was struck at two mints.

Fa - Fergana فرغانة

Kd - Khoqand خوقند

MUHAMMAD ALI KAHN
AH1238-1256/1822-1840AD

PUL

COPPER

C#	Date	VG	Fine	VF	XF
60	AH1249 (Kd)	6.00	12.50	20.00	35.00

63	AH1252(Fa)	15.00	35.00	50.00	70.00

TENGA

SILVER

65	AH1241	10.00	22.50	37.50	55.00
	1243	10.00	22.50	37.50	55.00
	1244	10.00	22.50	37.50	55.00

A66	ND(Kd)	—	—	—	—

Obv: Teardrop border. Rev: Hexagon.

66	AH1245	15.00	25.00	40.00	65.00

TILLA

GOLD

67	AH1247(Fa)				

C#	Date	VG	Fine	VF	XF
68	AH1252	75.00	100.00	150.00	250.00
	1254	75.00	100.00	150.00	250.00
	1255	75.00	100.00	150.00	250.00
	1256	75.00	100.00	150.00	250.00
	1257	75.00	100.00	150.00	250.00

SHER ALI
AH1258-1261/1842-1845AD
FALUS
COPPER

| — | AH1259 | — | — | — | — |

TILLA
GOLD

78	AH1259/1258	100.00	125.00	150.00	225.00
	1259	80.00	100.00	135.00	175.00
	1260	80.00	100.00	135.00	175.00

MUHAMMAD KHUDAYAR KHAN
2nd Reign
AH1261-1275/1845-1858AD
PUL
COPPER

| 87 | AH 1265 | 8.00 | 14.00 | 23.50 | 35.00 |
| | 1269 | 8.00 | 14.00 | 23.50 | 35.00 |

TENGA

SILVER

95	AH1266/1268	31.50	50.00	75.00	100.00
	1266	25.00	40.00	60.00	80.00
	1269	25.00	40.00	60.00	80.00
	1270	25.00	40.00	60.00	80.00
	1271	25.00	40.00	60.00	80.00
	1272	25.00	40.00	60.00	80.00
	1273	25.00	40.00	60.00	80.00
	1274	25.00	40.00	60.00	80.00
	1275	25.00	40.00	60.00	80.00

TILLA

GOLD

100	AH1260	75.00	100.00	150.00	250.00
	1261/1264	95.00	125.00	190.00	325.00
	1261	75.00	100.00	150.00	250.00
	1262/1261	95.00	125.00	190.00	325.00
	1263	75.00	100.00	150.00	250.00
	1264	75.00	100.00	150.00	250.00
	1265	75.00	100.00	150.00	250.00
	1266	75.00	100.00	150.00	250.00
	1270	75.00	100.00	150.00	250.00
	1272	75.00	100.00	150.00	250.00
	1273	75.00	100.00	150.00	250.00
	1274	75.00	100.00	150.00	250.00
	1275	75.00	100.00	150.00	250.00

| 100.5 | AH1261/1262 | — | — | — | — |

MUHAMMAD FULAD
Rebel
AH1275-1290/1858-1873AD

TENGA

SILVER

C#	Date	VG	Fine	VF	XF
105	AH1292	15.00	25.00	40.00	60.00
	1293	15.00	25.00	40.00	60.00

TILLA

GOLD

| 110 | AH1275-90 | 70.00 | 85.00 | 100.00 | 125.00 |

MALLA KHAN
AH1275-1278/1858-1862AD
PUL

COPPER, square

| 112 | AH1277 | 10.00 | 20.00 | 32.50 | 60.00 |

TENGA

SILVER

115	AH1275	27.50	55.00	70.00	85.00
	1276	27.50	55.00	70.00	85.00
	1277	27.50	55.00	70.00	85.00

TILLA

GOLD

118	AH1275	125.00	175.00	225.00	300.00
	1276	125.00	175.00	225.00	300.00
	1277	125.00	175.00	225.00	300.00
	1278	125.00	175.00	225.00	300.00

SHAH MURAD
AH1278-1279/1862AD
TILLA

GOLD

| 128 | AH1278 | 100.00 | 125.00 | 150.00 | 175.00 |

MUHAMMAD KHUDAYAR KHAN
3rd Reign
AH1279-1280/1862-1863AD
TENGA

SILVER
Obv. & rev: Teardrop borders.

C#	Date	VG	Fine	VF	XF
130	AH1279	30.00	60.00	100.00	150.00

TILLA
GOLD

| 135 | Dates unknown | 75.00 | 95.00 | 115.00 | 125.00 |

SAYYID SULTAN
AH1280-1282/1863-1865AD
TENGA

SILVER

140	AH1280	42.50	75.00	125.00	175.00
	1281	42.50	75.00	125.00	175.00
	1285	42.50	75.00	125.00	175.00

TILLA

GOLD

| 145 | AH1280 | 100.00 | 115.00 | 140.00 | 165.00 |
| | 1281 | 100.00 | 115.00 | 140.00 | 165.00 |

MUHAMMAD KHUDAYAR KHAN
4th Reign
AH1282-1292/1865-1875AD
PUL

COPPER

| 148 | AH1287 | 6.00 | 13.50 | 26.50 | 37.50 |

TENGA

SILVER

151	AH1282	25.00	40.00	60.00	80.00
	1283	25.00	40.00	60.00	80.00
	1284	25.00	40.00	60.00	80.00
	1285	25.00	40.00	60.00	80.00
	1286	25.00	40.00	60.00	80.00
	1287	25.00	40.00	60.00	80.00
	1289	25.00	40.00	60.00	80.00
	1291	25.00	40.00	60.00	80.00
	1292	25.00	40.00	60.00	80.00

TILLA

GOLD

155	AH1282	70.00	80.00	100.00	140.00
	1283	70.00	80.00	100.00	140.00
	1285	70.00	80.00	100.00	140.00

NASIR AL DIN
AH1292-1293/1875-1875AD
TILLA
GOLD

| 165 | AH1292 | — | Reported, not confirmed |

UNITED ARAB EMIRATES

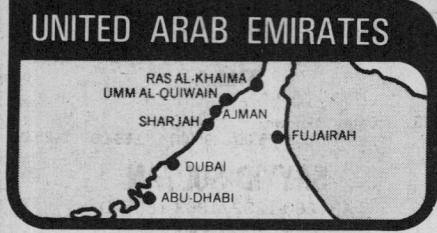

Five of the former Trucial States which comprise The United Arab Emirates, and which were formerly British treaty protectorates located along the southern shore of the Arabian Peninsula, have issued Non-Circulating Legal Tender Coins (NCLT). They are Ajman, Fujairah, Ras Al Khaimah, Sharjah and Umm Al-Quiwain. These coins have been declared legal tender by the issuing states but are not intended to circulate. No circulation strikes were minted, and none of the coins were available at face value.

AJMAN

Ajman is the smallest and poorest of the emirates in the United Arab Emirates. It has an estimated area of 100 sq. mi. (250 sq. km.) and a population of 6,000. Ajman's first act as an autonomous entity was a treaty with Great Britain in 1820. On December 2, 1971 Ajman became one of the six original members of the United Arab Emirates.

TITLES

Ajman اجمان

RULERS

Rashid III, 1928—

MONETARY SYSTEM

100 Dirhams = 1 Ryal

RIYAL

3.9500 g, .640 SILVER, .0812 oz ASW
Rev: 2 dates.

KM#	Date	Year	Mintage	VF	XF	Unc
1.1	AH1389	1969	.020	—	—	5.00

Rev: 3 dates.
| 1.2 | AH1390 | 1970 | — | — | — | 20.00 |

2 RIYALS

6.4500 g, .835 SILVER, .1731 oz ASW
Rev: 2 dates.
| 2.1 | AH1389 | 1969 | .020 | — | — | 10.00 |

Rev: 3 dates.
| 2.2 | AH1390 | 1970 | — | — | — | 30.00 |

5 RIYALS

15.0000 g, .835 SILVER, .4027 oz ASW
Rev: 2 dates.
| 3.1 | AH1389 | 1969 | .010 | — | — | 17.50 |

Rev: 3 dates.
| 3.2 | AH1390 | 1970 | — | — | — | 50.00 |

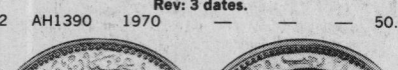

15.0000 g, .925 SILVER, .4460 oz ASW
Gamal Abdel Nassar
| 12 | AH1390 | 1970 | 5,000 | — | Proof | 17.50 |

Rev: Dag Hammarskjold
| 17 | ND | (1970) | 1,175 | — | Proof | 50.00 |

Rev: Mahatma Gandhi
| 18 | ND | (1970) | 1,175 | — | Proof | 50.00 |

Rev: Martin Luther King
KM#	Date	Year	Mintage	VF	XF	Unc
19	ND	(1970)	1,175	—	Proof	50.00

Rev: George C. Marshall
| 20 | ND | (1970) | 1,175 | — | Proof | 50.00 |

Rev: Bertrand A. Russell
| 21 | ND | (1970) | 1,175 | — | Proof | 50.00 |

Rev: Albert Schweitzer
| 22 | ND | (1970) | 1,175 | — | Proof | 50.00 |

Rev: Jan Palac
| 23 | ND | (1970) | 1,175 | — | Proof | 50.00 |

Rev: Albert J. Luthuli
| 24 | ND | (1970) | 1,175 | — | Proof | 50.00 |

F.A.O. Issue
| 26 | AH1390 | 1970 | 2,000 | — | Proof | 40.00 |

NOTE: This issue is not recognized by the FAO.

Save Venice
| 27 | ND | (1971) | 4,800 | — | Proof | 30.00 |

7-1/2 RIYALS

23.0000 g, .925 SILVER, .6840 oz ASW
Obv: Bonefish
| 5 | AH1389 | 1970 | 4,350 | — | — | 30.00 |
| | 1389 | 1970 | 650 pcs. | — | Proof | 70.00 |

Obv: Berber Falcon
KM#	Date	Year	Mintage	VF	XF	Unc
6	AH1389	1970	4,350	—	—	30.00
	1389	1970	650 pcs.	—	Proof	70.00

Obv: Gazelle
Rev: Similar to KM#6.
| 7 | AH1389 | 1970 | 4,350 | — | — | 30.00 |
| | 1389 | 1970 | 650 pcs. | — | Proof | 70.00 |

23.0000 g, .835 SILVER, .6175 oz ASW
Rev: Gamal Abdel Nassar
| 13 | AH1390 | 1970 | 6,000 | — | Proof | 27.50 |

10 RIYALS

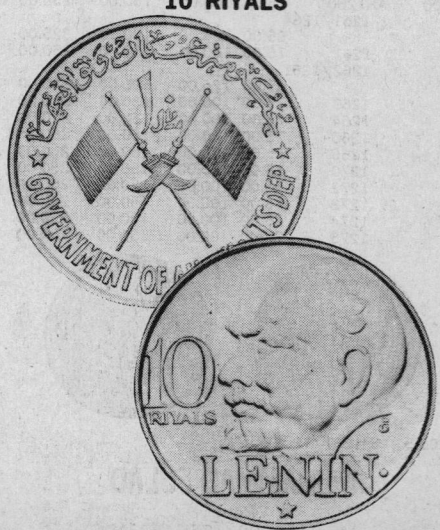

29.9000 g, .925 SILVER, .8892 oz ASW

KM#	Date	Year	Mintage	VF	XF	Unc
9.1	ND	(1970)	—	—	—	50.00

Obv: PROOF added.

| 9.2 | ND | (1970) | 3,200 | — | Proof | 40.00 |

25 RIYALS

5.1750 g, .900 GOLD, .1497 oz AGW
Rev: Gamal Abdel Nassar

| 15 | AH1390 | 1970 | 1,100 | — | Proof | 150.00 |

NOTE: Some of these coins have a serial number on the obverse below the bust.

Rev: Dag Hammarskjold
| 28 | ND | (1970) | — | — | Proof | 150.00 |

Rev: Mahatma Gandhi
| 29 | ND | (1970) | — | — | Proof | 150.00 |

Rev: Martin Luther King
| 30 | ND | (1970) | — | — | Proof | 150.00 |

Rev: George C. Marshall
| 31 | ND | (1970) | — | — | Proof | 150.00 |

Rev: Bertrand A. Russell
| 32 | ND | (1970) | — | — | Proof | 150.00 |

Rev: Albert Schweitzer
| 33 | ND | (1970) | — | — | Proof | 150.00 |

Rev: Jan Palac
| 34 | ND | (1970) | — | — | Proof | 150.00 |

Rev: Albert J. Luthuli
| 35 | ND | (1970) | — | — | Proof | 150.00 |

Rev. leg: Save Venice.
| 36 | ND | (1971) | — | — | Proof | 150.00 |

50 RIYALS

10.3500 g, .900 GOLD, .2995 oz AGW
Similar to 7.5 Riyals, KM#13.
| 16 | AH1390 | 1970 | 700 pcs. | — | Proof | 225.00 |

NOTE: Some of these coins have a serial number below the bust on the obverse.

Rev. leg: Save Venice.
| 39 | ND | (1971) | — | — | Proof | 225.00 |

75 RIYALS

15.5300 g, .900 GOLD, .4494 oz AGW
Obv: Fish
| 41 | AH1389 | 1970 | — | — | Proof | 300.00 |

100 RIYALS

20.7000 g, .900 GOLD, .5990 oz AGW
Rev: Nikolai Lenin
| 10 | ND | (1970) | 1,000 | — | Proof | 375.00 |

Rev. leg: Save Venice.
| 40 | ND | (1971) | — | — | Proof | 375.00 |

MINT SETS (MS)

KM#	Date	Mintage	Identification	Issue Price	Mkt. Val.
MS1	1969(3)	1,200	KM1-3	11.22	32.50
MS2	1970(3)	4,350	KM5-7	—	90.00

PROOF SETS (PS)

PS1	1970(8)	1,175	KM17-24	—	400.00
PS2	1970(8)	—	KM28-35	—	1200.
PS3	1970(4)	—	KM12,13,15,16	—	420.00
PS5	1970(3)	650	KM5-7	75.00	210.00
PS8	1970(2)	5,000	KM12,13	9.50	45.00
PS9	1970(3)	—	KM12,13,15	—	200.00
PS10	1971(4)	—	KM27,36,39,40	—	780.00

FUJAIRAH

Fujairah is the only emirate of the United Arab Emirates that does not have territory on the Persian Gulf. It is on the eastern side of the "horn" of Oman. It has an estimated area of 450 sq. mi. (1200 sq. km.) and a population of 27,000. Fujairah has been, historically a frequent rival of Sharjah. As recently as 1952 Great Britain recognized Fujairah as an autonomous state. An original member of the United Arab Emirates.

TITLES

الفجيره

Al-Fujairah

RULERS
Mohammad, 1952-74
Hamad, 1974-

RIYAL

3.0000 g, .999 SILVER, .0963 oz ASW
Obv: Arms.

KM#	Date	Year	Mintage	VF	XF	Unc
1	AH1388	1969	4,050	—	Proof	10.00
	1389	1970	Inc. Ab.	—	Proof	10.00

2 RIYALS

6.0000 g, .999 SILVER, .1926 oz ASW
| 2 | AH1388 | 1969 | 6,250 | — | Proof | 27.50 |
| | 1389 | 1970 | Inc. Ab. | — | Proof | 27.50 |

5 RIYALS

15.0000 g, .999 SILVER, .4818 oz ASW
Obv: Arms.
| 3 | AH1388 | 1969 | 6,450 | — | Proof | 45.00 |
| | 1389 | 1970 | Inc. Ab. | — | Proof | 45.00 |

10 RIYALS

30.0000 g, .999 SILVER, .9636 oz ASW
| 4 | AH1388 | 1969 | 6,050 | — | Proof | 50.00 |
| | 1389 | 1970 | 500 pcs. | — | Proof | 50.00 |

Obv: Similar to KM#4.
KM#	Date	Year	Mintage	VF	XF	Unc
5	AH1388	1969	6,250	—	Proof	50.00
	1389	1970	500 pcs.	—	Proof	50.00

Obv: Similar to KM#4.
| 19 | AH1389 | 1970 | 3,000 | — | Proof | 50.00 |

Obv: Similar to KM#4.
| 20 | AH1389 | 1970 | 300 pcs. | — | Proof | 50.00 |

Obv: Similar to KM#4.
| 21 | AH1389 | 1970 | 300 pcs. | — | Proof | 50.00 |

Obv: Similar to KM#4.
| 22 | AH1389 | 1971 | 400 pcs. | — | Proof | 50.00 |

Fujairah / UNITED ARAB EMIRATES 1718

25 RIYALS

5.1800 g, .900 GOLD, .1499 oz AGW

KM#	Date	Year	Mintage	VF	XF	Unc
7	AH1388	1969	3,280	—	Proof	110.00
	1389	1970	Inc. Ab.	—	Proof	110.00

NOTE: The 1969 issue has the fineness incuse, the 1970 issue has the fineness both raised and incuse.

50 RIYALS

10.3600 g, .900 GOLD, .2998 oz AGW
Obv: Similar to 25 Riyals, KM#7.
Rev: Similar to 5 Riyals, KM#3.

8	AH1388	1969	2,230	—	Proof	225.00
	1389	1970	Inc. Ab.	—	Proof	225.00

100 RIYALS

20.7300 g, .900 GOLD, .5999 oz AGW
Obv: Similar to KM#24.
Rev: Similar to 10 Riyals, KM#4.

9	AH1388	1969	2,140	—	Proof	375.00

Similar to 10 Riyals, KM#5.

10	AH1388	1969	3,040	—	Proof	375.00
	1389	1970	—	—	Proof	375.00

Obv: Similar to KM#24.
Rev: Similar to 10 Riyals, KM#19.

23	AH1389	1970	600 pcs.	—	Proof	400.00

24	AH1389	1970	290 pcs.	—	Proof	500.00

Obv: Similar to KM#24.
Rev: Similar to 10 Riyals, KM#21.

26	AH1389	1970	250 pcs.	—	Proof	500.00

Obv: Similar to KM#24.
Rev: Similar to 10 Riyals, KM#22.

25	AH1389	1971	550 pcs.	—	Proof	400.00

200 RIYALS

41.4600 g, .900 GOLD, 1.1998 oz AGW
Obv: Arms.

11	AH1388	1969	680 pcs.	—	Proof	725.00

NOTE: The above pieces are serially numbered on the obverse.

PROOF SETS (PS)

KM#	Date	Mintage	Identification	Issue Price	Mkt. Val.
PS1	Mixed 1969-71 (18)	—	—	—	—
PS2	Mixed 1969-71 (9)	—	KM1-5,19-22	—	385.00
PS3	Mixed 1969-71 (8)	—	KM4,5,19,22,9,10,23,25	—	1750.
PS4	1969(8)	—	KM1-4,7-9,11	—	1570.
PS5	1969(5)	2,550	KM1-5	40.00	185.00
PS6	1969(5)	5,000	KM7-11	280.00	1810.
PS7	1969(4)	—	KM1-4	—	135.00
PS8	1970(5)	200	KM1-5	40.00	185.00

RAS AL KHAIMA

Ras Al Khaima is only one of the coin issuing emirates that was not one of the original members of the United Arab Emirates. It was a part of Sharjah. It has an estimated area of 650 sq. mi. (1700 sq. km.) and a population of 30,000. Ras Al Khaima is the only member of the United Arab Emirates that has agriculture as its principal industry.

TITLES

Ras Al Khaima   راس الخيمه

RULERS

Saqr, 1948—

MONETARY SYSTEM

100 Dirhams = 1 Riyal

50 DIRHAMS

COPPER-NICKEL

KM#	Date	Year	Mintage	VF	XF	Unc
28	AH1390	1970	—	—	—	3.00

RIYAL

3.9500 g, .640 SILVER, .0812 oz ASW

1	AH1389	1969	1,500	—	—	5.00

2 RIYALS

6.4500 g, .835 SILVER, .1731 oz ASW

2	AH1389	1969	1,500	—	—	7.50

2 1/2 RIYALS

7.0000 g, .925 SILVER, .2081 oz ASW

29	AH1390	1970	—	—	—	10.00

5 RIYALS

15.0000 g, .835 SILVER, .4027 oz ASW

3	AH1389	1969	1,500	—	—	12.50

7 1/2 RIYALS

22.6000 g, .925 SILVER, .6721 oz ASW

KM#	Date	Year	Mintage	VF	XF	Unc
30	AH1390	1970	—	—	—	18.00

22.3100 g, .925 SILVER, .6634 oz ASW
Giacomo Agostini

5	ND	(1970)	*2,000	—	Proof	750.00

Centennial of Rome - Man Plowing

KM#	Date	Mintage	VF	XF	Unc
17	1970	*2,000	—	Proof	35.00

Rev: Jules Rimet cup.
Similar to 10 Riyals, KM#6.

32	1970	*2,000	—	Proof	150.00

10 RIYALS

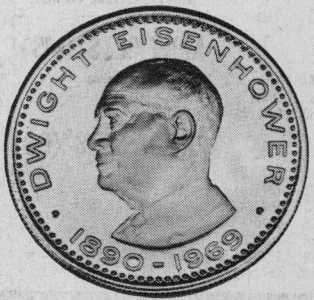

30.0000 g, .925 SILVER, .8921 oz ASW
Dwight Eisenhower

31	1970	4,500	—	—	15.00
	1970	1,400	—	Proof	25.00

Obv: Denomination.

KM#	Date	Mintage	VF	XF	Unc
6	1970	*2,000	—	Proof	225.00

Felice Gimondi
Obv: Denomination.

KM#	Date	Year	Mintage	VF	XF	Unc
7	ND	(1970)	*2,000	—	Proof	750.00

Centennial of Rome - Emperor

KM#	Date	Mintage	VF	XF	Unc
18	1970	*2,000	—	Proof	50.00

15 RIYALS

44.8700 g, .925 SILVER, 1.3345 oz ASW
Obv: Denomination.

| 8 | ND | | *2,000 | — | Proof | 275.00 |

Centennial of Rome - Founders

KM#	Date	Mintage	VF	XF	Unc
19	1970	*2,000	—	Proof	75.00

Rev: Jules Rimet cup.
Similar to 10 Riyals, KM#6.

| 33 | 1970 | | | — | Proof | 275.00 |

50 RIYALS

10.3500 g, .900 GOLD, .2995 oz AGW
Obv: Denomination. Rev: Bust of Gigi Riva.

KM#	Date	Year	Mintage	VF	XF	Unc
10	ND	(1970)	*2,000	—	Proof	300.00

Centennial of Rome - Vittorio Emanuele II

KM#	Date	Mintage	VF	XF	Unc
21	1970	*2,000	—	Proof	300.00

75 RIYALS

15.5300 g, .900 GOLD, .4494 oz AGW
Obv: Denomination. Rev: Bust of Gianni Rivera.

KM#	Date	Year	Mintage	VF	XF	Unc
11	ND	(1970)	*2,000	—	Proof	350.00

Centennial of Rome - Capitol

KM#	Date	Mintage	VF	XF	Unc
22	1970	*2,000	—	Proof	350.00

100 RIYALS

20.7000 g, .900 GOLD, .5990 oz AGW
Obv: Denomination. Rev: Jules Rimet cup.
Similar to 10 Riyals, KM#6.

| 12 | 1970 | | | — | Proof | 400.00 |

Centennial of Rome - WW I Victory

| 23 | 1970 | *2,000 | — | Proof | 400.00 |

150 RIYALS

31.0500 g, .900 GOLD, .8985 oz AGW
1972 Munich Olympics

KM#	Date	Year	Mintage	VF	XF	Unc
13	ND	(1970)	*2,000	—	Proof	600.00

Centennial of Rome - Standing Liberty

KM#	Date	Mintage	VF	XF	Unc
24	1970	*2,000	—	Proof	600.00

200 RIYALS

41.4000 g, .900 GOLD, 1.1980 oz AGW
Obv: Denomination. Rev: Soccer team.
Similar to 15 Riyals, KM#8.

KM#	Date	Year	Mintage	VF	XF	Unc
14	ND	(1970)	*2,000	—	Proof	750.00

Centennial of Rome - Romulus and Remus

KM#	Date	Mintage	VF	XF	Unc
25	1970	*2,000	—	Proof	750.00

MINT SETS (MS)

KM#	Date	Mintage	Identification	Issue Price	Mkt. Val.
MS1	1969(3)	1,500	KM1-3	10.80	25.00

PROOF SETS (PS)

PS1	(1970) (9)	—	KM5-8,10-14	—	4400.
PS2	1970(8)	—	KM17-19,21-25	—	2560.
PS3	(1970) (5)	—	KM10-14	—	2400.
PS4	1970(5)	—	KM21-25	—	2400.
PS5	(1970) (4)	—	KM5-8	41.50	2000.
PS6	1970(3)	—	KM17-19	—	160.00

SHARJAH

Sharjah is the only one of the emirates that shares boundaries with all of the others plus Oman. It has an area of 1,000 sq. mi. (2,600 sq. km.) and a population of 40,000. Sharjah was an important pirate base in the 18th and early 19th centuries. Most of the treaties and diplomatic relations were with Great Britain.

TITLES

الشارجة

Sharjah

RULERS

Saqr III, 1951-1965
Khalid III, 1965-1972

5 RUPEES

25.0000 g, .720 SILVER, .5787 oz ASW
John F. Kennedy Memorial

KM#	Date	Mintage	VF	XF	Unc
1	1964	—	—	—	12.50
	1964 PROOF below flags on rev.				
				Proof	20.00

NOTE: KM#1 was ordered by the Sheik, who according to the British had no authority to issue it.

RIYAL

3.0000 g, .999 SILVER, .0963 oz ASW
Mona Lisa

KM#	Date	Year	Mintage	VF	XF	Unc
2	AH1389	1970	3,850	—	Proof	12.50

2 RIYALS

6.0000 g, .999 SILVER, .1927 oz ASW

Sharjah/UNITED ARAB EMIRATES 1720

Mexico World Soccer Cup

KM#	Date	Year	Mintage	VF	XF	Unc
3	AH1389	1970	4,500	—	Proof	25.00

5 RIYALS

15.0000 g, .999 SILVER, .4818 oz ASW
Napoleon

| 4 | AH1389 | 1970 | 2,500 | — | Proof | 37.50 |

10 RIYALS

30.0000 g, .999 SILVER, .9636 oz ASW
Bolivar
Obv: Similar to 1 Riyal, KM#2.

| 5 | AH1389 | 1970 | 3,200 | — | Proof | 45.00 |

25 RIYALS

5.1800 g, .900 GOLD, .1499 oz AGW
Mona Lisa

| 7 | AH1389 | 1970 | 6,775 | — | Proof | 150.00 |

50 RIYALS

10.3600 g, .900 GOLD, .2998 oz AGW
Mexico World Soccer Cup
Obv: Similar to 25 Riyals, KM#7.

| 8 | AH1389 | 1970 | 1,815 | — | Proof | 225.00 |

100 RIYALS

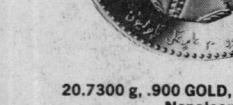

20.7300 g, .900 GOLD, .5999 oz AGW
Napoleon
Obv: Similar to KM#10.

| 9 | AH1389 | 1970 | — | — | Proof | 450.00 |

Bolivar

KM#	Date	Year	Mintage	VF	XF	Unc
10	AH1389	1970	—	—	Proof	400.00

200 RIYALS

41.4600 g, .900 GOLD, 1.1998 oz AGW
Khalid III
Obv: Similar to 25 Riyals, KM#7.

| 11 | AH1389 | 1970 | 435 pcs. | — | Proof | 750.00 |

PROOF SETS (PS)

KM#	Date	Mintage	Identification	Issue Price	Mkt. Val.
PS1	1970(9)	5,000	KM2-5,7-11	—	2100.
PS2	1970(5)	5,000	KM7-11	—	1975.
PS3	1970(4)	2,500	KM2-5	25.30	120.00

UMM AL QAIWAIN

This emirate is the second smallest, least developed and smallest in population. The area is 300 sq. mi. (800 sq. km.) and the population is 5,000. The first recognition by the West was in 1820. Most of the emirate is uninhabited desert. Native boat building is an important activity. One of the original members of the United Arab Emirates.

TITLES

ام القوين

Umm Al-Qaiwain

RULERS

Ahmed II, 1929—

RIYAL

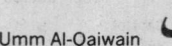

3.0000 g, .999 SILVER, .0963 oz ASW

KM#	Date	Year	Mintage	VF	XF	Unc
1	AH1389	1970	2,050	—	Proof	10.00

2 RIYALS

6.0000 g, .999 SILVER, .1927 oz ASW

| 2 | AH1389 | 1970 | 2,050 | — | Proof | 17.50 |

---

5 RIYALS

15.0000 g, .999 SILVER, .4818 oz ASW

KM#	Date	Year	Mintage	VF	XF	Unc
3	AH1389	1970	2,100	—	Proof	32.50

10 RIYALS

30.0000 g, .999 SILVER, .9636 oz ASW
Obv: Similar to 5 Riyals, KM#3.

| 4 | AH1389 | 1970 | 2,000 | — | Proof | 40.00 |

25 RIYALS

5.1800 g, .900 GOLD, .1499 oz AGW

| 6 | AH1389 | 1970 | 500 pcs. | — | Proof | 150.00 |

50 RIYALS

10.3600 g, .900 GOLD, .2998 oz AGW

| 7 | AH1389 | 1970 | 420 pcs. | — | Proof | 300.00 |

100 RIYALS

20.7300 g, .900 GOLD, .5999 oz AGW

| 8 | AH1389 | 1970 | 300 pcs. | — | Proof | 450.00 |

200 RIYALS

41.4600 g, .900 GOLD, 1.1998 oz AGW
Obv: Similar to 25 Riyals, KM#6.

KM#	Date	Year	Mintage	VF	XF	Unc
9	AH1389	1970	230 pcs.	—	Proof	700.00

PROOF SETS (PS)

KM#	Date	Mintage	Identification	Issue Price	Mkt. Val.
PS1	1970(4)	2,000	KM1-4	26.30	100.00
PS2	1970(4)	230	KM6-9	—	1600.
PS3	1970(8)	—	KM1-4,6-9	—	1700.

UNITED ARAB EMIRATES

The seven United Arab Emirates (formerly known as the Trucial Shaikhdoms or States), located along the southern shore of the Persian Gulf, are comprised of the Shaikhdoms of Abu Dhabi, Dubai, Sharjah, Ajman, Umm al Quawain, Ras al Khaimah and Fujairah. They have a combined area of about 32,000 sq. mi. (82,880 sq. km.) and a population of about 760,000. Capital: Abu Zaby (Abu Dhabi). Since the oil strikes of 1958-60, the economy has centered about petroleum.
The Trucial States came under direct British influence in 1892 when the Maritime Truce Treaty enacted after the supression of pirate activity along the Trucial Coast was enlarged to enjoin the states from disposing of any territory, or entering into any foreign agreements, without British consent in return for British protection from external aggression. In March of 1971 Britain reaffirmed its decision to terminate its treaty relationships with the Trucial Shaikhdoms, whereupon the seven states joined with Bahrain and Qatar in an effort to form a union of Arab Emirates under British protection. When the prospective members failed to agree on terms of union, Bahrain and Qatar declared their respective independence, Aug. and Sept. of 1971. Six of the shaikhdoms united to form the United Arab Emirates on Dec. 2, 1971. Ras al Khaimah joined a few weeks later.

TITLES

الامارات العربية المتحدة

El-Imara(t) El-Arabiya(t) El-Muttahidah

MONETARY SYSTEM
100 Fils = 1 Dirham
1000 Fils = 1 Dinar

FIL

BRONZE
F.A.O. Issue

KM#	Date	Year	Mintage	VF	XF	Unc
1	AH1393	1973	4.000	.10	.15	.20
	1395	1975	—	.10	.15	.20

5 FILS

BRONZE
F.A.O. Issue

KM#	Date	Year	Mintage	VF	XF	Unc
2	AH1393	1973	11.400	.10	.15	.25
	1402	1982	—	.10	.15	.25

10 FILS

BRONZE

KM#	Date	Year	Mintage	VF	XF	Unc
3	AH1393	1973	6.400	.15	.35	1.00
	1402	1982	—	.15	.35	1.00
	1404	1984	—	.15	.35	1.00

25 FILS

COPPER-NICKEL

KM#	Date	Year	Mintage	VF	XF	Unc
4	AH1393	1973	10.400	.25	.35	.50
	1402	1982	—	.25	.35	.50
	1404	1984	—	.25	.35	.50
	1406	1986	—	.25	.35	.50
	1407	1987	—	.25	.35	.50

50 FILS

COPPER-NICKEL

KM#	Date	Year	Mintage	VF	XF	Unc
5	AH1393	1973	8.400	.35	.50	2.00
	1402	1982	—	.35	.50	2.00
	1404	1984	—	.35	.50	2.00
	1407	1987	—	.35	.50	2.00

DIRHAM

COPPER-NICKEL

KM#	Date	Year	Mintage	VF	XF	Unc
6	AH1393	1973	13.000	.50	.75	2.00
	1402	1982	—	.50	.75	2.00
	1404	1984	—	.50	.75	2.00
	1406	1986	—	.50	.75	2.00
	1407	1987	—	.50	.75	2.00

27th Chess Olympiad in Dubai

KM#	Date	Mintage	VF	XF	Unc
10	1986	—	—	—	10.00

25th Anniversary of Off Shore Oil Drilling

KM#	Date	Mintage	VF	XF	Unc
11	1987	—	—	—	10.00

10th Anniversary of Al Ain University

KM#	Date	Mintage	VF	XF	Unc
14	1988	—	—	—	8.00

5 DIRHAMS

COPPER-NICKEL
1500th Anniversary of the Hegira

KM#	Date	Year	Mintage	VF	XF	Unc
9	AH1401	1981	—	—	—	5.50

50 DIRHAMS

27.2200 g, .925 SILVER, .8095 oz ASW
IYC and UNICEF

KM#	Date	Year	Mintage	VF	XF	Unc
7	AH1400	1980	8,031	—	Proof	25.00

500 DIRHAMS

19.9700 g, .917 GOLD, .5886 oz AGW
5th Anniversary of United Arab Emirates

KM#	Date	Mintage	VF	XF	Unc
12	1976	.011	—	Proof	500.00

750 DIRHAMS

17.1700 g, .900 GOLD, .4969 oz AGW
IYC and UNICEF

KM#	Date	Year	Mintage	VF	XF	Unc
8	AH1400	1980	3,063	—	Proof	325.00

1000 DIRHAMS

39.9400 g, .917 GOLD, 1.1771 oz AGW
5th Anniversary of United Arab Emirates
Similar to 500 Dirhams, KM#12.

KM#	Date	Mintage	VF	XF	Unc
13	1976	.010	—	Proof	1.000.

UNITED STATES

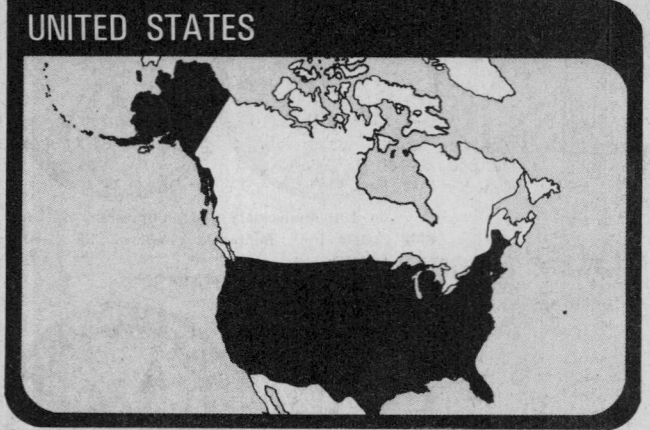

The United States of America as politcally organized under the Articles of Confederation consisted of the 13 original British-American colonies — New Hampshire, Massachusetts, Rhode Island, Connecticut, New York, New Jersey, Pennsylvania, Delaware, Virginia, North Carolina, South Carolina, Georgia and Maryland — clustered along the eastern seaboard of North America between the forests of Maine and the marshes of Georgia. Under the Articles of Confederation, the United States had no national capital; Philadelphia, where the "United States in Congress Assembled" met, was the "seat of government." The population during this political phase of America's history (1781-1789) was about 3 million, most of whom lived on self-sufficient family farms. Fishing, lumbering and the production of grains for export were major economic endeavors. Rapid strides were also being made in industry and manufacturing; by 1775, the (then) colonies were acccounting for one-seventh of the world's production of raw iron.

On the basis of the voyage of John Cabot to the North American mainland in 1497, England claimed the entire continent. The first permanent English settlement was established at Jamestown, Virginia, in 1607. France and Spain also claimed extensive territory in North America. At the end of the French and Indian Wars (1763), England acquired all of the territory east of the Mississippi River, including East and West Florida. From 1776 to 1781, the States were governed by the Continental Congress. From 1781 to 1789, they were organized under the Articles of Confederation, during which period the individual States had the right to issue money. Independence from Great Britain was attained by the American Revolution in 1776. The Constitution which organized and governs the present United States was ratified on Nov. 21, 1788.

U.S. MINT ISSUES OF 1792

The better part of a year passed between the establishment of the United States Mint and the introduction of regular half-cent and cent coinage in 1793. During this time several pattern issues, including a substantial issue of about 1500 half-dismes, were executed under the supervision of David Rittenhouse who was appointed as Mint Director by President Washington on April 14, 1792, just twelve days after the law establishing the Mint was enacted.

Rittenhouse did not actually accept the appointment until July 1, and sometime during the two weeks following the first U.S. coins — the 1792 half-dismes — were apparently struck. The dies for this coin were prepared by Robert Birch (the similar disme obverse, and apparently the reverse was executed by Adam Eckfeldt), and the actual striking did not take place in the first mint building, but in the cellar of a building where the mint's early equipment acquisitions were being stored, as its construction did not commence until July 31.

Those first half-dismes, which are reputed to carry a portrait of Martha Washington, were struck at the request of President Washington from silver which he presented for their execution, the popular opinion being that it was taken from his silver service.

Construction of the Mint building progressed rapidly, so that all was in readiness for the installation of two coining presses purchased abroad which arrived on September 21. In his annual address to Congress on November 6, President Washington remarked on the "small beginning" which had been made in the production of coins. The first coins actually struck at the Mint, however, were probably silver center cent patterns produced on December 17 from dies prepared by Henry Voight. These coins carried a silver plug worth three-quarters of a cent in the center of a copper planchet valued at one-quarter of a cent, while similar pieces were also prepared without the silver plug.

Three other patterns of 1792 exist. Chronologically the first was probably a cent created by Robert Birch which carries an obverse bust similar to that on the half-disme and bears the abbreviation "G.W.Pt." (George Washington President) at the base of the reverse. The second is a similar cent which has Birch's name signed to the bust and a reverse similar to that adopted in 1793, with the fraction 1/100 at the base. The final pattern was apparently intended for a quarter and engraved by Joseph Wright.

HALF DISME

KM#	Date	Good	Fine	VF
75	1792	1,000.	3,000.	5,000.
75a	1792 Copper (unique)	2,000.	3,500.	6,000.

DISME

76	1792 Silver (3 known)			
76a	1792 Copper (2 reeded edge, about 10 plain edge)		Garrett	54,000.

SILVER CENTER CENT

77	1792 Silver Center (about 8 known)	Garrett	95,000.
77a	1792 No Silver Center (copper or billon, 4 known)	Garrett	28,000.

BIRCH CENT

78	1792 Copper (known with plain and two types of lettered edges, about 15 known combined.)	Garrett	200,000.
78a	1792 "G.W. Pt." on reverse below wreath tie, White Metal (unique)	Garrett	90,000.

WRIGHT QUARTER

79	1792 Copper, Reeded Edge (2 known)		
79b	1792 White Metal Die-Trial	Garrett	12,000.

HALF CENTS

Liberty Cap

Type: Half Cents — Liberty Capped
Dates of issue: 1793
Designer: Adam Eckfeldt
Size: 22 MM
Weight: 6.74 Grams
Composition: 100% Copper

Date	Mintage	G-4	VG-8	F-12	VF-20	XF-40	MS-60
1793 Head L	35,334	1600.	1900.	2850.	4400.	6500.	—

Type: Half Cents — Liberty Capped
Dates of issue: 1794-1797
Designer: 1794 Robert Scot, 1795 John Smith Gardner
Size: 23.5 MM
Weight: 1794 & 1795, 6.74 Grams, 1795-97 thin planchet 5.44 Grams
Composition: 100% Copper

Date	Mintage	G-4	VG-8	F-12	VF-20	XF-40	MS-60
1794 Head R	81,600	265.	375.	700.	1250.	2100.	—
1795 Lettered Edge, Pole	25,600	245.	350.	550.	1000.	1900.	—
1795 Plain Edge, No Pole	109,000	225.	285.	540.	915.	1700.	—
1795 Lettered Edge, Punctuated Date	Inc. Ab.	245.	350.	550.	1000.	2100.	—
1795 Plain Edge, Punctuated Date	Inc. Ab.	240.	335.	535.	900.	1800.	—
1796 W/Pole	5,090	3900.	5300.	8000.	12,500.	20,000.	—
1796 No Pole	1,390	—	—	—	Rare	—	—
1797 Pl. Edge	119,215	265.	375.	575.	1000.	1900.	—
1797 Let. Edge	Inc. Ab.	1000.	1600.	2500.	5000.	—	—
1797 1 Above 1	Inc. Ab.	225.	285.	540.	915.	1700.	—

Draped Bust

  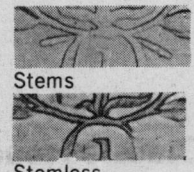

Stems
Stemless

Type: Half Cents — Draped Bust
Dates of issue: 1800-1808
Designer: Robert Scot
Size: 23.5 MM
Weight: 5.44 Grams
Composition: 100% Copper

Date	Mintage	G-4	VG-8	F-12	VF-20	XF-40	MS-60
1800	211,530	30.00	42.50	61.00	100.	250.	—
1802/0 Rev. 1800	14,366	5000.	8500.	12,000.	—	—	—
1802/0 Rev. 1802	Inc. Ab.	240.	315.	900.	2750.	—	—
1803	97,900	33.00	44.00	65.00	125.	325.	—
1804 Plain 4, Stemless Wreath	1,055,312	28.00	32.00	44.00	63.00	140.	690.
1804 Plain 4, Stems	Inc. Ab.	30.00	40.00	52.00	75.00	175.	690.
1804 Cross 4, Stemless	Inc. Ab.	30.00	40.00	52.00	75.00	175.	690.
1804 Cross 4, Stems	Inc. Ab.	30.00	40.00	52.00	75.00	175.	690.
1804 Spiked Chin	Inc.Ab.	28.00	32.00	44.00	63.00	140.	690.
1805 Small 5, Stemless	814,464	29.00	37.00	50.00	77.00	200.	—
1805 Small 5, Stems	Inc. Ab.	200.	325.	500.	750.	—	—
1805 Large 5, Stems	Inc. Ab.	29.00	37.00	50.00	77.00	200.	—

Date	Mintage	G-4	VG-8	F-12	VF-20	XF-40	MS-60
1806 Small 6, Stems	356,000	75.00	125.	200.	275.	—	—
1806 Small 6, Stemless	Inc. Ab.	28.00	32.00	44.00	63.00	185.	800.
1806 Large 6, Stems	Inc. Ab.	28.00	32.00	44.00	63.00	185.	—
1807	476,000	28.00	32.00	50.00	77.00	225.	690.
1808 Over 7	400,000	60.00	105.	200.	625.	—	—
1808	Inc. Ab.	29.00	37.00	50.00	77.00	330.	950.

Classic Head

Type: Half Cents — Classic Head
Dates of issue: 1809-1836
Designer: John Reich
Size: 23.5 MM
Weight: 5.44 Grams
Composition: 100% Copper

Date	Mintage	G-4	VG-8	F-12	VF-20	XF-40	MS-60
1809 Over 6	1,154,572	26.00	30.00	36.00	56.00	80.00	500.
1809	Inc. Ab.	21.00	27.00	36.00	53.00	75.00	475.
1810	215,000	31.00	36.00	45.00	105.	200.	1400.
1811	63,140	80.00	130.	325.	800.	1600.	—
1811 Restrike, Reverse of 1802, Uncirculated							6500.
1825	63,000	33.00	39.00	47.00	67.00	130.	800.
1826	234,000	28.00	33.00	40.00	56.00	83.00	700.
1828 13 Stars	606,000	21.00	27.00	32.00	44.00	57.00	285.
1828 12 Stars	Inc. Ab.	25.00	33.00	40.00	56.00	80.00	500.
1829	487,000	25.00	30.00	33.00	46.00	69.00	600.
1831 Original	2,200	—	—	—	4000.	5000.	7500.
1831 Restrike, Lg. Berries, Reverse of 1836, Proof						—	6000.
1831 Restrike, Sm. Berries, Reverse of 1852, Proof						—	7000.
1832	154,000	21.00	27.00	32.00	44.00	57.00	550.
1833	120,000	21.00	27.00	32.00	44.00	57.00	425.
1834	141,000	21.00	27.00	32.00	44.00	57.00	450.
1835	398,000	21.00	27.00	32.00	44.00	57.00	350.
1836 Original				Proof Only		—	6500.
1836 Restrike, Reverse of 1852, Proof Only						—	6500.

Braided Hair

Type: Half Cents — Braided Hair
Dates of issue: 1840-1854
Designer: Christian Gobrecht
Size: 23 MM
Weight: 5.44 Grams
Composition: 100% Copper

Date	Mintage	G-4	VG-8	F-12	VF-20	XF-40	MS-60	Prf-60
1840 Original	—	—	—	—	Proof Only	—	—	3800.
1840 Restrike	—	—	—	—	Proof Only	—	—	3200.
1841 Original	—	—	—	—	Proof Only	—	—	3800.
1841 Restrike	—	—	—	—	Proof Only	—	—	3000.
1842 Original	—	—	—	—	Proof Only	—	—	3800.
1842 Restrike	—	—	—	—	Proof Only	—	—	3200.
1843 Original	—	—	—	—	Proof Only	—	—	3800.
1843 Restrike	—	—	—	—	Proof Only	—	—	3200.
1844 Original	—	—	—	—	Proof Only	—	—	3800.
1844 Restrike	—	—	—	—	Proof Only	—	—	3200.
1845 Original	—	—	—	—	Proof Only	—	—	3800.
1845 Restrike	—	—	—	—	Proof Only	—	—	3200.
1846 Original	—	—	—	—	Proof Only	—	—	3800.
1846 Restrike	—	—	—	—	Proof Only	—	—	3200.
1847 Original	—	—	—	—	Proof Only	—	—	3800.
1847 Restrike	—	—	—	—	Proof Only	—	—	3200.
1848 Original	—	—	—	—	Proof Only	—	—	3800.
1848 Restrike	—	—	—	—	Proof Only	—	—	3200.
1849 Original Small Date	—	—	—	—	Proof Only	—	—	3800.
1849 Restrike Small Date	—	—	—	—	Proof Only	—	—	3200.

Date	Mintage	G-4	VG-8	F-12	VF-20	XF-40	MS-60
1849 Lg. Date	39,864	39.00	43.00	50.00	58.00	80.00	475.
1850	39,812	36.00	37.00	44.00	55.00	75.00	525.
1851	147,672	27.00	34.00	43.00	50.00	63.00	225.
1852					Proof Only		4250.
1853	129,694	27.00	34.00	43.00	50.00	63.00	225.
1854	55,358	29.00	37.00	44.00	52.00	69.00	225.
1855	56,500	29.00	37.00	44.00	52.00	69.00	225.
1856	40,430	36.00	39.00	45.00	55.00	75.00	285.
1857	35,180	50.00	55.00	65.00	80.00	110.	350.

LARGE CENTS

Flowing Hair

Type: Large Cents — Flowing Hair, Chain Type
Dates of issue: 1793
Designer: Henry Voigt
Size: 26-27 MM
Weight: 13.48 Grams
Composition: 100% Copper

Date	Mintage	G-4	VG-8	F-12	VF-20	XF-40	MS-60
1793 Chain	36,103	2100.	2750.	4500.	9100.	19,000.	—

Auction 80, Aug. 1980, MS-65 $120,000.

Type: Large Cents — Flowing Hair, Wreath Type
Dates of issue: 1793
Designer: Adam Eckfeldt
Size: 26-28 MM
Weight: 13.48 Grams
Composition: 100% Copper

Date	Mintage	G-4	VG-8	F-12	VF-20	XF-40	MS-60
1793 Wreath	63,353	975.	1250.	1950.	3450.	6950.	—

Liberty Cap

Type: Large Cents — Liberty Cap
Dates of issue: 1793-1796
Designer: 1793-1795 (thick planchet)
  Joseph Wright; 1795-1796 (thin planchet)
  John Smith Gardner
Size: 29 MM
Weight: Thick planchet 13.48 Grams; thin planchet 10.89 Grams
Composition: 100% Copper

Date	Mintage	G-4	VG-8	F-12	VF-20	XF-40	MS-60
1793 Cap	11,056	2450.	3200.	4500.	6000.	—	—
1794	918,521	165.	250.	425.	800.	1450.	—
1794 Head '93	Inc. Ab.	325.	500.	1100.	2000.		—
1795	501,500	160.	200.	415.	725.	1400.	—
1795 Lettered Edge, One Cent High In Wreath							
	37,000	180.	275.	450.	750.	1375.	—
1796 Lib. Cap	109,825	175.	260.	415.	900.	1650.	—

Draped Bust

Type: Large Cents — Draped Bust
Dates of issue: 1796-1807
Designer: Robert Scot
Size: 29 MM
Weight: 10.89 Grams
Composition: 100% Copper

Date	Mintage	G-4	VG-8	F-12	VF-20	XF-40	MS-60
1796	363,375	70.00	90.00	165.	335.	750.	—
1797	897,510	40.00	60.00	125.	325.	750.	—

Stems   Stemless

Date	Mintage	G-4	VG-8	F-12	VF-20	XF-40	MS-60
1797 Stemless	Inc. Ab.	60.00	100.	200.	1500.	2250.	—
1798	1,841,745	30.00	50.00	125.	325.	685.	—
1798/97	Inc. Ab.	70.00	115.	185.	450.	800.	—
1799	42,540	900.	1650.	3500.	5900.	—	—
1800	2,822,175	29.00	45.00	110.	300.	665.	—
1801	1,362,837	29.00	45.00	110.	300.	665.	—
1801 3 Errors 1/000, One Stem, IINITED							
	Inc. Ab.	37.00	65.00	140.	300.	685.	—
1802	3,435,100	21.00	35.00	90.00	285.	665.	2000.
1803	2,471,353	21.00	35.00	90.00	285.	665.	2000.
1804	756,838	450.	695.	1250.	2000.	3500.	—
1805	941,116	28.00	40.00	100.	290.	665.	—
1806	348,000	40.00	65.00	100.	285.	750.	—
1807	727,221	24.00	35.00	120.	290.	665.	—

Classic Head

Type: Large Cents — Classic Head
Dates of issue: 1808-1814
Designer: John Reich
Size: 29 MM
Weight: 10.89 Grams
Composition: 100% Copper

Date	Mintage	G-4	VG-8	F-12	VF-20	XF-40	MS-60
1808	1,109,000	33.00	55.00	125.	300.	770.	—
1809	222,867	70.00	125.	200.	490.	1500.	—
1810	1,458,500	28.00	38.00	120.	290.	760.	3000.
1811	218,025	65.00	105.	165.	445.	850.	—
1812	1,075,500	28.00	38.00	95.00	290.	760.	2200.
1813	418,000	45.00	72.00	130.	325.	800.	—
1814	357,830	28.00	38.00	120.	290.	760.	2200.

Coronet Type

Type: Large Cents — Coronet Type
Dates of issue: 1816-1839
Designer: Robert Scot
Size: 28-29 MM
Weight: 10.89 Grams
Composition: 100% Copper

Date	Mintage	G-4	VG-8	F-12	VF-20	XF-40	MS-60
1816	2,820,982	12.50	17.00	27.00	50.00	120.	300.
1817	3,948,400	11.00	13.00	21.00	40.00	100.	285.
1817 15 Stars	Inc. Ab.	12.00	20.00	30.00	60.00	155.	450.
1818	3,167,000	10.00	13.00	21.00	40.00	100.	350.
1819	2,671,000	11.00	13.00	21.00	40.00	100.	315.
1820	4,407,550	11.00	13.00	21.00	40.00	100.	265.
1821	389,000	17.50	30.00	45.00	100.	250.	—
1822	2,072,339	11.00	15.00	24.00	46.00	135.	350.
1823	Inc. 1824	30.00	50.00	90.00	235.	650.	—
1823/22	Inc. 1824	27.00	45.00	65.00	175.	350.	1750.
1824	1,262,000	11.50	16.00	28.00	60.00	80.00	575.
1824/22	Inc. Ab.	20.00	35.00	55.00	115.	275.	1500.
1825	1,461,100	10.50	14.00	24.00	55.00	150.	350.
1826	1,517,425	10.50	14.00	24.00	50.00	130.	600.
1826/25	Inc. Ab.	18.00	30.00	60.00	115.	250.	800.
1827	2,357,732	10.50	12.50	20.00	45.00	115.	600.
1828	2,260,624	10.00	12.50	20.00	50.00	115.	300.
1829	1,414,500	10.50	13.00	21.00	45.00	120.	350.
1830	1,711,500	10.50	13.00	20.00	40.00	110.	325.
1831	3,359,260	7.25	8.60	16.50	35.00	100.	325.
1832	2,362,000	7.25	8.60	16.50	40.00	100.	325.
1833	2,739,000	7.25	8.60	16.50	35.00	100.	325.
1834	1,855,100	7.25	8.60	16.50	40.00	100.	350.
1835	3,878,400	7.25	8.60	16.50	40.00	100.	325.
1836	2,111,000	7.25	8.60	16.50	40.00	95.00	300.
1837	5,558,300	7.25	8.60	16.50	33.00	90.00	300.
1838	6,370,200	7.25	8.60	16.50	33.00	80.00	265.
1839	3,128,661	7.25	8.60	16.50	42.00	100.	350.
1839/36	Inc. Ab.	135.	225.	300.	600.	1200.	—

Braided Hair

Type: Large Cents — Braided Hair
Dates of issue: 1840-1857
Designer: Christian Gobrecht
Size: 27.5 MM
Weight: 10.89 Grams
Composition: 100% Copper

Date	Mintage	G-4	VG-8	F-12	VF-20	XF-40	MS-60
1840	2,462,700	7.25	9.00	11.50	19.00	58.00	265.
1841	1,597,367	9.00	11.00	15.00	23.00	68.00	300.
1842	2,383,390	7.25	9.00	11.50	18.00	55.00	265.

Small Date — Large Date

Large cents of 1840 and 1842 are known with both small and large dates, with little differential in value.

Date	Mintage	G-4	VG-8	F-12	VF-20	XF-40	MS-60
1843	2,425,342	7.25	9.00	17.00	25.00	65.00	225.
1843 Obverse 1842 With Reverse of 1844							
	Inc. Ab.	13.00	18.00	35.00	45.00	80.00	350.
1844	2,398,752	8.00	9.75	11.00	17.00	49.00	190.
1844/81	Inc. Ab.	12.00	20.00	28.00	60.00	130.	450.
1845	3,894,804	6.00	6.95	10.00	14.00	40.00	190.
1846	4,120,800	6.00	6.95	10.00	14.00	40.00	190.
1847	6,183,669	6.00	6.95	10.00	14.00	40.00	190.
1848	6,415,799	6.00	6.95	10.00	14.00	40.00	190.
1849	4,178,500	6.00	6.95	10.00	14.00	40.00	275.
1850	4,426,844	6.00	6.95	10.00	14.00	40.00	275.
1851	9,889,707	6.00	6.95	10.00	14.00	40.00	275.
1851/81	Inc. Ab.	10.00	12.50	18.00	35.00	95.00	400.
1852	5,063,094	6.00	6.95	10.00	14.00	40.00	190.
1853	6,641,131	6.00	6.95	10.00	14.00	40.00	190.
1854	4,236,156	6.00	6.95	10.00	14.00	40.00	190.

Slanting 5's — Upright 5's

Large cents of 1855 and 1856 are known with both slanting and upright 5's, with little differential in value.

Date	Mintage	G-4	VG-8	F-12	VF-20	XF-40	MS-60
1855	1,574,829	6.00	6.95	10.00	14.00	40.00	190.
1856	2,690,463	6.00	6.95	10.00	14.00	40.00	190.
1857	333,456	20.00	25.00	35.00	55.00	85.00	300.

FLYING EAGLE CENTS

Type: Small Cents — Flying Eagle
Dates of issue: 1856-1858
Designer: James B. Longacre
Size: 19 MM
Weight: 4.67 Grams
Composition: 88% Copper, 12% Nickel

Date	Mintage	G-4	VG-8	F-12	VF-20	XF-40	AU-50	MS-60	MS-65	Prf-65
1856	Est. 1,000	1700.	1900.	2100.	2350.	2650.	2900.	3800.	6700	11,500.
1857	17,450,000	10.00	11.50	14.00	25.00	60.00	140.	225.	4600	11,500.

Large Letters — Small Letters
AM Connected — AM Separated

Date	Mintage	G-4	VG-8	F-12	VF-20	XF-40	AU-50	MS-60	MS-65	Prf-65
1858 LL	24,600,000	10.00	11.50	14.00	25.00	60.00	140.	225.	4600	11,500.
1858 SL	Inc. Ab.	10.00	11.50	14.00	25.00	60.00	140.	225.	4600	11,500.

INDIAN HEAD CENTS

Copper-Nickel

1859 — 1860-1909

Type: Small Cents — Indian Head, Copper Nickel
Dates of issue: 1859-1864
Designer: James B. Longacre
Size: 19 MM
Weight: 4.67 Grams
Composition: 88% Copper, 12% Nickel

Date	Mintage	G-4	VG-8	F-12	VF-20	XF-40	AU-50	MS-60	MS-65	Prf-65
1859	36,400,000	4.15	4.75	7.70	22.50	63.00	130.	170.	3400.	3150.
1860	20,566,000	4.25	5.50	7.00	15.00	30.00	40.00	130.	1900.	2650.
1861	10,100,000	10.00	13.00	18.00	30.00	50.00	75.00	200.	1900.	2650.
1862	28,075,000	2.40	3.00	5.75	12.00	23.00	35.00	90.00	1150.	2400.
1863	49,840,000	2.40	3.00	4.25	10.00	18.00	30.00	90.00	1150.	2400.
1864	13,740,000	7.00	10.00	14.00	25.00	45.00	55.00	130.	2100.	2650.

Bronze

Type: Small Cents — Indian Head, Bronze
Dates of issue: 1864-1909
Designer: James B. Longacre
Size: 19 MM
Weight: 3.11 Grams
Composition: 95% Copper, 5% Tin and Zinc

MINT MARKS:
S San Francisco

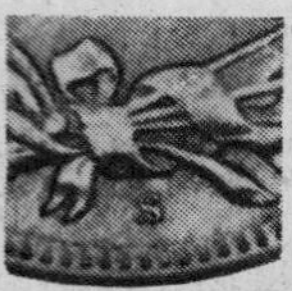
Mintmark

Date	Mintage	G-4	VG-8	F-12	VF-20	XF-40	AU-50	MS-60	MS-65	Prf-65
1864	39,233,714	3.00	4.75	9.00	18.00	30.00	50.00	95.00	650.	2600.
1864 L	Inc. Ab.	35.00	41.00	57.00	90.00	150.	200.	315.	1500	15,000.

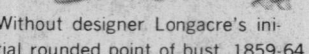

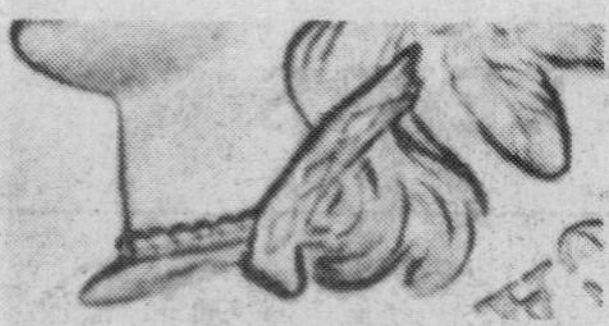
Without designer Longacre's initial rounded point of bust, 1859-64.

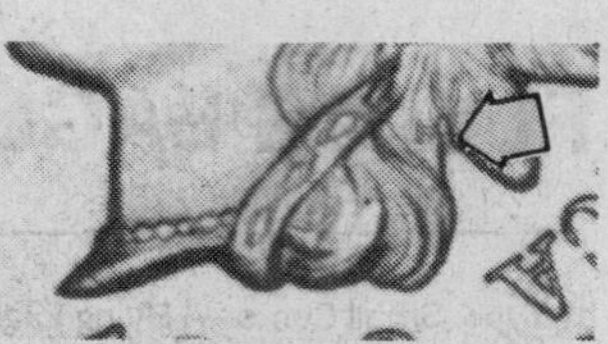
With designer Longacre's initial added, pointed bust, 1864-1909.

Date	Mintage	G-4	VG-8	F-12	VF-20	XF-40	AU-50	MS-60	MS-65	Prf-65
1865	35,429,286	4.50	6.00	7.50	18.00	25.00	45.00	75.00	425.	1400.
1866	9,826,500	22.00	28.00	35.00	60.00	90.00	110.	150.	600.	1350.
1867	9,821,000	22.00	28.00	35.00	60.00	90.00	110.	150.	600.	1350.
1868	10,266,500	22.00	28.00	35.00	60.00	90.00	110.	150.	600.	1350.
1869/8	6,420,000	100.	135.	225.	350.	525.	695.	880.	3500.	—
1869	Inc. Ab.	35.00	40.00	70.00	110.	160.	180.	380.	1300.	1350.
1870	5,275,000	25.00	38.00	60.00	95.00	120.	160.	275.	1100.	1350.
1871	3,929,500	35.00	45.00	80.00	115.	160.	185.	315.	1000.	1350.
1872	4,042,000	40.00	55.00	90.00	135.	190.	225.	390.	1500.	1400.
1873	11,676,500	10.00	17.50	24.00	38.00	60.00	85.00	150.	900.	1100.
1874	14,187,500	10.00	14.00	20.00	35.00	55.00	75.00	150.	650.	1100.
1875	13,528,000	10.00	12.00	18.00	32.00	60.00	85.00	150.	650.	1100.
1876	7,944,000	13.00	18.00	30.00	55.00	75.00	95.00	180.	700.	1100.
1877	852,500	180.	245.	350.	530.	750.	975.	1600.	4600.	3500.
1878	5,799,850	14.00	18.00	32.00	55.00	85.00	115.	200.	550.	950.
1879	16,231,200	4.00	5.00	7.00	12.00	25.00	40.00	80.00	475.	820.
1880	38,964,955	3.00	3.50	4.50	6.50	15.00	25.00	75.00	475.	820.
1881	39,211,575	3.00	3.50	4.50	6.50	15.00	25.00	75.00	425.	820.
1882	38,581,100	3.00	3.50	4.50	6.50	15.00	25.00	75.00	425.	820.
1883	45,589,109	3.00	3.50	4.50	6.50	15.00	25.00	75.00	425.	820.
1884	23,261,742	3.50	4.50	7.50	10.00	18.00	30.00	80.00	425.	820.
1885	11,765,384	4.00	5.00	10.00	18.00	30.00	40.00	90.00	425.	820.
1886	17,654,290	3.25	4.25	7.50	12.00	25.00	35.00	80.00	425.	820.
1887	45,226,483	1.50	1.75	2.50	4.50	11.00	22.00	70.00	425.	820.
1888	37,494,414	1.50	1.75	3.00	5.50	13.00	22.00	70.00	425.	820.
1889	48,869,361	1.20	1.25	2.50	4.50	11.00	18.00	35.00	425.	820.
1890	57,182,854	1.20	1.25	2.25	4.50	10.00	18.00	35.00	410.	820.
1891	47,072,350	1.20	1.25	2.25	4.50	10.00	18.00	35.00	410.	820.
1892	37,649,832	1.20	1.50	2.50	4.50	10.00	18.00	35.00	410.	820.
1893	46,642,195	1.20	1.25	2.25	4.50	10.00	18.00	35.00	410.	820.
1894	16,752,132	1.75	4.00	7.00	10.00	19.00	32.00	70.00	360.	820.
1895	38,343,636	1.00	1.25	3.00	4.50	8.50	18.00	35.00	315.	820.
1896	39,057,293	.90	1.20	1.75	3.75	8.50	18.00	35.00	315.	820.
1897	50,466,330	.90	1.10	1.50	3.00	8.50	18.00	35.00	315.	820.
1898	49,823,079	.95	1.15	1.50	3.00	8.50	18.00	35.00	315.	820.
1899	53,600,031	.90	1.10	1.50	3.00	8.50	18.00	35.00	315.	820.
1900	66,833,764	.55	.65	.90	2.00	7.00	15.00	22.00	210.	500.
1901	79,611,143	.55	.65	.90	2.00	7.00	15.00	22.00	210.	500.
1902	87,376,722	.55	.65	.90	2.00	7.00	15.00	22.00	210.	500.
1903	85,094,493	.55	.65	.90	2.00	7.00	15.00	22.00	210.	500.
1904	61,328,015	.55	.65	.90	2.00	7.00	15.00	22.00	210.	500.
1905	80,719,163	.55	.65	.90	2.00	7.00	15.00	22.00	210.	500.
1906	96,022,255	.55	.65	.90	2.00	7.00	15.00	22.00	210.	500.
1907	108,138,618	.55	.65	.90	2.00	7.00	15.00	22.00	210.	500.
1908	32,327,987	.55	.65	.90	2.00	7.00	15.00	22.00	210.	500.
1908S	1,115,000	20.00	22.00	25.00	32.00	45.00	95.00	150.	875.	—
1909	14,370,645	2.00	3.00	3.50	4.00	10.00	18.00	60.00	460.	950.
1909S	309,000	95.00	110.	125.	150.	180.	275.	325.	1500.	—

LINCOLN CENTS

Type: Small Cents — Lincoln Cents — Wheat Back
Dates of issue: 1909-1958
Designer: Victor D. Brenner
Size: 19 MM
Weight: 3.11 Grams
Composition: 95% Copper, 5% Tin and Zinc, 1944-1946 95% Copper, 5% Zinc . . Note: Shell case Copper

MINT MARKS:
D Denver
S San Francisco

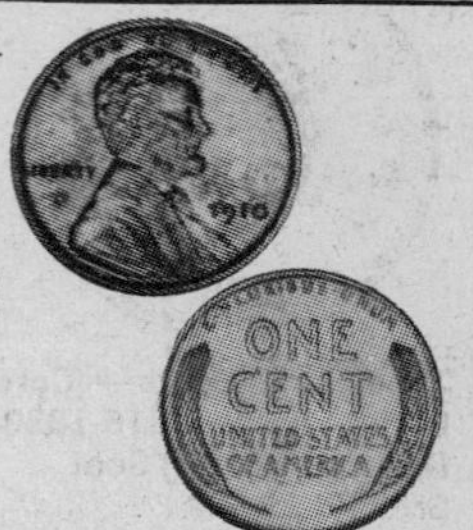

Date	Mintage	G-4	VG-8	F-12	VF-20	XF-40	AU-50	MS-60	MS-65	Prf-65
1909	72,702,618	.40	.45	.65	1.35	2.40	7.25	12.00	110.	1000.
1909VDB	27,995,000	1.60	1.90	2.25	2.50	3.25	7.50	11.50	60.00	3000.
1909S	1,825,000	35.00	39.00	45.00	54.00	95.00	115.	195.	575.	—
1909SVDB	484,000	245.	250.	265.	298.	385.	440.	500.	1400.	—
1910	146,801,218	.15	.20	.25	.60	2.25	4.75	12.00	60.00	950.
1910S	6,045,000	5.25	6.00	7.00	11.00	21.00	45.00	70.00	425.	—
1911	101,177,787	.25	.30	.50	1.95	4.90	7.00	15.00	90.00	850.
1911D	12,672,000	3.00	3.75	6.50	9.75	27.00	50.00	88.00	525.	—
1911S	4,026,000	13.50	14.50	18.50	20.00	37.00	57.00	125.	690.	—
1912	68,153,060	.75	.85	1.85	3.50	12.00	18.00	36.00	150.	750.
1912D	10,411,000	3.50	4.00	7.50	13.50	37.00	48.00	120.	540.	—
1912S	4,431,000	7.50	8.50	11.50	17.00	34.00	48.00	110.	600.	—
1913	76,532,352	.40	.50	1.60	3.00	8.50	11.00	20.00	140.	850.
1913D	15,804,000	1.50	1.75	3.00	7.00	24.00	40.00	70.00	465.	—
1913S	6,101,000	5.00	5.50	7.00	11.50	30.00	45.00	90.00	850.	—
1914	75,238,432	.30	..35	1.50	3.00	10.00	18.50	47.00	300.	1000.
1914D	1,193,000	65.00	75.00	90.00	150.	385.	540.	950.	2500.	—
1914S	4,137,000	8.00	9.00	11.00	17.00	36.00	59.00	160.	1900.	—
1915	29,092,120	1.25	1.40	5.50	10.00	40.00	60.00	100.	430.	1500.
1915D	22,050,000	.95	1.05	1.50	3.50	9.00	22.00	35.00	400.	—
1915S	4,833,000	6.00	7.00	7.50	9.50	29.00	42.00	95.00	750.	—
1916	131,833,677	.15	.20	.45	1.50	3.00	5.00	9.00	90.00	1750.
1916D	35,956,000	.25	.30	1.25	2.50	8.00	28.00	46.00	340.	—
1916S	22,510,000	.85	1.00	1.50	2.50	8.00	26.00	50.00	475.	—
1917	196,429,785	.10	.15	.25	.50	2.75	5.00	10.00	75.00	—
1917D	55,120,000	.25	.30	1.00	2.00	6.50	24.00	50.00	360.	—
1917S	32,620,000	.35	.55	.80	2.20	6.75	32.50	50.00	525.	—
1918	288,104,634	.10	.15	.35	.60	2.50	7.25	10.00	95.00	—
1918D	47,830,000	.30	.35	1.00	2.00	6.50	15.00	47.00	425.	—
1918S	34,680,000	.35	.50	.80	2.00	6.00	18.50	55.00	510.	—
1919	392,021,000	.10	.15	.20	.50	2.00	5.00	7.50	90.00	—
1919D	57,154,000	.30	.35	.60	2.20	6.75	10.00	39.00	225.	—
1919S	139,760,000	.20	.25	.50	.85	2.00	7.00	30.00	300.	—
1920	310,165,000	.10	.15	.20	.45	2.50	5.00	8.75	80.00	—
1920D	49,280,000	.30	.35	.75	2.00	6.50	13.00	50.00	315.	—
1920S	46,220,000	.20	.30	.40	1.25	4.00	14.00	56.00	450.	—
1921	39,157,000	.30	.35	.60	2.00	5.75	12.00	34.00	210.	—
1921S	15,274,000	.60	.85	1.50	3.50	12.00	50.00	115.	1175.	—
1922D	7,160,000	5.00	5.75	7.25	9.00	18.50	38.00	70.00	600.	—
1922	Inc. Ab.	180.	200.	250.	400.	1050.	1800.	3100	13,000.	—
1923	74,723,000	.25	.30	.35	1.80	5.00	7.00	9.00	80.00	—
1923S	8,700,000	1.50	1.90	2.75	5.00	19.00	70.00	185.	1185.	—
1924	75,178,000	—	.10	.15	1.25	5.00	7.00	20.00	180.	—
1924D	2,520,000	9.00	9.50	13.00	17.00	47.00	100.	210.	1200.	—
1924S	11,696,000	.60	.85	1.50	3.75	16.00	35.00	95.00	1020.	—
1925	139,949,000	.10	.15	.20	.85	3.00	4.50	8.25	65.00	—
1925D	22,580,000	.30	.35	.70	2.90	7.50	12.00	44.00	475.	—
1925S	26,380,000	.25	.30	.45	1.50	6.75	12.00	56.00	700.	—
1926	157,088,000	.10	.15	.20	.85	2.00	3.50	7.00	70.00	—
1926D	28,020,000	.20	.25	.65	1.75	4.50	10.00	45.00	475.	—
1926S	4,550,000	2.50	2.75	3.00	5.50	11.00	50.00	85.00	725.	—
1927	144,440,000	—	.15	.25	.85	2.00	3.75	7.25	60.00	—
1927D	27,170,000	.20	.25	.45	1.00	3.25	9.50	29.00	390.	—
1927S	14,276,000	.55	.65	1.75	3.00	10.50	20.00	65.00	435.	—
1928	134,116,000	.10	.15	.20	.80	2.50	3.75	7.00	65.00	—
1928D	31,170,000	.20	.25	.35	.75	3.50	7.00	20.00	195.	—
1928S	17,266,000	.45	.55	.70	2.00	4.00	9.00	46.00	570.	—
1929	185,262,000	.15	.20	.25	.80	1.50	3.75	5.50	50.00	—
1929D	41,730,000	.15	.20	.25	.45	2.00	5.00	16.00	85.00	—
1929S	50,148,000	.15	.20	.25	1.00	2.25	3.75	8.75	75.00	—
1930	157,415,000	.15	.20	.30	.45	1.50	2.50	6.00	40.00	—
1930D	40,100,000	.15	.20	.30	.50	1.75	5.75	12.00	50.00	—
1930S	24,286,000	.20	.25	.35	.70	1.75	4.00	7.00	60.00	—
1931	19,396,000	.50	.55	.65	1.00	2.50	6.00	13.50	85.00	—
1931D	4,480,000	2.50	2.75	3.00	3.50	7.00	24.00	45.00	325.	—
1931S	866,000	33.00	34.00	35.00	36.00	41.00	45.00	65.00	275.	—
1932	9,062,000	1.25	1.75	1.85	2.00	3.25	9.00	17.50	90.00	—
1932D	10,500,000	.65	.75	.85	1.25	2.00	9.00	17.00	100.	—
1933	14,360,000	1.15	1.25	1.50	1.80	3.50	9.00	18.00	100.	—
1933D	6,200,000	1.90	2.00	2.25	3.00	6.00	11.00	25.00	110.	—
1934	219,080,000	—	.10	.15	.20	.75	1.50	5.75	10.00	—
1934D	28,446,000	.10	.15	.20	.25	2.00	6.50	32.00	57.00	—
1935	245,338,000	—	.10	.15	.20	.75	1.00	2.50	4.50	—
1935D	47,000,000	—	.10	.15	.20	.75	3.00	6.00	11.00	—
1935S	38,702,000	—	.20	.25	.30	2.25	5.00	12.00	35.00	—

Date	Mintage	G-4	VG-8	F-12	VF-20	XF-40	AU-50	MS-60	MS-65	Prf-65
1936	309,637,569	—	.10	.15	.20	.75	1.00	1.75	3.25	460.
1936D	40,620,000	—	.10	.15	.25	.75	1.50	3.50	5.75	—
1936S	29,130,000	.10	.15	.25	.30	.75	2.25	3.50	5.50	—
1937	309,179,320	—	.10	.15	.20	.70	1.00	1.50	3.25	190.
1937D	50,430,000	—	.10	.15	.25	.70	1.00	2.50	3.50	—
1937S	34,500,000	—	.10	.15	.25	.60	1.50	2.80	4.50	—
1938	156,696,734	—	.10	.15	.20	.50	1.00	2.25	3.50	115.
1938D	20,010,000	—	.15	.25	.30	.75	2.25	2.75	5.25	—
1938S	15,180,000	.30	.35	.45	.60	.80	1.25	2.80	4.75	—
1939	316,479,520	—	.10	.15	.20	.25	.40	1.25	3.00	95.00
1939D	15,160,000	.35	.40	.50	.60	.75	2.25	3.75	7.00	—
1939S	52,070,000	—	.15	.20	.25	.45	1.50	2.25	3.50	—
1940	586,825,872	—	—	.15	.20	.25	.40	.85	1.25	85.00
1940D	81,390,000	—	.10	.15	.20	.25	.90	1.50	3.25	—
1940S	112,940,000	—	.10	.15	.20	.25	.90	1.50	2.50	—
1941	887,039,100	—	—	—	.10	.15	.30	1.60	2.35	75.00
1941D	128,700,000	—	—	—	.10	.15	1.00	3.25	5.50	—
1941S	92,360,000	—	—	—	.10	.15	1.25	4.50	11.50	—
1942	657,828,600	—	—	—	.10	.15	.25	.75	1.00	75.00
1942D	206,698,000	—	—	—	.10	.15	.25	1.00	1.40	—
1942S	85,590,000	—	—	—	.15	.25	1.50	5.50	10.00	—

Type: Small Cents — Lincoln — Steel
Dates of issue: 1943
Designer: Victor D. Brenner
Size: 19 MM
Weight: 2.70 Grams
Composition: Steel, coated with Zinc

MINT MARKS:
D Denver
S San Francisco

Date	Mintage	XF-40	MS-60	Prf-65
1943	684,628,670	.40	1.20	—
1943D	217,660,000	.45	2.20	—
1943S	191,550,000	.45	5.00	—
1944	1,435,400,000	.10	.50	—
1944D	430,578,000	.10	1.00	—
1944D,D/S		150.	340.	—
1944S	282,760,000	.15	.75	—
1945	1,040,515,000	.10	.80	—
1945D	226,268,000	.10	.80	—
1945S	181,770,000	.15	.70	—
1946	991,655,000	.10	.30	—
1946D	315,690,000	.10	.45	—
1946S	198,100,000	.15	.85	—
1947	190,555,000	.15	1.25	—
1947D	194,750,000	.10	.70	—
1947S	99,000,000	.15	.75	—
1948	317,570,000	.10	.75	—
1948D	172,637,000	.10	.80	—
1948S	81,735,000	.15	1.00	—
1949	217,775,000	.10	1.50	—
1949D	153,132,000	.10	1.50	—
1949S	64,290,000	.20	2.50	—
1950	272,686,386	—	.90	75.00
1950D	334,950,000	.10	.70	—
1950S	118,505,000	.15	.80	—
1951	295,633,500	.10	.90	45.00
1951D	625,355,000	.10	.50	—
1951S	136,010,000	.15	1.50	—
1952	186,856,980	.10	1.00	32.00
1952D	746,130,000	.10	.50	—
1952S	137,800,004	.15	1.00	—
1953	256,883,800	—	.50	19.00
1953D	700,515,000	.10	.50	—
1953S	181,835,000	.15	.45	—
1954	71,873,350	.15	.75	6.50
1954D	251,552,500	.10	.25	—
1954S	96,190,000	.15	.35	—
1955	330,958,000	.10	.20	5.00
1955 Doubled Die		400.	725.	—
1955D	563,257,500	.10	.20	—
1955S	44,610,000	.25	.60	—
1956	421,414,384	—	.15	2.00
1956D	1,098,201,100	—	.15	—
1957	283,787,952	—	.15	1.45
1957D	1,051,342,000	—	.15	—
1958	253,400,652	—	.15	1.75
1958D	800,953,300	—	.15	—

Type: Small Cents — Lincoln Memorial
Dates of issue: 1959 to Date
Designer: Obverse: Victor D. Brenner.
Reverse: Frank Gasparro
Size: 19 MM
Weight: 1959-1982 3.11 Grams, some 1982 and all 1983 2.5 Grams
Composition: 1959-1962 95% Copper, 5% Tin and Zinc, 1962-1982 95% Copper, 5% Zinc, some 1982 and all 1983 have a core of 99.2% Zinc and .8% Copper. Total content is 97.6% Zinc and 2.4% Copper

MINT MARKS:
D Denver
S San Francisco

Date	Mintage	XF-40	MS-65	Prf-65
1959	610,864,291	—	.20	1.10
1959D	1,279,760,000	—	.20	—
1960 SD	588,096,602	1.25	4.50	13.00
1960 LD	Inc. Ab.	—	.15	.75
1960D SD	1,580,884,000	—	.25	—
1960D LD	Inc. Ab.	—	.15	—
1961	756,373,244	—	.15	.65
1961D	1,753,266,700	—	.15	—
1962	609,263,019	—	.15	.65
1962D	1,793,148,400	—	.15	—
1963	757,185,645	—	.15	.65
1963D	1,774,020,400	—	.15	—
1964	2,652,525,762	—	.15	.65
1964D	3,799,071,500	—	.15	—
1965	1,497,224,900	—	.15	—
1966	2,188,147,783	—	.15	—
1967	3,048,667,100	—	.15	—
1968	1,707,880,970	—	.15	—
1968D	2,886,269,600	—	.15	—
1968S	261,311,510	—	.15	.70
1969	1,136,910,000	—	.25	—
1969D	4,002,832,200	—	.15	—
1969S	547,309,631	—	.15	.70

Date	Mintage	XF-40	MS-65	Prf-65
1970	1,898,315,000	—	.15	—
1970D	2,891,438,900	—	.15	—
1970S	693,192,814	—	.15	.75
1970S Small date	—	28.00	—	—
1971	1,919,490,000	—	.25	—
1971D	2,911,045,600	—	.25	—
1971S	528,354,192	—	.15	.70
1972	2,933,255,000	—	.15	—
1972 Doubled Die	—	140.	225.	—
1972D	2,665,071,400	—	.15	—
1972S	380,200,104	—	.15	.70
1973	3,728,245,000	—	.10	—
1973D	3,549,576,588	—	.10	—
1973S	319,937,634	—	.15	.75
1974	4,232,140,523	—	.10	—
1974D	4,235,098,000	—	.10	—
1974S	412,039,228	—	.15	.80
1975	5,451,476,142	—	.10	—
1975D	4,505,245,300	—	.10	—
1975S Proof Only	—	—	11.00	
1976	4,674,292,426	—	.10	—
1976D	4,221,592,455	—	.10	—
1976S Proof Only	—	—	3.50	
1977	4,469,930,000	—	.10	—
1977D	4,149,062,300	—	.10	—
1977S Proof Only	—	—	2.75	
1978	5,558,605,000	—	.10	—
1978D	4,280,233,400	—	.10	—
1978S Proof Only	—	—	5.00	
1979	6,018,515,000	—	.10	—
1979D	4,139,357,254	—	.10	—
1979S Proof Only	—	—	3.90	
1979S T-II Proof Only	—	—	4.50	
1980	7,414,705,000	—	.10	—
1980D	5,140,098,660	—	.10	—
1980S Proof Only	—	—	2.00	

Date	Mintage	XF-40	MS-65	Prf-65
1981	7,491,750,000	—	.10	—
1981D	5,373,235,677	—	.10	—
1981S Proof Only	—	—	1.75	
1982 Copper large date	10,712,525,000	—	.10	—
1982 Copper SD	—	.15	—	
1982 Zinc LD	—	.35	—	
1982 Zinc SD	—	.50	—	
1982D Copper LD	6,012,979,368	—	.10	—
1982D Zinc LD	—	.20	—	
1982D Zinc SD	—	—	—	
1982S Proof Only	—	.10	4.25	
1983	7,752,355,000	—	.10	—
1983 Doubled Die (Rev.)	—	175.	—	
1983D	6,467,199,428	—	.10	—
1983S Proof Only	—	—	9.50	
1984	8,151,079,000	—	.10	—
1984 Doubled Die	—	90.00	—	
1984D	5,569,238,906	—	.10	—
1984S Proof Only	—	—	13.50	
1985	5,648,489,887	—	.10	—
1985D	5,287,399,926	—	.10	—
1985S Proof Only	—	—	8.00	
1986	4,491,395,493	—	.10	—
1986D	4,442,866,698	—	.10	—
1986S Proof Only	—	—	7.25	
1987	4,682,466,931	—	.10	—
1987D	4,879,389,514	—	.10	—
1987S Proof Only	—	—	8.00	
1988	—	.10	—	
1988D	—	.10	—	
1988S Proof Only	—	—	8.00	
1989	—	.10	—	
1989D	—	.10	—	
1989S Proof Only	—	—	8.00	

UNITED STATES 1727

1955 Doubled Die

1972 Doubled Die

1960 SMALL DATE

1983 Doubled Die Reverse

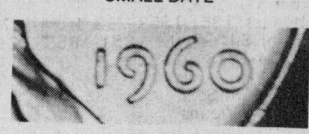
1960 LARGE DATE

1970 S LARGE DATE   1970 S SMALL DATE

1982 LARGE DATE

1982 SMALL DATE

TWO CENT

Type: Two-Cent Pieces
Dates of issue: 1864-1873
Designer: James B. Longacre
Size: 23 MM
Weight: 6.22 Grams
Composition: 95% Copper, 5% Tin and Zinc

Date	Mintage	G-4	VG-8	F-12	VF-20	XF-40	AU-50	MS-60	MS-65	Prf-65
1864 SM	19,847,500	55.00	80.00	100.	175.	275.	350.	500.	1900	15,000.
1864 LM	Inc. Ab.	5.00	5.50	9.50	16.00	35.00	63.00	115.	600.	2700.

SMALL MOTTO

LARGE MOTTO

Date	Mintage	G-4	VG-8	F-12	VF-20	XF-40	AU-50	MS-60	MS-65	Prf-65
1865	13,640,000	5.00	5.50	9.50	16.00	35.00	63.00	115.	600.	1400.
1866	3,177,000	5.00	6.50	10.00	16.00	35.00	70.00	115.	600.	1400.
1867	2,938,750	5.00	7.00	10.00	18.00	38.00	75.00	115.	600.	1400.
1868	2,803,750	6.00	7.50	10.50	18.00	40.00	75.00	115.	600.	1400.
1869	1,546,500	7.00	9.50	13.50	25.00	50.00	85.00	200.	1150.	1400.
1870	861,250	9.00	13.00	21.00	35.00	70.00	110.	300.	1350.	1400.
1871	721,250	11.00	15.00	24.00	42.00	75.00	140.	350.	1550.	1400.
1872	65,000	75.00	105.	150.	250.	350.	475.	1100.	3000.	2150.
1873	Est. 1100	—	—	Proof Only					—	3000.
	Impaired Proof			1150.	1250.	1350.	1650.			

THREE CENT SILVER

Type: Three Cent Pieces — Silver
Dates of issue: 1851-1873
Designer: James B. Longacre
Size: 14 MM
Weight: 1851-1853 .80 Grams, 1854-1873 .75 Grams
Composition: 1851-1853 75% Silver, 25% Copper, 1854-1873 90% Silver, 10% Copper
Fineness: 1851-1853 .750, 1854-1873 .900
Actual Silver wt.: 1851-1853 .0193 Oz., 1854-1873 .0218 Oz.

MINT MARKS:
O New Orleans

Mintmark

Type 1 - No Outlines To Star

Date	Mintage	G-4	VG-8	F-12	VF-20	XF-40	AU-50	MS-60	MS-65	Prf-65
1851	5,447,400	12.00	15.00	18.00	30.00	70.00	125.	225.	4000.	—
1851O	720,000	18.00	23.00	33.00	60.00	125.	225.	500.	4100.	—
1852	18,663,500	10.00	11.50	14.00	30.00	41.00	110.	155.	3800.	—
1853	11,400,000	10.00	11.50	14.00	30.00	41.00	110.	155.	3800.	—

Type 2 - Three Outlines To Star

Date	Mintage	G-4	VG-8	F-12	VF-20	XF-40	AU-50	MS-60	MS-65	Prf-65
1854	671,000	13.00	16.00	23.00	45.00	110.	210.	265.	7050.	—
1855	139,000	18.00	27.00	45.00	85.00	170.	450.	700.	7400	11,500.
1856	1,458,000	10.00	13.00	16.00	40.00	85.00	210.	265.	7050	11,000.
1857	1,042,000	11.00	14.00	17.00	41.00	85.00	210.	265.	7050.	9500.
1858	1,604,000	10.00	13.00	16.00	40.00	85.00	210.	265.	7050.	9500.

Type 3 - Two Outlines To Star

Date	Mintage	G-4	VG-8	F-12	VF-20	XF-40	AU-50	MS-60	MS-65	Prf-65
1859	365,000	10.00	12.50	16.00	35.00	70.00	115.	155.	3650.	2900.
1860	287,000	10.00	12.50	16.00	35.00	70.00	115.	155.	3650.	2900.
1861	498,000	10.00	12.50	16.00	35.00	70.00	115.	155.	3650.	2900.
1862	343,550	10.00	12.50	16.00	35.00	70.00	115.	155.	3650.	2900.
1863	21,460	325.	375.	425.	500.	600.	675.	950.	4800.	4400.
1864	12,470	250.	275.	325.	375.	485.	550.	700.	4900.	4400.
1865	8,500	260.	300.	350.	400.	500.	550.	725.	4700.	4600.

Date	Mintage	G-4	VG-8	F-12	VF-20	XF-40	AU-50	MS-60	MS-65	Prf-65
1866	22,725	225.	250.	300.	350.	400.	475.	700.	3600.	4400.
1867	4,625	285.	325.	375.	425.	525.	600.	750.	4500.	4100.
1868	4,100	285.	325.	375.	425.	525.	600.	750.	4500.	4100.
1869	5,100	285.	325.	375.	425.	525.	600.	750.	4500.	4100.
1870	4,000	285.	325.	375.	425.	525.	600.	750.	4500.	4200.
1871	4,360	285.	325.	375.	425.	525.	600.	750.	5500.	4200.
1872	1,950	325.	375.	450.	550.	650.	750.	950.	4750.	4700.
1873	600	—	—	Proof Only					—	4900.
	Impaired Proof			750.	850.	950.	1200.			

THREE CENT NICKEL

Type: Three Cent Pieces — Nickel
Dates of issue: 1865-1889
Designer: James B. Longacre
Size: 17.9 MM
Weight: 1.94 Grams
Composition: 75% Copper, 25% Nickel

Date	Mintage	G-4	VG-8	F-12	VF-20	XF-40	AU-50	MS-60	MS-65	Prf-65
1865	11,382,000	4.25	4.50	5.00	6.30	15.00	35.00	75.00	2650.	3600.
1866	4,801,000	4.25	4.50	5.00	6.30	15.00	35.00	75.00	2650.	3300.
1867	3,915,000	4.25	4.50	5.00	6.30	15.00	35.00	75.00	2650.	1750.
1868	3,252,000	4.25	4.50	5.00	6.30	15.00	35.00	75.00	2650.	1750.
1869	1,604,000	4.25	4.75	5.50	6.50	17.00	40.00	85.00	2700.	1750.
1870	1,335,000	4.25	4.75	5.50	6.50	17.00	40.00	85.00	2700.	1750.
1871	604,000	5.00	6.00	8.00	9.25	18.00	40.00	225.	2800.	1750.
1872	862,000	4.50	5.25	7.00	8.50	17.00	60.00	250.	2800.	1750.
1873	1,173,000	4.50	5.25	6.00	8.25	16.50	45.00	85.00	2700.	1750.
1874	790,000	5.25	5.50	7.00	8.50	17.00	50.00	250.	2800.	1750.
1875	228,000	8.00	9.00	12.00	18.00	31.00	95.00	275.	2900.	1750.
1876	162,000	10.00	12.50	17.00	24.00	38.00	100.	275.	2950.	1750.
1877	Est. 900	—	—	Proof Only				—	—	3900.
	Impaired Proof			1200.	1300.	1400.	1500.			
1878	2,350	—	—	Proof Only				—	—	3000.
	Impaired Proof			625.	675.	750.	850.			
1879	41,200	46.00	55.00	70.00	80.00	100.	150.	300.	2850.	3300.
1880	24,955	63.00	80.00	90.00	100.	130.	175.	325.	2900.	3300.
1881	1,080,575	4.25	5.00	6.50	9.00	20.00	35.00	150.	2700.	1750.
1882	25,300	63.00	70.00	80.00	90.00	125.	210.	500.	2850.	3300.
1883	10,609	125.	145.	200.	225.	250.	450.	650.	2900.	3300.
1884	5,642	290.	330.	375.	415.	475.	575.	800.	3100.	3400.
1885	4,790	350.	380.	500.	550.	600.	700.	1200.	3200.	3500.
1886	4,290	—	—	Proof Only				—	—	3350.
	Impaired Proof			525.	575.	650.	800.			
1887/6	7,961	—	—	Proof Only				—	—	3500.
	Impaired Proof			650.	725.	800.	875.			
1887	Inc. Ab.	240.	250.	275.	300.	325.	500.	600.	3000.	3350.
1888	41,083	55.00	60.00	70.00	80.00	100.	125.	425.	2850.	3350.
1889	21,561	63.00	70.00	90.00	105.	125.	150.	475.	2850.	3350.

HALF DIMES

Flowing Hair Half-Dimes

Type: Half Dimes, Flowing Hair Type
Dates of issue: 1794-1795
Designer: Robert Scot
Size: 16.5 MM
Weight: 1.35 Grams
Composition: 89.24% Silver & 10.76% Copper
Fineness: .8924
Actual Silver wt.: .0388 Oz. pure Silver

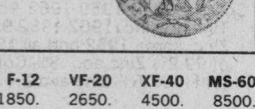

Date	Mintage	G-4	VG-8	F-12	VF-20	XF-40	MS-60
1794	86,416	1075.	1250.	1850.	2650.	4500.	8500.
1795	Inc. Ab.	500.	700.	1250.	1750.	2650.	6300.

Draped Bust Half-Dimes

Type: Half Dimes — Draped Bust, Small Eagle Reverse
Dates of issue: 1796-1797
Designer: Robert Scot
Size: 16.5 MM
Weight: 1.35 Grams
Composition: 89.24% Silver & 10.76% Copper
Fineness: .8924
Actual Silver wt.: .0388 Oz. pure Silver

Date	Mintage	G-4	VG-8	F-12	VF-20	XF-40	MS-60
1796	10,230	850.	925.	1350.	2150.	3350.	7850.
1796 Liberty	Inc. Ab.	850.	925.	1350.	2150.	3350.	—
1796/5	Inc. Ab.	1200.	1400.	1600.	2400.	3400.	9000.
1797 13 Stars	44,527	900.	975.	1400.	2200.	3350.	11,500.
1797 15 Stars	Inc. Ab.	850.	925.	1350.	2150.	3350.	7850.
1797 16 Stars	Inc. Ab.	875.	950.	1375.	2150.	3350.	7850.

Heraldic Eagle Introduced

Type: Half Dimes — Draped Bust, Heraldic Eagle
Dates of issue: 1800-1805
Designer: Robert Scot
Size: 16.5 MM
Weight: 1.35 Grams
Composition: 89.24% Silver & 10.76% Copper
Fineness: .8924
Actual Silver wt.: .0388 Oz. pure Silver

Date	Mintage	G-4	VG-8	F-12	VF-20	XF-40	MS-60
1800	24,000	675.	875.	1100.	1400.	2400.	6950.
1800 Libekty	Inc. Ab.	675.	875.	1100.	1400.	2400.	6950.
1801	33,910	750.	975.	1100.	1500.	2750.	10,000.
1802	13,010	10,500.	13,000.	23,000.	32,000.	45,000.	—
1803	37,850	625.	700.	1050.	1400.	2400.	6950.
1805	15,600	975.	1175.	1500.	1900.	3250.	—

Liberty Cap Half-Dimes

Type: Half Dimes — Capped Bust
Dates of issue: 1829-1837
Designer: William Kneass
Size: 15.5 MM
Weight: 1.35 Grams
Composition: 89.24% Silver & 10.76% Copper
Fineness: .8924
Actual Silver wt.: .0388 Oz. pure Silver

Date	Mintage	G-4	VG-8	F-12	VF-20	XF-40	AU-50	MS-60	MS-65
1829	1,230,000	12.00	18.00	25.00	50.00	125.	245.	350.	9000.
1830	1,240,000	12.00	18.00	25.00	50.00	125.	245.	350.	9000.
1831	1,242,700	12.00	18.00	25.00	50.00	125.	245.	350.	9000.
1832	965,000	12.00	18.00	25.00	50.00	125.	245.	350.	9000.
1833	1,370,000	12.00	18.00	25.00	50.00	125.	245.	350.	9000.
1834	1,480,000	12.00	18.00	25.00	50.00	125.	245.	350.	9000.
1835 Large Date, Large 5C.	2,760,000	12.00	18.00	25.00	50.00	125.	245.	350.	9000.
1835 Large Date, Small 5C.	Inc. Ab.	12.00	18.00	25.00	50.00	125.	245.	350.	9000.
1835 Small Date, Large 5C.	Inc. Ab.	12.00	18.00	25.00	50.00	125.	245.	350.	9000.
1835 Small Date, Small 5C.	Inc. Ab.	12.00	18.00	25.00	50.00	125.	245.	350.	9000.
1836 Large 5C.	1,900,000	12.00	18.00	25.00	50.00	125.	245.	350.	9000.
1836 Small 5C.	Inc. Ab.	12.00	18.00	25.00	50.00	125.	245.	350.	9000.
1837 Large 5C.	2,276,000	12.00	18.00	25.00	50.00	125.	245.	350.	9000.
1837 Small 5C.	Inc. Ab.	25.00	40.00	60.00	85.00	150.	350.	1250.	9500.

Liberty Seated Half-Dimes
Without Stars Around Rim

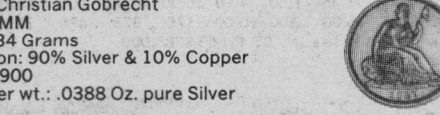

Type: Half Dimes — Liberty Seated — No Stars Obverse
Dates of issue: 1837-1838
Designer: Christian Gobrecht
Size: 15.5 MM
Weight: 1.34 Grams
Composition: 90% Silver & 10% Copper
Fineness: .900
Actual Silver wt.: .0388 Oz. pure Silver

MINT MARKS:
O New Orleans

Date	Mintage	G-4	VG-8	F-12	VF-20	XF-40	MS-60
1837 Sm. Date	Inc. Ab.	25.00	35.00	53.00	110.	225.	750.
1837 Lg. Date	Inc. Ab.	25.00	35.00	53.00	110.	225.	500.
1838O	70,000	100.	150.	225.	400.	700.	—

Stars Added Around Rim

Type: Half Dimes — Liberty Seated — with stars
Dates of issue: 1838-1853
MINT MARKS:
O New Orleans

Date	Mintage	G-4	VG-8	F-12	VF-20	XF-40	MS-60
1838	2,255,000	5.00	6.25	10.00	25.00	85.00	330.
1838 Sm.stars	Inc. Ab.	25.00	35.00	50.00	125.	250.	1200.
1839	1,069,150	8.00	10.00	13.00	29.00	70.00	330.
1839O	1,034,039	9.00	12.00	16.00	31.00	75.00	500
1839O Rev. 1838O	—	75.00	100.	175.	250.	500.	—
1840	1,344,085	5.00	6.25	10.00	21.00	57.00	450
1840O	935,000	10.00	13.00	18.00	35.00	85.00	600

Drapery Added To Liberty

Without Drapery   With Drapery

Date	Mintage	G-4	VG-8	F-12	VF-20	XF-40	MS-60
1840	Inc. Ab.	20.00	32.50	50.00	75.00	150.	1800
1840O	Inc. Ab.	30.00	50.00	80.00	120.	200.	—
1841	1,150,000	4.85	5.50	6.25	22.00	55.00	155.
1841O	815,000	10.00	15.00	22.50	40.00	85.00	650
1842	815,000	4.85	5.50	6.25	22.00	55.00	155.
1842O	350,000	28.00	45.00	65.00	140.	375.	—
1843	1,165,000	4.85	5.50	6.25	18.00	41.00	155.
1844	430,000	6.50	8.50	11.00	24.00	60.00	155.
1844O	220,000	60.00	100.	175.	350.	950.	—
1845	1,564,000	4.85	5.50	6.25	22.00	44.00	155
1845/1845	Inc. Ab.	8.00	11.00	15.00	30.00	75.00	350
1846	27,000	150.	200.	275.	450.	850.	—
1847	1,274,000	6.00	7.00	8.00	18.00	41.00	155
1848 Medium Date	668,000	7.00	8.50	11.00	32.00	60.00	175.
1848 Lg. Date	Inc. Ab.	20.00	26.00	35.00	75.00	175.	500.
1848O	600,000	12.00	17.50	25.00	42.50	90.00	600
1849/8	1,309,000	12.00	17.50	25.00	45.00	100.	500.
1849/6	Inc. Ab.	10.00	14.00	20.00	35.00	75.00	425.
1849	Inc. Ab.	6.00	8.00	11.00	18.00	45.00	600.
1849O	140,000	35.00	55.00	85.00	200.	500.	—
1850	955,000	4.85	5.50	6.25	18.00	41.00	400.
1850O	690,000	11.00	16.00	22.50	37.50	80.00	800
1851	781,000	4.85	5.50	6.25	18.00	41.00	400.
1851O	860,000	10.00	15.00	20.00	35.00	75.00	800
1852	1,000,500	6.00	7.00	10.00	18.00	41.00	175.
1852O	260,000	30.00	48.00	70.00	150.	400.	—
1853	135,000	25.00	38.00	55.00	85.00	200.	800.
1853O	160,000	135.	190.	275.	425.	850.	—

Arrows At Date

Type: Half Dimes — Liberty Seated — Arrows at Date
Dates of issue: 1853-1855
Designer: Christian Gobrecht
Size: 15.5 MM
Weight: 1.24 Grams
Composition: 90% Silver & 10% Copper
Fineness: .900
Actual Silver wt.: .0362 Oz. pure Silver
MINT MARKS:
O New Orleans

Date	Mintage	G-4	VG-8	F-12	VF-20	XF-40	MS-60	Prf-65
1853	13,210,020	4.85	5.50	6.25	17.00	50.00	160.	11,500.
1853O	2,200,000	6.00	8.00	11.00	24.00	60.00	325.	—
1854	5,740,000	5.00	6.50	8.50	17.00	50.00	250.	11,000.
1854O	1,560,000	7.00	9.00	12.00	27.00	70.00	700.	—
1855	1,750,000	5.50	7.00	10.00	22.00	55.00	250.	11,000.
1855O	600,000	12.00	17.00	25.00	45.00	100.	1000.	—

Arrows At Date Removed

Dates of issue: 1856-1859
MINT MARKS:
O New Orleans

Date	Mintage	G-4	VG-8	F-12	VF-20	XF-40	MS-60	Prf-65
1856	4,880,000	3.75	5.50	9.00	18.00	41.00	155.	8000.
1856O	1,100,000	8.00	10.00	12.00	27.00	70.00	600.	—
1857	7,280,000	3.50	4.50	6.25	18.00	45.00	155.	8000.
1857O	1,380,000	7.00	9.00	11.00	25.00	65.00	600.	—

UNITED STATES 1730

Date	Mintage	G-4	VG-8	F-12	VF-20	XF-40	MS-60	Prf-65
1858	3,500,000	4.25	5.50	6.25	18.00	45.00	155.	8000.
1858 Inverted Date								
Inc. Ab.	35.00	48.00	75.00	115.	200.	700.	—
1858 Double Date								
Inc. Ab.	40.00	55.00	80.00	120.	210.	1200.	—
1858O	1,660,000	7.00	9.00	12.00	26.00	65.00	600.	—
1859	340,000	9.00	12.00	15.00	33.00	85.00	250.	10,500.
1859O	560,000	8.00	10.00	13.00	30.00	80.00	700.	—

Transitional Patterns

Date	Mintage	G-4	VG-8	F-12	VF-20	XF-40	MS-60	Prf-65
1859 Obverse of 1859, Reverse 1860					—		15,000.
1860 Obverse of 1859, Reverse 1860					—	4000.	

Type: Half Dimes — Liberty Seated — Legend Obverse
Dates of issue: 1860-1873
Designer: Christian Gobrecht
Size: 15.5 MM
Weight: 1.24 Grams
Composition: 90% Silver & 10% Copper
Fineness: .900
Actual Silver wt.: .0362 Oz. pure Silver

MINT MARKS:
O New Orleans
S San Francisco

Mintmark ONLY 1871-72

Obverse Legend Replaces Stars

Date	Mintage	G-4	VG-8	F-12	VF-20	XF-40	MS-60	MS-65	Prf-65
1860	799,000	6.00	7.50	12.50	25.00	40.00	140.	3450.	3400.
1860O	1,060,000	6.00	7.50	12.50	25.00	40.00	350.	3450.	
1861	3,361,000	4.40	5.00	8.00	14.00	28.00	140.	3450.	3400.
1861/0	Inc. Ab.	20.00	35.00	60.00	120.	250.	800.	—	
1862	1,492,550	4.40	5.00	8.00	16.00	30.00	140.	3450.	3400.
1863	18,460	135.	165.	200.	260.	375.	800.	4000.	3550.
1863S	100,000	15.00	23.00	35.00	65.00	125.	900.	—	
1864	48,470	225.	290.	350.	450.	625.	950.	4000.	3550.
1864S	90,000	22.50	34.00	50.00	80.00	150.	1200.	—	
1865	13,500	225.	275.	350.	450.	625.	1300.	4250.	3550.
1865S	120,000	12.50	18.00	25.00	50.00	100.	975.	—	
1866	10,725	185.	225.	285.	375.	550.	1000.	4250.	3550.
1866S	120,000	12.50	18.00	25.00	50.00	100.	950.	—	
1867	8,625	365.	425.	475.	550.	675.	1300.	4250.	3550.
1867S	120,000	12.50	18.00	25.00	48.00	100.	900.	—	
1868	89,200	40.00	60.00	85.00	115.	175.	600.	4400.	3550.
1868S	280,000	10.00	14.00	20.00	33.00	60.00	500.	—	
1869	208,600	10.00	14.00	20.00	33.00	60.00	475.	4300.	3550.
1869S	230,000	10.00	14.00	20.00	33.00	60.00	500.	—	
1870	536,600	6.00	7.50	9.00	17.00	35.00	450.	3900.	3400.
1870S	Unique, Superior Galleries Sale, July, 1986 B.U. $253,000.								
1871	1,873,960	4.40	5.00	8.00	14.00	28.00	350.	3900.	3400.
1871S	161,000	15.00	19.00	25.00	45.00	85.00	675.	3450.	
1872	2,947,950	4.40	5.00	8.00	15.00	30.00	350.	3900.	
1872S Mintmark in Wreath									
	837,000	5.00	6.50	8.00	15.00	30.00	425.	3900.	
1872S Mintmark Below Wreath									
Inc. Ab.	5.00	6.50	8.00	15.00	30.00	450.	3900.		
1873	712,600	5.00	6.50	8.00	15.00	30.00	350.	3900.	3400.
1873S	324,000	7.50	9.50	12.50	20.00	38.00	350.	3900.	

SHIELD NICKELS

Type: Nickel Five Cent Pieces — Shield
Dates of issue: 1866-1883
Designer: James B. Longacre
Size: 20.5 MM
Weight: 5 Grams
Composition: 75% Copper, 25% Nickel

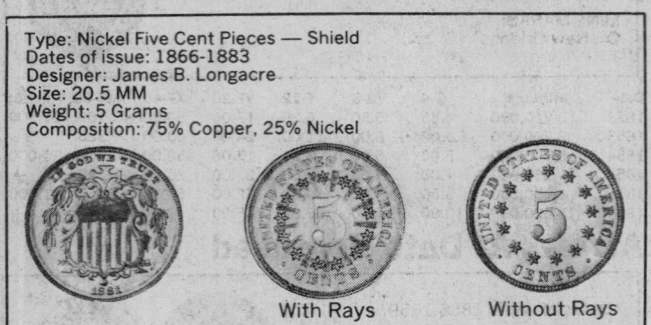

With Rays   Without Rays

Date	Mintage	G-4	VG-8	F-12	VF-20	XF-40	AU-50	MS-60	MS-65	Prf-65
1866	14,742,500	12.50	14.00	19.00	35.00	115.	165.	285.	7050.	7000.
1867 With Rays										
	2,019,000	17.00	20.00	32.00	40.00	115.	175.	550.	7200	10,500.
1867 Without Rays										
	28,890,500	6.00	7.50	9.00	12.50	30.00	45.00	100.	2400.	1750.
1868	28,817,000	6.00	7.50	9.00	12.50	30.00	45.00	100.	2400.	1750.
1869	16,395,000	6.00	7.50	9.50	13.00	30.00	45.00	100.	2400.	1750.

Date	Mintage	G-4	VG-8	F-12	VF-20	XF-40	AU-50	MS-60	MS-65	Prf-65
1870	4,806,000	7.50	8.50	10.00	16.50	43.00	59.00	175.	2750.	1750.
1871	561,000	25.00	30.00	40.00	75.00	110.	165.	300.	3200.	3250.
1872	6,036,000	8.00	9.00	10.50	16.50	40.00	65.00	175.	2750.	1750.
1873	4,550,000	8.00	9.00	11.00	17.00	43.00	65.00	175.	2750.	2500.
1874	3,538,000	9.00	10.00	11.50	18.00	48.00	70.00	200.	3150.	2450.
1875	2,097,000	10.00	12.00	16.00	25.00	58.00	90.00	200.	3100.	2450.
1876	2,530,000	10.00	12.00	15.50	24.00	52.00	85.00	200.	3250.	2500.
1877	Est. 900			Proof Only				—	—	5100.
	Impaired Proof	1350.	1450.	1600.	1700.					—
1878	2,350	—	—	Proof Only				—	—	3750.
	Impaired Proof		700.	750.	800.	850.				—
1879	29,100	275.	300.	350.	435.	490.	575.	750.	3150.	3350.
1880	19,995	300.	350.	415.	475.	575.	630.	800.	3200.	3350.
1881	72,375	150.	190.	275.	350.	440.	540.	700.	3100.	3350.
1882	11,476,600	7.00	9.50	11.00	15.00	30.00	45.00	250.	3000.	1750.
1883	1,456,919	12.00	14.00	17.50	22.50	32.50	45.00	250.	3100.	1750.
1883/2	—	75.00	90.00	115.	140.	175.	250.	350.	3100.	

LIBERTY HEAD NICKELS

With Cents   Without Cents

Type: Nickel Five Cent Pieces — Liberty Head
Dates of issue: 1883-1913
Designer: Charles E. Barber
Size: 21.2 MM
Weight: 5 Grams
Composition: 75% Copper, 25% Nickel

MINT MARKS:
D Denver
S San Francisco

Mintmark

Date	Mintage	G-4	VG-8	F-12	VF-20	XF-40	AU-50	MS-60	MS-65	Prf-65
1883 NC	5,479,519	2.50	3.50	4.00	5.50	7.50	11.50	29.00	1000.	2000.
1883 WC	16,032,983	5.50	6.25	10.50	19.00	33.00	65.00	65.00	2100.	1950.
1884	11,273,942	7.50	9.00	13.00	19.00	35.00	75.00	175.	2150.	1950.
1885	1,476,490	175.	230.	360.	475.	650.	900.	1100.	2600.	3450.
1886	3,330,290	48.00	60.00	110.	150.	215.	300.	500.	2200.	3150.
1887	15,263,652	6.00	8.00	12.00	16.00	35.00	80.00	145.	2000.	1500.
1888	10,720,483	8.00	10.00	15.00	25.00	46.00	100.	160.	2100.	1500.
1889	15,881,361	4.00	6.00	10.00	16.00	34.00	80.00	150.	2000.	1500.
1890	16,259,272	5.00	7.50	12.00	17.00	36.00	85.00	155.	2000.	1500.
1891	16,834,350	3.50	5.50	10.00	15.00	34.00	80.00	150.	2000.	1500.
1892	11,699,642	3.75	6.00	10.50	17.00	37.00	85.00	150.	2000.	1500.
1893	13,370,195	3.50	5.50	11.00	16.00	34.00	85.00	150.	2000.	1500.
1894	5,413,132	6.00	7.50	17.00	30.00	60.00	110.	200.	2200.	1500.
1895	9,979,884	2.60	3.50	8.00	14.00	31.00	80.00	140.	2000.	1500.
1896	8,842,920	4.00	6.00	10.50	18.00	37.00	90.00	155.	2100.	1500.
1897	20,428,735	2.00	2.50	4.00	8.00	21.00	70.00	130.	2050.	1500.
1898	12,532,087	1.50	2.00	4.50	8.50	22.00	73.00	135.	2050.	1500.
1899	26,029,031	1.00	1.25	3.50	7.50	18.00	50.00	125.	2050.	1500.
1900	27,255,995	.75	1.10	3.50	6.00	17.00	42.00	75.00	2000.	1500.
1901	26,480,213	.75	1.10	3.50	6.00	17.00	42.00	75.00	2000.	1500.
1902	31,480,579	.75	1.10	3.50	6.00	17.00	42.00	75.00	2000.	1500.
1903	28,006,725	.75	1.10	3.50	6.00	17.00	42.00	75.00	2000.	1500.
1904	21,404,984	.75	1.10	3.50	6.00	17.00	42.00	75.00	2000.	1500.
1905	29,827,276	.75	1.10	3.50	6.00	17.00	42.00	75.00	2000.	1500.
1906	38,613,725	.75	1.10	3.50	6.00	17.00	42.00	75.00	2000.	1500.
1907	39,214,800	.75	1.10	3.50	6.00	17.00	42.00	75.00	2000.	1500.
1908	22,686,177	.75	1.10	3.50	6.00	17.00	42.00	75.00	2000.	1500.
1909	11,590,526	1.00	1.25	3.75	6.75	20.00	48.00	100.	2000.	1500.
1910	30,169,353	.75	1.10	3.50	6.00	17.00	42.00	75.00	2000.	1500.
1911	39,559,372	.75	1.10	3.50	6.00	17.00	42.00	75.00	2000.	1500.
1912	26,236,714	.75	1.10	3.50	6.00	17.00	42.00	75.00	2000.	1500.
1912D	8,474,000	1.25	1.50	4.50	10.00	40.00	100.	250.	2200.	—
1912S	238,000	35.00	42.00	60.00	175.	375.	475.	725.	2700.	

1913 Only 5 known, Buss sale Jan. 85, Prf-63 $385,000.

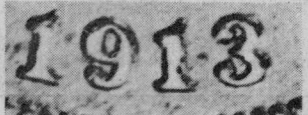 

Authentic   Altered Date

The above enlargements of the date areas of authentic and altered date 1913 Liberty Head nickels illustrate the normal differences in the configuration of the 3.

BUFFALO NICKELS

Mound Type   Line Type

Type: Nickel Five Cent Pieces — Buffalo or Indian Head
Dates of issue: 1913-1938
Designer: James Earl Fraser
Size: 21.2 MM
Weight: 5 Grams
Composition: 75% Copper, 25% Nickel

MINT MARKS:
D   Denver
S   San Francisco

Mound Type

Date	Mintage	G-4	VG-8	F-12	VF-20	XF-40	AU-50	MS-60	MS-65	Prf-65
1913	30,993,520	3.00	4.50	5.50	6.25	12.00	18.00	32.00	285.	1950.
1913D	5,337,000	5.00	7.50	9.50	13.50	24.00	45.00	70.00	750.	—
1913S	2,105,000	9.00	11.00	16.00	25.00	45.00	75.00	100.	880.	—

Line-Type

Date	Mintage	G-4	VG-8	F-12	VF-20	XF-40	AU-50	MS-60	MS-65	Prf-65
1913	29,858,700	3.50	4.50	5.50	8.00	13.50	25.00	32.00	640.	2950.
1913D	4,156,000	37.50	42.00	50.00	60.00	75.00	125.	240.	1700.	—
1913S	1,209,000	70.00	85.00	110.	125.	175.	250.	375.	2400.	—
1914	20,665,738	4.50	5.50	7.00	9.00	16.00	33.00	75.00	695.	3000.
1914D	3,912,000	32.00	37.50	45.00	65.00	105.	125.	275.	1500.	—
1914S	3,470,000	5.00	7.50	11.00	19.00	38.00	45.00	100.	1550.	—
1915	20,987,270	2.50	3.50	5.00	7.00	13.00	24.00	55.00	750.	3100.
1915D	7,569,500	7.00	10.00	20.00	40.00	55.00	85.00	150.	1500.	—
1915S	1,505,000	12.00	14.00	28.00	60.00	100.	145.	275.	1900.	—
1916	63,498,066	1.15	1.75	2.25	3.50	7.50	25.00	40.00	660.	3200.
1916/16	Inc. Ab.	800.	1100.	1600.	2000.	2800.	3500.	4700.	—	—
1916D	13,333,000	4.00	6.50	10.00	25.00	50.00	80.00	145.	1250.	—
1916S	11,860,000	3.50	5.00	7.00	19.00	50.00	80.00	130.	1250.	—
1917	51,424,029	1.25	1.75	2.50	4.50	11.00	30.00	45.00	725.	—
1917D	9,910,800	6.00	9.00	16.00	45.00	90.00	120.	220.	2000.	—
1917S	4,193,000	6.00	8.00	14.00	40.00	80.00	125.	230.	2450.	—
1918	32,086,314	1.25	2.00	3.50	7.50	19.00	35.00	75.00	915.	—

Mintmark   Overdate — 18D/17

Date	Mintage	G-4	VG-8	F-12	VF-20	XF-40	AU-50	MS-60	MS-65	Prf-65
1918D/17	8,362,314	475.	650.	800.	1300.	2750.	4750.	8500	27,000.	—
1918D	Inc. Ab.	6.50	10.00	18.00	65.00	115.	175.	300.	2750.	—
1918S	4,882,000	5.00	9.00	16.00	45.00	105.	145.	275.	2650.	—
1919	60,868,000	.75	1.00	1.50	3.50	10.00	20.00	40.00	725.	—
1919D	8,006,000	6.50	11.00	20.00	85.00	135.	160.	325.	2500.	—
1919S	7,521,000	4.00	6.50	12.00	50.00	115.	125.	275.	3700.	—
1920	63,093,000	.75	1.00	1.50	3.50	10.00	25.00	40.00	695.	—
1920D	9,418,000	5.00	8.50	15.00	65.00	125.	140.	325.	3700.	—
1920S	9,689,000	2.50	4.00	8.50	35.00	105.	125.	195.	4400.	—
1921	10,663,000	1.00	1.80	3.00	7.50	20.00	45.00	85.00	800.	—
1921S	1,557,000	17.00	25.00	50.00	225.	400.	500.	750.	3450.	—
1923	35,715,000	.50	.75	1.50	3.50	8.00	16.00	40.00	725.	—
1923S	6,142,000	1.50	2.50	5.00	25.00	50.00	75.00	130.	4400.	—
1924	21,620,000	.50	.75	1.25	4.50	12.00	35.00	55.00	725.	—
1924D	5,258,000	2.75	5.00	9.00	50.00	70.00	150.	200.	2000.	—
1924S	1,437,000	5.00	8.50	17.00	240.	350.	500.	850.	3000.	—
1925	35,565,100	.40	.60	1.00	3.50	10.00	19.00	40.00	700.	—
1925D	4,450,000	3.75	6.50	10.00	60.00	110.	125.	300.	2200.	—
1925S	6,256,000	1.75	4.00	7.00	25.00	45.00	80.00	200.	3400.	—
1926	44,693,000	.35	.50	.75	2.00	7.00	20.00	35.00	650.	—
1926D	5,638,000	4.00	7.50	15.00	60.00	120.	130.	140.	2500.	—
1926S	970,000	6.00	10.00	18.00	85.00	425.	550.	725.	4250.	—
1927	37,981,000	.30	.50	.80	1.75	7.00	16.00	30.00	680.	—
1927D	5,730,000	1.75	2.50	5.00	15.00	50.00	60.00	100.	1325.	—
1927S	3,430,000	.80	2.50	3.50	18.00	65.00	70.00	165.	1650.	—

Date	Mintage	G-4	VG-8	F-12	VF-20	XF-40	AU-50	MS-60	MS-65	Prf-65
1928	23,411,000	.30	.40	.75	2.00	7.00	16.00	35.00	660.	—
1928D	6,436,000	.60	.90	2.25	6.00	17.50	25.00	50.00	875.	—
1928S	6,936,000	.50	.80	1.25	4.00	15.00	30.00	70.00	1075.	—
1929	36,446,000	.30	.60	.75	1.75	8.00	15.00	29.00	500.	—
1929D	8,370,000	.45	.70	1.00	5.50	16.00	26.00	55.00	1075.	—
1929S	7,754,000	.40	.50	.75	2.50	10.00	20.00	40.00	975.	—
1930	22,849,000	.30	.50	.75	1.75	6.00	15.00	30.00	325.	—
1930S	5,435,000	.50	.60	1.00	2.00	9.50	25.00	50.00	695.	—
1931S	1,200,000	3.00	3.50	3.75	5.25	12.50	25.00	55.00	600.	—
1934	20,213,003	.30	.45	.65	2.00	6.00	12.00	30.00	350.	—
1934D	7,480,000	.45	.65	.90	3.00	8.50	20.00	50.00	425.	—
1935	58,264,000	.30	.40	.50	1.00	4.00	8.00	16.00	220.	—
1935D	12,092,000	.35	.55	.75	2.00	7.00	18.00	45.00	725.	—
1935S	10,300,000	.35	.40	.50	1.25	5.50	12.00	25.00	295.	—
1936	119,001,420	.30	.35	.50	1.00	3.50	7.50	13.00	180.	2150.
1936D	24,814,000	.30	.40	.50	1.25	4.00	8.50	16.00	210.	—
1936S	14,930,000	.30	.40	.50	1.25	4.00	11.00	18.00	265.	—
1937	79,485,769	.30	.35	.50	1.00	3.50	6.50	11.00	120.	2150.
1937D	17,826,000	.30	.40	.55	1.25	4.00	8.00	13.00	165.	—
1937D 3 Leg	Inc. Ab.	90.00	115.	135.	175.	210.	310.	750.	5900.	—

Three-Legged
Buffalo Enlargements

Date	Mintage	G-4	VG-8	F-12	VF-20	XF-40	AU-50	MS-60	MS-65	Prf-65
1937S	5,635,000	.40	.45	.70	1.75	4.00	8.00	13.00	180.	—
1938D	7,020,000	.40	.50	.75	1.75	4.00	7.50	12.00	120.	—
1938 D/D	—	1.00	2.00	3.00	4.00	5.00	10.00	16.00	120.	—
1938D/S	Inc. Ab.	3.50	5.00	8.00	10.00	12.50	16.00	25.00	140.	—

JEFFERSON NICKELS

Mintmarks

Reverse
1938-42, 46-64

Obverse
Since 1968

Type: Nickel Five Cent Pieces — Jefferson
Dates of issue: 1938 to present
Designer: Felix Schlag
Size: 21.2 MM
Weight: 5 Grams
Composition: 1938-1942, 1946 to date 75% Copper, 25% Nickel, 1942-1945 56% Copper, 35% Silver, 9% Manganese
Fineness: 1942-1945 .350
Actual Silver wt.: 1942-1945 .0563%

MINT MARKS:
D   Denver
S   San Francisco
P   Philadelphia (1942-45) (1980 to date)

Date	Mintage	G-4	VG-8	F-12	VF-20	XF-40	MS-60	MS-65	Prf-65
1938	19,515,365	—	.40	.50	1.00	1.50	3.50	7.00	85.00
1938D	5,376,000	.75	.90	1.00	1.25	1.75	4.25	7.50	—
1938S	4,105,000	1.00	1.50	1.75	2.00	2.50	5.00	8.00	—
1939	120,627,535	—	—	.15	.25	.30	1.75	2.00	75.00
Doubled Monticello			7.50	10.00	25.00	50.00	200.	—	—
1939D	3,514,000	2.50	3.00	3.50	4.50	6.75	28.00	50.00	—
1939S	6,630,000	.40	.45	.60	1.00	3.25	21.00	30.00	—
1940	176,499,158	—	—	—	.15	.25	1.00	1.25	55.00
1940D	43,540,000	—	—	.15	.30	.40	2.50	2.75	—
1940S	39,690,000	—	—	.15	.20	.50	2.25	2.75	—
1941	203,283,720	—	—	—	.15	.20	.75	1.00	55.00
1941D	53,432,000	—	—	.15	.25	.35	2.50	4.00	—
1941S	43,445,000	—	—	.15	.25	.40	3.75	5.75	—
1942	49,818,600	—	—	.15	.25	.40	1.50	1.75	50.00
1942D	13,938,000	—	.30	.40	.60	2.00	17.50	35.00	—

Silver Wartime Nickels

Date	Mintage	G-4	VG-8	F-12	VF-20	XF-40	MS-60	MS-65	Prf-65
1942P	57,900,600	—	.60	.85	1.00	1.75	12.50	20.00	345.
1942S	32,900,000	—	.70	1.00	1.10	1.75	9.50	15.00	—
1943P	271,165,000	—	.60	.85	1.00	1.50	4.00	6.50	—
1943P3/2	Inc. Ab.	20.00	30.00	45.00	70.00	110.	250.	600.	—
1943D	15,294,000	—	.90	1.10	1.50	1.75	3.75	5.50	—
1943S	104,060,000	—	.60	.85	1.00	1.50	4.25	5.75	—
1944P	119,150,000	—	.60	.85	1.00	1.50	4.75	6.00	—
1944D	32,309,000	—	.60	.85	1.00	1.75	9.25	12.00	—
1944S	21,640,000	—	.85	.95	1.25	3.00	8.00	15.00	—
1945P	119,408,100	—	.60	.85	1.00	1.75	6.25	7.50	—
1945D	37,158,000	—	.60	.85	1.00	1.50	5.65	6.50	—
1945S	58,939,000	—	.60	.85	1.00	1.50	3.75	7.50	—

Pre-War Composition

Date	Mintage	G-4	VG-8	F-12	VF-20	XF-40	MS-60	MS-65	Prf-65
1946	161,116,000	—	—	—	.15	.20	.40	.60	—
1946D	45,292,200	—	—	—	.25	.35	.75	.95	—
1946S	13,560,000	—	—	—	.30	.40	.60	.65	—
1947	95,000,000	—	—	—	.15	.20	.40	.55	—
1947D	37,822,000	—	—	—	.20	.30	.65	.70	—
1947S	24,720,000	—	—	—	.15	.20	.55	.65	—
1948	89,348,000	—	—	—	.15	.20	.35	.55	—
1948D	44,734,000	—	—	—	.25	.35	1.00	1.25	—
1948S	11,300,000	—	—	—	.25	.50	1.00	1.25	—
1949	60,652,000	—	—	—	.20	.25	.75	1.25	—
1949D	36,498,000	—	—	—	.30	.40	1.00	1.25	—
1949D D/S	Inc. Ab.	—	—	20.00	40.00	75.00	175.	350.	—
1949S	9,716,000	—	.15	.20	.35	1.50	2.00	2.50	—
1950	9,847,386	—	.25	.45	.50	.75	1.90	2.25	60.00
1950D	2,630,030	—	4.25	4.50	5.00	5.50	6.50	9.00	—
1951	28,609,500	—	.25	.30	.40	.50	1.00	1.50	42.00
1951D	20,460,000	—	.25	.30	.40	.50	1.25	1.50	—
1951S	7,776,000	—	.30	.40	.50	.75	1.75	4.00	—
1952	64,069,980	—	—	—	.15	.20	.55	.65	28.00
1952D	30,638,000	—	—	—	.20	.35	.75	1.75	—
1952S	20,572,000	—	—	—	.15	.20	.65	.90	—
1953	46,772,800	—	—	—	.15	.25	.35	.40	18.00
1953D	59,878,600	—	—	—	.15	.20	.30	.35	—
1953S	19,210,900	—	—	—	.15	.20	.35	.40	—
1954	47,917,350	—	—	—	—	.20	.30	.35	7.50
1954D	117,136,560	—	—	—	—	.30	.35	—	—
1954S	29,384,000	—	—	—	.15	.35	.40	—	—
1954S S/D	Inc. Ab.	—	—	3.50	7.00	11.00	25.00	37.50	—
1955	8,266,200	—	.25	.35	.40	.45	.75	1.25	6.50
1955D	74,464,100	—	—	—	—	.20	.30	—	—
1956	35,885,384	—	—	—	—	.25	.35	.35	2.25
1956D	67,222,940	—	—	—	—	—	.20	.35	—
1957	39,655,952	—	—	—	—	.25	.35	1.25	—
1957D	136,828,900	—	—	—	—	—	.20	.40	—
1958	17,963,652	—	—	—	.15	.20	.30	.55	2.25
1958D	168,249,120	—	—	—	—	—	.20	.35	—

Date	Mintage	MS-65	Prf-65	Date	Mintage	MS-65	Prf-65
1959	28,397,291	.35	1.10	1976S	Proof Only	—	.45
1959D	160,738,240	.25	—	1977	585,376,000	.15	—
1960	57,107,602	.25	.75	1977D	297,313,460	.20	—
1960D	192,582,180	.25	—	1977S	Proof Only	—	.45
1961	76,668,244	.25	.65	1978	391,308,000	.15	—
1961D	229,342,760	.25	—	1978D	313,092,780	.15	—
1962	100,602,019	.25	.65	1978S	Proof Only	—	.55
1962D	280,195,720	.25	—	1979	463,188,000	.15	—
1963	178,851,645	.25	.65	1979D	325,867,672	.15	—
1963D	276,829,460	.25	—	1979S	Proof Only	—	.70
1964	1,028,622,762	.25	.65	1979S T-II	Proof Only	—	1.65
1964D	1,787,297,160	.25	—	1980P	593,004,000	.15	—
1965	136,131,380	.25	—	1980D	502,323,448	.15	—
1966	156,208,283	.25	—	1980S	Proof Only	—	.45
1967	107,325,800	.25	—	1981P	657,504,000	.15	—
1968	None Minted	—	—	1981D	364,801,843	.15	—
1968D	91,227,880	.25	—	1981S	Proof Only	—	.45
1968S	103,437,510	.25	.35	1982P	292,355,000	.15	—
1969	None Minted	—	—	1982D	373,726,544	.15	—
1969D	202,807,500	.25	—	1982S	Proof Only	—	1.10
1969S	123,099,631	.25	.35	1983P	561,615,000	.15	—
1970	None Minted	—	—	1983D	536,726,276	.15	—
1970D	515,485,380	.25	—	1983S	Proof Only	—	1.65
1970S	241,464,814	.25	.40	1984P	746,769,000	.15	—
1971	106,884,000	.60	—	1984D	517,675,146	.15	—
1971D	316,144,800	.25	—	1984S	Proof Only	—	3.50
1971S	Proof Only	—	.85	1985P	647,114,962	.15	—
1972	202,036,000	.25	—	1985D	459,747,446	.15	—
1972D	351,694,600	.25	—	1985S	Proof Only	—	2.25
1972S	Proof Only	—	.85	1986P	536,883,483	.15	—
1973	384,396,000	.15	—	1986D	361,819,140	.15	—
1973D	261,405,000	.15	—	1986S	Proof Only	—	2.00
1973S	Proof Only	—	.95	1987P	371,499,481	.15	—
1974	601,752,000	.15	—	1987D	410,590,604	.15	—
1974D	277,373,000	.20	—	1987S	Proof Only	—	2.25
1974S	Proof Only	—	1.00	1988P	—	.15	—
1975	181,772,000	.15	—	1988D	—	.15	—
1975D	401,875,300	.15	—	1988S	Proof Only	—	2.25
1975S	Proof Only	—	1.10	1989P	—	.15	—
1976	367,124,000	.15	—	1989D	—	.15	—
1976D	563,964,147	.15	—	1989S	Proof Only	—	2.25

DIMES
Draped Bust Dimes

Type: Dimes — Draped Bust — Small Eagle Reverse
Dates of issue: 1796-1797
Designer: Robert Scot
Size: 19 MM
Weight: 2.70 Grams
Composition: 89.24% Silver & 10.76% Copper
Fineness: .8924
Actual Silver wt.: .0775 Oz. pure Silver

Date	Mintage	G-4	VG-8	F-12	VF-20	XF-40	MS-60
1796	22,135	950.	1150.	1550.	2400.	4150.	7000.
1797 13 Stars	25,261	1050.	1250.	1700.	2500.	4500.	7500.
1797 16 Stars	Inc. Ab.	1000.	1200.	1600.	2400.	4150.	7500.

Heraldic Eagle Introduced

Type: Dimes — Draped Bust — Heraldic Eagle
Dates of issue: 1798-1807
Designer: Robert Scot
Size: 19 MM
Weight: 2.70 Grams
Composition: 89.24% Silver & 10.76% Copper
Fineness: .8924
Actual Silver wt.: .0775 Oz. pure Silver

Date	Mintage	G-4	VG-8	F-12	VF-20	XF-40	MS-60
1798	27,550	550.	675.	950.	1300.	1900.	6000.
1798/97 13 Stars	Inc. Ab.	900.	1250.	1750.	2900.	4750.	—
1798/97 16 Stars	Inc. Ab.	550.	700.	900.	1300.	1900.	4400.
1798 Small 8	Inc. Ab.	900.	1300.	1800.	3000.	5000.	—
1800	21,760	550.	675.	900.	1250.	1800.	5400.
1801	34,640	525.	650.	875.	1200.	1750.	—
1802	10,975	700.	975.	1575.	2650.	4500.	—
1803	33,040	550.	675.	900.	1300.	1750.	5500.
1804 13 Stars	8,265	1000.	1400.	2250.	3500.	6000.	—
1804 14 Stars	Inc. Ab.	900.	1250.	2000.	3100.	5550.	—
1805 4 Berries	120,780	450.	575.	850.	1050.	1600.	4400.
1805 5 Berries	Inc. Ab.	450.	575.	850.	1050.	1600.	4400.
1807	165,000	450.	575.	850.	1050.	1600.	4400.

Liberty Capped Dimes

Type: Dimes — Capped Bust
Dates of issue: 1809-1837
Designer: John Reich
Size: 18.8 MM
Weight: 2.70 Grams
Composition: 89.24% Silver & 10.76% Copper
Fineness: .8924
Actual Silver wt.: .0775 Oz. pure Silver

Date	Mintage	G-4	VG-8	F-12	VF-20	XF-40	MS-60
1809	51,065	100.	180.	300.	475.	750.	4200.
1811/9	65,180	55.00	90.00	150.	285.	460.	4000.
1814 Sm. Dt.	421,500	40.00	60.00	90.00	185.	425.	1000.
1814 Lg. Dt.	Inc.Ab.	16.00	24.00	40.00	115.	335.	1000.
1820 Lg. O	942,587	15.00	21.00	35.00	105.	315.	1000.
1820 Sm. O	Inc.Ab.	15.00	21.00	35.00	105.	315.	1000.
1821 Lg. Dt.	1,186,512	15.00	21.00	35.00	105.	315.	1000.
1821 Sm. Dt.	Inc.Ab.	18.50	25.00	42.00	125.	350.	1000.
1822	100,000	325.	475.	675.	950.	1500.	5000.
1823/22 Lg.E's	440,000	15.00	20.00	33.00	100.	285.	1000.
1823/22 Sm.E's	Inc.Ab.	17.50	25.00	45.00	125.	360.	1000.
1824/22	Undetermined	30.00	40.00	60.00	165.	425.	1000.
1825	510,000	11.50	16.00	28.00	83.00	285.	1000.
1827	1,215,000	11.50	16.00	28.00	83.00	285.	1000.
1828 Lg.Dt.	125,000	35.00	45.00	60.00	165.	425.	3000.

Coin Size Reduced Slightly

Date	Mintage	G-4	VG-8	F-12	VF-20	XF-40	MS-60
1828 Sm.Dt.	I.A.	25.00	30.00	40.00	95.00	300.	1850.
1829 Lg. 10C.	770,000	16.00	21.00	40.00	75.00	265.	1700.
1829 Med.10C.	I.A.	17.50	25.00	35.00	85.00	285.	1500.
1829 Sm.10C.	I.A.	9.50	11.50	18.00	50.00	190.	1500.
1830 Lg.10C.	510,000	9.50	11.50	18.00	50.00	190.	1600.
1830 Sm.10C.	I.A.	13.50	18.00	25.00	63.00	225.	1600.
1830/29	I.A.	20.00	35.00	50.00	100.	275.	2100.
1831	771,350	9.50	11.50	18.00	50.00	190.	1800.
1832	522,500	9.50	11.50	18.00	50.00	190.	1750.
1833	485,000	9.50	11.50	18.00	50.00	190.	1700.
1833 High 3	I.A.	9.50	11.50	18.00	50.00	190.	1700.
1834 Lg. 4	635,000	9.50	11.50	18.00	50.00	190.	1600.
1834 Sm. 4	I.A.	9.50	11.50	18.00	50.00	190.	1600.
1835	1,410,000	9.50	11.50	18.00	50.00	190.	1000.
1836	1,190,000	9.50	11.50	18.00	50.00	190.	1000.
1837	1,042,000	9.50	11.50	18.00	50.00	190.	1100.

LIBERTY SEATED DIMES

Without Stars Around Rim

Mintmark Above And Below Wreath Tie

Type: Dimes — Liberty Seated — No Stars Obverse
Dates of issue: 1837-1838
Designer: Christian Gobrecht
Size: 17.9 MM
Weight: 2.67 Grams
Composition: 90% Silver & 10% Copper
Fineness: .900
Actual Silver wt.: .0773 Oz. pure Silver

MINT MARKS:
O New Orleans

Date	Mintage	G-4	VG-8	F-12	VF-20	XF-40	MS-60
1837 Sm.Date	Inc. Ab.	29.00	40.00	55.00	140.	350.	800.
1837 Lg.Date	Inc. Ab.	29.00	40.00	55.00	140.	350.	800.
1838O	406,034	40.00	50.00	80.00	190.	475.	3500.

Stars Added Around Rim

Dates of issue: 1838-1853
MINT MARKS:
O New Orleans

Date	Mintage	G-4	VG-8	F-12	VF-20	XF-40	MS-60
1838 Sm.Stars	1,992,500	20.00	30.00	45.00	75.00	150.	2000.
1838 Lg.Stars	Inc. Ab.	8.00	11.00	15.00	25.00	60.00	880.
1838 Partial Drapery	Inc. Ab.	40.00	65.00	100.	175.	400.	1500.
1839	1,053,115	8.00	11.00	15.00	25.00	60.00	250.
1839O	1,323,000	11.00	15.00	20.00	40.00	85.00	950.
1839O Rev. 1838O	—	120.	300.	450.	600.	1500.	—
1840	1,358,580	8.00	11.00	15.00	25.00	60.00	250.
1840O	1,175,000	11.00	15.00	20.00	40.00	85.00	1500.

Drapery Added To Liberty

Date	Mintage	G-4	VG-8	F-12	VF-20	XF-40	MS-60
1840	Inc. Ab.	25.00	45.00	75.00	135.	275.	—
1841	1,622,500	6.00	7.50	10.00	17.00	45.00	285.
1841O	2,007,500	8.00	11.00	15.00	28.00	60.00	1500.
1842	1,887,500	6.00	7.50	10.00	17.00	45.00	285.
1842O	2,020,000	8.00	11.00	15.00	28.00	60.00	—
1843	1,370,000	6.00	8.00	10.00	17.00	45.00	285.
1843/1843	—	15.00	20.00	30.00	70.00	150.	800.
1843O	150,000	45.00	75.00	125.	300.	650.	—
1844	72,500	30.00	50.00	85.00	175.	300.	2000.
1845	1,755,000	6.00	7.50	10.00	16.00	42.00	285.
1845/1845	Inc. Ab.	55.00	110.	175.	250.	500.	—
1845O	230,000	15.00	30.00	50.00	125.	500.	—
1846	31,300	90.00	110.	140.	250.	650.	—
1847	245,000	13.50	20.00	30.00	60.00	125.	1200.
1848	451,500	9.00	12.00	17.00	30.00	65.00	750.
1849	839,000	7.00	9.50	11.00	18.00	50.00	725.
1849/8	Inc. Ab.	30.00	70.00	125.	200.	350.	—
1849O	300,000	12.50	18.00	25.00	75.00	175.	—
1850	1,931,500	6.00	7.00	9.00	15.00	40.00	285.
1850O	510,000	10.00	14.00	20.00	40.00	80.00	1000.
1851	1,026,500	6.00	7.00	9.00	15.00	40.00	285.
1851O	400,000	10.00	15.00	25.00	45.00	90.00	1500.
1852	1,535,500	6.00	7.00	9.00	15.00	40.00	285.
1852O	430,000	14.00	19.00	30.00	85.00	225.	1800.
1853	95,000	65.00	80.00	100.	180.	300.	1000.

Arrows At Date

Type: Dimes — Liberty Seated — Arrows at Date
Dates of issue: 1853-1855
Designer: Christian Gobrecht
Size: 17.9 MM
Weight: 2.49 Grams
Composition: 90% Silver & 10% Copper
Fineness: .900
Actual Silver wt.: .0721 Oz. pure Silver

MINT MARKS:
O New Orleans

Date	Mintage	G-4	VG-8	F-12	VF-20	XF-40	MS-60	Prf-65
1853	12,078,010	4.00	5.25	6.25	14.00	44.00	350.	6800.
1853O	1,100,000	5.00	7.00	10.00	30.00	90.00	900.	—
1854	4,470,000	4.00	5.25	6.25	14.00	44.00	900.	11,000.
1854O	1,770,000	5.00	6.50	9.00	25.00	75.00	900.	—
1855	2,075,000	4.25	5.25	7.00	15.00	48.00	1000.	11,000.

Arrows At Date Removed

Dates of issue: 1856-1860
MINT MARKS:
O New Orleans
S San Francisco

Date	Mintage	G-4	VG-8	F-12	VF-20	XF-40	MS-60	Prf-65
1856 Small Date	5,780,000	5.00	6.50	8.00	12.50	32.00	565.	11,500.
1856 Large Date	Inc. Ab.	10.00	12.00	15.00	25.00	65.00	750.	—
1856O	1,180,000	7.00	9.00	12.00	25.00	60.00	750.	—
1856S	70,000	120.	145.	200.	285.	450.	—	—
1857	5,580,000	5.00	6.00	7.50	12.50	32.00	380.	11,500.
1857O	1,540,000	6.00	7.25	9.00	18.00	50.00	750.	—
1858	1,540,000	5.00	6.00	7.50	12.50	32.00	380.	12,000.
1858O	290,000	15.00	19.00	25.00	45.00	125.	1200.	—
1858S	60,000	95.00	115.	150.	250.	400.	—	—
1859	430,000	6.00	7.00	9.00	17.00	50.00	1000.	10,000.
1859O	480,000	7.50	9.50	12.50	25.00	70.00	1100.	—
1859S	60,000	100.	130.	175.	275.	425.	—	—
1860S	140,000	20.00	24.00	33.00	68.00	150.	—	—

Transitional Pattern

Date	Mintage	G-4	VG-8	F-12	VF-20	XF-40	MS-60	Prf-65
1859 Obverse of 1859, Reverse of 1860		—	—	—	—	—	—	25,000.

Legend Replaces Stars On Obverse

Dates of issue: 1860-1873
MINT MARKS:
CC Carson City
O New Orleans
S San Francisco

Mintmark

UNITED STATES 1734

Date	Mintage	G-4	VG-8	F-12	VF-20	XF-40	MS-60	Prf-65
1860	607,000	6.00	7.50	9.00	15.00	40.00	525.	3950.
1860O	40,000	300.	425.	650.	1100.	2000.	—	—
1861	1,884,000	4.50	5.50	7.00	12.00	28.00	325.	3950.
1861S	172,500	18.00	24.00	33.00	68.00	150.	—	—
1862	847,550	5.50	7.00	8.50	14.00	35.00	500.	3950.
1862S	180,750	15.00	21.00	30.00	60.00	125.	—	—
1863	14,460	300.	360.	450.	525.	600.	1200.	3950.
1863S	157,500	20.00	26.00	35.00	70.00	150.	1200.	—
1864	11,470	325.	400.	500.	575.	650.	1650.	3950.
1864S	230,000	12.50	19.00	28.00	50.00	100.	1200.	—
1865	10,500	350.	425.	525.	600.	700.	1300.	3950.
1865S	175,000	15.00	22.00	30.00	60.00	125.	—	—
1866	8,725	375.	450.	575.	675.	800.	1300.	3950.
1866S	135,000	20.00	28.00	40.00	75.00	150.	1500.	—
1867	6,625	475.	575.	700.	825.	1000.	1800.	3950.
1867S	140,000	20.00	28.00	40.00	70.00	140.	1200.	—
1868	464,600	7.00	8.00	10.00	18.00	50.00	700.	3950.
1868S	260,000	10.00	14.00	20.00	33.00	85.00	1000.	—
1869	256,600	12.00	16.00	28.00	40.00	85.00	725.	3950.
1869S	450,000	8.00	10.00	13.00	25.00	70.00	825.	—
1870	471,500	7.00	8.00	10.00	18.00	50.00	450.	3950.
1870S	50,000	90.00	125.	165.	260.	475.	2500.	—
1871	907,710	5.50	7.00	9.00	14.00	35.00	350.	3950.
1871CC	20,100	450.	625.	875.	1250.	2500.	—	—
1871S	320,000	13.00	20.00	30.00	60.00	125.	1000.	—
1872	2,396,450	5.00	6.00	7.00	11.00	25.00	350.	3950.
1872CC	35,480	300.	450.	650.	950.	2250.	—	—
1872S	190,000	25.00	38.00	55.00	85.00	175.	1100.	—
1873 Closed 3	1,568,600	7.00	8.50	10.00	18.00	50.00	350.	3950.
1873 Open 3	Inc. Ab.	15.00	18.00	23.00	40.00	100.	—	—
1873CC	12,400	—	—	Only One Known				

Arrows At Date

Type: Dimes — Liberty Seated — Arrows at Date
Dates of issue: 1873-1874
Designer: Christian Gobrecht
Size: 17.9 MM
Weight: 2.50 Grams
Composition: 90% Silver & 10% Copper
Fineness: .900
Actual Silver wt.: .0724 Oz. pure Silver

MINT MARKS:
CC Carson City
S San Francisco

Date	Mintage	G-4	VG-8	F-12	VF-20	XF-40	MS-60	Prf-65
1873	2,378,500	8.00	13.00	25.00	50.00	125.	410.	8550.
1873CC	18,791	500.	800.	1000.	1500.	2750.	13,000.	—
1873S	455,000	10.00	16.00	27.00	60.00	140.	1500.	—
1874	2,940,700	8.00	13.00	25.00	50.00	125.	410.	8550.
1874CC	10,817	900.	1350.	2000.	2500.	4300.	—	—
1874S	240,000	15.00	25.00	40.00	85.00	200.	1500.	—

Arrows At Date Removed

Dates of issue: 1875-1891
MINT MARKS:
CC Carson City
O New Orleans
S San Francisco

Date	Mintage	G-4	VG-8	F-12	VF-20	XF-40	MS-60	Prf-65
1875	10,350,700	4.00	5.00	6.50	10.00	22.00	140.	3950.
1875CC Mint mark in wreath	4,645,000	5.00	6.00	8.00	11.00	25.00	160.	—
1875CC Mint mark under wreath	Inc. Ab.	5.00	6.00	8.00	14.00	35.00	160.	—
1875S Mint mark in wreath	9,070,000	4.00	5.00	6.50	12.50	25.00	500.	—
1875S Mint mark under wreath	Inc. Ab.	4.00	5.00	6.25	9.00	22.00	140.	—
1876	11,461,150	2.65	3.25	6.25	9.00	22.00	140.	3950.
1876CC	8,270,000	4.00	5.00	6.25	10.00	25.00	140.	—
1876CC (Double obv.)	Inc. Ab.	20.00	30.00	70.00	250.	400.	—	—
1876S	10,420,000	2.65	4.00	8.00	12.00	22.00	140.	—
1877	7,310,510	2.65	3.25	6.25	9.50	22.00	140.	3950.
1877CC	7,700,000	3.25	4.50	7.00	10.00	25.00	140.	—
1877S	2,340,000	5.00	6.00	7.00	11.00	26.00	150.	—
1878	1,678,800	5.00	6.00	8.00	13.00	30.00	140.	3950.

Date	Mintage	G-4	VG-8	F-12	VF-20	XF-40	MS-60	Prf-65
1878CC	200,000	65.00	90.00	125.	175.	250.	900.	—
1879	15,100	175.	210.	250.	310.	400.	750.	3950.
1880	37,335	125.	165.	190.	240.	300.	675.	3950.
1881	24,975	150.	175.	215.	265.	350.	675.	3950.
1882	3,911,100	2.65	3.25	6.25	9.00	22.00	140.	3950.
1883	7,675,712	2.65	3.25	6.25	9.00	22.00	140.	3950.
1884	3,366,380	2.65	3.25	6.25	9.00	22.00	140.	3950.
1884S	564,969	14.00	17.00	23.00	33.00	65.00	450.	—
1885	2,533,427	2.65	3.25	6.25	9.00	22.00	140.	3950.
1885S	43,690	225.	250.	300.	400.	575.	3000.	—
1886	6,377,570	2.65	3.25	6.25	9.00	22.00	140.	3950.
1886S	206,524	20.00	25.00	40.00	70.00	90.00	500.	—
1887	11,283,939	2.65	3.25	6.25	9.00	22.00	140.	3950.
1887S	4,454,450	2.65	3.25	6.25	9.00	22.00	140.	—
1888	5,496,487	2.65	3.25	6.25	9.00	22.00	140.	3950.
1888S	1,720,000	5.00	6.00	8.00	14.00	35.00	140.	—
1889	7,380,711	2.65	3.25	6.25	9.00	22.00	140.	3950.
1889S	972,678	8.00	10.00	18.00	25.00	50.00	475.	—
1890	9,911,541	2.65	3.25	6.25	9.00	22.00	140.	4050.
1890S	1,423,076	8.00	10.00	13.50	25.00	45.00	475.	—
1890S/S	Inc. Ab.	75.00	100.	130.	185.	275.	—	—
1891	15,310,600	2.65	3.25	6.25	9.00	22.00	140.	4050.
1891O	4,540,000	4.50	6.00	7.00	9.00	22.00	475.	—
1891O/horz. O	Inc. Ab.	72.00	95.00	125.	175.	250.	—	—
1891S	3,196,116	3.00	3.75	7.00	12.00	28.00	500.	—

BARBER DIMES

Type: Dimes — Barber or Liberty Head Type
Dates of issue: 1892-1916
Designer: Charles E. Barber
Size: 17.9 MM
Weight: 2.50 Grams
Composition: 90% Silver & 10% Copper
Fineness: .900
Actual Silver wt.: .0724 Oz. pure Silver

MINT MARKS:
D Denver
O New Orleans
S San Francisco

Mintmark

Date	Mintage	G-4	VG-8	F-12	VF-20	XF-40	AU-50	MS-60	MS-65	Prf-65
1892	12,121,245	2.50	4.50	6.75	9.00	21.00	42.00	160.	2500.	3550.
1892O	3,841,700	5.50	7.50	10.50	14.00	30.00	60.00	180.	2950.	—
1892S	990,710	26.00	36.00	47.00	66.00	90.00	145.	240.	3900.	—
1893	3,340,792	5.25	7.50	11.00	15.00	26.00	48.00	160.	2500.	3550.
1893O	1,760,000	15.00	20.00	60.00	75.00	90.00	130.	240.	3800.	—
1893S	2,491,401	6.75	9.00	15.00	21.00	35.00	65.00	240.	3275.	—
1894	1,330,972	7.50	11.00	50.00	58.00	90.00	125.	230.	2800.	3550.
1894O	720,000	33.00	44.00	90.00	130.	250.	600.	850.	9500.	—
1894S	24	Norweb sale Oct. 87, Prf-65 $77,000.								
1895	690,880	57.00	75.00	145.	195.	250.	335.	525.	3450.	3550.
1895O	440,000	150.	200.	250.	325.	475.	650.	900.	6300.	—
1895S	1,120,000	16.00	22.00	34.00	45.00	56.00	90.00	235.	3300.	—
1896	2,000,762	6.00	9.00	18.00	23.00	40.00	65.00	185.	2700.	3550.
1896O	610,000	40.00	48.00	110.	175.	225.	375.	600.	6700.	—
1896S	575,056	35.00	46.00	75.00	100.	175.	280.	400.	3350.	—
1897	10,869,264	1.25	1.60	3.50	8.00	20.00	46.00	160.	2500.	3550.
1897O	666,000	36.00	43.00	80.00	110.	200.	360.	600.	6300.	—
1897S	1,342,844	8.00	12.00	20.00	35.00	60.00	105.	260.	3450.	—
1898	16,320,735	1.20	1.50	3.00	7.50	19.00	44.00	155.	2500.	3550.
1898O	2,130,000	4.00	7.50	13.50	24.00	55.00	90.00	300.	4900.	—
1898S	1,702,507	3.75	5.75	11.00	16.00	36.00	62.00	190.	2950.	—
1899	19,580,846	1.20	1.50	3.00	7.50	19.00	44.00	155.	2500.	3550.
1899O	2,650,000	3.60	5.75	11.50	23.00	55.00	90.00	300.	4400.	—
1899S	1,867,493	3.75	5.75	11.00	17.00	33.00	65.00	190.	2950.	—
1900	17,600,912	1.20	1.50	3.00	7.50	19.00	44.00	150.	2500.	3550.
1900O	2,010,000	5.50	8.50	15.00	28.00	60.00	120.	300.	5100.	—
1900S	5,168,270	2.40	3.25	6.00	10.00	24.00	55.00	175.	2950.	—
1901	18,860,478	1.20	1.50	3.00	7.50	19.00	44.00	150.	2500.	3550.
1901O	5,620,000	2.40	3.50	7.00	15.00	48.00	115.	295.	4700.	—
1901S	593,022	35.00	41.00	75.00	125.	225.	400.	700.	4700.	—
1902	21,380,777	1.10	1.50	2.90	7.25	18.00	44.00	150.	2500.	3550.
1902O	4,500,000	2.50	4.00	6.75	12.00	29.00	75.00	270.	3950.	—
1902S	2,070,000	4.00	7.00	13.50	25.00	55.00	105.	280.	3450.	—
1903	19,500,755	1.10	1.50	3.15	7.25	19.00	44.00	150.	2500.	3550.
1903O	8,180,000	2.30	3.10	5.50	9.00	27.00	75.00	250.	2950.	—
1903S	613,300	27.00	34.00	68.00	90.00	160.	325.	600.	5100.	—
1904	14,601,027	1.10	1.50	3.00	7.50	19.00	44.00	150.	2500.	3550.

Date	Mintage	G-4	VG-8	F-12	VF-20	XF-40	AU-50	MS-60	MS-65	Prf-65
1904S	800,000	21.00	28.00	44.00	80.00	145.	290.	540.	5100.	—
1905	14,552,350	1.10	1.50	3.20	7.25	19.00	45.00	155.	2500.	3550.
1905O	3,400,000	2.40	4.25	8.00	13.00	28.00	62.00	210.	2950.	—
1905S	6,855,199	2.30	3.60	6.25	10.50	24.00	55.00	230.	3050.	—
1906	19,958,406	1.00	1.35	2.90	6.75	18.00	42.00	125.	2200.	3550.
1906D	4,060,000	2.50	3.90	5.60	11.00	27.00	60.00	200.	2700.	—
1906O	2,610,000	2.65	5.25	12.50	18.00	30.00	62.00	210.	2700.	—
1906S	3,136,640	1.80	3.60	7.00	13.00	27.00	60.00	215.	2750.	—
1907	22,220,575	1.00	1.35	2.90	6.75	18.00	42.00	125.	2200.	3550.
1907D	4,080,000	1.80	2.75	6.50	10.00	26.00	62.00	205.	2900.	—
1907O	5,058,000	1.70	2.50	6.25	9.50	23.00	55.00	160.	2600.	—
1907S	3,178,470	2.20	4.25	6.75	12.00	30.00	68.00	250.	3450.	—
1908	10,600,545	1.10	1.50	3.00	7.25	19.00	44.00	125.	2200.	3550.
1908D	7,490,000	1.50	2.00	5.25	7.50	20.00	52.00	150.	2775.	—
1908O	1,789,000	2.40	4.50	11.50	18.00	37.00	90.00	250.	2700.	—
1908S	3,220,000	1.80	2.80	6.00	10.50	27.50	62.00	225.	3000.	—
1909	10,240,650	1.10	1.50	3.00	7.50	20.00	47.00	125.	2200.	3550.
1909D	954,000	3.00	6.50	14.00	23.00	41.00	90.00	250.	2700.	—
1909O	2,287,000	2.15	3.25	7.00	15.00	29.00	63.00	210.	2750.	—
1909S	1,000,000	3.10	6.75	16.50	30.00	50.00	95.00	260.	3000.	—
1910	11,520,551	1.15	1.45	3.25	7.50	19.00	45.00	135.	2250.	3550.
1910D	3,490,000	1.75	3.00	8.00	11.00	32.00	80.00	225.	3400.	—
1910S	1,240,000	2.25	3.25	9.00	15.00	30.00	70.00	205.	2800.	—
1911	18,870,543	1.00	1.30	3.00	7.00	18.00	42.00	125.	2000.	3550.
1911D	11,209,000	1.20	1.60	3.75	7.50	19.00	44.00	135.	2250.	—
1911S	3,520,000	1.50	2.25	5.25	9.00	23.00	60.00	155.	2800.	—
1912	19,350,700	1.10	1.40	2.90	6.75	18.00	42.00	125.	2200.	3550.
1912D	11,760,000	1.20	1.50	3.60	7.50	19.00	44.00	135.	2250.	—
1912S	3,420,000	1.50	2.25	5.25	9.00	23.00	60.00	152.	2800.	—
1913	19,760,622	1.10	1.30	2.75	6.50	18.00	42.00	125.	2200.	3550.
1913S	510,000	8.00	11.00	25.00	56.00	110.	190.	310.	4100.	—
1914	17,360,655	1.10	1.30	2.75	6.50	18.00	42.00	125.	2200.	4200.
1914D	11,908,000	1.10	1.40	3.25	7.00	19.00	43.00	135.	2250.	—
1914S	2,100,000	2.25	2.80	5.50	9.00	24.00	62.00	165.	2800.	—
1915	5,620,450	1.25	1.60	3.20	8.00	21.00	50.00	150.	2500.	4200.
1915S	960,000	1.75	2.50	8.00	14.00	31.00	76.00	210.	3000.	—
1916	18,490,000	1.00	1.30	2.75	6.50	18.00	42.00	125.	2200.	—
1916S	5,820,000	1.20	1.60	3.25	7.75	21.00	46.00	135.	2250.	—

MERCURY DIMES

Type: Dimes — Mercury
Dates of issue: 1916-1945
Designer: Adolph A. Weinman
Size: 17.9 MM
Weight: 2.50 Grams
Composition: 90% Silver & 10% Copper
Fineness: .900
Actual Silver wt.: .0724 Oz. pure Silver

MINT MARKS:
D Denver
S San Francisco

Mintmark

Date	Mintage	G-4	VG-8	F-12	VF-20	XF-40	MS-60	MS-65	65FSB	Prf-65
1916	22,180,080	2.00	2.75	4.75	7.25	10.00	32.00	175.	325.	—
1916D	264,000	300.	425.	850.	1100.	1550.	2300.	3250.	8500.	—
1916S	10,450,000	3.00	4.50	7.00	9.75	16.00	45.00	175.	650.	—
1917	55,230,000	1.60	2.10	2.75	5.50	7.50	45.00	160.	425.	—
1917D	9,402,000	3.50	5.25	8.00	15.00	38.00	95.00	675.	2350.	—
1917S	27,330,000	1.75	2.35	3.25	6.00	9.00	50.00	250.	2100.	—
1918	26,680,000	1.75	3.00	4.00	11.00	22.00	60.00	210.	600.	—
1918D	22,674,800	1.75	3.00	4.00	9.50	22.00	75.00	700.	4700.	—
1918S	19,300,000	1.75	2.50	4.50	6.50	14.00	40.00	465.	2750.	—
1919	35,740,000	1.60	2.25	3.25	5.50	8.00	38.00	275.	460.	—
1919D	9,939,000	3.00	4.25	6.00	15.00	32.50	140.	745.	2650.	—
1919S	8,850,000	2.40	3.60	5.00	12.00	27.00	140.	600.	4675.	—
1920	59,030,000	1.55	2.10	2.75	5.00	7.00	28.00	175.	390.	—
1920D	19,171,000	1.75	3.25	4.00	7.00	15.00	75.00	620.	1125.	—
1920S	13,820,000	1.75	2.80	4.00	6.50	13.50	65.00	515.	2150.	—
1921	1,230,000	19.00	27.00	64.00	120.	375.	735.	1550.	3600.	—
1921D	1,080,000	29.00	41.00	90.00	175.	350.	735.	1550.	3600.	—
1923	50,130,000	1.55	2.50	3.25	4.25	7.00	18.00	185.	390.	—
1923S	6,440,000	1.75	3.50	4.00	8.00	20.00	80.00	620.	3700.	—
1924	24,010,000	1.55	2.50	3.25	5.00	7.00	50.00	315.	460.	—
1924D	6,810,000	2.25	3.25	5.50	10.00	21.00	80.00	395.	1500.	—
1924S	7,120,000	2.00	2.80	4.00	7.00	17.50	80.00	700.	2500.	—
1925	25,610,000	1.60	2.50	2.75	4.25	7.50	35.00	270.	450.	—
1925D	5,117,000	4.00	5.75	8.50	24.00	60.00	225.	675.	3000.	—
1925S	5,850,000	2.00	2.80	4.00	8.00	20.00	100.	565.	3500.	—
1926	32,160,000	1.55	1.85	2.25	4.25	6.50	17.00	175.	400.	—
1926D	6,828,000	1.95	3.00	4.00	7.50	15.00	60.00	515.	800.	—
1926S	1,520,000	8.25	9.75	15.00	32.00	70.00	425.	1450.	4500.	—
1927	28,080,000	1.50	1.80	2.25	4.25	6.50	17.00	175.	375.	—
1927D	4,812,000	2.75	3.75	5.00	12.00	30.00	150.	575.	2450.	—
1927S	4,770,000	1.90	2.65	3.75	5.50	11.00	85.00	725.	2550.	—
1928	19,480,000	1.50	1.80	2.25	4.25	6.50	20.00	250.	375.	—
1928D	4,161,000	3.00	4.25	6.00	15.00	35.00	115.	410.	1900.	—
1928S	7,400,000	1.75	2.35	3.25	5.00	11.00	45.00	425.	1200.	—
1929	25,970,000	1.50	1.80	2.35	3.75	5.00	30.00	80.00	275.	—

Date	Mintage	G-4	VG-8	F-12	VF-20	XF-40	MS-60	MS-65	65FSB	Prf-65
1929D	5,034,000	2.65	3.60	5.00	8.00	12.00	44.00	145.	300.	—
1929S	4,730,000	1.65	1.90	2.25	4.25	6.50	40.00	165.	450.	—
1930	6,770,000	1.50	1.80	2.25	4.25	7.00	19.00	105.	475.	—
1930S	1,843,000	3.50	4.25	5.00	7.50	13.00	65.00	265.	550.	—
1931	3,150,000	1.95	2.50	3.50	5.00	11.00	37.50	125.	575.	—
1931D	1,260,000	5.50	7.50	11.00	18.00	32.00	100.	235.	450.	—
1931S	1,800,000	3.50	4.00	5.00	7.50	13.00	70.00	245.	650.	—
1934	24,080,000	1.20	1.45	1.75	3.00	5.00	20.00	63.00	135.	—
1934D	6,772,000	1.80	2.10	2.75	3.75	5.50	30.00	115.	425.	—
1935	58,830,000	1.10	1.20	1.50	2.15	4.25	11.50	65.00	125.	—
1935D	10,477,000	1.70	1.85	2.10	3.75	9.25	40.00	135.	500.	—
1935S	15,840,000	1.35	1.50	1.75	3.00	5.50	25.00	80.00	350.	—
1936	87,504,130	1.10	1.25	1.50	2.15	3.50	12.50	55.00	90.00	2150.
1936D	16,132,000	1.25	1.50	1.85	3.15	6.75	27.00	85.00	350.	—
1936S	9,210,000	1.25	1.45	1.75	2.75	4.75	18.00	57.00	175.	—
1937	56,865,756	1.10	1.25	1.50	1.90	3.25	12.50	55.00	115.	950.
1937D	14,146,000	1.25	1.50	1.85	3.00	5.50	24.00	100.	140.	—
1937S	9,740,000	1.25	1.50	1.85	3.00	5.50	17.50	70.00	300.	—
1938	22,198,728	1.10	1.25	1.50	2.15	3.50	12.00	51.00	115.	800.
1938D	5,537,000	1.75	1.95	2.25	3.75	5.75	24.00	100.	150.	—
1938S	8,090,000	1.35	1.55	1.85	2.35	3.75	15.00	60.00	165.	—
1939	67,749,321	1.10	1.25	1.50	1.90	3.25	11.50	45.00	150.	750.
1939D	24,394,000	1.25	1.45	1.75	2.15	3.50	11.50	50.00	80.00	—
1939S	10,540,000	1.35	1.55	1.85	2.35	4.25	16.00	68.00	625.	—
1940	65,361,827	.80	1.00	1.45	1.90	2.50	8.50	45.00	90.00	700.
1940D	21,198,000	.80	1.00	1.45	2.15	3.50	13.00	55.00	80.00	—
1940S	21,560,000	.80	1.00	1.45	1.90	2.75	8.50	48.00	175.	—
1941	175,106,557	.80	1.00	1.45	1.90	2.50	8.50	38.00	75.00	630.
1941D	45,634,000	.80	1.00	1.45	2.15	3.35	11.00	48.00	75.00	—
1941S	43,090,000	.80	1.00	1.45	1.90	3.75	12.00	50.00	100.	—

1942/1

1942/1D

Date	Mintage	G-4	VG-8	F-12	VF-20	XF-40	MS-60	MS-65	65FSB	Prf-65
1942/41	Unrecorded	160.	180.	225.	250.	300.	950.	2500.	4500.	—
1942	205,432,329	.80	1.00	1.45	1.90	2.50	8.50	38.00	75.00	630.
1942D	60,740,000	.80	1.00	1.45	1.90	2.50	10.00	47.00	75.00	—
1942/41D	Unrecorded	165.	185.	235.	270.	360.	1100.	2850.	4600.	—
1942S	49,300,000	.80	1.00	1.45	1.90	3.25	22.00	49.00	125.	—
1943	191,710,000	.80	1.00	1.45	1.90	2.50	8.50	44.00	125.	—
1943D	71,949,000	.80	1.00	1.45	1.90	3.75	8.50	40.00	75.00	—
1943S	60,400,000	.80	1.00	1.45	1.90	3.00	11.50	46.00	125.	—
1944	231,410,000	.80	1.00	1.45	1.90	2.50	8.50	65.00	250.	—
1944D	62,224,000	.80	1.00	1.45	1.90	3.75	11.50	40.00	105.	—
1944S	49,490,000	.80	1.00	1.45	1.90	3.75	11.50	48.00	115.	—
1945	159,130,000	.80	1.00	1.45	1.90	2.50	8.50	65.00	2500.	—
1945D	40,245,000	.80	1.00	1.45	1.90	3.75	11.50	41.00	115.	—
1945S	41,920,000	.80	1.00	1.45	1.90	3.75	11.50	40.00	200.	—
1945S Micro Inc.Ab.		1.50	1.65	1.85	3.00	4.25	15.00	70.00	650.	—

NOTE: All specimens listed as -65FSB are for fully struck MS-65 coins with fully split and rounded horizontal bands on the fasces.

FULLY SPLIT BANDS

ROOSEVELT DIMES

Mintmarks

1946-1964 Reverse

Since 1968 Obverse

Type: Dimes — Roosevelt
Dates of issue: 1946-1964
Designer: John R. Sinnock
Size: 17.9 MM
Weight: 2.50 Grams
Composition: 90% Silver & 10% Copper
Fineness: .900
Actual Silver wt.: .0724 Oz. pure Silver

MINT MARKS:
D Denver
S San Francisco

Date	Mintage	G-4	VG-8	F-12	VF-20	XF-40	AU-50	MS-60	MS-65	Prf-65
1946	225,250,000	—	—	—	.75	.95	1.10	1.60	2.50	—
1946D	61,043,500	—	—	—	.75	.95	1.10	3.20	4.50	—
1946S	27,900,000	—	—	—	.75	.95	1.10	2.90	5.25	—
1947	121,520,000	—	—	—	.75	.95	1.10	2.90	4.75	—
1947D	46,835,000	—	—	—	.75	.95	1.20	4.50	10.00	—
1947S	34,840,000	—	—	—	.75	.95	1.10	4.30	5.50	—
1948	74,950,000	—	—	—	.75	.95	1.10	8.25	11.00	—
1948D	52,841,000	—	—	—	.75	1.20	1.50	6.30	10.00	—
1948S	35,520,000	—	—	—	.75	.95	1.10	8.30	9.00	—
1949	30,940,000	—	—	—	1.00	1.50	4.50	16.00	29.00	—
1949D	26,034,000	—	—	.80	.95	1.25	2.00	8.30	12.50	—
1949S	13,510,000	—	1.25	1.70	2.75	4.25	7.50	31.00	55.00	—
1950	50,181,500	—	—	—	.75	.95	1.10	3.90	4.60	60.00
1950D	46,803,000	—	—	—	.75	.95	1.10	3.90	4.60	—
1950S	20,440,000	—	.85	1.00	1.10	1.25	5.00	15.00	35.00	—
1951	102,937,602	—	—	—	.75	.95	1.15	2.30	3.30	54.00
1951D	56,529,000	—	—	—	.75	.95	1.15	2.20	3.50	—
1951S	31,630,000	—	.80	.95	1.00	1.05	2.75	10.00	24.00	—
1952	99,122,073	—	—	—	.75	.95	1.10	2.10	3.30	32.00
1952D	122,100,000	—	—	—	.75	.95	1.10	1.80	3.80	—
1952S	44,419,500	—	—	.95	1.00	1.05	1.10	4.80	7.00	—
1953	53,618,920	—	—	—	.75	.95	1.10	1.90	3.60	22.00
1953D	136,433,000	—	—	—	.75	.95	1.10	1.40	3.50	—
1953S	39,180,000	—	—	—	.75	.95	1.10	1.20	2.25	—
1954	114,243,503	—	—	—	.75	.95	1.10	1.30	2.15	7.75
1954D	106,397,000	—	—	—	.75	.95	1.10	1.20	2.15	—
1954S	22,860,000	—	—	—	.75	.95	1.10	1.35	2.20	—
1955	12,828,381	—	—	.75	.95	1.00	1.10	2.00	3.00	7.25
1955D	13,959,000	—	—	.75	.95	1.10	1.20	1.60	2.25	—
1955S	18,510,000	—	—	—	.95	1.00	1.10	1.25	2.00	—
1956	109,309,384	—	—	—	.75	.85	.90	1.10	2.00	2.50
1956D	108,015,100	—	—	—	.75	.85	.90	1.10	1.65	—
1957	161,407,952	—	—	—	.75	.85	.90	1.10	1.60	2.00
1957D	113,354,330	—	—	—	.75	.85	.90	2.15	3.00	—
1958	32,785,652	—	—	—	.75	.85	.90	1.50	1.80	2.45
1958D	136,564,600	—	—	—	.75	.85	.90	1.30	1.50	—
1959	86,929,291	—	—	—	.75	.85	.90	1.10	1.50	1.60
1959D	164,919,790	—	—	—	.75	.85	.90	1.10	1.35	—
1960	72,081,602	—	—	—	.75	.85	.90	1.10	1.40	1.45
1960D	200,160,400	—	—	—	.75	.85	.90	1.00	1.35	—
1961	96,758,244	—	—	—	.75	.85	.90	1.00	1.35	1.25
1961D	209,146,550	—	—	—	.75	.85	.90	1.00	1.35	—
1962	75,668,019	—	—	—	.75	.85	.90	1.00	1.35	1.25
1962D	334,948,380	—	—	—	.75	.85	.90	1.00	1.35	—
1963	126,725,645	—	—	—	.75	.85	.90	1.00	1.35	1.25
1963D	421,476,530	—	—	—	.75	.85	.90	1.00	1.35	—
1964	933,310,762	—	—	—	.75	.85	.90	1.00	1.35	1.25
1964D	1,357,517,180	—	—	—	.75	.85	.90	1.00	1.35	—

Type: Dimes — Roosevelt — Clad
Dates of issue: 1965 to date
Designer: John R. Sinnock
Size: 17.9 MM
Weight: 2.27 Grams
Composition: 75% Copper & 25% Nickel

MINT MARKS:
D Denver
S San Francisco
P Philadelphia

Date	Mintage	G-4	VG-8	F-12	VF-20	XF-40	AU-50	MS-60	MS-65	Prf-65
1965	1,652,140,570	—	—	—	—	—	—	—	.40	—
1966	1,382,734,540	—	—	—	—	—	—	—	.40	—
1967	2,244,007,320	—	—	—	—	—	—	—	.30	—
1968	424,470,000	—	—	—	—	—	—	—	.25	—
1968D	480,748,280	—	—	—	—	—	—	—	.25	—
1968S	Proof Only									.75
1969	145,790,000	—	—	—	—	—	—	—	.40	—
1969D	563,323,870	—	—	—	—	—	—	—	.40	—
1969S	Proof Only									.7

Date	Mintage	G-4	VG-8	F-12	VF-20	XF-40	AU-50	MS-60	MS-65	Prf-65
1970	345,570,000	—	—	—	—	—	—	—	.30	—
1970D	754,942,100	—	—	—	—	—	—	—	.30	—
1970S	Proof Only									.55
1971	162,690,000	—	—	—	—	—	—	—	.25	—
1971D	377,914,240	—	—	—	—	—	—	—	.25	—
1971S	Proof Only									.50
1972	431,540,000	—	—	—	—	—	—	—	.20	—
1972D	330,290,000	—	—	—	—	—	—	—	.20	—
1972S	Proof Only									.60
1973	315,670,000	—	—	—	—	—	—	—	.20	—
1973D	455,032,426	—	—	—	—	—	—	—	.20	—
1973S	Proof Only									.40
1974	470,248,000	—	—	—	—	—	—	—	.20	—
1974D	571,083,000	—	—	—	—	—	—	—	.20	—
1974S	Proof Only									.50
1975	585,673,900	—	—	—	—	—	—	—	.25	—
1975D	313,705,300	—	—	—	—	—	—	—	.20	—
1975S	Proof Only									.55
1976	568,760,000	—	—	—	—	—	—	—	.20	—
1976D	695,222,774	—	—	—	—	—	—	—	.20	—
1976S	Proof Only									.35
1977	796,930,000	—	—	—	—	—	—	—	.20	—
1977D	376,607,228	—	—	—	—	—	—	—	.20	—
1977S	Proof Only									.30
1978	663,980,000	—	—	—	—	—	—	—	.20	—
1978D	282,847,540	—	—	—	—	—	—	—	.20	—
1978S	Proof Only									.50
1979	315,440,000	—	—	—	—	—	—	—	.20	—
1979D	390,921,184	—	—	—	—	—	—	—	.20	—
1979S	Proof Only									.60
1979S T-II	Proof Only									1.50
1980P	735,170,000	—	—	—	—	—	—	—	.20	—
1980D	719,354,321	—	—	—	—	—	—	—	.20	—
1980S	Proof Only									.45
1981P	676,650,000	—	—	—	—	—	—	—	.20	—
1981D	712,284,143	—	—	—	—	—	—	—	.20	—
1981S	Proof Only									.55
1982P	519,475,000	—	—	—	—	—	—	—	.30	—
1982 No mintmark		—	—	—	—	—	100.	110.	175.	—
1982D	542,713,584	—	—	—	—	—	—	—	.20	—
1982S	Proof Only									.85
1983P	647,025,000	—	—	—	—	—	—	—	.20	—
1983D	730,129,224	—	—	—	—	—	—	—	.20	—
1983S	Proof Only									1.25
1984P	856,669,000	—	—	—	—	—	—	—	.20	—
1984D	704,803,976	—	—	—	—	—	—	—	.20	—
1984S	Proof Only									1.80
1985P	705,200,962	—	—	—	—	—	—	—	.20	—
1985D	587,979,970	—	—	—	—	—	—	—	.20	—
1985S	Proof Only									1.80
1986P	682,649,693	—	—	—	—	—	—	—	.20	—
1986D	473,326,970	—	—	—	—	—	—	—	.20	—
1986S	Proof Only									1.15
1987P	762,709,481	—	—	—	—	—	—	—	.20	—
1987D	653,203,402	—	—	—	—	—	—	—	.20	—
1987S	Proof Only									1.80
1988P		—	—	—	—	—	—	—	.20	—
1988D		—	—	—	—	—	—	—	.20	—
1988S	Proof Only									1.80
1989P		—	—	—	—	—	—	—	.20	—
1989D		—	—	—	—	—	—	—	.20	—
1989S	Proof Only									1.80

TWENTY CENTS

Mintmark

Type: Twenty Cent Pieces
Dates of issue: 1875-1878
Designer: William Barber
Size: 22 MM
Weight: 5 Grams
Composition: 90% Silver & 10% Copper
Fineness: .900
Actual Silver wt.: .1447 Oz. pure Silver

MINT MARKS:
CC Carson City
S San Francisco

Date	Mintage	G-4	VG-8	F-12	VF-20	XF-40	AU-50	MS-60	MS-65	Prf-65
1875	39,700	50.00	70.00	100.	150.	275.	450.	1300	11,000	16,500.
1875S	1,155,000	33.00	41.00	60.00	85.00	170.	380.	800	10,500.	—
1875CC	133,290	45.00	65.00	100.	150.	275.	450.	1450	12,000.	—
1876	15,900	85.00	100.	130.	210.	400.	575.	1500	14,000	16,500.
1876CC	10,000	Norweb Sale Oct. 87 MS-64 $69,300.								
1877	510	Proof Only							—18,000.	
Impaired Proof				—	1350.	1850.	2450.			
1878	600	Proof Only							—18,000.	
Impaired Proof				—	1175.	1575.	2000.			

QUARTERS
Draped Bust Quarters

Type: Quarter Dollars — Draped Bust —
 Small Eagle Reverse
Dates of issue: 1796
Designer: Robert Scot
Size: 27.5 MM
Weight: 6.74 Grams
Composition: 89.24% Silver & 10.76% Copper
Fineness: .8924
Actual Silver wt.: .1935 Oz. pure Silver

Date	Mintage	G-4	VG-8	F-12	VF-20	XF-40	AU-50	MS-60	MS-65
1796	6,146	3700.	4050.	5650.	12,000.	17,500.	20,000.	23,000.	70,000.

Heraldic Eagle Introduced

Type: Quarter Dollars — Draped Bust —
 Heraldic Eagle Reverse
Dates of issue: 1804-1807
Designer: Robert Scot
Size: 27.5 MM
Weight: 6.74 Grams
Composition: 89.24% Silver & 10.76% Copper
Fineness: .8924
Actual Silver wt.: .1935 Oz. pure Silver

Date	Mintage	G-4	VG-8	F-12	VF-20	XF-40	AU-50	MS-60	MS-65
1804	6,738	975.	1650.	2750.	4250.	7250.	16,500.	22,000.	60,000.
1805	121,394	225.	275.	500.	1000.	1900.	4400.	5650.	56,500.
1806	206,124	225.	275.	500.	1000.	1900.	4150.	5650.	56,500.
1806/5	Inc. Ab.	225.	325.	550.	1075.	2000.	4400.	5650.	—
1807	220,643	225.	325.	550.	1075.	1900.	4150.	5650.	56,500.

Liberty Capped Quarters

Type: Quarter Dollars — Capped Bust —
 Large Size
Dates of issue: 1815-1828
Designer: John Reich
Size: 27 MM
Weight: 6.74 Grams
Composition: 89.24% Silver & 10.76% Copper
Fineness: .8924
Actual Silver wt.: .1935 Oz. pure Silver

Date	Mintage	G-4	VG-8	F-12	VF-20	XF-40	AU-50	MS-60	MS-65
1815	89,235	65.00	80.00	100.	300.	725.	2000.	3000.	25,000.
1818	361,174	39.00	50.00	90.00	235.	525.	1900.	2900.	25,000.
1818/15	Inc. Ab.	70.00	95.00	150.	425.	950.	2000.	3000.	25,000.
1819 Sm.9	144,000	44.00	55.00	100.	275.	600.	1900.	2900.	25,000.
1819 Lg.9	Inc. Ab.	44.00	55.00	100.	275.	600.	1900.	2900.	25,000.
1820 Sm.O	127,444	75.00	100.	165.	475.	1000.	—	2500.	25,000.
1820 Lg.O	Inc. Ab.	36.00	45.00	100.	225.	500.	1100.	2500.	25,000.
1821	216,851	36.00	45.00	100.	225.	500.	1100.	2500.	25,000.
1822	64,080	55.00	70.00	115.	350.	775.	1250.	2500.	25,000.
1822 25/50C.		600.	850.	1400.	2750.	4500.	8000.	15,000.	25,000.
1823/22	17,800	5250.	6500.	9000.	13,000.	18,000.			
		Stack's Auction, Aug. 1980 87,500.					—	Proof	
1824	Unrecorded	75.00	90.00	160.	425.	950.	1100.	2500.	25,000.
1825/22	168,000	70.00	85.00	125.	350.	800.	1500.	2700.	25,000.
1825/23	Inc. Ab.	40.00	50.00	100.	235.	550.	1500.	2700.	25,000.
1825/24	Inc. Ab.	44.00	55.00	100.	260.	575.	1500.	2700.	25,000.
1827 Original	4,000			Garrett Sale 1980		Proof		-190,000.	
1827 Restrike	I.A.			Stack's Auction 1977		Proof		-12,500.	
1828	102,000	36.00	45.00	85.00	250.	550.	1500.	2700.	25,000.
1828 25/50C.	I.A.	110.	165.	225.	450.	900.	2000.	3000.	

Motto Removed From Reverse

Type: Quarter Dollars — Capped Bust — No
 Motto Reverse — Small Size
Dates of issue: 1831-1838
Designer: William Kneass
Size: 24.3 MM
Weight: 6.74 Grams
Composition: 89.24% Silver & 10.76% Copper
Fineness: .8924
Actual Silver wt.: .1935 Oz. pure Silver

Date	Mintage	G-4	VG-8	F-12	VF-20	XF-40	AU-50	MS-60	MS-65
1831 Small Letters	398,000	35.00	38.00	50.00	100.	250.	500.	900.	19,000.
1831 Lg.Let.Inc. Ab.		35.00	38.00	50.00	100.	250.	500.	900.	19,000.
1832	320,000	40.00	45.00	55.00	155.	250.	500.	900.	19,000.
1833	156,000	44.00	54.00	65.00	120.	350.	500.	900.	19,000.
1834	286,000	40.00	45.00	55.00	100.	250.	500.	900.	19,000.
1835	1,952,000	35.00	38.00	50.00	100.	250.	500.	900.	19,000.
1836	472,000	35.00	38.00	50.00	100.	250.	500.	900.	19,000.
1837	252,400	37.00	42.00	50.00	100.	250.	500.	900.	19,000.
1838	832,000	35.00	38.00	50.00	100.	250.	500.	900.	19,000.

LIBERTY SEATED QUARTERS
Without Drapery On Liberty

Type: Quarter Dollars — Liberty Seated —
 No Motto above Eagle
Dates of issue: 1838-1853
Designer: Christian Gobrecht
Size: 24.3 MM
Weight: 6.68 Grams
Composition: 90% Silver & 10% Copper
Fineness: .900
Actual Silver wt.: .1934 Oz. pure Silver
MINT MARKS:
 O New Orleans

Without Drapery

Date	Mintage	G-4	VG-8	F-12	VF-20	XF-40	MS-60
1838	Inc. Ab.	9.50	15.00	22.00	44.00	190.	1250.
1839	491,146	9.50	15.00	22.00	44.00	190.	1250.
18400	425,200	9.50	15.00	22.00	44.00	190.	1250.

Drapery Added To Liberty

Mintmark

Date	Mintage	G-4	VG-8	F-12	VF-20	XF-40	MS-60
1840	188,127	45.00	65.00	100.	150.	250.	2500.
1840O	Inc. Ab.	30.00	50.00	75.00	110.	185.	1600.
1841	120,000	60.00	80.00	120.	200.	285.	1000.
1841O	452,000	25.00	40.00	60.00	100.	200.	1000.
1842 Sm Dt	88,000		Bowers Ruddy Sale, Aug, 1978, Proof				32,500.
1842 Lg Dt	Inc. Ab.	90.00	125.	150.	225.	425.	2700.
1842O Sm Dt	769,000	475.	625.	850.	1350.	3000.	
1842O Lg Dt	Inc. Ab.	10.00	16.00	30.00	50.00	100.	—
1843	645,600	9.50	10.00	12.50	40.00	80.00	350.
1843O	968,000	15.00	33.00	60.00	100.	200.	—
1844	421,200	12.50	16.00	26.00	43.00	80.00	350.
1844O	740,000	12.50	21.00	37.50	64.00	125.	1200.
1845	922,000	9.50	15.00	25.00	40.00	75.00	350.
1846	510,000	8.00	16.00	25.00	50.00	90.00	350.
1847	734,000	9.50	12.50	25.00	40.00	75.00	350.
1847O	368,000	25.00	48.00	80.00	130.	250.	725.
1848	146,000	30.00	42.00	70.00	95.00	175.	725.
1849	340,000	17.50	25.00	37.50	55.00	100.	600.
1849O	Unrecorded	350.	475.	750.	1350.	2500.	—
1850	190,800	23.00	45.00	55.00	85.00	150.	1000.
1850O	412,000	20.00	40.00	50.00	80.00	150.	1100.
1851	160,000	35.00	60.00	90.00	150.	250.	1000.
1851O	88,000	190.	260.	375.	625.	950.	—
1852	177,060	35.00	50.00	75.00	110.	210.	900.
1852O	96,000	185.	250.	350.	600.	900.	—
1853 Recut Date	44,200	175.	225.	300.	400.	600.	4500.

Arrows At Date

Type: Quarter Dollars — Liberty Seated — arrows at date
Dates of issue: 1853-1855
Designer: Christian Gobrecht
Size: 24.3 MM
Weight: 6.22 Grams
Composition: 90% Silver & 10% Copper
Fineness: .900
Actual Silver wt.: .1800 Oz. pure Silver

MINT MARKS:
O   New Orleans
S   San Francisco

With Rays, 1853 Only

Date	Mintage	G-4	VG-8	F-12	VF-20	XF-40	MS-60	Prf-65
1853 Rays	15,210,020	7.25	14.00	20.00	38.00	125.	800.	—
1853/4	Inc. Ab.	75.00	100.	125.	210.	400.	2000.	—
1853O Rays	1,332,000	10.00	26.00	30.00	75.00	160.	3000.	—
1854	12,380,000	7.50	14.00	21.00	32.00	115.	350.	9450.
1854O	1,484,000	8.00	14.00	23.00	35.00	115.	2500.	—
1854O Huge O	Inc. Ab.	50.00	75.00	125.	185.	275.	—	—
1855	2,857,000	7.50	12.50	18.00	24.00	115.	350.	9450.
1855O	176,000	40.00	70.00	100.	175.	285.	1850.	—
1855S	396,400	25.00	45.00	65.00	100.	200.	1750.	—

Arrows At Date Removed

Dates of issue: 1856-1866
MINT MARKS:
O   New Orleans
S   San Francisco

Date	Mintage	G-4	VG-8	F-12	VF-20	XF-40	MS-60	Prf-65
1856	7,264,000	7.50	12.50	17.50	28.00	54.00	350.	7700.
1856O	968,000	12.00	16.00	26.00	40.00	110.	850.	—
1856S	286,000	35.00	55.00	75.00	115.	225.	—	—
1856S/S	Inc. Ab.	75.00	100.	150.	300.	600.	—	—
1857	9,644,000	7.50	12.50	17.50	28.00	54.00	350.	7700.
1857O	1,180,000	13.00	17.00	25.00	40.00	80.00	900.	—
1857S	82,000	70.00	100.	140.	235.	385.	—	—
1858	7,368,000	7.50	12.50	21.00	28.00	54.00	350.	7700.
1858O	520,000	10.00	17.00	30.00	45.00	85.00	900.	—
1858S	121,000	60.00	90.00	120.	180.	275.	—	—
1859	1,344,000	8.50	14.00	23.00	30.00	63.00	700.	7700.
1859O	260,000	18.00	25.00	40.00	60.00	110.	900.	—
1859S	80,000	90.00	125.	175.	275.	400.	—	—
1860	805,400	9.50	13.00	23.00	30.00	64.00	900.	7700.

Date	Mintage	G-4	VG-8	F-12	VF-20	XF-40	MS-60	Prf-65
1860O	388,000	11.00	19.00	35.00	50.00	95.00	925.	—
1860S	56,000	145.	180.	275.	400.	600.	—	—
1861	4,854,600	7.50	12.50	17.50	28.00	54.00	350.	7700.
1861S	96,000	65.00	100.	175.	225.	300.	2600.	—
1862	932,550	8.00	12.50	18.00	35.00	80.00	350.	7700.
1862S	67,000	75.00	110.	160.	225.	375.	—	—
1863	192,060	25.00	35.00	45.00	75.00	150.	750.	7700.
1864	94,070	50.00	60.00	90.00	125.	200.	900.	7700.
1864S	20,000	175.	240.	300.	475.	750.	1800.	—
1865	59,300	65.00	90.00	110.	150.	250.	1250.	7700.
1865S	41,000	100.	125.	150.	225.	350.	2000.	—
1866	—		Unique		—	—	—	—

Motto Above Eagle

Dates of issue: 1866-1873
MINT MARKS:
CC   Carson City
S   San Francisco

Date	Mintage	G-4	VG-8	F-12	VF-20	XF-40	MS-60	Prf-65
1866	17,525	190.	225.	300.	385.	550.	1400.	5600.
1866S	28,000	185.	240.	310.	500.	700.	—	—
1867	20,625	175.	200.	225.	285.	500.	1300.	5600.
1867S	48,000	125.	175.	215.	300.	550.	3000.	—
1868	30,000	135.	165.	200.	275.	400.	1200.	5600.
1868S	96,000	60.00	70.00	100.	160.	250.	2300.	—
1869	16,600	200.	260.	325.	425.	550.	1400.	5600.
1869S	76,000	90.00	110.	150.	240.	400.	—	—
1870	87,400	40.00	48.00	65.00	80.00	125.	1000.	5350.
1870CC	8,340	1200.	1700.	2850.	3750.	5250.	—	—
1871	119,160	45.00	55.00	75.00	110.	195.	1000.	5350.
1871CC	10,890	800.	1100.	1400.	2250.	4250.	—	—
1871S	30,900	165.	225.	285.	450.	700.	3000.	—
1872	182,950	45.00	60.00	75.00	105.	175.	1000.	5350.
1872CC	22,850	375.	525.	750.	1250.	3000.	—	—
1872S	83,000	200.	295.	375.	500.	775.	4700.	—
1873 Clsd.3	212,600	50.00	70.00	100.	160.	250.	—	5600.
1873 Open 3	Inc. Ab.	40.00	45.00	60.00	80.00	125.	570.	—
1873CC	4,000		New England Sale, April, 1980 MS-65 205,000.					

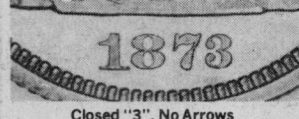
Closed "3", No Arrows

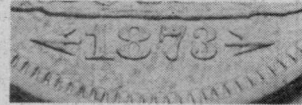
Open "3", Arrows

Arrows At Date

Dates of issue: 1873-1874
MINT MARKS:
CC   Carson City
S   San Francisco

Date	Mintage	G-4	VG-8	F-12	VF-20	XF-40	MS-60	Prf-65
1873	1,271,700	15.00	30.00	45.00	75.00	190.	550.	9450.
1873CC	12,462	1100.	1550.	2250.	3500.	5500.	—	—
1873S	156,000	40.00	60.00	90.00	145.	275.	550.	—
1874	471,900	15.00	30.00	45.00	75.00	200.	550.	9450.
1874S	392,000	24.00	40.00	65.00	140.	225.	550.	—

Arrows At Date Removed

Dates of issue: 1875-1891
MINT MARKS:
CC   Carson City
O   New Orleans
S   San Francisco

Date	Mintage	G-4	VG-8	F-12	VF-20	XF-40	MS-60	Prf-65
1875	4,293,500	7.50	12.50	19.50	28.00	70.00	250.	5350.
1875CC	140,000	50.00	80.00	145.	250.	400.	1400.	—
1875S	680,000	25.00	35.00	50.00	80.00	165.	500.	—
1876	17,817,150	7.50	12.50	19.50	28.00	70.00	250.	5350.
1876CC	4,944,000	9.00	15.00	22.50	35.00	70.00	320.	—
1876CC (Fine Reeding) Inc. Ab.		35.00	50.00	90.00	140.	275.	570.	—
1876S	8,596,000	7.50	12.50	19.50	28.00	70.00	250.	—
1877	10,911,710	7.50	12.50	19.50	28.00	70.00	250.	5350.
1877CC	4,192,000	7.50	15.00	25.00	35.00	70.00	825.	—
1877S	8,996,000	6.75	12.00	19.50	28.00	55.00	250.	—
1877S Over Horizontal S Inc. Ab.		40.00	60.00	85.00	125.	225.	1400.	—
1878	2,260,800	8.00	12.00	20.00	35.00	65.00	360.	5350.
1878CC	996,000	16.00	30.00	38.00	55.00	100.	360.	—
1878S	140,000	40.00	70.00	100.	150.	275.	1500.	—
1879	14,700	115.	145.	190.	235.	300.	600.	5350.
1880	14,955	115.	145.	190.	235.	300.	600.	5350.
1881	12,975	125.	150.	195.	250.	300.	600.	5350.
1882	16,300	125.	150.	195.	250.	300.	600.	5350.
1883	15,439	125.	150.	195.	250.	300.	600.	5350.
1884	8,875	165.	185.	200.	300.	375.	650.	5350.
1885	14,530	125.	150.	190.	250.	400.	600.	5350.
1886	5,886	265.	300.	350.	425.	525.	750.	5350.
1887	10,710	140.	170.	200.	275.	400.	650.	5350.
1888	10,833	125.	150.	175.	250.	300.	600.	5350.
1888S	1,216,000	8.00	14.00	22.00	30.00	65.00	320.	—
1889	12,711	115.	150.	195.	250.	325.	600.	5350.
1890	80,590	50.00	75.00	90.00	120.	200.	540.	5350.
1891	3,920,600	6.75	12.50	20.00	30.00	55.00	320.	5350.
1891O	68,000	125.	165.	225.	350.	600.	—	—
1891S	2,216,000	6.75	12.00	20.00	30.00	60.00	320.	—

BARBER QUARTERS

Type: Quarter Dollars — Barber
Dates of issue: 1892-1916
Designer: Charles E. Barber
Size: 24.3 MM
Weight: 6.25 Grams
Composition: 90% Silver & 10% Copper
Fineness: .900
Actual Silver wt.: .1809 Oz. pure Silver

MINT MARKS:
D Denver
O New Orleans
S San Francisco

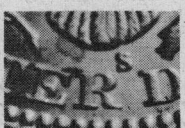
Mintmark

Date	Mintage	G-4	VG-8	F-12	VF-20	XF-40	AU-50	MS-60	MS-65	Prf-65
1892	8,237,245	3.25	4.75	12.50	19.00	52.00	120.	320.	4100.	5350.
1892O	2,640,000	5.25	9.00	14.50	27.00	63.00	160.	350.	4400.	—
1892S	964,079	15.00	19.00	33.00	50.00	85.00	215.	395.	5400.	—
1893	5,484,838	3.25	4.80	11.50	20.00	52.00	125.	325.	4200.	5350.
1893O	3,396,000	4.50	6.50	13.50	28.00	65.00	160.	360.	4700.	—
1893S	1,454,535	5.25	9.50	18.00	35.00	75.00	170.	375.	4800.	—
1894	3,432,972	3.25	4.80	13.00	24.00	56.00	125.	330.	4200.	5350.
1894O	2,852,000	4.50	7.25	14.00	25.00	68.00	170.	365.	4600.	—
1894S	2,648,821	4.50	7.25	13.50	26.00	68.00	165.	355.	4600.	—
1895	4,440,880	3.25	4.75	13.00	19.00	55.00	120.	310.	4300.	5350.
1895O	2,816,000	4.50	7.00	13.50	24.00	65.00	200.	400.	5000.	—
1895S	1,764,681	5.00	9.00	19.00	34.00	72.00	185.	350.	4650.	—
1896	3,874,762	3.30	5.30	12.50	22.00	57.00	125.	320.	4200.	5350.
1896O	1,484,000	4.75	9.00	21.00	45.00	115.	425.	775.	6300.	—
1896S	188,039	195.	250.	550.	850.	1125.	2500.	3500.	8500.	—
1897	8,140,731	2.90	3.50	11.50	21.00	50.00	115.	300.	4050.	5350.
1897O	1,414,800	7.25	11.50	21.00	45.00	115.	425.	800.	6000.	—
1897S	542,229	11.00	16.00	28.00	52.00	115.	275.	375.	4800.	—
1898	11,100,735	2.75	3.40	11.00	19.00	47.00	105.	225.	3900.	5350.
1898O	1,868,000	5.25	9.00	17.50	32.00	81.00	225.	475.	6300.	—
1898S	1,020,592	4.75	7.25	13.50	27.00	62.00	185.	365.	4500.	—
1899	12,624,846	2.75	3.40	11.00	19.00	47.00	105.	225.	4050.	5350.
1899O	2,644,000	5.50	9.00	17.00	30.00	66.00	220.	390.	5600.	—
1899S	708,000	9.00	12.50	22.00	37.00	75.00	195.	360.	4600.	—
1900	10,016,912	2.75	3.40	11.00	19.00	47.00	105.	300.	4050.	5350.
1900O	3,416,000	6.00	10.00	20.00	40.00	87.00	250.	410.	6300.	—
1900S	1,858,585	5.25	7.75	13.00	25.00	60.00	100.	325.	4600.	—
1901	8,892,813	2.75	3.40	11.00	19.00	47.00	105.	300.	4050.	5350.
1901O	1,612,000	13.00	20.00	37.50	72.00	155.	450.	775.	6900.	—
1901S	72,664	925.	1250.	2000.	2800.	4000.	6250.	8500.	38,000.	—
1902	12,197,744	2.75	3.40	11.00	19.00	47.00	105.	300.	4050.	5350.
1902O	4,748,000	4.75	6.25	15.00	31.00	62.00	185.	385.	5500.	—

Date	Mintage	G-4	VG-8	F-12	VF-20	XF-40	AU-50	MS-60	MS-65	Prf-65
1902S	1,524,612	9.25	11.50	18.00	37.00	90.00	205.	375.	4600.	—
1903	9,670,064	2.75	3.40	11.00	19.00	47.00	105.	300.	4050.	5350.
1903O	3,500,000	4.75	6.25	13.50	31.00	68.00	165.	335.	4800.	—
1903S	1,036,000	9.00	13.00	18.00	38.00	90.00	235.	380.	4800.	—
1904	9,588,813	2.75	3.40	11.00	19.00	47.00	105.	300.	4050.	5350.
1904O	2,456,000	5.50	9.00	20.00	40.00	110.	400.	700.	7550.	—
1905	4,968,250	2.75	3.40	11.00	19.00	47.00	105.	315.	4050.	5350.
1905O	1,230,000	5.25	9.00	20.00	35.00	70.00	165.	355.	4600.	—
1905S	1,884,000	5.50	9.00	17.50	32.00	60.00	155.	340.	4600.	—
1906	3,656,435	3.50	4.75	12.00	23.00	56.00	140.	325.	4050.	5350.
1906D	3,280,000	3.50	5.25	13.50	27.00	58.00	135.	330.	4300.	—
1906O	2,056,000	3.60	6.00	16.00	30.00	65.00	145.	345.	4300.	—
1907	7,192,575	2.75	3.25	10.00	18.00	45.00	100.	300.	4050.	5350.
1907D	2,484,000	3.25	4.75	13.50	26.00	54.00	135.	330.	4300.	—
1907O	4,560,000	3.25	4.50	11.00	20.00	55.00	130.	315.	4300.	—
1907S	1,360,000	4.25	5.50	14.00	26.00	64.00	150.	360.	4900.	—
1908	4,232,545	2.75	3.50	10.50	19.00	50.00	105.	300.	4050.	5350.
1908D	5,788,000	3.00	4.00	11.00	20.00	53.00	115.	300.	4300.	—
1908O	6,244,000	3.00	4.00	11.00	20.00	53.00	115.	300.	4300.	—
1908S	784,000	8.50	13.00	23.00	40.00	90.00	200.	390.	4900.	—
1909	9,268,650	2.75	3.25	10.00	19.00	48.00	105.	225.	4050.	5350.
1909D	5,114,000	2.90	3.50	11.00	19.00	50.00	115.	300.	4300.	—
1909O	712,000	10.00	14.00	40.00	75.00	170.	335.	565.	6300.	—
1909S	1,348,000	3.25	4.75	11.00	22.00	55.00	145.	370.	4750.	—
1910	2,244,551	3.00	4.00	11.50	21.00	52.00	115.	315.	4050.	5350.
1910D	1,500,000	3.50	5.00	12.00	24.00	55.00	140.	340.	4600.	—
1911	3,720,543	2.85	3.60	11.00	20.00	50.00	115.	300.	4050.	5350.
1911D	933,600	3.60	5.50	16.50	29.00	60.00	145.	330.	4300.	—
1911S	988,000	3.50	5.00	14.00	26.00	56.00	140.	320.	4300.	—
1912	4,400,700	2.75	3.50	11.00	19.00	47.00	105.	300.	4050.	5350.
1912S	708,000	3.50	5.00	13.50	28.00	60.00	140.	365.	4600.	—
1913	484,613	12.00	16.00	50.00	120.	385.	600.	1200.	6900.	7500.
1913D	1,450,800	3.40	4.75	13.50	28.00	58.00	130.	325.	4300.	—
1913S	40,000	260.	350.	725.	1175.	2000.	2750.	2500.	8700.	—
1914	6,244,610	2.60	3.10	9.50	18.00	46.00	100.	225.	4050.	5800.
1914D	3,046,000	2.75	3.50	10.00	19.00	48.00	105.	300.	4050.	—
1914S	264,000	17.00	23.00	50.00	125.	275.	450.	700.	6300.	—
1915	3,480,450	2.75	3.50	10.00	19.00	47.00	105.	300.	4050.	6000.
1915D	3,694,000	2.75	3.50	10.00	19.50	49.00	105.	300.	4050.	—
1915S	704,000	5.00	6.25	16.00	28.00	58.00	130.	335.	4650.	—
1916	1,788,000	3.00	3.60	11.00	21.00	52.00	110.	300.	4050.	—
1916D	6,540,800	2.75	3.25	9.50	18.00	46.00	100.	225.	4050.	—

STANDING LIBERTY QUARTERS

Variety I

Type: Quarter Dollars — Standing Liberty
Dates of issue: 1916-1930
Designer: Herman A. MacNeil
Size: 24.3 MM
Weight: 6.25 Grams
Composition: 90% Silver & 10% Copper
Fineness: .900
Actual Silver wt.: .1809 Oz. pure Silver

MINT MARKS:
D Denver
S San Francisco

Full Head Detail

Bare Breast
1916-1917

Date	Mintage	G-4	VG-8	F-12	VF-20	XF-40	AU-50	MS-60	MS-65	-65FH
1916	52,000	825.	1000.	1200.	1400.	1750.	2100.	2500.	9000	12,000.
1917	8,792,000	8.00	9.00	17.00	29.00	60.00	95.00	170.	1650.	2200.
1917D	1,509,200	15.00	18.00	24.00	48.00	95.00	125.	185.	2100.	2550.
1917S	1,952,000	14.00	17.00	20.00	43.00	88.00	130.	195.	2250.	2950.

Variety II

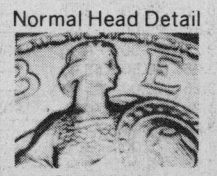
Normal Head Detail
Chain Mail Clad
1917-1930

Mintmark
Overdate — 18/17S

Date	Mintage	G-4	VG-8	F-12	VF-20	XF-40	AU-50	MS-60	MS-65	-65FH
1917	13,880,000	12.00	14.00	17.00	23.00	40.00	65.00	110.	1700.	2100.
1917D	6,224,400	20.00	26.00	45.00	60.00	85.00	110.	150.	1700.	4200.
1917S	5,522,000	19.00	24.00	30.00	53.00	80.00	115.	145.	1700.	4300.
1918	14,240,000	14.50	17.00	22.50	32.00	50.00	80.00	150.	1700.	2500.
1918D	7,380,000	20.00	24.00	37.00	54.00	90.00	120.	185.	1700.	5000.
1918S	11,072,000	14.00	17.00	22.00	31.00	50.00	80.00	150.	1700.	5300.
1918S/17	Inc.Ab.	900.	1100.	1500.	2000.	3200.	6000.	8100	35,000.	—
1919	11,324,000	24.00	30.00	40.00	50.00	70.00	100.	150.	1700.	2500.
1919D	1,944,000	45.00	65.00	100.	145.	200.	275.	400.	3000.	9450.
1919S	1,836,000	43.00	70.00	100.	135.	210.	275.	425.	3200.	9000.
1920	27,860,000	13.00	15.00	17.00	20.00	40.00	70.00	130.	1700.	2500.
1920D	3,586,400	24.00	32.00	50.00	75.00	110.	165.	225.	1800.	4000.
1920S	6,380,000	15.00	17.00	23.00	28.00	52.00	80.00	150.	2500.	6200.
1921	1,916,000	55.00	80.00	125.	165.	240.	340.	460.	2100.	4400.
1923	9,716,000	14.50	17.00	20.00	25.00	42.00	70.00	110.	1400.	3000.
1923S	1,360,000	95.00	135.	185.	240.	375.	460.	575.	1900.	5000.
1924	10,920,000	13.50	15.00	18.00	26.00	42.00	70.00	110.	1700.	2600.
1924D	3,112,000	22.00	30.00	45.00	65.00	95.00	115.	160.	1700.	3800.
1924S	2,860,000	16.50	19.00	22.00	27.00	50.00	80.00	160.	2100.	4800.
1925	12,280,000	2.50	3.00	8.00	12.50	25.00	60.00	110.	1700.	2400.
1926	11,316,000	2.50	3.00	8.00	12.50	25.00	60.00	110.	1700.	2400.
1926D	1,716,000	6.00	7.50	12.00	21.00	54.00	90.00	110.	1750.	5000.
1926S	2,700,000	3.25	5.00	11.00	21.00	55.00	100.	180.	2500.	9500.
1927	11,912,000	2.50	3.00	8.00	12.50	25.00	60.00	110.	1700.	2400.
1927D	976,400	6.00	8.00	13.50	27.00	65.00	105.	165.	1750.	3300.
1927S	396,000	7.50	11.00	50.00	125.	500.	900.	1400.	6500	13,000.
1928	6,336,000	2.50	3.00	8.00	12.50	25.00	60.00	110.	1700.	2400.
1928D	1,627,600	4.00	6.00	9.00	18.00	36.00	72.00	140.	1700.	2850.
1928S	2,644,000	3.00	3.75	8.00	12.50	25.00	60.00	110.	1700.	2400.
1929	11,140,000	2.50	3.00	8.00	12.50	25.00	60.00	110.	1700.	2400.
1929D	1,358,000	4.00	5.50	8.00	17.50	35.00	70.00	130.	1800.	4200.
1929S	1,764,000	3.00	3.75	6.75	16.00	32.00	65.00	110.	1700.	2400.
1930	5,632,000	2.50	3.00	8.00	12.50	25.00	60.00	110.	1700.	2400.
1930S	1,556,000	2.75	3.50	8.00	16.00	32.00	65.00	110.	1700.	2400.

NOTE: -65FH values are for MS-65 full head pieces.

WASHINGTON QUARTERS

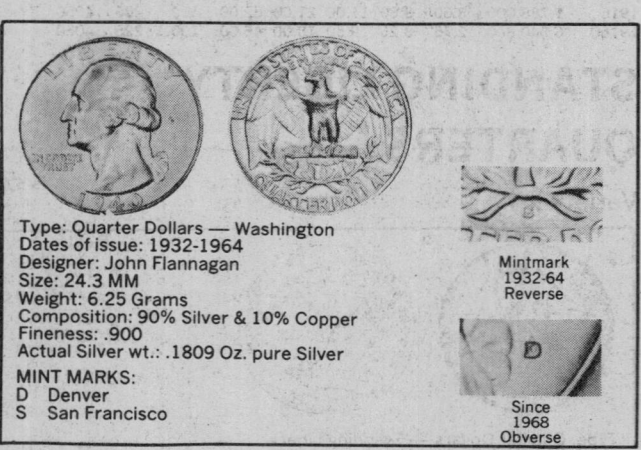

Mintmark
1932-64
Reverse

Type: Quarter Dollars — Washington
Dates of issue: 1932-1964
Designer: John Flannagan
Size: 24.3 MM
Weight: 6.25 Grams
Composition: 90% Silver & 10% Copper
Fineness: .900
Actual Silver wt.: .1809 Oz. pure Silver

MINT MARKS:
D Denver
S San Francisco

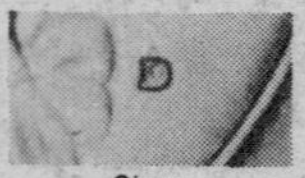

Since
1968
Obverse

Date	Mintage	G-4	VG-8	F-12	VF-20	XF-40	MS-60	MS-65	Prf-65
1932	5,404,000	3.00	3.25	4.50	6.75	9.00	28.00	600.	—
1932D	436,800	34.00	36.00	45.00	65.00	150.	410.	4200.	—
1932S	408,000	29.00	32.00	35.00	45.00	50.00	250.	3800.	—
1934	31,912,052	2.40	3.00	3.75	4.50	5.75	55.00	300.	—
1934D	3,527,200	3.25	4.00	6.00	7.00	10.00	80.00	800.	—
1935	32,484,000	2.40	3.00	3.75	4.50	5.75	35.00	225.	—
1935D	5,780,000	2.40	4.00	6.00	7.00	10.00	80.00	650.	—
1935S	5,660,000	2.40	3.00	4.50	5.00	7.50	60.00	475.	—
1936	41,303,837	2.40	3.00	4.00	4.50	6.00	32.00	225.	1800.
1936D	5,374,000	2.80	3.50	4.00	14.00	30.00	235.	1400.	—
1936S	3,828,000	2.80	3.00	4.00	7.00	10.00	60.00	275.	—
1937	19,701,542	2.40	3.00	4.00	5.75	7.50	35.00	215.	550.
1937D	7,189,600	2.75	3.00	4.00	7.00	9.00	32.00	295.	—
1937S	1,652,000	3.50	4.00	4.50	12.00	20.00	90.00	475.	—
1938	9,480,045	2.80	3.00	4.50	7.50	12.00	45.00	295.	500.
1938S	2,832,000	2.80	3.00	4.50	7.50	11.00	40.00	250.	—
1939	33,548,795	2.40	3.00	3.75	4.25	5.50	19.75	125.	320.
1939D	7,092,000	2.40	3.00	3.75	4.50	7.50	30.00	150.	—
1939S	2,628,000	3.75	4.00	5.00	6.00	10.00	50.00	295.	—
1940	35,715,246	2.40	3.00	3.75	4.00	4.50	18.50	55.00	215.
1940D	2,797,600	3.25	3.50	7.00	10.00	15.50	95.00	300.	—
1940S	8,244,000	2.40	3.00	3.75	4.25	5.50	25.00	115.	—
1941	79,047,287	—	—	1.40	2.00	3.25	7.50	70.00	190.
1941D	16,714,800	—	—	1.40	2.00	3.25	26.50	65.00	—
1941S	16,080,000	—	—	1.40	2.00	3.25	20.00	95.00	—
1942	102,117,123	—	—	1.40	2.00	3.25	8.25	70.00	190.
1942D	17,487,200	—	—	1.40	2.00	3.25	14.00	75.00	—
1942S	19,384,000	—	—	1.40	2.00	4.50	75.00	300.	—
1943	99,700,000	—	—	1.40	2.00	3.25	8.00	70.00	—
1943D	16,095,600	—	—	1.40	2.00	3.25	19.00	60.00	—
1943S	21,700,000	—	—	1.40	2.00	3.25	35.00	180.	—

Date	Mintage	G-4	VG-8	F-12	VF-20	XF-40	MS-60	MS-65	Prf-65
1944	104,956,000	—	—	1.40	2.00	3.25	6.65	24.00	—
1944D	14,600,800	—	—	1.40	2.00	3.25	13.00	50.00	—
1944S	12,560,000	—	—	1.40	2.00	3.25	14.50	35.00	—
1945	74,372,000	—	—	1.40	2.00	3.25	6.00	25.00	—
1945D	12,341,600	—	—	1.40	2.00	3.25	9.00	50.00	—
1945S	17,004,001	—	—	1.40	2.00	3.25	8.75	26.00	—
1946	53,436,000	—	—	1.40	2.00	3.25	6.00	15.00	—
1946D	9,072,800	—	—	2.00	3.00	3.75	6.00	10.00	—
1946S	4,204,000	—	—	2.40	3.50	4.50	6.65	33.00	—
1947	22,556,000	—	—	1.40	2.00	3.25	8.75	12.50	—
1947D	15,338,400	—	—	1.40	2.00	3.25	8.00	13.00	—
1947S	5,532,000	—	—	3.25	3.75	4.00	8.00	13.00	—
1948	35,196,000	—	—	1.40	2.00	3.25	6.00	10.00	—
1948D	16,766,800	—	—	1.40	2.00	3.25	7.50	12.00	—
1948S	15,960,000	—	—	1.40	2.00	3.25	8.75	14.00	—
1949	9,312,000	—	—	1.40	2.00	3.50	24.00	37.00	—
1949D	10,068,400	—	—	2.00	3.25	4.00	8.75	31.00	—
1950	24,971,512	—	—	1.40	3.00	3.25	6.00	8.00	150.
1950D	21,075,600	—	—	1.40	2.50	2.75	6.00	8.00	—
1950D D/S	Inc. Ab.	21.00	25.00	30.00	60.00	140.	250.	500.	—
1950S	10,284,004	—	—	1.40	3.00	3.25	9.25	13.50	—
1950S S/D	Inc. Ab.	21.00	25.00	30.00	60.00	170.	490.	625.	—
1951	43,505,602	—	—	1.40	1.45	1.50	5.25	6.00	72.00
1951D	35,354,800	—	—	1.40	1.45	1.50	4.75	5.50	—
1951S	9,048,000	—	—	1.40	1.45	4.25	12.75	18.50	—
1952	38,862,073	—	—	1.40	1.45	1.50	3.90	5.50	58.00
1952D	49,795,200	—	—	1.40	1.45	1.50	3.65	6.00	—
1952S	13,707,800	—	—	1.40	3.25	3.50	9.50	11.50	—
1953	18,664,920	—	—	1.40	1.45	1.50	4.50	5.25	36.00
1953D	56,112,400	—	—	1.40	1.45	1.50	3.50	5.25	—
1953S	14,016,000	—	—	1.40	1.45	1.50	4.90	6.50	—
1954	54,645,503	—	—	1.40	1.50	1.60	2.75	4.75	15.00
1954D	42,305,500	—	—	1.40	1.45	1.50	2.65	4.50	—
1954S	11,834,722	—	—	1.40	1.45	1.50	4.00	5.25	—
1955	18,558,381	—	—	1.40	1.45	1.50	3.50	6.00	12.00
1955D	3,182,400	—	—	3.00	3.75	4.00	5.50	7.50	—
1956	44,813,384	—	—	1.40	1.45	1.50	2.50	4.00	6.00
1956D	32,334,500	—	—	1.40	1.45	1.50	2.50	4.00	—
1957	47,779,952	—	—	1.40	1.45	1.50	2.65	4.25	4.00
1957D	77,924,160	—	—	1.40	1.45	1.50	2.50	4.50	—
1958	7,235,652	—	—	1.40	1.45	1.50	3.00	6.50	8.00
1958D	78,124,900	—	—	1.40	1.45	1.50	2.50	4.50	—
1959	25,533,291	—	—	1.40	1.45	1.50	2.25	4.00	3.80
1959D	62,054,232	—	—	1.40	1.45	1.50	2.25	4.00	—
1960	30,855,602	—	—	1.40	1.45	1.50	2.25	4.00	3.60
1960D	63,000,324	—	—	1.40	1.45	1.50	2.25	4.00	—
1961	40,064,244	—	—	1.40	1.45	1.50	1.90	4.00	3.25
1961D	83,656,928	—	—	1.40	1.45	1.50	2.40	4.00	—
1962	39,374,019	—	—	1.40	1.45	1.50	2.50	4.00	3.25
1962D	127,554,756	—	—	1.40	1.45	1.50	1.75	4.00	—
1963	77,391,645	—	—	1.40	1.45	1.50	1.75	3.75	3.25
1963D	135,288,184	—	—	1.40	1.45	1.50	1.75	3.75	—
1964	564,341,347	—	—	1.40	1.45	1.50	1.75	3.75	3.25
1964D	704,135,528	—	—	1.40	1.45	1.50	1.75	3.75	—

Type: Quarter Dollars — Washington — Clad
Dates of issue: 1965 to Present
Designer: John Flannagan
Size: 24.3 MM
Weight: 5.67 Grams
Composition: Clad layers of 75% Copper & 25% Nickel, bonded to pure Copper core

MINT MARKS:
D Denver
P Philadelphia
S San Francisco

Date	Mintage	G-4	VG-8	F-12	VF-20	XF-40	MS-60	MS-65	Prf-65
1965	1,819,717,540	—	—	—	—	—	—	.80	—
1966	821,101,500	—	—	—	—	—	—	.80	—
1967	1,524,031,848	—	—	—	—	—	—	.80	—
1968	220,731,500	—	—	—	—	—	—	.80	—
1968D	101,534,000	—	—	—	—	—	—	1.00	—
1968S	Proof Only	—	—	—	—	—	—	—	.55
1969	176,212,000	—	—	—	—	—	—	1.00	—
1969D	114,372,000	—	—	—	—	—	—	1.25	—
1969S	Proof Only	—	—	—	—	—	—	—	.55
1970	136,420,000	—	—	—	—	—	—	.50	—
1970D	417,341,364	—	—	—	—	—	—	.50	—
1970S	Proof Only	—	—	—	—	—	—	—	.50
1971	109,284,000	—	—	—	—	—	—	.50	—
1971D	258,634,428	—	—	—	—	—	—	.50	—
1971S	Proof Only	—	—	—	—	—	—	—	.60
1972	215,048,000	—	—	—	—	—	—	.40	—
1972D	311,067,732	—	—	—	—	—	—	.40	—
1972S	Proof Only	—	—	—	—	—	—	—	.50
1973	346,924,000	—	—	—	—	—	—	.40	—
1973D	232,977,400	—	—	—	—	—	—	.40	—
1973S	Proof Only	—	—	—	—	—	—	—	.50
1974	801,456,000	—	—	—	—	—	—	.40	—
1974D	353,160,300	—	—	—	—	—	—	.40	—
1974S	Proof Only	—	—	—	—	—	—	—	.60

Type: Quarter Dollars — Bicentennial — Date 1776-1976 — Silver
Dates of issue: 1975-1976
Designer: John Flannagan and Jack L. Ahr
Size: 24.3 MM
Weight: Silver Issues 5.75 Grams, Copper Nickel 5.67 Grams
Composition: Silver Clad Issues — 1976 Clad layers of 80% Copper and 20% Silver, bonded to core of 79.1% Copper and 20.9% Silver
Fineness: Silver Issues .400
Actual Silver wt.: .0740 Oz. pure Silver

MINT MARKS:
D   Denver
S   San Francisco

Date	Mintage	G-4	VG-8	F-12	VF-20	XF-40	MS-60	MS-65	Prf-65
1976	809,784,016	—	—	—	—	—	—	.60	—
1976D	860,118,839	—	—	—	—	—	—	.60	—
1976S		—	—	—	—	—	—	—	.65
1976S Silver		—	—	—	—	—	—	2.50	4.00
1977	468,556,000	—	—	—	—	—	—	.40	—
1977D	258,898,212	—	—	—	—	—	—	.40	—
1977S	Proof Only								.45
1978	521,452,000	—	—	—	—	—	—	.40	—
1978D	287,373,152	—	—	—	—	—	—	.40	—
1978S	Proof Only								.50
1979	515,708,000	—	—	—	—	—	—	.50	—
1979D	489,789,780	—	—	—	—	—	—	.50	—
1979S	Proof Only								.50
1979S T-II	Proof Only								1.95
1980P	635,832,000	—	—	—	—	—	—	.50	—
1980D	518,327,487	—	—	—	—	—	—	.50	—
1980S	Proof Only								.45
1981P	601,716,000	—	—	—	—	—	—	.50	—
1981D	575,722,833	—	—	—	—	—	—	.50	—
1981S	Proof Only								.50
1982P	500,931,000	—	—	—	—	—	—	2.00	—
1982D	480,042,788	—	—	—	—	—	—	1.00	—
1982S	Proof Only								.55
1983P	673,535,000	—	—	—	—	—	—	.50	—
1983D	617,806,446	—	—	—	—	—	—	.75	—
1983S	Proof Only								.90
1984P	676,545,000	—	—	—	—	—	—	.50	—
1984D	546,483,064	—	—	—	—	—	—	.50	—
1984S	Proof Only								1.50
1985P	775,818,962	—	—	—	—	—	—	.50	—
1985D	519,962,888	—	—	—	—	—	—	.50	—
1985S	Proof Only								1.00
1986P	551,199,333	—	—	—	—	—	—	.50	—
1986D	504,298,660	—	—	—	—	—	—	.50	—
1986S	Proof Only								.90
1987P	582,499,481	—	—	—	—	—	—	.50	—
1987D	655,594,696	—	—	—	—	—	—	.50	—
1987S	Proof Only								1.25
1988P		—	—	—	—	—	—	.50	—
1988D		—	—	—	—	—	—	.50	—
1988S	Proof Only								1.25
1989P		—	—	—	—	—	—	.50	—
1989D		—	—	—	—	—	—	.50	—
1989S	Proof Only								1.25

HALF DOLLARS

Flowing Hair Half Dollars

Type: Half Dollars — Flowing Hair
Dates of issue: 1794-1795
Designer: Robert Scot
Size: 32.5 MM
Weight: 13.48 Grams
Composition: 89.24% Silver & 10.76% Copper
Fineness: .8924
Actual Silver wt.: .3869 Oz. pure Silver

Date	Mintage	G-4	VG-8	F-12	VF-20	XF-40	MS-60
1794	23,464	1150.	1850.	2750.	3950.	6950.	—
1795	299,680	440.	500.	825.	1450.	2500.	13,000.
1795 Recut Date	Inc. Ab.	550.	625.	900.	1450.	2500.	13,000.
1795 3 Leaves	Inc. Ab.	1850.	2500.	3300.	5850.	11,000.	—

Draped Bust Half Dollars

Dates of issue: 1796-1797

Date	Mintage	G-4	VG-8	F-12	VF-20	XF-40	MS-60
1796 15 Stars	3,918	10,000.	12,000.	15,000.	27,000.	39,000.	—
1796 16 Stars	Inc. Ab.	10,000.	12,000.	15,000.	27,000.	39,000.	—
1797	Inc. Ab.	10,000.	12,000.	15,000.	27,000.	39,000.	—

Heraldic Eagle Introduced

Type: Half Dollars — Draped Bust — Heraldic Eagle Reverse
Dates of issue: 1801-1807
Designer: Robert Scot

Date	Mintage	G-4	VG-8	F-12	VF-20	XF-40	MS-60
1801	30,289	160.	325.	695.	950.	1250.	9500.
1802	29,890	175.	375.	695.	950.	1250.	9200.
1803 Sm. 3	188,234	150.	250.	400.	695.	1000.	6500.
1803 Lg. 3	Inc. Ab.	85.00	125.	200.	400.	900.	6500.
1805	211,722	70.00	100.	140.	400.	800.	6400.
1805/4	Inc. Ab.	175.	250.	475.	650.	1375.	6400.
1806 Round Top 6, Large Stars	839,576	70.00	90.00	140.	325.	625.	6300.
1806 Round Top 6, Small Stars	Inc. Ab.	70.00	90.00	140.	325.	625.	6300.
1806 Pointed Top 6, Stem Not Through Claw	Inc. Ab.	70.00	90.00	140.	325.	625.	6300.
1806 Pointed Top 6, Stem Through Claw	Inc. Ab.	70.00	90.00	140.	325.	625.	6300.
1806/5	Inc. Ab.	80.00	120.	200.	450.	775.	6300.
1806 Over Inverted 6	Inc. Ab.	175.	225.	325.	675.	1175.	6300.
1807	301,076	80.00	110.	165.	315.	575.	6300.

Liberty Capped Half Dollars

Type: Half Dollars — Capped Bust — Lettered Edge
Dates of issue: 1807-1836
Designer: John Reich
Size: 32.5 MM
Weight: 13.48 Grams
Composition: 89.24% Silver & 10.76% Copper
Fineness: .8924
Actual Silver wt.: .3869 Oz. pure Silver

Date	Mintage	G-4	VG-8	F-12	VF-20	XF-40	MS-60
1807 Sm. Stars	750,500	75.00	100.	175.	300.	550.	1250.
1807 Lg. Stars	Inc. Ab.	85.00	100.	125.	240.	500.	2500.
1807 50/20 C.	Inc. Ab.	45.00	60.00	75.00	140.	350.	1250.
1808	1,368,600	37.50	42.50	53.00	90.00	185.	650.
1808/7	Inc. Ab.	40.00	50.00	60.00	125.	200.	900.
1809	1,405,810	36.00	42.50	55.00	75.00	160.	650.
1810	1,276,276	34.50	38.00	46.00	70.00	145.	650.
1811 Sm. 8	1,203,644	32.00	37.50	45.00	70.00	145.	650.
1811 Lg. 8	Inc. Ab.	32.50	37.00	50.00	85.00	165.	650.
1811 Dt. 18.11	Inc. Ab.	35.00	40.00	60.00	95.00	185.	850.
1812	1,628,059	32.50	37.50	45.00	70.00	145.	650.
1812/11	Inc. Ab.	42.50	50.00	80.00	115.	225.	650.
1813	1,241,903	32.50	37.50	45.00	70.00	145.	650.
1814	1,039,075	34.50	38.00	47.00	70.00	145.	650.
1814/13	Inc. Ab.	42.50	52.50	69.00	100.	200.	650.
1815/12	47,150	750.	950.	1350.	1750.	2250.	4500.
1817	1,215,567	31.50	33.00	40.00	65.00	135.	650.
1817/13	Inc. Ab.	80.00	135.	185.	325.	500.	1500.
1817/14				5 Pieces Known - Rare			
1817 Dt. 181.7	Inc. Ab.	37.00	47.00	70.00	115.	195.	650.
1818	1,960,322	31.50	33.00	40.00	70.00	135.	650.
1818/17	Inc. Ab.	31.50	33.00	40.00	70.00	135.	650.
1819	2,208,000	31.50	33.00	40.00	70.00	135.	650.
1819/18 Sm. 9	Inc. Ab.	31.50	33.00	40.00	70.00	135.	650.
1819/18 Lg. 9	Inc. Ab.	31.50	33.00	40.00	70.00	135.	650.
1820 Sm. Dt.	751,122	39.00	49.00	67.00	135.	210.	650.
1820 Lg. Dt.	Inc. Ab.	39.00	50.00	67.00	135.	210.	650.
1820/19	Inc. Ab.	37.00	49.00	75.00	130.	225.	650.
1821	1,305,797	33.00	35.00	40.00	70.00	135.	650.
1822	1,559,573	32.00	34.00	40.00	65.00	135.	650.
1822/1	Inc. Ab.	50.00	69.00	110.	185.	300.	650.
1823	1,694,200	31.50	33.00	40.00	65.00	135.	650.
1823 Broken 3	Inc. Ab.	37.00	52.00	84.00	115.	220.	650.
1823 Patched 3	Inc. Ab.	37.00	50.00	75.00	95.00	195.	650.
1823 Ugly 3	Inc. Ab.	35.00	40.00	65.00	95.00	185.	650.
1824	3,504,954	31.00	33.00	40.00	50.00	95.00	650.
1824/21	Inc. Ab.	35.00	40.00	58.00	95.00	185.	650.
1824/Over Various Dates							
	Inc. Ab.	31.50	33.00	40.00	65.00	145.	650.
1825	2,943,166	31.50	33.00	40.00	50.00	95.00	650.
1826	4,004,180	31.50	33.00	40.00	50.00	95.00	650.
1827 Curled 2	5,493,400	33.00	36.00	42.50	85.00	150.	650.
1827 Square 2	Inc. Ab.	31.50	33.00	40.00	50.00	95.00	650.
1827/6	Inc. Ab.	35.00	40.00	60.00	90.00	145.	650.
1828 Curled Base 2, No Knob							
	3,075,200	30.00	33.00	37.50	50.00	95.00	650.
1828 Curled Base 2, Knobbed 2							
	Inc. Ab.	35.00	45.00	60.00	85.00	150.	650.
1828 Small 8's, Square Base 2, Large Letters							
	Inc. Ab.	27.50	32.00	34.00	43.00	90.00	650.
1828 Small 8's, Square Base 2, Small Letters							
	Inc. Ab.	27.50	32.00	65.00	125.	250.	800.
1828 Large 8's, Square Base 2							
	Inc. Ab.	27.50	32.00	34.00	43.00	90.00	650.
1829	3,712,156	27.50	32.00	34.00	43.00	90.00	650.
1829/27	Inc. Ab.	35.00	40.00	60.00	85.00	165.	650.
1830 Small 0 In Date							
	4,764,800	27.50	32.00	34.00	43.00	89.00	650.
1830 Large 0 In Date							
	Inc. Ab.	27.50	32.00	34.00	43.00	89.00	650.
1831	5,873,660	27.50	32.00	34.00	43.00	89.00	650.
1832 Sm. Lt.	4,797,000	27.50	32.00	34.00	43.00	89.00	650.
1832 Lg. Let.	Inc. Ab.	30.00	38.00	45.00	65.00	195.	1250.
1833	5,206,000	27.50	32.00	34.00	43.00	89.00	650.
1834 Small Date, Large Stars, Small Letters							
	6,412,004	27.50	32.00	34.00	43.00	89.00	650.
1834 Small Date, Small Stars, Small Letters							
	Inc. Ab.	27.50	32.00	34.00	43.00	89.00	650.
1834 Large Date, Small Letters							
	Inc. Ab.	27.50	31.50	34.00	43.00	89.00	650.
1834 Large Date, Large Letters							
	Inc. Ab.	27.50	31.50	34.00	43.00	89.00	650.
1835	5,352,006	27.50	31.50	34.00	43.00	89.00	650.
1836	6,545,000	27.50	31.50	34.00	43.00	89.00	650.
1836 50/00	Inc. Ab.	50.00	60.00	80.00	160.	225.	1100.

Reeded Edge - 50 Cents On Reverse

Type: Half Dollars — Capped Bust — Reed Edge — Reverse "50 Cents"
Dates of issue: 1836-1837
Designer: Christian Gobrecht
Size: 30 MM
Weight: 13.36 Grams
Composition: 90% Silver & 10% Copper
Fineness: .900
Actual Silver wt.: .3867 Oz. pure Silver

Date	Mintage	G-4	VG-8	F-12	VF-20	XF-40	MS-60
1836	1,200	500.	675.	900.	1450.	1875.	3500.
1837	3,629,820	32.00	38.00	41.00	60.00	125.	800.

Half Dol. On Reverse

Type: Half Dollar — Capped Bust — Reeded Eagle — reverse Half Dollar
Dates of issue: 1838-1839

MINT MARKS:
O New Orleans

Mintmark

Date	Mintage	G-4	VG-8	F-12	VF-20	XF-40	MS-60
1838	3,546,000	32.00	38.00	41.00	60.00	125.	900.
1838O	Est. 20				Auction 82 MS-63 47,000.		
1839	3,334,560	32.00	38.00	41.00	60.00	125.	800.
1839O	178,976	85.00	125.	185.	375.	595.	3250.

LIBERTY SEATED HALVES

Type: Half Dollars — Liberty Seated — No Motto Above Eagle
Dates of issue: 1839-1853
Designer: Christian Gobrecht
Size: 30.6 MM
Weight: 13.36 Grams
Composition: 90% Silver & 10% Copper
Fineness: .900
Actual Silver wt.: .3867 Oz. pure Silver

MINT MARKS:
O New Orleans

Mintmark

Date	Mintage	G-4	VG-8	F-12	VF-20	XF-40	MS-60
1839 No Drapery From Elbow							
	Inc. Ab.	38.00	65.00	110.	250.	650.	3650.
1839 Drapery	Inc. Ab.	20.00	25.00	40.00	70.00	115.	950.
1840 Sm. Let.	1,435,008	16.50	20.00	30.00	60.00	100.	950.
1840 Rev. 1838	Inc. Ab.	85.00	120.	175.	250.	450.	2000.
1840O	855,100	17.00	23.00	34.00	60.00	125.	1000.
1841	310,000	45.00	55.00	70.00	125.	265.	1300.
1841O	401,000	24.00	35.00	45.00	90.00	150.	1300.
1842 Sm. Date	2,012,764	27.00	32.00	40.00	75.00	125.	1300.
1842 Lg. Date	Inc. Ab.	16.00	21.00	33.00	50.00	75.00	1250.
1842O Sm. Date	957,000	700.	1000.	1400.	2500.	5000.	
1842O Lg. Date	Inc. Ab.	17.00	23.00	34.00	50.00	90.00	1000.
1843	3,844,000	16.00	21.00	30.00	42.00	70.00	950.
1843O	2,268,000	16.00	21.00	30.00	42.00	70.00	1000.
1844	1,766,000	16.00	21.00	30.00	42.00	70.00	950.
1844O	2,005,000	18.00	21.00	36.00	55.00	80.00	1000.
1845	589,000	30.00	40.00	50.00	90.00	165.	1200.
1845O	2,094,000	16.00	21.00	30.00	42.00	70.00	950.
1845O No Drapery							
	Inc. Ab.	40.00	60.00	90.00	120.	195.	1000.
1846 Med Dt	2,210,000	16.00	20.00	28.00	40.00	70.00	950.
1846 Tall Dt	Inc. Ab.	22.00	30.00	60.00	80.00	125.	950.
1846 Over Horizontal 6							
	Inc. Ab.	140.	185.	250.	375.	550.	2500.
1846O Med Dt	2,304,000	16.00	18.00	28.00	38.00	75.00	950.
1846O Tall Dt	Inc. Ab.	115.	150.	200.	325.	500.	2000.
1847/1846	1,156,000	1500.	1900.	2500.	3250.	4500.	—
1847	Inc. Ab.	16.00	30.00	45.00	60.00	110.	950.
1847O	2,584,000	15.00	25.00	35.00	50.00	95.00	950.
1848	580,000	30.00	35.00	55.00	85.00	140.	950.
1848O	3,180,000	18.00	25.00	32.00	40.00	75.00	950.
1849	1,252,000	25.00	35.00	50.00	85.00	125.	950.

Date	Mintage	G-4	VG-8	F-12	VF-20	XF-40	MS-60
1849O	2,310,000	15.00	18.00	21.00	35.00	63.00	950.
1850	227,000	175.	225.	285.	350.	450.	1500.
1850O	2,456,000	15.00	18.00	21.00	35.00	63.00	950.
1851	200,750	225.	265.	325.	415.	550.	1800.
1851O	402,000	37.00	45.00	57.00	90.00	175.	950.
1852	77,130	300.	350.	425.	475.	650.	2500.
1852O	144,000	65.00	80.00	125.	225.	350.	1500.
1853O	Unrecorded			Garrett Sale, 1979, VF 40,000.			

Arrows At Date

Type: Half Dollars — Liberty Seated — arrows at date
Dates of issue: 1853-1855
Designer: Christian Gobrecht
Size: 30.6 MM
Weight: 12.44 Grams
Composition: 90% Silver & 10% Copper
Fineness: .900
Actual Silver wt.: .3600 Oz. pure Silver

MINT MARKS:
O   New Orleans
S   San Francisco

Date	Mintage	G-4	VG-8	F-12	VF-20	XF-40	MS-60	Prf-65
1853 Rays On Reverse								
	3,532,708	16.50	30.00	45.00	90.00	250.	1900.	—
1853O Rays On Reverse								
	1,328,000	19.00	25.00	40.00	100.	290.	1900.	—
1854	2,982,000	15.00	20.00	29.00	50.00	100.	550.	—
1854O	5,240,000	15.00	20.00	29.00	50.00	100.	550.	—
1855	759,500	23.00	30.00	40.00	60.00	150.	900.	15,500.
1855O	3,688,000	15.00	20.00	29.00	50.00	100.	550.	—
1855S	129,950	300.	380.	550.	1000.	2250.	—	—

Arrows At Date Removed

Dates of issue: 1856-1866

MINT MARKS:
O   New Orleans
S   San Francisco

Date	Mintage	G-4	VG-8	F-12	VF-20	XF-40	MS-60	Prf-65
1856	938,000	16.00	25.00	32.00	47.50	90.00	500.	11,000.
1856O	2,658,000	15.00	21.00	28.00	45.00	82.00	500.	—
1856S	211,000	40.00	50.00	70.00	100.	225.	1500.	—
1857	1,988,000	15.00	18.00	28.00	45.00	82.00	350.	11,000.
1857O	818,000	18.00	21.00	25.00	55.00	100.	850.	—
1857S	158,000	45.00	65.00	110.	180.	290.	1400.	—
1858	4,226,000	15.00	18.00	35.00	60.00	80.00	350.	11,000.
1858O	7,294,000	16.00	19.00	35.00	45.00	75.00	350.	—
1858S	476,000	20.00	30.00	48.00	75.00	135.	550.	—
1859	748,000	16.50	27.00	42.00	55.00	90.00	350.	11,000.
1859O	2,834,000	15.00	25.00	40.00	50.00	85.00	550.	—
1859S	566,000	20.00	28.00	45.00	70.00	120.	750.	—
1860	303,700	18.00	21.00	27.00	70.00	145.	1000.	11,000.
1860O	1,290,000	15.00	18.00	21.00	35.00	75.00	350.	—
1860S	472,000	18.00	30.00	50.00	70.00	130.	850.	—
1861	2,888,400	15.00	25.00	35.00	45.00	75.00	350.	11,000.
1861O	2,532,633	15.00	25.00	35.00	45.00	75.00	350.	—
1861S	939,500	17.00	20.00	24.00	45.00	75.00	975.	—
1862	253,550	24.00	32.00	45.00	80.00	150.	750.	11,000.
1862S	1,352,000	16.00	27.00	35.00	60.00	90.00	350.	—
1863	503,660	18.00	25.00	40.00	70.00	130.	750.	11,000.
1863S	916,000	16.00	25.00	35.00	45.00	80.00	350.	—
1864	379,570	20.00	30.00	55.00	85.00	160.	750.	11,000.
1864S	658,000	16.50	20.00	40.00	50.00	85.00	350.	—
1865	511,900	18.00	23.00	40.00	55.00	105.	750.	11,000.
1865S	675,000	17.00	21.00	30.00	50.00	75.00	350.	—
1866	—	—	—	—	Proof, Unique			
1866S	60,000	60.00	80.00	150.	225.	335.	5000.	—

Motto Above Eagle

Dates of issue: 1866-1873

MINT MARKS:
CC Carson City
S   San Francisco

Date	Mintage	G-4	VG-8	F-12	VF-20	XF-40	MS-60	Prf-65
1866	745,625	15.00	24.00	29.00	39.00	63.00	800.	6950.
1866S	994,000	15.00	24.00	29.00	39.00	63.00	800.	—
1867	449,925	16.00	27.00	35.00	55.00	100.	1000.	6950.
1867S	1,196,000	15.00	24.00	29.00	39.00	63.00	800.	—
1868	418,200	21.00	28.00	35.00	70.00	135.	1000.	6950.
1868S	1,160,000	15.00	24.00	29.00	39.00	63.00	800.	—
1869	795,900	15.00	24.00	29.00	39.00	63.00	800.	6950.
1869S	656,000	15.00	27.00	35.00	47.00	80.00	800.	—
1870	634,900	17.00	27.00	35.00	47.00	80.00	800.	6950.
1870CC	54,617	600.	850.	1200.	2000.	3000.	—	—
1870S	1,004,000	15.00	24.00	29.00	42.00	75.00	800.	—
1871	1,204,560	16.00	24.00	29.00	39.00	63.00	800.	6950.
1871CC	153,950	115.	150.	200.	325.	600.	4000.	—
1871S	2,178,000	15.00	24.00	29.00	39.00	63.00	800.	—
1872	881,550	15.00	24.00	29.00	39.00	63.00	800.	6950.
1872CC	272,000	37.00	50.00	90.00	160.	350.	2500.	—
1872S	580,000	23.00	28.00	40.00	80.00	145.	900.	—
1873 Closed 3								
	801,800	15.00	24.00	38.00	50.00	95.00	760.	6950.
1873 Open 3								
	Inc. Ab.	2500.	3000.	4000.	5000.	6500.	—	—
1873CC	122,500	100.	120.	200.	310.	475.	3000.	6950.

1873S No Arrows - 5,000 Minted - No Specimens Known To Survive

Arrows At Date

Type: Half Dollars — Liberty Seated — Arrows at Date
Dates of issue: 1873-1874
Designer: Christian Gobrecht
Size: 30.6 MM
Weight: 12.50 Grams
Composition: 90% Silver & 10% Copper
Fineness: .900
Actual Silver wt.: .3618 Oz. pure Silver

MINT MARKS:
CC Carson City
S   San Francisco

Date	Mintage	G-4	VG-8	F-12	VF-20	XF-40	MS-60	Prf-65
1873	1,815,700	16.50	25.00	36.00	80.00	210.	650.	15,500.
1873CC	214,560	60.00	75.00	95.00	225.	450.	2500.	—
1873S	233,000	45.00	60.00	90.00	165.	300.	1850.	—
1874	2,360,300	16.50	25.00	36.00	80.00	210.	650.	15,500.
1874CC	59,000	165.	210.	325.	500.	925.	4500.	—
1874S	394,000	25.00	30.00	38.00	100.	275.	2000.	—

Arrows At Date Removed

Dates of issue: 1875-1891

MINT MARKS:
CC Carson City
S   San Francisco

Date	Mintage	G-4	VG-8	F-12	VF-20	XF-40	MS-60	Prf-65
1875	6,027,500	15.00	24.00	29.00	37.00	60.00	800.	6150.
1875CC	1,008,000	17.00	33.00	35.00	45.00	100.	850.	—
1875S	3,200,000	15.00	24.00	29.00	37.00	60.00	320.	—
1876	8,419,150	15.00	24.00	32.00	40.00	60.00	320.	6150.
1876CC	1,956,000	18.00	30.00	35.00	45.00	100.	850.	—
1876S	4,528,000	15.00	24.00	32.00	40.00	60.00	320.	—
1877	8,304,510	15.00	24.00	29.00	45.00	60.00	320.	6150
1877CC	1,420,000	17.00	33.00	35.00	45.00	95.00	800.	—
1877S	5,356,000	15.00	24.00	29.00	37.00	65.00	320.	—
1878	1,378,400	16.00	26.00	32.00	40.00	66.00	320.	6150.
1878CC	62,000	225.	260.	350.	450.	650.	1250.	3000.
1878S	12,000	5700.	7500.	8500.	12,500.	17,500.	25,000.	—
1879	5,900	250.	275.	300.	375.	475.	1600.	7550.
1880	9,755	200.	220.	275.	310.	400.	1500.	7550.

Date	Mintage	G-4	VG-8	F-12	VF-20	XF-40	MS-60	Prf-65
1881	10,975	185.	210.	265.	300.	390.	1400.	7550.
1882	5,500	250.	275.	300.	375.	475.	1600.	7550.
1883	9,039	200.	220.	275.	310.	400.	1600.	7550.
1884	5,275	280.	300.	370.	420.	525.	1700.	7550.
1885	6,130	275.	300.	350.	410.	525.	1700.	7550.
1886	5,886	285.	310.	350.	430.	550.	1700.	7550.
1887	5,710	300.	330.	375.	450.	575.	1700.	7550.
1888	12,833	175.	200.	235.	290.	375.	1100.	7550.
1889	12,711	185.	200.	235.	290.	395.	1100.	7550.
1890	12,590	185.	200.	235.	290.	375.	1100.	7550.
1891	200,600	30.00	35.00	55.00	80.00	115.	1000.	7550.

BARBER HALVES

Type: Half Dollars — Barber or Liberty Head
Dates of issue: 1892-1915
Designer: Charles E. Barber
Size: 30.6 MM
Weight: 12.50 Grams
Composition: 90% Silver & 10% Copper
Fineness: .900
Actual Silver wt.: .3618 Oz. pure Silver

Mintmark

MINT MARKS:
D Denver
O New Orleans
S San Francisco

Date	Mintage	G-4	VG-8	F-12	VF-20	XF-40	AU-50	MS-60	MS-65	Prf-65
1892	935,245	17.00	25.00	42.00	60.00	170.	350.	600.	5900.	6950.
1892O	390,000	100.	125.	170.	280.	400.	600.	1000.	6350.	—
1892S	1,029,028	105.	135.	175.	280.	410.	575.	1050.	8500.	—
1893	1,826,792	11.00	22.00	42.00	62.00	175.	360.	625.	6300.	6950.
1893O	1,389,000	17.50	25.00	50.00	110.	275.	425.	750.	7500.	—
1893S	740,000	45.00	66.00	105.	245.	400.	525.	1000.	7500.	—
1894	1,148,972	8.00	14.00	47.00	78.00	185.	350.	600.	6300.	6950.
1894O	2,138,000	8.50	16.00	45.00	85.00	245.	400.	700.	6500.	—
1894S	4,048,690	7.50	14.00	42.00	70.00	230.	380.	650.	6500.	—
1895	1,835,218	8.00	12.50	36.00	58.00	165.	340.	625.	6700.	6950.
1895O	1,766,000	8.50	14.00	40.00	75.00	225.	410.	700.	6500.	—
1895S	1,108,086	16.50	23.00	48.00	95.00	235.	410.	675.	6500.	—
1896	950,762	11.00	17.50	43.00	72.00	195.	375.	600.	6700.	6950.
1896O	924,000	16.50	24.00	62.00	140.	345.	600.	1000.	9750.	—
1896S	1,140,948	52.00	65.00	105.	210.	400.	650.	1050.	8400.	—
1897	2,480,731	5.75	9.00	27.00	52.00	150.	300.	500.	6200.	6950.
1897O	632,000	46.00	63.00	90.00	260.	475.	800.	1300.	10,000.	—
1897S	933,900	76.50	105.	150.	255.	450.	685.	1150.	8500.	—
1898	2,956,735	5.50	9.00	27.00	51.00	145.	290.	480.	5850.	6950.
1898O	874,000	14.50	21.00	50.00	125.	375.	560.	660.	8600.	—
1898S	2,358,550	8.00	17.00	35.00	63.00	210.	390.	615.	6500.	—
1899	5,538,846	5.50	8.75	27.00	50.00	145.	290.	500.	5900.	6950.
1899O	1,724,000	8.00	13.00	40.00	75.00	250.	400.	675.	8500.	—
1899S	1,686,411	8.50	16.00	38.00	58.00	210.	375.	615.	6500.	—
1900	4,762,912	5.50	9.00	27.00	50.00	145.	290.	480.	5850.	6950.
1900O	2,744,000	8.25	12.50	39.00	85.00	275.	425.	695.	10,000.	—
1900S	2,560,322	8.00	12.00	35.00	60.00	195.	345.	615.	6000.	—
1901	4,268,813	5.50	9.00	26.00	50.00	145.	290.	480.	5850.	6950.
1901O	1,124,000	8.00	13.00	36.00	74.00	325.	500.	1100.	10,000.	—
1901S	847,044	13.50	18.00	56.00	195.	510.	800.	1200.	9500.	—
1902	4,922,777	5.50	9.00	26.00	50.00	140.	290.	480.	5850.	6950.
1902O	2,526,000	7.25	11.00	31.00	60.00	205.	390.	695.	8000.	—
1902S	1,460,670	7.50	12.00	39.00	65.00	220.	400.	650.	6200.	—
1903	2,278,755	5.75	9.50	29.00	55.00	155.	300.	480.	5850.	6950.
1903O	2,100,000	6.25	12.00	31.00	62.00	195.	390.	650.	7500.	—
1903S	1,920,772	6.50	12.50	36.00	67.00	215.	410.	650.	6200.	—
1904	2,992,670	5.50	9.00	26.00	50.00	140.	290.	480.	5850.	6950.
1904O	1,117,600	9.75	13.50	41.00	90.00	310.	535.	1100.	11,000.	—
1904S	553,038	12.00	18.00	54.00	150.	385.	630.	1050.	9000.	—
1905	662,727	10.25	14.00	45.00	100.	265.	440.	650.	6300.	6950.
1905O	505,000	10.50	16.00	51.00	120.	290.	475.	695.	6500.	—
1905S	2,494,000	5.75	9.75	35.00	62.00	205.	390.	650.	6100.	—
1906	2,638,675	5.25	8.75	25.00	50.00	140.	290.	480.	5850.	6950.
1906D	4,028,000	5.25	9.75	30.00	51.00	160.	310.	580.	5900.	—
1906O	2,446,000	5.50	10.00	31.00	54.00	170.	320.	600.	6100.	—
1906S	1,740,154	5.75	10.50	38.00	63.00	200.	365.	625.	6200.	—
1907	2,598,575	5.25	9.00	25.00	50.00	140.	290.	480.	5850.	6950.
1907D	3,856,000	5.50	9.75	27.00	52.00	150.	310.	580.	6300.	—
1907O	3,946,000	5.50	9.60	27.00	52.00	150.	310.	600.	6300.	—
1907S	1,250,000	5.75	11.00	34.00	65.00	205.	350.	650.	8600.	—
1908	1,354,545	5.75	10.00	30.00	56.00	155.	335.	500.	5850.	6950.
1908D	3,280,000	5.50	9.00	24.00	50.00	140.	290.	580.	6000.	—
1908O	5,360,000	5.50	9.00	24.00	50.00	145.	290.	580.	6000.	—
1908S	1,644,828	5.75	11.00	34.00	63.00	220.	370.	620.	6200.	—
1909	2,368,650	5.25	8.75	24.00	50.00	140.	290.	480.	5850.	6950.
1909O	925,400	8.50	11.00	36.00	80.00	285.	525.	750.	9000.	—
1909S	1,764,000	5.50	9.75	30.00	55.00	185.	365.	620.	7000.	—
1910	418,551	9.75	14.50	43.00	85.00	280.	480.	675.	6100.	6950.
1910S	1,948,000	5.50	9.50	28.00	56.00	190.	340.	610.	6000.	—
1911	1,406,543	5.50	9.50	27.00	53.00	150.	290.	480.	5850.	6950.
1911D	695,080	6.00	11.00	34.00	65.00	200.	350.	600.	5900.	—
1911S	1,272,000	5.50	9.75	32.00	62.00	175.	335.	610.	6000.	—
1912	1,550,700	5.25	9.00	25.00	53.00	145.	290.	480.	5850.	6950.
1912D	2,300,800	5.25	9.00	24.00	50.00	140.	290.	480.	5850.	6950.
1912S	1,370,000	5.50	9.75	29.00	56.00	185.	335.	610.	6000.	—
1913	188,627	18.00	24.00	60.00	125.	300.	525.	850.	8000.	6950.
1913D	534,000	5.75	11.00	33.00	66.00	190.	345.	500.	6000.	—
1913S	604,000	5.75	11.00	34.00	78.00	210.	410.	650.	8000.	—
1914	124,610	22.00	32.00	85.00	200.	425.	650.	800.	7500.	8000.
1914S	992,000	5.75	9.75	30.00	63.00	200.	390.	610.	7500.	—
1915	138,450	19.50	27.00	67.00	140.	325.	550.	850.	9500.	8000.
1915D	1,170,400	5.25	8.75	24.00	50.00	140.	290.	480.	5850.	—
1915S	1,604,000	5.25	8.75	24.00	50.00	145.	300.	590.	5850.	—

WALKING LIBERTY HALVES

Type: Half Dollars — Walking Liberty
Dates of issue: 1916-1947
Designer: Adolph A. Weinman
Size: 30.6 MM
Weight: 12.50 Grams
Composition: 90% Silver & 10% Copper
Fineness: .900
Actual Silver wt.: .3618 Oz. pure Silver

Mintmarks

OBV.

REV.

MINT MARKS:
D Denver
S San Francisco

Mint Mark On Obverse

Date	Mintage	G-4	VG-8	F-12	VF-20	XF-40	AU-50	MS-60	MS-65	Prf-65
1916	608,000	12.00	20.00	60.00	120.	210.	300.	420.	2800.	—
1916D	1,014,400	10.00	17.00	35.00	70.00	160.	200.	380.	2525.	—
1916S	508,000	24.00	45.00	120.	265.	385.	500.	800.	4600.	—
1917D	765,400	9.00	16.00	35.00	90.00	175.	250.	500.	4425.	—
1917S	952,000	11.00	20.00	45.00	145.	350.	500.	1000.	7250.	—

Mint Mark On Reverse

Date	Mintage	G-4	VG-8	F-12	VF-20	XF-40	AU-50	MS-60	MS-65	Prf-65
1917	12,292,000	5.00	8.00	12.00	20.00	35.00	60.00	155.	1425.	—
1917D	1,940,000	6.00	12.50	25.00	50.00	140.	240.	550.	5050.	—
1917S	5,554,000	5.00	9.50	16.00	23.00	48.00	90.00	250.	5000.	—
1918	6,634,000	5.00	8.00	19.00	45.00	125.	230.	350.	3850.	—
1918D	3,853,040	6.00	12.00	20.00	55.00	135.	265.	700.	6650.	—
1918S	10,282,000	5.00	10.00	16.00	30.00	50.00	100.	275.	4700.	—
1919	962,000	12.00	19.00	35.00	125.	350.	550.	1075.	5800.	—
1919D	1,165,000	11.00	16.00	35.00	140.	410.	800.	2000.	13,800.	—
1919S	1,552,000	9.50	13.00	25.00	95.00	395.	725.	1850.	9775.	—
1920	6,372,000	5.00	8.00	13.00	25.00	60.00	110.	245.	3500.	—
1920D	1,551,000	8.50	12.50	25.00	125.	275.	485.	1000.	6200.	—
1920S	4,624,000	6.00	10.00	17.00	45.00	135.	335.	880.	5050.	—
1921	246,000	38.00	60.00	190.	495.	1050.	1400.	2100.	5750.	—
1921D	208,000	68.00	90.00	215.	475.	1050.	1550.	2250.	7250.	—
1921S	548,000	13.00	20.00	45.00	300.	1050.	2650.	6300.	22,500.	—
1923S	2,178,000	7.75	11.00	19.00	50.00	160.	350.	880.	6650.	—
1927S	2,392,000	7.00	8.50	11.00	28.00	90.00	235.	725.	5175.	—
1928S	1,940,000	7.50	9.00	12.50	35.00	115.	250.	800.	5300.	—
1929D	1,001,200	8.00	10.00	13.00	25.00	75.00	150.	365.	2350.	—
1929S	1,902,000	7.00	8.00	10.00	20.00	70.00	150.	350.	2475.	—
1933S	1,786,000	8.00	9.00	12.50	20.00	50.00	150.	330.	2475.	—
1934	6,964,000	4.50	6.25	7.50	9.50	15.00	40.00	85.00	840.	—
1934D	2,361,400	5.75	6.75	8.50	12.50	30.00	60.00	170.	1275.	—
1934S	3,652,000	5.75	6.50	7.50	10.00	23.00	60.00	325.	2000.	—
1935	9,162,000	4.50	6.00	7.00	8.50	13.00	23.00	65.00	500.	—
1935D	3,003,800	5.75	7.00	8.50	13.00	30.00	70.00	225.	2000.	—
1935S	3,854,000	5.50	6.50	7.50	10.00	25.00	60.00	215.	1575.	—
1936	12,617,901	4.50	6.00	7.00	8.50	12.50	25.00	60.00	465.	6100.
1936D	4,252,400	5.75	6.50	7.50	10.00	23.00	43.00	115.	780.	—
1936S	3,884,000	5.75	6.50	7.50	10.00	23.00	40.00	145.	1100.	—
1937	9,527,728	4.50	6.00	7.00	8.50	13.00	25.00	60.00	500.	2450.
1937D	1,676,000	6.00	7.50	9.00	15.00	32.00	75.00	225.	1000.	—
1937S	2,090,000	5.50	6.50	8.00	10.00	23.00	50.00	160.	1050.	—
1938	4,118,152	5.00	6.00	7.00	9.50	16.00	30.00	100.	850.	1850.
1938D	491,600	16.00	20.00	25.00	43.00	100.	225.	390.	1950.	—
1939	6,820,808	4.50	5.25	6.25	8.00	14.00	25.00	90.00	510.	1750.
1939D	4,267,800	4.50	5.25	6.25	8.50	16.00	25.00	82.00	525.	—
1939S	2,552,000	5.00	6.00	6.50	9.00	18.00	35.00	115.	750.	—
1940	9,167,279	3.75	4.75	5.75	6.75	11.00	14.00	50.00	410.	1500.
1940S	4,550,000	3.75	4.75	5.75	12.50	14.00	22.00	75.00	950.	—
1941	24,207,412	3.75	4.75	5.75	6.75	9.00	17.00	50.00	400.	1400.
1941D	11,248,400	3.75	4.75	5.75	6.75	11.00	17.00	63.00	450.	—
1941S	8,098,000	3.75	4.75	5.75	6.75	17.50	46.00	215.	2125.	—
1942	47,839,120	3.75	4.75	5.75	6.75	9.00	12.50	50.00	400.	1400.
1942D	10,973,800	3.75	4.75	5.75	6.75	11.50	17.00	69.00	450.	—

Date	Mintage	G-4	VG-8	F-12	VF-20	XF-40	AU-50	MS-60	MS-65	Prf-65
1942S	12,708,000	3.75	4.75	5.75	6.75	12.50	35.00	120.	700.	—
1943	53,190,000	3.75	4.75	5.75	6.75	9.00	12.50	50.00	400.	—
1943D	11,346,000	3.75	4.75	5.75	6.75	9.00	19.00	75.00	550.	—
1943S	13,450,000	3.75	4.75	5.75	6.75	10.00	35.00	115.	785.	—
1944	28,206,000	3.75	4.75	5.75	6.75	10.00	12.50	50.00	400.	—
1944D	9,769,000	3.75	4.75	5.75	6.75	9.00	16.00	63.00	450.	—
1944S	8,904,000	3.75	4.75	5.75	6.75	10.00	21.00	75.00	1400.	—
1945	31,502,000	3.75	4.75	5.75	6.75	10.00	12.50	50.00	400.	—
1945D	9,966,800	3.75	4.75	5.75	6.75	9.00	15.00	63.00	450.	—
1945S	10,156,000	3.75	4.75	5.75	6.75	10.00	19.00	75.00	525.	—
1946	12,118,000	3.75	4.75	5.75	6.75	10.00	12.50	50.00	465.	—
1946D	2,151,000	5.00	7.00	8.00	11.50	20.00	25.00	63.00	410.	—
1946S	3,724,000	3.75	4.75	5.75	6.75	10.00	21.00	75.00	450.	—
1947	4,094,000	3.75	4.75	5.75	6.75	7.50	26.00	82.00	465.	—
1947D	3,900,600	3.75	4.75	5.75	6.75	7.50	23.00	75.00	465.	—

FRANKLIN HALVES

Mintmark

Type: Half Dollars — Franklin
Dates of issue: 1948-1963
Designer: John R. Sinnock
Size: 30.6 MM
Weight: 12.50 Grams
Composition: 90% Silver & 10% Copper
Fineness: .900
Actual Silver wt.: .3618 Oz. pure Silver

MINT MARKS:
D Denver
S San Francisco

Date	Mintage	G-4	VG-8	F-12	VF-20	XF-40	AU-50	MS-60	MS-65	65FBL	Prf-65
1948	3,006,814	—	3.50	4.00	4.50	9.00	10.00	28.00	150.	150.	—
1948D	4,028,600	—	3.50	4.00	4.50	9.00	10.00	16.00	150.	150.	—
1949	5,614,000	—	3.50	4.00	6.00	11.00	15.00	63.00	235.	235.	—
1949D	4,120,600	—	3.50	4.00	6.00	12.00	19.00	53.00	265.	275.	—
1949S	3,744,000	4.25	4.50	4.75	9.00	25.00	50.00	155.	300.	575.	—
1950	7,793,509	—	—	4.00	4.50	9.00	12.00	53.00	140.	150.	800.
1950D	8,031,600	—	—	4.00	4.50	9.00	10.00	29.00	260.	260.	—
1951	16,859,602	—	—	4.00	4.50	9.00	10.00	17.00	125.	150.	425.
1951D	9,475,200	—	—	3.50	4.25	4.75	12.50	45.00	165.	250.	—
1951S	13,696,000	—	—	3.50	4.25	4.75	20.00	45.00	165.	450.	—
1952	21,274,073	—	—	3.50	4.25	4.75	10.00	14.25	125.	150.	290.
1952D	25,395,600	—	—	—	3.50	4.75	9.50	13.75	150.	150.	—
1952S	5,526,000	—	—	3.50	4.25	4.75	18.00	41.00	115.	500.	—
1953	2,796,920	3.75	4.00	4.25	5.00	6.00	14.00	29.00	150.	160.	215.
1953D	20,900,400	—	—	—	3.50	4.75	8.00	11.00	150.	150.	—
1953S	4,148,000	—	—	3.50	4.25	4.75	10.00	24.00	125.	875.	—
1954	13,421,503	—	—	—	3.50	4.75	6.00	8.75	125.	160.	125.
1954D	25,445,580	—	—	—	3.50	4.25	4.75	7.00	190.	190.	—
1954S	4,993,400	—	—	3.50	4.25	4.75	8.25	11.50	140.	165.	—
1955	2,876,381	5.50	6.00	7.50	8.00	8.50	9.00	11.00	125.	150.	100.
1956	4,701,384	—	—	3.50	4.25	4.75	8.00	10.50	115.	150.	72.00
1957	6,361,952	—	—	3.50	4.25	4.75	9.50	13.50	115.	140.	54.00
1957D	19,966,850	—	—	—	3.50	4.75	5.50	6.75	115.	150.	—
1958	4,917,652	—	—	3.50	4.25	4.75	7.50	10.50	125.	150.	72.00
1958D	23,962,412	—	—	—	3.00	3.50	4.50	6.00	125.	150.	—
1959	7,349,291	—	—	—	3.00	3.50	6.50	8.00	160.	160.	48.00
1959D	13,053,750	—	—	—	3.00	3.50	6.50	7.75	155.	155.	—
1960	7,715,602	—	—	—	3.00	3.50	4.00	6.00	160.	160.	42.00
1960D	18,215,812	—	—	—	3.00	3.50	4.00	5.00	165.	165.	—
1961	11,318,244	—	—	—	3.00	3.50	4.00	5.00	150.	150.	31.00
1961D	20,276,442	—	—	—	3.00	3.50	4.00	5.00	170.	170.	—
1962	12,932,019	—	—	—	3.00	3.50	4.00	5.00	150.	150.	31.00
1962D	35,473,281	—	—	—	3.00	3.50	4.00	5.00	150.	150.	—
1963	25,239,645	—	—	—	3.00	3.50	4.00	4.50	150.	150.	31.00
1963D	67,069,292	—	—	—	3.00	3.50	4.00	4.50	150.	150.	—

NOTE: All specimens listed as -65FBL are for Full Bell Lines.

KENNEDY HALVES

Date	Mintage	G-4	VG-8	F-12	VF-20	XF-40	AU-50	MS-60	MS-65	Prf-65
1964	277,254,766	—	—	—	—	2.50	3.25	3.75	7.50	16.00
1964D	156,205,446	—	—	—	—	2.50	3.25	3.75	7.50	—
1965	65,879,366	—	—	—	—	1.90	1.95	3.00	4.00	—
1966	108,984,932	—	—	—	—	1.50	1.60	3.00	4.00	—
1967	295,046,978	—	—	—	—	1.50	1.60	2.75	3.65	—
1968D	246,951,930	—	—	—	—	1.50	1.60	2.75	3.65	—
1968S	3,041,506	—	—	—	—	—	—	—	—	3.00
1969D	129,881,800	—	—	—	—	1.50	1.60	2.75	3.65	—
1969S	2,934,631	—	—	—	—	—	—	—	—	3.00
1970D	2,150,000	—	—	—	—	—	—	18.00	22.00	—
1970S	2,632,810	—	—	—	—	—	—	—	—	7.50
1971	155,640,000	—	—	—	—	—	—	1.00	1.50	—
1971D	302,097,424	—	—	—	—	—	—	1.00	1.50	—
1971S	3,244,183	—	—	—	—	—	—	—	—	1.60
1972	153,180,000	—	—	—	—	—	—	1.00	1.50	—
1972D	141,890,000	—	—	—	—	—	—	1.00	1.50	—
1972S	3,267,667	—	—	—	—	—	—	—	—	1.60
1973	64,964,000	—	—	—	—	—	—	—	1.00	—

Type: Half Dollars — Kennedy
Dates of issue: 1964 to Date
Designer: Gilroy Roberts, Frank Gasparro
Size: 30.6 MM
Weight: 1964 12.50 Grams, 1965-70 11.50 Grams, 1971- 11.34 Grams
Composition: Silver Clad Issues —
1965-1970 Clad layers of 80% Copper and 20% Silver, bonded to core of 79.1% Copper and 20.9% Silver, 1971- Clad layers of 75% Copper & 25% Nickel, bonded to pure Copper core, 1976 Silver Clad layers of 80% Copper and 20% Silver, bonded to core of 79.1% Copper and 20.9% Silver
Fineness: 1964 .900, 1965-70 .400
Actual Silver wt.: 1964 .3618 Oz. pure Silver, 1965-70 .1480 Oz. pure Silver

REV.
Mintmark 1964

OBV.
Mintmark 1968 to Date

MINT MARKS:
D Denver
S San Francisco

Date	Mintage	G-4	VG-8	F-12	VF-20	XF-40	MS-60	MS-65	Prf-65
1973D	83,171,400	—	—	—	—	—	—	1.00	—
1973S	Proof Only	—	—	—	—	—	—	—	3.00
1974	201,596,000	—	—	—	—	—	—	.80	—
1974D	79,066,300	—	—	—	—	—	—	.80	—
1974S	Proof Only	—	—	—	—	—	—	—	3.00
1976	234,308,000	—	—	—	—	—	—	1.00	—
1976D	287,565,248	—	—	—	—	—	—	1.00	—
1976S	—	—	—	—	—	—	—	—	3.00
1976S Silver	—	—	—	—	—	—	—	4.00	7.00
1977	43,598,000	—	—	—	—	—	—	1.50	—

Type: Half Dollars — Bicentennial — Dated 1776-1976
Dates of issue: 1975-1976
Designer: Gilroy Roberts and Seth Huntington
Size: 30.6 MM
Weight: Silver issues 11.50 Grams, Copper Nickel 11.34 Grams
Composition: Silver Issues — 40% Silver & 60% Copper, Copper Nickel — 75% Copper & 25% Nickel
Fineness: .400 — Silver Issues
Actual Silver wt.: .1480 Oz. pure Silver

MINT MARKS:
D Denver
P Philadelphia
S San Francisco

Date	Mintage	G-4	VG-8	F-12	VF-20	XF-40	MS-60	MS-65	Prf-65
1977D	31,449,106	—	—	—	—	—	—	1.50	—
1977S	Proof Only	—	—	—	—	—	—	—	3.00
1978	14,350,000	—	—	—	—	—	—	1.25	—
1978D	13,765,799	—	—	—	—	—	—	1.25	—
1978S	Proof Only	—	—	—	—	—	—	—	3.00
1979	68,312,000	—	—	—	—	—	—	.80	—
1979D	15,815,422	—	—	—	—	—	—	.80	—
1979S	Proof Only	—	—	—	—	—	—	—	2.00
1979S T-II Proof Only	—	—	—	—	—	—	—	—	14.00
1980P	44,134,000	—	—	—	—	—	—	.80	—
1980D	33,456,449	—	—	—	—	—	—	.80	—
1980S	Proof Only	—	—	—	—	—	—	—	1.20
1981P	29,544,000	—	—	—	—	—	—	.75	—
1981D	27,839,533	—	—	—	—	—	—	.75	—
1981S	Proof Only	—	—	—	—	—	—	—	1.40
1982P	10,819,000	—	—	—	—	—	—	.75	—
1982D	13,140,102	—	—	—	—	—	—	1.00	—
1982S	Proof Only	—	—	—	—	—	—	—	4.00
1983P	34,139,000	—	—	—	—	—	—	.75	—
1983D	32,472,244	—	—	—	—	—	—	1.00	—
1983S	Proof Only	—	—	—	—	—	—	—	5.50
1984P	26,029,000	—	—	—	—	—	—	.75	—
1984D	26,262,158	—	—	—	—	—	—	.75	—
1984S	Proof Only	—	—	—	—	—	—	—	8.50
1985P	18,706,962	—	—	—	—	—	—	.75	—
1985D	19,814,034	—	—	—	—	—	—	.75	—
1985S	Proof Only	—	—	—	—	—	—	—	11.00
1986P	13,107,633	—	—	—	—	—	—	.75	—
1986D	15,336,145	—	—	—	—	—	—	.75	—
1986S	Proof Only	—	—	—	—	—	—	—	5.50
1987P	—	—	—	—	—	—	—	4.50	—
1987D	—	—	—	—	—	—	—	4.50	—
1987S	Proof Only	—	—	—	—	—	—	—	6.50
1988P	—	—	—	—	—	—	—	1.00	—
1988D	—	—	—	—	—	—	—	1.00	—
1988S	Proof Only	—	—	—	—	—	—	—	6.50
1989P	—	—	—	—	—	—	—	1.00	—
1989D	—	—	—	—	—	—	—	1.00	—
1989S	Proof Only	—	—	—	—	—	—	—	6.50

SILVER DOLLARS

Flowing Hair Silver Dollars

Type: Silver Dollars — Flowing Hair
Dates of issue: 1794-1795
Designer: Robert Scot
Size: 39-40 MM
Weight: 26.96 Grams
Composition: 89.24% Silver & 10.76% Copper
Fineness: .8924
Actual Silver wt.: .7737 Oz. pure Silver

Date	Mintage	G-4	VG-8	F-12	VF-20	XF-40	MS-60
1794	1,758	8000.	11,000.	16,500.	25,000.	40,000.	—
1795 2 Leaves	203,033	750.	900.	1500.	2250.	3800.	40,000.
1795 3 Leaves	Inc. Ab.	750.	900.	1500.	2250.	3800.	40,000.

Draped Bust Silver Dollars
Small Eagle

Type: Silver Dollars — Draped Bust — Small Eagle Reverse
Dates of issue: 1795-1798
Designer: Robert Scot
Size: 39-40 MM
Weight: 26.96 Grams
Composition: 89.24% Silver & 10.76% Copper
Fineness: .8924
Actual Silver wt.: .7737 Oz. pure Silver

Date	Mintage	G-4	VG-8	F-12	VF-20	XF-40	MS-60
1795	Inc. Ab.	650.	800.	1075.	1650.	3000.	15,000.
1796 Small Date, Small Letters	72,920	575.	675.	900.	1900.	2750.	12,000.
1796 Small Date, Large Letters	Inc. Ab.	575.	675.	900.	1900.	2750.	12,000.
1796 Large Date, Small Letters	Inc. Ab.	575.	675.	900.	1900.	2750.	12,000.
1797 9 Stars Left, 7 Stars Right, Small Letters	7,776	1500.	1850.	2550.	4500.	7500.	22,000.
1797 9 Stars Left, 7 Stars Right, Large Letters	Inc. Ab.	575.	675.	900.	1900.	2750.	12,000.
1797 10 Stars Left, 6 Stars Right		575.	675.	900.	1900.	2750.	12,000.
1798 13 Stars	327,536	1000.	1500.	2000.	2900.	4250.	18,000.
1798 15 Stars	Inc. Ab.	1300.	1800.	2250.	3350.	5000.	18,000.

Heraldic Eagle

Date	Mintage	G-4	VG-8	F-12	VF-20	XF-40	MS-60
1798 Knob 9	Inc. Ab.	325.	400.	525.	800.	1400.	10,000.
1798 10 Arrows	Inc. Ab.	325.	400.	525.	800.	1400.	10,000.
1798 4 Berries	Inc. Ab.	325.	400.	525.	800.	1400.	10,000.
1798 5 Berries, 12 Arrows	Inc. Ab.	325.	400.	525.	800.	1400.	10,000.
1798 High 8	Inc. Ab.	325.	400.	525.	800.	1400.	10,000.
1798 13 Arrows	Inc. Ab.	325.	400.	525.	800.	1400.	10,000.
1799/98 13 Star Reverse	423,515	325.	400.	525.	800.	1400.	15,000.
1799/98 15 Star Reverse	Inc. Ab.	400.	500.	1000.	1250.	2200.	15,000.

Type: Silver Dollars — Heraldic Eagle Reverse
Dates of issue: 1798-1804
Designer: Robert Scot
Size: 39-40 MM
Weight: 26.96 Grams
Composition: 89.24% Silver & 10.76% Copper
Fineness: .8924
Actual Silver wt.: .7737 Oz. pure Silver

Date	Mintage	G-4	VG-8	F-12	VF-20	XF-40	MS-60
1799 Irregular Date, 13 Star Reverse	Inc. Ab.	325.	400.	525.	800.	1400.	10,000.
1799 Irregular Date, 15 Star Reverse	Inc. Ab.	325.	400.	525.	800.	1400.	10,000.
1799 Perfect Date, 7 and 6 Star Obverse, No Berries	Inc. Ab.	325.	400.	525.	800.	1400.	10,000.
1799 Perfect Date, 7 and 6 Star Obverse, Small Berries	Inc. Ab.	325.	400.	525.	800.	1400.	10,000.
1799 Perfect Date, 7 and 6 Star Obverse, Medium Large Berries	Inc. Ab.	325.	400.	525.	800.	1400.	10,000.
1799 Perfect Date, 7 and 6 Star Obverse, Extra Large Berries	Inc. Ab.	325.	400.	525.	800.	1400.	10,000.
1799 8 Stars Left, 5 Stars Right On Obverse	Inc. Ab.	425.	525.	900.	1200.	2150.	10,000.
1800 Liberty "R" Double Cut	220,920	325.	400.	525.	800.	1400.	10,000.
1800 States First "T" Double Cut	Inc. Ab.	325.	400.	525.	800.	1400.	10,000.
1800 Both Letters Double Cut	Inc. Ab.	325.	400.	525.	800.	1400.	10,000.
1800 United, "T" Double Cut	Inc. Ab.	325.	400.	525.	800.	1400.	10,000.
1800 Very Wide Date, Low 8	Inc. Ab.	325.	400.	525.	800.	1400.	10,000.
1800 Sm. Berries	Inc. Ab.	325.	400.	525.	800.	1400.	10,000.
1800 Dot Date	Inc. Ab.	325.	400.	525.	800.	1400.	10,000.
1800 12 Arrows	Inc. Ab.	325.	400.	525.	800.	1400.	10,000.
1800 10 Arrows	Inc. Ab.	325.	400.	525.	800.	1400.	10,000.
1800 "Americai"	Inc. Ab.	325.	400.	525.	800.	1400.	10,000.
1801	54,454	375.	450.	650.	900.	1850.	10,000.
1801	(Unrecorded)	Proof Restrike - Rare					
1802/1 Close	Inc. Ab.	350.	425.	600.	850.	1600.	10,000.
1802/1 Wide	Inc. Ab.	350.	425.	600.	850.	1600.	10,000.
1802 Close, Perfect Date	Inc. Ab.	375.	450.	650.	875.	1650.	10,000.
1802 Wide, Perfect Date	Inc. Ab.	375.	450.	650.	875.	1650.	10,000.
1802	(Unrecorded)	Proof Restrike - Rare					
1803 Lg. 3	85,634	350.	425.	600.	850.	1575.	10,000.
1803 Sm. 3	Inc. Ab.	375.	450.	650.	950.	1700.	10,000.
1803	(Unrecorded)	Proof Restrike - Rare					
1804	15 Known	(3 Varieties)					

Buss Sale Jan. 1985, MS-60 $308,000.

GOBRECHT PATTERNS

Stars Around Obverse Border (1838-1839) Stars in Reverse Field (1836)

Type: Dollars — Gobrecht
Dates of issue: 1836-1839
Designer: Christian Gobrecht
Size: 38.1 M.M.
Weight: 26.73 Grams
Composition: 90% Silver + 10% Copper
Fineness: .900
Actual Silver St.: .7736 Oz.
Coin struck in several metals

Date	Mintage	VF-20	XF-40	AU-50	Prf-60
1836 C. GOBRECHT F. below base. Rev. Eagle flying left amid stars. Plain edge.	—	—	—	—	—
1836 Obv: Same as above. Rev: Eagle flying in plain field. Plain edge.	—	—	—	—	—
1836 C. GOBRECHT F. on base. Rev: Eagle flying left amid stars. Plain edge.	—	2500.	3750.	4750.	7500.
1836 Same as above, reeded edge.	—	—	—	—	—
1836 Obv: Same as above. Rev: Eagle flying in plain field. Plain edge.	—	—	—	—	10,000.
1838 Similar obv., designer's name omitted, stars added around border. Rev: Eagle flying left in plain field. Reeded edge.	—	3000.	4500.	—	7500.
1838 Same as above. Plain edge. Restrikes only.	3 known				
1838 Obv: Same as above. Rev: Eagle flying left amid stars. Plain edge. Restrikes only.	2 known				
1839 Obv: Same as above. Rev: Eagle in plain field. Reeded edge. Also known with plain edge and plain edge with eagle amid stars.	—	—	3750.	—	15,000.

LIBERTY SEATED DOLLARS
No Motto

Type: Silver Dollars — Liberty Seated
Dates of issue: 1840-1873
Designer: Christian Gobrecht
Size: 38.1 MM
Weight: 26.73 Grams
Composition: 90% Silver & 10% Copper
Fineness: .900
Actual Silver wt.: .7736 Oz. pure Silver

MINT MARKS:
CC Carson City
S San Francisco

Date	Mintage	VG-8	F-12	VF-20	XF-40	AU-50	MS-60	MS-65	Prf-65
1840	61,005	225.	270.	350.	550.	625.	950.	—	—
1841	173,000	190.	250.	300.	425.	500.	950.	30,000.	—
1842	184,618	175.	250.	300.	400.	500.	950.	30,000.	—
1843	165,100	175.	250.	300.	400.	500.	950.	30,000.	—
1844	20,000	250.	300.	400.	575.	800.	1800.	—	—
1845	24,500	240.	285.	385.	550.	775.	1800.	—	—
1846	110,600	175.	250.	300.	400.	600.	1150.	30,000.	—
1846O	59,000	190.	270.	425.	600.	950.	4000.	—	—
1847	140,750	175.	250.	300.	400.	600.	1750.	30,000.	—
1848	15,000	350.	475.	620.	800.	1150.	2050.	30,000.	—
1849	62,600	180.	300.	400.	500.	750.	1750.	30,000.	—
1850	7,500	450.	600.	800.	1100.	1750.	3500.	—	—
1850O	40,000	280.	450.	625.	1000.	2000.	3500.	—	—
1851	1,300	—	7000.	8500.	11,000.	15,000.	—	—	—
1852	1,100	—	6000.	7500.	10,500.	14,000.	—	—	—
1853	46,110	210.	275.	365.	500.	625.	950.	—	—
1854	33,140	730.	1000.	1400.	2000.	3000.	4500.	—	—
1855	26,000	650.	900.	1250.	1700.	2800.	4000.	—	24,000.
1856	63,500	240.	300.	425.	600.	775.	1800.	—	24,000.
1857	94,000	220.	280.	400.	575.	750.	1700.	—	24,000.
1858	Est. 200	—	—	Proof	—	—	—	—	24,000.
				4500.	5700.	6900.			
1859	256,500	300.	400.	525.	700.	1000.	1900.	30,000.	24,000.
1859O	360,000	100.	165.	200.	315.	500.	950.	30,000.	—
1859S	20,000	300.	385.	585.	900.	1250.	—	—	—
1860	218,930	320.	450.	600.	800.	1150.	2000.	30,000.	24,000.
1860O	515,000	100.	165.	200.	315.	500.	1150.	30,000.	—
1861	78,500	375.	500.	645.	825.	1150.	2000.	30,000.	24,000.
1862	12,090	385.	515.	670.	875.	1250.	2200.	30,000.	24,000.
1863	27,660	230.	300.	380.	500.	700.	1800.	30,000.	24,000.
1864	31,170	215.	275.	360.	475.	650.	1600.	30,000.	24,000.
1865	47,000	210.	250.	340.	475.	600.	1500.	30,000.	24,000.
1866	Only 2 Known Without Motto								

Motto Added On Reverse

Mintmark

Date	Mintage	VG-8	F-12	VF-20	XF-40	AU-50	MS-60	MS-65	Prf-65
1866	49,625	210.	250.	340.	475.	575.	1500.	25,000.	22,000.
1867	47,525	230.	270.	350.	500.	600.	1500.	25,000.	22,000.
1868	162,700	175.	225.	300.	400.	525.	1450.	25,000.	22,000.
1869	424,300	150.	200.	280.	390.	550.	950.	25,000.	22,000.
1870	416,000	135.	190.	250.	350.	525.	950.	25,000.	22,000.
1870CC	12,462	275.	425.	550.	750.	1250.	2500.	—	—
1870S	Unrecorded			Aug. 1978 ANA Sale VF 39,000.				—	—
1871	1,074,760	95.00	160.	200.	315.	500.	1400.	25,000.	22,000.
1871CC	1,376	1950.	2600.	3200.	4800.	6000.	7500.	—	—
1872	1,106,450	95.00	160.	200.	315.	500.	950.	25,000.	22,000.
1872CC	3,150	1150.	1500.	2000.	2750.	3500.	4500.	—	—
1872S	9,000	200.	400.	575.	850.	1750.	3250.	—	—
1873	293,600	170.	225.	300.	450.	575.	1500.	25,000.	22,000.
1873CC	2,300	2500.	3400.	4500.	5800.	6750.	9500.	25,000.	—
1873S	700			Unknown				—	—

TRADE DOLLARS

Type: Silver Dollars — Trade
Dates of issue: 1873-1883
Designer: William Barber
Size: 38.1 MM
Weight: 27.22 Grams
Composition: 90% Silver & 10% Copper
Fineness: .900
Actual Silver wt.: .7878 Oz. pure Silver

MINT MARKS:
CC Carson City
S San Francisco

Date	Mintage	VG-8	F-12	VF-20	XF-40	AU-50	MS-60	MS-65	Prf-65
1873	397,500	95.00	115.	165.	250.	325.	1000.	14,000.	12,500.
1873CC	124,500	175.	200.	265.	400.	750.	1500.	14,000.	—
1873S	703,000	120.	130.	165.	250.	350.	1200.	14,000.	—
1874	987,800	90.00	110.	130.	225.	400.	630.	14,000.	12,500.
1874CC	1,373,200	90.00	105.	125.	225.	325.	1000.	14,000.	—
1874S	2,549,000	80.00	95.00	115.	200.	285.	525.	14,000.	—
1875	218,900	250.	350.	600.	900.	1250.	1850.	14,000.	12,500.
1875CC	1,573,700	85.00	100.	135.	250.	475.	900.	14,000.	—
1875S	4,487,000	65.00	80.00	95.00	165.	285.	525.	14,000.	—
1875S/CC	Inc.Ab.	275.	375.	500.	750.	900.	1500.	—	—
1876	456,150	80.00	95.00	115.	200.	285.	525.	14,000.	12,500.
1876CC	509,000	95.00	115.	165.	250.	375.	900.	14,000.	—
1876S	5,227,000	70.00	82.00	95.00	165.	250.	500.	14,000.	—
1877	3,039,710	55.00	80.00	90.00	165.	250.	500.	14,000.	12,500.
1877CC	534,000	140.	170.	225.	375.	500.	1200.	14,000.	—
1877S	9,519,000	63.00	76.00	85.00	140.	250.	500.	14,000.	—
1878	900			Proof Only			—	—	20,000.
1878CC	97,000	300.	375.	650.	1100.	1750.	2500.	—	—
1878S	4,162,000	63.00	76.00	85.00	140.	250.	500.	14,000.	—
1879	1,541			Proof Only			—	—	20,000.
1880	1,987			Proof Only	1100.	1300.	1500.	—	15,000.
1881	960			Proof Only	1050.	1250.	1450.	—	18,000.
1882	1,097			Proof Only	1150.	1400.	1650.	—	18,000.
1883	979			Proof Only	1200.	1450.	1750.	—	18,000.
1884	10		Proof Only, Hanks & Associates, May 1985					50,000.	
1885	5		Proof Only, Stacks, Jan. 1984					110,000.	

MORGAN DOLLARS

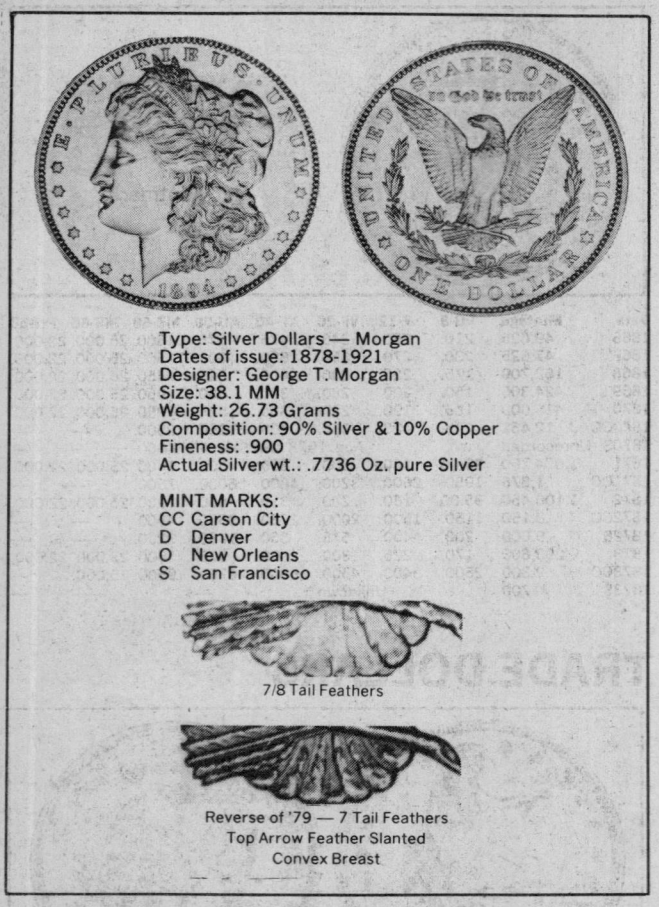

Type: Silver Dollars — Morgan
Dates of issue: 1878-1921
Designer: George T. Morgan
Size: 38.1 MM
Weight: 26.73 Grams
Composition: 90% Silver & 10% Copper
Fineness: .900
Actual Silver wt.: .7736 Oz. pure Silver

MINT MARKS:
CC Carson City
D   Denver
O   New Orleans
S   San Francisco

7/8 Tail Feathers

*Reverse of '79 — 7 Tail Feathers
Top Arrow Feather Slanted
Convex Breast*

Date	Mintage	F-12	VF-20	XF-40	AU-50	MS-60	MS-63	MS-65	Prf-65
1878 8 Tail Feathers									
	750,000	17.00	19.00	22.00	35.00	57.00	125.	3300.	10,000.
1878 7 Tail Feathers, Rev. of '78									
	Inc. Ab.	14.00	17.00	19.00	25.00	38.00	110.	3100.	10,000.
1878 7 Tail Feathers, Rev. of '79									
	Inc. Ab.	10.00	11.50	13.00	25.00	50.00	190.	4650.	—
1878 7 Over 8 Tail Feathers									
	9,759,550	22.00	25.00	28.00	45.00	63.00	190.	4900.	
1878CC	2,212,000	28.00	35.00	45.00	50.00	100.	160.	4050.	
1878S	9,744,000	11.50	13.00	17.00	20.00	36.00	65.00	850.	
1879	14,807,100	10.00	11.50	13.00	20.00	32.00	95.00	3850.	9000.
1879CC	756,000	39.00	70.00	250.	390.	1250.	3650.	26,000.	
1879O	2,887,000	10.00	11.50	13.00	24.00	50.00	195.	7200.	
1879S Rev. of '78									
	9,110,000	19.00	21.00	25.00	36.00	88.00	595.	19,000.	
1879S Rev. of '79									
	9,110,000	10.00	11.50	13.00	25.00	29.00	64.00	410.	
1880	12,601,335	10.00	11.50	13.00	21.00	31.00	75.00	4400.	9000.
1880CC Rev. of '78									
	591,000	39.00	53.00	88.00	110.	160.	245.	3650.	—
1880CC Rev. of '79									
	591,000	39.00	53.00	88.00	125.	155.	225.	2500.	—
1880O	5,305,000	10.00	11.50	13.00	28.00	45.00	380.	50,500.	—
1880S	8,900,000	10.00	11.50	13.00	25.00	28.00	64.00	410.	—
1881	9,163,975	10.00	11.50	13.00	20.00	31.00	75.00	3550.	9000.
1881CC	296,000	71.00	91.00	110.	145.	205.	225.	1250.	—
1881O	5,708,000	10.00	11.50	13.00	20.00	27.00	90.00	4700.	—
1881S	12,760,000	10.00	11.50	13.00	25.00	28.00	64.00	410.	—
1882	11,101,100	10.00	11.50	13.00	20.00	31.00	75.00	1750.	9000.
1882CC	1,133,000	34.00	35.00	42.00	66.00	85.00	125.	1050.	—
1882O	6,090,000	10.00	11.50	13.00	17.00	27.00	64.00	4400.	—
1882S	9,250,000	10.00	11.50	13.00	25.00	29.00	64.00	410.	—
1883	12,291,039	10.00	11.50	13.00	18.00	31.00	60.00	680.	9000.
1883CC	1,204,000	29.00	41.00	49.00	66.00	85.00	125.	920.	—
1883O	8,725,000	10.00	11.50	16.00	17.00	21.00	60.00	530.	—
1883S	6,250,000	19.00	20.00	25.00	95.00	350.	1650.	38,000.	—
1884	14,070,875	10.00	11.50	13.00	18.00	29.00	65.00	1050.	9000.
1884CC	1,136,000	70.00	75.00	80.00	85.00	90.00	120.	850.	—
1884O	9,730,000	10.00	11.50	13.00	17.00	21.00	60.00	410.	—
1884S	3,200,000	15.00	20.00	35.00	190.	3150.	15,000.	75,500.	—
1885	17,787,767	10.00	11.50	13.00	18.00	22.00	60.00	410.	9000.
1885CC	228,000	225.	240.	245.	250.	265.	300.	1800.	—
1885O	9,185,000	10.00	11.50	13.00	17.00	22.00	60.00	410.	—
1885S	1,497,000	15.00	17.00	21.00	50.00	115.	175.	4550.	—
1886	19,963,886	10.00	11.50	13.00	17.00	21.00	63.00	410.	9000.
1886O	10,710,000	11.00	15.00	18.00	48.00	350.	2200.	55,500.	—
1886S	750,000	25.00	30.00	35.00	38.00	120.	265.	4900.	—

Date	Mintage	F-12	VF-20	XF-40	AU-50	MS-60	MS-63	MS-65	Prf-65
1887	20,290,710	10.00	11.50	13.00	19.00	21.00	60.00	410.	9000.
1887O	11,550,000	10.00	11.50	13.00	27.00	45.00	155.	11,000.	—
1887S	1,771,000	14.00	15.00	19.00	31.00	80.00	215.	7450.	—
1888	19,183,833	10.00	11.50	13.00	19.00	21.00	63.00	930.	9000.
1888O	12,150,000	10.00	11.50	13.00	18.00	27.00	70.00	2200.	—
1888S	657,000	23.00	27.00	28.00	43.00	125.	265.	6850.	—
1889	21,726,811	10.00	11.50	13.00	18.00	21.00	60.00	2250.	9000.
1889CC	350,000	195.	315.	675.	2150.	6300.	16,500.	113,500.	—
1889O	11,875,000	12.50	14.00	18.00	28.00	76.00	265.	6050.	—
1889S	700,000	18.00	24.00	35.00	45.00	120.	250.	4300.	—
1890	16,802,590	10.00	11.50	13.00	18.00	27.00	85.00	5600.	9000.
1890CC	2,309,041	29.00	39.00	50.00	70.00	215.	415.	11,500.	—
1890CC Tail Bar Variety									
	Inc. Ab.	34.00	42.00	50.00	100.	215.	475.	7300.	—
1890O	10,701,000	10.00	11.50	13.00	25.00	45.00	120.	6150.	—
1890S	8,230,373	14.00	15.00	18.00	24.00	46.00	120.	2100.	—
1891	8,694,206	10.00	15.00	18.00	34.00	50.00	155.	10,000.	9000.
1891CC	1,618,000	29.00	39.00	50.00	70.00	195.	405.	6600.	—
1891O	7,954,529	14.00	15.00	18.00	32.00	57.00	225.	9500.	—
1891S	5,296,000	14.00	15.00	18.00	24.00	57.00	110.	3150.	—
1892	1,037,245	15.00	18.00	23.00	46.00	100.	250.	6050.	9000.
1892CC	1,352,000	34.00	50.00	84.00	170.	350.	950.	7700.	—
1892O	2,744,000	14.00	15.00	18.00	46.00	120.	250.	8000.	—
1892S	1,200,000	23.00	47.00	160.	700.	6500.	16,500.	88,000.	—
1893	378,792	41.00	50.00	85.00	140.	355.	460.	9500.	9000.
1893CC	677,000	55.00	125.	295.	495.	920.	3950.	40,500.	—
1893O	300,000	42.00	65.00	205.	315.	1100.	4600.	50,500.	—
1893S	100,000	950.	1450.	3300.	9000.	17,000.	39,000.	26,000.	—
1894	110,972	225.	260.	350.	540.	900.	1900.	20,000.	9000.
1894O	1,723,000	15.00	17.00	28.00	70.00	440.	1550.	36,000.	—
1894S	1,260,000	26.00	55.00	90.00	160.	350.	640.	7350.	—
1895	12,880	3000.	5000.	6500.	12,000.	—	—	—	36,500.
1895O	450,000	45.00	85.00	190.	380.	2000.	10,000.	56,500.	—
1895S	400,000	74.00	155.	440.	570.	900.	1750.	21,500.	—
1896	9,967,762	10.00	11.50	13.00	17.00	21.00	59.00	850.	9000.
1896O	4,900,000	14.00	15.00	19.00	83.00	730.	5300.	64,500.	—
1896S	5,000,000	20.00	39.00	90.00	225.	570.	1850.	21,000.	—
1897	2,822,731	10.00	11.50	13.00	17.00	21.00	59.00	1400.	9000.
1897O	4,004,000	14.00	15.00	19.00	45.00	415.	4400.	25,000.	—
1897S	5,825,000	15.00	16.00	18.00	22.00	45.00	105.	1300.	—
1898	5,884,735	10.00	11.50	13.00	17.00	21.00	59.00	1150.	9000.
1898O	4,440,000	16.00	16.50	17.00	21.00	24.00	59.00	460.	—
1898S	4,102,000	14.00	15.00	21.00	50.00	160.	310.	3350.	—
1899	330,846	25.00	31.00	45.00	66.00	90.00	140.	2450.	9000.
1899O	12,290,000	14.00	15.00	16.00	22.00	24.00	59.00	480.	—
1899S	2,562,000	15.00	16.00	24.00	60.00	100.	295.	4300.	—
1900	8,880,938	10.00	11.50	13.00	17.00	21.00	59.00	950.	9000.
1900O	12,590,000	10.00	12.00	14.00	18.00	25.00	59.00	530.	—
1900O/CC *Inc. Ab.		21.00	23.00	26.00	50.00	115.	280.	4150.	—
1900S	3,540,000	14.00	15.00	18.00	45.00	90.00	230.	3700.	—
1901	6,962,813	28.00	37.00	54.00	160.	1050.	8800.	53,500.	9000.
1901O	13,320,000	15.00	16.00	17.00	22.00	27.00	59.00	1000.	—
1901S	2,284,000	20.00	24.00	35.00	75.00	250.	530.	5350.	—
1902	7,994,777	10.00	11.50	13.00	28.00	38.00	85.00	1600.	9000.
1902O	8,636,000	14.00	15.00	16.00	21.00	24.00	59.00	980.	—
1902S	1,530,000	25.00	41.00	70.00	95.00	125.	220.	5400.	—
1903	4,652,755	12.00	13.00	14.00	21.00	32.00	65.00	1000.	9000.
1903O	4,450,000	160.	180.	195.	205.	215.	240.	1400.	—
1903S	1,241,000	28.00	47.00	165.	670.	1800.	2800.	6750.	—
1904	2,788,650	12.00	13.00	15.00	31.00	76.00	225.	7050.	9000.
1904O	3,720,000	15.00	16.00	17.00	21.00	24.00	59.00	550.	—
1904S	2,304,000	30.00	60.00	110.	440.	950.	1650.	11,000.	—
1921	44,690,000	8.50	9.50	10.50	11.00	17.00	31.00	600.	—
1921D	20,345,000	8.50	9.50	10.50	13.00	28.00	45.00	1650.	—
1921S	21,695,000	8.50	9.50	10.50	13.00	28.00	50.00	3350.	—

PEACE DOLLARS

Type: Silver Dollars — Peace
Dates of issue: 1921-1935
Designer: Anthony DeFrancisci
Size: 38.1 MM
Weight: 26.73 Grams
Composition: 90% Silver & 10% Copper
Fineness: .900
Actual Silver wt.: .7736 Oz. pure Silver

MINT MARKS:
D Denver
S San Francisco

Mintmark

Date	Mintage	F-12	VF-20	XF-40	AU-50	MS-60	MS-63	MS-65
1921	1,006,473	27.00	32.00	41.00	57.00	160.	380.	3850.
1922	51,737,000	8.50	9.00	9.50	11.00	15.00	45.00	750.
1922D	15,063,000	8.50	10.00	10.50	11.00	34.00	110.	2100.
1922S	17,475,000	8.50	10.00	10.50	11.00	34.00	125.	5050.
1923	30,800,000	8.50	9.00	9.50	11.00	15.00	45.00	650.
1923D	6,811,000	13.00	14.00	15.00	18.00	34.00	110.	2500.
1923S	19,020,000	13.00	14.00	15.00	12.00	29.00	140.	9700.
1924	11,811,000	13.00	14.00	15.00	17.50	21.00	45.00	750.
1924S	1,728,000	14.00	18.00	26.00	44.00	100.	560.	12,000.
1925	10,198,000	10.00	14.00	15.00	17.50	21.00	45.00	650.
1925S	1,610,000	15.50	18.00	20.00	31.50	90.00	355.	8400.
1926	1,939,000	9.50	14.00	15.00	22.00	32.00	105.	1750.
1926D	2,348,700	9.50	16.00	19.00	29.00	50.00	155.	2000.
1926S	6,980,000	9.50	14.00	15.00	19.00	45.00	125.	2650.
1927	848,000	19.00	22.00	24.00	30.00	65.00	160.	7350.
1927D	1,268,900	17.00	18.00	25.00	69.00	160.	1100	10,300.
1927S	866,000	21.00	23.00	30.00	57.00	120.	475.	13,000.
1928	360,649	100.	115.	125.	145.	215.	520.	7850.
1928S	1,632,000	15.50	18.00	21.00	45.00	100.	425.	14,500.
1934	954,057	18.00	21.00	23.00	30.00	85.00	195.	3500.
1934D	1,569,500	15.00	16.00	24.00	35.00	100.	285.	3800.
1934S	1,011,000	25.00	41.00	140.	540.	1250.	3650.	10,000.
1935	1,576,000	13.00	14.00	16.00	22.00	63.00	155.	2400.
1935S	1,964,000	15.00	17.00	20.00	50.00	105.	330.	3100.

EISENHOWER DOLLARS

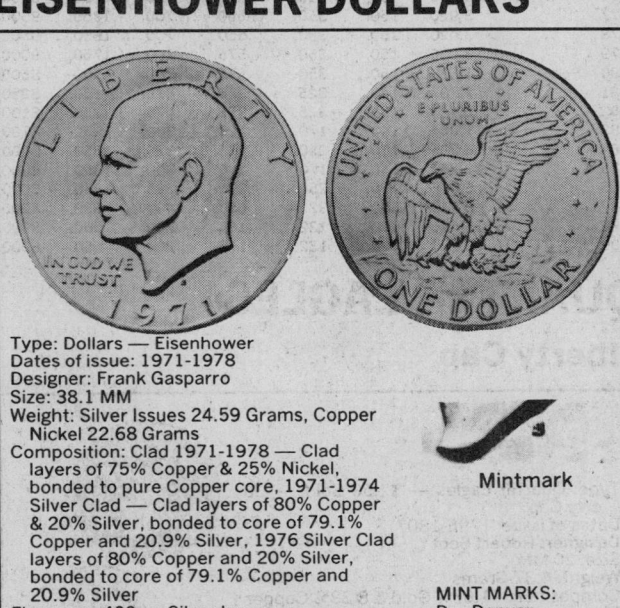

Type: Dollars — Eisenhower
Dates of issue: 1971-1978
Designer: Frank Gasparro
Size: 38.1 MM
Weight: Silver Issues 24.59 Grams, Copper Nickel 22.68 Grams
Composition: Clad 1971-1978 — Clad layers of 75% Copper & 25% Nickel, bonded to pure Copper core, 1971-1974 Silver Clad — Clad layers of 80% Copper & 20% Silver, bonded to core of 79.1% Copper and 20.9% Silver, 1976 Silver Clad layers of 80% Copper and 20% Silver, bonded to core of 79.1% Copper and 20.9% Silver
Fineness: .400 — Silver Issues
Actual Silver wt.: .3163 Oz. pure Silver

Mintmark

MINT MARKS:
D   Denver
S   San Francisco

Bicentennial

Type: Dollars — Bicentennial — Dated 1776-1976
Dates of issue: 1975-1976
Designer: Frank Gasparro and Dennis R. Williams
Size: 38.1 MM
Weight: Silver Issues 24.59 Grams, Copper Nickel 22.68 Grams
Composition: Silver Issues — 40% Silver & 60% Copper, Copper Nickel — 75% Copper & 25% Nickel
Fineness: .400 — Silver Issues
Actual Silver wt.: .3163 Oz. pure Silver

MINT MARKS:
D   Denver
S   San Francisco

Variety 1

Variety 2

Date	Mintage	MS-65	Date	Mintage	MS-65
1971	47,799,000	2.00	1974S Silver Prf	1,306,579	11.00
1971D	68,587,424	2.00	1974S Clad Prf	2,617,350	4.50
1971S Silver Unc	6,868,530	4.85	1976 Type I	117,337,000	1.90
1971S Silver Prf	4,265,234	7.70	1976 Type II	Inc. Ab.	1.90
1972	75,890,000	2.00	1976D Type I	103,228,274	1.90
1972D	92,548,511	1.80	1976D Type II	Inc. Ab.	1.90
1972S Silver Unc	2,193,056	6.00	1976S Cld Prf T-I	2,909,369	7.00
1972S Silver Prf	1,811,631	9.00	1976S Cld Prf T-II	4,149,730	4.40
1973	2,000,056	4.15	1976S Silver Unc	—	6.50
1973D	2,000,000	4.15	1976S Silver Prf	—	9.50
1973S Silver Unc	1,833,140	9.10	1977	12,596,000	1.45
1973S Silver Prf	1,005,617	39.00	1977D	32,983,000	1.70
1973S Clad Prf	2,769,624	5.00	1977S Clad Prf	3,251,152	4.15
1974	27,366,000	1.55	1978	25,702,000	1.70
1974D	35,466,000	1.55	1978D	33,012,890	1.70
1974S Silver Unc	1,720,000	6.40	1978S Clad Prf	3,127,788	4.15

ANTHONY DOLLARS

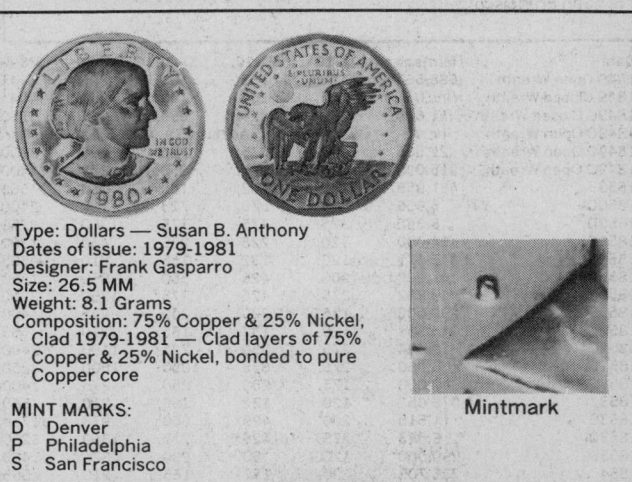

Type: Dollars — Susan B. Anthony
Dates of issue: 1979-1981
Designer: Frank Gasparro
Size: 26.5 MM
Weight: 8.1 Grams
Composition: 75% Copper & 25% Nickel, Clad 1979-1981 — Clad layers of 75% Copper & 25% Nickel, bonded to pure Copper core

MINT MARKS:
D   Denver
P   Philadelphia
S   San Francisco

Mintmark

Date	Mintage	MS-65	Date	Mintage	MS-65
1979P	360,222,000	1.45	1980S	20,422,000	1.40
1979D	288,015,744	1.45	1980S Prf	3,547,030	4.80
1979S	109,576,000	1.45	1981P	3,000,000	3.80
1979S Prf T-I	3,677,175	7.60	1981D	3,250,000	3.80
1979S Prf T-II	—	85.00	1981S	3,492,000	3.80
1980P	27,610,000	1.40	1981S Prf T-I	4,063,083	4.80
1980D	41,628,708	1.40	1981S Prf T-II	—	76.00

BICENTENNIAL COINAGE

The nation's quarter, half and dollar coinage was redesigned in 1975 to provide circulation issue commemoratives of the bicentennial of the American Revolution. While the obverses of these coins retained the familiar portraits of Washington, Kennedy and Eisenhower, with the addition of commemoratives — 1776 • 1976 — dual dating, the reverses were completely redesigned to feature themes reminiscent of the birth of the country.

To accomplish this change, assuring that sufficient quantities could be produced to attain active circulation and negate the possibility that a temporary shortage of any of the three denominations might develop, Congress authorized Mint officials to continue production of 1974 dated quarters, halves and dollars into mid-1975. The availability of this authority led to a decision not to produce 1975 dated counterparts of the regular issue designs.

The first bicentennial coin released to circulation was Seth G. Huntington's half dollar featuring a rendering of Philadelphia's Independence Hall. The release of 100 million of these coins on July 7, 1975, was followed on August 18 by the unveiling of Jack L. Ahr's "colonial drummer" quarter. The last coin released was Dennis R. Williams' time-capsule Liberty Bell and moon dollar, which was belatedly placed in the hands of the public on October 13.

All three coins were produced for circulation issue in the standard cupro-nickel clad copper composition, in which version they were also produced for inclusion in mint (uncirculated coin) and proof sets in combination with 1975 dated cents, nickels and dimes. Mint and proof sets were also produced containing 1976 dated coins of the lower denominations. They were also made available in .400 fine silver versions, in sets only, each of which contained one specimen of each of the three coins in uncirculated or proof quality.

All versions of the dollar coin exist in two distinct varieties. Both the obverse and reverse dies were revised to facilitate production.

Values for Bicentennial coins will be found in the listings of their respective denomination.

GOLD DOLLARS

Liberty Head

Type: Gold Dollars — Liberty Head
Dates of issue: 1849-1854
Designer: James B. Longacre
Size: 13 MM
Weight: 1.672 Grams
Composition: 90% Gold & 10% Copper
Fineness: .900
Actual Gold wt.: .0484 Oz. pure Gold

MINT MARKS
C Charlotte
D Dahlonega
O New Orleans
S San Francisco

Mintmark

Date	Mintage	F-12	VF-20	XF-40	AU-50	MS-60
1849 Open Wreath	688,567	135.	155.	190.	200.	645.
1849 Closed Wreath	Inc. Ab.	135.	155.	190.	200.	645.
1849C Closed Wreath	11,634	275.	425.	650.	975.	1750.
1849C Open Wreath	Inc. Ab.	Auction '79, XF 90,000.				Rare
1849D Open Wreath	21,588	350.	375.	725.	1200.	3000.
1849O Open Wreath	215,000	120.	195.	250.	375.	1400.
1850	481,953	120.	132.	165.	210.	565.
1850C	6,966	200.	375.	725.	1100.	2400.
1850D	8,382	375.	475.	775.	1350.	3250.
1850O	14,000	120.	225.	265.	450.	1300.
1851	3,317,671	120.	132.	165.	210.	565.
1851C	41,267	200.	425.	550.	850.	1550.
1851D	9,882	275.	425.	775.	1350.	3250.
1851O	290,000	175.	200.	250.	375.	1400.
1852	2,045,351	120.	132.	165.	210.	565.
1852C	9,434	275.	550.	725.	1100.	2400.
1852D	6,360	275.	675.	1050.	1500.	3250.
1852O	140,000	175.	200.	250.	375.	1400.
1853	4,076,051	120.	132.	165.	210.	565.
1853C	11,515	200.	425.	650.	975.	1750.
1853D	6,583	275.	425.	775.	1350.	3250.
1853O	290,000	120.	150.	230.	375.	1425.
1854	736,709	120.	132.	165.	210.	565.
1854D	2,935	350.	550.	1250.	1750.	5500.
1854S	14,632	120.	220.	425.	925.	2600.

Small Indian Head

Type: Gold Dollars — Indian Head — Small Head
Dates of issue: 1854-1856
Designer: James B. Longacre
Size: 15 MM
Weight: 1.672 Grams
Composition: 90% Gold & 10% Copper
Fineness: .900
Actual Gold wt.: .0484 Oz. pure Gold

MINT MARKS:
C Charlotte
D Dahlonega
O New Orleans
S San Francisco

Mintmark Below Wreath Tie

Date	Mintage	F-12	VF-20	XF-40	AU-50	MS-60
1854	902,736	175.	245.	450.	1500.	4500.
1855	758,269	175.	245.	450.	1500.	4500.
1855C	9,803	400.	625.	975.	2250.	8750.
1855D	1,811	1750.	3000.	5250.	7500.	17,500.
1855O	55,000	350.	575.	800.	1650.	8250.
1856S	24,600	350.	510.	950.	2500.	8000.

Large Indian Head

Type: Gold Dollars — Indian Head — Large Head
Dates of issue: 1856-1889
Designer: James B. Longacre
Size: 15 MM
Weight: 1.672 Grams
Composition: 90% Gold & 10% Copper
Fineness: .900
Actual Gold wt.: .0484 Oz. pure Gold

MINT MARKS:
C Charlotte
D Dahlonega
S San Francisco

Mintmark Below Wreath Tie

Date	Mintage	F-12	VF-20	XF-40	AU-50	MS-60	Prf-65
1856 Upright 5	1,762,936	120.	132.	165.	200.	550.	—
1856 Slant 5	Inc. Ab.	120.	132.	165.	200.	550.	—
1856D	1,460	1850.	3000.	4750.	7250.	14,500.	—
1857	774,789	120.	132.	165.	200.	550.	—
1857C	13,280	200.	475.	650.	1100.	2150.	—
1857D	3,533	350.	725.	1250.	1950.	3750.	—
1857S	10,000	150.	325.	355.	725.	1550.	—
1858	117,995	120.	132.	165.	200.	550.	13,000.
1858D	3,477	450.	725.	1250.	1900.	4250.	—
1858S	10,000	175.	240.	375.	575.	1400.	—
1859	168,244	120.	132.	165.	200.	550.	12,000.
1859C	5,235	200.	475.	750.	1200.	2350.	—
1859D	4,952	250.	725.	1250.	1900.	3500.	—
1859S	15,000	150.	210.	375.	950.	2250.	—
1860	36,668	120.	132.	165.	200.	550.	10,000.
1860D	1,566	1750.	2750.	4250.	5900.	15,000.	—
1860S	13,000	150.	325.	375.	575.	1325.	—
1861	527,499	120.	132.	165.	200.	550.	8500.
1861D	Unrecorded	3500.	6000.	11,000.	—	22,500.	—
1862	1,361,390	120.	132.	165.	200.	550.	8500.
1863	6,250	150.	325.	475.	850.	4500.	8500.
1864	5,950	150.	325.	475.	850.	3200.	8500.
1865	3,725	150.	325.	475.	850.	3500.	9250.
1866	7,130	150.	325.	425.	850.	1750.	8750.
1867	5,250	150.	325.	425.	800.	2200.	8500.
1868	10,525	150.	325.	400.	750.	1600.	9000.
1869	5,925	150.	330.	375.	600.	1800.	9000.
1870	6,335	150.	325.	375.	600.	1800.	8500.
1870S	3,000	350.	800.	1500.	2000.	3750.	—
1871	3,930	150.	350.	500.	850.	1750.	9000.
1872	3,530	150.	350.	500.	900.	1900.	9000.
1873 Clsd 3	125,125	150.	200.	550.	900.	1550.	9000.
1873 Open 3	Inc. Ab.	120.	132.	165.	200.	550.	—
1874	198,820	120.	132.	165.	200.	550.	11,500.
1875	420	—	2500.	3500.	4500.	9750.	15,000.
1876	3,245	150.	330.	375.	625.	1700.	8500.
1877	3,920	150.	325.	550.	700.	1850.	9500.
1878	3,020	150.	350.	550.	700.	1850.	9500.
1879	3,030	150.	350.	575.	700.	1750.	9000.
1880	1,636	150.	350.	575.	700.	1500.	8500.
1881	7,707	140.	325.	375.	475.	1150.	8250.
1882	5,125	150.	325.	375.	475.	1350.	8100.
1883	11,007	140.	170.	220.	300.	1350.	8100.
1884	6,236	150.	250.	275.	325.	1350.	8000.
1885	12,261	140.	170.	220.	300.	1350.	8000.
1886	6,016	150.	250.	275.	325.	1350.	8000.
1887	8,543	150.	325.	350.	400.	1350.	8000.
1888	16,580	120.	132.	165.	200.	550.	8000.
1889	30,729	120.	132.	165.	200.	550.	8000.

QUARTER EAGLES

Liberty Cap

Type: Quarter Eagles — $2.50 Gold — Liberty Cap
Dates of issue: 1796-1807
Designer: Robert Scot
Size: 20 MM
Weight: 4.37 Grams
Composition: 91.67% Gold & 8.33% Copper
Fineness: .9167
Actual Gold wt.: .1289 Oz. pure Gold

Date	Mintage	F-12	VF-20	XF-40	MS-60
1796 No Stars	963	9500.	15,000.	24,000.	40,000.
1796 Stars	432	6000.	9000.	14,000.	32,000.
1797	427	4500.	6750.	9500.	27,500.
1798	1,094	2500.	4000.	6250.	18,000.
1802 Over 1	3,035	2500.	3750.	5750.	16,000.
1804 13 Star Reverse	3,327	3400.	5200.	7750.	17,000.
1804 14 Star Reverse	Inc. Ab.	2500.	3750.	5750.	16,000.
1805	1,781	2500.	3750.	5750.	16,000.
1806 Over 4	1,616	2500.	3750.	5750.	16,000.
1806 Over 5	Inc. Ab.	4000.	6500.	10,000.	19,000.
1807	6,812	2500.	3750.	5750.	16,000.

Turban Head

Type: Quarter Eagles $2.50 Gold — Turban Head
Dates of issue: 1808-1834
Designer: John Reich
Size: 1808 20 MM, 1829-1834 18.5 MM
Weight: 4.37 Grams
Composition: 91.67% Gold & 8.33% Copper
Fineness: .9167
Actual Gold wt.: .1289 Oz. pure Gold

Date	Mintage	F-12	VF-20	XF-40	MS-60
1808 (20mm dia)	2,710	9000.	12,500.	17,000.	45,000.
1821 (18.5mm dia)	6,448	3250.	4000.	5750.	14,000.
1824 Over 21	2,600	3250.	4000.	5750.	15,000.

Date	Mintage	F-12	VF-20	XF-40	MS-60
1825	4,434	3250.	4000.	5750.	14,000.
1826 Over 25	760	3500.	5500.	10,000.	18,000.
1827	2,800	3250.	4000.	5750.	14,000.
1829	3,403	3250.	3750.	4750.	14,000.
1830	4,540	3250.	3750.	4750.	12,750.
1831	4,520	3250.	3750.	4750.	12,750.
1832	4,400	3250.	3750.	4750.	12,750.
1833	4,160	3250.	3750.	4750.	12,750.
1834	4,000	3500.	7000.	12,000.	25,000.

Liberty Without Turban

Type: Quarter Eagles — $2.50 Gold — Liberty Without Turban — Classic Head
Dates of issue: 1834-1839
Designer: William Kneass
Size: 18.2 MM
Weight: 4.18 Grams
Composition: 89.92% Gold & 10.08% Copper
Fineness: .8992
Actual Gold wt.: .1209 Oz. pure Gold

MINT MARKS:
C Charlotte
D Dahlonega
O New Orleans

Mintmark

Date	Mintage	VF-20	XF-40	AU-50	MS-60	MS-65
1834	112,234	255.	365.	815.	1900.	10,000.
1835	131,402	255.	365.	815.	1900.	10,000.
1836	547,986	255.	365.	815.	1900.	10,000.
1837	45,080	255.	365.	815.	1900.	10,000.
1838	47,030	255.	365.	815.	1900.	10,000.
1838C	7,880	650.	1000.	1500.	5000.	—
1839	27,021	255.	365.	815.	1900.	10,000.
1839C	18,140	550.	900.	1500.	5000.	—
1839D	13,674	850.	1500.	3000.	7500.	—
1839O	17,781	360.	750.	1150.	4500.	11,000.

Coronet Head

Type: Quarter Eagles — $2.50 Gold — Coronet Head
Dates of issue: 1840-1907
Designer: Christian Gobrecht
Size: 18 MM
Weight: 4.18 Grams
Composition: 90% Gold & 10% Copper
Fineness: .900
Actual Gold wt.: .1210 Oz. pure Gold

MINT MARKS:
C Charlotte
D Dahlonega
O New Orleans
S San Francisco

Mintmark

Date	Mintage	F-12	VF-20	XF-40	AU-50	MS-60	Prf-65
1840	18,859	200.	275.	350.	575.	—	—
1840C	12,822	265.	475.	750.	1150.	2800.	—
1840D	3,532	1350.	2500.	3750.	—	—	—
1840O	33,580	200.	225.	325.	500.	1900.	—
1841		Bowers Ruddy Sale Oct.1982 Prf-63 75,000.					—
1841C	10,281	225.	475.	750.	1200.	2850.	—
1841D	4,164	800.	1700.	2800.	4000.	—	—
1842	2,823	250.	500.	800.	1300.	—	—
1842C	6,729	350.	800.	1100.	1900.	—	—
1842D	4,643	800.	1500.	2500.	4000.	—	—
1842O	19,800	200.	300.	500.	800.	—	—
1843	100,546	200.	225.	250.	375.	1350.	—
1843C Sm Dt	26,064	750.	1600.	2500.	3750.	7500.	—
1843C Lg Dt	Inc. Ab.	225.	450.	675.	1000.	1850.	—
1843D	36,209	225.	475.	850.	1350.	2400.	—
1843O Sm Dt	288,002	200.	225.	250.	325.	1450.	—
1843O Lg Dt	76,000	200.	250.	325.	400.	1450.	—
1844	6,784	200.	350.	600.	900.	2200.	—
1844C	11,622	225.	475.	750.	1100.	2000.	—
1844D	17,332	225.	500.	850.	1400.	2300.	—
1845	91,051	175.	190.	215.	290.	1045.	—
1845D	19,460	225.	500.	850.	1400.	2300.	—
1845O	4,000	400.	950.	1500.	—	—	—
1846	21,598	200.	250.	300.	375.	1900.	—
1846C	4,808	275.	675.	950.	1250.	2250.	—
1846D	19,303	300.	600.	1000.	1400.	2300.	—
1846O	66,000	200.	250.	300.	375.	1600.	—
1847	29,814	200.	250.	300.	375.	1350.	—
1847C	23,226	275.	475.	700.	1000.	1800.	—
1847D	15,784	300.	475.	850.	1400.	2300.	—
1847O	124,000	200.	250.	300.	375.	1600.	—
1848	7,497	300.	500.	800.	1150.	2000.	—

Date	Mintage	F-12	VF-20	XF-40	AU-50	MS-60	Prf-65
1848 CAL.	1,389	3500.	4500.	8000.	—	17,500.	—
1848C	16,788	275.	475.	850.	1050.	1950.	—
1848D	13,771	300.	500.	850.	1500.	2500.	—
1849	23,294	200.	250.	300.	350.	1400.	—
1849C	10,220	275.	500.	850.	1150.	2500.	—
1849D	10,945	275.	600.	1000.	1400.	2500.	—
1850	252,923	175.	185.	210.	250.	950.	—
1850C	9,148	275.	500.	850.	1400.	2500.	—
1850D	12,148	275.	600.	1000.	1400.	2400.	—
1850O	84,000	200.	250.	300.	350.	1450.	—
1851	1,372,748	175.	185.	210.	250.	950.	—
1851C	14,923	275.	475.	850.	1100.	1950.	—
1851D	11,264	275.	600.	1000.	1400.	2400.	—
1851O	148,000	200.	250.	300.	425.	1450.	—
1852	1,159,681	175.	185.	210.	250.	950.	—
1852C	9,772	300.	500.	900.	1600.	3000.	—
1852D	4,078	275.	700.	1400.	2500.	3450.	—
1852O	140,000	200.	250.	300.	450.	1700.	—
1853	1,404,668	175.	185.	210.	275.	1015.	—
1853D	3,178	275.	700.	1300.	1900.	3000.	—
1854	596,258	175.	185.	210.	250.	950.	—
1854C	7,295	250.	550.	850.	1350.	2750.	—
1854D	1,760	2250.	3500.	5000.	—	—	—
1854O	153,000	200.	250.	300.	450.	1800.	—
1854S	246	10,000.	20,000.	30,000.	—	—	—
1855	235,480	175.	185.	210.	275.	1015.	—
1855C	3,677	500.	800.	1400.	2500.	—	—
1855D	1,123	2500.	3750.	5500.	—	7500.	—
1856	384,240	175.	185.	210.	275.	950.	22,000.
1856C	7,913	250.	550.	975.	1500.	—	—
1856D	874	4500.	7250.	9000.	—	15,000.	—
1856O	21,100	200.	250.	325.	400.	1750.	—
1856S	71,120	200.	250.	325.	400.	1800.	—
1857	214,130	175.	185.	210.	250.	950.	—
1857D	2,364	265.	900.	1400.	2300.	4500.	—
1857O	34,000	200.	250.	350.	575.	1900.	—
1857S	69,200	200.	250.	300.	600.	2500.	—
1858	47,377	200.	250.	300.	350.	1350.	19,000.
1858C	9,056	265.	500.	850.	1350.	1950.	—
1859	39,444	200.	250.	300.	350.	1350.	19,000.
1859D	2,244	265.	900.	1500.	2200.	3250.	—
1859S	15,200	200.	250.	400.	550.	2500.	—
1860	22,675	200.	250.	300.	400.	1400.	19,000.
1860C	7,469	265.	500.	850.	1350.	1950.	—
1860S	35,600	200.	250.	400.	800.	2500.	—
1861	1,283,878	150.	175.	200.	245.	565.	19,000.
1861S	24,000	200.	250.	400.	800.	3000.	—
1862	98,543	200.	250.	300.	340.	1045.	19,000.
1862 Over 1	Inc. Ab.	—	1000.	1500.	—	3500.	—
1862S	8,000	200.	325.	700.	1000.	2500.	—
1863	30	Bowers & Ruddy Oct. 1982, Proof only 39,600.					
1863S	10,800	200.	250.	400.	750.	2200.	—
1864	2,874	800.	1500.	2250.	3500.	6500.	19,000.
1865	1,545	450.	1400.	2200.	3250.	6000.	19,000.
1865S	23,376	200.	300.	450.	750.	2200.	—
1866	3,110	225.	300.	500.	900.	2500.	19,000.
1866S	38,960	200.	250.	400.	750.	2200.	—
1867	3,250	225.	275.	450.	650.	1750.	19,000.
1867S	28,000	200.	250.	450.	700.	2500.	—
1868	3,625	200.	300.	400.	650.	1750.	19,000.
1868S	34,000	200.	250.	325.	550.	1750.	—
1869	4,345	200.	300.	325.	700.	1650.	19,000.
1869S	29,500	200.	250.	300.	600.	1900.	—
1870	4,555	210.	260.	350.	500.	1900.	19,000.
1870S	16,000	200.	250.	300.	425.	1900.	—
1871	5,350	210.	275.	325.	500.	1600.	19,000.
1871S	22,000	200.	250.	300.	400.	1750.	—
1872	3,030	225.	275.	400.	575.	1900.	19,000.
1872S	18,000	200.	250.	300.	400.	1900.	—
1873 Clsd 3	178,025	200.	250.	300.	340.	750.	19,000.
1873 Open 3	Inc. Ab.	200.	250.	300.	340.	750.	—
1873S	27,000	200.	250.	300.	500.	2200.	—
1874	3,940	225.	300.	375.	500.	1500.	19,000.
1875	420	1500.	3000.	5500.	7250.	9000.	19,000.
1875S	11,600	200.	250.	300.	475.	1350.	—
1876	4,221	210.	250.	425.	750.	2500.	19,000.
1876S	5,000	210.	250.	325.	575.	1700.	—
1877	1,652	325.	450.	700.	950.	2250.	19,000.
1877S	35,400	110.	180.	210.	250.	1300.	—
1878	286,260	110.	155.	180.	215.	595.	19,000.
1878S	178,000	110.	155.	180.	215.	595.	—
1879	88,990	110.	155.	180.	215.	595.	19,000.
1879S	43,500	110.	155.	180.	215.	595.	—
1880	2,996	215.	250.	350.	500.	1500.	19,000.
1881	691	500.	1000.	1500.	2700.	4000.	19,000.
1882	4,067	110.	225.	325.	425.	1500.	19,000.

Date	Mintage	F-12	VF-20	XF-40	AU-50	MS-60	Prf-65
1883	2,002	110.	225.	400.	500.	1500	19,000.
1884	2,023	110.	225.	400.	500.	1500.	19,000.
1885	887	500.	800.	1200.	2000.	3000.	19,000.
1886	4,088	110.	210.	300.	400.	1100.	19,000.
1887	6,282	110.	190.	225.	400.	1100.	19,000.
1888	16,098	110.	190.	275.	450.	1100.	19,000.
1889	17,648	110.	190.	275.	450.	900.	19,000.
1890	8,813	110.	190.	300.	450.	1100.	19,000.
1891	11,040	110.	190.	275.	450.	1100.	19,000.
1892	2,545	180.	275.	475.	700.	1200.	19,000.
1893	30,106	110.	155.	200.	260.	950.	19,000.
1894	4,122	110.	155.	200.	400.	1125.	19,000.
1895	6,199	110.	155.	200.	400.	1125.	19,000.
1896	19,202	110.	155.	180.	215.	595.	19,000.
1897	29,904	110.	155.	180.	215.	595.	19,000.
1898	24,165	110.	155.	180.	215.	595.	19,000.
1899	27,350	110.	155.	180.	215.	595.	19,000.
1900	67,205	110.	155.	180.	215.	595.	19,000.
1901	91,322	110.	155.	180.	215.	595.	19,000.
1902	133,733	110.	155.	180.	215.	595.	19,000.
1903	201,257	110.	155.	180.	215.	595.	19,000.
1904	160,960	110.	155.	180.	215.	595.	19,000.
1905	217,944	110.	155.	180.	215.	595.	19,000.
1906	176,490	110.	155.	180.	215.	595.	19,000.
1907	336,448	110.	155.	180.	215.	595.	19,000.

Indian Head

Type: Quarter Eagles — $2.50 Gold — Indian Head
Dates of issue: 1908-1929
Designer: Bela Lyon Pratt
Size: 18 MM
Weight: 4.18 Grams
Composition: 90% Gold & 10% Copper
Fineness: .900
Actual Gold wt.: .1210 Oz. pure Gold

MINT MARKS:
D Denver

Mintmark

Date	Mintage	VF-20	XF-40	AU-50	MS-60	MS-63	MS-65	Prf-65
1908	565,057	145.	165.	190.	460.	1250.	9200.	18,000.
1909	441,899	145.	165.	190.	460.	1275.	9350.	18,000.
1910	492,682	145.	165.	190.	470.	1275.	9400.	18,000.
1911	704,191	145.	165.	190.	460.	1250.	9500.	18,000.
1911D	55,680	700.	1000.	1500.	3100.	5000.	28,500.	—
1912	616,197	145.	165.	190.	460.	1250.	9400.	18,000.
1913	722,165	145.	165.	190.	450.	1250.	9350.	18,000.
1914	240,117	145.	165.	205.	510.	1300.	9500.	18,000.
1914D	448,000	145.	165.	190.	460.	1275.	9200.	—
1915	606,100	145.	165.	190.	450.	1275.	9200.	18,000.
1925D	578,000	145.	165.	190.	280.	1200.	9000.	—
1926	446,000	145.	165.	190.	280.	1200.	9000.	—
1927	388,000	145.	165.	190.	280.	1200.	9000.	—
1928	416,000	145.	165.	190.	280.	1200.	9000.	—
1929	532,000	145.	180.	210.	375.	1250.	9250.	—

THREE DOLLARS

Type: Three Dollars — Gold
Dates of issue: 1854-1889
Designer: James B. Longacre
Size: 20.5 MM
Weight: 5.015 Grams
Composition: 90% Gold & 10% Copper
Fineness: .900
Actual Gold wt.: .1452 Oz. pure Gold

MINT MARKS:
D Dahlonega
O New Orleans
S San Francisco

Mintmark Below Wreath Tie

Date	Mintage	F-12	VF-20	XF-40	AU-50	MS-60	Prf-65
1854	138,618	365.	505.	650.	1070.	2800.	45,000.
1854D	1,120	—	9500.	14,000.	22,000.	49,000.	—
1854O	24,000	365.	600.	750.	1400.	4100.	—
1855	50,555	365.	505.	650.	1070.	2800.	—
1855S	6,600	550.	760.	925.	2200.	5800.	—
1856	26,010	365.	535.	690.	1200.	3200.	—
1856S	34,500	500.	760.	800.	1350.	4400.	—
1857	20,891	365.	535.	690.	1100.	2900.	45,000.
1857S	14,000	510.	760.	925.	1750.	5200.	—
1858	2,133	550.	800.	950.	1850.	4600.	45,000.
1859	15,638	365.	505.	725.	1150.	2900.	45,000.
1860	7,155	550.	760.	850.	1200.	3200.	45,000.
1860S	7,000	525.	760.	1050.	2100.	5750.	—
1861	6,072	550.	760.	875.	1450.	3700.	45,000.
1862	5,785	525.	760.	900.	1450.	3700.	45,000.
1863	5,039	600.	760.	925.	1650.	4500.	45,000.
1864	2,680	600.	760.	950.	1600.	4200.	45,000.
1865	1,165	700.	800.	1275.	2750.	7500.	45,000.
1866	4,030	525.	760.	1275.	1600.	4900.	45,000.
1867	2,650	575.	800.	975.	1600.	4300.	45,000.
1868	4,875	525.	760.	900.	1600.	4300.	45,000.
1869	2,525	575.	760.	900.	1700.	4900.	45,000.

Date	Mintage	F-12	VF-20	XF-40	AU-50	MS-60	Prf-65
1870	3,535	525.	760.	900.	1600.	4500.	45,000.
1870S	2	Bowers Ruddy Sale Oct. 1982 XF-40 625,000.					
1871	1,330	550.	880.	975.	1725.	4500.	45,000.
1872	2,030	525.	800.	950.	1600.	4300.	45,000.
1873 Open 3	25	Proof Only					
1873 Clsd 3	Unknown	—	4000.	5000.	5500.	10,500.	—
1874	41,820	365.	505.	650.	1070.	2900.	45,000.
1875	20	(Proofs Only)					
		Bowers & Ruddy Sale Oct. 1982					100,000.
1876	45	(Proofs Only)					
		Bowers & Ruddy Sale Oct. 1982					52,000.
1877	1,488	600.	900.	1450.	2750.	5200.	45,000.
1878	82,324	365.	505.	650.	1070.	2800.	45,000.
1879	3,030	550.	800.	900.	1550.	3450.	45,000.
1880	1,036	550.	900.	925.	1650.	3450.	45,000.
1881	554	900.	1200.	1650.	2800.	4500.	45,000.
1882	1,576	550.	800.	900.	1650.	3700.	45,000.
1883	989	550.	800.	925.	1700.	3700.	45,000.
1884	1,106	550.	800.	925.	1650.	3800.	45,000.
1885	910	550.	800.	1100.	1800.	4400.	45,000.
1886	1,142	550.	800.	925.	1650.	3900.	45,000.
1887	6,160	550.	625.	725.	1150.	3000.	45,000.
1888	5,291	525.	625.	725.	1150.	3000.	45,000.
1889	2,429	525.	625.	725.	1150.	3000.	45,000.

STELLA

Type: Four Dollars Gold Pattern — "Stella"
Dates of issue: 1879-1880
Designer: Charles E. Barber — Flowing Hair Type.
George T. Morgan — Coiled Hair Type

Date	Type	Mintage	VF-20	XF-40	AU-50	Prf-65
1879	Flowing Hair	415	—	—	—	50,000.
	Impaired Proofs	—	10,000.	13,500.	26,000.	
1879	Coiled Hair	10	—	—	—	85,000.
1880	Flowing Hair	15	—	—	—	65,000.
1880	Coiled Hair	10	—	—	—	85,000.

HALF EAGLES

Liberty Cap

Type: Half Eagles $5.00 Gold — Liberty Capped, Heraldic Eagle and Small Eagle
Dates of issue: 1795-1807
Designer: Robert Scot
Size: 25 MM
Weight: 8.75 Grams
Composition: 91.67% Gold & 8.33% Copper
Fineness: .9167
Actual Gold wt.: .2580 Oz. pure Gold

Date	Mintage	F-12	VF-20	XF-40	MS-60
1795 Sm. Eagle	8,707	5250.	7600.	9750.	25,000.
1795 Lg. Eagle	Inc. Ab.	4000.	7500.	12,500.	32,000.
1796 Over 95 Small Eagle	6,196	5250.	7750.	10,000.	25,000.
1797 Over 95 Large Eagle	3,609	4200.	5250.	8500.	18,500.
1797 15 Stars, Small Eagle	Inc. Ab.	5500.	8000.	10,500.	27,000.
1797 16 Stars, Small Eagle	Inc. Ab.	5500.	8000.	10,500.	27,000.
1798 Sm. Eagle	24,867	Bowers Ruddy Sale Oct.1982 VF 70,000.			
1798 Large Eagle, Small 8	Inc. Ab.	1200.	1850.	3700.	9500.
1798 Large Eagle, Large 8, 13 Star Reverse	Inc. Ab.	1200.	1850.	3700.	9500.
1798 Large Eagle, Large 8, 14 Star Reverse	Inc. Ab.	1600.	2750.	4750.	12,500.
1799	7,451	1000.	1800.	3700.	9500.
1800	37,628	1000.	1550.	2900.	9250.
1802 Over 1	53,176	1000.	1550.	2900.	9000.

Date	Mintage	F-12	VF-20	XF-40	MS-60
1803 Over 2	33,506	1000.	1550.	2900.	9000.
1804 Sm. 8	30,475	1000.	1550.	2900.	9000.
1804 Lg. 8	Inc. Ab.	1000.	1550.	2900.	9000.
1805	33,183	1000.	1550.	2900.	9000.
1806 Pointed 6	64,093	1000.	1550.	2900.	10,000.
1806 Round 6	Inc. Ab.	1000.	1550.	2900.	9000.
1807	32,488	1000.	1550.	2900.	9000.

Turban Head

Type: Half Eagles — $5.00 Gold — Turban Head
Dates of issue: 1807-1834
Designer: John Reich
Size: 25 MM
Weight: 8.75 Grams
Composition: 91.67% Gold & 8.33% Copper
Fineness: .9167
Actual Gold wt.: .2580 Oz. pure Gold

Date	Mintage	F-12	VF-20	XF-40	MS-60
1807	51,605	1250.	2000.	2750.	8000.
1808	55,578	1250.	2000.	2750.	8000.
1808 Over 7	Inc. Ab.	1400.	2100.	3200.	8500.
1809 Over 8	33,875	1250.	2000.	2750.	8000.
1810 Small Date, Sm 5	100,287	—	Rare	—	—
1810 Small Date, Lg. 5	Inc. Ab.	1300.	2000.	2750.	8000.
1810 Large Date, Sm. 5	Inc. Ab.	1650.	2750.	3250.	9000.
1810 Large Date, Lg. 5	Inc. Ab.	1250.	2000.	2750.	8000.
1811 Small 5	99,581	1250.	2000.	2750.	8000.
1811 Large 5	Inc. Ab.	1300.	2200.	2950.	8750.
1812	58,087	1300.	2000.	2750.	9000.

Large Head Type Introduced

Date	Mintage	F-12	VF-20	XF-40	MS-60
1813	95,428	1150.	1700.	2450.	11,000.
1814 Over 13	15,454	1200.	2000.	2700.	12,500.
1815	635	Norweb Sale Oct.1987 AU-55 $82,500.			
1818	48,588	1150.	1700.	2450.	12,000.
1819	51,723	—	Rare	—	—
1820 Curve Base 2, Small Letters	263,806	1150.	1700.	2450.	12,500.
1820 Curve Base 2, Large Letters	Inc. Ab.	1150.	1700.	2450.	12,500.
1820 Sq. Base 2	Inc. Ab.	1150.	1700.	2450.	12,500.
1821	34,641	3000.	4500.	7500.	15,000.
1822	(3 known) 17,796	Bowers Ruddy Sale Oct.1982 VF-30 625,000.			
1823	14,485	1800.	2800.	4000.	14,500.
1824	17,340	—	Rare	—	—
1825 Over 21	29,060	3250.	5000.	7500.	15,000.
1825 Over 24	Inc. Ab.	Bowers Ruddy Sale Oct.1982 Prf-60 200,000.			
1826	18,069	2750.	6000.	8500.	19,000.
1827	24,913	Superior Sale June, 1985 MS-65 $60,500.			
1828 8 Over 7	28,029	Bowers Ruddy Sale Oct.1982 AU-55 40,000.			
1828	Inc. Ab.	Bowers Ruddy Sale Oct.1982 AU-55 24,000.			
1829 Lg. Dt.	57,442	Superior Sale July, 1985 MS-65 $104,500.			
1829 Sm. Dt.	Inc. Ab.	Bowers Ruddy Sale Oct.1982 XF-45 26,000.			
1830 Sm. 5D.	126,351	2000.	3750.	5250.	15,000.
1830 Lg. 5D.	Inc. Ab.	2000.	3750.	5250.	15,000.
1831	140,594	2000.	3750.	5250.	15,000.
1832 Curve Base 2, 12 Stars	157,487	—	Rare	—	—
1832 Square Base 2, 13 Stars	Inc. Ab.	2500.	6500.	8750.	21,000.
1833	193,630	2000.	3750.	5250.	14,750.
1834 Plain 4	50,141	2000.	3750.	5250.	15,000.
1834 Crosslet 4	Inc. Ab.	2000.	3750.	5250.	15,000.

Liberty Without Turban

Mintmark Above Date

Type: Half Eagles — $5.00 Gold — Liberty Without Turban — Classic Head
Dates of issue: 1834-1838
Designer: William Kneass
Size: 22.5 MM
Weight: 8.36 MM
Composition: 89.92% Gold & 10.08 Copper
Fineness: .8992
Actual Gold wt.: .2418 Oz. pure Gold

MINT MARKS:
C Charlotte
D Dahlonega

Date	Mintage	VF-20	XF-40	AU-50	MS-60	MS-65
1834 Plain 4	658,028	265.	425.	1000.	2400.	11,500.
1834 Crosslet 4	Inc. Ab.	1000.	1500.	2250.	6500.	—
1835	371,534	265.	425.	1000.	2400.	11,500.
1836	553,147	265.	425.	1000.	2400.	11,500.
1837	207,121	265.	425.	1000.	2400.	11,500.
1838	286,588	265.	425.	1000.	2400.	11,500.
1838C	17,179	800.	1750.	2500.	6000.	—
1838D	20,583	1450.	2500.	3500.	8000.	—

HALF EAGLES
Coronet Head

Mintmarks:
Above Date 1839
Below Eagle From 1840

Type: Half Eagles $5.00 Gold — Coronet Type
Dates of issue: 1839-1908
Designer: Christian Gobrecht
Size: 21.6 MM
Weight: 8.359 Grams
Composition: 90% Gold & 10% Copper
Fineness: .900
Actual Gold wt.: .2420 Oz. pure Gold

MINT MARKS:
C   Charlotte
CC Carson City
D   Dahlonega (1839-1861)
D   Denver (1906 & 1907)
O   New Orleans
S   San Francisco

Date	Mintage	F-12	VF-20	XF-40	MS-60	Prf-65
1839	118,143	200.	325.	435.	2750.	—
1839 Over 8 Curved Date	Inc. Ab.	200.	300.	600.	1800.	—
1839C	17,205	350.	650.	1350.	3500.	—
1839D	18,939	350.	675.	1350.	5000.	—
1840	137,382	190.	210.	275.	2500.	—
1840C	18,992	325.	600.	900.	3250.	—
1840D	22,896	325.	650.	1100.	5000.	—
1840O	40,120	200.	425.	550.	2750.	—
1841	15,833	200.	325.	450.	2500.	—
1841C	21,467	300.	525.	900.	3500.	—
1841D	30,495	300.	600.	1000.	4500.	—
1841O	50	Only 2 Known		—	—	—
1842 Sm Let	27,578	200.	250.	500.	2500.	—
1842 Lg Let	Inc. Ab.	200.	250.	500.	2500.	—
1842C Sm Dt	28,184	1500.	3500.	5000.	—	—
1842C Lg Dt	Inc. Ab.	300.	525.	850.	3000.	—
1842D Sm Dt	59,608	300.	525.	850.	4500.	—
1842D Lg Dt	Inc. Ab.	1250.	2250.	3500.	—	—
1842O	16,400	225.	400.	650.	3000.	—
1843	611,205	150.	180.	210.	1465.	—
1843C	44,201	300.	500.	850.	2950.	—
1843D	98,452	300.	500.	850.	4500.	—
1843O Sm Let	19,075	200.	300.	500.	2750.	—
1843O Lg Let	82,000	200.	250.	350.	2450.	—
1844	340,330	150.	180.	210.	1465.	—

UNITED STATES 1754

Date	Mintage	F-12	VF-20	XF-40	MS-60	Prf-65
1844C	23,631	300.	525.	950.	3500.	—
1844D	88,982	300.	500.	850.	4500.	—
1844O	364,600	160.	195.	250.	2250.	—
1845	417,099	150.	180.	210.	1475.	—
1845D	90,629	300.	500.	850.	4500.	—
1845O	41,000	200.	350.	600.	3500.	—
1846	395,942	150.	180.	210.	1465.	—
1846C	12,995	300.	600.	1050.	4000.	—
1846D	80,294	300.	500.	850.	4500.	—
1846O	58,000	200.	300.	450.	2500.	—
1847	915,981	150.	180.	210.	1465.	—
1847C	84,151	250.	500.	850.	3500.	—
1847D	64,405	300.	500.	850.	4500.	—
1847O	12,000	250.	500.	1150.	—	—
1848	260,775	150.	180.	210.	2200.	—
1848C	64,472	250.	500.	900.	2750.	—
1848D	47,465	300.	500.	900.	5000.	—
1849	133,070	150.	180.	210.	2200.	—
1849C	64,823	250.	500.	850.	2750.	—
1849D	39,036	300.	525.	950.	4500.	—
1850	64,491	170.	200.	250.	2200.	—
1850C	63,591	250.	475.	750.	2750.	—
1850D	43,984	300.	500.	900.	4750.	—
1851	377,505	150.	180.	210.	1465.	—
1851C	49,176	250.	500.	850.	3200.	—
1851D	62,710	300.	525.	850.	4500.	—
1851O	41,000	200.	275.	450.	3000.	—
1852	573,901	150.	180.	210.	1465.	—
1852C	72,574	250.	500.	750.	2900.	—
1852D	91,584	300.	500.	800.	4000.	—
1853	305,770	150.	180.	210.	1465.	—
1853C	65,571	275.	475.	800.	2750.	—
1853D	89,678	300.	500.	850.	4500.	—
1854	160,675	160.	200.	250.	2250.	—
1854C	39,283	250.	550.	875.	3250.	—
1854D	56,413	250.	500.	800.	4500.	—
1854O	46,000	200.	300.	500.	2500.	—
1854S	268 Bowers Ruddy Sale Oct.1982 AU-55 170,000.					
1855	117,098	160.	200.	250.	2200.	—
1855C	39,454	250.	525.	850.	3000.	—
1855D	22,432	300.	600.	1000.	5500.	—
1855O	11,100	250.	550.	850.	3000.	—
1855S	61,000	200.	300.	500.	2500.	—
1856	197,990	160.	200.	250.	2200.	—
1856C	28,457	250.	550.	900.	4500.	—
1856D	19,786	250.	600.	1000.	5500.	—
1856O	10,000	275.	550.	850.	—	—
1856S	105,100	160.	250.	350.	2500.	—
1857	98,188	160.	200.	250.	2200.	40,000.
1857C	31,360	300.	525.	850.	3500.	—
1857D	17,046	300.	600.	1000.	5000.	—
1857O	13,000	200.	550.	850.	—	—
1857S	87,000	180.	250.	375.	2500.	—
1858	15,136	200.	230.	350.	2500.	40,000.
1858C	38,856	250.	525.	850.	3500.	—
1858D	15,362	300.	600.	1000.	6000.	—
1858S	18,600	250.	400.	800.	3500.	—
1859	16,814	200.	275.	450.	2500.	32,500.
1859C	31,847	300.	525.	850.	3500.	—
1859D	10,366	250.	625.	1200.	6000.	—
1859S	13,220	250.	475.	900.	3000.	—
1860	19,825	200.	300.	500.	2350.	30,000.
1860C	14,813	300.	550.	850.	4000.	—
1860D	14,635	300.	625.	1100.	6000.	—
1860S	21,200	200.	450.	800.	—	—
1861	688,150	150.	180.	210.	1465.	30,000.
1861C	6,879	700.	1100.	2200.	—	—
1861D	1,597	2500.	5250.	7500.	—	—
1861S	18,000	200.	400.	800.	—	—
1862	4,465	350.	700.	1000.	—	30,000.
1862S	9,500	350.	1100.	2200.	—	—
1863	2,472	500.	900.	1500.	—	30,000.
1863S	17,000	300.	750.	1500.	—	—
1864	4,220	400.	600.	950.	4000.	30,000.
1864S	3,888	1200.	1750.	2950.	—	—
1865	1,295	600.	900.	1500.	—	30,000.
1865S	27,612	300.	700.	1250.	—	—
1866S	9,000	300.	800.	1400.	—	—

Motto Added Over Eagle

Date	Mintage	VF-20	XF-40	AU-50	MS-60	MS-65	Prf-65
1866	6,730	600.	1000.	—	—	—	30,000.
1866S	34,920	550.	950.	—	—	—	—
1867	6,920	550.	950.	—	—	—	30,000.
1867S	29,000	600.	1000.	—	—	—	—
1868	5,725	450.	850.	—	—	—	22,500.

Date	Mintage	VF-20	XF-40	AU-50	MS-60	MS-65	Prf-65
1868S	52,000	450.	800.	—	—	—	—
1869	1,785	750.	1250.	—	—	—	22,500.
1869S	31,000	575.	900.	3700.	—	—	—
1870	4,035	600.	900.	—	—	—	22,500.
1870CC	7,675	2500.	4000.	7250.	—	—	—
1870S	17,000	700.	1100.	—	—	—	—
1871	3,230	700.	1100.	—	—	—	25,000.
1871CC	20,770	800.	1250.	—	—	—	—
1871S	25,000	400.	800.	—	—	—	—
1872	1,690	750.	1250.	—	2500.	—	18,500.
1872CC	16,980	850.	1400.	—	—	—	—
1872S	36,400	400.	750.	—	—	—	—
1873 Clsd 3	49,305	225.	235.	260.	475.	12,500.	18,500.
1873 Open 3	63,200	225.	235.	260.	475.	12,500.	—
1873CC	7,416	1000.	1500.	—	—	—	—
1873S	31,000	500.	800.	—	—	—	—
1874	3,508	500.	900.	—	—	—	25,000.
1874CC	21,198	600.	1000.	2000.	3500.	—	—
1874S	16,000	650.	1000.	—	—	—	—
1875	220	—	Rare	—	—	—	55,000.
1875CC	11,828	850.	1400.	—	—	—	—
1875S	9,000	600.	1200.	1500.	2000.	—	—
1876	1,477	850.	1350.	1650.	2250.	—	30,000.
1876CC	6,887	950.	1400.	—	2250.	—	—
1876S	4,000	1100.	2200.	—	—	—	—
1877	1,152	800.	1250.	—	2500.	—	30,000.
1877CC	8,680	875.	1500.	—	2750.	—	—
1877S	26,700	400.	650.	—	—	—	—
1878	131,740	120.	130.	145.	240.	11,500.	30,000.
1878CC	9,054	1500.	2500.	—	—	—	—
1878S	144,700	120.	130.	145.	240.	11,500.	—
1879	301,950	120.	130.	145.	240.	11,500.	30,000.
1879CC	17,281	350.	650.	950.	1900.	—	—
1879S	426,200	120.	130.	145.	240.	11,500.	—
1880	3,166,436	120.	130.	145.	240.	11,500.	30,000.
1880CC	51,017	300.	550.	700.	950.	—	—
1880S	1,348,900	120.	130.	145.	240.	11,500.	—
1881	5,708,802	120.	130.	145.	240.	11,500.	30,000.
1881/80	(Inc. Ab.)			Extremely Rare			
1881CC	13,886	350.	550.	700.	950.	—	—
1881S	969,000	120.	130.	145.	240.	11,500.	—
1882	2,514,568	120.	130.	145.	240.	11,500.	30,000.
1882CC	82,817	250.	500.	650.	950.	—	—
1882S	969,000	120.	130.	145.	240.	11,500.	—
1883	233,461	120.	130.	145.	240.	11,500.	30,000.
1883CC	12,958	225.	400.	650.	950.	—	—
1883S	83,200	195.	215.	250.	475.	11,500.	—
1884	191,078	125.	135.	225.	450.	11,500.	30,000.
1884CC	16,402	250.	500.	650.	850.	—	—
1884S	177,000	120.	130.	145.	240.	11,500.	—
1885	601,506	120.	130.	145.	240.	11,500.	30,000.
1885S	1,211,500	120.	130.	145.	240.	11,500.	—
1886	388,432	120.	130.	145.	240.	11,500.	30,000.
1886S	3,268,000	120.	130.	145.	240.	11,500.	—
1887	87	Proofs Only		—	—	—	40,000.
1887S	1,912,000	120.	130.	145.	240.	11,500.	—
1888	18,296	120.	130.	145.	240.	11,500.	30,000.
1888S	293,900	120.	130.	145.	240.	11,500.	—
1889	7,565	300.	375.	475.	700.	—	30,000.
1890	4,328	250.	400.	550.	800.	—	30,000.
1890CC	53,800	300.	425.	700.	900.	—	—
1891	61,413	120.	130.	145.	240.	11,500.	30,000.
1891CC	208,000	250.	375.	700.	900.	—	—
1892	753,572	120.	130.	145.	240.	11,500.	30,000.
1892CC	82,968	300.	600.	700.	900.	—	—
1892O	10,000	900.	1250.	1800.	3000.	—	—
1892S	298,400	120.	130.	145.	240.	11,500.	—
1893	1,528,197	120.	130.	145.	240.	11,500.	30,000.
1893CC	60,000	300.	600.	750.	900.	—	—
1893O	110,000	195.	300.	400.	700.	—	—
1893S	224,000	120.	130.	145.	240.	11,500.	—
1894	957,955	120.	130.	145.	240.	11,500.	30,000.
1894O	16,600	195.	300.	400.	750.	—	—
1894S	55,900	120.	130.	145.	240.	11,500.	—
1895	1,345,936	120.	130.	145.	240.	11,500.	30,000.
1895S	112,000	120.	130.	145.	240.	11,500.	—
1896	59,063	120.	130.	145.	240.	11,500.	30,000.
1896S	155,400	120.	130.	145.	240.	11,500.	—
1897	867,883	120.	130.	145.	240.	11,500.	30,000.
1897S	354,000	120.	130.	145.	240.	11,500.	—
1898	633,495	120.	130.	145.	240.	11,500.	30,000.
1898S	1,397,400	120.	130.	145.	240.	11,500.	—
1899	1,710,729	120.	130.	145.	240.	11,500.	30,000.
1899S	1,545,000	120.	130.	145.	240.	11,500.	—
1900	1,405,730	120.	130.	145.	240.	11,500.	30,000.
1900S	329,000	120.	130.	145.	240.	11,500.	—
1901	616,040	120.	130.	145.	240.	11,500.	30,000.
1901S	3,648,000	120.	130.	145.	240.	11,500.	—
1902	172,562	120.	130.	145.	240.	11,500.	30,000.
1902S	939,000	120.	130.	145.	240.	11,500.	—
1903	227,024	120.	130.	145.	240.	11,500.	30,000.
1903S	1,855,000	120.	130.	145.	240.	11,500.	—
1904	392,136	120.	130.	145.	240.	11,500.	30,000.
1904S	97,000	120.	130.	145.	240.	11,500.	—
1905	302,308	120.	130.	145.	240.	11,500.	30,000.
1905S	880,700	120.	130.	145.	240.	11,500.	—
1906	348,820	120.	130.	145.	240.	11,500.	30,000.
1906D	320,000	120.	130.	145.	240.	11,500.	—
1906S	598,000	120.	130.	145.	240.	11,500.	—
1907	626,192	120.	130.	145.	240.	11,500.	30,000.
1907D	888,000	120.	130.	145.	240.	11,500.	—
1908	421,874	120.	130.	145.	240.	11,500.	—

Indian Head

Mintmark At Point Of Fasces

Type: Half Eagles — $5.00 Gold — Indian Head
Dates of issue: 1908-1929
Designer: Bela Lyon Pratt
Size: 21.6 MM
Weight: 8.359 Grams
Composition: 90% Gold & 10% Copper
Fineness: .900
Actual Gold wt.: .2420 Oz. pure Gold

MINT MARKS:
D Denver
O New Orleans
S San Francisco

Date	Mintage	VF-20	XF-40	AU-50	MS-60	MS-63	MS-65	Prf-65
1908	578,012	190.	200.	250.	760.	4000.	21,000.	30,000.
1908D	148,000	190.	200.	250.	760.	4100.	21,000.	
1908S	82,000	250.	400.	525.	2500.	5200.	21,000.	—
1909	627,138	190.	200.	250.	850.	4100.	21,000.	30,000.
1909D	3,423,560	190.	200.	230.	615.	3900.	21,000.	
1909O	34,200	600.	900.	1200.	6600.	17,000.	52,000.	
1909S	297,200	250.	300.	475.	1250.	4700.	22,000.	
1910	604,250	250.	265.	300.	850.	4200.	21,000.	30,000.
1910D	193,600	250.	265.	300.	850.	4350.	21,000.	
1910S	770,200	250.	350.	600.	2000.	5700.	22,000.	—
1911	915,139	190.	200.	230.	615.	3900.	21,000.	30,000.
1911D	72,500	350.	500.	950.	4250.	9550.	29,000.	—
1911S	1,416,000	250.	265.	400.	950.	4250.	22,000.	—
1912	790,144	190.	200.	230.	615.	3900.	21,000.	30,000.
1912S	392,000	250.	265.	400.	1600.	5500.	24,000.	
1913	916,099	190.	200.	230.	615.	3900.	21,000.	30,000.
1913S	408,000	300.	350.	400.	2750.	6600.	27,000.	
1914	247,125	190.	200.	230.	615.	3900.	21,000.	30,000.
1914D	247,000	190.	200.	230.	615.	4250.	21,000.	
1914S	263,000	190.	200.	260.	1000.	5250.	21,000.	—
1915	588,075	190.	200.	235.	775.	3900.	21,000.	30,000.
1915S	164,000	300.	325.	400.	2550.	6050.	29,000.	—
1916S	240,000	190.	200.	260.	1000.	4775.	21,000.	—
1929	662,000	2000.	3000.	3700.	6800.	9400.	23,500.	—

EAGLES

Liberty Cap

Type: Eagles — $10.00 Gold — Liberty Cap, Small Eagle
Dates of issue: 1795-1797
Designer: Robert Scot
Size: 33 MM
Weight: 17.50 Grams
Composition: 91.67% Gold & 8.33% Copper
Fineness: .9167
Actual Gold wt.: .5159 Oz. pure Gold

Date	Mintage	F-12	VF-20	XF-40	MS-60
1795	5,583	—	8500.	11,000.	32,500.
1796	4,146	—	8500.	11,000.	32,500.
1797 Sm. Eagle	3,615	—	8500.	11,000.	32,500.

Heraldic Eagle Introduced

Dates of issue: 1797-1804

Date	Mintage	F-12	VF-20	XF-40	MS-60
1797 Lg. Eagle	10,940	2500.	3500.	5000.	16,000.
1798 Over 97, 9 Stars Left, 4 Right	900	Bowers Ruddy Sale Oct.1982 AU-55 30,000.			
1798 Over 97, 7 Stars Left, 6 Right	842	Bowers Ruddy Sale Oct.1982 XF-45 46,000.			
1799	37,449	2400.	3000.	4000.	14,000.
1800	5,999	2400.	3250.	4000.	14,000.
1801	44,344	2400.	3000.	4000.	14,000.
1803	15,017	2400.	3250.	4000.	14,000.
1804	3,757	2750.	4000.	5500.	17,500.

Coronet Head

Mintmark

Type: Eagles $10.00 Gold — Coronet Type
Dates of issue: 1838-1907
Designer: Christian Gobrecht
Size: 27 MM
Weight: 16.718 Grams
Composition: 90% Gold & 10% Copper
Fineness: .900
Actual Gold wt.: .4839 Oz. pure Gold

MINT MARKS:
CC Carson City
D Denver
O New Orleans
S San Francisco

Date	Mintage	F-12	VF-20	XF-40	MS-60	Prf-65
1838	7,200	450.	850.	1750.	7500.	—
1839 Lg. Lts.	38,248	450.	800.	1500.	6500.	—

OLD STYLE   NEW STYLE

New Type Liberty Head Introduced

Date	Mintage	F-12	VF-20	XF-40	MS-60	Prf-65
1839 Sm. Lts.	Inc. Ab.	700.	1200.	2000.	8500.	—
1840	47,338	350.	375.	450.	4700.	—
1841	63,131	350.	375.	450.	4700.	—
1841O	2,500	475.	1000.	2200.	6500.	—
1842 Sm. Dt.	81,507	350.	400.	600.	4700.	—
1842 Lg. Dt.	Inc. Ab.	350.	375.	550.	4700.	—
1842O	27,400	375.	400.	500.	4700.	—
1843	75,462	350.	375.	450.	4700.	—
1843O	175,162	350.	375.	450.	4700.	—
1844	6,361	350.	650.	1100.	5500.	—
1844O	118,700	350.	375.	450.	5500.	—
1845	26,153	350.	450.	600.	5500.	—
1845O	47,500	350.	400.	460.	5500.	—
1846	20,095	350.	450.	600.	5500.	—
1846O	81,780	350.	400.	460.	5500.	—
1847	862,258	250.	300.	340.	1915.	—
1847O	571,500	250.	300.	340.	5500.	—

UNITED STATES 1756

Date	Mintage	F-12	VF-20	XF-40	MS-60	Prf-65
1848	145,484	250.	300.	340.	1915.	—
1848O	38,850	400.	600.	1000.	5500.	—
1849	653,618	250.	300.	340.	1915.	—
1849O	23,900	350.	700.	1100.	5000.	—
1850	291,451	250.	300.	340.	1915.	—
1850O	57,500	350.	400.	460.	3600.	—
1851	176,328	250.	300.	340.	1915.	—
1851O	263,000	250.	300.	340.	1915.	—
1852	263,106	350.	400.	460.	2500.	—
1852O	18,000	300.	500.	700.	3600.	—
1853	201,253	250.	300.	340.	1915.	—
1853O	51,000	350.	400.	460.	3600.	—
1854	54,250	350.	400.	460.	3600.	—
1854O	52,500	350.	400.	460.	3600.	—
1854S	123,826	250.	300.	340.	1915.	—
1855	121,701	250.	300.	340.	1915.	—
1855O	18,000	350.	500.	700.	3600.	—
1855S	9,000	450.	950.	1750.	5250.	—
1856	60,490	350.	400.	460.	3600.	—
1856O	14,500	350.	475.	600.	3600.	—
1856S	68,000	350.	400.	600.	3600.	—
1857	16,606	350.	400.	650.	3600.	—
1857O	5,500	550.	1000.	1750.	—	—
1857S	26,000	350.	525.	650.	3600.	—
1858	2,521	2000.	3500.	5250.	—	45,000.
1858O	20,000	350.	400.	500.	3600.	—
1858S	11,800	475.	650.	1200.	3850.	—
1859	16,093	350.	500.	650.	3600.	45,000.
1859O	2,300	1275.	2350.	3500.	—	—
1859S	7,000	700.	1600.	2250.	3600.	—
1860	15,105	350.	475.	600.	3600.	43,000.
1860O	11,100	350.	500.	700.	4500.	—
1860S	5,000	750.	1750.	2500.	6000.	—
1861	113,233	250.	300.	340.	1915.	43,000.
1861S	15,500	400.	600.	1000.	3600.	—
1862	10,995	325.	475.	600.	3600.	43,000.
1862S	12,500	500.	900.	1600.	3600.	—
1863	1,248	2000.	3500.	5000.	9000.	43,000.
1863S	10,000	500.	900.	1500.	—	—
1864	3,580	600.	1200.	1900.	5500.	43,000.
1864S	2,500	2000.	3500.	5250.	—	—
1865	4,005	650.	1000.	1700.	5750.	43,000.
1865S	16,700	450.	925.	1500.	4750.	—
1865S Over Inverted 186	Inc. Ab.		Stack's Sale April 1982 XF 1425.			
1866S	8,500	950.	1650.	2350.	—	—

Motto Added Over Eagle

Date	Mintage	VF-20	XF-40	AU-50	MS-60	MS-65	Prf-65
1866	3,780	600.	1000.	1900.	—	—	43,000.
1866S	11,500	600.	1200.	2000.	—	—	—
1867	3,140	800.	1300.	2000.	—	—	43,000.
1867S	9,000	1400.	2500.	—	—	—	—
1868	10,655	550.	650.	1500.	—	—	43,000.
1868S	13,500	650.	1250.	2000.	—	—	—
1869	1,855	1200.	2000.	3000.	4000.	—	43,000.
1869S	6,430	750.	1250.	2750.	—	—	—
1870	4,025	750.	1250.	2250.	—	—	43,000.
1870CC	5,908	2500.	4250.	8000.	—	—	—
1870S	8,000	700.	1250.	2000.	—	—	—
1871	1,820	1500.	2250.	—	3500.	—	43,000.
1871CC	8,085	850.	1850.	—	—	—	—
1871S	16,500	650.	1200.	—	—	—	—
1872	1,650	1700.	2750.	—	—	—	43,000.
1872CC	4,600	1000.	2100.	—	—	—	—
1872S	17,300	650.	1200.	—	—	—	—
1873 Clsd 3	825	3500.	5250.	—	—	—	50,000.
1873CC	4,543	1400.	2400.	3500.	—	—	—
1873S	12,000	800.	1700.	2750.	—	—	—
1874	53,160	345.	375.	450.	650.	—	43,000.
1874CC	16,767	600.	1400.	2500.	—	—	—
1874S	10,000	700.	1300.	2100.	—	—	—
1875	120		Bowers & Ruddy Sale Oct. 1982				95,000.
1875CC	7,715	1100.	2200.	3500.	—	—	—
1876	732	2250.	4000.	5500.	8500.	—	43,000.
1876CC	4,696	1500.	2500.	3750.	—	—	—
1876S	5,000	800.	1400.	2500.	3500.	—	—
1877	817	2500.	4500.	5250.	7500.	—	43,000.
1877CC	3,332	1700.	2750.	3200.	4000.	—	—
1877S	17,000	550.	900.	1000.	2000.	—	—
1878	73,800	255.	265.	310.	425.	12,000.	43,000.
1878CC	3,244	1700.	2500.	4000.	—	—	—
1878S	26,100	450.	650.	900.	2000.	—	—
1879	384,770	255.	265.	275.	350.	12,000.	43,000.
1879CC	1,762	3700.	5000.	9000.	—	—	—
1879O	1,500	2200.	3500.	4600.	8000.	—	—
1879S	224,000	280.	290.	310.	425.	—	—
1880	1,644,876	215.	225.	230.	280.	11,500.	43,000.
1880CC	11,190	425.	700.	800.	2000.	—	—
1880O	9,200	400.	550.	1000.	1600.	—	—
1880S	506,250	230.	240.	230.	280.	11,500.	—
1881	3,877,260	215.	225.	230.	280.	11,500.	43,000.
1881CC	24,015	400.	500.	750.	1150.	—	—

Date	Mintage	VF-20	XF-40	AU-50	MS-60	MS-65	Prf-65
1881O	8,350	400.	550.	1100.	1700.	—	—
1881S	970,000	215.	225.	230.	280.	11,500.	—
1882	2,324,480	215.	225.	230.	280.	11,500.	43,000.
1882CC	6,764	475.	900.	1200.	2000.	—	—
1882O	10,820	400.	500.	950.	1500.	—	—
1882S	132,000	260.	270.	280.	425.	12,000.	—
1883	208,740	215.	225.	230.	280.	11,500.	43,000.
1883CC	12,000	400.	700.	950.	1600.	—	—
1883O	800	3200.	4200.	6250.	9000.	—	—
1883S	38,000	400.	500.	675.	1000.	12,000.	—
1884	76,905	275.	285.	310.	425.	12,000.	45,000.
1884CC	9,925	450.	750.	1100.	1800.	—	—
1884S	124,250	215.	225.	230.	280.	11,500.	—
1885	253,527	215.	225.	230.	280.	11,500.	43,000.
1885S	228,000	215.	225.	230.	280.	11,500.	—
1886	236,160	215.	225.	230.	280.	11,500.	43,000.
1886S	826,000	215.	225.	230.	280.	11,500.	—
1887	53,680	215.	290.	310.	425.	12,000.	43,000.
1887S	817,000	215.	225.	230.	280.	11,500.	—
1888	132,996	275.	280.	290.	425.	12,000.	43,000.
1888O	21,335	350.	400.	575.	750.	—	—
1888S	648,700	215.	225.	230.	280.	11,500.	—
1889	4,485	400.	450.	500.	800.	—	43,000.
1889S	425,400	215.	225.	230.	280.	11,500.	—
1890	58,043	275.	285.	310.	425.	12,000.	43,000.
1890CC	17,500	275.	450.	600.	950.	—	—
1891	91,868	275.	285.	310.	475.	12,000.	43,000.
1891CC	103,732	360.	450.	600.	950.	—	—
1892	797,552	215.	225.	230.	280.	11,500.	43,000.
1892CC	40,000	375.	600.	775.	950.	—	—
1892O	28,688	330.	375.	425.	650.	—	—
1892S	115,500	275.	285.	310.	425.	12,000.	—
1893	1,840,895	215.	225.	230.	280.	11,500.	43,000.
1893CC	14,000	380.	500.	700.	950.	—	—
1893O	17,000	340.	380.	500.	750.	—	—
1893S	141,350	275.	285.	310.	425.	12,000.	—
1894	2,470,778	215.	225.	230.	280.	11,500.	43,000.
1894O	107,500	275.	285.	310.	425.	12,000.	—
1894S	25,000	470.	600.	800.	1600.	12,000.	—
1895	567,826	215.	225.	230.	280.	11,500.	43,000.
1895O	98,000	275.	285.	310.	425.	12,000.	—
1895S	49,000	400.	600.	800.	1500.	—	—
1896	76,348	215.	225.	230.	280.	11,500.	43,000.
1896S	123,750	215.	225.	230.	280.	11,500.	—
1897	1,000,159	215.	225.	230.	280.	11,500.	43,000.
1897O	42,500	280.	290.	320.	450.	12,000.	—
1897S	234,750	215.	225.	230.	280.	11,500.	—
1898	812,197	215.	225.	230.	280.	11,500.	43,000.
1898S	473,600	215.	225.	230.	280.	11,500.	—
1899	1,262,305	215.	225.	230.	280.	11,500.	43,000.
1899O	37,047	280.	290.	320.	450.	12,000.	—
1899S	841,000	215.	225.	230.	280.	11,500.	—
1900	293,960	215.	225.	230.	280.	11,500.	43,000.
1900S	81,000	280.	290.	320.	450.	10,500.	—
1901	1,718,825	215.	225.	230.	280.	11,500.	43,000.
1901O	72,041	275.	290.	320.	450.	12,000.	—
1901S	2,812,750	215.	225.	230.	280.	11,500.	—
1902	82,513	275.	290.	310.	450.	11,500.	43,000.
1902S	469,500	215.	225.	230.	280.	11,500.	—
1903	125,926	215.	225.	230.	280.	11,500.	43,000.
1903O	112,771	215.	225.	230.	280.	11,500.	—
1903S	538,000	215.	225.	230.	280.	11,500.	—
1904	162,038	215.	225.	230.	280.	11,500.	43,000.
1904O	108,950	215.	225.	230.	280.	11,500.	—
1905	201,078	215.	225.	230.	280.	11,500.	43,000.
1905S	369,250	215.	225.	230.	280.	11,500.	—
1906	165,497	215.	225.	230.	280.	11,500.	43,000.
1906D	981,000	215.	225.	230.	280.	11,500.	—
1906O	86,895	280.	290.	310.	450.	12,000.	—
1906S	457,000	215.	225.	230.	280.	11,500.	—
1907	1,203,973	215.	225.	230.	280.	11,500.	43,000.
1907D	1,030,000	215.	225.	230.	280.	11,500.	—
1907S	210,500	215.	225.	230.	280.	11,500.	—

Indian Head

Mintmark At Point Of Fasces

Type: Eagles — $10.00 Gold — Indian Head
Dates of issue: 1907-1933
Designer: Augustus Saint-Gaudens
Size: 27 MM
Weight: 16.718 Grams
Composition: 90% Gold & 10% Copper
Fineness: .900
Actual Gold wt.: .4839 Oz. pure Gold

MINT MARKS:
D Denver
S San Francisco

Date	Mintage	VF-20	XF-40	AU-50	MS-60	MS-63	MS-65	Prf-65
1907 Wire edge, periods before & after leg.								
	500	—	3000.	—	9500.	15,750.	34,500.	37,500.
1907 Same, without stars on edge								
	—	Unique						
1907 Rolled edge, periods								
	42	—	—	—	—	—	—	—
1907 Without periods								
	239,406	525.	575.	625.	1000.	2400.	12,500.	—
1908 Without motto								
	33,500	535.	585.	750.	950.	3250.	13,000.	—
1908D Without motto								
	210,000	525.	575.	600.	700.	3150.	14,000.	—

IN GOD WE TRUST MOTTO ADDED

Date	Mintage	VF-20	XF-40	AU-50	MS-60	MS-63	MS-65	Prf-65
1908	341,486	425.	435.	445.	575.	2200.	12,000.	40,000.
1908D	836,500	475.	550.	575.	620.	2400.	14,000.	—
1908S	59,850	550.	700.	1250.	3100.	5100.	17,000.	—
1909	184,863	425.	435.	445.	580.	2700.	12,000.	37,500.
1909D	121,540	425.	435.	445.	580.	2300.	12,750.	—
1909S	292,350	475.	550.	600.	875.	3375.	13,000.	—
1910	318,704	425.	435.	445.	550.	1800.	12,000.	37,500.
1910D	2,356,640	425.	435.	445.	550.	1800.	12,000.	—
1910S	811,000	475.	500.	550.	1100.	3000.	14,000.	—
1911	505,595	425.	435.	445.	550.	1800.	12,000.	37,500.
1911D	30,100	550.	800.	950.	5200.	11,000.	37,000.	—
1911S	51,000	475.	500.	575.	2100.	4100.	13,500.	—
1912	405,083	490.	500.	510.	550.	1800.	13,500.	37,500.
1912S	300,000	475.	500.	550.	1575.	3100.	14,000.	—
1913	442,071	425.	435.	445.	550.	1800.	12,000.	38,000.
1913S	66,000	550.	750.	1000.	6900.	15,000.	—	—
1914	151,050	425.	435.	445.	550.	1800.	12,000.	37,500.
1914D	343,500	425.	435.	445.	550.	2200.	12,000.	—
1914S	208,000	430.	500.	575.	660.	2800.	14,000.	—
1915	351,075	425.	435.	445.	550.	2000.	13,000.	38,000.
1915S	59,000	525.	590.	950.	3000.	8000.	69,000.	—
1916S	138,500	490.	500.	700.	1150.	2400.	13,500.	—
1920S	126,500	6500.	8000.	9200.	14,500.	31,000.	75,000.	—
1926	1,014,000	425.	435.	445.	550.	1800.	11,500.	—
1930S	96,000	3500.	5000.	7500.	13,000.	18,500.	29,000.	—
1932	4,463,000	425.	435.	445.	550.	1800.	11,500.	—
1933	312,500	—	—	—	50,000.	73,000.	88,000.	—

DOUBLE EAGLES
Coronet Head

Type: Double Eagles — $20.00 Gold — Coronet
Dates of issue: 1849-1933
Designer: James B. Longacre
Size: 34 MM
Weight: 33.436 Grams
Composition: 90% Gold & 10% Copper
Fineness: .900
Actual Gold wt.: .9677 Oz. pure Gold

MINT MARKS:
CC Carson City
D Denver
O New Orleans
S San Francisco

Mintmark

Date	Mintage	VF-20	XF-40	AU-50	MS-60	MS-65	Prf-65
1849	1	Unique, In U. S. Mint Collection				—	—
1850	1,170,261	530.	575.	705.	2200.	44,000.	—
1850O	141,000	790.	940.	1150.	3750.	—	—
1851	2,087,155	470.	545.	705.	1350.	44,000.	—
1851O	315,000	790.	940.	1150.	3300.	—	—
1852	2,053,026	470.	545.	705.	1350.	44,000.	—
1852O	190,000	790.	940.	1150.	3250.	—	—
1853	1,261,326	470.	545.	705.	1350.	44,000.	—
1853O	71,000	740.	1000.	1800.	3750.	—	—
1854	757,899	470.	545.	705.	1350.	44,000.	—
1854O	3,250	Bowers Ruddy Sale Oct.1982 AU-50 40,000.					
1854S	141,468	550.	810.	1000.	2800.	—	—
1855	364,666	470.	545.	705.	1350.	44,000.	—
1855O	8,000	3000.	4500.	6500.	—	—	—
1855S	879,675	470.	545.	705.	1350.	—	—

Date	Mintage	VF-20	XF-40	AU-50	MS-60	MS-65	Prf-65
1856	329,878	470.	545.	705.	1350.	44,000.	—
1856O	2,250	Bowers Ruddy Sale, Oct.1982 EX-45 45,000.					
1856S	1,189,750	470.	545.	705.	1350.	44,000.	—
1857	439,375	470.	545.	705.	1350.	44,000.	—
1857O	30,000	850.	1300.	2500.	4000.	—	—
1857S	970,500	470.	545.	705.	1350.	44,000.	—
1858	211,714	470.	545.	705.	1350.	44,000.	—
1858O	35,250	850.	1300.	2400.	4000.	—	—
1858S	846,710	470.	545.	705.	1350.	44,000.	—
1859	43,597	900.	1500.	2000.	3500.	—	65,000.
1859O	9,100	2000.	3500.	5000.	7250.	—	—
1859S	636,445	470.	545.	705.	1350.	44,000.	—
1860	577,670	470.	545.	705.	1350.	44,000.	65,000.
1860O	6,600	3000.	4500.	5750.	9000.	—	—
1860S	544,950	470.	545.	705.	1350.	44,000.	—
1861	2,976,453	470.	545.	705.	1350.	44,000.	65,000.
1861 Paquet Rev.	Inc. Ab.	Bowers & Merina Sale, Nov.1988 MS-67 660,000.					—
1861O	17,741	1750.	2500.	3750.	7500.	—	—
1861S	768,000	470.	545.	705.	1350.	44,000.	—
1861S Paquet Rev.	Inc. Ab.	—	—	9500.	—	—	—
1862	92,133	550.	840.	1100.	3500.	—	65,000.
1862S	854,173	470.	545.	705.	1350.	44,000.	—

1861 Paquet Reverse

Date	Mintage	VF-20	XF-40	AU-50	MS-60	MS-65	Prf-65
1863	142,790	530.	900.	1500.	3300.	—	65,000.
1863S	966,570	470.	545.	705.	2000.	44,000.	—
1864	204,285	530.	900.	1500.	3300.	—	65,000.
1864S	793,660	470.	545.	705.	2250.	44,000.	—
1865	351,200	750.	900.	1400.	3200.	—	65,000.
1865S	1,042,500	470.	545.	705.	1350.	44,000.	—
1866S	Inc. Below	740.	1300.	1850.	4000.	—	—

Motto Added Over Eagle

Date	Mintage	VF-20	XF-40	AU-50	MS-60	MS-65	Prf-65
1866	698,775	425.	435.	630.	1500.	—	65,000.
1866S	842,250	425.	435.	630.	1500.	—	—
1867	251,065	425.	435.	590.	630.	—	65,000.
1867S	920,750	425.	435.	630.	1300.	—	—
1868	98,600	425.	435.	630.	1750.	—	65,000.
1868S	837,500	425.	435.	630.	1350.	—	—
1869	175,155	425.	435.	630.	1100.	—	65,000.
1869S	686,750	425.	435.	630.	1100.	—	—
1870	155,185	425.	435.	630.	1050.	—	65,000.
1870CC	3,789	Stacks Sale, Dec. 1988 EF-40 20,900.					—
1870S	982,000	425.	435.	630.	1050.	—	—
1871	80,150	700.	800.	1150.	2000.	—	65,000.
1871CC	17,387	1850.	3000.	3500.	5000.	—	—
1871S	928,000	425.	435.	590.	630.	46,000.	—
1872	251,880	425.	435.	590.	630.	—	65,000.
1872CC	26,900	765.	1000.	2600.	4000.	—	—
1872S	780,000	425.	435.	590.	630.	46,000.	—
1873 Clsd 3	Est. 208,925	750.	825.	950.	1750.	—	65,000.
1873 Open 3	Est. 1,500,900	425.	435.	590.	630.	46,000.	—
1873CC	22,410	800.	1300.	1750.	2800.	—	—
1873S	1,040,600	425.	435.	590.	630.	46,000.	—
1874	366,800	425.	435.	590.	630.	46,000.	65,000.
1874CC	115,085	665.	700.	1200.	1750.	—	—
1874S	1,214,000	425.	435.	590.	630.	46,000.	—
1875	295,740	670.	700.	785.	880.	46,000.	75,000.
1875CC	111,151	730.	900.	1200.	1800.	—	—
1875S	1,230,000	425.	435.	590.	630.	46,000.	—
1876	583,905	425.	435.	590.	630.	46,000.	65,000.
1876CC	138,441	675.	800.	900.	1250.	—	—
1876S	1,597,000	425.	435.	590.	630.	46,000.	—

Twenty Dollars Spelled Out

Date	Mintage	VF-20	XF-40	AU-50	MS-60	MS-65	Prf-65
1877	397,670	425.	435.	450.	500.	10,500.	65,000.
1877CC	42,565	800.	850.	1150.	2500.	—	—
1877S	1,735,000	425.	435.	450.	500.	10,500.	—
1878	543,645	425.	435.	450.	500.	10,500.	65,000.
1878CC	13,180	800.	850.	1250.	2750.	—	—
1878S	1,739,000	425.	435.	450.	500.	10,500.	—
1879	207,630	425.	435.	450.	500.	10,500.	65,000.
1879CC	10,708	850.	1500.	2250.	3750.	—	—
1879O	2,325	2500.	3500.	4750.	8000.	—	—
1879S	1,223,800	425.	435.	450.	500.	10,500.	—
1880	51,456	575.	590.	600.	750.	—	65,000.
1880S	836,000	425.	435.	450.	500.	10,500.	—
1881	2,260	2500.	4500.	7500.	14,000.	—	65,000.
1881S	727,000	425.	435.	450.	500.	10,500.	—
1882	630	8000.	15,000.	23,500.	35,000.	—	65,000.
1882CC	39,140	750.	800.	950.	1500.	—	—
1882S	1,125,000	425.	435.	450.	500.	10,500.	—
1883	92	Bowers Ruddy Sale Oct.1982 Prf-67 80,000.					
1883CC	59,962	750.	800.	950.	1500.	—	—
1883S	1,189,000	425.	435.	450.	500.	10,500.	—
1884	71	Bowers Ruddy Sale Oct. 1982					75,000.
1884CC	81,139	750.	800.	950.	1500.	—	—
1884S	916,000	425.	435.	450.	500.	10,500.	—
1885	828	6000.	10,000.	15,000.	27,500.	—	65,000.
1885CC	9,450	1000.	1500.	2250.	3500.	—	—
1885S	683,500	425.	435.	450.	500.	10,500.	—
1886	1,106	5000.	10,000.	13,500.	22,000.	—	65,000.
1887	121	Bowers Ruddy Sale Oct. 1982					42,500.
1887S	283,000	425.	435.	450.	500.	10,500.	—
1888	226,266	425.	435.	450.	500.	10,500.	65,000.
1888S	859,600	425.	435.	450.	500.	10,500.	—
1889	44,111	700.	735.	850.	1000.	—	65,000.
1889CC	30,945	850.	900.	1050.	1450.	—	—
1889S	774,700	425.	435.	450.	500.	10,500.	—
1890	75,995	690.	725.	750.	875.	—	65,000.
1890CC	91,209	710.	800.	910.	1125.	—	—
1890S	802,750	425.	435.	450.	500.	10,500.	—
1891	1,442	2500.	3500.	5000.	8500.	—	65,000.
1891CC	5,000	1900.	2500.	3200.	5500.	—	—
1891S	1,288,125	425.	435.	450.	500.	10,500.	—
1892	4,523	1200.	1750.	2400.	5000.	—	65,000.
1892CC	27,265	840.	1000.	1500.	2150.	—	—
1892S	930,150	425.	435.	450.	500.	10,500.	—
1893	344,339	425.	435.	450.	500.	10,500.	65,000.
1893CC	18,402	840.	1050.	1600.	2800.	—	—
1893S	996,175	425.	435.	450.	500.	10,500.	—
1894	1,368,990	425.	435.	450.	500.	10,500.	65,000.
1894S	1,048,550	425.	435.	450.	500.	10,500.	—
1895	1,114,656	425.	435.	450.	500.	10,500.	65,000.
1895S	1,143,500	425.	435.	450.	500.	10,500.	—
1896	792,663	425.	435.	450.	500.	10,500.	65,000.
1896S	1,403,925	425.	435.	450.	500.	10,500.	—
1897	1,383,261	425.	435.	450.	500.	10,500.	65,000.
1897S	1,470,250	425.	435.	450.	500.	10,500.	—
1898	170,470	425.	435.	450.	500.	10,500.	65,000.
1898S	2,575,175	425.	435.	450.	500.	10,500.	—
1899	1,669,384	425.	435.	450.	500.	10,500.	65,000.
1899S	2,010,300	425.	435.	450.	500.	10,500.	—
1900	1,874,584	425.	435.	450.	500.	10,500.	65,000.
1900S	2,459,500	425.	435.	450.	500.	10,500.	—
1901	111,526	425.	435.	450.	500.	10,500.	65,000.
1901S	1,596,000	425.	435.	450.	500.	10,500.	—
1902	31,254	740.	780.	810.	1025.	—	65,000.
1902S	1,753,625	425.	435.	450.	500.	10,500.	—
1903	287,428	425.	435.	450.	500.	10,500.	65,000.
1903S	954,000	425.	435.	450.	500.	10,500.	—
1904	6,256,797	425.	435.	450.	500.	10,500.	65,000.
1904S	5,134,175	425.	435.	450.	500.	10,500.	—
1905	59,011	600.	640.	800.	925.	—	65,000.
1905S	1,813,000	425.	435.	450.	500.	10,500.	—
1906	69,690	600.	640.	800.	925.	—	65,000.
1906D	620,250	425.	435.	450.	500.	10,500.	—
1906S	2,065,750	425.	435.	450.	500.	10,500.	—
1907	1,451,864	425.	435.	450.	500.	10,500.	65,000.
1907D	842,250	425.	435.	450.	500.	10,500.	—
1907S	2,165,800	425.	435.	450.	500.	10,500.	—

Saint-Gaudens

Roman Numeral Date — High Relief

Date	Mintage	VF-20	XF-40	AU-50	MS-60	MS-63	MS-65	Prf-65
1907 Extremely High Relief, Plain Edge								
					Unique			
1907 Extremely High Relief, Lettered Edge								
Unrecorded Bowers Ruddy Sale Oct.1982 Prf-67 220,000.								
1907 High Relief, Roman Numerals, Plain Edge								
					Rare			
1907 High Relief, Roman Numerals, Wire Rim								
	11,250	2500.	4850.	6500.	8000.	14,500.	39,000.	—
1907 High Relief, Roman Numerals, Flat Rim								
	Inc. Ab.	2500.	4850.	6500.	8000.	14,500.	39,000.	—

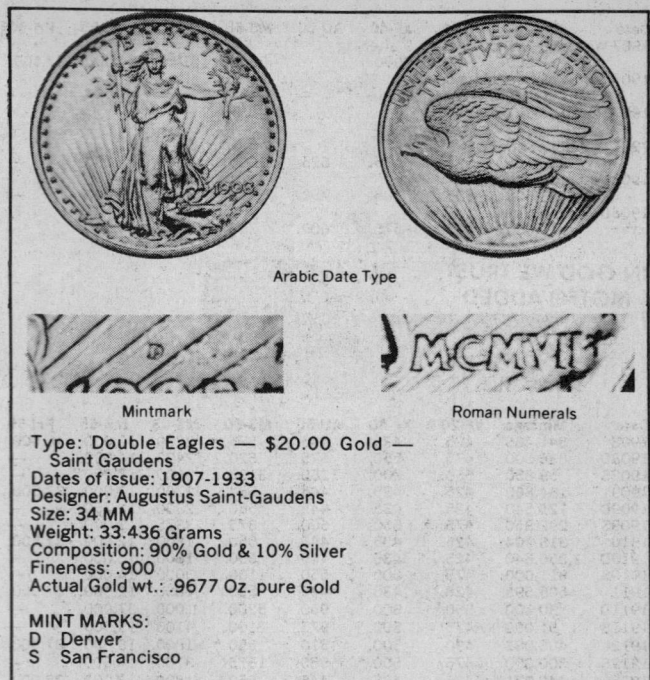

Arabic Date Type

Mintmark   Roman Numerals

Type: Double Eagles — $20.00 Gold —
  Saint Gaudens
Dates of issue: 1907-1933
Designer: Augustus Saint-Gaudens
Size: 34 MM
Weight: 33.436 Grams
Composition: 90% Gold & 10% Silver
Fineness: .900
Actual Gold wt.: .9677 Oz. pure Gold

MINT MARKS:
D   Denver
S   San Francisco

Date	Mintage	VF-20	XF-40	AU-50	MS-60	MS-63	MS-65	Prf-65
1907 Large Letters On Edge					Unique		—	—
1907 Small Letters On Edge								
	361,667	440.	445.	515.	600.	1125.	4350.	—
1908	4,271,551	440.	445.	515.	550.	920.	3800.	—
1908D	663,750	440.	445.	515.	700.	1250.	5750.	—

IN GOD WE TRUST

Date	Mintage	VF-20	XF-40	AU-50	MS-60	MS-63	MS-65	Prf-65
1908	156,359	440.	445.	515.	620.	1250.	7150.	47,500.
1908D	349,500	440.	445.	515.	620.	1325.	4800.	—
1908S	22,000	800.	1000.	1300.	3200.	5300.	20,000.	—
1909/8	161,282	500.	525.	550.	710.	1725.	12,500.	—
1909	Inc. Ab.	440.	445.	535.	740.	1575.	12,500.	47,500.
1909D	52,500	700.	800.	900.	2300.	5600.	16,000.	—
1909S	2,774,925	440.	445.	525.	590.	1050.	4700.	—
1910	482,167	440.	445.	525.	590.	1050.	7900.	47,500.
1910D	429,000	440.	445.	525.	590.	1125.	4100.	—
1910S	2,128,250	440.	445.	525.	590.	1150.	7000.	—
1911	197,350	440.	475.	535.	610.	1350.	12,000.	47,500.
1911D	846,500	440.	475.	535.	570.	920.	4000.	—
1911S	775,750	440.	475.	535.	610.	1050.	4500.	—
1912	149,824	440.	445.	535.	610.	1500.	14,000.	47,500.
1913	168,838	440.	445.	580.	610.	1550.	14,000.	47,500.
1913D	393,500	440.	445.	525.	590.	1150.	5500.	—
1913S	34,000	440.	445.	580.	1150.	2150.	13,500.	—
1914	95,320	440.	445.	580.	600.	1450.	17,000.	47,500.
1914D	453,000	440.	445.	525.	580.	1000.	4650.	—
1914S	1,498,000	440.	445.	525.	580.	930.	4000.	—
1915	152,050	440.	445.	580.	660.	1725.	14,000.	47,500.
1915S	567,500	440.	445.	525.	575.	930.	3850.	—
1916S	796,000	440.	445.	525.	575.	1200.	3850.	—
1920	228,250	440.	445.	580.	610.	1375.	11,000.	—
1920S	558,000	5000.	8500.	10,000.	14,750.	20,000.	51,000.	—
1921	528,500	8000.	12,000.	15,000.	21,000.	30,000.	69,000.	—
1922	1,375,500	440.	445.	455.	575.	920.	8000.	—
1922S	2,658,000	550.	650.	860.	1200.	2600.	8800.	—
1923	566,000	440.	445.	455.	525.	850.	7500.	—
1923D	1,702,250	560.	585.	610.	590.	1000.	4000.	—
1924	4,323,500	440.	445.	455.	525.	850.	3850.	—
1924D	3,049,500	700.	900.	1100.	1800.	3500.	31,000.	—
1924S	2,927,500	700.	900.	1100.	1950.	3100.	17,500.	—
1925	2,831,750	440.	445.	455.	525.	850.	3850.	—
1925D	2,938,500	875.	1150.	1400.	2200.	3200.	17,500.	—
1925S	3,776,500	875.	1150.	1400.	2300.	5750.	23,000.	—
1926	816,750	440.	445.	455.	525.	850.	3850.	—
1926D	481,000	1000.	1200.	1600.	2400.	4200.	20,000.	—
1926S	2,041,500	875.	1100.	1300.	1750.	2700.	10,500.	—
1927	2,946,750	440.	445.	455.	525.	850.	3850.	—
1927D	180,000	Stacks Sale Oct.1985 MS-65 275,000.						
1927S	3,107,000	2750.	4500.	5750.	8600.	15,000.	35,000.	—
1928	8,816,000	440.	445.	455.	525.	850.	3850.	—
1929	1,779,750	1750.	4500.	5500.	8000.	10,500.	25,000.	—
1930S	74,000	6000.	10,000.	12,750.	14,500.	20,000.	44,000.	—
1931	2,938,250	4250.	7500.	10,500.	12,000.	21,500.	36,000.	—
1931D	106,500	3750.	7250.	9750.	15,000.	19,000.	42,000.	—
1932	1,101,750	5000.	9000.	11,250.	15,500.	22,000.	47,000.	—
1933	445,500	None placed in circulation						

COMMEMORATIVES

Quarter

Date	Event	Mintage	AU-50	MS-60	MS-63	MS-64	MS-65
1893	Isabella Quarter	24,214	180.	390.	790.	1700.	5100.

Dollar

Date	Event	Mintage	AU-50	MS-60	MS-63	MS-64	MS-65
1900	Lafayette Dollar	36,026	250.	680.	2500.	5900.	16,000.

Half dollars

2x2 ADDED

Date	Event	Mintage	AU-50	MS-60	MS-63	MS-64	MS-65
1921	Alabama 2X2	6,006	125.	270.	510.	2500.	7100.
1921	Alabama	59,038	74.00	200.	410.	2500.	7300.

Date	Event	Mintage	AU-50	MS-60	MS-63	MS-64	MS-65
1936	Albany	17,671	265.	295.	370.	680.	1350.

Date	Event	Mintage	AU-50	MS-60	MS-63	MS-64	MS-65
1937	Antietam	18,028	340.	405.	540.	650.	1000.
1935	Arkansas PDS Set	5,505	—	255.	340.	1100.	3300.

Date	Event	Mintage	AU-50	MS-60	MS-63	MS-64	MS-65
1936	Arkansas PDS Set	9,660	—	255.	340.	1100.	3300.

Date	Event	Mintage	AU-50	MS-60	MS-63	MS-64	MS-65
1937	Arkansas PDS Set	5,505	—	270.	340.	1100.	3300.
1938	Arkansas PDS Set	3,155	—	430.	540.	1400.	3850.
1939	Arkansas PDS Set	2,104	—	840.	1000.	2500.	5750.
	Arkansas - Type Coin	—	74.00	85.00	115.	370.	1100.

See Also Robinson-Arkansas

Date	Event	Mintage	AU-50	MS-60	MS-63	MS-64	MS-65
1936	Bay Bridge	71,424	100.	180.	200.	280.	760.

1934 ADDED

Date	Event	Mintage	AU-50	MS-60	MS-63	MS-64	MS-65
1934	Boone	10,007	100.	115.	125.	200.	590.
1935	Boone - PDS Set w/1934	5,005	—	900.	1000.	1450.	2750.
1935	Boone - PDS Set	2,003	—	340.	370.	600.	1950.
1936	Boone - PDS Set	5,005	—	340.	370.	600.	1800.
1937	Boone - PDS Set	2,506	—	630.	730.	850.	2050.
1938	Boone - PDS Set	2,100	—	1050.	1200.	1600.	2400.
	Boone - Type Coin	—	96.00	115.	125.	200.	590.

Date	Event	Mintage	AU-50	MS-60	MS-63	MS-64	MS-65
1936	Bridgeport	25,015	125.	145.	170.	340.	1150.

Date	Event	Mintage	AU-50	MS-60	MS-63	MS-64	MS-65
1925S	California Jubilee	86,594	120.	140.	350.	540.	1800.

Date	Event	Mintage	AU-50	MS-60	MS-63	MS-64	MS-65
1936	Cincinnati - PDS Set	5,005	—	930.	1050.	1500.	7650.
1936	Cincinnati - Type Coin	—	280.	315.	350.	500.	1900.

COMMEMORATIVES

Date	Event	Mintage	AU-50	MS-60	MS-63	MS-64	MS-65
1936	Cleveland - Great Lakes	50,030	79.00	95.00	125.	230.	1150.

Date	Event	Mintage	AU-50	MS-60	MS-63	MS-64	MS-65
1936	Gettysburg	26,928	215.	255.	345.	480.	1650.

STAR ADDED

Date	Event	Mintage	AU-50	MS-60	MS-63	MS-64	MS-65
1936	Columbia PDS Set	9,007	—	840.	1000.	1100.	1850.
1936	Columbia - Type Coin	—	270.	280.	325.	360.	620.

Date	Event	Mintage	AU-50	MS-60	MS-63	MS-64	MS-65
1922	Grant-With Star	4,256	315.	630.	1800.	4950.	16,000.
1922	Grant	67,405	79.00	100.	370.	650.	2400.

Date	Event	Mintage	AU-50	MS-60	MS-63	MS-64	MS-65
1892	Columbian Expo	950,000	20.00	51.00	265.	930.	3350.
1893	Columbian Expo	1,550,405	12.50	51.00	265.	955.	4500.

Date	Event	Mintage	AU-50	MS-60	MS-63	MS-64	MS-65
1928	Hawaiian	10,008	675.	790.	1400.	2750.	10,150.

Date	Event	Mintage	AU-50	MS-60	MS-63	MS-64	MS-65
1935	Connecticut	25,018	205.	240.	315.	480.	1350.

Date	Event	Mintage	AU-50	MS-60	MS-63	MS-64	MS-65
1935	Hudson	10,008	395.	510.	650.	1450.	4550.

Date	Event	Mintage	AU-50	MS-60	MS-63	MS-64	MS-65
1936	Delaware	20,993	200.	255.	305.	450.	1350.

Date	Event	Mintage	AU-50	MS-60	MS-63	MS-64	MS-65
1924	Huguenot-Walloon	142,080	68.00	100.	240.	565.	2250.

Date	Event	Mintage	AU-50	MS-60	MS-63	MS-64	MS-65
1936	Elgin	20,015	270.	280.	305.	430.	900.

Date	Event	Mintage	AU-50	MS-60	MS-63	MS-64	MS-65
1918	Lincoln-Illinois	100,058	74.00	115.	180.	480.	1550.

Date	Event	Mintage	AU-50	MS-60	MS-63	MS-64	MS-65
1946	Iowa	100,057	79.00	90.00	140.	150.	390.

Date	Event	Mintage	AU-50	MS-60	MS-63	MS-64	MS-65
1925	Lexington-Concord	162,013	48.00	56.00	140.	480.	2100.

Date	Event	Mintage	AU-50	MS-60	MS-63	MS-64	MS-65
1936	Long Island	81,826	79.00	90.00	125.	280.	1450.

Date	Event	Mintage	AU-50	MS-60	MS-63	MS-64	MS-65
1936	Lynchburg	20,013	195.	215.	250.	370.	1050.

Date	Event	Mintage	AU-50	MS-60	MS-63	MS-64	MS-65
1920	Maine	50,028	70.00	100.	270.	560.	2400.

Date	Event	Mintage	AU-50	MS-60	MS-63	MS-64	MS-65
1934	Maryland	25,015	130.	150.	215.	390.	1200.

UNITED STATES 1761

2★4 ADDED

Date	Event	Mintage	AU-50	MS-60	MS-63	MS-64	MS-65
1921	Missouri - 2★4	5,000	200.	395.	1000.	2500.	8800.
1921	Missouri	15,428	170.	370.	750.	2500.	9900.

Date	Event	Mintage	AU-50	MS-60	MS-63	MS-64	MS-65
1923S	Monroe	274,077	22.50	51.00	235.	1300.	4600.

Date	Event	Mintage	AU-50	MS-60	MS-63	MS-64	MS-65
1938	New Rochelle	15,266	370.	405.	450.	480.	1000.

Date	Event	Mintage	AU-50	MS-60	MS-63	MS-64	MS-65
1936	Norfolk	16,936	540.	595.	620.	680.	750.

Date	Event	Mintage	AU-50	MS-60	MS-63	MS-64	MS-65
1926	Oregon	47,955	90.00	100.	180.	240.	680.
1926S	Oregon	83,055	90.00	100.	180.	240.	590.
1928	Oregon	6,028	130.	195.	240.	340.	1150.
1933D	Oregon	5,008	165.	215.	280.	370.	1200.
1934D	Oregon	7,006	115.	195.	270.	370.	1250.
1936	Oregon	10,006	115.	150.	195.	280.	590.
1936S	Oregon	5,006	125.	200.	250.	370.	600.
1937D	Oregon	12,008	108.	120.	195.	255.	590.
1938	Oregon - PDS Set	6,005	—	510.	675.	1000.	1850.
1939	Oregon - PDS Set	3,004	—	1200.	1600.	1950.	2900.
	Oregon - Type Coin	—	90.00	100.	180.	240.	590.

Date	Event	Mintage	AU-50	MS-60	MS-63	MS-64	MS-65
1915S	Panama - Pacific	27,134	180.	315.	930.	2100.	4650.

Date	Event	Mintage	AU-50	MS-60	MS-63	MS-64	MS-65
1926	Sesquicentennial	141,120	51.00	56.00	255.	1550.	6250.

1921 VERSION

Date	Event	Mintage	AU-50	MS-60	MS-63	MS-64	MS-65
1920	Pilgrim	152,112	41.50	53.00	140.	370.	1650.
1921	Pilgrim	20,053	79.00	120.	200.	590.	2250.

Date	Event	Mintage	AU-50	MS-60	MS-63	MS-64	MS-65
1935	Spanish Trail	10,008	575.	730.	820.	1100.	2050.

Date	Event	Mintage	AU-50	MS-60	MS-63	MS-64	MS-65
1936	Rhode Island - PDS Set	15,010	—	330.	390.	1000.	3650.
1936	Rhode Island - Type Coin	—	96.00	120.	125.	340.	1200.

Date	Event	Mintage	AU-50	MS-60	MS-63	MS-64	MS-65
1925	Stone Mountain	1,314,709	26.00	34.00	70.00	145.	650.

Date	Event	Mintage	AU-50	MS-60	MS-63	MS-64	MS-65
1937	Roanoke	29,030	215.	240.	280.	310.	750.

Date	Event	Mintage	AU-50	MS-60	MS-63	MS-64	MS-65
1934	Texas	61,463	110.	130.	195.	240.	540.
1935	Texas - PDS Set	9,994	—	390.	580.	700.	1600.
1936	Texas - PDS Set	8,911	—	390.	580.	700.	1600.
1937	Texas - PDS Set	6,571	—	430.	580.	700.	1600.
1938	Texas - PDS Set	3,775	—	590.	750.	950.	2050.
	Texas - Type Coins	—	110.	130.	195.	240.	540.

Date	Event	Mintage	AU-50	MS-60	MS-63	MS-64	MS-65
1936	Robinson-Arkansas	25,265	90.00	100.	145.	280.	1300.

(See Also Arkansas)

Date	Event	Mintage	AU-50	MS-60	MS-63	MS-64	MS-65
1925	Ft. Vancouver	14,994	200.	370.	450.	820.	2800.

Date	Event	Mintage	AU-50	MS-60	MS-63	MS-64	MS-65
1935S	San Diego	70,132	79.00	96.00	140.	155.	390.
1936D	San Diego	30,092	85.00	105.	145.	170.	450.

Date	Event	Mintage	AU-50	MS-60	MS-63	MS-64	MS-65
1927	Vermont	28,142	155.	200.	280.	620.	2400.

Date	Event	Mintage	AU-50	MS-60	MS-63	MS-64	MS-65
1946	B.T.W. - PDS Set	200,113	—	34.00	54.00	90.00	510.
1947	B.T.W. - PDS Set	100,017	—	44.00	65.00	90.00	590.
1948	B.T.W. - PDS Set	8,005	—	75.00	125.	280.	540.
1949	B.T.W. - PDS Set	6,004	—	90.00	140.	315.	600.
1950	B.T.W. - PDS Set	6,004	—	90.00	120.	225.	590.
1951	B.T.W. - PDS Set	7,004	—	75.00	100.	215.	560.
	B.T.W. - Type Coin	—	10.00	11.50	18.00	30.00	170.

Date	Event	Mintage	AU-50	MS-60	MS-63	MS-64	MS-65
1951	Wash.-Carv. - PDS Set	10,004	—	50.00	90.00	150.	1800.
1952	Wash.-Carv. - PDS Set	8,006	—	50.00	90.00	200.	2050.
1953	Wash.-Carv. - PDS Set	8,003	—	70.00	90.00	200.	2250.
1954	Wash.-Carv. - PDS Set	12,006	—	51.00	90.00	150.	2250.
	Wash.-Carver - Type Coin	—	10.00	12.50	19.50	40.00	340.

Date	Event	Mintage	AU-50	MS-60	MS-63	MS-64	MS-65
1936	Wisconsin	25,015	225.	250.	280.	380.	650.

Date	Event	Mintage	AU-50	MS-60	MS-63	MS-64	MS-65
1936	York County	25,015	200.	225.	280.	370.	650.

Gold dollars

Date	Event	Mintage	AU-50	MS-60	MS-63	MS-64	MS-65
1903	Louisiana, Jefferson	17,500	350.	760.	2150.	2850.	5900.
1903	Louisiana, McKinley	17,500	350.	760.	2050.	2850.	6050.

Date	Event	Mintage	AU-50	MS-60	MS-63	MS-64	MS-65
1904	Lewis and Clark Expo.	10,025	470.	1250.	4600.	6050.	14,900.
1905	Lewis and Clark Expo.	10,041	470.	1250.	5250.	8550.	20,600.

Date	Event	Mintage	AU-50	MS-60	MS-63	MS-64	MS-65
1915S	Pan-Pacific Expo.	15,000	325.	700.	1650.	2800.	5750.

Date	Event	Mintage	AU-50	MS-60	MS-63	MS-64	MS-65
1916	McKinley Memorial	9,977	325.	760.	1750.	2800.	5950.
1917	McKinley Memorial	10,000	350.	820.	2100.	2850.	6750.

Date	Event	Mintage	AU-50	MS-60	MS-63	MS-64	MS-65
1922	Grant Mem. w/o star	5,016	1750.	1800.	3750.	4700.	6800.
1922	Grant Mem. w/star	5,000	1750.	1800.	3900.	4850.	6800.

Gold Two And A Half Dollars

Date	Event	Mintage	AU-50	MS-60	MS-63	MS-64	MS-65
1915S	Pan-Pacific Expo.	6,749	880.	1800.	4200.	5300.	8950.

Date	Event	Mintage	AU-50	MS-60	MS-63	MS-64	MS-65
1926	Philadelphia Sesqui.	46,019	295.	620.	1230.	2350.	15,800.

Gold Fifty Dollars

Date	Event	Mintage	AU-50	MS-60	MS-63	MS-64	MS-65
1915S	Pan-Pacific Expo., Round	483	20,500.	30,000.	44,500.	59,500.	105,500.
1915S	Pan-Pacific Expo., Octagon	645	16,000.	22,000.	37,500.	50,500.	93,500.

MODERN COMMEMORATIVES
Half Dollars

Date	Mintage	(Proof)	MS-65	Prf-65
1982D Geo.Wash.	2,210,502	—	11.00	—
1982S Geo.Wash.	—	(4,894,044)	—	11.00

Date	Mintage	(Proof)	MS-65	Prf-65
1986D Statue of Liberty	—	—	7.00	—
1986S Statue of Liberty	—	—	—	8.00
1989D Congress	—	—	—	—

Silver Dollars

Date	Mintage	(Proof)	MS-65	Prf-65
1983P Olympic	294,543	—	25.00	—
1983D Olympic	174,014	—	42.00	—
1983S Olympic	174,014	(1,577,025)	28.00	24.00

Date	Mintage	(Proof)	MS-65	Prf-65
1984P Olympic	217,954	—	24.00	—
1984D Olympic	116,675	—	90.00	—
1984S Olympic	116,675	(1,801,210)	69.00	25.00

Date	Mintage	(Proof)	MS-65	Prf-65
1986P Statue of Liberty	—	—	24.00	—
1986S Statue of Liberty	—	—	—	28.00

Date	Mintage	(Proof)	MS-65	Prf-65
1987P Constitution	—	—	16.00	—
1987S Constitution	—	—	—	20.00
1988D Olympic	—	—	30.00	—
1988S Olympic	—	—	—	35.00
1989D Congress	—	—	—	—
1989S Congress	—	—	—	—

Half Eagles

Date	Mintage	(Proof)	MS-65	Prf-65
1986W Statue of Liberty	—	—	230.	220.

Date	Mintage	(Proof)	MS-65	Prf-65
1987W Constitution	—	—	150.	150.
1988W Olympic	—	—	210.	220.
1989W Congress	—	—	—	—

Eagles

Date	Mintage	(Proof)	MS-65	Prf-65
1984W Olympic	75,886	(381,085)	295.	260.
1984P Olympic	33,309	—	—	610.
1984D Olympic	34,533	—	—	385.
1984S Olympic	48,551	—	—	310.

COIN SETS

Olympic

Date	Price
1983 & 1984 Proof Dollars.	51.00
1983 & 1984 6 Coin Set. One 1983 and one 1984 uncirculated and proof dollar. One uncirculated and one proof $10 gold piece.	690.
1983 Collectors Set- 1983 PDS uncirculated dollars.	100.
1984 Collectors Set- 1984 PDS uncirculated dollars.	185.
1983 Silver Proof dollar in case.	26.00
1984 Silver Proof dollar in case.	27.00
1983 & 1984 Gold and Silver Proof Set. One 1983 and one 1984 proof dollar and one 1984 proof $10 gold piece.	275.

Statue of Liberty

Date	Price
1986 2 Coin set: Proof silver dollar and clad half dollar.	38.00
1986 3 Coin set: Proof silver dollar, clad half dollar and half eagle.	265.
1986 2 Coin set: Uncirculated silver dollar and clad half dollar.	33.00
1986 3 Coin set: Uncirculated silver dollar, clad half dollar and half eagle.	305.
1986 6 Coin set: 1 each of the proof and uncirculated issues.	645.

Constitution

Date	Price
1987 2 Coin set: Uncirculated silver dollar and half eagle.	155.
1987 2 Coin set: Proof silver dollar and half eagle.	157.
1987 4 Coin set: 1 each of the proof and uncirculated issues.	314.

AMERICAN EAGLES

Prices based on $393.00 spot gold.

The American Eagle gold coin series was minted to compete with other bullion coins of the world. The weight of 1, 1/2, 1/4 and 1/10th ounce indicates the total gold weight of the coin. The composition of all four gold bullion coins is an alloy containing 91.67 percent gold, 3.0 percent silver, and 5.33 percent copper.

Fifty Dollars - 1 oz

Date	Mintage	Unc	Prf.
1986	1,362,650	400.	—
1986W	446,290	—	480.
1987	1,045,500	400.	—
1987W	147,498	—	500.
1988	465,000	400.	—
1988W	87,133	—	700.
1989	—	—	—
1989W	—	—	—

Twenty Five Dollars - 1/2 oz

Date	Mintage	Unc	Prf.
1986	599,566	207.50	—
1987	131,255	207.50	—
1987P	143,398	—	240.
1988	45,000	218.	—
1988P	76,528	—	340.
1989	—	—	—
1989P	—	—	—

Ten Dollars - 1/4 oz

Date	Mintage	Unc	Prf.
1986	726,031	107.25	—
1987	269,255	107.25	—
1988	49,000	140.00	—
1988P	98,028	—	180.
1989	—	—	—
1989P	—	—	—

Five Dollars - 1/10 oz

Date	Mintage	Unc	Prf.
1986	912,609	45.50	—
1987	580,266	45.50	—
1988	159,500	45.50	—
1988P	143,881	—	70.00
1989	—	—	—
1989P	—	—	—

SILVER EAGLES

Prices based on $6.03 spot silver

The Silver American Eagle like the gold Eagles was struck primarily to compete with other bullion coins. The $1.00 face value coin contains one troy ounce of .999 fine silver and .001 troy ounces of copper.

1 Dollar - 1 oz

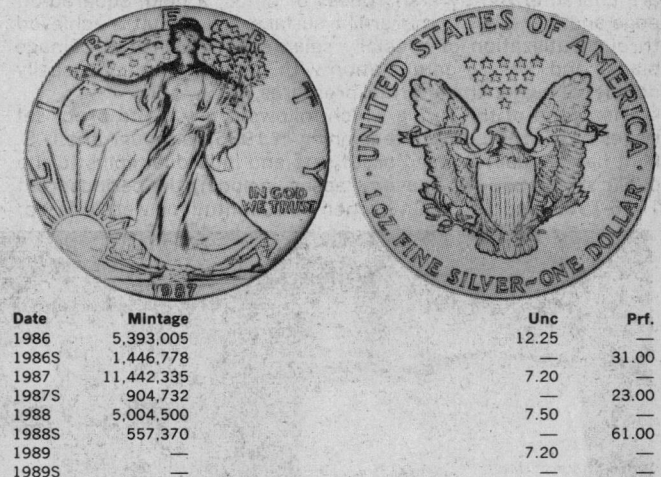

Date	Mintage	Unc	Prf.
1986	5,393,005	12.25	—
1986S	1,446,778	—	31.00
1987	11,442,335	7.20	—
1987S	904,732	—	23.00
1988	5,004,500	7.50	—
1988S	557,370	—	61.00
1989	—	7.20	—
1989S	—	—	—

MINT SETS

Mint sets by definition consist of one uncirculated coin of each denomination, from each mint, produced during a given year. In the following listing the production figures and valuations indicated are for "official" sets assembled and sold to collectors by the Treasury's Bureau of the Mint. Official Mint-assembled sets through 1958 actually contained two examples of each coin of regular issue mounted in cardboard holders that caused the coins to tarnish. Commencing in 1959, the Treasury's sets, packaged in sealed pliofilm packets, include only one specimen of each coin struck for the year.

During the years 1965-1967 when the Mint was offering neither mint nor proof sets, it made available "Special Mint Sets." The quality of the 1965 sets in pliofilm packets was quite low, but an improvement was made in 1966-1967 when the sets were offered in plastic cases, and possessed a proof-like appearance. The Mint renewed the offering of officially packaged mint sets in 1968, and continued to the present, excepting the years 1982-1983, during which time the issue of officially packaged sets was again suspended.

Date	Sets Sold	Issue Price	Value
1947	(Est.) 5,000	4.87	820.
1948	(Est.) 6,000	4.92	230.
1949	(Est.) 5,200	5.45	755.
1950	None Issued		
1951	8,654	6.75	380.
1952	11,499	6.14	250.
1953	15,538	6.14	225.
1954	52,599	6.19	130.
1955	49,656	3.57	78.00
1956	45,475	3.34	62.00
1957	32,324	4.40	84.00
1958	50,315	4.43	81.00
1959	187,000	2.40	22.00
1960	260,485	2.40	17.50
1961	223,704	2.40	19.50
1962	385,285	2.40	23.00
1963	606,622	2.40	21.00
1964	978,157	2.40	14.50
1965 SMS	2,360,000	4.00	12.90
1966 SMS	2,261,583	4.00	8.80
1967 SMS	1,863,344	4.00	16.40
1968	2,105,128	2.50	6.30
1969	1,306,723	2.50	16.40
1970 Lg. date	2,150,000	2.50	21.00
1970 Sm. date	Inc. Ab.	2.50	24.00
1971	2,193,396	3.50	5.30
1972	2,750,000	3.50	5.45
1973	1,767,691	6.00	11.00
1974	1,975,981	6.00	8.25
1975	1,921,488	6.00	7.85
1976 3 pc.	4,908,319	9.00	13.00
1976	1,892,513	6.00	8.25
1977	2,006,869	7.00	8.25
1978	2,162,609	7.00	8.25
1979 No "S" Dollar	2,526,000	8.00	6.60
1980	2,813,118	9.00	7.00
1981	2,908,145	11.00	10.50
1982 & 1983	None issued	—	—
1984	1,832,857	7.00	10.80
1985	1,710,571	7.00	13.60
1986	1,153,536	7.00	40.00
1987	2,890,758	7.00	13.30
1988		7.00	9.10
1989		7.00	10.80

PROOF SETS

Proof sets are composed of specially struck coins representing the ultimate in the minter's art. Proof coins — the term relates to the method of manufacture, not the condition of the coin — are characterized by a sharpness of detail, a bold, squared-off edge and, generally, a mirror-like surface. This result is achieved through utilization of specially selected and polished coinage blanks and dies, in combination with multiple striking (usually double) at higher-than-normal pressures.

The scope of the listing which follows is limited to proof set issues of the modern era (beginning in 1936), although the U.S. Mint has annually offered proof sets and individual coins to the public since 1858, with several lapses, including the periods from 1916-1935, and 1943-1949, when no substitutions were offered, and 1965-1967, when the Mint prepared "Special Mint Sets" in lieu of both their conventional proof and uncirculated coin set offerings. Valuations for the earlier proof coins are incorporated in the regular date listings in this guide.

The proof issued since 1936 are generally termed "brilliant proofs," most of the individual coins possessing uniformly brilliant mirror-like surfaces. Sometimes one or more coins in the set may feature the raised surfaces of the design in a frosted finish. These represent early strikes from new proof dies and command a premium value in excess of that for standard proof strikes.

Prior to 1968 all regular proof coins were produced at the Philadelphia Mint, but since that time they have been offered as products of the San Francisco Assay Office minting facility.

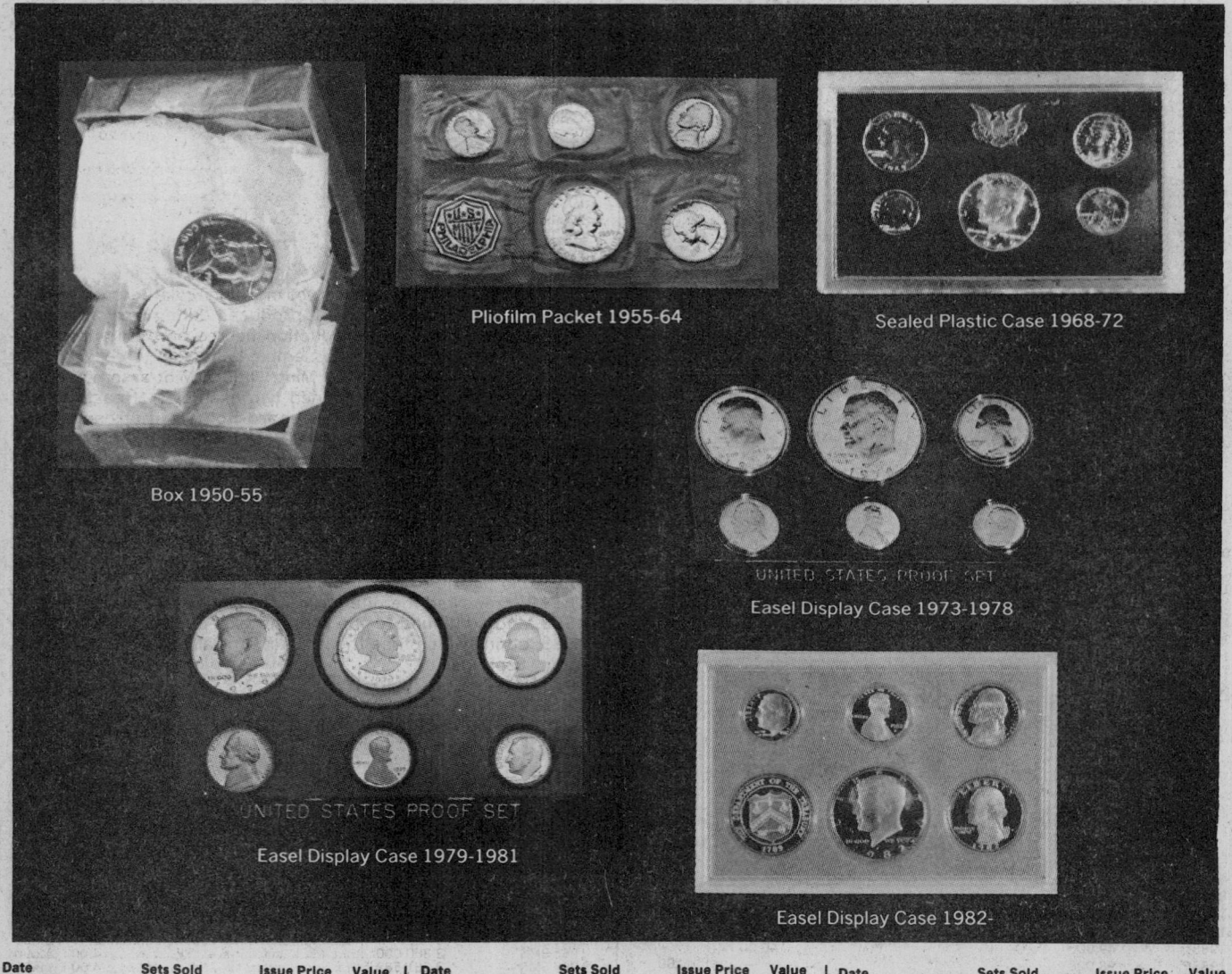

Box 1950-55
Pliofilm Packet 1955-64
Sealed Plastic Case 1968-72
Easel Display Case 1973-1978
Easel Display Case 1979-1981
Easel Display Case 1982-

Date	Sets Sold	Issue Price	Value	Date	Sets Sold	Issue Price	Value	Date	Sets Sold	Issue Price	Value
1936	3,837	1.89	5050.	1961	3,028,244	2.10	16.00	1979S Type II	Inc.Ab.	9.00	95.00
1937	5,542	1.89	3500.	1962	3,218,019	2.10	16.00	1980S	3,547,030	10.00	6.95
1938	8,045	1.89	1850.	1963	3,075,645	2.10	16.00	1981S	4,063,083	11.00	6.95
1939	8,795	1.89	1650.	1964	3,950,762	2.10	17.00	1981S Type II	—	11.00	260.
1940	11,246	1.89	1450.	1968S	3,041,509	5.00	5.00	1982S	3,857,479	11.00	6.00
1941	15,287	1.89	1300.	1968 S No S 10C	—	5.00	8350.	1983S Pres.	—	59.00	90.00
1942 5 coins	Inc. Bl.	1.89	1300.	1969S	2,934,631	5.00	5.00	1983S	3,138,765	11.00	10.00
1942 both 5C	21,120	1.89	1450.	1970S lg. date	2,632,810	5.00	12.50	1983S No S 10¢	—	11.00	1380.
1950	51,386	2.10	610.	1970S sm. date	Inc. Ab.	5.00	88.00	1984S Pres.	316,680	59.00	55.00
1951	57,500	2.10	385.	1970S No S 10 C	Est. 2,200	5.00	775.	1984S	2,748,430	11.00	29.00
1952	81,980	2.10	250.	1971S	3,224,138	5.00	5.00	1985S	3,362,821	11.00	24.00
1953	128,800	2.10	150.	1971S No S 5C	Est. 1,655	5.00	1100.	1986S Pres.	599,317	48.50	50.00
1954	233,300	2.10	83.00	1972S	3,267,667	5.00	5.00	1986S	2,411,180	11.00	29.00
1955 box	378,200	2.10	76.00	1973S	2,769,624	7.00	9.80	1987S	3,972,233	11.00	15.00
1955 flat pack	Inc. Ab.	2.10	78.00	1974S	2,617,350	7.00	8.20	1987S Pres.	435,495	45.00	41.00
1956	669,384	2.10	45.00	1975S	2,909,369	7.00	10.00	1988S	—	11.00	12.00
1957	1,247,952	2.10	22.00	1976S 3 pc.	3,998,621	12.00	18.00	1988S Pres.	—	45.00	57.00
1958	875,652	2.10	32.00	1976S	4,149,730	7.00	9.20	1989S	—	11.00	—
1959	1,149,291	2.10	20.00	1977S	3,251,152	9.00	7.60	1989S Pres.	—	45.00	—
1960 lg. date	1,691,602	2.10	18.00	1978S	3,127,788	9.00	7.60				
1960 sm. date	Inc. Ab.	2.10	25.00	1979S	3,677,175	9.00	12.00				

TERRITORIAL GOLD

Territorial gold pieces (also referred to as "Private" and "Pioneer" gold) are those struck outside the U.S. Mint and not recognized as official issues by the federal government. The pieces so identified are of various shapes, denominations, and degrees of intrinsic value, and were locally required because of the remoteness of the early gold fields from a federal mint and/or an insufficient quantity of official coinage in frontier areas.

The legality of these privately issued pieces derives from the fact that federal law prior to 1864 prohibited a state from coining money, but did not specifically deny that right to an individual, providing that the privately issued coins did not closely resemble those of the United States.

In addition to coin-like gold pieces, the private minters of the gold rush days also issued gold in ingot and bar form. Ingots were intended for circulation and were cast in regular values and generally in large denominations. Bars represent a miner's deposit after it had been assayed, refined, cast into convenient form (generally rectangular), and stamped with the appropriate weight, fineness, and value. Although occasionally cast in even values for the convenience of banks, bars were more often of odd denomination, and when circulated were rounded off to the nearest figure. Ingots and bars are omitted from this listing.

Georgia and North Carolina

The first territorial gold pieces were struck in 1830 by **Templeton Reid**, a goldsmith and assayer who established a private mint at Gainesville, Georgia, at the time gold was being mined on a relatively large scale in Georgia and North Carolina. Reid's pieces were issued in denominations of $2.50, $5, and $10. Except for an undated variety of the $10 piece, all are dated 1830.

The southern Appalachians were also the scene of a private gold minting operation conducted by Christopher Bechtler Sr., his son August, and nephew Christopher Jr. The Bechtlers, a family of German metallurgists, established a mint at Rutherfordton, North Carolina, which produced territorial gold coins for a longer period than any other private mint in American history. Christopher Bechtler Sr. ran the Bechtler mint from July 1831 until his death in 1842, after which the mint was taken over by his son August who ran it until 1852.

The Bechtler coinage includes but three denominations -- $1, $2.50, and $5 -- but they were issued in a wide variety of weights and sizes. The coinage is undated, except for three varieties of the $5 piece which carry the inscription "Aug. 1, 1834" to indicate that they conform to the new weight standard adopted by the U.S. Treasury for official gold coins. **Christopher Bechtler Sr.** produced $2.50 and $5 gold coins for Georgia, and $1, $2.50, and $5 coins for North Carolina. The dollar coins have the distinction of being the first gold coins of that denomination to be produced in the United States. While under the supervision of **August Bechtler**, the Bechtler mint issued $1 and $5 coins for North Carolina.

California

Norris, Grieg & Norris produced the first territorial gold coin struck in California, a $5 piece struck in 1849 at Benicia City, though it bears the imprint of San Francisco. The coining facility was owned by Thomas H. Norris, Charles Greig, and Hiram A. Norris, members of a New York engineering firm. A unique 1850 variety of this coin has the name STOCKTON beneath the date, instead of SAN FRANCISCO.

Early in 1849, John Little Moffat, a New York assayer, established an assay office at San Francisco in association with Joseph R. Curtis, Philo H. Perry, and Samuel Ward. The first issues of the **Moffat & Co.** assay office consisted of rectangular $16 ingots and assay bars of various and irregular denominations. In early August, the firm began striking $5 and $10 gold coins which resemble those of the U.S. Mint in design, but carry the legend S.M.V. (Standard Mint Value) CALIFORNIA GOLD on the reverse. Five-dollar pieces of the same design were also issued in 1850.

On Sept. 30, 1850, Congress directed the Secretary of the Treasury to establish an official Assay Office in California. Moffat & Co. obtained a contract to perform the duties of the U.S. Assay Office. **Augustus Humbert**, a New York watchcase maker, was appointed **U.S. Assayer** of Gold in California. Humbert stamped the first octagonal coin-ingots of the Provisional Government Mint on Jan. 31, 1851. The $50 pieces were accepted at par with standard U.S. gold coins, but were not officially recognized as coins. Officially, they were designated as "ingots." Colloquially, they were known as slugs, quintuple eagles, or five-eagle pieces.

The $50 ingots failed to alleviate the need of California for gold coins. The banks regarded them as disadvantageous to their interests and utilized them only when compelled to do so by public need or convenience. Being of sound value, the ingots drove the overvalued $5, $10, and $20 territorial gold coins from circulation, bringing about a return to the use of gold dust for everyday transactions. Eventually, the slugs became so great a nuisance that they were discounted 3 percent when accepted. This unexpected turn of events forced Moffat & Co. to resume the issuing of $10 and $20 gold coins in 1852. The $10 piece was first issued with the Moffat & Co. imprint on Liberty's coronet, and later with the official imprint of Augustus Humbert on reverse. The $20 piece was issued with the Humbert imprint.

On Feb. 14, 1852, John L. Moffat withdrew from Moffat & Co. to enter the diving bell business, and Moffat & Co. was reorganized as the **United States Assay Office of Gold**, composed of Joseph R. Curtis, Philo H. Perry, and Samuel Ward. The U.S. Assay Office of Gold issued gold coins in denominations of $50 and $10 in 1852, and $20 and $10 in 1853. With the exception of the $50 slugs, they carry the imprint of the Assay Office on reverse. The .900 fine issues of this facility reflect an attempt to bring the issues of the U.S. Assay Office into conformity with the U.S. Mint standard.

The last territorial gold coins to bear the imprint of Moffat & Co. are $20 pieces issued in 1853, after the retirement of John L. Moffat. These coins do not carry a mark of fineness, and generally assay below the U.S. Mint standard.

Templeton Reid, previously mentioned in connection with the private gold issues of Georgia, moved his coining equipment to California when gold was discovered there, and in 1849 issued $10 and $25 gold pieces. No specimens are available to present-day collectors. The only known $10 piece is in the Smithsonian Collection. The only known specimen of the $25 piece was stolen from the U.S. Mint Cabinet Collection in 1858 and was never recovered.

Little is known of the origin and location of the **Cincinnati Mining & Trading Co.** It is believed that the firm was organized in the East and was forced to abandon most of its equipment while enroute to California. A few $5 and $10 gold coins were struck in 1849. Base metal counterfeits exist.

The **Massachusetts & California Co.** was organized in Northampton, Mass., in May 1849 by Josiah Hayden, S. S. Wells, Miles G. Moies, and others. Coining equipment was taken to San Francisco where $5 gold pieces were struck in 1849. The few pieces extant are heavily alloyed with copper.

Wright & Co., a brokerage firm located in Portsmouth Square, San Francisco, issued an undated $10 gold piece in the autumn of 1849 under the name of **Miners' Bank**. Unlike most territorial gold pieces, the Miners' Bank eagle was alloyed with copper. The coinage proved to be unpopular because of its copper-induced color and low intrinsic value. The firm was dissolved on Jan. 14, 1850.

In 1849, Dr. **J. S. Ormsby** and Major William M. Ormsby struck gold coins of $5 and $10 denominations at Sacramento under the name of Ormsby & Co. The coinage, which is identified by the initials J. S. O., is undated. Ormsby & Co. coinage was greatly over-valued, the eagle assaying at as little as $9.37.

The **Pacific Co.** of San Francisco issued $5 and $10 gold coins in 1849. The clouded story of this coinage is based on conjecture. It is believed that the well-struck pattern coins of this type were struck in the East by the Pacific Co. that organized in Boston and set sail for California on Feb. 20, 1849, and that the crudely hand-struck pieces were made by the jewelry firm of Broderick and Kohler after the dies passed into their possession. In any event, the intrinsic value of the initial coinage exceeded face value, but by the end of 1849, when they passed out of favor, the coins had been debased so flagrantly that the eagles assayed for as little as $7.86.

Dubosq & Co., a Philadelphia jewelry firm owned by Theodore Dubosq Sr. and Jr. and Henry Dubosq, took melting and coining equipment to San Francisco in 1849, and in 1850 issued $5 and $10 gold coins struck with dies allegedly made by U.S. Mint Engraver James B. Longacre. Dubosq & Co. coinage was immensely popular with the forty-niners because its intrinsic worth was in excess of face value.

The minting equipment of David C. Broderick and Frederick D. Kohler (see Pacific Co.) was acquired in May 1850 by San Francisco jewelers George C. Baldwin and Thomas S. Holman, who organized a private minting venture under the name of **Baldwin & Co**. The firm produced a $5 piece of Liberty Head design and a $10 piece with Horseman device in 1850. Liberty Head $10 and $20 pieces were coined in 1851. Baldwin & Co. produced the first $20 piece issued in California.

Schultz & Co. of San Francisco, a brass foundry located in the rear of the Baldwin & Co. establishment, and operated by Judge G. W. Schultz and William T. Garratt, issued $5 gold coins from early 1851 until April of that year. The inscription "SHULTS & CO." is a misspelling of SCHULTZ & CO.

Dunbar & Co. of San Francisco issued a $5 gold piece in 1851, after Edward E. Dunbar, owner of the California Bank in San Francisco, purchased the coining equipment of the defunct Baldwin & Co.

The San Francisco-based firm of **Wass, Molitor & Co.** was owned by two Hungarian exiles, Count S. C. Wass and A. P. Molitor, who initially founded the firm as a gold smelting and assaying plant. In response to a plea from the commercial community for small gold coins, Wass, Molitor & Co. issued $5 and $10 gold coins in 1852. The $5 piece was coined with small head and large head varieties, and the $10 piece with small head, large head, and small close-date varieties. The firm produced a second issue of gold coins in 1855, in denominations of $10, $20, and $50.

The U.S. Assay Office in California closed its doors on Dec. 14, 1853, to make way for the newly established San Francisco Branch Mint. The Mint, however, was unable to start immediate quantity production due to the lack of refining acids. During the interim, John G. Kellogg, a former employee of Moffat & Co., and John Glover Richter, a former assayer in the U.S. Assay Office, formed **Kellogg & Co.** for the purpose of supplying businessmen with urgently needed coinage. The firm produced $20 coins dated 1854 and 1855, after which Augustus Humbert replaced Richter, and the enterprise reorganized as Kellogg & Humbert, Melters, Assayers & Coiners. Kellogg & Humbert endured until 1860, but issued coins, $20 pieces, only in 1855.

Oregon

The Oregon Exchange Co., a private mint located at Oregon City, Oregon Territory, issued $5 and $10 pieces of local gold in 1849. The initials K., M., T., A., W., R., C. (G on the $5 piece), and S. on the obverse represent the eight founders of the **Oregon Exchange Co.**: William Kilborne, Theophilus Magruder, James Taylor, George Abernathy, William Willson, William Rector, John Campbell, and Noyes Smith. Campbell is erroneously represented by a G on the $5 coin. For unknown reasons, the initials A and W are omitted from the $10 piece. O.T. (Oregon Territory) is erroneously presented as T.O. on the $5 coin.

Utah

In 1849, the **Mormons** settled in the Great Salt Lake Valley of Utah and established the Deseret Mint in a small adobe building in Salt Lake City. Operating under the direct supervision of Brigham Young, the Deseret Mint issued $2.50, $5, $10, and $20 gold coins in 1849. Additional $5 pieces were struck in 1850 and 1860, the latter in a temporary mint set up in Barlow's jewelry shop. The Mormon $20 piece was the first of that denomination to be struck in the United States. The initials G.S.L.C.P.G. on Mormon coins denotes "Great Salt Lake City Pure Gold." It was later determined that the coinage was grossly deficient in value, mainly because no attempt was made to assay or refine the gold.

Colorado

The discovery of gold in Colorado Territory was accompanied by the inevitable need for coined money. Austin M. Clark, Milton E. Clark, and Emanuel H. Gruber, bankers of Leavenworth, Kansas, moved to Denver where they established a bank and issued $2.50, $5, $10, and $20 gold coins in 1860 and 1861. To protect the holder from loss by abrasion, **Clark, Gruber & Co.** made their coins slightly heavier than full value required. The 1860 issues carry the inscription PIKE'S PEAK GOLD on reverse. CLARK, GRUBER & CO. appears on the reverse of the 1861 issues, and PIKE'S PEAK on the coronet of Liberty. The government purchased the plant of Clark, Gruber & Co. in 1863 and operated it as a federal Assay Office until 1906.

In the summer of 1861, **John Parsons**, an assayer whose place of business was located in South Park at the Tarryall Mines, Colorado, issued undated gold coins in the denominations of $2.50 and $5. They, too, carry the inscription PIKE'S PEAK GOLD on reverse.

J. J. Conway & Co., bankers of Georgia Gulch, Colorado, operated the Conway Mint for a short period in 1861. Undated gold coins in the denominations of $2.50, $5, and $10 were issued. A variety of the $5 coin does not carry the numeral 5 on reverse. The issues of the Conway Mint were highly regarded for their scrupulously maintained value.

NOTE: The above introduction is organized chronologically by geographical region. However, for ease of use the following listings appear alphabetically by state and issuer, except for small California gold.

Small California Gold

During the California gold rush, a wide variety of U.S. and foreign coins was used for small change, but their number was extremely limited. More common was the use of gold dust, though this offered the miner relatively low value for his gold.

By 1852 California jewelers had begun to manufacture 25¢, 50¢ and $1 gold pieces in round and octagonal shapes. Makers included Antonio Louis Nouizillet, Isadore Routhier, Robert B. Gray, Pierre Frontier, Eugene Diviercy, Herman J. Brand, Herman and Jacob Levison, Reuben N. Hershfield and Noah Mitchell. M. Deriberpie was an engraver who cut dies for Nouizillet. Only two or three of these companies were in production at any one time. Many varieties bear the maker's initials. In general, the large Liberty Head types, Eagle reverses and Washington Head types were made by Frontier and his partners. The small Liberty Head types were generally made by Nouizillet and later by Gray and then the Levison brothers and the California Jewelry Co. Coins initialed "G.G." are apparently patterns made by Frontier and Diviercy for the New York firm of Gaime, Guillemot & Co., that never went into production.

The gold rush era coins were generally struck from unrefined native gold-silver alloy. Some were hand struck from hand engraved dies. Others were pressed from high quality hubbed dies into reeded collars. After establishment of the San Francisco Mint in 1854, private coinage gradually died out. By 1857-1858, almost no private gold coins were being made. Production resumed, however, in 1859 as the small denomination gold pieces proved popular as souvenirs and for use in jewelry. By then intrinsic value was generally ignored. Planchets were thinner and were often low-grade surfaced with pure gold. New designs such as the Indian Heads were introduced and the use of polished dies to impart proof-like surfaces became common.

Though all private coinage was outlawed by the Private Coinages Act of 1864, this law was unenforced in California and production of small denominated gold continued through 1882. In the spring of 1883, Col. Henry Finnegass of the U.S. Secret Service halted production of the private gold pieces. Undenominated tokens (lacking DOLLARS, CENTS or the equivalent on reverse) were also made during this latter period, sometimes by the same manufacturing jeweler using the same obverse die as the small denomination gold coins.

Approximately 15,000 pieces of California small denomination gold are estimated to exist, in a total of over 500 varieties. A few varieties are undated, mostly gold rush era pieces; and a few are back-dated. Major varieties are listed here. Individual listings may consist of several varieties; prices quoted are for the most common variety. True MS-65 coins are rare and bring substantial premiums. Walter Breen has established that Period One pieces (1852-1856) were "circulating issues", unlike those made 1859-1882 or later which were souvenirs or jewelry pieces. Public awareness to these differences will no doubt eventually place premium values on Period One coins. For further information consult W. Breen and R.J. Gillio CALIFORNIA PIONEER FRACTIONAL GOLD, 1983.

1/4 DOLLAR - OCTAGONAL

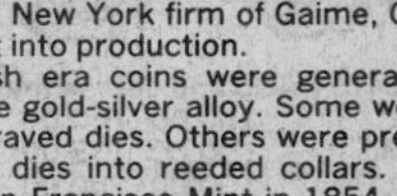

Obv: Large Liberty head.
Rev: Value and date within beaded circle.

KM#	Date	VF	XF	AU	Unc
1.1	1853	75.00	125.00	150.00	225.00
	1854	75.00	125.00	150.00	225.00
	1855	75.00	125.00	175.00	250.00
	1856	75.00	125.00	175.00	250.00

Rev: Value and date within wreath.

KM#	Date	VF	XF	AU	Unc
1.2	1859	75.00	125.00	190.00	275.00
	1864	120.00	150.00	200.00	350.00
	1866	120.00	150.00	200.00	350.00
	1867	75.00	110.00	190.00	275.00
	1868	90.00	135.00	200.00	350.00
	1869	90.00	135.00	200.00	350.00
	1870	75.00	110.00	190.00	275.00
	1871	75.00	110.00	190.00	275.00

Obv: Large Liberty head over date.
Rev: Value and CAL within wreath.

KM#	Date	VF	XF	AU	Unc
1.3	1872	85.00	125.00	195.00	325.00
	1873	65.00	90.00	150.00	225.00

Obv: Small Liberty head.
Rev: Value and date within beaded circle.

KM#	Date	VF	XF	AU	Unc
1.4	1853	85.00	125.00	175.00	275.00

Obv: Small Liberty head over date.
Rev: Value within wreath.

KM#	Date	VF	XF	AU	Unc
1.5	1854	85.00	125.00	175.00	275.00

Obv: Small Liberty head.
Rev: Value and date within wreath.

KM#	Date	VF	XF	AU	Unc
1.6	1855	90.00	135.00	195.00	275.00
	1856	90.00	135.00	195.00	275.00
	1857*	75.00	110.00	150.00	250.00
	1860	90.00	120.00	175.00	295.00
	1870	100.00	150.00	200.00	325.00

*Modern restrikes exist.

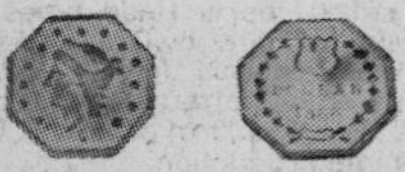

Rev: Value in shield and date within wreath.

KM#	Date	VF	XF	AU	Unc
1.7	1863	100.00	150.00	225.00	325.00
	1864	90.00	135.00	190.00	325.00
	1865/4	100.00	200.00	300.00	475.00
	1866	100.00	200.00	300.00	475.00
	1867	100.00	160.00	250.00	395.00
	1868	100.00	160.00	250.00	395.00
	1869	100.00	160.00	250.00	395.00
	1870	100.00	160.00	270.00	425.00

Obv: Small Liberty head over date.
Rev: Value and CAL within wreath.

KM#	Date	VF	XF	AU	Unc
1.8	1870	85.00	110.00	150.00	250.00
	1871	85.00	110.00	150.00	250.00
	1873	125.00	175.00	275.00	395.00
	1874	90.00	135.00	225.00	300.00
	1875/3	140.00	185.00	225.00	375.00
	1876	80.00	120.00	195.00	315.00

Obv: Goofy Liberty head.
Rev: Value and date within wreath.

KM#	Date	VF	XF	AU	Unc
1.9	1870	90.00	135.00	250.00	425.00

Obv: Oriental Liberty head over date.
Rev: 1/4 CALDOLL within wreath.

KM#	Date	VF	XF	AU	Unc
1.10	1881	—	—	Rare	—

Obv: Large Liberty head over 1872.
Rev: Value and 1871 within wreath.

KM#	Date	VF	XF	AU	Unc
1.11	1872-71	500.00	1000.	1500.	2200.

Obv: Large Indian head over date.
Rev: Value within wreath.

KM#	Date	VF	XF	AU	Unc
2.1	1852	120.00	200.00	295.00	475.00
	1868	130.00	225.00	350.00	550.00
	1874	120.00	200.00	325.00	525.00
	1876	100.00	150.00	275.00	450.00
	1880	85.00	125.00	195.00	295.00
	1881	85.00	125.00	195.00	295.00

Rev: Value and CAL within wreath.

KM#	Date	VF	XF	AU	Unc
2.2	1872	75.00	110.00	175.00	250.00
	1873	130.00	200.00	300.00	395.00
	1874	75.00	110.00	175.00	250.00
	1875	75.00	110.00	175.00	250.00
	1876	75.00	110.00	175.00	250.00

Obv: Small Indian head over date.

KM#	Date	VF	XF	AU	Unc
2.3	1875	95.00	175.00	295.00	425.00
	1876	95.00	175.00	295.00	425.00
	1881	95.00	175.00	295.00	425.00

Obv: Aztec Indian head over date.

KM#	Date	VF	XF	AU	Unc
2.4	1880	90.00	150.00	250.00	425.00

Obv: Dumb Indian head over date.
Rev: Value and CAL within wreath.

KM#	Date	VF	XF	AU	Unc
2.6	1881	250.00	500.00	750.00	1250.

Obv: Young Indian head over date.
Rev: Value within wreath.

KM#	Date	VF	XF	AU	Unc
2.7	1881	250.00	500.00	750.00	1250.

Rev: Value and CAL within wreath.

KM#	Date	VF	XF	AU	Unc
2.8	1882	200.00	300.00	500.00	750.00

Obv: Washington head over date.

KM#	Date	VF	XF	AU	Unc
3	1872	200.00	425.00	750.00	1250.

1/4 DOLLAR - ROUND

Obv: Defiant eagle over date.
Rev: 25¢ within wreath.

KM#	Date	VF	XF	AU	Unc
4	1854	5000.	7000.	9000.	13,500.

Superior Sale Sept. 1988 Gem Unc $44,000.

Obv: Large Liberty head.
Rev: Value and date within wreath.

KM#	Date	VF	XF	AU	Unc
5.1	1853	—	—	Rare	—
	1854	400.00	500.00	750.00	1250.
	1859	90.00	110.00	175.00	275.00
	1865	90.00	175.00	225.00	350.00
	1866	90.00	135.00	225.00	350.00
	1867	60.00	90.00	150.00	250.00
	1868	60.00	90.00	150.00	250.00
	1870	60.00	90.00	150.00	250.00
	1871	60.00	90.00	150.00	250.00

Obv: Large Liberty head over date.
Rev: Value and CAL within wreath.

KM#	Date	VF	XF	AU	Unc
5.2	1871	75.00	110.00	150.00	225.00
5.2	1872	90.00	175.00	225.00	375.00
	1873	75.00	110.00	150.00	225.00

Obv: Small Liberty head.
Rev: 25¢ in wreath.

KM#	Date	VF	XF	AU	Unc
5.3	ND	1000.	1350.	1750.	2750.

Rev: 1/4 DOLL. or DOLLAR and date in wreath.

KM#	Date	VF	XF	AU	Unc
5.4	ND	110.00	165.00	275.00	450.00
	1853	275.00	400.00	550.00	750.00
	1855	90.00	110.00	150.00	250.00
	1856	90.00	135.00	225.00	375.00
	1860	90.00	110.00	150.00	275.00
	1863/1860	250.00	500.00	750.00	950.00
	1864	90.00	135.00	225.00	360.00
	1865	90.00	110.00	150.00	275.00
	1866	120.00	195.00	350.00	525.00
	1867	90.00	110.00	150.00	275.00
	1869	90.00	110.00	150.00	275.00
	1870	120.00	195.00	350.00	525.00

Rev: Value in shield and date within wreath.

KM#	Date	VF	XF	AU	Unc
5.5	1863	150.00	225.00	375.00	550.00

Obv: Small Liberty head over date.
Rev: Value and CAL within wreath.

KM#	Date	VF	XF	AU	Unc
5.6	ND	120.00	180.00	300.00	525.00
	1870	90.00	110.00	150.00	225.00
	1871	90.00	110.00	150.00	225.00
	1873	120.00	225.00	350.00	500.00
	1874	120.00	200.00	300.00	400.00
	1875	120.00	180.00	300.00	525.00
	1876	95.00	120.00	195.00	325.00

Obv: Goofy Liberty head.
Rev: Value and date within wreath.

KM#	Date	VF	XF	AU	Unc
5.7	1870	95.00	150.00	225.00	350.00

Obv: Liberty head with H and date below.
Rev: Value and CAL in wreath.

KM#	Date	VF	XF	AU	Unc
5.8	1871	80.00	120.00	195.00	325.00

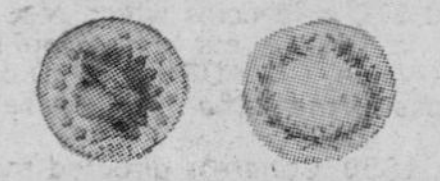

Obv: Large Indian head over date.
Rev: Value within wreath.

KM#	Date	VF	XF	AU	Unc
6.1	1852	100.00	150.00	250.00	425.00
	1868	125.00	200.00	325.00	495.00
	1874	125.00	200.00	325.00	495.00
	1876	75.00	120.00	175.00	275.00
	1880	75.00	120.00	175.00	275.00
	1881	75.00	120.00	175.00	275.00

Rev: Value and CAL within wreath.

KM#	Date	VF	XF	AU	Unc
6.2	1872	90.00	120.00	175.00	295.00
	1873	100.00	150.00	250.00	395.00
	1874	90.00	120.00	175.00	295.00
	1875	75.00	115.00	165.00	250.00
	1876	90.00	120.00	175.00	295.00

Obv: Small Indian head over date.

KM#	Date	VF	XF	AU	Unc
6.3	1875	85.00	115.00	195.00	295.00
	1876	100.00	150.00	275.00	450.00

Obv: Young Indian head over date.

KM#	Date	VF	XF	AU	Unc
6.4	1882	500.00	750.00	1000.	1500.

Obv: Washington head over date.

KM#	Date	VF	XF	AU	Unc
7	1872	250.00	375.00	625.00	1250.

1/2 DOLLAR - OCTAGONAL

Obv: Liberty head over date.
Rev: 1/2 DOLLAR in beaded circle. CALIFORNIA GOLD around circle.

8.1	1853	100.00	200.00	275.00	395.00
	1854	100.00	200.00	275.00	395.00
	1856	200.00	250.00	450.00	675.00

Rev: Small eagle with rays ("peacock").

8.2	1853	550.00	700.00	1200.	1750.

Obv: Large Liberty head.
Rev: Large eagle with date.

8.3	1853	750.00	1250.	2250.	3500.

Rev: Value and date within wreath.

8.4	1859	100.00	150.00	265.00	395.00
	1866	125.00	200.00	295.00	450.00
	1867	125.00	200.00	295.00	450.00
	1868	125.00	200.00	295.00	450.00
	1869	125.00	200.00	295.00	450.00
	1870	125.00	200.00	295.00	450.00
	1871	85.00	115.00	195.00	325.00

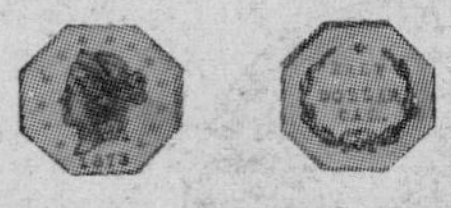

Obv: Large Liberty head over date.
Rev: Value and CAL within wreath.

8.5	1872	75.00	115.00	175.00	275.00
	1873	75.00	115.00	175.00	275.00

Obv: Liberty head.
Rev: Date in wreath, HALF DOL. CALIFORNIA GOLD around wreath.

8.6	1854	150.00	225.00	350.00	475.00
	1855	120.00	180.00	295.00	425.00
	1856	120.00	180.00	295.00	425.00
	1868	75.00	100.00	175.00	275.00

Obv: Small Liberty head.
Rev: HALF DOLLAR and date in wreath.

8.7	1864	75.00	110.00	175.00	275.00
	1870	95.00	175.00	295.00	475.00

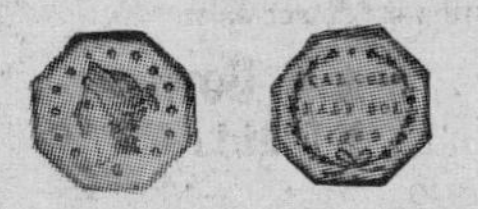

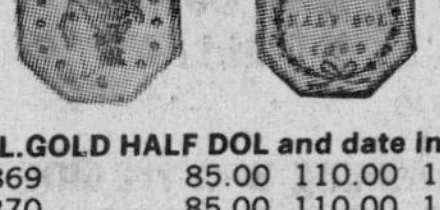

Rev: CAL.GOLD HALF DOL and date in wreath.

8.8	1869	85.00	110.00	175.00	275.00
	1870	85.00	110.00	175.00	275.00

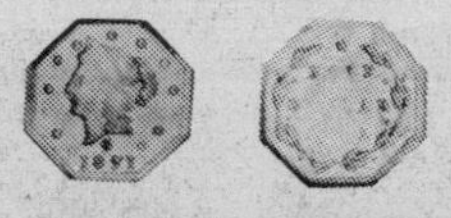

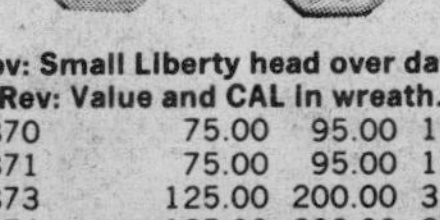

Obv: Small Liberty head over date.
Rev: Value and CAL in wreath.

8.9	1870	75.00	95.00	150.00	275.00
	1871	75.00	95.00	150.00	275.00
	1873	125.00	200.00	350.00	475.00
	1874	125.00	200.00	350.00	475.00

KM#	Date	VF	XF	AU	Unc
8.9	1875	400.00	500.00	750.00	1000.
	1876	130.00	200.00	350.00	550.00

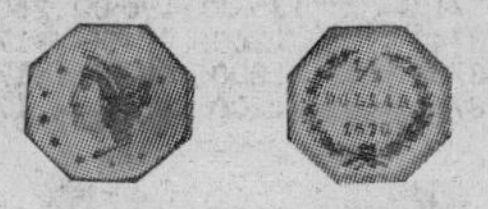

Obv: Goofy Liberty head.
Rev: Value and date within wreath.

8.10	1870	85.00	130.00	250.00	425.00

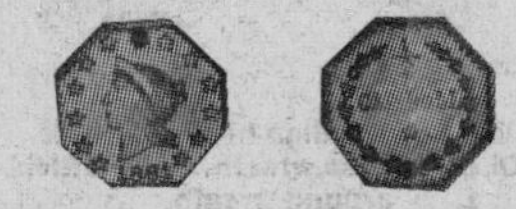

Obv: Oriental Liberty head over date.
Rev: 1/2 CALDOLL within wreath.

8.11	1881	200.00	300.00	525.00	850.00

Obv: Large Indian head over date.
Rev: Value within wreath.

9.1	1852	500.00	750.00	950.00	1450.
	1868	200.00	350.00	550.00	850.00
	1874	200.00	350.00	550.00	850.00
	1876	200.00	250.00	450.00	750.00
	1880	125.00	150.00	250.00	395.00
	1881	500.00	750.00	950.00	1450.

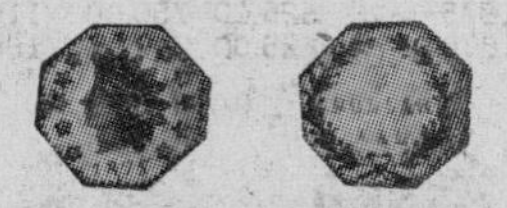

Rev: Value and CAL within wreath.

9.2	1852	175.00	225.00	395.00	575.00
	1868	175.00	225.00	395.00	575.00
	1872	100.00	125.00	225.00	450.00
	1873	150.00	200.00	350.00	450.00
	1874/3	100.00	125.00	225.00	450.00
	1874	150.00	185.00	325.00	500.00
	1875	90.00	110.00	200.00	450.00
	1876	100.00	125.00	225.00	450.00
	1878	150.00	200.00	325.00	500.00
	1880	150.00	200.00	325.00	500.00
	1881	150.00	200.00	325.00	500.00

Obv: Small Indian head over date.

9.3	1875	125.00	225.00	350.00	550.00
	1876	125.00	225.00	350.00	550.00

Obv: Young Indian head over date.

9.4	1881	200.00	250.00	400.00	750.00
	1882	250.00	400.00	550.00	850.00

1/2 DOLLAR - ROUND

Obv: Arms of California and date.
Rev: Eagle and legends.

10	1853	1500.	3000.	4500.	6500.

Obv: Liberty head.
Rev: Large eagle and legends.

11.1	1854	1000.	2000.	3500.	5000.

Obv: Liberty head and date.
Rev: HALF DOL. CALIFORNIA GOLD around wreath.

11.2	1854	120.00	180.00	295.00	500.00

Obv: Liberty head.

Rev: Date in wreath. Value and CALIFORNIA GOLD around wreath.

KM#	Date	VF	XF	AU	Unc
11.3	1852	95.00	175.00	275.00	495.00
	1853	95.00	175.00	275.00	495.00
	1854*	60.00	90.00	125.00	225.00
	1855	200.00	250.00	450.00	725.00
	1856	120.00	195.00	275.00	525.00
	1860	85.00	150.00	250.00	425.00

*Beware of Kroll type counterfeits.

Rev: Small eagle and legends.

11.4	1853	1500.	3000.	4500.	6500.

Rev: Value in wreath. CALIFORNIA GOLD and date around wreath.

11.5	1853	200.00	250.00	500.00	800.00

Rev: Value and date within wreath.

11.6	1854	750.00	1000.	1500.	2250.
	1855	200.00	250.00	450.00	750.00
	1859	85.00	125.00	175.00	275.00
	1865	130.00	200.00	295.00	550.00
	1866	130.00	200.00	295.00	550.00
	1867	100.00	150.00	250.00	425.00
	1868	100.00	150.00	250.00	425.00
	1869	130.00	200.00	295.00	550.00
	1870	85.00	125.00	175.00	275.00
	1871	85.00	125.00	175.00	275.00
	1873	130.00	200.00	295.00	550.00

Obv: Liberty head over date.
Rev: Value and CAL within wreath.

11.7	1870	85.00	125.00	175.00	250.00
	1871	85.00	125.00	175.00	250.00
	1872	130.00	200.00	350.00	550.00
	1873	150.00	200.00	295.00	475.00
	1874	125.00	200.00	295.00	425.00
	1875	125.00	200.00	295.00	425.00
	1876	125.00	200.00	295.00	425.00

Obv: Liberty head.
Rev: Value and date within wreath. CALIFORNIA GOLD outside.

11.8	1863	350.00	500.00	750.00	1225.

Obv: Liberty head.
Rev: HALF DOLLAR and date in wreath.

11.9	1864	85.00	100.00	175.00	275.00
	1866	—	—	Rare	—
	1867	85.00	125.00	195.00	325.00
	1868	85.00	125.00	195.00	325.00
	1869	85.00	125.00	195.00	325.00
	1870	150.00	200.00	225.00	450.00

Obv: Goofy Liberty head.
Rev: Value and date within wreath.

11.11	1870	130.00	200.00	350.00	550.00

Obv: Liberty head with H and date below.
Rev: Value and CAL within wreath.

11.12	1871	100.00	150.00	275.00	475.00

Obv: Large Indian head over date.
Rev: Value within wreath.

KM#	Date	VF	XF	AU	Unc
12.1	1852	200.00	250.00	425.00	650.00
	1868	200.00	250.00	425.00	650.00
	1874	200.00	250.00	425.00	650.00
	1876	125.00	175.00	300.00	500.00
	1878/6	250.00	500.00	750.00	1100
	1880	125.00	175.00	275.00	425.00
	1881	125.00	175.00	275.00	425.00

Rev: Value and CAL within wreath.

12.2	1872	125.00	175.00	300.00	475.00
	1873	125.00	175.00	300.00	475.00
	1874/3	150.00	195.00	350.00	575.00
	1874	125.00	175.00	300.00	475.00
	1875/3	125.00	175.00	325.00	525.00
	1875	150.00	195.00	350.00	575.00
	1876/5/3	125.00	175.00	325.00	525.00
	1876	200.00	250.00	450.00	750.00

Obv: Small Indian head over date.

12.3	1875	140.00	175.00	325.00	425.00
	1876	150.00	185.00	350.00	575.00

Obv: Young Indian head over date.

| 12.4 | 1882 | 350.00 | 500.00 | 750.00 | 1000. |

DOLLAR - OCTAGONAL

Obv: Liberty head.
Rev: Large eagle and legends.

13.1	ND	1300.	2000.	2750.	4500.
	1853	2000.	3000.	3750.	5500.
	1854	1300.	2000.	2750.	4500.

Rev: Value and date in beaded circle. CALIFORNIA GOLD initials around circle.

13.2	1853 DERI	250.00	350.00	500.00	700.00
	1853 FD	195.00	295.00	375.00	550.00
	1853 N	330.00	480.00	700.00	950.00
	1854 DERI	375.00	575.00	825.00	1150.
	1854 FD	210.00	290.00	375.00	550.00
	1855 FD	210.00	290.00	375.00	550.00
	1856	1300	1550.	2950.	4500.
	1863*	95.00	150.00	225.00	325.00

*Modern restrikes exist.

Rev: Value and date inside wreath. Legends outside wreath.

13.3	1854	225.00	325.00	525.00	750.00
	1855 NR	225.00	325.00	525.00	750.00
	1858 K	120.00	175.00	250.00	350.00
	1859 FD	825.00	1100.	1650.	2500.
	1860	135.00	190.00	275.00	395.00
	1868 G	185.00	260.00	370.00	525.00
	1869 G	135.00	190.00	275.00	395.00
	1870 G	275.00	350.00	450.00	650.00
	1871	275.00	350.00	450.00	650.00

Obv: Goofy Liberty head.
Rev: Value and date inside wreath.

| 13.4 | 1870 | 135.00 | 190.00 | 275.00 | 425.00 |

Obv: Liberty head over date.
Rev: Value and date within wreath. CALIFORNIA GOLD around wreath.

KM#	Date	VF	XF	AU	Unc
13.5	1871 G	135.00	190.00	250.00	350.00
	1874	1200.	1400.	1750.	2750.
	1875	1200.	1400.	1750.	2750.
	1876	1200.	1400.	1750.	2750.

Obv: Large Indian head over date.
Rev: 1 DOLLAR inside wreath. CALIFORNIA GOLD around wreath.

14.1	1872	500.00	750.00	1250.	1750.
	1873/2	825.00	1100.	1650.	2750.
	1873	350.00	500.00	750.00	1150.
	1874	275.00	350.00	450.00	750.00
	1875	275.00	350.00	450.00	750.00
	1876	275.00	350.00	450.00	750.00

Obv: Small Indian head over date.
Rev: 1 DOLLAR CAL inside wreath.

14.2	1875	525.00	750.00	1100.	1650.
	1876	825.00	1100.	1650.	2500.

Rev: 1 DOLLAR inside wreath. CALIFORNIA GOLD around wreath.

| 14.3 | 1876 | 750.00 | 950.00 | 1475. | 2250. |

DOLLAR - ROUND

Obv: Liberty head.
Rev: Large eagle and legends.

| 15.1 | 1853 | 9,500. | 12,000. | 14,500. | 19,500. |

Rev: Value and date inside wreath. CALIFORNIA GOLD around wreath.

15.2	1854 GL	1750.	2750.	3750.	5250.
	1854 FD	3300.	3850.	4750.	6500.
	1854	3300.	3850.	4750.	6500.
	1857	3300.	3850.	4750.	6500.
	1870 G	1250.	1750.	2450.	3250.
	1871	3300.	3850.	4950.	6500.

Obv: Liberty head over date. Rev: Value inside wreath. CALIFORNIA GOLD around wreath.

15.3	1870 G	750.00	1000.	1500.	2000.
	1871 G	950.00	1350.	1750.	2750.

Obv: Goofy Liberty head.
Rev: Value and date inside wreath. CALIFORNIA GOLD around wreath.

| 15.4 | 1870 | 750.00 | 1000. | 1500. | 2150. |

Obv: Large Indian head over date.
Rev: Value inside wreath. CALIFORNIA GOLD outside wreath.

| 16 | 1872 | 750.00 | 1000. | 1750. | 2500. |

Regular Issues
CALIFORNIA

Baldwin & Company
5 DOLLARS

KM#	Date	Fine	VF	XF	Unc
17	1850	4500.	6500.	8500.	17,500.

10 DOLLARS

| 18 | 1850 Horseman | 15,000. | 27,500. | 37,500. | 59,500. |

| 19 | 1851 | 9500. | 14,000. | 28,000. | — |

20 DOLLARS

| 20 | 1851 | — | — | — | — |

Garrett Sale March 1980, VF-30 $110,000.
NOTE: Beware of copies cast in base metals.

Blake & Company
20 DOLLARS

| 21 | 1855 | — | — | — | — |

NOTE: Many modern copies exist.

J. H. Bowie
5 DOLLARS

| 22 | 1849 | — | — | — | — |

Cincinnati Mining and Trading Company
5 DOLLARS

| 23 | 1849 | — | — | Rare | |

Territorial Gold / UNITED STATES 1771

10 DOLLARS

KM#	Date	Fine	VF	XF	Unc
24	1849			Rare	—

Brand Sale 1984, XF $104,500.

Dubosq & Company
5 DOLLARS

| 26 | 1850 | 25,000. | 42,500. | Rare | — |

10 DOLLARS

| 27 | 1850 | 37,500. | 55,000. | Rare | — |

Dunbar & Company
5 DOLLARS

| 28 | 1851 | 22,500. | 32,500. | 52,500. | — |

Spink & Son Sale 1988, AU $62,000.

Augustus Humbert
United States Assayer
10 DOLLARS

AUGUSTUS HUMBERT Imprint

| 29.1 | 1852/1 | 2000. | 3500. | 5500. | 15,000. |
| | 1852 | 1500. | 2500. | 4750. | 11,500. |

Error: IINITED.

| 29.2 | 1852/1 | — | — | Rare | — |
| | 1852 | — | — | Rare | — |

20 DOLLARS

| 30 | 1852/1 | 4500. | 6000. | 9500. | — |

Garrett Sale March 1980, Humberts Proof $325,000.

50 DOLLARS

Obv: 50 D C 880 THOUS, eagle.

Edge: Lettered. Rev: 50 in center.

KM#	Date	Fine	VF	XF	Unc
31.1	1851	9500.	12,000.	22,000.	—

Obv: 887 THOUS.

| 31.1a | 1851 | 8000. | 11,000. | 20,000. | 45,000. |

Obv: 880 THOUS. Rev: Without 50.

| 31.2 | 1851 | 6500. | 10,000. | 20,000. | 50,000. |

Obv: 887 THOUS.

| 31.2a | 1851 | — | 12,500. | 22,500. | — |

ASSAYER inverted

| 31.3 | 1851 | — | — | Unique | |

Obv: 880 THOUS. Rev: Rays from central star.

| 31.4 | 1851 | — | — | Unique | |

Obv: 880 THOUS. Rev: "Target".

| 32.1 | 1851 | 8000. | 12,500. | 18,000. | 45,000. |

Obv: 887 THOUS.

| 32.1a | 1851 | 8000. | 12,500. | 18,000. | 45,000. |

Garrett Sale March 1980, Humberts Proof $500,000.

Rev: Small design.

| 32.2 | 1851 | 8000. | 12,500. | 16,000. | — |
| | 1852 | 6500. | 9500. | 21,000. | 55,000. |

Kellogg & Company
20 DOLLARS

Obv: Thick date. Rev: Short arrows.

KM#	Date	Fine	VF	XF	Unc
33.1	1854	2000.	3000.	5500.	12,500.

Obv: Medium date.

| 33.2 | 1854 | 2000. | 3000. | 5500. | 12,500. |

Obv: Thin date.

| 33.3 | 1854 | 2000. | 3000. | 4500. | 11,500. |

Rev: Long arrows.

| 33.4 | 1854 | 2000. | 3000. | 4500. | 11,500. |
| | 1855 | 2500. | 3500. | 5500. | 14,000. |

Garrett Sale March 1980, Proof $230,000.

Rev: Medium arrows.

| 33.5 | 1855 | 2500. | 3500. | 4500. | 14,000. |

Rev: Short arrows.

| 33.6 | 1855 | 2500. | 3500. | 4500. | 14,000. |

50 DOLLARS

| 34 | 1855 | — | — | — | — |

Bowers & Merena Sale Sept. 1984, Proof $165,000.

Massachusetts and California Company
5 DOLLARS

| 35 | 1849 | 35,000. | 55,000. | Rare | — |
| | | | | Proof | 110,000. |

Miners Bank
10 DOLLARS

RED GOLD

KM#	Date	Fine	VF	XF	Unc
36	ND(1849)	—	8500.	14,500.	35,000.

Garrett Sale March 1980, MS-65 $135,000.

YELLOW GOLD

| 36a | ND(1849) | | | | |

Rare as most specimens have heavy copper alloy.

Moffat & Co.
5 DOLLARS

37.1	1849	800.00	1200.	2500.	6500.

Rev: Die break at DOL.
| 37.2 | 1849 | 800.00 | 1200. | 2500. | 6500. |

Rev: Die break on shield.
| 37.3 | 1849 | 800.00 | 1200. | 2500. | 6500. |

Rev: Small letters.
| 37.4 | 1850 | 800.00 | 1500. | 4000. | 9500. |

Rev: Large letters.
| 37.5 | 1850 | 800.00 | 1500. | 3500. | 9000. |

Garrett Sale March 1980, MS-60 $21,000.

10 DOLLARS

Rev. val: TEN DOL., arrow under period.
| 38.1 | 1849 | 1800. | 3500. | 6000. | 11,500. |

Rev: Arrow over period.
| 38.2 | 1849 | 1800. | 3500. | 6000. | 11,500. |

Rev. val: TEN D., large letters.
| 38.3 | 1849 | 2250. | 5000. | 7500. | 14,500. |

Rev: Small letters.
| 38.4 | 1849 | 2250. | 5000. | 7500. | 14,500. |

MOFFAT & CO. imprint, wide date.
| 39.1 | 1852 | 2000. | 4250. | 8500. | 15,000. |

Close date
| 39.2 | 1852 | 1800. | 4000. | 8500. | 15,000. |

NOTE: Struck by Augustus Humbert.

20 DOLLARS

KM#	Date	Fine	VF	XF	Unc
40	1853	2250.	4000.	6500.	12,500.

NOTE: Struck by Curtis, Perry & Ward.

Norris, Greig & Norris
HALF EAGLE

Obv: Period after ALLOY. Plain edge.
| 41.1 | 1849 | 2200. | 3750. | 8500. | 22,000. |

Obv: W/o period after ALLOY.
| 41.2 | 1849 | 2200. | 3750. | 8500. | 22,000. |

Obv: Period after ALLOY. Reeded edge.
| 41.3 | 1849 | 1950. | 4500. | 9500. | 27,500. |

Obv: W/o period after ALLOY.
| 41.4 | 1849 | 4500. | 9500. | 27,500. | |

Rev: STOCKTON beneath date.
| 42 | 1850 | — | — | Unique | — |

J.S. Ormsby
5 DOLLARS

| 43 | ND(1849) | — | — | Unique | — |

10 DOLLARS

| 44 | ND(1849) | | | | |

Garrett Sale March 1980, F-12 $100,000.

Pacific Company
5 DOLLARS

| 45 | 1849 | | | | |

Garrett Sale March 1980, VF-30 $180,000.

10 DOLLARS

Plain edge

KM#	Date	Fine	VF	XF	Unc
46.1	1849	—	—	Rare	

Waldorf Sale 1964, $24,000.

Reeded edge
| 46.2 | 1849 | — | — | Rare | |

Templeton Reid
10 DOLLARS

| 47 | 1849 | — | — | Unique | — |

20 DOLLARS

| 48 | 1849 | | | Unknown | |

NOTE: Only known specimen of above stolen from U.S. Mint in 1858 and never recovered. Also see listings under Georgia.

Schultz & Company
5 DOLLARS

| 49 | 1851 | — | — | 45,000. | |

Stacks Sale July 1984, EF $36,300.

United States Assay Office of Gold
10 DOLLARS

Obv: TEN DOLS 884 THOUS.
Rev: O of OFFICE under I of UNITED.
| 50.1 | 1852 | 1750. | 2500. | 3750. | 9500. |

Garrett Sale March 1980, MS-60 $18,000.

Rev: O under N, strong beads.
| 51.2 | 1852 | 1750. | 2500. | 3750. | 9500. |

Rev: Weak beads.
| 51.3 | 1852 | 1750. | 2500. | 3750. | 9500. |

Obv: TEN D, 884 THOUS.
| 52 | 1853 | 5000. | 7750. | 14,500. | — |

Obv: 900 THOUS.

KM#	Date	Fine	VF	XF	Unc
52a	1853	2700.	4200.	6500.	—

Garrett Sale March 1980, MS-60 $35,000.

20 DOLLARS

Obv: 884/880 THOUS.

| 53 | 1853 | 9500. | 15,000. | 23,000. | 27,000. |

Obv: 900/880 THOUS.

| 53a | 1853 | 1650. | 3000. | 6500. | 11,500. |

NOTE: 1853 Liberty Head listed under Moffat & Co.

50 DOLLARS

Obv: 887 THOUS.

| 54 | 1852 | 4000. | 6500. | 16,000. | 50,000. |

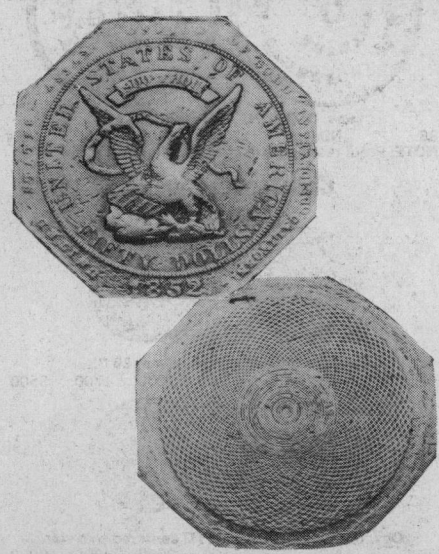

Obv: 900 THOUS.

| 54a | 1852 | 6000. | 7500. | 19,500. | 60,000. |

Wass, Molitor & Co.
5 DOLLARS

Obv: Small head, rounded bust.

KM#	Date	Fine	VF	XF	Unc
55.1	1852	2500.	5000.	7500.	17,500.

Thick planchet.

| 55.2 | 1852 | — | — | Unique | — |

Obv: Large head, pointed bust.

| 56 | 1852 | 2000. | 4500. | 7500. | 17,500. |

10 DOLLARS

Obv: Long neck, large date.

| 57 | 1852 | 4000. | 6750. | 9000. | 15,000. |

Obv: Short neck, wide date.

| 58 | 1852 | 1800. | 3500. | 5500. | — |

Obv: Short neck, small date.

| 59.1 | 1852 | — | — | Unique | — |

Obv: Plugged date.

| 59.2 | 1855 | 7000. | 11,000. | 18,000. | — |

20 DOLLARS

Obv: Large head.

| 60 | 1855 | — | — | Rare | — |

Obv: Small head.

| 61 | 1855 | 6000. | 11,500. | 17,000. | — |

50 DOLLARS

KM#	Date	Fine	VF	XF	Unc
62	1855	8500.	11,500.	21,500.	—

Garrett Sale March 1980, MS-65 $275,000.

COLORADO
Clark, Gruber & Co.
2-1/2 DOLLARS

| 63 | 1860 | 850.00 | 1500. | 3200. | 8500. |

Garrett Sale March 1980, MS-65 $12,000.

| 64.1 | 1861 | 850.00 | 1500. | 2500. | 7500. |

Ex. high edge.

| 64.2 | 1861 | 850.00 | 1750. | 3500. | 9500. |

5 DOLLARS

| 65 | 1860 | 1200. | 2200. | 3750. | 10,000. |

Garrett Sale March 1980, MS-63 $9,000.

| 66 | 1861 | 1500. | 2500. | 3250. | 9500. |

10 DOLLARS

| 67 | 1860 | 2750. | 3950. | 6500. | 15,000. |

Territorial Gold / UNITED STATES 1774

KM#	Date	Fine	VF	XF	Unc
68	1861	1500.	2250.	3250.	10,000.

20 DOLLARS

69	1860	12,000.	17,000.	24,000.	59,000.

70	1861	4000.	5400.	11,000.	—

J.J. Conway
2-1/2 DOLLARS

71	ND(1861)	—	40,000.	65,000.	—

5 DOLLARS

72.1	ND(1861)				
	Brand Sale June 1984, XF-40 $44,000.				
	Rev: Numeral 5 omitted.				
72.2	ND(1861)			Unique	—

10 DOLLARS

73	ND(1861)	—	50,000.	Rare	—

John Parsons
2-1/2 DOLLARS

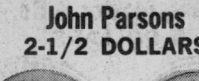

KM#	Date	Fine	VF	XF	Unc
74	ND(1861)	—	—	—	—
	Garrett Sale March 1980, VF-20 $85,000.				

5 DOLLARS

75	ND(1861)				
	Garrett Sale March 1980, VF-20 $100,000.				

GEORGIA
Christopher Bechtler
2-1/2 DOLLARS

Rev: GEORGIA, 64 G, 22 CARATS.
76.1	ND	1250.	2250.	3000.	6500.

Rev: GEORGIA, 64 G, 22 CARATS, even 22.
76.2	ND	1800.	2500.	3700.	7500.

5 DOLLARS

Obv: RUTHERF. Rev: 128 G, 22 CARATS.
77	ND	2200.	2900.	4500.	8750.

Obv: RUTHERFORD.
78.1	ND	1800.	2750.	3700.	8000.

Rev: Colon after 128 G:
78.2	ND	1800.	2750.	3700.	8000.

Templeton Reid
2-1/2 DOLLARS

79	1830	15,000.	42,000.	55,000.	—

5 DOLLARS

80	1830	—	—	—	—
	Garrett Sale Nov. 1979, XF-40 $200,000.				

10 DOLLARS

Obv: With date.
KM#	Date	Fine	VF	XF	Unc
81	1830	—	—	VG	50,000.

Obv: Undated.
82	ND(1830)	—	—	—	—

NOTE: Also see listings under California.

NORTH CAROLINA
August Bechtler
DOLLAR

Rev: CAROLINA, 27 G. 21C., plain edge.
83.1	ND	450.00	800.00	1250.	2750.

Reeded edge
83.2	ND	450.00	800.00	1250.	2750.

5 DOLLARS

Rev: CAROLINA, 134 G. 21 CARATS.
84	ND	1200.	2100.	3500.	6500.

Rev: CAROLINA, 128 G. 22 CARATS.
85	ND	2200.	3500.	5500.	10,000.

Rev: CAROLINA, 141 G:20 CARATS.
86	ND	2000.	3200.	5000.	9000.

NOTE: Proof restrikes exist from original dies.

Christopher Bechtler
DOLLAR

Obv: CAROLINA, N reversed, 28 G.
87	ND	900.00	1200.	1700.	3500.

Obv: N. CAROLINA. Rev: 28 G centered w/o star.
88.1	ND	1500.	2200.	4000.	8000.

Obv: N. CAROLINA. Rev: 28 G high w/o star. . . .
88.2	ND	2000.	3000.	4500.	8500.

Territorial Gold / UNITED STATES 1775

Obv: N CAROLINA. Rev: 30 G.

KM#	Date	Fine	VF	XF	Unc
89	ND	850.00	1100.	1800.	3700.

2-1/2 DOLLARS

Rev: CAROLINA, 67 G. 21 CARATS.

| 90.1 | ND | 1200. | 1700. | 2900. | 5500. |

Rev: 64 G 22 CARATS, uneven 22.

| 90.2 | ND | 1300. | 1850. | 3200. | 6400. |

Rev: Even 22.

| 90.3 | ND | 1450. | 2000. | 3500. | 7000. |

Rev: CAROLINA, 70 G. 20 CARATS.

| 91 | ND | 1500. | 2000. | 3200. | 7000. |

Obv: NORTH CAROLINA, 20 C. 75 G.
Rev: RUTHERFORD in a circle. Border of large beads.

| 92.1 | ND | — | 4500. | 6750. | 12,000. |

Obv: NORTH CAROLINA, w/o 75 G, wide 20 C.

| 92.2 | ND | 2800. | 4500. | 6500. | 11,500. |

Obv: Narrow 20 C.

| 92.3 | ND | 2800. | 4500. | 6500. | 11,500. |

Obv: NORTH CAROLINA w/o 75 G,
CAROLINA above 250 instead of GOLD.

| 93.1 | ND | — | — | Unique | — |

Obv: NORTH CAROLINA, 20 C.
Rev: 75 G. Border finely serrated.

| 93.2 | ND | 3000. | 5000. | 7500. | |

5 DOLLARS

Rev: CAROLINA, 134 G. star 21 CARATS.

| 94 | ND | 1500. | 2200. | 3000. | 6200. |

Rev: 21 above CARATS, w/o star.

| 95 | ND | 1500. | 2200. | 3000. | 6200. |

Obv: RUTHERFORD. Rev: CAROLINA, 140 G. 20 CARATS.

Plain edge.

KM#	Date	Fine	VF	XF	Unc
96.1	1834	1400.	2500.	3500.	6000.

Reeded edge

| 96.2 | 1834 | 1600. | 3000. | 4500. | 6500. |

Obv: RUTHERF. Rev: CAROLINA. 140 G. 20 CARATS.
20 close to CARATS.

| 97.1 | 1834 | 1800. | 2750. | 5000. | 7500. |

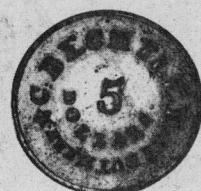 

Rev: 20 away from CARATS.

| 97.2 | 1834 | 1800. | 2750. | 5000. | 7500. |

Obv: RUTHERF. Rev: CAROLINA, 141 G, 20 CARATS.

| 98 | ND | — | Proof restrike | — |

Rev: NORTH CAROLINA, 150 G, below 20 CARATS.

| 99.1 | ND | 2200. | 3200. | 6000. | 12,500. |

Rev: Without 150 G.

| 99.2 | ND | 2800. | 4500. | 6500. | 13,500. |

OREGON

Oregon Exchange Co.
5 DOLLARS

| 100 | 1849 | 8500. | 13,500. | 18,500. | — |

10 DOLLARS

| 101 | 1849 | 17,500. | 29,500. | 42,500. | — |

UTAH

Mormon Issues
2-1/2 DOLLARS

| 102 | 1849 | 5000. | 7000. | 9500. | — |

5 DOLLARS

KM#	Date	Fine	VF	XF	Unc
103	1849	4500.	5500.	7000.	12,000.

| 104 | 1850 | 3000. | 4500. | 6500. | — |

| 105 | 1860 | 5500. | 9000. | 14,000. | 24,000. |

10 DOLLARS

| 106 | 1849 | 65,000. | 90,000. | | |

20 DOLLARS

| 107 | 1849 | 25,000. | 37,500. | 57,500. | — |

HAWAII

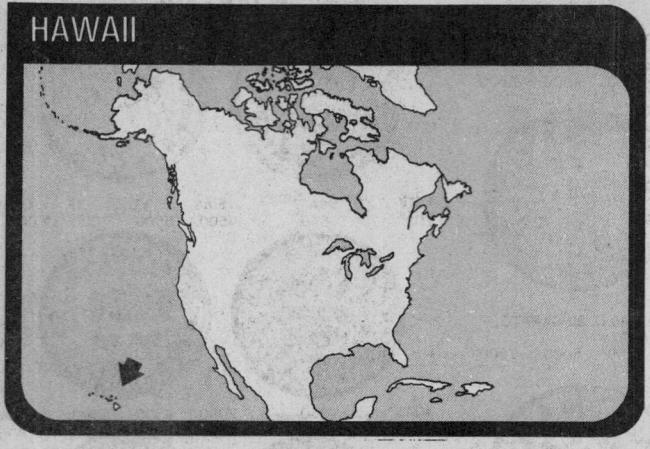

The 50th state of Hawaii, called the 'Aloha State', consists of eight main islands and numerous smaller islets of coral and volcanic origin. Situated in the central Pacific Ocean 2,400 miles from San Francisco, the Hawaiian archipelago has an area of 6,450 sq. mi. and a population of 1,083,000. Capitol: Honolulu. The principal sources of income are, in order: tourism, defense, and agriculture. The main exports are sugar cane and pineapple.

The islands, originally populated by Polynesians from the Society Islands, were rediscovered by British navigator Capt. James Cook in 1778. He named them the Sandwich Islands. King Kamehameha I (the Great) united the islands under one kingdom which endured until 1893, when Queen Lilioukalani was deposed and a provisional government established. This was followed in 1894 by a republic which governed Hawaii until 1898, when the islands were ceded to the United States. Hawaii was organized as a territory in 1900, and attained statehood on August 21, 1959.

RULERS

Kamehameha I, 1795-1819
Kamehameha II, 1819-24
Kamehameha III, 1825-54
Kamehameha IV, 1854-63
Kamehameha V, 1863-72
Lunalilo, 1873-74
Kalakaua, 1874-91
Liliuokalani, 1891-93
Provisional Govt., 1893-94
Republic, 1894-98
Annexed to U.S., 1898-1900
Territory, 1900-59

MONETARY SYSTEM

100 Hapa Haneri   Akahi Dala
100 Cents   1 Dollar (Dala)

CENT

Copper

KM#	Date	Mintage	VG	Fine	VF	XF	AU	MS-60	MS-65
1a	1847 plain 4, 13 berries (6 left, 7 right)								
		.100	150.00	200.00	250.00	350.00	500.00	800.00	2500.
1b	1847 plain 4, 15 berries (8 left, 7 right)								
		Inc. Ab.	150.00	200.00	250.00	350.00	550.00	850.00	2500.
1f	1847 plain 4, 15 berries (7 left, 8 right)								
		Inc. Ab.	150.00	200.00	250.00	350.00	550.00	850.00	2500.
1c	1847 plain 4, 17 berries (8 left, 9 right)								
		Inc. Ab.	160.00	225.00	275.00	450.00	700.00	1100.	2750.
1d	1847 crosslet 4, 15 berries (7 left, 8 right)								
		Inc. Ab.	150.00	200.00	250.00	350.00	500.00	850.00	2500.
1e	1847 crosslet 4, 18 berries (9 left, 9 right)								
		Inc. Ab.	170.00	235.00	300.00	500.00	1000.	1500.	3500.

SOUVENIR CENT

Modern replicas of the 1847 cent have been produced in several varieties, struck of brass oroide since the late 1940's for sale to tourists as souvenirs of their visits to the islands.

10 CENTS (UMI KENETA)

.900 Silver

KM#	Date	Mintage	VG	Fine	VF	XF	AU	MS-60	MS-65
3	1883	.250	35.00	45.00	75.00	200.00	500.00	1500.	3000.
	1883	26 pcs.	—	—	—	—	Proof	4500.	7500.

1/4 DOLLAR (HAPAHA)

.900 Silver

KM#	Date	Mintage	VG	Fine	VF	XF	AU	MS-60	MS-65
5	1883	.500	35.00	45.00	50.00	90.00	150.00	275.00	450.00
	1883/1383	Inc. Ab.	35.00	45.00	50.00	90.00	150.00	375.00	600.00
	1883	26 pcs.	—	—	—	—	Proof	2500.	5000.

Copper

KM#	Date	Mintage	VG	Fine	VF	XF	AU	MS-60	MS-65
5a	1883	18 pcs.	—	—	—	—	Proof	2500.	4500.

1/2 DOLLAR (HAPULA)

.900 Silver

KM#	Date	Mintage	VG	Fine	VF	XF	AU	MS-60	MS-65
6	1883	.700	40.00	55.00	75.00	150.00	350.00	800.00	2500.
	1883	26 pcs.	—	—	—	—	Proof	3000.	6000.

Copper

KM#	Date	Mintage	VG	Fine	VF	XF	AU	MS-60	MS-65
6a	1883	18 pcs.	—	—	—	—	Proof	3000.	5500.

DOLLAR (AKAHI DALA)

.900 Silver

KM#	Date	Mintage	VG	Fine	VF	XF	AU	MS-60	MS-65
7	1883	.500	160.00	200.00	250.00	450.00	1000.	5000.	9500.
	1883	26 pcs.	—	—	—	—	Proof	6000.	15,000.

Copper

KM#	Date	Mintage	VG	Fine	VF	XF	AU	MS-60	MS-65
7a	1883	18 pcs.	—	—	—	—	Proof	4000.	9000.

NOTE: Official records indicate the following quantities of the above issues were redeemed and melted: KM#1, 88,305; KM#3, 79; KM#5, 257,400; KM#6, 612,245; KM#7, 453,652. That leaves approximate net mintages of: KM#1, 11,600; KM#3, 250,000; KM#5, (regular date) 202,600, (overdate) 40,000; KM#6, 87,700; KM#7, 46,300.

URUGUAY

The Oriental Republic of Uruguay (so called because of its location on the east bank of the Uruguay River) is situated on the Atlantic coast of South America between Argentina and Brazil. This most advanced of South American countries has an area of 68,536 sq. mi. (177,508 sq. km.) and a population of *3 million. Capital: Montevideo. Uruguay's chief economic asset is its rich, rolling grassy plains. Meat, wool, hides and skins are exported.

Uruguay was discovered in 1516 by Juan Diaz de Solis, a Spaniard, but settled by the Portuguese who founded Colonia in 1680. Spain contested Portuguese possession and, after a long struggle, gained control of the country in 1778. During the general South American struggle for independence, Uruguay cast off the Spanish bond, only to be reconquered by the Portuguese from Brazil in the struggle of 1816-20. Revolt flared anew in 1825 and independence was reasserted in 1828 with the help of Argentina. The Uruguayan Republic was established in 1830.

MINT MARKS
A - Paris, Berlin, Vienna
(a) Paris, privy marks only
D - Lyon (France)
H - Birmingham
Mo,Mx - Mexico City
(p) Poissy, France
So - Santiago (Small O above S)
(u) - Utrecht

MONETARY SYSTEM
100 Centesimo = 1 Peso
Commencing 1975
1000 Old Pesos = 1 New Peso

CENTESIMO

BRONZE, 5.00 g

KM#	Date	Mintage	Fine	VF	XF	Unc
11	1869A	1.000	1.00	2.00	10.00	30.00
	1869H	1.000	1.00	2.00	10.00	30.00

COPPER-NICKEL, 2.00 g

19	1901A	5.000	.45	.75	3.00	18.00
	1901A	—	—	—	Proof	225.00
	1909A	5.000	.45	.75	3.00	12.00
	1924(p)	3.000	.75	1.50	3.50	12.50
	1936A	2.000	1.25	2.00	5.00	20.00

1.50 g

32	1953	5.000	.20	.30	.50	1.00
	1953	—	—	—	Proof	60.00

2 CENTESIMOS

BRONZE, 10.00 g

12	1869A	3.000	1.00	2.50	10.00	27.50
	1869H	2.000	1.00	2.50	10.00	27.50

COPPER-NICKEL, 3.50 g

KM#	Date	Mintage	Fine	VF	XF	Unc
20	1901A	7.500	.50	1.00	2.50	14.00
	1909A	10.000	.50	1.00	2.00	7.00
	1924(p)	11.000	.50	1.00	2.75	8.00
	1936A	6.500	.75	1.50	3.50	12.00
	1941So	10.000	.50	1.00	2.50	7.50

COPPER, 3.50 g

20a	1943So	5.000	.25	.50	1.75	6.00
	1944So	3.500	.35	.75	1.25	5.00
	1945So	2.500	.35	.75	1.50	7.00
	1946So	2.500	.35	.75	1.50	7.00
	1947So	5.000	.35	.75	1.00	4.50
	1948So	7.500	.25	.50	.75	3.00
	1949So	7.400	.25	.50	.75	3.00
	1951So	12.500	.25	.50	.75	2.50

COPPER-NICKEL, 2.50 g

33	1953	50.000	.20	.30	.50	1.25
	1953	—	—	—	Proof	65.00

NICKEL-BRASS, 2.00 g

37	1960	17.500		.15	.25	.50
	1960	—		—	Proof	40.00

4 CENTESIMOS

BRONZE, 20.00 g

13	1869A	2.000	2.00	4.00	12.50	75.00
	1869H	6.250	2.00	4.00	12.50	60.00

5 CENTESIMOS

COPPER, 4.25 g

KM#	Date	Mintage	VG	Fine	VF	XF
1	1840	1,500	125.00	250.00	400.00	650.00
	1844/0	—	95.00	190.00	325.00	475.00
	1844	—	85.00	175.00	300.00	425.00
	1854/40	—	20.00	30.00	50.00	100.00
	1854/44	—	20.00	30.00	50.00	100.00

4.35 g

KM#	Date	Mintage	VG	Fine	VF	XF
6	1855	—	75.00	125.00	225.00	500.00

KM#	Date	Mintage	Fine	VF	XF	Unc
8	1857D	—	5.00	10.00	20.00	50.00

COPPER-NICKEL, 5.00 g

21	1901A	6.000	.25	.75	2.00	10.00
	1901A	—	—	—	Proof	325.00
	1909A	5.000	.25	.75	2.00	10.00
	1909A	—	—	—	Proof	125.00
	1924(p)	5.000	.35	1.00	3.50	8.00
	1936A	3.000	.35	1.00	3.00	8.00
	1941So	26.000	.25	.75	1.50	4.00
	1941S(O)	—	—	—	Proof	200.00

COPPER, 5.00 g

21a	1944So	4.000	.20	.65	1.00	7.00
	1946So	2.000	.20	.50	1.50	8.00
	1947So	2.000	.20	.50	1.50	8.00
	1948So	3.000	.20	.50	1.00	7.00
	1949So	2.800	.20	.50	1.00	7.00
	1951So	15.000	.20	.50	1.00	4.50

COPPER-NICKEL, 3.50 g

34	1953	17.500	.20	.30	.50	1.00
	1953	—	—	—	Proof	75.00

NICKEL-BRASS, 3.50 g

38	1960	88.000		.15	.25	.50
	1960	—		—	Proof	40.00

10 CENTESIMOS

2.5000 g, .900 SILVER, .0723 oz ASW

14	1877A privy mark anchor points to left					
		3.000	3.50	6.00	10.00	35.00
	1877A privy mark anchor points to right					
	Inc. Ab.	—	—	—	—	
	1893/77So	—	—	—	—	
	1893 w/o mm	—	50.00	70.00	110.00	250.00
	1893So	1.000	2.50	7.00	15.00	50.00

ALUMINUM-BRONZE, 8.00 g

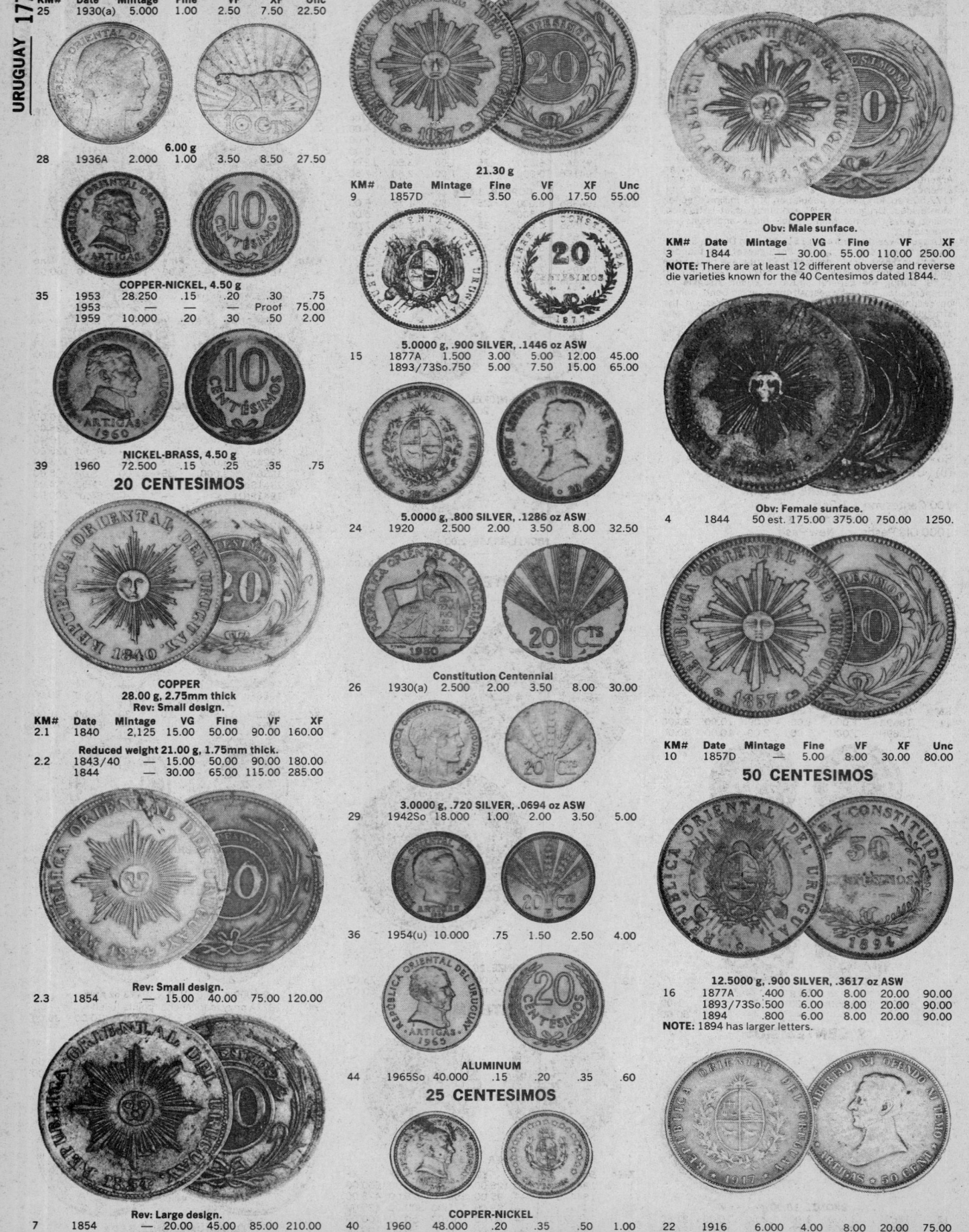

URUGUAY 1778

Constitution Centennial

KM#	Date	Mintage	Fine	VF	XF	Unc
25	1930(a)	5.000	1.00	2.50	7.50	22.50

6.00 g

| 28 | 1936A | 2.000 | 1.00 | 3.50 | 8.50 | 27.50 |

COPPER-NICKEL, 4.50 g

35	1953	28.250	.15	.20	.30	.75
	1953		—	—	Proof	75.00
	1959	10.000	.20	.30	.50	2.00

NICKEL-BRASS, 4.50 g

| 39 | 1960 | 72.500 | .15 | .25 | .35 | .75 |

20 CENTESIMOS

COPPER
28.00 g, 2.75mm thick
Rev: Small design.

KM#	Date	Mintage	VG	Fine	VF	XF
2.1	1840	2,125	15.00	50.00	90.00	160.00

Reduced weight 21.00 g, 1.75mm thick.

| 2.2 | 1843/40 | — | 15.00 | 50.00 | 90.00 | 180.00 |
| | 1844 | — | 30.00 | 65.00 | 115.00 | 285.00 |

Rev: Small design.

| 2.3 | 1854 | — | 15.00 | 40.00 | 75.00 | 120.00 |

Rev: Large design.

| 7 | 1854 | — | 20.00 | 45.00 | 85.00 | 210.00 |
| (2.4) | 1855 | — | 20.00 | 45.00 | 85.00 | 210.00 |

21.30 g

KM#	Date	Mintage	Fine	VF	XF	Unc
9	1857D	—	3.50	6.00	17.50	55.00

5.0000 g, .900 SILVER, .1446 oz ASW

| 15 | 1877A | 1.500 | 3.00 | 5.00 | 12.00 | 45.00 |
| | 1893/73So | .750 | 5.00 | 7.50 | 15.00 | 65.00 |

5.0000 g, .800 SILVER, .1286 oz ASW

| 24 | 1920 | 2.500 | 2.00 | 3.50 | 8.00 | 32.50 |

Constitution Centennial

| 26 | 1930(a) | 2.500 | 2.00 | 3.50 | 8.00 | 30.00 |

3.0000 g, .720 SILVER, .0694 oz ASW

| 29 | 1942So | 18.000 | 1.00 | 2.00 | 3.50 | 5.00 |

| 36 | 1954(u) | 10.000 | .75 | 1.50 | 2.50 | 4.00 |

ALUMINUM

| 44 | 1965So | 40.000 | .15 | .20 | .35 | .60 |

25 CENTESIMOS

COPPER-NICKEL

| 40 | 1960 | 48.000 | .20 | .35 | .50 | 1.00 |
| | 1960 | | — | — | Proof | 60.00 |

40 CENTESIMOS

COPPER
Obv: Male sunface.

KM#	Date	Mintage	VG	Fine	VF	XF
3	1844	—	30.00	55.00	110.00	250.00

NOTE: There are at least 12 different obverse and reverse die varieties known for the 40 Centesimos dated 1844.

Obv: Female sunface.

| 4 | 1844 | 50 est. | 175.00 | 375.00 | 750.00 | 1250. |

KM#	Date	Mintage	Fine	VF	XF	Unc
10	1857D	—	5.00	8.00	30.00	80.00

50 CENTESIMOS

12.5000 g, .900 SILVER, .3617 oz ASW

16	1877A	.400	6.00	8.00	20.00	90.00
	1893/73So	.500	6.00	8.00	20.00	90.00
	1894	.800	6.00	8.00	20.00	90.00

NOTE: 1894 has larger letters.

| 22 | 1916 | 6.000 | 4.00 | 8.00 | 20.00 | 75.00 |
| | 1917 | Inc. Ab. | 4.00 | 6.00 | 17.50 | 60.00 |

URUGUAY 1779

ALUMINUM-BRONZE

KM#	Date	Mintage	Fine	VF	XF	Unc
53	1969So	42,320	—	—	.10	.25

7.0000 g, .720 SILVER, .1620 oz ASW

KM#	Date	Mintage	Fine	VF	XF	Unc
31	1943So	10,800	BV	2.00	3.00	9.00

9.0000 g, .720 SILVER, .2083 oz ASW

KM#	Date	Mintage	Fine	VF	XF	Unc
30	1942So	9,000	BV	2.25	4.50	12.50

10 PESOS

COPPER-NICKEL

41	1960	18,000	.20	.40	.60	1.00
	1960	—	—	—	Proof	60.00

COPPER-NICKEL

42	1960	8,000	.25	.50	.75	1.25
	1960	—	—	—	Proof	75.00

12.5000 g, .900 SILVER, .3617 oz ASW
Gaucho Heroes Sesquicentennial

43	1961	3,000	—	BV	4.00	8.50
	1961	—	—	—	Proof	600.00

ALUMINUM

45	1965So	50,000	—	.15	.25	.40	.70

PESO

ALUMINUM-BRONZE

46	1965So	60,000	—	—	.15	.35	.60
	1965So	25 pcs.	—	—	—	Proof	65.00

ALUMINUM-BRONZE

48	1965So	18,000	—	.15	.20	.35	1.00

27.0000 g, .875 SILVER, .7596 oz ASW

5	1844	1,500	200.00	350.00	700.00	1850.

NOTE: KM#5 exists both with coin and medal reverse alignments.

NICKEL-BRASS

49	1968So	103,200	—	—	.15	.30
	1968So	50 pcs.	—	—	—	Proof	50.00

NICKEL-BRASS

51	1968So	75,000	—	.15	.20	.35	.50
	1968So	50 pcs.	—	—	—	Proof	80.00

ALUMINUM-BRONZE

52	1969So	51,800	—	—	.15	.30

5 PESOS

25.5000 g, .917 SILVER, .7518 oz ASW

17	1877A	.300	25.00	45.00	100.00	400.00
	1877A	—	—	—	Proof	1000.

25.0000 g, .900 SILVER, .7235 oz ASW

17a	1878A	*.100	125.00	350.00	800.00	1500.
	1893/73So	.500	25.00	50.00	100.00	425.00
	1893So	Inc. Ab.	20.00	35.00	85.00	400.00
	1893	.600	20.00	35.00	75.00	350.00
	1895	1.000	15.00	25.00	65.00	300.00

***NOTE:** 43,200 melted after they were recovered from salt water.

8.4850 g, .917 GOLD, .2501 oz AGW
Constitution Centennial

27	1930(a)	*.100	125.00	150.00	175.00	250.00

NOTE: Only 14,415 were released. Remainder withheld.

ALUMINUM-BRONZE

47	1965So	18,000	.20	.30	.50	1.00
	1965So	25 pcs.	—	—	—	Proof	75.00

ALUMINUM-BRONZE

54	1969So	25,000	—	.15	.20	.35	.50

20 PESOS

COPPER-NICKEL

56	1970So	50,000	—	.15	.25	.40	.75
	1970So	—	—	—	—	Proof	80.00

50 PESOS

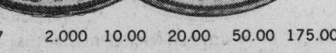

23	1917	2,000	10.00	20.00	50.00	175.00

NICKEL-BRASS

50	1968So	42,680	.10	.20	.30	.40
	1968So	50 pcs.	—	—	—	Proof	65.00

COPPER-NICKEL

57	1970So	20,000	—	.20	.35	.50	1.50
	1970So	—	—	—	—	Proof	80.00

URUGUAY

NICKEL-BRASS
Centennial Birth of Rodo

KM#	Date	Mintage	Fine	VF	XF	Unc
58	1971So	15.000	.20	.50	1.00	2.00

6.0200 g, .900 SILVER, .1742 oz ASW
| 58a | 1971So | 1,000 | — | — | Proof | 17.50 |

GOLD
| 58b | 1971So | 100 pcs. | — | — | Proof | 350.00 |

100 PESOS

COPPER-NICKEL
| 59 | 1973Mx | 20.000 | .25 | .50 | 1.00 | 2.50 |

1000 PESOS

25.0000 g, .900 SILVER, .7234 oz ASW
F.A.O. Issue
| 55 | 1969So | .500 | — | BV | 8.00 | 12.50 |
| | 1969So | 250 pcs. | — | — | Proof | 80.00 |

BRONZE (OMS)
| 55a | 1969So | .011 | — | — | 25.00 | 40.00 |

COUNTERSTAMPED COINAGE
PESO

SILVER
| 18 | 1895 | — | 75.00 | 125.00 | 200.00 | — |

NOTE: Dies were made in the Paysandu area of Uruguay, and Brazil 2,000 reis were overstruck to create an 1895 1 peso coin. These coins are considered by some to be a contemporary counterfeit and probably have no official standing.

MONETARY REFORM
1000 Old Pesos = 1 New Peso

CENTESIMO

ALUMINUM
KM#	Date	Mintage	Fine	VF	XF	Unc
71	1977So	10.000	—	—	.15	.35

3.7000 g, .900 SILVER, .1071 oz ASW
| 71a | 1979So | 202 pcs. | — | — | Proof | 15.00 |

6.2600 g, .900 GOLD, .1811 oz AGW
| 71b | 1979So | 50 pcs. | — | — | Proof | 175.00 |

2 CENTESIMOS

ALUMINUM
| 72 | 1977So | 13.800 | — | — | .15 | .35 |
| | 1978So | 6.200 | — | — | .15 | .35 |

5.2000 g, .900 SILVER, .1505 oz ASW
| 72a | 1979So | 202 pcs. | — | — | Proof | 20.00 |

9.2500 g, .900 GOLD, .2676 oz AGW
| 72b | 1979So | 52 pcs. | — | — | Proof | 275.00 |

5 CENTESIMOS

ALUMINUM
| 73 | 1977So | 8.500 | — | — | .15 | .35 |
| | 1978So | 21.500 | — | — | .15 | .35 |

7.4000 g, .900 SILVER, .2141 oz ASW
| 73a | 1979So | 202 pcs. | — | — | Proof | 20.00 |

12.5500 g, .900 GOLD, .3631 oz AGW
| 73b | 1979So | 52 pcs. | — | — | Proof | 350.00 |

10 CENTESIMOS

ALUMINUM-BRONZE
66	1976So	127.400	—	—	.15	.35
	1977So	12.700	—	—	.20	.40
	1978So	19.900	—	—	.20	.40
	1981So	—	—	—	.20	.40

3.8000 g, .900 SILVER, .1100 oz ASW
| 66a | 1976So | 200 pcs. | — | — | Proof | 20.00 |
| | 1977So | 200 pcs. | — | — | Proof | 20.00 |

6.0000 g, .900 GOLD, .1736 oz AGW
| 66b | 1976So | 50 pcs. | — | — | Proof | 175.00 |

20 CENTESIMOS

ALUMINUM-BRONZE
67	1976So	40.000	—	—	.20	.45
	1977So	4.700	—	—	.20	.60
	1978So	15.300	—	—	.20	.45
	1981So	—	—	—	.20	.45

6.4000 g, .900 SILVER, .1852 oz ASW
| 67a | 1976So | 200 pcs. | — | — | Proof | 22.50 |
| | 1977So | 200 pcs. | — | — | Proof | 22.50 |

10.5000 g, .900 GOLD, .3038 oz AGW
| 67b | 1976So | 50 pcs. | — | — | Proof | 350.00 |

50 CENTESIMOS

ALUMINUM-BRONZE
KM#	Date	Mintage	Fine	VF	XF	Unc
68	1976So	30.000	—	—	.20	.50
	1977So	9.800	—	—	.20	.50
	1978So	.200	—	—	.20	.55
	1981So	—	—	—	.20	.50

9.0000 g, .900 SILVER, .2604 oz ASW
| 68a | 1976So | 200 pcs. | — | — | Proof | 35.00 |
| | 1977So | 200 pcs. | — | — | Proof | 35.00 |

15.0000 g, .900 GOLD, .4340 oz AGW
| 68b | 1976So | 50 pcs. | — | — | Proof | 500.00 |

NEW PESO

ALUMINUM-BRONZE
69	1976So	65.540	—	—	.30	.60
	1977So	7.360	—	—	.30	.65
	1978So	27.100	—	—	.30	.65

13.5000 g, .900 SILVER, .3906 oz ASW
| 69a | 1976So | 200 pcs. | — | — | Proof | 40.00 |

23.0000 g, .900 GOLD, .6655 oz AGW
| 69b | 1976So | 50 pcs. | — | — | Proof | 600.00 |

COPPER-NICKEL
| 74 | 1980So | — | — | .20 | .35 | .50 |
| | 1981So | — | — | .20 | .35 | .50 |

7.0000 g, .900 SILVER, .2026 oz ASW
| 74a | 1980So | 300 pcs. | — | — | Proof | 25.00 |

11.6500 g, .900 GOLD, .3371 oz AGW
| 74b | 1980So | 100 pcs. | — | — | Proof | 300.00 |

6.9400 g, .900 SILVER, .2008 oz ASW
Obv: National flag.
| 76 | 1981 | 100 pcs. | — | — | Proof | 30.00 |

2 NEW PESOS

COPPER-NICKEL-ZINC
World Food Day
| 77 | 1981 | 95.000 | — | — | .20 | .35 | .75 |

14.5300 g, .900 GOLD, .4204 oz AGW
| 77a | 1981 | 100 pcs. | — | — | Proof | 400.00 |

5 NEW PESOS

COPPER-NICKEL-ALUMINUM

URUGUAY 1781

150th Anniversary of Revolutionary Movement

KM#	Date	Mintage	Fine	VF	XF	Unc
65	ND(1975)So	3,000	.50	.75	1.25	2.50

18.4300 g, .900 SILVER, .5332 oz ASW
| 65a | ND(1975)So | 2,000 | — | — | Proof | 15.00 |

GOLD
| 65b | ND(1975)So | 1,000 | — | — | Proof | 500.00 |

NOTE: 50 pieces each in aluminum, alpaca and copper are reported to have been struck.

COPPER-ALUMINUM
250th Anniversary Founding of Montevideo
| 70 | 1976So | .300 | .75 | 1.00 | 1.50 | 4.00 |

SILVER
| 70b | 1976So | — | — | Reported, not confirmed | | |

30.0000 g, .900 GOLD, .8681 oz AGW
| 70a | 1976So | 100 pcs. | — | — | Proof | 725.00 |

COPPER-NICKEL
| 75 | 1980 | — | — | .20 | .40 | 1.25 |
| | 1981 | — | — | .20 | .40 | 1.25 |

9.3000 g, .900 SILVER, .2691 oz ASW
| 75a | 1980So | 300 pcs. | — | — | Proof | 30.00 |

15.6000 g, .900 GOLD, .4514 oz AGW
| 75b | 1980So | 100 pcs. | — | — | Proof | 450.00 |

9.3000 g, .900 SILVER, .2691 oz ASW
Obv: Coat of arms.
| 78 | 1981 | — | — | — | Proof | 30.00 |

10 NEW PESOS

COPPER-NICKEL
| 79 | 1981So | — | — | .20 | .50 | 1.50 |

11.6300 g, .900 SILVER, .3365 oz ASW
| 79a | 1981So | 100 pcs. | — | — | Proof | 35.00 |

19.4800 g, .900 GOLD, .5637 oz AGW
| 79b | 1981So | 100 pcs. | — | — | Proof | 500.00 |

20 NEW PESOS

COPPER-NICKEL
World Fisheries Conference
| 86 | 1984 | .101 | — | — | — | 5.00 |

11.6600 g, .925 SILVER, .3468 oz ASW
| 86a | 1984 | .025 | — | — | Proof | 15.00 |

19.6000 g, .917 GOLD, .5776 oz AGW
| 86b | 1984 | 100 pcs. | — | — | Proof | 600.00 |

100 NEW PESOS

12.0000 g, .900 SILVER, .3472 oz ASW
Hydroelectric Dam
KM#	Date	Mintage	Fine	VF	XF	Unc
80	1981So	.025	—	—	6.00	12.50

20.0000 g, .900 GOLD, .5787 oz AGW
| 80a | 1981So | 300 pcs. | — | — | Proof | 375.00 |

500 NEW PESOS

12.0000 g, .900 SILVER, .3472 oz ASW
Hydroelectric Dam
| 82 | 1983 | .015 | — | — | — | 15.00 |

20.0000 g, .900 GOLD, .5787 oz AGW
| 82a | 1983 | 100 pcs. | — | — | Proof | 500.00 |

12.0000 g, .900 SILVER, .3473 oz ASW
General Leandro Gomez
| 90 | 1986 | 6,000 | — | — | Proof | 25.00 |

2000 NEW PESOS

65.0000 g, .900 SILVER, 1.8810 oz ASW
Royal Visit of Spanish King and Queen
| 83 | 1983 | .020 | — | — | Proof | 32.50 |

25.0000 g, .900 SILVER, .7234 oz ASW
140th Anniversary of Silver Coinage and
25th Meeting of Interamerican Bank Governors
KM#	Date	Mintage	Fine	VF	XF	Unc
87	1984	.015	—	—	Proof	40.00

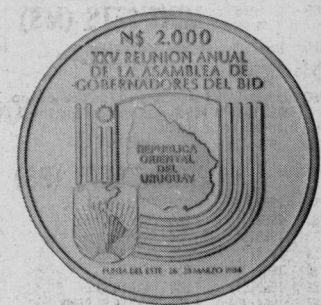

25th Meeting of Interamerican Bank Governors
| 88 | 1984 | .015 | — | — | Proof | 40.00 |

5000 NEW PESOS

12.0000 g, .900 SILVER, .3472 oz ASW
Hydroelectric Dam
| 81 | 1981So | .015 | — | — | Proof | 22.50 |

20.0000 g, .900 GOLD, .5787 oz AGW
| 81a | 1981So | 3,000 | — | — | Proof | 325.00 |

URUGUAY 1782

20000 NEW PESOS

20.0000 g, .900 GOLD, .5787 oz AGW
Royal Visit

KM#	Date	Mintage	Fine	VF	XF	Unc
84	1983	1,500	—	—	Proof	375.00

12.0000 g, .900 SILVER, .3472 oz ASW

| 84a | 1983 | 100 pcs. | — | — | Proof | 75.00 |

20.0000 g, .900 GOLD, .5787 oz AGW
Hydroelectric Dam

| 85 | 1983 | 2,500 | — | — | Proof | 375.00 |

130th Anniversary of Gold Coinage and 25th Meeting of Interamerican Bank Governors

| 89 | 1984 | 1,500 | — | — | Proof | 375.00 |

MINT SETS (MS)

KM#	Date	Mintage	Identification	Issue Price	Mkt. Val.
MS1	1969/70(5)	—	KM52-54,56-57	—	3.50
MS2	1969/70(5)	—	KM52-54,56-57	—	3.50

NOTE: KM#MS1 was issued for the law no. 13,637 of Dec. 21, 1967 while MS2 was issued for the 11th Assembly of the Interamerica Bank.

| MS3 | 1976(4) | — | KM66-69 | — | 2.50 |

PROOF SETS (PS)

PS1	1953(4)	100	KM32-35	—	275.00
PS2	1968(5)	1,000	Pn79,81,83-85	—	78.00
PS3	1968(3)	50	KM49-51	—	200.00
PS4	1968(3)	*100	Pn78,80,82	—	90.00
PS5	1969(3)	*50	Pn86,88,90	—	75.00
PS6	1969(3)	1,000	Pn87,89,91	—	30.00
PS7	1969/70(5)	1,000	Pn87,89,91,96,98	—	50.00

VANUATU

The Republic of Vanuatu, formerly New Hebrides Condominium, a group of islands located in the South Pacific 500 miles (800 km.) west of Fiji, are under the joint sovereignty of Great Britain and France. The islands have an area of 5,700 sq. mi. (14,763 sq. km.) and a population of *150,000, mainly Melanesians of mixed blood. Capital: Port-Vila. The volcanic and coral islands, while malarial and subject to frequent earthquakes, are extremely fertile, and produce copra, coffee, tropical fruits and timber for export.

The New Hebrides were discovered by Portuguese navigator Pedro de Quiros in 1606, visited by French explorer Bougainville in 1768, and named by British navigator Capt. James Cook in 1774. Ships of all nations converged on the islands to trade for sandalwood, prompting France and Britain to relinquish their individual claims and declare the islands a neutral zone in 1878. The New Hebrides were placed under the control of a mixed Anglo-French commission of naval officers during the native uprisings of 1887, and established as a condominium under the joint sovereignty of France and Great Britain in 1906.

MINT MARKS
(a) - Paris, privy marks only

MONETARY SYSTEM
100 Centimes = 1 Franc

NEW HEBRIDES
FRANC

NICKEL-BRASS

KM#	Date	Mintage	VF	XF	Unc
4.1	1970(a)	.435	.25	.50	.75

Obv. leg: I.E.O.M. added.

4.2	1975(a)	.350	.20	.40	.60
	1978(a)	.200	.20	.40	.60
	1979(a)	—	.20	.40	.60

2 FRANCS

NICKEL-BRASS

| 5.1 | 1970(a) | .264 | .60 | 1.25 | 2.00 |

Obv. leg: I.E.O.M. added.

5.2	1973(a)	.200	.20	.40	.60
	1975(a)	.300	.20	.40	.60
	1978(a)	.150	.20	.40	.60
	1979(a)	—	.20	.40	.60

5 FRANCS

NICKEL-BRASS

| 6.1 | 1970(a) | .375 | .50 | .75 | 1.50 |

Obv. leg: I.E.O.M. added.

KM#	Date	Mintage	VF	XF	Unc
6.2	1975(a)	.350	.30	.60	1.00
	1979(a)	—	.30	.60	1.00

10 FRANCS

NICKEL

| 2.1 | 1967(a) | .250 | .30 | .60 | 1.25 |
| | 1970(a) | .400 | .30 | .60 | 1.25 |

Obv. leg: I.E.O.M. added.

2.2	1973(a)	.200	.30	.60	1.25
	1975(a)	.300	.30	.60	1.25
	1979(a)	—	.30	.60	1.25

20 FRANCS

NICKEL

| 3.1 | 1967(a) | .250 | .60 | 1.00 | 2.00 |
| | 1970(a) | .300 | .60 | 1.00 | 2.00 |

Obv. leg: I.E.O.M. added.

3.2	1973(a)	.200	.60	1.00	2.00
	1975(a)	.150	.60	1.00	2.00
	1979(a)	—	.60	1.00	2.00

50 FRANCS

NICKEL

KM#	Date	Mintage	VF	XF	Unc
7	1972(a)	.200	1.50	2.50	3.50
	1979(a)	—	1.50	2.50	3.50

100 FRANCS

25.0000 g, .835 SILVER, .6712 oz ASW

1	1966(a)	.200	—	—	16.00
	1979(a)	—	—	—	20.00

FLEUR DE COIN SETS (SS)

KM#	Date	Mintage	Identification	Issue Price	Mkt. Val.
SS1	1967(3)	2,200	Y1,2,3(1966)	10.00	10.00

NOTE: These sets were issued with New Caledonia and French Polynesia 1967 sets.

VANUATU

VATU

NICKEL-BRASS

KM#	Date	Mintage	VF	XF	Unc
3	1983	—	—	.10	.35
	1983	—	—	Proof	3.00

2 VATU

NICKEL-BRASS

4	1983	—	—	.10	.45
	1983	—	—	Proof	3.00

5 VATU

NICKEL-BRASS

5	1983	—	—	.15	.60
	1983	—	—	Proof	4.00

10 VATU

COPPER-NICKEL

6	1983	—	—	.15	.75
	1983	—	—	Proof	4.00

20 VATU

COPPER-NICKEL

KM#	Date	Mintage	VF	XF	Unc
7	1983	—	—	.30	1.25
	1983	—	—	Proof	6.00

50 VATU

NICKEL
1st Anniversary of Independence

1	1981	—	—	1.00	2.00

15.0000 g, .925 SILVER, .4461 oz ASW

1a	1981	846 pcs.	—	Proof	50.00

COPPER-NICKEL

8	1983	—	—	1.00	2.00
	1983	—	—	Proof	10.00

100 VATU

NICKEL-BRASS

9	1988	—	—	—	3.75

10,000 VATU

15.9800 g, .917 GOLD, .4712 oz AGW
1st Anniversary of Independence

KM#	Date	Mintage	VF	XF	Unc
2	1981	538 pcs.	—	—	350.00
	1981	1,054	—	Proof	350.00

PROOF SETS (PS)

KM#	Date	Mintage	Identification	Issue Price	Mkt. Val.
PS1	1983(6)	—	KM3-8	—	30.00

VATICAN PAPAL CITY STATES

The 21 Papal City States spanned the Papal states from one end to the other. Most of the cities had been the holy see for hundreds of years. Many of them housed religious architecture and relics that were a veritable history of the church. Many had strong local families that helped administrate the city and occassionally opposed the Papal authority. Most of these cities stayed in the Papal states until 1860 when Papal territories began to crumble due to the move for unification of all Italy.

MINTS
17 of the mints functioned only during the Napoleonic period.

1 - Ancona
2 - Ascoli
3 - Bologna
4 - Civitavecchia
5 - Fano
6 - Fermo
7 - Ferrara
8 - Foligno
9 - Gubbio
10 - Macerata
11 - Matelica
12 - Montalto
13 - Pergola
14 - Perugia
15 - Ravenna
16 - Ronciglione
17 - San Severino
18 - Spoleto
19 - Terni
20 - Tivoli
21 - Viterbo

EXTRINSIC MINT
Avignon (Southern France)

PONTIFFS
Pius VII, 1800-1823
Sede Vacante, Aug. 20-Sept. 28, 1823
Leo XII, 1823-1829
Sede Vacante, Feb. 10-Mar. 31, 1829
Pius VIII, 1829-1830
Sede Vacante, Nov. 30, 1830-Feb. 2, 1831
Gregory XVI, 1831-1846
Sede Vacante, June 1-16, 1846
Pius IX, 1846-1878

MONETARY SYSTEM
6 Quattrini = 1 Bolognino or Baiocco
5 Baiocchi = 1 Grossi
2 Grossi = 1 Giuli = 1 Paoli
3 Giuli = 3 Paoli = 1 Testone
10 Giuli = 10 Paoli = 1 Scudo
3 Scudi = 1 Doppia

ANCONA
Anconna

A city in the Marches, was founded by Syracusan refugees about 390 B.C. It became a semi-independent republic under papal protection in the 14th century, and a papal state in 1532. From 1797 until the formation of the United Kingdom of Italy it was part of the Roman Republic (1798-99), a papal state (1799-1808), part of the Italian Kingdom of Napoleon (1808-14), a papal state (1814-48), a part of the Roman Republic (1848-49), and a papal state (1849-60).

MINT MARKS
A - Ancona

MONETARY SYSTEM
100 Baiocchi = 1 Scudo

ROMAN REPUBLIC
1798-1799, 1848-1849

BAIOCCO

CAST COPPER
Rev: A below date.

C#	Date	Year	VG	Fine	VF	XF
12	1849A	—	5.50	10.00	20.00	32.50

3 BAIOCCHI
CAST COPPER
Obv: Fasces, REPUBBLICA ROMANA.
Rev: Value, date, mm.

13	1848A	—	30.00	60.00	100.00	150.00

ROMAN REPUBLIC
Repubblica Romana

A short-lived Republican movement fostered by the French Revolution, submerged the Papal States in 1798-99. They reappeared in 1814, and except for the Republican movement of 1848-49, maintained their authority until 1860.

MINT MARKS
R - Rome

1848-1849
1/2 BAIOCCO

COPPER

C#	Date	Year	Good	VG	Fine	VF
21	1849R	—	2.00	4.00	6.50	10.00

BAIOCCO

COPPER

| 22 | 1849R | — | 2.00 | 4.00 | 6.50 | 10.00 |

3 BAIOCCHI

COPPER
Obv: Round 3.

| 23 | 1849R | — | 4.00 | 8.00 | 15.00 | 20.00 |

Obv: Flat topped 3.

C#	Date	Year	Good	VG	Fine	VF
23.1	1849B	—	5.00	10.00	18.00	30.00
	1849R	—	4.00	8.00	15.00	20.00

4 BAIOCCHI

1.9500 g, .200 SILVER, .0125 oz ASW

| 24 | 1849B | — | 5.00 | 10.00 | 18.00 | 30.00 |
| | 1849R | — | 4.00 | 8.00 | 13.00 | 20.00 |

8 BAIOCCHI

3.9000 g, .200 SILVER, .0251 oz ASW

| 25 | 1849R | — | 7.50 | 15.00 | 25.00 | 40.00 |

16 BAIOCCHI

7.8000 g, .200 SILVER, .0502 oz ASW

| 26 | 1849R | — | 9.00 | 18.00 | 25.00 | 45.00 |

40 BAIOCCHI

20.0000 g, .200 SILVER, .1286 oz ASW

| 27 | 1849R | — | 15.00 | 30.00 | 50.00 | 80.00 |

VATICAN-PAPAL STATES

During many centuries prior to the formation of the unified Kingdom of Italy, when Italy was divided into numerous independent papal and ducal states, the Popes held temporal sovereignty over an area in central Italy comprising some 17,000 sq. mi. (44,030 sq. km.) including the city of Rome. At the time of the general unification of Italy under the Kingdom of Sardinia, 1861, the papal dominions beyond Rome were acquired by that kingdom, diminishing the Pope's sovereignty to Rome and its environs. In 1870, while France's opposition to papal dispossession was neutralized by its war with Prussia, the Italian army seized weakly defended Rome and made it the capital of Italy, thereby abrogating the last vestige of papal temporal power. In 1871, the Italian Parliament enacted the Law of Guarantees, which guaranteed a special status for the Vatican area, and spiritual freedom and a generous income for the Pope. Pope Pius IX and his successors adamantly refused to acknowledge the validity of these laws, and voluntarily "imprisoned" themselves in the Vatican. The impasse between State and Church lasted until the signing of the Lateran Treaty, Feb. 11, 1929, by which Italy recognized the sovereignty and independence of the new Vatican City state.

PONTIFFS

Pius VII, 1800-1823
  Sede Vacante, Aug. 20-Sept. 28, 1823
Leo XII, 1823-1829
  Sede Vacante, Feb. 10-Mar. 31, 1829
Pius VIII, 1829-1830
  Sede Vacante, Nov. 30, 1830-Feb. 2, 1831
Gregory XVI, 1831-1846
  Sede Vacante, June 1-16, 1846
Pius IX, 1846-1878

MINT MARKS

B - Bologna
R - Rome

MONETARY SYSTEM
(Until 1860)

150 Quattrini = 30 Baiocchi =
  6 Grossi = 4 Carlini = 3 Giulio =
  3 Paoli = 1 Testone.
100 Baiocchi = 1 Scudo
30 Paoli = Doppia

QUATTRINO

COPPER

C#	Date	Year	VG	Fine	VF	XF
106	1801R	—	6.00	12.00	25.00	45.00

C#	Date	Year	VG	Fine	VF	XF
107	1802R	II	4.00	7.50	12.50	25.00

Obv. value: QVATTRINO.

C#	Date	Year	VG	Fine	VF	XF
107a	1816B	XVI	4.00	7.50	12.50	25.00
	1816R	XVI	4.00	7.50	12.50	25.00
	1816R	XVII	4.00	7.50	12.50	25.00
	1821B	XXII	5.00	8.50	14.00	28.00
	1821R	XXII	4.00	7.50	12.50	25.00
	1822B	XXII	4.00	7.50	12.50	25.00

Obv. value: VN QVATTRINO.

107.5	1816B	XVI	15.00	25.00	40.00	70.00

125.5	1824(B)	I	4.00	7.50	12.50	25.00

126	1824R	I	3.00	5.00	8.50	15.00
	1825R	II	3.00	5.00	8.50	15.00

126a	1826R	IV	3.00	5.00	8.50	15.00

135	1829R	I	4.00	7.50	12.50	25.00

144	1831R	I	2.00	4.00	7.50	15.00

144a	1835R	V	2.00	4.00	7.50	15.00
	1836B	VI	2.00	4.00	7.50	15.00
	1838B	VIII	2.00	4.00	7.50	15.00
	1839B	IX	4.00	7.50	12.50	25.00
	1839R	IX	2.00	4.00	7.50	15.00
	1840B	X	4.00	7.50	12.50	25.00
	1841R	X	3.00	5.00	8.50	15.00
	1841R	XI	2.00	4.00	7.50	15.00
	1843B	XIII	2.00	4.00	7.50	15.00
	1843R	XIII	2.00	4.00	7.50	15.00
	1844B	XIV	2.00	4.00	7.50	15.00
	1844R	XIV	2.00	4.00	7.50	15.00

C#	Date	Mintage	VG	Fine	VF	XF
164	1851R yr.VI.090		3.00	5.00	8.50	15.00
	1854B yr.IX.173		3.00	5.00	8.50	15.00

MEZZO (1/2) BAIOCCO

COPPER

C#	Date	Year	VG	Fine	VF	XF
108	1801R	—	5.00	8.50	14.00	28.00

NOTE: Varieties exist.

109	1802R	II	3.00	5.00	8.50	15.00

109a	1816R	XVI	5.00	10.00	17.50	30.00
	1816R	XVII	5.00	10.00	17.50	30.00

109a.1	1816B	XVI	3.00	5.00	8.50	15.00
	1816B	XVII	3.00	5.00	8.50	15.00
	1822B	XXII	5.00	8.50	14.00	28.00
	1822R	XXII	5.00	8.50	14.00	28.00

109a.2	1822R	XXII	10.00	20.00	35.00	50.00

127	1824B	I	6.00	10.00	17.50	30.00

127a	1825R	II	4.00	7.50	12.50	25.00
	1826R	III	4.00	7.50	12.50	25.00

Papal States / VATICAN 1786

C#	Date	Year	VG	Fine	VF	XF
136	1829B	I	5.00	10.00	17.50	30.00
	1829R	I	5.00	10.00	17.50	30.00

145	1831R	I	2.00	4.00	7.50	15.00
	1832B	II	4.00	7.50	15.00	30.00
	1832B	III	3.50	6.50	12.50	17.50
	1833B	III	2.00	4.00	7.50	15.00
	1834B	IV	2.00	4.00	7.50	15.00

145a	1835B	V	2.00	4.00	7.50	15.00
	1835R	V	2.00	4.00	7.50	15.00
	1836B	VI	2.00	4.00	7.50	15.00
	1836R	VI	2.00	4.00	7.50	15.00
	1837B	VII	2.00	4.00	7.50	15.00
	1837R	VII	3.50	6.50	12.50	17.50
	1838B	VIII	3.50	6.50	12.50	17.50
	1838R	VIII	3.50	6.50	12.50	17.50
	1839B	IX	2.00	4.00	7.50	15.00
	1839R	IX	3.50	6.50	12.50	17.50
	1840R	IX	3.50	6.50	12.50	17.50
	1840B	X	3.00	5.00	8.50	15.00
	1840R	X	2.00	4.00	7.50	15.00
	1841B	X	3.00	6.00	9.00	17.50
	1841R	XI	2.00	4.00	7.50	15.00
	1842B	XI	2.00	4.00	7.50	15.00
	1842R	XII	2.00	4.00	7.50	15.00
	1843B	XII	2.00	4.00	7.50	15.00
	1843R	XIII	2.00	4.00	7.50	15.00
	1844B	XIII	2.00	4.00	7.50	15.00
	1844B	XIV	2.00	4.00	7.50	15.00
	1844R	XIV	2.00	4.00	7.50	15.00
	1845B	XV	2.00	4.00	7.50	15.00
	1845R	XV	2.00	4.00	7.50	15.00

C#	Date	Mintage	VG	Fine	VF	XF
165	1847B yr.II	.074	2.00	4.00	7.50	15.00
	1847R yr.II					
		9,000	3.50	6.50	12.50	17.50
	1848/7B yr.II					
		.049	2.50	5.00	8.00	15.00
	1848B yr.II I.A.	3.50	6.50	12.50	17.50
	1848R yr.II .644	2.00	4.00	7.50	15.00
	1848B yr.III I.A.	2.00	4.00	7.50	15.00
	1848R yr.IIII I.A.	3.50	6.50	12.50	17.50
	1849B yr.III .104	2.00	4.00	7.50	15.00
	1849B yr.IV I.A.	2.00	4.00	7.50	15.00
	1849R yr.IIII					
		1.921	2.00	4.00	7.50	15.00
	1849R yr.IV I.A.	2.00	4.00	7.50	15.00

166	1850B yr.IV	.176	2.00	4.00	7.50	15.00
	1850R yr.IV					
		5.552	2.00	4.00	7.50	15.00
	1850B yr.V I.A.	2.00	4.00	7.50	15.00

C#	Date	Mintage	VG	Fine	VF	XF
166	1850R yr.V I.A.	2.00	4.00	7.50	15.00
	1851B yr.V					
		1.257	2.00	4.00	7.50	15.00
	1851R yr.V					
		4.001	2.00	4.00	7.50	15.00
	1851B yr.VI I.A.	2.00	4.00	7.50	15.00
	1851R yr.VI I.A.	2.00	4.00	7.50	15.00
	1852B yr.VI .706	2.00	4.00	7.50	15.00

BAIOCCO
COPPER

C#	Date	Year	VG	Fine	VF	XF
166	1801R	I	20.00	35.00	50.00	75.00

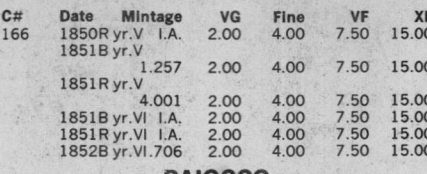

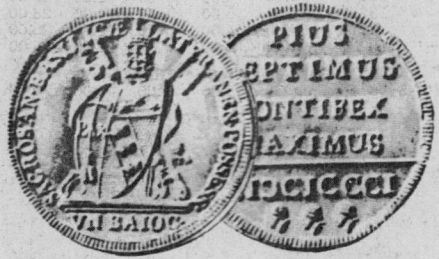

COPPER

| 111 | 1801R | — | 3.00 | 6.00 | 9.00 | 17.50 |

| 111.1 | 1801R | — | 5.00 | 10.00 | 15.00 | 25.00 |

Rev: G. PASINATES S. C. below date

| 111.2 | 1801R | — | 15.00 | 25.00 | 40.00 | 80.00 |

112	1802R	II	3.00	6.00	9.00	17.50
	1815B	XVI	5.00	10.00	15.00	25.00

112.1	1816B	XVI	5.00	10.00	18.00	30.00
	1816R	XVI	5.00	10.00	18.00	30.00
	1816B	XVII	5.00	10.00	18.00	30.00
	1816R	XVII	10.00	20.00	35.00	50.00

C#	Date	Year	VG	Fine	VF	XF
137	1829R	I	7.50	12.50	20.00	35.00

NOTE: Two varieties of edge inscription exist.

146	1831R	I	5.00	10.00	15.00	25.00
	1832B	I	15.00	25.00	45.00	70.00
	1832R	II	7.50	12.50	20.00	35.00

146a	1835B	V	2.00	4.00	7.50	15.00
	1835R	V	2.00	4.00	7.50	15.00
	1836B	VI	2.00	4.00	7.50	15.00
	1836R	VI	2.00	4.00	7.50	15.00
	1837B	VII	2.00	4.00	7.50	15.00
	1837R	VII	2.00	4.00	7.50	15.00
	1838B	VIII	10.00	20.00	35.00	50.00
	1838R	VIII	5.00	10.00	15.00	25.00
	1839R	VIII	7.50	12.50	20.00	35.00
	1839B	IX	2.00	4.00	7.50	15.00
	1839R	IX	5.00	10.00	15.00	25.00
	1840B	X	2.00	4.00	7.50	15.00
	1840R	X	2.00	4.00	7.50	15.00
	1841B	X	5.00	10.00	15.00	25.00
	1841B	XI	10.00	20.00	35.00	50.00
	1841R	XI	3.50	6.50	12.50	17.50
	1842B	XI	3.50	6.50	12.50	17.50
	1842B	XII	2.00	4.00	7.50	15.00
	1842R	XII	3.50	6.50	12.50	17.50
	1843B	XII	3.50	6.50	12.50	17.50
	1843B	XIII	3.50	6.50	12.50	17.50
	1843R	XIII	3.50	6.50	12.50	17.50
	1844B	XIII	2.00	4.00	7.50	15.00
	1844B	XIV	2.00	4.00	7.50	15.00
	1844R	XIV	2.00	4.00	7.50	15.00
	1845B	XV	2.00	4.00	7.50	15.00
	1845R	XV	3.50	6.50	12.50	17.50

C#	Date	Mintage	VG	Fine	VF	XF
167	1846B yr.I	—	6.00	10.00	17.50	30.00
	1846R yr.I					
		7,500	4.00	7.50	12.50	25.00
	1847B yr.I .058	4.00	7.50	12.50	25.00
	1847R yr.I .014	7.50	12.50	20.00	35.00
	1847R yr.II I.A.	4.00	7.50	12.50	25.00
	1848R yr.II .494	3.50	6.50	12.50	25.00
	1848R yr.III					
		I.A.	2.00	4.00	7.50	15.00
	1848R yr.IV I.A.	2.00	4.00	7.50	15.00

NOTE: Varieties of date wording exist.

167.1	1849R yr.IV				
		1.080	2.00	4.00	7.50	15.00

Papal States / VATICAN 1787

C#	Date	Mintage	VG	Fine	VF	XF
168	1849B yr.IV	.061	6.00	10.00	17.50	30.00
	1850B yr.IV	.402	4.00	7.50	12.50	25.00
	1850R yr.IV	4.681	3.00	6.00	9.00	17.50
	1850B yr.V	I.A.	4.00	7.50	12.50	25.00
	1850R yr.V	I.A.	3.00	6.00	9.00	17.50
	1851B yr.V	.899	3.00	6.00	9.00	17.50
	1851R yr.V	5.706	4.00	7.50	12.50	25.00
	1851B yr.VI	I.A.	2.00	4.00	7.50	15.00
	1851R yr.VI	I.A.	4.00	7.50	12.50	25.00
	1852B yr.VI	.655	2.00	4.00	7.50	15.00
	1852R yr.VI	1.211	7.50	15.00	20.00	35.00
	1853R yr.VII	.035	7.50	15.00	20.00	35.00

2 BAIOCCHI

BILLON

169	1848B yr.III	.644	3.00	6.00	9.00	17.50
	1848R yr.III	.227	3.00	6.00	9.00	17.50
	1849R yr.IV	1.117	3.00	6.00	9.00	17.50
	1849B yr.III	—	3.00	6.00	9.00	17.50
	1849B yr.IV	—	3.00	6.00	9.00	17.50

169a	1850B yr.IV	—	3.00	6.00	9.00	17.50
	1850R yr.IV	3.784	3.00	6.00	9.00	17.50
	1850B yr.V	—	7.50	12.50	20.00	35.00
	1850R yr.V	I.A.	2.00	4.00	7.50	15.00
	1851B yr.V		2.00	4.00	7.50	15.00
	1851R yr.V	2.557	2.00	4.00	7.50	15.00
	1851B yr.VI	—	2.00	4.00	7.50	15.00
	1851R yr.VI	I.A.	2.00	4.00	7.50	15.00
	1852B yr.V	—	5.00	10.00	17.50	30.00
	1852R yr.VI	1.727	4.00	7.50	15.00	25.00
	1852B yr.VI	—	2.00	4.00	7.50	15.00
	1852R yr.VI	I.A.	2.00	4.00	7.50	15.00
	1852R yr.VII	I.A.	4.00	7.50	15.00	30.00
	1853R yr.VII	1.460	4.00	7.50	15.00	30.00
	1853B yr.VII	—	3.50	7.00	12.50	22.50
	1853R yr.VII	I.A.	2.00	4.00	7.50	15.00
	1853R yr.VIII	I.A.	2.00	4.00	7.50	15.00
	1854R yr.VIII	5,000	35.00	75.00	100.00	140.00

GROSSO

1.3210 g, .917 SILVER, .0389 oz ASW

C#	Date	Year	VG	Fine	VF	XF
113	1815R	XVI	7.50	15.00	22.50	40.00
113	1816B	XVI	15.00	25.00	40.00	70.00
	1816B	XVII	7.50	15.00	22.50	40.00
	1817B	XVII	7.50	15.00	22.50	40.00

5 BAIOCCHI

1.3430 g, .900 SILVER, .0388 oz ASW

147	1835R	V	4.00	7.50	15.00	30.00
	1836R	VI	4.00	7.50	15.00	30.00
	1839R	IX	6.00	10.00	17.50	35.00
	1840B	X	4.00	7.50	15.00	30.00
	1841R	X	10.00	20.00	35.00	50.00
	1841B	XI	4.00	7.50	15.00	30.00
	1841R	XI	15.00	25.00	40.00	70.00
	1842B	XI	4.00	7.50	15.00	30.00
	1842R	XI	15.00	25.00	40.00	70.00
	1842B	XII	4.00	7.50	15.00	30.00
	1842R	XII	4.00	7.50	15.00	30.00
	1843B	XIII	4.00	7.50	15.00	30.00
	1843R	XIII	4.00	7.50	15.00	30.00
	1844B	XIII	4.00	7.50	15.00	30.00
	1844B	XIV	4.00	7.50	15.00	30.00
	1844/3R	—	5.00	8.00	17.50	32.50
	1844R	XIV	4.00	7.50	15.00	30.00
	1845B	XV	4.00	7.50	15.00	30.00
	1845R	XV	4.00	7.50	15.00	30.00
	1846R	XVI	4.00	7.50	15.00	30.00

C#	Date	Mintage	VG	Fine	VF	XF
171	1847B yr.I	2.387	4.00	7.50	15.00	30.00
	1847R yr.II	1.191	4.00	7.50	15.00	30.00
	1848R yr.II	2,122	20.00	40.00	75.00	125.00
	1849R yr.IV	.021	4.00	7.50	15.00	30.00
	1850R yr.V	.010	4.00	7.50	15.00	30.00
	1851R yr.V	.011	4.00	7.50	15.00	30.00
	1851R yr.VI	I.A.	4.00	7.50	15.00	30.00
	1852R yr.VII	.020	4.00	7.50	15.00	30.00
	1853R yr.VII	.014	4.00	7.50	15.00	30.00
	1855R yr.IX	9,200	20.00	40.00	75.00	120.00
	1855R yr.X I.A.	20.00	40.00	75.00	120.00

1.4280 g, .800 SILVER, .0367 oz ASW

171a	1856R yr.X	3,440	20.00	40.00	75.00	120.00
	1857R yr.XI	.023	4.00	7.50	15.00	30.00
	1858R yr.XII	1.573	4.00	7.50	15.00	30.00
	1858R yr.XIII	.224	12.50	25.00	40.00	75.00
	1858R yr.XIII Inc. Ab.	4.00	7.50	15.00	30.00
	1859B yr.XIII	.173	12.50	25.00	40.00	75.00
	1859R yr.XIII	.083	4.00	7.50	15.00	30.00
	1860R yr.XV	.169	4.00	7.50	15.00	30.00
	1861R yr.XVI	.147	4.00	7.50	15.00	30.00
	1862R yr.XVII	.135	4.00	7.50	15.00	30.00
	1863R yr.XVIII	.044	4.00	7.50	15.00	30.00
	1864R yr.XIX	.101	4.00	7.50	15.00	30.00

1.3330 g, .835 SILVER, .0357 oz ASW

171b	1865R yr.XIX	.106	9.00	15.00	25.00	45.00
	1865R yr.XX I.A.	4.00	7.50	15.00	30.00
	1866R yr.XX	.040	6.00	10.00	17.50	35.00

COPPER

C#	Date	Mintage	VG	Fine	VF	XF
170	1849B yr.IV	—	5.00	10.00	15.00	25.00
	1849R yr.IV	.938	5.00	10.00	15.00	25.00
	1850B yr.IV	—	5.00	10.00	15.00	25.00
	1850R yr.IV	10.164	5.00	10.00	15.00	25.00
	1850B yr.V	—	5.00	10.00	15.00	25.00
	1850R yr.V I.A.	5.00	10.00	15.00	25.00

Rev: Similar to C#170.

170a	1850B yr.V	—	5.00	10.00	15.00	25.00
	1850R yr.V I.A.	5.00	10.00	15.00	25.00
	1851B yr.V	—	5.00	10.00	15.00	25.00
	1851R yr.V	7.949	5.00	10.00	15.00	30.00
	1851B yr.VI	—	4.00	7.50	15.00	25.00
	1851R yr.VI I.A.	4.00	7.50	15.00	25.00
	1852B yr.VI	—	4.00	7.50	15.00	25.00
	1852R yr.VI	9.746	4.00	7.50	15.00	25.00
	1852B yr.VII	—	4.00	7.50	15.00	25.00
	1852R yr.VII Inc. Ab.	4.00	7.50	15.00	25.00
	1853B yr.VII	—	4.00	7.50	15.00	25.00
	1853R yr.VII	8.428	4.00	7.50	15.00	25.00
	1853B yr.VIII Inc. Ab.	4.00	7.50	15.00	25.00
	1854B yr.VIII	—				
	1854R yr.VIII	1.977	9.00	17.50	25.00	45.00
	1854B yr.IX	—	4.00	7.50	15.00	25.00
	1854R yr.IX I.A.	9.00	17.50	25.00	45.00

GIULIO

2.6420 g, .917 SILVER, .0779 oz ASW

C#	Date	Year	VG	Fine	VF	XF
114	1817/6B	XVIII	20.00	40.00	75.00	100.00
	1817B	XVIII	20.00	40.00	75.00	100.00

10 BAIOCCHI

2.6870 g, .900 SILVER, .0777 oz ASW

148	1836B	VI	12.50	25.00	40.00	75.00
	1836R	VI	7.50	15.00	22.50	40.00
	1839B	IX	7.50	15.00	22.50	40.00
	1839R	IX	7.50	15.00	22.50	40.00
	1841B	XI	5.00	10.00	17.50	30.00
	1841R	XI	10.00	20.00	35.00	50.00
	1842B	XI	7.50	15.00	22.50	40.00
	1842B	XII	5.00	10.00	17.50	30.00
	1842R	XII	12.50	25.00	40.00	75.00

Papal States / VATICAN 1788

C#	Date	Year	VG	Fine	VF	XF
148	1843B	XIII	7.50	15.00	22.50	40.00
	1844B	XIV	7.50	15.00	22.50	40.00
	1846R	XVI	10.00	20.00	35.00	50.00

C#	Date	Mintage	VG	Fine	VF	XF
172	1847B yr.I	.011	12.50	25.00	40.00	75.00
	1847B yr.II	I.A.	12.50	25.00	40.00	75.00
	1847R yr.II	.012	5.00	10.00	15.00	30.00
	1848B yr.II	.017	12.50	25.00	40.00	75.00
	1848R yr.II	.033	5.00	10.00	15.00	30.00
	1848B yr.III	I.A.	12.50	25.00	40.00	75.00
	1848R yr.III	I.A.	5.00	10.00	15.00	30.00
	1849R yr.IIII					
		1.274	25.00	45.00	75.00	125.00
	1850R yr.IIII					
		.089	5.00	10.00	15.00	30.00
	1850R yr.V	I.A.	5.00	10.00	15.00	30.00
	1852R yr.VII					
		.033	5.00	10.00	15.00	30.00
	1853R yr.VII					
		.041	5.00	10.00	15.00	30.00
	1854R yr.VIII					
		5,570	40.00	75.00	100.00	175.00
	1855R yr.IX					
		4,400	40.00	75.00	100.00	175.00
	1856R yr.X					
		1,140	45.00	80.00	125.00	175.00

2.8570 g, .800 SILVER, .0734 oz ASW

C#	Date		VG	Fine	VF	XF
172a	1858R yr.XII					
		2.548	3.00	6.00	10.00	20.00
	1858R yr.XIII		4.00	7.50	15.00	25.00
	1858B yr. XIII					
		Inc. Ab.	12.50	25.00	40.00	75.00
	1859R yr.XIII					
		.088	10.00	20.00	35.00	50.00
	1860R yr.XIV					
		.150	10.00	20.00	35.00	50.00
	1861R yr.XVI					
		.327	4.00	7.50	15.00	25.00
	1862R yr.XVI					
		7.417	2.50	5.00	10.00	15.00
	1862R yr.XVII					
		Inc. Ab.	2.50	5.00	10.00	15.00
	1863R yr.XVI	—	75.00	125.00	175.00	225.00
	1863R yr.XVII					
		1.084	4.00	7.50	15.00	25.00
	1863R yr.XVIII					
		Inc. Ab.	4.00	7.50	15.00	25.00
	1864R yr.XVIII					
		1.147	10.00	20.00	35.00	50.00
	1864R yr.XIX					
		Inc. Ab.	10.00	20.00	35.00	50.00

2.6660 g, .835 SILVER, .0715 oz ASW

C#	Date		VG	Fine	VF	XF
172b	1865R yr.XIX					
		.409	8.00	15.00	22.50	40.00
	1865R yr.XX I.A.		8.00	15.00	22.50	40.00

DOPPIO (2) GIULIO
(1/5 Scudo)

5.2850 g, .917 SILVER, .1558 oz ASW

C#	Date	Year	VG	Fine	VF	XF
115	1816B	XVII	20.00	40.00	75.00	100.00
	1816B	XVIII	20.00	40.00	75.00	100.00
	1818B	XVII	10.00	20.00	35.00	50.00
	1818B	XVIII	10.00	20.00	35.00	50.00

Sede Vacante

C#	Date	Year	VG	Fine	VF	XF
122	1823B	—	40.00	75.00	100.00	175.00

20 BAIOCCHI

5.2850 g, .917 SILVER, .1558 oz ASW

149	1834R	IV	10.00	20.00	35.00	50.00

5.3740 g, .900 SILVER, .1555 oz ASW

150	1835B	V	8.00	15.00	22.50	40.00
	1835R	V	10.00	20.00	35.00	50.00
	1836B	V	80.00	125.00	200.00	350.00
	1836B	VI	8.00	15.00	22.50	40.00
	1836R	VI	40.00	75.00	100.00	175.00
	1837R	VII	20.00	40.00	75.00	120.00
	1838B	VIII	8.00	15.00	22.50	40.00
	1838R	VIII	10.00	20.00	35.00	50.00
	1839R	IX	10.00	20.00	35.00	50.00
	1840B	X	8.00	15.00	22.50	40.00
	1841B	XI	8.00	15.00	22.50	40.00
	1841R	XI	10.00	20.00	35.00	50.00
	1842B	XII	25.00	45.00	75.00	125.00
	1842R	XII	10.00	20.00	35.00	50.00
	1844B	XII	8.00	15.00	22.50	40.00
	1844R	XIII	100.00	200.00	350.00	650.00
	1844B	XIV	8.00	15.00	22.50	40.00
	1845B	XV	8.00	15.00	22.50	40.00
	1846R	XVI	10.00	20.00	35.00	50.00

C#	Date	Mintage	VG	Fine	VF	XF
173	1848R yr. II	—	10.00	20.00	35.00	50.00
	1848R yr. III	—	10.00	20.00	35.00	50.00
	1849B yr. III	—	12.50	25.00	40.00	75.00
	1849B yr. IV	—	15.00	25.00	40.00	75.00
	1849R yr. V	—	10.00	20.00	35.00	50.00
	1850B yr. IV	—	15.00	25.00	40.00	75.00
	1850R yr. IV	—	8.00	15.00	22.50	40.00
	1850R yr. V	—	8.00	15.00	25.00	40.00
	1851B yr. V	—	15.00	25.00	40.00	75.00
	1852B yr. VII	—	30.00	60.00	90.00	125.00
	1852R yr. VII					
		.010	25.00	40.00	65.00	75.00
	1853R yr. VII	—	10.00	20.00	35.00	60.00
		.126	12.50	25.00	40.00	75.00
	1854R yr. VIII	—	10.00	20.00	35.00	50.00
	1856R yr. X	—	12.50	25.00	40.00	75.00
	1858B yr. XII	—	12.50	25.00	40.00	75.00
	1858R yr. XII	—	8.00	15.00	22.50	40.00

NOTE: Two varieties of ANNO III exist.

5.7140 g, .800 SILVER, .1469 oz ASW

173a	1858B yr.XIII	—	10.00	20.00	35.00	60.00
	1858R yr.XIII	—	5.00	10.00	15.00	25.00
	1859B yr.XIII					
		.604	10.00	20.00	35.00	60.00
	1859R yr.XIII					
		1.104	7.50	12.50	20.00	35.00
	1859R yr.XIV					
		Inc. Ab.	7.50	12.50	20.00	35.00
	1860/50R	—	5.00	10.00	15.00	25.00
	1860R yr.XIV					
		3.656	5.00	10.00	15.00	25.00
	1860R yr.XV I.A.		5.00	10.00	15.00	25.00
	1861R yr.XV					
		2.987	7.50	12.50	20.00	35.00
	1861R yr.XVI					
		Inc. Ab.	7.50	12.50	20.00	35.00
	1862R yr.XVI					
		1.150	7.50	12.50	20.00	35.00
	1862R yr.XVII					
		Inc. Ab.	7.50	12.50	20.00	35.00

C#	Date	Mintage	VG	Fine	VF	XF
173a	1863R yr.XVII					
		3.155	7.50	12.50	20.00	35.00
	1863R yr.XVIII					
		Inc. Ab.	7.50	12.50	20.00	35.00
	1864R yr.XVIII					
		2.100	7.50	12.50	20.00	35.00
	1864R yr.XIX					
		Inc. Ab.	10.00	20.00	35.00	60.00
	1865R yr.XIX					
		7.346	5.00	10.00	15.00	25.00
	1865R yr.XX I.A.		5.00	10.00	15.00	25.00
	1866R yr.XX					
		5.600	5.00	10.00	15.00	25.00

30 BAIOCCHI
(Testone)

7.9280 g, .917 SILVER, .2337 oz ASW

C#	Date	Year	VG	Fine	VF	XF
116	1802R	III	17.50	35.00	60.00	90.00
	1803R	III	17.50	35.00	60.00	90.00

138	1830R	II	15.00	30.00	55.00	85.00

Sede Vacante

141	1830B	—	20.00	40.00	65.00	90.00
	1830R	—	25.00	45.00	75.00	100.00

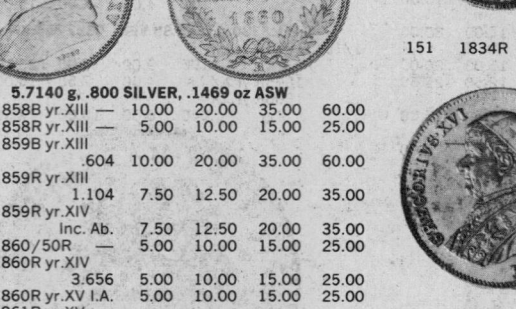

151	1834R	IV	15.00	30.00	45.00	75.00

8.0610 g, .900 SILVER, .2332 oz ASW

152	1836B	VI	25.00	45.00	75.00	100.00
	1836R	VI	37.50	75.00	125.00	200.00
	1837B	VII	25.00	45.00	75.00	100.00
	1837R	VII	37.50	75.00	125.00	200.00
	1838R	VIII	25.00	45.00	75.00	100.00
	1846R	XVI	25.00	45.00	75.00	100.00

50 BAIOCCHI

13.2140 g, .917 SILVER, .3896 oz ASW

C#	Date	Year	VG	Fine	VF	XF
153	1832B	II	20.00	40.00	65.00	90.00
	1832R	II	25.00	45.00	75.00	100.00
	1834R	IV	25.00	45.00	75.00	100.00

NOTE: Two varieties of 1832B exist.

13.4350 g, .900 SILVER, .3887 oz ASW

154	1835R	V	25.00	45.00	75.00	100.00
	1836B	VI	25.00	45.00	75.00	100.00
	1836R	VI	50.00	75.00	110.00	175.00
	1837B	VII	25.00	45.00	75.00	100.00
	1840B	X	50.00	75.00	110.00	175.00
	1841B	XI	25.00	45.00	75.00	100.00
	1842B	XII	50.00	75.00	110.00	175.00
	1843R	XIII	25.00	45.00	75.00	100.00
	1845R	XV	25.00	45.00	75.00	100.00
	1846R	XVI	25.00	45.00	75.00	100.00

C#	Date	Mintage	VG	Fine	VF	XF
174	1850R yr.IV	104	25.00	45.00	75.00	100.00
	1850R yr.V	I.A.	25.00	45.00	75.00	100.00
	1853R yr.VII	.684	50.00	75.00	110.00	175.00
	1853R yr.VIII	Inc. Ab.	25.00	45.00	75.00	100.00
	1854B yr.IX	2,718	25.00	45.00	75.00	100.00
	1856B yr.X	4,226	25.00	45.00	75.00	100.00
	1857B yr.XII	8,711	50.00	75.00	110.00	175.00

1/2 SCUDO

13.2500 g, .917 SILVER, .3907 oz ASW

C#	Date	Year	VG	Fine	VF	XF
117	1800R	I	45.00	90.00	125.00	175.00
	1802R	II	35.00	70.00	100.00	140.00
	1802R	III	35.00	70.00	100.00	140.00
	1803R	III	35.00	70.00	100.00	140.00
	1816B	XVII	35.00	70.00	100.00	140.00

Sede Vacante

C#	Date	Year	VG	Fine	VF	XF
123	1823B	—	40.00	75.00	110.00	150.00

Sede Vacante

132	1829B	—	35.00	70.00	100.00	140.00
	1829R	—	35.00	70.00	100.00	140.00

2 ZECCHINI

6.9040 g, .998 GOLD, .2215 oz AGW

C#	Date	Year	Fine	VF	XF	Unc
130	1825R	III	500.00	900.00	1500.	3000.

131	1828R	V	500.00	900.00	1500.	3000.

SCUDO

26.2500 g, .917 SILVER, .7739 oz ASW

C#	Date	Mintage	VG	Fine	VF	XF
119	1802R	II	50.00	85.00	110.00	200.00
	1802R	III	60.00	100.00	140.00	250.00
	1802R	IV	50.00	85.00	110.00	200.00
	1803R	IV	75.00	125.00	175.00	300.00
	1805R	VI	50.00	85.00	110.00	200.00
	1807R	VIII	50.00	85.00	110.00	200.00

26.4280 g, .917 SILVER, .7792 oz ASW
Rev: Similar to C#120.

C#	Date	Mintage	VG	Fine	VF	XF
119.1	1815R	XVI	50.00	85.00	110.00	200.00
	1816B	XVII	40.00	70.00	100.00	200.00
	1817B	XVII	60.00	100.00	150.00	225.00
	1818B	XVIII	50.00	85.00	110.00	200.00

120	1816R	XVII	—	—	Rare	—

Sede Vacante

124	1823B	—	100.00	150.00	300.00	500.00

Papal States / VATICAN 1790

Sede Vacante

C#	Date	Mintage	VG	Fine	VF	XF
124.1	1823R	—	300.00	500.00	1000.	1500.

128	1825R	II	100.00	175.00	250.00	325.00
	1825B	III	75.00	125.00	175.00	250.00
	1826R	III	100.00	175.00	250.00	325.00

128.1	1826R	III	100.00	175.00	250.00	325.00

Sede Vacante

133	1829B	—	75.00	150.00	250.00	325.00
	1829R	—	125.00	200.00	275.00	400.00

C#	Date	Mintage	VG	Fine	VF	XF
139	1830B	I	85.00	150.00	185.00	300.00
	1830ROMA	I	65.00	120.00	145.00	175.00

Sede Vacante

142	1830B	—	65.00	125.00	150.00	225.00
	1830ROMA	—	85.00	150.00	185.00	300.00

C#	Date	Year	VG	Fine	VF	XF
155	1831B	An. I	60.00	100.00	150.00	200.00
	1831R	An. I	50.00	75.00	110.00	175.00

C#	Date	Year	VG	Fine	VF	XF
155	1833B	An. III	100.00	175.00	250.00	325.00
	1833R	An. III	60.00	100.00	150.00	200.00
	1833R	A. III	90.00	175.00	250.00	350.00
	1834R	An. IV	50.00	75.00	110.00	175.00
	1834R	A. IV	100.00	175.00	250.00	325.00

26.8710 g, .900 SILVER, .7776 oz ASW

156	1835B	V	50.00	75.00	110.00	175.00
	1835R	V	75.00	125.00	175.00	225.00
	1836R	VI	75.00	125.00	175.00	225.00
	1837R	VII	50.00	75.00	110.00	175.00
	1838B	VIII	75.00	125.00	175.00	225.00
	1838R	VIII	75.00	125.00	175.00	225.00
	1839R	VIII	75.00	125.00	175.00	225.00
	1839R	IX	75.00	125.00	175.00	225.00
	1840R	X	60.00	100.00	150.00	200.00
	1841R	XI	75.00	125.00	175.00	225.00
	1842R	XI	90.00	175.00	250.00	350.00
	1842R	XII	125.00	300.00	500.00	1000.
	1843R	XIII	50.00	75.00	110.00	175.00
	1844R	XIV	75.00	125.00	175.00	225.00
	1845R	XV	45.00	75.00	100.00	175.00
	1846R	XVI	45.00	75.00	100.00	175.00

Sede Vacante

162	1846R	—	90.00	175.00	250.00	350.00

Obv: NIC. CER. BARA below bust.

C#	Date	Mintage	VG	Fine	VF	XF
175	1846B yr.I					
		2,073	75.00	125.00	175.00	225.00
	1846R yr.I					
		1,820	125.00	200.00	275.00	400.00
	1847B yr.II	.020	60.00	100.00	150.00	200.00
	1847R yr.II	.012	75.00	125.00	175.00	225.00
	1848R yr.II	.029	60.00	100.00	150.00	200.00
	1848R yr.III I.A.		75.00	125.00	175.00	225.00

Obv: W/o NIC. CER. BARA below bust.

175.1	1850R yr.IV					
		9,222	35.00	50.00	100.00	135.00
	1853R yr.VII					
		.527	35.00	50.00	100.00	135.00
	1853B yr.VIII					

Papal States / VATICAN 1791

C#	Date	Mintage	VG	Fine	VF	XF
175.1		2,310	100.00	200.00	300.00	500.00
	1853R yr.VIII	Inc. Ab.	35.00	50.00	100.00	135.00
	1854B yr.IX	3,715	100.00	200.00	300.00	500.00
	1854R yr.IX	.146	35.00	50.00	100.00	135.00
	1856R yr.XI	1,050	100.00	200.00	300.00	500.00

1.7330 g, .900 GOLD, .0501 oz AGW, 14.4mm

C#	Date	Mintage	Fine	VF	XF	Unc
176	1853B yr.VIII	3,306	75.00	125.00	175.00	275.00
	1853R yr.VIII	.209	60.00	100.00	135.00	200.00
	1854B yr.VIII	5,539	75.00	125.00	175.00	275.00
	1854R yr.VIII	.097	60.00	100.00	150.00	200.00
	1854R yr.IX	Inc. Ab.	60.00	100.00	150.00	200.00
	1857R yr.XII	.016	75.00	125.00	175.00	275.00

16.3mm

176a	1858R yr.XII	.359	60.00	100.00	135.00	200.00
	1858R yr.XIII	Inc. Ab.	60.00	100.00	135.00	200.00
	1859R yr.XIII	.103	60.00	100.00	135.00	200.00
	1861R yr.XV	.084	60.00	100.00	135.00	200.00
	1861R yr.XVI	Inc. Ab.	60.00	100.00	135.00	200.00
	1862R yr.XVI	.226	60.00	100.00	135.00	200.00
	1862R yr.XVII	Inc. Ab.	60.00	100.00	135.00	200.00
	1863R yr.XVII	.149	60.00	100.00	135.00	200.00
	1863R yr.XVIII	Inc. Ab.	60.00	100.00	135.00	200.00
	1864R yr.XIX	5,735	75.00	125.00	175.00	250.00
	1865R yr.XIX	.021	60.00	100.00	135.00	200.00

2-1/2 SCUDI

4.3340 g, .900 GOLD, .1254 oz AGW

C#	Date	Year	Fine	VF	XF	Unc
158	1835B	V	150.00	250.00	350.00	450.00
	1835R	V	150.00	250.00	350.00	450.00
	1836B	V	150.00	250.00	350.00	450.00
	1836B	VI	100.00	150.00	225.00	325.00
	1836R	VI	100.00	150.00	225.00	325.00
	1837R	VII	150.00	250.00	350.00	450.00
	1839R	IX	150.00	250.00	350.00	450.00
	1840B	X	100.00	150.00	225.00	325.00
	1841R	XI	150.00	250.00	350.00	500.00
	1842B	XII	100.00	150.00	225.00	325.00
	1842R	XII	175.00	275.00	400.00	600.00
	1843B	XIII	100.00	150.00	225.00	325.00
	1844B	XIII	150.00	250.00	350.00	450.00
	1845B	XV	175.00	275.00	400.00	600.00
	1845R	XV	150.00	250.00	350.00	500.00
	1846B	XVI	100.00	150.00	225.00	325.00

C#	Date	Mintage	Fine	VF	XF	Unc
177	1848R yr.II	3,197	175.00	275.00	375.00	500.00
	1853R yr.VII	.117	100.00	175.00	250.00	325.00
	1853R yr.VIII	Inc. Ab.	100.00	150.00	225.00	325.00
	1854R yr.VIII	.276	80.00	110.00	150.00	225.00
	1854B yr.IX	.032	90.00	125.00	175.00	275.00
	1854R yr.IX					

C#	Date	Mintage	Fine	VF	XF	Unc
177		Inc. Ab.	80.00	110.00	150.00	225.00
	1855R yr.IX	.059	80.00	110.00	150.00	225.00
	1855R yr.X	Inc. Ab.	80.00	110.00	150.00	225.00
	1856B yr.X	8,040	100.00	175.00	250.00	350.00
	1856R yr.X	.104	85.00	110.00	150.00	225.00
	1856R yr.XI	Inc. Ab.	85.00	110.00	150.00	225.00
	1857R yr.X	—	100.00	150.00	225.00	325.00
	1857R yr.XI	—	175.00	275.00	375.00	500.00
	1857B yr.XII	6,284	150.00	250.00	325.00	400.00
	1857R yr.XII	—	90.00	125.00	175.00	275.00
	1858R yr.XII	—	100.00	150.00	225.00	325.00
	1858B yr.XIII	2,787	175.00	275.00	375.00	500.00
	1858R yr.XIII	—	90.00	125.00	175.00	275.00
	1859B yr.XIII	.066	100.00	150.00	225.00	325.00
	1859R yr.XIII	—	80.00	125.00	175.00	250.00
	1859R yr.XIV	—	80.00	125.00	175.00	250.00
	1860R yr.XIV	—	80.00	125.00	175.00	250.00
	1860R yr.XV	—	80.00	125.00	175.00	250.00
	1861R yr.XV	—	80.00	125.00	175.00	250.00
	1861R yr.XVI	—	80.00	125.00	175.00	250.00
	1862R yr.XVI	—	80.00	125.00	175.00	250.00
	1862R yr.XVII	—	80.00	125.00	175.00	250.00
	1863R yr.XVII	—	80.00	125.00	175.00	250.00

5 SCUDI

8.6680 g, .900 GOLD, .2508 oz AGW

C#	Date	Year	Fine	VF	XF	Unc
159	1834R	IV	1250.	2500.	3000.	4000.

160	1835B	V	275.00	475.00	700.00	1000.
	1835R	V	275.00	475.00	700.00	1000.
	1836R	VI	275.00	475.00	700.00	1000.
	1837R	VI	400.00	800.00	1200.	1800.
	1837R	VII	275.00	475.00	700.00	1000.
	1838R	VII	275.00	475.00	700.00	1000.
	1838R	VIII	275.00	475.00	700.00	1000.
	1839R	VIII	350.00	725.00	1000.	1500.
	1839R	IX	350.00	725.00	1000.	1500.
	1840R	IX	350.00	725.00	1000.	1500.
	1841B	XI	400.00	650.00	950.00	1750.
	1841R	XI	275.00	475.00	700.00	1000.
	1842B	XII	275.00	475.00	700.00	1000.
	1842R	XII	275.00	475.00	700.00	1000.
	1843B	XIII	400.00	650.00	950.00	1750.
	1843R	XIII	275.00	475.00	700.00	1000.
	1845R	XV	275.00	475.00	700.00	1000.
	1846R	XVI	275.00	475.00	700.00	1000.

Sede Vacante

163	1846R	—	725.00	1200.	1600.	2500.

C#	Date	Mintage	Fine	VF	XF	Unc
178	1846B yr.I	.011	275.00	475.00	725.00	1000.
	1846R yr.I	5,755	325.00	575.00	900.00	1300.
	1847R yr.II	1,399	400.00	725.00	1000.	1400.
	1848R yr.III	1,633	325.00	575.00	800.00	1200.
	1850R yr.IV	6,473	350.00	725.00	1000.	1400.
	1854R yr.IX	.104	250.00	450.00	650.00	900.00

10 SCUDI

17.3360 g, .900 GOLD, .5016 oz AGW

C#	Date	Year	Fine	VF	XF	Unc
161	1835B	V	400.00	725.00	1000.	1350.
	1835R	V	300.00	475.00	725.00	1100.
	1836R	V	300.00	475.00	725.00	1100.
	1836B	V	300.00	475.00	725.00	1100.
	1836R	VI	350.00	725.00	1000.	1400.
	1837R	VI	350.00	725.00	1000.	1400.
	1837R	VII	300.00	475.00	725.00	1100.
	1838R	VII	325.00	575.00	800.00	1250.
	1838R	VIII	325.00	575.00	800.00	1250.
	1839R	VIII	325.00	575.00	800.00	1250.
	1839R	IX	350.00	725.00	1000.	1400.
	1840B	X	350.00	725.00	1000.	1400.
	1840R	X	325.00	575.00	800.00	1250.
	1841R	X	325.00	575.00	800.00	1250.
	1841B	XI	325.00	575.00	800.00	1250.
	1841R	XI	325.00	575.00	800.00	1250.
	1842R	XI	325.00	575.00	800.00	1250.
	1842B	XII	325.00	575.00	800.00	1250.
	1842R	XII	325.00	575.00	800.00	1250.
	1843R	XIII	350.00	725.00	1000.	1400.
	1844R	XIV	350.00	725.00	1000.	1400.
	1845B	XV	325.00	575.00	800.00	1250.
	1845R	XV	350.00	725.00	1000.	1400.

C#	Date	Mintage	Fine	VF	XF	Unc
179	1850R yr.IV	5,875	650.00	1250.	1750.	2750.
	1850R yr.V	I.A.	400.00	750.00	1000.	1500.
	1856R yr.XI	2,483	650.00	1000.	1500.	2500.

DOPPIA

5.4500 g, .917 GOLD, .1606 oz AGW
Mint: Rome

C#	Date	Year	Fine	VF	XF	Unc
121	(1800/1)	I	125.00	175.00	275.00	425.00
	(1801/2)	II	125.00	175.00	275.00	425.00
	(1802/3)	III	125.00	175.00	275.00	425.00
	(1803/4)	IV	125.00	175.00	275.00	425.00
	(1804/5)	V	125.00	175.00	275.00	425.00
	(1807/8)	VIII	125.00	175.00	275.00	425.00
	(1809/10)	X	125.00	175.00	275.00	425.00

Modified design

121.1	(1815/6)	XVI	125.00	175.00	275.00	425.00
	(1817/8)	XVIII	175.00	250.00	325.00	500.00
	(1823/4)	XXIV	125.00	175.00	275.00	425.00

Mint: Bologna

121.2	(1815/6)B	XVI	125.00	200.00	300.00	500.00
	(1816/7)B	XVII	125.00	200.00	300.00	500.00

Papal States / VATICAN 1792

C#	Date	Year	Fine	VF	XF	Unc
121.2	(1820/1)B	XXI	150.00	250.00	375.00	600.00
	(1821/2)B	XXII	150.00	250.00	375.00	600.00

Sede Vacante

125	1823B	—	175.00	250.00	350.00	550.00
	1823R	—	175.00	250.00	350.00	550.00

129	(1823/4)R	I	150.00	200.00	350.00	550.00
	(1824/5)B	II	150.00	200.00	350.00	550.00
	(1824/5)R	II	150.00	200.00	350.00	550.00

Sede Vacante

134	1829B	—	300.00	500.00	900.00	1400.
	1829R	—	300.00	500.00	900.00	1400.

Sede Vacante

143	1830R	—	325.00	650.00	1000.	1500.

157	1833R	III	275.00	450.00	650.00	900.00
	1834B	III	275.00	450.00	650.00	900.00

DECIMAL COINAGE
5 Centesimi = 1 Soldi
20 Soldi = 1 Lira

CENTESIMO

COPPER

C#	Date	Mintage	Fine	VF	XF	Unc
180	1866R yr.XXI	.525	3.00	6.00	10.00	20.00
	1867R yr.XXII	2.930	3.00	6.00	9.00	17.50
	1868R yr.XXII	1.960	6.00	10.00	17.50	30.00

1/2 SOLDO
(2-1/2 Centesimi)

COPPER

C#	Date	Mintage	Fine	VF	XF	Unc
181	1866R yr.XXI	.189	3.00	6.00	10.00	20.00
	1867R yr.XXI	7.892	2.00	3.50	6.00	15.00
	1867R yr.XXII Inc. Ab.		2.00	4.00	7.50	18.00

SOLDO
(5 Centesimi)

COPPER
Obv: Small bust.

182	1866R yr.XXI	1.280	1.75	2.50	6.00	15.00

Obv: Large bust.

182a	1866R yr.XXI Inc. Ab.		1.75	2.50	6.00	15.00
	1867R yr.XXI lg. date	8.544	1.75	2.50	6.00	15.00
	1867R yr.XXI sm. date Inc. Ab.		1.75	2.50	6.00	15.00

2 SOLDI
(10 Centesimi)

COPPER

183	1866R yr.XXI	3.410	2.00	4.00	7.50	18.00
	1867R yr.XXI	3.188	2.00	4.00	7.50	18.00

4 SOLDI
(20 Centesimi)

COPPER

184	1866R yr.XXI	2.465	3.00	6.00	10.00	20.00
	1867R yr.XXI	2.039	3.00	6.00	10.00	20.00
	1867R yr.XXII Inc. Ab.		3.00	6.00	10.00	20.00
	1868R yr.XXII	5.602	3.00	6.00	10.00	20.00
	1868R yr.XXIII Inc. Ab.		3.00	6.00	10.00	20.00
	1869R yr.XXIII					

184	1869R yr.XXIV	2.760	3.00	6.00	10.00	20.00
	Inc. Ab.		3.00	6.00	10.00	20.00

5 SOLDI
(25 Centesimi)

1.2500 g, .835 SILVER, .0335 oz ASW

186	1866R yr.XXI	.964	4.00	7.50	15.00	30.00
	1867R yr.XXI	1.920	4.00	7.50	15.00	30.00
	1867R yr.XXII Inc. Ab.		4.00	7.50	15.00	30.00

10 SOLDI
(50 Centesimi)

2.5000 g, .835 SILVER, .0671 oz ASW
Obv. leg: PIUS IX PON. MAX. A.....

187	1866R yr.XXI	.292	15.00	22.50	40.00	60.00
	1867R yr.XXI	4.402	4.00	7.50	12.50	30.00
	1867R yr.XXII Inc. Ab.		4.00	7.50	12.50	30.00
	1868R yr.XXII	8.204	4.00	7.50	12.50	30.00

Obv. leg: PIUS IX P.M.A.....

187a	1868R yr.XXIII Inc. Ab.		4.00	7.50	12.50	30.00
	1869R yr.XXIII	4.433	4.00	7.50	12.50	30.00
	1869R yr.XXIV Inc. Ab.		4.00	7.50	12.50	30.00

LIRA

5.0000 g, .835 SILVER, .1342 oz ASW
Obv: Small bust w/o ornament below.

188	1866R yr.XX	7.634	45.00	75.00	100.00	175.00

Obv: Ornament below bust.

188b	1866R yr.XX I.A.		45.00	75.00	100.00	175.00
	1866R yr.XXI Inc. Ab.		5.00	10.00	15.00	30.00

Medium bust

188d	1866R yr.XXI Inc. Ab.		5.00	10.00	15.00	30.00

Obv: Large bust, PIUS IX PON. MAX. AN...

C#	Date	Mintage	Fine	VF	XF	Unc
188a	1866R yr.XXI	Inc. Ab.	5.00	7.50	15.00	30.00
	1867R yr.XXI	5.339	4.00	6.00	12.50	30.00
	1867R yr.XXII	Inc. Ab.	4.00	6.00	12.50	30.00
	1868R yr.XXII	2.050	4.00	6.00	12.50	30.00

Obv. leg: PIUS IX PON.M.A....

188c	1868R yr.XXIII	Inc. Ab.	4.00	6.00	12.50	30.00
	1869R yr.XXIII	1.144	5.00	10.00	15.00	30.00
	1869R yr.XXIV	Inc. Ab.	5.00	10.00	15.00	30.00

2 LIRE

10.0000 g, .835 SILVER, .2684 oz ASW
Obv. leg: PIUS IX PON MAX.A....

189	1866R yr.XX	.367	75.00	100.00	175.00	225.00
	1866R yr.XXI	Inc. Ab.	12.50	20.00	40.00	75.00
	1867R yr.XXI	1.124	15.00	25.00	45.00	90.00
	1867R yr.XXII	Inc. Ab.	12.50	20.00	40.00	75.00
	1868R yr.XXII	.530	15.00	25.00	45.00	90.00

Obv. leg: PIUS IX PON.M.A....

189a	1868R yr.XXIII	Inc. Ab.	15.00	25.00	45.00	90.00
	1869R yr.XXIV	.111	12.50	20.00	40.00	75.00
	1870R yr.XXIV	.183	15.00	25.00	45.00	90.00

2-1/2 LIRE

12.5000 g, .900 SILVER, .3617 oz ASW

190	1867R yr.XXI	.257	35.00	60.00	90.00	175.00

5 LIRE

1.6120 g, .900 GOLD, .0466 oz AGW

192	1866R yr.XXI	3,226	250.00	325.00	500.00	750.00
	1867R yr.XXII	3,787	250.00	325.00	500.00	750.00

25.0000 g, .900 SILVER, .7234 oz ASW

C#	Date	Mintage	Fine	VF	XF	Unc
191	1867R yr.XXI	5,804	60.00	100.00	150.00	375.00
	1870R yr.XXIV	.099	50.00	75.00	125.00	350.00
	1870R yr.XXV	Inc. Ab.	50.00	75.00	125.00	350.00

10 LIRE

3.2250 g, .900 GOLD, .0933 oz AGW
Obv. leg: PIUS IX PON. MAX.A....

193	1866R yr.XXI	8,578	150.00	200.00	300.00	450.00
	1867R yr.XXI	8,570	150.00	200.00	300.00	450.00
	1867R yr.XXII	Inc. Ab.	150.00	200.00	300.00	450.00

Obv. leg: PIUS IX P.M.A.....

193a	1869R yr.XXIV	5,945	300.00	400.00	600.00	800.00

20 LIRE

6.4510 g, .900 GOLD, .1866 oz AGW
Plain edge, small bust

194	1866R yr.XX	.103	400.00	525.00	675.00	1000.

Reeded edge

194.1	1866R yr.XX I.A.	100.00	150.00	175.00	225.00
	1866R yr.XXI Inc. Ab.	100.00	150.00	175.00	225.00
	1867R yr.XXI .039	100.00	150.00	175.00	225.00

Medium bust

194.2	1867R yr.XXII Inc. Ab.	100.00	150.00	175.00	225.00
	1868R yr.XXII .038	100.00	150.00	175.00	225.00
	1868R yr.XXIII Inc. Ab.	100.00	150.00	175.00	225.00

Large bust

194.3	1868R yr.XXIII					

C#	Date	Mintage	Fine	VF	XF	Unc
194.3		.039	100.00	150.00	175.00	225.00
	1869R yr.XXIII	.054	100.00	150.00	175.00	225.00
	1869R yr.XXIV	Inc. Ab.	100.00	150.00	175.00	225.00
	1870R yr.XXIV	.024	100.00	150.00	175.00	225.00
	1870R yr.XXV	Inc. Ab.	100.00	150.00	175.00	225.00

50 LIRE

16.1290 g, .900 GOLD, .4667 oz AGW

195	1868R yr.XXII	1,173	600.00	1000.	1800.	3000.
	1868R yr.XXIII	Inc. Ab.	800.00	1500.	2500.	4000.
	1870R yr.XXIV	1,459	600.00	1000.	1800.	3000.

100 LIRE

32.2580 g, .900 GOLD, .9335 oz AGW

196	1866R yr.XXI	1,115	500.00	750.00	1250.	2500.
	1868R yr.XXIII	440 pcs.	500.00	750.00	1250.	2500.
	1869T yr.XXIII	624 pcs.	500.00	750.00	1250.	2500.
	1869R yr.XXIV	Inc. Ab.	500.00	750.00	1250.	2500.

VATICAN CITY

The State of the Vatican City, a papal state on the right bank of the Tiber River within the boundaries of Rome, has an area of 0.17 sq. mi. (44 sq. km.) and a population of *1,000. Capital: Vatican City.

Vatican City State, comprising the Vatican, St. Peter's and extraterritorial right to Castel Gandolfo and 13 buildings in Rome, is all that remains of the extensive papal states over which the Pope exercised temporal power in central Italy. During the struggle for Italian unification, the papal states, including Rome, were forcibly incorporated into the Kingdom of Italy in 1870. The resultant confrontation of crozier and sword remained unresolved until the signing of the Lateran Treaty, Feb. 11, 1929, between the Vatican and the Kingdom of Italy which recognized the independence and sovereignty of the State of the Vatican City, defined the relationship between the government and the church within Italy, and financially compensated the Holy See for its territorial losses in 1870.

Today the Pope exercises supreme legislative, executive and judicial power within the Vatican City, and the State of the Vatican City is recognized by many nations as an independent sovereign state under the temporal jurisdiction of the Pope, even to the extent of ambassadorial exchange.

PONTIFFS
Pius XI, 1922-1939
Sede Vacante, Feb. 10 - Mar. 2, 1939
Pius XII, 1939-1958
Sede Vacante, Oct. 9 -28, 1958
John XXIII, 1958-1963
Sede Vacante, June 3 - 21,1963
Paul VI, 1963-1978
Sede Vacante, Aug. 6 - 26, 1978
John Paul I, Aug. 26 - Sept. 28, 1978
Sede Vacante, Sept. 28 - Oct. 16, 1978
John Paul II, 1978—

MONETARY SYSTEM
100 Centesimi = 1 Lira

5 CENTESIMI

COPPER

Y#	Date	Mintage	Fine	VF	XF	Unc
1	1929	.010	2.50	5.00	7.50	16.00
	1930	.100	1.00	2.50	4.00	6.00
	1931	.100	1.00	2.50	4.00	6.00
	1932	.100	1.00	2.50	4.00	6.00
	1934	.100	1.00	2.50	4.00	6.00
	1935	.044	2.50	5.00	10.00	20.00
	1936	.062	1.00	2.50	4.00	6.00
	1937	.062	1.00	2.50	4.00	6.00
	1938	—	—	—	Rare	—

Jubilee

11	1933-34	.100	2.50	5.00	10.00	20.00

ALUMINUM-BRONZE

22	1939	.062	1.00	2.50	4.00	7.50
	1940	.062	1.00	2.50	4.00	7.50
	1941	5,000	4.00	7.50	15.00	25.00

BRASS

Y#	Date	Mintage	Fine	VF	XF	Unc
31	1942	5,000	5.00	10.00	17.50	35.00
	1943	1,000	15.00	25.00	40.00	85.00
	1944	1,000	15.00	25.00	40.00	85.00
	1945	1,000	15.00	25.00	40.00	85.00
	1946	1,000	15.00	25.00	40.00	85.00

10 CENTESIMI

COPPER

2	1929	.010	2.50	5.00	7.50	18.00
	1930	.090	1.00	2.00	4.00	6.00
	1931	.090	1.00	2.00	4.00	6.00
	1932	.090	1.00	2.00	4.00	6.00
	1934	.090	1.00	2.00	4.00	6.00
	1935	.090	1.00	2.00	4.00	6.00
	1936	.081	1.00	2.00	4.00	8.00
	1937	.081	1.00	2.00	4.00	8.00
	1938	—	—	—	Rare	—

Jubilee

12	1933-34	.090	2.50	5.00	10.00	20.00

ALUMINUM-BRONZE

23	1939	.081	1.25	2.50	5.00	10.00
	1940	.081	1.25	2.50	5.00	10.00
	1941	7,500	4.00	7.50	15.00	25.00

BRASS

32	1942	7,500	4.00	7.50	15.00	25.00
	1943	1,000	20.00	40.00	60.00	85.00
	1944	1,000	20.00	40.00	60.00	85.00
	1945	1,000	20.00	40.00	60.00	85.00
	1946	1,000	20.00	40.00	60.00	85.00

20 CENTESIMI

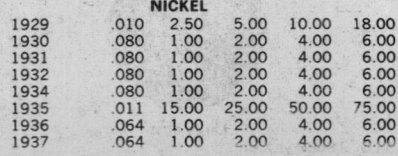

NICKEL

3	1929	.010	2.50	5.00	10.00	18.00
	1930	.080	1.00	2.00	4.00	6.00
	1931	.080	1.00	2.00	4.00	6.00
	1932	.080	1.00	2.00	4.00	6.00
	1934	.080	1.00	2.00	4.00	6.00
	1935	.011	15.00	25.00	50.00	75.00
	1936	.064	1.00	2.00	4.00	6.00
	1937	.064	1.00	2.00	4.00	6.00

Jubilee

Y#	Date	Mintage	Fine	VF	XF	Unc
13	1933-34	.080	2.50	5.00	10.00	20.00

24	1939	.064	1.00	2.00	4.00	6.00

STAINLESS STEEL

24a	1940	.064	1.00	2.00	4.00	5.50
	1941	.125	1.00	2.00	4.00	5.50

33	1942	.125	1.00	2.00	4.00	5.50
	1943	1,000	20.00	40.00	60.00	85.00
	1944	1,000	20.00	40.00	60.00	85.00
	1945	1,000	20.00	40.00	60.00	85.00
	1946	1,000	20.00	40.00	60.00	85.00

50 CENTESIMI

NICKEL

4	1929	.010	2.50	5.00	10.00	18.00
	1930	.080	1.00	2.00	4.00	6.00
	1931	.080	1.00	2.00	4.00	6.00
	1932	.080	1.00	2.00	4.00	6.00
	1934	.080	1.00	2.00	4.00	6.00
	1935	.014	3.00	6.00	12.00	25.00
	1936	.052	1.00	2.00	4.00	6.00
	1937	.052	1.00	2.00	4.00	6.00

Jubilee

14	1933-34	.080	2.00	4.00	8.00	16.00

25	1939	.052	1.00	2.00	4.00	6.00

STAINLESS STEEL

25a	1940	.052	1.00	2.00	4.00	5.50
	1941	.180	1.00	2.00	4.00	5.50

34	1942	.180	1.00	2.00	4.00	5.50

VATICAN CITY

Y#	Date	Mintage	Fine	VF	XF	Unc
34	1943	1,000	20.00	40.00	60.00	85.00
	1944	1,000	20.00	40.00	60.00	85.00
	1945	1,000	20.00	40.00	60.00	85.00
	1946	1,000	20.00	40.00	60.00	85.00

LIRA

NICKEL

Y#	Date	Mintage	Fine	VF	XF	Unc
5	1929	.010	2.50	5.00	10.00	18.00
	1930	.080	1.00	2.00	4.00	6.00
	1931	.080	1.00	2.00	4.00	6.00
	1932	.080	1.00	2.00	4.00	6.00
	1934	.080	1.00	2.00	4.00	6.00
	1935	.040	1.00	2.00	4.00	6.00
	1936	.040	1.00	2.00	4.00	6.00
	1937	.070	1.00	2.00	4.00	6.00

Jubilee, enlargement of date area

Y#	Date	Mintage	Fine	VF	XF	Unc
15	1933-34	.080	3.00	5.00	10.00	20.00
26	1939	.070	1.75	3.00	5.00	10.00

STAINLESS STEEL

Y#	Date	Mintage	Fine	VF	XF	Unc
26a	1940	.070	1.75	3.00	5.00	7.50
	1941	.284	.50	1.00	2.00	4.00
35	1942	.284	.50	1.00	2.00	4.00
	1943	1,000	20.00	40.00	60.00	85.00
	1944	1,000	20.00	40.00	60.00	85.00
	1945	1,000	20.00	40.00	60.00	85.00
	1946	1,000	20.00	40.00	60.00	85.00

ALUMINUM

Y#	Date	Mintage	Fine	VF	XF	Unc
40	1947	.120	.50	1.00	2.00	4.00
	1948	.010	.75	2.00	4.00	7.00
	1949	.010	.75	2.00	4.00	7.00

Holy Year

Y#	Date	Mintage	Fine	VF	XF	Unc
44	1950	.050	.50	1.00	2.00	4.00
49	1951	.400	.15	.25	.50	1.50
	1952	.400	.15	.25	.50	1.50
	1953	.400	.15	.25	.50	1.50
	1955	.010	.75	1.50	3.00	6.00
	1956	.010	.75	1.50	3.00	6.00
	1957	.030	.50	1.00	2.00	4.00
	1958	.030	.50	1.00	2.00	4.00
58	1959	.025	1.00	2.00	4.00	10.00
	1960	.025	.50	1.25	2.50	5.00
	1961	.025	.50	1.25	2.50	5.00
	1962	.025	.50	1.25	2.50	5.00

Ecumenical Council

Y#	Date	Mintage	Fine	VF	XF	Unc
67	1962	.050	.50	1.00	1.50	3.00
76	1963	.060	.50	1.00	2.00	5.00
	1964	.060	.25	.50	1.00	2.00
	1965	.060	.25	.50	1.00	2.00
84	1966	.090	.20	.40	.75	1.25

Fifth Year

Y#	Date	Mintage	Fine	VF	XF	Unc
92	1967	.100	.20	.40	.75	1.25

F.A.O. Issue

Y#	Date	Mintage	Fine	VF	XF	Unc
100	ND(1968)	.100	.20	.40	.75	1.25
108	1969	.100	.20	.40	.75	1.25
116	1970	.100	.20	.40	.75	1.25
	1971	.110	.20	.40	.75	1.25
	1972	.110	.20	.40	.75	1.25
	1973	.132	.20	.40	.75	1.25
	1974	.132	.15	.25	.50	1.00
	1975	.150	.15	.25	.50	1.00
	1976	.150	.15	.25	.50	1.00
	1977	.135	.15	.25	.50	1.00

Holy Year

Y#	Date	Mintage	Fine	VF	XF	Unc
124	1975	.180	.10	.25	.50	1.00

2 LIRE

NICKEL

Y#	Date	Mintage	Fine	VF	XF	Unc
6	1929	.010	2.50	5.00	10.00	18.00
	1930	.050	1.00	2.00	4.00	6.00
	1931	.050	1.00	2.00	4.00	6.00
	1932	.050	1.00	2.00	4.00	6.00
	1934	.050	1.00	2.00	4.00	6.00
	1935	.070	1.00	2.00	4.00	6.00
	1936	.040	1.00	2.00	4.00	6.00
	1937	.070	1.00	2.00	4.00	6.00

Jubilee

Y#	Date	Mintage	Fine	VF	XF	Unc
16	1933-34	.050	2.00	4.00	6.00	10.00
27	1939	.040	1.50	3.00	5.00	10.00

STAINLESS STEEL

Y#	Date	Mintage	Fine	VF	XF	Unc
27a	1940	.040	.50	.75	1.50	4.00
	1941	.270	.25	.50	1.00	3.00
36	1942	.270	.25	.50	1.00	3.00
	1943	1,000	20.00	40.00	60.00	85.00
	1944	1,000	20.00	40.00	60.00	85.00
	1945	1,000	20.00	40.00	60.00	85.00
	1946	1,000	20.00	40.00	60.00	85.00

ALUMINUM

Y#	Date	Mintage	Fine	VF	XF	Unc
41	1947	.065	1.00	2.00	4.00	8.00
	1948	.110	.75	1.50	3.50	5.00
	1949	.010	2.00	4.00	6.00	10.00

1795

VATICAN CITY 1796

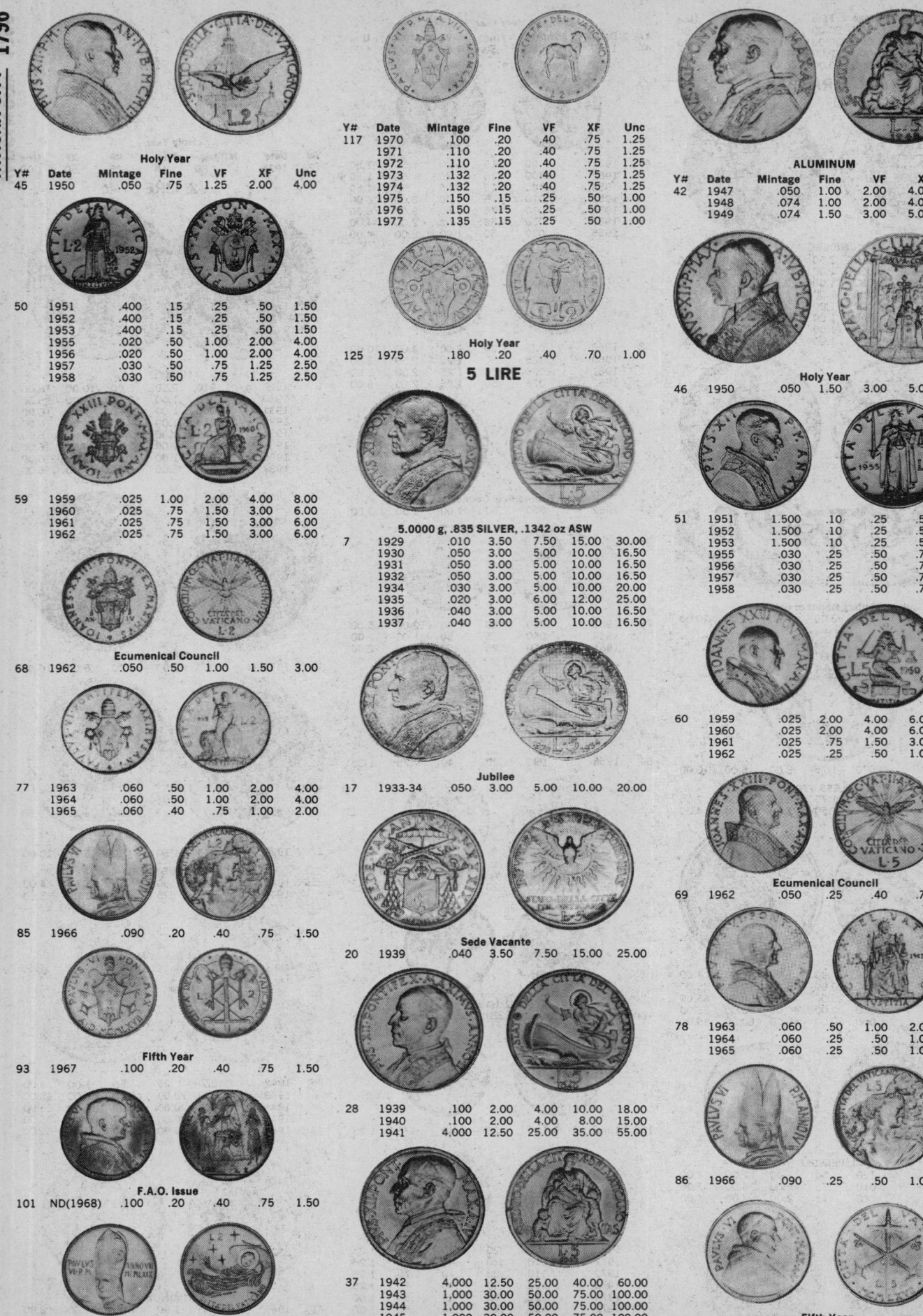

Holy Year

Y#	Date	Mintage	Fine	VF	XF	Unc
45	1950	.050	.75	1.25	2.00	4.00

50	1951	.400	.15	.25	.50	1.50
	1952	.400	.15	.25	.50	1.50
	1953	.400	.15	.25	.50	1.50
	1955	.020	.50	1.00	2.00	4.00
	1956	.020	.50	1.00	2.00	4.00
	1957	.030	.50	.75	1.25	2.50
	1958	.030	.50	.75	1.25	2.50

59	1959	.025	1.00	2.00	4.00	8.00
	1960	.025	.75	1.50	3.00	6.00
	1961	.025	.75	1.50	3.00	6.00
	1962	.025	.75	1.50	3.00	6.00

Ecumenical Council

68	1962	.050	.50	1.00	1.50	3.00

77	1963	.060	.50	1.00	2.00	4.00
	1964	.060	.50	1.00	2.00	4.00
	1965	.060	.40	.75	1.00	2.00

85	1966	.090	.20	.40	.75	1.50

Fifth Year

93	1967	.100	.20	.40	.75	1.50

F.A.O. Issue

101	ND(1968)	.100	.20	.40	.75	1.50

109	1969	.100	.20	.40	.75	1.50

Y#	Date	Mintage	Fine	VF	XF	Unc
117	1970	.100	.20	.40	.75	1.25
	1971	.110	.20	.40	.75	1.25
	1972	.110	.20	.40	.75	1.25
	1973	.132	.20	.40	.75	1.25
	1974	.132	.20	.40	.75	1.25
	1975	.150	.15	.25	.50	1.00
	1976	.150	.15	.25	.50	1.00
	1977	.135	.15	.25	.50	1.00

Holy Year

125	1975	.180	.20	.40	.70	1.00

5 LIRE

5.0000 g, .835 SILVER, .1342 oz ASW

7	1929	.010	3.50	7.50	15.00	30.00
	1930	.050	3.00	5.00	10.00	16.50
	1931	.050	3.00	5.00	10.00	16.50
	1932	.050	3.00	5.00	10.00	16.50
	1934	.030	3.00	5.00	10.00	20.00
	1935	.020	3.00	6.00	12.00	25.00
	1936	.040	3.00	5.00	10.00	16.50
	1937	.040	3.00	5.00	10.00	16.50

Jubilee

17	1933-34	.050	3.00	5.00	10.00	20.00

Sede Vacante

20	1939	.040	3.50	7.50	15.00	25.00

28	1939	.100	2.00	4.00	10.00	18.00
	1940	.100	2.00	4.00	8.00	15.00
	1941	4,000	12.50	25.00	35.00	55.00

37	1942	4,000	12.50	25.00	40.00	60.00
	1943	1,000	30.00	50.00	75.00	100.00
	1944	1,000	30.00	50.00	75.00	100.00
	1945	1,000	30.00	50.00	75.00	100.00
	1946	1,000	30.00	50.00	75.00	100.00

ALUMINUM

Y#	Date	Mintage	Fine	VF	XF	Unc
42	1947	.050	1.00	2.00	4.00	7.50
	1948	.074	1.00	2.00	4.00	7.50
	1949	.074	1.50	3.00	5.00	8.00

Holy Year

46	1950	.050	1.50	3.00	5.00	8.00

51	1951	1.500	.10	.25	.50	1.50
	1952	1.500	.10	.25	.50	1.50
	1953	1.500	.10	.25	.50	1.50
	1955	.030	.25	.50	.75	2.00
	1956	.030	.25	.50	.75	2.00
	1957	.030	.25	.50	.75	2.00
	1958	.030	.25	.50	.75	2.00

60	1959	.025	2.00	4.00	6.00	10.00
	1960	.025	2.00	4.00	6.00	10.00
	1961	.025	.75	1.50	3.00	4.50
	1962	.025	.25	.50	1.00	2.50

Ecumenical Council

69	1962	.050	.25	.40	.75	1.50

78	1963	.060	.50	1.00	2.00	4.00
	1964	.060	.25	.50	1.00	2.00
	1965	.060	.25	.50	1.00	2.00

86	1966	.090	.25	.50	1.00	2.00

Fifth Year

94	1967	.100	.20	.40	.60	1.00

VATICAN CITY 1797

F.A.O. Issue

Y#	Date	Mintage	Fine	VF	XF	Unc
102	ND(1968)	.100	.20	.40	.60	1.00

110	1969	.100	.20	.40	.60	1.00

118	1970	.100	.20	.40	.60	1.00
	1971	.110	.20	.40	.60	1.00
	1972	.110	.20	.40	.60	1.00
	1973	.132	.20	.40	.60	1.00
	1974	.132	.20	.40	.60	1.00
	1975	.150	.20	.40	.60	1.00
	1976	.150	.20	.40	.60	1.00
	1977	.135	.20	.40	.60	1.00

Holy Year

126	1975	.380	.15	.25	.35	1.00

16th Year

133	1978	.120	.15	.25	.40	1.00
A143	1979	.120	.15	.25	.40	1.00

10 LIRE

10.0000 g, .835 SILVER, .2684 oz ASW

8	1929	.010	3.50	7.50	17.50	35.00
	1930	.050	5.00	8.00	12.50	20.00
	1931	.050	5.00	8.00	12.50	20.00
	1932	.050	5.00	8.00	12.50	20.00
	1934	.060	5.00	8.00	12.50	20.00
	1935	.050	5.00	8.00	12.50	20.00
	1936	.040	5.00	8.00	12.50	20.00
	1937	.040	5.00	8.00	12.50	20.00

Jubilee

18	1933-34	.050	5.00	8.00	12.50	20.00

Sede Vacante

Y#	Date	Mintage	Fine	VF	XF	Unc
21	1939	.030	5.00	10.00	17.50	35.00

29	1939	.010	7.50	12.00	25.00	40.00
	1940	.010	7.50	12.00	25.00	40.00
	1941	4,000	10.00	20.00	40.00	80.00

38	1942	4,000	15.00	25.00	50.00	90.00
	1943	1,000	40.00	60.00	85.00	125.00
	1944	1,000	40.00	60.00	85.00	125.00
	1945	1,000	40.00	60.00	85.00	125.00
	1946	1,000	40.00	60.00	85.00	125.00

ALUMINUM

43	1947	.050	1.50	3.00	5.00	8.00
	1948	.060	1.50	3.00	5.00	8.00
	1949	.060	2.00	3.50	5.50	10.00

Holy Year

47	1950	.060	1.50	3.00	5.00	8.00

52	1951	1.130	.25	.50	.75	1.50
	1952	1.130	.25	.50	.75	1.50
	1953	1.130	.25	.50	.75	1.50
	1955	.080	.50	.75	1.50	3.50
	1956	.080	.50	.75	1.50	3.50
	1957	.036	.50	.75	1.50	3.50
	1958	.030	.50	.75	1.50	3.50

Y#	Date	Mintage	Fine	VF	XF	Unc
61	1959	.050	1.00	2.50	4.00	7.50
	1960	.050	.50	2.00	3.00	6.00
	1961	.050	.50	2.00	3.00	6.00
	1962	.050	.50	1.00	2.00	4.00

Ecumenical Council

70	1962	.100	.50	1.00	1.50	3.00

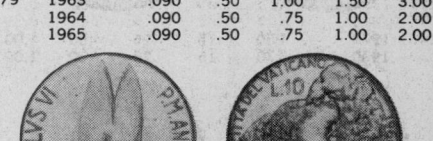

79	1963	.090	.50	1.00	2.00	3.00
	1964	.090	.50	.75	1.00	2.00
	1965	.090	.50	.75	1.00	2.00

87	1966	.100	.15	.30	.75	1.50

Fifth Year

95	ND(1967)	.110	.15	.30	.75	1.50

F.A.O. Issue

103	ND(1968)	.110	.20	.40	.80	1.50

111	1969	.110	.15	.30	.60	1.25

119	1970	.110	.15	.25	.55	1.25
	1971	.160	.15	.25	.50	1.00
	1972	.160	.15	.25	.50	1.00
	1973	.170	.15	.25	.50	1.00
	1974	.170	.15	.25	.50	1.00
	1975	.200	.15	.25	.50	1.00
	1976	.200	.15	.25	.50	1.00
	1977	.200	.15	.25	.50	1.00

VATICAN CITY 1798

Holy Year

Y#	Date	Mintage	Fine	VF	XF	Unc
127	1975	.400	.15	.25	.75	1.50

16th Year

134	1978	.250	.15	.25	.50	1.00
143	1979	.250	.15	.25	.50	1.00
	1980	.170	.15	.25	.50	1.00
155	1981	.170	.15	.25	.50	1.00

Creation of Woman
Obv: Similar to 1000 Lire, Y#167.

161	1982	.220	.15	.25	.50	1.00

Work and Teaching

170	1983	.110	.15	.25	.50	1.00

Obv: Similar to 1000 Lire, Y#183.

177	1984	.110	.15	.25	.50	1.00
185	1985	—	.15	.25	.50	1.00

Obv: Similar to 200 Lire, Y#196.

Y#	Date	Mintage	Fine	VF	XF	Unc
192	1986	—	.15	.25	.50	1.00

Obv: Similar to 200 Lire, Y#203.
Rev: Basilica Pieta Statue.

199	1987	—	.15	.25	.50	1.00

Temptation of Adam and Eve
Obv: Similar to 200 Lire, Y#210.

206	1988	—	.15	.25	.50	1.00

20 LIRE

ALUMINUM-BRONZE

A52	1957	.020	.50	.75	1.25	2.50
	1958	.060	.50	.75	1.25	2.50
62	1959	.050	.50	.75	1.25	2.50
	1960	.050	.50	.75	1.25	2.50
	1961	.050	.50	.75	1.00	2.50
	1962	.050	.50	.75	1.00	2.50

Ecumenical Council

71	1962	.100	.25	.75	1.00	2.00
80	1963	.090	.50	1.00	2.00	4.00
	1964	.090	.50	.75	1.00	2.00
	1965	.090	.50	.75	1.00	2.00
88	1966	.100	.15	.30	.75	1.50

Fifth Year

Y#	Date	Mintage	Fine	VF	XF	Unc
96	ND(1967)	.105	.15	.30	.75	1.25

F.A.O. Issue

104	ND(1968)	.105	.15	.25	.75	1.50
112	1969	.105	.15	.25	.60	1.25
120	1970	.105	.15	.25	.50	1.25
	1971	.170	.15	.25	.50	1.25
	1972	.170	.15	.25	.50	1.00
	1973	—	.15	.25	.50	1.00
	1974	—	.15	.25	.50	1.00
	1975	.250	.15	.25	.50	1.00
	1976	.250	.15	.25	.50	1.00
	1977	.250	.15	.25	.50	1.00

Holy Year

128	1975	.400	.15	.25	.50	1.25

16th Year

135	1978	.120	.15	.25	.50	1.25
144	1979	.120	.15	.25	.50	1.00
	1980	.265	.15	.25	.50	1.00
156	1981	.265	.15	.25	.50	1.00

VATICAN CITY 1799

Marriage
Obv: Similar to 1000 Lire, Y#167.

Y#	Date	Mintage	Fine	VF	XF	Unc
162	1982	.360	.15	.25	.50	1.00

Incarnation of the Word

171	1983	.170	.15	.25	.50	1.00

Obv: Similar to 1000 Lire, Y#183.

178	1984	.170	.15	.25	.50	1.00

186	1985	—	.15	.25	.50	1.00

Obv: Similar to 200 Lire, Y#196.

193	1986	—	.15	.25	.50	1.00

Obv: Similar to 200 Lire, Y#203.
Rev: Assumption of Mother Mary into Heaven.

200	1987		.15	.25	.50	1.00

Forbidding of the Fruit to Adam and Eve
Similar to 200 Lire, Y#210.

207	1988		.15	.25	.50	1.00

50 LIRE

STAINLESS STEEL

Y#	Date	Mintage	Fine	VF	XF	Unc
54	1955	.180	.50	1.00	1.50	3.00
	1956	.180	.50	1.00	1.50	3.00
	1957	.180	.50	1.00	1.50	3.00
	1958	.060	.50	1.00	1.50	3.00

Obv: Continuous leg.

Y#	Date	Mintage	Fine	VF	XF	Unc
63	1959	.100	.40	1.00	2.50	7.00

63.1	1960	.100	.40	1.00	2.50	7.50
	1961	.100	.40	1.00	2.00	3.50
	1962	.100	.40	1.00	2.00	3.50

Ecumenical Council

72	1962	.200	.25	.50	1.25	2.50

81	1963	.120	.50	1.00	2.00	4.00
	1964	.120	.25	.75	1.50	3.00
	1965	.120	.25	.50	1.00	2.00

89	1966	.150	.25	.50	1.00	2.00

Fifth Year

97	1967	.190	.25	.50	1.00	2.00

F.A.O. Issue

105	ND(1968)	.190	.25	.50	1.00	2.00

113	1969	.190	.25	.50	1.00	2.00

Y#	Date	Mintage	Fine	VF	XF	Unc
121	1970	.190	.15	.30	.75	1.50
	1971	.700	.15	.30	.75	1.50
	1972	.700	.15	.30	.75	1.25
	1973	.750	.15	.30	.75	1.25
	1974	.750	.15	.30	.75	1.25
	1975	.600	.15	.30	.75	1.25
	1976	.600	.15	.30	.75	1.25

Holy Year

129	1975	.500	.20	.40	.75	1.25

A121	1977	.600	.15	.20	.35	1.00

16th Year

136	1978	.223	.15	.25	.50	1.00

145	1979	.223	.15	.25	.50	1.00
	1980	.250	.15	.25	.50	1.00

157	1981	.240	.15	.25	.50	1.00

Maternity
Obv: Similar to 1000 Lire, Y#167.

163	1982	.400	.15	.25	.50	.75

VATICAN CITY 1800

Banishment of Adam and Eve

Y#	Date	Mintage	Fine	VF	XF	Unc
172	1983	.300	.15	.25	.50	1.00

Jubilee

Y#	Date	Mintage	VF	XF	Unc
19	1933-34	.023	150.00	200.00	275.00

5.1900 g, .900 GOLD, .1501 oz AGW

Y#	Date	Mintage	Fine	VF	XF	Unc
A53	1957	2,000	—	200.00	250.00	300.00
	1958	3,000	—	200.00	250.00	300.00

5.1900 g, .900 GOLD, .1501 oz AGW

Y#	Date	Mintage	VF	XF	Unc
10	1936	8,239	175.00	225.00	275.00
	1937	2,000	1000.00	2000.	3000.
	1938	6 pcs.	—	Rare	

Obv: Similar to 1000 Lire, Y#183.

| 179 | 1984 | .300 | .15 | .25 | .50 | 1.00 |

| 66 | 1959 | 3,000 | — | 500.00 | 700.00 | 1000. |

30	1939	2,700	175.00	225.00	325.00
	1940	2,000	175.00	225.00	375.00
	1941	2,000	175.00	225.00	375.00

STAINLESS STEEL

| 187 | 1985 | — | .15 | .25 | .50 | 1.00 |

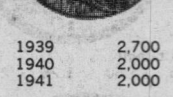

| 64 | 1959 | .783 | .60 | 1.25 | 2.00 | 4.00 |

39	1942	2,000	200.00	250.00	400.00
	1943	1,000	300.00	400.00	500.00
	1944	1,000	300.00	400.00	500.00
	1945	1,000	300.00	400.00	500.00
	1946	1,000	300.00	400.00	500.00
	1947	1,000	300.00	400.00	500.00
	1948	5,000	150.00	200.00	250.00
	1949	1,000	300.00	400.00	500.00

Obv: Similar to 200 Lire, Y#196.

| 194 | 1986 | — | .15 | .25 | .50 | 1.00 |

64.1	1960	.783	.80	1.75	3.00	7.50
	1961	.783	.40	.75	1.00	2.50
	1962	.783	.40	.75	1.00	2.00

Obv: Similar to 200 Lire, Y#203.
Rev: Mother Mary protecting kneeling sinners.

| 201 | 1987 | — | .15 | .25 | .50 | 1.00 |

Holy Year

| 48 | 1950 | .020 | 150.00 | 200.00 | 250.00 |

Ecumenical Council

| 73 | 1962 | 1.566 | .25 | .40 | .75 | 1.50 |

53	1951	1,000	300.00	400.00	600.00
	1952	1,000	300.00	400.00	600.00
	1953	1,000	300.00	400.00	600.00
	1954	1,000	350.00	500.00	650.00
	1955	1,000	300.00	400.00	600.00
	1956	1,000	300.00	400.00	600.00

Creation of Eve From Adam's Rib
Obv: Similar to 200 Lire, Y#210.

| 208 | 1988 | — | .15 | .25 | .50 | 1.00 |

100 LIRE

82	1963	.558	.50	1.00	2.00	4.00
	1964	.558	.25	.50	1.00	2.00
	1965	.558	.25	.50	1.00	2.00

8.8000 g, .900 GOLD, .2546 oz AGW

Y#	Date	Mintage	VF	XF	Unc
9	1929	10,000	150.00	200.00	300.00
	1930	2,621	300.00	500.00	750.00
	1931	3,343	200.00	300.00	500.00
	1932	5,073	200.00	300.00	400.00
	1934	2,533	250.00	350.00	500.00
	1935	2,015	250.00	350.00	500.00

STAINLESS STEEL

Y#	Date	Mintage	Fine	VF	XF	Unc
55	1955	1.300	.25	.50	1.00	2.00
	1956	1.400	.25	.50	1.00	2.00
	1957	.900	.25	.50	1.00	2.00
	1958	.852	.25	.50	1.00	2.00

| 90 | 1966 | .388 | .25 | .50 | 1.00 | 2.00 |

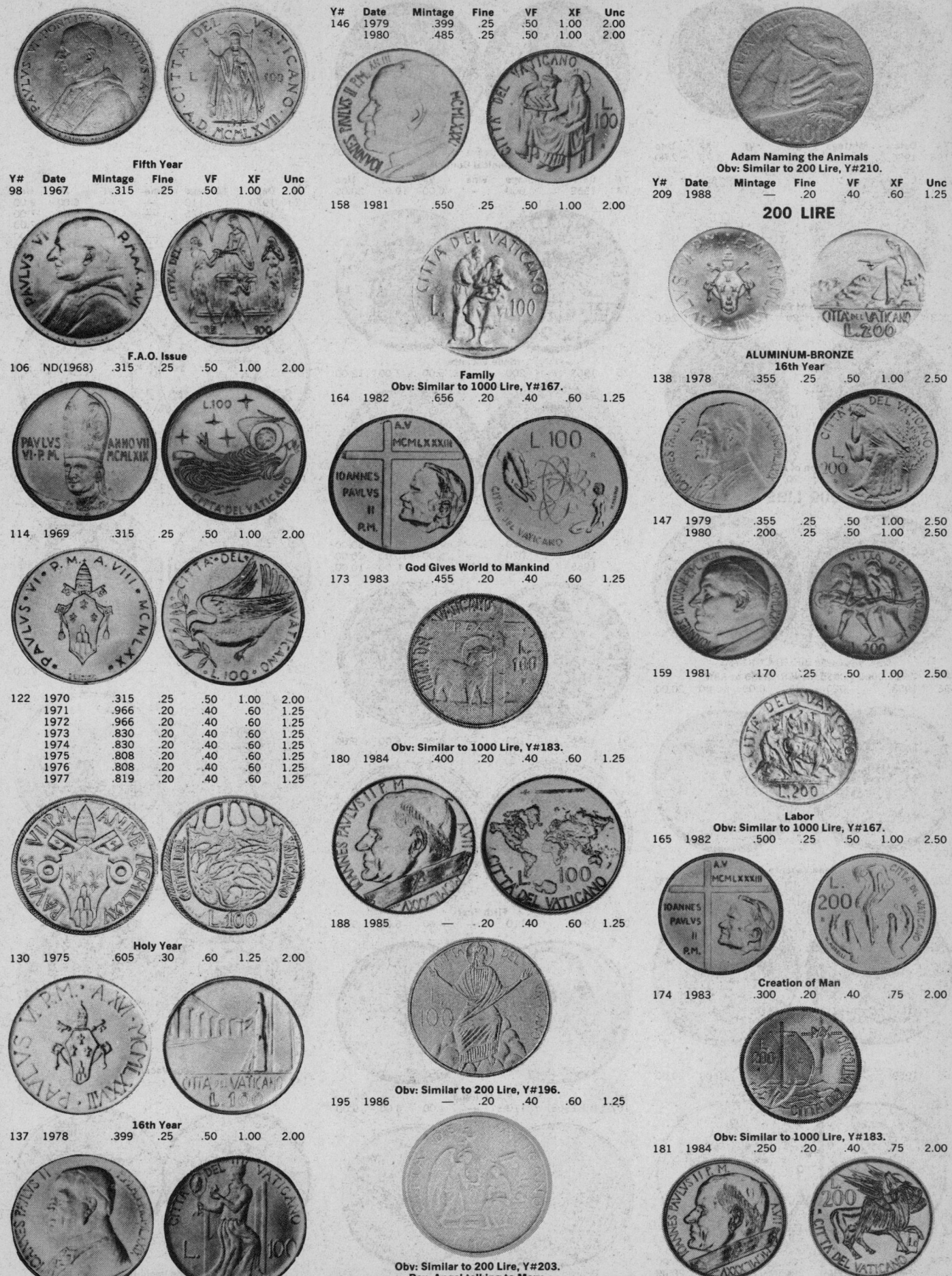

VATICAN CITY 1801

Fifth Year

Y#	Date	Mintage	Fine	VF	XF	Unc
98	1967	.315	.25	.50	1.00	2.00

F.A.O. Issue
| 106 | ND(1968) | .315 | .25 | .50 | 1.00 | 2.00 |

| 114 | 1969 | .315 | .25 | .50 | 1.00 | 2.00 |

122	1970	.315	.25	.50	1.00	2.00
	1971	.966	.20	.40	.60	1.25
	1972	.966	.20	.40	.60	1.25
	1973	.830	.20	.40	.60	1.25
	1974	.830	.20	.40	.60	1.25
	1975	.808	.20	.40	.60	1.25
	1976	.808	.20	.40	.60	1.25
	1977	.819	.20	.40	.60	1.25

Holy Year
| 130 | 1975 | .605 | .30 | .60 | 1.25 | 2.00 |

16th Year
| 137 | 1978 | .399 | .25 | .50 | 1.00 | 2.00 |

Y#	Date	Mintage	Fine	VF	XF	Unc
146	1979	.399	.25	.50	1.00	2.00
	1980	.485	.25	.50	1.00	2.00

| 158 | 1981 | .550 | .25 | .50 | 1.00 | 2.00 |

Family
Obv: Similar to 1000 Lire, Y#167.
| 164 | 1982 | .656 | .20 | .40 | .60 | 1.25 |

God Gives World to Mankind
| 173 | 1983 | .455 | .20 | .40 | .60 | 1.25 |

Obv: Similar to 1000 Lire, Y#183.
| 180 | 1984 | .400 | .20 | .40 | .60 | 1.25 |

| 188 | 1985 | — | .20 | .40 | .60 | 1.25 |

Obv: Similar to 200 Lire, Y#196.
| 195 | 1986 | — | .20 | .40 | .60 | 1.25 |

Obv: Similar to 200 Lire, Y#203.
Rev: Angel talking to Mary.
| 202 | 1987 | — | .20 | .40 | .60 | 1.25 |

Adam Naming the Animals
Obv: Similar to 200 Lire, Y#210.
Y#	Date	Mintage	Fine	VF	XF	Unc
209	1988	—	.20	.40	.60	1.25

200 LIRE

ALUMINUM-BRONZE
16th Year
| 138 | 1978 | .355 | .25 | .50 | 1.00 | 2.50 |

| 147 | 1979 | .355 | .25 | .50 | 1.00 | 2.50 |
| | 1980 | .200 | .25 | .50 | 1.00 | 2.50 |

| 159 | 1981 | .170 | .25 | .50 | 1.00 | 2.50 |

Labor
Obv: Similar to 1000 Lire, Y#167.
| 165 | 1982 | .500 | .25 | .50 | 1.00 | 2.50 |

Creation of Man
| 174 | 1983 | .300 | .20 | .40 | .75 | 2.00 |

Obv: Similar to 1000 Lire, Y#183.
| 181 | 1984 | .250 | .20 | .40 | .75 | 2.00 |

| 189 | 1985 | — | .20 | .40 | .75 | 2.00 |

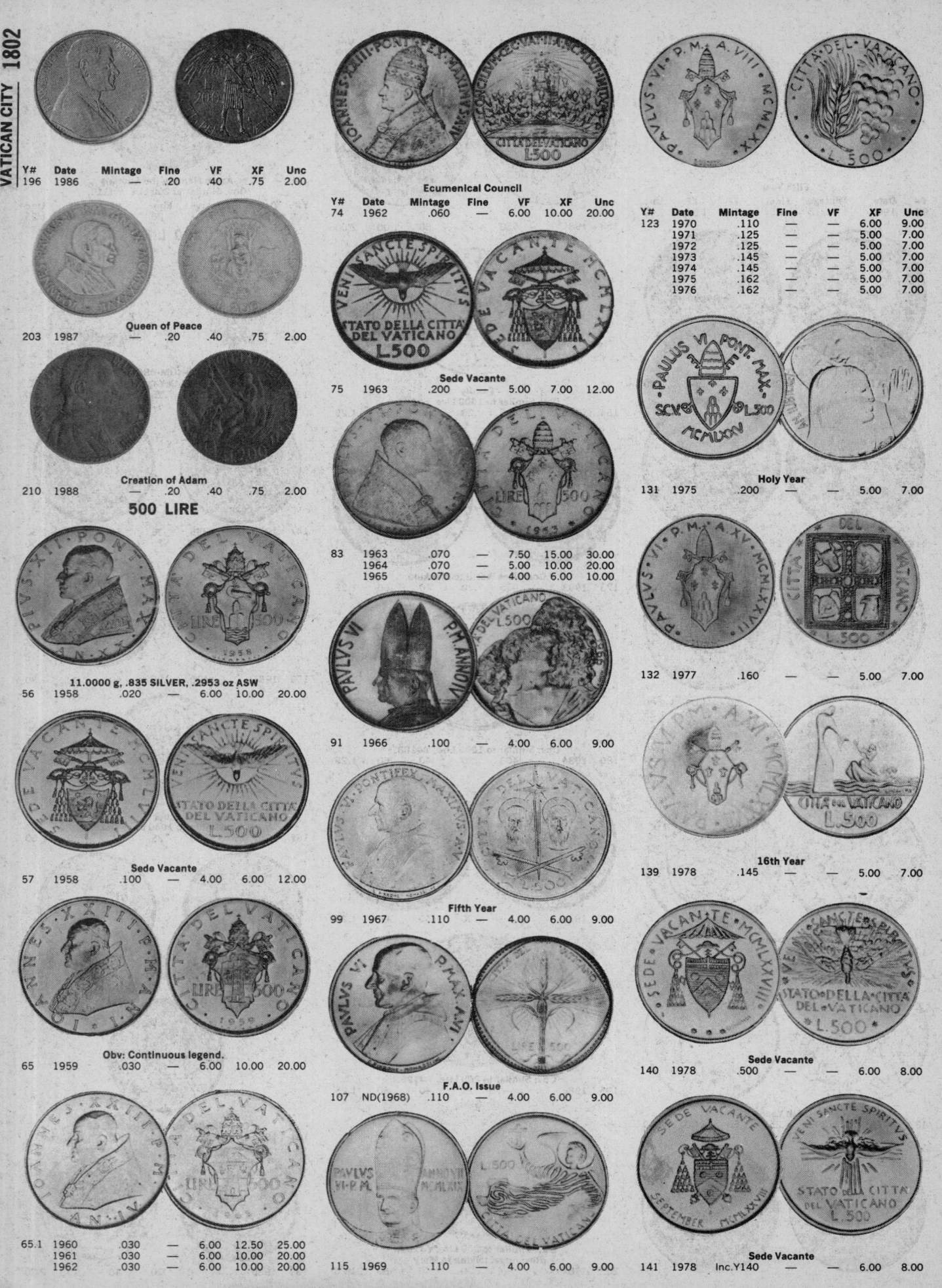

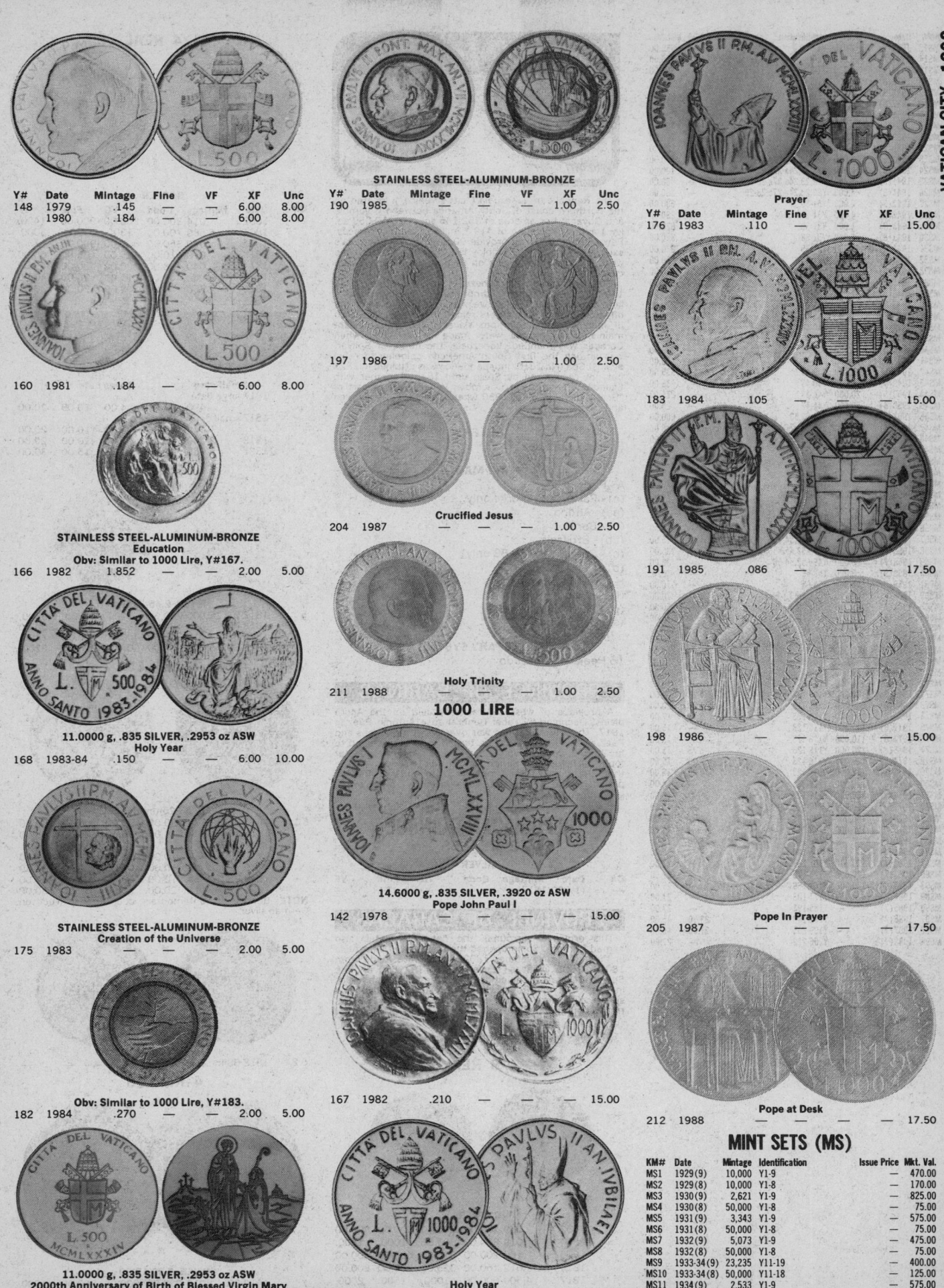

VATICAN CITY

KM#	Date	Mintage	Identification	Issue Price	Mkt. Val.
MS13	1935(9)	2,015	Y1-9	—	685.00
MS14	1935(8)	9,000	Y1-8	—	250.00
MS15	1936(9)	8,239	Y1-8,10	—	350.00
MS16	1936(8)	40,000	Y1-8	—	75.00
MS17	1937(9)	2,000	Y1-8,10	—	3075.00
MS18	1937(8)	20,000	Y1-8	—	75.00
MS19	1938(3)	—	Y1-2,10	—	Rare
MS20	1939(9)	2,700	Y22-30	—	435.00
MS21	1939(8)	10,000	Y22-29	—	110.00
MS22	1939(2)	30,000	Y20,21	—	60.00
MS23	1940(9)	2,000	Y22,23,24a-27a,28-30	—	470.00
MS24	1940(8)	10,000	Y22,23,24a-27a,28-29	—	100.00
MS25	1941(9)	2,000	Y22,23,24a-27a,28-30	—	580.00
MS26	1941(8)	4,000	Y22,23,24a-27a,28-29	—	200.00
MS27	1942(9)	2,000	Y31-39	—	630.00
MS28	1942(8)	4,000	Y31-38	—	230.00
MS29	1943(9)	1,000	Y31-39	—	820.00
MS30	1943(8)	1,000	Y31-38	—	320.00
MS31	1944(9)	1,000	Y31-39	—	820.00
MS32	1944(8)	1,000	Y31-38	—	320.00
MS33	1945(9)	1,000	Y31-39	—	820.00
MS34	1945(8)	1,000	Y31-38	—	320.00
MS35	1946(9)	1,000	Y31-39	—	820.00
MS36	1946(8)	1,000	Y31-38	—	320.00
MS37	1947(5)	1,000	Y39-43	—	530.00
MS38	1947(4)	50,000	Y40-43	—	28.00
MS39	1947(2)	—	Y42-43	—	16.00
MS40	1948(5)	5,000	Y39-43	—	280.00
MS41	1948(4)	10,000	Y40-43	—	28.00
MS42	1949(5)	1,000	Y39-43	—	535.00
MS43	1949(4)	10,000	Y40-43	—	35.00
MS44	1950(5)	20,000	Y44-48	—	275.00
MS45	1950(4)	50,000	Y44-47	—	25.00
MS46	1951(5)	1,000	Y49-52,53	—	600.00
MS47	1951(4)	400,000	Y49-52	—	6.00
MS48	1952(5)	1,000	Y49-52,53	—	600.00
MS49	1952(4)	400,000	Y49-52	—	6.00
MS50	1953(5)	1,000	Y49-52,53	—	600.00
MS51	1953(4)	400,000	Y49-52	—	6.00
MS52	1955(7)	1,000	Y49-55	—	620.00
MS53	1955(6)	10,000	Y49-52,54,55	—	20.00
MS54	1956(7)	1,000	Y49-55	—	620.00
MS55	1956(6)	10,000	Y49-52,54,55	—	20.00
MS56	1957(7)	2,000	Y49-A52,A53,54,55	—	315.00
MS57	1957(7)	20,000	Y49-A52,54,55	—	15.00
MS58	1958(7)	3,000	Y49-A52,A53-56	—	335.00
MS59	1958(7)	20,000	Y49-A52,54-56	—	35.00
MS60	1959(9)	3,000	Y58-66	—	1070.
MS61	1959(8)	25,000	Y58-65	—	70.00
MS62	1960(8)	25,000	Y58-62,63.1-65.1	—	70.00
MS63	1961(8)	25,000	Y58-62,63.1-65.1	—	50.00
MS64	1962(8)	25,000	Y58-62,63.1-65.1	—	45.00
MS65	1962(8)	50,000	Y67-74	—	37.00
MS66	1963(8)	60,000	Y76-83	—	58.00
MS67	1963(8)	60,000	Y76-83	—	37.00
MS68	1964(8)	60,000	Y76-83	—	37.00
MS69	1965(8)	60,000	Y76-83	—	25.00
MS70	1966(8)	90,000	Y84-91	—	20.00
MS71	1967(8)	100,000	Y92-99	3.25	20.00
MS72	1968(8)	100,000	Y100-107	4.20	20.00
MS73	1969(8)	100,000	Y108-115	4.20	20.00
MS74	1970(8)	100,000	Y116-123	5.00	17.00
MS75	1971(8)	110,000	Y116-123	—	15.00
MS76	1972(8)	110,000	Y116-123	6.00	15.00
MS77	1973(8)	120,000	Y116-123	6.75	15.00
MS78	1974(8)	120,000	Y116-123	7.25	15.00
MS79	1975(8)	132,000	Y116-123	9.00	15.00
MS80	1975(8)	170,000	Y124-131	—	15.00
MS81	1976(8)	180,000	Y116-123	—	15.00
MS82	1977(8)	180,000	Y116-122,132	—	15.00
MS83	1978(7)	180,000	Y133-139	—	16.00
MS84	1979(8)	156,000	Y143-148	—	16.00
MS85	1980(6)	—	Y143-148	18.00	16.00
MS86	1981(6)	—	Y155-160	—	16.00
MS87	1982(7)	120,000	Y161-167	—	27.00
MS88	1983(7)	120,000	Y170-176	—	27.00
MS93	1983/84(2)	130,000	Y168-169	—	25.00
MS89	1984(7)	—	Y177-183	—	27.00
MS90	1985(7)	—	Y185-191	—	27.00
MS91	1986(7)	—	Y192-198	23.50	45.00
MS92	1987(7)	—	Y199-205	27.00	45.00
MS94	1988(7)	—	Y206-212	—	27.00

VENEZUELA

The Republic of Venezuela ("Little Venice"), located on the northern coast of South America between Colombia and Guyana, has an area of 352,145 sq. mi. (912,050 sq. km.) and a population of *19.2 million. Capital: Caracas. Petroleum and mining provide 90 percent of Venezuela's exports although they employ less than 2 percent of the work force. Coffee, grown on 60,000 plantations, is the chief crop.

Columbus discovered Venezuela on his third voyage in 1498. Initial exploration did not reveal Venezuela to be a land of great wealth. An active pearl trade operated on the off-shore islands and slavers raided the interior in search of Indians to be sold into slavery, but no significant mainland settlements were made before 1567 when Caracas was founded. Venezuela, the home of Bolivar, was among the first South American colonies to rebel against Spain in 1810. Independence was attained in 1821 but not recognized by Spain until 1845. Together with Ecuador, Panama and Colombia, Venezuela was part of "Gran Colombia" until 1830 when it became a sovereign and independent state.

RULERS
Spanish, until 1821

MINT MARKS
A - Paris
(a) - Paris, privy marks only
(aa) - Altona
(b) - Berlin
(bb) - Brussels
(c) - Caracas (1886-89 only)
(d) - Denver
H - Heaton, Birmingham
(l) - London
(p) - Philadelphia
(s) - San Francisco

MONETARY SYSTEM
16 Reales = 1 Escudo

PROVINCE OF BARINAS

A province of west central Venezuela on the Apure plains. Occupied by rebel General Jose Antonio Paez in 1817. The city of Barinas was overrun with refugees and Paez asked that all silver be turned in to be recoined to facilitate commerce and trade. The coins were made but found disfavor with Simon Bolivar who issued a decree that the coins should not circulate outside Barinas province and would be redeemed by the central government.

REPUBLICAN COINAGE
2 REALES
SILVER

C#	Date	Mintage	Good	VG	Fine	VF
—	(1)800(1817)	—	—	—	—	—

PROVINCE OF CARACAS

This province surrounds the national capital, also named Caracas. Spain opened the first mint in Venezuela in that city in November 1802. Coins were made from 1802 to 1805. Caracas rebelled on April 19, 1810, and the Spanish retreated. The city surrendered to Spanish forces in July, 1812, and Royalist coinage resumed. Copper and silver coins were struck through 1821, when Bolivar's troops defeated the Spanish.

ROYALIST COINAGE
1/8 REAL

COPPER

	Date	Mintage	Good	VG	Fine	VF
1	1802	.059	170.00	350.00	500.00	800.00
	1804	.019	300.00	600.00	1000.	1500.
	1805	.100	200.00	375.00	600.00	900.00
	1814	.012	150.00	325.00	500.00	800.00
	1817	4,500	600.00	1000.	1500.	2000.
	1818	.094	75.00	100.00	175.00	250.00

1/4 REAL

COPPER

C#	Date	Mintage	Good	VG	Fine	VF
2	1802	.014	300.00	500.00	900.00	1400.
	1804	6,589	600.00	1300.	1700.	3000.
	1805	.070	350.00	600.00	900.00	1750.
	1813	.010	10.00	25.00	35.00	60.00
	1814/3	.040	8.00	20.00	30.00	45.00
	1814	Inc. Ab.	8.00	15.00	25.00	40.00
	1816	.750	4.00	8.00	20.00	30.00

	Small date		Large date	
1817 large date	.490	2.00	4.00	10.00	20.00
1817 small date	1.640	2.00	4.00	10.00	20.00
1818	2.240	2.00	4.00	10.00	20.00
1821	.650	2.00	4.00	15.00	30.00

REAL

SILVER, 2.45-3.25 g

	Date	Mintage	Good	VG	Fine	VF
5	1817 BS	6,500	700.00	1200.	1800.	3500.
	1818 BS	.014	125.00	250.00	400.00	800.00
	1820 BS	.011	300.00	400.00	700.00	1400.
	1821 BS	8,000	300.00	500.00	900.00	2200.

2 REALES

SILVER, 23-25mm, 4.3-5.3 g

	Date	Mintage	Good	VG	Fine	VF
6.1	1817 BS	.076	30.00	60.00	100.00	150.00
	1818 BS	.777	8.00	15.00	25.00	45.00
	1819/8 BS	1.450	10.00	15.00	22.50	37.50
	1819 BS	Inc. Ab.	10.00	15.00	22.50	37.50
	1820 BS	.755	10.00	20.00	30.00	50.00
	1821 BS	.110	20.00	30.00	50.00	80.00

NOTE: Beware of contemporary counterfeits struck on German silver.

| 6.2 | 1818 BS | Inc. Ab. | — | — | — | — |

4 REALES

SILVER, 9.50-10.30 g

| 7 | 1819 BS | .018 | 250.00 | 500.00 | 800.00 | 1200. |
| | 1820 BS | .029 | 250.00 | 500.00 | 800.00 | 1200. |

ROYALIST and/or REPUBLICAN COINAGE
REAL

SILVER, 2.4-3.0 g
Resembles Lima cob of 18th century.
Obv: L-M. Rev: M-L.

C#	Date	Good	VG	Fine	VF
12	(1810-21) LM*	25.00	50.00	90.00	150.00

2 REALES

SILVER
Obv: L-M. Rev: M-L.

13	(1810-21) LM*	15.00	25.00	40.00	70.00

NOTE: Of the many actual, false and blundered dates, the following have been noted 184, 231, 816, 471, 817, 814, 751, 142, 182, 1816, 1817, 931, 781, 172, 174.

REPUBLICAN COINAGE
1812

19 refers to 19 April 1810, date of the Declaration of Independence.

1/8 REAL

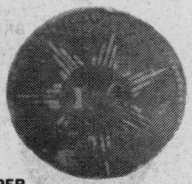

COPPER
Caracas Mint

C#	Date	Mintage	Good	VG	Fine	VF
21	1812	7,000	150.00	225.00	500.00	800.00

1/4 REAL

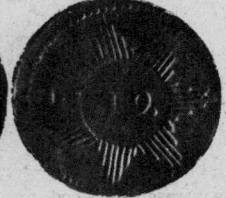

COPPER, 26-30mm

22	1812	.030	30.00	60.00	85.00	150.00

1/2 REAL

SILVER
Obv: Large "1/2".

25.1	Ano 2(1812)	.016	300.00	500.00	800.00	1250.

Obv: Small "1/2".

25.2	Ano 2(1812) 2 pcs. known	—	—	Rare	—

REAL

SILVER

26	Ano 2(1812)	.020	300.00	500.00	800.00	1500.

Under Gran Colombia
1/4 REAL

SILVER

C#	Date	Mintage	Good	VG	Fine	VF
31	1821	.090	75.00	125.00	250.00	450.00
	1822	.540	30.00	50.00	100.00	200.00

34	1829	.750	12.00	20.00	30.00	60.00
	1830	.650	12.00	25.00	35.00	70.00

1/2 REAL

SILVER

35	1829 O 1 known	—	—	—	—

PROVINCE OF GUAYANA

Province in eastern Venezuela. Legislation was passed on October 26, 1813 to authorize the striking of coins. This was to alleviate the coin shortage caused by the isolated geographical location of the province relative to other Spanish forces. Around 1900, this area was incorporated into British Guiana.

ROYALIST COINAGE
1/4 REAL

COPPER

40	1813	—	500.00	800.00	1200.	1600.
	1815	—	—	Reported, not confirmed		

1/2 REAL

COPPER

41	1813	—	30.00	50.00	70.00	130.00
	1814	—	4.00	10.00	22.50	50.00
	1815	—	4.00	10.00	22.50	50.00
	1816	—	8.00	12.00	30.00	50.00
	1817	—	4.00	10.00	22.50	50.00

PROVINCE OF MARACAIBO

A province in northwestern Venezuela including the city of Maracaibo, on the channel between Lake Maracaibo and the Caribbean Sea. This crude coinage was presumably necessary because of the temporary isolation of the Royalist forces from the main Spanish armies.

ROYALIST COINAGE
1/2 REAL

COPPER

10	1813	—	175.00	325.00	450.00	650.00

2/4 REAL

COPPER

KM#	Date	Mintage	Good	VG	Fine	VF
3 (C49)	ND	—	40.00	75.00	135.00	225.00

NOTE: Varieties exist.

REPUBLIC OF VENEZUELA
MONETARY SYSTEM
10 Centavos = 1 Real
10 Reales = 1 Peso

1/4 CENTAVO

COPPER, 2.9-3.0 g

Y#	Date	Mintage	VG	Fine	VF	XF
1	1843WW	3.840	2.00	4.00	10.00	35.00
	1852H	2.000	3.00	8.00	25.00	60.00

2.7 g

4	1852	4.000	2.00	4.00	15.00	35.00

1/2 CENTAVO

COPPER, 24mm, 5.7-6.0 g

2	1843WW	.960	3.00	7.00	20.00	50.00
	1843WW				Proof	225.00
	1852H	.500	5.00	10.00	30.00	90.00

22mm, 5.4 g

5	1852	1.000	3.00	7.00	20.00	50.00

CENTAVO

COPPER, 32mm, 11.4-12.1 g

3	1843WWYON	.480	10.00	25.00	60.00	100.00
	1852HEATON	.250	7.00	15.00	30.00	65.00

30mm, 10.9 g

6	1852	.500	3.00	6.00	14.00	50.00

VENEZUELA 1806

Engrailed edge, thick planchet, 7.5 g.

Y#	Date	Mintage	VG	Fine	VF	XF
7	1858 HEATON w/LIBERTAD incuse					
		1.000	2.50	4.50	9.00	18.50
	1858 HEATON w/LIBERTAD in relief					
		1.000	2.50	4.50	9.00	18.50
	1862 HEATON					
		1.500	2.50	4.50	9.00	20.00
	1863 HEATON					
		.500	3.00	6.00	12.50	30.00

1/2 REAL
.900 SILVER
Similar to 2 Reales, Y#10 but value shown as 1-1/2 Real, erroneously.

| 8 | 1858A | .040 | 150.00 | 300.00 | 750.00 | 1800. |

REAL
.900 SILVER
Similar to 2 Reales, Y#10.

| 9 | 1858A | .042 | 40.00 | 80.00 | 225.00 | 700.00 |

2 REALES
SILVER
Rev: Similar to C#6.2.

C#	Date	Mintage	Good	VG	Fine	VF
36	1818(1830)BS	.268	10.00	18.50	37.50	70.00

.900 SILVER

Y#	Date	Mintage	VG	Fine	VF	XF
10	1858A	.030	35.00	75.00	150.00	375.00

5 REALES

.900 SILVER

| 11 | 1858A | .026 | 65.00 | 150.00 | 325.00 | 600.00 |

10 REALES

SILVER

Y#	Date	Mintage	Fine	VF	XF	Unc
A11	1863A	*.300	—	—	4000.	7000.

*NOTE: Almost entire issue melted, estimated 300 pcs. survived.

MONETARY REFORM
(1871-79)
100 Centavos = 1 Venezolano

CENTAVO

COPPER-NICKEL

Y#	Date	Mintage	VG	Fine	VF	XF
25	1876(P)	8.000	3.00	4.00	7.00	20.00
	1877(P)	2.000	4.00	7.00	12.50	30.00

2-1/2 CENTAVOS

COPPER-NICKEL

| 26 | 1876(P) | 1.500 | 4.00 | 8.00 | 20.00 | 40.00 |
| | 1877(P) | .500 | 5.00 | 12.00 | 30.00 | 70.00 |

5 CENTAVOS

1.2500 g, .835 SILVER, .0336 oz ASW

| 12 | 1874A | .800 | 3.50 | 9.00 | 15.00 | 35.00 |
| | 1876A | .520 | 4.00 | 9.00 | 20.00 | 50.00 |

10 CENTAVOS

2.5000 g, .835 SILVER, .0671 oz ASW

| 13 | 1874A | .800 | 4.50 | 12.00 | 22.00 | 50.00 |
| | 1876A | .280 | 7.50 | 20.00 | 40.00 | 80.00 |

20 CENTAVOS

5.0000 g, .835 SILVER, .1342 oz ASW

| 14 | 1874A | .400 | 7.50 | 18.00 | 35.00 | 100.00 |
| | 1876A | .136 | 18.00 | 35.00 | 75.00 | 170.00 |

50 CENTAVOS

12.5000 g, .835 SILVER, .3356 oz ASW

15	1873A	.200	15.00	40.00	80.00	300.00
	1874A	.200	15.00	35.00	75.00	280.00
	1876A	.158	20.00	40.00	80.00	300.00

VENEZOLANO

25.0000 g, .900 SILVER, .7234 oz ASW

| 16 | 1876A | .035 | 30.00 | 90.00 | 200.00 | 1000. |
| | 1876A | — | — | Proof | | 7500. |

5 VENEZOLANOS

8.0645 g, .900 GOLD, .2333 oz AGW

Y#	Date	Mintage	Fine	VF	XF	Unc
17	1875A	.069	140.00	200.00	275.00	550.00

MONETARY REFORM
100 Centimos = 1 Bolivar

5 CENTIMOS

COPPER-NICKEL

27	1896(B)	4.000	.50	2.00	10.00	45.00
	1915(P)	2.000	1.00	4.00	30.00	125.00
	1921(P)	2.000	.50	2.00	8.00	30.00
	1925(P)	2.000	.30	1.00	6.00	15.00
	1927(P)	2.000	.30	1.00	6.00	15.00
	1929(P)	2.000	.25	1.00	6.00	15.00
	1936(P)	5.000	.15	.50	3.00	5.00
	1938(P)	6.000	.10	.20	3.00	5.00

BRASS

| 29 | 1944(D) | 4.000 | .50 | 1.00 | 3.00 | 7.00 |

COPPER-NICKEL

29a	1945(P)	12.000	.10	.20	.40	1.50
	1946(P)	12.000	.10	.20	.40	1.50
	1948(P)	18.000	.10	.20	.30	1.50

| 38 | 1958(P) | 25.000 | — | — | .10 | .30 |

38.1	1964	40.000	—	—	.10	.20
	1965	60.000	—	—	.10	.20
38.2	1971	40.000	—	—	.10	.20

COPPER-CLAD STEEL

49	1974	200.000	—	—	—	.15
	1976	200.000	—	—	—	.15
	1977	600.000	—	—	—	.15
	1982	600.000	—	—	—	.10

NICKEL-CLAD STEEL

49a	1982		—	—	—	.10
	1983	600.000	—	—	—	.10
	1986	500.000	—	—	—	.10

10 CENTIMOS

COPPER-NICKEL

Y#	Date	Mintage	Fine	VF	XF	Unc
A40	1971	60.000	—	—	.10	.25

12-1/2 CENTIMOS

COPPER-NICKEL

Y#	Date	Mintage	Fine	VF	XF	Unc
28	1896(B)	6.000	1.00	4.00	10.00	45.00
	1925(P)	.800	2.00	5.00	20.00	75.00
	1927(P)	.800	1.00	2.00	8.00	30.00
	1929(P)	.800	.15	.50	5.00	20.00
	1936(P)	1.200	.15	.30	1.00	8.00
	1938(P)	1.600	.15	.30	.65	6.00

NOTE: Varieties exist.

BRASS

Y#	Date	Mintage	Fine	VF	XF	Unc
30	1944(D)	.800	2.00	4.00	8.00	40.00

COPPER-NICKEL

30a	1945(P)	11.200	.10	.20	.35	2.00
	1946(P)	9.200	.10	.20	.35	3.00
	1948(S)	6.000	.10	.20	.35	2.00

39	1958(P)	10.000	—	—	.10	.50
	1969	2.000		Not released		60.00

25 CENTIMOS

1.2500 g, .835 SILVER, .0336 oz ASW

35	1954(P)	36.000	—	—	BV	1.00

35a	1960(a)	48.000	—	—	BV	.50

NICKEL

40	1965(aa)	240.000	—	—	.10	.30

26.8000 g, 1.18mm thick

50	1977	240.000	—	—	.10	.20

26.5000 g, 1.07mm thick

50a	1978	200.000	—	—	.10	.20
	1987	—	—	—	.10	.20

50 CENTIMOS

2.5000 g, .835 SILVER, .0671 OZ ASW

36	1954(P)	15.000	—	—	BV	2.00

Y#	Date	Mintage	Fine	VF	XF	Unc
36a	1960(a)	20.000	—	—	BV	1.50

NICKEL

41	1965(L)	180.000	—	.10	.15	.25
	1985	50.000	—	.10	.15	.25

1/5 BOLIVAR

1.0000 g, .835 SILVER, .0268 oz ASW

Y#	Date	Mintage	VG	Fine	VF	XF
19	1879(BB)	.125	100.00	175.00	350.00	750.00

NOTE: Coin recalled and many melted upon issuance of the 1/4 Bolivar in 1894.

1/4 BOLIVAR

1.2500 g, .835 SILVER, .0336 oz ASW

Y#	Date	Mintage	Fine	VF	XF	Unc
20	1894A	2.000	1.50	3.00	8.00	20.00
	1900(a)	.407	4.00	12.00	20.00	65.00
	1901(a)	.393	5.00	15.00	35.00	100.00
	1903(P)	.400	5.00	15.00	35.00	100.00
	1911(a)	.600	2.00	3.00	10.00	40.00
	1912(a)	.800	3.00	5.00	15.00	50.00
	1919(P)	.400	2.00	3.00	10.00	40.00
	1921(P)	.800	1.50	3.00	8.00	25.00
	1924(P)	.400	1.50	3.00	8.00	25.00
	1929(P)	1.200	—	—	BV	1.00	6.00
	1935(P)	3.400	—	—	BV	1.00	3.00
	1936(P)	2.800	—	—	BV	1.00	3.00
	1944(P)	1.800	—	—	BV	1.00	2.00
	1945(P)	8.000	—	—	—	BV	1.50
	1946(P)	8.000	—	—	—	BV	1.00
	1948(S)	8.638	—	—	—	BV	1.00

1/2 BOLIVAR

2.5000 g, .835 SILVER, .0671 oz ASW

21	1879(BB)	.200	20.00	50.00	150.00	400.00
	1886(C)	.300	10.00	20.00	65.00	180.00
	1887(C)	.310	50.00	100.00	150.00	350.00
	1888(C)	.230	350.00	550.00	900.00	1750.
	1889(C)	.080	—	—	Rare	—
	1893A	.500	10.00	15.00	50.00	150.00
	1900A	.600	15.00	30.00	65.00	175.00
	1900(a)	—	30.00	50.00	115.00	350.00
	1901(a)	.600	15.00	30.00	65.00	175.00
	1903(P)	.200	30.00	70.00	160.00	400.00
	1911(a)	.300	25.00	50.00	100.00	200.00
	1912(a)	1.920	4.00	8.00	25.00	90.00
	1919(P)	.400	5.00	10.00	35.00	100.00
	1921(P)	.600	2.00	6.00	15.00	50.00
	1924(P)	.800	2.00	5.00	10.00	35.00
	1929(P)	.400	1.00	2.00	7.50	20.00
	1935(P)	1.000	—	BV	1.00	7.00
	1936(P)	.600	1.00	2.00	5.00	15.00

21a	1944(D)	.500	—	BV	1.00	3.00	6.00
	1945(P)	4.000	—	—	BV	1.00	4.00
	1946(P)	2.500	—	—	BV	1.00	4.00

BOLIVAR

5.0000 g, .835 SILVER, .1342 oz ASW

Y#	Date	Mintage	Fine	VF	XF	Unc
22	1879(BB)	.375	20.00	50.00	200.00	700.00
	1886(C)	.600	15.00	25.00	100.00	500.00
	1887(C)	.280	100.00	250.00	500.00	1000.
	1888(C)	.197	130.00	300.00	700.00	1300.
	1889(C)	.118	100.00	250.00	500.00	1200.
	1893(a)	.500	10.00	25.00	60.00	175.00
	1900(a)	.380	15.00	40.00	85.00	250.00
	1901(a)	.323	20.00	40.00	100.00	300.00
	1903(P)	.800	5.00	10.00	40.00	125.00
	1911(a)	1.500	3.00	5.00	25.00	60.00
	1912(a)	.820	5.00	15.00	70.00	250.00
	1919(P)	1.000	2.00	4.00	10.00	45.00
	1921(P)	1.000	2.00	4.00	10.00	40.00
	1924(P)	1.500	BV	1.50	5.00	20.00
	1926(P)	1.000	BV	1.50	5.00	20.00
	1929(P)	2.500	—	BV	1.50	7.00
	1935(P)	5.000	—	BV	1.50	4.00
	1936(P)	5.000	—	BV	1.50	4.00

22a	1945(P)	8.000	—	—	BV	3.00

37	1954(P)	13.500	—	—	BV	2.00

37a	1960(a)	30.000	—	—	BV	1.25
	1965(a)	20.000	—	—	BV	1.25

NICKEL

42	1967	180.000	—	.10	.15	.50

52	1977	200.000	—	.10	.15	.50
	1986	—	—	.10	.15	.50

2 BOLIVARES

10.0000 g, .835 SILVER, .2685 oz ASW

VENEZUELA 1808

Y#	Date	Mintage	Fine	VF	XF	Unc
23	1879(BB)	.375	20.00	75.00	300.00	750.00
	1886(C)	.240	50.00	200.00	500.00	1200.
	1887(C)	.200	10.00	50.00	100.00	250.00
	1888(C)	.141	50.00	200.00	500.00	1200.
	1889(C)	.050	50.00	200.00	500.00	1200.
	1894(a)	.250	15.00	40.00	250.00	600.00
	1900(a)	.350	10.00	25.00	85.00	200.00
	1902(P)	.500	10.00	30.00	120.00	375.00
	1903(P)	.500	10.00	15.00	75.00	300.00
	1904(a)	.500	5.00	15.00	75.00	300.00
	1905(a)	.750	5.00	15.00	75.00	250.00
	1911(a)	.750	3.00	15.00	50.00	125.00
	1912(a)	.500	3.00	15.00	100.00	300.00
	1913(a)	.210	15.00	30.00	150.00	400.00
	1919(P)	1.000	BV	3.00	10.00	45.00
	1922(P)	1.000	BV	3.00	10.00	40.00
	1924(P)	1.250	BV	3.00	10.00	40.00
	1926(P)	1.000	BV	3.00	10.00	40.00
	1929(P)	1.500	BV	2.50	8.00	20.00
	1930(P)	.425	2.50	7.00	25.00	130.00
	1935(P)	3.000	BV	2.50	3.50	6.00
	1936(P)	2.500	BV	2.50	3.50	6.00

| 23a | 1945(P) | 3.000 | — | BV | 2.50 | 3.50 |

| A37 | 1960(a) | 4.000 | — | — | BV | 3.00 |
| | 1965(a) | 7.170 | — | — | BV | 3.00 |

NICKEL

43	1967	50.000	—	.15	.25	1.00
	1986	—	—	.15	.25	1.00
	1988	—	—	.15	.25	1.00

5 BOLIVARES

25.0000 g, .900 SILVER, .7234 oz ASW

24	1879(BB)	.250	10.00	60.00	225.00	650.00
	1886(C)	.470	10.00	30.00	150.00	350.00
	1887(C)	.500	10.00	35.00	225.00	500.00
	1888(C)	.281	10.00	35.00	225.00	600.00
	1889(C)	.329	10.00	35.00	225.00	600.00
	1900(a)	.270	10.00	25.00	150.00	400.00
	1901(a)	.090	15.00	100.00	400.00	900.00
	1902(P)	.500	8.00	15.00	100.00	400.00
	1903(P)	.200	10.00	15.00	100.00	400.00
	1904(a)	.200	8.00	15.00	125.00	500.00
	1905(a)	.300	8.00	15.00	100.00	350.00
	1910(a)	.400	BV	10.00	75.00	250.00
	1911(a)	1.104	BV	10.00	40.00	175.00
	1912(a)	.696	BV	10.00	40.00	175.00
	1919(P)	.400	BV	10.00	25.00	150.00
	1921(P)	.500	BV	10.00	20.00	80.00
	1924(P)	.500	BV	10.00	20.00	60.00
	1926(P)	.800	BV	10.00	20.00	50.00
	1929(P)	.800	BV	10.00	20.00	50.00
	1935(P)	1.600	BV	10.00	15.00	35.00
	1936(P)	2.000	BV	10.00	15.00	35.00

NICKEL

Y#	Date	Mintage	Fine	VF	XF	Unc
44	1973	20.000	—	.50	.75	1.50

| 53 | 1977 | 60.000 | — | .25 | .50 | 1.00 |
| | 1987 | — | — | .25 | .50 | 1.00 |

10 BOLIVARES

3.2258 g, .900 GOLD, .0933 oz AGW

| 31 | 1930 | .500 | BV | 50.00 | 60.00 | 85.00 |

NOTE: Only 6,000 pcs. of the total mintage were released. The balance remaining as part of the nation's gold reserve.

30.0000 g, .900 SILVER, .8681 oz ASW
Centennial of Bolivar Portrait on Coinage

| 45 | 1973 | 2.000 | — | — | 8.00 | 12.00 |

20 BOLIVARES

6.4516 g, .900 GOLD, .1867 oz AGW

32	1879	.041	BV	100.00	150.00	300.00
	1880	.084	BV	100.00	110.00	300.00
	1886	.023	BV	130.00	150.00	200.00
	1887	.132	115.00	160.00	220.00	500.00
	1888	.081	100.00	150.00	200.00	450.00
	1904(a)	.100	BV	100.00	110.00	130.00
	1905(a)	.100	BV	100.00	110.00	130.00
	1910(a)	.070	BV	100.00	110.00	130.00
	1911(a)	.080	BV	100.00	110.00	130.00
	1912(a)	.150	BV	100.00	110.00	130.00

25 BOLIVARES

28.2800 g, .925 SILVER, .8411 oz ASW
Conservation Series
Rev: Jaguar.

Y#	Date	Mintage	VF	XF	Unc
46	1975	.200	—	—	20.00
	1975	.030	—	Proof	30.00

50 BOLIVARES

35.0000 g, .925 SILVER, 1.0409 oz ASW
Conservation Series
Obv: Similar to 25 Bolivares, Y#46.
Rev: Giant armadillo.

| 47 | 1975 | .200 | — | — | 25.00 |
| | 1975 | .030 | — | Proof | 30.00 |

75 BOLIVARES

17.0000 g, .900 SILVER, .4920 oz ASW
150th Anniversary of Sucre's Death

Y#	Date	Mintage	Fine	VF	XF	Unc
55	1980	.500	—	—	—	7.50

100 BOLIVARES

32.2580 g, .900 GOLD, .9334 oz AGW

| 34 | 1886 | 4.250 | BV | 600.00 | 700.00 | 1000. |
| | 1887 | .028 | BV | 600.00 | 700.00 | 1000. |

Y#	Date	Mintage	Fine	VF	XF	Unc
34	1888	.032	BV	600.00	700.00	1000.
	1889	.023	BV	600.00	700.00	1000.

22.0000 g, .900 SILVER, .6367 oz ASW
150th Anniversary of Bolivar's Death

| 56 | 1980 | .500 | — | — | 10.00 |

27.0000 g, .835 SILVER, .7249 oz ASW
Andres Bello

| 57 | 1981 | .500 | — | Proof | 10.00 |

31.1000 g, .900 SILVER, .9000 oz ASW
Simon Bolivar

| 58 | 1983 | .300 | — | Proof | 15.00 |

200th Birthday of Jose M. Vargas

Y#	Date	Mintage	Fine	VF	XF	Unc
60	1986	.500	—	—	12.50
	1986	500 pcs.	—	—	Proof 200.00

500 BOLIVARES

18.0000 g, .900 GOLD, .5209 oz AGW
Nationalization of Oil Industry

Y#	Date	Mintage	VF	XF	Unc
54	1975	100 pcs.	—	—	6750.

1000 BOLIVARES

33.4370 g, .900 GOLD, .9676 oz AGW
Conservation Series
Rev: Cock of the Rock.

| 48 | 1975 | .010 | — | — | 500.00 |
| | 1975 | *3,000 | — | Proof | 900.00 |

3000 BOLIVARES

31.1000 g, .900 GOLD, .9000 oz AGW
Simon Bolivar

| 59 | 1983 | .010 | — | Proof | 500.00 |

5000 BOLIVARES

15.4900 g, .900 GOLD, .4483 oz AGW
Rafael Urdaneta

Y#	Date	Mintage	VF	XF	Unc
62	1988	.025	—	Proof	275.00

15.5700 g, .900 GOLD, .4506 oz AGW
Santiago Marino

| 63 | 1988 | .025 | — | Proof | 275.00 |

10,000 BOLIVARES

31.1000 g, .900 GOLD, .9000 oz AGW

| 61 | 1987 | .050 | — | Proof | 500.00 |

MINT SETS (MS)

KM#	Date	Mintage	Identification	Issue Price	Mkt. Val.
MS1	1975(3)	—	Y46-48	250.00	545.00

PROOF SETS (PS)

| PS1 | 1975(3) | — | Y46-48 | — | 960.00 |

LEPROSARIA COINAGE (L)

The Venezuelan Government maintained a large leper colony on Providencia Island, in Lake Maracaibo, where several hundred persons suffering from Hansen's disease were cared for. To provide for monetary transactions on the island, and to prevent ordinary coins from returning to general circulation after being handled by lepers, the Venezuelan Government formerly provided a distinctive currency. They had value only on the island until 30 years ago, when the illness was almost extinguished in South America and medical research revealed that little risk was involved in handling these coins.

MARACAIBO LAZARETO NACIONAL
5 CENTIMOS

BRASS

KM#	Date	Mintage	VG	Fine	VF	XF
L8	1916	—	7.00	13.50	20.00	37.50

1/8 BOLIVAR

VENEZUELA – Maracaibo Lazareto Nacional

BRASS

KM#	Date	Mintage	VG	Fine	VF	XF
L1	1913	—	9.00	15.00	22.50	40.00

1/2 BOLIVAR
BRASS
Similar to 1/8 Bolivar, KM#L1.

KM#	Date	Mintage	VG	Fine	VF	XF
L2	1913	—	—	—	—	—

BOLIVAR
BRASS
Similar to 1/8 Bolivar, KM#L1.

KM#	Date	Mintage	VG	Fine	VF	XF
L3	1913	—	—	—	—	—

2 BOLIVARES

BRASS
Obv: Similar to 20 Bolivares, KM#L7.

KM#	Date	Mintage	VG	Fine	VF	XF
L4	1913	—	—	—	—	—

5 BOLIVARES
BRASS
Similar to 1/8 Bolivar, KM#L1.

KM#	Date	Mintage	VG	Fine	VF	XF
L5	1913	—	—	—	—	—

10 BOLIVARES
BRASS
Similar to 1/8 Bolivar, KM#L1.

KM#	Date	Mintage	VG	Fine	VF	XF
L6	1913	—	—	—	—	—

20 BOLIVARES

BRASS
Rev: Similar to 2 Bolivares, KM#L4.

KM#	Date	Mintage	VG	Fine	VF	XF
L7	1913	—	—	—	—	—

CABO BLANCO
A leper colony located near the capitol city of Caracas. Coins were struck in 1936 for this colony.

ISLA DE PROVIDENCIA

0.05 BOLIVARES
(5 Centimos)

BRASS

KM#	Date	Mintage	VG	Fine	VF	XF
L20	1939	—	5.00	9.50	13.50	25.00

0.12-1/2 BOLIVARES
(12-1/2 Centimos)

BRASS

KM#	Date	Mintage	VG	Fine	VF	XF
L21	1939	—	6.50	11.50	17.50	27.50

VIETNAM/ANNAM

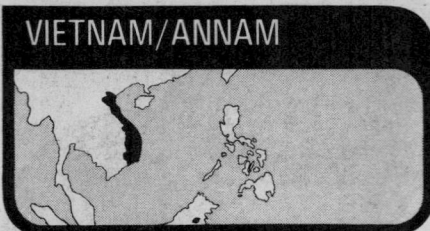

In 207 B.C. a Chinese general set up the Kingdom of Nam-Viet on the Red River. This kingdom was overthrown by the Chinese under the Han Dynasty in 111 B.C., whereupon the country became a Chinese province under the name of Giao-Chi, which was later changed to Annam or peaceful or pacified of the South. Chinese rule was maintained until 968, when the Vietnamese became independent until 1407 when China again invaded Vietnam. The Chinese were driven out in 1428 and the country became independent and named Dai-Viet. Gia Long renamed the country Dai Nam in 1802.

The former French Protectorate of Annam, now part of Vietnam, had an area of 57,840 sq. mi. (141,806 sq. km.) and supported a population of about 6 million. It was bounded on the North by Tonkin and on the South by Cochin China. Former capital: Hue. Chief products of the area are silk, cinnamon and rice. There are important mineral deposits in the mountainous inland.

United Dai Nam
EMPERORS

Gia Long, 1802-1820	嘉隆
Minh Mang, 1820-1841	明命
Thieu Tri, 1841-1847	紹治
Tu Duc, 1848-1883	嗣德
Kien Phuc, 1883-1884	建福
Ham Nghi, 1884-1885	咸宜

Protectorate of Annam
EMPERORS

Dong Khanh, 1885-1888	同慶
Thanh Thai, 1888-1907	成泰
Duy Tan, 1907-1916	維新
Khai Dinh, 1916-1925	啟定
Bao Dai, 1926-1945	保大

REBELS and INVADERS

Bao Hung, 1801-1802	寶興
Tri Nguyen, 1831-1834	治元
Nguyen Long, 1832-1833	元隆

IDENTIFICATION

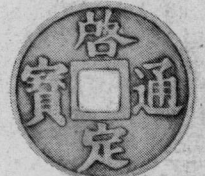

Khai — 啟
Bao — 寶
Thong — 通
Dinh — 定

Khai Dinh Thong Bao

The square holed cash coins of Annam are easily identified by reading the characters top-bottom (emperor's name) and right-left ("Thong Bao" general currency). The character at right will change with some emperors.

NUMERALS
Column A, conventional; Column B, formal.

NUMBER	CONVENTIONAL	FORMAL	COMMERCIAL
1	一 元	壹 弌	1
2	二	弍 貳	11
3	三	叄 弎	111
4	四	肆	X
5	五	伍	8
6	六	陸	上
7	七	柒	上
8	八	捌	上
9	九	玖	夕
10	十	拾 什	十
20	十二 or 廿	拾貳	11十
25	五十二 or 五廿	伍拾貳	11十8
30	十三 or 卅	拾叄	111十
100	百一	佰壹	1百
1,000	千一	仟壹	1千
10,000	萬一	萬壹	1万
100,000	萬十 億一	萬拾 億壹	十万
1,000,000	萬百一	萬佰壹	1百万

NOTE: This table has been adapted from *Chinese Bank Notes* by Ward Smith and Brian Matravers.

MONETARY SYSTEM
COPPER AND ZINC
10 Dong (zinc) = 1 Dong (copper)
600 Dong (zinc) = 1 Quan (string of cash)
Approx. 2600 Dong (zinc) = 1 Piastre

NOTE: Ratios between metals changed frequently, therefore the above is given as an approximate relationship.

PHAN SYSTEM
1 Phan .3778 grams
5 Phan (or 1/2 Tien) 1.8892 grams
10 Phan (or 1 Tien) 3.7783 grams

NOTE: The Van and Quan pieces are denominations for fiat money. A 10 Van coin was officially worth 10 full weight 1 Tien coins of copper, but, of course, weighed less and less during the inflationary times of their period of issue. The 3 Quan silver bar was officially worth 3 full weight strings of copper coins. The weight of these Van and Quan coins and bars varied considerably and are specified at their listing. The heavier weight pieces are generally the earliest issues with the lighter ones the latest.

PALACE ISSUES

C#53 "1 Mach or 60 Dong"

There are many dollar size and larger copper and brass tokens with obverses similar to the small square holed cash coins listed here with eight, four, or two characters or dragon and fish on the reverse. These were believed to have been given as gifts or bestowed as rewards and circulated to some extent although they do not carry any designation of weight or denomination.

CHARACTER IDENTIFICATION

The Vietnamese used Chinese-style characters for official documents and coins and bars. Some were modified to their liking and will sometimes not match the Chinese character for the same word. The above identification and this table will translate most of the Vietnamese characters (Chinese-style) on their coins and bars described herein.

Chinese/French
Vietnamese/English

安南　An Nam = name of the French protectorate

大南　Dai Nam = name of the country under Gia Long's Nguyen dynasty

越南　Viet Nam = name used briefly during Minh Mang's reign and became the modern name of the country

貫　Quan = a string of cash-style coins

分　Phan = a weight of about .38 grams

文　Van = cash-style coins

COPPER, BRASS and ZINC 'CASH' COINAGE
(1 Phan)

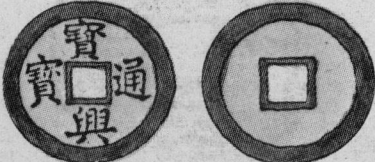

BRASS
Rev: Plain.

C#	Date	Emperor	Good	VG	Fine	VF
57	(1801-02)	Bao Hung	—	—	Rare	—

 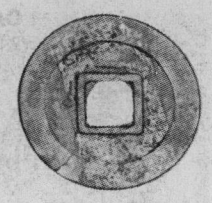

COPPER ALLOYS, 24-25mm
Rev: Plain.

C#	Date	Emperor	Good	VG	Fine	VF
61.1	(1802-20)	Gia Long	1.25	2.00	3.50	6.00

23-24mm
| 61.2 | (1802-20) | Gia Long | .85 | 1.50 | 2.75 | 4.50 |

Rev: Dot.
| 61.3 | (1802-20) | Gia Long | 2.00 | 3.50 | 5.50 | 9.00 |

Rev: Circle.
| 61.3a | (1802-20) | Gia Long | 2.00 | 3.50 | 5.50 | 9.00 |

Obv: Double rim.
| 61.3b | (1802-20) | Gia Long | 2.00 | 3.50 | 5.50 | 9.00 |

 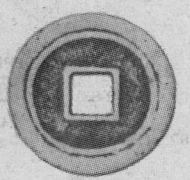

Obv. & rev: Double rim.
| 61.3c | (1802-20) | Gia Long | 2.00 | 3.50 | 5.50 | 9.00 |

Rev: Crescent.
| 61.4 | (1802-20) | Gia Long | 2.75 | 4.50 | 7.50 | 12.50 |

ZINC
Rev: Plain.
| 73 | (1802-20) | Gia Long | 4.50 | 7.50 | 12.50 | 20.00 |

COPPER ALLOYS, 24-25mm
| 81.1 | (1820-41) | Minh Mang | 1.00 | 1.75 | 2.75 | 4.50 |

23-24mm
| 81.2 | (1820-41) | Minh Mang | .75 | 1.25 | 2.00 | 3.50 |

ZINC
| 79 | (1820-41) | Minh Mang | 1.25 | 2.00 | 3.50 | 8.00 |

COPPER ALLOYS
Nguy Khoi Rebellion
Obv. leg: *Tri Nguyen Thong Bao.*
| 137 | (1831-34) | Tri Nguyen | 8.50 | 13.50 | 21.50 | 35.00 |

 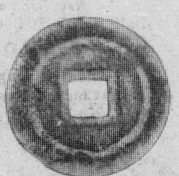

Nung Rebellion
Obv. leg: *Nguyen Long Thong Bao,* **cursive** *Nguyen.*
| 138.1 | (1832-33) | Nguyen Long | 8.50 | 13.50 | 21.50 | 35.00 |

Obv: Conventional *Nguyen.*
| 138.2 | (1823-33) | Nguyen Long | 10.50 | 18.00 | 30.00 | 45.00 |

Obv: Cursive *Nguyen.* **Rev: Double rim.**
| 139.1 | (1832-33) | Nguygen Long | 10.50 | 18.00 | 30.00 | 45.00 |

 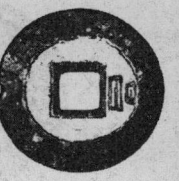

Rev: Character *Xuong.*
C#	Date	Emperor	Good	VG	Fine	VF
139.2	(1832-33)	Nguyen Long	10.50	18.00	30.00	45.00

COPPER ALLOYS, 24-25mm
| 141.1 | (1841-47) | Thieu Tri | .60 | 1.00 | 1.75 | 3.00 |

23-24mm
| 141.2 | (1841-47) | Thieu Tri | .60 | 1.00 | 1.75 | 3.00 |

ZINC
| 140 | (1841-47) | Thieu Tri | 2.75 | 4.50 | 7.50 | 12.50 |

COPPER ALLOYS, 24-25mm
| 201.1 | (1848-83) | Tu Duc | 1.25 | 2.00 | 3.50 | 6.00 |

23-24mm
| 201.2 | (1848-83) | Tu Duc | 1.25 | 2.00 | 3.50 | 6.00 |

ZINC
Obv: *Kien Phuc Thong Bao.*
| 271.1 | (1883-84) | Kien Phuc | 18.50 | 30.00 | 50.00 | 80.00 |

Obv: *Phuc* **written differently.**
| 271.2 | (1883-84) | Kien Phuc | 18.50 | 30.00 | 50.00 | 80.00 |

COPPER ALLOYS
Obv: *Ham Nghi Thong Bao.*
| 281 | (1884-85) | Ham Nghi | 35.00 | 60.00 | 100.00 | 165.00 |

24mm
| 301.1 | (1885-88) | Dong Khanh | 2.75 | 4.50 | 7.50 | 12.50 |

Annam / VIETNAM 1812

26mm

C#	Date	Emperor	Good	VG	Fine	VF
301.2	(1885-88)	Dong Khanh	11.50	18.50	30.00	50.00

 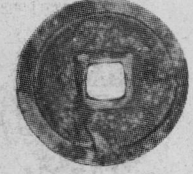
Rev: Blank.

Y#	Date	Emperor	Good	VG	Fine	VF
1	(1888-1907)	Than Thai	2.00	3.50	5.50	9.00

Similar to Y#5.1 but cast.

| 4 | (1916-25) | Khai Dinh | 5.50 | 9.00 | 15.00 | 25.00 |

 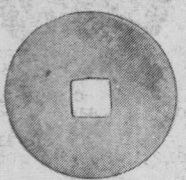
Struck, 22mm. Some pieces are uniface.

| 5.1 | (1916-25) | Khai Dinh | 1.75 | 2.75 | 4.50 | 7.50 |

 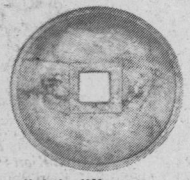
Larger size, characters slightly different.

| 5.2 | (1916-25) | Khai Dinh | 2.00 | 3.50 | 6.00 | 10.00 |

18mm

| 6 | (1926-45) | Bao Dai | 4.50 | 7.50 | 12.50 | 20.00 |

 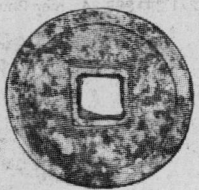
Rev: Plain, 24mm.

| 6a | (1926-45) | Bao Dai | 4.50 | 7.50 | 12.50 | 20.00 |

CASH
(6 Phan)

COPPER ALLOYS
Rev: *Luc Phan* in seal script.

C#	Date	Emperor	Good	VG	Fine	VF
62	(1802-20)	Gia Long	2.75	4.50	7.50	12.50

CASH
(7 Phan)

 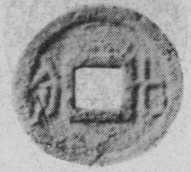
ZINC
Rev: *That Phan.*

C#	Date	Emperor	Good	VG	Fine	VF
63	(1802-20)	Gia Long	5.50	9.00	15.00	25.00

6 VAN

 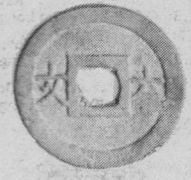
COPPER ALLOYS
Rev: *Luc Van.*

| 202 | (1848-83) | Tu Duc | 1.25 | 2.00 | 3.50 | 6.00 |

24-26mm

| 202.1 | (1848-83) | Tu Duc | 1.25 | 2.00 | 3.50 | 6.00 |

| 282 | (1884-85) | Ham Nghi | 35.00 | 60.00 | 100.00 | 165.00 |

Y#	Date	Emperor	Good	VG	Fine	VF
1a	(1888-1907)	Than Thoi	—	—	Rare	—

8 VAN
ZINC
Rev: Plain.

C#	Date	Emperor	Good	VG	Fine	VF
191	(1848-83)	Tu Duc	2.00	3.50	5.50	9.00

 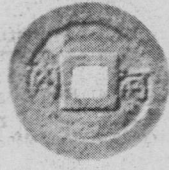
Rev: *Ha Noi.*

| 192.1 | (1848-83) | Tu Duc | 5.00 | 8.50 | 13.50 | 21.50 |

Rev: *Son Tay.*

| 192.2 | (1848-83) | Tu Duc | 6.00 | 10.00 | 16.50 | 25.00 |

COPPER ALLOYS
Obv: *Trung Bao* (heavy currency).
Rev: *Bat Van* and *An Nam.*

| 203 | (1848-83) | Tu Duc | — | — | Rare | — |

10 VAN
COPPER ALLOYS
Rev: Four Chinese characters *Tang.....Shih Wen.*

| 65 | (1802-20) | Gia Long | 11.50 | 18.50 | 30.00 | 50.00 |

Rev: *Chuan Thap Van.*

| 204 | (1848-83) | Tu Duc | 11.50 | 18.50 | 30.00 | 50.00 |

Rev: *Chuan Nhat Thap Van.*

C#	Date	Emperor	Good	VG	Fine	VF
204a	(1848-83)	Tu Duc	11.50	18.50	30.00	50.00

Rev: *Thap Van.*

Y#	Date	Emperor	Good	VG	Fine	VF
2	(1888-1907)	Than Thoi	.50	.75	1.25	2.50

| 3 | (1907-16) | Duy Tan | .50 | .75 | 1.25 | 2.50 |

| 7 | (1926-45) | Bao Dai | 2.00 | 3.50 | 6.00 | 10.00 |

20 VAN

COPPER or BRASS
Rev: *Chuan Nhi Thap Van.*

C#	Date	Emperor	Good	VG	Fine	VF
205	(1848-83)	Tu Duc	70.00	100.00	140.00	200.00

30 VAN

COPPER or BRASS
Rev: *Chuan Tam Thap Van.*

| 205.5 | (1848-83) | Tu Duc | 85.00 | 120.00 | 170.00 | 240.00 |

40 VAN

COPPER or BRASS
Rev: Chuan Tu Thap Van.

C#	Date	Emperor	Good	VG	Fine	VF
206	(1848-83)	Tu Duc	85.00	120.00	170.00	240.00

50 VAN

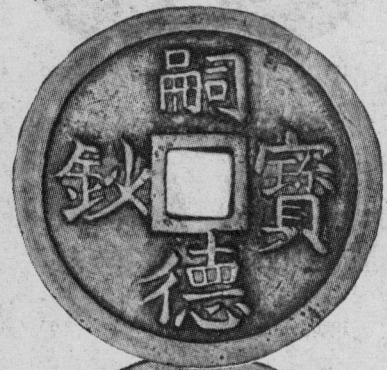

COPPER or BRASS
Rev: Chuan Ngu Thap Van.

206.5	(1848-83)	Tu Duc	70.00	100.00	140.00	200.00

60 VAN

COPPER or BRASS, 43mm
Rev: Chuan Luc Thap Van.

207.1	(1848-83)	Tu Duc	42.50	60.00	85.00	120.00

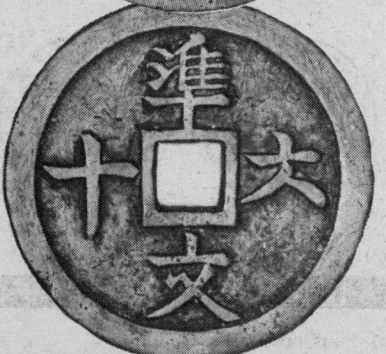

47-49mm

207.2	(1848-83)	Tu Duc	42.50	60.00	85.00	120.00

VIETNAM/FRENCH COCHIN CHINA

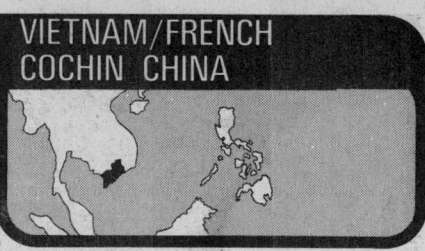

Cochin-China, a colony of France in Indo-China, now part of Vietnam, occupied an alluvial plain of the Mekong Delta along the South China Sea. In its colonial period, Cochin-China had an area of 24,981 sq. mi. (63,701 sq. km.) and a population of about 5 million. Capital: Saigon. The region was (and is) one of Asia's chief rice-growing areas. Fishing is also an important economic activity. French Cochin-China exported rice, fish and timber.

The region, inhabited mainly by Vietnamese, was formerly part of the ancient Khmer empire and later of the Empire of Dai Viet. It was brought under French control in 1862-67 and made a colony. The Japanese occupied the area before World War II to use as a base for the invasion of Malaya. When France regained power of the area following World War II, Cochin-China was included in the Federation of Indo-China as an autonomous republic. It was attached to Vietnam in 1949.

MINT MARKS
A - Paris
K - Bordeaux

MONETARY SYSTEM
5 Sapeques = 1 Cent
100 Cents = 1 Piastre

SAPEQUE

BRONZE
Center hole punched in France 1 Centime Y#41

KM#	Date	Mintage	Fine	VF	XF	Unc
1 (Y-A1)	1875K	1.000	5.00	10.00	20.00	50.00

2 (Y1)	1879A	20.000	3.00	6.00	12.50	25.00
	1885A	100 pcs.	—	—	Proof	250.00

NOTE: The above coin has 2/1000 on the reverse and thus is often mistaken for a 2 Sapeque.

CENT

BRONZE

3 (Y2)	1879A	.500	5.00	15.00	40.00	150.00
	1884A	.444	6.00	25.00	50.00	200.00
	1885A	.255	7.00	30.00	75.00	225.00
	1885A	100 pcs.	—	—	Proof	300.00

10 CENTS

2.7216 g, .900 SILVER, .0787 oz ASW

4 (Y3)	1879A	.400	20.00	30.00	70.00	250.00
	1884A	.510	25.00	50.00	100.00	350.00
	1885A	100 pcs.	—	—	Proof	650.00

20 CENTS

5.4431 g, .900 SILVER, .1575 oz ASW

KM#	Date	Mintage	Fine	VF	XF	Unc
5 (Y4)	1879A	.350	25.00	50.00	120.00	350.00
	1884A	.320	35.00	60.00	150.00	375.00
	1885A	100 pcs.	—	—	Proof	750.00

50 CENTS

13.6078 g, .900 SILVER, .3937 oz ASW

6 (Y5)	1879A	.180	75.00	125.00	250.00	600.00
	1884A	.010	400.00	600.00	800.00	2500.
	1885A	100 pcs.	—	—	Proof	1200.

PIASTRE

27.2156 g, .900 SILVER, .7875 oz ASW

7 (Y6)	1885A	100 pcs.	—	—	Proof	8000.

PROOF SETS (PS)

KM#	Date	Mintage	Identification	Issue Price	Mkt. Val.
PS1	1879A	—	KM-E6-E10	—	2100.
PS2	1885A(5)	100	KM3-7	—	11,000.

VIETNAM-TONKIN

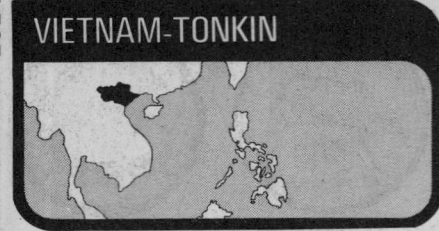

Tonkin, a former French protectorate in North Indo-China, comprises the greater part of present North Vietnam. It had an area of 44,672 sq. mi. (75,700 sq. km.) and a population of about 4 million. Capital: Hanoi. The initial value of Tonkin to France was contained in the access it afforded to the trade of China's Yunnan province.

France established a protectorate over Annam and Tonkin by the treaties of Tientsin and Hue negotiated in 1884. Tonkin was incorporated in the independent state of Vietnam (within the French Union) and upon the defeat of France by the Viet Minh became the body of North Vietnam.

MINT MARKS
(a) - Paris, privy marks only

1/600 PIASTRE

ZINC

KM#	Date	Mintage	Fine	VF	XF	Unc
1 (Y1)	1905(a)	60,000	3.00	7.00	15.00	32.00

NOTE: Previously it had been thought that genuine specimens of this coin were 1.5mm thick while thinner pieces were counterfeits. Recent evidence however indicates that the genuine coin is about 0.9 mm thick and weighs 2.14 grams while the 1.5 mm thick piece is a piefort weighing about 4.8 grams.

VIETNAM

The Socialist Republic of Vietnam, located in Southeast Asia west of the South China Sea, has an area of 127,300 sq. mi. (329,707 sq. km.) and a population of *66.7 million. Capital: Hanoi. Agricultural products, coal, and mineral ores are exported.

At the start of World War II, Vietnamese Nationalists fled to China's Kwangsi provinces where Ho Chi Minh organized the Revolution to free Vietnam of French rule. The Japanese occupied Vietnam during World War II. As the end of the war drew near, they ousted the Vichy French administration and granted Vietnam independence under a puppet government headed by Bao Dai, emperor of Annam. The Bao Dai government collapsed at the end of the war, and on Sept. 2, 1945, Ho Chi Minh proclaimed the existence of an independent Vietnam consisting of Cochin-China, Annam, and Tonkin, and set up a Communist government. France recognized the new government as a free state, but reneged and in 1949 reinstalled Bao Dai as Ruler of Vietnam and extended the regime independence within the French Union. Ho Chi Minh led a guerrilla war, in the first Indochina war, against the French puppet state that raged on to the disastrous defeat of the French by the Viet Minh at Dien Bien Phu on May 7, 1954.

An agreement signed at Geneva on July 21, 1954, provided for a temporary division of Vietnam at the 17th parallel of latitude, between a Communist-dominated north and a U.S.-supported south. In Oct. 1955, South Vietnam deposed Bao Dai by referendum and authorized the establishment of a republic with Ngo Dinh Diem as president. The Republic of South Vietnam was proclaimed on Oct. 26, 1955, and was immediately recognized by some Western Powers.

The activities of Communists in South Vietnam led to U.S. intervention and the second Indochina war which came to a brief halt in 1973 (when a cease-fire was arranged and U.S. forces withdrawn), but didn't end until April 30, 1975 when South Vietnam surrendered unconditionally. The People's Revolutionary Party assumed power in the government of South Vietnam until July 2, 1976, when the two Vietnams were reunited as the Socialist Republic of Vietnam.

For earlier coinage refer to French Indo-China.

MONETARY SYSTEM
10 Xu = 1 Hao
10 Hao = 1 Dong

20 XU

ALUMINUM

KM#	Date	Mintage	Fine	VF	XF	Unc
1 (Y1)	1945	—	50.00	75.00	100.00	150.00

5 HAO

ALUMINUM
Value in incuse lettering

2.1 (Y2)	1946	—	15.00	30.00	60.00	100.00

NOTE: Common with rotated dies.

Value in raised lettering

KM#	Date	Mintage	Fine	VF	XF	Unc
2.2 (Y2a)	1946	—	5.00	8.00	12.50	25.00

DONG

ALUMINUM

3 (Y3)	1946	—	50.00	100.00	150.00	250.00

2 DONG

BRONZE

4 (Y4)	1946	—	15.00	30.00	50.00	125.00

NORTH VIETNAM

XU

ALUMINUM

5 (Y5)	1958	—	.75	1.50	2.50	4.00

2 XU

ALUMINUM

6 (Y6)	1958	—	.75	1.50	2.50	4.00

5 XU

ALUMINUM

7 (Y7)	1958	—	1.00	2.00	3.50	5.00

SOUTH VIETNAM

MINT MARKS
(a) - Paris, privy marks only

MONETARY SYSTEM
100 Xu (Su) = 1 Dong

VIETNAM 1815

10 SU

ALUMINUM

KM#	Date	Mintage	Fine	VF	XF	Unc
1 (Y1)	1953(a)	20.000	.15	.25	.45	.75

20 SU

ALUMINUM

| 2 (Y2) | 1953(a) | 15.000 | .30 | .50 | .75 | 1.25 |

50 XU

ALUMINUM

| 3 (Y3) | 1953(a) | 15.000 | 1.50 | 3.00 | 6.00 | 12.50 |

50 SU

ALUMINUM

| 4 (Y4) | 1960 | 10.000 | .25 | .50 | 1.25 | 2.50 |
| | 1960 | — | — | — | Proof | — |

50 XU

ALUMINUM

| 6 (Y6) | 1963 | 20.000 | .20 | .40 | .75 | 1.50 |

DONG

COPPER-NICKEL

| 5 (Y5) | 1960 | 105.000 | .15 | .25 | .35 | .75 |
| | 1960 | — | — | — | Proof | — |

KM#	Date	Mintage	Fine	VF	XF	Unc
7 (Y7)	1964	44.000	.15	.25	.35	.75
	1964	—	—	—	Proof	—

NICKEL-CLAD STEEL

| 7a (Y7a) | 1971 | — | .10 | .15 | .25 | .50 |

ALUMINUM F.A.O. Issue

| 12 (Y12) | 1971 | 30.000 | .10 | .15 | .25 | .50 |

5 DONG

COPPER-NICKEL

| 9 (Y8) | 1966 | 100.000 | .10 | .20 | .40 | .80 |

NICKEL-CLAD STEEL

| 9a (Y8a) | 1971 | 15.000 | .10 | .50 | 1.00 | |

10 DONG

COPPER-NICKEL

| 8 (Y9) | 1964 | 15.000 | .20 | .40 | .60 | 1.25 |

NICKEL-CLAD STEEL

| 8a (Y9a) | 1968 | 30.000 | .10 | .15 | .25 | .60 |
| | 1970 | 50.000 | .10 | .15 | .25 | .60 |

BRASS-CLAD STEEL F.A.O. Issue

| 13 (Y13) | 1974 | 30.000 | .10 | .15 | .30 | .60 |

20 DONG

NICKEL-CLAD STEEL F.A.O. Issue

KM#	Date	Mintage	Fine	VF	XF	Unc
11 (Y11)	1968	.500	.25	.50	1.00	2.00

50 DONG

NICKEL CLAD STEEL F.A.O. Issue

| 14 (Y14) | 1975 | 1.010 | — | — | — | 600.00 |

NOTE: It is reported that all but a few examples were "disposed of as scrap metal".

PROVISIONAL COINAGE
(South)

XU

ALUMINUM

| 8 (Y8) | ND(1976) | — | .50 | 1.50 | 3.00 | 9.00 |

2 XU

ALUMINUM

| 9 (Y9) | 1975 | — | .50 | 1.50 | 3.00 | 9.00 |

5 XU

ALUMINUM

| 10 (Y10) | ND(1976) | — | .50 | 1.50 | 3.00 | 9.00 |

VIETNAM

MINT MARKS

(h) - Key - Habana, Cuba

HAO

ALUMINUM

| 11 (Y11) | 1976 | — | .50 | 1.00 | 2.50 | 5.00 |

NICKEL-CLAD STEEL

| 10 | 1968 | — | .25 | .45 | .85 | 1.85 |

VIETNAM 1816

2 HAO

ALUMINUM

KM#	Date	Mintage	Fine	VF	XF	Unc
12 (Y12)	1976	—	.50	1.00	2.50	5.00

5 HAO

ALUMINUM

KM#	Date	Mintage	Fine	VF	XF	Unc
13 (Y13)	1976	—	.75	1.50	3.00	6.00

DONG

ALUMINUM

KM#	Date	Mintage	Fine	VF	XF	Unc
14 (Y14)	1976	—	7.00	12.00	20.00	40.00

10 DONG

COPPER-NICKEL
Nature - Water Buffalo

KM#	Date	Mintage	Fine	VF	XF	Unc
15	1986(h)	—				7.50

Nature - Peacock

| 16 | 1986(h) | — | | | | 7.50 |

Nature - Elephant

| 17 | 1986(h) | — | | | | 7.50 |

100 DONG

12.0000 g, .999 SILVER, .3855 oz ASW
Junk Under Sail

KM#	Date	Mintage	Fine	VF	XF	Unc
18	1986	—				30.00

Wildlife - Buffalo

| 19 | 1986 | 5,000 | | | | 45.00 |

Wildlife - Peacock

| 20 | 1986 | 5,000 | | | | 45.00 |

Wildlife - Elephant

| 21 | 1986 | 5,000 | | | | 45.00 |

100 Years of the Automobile

| 22 | 1986 | 2,000 | | | | 20.00 |

Calgary Olympics - Skier

| 23 | 1986 | 2,000 | | | | 50.00 |

Calgary Olympics - Fencer

KM#	Date	Mintage	Fine	VF	XF	Unc
24	1986	—				50.00

15.9900 g, .980 SILVER, .5039 oz ASW

| 25 | 1988(h) | — | | | | 35.00 |

Listings For
VISCAYAN REPUBLIC: refer to Spain

WEST AFRICAN STATES

The West African States, a former federation of eight French colonial territories on the northwest coast of Africa, had an area of 1,831,079 sq. mi. (4,742,495 sq. km.) and a population of about 17 million. Capital: Dakar. The constituent territories were Mauritania, Senegal, Dahomey, French Sudan, Ivory Coast, Upper Volta, Niger and French Guinea.

The members of the federation were overseas territories within the French Union until Sept. of 1958 when all but French Guinea approved the constitution of the Fifth French Republic, thereby electing to become autonomous members of the new French Community. French Guinea voted to become the fully independent Republic of Guinea. The other seven attained independence in 1960. The French West Africa territories were provided with a common currency, a practice which was continued as the monetary union of the West African States which provides a common currency to the autonomous republics of Dahomey (now Benin), Senegal, Upper Volta (now Burkina Faso), Ivory Coast, Togo and Niger.

For earlier coinage refer to Togo, and French West Africa.

MINT MARKS
(a) - Paris, privy marks only

MONETARY SYSTEM
100 Centimes = 1 Franc

FRANC

ALUMINUM

KM#	Date	Mintage	VF	XF	Unc
3	1961(a)	3.000	.15	.30	.60
(Y1)	1962(a)	2.000	3.00	8.00	12.00
	1963(a)	4.500	3.00	8.00	12.00
	1964(a)	5.000	.10	.30	.60
	1965(a)	6.000	.10	.20	.40
	1967(a)	2.500	.15	.30	.60
	1970(a)	4.000	Reported, not confirmed		
	1971(a)	4.000	.15	.30	.60
	1972(a)	4.000	.10	.20	.40
	1973(a)	4.500	.10	.20	.40
	1974(a)	—	.10	.20	.40
	1975(a)	10.080	.15	.30	.60
	1976(a)	8.000	.10	.20	.40

NOTE: The 1962 and 1963 issue have the engraver general's name on the obverse.

STEEL

8	1976(a)	8.000	—	.10	.35
(Y7)	1977(a)	14.700	—	.10	.35
	1978(a)	—	—	.10	.35
	1980(a)	—	—	.10	.35
	1981(a)	—	—	.10	.35
	1982(a)	—	—	.10	.35

5 FRANCS

ALUMINUM-BRONZE

2	1960(a)	5.000	.20	.40	.70
(Y2)	1962(a)	5.000	—	—	—
	1963(a)	—	—	—	—
	1965(a)	6.510	.20	.45	.75
	1966(a)	6.000	Reported, not confirmed		
	1967(a)	6.010	.20	.40	.70
	1968(a)	6.000	.20	.45	.75
	1969(a)	8.000	.20	.40	.70
	1970(a)	10.005	.20	.40	.70
	1971(a)	10.000	.20	.40	.70
	1972(a)	5.000	.20	.40	.70
	1973(a)	6.000	.20	.45	.75
	1974(a)	13.326	.10	.15	.30
	1975(a)	16.840	.20	.40	.70
(Y2)	1976(a)	20.010	.20	.30	.60
	1977(a)	16.840	.20	.30	.60
	1978(a)	—	.20	.30	.60
	1979(a)	—	.10	.20	.40
	1980(a)	—	.10	.20	.40
	1981(a)	—	.10	.20	.40
	1982(a)	—	.10	.20	.40
	1985(a)	—	.10	.20	.40
	1987(a)	—	.10	.20	.40

10 FRANCS

ALUMINUM-BRONZE

1	1959(a)	10.000	.15	.30	.60
(Y3)	1961(a)	—	—	—	—
	1962(a)	—	—	—	—
	1964(a)	10.000	.20	.40	.70
	1965(a)	6.000	Reported, not confirmed		
	1966(a)	6.000	.20	.40	.70
	1967(a)	3.500	.25	.50	.90
	1968(a)	6.000	.20	.40	.70
	1969(a)	7.000	.25	.50	.90
	1970(a)	7.000	.15	.30	.60
	1971(a)	8.000	.15	.30	.60
	1972(a)	5.500	.20	.40	.70
	1973(a)	3.000	.20	.40	.70
	1974(a)	10.000	.10	.20	.35
	1975(a)	17.000	.15	.30	.60
	1976(a)	18.000	.15	.30	.60
	1977(a)	9.050	.15	.25	.50
	1978(a)	—	.15	.25	.50
	1979(a)	—	.15	.25	.50
	1980(a)	—	.15	.25	.50
	1981(a)	—	.15	.25	.50

BRASS
F.A.O. Issue

10	1981(a)	—	.25	.50	1.00
(Y9)	1982(a)	—	.25	.50	1.00
	1983(a)	—	.25	.50	1.00
	1984(a)	—	.25	.50	1.00
	1985(a)	—	.25	.50	1.00
	1986(a)	—	.25	.50	1.00

25 FRANCS

ALUMINUM-BRONZE

5	1970(a)	7.000	.25	.45	.80
(Y-A3)	1971(a)	7.000	.50	.75	1.25
	1972(a)	2.000	1.00	1.50	3.00
	1975(a)	5.035	.25	.45	.80
	1976(a)	3.365	.25	.45	.80
	1977(a)	3.288	.25	.45	.80
	1978(a)	—	.25	.45	.80
	1979(a)	—	.25	.45	.80

F.A.O. Issue

9	1980(a)	—	.25	1.00	2.50
(Y8)	1981(a)	—	.25	1.00	2.50
	1982(a)	—	.25	1.00	2.50
	1987(a)	—	.25	1.00	2.50

50 FRANCS

COPPER-NICKEL
F.A.O. Issue

KM#	Date	Mintage	VF	XF	Unc
6	1972(a)	20.000	.35	.50	1.25
(Y5)	1974(a)	3.000	.50	.75	1.50
	1975(a)	9.000	.25	.40	.75
	1976(a)	6.002	.35	.50	1.00
	1977(a)	4.832	.35	.50	1.00
	1978(a)	—	.35	.50	1.00
	1979(a)	—	.35	.50	1.00
	1980(a)	—	.35	.50	1.00
	1981(a)	—	.35	.50	1.00
	1982(a)	—	.35	.50	1.00
	1984(a)	—	.35	.50	1.00
	1985(a)	—	.35	.50	1.00

100 FRANCS

NICKEL

4	1967(a)	—	.75	.90	1.50
(Y4)	1968(a)	25.000	.75	.90	1.50
	1969(a)	25.000	.75	.90	1.50
	1970(a)	4.510	.80	.90	1.50
	1971(a)	12.000	.50	.75	1.25
	1972(a)	5.000	.60	.75	1.25
	1973(a)	5.000	.60	.75	1.25
	1974(a)	8.500	.60	.75	1.25
	1975(a)	16.000	.60	.75	1.25
	1976(a)	11.575	.60	.75	1.25
	1977(a)	9.355	.60	.75	1.25
	1978(a)	—	.60	.75	1.25
	1979(a)	—	.60	.75	1.25
	1980(a)	—	.60	.75	1.25
	1981(a)	—	.60	.75	1.25
	1982(a)	—	.60	.75	1.25
	1984(a)	—	.60	.75	1.25

500 FRANCS

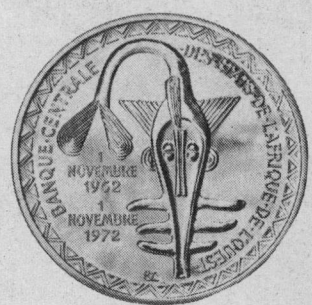

25.0000 g, .900 SILVER, .7234 oz ASW
10th Anniversary of Monetary Union

7	1972(a)	.100	—	25.00	35.00
(Y6)					

WEST AFRICAN STATES

5000 FRANCS

24.9500 g, .900 SILVER, .7220 oz ASW, 37mm
20th Anniversary of Monetary Union

KM#	Date	Mintage	VF	XF	Unc
11 (Y10)	1982(a)	.200	—	20.00	30.00

14.4900 g, .900 GOLD, .4193 oz AGW

| 12 (Y10a) | 1982(a) | — | — | — | 425.00 |

FLEUR DE COIN SETS (SS)

KM#	Date	Mintage	Identification	Mkt.Val.
SS1	1968(a)	—	KM1-2,4	7.50

Listings For
WEST GERMANY: refer to Germany
WEST IRIAN: refer to Indonesia
WEST NEW GUINEA: refer to Indonesia

WESTERN SAMOA

The Independent State of Western Samoa, located in the Pacific Ocean 1,600 miles (2,574 km.) northeast of New Zealand, has an area of 1,097 sq. mi. (2,842 sq. km.) and a population of *169,000. Capital: Apia. The economy is based on agriculture, fishing and tourism. Copra, cocoa and bananas are exported.

The first European to sight the Samoan group of islands was the Dutch navigator Jacob Roggeveen in 1772. Great Britain, the United States and Germany established consular representation at Apia in 1847, 1853 and 1861 respectively. The conflicting interests of the three powers produced the Berlin agreement of 1889 which declared Samoa neutral and had the effect of establishing a tripartite protectorate over the islands. A further agreement, 1899, recognized the rights of the United States in those islands east of 171 deg. west longitude (American Samoa) and of Germany in the other islands (Western Samoa). New Zealand occupied Western Samoa at the start of World War I and administered it as a League of Nations mandate and U. N. trusteeship until Jan. 1, 1962, when it became an independent state.

Western Samoa is a member of the Commonwealth of Nations. The Chief Executive is Chief of State. The prime minister is the Head of Government. The present Head of State, Malietoa Tanumafili II, holds his position for life. Future Heads of State will be elected by the Legislative Assembly for five-year terms.

Western Samoa, which had used New Zealand coinage, converted to a decimal coinage in 1967.

RULERS
British, until 1962
Malietoa Tanumafili II, 1962 -

MONETARY SYSTEM
100 Sene = 1 Tala

SENE

BRONZE

KM#	Date	Mintage	VF	XF	Unc
1	1967	.915	.10	.15	.20
	1967	.015	—	Proof	.50

| 12 | 1974 | 3.380 | — | .10 | .15 |

1.9500 g, .925 SILVER, .0579 oz ASW

| 12a | 1974 | 5,578 | — | Proof | 2.50 |

2 SENE

BRONZE

2	1967	.465	.10	.15	.25
	1967	.015	—	Proof	.50

| 13 | 1974 | 1.640 | .10 | .15 | .20 |

3.8000 g, .925 SILVER, .1130 oz ASW

| 13a | 1974 | 5,578 | — | Proof | 3.25 |

5 SENE

COPPER-NICKEL

KM#	Date	Mintage	VF	XF	Unc
3	1967	.495	.15	.25	.35
	1967	.015	—	Proof	1.00

| 14 | 1974 | 1.736 | .10 | .20 | .30 |

3.2500 g, .925 SILVER, .0966 oz ASW

| 14a | 1974 | 5,578 | — | Proof | 4.00 |

10 SENE

COPPER-NICKEL

4	1967	.400	.20	.35	.50
	1967	.015	—	Proof	1.00

| 15 | 1974 | 1.580 | .15 | .30 | .45 |

6.3700 g, .925 SILVER, .1894 oz ASW

| 15a | 1974 | 5,578 | — | Proof | 4.50 |

20 SENE

COPPER-NICKEL

5	1967	.400	.25	.50	1.00
	1967	.015	—	Proof	1.50

| 16 | 1974 | 1.380 | .20 | .40 | .75 |

12.7000 g, .925 SILVER, .3776 oz ASW

| 16a | 1974 | 5,578 | — | Proof | 5.50 |

50 SENE

COPPER-NICKEL

6	1967	.080	.75	1.25	1.75
	1967	.015	—	Proof	2.00

WESTERN SAMOA 1819

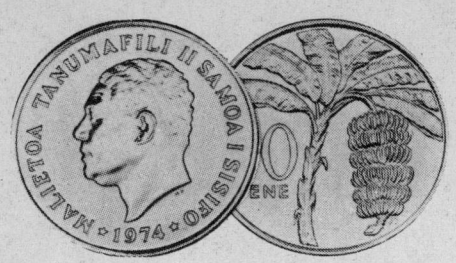

KM#	Date	Mintage	VF	XF	Unc
17	1974	.050	.75	1.25	1.75

15.4000 g, .925 SILVER, .4579 oz ASW

| 17a | 1974 | 5,578 | — | Proof | 6.50 |

TALA

Visit Of Pope Paul VI
Obv: Similar to KM#8.

KM#	Date	Mintage	VF	XF	Unc
10	1970	.035	—	—	3.50
	1970	3,000	—	Proof	17.50

COPPER-NICKEL
U.S. Bicentennial

KM#	Date	Mintage	VF	XF	Unc
20	1976	.040	—	—	5.00

30.4000 g, .925 SILVER, .9040 oz ASW

| 20a | 1976 | 4,127 | — | Proof | 22.50 |

COPPER-NICKEL
Obv: Similar to 50 Sene, KM#6.

7	1967	.020	—	—	4.00
	1967	.015	—	Proof	10.00

Roggeveen's Pacific Voyage
Obv: Similar to KM#8.

11	1972	.035	—	—	3.50
	1972	3,000	—	Proof	30.00

COPPER-NICKEL
Montreal Olympics
Obv: Similar to KM#8.

| 22 | 1976 | .040 | — | — | 5.00 |

30.4000 g, .925 SILVER, .9040 oz ASW

| 22a | 1976 | 6,000 | — | Proof | 22.50 |

10th British Commonwealth Games
Obv: Similar to KM#8.

| 18 | 1974 | .040 | — | — | 5.00 |

30.4000 g, .925 SILVER, .9040 oz ASW

| 18a | 1974 | 1,500 | — | Proof | 100.00 |

75th Anniversary Death of Robert Louis Stevenson

8	1969	.025	—	—	5.00
	1969	1,500	—	Proof	50.00

COPPER-NICKEL
Obv: Similar to 50 Sene, KM#17.

| 19 | 1974 | .024 | — | — | 4.50 |

31.1500 g, .925 SILVER, .9263 oz ASW

| 19a | 1974 | .011 | — | Proof | 12.50 |

200th Anniversary Captain Cook Voyages
Obv: Similar to KM#8.

9	1970	.032	—	—	3.50
	1970	3,000	—	Proof	17.50

COPPER-NICKEL
Queen's Silver Jubilee
Obv: Similar to KM#8.

| 24 | 1977 | .027 | — | — | 5.00 |

30.4000 g, .925 SILVER, .9040 oz ASW

| 24a | 1977 | 6,171 | — | Proof | 17.50 |

COPPER-NICKEL
Lindbergh's New York to Paris Flight
Obv: Similar to KM#8.

| 26 | 1977 | .017 | — | — | 5.00 |

30.4000 g, .925 SILVER, .9040 oz ASW

| 26a | 1977 | 4,522 | — | Proof | 20.00 |

WESTERN SAMOA 1820

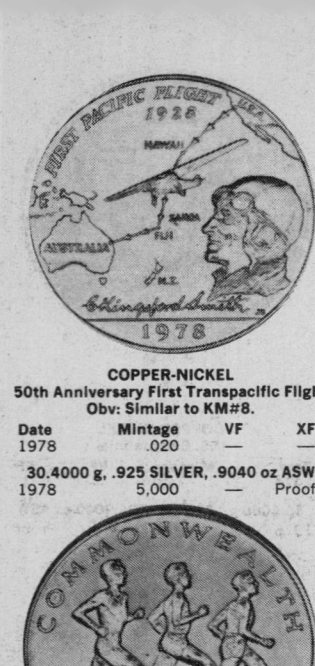

COPPER-NICKEL
50th Anniversary First Transpacific Flight
Obv: Similar to KM#8.

KM#	Date	Mintage	VF	XF	Unc
28	1978	.020	—	—	5.00

30.4000 g, .925 SILVER, .9040 oz ASW

28a	1978	5,000	—	Proof	17.50

COPPER-NICKEL
XI Commonwealth Games
Obv: Similar to KM#8.

30	1978	7,710	—	—	6.50

30.4000 g, .925 SILVER, .9040 oz ASW

30a	1978	5,000	—	Proof	17.50

COPPER-NICKEL
Bicentenary of the Death of Cook
Obv: Similar to KM#8.

32	1979	5,000	—	—	5.00

1980 Olympics - Hurdles
Obv: Similar to KM#8.

35	1980	5,000	—	—	5.00

F.A.O. Issue
Obv: Similar to KM#8.

38	1980	.010	—	—	5.00

Governor Wilhelm Solf
Obv: Similar to KM#8.

KM#	Date	Mintage	VF	XF	Unc
40	1980	5,000	—	—	5.50

Wedding of Prince Charles and Lady Diana
Obv: Similar to KM#8.

43	1981	.012	—	—	5.25

I.Y.D.P. - President Roosevelt
Obv: Similar to KM#8.

47	1981	8,000	—	—	3.50

Commonwealth Games - Javelin Thrower
Obv: Similar to KM#8.

50	1982	6,000	—	—	3.50

South Pacific Games - Runner
Obv: Similar to KM#8.

53	1983	8,000	—	—	3.50

ALUMINUM-BRONZE
Circulation Coinage

KM#	Date	Mintage	VF	XF	Unc
57	1984	1.000	.60	1.00	1.50

COPPER-NICKEL

57a	1984	5,000	—	—	3.50

1984 Olympics

58	1984	5,000	—	—	3.50

Prince Andrew's Marriage

63	1986	.010	—	—	3.50

World Wildlife Fund - Bird

75	1986	—	—	—	3.50

10 TALA

WESTERN SAMOA 1821

31.3300 g, .500 SILVER, .5036 oz ASW
Bicentenary of the Death of Cook

KM#	Date	Mintage	VF	XF	Unc
33	1979	3,000	—	—	12.50

31.4700 g, .925 SILVER, .9359 oz ASW

| 33a | 1979 | 5,000 | — | Proof | 20.00 |

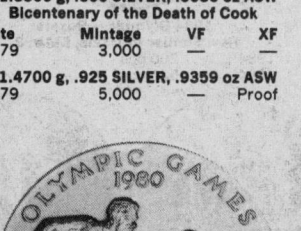

31.3300 g, .500 SILVER, .5036 oz ASW
1980 Olympics - Hurdles
Obv: Similar to KM#33.

| 36 | 1980 | 3,000 | — | — | 12.50 |

31.4700 g, .925 SILVER, .9359 oz ASW

| 36a | 1980 | 4,000 | — | Proof | 30.00 |

31.3300 g, .500 SILVER, .5036 oz ASW
Obv: Similar to KM#33.

| 39 | 1980 | 3,000 | — | Proof | 17.50 |

Governor Wilhelm Solf
Obv: Similar to KM#33.

| 41 | 1980 | 3,000 | — | — | 20.00 |

31.4700 g, .925 SILVER, .9359 oz ASW

| 41a | 1980 | 4,000 | — | Proof | 25.00 |

Wedding of Prince Charles and Lady Diana
Rev: Similar to 1 Tala, KM#43.

| 44 | 1981 | 5,000 | — | Proof | 22.50 |

IYDP - President Roosevelt
Rev: Similar to 1 Tala, KM#47.

| 48 | 1981 | 5,000 | — | Proof | 25.00 |

Commonwealth Games - Javelin Thrower
Obv: Similar to KM#33.

KM#	Date	Mintage	VF	XF	Unc
51	1982	4,000	—	Proof	25.00

South Pacific Games - Runner
Obv: Similar to KM#33.

| 54 | 1983 | 3,000 | — | Proof | 27.50 |

1984 Olympics - Boxers

| 59 | 1984 | 2,500 | — | Proof | 27.50 |

Prince Andrew's Marriage
Similar to 1 Tala, KM#63.

| 64 | 1986 | 2,500 | — | Proof | 35.00 |

31.1000 g, .999 SILVER, 1.0000 oz ASW
America's Cup Race

| 66 | 1987 | *.050 | — | Proof | 30.00 |

31.4700 g, .925 SILVER, .9360 oz ASW
Wildlife Fund

KM#	Date	Mintage	VF	XF	Unc
72	1986	*.025	—	Proof	25.00

1988 Olympics - 3 Torches & Athletes

| 70 | 1988 | .020 | — | — | 35.00 |

31.1030 g, .999 SILVER, 1.0000 oz ASW
Kon-Tiki-Raft and Map

| 75 | 1988 | *.020 | — | Proof | 25.00 |

25 TALA

155.5000 g, .999 SILVER, 5.0000 oz ASW
Kon-Tiki
Reduced size. Actual size: 65mm.

| 62 | 1986 | *.025 | — | Proof | 100.0 |

WESTERN SAMOA 1822

America's Cup Race
Reduced size. Actual size: 65mm.

KM#	Date	Mintage	VF	XF	Unc
67	1987	*.035	—	Proof	75.00

50 TALA

31.1030 g, .999 PALLADIUM, 1.0000 oz APW
Kon-Tiki-Raft and Bamboo Poles

| 76 | 1988 | *.010 | — | Proof | 200.00 |

7.7700 g, .999 GOLD, .2500 oz AGW
Trans-Antartica Expedition

| 78 | 1988 | *.030 | — | Proof | 125.00 |

100 TALA

15.5500 g, .917 GOLD, .4583 oz AGW
U.S. Bicentennial

| | 1976 | 2,000 | — | Proof | 250.00 |

Montreal Olympics - Weight Lifter
Similar to 1 Tala, KM#22.

| | 1976 | 2,500 | — | Proof | 250.00 |

Queen's Silver Jubilee

KM#	Date	Mintage	VF	XF	Unc
25	1977	2,500	—	Proof	250.00

Lindbergh's New York to Paris Flight

| 27 | 1977 | 660 pcs. | — | Proof | 350.00 |

50th Anniversary Transpacific Flight
Similar to 1 Tala, KM#28.

| 29 | 1978 | 1,500 | — | Proof | 300.00 |

XI Commonwealth Games
Similar to 1 Tala, KM#30.

| 31 | 1978 | 1,000 | — | Proof | 275.00 |

12.5000 g, .917 GOLD, .3686 oz AGW
Bicentenary of the Death of Captain James Cook
Similar to 10 Tala, KM#33.

| 34 | 1979 | 1,000 | — | Proof | 275.00 |

7.5000 g, .917 GOLD, .2211 oz AGW
1980 Olympics - Hurdles

| 37 | 1980 | 250 pcs. | — | — | 125.00 |
| | 1980 | 1,000 | — | Proof | 150.00 |

Governor Wilhelm Solf

| 42 | 1980 | 250 pcs. | — | — | 125.00 |
| | 1980 | 1,000 | — | Proof | 150.00 |

Wedding of Prince Charles and Lady Diana

| 45 | 1981 | 250 pcs. | — | — | 125.00 |
| | 1981 | 1,500 | — | Proof | 150.00 |

IYDP - President Roosevelt
Similar to 1 Tala, KM#47.

| 49 | 1981 | 250 pcs. | — | — | 125.00 |
| | 1981 | 1,500 | — | Proof | 150.00 |

Commonwealth Games - Javelin Thrower

KM#	Date	Mintage	VF	XF	Unc
52	1982	250 pcs.	—	—	125.00
	1982	1,000	—	Proof	150.00

South Pacific Games - Runner
Similar to 10 Tala, KM#54.

| 55 | 1983 | 1,000 | — | Proof | 175.00 |

1984 Olympics - Boxers
Rev: Similar to 1 Tala, KM#58.

| 60 | 1984 | 200 pcs. | — | — | 175.00 |
| | 1984 | 500 pcs. | — | Proof | 200.00 |

7.5000 g, .900 GOLD, .2170 oz AGW
America's Cup Race

| 68 | 1987 | *5,000 | — | Proof | 150.00 |

Kon-Tiki - Raft and Inscription

| 77 | 1988 | *5,000 | — | Proof | 150.00 |

1000 TALA

33.9500 g, .917 GOLD, 1.0010 oz AGW
Wedding of Prince Charles and Lady Diana
Similar to 100 Tala, KM#45.

| 46 | 1981 | 100 pcs. | — | Proof | 900.00 |

31.1000 g, .917 GOLD, .9170 oz AGW
South Pacific Games - Runner
Similar to 10 Tala, KM#54.

| 56 | 1983 | 100 pcs. | — | Proof | 900.00 |

1984 Olympics - Boxers

| 61 | 1984 | 100 pcs. | — | Proof | 900.00 |

33.9500 g, .917 GOLD, 1.0010 oz AGW
Prince Andrew's Marriage
Obv: Similar to 1 Tala, KM#8.
Rev: Similar to 1 Tala, KM#63.

| 65 | 1986 | 50 pcs. | — | — | 1100. |

MINT SETS (MS)

KM#	Date	Mintage	Identification	Issue Price	Mkt. Val.
MS1	1967(6)	—	KM1-6		4.00
MS2	1974(7)	10,740	KM12-17,19	5.30	7.50

PROOF SETS (PS)

| PS1 | 1967(7) | 15,000 | KM1-7 | 10.00 | 11.50 |
| PS2 | 1974(7) | 5,578 | KM12a-17a,19a | 53.00 | 40.00 |

YEMEN ARAB REP.

The Yemen Arab Republic, located in the southwestern corner of the Arabian Peninsula, has an area of 75,290 sq. mi. (195,000 sq. km.) and a population of 6.0 million. Capital: San'a. The industries of Yemen, one of the world's poorest countries, are agriculture and local handicrafts. Qat (a mildly narcotic leaf), coffee, cotton and rock salt are exported.

One of the oldest centers of civilization in the Near East, Yemen was once part of the Minaean Kingdom and of the ancient Kingdom of Sheba, after which it was captured successively by Egyptians, Ethiopians and Romans. It was converted to the Moslem religion in 628 A.D. and administered as a caliphate until 1538, when it came under Turkish occupation which was maintained until 1918 when autonomy was achieved through revolution.

Provoked by the harsh rule of Imam Mohammed al-Badr, last ruler of the Kingdom of Mutawwakkilite, the National Liberation Front seized control of the government on Sept. 27, 1962. Badr fled to Saudi Arabia, and to maintain a pretense of sovereignty issued a coinage for the Royalist government in exile.

TITLES

Dar El-Khilafat   دار الخلافة

El-Muttahidah   المتحدة

El-Yemeniyat   اليمنية

RULERS

Imam Yahya, AH1322-1367/1904-1948AD
Imam Ahmad, AH1367-1382/
   1948-1962AD
Imam al-Badr, AH1382-1388/
   1962-1968AD (mostly in exile)

MINTNAME

San'a

MONETARY SYSTEM

2 Zalat = 1 Halala
2 Halala = 1 Buqsha
40 Buqsha = 1 Riyal

NOTE: The Riyal was called an IMADI RIYAL during the reign of Imam Yahya, and an AHMADI RIYAL during the reign of Imam Ahmad. Except for the 1 Zalat, which bears no indication of value, all of the Mutawakkilite coins bear the denomination expressed as a fraction of the Riyal.

DATING: All coins of Imam Yahya have accession date AH 1322 on obverse and actual date of issue on reverse. All coins of Imam Ahmad bear accession date AH1367 on obverse and actual date on reverse.

NOTE: Coins struck during the Mutawakkilite kingdom, as well as the early issues of the Republic (Y-20 through Y-A25 and Y-32), were struck at the mint in San'a. The San'a Mint was essentially a medieval mint, using hand-cut dies and crudely machined blanks. There is a large amount of variation from one die to the next, and literally hundreds of subtypes could be identified. Types are divided only when there are changes in the inscriptions, or major variations in the basic type, such as the use of open and closed crescents in which the ruler's name was written.

MUTAWWAKKILITE KINGDOM

TITLES

المملكة المتوكلية اليمنية

El-Mamlakat El-Mutawakeliyat El-Yemeniat

IMAM YAHYA
AH1322-1367/1904-1948AD

ZALAT

BRONZE
Accession Date: AH1322

Y#	Date	Mintage	Good	VG	Fine	VF
B1	ND	—	30.00	60.00	125.00	200.00

NOTE: Dated accessionally on obverse. Probably struck about 1925. Dies have been prepared in Italy.

Obv: Similar to Y#10.3. W/o denomination.

Y#	Date	Mintage	Good	VG	Fine	VF
1a.1	AH1341	—	Reported, not confirmed			
	1342	—	Reported, not confirmed			

Obv: W/o crescent. Rev: Date in margin.

| 1a.2 | AH1342 | — | Reported, not confirmed | | | |

Rev: Date within circle.

1a.3	AH1340	—	10.00	25.00	75.00	125.00
	1342	—	5.00	12.00	30.00	50.00
	1343	—	5.00	10.00	20.00	40.00
	1344	—	5.00	12.00	30.00	50.00
	1345	—	10.00	25.00	75.00	125.00
	1346	—	5.00	10.00	20.00	40.00

1/80 RIYAL
(1 Halala)

BRONZE (Yellow or Red)
Accession Date AH1322

| 2.1 | AH1322 (accessional date only; w/o actual date) |
| | — | 12.50 | 25.00 | 50.00 | 75.00 |

Rev: Denomination added w/o mintname.

2.2	AH1330	—	20.00	35.00	60.00	100.00
	1331	—	20.00	35.00	75.00	150.00
	1332	—	10.00	15.00	25.00	40.00
	1333	—	10.00	15.00	25.00	40.00
	1338	—	10.00	15.00	25.00	40.00
	ND Mule	—	20.00	30.00	60.00	100.00

NOTE: The number of stars on the reverse as well as the exact arrangement of the legend, varies within each year. The mule consists of 2 obverses.

Obv. leg: Rabb al-Alamin.
Rev: Struck at Sana added.

| 2.3 | AH1340 | — | 10.00 | 20.00 | 40.00 | 75.00 |
| | 1341 | — | 10.00 | 20.00 | 40.00 | 75.00 |

Obv: W/o Rabb al-Alamin.
Rev: Sana below date.

| 2.4 | AH1341 | — | 12.00 | 25.00 | 50.00 | 85.00 |
| | 1342 | — | 12.00 | 25.00 | 50.00 | 85.00 |

Obv: Rabb al-Alamin.

2.5	AH1341	—	7.00	12.00	25.00	40.00
	1342	—	2.00	5.00	12.00	20.00
	1343	—	2.00	5.00	12.00	20.00
	1344	—	2.00	5.00	12.00	20.00
	1345	—	1.50	4.00	8.00	15.00
	1346	—	1.50	3.00	6.00	12.00
	1347	—	1.50	4.00	8.00	15.00
	1348	—	1.50	4.00	8.00	15.00
	1349	—	1.50	4.00	8.00	15.00
	1350	—	1.50	4.00	8.00	15.00
	1351	—	2.00	6.00	12.00	20.00
	1352	—	2.00	6.00	12.00	20.00
	1353	—	2.00	6.00	12.00	20.00
	1358	—	10.00	15.00	25.00	40.00
	1359	—	2.50	6.00	12.00	20.00
	1360	—	2.50	4.00	8.00	15.00
	1361	—	4.00	8.00	15.00	25.00

NOTE: Number of stars on reverse varies. Some examples of 1346 show the 6 reengraved over low 6.

1/40 RIYAL
(1 Buqsha)

BRONZE (Yellow or Red)
Accession Date: AH1322
Obv: W/o *Rabb al-Alamin*.

Y#	Date	Mintage	VG	Fine	VF	XF
3.1	AH1341	—	10.00	20.00	40.00	80.00

Obv: *Rabb al-Alamin* added.

3.2	AH1342	—	4.00	10.00	20.00	60.00
	1343	—	4.00	10.00	20.00	60.00
	1344	—	15.00	30.00	50.00	75.00
	13442 (error)				Rare	—
	1345	—	12.00	20.00	35.00	100.00
	1349	—	1.50	3.50	10.00	25.00
	1353	—	Reported, not confirmed			
	1358	—	2.00	4.00	10.00	25.00
	1359	—	2.00	4.00	10.00	25.00
	1360	—	2.00	4.00	10.00	25.00
	1361/0	—	10.00	20.00	50.00	75.00
	1362/0	—	2.50	5.00	10.00	35.00
	1362	—	1.50	3.50	10.00	30.00
	1363	—	1.50	5.00	12.00	35.00
	1364	—	1.50	5.00	12.00	35.00
	1365/4	—	2.25	5.00	12.00	35.00
	1366	—	1.50	3.50	12.00	30.00
	1367	—	10.00	20.00	50.00	75.00

1/20 IMADI RIYAL

SILVER
Accession Date: AH1322
Obv: Narrow crescent. Rev W/o *Sana*.

4.1	AH1337	—	40.00	80.00	150.00	250.00
	1338	—			Rare	—
	1339	—	40.00	80.00	150.00	250.00
	1340	—	20.00	30.00	60.00	100.00

NOTE: The number of stars on reverse varies.

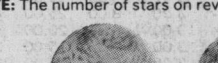

Rev: *Sana* below date.

| 4.2 | AH1341 | — | 40.00 | 80.00 | 150.00 | 250.00 |

Obv: Redesigned; wide crescent.

4.3	AH1342	—	5.00	12.00	30.00	60.00
	1343	—	4.00	10.00	25.00	50.00
	1344	—	4.00	10.00	25.00	50.00
	1345	—	4.00	10.00	25.00	50.00
	1347	—	5.00	12.00	30.00	50.00
	1348	—	4.00	10.00	25.00	50.00
	1349	—	4.00	10.00	25.00	50.00
	1350	—	4.00	12.00	30.00	60.00
	1351	—	5.00	15.00	35.00	75.00
	1352	—	4.00	12.00	30.00	60.00
	1353	—	4.00	12.00	30.00	60.00
	1358	—	3.00	8.00	20.00	40.00
	1359	—	3.00	8.00	20.00	40.00
	1362/59	—	5.00	15.00	30.00	60.00
	1363	—	4.00	10.00	25.00	60.00
	1364/40	—	3.00	8.00	20.00	40.00
	1364	—	3.00	8.00	20.00	40.00
	1365	—	3.00	10.00	25.00	50.00
	1366/4	—	4.00	12.00	30.00	60.00
	1366	—	4.00	12.00	30.00	60.00

NOTE: Y#4.1, 4.2 and 4.3 are all without *Rabb al-Alamin* on obverse.

YEMEN ARAB REPUBLIC

1/10 IMADI RIYAL

SILVER
Accession Date: AH1322
Obv: Narrow crescent, *Rabb al Alamin*.
Rev: W/o *Sana*.

Y#	Date	Mintage	VG	Fine	VF	XF
5.1	AH1337 5 stars	—	30.00	60.00	100.00	175.00
	1337 3 stars	—	30.00	60.00	100.00	175.00

Obv: W/o *Rabb al-Alamin*.

5.2	AH1339	—	20.00	40.00	75.00	150.00
	1340	—	20.00	40.00	75.00	150.00

Rev: *Sana* below date.

5.3	AH1341	—	20.00	40.00	75.00	150.00

Rev: *Sana* above date.

5.4	AH1342	—	20.00	40.00	75.00	150.00

Obv: W/o *Rabb al-Alamin*.

5.5	AH1342	—	4.00	10.00	25.00	50.00
	1343	—	4.00	10.00	25.00	50.00
	1344	—	3.00	8.00	20.00	40.00
	1345	—	3.00	8.00	20.00	40.00
	1347	—	3.00	8.00	20.00	40.00
	1348	—	3.00	8.00	20.00	35.00
	1349	—	3.00	6.00	15.00	30.00
	1350	—	—	—	—	—
	1351	—	4.00	10.00	25.00	40.00
	1352	—	4.00	10.00	25.00	40.00
	1358/49	—	3.00	8.00	15.00	30.00
	1358	—	3.00	8.00	15.00	30.00
	1359/49	—	3.00	8.00	15.00	30.00
	1363	—	3.00	8.00	25.00	45.00
	1364/3	—	3.00	8.00	20.00	40.00
	1364	—	3.00	8.00	15.00	35.00
	1365	—	3.00	8.00	15.00	35.00
	1366/5	—	4.00	10.00	20.00	50.00

NOTE: Number of stars on reverse and arrangement of obverse inscription varies considerably.

1/8 IMADI RIYAL

SILVER
Accession Date: AH1322
Rev: *Thumn* in place of *Ushr* below date.

8	AH1339	—	300.00	500.00	1000.	1500.

1/4 IMADI RIYAL

SILVER
Accession Date: AH1322
Obv: Closed crescent. Rev: *Sana* below date.

6.1	AH1341	—	20.00	45.00	75.00	150.00
	1342	—	25.00	50.00	100.00	175.00

Obv: Open crescent, *Rabb al-Alamin*.
Rev: *Sana* above date.

Y#	Date	Mintage	VG	Fine	VF	XF
6.2	AH1342	—	30.00	50.00	100.00	175.00

Obv: Crescents and stars in border.

6.3	AH1342	—	30.00	50.00	100.00	175.00

Obv: W/crescents only in border.

6.4	AH1342	—	20.00	40.00	75.00	150.00
	1343	—	20.00	40.00	75.00	150.00

NOTE: Number of crescents on obverse varies.

Rev: Redesigned, date moved to margin.

10	AH1343	—	20.00	60.00	100.00	175.00
	1344	—	4.25	10.00	25.00	75.00
	1345	—	4.25	10.00	25.00	60.00
	1349	—	—	Reported, not confirmed		
	1351	—	20.00	30.00	50.00	100.00
	1352	—	5.00	12.00	20.00	40.00
	1358	—	3.50	5.50	15.00	35.00
	1359	—	3.50	5.50	15.00	35.00
	1363	—	3.50	8.00	20.00	40.00
	1364/3	—	4.25	8.00	20.00	40.00
	1364	—	3.50	5.00	20.00	40.00
	1365/4	—	4.25	6.00	20.00	40.00
	1365	—	3.50	5.00	20.00	40.00
	1366	—	3.50	5.00	20.00	40.00

NOTE: The size of the reverse inner circle varies. Also, the number of crescents on obverse varies from 12 to 16.

IMADI RIYAL

SILVER
Accession Date: AH1322

Y#	Date	Mintage	VG	Fine	VF	XF
7	AH1344	—	8.00	10.00	15.00	25.00
	1365 (1 known)	—	—	—	Unc	1850.

NOTE: Several varieties exist, possibly struck over a number of years with frozen date.

GOLD 1/40 RIYAL

GOLD, 0.92 g
Accession Date: AH1322

A10	AH(13)44	—	—	—	—	1350.

GOLD 1/20 RIYAL

GOLD, 1.70 g
Accession Date: AH1322

B10	AH(13)44	—	—	—	—	1500.

GOLD 1/10 RIYAL

GOLD, 3.31 g
Accession Date: AH1322

C10	AH(13)44	—	—	—	—	1650.

GOLD 1/5 RIYAL

GOLD, 6.80 g
Accession Date: AH1322

D10 (A10)	AH(13)44	—	—	—	—	2000.

GOLD 1/2 RIYAL

GOLD, 17.70 g
Accession Date: AH1322

E10	AH(13)44	—	—	—	—	2500.

17.44-17.82 g

K10	AH1352	—	—	—	—	2000.

GOLD RIYAL

GOLD, 35.50 g
Accession Date: AH1322

F10 (G7)	AH1344	—	—	—	Rare	—

GOLD 2 RIYALS

GOLD, 69.83 g
Accession Date: AH1322

Y#	Date	Mintage	VG	Fine	VF	XF
M10	AH1352	—	—	—	—	6000.

NOTE: The Yemeni gold coins listed above are believed to be presentation pieces.

IMAM AHMAD
AH1367-1382/1948-1962AD

1/80 RIYAL

BRONZE
Accession Date: AH1367

Y#	Date	Mintage	VG	Fine	VF	XF
11	AH1368	—	1.00	2.00	5.00	10.00
	1371	—	.30	1.00	3.00	8.00
	1372	—	.30	1.00	3.00	8.00
	1373	—	.30	.60	1.00	3.00
	1373 w/o sanat	—	—	—	Rare	—
	1374	—	.30	1.00	3.00	8.00
	1275 (error for 1375)					
		—	1.00	2.00	6.00	12.00
	1386/76	—	1.00	2.00	4.00	8.00
	1378	—	.30	1.00	3.00	6.00
	1379	—	.50	1.00	3.00	6.00
	1380/79	—	.50	1.00	3.00	6.00
	1380/9	—	.50	1.00	3.00	6.00
	1381/80/78					
		—	.40	.85	1.50	2.50
	1381/79	—	.40	.85	1.50	2.50
	1381	—	.20	.40	.75	1.25
	1382	—	—	—	Rare	—

NOTE: There is a variation in the number of stars on reverse, as follows AH1368 - 8 stars AH1371-74 and some AH1381 not overdate have 7 stars AH1375-1381 including some AH1381 not overdate, and all AH1381 overdates have 8 stars.

NOTE: Formerly listed AH1386 is now listed as AH1386/76.

ALUMINUM

11a	AH1374	—	.25	1.00	2.50	5.00
	1375	—	—	Reported, not confirmed		
	1376	—	.25	1.50	4.00	8.00
	1377	—	.75	2.50	5.50	10.00
	1378	—	.25	1.00	2.50	5.00
	1379/5	—	.75	2.50	5.50	10.00
	1379/8	—	.75	2.50	5.50	10.00
	1379	—	.25	1.00	2.50	5.00

NOTE: AH1374 has 7 stars, the rest have 8 stars on reverse.

18	AH1367 (accessional year only)					
		—	.15	.25	.50	1.00

NOTE: Y#18 and 19 were struck privately in Lebanon.

1/40 RIYAL

BRONZE or BRASS

Accession Date: AH1367

Y#	Date	Mintage	VG	Fine	VF	XF
12	AH1368	—	.50	1.00	4.00	12.00
	1369	—	.75	1.25	5.00	15.00
	1370	—	.35	.75	3.00	6.00
	1371	—	.35	.75	3.00	6.00
	1372	—	.35	.75	2.00	5.00
	1373/2	—	.85	1.80	3.00	6.00
	1373	—	.35	.75	2.00	5.00
	1374	—	.35	.75	2.00	5.00
	1375/4	—	.50	1.00	3.00	6.00
	1375	—	.35	.75	2.00	5.00
	1376	—	.50	1.00	5.00	12.00
	1377/6	—	.85	1.75	4.00	10.00
	1379/7	—	.85	1.75	4.00	10.00
	1380/79	—	10.00	20.00	50.00	75.00

ALUMINUM

12a	AH1374	—	.50	1.00	4.00	12.00
	1375	—	.50	1.00	4.00	12.00
	1376	—	.50	1.00	4.00	12.00
	1377/6	—	10.00	20.00	40.00	75.00
	1377	—	15.00	30.00	50.00	90.00

NOTE: AH1377 plain date has 1376 instead of 1367 on obverse.

19	AH1367 (accessional date)					
		—	.15	.25	.35	.60

1/16 AHMADI RIYAL

SILVER
Accession Date: AH1367
Obv. leg: Amir al-Mu'minin

13	AH1367	—	.75	1.50	6.00	12.00
	1368	—	.75	1.50	5.00	10.00
	1371	—	.75	1.50	5.00	10.00
	1374	—	.75	1.50	4.00	8.00

NOTE: Size of inner circle on reverse varies.

Obv. leg: *Al-Amir.*

| 13.1 | AH1374 | — | 60.00 | 150.00 | 250.00 | 350.00 |

1/10 IMADI RIYAL

SILVER
Accession Date: AH1367

| A14 | AH1370 | — | 400.00 | 750.00 | 1250. | 1500. |

1/8 AHMADI RIYAL

SILVER
Accession Date: AH1367
Pentagonal planchet

14	AH1367	—	4.00	8.00	15.00	30.00
	1368	—	2.75	3.50	8.00	20.00
	1370	—	2.75	3.50	8.00	20.00
	1371	—	1.75	2.50	6.00	15.00
	1372	—	1.75	2.50	4.00	10.00
	1373	—	1.75	2.50	4.00	10.00
	1374	—	1.75	2.50	5.00	15.00
	1375/1	—	1.75	2.50	5.00	15.00
	1379	—	1.75	2.50	6.00	15.00
	1380	—	1.75	2.50	7.00	20.00

NOTE: Size of inner circle on reverse varies.

Hexagonal planchet

| 14a | AH1368 | — | 250.00 | 500.00 | 1000. | 1500. |

1/4 AHMADI RIYAL

SILVER
Accession Date: AH1367

15	AH1367	—	3.50	5.00	7.50	15.00
	1368	—	3.50	5.00	7.50	15.00
	1370	—	3.00	4.00	6.00	12.00
	1371/68	—	6.00	8.00	12.50	20.00
	1371/0	—	4.50	6.00	9.00	15.00
	1371	—	3.00	4.00	6.00	10.00
	1372	—	3.00	4.00	6.00	10.00
	1374	—	3.00	4.00	6.00	10.00
	1375/3	—	4.50	6.00	9.00	15.00
	1375	—	3.00	4.00	6.00	10.00
	1376	—	—	Reported, not confirmed		
	1377/5	—	4.50	6.00	9.00	15.00
	1380	—	30.00	60.00	100.00	175.00

NOTE: The size of reverse inner circle varies considerably. All dates have only the final 2 digits on the coin.

1/2 AHMADI RIYAL

SILVER
Accession Date: AH1367

Rev: Full dates, denomination and mint name face inward.

16.1	AH1367	—	6.00	10.00	15.00	35.00
	1368	—	6.00	10.00	15.00	35.00
	1369	—	5.00	8.00	12.50	20.00
	1370	—	7.50	12.50	20.00	40.00
	1372/68	—	6.00	10.00	15.00	30.00
	1373	—	9.00	15.00	25.00	45.00

NOTE: These coins were struck over blanks punched from Maria Theresa Thalers. The outer rings are reported to have circulated as currency, but this is doubtful, as they are found only counterstamped *Void* in Arabic. Refer to *Unusual World Coins*, 2nd edition, Krause Publications.

Similar to Y#16.1 but w/partial date; last two digits only.

| 16.2 | AH(13)75 | — | 6.00 | 10.00 | 15.00 | 22.50 |

YEMEN ARAB REPUBLIC

Full date; denomination and mint name face outward.

Y#	Date	Mintage	VG	Fine	VF	XF
16.3	AH1377	—	5.00	8.00	12.50	20.00
	1378	—	6.00	10.00	15.00	25.00
	1379	—	5.00	8.00	12.50	20.00
	1380	—	17.50	30.00	40.00	75.00
	1381	—	12.50	22.50	30.00	50.00
	1382	—	7.50	12.50	25.00	40.00

AHMADI RIYAL

SILVER
Accession Date: AH1367

Y#	Date	Mintage	VG	Fine	VF	XF
17	AH1367	—	17.50	30.00	40.00	60.00
	1370	—	12.50	20.00	25.00	40.00
	1371	—	12.50	20.00	25.00	40.00
	1372/68	—	—	Reported, not confirmed		
	1373	—	10.00	17.50	20.00	25.00
	1374	—	12.50	20.00	20.00	40.00
	1375	—	10.00	17.50	22.50	40.00
	1378	—	12.50	20.00	25.00	35.00
	1380	—	10.00	17.50	22.50	30.00

NOTE: These are usually found struck over Austrian Maria Theresa Talers and occasionally over other foreign crowns. Most AH1373 Riyals appear to be recut from AH1372 dies, and the dates are easily confused.

NOTE: Maria Theresa Talers and Eritrea Talleros exist c/s with obv. and rev. of the 1/16 Ahmadi Riyal (Y#13). Refer to "Unusual World Coins" second edition.

GOLD 1/4 RIYAL
(Sovereign)

GOLD, 8.88 g
Accession Date: AH1367

Y#	Date	Mintage	Fine	VF	XF	Unc
G15	AH(13)71	—	—	350.00	550.00	850.00
	(13)75/3	—	—	350.00	550.00	850.00
	(13)75	—	—	350.00	550.00	850.00
	(13)77/5	—	—	350.00	550.00	850.00

NOTE: The above may be encountered with an additional c/m of an Arabic 1 indicating the equivalence to an English Sovereign.

GOLD 1/2 RIYAL
(2 Sovereigns)

GOLD, 17.75 g
Accession Date: AH1367

Y#	Date	Mintage	Fine	VF	XF	Unc
G16	AH1370	—	—	650.00	900.00	1350.
	1371	—	—	650.00	900.00	1350.
	1375	—	—	650.00	900.00	1350.
	1378	—	—	650.00	900.00	1350.
	1379	—	—	650.00	900.00	1350.
	1380	—	—	650.00	900.00	1350.
	1381	—	—	650.00	900.00	1350.

NOTE: The above may be encountered with an additional c/m of an Arabic 2 indicating the equivalence to two English Sovereigns.

GOLD RIYAL
(4 Sovereigns)

GOLD, 35.50 g
Accession Date: AH1367

Y#	Date	Mintage	Fine	VF	XF	Unc
G17	AH1371	—	—	—	Rare	—
	1373	—	—	700.00	900.00	1100.
	1374	—	—	700.00	900.00	1100.
	1375	—	—	650.00	850.00	1000.
	1377	—	—	700.00	900.00	1100.
	1378	—	—	700.00	900.00	1100.
	1381	—	—	650.00	850.00	1000.

NOTE: The above may be encountered with an additional c/m of an Arabic 4 indicating the equivalence to four English Sovereigns.

REPUBLIC

1/80 RIYAL
(1/2 Buqsha)

BRONZE

Y#	Date	Mintage	VF	XF	Unc
20	AH1382	—	.50	2.00	5.00

NOTE: 2 varieties exist.

21	AH1382	—	2.00	6.00	15.00

NOTE: 4 varieties known to exist.

1/2 BUQSHA

BRONZE

Y#	Date	Mintage	VF	XF	Unc
32	AH1382	—	3.00	5.00	8.50

COPPER-ALUMINUM

Y#	Date	Year	Mintage	VF	XF	Unc
26	AH1382	1963	10.000	.15	.20	.30

NOTE: Y#26-31 were struck at Cairo.

1/40 RIYAL
(1 Buqsha)

BRASS or BRONZE

Y#	Date	Mintage	VF	XF	Unc
22	AH1382	—	.75	1.00	1.50
	1383	—	1.50	2.25	6.00
	1384/284	—	—	—	—
	1384	—	4.00	7.50	20.00

NOTE: Dated both sides; AH1382 and AH1383 are dated AH1382 on obverse, actual date on reverse; AH1384 dated AH1384 on both sides. There are many varieties of date size, inner circle size, calligraphy, etc.

BUQSHA

COPPER-ALUMINUM

Y#	Date	Year	Mintage	VF	XF	Unc
27	AH1382	1963	10.377	.20	.30	.50

1/20 RIAL
(2 Buqsha)

.720 SILVER
Thick variety, 1.10-1.60 g
Rev: Two stones in top row of wall.

Y#	Date	Mintage	VF	XF	Unc
23.1 (Y23)	AH1382	—	6.00	10.00	30.00

Thin variety, 0.60-0.90 g
Rev: Three stones in top row of wall.

23.2 (Y23.1)	AH1382	—	2.00	4.00	10.00

2 BUQSHA

COPPER-ALUMINUM

Y#	Date	Year	Mintage	VF	XF	Unc
A27	AH1382	1963	—	.25	.60	.75

1/10 RIYAL
(4 Buqsha)

YEMEN ARAB REPUBLIC

.720 SILVER
Thick variety, 2.40-3.00 g
Rev: Three stones in top row of wall.

Y#	Date	Mintage	VF	XF	Unc
24.1 (Y24)	AH1382	—	5.00	10.00	20.00

Thin variety, 1.40-1.80 g
Rev: Four stones in top row of wall.

| 24.2 (Y24.1) | AH1382 | — | 2.00 | 4.00 | 10.00 |

5 BUQSHA

.720 SILVER

Y#	Date	Year	Mintage	VF	XF	Unc
28	AH1382	1963	1.600	1.25	1.50	2.00

2/10 RIYAL
(8 Buqsha)

.720 SILVER
Thick variety, 5.80-6.50 g

Y#	Date	Mintage	VF	XF	Unc
25.1 (Y25)	AH1382	—	8.00	15.00	25.00

Thin variety, 5.001 g

| 25.2 (Y25.1) | AH1382 | — | 60.00 | 100.00 | 150.00 |

NOTE: The weight of this coin corresponds to the proper weight of the 1/4 Riyal, but bears the denomination USHRAN (two tenths), probably in error.

1/4 RIAL
(10 Buqsha)

.720 SILVER
Thick variety, 6.00-7.00 g

| A25.1 (Y-A25) | AH1382 | — | 40.00 | 65.00 | 150.00 |

Thin variety, 4.00-4.60 g

| A25.2 (Y-A25a) | AH1382 | — | 40.00 | 65.00 | 150.00 |

10 BUQSHA

5.0000 g, .720 SILVER, .1157 oz ASW

Y#	Date	Year	Mintage	VF	XF	Unc
29	AH1382	1963	1.024	2.00	2.25	2.75

20 BUQSHA

9.8500 g, .720 SILVER, .2280 oz ASW

Y#	Date	Year	Mintage	VF	XF	Unc
30	AH1382	1963	1.016	4.00	5.00	6.50

RIAL

19.7500 g, .720 SILVER, .4571 oz ASW

| 31 | AH1382 | 1963 | 4.614 | 5.00 | 6.00 | 8.00 |

DECIMAL COINAGE
100 Fils = 1 Riyal

FILS

ALUMINUM

33	AH1394	1974	*1.000	10.00	20.00	40.00
	1394	1974	5,024	—	Proof	1.50
	1400	1980	.010	—	Proof	1.50

*NOTE: It is doubtful that the entire mintage was released to circulation.

F.A.O. Issue

| 43 (42) | AH1398 | 1978 | 7,050 | — | 1.25 | 3.00 |

5 FILS

BRASS

34	AH1394	1974	10.000	.50	1.00	2.50
	1394	1974	5,024	—	Proof	2.00
	1400	1980	.010	—	Proof	1.75

F.A.O. Issue

| 38 | AH1394 | 1974 | .500 | — | .10 | .25 |

10 FILS

BRASS

Y#	Date	Year	Mintage	VF	XF	Unc
35	AH1394	1974	20.000	.50	1.00	2.50
	1394	1974	5,024	—	Proof	2.50
	1400	1980	.010	—	Proof	2.00

F.A.O. Issue

| 39 | AH1394 | 1974 | .200 | — | .10 | .25 |

25 FILS

COPPER-NICKEL

36	AH1394	1974	15.000	.15	.30	.75
	1394	1974	5,024	—	Proof	3.00
	1399	1979	11.000	.15	.30	.75
	1400	1980	.010	—	Proof	2.25

F.A.O. Issue

| 40 | AH1394 | 1974 | .040 | — | .20 | .50 |

50 FILS

COPPER-NICKEL

37	AH1394	1974	10.000	.20	.40	1.00
	1394	1974	5,024	—	Proof	3.50
	1399	1979	4.000	.20	.40	1.00
	1400	1980	.010	—	Proof	2.50
	1405	1985	—	.20	.40	1.00

F.A.O. Issue

| 41 | AH1394 | 1974 | .025 | — | .25 | .75 |

RIYAL

12.0000 g, .925 SILVER, .3569 oz ASW

KM#	Date	Year	Mintage	VF	XF	Unc
1	—	1969	3,200	—	—	12.50

20.4800 g, .900 GOLD, .5926 oz AGW

| 1a | | 1969 | 100 pcs. | — | Proof | 650.00 |

1827

YEMEN ARAB REPUBLIC

COPPER-NICKEL

Y#	Date	Year	Mintage	VF	XF	Unc
42	AH1396	1976	7,800	.50	1.25	3.75
	1400	1980	—	—	Proof	5.00
	1405	1985	—	.50	1.25	3.75

44	AH1398	1978	7,050	—	2.00	4.00
(43)		**F.A.O. Issue**				

2 RIYALS

25.0000 g, .925 SILVER, .7435 oz ASW
Apollo II

KM#	Date	Year	Mintage	VF	XF	Unc
2	—	1969	7,583	—	—	20.00
	—	1969	200 pcs.	—	Proof	40.00

Apollo II
Obv: Similar to KM#2.

3	—	1969	7,583	—	—	20.00
		1969	200 pcs.	—	Proof	40.00

KM#	Date	Year	Mintage	VF	XF	Unc
4	—	1969	4,200	—	Proof	25.00

42.2900 g, .900 GOLD, 1.2238 oz AGW

4a	—	1969	100 pcs.	—	Proof	1300.

2-1/2 RIYALS

9.0000 g, .925 SILVER, .2676 oz ASW

14	AH1395	1975	*.205	—	—	10.00
	AH1395	1975	*5,000	—	Proof	20.00

*NOTE: Projected mintage.

5 RIYALS

4.9000 g, .900 GOLD, .1418 oz AGW

KM#	Date	Mintage	VF	XF	Unc
6	1969	—	—	Proof	150.00

18.0000 g, .925 SILVER, .5353 oz ASW

KM#	Date	Year	Mintage	VF	XF	Unc
15	AH1395	1975	.235	—	—	17.50
	1395	1975	5,000	—	Proof	35.00

10 RIYALS

9.8000 g, .900 GOLD, .2836 oz AGW

KM#	Date	Mintage	VF	XF	Unc
7	1969	—	—	Proof	250.00

12.0800 g, .925 SILVER, .3569 oz ASW
Mule. Obv: KM#7. Rev: KM#1.

23	1969				

36.0000 g, .925 SILVER, 1.0707 oz ASW

KM#	Date	Year	Mintage	VF	XF	Unc
16	AH1395	1975	8,000	—	—	40.00
	1395	1975	4,000	—	Proof	70.00

15 RIYALS

54.0000 g, .925 SILVER, 1.6061 oz ASW

17	AH1395	1975	.070	—	—	30.00
	1395	1975	5,000	—	Proof	60.00

20 RIYALS

19.6000 g, .900 GOLD, .5672 oz AGW
Obv: Arms. Rev: Apollo 11 landing.

KM#	Date	Mintage	VF	XF	Unc
8	1969	—	—	Proof	350.00

9	1969	—	—	Proof	450.00

KM#	Date	Year	Mintage	VF	XF	Unc
18	AH1395	1975	—	—	—	200.00
	1395	1975	3,500	—	Proof	350.00

25 RIYALS

.900 GOLD

KM#	Date	Year	Mintage	VF	XF	Unc
19	AH1395	1975	—	—	—	200.00
	1395	1975	3,500	—	Proof	375.00

28.2800 g, .925 SILVER, .8411 oz ASW
International Year of Disabled Persons

Y#	Date	Year	Mintage	VF	XF	Unc
46	AH1401	1981	.010	—	—	25.00
	1401	1981	.010	—	Proof	25.00

20th Anniversary of Independence

| 47 | AH1402 | 1982 | 2,000 | — | Proof | 45.00 |

28.2500 g, .925 SILVER, .8402 oz ASW
International Year of the Child

| 45 | AH1403 | 1983 | 6,604 | — | Proof | 35.00 |

Decade for Women

Y#	Date	Year	Mintage	VF	XF	Unc
49	AH1405	1985	1,000	—	Proof	25.00

30 RIYALS

29.4000 g, .900 GOLD, .8508 oz AGW

KM#	Date	Mintage	VF	XF	Unc
10	1969	—	—	Proof	600.00

50 RIYALS

49.0000 g, .900 GOLD, 1.4180 oz AGW

| 11 | 1969 | — | — | Proof | 1000. |

9.1000 g, .900 GOLD, .2633 oz AGW

KM#	Date	Year	Mintage	VF	XF	Unc
20	AH1395	1975	—	—	—	250.00
	1395	1975	3,500	—	Proof	250.00

75 RIYALS

13.6500 g, .900 GOLD, .3950 oz AGW
Obv: Arms. Rev: XXI Olympiad.

| 21 | AH1395 | 1975 | — | — | — | 300.00 |
| | 1395 | 1975 | 3,500 | — | Proof | 400.00 |

100 RIYALS

18.2000 g, .900 GOLD, .5266 oz AGW

KM#	Date	Year	Mintage	VF	XF	Unc
22	AH1395	1975	—	—	—	350.00
	1395	1975	3,500	—	Proof	425.00

500 RIYALS

15.9000 g, .917 GOLD, .4686 oz AGW
20th Anniversary of Independence

| 48 | AH1402 | 1982 | 1,000 | — | Proof | 350.00 |

MINT SETS (MS)

KM#	Date	Mintage	Identification	Issue Price	Mkt. Val.
MS1	1975(4)	—	KM14-17	50.00	70.00
MS2	1975(5)	—	KM18-22	360.00	1925.

PROOF SETS (PS)

PS1	1969(7)	*2,000	KM1,4,6,7,9-11	375.00	2450.
PS2	1969(4)	1,500	KM1-4	—	110.00
PS3	1969(4)	—	KM1-2,1a-2a	—	2000.
PS4	1969(3)	—	KM2,3,6	78.00	150.00
PS5	1974(5)	5,024	Y33-37	15.00	12.50
PS6	1975(5)	3,500	KM18-22	485.00	1800.
PS7	1975(4)	5,000	KM14-17	75.00	175.00
PS8	1980(6)	10,000	Y33-37,42	31.00	15.00

YEMEN

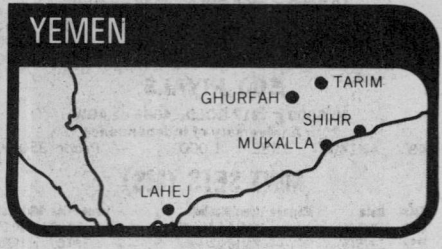

The states of Britain's former Eastern and Western Aden Protectorates, now a part of the People's Democratic Republic of Yemen, were coin issuing entities of interest to numismatists.

ADEN-PROTECTORATE STATES

GHURFAH

A city sultanate of Eastern Aden Protectorate was an oasis settlement located in the Hadramaut Wadi region on the southern coast of Arabia.

TITLES

Al-Khurfah

RULERS

Abdat Umar bin Abdat, 1928-1939
Ubayd bin Saht bin Abdat, 1939-1945

4 CHOMSIHS

.6500 g, .900 SILVER, .0188 oz ASW

Y#	Date	Mintage	VG	Fine	VF	XF
4	AH1344	5,000	15.00	35.00	45.00	65.00

8 CHOMSIHS

1.1000 g, .900 SILVER, .0318 oz ASW

6	AH1344	5,000	12.50	32.50	40.00	50.00

15 CHOMSIHS

2.0000 g, .900 SILVER, .0578 oz ASW

8	AH1344	.010	7.50	12.00	17.50	27.50

30 CHOMSIHS

3.9500 g, .900 SILVER, .1142 oz ASW

10	AH1344	.010	11.00	17.50	25.00	32.50

45 CHOMSIHS

5.9000 g, .900 SILVER, .1707 oz ASW

11	AH1344	.010	120.00	200.00	300.00	450.00

60 CHOMSIHS

7.8000 g, .900 SILVER, .2257 oz ASW

Y#	Date	Mintage	VG	Fine	VF	XF
12	AH1344	.010	25.00	37.50	55.00	80.00

LAHEJ

A sultanate situated north of the port city of Aden, was comprised in Western Aden Protectorate located in southern Arabia near the entrance of the Red Sea. Lahej entered into a protective treaty relationship with Britain following Britain's capture of Aden in 1839.

TITLES

Lahej

RULERS

Ali bin Muhsin,
 AH1265-1279/1849-1863AD
Fadl III bin Ali,
 AH1282,1291-1315/1863,1874-1898AD

1/2 PESSA

COPPER

1	ND(1860)	—	7.50	15.00	27.50	40.00

2	AH1291(1896)	.678	10.00	17.50	35.00	50.00

The date AH1291-1874 appears on Y#2 coins and refers to the date the Sultan began his first reign.

KASADI OF MUKALLA

A port, city sultanate and capital of the Quaiti state of Shihr and Mukalla in Eastern Aden Protectorate in southern Arabia, was a principal port servicing trade between the Near East and India and Java.

TITLES

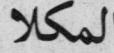

Al-Mukala

RULERS

Salah bin Muhammad,
 AH1290/1873AD
Umar bin Salah,
 AH1290-1298/1873-1881AD

1/2 CHOMSIH

BRONZE

Y#	Date	Year	Good	VG	Fine	VF
1	AH1276	(1859)	25.00	45.00	75.00	120.00

CHOMSIH

BRONZE

2	AH1276	(1859)	20.00	40.00	65.00	100.00

QUAITI STATE

The Quaiti State of Shihr and Mukalla was comprised in Eastern Aden Protectorate located in southern Arabia near the entrance to the Red Sea.

TITLES

Quaiti قيطي

RULERS

Munasir bin Abdullah bin Umar, 1830-1866
Awadh bin Umar, 1866-1909

COUNTERMARKED COINAGE

1/12 ANNA

COPPER

c/m: Arabic in 10mm circle on India 1/12 Anna, KM#445.

Y#	Date	Year	Good	VG	Fine	VF
A1	AH1307	—	8.50	13.50	18.50	27.50

1/4 ANNA

COPPER

c/m: Arabic in 15mm circle on India 1/4 Anna, KM#232.

B1	AH1307	AH1249	8.50	13.50	18.50	27.50

c/m: Arabic in 10mm circle on India 1/4 Anna, KM#231.

1	AH1307	(1830-33)	4.50	7.50	12.50	20.00

c/m: Arabic in 10mm circle on India 1/4 Anna, KM#446.

1.1	AH1307	(1833-58)	4.50	7.50	12.50	20.00

c/m: Arabic in 15mm circle on India 1/4 Anna, KM#467.

1.2	AH1307	(1862-76)	4.50	7.50	12.50	20.00

c/m: Arabic in 10mm circle on Mombasa 1/4 Anna, KM#1.

1.3	AH1307	AH1388	7.50	12.50	17.50	25.00

c/m: Arabic in 10mm circle on Zanzibar Pysa, KM#1.

1.4	AH1307	AH1299	7.50	12.50	17.50	25.00

1/2 ANNA

COPPER

c/m: Arabic in 15mm circle on India 1/2 Anna, KM#251.

2	AH1307	(1834)	8.50	13.50	18.50	27.50

c/m: Arabic in 15mm circle on India 1/2 Anna, KM#447.

2.1	AH1307	(1833-45)	8.50	13.50	18.50	27.50

c/m: in 15mm circle on India 1/2 Anna, KM#468.

Y#	Date	Year	Good	VG	Fine	VF
2.2	AH1307	(1862-76)	8.50	13.50	18.50	27.50

1/4 RUPEE
SILVER
c/m: Arabic in 10mm circle on India 1/4 Rupee, KM#96.

A3	AH1307	AH1204	8.50	13.50	18.50	27.50

1/2 RUPEE
SILVER
c/m: Arabic in 10mm circle on India 1/2 Rupee.

3	AH1307	—	7.50	12.50	17.50	25.00

c/m: Arabic in 10mm circle on English 1 Shilling, KM#734.

3.1	AH1307	(1862)	7.50	12.50	17.50	25.00

c/m: Arabic in 15mm circle on India 1/2 Rupee.

4	AH1307	—	10.00	15.00	22.50	30.00

c/m: Arabic in 15mm circle on Mexico 2 Reales, KM#88.

4.1	AH1307	(1785)	10.00	15.00	22.50	30.00

RUPEE

SILVER
c/m: Arabic in 10mm circle on India Rupee, KM#457.

5	AH1307	(1840)	10.00	15.00	22.50	30.00

PRICES - Single c/m on coin. Add 15 percent for each additional c/m.

c/m: Arabic in 15mm circle on India Rupee, KM#458.

6	AH1307	(1840)	11.50	17.50	25.00	35.00

RYAL

SILVER
c/m: Arabic in 10mm circle on Austria MTT, Y#55.

7	AH1307	(1780)	25.00	35.00	45.00	55.00

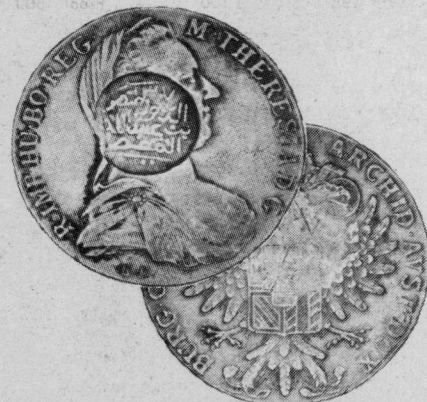

c/m: Arabic in 15mm circle on Austria MTT, Y#55.

7a	AH1307	(1780)	30.00	40.00	50.00	65.00

SOVEREIGN
GOLD
c/m: Arabic on English Sovereign, KM#767.

Y#	Date	Year	Good	VG	Fine	VF
A8	AH1307	(1889)	—	—	Rare	—

REGULAR COINAGE
5 CHOMSIHS

COPPER and BRONZE

8	AH1315	1897	4.50	7.50	15.00	25.00

9	AH1318	1900	4.00	6.50	12.50	20.00

1/3 RYAL

SILVER

KM#	Date	Good	VG	Fine	VF
10	AH1315	150.00	250.00	350.00	500.00

1/2 RYAL

SILVER

11	AH1316	175.00	300.00	450.00	600.00

SEIYUN & TARIM

Kathiri State of Seiyun and Tarim, a city sultanate in Eastern Aden Protectorate, was an important oasis settlement in the Hadramaut Wadi region on the southern coast of Arabia. It became a British treaty protectorate in the 1880's.

TITLES

تريم

Tarim

RULERS
Syed Hussein Bin Sahil, 1842

MINT MARKS
H - Heaton, Birmingham

MONETARY SYSTEM
120 Chomsihs = 1 Ryal

CHOMSIH

COPPER, thin

Y#	Date	Year	Mintage	VG	Fine	VF
A1	AH1258	1842	—	10.00	17.50	27.50

3 CHOMSIHS

COPPER, thick

Y#	Date	Year	Mintage	VG	Fine	VF
A2	AH1258	1842	—	15.00	25.00	45.00

4 CHOMSIHS

.8000 g, .900 SILVER, .0231 oz ASW

Y#	Date	Year	Mintage	Fine	VF	XF
A4	AH1270	1853	—	55.00	85.00	125.00

6 CHOMSIHS

.9000 g, .900 SILVER, .0260 oz ASW

1	AH1315H	1897	.335	3.00	6.50	12.50

8 CHOMSIHS

1.6500 g, .900 SILVER, .0477 oz ASW

A5	AH1270	1853	—	55.00	85.00	125.00

12 CHOMSIHS

1.5000 g, .900 SILVER, .0434 oz ASW

2	AH1315H	1897	.167	6.00	10.00	15.00
	1315H	1897	—	—	Proof	75.00

16 CHOMSIHS

3.3500 g, .900 SILVER, .0969 oz ASW

A6	AH1270	1853	—	65.00	100.00	150.00

24 CHOMSIHS

3.1500 g, .900 SILVER, .0911 oz ASW

3	AH1315H	1897	.083	5.00	10.00	15.00
	1315H	1897	—	—	Proof	125.00

30 CHOMSIHS

7.6500 g, .900 SILVER, .2213 oz ASW

A3	AH1258	1842	—	100.00	150.00	250.00

YEMEN DEMOCRATIC REPUBLIC

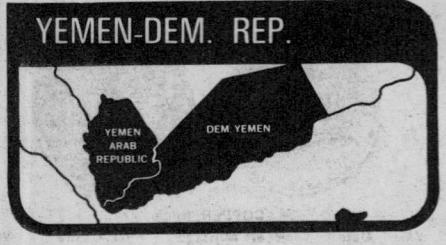

The People's Democratic Republic of Yemen, located on the southern coast of the Arabian Peninsula, has an area of 128,560 sq. mi. (332,968 sq. km.) and a population of *2.5 million. Capital: Aden. It consists of the port city of Aden, 17 states of the former South Arabian Federation, 3 small shaikhdoms, 3 large sultanates, Quaiti, Kathiri, and Mahri, which made up the Eastern Aden Protectorate, and Socotra, the largest island in the Arabian Sea. The port of Aden is the area's most valuable natural resource. Cotton, fish, coffee and hides are exported.

Between 1200 B.C. and the 6th century A.D., what is now the People's Democratic Republic of Yemen was part of the Minaean kingdom. In subsequent years it was controlled by Persians, Egyptians and Turks. Aden, one of the cities mentioned in the Bible, had been a port for trade between the East and West for 2,000 years. British rule began in 1839 when the British East India Co. seized control to put an end to the piracy threatening trade with India. To protect their foothold in Aden, the British found it necessary to extend their control into the area known historically as the Hadramaut, and to sign protection treaties with the shaikhs of the hinterland. Eventually, 15 of the 16 Western Protectorate States, the Wahidi State of the Eastern Protectorate, and Aden Colony joined to form the Federation of South Arabia.

In 1959, Britain agreed to prepare South Arabia for full independence, which was achieved on Nov. 30, 1967, at which time South Arabia, including Aden, changed its name to the People's Republic of Southern Yemen. On Dec. 1, 1970, following the overthrowing of the new government by the National Liberation Front, Southern Yemen changed its name to the People's Democratic Republic of Yemen.

SOUTH ARABIA

MONETARY SYSTEM
1000 Fils = 1 Dinar

FILS

ALUMINUM

KM#	Date	Mintage	VF	XF	Unc
1	1964	10.000	—	.10	.15
(Y1)	1964	—	—	Proof	1.25

5 FILS

		BRONZE			
2	1964	10.000	.15	.25	.50
(Y2)	1964	—	—	Proof	1.50

25 FILS

		COPPER-NICKEL			
3	1964	4.000	.25	.45	.85
(Y3)	1964	—	—	Proof	2.00

50 FILS

COPPER-NICKEL

KM#	Date	Mintage	VF	XF	Unc
4	1964	6.000	.45	.65	1.25
(Y4)	1964	—	—	Proof	3.25

PROOF SETS (PS)

KM#	Date	Mintage	Identification	Issue Price	Mkt. Val.
PS1	1964(4)	10,500	KM1-4	9.90	8.00

PEOPLE'S DEMOCRATIC REPUBLIC OF YEMEN

MONETARY SYSTEM
1000 Fils = 1 Dinar

2-1/2 FILS

ALUMINUM

KM#	Date	Year	Mintage	VF	XF	Unc
3 (Y3)	AH1393	1973	20.000	.10	.15	.25

5 FILS

BRONZE

KM#	Date	Mintage	VF	XF	Unc
2 (Y2)	1971	2.000	.30	.60	1.00

ALUMINUM

KM#	Date	Year	Mintage	VF	XF	Unc
4 (Y4)	AH1393	1973	20.000	.15	.30	.50

10 FILS

ALUMINUM

KM#	Date	Mintage	VF	XF	Unc
9 (Y9)	1981	—	.35	.75	2.75

25 FILS

COPPER-NICKEL

5	1976	2.000	.25	.50	1.25
(Y5)	1977	1.000	.25	.50	1.75
	1982	—	.25	.50	1.75

50 FILS

COPPER-NICKEL

6	1976	2.000	.35	.75	2.50
(Y6)	1977	2.000	.35	.75	2.50
	1979	—	—	.35	.75	2.50

100 FILS

COPPER-NICKEL

10 (Y10)	1981	—	.50	1.00	3.25

250 FILS

COPPER-NICKEL

KM#	Date	Mintage	VF	XF	Unc
7 (Y7)	1977	.030	—	—	6.00

11 (Y11)	1981	—	—	—	10.00

2 DINARS

28.2800 g, .925 SILVER, .8411 oz ASW
IYDP - Abdulla Baradoni

12	1981	.010	—	—	25.00
(Y12)	1981	.010	—	Proof	30.00

5 DINARS

12.5000 g, .925 SILVER, .3718 oz ASW

8 (Y8)	1977	6,000	—	Proof	40.00

50 DINARS

15.9800 g, .917 GOLD, .4712 oz AGW
International Year of Disabled Persons
Obv: Similar to 2 Dinars, KM#12. Rev: Eagle crest.

13	1981	2,100	—	—	400.00
(Y13)	1981	1,100	—	Proof	500.00

YUGOSLAVIA

The Socialist Federal Republic of Yugoslavia, a Balkan country located on the east shore of the Adriatic Sea, has an area of 98,766 sq. mi. (255,804 sq. km.) and a population of *23.8 million. Capital: Belgrade. The chief industries are agriculture, mining, manufacturing and tourism. Machinery, nonferrous metals, meat and fabrics are exported.

Yugoslavia was proclaimed on Dec. 1, 1918, after the union of the Kingdom of Serbia, Montenegro and the South Slav territories of Austria-Hungary; and changed its official name from the Kingdom of the Serbs, Croats and Slovenes to the Kingdom of Yugoslavia on Oct. 3, 1929. The republic is currently composed of six autonomous republics - Serbia, Croatia, Slovenia, Bosnia-Herzegovina, Macedonia and Montenegro - and two autonomous provinces within Serbia: Kosovo-Melohija and Vojvodina. The government of Yugoslavia attempted to remain neutral in World War II but, yielding to German pressure, aligned itself with the Axis powers in March of 1941; a few days later it was overthrown by revolutionary forces and its neutrality reasserted. The Nazis occupied the country on April 6, and throughout the remaining war years were resisted by a number of guerrilla armies, notably that of Marshal Josip Broz Tito. After the defeat of the Axis powers, a leftist coalition headed by Tito abolished the monarchy and, on Jan. 31, 1946, established a "People's Republic."

The name Yugoslavia appears on the coinage in letters of the Cyrillic alphabet alone until formation of the Federated People's Republic of Yugoslavia in 1953, after which both the Cyrillic and Latin alphabets are employed. From 1965, the coin denomination appears in the four different languages of the federated republics in letters of both the Cyrillic and Latin alphabets.

Para ПАРА
Dinar ДИНАР, Dinara ДИНАРА
Dinari ДИНАРИ, Dinarjev

RULERS
Petar I, 1918-1921
Alexander I, 1921-1934
Petar II, 1934-1945

MINT MARKS
(a) - Paris, privy marks only
(k) - КОВНИЦА, А.Д. - Kovnica, A.D. (Akcionarno Drustvo) Belgrade
(l) - London
(p) - Poissy (thunderbolt)
(v) - Vienna

MONETARY SYSTEM
100 Para = 1 Dinar

KINGDOM OF THE SERBS, CROATS AND SLOVENES
5 PARA

ZINC

KM#	Date	Mintage	Fine	VF	XF	Unc
1 (Y1)	1920(v)	3.826	3.00	7.50	15.00	35.00

10 PARA

ZINC

2 (Y2)	1920(v)	58.946	1.50	4.00	7.00	16.00

25 PARA

NICKEL-BRONZE

KM#	Date	Mintage	Fine	VF	XF	Unc
3 (Y3)	1920(v)	48.173	1.00	2.50	6.00	14.00

50 PARA

NICKEL-BRONZE

4 (Y4)	1925	25.000	.50	1.00	2.00	5.00
	1925(p)	24.500	.50	1.50	3.00	6.00

DINAR

NICKEL-BRONZE

5 (Y5)	1925	37.000	.50	1.00	2.00	5.00
	1925(p)	37.500	.75	1.50	3.00	6.00

2 DINARA

NICKEL-BRONZE

6 (Y6)	1925	25.004	1.00	2.00	4.50	9.00
	1925(p)	29.500	1.00	2.50	5.00	11.00

20 DINARA

6.4516 g, .900 GOLD, .1867 oz AGW

7 (Y10)	1925(a)	1,000	125.00	150.00	200.00	250.00
	1925(a)	—	—	—	—	Proof

KINGDOM OF YUGOSLAVIA
25 PARA

BRONZE

17 (Y13)	1938	40.000	1.25	2.00	4.00	9.00
	1938	—	—	—	—	Proof

50 PARA

ALUMINUM-BRONZE

18 (Y14)	1938	100.000	.35	.75	2.00	5.00

DINAR

ALUMINUM-BRONZE

KM#	Date	Mintage	Fine	VF	XF	Unc
19 (Y15)	1938	100.000	.50	.75	1.75	4.50
	1938	—	—	—	—	Proof

2 DINARA

ALUMINUM-BRONZE, 14mm crown

20 (Y16)	1938	74.250	.50	1.00	2.50	6.00
	1938	—	—	—	—	Proof

12mm crown

21 (Y17)	1938	.750	4.00	8.00	16.00	32.00
	1938	—	—	—	—	Proof

10 DINARA

7.0000 g, .500 SILVER, .1125 oz ASW

10 (Y7)	1931(l)	16.000	2.00	4.00	8.00	16.00
	1931(l)	—	—	—	—	Proof
	1931(a)	4.000	3.50	7.00	15.00	27.50
	1931(a)	—	—	—	—	Proof

NICKEL

22 (Y18)	1938	25.000	.50	1.00	2.50	6.00

20 DINARA

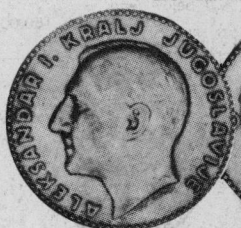 

14.0000 g, .500 SILVER, .2250 oz ASW

11 (Y8)	1931	12.500	BV	6.00	12.50	32.00
	1931	—	—	—	—	Proof

YUGOSLAVIA 1834

9.0000 g, .750 SILVER, .2170 oz ASW

KM#	Date	Mintage	Fine	VF	XF	Unc
23 (Y19)	1938	15.000	BV	3.00	6.50	14.00

50 DINARA

23.3300 g, .750 SILVER, .5626 oz ASW

16 (Y9)	1932(k) signature at truncation					
	1932(l) w/o signature at truncation	5.500	10.00	20.00	35.00	80.00
	1932(l)	5.500	10.00	22.00	37.50	90.00
		—	—	—	—	Proof

15.0000 g, .750 SILVER, .3617 oz ASW

| 24 (Y20) | 1938 | 10.000 | 4.00 | 6.00 | 10.00 | 15.00 |

COUNTERMARKED COINAGE
DUKAT

3.4900 g, .986 GOLD, .1106 oz AGW
c/m: Sword.
Obv. and rev: Small leg. w/
КОВНИЦА. А.Д. below head.

| 12.1 (Y-A11.1) | 1931(k) | *.050 | — | 95.00 | 120.00 | 150.00 |
| | 1932(k) Inc. Be. | — | — | Rare | | |

c/m: Ear of corn.

12.2 (Y-A11.2)	1931(k)	*.150	—	80.00	110.00	140.00
	1932(k)	*.070	—	90.00	115.00	150.00
	1933(k)	*.040	—	150.00	200.00	275.00
	1934(k)	*2,000	—	500.00	800.00	1200.

c/m: Sword.
Obv. and rev: Large leg. w/o
КОВНИЦА, А.Д. below head.

| 13 (Y-B11) | 1931(v) | 2,869 | | | | |

NOTE: Countermarks are a sword for Bosnia and an ear of corn for Serbia.

4 DUKATA

13.9600 g, .986 GOLD, .4425 oz AGW
c/m: Sword.
Obv. and rev: Small leg.

KM#	Date	Mintage	Fine	VF	XF	Unc
14.1 (Y12.1)	1931(k)	*.010	—	350.00	500.00	750.00
	1932(k) Inc. Be.				Rare	

c/m: Ear of corn.

14.2 (Y12.2)	1931(k)	*.015	—	350.00	500.00	800.00
	1932(k)	*.010	—	350.00	550.00	850.00
	1933(k)	*2,000	—	1000.	1400.	1900.
	1934(k)		—	1600.	2400.	3200.

Obv. and rev: Large leg. w/o
КОВНИЦА. А. Д. below busts.

| A15.1 (Y-A12.1) | 1931(v) 51 pcs. | — | — | Rare | |

c/m: Sword.

| A15.2 (YA12.2) | 1931(v) Inc. Ab. | — | — | Rare | |

PEOPLE'S REPUBLIC
5 PARA

COPPER-ZINC

| 42 (Y36) | 1965 | | | .10 | .15 | .25 |

43 (Y38)	1965	16.200	—	—	.10	.20
	1973	36.384	—	—	.10	.15
	1974	3.628	—	—	.10	.25
	1975	20.272	—	—	.10	.15
	1976	30.490	—	—	.10	.15
	1977	10.270	—	—	.10	.15
	1978	12.000	—	—	.10	.15
	1979	20.414	—	—	.10	.15
	1980	22.412	—	—	.10	.15
	1981	.630	—	—	.10	.25

10 PARA

COPPER-ZINC

44 (Y39)	1965	15.400	—	—	.10	.20
	1973	16.647	—	—	.10	.15
	1974	60.139	—	—	.10	.15
	1975	36.079	—	—	.10	.15
	1976	36.111	—	—	.10	.15
	1977	40.451	—	—	.10	.15
	1978	50.129	—	—	.10	.15
	1979	89.738	—	—	.10	.15

KM#	Date	Mintage	Fine	VF	XF	Unc
Y39	1980	90.111	—	—	.10	.15
	1981	14.090	—	—	.10	.15

20 PARA

COPPER-ZINC

45 (Y40)	1965		—	—	.10	.30
	1973	30.448	—	—	.10	.30
	1974	31.364	—	—	.10	.30
	1975	44.683	—	—	.10	.30
	1976	33.312	—	—	.10	.30
	1977	40.782	—	—	.10	.30
	1978	39.994	—	—	.10	.30
	1979	49.121	—	—	.10	.30
	1980	73.757	—	—	.10	.30
	1981	96.144	—	—	.10	.30

25 PARA

BRONZE

| 84 (Y78) | 1982 | 185.316 | — | — | .10 | .20 |
| | 1983 | 65.290 | — | — | .10 | .20 |

50 PARA

ZINC

| 25 (Y21) | 1945 | 40.000 | .50 | 1.00 | 2.00 | 4.00 |

ALUMINUM

| 29 (Y25) | 1953 | | | | .10 | .25 |

COPPER-ZINC

46 (Y41)	1965		—	—	.10	.20	.65
	1973	23.739	—	—	.10	.20	.65
	1974	.033	1.00	1.50	2.50	5.00
	1975	10.220	—	—	.10	.20	.65
	1976	8.438	—	—	.10	.20	.65
	1977	17.864	—	—	.10	.20	.65
	1978	40.177	—	—	.10	.20	.65
	1979	15.299	—	—	.10	.20	.65
	1980	24.974	—	—	.10	.20	.65
	1981	40.319	—	—	.10	.20	.65

BRONZE

85 (Y79)	1982	79.584	—	—	.10	.20
	1983	72.100	—	—	.10	.20
	1984	59.642	.25	.50	1.00	1.50

DINAR

YUGOSLAVIA 1835

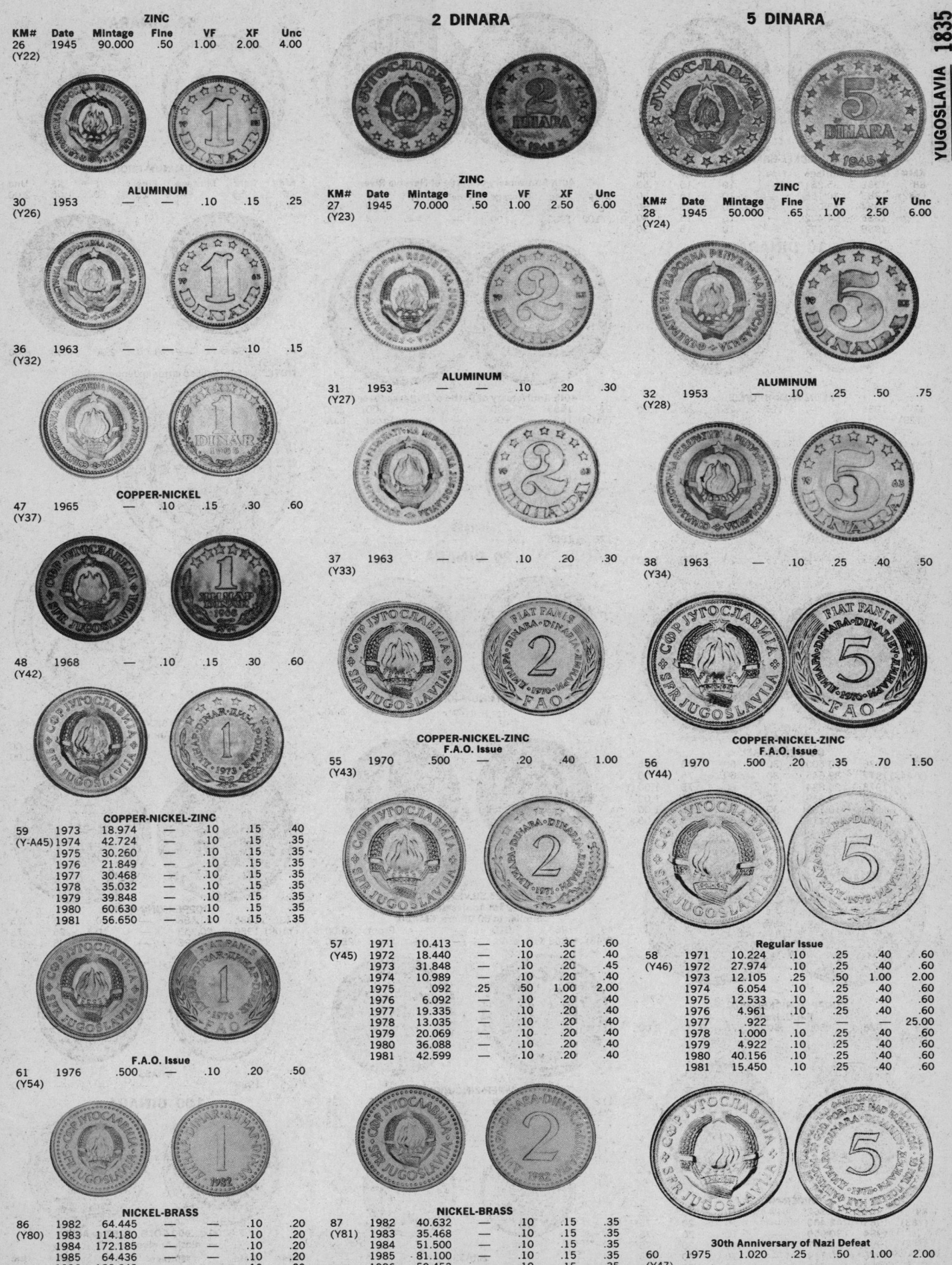

1 DINAR

ZINC

KM#	Date	Mintage	Fine	VF	XF	Unc
26 (Y22)	1945	90.000	.50	1.00	2.00	4.00

ALUMINUM

| 30 (Y26) | 1953 | — | — | .10 | .15 | .25 |
| 36 (Y32) | 1963 | — | — | — | .10 | .15 |

COPPER-NICKEL

| 47 (Y37) | 1965 | — | .10 | .15 | .30 | .60 |
| 48 (Y42) | 1968 | — | .10 | .15 | .30 | .60 |

COPPER-NICKEL-ZINC

59 (Y-A45)	1973	18.974	—	.10	.15	.40
	1974	42.724	—	.10	.15	.35
	1975	30.260	—	.10	.15	.35
	1976	21.849	—	.10	.15	.35
	1977	30.468	—	.10	.15	.35
	1978	35.032	—	.10	.15	.35
	1979	39.848	—	.10	.15	.35
	1980	60.630	—	.10	.15	.35
	1981	56.650	—	.10	.15	.35

F.A.O. Issue

| 61 (Y54) | 1976 | .500 | — | .10 | .20 | .50 |

NICKEL-BRASS

86 (Y80)	1982	64.445	—	—	.10	.20
	1983	114.180	—	—	.10	.20
	1984	172.185	—	—	.10	.20
	1985	64.436	—	—	.10	.20
	1986	122.643	—	—	.10	.20

2 DINARA

ZINC

KM#	Date	Mintage	Fine	VF	XF	Unc
27 (Y23)	1945	70.000	.50	1.00	2.50	6.00

ALUMINUM

| 31 (Y27) | 1953 | — | — | .10 | .20 | .30 |
| 37 (Y33) | 1963 | — | — | .10 | .20 | .30 |

COPPER-NICKEL-ZINC
F.A.O. Issue

| 55 (Y43) | 1970 | .500 | — | .20 | .40 | 1.00 |

57 (Y45)	1971	10.413	—	.10	.30	.60
	1972	18.440	—	.10	.20	.40
	1973	31.848	—	.10	.20	.45
	1974	10.989	—	.10	.20	.40
	1975	.092	.25	.50	1.00	2.00
	1976	6.092	—	.10	.20	.40
	1977	19.335	—	.10	.20	.40
	1978	13.035	—	.10	.20	.40
	1979	20.069	—	.10	.20	.40
	1980	36.088	—	.10	.20	.40
	1981	42.599	—	.10	.20	.40

NICKEL-BRASS

87 (Y81)	1982	40.632	—	.10	.15	.35
	1983	35.468	—	.10	.15	.35
	1984	51.500	—	.10	.15	.35
	1985	81.100	—	.10	.15	.35
	1986	50.453	—	.10	.15	.35

5 DINARA

ZINC

KM#	Date	Mintage	Fine	VF	XF	Unc
28 (Y24)	1945	50.000	.65	1.00	2.50	6.00

ALUMINUM

| 32 (Y28) | 1953 | — | .10 | .25 | .50 | .75 |
| 38 (Y34) | 1963 | — | .10 | .25 | .40 | .50 |

COPPER-NICKEL-ZINC
F.A.O. Issue

| 56 (Y44) | 1970 | .500 | .20 | .35 | .70 | 1.50 |

Regular Issue

58 (Y46)	1971	10.224	.10	.25	.40	.60
	1972	27.974	.10	.25	.40	.60
	1973	12.105	.25	.50	1.00	2.00
	1974	6.054	.10	.25	.40	.60
	1975	12.533	.10	.25	.40	.60
	1976	4.961	.10	.25	.40	.60
	1977	.922	—	—	—	25.00
	1978	1.000	.10	.25	.40	.60
	1979	4.922	.10	.25	.40	.60
	1980	40.156	.10	.25	.40	.60
	1981	15.450	.10	.25	.40	.60

30th Anniversary of Nazi Defeat

| 60 (Y47) | 1975 | 1.020 | .25 | .50 | 1.00 | 2.00 |

YUGOSLAVIA 1836

NICKEL-BRASS

KM#	Date	Mintage	Fine	VF	XF	Unc
88	1982	35.281	—	.10	.15	.50
(Y82)	1983	40.156	—	.10	.15	.50
	1984	33.023	—	.10	.15	.50
	1985	94.422	—	.10	.15	.50
	1986	37.199	—	.10	.15	.50

10 DINARA

40th Anniversary of Battle of Neretva River

KM#	Date	Mintage	Fine	VF	XF	Unc
96	1983	.900	—	—	1.00	2.00
(Y102)	1983	.100	—	—	Proof	5.00

50 DINARA

ALUMINUM-BRONZE

KM#	Date	Mintage	Fine	VF	XF	Unc
35	1955	—	.25	.50	1.00	2.00
(Y31)						

41	1963	—	1.00	2.00	4.00	8.00
(Y-B35)						

NOTE: Exists with filled letter in denomination.

ALUMINUM-BRONZE

33	1955	—	.15	.25	.50	1.00
(Y29)						

40th Anniversary of Battle of Sutjeska River

97	1983	.900	—	—	1.00	2.00
(Y103)	1983	.100	—	—	Proof	5.00

BRASS

123	1988	—	—	—	—	.10

20 DINARA

39	1963	—	.15	.25	.50	1.00
(Y35)						

COPPER-NICKEL

62	1976	10.500	.30	.60	.75	1.25
(Y-A47)	1977	39.645	.30	.60	.75	1.00
	1978	29.834	.30	.60	.75	1.00
	1979	4.969	.30	.60	.75	1.00
	1980	10.139	.30	.60	.75	1.00
	1981	20.116	.30	.60	.75	1.00

COPPER-NICKEL-ZINC
F.A.O. Issue

63	1976	.500	.50	.75	1.00	2.00
(Y55)						

COPPER-NICKEL

89	1982	8.862	—	.10	.20	.75
(Y83)	1983	42.400	—	.10	.20	.75
	1984	30.900	—	.10	.20	.75
	1985	31.647	—	.10	.20	.75
	1986	40.739	—	.10	.20	.75
	1987	104.988	—	.10	.20	.75

ALUMINUM-BRONZE

34	1955	—	.25	.50	1.00	2.00
(Y30)						

40	1963	—	.75	1.25	2.00	4.00
(Y-A35)						

9.0000 g, .925 SILVER, .2676 oz ASW
25th Anniversary
Similar to 50 Dinara, KM#50.

49	1968	.010	—	—	Proof	25.00
(Y48)	1968 NI Inc. Ab.	—	—	—	Proof	25.00

COPPER-ZINC-NICKEL

112	1985	5.000	—	.10	.15	.35
(Y108)	1986	20.937	—	.10	.15	.35
	1987	39.514	—	.10	.15	.35

BRASS

124	1988	—	—	—	—	.10

20.0000 g, .925 SILVER, .5948 oz ASW
25th Anniversary

50	1968	.010	—	—	Proof	50.00
(Y49)	1968 NI Inc. Ab.	—	—	—	Proof	50.00

COPPER-ZINC-NICKEL

113	1985	25.488	—	.10	.25	.75
(Y109)	1986	20.353	—	.10	.25	.75
	1987	21.792	—	.10	.25	.75

BRASS

125	1988	—	—	—	—	.10

100 DINARA

7.8200 g, .900 GOLD, .2263 oz AGW
25th Anniversary

KM#	Date	Mintage	VF	XF	Unc
51	1968	.010	—	Proof	150.00

YUGOSLAVIA 1837

KM#	Date	Mintage	VF	XF	Unc
(Y50)	1968 NI	Inc. Ab.	—	Proof	150.00

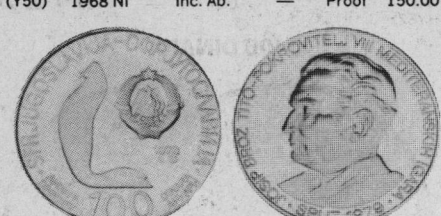

10.0600 g, .925 SILVER, .2991 oz ASW
8th Mediterranean Games at Split

65 (Y57)	1979	.071	—	Proof	16.00

COPPER-ZINC-NICKEL

KM#	Date	Mintage	VF	XF	Unc
114 (Y110)	1985	18.684	.25	.50	1.50
	1986	17.905	—	.40	.60
	1987	94.069	—	.40	.60

15.6400 g, .900 GOLD, .4526 oz AGW
25th Anniversary

KM#	Date	Mintage	VF	XF	Unc
52 (Y51)	1968	.010	—	Proof	275.00
	1968 NI	Inc. Ab.	—	Proof	275.00

13.0000 g, .925 SILVER, .3867 oz ASW
1984 Winter Olympics - Ice Hockey

90 (Y84)	1982	.110	—	Proof	14.00

COPPER-NICKEL-ZINC
40th Anniversary of Liberation from Fascism

115 (Y115)	1985	.200	—	Proof	3.00

1984 Winter Olympics - Figure Skating

98 (Y88)	1983	.110	—	Proof	14.00

COPPER-NICKEL
200th Anniversary of Birth of Karajich

127 (Y111)	1987	*.200	—	Proof	3.00

14.9600 g, .750 SILVER, .3607 oz ASW
85th Birthday of Tito
Upper edge inscription in Cyrillic.

64.1 (Y56.1)	1977	.500	—	Proof	16.00

14.0000 g, .600 SILVER, .2701 oz ASW

64.1a (Y56.1a)	1977	.300	—	—	11.00

14.9600 g, .750 SILVER, .3607 oz ASW
Upper edge inscription in western letters.

64.2 (Y56.2)	1977	Inc. Ab.	—	Proof	16.00

14.0000 g, .600 SILVER, .2701 oz ASW

64.2a (Y56.2a)	1977	Inc. Ab.	—	—	11.00

1984 Winter Olympics - Bobsledding

99 (Y92)	1983	.110	—	Proof	14.00

BRASS

126	1988	—	—	—	.10

150 DINARA

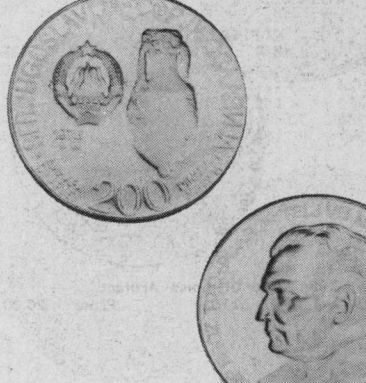

1984 Winter Olympics - Speed Skating

105 (Y96)	1984	.110	—	Proof	14.00

12.5000 g, .925 SILVER, .3717 oz ASW
8th Mediterranean Games at Split

66 (Y58)	1979	.070	—	Proof	16.00

200 DINARA

15.0000 g, .925 SILVER, .4461 oz ASW
8th Mediterranean Games at Split

67 (Y59)	1979	.058	—	Proof	25.00

250 DINARA

1984 Winter Olympics - Pairs Figure Skating

106 (Y99)	1984	.110	—	Proof	14.00

YUGOSLAVIA 1838

17.5700 g, .925 SILVER, .5225 oz ASW
8th Mediterranean Games at Split

KM#	Date	Mintage	VF	XF	Unc
68 (Y60)	1978	.048	—	Proof	30.00

17.0000 g, .925 SILVER, .5056 oz ASW
1984 Winter Olympics - Sarajevo View
91 (Y85)   1982   .110   —   Proof   20.00

1984 Winter Olympics - Artifact
100 (Y89)   1983   .110   —   Proof   20.00

1984 Winter Olympics - Radimlja Tombs

KM#	Date	Mintage	VF	XF	Unc
101 (Y93)	1983	.110	—	Proof	20.00

1984 Winter Olympics - Jajce Village
107 (Y97)   1984   .110   —   Proof   20.00

1984 Winter Olympics - Tito
108 (Y100)   1984   .110   —   Proof   20.00

300 DINARA

20.1200 g, .925 SILVER, .5983 oz ASW
8th Mediterranean Games at Split
69 (Y61)   1978   .036   —   Proof   30.00

350 DINARA

22.5300 g, .925 SILVER, .6700 oz ASW
8th Mediterranean Games at Split

KM#	Date	Mintage	VF	XF	Unc
70 (Y62)	1978	.024	—	Proof	30.00

400 DINARA

25.1200 g, .925 SILVER, .7470 oz ASW
8th Mediterranean Games at Split
71 (Y63)   1978   .024   —   Proof   35.00

500 DINARA

39.1000 g, .900 GOLD, 1.1315 oz AGW
25th Anniversary
53 (Y52)   1968   .010   —   Proof   650.00
        1968 NI   Inc. Ab.   —   Proof   650.00

8.0000 g, .925 SILVER, .2379 oz ASW
Vukovar Congress
76 (Y68)   1980   .018   —   Proof   22.50

8.1000 g, .750 SILVER, .1953 oz ASW
Table Tennis
80 (Y72)   1981   .018   —   Proof   27.50

1000 DINARA

YUGOSLAVIA 1839

23.0000 g, .925 SILVER, .6841 oz ASW
1984 Winter Olympics - Downhill Skiing

KM#	Date	Mintage	VF	XF	Unc
92 (Y86)	1982	.110	—	Proof	22.50

1984 Winter Olympics - Cross Country Skiing

KM#	Date	Mintage	VF	XF	Unc
109 (Y98)	1984	.110	—	Proof	22.50

1984 Winter Olympics - Ski Jumping

| 102 (Y90) | 1983 | .110 | — | Proof | 22.50 |

1984 Winter Olympics - Slalom

| 110 (Y101) | 1984 | .110 | — | Proof | 22.50 |

1984 Winter Olympics - Biathalon

| 103 (Y94) | 1983 | .110 | — | Proof | 22.50 |

13.0000 g, .925 SILVER, .3867 oz ASW
Ski Jumping Championship - Herons
Obv: Similar to 10,000 Dinara, KM#123.

| 116 (Y104) | 1985 | .050 | — | Proof | 12.50 |

78.2000 g, .900 GOLD, 2.2630 oz AGW
25th Anniversary

KM#	Date	Mintage	VF	XF	Unc
54 (Y53)	1968	.010	—	Proof	1250.
	1968 NI	Inc. Ab.	—	Proof	1250.

14.0000 g, .925 SILVER, .4164 oz ASW
Vukovar Congress

| 77 (Y69) | 1980 | .016 | — | Proof | 30.00 |

25.9000 g, .750 SILVER, .6245 oz ASW
Tito's Death

YUGOSLAVIA 1840

NOTE: Eyes with and without pupils.

26.0000 g, .925 SILVER, .7733 oz ASW

KM#	Date	Mintage	VF	XF	Unc
78a	1980	.200	—	Proof	35.00
(Y71a)	1980 ZM	Inc. Ab.	—	Proof	35.00

14.0500 g, .750 SILVER, .3388 oz ASW
Table Tennis

81	1981	.016	—	Proof	30.00
(Y73)					

40th Anniversary of Uprising and Revolution

82	1981	.100	—	Proof	17.50
(Y75)					

18.0000 g, .925 SILVER, .5354 oz ASW
Canoeing Championships - City View

93	1982	.046	—	Proof	25.00
(Y76)					

23.0000 g, .925 SILVER, .6841 oz ASW
Ski Jumping Championship - Bloudek
Obv: Similar to 10,000 Dinara, KM#123.

117	1985	.020	—	Proof	25.00
(Y105)					

Ski Jumping Championship - Slovenian Cradle
Obv: Similar to 10,000 Dinara, KM#123.

KM#	Date	Mintage	VF	XF	Unc
118	1985	.020	—	Proof	25.00
(Y106)					

6.0000 g, .925 SILVER, .1784 oz ASW
Sinjska Alka

119	1985	.060	—	Proof	15.00
(Y117)					

1500 DINARA

8.8000 g, .900 GOLD, .2546 oz AGW
8th Mediterranean Games at Split

72	1978	.035	—	Proof	175.00
(Y64)					

22.0000 g, .925 SILVER, .6542 oz ASW
Vukovar Congress

79	1980	.016	—	Proof	35.00
(Y70)					

22.1000 g, .750 SILVER, .5329 oz ASW
Table Tennis

83	1981	.016	—	Proof	35.00
(Y74)					

22.1000 g, .925 SILVER, .6572 oz ASW
Canoeing Championships - Tito

KM#	Date	Mintage	VF	XF	Unc
94	1982	.036	—	Proof	25.00
(Y77)					

2000 DINARA

11.8000 g, .900 GOLD, .3414 oz AGW
8th Mediterranean Games at Split

73	1978	.035	—	Proof	225.00
(Y65)					

14.0000 g, .925 SILVER, .4164 oz ASW
Sinjska Alka

120	1985	.020	—	Proof	25.00
(Y118)					

2500 DINARA

14.7000 g, .900 GOLD, .4254 oz AGW
8th Mediterranean Games at Split

74	1978	.035	—	Proof	275.00
(Y66)					

3000 DINARA

26.0000 g, .925 SILVER, .7733 oz ASW
Sinjska Alka

121	1985	.020	—	Proof	35.00
(Y119)					

YUGOSLAVIA 1841

13.0000 g, .925 SILVER, .3867 oz ASW
200th Anniversary of Birth of Karajich
Rev: Similar to 100 Dinara, KM#127.

KM#	Date	Mintage	VF	XF	Unc
128 (Y112)	1987	*.050	—	Proof	22.50

5000 DINARA

29.5000 g, .900 GOLD, .8536 oz AGW
8th Mediterranean Games at Split

| 75 (Y67) | 1978 | .012 | — | Proof | 450.00 |

8.0000 g, .900 GOLD, .2315 oz AGW
1984 Winter Olympics - Emblem

| 95 (Y87) | 1982 | .055 | — | Proof | 175.00 |

1984 Winter Olympics - Tito

| 104 (Y91) | 1983 | .055 | — | Proof | 175.00 |

1984 Winter Olympics - Flame

| 111 (Y95) | 1984 | .055 | — | Proof | 175.00 |

23.5000 g, .925 SILVER, .6989 oz ASW
40th Anniversary of Liberation from Fascism
Similar to 100 Dinara, KM#115.

| 122 (Y116) | 1985 | .100 | — | Proof | 35.00 |

17.0000 g, .925 SILVER, .5056 oz ASW
200th Anniversary of Birth of Karajich

KM#	Date	Mintage	VF	XF	Unc
129 (Y113)	1987	*.050	—	Proof	30.00

10000 DINAR

8.0000 g, .900 GOLD, .2315 oz AGW
World Ski Jumping Championship

| 123 (Y107) | 1985 | .010 | — | Proof | 175.00 |

5.0000 g, .900 GOLD, .1447 oz AGW
Sinjska Alka

| 124 (Y120) | 1985 | .012 | — | Proof | 175.00 |

20000 DINARA

8.0000 g, .900 GOLD, .2315 oz AGW
Sinjska Alka

| 125 (Y121) | 1985 | 8,000 | — | Proof | 275.00 |

40000 DINARA

14.0000 g, .900 GOLD, .4083 oz AGW
Sinjska Alka

| 126 (Y122) | 1985 | 5,000 | — | Proof | 475.00 |

50000 DINAR

8.0000 g, .900 GOLD, .2315 oz AGW
200th Anniversary of Birth of Karajich
Similar to 5,000 Dinar, KM#129.

| 130 (Y114) | 1987 | *.010 | — | Proof | 175.00 |

MINT SETS (MS)

KM#	Date	Mintage	Identification	Issue Price	Mkt. Val.
MS1	1953/55(7)	—	KM29-35	—	4.50
MS2	1963(6)	—	KM36-41	—	7.50
MS3	1965(5)	—	KM43-47	—	3.50
MS4	1982(6)	—	KM84-89	—	2.50
MS5	1983(6)	—	KM84-89	—	2.50

PROOF SETS (PS)

PS1	1968(6)	*10,000	KM49-54	—	2400.
PS2	1968(4)	*10,000	KM51-54	—	2325.
PS3	1968(2)	*10,000	KM49-50	15.00	75.00
PS4	1978(7)	6,000	KM65-71	—	185.00
PS5	1978(11)	12,000	KM65-75	—	1310.
PS6	1980(3)	—	KM76-77,79	—	90.00
PS7	1981(3)	—	KM80-81,83	—	95.00
PS8	1982(3)	—	KM90-92	—	57.50
PS9	1982(2)	—	KM93-94	—	50.00
PS10	1983(3)	—	KM98,100,102	—	57.50
PS11	1983(3)	—	KM99,101,103	—	57.50
PS12	1984(3)	—	KM105,107,109	—	57.50
PS13	1984(3)	—	KM106,108,110	—	57.50
PS14	Mixed dates	—	KM95,104,111	—	525.00

*NOTE: Authorized mintages.

YUGOSLAVIA-CATTARO, RAGUSA, & ZARA

CATTARO

A seaport of Montenegro, Yugoslavia, occupies a ledge between the Montenegrin mountains and an inlet of the Adriatic Sea which forms one of the finest natural harbors in the world. It has at various times been occupied by Turks, Venetians, Spaniards, French, English and Austrians. It became a part of Yugoslavia in 1918. Cattaro was united to the French Empire during the period of 1807-13. In 1813, while the city was besieged by Montenegrins and a British fleet, the French defenders issued an emergency cast silver coinage.

FRENCH SEIGE COINAGE
FRANC

CAST SILVER

KM#	Date	Mintage	Good	VG	Fine	VF
1 (C1)	1813	—	50.00	75.00	125.00	200.00

5 FRANCS

CAST SILVER

	Date	Mintage	Good	VG	Fine	VF
2 (C2)	1813	—	250.00	450.00	700.00	1000.

10 FRANCS

CAST SILVER

KM#	Date	Mintage	Good	VG	Fine	VF
3 (C3)	1813	—	400.00	800.00	1200.	1875.

RAGUSA

A port city on the Dalmatian coast of Yugoslavia. Upon its incorporation in Yugoslavia in 1918, its name was officially changed to Dubrovnik. Ragusa was once a great mercantile power, the merchant fleets of which sailed as far abroad as India and America. The city's present industries include oil-refining, slate mining, and the manufacture of liquers, cheese, silk, leather and soap.

The island rock of Ragusa was colonized during the 7th century by refugees from the destroyed Latin communities of Salona and Epidaurus, and a colony of Slavs. For four centuries Ragusa successfully defended itself against attacks by foreign powers, but from 1205 to 1358 recognized Venetian suzerainty. From 1358 to 1526, Ragusa was a vassal state of Hungary. The fall of Hungary in 1526 freed Ragusa, permitting it to become one of the foremost commercial powers of the Mediterranean and a leader in the development of literature and art. After this period its importance declined, due in part to the discovery of America which reduced the importance of Mediterranean ports. A measure of its former economic importance was regained during the Napoleonic Wars when the republic, by adopting a policy of neutrality (1800-1805), became the leading carrier of the Mediterranean. This favored position was terminated by French seizure in 1805. In 1814 Ragusa was annexed by Austria, remaining a part of the Austrian Empire until its incorporation in the newly formed state of Yugoslavia in 1918.

MONETARY SYSTEM
6 Soldi = 1 Grosetto
12 Grosetti = 1 Perpero
40 Grosetti = 1 Ducato
60 Grosetti = 1 Tallero

VI (6) GROSSETTI
BILLON
Obv: St. Blaze. Rev: Value.

C#	Date	Mintage	VG	Fine	VF	XF
4	1801	—	8.00	15.00	25.00	45.00

PERPERO
BILLON
Obv: St. Blaze. Rev: Christ.

	Date	Mintage	VG	Fine	VF	XF
5	1801-03	—	12.00	20.00	27.50	50.00

ZARA

Zara, a port and fortress in Dalmatia, was occupied by the French during the period of 1807-13. While the French defenders of the city were under siege in 1813, they issued a silver emergency coinage.

FRENCH SEIGE COINAGE
4 FRANCS - 60 CENTIMES

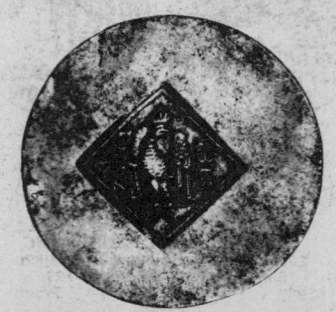

SILVER

KM#	Date	Mintage	VG	Fine	VF	XF
1 (C1)	1813	—	200.00	400.00	650.00	1000.

9 FRANCS - 20 CENTIMES

SILVER

	Date	Mintage	VG	Fine	VF	XF
2 (C2)	1813	—	300.00	600.00	800.00	1200.

18 FRANCS - 40 CENTIMES

SILVER

	Date	Mintage	VG	Fine	VF	XF
3 (C3)	1813	—	600.00	1500.	2750.	5000.

YUGOSLAVIA/Croatia

Croatia, a federal republic of the Socialist Federal Republic of Yugoslavia, has an area of 21,829 sq. mi. (56,538 sq. km.) and a population of about 5 million. Capital: Zagreb.

The country was attached to the Kingdom of Hungary until Dec. 1, 1918, when it joined with Serbia, Slovenia, Bosnia-Herzegovina, Macedonia and Montenegro to form the Kingdom of the Serbs, Croats and Slovenes, which changed its name to the Kingdom of Yugoslavia on Oct. 3, 1929. On April 6, 1941, Hitler, angered by the coup d' etat that overthrew the pro-Nazi regime of regent Prince Paul, sent the Nazi armies crashing across the Yugoslav borders from Germany, Hungary, Romania and Bulgaria. Within a week the army of the Balkan Kingdom was prostrate and broken. Yugoslavia was dismembered to award Hitler's Balkan allies. Croatia, reconstituted as a nominal kingdom, was given to the administration of an Italian princeling, who wisely decided to remain in Italy.

The word 'kunas', derived from the Russian 'cunica' which means marten, reflects the use of furs for money in medieval eastern Europe.

MONETARY SYSTEM
100 Banica = 1 Kuna

KUNA
ZINC
Similar to 2 Kune, Y#1.

KM#	Date	Mintage	Fine	VF	XF	Unc
1 (Y-A1)	1941	—	—	—	Rare	—

2 KUNE

ZINC

2 (Y1)	1941	—	2.50	5.00	7.50	12.00
	1941	—	—	—	Proof	75.00

YUGOSLAVIA/Montenegro

The former independent kingdom of Montenegro, now one of the nominally autonomous federated units of Yugoslavia, was located in southeastern Europe north of Albania. As a kingdom, it had an area of 5,333 sq. mi. (13,812 sq. km.) and a population of about 250,000. Capital: Titograd. The predominantly pastoral kingdom had few industries.

Montenegro became an independent state in 1355 following the break-up of the Serb empire. During the Turkish invasion of Albania and Herzegovina in the 15th century, the Montenegrins moved their capital to the remote mountain village of Cetinje where they maintained their independence through two centuries of intermittent attack, emerging as the only one of the Balkan states not subjugated by the Turks. When World War I began, Montenegro joined with Serbia and was subsequently invaded and occupied by the Austrians. Austria withdrew upon the defeat of the Central Powers, permitting the Serbians to move in and maintain the occupation. Montenegro then joined the kingdom of the Serbs, Croats and Slovenes, which later became Yugoslavia.

The coinage, issued under the autocratic rule of Prince Nicholas, is obsolete.

RULERS
Nicholas I, as Prince, 1860-1910
 as King, 1910-1918

MINT MARKS
(a) - Paris, privy marks only

MONETARY SYSTEM
100 Para, ΠΑΡΑ = 1 Perper, ПЕРПЕР

PARA

BRONZE

KM#	Date	Mintage	Fine	VF	XF	Unc
1 (Y1)	1906	.200	8.00	15.00	32.00	65.00

| 16 (Y11) | 1913 | .100 | 12.50 | 25.00 | 50.00 | 100.00 |
| | 1914 | .200 | 6.00 | 12.00 | 25.00 | 55.00 |

2 PARE

BRONZE

| 2 (Y2) | 1906 | .600 | 4.00 | 8.00 | 17.50 | 32.00 |
| | 1908 | .250 | 8.00 | 17.50 | 27.50 | 60.00 |

| 17 (Y12) | 1913 | .500 | 4.00 | 7.50 | 15.00 | 30.00 |
| | 1914 | .400 | 4.50 | 9.00 | 18.00 | 40.00 |

10 PARA

NICKEL

| 3 (Y3) | 1906 | .750 | 2.25 | 5.00 | 12.00 | 25.00 |
| | 1908 | .250 | — | 7.50 | 15.00 | 30.00 |

| 18 (Y13) | 1913 | .200 | 4.00 | 8.00 | 16.00 | 32.00 |
| | 1914 | .800 | 3.00 | 6.00 | 12.00 | 25.00 |

20 PARA

NICKEL

| 4 (Y4) | 1906 | .600 | 3.00 | 6.00 | 12.00 | 25.00 |
| | 1908 | .400 | 3.00 | 7.00 | 14.00 | 30.00 |

| 19 (Y14) | 1913 | .200 | 4.00 | 8.00 | 16.00 | 32.00 |
| | 1914 | .800 | 3.00 | 6.00 | 12.00 | 25.00 |

PERPER

5.0000 g, .835 SILVER, .1342 oz ASW

| 5 (Y5) | 1909(a) | *.500 | 8.50 | 16.00 | 32.00 | 90.00 |

*NOTE: Approximately 30% melted.

| 14 (Y15) | 1912 | .520 | 8.00 | 14.00 | 30.00 | 80.00 |
| | 1914 | .500 | 9.00 | 18.00 | 35.00 | 90.00 |

2 PERPERA

10.0000 g, .835 SILVER, .2685 oz ASW

| 7 (Y6) | 1910 | .300 | 15.00 | 30.00 | 60.00 | 140.00 |

| 20 (Y16) | 1914 | .200 | 15.00 | 35.00 | 75.00 | 160.00 |

5 PERPERA

25.0000 g, .900 SILVER, .7234 oz ASW

KM#	Date	Mintage	Fine	VF	XF	Unc
6 (Y7)	1909(a)	*.060	60.00	120.00	240.00	500.00

*NOTE: Approximately 50% melted.

15 (Y17)	1912	.040	75.00	150.00	250.00	520.00
	1914	.020	85.00	160.00	275.00	600.00

10 PERPERA

3.3875 g, .900 GOLD, .0980 oz AGW

| 8 (Y8) | 1910 | .040 | 125.00 | 250.00 | 325.00 | 500.00 |

50th Year of Reign

| 9 (Y18) | 1910 | .035 | 125.00 | 250.00 | 325.00 | 500.00 |

20 PERPERA

6.7751 g, .900 GOLD, .1960 oz AGW

| 10 (Y9) | 1910 | .030 | 150.00 | 275.00 | 450.00 | 650.00 |

50th Year of Reign

KM#	Date	Mintage	Fine	VF	XF	Unc
11 (Y19)	1910	.030	150.00	275.00	450.00	650.00

100 PERPERA

33.8753 g, .900 GOLD, .9802 oz AGW

12 (Y10)	1910	300 pcs.	—	4500.	6500.	10,000.
	1910	25 pcs.	—	—	Proof	12,500.

13 (Y20)	1910	500 pcs.	—	4500.	6500.	10,000.
	1910	Inc. Ab.	Proof	Reported, not confirmed		

YUGOSLAVIA/Serbia

Serbia, a former inland Balkan kingdom (now a federated republic of Yugoslavia) had an area of 34,116 sq. mi. (88,361 sq. km.). Capital: Belgrade.
Serbia emerged as a separate kingdom in the 12th century and attained its greatest expansion and political influence in the mid-14th century. After the Battle of Kosovo, 1389, Serbia became a vassal principality of Turkey and remained under Turkish suzeranity until it was re-established as an independent kingdom by the 1887 Treaty of Berlin. Following World War I, which had its immediate cause in the assassination of Austrian Archduke Francis Ferdinand by a Serbian nationalist, Serbia joined with the Croats and Slovenes to form the new Kingdom of the South Slavs with Peter I of Serbia as king. The name of the kingdom was later changed to Yugoslavia. Invaded by Germany, during World War II, Serbia emerged as a constituent republic of the Socialist Federal Republic of Yugoslavia.

RULERS
Michael, Obrenovich III
  as Prince 1839-1842, 1860-1868
Milan, Obrenovich IV,
  as Prince, 1868-1882
Alexander I, 1889-1902
Peter I, 1903-1918

MINT MARKS
A - Paris
(a) - Paris, privy mark only
(g) - Gorham Mfg. Co., Providence, R.I.
H - Birmingham
V - Vienna
БП - (BP) Budapest

MONETARY SYSTEM
100 Para = 1 Dinara

DENOMINATIONS
ПАРА = Para
ПАРЕ = Pare
ДИНАР = Dinar
ДИНАРА = Dinara

KINGDOM
PARA

BRONZE
SERBIA spelled СРБСКИ

KM#	Date	Mintage	Fine	VF	XF	Unc
1.1 (Y1.1)	1868	7.500	5.00	12.00	27.50	65.00

SERBIA spelled СРѢСКИ

| 1.2 (Y1.2) | 1868 | Inc. Ab. | 6.00 | 15.00 | 35.00 | 70.00 |

2 PARE

BRONZE

| 23 (Y13) | 1904 | 12.500 | 1.00 | 3.00 | 9.00 | 24.00 |

5 PARA

BRONZE

| 2 (Y2) | 1868 | 7.420 | 4.00 | 12.00 | 35.00 | 85.00 |

Serbia / YUGOSLAVIA 1845

KM#	Date	Mintage	Fine	VF	XF	Unc
7	1879	6.000	2.00	8.00	22.00	50.00
(Y7)	1879	—	—	—	Proof	120.00

COPPER-NICKEL

18	1883	5.000	1.00	3.00	7.00	18.00
(Y14)	1884H	3.000	1.00	2.00	6.50	15.00
	1884H	—	—	—	Proof	125.00
	1904*	8.000	1.00	2.00	3.50	10.00
	1904	Inc. Ab.	—	—	Proof	100.00
	1912	10.000	.75	1.50	3.50	9.00
	1912	—	—	—	Proof	75.00
	1917(g)	5.000	5.00	10.00	18.00	27.50

*NOTE: Medallic struck.

10 PARA

BRONZE

3	1868	6.590	5.00	16.00	35.00	80.00
(Y3)						

8	1879	9.000	4.00	9.00	27.50	65.00
(Y8)	1879	—	—	—	Proof	150.00

COPPER-NICKEL

19	1883	5.000	.75	1.75	4.00	12.00
(Y15)	1884H	6.500	.75	1.75	3.50	9.00
	1884H	—	—	—	Proof	150.00
	1904	—	—	—	Proof	175.00
	1912*	7.700	.75	1.50	3.50	8.00
	1912	—	—	—	Proof	75.00
	1917(g)	5.000	1.00	2.00	5.00	18.00
	1917(g)	—	—	—	Proof	80.00

*NOTE: Medallic struck.

20 PARA

COPPER-NICKEL

20	1883	2.500	1.00	3.00	9.00	20.00
(Y16)	1884H	6.000	1.00	2.00	7.00	13.50
	1884H	—	—	—	Proof	150.00
	1904	—	—	—	Proof	175.00
	1912*	5.650	.75	1.75	5.00	10.00
	1912	—	—	—	Proof	100.00
	1917(g)	5.000	1.00	2.00	7.00	22.00

*NOTE: Medallic struck.

50 PARA

2.5000 g, .835 SILVER, .0671 oz ASW

KM#	Date	Mintage	Fine	VF	XF	Unc
4	1875	2.000	8.00	17.50	45.00	130.00
(Y4)	1875	—	—	—	Proof	300.00

9	1879	.600	5.00	12.00	25.00	75.00
(Y4a)	1879	—	—	—	Proof	250.00

Obv: Designer's signature below neck.

24.1	1904	1.400	2.00	4.00	9.00	22.00
(Y19)	1912	.800	2.00	4.00	12.00	25.00
	1915(a)	7.901	1.00	2.00	4.00	12.00

Obv: W/o designer's signature.

24.2	1915(a)	12.138	5.00	10.00	25.00	80.00
(Y19a)						

DINAR

5.0000 g, .835 SILVER, .1342 oz ASW

5	1875	3.000	12.00	25.00	80.00	250.00
(Y5)	1875	—	—	—	Proof	400.00

10	1879	4.800	6.00	15.00	37.50	90.00
(Y5a)	1879	—	—	—	Proof	250.00

21	1897	4.001	3.00	6.00	14.00	45.00
(Y17)						

Obv: Designer's signature below neck.

25.1	1904	.994	4.00	9.00	20.00	60.00
(Y20)	1912	8.000	3.00	5.00	12.00	32.50
	1915(a)	10.688	2.00	4.00	8.00	16.00

Obv: W/o designer's signature.

25.2	1915(a)	2.322	4.50	12.00	28.00	65.00
(Y20a)						

2 DINARA

10.0000 g, .835 SILVER, .2684 oz ASW

6	1875	1.000	25.00	65.00	140.00	350.00
(Y6)	1875	—	—	—	Proof	450.00

KM#	Date	Mintage	Fine	VF	XF	Unc
11	1879	1.750	7.50	22.00	55.00	160.00
(Y6a)	1879	—	—	—	Proof	450.00

22	1897	.500	6.00	14.00	32.00	65.00
(Y18)						

Obv: Designer's signature below neck.

26.1	1904	1.150	8.00	16.00	35.00	80.00
(Y21)	1912	.800	7.00	14.00	25.00	55.00
	1915(a)	4.174	5.00	10.00	20.00	40.00

Obv: W/o designer's signature.

26.2	1915(a)	.826	5.00	15.00	35.00	75.00
(Y21a)						

5 DINARA

25.0000 g, .900 SILVER, .7234 oz ASW
Edge Type 1: БОГ*ЧУВА*СРБИЈУ*

12	1879	.200	30.00	65.00	140.00	350.00
(Y9.1)	1879	—	—	—	Proof	600.00

Edge Type 2: БОГ*СРБИЈУ*ЧУВА*

13	1879	Inc. Ab.	40.00	80.00	175.00	450.00
(Y9.2)						

Serbia / YUGOSLAVIA

25.0000 g, .835 SILVER, .6712 oz ASW
Karageorgevich Dynasty 100th Anniversary
Edge Type 1: БОГ*ЧУВА*СРБИЈУ***

KM#	Date	Mintage	Fine	VF	XF	Unc
27 (Y22.1)	1904	.200	35.00	75.00	150.00	420.00
	1904				Proof	650.00

Edge Type 2: БОГ*СРБИЈУ*ЧУВА***

| 28 (Y22.2) | 1904 | Inc. Ab. | — | — | — | — |

10 DINARA

3.2258 g, .900 GOLD, .0933 oz AGW

| 16 (Y11) | 1882V | .300 | 75.00 | 125.00 | 150.00 | 250.00 |

20 DINARA

6.4516 g, .900 GOLD, .1867 oz AGW
Obv. leg: Full title.

| 14 (Y10) | 1879A | .050 | 125.00 | 160.00 | 300.00 | 550.00 |

Obv. leg: Short title.

| 17 (Y12) | 1882V | .300 | 110.00 | 135.00 | 180.00 | 300.00 |

GERMAN OCCUPATION WW II
50 PARA

ZINC

| 30 (Y23) | 1942БП | — | 2.00 | 3.50 | 7.50 | 16.00 |

DINAR

ZINC

| 31 (Y24) | 1942БП | — | .50 | 1.50 | 4.00 | 8.00 |

2 DINARA

ZINC

KM#	Date	Mintage	Fine	VF	XF	Unc
32 (Y25)	1942БП	—	.50	1.50	4.50	9.50

10 DINARA

ZINC

| 33 (Y26) | 1943БП | 1.750 | 1.00 | 2.50 | 6.00 | 14.00 |

ZAIRE

The Republic of Zaire (formerly the Belgian Congo), located in the south-central part of Africa, has an area of 905,568 sq. mi. (2,345,409 sq. km.) and a population of *34 million. Capital: Kinshasa. The mineral-rich country produces copper, tin, diamonds, gold, zinc, cobalt and uranium.

In ancient times the territory comprising Zaire was occupied by Negrito peoples (Pygmies) pushed into the mountains by Bantu and Nilotic invaders. The interior was first explored by the American correspondent Henry Stanley, who was subsequently commissioned by King Leopold II of Belgium to conclude development treaties with the local chiefs. The Berlin conference of 1885 awarded the area to Leopold, who administered and exploited it as his private property until it was annexed to Belgium in 1908. Following the eruption of bloody independence riots in 1959, Belgium granted the Belgian Congo independence as the Republic of the Congo on June 30, 1960. The nation officially changed its name to Zaire on Oct. 27, 1971.

BELGIAN CONGO

The Belgian Congo attained independence (as Republic of Zaire) with the distinction of being the most ill-prepared country to ever undertake self-government. Without a single doctor, lawyer or engineer, with no organized unit capable of maintaining law and order, independence disintegrated into an orgy of anarchy. Provinces seceded. Intertribal warfare erupted. Belgian troops intervened to protect Belgian citizens from retributive massacre. By 1961 four groups were fighting for political dominance. The most serious threat to the viability of the country was posed by the secession of mineral-rich Katanga province on July 11, 1960. After two and one-half years of sporadic warfare with a U.N. military force, Katanga's leaders capitulated, Jan. 14, 1963, and the rebellious province was partitioned into three provinces.

RULERS
Belgian, until 1960

MINT MARKS
H - Heaton, Birmingham

MONETARY SYSTEM
100 Centimes = 1 Franc

CENTIME

COPPER

KM#	Date	Mintage	Fine	VF	XF	Unc
1 (Y1)	1887	.180	1.00	2.50	4.00	9.00
	1888	Inc. Ab.	1.00	2.50	4.00	9.00

| 15 (Y15) | 1910 | 2.000 | 1.00 | 2.00 | 3.00 | 6.00 |
| | 1919 | .500 | 1.00 | 2.00 | 3.00 | 7.00 |

2 CENTIMES

COPPER

| 2 (Y2) | 1887 | .130 | 1.00 | 2.00 | 4.50 | 9.00 |
| | 1888 | Inc. Ab. | 1.00 | 2.00 | 4.50 | 9.00 |

| 16 (Y16) | 1910 | 1.500 | 1.00 | 2.00 | 6.00 | 20.00 |
| | 1919 | .500 | 1.25 | 2.50 | 7.50 | 25.00 |

5 CENTIMES

COPPER

KM#	Date	Mintage	Fine	VF	XF	Unc
3 (Y3)	1887	.180	1.00	3.00	5.00	10.00
	1888/7	Inc. Ab.	1.00	3.00	5.00	12.50
	1888	Inc. Ab.	1.00	2.00	3.00	12.00
	1894	.150	1.50	3.00	5.00	15.00

COPPER-NICKEL

9 (Y9)	1906	.100	5.00	10.00	20.00	35.00
	1908	.180	4.00	7.50	17.50	32.50

12 (Y12)	1909	1.800	5.00	12.50	35.00	75.00

KM#	Date	Mintage	Fine	VF	XF	Unc
17 (Y17)	1910	6.000	.75	1.50	2.50	5.00
	1911	5.000	.75	1.50	2.50	5.00
	1917H	1.000	1.00	3.00	6.00	15.00
	1919H	3.000	1.00	2.00	4.00	12.00
	1919	6.850	.25	.75	1.50	4.00
	1920	2.740	.50	.75	1.75	5.00
	1921	17.260	.25	.75	1.50	4.00
	1921H	3.000	1.00	2.00	4.00	10.00
	1925	11.000	.25	.75	1.50	4.00
	1926/5	5.770	2.25	4.50	—	—
	1926	Inc. Ab.	.25	.75	1.75	4.00
	1927	2.000	.50	1.00	1.75	4.00
	1928/6	1.500	2.00	4.00	8.00	15.00
	1928	Inc. Ab.	.75	1.25	2.00	5.00

10 CENTIMES

COPPER

4 (Y4)	1887	.040	2.00	3.50	7.50	15.00
	1888	Inc. Ab.	2.00	3.50	7.50	20.00
	1889	.100	2.00	3.50	7.50	20.00
	1894	.150	2.00	3.50	7.50	20.00

COPPER-NICKEL

KM#	Date	Mintage	Fine	VF	XF	Unc
10 (Y10)	1906	.100	4.00	10.00	25.00	60.00
	1908	.800	3.00	7.50	20.00	50.00

13 (Y13)	1909	1.500	6.00	15.00	35.00	75.00

18 (Y18)	1910	5.000	.50	1.00	2.00	4.50
	1911	5.000	.50	1.00	2.00	4.50
	1917H	.500	1.00	2.50	6.00	40.00
	1919	3.430	.50	1.00	3.00	6.00
	1919H	1.500	.75	1.25	3.25	6.00
	1920	1.510	.75	1.25	3.25	6.00
	1921	13.540	.25	.75	2.00	4.00
	1921H	3.000	.75	1.50	3.50	8.00
	1922	14.950	.25	1.00	2.50	6.00
	1924	3.600	.50	1.50	3.00	6.00
	1925/4	4.800	2.00	4.00	8.00	50.00
	1925	Inc. Ab.	.25	.75	2.00	4.00
	1927	2.020	.25	.75	2.00	4.00
	1928/7	5.600	.75	1.50	4.50	40.00
	1928	Inc. Ab.	.25	.75	2.00	4.00

20 CENTIMES

 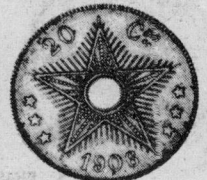

COPPER-NICKEL

11 (Y11)	1906	.100	5.00	12.50	25.00	60.00
	1908	.400	4.00	7.50	15.00	40.00

14 (Y14)	1909	.300	7.00	17.50	35.00	100.00

19 (Y19)	1910	1.000	.75	1.50	3.00	10.00
	1911	1.250	.75	1.50	3.00	10.00

50 CENTIMES

2.5000 g .835 SILVER, .0671 oz ASW

5 (Y5)	1887	.020	7.00	11.00	27.00	60.00
	1887	—	—	—	Proof	125.00

KM#	Date	Mintage	Fine	VF	XF	Unc
(Y5)	1891	.060	8.00	12.00	35.00	75.00
	1894	.040	8.00	12.00	40.00	100.00
	1896	.200	8.00	12.00	30.00	65.00

COPPER-NICKEL
Rev: French leg. CONGO BELGE

22 (Y20)	1921	4.000	.50	1.00	2.50	25.00
	1922	6.000	.50	1.00	2.50	25.00
	1923	7.200	.50	1.00	2.50	25.00
	1924	1.096	.50	1.00	2.50	25.00
	1925	16.104	.50	1.00	2.50	20.00
	1926/5	16.000	.50	4.00	7.00	30.00
	1926	Inc. Ab.	.50	1.00	2.50	25.00
	1927	10.000	.50	1.00	2.50	25.00
	1929/7	7.504	.50	1.00	2.50	30.00
	1929/8	Inc. Ab.	.50	4.00	7.00	85.00
	1929	Inc. Ab.	.50	1.00	2.50	20.00

Rev: Flemish leg. BELGISCH CONGO

23 (Y20.1)	1921	4.000	.50	1.00	2.50	25.00
	1922	5.592	.50	1.00	2.50	20.00
	1923/1	7.208	.50	2.50	5.00	65.00
	1923	Inc. Ab.	.50	1.00	2.50	20.00
	1924	7.000	.50	1.00	2.50	25.00
	1925/4	10.600	.50	2.50	5.00	75.00
	1925	Inc. Ab.	.50	1.00	2.50	25.00
	1926	25.200	.50	1.00	2.50	20.00
	1927	4.800	.50	1.00	2.50	20.00
	1928	7.484	.50	1.00	2.50	20.00
	1929/8	.116	.50	2.50	5.00	65.00
	1929	Inc. Ab.	.50	1.00	2.50	20.00

FRANC

5.0000 g, .835 SILVER, .1342 oz ASW

6 (Y6)	1887	.020	7.00	15.00	30.00	80.00
	1891	.070	7.00	17.00	35.00	95.00
	1894	.070	7.00	17.00	40.00	110.00
	1896	.160	7.00	17.00	35.00	100.00

COPPER-NICKEL
Rev: French leg. CONGO BELGE

20 (Y21)	1920	4.000	.75	1.25	3.00	30.00
	1922	5.000	.75	1.25	3.00	30.00
	1923/2	5.000	.75	1.25	3.00	30.00
	1923	Inc. Ab.	.75	1.25	3.00	30.00
	1924	6.030	.75	1.25	3.00	30.00
	1925	10.470	.75	1.25	3.00	30.00
	1926/5	12.500	.75	1.25	3.00	30.00
	1926	Inc. Ab.	.75	1.25	3.00	30.00
	1927	15.250	.75	1.25	3.00	30.00
	1929	5.763	.75	1.25	3.00	30.00
	1930	5.000	.75	1.25	3.00	30.00

Rev: Flemish leg. BELGISCH CONGO

21 (Y21.1)	1920	.475	.75	1.25	3.00	30.00
	1921	3.525	.75	1.25	3.00	30.00
	1922	5.000	.75	1.25	3.00	30.00
	1923	7.362	.75	1.25	3.00	30.00
	1924	4.608	.75	1.25	3.00	30.00
	1925	9.530	.75	1.25	3.00	30.00
	1926/5	17.000	.75	1.25	3.00	30.00
	1926	Inc. Ab.	.75	1.25	3.00	30.00
	1928	9.250	.75	1.25	3.00	30.00
	1929	4.250	.75	1.25	3.00	30.00

BRASS

KM#	Date	Mintage	Fine	VF	XF	Unc
26	1944	25.000	.25	.75	2.25	5.00
(Y22)	1946	15.000	.50	1.00	2.50	6.00
	1949	15.000	.50	1.00	2.50	3.50

2 FRANCS

10.0000 g, .835 SILVER, .2685 oz ASW

7	1887	.020	25.00	45.00	100.00	200.00
(Y7)	1891	.030	30.00	50.00	120.00	250.00
	1894	.080	30.00	50.00	120.00	250.00
	1896	.100	30.00	50.00	120.00	250.00

BRASS

25 (Y24)	1943	25.000	1.50	3.00	6.00	20.00

28	1946	13.000	.75	1.50	2.50	8.00
(Y23)	1947	12.000	.75	1.50	2.00	7.00

5 FRANCS

25.0000 g, .900 SILVER, .7234 oz ASW

Obv. leg: LEOPOLD II R.D.BELGES. . . . .

8.1	1887	8,000	100.00	175.00	225.00	510.00
(Y8.1)	1891	.030	100.00	175.00	225.00	510.00
	1894	.050	100.00	175.00	225.00	510.00
	1896	.110	100.00	175.00	225.00	510.00

Obv. leg: LEOPOLD II ROI DES BELGES

KM#	Date	Mintage	Fine	VF	XF	Unc
8.2 (Y8.2)	1887	100 pcs.	1000.	2500.	4250.	6250.

NICKEL-BRONZE

24	1936	2.600	5.00	10.00	20.00	90.00
(Y26)	1937	11.400	4.00	8.00	17.50	80.00

BRASS

29 (Y25)	1947	10.000	2.00	5.00	10.00	35.00

50 FRANCS

17.4000 g, .835 SILVER, .4671 oz ASW

27 (Y27)	1944	1.000	30.00	50.00	85.00	125.00

RUANDA-URUNDI

The Belgian Congo and Ruanda-Urundi were united administratively from 1925 to 1960. Ruanda-Urundi was made a U.N. Trust territory in 1946. Coins for these 2 areas were made jointly between 1952 and 1960. Ruanda-Urundi became the Republic of Rwanda on June 1, 1962.

For later coinage refer to Rwanda and Burundi, Rwanda, and Burundi.

MONETARY SYSTEM

100 Centimes = 1 Franc

50 CENTIMES

ALUMINUM

KM#	Date	Mintage	VF	XF	Unc
2	1954 DB	4.700	.35	.75	2.50
(Y29)	1955 DB	20.300	.15	.60	1.50

FRANC

ALUMINUM

4	1957	10.000	.50	1.25	2.50
(Y30)	1958	20.000	.50	1.00	2.00
	1959	20.000	.50	1.00	2.00
	1960	20.000	.50	1.25	2.50

5 FRANCS

BRASS

1 (Y28)	1952	10.000	1.00	3.50	10.00

ALUMINUM

3	1956 DB	10.000	1.00	2.00	3.75
(Y31)	1958 DB	26.110	.75	1.75	3.00
	1959 DB	3.890	1.00	2.50	4.00

CONGO DEM REP.

Democratic Republic of the Congo achieved independence on June 30, 1960. It followed the same monetary system as when under the Belgians. Monetary Reform of 1967 introduced new denominations and coins. The name of the country was changed to Zaire in 1971.

MINT MARKS

(b) - Brussels, privy marks only

10 FRANCS

ALUMINUM

KM#	Date	Mintage	Fine	VF	XF	Unc
1	1965(b)	100.000*	.50	1.00	2.25	4.50

*NOTE: Most recalled and melted down.

3.1900 g, .900 GOLD, .0923 oz AGW

Obv: Similar to 100 Francs, KM#6.

KM#	Date	Mintage	Fine	VF	XF	Unc
2	1965	3,000*	—	—	—	85.00

*NOTE: Approximately 70 per cent melted.

20 FRANCS

6.3400 g, .900 GOLD, .1834 oz AGW
Obv: Similar to 100 Francs, KM#6.

3	1965	3,000*	—	—	Proof	145.00

*NOTE: Approximately 70 per cent melted.

25 FRANCS

8.0000 g, .900 GOLD, .2315 oz AGW
Obv: Similar to 100 Francs, KM#6.

4	1965	3,000*	—	—	Proof	175.00

*NOTE: Approximately 70 per cent melted.

SILVER (OMS)

4a	1965	—	—	—	Proof	60.00

50 FRANCS

15.9800 g, .900 GOLD, .4624 oz AGW
Obv: Similar to 100 Francs, KM#6.

5	1965	3,000*	—	—	Proof	350.00

*NOTE: Approximately 70 per cent melted.

100 FRANCS

32.2300 g, .900 GOLD, .9327 oz AGW
Rev: Similar to 50 Francs, KM#5.

6	1965	3,000*	—	—	Proof	650.00

*NOTE: Approximately 70 per cent melted.

SILVER (OMS)

6a	1965	—	—	—	Proof	100.00

MONETARY REFORM

100 Sengi = 1 Likuta
100 Makuta (plural of Likuta) = 1 Zaire

10 SENGI

ALUMINUM

7	1967	90.996	—	.15	.40	.85

3.4300 g, .900 GOLD, .0990 oz AGW
Obv: Bust of President Mobutu.
Rev: Tiger head above crossed spears.

10	1970	1,000	—	—	Proof	100.00

LIKUTA

ALUMINUM

KM#	Date	Mintage	Fine	VF	XF	Unc
8	1967	36.290	—	.10	.30	.60
	1968	36.290	—	.10	.30	.60
	1969	12.890	—	.10	.30	.75

5 MAKUTA

COPPER-NICKEL

9	1967	1.980	.25	.50	1.00	2.00
	1968	1.980	.25	.50	1.00	2.00
	1969	.490	.25	.50	1.00	2.75

25 MAKUTAS

7.8400 g, .900 GOLD, .2260 oz AGW
Obv: Arms. Rev: Portrait of President Mobutu.

11	1970	1,000	—	—	Proof	175.00

50 MAKUTAS

15.8800 g, .900 GOLD, .4590 oz AGW
Obv: Arms. Rev: Portrait of President Mobutu.

12	1970	1,000	—	—	Proof	300.00

ZAIRE

20.0000 g, .900 GOLD, .5790 oz AGW
Obv: Arms. Rev: Portrait of President Mobutu.

13	1970	1,000	—	—	Proof	425.00

MINT SETS (MS)

KM#	Date	Mintage	Identification	Issue Price	Mkt. Val.
MS1	1970(4)	1,000	KM10-13	—	1300.	1100.

PROOF SETS (PS)

PS1	1965(5)	*3,000	KM2-6	490.00	1400.

*NOTE: Approximately 70 per cent melted.

PS2	1970(4)	1,000	KM10-13	—	1000.

KATANGA

Katanga, the southern province of the former Belgian Congo, had an area of 191,873 sq. mi. (496,951 sq. km.) and was noted for its mineral wealth.

MONETARY SYSTEM
100 Centimes = 1 Franc

FRANC

BRONZE

KM#	Date	Mintage	VF	XF	Unc
1	1961	—	1.00	1.50	3.50

5 FRANCS

BRONZE

2	1961	—	1.50	2.50	5.00

13.3300 g, .900 GOLD, .3857 oz AGW

2a	1961	.020	—	—	225.00

REPUBLIC OF ZAIRE

MONETARY SYSTEM
100 Makuta = 1 Zaire

5 MAKUTA

COPPER-NICKEL

KM#	Date	Mintage	VF	XF	Unc
12 (Y3)	1977	8.000	.50	1.00	2.00

10 MAKUTA

COPPER-NICKEL

7 (Y4)	1973	5.000	2.00	4.00	7.50
	1975	—	2.00	3.75	7.00
	1976	—	1.50	3.50	6.00
	1978	—	1.50	3.50	6.00

20 MAKUTA

COPPER-NICKEL

8 (Y5)	1973	—	3.00	5.00	9.00
	1976	—	2.50	4.50	8.50

ZAIRE

BRASS

13	1987	—	—	—	2.00

2-1/2 ZAIRES

ZAIRE 1849

ZAIRE 1850

28.2800 g, .925 SILVER, .8411 oz ASW
Conservation Series
Rev: Mountain Gorilla.

KM#	Date	Mintage	VF	XF	Unc
9	1975	5,735	—	—	35.00
(Y8)	1975	6,629	—	Proof	45.00

5 ZAIRES

27.8400 g, .925 SILVER, .8280 oz ASW
Hotel Intercontinental

| 1 | 1971 | — | — | Proof | 30.00 |

35.0000 g, .925 SILVER, 1.0409 oz ASW
Conservation Series
Obv: Similar to 2-1/2 Zaires, Y#8.
Rev: Okapi.

| 10 | 1975 | 5,734 | — | — | 30.00 |
| (Y9) | 1975 | 6,431 | — | Proof | 40.00 |

BRASS
| 14 | 1987 | — | — | — | 3.50 |

10 ZAIRES

.900 GOLD, .2882 oz AGW
Intercontinental
| | | — | — | Proof | 140.00 |

6.0400 g, .999 PLATINUM, .1940 oz APW
KM#	Date	Mintage	VF	XF	Unc
3	1971	—	—	Proof	125.00

20 ZAIRES

20.9000 g, .900 GOLD, .6048 oz AGW
Hotel Intercontinental
| 4 | 1971 | — | — | Proof | 300.00 |

3.8900 g, .999 PLATINUM, .1250 oz APW
| 5 | 1971 | — | — | Proof | 80.00 |

50 ZAIRES

46.9600 g, .900 GOLD, 1.3590 oz AGW
Hotel Intercontinental
| 6 | 1971 | — | — | Proof | 675.00 |

100 ZAIRES

33.4370 g, .900 GOLD, .9676 oz AGW
Conservation Series
Rev: Leopard.
| 11 | 1975 | 1,415 | — | — | 600.00 |
| (Y10) | 1975 | 279 pcs. | — | Proof | 900.00 |

PROOF SETS (PS)

KM#	Date	Mintage	Identification	Issue Price	Mkt. Val.
PS1	1971(6)	—	KM1-6	—	1350.
PS2	1975(2)	500	KM9-10	60.00	85.00

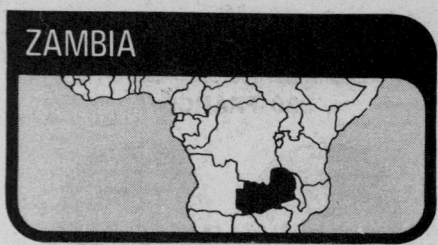

ZAMBIA

The Republic of Zambia (formerly Northern Rhodesia), a landlocked country in south-central Africa, has an area of 290,586 sq. mi. (752,614 sq. km.) and a population of *7.8 million. Capital: Lusaka. The economy of Zambia is based principally on copper, of which Zambia is the world's third largest producer. Copper, zinc, lead, cobalt and tobacco are exported.

The area that is now Zambia was brought within the British sphere of influence in 1888 by empire builder Cecil Rhodes, who obtained mining concessions in southcentral Africa from indigenous chiefs. The territory was ruled by the British South Africa Company, which Rhodes established, until 1924 when its administration was transferred to the British government as a protectorate. In 1953, Northern Rhodesia was joined with Nyasaland and the colony of Southern Rhodesia to form the Federation of Rhodesia and Nyasaland. Northern Rhodesia seceded from the Federation on Oct. 24, 1964, and became the independent Republic of Zambia. Zambia is a member of the Commonwealth of Nations. The president is Chief of State.

Zambia converted to a decimal coinage on January 16, 1969.

For earlier coinage refer to Rhodesia and Nyasaland.

RULERS
British, until 1964

MONETARY SYSTEM
12 Pence = 1 Shilling
20 Shillings = 1 Pound
100 Ngwee = 1 Kwacha

PENNY

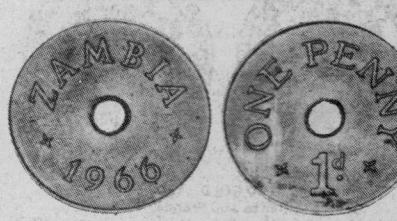

BRONZE
KM#	Date	Mintage	Fine	VF	XF	Unc
5	1966	7.200	.10	.30	.70	1.50
	1966	60 pcs.	—	—	Proof	

SIXPENCE

COPPER-NICKEL-ZINC
| 1 | 1964 | 3.500 | .15 | .30 | .60 | 1.00 |
| | 1964 | 5,000 | — | — | Proof | 1.50 |

| 6 | 1966 | 7.200 | .15 | .30 | .50 | .75 |
| | 1966 | 60 pcs. | — | — | Proof | |

SHILLING

COPPER-NICKEL
| 2 | 1964 | 3.510 | .35 | .75 | 1.25 | 2.00 |
| | 1964 | 5,000 | — | — | Proof | 2.50 |

ZAMBIA

KM#	Date	Mintage	Fine	VF	XF	Unc
7	1966	5.000	.25	.40	.75	2.00
	1966	60 pcs.	—	—	Proof	—

2 SHILLINGS

COPPER-NICKEL

3	1964	3.770	.50	1.00	1.75	3.25
	1964	5,000	—	—	Proof	4.50

8	1966	5.000	.50	1.00	1.50	3.00
	1966	60 pcs.	—	—	Proof	—

5 SHILLINGS

COPPER-NICKEL

4	1965	.010	—	2.00	3.00	4.00
	1965	.020	—	—	Proof	6.00

DECIMAL COINAGE
100 Ngwee = 1 Kwacha

NGWEE

BRONZE

KM#	Date	Mintage	VF	XF	Unc
9	1968	8.000	.10	.15	.35
	1968	4,000	—	Proof	1.25
	1969	16.000	.10	.15	.35
	1972	21.000	.10	.15	.35
	1978	23.976	.10	.15	.35
	1978	.024	—	Proof	2.00

COPPER-CLAD-STEEL

KM#	Date	Mintage	VF	XF	Unc
9a	1982	10.000	—	.10	.25
	1983	60.000	—	.10	.25

2 NGWEE

BRONZE

10	1968	19.000	.10	.20	.40
	1968	4,000	—	Proof	1.50
	1978	—	.10	.20	.40
	1978	.024	—	Proof	2.00

COPPER-CLAD-STEEL

10a	1982	7.500	.10	.15	.35
	1983	60.000	.10	.15	.35

5 NGWEE

COPPER-NICKEL

11	1968	12.000	.20	.30	.60
	1968	4,000	—	Proof	1.75
	1972	9.000	.20	.30	.60
	1978	1.976	.20	.30	.60
	1978	.024	—	Proof	2.50
	1982	12.000	.20	.30	.60

10 NGWEE

COPPER-NICKEL-ZINC

12	1968	1.000	.35	.75	1.50
	1968	4,000	—	Proof	2.00
	1972	1.000	.35	.65	1.00
	1978	1.976	.35	.65	1.00
	1978	.024	—	Proof	3.00
	1982	8.000	.35	.65	1.00

20 NGWEE

COPPER-NICKEL

13	1968	1.500	.50	1.50	3.00
	1968	4,000	—	Proof	2.50
	1972	7.500	.50	1.00	2.00
	1978	.024	—	Proof	3.50

World Food Day

22	1981	.970	.50	1.25	2.00

Bank of Zambia

23	1985	—	.50	1.00	1.50

50 NGWEE

COPPER-NICKEL
F.A.O. issue

KM#	Date	Mintage	VF	XF	Unc
14	1969	.070	.75	1.50	3.75

F.A.O. Issue

15	1972	.510	.50	—	2.50

Second Republic 13th December 1972

16	1972	6.000	1.00	2.00	4.00
	1972	2.000	—	Proof	9.00
	1978	.024	—	Proof	7.00

United Nations

24	1985	—	1.00	1.25	2.25

KWACHA

COPPER-NICKEL
10th Anniversary of Independence

17	1974	1,500	—	—	Proof

ZAMBIA 1851

ZAMBIA

5 KWACHA

25.3100 g, .925 SILVER, .7527 oz ASW
Conservation Series
Obv: Similar to 20 Ngwee, KM#13.
Rev: Kafue Lechwe.

KM#	Date	Mintage	VF	XF	Unc
18	1979	3,250	—	—	25.00

28.2800 g, .925 SILVER, .8411 oz ASW

| 18a | 1979 | 3,407 | — | Proof | 50.00 |

10 KWACHA

31.6500 g, .925 SILVER, .9398 oz ASW
Conservation Series
Obv: Similar to 20 Ngwee, KM#13.
Rev: Taita Falcon.

| 19 | 1979 | 3,250 | — | — | 30.00 |

35.0000 g, .925 SILVER, 1.0409 oz ASW

| 19a | 1979 | 3,256 | — | Proof | 65.00 |

27.2200 g, .925 SILVER, .8095 oz ASW
International year of the Child
Obv: Similar to 20 Ngwee, KM#13.

| 21 | 1980 | .012 | — | Proof | 18.00 |

Conservation - Bird
.025 — Proof 25.00 35.00

200 KWACHA

33.4370 g, .900 GOLD, .9676 oz AGW
Conservation Series
Obv: Similar to 20 Ngwee, KM#13.
Rev: African Wild Dog.

KM#	Date	Mintage	VF	XF	Unc
20	1979	455 pcs.	—	—	600.00
	1979	245 pcs.	—	Proof	900.00

MINT SETS (MS)

KM#	Date	Mintage	Identification	Issue Price	Mkt. Val.
MS1	1968(5)	—	KM9-13	2.00	6.00

PROOF SETS (PS)

PS1	1964(3)	5,000	KM1-3	—	8.50
PS2	1965(2)	100	KM4 (2 pcs.)	—	12.00
PS3	1966(8)	30	KM5-8, double sets	—	—
PS4	1968(5)	4,000	KM9-13	10.00	9.00
PS5	1978(6)	20,000	KM9-13,16	21.00	20.00

Listings For
ZANZIBAR: refer to Tanzania

ZIMBABWE

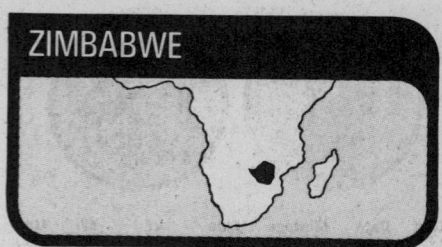

The Republic of Zimbabwe (formerly the Republic of Rhodesia), located in the east-central part of southern Africa, has an area of 150,804 sq. mi. (390,580 sq. km.) and a population of *10 million. Capital: Harare (formerly Salisbury). The economy is based on agriculture and mining. Tobacco, sugar, asbestos, copper and chrome, ore and coal are exported.

The Rhodesian area, the habitat of paleolithic man, contains extensive evidence of earlier civilizations, notably the world-famous ruins of Zimbabwe, a gold-trading center that flourished about the 14th or 15th century A.D. The Portuguese of the 16th century were the first Europeans to attempt to develop south-central Africa, but it remained for Cecil Rhodes and the British South Africa Co. to open the hinterlands. Rhodes obtained a concession for mineral rights from local chiefs in 1888 and administered his African empire (named Southern Rhodesia in 1895) through the British South Africa Co. until 1923, when the British government annexed the area after the white settlers voted for existence as a separate entity, rather than for incorporation into the Union of South Africa. From Sept. of 1953 through 1963 Southern Rhodesia was joined with the British Protectorates of Northern Rhodesia and Nyasaland into a multiracial federation, known as the Federation of Rhodesia and Nyasaland. When the federation was dissolved at the end of 1963, Northern Rhodesia and Nyasaland became the independent states of Zambia and Malawi.

Britain was prepared to grant independence to Southern Rhodesia but declined to do so when the politically dominant white Rhodesians refused to give assurances of representative government. On May 11, 1965, following two years of unsuccessful negotiation with the British government, Prime Minister Ian Smith issued an unilateral declaration of independence. Britain responded with economic sanctions supported by the United Nations. After further futile attempts to effect an accommodation, the Rhodesian Parliament severed all ties with Britain, and on March 2, 1970, established the Republic of Rhodesia.

On March 3, 1978, Prime Minister Ian Smith and three moderate black nationalist leaders signed an agreement providing for black majority rule. The name of the country was changed to Zimbabwe Rhodesia. This arrangement was not accepted by Britain and following further negotiations, an acceptable form of independence was attained on April 18, 1980. The name of the country was changed to Zimbabwe which remains a member of the British Commonwealth of Nations.

SOUTHERN RHODESIA
RULERS
British until 1970

MONETARY SYSTEM
12 Pence = 1 Shilling
2 Shillings = 1 Florin
5 Shillings = 1 Crown
20 Shillings = 1 Pound

1/2 PENNY

COPPER-NICKEL

KM#	Date	Mintage	Fine	VF	XF	Unc
6	1934	.240	.75	2.25	9.00	30.00
	1934	—	—	—	Proof	500.00
	1936	.240	4.00	8.00	25.00	125.00
	1936	—	—	—	Proof	—

14	1938	.240	.75	1.75	6.50	30.00
	1938	—	—	—	Proof	500.00
	1939	.480	.75	1.75	9.00	60.00
	1939	—	—	—	Proof	500.00

BRONZE

14a	1942	.480	.75	1.75	4.50	30.00
	1942	—	—	—	Proof	500.00
	1943	.960	.40	.80	2.25	8.00
	1944	.960	.40	.80	2.50	10.00
	1944	—	—	—	Proof	—

Obv. leg: KING GEORGE THE SIXTH

KM#	Date	Mintage	Fine	VF	XF	Unc
26	1951	.480	.75	1.25	2.25	7.50
	1951	—	—	—	Proof	—
	1952	.480	.75	1.25	2.50	12.50
	1952	—	—	—	Proof	300.00

KM#	Date	Mintage	Fine	VF	XF	Unc
28	1954	.960	.75	2.25	10.00	75.00
	1954	20 pcs.	—	—	Proof	500.00

PENNY

COPPER-NICKEL

KM#	Date	Mintage	Fine	VF	XF	Unc
7	1934	.360	.75	1.50	3.50	35.00
	1934	—	—	—	Proof	450.00
	1935	.492	.75	2.50	12.00	125.00
	1935	—	—	—	Proof	—
	1936	1.044	.60	1.25	3.50	40.00
	1936	—	—	—	Proof	—

KM#	Date	Mintage	Fine	VF	XF	Unc
8	1937	.908	.75	1.25	3.50	25.00
	1937	—	—	—	Proof	375.00
	1938	.240	1.75	3.25	10.00	40.00
	1938	—	—	—	Proof	—
	1939	1.284	.50	1.00	3.50	40.00
	1939	—	—	—	Proof	—
	1940	1.080	.60	1.25	3.50	40.00
	1940	—	—	—	Proof	—
	1941	.720	.60	1.25	4.50	45.00
	1941	—	—	—	Proof	—
	1942	.960	.60	1.25	4.50	70.00
	1942	—	—	—	—	—

BRONZE

KM#	Date	Mintage	Fine	VF	XF	Unc
8a	1942	.480	4.00	6.50	22.50	150.00
	1942	—	—	—	Proof	500.00
	1943	3.120	.50	.80	2.50	15.00
	1944	2.400	.50	.80	2.50	20.00
	1944	—	—	—	Proof	—
	1947	3.600	.75	1.25	3.50	20.00
	1947	—	—	—	Proof	—

KM#	Date	Mintage	Fine	VF	XF	Unc
25	1949	1.440	.50	1.00	2.00	40.00
	1949	—	—	—	Proof	500.00
	1950	.720	1.00	1.75	5.00	45.00
	1950	—	—	—	Proof	500.00
	1951	4.896	.50	.75	1.25	10.00
	1951	—	—	—	Proof	500.00
	1952	2.400	.50	.75	1.75	15.00
	1952	—	—	—	Proof	—

KM#	Date	Mintage	Fine	VF	XF	Unc
29	1954	.960	4.00	8.00	25.00	175.00
	1954	20 pcs.	—	—	Proof	500.00

3 PENCE

1.4100 g, .925 SILVER, .0419 oz ASW

KM#	Date	Mintage	Fine	VF	XF	Unc
1	1932	.688	1.00	2.00	6.50	35.00
	1932	—	—	—	Proof	100.00
	1934	.628	1.00	3.00	12.00	90.00
	1934	—	—	—	Proof	—
	1935	.840	1.00	3.00	12.00	65.00
	1935	—	—	—	Proof	—
	1936	1.052	1.00	2.50	10.00	55.00
	1936	—	—	—	Proof	—

KM#	Date	Mintage	Fine	VF	XF	Unc
9	1937	1.228	1.00	3.50	8.00	40.00
	1937	—	—	—	Proof	250.00

Obv: KING moved right of head

KM#	Date	Mintage	Fine	VF	XF	Unc
16	1939	.160	6.00	10.00	25.00	150.00
	1939	—	—	—	Proof	600.00
	1940	1.200	.75	2.50	10.00	50.00
	1940	—	—	—	Proof	—
	1941	.600	3.50	6.50	12.00	80.00
	1941	—	—	—	Proof	—
	1942	2.000	.75	1.50	7.00	40.00
	1942	—	—	—	Proof	—

1.4100 g, .500 SILVER, .0226 oz ASW

KM#	Date	Mintage	Fine	VF	XF	Unc
16a	1944	1.600	.75	1.50	10.00	65.00
	1945	.800	1.50	4.00	25.00	70.00
	1945	—	—	—	Proof	—
	1946	2.400	1.00	2.50	8.00	45.00
	1946	—	—	—	Proof	—

COPPER-NICKEL

KM#	Date	Mintage	Fine	VF	XF	Unc
16b	1947	8.000	.40	.80	2.50	20.00
	1947	—	—	—	Proof	500.00

KM#	Date	Mintage	Fine	VF	XF	Unc
20	1948	2.000	.40	.80	3.50	30.00
	1948	—	—	—	Proof	—
	1949	4.000	.40	.80	3.00	25.00
	1949	—	—	—	Proof	500.00
	1951	5.600	.40	.80	2.50	20.00
	1951	—	—	—	Proof	—
	1952	4.800	.40	.80	2.50	30.00
	1952	—	—	—	Proof	400.00

6 PENCE

2.8300 g, .925 SILVER, .0841 oz ASW

KM#	Date	Mintage	Fine	VF	XF	Unc
2	1932	.544	2.50	4.00	10.00	60.00
	1932	—	—	—	Proof	150.00
	1934	.214	3.50	7.50	30.00	100.00
	1935	.380	2.50	6.00	30.00	150.00
	1935	—	—	—	Proof	—
	1936	.675	2.00	4.00	17.50	70.00
	1936	—	—	—	Proof	—

KM#	Date	Mintage	Fine	VF	XF	Unc
10	1937	.823	4.00	8.00	17.50	65.00
	1937	—	—	—	Proof	250.00

Obv: KING moved right of head

KM#	Date	Mintage	Fine	VF	XF	Unc
17	1939	.200	4.00	10.00	45.00	200.00
	1939	—	—	—	Proof	900.00
	1940	.600	2.00	4.00	20.00	75.00
	1940	—	—	—	Proof	—
	1941	.300	2.50	5.00	17.50	65.00
	1941	—	—	—	Proof	—
	1942	1.200	1.25	2.50	10.00	55.00
	1942	—	—	—	Proof	—

2.8300 g, .500 SILVER, .0454 oz ASW

KM#	Date	Mintage	Fine	VF	XF	Unc
17a	1944	.800	1.75	4.00	15.00	90.00
	1945	.400	15.00	25.00	65.00	150.00
	1945	—	—	—	Proof	—
	1946	1.600	1.75	4.00	15.00	70.00
	1946	—	—	—	Proof	—

COPPER-NICKEL

KM#	Date	Mintage	Fine	VF	XF	Unc
17b	1947	5.000	.50	1.00	4.00	20.00
	1947	—	—	—	Proof	600.00

KM#	Date	Mintage	Fine	VF	XF	Unc
21	1948	1.000	.50	1.25	4.50	27.50
	1948	—	—	—	Proof	—
	1949	2.000	.50	1.00	3.50	30.00
	1949	—	—	—	Proof	450.00
	1950	2.000	.50	1.00	4.50	45.00
	1950	—	—	—	Proof	450.00
	1951	2.800	.50	1.00	2.50	22.50
	1951	—	—	—	Proof	—
	1952	1.200	.50	1.50	3.50	45.00
	1952	—	—	—	Proof	—

SHILLING

5.6600 g, .925 SILVER, .1683 oz ASW

KM#	Date	Mintage	Fine	VF	XF	Unc
3	1932	.896	2.50	5.00	22.50	100.00
	1932	—	—	—	Proof	200.00
	1934	.333	4.00	8.00	45.00	175.00
	1935	.830	2.50	5.50	17.50	125.00
	1935	—	—	—	Proof	—
	1936	1.663	2.00	4.50	17.50	125.00
	1936	—	—	—	Proof	—

KM#	Date	Mintage	Fine	VF	XF	Unc
11	1937	1.700	2.50	6.00	17.50	90.00
	1937	—	—	—	Proof	250.00

Obv: KING moved right of head

KM#	Date	Mintage	Fine	VF	XF	Unc
18	1939	.420	8.00	17.50	70.00	300.00
	1939	—	—	—	Proof	1500.
	1940	.750	6.50	15.00	50.00	175.00
	1940	—	—	—	Proof	—
	1941	.800	7.50	15.00	45.00	150.00

Southern Rhodesia / ZIMBABWE 1854

KM#	Date	Mintage	Fine	VF	XF	Unc
18	1941	—	—	—	—	—
	1942	2.100	2.50	5.00	15.00	55.00
	1942	—	—	—	Proof	—

5.6600 g, .500 SILVER, .0909 oz ASW

18a	1944	1.600	3.00	—	12.50	80.00
	1946	1.700	4.50	12.00	50.00	120.00
	1946	—	—	—	Proof	—

COPPER-NICKEL

18b	1947	8.000	.75	1.50	4.50	40.00
	1947	—	—	—	Proof	500.00

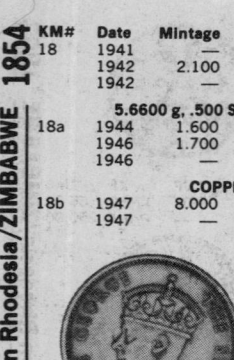

22	1948	1.500	.75	1.50	6.50	30.00
	1948	—	—	—	Proof	—
	1949	4.000	.75	1.25	4.50	30.00
	1949	—	—	—	Proof	600.00
	1950	2.000	1.00	3.00	10.00	55.00
	1950	—	—	—	Proof	600.00
	1951	3.000	.75	1.25	4.50	20.00
	1951	—	—	—	Proof	—
	1952	2.600	.75	1.50	4.50	55.00
	1952	—	—	—	Proof	—

2 SHILLINGS

11.3100 g, .925 SILVER, .3363 oz ASW

4	1932	.498	5.00	12.00	30.00	120.00
	1932	—	—	—	Proof	175.00
	1934	.154	12.50	20.00	125.00	300.00
	1935	.365	6.00	12.50	40.00	125.00
	1935	—	—	—	Proof	—
	1936	.683	6.00	12.50	40.00	125.00
	1936	—	—	—	Proof	—

12	1937	.552	8.50	15.00	35.00	125.00
	1937	—	—	—	Proof	250.00

Obv: KING moved right of head

19	1939	.120	100.00	200.00	750.00	1200.
	1939	—	—	—	Proof	2500.
	1940	.525	10.00	20.00	75.00	250.00
	1940	—	—	—	Proof	—
	1941	.400	10.00	20.00	100.00	300.00
	1941	—	—	—	Proof	—
	1942	.850	5.00	10.00	25.00	90.00

11.3100 g, .500 SILVER, .1818 oz ASW

	1944	1.300	7.50	12.50	40.00	135.00
	1946	.700	100.00	200.00	300.00	800.00
	1946	—	—	—	Proof	—

COPPER-NICKEL

	1947	3.750	1.75	4.00	12.50	55.00
	1947	—	—	—	Proof	—

KM#	Date	Mintage	Fine	VF	XF	Unc
23	1948	.750	1.00	3.00	10.00	40.00
	1948	—	—	—	Proof	—
	1949	2.000	1.00	3.00	10.00	50.00
	1949	—	—	—	Proof	700.00
	1950	1.000	1.00	4.00	15.00	75.00
	1950	—	—	—	Proof	700.00
	1951	2.600	1.00	3.00	6.00	27.50
	1951	—	—	—	Proof	—
	1952	1.800	1.00	3.00	10.00	75.00
	1952	—	—	—	Proof	—

30	1954	.300	30.00	75.00	225.00	650.00
	1954	20 pcs.	—	—	Proof	1750.

1/2 CROWN

14.1400 g, .925 SILVER, .4205 oz ASW

5	1932	.634	6.00	10.00	40.00	165.00
	1932	—	—	—	Proof	225.00
	1934	.419	7.00	12.00	50.00	250.00
	1934	—	—	—	Proof	—
	1935	.512	6.00	10.00	40.00	175.00
	1935	—	—	—	Proof	—
	1936	.518	6.00	10.00	40.00	175.00
	1936	—	—	—	Proof	—

13	1937	1.174	5.00	10.00	27.50	150.00
	1937	—	—	—	Proof	300.00

15	1938	.400	6.00	8.50	32.00	150.00
	1938	—	—	—	Proof	—
	1939	.224	10.00	20.00	65.00	300.00
	1939	—	—	—	Proof	2000.
	1940	.800	6.00	8.50	27.50	80.00
	1940	—	—	—	Proof	—
	1941	1.240	4.00	7.00	15.00	70.00
	1941	—	—	—	Proof	—
	1942	2.008	4.00	7.00	15.00	75.00
	1942	—	—	—	Proof	—

14.1400 g, .500 SILVER, .2273 oz ASW

15a	1944	.800	4.00	8.00	22.50	80.00
	1946	1.400	4.00	10.00	27.50	150.00
	1946	—	—	—	Proof	—

COPPER-NICKEL

KM#	Date	Mintage	Fine	VF	XF	Unc
15b	1947	6.000	1.50	3.00	5.00	20.00
	1947	—	—	—	Proof	—

24	1948	.800	1.50	3.00	10.00	50.00
	1948	—	—	—	Proof	—
	1949	1.600	1.50	3.00	8.00	50.00
	1949	—	—	—	Proof	700.00
	1950	1.200	1.50	3.00	10.00	75.00
	1950	—	—	—	Proof	700.00
	1951	3.200	1.50	3.00	6.50	25.00
	1951	—	—	—	Proof	500.00
	1952	2.800	1.50	3.00	6.50	75.00
	1952	—	—	—	Proof	700.00

31	1954	1.200	6.00	12.00	30.00	70.00
	1954	20 pcs.	—	—	Proof	1750.

CROWN

28.2800 g, .500 SILVER, .4546 oz ASW
Cecil Rhodes Centennial

27	1953	.124	5.00	7.50	10.00	15.00
	1953	1,500	—	—	Proof	135.00

PROOF SETS (PS)

KM#	Date	Mintage	Identification	Issue Price	Mkt. Val.
PS1	1932(5)	496	KM1-5	—	550.00
PS2	1937(6)	40	KM8-13	—	1700.
PS3	1939(5)	10	KM15-19	—	5000.
PS4	1953(2)	3	KM27 double set	—	Rare
PS5	1954(4)	20	KM28-31	—	4500.

RHODESIA & NYASALAND

The Federation of Rhodesia and Nyasaland (or the Central African Federation), comprising the British protectorates of Northern Rhodesia and Nyasaland and the self-governing colony of Southern Rhodesia, was located in the east-central part of southern Africa. The multiracial federation had an area of about 487,000 sq. mi. (1,261,330 sq. km.) and a population of 6.8 million. Capital: Salisbury, in Southern Rhodesia.

The geographical unity of the three British possessions suggested the desirability of political and economic union as early as 1924. Despite objections by the African constituency of Northern Rhodesia and Nyasaland, who feared that African self-determination would be retarded by the dominant influence of prosperous and self-governing Southern Rhodesia, the Central African

Federation was established in Sept. of 1953. As feared, the Federation was effectively and profitably dominated by the European constituency of Southern Rhodesia despite the fact that the three component countries largely retained their prefederation political structure. It was dissolved at the end of 1963, largely because of the effective opposition of the Nyasaland African Congress. Northern Rhodesia and Nyasaland became independent states in 1964. Southern Rhodesia unilaterally declared its independence the following year.

The coinage is obsolete.

For earlier coinage refer to Southern Rhodesia. For later coinage refer to Malawi and Zambia and Rhodesia.

RULERS
Elizabeth II, 1952-1964

MONETARY SYSTEM
12 Pence = 1 Shilling
5 Shillings = 1 Crown

1/2 PENNY

BRONZE

KM#	Date	Mintage	Fine	VF	XF	Unc
1	1955	.720	.15	.25	.50	2.50
	1955	2,010	—	—	Proof	5.00
	1956	.480	.20	.50	1.00	3.50
	1956	—	—	—	Proof	450.00
	1957	1,920	.10	.15	.25	2.50
	1957	—	—	—	Proof	450.00
	1958	2,400	.10	.15	.25	2.50
	1958	—	—	—	Proof	450.00
	1964	1,440	.10	.15	.25	1.00

PENNY

BRONZE

KM#	Date	Mintage	Fine	VF	XF	Unc
2	1955	2,040	.15	.25	.75	4.00
	1955	2,010	—	—	Proof	5.00
	1956	4,800	.15	.25	.50	4.00
	1956	—	—	—	Proof	450.00
	1957	7,200	.10	.15	.25	3.00
	1957	—	—	—	Proof	—
	1958	2,880	.10	.15	.25	3.00
	1958	—	—	—	Proof	450.00
	1961	4,800	.10	.15	.25	2.00
	1961	—	—	—	Proof	—
	1962	6,000	.10	.15	.25	2.00
	1963	6,000	.10	.15	.25	2.00
	1963	—	—	—	Proof	450.00

3 PENCE

COPPER-NICKEL

KM#	Date	Mintage	Fine	VF	XF	Unc
3	1955	1,200	.20	.50	1.00	5.00
	1955	10 pcs.	—	—	Proof	500.00
	1956	3,200	.50	1.00	2.50	20.00
	1956	—	—	—	Proof	325.00
	1957	6,000	.20	.50	1.00	4.00
	1957	—	—	—	Proof	500.00
	1962	4,000	.20	.50	1.00	4.00
	1962	—	—	—	Proof	—
	1963	2,000	.20	.50	1.00	4.00
	1963	—	—	—	Proof	—
	1964	3,600	.15	.25	.50	1.50

1.4100 g, .500 SILVER, .0226 oz ASW

| 3a | 1955 | 2,000 | — | — | Proof | 7.50 |

6 PENCE

COPPER-NICKEL

4	1955	.400	.50	1.00	3.00	12.00
	1955	10 pcs.	—	—	Proof	325.00
	1956	.800	.75	2.00	7.00	50.00
	1956	—	—	—	Proof	—

KM#	Date	Mintage	Fine	VF	XF	Unc
4	1957	4,000	.20	.50	1.00	4.00
	1957	—	—	—	Proof	—
	1962	2,800	.20	.50	1.00	3.00
	1962	—	—	—	Proof	—
	1963	.800	5.00	10.00	35.00	60.00
	1963	—	—	—	Proof	—

2.8300 g, .500 SILVER, .0454 oz ASW

| 4a | 1955 | 2,000 | — | — | Proof | 12.50 |

SHILLING

COPPER-NICKEL

5	1955	.200	2.00	5.00	10.00	25.00
	1955	10 pcs.	—	—	Proof	400.00
	1956	1,700	.75	2.00	5.00	40.00
	1956	—	—	—	Proof	—
	1957	3,500	.50	1.50	3.00	8.50
	1957	—	—	—	Proof	—

5.6600 g, .500 SILVER, .0909 oz ASW

| 5a | 1955 | 2,000 | — | — | Proof | 15.00 |

2 SHILLINGS

COPPER-NICKEL

6	1955	1,750	1.50	3.00	6.00	15.00
	1955	10 pcs.	—	—	Proof	550.00
	1956	1,850	1.00	2.50	5.00	12.00
	1956	—	—	—	Proof	—
	1957	1,500	1.00	2.50	5.00	12.00
	1957	—	—	—	Proof	—

11.3100 g, .500 SILVER, .1818 oz ASW

| 6a | 1955 | 2,000 | — | — | Proof | 20.00 |

1/2 CROWN

COPPER-NICKEL

7	1955	1,600	1.00	2.50	5.00	15.00
	1955	10 pcs.	—	—	Proof	550.00
	1956	.160	6.00	12.50	35.00	250.00
	1956	—	—	—	Proof	—
	1957	2,400	8.00	17.50	35.00	100.00
	1957	—	—	—	Proof	—

14.1400 g, .500 SILVER, .2273 oz ASW

| 7a | 1955 | 2,000 | — | — | Proof | 25.00 |

NOTE: For later coinage see Malawi, Rhodesia and Zambia.

PROOF SETS (PS)

KM#	Date	Mintage	Identification	Issue Price	Mkt. Val.
PS1	1955(7)	10	KM1-7	—	2150.
PS2	1955(7)	2,000	KM1-2,3a-7a	—	90.00

RHODESIA

MONETARY SYSTEM
12 Pence = 1 Shilling
20 Shillings = 1 Pound

3 PENCE

COPPER-NICKEL

KM#	Date	Mintage	Fine	VF	XF	Unc
8	1968	2,400	.25	.50	.75	2.50
	1968	10 pcs.	—	—	Proof	2000.00

6 PENCE = 5 CENTS

COPPER-NICKEL

1	1964	13,500	.15	—	.40	1.50
	1964	2,060	—	—	Proof	7.50

SHILLING = 10 CENTS

COPPER-NICKEL

2	1964	15,500	.15	.25	.75	1.75
	1964	2,060	—	—	Proof	7.50

2 SHILLINGS = 20 CENTS

COPPER-NICKEL

3	1964	10,500	.25	.50	1.25	3.00
	1964	2,060	—	—	Proof	15.00

2-1/2 SHILLINGS = 25 CENTS

COPPER-NICKEL

4	1964	11,500	.50	.75	1.75	3.50
	1964	2,060	—	—	Proof	20.00

10 SHILLINGS

3.9940 g, .916 GOLD, .1177 oz AGW

| 5 | 1966 | 6,000 | — | — | Proof | 115.00 |

POUND

7.9881 g, .916 GOLD, .2354 oz AGW

| 6 | 1966 | 5,000 | — | — | Proof | 215.00 |

Rhodesia / ZIMBABWE

5 POUNDS

39.9403 g, .916 GOLD, 1.1772 oz AGW

KM#	Date	Mintage	Fine	VF	XF	Unc
7	1966	3,000	—	—	Proof	820.00

DECIMAL COINAGE
100 Cents = 1 Dollar

1/2 CENT

BRONZE

KM#	Date	Mintage	Fine	VF	XF	Unc
9	1970	10.000	—	.10	.20	.50
	1970	*12 pcs.	—	—	Proof	1500.
	1971	2.000	—	.10	.25	1.00
	1972	2.000	—	.10	.25	1.00
	1973	*28 pcs.	—	—	Proof	1250.
	1975	10.001	—	.10	.20	.50
	1977	*8-10 pcs.	—	—	Proof	1500.

*NOTE: Original mintage melted.

CENT

BRONZE

KM#	Date	Mintage	Fine	VF	XF	Unc
10	1970	25.000	—	.10	.20	.50
	1970	*12 pcs.	—	—	Proof	1500.
	1971	15.000	—	.10	.20	.50
	1972	10.000	—	.10	.20	.50
	1973	5.000	—	.10	.20	.75
	1973	*25 pcs.	—	—	Proof	1250.
	1974	—	—	.10	.20	.50
	1975	10.000	—	.10	.20	.50
	1976	20.000	—	.10	.20	.50
	1977	10.000	—	.10	.20	.50

2-1/2 CENTS

COPPER-NICKEL

KM#	Date	Mintage	Fine	VF	XF	Unc
11	1970	4.000	.15	.25	.40	1.00
	1970	*12 pcs.	—	—	Proof	1500.

5 CENTS

COPPER-NICKEL

KM#	Date	Mintage	Fine	VF	XF	Unc
12	1973	—	.25	1.00	1.75	3.50
	1973	*25 pcs.	—	—	Proof	1250.

13	1975	3.500	.15	.25	.40	.75
	1976	8.038	.15	.25	.40	.75
	1977	3.015	.25	.75	1.50	4.00

10 CENTS

COPPER-NICKEL

KM#	Date	Mintage	Fine	VF	XF	Unc
14	1975	1.874	.15	.30	.60	1.50
	1976	.129	.50	.75	1.25	3.50

20 CENTS

COPPER-NICKEL

KM#	Date	Mintage	Fine	VF	XF	Unc
15	1975	—	.50	.75	1.00	3.00
	1976	1.937	.50	.75	1.00	3.00
	1977	—	.75	1.00	1.50	4.00

25 CENTS

COPPER-NICKEL

KM#	Date	Mintage	Fine	VF	XF	Unc
16	1975	—	.50	1.00	1.75	4.00
	1976	1.011	.50	1.00	1.75	4.00

PROOF SETS (PS)

KM#	Date	Mintage	Identification	Issue Price	Mkt. Val.
PS1	1964(8)	10	KM1-4 double set	—	750.00
PS2	1964(4)	2,060	KM1-4	—	50.00
PS3	1966(3)	2,000	KM5-7	280.00	1150.
PS4	1970(6)	6	KM9-11 double set	—	9000.

ZIMBABWE

MONETARY SYSTEM
100 Cents = 1 Dollar

CENT

BRONZE

KM#	Date	Mintage	VF	XF	Unc
1	1980	10.000	.10	.25	.50
	1980	.015	—	Proof	2.00
	1982	—	.10	.25	.50
	1983	—	.10	.25	.50
	1986	—	.10	.25	.50

5 CENTS

COPPER-NICKEL

KM#	Date	Mintage	VF	XF	Unc
2	1980	—	.15	.30	.75
	1980	.015	—	Proof	2.00
	1982	—	.15	.30	.75
	1983	—	.15	.30	.75

10 CENTS

COPPER-NICKEL

KM#	Date	Mintage	VF	XF	Unc
3	1980	—	.15	.30	1.25
	1980	.015	—	Proof	3.00

20 CENTS

COPPER-NICKEL

	1980	—	.25	.50	1.50
4	1980	.015	—	Proof	3.00
	1983	—	.25	.50	1.50

50 CENTS

COPPER-NICKEL

	1980	—	.50	1.00	2.00
5	1980	.015	—	Proof	5.00

DOLLAR

COPPER-NICKEL

	1980	—	1.00	1.25	3.00
6	1980	.015	—	Proof	10.00

PROOF SETS (PS)

KM#	Date	Mintage	Identification	Issue Price	Mkt. Val.
PS1	1980	15,000	KM1-6	29.00	25.00